The Guinness World Car Record

Ivan Berg

GUINNESS PUBLISHING

First published in 1992 by Guinness Publishing Ltd

Typeset in Helvetica Medium
by Ace Filmsetting Ltd, Frome, Somerset
Printed and bound in Great Britain by The Bath Press, Bath

A catalogue record for this book is available from the British Library

ISBN 0–85112–529–8

Contents

About the author

Ivan Berg joined the Merchant Navy in 1952 at the age of 16 with the romantic notion of emulating the adventurous lives of writers such as Hemingway, W.W. Jacobs and Jack London. The life was sufficiently adventurous, particularly on the north Atlantic run on both of Cunard's Queens, but left him too tired to write. It was not until National Service in the Royal Air Force that he began to produce in earnest.

Eighteen months as a medic in the ENT department at the Central Medical Establishment provided the time to create, not the adventure novel of early dreams, but the first motor racing series on British television; 'The Chequered Flag' - for Rediffusion TV in 1960.

The next 10 years were spent variously as a screenwriter, author and journalist. Apart from 'The Chequered Flag' his credits included 'Moonstrike' - BBC1, 'A Touch of Brass' - Worldwide Films, *Tackle Karting This Way* and *Tackle Motor Sport This Way* for Hutchinson Stanley Paul and *TRAD*, a reference book on the UK Trad Jazz scene for Foulsham. Weekly adventure stories and a comic strip featuring his fictional motoring hero Revs Ransome were produced for *TV Express*, and he contributed features to *TV Times*, *Daily Mail*, *Honey* magazine and the provincial press.

In 1970 Berg started a recording studio with his wife Inge, and between 1970 and 1982 produced radio commercials and documentaries and published a very large range of spoken word cassettes. In 1982, intrigued by the publishing challenge offered by the fledgling home computer market, he bought a Commodore VIC 20 computer. The result was the publishing with Commodore Computers of a range of enormously successful home and educational software during the home computer boom years of '83 and '84.

In 1990 with both children doing well in the media (Sanchia is a BBC Television producer and reporter and Nik is a reporter with *Auto Express* magazine), Berg decided there was a case for 'following in his son's/daughter's footsteps' and returned to writing and production with 'Austins of the 1930s', a film shot in the summer.

The *Sunday Times* said it was "...an outstanding new production" featuring "four cars that, with an excellent script, electrify the small screen."

Flattered and encouraged by this reception he began work on a project which combined his computer knowledge with his love of cars and the old-found writing skills. The result is this book and its smaller sister, *The Guinness Current Car Index*.

Preface

After a year-and-a-half of research and data collection, I now have, or have access to, complete and incomplete information on upwards of 10,000 cars dating from the end of the last century to the present day. At the time of writing more than half a million items of data have been entered in the computer database set up for the project.

Information has been gathered from the archivists of one-make car clubs, from manufacturers' historians, from motoring organisations and from publications dating back to 1880.

As might be expected, the information on old cars tends to be inconsistent and incomplete and it is one of the aims of this project to request, search for, and add data to the database continuously. In this respect, reader's contributions and substantiated corrections are welcome. (Write to me c/o Guinness Publishing.)

The 5,008 cars included in this first edition were, as is made clear in the introduction, selected on the basis of consistency and compatibility of information.

Acknowledgements and thanks

Top of this list is DataEase UK Limited, part of the DataEase International group, which provided the superbly flexible and friendly DataEase 4.2 database software that made this project viable. Particular mention must be made of DataEase Senior Analyst Lee Cox for a yearful of tuition and trouble-shooting.

Next comes the world's longest running motoring magazine for the supply of and permission to use road-test data. *Autocar*, now *Autocar & Motor*, was first published in 1895 and introduced the 'Autocar Road Test' in 1928.

Road & Track road-tests have been keeping American enthusiasts informed for 45 years, both on US built and 'imported' or 'foreign' cars. Thank you *R&T* for permission to use the data from over eight-hundred US and more than fifteen hundred foreign car road-tests.

Thank you to the Automobile Association and AA librarian Mike Passmore for searching out road-tests from 1928 to 1950 from the AA's complete collection of *Autocar*.

To the RAC Motor Sports Association and Neil Eason Gibson for technical advice. Likewise Roy Jackson-Moore of Austin-Healey Bonneville and 50s Aston Martins fame, *Auto Express* Motoring Editor Lawrence Pearce, and consultant Ravi Sikka.

Thank you to all the motor manufacturers who have provided information packs, brochures and books.

Thank you very much co-author and wife Inge. She refuses, for reasons of modesty, a joint credit. I hope that she will accept acknowledgment here for the database design and the entry and husbanding of the half million or more items of data used to produce this book and its smaller sister *The Guinness Current Car Index*.

Members of more than one-hundred-and-seventy one-make car clubs in the US and the UK took the time to fill in 1,500 data sheets. Thanks in particular to Bob Whyte, Daimler & Lanchester Owners Club, Stan Smith, Mercedes Benz Club, and in alphabetical order:

Alfa Romeo 1900 Register ■ *Alfa Romeo Section VSCC* ■ *Alvis Owners Club* ■ *AMC World Clubs Inc* ■ *American Auto Club* ■ *Armstrong-Siddeley Owners Club* ■ *Ashley Register* ■ *Association of Healey Owners* ■ *Aston Martin Owners Club* ■

Aussie Chargers Club ■ Austin 3-litre Drivers Register ■ Austin A30-A35 Owners Club ■ Austin A40 Farina Club ■ Austin Atlantic Owners Club ■ Austin Big 7 Register ■ Austin Counties Car Club ■ Austin Gipsy Register ■ Austin Seven Clubs Association ■ Avenger & Sunbeam Owners Club ■ Bentley Drivers Club ■ Berkeley Enthusiasts Club ■ BMC Cambridge-Oxford Owners Club ■ Bond Owners Club ■ Bristol Owners Club ■ British Saab Enthusiasts ■ British Salmson Owners Club ■ BSA Frontwheel Drive Club ■ Buckler Car Register ■ Buick Club of America ■ Buick GS Club of America ■ Capri Club International ■ Chrysler 300 Club International ■ Citroen Deux Chevaux Club of Great Britain ■ Classic Thunderbird Club International ■ Club Alfa Romeo 2600/2000 International ■ Club Alpine Renault Great Britain ■ Club Elite ■ Club Lotus ■ Club Triumph North London ■ Clyno Register ■ Continental Mark II Owners Association ■ Cougar Club of America ■ Crown Victoria Association ■ DAF Owners Club ■ Datsun Classic Z Register ■ De Tomaso Drivers Club ■ Dellow Register ■ Desoto Club of America ■ Early Ford V8 of America ■ East Yorkshire Micro Maniacs ■ EB Register ■ Edsel Owners Club ■ F & FB (Vauxhall) Victor Owners Club ■ Facel Vega Owners Club ■ Falcon Register ■ Fiat X1/9 Owners Club ■ Fiero Owners Club of America ■ Ford 105E Owners Club ■ Ford Corsair Owners Club ■ Ford Cortina 1600E Owners Club ■ Ford Cortina Mark II Register ■ Ford Executive Owners Register ■ Ford Galaxie Club of America ■ Ford Mark 1/Consul/Zephyr & Zodiac Club ■ Ford Mark II Independent Owners Club ■ Ford Mark II/Consul/Zephyr/Zodiac Club ■ Ford Mk III Zephyr & Zodiac Owners Club ■ Ford Mk IV Zephyr & Zodiac Owners Club ■ Ford Savage Register ■ Ford Sidevalve Owners Club ■ Frazer-Nash Section VSCC ■ Frisky Register ■ Gilbern Owners Club ■ Ginetta Owners Club ■ Gordon Keeble Owners Club ■ GTO Association of America ■ Heinkel Trojan Owners Club ■ Historic Lotus Register ■ Historic Volkswagen Club ■ Holden UK Register ■ Imp Club ■ Imperial Owners Club International ■ International Camaro Club ■ Isetta Owners Club of Great Britain ■ ISO/Bizzarrini Club ■ Jensen Owners Club ■ Jowett Car Club ■ Karmann Ghia Owners Club ■ Lagonda Club ■ Land-Rover Series Two Club ■ Lea-Francis Owners Club ■ Lincoln and Continental Owners Club ■ London Vintage Taxi Association ■ Lotus Seven Club ■ Manta A Series Register ■ Marcos Owners Club ■ Marendaz Special Car Register ■ Markham Peasey Register ■ Marlin Owners Club ■ Matra Enthusiasts' Club ■ Messerschmitt Owners Club ■ Metropolitan Owners Club ■ MG Octagon Car Club ■ Mid-Century Mercury Car Club ■ Midget & Sprite Club ■ Mini Seven Racing Club ■ Morgan Sports Car Club ■ Morris Cowley & Oxford Club ■ Morris Marina Owners Club ■ Morris Minor Owners Club ■ Morris Register ■ Mustang Owners Club International ■ Mustang Owners Club ■ Nineteen Thirty-Two Buick Registry ■ North-East Club for Pre-War Austin ■ NSU Owners Club ■ NSU RO80 Club of Great Britain ■ Ogle

Register ■ Opel Manta Club ■ P6 Rover Owners Club ■ Piper Sports & Racing Club ■ Radford Register ■ Railton Owners Club ■ Raleigh Safety Seven Owners Club ■ Range Rover Register Limited ■ Rapier Register ■ Rear Engine Renault Club ■ Reliant Rebel Register ■ Reliant Sabre & Scimitar Owners Club ■ Reliant Scimitar Drivers Club ■ Reo Club of America ■ Riley Motor Club ■ Riley Register ■ Rochdale Owners Club ■ Rover P5 Owners Club ■ Scootacar Register ■ Simca Owners Register ■ Singer Owners Club ■ Stag Owners Club ■ Star,Starling,Stuart & Briton Register ■ Stevens-Duryea Associates ■ Sunbeam Rapier Owners Club ■ Sunbeam Talbot Darracq Register ■ The 1100 Club ■ The Datsun Z Club ■ The Diva Register ■ The Judge GTO International ■ The Sunbeam Tiger Owners Club ■ Tornado Register ■ TR Register ■ Trident Car Club ■ Triumph 1300 Register ■ Triumph 2000/2500/2.5 Register ■ Triumph Dolomite Sprint Register ■ Triumph Mayflower Club ■ Triumph Razoredge Owners Club ■ Triumph Roadster Club ■ Tucker Automobile Club of America ■ Turner Register ■ TVR Car Club ■ Unipower Owners Club ■ Vauxhall Droop Snoot Group ■ Vauxhall Owners Club ■ Vauxhall PA/PB/PC/E Series Owners Club ■ Vauxhall Viva Owners Club ■ Vauxhall VX4/90 Drivers Club ■ Vintage Austin Register ■ Volkswagen Cabriolet Owners Club ■ Volvo Owners Club ■ VW Type 3 and 4 Club ■ Wolseley 6/80 & Morris Oxford Club ■ Wolseley Hornet Special Club

Ivan Berg May 1992

Introduction

When cycling to school in the late forties I devised and played a car recognition and facts game. If I could name a parked car or a car that passed me I gave myself one point. If I knew the number of cylinders in the engine, there was another point, top speed, one more, and so on to a maximum of ten.

It got so that I could name any car of that period at a distance of a hundred yards. Humber Super Snipe and Pullman, Vauxhall Velox and Wyvern; Standard, Morris, Austin, Rolls-Royce, Daimler, Armstrong Siddeley, Wolseley, Rover; the very occasional Chevrolet, Buick and Nash. Once or twice a Cadillac. Even a 'requisitioned' Mercedes or two.

The game developed into a lifelong habit. I must have produced a special set of synapses to recognise cars and file my ten facts automatically, because it is certainly something I have never done consciously since the age of 13.

I have no way of knowing how many cars and how many facts I have stored in more than forty years. I am not about to issue any challenges but I cannot recall not being able to recognise a car made after World War 2 and come up with a fact or two about it.

Of course I am not alone in this pastime. Since piston first turned crank there has been a fascination with car facts and figures. As a schoolboy I tuned in automatically to the most quoted and most popular. How fast, how powerful, how quick to fifty or sixty, and how many miles to the gallon ? I admired style too but this could only be measured subjectively.

My sources of information were motoring magazines, manufacturer's brochures collected during visits to the post-war London Motor Shows, and the occasional reference book from the library.

The motoring magazines sometimes compared one car with another and even listed the performance figures of a few comparable models. It seemed natural to me to re-assemble these as lists by maximum speed, by nought to sixty times, by miles per gallon.

I never found a book then which did this. I never ever did. It was never a practical proposition to sort more than a few figures. Look at the numbers involved. Take just five interesting figures for a thousand cars, say maximum speed, nought to sixty time, engine brake horse-power, power-to-weight ratio, and bhp per litre. Put each figure on one index card so it can be sorted. That's five thousand index cards. Now sort them in order of maximum speed. Forget it.

Today it is practical. The electronic equivalent of those five thousand cards can be sorted in the order required in just a few minutes on a computer most authors can afford to have at home.

I have one. Hence *The Guinness World Car Record.*

The figures I find interesting start to get reliable after 1928 when the British motoring journal *Autocar* introduced the 'Autocar Road Test'. (Which is why, with a few of notable exceptions, this book deals with cars from 1928.) Many magazines followed suit. Even then the performance figures were somewhat perfunctory, consisting of maximum speeds attained in each gear, and fuel consumption figures provided by the manufacturer which usually turned out to be remarkably similar to that of any comparable car.

In 1934 *Autocar* added acceleration times and timed maximum speeds over the quarter-mile to the road-test data and from 1952 the fuel consumption during the road-test was actually measured and shown as 'overall'.

Road & Track magazine began road-testing in America in 1947. The test format had a good deal in common with *Autocar*'s road-test. Compatibility and consistency of data is of obvious importance if comparisons are to be meaningful, so all the performance figures here are sourced from *Autocar* (*Autocar & Motor* since 1988) and *Road & Track.*

The 'notable exceptions' mentioned in parenthesis above include a 1915 Model T Ford and a 1926 Bugatti which were the subjects, among other early cars, of *R&T* retrospective road-tests.

Being suitably superlative, (this is a Guinness publication after all) there are five thousand and eight cars described in these pages, built between 1928 and March 1992. Each car has up to forty-three dynamic and static facts and figures which are available for comparison with the up to forty-three facts and figures of every other car.

I say *up to* forty-three items. Some cars, particularly those built prior to 1950 will have a lot less, because the information was not available at the time the data was entered. (I hope to fill the gaps with your help in each edition - see preface.)

I make no claims that the facts and figures used are complete or definitive. Simply that they are the best available for the purpose. In a number of cases calculated or claimed figures have been used so that some rare and interesting cars could be included.

Many models have been tested several times through their production lives and the differences, and indeed the similarities, are often surprising.

In the specifications section, readable type and a finite number of pages means around forty lines per car. What is fitted into those forty lines is a mix of personal preference, consultation, and what makes a good component for a comparison list.

The Lists

As readers familiar with computers will know, data can be manipulated in manifold ways. The number and variety of comparative lists which could be produced from the data used in this book is virtually limitless. More lists may be produced than there are stars in the galaxy.

Not all of them would be interesting. How many of us would wish to know the number of cars with leaf springs on the rear suspension which had a ground clearance of less than five inches and where and when and by whom they were built? Or which particular cars made in 1961 have bodies which are between thirty-six and seventy inches longer than their wheelbase?

There are more than a thousand lists here which I hope are interesting. I think they speak for themselves and make no comments other than that I was very surprised at the number of small six-cylinder engines fitted to family cars in the 1930s and the number of straight-eights and V-12s in the same period. You may be astonished to see which cars head some of the lists, how the older cars can still joust with the new, how little fuel consumption has changed over the decades and how much engine power has increased.

The lists mostly have to do with performance. With the figures from more than five thousand cars available, the list size has had to be limited by appropriate criteria. For example more than five hundred cars take seven seconds or less to reach sixty miles-an-hour, so the seven second criterion is reduced to five. The resultant figure of around a hundred is more manageable. The factor used to limit the list size is stated at the top of each list and is either meaningful or arbitrary - depending on the number of cars meeting the initial criteria.

To avoid masses of redundant zeros in the lists all figures have been limited to one decimal place. Where figures appear to be duplicated the ranking order is nevertheless correct because it has been computed by the additional decimal place held in the computer database.

A list can be produced according to one or any number of criteria. One example should suffice. First, the query:

'Make a list comprising cars built between 1925 and 1940 which had a maximum speed of 100mph or more. Order the list by maximum speed and give maximum speed, make, model, year - and because the more sceptical reader will wish to check - the car's reference in the specifications section of this book. Finally give the total number of cars in the list.'

Run the computer.

And the 100mph plus cars built between 1925 and 1940 are:

1 121.0mph 194.7kmh Bugatti 50S 1926: 648
2 120.0mph 193.1kmh Mercedes-Benz SSKL 1929: 2776
3 115.0mph 185.0kmh Duesenberg J Coupe 1930: 1352
Talbot Figoni et Falaschi 1938: 4343
4 112.0mph 180.2kmh Cord 812-S 1937: 1101
5 110.1mph 177.2kmh Lagonda Rapide 1939: 2445
6 110.0mph 177.0kmh Alfa Romeo 8C2300 1932: 41
Bugatti 55 1932: 651
Lagonda Le Mans 1934: 2437
7 108.0mph 173.8kmh Alfa Romeo 2.3 Mille Miglia 1933: 42
Mercedes-Benz 36/220-S 1928: 2774
8 106.8mph 171.8kmh Alfa Romeo Supercharged Straight Eight 1931: 39
9 106.0mph 170.6kmh Duesenberg SJ Town Car 1938: 1353
10 105.0mph 168.9kmh Marmon 16 1932: 2651
Squire X101 1935: 4190
11 104.6mph 168.3kmh Mercedes-Benz Type 540 1938: 2785
12 104.2mph 167.7kmh Lagonda Rapide 1937: 2441
13 104.0mph 167.3kmh Auburn 8-52 Speedster 1936: 264
14 103.4mph 166.4kmh Frazer-Nash BMW Grand Prix 1937: 1989
Lagonda 4.5-litre 12 Cylinder Saloon 1938: 2443
15 102.3mph 164.6kmh Cord 812 1937: 1100
16 102.2mph 164.4kmh Cord Supercharged Saloon 1937: 1102
17 101.1mph 162.7kmh Bentley 8-litre Saloon 1930: 463
Jaguar SS 100 3.5-litre 1938: 2267
18 100.5mph 161.7kmh Lagonda Rapide Tourer 1935: 2439
Mercedes-Benz Type 500 Supercharged 1936: 2782
Railton Light Sports Tourer 1935: 3757
19 100.0mph 160.9kmh Alvis 4.3-litre 1939: 162
Hispano-Suiza 54/220 1934: 2084
Lagonda Saloon de Ville 1938: 2444

Number of cars in list : 30

Bearing in mind the name of my publisher and the reputation of their major work, *The Guinness Book of Records*, I found it difficult to resist the temptation to introduce some oddities. For example, we have power-to-weight ratio, so why not power-to-length ratio expressed as bhp/ft ? And a bhp/ft list. Or speed-to-weight ratio, mph/ton, and list. I shall no doubt receive suggestions aplenty and will include the most original, amusing or practical in the next edition.

LIST OF LISTS

48 ranked lists in sets of eight over time - incorporating means (averages): p. 277.

Using the lists

The list layout is standardised throughout. In ranked lists the first number in each column is the individual car's or group of cars' position in the list, next are the list subject figures followed by make and model or model. The figure after the colon is the car's reference or look-up number in the specifications section of the book.

List of makes in A-Z of Specifications

Car specifications

All figures are to one decimal place.

Each complete car specification consists of:

Car Reference Number
Make
Model
Year made
Country of origin
Maximum speed in mph and kmh
0-50mph and 80.5kmh to 1/10th of a second
0-60mph and 96.5kmh to 1/10th of a second
0-1/4mile to 1/10th of a second
0-1km to 1/10th of a second
bhp, kW and PS and rpm at maximum power
lbft and Nm and rpm at for maximum torque
bhp/ton and bhp/tonne (power-to-weight ratio)
bhp/litre, kW/litre and PS/litre (specific output)
ft/sec and m/sec for piston speed at peak power
mpg mpgUS and L/100km
Engine type and if supercharged or turbocharged
Engine capacity in cc and cu in
Cylinder configuration and fuel system (injection or carburettor)
Compression ratio
Cylinder bore
Cylinder stroke
Valve type and number of valves
Transmission
Number of forward speeds
Wheels driven
Spring type front and rear
Brake system if power-assisted and/or anti-lock
Brake type front and rear
Steering type
Wheelbase in and cm
Front track in and cm
Rear track in and cm
Length in and cm
Width in and cm

Height in and cm
Ground clearance in and cm
Kerb weight kg and lb
Fuel tank capacity in L, gal and galUS

Abbreviations

ABS anti-lock brakes
bhp brake horsepower
bhp/L brake horsepower per litre
bhp/ton brake horsepower per Imperial ton
bhp/tonne brake horsepower per metric tonne
cc cubic centimetres
cm centimetre
cu in cubic inches
F front
ft/sec feet per second
gal gallon
galUS US gallon
in inches
kg kilogrammes
km kilometre
kmh kilometres per hour
kW kilowatts
kW/L kilowatts per litre
L litre
lb pounds
lbft pounds force feet
mpg miles per gallon
mpgUS miles per US gallon
mph miles per hour
mm millimetres
m/sec metres per second
Nm Newton metres
PA power-assisted
PS pferdestarke
PS/L pferdestarke per litre
R rear
rpm revolutions per minute
sec seconds

Explanation of car specifications

Some of the specification items will not be shown for older cars. For example, in the early days brake horse-power and torque and the engine revolutions at which they were obtained were not stated. (If you can fill the knowledge gaps, please do - see preface.)

Reference number:

Cars are ordered alphabetically by make, then by year of manufacture and then by model name. The reference or look-up number will also appear when a car has a place in one of the comparison lists in the lists section of the book.

Make:

In alphabetical order. In recent times some European and Japanese cars have been marketed in the United States under different make names; examples are Acura (Honda), and Sterling (Rover). As the Sterling is not marketed in the US at the time of writing, it has been included with the other Rovers. All Land-Rover and Range Rover vehicles are marketed as Range Rover in the US. An American tested Land-Rover County will therefore appear under Range Rover.

Model:

In alphabetical order by year. The choice of models included is determined by the cars tested in that year in both the UK and the US. Model duplication will occur when a popular car has been tested regularly throughout its production life. Nevertheless the figures will generally be different year by year, and not always in the same direction ! There may also be occasions where the same model appears twice in the same year. This will occur when the car has been tested both in the US and the UK.

Many of the post 1960 model name suffixes will not be familiar to European eyes. These will probably be US modified and have been included because they are or were based upon production cars and are and were available for purchase. Their performance figures will often appear outrageous.

Year:

Cars included in this book were tested between 1928 and March 1992.

Country:

Generally, the country where the vehicle was built. Some modern American joint-venture models will be shown as built in the far east. Japanese cars built or assembled in the UK or USA are listed as Japanese.

Maximum speed:
In miles per hour and kilometres per hour, to one decimal place. This is the maximum speed the vehicle achieved during the road test and is not necessarily the mean of two or more runs.

Older cars' maximum speeds were generally arrived at by timing the vehicle over a quarter-mile.

0-50mph 80.5kmh, 0-60mph 96.5kmh, 0-1/4 mile and 0-1km:

The time in seconds to one decimal place taken by the car to accelerate from standstill to the measured speed or distance from a standing start. Usually the best of several starts. Nowadays a brutal test conducted by taking the engine revolutions to peak power and dropping the clutch. Wheelspin replaces clutch-slip. Tests hardiness of complete drive-train. Not at all appropriate for the older cars.

Maximum power:
The maximum power produced by the engine of the car when tested by the manufacturer (usually) on a dynamometer. Shown in brake horse-power, kilowatts and the EC PS measure to one decimal place. The engine revolutions per minute, (rpm) at which the maximum power was achieved is also given. Maximum or peak power does not necessarily correlate with the engine's maximum rpm.

Maximum torque:
This figure is also measured by the manufacturer and represents the maximum twisting force or pulling power of the engine. Shown in pounds/feet (lbft) and Newton/metres (Nm). The rpm at which this maximum figure was achieved is also given. There is not necessarily any correlation between maximum rpm and maximum torque.

Power to weight ratio:
Here expressed as bhp/ton (Imperial) and bhp/tonne (Metric). Often stated in other publications as bhp/pound and bhp/kilo. This is an interesting figure, produced by dividing the bhp by the kerb weight and multiplying the result by either 2240 for bhp ton or 1000 for bhp tonne. The figure is interesting because, unlike specific output, (bhp per litre), it can bear a direct relationship to the accelerative power of the car.

Specific output:
This has to do with engine efficiency. The more power that can be squeezed from each cubic centimetre of engine capacity the better. Expressed here as bhp/litre,

kW/litre and PS/litre. The figure is produced by dividing the power figure by the engine metric cubic capacity and multiplying the result by 1000 (ccs per litre).

There are many ways of improving an engine's specific output, and they tend to come in fashions. Superchargers were the bee's knees in the 1930s and have since regained favour, notably with Volkswagen. Turbocharging was in during the late 1970s and for most of the 1980s. In the 1950s the done thing was to increase compression ratios, add or change carburettors and polish ports. The latter part of the 1980s saw a trend towards more valves - up to five per cylinder, (eight per cylinder in the case of Honda's oval-piston NR750 motor-cycle engine) and the fitting of variable air intake systems.

The keen-eyed will note that Mazda RX-7s and NSU Ro80s and Spyders come high on the lists for specific output for normally aspirated engines. (Not turbocharged or supercharged.) This is because they have Wankel rotary engines, and as these produce three power-strokes per rotor on every revolution of the crankshaft, they need less capacity then a conventional four-stroke engine for a similar power output.

In the UK and Europe rotary engine capacity is usually increased artificially by multiplying by 1.8. The accepted method of measuring the capacity of a Wankel rotary engine, used by most engineers and in the US, is to take the difference between the largest and smallest volume of one rotor chamber and multilply that by the number of chambers. Not dissimilar to the way a piston engine's capacity is measured.

Piston speed at peak power:
Expressed in feet and metres per second. In the days when very long-stroke (piston stroke greater than cylinder bore) engines were the norm piston speeds in excess of 2500 feet per minute (41.6ftsec here) were deemed to produce excessive main-bearing loads. There was a preoccupation with 'big-ends' as they were known, right up until the 1960s, the failure of which caused no end of head-shaking.

Today's high-revving engines suffer to a far lesser degree and piston speeds are very much higher. Main bearings these days fail more from lack of lubrication caused by poor maintenance than from excessive loading.

Nevertheless the figure is interesting because of its relationship with bore and stroke and engine rpm. It is produced by doubling the cylinder stroke, multiplying the result by the engine rpm at peak power and dividing that result first by 1000 and then by 60.

Fuel consumption:
Autocar & Motor and *Road & Track* are incompatible on this one. *Road & Track*

quotes an 'average' or 'normal driving' figure, while *Autocar & Motor*'s 'overall' fuel consumption figure is the result of dividing the number of miles driven on the test by the amount of fuel used.

(On the basis that only like can be compared with like if comparisons are to be meaningful, there are two lists for fuel consumption, one according to *Autocar & Motor*, the other according to *Road & Track*.)

These figures are by no means definitive and they may bear no relation to manufacturer's figures, other road tests, or your own experience. They are different from the constant speed measurements and 'Urban' figures produced using the EC criteria.

In the case of *Autocar & Motor* they are nevertheless figures achieved by the driving of the car throughout a reasonably standardised road test, one which has stayed pretty much in its present form since 1952. The figures may well be lower than figures found elsewhere, sometimes alarmingly so as the car will have been driven hard throughout.

Engine type:
With the exceptions of the two electrically engined cars, all engines are diesel or petrol, two-stroke, four-stroke or rotary, and may be turbocharged or supercharged.

Engine capacity:
This is the capacity of an engine cylinder chamber, measured with the piston at the bottom of its stroke, multiplied by the number of cylinders. (For Wankel rotary engines see Specific output, above). Nearly always measured in cubic centimetres, though most Americans remain loyal to the cubic inch. Both are found here. If specified, a turbocharger or supercharger is also listed here.

Configuration:
Consists of cylinder configuration, number of cylinders, number of carburettors or fuel injection.

An engine which has its cylinders arranged one behind the other is called IN-LINE. If the cylinders are horizontally opposed, as in the Porsche 911, VW Beetle, and some Ferraris and Lancias, the engine is FLAT. In a VEE configuration two banks of one, two, three, four, five, six, or eight cylinders are set at an angle to each other. VEE engines cram a lot of power into a little space.

Compression ratio:
The amount by which the fuel mixture is compressed during the cylinder or rotor compression stroke prior to its ignition. Ratios in petrol engines rarely exceed

12.5:1. Diesel engines which rely on the compression of the fuel mixture for ignition can have ratios as high as 25:1

Bore and stroke:
Normally measured in millimetres, also in inches here. Not given for rotary engines. The bore is the diameter of the cylinder, and the stroke is the distance travelled by the piston during half a revolution of the crankshaft. The terminologies are OVERSQUARE, when the bore is greater than the stroke (short-stroke), SQUARE, when the bore is equal to the stroke, and UNDERSQUARE, when the stroke is greater than the bore (long-stroke). As a rule, long-stroke engines produce high torque at low engine revolutions and short-stroke engines produce high power at high revolutions.

Valve type and No:
Virtually all modern four-stroke piston engines employ overhead-valves, to inlet the fuel charge and exhaust the spent gas. Rotary engines have inlet and exhaust ports which are opened and closed for the same purpose by the motion of the rotor.

Overhead valves can be operated indirectly by pushrods and rockers actuated by a gear driven camshaft in the engine block, or directly by overhead camshafts. High performance engines, almost always those with multi-valve cylinder heads, use one or more overhead camshafts - one camshaft to operate the inlet valves, the other the exhaust valves. Thus a twin-overhead camshaft VEE 8 engine will have 4 camshafts, 2 for each bank of cylinders.

The number of valves on most production engines used to be two per cylinder - one inlet valve, one exhaust valve. Then, in the cause of greater efficiency another inlet valve was introduced, then another exhaust valve, then another inlet valve. Currently very few engines have more than five valves per cylinder, the exception being the eight-valve Honda NR750 mentioned earlier. The highest number of valves here is 64, comprising four valves per cylinder on a sixteen cylinder engine.

Transmission:
Categorised as manual, manual with overdrive, automatic, pre- selector, and continously variable.

No. of forward speeds: (gears)
Where specified, the number of overdrive speeds (gears) has been added to the total. Thus, a car with a four-speed gearbox with overdrive available on third and top, is shown as having six forward speeds.

Wheels driven:
Shown as front, rear, 4-wheel drive and 4-wheel engageable.

Springs Front/Rear:

Spring types are classified as leaf, coil, torsion-bar and gas - which also covers air springs, hydro-pneumatic and hydragas systems.

Brake system:

Power-assisted (PA) and anti-lock (ABS) if specified.

Brakes Front/Rear:

Shown as Disc/Disc, Disc/Drum or Drum/Drum.

Steering:

Type of steering, i.e., rack and pinion, re-circulating ball, ball and nut etc., and whether power-assisted (PA). The two most popular systems in modern cars are rack and pinion and re-circulating ball. The enthusiast will claim that rack and pinion gives the best steering feel and response.

Wheelbase:

The distance between front and rear wheels measured from the centre of the wheels. Long wheelbase, narrow track cars tend to be good in a straight line. Short wheelbase, wide track cars can be very good at changing direction, often when you don't want them to.

Track Front/Rear:

The distance between the front/rear wheels measured from the centre of the tyre tread.

Length:

Overall. Measured from bumper to bumper. Foreign cars specified for the US market have often been longer overall in order to meet bumper regulations.

Width:

Overall. Some discrepancies may have crept in here as width overall can (in some difficult to identify cases) mean either including or excluding mirrors.

Height:

Overall. Normally measured without passengers.

Kerb weight:

Weight at the time of test, generally with a half-full fuel tank and no passengers.

Fuel tank capacity:

As specified by the manufacturer.

LISTS

21 lists by country

5008 cars ordered by year made, make and model, with country totals.

Australia

1952 Holden Saloon: 2085

1960 Chrysler Valiant: 974

1966 Chrysler Valiant Premium Auto: 986

1969 Holden Brougham: 2086

1970 Chrysler Charger: 990

1990 Mercury Capri XR-2: 2961

Australia total: 6

Austria

1931 Austro Daimler 32/100 Saloon: 448

1957 Denzel 1300: 1255

Austria total: 2

Brazil

1973 Volkswagen SP-2: 4791

1987 Volkswagen Fox GL: 4861

Brazil total: 2

Czechoslovakia

1932 Tatra 12hp Drop-head Coupe: 4349

1960 Skoda Octavia: 4182

1961 Skoda Felicia: 4183

1965 Skoda 1000MB: 4184

1970 Skoda S100L: 4185

1972 Skoda S110LS: 4186

1977 Skoda 120L: 4187

1986 Skoda Estelle 120 LSE: 4188

1989 Skoda 136 Rapide Coupe: 4189

Czechoslovakia total: 9

E. Germany

1967 Wartburg Knight: 4970

1973 Wartburg Knight: 4971

E. Germany total: 2

France

1926 Bugatti 50S: 648

1928 Delage 21hp Weymann Saloon: 1245

1929 Delaunay-Belleville 21hp Saloon: 1253

1930 Amilcar Straight Eight Saloon: 207
Bugatti 49: 649
Citroen Six Saloon: 1010
Delage 18.2hp Saloon: 1246
Delage Straight Eight Sports Saloon: 1247
Panhard 18hp Saloon: 3364
Renault Vivasix Saloon: 3797
Tracta Sports Two-seater: 4484

1931 Bugatti 5-litre Saloon: 650
Delage Super Sports Straight Eight: 1248

1932 Bugatti 55: 651
Darracq Straight Eight Saloon: 1156

1933 Delage D6-11 Sports Saloon: 1249
Hotchkiss 3.5-litre Coupe: 2161

1934 Hotchkiss Paris-Nice Speed Model: 2162

1935 Hotchkiss Paris-Nice Saloon: 2163
Renault 12.1hp Airline Saloon: 3798
Renault 24hp Big Six Saloon: 3799

1936 Citroen Super Model Twelve: 1011
Citroen Super Modern Fifteen Saloon: 1012
Delahaye 23.8hp Drop-head Coupe: 1252

1937 Citroen Sports Twelve Saloon: 1013
Delage D6-70 Sports Coupe: 1250
Hotchkiss 28hp Cabourg Saloon: 2164
Renault 17.9hp Touring Saloon: 3800

1938 Delage D8-120 Super Sports: 1251
Hotchkiss 3.5-litre Saloon: 2165
Talbot Figoni et Falaschi: 4343

1940 Citroen Light Fifteen Roadster: 1014

1948 Citroen Light Fifteen: 1015
Renault 4CV: 3801

1949 Citroen Six Saloon: 1016

1951 Simca 8 Sport: 4129

1952 Citroen Light Fifteen: 1017
Ford Comete: 1625
Simca Aronde: 4130

1953 Citroen 11CV: 1018
Citroen 2CV Cabriolet: 1019
Citroen Big Fifteen: 1020
Renault 750: 3802

1954 Citroen Six: 1021
Panhard Dyna: 3365
Panhard Dyna Junior Sports: 3366
Simca Aronde: 4131

1955 Citroen 2CV: 1022
Peugeot 203: 3384
Peugeot 403: 3385
Renault 4CV: 3803
Renault 750: 3804
Simca Aronde: 4132

1956 Citroen DS19: 1023
Facel Vega Coupe: 1364
Panhard Dyna Sedan: 3367
Renault Dauphine: 3805
Simca Elysee: 4133
Simca Sports Coupe: 4134

1957 Citroen DS19: 1024
Deutsch-Bonnet Coupe: 1256
Renault Dauphine: 3806
Simca Versailles V8: 4135

1958 Citroen ID19: 1025
Facel Vega FVS: 1365
Renault Dauphine Ferry: 3807
Renault Fregate Transfluide: 3808
Simca Aronde Montlhery: 4136
Simca Vedette Beaulieu: 4137

1959 Lago America: 2431
Panhard Dyna: 3368
Panhard PL17: 3369
Renault Carvelle: 3809
Renault Dauphine: 3810
Renault Dauphine Gordini: 3811
Simca Elysee: 4138

1960 Citroen ID Safari: 1026
Citroen ID19: 1027
Facel Vega HK-500: 1366
Peugeot 403: 3386
Peugeot 404: 3387
Renault Caravelle: 3812
Renault Floride: 3813
Simca Etoile: 4139
Simca Oceane: 4140
Simca Vedette V8: 4141

1961 Citroen Bijou: 1028
Citroen DS: 1029
Facel Vega Facellia 1600: 1367
Peugeot 404: 3388

Renault Dauphine Gordini: 3814
Simca Aronde Montlhery: 4142

1962 Citroen Ami 6: 1030
Facel Vega Facel II: 1368
Panhard PL17 Tiger: 3370
Peugeot 403 B Estate Car: 3389
Peugeot 404 U6 Estate Car: 3390
Renault Caravelle S: 3815
Renault Dauphine: 3816
Renault Dauphine Gordini de Luxe: 3817
Renault R8: 3818
Simca 1000: 4143
Simca 5: 4144

1963 Citroen DS: 1031
Renault 4 L Estate Car: 3819
Renault Dauphine Automatic: 3820
Renault Floride Caravelle: 3821
Renault R8: 3822
Simca 1000: 4145
Simca 1000 Special: 4146
Simca 1300GL: 4147

1964 Panhard 24CT Sports Coupe: 3371
Renault R8 1100: 3823
Simca 1500: 4148

1965 Citroen DS21 Pallas M: 1032
Citroen DSM: 1033
Peugeot 404: 3391
Peugeot 404 Diesel: 3392
Peugeot 404 KF2: 3393
Renault 8 Gordini: 3824
Renault Caravelle: 3825
Renault R8 Rally: 3826
Simca 1500GL Estate: 4149

1966 Citroen DS21: 1034
Peugeot 204: 3394
Renault 1100 Automatic: 3827
Renault 16 GL: 3828
Renault 4 Estate Car: 3829
Simca 1000GLS: 4150

1967 Citroen Ami 6 Break: 1035
Peugeot 404 Automatique: 3395
Peugeot 404 L Estate: 3396
Renault 10: 3830
Renault 8 Gordini 1300: 3831
Simca 1000GLS: 4151
Simca 1301: 4152

1968 Citroen DS21 Safari: 1036
Peugeot 204 Coupe: 3397
Peugeot 404 Station Wagon: 3398
Peugeot 504 Injection: 3399
Renault 16: 3832
Simca 1100GLS: 4153

1969 Matra M530A: 2682
Peugeot 404 Automatic: 3400
Renault 16 TS: 3833
Renault 6: 3834
Simca 1204: 4154
Simca 1501 Special Estate: 4155

1970 Citroen Ami 8 Club: 1037
Citroen DS21 EFI 139 Pallas: 1038
Peugeot 504: 3401
Renault 10: 3835
Renault 12 TL: 3836
Simca 1204 Special: 4156

1971 Citroen GS: 1039
Citroen Safari 21: 1040
Citroen Safari SM: 1041
Peugeot 304: 3402
Peugeot 504 Automatic: 3403
Renault 16 TL Automatic: 3837
Renault 6 1100: 3838

1972 Citroen GS: 1042
Citroen SM: 1043
Peugeot 204: 3404
Peugeot 304 Estate Car: 3405
Peugeot 504 Family Estate: 3406
Renault 12 Estate: 3839
Renault 12 TL: 3840
Renault 15 Coupe: 3841
Renault 15 TL: 3842
Renault 16 TS: 3843

1973 Citroen GS 1220: 1044
Citroen Safari SM: 1045
Peugeot 104: 3407
Peugeot 504: 3408
Peugeot 504 Diesel: 3409
Renault 17: 3844
Renault 5 TL: 3845

1974 Peugeot 504 L Diesel: 3410
Peugeot 504 Station Wagon: 3411
Renault 6 TL: 3846
Simca 1100 Special: 4157

1975 Citroen 2CV6: 1046
Citroen CX 2000: 1047
Citroen GS Pallas: 1048
Matra-Simca Bagheera: 2684
Peugeot 504: 3412
Peugeot 604: 3413
Renault 12: 3847
Renault 17 Gordini: 3848
Renault 5 TS: 3849

1976 Citroen CX 2200 Pallas: 1049
Citroen GS X2: 1050
Peugeot 104: 3414
Peugeot 104 ZS: 3415
Renault 15 GTL: 3850
Renault 17 Gordini: 3851
Renault 20 TL: 3852
Renault 30 TS: 3853
Renault 5 GTL: 3854

1977 Citroen CX 2200 Diesel: 1051
Citroen CX 2400: 1052
Citroen CX 2400 GTi: 1053
Peugeot 504 Diesel Automatique: 3416
Peugeot 604 SLV-6: 3417
Renault 12 TL: 3855
Renault 14: 3856
Renault 17 TS: 3857
Renault 20 TS: 3858
Simca 1000LS: 4158

1978 Citroen CX Pallas C-Matic Injection: 1054
Matra Rancho: 2683
Peugeot 305 SR: 3418
Renault 30 TS: 3859
Renault 5 Automatic: 3860

1979 Citroen Athena: 1055
Citroen CX 2500 Diesel Super: 1056
Citroen Visa Club: 1057
Peugeot 504: 3419
Peugeot 505 STI: 3420
Peugeot 604: 3421
Renault 18 GTS: 3861
Renault 18 TS Estate: 3862
Renault 30 TX: 3863
Renault 5 Gordini: 3864
Renault 5 Racer: 3865
Renault 5 TL: 3866
Renault Gordini: 3867
Renault Le Car: 3868

1980 Peugeot 505 S: 3422
Peugeot 505 SD: 3423
Peugeot 604 D Turbo: 3424

1981 Citroen CX Pallas: 1058
Peugeot 305 S: 3425
Peugeot 505 S Turbodiesel: 3426
Renault 14 TS: 3869
Renault 18 Turbo: 3870
Renault 18i: 3871
Renault 20 TX: 3872
Renault 5 Turbo: 3873
Renault Le Car Turbo: 3874

1982 Peugeot 505 GR Estate: 3427
Peugeot 505 STI: 3428
Renault 18 GTX Estate: 3875
Renault 5 Gordini Turbo: 3876
Renault 9 GLT: 3877
Renault 9 TC: 3878
Renault 9 TSE: 3879
Renault Alliance DL: 3880
Renault Fuego GTS: 3881
Renault Fuego Turbo: 3882

1983 Citroen BX14 RE: 1059
Citroen BX16 TRS: 1060
Peugeot 205 GR: 3429
Peugeot 305 SR: 3430
Renault 11 TSE: 3883
Renault Fuego Turbo: 3884

1984 Citroen BX19 RD Diesel: 1061
Citroen CX GTi Turbo: 1062
Citroen LNA 11RE: 1063
Citroen Visa Convertible: 1064
Peugeot 205 GTi: 3431
Peugeot 505 GRi: 3432
Peugeot 505 S Wagon: 3433
Renault 25 V6: 3885
Renault 5 Turbo 2: 3886
Renault Fuego: 3887
Renault Fuego 2.2: 3888

1985 Citroen 2CV6 Charleston: 1065
Citroen BX16 TRS Automatic: 1066
Citroen CX22 TRS: 1067
Citroen Visa 14TRS: 1068
Citroen Visa 17RD: 1069
Citroen Visa GTi: 1070
Peugeot 205 XL: 3434
Peugeot 305 GRD Estate: 3435
Peugeot 309 1.3 GL: 3436
Peugeot 505 Turbo: 3437
Renault 25 V6 Turbo: 3889
Renault 5 TSE: 3890
Renault Encore GS: 3891
Renault Espace 2000 TSE: 3892

1986 Citroen BX19 RD Estate: 1071
Citroen CX25 Ri Familiale Auto: 1072
Citroen Visa GTi: 1073
Peugeot 205 GTi: 3438
Peugeot 309 1.6 GR: 3439
Peugeot 309 SR Injection: 3440
Peugeot 505 GTi Family Estate: 3441
Peugeot 505 Turbo: 3442
Renault 21 GTS: 3893
Renault 21 Savanna GTX: 3894
Renault 5 GT Turbo: 3895
Renault 5 GTL 5-door: 3896
Renault 9 Turbo: 3897
Renault Alliance 1.7L: 3898
Renault GTA V6 Turbo: 3899

1987 Citroen AX GT: 1074
Citroen AX11 TRE: 1075
Citroen AX14 TRS: 1076
Citroen BX GTi 16v: 1077
Citroen CX25 DTR Turbo 2: 1078
MVS Venturi GT: 3190
Peugeot 205 GTi 1.9: 3443
Peugeot 309 GTi: 3444
Peugeot 505 STX: 3445
Renault 11 Turbo: 3900
Renault 5 GT Turbo: 3901
Renault 5 GTX 3-DR: 3902
Renault Alliance GTA: 3903

1988 Citroen AX11 TRE 5DR: 1079
Citroen BX DTR Turbo: 1080
Peugeot 405 1.6 GL: 3446
Peugeot 405 GRD: 3447
Peugeot 405 Mi16: 3448
Peugeot 405 SRi: 3449
Renault 21 Ti: 3904
Renault 21 Turbo: 3905
Renault GTA V6: 3906

1989 Citroen AX14 DTR: 1081
Citroen BX14 TGE: 1082
Peugeot 205 1.1GL: 3450
Peugeot 205 CJ: 3451
Peugeot 309 GLX: 3452
Peugeot 309 GTi: 3453
Peugeot 405 GTD Turbo: 3454
Peugeot 405 Mi16: 3455
Renault 19 TSE: 3907
Renault 19 TXE: 3908
Renault 21 GTS Hatchback: 3909
Renault 25 TXi: 3910
Renault 5 Campus: 3911
Renault Espace TXE: 3912

1990 Citroen AX GT5: 1083
Citroen BX GTi 4x4: 1084
Citroen CX25 GTi Turbo 2 CX Auto: 1085
Citroen XM 2.0SEi: 1086
MVS Venturi: 3191
Peugeot 309 Style 5-door: 3456
Peugeot 405 GLx4: 3457
Peugeot 405 GR Injection Auto: 3458
Peugeot 405 Mi16x4: 3459
Peugeot 405 Turbo 16 Pike's Peak: 3460
Peugeot 605 SRi: 3461
Renault 19 TXE Chamade: 3913
Renault 21 Turbo Quadra: 3914
Renault 21 TXi: 3915
Renault 25 V6 2.9 Auto: 3916

1991 Citroen AX11 TZX: 1087
Citroen XM 3.0 SEi Auto: 1088
Citroen XM V6.24: 1089
Citroen ZX 1.4 Avantage: 1090
Citroen ZX Volcane: 1091
Peugeot 106 XR: 3462

Peugeot 106 XSi: 3463
Peugeot 205 D Turbo: 3464
Peugeot 605 SR TD: 3465
Peugeot 605 SV 3.0 Auto: 3466
Peugeot 605 SVE 24: 3467
Renault 19 16v: 3917
Renault Alpine A610 Turbo: 3918
Renault Clio 1.2 RN: 3919
Renault Clio 1.4RT: 3920
Renault Espace V6: 3921

1992 Citroen AX GTi: 1092
Citroen XM Turbo SD Estate: 1093
Peugeot 106 XT: 3468
Renault 19 16v Cabriolet: 3922
Renault Cleo 16v: 3923

France total: 369

Germany

1928 Mercedes-Benz 36/220-S: 2774

1929 Mercedes-Benz 32/90 Saloon: 2775
Mercedes-Benz SSKL: 2776

1930 Mercedes-Benz 32/90 Limousine: 2777

1931 Mercedes-Benz 21/60 Coupe: 2778

1934 DKW 7.1hp Cabriolet: 1259
Mercedes-Benz 12hp Rear-engined Saloon: 2779

1935 British Adler 13.67 Cabriolet: 641
Frazer-Nash BMW 12.5hp Saloon: 1987
Frazer-Nash BMW Type 55 Cabriolet: 1988
Mercedes-Benz Type 290 Cabriolet: 2780

1936 Mercedes-Benz 20.8hp Diesel Saloon: 2781
Mercedes-Benz Type 500 Supercharged: 2782

1937 DKW 7.1hp Cabriolet: 1260
Frazer-Nash BMW Grand Prix Two-seater: 1989
Mercedes-Benz Type 230 Saloon: 2783
Opel Kadet Saloon: 3306

1938 Frazer-Nash BMW Type 326 Saloon: 1990
Mercedes-Benz Type 320 Saloon: 2784
Mercedes-Benz Type 540: 2785
Opel Olympia Saloon: 3307

1939 Frazer-Nash BMW Type 327 Cabriolet: 1991

1952 Mercedes-Benz 170S: 2786
Mercedes-Benz 300: 2787
Mercedes-Benz 300SL Carrera Panamericana: 2788
Porsche 356 4: 3601
Volkswagen Sedan de Luxe: 4738

1953 Mercedes-Benz 300 Sedan: 2789
Volkswagen Export Saloon: 4739

1954 DKW Sonderklasse: 1261
Mercedes-Benz 180 Saloon: 2790
Porsche 356: 3602
Porsche Super Coupe: 3603
Volkswagen De Luxe: 4740
Volkswagen Sedan: 4741
Volkswagen Sedan TC: 4742

1955 Borgward Isabella 1500: 630
DKW 3-6: 1262
Mercedes-Benz 190SL: 2791
Mercedes-Benz 300B: 2792
Mercedes-Benz 300SL: 2793
Mercedes-Benz 300SL Coupe: 2794
Mercedes-Benz 300SLR: 2795
Porsche 1500 S Speedster: 3604
Volkswagen Sedan Supercharged: 4743

1956 BMW 501: 498
BMW Isetta Motocoupe: 499
Borgward Isabella TS: 631
DKW 3-6: 1263
DKW Karavan: 1264
Ford Taunus 15M: 1640
Porsche 1600: 3605
Porsche Carrera Coupe: 3606
Porsche Continental Coupe: 3607
Porsche Continental Speedster: 3608
Volkswagen Karmann-Ghia: 4744
Volkswagen Micro Bus: 4745
Volkswagen Sedan: 4746

1957 BMW 507: 500
Goliath 1100 Sedan: 2005
Goliath 900: 2006
Mercedes-Benz 219: 2796
Porsche 1600 Coupe: 3609
Porsche 550 Spyder: 3610
Volkswagen Karmann-Ghia Okrasa: 4747
Volkswagen Sedan Judson: 4748

1958 Auto Union 1000: 449
BMW 600: 501
BMW Isetta 300: 502
Borgward Isabella Coupe: 632
Borgward Isabella TS: 633
DKW 3-6 Sonderklasse Coupe: 1265
Ford Taunus 17M: 1647
Lloyd LP 600: 2588
Mercedes-Benz 180D: 2797
Mercedes-Benz 190SL: 2798
Mercedes-Benz 220S: 2799
Mercedes-Benz 300SL Roadster: 2800
Messerschmitt (FMR) Tg 500: 2966
Opel Rekord: 3308
Porsche 1600: 3611
Porsche 1600 Super Speedster: 3612
Porsche RSK: 3613
Volkswagen De Luxe Saloon: 4750

1959 Auto Union 1000: 450
Ford Taunus 17M Estate: 1652
Goggomobil TS400: 2004
Goliath Tiger: 2007
Mercedes-Benz 220SE: 2801
NSU Prinz 34hp: 3256
NSU Prinz II: 3257
Porsche 1600 Convertible D: 3614

1960 BMW 700: 503
Borgward 2.3 Grosse: 634
Borgward Isabella TS: 635
Borgward Isabella TS Coupe: 636
DKW 750: 1266
Ford Taunus 17M: 1659
Mercedes-Benz 190SL: 2802
Mercedes-Benz 220: 2803
Mercedes-Benz 220SE: 2804
NSU Sport-Prinz: 3258
Porsche Super 75: 3615
Porsche Super 90 Cabriolet: 3616
Volkswagen De Luxe: 4751
Volkswagen Sedan: 4752

1961 Auto Union Universal: 451
DKW Junior: 1267
Ford Taunus 17M: 1664
Mercedes-Benz 190: 2805
Mercedes-Benz 220SE Coupe: 2806
Mercedes-Benz 300SL Roadster: 2807
Porsche 1600 N: 3617
Volkswagen 1500: 4753
Volkswagen Karmann Ghia: 4754
Volkswagen Sedan: 4755
Volkswagen Station Wagon: 4756
Volkswagen Van: 4757

1962 BMW 700 Coupe: 504
DKW Junior de Luxe: 1268
Mercedes-Benz 300SE: 2808
NSU Prinz 4: 3259
Porsche Carrera 2-litre: 3618
Porsche Super 90 Cabriolet: 3619
Volkswagen 1200 de Luxe: 4758
Volkswagen 1500: 4759
Volkswagen Karmann-Ghia: 4760
Volkswagen Sedan EMPI: 4761

1963 BMW 1500: 505
BMW 1800 Saloon: 506
Mercedes-Benz 190C Automatic: 2809
Mercedes-Benz 230SL: 2810
Volkswagen 1500 Estate: 4762
Volkswagen Karmann-Ghia 1500: 4763

1964 BMW 700 LS: 507
Mercedes-Benz 230SL: 2811
Mercedes-Benz 300SE LWB: 2812
Opel Kadett: 3309
Porsche 356 C: 3620
Porsche 904 Carrera GTS: 3621
Volkswagen 1500S: 4764

1965 BMW 1800 Ti: 508
Ford Taunus 20M: 1726
Glas 1300GT: 1999
Mercedes-Benz 190D: 2813
Mercedes-Benz 220SE: 2814
Mercedes-Benz 230SL Automatic: 2815
Mercedes-Benz 600: 2816
NSU Prinz 1000L: 3260
NSU Spider: 3261
NSU Wankel Spider: 3262
Opel Diplomat: 3310
Porsche 911: 3622
Porsche 912: 3623
Volkswagen 1200: 4765
Volkswagen 1300: 4766

1966 Auto Union Audi: 452
BMW 2000: 509
BMW 2000 CS: 510
BMW 2000 Ti: 511
Glas 1700GT: 2000
Mercedes-Benz 230 Automatic: 2817
Mercedes-Benz 250S: 2818
Mercedes-Benz 300D: 2819
NSU Typ 110: 3263
Opel Kadett S: 3311
Porsche 911 S: 3624
Porsche 912: 3625
Volkswagen 1300: 4767
Volkswagen 1300 de Luxe: 4768
Volkswagen 1500: 4769
Volkswagen 1600 Fastback: 4770
Volkswagen 1600 TL: 4771

1967 Auto Union Audi Super 90: 453
BMW 1600 Coupe: 512
BMW 1600-2: 513
BMW 2000 TiLux: 514
Frazer-Nash BMW 2000TI: 1992
Mercedes-Benz 250SE: 2820
Mercedes-Benz 600: 2821
Opel Kadett Rallye: 3312
Opel Rekord Coupe: 3313
Porsche 911 S: 3626
Volkswagen 1500: 4772
Volkswagen Beetle 1500: 4773

1968 BMW 2000 CS: 515
BMW 2002: 516
Mercedes-Benz 220: 2822
Mercedes-Benz 250: 2823
Mercedes-Benz 250 Automatic: 2824
Mercedes-Benz 280SL: 2825
NSU Ro80: 3264
NSU Super Prinz: 3265
Opel Kadette Rallye 1.9: 3314
Opel Station Wagon 1.1: 3315
Opel Station Wagon 1.5: 3316
Opel Station Wagon 1.9: 3317
Porsche 911 E Sportomatic: 3627
Porsche 911 Sportomatic: 3628
Volkswagen 1500 Automatic: 4774
Volkswagen 1500 Semi-automatic: 4775
Volkswagen 1600 Squareback: 4776
Volkswagen 1600 TL Automatic: 4777
Volkswagen 411 L: 4778
Volkswagen Derby LS: 4779

1969 Auto Union 100 LS: 454
BMW 2000 Tilux: 517
BMW 2002: 518
BMW 2500: 519
Mercedes-Benz 220: 2826
Mercedes-Benz 280SL: 2827
Mercedes-Benz 300SEL 6.3: 2828
Opel Commodore GS Coupe: 3318
Opel GT: 3319
Opel GT 1.9: 3320
Opel GT 1900: 3321
Opel Kadett Rallye 1.9: 3322
Porsche 911 E: 3629
Porsche 911 T: 3630
Volkswagen 1600 Squareback: 4780

1970 Audi 100 LS: 265
BMW 2002 Automatic: 520
BMW 2800 CS: 521
Ford Capri Plus 50: 1782
Ford Maverick: 1786
Mercedes-Benz 250 Coupe: 2829
Mercedes-Benz 280SE: 2830
Mercedes-Benz 280SE 3.5: 2831
Mercedes-Benz 280SL: 2832
Opel Diplomat: 3323
Opel Manta Rallye 1.9: 3324
Opel Senator: 3325
Porsche 911 S 2.2-litre: 3631
Porsche 911 T: 3632
Porsche 914: 3633
Porsche 914 6: 3634

Volkswagen 411 LE Variant: 4781
Volkswagen Porsche 914: 4782
Volkswagen Super Beetle: 4783

1971 Audi 100 LS Auto: 266
BMW 2002: 522
BMW 2002 Tii: 523
BMW 3.0 CS: 524
BMW 3.0S: 525
BMW Bavaria: 526
Ford Capri 2000: 1791
Mercedes-Benz 220D: 2833
Mercedes-Benz 300SL: 2834
Opel Ascona Voyage: 3326
Opel GT: 3327
Opel Rallye 1900: 3328
Porsche 911 E 2.4-litre: 3635
Porsche 911 T Sportomatic: 3636
Volkswagen 411: 4784
Volkswagen Porsche 914/b: 4785
Volkswagen Super Beetle: 4786
Volkswagen Van: 4787

1972 Audi 100 Coupe S: 267
BMW 2002 Tii: 527
BMW 2002 TransAm: 528
Ford Capri 2600 V6: 1803
Ford Capri RS2600: 1805
Mercedes-Benz 280SE 3.5: 2835
Mercedes-Benz 280SEL: 2836
Mercedes-Benz 350SL: 2837
Opel Rekord 1900: 3329
Porsche 911 E: 3637
Volkswagen K70: 4788

1973 Audi 100 LS: 268
Audi 80 LS: 269
Audi Fox: 270
BMW 3.0 CS: 529
BMW 3.0 CSL: 530
BMW 520i: 531
BMW Bavaria: 532
Mercedes-Benz 230/4: 2838
Mercedes-Benz 280: 2839
Mercedes-Benz 280CE Auto: 2840
Mercedes-Benz 280SE: 2841
Mercedes-Benz 450SE: 2842
Mercedes-Benz 450SLC: 2843
Opel 1900 Station Wagon: 3330
Opel Ascona 1900SR: 3331
Opel Commodore GS Coupe: 3332
Opel GT: 3333
Opel Manta: 3334
Opel Manta Berlinetta Auto: 3335
Porsche 911 S: 3638
Porsche 914 1.7-litre: 3639
Porsche 914 2-litre: 3640
Porsche Carrera RS Touring: 3641
Porsche Carrera RSR: 3642
Volkswagen Karmann-Ghia: 4789
Volkswagen Passat LS: 4790
Volkswagen Sports Bug: 4792
Volkswagen Type III: 4793

1974 Audi 80 GT: 271
BMW 2002 Tii: 533
BMW 2002 Turbo: 534
BMW 3.3L: 535
BMW 525: 536
Ford Capri 2800 V6: 1821
Glas 1700: 2001
Mercedes-Benz 280E: 2844
Mercedes-Benz 450SEL: 2845
Mercedes-Benz 450SL: 2846
NSU Ro80: 3266
Opel Commodore GS 2.8: 3336
Opel Commodore GSE: 3337
Opel Kadett Coupe: 3338
Porsche 911 Carrera: 3643
Porsche 911 Targa: 3644
Porsche 911S 2.7-litre: 3645
Volkswagen 181: 4794
Volkswagen 412: 4795
Volkswagen Dasher: 4796
Volkswagen Sciroco TS: 4797

1975 Audi 100 GL Automatic: 272
Audi 80 Estate: 273
Audi Fox: 274
BMW 1602L: 537
BMW 525: 538
BMW 530i: 539
Mercedes-Benz 280S: 2847
Mercedes-Benz 300D: 2848
Mercedes-Benz 450SLC: 2849
Opel 1900: 3339
Opel Ascona 1900SR: 3340
Opel Manta: 3341
Porsche 911 Carrera: 3646
Porsche Carrera RS 3-litre: 3647
Porsche Turbo 3-litre: 3648
Volkswagen Beetle: 4798
Volkswagen Golf 1100L: 4799
Volkswagen Polo: 4800
Volkswagen Rabbit: 4801
Volkswagen Scirocco: 4802

1976 Audi 80 GTE: 275
BMW 633 CSi: 540
Ford Capri II 2.8 V6: 1839
Ford Capri V6 Black Gold: 1840
Mercedes-Benz 280E: 2850
Mercedes-Benz 450SL: 2851
Opel Rekord 2100D: 3342
Opel Rekord Berlina Pacesetter: 3343
Porsche 911 S: 3649
Porsche 911 Turbo Carrera: 3650
Porsche 912 E: 3651
Porsche 914 2.0-litre: 3652
Porsche 924: 3653
Volkswagen Golf 1600 LS: 4803
Volkswagen Sciroco TS: 4804

1977 Audi 100 5E: 276
Audi 100 GLS: 277
Audi Fox: 278
BMW 320: 541
BMW 320i: 542
BMW 528: 543
BMW 630 CSi: 544
BMW 733i: 545
Ford Fiesta Ghia: 1855
Mercedes-Benz 230C: 2852
Mercedes-Benz 280E: 2853
Mercedes-Benz 600SE: 2854
Porsche 911 SC: 3654
Porsche 911 Turbo: 3655
Porsche 924: 3656
Porsche 935 Group 4 Holbert: 3657
Volkswagen Dasher: 4805
Volkswagen Golf GTi: 4806
Volkswagen Passat GLS: 4807
Volkswagen Polo LS: 4808
Volkswagen Rabbit Diesel: 4809
Volkswagen Scirocco Fi: 4810
Volkswagen Sciroco GTi: 4811

1978 Audi 100 L Avant: 279
Audi 5000: 280
BMW 320i Alpina: 546
BMW 323i: 547
BMW 333i Alpina: 548
BMW 528i: 549
BMW 733i: 550
Mercedes-Benz 200: 2855
Mercedes-Benz 300CD: 2856
Mercedes-Benz 300SD: 2857
Mercedes-Benz 450SEL: 2858
Opel Rekord 2.0S: 3344
Porsche 911 SC: 3658
Porsche 911 Turbo: 3659
Porsche 924 Lux: 3660
Porsche 928: 3661
Porsche 928 Automatic: 3662
Volkswagen Beetle Convertible: 4812
Volkswagen Golf GLS: 4813
Volkswagen Golf LD: 4814

1979 Audi 100 GL5S: 281
Audi 80 GLS: 282
BMW 528i: 551
BMW 635 CSi: 552
BMW 732i: 553
Ford Fiesta Healey: 1864
Mercedes-Benz 250T: 2859
Mercedes-Benz 280CE: 2860
Mercedes-Benz 300TD: 2861
Mercedes-Benz 450SEL 6.9: 2862
Mercedes-Benz 450SL: 2863
Opel Kadett 1.3S Berlina: 3345
Porsche 924: 3663
Porsche 924 Turbo: 3664
Porsche 928 Automatic: 3665
Volkswagen Scirocco: 4815
Volkswagen Sciroco GLi: 4816
Volkswagen Sciroco GLS: 4817

1980 Audi 4000: 283
Audi 5000 S Diesel: 284
BMW 320i: 554
BMW 633 CSi: 555
BMW M1: 556
Ford Fiesta: 1869
Mercedes-Benz 450SL: 2864
Porsche 911 SC: 3666
Porsche 924: 3667
Porsche 924 S Turbo: 3668
Porsche 928: 3669
Volkswagen Dasher Diesel: 4818
Volkswagen Jetta: 4819
Volkswagen Jetta GLS: 4820
Volkswagen Rabbit: 4821
Volkswagen Scirocco: 4822
Volkswagen Vanagon: 4823

1981 Audi 200 5E: 285
Audi 4000 Automatic: 286
Audi 5000 Turbo: 287
Audi Coupe: 288
Audi Quattro: 289
BMW 323i Hardy & Beck: 557
BMW 528i: 558
Mercedes-Benz 230E: 2865
Mercedes-Benz 230TE: 2866
Mercedes-Benz 300GD: 2867
Mercedes-Benz 300TD: 2868
Mercedes-Benz 380SEL: 2869
Opel Manta GTJ: 3346
Opel Manta Monza S3.0E: 3347
Porsche 911 SC: 3670
Porsche 924 Turbo: 3671
Volkswagen Golf 1300 LS: 4824
Volkswagen Passat CL Formel E: 4825
Volkswagen Passat GL 5S Estate: 4826
Volkswagen Rabbit: 4827
Volkswagen Rabbit Convertible: 4828
Volkswagen Rabbit Diesel: 4829
Volkswagen Scirocco GT-3 Davey: 4830
Volkswagen Scirocco S: 4831

1982 Audi 100 CD: 290
Audi 80 Turbo Diesel: 291
Audi Quattro: 292
BMW 316: 559
BMW 528e: 560
BMW 635 CSi: 561
BMW 745i: 562
Mercedes-Benz 380SEC: 2870
Mercedes-Benz 380SL: 2871
Porsche 924 Weissach: 3672
Porsche 944: 3673
Porsche 944 Lux: 3674
Volkswagen Golf GTi 1800: 4832
Volkswagen Polo C: 4833
Volkswagen Polo C Formel E: 4834
Volkswagen Quantum: 4835
Volkswagen Santana GX5: 4836
Volkswagen Scirocco GL: 4837

1983 Audi 200 Turbo: 293
Audi 5000 S: 294
Audi 80 Quattro: 295
Audi Coupe Injection: 296
BMW 318i: 563
BMW 320i: 564
BMW 525E: 565
BMW 533i: 566
BMW 735i: 567
Mercedes-Benz 190: 2872
Mercedes-Benz 190E: 2873
Mercedes-Benz 280SE: 2874
Mercedes-Benz 380SL: 2875
Opel Manta Berlinetta 1.8S: 3348
Opel Manta GTE: 3349
Porsche 911 Cabriolet: 3675
Porsche 911 Turbo: 3676
Porsche 928 S: 3677
Porsche 944: 3678
Volkswagen Quantum GL5: 4838
Volkswagen Rabbit GTi: 4839
Volkswagen Scirocco: 4840
Volkswagen Scirocco GTi: 4841
Volkswagen Vanagon Wasserboxer: 4842

1984 Audi 200 Quattro Turbo: 297
Audi 4000 S Quattro: 298
Audi 5000 S Avant: 299
Audi 5000 S Turbo: 300
Audi 80 GL: 301
Audi Coupe GT: 302
Bitter SC: 492
BMW 318i: 568
BMW 325E: 569
BMW 633 CSi: 570
BMW 735i Automatic: 571
BMW M635 CSi: 572
Ford Sierra XR4i: 1898
Mercedes-Benz 190E: 2876
Mercedes-Benz 500SEC: 2877
Opel Manta Monza GSE: 3350
Porsche 911 Carrera: 3679
Porsche 911 Turbo Cabriolet Ruf: 3680
Porsche 944: 3681
Volkswagen Jetta GLi: 4843

Volkswagen Jetta GLX: 4844
Volkswagen Passat CL Turbo Diesel Estate: 4845
Volkswagen Scirocco: 4846
Volkswagen Scirocco 16v: 4847

1985 Audi 100 Quattro: 303
Audi 200 Avant Quattro: 304
Audi 5000 S Turbo Quattro: 305
Audi 90 Quattro: 306
Audi Coupe GT: 307
Audi Quattro: 308
Audi Quattro Sport: 309
BMW 325i: 573
BMW 327S Hardy & Beck: 574
BMW 732i: 575
BMW M535i: 576
BMW M635 CSi Hardy & Beck: 577
Mercedes-Benz 190E 2.3: 2878
Mercedes-Benz 190E 2.3-16: 2879
Mercedes-Benz 190E BBS/Callaway Turbo: 2880
Mercedes-Benz 300E: 2881
Mercedes-Benz 500SEL: 2882
Merkur XR4Ti: 2963
Porsche 911 Carrera: 3682
Porsche 928 S: 3683
Porsche 928 S Series II: 3684
Porsche 944 Lux: 3685
Porsche 944 Turbo: 3686
Volkswagen Cabriolet Wolfsburg: 4848
Volkswagen Golf: 4849
Volkswagen Golf GTi: 4850
Volkswagen Jetta GLi: 4851
Volkswagen Scirocco: 4852
Volkswagen Scirocco 16v: 4853
Volkswagen Scirocco GTX: 4854

1986 Audi 100 Turbo Diesel: 310
Audi 5000 S: 311
Audi 80 1.8S: 312
Audi 90: 313
Audi Coupe GT: 314
Audi Coupe GT 2.2: 315
Audi Coupe Quattro: 316
Bitter SC: 493
BMW 325 ES: 578
BMW 325i Convertible: 579
BMW 520i: 580
BMW 524 TD: 581
BMW 535i: 582
BMW 635 CSi: 583
BMW 735i: 584
BMW 735i Automatic: 585
Mercedes-Benz 190E 2.3-16: 2883
Mercedes-Benz 200: 2884
Mercedes-Benz 300E: 2885
Mercedes-Benz 300TE: 2886
Mercedes-Benz 420SE: 2887
Mercedes-Benz 560SEC: 2888
Mercedes-Benz 560SEL: 2889
Mercedes-Benz 560SL: 2890
Porsche 911 Cabriolet: 3687
Porsche 911 Carrera SE: 3688
Porsche 911 Turbo: 3689
Porsche 924 S: 3690
Porsche 928 S: 3691
Porsche 928 S4 Automatic: 3692
Porsche 944: 3693
Porsche 944 S: 3694
Porsche 944 Turbo: 3695
Volkswagen Caravelle Syncro: 4855
Volkswagen Golf GTi 16v: 4856
Volkswagen Jetta GT: 4857
Volkswagen Quantum Synchro Wagon: 4858
Volkswagen Scirocco 16v: 4859
Volkswagen Scirocco GTX 16v: 4860

1987 Audi 90 2.2E: 317
Audi 90 Quattro: 318
BMW 318i 2-door: 586
BMW 325i Cabriolet: 587
BMW 730i SE: 588
BMW 750i L: 589
BMW M3: 590
Mercedes-Benz 190E 2.6: 2891
Mercedes-Benz 300CE: 2892
Mercedes-Benz 300TD: 2893
Mercedes-Benz 420SEL: 2894
Mercedes-Benz 560SEC Cabriolet Straman: 2895
Merkur Scorpio: 2964
Porsche 911 Carrera: 3696
Porsche 911 Turbo Gemballa Avalanche: 3697
Porsche 911 Turbo Ruf 3.4: 3698
Porsche 911 Turbo Slant-Nose: 3699
Porsche 924 S: 3700
Porsche 944 S: 3701
Porsche 959 S: 3702
Volkswagen Golf Cabriolet Clipper: 4862
Volkswagen GTi 16v: 4863
Volkswagen Jetta GTi 16v: 4864
Volkswagen Passat GT 5-door: 4865

1988 Audi 100 Avant Quattro: 319
Audi 100 Sport: 320
Audi 80 1.8E: 321
Audi 90 Quattro: 322
Audi Quattro: 323
BMW 325i S: 591
BMW 325i X: 592
BMW 535i SE: 593
BMW 635 CSi: 594
BMW 735i: 595
BMW 750i L: 596
BMW M6: 597
Isdera Imperator: 2244
Mercedes-Benz 260E Auto: 2896
Mercedes-Benz 300CE: 2897
Mercedes-Benz 300E 4Matic: 2898
Mercedes-Benz 300E AMG Hammer: 2899
Merkur XR4Ti: 2965
Porsche 911 Cabriolet: 3703
Porsche 911 Carrera: 3704

Porsche 911 Carrera Club Sport: 3705
Porsche 911 Club Sport: 3706
Porsche 911 Speedster: 3707
Porsche 911 Turbo: 3708
Porsche 911 Turbo Koenig RS: 3709
Porsche 911 Turbo Ruf Twin Turbo: 3710
Porsche 924 S: 3711
Porsche 928 S4: 3712
Porsche 944: 3713
Porsche 944 S: 3714
Porsche 944 Turbo: 3715
Porsche 944 Turbo SE: 3716
Porsche 959 Comfort: 3717
Porsche 959 Sport: 3718
Volkswagen GTi 16v: 4866
Volkswagen Jetta GLi 16v: 4867
Volkswagen Jetta Turbo Diesel: 4868
Volkswagen Passat GT: 4869
Volkswagen Polo C Saloon: 4870
Volkswagen Quantum GLS Synchro Wagon: 4871
Volkswagen Scirocco 16v: 4872

1989 Audi 90: 324
Audi 90 Quattro 20v: 325
Audi Coupe 2.2E: 326
Audi Coupe Quattro: 327
BMW 316i 4-door: 598
BMW 325i S: 599
BMW 535i: 600
BMW 535i Automatic: 601
BMW 735i Alpina B11: 602
BMW M3: 603
BMW M3 Evolution: 604
BMW M3 Hor Technologie: 605
BMW M5: 606
BMW M635 CSi: 607
BMW Z1: 608
Irmsher GT: 2243
Koenig Competition: 2417
Mercedes-Benz 190: 2900
Mercedes-Benz 190E 2.5-16: 2901
Mercedes-Benz 190E 2.6: 2902
Mercedes-Benz 190E AMG Baby Hammer: 2903
Mercedes-Benz 200E Automatic: 2904
Mercedes-Benz 300CE Cabriolet Straman: 2905
Mercedes-Benz 300E: 2906
Mercedes-Benz 560SL: 2907
Porsche 911 3.3 Turbo: 3719
Porsche 911 Carrera 4: 3720
Porsche 911 Carrera Cabriolet: 3721
Porsche 911 Club Sport: 3722
Porsche 911 Turbo: 3723
Porsche 911 Turbo Motorsport Design: 3724
Porsche 928 Cabrio Strosek: 3725
Porsche 928 S4 Koenig: 3726
Porsche 928 S4 SE: 3727
Porsche 944: 3728
Porsche 944 S2: 3729
Porsche 944 Turbo: 3730
Porsche 959: 3731
Treser T1: 4485
Volkswagen Caravelle Carat Automatic: 4873
Volkswagen Corrado: 4874
Volkswagen Corrado 16v: 4875
Volkswagen Golf CL Catalyst: 4876
Volkswagen Jetta Syncro: 4877
Volkswagen Passat GT 16v: 4878
Zender Vision 3: 5007

1990 Audi 80 2.0E: 328
Audi 90 Quattro: 329
Audi Quattro 20v: 330
Audi V8 Quattro: 331
Audi V8 Quattro Automatic: 332
Bitter Type 3 Cabrio: 494
BMW 318i S: 609
BMW 325i Convertible: 610
BMW 735i Koenig: 611
BMW 750i: 612
BMW 750i Alpina B12: 613
Koenig Competition Evolution: 2418
Mercedes-Benz 190E 2.5-16 Evolution II: 2908
Mercedes-Benz 300CE: 2909
Mercedes-Benz 300CE AMG Hammer: 2910
Mercedes-Benz 300D: 2911
Mercedes-Benz 300E-24: 2912
Mercedes-Benz 500SL: 2913
Porsche 911 Carrera 2: 3732
Porsche 911 Carrera 2 Tiptronic: 3733
Porsche 911 Carrera 4: 3734
Porsche 911 Speedster: 3735
Porsche 911 Turbo: 3736
Porsche 911 Turbo RS Tuning: 3737
Porsche 928: 3738
Porsche 928 Automatic: 3739
Porsche 928 Gemballa: 3740
Porsche 944 Cabriolet: 3741
Porsche 944 S2: 3742
Porsche 944 S2 Cabriolet: 3743
Porsche Carrera 2 Cabriolet Tiptronic: 3744
Porsche Panamericana: 3745
Volkswagen Corrado G60: 4879
Volkswagen Passat CL TD Estate: 4880
Volkswagen Passat GL: 4881
Zender Fact 4: 5008

1991 Audi 100 2.8E Auto: 333
Audi 200 Quattro: 334
Audi 80 16v Sport: 335
Audi 90 Quattro 20v: 336
Audi Coupe S2: 337
Audi V8 Quattro: 338
BMW 318i: 614
BMW 325i SE: 615
BMW 520i: 616
BMW 525i: 617
BMW 525i SE 24v: 618
BMW 535i Alpina B10 Bi-Turbo: 619
BMW 850i: 620
BMW M3 Sport Evolution: 621
BMW M5: 622
Koenig C62: 2419
Mercedes-Benz 190E 1.8 Auto: 2914
Mercedes-Benz 190E 2.3: 2915
Mercedes-Benz 190E 2.5-16 Evolution II: 2916
Mercedes-Benz 300SL-24 5-speed Auto: 2917
Mercedes-Benz 400SE: 2918
Mercedes-Benz 500E: 2919
Mercedes-Benz 500SL: 2920
Mercedes-Benz G-Wagen 300 GD LWB: 2921
Opel Calibra 2.0i 16v: 3351
Opel Omega Lotus: 3352
Porsche 911 Carrera Turbo: 3746
Porsche 911 Ruf: 3747
Porsche 911 Ruf CTR: 3748
Porsche 911 Ruf TR2: 3749
Porsche 911 Turbo: 3750
Porsche 911 Turbo Gemballa Mirage: 3751
Porsche 928: 3752
Volkswagen Corrado G60: 4882
Volkswagen Corrado Neuspeed: 4883
Volkswagen GTi 16v: 4884
Volkswagen Jetta GLi 16v: 4885
Volkswagen Polo 1.3 CL Coupe: 4886
Volkswagen Polo G40: 4887
Volkswagen Polo GT Coupe: 4888

1992 Audi 80 2.8E V6 Quattro: 339
BMW 325i: 623
BMW 520i SE Touring: 624
BMW 850i Manual: 625
Mercedes-Benz 500SEL: 2922
Mercedes-Benz 600SEL: 2923
Porsche 911 Carrera RS: 3753
Volkswagen Golf 1.8 GL: 4889
Volkswagen Golf GTi: 4890

Germany total: 785

Italy

1928 Fiat 17/50 Saloon: 1454

1931 Alfa Romeo Supercharged Straight Eight: 39
Bianchi Straight Eight Saloon: 490

1932 Alfa Romeo 1750: 40
Alfa Romeo 8C2300: 41

1933 Alfa Romeo 2.3 Mille Miglia: 42

1934 Fiat Balilla Pillarless Saloon: 1455
Lancia 27.6hp Astura Saloon: 2485
Lancia Augusta Saloon: 2486

1935 Fiat 1500 Saloon: 1456
Fiat Balilla Sports Two-seater: 1457

1936 Fiat 500 Convertible Saloon: 1458

1937 Bianchi 12hp Pillarless Saloon: 491
Fiat 1500 Pillarless Saloon: 1459
Fiat Balilla Pillarless Saloon: 1460
Lancia Aprilia Pillarless Saloon: 2487

1938 Lancia Aprilia Saloon: 2488

1947 Cisitalia Aerodinamica Mille Miglia: 1009

1948 Ferrari 166 Mille Miglia Barchetta: 1371

1950 Fiat 1400 Saloon: 1461

1951 Fiat 500C Convertible (Topolino): 1462

1952 Ferrari 212 Touring: 1372
Ferrari 375 Indianapolis: 1373
Fiat 1400: 1463
Fiat 500C Convertible: 1464
Lancia Aurelia 2-litre Saloon: 2489

1953 Alfa Romeo 1900: 43
Ferrari 212 Coupe: 1374
Ferrari 4.1 Coupe: 1375
Fiat 1100: 1465
Fiat 1900: 1466
Siata Spyder V8: 4127

1954 Alfa Romeo B.A.T.7 Scaglione: 44
Ferrari 250 Mille Miglia: 1376
Fiat 1100 TV Saloon: 1467
Fiat 8V: 1468
Maserati A6G/54 Frua Gran Sport: 2652
Moretti 750 Grand Sport Berlinetta Coupe: 3119

1955 Fiat 600: 1469
Lancia Aurelia Gran Turismo 2500: 2490
Lancia Spyder: 2491
Nardi Blue Ray 1: 3192
Osca 1490cc Spyder: 3353

1956 Alfa Romeo Giulietta Spyder: 45
Ferrari 412 MI: 1377

1957 Ferrari 250 Testa Rossa: 1378
Ferrari TRC 2500 Testa Rossa: 1379
Fiat 1100: 1470
Fiat 1100 Saloon: 1471
Fiat 600: 1472
Fiat 600 Multipla: 1473
Fiat Multipla: 1474

1958 Abarth Zagato 750 GT: 1
Alfa Romeo 1300 SV Spider: 46
Ferrari 250 GT Cabriolet: 1380
Ferrari 250 GT Coupe: 1381
Ferrari 250 Testa Rossa: 1382
Fiat 1200 Gran Luce: 1475
Fiat 1200 TV Spyder: 1476
Fiat 500: 1477
Fiat 750 Abarth: 1478
Fiat Abarth 750GT Zagato: 1479
Fiat Abarth Zagato: 1480
Lancia Aurelia GT 2500: 2492
Lancia Flaminia: 2493
Nardi Blue Ray 2: 3193

1959 Alfa Romeo 2000 Spider: 47
Alfa Romeo Super Spider: 48
Fiat 1200 Gran Luce: 1481
Fiat 500: 1482
Fiat 500 Nuova: 1483
Lancia Appia Sedan: 2494
Lancia Flaminia: 2495
Maserati GT Coupe: 2653

1960 Alfa Romeo 2000: 49
ASA 1000GT: 221
Ferrari 250 GT Berlinetta SWB: 1383
Ferrari 250 GT Coupe: 1384
Fiat 1500: 1484
Fiat 2100: 1485
Fiat 600: 1486
Fiat Abarth 850: 1487
Fiat Abarth Twin Cam: 1488
Lancia Flaminia Coupe: 2496
Lancia Zagato: 2497

1961 Alfa Romeo Giulia SS: 50
Alfa Romeo Giulietta Sprint: 51
Alfa Romeo Giulietta ti: 52
Alfa Romeo Sprint Speciale: 53
Alfa Romeo Sprint Zagato: 54
Fiat 1200 Spider: 1489
Fiat 1300: 1490
Fiat 1500: 1491
Fiat 500 Giardiniera: 1492
Fiat 600D: 1493
Lancia Flavia: 2498
Maserati 3500GT: 2654

1962 Alfa Romeo 2600: 55
Ferrari 250 GT 2+2: 1385
Ferrari 250 GTO: 1386
Ferrari 4.9: 1387
Fiat 2300: 1494
Lancia Appia III: 2499
Lancia Flaminia Sedan: 2500

1963 Alfa Romeo 2600 Saloon: 56
Alfa Romeo Giulia ti: 57
Ferrari 250 GT Berlinetta Lusso: 1388
Ferrari 400 Super America: 1389
Fiat 1100: 1495
Fiat 1100D: 1496
Iso Grifo A3L Berlinetta: 2245
Maserati 3500 GTI Sebring: 2655

1964 Alfa Romeo Giulia 1600 Spider: 58
Alfa Romeo Sprint GT: 59
Fiat 1500L: 1497
Fiat 500D: 1498
Fiat 850 Super: 1499
Innocenti S: 2233
Iso GT: 2246
Iso Rivolta IR-340: 2247
Lancia Flavia Coupe: 2501
Lancia Fulvia: 2502
Lancia Fulvia 2C: 2503

1965 Alfa Romeo Giulia ti: 60
Alfa Romeo Giulia Veloce: 61
Bizzarrini 5300 Spyder: 495
Ferrari 365 GTC: 1390
Fiat 1500: 1500
Fiat 1500 Spider: 1501
Fiat Abarth OT 1600: 1502
Lamborghini 350GT: 2449
Lancia Flaminia Coupe 3B: 2504
Lancia Flavia Zagato Sport: 2505

1966 Alfa Romeo 1600 Spider: 62
Alfa Romeo 2600 Sprint: 63
Alfa Romeo Giulia Sprint GTV: 64
Alfa Romeo Sprint Speciale: 65
Bizzarrini GT America: 496
Bizzarrini P538: 497
Ferrari 275 GTS: 1391
Fiat 1100R: 1503
Fiat 500F: 1504
Fiat 850 Coupe: 1505
Fiat Abarth 595: 1506
Iso Grifo GL 365: 2248
Lamborghini 400GT: 2450
Lancia Fulvia Coupe: 2506

1967 Alfa Romeo 33 2.0 Stradale: 66
Alfa Romeo Duetto Spider: 67
Alfa Romeo Giulia 1300 ti: 68
Alfa Romeo GTV: 69
Ferrari 275 GTS/4 NART: 1392
Fiat 124: 1507
Fiat 125: 1508
Lamborghini Miura: 2451
Lancia Flavia Injection: 2507
Lancia Fulvia 1.3 Rallye: 2508
Lancia Fulvia 1.3 Zagato: 2509

1968 Alfa Romeo 1750 Berlina: 70
Alfa Romeo 1750 GT Veloce: 71
Alfa Romeo Giulia Super: 72
Ferrari 330 GTS: 1393
Fiat 124 Sport Coupe: 1509
Fiat 124 Sport Spider: 1510
Fiat 124 Station Wagon: 1511
Fiat 850 Idromatic: 1512
Fiat 850 Special: 1513
Fiat 850 Spider: 1514
Lamborghini Miura: 2452
Maserati Quattroporte: 2656

1969 Alfa Romeo 1750 Berlina: 73
Alfa Romeo 1750 Spider: 74
Alfa Romeo GT 1300 Junior: 75
De Tomaso Mangusta: 1235
Ferrari 365 GTS 2+2: 1394
Ferrari Daytona Sportwagen: 1395
Fiat 124 Coupe: 1515
Fiat 124 Estate Car: 1516
Fiat 125 Special: 1517
Fiat 850 Coupe: 1518
Fiat Abarth 1300: 1519
Iso Rivolta S4: 2249
Lamborghini Espada: 2453
Lancia Fulvia Coupe: 2510
Siata Spring 850: 4128

1970 Ferrari 365 GTB/4 Daytona: 1396
Fiat 124 Coupe 1600: 1520
Fiat 124 Special: 1521
Fiat 124 Spider: 1522
Fiat 128 4-door: 1523
Fiat 850 Racer: 1524
Lamborghini Espada: 2454
Lamborghini Miura P400S: 2455
Lamborghini Miura S: 2456
Lancia Fulvia Sedan: 2511
Maserati Indy: 2657

1971 Alfa Romeo 1750 Spider Veloce: 76
De Tomaso Pantera: 1236
Ferrari Daytona: 1397
Ferrari Daytona Cannonball: 1398
Fiat 124 Special T: 1525
Fiat 124 Spider 1600: 1526
Fiat 124 Sport Coupe: 1527
Fiat 127: 1528
Fiat 128: 1529
Iso Grifo GL: 2250
Lancia Fulvia Sedan: 2512
Maserati Ghibli: 2658
Maserati Indy: 2659

1972 Alfa Romeo 1750 Berlina: 77
Alfa Romeo 1750 GTV TransAm: 78
Alfa Romeo 2000 GTV: 79
Alfa Romeo 2000 GTV Injection: 80
Alfa Romeo Alfasud: 81
Alfa Romeo Montreal: 82
De Tomaso Pantera: 1237
Ferrari 246 GT Dino: 1399
Ferrari 365 GTC4: 1400
Fiat 124: 1530
Fiat 128 Coupe 1300: 1531
Fiat 128 SL 1300 Coupe: 1532
Fiat 130 Automatic: 1533
Lamborghini Jarama 400GT: 2457
Lancia 2000: 2513

1973 Alfa Romeo 2000: 83
Alfa Romeo Alfasud: 84
Alfa Romeo Alfetta: 85
Alfa Romeo Giulia 1600 Sprint: 86
Alfa Romeo Montreal: 87
De Tomaso Pantera: 1238
Fiat 124 Spider: 1534
Fiat 124 Spider 1600: 1535
Fiat 124 Sport Coupe 1800: 1536
Fiat 124 Station Wagon: 1537
Fiat 124S Automatic: 1538
Fiat 126: 1539
Fiat 128 Station Wagon: 1540
Fiat 132 1800 Special: 1541
Lamborghini Bravo: 2458
Lamborghini Jarama 400GT: 2459
Lancia Beta 1800: 2514
Maserati Bora: 2660

1974 Alfa Romeo Alfasud ti: 88
Alfa Romeo Alfetta: 89
De Tomaso Pantera GTS: 1239
De Tomaso Pantera L: 1240
Ferrari 246 GTS Dino: 1401
Ferrari 308 GT4 Dino: 1402
Ferrari 365 GTB/4 Competitione: 1403
Ferrari 365 GTB/4 Daytona: 1404
Fiat 132 GLS: 1542
Fiat X1/9: 1543
Iso Rivolta Fidia: 2251
Lamborghini Urraco S: 2460

Lancia Fulvia Coupe S3: 2515
Maserati Merak: 2661

1975 Alfa Romeo Alfetta GT: 90
Ferrari 308 Dino GT4: 1405
Ferrari 365 GT4 2+2: 1406
Ferrari 512 BB: 1407
Fiat 124 Special TC: 1544
Fiat 124 Sport Coupe 1800: 1545
Fiat 128: 1546
Fiat 128 Special: 1547
Fiat 131 1300S: 1548
Fiat 133: 1549
Lancia Beta 1600 Coupe: 2516
Lancia Beta Monte Carlo: 2517
Maserati Khamsin Automatic: 2662
Maserati Merak: 2663

1976 Alfa Romeo Alfetta 1.6: 91
Alfa Romeo Alfetta GT: 92
Alfa Romeo Alfetta GTV: 93
Alfa Romeo Spider Veloce 2000: 94
Ferrari 308 GT4 Dino: 1408
Ferrari 308 GTB: 1409
Ferrari Dino 308 GT4 2+2: 1410
Fiat 124 Spider: 1550
Fiat 124 Sport Spider: 1551
Fiat 128 3P: 1552
Fiat 128 Estate: 1553
Fiat 131: 1554
Lamborghini Countach: 2461
Lamborghini Silhouette 3000: 2462
Lamborghini Urraco: 2463
Lancia Beta 1300: 2518
Lancia Beta 2000: 2519
Lancia Beta Coupe: 2520
Lancia Beta Sedan: 2521
Maserati Bora: 2664
Maserati Khamsin: 2665

1977 Alfa Romeo Alfasud 1200ti: 95
Alfa Romeo Alfasud 1300ti: 96
Alfa Romeo Alfasud 5M: 97
Alfa Romeo Alfetta: 98
Alfa Romeo Spider: 99
Ferrari 308 GTB: 1411
Fiat 127 1050 CL: 1555
Fiat 131: 1556
Fiat X1/9: 1557
Lancia Beta: 2522
Lancia Beta HPE 2000: 2523
Lancia Beta Scorpion: 2524
Lancia Gamma: 2525

1978 Alfa Romeo Alfasud Sprint 1.5: 100
Alfa Romeo Alfetta 2.0: 101
Alfa Romeo Giulietta 1.6: 102
Alfa Romeo Sport Sedan: 103
Ferrari 308 GTS: 1412
Ferrari 512 BB: 1413
Fiat 127 Sport: 1558
Fiat 131 Supermirafiori: 1559
Fiat 132 2000 GLS: 1560
Fiat Super Brava: 1561
Lancia Gamma Berlina: 2526
Maserati Khamsin: 2666
Maserati Kyalami: 2667
Maserati Merak: 2668

1979 Alfa Romeo Alfasud 1.5 Sprint Veloce: 104
Alfa Romeo Sport Sedan Automatic: 105
Alfa Romeo Sprint Veloce: 106
Fiat 124 Spider: 1562
Fiat 124 Sports Spider: 1563
Fiat 126 de Ville: 1564
Fiat Mirafiori Sport: 1565
Fiat Strada: 1566
Fiat Strada 65CL: 1567
Fiat Strada 75CL: 1568
Fiat X1/9 1300: 1569
Fiat X1/9 1500: 1570
Lamborghini Countach S: 2464
Lancia Beta 2000 Automatic: 2527
Lancia Beta HPE 1600: 2528
Lancia HPE: 2529
Maserati Khamsin: 2669

1980 Alfa Romeo Spider: 107
Ferrari 308 GT4 Dino: 1414
Fiat Brava Abarth Rally: 1571
Lancia Zagato: 2530

1981 Alfa Romeo Alfasud 1.5: 108
Alfa Romeo GTV6: 109
Ferrari 308 GTSi: 1415
Fiat 127 1050 Super: 1572
Fiat Brava: 1573
Fiat Panda: 1574
Lancia Montecarlo Group 5 Turbo: 2531
Lancia Montecarlo Spyder: 2532
Lancia Trevi 2000: 2533
Maserati Merak SS: 2670

1982 Alfa Romeo Spider Veloce: 110
Alfa Romeo Spider Veloce 2000: 111
Ferrari 288 GTO: 1416
Ferrari 512 BB: 1417
Ferrari Mondial 8: 1418
Fiat Mirafiori 1400CL: 1575
Fiat Spider 2000: 1576
Fiat Spider Turbo: 1577
Fiat Strada Super 85: 1578
Fiat X1/9: 1579
Lamborghini Countach LP 500S: 2465
Lamborghini Countach S: 2466
Lamborghini Jalpa: 2467
Lancia Beta Coupe: 2534
Lancia Delta Automatic: 2535

1983 Alfa Romeo Alfa 33 1.5: 112
Ferrari 308 GTBi Quattrovalvole: 1419
Ferrari 308 GTSi Targa: 1420
Fiat Spider 2000: 1580
Fiat Strada 60 Comfort ES: 1581
Fiat Uno 55 S: 1582
Fiat Uno 70 SX: 1583
Lancia Prisma 1600: 2536
Maserati Quattroporte: 2671

1984 Alfa Romeo Alfetta Gold Cloverleaf: 113
Alfa Romeo GTV6: 114
Alfa Romeo Spider: 115
Alfa Romeo Sprint Green Cloverleaf: 116
De Tomaso Pantera GT5: 1241
Ferrari 288 GTO: 1421
Ferrari 512 BBi: 1422
Ferrari GTO: 1423
Ferrari Mondial Cabriolet Quattrovalvole: 1424
Fiat Regata 100 S: 1584
Fiat Regata 70 ES: 1585
Fiat Strada Abarth 130TC: 1586
Fiat X1/9: 1587
Lancia Rally: 2537
Pininfarina Azzurra: 3469
Pininfarina Spider: 3470

1985 Alfa Romeo Alfa 33 1.5 4x4 Estate: 117
Alfa Romeo Alfa 90 2.5 Gold Cloverleaf: 118
Alfa Romeo Arna 1.3SL: 119
Alfa Romeo Arna ti: 120
Alfa Romeo Graduate: 121
Alfa Romeo GTV Callaway Twin Turbo: 122
Ferrari 365 GTB Goldsmith: 1425
Ferrari Testa Rossa: 1426
Fiat Uno 70 SX: 1588
Fiat Uno Turbo ie: 1589
Fiat X1/9: 1590
Fiat X1/9VS: 1591
Lamborghini Countach: 2468
Lancia Coupe 2000ie: 2538
Lancia Thema 2.0 ie LX Turbo: 2539
Lancia Y10 Turbo: 2540
Maserati Biturbo: 2672
Maserati Biturbo Automatic: 2673
Maserati Biturbo E: 2674

1986 Alfa Romeo Alfa 33 1.3 S: 123
Alfa Romeo Alfa 75 1.8: 124
Alfa Romeo Alfa 75 2.5 Green Cloverleaf: 125
Alfa Romeo GTV6: 126
Alfa Romeo Milano Platinum: 127
Alfa Romeo Spider Quadrifoglio: 128
De Tomaso Pantera GT5-S: 1242
Ferrari 3.2 Mondial: 1427
Ferrari 328 GTB: 1428
Ferrari Mondial 3.2: 1429
Ferrari Mondial 3.2QV: 1430
Fiat Panda 1000 S: 1592
Fiat Panda 750 L: 1593
Fiat Regata DS: 1594
Lamborghini Countach 5000S: 2469
Lamborghini Jalpa 3500: 2470
Lancia Delta HF 4WD: 2541
Lancia Delta HF Turbo ie: 2542
Lancia Prisma 1600ie LX: 2543
Lancia Thema 2.0ie: 2544
Lancia Y10 Fire: 2545

1987 Alfa Romeo 33 1.7 Veloce: 129
Alfa Romeo Alfa 33 1.7 Sportwagon Veloce: 130
Alfa Romeo Alfa 75 2.0i Twin Spark: 131
Alfa Romeo Alfa 75 V6 3.0: 132
Alfa Romeo Milano Verde 3.0: 133
Ferrari 328 GTS: 1431
Ferrari 412: 1432
Ferrari Mondial Cabriolet 3.2: 1433
Fiat Croma ie Super: 1595
Fiat Regata 100S ie: 1596
Fiat Uno Selecta: 1597
Lancia Thema 8.32: 2546
Maserati Biturbo Spyder: 2675

1988 Alfa Romeo 75 2.5 Auto: 134
Alfa Romeo 75 Evoluzione: 135
Alfa Romeo Spider: 136
Alfa Romeo Sprint 1.7 Cloverleaf: 137
Ferrari 308 Norwood Bonneville GTO: 1434
Ferrari F40: 1435
Ferrari Mondial Cabriolet: 1436
Ferrari Testa Rossa: 1437
Ferrari Testa Rossa Straman Spyder: 1438
Fiat Tipo 1.4: 1598
Fiat X1/9: 1599
Lamborghini Jalpa: 2471
Lamborghini LM129: 2472
Lancia Delta HF Integrale: 2547
Lancia Thema 8.32: 2548
Maserati 430: 2676
Maserati Biturbo: 2677

1989 Alfa Romeo 164 3.0 Lusso: 138
Alfa Romeo 164 Automatic: 139
Alfa Romeo Milano 3.0: 140
Alfa Romeo Spider Quadrifoglio: 141
Chrysler TC by Maserati: 1008
De Tomaso Pantera Group 3: 1243
Ferrari 308 Norwood: 1439
Ferrari Mondial 3.2 Cabriolet: 1440
Ferrari Mondial t: 1441
Ferrari Testa Rossa: 1442
Ferrari Testa Rossa Gemballa: 1443
Ferrari Testa Rossa Norwood: 1444
Fiat Tipo 1.6 DGT SX: 1600
Fiat X1/9: 1601
Lamborghini Countach 25th Anniversary: 2473
Lancia Delta Integrale 16v: 2549
Lancia Thema 2.0ie 16v: 2550
Maserati 430: 2678
Maserati Spyder: 2679

1990 Alfa Romeo 164 Twin Spark Lusso: 142
Alfa Romeo 164S: 143
Alfa Romeo 33 Boxer 16v: 144
Bertone Zabrus: 488
Cizeta Moroder V16T: 1094
De Tomaso Pantera GT5 S: 1244
Ferrari 348tb: 1445
Ferrari F40: 1446
Ferrari Mondial: 1447
Ferrari Pininfarina Mythos: 1448
Fiat Croma CHT: 1602
Fiat Tempra 1.6 SX: 1603
Fiat Uno 60S: 1604
Fiat Uno Turbo ie: 1605
Ital Design Aztec: 2262
Lamborghini Diablo: 2474
Lancia Dedra 1.8i: 2551
Lancia Dedra 2.0ie: 2552
Lancia Thema 2.0ie 16v SE Turbo: 2553
Lancia Y10 GTie: 2554
Maserati 228: 2680
Maserati Shamal: 2681

1991 Alfa Romeo 164 Cloverleaf: 145
Alfa Romeo 164L: 146
Alfa Romeo Spider Veloce: 147
Bertone Emotion Lotus: 489
Bugatti EB110: 652
Ferrari 348tb: 1449
Ferrari F40: 1450
Ferrari GTO Norwood: 1451
Ferrari Mondial t: 1452
Ferrari Mondial t Cabriolet: 1453
Lamborghini Diablo: 2475
Lancia Dedra 2000 Turbo: 2555

1992 Fiat Tipo 1.8ie DGT SX: 1606

Italy total: 512

Japan

1958 Datsun 1000: 1157
Toyota Toyopet Crown de Luxe: 4350

1960 Toyota Toyopet Tiara: 4351

1961 Datsun Bluebird Station Wagon: 1158

1964 Datsun SPL-310: 1159
Toyota 1900: 4352

1965 Daihatsu Compagno Berlina: 1115
Honda S600: 2087

1966 Toyota Corona: 4353
Toyota Corona 1900: 4354
Toyota Crown Custom: 4355

1967 Datsun 1600 Sedan: 1160
Datsun 1600 Sports: 1161
Datsun 2000 Sports: 1162
Honda S800: 2088
Toyota 2000GT: 4356
Toyota Corona Coupe: 4357
Toyota Land Cruiser: 4358

1968 Datsun 1600: 1163
Datsun 510 Sedan: 1166
Honda N360: 2089
Mazda 110S Coupe: 2685
Mazda 1500 de Luxe: 2686
Mitsubishi Colt 1100F: 3061
Toyota Corolla: 4359
Toyota Corolla de Luxe: 4360
Toyota Corona: 4361

1969 Datsun 1000 de Luxe: 1168
Subaru 360: 4243
Subaru Star: 4244
Toyota Crown Toyoglide: 4362

1970 Datsun 1200: 1169
Datsun 1600 Pickup: 1170
Datsun 240Z: 1171
Honda 600: 2090
Mazda 1200 de Luxe: 2687
Toyota Corona Mk II: 4363
Toyota Corona Mk II 1900: 4364
Toyota Crown: 4365

1971 Datsun 100A: 1172
Datsun 1200 Coupe: 1173
Datsun 1200 Estate: 1174
Datsun 240Z: 1175
Datsun 240Z Automatic: 1176
Datsun 510: 1177
Dodge Colt: 1316
Mazda 1800: 2688
Mazda Rotary: 2689
Mazda RX-2: 2690
Subaru Hapi Van 360: 4245
Suzuki Brute: 4320
Toyota 1900SL: 4366
Toyota Celica: 4367
Toyota Corolla: 4368
Toyota Corolla 1200SL: 4369
Toyota Corolla 1600: 4370
Toyota Corona de Luxe: 4371
Toyota Land Cruiser: 4372
Toyota Land Cruiser Wagon: 4373

1972 Datsun 180B: 1178
Datsun 240C: 1179
Datsun 510 TransAm: 1180
Honda 600 Coupe: 2091
Mazda RX-2: 2691
Mazda RX-3: 2692
Subaru FF-1 1300: 4246
Toyota Carina: 4374
Toyota Crown 2600: 4375
Toyota Custom Crown Estate: 4376

1973 Datsun 200L: 1181
Datsun 240Z: 1182
Datsun 610 1800: 1183
Datsun 610 Station Wagon: 1184
Dodge Colt Station Wagon: 1319
Honda Civic: 2092
Honda Civic Hondamatic: 2093
Mazda RX-3 Station Wagon: 2693
Mazda RX-4: 2694
Subaru 1300 GL Coupe: 4247
Subaru 1400 DL: 4248
Toyota Celica: 4377
Toyota Corolla: 4378
Toyota Corolla SR5: 4379
Toyota Corona: 4380
Toyota Mk II: 4381
Toyota Mk II 2.6: 4382

1974 Datsun 120Y: 1185
Datsun 260Z: 1186
Datsun 260Z 2+2: 1187
Datsun 710: 1188
Datsun B210: 1189
Dodge Colt GT 2-litre: 1320
Mazda 1300: 2695
Mazda 929: 2696
Mazda Rotary Pickup: 2697
Mazda RX-4 Coupe: 2698
Mazda RX-4 Station Wagon: 2699
Toyota Celica GT: 4383
Toyota Corona 2000 Mk II Automatic: 4384
Toyota Corona SR: 4385
Toyota Mk II Station Wagon: 4386

1975 Datsun 240Z Sharp: 1190
Datsun 260C Estate: 1191
Datsun 280Z: 1192
Datsun 710: 1193
Datsun B210: 1194
Dodge Colt GT: 1321
Honda Civic CVCC: 2094
Mazda 808: 2700
Mitsubishi Colt Galant 2000: 3062
Subaru DL: 4249
Toyota Celica GT: 4387
Toyota Corolla: 4388
Toyota Corolla 30: 4389
Toyota Corolla SR5: 4390
Toyota Crown Super: 4391
Toyota Pickup SR5: 4392

1976 Buick Opel by Isuzu: 689
Datsun 140J Violet: 1195
Datsun 200L-6: 1196
Datsun B210: 1197
Datsun B210 Electramotive: 1198
Datsun F10: 1199
Honda Accord: 2095
Mazda Cosmo: 2701
Mitsubishi Colt Celeste 2000: 3063
Plymouth Arrow GT: 3512
Subaru 4WD Station Wagon: 4250
Toyota 1000: 4393
Toyota Carina: 4394
Toyota Celica Liftback: 4395
Toyota Corolla Liftback: 4396

1977 Datsun 180B Bluebird: 1200
Datsun 200SX: 1201
Datsun 260Z: 1202
Datsun 810 Sedan: 1203
Datsun Cherry F11: 1204
Dodge Colt Lancer: 1322
Honda Accord: 2096
Honda Civic 1500: 2097
Mazda 323: 2702
Mazda GLC: 2703
Mazda RX-4: 2704
Mitsubishi Colt Sigma 2000: 3064
Subaru 1600 4WD Estate: 4251
Toyota Corolla 1200: 4397
Toyota Corona Cressida: 4398

1978 Datsun 280Z Scarab: 1205
Datsun 510: 1206
Datsun Laurel Six: 1207
Honda Accord: 2098
Honda Civic: 2099
Mazda RX-7: 2705
Mitsubishi Colt Lancer Estate: 3065
Mitsubishi Colt Sappore 2000 GSR: 3066
Plymouth Sapporo: 3515
Subaru 1600 Coupe: 4252
Subaru DL: 4253
Toyota Celica: 4399
Toyota Celica 2000GT: 4400
Toyota Celica GT Liftback: 4401
Toyota Cressida: 4402

1979 Daihatsu Charade XTE: 1116
Datsun 2.4 Laurel Six: 1208
Datsun 210: 1209
Datsun 240K: 1210
Datsun 280ZX: 1211
Datsun 280ZX 2+2 Automatic: 1212
Datsun 280ZX Automatic: 1213
Datsun 310 Coupe: 1214
Datsun 810 Coupe: 1215
Datsun New Sunny: 1216
Dodge Colt Hatchback: 1323
Honda Accord 4-door: 2100
Honda Prelude: 2101
Mazda 1.4 SP: 2706
Mazda 626 Coupe: 2707
Mazda GLC Wagon: 2708
Mazda Montrose 1600 GLS: 2709
Mazda RX-7: 2710
Mazda RX-7 GS: 2711
Mitsubishi Colt 1400 GLX: 3067
Plymouth Fire Arrow: 3516
Toyota Celica Supra: 4403
Toyota Corona 5-door: 4404
Toyota Corona Liftback: 4405

1980 Datsun 200SX: 1217
Datsun 280ZX: 1218
Datsun 280ZX Automatic: 1219
Datsun 280ZX Electramotive: 1220
Datsun 280ZX Sharp: 1221
Datsun 510: 1222
Honda Civic: 2102
Honda Civic GL 1500: 2103
Honda Prelude: 2104
Mazda 626: 2712
Mazda Montrose GLS Coupe: 2713
Mazda RX-7: 2714
Mazda RX-7 Racer: 2715
Plymouth Champ: 3517
Subaru DL-5: 4254
Suzuki SC 100: 4321
Toyota Celica GT: 4406
Toyota Corolla Sport Coupe: 4407
Toyota Corolla Tercel SR5: 4408

1981 Daihatsu Domino: 1117
Datsun 280ZX Turbo: 1223
Datsun 810 Maxima: 1224
Honda Accord: 2105
Honda Civic 4-door Sedan: 2106
Honda Prelude: 2107
Honda Quintet: 2108
Mazda 323 1300: 2716
Mazda GLC: 2717
Mazda GLC Sport: 2718
Mazda RX-7 GSL: 2719
Mitsubishi Colt Lancer 2000 Turbo: 3068
Subaru 1800 4WD Estate: 4255
Suzuki Alto FX: 4322
Toyota Cressida: 4409
Toyota Cressida DX Estate: 4410
Toyota Starlet: 4411

1982 Daihatsu Charmant 1600LE: 1118
Datsun 280ZX: 1225
Datsun Stanza 1.6 GL: 1226
Datsun Sunny 1.5 DX: 1227
Dodge Challenger: 1325
Honda Accord: 2109
Honda Accord LX: 2110
Mazda RX-7: 2720
Mitsubishi Colt Cordia Turbo: 3069
Mitsubishi Colt Hatchback Turbo: 3070
Mitsubishi Colt Starion Turbo: 3071
Mitsubishi Cordia LS: 3072
Nissan Sentra: 3204
Nissan Stanza XE: 3205
Subaru GL: 4256
Toyota Celica: 4412
Toyota Celica 2.0ST: 4413
Toyota Celica GTA: 4414
Toyota Celica Supra: 4415

1983 Daihatsu Charade CX: 1119
Daihatsu Charade Diesel: 1120
Datsun 200SX: 1228
Datsun 280ZX: 1229
Datsun 280ZX Electramotive: 1230
Datsun 280ZX Turbo: 1231
Datsun Micra GL: 1232
Honda CRX 1.5: 2111
Honda Prelude EX ALB: 2112
Isuzu I-Mark LS: 2252
Mazda 626: 2721
Mazda 626 1600 LX: 2722
Mazda RX-7: 2723
Mitsubishi Colt Shogun: 3073
Mitsubishi Starion: 3074
Mitsubishi Starion Turbo: 3075
Mitsubishi Tredia Turbo: 3076
Nissan Pulsar NX: 3206
Subaru GL Turbo Traction Wagon: 4257
Suzuki Alto FX Automatic: 4323
Toyota Camry LE: 4416
Toyota Celica GTS: 4417
Toyota Corolla GL: 4418
Toyota Corolla SR5 Hardtop: 4419
Toyota Cressida: 4420
Toyota Supra: 4421
Toyota Tercel 4WD Wagon: 4422
Toyota Tercel GL: 4423

1984 Chevrolet Sprint: 895
Dodge Colt Vista: 1329
Dodge Conquest: 1330
Honda Civic CRX: 2113
Honda Civic DL: 2114
Honda Jazz: 2115
Honda Prelude: 2116

Isuzu Impulse: 2253
Mazda RX-7: 2724
Mazda RX-7 GSL SE: 2725
Mitsubishi Colt 1600 Turbo: 3077
Mitsubishi Cordia Turbo 1.8: 3078
Mitsubishi Galant 1600 GL: 3079
Mitsubishi Mirage Turbo: 3080
Nissan 200SX Turbo: 3207
Nissan 300ZX: 3208
Nissan 300ZX Turbo: 3209
Nissan Pulsar NX Turbo: 3210
Nissan Silvia Turbo ZX: 3211
Plymouth Colt GTS Turbo: 3518
Toyota Carina II 116GL: 4424
Toyota Celica 2.8i Supra: 4425
Toyota Corolla GT Coupe: 4426
Toyota Corolla GTS: 4427
Toyota Corolla LE: 4428
Toyota Supra: 4429
Toyota Van LE: 4430

1985 Daihatsu Charmant 1300LC: 1121
Honda Accord 2.0 EXi: 2117
Honda Accord EX Automatic: 2118
Honda Accord SEi: 2119
Honda Civic GT: 2120
Honda Civic S: 2121
Honda Civic Shuttle: 2122
Honda Civic Wagon: 2123
Honda CRX Si: 2124
Honda Prelude: 2125
Mazda 323 1.5 GLX: 2726
Mazda 323 1.6i: 2727
Mazda RX-7 GSL: 2728
Mitsubishi Colt Starion Turbo: 3081
Mitsubishi Galant: 3082
Mitsubishi Galant Turbo: 3083
Mitsubishi Space Wagon 1800GLX: 3084
Mitsubishi Starion: 3085
Mitsubishi Starion ESI: 3086
Nissan Bluebird Turbo ZX: 3212
Nissan Cherry 1.3 SGT: 3213
Nissan Maxima SE: 3214
Subaru 1.8 GTi: 4258
Subaru 1.8 RX Turbo: 4259
Subaru 4WD Turbo: 4260
Subaru 4WD Turbo XT Coupe: 4261
Subaru Turbo 4WD Estate: 4262
Subaru XT Coupe DL: 4263
Subaru XT Turbo Coupe: 4264
Suzuki Swift 1.3GS: 4324
Toyota Celica GTS: 4431
Toyota Corolla GT Hatchback: 4432
Toyota MR2: 4433
Toyota Space Cruiser: 4434
Toyota Starlet 1.0GL: 4435
Toyota Supra: 4436
Toyota Tercel 4WD Estate: 4437

1986 Acura Integra RS: 28
Acura Legend: 29
Chevrolet Sprint: 904
Daihatsu Domino: 1122
Dodge Colt Turbo: 1333
Honda Accord LXi: 2126
Honda Civic Hatchback: 2127
Honda CRX Coupe 1.6i 16: 2128
Honda CRX Si: 2129
Honda CRX Si Jackson Turbo: 2130
Honda Integra 1.5: 2131
Honda Integra EX 16: 2132
Honda Legend: 2133
Honda Prelude 2.0 Si: 2134
Isuzu I-Mark: 2254
Isuzu Impulse Sports Coupe: 2255
Isuzu Impulse Turbo: 2256
Mazda 323 1.5 GLX Estate: 2729
Mazda 323 1.6i: 2730
Mazda 323 LX: 2731
Mazda 323 Turbo 4x4 Lux: 2732
Mazda 626 2.0i 5-door: 2733
Mazda 626 GT: 2734
Mazda RX-7: 2735
Mazda RX-7 GXL: 2736
Mazda RX-7 Turbo: 2737
Mitsubishi Cordia Turbo: 3087
Mitsubishi Lancer 1.5 GLX Estate: 3088
Mitsubishi Mirage: 3089
Mitsubishi Starion ESI-R: 3090
Nissan 300ZX: 3215
Nissan 300ZX Turbo: 3216
Nissan Bluebird 1.8 ZX: 3217
Nissan Laurel 2.4 SGL Automatic: 3218
Nissan Sentra: 3219
Nissan Sentra Sport Coupe SE: 3220
Nissan Sunny 1.3 LX 5-door: 3221
Subaru 4WD 3-door Turbo Coupe: 4265
Subaru Hatchback: 4266
Suzuki Alto GLA: 4325
Suzuki Swift 1.3 GTi: 4326
Toyota Celica 2.0GT: 4438
Toyota Celica GTS: 4439
Toyota MR2: 4440
Toyota MR2 T-Bar: 4441
Toyota Supra: 4442
Toyota Supra 3.0i: 4443
Toyota Tercel DX: 4444

1987 Acura Integra LS: 30
Daihatsu Charade CX Diesel Turbo: 1123
Daihatsu Charade GT ti: 1124
Daihatsu Fourtrak Estate DT EL: 1125
Ford Festiva L: 1919
Honda Ballade EX: 2135
Honda Civic 1.4 GL 3-door: 2136
Honda Legend Coupe: 2137
Honda Prelude 2.0 Si: 2138
Honda Prelude 2.0i 16: 2139
Isuzu Trooper 3-door TD: 2257
Mazda 323 1.5 GLX: 2738
Mazda 626 2.0 GLS Executive: 2739
Mazda RX-7 Turbo: 2740
Mercury Tracer: 2959
Mitsubishi Colt 1500 GLX 5-door: 3091
Mitsubishi Galant 2000 GLS Automatic: 3092
Mitsubishi Galant Sapporo: 3093
Mitsubishi Shogun Turbo Diesel 5-door: 3094
Mitsubishi Starion 2000 Turbo: 3095
Mitsubishi Starion ESI-R: 3096
Nissan 200SX SE V6: 3222
Nissan 300ZX: 3223
Nissan 300ZX Turbo: 3224
Nissan Micra SGL 5-DR: 3225
Nissan Pulsar NX SE: 3226

Nissan Sunny ZX Coupe: 3227
Nissan Sunny 1.6 SLX Coupe: 3228
Subaru Justy: 4267
Subaru XT Turbo 4WD: 4268
Suzuki SJ413V JX: 4327
Suzuki Swift 1.3 GLX: 4328
Suzuki Swift 1.3 GLX Executive: 4329
Toyota Camry 2.0 GLi: 4445
Toyota Camry 2.0 GLi Estate: 4446
Toyota Celica GT Cabriolet: 4447
Toyota Corolla Executive: 4448
Toyota Corolla FX-16 GTS: 4449
Toyota Landcruiser: 4450
Toyota MR2 Supercharged: 4451
Toyota Supra: 4452

1988 Acura Integra LS Special Edition: 31
Chevrolet Nova Twin Cam: 923
Chevrolet Sprint: 924
Chrysler Conquest TSi: 1007
Daihatsu Charade CLX: 1126
Daihatsu Charade Turbo: 1127
Honda Civic CRX: 2140
Honda CRX Si: 2141
Honda CRX Si Jackson: 2142
Honda Legend Saloon Automatic: 2143
Honda Shuttle 1.6i RT4 4WD: 2144
Isuzu I-Mark RS Turbo: 2258
Isuzu Impulse Turbo: 2259
Mazda 121 1.3 LX Sun Top: 2741
Mazda 323 GTX: 2742
Mazda 323 Turbo 4x4: 2743
Mazda 626 2.0 GLX Executive Estate: 2744
Mazda 626 2.0i GT 4WS: 2745
Mazda 929: 2746
Mazda MX-6: 2747
Mazda MX-6 GT: 2748
Mazda RX-7 Convertible: 2749
Mazda RX-7 GTU: 2750
Mazda RX-7 Turbo: 2751
Mitsubishi Cordia Turbo: 3097
Mitsubishi Galant 2000 GLSi: 3098
Mitsubishi Galant GTi-16v: 3099
Mitsubishi Lancer GTi 16v: 3100
Mitsubishi Mirage Turbo: 3101
Nissan 200SX SE V6: 3229
Nissan 240SX: 3230
Nissan 300ZX: 3231
Subaru 4WD Turbo Estate: 4269
Subaru Justy 4WD GL: 4270
Subaru Justy GL: 4271
Subaru XT6 4WD: 4272
Toyota Carina 1.6 GL: 4453
Toyota Celica All-Trac Turbo: 4454
Toyota Celica GT4: 4455
Toyota Corolla 1.3 GL: 4456
Toyota Corolla 4WD Estate: 4457
Toyota Landcruiser II TD: 4458
Toyota Supra: 4459
Toyota Supra Turbo: 4460

1989 Acura Integra LS: 32
Acura Legend Coupe L: 33
Daihatsu Charade 1.3 CX: 1128
Daihatsu Charade CLS: 1129
Daihatsu Sportrak EL: 1130
Honda Civic Si: 2145
Honda Civic Si HKS: 2146
Honda CRX Si HKS: 2147
Honda Prelude Si 4WS: 2148
Honda Shuttle 1.4 GL Automatic: 2149
Mazda 323 1.6i: 2752
Mazda 323 1.8 GT: 2753
Mazda MPV: 2754
Mazda MX-5 Miata: 2755
Mazda MX-6 GT 4WS: 2756
Mazda RX-7 Convertible Racing Beat: 2757
Mazda RX-7 GTUs: 2758
Mazda RX-7 Turbo II: 2759
Mitsubishi Eclipse: 3102
Mitsubishi Eclipse GSX: 3103
Mitsubishi Galant GS: 3104
Mitsubishi Shogun V6 5-door: 3105
Mitsubishi Starion 2.6 Turbo: 3106
Mitsubishi Starion ESI-R: 3107
Nissan 200SX: 3232
Nissan 240SX Turbo Tokico/Cartech: 3233
Nissan 300ZX: 3234
Nissan Maxima: 3235
Nissan Maxima SE: 3236
Nissan Micra 1.2 GSX: 3237
Nissan Prairie: 3238
Nissan Sunny 1.4 LS: 3239
Plymouth Laser RS: 3521
Subaru Justy GL II 5-door 4WD: 4273
Subaru Legacy FIA Record: 4274
Subaru XT6: 4275
Suzuki Swift 1.3 GLX: 4330
Suzuki Swift 1.3 GTi: 4331
Suzuki Vitara JLX: 4332
Toyota Camry V6 GXi: 4461
Toyota Carina II 1.6 GL Liftback: 4462
Toyota Corolla GTS: 4463
Toyota MR2 Supercharged: 4464
Toyota Supra 3.0i Turbo: 4465
Toyota Supra Turbo: 4466
Toyota Supra Turbo TRD: 4467

1990 Acura Integra GS: 34
Acura Legend Coupe: 35
Acura NSX: 36
Daihatsu Applause 16 Xi: 1131
Honda Accord 2.0 EXi: 2150
Honda Concerto 1.6i 16: 2151
Honda CRX 1.6i VT: 2152
Infiniti M30: 2230
Infiniti Q45: 2231
Isuzu Impulse XS: 2260
Lexus LS400: 2570
Mazda MX-5 Miata Millen: 2760
Mazda MX-6 GT: 2761
Mazda Protege: 2762
Mazda RX-7 Convertible: 2763
Mazda RX-7 Turbo: 2764
Mitsubishi Galant 2000 GLSi Coupe: 3108
Mitsubishi Lancer GLXi 4WD Liftback: 3109
Mitsubishi Lancer Liftback 1800 GTi-16v: 3110
Nissan 300ZX: 3240
Nissan 300ZX Turbo: 3241
Nissan Skyline GT-R: 3243
Subaru Legacy 2.2 GX 4WD: 4276
Suzuki Swift GT: 4333
Toyota Celica 2.0 GT: 4468
Toyota Celica All-Trac Turbo: 4469
Toyota Celica GTS: 4470
Toyota MR2: 4471
Toyota MR2 GT: 4472
Toyota MR2 Turbo: 4473
Toyota Previa LE: 4474
Toyota Starlet GL: 4475

1991 Acura Legend LS: 37
Dodge Stealth R/T Turbo: 1347
Geo Storm GSi: 1994
Honda Civic 1.5 VEi: 2153
Honda Civic 1.6i VT: 2154
Honda Legend: 2155
Honda NSX: 2156
Honda Prelude Si: 2157
Infiniti G20: 2232
Isuzu Impulse RS: 2261
Lexus SC400: 2571
Mazda 121 GSX: 2765
Mazda 323 1.8 GT: 2766
Mazda MX-3 V6: 2767
Mazda RX-7 Cartech: 2768
Mazda RX-7 Infini IV: 2769

Mazda RX-7 Mariah Mode Six: 2770
Mazda RX-7 Turbo: 2771
Mitsubishi 3000GT VR-4: 3111
Mitsubishi Colt 1800 GTI-16v: 3112
Mitsubishi Diamante LS: 3113
Mitsubishi Galant VR-4: 3114
Mitsubishi Shogun V6 LWB: 3115
Mitsubishi Sigma: 3116
Mitsubishi Space Runner 1800-16v GLXi: 3117
Nissan 100NX: 3244
Nissan 240SX: 3245
Nissan 300ZX Motor Sports International SR-71: 3246
Nissan 300ZX Turbo Millen Super GTZ: 3247
Nissan 300ZX Twin Turbo: 3248
Nissan NX2000: 3249
Nissan Sentra SE-R: 3252
Nissan Sunny 1.6 GS 5-door: 3253
Subaru Legacy 2.0 4Cam Turbo Estate: 4277
Subaru Legacy Sports Sedan: 4278
Toyota Camry 2.2 GL: 4476
Toyota Celica GT Convertible: 4477
Toyota Landcruiser VX: 4478
Toyota MR2: 4479
Toyota MR2 HKS: 4480
Toyota Previa: 4481
Toyota Tercel LE: 4482

1992 Honda Legend Coupe: 2158
Honda NSX Auto: 2159
Honda Prelude Si 4WS: 2160
Lexus ES300: 2572
Mazda MX-3 1.6 Auto: 2772
Mazda MX-3 GS: 2773
Nissan 200SX: 3254
Nissan Sunny 2.0 GTi: 3255
Subaru SVX: 4279
Toyota Paseo: 4483

Japan total: 596

Korea

1982 Hyundai Pony 1400 TLS: 2219

1984 Hyundai Stellar 1600 GSL: 2220

1985 Hyundai Pony 1.5 GLS: 2221

1986 Hyundai Excel GL: 2222
Hyundai Excel GLS: 2223

1987 Pontiac Le Mans: 3583

1989 Hyundai Sonata 2.0i GLS: 2224

1990 Hyundai Sonata 2.4i GLS: 2225

1991 Hyundai Lantra 1.6 Cdi: 2226
Hyundai S Coupe GSi: 2227
Hyundai X2 1.5 GSi: 2228

Korea total: 11

Malaysia

1989 Proton 1.5 SE Aeroback: 3754

1991 Proton 1.5 SE Triple Valve Aeroback: 3755

Malaysia total: 2

Nederlands

1930 Minerva 22/28hp Limousine: 3042

1958 DAF 55: 1107

1960 DAF 600 de Luxe: 1108

1962 DAF Daffodil: 1109
DAF Daffodil de Luxe Extra: 1110

1967 DAF 44: 1111

1971 DAF 55 Estate: 1112

1973 DAF 66SL: 1113

1974 DAF 66SL 1300: 1114

Nederlands total: 9

Poland

1975 Polski Fiat 125P: 3525

1979 Polonez 1500: 3524

Poland total: 2

Romania

1985 Dacia Duster GLX: 1106

Romania total: 1

Spain

1934 Hispano-Suiza 30/120 Saloon: 2083
Hispano-Suiza 54/220: 2084

1976 Seat 1200 Sport: 4110

1985 Seat 1.5 GLX: 4111

1986 Seat Malaga 1.2L: 4112

1989 Seat Ibiza SXi: 4113

1992 Seat Toledo 1.9 CL Diesel: 4114
Seat Toledo 2.0 GTi: 4115

Spain total: 8

Sweden

1954 Volvo 444: 4891

1956 Saab 93: 4053
Volvo PV444 California: 4892

1957 Saab 93: 4054
Volvo PV444: 4893
Volvo PV444 Sports: 4894
Volvo PV444L: 4895

1958 Saab Gran Turismo: 4055
Volvo 4-speed: 4896
Volvo Amazon: 4897

1959 Volvo 122S: 4898

1960 Saab 96: 4056

1961 Saab 96 Sedan: 4057
Volvo 122S: 4899
Volvo P1800: 4900

1962 Volvo 122: 4901
Volvo 122S B18: 4902
Volvo P1800: 4903

1963 Saab 95: 4058
Volvo 121 Estate: 4904
Volvo PV544: 4905

1964 Saab 850GT: 4059

1965 Volvo 122 Automatic: 4906
Volvo 131: 4907

1966 Saab 96: 4060
Volvo 1800S: 4908

1967 Saab 96 V4: 4061
Saab V4: 4062
Volvo 144S: 4909

1968 Saab Sonnet V4: 4063
Saab Station Wagon V4: 4064
Volvo 145S Estate: 4910
Volvo 145S Wagon: 4911

1969 Saab 99: 4065
Saab Sport: 4066
Volvo 142S 2.0: 4912
Volvo 144S: 4913
Volvo 164: 4914

1970 Saab 99: 4067
Saab 99E: 4068
Saab Sonnet III: 4069
Volvo 164 Automatic: 4915
Volvo 1800E: 4916

1971 Saab 99: 4070
Volvo 142E: 4917
Volvo 144 Grand Luxe: 4918
Volvo 145E Estate: 4919

1972 Saab 99CM4 2.0: 4071
Saab 99E 1.85: 4072
Saab 99EA: 4073
Saab Sonnet III: 4074
Volvo 164E: 4920
Volvo 1800 ES: 4921

1973 Saab 99E: 4075
Saab Sonnet: 4076
Volvo 144 de Luxe: 4922
Volvo 144E: 4923
Volvo 164E: 4924

1974 Saab 99LE Wagonback: 4077
Volvo 142 GL: 4925
Volvo 145: 4926

1975 Saab 99EMS: 4078
Volvo 242 GL: 4927
Volvo 244 GL: 4928
Volvo 264 GL: 4929

1976 Saab 99GL Super Combi: 4079
Volvo 242 GL: 4930
Volvo 265 DL: 4931

1977 Saab 99EMS: 4080
Volvo 244 DL: 4932
Volvo 343: 4933

1978 Saab Turbo: 4081
Volvo 242 GT: 4934
Volvo 242 IPD: 4935
Volvo 262C: 4936
Volvo 265 GLE Estate: 4937
Volvo 343: 4938

1979 Saab 900 Turbo: 4082
Saab 900GL: 4083

1980 Saab 900GLE: 4084
Volvo Diesel: 4939
Volvo GL: 4940

1981 Saab 900 Turbo: 4085
Saab 900GLS: 4086
Volvo 265 GLE: 4941

1982 Saab 900: 4087
Saab 900 Turbo: 4088
Volvo 240 GL: 4942
Volvo 360 GLT: 4943
Volvo 760 GLE: 4944
Volvo GLT Turbo: 4945

1983 Volvo 760 GLE: 4946
Volvo 760 Turbo: 4947

1984 Volvo 740 GLT: 4948
Volvo 760 GLE: 4949
Volvo GLT Wagon: 4950

1985 Saab 900 Turbo: 4089
Saab 9000 Turbo 16v: 4090
Saab 900i: 4091
Volvo 740 Turbo Wagon: 4951
Volvo 760 Turbo Estate: 4952

1986 Saab 9000: 4092
Saab 9000i: 4093
Volvo 340 GLE: 4953

1987 Volvo 480 ES: 4954
Volvo 740 Turbo: 4955
Volvo 760 GLE: 4956

1988 Saab 9000CD: 4094

1989 Saab 900 Turbo S: 4095
Saab 9000 Turbo: 4096
Saab Carlsson: 4097

Volvo 440 Turbo: 4957
Volvo 740 GLE: 4958
Volvo 740 Turbo: 4959

1990 Saab 9000CD: 4098
Saab 900SPG: 4099
Saab CDS 2.3: 4100
Volvo 440 GLE: 4960
Volvo 460 GLi: 4961
Volvo 460 Turbo: 4962
Volvo 740 GLT 16v Estate: 4963
Volvo 740 Turbo: 4964

1991 Saab 9000 2.3 Turbo TCS: 4101
Saab 9000 Turbo: 4102
Saab 9000CS Turbo S: 4103
Saab 9000S: 4104
Volvo 940 SE: 4965
Volvo 940 SE Turbo: 4966
Volvo 940 Turbo: 4967
Volvo 960 24v: 4968

1992 Saab 9000 2.3CS: 4105
Volvo 960: 4969

Sweden total: 132

Switzerland

1969 Monteverdi 375L: 3118

1990 Sbarro Chrono 3.5: 4108

Switzerland total: 2

UK

1927 Rolls-Royce Phantom I Phaeton: 3946

1928 Hillman Safety Saloon: 2022
Invicta 4.5-litre: 2241
Morris Minor Saloon: 3138

1929 Aston Martin Super Sports: 222
Austin 7 Tourer: 340
Bentley 4.5-litre: 461
Crossley 2-litre Saloon: 1103
Daimler 30hp Double-six Saloon: 1132
HE 16/60 Sports Four-seater: 2017
Hillman Segrave Saloon: 2023
Hillman Straight Eight Saloon: 2024
Humber Snipe: 2180
Lagonda 3-litre Tourer: 2432
Lea-Francis 12/40 Saloon: 2566
Lea-Francis Hyper-sports: 2567
MG Midget: 2968
MG Six Sports: 2969
Morris Isis: 3139
Rolls-Royce 20 Saloon: 3947
Sunbeam Weymann Saloon: 4280
Vauxhall 20/60 Limousine: 4609

1930 AJS 9hp Saloon: 38
Bentley 4.5-litre Supercharged: 462

Bentley 8-litre Saloon: 463
Bentley Speed Six Weymann: 464
Ford 24 Saloon: 1609
Frazer-Nash Super Sports: 1979
HE Supercharged Six Coupe: 2018
Lagonda 2-litre Supercharged: 2433
Morris 8 Minor: 3140
Triumph Super 7 Saloon: 4487
Triumph Supercharged 7: 4488
Wolseley Hornet: 4977

1931 AC Acedes Magna Coupe: 2
Alvis 12/60 Sports: 154
Armstrong Siddeley 15 Saloon: 209
Aston Martin Sports Four-seater: 223
Austin 7 Saloon: 341
Austin 7 Sports Two-seater: 342
Austin 7 Sunshine Saloon: 343
Frazer-Nash Boulogne II: 1980
Invicta 4.5-litre: 2242
Jaguar SS1 Sports Tourer: 2263
Lagonda 3-litre Special Tourer: 2434
MG Mk II Montlhery Supercharged: 2970
Morris Major Six Saloon: 3141
Rolls-Royce 25 Saloon: 3948
Rover Light Six Speed Model: 3973
Vauxhall Cadet Saloon: 4610
Wolseley Viper Saloon: 4978

1932 Alvis Speed 20 (72bhp): 155
Alvis Speed 20 (87bhp): 156
Armstrong Siddeley Rally Tourer: 210
Aston Martin 1.5-litre: 224
BSA FWD Tourer: 646
Ford V8: 1610
Hillman Minx Sports Tourer: 2025
Hillman Wizard 65 Saloon de Luxe: 2026
Humber 16/60 Saloon: 2181
Humber Pullman Limousine: 2182
Lanchester 15/18 Saloon: 2477
Rolls-Royce Phantom II: 3949
Rover Pilot: 3974
Singer 14/6 Saloon: 4159
Talbot 65 Saloon: 4335

1933 AC Ace Fixed-head Coupe: 3
Armstrong Siddeley Long 15hp Saloon: 211
Aston Martin Le Mans: 225
Daimler 15hp Saloon: 1133
Ford 8 Tudor Saloon: 1611
Frazer-Nash 1.5-litre: 1981
Frazer-Nash TT Replica: 1982
Lagonda 16/80 Tourer: 2435
Lea-Francis 2-litre Saloon: 2568
Morris 10/4: 3142
Morris 10/6: 3143
Morris Cowley Saloon: 3144
Morris Cowley Six: 3145
Rolls-Royce Phantom II: 3950
Singer 9 Sports: 4160
Standard 16 Special Saloon: 4191
Standard Avon 16 Open Four-Seater: 4192
Standard Avon Coupe: 4193
Talbot 105 Speed Model: 4336

1934 AC Ace Sports Four-seater: 4
AC Greyhound Close-coupled Saloon: 5
Aston Martin 1.5-litre Mk II: 226
Austin 10/4 Saloon: 344
Austin 12/6: 345
Austin 15.9hp Ascot Saloon: 346
Austin 20 Ranelagh Landaulet: 347
Bentley Sedan: 465
British Salmson Closed-coupled Saloon: 642
Crossley 10hp Torquay: 1104
Ford 10 de Luxe Saloon: 1612
Frazer-Nash 14hp Sports Tourer: 1983
Hillman 20/70 Limousine: 2027
Hillman Aero Minx Coupe: 2028
Humber 12 Vogue: 2183
Lagonda 3.5-litre Tourer: 2436
Lagonda Le Mans: 2437
Lagonda Rapier Four-seater Tourer: 2438
MG Magna Continental Coupe: 2971
MG Magnette N Two-seater: 2972
MG Midget P Type: 2973
Morris 15/6 Saloon: 3146
Morris 8 Saloon: 3147
Railton Terraplane: 3756
Riley 12 Mentone Saloon: 3924
Rover 12 Saloon: 3975
Talbot 75 Saloon: 4337
Triumph Gloria 6 Vitesse: 4489
Vauxhall 20 Saloon: 4611

1935 AC Ace Drop-head Coupe: 6
Alvis Firebird Saloon: 157
Armstrong Siddeley 17hp Sports Foursome: 212
Armstrong Siddeley 30 Special Sports Saloon: 213
Aston Martin 1.5-litre: 227
Austin 16 Hertford Saloon: 348
Austin 7 Ruby Saloon: 349
Crossley 10hp Regis Sports Saloon: 1105
Hillman 20/27 Sports Saloon: 2029
Hillman Aero Minx Cresta Saloon: 2030
Humber 12 Six-light Saloon: 2184
Humber Snipe Sports Saloon: 2185
Jowett 7hp Curlew de Luxe: 2406
Lagonda Rapide Tourer: 2439
Lanchester 18 Saloon: 2478
Marendaz 15/90 Special Tourer: 2647
MG Magnette KN Saloon: 2974
Morris 10/6 Sports Tourer: 3148
Morris 16 Series II Saloon: 3149
Morris 21 Series II Saloon: 3150
Railton Light Sports Tourer: 3757
Riley 1.5 Kestrel Special: 3925
Rolls-Royce 20/25 Touring Saloon: 3951
Rover Speed 14 Streamline Coupe: 3976
Singer Le Mans Special Speed Model: 4161
Squire X101: 4190
Sunbeam 20 Saloon: 4281
Talbot 75 Drop-frame Sports Saloon: 4338
Triumph 2-litre Southern Cross: 4490
Vauxhall 27 Saloon: 4612
Wolseley 14 Hornet Special: 4979

1936 AC 2-litre Aero Saloon: 7
AC Ace: 8
Armstrong Siddeley 17hp Touring Saloon: 214
Aston Martin Sports Saloon: 228
Austin 20 Mayfair Limousine: 350
Austin 7 Ruby Saloon: 351
Bentley 4.25-litre: 466
British Salmson 12hp Four-seater Tourer: 643
British Salmson 20.8hp Sports Two-seater: 644
Daimler 15hp Saloon: 1134
Daimler 25.7hp Light Straight Eight Coupe: 1135
Ford V8 Touring Saloon: 1614
Hillman Hawk Sports Saloon: 2031
Humber Pullman Limousine: 2186
Humber Snipe Sports Saloon: 2187
Jaguar SS 2.5-litre: 2264
Jensen 3.5-litre Saloon: 2384
Lagonda 4.5-litre Tourer: 2440
MG Midget PB: 2975
MG Midget Series T: 2976
Morgan 4/4: 3120
Railton Straight Eight Saloon: 3758
Riley 1.5 Falcon Saloon: 3926
Rolls-Royce Phantom III: 3952
Talbot 105 Airline Saloon: 4339
Talbot 3.5-litre Speed Saloon: 4340
Triumph 14/60 Dolomite Saloon: 4491
Triumph Gloria 6 Vitesse: 4492
Triumph Vitesse: 4493
Wolseley Super 6: 4980

1937 AC 2-litre Fixed-head Coupe: 9
Alvis 4.3-litre Vanden Plas Saloon: 158
Alvis Crested Eagle 25: 159
Armstrong Siddeley 25.3hp Town and Country Saloon: 215
Armstrong Siddeley Six-light Saloon: 216
Aston Martin 2-litre: 229
Austin 10 Cambridge: 352
Austin 14 Goodwood Saloon: 353
Austin Big 7: 354
Bentley 4.5-litre: 467
British Salmson 14hp Saloon: 645
Ford 10: 1615
Frazer-Nash 1.5-litre: 1984
Hillman 80 Limousine: 2032
Hillman Minx Saloon de Luxe: 2033
HRG 12hp Sports Two-seater: 2166
Humber Snipe Drop-head Foursome: 2188
Jaguar SS 100 2.5-litre: 2265
Jowett De Luxe Saloon: 2407
Lagonda Rapide: 2441
Lammas-Graham Drop-head Coupe: 2476
Lanchester 18: 2479
Lanchester SS 2.5-litre: 2480
Morris 10 Series II: 3151
Railton Cobham Saloon: 3759
Riley 8/90 Adelphi Saloon: 3927
Riley 9 Monaco: 3928
Riley Kestrel Sprite: 3929
Riley Sprite: 3930
Rover 16 Sports Saloon: 3977
Standard Flying 10: 4194
Triumph Gloria 12: 4494
Vauxhall 10/4 de Luxe Saloon: 4613
Vauxhall 14 de Luxe: 4614
Wolseley Salon de Ville: 4981

1938 AC 2-litre Sports: 10
Alvis 12/70 Tourer: 160
Alvis Speed 25: 161
Armstrong Siddeley 16 Saloon: 217
Aston Martin Drop-head Coupe: 230

Austin 14: 355
Bentley 4.25-litre: 468
Daimler 18hp 2.5-litre: 1136
Daimler 24hp Limousine: 1137
Ford Prefect: 1616
Ford V8 30: 1617
HRG 1.5-litre: 2167
Humber 16.9hp Saloon: 2189
Humber Snipe Sports Saloon: 2190
Jaguar SS 1.5-litre: 2266
Jaguar SS 100 3.5-litre: 2267
Jensen 3.5-litre Tourer: 2385
Lagonda 4.5-litre: 2442
Lagonda 4.5-litre 12 Cylinder Saloon: 2443

Lagonda Saloon de Ville: 2444
Lanchester 11 Saloon: 2481
Lanchester Roadrider de Luxe Saloon: 2482
Morgan 4/4: 3121
Morris 10 Series III: 3152
Morris 8 Tourer: 3153
Morris 8hp Tourer: 3154
Railton 10 Drop-head Coupe: 3760
Riley 16 2.5: 3931
Rover 14: 3978
Rover 16 Saloon: 3979
Standard Flying 20: 4195
Talbot 10hp Drop-head Coupe: 4341
Talbot 3-litre Saloon: 4342
Vauxhall 10 Saloon de Luxe: 4615
Vauxhall 12/4 de Luxe Saloon: 4616
Vauxhall 25 Saloon: 4617
Wolseley 14/56 Salon de Ville: 4982
Wolseley Drop-head Coupe: 4983
Wolseley Super 6: 4984

1939 AC 2-litre: 11
Alvis 4.3-litre: 162
Aston Martin 2-litre: 231
Austin 8 Saloon: 356
Bentley 4.5-litre: 469
BSA Scout: 647
Ford 8: 1618
Jowett 8hp: 2408
Lagonda Rapide: 2445
Morgan SS: 3122
Morris 8 Series E Tourer: 3155
Morris 8hp Series E Tourer: 3156
Sunbeam-Talbot 2-litre Sports Tourer: 4314
Triumph 2-litre Dolomite: 4495
Wolseley 12/48: 4985

1940 Jaguar SS 2.5-litre: 2268
Jaguar SS1 2.5-litre: 2269
Lagonda Drop-head Coupe: 2446
Lanchester Roadrider de Luxe Saloon: 2483
Singer Super 10 Saloon: 4162
Vauxhall 12 Saloon: 4618

1946 Daimler Twenty-Seven Limousine: 1138

1947 Austin 16 Saloon: 357
Austin 8 Saloon: 358
Bentley 4.5-litre Mk VI Saloon: 470
Hillman Minx Saloon: 2034
Humber Hawk Saloon: 2191
MG TC Midget: 2977
Riley 1.5: 3932
Riley 2.5 Saloon: 3933
Standard 12 Saloon: 4196
Sunbeam-Talbot 10 Sports Saloon: 4315
Sunbeam-Talbot 2-litre Sports Saloon: 4316
Triumph 1800 Roadster: 4496
Triumph 1800 Saloon: 4497
Vauxhall 12 Saloon: 4619

1948 Allard Drop-head Coupe: 148
Allard V8: 149
Armstrong Siddeley 2-litre Saloon: 218
Austin A125 Sheerline: 359
Austin A40: 360
Bristol 400: 638
Daimler Straight Eight: 1139
Ford Prefect: 1620
Ford V8 Pilot: 1621
Healey 2.4-litre Roadster: 2019
HRG 1.5-litre: 2168
Jaguar 3.5-litre: 2270
Jaguar Mk IV: 2271
Jowett Javelin: 2409
Lea-Francis Sports: 2569
Morris Minor: 3157
Morris Oxford: 3158
Riley 2.5 Sports: 3934
Standard 8: 4197
Standard Vanguard: 4198
Sunbeam-Talbot 90 Sports Saloon: 4317
Vauxhall 14: 4620
Vauxhall Velox: 4621

1949 AC 2-litre Saloon: 12
Austin A135 Princess: 361
Austin A70: 362
Austin A90 Atlantic: 363
Ford Anglia 10 Saloon: 1622
Ford Anglia 8 Saloon: 1623
Hillman Minx Saloon: 2035
Humber Hawk: 2192
Humber Imperial: 2193
Humber Imperial Saloon: 2194
Humber Super Snipe: 2195
Jaguar 3.5-litre Mk V: 2272
Lagonda 2.5-litre Saloon: 2447
Lanchester 10: 2484
MG TC: 2978
Riley 2.5 Saloon: 3935
Rolls-Royce Silver Wraith: 3953
Rover 75: 3980
Rover 75 Saloon: 3981
Singer 9 Roadster: 4163
Singer SM1500 Saloon: 4164
Sunbeam-Talbot 80 Saloon: 4318
Triumph 2000 Saloon: 4498
Triumph Roadster: 4499
Vauxhall Wyvern: 4622
Wolseley 4/50: 4986

1950 Jaguar XK120: 2273
MG TD: 2979
Morris Minor Tourer: 3159
Morris Oxford Saloon: 3160
Rover 75: 3982
Vauxhall Velox: 4623
Wolseley 6/80: 4987

1951 Aston Martin DB2: 232
Austin A40: 364
Austin A40 Sport: 365
Ford Consul: 1624
Hillman Minx Estate: 2036
Hillman Minx Sedan: 2037
Humber Hawk: 2196
Jaguar C Type: 2274
Jaguar XK120: 2275
Jaguar XK140: 2276
Jensen Interceptor Cabriolet: 2386
MG TD: 2980
Sunbeam Talbot 90: 4282
Vauxhall Velox: 4624

1952 Allard K2: 150
Alvis 3-litre: 163
Austin A40 Somerset: 366
Austin Princess: 367
Bentley Continental: 471
Bentley Mk VI: 472
Bentley Sports Saloon: 473
Bristol 401: 639
Healey Tickford Saloon: 2020
Hillman Minx Convertible: 2038
Humber Pullman Limousine: 2197
Humber Super Snipe: 2198
Jaguar Mk VII: 2277
MG 1.25-litre Saloon: 2981
Morgan Plus 4: 3123
Riley 2.5: 3936
Rover 75: 3983
Singer SM Roadster: 4165
Singer SM1500 Saloon: 4166
Standard Vanguard: 4199
Vauxhall Velox: 4625
Vauxhall Wyvern: 4626
Wolseley 6/80: 4988

1953 AC 2-litre: 13
Alvis 3-litre: 164
Armstrong Siddeley Sapphire Saloon: 219
Aston Martin DB2/4 Saloon: 233
Austin A30: 368
Austin-Healey 100: 428
Daimler Conquest: 1140
Ford Zephyr Sedan: 1628
Ford Zephyr Sedan Modified: 1629
Frazer-Nash Targa Florio Turismo: 1985
Healey Sports Convertible: 2021
Hillman Minx Califonian Coupe: 2039
Humber Super Snipe: 2199
Humber Super Snipe Mk IV: 2200
Jaguar Mk VII: 2278
Jaguar XK120 Coupe: 2279
Jaguar XK120C: 2280
Jaguar XK120M: 2281
Jowett Jupiter: 2410
Jowett Jupiter Mk IA: 2411
MG Midget: 2982
MG TD: 2983
MG TDC Mk II: 2984
Morris Minor Series II: 3161
Morris Oxford Travellers' Car: 3162
Riley 1.5: 3937
Riley 2.5: 3938
Rolls-Royce Silver Dawn: 3954
Rover Jet: 3984
Singer Roadster: 4167
Singer SM1500 Saloon: 4168
Standard 8: 4200
Standard Vanguard Estate: 4201
Standard Vanguard Phase II: 4202
Sunbeam-Talbot 90 Mk IIA: 4319
Wolseley 4/44: 4989

1954 Allard K3 Convertible: 151
Allard Palm Beach: 152
Aston Martin DB2: 234
Austin A30: 369
Austin A40 Somerset Coupe: 370
Austin Princess: 371
Austin-Healey 100: 429
Bentley Sports: 474
Ford Anglia Saloon: 1630
Ford Popular: 1631
Hillman Minx Supercharged: 2040
Humber Hawk Mk VI: 2201
MG Magnette: 2985
MG TD Laystall: 2986
MG TF: 2987
MG TF 1500: 2988
MG TF Supercharged: 2989
Morgan Plus 4: 3124
Morris Minor: 3163
Morris Oxford Saloon: 3164
Nash Metropolitan: 3197
Nash Nash-Healey Roadster: 3198
Rolls-Royce Silver Dawn: 3955
Rover 60: 3985
Rover 90: 3986
Singer SM Roadster: 4169
Sunbeam Alpine: 4283
Sunbeam Alpine II: 4284
Triumph TR2: 4500
Triumph TR2 Sports: 4501
Vauxhall Velox: 4627

1955 Austin A50 Cambridge: 372
Austin A90 Westminster: 373
Austin-Healey 100S: 430
Daimler One-O-Four Ladies' Model: 1141
Daimler Regency Mk II: 1142
Ford Anglia: 1632
Ford Prefect: 1633
Ford Prefect 1172cc: 1634
Ford Zodiac: 1636
Frazer-Nash Targa Florio Fast Roadster: 1986
Hillman Husky: 2041
Hillman Minx de Luxe: 2042
Jaguar Mk VII: 2282
Jaguar XK140MC: 2283
Land Rover Station Wagon: 2556
MG A: 2990
MG Magnette: 2991
Morgan Plus 4: 3125
Morris Cowley: 3165
Nash Metropolitan: 3199
Nash Nash-Healey Roadster Supercharged: 3200
Riley Pathfinder: 3939
Rover 75: 3987
Singer Hunter: 4170
Standard 10: 4203
Sunbeam Mk III: 4285
Swallow Doretti: 4334
Triumph TR2 Hardtop: 4502
Vauxhall Cresta: 4628
Vauxhall Wyvern: 4629
Wolseley 6/90: 4990

1956 AC Ace Roadster: 14
AC Aceca: 15
Aston Martin Spyder Touring: 235
Austin A105: 374
Austin A30 Countryman: 375
Austin-Healey 100M: 431
Bentley Continental Park Ward DH Coupe: 475
Bentley Series S: 476
Dellow Mk V: 1254
Ford Anglia: 1637
Ford Consul Mk II: 1638
Ford Zephyr: 1642
Hillman Minx de Luxe: 2043
Humber Hawk Estate: 2202
Jaguar 2.4 Sedan: 2284
Jaguar D Type: 2285
Jaguar Mk VII Auto: 2286
Jaguar XK 140: 2287
Jensen 541: 2387
Lagonda 3-litre Saloon: 2448
MG A: 2992
Morris Isis: 3166
Paramount Roadster: 3381
Riley Pathfinder: 3939
Rover 60: 3988
Rover 90: 3989
Standard Vanguard III: 4204
Standard Vanguard Sportsman: 4205

Sunbeam Rapier: 4286
Triumph TR3: 4503

1957 AC Ace Bristol: 16
Alvis 3-litre Graber: 165
Austin A55: 376
Austin A95 Westminster: 377
Austin-Healey 100/6: 432
Berkeley Sports: 484
Daimler One-O-Four: 1143
Ford Zodiac Automatic: 1643
Hillman Minx Convertible: 2044
Humber Hawk: 2203
Jaguar 2.4 Saloon: 2288
Jaguar Mk VIII: 2289
Jaguar XK150: 2290
Jaguar XKSS: 2291
Lotus 11 Le Mans: 2589
Lotus Mk XI: 2590
Lotus Sports: 2591
MG A Coupe: 2993
Morgan 4/4 Modified: 3126
Morris Minor 1000: 3167
Morris Minor 1100: 3168
Morris Oxford Series III: 3169
Rover 105S: 3990
Standard Vanguard III: 4206
Sunbeam Rapier: 4287
Triumph TR2 Hardtop: 4504
Triumph TR3: 4505
Wolseley 15/50: 4991
Wolseley 6/90: 4992

1958 AC AC-Bristol Zagato: 17
AC Aceca-Bristol Coupe: 18
AC Bristol: 19
AC Bristol D-2: 20
Aston Martin Mk III: 236
Austin A105 Automatic: 378
Austin A35 4-door: 379
Austin A40: 380
Austin A55: 381
Austin A95 Countryman: 382
Austin-Healey 100/6: 433
Austin-Healey Mille Miglia: 434
Austin-Healey Sprite: 435
Berkeley Sports: 485
Berkeley Sports 4: 486
Daimler Majestic: 1144
Elva Courier: 1358
Ford Anglia de Luxe: 1644
Ford Consul: 1645
Ford Zephyr Estate: 1648
Frisky Coupe: 1993
Hillman Hunter Husky: 2045
Hillman Husky: 2046
Hillman Minx Estate: 2047
Hillman Minx Series II: 2048
Hillman Minx Series III Convertible: 2049
Humber Hawk Estate: 2204
Humber Super Snipe: 2205
Jaguar 3.4: 2292
Jaguar XK150: 2293
Jaguar XK150S: 2294
Jensen 541R: 2388
MG A Judson: 2994
MG A Twin Cam: 2995
MG Magnette: 2996
MG Twin Cam MGA: 2997
Morris Minor 1000 Traveller: 3170
Morris Oxford Traveller Series III: 3171
Nash Metropolitan 1500: 3202
Riley 1.5: 3941
Rolls-Royce Silver Cloud: 3956
Rolls-Royce Silver Cloud "S": 3957
Rover 105R de Luxe: 3991
Singer Gazelle IIA Convertible: 4171
Standard 8: 4207
Standard Ensign: 4208
Standard Pennant: 4209
Standard Super 10: 4210
Standard Vanguard III Automatic: 4211
Sunbeam Rapier: 4288
Sunbeam Rapier Series II: 4289
Triumph Station Wagon: 4506
Vauxhall Cresta: 4630
Vauxhall Victor: 4631
Vauxhall Victor Estate: 4632
Wolseley 1500: 4993

1959 Allard GT Coupe: 153
Alvis 3-litre TD21: 166
Armstrong Siddeley Star Sapphire: 220
Aston Martin DB4: 237
Austin A105 Vanden Plas: 383
Austin A55 Cambridge Mk II: 384
Austin A99: 385
Austin Gipsy: 386
Austin-Healey 3000: 436
Austin-Healey Sprite Hardtop: 437
Daimler DK 400B: 1145
Daimler V8 SP250: 1146
Ford Anglia: 1649
Ford Popular II: 1651
Hillman Minx Series IIIA Easidrive: 2050
Humber Super Snipe: 2206
Jaguar XK150S: 2295
MG A 1600: 2998
MG Magnette Mk III: 2999
Mini Minor de Luxe: 3043
Morgan Plus 4: 3127
Peerless GT Coupe: 3383
Rover 3-litre: 3992
Rover 80: 3993
Sunbeam Alpine: 4290
Sunbeam Rapier III: 4291
Triumph Herald Coupe: 4507
Triumph Herald Saloon: 4508
Vauxhall Friary Estate Car: 4633
Vauxhall Victor de Luxe: 4634
Wolseley 15/60: 4994
Wolseley 6/99: 4995

1960 AC Aceca-Bristol: 21
Austin A40 Countryman: 387
Austin A99: 388
Austin A99 Automatic: 389
Austin-Healey Sebring Sprite: 438
Austin-Healey Sprite Supercharged: 439
Bentley S2 Continental: 477
Berkeley B95: 487
Daimler SP250: 1147
Ford Anglia: 1654
Ford Consul Mk II: 1655
Ford Zephyr: 1660
Gordon GT: 2008
Hillman Easidrive: 2051
Hillman Hunter Husky Series II: 2052
Humber Super Snipe Estate: 2207
Jaguar 3.4: 2296
Jaguar 3.8 Sedan: 2297
Lotus Elite: 2592
Mini Minor: 3044
Mini Traveller: 3045
Riley 4/68: 3942
Rolls-Royce Silver Cloud II: 3958
Rolls-Royce Silver Cloud II V8: 3959
Rover 100: 3994
Rover 3-litre: 3995
Sunbeam Alpine: 4292
Triumph Herald Convertible: 4509
Triumph Herald Coupe: 4510
Turner Turner-Climax: 4582
Vanden Plas Princess: 4604
Vauxhall Cresta: 4635
Vauxhall Cresta Overdrive: 4636
Vauxhall Velox III: 4637

1961 AC Greyhound: 22
Aston Martin DB4: 238
Austin A55 Countryman: 390
Austin Seven 850: 391
Austin-Healey 3000: 440
Austin-Healey Sprite Mk II: 441
Bristol 407: 640
Daimler Majestic Major: 1148
Fairthorpe Zeta: 1369
Ford Consul Capri: 1661
Gilbern GT: 1995
Humber 3-litre: 2208
Humber Super Snipe Series III: 2209
Jaguar E Type Coupe: 2298
Jaguar XKE: 2299
Jensen 541S Automatic: 2389
Lotus 7: 2593
Lotus Super 7: 2594
MG A 1600 Mk II: 3000
MG A Mk II: 3001
MG Midget: 3002
Mini Cooper: 3046
Morris Minor 1000: 3172
Ogle 1.5: 3267
Riley 1.5: 3943
Rover 100: 3996
Rover 3-litre Automatic: 3997
Singer Gazelle Series IIIB: 4172
Singer Vogue: 4173
Standard Vanguard: 4212
Sunbeam Alpine Mk II: 4293
Triumph Herald 1200: 4511
Turner Sports: 4583
TVR Grantura: 4584
Vauxhall Victor Estate: 4638
Warwick GT: 4972

1962 AC Aceca-Buick: 23
AC Greyhound: 24
Alvis 3-litre TD21 Series II Automatic: 167
Aston Martin DB4: 239
Aston Martin DB4 GT Zagato: 240
Austin A40 Mk II: 392
Austin A60 Cambridge: 393
Austin-Healey 3000: 442
Austin-Healey 3000 Mk II: 443
Ford Anglia de Luxe Estate: 1666
Ford Anglia Super: 1667
Ford Consul Capri: 1668
Ford Consul Cortina: 1669
Ford Zephyr 4: 1681
Ford Zephyr 4 Automatic: 1682
Ford Zodiac Mk III: 1683
Hillman Super Minx: 2053
Hillman Super Minx Mk II: 2054

Jaguar Mk X: 2300
Lotus Super 7: 2595
MG 1100: 3003
MG B 1800: 3004
Ogle Austin Mini Cooper GT: 3268
Reliant Sabre Sports: 3782
Riley Elf: 3944
Rover 3-litre: 3998
Standard Ensign de Luxe Estate: 4213
Sunbeam Harrington Le Mans: 4294
Sunbeam Le Mans: 4295
Triumph Herald: 4512
Triumph Herald 1200 Estate: 4513
Triumph Spitfire 4: 4514
Triumph Sports 6: 4515
Triumph TR4: 4516
Vauxhall Victor Super: 4639
Vauxhall VX4/90: 4640
Wolseley 16/60 Automatic: 4996
Wolseley 6/110: 4997

1963 Austin-Healey Sprite 1100: 444
Daimler 2.5-litre V8 Saloon: 1149
Daimler Limousine: 1150
Dove GTR4: 1349
Ford Capri GT: 1684
Ford Consul Corsair GT: 1685
Ford Consul Cortina: 1686
Ford Consul Cortina 1500: 1687
Ford Cortina Estate de Luxe: 1688
Ford Cortina Lotus: 1689
Ford Cortina Super: 1690
Ford Zephyr 6 Estate: 1700
Hillman Hunter Husky III: 2055
Hillman Imp de Luxe: 2056
Humber Hawk III: 2210
Humber Sceptre: 2211
Jaguar 3.8 Mk II: 2301
Jaguar 3.8 Mk II Automatic: 2302
Jaguar E Type Coupe: 2303
Jensen CV8: 2390
Lotus Elan 1600: 2596
Lotus Elite: 2597
MG 1100: 3005
MG Magnette Mk IV: 3006
MG Midget: 3007
Mini Cooper S: 3047
Mini Super de Luxe: 3048
Morgan 4/4: 3128
Morris 1100: 3173
Rolls-Royce Silver Cloud III: 3960
Rover 2000: 3999
Rover 3-litre Coupe: 4000
Rover Coupe: 4001
Singer Vogue Mk II: 4174
Sunbeam Alpine GT: 4296
Sunbeam Alpine Series III: 4297
Triumph Herald 12/50: 4517
Triumph Spitfire 4: 4518
Triumph Vitesse 6: 4519
Vanden Plas Princess 3-litre Automatic: 4605
Vauxhall Cresta Series PB: 4641
Vauxhall Viva de Luxe: 4642
Wolseley Hornet: 4998

1964 Aston Martin DB5: 241
Austin 1800: 394
Austin-Healey 3000 Mk III: 445
Bond Equipe GT: 626
Daimler Conquest Century Saloon: 1151
Ford Consul Corsair: 1701
Ford Cortina Super: 1702
Ford Zephyr 6: 1709
Hillman Minx Series V Automatic: 2057
Hillman Super Minx Convertible: 2058
Hillman Super Minx III: 2059
Jaguar 3.8S Sedan: 2304
Jaguar 4.2 litre Mk X: 2305
Jaguar XKE: 2306

Vauxhall Victor 2300 SL: 4667
Vauxhall Viva 1800: 4668
Vauxhall Viva HC Estate: 4669
Vauxhall VX4/90: 4670

1973 Aston Martin V8 Automatic: 245
Austin Allegro 1300 Super: 406
Austin Marina GT: 407
Chrysler 2-litre: 992
Ford Capri 3000 GXL: 1811
Ford Consul 3000 GT: 1812
Ford Cortina 1600 XL: 1813
Ford Cortina 1600 XL Estate: 1814
Ford Cortina 2000 Estate: 1815
Ford Cortina 2000E: 1816
Ford Escort RS2000: 1817
Ford Granada Estate Auto: 1818
Hillman Avenger DL: 2076
Hillman Avenger GLS: 2077
Jaguar XJ12: 2324
Jensen Healey: 2398
Land Rover SWB: 2558
Lotus Europa Special 5-speed: 2616
MG B: 3023
MG B GT: 3024
MG B GT V8: 3025
MG Midget: 3026
Mini 850: 3055
Reliant Scimitar GTE: 3788
Rover 2000SC: 4013
Rover 2200SC Automatic: 4014
Triumph 1500TC: 4554
Triumph Dolomite Automatic: 4555
Triumph GT6: 4556
Triumph Spitfire: 4557
Triumph Spitfire 1500: 4558
Triumph TR6: 4559
TVR Vixen 2500M: 4588
Vauxhall Victor Estate: 4671

1974 Austin Allegro 1500 Special Automatic: 408
Austin Allegro HL: 409
Austin Vanden Plas 1500: 410
Daimler Sovereign LWB Automatic: 1154
Ford Capri II 1600 GT: 1822
Ford Escort 1100L: 1823
Ford Granada Ghia Coupe: 1824
Ford Granada GXL: 1825
Hillman Avenger 1300 GL: 2078
Hillman Avenger 1600 GLS: 2079
Humber Sceptre Estate: 2215
Jaguar XKE V12: 2325
Jensen Healey Huffaker: 2399
Jensen Interceptor III: 2400
Jensen Interceptor III Convertible: 2401
Mini 1275GT: 3056
Rolls-Royce Corniche: 3964
Rover 2200TC: 4015
Triumph 2500TC: 4560
Triumph Spitfire: 4561
Triumph Toledo: 4562
TVR 3000M: 4589
Vanden Plas 1500: 4607
Vanden Plas Princess R: 4608
Vauxhall Firenza: 4672
Vauxhall Magnum 2300: 4673
Vauxhall Viva 1256 DL: 4674
Vauxhall VX4/90: 4675

1975 Aston Martin V8: 246
Austin 2200 HL: 411
Austin Allegro 1300 Estate: 412
Caterham Super 7: 722
Ford Capri 2000S GT: 1828
Ford Consul 2000L: 1829
Ford Cortina 1300L: 1830
Ford Cortina 2000E Estate: 1831
Ford Escort 1.3 Ghia: 1832
Ford Escort RS1800: 1833
Ford Granada 2000 GL: 1834
Hillman Avenger GLS: 2080
Hillman Hunter Super: 2081
Jaguar XJ12L: 2326
Jaguar XJ3.4: 2327
Jaguar XJ5.3C: 2328
Lotus Elite: 2617
Lotus Elite 503: 2618
MG B: 3027
MG Midget 1500: 3028
Mini 1000: 3057
Mini Automatic: 3058
Panther De Ville: 3373
Panther J72: 3374
Range Rover V8: 3772
Reliant Kitten: 3789
Sunbeam Rapier: 4313
Triumph 2500S: 4563
Triumph Dolomite: 4564
Triumph Dolomite Sprint: 4565
Triumph Spitfire 1500: 4566
Triumph TR7: 4567
Vauxhall Chevette L: 4676
Vauxhall Magnum 1800: 4677

1976 Austin Allegro 1100: 413
Austin Princess 2200 HLS: 414
Chrysler Alpine S: 993
Chrysler Avenger Super 1300: 994
Enfield 8000 Electric: 1359
Ford Capri 1300: 1837
Ford Capri 3000S: 1838
Ford Cortina 2.0 Ghia: 1842
Ford Escort 1300 GL: 1843
Ford Escort RS2000: 1844
Ford Fiesta: 1845
Ford Granada 3000 S: 1846
Ginetta G21S: 1997
Hillman Avenger 1600 Super: 2082
Jaguar XJ12C: 2329
Jaguar XJS: 2330
Jensen GT: 2402
Jensen Interceptor III Convertible: 2403
MG B: 3029
MG Midget: 3030
MG Midget Mk IV: 3031
Mini Clubman 1100: 3059
Morris Marina 1.8 HL: 3183
Reliant Kitten DL Estate: 3790
Reliant Scimitar GTE: 3791
Rolls-Royce Silver Shadow: 3965
Rover 3500: 4016
Rover 3500 Automatic: 4017
Triumph Dolomite 1500HL: 4568
Triumph Spitfire: 4569
Triumph TR7: 4570
TVR 1600M: 4590
Vauxhall Blydenstein Chevette 1500: 4678
Vauxhall Cavalier 1600 GL: 4679
Vauxhall Cavalier GL Coupe: 4680
Vauxhall Chevette L: 4681
Vauxhall VX1800: 4682

1977 Aston Martin V8 Coupe: 247
Aston Martin V8 Vantage: 248
Austin Allegro 1750 HL: 415
Austin Maxi 1750: 416
Chrysler Alpine GL: 995
Chrysler Avenger 1600 Estate: 996
Chrysler Sunbeam 1.0LS: 997
Chrysler Sunbeam 1.6S: 998
Ford Cortina 2.3 Ghia: 1849
Ford Escort 1300 GL: 1850
Ford Escort 1600 Sport: 1851
Ford Fiesta 1000: 1852
Ford Fiesta 1100 Ghia: 1853
Ford Fiesta 1300 S: 1854
Ford Granada 2.3 GL Auto: 1856
Jaguar XJ4.2: 2331
Jaguar XJS Automatic: 2332
Jaguar XJS Tullius: 2333
Jensen GT: 2404
Lotus Eclat 523: 2619
Lotus Esprit: 2620
Lotus Esprit 16v: 2621
Lotus Sprint: 2622
MG B GT: 3032
Morris Marina 1.3 Super Coupe: 3184
Panther Lima: 3375
Reliant Scimitar GTE: 3792
Rolls-Royce Silver Shadow: 3966
Rover 2600: 4018
Triumph TR7: 4571
Triumph TR7 Tullius: 4572
TVR 2500M: 4591
TVR Taimar: 4592
Vauxhall Cavalier 1300L: 4683
Vauxhall Magnum 1800: 4684
Vauxhall VX2300 Estate: 4685

1978 Aston Martin V8: 249
Austin Princess II 2000 HL: 417
Chrysler 1300 GL: 999
Chrysler Alpine GLS: 1000
Chrysler Horizon GL: 1001
Ford Capri 1600S: 1857
Ford Granada 2.0L: 1858
Ford Granada 2.1D: 1859
Ford Granada 2.8i S: 1860
Jaguar XJ12L: 2334
Jaguar XJ5.3 Automatic: 2335
Lotus Elite V8: 2623
Morgan Plus 8: 3131
Morris Marina 1700HL: 3185
Range Rover V8: 3773
Rolls-Royce Silver Wraith II: 3967
Rover 2300: 4019
Vauxhall Carlton: 4686
Vauxhall Cavalier 2000 GLS: 4687
Vauxhall Chevette 2300 HS: 4688

1979 Bentley T2: 478
Chrysler Sunbeam 1600 Ti: 1002
Ford Capri 2000S: 1861
Ford Cortina 1600L: 1862
Ford Cortina 2.3 Ghia S: 1863
Ford Granada 2.8i GLS Estate: 1865
Jaguar XJ6 4.2: 2336
Jaguar XJ6L: 2337
Jaguar XJS: 2338
Lotus Elite: 2624
Lotus Esprit S2: 2625
MG B: 3033
MG Midget: 3034
Mini 850 Super de Luxe: 3060
Triumph Dolomite 1850HL: 4573
Triumph Spitfire: 4574
Triumph TR7: 4575
TVR Convertible Turbo: 4593
TVR Taimar Roadster: 4594
Vauxhall Royale Coupe: 4689

1980 Aston Martin Lagonda: 250
Jaguar XJ6 Series III: 2339
Lotus Eclat: 2626
MG B: 3035
Morgan Plus 8 Turbo: 3132
Rolls-Royce Silver Shadow II: 3968
Rover 3500: 4020
Triumph Spitfire: 4576
Triumph TR8: 4577
Triumph TR8 Group 44: 4578
Triumph TR8 Libra Rally: 4579
TVR 3000S Roadster: 4595

1981 Austin Metro Automatic: 418
Austin Mini Metro: 419
Daimler Double-Six HE: 1155
Ford Capri 2.8 Injection: 1871
Ford Cortina 2.0 GL: 1872
Ford Escort 1.6L Estate: 1874
Ford Fiesta Popular: 1875
Ford Fiesta XR2: 1876
Ford Granada 2.8i: 1877
Jaguar XJS: 2340
Jaguar XJS Automatic: 2341
Lotus Esprit Turbo: 2627
Morris Ital 2.0 HLS Automatic: 3186
Reliant Scimitar GTE: 3793
Rolls-Royce Silver Spirit: 3969
Rover Vanden Plas: 4021
Talbot Solara GLS: 4344
Talbot Tagora 2.2GLS: 4345
Triumph Acclaim HL: 4580
TVR Tasmin: 4596
Vauxhall Cavalier 1.6S GL: 4690

1982 Aston Martin Lagonda: 251
Aston Martin V8: 252
Austin Ambassador 2.0 HL: 420
Bentley Mulsanne Turbo: 479
De Lorean DMC 2.8-litre Coupe: 1233
Ford Escort 1600 GL: 1878
Ford Granada 2.3L Estate: 1879
Ford Sierra 1.6L: 1882
Ford Sierra 2.3 Ghia Automatic: 1883
Jaguar XJS HE: 2342
Land Rover County: 2559
MG Metro 1300: 3036
Rolls-Royce Corniche: 3970
Rolls-Royce Silver Spur: 3971
Rover 2000: 4022
Rover SD Turbo: 4023
Talbot Samba Cabriolet: 4346
Talbot Samba GL: 4347
Triumph TR7 Convertible: 4581
Vauxhall Astra 1600 GL: 4691
Vauxhall Cavalier GLS: 4692
Vauxhall Cavalier LD: 4693

1983 Aston Martin Volante: 253
Austin Maestro 1.6 HLS: 421
Austin Maestro 1600: 422
Ford Escort 1.6 GL Automatic: 1884
Ford Escort XR3i: 1885
Ford Fiesta 1.1 Ghia: 1886
Ford Granada 2.5 Diesel Estate: 1887
Ford Orion 1.6 GL: 1889
Ford Sierra XR4i: 1890
Jaguar XJS: 2343
Lotus Eclat Excel: 2628
Lotus Esprit Turbo: 2629
MG Metro Turbo: 3037
Panther Kallista 2.8: 3376
Rover Vitesse: 4024

Talbot Horizon 1.9LD: 4348
TVR Tasmin Convertible: 4597
Vauxhall Astra GTE: 4694
Vauxhall Carlton 2.0 GL: 4695
Vauxhall Cavalier CD: 4696
Vauxhall Nova 1.2L: 4697

1984 Aston Martin Lagonda: 254
Aston Martin Vantage: 255
Austin Montego 1.6L: 423
Ford Fiesta 1.3L CVH: 1892
Ford Fiesta 1.6L Diesel: 1893
Ford Fiesta XR2: 1894
Jaguar XJ6 Vanden Plas: 2344
Jaguar XJS 3.6: 2345
Jaguar XJS HE: 2346
MG Montego EFi: 3038
Morgan 4/4: 3133
Panther Kallista 2.8: 3377
Rover 213 Vanden Plas: 4025
Vauxhall Astra GTE: 4698

1985 Austin Montego 2.0 HL: 424
Autokraft AC Cobra Mk IV: 455
Bentley Mulsanne Turbo: 480
Caterham 1700 Super Sprint: 723
Caterham 7: 724
Ford Escort RS Turbo: 1901
Ford Fiesta XR2: 1902
Ford Granada Scorpio: 1903
Ford Granada Scorpio 4x4: 1904
Ford Sierra 1.8 Ghia: 1906
Ford Sierra 2.0i S: 1907
Jaguar XJS HE Cabriolet: 2347
MG Montego Turbo: 3039
Naylor TF 1700: 3203
Panther Kallista 1.6L: 3378
Reliant Scimitar SS1 1600: 3794
Rover 216 Vitesse: 4026
TVR 350i Series II: 4598
Vauxhall Astra 1.3 GL: 4699
Vauxhall Astra 1.6 SR: 4700
Vauxhall Cavalier SRi: 4701
Vauxhall Senator 3.0i CD: 4702

1986 Aston Martin Volante: 256
Austin Montego 2.0 Vanden Plas EFI: 425
Ford Escort 1.4 GL: 1909
Ford Escort RS Turbo: 1911
Ford Escort XR3i: 1912
Ford Orion 1.4 GL: 1916
Ford RS200: 1917
Ford Sierra Ghia 4x4 Estate: 1918
Jaguar XJ6 3.6: 2348
Jaguar XJS: 2349
Jaguar XJSC: 2350
Jaguar XJSC HE: 2351
Lotus Esprit Turbo: 2630
Lotus Excel SE: 2631
Range Rover Vogue: 3774
Reliant Scimitar Ti: 3795
Rover 825i: 4027
Vauxhall Belmont 1.8 GLSi: 4703
Vauxhall Carlton CD 2.0i: 4704
Vauxhall Nova 1.3 GL 5-door: 4705

1987 Austin Metro 1.3L 3-door: 426
Autokraft AC Cobra Mk IV: 456
Bentley Turbo R: 481
Ford Fiesta 1.1 Ghia Auto: 1920
Ford Granada 2.4i Ghia: 1921
Ford Granada Scorpio 2.9 EX: 1922
Ford Sierra Sapphire 2.0 Ghia: 1925
Jaguar XJ6: 2352
Jaguar XJ6 2.9: 2353
Jaguar XJS 3.6 Automatic: 2354
Land Rover Ninety County Turbo Diesel: 2560
Land Rover One Ten County V8: 2561
Lotus Elan Autocrosser: 2632
Lotus Esprit Turbo HC: 2633
Lotus Excel SA: 2634
Lynx D Type: 2642
Morgan Plus 8: 3134
Range Rover V8: 3775
Rover 820SE: 4028
Rover Montego 1.6L: 4029
Rover Sterling Automatic: 4030
TVR 390 SE: 4599
TVR S Convertible: 4600
Vauxhall Astra GTE 2.0i: 4706
Vauxhall Belmont 1.6 GL: 4707
Vauxhall Carlton 3000 GSi: 4708
Vauxhall Cavalier 2.0i CD: 4709
Vauxhall Cavalier SRi 130 4-door: 4710
Vauxhall Senator 3.0i CD: 4711

1988 Aston Martin Zagato: 257
Ford Sierra RS Cosworth: 1934
Jaguar XJS: 2355
Jaguar XJS Koenig: 2356
Jaguar XJS V12 Convertible: 2357
Lotus Esprit Turbo: 2635
Lynx XJS Eventer: 2643
Morgan Plus 8: 3135
Range Rover Vogue Turbo D: 3776
Rover 820 Fastback: 4031
Rover 827 SLi Auto: 4032
Rover Vitesse: 4033
Vauxhall Carlton L 1.8i: 4712
Vauxhall Carlton L 2.3D: 4713
Vauxhall Cavalier 4x4: 4714
Vauxhall Nova GTE: 4715

1989 Aston Martin Virage: 258
Aston Martin Volante: 259
Aston Martin Zagato Volante: 260
Austin Metro GTa: 427
Carbodies Fairway 2.7 Silver: 721
Ford Escort 1.3L 3-door: 1936
Ford Fiesta 1.1LX 5-door: 1937
Ford Fiesta 1.4 Ghia: 1938
Ford Fiesta 1.6S: 1939
Ford Sierra Sapphire 2000E: 1944
Ford Sierra XR 4x4: 1945
Jaguar 4.0 Sovereign: 2358
Jaguar XJ220: 2359
Jaguar XJS Convertible: 2360
Jaguar XJS V12 Convertible: 2361
Land Rover Ninety County V8: 2562
Lotus Esprit Turbo: 2636
Lotus Esprit Turbo SE: 2637
MG Maestro Turbo: 3040
Range Rover Vogue: 3777
Range Rover Vogue SE: 3778
Rover Montego 2.0 DSL Turbo: 4034
Rover Sterling Catalyst: 4035
Rover Vitesse: 4036
TVR 420 SEAC: 4601
TVR S Convertible: 4602
Vauxhall Astra 1.7 DL: 4716
Vauxhall Cavalier 1.4L: 4717
Vauxhall Cavalier 1.6L: 4718
Vauxhall Cavalier SRi: 4719
Vauxhall Senator 2.5i: 4720
Vauxhall Senator 3.0i CD: 4721

1990 Bentley Turbo R: 482
Caterham 7 HPC: 725
Ford Fiesta RS Turbo: 1949
Ford Fiesta XR2i: 1950
Ford Granada 2.5 GL Diesel: 1951
Ford Granada Ghia X 2.9 EFi Saloon: 1952
Ford Granada Scorpio 2.0i Auto: 1953
Ford Sierra Sapphire Cosworth 4x4: 1958
Ginetta G32: 1998
IAD Venus: 2229
Jaguar XJ6 Vanden Plas: 2362
Jaguar XJR 4.0: 2363
Jaguar XJRS: 2364
Jaguar XJS: 2365
Jaguar XJS Lister Le Mans: 2366
Jaguar XJS Railton: 2367
Land Rover Discovery TDi: 2563
Land Rover Discovery V8: 2564
Lotus Elan: 2638
Lotus Elan SE: 2639
Lotus Esprit Turbo SE: 2640
MG B British Motor Heritage: 3041
Morgan Plus 4 Mk III: 3136
Nissan Primera 1.6 LS: 3242
Panther Kallista: 3379
Panther Solo: 3380
Range Rover County: 3779
Range Rover Vogue SE: 3780
Reliant Scimitar SST 1800Ti: 3796
Rover 214 GSi: 4037
Rover 216 GSi: 4038
Rover 414 Si: 4039
Rover 416 GTi: 4040
Rover Metro 1.4SL: 4041
Rover Metro GTi 16v: 4042
Vauxhall Calibra 2.0i 16v: 4722
Vauxhall Carlton 3.0i CDX Estate: 4723
Vauxhall Carlton GSi 3000 24v: 4724
Vauxhall Cavalier GSi 2000 16v: 4725
Vauxhall Cavalier GSi 2000 16v 4x4: 4726
Vauxhall Nova 1.5TD Merit: 4727

1991 Aston Martin Virage: 261
Bentley Turbo R: 483
Caterham Super 7: 726
Ford Escort 1.4LX: 1960
Ford Escort 1.6 Ghia Estate: 1961
Ford Escort Cabriolet: 1962
Ford Orion 1.6i Ghia: 1968
Ford Scorpio 24v: 1970
Jaguar XJ6 3.2: 2368
Jaguar XJR15: 2369
Jaguar XJS: 2370
Jaguar XJS 4.0 Auto: 2371
Jaguar XJS Convertible: 2372
Land Rover Discovery V8i 5DR: 2565
Lotus Elan SE: 2641
Morgan Plus 8: 3137
Nissan Primera 2.0 GSX: 3250
Nissan Primera 2.0E ZX: 3251
Parradine V-12: 3382
Rolls-Royce Silver Spirit II: 3972
Rover 214S: 4043
Rover 216 GTi: 4044
Rover 218 SD: 4045
Rover 220 GTi: 4046
Rover 825 TD: 4047
Rover Mini Cooper S: 4048
Rover Sterling 827SL: 4049
Safir GT40: 4106
TVR V8 S: 4603
Vauxhall Calibra 2.0i: 4728
Vauxhall Calibra 4x4: 4729
Vauxhall Nova 1.2 Luxe: 4730
Vauxhall Senator 3.0i 24v: 4731
Westfield SEight: 4973

1992 Ford Escort RS2000: 1973
Ford Escort XR3i: 1974
Range Rover Vogue SE: 3781
Rover 820i: 4050
Rover Sterling Automatic: 4051
Vauxhall 1.4i GLS: 4732
Vauxhall Cavalier 1.7 GL TD: 4733
Vauxhall Frontera 2.3 TD Estate: 4734

UK total: 1,577

USA

1915 Ford Model T: 1608

1926 Wills Sainte Claire Six: 4974

1927 Kissel 8-65 Gold Bug: 2416

1928 Buick Empire Saloon: 653
Stutz Roadster: 4239

1929 Auburn 8-120 Speedster: 262
Chrysler 65 Saloon: 960
Chrysler 75 Saloon: 961
Dodge New Six Saloon: 1269
Du Pont Speedster: 1350
Franklin 29.4hp Saloon: 1977
Graham-Paige 21.6hp Saloon: 2015
Graham-Paige Straight Eight: 2016
Marmon Roosevelt Saloon: 2648
Packard 32.5hp Saloon: 3354
Studebaker Double-twelve Open Tourer: 4214
Stutz 36.4hp Saloon: 4240

1930 Buick 28.4hp Saloon: 654
Buick Light Eight Saloon: 655
Cadillac V16 "Madame X": 699
Chrysler 77 Saloon: 962
Chrysler Eight Saloon: 963
Cord L-29: 1097
Dodge Eight Saloon: 1270
Du Pont Town Car: 1351
Duesenberg J Coupe: 1352
Hudson Straight Eight Roadster: 2169
Hupmobile Straight Eight Limousine: 2216
La Salle Enclosed Drive Limousine: 2421
Lincoln 39.2hp Town Saloon: 2573
Marmon 69 Saloon: 2649
Marmon 79 Saloon: 2650
Nash Straight Eight Saloon: 3194
Packard 7-34 Phaeton: 3355
Studebaker Commander Brougham: 4215
Studebaker Erskine Saloon: 4216

1931 Cadillac V16 Fleetwood Roadster: 700
Chrysler Custom Imperial Le Baron: 964
Cord Front Wheel Drive Phaeton: 1098
De Soto Straight Eight Saloon: 1234
Lincoln 39.2hp Saloon: 2574
Studebaker President Limousine: 4217
Stutz Straight Eight Saloon: 4241

1932 Essex Terraplane Tourer: 1360
Graham Blue Streak Saloon: 2010
Lincoln Twelve Cylinder Town Sedan: 2575

Ford Galaxie 500 XL: 1699
International 900 Pickup: 2236
Mercury Comet S-22 Sportster: 2931
Mercury Super Marauder S-55: 2932
Oldsmobile F-85 Jetfire: 3279
Oldsmobile Starfire: 3280
Plymouth Fury: 3482
Plymouth Sport Fury: 3483
Plymouth Valiant V-100: 3484
Pontiac Catalina: 3537
Pontiac Grand Prix: 3538
Pontiac Tempest Le Mans V8: 3539
Studebaker Avanti: 4236
Studebaker Regal Wagonaire Supercharged: 4237
Willys Wagoneer 4WD: 4976

1964 AMC Rambler American 440: 177
AMC Rambler Classic 770: 178
AMC Rambler Classic Typhoon: 179
Buick Electra 225: 669
Buick Skylark Sports Wagon: 670
Buick Special: 671
Buick Wildcat: 672
Cadillac Coupe de Ville: 705
Cadillac Sedan de Ville: 706
Chevrolet Chevelle 300: 780
Chevrolet Chevelle Malibu: 781
Chevrolet Chevelle Super Sport: 782
Chevrolet Chevy II V8 Station Wagon: 783
Chevrolet Corvair Monza: 784
Chevrolet Corvair Sprint: 785
Chevrolet Corvette Sting Ray: 786
Chevrolet Corvette Sting Ray Automatic: 787
Chevrolet Corvette Sting Ray Injection: 788
Chevrolet El Camino: 789
Chrysler Imperial Le Baron: 982
Dodge Dart GT: 1288
Dodge Polara: 1289
Dodge Polara 500: 1290
Dodge Safari Super Sport: 1291
Excalibur SS: 1363
Ford Custom 500: 1703
Ford Falcon Sprint: 1704
Ford Galaxie 500: 1705
Ford Mustang: 1706
Ford Mustang 271hp: 1707
Ford Mustang Convertible: 1708
Jeep Wagoneer: 2373
Lincoln Continental: 2581
Mercury Comet A/FX: 2933
Mercury Comet Caliente: 2934
Mercury Comet Cyclone 4-speed: 2935
Mercury Comet Cyclone Automatic: 2936
Mercury Park Lane: 2937
Oldsmobile Cutlass 442: 3281
Oldsmobile F-85 Cutlass Holiday: 3282
Oldsmobile Jetstar I: 3283
Plymouth Barracuda: 3485
Pontiac Tempest GTO: 3540
Rambler 770 Six: 3767
Shelby AC Ford Cobra: 4117
Shelby Cobra USRRC: 4118
Studebaker Daytona R-4: 4238

1965 AMC Rambler American 440-H: 180
Buick LeSabre 400: 673
Buick Riviera: 674
Buick Skylark: 675
Buick Skylark Gran Sport: 676
Chevrolet Caprice Custom 396: 790
Chevrolet Chevelle Malibu: 791
Chevrolet Chevelle Malibu 396: 792
Chevrolet Corvair Corsa IECO: 793
Chevrolet Corvair Monza: 794
Chevrolet Corvette: 795
Chevrolet Corvette 396: 796
Chevrolet Corvette Injection: 797
Chevrolet Corvette Sting Ray 396: 798
Chevrolet Impala SS: 799
Chrysler Newport: 983
Dodge A-100 Super/Surfer: 1292
Dodge Coronet: 1293
Dodge Coronet 426-S: 1294
Dodge Coronet 440: 1295
Dodge Coronet 500: 1296
Dodge Dart GT: 1297
Ford Fairlane 500: 1713
Ford Galaxie 500 XL 427: 1714
Ford Galaxie LTD: 1715
Ford Mustang: 1716
Ford Mustang 6: 1717
Ford Mustang Convertible: 1718
Ford Mustang Convertible V8: 1719
Ford Mustang Coupe: 1720
Ford Mustang Coupe Automatic: 1721
Ford Mustang Fastback: 1722
Ford Mustang High Performance: 1723
Ford Mustang V8 4.2-litre: 1724
Ford Mustang V8 4.7-litre: 1725
Ford Thunderbird: 1727
Mercury Monterey: 2938
Mercury Park Lane: 2939
Meyers Manx: 2967
Oldsmobile Cutlass Holiday 442: 3284
Oldsmobile Dynamic Delta 88 Holiday: 3285
Oldsmobile Toronado: 3286
Plymouth Barracuda S: 3486
Plymouth Belvedere Satellite: 3487
Plymouth Fury Station Wagon: 3488
Pontiac Bonneville Vista: 3541
Pontiac Catalina 2+2: 3542
Pontiac Tempest GTO: 3543
Shelby Cobra Daytona Coupe: 4119
Shelby GT 350: 4120

1966 AMC Ambassador DPL: 181
AMC Rogue V8: 182
Avanti II: 458
Buick Riviera Gran Sport: 677
Cadillac Calais: 707
Chevrolet Bel Air Six: 800
Chevrolet Chevy II Nova SS: 801
Chevrolet Corvette: 802
Chevrolet Corvette Convertible: 803
Chrysler 300: 984
Chrysler Turbine: 985
Dodge Charger: 1298
Ford Bronco: 1729
Ford Custom 500: 1734
Ford Fairlane GTA: 1735
Ford Falcon Ranchero Custom: 1736
Ford Galaxie 7-litre: 1737
Ford Thunderbird Town Landau: 1739
Mercury Comet Cyclone GT: 2940
Oldsmobile Cutlass 442: 3287
Oldsmobile Toronado: 3288
Plymouth Barracuda S: 3489
Plymouth Satellite: 3490
Plymouth Satellite Street Hemi: 3491
Plymouth VIP: 3492
Pontiac GTO: 3544
Pontiac Le Mans OHC: 3545
Pontiac Tempest GTO: 3546
Pontiac Tempest Sprint: 3547
Pontiac Tempest Sprint Automatic: 3548
Rambler 770 V8 Convertible: 3768
Shelby GT 350-S: 4121

1967 AMC Javelin SST 343: 183
AMC Marlin: 184
AMC Rambler American 220: 185
AMC Rambler Rebel 770: 186
AMC Rambler Rebel SST: 187
Buick California GS: 678
Buick GS400: 679
Buick Wildcat: 680
Cadillac Eldorado: 708
Chevrolet Camaro: 804
Chevrolet Camaro 427 Dana: 805
Chevrolet Camaro Six: 806
Chevrolet Camaro SS350: 807
Chevrolet Corvette: 808
Chevrolet Impala SS427: 809
Chrysler Imperial Crown: 987
Dodge Charger: 1299
Dodge Coronet R/T: 1300
Dodge Dart 270: 1301
Dodge Monaco Wagon: 1302
Ford Fairlane Ranchero: 1746
Ford Mustang: 1747
Ford Mustang 390 Fastback: 1748
Ford Thunderbird: 1749
Kaiser Jeepster: 2415
Mercury Cougar: 2941
Mercury Cougar Group 2: 2942
Mercury Cougar GT: 2943
Mercury Marquis: 2944
Oldsmobile F-85 Cutlass Cruiser: 3289
Plymouth Barracuda: 3493
Plymouth Barracuda 6: 3494
Plymouth Barracuda Fastback V8: 3495
Plymouth Fury III: 3496
Plymouth GTX: 3497
Pontiac Firebird 440: 3549
Pontiac Firebird Sprint: 3550
Pontiac Grand Prix: 3551
Pontiac GTO Ram Air: 3552
Rambler Rebel 6 Estate Car: 3769
Shelby GT 500: 4122

1968 AMC Ambassador: 188
AMC AMX: 189
AMC AMX Automatic: 190
AMC Javelin: 191
AMC Javelin SST: 192
Buick GS400: 681
Buick Riviera: 682
Cadillac Coupe de Ville: 709
Checker Marathon: 727
Chevrolet Camaro SS396: 810
Chevrolet Camaro Z/28: 811
Chevrolet Chevelle Malibu: 812
Chevrolet Chevelle SS396: 813
Chevrolet Chevy II: 814
Chevrolet Corvair Monza: 815
Chevrolet Corvair Sport Coupe: 816
Chevrolet Corvette: 817
Chevrolet Corvette Convertible: 818
Chevrolet Corvette Coupe: 819
Chevrolet Corvette L88: 820
Chevrolet El Camino: 821
Chevrolet Impala: 822
Chevrolet Malibu 327: 823
Datsun 2000 Sports: 1164
Datsun 510: 1165
Datsun 510 Station Wagon: 1167
Dodge Charger R/T: 1303
Dodge Coronet R/T: 1304
Dodge Dart GTS: 1305
Dodge Dart GTS 340: 1306
Ford Galaxie: 1759
Ford Mustang 428 Cobra Jet: 1761
Ford Mustang Fastback: 1762
Ford Torino: 1763
Ford XL Fastback 428: 1764
Mercury Cougar: 2945
Mercury Cougar XR-7: 2946
Mercury Cyclone: 2947
Oldsmobile 4-4-2: 3290
Oldsmobile Delmont: 3291
Oldsmobile Toronado: 3292
Plymouth Barracuda 340-S: 3498
Plymouth Barracuda Fastback: 3499
Plymouth Fury III: 3500
Plymouth GTX: 3501
Plymouth GTX Hemi: 3502
Plymouth Road Runner: 3503
Pontiac Firebird RA400: 3553
Pontiac GTO: 3554
Rambler Javelin Hardtop SST: 3770
Shelby GT 350: 4123
Shelby GT 500-KR: 4124

1969 AMC Ambassador SST Wagon: 193
AMC Rambler Scrambler: 194
Avanti II: 459
Buick Riviera: 683
Buick Skylark: 684
Buick Sportswagon: 685
Buick Wildcat: 686
Checker Marathon: 728
Chevrolet Camaro SS 396: 824
Chevrolet Camaro Z/28: 825
Chevrolet Camaro Z/28 Yenko/SC: 826
Chevrolet Caprice: 827
Chevrolet Chevelle Malibu: 828
Chevrolet Corvette 435hp: 829
Chevrolet Corvette L36: 830
Chevrolet Corvette L46: 831
Chevrolet Corvette L68: 832
Chevrolet Corvette L71: 833
Chevrolet Corvette L71/89: 834
Chevrolet Corvette L88: 835
Chevrolet Corvette LT-1: 836
Chevrolet Corvette Stingray: 837
Chevrolet Corvette ZQ3: 838
Chevrolet Kingswood Estate Wagon: 839
Chrysler 300: 988
Dodge Coronet 500 Station Wagon: 1307
Dodge Hemi Charger 500 Automatic: 1308
Dodge Hemi Charger 500 Manual: 1309
Dodge Monaco: 1310
Dodge Super Bee: 1311
Dodge Super Bee Six-Pack: 1312
Dodge Swinger: 1313
Fiberfab Jamaican Buick V8: 1607
Ford Fairlane 351: 1771
Ford Fairlane Cobra: 1772
Ford LTD: 1773
Ford Maverick: 1774
Ford Mustang 428 Mach I: 1775
Ford Mustang Boss 302: 1776
Ford Mustang Boss 429: 1777
Ford Mustang Grande: 1778
Ford Thunderbird: 1779
Mercury Marquis Brougham: 2948
Mercury Marquis Marauder X-100: 2949
Oldsmobile 442 Hurst: 3293
Oldsmobile 88 Delta Royale: 3294
Oldsmobile Cutlass W-31: 3295
Plymouth Cuda 340: 3504

Chevrolet Camaro IROC-Z: 927
Chevrolet Camaro IROC-Z Automatic: 928
Chevrolet Camaro IROC-Z Chevrolet Engineering: 929
Chevrolet Corvette: 930
Chevrolet Corvette Callaway: 931
Chevrolet Corvette Guldstrand Grand Sport 80: 932
Chevrolet Corvette L98: 933
Chevrolet Corvette ZR-1: 934
Dodge Daytona Shelby: 1339
Dodge Shadow ES Turbo: 1340
Dodge Shelby CSX: 1341
Dodge Shelby CSX VNT: 1342
Ford Mustang 5.0 Cartech Turbo: 1940
Ford Mustang Saleen SSC: 1941
Ford Mustang SVO J Bittle American: 1942
Ford Probe GT Suspension Techniques/ HKS: 1943
Ford Taurus SHO: 1946
Ford Thunderbird Super Coupe: 1947
Ford Thunderbird Super Coupe Ford Engineering: 1948
Lincoln Continental Mk VII: 2586
Mercury Cougar XR-7: 2960
Oldsmobile Calais HO Quad 4: 3303
Oldsmobile Cutlass Calais International Series HO: 3304
Pontiac Firebird T/A Turbo Pontiac Engineering: 3588
Pontiac Firebird TransAm 20th Anniversary: 3589
Pontiac Firebird TransAm Turbo: 3590
Pontiac Grand Am Turbo: 3591
Pontiac Grand Prix McLaren Turbo: 3592

1990 Cadillac Allante: 716
Cadillac Aurora: 717
Cadillac Eldorado Touring Coupe: 718
Chevrolet Beretta GT: 935
Chevrolet Beretta GTZ: 936
Chevrolet Camaro IROC-Z Convertible: 937
Chevrolet Camaro Z/28: 938
Chevrolet Cavalier Z24: 939
Chevrolet Corvette Callaway: 940
Chevrolet Corvette Callaway Sledgehammer: 941
Chevrolet Corvette Convertible: 942
Chevrolet Corvette Coupe: 943
Chevrolet Corvette L98: 944
Chevrolet Lumina APV: 945
Consulier GTP LX: 1096
Dodge Daytona ES: 1343
Dodge Daytona Shelby: 1344
Dodge Shadow ES VNT: 1345
Eagle Talon: 1355
Evans Series I: 1362
Ford Mustang GT Convertible: 1954
Ford Mustang LX 5.0L: 1955
Ford Probe GT: 1956
Ford Probe LX: 1957
GM Impact: 2002
Lincoln Continental Mk VII LSC: 2587
Oldsmobile Toronado Trofeo: 3305
Plymouth Laser RS Turbo: 3522
Pontiac Firebird Formula: 3593
Pontiac Firebird TransAm GTA: 3594
Pontiac Grand Prix STE Turbo: 3595
Vector W2: 4735

1991 Buick Reatta Convertible: 698
Cadillac Allante: 719
Cadillac Seville Touring Sedan: 720
Chevrolet Baretta GTZ: 946
Chevrolet Camaro Z/28 Convertible: 947
Chevrolet Corvette Callaway: 948
Chevrolet Corvette Callaway Speedster: 949
Chevrolet Corvette Callaway Twin Turbo: 950
Chevrolet Corvette Lingenfelter: 951
Chevrolet Corvette Rick Mears: 952
Chevrolet Corvette ZR-1: 953
Chevrolet Corvette ZR-1 Geiger: 954
Chevrolet Corvette ZR-1 SS: 955
Chevrolet Corvette ZR-2: 956
Chevrolet Lumina Z34: 957
Dodge Spirit R/T: 1346
Eagle GTP: 1356
Eagle Talon TSi 4WD: 1357
Ford Crown Victoria LX: 1959
Ford Escort GT: 1963
Ford Escort Millen: 1964
Ford Festiva Shogun: 1965
Ford Mustang Holdener: 1966
Ford Mustang NOS/Saleen: 1967
Ford Probe GT: 1969
Ford Taurus SHO: 1971
Ford Thunderbird LX: 1972
Mercury Tracer LTS: 2962
Plymouth Laser RS Turbo: 3523
Pontiac Firebird GTA: 3596
Pontiac Firebird TDM Technologies: 3597
Pontiac Firebird TransAm Convertible: 3598
Pontiac Grand Prix GTP: 3599
Saturn Sports Coupe: 4107
Vector W8 Twin Turbo: 4736

1992 Chevrolet Camaro Z28: 958
Chevrolet Corvette LT1: 959
Dodge Viper: 1348
Ford Mustang LX: 1975
Ford Taurus LX: 1976
Pontiac Bonneville SSEi: 3600

USA total: 965

USSR

1960 Volga M21K: 4737

1967 Moskvich De Luxe: 3187

1975 Lada 1200: 2423

Moskvich 1500: 3188

1976 Lada 1500: 2424

1978 Lada 1300 ES: 2425

1979 Lada Niva 1600: 2426

1986 Lada Riva 1500 Estate: 2427

1987 Lada Niva Cossack Cabrio: 2428
Lada Samara 1300 SL: 2429

1989 Lada Samara 1300L 5-door: 2430

USSR total: 11

Yugoslavia

1981 Zastava 1300 ZLX-E: 5006

1986 Yugo GV: 5002

1987 Yugo 45 GLS: 5003

1988 Yugo 65A GLX: 5004

1990 Yugo Sana 1.4: 5005

Yugoslavia total: 5

Total No. of cars listed: 5,008

Maximum speed

246 lists of makes ordered by make, maximum speed in mph and kmh, year and model.

Abarth

	mph	kmh		
1	96.5	155.3	1958	Zagato 750 GT: 1

AC

	mph	kmh		
1	143.0	230.1	1968	428 Fastback: 26
2	140.0	225.3	1965	Cobra: 25
3	121.0	194.7	1958	AC-Bristol Zagato: 17
4	118.0	189.9	1958	Bristol: 19
5	116.0	186.6	1960	Aceca-Bristol: 21
6	115.2	185.4	1957	Ace Bristol: 16
7	115.0	185.0	1962	Aceca-Buick: 23
			1958	Bristol D-2: 20
8	107.0	172.2	1961	Greyhound: 22
9	105.0	168.9	1962	Greyhound: 24
10	104.0	167.3	1956	Aceca: 15
11	103.8	167.0	1958	Aceca-Bristol Coupe: 18
12	101.9	164.0	1956	Ace Roadster: 14
13	90.0	144.8	1938	2-litre Sports: 10
14	85.7	137.9	1936	Ace: 8
15	84.0	135.2	1939	2-litre: 11
			1953	2-litre: 13
16	83.0	133.5	1949	2-litre Saloon: 12
17	81.0	130.3	1936	2-litre Aero Saloon: 7
18	80.0	128.7	1934	Ace Sports Four-seater: 4
19	79.6	128.1	1937	2-litre Fixed-head Coupe: 9
20	77.5	124.7	1934	Greyhound Close-coupled Saloon: 5
21	72.5	116.7	1935	Ace Drop-head Coupe: 6
			1933	Ace Fixed-head Coupe: 3
22	61.6	99.1	1931	Acedes Magna Coupe: 2

Acura

	mph	kmh		
1	168.0	270.3	1990	NSX: 36
2	135.0	217.2	1991	Legend LS: 37
3	130.0	209.2	1990	Integra GS: 34
			1990	Legend Coupe: 35
			1989	Legend Coupe L: 33
4	129.0	207.6	1986	Legend: 29
5	120.0	193.1	1986	Integra RS: 28
6	112.0	180.2	1989	Integra LS: 32
			1988	Integra LS Special Edition: 31
7	110.0	177.0	1987	Integra LS: 30

AJS

	mph	kmh		
1	56.9	91.6	1930	9hp Saloon: 38

Alfa Romeo

	mph	kmh		
1	161.0	259.0	1967	33 2.0 Stradale: 66
2	144.0	231.7	1991	164 Cloverleaf: 145
3	140.0	225.3	1989	164 3.0 Lusso: 138
			1990	164S: 143
			1972	Montreal: 82
4	138.0	222.0	1987	Alfa 75 V6 3.0: 132
5	137.0	220.4	1989	164 Automatic: 139
			1985	GTV Callaway Twin Turbo: 122
6	136.0	218.8	1987	Milano Verde 3.0: 133
7	133.0	214.0	1988	75 Evoluzione: 135
			1986	GTV6: 126
8	132.0	212.4	1981	GTV6: 109
			1973	Montreal: 87
9	130.0	209.2	1986	Alfa 75 2.5 Green Cloverleaf: 125
			1984	GTV6: 114
10	129.0	207.6	1990	33 Boxer 16v: 144
			1986	Milano Platinum: 127
11	128.0	206.0	1987	Alfa 75 2.0i Twin Spark: 131
			1985	Alfa 90 2.5 Gold Cloverleaf: 118
12	127.0	204.3	1990	164 Twin Spark Lusso: 142
13	126.0	202.7	1988	75 2.5 Auto: 134
14	125.0	201.1	1989	Milano 3.0: 140
15	124.0	199.5	1962	2600: 55
16	122.0	196.3	1972	2000 GTV: 79
			1975	Alfetta GT: 90
17	121.0	194.7	1972	1750 GTV TransAm: 78
18	120.0	193.1	1986	Alfa 75 1.8: 124
			1976	Alfetta GTV: 93
			1961	Sprint Speciale: 53
			1961	Sprint Zagato: 54
19	119.0	191.5	1966	2600 Sprint: 63
			1976	Spider Veloce 2000: 94
20	118.0	189.9	1968	1750 GT Veloce: 71
			1973	2000: 83
			1987	33 1.7 Veloce: 129
			1987	Alfa 33 1.7 Sportwagon Veloce: 130
21	117.0	188.3	1968	1750 Berlina: 70
22	116.0	186.6	1978	Sport Sedan: 103
			1988	Sprint 1.7 Cloverleaf: 137
			1979	Sprint Veloce: 106
23	115.0	185.0	1969	1750 Spider: 74

			1954	B.A.T.7 Scaglione: 44
			1966	Giulia Sprint GTV: 64
24	114.0	183.4	1971	1750 Spider Veloce: 76
			1978	Alfetta 2.0: 101
25	113.0	181.8	1966	1600 Spider: 62
			1974	Alfetta: 89
			1967	Duetto Spider: 67
26	112.0	180.2	1985	Alfa 33 1.5 4x4 Estate: 117
			1973	Alfetta: 85
			1984	Alfetta Gold Cloverleaf: 113
			1976	Alfetta GT: 92
			1973	Giulia 1600 Sprint: 86
			1961	Giulia SS: 50
			1967	GTV: 69
			1964	Sprint GT: 59
			1966	Sprint Speciale: 65
27	111.3	179.1	1959	2000 Spider: 47
28	111.0	178.6	1984	Sprint Green Cloverleaf: 116
29	110.0	177.0	1969	1750 Berlina: 73
			1972	2000 GTV Injection: 80
			1932	8C2300: 41
			1984	Spider: 115
			1980	Spider: 107
			1986	Spider Quadrifoglio: 128
			1982	Spider Veloce: 110
			1979	Sport Sedan Automatic: 105
30	109.0	175.4	1963	2600 Saloon: 56
			1986	Alfa 33 1.3 S: 123
			1985	Arna ti: 120
			1965	Giulia Veloce: 61
31	108.0	173.8	1972	1750 Berlina: 77
			1933	2.3 Mille Miglia: 42
			1964	Giulia 1600 Spider: 58
			1968	Giulia Super: 72
			1978	Giulietta 1.6: 102
			1982	Spider Veloce 2000: 111
32	107.5	173.0	1963	Giulia ti: 57
33	106.8	171.8	1931	Supercharged Straight Eight: 39
34	106.0	170.6	1981	Alfasud 1.5: 108
			1979	Alfasud 1.5 Sprint Veloce: 104
			1977	Alfasud 1200ti: 95
35	105.5	169.7	1953	1900: 43
36	105.0	168.9	1983	Alfa 33 1.5: 112
			1976	Alfetta 1.6: 91
37	104.6	168.3	1958	1300 SV Spider: 46
38	104.0	167.3	1978	Alfasud Sprint 1.5: 100
			1969	GT 1300 Junior: 75
			1977	Spider: 99
39	103.0	165.7	1977	Alfasud 1300ti: 96
			1961	Giulietta Sprint: 51
			1985	Graduate: 121
			1988	Spider: 136
			1989	Spider Quadrifoglio: 141
			1991	Spider Veloce: 147
40	102.0	164.1	1974	Alfasud ti: 88
			1965	Giulia ti: 60
41	101.0	162.5	1985	Arna 1.3SL: 119
			1967	Giulia 1300 ti: 68
42	100.0	160.9	1960	2000: 49
			1956	Giulietta Spyder: 45
43	97.0	156.1	1977	Alfetta: 98
			1961	Giulietta ti: 52
44	96.0	154.5	1972	Alfasud: 81
45	94.0	151.2	1973	Alfasud: 84
			1977	Alfasud 5M: 97
46	91.0	146.4	1932	1750: 40

Allard

1	120.0	193.1	1959	GT Coupe: 153
2	115.0	185.0	1954	K3 Convertible: 151
3	102.0	164.1	1952	K2: 150
4	90.0	144.8	1948	Drop-head Coupe: 148
5	87.0	140.0	1954	Palm Beach: 152
6	86.0	138.4	1948	V8: 149

Alvis

1	108.0	173.8	1965	3-litre Series III: 168
			1965	TE21S: 169
2	106.0	170.6	1959	3-litre TD21: 166
3	103.0	165.7	1957	3-litre Graber: 165
			1962	3-litre TD21 Series II Automatic: 167
4	101.1	162.7	1953	3-litre: 164
5	100.0	160.9	1939	4.3-litre: 162
6	96.7	155.6	1938	Speed 25: 161
7	91.8	147.7	1937	4.3-litre Vanden Plas Saloon: 158
8	89.1	143.4	1932	Speed 20 (87bhp): 156
9	86.0	138.4	1952	3-litre: 163
10	84.1	135.3	1937	Crested Eagle 25: 159
11	81.8	131.6	1938	12/70 Tourer: 160
12	80.0	128.7	1932	Speed 20 (72bhp): 155
13	71.4	114.9	1931	12/60 Sports: 154
14	70.8	113.9	1935	Firebird Saloon: 157

AMC

1	121.0	194.7	1969	Ambassador SST Wagon: 193
2	120.0	193.1	1970	Javelin 390: 198
3	116.0	186.6	1967	Marlin: 184
			1974	Matador X: 200
4	114.0	183.4	1963	Ambassador 990: 175
			1968	Javelin SST: 192
5	112.0	180.2	1970	Hornet 4.9-litre: 197
6	111.0	178.6	1967	Javelin SST 343: 183
7	110.0	177.0	1968	AMX: 189
			1967	Rambler Rebel SST: 187
8	108.0	173.8	1973	Hornet Hatchback: 199
			1968	Javelin: 191
			1969	Rambler Scrambler: 194
9	107.0	172.2	1968	AMX Automatic: 190
10	106.0	170.6	1966	Rogue V8: 182
11	105.0	168.9	1962	Ambassador 400: 173
			1977	Pacer Wagon: 205
12	102.0	164.1	1966	Ambassador DPL: 181
13	101.0	162.5	1970	Hornet 3.8-litre: 196
14	100.0	160.9	1964	Rambler Classic 770: 178
			1961	Rambler Classic V8: 172
15	98.0	157.7	1968	Ambassador: 188
			1967	Rambler American 220: 185
16	97.0	156.1	1977	Gremlin 2-litre: 204
			1976	Pacer: 203
17	95.0	152.9	1970	Gremlin: 195
			1964	Rambler American 440: 177
			1964	Rambler Classic Typhoon: 179
18	94.0	151.2	1967	Rambler Rebel 770: 186
19	92.0	148.0	1980	Eagle: 206
			1963	Rambler 660: 176
20	90.0	144.8	1961	Rambler American: 170
			1965	Rambler American 440-H: 180
			1961	Rambler Classic Super 6: 171
21	88.0	141.6	1975	Pacer: 202
			1962	Rambler American: 174

Amilcar

1	73.7	118.6	1930	Straight Eight Saloon: 207

Apollo

1	104.0	167.3	1963	GT: 208

Armstrong Siddeley

1	102.2	164.4	1959	Star Sapphire: 220
2	91.5	147.2	1953	Sapphire Saloon: 219
3	85.7	137.9	1935	30 Special Sports Saloon: 213
4	76.2	122.6	1937	25.3hp Town and Country Saloon: 215
5	73.7	118.6	1938	16 Saloon: 217
6	72.5	116.7	1935	17hp Sports Foursome: 212
7	70.8	113.9	1932	Rally Tourer: 210
			1937	Six-light Saloon: 216
8	70.0	112.6	1948	2-litre Saloon: 218
9	67.1	108.0	1936	17hp Touring Saloon: 214
10	61.6	99.1	1933	Long 15hp Saloon: 211
11	60.8	97.8	1931	15 Saloon: 209

ASA

1	115.0	185.0	1960	1000GT: 221

Aston Martin

1	183.0	294.4	1988	Zagato: 257
2	170.0	273.5	1977	V8 Vantage: 248
3	165.0	265.5	1989	Zagato Volante: 260
4	162.0	260.7	1971	DBS V8: 244
5	160.0	257.4	1991	Virage: 261
6	155.0	249.4	1989	Virage: 258
7	153.5	247.0	1962	DB4 GT Zagato: 240
8	148.0	238.1	1962	DB4: 239
			1966	DB6: 242
			1982	V8: 252
9	147.0	236.5	1978	V8: 249
			1975	V8: 246
			1973	V8 Automatic: 245
10	145.0	233.3	1986	Volante: 256
11	144.0	231.7	1980	Lagonda: 250
12	143.0	230.1	1968	DBS: 243
13	142.6	229.4	1964	DB5: 241
14	142.0	228.5	1983	Volante: 253
15	141.0	226.9	1961	DB4: 238
16	140.2	225.6	1959	DB4: 237
17	140.0	225.3	1982	Lagonda: 251
			1977	V8 Coupe: 247
18	135.0	217.2	1989	Volante: 259
19	132.0	212.4	1956	Spyder Touring: 235
20	126.0	202.7	1984	Lagonda: 254
21	120.0	193.1	1953	DB2/4 Saloon: 233
			1958	Mk III: 236

22	110.0	177.0	1954	DB2: 234
23	106.0	170.6	1951	DB2: 232
24	97.8	157.4	1939	2-litre: 231
25	84.9	136.6	1934	1.5-litre Mk II: 226
			1938	Drop-head Coupe: 230
			1933	Le Mans: 225
26	84.1	135.3	1937	2-litre: 229
27	82.5	132.7	1935	1.5-litre: 227
28	81.0	130.3	1929	Super Sports: 222
29	78.9	127.0	1936	Sports Saloon: 228
30	75.0	120.7	1931	Sports Four-seater: 223
31	74.3	119.5	1932	1.5-litre: 224

Auburn

1	104.0	167.3	1936	8-52 Speedster: 264
2	90.0	144.8	1929	8-120 Speedster: 262
3	86.5	139.2	1936	38hp Saloon: 263

Audi

1	155.0	249.4	1985	Quattro Sport: 309
2	153.0	246.2	1991	Coupe S2: 337
3	152.0	244.6	1991	V8 Quattro: 338
4	150.0	241.4	1991	200 Quattro: 334
5	145.0	233.3	1984	200 Quattro Turbo: 297
6	144.0	231.7	1990	V8 Quattro: 331
			1990	V8 Quattro Automatic: 332
7	142.0	228.5	1983	200 Turbo: 293
			1990	Quattro 20v: 330
8	140.0	225.3	1985	200 Avant Quattro: 304
9	138.9	223.5	1989	90 Quattro 20v: 325
10	137.0	220.4	1981	Quattro: 289
11	136.0	218.8	1991	100 2.8E Auto: 333
			1988	Quattro: 323
12	134.0	215.6	1992	80 2.8E V6 Quattro: 339
13	132.0	212.4	1985	5000 S Turbo Quattro: 305
			1991	80 16v Sport: 335
			1989	Coupe 2.2E: 326
14	130.0	209.2	1990	90 Quattro: 329
15	129.0	207.6	1982	100 CD: 290
16	128.0	206.0	1988	90 Quattro: 322
			1985	Quattro: 308
			1982	Quattro: 292
17	127.0	204.3	1987	90 2.2E: 317
			1987	90 Quattro: 318
18	126.0	202.7	1986	Coupe GT 2.2: 315
19	124.0	199.5	1984	5000 S Turbo: 300
20	123.9	199.4	1989	Coupe Quattro: 327
21	123.0	197.9	1988	100 Avant Quattro: 319
22	122.0	196.3	1988	100 Sport: 320
			1988	80 1.8E: 321
			1986	Coupe Quattro: 316
23	121.0	194.7	1990	80 2.0E: 328
			1983	80 Quattro: 295
			1983	Coupe Injection: 296
24	120.0	193.1	1989	90: 324
			1985	90 Quattro: 306
			1985	Coupe GT: 307
25	119.0	191.5	1985	100 Quattro: 303
26	116.0	186.6	1984	4000 S Quattro: 298
27	115.0	185.0	1986	90: 313
			1986	Coupe GT: 314
28	114.0	183.4	1972	100 Coupe S: 267
			1984	5000 S Avant: 299
			1986	80 1.8S: 312
29	113.0	181.8	1986	100 Turbo Diesel: 310
			1981	200 5E: 285
			1986	5000 S: 311
			1981	5000 Turbo: 287
			1976	80 GTE: 275
30	112.0	180.2	1977	100 5E: 276
			1984	Coupe GT: 302
31	111.0	178.6	1981	Coupe: 288
32	110.0	177.0	1979	100 GL5S: 281
			1977	100 GLS: 277
			1983	5000 S: 294
33	107.0	172.2	1975	100 GL Automatic: 272
			1971	100 LS Auto: 266
			1974	80 GT: 271
34	106.0	170.6	1984	80 GL: 301
35	105.0	168.9	1981	4000 Automatic: 286
			1975	80 Estate: 273
36	104.0	167.3	1980	4000: 283
37	103.0	165.7	1970	100 LS: 265
			1982	80 Turbo Diesel: 291
38	101.0	162.5	1978	100 L Avant: 279
39	100.0	160.9	1978	5000: 280
			1979	80 GLS: 282
			1973	Fox: 270
40	97.0	156.1	1977	Fox: 278
41	96.0	154.5	1973	80 LS: 269
42	94.0	151.2	1975	Fox: 274

Austin

1	112.0	180.2	1983	Maestro 1600: 422
			1986	Montego 2.0 Vanden Plas EFI: 425
2	111.0	178.6	1985	Montego 2.0 HL: 424
3	108.0	173.8	1972	2200: 404
4	105.0	168.9	1975	2200 HL: 411
			1977	Allegro 1750 HL: 415
			1983	Maestro 1.6 HLS: 421
5	104.0	167.3	1974	Allegro HL: 409
			1989	Metro GTa: 427
6	103.0	165.7	1984	Montego 1.6L: 423
7	102.0	164.1	1982	Ambassador 2.0 HL: 420
8	101.0	162.5	1970	3-litre: 401
			1968	3-litre Automatic: 396
			1972	Maxi High Line: 405
9	100.0	160.9	1960	A99: 388
			1978	Princess II 2000 HL: 417
10	98.0	157.7	1959	A99: 385
			1976	Princess 2200 HLS: 414
11	97.5	156.9	1960	A99 Automatic: 389
12	97.0	156.1	1959	A105 Vanden Plas: 383
13	96.0	154.5	1969	1300 GT: 398
			1968	1800 Mk II: 395
			1958	A105 Automatic: 378
			1973	Marina GT: 407
14	95.7	154.0	1949	A90 Atlantic: 363
15	95.0	152.9	1956	A105: 374
			1987	Metro 1.3L 3-door: 426
16	93.0	149.6	1971	1300 Mk III: 403
			1977	Maxi 1750: 416
17	92.8	149.3	1958	A95 Countryman: 382
18	92.0	148.0	1969	1300 Super: 399
			1970	Maxi 1750: 402
			1981	Metro Automatic: 418
19	91.0	146.4	1955	A90 Westminster: 373
			1957	A95 Westminster: 377
			1974	Vanden Plas 1500: 410
20	90.0	144.8	1964	1800: 394
21	89.0	143.2	1949	A135 Princess: 361
			1975	Allegro 1300 Estate: 412
22	88.0	141.6	1976	Allegro 1100: 413
			1969	Maxi: 400
23	87.0	140.0	1981	Mini Metro: 419
24	86.0	138.4	1952	Princess: 367
25	85.0	136.8	1974	Allegro 1500 Special Automatic: 408
26	84.0	135.2	1962	A60 Cambridge: 393
			1973	Allegro 1300 Super: 406
27	83.0	133.5	1948	A125 Sheerline: 359
28	82.5	132.7	1962	A40 Mk II: 392
29	81.0	130.3	1959	A55 Cambridge Mk II: 384
			1968	America: 397
30	80.0	128.7	1949	A70: 362
31	78.0	125.5	1961	A55 Countryman: 390
32	76.5	123.1	1957	A55: 376
33	76.0	122.3	1958	A55: 381
			1954	Princess: 371
34	75.0	120.7	1947	16 Saloon: 357
			1958	A35 4-door: 379
			1954	A40 Somerset Coupe: 370
			1955	A50 Cambridge: 372
			1961	Seven 850: 391
35	73.0	117.5	1958	A40: 380
			1960	A40 Countryman: 387
36	71.0	114.2	1952	A40 Somerset: 366
37	68.4	110.1	1938	14: 355
38	68.1	109.6	1934	12/6: 345
39	67.1	108.0	1936	20 Mayfair Limousine: 350
40	65.6	105.6	1931	7 Sports Two-seater: 342
41	65.0	104.6	1959	Gipsy: 386
42	63.0	101.4	1953	A30: 368
			1954	A30: 369
			1956	A30 Countryman: 375
43	62.9	101.2	1937	14 Goodwood Saloon: 353
44	61.6	99.1	1934	20 Ranelagh Landaulet: 347
45	61.0	98.1	1947	8 Saloon: 358
46	60.8	97.8	1937	10 Cambridge: 352
			1935	16 Hertford Saloon: 348
47	60.7	97.7	1934	15.9hp Ascot Saloon: 346
48	60.0	96.5	1948	A40: 360
49	57.3	92.2	1937	Big 7: 354
50	56.9	91.6	1939	8 Saloon: 356
51	54.0	86.9	1934	10/4 Saloon: 344
52	52.9	85.1	1936	7 Ruby Saloon: 351
53	52.6	84.6	1931	7 Sunshine Saloon: 343
54	51.0	82.1	1929	7 Tourer: 340
55	50.8	81.7	1935	7 Ruby Saloon: 349
56	47.6	76.6	1931	7 Saloon: 341

Austin-Healey

1	122.0	196.3	1964	3000 Mk III: 445
2	120.0	193.1	1962	3000 Mk II: 443
3	119.0	191.5	1953	100: 428
4	118.6	190.8	1955	100S: 430
5	116.0	186.6	1959	3000: 436
			1965	3000 Mk III: 446
6	115.0	185.0	1961	3000: 440
			1962	3000: 442

7	111.0	178.6	1958	100/6: 433
8	109.0	175.4	1956	100M: 431
			1958	Mille Miglia: 434
9	105.0	168.9	1957	100/6: 432
10	102.3	164.6	1954	100: 429
11	93.0	149.6	1968	Sprite: 447
12	90.0	144.8	1960	Sprite Supercharged: 439
13	87.4	140.6	1960	Sebring Sprite: 438
14	86.0	138.4	1959	Sprite Hardtop: 437
15	85.5	137.6	1961	Sprite Mk II: 441
16	85.0	136.8	1963	Sprite 1100: 444
17	81.0	130.3	1958	Sprite: 435

Austro Daimler

1	81.8	131.6	1931	32/100 Saloon: 448

Auto Union

1	108.0	173.8	1969	100 LS: 454
2	102.0	164.1	1967	Audi Super 90: 453
3	97.0	156.1	1966	Audi: 452
4	80.8	130.0	1958	1000: 449
5	80.3	129.2	1959	1000: 450
6	74.0	119.1	1961	Universal: 451

Autokraft

1	129.0	207.6	1987	AC Cobra Mk IV: 456

Avanti

1	135.0	217.2	1963	R2: 457
2	130.0	209.2	1984	II: 460
3	125.0	201.1	1966	II: 458
4	124.0	199.5	1969	II: 459

Bentley

1	146.0	234.9	1987	Turbo R: 481
2	145.0	233.3	1990	Turbo R: 482
3	135.0	217.2	1982	Mulsanne Turbo: 479
4	134.0	215.6	1985	Mulsanne Turbo: 480
5	128.0	206.0	1991	Turbo R: 483
6	120.5	193.9	1956	Continental Park Ward DH Coupe: 475
7	120.0	193.1	1979	T2: 478
8	116.9	188.1	1952	Continental: 471
9	114.5	184.2	1960	S2 Continental: 477
10	106.5	171.4	1954	Sports: 474
			1952	Sports Saloon: 473
11	101.1	162.7	1930	8-litre Saloon: 463
12	101.0	162.5	1956	Series S: 476
13	100.0	160.9	1952	Mk VI: 472
14	97.8	157.4	1930	4.5-litre Supercharged: 462
15	96.0	154.5	1938	4.25-litre: 468
16	94.7	152.4	1936	4.25-litre: 466
17	94.0	151.2	1947	4.5-litre Mk VI Saloon: 470
18	92.7	149.2	1939	4.5-litre: 469
19	92.0	148.0	1929	4.5-litre: 461
20	91.8	147.7	1937	4.5-litre: 467
21	91.0	146.4	1934	Sedan: 465
22	85.7	137.9	1930	Speed Six Weymann: 464

Berkeley

1	83.0	133.5	1958	Sports 4: 486
2	82.5	132.7	1960	B95: 487
3	65.0	104.6	1957	Sports: 484
4	58.0	93.3	1958	Sports: 485

Bertone

1	170.0	273.5	1991	Emotion Lotus: 489
2	138.0	222.0	1990	Zabrus: 488

Bianchi

1	71.4	114.9	1931	Straight Eight Saloon: 490
2	59.2	95.3	1937	12hp Pillarless Saloon: 491

Bitter

1	141.0	226.9	1990	Type 3 Cabrio: 494
2	130.0	209.2	1986	SC: 493

Bizzarini

1	180.0	289.6	1966	P538: 497
2	165.0	265.5	1965	5300Spyder: 495
3	145.0	233.3	1966	GT America: 496

BMW

1	179.0	288.0	1991	535i Alpina B10 Bi-Turbo: 619
2	171.0	275.1	1990	750i Alpina B12: 613
3	161.0	259.0	1991	850i: 620
4	160.0	257.4	1992	850i Manual: 625
5	158.0	254.2	1990	735i Koenig: 611
			1987	750i L: 589
			1984	M635 CSi: 572
6	156.0	251.0	1980	M1: 556
7	155.0	249.4	1988	750i L: 596
			1989	M5: 606
			1991	M5: 622
8	154.0	247.8	1989	735i Alpina B11: 602
9	153.0	246.2	1990	750i: 612
10	150.0	241.4	1989	M635 CSi: 607
11	148.0	238.1	1989	M3 Evolution: 604
12	147.0	236.5	1986	735i Automatic: 585
			1988	M6: 597
13	146.0	234.9	1985	M535i: 576
14	145.0	233.3	1988	535i SE: 593
			1985	M635 CSi Hardy & Beck: 577
15	143.0	230.1	1991	325i SE: 615
			1989	535i: 600
			1989	535i Automatic: 601
			1989	M3: 603
16	141.0	226.9	1991	525i SE 24v: 618
			1982	635 CSi: 561
17	140.0	225.3	1979	635 CSi: 552
			1987	M3: 590
18	139.0	223.7	1989	Z1: 608
19	137.0	220.4	1988	735i: 595
20	135.0	217.2	1986	325i Convertible: 579
			1985	327S Hardy & Beck: 574
			1988	635 CSi: 594
21	134.0	215.6	1973	3.0 CSL: 530
			1981	528i: 558
			1983	533i: 566
22	133.0	214.0	1988	325i S: 591
23	132.0	212.4	1971	3.0 CS: 524
			1985	325i: 573
			1992	520i SE Touring: 624
			1976	633 CSi: 540
			1987	730i SE: 588
			1984	735i Automatic: 571
24	131.0	210.8	1978	528i: 549
			1986	535i: 582
			1986	635 CSi: 583
			1983	735i: 567
25	130.0	209.2	1974	2002 Turbo: 534
			1987	325i Cabriolet: 587
			1991	520i: 616
			1979	732i: 553
26	129.0	207.6	1978	333i Alpina: 548
27	128.0	206.0	1971	3.0S: 525
			1992	325i: 623
			1991	525i: 617
28	127.0	204.3	1988	325i X: 592
29	126.0	202.7	1970	2800 CS: 521
			1978	323i: 547
			1977	528: 543
30	125.0	201.1	1973	3.0 CS: 529
			1990	318i S: 609
			1981	323i Hardy & Beck: 557
			1979	528i: 551
			1984	633 CSi: 570
			1985	732i: 575
31	124.0	199.5	1974	3.3L: 535
			1986	325 ES: 578
			1957	507: 500
			1980	633 CSi: 555
			1982	745i: 562
			1973	Bavaria: 532
32	123.0	197.9	1991	318i: 614
33	122.0	196.3	1984	325E: 569
			1977	630 CSi: 544
			1977	733i: 545
			1971	Bavaria: 526
34	121.0	194.7	1969	2500: 519
			1983	320i: 564
			1986	520i: 580
35	120.0	193.1	1971	2002 Tii: 523
			1975	530i: 539
36	119.0	191.5	1978	320i Alpina: 546
			1974	525: 536
			1975	525: 538
			1986	735i: 584
37	118.0	189.9	1971	2002: 522
			1972	2002 TransAm: 528
			1978	733i: 550
38	116.0	186.6	1987	318i 2-door: 586
			1973	520i: 531
39	115.0	185.0	1966	2000 CS: 510
			1972	2002 Tii: 527
40	114.0	183.4	1989	316i 4-door: 598
			1977	320: 541
			1982	528e: 560
41	113.0	181.8	1968	2000 CS: 515
			1983	525E: 565
42	112.0	180.2	1974	2002 Tii: 533
43	111.0	178.6	1969	2000 Tilux: 517

			1984	318i: 568
			1983	318i: 563
44	110.0	177.0	1967	2000 TiLux: 514
45	109.0	175.4	1966	2000 Ti: 511
			1980	320i: 554
46	108.0	173.8	1965	1800 Ti: 508
			1968	2002: 516
47	106.0	170.6	1967	1600 Coupe: 512
48	105.0	168.9	1966	2000: 509
49	104.0	167.3	1969	2002: 518
			1977	320i: 542
50	103.0	165.7	1982	316: 559
51	102.0	164.1	1970	2002 Automatic: 520
			1986	524 TD: 581
52	101.0	162.5	1956	501: 498
53	100.6	161.9	1963	1800 Saloon: 506
54	100.0	160.9	1967	1600-2: 513
55	96.0	154.5	1975	1602L: 537
56	95.0	152.9	1963	1500: 505
57	82.0	131.9	1962	700 Coupe: 504
58	78.0	125.5	1964	700 LS: 507
59	75.0	120.7	1960	700: 503
60	62.8	101.0	1958	600: 501
61	54.0	86.9	1956	Isetta Motocoupe: 499
62	49.7	80.0	1958	Isetta 300: 502

Bond

1	92.0	148.0	1965	Equipe GT 4S: 627
2	83.0	133.5	1964	Equipe GT: 626
3	82.0	131.9	1966	875: 628
4	77.0	123.9	1970	Bug: 629

Borgward

1	101.0	162.5	1960	2.3 Grosse: 634
2	98.0	157.7	1960	Isabella TS Coupe: 636
3	92.8	149.3	1960	Isabella TS: 635
			1956	Isabella TS: 631
4	91.0	146.4	1958	Isabella TS: 633
5	90.2	145.1	1958	Isabella Coupe: 632
6	80.6	129.7	1955	Isabella 1500: 630

Bricklin

1	111.0	178.6	1975	SV-1: 637

Bristol

1	122.0	196.3	1961	407: 640
2	93.7	150.8	1952	401: 639
3	92.0	148.0	1948	400: 638

British Adler

1	61.2	98.5	1935	13.67 Cabriolet: 641

British Salmson

1	88.2	141.9	1936	20.8hp Sports Two-seater: 644
2	75.6	121.6	1936	12hp Four-seater Tourer: 643
3	73.1	117.6	1937	14hp Saloon: 645
4	70.3	113.1	1934	Closed-coupled Saloon: 642

BSA

1	65.0	104.6	1939	Scout: 647
2	58.4	94.0	1932	FWD Tourer: 646

Bugatti

1	214.0	344.3	1991	EB110: 652
2	121.0	194.7	1926	50S: 648
3	110.0	177.0	1932	55: 651
4	88.2	141.9	1931	5-litre Saloon: 650
5	81.0	130.3	1930	49: 649

Buick

1	129.5	208.4	1970	GS455 Stage 1: 687
2	125.0	201.1	1988	Reatta: 695
			1991	Reatta Convertible: 698
			1967	Wildcat: 680
3	124.0	199.5	1969	Riviera: 683
4	123.0	197.9	1963	Riviera: 668
5	122.0	196.3	1965	Riviera: 674
			1969	Wildcat: 686
6	121.0	194.7	1965	Skylark Gran Sport: 676
7	120.0	193.1	1964	Electra 225: 669
			1966	Riviera Gran Sport: 677
8	118.0	189.9	1968	Riviera: 682
9	115.0	185.0	1962	Invicta: 663
			1964	Wildcat: 672
10	113.0	181.8	1969	Sportswagon: 685
			1962	Wildcat: 667
11	110.0	177.0	1967	GS400: 679
			1968	GS400: 681
12	109.0	175.4	1969	Skylark: 684
13	107.1	172.3	1978	Century: 691
14	107.0	172.2	1962	Skylark: 664
15	106.0	170.6	1965	LeSabre 400: 673
			1965	Skylark: 675
16	105.0	168.9	1967	California GS: 678
			1962	Skylark Automatic: 665
			1960	Special: 661
17	102.0	164.1	1979	Riviera S-type: 692
18	101.0	162.5	1976	Skyhawk: 690
			1975	Skylark: 688
			1961	Special: 662
19	100.0	160.9	1954	Roadmaster: 660
20	99.0	159.3	1964	Skylark Sports Wagon: 670
21	98.0	157.7	1976	Opel by Isuzu: 689
22	97.0	156.1	1983	Century T-type: 693
23	95.0	152.9	1962	Special V6: 666
24	93.0	149.6	1964	Special: 671
25	84.9	136.6	1938	Viceroy Saloon: 659
26	81.8	131.6	1936	Century Saloon: 658
27	73.7	118.6	1935	Light Eight Viceroy Saloon: 657
28	72.5	116.7	1933	Straight Eight Saloon: 656
29	70.0	112.6	1928	Empire Saloon: 653
30	67.1	108.0	1930	28.4hp Saloon: 654
			1930	Light Eight Saloon: 655

Cadillac

1	130.0	209.2	1990	Allante: 716
			1991	Allante: 719
2	125.0	201.1	1990	Eldorado Touring Coupe: 718
			1991	Seville Touring Sedan: 720
3	123.0	197.9	1964	Coupe de Ville: 705
4	121.0	194.7	1964	Sedan de Ville: 706
5	120.0	193.1	1968	Coupe de Ville: 709
			1967	Eldorado: 708
			1961	Fleetwood: 703
6	119.0	191.5	1988	Allante: 715
7	115.0	185.0	1966	Calais: 707
			1961	Coupe de Ville: 702
			1959	Eldorado Convertible: 701
8	114.0	183.4	1963	Park Avenue: 704
9	109.0	175.4	1976	Seville: 710
10	95.0	152.9	1978	Seville Diesel: 711
			1981	Seville Diesel: 712
11	94.0	151.2	1982	Cimarron: 713
12	88.8	142.9	1931	V16 Fleetwood Roadster: 700
13	87.0	140.0	1930	V16 "Madame X": 699

Carbodies

1	81.0	130.3	1989	Fairway 2.7 Silver: 721

Caterham

1	126.0	202.7	1990	7 HPC: 725
2	116.0	186.6	1985	1700 Super Sprint: 723
3	114.0	183.4	1975	Super 7: 722
4	112.0	180.2	1991	Super 7: 726
5	100.0	160.9	1985	7: 724

Checker

1	109.0	175.4	1969	Marathon: 728
2	103.0	165.7	1968	Marathon: 727

Chevrolet

1	255.0	410.3	1990	Corvette Callaway Sledgehammer: 941
2	221.0	355.6	1976	Corvette Greenwood: 870
3	204.0	328.2	1991	Corvette Lingenfelter: 951
4	203.0	326.6	1989	Camaro Gottlieb 1969: 926
5	201.0	323.4	1991	Corvette Callaway Speedster: 949
6	193.0	310.5	1989	Camaro IROC-Z Chevrolet Engineering: 929
7	191.0	307.3	1988	Corvette Callaway: 918
			1989	Corvette Callaway: 931
8	186.0	299.3	1991	Corvette ZR-1 Geiger: 954
9	185.0	297.7	1991	Corvette ZR-2: 956
10	184.0	296.1	1991	Corvette Callaway: 948
11	178.0	286.4	1986	Corvette Callaway: 901
12	172.0	276.7	1988	Corvette Guldstrand Grand Sport 80: 920
13	171.0	275.1	1989	Corvette Guldstrand Grand Sport 80: 932
14	170.0	273.5	1990	Corvette Callaway: 940
			1989	Corvette ZR-1: 934
15	169.0	271.9	1988	Corvette Bakeracing SCCA Escort: 917
16	163.0	262.3	1992	Corvette LT1: 959
17	158.0	254.2	1988	Corvette Convertible: 919
			1988	Corvette Z51: 922
18	155.0	249.4	1988	Corvette: 916
			1989	Corvette L98: 933

19	154.0	247.8	1986	Corvette: 900
			1987	Corvette: 908
			1987	Corvette ASC Geneve: 909
			1986	Corvette Z51: 902
			1991	Corvette ZR-1: 953
			1976	Monza Mike Keyser: 874
20	152.0	244.6	1978	Camaro IROC: 877
			1985	Corvette: 897
21	151.0	243.0	1968	Corvette L88: 820
			1969	Corvette L88: 835
22	150.0	241.4	1987	Camaro IROC-Z: 906
			1987	Corvette Convertible: 910
			1963	Corvette Grand Sport Roadster: 776
23	149.0	239.7	1987	Camaro IROC-Z L98: 907
			1989	Corvette: 930
			1990	Corvette L98: 944
24	148.0	238.1	1956	Corvette Sebring: 738
			1964	Corvette Sting Ray: 786
25	147.0	236.5	1991	Corvette Rick Mears: 952
26	145.0	233.3	1989	Camaro IROC-Z: 927
			1989	Camaro IROC-Z Automatic: 928
			1990	Camaro Z/28: 938
			1984	Corvette: 894
27	144.0	231.7	1970	Corvette 454: 844
28	142.0	228.5	1963	Corvette: 775
			1968	Corvette Convertible: 818
			1963	Corvette Sting Ray: 777
29	141.0	226.9	1969	Corvette L71/89: 834
30	140.0	225.3	1992	Camaro Z28: 958
31	138.0	222.0	1965	Corvette Sting Ray 396: 798
			1964	Corvette Sting Ray Injection: 788
32	137.0	220.4	1983	Corvette: 891
			1969	Corvette L68: 832
33	136.0	218.8	1965	Corvette: 795
			1965	Corvette 396: 796
34	135.0	217.2	1985	Camaro IROC-Z: 896
			1969	Corvette LT-1: 836
35	134.0	215.6	1969	Corvette L36: 830
36	133.0	214.0	1968	Camaro Z/28: 811
37	132.0	212.4	1957	Corvette: 739
			1979	Corvette: 881
			1957	Corvette Injection: 740
			1957	Corvette RPO 684/579E: 741
			1977	Corvette Sting Ray: 875
			1969	Corvette Stingray: 837
			1968	El Camino: 821
			1970	Monte Carlo: 847
38	131.0	210.8	1962	Chevy II Corvette: 757
			1961	Corvette 270: 752
39	130.0	209.2	1967	Camaro 427 Dana: 805
			1965	Chevelle Malibu 396: 792
			1980	Corvette: 884
			1966	Corvette Convertible: 803
			1964	Corvette Sting Ray Automatic: 787
			1963	Corvette Sting Ray Automatic: 778
40	129.1	207.7	1956	Corvette: 737
41	128.0	206.0	1961	Corvette: 750
			1968	Corvette: 817
			1959	Corvette: 743
			1961	Corvette 315: 753
			1968	Corvette Coupe: 819
42	127.0	204.3	1965	Corvette Injection: 797
			1988	Corvette Morrison/Baker Nelson Ledges: 921
43	126.0	202.7	1969	Camaro SS 396: 824
			1969	Caprice: 827
			1969	Corvette ZQ3: 838
44	125.0	201.1	1991	Baretta GTZ: 946
			1990	Beretta GT: 935
			1990	Beretta GTZ: 936
			1983	Camaro: 887
			1983	Camaro Z/28: 888
			1990	Cavalier Z24: 939
			1962	Corvette: 766
			1962	Impala SS 409: 768
			1967	Impala SS427: 809
45	124.0	199.5	1972	Camaro Z/28: 857
			1970	Chevelle SS396: 843
			1982	Corvette: 886
			1974	Corvette: 862
			1973	Corvette LT-1: 858
			1963	Impala Super Sport 409: 779
			1969	Kingswood Estate Wagon: 839
46	123.0	197.9	1966	Chevy II Nova SS: 801
47	122.0	196.3	1969	Corvette 435hp: 829
			1970	Corvette LT-1: 845
48	121.0	194.7	1968	Camaro SS396: 810
			1967	Corvette: 808
49	120.0	193.1	1967	Camaro: 804
			1990	Camaro IROC-Z Convertible: 937
			1967	Camaro SS350: 807
			1969	Camaro Z/28: 825
			1991	Camaro Z/28 Convertible: 947
			1988	Cavalier Z24 Convertible: 915
			1968	Chevelle SS396: 813
			1964	Corvair Sprint: 785
50	119.0	191.5	1970	Camaro Z/28: 841
			1969	Corvette L46: 831
			1969	Corvette L71: 833
51	118.0	189.9	1970	Camaro Z/28 RS: 842
			1970	Impala: 846
52	117.0	188.3	1973	Monte Carlo: 859
			1970	Nova SS350: 848
53	116.9	188.1	1955	Corvette V8: 735
54	116.0	186.6	1962	Bel Air 409 SS/S: 755
			1968	Chevy II: 814
55	115.0	185.0	1987	Beretta GT: 905
			1970	Camaro: 840
			1982	Camaro Z/28: 885
			1969	Chevelle Malibu: 828
			1983	Citation X11 HO: 890
			1966	Corvette: 802
			1961	Impala: 754
			1968	Malibu 327: 823
56	114.0	183.4	1965	Caprice Custom 396: 790
57	113.0	181.8	1986	Cavalier Z24: 898
			1991	Lumina Z34: 957
58	112.0	180.2	1968	Chevelle Malibu: 812
			1976	Cosworth Vega: 871
59	111.0	178.6	1956	210: 736
			1962	Impala Station Wagon: 769
60	110.0	177.0	1989	Baretta GTU: 925
			1972	Camaro Budget: 855
			1984	Camaro Z/28: 893
			1986	Celebrity CL Eurosport: 899
			1964	Chevelle Super Sport: 782
			1964	El Camino: 789
			1988	Nova Twin Cam: 923
61	109.0	175.4	1961	Corvette 230: 751
			1975	Nova LN: 865
62	108.0	173.8	1979	Citation X11: 880
63	107.1	172.3	1953	Corvette: 732
64	107.0	172.2	1976	Camaro: 867
			1972	Camaro Luxury: 856
			1965	Impala SS: 799
65	106.4	171.2	1954	Corvette: 733
66	106.0	170.6	1965	Corvair Corsa IECO: 793
			1968	Corvair Sport Coupe: 816
67	105.0	168.9	1963	Biscayne V8: 771
			1962	Corvair Spyder: 765
			1990	Lumina APV: 945
68	104.7	168.5	1955	210 Coupe Club V8: 734
69	104.0	167.3	1967	Camaro Six: 806
			1964	Chevy II V8 Station Wagon: 783
70	103.0	165.7	1975	Monza 2+2 V8: 864
			1976	Monza 2+2 V8: 873
71	102.0	164.1	1971	Vega L11: 854
72	100.0	160.9	1983	Cavalier CS: 889
			1974	Vega: 863
			1973	Vega: 860
73	98.0	157.7	1971	Blazer: 850
			1968	Corvair Monza: 815
			1964	Corvair Monza: 784
			1962	Corvair Navarro: 764
			1971	Vega 2300: 853
74	97.0	156.1	1978	Blazer: 876
75	96.0	154.5	1968	Impala: 822
76	95.0	152.9	1966	Bel Air Six: 800
			1986	Nova CL: 903
77	93.0	149.6	1963	Corvair Monza EMPI: 774
78	92.0	148.0	1964	Chevelle Malibu: 781
			1962	Chevy II: 756
			1962	Chevy II Six Automatic: 760
			1962	Chevy II Six Manual: 761
			1961	Corvair Monza 4-speed: 749
79	91.5	147.2	1965	Chevelle Malibu: 791
80	91.0	146.4	1976	Chevette Rally 1.6: 868
81	90.0	144.8	1964	Chevelle 300: 780
			1962	Corvair Monza: 762
			1965	Corvair Monza: 794
			1963	Corvair Monza Convertible: 773
			1962	Corvair Monza Coupe: 763
			1971	Pickup Cheyenne Fleetside: 851
			1975	Vega GT: 866
82	88.0	141.6	1959	Corvair: 742
			1978	Malibu: 879
			1971	Vega: 852
83	87.5	140.8	1960	Corvair 4-speed: 744
84	87.0	140.0	1984	Sprint: 895
85	85.5	137.6	1960	Corvair Automatic: 745
86	85.0	136.8	1963	Bel Air: 770
			1963	C-10 Fleetside Pickup: 772
			1961	Corvair Monza: 748
87	84.6	136.1	1961	Corvair 700: 746
88	84.1	135.3	1938	Master de Luxe Saloon: 731
89	84.0	135.2	1962	Chevy II Four Manual: 759

90	82.0	131.9	1962	Chevy II Four Automatic: 758
91	79.6	128.1	1935	26.3hp Saloon de Luxe: 729
92	78.9	127.0	1937	Master de Luxe Sports Sedan: 730
93	70.0	112.6	1961	Corvair Greenbrier: 747

Chrysler

1	135.0	217.2	1958	300-D: 973
			1989	TC by Maserati: 1008
2	133.0	214.0	1962	300-H: 980
3	131.0	210.8	1961	300-G: 975
4	130.0	209.2	1963	300-J: 981
			1961	Enforcer: 976
5	127.0	204.3	1970	300-H: 989
			1988	Conquest TSi: 1007
6	121.0	194.7	1964	Imperial Le Baron: 982
7	120.0	193.1	1962	300: 979
			1966	300: 984
			1961	Imperial: 977
			1987	Le Baron Coupe: 1006
			1985	Le Baron GTS: 1004
8	119.0	191.5	1969	300: 988
9	118.0	189.9	1986	Laser XT: 1005
10	117.0	188.3	1967	Imperial Crown: 987
			1961	Newport: 978
11	116.0	186.6	1970	Charger: 990
12	113.0	181.8	1984	Laser XE: 1003
13	112.0	180.2	1979	Sunbeam 1600 Ti: 1002
14	110.0	177.0	1965	Newport: 983
15	109.0	175.4	1966	Valiant Premium Auto: 986
16	107.0	172.2	1953	New Yorker Saloon: 971
17	105.0	168.9	1973	2-litre: 992
			1976	Alpine S: 993
18	104.5	168.1	1955	Windsor de Luxe: 972
19	104.0	167.3	1951	Saratoga Club Coupe: 970
20	102.0	164.1	1978	Alpine GLS: 1000
21	101.0	162.5	1971	180: 991
			1977	Sunbeam 1.6S: 998
22	100.0	160.9	1978	Horizon GL: 1001
23	96.0	154.5	1978	1300 GL: 999
			1931	Custom Imperial Le Baron: 964
			1960	Valiant: 974
24	94.7	152.4	1937	Super Power Saloon: 968
25	94.0	151.2	1977	Avenger 1600 Estate: 996
26	93.0	149.6	1977	Alpine GL: 995
27	91.0	146.4	1976	Avenger Super 1300: 994
28	88.6	142.6	1935	Heston Airflow Saloon: 965
29	83.3	134.0	1938	Royal Saloon: 969
30	80.0	128.7	1977	Sunbeam 1.0LS: 997
31	78.9	127.0	1937	Richmond Touring Saloon: 967
32	77.5	124.7	1936	23.4hp Wimbledon Saloon: 966
33	75.0	120.7	1930	77 Saloon: 962
34	73.1	117.6	1930	Eight Saloon: 963
35	70.0	112.6	1929	75 Saloon: 961
36	64.0	103.0	1929	65 Saloon: 960

Cisitalia

1	125.0	201.1	1947	Aerodinamica Mille Miglia: 1009

Citroen

1	145.0	233.3	1991	XM V6.24: 1089
2	140.0	225.3	1973	Safari SM: 1045
3	135.0	217.2	1971	Safari SM: 1041
			1972	SM: 1043
			1991	XM 3.0 SEi Auto: 1088
4	133.0	214.0	1987	BX GTi 16v: 1077
5	128.0	206.0	1984	CX GTi Turbo: 1062
6	125.0	201.1	1991	ZX Volcane: 1091
7	122.0	196.3	1990	XM 2.0SEi: 1086
8	118.0	189.9	1977	CX 2400 GTi: 1053
9	116.0	186.6	1990	BX GTi 4x4: 1084
			1977	CX 2400: 1052
			1981	CX Pallas: 1058
			1986	CX25 Ri Familiale Auto: 1072
10	115.0	185.0	1992	AX GTi: 1092
			1976	CX 2200 Pallas: 1049
			1986	Visa GTi: 1073
11	114.0	183.4	1970	DS21 EFI 139 Pallas: 1038
12	113.0	181.8	1978	CX Pallas C-Matic Injection: 1054
			1985	CX22 TRS: 1067
			1987	CX25 DTR Turbo 2: 1078
13	112.0	180.2	1983	BX16 TRS: 1060
			1975	CX 2000: 1047
			1985	Visa GTi: 1070
			1992	XM Turbo SD Estate: 1093
14	110.0	177.0	1979	Athena: 1055
15	109.0	175.4	1990	AX GT5: 1083
			1985	BX16 TRS Automatic: 1066
			1971	Safari 21: 1040
16	108.0	173.8	1987	AX GT: 1074
			1965	DS21 Pallas M: 1032
17	107.0	172.2	1991	ZX 1.4 Avantage: 1090
18	106.0	170.6	1988	BX DTR Turbo: 1080
			1966	DS21: 1034
19	105.0	168.9	1965	DSM: 1033
20	102.0	164.1	1989	BX14 TGE: 1082
21	101.0	162.5	1987	AX11 TRE: 1075
			1987	AX14 TRS: 1076
22	100.0	160.9	1984	BX19 RD Diesel: 1061
			1968	DS21 Safari: 1036
			1975	GS Pallas: 1048
			1976	GS X2: 1050
23	99.0	159.3	1983	BX14 RE: 1059
			1979	CX 2500 Diesel Super: 1056
24	98.0	157.7	1988	AX11 TRE 5DR: 1079
			1963	DS: 1031
			1985	Visa 14TRS: 1068
25	96.0	154.5	1973	GS 1220: 1044
26	95.0	152.9	1991	AX11 TZX: 1087
			1961	DS: 1029
27	94.0	151.2	1986	BX19 RD Estate: 1071
28	93.0	149.6	1985	Visa 17RD: 1069
29	92.0	148.0	1989	AX14 DTR: 1081
			1971	GS: 1039
30	90.0	144.8	1977	CX 2200 Diesel: 1051
			1972	GS: 1042
31	88.4	142.2	1956	DS19: 1023
32	88.0	141.6	1958	ID19: 1025
33	87.5	140.8	1957	DS19: 1024
34	87.4	140.6	1960	ID19: 1027
35	87.0	140.0	1960	ID Safari: 1026
36	85.0	136.8	1984	LNA 11RE: 1063
			1984	Visa Convertible: 1064
37	84.0	135.2	1954	Six: 1021
38	83.0	133.5	1949	Six Saloon: 1016
39	76.0	122.3	1948	Light Fifteen: 1015
			1952	Light Fifteen: 1017
40	75.0	120.7	1953	11CV: 1018
			1940	Light Fifteen Roadster: 1014
41	73.0	117.5	1970	Ami 8 Club: 1037
42	72.5	116.7	1936	Super Modern Fifteen Saloon: 1012
43	72.0	115.8	1953	Big Fifteen: 1020
			1979	Visa Club: 1057
44	71.0	114.2	1975	2CV6: 1046
			1985	2CV6 Charleston: 1065
45	69.5	111.8	1962	Ami 6: 1030
46	68.7	110.5	1937	Sports Twelve Saloon: 1013
47	68.0	109.4	1967	Ami 6 Break: 1035
48	63.3	101.8	1936	Super Model Twelve: 1011
49	60.8	97.8	1930	Six Saloon: 1010
50	50.5	81.3	1961	Bijou: 1028
51	49.2	79.2	1955	2CV: 1022
52	41.0	66.0	1953	2CV Cabriolet: 1019

Cizeta

1	204.0	328.2	1990	Moroder V16T: 1094

Clan

1	102.0	164.1	1971	Crusader: 1095

Consulier

1	140.0	225.3	1990	GTP LX: 1096

Cord

1	112.0	180.2	1937	812-S: 1101
2	102.3	164.6	1937	812: 1100
3	102.2	164.4	1937	Supercharged Saloon: 1102
4	92.4	148.7	1936	Front Wheel Drive Saloon: 1099
5	77.0	123.9	1930	L-29: 1097
6	76.9	123.7	1931	Front Wheel Drive Phaeton: 1098

Crossley

1	77.0	123.9	1929	2-litre Saloon: 1103
2	65.6	105.6	1935	10hp Regis Sports Saloon: 1105
3	60.0	96.5	1934	10hp Torquay: 1104

Dacia

1	74.0	119.1	1985	Duster GLX: 1106

DAF

1	89.0	143.2	1974	66SL 1300: 1114
2	83.0	133.5	1973	66SL: 1113
3	82.0	131.9	1958	55: 1107
			1971	55 Estate: 1112

4	75.0	120.7	1967	44: 1111
5	63.5	102.2	1962	Daffodil: 1109
			1962	Daffodil de Luxe Extra: 1110
6	57.0	91.7	1960	600 de Luxe: 1108

Daihatsu

1	116.0	186.6	1987	Charade GT ti: 1124
2	111.0	178.6	1990	Applause 16 Xi: 1131
3	102.0	164.1	1989	Charade 1.3 CX: 1128
4	96.0	154.5	1988	Charade Turbo: 1127
			1982	Charmant 1600LE: 1118
5	95.0	152.9	1989	Charade CLS: 1129
			1985	Charmant 1300LC: 1121
6	91.0	146.4	1989	Sportrak EL: 1130
7	88.0	141.6	1983	Charade CX: 1119
			1986	Domino: 1122
8	85.0	136.8	1979	Charade XTE: 1116
			1987	Fourtrak Estate DT EL: 1125
9	82.0	131.9	1983	Charade Diesel: 1120
10	81.0	130.3	1987	Charade CX Diesel Turbo: 1123
11	76.0	122.3	1981	Domino: 1117
12	70.0	112.6	1965	Compagno Berlina: 1115

Daimler

1	151.0	243.0	1981	Double-Six HE: 1155
2	127.0	204.3	1960	SP250: 1147
3	122.0	196.3	1959	V8 SP250: 1146
4	120.0	193.1	1961	Majestic Major: 1148
			1972	Sovereign: 1153
			1974	Sovereign LWB Automatic: 1154
5	115.0	185.0	1966	2.5-litre V8: 1152
6	114.0	183.4	1963	Limousine: 1150
7	112.5	181.0	1963	2.5-litre V8 Saloon: 1149
8	103.5	166.5	1958	Majestic: 1144
9	102.5	164.9	1955	One-O-Four Ladies' Model: 1141
10	98.0	157.7	1957	One-O-Four: 1143
11	93.8	150.9	1959	DK 400B: 1145
12	90.0	144.8	1936	25.7hp Light Straight Eight Coupe: 1135
13	88.0	141.6	1964	Conquest Century Saloon: 1151
14	85.0	136.8	1955	Regency Mk II: 1142
			1948	Straight Eight: 1139
15	81.0	130.3	1953	Conquest: 1140
			1946	Twenty-Seven Limousine: 1138
16	75.0	120.7	1938	24hp Limousine: 1137
			1929	30hp Double-six Saloon: 1132
17	73.7	118.6	1938	18hp 2.5-litre: 1136
18	70.3	113.1	1936	15hp Saloon: 1134
19	66.6	107.2	1933	15hp Saloon: 1133

Darracq

1	80.1	128.9	1932	Straight Eight Saloon: 1156

Datsun

1	147.0	236.5	1975	240Z Sharp: 1190
2	145.0	233.3	1983	280ZX Electramotive: 1230
3	130.0	209.2	1978	280Z Scarab: 1205
4	129.0	207.6	1983	280ZX Turbo: 1231
			1981	280ZX Turbo: 1223
5	127.0	204.3	1972	510 TransAm: 1180
6	126.0	202.7	1971	240Z: 1175
7	124.0	199.5	1983	280ZX: 1229
			1980	280ZX Sharp: 1221
			1976	B210 Electramotive: 1198
8	123.0	197.9	1982	280ZX: 1225
9	122.0	196.3	1970	240Z: 1171
			1980	280ZX Electramotive: 1220
10	121.0	194.7	1974	260Z 2+2: 1187
			1979	280ZX: 1211
11	120.0	193.1	1971	240Z Automatic: 1176
12	119.0	191.5	1975	280Z: 1192
13	115.0	185.0	1973	240Z: 1182
			1977	260Z: 1202
14	114.0	183.4	1968	2000 Sports: 1164
			1967	2000 Sports: 1162
			1979	280ZX 2+2 Automatic: 1212
15	113.0	181.8	1974	260Z: 1186
			1981	810 Maxima: 1224
16	112.0	180.2	1979	240K: 1210
17	111.0	178.6	1980	280ZX Automatic: 1219
			1977	810 Sedan: 1203
18	110.0	177.0	1980	200SX: 1217
19	108.0	173.8	1983	200SX: 1228
			1979	810 Coupe: 1215
20	107.0	172.2	1972	180B: 1178
21	104.0	167.3	1973	200L: 1181
			1972	240C: 1179
22	103.0	165.7	1977	180B Bluebird: 1200
			1976	200L-6: 1196
23	102.0	164.1	1980	510: 1222
24	101.0	162.5	1967	1600 Sports: 1161
			1979	2.4 Laurel Six: 1208
25	100.0	160.9	1976	140J Violet: 1195
			1975	260C Estate: 1191
			1973	610 1800: 1183
26	98.0	157.7	1977	200SX: 1201
			1978	510: 1206
			1968	510: 1165
			1971	510: 1177
			1968	510 Sedan: 1166
			1982	Sunny 1.5 DX: 1227
27	97.0	156.1	1979	310 Coupe: 1214
			1982	Stanza 1.6 GL: 1226
28	96.0	154.5	1974	120Y: 1185
			1974	710: 1188
29	95.0	152.9	1970	1200: 1169
			1968	1600: 1163
			1975	710: 1193
			1978	Laurel Six: 1207
30	94.0	151.2	1976	F10: 1199
31	93.0	149.6	1971	1200 Coupe: 1173
			1979	210: 1209
32	91.0	146.4	1974	B210: 1189
33	90.0	144.8	1970	1600 Pickup: 1170
34	89.5	144.0	1968	510 Station Wagon: 1167
35	89.0	143.2	1971	1200 Estate: 1174
36	88.0	141.6	1983	Micra GL: 1232
37	87.5	140.8	1964	SPL-310: 1159
38	87.0	140.0	1971	100A: 1172
39	86.0	138.4	1979	New Sunny: 1216
40	85.0	136.8	1967	1600 Sedan: 1160
			1977	Cherry F11: 1204
41	78.0	125.5	1969	1000 de Luxe: 1168
42	75.0	120.7	1961	Bluebird Station Wagon: 1158
43	65.6	105.6	1958	1000: 1157

De Lorean

1	109.0	175.4	1982	DMC 2.8-litre Coupe: 1233

De Soto

1	68.1	109.6	1931	Straight Eight Saloon: 1234

De Tomaso

1	168.0	270.3	1989	Pantera Group 3: 1243
2	167.0	268.7	1990	Pantera GT5 S: 1244
3	165.0	265.5	1986	Pantera GT5-S: 1242
4	159.0	255.8	1972	Pantera: 1237
			1974	Pantera GTS: 1239
5	143.0	230.1	1973	Pantera: 1238
			1974	Pantera L: 1240
6	137.0	220.4	1984	Pantera GT5: 1241
7	129.0	207.6	1971	Pantera: 1236
8	118.0	189.9	1969	Mangusta: 1235

Delage

1	98.9	159.1	1931	Super Sports Straight Eight: 1248
2	96.5	155.3	1938	D8-120 Super Sports: 1251
3	86.5	139.2	1930	Straight Eight Sports Saloon: 1247
4	83.3	134.0	1937	D6-70 Sports Coupe: 1250
5	73.7	118.6	1933	D6-11 Sports Saloon: 1249
6	70.0	112.6	1928	21hp Weymann Saloon: 1245
7	64.7	104.1	1930	18.2hp Saloon: 1246

Delahaye

1	98.9	159.1	1936	23.8hp Drop-head Coupe: 1252

Delaunay-Belleville

1	66.0	106.2	1929	21hp Saloon: 1253

Dellow

1	74.0	119.1	1956	Mk V: 1254

Denzel

1	99.0	159.3	1957	1300: 1255

Deutsch-Bonnet

1	88.0	141.6	1957	Coupe: 1256

Devin

1	131.0	210.8	1959	Super Sports: 1257
2	72.2	116.2	1960	VW: 1258

DKW

1 82.0 131.9 1958 3-6 Sonderklasse Coupe: 1265
2 77.7 125.0 1956 3-6: 1263
3 74.5 119.9 1954 Sonderklasse: 1261
4 73.8 118.7 1955 3-6: 1262
5 73.0 117.5 1961 Junior: 1267
6 71.0 114.2 1962 Junior de Luxe: 1268
7 70.5 113.4 1960 750: 1266
8 61.9 99.6 1956 Karavan: 1264
9 56.6 91.1 1937 7.1hp Cabriolet: 1260
10 53.5 86.1 1934 7.1hp Cabriolet: 1259

Dodge

1 190.0 305.7 1992 Viper: 1348
2 159.0 255.8 1991 Stealth R/T Turbo: 1347
3 140.0 225.3 1989 Shelby CSX: 1341
1991 Spirit R/T: 1346
4 136.0 218.8 1969 Hemi Charger 500 Automatic: 1308
5 135.0 217.2 1990 Daytona Shelby: 1344
1988 Shelby CSX: 1338
6 134.0 215.6 1967 Charger: 1299
1969 Hemi Charger 500 Manual: 1309
7 132.0 212.4 1968 Charger R/T: 1303
8 130.0 209.2 1990 Shadow ES VNT: 1345
9 128.0 206.0 1970 Challenger R/T: 1314
10 127.0 204.3 1969 Monaco: 1310
11 126.0 202.7 1969 Coronet 500 Station Wagon: 1307
12 125.0 201.1 1990 Daytona ES: 1343
1989 Daytona Shelby: 1339
1964 Polara 500: 1290
13 123.0 197.9 1968 Coronet R/T: 1304
14 122.0 196.3 1968 Dart GTS: 1305
1968 Dart GTS 340: 1306
15 121.0 194.7 1969 Swinger: 1313
16 120.0 193.1 1966 Charger: 1298
1965 Coronet 426-S: 1294
1988 Daytona Shelby Z: 1336
1989 Shelby CSX VNT: 1342
1986 Shelby GLH-S: 1335
17 119.0 191.5 1962 Custom 880: 1279
18 118.0 189.9 1988 Lancer Shelby: 1337
1964 Polara: 1289
19 117.0 188.3 1969 Super Bee Six-Pack: 1312
20 115.0 185.0 1970 Charger R/T: 1315
1965 Coronet 500: 1296
1961 Dart: 1275
1965 Dart GT: 1297
1963 Polara: 1286
1963 Ramcharger 426 Super/Stock: 1287
1989 Shadow ES Turbo: 1340
21 113.0 181.8 1967 Coronet R/T: 1300
22 111.0 178.6 1983 Shelby Charger: 1328
23 110.2 177.3 1969 Super Bee: 1311
24 110.0 177.0 1959 Custom Royal: 1274
1985 Omni GLH: 1332
25 109.0 175.4 1982 Challenger: 1325
1961 Dart Phoenix: 1276
1961 Lancer 225 Hyper-Pack: 1278
26 108.0 173.8 1958 Custom Royal: 1273
1967 Monaco Wagon: 1302
27 107.0 172.2 1962 Dart 413: 1280
28 105.0 168.9 1982 Charger 2.2: 1326
1965 Coronet 440: 1295
29 102.0 164.1 1974 Colt GT 2-litre: 1320
1964 Dart GT: 1288
30 101.0 162.5 1984 Daytona Turbo Z: 1331
31 100.0 160.9 1983 600ES: 1327
1981 Aires Wagon: 1324
1963 Dart GT 225 Smogburner: 1285
1961 Lancer: 1277
1962 Lancer Gran Turismo: 1282
32 99.0 159.3 1965 Coronet: 1293
33 97.0 156.1 1975 Colt GT: 1321
1984 Colt Vista: 1329
34 96.0 154.5 1971 Colt: 1316
1977 Colt Lancer: 1322
1967 Dart 270: 1301
35 95.0 152.9 1979 Colt Hatchback: 1323
1963 Dart 270: 1284
36 91.0 146.4 1963 D-100 Sweptline Pickup: 1283
37 90.0 144.8 1965 A-100 Super/Surfer: 1292
38 82.0 131.9 1971 Pickup Power Wagon: 1317
39 80.0 128.7 1962 Dreamer: 1281
40 76.9 123.7 1937 Victory Six Touring Saloon: 1271
41 76.2 122.6 1938 De Luxe Saloon: 1272
42 69.2 111.3 1930 Eight Saloon: 1270
43 64.0 103.0 1929 New Six Saloon: 1269
44 50.2 80.8 1964 Safari Super Sport: 1291

Dove

1 110.0 177.0 1963 GTR4: 1349

Du Pont

1 97.0 156.1 1929 Speedster: 1350
2 76.0 122.3 1930 Town Car: 1351

Duesenberg

1 115.0 185.0 1930 J Coupe: 1352
2 106.0 170.6 1938 SJ Town Car: 1353

Eagle

1 200.0 321.8 1991 GTP: 1356
2 143.0 230.1 1990 Talon: 1355
1991 Talon TSi 4WD: 1357
3 125.0 201.1 1988 Premier ES: 1354

Elva

1 98.5 158.5 1958 Courier: 1358

Enfield

1 37.0 59.5 1976 8000 Electric: 1359

Essex

1 82.5 132.7 1933 Terraplane Straight Eight: 1361
2 73.7 118.6 1932 Terraplane Tourer: 1360

Excalibur

1 125.0 201.1 1964 SS: 1363

Facel Vega

1 135.5 218.0 1958 FVS: 1365
2 133.0 214.0 1962 Facel II: 1368
3 130.0 209.2 1960 HK-500: 1366
4 121.1 194.8 1956 Coupe: 1364
5 114.0 183.4 1961 Facellia 1600: 1367

Fairthorpe

1 119.0 191.5 1961 Zeta: 1369

Ferguson

1 104.0 167.3 1966 R5: 1370

Ferrari

1 210.0 337.9 1989 Testa Rossa Norwood: 1444
2 201.0 323.4 1988 F40: 1435
3 200.0 321.8 1990 F40: 1446
4 199.0 320.2 1991 GTO Norwood: 1451
5 198.0 318.6 1988 308 Norwood Bonneville GTO: 1434
6 196.0 315.4 1991 F40: 1450
7 189.0 304.1 1984 288 GTO: 1421
8 186.0 299.3 1974 365 GTB/4 Competitione: 1403
9 185.0 297.7 1989 Testa Rossa Gemballa: 1443
10 182.0 292.8 1989 308 Norwood: 1439
11 181.0 291.2 1988 Testa Rossa: 1437
1988 Testa Rossa Straman Spyder: 1438
12 180.0 289.6 1982 288 GTO: 1416
1952 375 Indianapolis: 1373
1963 400 Super America: 1389
1984 GTO: 1423
1990 Pininfarina Mythos: 1448
13 178.0 286.4 1985 Testa Rossa: 1426
14 177.0 284.8 1985 365 GTB Goldsmith: 1425
15 175.0 281.6 1962 250 GTO: 1386
1975 512 BB: 1407
1971 Daytona: 1397
16 174.0 280.0 1956 412 MI: 1377
1989 Testa Rossa: 1442
17 173.0 278.4 1970 365 GTB/4 Daytona: 1396
1971 Daytona Cannonball: 1398
1969 Daytona Sportwagen: 1395
18 171.0 275.1 1991 348tb: 1449
19 168.0 270.3 1957 250 Testa Rossa: 1378
1982 512 BB: 1417
20 165.0 265.5 1962 4.9: 1387
21 164.0 263.9 1990 348tb: 1445
22 163.0 262.3 1978 512 BB: 1413
23 155.0 249.4 1967 275 GTS/4 NART: 1392
1986 328 GTB: 1428

24	154.0	247.8	1976	308 GTB: 1409
			1976	Dino 308 GT4 2+2: 1410
			1990	Mondial: 1447
			1991	Mondial t: 1452
			1991	Mondial t Cabriolet: 1453
25	152.0	244.6	1974	308 GT4 Dino: 1402
			1972	365 GTC4: 1400
			1969	365 GTS 2+2: 1394
26	151.0	243.0	1965	365 GTC: 1390
27	150.0	241.4	1962	250 GT 2+2: 1385
			1963	250 GT Berlinetta Lusso: 1388
			1975	365 GT4 2+2: 1406
			1953	4.1 Coupe: 1375
28	149.0	239.7	1987	328 GTS: 1431
			1986	Mondial 3.2: 1429
29	147.0	236.5	1981	308 GTSi: 1415
			1987	412: 1432
30	146.0	234.9	1968	330 GTS: 1393
31	145.0	233.3	1966	275 GTS: 1391
			1986	3.2 Mondial: 1427
			1978	308 GTS: 1412
			1989	Mondial 3.2 Cabriolet: 1440
			1988	Mondial Cabriolet: 1436
			1987	Mondial Cabriolet 3.2: 1433
32	144.0	231.7	1986	Mondial 3.2QV: 1430
33	142.0	228.5	1983	308 GTBi Quattrovalvole: 1419
34	141.0	226.9	1972	246 GT Dino: 1399
			1974	246 GTS Dino: 1401
35	140.0	225.3	1958	250 Testa Rossa: 1382
			1983	308 GTSi Targa: 1420
36	138.0	222.0	1975	308 Dino GT4: 1405
			1976	308 GT4 Dino: 1408
			1980	308 GT4 Dino: 1414
			1984	Mondial Cabriolet Quattrovalvole: 1424
37	135.0	217.2	1954	250 Mille Miglia: 1376
			1982	Mondial 8: 1418
38	132.0	212.4	1977	308 GTB: 1411
39	130.0	209.2	1957	TRC 2500 Testa Rossa: 1379
40	128.0	206.0	1953	212 Coupe: 1374
41	126.0	202.7	1958	250 GT Cabriolet: 1380
			1960	250 GT Coupe: 1384
			1958	250 GT Coupe: 1381
42	125.0	201.1	1948	166 Mille Miglia Barchetta: 1371
43	123.0	197.9	1952	212 Touring: 1372

Fiat

1	136.0	218.8	1965	Abarth OT 1600: 1502
2	128.0	206.0	1990	Uno Turbo ie: 1605
3	123.0	197.9	1984	Strada Abarth 130TC: 1586
4	122.0	196.3	1985	Uno Turbo ie: 1589
5	121.0	194.7	1987	Croma ie Super: 1595
6	120.0	193.1	1954	8V: 1468
			1992	Tipo 1.8ie DGT SX: 1606
7	117.0	188.3	1985	X1/9VS: 1591
8	116.0	186.6	1990	Croma CHT: 1602
9	115.0	185.0	1982	Spider 2000: 1576
10	114.0	183.4	1972	130 Automatic: 1533
11	113.0	181.8	1980	Brava Abarth Rally: 1571
			1990	Tempra 1.6 SX: 1603
12	112.0	180.2	1970	124 Coupe 1600: 1520
			1971	124 Spider 1600: 1526
			1971	124 Sport Coupe: 1527
			1979	Mirafiori Sport: 1565
			1979	X1/9 1500: 1570
13	110.0	177.0	1984	Regata 100 S: 1584
14	109.0	175.4	1983	Spider 2000: 1580
15	108.0	173.8	1973	124 Sport Coupe 1800: 1536
			1979	124 Sports Spider: 1563
			1978	132 2000 GLS: 1560
			1981	Brava: 1573
			1982	X1/9: 1579
			1984	X1/9: 1587
16	107.0	172.2	1975	124 Sport Coupe 1800: 1545
			1974	132 GLS: 1542
			1987	Regata 100S ie: 1596
			1979	Strada: 1566
			1989	Tipo 1.6 DGT SX: 1600
			1988	X1/9: 1599
			1989	X1/9: 1601
17	106.0	170.6	1970	124 Spider: 1522
			1973	124 Spider 1600: 1535
			1968	124 Sport Spider: 1510
			1969	125 Special: 1517
			1973	132 1800 Special: 1541
			1969	Abarth 1300: 1519
18	105.0	168.9	1968	124 Sport Coupe: 1509
			1978	131 Supermirafiori: 1559
			1985	Uno 70 SX: 1588
			1985	X1/9: 1590
19	104.0	167.3	1969	124 Coupe: 1515
			1960	1500: 1484
			1982	Spider Turbo: 1577
20	103.0	165.7	1983	Uno 70 SX: 1583
21	102.0	164.1	1971	124 Special T: 1525
			1979	124 Spider: 1562
			1976	128 3P: 1552
			1960	Abarth Twin Cam: 1488
			1978	Super Brava: 1561
22	101.0	162.5	1973	124 Spider: 1534
			1972	128 Coupe 1300: 1531
			1962	2300: 1494
			1988	Tipo 1.4: 1598
23	100.0	160.9	1976	124 Spider: 1550
			1967	125: 1508
			1960	Abarth 850: 1487
			1984	Regata 70 ES: 1585
			1977	X1/9: 1557
24	99.0	159.3	1976	131: 1554
			1979	Strada 75CL: 1568
			1982	Strada Super 85: 1578
25	98.0	157.7	1978	127 Sport: 1558
			1977	131: 1556
26	97.0	156.1	1990	Uno 60S: 1604
27	96.0	154.5	1972	124: 1530
			1986	Regata DS: 1594
			1983	Strada 60 Comfort ES: 1581
28	95.0	152.9	1976	124 Sport Spider: 1551
			1969	850 Coupe: 1518
			1983	Uno 55 S: 1582
29	94.0	151.2	1973	124S Automatic: 1538
			1975	131 1300S: 1548
			1965	1500: 1500
			1965	1500 Spider: 1501
30	93.0	149.6	1960	2100: 1485
			1974	X1/9: 1543
31	92.4	148.7	1961	1500: 1491
32	92.0	148.0	1975	124 Special TC: 1544
			1975	128 Special: 1547
			1982	Mirafiori 1400CL: 1575
33	91.0	146.4	1987	Uno Selecta: 1597
34	90.5	145.6	1961	1300: 1490
35	90.0	144.8	1961	1200 Spider: 1489
			1970	124 Special: 1521
			1964	1500L: 1497
			1966	850 Coupe: 1505
			1979	X1/9 1300: 1569
36	89.2	143.5	1958	1200 TV Spyder: 1476
37	89.0	143.2	1958	1200 Gran Luce: 1475
			1976	128 Estate: 1553
			1981	Panda: 1574
			1986	Panda 1000 S: 1592
38	88.0	141.6	1977	127 1050 CL: 1555
			1981	127 1050 Super: 1572
			1979	Strada 65CL: 1567
39	87.5	140.8	1972	128 SL 1300 Coupe: 1532
40	87.1	140.1	1958	Abarth 750GT Zagato: 1479
			1958	Abarth Zagato: 1480
41	87.0	140.0	1970	128 4-door: 1523
42	86.0	138.4	1969	124 Estate Car: 1516
			1953	1900: 1466
43	85.0	136.8	1967	124: 1507
			1968	124 Station Wagon: 1511
			1971	127: 1528
			1971	128: 1529
44	84.1	135.3	1959	1200 Gran Luce: 1481
45	84.0	135.2	1954	1100 TV Saloon: 1467
			1970	850 Racer: 1524
			1968	850 Special: 1513
			1968	850 Spider: 1514
46	83.0	133.5	1963	1100: 1495
47	81.0	130.3	1963	1100D: 1496
			1966	1100R: 1503
48	80.0	128.7	1986	Panda 750 L: 1593
49	78.0	125.5	1975	133: 1549
			1964	850 Super: 1499
50	77.0	123.9	1957	1100 Saloon: 1471
			1968	850 Idromatic: 1512
51	76.9	123.7	1950	1400 Saloon: 1461
52	76.3	122.8	1952	1400: 1463
53	76.0	122.3	1953	1100: 1465
			1958	750 Abarth: 1478
			1966	Abarth 595: 1506
54	75.0	120.7	1937	1500 Pillarless Saloon: 1459
55	73.7	118.6	1957	1100: 1470
			1935	Balilla Sports Two-seater: 1457
56	72.0	115.8	1937	Balilla Pillarless Saloon: 1460
57	71.4	114.9	1935	1500 Saloon: 1456
58	68.0	109.4	1979	126 de Ville: 1564
			1961	600D: 1493
59	66.6	107.2	1959	500 Nuova: 1483
60	66.0	106.2	1960	600: 1486
61	65.0	104.6	1973	126: 1539
62	61.0	98.1	1959	500: 1482
			1964	500D: 1498
			1966	500F: 1504
63	60.3	97.0	1952	500C Convertible: 1464
			1951	500C Convertible (Topolino): 1462
			1957	600: 1472
64	60.0	96.5	1961	500 Giardiniera: 1492

65	59.5	95.7	1955	600: 1469
66	58.8	94.6	1957	Multipla: 1474
67	57.5	92.5	1934	Balilla Pillarless Saloon: 1455
68	55.0	88.5	1928	17/50 Saloon: 1454
			1957	600 Multipla: 1473
69	54.0	86.9	1958	500: 1477
70	52.6	84.6	1936	500 Convertible Saloon: 1458

Fiberfab

1	100.0	160.9	1969	Jamaican Buick V8: 1607

Ford

1	205.0	329.8	1968	GT40: 1760
2	186.0	299.3	1991	Mustang NOS/Saleen: 1967
3	185.0	297.7	1989	Mustang 5.0 Cartech Turbo: 1940
4	177.0	284.8	1988	Mustang Cartech Turbo: 1928
5	174.0	280.0	1991	Mustang Holdener: 1966
6	173.0	278.4	1989	Mustang SVO J Bittle American: 1942
7	164.0	263.9	1966	GT40 Super Street: 1738
8	160.0	257.4	1989	Thunderbird Super Coupe Ford Engineering: 1948
9	155.0	249.4	1963	Fastback NASCAR: 1698
10	153.0	246.2	1976	Cobra II Kemp: 1841
11	151.0	243.0	1971	Mustang TransAm: 1796
12	149.0	239.7	1988	Mustang Convertible Saleen: 1929
13	148.0	238.1	1987	Mustang GT: 1923
			1988	Mustang GT: 1930
			1990	Mustang LX 5.0L: 1955
14	146.0	234.9	1990	Sierra Sapphire Cosworth 4x4: 1958
15	145.0	233.3	1991	Thunderbird LX: 1972
16	143.0	230.1	1988	Sierra RS Cosworth: 1934
17	140.0	225.3	1992	Mustang LX: 1975
			1986	RS200: 1917
			1991	Scorpio 24v: 1970
			1989	Taurus SHO: 1946
			1991	Taurus SHO: 1971
			1989	Thunderbird Super Coupe: 1947
18	139.0	223.7	1987	Thunderbird Bondurant 5.0: 1926
19	136.0	218.8	1965	Galaxie 500 XL 427: 1714
20	135.0	217.2	1985	Mustang GT: 1905
			1986	Mustang GT 5.0: 1913
			1990	Mustang GT Convertible: 1954
21	134.0	215.6	1986	Mustang SVO: 1915
			1984	Mustang SVO: 1897
22	132.0	212.4	1990	Fiesta RS Turbo: 1949
23	131.1	211.0	1992	Escort RS2000: 1973
24	131.0	210.8	1988	Probe GT: 1933
			1990	Probe GT: 1956
			1987	Thunderbird Turbo Coupe: 1927
25	130.0	209.2	1976	Capri V6 Black Gold: 1840
			1962	Galaxie 406: 1679
			1990	Probe LX: 1957
			1989	Sierra XR 4x4: 1945
26	129.0	207.6	1981	Capri 2.8 Injection: 1871
			1983	Sierra XR4i: 1890
27	128.0	206.0	1985	Escort RS Turbo: 1901
28	127.0	204.3	1985	Granada Scorpio: 1903
29	126.0	202.7	1972	Capri RS2600: 1805
			1987	Granada Scorpio 2.9 EX: 1922
			1992	Taurus LX: 1976
			1969	Thunderbird: 1779
30	125.5	201.9	1969	Fairlane Cobra: 1772
31	125.0	201.1	1991	Crown Victoria LX: 1959
			1986	Escort RS Turbo: 1911
			1992	Escort XR3i: 1974
			1990	Granada Ghia X 2.9 EFi Saloon: 1952
			1985	Granada Scorpio 4x4: 1904
			1983	Mustang GT 5.0: 1888
			1984	Sierra XR4i: 1898
32	124.0	199.5	1986	Sierra Ghia 4x4 Estate: 1918
33	123.0	197.9	1963	Falcon Futura V8: 1695
			1963	Falcon V8: 1697
			1969	LTD: 1773
			1973	Pinto Pangra: 1819
			1968	XL Fastback 428: 1764
34	122.0	196.3	1973	Capri 3000 GXL: 1811
			1972	Capri 3000E: 1804
			1961	Galaxie: 1663
			1987	Granada 2.4i Ghia: 1921
35	121.0	194.7	1969	Mustang 428 Mach I: 1775
			1979	Mustang Turbo: 1867
			1980	Mustang Turbo: 1870
			1991	Orion 1.6i Ghia: 1968
36	120.0	193.1	1991	Escort GT: 1963
			1990	Fiesta XR2i: 1950
			1964	Galaxie 500: 1705
			1964	Mustang 271hp: 1707
			1965	Mustang Fastback: 1722
			1965	Mustang High Performance: 1723
			1991	Probe GT: 1969
			1989	Sierra Sapphire 2000E: 1944
			1967	Thunderbird: 1749
			1961	Thunderbird: 1665
			1959	Thunderbird: 1653
37	119.2	191.8	1969	Mustang Grande: 1778
38	119.0	191.5	1969	Fairlane 351: 1771
			1981	Granada 2.8i: 1877
			1962	Thunderbird Sports Roadster: 1680
			1983	Thunderbird Turbo Coupe: 1891
39	118.0	189.9	1976	Capri 3000S: 1838
			1983	Escort XR3i: 1885
			1986	Escort XR3i: 1912
			1969	Mustang Boss 302: 1776
			1969	Mustang Boss 429: 1777
			1982	Mustang GT 5.0: 1881
			1985	Sierra 2.0i S: 1907
40	117.0	188.3	1978	Granada 2.8i S: 1860
			1987	Sierra Sapphire 2.0 Ghia: 1925
			1966	Thunderbird Town Landau: 1739
41	116.5	187.4	1964	Mustang Convertible: 1708
42	116.0	186.6	1991	Escort Cabriolet: 1962
			1985	Fiesta XR2: 1902
			1966	Galaxie 7-litre: 1737
			1965	Galaxie LTD: 1715
			1976	Granada 3000 S: 1846
			1956	Thunderbird: 1641
43	115.0	185.0	1969	Capri 3000 GT XLR: 1768
			1966	Fairlane GTA: 1735
			1962	Galaxie: 1678
			1982	Sierra 2.3 Ghia Automatic: 1883
			1988	Taurus 3.8: 1935
			1965	Thunderbird: 1727
			1970	Torino GT: 1788
44	114.0	183.4	1973	Consul 3000 GT: 1812
			1975	Escort RS1800: 1833
			1990	Granada Scorpio 2.0i Auto: 1953
			1982	Mustang 4.2: 1880
45	113.0	181.8	1970	Escort 1600 RS: 1785
			1968	Escort Twin Cam: 1758
			1972	Granada GXL: 1808
			1967	Mustang 390 Fastback: 1748
			1968	Mustang Fastback: 1762
			1983	Orion 1.6 GL: 1889
46	112.0	180.2	1976	Escort RS2000: 1844
			1984	Fiesta XR2: 1894
47	111.0	178.6	1974	Capri 2800 V6: 1821
			1973	Escort RS2000: 1817
			1979	Granada 2.8i GLS Estate: 1865
			1974	Granada Ghia Coupe: 1824
			1956	Interceptor Coupe: 1639
			1965	Mustang Convertible V8: 1719
			1984	Mustang GT: 1895
			1968	Torino: 1763
48	110.1	177.2	1955	Thunderbird: 1635
49	110.0	177.0	1975	Capri 2000S GT: 1828
			1972	Capri 2600 V6: 1803
			1989	Fiesta 1.6S: 1939
			1974	Granada GXL: 1825
			1972	LTD: 1809
			1964	Mustang: 1706
			1967	Mustang: 1747
			1965	Mustang Coupe Automatic: 1721
			1972	Mustang Grande: 1810
			1965	Mustang V8 4.7-litre: 1725
50	109.0	175.4	1979	Cortina 2.3 Ghia S: 1863
			1973	Granada Estate Auto: 1818
			1965	Mustang Coupe: 1720
51	108.0	173.8	1971	Capri 2000: 1791
			1976	Capri II 2.8 V6: 1839
			1970	Capri Plus 50: 1782
			1968	Cortina Race-proved Savage: 1754
			1991	Escort 1.4LX: 1960
			1991	Escort 1.6 Ghia Estate: 1961
			1967	Fairlane Ranchero: 1746
			1979	Fiesta Healey: 1864
			1960	Galaxie: 1658
52	107.5	173.0	1963	Cortina Lotus: 1689
53	107.0	172.2	1969	Capri 2000 GT: 1767
			1979	Capri 2000S: 1861
			1963	Falcon Sprint Convertible: 1696
			1990	Granada 2.5 GL Diesel: 1951
54	106.0	170.6	1974	Capri II 1600 GT: 1822
			1981	Fiesta XR2: 1876
			1976	Mustang II V8: 1848

			1986	Orion 1.4 GL: 1916
55	105.0	168.9	1970	Cortina 2000 GXL: 1783
			1973	Cortina 2000E: 1816
			1967	Cortina Lotus: 1744
			1964	Custom 500: 1703
			1964	Falcon Sprint: 1704
			1963	Galaxie 500 XL: 1699
56	104.0	167.3	1977	Cortina 2.3 Ghia: 1849
			1986	Escort 1.4 GL: 1909
			1983	Escort 1.6 GL Automatic: 1884
			1981	Escort 1.6L Estate: 1874
			1977	Escort 1600 Sport: 1851
			1984	Fiesta 1.3L CVH: 1892
			1982	Sierra 1.6L: 1882
57	103.5	166.5	1962	Zodiac Mk III: 1683
58	103.0	165.7	1976	Cortina 2.0 Ghia: 1842
			1981	Cortina 2.0 GL: 1872
			1975	Cortina 2000E Estate: 1831
			1982	Escort 1600 GL: 1878
			1962	Fairlane 500 Sports Coupe: 1672
			1978	Granada 2.0L: 1858
			1985	Sierra 1.8 Ghia: 1906
59	102.0	164.1	1968	Cortina GT: 1752
			1979	Mustang Ghia Turbo: 1866
			1974	Mustang II Ghia: 1826
			1971	Pinto 2-litre: 1800
			1966	Zephyr 6 Mk IV: 1740
			1967	Zodiac Executive: 1750
60	101.0	162.5	1978	Capri 1600S: 1857
			1973	Cortina 2000 Estate: 1815
			1977	Fiesta Ghia: 1855
			1982	Granada 2.3L Estate: 1879
			1975	Granada 5-litre: 1835
			1965	Mustang Convertible: 1718
			1965	Mustang V8 4.2-litre: 1724
61	100.0	160.9	1971	1600 GT: 1789
			1972	Capri 1600 XL: 1802
			1975	Consul 2000L: 1829
			1967	Cortina 1600E: 1742
			1966	Cortina Lotus: 1732
			1989	Fiesta 1.4 Ghia: 1938
			1977	Fiesta 1300 S: 1854
			1977	Granada 2.3 GL Auto: 1856
			1965	Taunus 20M: 1726
			1984	Tempo GLX: 1899
62	99.0	159.3	1970	Maverick: 1786
			1974	Mustang II Mach I: 1827
			1968	Zephyr de Luxe: 1765
63	98.0	157.7	1969	Capri 1600 GT: 1766
			1972	Consul 2000L: 1806
			1967	Corsair 2000E: 1741
			1971	Escort 1300 GT: 1793
64	97.0	156.1	1963	Capri GT: 1684
			1968	Cortina GT Estate: 1753
			1989	Escort 1.3L 3-door: 1936
			1965	Zodiac Executive: 1728
65	96.0	154.5	1963	Consul Corsair GT: 1685
			1969	Cortina 1600 GT: 1770
			1973	Cortina 1600 XL Estate: 1814
			1975	Escort 1.3 Ghia: 1832
			1971	Escort Sport: 1795
			1965	Fairlane 500: 1713
			1975	Granada 2000 GL: 1834
66	95.0	152.9	1966	Custom 500: 1734
			1966	Falcon Ranchero Custom: 1736
			1987	Festiva L: 1919
			1968	Galaxie: 1759
			1969	Maverick: 1774
			1964	Zephyr 6: 1709
67	94.0	151.2	1970	Capri 1300 GT: 1780
			1966	Corsair GT Estate: 1730
			1979	Cortina 1600L: 1862
			1965	Cortina GT: 1712
			1962	Fairlane 500: 1671
			1962	Fairlane V8: 1673
68	93.0	149.6	1973	Cortina 1600 XL: 1813
			1977	Escort 1300 GL: 1850
			1989	Fiesta 1.1LX 5-door: 1937
			1975	Pinto 2300: 1836
69	92.0	148.0	1975	Cortina 1300L: 1830
			1976	Escort 1300 GL: 1843
			1958	Fairlane 500: 1646
			1984	Fiesta 1.6L Diesel: 1893
70	91.4	147.1	1953	Zephyr Sedan Modified: 1629
71	91.0	146.4	1967	Cortina GT: 1743
			1960	Falcon: 1656
			1976	Fiesta: 1845
			1960	Zephyr: 1660
			1963	Zephyr 6 Estate: 1700
72	90.0	144.8	1986	Aerostar XLT: 1908
			1971	Bronco: 1790
			1970	Capri 1600: 1781
			1962	Country Sedan: 1670
			1963	Fairlane Squire Wagon: 1693
			1962	Falcon 170 Manual: 1677
			1983	Fiesta 1.1 Ghia: 1886
			1965	Mustang: 1716
			1965	Mustang 6: 1717
73	89.0	143.2	1965	Corsair GT: 1711
			1983	Granada 2.5 Diesel Estate: 1887
74	88.0	141.6	1976	Capri 1300: 1837
			1987	Fiesta 1.1 Ghia Auto: 1920
			1977	Fiesta 1100 Ghia: 1853
			1978	Granada 2.1D: 1859
75	87.3	140.5	1938	V8 30: 1617
			1936	V8 Touring Saloon: 1614
76	87.1	140.1	1964	Consul Corsair: 1701
77	87.0	140.0	1972	1600 XL Auto: 1801
			1972	Cortina 1300L: 1807
			1971	Escort 1300 XL: 1794
			1959	Falcon: 1650
			1961	Taunus 17M: 1664
78	86.0	138.4	1968	Cortina 1300 de Luxe: 1751
			1960	Falcon Automatic: 1657
			1956	Zephyr: 1642
79	85.0	136.8	1968	Cortina Station Wagon: 1755
			1968	Escort 1300: 1757
			1963	F-100 Styleside Pickup: 1692
80	84.6	136.1	1957	Zodiac Automatic: 1643
81	84.5	136.0	1962	Zephyr 4: 1681
82	84.0	135.2	1962	Anglia Super: 1667
			1952	Comete: 1625
			1974	Escort 1100L: 1823
			1962	Falcon 170 Automatic: 1676
			1958	Zephyr Estate: 1648
			1955	Zodiac: 1636
83	83.3	134.0	1952	Customline 8: 1627
84	83.2	133.9	1952	Customline 6: 1626
85	83.0	133.5	1966	Cortina 1300 de Luxe: 1731
			1966	Cortina Super Estate: 1733
			1970	Escort 1300 Super Estate: 1784
86	82.5	132.7	1961	Consul Capri: 1661
			1964	Cortina Super: 1702
			1959	Taunus 17M Estate: 1652
			1948	V8 Pilot: 1621
87	82.0	131.9	1962	Consul Capri: 1668
			1963	Cortina Super: 1690
			1967	Cortina Super Estate: 1745
			1962	Falcon 144 Manual: 1675
			1963	Falcon Futura: 1694
			1971	Pinto 1600: 1799
88	81.3	130.8	1947	Tudor Sedan: 1619
89	81.0	130.3	1963	Consul Cortina 1500: 1687
			1977	Fiesta 1000: 1852
			1981	Fiesta Popular: 1875
90	80.6	129.7	1958	Consul: 1645
91	80.0	128.7	1968	Escort: 1756
92	79.5	127.9	1953	Zephyr Sedan: 1628
93	79.0	127.1	1959	Anglia: 1649
			1965	Anglia Estate: 1710
			1956	Consul Mk II: 1638
			1960	Taunus 17M: 1659
			1958	Taunus 17M: 1647
94	78.6	126.5	1960	Consul Mk II: 1655
95	78.5	126.3	1963	Cortina Estate de Luxe: 1688
			1956	Taunus 15M: 1640
96	78.2	125.8	1932	V8: 1610
97	78.0	125.5	1971	Pinto: 1798
98	77.0	123.9	1962	Consul Cortina: 1669
			1971	Pickup 4WD: 1797
			1962	Zephyr 4 Automatic: 1682
99	76.4	122.9	1962	Falcon 144 Automatic: 1674
100	75.0	120.7	1963	Consul Cortina: 1686
			1961	Econoline: 1662
101	74.0	119.1	1960	Anglia: 1654
			1966	Bronco: 1729
102	73.0	117.5	1962	Anglia de Luxe Estate: 1666
			1955	Prefect: 1633
103	72.0	115.8	1958	Anglia de Luxe: 1644
			1969	Cortina 1100: 1769
104	71.1	114.4	1955	Anglia: 1632
105	70.0	112.6	1954	Anglia Saloon: 1630
			1955	Prefect 1172cc: 1634
106	69.5	111.8	1956	Anglia: 1637
107	69.0	111.0	1959	Popular II: 1651
108	66.1	106.4	1934	10 de Luxe Saloon: 1612
109	65.6	105.6	1937	10: 1615
110	65.2	104.9	1938	Prefect: 1616
111	64.2	103.3	1930	24 Saloon: 1609
112	63.0	101.4	1949	Anglia 10 Saloon: 1622
113	62.0	99.8	1934	Model A: 1613
114	61.0	98.1	1954	Popular: 1631
			1948	Prefect: 1620
115	60.4	97.2	1939	8: 1618
116	59.0	94.9	1949	Anglia 8 Saloon: 1623
117	58.8	94.6	1933	8 Tudor Saloon: 1611
118	44.0	70.8	1915	Model T: 1608

Franklin

1	64.0	103.0	1929	29.4hp Saloon: 1977

Frazer

1	83.0	133.5	1949	Saloon: 1978

Frazer-Nash

1	116.0	186.6	1953	Targa Florio Turismo: 1985
2	114.0	183.4	1955	Targa Florio Fast Roadster: 1986
3	87.3	140.5	1933	1.5-litre: 1981
			1937	1.5-litre: 1984
			1931	Boulogne II: 1980
4	86.5	139.2	1933	TT Replica: 1982
5	84.5	136.0	1934	14hp Sports Tourer: 1983
6	77.2	124.2	1930	Super Sports: 1979

Frazer-Nash BMW

1	110.0	177.0	1967	2000TI: 1992
2	103.4	166.4	1937	Grand Prix Two-seater: 1989
3	96.7	155.6	1939	Type 327 Cabriolet: 1991
4	80.3	129.2	1935	Type 55 Cabriolet: 1988
5	76.2	122.6	1938	Type 326 Saloon: 1990
6	75.0	120.7	1935	12.5hp Saloon: 1987

Frisky

1	56.0	90.1	1958	Coupe: 1993

Geo

1	120.0	193.1	1991	Storm GSi: 1994

Gilbern

1	116.0	186.6	1969	Invader: 1996
2	91.0	146.4	1961	GT: 1995

Ginetta

1	119.0	191.5	1976	G21S: 1997
2	116.0	186.6	1990	G32: 1998

Glas

1	112.0	180.2	1966	1700GT: 2000
2	98.0	157.7	1965	1300GT: 1999
3	91.0	146.4	1974	1700: 2001

GM

1	75.0	120.7	1990	Impact: 2002

GMC

1	95.0	152.9	1985	Safari Cargo Mover: 2003

Goggomobil

1	61.0	98.1	1959	TS400: 2004

Goliath

1	84.0	135.2	1959	Tiger: 2007
2	75.6	121.6	1957	1100 Sedan: 2005
3	72.0	115.8	1957	900: 2006

Gordon

1	142.0	228.5	1960	GT: 2008

Gordon Keeble

1	137.0	220.4	1965	GK1: 2009

Graham

1	91.8	147.7	1938	26hp Supercharged Saloon: 2014
			1935	33.8hp Supercharged Saloon: 2012
2	89.1	143.4	1936	26hp Supercharged Saloon: 2013
3	80.3	129.2	1932	Blue Streak Saloon: 2010
4	75.6	121.6	1935	21.6hp Saloon: 2011

Graham-Paige

1	76.0	122.3	1929	Straight Eight: 2016
2	62.0	99.8	1929	21.6hp Saloon: 2015

HE

1	78.0	125.5	1929	16/60 Sports Four-seater: 2017
2	66.4	106.8	1930	Supercharged Six Coupe: 2018

Healey

1	104.6	168.3	1952	Tickford Saloon: 2020
2	102.0	164.1	1948	2.4-litre Roadster: 2019
3	100.0	160.9	1953	Sports Convertible: 2021

Hillman

1	110.0	177.0	1972	Hunter GLS: 2075
2	102.0	164.1	1975	Avenger GLS: 2080
3	98.0	157.7	1973	Avenger GLS: 2077
			1970	Avenger GT: 2070
4	97.0	156.1	1976	Avenger 1600 Super: 2082
			1970	Avenger GL: 2069
5	96.0	154.5	1969	GT: 2067
6	94.0	151.2	1974	Avenger 1600 GLS: 2079
			1975	Hunter Super: 2081
7	92.0	148.0	1957	Minx Convertible: 2044
8	91.0	146.4	1969	Hunter Mk II: 2068
9	89.0	143.2	1967	Estate: 2063
			1971	Hunter Super: 2072
10	88.0	141.6	1973	Avenger DL: 2076
11	87.0	140.0	1974	Avenger 1300 GL: 2078
			1972	Avenger Estate: 2074
12	86.0	138.4	1967	Minx: 2066
			1962	Super Minx: 2053
			1966	Super Minx Estate: 2062
13	85.0	136.8	1962	Super Minx Mk II: 2054
14	84.0	135.2	1970	Avenger Super: 2071
			1965	Minx Series VI de Luxe: 2060
15	83.6	134.5	1964	Super Minx III: 2059
16	83.0	133.5	1963	Imp de Luxe: 2056
17	82.7	133.1	1956	Minx de Luxe: 2043
18	82.0	131.9	1958	Minx Series III Convertible: 2049
19	81.0	130.3	1967	Imp Californian: 2065
			1971	Imp de Luxe: 2073
			1965	Super Imp: 2061
20	80.0	128.7	1954	Minx Supercharged: 2040
			1964	Super Minx Convertible: 2058
21	79.5	127.9	1958	Minx Estate: 2047
22	79.0	127.1	1967	Hunter Husky: 2064
			1959	Minx Series IIIA Easidrive: 2050
			1964	Minx Series V Automatic: 2057
23	78.5	126.3	1960	Easidrive: 2051
24	76.0	122.3	1963	Hunter Husky III: 2055
			1958	Minx Series II: 2048
25	75.0	120.7	1936	Hawk Sports Saloon: 2031
			1960	Hunter Husky Series II: 2052
26	74.5	119.9	1955	Minx de Luxe: 2042
27	74.0	119.1	1958	Hunter Husky: 2045
28	73.8	118.7	1958	Husky: 2046
29	73.7	118.6	1937	80 Limousine: 2032
30	72.5	116.7	1934	Aero Minx Coupe: 2028
31	72.0	115.8	1935	20/27 Sports Saloon: 2029
32	71.4	114.9	1935	Aero Minx Cresta Saloon: 2030
33	70.5	113.4	1953	Minx Califonian Coupe: 2039
34	70.0	112.6	1952	Minx Convertible: 2038
35	69.0	111.0	1951	Minx Estate: 2036
36	68.4	110.1	1934	20/70 Limousine: 2027
37	68.0	109.4	1955	Husky: 2041
38	67.0	107.8	1949	Minx Saloon: 2035
39	66.1	106.4	1932	Wizard 65 Saloon de Luxe: 2026
40	65.0	104.6	1929	Straight Eight Saloon: 2024
41	63.0	101.4	1947	Minx Saloon: 2034
42	62.5	100.6	1937	Minx Saloon de Luxe: 2033
43	60.8	97.8	1932	Minx Sports Tourer: 2025
44	57.0	91.7	1929	Segrave Saloon: 2023
45	56.0	90.1	1928	Safety Saloon: 2022

Hispano-Suiza

1	100.0	160.9	1934	54/220: 2084
2	82.9	133.4	1934	30/120 Saloon: 2083

Holden

1	106.0	170.6	1969	Brougham: 2086
2	80.0	128.7	1952	Saloon: 2085

Honda

1	162.0	260.7	1991	NSX: 2156
2	158.0	254.2	1992	NSX Auto: 2159
3	143.0	230.1	1992	Legend Coupe: 2158
4	142.0	228.5	1991	Legend: 2155
5	133.0	214.0	1987	Legend Coupe: 2137
6	132.0	212.4	1990	CRX 1.6i VT: 2152
7	130.0	209.2	1991	Prelude Si: 2157
8	128.0	206.0	1991	Civic 1.6i VT: 2154
			1988	Legend Saloon Automatic: 2143
			1987	Prelude 2.0i 16: 2139
9	127.0	204.3	1986	Legend: 2133
			1987	Prelude 2.0 Si: 2138
			1989	Prelude Si 4WS: 2148
10	126.0	202.7	1992	Prelude Si 4WS: 2160
11	125.0	201.1	1990	Accord 2.0 EXi: 2150
			1988	Civic CRX: 2140
			1986	CRX Coupe 1.6i 16: 2128
			1988	CRX Si: 2141
			1988	CRX Si Jackson: 2142
12	121.0	194.7	1990	Concerto 1.6i 16: 2151
13	119.0	191.5	1986	Integra EX 16: 2132
14	117.0	188.3	1985	Accord 2.0 EXi: 2117
15	116.0	186.6	1986	CRX Si: 2129

16	115.0	185.0	1984	Civic CRX: 2113
			1989	Civic Si: 2145
			1985	CRX Si: 2124
17	112.0	180.2	1991	Civic 1.5 VEi: 2153
			1985	Civic GT: 2120
			1985	Prelude: 2125
18	108.0	173.8	1986	Accord LXi: 2126
			1985	Accord SEi: 2119
			1987	Civic 1.4 GL 3-door: 2136
			1984	Prelude: 2116
19	107.0	172.2	1985	Civic Shuttle: 2122
			1983	Prelude EX ALB: 2112
			1988	Shuttle 1.6i RT4 4WD: 2144
20	106.0	170.6	1979	Accord 4-door: 2100
21	104.0	167.3	1985	Accord EX Automatic: 2118
			1983	CRX 1.5: 2111
22	103.0	165.7	1981	Prelude: 2107
23	102.0	164.1	1986	Integra 1.5: 2131
24	101.0	162.5	1980	Prelude: 2104
			1979	Prelude: 2101
25	100.0	160.9	1985	Civic S: 2121
			1989	Shuttle 1.4 GL Automatic: 2149
26	99.0	159.3	1987	Ballade EX: 2135
			1980	Civic GL 1500: 2103
27	98.0	157.7	1982	Accord: 2109
			1982	Accord LX: 2110
			1984	Civic DL: 2114
			1985	Civic Wagon: 2123
28	97.0	156.1	1977	Civic 1500: 2097
29	96.0	154.5	1981	Quintet: 2108
			1967	S800: 2088
30	95.0	152.9	1977	Accord: 2096
			1978	Civic: 2099
31	91.0	146.4	1973	Civic: 2092
			1975	Civic CVCC: 2094
32	90.0	144.8	1976	Accord: 2095
			1978	Accord: 2098
			1981	Civic 4-door Sedan: 2106
			1965	S600: 2087
33	89.0	143.2	1984	Jazz: 2115
34	86.0	138.4	1973	Civic Hondamatic: 2093
35	78.0	125.5	1972	600 Coupe: 2091
36	74.0	119.1	1968	N360: 2089
37	73.0	117.5	1970	600: 2090

Hotchkiss

1	95.7	154.0	1935	Paris-Nice Saloon: 2163
2	94.7	152.4	1938	3.5-litre Saloon: 2165
3	93.2	150.0	1934	Paris-Nice Speed Model: 2162
4	88.2	141.9	1937	28hp Cabourg Saloon: 2164
5	80.3	129.2	1933	3.5-litre Coupe: 2161

HRG

1	86.5	139.2	1938	1.5-litre: 2167
2	85.7	137.9	1937	12hp Sports Two-seater: 2166
3	83.0	133.5	1948	1.5-litre: 2168

Hudson

1	92.9	149.5	1952	Hornet: 2177
2	91.0	146.4	1949	Commodore: 2176
3	88.5	142.4	1953	Super Jet: 2178
4	87.3	140.5	1935	Eight Saloon: 2171
5	84.9	136.6	1934	Terraplane: 2170
6	84.0	135.2	1956	Rambler: 2179
7	82.5	132.7	1936	22hp Six Saloon: 2173
8	81.8	131.6	1938	22hp Six Special Saloon: 2175
9	80.3	129.2	1935	Terraplane Big Six Saloon: 2172
10	75.6	121.6	1937	Terraplane Saloon: 2174
11	69.2	111.3	1930	Straight Eight Roadster: 2169

Humber

1	102.0	164.1	1965	Imperial: 2212
			1967	Sceptre: 2214
2	101.5	163.3	1961	Super Snipe Series III: 2209
3	100.0	160.9	1961	3-litre: 2208
4	97.0	156.1	1974	Sceptre Estate: 2215
5	96.0	154.5	1960	Super Snipe Estate: 2207
6	94.5	152.1	1958	Super Snipe: 2205
7	91.0	146.4	1966	Sceptre II Automatic: 2213
			1953	Super Snipe Mk IV: 2200
8	90.0	144.8	1963	Sceptre: 2211
			1959	Super Snipe: 2206
9	87.8	141.3	1953	Super Snipe: 2199
10	86.5	139.2	1936	Snipe Sports Saloon: 2187
11	86.0	138.4	1963	Hawk III: 2210
12	84.0	135.2	1957	Hawk: 2203
			1954	Hawk Mk VI: 2201
			1952	Super Snipe: 2198
13	82.0	131.9	1952	Pullman Limousine: 2197
14	81.8	131.6	1937	Snipe Drop-head Foursome: 2188
15	81.7	131.5	1956	Hawk Estate: 2202
16	81.0	130.3	1958	Hawk Estate: 2204
17	80.5	129.5	1949	Super Snipe: 2195
18	80.3	129.2	1935	Snipe Sports Saloon: 2185
19	79.0	127.1	1949	Imperial: 2193
			1949	Imperial Saloon: 2194
20	78.9	127.0	1938	Snipe Sports Saloon: 2190
21	78.2	125.8	1936	Pullman Limousine: 2186
22	75.0	120.7	1929	Snipe: 2180
23	72.2	116.2	1951	Hawk: 2196
24	72.0	115.8	1949	Hawk: 2192
25	70.8	113.9	1938	16.9hp Saloon: 2189
26	68.7	110.5	1935	12 Six-light Saloon: 2184
27	67.1	108.0	1932	Pullman Limousine: 2182
28	66.1	106.4	1934	12 Vogue: 2183
29	64.7	104.1	1932	16/60 Saloon: 2181
30	64.0	103.0	1947	Hawk Saloon: 2191

Hupmobile

1	78.2	125.8	1935	29.4hp Saloon: 2217
			1935	32.5hp Saloon: 2218
2	70.8	113.9	1930	Straight Eight Limousine: 2216

Hyundai

1	115.0	185.0	1990	Sonata 2.4i GLS: 2225
2	114.0	183.4	1991	Lantra 1.6 Cdi: 2226
3	108.0	173.8	1989	Sonata 2.0i GLS: 2224
4	105.0	168.9	1991	S Coupe GSi: 2227
5	100.0	160.9	1984	Stellar 1600 GSL: 2220
			1991	X2 1.5 GSi: 2228
6	98.0	157.7	1985	Pony 1.5 GLS: 2221
7	92.0	148.0	1986	Excel GLS: 2223
8	91.0	146.4	1982	Pony 1400 TLS: 2219

IAD

1	165.0	265.5	1990	Venus: 2229

Infiniti

1	150.0	241.4	1990	Q45: 2231
2	130.0	209.2	1991	G20: 2232
3	128.0	206.0	1990	M30: 2230

Innocenti

1	85.0	136.8	1964	S: 2233

International

1	95.0	152.9	1972	Scout: 2240
2	92.0	148.0	1971	Scout: 2238
3	90.0	144.8	1971	Pickup 4WD 1210 Camper Special: 2237
			1971	Travelall 1210: 2239
4	85.0	136.8	1962	Travelall: 2235
5	81.0	130.3	1963	900 Pickup: 2236
6	80.0	128.7	1961	Scout: 2234

Invicta

1	92.0	148.0	1931	4.5-litre: 2242
2	68.0	109.4	1928	4.5-litre: 2241

Irmsher

1	150.0	241.4	1989	GT: 2243

Isdera

1	176.0	283.2	1988	Imperator: 2244

Iso

1	163.0	262.3	1966	Grifo GL 365: 2248
2	157.0	252.6	1971	Grifo GL: 2250
3	153.0	246.2	1963	Grifo A3L Berlinetta: 2245
4	142.0	228.5	1964	Rivolta IR-340: 2247
5	135.0	217.2	1964	GT: 2246
6	123.0	197.9	1969	Rivolta S4: 2249

Isuzu

1	130.0	209.2	1986	Impulse Turbo: 2256
2	125.0	201.1	1988	Impulse Turbo: 2259
3	120.0	193.1	1991	Impulse RS: 2261
			1990	Impulse XS: 2260
4	100.0	160.9	1984	Impulse: 2253
			1986	Impulse Sports Coupe: 2255
5	84.0	135.2	1983	I-Mark LS: 2252
6	80.0	128.7	1987	Trooper 3-door TD: 2257

Ital Design

1	150.0	241.4	1990	Aztec: 2262

Jaguar

1	200.0	321.8	1989	XJ220: 2359
			1990	XJS Lister Le Mans: 2366
2	192.0	308.9	1956	D Type: 2285
3	185.0	297.7	1991	XJR15: 2369
4	184.0	296.1	1967	XJ13: 2313
5	180.0	289.6	1977	XJS Tullius: 2333
6	157.0	252.6	1982	XJS HE: 2342
7	156.0	251.0	1965	E Type 4.2: 2309
8	155.0	249.4	1963	E Type Coupe: 2303
9	154.0	247.8	1976	XJS: 2330
			1981	XJS Automatic: 2341
10	151.7	244.1	1961	E Type Coupe: 2298
11	151.0	243.0	1951	C Type: 2274
12	150.0	241.4	1990	XJRS: 2364
			1989	XJS Convertible: 2360
			1988	XJS Koenig: 2356
			1986	XJSC HE: 2351
			1964	XKE: 2306
			1961	XKE: 2299
13	149.0	239.7	1957	XKSS: 2291
14	148.0	238.1	1973	XJ12: 2324
			1978	XJ5.3 Automatic: 2335
			1975	XJ5.3C: 2328
15	147.0	236.5	1991	XJS: 2370
16	146.0	234.9	1985	XJS HE Cabriolet: 2347
			1988	XJS V12 Convertible: 2357
17	143.0	230.1	1971	E Type V12: 2319
			1990	XJR 4.0: 2363
			1977	XJS Automatic: 2332
18	142.0	228.5	1972	XJ12: 2321
			1984	XJS 3.6: 2345
19	141.0	226.9	1989	4.0 Sovereign: 2358
			1967	E Type Roadster: 2312
			1989	XJS V12 Convertible: 2361
			1986	XJSC: 2350
			1953	XK120C: 2280
20	140.0	225.3	1986	XJ6 3.6: 2348
			1983	XJS: 2343
			1988	XJS: 2355
			1984	XJS HE: 2346
21	139.0	223.7	1976	XJ12C: 2329
			1981	XJS: 2340
22	138.0	222.0	1991	XJS 4.0 Auto: 2371
			1974	XKE V12: 2325
23	137.0	220.4	1979	XJS: 2338
24	136.0	218.8	1991	XJ6 3.2: 2368
			1990	XJ6 Vanden Plas: 2362
			1958	XK150S: 2294
			1959	XK150S: 2295
25	135.0	217.2	1990	XJS: 2365
			1991	XJS Convertible: 2372
			1990	XJS Railton: 2367
			1972	XKE V12: 2323
26	134.0	215.6	1987	XJS 3.6 Automatic: 2354
27	132.0	212.4	1986	XJS: 2349
28	131.0	210.8	1975	XJ12L: 2326
29	130.0	209.2	1987	XJ6: 2352
			1979	XJ6 4.2: 2336
30	129.5	208.4	1956	XK 140: 2287
31	128.0	206.0	1978	XJ12L: 2334
			1966	XKE 4.2 2+2: 2310
32	126.0	202.7	1963	3.8 Mk II: 2301
			1967	420: 2311
			1950	XK120: 2273
33	125.5	201.9	1958	XK150: 2293
34	125.0	201.1	1960	3.8 Sedan: 2297
			1951	XK140: 2276
35	124.0	199.5	1965	4.2 litre Mk X Overdrive: 2308
36	123.0	197.9	1965	3.8S: 2307
			1964	4.2 litre Mk X: 2305
			1971	XJ6 4.2: 2320
37	122.0	196.3	1951	XK120: 2275
38	121.6	195.7	1957	XK150: 2290
39	121.0	194.7	1958	3.4: 2292
			1953	XK120 Coupe: 2279
40	120.8	194.4	1953	XK120M: 2281
41	120.6	194.0	1963	3.8 Mk II Automatic: 2302
42	120.3	193.6	1955	XK140MC: 2283
43	120.0	193.1	1960	3.4: 2296
			1968	420 Sedan: 2315
			1962	Mk X: 2300
			1975	XJ3.4: 2327
			1970	XJ6: 2318
			1969	XJ6 4.2 Automatic: 2316
44	119.0	191.5	1977	XJ4.2: 2331
			1969	XKE Coupe: 2317
45	118.0	189.9	1987	XJ6 2.9: 2353
46	117.0	188.3	1980	XJ6 Series III: 2339
			1984	XJ6 Vanden Plas: 2344
47	116.0	186.6	1964	3.8S Sedan: 2304
			1979	XJ6L: 2337
48	115.0	185.0	1972	XJ6: 2322
49	109.0	175.4	1957	Mk VIII: 2289
50	107.0	172.2	1968	240: 2314
51	106.3	171.0	1955	Mk VII: 2282
52	104.0	167.3	1957	2.4 Saloon: 2288
			1953	Mk VII: 2278
53	103.0	165.7	1952	Mk VII: 2277
			1956	Mk VII Auto: 2286
54	101.1	162.7	1956	2.4 Sedan: 2284
			1938	SS 100 3.5-litre: 2267
55	94.7	152.4	1937	SS 100 2.5-litre: 2265
56	91.0	146.4	1948	3.5-litre: 2270
			1949	3.5-litre Mk V: 2272
			1948	Mk IV: 2271
57	90.0	144.8	1940	SS 2.5-litre: 2268
58	88.2	141.9	1936	SS 2.5-litre: 2264
59	84.5	136.0	1931	SS1 Sports Tourer: 2263
60	83.3	134.0	1940	SS1 2.5-litre: 2269
61	74.3	119.5	1938	SS 1.5-litre: 2266

Jeep

1	97.0	156.1	1971	Wagoneer 1414C: 2378
2	94.0	151.2	1971	Commando: 2375
3	92.0	148.0	1978	Cherokee Chief: 2383
			1971	CJ-5: 2374
			1964	Wagoneer: 2373
4	91.0	146.4	1971	Wagoneer: 2377
5	90.0	144.8	1974	Wagoneer: 2382
6	88.0	141.6	1972	Commando: 2380
			1971	Gladiator Pickup J-2500 Townside: 2376
7	82.0	131.9	1972	CJ-5 V8: 2379
			1974	CJ6: 2381

Jensen

1	145.0	233.3	1971	SP: 2397
2	141.0	226.9	1970	FF II: 2394
3	137.0	220.4	1969	Interceptor: 2393
4	136.0	218.8	1971	Interceptor: 2396
5	134.0	215.6	1974	Healey Huffaker: 2399
6	133.0	214.0	1963	CV8: 2390
			1967	Interceptor: 2391
			1974	Interceptor III: 2400
7	130.0	209.2	1968	FF: 2392
8	127.5	205.1	1958	541R: 2388
9	126.0	202.7	1974	Interceptor III Convertible: 2401
10	125.0	201.1	1973	Healey: 2398
11	122.0	196.3	1970	Interceptor II: 2395
12	120.0	193.1	1976	GT: 2402
			1976	Interceptor III Convertible: 2403
13	113.0	181.8	1977	GT: 2404
14	112.0	180.2	1956	541: 2387
15	110.0	177.0	1961	541S Automatic: 2389
16	102.0	164.1	1951	Interceptor Cabriolet: 2386
17	89.1	143.4	1938	3.5-litre Tourer: 2385
18	82.5	132.7	1936	3.5-litre Saloon: 2384

Jensen-Healey

1	120.0	193.1	1972	2-litre: 2405

Jowett

1	86.2	138.7	1953	Jupiter: 2410
2	85.0	136.8	1953	Jupiter Mk IA: 2411
3	76.0	122.3	1948	Javelin: 2409
4	61.6	99.1	1937	De Luxe Saloon: 2407
5	56.2	90.4	1939	8hp: 2408
6	54.5	87.7	1935	7hp Curlew de Luxe: 2406

Kaiser

1	87.0	140.0	1967	Jeepster: 2415
2	82.0	131.9	1952	Henry J 6: 2414

Kissel

1	78.0	125.5	1927	8-65 Gold Bug: 2416

Koenig

1	235.0	378.1	1991	C62: 2419
2	230.0	370.1	1990	Competition Evolution: 2418
3	217.0	349.2	1989	Competition: 2417

Kurtis

1	101.1	162.7	1953	Hornet Roadster: 2420

La Salle

1	88.2	141.9	1938	37-50 V8 Saloon: 2422
2	70.3	113.1	1930	Enclosed Drive Limousine: 2421

Lada

1	96.0	154.5	1976	1500: 2424
			1987	Samara 1300 SL: 2429
2	94.0	151.2	1989	Samara 1300L 5-door: 2430

3	90.0	144.8	1975	1200: 2423
4	89.0	143.2	1978	1300 ES: 2425
			1986	Riva 1500 Estate: 2427
5	81.0	130.3	1987	Niva Cossack Cabrio: 2428
6	78.0	125.5	1979	Niva 1600: 2426

Lago

1	118.0	189.9	1959	America: 2431

Lagonda

1	110.1	177.2	1939	Rapide: 2445
2	110.0	177.0	1934	Le Mans: 2437
3	104.2	167.7	1937	Rapide: 2441
4	103.4	166.4	1938	4.5-litre 12 Cylinder Saloon: 2443
5	101.0	162.5	1956	3-litre Saloon: 2448
6	100.5	161.7	1935	Rapide Tourer: 2439
7	100.0	160.9	1938	Saloon de Ville: 2444
8	96.7	155.6	1936	4.5-litre Tourer: 2440
9	95.7	154.0	1938	4.5-litre: 2442
10	94.7	152.4	1940	Drop-head Coupe: 2446
11	91.0	146.4	1949	2.5-litre Saloon: 2447
12	88.2	141.9	1930	2-litre Supercharged: 2433
13	83.7	134.7	1934	3.5-litre Tourer: 2436
14	82.9	133.4	1931	3-litre Special Tourer: 2434
15	80.0	128.7	1929	3-litre Tourer: 2432
16	77.5	124.7	1933	16/80 Tourer: 2435
17	74.0	119.1	1934	Rapier Four-seater Tourer: 2438

Lamborghini

1	202.0	325.0	1991	Diablo: 2475
			1990	Diablo: 2474
2	192.0	308.9	1976	Countach: 2461
3	180.0	289.6	1967	Miura: 2451
4	179.0	288.0	1985	Countach: 2468
			1989	Countach 25th Anniversary: 2473
5	173.0	278.4	1986	Countach 5000S: 2469
			1970	Miura P400S: 2455
6	170.0	273.5	1973	Bravo: 2458
7	168.0	270.3	1970	Miura S: 2456
8	165.0	265.5	1982	Countach LP 500S: 2465
9	164.0	263.9	1979	Countach S: 2464
10	163.0	262.3	1968	Miura: 2452
11	158.0	254.2	1969	Espada: 2453
12	156.0	251.0	1966	400GT: 2450
13	154.0	247.8	1988	Jalpa: 2471
14	152.0	244.6	1965	350GT: 2449
			1972	Jarama 400GT: 2457
			1973	Jarama 400GT: 2459
15	150.0	241.4	1982	Countach S: 2466
			1970	Espada: 2454
16	147.0	236.5	1976	Silhouette 3000: 2462
17	145.0	233.3	1986	Jalpa 3500: 2470
18	144.0	231.7	1974	Urraco S: 2460
19	133.0	214.0	1982	Jalpa: 2467
20	124.0	199.5	1988	LM129: 2472
			1976	Urraco: 2463

Lammas-Graham

1	94.7	152.4	1937	Drop-head Coupe: 2476

Lanchester

1	89.1	143.4	1937	SS 2.5-litre: 2480
2	73.7	118.6	1938	Roadrider de Luxe Saloon: 2482
3	71.4	114.9	1932	15/18 Saloon: 2477
			1935	18 Saloon: 2478
4	70.8	113.9	1937	18: 2479
5	69.0	111.0	1949	10: 2484
6	68.0	109.4	1940	Roadrider de Luxe Saloon: 2483
7	63.3	101.8	1938	11 Saloon: 2481

Lancia

1	149.0	239.7	1987	Thema 8.32: 2546
2	143.0	230.1	1990	Thema 2.0ie 16v SE Turbo: 2553
3	140.0	225.3	1981	Montecarlo Group 5 Turbo: 2531
			1985	Thema 2.0 ie LX Turbo: 2539
			1988	Thema 8.32: 2548
4	133.0	214.0	1991	Dedra 2000 Turbo: 2555
5	130.0	209.2	1986	Delta HF 4WD: 2541
			1988	Delta HF Integrale: 2547
6	129.0	207.6	1989	Delta Integrale 16v: 2549
7	128.0	206.0	1984	Rally: 2537
8	126.0	202.7	1990	Dedra 2.0ie: 2552
			1989	Thema 2.0ie 16v: 2550
9	122.0	196.3	1986	Delta HF Turbo ie: 2542
10	121.0	194.7	1977	Gamma: 2525
11	120.0	193.1	1975	Beta Monte Carlo: 2517
			1978	Gamma Berlina: 2526
			1981	Montecarlo Spyder: 2532
12	119.0	191.5	1986	Prisma 1600ie LX: 2543
13	118.0	189.9	1990	Dedra 1.8i: 2551
			1986	Thema 2.0ie: 2544
			1960	Zagato: 2497
14	116.0	186.6	1972	2000: 2513
			1977	Beta HPE 2000: 2523
			1974	Fulvia Coupe S3: 2515
15	115.0	185.0	1965	Flaminia Coupe 3B: 2504
			1965	Flavia Zagato Sport: 2505
16	114.0	183.4	1976	Beta 2000: 2519
			1981	Trevi 2000: 2533
17	113.0	181.8	1958	Aurelia GT 2500: 2492
			1975	Beta 1600 Coupe: 2516
			1985	Coupe 2000ie: 2538
18	112.0	180.2	1955	Aurelia Gran Turismo 2500: 2490
19	111.0	178.6	1982	Beta Coupe: 2534
			1985	Y10 Turbo: 2540
			1980	Zagato: 2530
20	109.0	175.4	1973	Beta 1800: 2514
			1979	Beta 2000 Automatic: 2527
			1976	Beta Coupe: 2520
			1967	Fulvia 1.3 Zagato: 2509
			1969	Fulvia Coupe: 2510
			1983	Prisma 1600: 2536
21	108.0	173.8	1955	Spyder: 2491
22	107.0	172.2	1960	Flaminia Coupe: 2496
			1964	Flavia Coupe: 2501
			1990	Y10 GTie: 2554
23	106.0	170.6	1979	Beta HPE 1600: 2528
24	105.0	168.9	1962	Flaminia Sedan: 2500
			1967	Flavia Injection: 2507
25	104.0	167.3	1977	Beta Scorpion: 2524
			1976	Beta Sedan: 2521
			1967	Fulvia 1.3 Rallye: 2508
			1966	Fulvia Coupe: 2506
26	103.0	165.7	1958	Flaminia: 2493
27	102.0	164.1	1977	Beta: 2522
			1976	Beta 1300: 2518
			1970	Fulvia Sedan: 2511
			1971	Fulvia Sedan: 2512
28	101.0	162.5	1979	HPE: 2529
29	100.0	160.9	1959	Flaminia: 2495
30	97.0	156.1	1982	Delta Automatic: 2535
31	96.0	154.5	1961	Flavia: 2498
32	94.0	151.2	1964	Fulvia 2C: 2503
			1986	Y10 Fire: 2545
33	92.0	148.0	1952	Aurelia 2-litre Saloon: 2489
34	85.0	136.8	1964	Fulvia: 2502
35	83.1	133.7	1934	27.6hp Astura Saloon: 2485
36	82.0	131.9	1962	Appia III: 2499
37	81.8	131.6	1959	Appia Sedan: 2494
			1938	Aprilia Saloon: 2488
38	81.0	130.3	1937	Aprilia Pillarless Saloon: 2487
39	66.1	106.4	1934	Augusta Saloon: 2486

Land Rover

1	107.0	172.2	1991	Discovery V8i 5DR: 2565
2	99.0	159.3	1990	Discovery V8: 2564
3	92.0	148.0	1990	Discovery TDi: 2563
			1989	Ninety County V8: 2562
4	88.0	141.6	1987	One Ten County V8: 2561
5	86.0	138.4	1982	County: 2559
6	76.0	122.3	1987	Ninety County Turbo Diesel: 2560
7	73.0	117.5	1971	Series III: 2557
8	68.0	109.4	1973	SWB: 2558
9	59.5	95.7	1955	Station Wagon: 2556

Lea-Francis

1	87.0	140.0	1948	Sports: 2569
2	85.0	136.8	1929	Hyper-sports: 2567
3	72.5	116.7	1933	2-litre Saloon: 2568
4	60.0	96.5	1929	12/40 Saloon: 2566

Lexus

1	150.0	241.4	1991	SC400: 2571
2	148.0	238.1	1990	LS400: 2570
3	135.0	217.2	1992	ES300: 2572

Lincoln

1	125.0	201.1	1989	Continental Mk VII: 2586
			1990	Continental Mk VII LSC: 2587
2	121.0	194.7	1964	Continental: 2581
3	120.0	193.1	1985	Continental Mk VII LSC: 2584
4	117.0	188.3	1961	Continental: 2580
5	116.0	186.6	1958	Continental Mk III: 2579
6	108.1	173.9	1953	Cosmopolitan Sedan: 2578
7	104.0	167.3	1976	Continental Limousine: 2582
8	95.7	154.0	1932	Twelve Cylinder Town Sedan: 2575
9	90.9	146.3	1936	Zephyr Saloon: 2576
10	90.0	144.8	1938	Zephyr Saloon: 2577
11	84.9	136.6	1931	39.2hp Saloon: 2574
12	79.6	128.1	1930	39.2hp Town Saloon: 2573

Lloyd

1	63.4	102.0	1958	LP 600: 2588

Lotus

1	165.0	265.5	1990	Esprit Turbo SE: 2640
2	161.0	259.0	1989	Esprit Turbo SE: 2637
3	156.0	251.0	1989	Esprit Turbo: 2636
4	153.0	246.2	1988	Esprit Turbo: 2635
5	152.0	244.6	1986	Esprit Turbo: 2630
6	149.0	239.7	1981	Esprit Turbo: 2627
7	148.0	238.1	1978	Elite V8: 2623
			1983	Esprit Turbo: 2629
8	146.0	234.9	1987	Esprit Turbo HC: 2633
9	137.0	220.4	1990	Elan: 2638
			1991	Elan SE: 2641
			1990	Elan SE: 2639
10	135.0	217.2	1979	Esprit S2: 2625
11	134.0	215.6	1986	Excel SE: 2631
12	131.0	210.8	1983	Eclat Excel: 2628
13	129.0	207.6	1977	Eclat 523: 2619
14	128.0	206.0	1987	Excel SA: 2634
15	126.0	202.7	1975	Elite 503: 2618
16	125.0	201.1	1980	Eclat: 2626
			1979	Elite: 2624
17	124.0	199.5	1969	Elan S4 Drophead SE: 2603
			1977	Esprit: 2620
18	123.0	197.9	1967	Elan Coupe SE: 2600
19	121.0	194.7	1971	Plus 2S 130: 2610
			1972	Plus 2S 130/5: 2615
20	120.0	193.1	1977	Esprit 16v: 2621
			1972	Europa Twin Cam: 2614
			1977	Sprint: 2622
21	119.0	191.5	1967	Elan SE: 2601
			1975	Elite: 2617
22	118.0	189.9	1968	Elan +2: 2602
			1971	Elan Sprint: 2608
23	117.0	188.3	1973	Europa Special 5-speed: 2616
24	115.0	185.0	1964	Elan 1600: 2599
			1987	Elan Autocrosser: 2632
			1963	Elite: 2597
			1960	Elite: 2592
25	114.0	183.4	1972	Europa: 2613
26	112.5	181.0	1957	11 Le Mans: 2589
27	112.0	180.2	1972	Elan Sprint: 2612
28	110.0	177.0	1972	Elan Plus 2S 130: 2611
			1969	Elan S4 SE: 2604
			1971	Europa S2: 2609
29	109.0	175.4	1970	Europa S2: 2606
30	107.0	172.2	1963	Elan 1600: 2596
31	106.0	170.6	1970	7 Twin Cam SS: 2605
			1964	Cortina: 2598
32	103.6	166.7	1961	Super 7: 2594
33	102.0	164.1	1962	Super 7: 2595
34	97.8	157.4	1957	Sports: 2591
35	96.0	154.5	1970	Super 7 Twincam: 2607
36	85.0	136.8	1961	7: 2593

Lynx

1	151.0	243.0	1988	XJS Eventer: 2643
2	150.0	241.4	1987	D Type: 2642

Marcos

1	120.0	193.1	1971	3-litre Volvo: 2646
2	118.0	189.9	1965	1800: 2644
3	112.0	180.2	1968	1600GT: 2645

Marendaz

1	84.1	135.3	1935	15/90 Special Tourer: 2647

Marmon

1	105.0	168.9	1932	16: 2651
2	72.5	116.7	1930	79 Saloon: 2650
3	68.4	110.1	1930	69 Saloon: 2649
4	65.0	104.6	1929	Roosevelt Saloon: 2648

Maserati

1	163.0	262.3	1976	Bora: 2664
2	162.0	260.7	1973	Bora: 2660
3	160.0	257.4	1978	Khamsin: 2666
			1990	Shamal: 2681
4	157.0	252.6	1971	Indy: 2659
5	154.0	247.8	1971	Ghibli: 2658
6	147.0	236.5	1978	Kyalami: 2667
			1981	Merak SS: 2670
7	145.0	233.3	1989	430: 2678
8	142.0	228.5	1990	228: 2680
9	141.0	226.9	1978	Merak: 2668
10	140.0	225.3	1979	Khamsin: 2669
			1976	Khamsin: 2665
11	138.0	222.0	1963	3500 GTI Sebring: 2655
12	136.0	218.8	1970	Indy: 2657
13	135.0	217.2	1975	Merak: 2663
14	133.0	214.0	1974	Merak: 2661
15	130.0	209.2	1988	430: 2676
			1975	Khamsin Automatic: 2662
			1968	Quattroporte: 2656
			1989	Spyder: 2679
16	129.0	207.6	1988	Biturbo: 2677
			1985	Biturbo E: 2674
			1959	GT Coupe: 2653
17	128.0	206.0	1987	Biturbo Spyder: 2675
18	127.0	204.3	1961	3500GT: 2654
19	125.0	201.1	1954	A6G/54 Frua Gran Sport: 2652
			1985	Biturbo: 2672
20	123.0	197.9	1983	Quattroporte: 2671

Matra

1	97.0	156.1	1969	M530A: 2682
2	92.0	148.0	1978	Rancho: 2683

Matra-Simca

1	102.0	164.1	1975	Bagheera: 2684

Mazda

1	178.0	286.4	1991	RX-7 Cartech: 2768
2	170.0	273.5	1991	RX-7 Mariah Mode Six: 2770
3	150.0	241.4	1986	RX-7 Turbo: 2737
			1989	RX-7 Turbo II: 2759
4	149.0	239.7	1991	RX-7 Turbo: 2771
5	140.0	225.3	1988	RX-7 Turbo: 2751
			1990	RX-7 Turbo: 2764
6	135.0	217.2	1986	RX-7: 2735
7	133.0	214.0	1980	RX-7 Racer: 2715
8	131.0	210.8	1988	MX-6: 2747
			1988	MX-6 GT: 2748
9	130.0	209.2	1990	Protege: 2762
			1989	RX-7 GTUs: 2758
10	128.0	206.0	1989	323 1.8 GT: 2753
			1988	RX-7 GTU: 2750
			1986	RX-7 GXL: 2736
11	126.0	202.7	1990	MX-5 Miata Millen: 2760
			1982	RX-7: 2720
			1984	RX-7: 2724
12	125.0	201.1	1986	323 Turbo 4x4 Lux: 2732
			1991	MX-3 V6: 2767
			1988	RX-7 Convertible: 2749
13	124.0	199.5	1988	323 Turbo 4x4: 2743
			1988	626 2.0i GT 4WS: 2745
			1990	MX-6 GT: 2761
			1989	MX-6 GT 4WS: 2756
14	123.0	197.9	1991	323 1.8 GT: 2766
15	122.0	196.3	1980	RX-7: 2714
			1978	RX-7: 2705
16	121.0	194.7	1986	626 2.0i 5-door: 2733
			1988	929: 2746
17	120.0	193.1	1986	626 GT: 2734
			1992	MX-3 GS: 2773
			1985	RX-7 GSL: 2728
18	119.0	191.5	1988	323 GTX: 2742
			1971	RX-2: 2690
19	118.0	189.9	1968	110S Coupe: 2685
			1983	RX-7: 2723
			1981	RX-7 GSL: 2719
20	117.0	188.3	1989	MX-5 Miata: 2755
			1974	RX-4 Coupe: 2698
21	116.0	186.6	1989	323 1.6i: 2752
			1972	RX-2: 2691
22	115.0	185.0	1985	323 1.6i: 2727
			1979	RX-7: 2710
23	113.0	181.8	1987	626 2.0 GLS Executive: 2739
24	112.0	180.2	1972	RX-3: 2692
			1977	RX-4: 2704
			1991	RX-7 Infini IV: 2769
25	111.0	178.6	1976	Cosmo: 2701
26	110.0	177.0	1988	626 2.0 GLX Executive Estate: 2744
			1989	MPV: 2754
27	109.0	175.4	1973	RX-4: 2694
28	108.0	173.8	1980	Montrose GLS Coupe: 2713
29	106.0	170.6	1984	RX-7 GSL SE: 2725
30	105.0	168.9	1983	626: 2721
			1979	626 Coupe: 2707
31	104.0	167.3	1986	323 LX: 2731
32	103.0	165.7	1974	Rotary Pickup: 2697
33	102.0	164.1	1983	626 1600 LX: 2722
			1992	MX-3 1.6 Auto: 2772
34	101.0	162.5	1987	323 1.5 GLX: 2738
			1979	Montrose 1600 GLS: 2709
35	98.0	157.7	1985	323 1.5 GLX: 2726
			1986	323 1.5 GLX Estate: 2729
36	97.0	156.1	1975	808: 2700
37	96.0	154.5	1981	GLC Sport: 2718
			1979	GLC Wagon: 2708
38	94.0	151.2	1974	1300: 2695
			1981	323 1300: 2716

			1974	929: 2696
			1971	Rotary: 2689
39	92.0	148.0	1988	121 1.3 LX Sun Top: 2741
			1968	1500 de Luxe: 2686
40	91.0	146.4	1991	121 GSX: 2765
			1977	GLC: 2703
41	90.0	144.8	1977	323: 2702
			1981	GLC: 2717
42	88.0	141.6	1979	1.4 SP: 2706
43	87.0	140.0	1970	1200 de Luxe: 2687
44	85.0	136.8	1971	1800: 2688

Mercedes-Benz

1	185.0	297.7	1990	300CE AMG Hammer: 2910
2	183.0	294.4	1988	300E AMG Hammer: 2899
3	180.0	289.6	1955	300SLR: 2795
4	160.0	257.4	1990	500SL: 2913
5	159.0	255.8	1991	500E: 2919
6	155.0	249.4	1990	190E 2.5-16 Evolution II: 2908
			1992	500SEL: 2922
			1991	500SL: 2920
			1992	600SEL: 2923
7	151.0	243.0	1990	300CE: 2909
			1986	560SEL: 2889
8	150.0	241.4	1952	300SL Carrera Panamericana: 2788
9	148.0	238.1	1990	300E-24: 2912
10	146.0	234.9	1955	300SL Coupe: 2794
			1991	400SE: 2918
			1987	560SEC Cabriolet Straman: 2895
11	145.0	233.3	1985	190E 2.3-16: 2879
			1986	560SEC: 2888
12	144.0	231.7	1989	190E 2.5-16: 2901
13	143.0	230.1	1985	300E: 2881
14	141.0	226.9	1987	300CE: 2892
15	140.0	225.3	1989	190E AMG Baby Hammer: 2903
			1986	300E: 2885
			1989	300E: 2906
			1979	450SEL 6.9: 2862
16	139.0	223.7	1986	190E 2.3-16: 2883
17	138.0	222.0	1986	420SE: 2887
18	137.0	220.4	1988	300CE: 2897
			1989	300CE Cabriolet Straman: 2905
			1989	560SL: 2907
			1977	600SE: 2854
19	136.0	218.8	1988	300E 4Matic: 2898
			1974	450SEL: 2845
			1975	450SLC: 2849
			1984	500SEC: 2877
20	135.0	217.2	1955	300SL: 2793
			1991	300SL-24 5-speed Auto: 2917
21	134.0	215.6	1987	190E 2.6: 2891
			1988	260E Auto: 2896
			1969	300SEL 6.3: 2828
22	133.0	214.0	1985	500SEL: 2882
23	132.0	212.4	1982	380SEC: 2870
			1967	600: 2821
24	131.0	210.8	1987	420SEL: 2894
25	130.0	209.2	1958	300SL Roadster: 2800
			1961	300SL Roadster: 2807
			1986	560SL: 2890
26	129.0	207.6	1989	190E 2.6: 2902
			1979	280CE: 2860
			1983	280SE: 2874
			1978	450SEL: 2858
27	128.0	206.0	1974	280E: 2844
			1972	280SE 3.5: 2835
28	127.0	204.3	1986	300TE: 2886
			1973	450SE: 2842
29	126.0	202.7	1973	280CE Auto: 2840
			1971	300SL: 2834
30	125.0	201.1	1970	280SE 3.5: 2831
31	124.0	199.5	1963	230SL: 2810
			1972	350SL: 2837
			1974	450SL: 2846
			1973	450SLC: 2843
32	123.0	197.9	1983	190E: 2873
33	121.0	194.7	1986	200: 2884
			1964	230SL: 2811
			1973	280SE: 2841
			1970	280SL: 2832
34	120.0	193.1	1991	190E 1.8 Auto: 2914
			1989	200E Automatic: 2904
			1929	SSKL: 2776
35	118.0	189.9	1976	280E: 2850
			1972	280SEL: 2836
36	117.0	188.3	1979	450SL: 2863
			1976	450SL: 2851
37	116.0	186.6	1967	250SE: 2820
			1970	280SE: 2830
38	115.3	185.5	1964	300SE LWB: 2812
39	115.0	185.0	1965	230SL Automatic: 2815
			1970	250 Coupe: 2829
			1990	300D: 2911
			1987	300TD: 2893
			1981	380SEL: 2869
			1965	600: 2816
40	114.0	183.4	1984	190E: 2876
			1985	190E 2.3: 2878
			1968	280SL: 2825
			1969	280SL: 2827
41	113.0	181.8	1981	230E: 2865
			1979	250T: 2859
42	112.0	180.2	1973	230/4: 2838
			1980	450SL: 2864
43	110.0	177.0	1983	190: 2872
			1989	190: 2900
			1968	250 Automatic: 2824
			1966	250S: 2818
			1973	280: 2839
			1978	300SD: 2857
			1983	380SL: 2875
			1982	380SL: 2871
44	109.2	175.7	1958	190SL: 2798
45	109.0	175.4	1968	250: 2823
			1962	300SE: 2808
46	108.0	173.8	1961	220SE Coupe: 2806
			1981	230TE: 2866
			1977	280E: 2853
			1928	36/220-S: 2774
47	107.6	173.1	1959	220SE: 2801
48	106.0	170.6	1960	190SL: 2802
			1965	220SE: 2814
49	105.5	169.7	1960	220SE: 2804
50	105.0	168.9	1952	300: 2787
51	104.6	168.3	1938	Type 540: 2785
52	103.0	165.7	1975	280S: 2847
53	102.0	164.1	1969	220: 2826
			1955	300B: 2792
			1981	300TD: 2868
54	101.0	162.5	1958	220S: 2799
			1977	230C: 2852
55	100.5	161.7	1936	Type 500 Supercharged: 2782
56	99.8	160.6	1955	190SL: 2791
57	98.5	158.5	1953	300 Sedan: 2789
58	97.0	156.1	1978	200: 2855
			1979	300TD: 2861
59	96.0	154.5	1960	220: 2803
			1966	230 Automatic: 2817
60	95.0	152.9	1968	220: 2822
			1978	300CD: 2856
61	91.0	146.4	1966	300D: 2819
62	90.8	146.1	1957	219: 2796
63	89.0	143.2	1975	300D: 2848
64	88.0	141.6	1961	190: 2805
65	85.0	136.8	1963	190C Automatic: 2809
66	84.0	135.2	1971	220D: 2833
			1991	G-Wagen 300 GD LWB: 2921
67	83.0	133.5	1981	300GD: 2867
68	80.0	128.7	1965	190D: 2813
69	77.5	124.7	1938	Type 320 Saloon: 2784
70	77.0	123.9	1954	180 Saloon: 2790
71	75.0	120.7	1929	32/90 Saloon: 2775
72	72.5	116.7	1935	Type 290 Cabriolet: 2780
73	70.4	113.3	1952	170S: 2786
74	70.3	113.1	1937	Type 230 Saloon: 2783
75	68.1	109.6	1958	180D: 2797
76	62.5	100.6	1931	21/60 Coupe: 2778
			1930	32/90 Limousine: 2777
77	56.2	90.4	1936	20.8hp Diesel Saloon: 2781
78	55.5	89.3	1934	12hp Rear-engined Saloon: 2779

Mercury

1	143.0	230.1	1989	Cougar XR-7: 2960
2	133.0	214.0	1964	Comet A/FX: 2933
3	130.0	209.2	1962	S-55 406: 2930
4	126.0	202.7	1983	Capri: 2957
			1969	Marquis Marauder X-100: 2949
5	125.0	201.1	1967	Cougar Group 2: 2942
			1991	Tracer LTS: 2962
6	124.0	199.5	1990	Capri XR-2: 2961
7	122.0	196.3	1968	Cougar XR-7: 2946
8	120.0	193.1	1966	Comet Cyclone GT: 2940
			1967	Marquis: 2944
9	117.0	188.3	1968	Cyclone: 2947
10	116.0	186.6	1964	Park Lane: 2937
11	115.0	185.0	1967	Cougar GT: 2943
			1965	Park Lane: 2939
			1986	Sable LS: 2958
12	114.0	183.4	1969	Marquis Brougham: 2948
13	113.0	181.8	1963	Super Marauder S-55: 2932
14	110.0	177.0	1967	Cougar: 2941
15	109.0	175.4	1964	Comet Caliente: 2934
			1964	Comet Cyclone 4-speed: 2935
16	108.0	173.8	1975	Capri II 2.8 V6: 2952
17	107.0	172.2	1968	Cougar: 2945
18	106.0	170.6	1965	Monterey: 2938
19	105.0	168.9	1987	Tracer: 2959
20	104.0	167.3	1970	Cougar Eliminator: 2950
21	103.0	165.7	1963	Comet S-22 Sportster: 2931
22	100.0	160.9	1961	Meteor 800: 2928
			1977	Monarch: 2953
23	98.0	157.7	1981	Lynx Hatchback RS: 2956
24	96.0	154.5	1977	Zephyr: 2954

25	93.0	149.6	1962	Meteor: 2929
26	92.0	148.0	1975	Bobcat 2.3-litre: 2951
27	91.0	146.4	1981	LN7: 2955
28	89.0	143.2	1961	Comet 170: 2927
29	86.5	139.2	1949	Coupe: 2924
30	85.0	136.8	1961	Comet: 2926
31	79.0	127.1	1960	Comet: 2925

Merkur

1	130.0	209.2	1987	Scorpio: 2964
2	120.0	193.1	1988	XR4Ti: 2965
			1985	XR4Ti: 2963

Messerschmitt (FMR)

1	68.0	109.4	1958	Tg 500: 2966

Meyers

1	70.0	112.6	1965	Manx: 2967

MG

1	131.0	210.8	1989	Maestro Turbo: 3040
2	130.0	209.2	1972	Costello B GT V8: 3022
3	127.0	204.3	1985	Montego Turbo: 3039
4	125.4	201.8	1973	B GT V8: 3025
5	121.0	194.7	1967	C: 3011
6	118.0	189.9	1969	C: 3017
7	117.0	188.3	1968	C GT Automatic: 3016
8	116.0	186.6	1984	Montego EFi: 3038
9	114.0	183.4	1958	Twin Cam MGA: 2997
10	113.0	181.8	1958	A Twin Cam: 2995
11	111.0	178.6	1975	B: 3027
			1983	Metro Turbo: 3037
12	106.0	170.6	1965	B: 3008
			1970	B Automatic: 3018
13	105.0	168.9	1958	A Judson: 2994
			1961	A Mk II: 3001
			1962	B 1800: 3004
			1990	B British Motor Heritage: 3041
			1971	B GT: 3020
			1966	B GT: 3009
14	104.0	167.3	1968	B All-Synchro: 3015
			1977	B GT: 3032
			1970	B Mk II: 3019
15	103.0	165.7	1982	Metro 1300: 3036
16	102.3	164.6	1961	A 1600 Mk II: 3000
17	102.0	164.1	1957	A Coupe: 2993
			1966	B GT Coupe: 3010
			1975	Midget 1500: 3028
18	101.4	163.2	1959	A 1600: 2998
19	101.0	162.5	1968	1300 Mk II: 3013
20	100.0	160.9	1973	B: 3023
21	99.0	159.3	1956	A: 2992
22	96.0	154.5	1973	B GT: 3024
			1971	Midget Mk III: 3021
23	95.1	153.0	1955	A: 2990
24	95.0	152.9	1968	1300 Mk II Auto: 3014
			1967	Midget Mk III: 3012
25	94.0	151.2	1980	B: 3035
26	93.0	149.6	1979	B: 3033
27	90.0	144.8	1976	B: 3029
			1973	Midget: 3026
			1963	Midget: 3007
28	89.0	143.2	1962	1100: 3003
29	88.0	141.6	1958	Magnette: 2996
30	87.9	141.4	1954	TD Laystall: 2986
31	87.8	141.3	1931	Mk II Montlhery Supercharged: 2970
32	87.0	140.0	1954	TF Supercharged: 2989
33	86.5	139.2	1963	Magnette Mk IV: 3006
34	86.0	138.4	1959	Magnette Mk III: 2999
			1961	Midget: 3002
35	85.4	137.4	1954	TF 1500: 2988
36	85.0	136.8	1979	Midget: 3034
37	83.0	133.5	1954	Magnette: 2985
			1976	Midget: 3030
			1976	Midget Mk IV: 3031
38	81.3	130.8	1953	TDC Mk II: 2984
39	81.0	130.3	1955	Magnette: 2991
			1951	TD: 2980
40	80.7	129.8	1934	Magnette N Two-seater: 2972
41	80.1	128.9	1954	TF: 2987
42	80.0	128.7	1963	1100: 3005
43	79.6	128.1	1936	Midget Series T: 2976
44	78.9	127.0	1950	TD: 2979
			1953	TD: 2983
45	78.0	125.5	1929	Six Sports: 2969
			1947	TC Midget: 2977
46	75.3	121.2	1935	Magnette KN Saloon: 2974
47	75.0	120.7	1952	1.25-litre Saloon: 2981
			1953	Midget: 2982
			1936	Midget PB: 2975
48	74.3	119.5	1934	Midget P Type: 2973
49	73.0	117.5	1949	TC: 2978
50	72.5	116.7	1934	Magna Continental Coupe: 2971
51	64.0	103.0	1929	Midget: 2968

Minerva

1	72.0	115.8	1930	22/28hp Limousine: 3042

Mini

1	98.0	157.7	1965	Cooper 1275S: 3051
2	97.5	156.9	1964	Cooper 1275S: 3049
3	91.0	146.4	1971	1275GT: 3054
			1963	Cooper S: 3047
4	90.0	144.8	1974	1275GT: 3056
			1965	Cooper: 3050
5	88.0	141.6	1969	1275GT: 3053
6	87.4	140.6	1961	Cooper: 3046
7	83.0	133.5	1973	850: 3055
			1976	Clubman 1100: 3059
8	82.0	131.9	1975	1000: 3057
9	80.0	128.7	1979	850 Super de Luxe: 3060
10	79.0	127.1	1967	Super de Luxe Mk II: 3052
11	75.0	120.7	1960	Minor: 3044
12	74.5	119.9	1959	Minor de Luxe: 3043
13	74.0	119.1	1963	Super de Luxe: 3048
14	72.0	115.8	1975	Automatic: 3058
15	68.5	110.2	1960	Traveller: 3045

Mitsubishi

1	163.0	262.3	1985	Galant: 3082
2	159.0	255.8	1991	3000GT VR-4: 3111
3	143.0	230.1	1989	Eclipse: 3102
4	140.0	225.3	1985	Colt Starion Turbo: 3081
5	136.0	218.8	1987	Starion 2000 Turbo: 3095
6	134.0	215.6	1982	Colt Starion Turbo: 3071
7	132.0	212.4	1981	Colt Lancer 2000 Turbo: 3068
8	130.0	209.2	1991	Diamante LS: 3113
			1991	Galant VR-4: 3114
			1991	Sigma: 3116
			1989	Starion 2.6 Turbo: 3106
9	127.0	204.3	1985	Starion ESI: 3086
			1989	Starion ESI-R: 3107
10	126.0	202.7	1985	Galant Turbo: 3083
11	122.0	196.3	1988	Galant GTi-16v: 3099
			1990	Lancer Liftback 1800 GTi-16v: 3110
12	121.0	194.7	1991	Colt 1800 GTI-16v: 3112
13	120.0	193.1	1989	Galant GS: 3104
			1983	Starion: 3074
			1985	Starion: 3085
			1983	Starion Turbo: 3075
14	118.0	189.9	1988	Mirage Turbo: 3101
15	116.0	186.6	1982	Colt Cordia Turbo: 3069
			1988	Lancer GTi 16v: 3100
16	115.0	185.0	1984	Colt 1600 Turbo: 3077
			1988	Cordia Turbo: 3097
			1986	Cordia Turbo: 3087
			1984	Cordia Turbo 1.8: 3078
			1987	Galant Sapporo: 3093
			1991	Space Runner 1800-16v GLXi: 3117
17	113.0	181.8	1990	Galant 2000 GLSi Coupe: 3108
			1983	Tredia Turbo: 3076
18	112.0	180.2	1988	Galant 2000 GLSi: 3098
19	109.0	175.4	1976	Colt Celeste 2000: 3063
20	108.0	173.8	1984	Mirage Turbo: 3080
21	106.0	170.6	1978	Colt Sappore 2000 GSR: 3066
22	105.0	168.9	1982	Colt Hatchback Turbo: 3070
			1987	Galant 2000 GLS Automatic: 3092
			1990	Lancer GLXi 4WD Liftback: 3109
			1991	Shogun V6 LWB: 3115
23	103.0	165.7	1984	Galant 1600 GL: 3079
24	102.0	164.1	1975	Colt Galant 2000: 3062
			1989	Shogun V6 5-door: 3105
25	101.0	162.5	1982	Cordia LS: 3072
26	99.0	159.3	1977	Colt Sigma 2000: 3064
			1985	Space Wagon 1800GLX: 3084
27	97.0	156.1	1986	Lancer 1.5 GLX Estate: 3088
28	96.0	154.5	1979	Colt 1400 GLX: 3067
29	95.0	152.9	1987	Colt 1500 GLX 5-door: 3091
30	94.0	151.2	1978	Colt Lancer Estate: 3065
31	90.0	144.8	1983	Colt Shogun: 3073
32	83.0	133.5	1968	Colt 1100F: 3061
			1987	Shogun Turbo Diesel 5-door: 3094

Monteverdi

1	152.0	244.6	1969	375L: 3118

Moretti

1	100.0	160.9	1954	750 Grand Sport Berlinetta Coupe: 3119

Morgan

1	128.0	206.0	1980	Plus 8 Turbo: 3132
2	126.0	202.7	1987	Plus 8: 3134
3	125.0	201.1	1988	Plus 8: 3135

1968 Plus 8: 3129
4 124.0 199.5 1978 Plus 8: 3131
5 122.0 196.3 1991 Plus 8: 3137
6 105.0 168.9 1970 Plus 8: 3130
7 103.0 165.7 1984 4/4: 3133
8 102.1 164.3 1959 Plus 4: 3127
9 102.0 164.1 1954 Plus 4: 3124
10 98.4 158.3 1955 Plus 4: 3125
11 85.0 136.8 1939 SS: 3122
12 81.4 131.0 1952 Plus 4: 3123
13 80.0 128.7 1963 4/4: 3128
1957 4/4 Modified: 3126
14 78.2 125.8 1938 4/4: 3121
15 77.5 124.7 1936 4/4: 3120

Morris

1 104.0 167.3 1976 Marina 1.8 HL: 3183
2 103.0 165.7 1971 Marina TC: 3181
3 102.0 164.1 1981 Ital 2.0 HLS Automatic: 3186
4 101.0 162.5 1969 1800S: 3177
1978 Marina 1700HL: 3185
5 100.0 160.9 1971 Marina 1.8TC: 3180
6 96.0 154.5 1972 Marina Estate: 3182
7 92.0 148.0 1966 1800: 3176
8 88.0 141.6 1956 Isis: 3166
1971 Marina 1.3 Super Coupe: 3179
1977 Marina 1.3 Super Coupe: 3184
9 80.5 129.5 1964 Oxford VI Traveller: 3175
10 80.0 128.7 1970 1100 Mk II: 3178
11 78.5 126.3 1963 1100: 3173
12 78.0 125.5 1958 Oxford Traveller Series III: 3171
13 77.0 123.9 1964 Minor 1000 de Luxe: 3174
14 76.0 122.3 1961 Minor 1000: 3172
1954 Oxford Saloon: 3164
15 75.5 121.5 1957 Oxford Series III: 3169
16 75.2 121.0 1957 Minor 1000: 3167
17 73.7 118.6 1935 21 Series II Saloon: 3150
18 73.2 117.8 1957 Minor 1100: 3168
19 70.0 112.6 1958 Minor 1000 Traveller: 3170
1948 Oxford: 3158
20 69.2 111.3 1935 16 Series II Saloon: 3149
21 67.0 107.8 1955 Cowley: 3165
1950 Oxford Saloon: 3160
22 66.6 107.2 1935 10/6 Sports Tourer: 3148
23 66.0 106.2 1953 Oxford Travellers' Car: 3162
24 65.2 104.9 1938 10 Series III: 3152
25 63.8 102.7 1939 8 Series E Tourer: 3155
1939 8hp Series E Tourer: 3156
26 62.7 100.9 1954 Minor: 3163
27 62.0 99.8 1948 Minor: 3157
1953 Minor Series II: 3161
28 61.2 98.5 1933 Cowley Six: 3145
29 61.0 98.1 1950 Minor Tourer: 3159
30 60.0 96.5 1929 Isis: 3139
31 59.3 95.4 1934 15/6 Saloon: 3146
32 59.2 95.3 1937 10 Series II: 3151
1933 10/6: 3143
1938 8 Tourer: 3153
1938 8hp Tourer: 3154
33 58.0 93.3 1934 8 Saloon: 3147
1931 Major Six Saloon: 3141
34 57.3 92.2 1933 10/4: 3142
35 56.9 91.6 1933 Cowley Saloon: 3144
36 55.2 88.8 1930 8 Minor: 3140
37 55.0 88.5 1928 Minor Saloon: 3138

Moskvich

1 95.0 152.9 1975 1500: 3188
2 81.0 130.3 1967 De Luxe: 3187

Muntz

1 108.0 173.8 1951 Jet: 3189

MVS

1 153.0 246.2 1987 Venturi GT: 3190

Nardi

1 140.0 225.3 1955 Blue Ray 1: 3192
2 125.0 201.1 1958 Blue Ray 2: 3193

Nash

1 112.8 181.5 1955 Nash-Healey Roadster Supercharged: 3200
2 104.6 168.3 1954 Nash-Healey Roadster: 3198
3 87.3 140.5 1938 Ambassador Six Saloon: 3195
4 79.0 127.1 1952 Rambler Station Wagon: 3196
5 78.0 125.5 1956 Rambler Station Wagon: 3201
6 76.0 122.3 1955 Metropolitan: 3199
7 75.5 121.5 1958 Metropolitan 1500: 3202
8 74.0 119.1 1954 Metropolitan: 3197
9 72.5 116.7 1930 Straight Eight Saloon: 3194

Naylor

1 93.0 149.6 1985 TF 1700: 3203

Nissan

1 166.0 267.1 1991 300ZX Turbo Millen Super GTZ: 3247
2 158.0 254.2 1990 300ZX: 3240
3 156.0 251.0 1990 Skyline GT-R: 3243
4 155.0 249.4 1990 300ZX Turbo: 3241
1991 300ZX Twin Turbo: 3248
5 148.0 238.1 1989 300ZX: 3234
6 144.0 231.7 1987 300ZX Turbo: 3224
7 141.0 226.9 1989 200SX: 3232
8 140.0 225.3 1992 200SX: 3254
9 138.0 222.0 1984 300ZX Turbo: 3209
10 133.0 214.0 1986 300ZX Turbo: 3216
11 132.0 212.4 1991 Primera 2.0E ZX: 3251
1992 Sunny 2.0 GTi: 3255
12 130.0 209.2 1991 NX2000: 3249
13 128.0 206.0 1984 300ZX: 3208
1986 300ZX: 3215
14 126.0 202.7 1984 Silvia Turbo ZX: 3211
15 125.0 201.1 1988 240SX: 3230
1987 300ZX: 3223
1988 300ZX: 3231
1991 Primera 2.0 GSX: 3250
1991 Sentra SE-R: 3252
16 122.0 196.3 1989 Maxima: 3235
17 120.0 193.1 1985 Bluebird Turbo ZX: 3212
1985 Maxima SE: 3214
1989 Maxima SE: 3236
18 119.0 191.5 1988 200SX SE V6: 3229
19 118.0 189.9 1986 Bluebird 1.8 ZX: 3217
1987 Sunny ZX Coupe: 3227
20 116.0 186.6 1991 100NX: 3244
1984 200SX Turbo: 3207
21 115.0 185.0 1991 240SX: 3245
1987 Pulsar NX SE: 3226
22 112.8 181.5 1990 Primera 1.6 LS: 3242
23 112.0 180.2 1991 Sunny 1.6 GS 5-door: 3253
24 105.0 168.9 1986 Laurel 2.4 SGL Automatic: 3218
1982 Stanza XE: 3205
1989 Sunny 1.4 LS: 3239
1987 Sunny 1.6 SLX Coupe: 3228
25 101.0 162.5 1983 Pulsar NX: 3206
26 100.0 160.9 1986 Sentra Sport Coupe SE: 3220
27 98.0 157.7 1989 Prairie: 3238
28 94.0 151.2 1985 Cherry 1.3 SGT: 3213
29 93.0 149.6 1989 Micra 1.2 GSX: 3237
1986 Sunny 1.3 LX 5-door: 3221
30 90.0 144.8 1982 Sentra: 3204
31 89.0 143.2 1987 Micra SGL 5-DR: 3225

NSU

1 112.0 180.2 1974 Ro80: 3266
2 108.0 173.8 1968 Ro80: 3264
3 98.0 157.7 1965 Wankel Spider: 3262
4 96.0 154.5 1965 Spider: 3261
5 87.0 140.0 1966 Typ 110: 3263
6 80.0 128.7 1965 Prinz 1000L: 3260
7 76.0 122.3 1960 Sport-Prinz: 3258
8 74.0 119.1 1968 Super Prinz: 3265
9 73.5 118.3 1962 Prinz 4: 3259
10 70.4 113.3 1959 Prinz 34hp: 3256
11 64.0 103.0 1959 Prinz II: 3257

Ogle

1 99.0 159.3 1962 Austin Mini Cooper GT: 3268
2 93.0 149.6 1961 1.5: 3267

Oldsmobile

1 132.0 212.4 1969 442 Hurst: 3293
2 130.0 209.2 1967 F-85 Cutlass Cruiser: 3289
3 128.0 206.0 1969 Cutlass W-31: 3295
4 127.0 204.3 1966 Toronado: 3288
5 125.0 201.1 1989 Calais HO Quad 4: 3303
1989 Cutlass Calais International Series HO: 3304
1990 Toronado Trofeo: 3305
6 124.0 199.5 1965 Toronado: 3286
7 123.0 197.9 1968 Toronado: 3292
8 122.0 196.3 1962 98 Holiday Sports Sedan: 3275
1970 Rallye 350: 3297
9 121.0 194.7 1966 Cutlass 442: 3287
10 120.0 193.1 1964 Cutlass 442: 3281
1988 Cutlass Calais International Series: 3301
1968 Delmont: 3291
11 118.0 189.9 1969 88 Delta Royale: 3294
1965 Cutlass Holiday 442: 3284
12 117.0 188.3 1964 Jetstar I: 3283
13 116.0 186.6 1970 4-4-2 W30: 3296
14 115.0 185.0 1968 4-4-2: 3290

			1962	Dynamic 88 Celebrity Sedan: 3276
			1958	Super 88: 3272
15	112.0	180.2	1963	Starfire: 3280
16	111.0	178.6	1964	F-85 Cutlass Holiday: 3282
17	110.0	177.0	1973	Cutlass Salon: 3298
			1965	Dynamic Delta 88 Holiday: 3285
18	107.0	172.2	1962	F-85 Jetfire Sports Coupe: 3277
19	102.0	164.1	1961	F-85: 3273
			1961	F-85 Station Wagon: 3274
			1962	F-85 V8: 3278
20	101.0	162.5	1955	Super 88: 3271
21	100.0	160.9	1963	F-85 Jetfire: 3279
22	87.0	140.0	1976	Starfire: 3299
23	80.3	129.2	1936	28.8hp Saloon: 3270
24	79.6	128.1	1935	26.3hp Saloon: 3269

Opel

1	174.0	280.0	1991	Omega Lotus: 3352
2	137.0	220.4	1991	Calibra 2.0i 16v: 3351
3	135.0	217.2	1981	Manta Monza S3.0E: 3347
4	134.0	215.6	1984	Manta Monza GSE: 3350
5	123.0	197.9	1965	Diplomat: 3310
6	122.0	196.3	1983	Manta GTE: 3349
7	120.0	193.1	1970	Senator: 3325
8	118.0	189.9	1974	Commodore GSE: 3337
9	116.0	186.6	1969	Commodore GS Coupe: 3318
			1969	GT 1900: 3321
10	115.0	185.0	1974	Commodore GS 2.8: 3336
11	114.0	183.4	1973	Commodore GS Coupe: 3332
			1970	Diplomat: 3323
12	113.0	181.8	1969	GT 1.9: 3320
13	111.0	178.6	1969	GT: 3319
14	110.0	177.0	1971	GT: 3327
			1983	Manta Berlinetta 1.8S: 3348
15	109.0	175.4	1981	Manta GTJ: 3346
			1970	Manta Rallye 1.9: 3324
16	105.0	168.9	1978	Rekord 2.0S: 3344
17	104.0	167.3	1979	Kadett 1.3S Berlina: 3345
			1975	Manta: 3341
18	103.0	165.7	1975	Ascona 1900SR: 3340
			1972	Rekord 1900: 3329
19	102.0	164.1	1976	Rekord Berlina Pacesetter: 3343
			1967	Rekord Coupe: 3313
20	101.0	162.5	1973	Ascona 1900SR: 3331
			1969	Kadett Rallye 1.9: 3322
			1968	Kadette Rallye 1.9: 3314
21	100.0	160.9	1973	GT: 3333
			1973	Manta Berlinetta Auto: 3335
			1968	Station Wagon 1.9: 3317
22	96.0	154.5	1975	1900: 3339
			1971	Ascona Voyage: 3326
			1974	Kadett Coupe: 3338
23	93.0	149.6	1973	Manta: 3334
			1971	Rallye 1900: 3328
24	91.0	146.4	1967	Kadett Rallye: 3312
25	90.0	144.8	1968	Station Wagon 1.5: 3316
26	85.0	136.8	1966	Kadett S: 3311
27	82.0	131.9	1976	Rekord 2100D: 3342
28	78.2	125.8	1958	Rekord: 3308
29	76.0	122.3	1964	Kadett: 3309
30	75.0	120.7	1968	Station Wagon 1.1: 3315
31	69.2	111.3	1938	Olympia Saloon: 3307
32	59.2	95.3	1937	Kadet Saloon: 3306

Packard

1	92.5	148.8	1930	7-34 Phaeton: 3355
2	88.0	141.6	1934	Twelve Victoria: 3359
3	86.1	138.5	1934	32.5hp Saloon: 3358
4	85.0	136.8	1932	Super 8 Phaeton: 3356
5	84.9	136.6	1935	120 Saloon: 3360
			1937	120 Saloon: 3362
			1936	32.5hp Standard Eight Saloon: 3361
6	80.3	129.2	1933	Straight Eight Saloon: 3357
7	77.5	124.7	1938	30hp Six Saloon: 3363
8	70.0	112.6	1929	32.5hp Saloon: 3354

Panhard

1	92.0	148.0	1964	24CT Sports Coupe: 3371
2	81.0	130.3	1962	PL17 Tiger: 3370
3	80.2	129.0	1956	Dyna Sedan: 3367
4	79.0	127.1	1959	Dyna: 3368
			1959	PL17: 3369
5	76.9	123.7	1954	Dyna Junior Sports: 3366
6	75.5	121.5	1954	Dyna: 3365
7	66.1	106.4	1930	18hp Saloon: 3364

Panther

1	146.0	234.9	1990	Solo: 3380
2	120.0	193.1	1977	Lima: 3375
3	115.0	185.0	1972	J72: 3372
4	112.0	180.2	1983	Kallista 2.8: 3376
			1984	Kallista 2.8: 3377
5	108.0	173.8	1975	J72: 3374
6	92.0	148.0	1985	Kallista 1.6L: 3378

Paramount

1	72.0	115.8	1956	Roadster: 3381

Parradine

1	170.0	273.5	1991	V-12: 3382

Peerless

1	110.0	177.0	1959	GT Coupe: 3383

Peugeot

1	144.0	231.7	1991	605 SVE 24: 3467
2	134.0	215.6	1988	405 Mi16: 3448
3	133.0	214.0	1991	605 SV 3.0 Auto: 3466
4	130.0	209.2	1989	405 Mi16: 3455
5	127.0	204.3	1990	405 Mi16x4: 3459
6	125.0	201.1	1989	309 GTi: 3453
			1990	405 Turbo 16 Pike's Peak: 3460
			1987	505 STX: 3445
7	123.0	197.9	1987	205 GTi 1.9: 3443
			1990	605 SRi: 3461
8	122.0	196.3	1986	205 GTi: 3438
			1987	309 GTi: 3444
			1986	309 SR Injection: 3440
9	121.0	194.7	1990	405 GR Injection Auto: 3458
10	120.0	193.1	1984	205 GTi: 3431
11	119.0	191.5	1985	505 Turbo: 3437
12	118.0	189.9	1991	106 XSi: 3463
			1988	405 SRi: 3449
13	117.0	188.3	1990	405 GLx4: 3457
14	116.0	186.6	1991	605 SR TD: 3465
15	113.0	181.8	1975	604: 3413
16	112.0	180.2	1979	604: 3421
17	111.0	178.6	1977	604 SLV-6: 3417
18	109.0	175.4	1992	106 XT: 3468
			1989	405 GTD Turbo: 3454
			1986	505 GTi Family Estate: 3441
19	108.0	173.8	1988	405 1.6 GL: 3446
			1984	505 GRi: 3432
20	107.0	172.2	1968	504 Injection: 3399
21	103.0	165.7	1991	205 D Turbo: 3464
			1983	305 SR: 3430
			1980	505 S: 3422
			1979	505 STI: 3420
22	102.0	164.1	1988	405 GRD: 3447
			1982	505 GR Estate: 3427
23	101.0	162.5	1989	205 CJ: 3451
			1965	404 KF2: 3393
			1982	505 STI: 3428
24	100.0	160.9	1976	104 ZS: 3415
			1983	205 GR: 3429
			1971	504 Automatic: 3403
			1972	504 Family Estate: 3406
25	99.0	159.3	1989	205 1.1GL: 3450
			1986	309 1.6 GR: 3439
			1979	504: 3419
26	98.0	157.7	1985	309 1.3 GL: 3436
			1970	504: 3401
27	97.0	156.1	1991	106 XR: 3462
			1981	305 S: 3425
			1984	505 S Wagon: 3433
28	96.0	154.5	1978	305 SR: 3418
			1990	309 Style 5-door: 3456
			1975	504: 3412
			1980	604 D Turbo: 3424
29	95.0	152.9	1989	309 GLX: 3452
30	93.0	149.6	1985	305 GRD Estate: 3435
31	92.0	148.0	1972	304 Estate Car: 3405
			1960	404: 3387
32	91.0	146.4	1966	204: 3394
			1969	404 Automatic: 3400
33	90.0	144.8	1965	404: 3391
			1967	404 L Estate: 3396
			1981	505 S Turbodiesel: 3426
34	89.0	143.2	1968	204 Coupe: 3397
35	88.4	142.2	1961	404: 3388
36	88.0	141.6	1985	205 XL: 3434
			1971	304: 3402
37	87.0	140.0	1967	404 Automatique: 3395
38	86.0	138.4	1973	104: 3407
			1977	504 Diesel Automatique: 3416
39	85.0	136.8	1976	104: 3414
			1968	404 Station Wagon: 3398
			1962	404 U6 Estate Car: 3390
			1974	504 L Diesel: 3410
40	84.0	135.2	1972	204: 3404
41	83.0	133.5	1962	403 B Estate Car: 3389
			1973	504 Diesel: 3409
42	82.0	131.9	1965	404 Diesel: 3392
43	80.8	130.0	1960	403: 3386
44	77.0	123.9	1955	403: 3385
45	70.5	113.4	1955	203: 3384

Pininfarina

1 106.0 170.6 1984 Azzurra: 3469

Plymouth

1 144.0 231.7 1968 GTX Hemi: 3502
2 143.0 230.1 1989 Laser RS: 3521
1990 Laser RS Turbo: 3522
3 130.0 209.2 1966 Satellite Street Hemi: 3491
4 127.0 204.3 1968 Barracuda 340-S: 3498
5 125.4 201.8 1970 Barracuda: 3509
6 125.0 201.1 1991 Laser RS Turbo: 3523
7 122.0 196.3 1968 Road Runner: 3503
8 121.0 194.7 1968 GTX: 3501
9 120.6 194.0 1958 Fury: 3474
10 120.0 193.1 1970 Duster 340: 3510
1967 GTX: 3497
1966 Satellite: 3490
1962 Sport Fury: 3481
11 119.6 192.4 1969 Cuda 340: 3504
12 119.0 191.5 1963 Sport Fury: 3483
13 118.0 189.9 1968 Barracuda Fastback: 3499
1967 Barracuda Fastback V8: 3495
1965 Barracuda S: 3486
1969 Cuda 440: 3505
14 115.0 185.0 1966 Barracuda S: 3489
1965 Belvedere Satellite: 3487
1969 Fury III: 3506
1967 Fury III: 3496
15 114.8 184.7 1956 Fury: 3472
16 113.0 181.8 1965 Fury Station Wagon: 3488
1969 Road Runner: 3507
1969 Satellite Sport: 3508
17 110.0 177.0 1968 Fury III: 3500
1962 Savoy V8: 3480
18 109.5 176.2 1963 Fury: 3482
19 108.0 173.8 1967 Barracuda: 3493
1979 Fire Arrow: 3516
1978 Sapporo: 3515
20 106.0 170.6 1984 Colt GTS Turbo: 3518
1959 Fury: 3475
21 105.0 168.9 1964 Barracuda: 3485
22 104.0 167.3 1966 VIP: 3492
23 102.0 164.1 1976 Arrow GT: 3512
1962 Savoy Station Wagon: 3479
1984 Voyager: 3519
24 99.0 159.3 1976 Volare Station Wagon: 3513
25 98.0 157.7 1963 Valiant V-100: 3484
26 97.0 156.1 1967 Barracuda 6: 3494
27 96.0 154.5 1978 Horizon: 3514
28 95.2 153.2 1960 Valiant: 3476
29 95.0 152.9 1956 Savoy: 3473
1960 Valiant Automatic: 3477
30 93.5 150.4 1961 Savoy 6: 3478
31 86.5 139.2 1952 Cambridge: 3471
32 85.0 136.8 1971 Cricket: 3511

Polonez

1 92.0 148.0 1979 1500: 3524

Polski Fiat

1 93.0 149.6 1975 125P: 3525

Pontiac

1 192.0 308.9 1991 Firebird TDM Technologies: 3597
2 183.0 294.4 1982 Petty Grand National: 3571
3 178.0 286.4 1989 Firebird T/A Turbo Pontiac Engineering: 3588
4 155.0 249.4 1989 Firebird TransAm 20th Anniversary: 3589
5 150.0 241.4 1991 Firebird GTA: 3596
1989 Firebird TransAm Turbo: 3590
6 144.0 231.7 1978 Firebird TransAm Silverbird: 3566
7 136.0 218.8 1990 Firebird TransAm GTA: 3594
8 135.0 217.2 1990 Firebird Formula: 3593
1962 Grand Prix 421: 3533
9 130.0 209.2 1991 Firebird TransAm Convertible: 3598
10 129.0 207.6 1969 Grand Prix: 3556
11 128.0 206.0 1992 Bonneville SSEi: 3600
1989 Grand Prix McLaren Turbo: 3592
12 127.0 204.3 1961 Tempest Supercharged: 3532
13 125.0 201.1 1987 Fiero Formula: 3580
1985 Fiero GT: 3577
1986 Fiero GT: 3578
1991 Grand Prix GTP: 3599
1988 Sunbird GT: 3587
1966 Tempest GTO: 3546
14 124.0 199.5 1990 Grand Prix STE Turbo: 3595
1969 GTO Judge: 3557
15 123.0 197.9 1970 Formula 400: 3559
16 122.0 196.3 1964 Tempest GTO: 3540
17 121.0 194.7 1966 GTO: 3544
1970 GTO 400: 3560
18 120.0 193.1 1987 Bonneville SE: 3579
1965 Catalina 2+2: 3542
1989 Grand Am Turbo: 3591
19 119.0 191.5 1965 Bonneville Vista: 3541
20 118.0 189.9 1970 GTO 455: 3561
21 117.0 188.3 1963 Catalina: 3537
1962 Royal Bobcat: 3535
22 115.0 185.0 1988 Bonneville SE: 3585
1967 Firebird 440: 3549
1963 Tempest Le Mans V8: 3539
23 114.0 183.4 1959 Bonneville: 3528
1961 Catalina Super Stock: 3529
1967 Firebird Sprint: 3550
1963 Grand Prix: 3538
1965 Tempest GTO: 3543
24 113.0 181.8 1966 Le Mans OHC: 3545
1966 Tempest Sprint: 3547
25 112.0 180.2 1968 GTO: 3554
26 110.0 177.0 1976 Firebird TransAm: 3563
1973 Grand Am: 3562
1967 Grand Prix: 3551
27 108.0 173.8 1984 Firebird TransAm: 3575
28 107.0 172.2 1968 Firebird RA400: 3553
1967 GTO Ram Air: 3552
29 106.0 170.6 1982 Firebird TransAm: 3570
1980 Firebird TransAm Turbo: 3567
30 105.0 168.9 1983 6000STE: 3572
1969 Tempest: 3558
31 103.0 165.7 1977 Bonneville: 3564
1984 Fiero: 3573
1984 Fiero SE: 3574
32 102.0 164.1 1961 Tempest Automatic: 3531
33 100.0 160.9 1987 Le Mans: 3583
1962 Parisienne: 3534
1966 Tempest Sprint Automatic: 3548
34 99.0 159.3 1980 Phoenix: 3568
35 92.0 148.0 1962 Tempest 4: 3536
36 85.7 137.9 1937 Eight Fixed-head Coupe: 3527
37 85.0 136.8 1981 J2000: 3569
1961 Tempest: 3530
38 80.3 129.2 1936 Touring Saloon de Luxe: 3526

Porsche

1 216.0 347.5 1990 911 Turbo RS Tuning: 3737
2 211.0 339.5 1988 911 Turbo Ruf Twin Turbo: 3710
3 208.0 334.7 1991 911 Ruf CTR: 3748
4 205.0 329.8 1991 911 Turbo Gemballa Mirage: 3751
5 201.0 323.4 1988 911 Turbo Koenig RS: 3709
1987 959S: 3702
6 198.0 318.6 1989 959: 3731
1988 959 Comfort: 3717
1988 959 Sport: 3718
7 196.1 315.5 1991 911 Ruf TR2: 3749
8 196.0 315.4 1991 911 Ruf: 3747
9 186.0 299.3 1989 928 S4 Koenig: 3726
10 183.0 294.4 1989 911 Turbo Motorsport Design: 3724
11 178.0 286.4 1973 Carrera RSR: 3642
12 171.0 275.1 1991 911 Turbo: 3750
13 168.0 270.3 1991 911 Carrera Turbo: 3746
14 165.0 265.5 1983 911 Turbo: 3676
1987 911 Turbo Gemballa Avalanche: 3697
1988 928 S4: 3712
15 163.0 262.3 1977 935 Group 4 Holbert: 3657
16 162.0 260.7 1989 928 S4 SE: 3727
1989 944 Turbo: 3730
17 161.0 259.0 1990 911 Carrera 4: 3734
1989 911 Carrera 4: 3720
1992 911 Carrera RS: 3753
1986 928 S4 Automatic: 3692
18 160.0 257.4 1990 911 Carrera 2: 3732
1984 911 Turbo Cabriolet Ruf: 3680
19 159.0 255.8 1990 911 Carrera 2 Tiptronic: 3733
1990 911 Turbo: 3736
1989 911 Turbo: 3723
1990 Carrera 2 Cabriolet Tiptronic: 3744
20 158.0 254.2 1989 911 3.3 Turbo: 3719
1987 911 Turbo Ruf 3.4: 3698
1986 944 Turbo: 3695
21 157.0 252.6 1987 911 Turbo Slant-Nose: 3699
22 156.0 251.0 1978 911 Turbo: 3659
1976 911 Turbo Carrera: 3650
23 155.0 249.4 1988 911 Speedster: 3707
1988 911 Turbo: 3708
1989 928 Cabrio Strosek: 3725
1988 944 Turbo: 3715
1958 RSK: 3613
24 154.0 247.8 1989 911 Club Sport: 3722
1988 944 Turbo SE: 3716
25 153.0 246.2 1986 911 Turbo: 3689
1985 944 Turbo: 3686
1975 Turbo 3-litre: 3648
26 152.0 244.6 1988 911 Carrera Club Sport: 3705
1986 928 S: 3691
27 151.0 243.0 1985 911 Carrera: 3682
1985 928 S Series II: 3684
28 150.0 241.4 1964 904 Carrera GTS: 3621
29 149.0 239.7 1988 911 Cabriolet: 3703

			1988	911 Carrera: 3704
			1989	911 Carrera Cabriolet: 3721
			1986	911 Carrera SE: 3688
			1988	911 Club Sport: 3706
			1990	911 Speedster: 3735
			1990	944 S2: 3742
			1990	944 S2 Cabriolet: 3743
			1975	Carrera RS 3-litre: 3647
			1973	Carrera RS Touring: 3641
30	147.0	236.5	1989	944 S2: 3729
31	146.0	234.9	1984	911 Carrera: 3679
			1981	911 SC: 3670
32	144.0	231.7	1974	911 Carrera: 3643
			1970	911 S 2.2-litre: 3631
			1979	924 Turbo: 3664
33	143.0	230.1	1978	928: 3661
			1985	928 S: 3683
34	142.0	228.5	1973	911 S: 3638
			1974	911S 2.7-litre: 3645
35	141.0	226.9	1967	911 S: 3626
			1977	911 SC: 3654
			1986	944 S: 3694
36	140.0	225.3	1971	911 E 2.4-litre: 3635
			1980	928: 3669
			1988	944 S: 3714
37	139.0	223.7	1989	944: 3728
38	138.0	222.0	1972	911 E: 3637
			1976	911 S: 3649
			1980	911 SC: 3666
			1988	924 S: 3711
			1978	928 Automatic: 3662
39	137.0	220.4	1966	911 S: 3624
			1982	944 Lux: 3674
			1985	944 Lux: 3685
40	136.0	218.8	1987	924 S: 3700
			1983	928 S: 3677
41	134.0	215.6	1975	911 Carrera: 3646
			1968	911 E Sportomatic: 3627
42	133.0	214.0	1979	928 Automatic: 3665
43	132.0	212.4	1965	911: 3622
			1986	924 S: 3690
			1988	944: 3713
			1982	944: 3673
44	131.0	210.8	1970	911 T: 3632
45	130.0	209.2	1986	911 Cabriolet: 3687
			1969	911 E: 3629
46	129.0	207.6	1980	924 S Turbo: 3668
47	127.0	204.3	1974	911 Targa: 3644
			1978	924 Lux: 3660
			1981	924 Turbo: 3671
48	126.0	202.7	1978	911 SC: 3658
			1977	924: 3656
49	125.0	201.1	1983	944: 3678
50	124.0	199.5	1983	911 Cabriolet: 3675
51	123.0	197.9	1970	914 6: 3634
			1980	924: 3667
			1982	924 Weissach: 3672
			1986	944: 3693
52	122.7	197.4	1962	Carrera 2-litre: 3618
53	122.0	196.3	1969	911 T: 3630
			1971	911 T Sportomatic: 3636
54	121.6	195.7	1957	550 Spyder: 3610
55	121.0	194.7	1965	912: 3623
56	120.0	193.1	1956	Carrera Coupe: 3606
57	119.0	191.5	1966	912: 3625
			1973	914 2-litre: 3640
58	117.0	188.3	1968	911 Sportomatic: 3628
			1979	924: 3663
			1960	Super 90 Cabriolet: 3616
59	115.0	185.0	1976	912 E: 3651
60	112.5	181.0	1962	Super 90 Cabriolet: 3619
61	111.0	178.6	1976	924: 3653
62	110.0	177.0	1984	944: 3681
			1960	Super 75: 3615
63	109.0	175.4	1970	914: 3633
64	107.6	173.1	1954	Super Coupe: 3603
65	107.0	172.2	1976	914 2.0-litre: 3652
66	105.2	169.3	1958	1600 Super Speedster: 3612
67	103.0	165.7	1958	1600: 3611
			1952	356 4: 3601
68	102.0	164.1	1956	1600: 3605
69	101.4	163.2	1957	1600 Coupe: 3609
70	100.5	161.7	1955	1500 S Speedster: 3604
71	100.0	160.9	1961	1600 N: 3617
			1964	356 C: 3620
72	98.1	157.8	1956	Continental Coupe: 3607
73	98.0	157.7	1959	1600 Convertible D: 3614
74	96.0	154.5	1973	914 1.7-litre: 3639
75	95.4	153.5	1956	Continental Speedster: 3608
76	91.0	146.4	1954	356: 3602

Proton

1	100.0	160.9	1991	1.5 SE Triple Valve Aeroback: 3755
2	99.0	159.3	1989	1.5 SE Aeroback: 3754

Railton

1	100.5	161.7	1935	Light Sports Tourer: 3757
2	91.8	147.7	1936	Straight Eight Saloon: 3758
3	88.2	141.9	1937	Cobham Saloon: 3759
			1934	Terraplane: 3756
4	68.7	110.5	1938	10 Drop-head Coupe: 3760

Rambler

1	120.0	193.1	1968	Javelin Hardtop SST: 3770
2	110.0	177.0	1960	Rebel V8: 3762
3	107.0	172.2	1966	770 V8 Convertible: 3768
4	99.0	159.3	1967	Rebel 6 Estate Car: 3769
5	95.0	152.9	1964	770 Six: 3767
6	91.5	147.2	1961	Estate: 3766
7	91.0	146.4	1960	Super 6 Station Wagon: 3764
8	88.2	141.9	1960	Six: 3763
9	85.0	136.8	1961	American: 3765
10	84.0	135.2	1959	American: 3761

Range Rover

1	110.0	177.0	1990	Vogue SE: 3780
2	109.0	175.4	1990	County: 3779
3	108.0	173.8	1992	Vogue SE: 3781
4	106.0	170.6	1986	Vogue: 3774
			1989	Vogue: 3777
5	105.0	168.9	1975	V8: 3772
6	102.0	164.1	1989	Vogue SE: 3778
7	100.0	160.9	1978	V8: 3773
8	93.0	149.6	1988	Vogue Turbo D: 3776
9	92.0	148.0	1970	V8: 3771
10	90.0	144.8	1987	V8: 3775

Reliant

1	132.0	212.4	1990	Scimitar SST 1800Ti: 3796
2	124.0	199.5	1986	Scimitar Ti: 3795
3	123.0	197.9	1973	Scimitar GTE: 3788
4	122.0	196.3	1967	Scimitar GT: 3785
5	119.0	191.5	1976	Scimitar GTE: 3791
			1977	Scimitar GTE: 3792
6	118.0	189.9	1965	Scimitar: 3784
7	117.0	188.3	1981	Scimitar GTE: 3793
8	116.0	186.6	1970	Scimitar GTE Automatic: 3787
9	110.5	177.8	1964	Sabre Six GT: 3783
10	110.0	177.0	1985	Scimitar SS1 1600: 3794
11	90.8	146.1	1962	Sabre Sports: 3782
12	80.0	128.7	1975	Kitten: 3789
			1976	Kitten DL Estate: 3790
13	70.0	112.6	1968	Rebel 700 Estate: 3786

Renault

1	165.0	265.5	1991	Alpine A610 Turbo: 3918
2	158.0	254.2	1981	Le Car Turbo: 3874
3	152.0	244.6	1986	GTA V6 Turbo: 3899
4	141.0	226.9	1988	GTA V6: 3906
5	140.0	225.3	1990	21 Turbo Quadra: 3914
6	139.0	223.7	1988	21 Turbo: 3905
			1985	25 V6 Turbo: 3889
7	130.0	209.2	1991	19 16v: 3917
			1984	25 V6: 3885
8	129.0	207.6	1992	19 16v Cabriolet: 3922
			1990	25 V6 2.9 Auto: 3916
9	128.0	206.0	1989	25 TXi: 3910
10	126.8	204.0	1992	Cleo 16v: 3923
11	126.0	202.7	1990	21 TXi: 3915
			1986	5 GT Turbo: 3895
			1984	5 Turbo 2: 3886
12	123.0	197.9	1987	11 Turbo: 3900
13	122.0	196.3	1986	21 Savanna GTX: 3894
			1988	21 Ti: 3904
			1987	5 GT Turbo: 3901
			1981	5 Turbo: 3873
14	120.0	193.1	1975	17 Gordini: 3848
15	119.0	191.5	1978	30 TS: 3859
16	118.0	189.9	1991	Espace V6: 3921
17	117.0	188.3	1979	30 TX: 3863
18	116.0	186.6	1976	30 TS: 3853
			1986	9 Turbo: 3897
			1983	Fuego Turbo: 3884
19	115.0	185.0	1982	5 Gordini Turbo: 3876
20	114.0	183.4	1981	18 Turbo: 3870
			1986	21 GTS: 3893
21	113.0	181.8	1985	Espace 2000 TSE: 3892
22	112.0	180.2	1989	19 TXE: 3908
			1989	21 GTS Hatchback: 3909
			1979	5 Gordini: 3864
			1987	5 GTX 3-DR: 3902
			1982	Fuego GTS: 3881
23	111.0	178.6	1990	19 TXE Chamade: 3913
24	110.0	177.0	1982	18 GTX Estate: 3875
			1965	8 Gordini: 3824
			1987	Alliance GTA: 3903
25	109.0	175.4	1979	5 Racer: 3865

			1989	Espace TXE: 3912
26	108.0	173.8	1976	17 Gordini: 3851
			1981	18i: 3871
			1989	19 TSE: 3907
			1967	8 Gordini 1300: 3831
27	107.0	172.2	1981	20 TX: 3872
			1991	Clio 1.4RT: 3920
28	106.0	170.6	1985	5 TSE: 3890
29	104.0	167.3	1969	16 TS: 3833
30	103.0	165.7	1973	17: 3844
31	102.0	164.1	1976	15 GTL: 3850
			1977	17 TS: 3857
			1975	5 TS: 3849
			1982	Fuego Turbo: 3882
32	101.0	162.5	1981	14 TS: 3869
			1976	20 TL: 3852
33	100.1	161.0	1991	Clio 1.2 RN: 3919
34	100.0	160.9	1972	16 TS: 3843
			1979	18 GTS: 3861
			1977	20 TS: 3858
			1985	Encore GS: 3891
			1979	Gordini: 3867
35	99.0	159.3	1986	5 GTL 5-door: 3896
36	98.0	157.7	1965	R8 Rally: 3826
37	97.0	156.1	1979	18 TS Estate: 3862
38	96.0	154.5	1983	11 TSE: 3883
			1972	15 TL: 3842
			1982	9 GLT: 3877
			1982	9 TSE: 3879
39	93.0	149.6	1977	14: 3856
			1968	16: 3832
			1982	9 TC: 3878
40	92.0	148.0	1972	15 Coupe: 3841
			1971	16 TL Automatic: 3837
			1989	5 Campus: 3911
41	90.0	144.8	1970	12 TL: 3836
			1966	16 GL: 3828
			1978	5 Automatic: 3860
			1976	5 GTL: 3854
			1982	Alliance DL: 3880
			1965	Caravelle: 3825
42	89.0	143.2	1972	12 Estate: 3839
			1972	12 TL: 3840
43	88.0	141.6	1970	10: 3835
			1977	12 TL: 3855
44	87.0	140.0	1973	5 TL: 3845
			1974	6 TL: 3846
45	85.0	136.8	1962	Caravelle S: 3815
46	84.0	135.2	1979	5 TL: 3866
			1964	R8 1100: 3823
47	83.5	134.4	1962	R8: 3818
48	83.0	133.5	1960	Floride: 3813
49	82.0	131.9	1966	1100 Automatic: 3827
			1958	Fregate Transfluide: 3808
50	81.0	130.3	1971	6 1100: 3838
			1963	Floride Caravelle: 3821
51	80.0	128.7	1961	Dauphine Gordini: 3814
52	79.2	127.4	1958	Dauphine Ferry: 3807
53	79.0	127.1	1967	10: 3830
			1962	Dauphine Gordini de Luxe: 3817
			1963	R8: 3822
54	77.5	124.7	1960	Caravelle: 3812
55	76.9	123.7	1935	24hp Big Six Saloon: 3799
56	75.6	121.6	1959	Caravelle: 3809
57	75.0	120.7	1969	6: 3834
58	73.4	118.1	1959	Dauphine Gordini: 3811
59	72.2	116.2	1963	Dauphine Automatic: 3820
60	72.1	116.0	1956	Dauphine: 3805
61	70.3	113.1	1937	17.9hp Touring Saloon: 3800
62	70.0	112.6	1963	4 L Estate Car: 3819
63	69.5	111.8	1962	Dauphine: 3816
64	69.0	111.0	1959	Dauphine: 3810
65	68.0	109.4	1966	4 Estate Car: 3829
66	67.5	108.6	1957	Dauphine: 3806
67	65.3	105.1	1955	4CV: 3803
68	64.0	103.0	1955	750: 3804
69	60.0	96.5	1948	4CV: 3801
			1953	750: 3802
			1930	Vivasix Saloon: 3797
70	58.0	93.3	1935	12.1hp Airline Saloon: 3798

Riley

1	102.0	164.1	1955	Pathfinder: 3939
2	100.2	161.2	1956	Pathfinder: 3940
3	94.5	152.1	1952	2.5: 3936
4	94.0	151.2	1953	2.5: 3938
5	92.0	148.0	1949	2.5 Saloon: 3935
6	91.0	146.4	1960	4/68: 3942
			1967	Kestrel: 3945
7	90.0	144.8	1947	2.5 Saloon: 3933
			1948	2.5 Sports: 3934
8	86.5	139.2	1937	Sprite: 3930
9	86.0	138.4	1961	1.5: 3943
10	85.0	136.8	1958	1.5: 3941
11	84.1	135.3	1938	16 2.5: 3931
12	81.8	131.6	1935	1.5 Kestrel Special: 3925
			1937	8/90 Adelphi Saloon: 3927
13	81.0	130.3	1947	1.5: 3932
14	78.9	127.0	1937	Kestrel Sprite: 3929
15	75.5	121.5	1953	1.5: 3937
16	73.5	118.3	1962	Elf: 3944
17	73.1	117.6	1936	1.5 Falcon Saloon: 3926
18	67.1	108.0	1934	12 Mentone Saloon: 3924
19	63.8	102.7	1937	9 Monaco: 3928

Rolls-Royce

1	129.0	207.6	1982	Corniche: 3970
2	128.0	206.0	1991	Silver Spirit II: 3972
3	122.0	196.3	1974	Corniche: 3964
4	120.0	193.1	1976	Silver Shadow: 3965
			1978	Silver Wraith II: 3967
5	119.0	191.5	1972	Silver Shadow: 3963
			1981	Silver Spirit: 3969
6	118.0	189.9	1966	Silver Shadow: 3961
7	117.0	188.3	1963	Silver Cloud III: 3960
8	115.0	185.0	1960	Silver Cloud II: 3958
9	114.0	183.4	1969	Silver Shadow: 3962
			1980	Silver Shadow II: 3968
10	112.0	180.2	1960	Silver Cloud II V8: 3959
11	108.0	173.8	1982	Silver Spur: 3971
12	106.0	170.6	1958	Silver Cloud: 3956
			1977	Silver Shadow: 3966
13	102.5	164.9	1958	Silver Cloud "S": 3957
14	92.5	148.8	1936	Phantom III: 3952
15	92.3	148.5	1933	Phantom II: 3950
16	88.0	141.6	1932	Phantom II: 3949
17	87.8	141.3	1953	Silver Dawn: 3954
18	87.5	140.8	1954	Silver Dawn: 3955
19	80.0	128.7	1927	Phantom I Phaeton: 3946
20	76.2	122.6	1935	20/25 Touring Saloon: 3951
21	69.5	111.8	1949	Silver Wraith: 3953
22	67.6	108.8	1931	25 Saloon: 3948
23	65.0	104.6	1929	20 Saloon: 3947

Rover

1	151.0	243.0	1953	Jet: 3984
2	142.0	228.5	1966	Rover-BRM Turbine: 4006
3	138.0	222.0	1989	Vitesse: 4036
4	134.0	215.6	1988	Vitesse: 4033
5	133.0	214.0	1983	Vitesse: 4024
6	132.0	212.4	1988	827 SLi Auto: 4032
			1989	Sterling Catalyst: 4035
7	131.0	210.8	1992	Sterling Automatic: 4051
8	130.0	209.2	1986	825i: 4027
9	128.0	206.0	1991	220 GTi: 4046
10	127.0	204.3	1987	Sterling Automatic: 4030
11	126.0	202.7	1991	216 GTi: 4044
			1976	3500: 4016
			1992	820i: 4050
			1981	Vanden Plas: 4021
12	125.0	201.1	1971	3500S: 4012
13	121.0	194.7	1990	416 GTi: 4040
14	119.0	191.5	1976	3500 Automatic: 4017
15	118.0	189.9	1977	2600: 4018
			1987	820SE: 4028
16	117.0	188.3	1990	216 GSi: 4038
			1970	3500S: 4010
			1991	825 TD: 4047
17	116.0	186.6	1966	2000TC: 4004
			1980	3500: 4020
18	115.0	185.0	1988	820 Fastback: 4031
			1990	Metro GTi 16v: 4042
19	113.0	181.8	1970	3500: 4009
20	112.0	180.2	1974	2200TC: 4015
			1966	3-litre Coupe Mk III: 4005
21	111.0	178.6	1978	2300: 4019
22	110.3	177.5	1963	3-litre Coupe: 4000
23	109.0	175.4	1967	3.5-litre: 4007
24	108.0	173.8	1971	2000TC: 4011
			1990	214 GSi: 4037
			1985	216 Vitesse: 4026
25	106.0	170.6	1969	2000TC: 4008
			1990	Metro 1.4SL: 4041
			1987	Montego 1.6L: 4029
			1982	SD Turbo: 4023
26	105.0	168.9	1982	2000: 4022
			1990	414 Si: 4039
			1963	Coupe: 4001
27	104.5	168.1	1963	2000: 3999
28	104.0	167.3	1973	2000SC: 4013
29	103.0	165.7	1973	2200SC Automatic: 4014
			1961	3-litre Automatic: 3997
30	102.0	164.1	1991	214S: 4043
			1989	Montego 2.0 DSL Turbo: 4034
31	101.0	162.5	1964	2000: 4002
32	100.0	160.9	1962	3-litre: 3998
			1960	3-litre: 3995
33	98.0	157.7	1984	213 Vanden Plas: 4025
			1991	Mini Cooper S: 4048
34	97.5	156.9	1959	3-litre: 3992
35	97.0	156.1	1991	218 SD: 4045
36	96.0	154.5	1957	105S: 3990
37	95.0	152.9	1961	100: 3996

			1960	100: 3994
38	94.0	151.2	1966	2000 Automatic: 4003
39	91.0	146.4	1958	105R de Luxe: 3991
			1956	90: 3989
40	90.0	144.8	1954	90: 3986
41	87.0	140.0	1955	75: 3987
			1959	80: 3993
42	82.5	132.7	1935	Speed 14 Streamline Coupe: 3976
43	82.0	131.9	1950	75: 3982
44	81.8	131.6	1931	Light Six Speed Model: 3973
45	80.5	129.5	1952	75: 3983
46	79.0	127.1	1954	60: 3985
47	78.0	125.5	1956	60: 3988
48	77.5	124.7	1937	16 Sports Saloon: 3977
49	75.6	121.6	1938	16 Saloon: 3979
50	75.0	120.7	1949	75: 3980
			1949	75 Saloon: 3981
51	72.0	115.8	1938	14: 3978
52	69.7	112.1	1934	12 Saloon: 3975
53	60.8	97.8	1932	Pilot: 3974

Ruger

1	116.0	186.6	1970	Bentley Clone: 4052

Saab

1	148.0	238.1	1989	Carlsson: 4097
2	142.0	228.5	1991	9000 2.3 Turbo TCS: 4101
3	140.0	225.3	1988	9000CD: 4094
4	139.0	223.7	1985	9000 Turbo 16v: 4090
5	138.6	223.0	1991	9000CS Turbo S: 4103
6	135.0	217.2	1989	9000 Turbo: 4096
			1991	9000 Turbo: 4102
7	129.0	207.6	1992	9000 2.3CS: 4105
8	127.0	204.3	1990	CDS 2.3: 4100
9	125.0	201.1	1990	9000CD: 4098
			1990	900SPG: 4099
10	124.0	199.5	1985	900 Turbo: 4089
			1989	900 Turbo S: 4095
			1986	9000: 4092
11	123.0	197.9	1978	Turbo: 4081
12	121.0	194.7	1986	9000i: 4093
13	119.0	191.5	1979	900 Turbo: 4082
14	116.0	186.6	1982	900 Turbo: 4088
15	110.0	177.0	1975	99EMS: 4078
16	108.0	173.8	1974	99LE Wagonback: 4077
17	107.0	172.2	1981	900 Turbo: 4085
18	106.0	170.6	1981	900GLS: 4086
			1985	900i: 4091
19	105.0	168.9	1982	900: 4087
			1979	900GL: 4083
			1976	99GL Super Combi: 4079
20	103.0	165.7	1972	99CM4 2.0: 4071
21	102.0	164.1	1977	99EMS: 4080
22	100.0	160.9	1970	Sonnet III: 4069
23	98.0	157.7	1972	99E 1.85: 4072
24	97.0	156.1	1971	99: 4070
			1972	99EA: 4073
			1968	Sonnet V4: 4063
25	95.0	152.9	1972	Sonnet III: 4074
26	93.0	149.6	1967	96 V4: 4061
			1967	V4: 4062
27	92.0	148.0	1970	99: 4067
			1970	99E: 4068
28	91.0	146.4	1969	99: 4065
29	90.0	144.8	1968	Station Wagon V4: 4064
30	88.0	141.6	1958	Gran Turismo: 4055
			1969	Sport: 4066
31	87.0	140.0	1964	850GT: 4059
32	80.0	128.7	1961	96 Sedan: 4057
33	79.0	127.1	1966	96: 4060
34	76.0	122.3	1956	93: 4053
35	74.8	120.4	1957	93: 4054
36	74.0	119.1	1960	96: 4056
37	68.0	109.4	1963	95: 4058

Safir

1	193.0	310.5	1991	GT40: 4106

Saturn

1	124.0	199.5	1991	Sports Coupe: 4107

Sbarro

1	124.0	199.5	1990	Chrono 3.5: 4108

Scarab

1	161.0	259.0	1959	Mk II: 4109

Seat

1	124.0	199.5	1992	Toledo 2.0 GTi: 4115
2	109.0	175.4	1985	1.5 GLX: 4111
3	108.0	173.8	1989	Ibiza SXi: 4113
4	103.0	165.7	1992	Toledo 1.9 CL Diesel: 4114
5	99.0	159.3	1976	1200 Sport: 4110
6	94.0	151.2	1986	Malaga 1.2L: 4112

Shelby

1	190.0	305.7	1965	Cobra Daytona Coupe: 4119
2	162.0	260.7	1974	Cobra 427: 4126
3	153.0	246.2	1962	AC Ford Cobra: 4116
4	139.0	223.7	1964	AC Ford Cobra: 4117
5	132.0	212.4	1967	GT 500: 4122
6	130.0	209.2	1969	GT 500: 4125
			1968	GT 500-KR: 4124
7	127.0	204.3	1966	GT 350-S: 4121
8	124.0	199.5	1965	GT 350: 4120
9	119.0	191.5	1968	GT 350: 4123

Siata

1	104.8	168.6	1953	Spyder V8: 4127
2	73.0	117.5	1969	Spring 850: 4128

Simca

1	97.0	156.1	1970	1204 Special: 4156
2	94.0	151.2	1964	1500: 4148
			1965	1500GL Estate: 4149
3	93.0	149.6	1969	1501 Special Estate: 4155
4	92.0	148.0	1974	1100 Special: 4157
			1958	Vedette Beaulieu: 4137
5	91.0	146.4	1960	Vedette V8: 4141
6	87.4	140.6	1957	Versailles V8: 4135
7	87.0	140.0	1969	1204: 4154
8	85.0	136.8	1968	1100GLS: 4153
			1961	Aronde Montlhery: 4142
9	84.6	136.1	1958	Aronde Montlhery: 4136
10	84.5	136.0	1963	1300GL: 4147
11	84.3	135.6	1956	Sports Coupe: 4134
12	82.3	132.4	1951	8 Sport: 4129
13	82.0	131.9	1966	1000GLS: 4150
			1977	1000LS: 4158
			1967	1301: 4152
14	81.0	130.3	1963	1000 Special: 4146
			1967	1000GLS: 4151
15	80.0	128.7	1962	5: 4144
			1960	Etoile: 4139
16	79.5	127.9	1960	Oceane: 4140
17	76.5	123.1	1955	Aronde: 4132
18	76.0	122.3	1954	Aronde: 4131
			1959	Elysee: 4138
			1956	Elysee: 4133
19	75.0	120.7	1963	1000: 4145
20	73.5	118.3	1952	Aronde: 4130
21	73.0	117.5	1962	1000: 4143

Singer

1	95.0	152.9	1966	Vogue: 4178
2	90.0	144.8	1965	Vogue Mk III Estate: 4177
3	87.0	140.0	1967	Gazelle: 4180
4	86.0	138.4	1966	Vogue Automatic: 4179
5	85.0	136.8	1961	Gazelle Series IIIB: 4172
			1961	Vogue: 4173
			1963	Vogue Mk II: 4174
6	84.0	135.2	1964	Chamois: 4175
			1958	Gazelle IIA Convertible: 4171
7	83.3	134.0	1953	Roadster: 4167
8	80.0	128.7	1964	Gazelle Series V: 4176
9	79.5	127.9	1953	SM1500 Saloon: 4168
10	78.0	125.5	1969	Chamois: 4181
11	76.0	122.3	1955	Hunter: 4170
12	75.6	121.6	1935	Le Mans Special Speed Model: 4161
13	75.0	120.7	1954	SM Roadster: 4169
			1952	SM Roadster: 4165
			1952	SM1500 Saloon: 4166
14	72.0	115.8	1949	SM1500 Saloon: 4164
15	70.0	112.6	1949	9 Roadster: 4163
16	66.1	106.4	1933	9 Sports: 4160
17	62.5	100.6	1940	Super 10 Saloon: 4162
18	60.8	97.8	1932	14/6 Saloon: 4159

Skoda

1	92.0	148.0	1989	136 Rapide Coupe: 4189
2	88.0	141.6	1986	Estelle 120 LSE: 4188
3	86.0	138.4	1977	120L: 4187
			1972	S110LS: 4186
4	83.0	133.5	1961	Felicia: 4183
5	80.0	128.7	1970	S100L: 4185
6	76.0	122.3	1965	1000MB: 4184
			1960	Octavia: 4182

Squire

1	105.0	168.9	1935	X101: 4190

Standard

1	94.0	151.2	1962	Ensign de Luxe Estate: 4213
2	90.0	144.8	1956	Vanguard Sportsman: 4205
3	85.0	136.8	1961	Vanguard: 4212
4	82.6	132.9	1958	Vanguard III Automatic: 4211
5	81.5	131.1	1952	Vanguard: 4199
			1957	Vanguard III: 4206
6	81.0	130.3	1953	Vanguard Phase II: 4202
7	80.0	128.7	1953	Vanguard Estate: 4201
			1956	Vanguard III: 4204
8	79.0	127.1	1958	Ensign: 4208
9	78.0	125.5	1948	Vanguard: 4198
10	76.9	123.7	1938	Flying 20: 4195
11	75.0	120.7	1933	Avon Coupe: 4193
12	73.7	118.6	1933	Avon 16 Open Four-Seater: 4192
13	72.0	115.8	1947	12 Saloon: 4196
14	67.0	107.8	1955	10: 4203
			1958	Pennant: 4209
15	65.5	105.4	1958	Super 10: 4210
16	65.0	104.6	1958	8: 4207
17	63.8	102.7	1937	Flying 10: 4194
18	63.0	101.4	1953	8: 4200
19	61.6	99.1	1933	16 Special Saloon: 4191
20	61.0	98.1	1948	8: 4197

Studebaker

1	132.0	212.4	1964	Daytona R-4: 4238
2	121.0	194.7	1963	Regal Wagonaire Supercharged: 4237
3	120.0	193.1	1963	Avanti: 4236
4	117.0	188.3	1962	Avanti: 4233
5	115.0	185.0	1961	Hawk 4-speed: 4230
6	107.1	172.3	1953	Commander Supercharged: 4225
7	105.0	168.9	1961	Lark Cruiser: 4232
			1960	Lark V8: 4229
8	103.0	165.7	1962	Hawk Gran Turismo: 4234
9	100.0	160.9	1962	Lark Daytona: 4235
10	95.3	153.3	1953	Commander Coupe: 4224
11	94.0	151.2	1954	Commander Coupe: 4226
12	92.8	149.3	1951	Land Cruiser: 4223
13	91.0	146.4	1929	Double-twelve Open Tourer: 4214
14	90.0	144.8	1961	Lark 6: 4231
15	87.3	140.5	1935	President Saloon: 4219
16	82.0	131.9	1960	Lark 6: 4228
17	81.0	130.3	1936	De Luxe Saloon: 4220
18	80.0	128.7	1959	Lark 6: 4227
19	78.2	125.8	1937	Dictator de Luxe Saloon: 4221
20	77.5	124.7	1949	Champion: 4222
			1935	Dictator Saloon de Luxe: 4218
21	72.0	115.8	1931	President Limousine: 4217
22	70.3	113.1	1930	Commander Brougham: 4215
23	62.5	100.6	1930	Erskine Saloon: 4216

Stutz

1	90.0	144.8	1932	DV32 Sports Saloon: 4242
2	80.0	128.7	1928	Roadster: 4239
3	77.5	124.7	1931	Straight Eight Saloon: 4241
4	72.0	115.8	1929	36.4hp Saloon: 4240

Subaru

1	161.0	259.0	1989	Legacy FIA Record: 4274
2	143.0	230.1	1992	SVX: 4279
3	134.0	215.6	1991	Legacy 2.0 4Cam Turbo Estate: 4277
4	129.0	207.6	1991	Legacy Sports Sedan: 4278
5	121.0	194.7	1987	XT Turbo 4WD: 4268
6	120.0	193.1	1985	1.8 RX Turbo: 4259
			1985	4WD Turbo XT Coupe: 4261
			1985	XT Turbo Coupe: 4264
7	119.0	191.5	1990	Legacy 2.2 GX 4WD: 4276
8	116.0	186.6	1988	4WD Turbo Estate: 4269
9	115.0	185.0	1985	XT Coupe DL: 4263
			1989	XT6: 4275
10	114.0	183.4	1986	4WD 3-door Turbo Coupe: 4265
11	112.0	180.2	1985	Turbo 4WD Estate: 4262
12	105.0	168.9	1985	1.8 GTi: 4258
13	101.0	162.5	1978	1600 Coupe: 4252
			1985	4WD Turbo: 4260
14	96.0	154.5	1983	GL Turbo Traction Wagon: 4257
15	95.0	152.9	1982	GL: 4256
16	93.0	149.6	1973	1300 GL Coupe: 4247
			1978	DL: 4253
			1972	FF-1 1300: 4246
			1989	Justy GL II 5-door 4WD: 4273
17	91.0	146.4	1981	1800 4WD Estate: 4255
			1980	DL-5: 4254
			1987	Justy: 4267
18	88.0	141.6	1977	1600 4WD Estate: 4251
19	83.0	133.5	1976	4WD Station Wagon: 4250
			1969	Star: 4244
20	56.0	90.1	1969	360: 4243

Sunbeam

1	122.0	196.3	1967	Tiger II: 4307
2	118.0	189.9	1964	Tiger: 4301
			1965	Tiger 260: 4302
3	106.0	170.6	1968	Rapier: 4309
			1969	Rapier H120: 4312
4	105.8	170.2	1962	Harrington Le Mans: 4294
5	102.0	164.1	1975	Rapier: 4313
6	101.0	162.5	1959	Alpine: 4290
7	100.0	160.9	1961	Alpine Mk II: 4293
			1963	Alpine Series III: 4297
			1966	Alpine Series V: 4304
			1962	Le Mans: 4295
8	98.0	157.7	1963	Alpine GT: 4296
			1954	Alpine II: 4284
9	96.0	154.5	1954	Alpine: 4283
			1966	Alpine 1.7: 4303
10	95.0	152.9	1960	Alpine: 4292
			1955	Mk III: 4285
11	94.0	151.2	1969	Alpine GT: 4311
12	93.0	149.6	1959	Rapier III: 4291
13	92.0	148.0	1969	Alpine: 4310
			1964	Alpine GT Series IV Automatic: 4298
14	91.0	146.4	1958	Rapier Series II: 4289
15	90.0	144.8	1964	Alpine Series IV: 4299
			1968	Arrow Station Wagon: 4308
			1966	Imp Sport: 4305
16	89.0	143.2	1967	Stiletto: 4306
17	87.0	140.0	1958	Rapier: 4288
			1951	Talbot 90: 4282
18	85.7	137.9	1957	Rapier: 4287
19	85.0	136.8	1956	Rapier: 4286
20	76.0	122.3	1964	Imp: 4300
21	70.0	112.6	1929	Weymann Saloon: 4280
22	66.6	107.2	1935	20 Saloon: 4281

Sunbeam-Talbot

1	83.0	133.5	1953	90 Mk IIA: 4319
2	80.0	128.7	1939	2-litre Sports Tourer: 4314
			1948	90 Sports Saloon: 4317
3	74.0	119.1	1949	80 Saloon: 4318
4	72.0	115.8	1947	2-litre Sports Saloon: 4316
5	68.0	109.4	1947	10 Sports Saloon: 4315

Suzuki

1	116.0	186.6	1989	Swift 1.3 GTi: 4331
2	112.0	180.2	1986	Swift 1.3 GTi: 4326
3	105.0	168.9	1990	Swift GT: 4333
4	103.0	165.7	1989	Swift 1.3 GLX: 4330
			1985	Swift 1.3GS: 4324
5	102.0	164.1	1987	Swift 1.3 GLX: 4328
6	97.0	156.1	1987	Swift 1.3 GLX Executive: 4329
7	90.0	144.8	1989	Vitara JLX: 4332
8	84.0	135.2	1981	Alto FX: 4322
9	80.0	128.7	1986	Alto GLA: 4325
10	78.0	125.5	1983	Alto FX Automatic: 4323
			1980	SC 100: 4321
11	76.0	122.3	1987	SJ413V JX: 4327
12	48.0	77.2	1971	Brute: 4320

Swallow

1	101.0	162.5	1955	Doretti: 4334

Talbot

1	115.0	185.0	1938	Figoni et Falaschi: 4343
2	107.0	172.2	1981	Tagora 2.2GLS: 4345
3	98.0	157.7	1983	Horizon 1.9LD: 4348
			1981	Solara GLS: 4344
4	96.0	154.5	1982	Samba Cabriolet: 4346
5	95.0	152.9	1982	Samba GL: 4347
6	92.7	149.2	1936	3.5-litre Speed Saloon: 4340
7	89.1	143.4	1936	105 Airline Saloon: 4339
8	88.2	141.9	1933	105 Speed Model: 4336
9	84.9	136.6	1938	3-litre Saloon: 4342
10	73.7	118.6	1935	75 Drop-frame Sports Saloon: 4338
11	70.3	113.1	1934	75 Saloon: 4337
12	69.2	111.3	1938	10hp Drop-head Coupe: 4341
13	65.6	105.6	1932	65 Saloon: 4335

Tatra

1	57.6	92.7	1932	12hp Drop-head Coupe: 4349

Toyota

1	146.0	234.9	1989	Supra 3.0i Turbo: 4465
2	145.0	233.3	1990	MR2 Turbo: 4473
3	140.0	225.3	1989	Supra Turbo: 4466
			1988	Supra Turbo: 4460
4	139.0	223.7	1990	MR2 GT: 4472
5	138.0	222.0	1986	Supra 3.0i: 4443
6	137.0	220.4	1988	Celica GT4: 4455
7	135.0	217.2	1989	MR2 Supercharged: 4464
			1987	MR2 Supercharged: 4451

8	134.0	215.6	1990	Celica 2.0 GT: 4468
			1988	Celica All-Trac Turbo: 4454
9	133.0	214.0	1986	Celica 2.0GT: 4438
			1988	Supra: 4459
			1986	Supra: 4442
10	132.0	212.4	1982	Celica Supra: 4415
11	130.0	209.2	1984	Supra: 4429
			1987	Supra: 4452
12	128.0	206.0	1967	2000GT: 4356
			1984	Celica 2.8i Supra: 4425
13	127.0	204.3	1987	Celica GT Cabriolet: 4447
			1983	Supra: 4421
			1985	Supra: 4436
14	126.0	202.7	1991	Camry 2.2 GL: 4476
15	125.0	201.1	1990	Celica All-Trac Turbo: 4469
			1990	Celica GTS: 4470
			1992	Paseo: 4483
16	124.0	199.5	1985	MR2: 4433
17	123.0	197.9	1986	Celica GTS: 4439
			1991	MR2: 4479
18	122.0	196.3	1986	MR2 T-Bar: 4441
19	121.0	194.7	1985	Corolla GT Hatchback: 4432
			1986	MR2: 4440
20	120.0	193.1	1975	Celica GT: 4387
			1991	Celica GT Convertible: 4477
			1984	Corolla GT Coupe: 4426
21	119.0	191.5	1989	Camry V6 GXi: 4461
22	118.0	189.9	1987	Camry 2.0 GLi: 4445
23	115.0	185.0	1989	Corolla GTS: 4463
			1984	Corolla GTS: 4427
24	113.0	181.8	1978	Celica: 4399
			1978	Celica 2000GT: 4400
			1978	Celica GT Liftback: 4401
			1983	Cressida: 4420
25	112.0	180.2	1987	Camry 2.0 GLi Estate: 4446
			1979	Celica Supra: 4403
26	111.0	178.6	1982	Celica: 4412
27	110.0	177.0	1989	Carina II 1.6 GL Liftback: 4462
			1982	Celica 2.0ST: 4413
			1980	Celica GT: 4406
			1985	Celica GTS: 4431
			1991	Previa: 4481
28	109.0	175.4	1988	Carina 1.6 GL: 4453
29	108.0	173.8	1971	Celica: 4367
30	107.0	172.2	1990	Previa LE: 4474
31	106.0	170.6	1981	Cressida DX Estate: 4410
32	105.0	168.9	1983	Celica GTS: 4417
			1976	Celica Liftback: 4395
			1987	Corolla FX-16 GTS: 4449
			1991	Tercel LE: 4482
33	104.0	167.3	1971	1900SL: 4366
			1983	Camry LE: 4416
			1984	Carina II 116GL: 4424
			1974	Celica GT: 4383
			1987	Corolla Executive: 4448
			1979	Corona Liftback: 4405
			1991	Landcruiser VX: 4478
34	103.0	165.7	1982	Celica GTA: 4414
35	102.0	164.1	1970	Corona Mk II 1900: 4364
			1972	Custom Crown Estate: 4376
36	101.0	162.5	1975	Crown Super: 4391
			1973	Mk II 2.6: 4382
37	100.0	160.9	1979	Corona 5-door: 4404
			1981	Cressida: 4409
			1969	Crown Toyoglide: 4362
38	99.0	159.3	1983	Corolla SR5 Hardtop: 4419
			1983	Tercel GL: 4423
39	98.0	157.7	1983	Corolla GL: 4418
			1980	Corolla Sport Coupe: 4407
			1975	Corolla SR5: 4390
			1971	Corona de Luxe: 4371
			1970	Corona Mk II: 4363
40	97.0	156.1	1976	Carina: 4394
			1973	Celica: 4377
			1988	Corolla 1.3 GL: 4456
			1971	Corolla 1200SL: 4369
			1988	Corolla 4WD Estate: 4457
			1984	Corolla LE: 4428
			1974	Corona 2000 Mk II Automatic: 4384
			1977	Corona Cressida: 4398
41	96.0	154.5	1974	Corona SR: 4385
			1973	Mk II: 4381
42	95.0	152.9	1971	Corolla 1600: 4370
43	94.0	151.2	1972	Carina: 4374
			1975	Pickup SR5: 4392
			1985	Tercel 4WD Estate: 4437
44	93.0	149.6	1976	Corolla Liftback: 4396
			1978	Cressida: 4402
			1970	Crown: 4365
			1981	Starlet: 4411
			1984	Van LE: 4430
45	92.0	148.0	1964	1900: 4352
			1966	Crown Custom: 4355
46	91.0	146.4	1980	Corolla Tercel SR5: 4408
			1968	Corona: 4361
			1990	Starlet GL: 4475
47	90.0	144.8	1975	Corolla 30: 4389
			1966	Corona 1900: 4354
			1967	Corona Coupe: 4357
			1972	Crown 2600: 4375
			1985	Space Cruiser: 4434
48	89.0	143.2	1971	Corolla: 4368
49	88.0	141.6	1976	1000: 4393
			1985	Starlet 1.0GL: 4435
50	87.0	140.0	1966	Corona: 4353
			1987	Landcruiser: 4450
51	86.0	138.4	1968	Corolla de Luxe: 4360
			1973	Corolla SR5: 4379
52	85.0	136.8	1977	Corolla 1200: 4397
			1983	Tercel 4WD Wagon: 4422
53	83.0	133.5	1968	Corolla: 4359
54	82.0	131.9	1971	Land Cruiser: 4372
			1971	Land Cruiser Wagon: 4373
55	81.0	130.3	1988	Landcruiser II TD: 4458
56	80.3	129.2	1960	Toyopet Tiara: 4351
57	77.0	123.9	1967	Land Cruiser: 4358
58	72.0	115.8	1958	Toyopet Crown de Luxe: 4350

Tracta

1	71.4	114.9	1930	Sports Two-seater: 4484

Treser

1	130.0	209.2	1989	T1: 4485

Trihawk

1	94.0	151.2	1982	304: 4486

Triumph

1	150.0	241.4	1980	TR8 Group 44: 4578
2	132.0	212.4	1977	TR7 Tullius: 4572
3	121.0	194.7	1968	TR5 PI: 4536
			1969	TR6: 4541
4	120.0	193.1	1980	TR8: 4577
5	117.0	188.3	1975	Dolomite Sprint: 4565
			1970	Stag: 4544
6	113.0	181.8	1971	Stag Automatic: 4551
7	112.0	180.2	1971	GT6 Mk III: 4547
			1971	Stag: 4550
8	111.0	178.6	1965	TR4A IRS: 4525
9	110.0	177.0	1977	TR7: 4571
			1976	TR7: 4570
			1979	TR7: 4575
10	109.0	175.4	1969	GT6: 4539
			1970	TR6: 4546
			1982	TR7 Convertible: 4581
11	108.0	173.8	1975	2500S: 4563
			1974	2500TC: 4560
			1967	GT6: 4530
			1975	TR7: 4567
12	107.0	172.2	1969	2.5PI: 4537
			1972	2.5PI Mk II: 4552
			1969	GT6 Mk II: 4540
			1955	TR2 Hardtop: 4502
			1968	TR250: 4535
			1965	TR4A: 4524
			1980	TR8 Libra Rally: 4579
13	106.0	170.6	1957	TR3: 4505
			1973	TR6: 4559
14	105.0	168.9	1954	TR2 Sports: 4501
15	104.7	168.5	1956	TR3: 4503
16	104.0	167.3	1973	GT6: 4556
			1962	TR4: 4516
17	103.0	165.7	1972	Dolomite: 4553
			1954	TR2: 4500
			1957	TR2 Hardtop: 4504
18	102.0	164.1	1975	Dolomite: 4564
			1969	Vitesse 2-litre Mk II: 4542
19	101.0	162.5	1975	Spitfire 1500: 4566
			1964	TR4: 4521
20	100.0	160.9	1968	Spitfire: 4534
			1967	Spitfire Mk III: 4532
21	99.0	159.3	1979	Dolomite 1850HL: 4573
22	98.0	157.7	1969	2000 Mk II: 4538
23	97.0	156.1	1973	Dolomite Automatic: 4555
24	95.0	152.9	1976	Dolomite 1500HL: 4568
25	94.0	151.2	1964	2000: 4520
			1966	2000 Estate Car: 4528
			1974	Spitfire: 4561
			1973	Spitfire 1500: 4558
			1962	Spitfire 4: 4514
			1966	Spitfire Mk II: 4529
26	93.0	149.6	1973	1500TC: 4554
			1965	2000: 4522
			1971	Spitfire 4: 4548
27	92.0	148.0	1981	Acclaim HL: 4580
			1965	Spitfire Mk II: 4523
28	91.0	146.4	1965	Vitesse Convertible: 4526
29	90.0	144.8	1980	Spitfire: 4576
			1963	Spitfire 4: 4518
			1974	Toledo: 4562
30	89.0	143.2	1979	Spitfire: 4574

31	88.0	141.6	1970	1500: 4543
			1963	Vitesse 6: 4519
32	86.0	138.4	1966	1300: 4527
			1973	Spitfire: 4557
			1976	Spitfire: 4569
			1971	Spitfire Mk IV: 4549
			1970	Toledo: 4545
33	85.0	136.8	1968	Herald 13/60 Convertible: 4533
34	83.3	134.0	1935	2-litre Southern Cross: 4490
35	82.0	131.9	1962	Sports 6: 4515
36	81.0	130.3	1939	2-litre Dolomite: 4495
37	80.0	128.7	1947	1800 Roadster: 4496
			1967	Herald 1200: 4531
			1960	Herald Coupe: 4510
			1959	Herald Coupe: 4507
38	79.0	127.1	1960	Herald Convertible: 4509
39	78.2	125.8	1936	Gloria 6 Vitesse: 4492
			1936	Vitesse: 4493
40	78.0	125.5	1963	Herald 12/50: 4517
41	77.0	123.9	1949	Roadster: 4499
42	76.0	122.3	1961	Herald 1200: 4511
43	75.0	120.7	1947	1800 Saloon: 4497
			1949	2000 Saloon: 4498
			1934	Gloria 6 Vitesse: 4489
44	74.5	119.9	1962	Herald 1200 Estate: 4513
45	72.8	117.1	1958	Station Wagon: 4506
46	72.5	116.7	1936	14/60 Dolomite Saloon: 4491
47	72.0	115.8	1962	Herald: 4512
48	71.5	115.0	1959	Herald Saloon: 4508
49	69.7	112.1	1937	Gloria 12: 4494
50	67.6	108.8	1930	Supercharged 7: 4488
51	52.9	85.1	1930	Super 7 Saloon: 4487

Turner

1	104.0	167.3	1960	Turner-Climax: 4582
2	80.0	128.7	1961	Sports: 4583

TVR

1	165.0	265.5	1989	420 SEAC: 4601
2	150.0	241.4	1991	V8 S: 4603
3	144.0	231.7	1987	390 SE: 4599
4	140.0	225.3	1979	Convertible Turbo: 4593
			1989	S Convertible: 4602
5	138.0	222.0	1985	350i Series II: 4598
6	130.0	209.2	1987	S Convertible: 4600
7	126.0	202.7	1981	Tasmin: 4596
8	125.0	201.1	1980	3000S Roadster: 4595
			1979	Taimar Roadster: 4594
9	124.0	199.5	1974	3000M: 4589
10	119.0	191.5	1977	Taimar: 4592
			1970	Tuscan: 4586
11	111.0	178.6	1973	Vixen 2500M: 4588
			1969	Vixen S2: 4585
12	109.0	175.4	1977	2500M: 4591
13	108.0	173.8	1983	Tasmin Convertible: 4597
14	106.0	170.6	1976	1600M: 4590
15	101.0	162.5	1961	Grantura: 4584
16	100.0	160.9	1970	Vixen: 4587

Vanden Plas

1	107.5	173.0	1974	Princess R: 4608
2	106.0	170.6	1963	Princess 3-litre Automatic: 4605
3	98.0	157.7	1960	Princess: 4604
4	91.0	146.4	1974	1500: 4607
5	86.0	138.4	1965	Princess 1100: 4606

Vauxhall

1	148.0	238.1	1990	Carlton GSi 3000 24v: 4724
2	140.0	225.3	1991	Senator 3.0i 24v: 4731
3	139.0	223.7	1990	Calibra 2.0i 16v: 4722
4	135.0	217.2	1987	Carlton 3000 GSi: 4708
5	134.0	215.6	1990	Cavalier GSi 2000 16v: 4725
6	132.0	212.4	1991	Calibra 4x4: 4729
			1990	Carlton 3.0i CDX Estate: 4723
			1989	Senator 3.0i CD: 4721
7	129.0	207.6	1990	Cavalier GSi 2000 16v 4x4: 4726
8	128.0	206.0	1991	Calibra 2.0i: 4728
			1989	Senator 2.5i: 4720
9	126.0	202.7	1989	Cavalier SRi: 4719
			1987	Senator 3.0i CD: 4711
10	125.0	201.1	1987	Astra GTE 2.0i: 4706
			1985	Senator 3.0i CD: 4702
11	124.0	199.5	1984	Astra GTE: 4698
			1988	Cavalier 4x4: 4714
12	123.0	197.9	1986	Carlton CD 2.0i: 4704
13	122.0	196.3	1988	Carlton L 1.8i: 4712
14	120.0	193.1	1986	Belmont 1.8 GLSi: 4703
15	119.0	191.5	1974	Firenza: 4672
			1988	Nova GTE: 4715
16	118.0	189.9	1983	Astra GTE: 4694
17	117.0	188.3	1987	Cavalier SRi 130 4-door: 4710
			1977	Chevette 2300 HS: 4688
18	116.0	186.6	1983	Carlton 2.0 GL: 4695
			1983	Cavalier CD: 4696
			1985	Cavalier SRi: 4701
			1979	Royale Coupe: 4689
19	115.0	185.0	1987	Cavalier 2.0i CD: 4709
20	112.0	180.2	1987	Belmont 1.6 GL: 4707
			1978	Cavalier 2000 GLS: 4687
21	111.0	178.6	1978	Carlton: 4686
			1989	Cavalier 1.6L: 4718
			1992	Cavalier 1.7 GL TD: 4733
22	110.0	177.0	1976	Cavalier GL Coupe: 4680
23	108.0	173.8	1992	1.4i GLS: 4732
			1982	Astra 1600 GL: 4691
			1981	Cavalier 1.6S GL: 4690
24	107.0	172.2	1989	Cavalier 1.4L: 4717
			1972	Ventora: 4666
			1970	Ventora II: 4661
25	105.0	168.9	1985	Astra 1.3 GL: 4699
			1985	Astra 1.6 SR: 4700
			1988	Carlton L 2.3D: 4713
			1982	Cavalier GLS: 4692
26	104.0	167.3	1972	Firenza Sport SL: 4665
			1968	Ventora: 4656
			1974	VX4/90: 4675
27	103.0	165.7	1967	Cresta Estate: 4653
			1977	Magnum 1800: 4684
			1974	Magnum 2300: 4673
28	102.0	164.1	1965	Cresta de Luxe Powerglide: 4646
			1986	Nova 1.3 GL 5-door: 4705
			1990	Nova 1.5TD Merit: 4727
			1965	Velox: 4647
			1970	Viva GT: 4662
			1968	Viva GT: 4658
			1977	VX2300 Estate: 4685
			1972	VX4/90: 4670
29	101.0	162.5	1976	VX1800: 4682
30	100.0	160.9	1976	Blydenstein Chevette 1500: 4678
			1976	Cavalier 1600 GL: 4679
			1972	Victor 2300 SL: 4667
			1972	Viva 1800: 4668
31	99.0	159.3	1971	Firenza: 4663
32	98.0	157.7	1983	Nova 1.2L: 4697
			1967	Victor 2000: 4655
			1966	Viscount Automatic: 4651
33	97.0	156.1	1960	Cresta Overdrive: 4636
34	96.0	154.5	1989	Astra 1.7 DL: 4716
			1965	VX4/90: 4650
35	94.0	151.2	1975	Magnum 1800: 4677
			1991	Nova 1.2 Luxe: 4730
			1964	VX4/90: 4645
36	93.0	149.6	1982	Cavalier LD: 4693
			1963	Cresta Series PB: 4641
			1973	Victor Estate: 4671
37	92.0	148.0	1977	Cavalier 1300L: 4683
			1960	Velox III: 4637
38	91.5	147.2	1959	Friary Estate Car: 4633
39	91.0	146.4	1975	Chevette L: 4676
			1976	Chevette L: 4681
40	90.0	144.8	1960	Cresta: 4635
			1958	Cresta: 4630
			1969	Victor: 4660
			1968	Victor 2000 Estate Automatic: 4657
41	88.0	141.6	1974	Viva 1256 DL: 4674
			1962	VX4/90: 4640
42	87.0	140.0	1964	Victor Estate: 4644
			1972	Viva HC Estate: 4669
43	86.0	138.4	1952	Velox: 4625
44	85.5	137.6	1965	Victor 101 Estate: 4648
45	85.1	137.0	1992	Frontera 2.3 TD Estate: 4734
46	83.5	134.4	1955	Cresta: 4628
47	83.0	133.5	1967	Victor 101 de Luxe: 4654
48	82.0	131.9	1954	Velox: 4627
			1966	Viva de Luxe: 4652
			1965	Viva SL90: 4649
			1968	Viva SL90 Estate: 4659
49	81.0	130.3	1938	25 Saloon: 4617
			1971	Viva de Luxe: 4664
50	80.5	129.5	1963	Viva de Luxe: 4642
51	80.0	128.7	1959	Victor de Luxe: 4634
52	78.5	126.3	1951	Velox: 4624
53	78.0	125.5	1961	Victor Estate: 4638
54	77.0	123.9	1962	Victor Super: 4639
55	76.0	122.3	1948	Velox: 4621
56	75.2	121.0	1958	Victor: 4631
57	75.0	120.7	1950	Velox: 4623
58	73.0	117.5	1964	Bedford Beagle: 4643
			1958	Victor Estate: 4632
59	71.4	114.9	1935	27 Saloon: 4612
60	71.0	114.2	1948	14: 4620
			1955	Wyvern: 4629
			1952	Wyvern: 4626
61	69.7	112.1	1934	20 Saloon: 4611
62	68.1	109.6	1937	14 de Luxe: 4614
63	67.1	108.0	1938	12/4 de Luxe Saloon: 4616
64	65.0	104.6	1947	12 Saloon: 4619
			1929	20/60 Limousine: 4609
65	63.3	101.8	1938	10 Saloon de Luxe: 4615
			1940	12 Saloon: 4618
66	62.0	99.8	1949	Wyvern: 4622

67	61.2	98.5	1931	Cadet Saloon: 4610
68	60.4	97.2	1937	10/4 de Luxe Saloon: 4613

Vector

1	218.0	350.8	1991	W8 Twin Turbo: 4736
2	200.0	321.8	1990	W2: 4735

Volga

1	79.5	127.9	1960	M21K: 4737

Volkswagen

1	140.0	225.3	1989	Corrado: 4874
2	139.0	223.7	1991	Corrado G60: 4882
3	137.0	220.4	1990	Corrado G60: 4879
4	132.0	212.4	1989	Corrado 16v: 4875
5	131.0	210.8	1985	Scirocco 16v: 4853
6	130.0	209.2	1987	Jetta GTi 16v: 4864
7	129.0	207.6	1989	Passat GT 16v: 4878
			1981	Scirocco GT-3 Davey: 4830
8	125.0	201.1	1986	Golf GTi 16v: 4856
			1991	Jetta GLi 16v: 4885
			1990	Passat GL: 4881
			1971	Porsche 914/b: 4785
			1988	Scirocco 16v: 4872
			1986	Scirocco 16v: 4859
9	122.0	196.3	1991	GTi 16v: 4884
			1987	GTi 16v: 4863
			1988	GTi 16v: 4866
			1988	Passat GT: 4869
			1985	Scirocco GTX: 4854
10	121.0	194.7	1992	Golf GTi: 4890
			1988	Jetta GLi 16v: 4867
			1983	Scirocco GTi: 4841
11	120.0	193.1	1991	Polo G40: 4887
			1986	Scirocco GTX 16v: 4860
12	119.0	191.5	1986	Jetta GT: 4857
13	116.0	186.6	1982	Golf GTi 1800: 4832
			1982	Santana GX5: 4836
14	115.0	185.0	1985	Jetta GLi: 4851
			1979	Scirocco GLi: 4816
			1977	Scirocco GTi: 4811
15	113.0	181.8	1984	Jetta GLX: 4844
			1981	Passat GL 5S Estate: 4826
			1986	Quantum Synchro Wagon: 4858
16	112.0	180.2	1984	Jetta GLi: 4843
17	110.0	177.0	1977	Golf GTi: 4806
			1982	Scirocco GL: 4837
18	109.0	175.4	1985	Scirocco: 4852
			1984	Scirocco: 4846
			1981	Scirocco S: 4831
19	108.0	173.8	1989	Jetta Syncro: 4877
			1980	Scirocco: 4822
20	107.0	172.2	1985	Golf: 4849
			1992	Golf 1.8 GL: 4889
			1985	Golf GTi: 4850
			1983	Rabbit GTi: 4839
			1976	Scirocco TS: 4804
21	106.0	170.6	1987	Golf Cabriolet Clipper: 4862
22	105.0	168.9	1983	Quantum GL5: 4838
			1974	Scirocco TS: 4797
23	104.0	167.3	1988	Jetta Turbo Diesel: 4868
			1981	Passat CL Formel E: 4825
			1984	Passat CL Turbo Diesel Estate: 4845
			1977	Passat GLS: 4807
			1987	Passat GT 5-door: 4865
			1991	Polo GT Coupe: 4888
			1970	Porsche 914: 4782
			1979	Scirocco: 4815
			1983	Scirocco: 4840
24	103.0	165.7	1990	Passat CL TD Estate: 4880
			1982	Quantum: 4835
25	102.0	164.1	1975	Scirocco: 4802
			1977	Scirocco Fi: 4810
			1979	Scirocco GLS: 4817
26	101.0	162.5	1980	Jetta GLS: 4820
			1973	Passat LS: 4790
27	100.0	160.9	1974	Dasher: 4796
			1987	Fox GL: 4861
			1978	Golf GLS: 4813
			1980	Jetta: 4819
28	99.0	159.3	1970	411 LE Variant: 4781
			1976	Golf 1600 LS: 4803
			1989	Golf CL Catalyst: 4876
			1991	Polo 1.3 CL Coupe: 4886
29	97.0	156.1	1973	SP-2: 4791
30	96.0	154.5	1977	Dasher: 4805
31	95.0	152.9	1981	Rabbit Convertible: 4828
32	94.0	151.2	1980	Dasher Diesel: 4818
33	93.0	149.6	1989	Caravelle Carat Automatic: 4873
			1972	K70: 4788
34	92.0	148.0	1975	Golf 1100L: 4799
			1973	Karmann-Ghia: 4789
35	91.0	146.4	1982	Polo C Formel E: 4834
36	90.0	144.8	1981	Golf 1300 LS: 4824
			1977	Rabbit Diesel: 4809
37	89.0	143.2	1988	Polo C Saloon: 4870
38	88.0	141.6	1980	Vanagon: 4823
			1983	Vanagon Wasserboxer: 4842
39	87.0	140.0	1968	411 L: 4778
			1963	Karmann-Ghia 1500: 4763
			1977	Polo LS: 4808
40	86.5	139.2	1957	Karmann-Ghia Okrasa: 4747
41	86.0	138.4	1964	1500S: 4764
			1968	1600 TL Automatic: 4777
			1968	Derby LS: 4779
			1982	Polo C: 4833
42	85.0	136.8	1968	1600 Squareback: 4776
			1966	1600 TL: 4771
			1978	Golf LD: 4814
43	84.0	135.2	1966	1500: 4769
			1971	411: 4784
			1975	Polo: 4800
44	83.8	134.8	1957	Sedan Judson: 4748
45	83.0	133.5	1978	Beetle Convertible: 4812
46	82.4	132.6	1962	1500: 4759
47	82.0	131.9	1961	1500: 4753
			1967	1500: 4772
			1963	1500 Estate: 4762
			1966	1600 Fastback: 4770
			1969	1600 Squareback: 4780
			1986	Caravelle Syncro: 4855
			1970	Super Beetle: 4783
48	81.0	130.3	1973	Sports Bug: 4792
49	80.0	128.7	1968	1500 Semi-automatic: 4775
			1962	Sedan EMPI: 4761
50	79.0	127.1	1966	1300: 4767
			1981	Rabbit Diesel: 4829
			1971	Super Beetle: 4786
51	78.0	125.5	1967	Beetle 1500: 4773
			1961	Karmann Ghia: 4754
52	76.0	122.3	1966	1300 de Luxe: 4768
			1956	Karmann-Ghia: 4744
53	75.0	120.7	1965	1300: 4766
			1968	1500 Automatic: 4774
			1962	Karmann-Ghia: 4760
54	74.5	119.9	1955	Sedan Supercharged: 4743
55	74.0	119.1	1960	De Luxe: 4751
56	73.0	117.5	1962	1200 de Luxe: 4758
			1974	181: 4794
57	72.0	115.8	1965	1200: 4765
58	71.5	115.0	1960	Sedan: 4752
59	71.4	114.9	1961	Sedan: 4755
60	70.8	113.9	1958	Alken-VW: 4749
61	70.2	113.0	1956	Sedan: 4746
62	69.0	111.0	1954	De Luxe: 4740
			1954	Sedan TC: 4742
63	66.1	106.4	1952	Sedan de Luxe: 4738
64	65.9	106.0	1953	Export Saloon: 4739
65	65.0	104.6	1958	De Luxe Saloon: 4750
			1954	Sedan: 4741
66	60.0	96.5	1961	Station Wagon: 4756
67	59.0	94.9	1956	Micro Bus: 4745

Volvo

1	135.0	217.2	1992	960: 4969
2	129.0	207.6	1991	960 24v: 4968
3	128.0	206.0	1987	740 Turbo: 4955
			1985	760 Turbo Estate: 4952
4	127.0	204.3	1989	440 Turbo: 4957
5	126.0	202.7	1990	460 Turbo: 4962
6	125.0	201.1	1989	740 GLE: 4958
			1989	740 Turbo: 4959
7	124.0	199.5	1991	940 SE: 4965
			1991	940 SE Turbo: 4966
8	122.0	196.3	1983	760 Turbo: 4947
9	121.0	194.7	1978	242 IPD: 4935
10	120.0	193.1	1973	164E: 4924
			1990	740 Turbo: 4964
			1982	760 GLE: 4944
11	119.0	191.5	1990	740 GLT 16v Estate: 4963
12	116.0	186.6	1972	1800 ES: 4921
13	115.0	185.0	1972	164E: 4920
			1970	1800E: 4916
			1985	740 Turbo Wagon: 4951
14	114.0	183.4	1984	740 GLT: 4948
			1987	760 GLE: 4956
			1982	GLT Turbo: 4945
15	113.0	181.8	1970	164 Automatic: 4915
16	112.0	180.2	1981	265 GLE: 4941
			1982	360 GLT: 4943
			1987	480 ES: 4954
17	111.0	178.6	1966	1800S: 4908
18	110.0	177.0	1969	164: 4914
19	109.0	175.4	1978	242 GT: 4934
			1978	262C: 4936
			1990	460 GLi: 4961
20	108.0	173.8	1975	264 GL: 4929
			1976	265 DL: 4931
			1984	GLT Wagon: 4950
21	107.0	172.2	1971	144 Grand Luxe: 4918
			1986	340 GLE: 4953

			1990	440 GLE: 4960
22	106.0	170.6	1971	142E: 4917
			1975	244 GL: 4928
23	105.0	168.9	1983	760 GLE: 4946
			1961	P1800: 4900
24	104.0	167.3	1971	145E Estate: 4919
			1962	P1800: 4903
25	103.0	165.7	1969	142S 2.0: 4912
			1967	144S: 4909
26	102.0	164.1	1974	142 GL: 4925
			1969	144S: 4913
			1982	240 GL: 4942
			1978	265 GLE Estate: 4937
27	100.0	160.9	1968	145S Wagon: 4911
28	99.5	160.1	1962	122: 4901
29	99.0	159.3	1968	145S Estate: 4910
30	98.0	157.7	1976	242 GL: 4930
			1977	244 DL: 4932
31	96.0	154.5	1978	343: 4938
32	95.0	152.9	1975	242 GL: 4927
33	94.0	151.2	1973	144 de Luxe: 4922
			1958	Amazon: 4897
34	93.8	150.9	1957	PV444L: 4895
35	93.5	150.4	1958	4-speed: 4896
36	93.0	149.6	1962	122S B18: 4902
37	92.0	148.0	1965	131: 4907
			1963	PV544: 4905
38	91.9	147.9	1959	122S: 4898
39	91.0	146.4	1957	PV444 Sports: 4894
40	90.0	144.8	1965	122 Automatic: 4906
			1961	122S: 4899
			1957	PV444: 4893
			1956	PV444 California: 4892
41	89.0	143.2	1963	121 Estate: 4904
42	88.0	141.6	1977	343: 4933
43	78.0	125.5	1954	444: 4891

Wartburg

1	87.0	140.0	1973	Knight: 4971
2	73.0	117.5	1967	Knight: 4970

Warwick

1	104.0	167.3	1961	GT: 4972

Westfield

1	140.0	225.3	1991	SEight: 4973

Wills Sainte Claire

1	73.0	117.5	1926	Six: 4974

Willys

1	88.0	141.6	1963	Wagoneer 4WD: 4976
2	81.3	130.8	1952	Aero Wing: 4975

Wolseley

1	105.0	168.9	1962	6/110: 4997
2	101.6	163.5	1959	6/99: 4995
3	100.0	160.9	1969	18/85 Mk II: 5001
4	94.5	152.1	1955	6/90: 4990
5	91.0	146.4	1967	18/85: 5000
6	90.0	144.8	1957	6/90: 4992
			1938	Drop-head Coupe: 4983
7	87.0	140.0	1965	1100: 4999
8	84.0	135.2	1952	6/80: 4988
9	81.0	130.3	1936	Super 6: 4980
10	80.0	128.7	1938	Super 6: 4984
11	79.2	127.4	1958	1500: 4993
12	79.0	127.1	1959	15/60: 4994
			1962	16/60 Automatic: 4996
13	78.5	126.3	1950	6/80: 4987
14	78.0	125.5	1957	15/50: 4991
			1963	Hornet: 4998
15	76.9	123.7	1937	Salon de Ville: 4981
16	75.0	120.7	1935	14 Hornet Special: 4979
17	72.0	115.8	1953	4/44: 4989
18	71.0	114.2	1949	4/50: 4986
19	70.5	113.4	1939	12/48: 4985
20	69.2	111.3	1938	14/56 Salon de Ville: 4982
21	62.2	100.1	1930	Hornet: 4977
22	60.0	96.5	1931	Viper Saloon: 4978

Yugo

1	99.0	159.3	1990	Sana 1.4: 5005
2	97.0	156.1	1988	65A GLX: 5004
3	90.0	144.8	1986	GV: 5002
4	83.0	133.5	1987	45 GLS: 5003

Zastava

1	92.0	148.0	1981	1300 ZLX-E: 5006

Zender

1	186.0	299.3	1990	Fact 4: 5008
2	175.0	281.6	1989	Vision 3: 5007

Acceleration

246 lists of makes ordered by make, acceleration time to 60mph/96.5kmh, year and model.

Abarth

	seconds	
1	15.8	1958 Zagato 750 GT: 1

AC

	seconds	
1	3.5	1989 Cobra 427 Modified 1965: 27
2	5.5	1965 Cobra: 25
3	6.2	1968 428 Fastback: 26
4	7.7	1962 Aceca-Buick: 23
5	7.8	1958 Bristol D-2: 20
6	8.2	1957 Ace Bristol: 16
7	9.0	1958 AC-Bristol Zagato: 17
8	9.1	1958 Bristol: 19
9	9.4	1958 Aceca-Bristol Coupe: 18
10	10.3	1960 Aceca-Bristol: 21
11	11.0	1956 Ace Roadster: 14
12	12.7	1961 Greyhound: 22
13	13.4	1956 Aceca: 15
14	13.5	1962 Greyhound: 24
15	18.1	1936 Ace: 8
16	18.3	1938 2-litre Sports: 10
17	19.4	1934 Ace Sports Four-seater: 4
18	20.6	1937 2-litre Fixed-head Coupe: 9
19	21.0	1953 2-litre: 13
20	21.8	1934 Greyhound Close-coupled Saloon: 5
21	22.6	1949 2-litre Saloon: 12
22	23.2	1936 2-litre Aero Saloon: 7
23	28.0	1935 Ace Drop-head Coupe: 6
24	28.8	1933 Ace Fixed-head Coupe: 3

Acura

	seconds	
1	5.7	1990 NSX: 36
2	7.9	1991 Legend LS: 37
3	8.0	1990 Legend Coupe: 35
		1989 Legend Coupe L: 33
4	8.1	1986 Legend: 29
5	9.1	1988 Integra LS Special Edition: 31
6	9.3	1987 Integra LS: 30
		1986 Integra RS: 28
7	9.4	1990 Integra GS: 34
8	9.7	1989 Integra LS: 32

Alfa Romeo

	seconds	
1	6.2	1985 GTV Callaway Twin Turbo: 122
2	7.0	1972 1750 GTV TransAm: 78
3	7.5	1988 75 Evoluzione: 135
		1987 Alfa 75 V6 3.0: 132
		1987 Milano Verde 3.0: 133
4	7.6	1990 164S: 143
		1972 Montreal: 82
5	7.8	1991 164 Cloverleaf: 145
6	7.9	1989 164 3.0 Lusso: 138
		1989 Milano 3.0: 140
7	8.0	1973 Montreal: 87
8	8.2	1986 GTV6: 126
9	8.3	1991 164L: 146
10	8.6	1973 Alfetta: 85
11	8.8	1981 GTV6: 109
12	8.9	1990 33 Boxer 16v: 144
		1986 Alfa 75 2.5 Green Cloverleaf: 125
		1976 Alfetta GTV: 93
13	9.0	1989 164 Automatic: 139
		1985 Alfa 90 2.5 Gold Cloverleaf: 118
		1986 Milano Platinum: 127
14	9.1	1987 33 1.7 Veloce: 129
		1984 GTV6: 114
15	9.2	1972 2000 GTV: 79
16	9.3	1987 Alfa 75 2.0i Twin Spark: 131
17	9.4	1933 2.3 Mille Miglia: 42
		1975 Alfetta GT: 90
18	9.5	1990 164 Twin Spark Lusso: 142
		1987 Alfa 33 1.7 Sportwagon Veloce: 130
		1988 Sprint 1.7 Cloverleaf: 137
19	9.6	1972 2000 GTV Injection: 80
20	9.8	1988 75 2.5 Auto: 134
		1984 Alfetta Gold Cloverleaf: 113
		1976 Spider Veloce 2000: 94
21	9.9	1969 1750 Spider: 74
		1971 1750 Spider Veloce: 76
		1973 2000: 83
22	10.0	1977 Spider: 99
23	10.1	1978 Alfetta 2.0: 101
		1978 Sport Sedan: 103
		1979 Sprint Veloce: 106
24	10.2	1985 Arna ti: 120
25	10.3	1986 Alfa 75 1.8: 124
26	10.4	1985 Graduate: 121
		1988 Spider: 136
27	10.5	1965 Giulia Veloce: 61
		1967 GTV: 69
28	10.6	1964 Sprint GT: 59
29	10.7	1980 Spider: 107
30	10.8	1968 1750 Berlina: 70

		1932 8C2300: 41
		1983 Alfa 33 1.5: 112
		1974 Alfetta: 89
		1989 Spider Quadrifoglio: 141
		1991 Spider Veloce: 147
		1984 Sprint Green Cloverleaf: 116
31	10.9	1985 Alfa 33 1.5 4x4 Estate: 117
		1979 Alfasud 1.5 Sprint Veloce: 104
32	11.0	1969 1750 Berlina: 73
		1972 1750 Berlina: 77
		1986 Spider Quadrifoglio: 128
		1959 Super Spider: 48
33	11.1	1962 2600: 55
		1966 Giulia Sprint GTV: 64
34	11.2	1968 1750 GT Veloce: 71
		1978 Alfasud Sprint 1.5: 100
		1961 Sprint Zagato: 54
35	11.3	1966 1600 Spider: 62
		1967 Duetto Spider: 67
36	11.5	1976 Alfetta 1.6: 91
		1968 Giulia Super: 72
37	11.6	1981 Alfasud 1.5: 108
38	11.7	1966 2600 Sprint: 63
		1986 Alfa 33 1.3 S: 123
		1984 Spider: 115
		1982 Spider Veloce: 110
39	11.8	1977 Alfasud 1300ti: 96
40	12.0	1976 Alfetta GT: 92
		1961 Giulia SS: 50
		1966 Sprint Speciale: 65
41	12.2	1978 Giulietta 1.6: 102
42	12.3	1961 Sprint Speciale: 53
43	12.9	1964 Giulia 1600 Spider: 58
44	13.0	1963 2600 Saloon: 56
45	13.1	1985 Arna 1.3SL: 119
		1963 Giulia ti: 57
46	13.2	1973 Giulia 1600 Sprint: 86
		1965 Giulia ti: 60
		1961 Giulietta Sprint: 51
		1969 GT 1300 Junior: 75
		1982 Spider Veloce 2000: 111
47	13.3	1979 Sport Sedan Automatic: 105
48	13.5	1972 Alfasud: 81
49	13.8	1977 Alfasud 1200ti: 95
50	13.9	1932 1750: 40
51	14.0	1974 Alfasud ti: 88
52	14.1	1958 1300 SV Spider: 46
53	14.2	1959 2000 Spider: 47
54	14.4	1977 Alfetta: 98
55	14.8	1956 Giulietta Spyder: 45
56	15.1	1973 Alfasud: 84
57	15.2	1960 2000: 49
58	15.3	1967 Giulia 1300 ti: 68
59	16.6	1977 Alfasud 5M: 97
60	17.1	1953 1900: 43
61	17.6	1961 Giulietta ti: 52

Allard

1	8.6	1954 K3 Convertible: 151
2	9.6	1959 GT Coupe: 153
3	11.6	1952 K2: 150
4	13.6	1948 V8: 149
5	16.9	1954 Palm Beach: 152
6	17.1	1948 Drop-head Coupe: 148

Alvis

1	12.5	1965 3-litre Series III: 168
		1965 TE21S: 169
2	13.1	1939 4.3-litre: 162
3	13.5	1957 3-litre Graber: 165
4	13.9	1959 3-litre TD21: 166
5	15.0	1938 Speed 25: 161
6	15.3	1937 4.3-litre Vanden Plas Saloon: 158
7	16.5	1953 3-litre: 164
8	16.6	1962 3-litre TD21 Series II Automatic: 167
9	19.4	1937 Crested Eagle 25: 159
10	19.8	1952 3-litre: 163
11	20.3	1938 12/70 Tourer: 160
12	22.0	1932 Speed 20 (72bhp): 155
13	36.4	1935 Firebird Saloon: 157

AMC

1	6.3	1969 Rambler Scrambler: 194
2	7.0	1968 Javelin: 191
3	7.2	1968 AMX: 189
		1968 AMX Automatic: 190
4	7.6	1970 Javelin 390: 198
5	7.9	1967 Javelin SST 343: 183
6	8.1	1968 Javelin SST: 192
7	8.2	1969 Ambassador SST Wagon: 193
8	8.9	1974 Matador X: 200
9	9.0	1967 Rambler Rebel SST: 187
10	9.1	1973 Hornet Hatchback: 199
11	9.3	1967 Marlin: 184
12	9.7	1974 Sportabout: 201
13	9.9	1966 Rogue V8: 182
14	10.1	1970 Hornet 4.9-litre: 197
15	10.6	1963 Ambassador 990: 175
16	10.9	1965 Rambler American 440-H: 180
17	11.6	1964 Rambler Classic 770: 178
18	12.0	1968 Ambassador: 188
19	12.3	1966 Ambassador DPL: 181
20	12.5	1970 Gremlin: 195
21	12.6	1964 Rambler Classic Typhoon: 179
22	13.7	1977 Pacer Wagon: 205
23	13.8	1967 Rambler American 220: 185
24	14.0	1962 Ambassador 400: 173
25	14.8	1976 Pacer: 203
26	15.3	1964 Rambler American 440: 177
27	15.4	1980 Eagle: 206
28	15.7	1977 Gremlin 2-litre: 204
		1970 Hornet 3.8-litre: 196
29	15.8	1975 Pacer: 202
		1961 Rambler Classic V8: 172
30	17.3	1967 Rambler Rebel 770: 186
31	18.2	1962 Rambler American: 174
32	18.5	1961 Rambler Classic Super 6: 171
33	18.7	1961 Rambler American: 170
34	19.8	1963 Rambler 660: 176

Apollo

1	8.4	1963 GT: 208

Armstrong Siddeley

1	14.2	1959 Star Sapphire: 220
2	15.5	1953 Sapphire Saloon: 219
3	19.8	1935 30 Special Sports Saloon: 213
4	26.9	1938 16 Saloon: 217
5	28.2	1935 17hp Sports Foursome: 212
6	29.7	1948 2-litre Saloon: 218
7	31.7	1937 25.3hp Town and Country Saloon: 215
8	33.2	1937 Six-light Saloon: 216
9	46.7	1936 17hp Touring Saloon: 214

Aston Martin

1	4.8	1988 Zagato: 257
2	5.4	1977 V8 Vantage: 248
3	5.6	1989 Zagato Volante: 260
4	6.0	1971 DBS V8: 244
		1989 Virage: 258
5	6.1	1962 DB4 GT Zagato: 240
6	6.2	1973 V8 Automatic: 245
7	6.5	1966 DB6: 242
8	6.6	1982 V8: 252
9	6.8	1991 Virage: 261
10	7.2	1978 V8: 249
11	7.4	1977 V8 Coupe: 247
12	7.5	1959 DB4: 237
		1975 V8: 246
13	7.8	1989 Volante: 259
14	8.1	1964 DB5: 241
15	8.2	1986 Volante: 256
16	8.4	1962 DB4: 239
17	8.5	1961 DB4: 238
18	8.6	1968 DBS: 243
19	8.8	1980 Lagonda: 250
20	8.9	1982 Lagonda: 251
		1984 Vantage: 255
		1983 Volante: 253
21	9.3	1958 Mk III: 236
22	10.1	1984 Lagonda: 254
23	12.4	1954 DB2: 234
24	12.6	1953 DB2/4 Saloon: 233
25	15.4	1939 2-litre: 231
26	19.6	1937 2-litre: 229
27	19.8	1938 Drop-head Coupe: 230
28	21.8	1934 1.5-litre Mk II: 226
29	24.6	1933 Le Mans: 225
30	25.6	1935 1.5-litre: 227
31	28.4	1936 Sports Saloon: 228

Auburn

1	15.0	1936 8-52 Speedster: 264
2	16.5	1929 8-120 Speedster: 262
3	20.4	1936 38hp Saloon: 263

Audi

1	4.8	1985 Quattro Sport: 309
2	5.9	1991 Coupe S2: 337
3	6.3	1988 Quattro: 323
		1990 Quattro 20v: 330
4	7.2	1991 200 Quattro: 334
5	7.3	1985 200 Avant Quattro: 304
		1981 Quattro: 289
6	7.4	1984 200 Quattro Turbo: 297
7	7.5	1991 V8 Quattro: 338
8	8.2	1982 Quattro: 292

		1985 Quattro: 308
9	8.3	1985 5000 S Turbo Quattro: 305
		1992 80 2.8E V6 Quattro: 339
10	8.4	1983 200 Turbo: 293
11	8.5	1989 90 Quattro 20v: 325
12	8.6	1986 Coupe Quattro: 316
13	8.7	1991 80 16v Sport: 335
14	8.8	1983 80 Quattro: 295
		1986 Coupe GT 2.2: 315
		1983 Coupe Injection: 296
15	8.9	1985 Coupe GT: 307
16	9.0	1985 90 Quattro: 306
		1990 90 Quattro: 329
		1990 V8 Quattro: 331
		1990 V8 Quattro Automatic: 332
17	9.3	1991 100 2.8E Auto: 333
		1985 100 Quattro: 303
		1989 90: 324
18	9.4	1981 5000 Turbo: 287
		1991 90 Quattro 20v: 336
19	9.5	1982 100 CD: 290
		1974 80 GT: 271
		1987 90 2.2E: 317
		1987 90 Quattro: 318
		1988 90 Quattro: 322
		1989 Coupe Quattro: 327
20	9.6	1976 80 GTE: 275
		1986 90: 313
		1986 Coupe GT: 314
21	9.7	1989 Coupe 2.2E: 326
22	9.8	1988 80 1.8E: 321
23	10.0	1988 100 Sport: 320
24	10.2	1984 4000 S Quattro: 298
25	10.5	1981 200 5E: 285
		1984 Coupe GT: 302
26	10.6	1988 100 Avant Quattro: 319
		1972 100 Coupe S: 267
		1984 5000 S Turbo: 300
		1990 80 2.0E: 328
27	10.7	1979 100 GL5S: 281
28	10.8	1984 80 GL: 301
29	10.9	1977 100 GLS: 277
30	11.1	1986 80 1.8S: 312
31	11.2	1984 5000 S Avant: 299
		1981 Coupe: 288
32	11.5	1980 4000: 283
33	11.6	1986 5000 S: 311
34	11.8	1977 100 5E: 276
		1971 100 LS Auto: 266
		1983 5000 S: 294
35	11.9	1975 100 GL Automatic: 272
36	12.1	1979 80 GLS: 282
37	12.2	1975 80 Estate: 273
38	12.6	1978 100 L Avant: 279
		1986 100 Turbo Diesel: 310
39	12.7	1973 Fox: 270
40	12.8	1982 80 Turbo Diesel: 291
		1977 Fox: 278
41	12.9	1981 4000 Automatic: 286
		1978 5000: 280
42	13.1	1975 Fox: 274
43	13.2	1973 80 LS: 269
44	13.6	1970 100 LS: 265
45	13.7	1973 100 LS: 268
46	20.5	1980 5000 S Diesel: 284

Austin

1	9.6	1983 Maestro 1600: 422
2	10.1	1985 Montego 2.0 HL: 424
3	10.9	1986 Montego 2.0 Vanden Plas EFI: 425
4	11.0	1974 Allegro HL: 409
5	11.4	1977 Allegro 1750 HL: 415
6	11.8	1989 Metro GTa: 427
7	11.9	1984 Montego 1.6L: 423
8	12.0	1983 Maestro 1.6 HLS: 421
9	13.0	1987 Metro 1.3L 3-door: 426
10	13.1	1972 2200: 404
11	13.2	1972 Maxi High Line: 405
12	13.5	1975 2200 HL: 411
13	14.2	1976 Princess 2200 HLS: 414
14	14.3	1982 Ambassador 2.0 HL: 420
15	14.6	1978 Princess II 2000 HL: 417
16	14.8	1968 3-litre Automatic: 396
17	15.0	1960 A99: 388
18	15.1	1960 A99 Automatic: 389
19	15.5	1973 Marina GT: 407
20	15.6	1969 1300 GT: 398
		1956 A105: 374
21	15.7	1970 3-litre: 401
22	15.8	1959 A99: 385
		1977 Maxi 1750: 416
		1970 Maxi 1750: 402
23	16.2	1971 1300 Mk III: 403
24	16.3	1968 1800 Mk II: 395
25	16.4	1969 1300 Super: 399
26	16.5	1975 Allegro 1300 Estate: 412
27	16.6	1969 Maxi: 400
28	16.7	1974 Vanden Plas 1500: 410
29	17.1	1964 1800: 394
30	17.3	1974 Allegro 1500 Special Automatic: 408
31	17.8	1959 A105 Vanden Plas: 383
32	18.0	1968 America: 397
33	18.1	1955 A90 Westminster: 373
34	18.3	1958 A105 Automatic: 378
35	18.4	1949 A90 Atlantic: 363
		1973 Allegro 1300 Super: 406
36	18.9	1981 Mini Metro: 419
37	19.1	1958 A95 Countryman: 382
38	19.4	1976 Allegro 1100: 413
		1981 Metro Automatic: 418
39	19.5	1952 Princess: 367
40	19.8	1957 A95 Westminster: 377
41	20.0	1949 A135 Princess: 361
42	20.6	1948 A125 Sheerline: 359
43	21.4	1962 A60 Cambridge: 393
44	22.9	1949 A70: 362
45	23.6	1959 A55 Cambridge Mk II: 384
46	23.9	1962 A40 Mk II: 392
47	25.5	1961 A55 Countryman: 390
48	26.0	1955 A50 Cambridge: 372
		1954 Princess: 371
49	29.3	1947 16 Saloon: 357
		1958 A55: 381
50	29.4	1951 A40: 364
51	29.6	1961 Seven 850: 391
52	31.0	1958 A35 4-door: 379
53	31.8	1957 A55: 376
54	33.9	1954 A40 Somerset Coupe: 370
55	35.4	1938 14: 355
56	35.6	1958 A40: 380
57	36.6	1952 A40 Somerset: 366
58	43.2	1960 A40 Countryman: 387
59	45.4	1936 20 Mayfair Limousine: 350

Austin-Healey

1	7.8	1955 100S: 430
2	9.6	1956 100M: 431
3	9.8	1965 3000 Mk III: 446
		1964 3000 Mk III: 445
4	10.3	1953 100: 428
5	10.4	1962 3000 Mk II: 443
		1958 Mille Miglia: 434
6	11.2	1958 100/6: 433
		1962 3000: 442
7	11.4	1959 3000: 436
8	11.5	1961 3000: 440
9	11.7	1954 100: 429
10	12.2	1957 100/6: 432
11	14.2	1960 Sebring Sprite: 438
12	14.7	1968 Sprite: 447
13	15.3	1960 Sprite Supercharged: 439
14	18.3	1963 Sprite 1100: 444
15	19.8	1961 Sprite Mk II: 441
16	20.9	1958 Sprite: 435
17	23.7	1959 Sprite Hardtop: 437

Auto Union

1	11.9	1969 100 LS: 454
2	12.8	1967 Audi Super 90: 453
3	16.5	1966 Audi: 452
4	21.7	1958 1000: 449
5	23.0	1959 1000: 450
6	35.7	1961 Universal: 451

Autokraft

1	5.0	1987 AC Cobra Mk IV: 456
2	5.2	1985 AC Cobra Mk IV: 455

Avanti

1	7.5	1969 II: 459
2	7.9	1963 R2: 457
3	8.4	1984 II: 460
4	8.8	1966 II: 458

Bentley

1	6.7	1990 Turbo R: 482
2	6.9	1985 Mulsanne Turbo: 480
3	7.0	1982 Mulsanne Turbo: 479
		1987 Turbo R: 481
4	7.1	1991 Turbo R: 483
5	9.4	1979 T2: 478
6	12.1	1960 S2 Continental: 477
7	12.9	1956 Continental Park Ward DH Coupe: 475
8	13.5	1952 Continental: 471
9	13.8	1954 Sports: 474
		1952 Sports Saloon: 473
10	14.2	1938 4.25-litre: 468
		1956 Series S: 476
11	15.2	1952 Mk VI: 472

12	15.5	1936 4.25-litre: 466
13	16.1	1939 4.5-litre: 469
14	17.1	1937 4.5-litre: 467
15	18.8	1934 Sedan: 465
16	25.8	1947 4.5-litre Mk VI Saloon: 470

Berkeley

1	17.2	1960 B95: 487
2	21.8	1958 Sports 4: 486
3	38.3	1957 Sports: 484

Bertone

1	5.0	1991 Emotion Lotus: 489

Bitter

1	7.6	1990 Type 3 Cabrio: 494
2	8.3	1986 SC: 493
3	9.2	1984 SC: 492

Bizzarini

1	6.4	1965 5300 Spyder: 495
		1966 GT America: 496

BMW

1	5.1	1991 535i Alpina B10 Bi-Turbo: 619
2	6.0	1990 735i Koenig: 611
		1989 M635 CSi: 607
3	6.1	1984 M635 CSi: 572
4	6.2	1980 M1: 556
5	6.3	1989 M5: 606
6	6.4	1991 M5: 622
		1985 M635 CSi Hardy & Beck: 577
7	6.5	1991 M3 Sport Evolution: 621
8	6.6	1989 M3 Evolution: 604
9	6.9	1985 327S Hardy & Beck: 574
		1990 750i Alpina B12: 613
		1988 750i L: 596
10	7.0	1978 333i Alpina: 548
11	7.1	1992 850i Manual: 625
		1987 M3: 590
		1989 M3: 603
12	7.2	1972 2002 TransAm: 528
		1991 850i: 620
		1988 M6: 597
13	7.3	1974 2002 Turbo: 534
		1973 3.0 CSL: 530
		1991 325i SE: 615
		1982 635 CSi: 561
		1990 750i: 612
14	7.4	1985 325i: 573
		1988 535i SE: 593
		1989 735i Alpina B11: 602
		1985 M535i: 576
15	7.5	1987 325i Cabriolet: 587
		1990 325i Convertible: 610
		1988 325i S: 591
		1989 325i S: 599
16	7.7	1989 535i: 600
		1987 750i L: 589
17	7.8	1983 735i: 567
18	7.9	1992 325i: 623
		1988 325i X: 592
		1986 535i: 582
		1989 Z1: 608
19	8.0	1971 3.0 CS: 524
		1971 3.0S: 525
		1983 320i: 564
		1979 732i: 553
20	8.1	1986 325i Convertible: 579
		1976 633 CSi: 540
21	8.2	1971 2002 Tii: 523
		1979 528i: 551
		1984 735i Automatic: 571
22	8.3	1971 2002: 522
		1978 323i: 547
		1983 533i: 566
		1989 M3 Hor Technologie: 605
23	8.4	1980 633 CSi: 555
		1984 633 CSi: 570
		1988 635 CSi: 594
24	8.5	1978 320i Alpina: 546
		1991 525i: 617
		1979 635 CSi: 552
		1986 635 CSi: 583
		1982 745i: 562
25	8.6	1989 535i Automatic: 601
		1978 733i: 550
26	8.7	1991 525i SE 24v: 618
		1981 528i: 558
		1978 528i: 549
27	8.8	1957 507: 500
28	8.9	1984 325E: 569
		1977 733i: 545
29	9.0	1986 325 ES: 578
		1977 528: 543
		1986 735i Automatic: 585
30	9.1	1985 732i: 575
		1986 735i: 584
31	9.2	1992 520i SE Touring: 624
32	9.3	1969 2500: 519
		1970 2800 CS: 521
		1987 318i 2-door: 586
		1990 318i S: 609
		1981 323i Hardy & Beck: 557
		1988 735i: 595
		1971 Bavaria: 526
33	9.5	1974 2002 Tii: 533
34	9.6	1991 520i: 616
35	9.7	1977 630 CSi: 544
36	9.8	1972 2002 Tii: 527
		1977 320: 541
37	9.9	1974 3.3L: 535
38	10.0	1966 2000 Ti: 511
		1969 2002: 518
		1973 3.0 CS: 529
39	10.1	1969 2000 Tilux: 517
		1989 316i 4-door: 598
40	10.2	1991 318i: 614
		1983 525E: 565
		1975 530i: 539
41	10.3	1982 528e: 560
42	10.5	1973 520i: 531
		1986 520i: 580
		1975 525: 538
		1987 730i SE: 588
43	10.6	1974 525: 536
44	10.7	1968 2000 CS: 515
		1967 2000 TiLux: 514
		1973 Bavaria: 532
45	10.9	1965 1800 Ti: 508
		1984 318i: 568
46	11.0	1986 524 TD: 581
47	11.1	1980 320i: 554
48	11.3	1966 2000 CS: 510
		1968 2002: 516
49	11.6	1967 1600-2: 513
		1983 318i: 563
50	11.7	1966 2000: 509
51	12.0	1977 320i: 542
52	12.1	1982 316: 559
53	12.5	1967 1600 Coupe: 512
54	13.3	1970 2002 Automatic: 520
55	13.7	1963 1800 Saloon: 506
56	14.1	1975 1602L: 537
57	15.0	1963 1500: 505
58	16.8	1956 501: 498
59	23.4	1962 700 Coupe: 504
60	28.0	1964 700 LS: 507
61	29.0	1960 700: 503

Bond

1	17.4	1966 875: 628
2	17.6	1964 Equipe GT: 626
3	20.0	1965 Equipe GT 4S: 627
4	23.2	1970 Bug: 629

Borgward

1	14.8	1960 2.3 Grosse: 634
2	16.0	1960 Isabella TS: 635
		1956 Isabella TS: 631
3	17.4	1960 Isabella TS Coupe: 636
4	17.5	1958 Isabella Coupe: 632
5	19.7	1958 Isabella TS: 633
6	22.4	1955 Isabella 1500: 630

Bricklin

1	9.9	1975 SV-1: 637

Bristol

1	9.9	1961 407: 640
2	17.4	1952 401: 639
3	19.1	1948 400: 638

British Salmson

1	19.4	1936 20.8hp Sports Two-seater: 644
2	27.2	1934 Closed-coupled Saloon: 642
3	31.0	1936 12hp Four-seater Tourer: 643
4	38.5	1937 14hp Saloon: 645

Bugatti

1	3.9	1991 EB110: 652
2	8.0	1926 50S: 648

3 17.3 1932 55: 651
4 20.2 1930 49: 649

Buick

1 6.0 1967 GS400: 679
2 6.1 1968 GS400: 681
3 6.5 1970 GS455 Stage 1: 687
4 6.8 1989 Reatta Turbo Buick Engineering: 697
5 7.4 1965 Riviera: 674
1965 Skylark Gran Sport: 676
6 7.7 1963 Riviera: 668
1964 Wildcat: 672
7 8.2 1966 Riviera Gran Sport: 677
8 8.4 1967 Wildcat: 680
9 8.5 1962 Invicta: 663
10 8.9 1988 Reatta: 695
1991 Reatta Convertible: 698
1962 Wildcat: 667
11 9.0 1969 Sportswagon: 685
12 9.2 1964 Electra 225: 669
1965 LeSabre 400: 673
13 9.3 1967 California GS: 678
14 9.5 1979 Riviera S-type: 692
15 9.9 1965 Skylark: 675
1969 Wildcat: 686
16 10.0 1969 Riviera: 683
1964 Skylark Sports Wagon: 670
17 10.2 1962 Skylark: 664
18 10.7 1968 Riviera: 682
1962 Skylark Automatic: 665
19 11.2 1988 Regal Custom: 696
1960 Special: 661
20 11.6 1969 Skylark: 684
21 11.9 1978 Century: 691
22 12.5 1986 Electra T-type: 694
23 12.6 1954 Roadmaster: 660
24 12.9 1961 Special: 662
25 13.2 1976 Opel by Isuzu: 689
26 14.1 1983 Century T-type: 693
27 14.2 1976 Skyhawk: 690
1975 Skylark: 688
28 14.8 1962 Special V6: 666
29 16.4 1936 Century Saloon: 658
30 16.9 1964 Special: 671
31 17.3 1938 Viceroy Saloon: 659
32 25.0 1935 Light Eight Viceroy Saloon: 657
33 26.8 1933 Straight Eight Saloon: 656

Cadillac

1 8.3 1990 Allante: 716
1991 Allante: 719
2 8.5 1990 Eldorado Touring Coupe: 718
1964 Sedan de Ville: 706
3 8.6 1991 Seville Touring Sedan: 720
4 9.2 1967 Eldorado: 708
5 9.3 1988 Allante: 715
6 9.4 1966 Calais: 707
7 9.5 1961 Coupe de Ville: 702
8 9.7 1964 Coupe de Ville: 705
9 9.9 1968 Coupe de Ville: 709
10 10.0 1990 Aurora: 717
1963 Park Avenue: 704
11 10.5 1985 Cimarron: 714
12 10.6 1959 Eldorado Convertible: 701
13 11.2 1961 Fleetwood: 703
14 13.3 1976 Seville: 710
15 15.7 1978 Seville Diesel: 711
16 15.9 1982 Cimarron: 713
17 18.8 1931 V16 Fleetwood Roadster: 700
18 20.0 1930 V16 "Madame X": 699
19 21.0 1981 Seville Diesel: 712

Carbodies

1 23.6 1989 Fairway 2.7 Silver: 721

Caterham

1 5.2 1990 7 HPC: 725
2 5.6 1985 1700 Super Sprint: 723
1991 Super 7: 726
3 6.2 1975 Super 7: 722
4 7.6 1985 7: 724

Checker

1 10.3 1969 Marathon: 728
2 13.9 1968 Marathon: 727

Chevrolet

1 3.4 1991 Corvette Lingenfelter: 951
2 3.9 1990 Corvette Callaway Sledgehammer: 941
3 4.0 1962 Bel Air 409 SS/S: 755
4 4.2 1991 Corvette ZR-1 SS: 955
5 4.4 1991 Corvette Callaway Speedster: 949
6 4.5 1989 Camaro IROC-Z Chevrolet Engineering: 929
1988 Corvette Bakeracing SCCA Escort: 917
7 4.6 1988 Corvette Callaway: 918
8 4.7 1976 Monza Mike Keyser: 874
9 4.8 1989 Camaro Gottlieb 1969: 926
10 4.9 1989 Corvette Callaway: 931
1991 Corvette Callaway: 948
1991 Corvette Callaway Twin Turbo: 950
1988 Corvette Morrison/Baker Nelson Ledges: 921
1991 Corvette ZR-1: 953
1989 Corvette ZR-1: 934
1991 Corvette ZR-1 Geiger: 954
1991 Corvette ZR-2: 956
11 5.0 1986 Corvette Callaway: 901
1963 Corvette Grand Sport Roadster: 776
12 5.1 1990 Corvette Callaway: 940
1989 Corvette Guldstrand Grand Sport 80: 932
13 5.2 1978 Camaro IROC: 877
1988 Corvette Guldstrand Grand Sport 80: 920
14 5.3 1962 Corvette Sebring: 767
15 5.5 1961 Corvette 315: 753
16 5.7 1957 Corvette: 739
1965 Corvette: 795
1965 Corvette 396: 796
1966 Corvette Convertible: 803
1957 Corvette Injection: 740
1970 Corvette LT-1: 845
1992 Corvette LT1: 959
1957 Corvette RPO 684/579E: 741
17 5.8 1970 Camaro Z/28 RS: 842
1986 Corvette: 900
1987 Corvette ASC Geneve: 909
1986 Corvette Z51: 902
18 5.9 1987 Corvette: 908
1962 Corvette: 766
1963 Corvette: 775
1961 Corvette 270: 752
1963 Corvette Sting Ray: 777
19 6.0 1985 Corvette: 897
1988 Corvette: 916
1988 Corvette Convertible: 919
1965 Corvette Sting Ray 396: 798
1988 Corvette Z51: 922
20 6.1 1969 Corvette 435hp: 829
21 6.2 1989 Corvette: 930
1990 Corvette Coupe: 943
1976 Corvette Greenwood: 870
22 6.3 1967 Camaro 427 Dana: 805
1990 Corvette Convertible: 942
1987 Corvette Convertible: 910
1965 Corvette Injection: 797
1990 Corvette L98: 944
1991 Corvette Rick Mears: 952
1956 Corvette Sebring: 738
1964 Corvette Sting Ray Injection: 788
23 6.4 1969 Corvette L46: 831
24 6.5 1970 Camaro Z/28: 841
1965 Chevelle Malibu 396: 792
1979 Corvette: 881
1968 Corvette Convertible: 818
1964 Corvette Sting Ray: 786
25 6.6 1987 Camaro IROC-Z: 906
1989 Camaro IROC-Z: 927
1988 Camaro IROC-Z 5.7: 913
1989 Camaro IROC-Z Automatic: 928
1990 Camaro Z/28: 938
1968 Chevelle SS396: 813
1961 Corvette: 750
1984 Corvette: 894
1959 Corvette: 743
1979 Corvette Automatic: 882
1969 Corvette L71/89: 834
1989 Corvette L98: 933
1963 Impala Super Sport 409: 779
26 6.7 1992 Camaro Z28: 958
27 6.8 1987 Camaro IROC-Z L98: 907
1969 Camaro SS 396: 824
1968 Corvette L88: 820
1969 Corvette L88: 835
1977 Corvette Sting Ray: 875
1968 El Camino: 821
28 6.9 1988 Camaro IROC-Z 5.0: 912
29 7.0 1970 Corvette 454: 844
1969 Corvette L71: 833
30 7.1 1983 Corvette: 891
31 7.2 1966 Chevy II Nova SS: 801
1969 Corvette LT-1: 836
1973 Corvette LT-1: 858
1963 Corvette Sting Ray Automatic: 778
32 7.3 1978 Camaro Z/28: 878
1962 Chevy II Corvette: 757
1956 Corvette: 737
1969 Corvette L68: 832
1962 Impala SS 409: 768
33 7.4 1968 Camaro Z/28: 811
1969 Camaro Z/28: 825

		1974 Corvette: 862
34	7.5	1972 Camaro Z/28: 857
35	7.6	1968 Camaro SS396: 810
		1969 Corvette L36: 830
36	7.7	1969 Caprice: 827
		1980 Corvette: 884
		1968 Corvette: 817
		1961 Corvette 230: 751
		1970 Monte Carlo: 847
37	7.8	1967 Camaro SS350: 807
		1969 Chevelle Malibu: 828
		1967 Corvette: 808
38	7.9	1984 Camaro Z/28: 893
39	8.0	1991 Baretta GTZ: 946
		1990 Beretta GTZ: 936
		1964 Corvette Sting Ray Automatic: 787
		1991 Lumina Z34: 957
40	8.1	1985 Camaro IROC-Z: 896
		1990 Cavalier Z24: 939
		1970 Chevelle SS396: 843
		1976 Corvette: 869
41	8.2	1988 Cavalier Z24 Convertible: 915
42	8.3	1987 Beretta GT: 905
		1966 Corvette: 802
43	8.4	1965 Caprice Custom 396: 790
		1969 Corvette Stingray: 837
		1969 Corvette ZQ3: 838
		1967 Impala SS427: 809
44	8.5	1986 Cavalier Z24: 898
45	8.6	1990 Beretta GT: 935
		1990 Camaro IROC-Z Convertible: 937
		1991 Camaro Z/28 Convertible: 947
		1968 Corvette Coupe: 819
		1973 Monte Carlo: 859
46	8.7	1964 Chevelle Super Sport: 782
		1968 Chevy II: 814
		1955 Corvette V8: 735
47	8.8	1970 Camaro: 840
48	8.9	1988 Nova Twin Cam: 923
49	9.0	1956 210: 736
		1989 Baretta GTU: 925
		1970 Impala: 846
		1969 Kingswood Estate Wagon: 839
50	9.1	1967 Camaro: 804
		1968 Chevelle Malibu: 812
		1964 El Camino: 789
51	9.2	1982 Corvette: 886
52	9.3	1988 Camaro: 911
		1962 Corvair Navarro: 764
		1968 Malibu 327: 823
		1970 Nova SS350: 848
53	9.5	1983 Camaro: 887
		1984 Camaro: 892
		1983 Camaro Z/28: 888
		1962 Impala Station Wagon: 769
54	9.6	1979 Citation X11: 880
55	9.7	1955 210 Coupe Club V8: 734
		1982 Camaro Z/28: 885
56	9.8	1972 Camaro Budget: 855
		1965 Impala SS: 799
57	9.9	1983 Citation X11 HO: 890
58	10.1	1976 Camaro: 867
59	10.3	1980 Citation: 883
		1975 Nova LN: 865
60	10.4	1976 Monza: 872
61	10.5	1972 Camaro Luxury: 856
62	10.6	1961 Impala: 754
63	10.7	1963 Biscayne V8: 771
		1986 Celebrity CL Eurosport: 899
64	10.8	1962 Corvair Spyder: 765
65	11.0	1954 Corvette: 733
		1953 Corvette: 732
66	11.4	1967 Camaro Six: 806
		1965 Corvair Corsa IECO: 793
		1968 Corvair Sport Coupe: 816
		1978 Malibu: 879
67	11.9	1964 Corvair Sprint: 785
68	12.3	1976 Cosworth Vega: 871
69	12.4	1974 Vega: 863
70	12.6	1990 Lumina APV: 945
71	12.7	1971 Beauville: 849
72	13.0	1962 Chevy II Six Manual: 761
		1986 Nova CL: 903
73	13.1	1983 Cavalier CS: 889
74	13.4	1964 Chevelle Malibu: 781
		1976 Monza 2+2 V8: 873
		1975 Monza 2+2 V8: 864
		1986 Sprint: 904
75	13.5	1973 Vega: 860
76	13.8	1968 Impala: 822
77	14.0	1962 Chevy II: 756
		1964 Corvair Monza: 784
78	14.2	1963 C-10 Fleetside Pickup: 772
		1964 Chevy II V8 Station Wagon: 783
		1971 Vega L11: 854
79	14.3	1964 Chevelle 300: 780
80	14.5	1978 Blazer: 876
		1962 Chevy II Six Automatic: 760
		1984 Sprint: 895
81	14.6	1988 Sprint: 924
		1973 Vega Station Wagon: 861
82	14.9	1971 Blazer: 850
		1971 Pickup Cheyenne Fleetside: 851
83	15.0	1963 Corvair Monza EMPI: 774
84	15.1	1965 Chevelle Malibu: 791
85	15.3	1963 Corvair Monza Convertible: 773
86	15.5	1966 Bel Air Six: 800
		1961 Corvair Monza 4-speed: 749
87	15.6	1968 Corvair Monza: 815
88	15.8	1975 Vega GT: 866
89	16.4	1960 Corvair 4-speed: 744
		1971 Vega 2300: 853
90	16.5	1971 Vega: 852
91	16.9	1976 Chevette Rally 1.6: 868
92	17.0	1963 Bel Air: 770
		1962 Chevy II Four Manual: 759
93	17.5	1960 Corvair Automatic: 745
		1965 Corvair Monza: 794
94	19.5	1959 Corvair: 742
95	19.7	1961 Corvair Monza: 748
96	20.0	1962 Chevy II Four Automatic: 758
97	20.4	1935 26.3hp Saloon de Luxe: 729
		1938 Master de Luxe Saloon: 731
98	20.6	1961 Corvair 700: 746
99	21.6	1962 Corvair Monza: 762
		1962 Corvair Monza Coupe: 763
100	22.6	1937 Master de Luxe Sports Sedan: 730
101	32.2	1961 Corvair Greenbrier: 747

Chrysler

1	6.9	1989 TC by Maserati: 1008
2	7.1	1970 300-H: 989
3	7.3	1988 Conquest TSi: 1007
4	7.7	1966 300: 984
		1962 300-H: 980
5	7.9	1963 300-J: 981
6	8.1	1986 Laser XT: 1005
7	8.2	1985 Le Baron GTS: 1004
8	8.3	1961 Enforcer: 976
9	8.4	1958 300-D: 973
		1961 300-G: 975
10	8.5	1969 300: 988
11	8.6	1984 Laser XE: 1003
12	8.7	1962 300: 979
13	8.8	1987 Le Baron Coupe: 1006
14	9.3	1970 Charger: 990
15	9.6	1967 Imperial Crown: 987
		1965 Newport: 983
16	10.0	1961 Imperial: 977
		1951 Saratoga Club Coupe: 970
		1966 Turbine: 985
17	10.4	1964 Imperial Le Baron: 982
18	10.7	1979 Sunbeam 1600 Ti: 1002
19	10.9	1961 Newport: 978
20	11.3	1966 Valiant Premium Auto: 986
21	12.6	1978 Alpine GLS: 1000
22	12.8	1973 2-litre: 992
23	12.9	1977 Sunbeam 1.6S: 998
24	13.1	1955 Windsor de Luxe: 972
25	13.3	1976 Alpine S: 993
26	13.6	1971 180: 991
		1953 New Yorker Saloon: 971
27	14.1	1977 Avenger 1600 Estate: 996
28	14.8	1978 1300 GL: 999
29	15.3	1978 Horizon GL: 1001
30	16.9	1977 Alpine GL: 995
		1937 Super Power Saloon: 968
31	17.5	1976 Avenger Super 1300: 994
32	17.7	1960 Valiant: 974
33	19.0	1935 Heston Airflow Saloon: 965
34	20.0	1931 Custom Imperial Le Baron: 964
35	20.2	1938 Royal Saloon: 969
36	22.6	1936 23.4hp Wimbledon Saloon: 966
37	23.9	1937 Richmond Touring Saloon: 967
38	24.3	1977 Sunbeam 1.0LS: 997

Citroen

1	7.5	1991 XM V6.24: 1089
2	7.9	1987 BX GTi 16v: 1077
3	8.6	1984 CX GTi Turbo: 1062
		1990 CX25 GTi Turbo 2 CX Auto: 1085
4	9.0	1987 AX GT: 1074
		1971 Safari SM: 1041
5	9.1	1986 Visa GTi: 1073
		1991 ZX Volcane: 1091
6	9.3	1992 AX GTi: 1092
		1973 Safari SM: 1045
		1972 SM: 1043
7	9.5	1991 XM 3.0 SEi Auto: 1088
8	9.7	1985 Visa GTi: 1070
9	10.1	1990 AX GT5: 1083
		1977 CX 2400 GTi: 1053
		1987 CX25 DTR Turbo 2: 1078
10	10.6	1990 BX GTi 4x4: 1084

11	10.7	1983 BX16 TRS: 1060
12	10.8	1985 CX22 TRS: 1067
13	11.0	1987 AX14 TRS: 1076
14	11.2	1990 XM 2.0SEi: 1086
15	11.6	1976 CX 2200 Pallas: 1049
		1981 CX Pallas: 1058
16	11.8	1977 CX 2400: 1052
		1970 DS21 EFI 139 Pallas: 1038
17	11.9	1988 BX DTR Turbo: 1080
		1986 CX25 Ri Familiale Auto: 1072
		1991 ZX 1.4 Avantage: 1090
18	12.2	1975 CX 2000: 1047
		1978 CX Pallas C-Matic Injection: 1054
19	12.5	1979 Athena: 1055
20	12.6	1987 AX11 TRE: 1075
		1988 AX11 TRE 5DR: 1079
21	13.1	1992 XM Turbo SD Estate: 1093
22	13.5	1991 AX11 TZX: 1087
		1985 BX16 TRS Automatic: 1066
23	13.9	1971 Safari 21: 1040
24	14.3	1989 BX14 TGE: 1082
25	14.4	1965 DS21 Pallas M: 1032
26	14.8	1966 DS21: 1034
27	14.9	1973 GS 1220: 1044
		1985 Visa 14TRS: 1068
28	15.0	1965 DSM: 1033
29	15.3	1983 BX14 RE: 1059
30	15.4	1976 GS X2: 1050
31	15.6	1984 BX19 RD Diesel: 1061
32	15.9	1975 GS Pallas: 1048
33	16.0	1984 LNA 11RE: 1063
34	16.2	1989 AX14 DTR: 1081
35	17.0	1979 CX 2500 Diesel Super: 1056
36	17.9	1986 BX19 RD Estate: 1071
37	18.0	1971 GS: 1039
38	18.2	1972 GS: 1042
39	18.4	1961 DS: 1029
40	18.6	1956 DS19: 1023
41	19.1	1960 ID19: 1027
		1985 Visa 17RD: 1069
42	19.3	1954 Six: 1021
43	20.1	1984 Visa Convertible: 1064
44	20.6	1948 Light Fifteen: 1015
45	20.8	1977 CX 2200 Diesel: 1051
46	21.1	1958 ID19: 1025
47	21.2	1963 DS: 1031
48	21.5	1953 11CV: 1018
49	21.9	1949 Six Saloon: 1016
50	22.1	1957 DS19: 1024
		1952 Light Fifteen: 1017
51	25.2	1960 ID Safari: 1026
52	27.3	1985 2CV6 Charleston: 1065
53	27.9	1979 Visa Club: 1057
54	29.1	1953 Big Fifteen: 1020
55	31.7	1970 Ami 8 Club: 1037
56	32.7	1975 2CV6: 1046
57	34.9	1940 Light Fifteen Roadster: 1014
58	36.1	1937 Sports Twelve Saloon: 1013
59	37.7	1936 Super Modern Fifteen Saloon: 1012
60	44.0	1962 Ami 6: 1030
61	54.7	1967 Ami 6 Break: 1035

Cizeta

1	4.5	1990 Moroder V16T: 1094

Clan

1	12.5	1971 Crusader: 1095

Consulier

1	5.7	1990 GTP LX: 1096

Cord

1	13.2	1937 Supercharged Saloon: 1102
2	13.5	1937 812: 1100
3	13.7	1937 812-S: 1101
4	20.1	1936 Front Wheel Drive Saloon: 1099
5	23.9	1930 L-29: 1097

Dacia

1	22.7	1985 Duster GLX: 1106

DAF

1	19.4	1974 66SL 1300: 1114
2	22.5	1958 55: 1107
3	23.1	1971 55 Estate: 1112
4	24.0	1973 66SL: 1113
5	31.2	1967 44: 1111
6	41.5	1960 600 de Luxe: 1108
7	52.0	1962 Daffodil: 1109

Daihatsu

1	7.9	1987 Charade GT ti: 1124
2	10.1	1990 Applause 16 Xi: 1131
3	11.2	1989 Charade 1.3 CX: 1128
4	11.3	1988 Charade Turbo: 1127
5	11.5	1989 Charade CLS: 1129
6	13.2	1982 Charmant 1600LE: 1118
7	14.2	1985 Charmant 1300LC: 1121
8	14.7	1986 Domino: 1122
9	15.2	1988 Charade CLX: 1126
10	15.6	1983 Charade CX: 1119
11	16.1	1979 Charade XTE: 1116
		1989 Sportrak EL: 1130
12	17.9	1987 Fourtrak Estate DT EL: 1125
13	20.8	1983 Charade Diesel: 1120
14	20.9	1987 Charade CX Diesel Turbo: 1123
15	26.6	1981 Domino: 1117

Daimler

1	8.1	1981 Double-Six HE: 1155
2	9.1	1960 SP250: 1147
3	10.2	1959 V8 SP250: 1146
4	10.3	1961 Majestic Major: 1148
		1974 Sovereign LWB Automatic: 1154
5	10.4	1972 Sovereign: 1153
6	11.3	1963 Limousine: 1150
7	13.8	1963 2.5-litre V8 Saloon: 1149
8	14.7	1966 2.5-litre V8: 1152
9	15.3	1958 Majestic: 1144
10	16.3	1964 Conquest Century Saloon: 1151
		1959 DK 400B: 1145
11	16.7	1955 One-O-Four Ladies' Model: 1141
12	17.3	1957 One-O-Four: 1143
13	18.8	1936 25.7hp Light Straight Eight Coupe: 1135
14	19.1	1955 Regency Mk II: 1142
15	20.4	1953 Conquest: 1140
16	26.0	1948 Straight Eight: 1139
17	28.7	1946 Twenty-Seven Limousine: 1138
18	31.0	1938 18hp 2.5-litre: 1136
19	35.9	1938 24hp Limousine: 1137
20	39.8	1936 15hp Saloon: 1134

Datsun

1	3.8	1983 280ZX Electramotive: 1230
2	5.6	1980 280ZX Sharp: 1221
3	5.7	1980 280ZX Electramotive: 1220
4	6.2	1978 280Z Scarab: 1205
5	6.7	1976 B210 Electramotive: 1198
6	7.0	1975 240Z Sharp: 1190
		1972 510 TransAm: 1180
7	7.4	1981 280ZX Turbo: 1223
8	7.9	1983 280ZX Turbo: 1231
9	8.0	1971 240Z: 1175
10	8.7	1970 240Z: 1171
11	9.1	1982 280ZX: 1225
12	9.2	1979 280ZX: 1211
		1980 280ZX: 1218
13	9.4	1975 280Z: 1192
14	9.7	1983 280ZX: 1229
15	9.9	1974 260Z 2+2: 1187
16	10.0	1974 260Z: 1186
17	10.1	1973 240Z: 1182
		1977 260Z: 1202
18	10.2	1967 2000 Sports: 1162
		1980 280ZX Automatic: 1219
		1979 280ZX Automatic: 1213
19	10.3	1968 2000 Sports: 1164
20	10.4	1971 240Z Automatic: 1176
21	11.0	1979 240K: 1210
		1982 Sunny 1.5 DX: 1227
22	11.3	1979 280ZX 2+2 Automatic: 1212
23	11.5	1983 200SX: 1228
24	11.6	1980 200SX: 1217
25	11.8	1979 2.4 Laurel Six: 1208
26	11.9	1979 810 Coupe: 1215
27	12.0	1982 Stanza 1.6 GL: 1226
28	12.2	1977 810 Sedan: 1203
29	12.3	1972 240C: 1179
		1981 810 Maxima: 1224
30	12.5	1972 180B: 1178
31	12.6	1973 200L: 1181
		1980 510: 1222
32	12.7	1978 510: 1206
33	12.8	1979 310 Coupe: 1214
34	13.3	1967 1600 Sports: 1161
		1977 200SX: 1201
35	13.5	1968 510 Sedan: 1166
36	13.6	1977 180B Bluebird: 1200
37	13.9	1971 510: 1177
38	14.0	1979 210: 1209
		1968 510: 1165
		1973 610 1800: 1183
39	14.4	1975 260C Estate: 1191
40	14.6	1974 710: 1188
41	14.7	1978 Laurel Six: 1207

42 14.8 1976 200L-6: 1196
43 14.9 1975 710: 1193
44 15.0 1983 Micra GL: 1232
45 15.1 1971 1200 Coupe: 1173
46 15.3 1970 1200: 1169
1976 B210: 1197
47 15.4 1968 1600: 1163
48 15.5 1976 F10: 1199
1964 SPL-310: 1159
49 15.6 1970 1600 Pickup: 1170
50 15.8 1976 140J Violet: 1195
51 16.0 1974 120Y: 1185
52 16.4 1971 1200 Estate: 1174
53 16.7 1974 B210: 1189
54 16.8 1971 100A: 1172
55 17.3 1975 B210: 1194
56 18.5 1973 610 Station Wagon: 1184
57 18.7 1968 510 Station Wagon: 1167
58 19.1 1979 New Sunny: 1216
59 19.4 1967 1600 Sedan: 1160
60 20.3 1977 Cherry F11: 1204
61 21.7 1969 1000 de Luxe: 1168
62 27.6 1961 Bluebird Station Wagon: 1158
63 46.0 1958 1000: 1157

De Lorean

1 10.5 1982 DMC 2.8-litre Coupe: 1233

De Tomaso

1 4.3 1989 Pantera Group 3: 1243
2 5.4 1986 Pantera GT5-S: 1242
3 5.5 1984 Pantera GT5: 1241
4 6.2 1972 Pantera: 1237
5 6.5 1974 Pantera GTS: 1239
6 6.8 1971 Pantera: 1236
7 7.0 1969 Mangusta: 1235
8 7.6 1973 Pantera: 1238
1974 Pantera L: 1240

Delage

1 17.6 1938 D8-120 Super Sports: 1251
2 23.3 1937 D6-70 Sports Coupe: 1250
3 31.6 1933 D6-11 Sports Saloon: 1249

Delahaye

1 13.7 1936 23.8hp Drop-head Coupe: 1252

Dellow

1 20.4 1956 Mk V: 1254

Denzel

1 13.7 1957 1300: 1255

Deutsch-Bonnet

1 21.3 1957 Coupe: 1256

Devin

1 5.7 1959 Super Sports: 1257
2 22.8 1960 VW: 1258

DKW

1 22.5 1958 3-6 Sonderklasse Coupe: 1265
2 24.2 1962 Junior de Luxe: 1268
3 25.5 1956 3-6: 1263
4 26.7 1954 Sonderklasse: 1261
5 28.4 1955 3-6: 1262
1960 750: 1266
6 37.6 1961 Junior: 1267
7 60.0 1956 Karavan: 1264

Dodge

1 4.1 1992 Viper: 1348
2 4.2 1963 Ramcharger 426 Super/Stock: 1287
3 5.7 1969 Hemi Charger 500 Automatic: 1308
1969 Hemi Charger 500 Manual: 1309
4 6.3 1968 Dart GTS: 1305
1968 Dart GTS 340: 1306
1991 Stealth R/T Turbo: 1347
1969 Super Bee Six-Pack: 1312
5 6.4 1967 Charger: 1299
6 6.5 1969 Coronet 500 Station Wagon: 1307
1991 Spirit R/T: 1346
7 6.6 1968 Coronet R/T: 1304
1969 Super Bee: 1311
8 6.7 1986 Shelby GLH-S: 1335
9 6.9 1988 Shelby CSX: 1338
1969 Swinger: 1313
10 7.1 1970 Challenger R/T: 1314
11 7.2 1966 Charger: 1298
1970 Charger R/T: 1315
1988 Daytona Shelby Z: 1336
1964 Polara 500: 1290
1989 Shelby CSX VNT: 1342
12 7.3 1990 Shadow ES VNT: 1345
13 7.4 1962 Dart 413: 1280
14 7.5 1989 Daytona Shelby: 1339
15 7.6 1968 Charger R/T: 1303
1990 Daytona Shelby: 1344
1988 Lancer Shelby: 1337
1969 Monaco: 1310
1989 Shelby CSX: 1341
16 7.7 1989 Shadow ES Turbo: 1340
17 7.8 1965 Coronet 426-S: 1294
18 8.0 1965 Coronet 500: 1296
19 8.1 1986 Omni GLH: 1334
20 8.4 1990 Daytona ES: 1343
1964 Polara: 1289
21 8.6 1967 Coronet R/T: 1300
1984 Daytona Turbo Z: 1331
1961 Lancer 225 Hyper-Pack: 1278
22 9.2 1986 Colt Turbo: 1333
1984 Conquest: 1330
23 9.3 1965 Coronet 440: 1295
1965 Dart GT: 1297
24 9.4 1985 Omni GLH: 1332
25 9.6 1963 Polara: 1286
26 10.0 1983 Shelby Charger: 1328
27 10.1 1982 Charger 2.2: 1326
28 10.3 1963 D-100 Sweptline Pickup: 1283
29 10.4 1979 Colt Hatchback: 1323
1961 Dart: 1275
30 10.5 1959 Custom Royal: 1274
31 10.8 1962 Custom 880: 1279
32 11.5 1958 Custom Royal: 1273
1967 Monaco Wagon: 1302
33 11.8 1983 600ES: 1327
1965 Coronet: 1293
1961 Dart Phoenix: 1276
34 12.1 1982 Challenger: 1325
1964 Dart GT: 1288
35 12.8 1977 Colt Lancer: 1322
36 13.1 1965 A-100 Super/Surfer: 1292
1981 Aires Wagon: 1324
37 13.2 1984 Colt Vista: 1329
1962 Lancer Gran Turismo: 1282
38 13.3 1963 Dart 270: 1284
39 13.4 1971 Colt: 1316
40 13.7 1961 Lancer: 1277
41 14.1 1974 Colt GT 2-litre: 1320
42 14.4 1973 Colt Station Wagon: 1319
1963 Dart GT 225 Smogburner: 1285
43 15.1 1967 Dart 270: 1301
44 16.7 1975 Colt GT: 1321
45 19.3 1962 Dreamer: 1281
46 23.0 1971 Pickup Power Wagon: 1317
47 24.8 1938 De Luxe Saloon: 1272
48 26.2 1937 Victory Six Touring Saloon: 1271

Dove

1 12.0 1963 GTR4: 1349

Du Pont

1 16.2 1929 Speedster: 1350
2 22.5 1930 Town Car: 1351

Duesenberg

1 8.6 1930 J Coupe: 1352
2 9.8 1938 SJ Town Car: 1353

Eagle

1 5.0 1991 GTP: 1356
2 6.8 1990 Talon: 1355
1991 Talon TSi 4WD: 1357
3 10.5 1988 Premier ES: 1354

Elva

1 12.7 1958 Courier: 1358

Essex

1 16.0 1933 Terraplane Straight Eight: 1361

Evans

1 4.6 1990 Series I: 1362

Excalibur

1	7.0	1964 SS: 1363

Facel Vega

1	7.8	1962 Facel II: 1368
2	9.3	1956 Coupe: 1364
3	9.6	1958 FVS: 1365
4	9.7	1960 HK-500: 1366
5	13.7	1961 Facellia 1600: 1367

Fairthorpe

1	7.9	1961 Zeta: 1369

Ferguson

1	14.7	1966 R5: 1370

Ferrari

1	3.7	1988 308 Norwood Bonneville GTO: 1434
2	3.8	1991 F40: 1450
3	4.5	1957 250 Testa Rossa: 1378
		1990 F40: 1446
4	4.7	1989 308 Norwood: 1439
		1989 Testa Rossa Norwood: 1444
5	5.0	1984 288 GTO: 1421
		1982 288 GTO: 1416
		1984 GTO: 1423
6	5.1	1954 250 Mille Miglia: 1376
		1985 365 GTB Goldsmith: 1425
		1982 512 BB: 1417
7	5.2	1956 412 MI: 1377
		1989 Testa Rossa: 1442
8	5.3	1988 Testa Rossa: 1437
		1985 Testa Rossa: 1426
		1989 Testa Rossa Gemballa: 1443
		1988 Testa Rossa Straman Spyder: 1438
9	5.4	1971 Daytona: 1397
10	5.6	1990 348tb: 1445
		1971 Daytona Cannonball: 1398
11	5.8	1974 365 GTB/4 Competitione: 1403
		1952 375 Indianapolis: 1373
		1957 TRC 2500 Testa Rossa: 1379
12	5.9	1962 250 GTO: 1386
		1987 328 GTS: 1431
		1970 365 GTB/4 Daytona: 1396
		1969 Daytona Sportwagen: 1395
		1989 Mondial t: 1441
13	6.0	1958 250 Testa Rossa: 1382
		1991 348tb: 1449
		1984 512 BBi: 1422
14	6.1	1953 4.1 Coupe: 1375
15	6.2	1978 512 BB: 1413
		1990 Pininfarina Mythos: 1448
16	6.3	1960 250 GT Berlinetta SWB: 1383
		1965 365 GTC: 1390
17	6.4	1974 308 GT4 Dino: 1402
18	6.5	1976 308 GTB: 1409
19	6.6	1986 328 GTB: 1428
		1962 4.9: 1387
		1990 Mondial: 1447
		1991 Mondial t: 1452
		1991 Mondial t Cabriolet: 1453
20	6.7	1967 275 GTS/4 NART: 1392
		1987 412: 1432
21	6.8	1983 308 GTBi Quattrovalvole: 1419
		1986 Mondial 3.2QV: 1430
22	6.9	1968 330 GTS: 1393
		1976 Dino 308 GT4 2+2: 1410
23	7.0	1989 Mondial 3.2 Cabriolet: 1440
		1988 Mondial Cabriolet: 1436
		1987 Mondial Cabriolet 3.2: 1433
24	7.1	1952 212 Touring: 1372
		1958 250 GT Cabriolet: 1380
		1958 250 GT Coupe: 1381
		1960 250 GT Coupe: 1384
		1986 3.2 Mondial: 1427
		1975 365 GT4 2+2: 1406
		1969 365 GTS 2+2: 1394
25	7.2	1966 275 GTS: 1391
		1974 365 GTB/4 Daytona: 1404
		1975 512 BB: 1407
26	7.3	1978 308 GTS: 1412
		1972 365 GTC4: 1400
27	7.4	1986 Mondial 3.2: 1429
28	7.6	1984 Mondial Cabriolet Quattrovalvole: 1424
29	7.8	1980 308 GT4 Dino: 1414
		1963 400 Super America: 1389
30	7.9	1972 246 GT Dino: 1399
		1981 308 GTSi: 1415
		1983 308 GTSi Targa: 1420
31	8.0	1974 246 GTS Dino: 1401
		1962 250 GT 2+2: 1385
		1963 250 GT Berlinetta Lusso: 1388
		1975 308 Dino GT4: 1405
		1976 308 GT4 Dino: 1408
32	8.2	1953 212 Coupe: 1374
33	9.4	1977 308 GTB: 1411
		1982 Mondial 8: 1418
34	10.0	1948 166 Mille Miglia Barchetta: 1371

Fiat

1	6.9	1980 Brava Abarth Rally: 1571
2	7.3	1965 Abarth OT 1600: 1502
3	8.2	1984 Strada Abarth 130TC: 1586
4	8.3	1990 Uno Turbo ie: 1605
5	9.1	1985 Uno Turbo ie: 1589
6	9.4	1982 Spider Turbo: 1577
7	9.9	1987 Croma ie Super: 1595
		1984 Regata 100 S: 1584
		1982 Spider 2000: 1576
8	10.0	1978 132 2000 GLS: 1560
9	10.4	1974 132 GLS: 1542
10	10.5	1973 124 Sport Coupe 1800: 1536
		1992 Tipo 1.8ie DGT SX: 1606
11	10.6	1979 124 Spider: 1562
		1973 132 1800 Special: 1541
12	10.7	1970 124 Coupe 1600: 1520
		1979 Mirafiori Sport: 1565
13	10.8	1985 X1/9VS: 1591
14	10.9	1983 Spider 2000: 1580
15	11.0	1979 X1/9 1500: 1570
16	11.2	1960 Abarth Twin Cam: 1488
17	11.3	1989 Tipo 1.6 DGT SX: 1600
		1985 Uno 70 SX: 1588
18	11.4	1972 130 Automatic: 1533
19	11.5	1979 124 Sports Spider: 1563
20	11.6	1990 Croma CHT: 1602
21	11.7	1976 128 3P: 1552
22	11.9	1970 124 Spider: 1522
		1968 124 Sport Spider: 1510
		1969 125 Special: 1517
		1978 131 Supermirafiori: 1559
23	12.0	1971 124 Special T: 1525
		1987 Regata 100S ie: 1596
		1988 X1/9: 1599
24	12.1	1978 Super Brava: 1561
		1983 Uno 70 SX: 1583
25	12.2	1971 124 Spider 1600: 1526
		1973 124 Spider 1600: 1535
		1990 Tempra 1.6 SX: 1603
26	12.3	1962 2300: 1494
		1979 Strada: 1566
		1985 X1/9: 1590
		1989 X1/9: 1601
		1984 X1/9: 1587
27	12.4	1971 124 Sport Coupe: 1527
		1982 Strada Super 85: 1578
		1982 X1/9: 1579
28	12.5	1973 124 Spider: 1534
		1969 Abarth 1300: 1519
29	12.6	1968 124 Sport Coupe: 1509
		1954 8V: 1468
30	12.7	1977 X1/9: 1557
31	12.9	1981 Brava: 1573
32	13.1	1972 128 Coupe 1300: 1531
		1988 Tipo 1.4: 1598
33	13.2	1975 124 Sport Coupe 1800: 1545
		1984 Regata 70 ES: 1585
34	13.3	1979 Strada 75CL: 1568
		1979 X1/9 1300: 1569
35	13.4	1967 125: 1508
		1977 131: 1556
36	13.7	1976 131: 1554
37	13.8	1973 124 Station Wagon: 1537
		1978 127 Sport: 1558
38	13.9	1975 128 Special: 1547
39	14.1	1983 Uno 55 S: 1582
40	14.2	1969 124 Coupe: 1515
		1990 Uno 60S: 1604
41	14.3	1970 124 Special: 1521
42	14.5	1960 2100: 1485
		1982 Mirafiori 1400CL: 1575
43	14.6	1972 124: 1530
44	14.7	1975 128: 1546
		1983 Strada 60 Comfort ES: 1581
45	14.8	1976 124 Spider: 1550
		1973 124S Automatic: 1538
46	15.2	1975 124 Special TC: 1544
		1972 128 SL 1300 Coupe: 1532
		1960 1500: 1484
47	15.3	1976 128 Estate: 1553
		1961 1500: 1491
		1974 X1/9: 1543
48	15.6	1969 850 Coupe: 1518
		1986 Regata DS: 1594
		1979 Strada 65CL: 1567
49	15.9	1967 124: 1507
50	16.0	1986 Panda 1000 S: 1592
51	16.1	1981 127 1050 Super: 1572
		1975 131 1300S: 1548
52	16.2	1965 1500: 1500
		1981 Panda: 1574

53	16.3	1970 128 4-door: 1523
54	16.6	1987 Uno Selecta: 1597
55	17.0	1971 128: 1529
		1965 1500 Spider: 1501
56	17.1	1973 128 Station Wagon: 1540
57	17.3	1958 Abarth 750GT Zagato: 1479
		1958 Abarth Zagato: 1480
58	17.4	1971 127: 1528
59	17.6	1977 127 1050 CL: 1555
		1960 Abarth 850: 1487
60	17.8	1969 124 Estate Car: 1516
61	17.9	1970 850 Racer: 1524
62	18.2	1966 850 Coupe: 1505
63	18.8	1958 1200 TV Spyder: 1476
64	19.0	1964 1500L: 1497
		1968 850 Special: 1513
65	19.1	1961 1200 Spider: 1489
66	19.2	1961 1300: 1490
67	19.6	1958 750 Abarth: 1478
68	19.9	1958 1200 Gran Luce: 1475
69	20.0	1959 1200 Gran Luce: 1481
		1968 850 Spider: 1514
70	20.6	1986 Panda 750 L: 1593
71	21.5	1954 1100 TV Saloon: 1467
72	21.6	1966 1100R: 1503
73	22.2	1953 1900: 1466
74	22.5	1963 1100D: 1496
75	24.8	1976 124 Sport Spider: 1551
76	25.4	1963 1100: 1495
77	25.5	1968 850 Idromatic: 1512
78	26.8	1964 850 Super: 1499
79	27.2	1966 Abarth 595: 1506
80	27.5	1950 1400 Saloon: 1461
81	28.9	1975 133: 1549
82	29.5	1957 1100: 1470
83	29.8	1957 1100 Saloon: 1471
84	30.4	1935 Balilla Sports Two-seater: 1457
85	32.7	1953 1100: 1465
86	36.6	1937 1500 Pillarless Saloon: 1459
87	37.2	1959 500 Nuova: 1483
88	39.5	1937 Balilla Pillarless Saloon: 1460
89	42.1	1979 126 de Ville: 1564
90	54.0	1957 600: 1472
91	62.2	1973 126: 1539

Fiberfab

1	9.2	1969 Jamaican Buick V8: 1607

Ford

1	4.1	1976 Cobra II Kemp: 1841
2	4.8	1965 Galaxie 500 XL 427: 1714
3	4.9	1988 Mustang Cartech Turbo: 1928
		1991 Mustang Holdener: 1966
4	5.0	1968 GT40: 1760
5	5.2	1989 Mustang SVO J Bittle American: 1942
		1989 Thunderbird Super Coupe Ford Engineering: 1948
6	5.3	1991 Festiva Shogun: 1965
		1966 GT40 Super Street: 1738
7	5.4	1989 Mustang 5.0 Cartech Turbo: 1940
8	5.5	1969 Mustang 428 Mach I: 1775
		1971 Mustang TransAm: 1796
9	5.7	1991 Mustang NOS/Saleen: 1967
10	5.8	1970 Mustang Boss 302: 1787
		1988 Sierra RS Cosworth: 1934
11	5.9	1968 Mustang 428 Cobra Jet: 1761
12	6.0	1988 Mustang Convertible Saleen: 1929
		1988 Mustang GT: 1930
		1987 Mustang LX 5.0: 1924
13	6.1	1986 RS200: 1917
14	6.2	1991 Escort Millen: 1964
15	6.3	1963 Fastback NASCAR: 1698
		1989 Mustang Saleen SSC: 1941
16	6.6	1990 Mustang LX 5.0L: 1955
		1990 Sierra Sapphire Cosworth 4x4: 1958
		1989 Taurus SHO: 1946
17	6.7	1987 Mustang GT: 1923
		1989 Probe GT Suspension Techniques/HKS: 1943
18	6.8	1987 Thunderbird Bondurant 5.0: 1926
19	6.9	1969 Mustang Boss 302: 1776
		1986 Mustang GT 5.0: 1913
20	7.0	1962 Galaxie 406: 1679
		1984 Mustang GT 5.0: 1896
		1986 Mustang Saleen: 1914
21	7.1	1969 Mustang Boss 429: 1777
		1992 Mustang LX: 1975
		1986 Mustang SVO: 1915
22	7.2	1985 Mustang GT: 1905
23	7.3	1972 Capri RS2600: 1805
		1969 Fairlane Cobra: 1772
		1988 Probe GT: 1933
24	7.4	1991 Probe GT: 1969
		1989 Thunderbird Super Coupe: 1947
25	7.5	1984 Mustang GT: 1895
26	7.6	1990 Probe GT: 1956
		1991 Taurus SHO: 1971
27	7.7	1976 Capri V6 Black Gold: 1840
		1984 Mustang SVO: 1897
		1973 Pinto Pangra: 1819
		1983 Sierra XR4i: 1890
		1968 Torino: 1763
28	7.8	1967 Mustang 390 Fastback: 1748
		1983 Mustang GT 5.0: 1888
29	7.9	1981 Capri 2.8 Injection: 1871
		1990 Fiesta RS Turbo: 1949
30	8.0	1966 Galaxie 7-litre: 1737
		1969 Mustang Grande: 1778
		1982 Mustang GT 5.0: 1881
		1990 Mustang GT Convertible: 1954
31	8.1	1985 Escort RS Turbo: 1901
		1970 Torino GT: 1788
32	8.2	1964 Mustang Convertible: 1708
		1990 Probe LX: 1957
		1959 Thunderbird: 1653
		1968 XL Fastback 428: 1764
33	8.3	1973 Capri 3000 GXL: 1811
		1992 Escort RS2000: 1973
		1964 Mustang 271hp: 1707
		1965 Mustang Fastback: 1722
		1965 Mustang High Performance: 1723
		1984 Sierra XR4i: 1898
34	8.4	1972 Capri 3000E: 1804
35	8.5	1963 Falcon V8: 1697
		1965 Mustang Coupe Automatic: 1721
		1965 Mustang V8 4.7-litre: 1725
		1991 Scorpio 24v: 1970
		1987 Thunderbird Turbo Coupe: 1927
36	8.6	1976 Capri 3000S: 1838
		1976 Escort RS2000: 1844
		1992 Escort XR3i: 1974
		1983 Escort XR3i: 1885
		1966 Fairlane GTA: 1735
		1989 Sierra XR 4x4: 1945
37	8.7	1968 Mustang Fastback: 1762
38	8.8	1956 Interceptor Coupe: 1639
39	8.9	1970 Escort 1600 RS: 1785
		1991 Escort GT: 1963
		1990 Fiesta XR2i: 1950
		1978 Granada 2.8i S: 1860
		1965 Mustang Convertible V8: 1719
40	9.0	1973 Consul 3000 GT: 1812
		1975 Escort RS1800: 1833
		1973 Escort RS2000: 1817
		1964 Mustang: 1706
		1965 Mustang Coupe: 1720
		1991 Thunderbird LX: 1972
41	9.1	1972 Granada GXL: 1808
		1969 LTD: 1773
42	9.2	1970 Capri Plus 50: 1782
		1968 Cortina Race-proved Savage: 1754
		1986 Escort RS Turbo: 1911
		1981 Granada 2.8i: 1877
		1976 Granada 3000 S: 1846
		1985 Sierra 2.0i S: 1907
43	9.3	1963 Falcon Futura V8: 1695
		1985 Fiesta XR2: 1902
		1988 Taurus 3.8: 1935
		1961 Thunderbird: 1665
44	9.4	1981 Fiesta XR2: 1876
		1965 Galaxie LTD: 1715
		1985 Granada Scorpio 4x4: 1904
		1966 Thunderbird Town Landau: 1739
45	9.5	1961 Galaxie: 1663
		1964 Galaxie 500: 1705
		1987 Granada 2.4i Ghia: 1921
		1990 Granada Ghia X 2.9 EFi Saloon: 1952
		1985 Granada Scorpio: 1903
		1986 Sierra Ghia 4x4 Estate: 1918
		1955 Thunderbird: 1635
46	9.6	1986 Escort XR3i: 1912
		1979 Fiesta Healey: 1864
		1987 Sierra Sapphire 2.0 Ghia: 1925
47	9.7	1966 Cortina Lotus: 1732
		1967 Mustang: 1747
		1983 Thunderbird Turbo Coupe: 1891
48	9.8	1967 Fairlane Ranchero: 1746
		1987 Granada Scorpio 2.9 EX: 1922
		1967 Thunderbird: 1749
		1969 Thunderbird: 1779
49	9.9	1963 Cortina Lotus: 1689
		1991 Crown Victoria LX: 1959
		1968 Escort Twin Cam: 1758
50	10.0	1979 Granada 2.8i GLS Estate: 1865
		1991 Orion 1.6i Ghia: 1968
		1989 Sierra Sapphire 2000E: 1944
51	10.1	1969 Fairlane 351: 1771
52	10.2	1991 Escort Cabriolet: 1962
		1987 Festiva L: 1919
		1989 Fiesta 1.6S: 1939
		1984 Fiesta XR2: 1894
		1956 Thunderbird: 1641
53	10.3	1969 Capri 3000 GT XLR: 1768
		1981 Cortina 2.0 GL: 1872
		1966 Falcon Ranchero Custom: 1736
		1974 Granada Ghia Coupe: 1824
		1965 Thunderbird: 1727

54	10.4	1975 Capri 2000S GT: 1828
		1972 Capri 2600 V6: 1803
		1972 Mustang Grande: 1810
		1976 Mustang II: 1847
		1979 Mustang Turbo: 1867
		1980 Mustang Turbo: 1870
		1983 Orion 1.6 GL: 1889
		1992 Taurus LX: 1976
55	10.5	1979 Cortina 2.3 Ghia S: 1863
		1980 Fiesta: 1869
		1962 Galaxie: 1678
		1976 Mustang II V8: 1848
56	10.6	1969 Capri 2000 GT: 1767
		1976 Capri II 2.8 V6: 1839
		1973 Cortina 2000E: 1816
57	10.7	1970 Cortina 2000 GXL: 1783
58	10.8	1979 Capri 2000S: 1861
		1974 Capri 2800 V6: 1821
59	11.0	1976 Cortina 2.0 Ghia: 1842
		1967 Cortina Lotus: 1744
60	11.1	1982 Escort 1600 GL: 1878
61	11.2	1963 Falcon Sprint Convertible: 1696
		1965 Mustang Convertible: 1718
		1965 Mustang V8 4.2-litre: 1724
62	11.4	1974 Capri II 1600 GT: 1822
		1986 Escort L: 1910
		1971 Pinto 2-litre: 1800
63	11.5	1971 Capri 2000: 1791
		1977 Fiesta Ghia: 1855
		1973 Granada Estate Auto: 1818
64	11.6	1990 Granada Scorpio 2.0i Auto: 1953
65	11.7	1985 Escort GL: 1900
		1974 Granada GXL: 1825
66	11.8	1972 LTD: 1809
67	11.9	1981 Escort 1.6L Estate: 1874
		1965 Fairlane 500: 1713
		1978 Granada 2.0L: 1858
		1982 Sierra 2.3 Ghia Automatic: 1883
68	12.0	1975 Consul 2000L: 1829
		1968 Galaxie: 1759
		1975 Granada 5-litre: 1835
		1979 Mustang Ghia Turbo: 1866
69	12.1	1962 Fairlane 500 Sports Coupe: 1672
		1964 Falcon Sprint: 1704
		1984 Fiesta 1.3L CVH: 1892
70	12.2	1977 Cortina 2.3 Ghia: 1849
		1983 Escort 1.6 GL Automatic: 1884
		1985 Sierra 1.8 Ghia: 1906
71	12.3	1991 Escort 1.6 Ghia Estate: 1961
		1977 Escort 1600 Sport: 1851
		1963 Galaxie 500 XL: 1699
72	12.4	1986 Escort 1.4 GL: 1909
		1971 Escort 1300 GT: 1793
		1982 Mustang 4.2: 1880
		1962 Thunderbird Sports Roadster: 1680
73	12.5	1965 Mustang 6: 1717
74	12.6	1975 Cortina 2000E Estate: 1831
		1982 Granada 2.3L Estate: 1879
75	12.7	1978 Capri 1600S: 1857
76	12.8	1991 Escort 1.4LX: 1960
		1986 Orion 1.4 GL: 1916
77	12.9	1972 Capri 1600 XL: 1802
		1973 Cortina 2000 Estate: 1815
78	13.0	1974 Mustang II Ghia: 1826
		1982 Sierra 1.6L: 1882
79	13.1	1967 Cortina 1600E: 1742
		1953 Zephyr Sedan Modified: 1629
		1967 Zodiac Executive: 1750
80	13.3	1971 1600 GT: 1789
81	13.4	1969 Capri 1600 GT: 1766
		1989 Fiesta 1.4 Ghia: 1938
		1990 Granada 2.5 GL Diesel: 1951
82	13.5	1967 Corsair 2000E: 1741
		1975 Escort 1.3 Ghia: 1832
		1962 Zodiac Mk III: 1683
83	13.6	1979 Cortina 1600L: 1862
		1960 Galaxie: 1658
		1984 Tempo GLX: 1899
84	13.7	1963 Capri GT: 1684
		1977 Fiesta 1300 S: 1854
85	13.8	1971 Escort Sport: 1795
		1980 Fairmont: 1868
		1974 Mustang II Mach I: 1827
86	13.9	1965 Cortina GT: 1712
		1981 Escort: 1873
87	14.1	1972 Consul 2000L: 1806
		1989 Escort 1.3L 3-door: 1936
88	14.2	1969 Cortina 1600 GT: 1770
		1968 Cortina GT Estate: 1753
89	14.3	1963 Consul Corsair GT: 1685
		1962 Country Sedan: 1670
		1970 Maverick: 1786
90	14.4	1986 Aerostar XLT: 1908
91	14.5	1971 Bronco: 1790
		1967 Cortina GT: 1743
		1977 Granada 2.3 GL Auto: 1856
		1969 Maverick: 1774
92	14.6	1966 Zephyr 6 Mk IV: 1740
93	14.7	1965 Corsair GT: 1711
		1973 Cortina 1600 XL: 1813
		1975 Granada 2000 GL: 1834
94	14.8	1970 Capri 1300 GT: 1780
		1962 Fairlane 500: 1671
		1965 Taunus 20M: 1726
95	14.9	1968 Cortina GT: 1752
96	15.0	1966 Corsair GT Estate: 1730
		1963 F-100 Styleside Pickup: 1692
97	15.1	1973 Cortina 1600 XL Estate: 1814
		1958 Fairlane 500: 1646
		1965 Mustang: 1716
98	15.2	1964 Custom 500: 1703
		1975 Pinto 2300: 1836
		1965 Zodiac Executive: 1728
99	15.3	1971 Econoline Chateau Wagon: 1792
		1989 Fiesta 1.1LX 5-door: 1937
100	15.4	1973 Pinto Station Wagon: 1820
101	15.5	1962 Fairlane V8: 1673
102	15.7	1977 Fiesta 1100 Ghia: 1853
103	15.8	1987 Fiesta 1.1 Ghia Auto: 1920
		1984 Fiesta 1.6L Diesel: 1893
104	16.0	1977 Escort 1300 GL: 1850
105	16.1	1963 Zephyr 6 Estate: 1700
106	16.3	1966 Custom 500: 1734
107	16.4	1975 Cortina 1300L: 1830
		1976 Escort 1300 GL: 1843
		1963 Fairlane Squire Wagon: 1693
108	16.5	1960 Zephyr: 1660
		1964 Zephyr 6: 1709
109	16.8	1983 Fiesta 1.1 Ghia: 1886
110	17.3	1970 Capri 1600: 1781
111	17.4	1938 V8 30: 1617
112	17.5	1962 Falcon 170 Manual: 1677
		1983 Granada 2.5 Diesel Estate: 1887
		1936 V8 Touring Saloon: 1614
113	17.6	1971 Escort 1300 XL: 1794
114	17.7	1959 Falcon: 1650
		1962 Falcon 170 Automatic: 1676
		1968 Zephyr de Luxe: 1765
115	17.8	1964 Consul Corsair: 1701
116	17.9	1956 Zephyr: 1642
117	18.0	1971 Pinto 1600: 1799
118	18.2	1968 Cortina 1300 de Luxe: 1751
119	18.5	1960 Taunus 17M: 1659
		1958 Taunus 17M: 1647
120	18.6	1960 Falcon: 1656
121	18.7	1958 Zephyr Estate: 1648
122	18.8	1976 Capri 1300: 1837
123	19.0	1963 Consul Cortina 1500: 1687
		1963 Cortina Super: 1690
		1962 Falcon 144 Manual: 1675
		1977 Fiesta 1000: 1852
124	19.4	1968 Escort 1300: 1757
125	19.6	1976 Fiesta: 1845
		1981 Fiesta Popular: 1875
		1962 Zephyr 4: 1681
126	19.7	1961 Taunus 17M: 1664
127	19.8	1972 Cortina 1300L: 1807
		1974 Escort 1100L: 1823
128	20.0	1971 Pinto: 1798
129	20.1	1970 Escort 1300 Super Estate: 1784
		1953 Zephyr Sedan: 1628
130	20.4	1972 1600 XL Auto: 1801
		1955 Zodiac: 1636
131	20.5	1966 Cortina Super Estate: 1733
		1948 V8 Pilot: 1621
132	20.8	1962 Anglia Super: 1667
		1962 Consul Capri: 1668
133	20.9	1957 Zodiac Automatic: 1643
134	21.0	1947 Tudor Sedan: 1619
135	21.3	1961 Consul Capri: 1661
136	21.4	1966 Cortina 1300 de Luxe: 1731
137	21.6	1963 Falcon Futura: 1694
138	21.8	1964 Cortina Super: 1702
139	22.3	1968 Escort: 1756
140	22.5	1962 Consul Cortina: 1669
		1960 Consul Mk II: 1655
141	22.6	1966 Bronco: 1729
142	22.8	1956 Taunus 15M: 1640
143	22.9	1960 Falcon Automatic: 1657
144	23.3	1962 Zephyr 4 Automatic: 1682
145	23.5	1959 Taunus 17M Estate: 1652
146	24.2	1965 Anglia Estate: 1710
147	24.4	1963 Consul Cortina: 1686
148	24.5	1952 Comete: 1625
		1962 Falcon 144 Automatic: 1674
149	24.6	1967 Cortina Super Estate: 1745
150	25.0	1956 Consul Mk II: 1638
151	25.4	1958 Consul: 1645
152	25.5	1963 Cortina Estate de Luxe: 1688
153	25.8	1961 Econoline: 1662
154	27.1	1969 Cortina 1100: 1769
155	27.2	1978 Granada 2.1D: 1859
156	29.0	1934 Model A: 1613
157	29.1	1960 Anglia: 1654
158	29.4	1959 Anglia: 1649
159	29.8	1955 Anglia: 1632
160	30.0	1956 Anglia: 1637
161	31.0	1955 Prefect: 1633

162	31.6	1951 Consul: 1624
163	32.4	1958 Anglia de Luxe: 1644
164	33.2	1954 Anglia Saloon: 1630
165	33.4	1934 10 de Luxe Saloon: 1612
166	36.4	1962 Anglia de Luxe Estate: 1666
		1959 Popular II: 1651
167	38.9	1955 Prefect 1172cc: 1634
168	47.9	1937 10: 1615

Frazer

1	21.8	1949 Saloon: 1978

Frazer-Nash

1	9.6	1955 Targa Florio Fast Roadster: 1986
2	10.4	1953 Targa Florio Turismo: 1985
3	13.8	1937 1.5-litre: 1984
4	14.0	1934 14hp Sports Tourer: 1983
5	16.0	1933 1.5-litre: 1981
6	18.0	1933 TT Replica: 1982

Frazer-Nash BMW

1	9.5	1937 Grand Prix Two-seater: 1989
2	10.8	1967 2000TI: 1992
3	15.2	1939 Type 327 Cabriolet: 1991
4	17.6	1935 Type 55 Cabriolet: 1988
5	26.2	1935 12.5hp Saloon: 1987
6	29.5	1938 Type 326 Saloon: 1990

Geo

1	9.3	1991 Storm GSi: 1994

Gilbern

1	10.7	1969 Invader: 1996
2	17.4	1961 GT: 1995

Ginetta

1	9.0	1990 G32: 1998
2	9.2	1976 G21S: 1997

Glas

1	11.2	1966 1700GT: 2000
2	12.5	1965 1300GT: 1999
3	17.1	1974 1700: 2001

GM

1	8.0	1990 Impact: 2002

GMC

1	11.9	1985 Safari Cargo Mover: 2003

Goliath

1	18.5	1959 Tiger: 2007
2	24.6	1957 1100 Sedan: 2005
3	32.0	1957 900: 2006

Gordon

1	7.7	1960 GT: 2008

Gordon Keeble

1	7.5	1965 GK1: 2009

Graham

1	14.5	1936 26hp Supercharged Saloon: 2013
2	15.8	1935 33.8hp Supercharged Saloon: 2012
3	16.4	1938 26hp Supercharged Saloon: 2014
4	24.0	1935 21.6hp Saloon: 2011

Healey

1	13.5	1953 Sports Convertible: 2021
2	14.6	1952 Tickford Saloon: 2020
3	14.7	1948 2.4-litre Roadster: 2019

Hillman

1	10.5	1972 Hunter GLS: 2075
2	12.2	1975 Avenger GLS: 2080
3	12.5	1970 Avenger GT: 2070
4	13.2	1976 Avenger 1600 Super: 2082
5	13.5	1973 Avenger GLS: 2077
6	13.6	1969 Hunter Mk II: 2068
7	13.9	1969 GT: 2067
8	14.3	1975 Hunter Super: 2081
9	14.5	1974 Avenger 1600 GLS: 2079
10	15.6	1970 Avenger GL: 2069
11	16.2	1971 Hunter Super: 2072
12	16.6	1972 Avenger Estate: 2074
13	17.0	1973 Avenger DL: 2076
14	17.5	1974 Avenger 1300 GL: 2078
15	17.8	1967 Minx: 2066
16	18.9	1957 Minx Convertible: 2044
17	19.2	1966 Super Minx Estate: 2062
18	19.8	1970 Avenger Super: 2071
19	19.9	1967 Estate: 2063
20	20.2	1954 Minx Supercharged: 2040
21	20.5	1965 Minx Series VI de Luxe: 2060
22	21.1	1971 Imp de Luxe: 2073
23	22.1	1967 Imp Californian: 2065
24	22.2	1962 Super Minx: 2053
25	22.5	1962 Super Minx Mk II: 2054
26	22.6	1964 Super Minx Convertible: 2058
27	22.9	1964 Super Minx III: 2059
28	23.7	1958 Husky: 2046
		1963 Imp de Luxe: 2056
29	24.0	1935 20/27 Sports Saloon: 2029
30	24.2	1967 Hunter Husky: 2064
31	25.0	1960 Easidrive: 2051
32	25.4	1965 Super Imp: 2061
33	26.4	1937 80 Limousine: 2032
34	26.6	1958 Minx Series III Convertible: 2049
35	26.7	1959 Minx Series IIIA Easidrive: 2050
36	27.7	1956 Minx de Luxe: 2043
37	27.9	1936 Hawk Sports Saloon: 2031
38	28.4	1958 Minx Estate: 2047
39	28.6	1934 20/70 Limousine: 2027
40	28.8	1964 Minx Series V Automatic: 2057
41	29.2	1958 Minx Series II: 2048
42	29.7	1955 Minx de Luxe: 2042
43	30.0	1960 Hunter Husky Series II: 2052
44	31.4	1958 Hunter Husky: 2045
45	32.3	1952 Minx Convertible: 2038
46	34.7	1953 Minx Californian Coupe: 2039
47	35.9	1963 Hunter Husky III: 2055
48	37.8	1935 Aero Minx Cresta Saloon: 2030
49	40.0	1951 Minx Sedan: 2037
50	40.2	1949 Minx Saloon: 2035

Hispano-Suiza

1	12.0	1934 54/220: 2084
2	19.6	1934 30/120 Saloon: 2083

Holden

1	11.9	1969 Brougham: 2086
2	20.7	1952 Saloon: 2085

Honda

1	5.7	1986 CRX Si Jackson Turbo: 2130
2	5.8	1991 NSX: 2156
3	6.8	1992 NSX Auto: 2159
4	7.4	1989 CRX Si HKS: 2147
5	7.6	1991 Civic 1.6i VT: 2154
6	7.9	1992 Prelude Si 4WS: 2160
7	8.0	1988 Civic CRX: 2140
		1989 Civic Si HKS: 2146
		1990 CRX 1.6i VT: 2152
		1986 CRX Coupe 1.6i 16: 2128
		1988 CRX Si Jackson: 2142
		1986 Legend: 2133
		1987 Legend Coupe: 2137
8	8.1	1992 Legend Coupe: 2158
9	8.2	1988 CRX Si: 2141
		1991 Legend: 2155
10	8.5	1984 Civic CRX: 2113
		1987 Prelude 2.0i 16: 2139
11	8.6	1986 Integra EX 16: 2132
		1988 Legend Saloon Automatic: 2143
12	8.7	1985 CRX Si: 2124
13	8.8	1991 Prelude Si: 2157
14	8.9	1986 CRX Si: 2129
15	9.1	1986 Prelude 2.0 Si: 2134
16	9.3	1990 Concerto 1.6i 16: 2151
		1987 Prelude 2.0 Si: 2138
17	9.4	1989 Civic Si: 2145
		1985 Prelude: 2125
		1989 Prelude Si 4WS: 2148
18	9.7	1987 Civic 1.4 GL 3-door: 2136
		1984 Prelude: 2116
19	9.8	1986 Accord LXi: 2126
		1985 Accord SEi: 2119
20	9.9	1990 Accord 2.0 EXi: 2150
		1985 Accord 2.0 EXi: 2117
		1985 Civic GT: 2120
21	10.0	1988 Shuttle 1.6i RT4 4WD: 2144
22	10.1	1983 CRX 1.5: 2111
23	10.7	1984 Civic DL: 2114

24	10.8	1980 Civic: 2102
25	10.9	1983 Prelude EX ALB: 2112
26	11.1	1987 Ballade EX: 2135
		1985 Civic S: 2121
27	11.2	1991 Civic 1.5 VEi: 2153
		1985 Civic Shuttle: 2122
28	11.3	1979 Prelude: 2101
29	11.5	1980 Prelude: 2104
		1981 Prelude: 2107
30	11.8	1986 Integra 1.5: 2131
31	11.9	1985 Civic Wagon: 2123
32	12.0	1979 Accord 4-door: 2100
		1985 Accord EX Automatic: 2118
		1980 Civic GL 1500: 2103
33	12.2	1981 Quintet: 2108
		1989 Shuttle 1.4 GL Automatic: 2149
34	13.0	1982 Accord: 2109
		1982 Accord LX: 2110
35	13.4	1981 Accord: 2105
		1984 Jazz: 2115
		1967 S800: 2088
36	13.6	1986 Civic Hatchback: 2127
37	13.7	1977 Civic 1500: 2097
38	13.8	1978 Accord: 2098
39	14.1	1973 Civic: 2092
40	14.5	1978 Civic: 2099
41	15.0	1975 Civic CVCC: 2094
42	15.1	1981 Civic 4-door Sedan: 2106
43	15.4	1976 Accord: 2095
44	17.0	1977 Accord: 2096
45	17.8	1965 S600: 2087
46	18.3	1973 Civic Hondamatic: 2093
47	23.4	1970 600: 2090
48	23.6	1972 600 Coupe: 2091
49	29.3	1968 N360: 2089

Hotchkiss

1	13.7	1938 3.5-litre Saloon: 2165
2	13.8	1935 Paris-Nice Saloon: 2163
3	14.0	1934 Paris-Nice Speed Model: 2162
4	18.1	1937 28hp Cabourg Saloon: 2164
5	25.0	1933 3.5-litre Coupe: 2161

HRG

1	14.3	1937 12hp Sports Two-seater: 2166
2	16.2	1938 1.5-litre: 2167
3	18.1	1948 1.5-litre: 2168

Hudson

1	15.1	1953 Super Jet: 2178
2	17.0	1934 Terraplane: 2170
3	17.6	1935 Eight Saloon: 2171
4	18.4	1949 Commodore: 2176
5	18.9	1956 Rambler: 2179
6	20.5	1938 22hp Six Special Saloon: 2175
7	23.0	1936 22hp Six Saloon: 2173
		1935 Terraplane Big Six Saloon: 2172
8	28.5	1937 Terraplane Saloon: 2174

Humber

1	13.1	1967 Sceptre: 2214
2	13.5	1974 Sceptre Estate: 2215
3	14.3	1961 Super Snipe Series III: 2209
4	16.0	1953 Super Snipe Mk IV: 2200
5	16.2	1965 Imperial: 2212
6	16.9	1966 Sceptre II Automatic: 2213
7	17.1	1963 Sceptre: 2211
8	17.5	1953 Super Snipe: 2199
9	18.0	1959 Super Snipe: 2206
10	18.7	1960 Super Snipe Estate: 2207
11	19.0	1958 Super Snipe: 2205
12	20.5	1961 3-litre: 2208
13	21.2	1952 Super Snipe: 2198
14	21.3	1963 Hawk III: 2210
15	22.7	1949 Super Snipe: 2195
16	23.4	1957 Hawk: 2203
17	23.7	1937 Snipe Drop-head Foursome: 2188
18	23.8	1954 Hawk Mk VI: 2201
19	24.4	1938 Snipe Sports Saloon: 2190
20	24.8	1936 Snipe Sports Saloon: 2187
21	25.7	1958 Hawk Estate: 2204
22	25.8	1935 Snipe Sports Saloon: 2185
23	26.2	1952 Pullman Limousine: 2197
24	26.5	1949 Imperial: 2193
		1949 Imperial Saloon: 2194
25	26.7	1956 Hawk Estate: 2202
26	27.2	1936 Pullman Limousine: 2186
27	27.9	1951 Hawk: 2196
28	31.2	1938 16.9hp Saloon: 2189
29	34.4	1949 Hawk: 2192
30	38.8	1935 12 Six-light Saloon: 2184

Hupmobile

1	16.6	1935 29.4hp Saloon: 2217
2	20.0	1935 32.5hp Saloon: 2218

Hyundai

1	10.9	1991 Lantra 1.6 Cdi: 2226
2	11.7	1989 Sonata 2.0i GLS: 2224
3	12.3	1990 Sonata 2.4i GLS: 2225
4	12.5	1991 S Coupe GSi: 2227
5	12.9	1986 Excel GLS: 2223
6	13.7	1991 X2 1.5 GSi: 2228
7	14.0	1986 Excel GL: 2222
8	14.4	1985 Pony 1.5 GLS: 2221
9	14.7	1984 Stellar 1600 GSL: 2220
10	14.8	1982 Pony 1400 TLS: 2219

IAD

1	5.0	1990 Venus: 2229

Infiniti

1	6.9	1990 Q45: 2231
2	10.0	1991 G20: 2232
3	10.4	1990 M30: 2230

Innocenti

1	18.4	1964 S: 2233

International

1	12.5	1971 Scout: 2238
2	14.2	1972 Scout: 2240
3	16.3	1971 Travelall 1210: 2239
4	18.0	1971 Pickup 4WD 1210 Camper Special: 2237
5	18.2	1962 Travelall: 2235
6	20.1	1961 Scout: 2234
7	27.5	1963 900 Pickup: 2236

Invicta

1	14.8	1931 4.5-litre: 2242

Irmsher

1	7.9	1989 GT: 2243

Isdera

1	5.0	1988 Imperator: 2244

Iso

1	6.2	1963 Grifo A3L Berlinetta: 2245
2	7.2	1971 Grifo GL: 2250
3	7.4	1966 Grifo GL 365: 2248
4	7.8	1969 Rivolta S4: 2249
5	8.0	1964 Rivolta IR-340: 2247
6	8.1	1974 Rivolta Fidia: 2251
7	8.2	1964 GT: 2246

Isuzu

1	8.5	1986 Impulse Turbo: 2256
2	8.6	1991 Impulse RS: 2261
3	8.8	1988 Impulse Turbo: 2259
4	8.9	1988 I-Mark RS Turbo: 2258
5	9.3	1990 Impulse XS: 2260
6	12.0	1986 I-Mark: 2254
7	12.9	1984 Impulse: 2253
		1986 Impulse Sports Coupe: 2255
8	19.9	1983 I-Mark LS: 2252
9	26.1	1987 Trooper 3-door TD: 2257

Jaguar

1	3.5	1989 XJ220: 2359
2	4.4	1990 XJS Lister Le Mans: 2366
3	4.7	1956 D Type: 2285
4	5.0	1977 XJS Tullius: 2333
5	5.2	1957 XKSS: 2291
6	6.5	1982 XJS HE: 2342
7	6.6	1951 C Type: 2274
		1981 XJS Automatic: 2341
		1953 XK120C: 2280
8	6.8	1971 E Type V12: 2319
9	6.9	1961 E Type Coupe: 2298
		1976 XJS: 2330
10	7.2	1963 E Type Coupe: 2303
		1986 XJSC HE: 2351
11	7.3	1958 XK150S: 2294
12	7.4	1967 E Type Roadster: 2312

		1973 XJ12: 2324
		1979 XJ6L: 2337
		1984 XJS 3.6: 2345
		1961 XKE: 2299
		1964 XKE: 2306
		1972 XKE V12: 2323
13	7.5	1977 XJS Automatic: 2332
		1988 XJS Koenig: 2356
14	7.6	1965 E Type 4.2: 2309
15	7.7	1990 XJRS: 2364
		1985 XJS HE Cabriolet: 2347
16	7.8	1978 XJ5.3 Automatic: 2335
		1981 XJS: 2340
		1991 XJS: 2370
		1987 XJS 3.6 Automatic: 2354
17	8.0	1988 XJS V12 Convertible: 2357
		1969 XKE Coupe: 2317
		1974 XKE V12: 2325
18	8.2	1983 XJS: 2343
		1984 XJS HE: 2346
19	8.3	1989 4.0 Sovereign: 2358
		1972 XJ12: 2321
		1975 XJ5.3C: 2328
		1991 XJ6 3.2: 2368
		1990 XJR 4.0: 2363
		1966 XKE 4.2 2+2: 2310
20	8.4	1951 XK140: 2276
		1955 XK140MC: 2283
21	8.5	1963 3.8 Mk II: 2301
		1953 XK120M: 2281
		1958 XK150: 2293
22	8.6	1988 XJS: 2355
		1979 XJS: 2338
23	8.7	1971 XJ6 4.2: 2320
		1986 XJS: 2349
		1991 XJS 4.0 Auto: 2371
		1989 XJS Convertible: 2360
24	8.8	1976 XJ12C: 2329
		1978 XJ12L: 2334
		1986 XJSC: 2350
25	8.9	1959 XK150S: 2295
26	9.1	1958 3.4: 2292
		1975 XJ12L: 2326
27	9.2	1960 3.8 Sedan: 2297
		1990 XJ6 Vanden Plas: 2362
28	9.5	1957 XK150: 2290
29	9.8	1963 3.8 Mk II Automatic: 2302
		1986 XJ6 3.6: 2348
30	9.9	1964 4.2 litre Mk X: 2305
		1967 420: 2311
		1987 XJ6 2.9: 2353
		1990 XJS: 2365
		1991 XJS Convertible: 2372
		1990 XJS Railton: 2367
		1989 XJS V12 Convertible: 2361
		1953 XK120 Coupe: 2279
31	10.0	1979 XJ6 4.2: 2336
32	10.1	1970 XJ6: 2318
		1969 XJ6 4.2 Automatic: 2316
33	10.4	1960 3.4: 2296
		1965 3.8S: 2307
		1965 4.2 litre Mk X Overdrive: 2308
		1938 SS 100 3.5-litre: 2267
34	10.6	1977 XJ4.2: 2331
		1980 XJ6 Series III: 2339
35	10.7	1972 XJ6: 2322
36	10.9	1975 XJ3.4: 2327
37	11.0	1968 420 Sedan: 2315
		1956 XK 140: 2287
38	11.5	1964 3.8S Sedan: 2304
		1987 XJ6: 2352
39	11.6	1955 Mk VII: 2282
		1957 Mk VIII: 2289
40	11.7	1951 XK120: 2275
41	12.0	1950 XK120: 2273
42	12.1	1962 Mk X: 2300
43	12.3	1984 XJ6 Vanden Plas: 2344
44	12.5	1968 240: 2314
45	13.1	1956 2.4 Sedan: 2284
46	13.4	1952 Mk VII: 2277
47	13.6	1953 Mk VII: 2278
48	14.3	1956 Mk VII Auto: 2286
49	15.8	1957 2.4 Saloon: 2288
50	16.8	1948 3.5-litre: 2270
		1948 Mk IV: 2271
51	17.4	1936 SS 2.5-litre: 2264
52	18.3	1937 SS 100 2.5-litre: 2265
53	18.9	1949 3.5-litre Mk V: 2272
54	19.5	1940 SS 2.5-litre: 2268
55	23.0	1931 SS1 Sports Tourer: 2263
56	24.0	1940 SS1 2.5-litre: 2269
57	25.1	1938 SS 1.5-litre: 2266

Jeep

1	11.2	1971 CJ-5: 2374
2	11.9	1971 Gladiator Pickup J-2500 Townside: 2376
		1974 Wagoneer: 2382
3	12.2	1978 Cherokee Chief: 2383
4	12.9	1971 Wagoneer: 2377
5	13.0	1972 CJ-5 V8: 2379
6	13.8	1972 Commando: 2380
7	14.2	1971 Wagoneer 1414C: 2378
8	15.5	1964 Wagoneer: 2373
9	16.4	1971 Commando: 2375
10	16.5	1974 CJ6: 2381

Jensen

1	6.4	1969 Interceptor: 2393
2	6.9	1971 SP: 2397
3	7.1	1970 Interceptor II: 2395
4	7.2	1974 Healey Huffaker: 2399
5	7.3	1967 Interceptor: 2391
6	7.4	1971 Interceptor: 2396
7	7.6	1974 Interceptor III Convertible: 2401
8	8.1	1970 FF II: 2394
9	8.4	1963 CV8: 2390
		1968 FF: 2392
10	8.7	1976 GT: 2402
11	9.3	1976 Interceptor III Convertible: 2403
12	9.7	1973 Healey: 2398
13	10.4	1974 Interceptor III: 2400
14	10.6	1958 541R: 2388
15	11.2	1977 GT: 2404
16	12.1	1956 541: 2387
17	12.4	1961 541S Automatic: 2389
18	13.7	1951 Interceptor Cabriolet: 2386
19	19.2	1938 3.5-litre Tourer: 2385
20	20.0	1936 3.5-litre Saloon: 2384

Jensen-Healey

1	7.8	1972 2-litre: 2405

Jowett

1	15.1	1953 Jupiter: 2410
2	16.8	1953 Jupiter Mk IA: 2411
3	25.4	1948 Javelin: 2409

Kaiser

1	12.6	1967 Jeepster: 2415
2	24.0	1952 Henry J 6: 2414

Kissel

1	23.5	1927 8-65 Gold Bug: 2416

Koenig

1	3.5	1991 C62: 2419
		1990 Competition Evolution: 2418
2	4.0	1989 Competition: 2417

Kurtis

1	7.7	1953 Hornet Roadster: 2420

La Salle

1	18.7	1938 37-50 V8 Saloon: 2422

Lada

1	13.4	1989 Samara 1300L 5-door: 2430
2	13.8	1976 1500: 2424
3	14.0	1987 Samara 1300 SL: 2429
4	16.4	1986 Riva 1500 Estate: 2427
5	16.6	1978 1300 ES: 2425
6	18.4	1975 1200: 2423
7	18.9	1987 Niva Cossack Cabrio: 2428
8	22.4	1979 Niva 1600: 2426

Lago

1	10.6	1959 America: 2431

Lagonda

1	12.5	1939 Rapide: 2445
2	12.9	1938 4.5-litre 12 Cylinder Saloon: 2443
3	13.1	1940 Drop-head Coupe: 2446
		1937 Rapide: 2441
4	14.6	1935 Rapide Tourer: 2439
5	14.8	1938 Saloon de Ville: 2444
6	15.5	1934 Le Mans: 2437
7	15.8	1956 3-litre Saloon: 2448
8	16.4	1938 4.5-litre: 2442
9	17.2	1936 4.5-litre Tourer: 2440
10	18.2	1949 2.5-litre Saloon: 2447
11	26.2	1933 16/80 Tourer: 2435

12	27.2	1934 3.5-litre Tourer: 2436
13	27.4	1934 Rapier Four-seater Tourer: 2438

Lamborghini

1	4.5	1991 Diablo: 2475
2	4.7	1989 Countach 25th Anniversary: 2473
3	4.9	1985 Countach: 2468
4	5.2	1986 Countach 5000S: 2469
5	5.5	1967 Miura: 2451
		1970 Miura S: 2456
6	5.6	1982 Countach LP 500S: 2465
7	5.7	1982 Countach S: 2466
8	5.9	1979 Countach S: 2464
9	6.2	1986 Jalpa 3500: 2470
10	6.3	1968 Miura: 2452
11	6.5	1969 Espada: 2453
12	6.7	1970 Miura P400S: 2455
13	6.8	1965 350GT: 2449
		1976 Countach: 2461
		1988 Jalpa: 2471
		1976 Silhouette 3000: 2462
14	7.2	1973 Jarama 400GT: 2459
		1972 Jarama 400GT: 2457
15	7.3	1982 Jalpa: 2467
16	7.5	1966 400GT: 2450
17	7.8	1970 Espada: 2454
		1988 LM129: 2472
18	8.5	1974 Urraco S: 2460
19	10.1	1976 Urraco: 2463

Lammas-Graham

1	16.2	1937 Drop-head Coupe: 2476

Lanchester

1	16.5	1937 SS 2.5-litre: 2480
2	33.1	1938 Roadrider de Luxe Saloon: 2482
3	33.2	1940 Roadrider de Luxe Saloon: 2483
4	36.8	1937 18: 2479
		1935 18 Saloon: 2478
5	44.7	1949 10: 2484

Lancia

1	3.6	1981 Montecarlo Group 5 Turbo: 2531
2	6.3	1989 Delta Integrale 16v: 2549
3	6.4	1988 Delta HF Integrale: 2547
4	6.6	1986 Delta HF 4WD: 2541
5	6.8	1990 Thema 2.0ie 16v SE Turbo: 2553
		1987 Thema 8.32: 2546
6	7.1	1984 Rally: 2537
7	7.2	1988 Thema 8.32: 2548
8	7.4	1991 Dedra 2000 Turbo: 2555
9	7.6	1985 Thema 2.0 ie LX Turbo: 2539
10	8.5	1986 Delta HF Turbo ie: 2542
11	8.6	1981 Montecarlo Spyder: 2532
12	8.8	1989 Thema 2.0ie 16v: 2550
13	9.2	1985 Coupe 2000ie: 2538
14	9.5	1986 Prisma 1600ie LX: 2543
15	9.7	1977 Gamma: 2525
16	9.8	1975 Beta Monte Carlo: 2517
17	9.9	1969 Fulvia Coupe: 2510
18	10.0	1990 Dedra 2.0ie: 2552
19	10.1	1976 Beta 2000: 2519
		1978 Gamma Berlina: 2526
20	10.3	1986 Thema 2.0ie: 2544
21	10.4	1972 2000: 2513
		1975 Beta 1600 Coupe: 2516
		1974 Fulvia Coupe S3: 2515
22	10.6	1977 Beta HPE 2000: 2523
23	10.7	1973 Beta 1800: 2514
24	10.8	1983 Prisma 1600: 2536
25	11.1	1981 Trevi 2000: 2533
26	11.3	1979 Beta HPE 1600: 2528
27	11.4	1979 Beta 2000 Automatic: 2527
28	11.5	1990 Dedra 1.8i: 2551
		1990 Y10 GTie: 2554
29	11.6	1982 Beta Coupe: 2534
30	11.8	1985 Y10 Turbo: 2540
31	11.9	1965 Flavia Zagato Sport: 2505
32	12.3	1955 Aurelia Gran Turismo 2500: 2490
33	12.5	1955 Spyder: 2491
		1980 Zagato: 2530
34	12.6	1967 Fulvia 1.3 Rallye: 2508
35	12.7	1965 Flaminia Coupe 3B: 2504
36	13.0	1967 Fulvia 1.3 Zagato: 2509
37	13.2	1976 Beta Coupe: 2520
		1964 Flavia Coupe: 2501
		1960 Zagato: 2497
38	13.3	1979 HPE: 2529
39	13.4	1977 Beta Scorpion: 2524
40	13.6	1976 Beta Sedan: 2521
		1960 Flaminia Coupe: 2496
41	13.8	1977 Beta: 2522
		1976 Beta 1300: 2518
42	13.9	1971 Fulvia Sedan: 2512
43	14.0	1958 Aurelia GT 2500: 2492
		1982 Delta Automatic: 2535
44	14.5	1962 Flaminia Sedan: 2500
45	15.0	1967 Flavia Injection: 2507
46	15.5	1959 Flaminia: 2495
47	15.6	1958 Flaminia: 2493
		1970 Fulvia Sedan: 2511
48	15.8	1966 Fulvia Coupe: 2506
49	16.7	1986 Y10 Fire: 2545
50	18.0	1952 Aurelia 2-litre Saloon: 2489
51	18.2	1964 Fulvia 2C: 2503
52	18.7	1961 Flavia: 2498
53	19.6	1934 27.6hp Astura Saloon: 2485
54	22.8	1938 Aprilia Saloon: 2488
55	23.0	1959 Appia Sedan: 2494
56	23.5	1964 Fulvia: 2502
57	23.7	1962 Appia III: 2499
58	25.2	1937 Aprilia Pillarless Saloon: 2487

Land-Rover

1	11.7	1991 Discovery V8i 5DR: 2565
2	12.8	1990 Discovery V8: 2564
3	13.6	1989 Ninety County V8: 2562
4	15.1	1987 One Ten County V8: 2561
5	17.1	1990 Discovery TDi: 2563
6	22.3	1987 Ninety County Turbo Diesel: 2560
7	26.1	1982 County: 2559
8	29.1	1973 SWB: 2558
9	31.7	1971 Series III: 2557

Lea-Francis

1	19.2	1948 Sports: 2569

Lexus

1	6.9	1991 SC400: 2571
2	8.3	1990 LS400: 2570
3	9.0	1992 ES300: 2572

Lincoln

1	8.0	1989 Continental Mk VII: 2586
2	8.3	1990 Continental Mk VII LSC: 2587
3	8.4	1986 Continental Mk VII LSC: 2585
4	8.7	1958 Continental Mk III: 2579
5	8.9	1985 Continental Mk VII LSC: 2584
6	11.2	1961 Continental: 2580
7	11.6	1976 Continental Limousine: 2582
8	11.8	1964 Continental: 2581
9	13.0	1984 Continental Mk VII: 2583
10	14.4	1953 Cosmopolitan Sedan: 2578
11	15.5	1938 Zephyr Saloon: 2577
12	16.0	1936 Zephyr Saloon: 2576

Lotus

1	4.9	1989 Esprit Turbo SE: 2637
2	5.1	1990 Esprit Turbo SE: 2640
3	5.2	1989 Esprit Turbo: 2636
4	5.3	1987 Elan Autocrosser: 2632
5	5.4	1988 Esprit Turbo: 2635
6	5.6	1986 Esprit Turbo: 2630
		1987 Esprit Turbo HC: 2633
7	6.1	1981 Esprit Turbo: 2627
8	6.5	1990 Elan SE: 2639
9	6.6	1991 Elan SE: 2641
		1983 Esprit Turbo: 2629
10	6.7	1990 Elan: 2638
11	6.8	1986 Excel SE: 2631
12	7.0	1971 Elan Sprint: 2608
		1972 Europa Twin Cam: 2614
13	7.1	1970 7 Twin Cam SS: 2605
		1983 Eclat Excel: 2628
14	7.4	1971 Plus 2S 130: 2610
15	7.5	1972 Plus 2S 130/5: 2615
16	7.6	1967 Elan Coupe SE: 2600
		1961 Super 7: 2594
17	7.7	1978 Elite V8: 2623
		1970 Super 7 Twincam: 2607
18	7.8	1969 Elan S4 Drophead SE: 2603
		1975 Elite 503: 2618
19	7.9	1977 Eclat 523: 2619
20	8.0	1967 Elan SE: 2601
		1979 Esprit S2: 2625
21	8.2	1987 Excel SA: 2634
22	8.3	1972 Europa: 2613
23	8.4	1972 Elan Sprint: 2612
		1977 Esprit: 2620
24	8.5	1963 Elan 1600: 2596
25	8.7	1964 Elan 1600: 2599
26	8.9	1968 Elan +2: 2602
27	9.0	1957 Mk XI: 2590
28	9.2	1977 Esprit 16v: 2621
29	9.4	1969 Elan S4 SE: 2604

30	9.6	1973 Europa Special 5-speed: 2616
31	9.7	1980 Eclat: 2626
		1979 Elite: 2624
		1977 Sprint: 2622
32	9.8	1972 Elan Plus 2S 130: 2611
33	9.9	1962 Super 7: 2595
34	10.5	1964 Cortina: 2598
35	10.7	1971 Europa S2: 2609
36	10.9	1957 11 Le Mans: 2589
37	11.1	1975 Elite: 2617
38	11.2	1970 Europa S2: 2606
39	11.8	1963 Elite: 2597
40	12.2	1960 Elite: 2592
41	14.2	1957 Sports: 2591
42	14.3	1961 7: 2593

Lynx

1	5.3	1987 D Type: 2642
2	7.6	1988 XJS Eventer: 2643

Marcos

1	7.5	1971 3-litre Volvo: 2646
2	9.1	1965 1800: 2644
3	11.4	1968 1600GT: 2645

Marendaz

1	15.8	1935 15/90 Special Tourer: 2647

Marmon

1	14.0	1932 16: 2651

Maserati

1	6.3	1989 430: 2678
		1985 Biturbo E: 2674
2	6.5	1988 430: 2676
		1973 Bora: 2660
		1978 Khamsin: 2666
3	6.7	1990 228: 2680
		1989 Spyder: 2679
4	6.9	1988 Biturbo: 2677
5	7.2	1985 Biturbo: 2672
		1987 Biturbo Spyder: 2675
		1976 Bora: 2664
6	7.3	1985 Biturbo Automatic: 2673
		1979 Khamsin: 2669
7	7.4	1970 Indy: 2657
8	7.5	1959 GT Coupe: 2653
		1971 Indy: 2659
		1975 Khamsin Automatic: 2662
9	7.6	1978 Kyalami: 2667
10	7.7	1981 Merak SS: 2670
11	8.0	1976 Khamsin: 2665
12	8.1	1961 3500GT: 2654
13	8.2	1975 Merak: 2663
14	8.3	1968 Quattroporte: 2656
15	8.4	1963 3500 GTI Sebring: 2655
16	9.1	1978 Merak: 2668
17	9.3	1983 Quattroporte: 2671
18	9.5	1971 Ghibli: 2658
		1974 Merak: 2661

Matra

1	14.9	1978 Rancho: 2683
2	15.6	1969 M530A: 2682

Matra-Simca

1	12.3	1975 Bagheera: 2684

Mazda

1	4.8	1991 RX-7 Mariah Mode Six: 2770
2	5.3	1980 RX-7 Racer: 2715
3	5.5	1991 RX-7 Cartech: 2768
4	5.8	1989 RX-7 Convertible Racing Beat: 2757
5	6.4	1990 MX-5 Miata Millen: 2760
		1990 RX-7 Turbo: 2764
		1991 RX-7 Turbo: 2771
6	6.6	1987 RX-7 Turbo: 2740
		1986 RX-7 Turbo: 2737
		1988 RX-7 Turbo: 2751
7	6.7	1989 RX-7 Turbo II: 2759
8	7.0	1991 RX-7 Infini IV: 2769
9	7.2	1988 MX-6 GT: 2748
10	7.5	1988 MX-6: 2747
11	7.8	1991 323 1.8 GT: 2766
		1988 323 Turbo 4x4: 2743
		1986 626 GT: 2734
12	7.9	1986 323 Turbo 4x4 Lux: 2732
		1986 RX-7 GXL: 2736
13	8.2	1990 MX-6 GT: 2761
		1989 MX-6 GT 4WS: 2756
14	8.5	1986 RX-7: 2735
		1984 RX-7: 2724
		1984 RX-7 GSL SE: 2725
		1988 RX-7 GTU: 2750
15	8.6	1989 323 1.8 GT: 2753
		1982 RX-7: 2720
		1989 RX-7 GTUs: 2758
16	8.7	1988 323 GTX: 2742
17	8.8	1989 323 1.6i: 2752
18	8.9	1991 MX-3 V6: 2767
19	9.1	1990 Protege: 2762
		1990 RX-7 Convertible: 2763
20	9.2	1992 MX-3 GS: 2773
		1978 RX-7: 2705
		1980 RX-7: 2714
21	9.4	1988 626 2.0i GT 4WS: 2745
22	9.5	1989 MX-5 Miata: 2755
23	9.7	1974 RX-4 Coupe: 2698
		1983 RX-7: 2723
		1988 RX-7 Convertible: 2749
		1979 RX-7 GS: 2711
		1981 RX-7 GSL: 2719
24	9.8	1985 323 1.6i: 2727
		1986 626 2.0i 5-door: 2733
25	9.9	1985 RX-7 GSL: 2728
26	10.0	1986 323 1.6i: 2730
		1971 RX-2: 2690
27	10.1	1979 RX-7: 2710
28	10.2	1968 110S Coupe: 2685
29	10.3	1972 RX-2: 2691
30	10.4	1987 626 2.0 GLS Executive: 2739
31	10.5	1988 929: 2746
32	10.7	1979 626 Coupe: 2707
33	10.8	1973 RX-4: 2694
34	10.9	1972 RX-3: 2692
35	11.0	1988 121 1.3 LX Sun Top: 2741
		1974 Rotary Pickup: 2697
36	11.1	1987 323 1.5 GLX: 2738
		1986 323 LX: 2731
37	11.2	1976 Cosmo: 2701
38	11.7	1988 626 2.0 GLX Executive Estate: 2744
		1989 MPV: 2754
		1974 RX-4 Station Wagon: 2699
39	12.1	1973 RX-3 Station Wagon: 2693
40	12.3	1986 323 1.5 GLX Estate: 2729
		1983 626 1600 LX: 2722
41	12.4	1983 626: 2721
		1977 RX-4: 2704
42	12.9	1980 Montrose GLS Coupe: 2713
43	13.0	1985 323 1.5 GLX: 2726
44	13.1	1981 323 1300: 2716
45	13.4	1992 MX-3 1.6 Auto: 2772
46	13.5	1979 GLC Wagon: 2708
		1971 Rotary: 2689
47	13.6	1979 Montrose 1600 GLS: 2709
48	13.9	1981 GLC Sport: 2718
49	14.0	1974 929: 2696
50	14.3	1981 GLC: 2717
51	14.4	1979 1.4 SP: 2706
		1980 626: 2712
52	14.7	1977 323: 2702
53	15.1	1974 1300: 2695
54	15.3	1991 121 GSX: 2765
55	15.6	1975 808: 2700
56	16.2	1977 GLC: 2703
57	17.2	1970 1200 de Luxe: 2687
58	17.5	1971 1800: 2688
59	18.0	1968 1500 de Luxe: 2686

Mercedes-Benz

1	5.0	1990 300CE AMG Hammer: 2910
2	5.2	1988 300E AMG Hammer: 2899
3	5.9	1990 500SL: 2913
4	6.1	1992 600SEL: 2923
5	6.3	1991 500E: 2919
6	6.4	1991 500SL: 2920
7	6.8	1989 560SL: 2907
8	6.9	1991 190E 2.5-16 Evolution II: 2916
		1987 560SEC Cabriolet Straman: 2895
9	7.0	1989 190E AMG Baby Hammer: 2903
		1958 300SL Roadster: 2800
		1986 560SEC: 2888
10	7.1	1990 190E 2.5-16 Evolution II: 2908
		1969 300SEL 6.3: 2828
		1986 560SEL: 2889
11	7.2	1989 190E 2.5-16: 2901
12	7.3	1979 450SEL 6.9: 2862
13	7.5	1987 300CE: 2892
		1986 300E: 2885
		1992 500SEL: 2922
		1986 560SL: 2890
14	7.6	1961 300SL Roadster: 2807
		1986 420SE: 2887
15	7.8	1986 190E 2.3-16: 2883
		1990 300E-24: 2912

		1952 300SL Carrera Panamericana: 2788
16	8.0	1985 190E 2.3-16: 2879
		1988 300CE: 2897
		1985 500SEL: 2882
17	8.2	1955 300SL Coupe: 2794
		1977 600SE: 2854
18	8.3	1987 190E 2.6: 2891
		1989 300E: 2906
		1988 300E 4Matic: 2898
19	8.4	1972 280SE 3.5: 2835
		1985 300E: 2881
		1991 400SE: 2918
20	8.5	1990 300CE: 2909
		1989 300CE Cabriolet Straman: 2905
21	8.6	1991 300SL-24 5-speed Auto: 2917
22	8.7	1989 190E 2.6: 2902
		1983 280SE: 2874
		1986 300TE: 2886
		1987 420SEL: 2894
23	8.8	1988 260E Auto: 2896
		1955 300SL: 2793
24	8.9	1973 280CE Auto: 2840
25	9.0	1975 450SLC: 2849
		1984 500SEC: 2877
26	9.1	1982 380SEC: 2870
		1974 450SEL: 2845
27	9.2	1985 190E BBS/Callaway Turbo: 2880
28	9.3	1970 280SE 3.5: 2831
		1970 280SL: 2832
		1971 300SL: 2834
		1978 450SEL: 2858
29	9.5	1929 SSKL: 2776
30	9.7	1983 190E: 2873
		1963 230SL: 2810
		1973 280SE: 2841
		1967 600: 2821
31	9.9	1985 190E 2.3: 2878
		1969 280SL: 2827
32	10.0	1979 450SL: 2863
		1965 600: 2816
33	10.1	1974 280E: 2844
		1981 380SEL: 2869
34	10.2	1974 450SL: 2846
35	10.3	1981 230E: 2865
		1968 280SL: 2825
		1987 300TD: 2893
36	10.4	1979 280CE: 2860
		1964 300SE LWB: 2812
37	10.5	1972 350SL: 2837
38	10.6	1973 450SE: 2842
39	10.7	1964 230SL: 2811
40	10.8	1967 250SE: 2820
41	10.9	1983 380SL: 2875
		1976 450SL: 2851
		1973 450SLC: 2843
42	11.0	1965 230SL Automatic: 2815
		1976 280E: 2850
43	11.2	1989 190: 2900
		1984 190E: 2876
		1970 280SE: 2830
		1972 280SEL: 2836
44	11.4	1991 190E 2.3: 2915
		1977 280E: 2853
		1962 300SE: 2808
45	11.5	1982 380SL: 2871
46	11.7	1973 280: 2839
		1980 450SL: 2864
47	11.9	1959 220SE: 2801
48	12.2	1960 220SE: 2804
49	12.3	1991 190E 1.8 Auto: 2914
		1989 200E Automatic: 2904
50	12.4	1961 220SE Coupe: 2806
		1979 250T: 2859
51	12.5	1965 220SE: 2814
52	12.7	1968 250 Automatic: 2824
		1978 300SD: 2857
53	12.9	1981 230TE: 2866
54	13.0	1955 190SL: 2791
		1986 200: 2884
55	13.2	1981 300TD: 2868
56	13.3	1958 190SL: 2798
57	13.4	1983 190: 2872
		1973 230/4: 2838
58	13.5	1960 190SL: 2802
59	13.6	1969 220: 2826
		1970 250 Coupe: 2829
60	13.8	1968 250: 2823
61	14.0	1977 230C: 2852
		1966 250S: 2818
		1928 36/220-S: 2774
62	15.0	1957 219: 2796
		1960 220: 2803
63	15.1	1966 230 Automatic: 2817
64	15.3	1978 200: 2855
65	15.5	1990 300D: 2911
66	15.8	1968 220: 2822
		1958 220S: 2799
67	15.9	1955 300B: 2792
68	16.1	1953 300 Sedan: 2789
69	16.3	1975 280S: 2847
70	16.4	1952 300: 2787
		1938 Type 540: 2785
71	16.5	1936 Type 500 Supercharged: 2782
72	17.1	1978 300CD: 2856
73	17.8	1961 190: 2805
74	18.1	1979 300TD: 2861
75	19.5	1963 190C Automatic: 2809
76	20.3	1975 300D: 2848
77	20.8	1966 300D: 2819
78	23.7	1981 300GD: 2867
79	25.4	1991 G-Wagen 300 GD LWB: 2921
80	27.5	1971 220D: 2833
81	29.9	1954 180 Saloon: 2790
82	32.0	1938 Type 320 Saloon: 2784
83	32.3	1958 180D: 2797
84	38.7	1965 190D: 2813
85	39.3	1937 Type 230 Saloon: 2783
86	44.4	1935 Type 290 Cabriolet: 2780

Mercury

1	4.2	1964 Comet A/FX: 2933
2	6.2	1968 Cyclone: 2947
3	6.6	1966 Comet Cyclone GT: 2940
4	7.0	1963 Super Marauder S-55: 2932
5	7.1	1968 Cougar XR-7: 2946
6	7.2	1967 Cougar Group 2: 2942
7	7.4	1989 Cougar XR-7: 2960
8	7.5	1969 Marquis Marauder X-100: 2949
9	7.6	1970 Cougar Eliminator: 2950
10	7.7	1967 Cougar GT: 2943
11	7.8	1983 Capri: 2957
12	8.0	1962 S-55 406: 2930
13	8.2	1969 Marquis Brougham: 2948
14	8.3	1990 Capri XR-2: 2961
15	9.1	1991 Tracer LTS: 2962
16	9.3	1964 Park Lane: 2937
17	9.4	1967 Marquis: 2944
18	9.5	1965 Park Lane: 2939
19	10.0	1968 Cougar: 2945
20	10.2	1964 Comet Cyclone 4-speed: 2935
21	10.3	1987 Tracer: 2959
22	10.6	1975 Capri II 2.8 V6: 2952
23	10.7	1967 Cougar: 2941
24	11.3	1977 Monarch: 2953
25	11.7	1986 Sable LS: 2958
26	11.8	1964 Comet Caliente: 2934
		1964 Comet Cyclone Automatic: 2936
27	12.2	1965 Monterey: 2938
28	13.9	1981 Lynx Hatchback RS: 2956
29	14.5	1963 Comet S-22 Sportster: 2931
30	15.0	1981 LN7: 2955
		1962 Meteor: 2929
31	15.2	1961 Comet: 2926
32	15.4	1975 Bobcat 2.3-litre: 2951
33	15.8	1977 Zephyr: 2954
34	16.6	1961 Meteor 800: 2928
35	19.2	1961 Comet 170: 2927
		1949 Coupe: 2924
36	21.0	1960 Comet: 2925

Merkur

1	7.9	1985 XR4Ti: 2963
2	8.1	1988 XR4Ti: 2965
3	10.1	1987 Scorpio: 2964

Messerschmitt (FMR)

1	27.8	1958 Tg 500: 2966

Meyers

1	22.7	1965 Manx: 2967

MG

1	6.9	1989 Maestro Turbo: 3040
2	7.5	1985 Montego Turbo: 3039
3	7.8	1972 Costello B GT V8: 3022
4	8.6	1973 B GT V8: 3025
5	9.4	1983 Metro Turbo: 3037
6	9.6	1984 Montego EFi: 3038
7	9.9	1958 A Twin Cam: 2995
8	10.0	1967 C: 3011
9	10.1	1969 C: 3017
10	10.9	1968 C GT Automatic: 3016
11	12.1	1975 B: 3027
		1968 B All-Synchro: 3015
		1970 B Mk II: 3019
12	12.2	1962 B 1800: 3004
		1982 Metro 1300: 3036
13	12.3	1975 Midget 1500: 3028
14	12.5	1958 A Judson: 2994
15	12.8	1961 A Mk II: 3001

		1990 B British Motor Heritage: 3041
16	12.9	1965 B: 3008
17	13.0	1971 B GT: 3020
18	13.3	1958 Twin Cam MGA: 2997
19	13.6	1980 B: 3035
		1970 B Automatic: 3018
		1966 B GT: 3009
		1966 B GT Coupe: 3010
20	13.7	1961 A 1600 Mk II: 3000
		1973 B: 3023
21	13.9	1979 B: 3033
22	14.0	1977 B GT: 3032
23	14.1	1968 1300 Mk II: 3013
		1971 Midget Mk III: 3021
24	14.2	1959 A 1600: 2998
25	14.3	1968 1300 Mk II Auto: 3014
		1979 Midget: 3034
26	14.5	1955 A: 2990
27	14.6	1973 B GT: 3024
		1967 Midget Mk III: 3012
28	15.0	1957 A Coupe: 2993
29	15.5	1973 Midget: 3026
		1976 Midget: 3030
		1976 Midget Mk IV: 3031
		1954 TF Supercharged: 2989
30	15.6	1956 A: 2992
31	16.3	1954 TF 1500: 2988
32	16.5	1953 TDC Mk II: 2984
33	17.2	1963 Midget: 3007
34	18.0	1954 TD Laystall: 2986
35	18.3	1976 B: 3029
36	18.4	1962 1100: 3003
37	18.5	1958 Magnette: 2996
38	18.9	1954 TF: 2987
39	19.4	1950 TD: 2979
		1953 TD: 2983
40	19.5	1963 Magnette Mk IV: 3006
41	20.2	1961 Midget: 3002
42	20.6	1959 Magnette Mk III: 2999
43	21.2	1949 TC: 2978
44	22.0	1954 Magnette: 2985
45	22.6	1955 Magnette: 2991
46	22.7	1947 TC Midget: 2977
47	22.8	1963 1100: 3005
		1934 Magnette N Two-seater: 2972
48	23.1	1936 Midget Series T: 2976
49	23.9	1953 Midget: 2982
50	27.4	1936 Midget PB: 2975
51	28.6	1935 Magnette KN Saloon: 2974
52	30.4	1952 1.25-litre Saloon: 2981
53	32.2	1934 Midget P Type: 2973

Mini

1	10.5	1965 Cooper 1275S: 3051
2	11.2	1964 Cooper 1275S: 3049
3	13.3	1971 1275GT: 3054
4	13.5	1963 Cooper S: 3047
5	14.6	1974 1275GT: 3056
6	14.7	1969 1275GT: 3053
7	16.8	1965 Cooper: 3050
8	17.9	1976 Clubman 1100: 3059
9	18.0	1961 Cooper: 3046
10	18.7	1975 1000: 3057
11	20.3	1979 850 Super de Luxe: 3060
12	26.2	1967 Super de Luxe Mk II: 3052
13	26.5	1959 Minor de Luxe: 3043
14	27.0	1960 Minor: 3044
15	27.5	1973 850: 3055
16	29.7	1963 Super de Luxe: 3048
17	32.0	1975 Automatic: 3058
18	33.8	1960 Traveller: 3045

Mitsubishi

1	6.3	1991 3000GT VR-4: 3111
2	6.6	1985 Colt Starion Turbo: 3081
3	6.8	1989 Eclipse GSX: 3103
4	6.9	1987 Starion 2000 Turbo: 3095
5	7.2	1989 Eclipse: 3102
6	7.5	1982 Colt Starion Turbo: 3071
		1985 Starion ESI: 3086
7	7.8	1989 Starion 2.6 Turbo: 3106
8	7.9	1991 Galant VR-4: 3114
9	8.0	1989 Starion ESI-R: 3107
10	8.2	1988 Mirage Turbo: 3101
11	8.3	1991 Colt 1800 GTI-16v: 3112
		1986 Starion ESI-R: 3090
		1987 Starion ESI-R: 3096
12	8.4	1988 Cordia Turbo: 3097
13	8.5	1986 Cordia Turbo: 3087
		1990 Lancer Liftback 1800 GTi-16v: 3110
14	8.6	1981 Colt Lancer 2000 Turbo: 3068
		1985 Galant Turbo: 3083
15	8.7	1984 Colt 1600 Turbo: 3077
		1988 Galant GTi-16v: 3099
16	9.0	1991 Diamante LS: 3113
		1988 Lancer GTi 16v: 3100
		1983 Tredia Turbo: 3076
17	9.2	1982 Colt Cordia Turbo: 3069
		1983 Starion: 3074
		1985 Starion: 3085
		1983 Starion Turbo: 3075
18	9.3	1991 Sigma: 3116
19	9.5	1984 Cordia Turbo 1.8: 3078
20	9.7	1989 Galant GS: 3104
21	9.9	1982 Colt Hatchback Turbo: 3070
22	10.0	1991 Space Runner 1800-16v GLXi: 3117
23	10.4	1990 Galant 2000 GLSi Coupe: 3108
		1987 Galant Sapporo: 3093
		1984 Mirage Turbo: 3080
24	10.9	1988 Galant 2000 GLSi: 3098
25	11.2	1976 Colt Celeste 2000: 3063
26	11.7	1990 Lancer GLXi 4WD Liftback: 3109
27	11.9	1975 Colt Galant 2000: 3062
28	12.0	1986 Mirage: 3089
29	12.2	1987 Colt 1500 GLX 5-door: 3091
30	12.5	1985 Space Wagon 1800GLX: 3084
31	12.7	1978 Colt Sappore 2000 GSR: 3066
32	12.8	1984 Galant 1600 GL: 3079
		1989 Shogun V6 5-door: 3105
33	13.1	1987 Galant 2000 GLS Automatic: 3092
		1991 Shogun V6 LWB: 3115
34	13.2	1978 Colt Lancer Estate: 3065
		1982 Cordia LS: 3072
35	13.4	1977 Colt Sigma 2000: 3064
36	13.8	1979 Colt 1400 GLX: 3067
37	14.0	1986 Lancer 1.5 GLX Estate: 3088
38	14.4	1985 Galant: 3082
39	14.5	1983 Colt Shogun: 3073
40	17.5	1968 Colt 1100F: 3061
41	17.8	1987 Shogun Turbo Diesel 5-door: 3094

Monteverdi

1	6.3	1969 375L: 3118

Moretti

1	15.5	1954 750 Grand Sport Berlinetta Coupe: 3119

Morgan

1	5.6	1987 Plus 8: 3134
2	6.1	1991 Plus 8: 3137
3	6.5	1978 Plus 8: 3131
4	6.7	1968 Plus 8: 3129
5	6.8	1980 Plus 8 Turbo: 3132
6	7.4	1988 Plus 8: 3135
7	7.7	1990 Plus 4 Mk III: 3136
8	8.5	1970 Plus 8: 3130
9	9.9	1959 Plus 4: 3127
10	10.4	1984 4/4: 3133
11	10.8	1955 Plus 4: 3125
12	13.3	1954 Plus 4: 3124
13	14.0	1939 SS: 3122
14	16.5	1963 4/4: 3128
15	17.1	1952 Plus 4: 3123
16	20.5	1957 4/4 Modified: 3126
17	28.3	1938 4/4: 3121
18	28.4	1936 4/4: 3120

Morris

1	11.4	1976 Marina 1.8 HL: 3183
2	11.7	1981 Ital 2.0 HLS Automatic: 3186
3	12.1	1971 Marina TC: 3181
4	12.3	1971 Marina 1.8TC: 3180
5	12.5	1978 Marina 1700HL: 3185
6	13.5	1972 Marina Estate: 3182
7	13.7	1969 1800S: 3177
8	17.3	1971 Marina 1.3 Super Coupe: 3179
9	17.4	1966 1800: 3176
10	17.8	1956 Isis: 3166
11	18.2	1977 Marina 1.3 Super Coupe: 3184
12	22.2	1963 1100: 3173
13	24.0	1970 1100 Mk II: 3178
14	24.8	1964 Minor 1000 de Luxe: 3174
15	25.1	1964 Oxford VI Traveller: 3175
16	27.1	1957 Oxford Series III: 3169
17	29.0	1954 Oxford Saloon: 3164
18	29.9	1958 Oxford Traveller Series III: 3171
19	31.2	1957 Minor 1100: 3168
20	31.3	1957 Minor 1000: 3167
21	32.6	1961 Minor 1000: 3172
22	34.1	1958 Minor 1000 Traveller: 3170
23	37.5	1955 Cowley: 3165
24	39.4	1935 21 Series II Saloon: 3150
25	41.4	1948 Oxford: 3158
26	42.8	1935 10/6 Sports Tourer: 3148
27	45.8	1953 Oxford Travellers' Car: 3162
28	46.7	1950 Oxford Saloon: 3160
29	52.5	1954 Minor: 3163

Moskvich

1 14.5 1975 1500: 3188
2 27.5 1967 De Luxe: 3187

Muntz

1 12.3 1951 Jet: 3189

MVS

1 6.0 1987 Venturi GT: 3190
2 6.5 1990 Venturi: 3191

Nash

1 9.8 1955 Nash-Healey Roadster Supercharged: 3200
2 11.5 1954 Nash-Healey Roadster: 3198
3 20.2 1938 Ambassador Six Saloon: 3195
4 20.7 1956 Rambler Station Wagon: 3201
5 21.9 1952 Rambler Station Wagon: 3196
6 22.4 1954 Metropolitan: 3197
7 22.9 1958 Metropolitan 1500: 3202
8 27.0 1955 Metropolitan: 3199

Naylor

1 12.5 1985 TF 1700: 3203

Nissan

1 5.0 1991 300ZX Turbo Millen Super GTZ: 3247
2 5.6 1990 300ZX: 3240
1991 300ZX Motor Sports International SR-71: 3246
1990 Skyline GT-R: 3243
3 6.3 1989 240SX Turbo Tokico/Cartech: 3233
4 6.5 1990 300ZX Turbo: 3241
1991 300ZX Twin Turbo: 3248
5 6.8 1992 200SX: 3254
6 7.0 1987 300ZX Turbo: 3224
7 7.1 1989 300ZX: 3234
8 7.2 1989 200SX: 3232
1986 300ZX Turbo: 3216
1984 300ZX Turbo: 3209
9 7.4 1988 300ZX: 3231
10 7.5 1992 Sunny 2.0 GTi: 3255
11 7.9 1987 200SX SE V6: 3222
12 8.1 1991 NX2000: 3249
1991 Sentra SE-R: 3252
13 8.2 1984 300ZX: 3208
14 8.4 1988 200SX SE V6: 3229
15 8.5 1989 Maxima SE: 3236
16 8.6 1986 Bluebird 1.8 ZX: 3217
1988 Maxima SE: 3214
17 8.7 1991 Primera 2.0E ZX: 3251
18 8.8 1991 240SX: 3245
1988 240SX: 3230
1987 300ZX: 3223
1985 Bluebird Turbo ZX: 3212
19 8.9 1991 Primera 2.0 GSX: 3250
1984 Silvia Turbo ZX: 3211
20 9.1 1986 300ZX: 3215
21 9.2 1987 Sunny ZX Coupe: 3227
22 9.4 1989 Maxima: 3235
23 9.5 1984 200SX Turbo: 3207
24 10.1 1991 100NX: 3244
25 10.3 1987 Pulsar NX SE: 3226
26 10.5 1991 Sunny 1.6 GS 5-door: 3253
27 10.6 1984 Pulsar NX Turbo: 3210
28 11.3 1982 Stanza XE: 3205
29 11.6 1986 Laurel 2.4 SGL Automatic: 3218
1987 Sunny 1.6 SLX Coupe: 3228
30 11.8 1986 Sentra: 3219
31 12.0 1989 Sunny 1.4 LS: 3239
32 12.4 1990 Primera 1.6 LS: 3242
33 12.8 1985 Cherry 1.3 SGT: 3213
1983 Pulsar NX: 3206
34 13.3 1986 Sentra Sport Coupe SE: 3220
35 13.7 1986 Sunny 1.3 LX 5-door: 3221
36 14.0 1989 Micra 1.2 GSX: 3237
37 14.4 1989 Prairie: 3238
38 14.5 1987 Micra SGL 5-DR: 3225
39 15.0 1982 Sentra: 3204

NSU

1 13.1 1974 Ro80: 3266
2 13.9 1968 Ro80: 3264
3 14.2 1965 Spider: 3261
4 16.7 1965 Wankel Spider: 3262
5 18.4 1966 Typ 110: 3263
6 20.5 1965 Prinz 1000L: 3260
7 26.5 1959 Prinz 34hp: 3256
8 27.7 1962 Prinz 4: 3259
1960 Sport-Prinz: 3258
9 35.7 1968 Super Prinz: 3265

Ogle

1 16.2 1962 Austin Mini Cooper GT: 3268
2 20.1 1961 1.5: 3267

Oldsmobile

1 5.7 1970 4-4-2 W30: 3296
2 6.2 1969 442 Hurst: 3293
3 6.3 1966 Cutlass 442: 3287
4 6.6 1969 Cutlass W-31: 3295
5 7.0 1968 4-4-2: 3290
1970 Rallye 350: 3297
6 7.4 1964 Cutlass 442: 3281
7 7.5 1964 Jetstar I: 3283
8 7.6 1989 Calais HO Quad 4: 3303
1989 Cutlass Calais International Series HO: 3304
9 7.8 1965 Cutlass Holiday 442: 3284
10 8.0 1968 Toronado: 3292
11 8.2 1988 Cutlass Calais International Series: 3301
1967 F-85 Cutlass Cruiser: 3289
12 8.5 1962 F-85 Jetfire Sports Coupe: 3277
1963 Starfire: 3280
13 8.7 1966 Toronado: 3288
14 9.4 1969 88 Delta Royale: 3294
1962 98 Holiday Sports Sedan: 3275
1964 F-85 Cutlass Holiday: 3282
15 9.7 1968 Delmont: 3291
16 9.8 1965 Dynamic Delta 88 Holiday: 3285
1963 F-85 Jetfire: 3279
17 9.9 1965 Toronado: 3286
18 10.2 1958 Super 88: 3272
19 10.4 1990 Toronado Trofeo: 3305
20 11.1 1973 Cutlass Salon: 3298
21 11.4 1988 Cutlass International Series: 3302
22 12.1 1955 Super 88: 3271
23 12.8 1962 Dynamic 88 Celebrity Sedan: 3276
24 14.0 1962 F-85 V8: 3278
25 14.2 1961 F-85 Station Wagon: 3274
26 14.5 1961 F-85: 3273
27 17.2 1976 Starfire: 3299
28 18.2 1980 Cutlass Diesel: 3300
29 21.7 1936 28.8hp Saloon: 3270
30 22.4 1935 26.3hp Saloon: 3269

Opel

1 4.9 1991 Omega Lotus: 3352
2 7.6 1991 Calibra 2.0i 16v: 3351
3 8.5 1981 Manta Monza S3.0E: 3347
4 8.7 1984 Manta Monza GSE: 3350
5 9.0 1983 Manta GTE: 3349
6 9.2 1970 Senator: 3325
7 10.2 1969 GT: 3319
8 10.7 1974 Commodore GS 2.8: 3336
1974 Commodore GSE: 3337
9 10.8 1965 Diplomat: 3310
1969 GT 1.9: 3320
10 11.0 1981 Manta GTJ: 3346
1978 Rekord 2.0S: 3344
11 11.1 1970 Diplomat: 3323
1983 Manta Berlinetta 1.8S: 3348
12 11.4 1973 Commodore GS Coupe: 3332
13 11.6 1975 Ascona 1900SR: 3340
14 11.9 1971 GT: 3327
15 12.0 1969 GT 1900: 3321
16 12.1 1968 Kadette Rallye 1.9: 3314
17 12.2 1970 Manta Rallye 1.9: 3324
18 12.3 1969 Kadett Rallye 1.9: 3322
1972 Rekord 1900: 3329
19 12.5 1973 Ascona 1900SR: 3331
20 12.7 1975 Manta: 3341
1967 Rekord Coupe: 3313
21 12.8 1969 Commodore GS Coupe: 3318
22 13.2 1973 GT: 3333
1973 Manta Berlinetta Auto: 3335
23 13.3 1973 Manta: 3334
24 13.6 1971 Rallye 1900: 3328
25 13.9 1976 Rekord Berlina Pacesetter: 3343
26 14.0 1975 1900: 3339
27 14.2 1973 1900 Station Wagon: 3330
1979 Kadett 1.3S Berlina: 3345
28 14.5 1971 Ascona Voyage: 3326
29 15.5 1974 Kadett Coupe: 3338
30 15.9 1967 Kadett Rallye: 3312
31 17.8 1966 Kadett S: 3311
32 19.6 1958 Rekord: 3308
33 23.0 1964 Kadett: 3309
34 27.4 1976 Rekord 2100D: 3342
35 34.2 1938 Olympia Saloon: 3307

Osca

1 7.0 1955 1490cc Spyder: 3353

Packard

1 17.2 1930 7-34 Phaeton: 3355

2	18.8	1932 Super 8 Phaeton: 3356
3	19.2	1934 Twelve Victoria: 3359
4	19.9	1937 120 Saloon: 3362
5	20.2	1935 120 Saloon: 3360
6	20.4	1936 32.5hp Standard Eight Saloon: 3361
7	21.2	1934 32.5hp Saloon: 3358
8	23.0	1933 Straight Eight Saloon: 3357
9	23.3	1938 30hp Six Saloon: 3363

Panhard

1	22.3	1964 24CT Sports Coupe: 3371
2	22.8	1962 PL17 Tiger: 3370
3	23.7	1956 Dyna Sedan: 3367
4	24.0	1959 Dyna: 3368
5	26.1	1954 Dyna: 3365
6	26.2	1954 Dyna Junior Sports: 3366
7	28.6	1959 PL17: 3369

Panther

1	6.4	1972 J72: 3372
2	6.7	1977 Lima: 3375
3	6.8	1990 Solo: 3380
4	7.7	1984 Kallista 2.8: 3377
5	7.8	1983 Kallista 2.8: 3376
6	8.9	1990 Kallista: 3379
7	10.7	1975 J72: 3374
8	12.0	1975 De Ville: 3373
9	12.6	1985 Kallista 1.6L: 3378

Paramount

1	30.6	1956 Roadster: 3381

Parradine

1	5.4	1991 V-12: 3382

Peerless

1	12.4	1959 GT Coupe: 3383

Peugeot

1	6.2	1990 405 Turbo 16 Pike's Peak: 3460
2	7.8	1987 205 GTi 1.9: 3443
3	7.9	1991 605 SVE 24: 3467
4	8.0	1988 405 Mi16: 3448
5	8.6	1984 205 GTi: 3431
6	8.7	1986 205 GTi: 3438
		1987 309 GTi: 3444
7	8.8	1989 309 GTi: 3453
8	8.9	1986 505 Turbo: 3442
9	9.0	1989 405 Mi16: 3455
10	9.4	1975 604: 3413
11	9.5	1990 405 Mi16x4: 3459
12	9.7	1991 106 XSi: 3463
		1986 309 SR Injection: 3440
13	9.8	1987 505 STX: 3445
14	10.1	1984 505 GRi: 3432
		1985 505 Turbo: 3437
15	10.3	1988 405 SRi: 3449
16	10.5	1986 505 GTi Family Estate: 3441
17	10.6	1991 605 SV 3.0 Auto: 3466
18	10.7	1979 604: 3421
19	10.9	1988 405 1.6 GL: 3446
		1990 405 GLx4: 3457
20	11.0	1992 106 XT: 3468
21	11.7	1989 205 CJ: 3451
22	11.8	1990 605 SRi: 3461
23	11.9	1990 405 GR Injection Auto: 3458
24	12.2	1989 405 GTD Turbo: 3454
		1977 604 SLV-6: 3417
25	12.3	1991 205 D Turbo: 3464
		1979 505 STI: 3420
26	12.4	1982 505 GR Estate: 3427
27	12.5	1983 205 GR: 3429
28	12.6	1968 504 Injection: 3399
29	12.7	1983 305 SR: 3430
30	12.8	1981 305 S: 3425
		1991 605 SR TD: 3465
31	12.9	1986 309 1.6 GR: 3439
32	13.0	1978 305 SR: 3418
		1980 505 S: 3422
33	13.2	1985 309 1.3 GL: 3436
34	13.3	1989 205 1.1GL: 3450
35	13.4	1979 504: 3419
36	13.6	1976 104 ZS: 3415
37	13.8	1991 106 XR: 3462
38	13.9	1965 404 KF2: 3393
39	14.1	1972 504 Family Estate: 3406
40	14.3	1982 505 STI: 3428
41	14.6	1972 304 Estate Car: 3405
42	14.7	1990 309 Style 5-door: 3456
43	14.8	1971 504 Automatic: 3403
44	15.4	1988 405 GRD: 3447
45	15.9	1973 504: 3408
		1970 504: 3401
46	16.1	1985 205 XL: 3434
47	16.2	1984 505 S Wagon: 3433
48	16.5	1971 304: 3402
		1989 309 GLX: 3452
49	16.7	1975 504: 3412
50	16.8	1985 305 GRD Estate: 3435
51	17.0	1980 604 D Turbo: 3424
52	17.4	1972 204: 3404
53	17.6	1981 505 S Turbodiesel: 3426
54	18.1	1965 404: 3391
		1974 504 Station Wagon: 3411
55	18.3	1966 204: 3394
56	18.4	1961 404: 3388
57	18.5	1973 104: 3407
58	19.0	1976 104: 3414
59	19.2	1967 404 L Estate: 3396
60	19.3	1969 404 Automatic: 3400
61	19.9	1968 204 Coupe: 3397
		1960 404: 3387
62	20.0	1967 404 Automatique: 3395
63	20.5	1960 403: 3386
		1962 404 U6 Estate Car: 3390
64	21.7	1977 504 Diesel Automatique: 3416
		1974 504 L Diesel: 3410
65	23.1	1980 505 SD: 3423
66	24.0	1955 403: 3385
67	25.2	1962 403 B Estate Car: 3389
68	25.4	1965 404 Diesel: 3392
69	28.1	1973 504 Diesel: 3409
70	34.5	1955 203: 3384

Pininfarina

1	10.9	1984 Spider: 3470
2	11.2	1984 Azzurra: 3469

Plymouth

1	5.1	1969 Road Runner: 3507
2	5.6	1969 Cuda 440: 3505
3	6.2	1970 Duster 340: 3510
4	6.3	1968 GTX Hemi: 3502
5	6.6	1967 GTX: 3497
6	6.8	1968 GTX: 3501
7	6.9	1990 Laser RS Turbo: 3522
8	7.0	1968 Barracuda 340-S: 3498
9	7.1	1969 Cuda 340: 3504
		1966 Satellite: 3490
		1966 Satellite Street Hemi: 3491
10	7.2	1989 Laser RS: 3521
11	7.3	1968 Road Runner: 3503
12	7.5	1970 Barracuda: 3509
13	8.0	1958 Fury: 3474
		1991 Laser RS Turbo: 3523
		1963 Sport Fury: 3483
14	8.2	1965 Barracuda S: 3486
		1962 Sport Fury: 3481
15	8.6	1969 Satellite Sport: 3508
16	8.7	1965 Belvedere Satellite: 3487
		1967 Fury III: 3496
17	8.9	1966 VIP: 3492
18	9.0	1956 Fury: 3472
19	9.2	1967 Barracuda Fastback V8: 3495
20	9.4	1968 Barracuda Fastback: 3499
		1984 Colt GTS Turbo: 3518
21	9.6	1979 Fire Arrow: 3516
22	9.7	1969 Fury III: 3506
23	10.2	1986 Horizon America: 3520
24	10.3	1966 Barracuda S: 3489
25	10.4	1980 Champ: 3517
26	10.5	1962 Savoy V8: 3480
27	10.7	1968 Fury III: 3500
28	10.8	1959 Fury: 3475
29	10.9	1967 Barracuda: 3493
30	11.1	1965 Fury Station Wagon: 3488
31	11.5	1963 Fury: 3482
32	12.0	1962 Savoy Station Wagon: 3479
33	12.1	1978 Sapporo: 3515
34	12.7	1963 Valiant V-100: 3484
35	12.9	1964 Barracuda: 3485
36	13.6	1967 Barracuda 6: 3494
37	13.7	1956 Savoy: 3473
38	13.9	1960 Valiant: 3476
39	14.0	1976 Arrow GT: 3512
		1978 Horizon: 3514
40	14.6	1976 Volare Station Wagon: 3513
41	14.7	1984 Voyager: 3519
42	15.3	1961 Savoy 6: 3478
43	16.0	1960 Valiant Automatic: 3477
44	18.5	1971 Cricket: 3511

Polonez

1	17.0	1979 1500: 3524

Polski Fiat

1	15.6	1975 125P: 3525

Pontiac

1	4.0	1978 Firebird TransAm Silverbird: 3566
2	4.1	1991 Firebird TDM Technologies: 3597
3	4.6	1961 Catalina Super Stock: 3529
4	5.1	1989 Firebird TransAm 20th Anniversary: 3589
5	5.2	1982 Petty Grand National: 3571
6	5.3	1989 Firebird TransAm Turbo: 3590
7	5.8	1969 Firebird TransAm: 3555
		1965 Tempest GTO: 3543
8	6.0	1962 Grand Prix 421: 3533
		1970 GTO 400: 3560
9	6.1	1967 GTO Ram Air: 3552
10	6.2	1969 GTO Judge: 3557
11	6.3	1987 Firebird Formula 5.0: 3582
12	6.4	1970 Formula 400: 3559
13	6.5	1967 Firebird 440: 3549
		1989 Firebird T/A Turbo Pontiac Engineering: 3588
		1978 Firebird TransAm: 3565
		1962 Royal Bobcat: 3535
14	6.6	1990 Firebird Formula: 3593
		1991 Firebird GTA: 3596
		1968 GTO: 3554
		1970 GTO 455: 3561
15	6.7	1968 Firebird RA400: 3553
16	6.8	1969 Grand Prix: 3556
		1966 Tempest GTO: 3546
17	6.9	1964 Tempest GTO: 3540
18	7.0	1989 Grand Prix McLaren Turbo: 3592
		1961 Tempest Supercharged: 3532
19	7.1	1990 Firebird TransAm GTA: 3594
20	7.4	1965 Catalina 2+2: 3542
21	7.7	1986 Fiero GT: 3578
		1987 Fiero GT: 3581
		1990 Grand Prix STE Turbo: 3595
22	7.8	1991 Firebird TransAm Convertible: 3598
		1988 Sunbird GT: 3587
23	7.9	1984 Firebird TransAm HO: 3576
		1989 Grand Am Turbo: 3591
		1966 GTO: 3544
24	8.0	1987 Fiero Formula: 3580
25	8.2	1966 Tempest Sprint: 3547
26	8.4	1985 Fiero GT: 3577
		1976 Firebird TransAm: 3563
		1991 Grand Prix GTP: 3599
27	8.6	1984 Firebird TransAm: 3575
28	8.8	1965 Bonneville Vista: 3541
29	9.0	1992 Bonneville SSEi: 3600
30	9.2	1982 Firebird TransAm: 3570
31	9.4	1967 Grand Prix: 3551
32	9.5	1988 Bonneville SE: 3585
		1963 Grand Prix: 3538
		1963 Tempest Le Mans V8: 3539
33	9.7	1959 Bonneville: 3528
		1987 Bonneville SE: 3579
		1988 Grand Prix SE: 3586
34	9.8	1980 Firebird TransAm Turbo: 3567
35	10.0	1966 Le Mans OHC: 3545
36	10.1	1963 Catalina: 3537
		1967 Firebird Sprint: 3550
37	10.3	1973 Grand Am: 3562
38	10.9	1984 Fiero: 3573
39	11.2	1983 6000STE: 3572
40	11.4	1969 Tempest: 3558
41	11.6	1984 Fiero SE: 3574
42	12.1	1987 Le Mans: 3583
		1980 Phoenix: 3568
43	12.7	1966 Tempest Sprint Automatic: 3548
44	14.6	1961 Tempest Automatic: 3531
45	14.8	1977 Bonneville: 3564
		1962 Parisienne: 3534
46	15.0	1961 Tempest: 3530
47	15.9	1962 Tempest 4: 3536
48	16.3	1981 J2000: 3569
49	19.3	1937 Eight Fixed-head Coupe: 3527
50	24.4	1936 Touring Saloon de Luxe: 3526

Porsche

1	3.6	1989 959: 3731
		1988 959 Sport: 3718
2	3.8	1991 911 Ruf: 3747
		1991 911 Ruf TR2: 3749
3	3.9	1991 911 Ruf CTR: 3748
4	4.0	1988 911 Turbo Koenig RS: 3709
		1989 911 Turbo Motorsport Design: 3724
		1988 911 Turbo Ruf Twin Turbo: 3710
		1988 959 Comfort: 3717
5	4.1	1991 911 Turbo Gemballa Mirage: 3751
6	4.5	1987 911 Turbo Ruf 3.4: 3698
7	4.6	1991 911 Carrera Turbo: 3746
		1990 911 Turbo RS Tuning: 3737
8	4.7	1991 911 Turbo: 3750
		1987 959 S: 3702
9	4.8	1989 911 Turbo: 3723
		1989 928 S4 Koenig: 3726
10	4.9	1989 911 3.3 Turbo: 3719
		1989 911 Carrera 4: 3720
		1992 911 Carrera RS: 3753
		1987 911 Turbo Gemballa Avalanche: 3697
11	5.0	1978 911 Turbo: 3659
		1988 911 Turbo: 3708
		1986 911 Turbo: 3689
		1987 911 Turbo Slant-Nose: 3699
		1958 RSK: 3613
12	5.1	1990 911 Carrera 2: 3732
		1983 911 Turbo: 3676
		1990 911 Turbo: 3736
13	5.2	1988 911 Carrera Club Sport: 3705
		1975 Carrera RS 3-litre: 3647
14	5.3	1989 911 Club Sport: 3722
		1984 911 Turbo Cabriolet Ruf: 3680
15	5.5	1985 911 Carrera: 3682
		1989 928 Cabrio Strosek: 3725
		1988 928 S4: 3712
		1989 928 S4 SE: 3727
		1989 944 Turbo: 3730
		1973 Carrera RS Touring: 3641
16	5.6	1986 911 Carrera SE: 3688
		1973 Carrera RSR: 3642
17	5.7	1986 911 Cabriolet: 3687
		1987 911 Carrera: 3696
		1988 911 Club Sport: 3706
		1988 944 Turbo SE: 3716
18	5.8	1990 911 Carrera 4: 3734
		1981 911 SC: 3670
		1977 935 Group 4 Holbert: 3657
		1990 Panamericana: 3745
19	5.9	1985 928 S: 3683
20	6.0	1990 911 Speedster: 3735
		1989 944 S2: 3729
		1988 944 Turbo: 3715
		1986 944 Turbo: 3695
21	6.1	1989 911 Carrera Cabriolet: 3721
		1974 911S 2.7-litre: 3645
		1990 928: 3738
		1990 928 Gemballa: 3740
		1975 Turbo 3-litre: 3648
22	6.2	1984 911 Carrera: 3679
		1986 928 S4 Automatic: 3692
		1990 Carrera 2 Cabriolet Tiptronic: 3744
23	6.3	1978 911 SC: 3658
		1991 928: 3752
		1990 928 Automatic: 3739
		1986 928 S: 3691
		1985 944 Turbo: 3686
24	6.4	1964 904 Carrera GTS: 3621
		1971 911 E 2.4-litre: 3635
25	6.5	1988 911 Cabriolet: 3703
		1977 911 SC: 3654
		1988 911 Speedster: 3707
26	6.6	1972 911 E: 3637
27	6.7	1980 911 SC: 3666
		1977 911 Turbo: 3655
		1976 911 Turbo Carrera: 3650
		1985 928 S Series II: 3684
		1986 944 S: 3694
		1990 944 S2: 3742
28	6.9	1990 911 Carrera 2 Tiptronic: 3733
		1979 924 Turbo: 3664
29	7.0	1983 911 Cabriolet: 3675
		1988 911 Carrera: 3704
		1983 928 S: 3677
		1989 944: 3728
30	7.1	1990 944 Cabriolet: 3741
		1990 944 S2 Cabriolet: 3743
31	7.2	1987 944 S: 3701
32	7.3	1970 911 S 2.2-litre: 3631
33	7.4	1982 944 Lux: 3674
34	7.5	1974 911 Carrera: 3643
		1976 911 S: 3649
		1988 924 S: 3711
		1978 928: 3661
		1988 944 S: 3714
35	7.8	1973 911 S: 3638
		1986 924 S: 3690
36	8.0	1966 911 S: 3624
		1987 924 S: 3700
		1978 928 Automatic: 3662
37	8.1	1967 911 S: 3626
		1970 911 T: 3632
		1980 928: 3669
38	8.2	1957 550 Spyder: 3610
		1975 911 Carrera: 3646
		1985 944 Lux: 3685
39	8.3	1979 928 Automatic: 3665
		1982 944: 3673
		1984 944: 3681
40	8.4	1969 911 E: 3629
41	8.5	1974 911 Targa: 3644
42	8.7	1970 914 6: 3634
		1988 944: 3713

43	8.8	1969 911 T: 3630
44	8.9	1986 944: 3693
45	9.0	1965 911: 3622
		1983 944: 3678
46	9.1	1971 911 T Sportomatic: 3636
47	9.2	1981 924 Turbo: 3671
		1962 Carrera 2-litre: 3618
48	9.3	1980 924 S Turbo: 3668
49	9.5	1978 924 Lux: 3660
50	9.7	1977 924: 3656
51	9.8	1968 911 E Sportomatic: 3627
52	10.3	1955 1500 S Speedster: 3604
		1968 911 Sportomatic: 3628
		1973 914 2-litre: 3640
53	10.5	1958 1600 Super Speedster: 3612
54	10.6	1980 924: 3667
		1982 924 Weissach: 3672
55	11.0	1979 924: 3663
56	11.3	1976 912 E: 3651
57	11.4	1960 Super 75: 3615
58	11.5	1956 Carrera Coupe: 3606
		1962 Super 90 Cabriolet: 3619
59	11.6	1966 912: 3625
60	11.9	1965 912: 3623
		1976 924: 3653
61	12.4	1954 Super Coupe: 3603
62	12.5	1960 Super 90 Cabriolet: 3616
63	12.7	1973 914 1.7-litre: 3639
		1976 914 2.0-litre: 3652
64	13.5	1964 356 C: 3620
65	13.8	1952 356 4: 3601
66	13.9	1970 914: 3633
		1956 Continental Speedster: 3608
67	14.0	1959 1600 Convertible D: 3614
68	14.1	1958 1600: 3611
69	14.4	1957 1600 Coupe: 3609
		1961 1600 N: 3617
70	15.0	1956 Continental Coupe: 3607
71	15.3	1956 1600: 3605
72	17.0	1954 356: 3602

Proton

1	12.4	1991 1.5 SE Triple Valve Aeroback: 3755
2	14.4	1989 1.5 SE Aeroback: 3754

Railton

1	9.2	1934 Terraplane: 3756
2	9.8	1935 Light Sports Tourer: 3757
3	11.2	1936 Straight Eight Saloon: 3758
4	15.6	1937 Cobham Saloon: 3759
5	35.6	1938 10 Drop-head Coupe: 3760

Rambler

1	9.4	1968 Javelin Hardtop SST: 3770
2	11.0	1960 Rebel V8: 3762
3	12.6	1966 770 V8 Convertible: 3768
4	14.2	1967 Rebel 6 Estate Car: 3769
5	14.7	1964 770 Six: 3767
6	14.9	1960 Six: 3763
7	17.3	1960 Super 6 Station Wagon: 3764
8	17.7	1959 American: 3761
9	18.4	1961 Estate: 3766
10	19.6	1961 American: 3765

Range Rover

1	10.8	1992 Vogue SE: 3781
2	11.3	1990 Vogue SE: 3780
3	11.7	1989 Vogue SE: 3778
4	11.9	1986 Vogue: 3774
5	12.1	1989 Vogue: 3777
6	12.3	1990 County: 3779
7	12.6	1987 V8: 3775
8	13.9	1970 V8: 3771
9	14.3	1978 V8: 3773
10	14.6	1975 V8: 3772
11	16.5	1988 Vogue Turbo D: 3776

Reliant

1	7.0	1990 Scimitar SST 1800Ti: 3796
2	7.2	1986 Scimitar Ti: 3795
3	8.9	1973 Scimitar GTE: 3788
4	9.4	1977 Scimitar GTE: 3792
5	10.0	1967 Scimitar GT: 3785
		1976 Scimitar GTE: 3791
6	10.7	1970 Scimitar GTE Automatic: 3787
7	10.8	1981 Scimitar GTE: 3793
8	11.4	1965 Scimitar: 3784
9	11.5	1985 Scimitar SS1 1600: 3794
10	12.2	1964 Sabre Six GT: 3783
11	16.6	1962 Sabre Sports: 3782
12	19.6	1975 Kitten: 3789
13	20.2	1976 Kitten DL Estate: 3790
14	35.9	1968 Rebel 700 Estate: 3786

Renault

1	4.8	1981 Le Car Turbo: 3874
2	5.7	1991 Alpine A610 Turbo: 3918
3	6.3	1986 GTA V6 Turbo: 3899
4	6.7	1984 5 Turbo 2: 3886
5	7.1	1986 5 GT Turbo: 3895
6	7.3	1987 5 GT Turbo: 3901
7	7.4	1979 5 Racer: 3865
8	7.5	1988 GTA V6: 3906
9	7.7	1981 5 Turbo: 3873
10	7.8	1990 21 Turbo Quadra: 3914
11	7.9	1987 11 Turbo: 3900
		1988 21 Turbo: 3905
12	8.1	1985 25 V6 Turbo: 3889
13	8.6	1992 Cleo 16v: 3923
14	8.8	1992 19 16v Cabriolet: 3922
15	9.0	1984 25 V6: 3885
		1986 9 Turbo: 3897
16	9.4	1991 Espace V6: 3921
17	9.5	1991 19 16v: 3917
		1990 25 V6 2.9 Auto: 3916
		1987 5 GTX 3-DR: 3902
18	9.8	1975 17 Gordini: 3848
		1986 21 Savanna GTX: 3894
		1990 21 TXi: 3915
		1978 30 TS: 3859
		1982 5 Gordini Turbo: 3876
19	10.0	1989 25 TXi: 3910
20	10.3	1988 21 Ti: 3904
		1979 30 TX: 3863
21	10.5	1981 20 TX: 3872
22	10.6	1982 18 GTX Estate: 3875
23	10.7	1979 5 Gordini: 3864
		1983 Fuego Turbo: 3884
		1982 Fuego Turbo: 3882
24	10.8	1981 18 Turbo: 3870
		1989 Espace TXE: 3912
25	10.9	1986 21 GTS: 3893
		1967 8 Gordini 1300: 3831
26	11.0	1984 Fuego: 3887
		1984 Fuego 2.2: 3888
27	11.1	1987 Alliance GTA: 3903
28	11.2	1982 Fuego GTS: 3881
29	11.4	1977 17 TS: 3857
		1990 19 TXE Chamade: 3913
		1985 5 TSE: 3890
		1986 Alliance 1.7L: 3898
30	11.5	1985 Encore GS: 3891
31	11.6	1989 21 GTS Hatchback: 3909
32	11.7	1989 19 TXE: 3908
		1976 30 TS: 3853
33	11.9	1979 Gordini: 3867
34	12.0	1991 Clio 1.4RT: 3920
35	12.1	1985 Espace 2000 TSE: 3892
36	12.2	1965 R8 Rally: 3826
37	12.3	1965 8 Gordini: 3824
38	12.4	1969 16 TS: 3833
39	12.5	1981 14 TS: 3869
		1973 17: 3844
40	12.6	1976 20 TL: 3852
		1982 9 TSE: 3879
		1979 Le Car: 3868
41	12.8	1983 11 TSE: 3883
		1989 19 TSE: 3907
42	13.0	1981 18i: 3871
43	13.2	1976 17 Gordini: 3851
44	13.4	1979 18 GTS: 3861
		1975 5 TS: 3849
45	13.6	1972 15 TL: 3842
46	14.0	1991 Clio 1.2 RN: 3919
47	14.2	1982 9 GLT: 3877
48	14.3	1979 18 TS Estate: 3862
49	14.8	1977 20 TS: 3858
		1986 5 GTL 5-door: 3896
50	14.9	1972 16 TS: 3843
51	15.1	1976 15 GTL: 3850
52	15.3	1977 14: 3856
53	15.4	1982 Alliance DL: 3880
54	15.7	1972 15 Coupe: 3841
		1979 5 TL: 3866
55	15.9	1972 12 TL: 3840
56	16.2	1968 16: 3832
57	16.3	1989 5 Campus: 3911
58	16.5	1972 12 Estate: 3839
		1970 12 TL: 3836
59	16.7	1977 12 TL: 3855
		1966 16 GL: 3828
60	16.8	1971 16 TL Automatic: 3837
61	17.2	1974 6 TL: 3846
62	17.5	1975 12: 3847
63	17.6	1976 5 GTL: 3854
		1965 Caravelle: 3825
64	18.3	1982 9 TC: 3878
65	18.9	1970 10: 3835
66	19.0	1967 10: 3830
67	19.4	1962 Caravelle S: 3815

68 20.1 1978 5 Automatic: 3860
69 20.6 1973 5 TL: 3845
1964 R8 1100: 3823
70 20.7 1971 6 1100: 3838
71 21.4 1963 R8: 3822
72 21.5 1958 Dauphine Ferry: 3807
73 22.0 1962 R8: 3818
74 22.3 1961 Dauphine Gordini: 3814
75 22.4 1959 Caravelle: 3809
76 22.5 1960 Caravelle: 3812
77 22.8 1962 Dauphine Gordini de Luxe: 3817
78 23.8 1960 Floride: 3813
79 24.8 1966 1100 Automatic: 3827
80 25.4 1963 Floride Caravelle: 3821
81 29.8 1969 6: 3834
82 30.8 1956 Dauphine: 3805
83 31.4 1959 Dauphine Gordini: 3811
84 31.5 1958 Fregate Transfluide: 3808
85 31.6 1935 24hp Big Six Saloon: 3799
86 31.9 1955 4CV: 3803
87 34.5 1962 Dauphine: 3816
88 38.1 1966 4 Estate Car: 3829
89 39.9 1963 Dauphine Automatic: 3820
90 40.5 1963 4 L Estate Car: 3819
91 43.9 1959 Dauphine: 3810
92 45.5 1937 17.9hp Touring Saloon: 3800
93 45.7 1957 Dauphine: 3806

Riley

1 16.4 1953 2.5: 3938
2 16.7 1955 Pathfinder: 3939
3 17.3 1967 Kestrel: 3945
4 17.4 1958 1.5: 3941
5 18.4 1949 2.5 Saloon: 3935
6 18.8 1938 16 2.5: 3931
1947 2.5 Saloon: 3933
1956 Pathfinder: 3940
1937 Sprite: 3930
7 19.0 1948 2.5 Sports: 3934
8 19.8 1961 1.5: 3943
9 20.5 1960 4/68: 3942
10 21.8 1935 1.5 Kestrel Special: 3925
11 23.8 1937 8/90 Adelphi Saloon: 3927
12 25.1 1953 1.5: 3937
13 29.4 1937 Kestrel Sprite: 3929
14 31.2 1947 1.5: 3932
15 32.3 1962 Elf: 3944

Rolls-Royce

1 9.6 1974 Corniche: 3964
2 9.7 1982 Corniche: 3970
3 10.0 1981 Silver Spirit: 3969
4 10.1 1978 Silver Wraith II: 3967
5 10.2 1972 Silver Shadow: 3963
6 10.4 1991 Silver Spirit II: 3972
7 10.6 1976 Silver Shadow: 3965
8 10.8 1963 Silver Cloud III: 3960
9 10.9 1966 Silver Shadow: 3961
10 11.0 1969 Silver Shadow: 3962
11 11.3 1980 Silver Shadow II: 3968
12 11.4 1960 Silver Cloud II V8: 3959
13 11.5 1960 Silver Cloud II: 3958
14 11.8 1977 Silver Shadow: 3966
15 12.1 1958 Silver Cloud "S": 3957
16 12.6 1982 Silver Spur: 3971
17 13.0 1958 Silver Cloud: 3956
18 16.2 1954 Silver Dawn: 3955
19 16.5 1936 Phantom III: 3952
20 17.0 1953 Silver Dawn: 3954
21 19.6 1933 Phantom II: 3950
22 21.0 1932 Phantom II: 3949
23 24.0 1927 Phantom I Phaeton: 3946
1949 Silver Wraith: 3953
24 31.4 1935 20/25 Touring Saloon: 3951

Rover

1 6.5 1953 Jet: 3984
2 7.6 1983 Vitesse: 4024
3 8.0 1986 825i: 4027
1989 Vitesse: 4036
4 8.4 1976 3500: 4016
1988 827 SLi Auto: 4032
5 8.8 1991 216 GTi: 4044
1991 220 GTi: 4046
6 9.1 1971 3500S: 4012
7 9.2 1992 820i: 4050
8 9.3 1989 Sterling Catalyst: 4035
9 9.4 1985 216 Vitesse: 4026
1991 Sterling 827SL: 4049
1992 Sterling Automatic: 4051
10 9.7 1981 Vanden Plas: 4021
1988 Vitesse: 4033
11 9.8 1990 Metro GTi 16v: 4042
12 10.0 1980 3500: 4020
1990 416 GTi: 4040
13 10.1 1987 Sterling Automatic: 4030
14 10.2 1987 820SE: 4028
15 10.3 1976 3500 Automatic: 4017
16 10.7 1977 2600: 4018
17 10.8 1970 3500: 4009
18 10.9 1990 216 GSi: 4038
19 11.0 1991 Mini Cooper S: 4048
20 11.3 1966 Rover-BRM Turbine: 4006
21 11.4 1974 2200TC: 4015
22 11.5 1990 414 Si: 4039
1987 Montego 1.6L: 4029
23 11.6 1988 820 Fastback: 4031
24 11.7 1990 214 GSi: 4037
1991 825 TD: 4047
25 11.9 1978 2300: 4019
1970 3500S: 4010
26 12.0 1990 Metro 1.4SL: 4041
27 12.2 1971 2000TC: 4011
28 12.4 1982 2000: 4022
1967 3.5-litre: 4007
29 12.6 1966 2000TC: 4004
30 13.0 1984 213 Vanden Plas: 4025
31 13.2 1969 2000TC: 4008
1989 Montego 2.0 DSL Turbo: 4034
32 13.3 1991 214S: 4043
33 14.3 1982 SD Turbo: 4023
34 14.5 1973 2200SC Automatic: 4014
35 14.7 1973 2000SC: 4013
36 15.0 1963 3-litre Coupe: 4000
1966 3-litre Coupe Mk III: 4005
37 15.1 1963 2000: 3999
38 15.3 1964 2000: 4002
39 15.5 1963 Coupe: 4001
40 16.2 1959 3-litre: 3992
41 16.9 1991 218 SD: 4045
42 17.1 1961 3-litre Automatic: 3997
43 17.7 1960 3-litre: 3995
44 17.9 1960 100: 3994
1957 105S: 3990
45 18.0 1966 2000 Automatic: 4003
46 18.1 1961 100: 3996
47 18.6 1962 3-litre: 3998
48 19.3 1956 90: 3989
49 19.8 1954 90: 3986
50 20.8 1955 75: 3987
51 21.4 1935 Speed 14 Streamline Coupe: 3976
52 22.8 1959 80: 3993
53 23.1 1950 75: 3982
54 23.2 1954 60: 3985
55 24.7 1952 75: 3983
56 25.2 1958 105R de Luxe: 3991
57 27.9 1956 60: 3988
58 28.0 1937 16 Sports Saloon: 3977
59 28.3 1938 16 Saloon: 3979
60 29.4 1949 75: 3980
1949 75 Saloon: 3981
61 29.8 1934 12 Saloon: 3975
62 41.3 1938 14: 3978

Ruger

1 7.7 1970 Bentley Clone: 4052

Saab

1 6.8 1991 9000 Turbo: 4102
2 6.9 1988 9000CD: 4094
3 7.3 1989 Carlsson: 4097
4 7.5 1991 9000 2.3 Turbo TCS: 4101
5 7.7 1989 9000 Turbo: 4096
6 8.0 1991 9000CS Turbo S: 4103
7 8.3 1985 9000 Turbo 16v: 4090
8 8.6 1985 900 Turbo: 4089
1986 9000: 4092
9 8.9 1989 900 Turbo S: 4095
1978 Turbo: 4081
10 9.1 1990 900SPG: 4099
11 9.3 1990 CDS 2.3: 4100
12 9.5 1992 9000 2.3CS: 4105
13 9.6 1979 900 Turbo: 4082
1986 9000i: 4093
14 9.7 1990 9000CD: 4098
15 10.0 1982 900 Turbo: 4088
1991 9000S: 4104
16 10.3 1975 99EMS: 4078
17 11.4 1981 900 Turbo: 4085
18 11.8 1977 99EMS: 4080
19 12.0 1972 99CM4 2.0: 4071
1974 99LE Wagonback: 4077
20 12.7 1985 900i: 4091
1973 99E: 4075
1972 99E 1.85: 4072
21 12.8 1971 99: 4070
22 13.2 1980 900GLE: 4084
23 13.3 1979 900GL: 4083
24 13.4 1972 Sonnet III: 4074
25 13.7 1968 Sonnet V4: 4063

26	13.8	1982 900: 4087
27	13.9	1981 900GLS: 4086
28	14.3	1972 99EA: 4073
29	14.4	1976 99GL Super Combi: 4079
		1970 Sonnet III: 4069
30	14.8	1970 99E: 4068
31	15.2	1958 Gran Turismo: 4055
32	15.7	1969 99: 4065
33	16.5	1967 96 V4: 4061
34	17.4	1970 99: 4067
35	17.5	1967 V4: 4062
36	19.1	1969 Sport: 4066
37	21.2	1964 850GT: 4059
38	24.1	1966 96: 4060
39	24.5	1961 96 Sedan: 4057
40	26.6	1960 96: 4056
41	27.2	1957 93: 4054
42	44.0	1963 95: 4058

Safir

1	4.0	1991 GT40: 4106

Saturn

1	8.6	1991 Sports Coupe: 4107

Sbarro

1	3.5	1990 Chrono 3.5: 4108

Scarab

1	4.2	1959 Mk II: 4109

Seat

1	10.3	1989 Ibiza SXi: 4113
2	10.6	1992 Toledo 2.0 GTi: 4115
3	10.9	1985 1.5 GLX: 4111
4	13.0	1976 1200 Sport: 4110
5	15.6	1992 Toledo 1.9 CL Diesel: 4114
6	15.7	1986 Malaga 1.2L: 4112

Shelby

1	4.2	1962 AC Ford Cobra: 4116
2	5.1	1964 Cobra USRRC: 4118
3	5.3	1974 Cobra 427: 4126
4	6.2	1966 GT 350-S: 4121
5	6.3	1968 GT 350: 4123
6	6.6	1964 AC Ford Cobra: 4117
7	6.8	1965 GT 350: 4120
8	6.9	1969 GT 500: 4125
		1968 GT 500-KR: 4124
9	7.2	1967 GT 500: 4122

Siata

1	12.4	1953 Spyder V8: 4127
2	25.0	1969 Spring 850: 4128

Simca

1	13.1	1974 1100 Special: 4157
2	13.6	1970 1204 Special: 4156
3	15.1	1964 1500: 4148
4	16.6	1969 1204: 4154
5	16.7	1965 1500GL Estate: 4149
6	17.2	1957 Versailles V8: 4135
7	18.4	1958 Vedette Beaulieu: 4137
		1960 Vedette V8: 4141
8	19.0	1968 1100GLS: 4153
9	19.2	1969 1501 Special Estate: 4155
10	19.3	1956 Sports Coupe: 4134
11	20.0	1962 5: 4144
12	20.6	1958 Aronde Montlhery: 4136
13	20.7	1960 Oceane: 4140
14	21.1	1959 Elysee: 4138
15	21.5	1967 1301: 4152
16	21.7	1967 1000GLS: 4151
		1977 1000LS: 4158
17	21.9	1961 Aronde Montlhery: 4142
18	22.3	1963 1000: 4145
19	22.5	1963 1000 Special: 4146
20	23.3	1963 1300GL: 4147
21	24.0	1951 8 Sport: 4129
22	24.6	1966 1000GLS: 4150
23	24.7	1956 Elysee: 4133
24	25.7	1960 Etoile: 4139
25	26.6	1962 1000: 4143
26	27.9	1955 Aronde: 4132
27	29.4	1954 Aronde: 4131

Singer

1	15.4	1966 Vogue: 4178
2	17.0	1953 Roadster: 4167
3	17.4	1966 Vogue Automatic: 4179
4	17.7	1965 Vogue Mk III Estate: 4177
5	18.5	1967 Gazelle: 4180
6	20.8	1952 SM Roadster: 4165
7	20.9	1961 Vogue: 4173
8	21.4	1958 Gazelle IIA Convertible: 4171
9	22.9	1964 Chamois: 4175
10	23.1	1953 SM1500 Saloon: 4168
11	23.3	1963 Vogue Mk II: 4174
12	23.9	1961 Gazelle Series IIIB: 4172
13	24.9	1964 Gazelle Series V: 4176
14	26.2	1969 Chamois: 4181
15	26.3	1955 Hunter: 4170
16	27.9	1952 SM1500 Saloon: 4166
17	29.1	1954 SM Roadster: 4169
18	34.8	1935 Le Mans Special Speed Model: 4161
19	36.7	1949 SM1500 Saloon: 4164

Skoda

1	14.9	1989 136 Rapide Coupe: 4189
2	18.9	1977 120L: 4187
3	19.6	1972 S110LS: 4186
4	19.9	1986 Estelle 120 LSE: 4188
5	24.5	1961 Felicia: 4183
6	29.0	1970 S100L: 4185
7	30.8	1965 1000MB: 4184
8	33.1	1960 Octavia: 4182

Squire

1	10.9	1935 X101: 4190

Standard

1	17.6	1956 Vanguard Sportsman: 4205
2	18.7	1962 Ensign de Luxe Estate: 4213
3	19.7	1961 Vanguard: 4212
4	20.8	1953 Vanguard Phase II: 4202
5	22.0	1953 Vanguard Estate: 4201
6	22.2	1956 Vanguard III: 4204
7	24.5	1952 Vanguard: 4199
8	24.8	1948 Vanguard: 4198
9	25.4	1958 Ensign: 4208
10	25.6	1938 Flying 20: 4195
11	25.9	1957 Vanguard III: 4206
12	27.5	1958 Vanguard III Automatic: 4211
13	33.8	1955 10: 4203
14	34.9	1958 Pennant: 4209
15	36.0	1947 12 Saloon: 4196
16	38.1	1958 Super 10: 4210
17	49.7	1937 Flying 10: 4194
18	52.0	1953 8: 4200
19	54.4	1958 8: 4207

Studebaker

1	7.3	1962 Avanti: 4233
2	7.8	1964 Daytona R-4: 4238
		1963 Regal Wagonaire Supercharged: 4237
3	9.1	1963 Avanti: 4236
4	10.0	1961 Lark Cruiser: 4232
5	10.2	1961 Hawk 4-speed: 4230
6	10.5	1960 Lark V8: 4229
7	11.4	1962 Hawk Gran Turismo: 4234
8	11.9	1953 Commander Supercharged: 4225
9	12.9	1962 Lark Daytona: 4235
10	14.0	1961 Lark 6: 4231
11	14.9	1953 Commander Coupe: 4224
12	15.4	1951 Land Cruiser: 4223
13	16.9	1954 Commander Coupe: 4226
14	17.9	1960 Lark 6: 4228
15	19.6	1936 De Luxe Saloon: 4220
16	20.4	1935 President Saloon: 4219
17	21.0	1959 Lark 6: 4227
18	22.4	1937 Dictator de Luxe Saloon: 4221
19	24.4	1935 Dictator Saloon de Luxe: 4218
20	25.9	1949 Champion: 4222

Stutz

1	20.5	1928 Roadster: 4239

Subaru

1	6.2	1989 Legacy FIA Record: 4274
2	7.0	1991 Legacy 2.0 4Cam Turbo Estate: 4277
3	7.3	1992 SVX: 4279
4	8.1	1991 Legacy Sports Sedan: 4278
5	8.5	1988 4WD Turbo Estate: 4269
6	8.7	1987 XT Turbo 4WD: 4268
7	9.2	1988 XT6 4WD: 4272
8	9.5	1985 XT Turbo Coupe: 4264

9	9.7	1985 4WD Turbo XT Coupe: 4261
		1989 XT6: 4275
10	9.9	1985 1.8 RX Turbo: 4259
11	10.1	1985 1.8 GTi: 4258
		1986 4WD 3-door Turbo Coupe: 4265
		1985 4WD Turbo: 4260
12	10.3	1985 XT Coupe DL: 4263
13	10.7	1985 Turbo 4WD Estate: 4262
14	10.8	1990 Legacy 2.2 GX 4WD: 4276
15	11.1	1988 Justy GL: 4271
16	12.0	1988 Justy 4WD GL: 4270
17	12.3	1978 DL: 4253
18	13.0	1983 GL Turbo Traction Wagon: 4257
		1987 Justy: 4267
19	13.2	1986 Hatchback: 4266
20	13.4	1978 1600 Coupe: 4252
		1980 DL-5: 4254
21	14.4	1989 Justy GL II 5-door 4WD: 4273
22	14.7	1972 FF-1 1300: 4246
23	14.8	1982 GL: 4256
24	15.6	1973 1300 GL Coupe: 4247
25	16.0	1975 DL: 4249
26	16.2	1973 1400 DL: 4248
27	16.3	1981 1800 4WD Estate: 4255
28	16.7	1977 1600 4WD Estate: 4251
29	18.8	1969 Star: 4244
30	23.3	1976 4WD Station Wagon: 4250

Sunbeam

1	7.5	1967 Tiger II: 4307
2	7.8	1964 Tiger: 4301
3	9.5	1965 Tiger 260: 4302
4	11.1	1969 Rapier H120: 4312
5	12.2	1962 Le Mans: 4295
6	12.3	1969 Alpine GT: 4311
7	12.8	1968 Rapier: 4309
		1975 Rapier: 4313
8	13.0	1962 Harrington Le Mans: 4294
9	13.6	1966 Alpine Series V: 4304
10	14.0	1959 Alpine: 4290
		1966 Alpine 1.7: 4303
		1961 Alpine Mk II: 4293
11	14.6	1969 Alpine: 4310
12	14.8	1954 Alpine II: 4284
13	14.9	1963 Alpine GT: 4296
14	15.2	1960 Alpine: 4292
15	16.3	1966 Imp Sport: 4305
16	16.5	1964 Alpine Series IV: 4299
17	17.6	1967 Stiletto: 4306
18	18.1	1963 Alpine Series III: 4297
19	18.4	1955 Mk III: 4285
20	18.8	1964 Alpine GT Series IV Automatic: 4298
21	18.9	1954 Alpine: 4283
22	19.4	1958 Rapier: 4288
23	20.2	1958 Rapier Series II: 4289
		1951 Talbot 90: 4282
24	20.6	1957 Rapier: 4287
25	21.7	1956 Rapier: 4286
26	24.9	1959 Rapier III: 4291
27	25.2	1964 Imp: 4300
28	37.0	1935 20 Saloon: 4281

Sunbeam-Talbot

1	20.8	1953 90 Mk IIA: 4319
2	22.1	1939 2-litre Sports Tourer: 4314
3	26.8	1948 90 Sports Saloon: 4317
4	35.2	1947 10 Sports Saloon: 4315
5	36.4	1949 80 Saloon: 4318

Suzuki

1	8.7	1989 Swift 1.3 GTi: 4331
2	9.1	1986 Swift 1.3 GTi: 4326
3	9.5	1990 Swift GT: 4333
4	10.3	1985 Swift 1.3GS: 4324
5	11.3	1987 Swift 1.3 GLX: 4328
6	11.6	1989 Swift 1.3 GLX: 4330
7	14.5	1987 Swift 1.3 GLX Executive: 4329
		1989 Vitara JLX: 4332
8	15.8	1981 Alto FX: 4322
9	19.4	1987 SJ413V JX: 4327
10	21.2	1980 SC 100: 4321
11	22.5	1983 Alto FX Automatic: 4323
12	24.4	1986 Alto GLA: 4325

Swallow

1	13.4	1955 Doretti: 4334

Talbot

1	11.3	1981 Tagora 2.2GLS: 4345
2	12.0	1981 Solara GLS: 4344
3	12.5	1982 Samba Cabriolet: 4346
4	13.8	1983 Horizon 1.9LD: 4348
5	16.0	1982 Samba GL: 4347
6	16.8	1936 3.5-litre Speed Saloon: 4340
7	19.4	1933 105 Speed Model: 4336
8	19.8	1936 105 Airline Saloon: 4339
9	20.1	1938 3-litre Saloon: 4342
10	34.4	1935 75 Drop-frame Sports Saloon: 4338

Toyota

1	5.8	1991 MR2 HKS: 4480
		1989 Supra Turbo TRD: 4467
2	6.2	1990 MR2 Turbo: 4473
3	6.6	1989 Supra Turbo: 4466
4	6.7	1990 MR2 GT: 4472
5	6.9	1989 Supra 3.0i Turbo: 4465
6	7.0	1987 MR2 Supercharged: 4451
		1986 Supra: 4442
		1988 Supra Turbo: 4460
7	7.5	1988 Supra: 4459
8	7.6	1988 Celica GT4: 4455
9	7.7	1988 Celica All-Trac Turbo: 4454
		1985 MR2: 4433
		1989 MR2 Supercharged: 4464
		1986 MR2 T-Bar: 4441
		1986 Supra 3.0i: 4443
10	7.9	1987 Supra: 4452
11	8.1	1990 Celica 2.0 GT: 4468
		1984 Celica 2.8i Supra: 4425
12	8.2	1986 Celica 2.0GT: 4438
13	8.4	1986 MR2: 4440
		1985 Supra: 4436
14	8.5	1985 Corolla GT Hatchback: 4432
		1990 MR2: 4471
15	8.6	1987 Celica GT Cabriolet: 4447
		1986 Celica GTS: 4439
		1984 Corolla GT Coupe: 4426
16	8.7	1982 Celica Supra: 4415
		1984 Supra: 4429
17	8.8	1978 Celica 2000GT: 4400
18	8.9	1983 Supra: 4421
19	9.0	1987 Camry 2.0 GLi: 4445
20	9.2	1987 Corolla FX-16 GTS: 4449
21	9.3	1975 Celica GT: 4387
		1989 Corolla GTS: 4463
		1991 MR2: 4479
22	9.5	1990 Celica All-Trac Turbo: 4469
23	9.7	1991 Camry 2.2 GL: 4476
24	10.0	1967 2000GT: 4356
25	10.1	1987 Camry 2.0 GLi Estate: 4446
26	10.2	1979 Celica Supra: 4403
		1983 Cressida: 4420
27	10.3	1992 Paseo: 4483
28	10.4	1978 Celica: 4399
		1978 Celica GT Liftback: 4401
29	10.5	1988 Carina 1.6 GL: 4453
		1982 Celica 2.0ST: 4413
		1990 Celica GTS: 4470
		1984 Corolla GTS: 4427
30	10.6	1980 Celica GT: 4406
31	10.8	1991 Celica GT Convertible: 4477
32	11.1	1989 Camry V6 GXi: 4461
		1987 Corolla Executive: 4448
33	11.3	1981 Cressida DX Estate: 4410
34	11.4	1978 Cressida: 4402
		1986 Tercel DX: 4444
35	11.5	1971 Celica: 4367
		1985 Celica GTS: 4431
36	11.8	1983 Celica GTS: 4417
37	12.0	1971 Corolla 1600: 4370
		1980 Corolla Sport Coupe: 4407
		1979 Corona 5-door: 4404
38	12.1	1988 Corolla 4WD Estate: 4457
		1981 Cressida: 4409
		1972 Custom Crown Estate: 4376
39	12.2	1989 Carina II 1.6 GL Liftback: 4462
		1982 Celica: 4412
		1991 Tercel LE: 4482
40	12.4	1973 Mk II 2.6: 4382
41	12.5	1990 Previa LE: 4474
42	12.6	1983 Camry LE: 4416
		1984 Carina II 116GL: 4424
		1991 Landcruiser VX: 4478
43	12.7	1976 Celica Liftback: 4395
44	12.8	1988 Corolla 1.3 GL: 4456
45	12.9	1971 1900SL: 4366
		1977 Corona Cressida: 4398
		1991 Previa: 4481
46	13.0	1973 Corona: 4380
47	13.1	1984 Corolla LE: 4428
48	13.2	1979 Corona Liftback: 4405
49	13.3	1974 Celica GT: 4383
		1975 Crown Super: 4391
50	13.5	1972 Carina: 4374
		1982 Celica GTA: 4414
		1971 Corona de Luxe: 4371
		1970 Corona Mk II 1900: 4364
		1983 Tercel GL: 4423
51	13.6	1973 Celica: 4377

52 13.7 1973 Corolla SR5: 4379
1983 Corolla SR5 Hardtop: 4419
53 13.9 1973 Corolla: 4378
1975 Pickup SR5: 4392
54 14.0 1968 Corona: 4361
55 14.1 1972 Crown 2600: 4375
56 14.2 1983 Corolla GL: 4418
1973 Mk II: 4381
1981 Starlet: 4411
57 14.3 1976 Carina: 4394
1975 Corolla: 4388
1971 Corolla 1200SL: 4369
58 14.4 1974 Mk II Station Wagon: 4386
59 14.5 1970 Corona Mk II: 4363
60 14.7 1990 Starlet GL: 4475
61 14.8 1976 Corolla Liftback: 4396
1980 Corolla Tercel SR5: 4408
1985 Starlet 1.0GL: 4435
62 14.9 1985 Tercel 4WD Estate: 4437
63 15.3 1970 Crown: 4365
1984 Van LE: 4430
64 15.9 1975 Corolla SR5: 4390
1966 Crown Custom: 4355
65 16.0 1974 Corona SR: 4385
1969 Crown Toyoglide: 4362
66 16.1 1985 Space Cruiser: 4434
67 16.3 1968 Corolla de Luxe: 4360
68 16.4 1974 Corona 2000 Mk II Automatic: 4384
69 16.5 1983 Tercel 4WD Wagon: 4422
70 16.9 1976 1000: 4393
1964 1900: 4352
1975 Corolla 30: 4389
71 17.0 1968 Corolla: 4359
72 17.1 1977 Corolla 1200: 4397
73 17.2 1966 Corona: 4353
74 18.0 1971 Land Cruiser: 4372
75 18.3 1967 Corona Coupe: 4357
76 18.8 1966 Corona 1900: 4354
77 19.0 1971 Corolla: 4368
78 19.6 1971 Land Cruiser Wagon: 4373
79 20.6 1967 Land Cruiser: 4358
80 20.7 1960 Toyopet Tiara: 4351
81 21.6 1987 Landcruiser: 4450
82 23.5 1988 Landcruiser II TD: 4458
83 26.0 1958 Toyopet Crown de Luxe: 4350

Treser

1 8.5 1989 T1: 4485

Trihawk

1 10.2 1982 304: 4486

Triumph

1 4.3 1980 TR8 Group 44: 4578
2 5.3 1980 TR8 Libra Rally: 4579
3 6.9 1977 TR7 Tullius: 4572
4 8.2 1969 TR6: 4541
5 8.4 1980 TR8: 4577
6 8.7 1975 Dolomite Sprint: 4565
7 8.8 1968 TR5 PI: 4536
8 9.1 1976 TR7: 4570
9 10.0 1969 GT6 Mk II: 4540
10 10.1 1971 GT6 Mk III: 4547
11 10.4 1969 2.5PI: 4537
1975 2500S: 4563
1971 Stag Automatic: 4551
12 10.5 1965 TR4A: 4524
13 10.6 1968 TR250: 4535
14 10.7 1964 TR4: 4521
1970 TR6: 4546
15 10.9 1962 TR4: 4516
16 11.0 1969 GT6: 4539
17 11.2 1977 TR7: 4571
1979 TR7: 4575
18 11.3 1975 TR7: 4567
19 11.4 1972 2.5PI Mk II: 4552
1957 TR3: 4505
1965 TR4A IRS: 4525
20 11.5 1971 Stag: 4550
1982 TR7 Convertible: 4581
21 11.6 1972 Dolomite: 4553
1970 Stag: 4544
1973 TR6: 4559
22 11.8 1974 2500TC: 4560
1975 Dolomite: 4564
23 11.9 1954 TR2 Sports: 4501
1969 Vitesse 2-litre Mk II: 4542
24 12.0 1967 GT6: 4530
1956 TR3: 4503
25 12.2 1954 TR2: 4500
26 12.5 1957 TR2 Hardtop: 4504
27 12.6 1973 GT6: 4556
1955 TR2 Hardtop: 4502
28 12.9 1981 Acclaim HL: 4580
1979 Dolomite 1850HL: 4573
29 13.2 1973 1500TC: 4554
1975 Spitfire 1500: 4566
30 13.5 1965 2000: 4522
1973 Dolomite Automatic: 4555
31 13.6 1968 Spitfire: 4534
1967 Spitfire Mk III: 4532
32 14.1 1964 2000: 4520
33 14.2 1976 Dolomite 1500HL: 4568
34 14.3 1980 Spitfire: 4576
1979 Spitfire: 4574
35 14.9 1969 2000 Mk II: 4538
36 15.0 1965 Spitfire Mk II: 4523
37 15.3 1976 Spitfire: 4569
38 15.4 1974 Spitfire: 4561
1973 Spitfire 1500: 4558
39 15.5 1963 Spitfire 4: 4518
1966 Spitfire Mk II: 4529
1965 Vitesse Convertible: 4526
40 15.6 1966 2000 Estate Car: 4528
41 15.9 1971 Spitfire Mk IV: 4549
42 16.0 1973 Spitfire: 4557
43 16.2 1971 Spitfire 4: 4548
44 17.1 1970 1500: 4543
1974 Toledo: 4562
45 17.3 1962 Spitfire 4: 4514
46 17.6 1970 Toledo: 4545
47 17.7 1968 Herald 13/60 Convertible: 4533
1962 Sports 6: 4515
48 17.8 1963 Vitesse 6: 4519
49 19.0 1966 1300: 4527
1935 2-litre Southern Cross: 4490
50 22.0 1934 Gloria 6 Vitesse: 4489
51 22.6 1962 Herald: 4512
52 23.0 1939 2-litre Dolomite: 4495
53 23.2 1959 Herald Coupe: 4507
54 24.0 1960 Herald Coupe: 4510
55 25.2 1963 Herald 12/50: 4517
56 25.4 1936 Vitesse: 4493
57 25.8 1967 Herald 1200: 4531
58 26.5 1960 Herald Convertible: 4509
59 26.6 1936 Gloria 6 Vitesse: 4492
60 27.9 1949 Roadster: 4499
61 28.4 1949 2000 Saloon: 4498
62 28.6 1961 Herald 1200: 4511
63 28.7 1962 Herald 1200 Estate: 4513
64 29.1 1947 1800 Saloon: 4497
65 29.2 1958 Station Wagon: 4506
66 30.4 1959 Herald Saloon: 4508
67 32.2 1936 14/60 Dolomite Saloon: 4491
68 34.4 1947 1800 Roadster: 4496
69 40.7 1937 Gloria 12: 4494

Turner

1 12.8 1960 Turner-Climax: 4582
2 21.3 1961 Sports: 4583

TVR

1 5.0 1989 420 SEAC: 4601
2 5.2 1991 V8 S: 4603
3 5.7 1987 390 SE: 4599
4 5.8 1979 Convertible Turbo: 4593
5 6.6 1985 350i Series II: 4598
6 7.0 1989 S Convertible: 4602
7 7.2 1970 Tuscan: 4586
8 7.6 1987 S Convertible: 4600
9 7.7 1974 3000M: 4589
1980 3000S Roadster: 4595
1979 Taimar Roadster: 4594
10 7.8 1977 Taimar: 4592
1981 Tasmin: 4596
11 9.3 1977 2500M: 4591
12 10.4 1976 1600M: 4590
13 10.5 1969 Vixen S2: 4585
14 10.6 1973 Vixen 2500M: 4588
15 10.8 1961 Grantura: 4584
16 11.4 1970 Vixen: 4587
17 11.8 1983 Tasmin Convertible: 4597

Vanden Plas

1 12.7 1974 Princess R: 4608
2 16.7 1974 1500: 4607
3 16.9 1963 Princess 3-litre Automatic: 4605
4 17.9 1960 Princess: 4604
5 21.1 1965 Princess 1100: 4606

Vauxhall

1 7.0 1990 Carlton GSi 3000 24v: 4724
2 7.9 1990 Cavalier GSi 2000 16v: 4725
3 8.1 1990 Calibra 2.0i 16v: 4722
4 8.2 1987 Carlton 3000 GSi: 4708
1987 Cavalier SRi 130 4-door: 4710
5 8.4 1987 Astra GTE 2.0i: 4706

		1990 Carlton 3.0i CDX Estate: 4723
6	8.5	1990 Cavalier GSi 2000 16v 4x4: 4726
		1978 Chevette 2300 HS: 4688
7	8.6	1988 Cavalier 4x4: 4714
8	8.9	1989 Cavalier SRi: 4719
9	9.0	1984 Astra GTE: 4698
		1991 Calibra 4x4: 4729
10	9.1	1988 Nova GTE: 4715
		1991 Senator 3.0i 24v: 4731
11	9.2	1983 Astra GTE: 4694
		1986 Belmont 1.8 GLSi: 4703
		1978 Cavalier 2000 GLS: 4687
12	9.3	1987 Cavalier 2.0i CD: 4709
		1983 Cavalier CD: 4696
		1989 Senator 2.5i: 4720
		1989 Senator 3.0i CD: 4721
13	9.4	1974 Firenza: 4672
14	9.5	1991 Calibra 2.0i: 4728
		1985 Cavalier SRi: 4701
15	10.0	1983 Carlton 2.0 GL: 4695
		1974 Magnum 2300: 4673
16	10.4	1986 Carlton CD 2.0i: 4704
		1985 Senator 3.0i CD: 4702
17	10.6	1987 Belmont 1.6 GL: 4707
18	10.8	1982 Astra 1600 GL: 4691
		1988 Carlton L 1.8i: 4712
		1982 Cavalier GLS: 4692
19	10.9	1987 Senator 3.0i CD: 4711
20	11.1	1974 VX4/90: 4675
21	11.2	1978 Carlton: 4686
		1976 Cavalier GL Coupe: 4680
22	11.4	1976 Blydenstein Chevette 1500: 4678
		1972 Firenza Sport SL: 4665
23	11.6	1965 Velox: 4647
24	11.8	1985 Astra 1.6 SR: 4700
		1971 Firenza: 4663
		1986 Nova 1.3 GL 5-door: 4705
		1968 Ventora: 4656
25	11.9	1968 Viva GT: 4658
26	12.0	1981 Cavalier 1.6S GL: 4690
27	12.1	1985 Astra 1.3 GL: 4699
		1989 Cavalier 1.6L: 4718
		1979 Royale Coupe: 4689
		1970 Ventora II: 4661
		1970 Viva GT: 4662
28	12.2	1990 Nova 1.5TD Merit: 4727
29	12.4	1972 Victor 2300 SL: 4667
30	12.5	1972 VX4/90: 4670
31	12.6	1977 Magnum 1800: 4684
		1972 Ventora: 4666
32	12.8	1992 1.4i GLS: 4732
		1992 Cavalier 1.7 GL TD: 4733
33	12.9	1989 Cavalier 1.4L: 4717
		1977 VX2300 Estate: 4685
34	13.1	1972 Viva 1800: 4668
35	13.7	1967 Cresta Estate: 4653
		1976 VX1800: 4682
36	14.0	1965 Cresta de Luxe Powerglide: 4646
37	14.2	1983 Nova 1.2L: 4697
38	14.5	1975 Chevette L: 4676
		1991 Nova 1.2 Luxe: 4730
39	14.8	1976 Cavalier 1600 GL: 4679
40	15.0	1967 Victor 2000: 4655
41	15.1	1989 Astra 1.7 DL: 4716
42	15.6	1975 Magnum 1800: 4677
43	15.7	1964 VX4/90: 4645
44	15.9	1966 Viscount Automatic: 4651
45	16.2	1988 Carlton L 2.3D: 4713
46	16.3	1960 Cresta Overdrive: 4636
47	16.8	1963 Cresta Series PB: 4641
48	16.9	1965 VX4/90: 4650
		1962 VX4/90: 4640
49	17.1	1968 Victor 2000 Estate Automatic: 4657
50	17.3	1973 Victor Estate: 4671
51	17.4	1960 Velox III: 4637
52	17.5	1976 Chevette L: 4681
53	17.8	1977 Cavalier 1300L: 4683
		1982 Cavalier LD: 4693
54	18.0	1960 Cresta: 4635
		1958 Cresta: 4630
55	18.1	1992 Frontera 2.3 TD Estate: 4734
		1974 Viva 1256 DL: 4674
		1972 Viva HC Estate: 4669
56	18.2	1965 Viva SL90: 4649
57	18.4	1959 Friary Estate Car: 4633
58	18.8	1965 Victor 101 Estate: 4648
59	19.3	1969 Victor: 4660
60	19.4	1968 Viva SL90 Estate: 4659
61	19.7	1955 Cresta: 4628
		1964 Victor Estate: 4644
		1966 Viva de Luxe: 4652
62	20.4	1967 Victor 101 de Luxe: 4654
63	20.9	1952 Velox: 4625
64	21.2	1954 Velox: 4627
65	21.3	1971 Viva de Luxe: 4664
66	21.9	1938 25 Saloon: 4617
67	22.1	1963 Viva de Luxe: 4642
68	22.4	1951 Velox: 4624
69	23.3	1948 Velox: 4621
70	23.4	1962 Victor Super: 4639
71	23.7	1961 Victor Estate: 4638
72	25.3	1958 Victor: 4631
73	27.4	1958 Victor Estate: 4632
74	28.1	1959 Victor de Luxe: 4634
75	28.6	1935 27 Saloon: 4612
76	29.1	1964 Bedford Beagle: 4643
77	30.6	1950 Velox: 4623
78	31.1	1955 Wyvern: 4629
79	31.5	1952 Wyvern: 4626
80	38.0	1937 14 de Luxe: 4614

Vector

1	4.0	1990 W2: 4735
2	4.2	1991 W8 Twin Turbo: 4736

Volga

1	30.3	1960 M21K: 4737

Volkswagen

1	6.7	1981 Scirocco GT-3 Davey: 4830
2	7.1	1987 Jetta GTi 16v: 4864
3	7.4	1991 Corrado Neuspeed: 4883
4	7.7	1986 Scirocco 16v: 4859
5	7.8	1989 Corrado: 4874
6	7.9	1984 Scirocco 16v: 4847
7	8.0	1986 Golf GTi 16v: 4856
		1986 Scirocco GTX 16v: 4860
8	8.3	1982 Golf GTi 1800: 4832
		1971 Porsche 914/b: 4785
		1988 Scirocco 16v: 4872
9	8.4	1991 GTi 16v: 4884
		1991 Polo G40: 4887
		1985 Scirocco 16v: 4853
10	8.5	1988 GTi 16v: 4866
		1987 GTi 16v: 4863
		1986 Jetta GT: 4857
11	8.7	1989 Corrado 16v: 4875
12	8.8	1988 Jetta GLi 16v: 4867
		1989 Passat GT 16v: 4878
		1977 Scirocco GTi: 4811
13	8.9	1991 Corrado G60: 4882
		1990 Corrado G60: 4879
		1979 Scirocco GLi: 4816
14	9.0	1985 Golf GTi: 4850
		1983 Scirocco GTi: 4841
		1985 Scirocco GTX: 4854
15	9.1	1991 Jetta GLi 16v: 4885
16	9.6	1986 Quantum Synchro Wagon: 4858
17	9.8	1977 Golf GTi: 4806
		1988 Quantum GLS Synchro Wagon: 4871
18	9.9	1992 Golf GTi: 4890
19	10.0	1985 Golf: 4849
20	10.3	1984 Jetta GLX: 4844
		1988 Passat GT: 4869
		1982 Scirocco GL: 4837
		1976 Scirocco TS: 4804
21	10.4	1985 Jetta GLi: 4851
		1979 Scirocco: 4815
		1979 Sciroco GLS: 4817
22	10.5	1987 Golf Cabriolet Clipper: 4862
23	10.6	1983 Rabbit GTi: 4839
24	10.7	1984 Scirocco: 4846
25	10.8	1987 Fox GL: 4861
		1982 Santana GX5: 4836
26	10.9	1990 Passat GL: 4881
		1987 Passat GT 5-door: 4865
27	11.1	1985 Cabriolet Wolfsburg: 4848
		1974 Scirocco TS: 4797
28	11.2	1984 Jetta GLi: 4843
		1980 Scirocco: 4822
29	11.3	1989 Jetta Syncro: 4877
30	11.4	1978 Golf GLS: 4813
31	11.5	1989 Golf CL Catalyst: 4876
32	11.6	1981 Passat GL 5S Estate: 4826
		1985 Scirocco: 4852
		1981 Scirocco S: 4831
33	11.7	1991 Polo GT Coupe: 4888
		1983 Scirocco: 4840
34	11.8	1977 Passat GLS: 4807
35	11.9	1981 Passat CL Formel E: 4825
36	12.0	1976 Golf 1600 LS: 4803
37	12.1	1980 Jetta: 4819
		1980 Rabbit: 4821
38	12.2	1977 Scirocco Fi: 4810
39	12.4	1973 Passat LS: 4790
40	12.6	1983 Quantum GL5: 4838
		1981 Rabbit: 4827
41	12.7	1974 Dasher: 4796
		1992 Golf 1.8 GL: 4889
		1975 Rabbit: 4801
		1975 Scirocco: 4802
42	12.9	1988 Jetta Turbo Diesel: 4868

1972 K70: 4788
43 13.0 1980 Jetta GLS: 4820
1982 Quantum: 4835
44 13.2 1977 Dasher: 4805
45 13.5 1991 Polo 1.3 CL Coupe: 4886
46 13.6 1984 Passat CL Turbo Diesel Estate: 4845
47 14.0 1981 Rabbit Convertible: 4828
48 14.7 1981 Golf 1300 LS: 4824
49 14.8 1970 Porsche 914: 4782
50 15.5 1975 Golf 1100L: 4799
51 15.6 1990 Passat CL TD Estate: 4880
52 15.8 1977 Rabbit Diesel: 4809
53 15.9 1970 411 LE Variant: 4781
54 16.0 1977 Polo LS: 4808
55 16.1 1968 Derby LS: 4779
1973 SP-2: 4791
56 16.3 1971 411: 4784
57 16.5 1968 411 L: 4778
58 16.7 1982 Polo C Formel E: 4834
59 16.8 1974 412: 4795
60 16.9 1989 Caravelle Carat Automatic: 4873
1988 Polo C Saloon: 4870
61 17.0 1978 Beetle Convertible: 4812
62 17.5 1973 Karmann-Ghia: 4789
63 17.9 1982 Polo C: 4833
64 18.0 1975 Polo: 4800
1957 Sedan Judson: 4748
65 18.1 1975 Beetle: 4798
66 18.2 1978 Golf LD: 4814
1973 Sports Bug: 4792
1973 Type III: 4793
67 18.3 1970 Super Beetle: 4783
1983 Vanagon Wasserboxer: 4842
68 18.4 1957 Karmann-Ghia Okrasa: 4747
1971 Super Beetle: 4786
69 18.9 1966 1600 Fastback: 4770
70 19.1 1964 1500S: 4764
71 19.3 1962 Sedan EMPI: 4761
72 19.4 1980 Dasher Diesel: 4818
73 20.3 1966 1600 TL: 4771
74 20.7 1961 1500: 4753
1967 1500: 4772
75 20.8 1969 1600 Squareback: 4780
76 21.2 1980 Vanagon: 4823
77 21.7 1963 Karmann-Ghia 1500: 4763
78 21.9 1966 1500: 4769
79 22.0 1955 Sedan Supercharged: 4743
80 22.1 1963 1500 Estate: 4762
81 22.2 1968 1500 Automatic: 4774
82 22.3 1968 1600 TL Automatic: 4777
1958 Alken-VW: 4749
83 22.5 1967 Beetle 1500: 4773
84 22.9 1981 Rabbit Diesel: 4829
85 23.0 1966 1300: 4767
86 23.2 1974 181: 4794
87 23.7 1966 1300 de Luxe: 4768
88 24.0 1962 1500: 4759
89 24.7 1986 Caravelle Syncro: 4855
90 25.4 1965 1300: 4766
91 26.5 1961 Karmann Ghia: 4754
92 26.8 1968 1500 Semi-automatic: 4775
93 27.5 1962 1200 de Luxe: 4758
94 27.7 1961 Sedan: 4755
95 27.8 1960 Sedan: 4752
96 28.0 1956 Sedan: 4746
97 28.8 1956 Karmann-Ghia: 4744
98 29.4 1965 1200: 4765
99 30.0 1962 Karmann-Ghia: 4760
100 32.1 1960 De Luxe: 4751
101 35.0 1954 Sedan TC: 4742
102 37.2 1952 Sedan de Luxe: 4738
103 38.4 1971 Van: 4787
104 39.2 1954 Sedan: 4741

Volvo

1 7.7 1985 760 Turbo Estate: 4952
2 7.8 1989 740 Turbo: 4959
3 8.3 1987 740 Turbo: 4955
4 8.4 1985 740 Turbo Wagon: 4951
5 8.8 1978 242 IPD: 4935
1990 740 Turbo: 4964
6 8.9 1990 460 Turbo: 4962
1991 940 Turbo: 4967
7 9.2 1991 940 SE: 4965
8 9.3 1991 940 SE Turbo: 4966
1991 960 24v: 4968
9 9.4 1984 740 GLT: 4948
1990 740 GLT 16v Estate: 4963
10 9.5 1969 164: 4914
1983 760 Turbo: 4947
11 9.6 1989 440 Turbo: 4957
1989 740 GLE: 4958
1987 760 GLE: 4956
12 10.0 1973 164E: 4924
13 10.1 1970 1800E: 4916
1982 760 GLE: 4944
1992 960: 4969
1984 GLT Wagon: 4950
14 10.2 1982 GLT Turbo: 4945
15 10.3 1987 480 ES: 4954
16 10.5 1971 142E: 4917
17 10.8 1981 265 GLE: 4941
18 11.1 1978 262C: 4936
1982 360 GLT: 4943
1990 460 GLi: 4961
19 11.3 1972 1800 ES: 4921
1978 242 GT: 4934
20 11.4 1975 244 GL: 4928
1984 760 GLE: 4949
21 11.5 1971 145E Estate: 4919
22 11.6 1971 144 Grand Luxe: 4918
23 11.9 1966 1800S: 4908
24 12.0 1972 164E: 4920
25 12.3 1969 142S 2.0: 4912
1983 760 GLE: 4946
26 12.4 1990 440 GLE: 4960
1961 P1800: 4900
27 12.6 1967 144S: 4909
28 12.7 1974 142 GL: 4925
1975 264 GL: 4929
29 12.8 1970 164 Automatic: 4915
30 12.9 1969 144S: 4913
31 13.0 1982 240 GL: 4942
1976 242 GL: 4930
1958 4-speed: 4896
32 13.2 1962 P1800: 4903
33 13.4 1986 340 GLE: 4953
34 13.5 1976 265 DL: 4931
1978 265 GLE Estate: 4937
35 13.6 1977 244 DL: 4932
36 13.9 1973 144 de Luxe: 4922
37 14.0 1958 Amazon: 4897
38 14.1 1963 PV544: 4905
39 14.2 1975 242 GL: 4927
1980 GL: 4940
40 14.3 1957 PV444L: 4895
41 14.4 1962 122: 4901
42 14.5 1962 122S B18: 4902
1973 144E: 4923
1968 145S Estate: 4910
1957 PV444: 4893
43 15.0 1978 343: 4938
44 15.8 1965 122 Automatic: 4906
45 15.9 1957 PV444 Sports: 4894
46 16.2 1959 122S: 4898
47 16.3 1974 145: 4926
48 16.6 1961 122S: 4899
49 17.0 1977 343: 4933
50 17.6 1965 131: 4907
51 18.5 1980 Diesel: 4939
52 19.6 1956 PV444 California: 4892
53 21.1 1963 121 Estate: 4904
54 29.6 1954 444: 4891

Wartburg

1 18.7 1973 Knight: 4971
2 25.1 1967 Knight: 4970

Warwick

1 12.8 1961 GT: 4972

Westfield

1 4.3 1991 SEight: 4973

Wills Sainte Claire

1 26.0 1926 Six: 4974

Willys

1 15.9 1963 Wagoneer 4WD: 4976

Wolseley

1 13.3 1962 6/110: 4997
2 15.2 1969 18/85 Mk II: 5001
3 17.2 1959 6/99: 4995
4 18.0 1967 18/85: 5000
5 18.1 1955 6/90: 4990
6 19.1 1938 Drop-head Coupe: 4983
7 20.3 1957 6/90: 4992
8 20.4 1938 Super 6: 4984
9 20.6 1965 1100: 4999
10 20.8 1952 6/80: 4988
11 21.0 1935 14 Hornet Special: 4979
1936 Super 6: 4980
12 24.1 1963 Hornet: 4998
13 24.3 1959 15/60: 4994
14 24.4 1958 1500: 4993
1950 6/80: 4987
1937 Salon de Ville: 4981
15 28.1 1962 16/60 Automatic: 4996

16	29.8	1957 15/50: 4991
17	32.6	1953 4/44: 4989
18	35.7	1938 14/56 Salon de Ville: 4982
19	36.1	1949 4/50: 4986

Yugo

1	11.7	1988 65A GLX: 5004
2	13.2	1990 Sana 1.4: 5005
3	13.9	1986 GV: 5002
4	21.6	1987 45 GLS: 5003

Zastava

1	16.0	1981 1300 ZLX-E: 5006

Zender

1	4.3	1990 Fact 4: 5008
2	6.0	1989 Vision 3: 5007

Fuel economy

226 lists ordered by make, fuel consumption in mpg, mpgUS and L/100km, year and model.
Autocar & Motor **'overall' figures from1952.**

Abarth

	mpg	mpg US	L/ 100km		
1	42.6	35.5	6.6	1958	Zagato 750 GT: 1

AC

	mpg	mpg US	L/ 100km		
1	21.6	18.0	13.1	1958	Bristol: 19
2	20.5	17.1	13.8	1956	Aceca: 15
				1960	Aceca-Bristol: 21
3	19.1	15.9	14.8	1953	2-litre: 13
4	18.5	15.4	15.3	1961	Greyhound: 22
5	17.0	14.2	16.6	1968	428 Fastback: 26
6	15.1	12.6	18.7	1965	Cobra: 25

Alfa Romeo

	mpg	mpg US	L/ 100km		
1	30.5	25.4	9.3	1977	Alfasud 5M: 97
2	29.7	24.7	9.5	1990	33 Boxer 16v: 144
3	29.6	24.6	9.5	1977	Alfasud 1300ti: 96
4	29.4	24.5	9.6	1983	Alfa 33 1.5: 112
				1985	Arna 1.3SL: 119
5	29.0	24.1	9.7	1977	Alfasud 1200ti: 95
6	28.8	24.0	9.8	1961	Giulietta ti: 52
7	28.6	23.8	9.9	1985	Alfa 33 1.5 4x4 Estate: 117
8	28.5	23.7	9.9	1964	Giulia 1600 Spider: 58
9	28.2	23.5	10.0	1981	Alfasud 1.5: 108
10	27.4	22.8	10.3	1963	Alfasud: 84
11	27.2	22.6	10.4	1986	Alfa 33 1.3 S: 123
12	26.7	22.2	10.6	1963	Giulia 1600 Sprint: 86
13	26.6	22.1	10.6	1963	Giulia ti: 57
14	26.2	21.8	10.8	1987	33 1.7 Veloce: 129
				1974	Alfasud ti: 88
15	25.9	21.6	10.9	1989	164 3.0 Lusso: 138
16	25.8	21.5	10.9	1987	Alfa 33 1.7 Sportwagon Veloce: 130
17	25.7	21.4	11.0	1979	Alfasud 1.5 Sprint Veloce: 104
				1988	Sprint 1.7 Cloverleaf: 137
18	25.6	21.3	11.0	1987	Alfa 75 2.0i Twin Spark: 131
19	25.1	20.9	11.3	1978	Alfasud Sprint 1.5: 100
20	25.0	20.8	11.3	1984	Alfetta Gold Cloverleaf: 113
21	24.8	20.7	11.4	1976	Spider Veloce 2000: 94
22	24.6	20.5	11.5	1953	1900: 43
				1976	Alfetta 1.6: 91
23	24.5	20.4	11.5	1986	Alfa 75 1.8: 124
24	24.4	20.3	11.6	1969	GT 1300 Junior: 75
25	24.3	20.2	11.6	1985	Arna ti: 120
26	23.9	19.9	11.8	1968	1750 GT Veloce: 71
				1984	Sprint Green Cloverleaf: 116
27	23.7	19.7	11.9	1975	Alfetta GT: 90
28	23.5	19.6	12.0	1974	Alfetta: 89
29	23.4	19.5	12.1	1990	164 Twin Spark Lusso: 142
				1978	Alfetta 2.0: 101
30	23.3	19.4	12.1	1976	Alfetta GTV: 93
31	23.2	19.3	12.2	1981	GTV6: 109
32	23.1	19.2	12.2	1968	1750 Berlina: 70
33	22.8	19.0	12.4	1989	164 Automatic: 139
				1986	Alfa 75 2.5 Green Cloverleaf: 125
34	22.4	18.7	12.6	1988	75 2.5 Auto: 134
35	22.2	18.5	12.7	1985	Alfa 90 2.5 Gold Cloverleaf: 118
36	21.9	18.2	12.9	1966	Giulia Sprint GTV: 64
				1978	Giulietta 1.6: 102
37	21.8	18.2	13.0	1963	2000: 83
38	21.4	17.8	13.2	1991	164 Cloverleaf: 145
39	21.3	17.7	13.3	1967	Giulia 1300 ti: 68
40	21.1	17.6	13.4	1972	2000 GTV: 79
41	20.5	17.1	13.8	1987	Alfa 75 V6 3.0: 132
42	19.3	16.1	14.6	1963	2600 Saloon: 56
43	17.7	14.7	16.0	1966	2600 Sprint: 63
44	14.9	12.4	19.0	1972	Montreal: 82

Allard

	mpg	mpg US	L/ 100km		
1	21.6	18.0	13.1	1954	Palm Beach: 152
2	16.3	13.6	17.3	1959	GT Coupe: 153
3	12.3	10.2	23.0	1952	K2: 150

Alvis

	mpg	mpg US	L/ 100km		
1	19.0	15.8	14.9	1952	3-litre: 163
2	18.5	15.4	15.3	1962	3-litre TD21 Series II Automatic: 167
3	18.3	15.2	15.4	1959	3-litre TD21: 166
4	18.0	15.0	15.7	1953	3-litre: 164
				1957	3-litre Graber: 165
5	15.9	13.2	17.8	1965	3-litre Series III: 168
				1965	TE21S: 169

AMC

	mpg	mpg US	L/ 100km		
1	15.8	13.2	17.9	1976	Pacer: 203

Armstrong Siddelely

	mpg	mpg US	L/ 100km		
1	18.0	15.0	15.7	1953	Sapphire Saloon: 219
2	14.1	11.7	20.0	1959	Star Sapphire: 220

Aston Martin

1	20.3	16.9	13.9	1953	DB2/4 Saloon: 233
2	18.0	15.0	15.7	1954	DB2: 234
3	16.4	13.7	17.2	1961	DB4: 238
4	15.6	13.0	18.1	1991	Virage: 261
5	14.7	12.2	19.2	1964	DB5: 241
6	14.0	11.7	20.2	1982	V8: 252
7	13.9	11.6	20.3	1962	DB4 GT Zagato: 240
8	13.7	11.4	20.6	1980	Lagonda: 250
9	13.5	11.2	20.9	1977	V8 Vantage: 248
10	13.0	10.8	21.7	1978	V8: 249
11	12.7	10.6	22.2	1968	DBS: 243
12	12.6	10.5	22.4	1966	DB6: 242
13	12.4	10.3	22.8	1963	V8 Automatic: 245
14	12.2	10.2	23.2	1971	DBS V8: 244
15	11.7	9.7	24.1	1975	V8: 246

Audi

1	37.3	31.1	7.6	1982	80 Turbo Diesel: 291
2	31.9	26.6	8.9	1984	80 GL: 301
3	31.0	25.8	9.1	1975	80 Estate: 273
4	30.8	25.6	9.2	1986	80 1.8S: 312
5	30.4	25.3	9.3	1963	80 LS: 269
6	29.7	24.7	9.5	1987	90 2.2E: 317
7	29.5	24.6	9.6	1974	80 GT: 271
8	29.4	24.5	9.6	1982	100 CD: 290
9	29.1	24.2	9.7	1976	80 GTE: 275
10	28.9	24.1	9.8	1986	100 Turbo Diesel: 310
11	28.7	23.9	9.8	1987	90 Quattro: 318
12	28.1	23.4	10.1	1988	80 1.8E: 321
				1979	80 GLS: 282
13	28.0	23.3	10.1	1991	80 16v Sport: 335
14	27.4	22.8	10.3	1988	100 Sport: 320
				1986	Coupe GT 2.2: 315
15	27.0	22.5	10.5	1989	Coupe Quattro: 327
16	26.9	22.4	10.5	1978	100 L Avant: 279
17	26.1	21.7	10.8	1989	Coupe 2.2E: 326
18	25.5	21.2	11.1	1983	80 Quattro: 295
				1983	Coupe Injection: 296
19	25.4	21.1	11.1	1990	80 2.0E: 328
20	25.2	21.0	11.2	1986	90: 313
21	24.7	20.6	11.4	1985	Coupe GT: 307
22	24.2	20.2	11.7	1986	Coupe Quattro: 316
23	23.9	19.9	11.8	1985	90 Quattro: 306
24	23.6	19.7	12.0	1972	100 Coupe S: 267
25	23.4	19.5	12.1	1975	100 GL Automatic: 272
26	23.3	19.4	12.1	1977	100 5E: 276
27	23.2	19.3	12.2	1971	100 LS Auto: 266
28	22.7	18.9	12.4	1985	100 Quattro: 303
29	22.2	18.5	12.7	1989	90 Quattro 20v: 325
30	21.5	17.9	13.1	1983	200 Turbo: 293
31	21.4	17.8	13.2	1988	100 Avant Quattro: 319
				1979	100 GL5S: 281
				1977	100 GLS: 277
32	20.7	17.2	13.6	1981	200 5E: 285
33	20.0	16.7	14.1	1992	80 2.8E V6 Quattro: 339
34	19.8	16.5	14.3	1984	200 Quattro Turbo: 297
35	19.7	16.4	14.3	1988	Quattro: 323
36	19.1	15.9	14.8	1981	Quattro: 289
				1990	Quattro 20v: 330
37	19.0	15.8	14.9	1991	100 2.8E Auto: 333
				1985	200 Avant Quattro: 304
38	18.2	15.2	15.5	1991	Coupe S2: 337
39	15.3	12.7	18.5	1985	Quattro Sport: 309
				1990	V8 Quattro: 331
				1990	V8 Quattro Automatic: 332

Austin

1	42.8	35.6	6.6	1954	A30: 369
2	42.0	35.0	6.7	1953	A30: 368
3	41.8	34.8	6.8	1958	A35 4-door: 379
4	40.2	33.5	7.0	1956	A30 Countryman: 375
5	38.0	31.6	7.4	1958	A40: 380
6	37.8	31.5	7.5	1960	A40 Countryman: 387
7	36.9	30.7	7.7	1987	Metro 1.3L 3-door: 426
8	35.7	29.7	7.9	1958	A55: 381
9	35.2	29.3	8.0	1981	Mini Metro: 419
10	34.4	28.6	8.2	1971	1300 Mk III: 403
11	33.6	28.0	8.4	1957	A55: 376
12	32.8	27.3	8.6	1983	Maestro 1.6 HLS: 421
13	32.5	27.1	8.7	1976	Allegro 1100: 413
14	31.9	26.6	8.9	1984	Montego 1.6L: 423
15	31.2	26.0	9.1	1975	Allegro 1300 Estate: 412
16	30.8	25.6	9.2	1963	Allegro 1300 Super: 406
17	30.7	25.6	9.2	1989	Metro GTa: 427
18	30.5	25.4	9.3	1962	A40 Mk II: 392
19	30.2	25.1	9.4	1969	1300 Super: 399
20	30.1	25.1	9.4	1954	A40 Somerset Coupe: 370
21	29.4	24.5	9.6	1985	Montego 2.0 HL: 424
22	28.8	24.0	9.8	1977	Maxi 1750: 416
23	28.5	23.7	9.9	1952	A40 Somerset: 366
24	28.4	23.6	9.9	1955	A50 Cambridge: 372
25	27.9	23.2	10.1	1986	Montego 2.0 Vanden Plas EFI: 425
26	27.7	23.1	10.2	1981	Metro Automatic: 418
27	27.2	22.6	10.4	1974	Vanden Plas 1500: 410
28	27.0	22.5	10.5	1969	1300 GT: 398
				1959	A55 Cambridge Mk II: 384
29	26.9	22.4	10.5	1968	1800 Mk II: 395
30	26.8	22.3	10.5	1983	Maestro 1600: 422
31	26.7	22.2	10.6	1977	Allegro 1750 HL: 415
32	26.5	22.1	10.7	1982	Ambassador 2.0 HL: 420
33	26.2	21.8	10.8	1962	A60 Cambridge: 393
34	26.0	21.6	10.9	1974	Allegro HL: 409
35	24.8	20.7	11.4	1972	Maxi High Line: 405
36	24.5	20.4	11.5	1970	Maxi 1750: 402
37	24.1	20.1	11.7	1978	Princess II 2000 HL: 417
38	24.0	20.0	11.8	1969	Maxi: 400
39	23.5	19.6	12.0	1964	1800: 394
40	23.4	19.5	12.1	1974	Allegro 1500 Special Automatic: 408
41	23.0	19.2	12.3	1961	A55 Countryman: 390
42	22.5	18.7	12.6	1956	A105: 374
43	22.3	18.6	12.7	1972	2200: 404
44	22.0	18.3	12.8	1955	A90 Westminster: 373
45	21.8	18.2	13.0	1976	Princess 2200 HLS: 414
46	21.2	17.7	13.3	1958	A95 Countryman: 382
47	20.8	17.3	13.6	1958	A105 Automatic: 378
48	20.7	17.2	13.6	1975	2200 HL: 411
49	20.4	17.0	13.8	1957	A95 Westminster: 377
50	20.3	16.9	13.9	1959	A105 Vanden Plas: 383
51	17.8	14.8	15.9	1959	Gipsy: 386
52	17.3	14.4	16.3	1959	A99: 385
53	15.8	13.2	17.9	1970	3-litre: 401
54	15.0	12.5	18.8	1952	Princess: 367
55	14.9	12.4	19.0	1968	3-litre Automatic: 396
56	14.2	11.8	19.9	1954	Princess: 371

Austin-Healey

1	40.3	33.6	7.0	1959	Sprite Hardtop: 437
2	34.0	28.3	8.3	1958	Sprite: 435
3	33.2	27.6	8.5	1961	Sprite Mk II: 441
4	28.3	23.6	10.0	1960	Sprite Supercharged: 439
5	24.5	20.4	11.5	1953	100: 428
6	21.2	17.7	13.3	1958	100/6: 433
7	20.3	16.9	13.9	1964	3000 Mk III: 445
8	20.0	16.7	14.1	1959	3000: 436
9	17.7	14.7	16.0	1961	3000: 440
10	17.1	14.2	16.5	1962	3000 Mk II: 443

Auto Union

1	26.4	22.0	10.7	1959	1000: 450
2	24.5	20.4	11.5	1966	Audi: 452
3	23.7	19.7	11.9	1969	100 LS: 454
4	23.1	19.2	12.2	1961	Universal: 451
5	21.3	17.7	13.3	1967	Audi Super 90: 453

Bentley

1	19.4	16.2	14.6	1952	Continental: 471
2	16.0	13.3	17.7	1954	Sports: 474
3	15.2	12.7	18.6	1956	Continental Park Ward DH Coupe: 475
4	15.0	12.5	18.8	1952	Mk VI: 472
5	14.2	11.8	19.9	1987	Turbo R: 481
6	14.0	11.7	20.2	1956	Series S: 476
7	13.6	11.3	20.8	1979	T2: 478
8	13.4	11.2	21.1	1985	Mulsanne Turbo: 480
9	13.0	10.8	21.7	1960	S2 Continental: 477
10	12.3	10.2	23.0	1952	Sports Saloon: 473
11	12.1	10.1	23.3	1982	Mulsanne Turbo: 479

Berkeley

1	44.7	37.2	6.3	1957	Sports: 484
2	33.1	27.6	8.5	1958	Sports 4: 486

BMW

1	61.0	50.8	4.6	1956	Isetta Motocoupe: 499
2	45.6	38.0	6.2	1958	600: 501
3	35.5	29.6	8.0	1962	700 Coupe: 504
4	32.3	26.9	8.7	1964	700 LS: 507
5	28.5	23.7	9.9	1984	318i: 568
6	27.6	23.0	10.2	1991	318i: 614
7	27.5	22.9	10.3	1990	318i S: 609
8	27.4	22.8	10.3	1987	318i 2-door: 586
9	27.2	22.6	10.4	1963	1800 Saloon: 506
10	26.7	22.2	10.6	1982	316: 559
11	26.6	22.1	10.6	1991	325i SE: 615
12	26.5	22.1	10.7	1986	325i Convertible: 579
13	26.3	21.9	10.7	1967	1600 Coupe: 512
14	26.2	21.8	10.8	1983	525E: 565
15	26.0	21.6	10.9	1983	320i: 564
				1989	M3 Evolution: 604
16	25.6	21.3	11.0	1975	1602L: 537
17	25.4	21.1	11.1	1971	2002: 522
18	25.3	21.1	11.2	1989	316i 4-door: 598
19	24.6	20.5	11.5	1977	320: 541
				1985	325i: 573

20	24.0	20.0	11.8	1971	2002 Tii: 523
				1989	Z1: 608
21	23.8	19.8	11.9	1986	520i: 580
22	23.7	19.7	11.9	1974	525: 536
23	23.3	19.4	12.1	1966	2000: 509
				1981	528i: 558
24	22.4	18.7	12.6	1963	520i: 531
25	22.3	18.6	12.7	1988	535i SE: 593
26	22.0	18.3	12.8	1991	520i: 616
27	21.8	18.2	13.0	1969	2500: 519
				1982	635 CSi: 561
28	21.7	18.1	13.0	1974	2002 Turbo: 534
				1991	525i SE 24v: 618
29	21.3	17.7	13.3	1971	3.0S: 525
30	21.2	17.7	13.3	1969	2000 Tilux: 517
31	20.8	17.3	13.6	1971	3.0 CS: 524
				1992	520i SE Touring: 624
32	20.6	17.2	13.7	1976	633 CSi: 540
				1989	M635 CSi: 607
33	20.3	16.9	13.9	1985	732i: 575
				1987	M3: 590
34	20.0	16.7	14.1	1987	730i SE: 588
35	19.8	16.5	14.3	1979	732i: 553
36	19.7	16.4	14.3	1978	323i: 547
37	19.6	16.3	14.4	1983	735i: 567
38	19.4	16.2	14.6	1977	733i: 545
39	19.3	16.1	14.6	1956	501: 498
40	19.2	16.0	14.7	1978	528i: 549
41	18.8	15.7	15.0	1984	735i Automatic: 571
42	18.5	15.4	15.3	1987	750i L: 589
43	18.1	15.1	15.6	1977	528: 543
44	17.7	14.7	16.0	1974	3.3L: 535
				1985	M535i: 576
45	17.5	14.6	16.1	1979	635 CSi: 552
				1986	735i Automatic: 585
46	17.2	14.3	16.4	1988	635 CSi: 594
47	17.1	14.2	16.5	1965	1800 Ti: 508
48	17.0	14.2	16.6	1984	M635 CSi: 572
49	16.7	13.9	16.9	1963	3.0 CSL: 530
50	16.2	13.5	17.4	1990	750i: 612
51	14.7	12.2	19.2	1992	850i Manual: 625
52	14.4	12.0	19.6	1991	850i: 620

Bond

1	35.0	29.1	8.1	1970	Bug: 629
2	34.5	28.7	8.2	1966	875: 628
3	30.3	25.2	9.3	1964	Equipe GT: 626
4	26.7	22.2	10.6	1965	Equipe GT 4S: 627

Borgward

1	33.0	27.5	8.6	1958	Isabella TS: 633
2	27.8	23.1	10.2	1960	Isabella TS Coupe: 636
3	19.6	16.3	14.4	1960	2.3 Grosse: 634

Bristol

1	22.7	18.9	12.4	1952	401: 639
2	14.1	11.7	20.0	1961	407: 640

Buick

1	17.5	14.6	16.1	1961	Special: 662
2	16.9	14.1	16.7	1978	Century: 691
3	16.0	13.3	17.7	1954	Roadmaster: 660
4	10.8	9.0	26.2	1965	Riviera: 674

Cadillac

1	10.9	9.1	25.9	1964	Coupe de Ville: 705
				1961	Fleetwood: 703
2	10.4	8.7	27.2	1968	Coupe de Ville: 709

Carbodies

1	23.0	19.2	12.3	1989	Fairway 2.7 Silver: 721

Caterham

1	28.3	23.6	10.0	1975	Super 7: 722
2	23.5	19.6	12.0	1985	1700 Super Sprint: 723
3	17.3	14.4	16.3	1990	7 HPC: 725

Chevrolet

1	22.3	18.6	12.7	1971	Vega 2300: 853
2	18.8	15.7	15.0	1961	Corvair 700: 746
3	17.6	14.7	16.1	1985	Corvette: 897
4	16.7	13.9	16.9	1984	Corvette: 894
5	16.4	13.7	17.2	1965	Chevelle Malibu: 791
6	14.6	12.2	19.3	1964	Corvette Sting Ray: 786
7	10.6	8.8	26.6	1978	Blazer: 876
8	10.3	8.6	27.4	1970	Impala: 846

Chrysler

1	32.6	27.1	8.7	1976	Avenger Super 1300: 994
2	31.5	26.2	9.0	1977	Sunbeam 1.0LS: 997
3	30.9	25.7	9.1	1978	Horizon GL: 1001
4	30.6	25.5	9.2	1977	Sunbeam 1.6S: 998
5	29.4	24.5	9.6	1978	1300 GL: 999
6	29.3	24.4	9.6	1976	Alpine S: 993
7	29.2	24.3	9.7	1977	Alpine GL: 995
8	28.2	23.5	10.0	1977	Avenger 1600 Estate: 996
9	27.7	23.1	10.2	1978	Alpine GLS: 1000
10	23.5	19.6	12.0	1971	180: 991
11	23.1	19.2	12.2	1963	2-litre: 992
12	22.3	18.6	12.7	1979	Sunbeam 1600 Ti: 1002
13	19.1	15.9	14.8	1960	Valiant: 974
14	18.1	15.1	15.6	1966	Valiant Premium Auto: 986
15	16.2	13.5	17.4	1953	New Yorker Saloon: 971
16	14.1	11.7	20.0	1955	Windsor de Luxe: 972
17	14.0	11.7	20.2	1970	Charger: 990

Citroen

1	63.2	52.6	4.5	1953	2CV Cabriolet: 1019
2	54.7	45.5	5.2	1989	AX14 DTR: 1081
3	49.2	41.0	5.7	1961	Bijou: 1028
4	45.9	38.2	6.2	1975	2CV6: 1046
5	44.5	37.1	6.3	1962	Ami 6: 1030
6	43.9	36.6	6.4	1985	Visa 17RD: 1069
7	42.1	35.1	6.7	1984	BX19 RD Diesel: 1061
8	38.9	32.4	7.3	1987	AX11 TRE: 1075
9	38.8	32.3	7.3	1991	AX11 TZX: 1087
10	38.4	32.0	7.4	1986	BX19 RD Estate: 1071
11	36.2	30.1	7.8	1988	BX DTR Turbo: 1080
12	36.1	30.1	7.8	1979	Visa Club: 1057
13	35.9	29.9	7.9	1990	AX GT5: 1083
14	35.2	29.3	8.0	1984	LNA 11RE: 1063
15	35.0	29.1	8.1	1967	Ami 6 Break: 1035
16	34.7	28.9	8.1	1987	AX14 TRS: 1076
17	34.0	28.3	8.3	1989	BX14 TGE: 1082
18	32.7	27.2	8.6	1988	AX11 TRE 5DR: 1079
19	32.2	26.8	8.8	1970	Ami 8 Club: 1037
20	32.0	26.6	8.8	1992	XM Turbo SD Estate: 1093
21	31.8	26.5	8.9	1977	CX 2200 Diesel: 1051
22	31.5	26.2	9.0	1979	CX 2500 Diesel Super: 1056
23	31.3	26.1	9.0	1985	Visa 14TRS: 1068
24	30.6	25.5	9.2	1984	Visa Convertible: 1064
25	30.5	25.4	9.3	1983	BX14 RE: 1059
26	30.4	25.3	9.3	1987	AX GT: 1074
27	30.3	25.2	9.3	1983	BX16 TRS: 1060
28	30.1	25.1	9.4	1987	CX25 DTR Turbo 2: 1078
29	29.8	24.8	9.5	1987	BX GTi 16v: 1077
30	29.2	24.3	9.7	1961	DS: 1029
31	29.0	24.1	9.7	1976	GS X2: 1050
32	28.8	24.0	9.8	1985	Visa GTi: 1070
33	28.6	23.8	9.9	1975	GS Pallas: 1048
34	26.5	22.1	10.7	1985	BX16 TRS Automatic: 1066
				1991	ZX 1.4 Avantage: 1090
35	26.3	21.9	10.7	1990	BX GTi 4x4: 1084
				1958	ID19: 1025
36	26.2	21.8	10.8	1979	Athena: 1055
				1985	CX22 TRS: 1067
				1986	Visa GTi: 1073
37	26.0	21.6	10.9	1992	AX GTi: 1092
38	25.8	21.5	10.9	1990	XM 2.0SEi: 1086
39	25.3	21.1	11.2	1991	ZX Volcane: 1091
40	24.8	20.7	11.4	1963	GS 1220: 1044
41	24.4	20.3	11.6	1952	Light Fifteen: 1017
42	24.2	20.2	11.7	1957	DS19: 1024
43	24.1	20.1	11.7	1963	DS: 1031
44	23.6	19.7	12.0	1953	Big Fifteen: 1020
45	23.5	19.6	12.0	1976	CX 2200 Pallas: 1049
				1977	CX 2400: 1052
46	23.3	19.4	12.1	1971	GS: 1039
47	23.2	19.3	12.2	1975	CX 2000: 1047
48	23.1	19.2	12.2	1971	Safari 21: 1040
49	22.0	18.3	12.8	1965	DS21 Pallas M: 1032
50	21.9	18.2	12.9	1981	CX Pallas: 1058
51	21.6	18.0	13.1	1977	CX 2400 GTi: 1053
				1960	ID Safari: 1026
52	20.9	17.4	13.5	1978	CX Pallas C-Matic Injection: 1054
				1970	DS21 EFI 139 Pallas: 1038
53	20.8	17.3	13.6	1991	XM V6.24: 1089
54	20.4	17.0	13.8	1986	CX25 Ri Familiale Auto: 1072
55	20.1	16.7	14.1	1984	CX GTi Turbo: 1062
56	18.8	15.7	15.0	1991	XM 3.0 SEi Auto: 1088
57	18.5	15.4	15.3	1954	Six: 1021
58	17.9	14.9	15.8	1963	Safari SM: 1045
59	16.0	13.3	17.7	1971	Safari SM: 1041

Clan

1	34.3	28.6	8.2	1971	Crusader: 1095

Dacia

1	31.1	25.9	9.1	1985	Duster GLX: 1106

DAF

1	34.5	28.7	8.2	1962	Daffodil de Luxe Extra: 1110
2	34.3	28.6	8.2	1967	44: 1111
3	33.6	28.0	8.4	1962	Daffodil: 1109
4	28.5	23.7	9.9	1958	55: 1107
5	27.1	22.6	10.4	1974	66SL 1300: 1114
6	26.4	22.0	10.7	1963	66SL: 1113
7	25.7	21.4	11.0	1971	55 Estate: 1112

Daihatsu

1	48.5	40.4	5.8	1983	Charade Diesel: 1120
2	45.5	37.9	6.2	1987	Charade CX Diesel Turbo: 1123
3	40.2	33.5	7.0	1983	Charade CX: 1119
4	39.1	32.6	7.2	1981	Domino: 1117
5	37.2	31.0	7.6	1986	Domino: 1122
6	36.5	30.4	7.7	1979	Charade XTE: 1116
7	34.8	29.0	8.1	1965	Compagno Berlina: 1115
8	30.9	25.7	9.1	1985	Charmant 1300LC: 1121
9	29.3	24.4	9.6	1982	Charmant 1600LE: 1118
10	29.2	24.3	9.7	1988	Charade Turbo: 1127
11	29.0	24.1	9.7	1990	Applause 16 Xi: 1131
12	28.8	24.0	9.8	1987	Charade GT ti: 1124
13	25.8	21.5	10.9	1989	Charade 1.3 CX: 1128
14	23.0	19.2	12.3	1987	Fourtrak Estate DT EL: 1125
15	21.4	17.8	13.2	1989	Sportrak EL: 1130

Daimler

1	29.1	24.2	9.7	1959	V8 SP250: 1146
2	19.7	16.4	14.3	1953	Conquest: 1140
3	19.3	16.1	14.6	1966	2.5-litre V8: 1152
4	19.0	15.8	14.9	1957	One-O-Four: 1143
5	18.8	15.7	15.0	1964	Conquest Century Saloon: 1151
6	18.0	15.0	15.7	1955	One-O-Four Ladies' Model: 1141
7	17.6	14.7	16.1	1958	Majestic: 1144
8	17.3	14.4	16.3	1963	2.5-litre V8 Saloon: 1149
9	17.0	14.2	16.6	1955	Regency Mk II: 1142
10	16.4	13.7	17.2	1981	Double-Six HE: 1155
				1972	Sovereign: 1153
11	14.8	12.3	19.1	1961	Majestic Major: 1148
12	14.7	12.2	19.2	1963	Limousine: 1150
13	14.3	11.9	19.8	1974	Sovereign LWB Automatic: 1154
14	12.3	10.2	23.0	1959	DK 400B: 1145

Datsun

1	43.7	36.4	6.5	1983	Micra GL: 1232
2	37.2	31.0	7.6	1977	Cherry F11: 1204
3	36.7	30.6	7.7	1982	Sunny 1.5 DX: 1227
4	34.8	29.0	8.1	1971	100A: 1172
5	31.9	26.6	8.9	1974	120Y: 1185
6	31.8	26.5	8.9	1982	Stanza 1.6 GL: 1226
7	31.6	26.3	8.9	1979	New Sunny: 1216
8	31.5	26.2	9.0	1976	140J Violet: 1195
9	31.2	26.0	9.1	1970	1200: 1169
10	29.3	24.4	9.6	1969	1000 de Luxe: 1168
11	28.9	24.1	9.8	1968	1600: 1163
12	27.7	23.1	10.2	1977	180B Bluebird: 1200
13	27.3	22.7	10.3	1971	1200 Estate: 1174
14	24.9	20.7	11.3	1972	180B: 1178
15	24.6	20.5	11.5	1963	200L: 1181
16	23.9	19.9	11.8	1974	260Z 2+2: 1187
17	23.3	19.4	12.1	1979	2.4 Laurel Six: 1208
18	22.4	18.7	12.6	1977	260Z: 1202
19	22.2	18.5	12.7	1976	200L-6: 1196
20	21.6	18.0	13.1	1972	240C: 1179
21	21.4	17.8	13.2	1971	240Z: 1175
22	21.3	17.7	13.3	1979	240K: 1210
23	21.1	17.6	13.4	1978	Laurel Six: 1207
24	20.2	16.8	14.0	1975	260C Estate: 1191
25	18.4	15.3	15.4	1979	280ZX 2+2 Automatic: 1212

De Tomaso

1	16.0	13.3	17.7	1986	Pantera GT5-S: 1242
2	13.0	10.8	21.7	1972	Pantera: 1237

DKW

1	33.2	27.6	8.5	1958	3-6 Sonderklasse Coupe: 1265
2	31.5	26.2	9.0	1954	Sonderklasse: 1261
3	30.1	25.1	9.4	1961	Junior: 1267

Dodge

1	17.3	14.4	16.3	1961	Dart Phoenix: 1276
2	15.9	13.2	17.8	1959	Custom Royal: 1274
3	14.5	12.1	19.5	1958	Custom Royal: 1273

Dove

1	24.1	20.1	11.7	1963	GTR4: 1349

Elva

1	29.8	24.8	9.5	1958	Courier: 1358

Facel Vega

1	14.4	12.0	19.6	1958	FVS: 1365
2	13.1	10.9	21.6	1962	Facel II: 1368

Fairthorpe

1	18.1	15.1	15.6	1961	Zeta: 1369

Ferguson

1	18.6	15.5	15.2	1966	R5: 1370

Ferrari

1	19.8	16.5	14.3	1976	Dino 308 GT4 2+2: 1410
2	19.2	16.0	14.7	1976	308 GTB: 1409
3	18.4	15.3	15.4	1990	348tb: 1445
4	16.8	14.0	16.8	1986	Mondial 3.2QV: 1430
5	16.6	13.8	17.0	1989	Testa Rossa: 1442
6	15.7	13.1	18.0	1978	512 BB: 1413
7	12.4	10.3	22.8	1971	Daytona: 1397
8	11.9	9.9	23.7	1965	365 GTC: 1390
9	11.0	9.2	25.7	1975	365 GT4 2+2: 1406

Fiat

1	55.5	46.2	5.1	1958	500: 1477
2	53.2	44.3	5.3	1959	500: 1482
3	49.0	40.8	5.8	1955	600: 1469
4	46.8	39.0	6.0	1961	500 Giardiniera: 1492
5	46.0	38.3	6.1	1964	500D: 1498
6	42.8	35.6	6.6	1966	500F: 1504
7	41.8	34.8	6.8	1986	Regata DS: 1594
8	41.0	34.1	6.9	1952	500C Convertible: 1464
9	39.4	32.8	7.2	1957	600 Multipla: 1473
10	39.0	32.5	7.2	1990	Uno 60S: 1604
11	38.9	32.4	7.3	1983	Strada 60 Comfort ES: 1581
12	38.8	32.3	7.3	1960	600: 1486
13	38.7	32.2	7.3	1981	127 1050 Super: 1572
				1981	Panda: 1574
14	38.0	31.6	7.4	1961	600D: 1493
15	37.1	30.9	7.6	1979	126 de Ville: 1564
16	36.8	30.6	7.7	1963	126: 1539
17	36.2	30.1	7.8	1953	1100: 1465
18	36.0	30.0	7.8	1975	133: 1549
19	35.8	29.8	7.9	1983	Uno 55 S: 1582
20	35.7	29.7	7.9	1985	Uno 70 SX: 1588
21	35.5	29.6	8.0	1964	850 Super: 1499
				1986	Panda 750 L: 1593
				1984	Regata 70 ES: 1585
22	35.4	29.5	8.0	1983	Uno 70 SX: 1583
23	34.9	29.1	8.1	1987	Uno Selecta: 1597
24	34.5	28.7	8.2	1958	1200 Gran Luce: 1475
25	34.2	28.5	8.3	1957	1100 Saloon: 1471
26	34.1	28.4	8.3	1978	127 Sport: 1558
				1969	850 Coupe: 1518
27	34.0	28.3	8.3	1986	Panda 1000 S: 1592
28	33.6	28.0	8.4	1966	Abarth 595: 1506
29	33.5	27.9	8.4	1954	1100 TV Saloon: 1467
30	32.7	27.2	8.6	1976	128 3P: 1552
31	32.6	27.1	8.7	1975	128 Special: 1547
32	32.5	27.1	8.7	1976	128 Estate: 1553
				1966	850 Coupe: 1505
33	32.2	26.8	8.8	1988	Tipo 1.4: 1598
34	32.0	26.6	8.8	1971	127: 1528
35	31.3	26.1	9.0	1982	Strada Super 85: 1578
36	30.7	25.6	9.2	1977	127 1050 CL: 1555
				1977	X1/9: 1557
37	30.4	25.3	9.3	1989	Tipo 1.6 DGT SX: 1600
38	29.2	24.3	9.7	1970	128 4-door: 1523
39	29.1	24.2	9.7	1984	Regata 100 S: 1584
40	29.0	24.1	9.7	1968	850 Special: 1513
				1987	Croma ie Super: 1595
41	28.6	23.8	9.9	1979	Strada 75CL: 1568
				1992	Tipo 1.8ie DGT SX: 1606
42	28.5	23.7	9.9	1972	128 Coupe 1300: 1531
43	28.3	23.6	10.0	1990	Croma CHT: 1602
44	28.2	23.5	10.0	1963	1100D: 1496
45	28.1	23.4	10.1	1990	Tempra 1.6 SX: 1603
46	27.6	23.0	10.2	1979	Strada 65CL: 1567
47	26.8	22.3	10.5	1967	124: 1507
				1965	1500: 1500
				1982	Mirafiori 1400CL: 1575
				1985	X1/9VS: 1591
48	26.6	22.1	10.6	1963	124S Automatic: 1538
49	26.5	22.1	10.7	1972	124: 1530
50	26.3	21.9	10.7	1984	Strada Abarth 130TC: 1586
51	26.2	21.8	10.8	1969	124 Estate Car: 1516
52	26.1	21.7	10.8	1985	Uno Turbo ie: 1589
				1979	X1/9 1500: 1570
53	25.9	21.6	10.9	1987	Regata 100S ie: 1596
				1990	Uno Turbo ie: 1605

54	25.5	21.2	11.1	1975	131 1300S: 1548
				1961	1500: 1491
55	25.0	20.8	11.3	1953	1900: 1466
56	24.7	20.6	11.4	1961	1300: 1490
57	24.6	20.5	11.5	1963	124 Sport Coupe 1800: 1536
58	24.5	20.4	11.5	1967	125: 1508
59	24.2	20.2	11.7	1971	124 Special T: 1525
60	24.1	20.1	11.7	1960	1500: 1484
61	23.8	19.8	11.9	1974	132 GLS: 1542
62	23.7	19.7	11.9	1964	1500L: 1497
63	23.6	19.7	12.0	1970	124 Coupe 1600: 1520
64	23.2	19.3	12.2	1978	131 Supermirafiori: 1559
				1963	132 1800 Special: 1541
65	23.1	19.2	12.2	1969	125 Special: 1517
66	22.5	18.7	12.6	1978	132 2000 GLS: 1560
				1979	Mirafiori Sport: 1565
67	22.2	18.5	12.7	1968	124 Sport Coupe: 1509
68	21.3	17.7	13.3	1962	2300: 1494
69	15.7	13.1	18.0	1972	130 Automatic: 1533
70	15.5	12.9	18.2	1954	8V: 1468

Ford

1	46.8	39.0	6.0	1984	Fiesta 1.6L Diesel: 1893
2	37.2	31.0	7.6	1983	Fiesta 1.1 Ghia: 1886
3	36.1	30.1	7.8	1959	Anglia: 1649
				1989	Escort 1.3L 3-door: 1936
4	35.2	29.3	8.0	1977	Fiesta 1000: 1852
5	35.0	29.1	8.1	1987	Fiesta 1.1 Ghia Auto: 1920
				1954	Popular: 1631
6	34.6	28.8	8.2	1986	Escort 1.4 GL: 1909
7	34.3	28.6	8.2	1977	Escort 1600 Sport: 1851
8	34.1	28.4	8.3	1955	Prefect: 1633
9	33.8	28.1	8.4	1955	Prefect 1172cc: 1634
10	33.5	27.9	8.4	1977	Fiesta 1100 Ghia: 1853
11	33.2	27.6	8.5	1989	Fiesta 1.1LX 5-door: 1937
				1983	Orion 1.6 GL: 1889
12	33.0	27.5	8.6	1982	Sierra 1.6L: 1882
13	32.9	27.4	8.6	1965	Anglia Estate: 1710
14	32.5	27.1	8.7	1977	Escort 1300 GL: 1850
15	32.1	26.7	8.8	1981	Escort 1.6L Estate: 1874
				1982	Escort 1600 GL: 1878
16	31.8	26.5	8.9	1976	Fiesta: 1845
17	31.6	26.3	8.9	1977	Fiesta 1300 S: 1854
18	31.5	26.2	9.0	1956	Taunus 15M: 1640
19	31.4	26.1	9.0	1962	Anglia Super: 1667
				1958	Consul: 1645
				1981	Fiesta Popular: 1875
20	31.0	25.8	9.1	1985	Fiesta XR2: 1902
				1986	Orion 1.4 GL: 1916
21	30.8	25.6	9.2	1962	Anglia de Luxe Estate: 1666
				1986	Escort XR3i: 1912
22	30.6	25.5	9.2	1990	Granada 2.5 GL Diesel: 1951
23	30.5	25.4	9.3	1983	Escort XR3i: 1885
				1961	Taunus 17M: 1664
24	30.2	25.1	9.4	1962	Consul Cortina: 1669
25	30.1	25.1	9.4	1958	Anglia de Luxe: 1644
				1978	Granada 2.1D: 1859
26	29.9	24.9	9.4	1984	Fiesta XR2: 1894
27	29.7	24.7	9.5	1954	Anglia Saloon: 1630
28	29.6	24.6	9.5	1959	Popular II: 1651
29	29.5	24.6	9.6	1963	Cortina Estate de Luxe: 1688
30	29.4	24.5	9.6	1974	Escort 1100L: 1823
31	29.3	24.4	9.6	1979	Cortina 1600L: 1862
				1975	Escort 1.3 Ghia: 1832
32	29.2	24.3	9.7	1981	Cortina 2.0 GL: 1872
				1991	Orion 1.6i Ghia: 1968
33	29.0	24.1	9.7	1956	Consul Mk II: 1638
				1991	Escort 1.4LX: 1960
				1989	Fiesta 1.6S: 1939
34	28.8	24.0	9.8	1981	Fiesta XR2: 1876
				1989	Sierra Sapphire 2000E: 1944
35	28.7	23.9	9.8	1976	Capri 1300: 1837
36	28.6	23.8	9.9	1964	Consul Corsair: 1701
				1991	Escort Cabriolet: 1962
				1992	Escort XR3i: 1974
37	28.4	23.6	9.9	1990	Fiesta XR2i: 1950
38	28.3	23.6	10.0	1970	Escort 1300 Super Estate: 1784
39	28.1	23.4	10.1	1984	Fiesta 1.3L CVH: 1892
				1989	Fiesta 1.4 Ghia: 1938
40	27.9	23.2	10.1	1961	Consul Capri: 1661
41	27.8	23.1	10.2	1991	Escort 1.6 Ghia Estate: 1961
42	27.6	23.0	10.2	1978	Capri 1600S: 1857
				1968	Escort: 1756
				1976	Escort 1300 GL: 1843
43	27.5	22.9	10.3	1983	Granada 2.5 Diesel Estate: 1887
44	27.4	22.8	10.3	1972	Capri 1600 XL: 1802
				1974	Capri II 1600 GT: 1822
				1986	Escort RS Turbo: 1911
45	27.2	22.6	10.4	1963	Cortina Super: 1690
46	27.0	22.5	10.5	1975	Cortina 1300L: 1830
				1959	Taunus 17M Estate: 1652
47	26.8	22.3	10.5	1966	Cortina 1300 de Luxe: 1731
				1985	Escort RS Turbo: 1901
				1985	Sierra 1.8 Ghia: 1906
				1987	Sierra Sapphire 2.0 Ghia: 1925
48	26.7	22.2	10.6	1963	Capri GT: 1684
				1971	Escort 1300 XL: 1794
49	26.6	22.1	10.6	1963	Escort RS2000: 1817
50	26.5	22.1	10.7	1975	Escort RS1800: 1833
51	26.4	22.0	10.7	1992	Escort RS2000: 1973
52	26.2	21.8	10.8	1965	Cortina GT: 1712
53	25.9	21.6	10.9	1963	Consul Corsair GT: 1685
54	25.6	21.3	11.0	1979	Capri 2000S: 1861
				1983	Escort 1.6 GL Automatic: 1884
55	25.4	21.1	11.1	1971	Escort 1300 GT: 1793
56	25.3	21.1	11.2	1971	1600 GT: 1789
				1975	Cortina 2000E Estate: 1831
57	25.2	21.0	11.2	1990	Granada Scorpio 2.0i Auto: 1953
58	25.1	20.9	11.3	1967	Cortina 1600E: 1742
				1970	Cortina 2000 GXL: 1783
59	25.0	20.8	11.3	1968	Escort 1300: 1757
				1971	Escort Sport: 1795
				1958	Zephyr Estate: 1648
60	24.9	20.7	11.3	1968	Cortina 1300 de Luxe: 1751
61	24.8	20.7	11.4	1969	Capri 1600 GT: 1766
				1966	Corsair GT Estate: 1730
				1972	Cortina 1300L: 1807
				1964	Cortina Super: 1702
62	24.7	20.6	11.4	1966	Cortina Super Estate: 1733
				1976	Escort RS2000: 1844
63	24.6	20.5	11.5	1963	Cortina 1600 XL: 1813
64	24.3	20.2	11.6	1970	Capri 1300 GT: 1780
65	24.1	20.1	11.7	1976	Cortina 2.0 Ghia: 1842
				1963	Cortina 2000E: 1816
				1956	Zephyr: 1642
66	24.0	20.0	11.8	1975	Capri 2000S GT: 1828
				1987	Granada Scorpio 2.9 EX: 1922
67	23.8	19.8	11.9	1981	Granada 2.8i: 1877
				1962	Zephyr 4: 1681
68	23.7	19.7	11.9	1963	Cortina 1600 XL Estate: 1814
				1960	Zephyr: 1660
				1955	Zodiac: 1636
69	23.6	19.7	12.0	1968	Cortina GT Estate: 1753
				1990	Fiesta RS Turbo: 1949
70	23.4	19.5	12.1	1985	Sierra 2.0i S: 1907
71	23.3	19.4	12.1	1972	Consul 2000L: 1806
				1963	Cortina 2000 Estate: 1815
				1960	Falcon: 1656
72	23.2	19.3	12.2	1975	Consul 2000L: 1829
73	23.1	19.2	12.2	1962	Zephyr 4 Automatic: 1682
				1957	Zodiac Automatic: 1643
74	22.8	19.0	12.4	1965	Corsair GT: 1711
				1977	Cortina 2.3 Ghia: 1849
75	22.7	18.9	12.4	1972	1600 XL Auto: 1801
76	22.6	18.8	12.5	1979	Cortina 2.3 Ghia S: 1863
77	22.4	18.7	12.6	1967	Cortina Super Estate: 1745
78	22.3	18.6	12.7	1969	Cortina 1100: 1769
79	22.2	18.5	12.7	1967	Cortina Lotus: 1744
80	22.1	18.4	12.8	1960	Falcon Automatic: 1657
81	22.0	18.3	12.8	1969	Capri 2000 GT: 1767
82	21.9	18.2	12.9	1985	Granada Scorpio: 1903
83	21.6	18.0	13.1	1990	Sierra Sapphire Cosworth 4x4: 1958
84	21.5	17.9	13.1	1972	Capri 3000E: 1804
				1970	Escort 1600 RS: 1785
				1968	Escort Twin Cam: 1758
				1987	Granada 2.4i Ghia: 1921
85	21.4	17.8	13.2	1983	Sierra XR4i: 1890
86	21.3	17.7	13.3	1981	Capri 2.8 Injection: 1871
				1976	Granada 3000 S: 1846
87	21.2	17.7	13.3	1978	Granada 2.0L: 1858
88	21.1	17.6	13.4	1968	Zephyr de Luxe: 1765
89	21.0	17.5	13.5	1991	Scorpio 24v: 1970
				1986	Sierra Ghia 4x4 Estate: 1918
90	20.9	17.4	13.5	1982	Sierra 2.3 Ghia Automatic: 1883
91	20.8	17.3	13.6	1963	Cortina Lotus: 1689
				1978	Granada 2.8i S: 1860
92	20.7	17.2	13.6	1963	Capri 3000 GXL: 1811
				1968	Cortina Race-proved Savage: 1754
				1974	Mustang II Ghia: 1826
93	20.6	17.2	13.7	1977	Granada 2.3 GL Auto: 1856
94	20.5	17.1	13.8	1967	Corsair 2000E: 1741
				1979	Granada 2.8i GLS Estate: 1865
95	20.3	16.9	13.9	1988	Sierra RS Cosworth: 1934
96	20.2	16.8	14.0	1965	Taunus 20M: 1726
97	20.1	16.7	14.1	1975	Granada 2000 GL: 1834
98	20.0	16.7	14.1	1952	Comete: 1625
				1963	Consul 3000 GT: 1812
99	19.7	16.4	14.3	1982	Granada 2.3L Estate: 1879
100	19.5	16.2	14.5	1976	Capri 3000S: 1838
101	19.4	16.2	14.6	1966	Zephyr 6 Mk IV: 1740
102	19.3	16.1	14.6	1969	Capri 3000 GT XLR: 1768
103	19.2	16.0	14.7	1985	Granada Scorpio 4x4: 1904
104	19.1	15.9	14.8	1972	Granada GXL: 1808
				1964	Zephyr 6: 1709
				1962	Zodiac Mk III: 1683
105	18.9	15.7	14.9	1990	Granada Ghia X 2.9 EFi Saloon: 1952
				1979	Mustang Ghia Turbo: 1866
				1963	Zephyr 6 Estate: 1700
106	18.8	15.7	15.0	1970	Maverick: 1786
107	18.7	15.6	15.1	1974	Granada Ghia Coupe: 1824
108	18.3	15.2	15.4	1986	RS200: 1917
109	17.7	14.7	16.0	1965	Zodiac Executive: 1728

110	17.4	14.5	16.2	1963	Granada Estate Auto: 1818
111	17.2	14.3	16.4	1967	Zodiac Executive: 1750
112	17.0	14.2	16.6	1989	Sierra XR 4x4: 1945
113	16.5	13.7	17.1	1960	Galaxie: 1658
				1956	Thunderbird: 1641
114	16.1	13.4	17.5	1958	Fairlane 500: 1646
				1963	Falcon Sprint Convertible: 1696
115	15.7	13.1	18.0	1962	Fairlane 500: 1671
116	15.1	12.6	18.7	1972	Mustang Grande: 1810
117	13.7	11.4	20.6	1961	Thunderbird: 1665
118	12.8	10.7	22.1	1964	Mustang Convertible: 1708
119	11.7	9.7	24.1	1964	Galaxie 500: 1705

Frazer-Nash

1	21.2	17.7	13.3	1953	Targa Florio Turismo: 1985
2	20.5	17.1	13.8	1955	Targa Florio Fast Roadster: 1986

Frazer-Nash BMW

1	21.1	17.6	13.4	1967	2000TI: 1992

Frisky

1	56.5	47.0	5.0	1958	Coupe: 1993

Gilbern

1	28.3	23.6	10.0	1961	GT: 1995
2	19.6	16.3	14.4	1969	Invader: 1996

Ginetta

1	25.5	21.2	11.1	1976	G21S: 1997
2	23.3	19.4	12.1	1990	G32: 1998

Glas

1	28.9	24.1	9.8	1974	1700: 2001

Goggomobil

1	47.8	39.8	5.9	1959	TS400: 2004

Gordon

1	14.2	11.8	19.9	1960	GT: 2008

Gordon Keeble

1	14.5	12.1	19.5	1965	GK1: 2009

Healey

1	23.8	19.8	11.9	1953	Sports Convertible: 2021
2	22.0	18.3	12.8	1952	Tickford Saloon: 2020

Hillman

1	38.1	31.7	7.4	1963	Imp de Luxe: 2056
2	35.5	29.6	8.0	1965	Super Imp: 2061
3	34.7	28.9	8.1	1955	Husky: 2041
				1955	Minx de Luxe: 2042
4	34.6	28.8	8.2	1967	Imp Californian: 2065
5	34.3	28.6	8.2	1956	Minx de Luxe: 2043
6	33.8	28.1	8.4	1967	Hunter Husky: 2064
7	33.6	28.0	8.4	1958	Hunter Husky: 2045
8	32.5	27.1	8.7	1958	Minx Series II: 2048
9	32.4	27.0	8.7	1971	Imp de Luxe: 2073
10	29.8	24.8	9.5	1963	Avenger DL: 2076
11	29.0	24.1	9.7	1953	Minx Califonian Coupe: 2039
				1958	Minx Estate: 2047
12	28.7	23.9	9.8	1967	Estate: 2063
13	28.6	23.8	9.9	1958	Minx Series III Convertible: 2049
14	28.3	23.6	10.0	1976	Avenger 1600 Super: 2082
				1975	Avenger GLS: 2080
15	28.1	23.4	10.1	1959	Minx Series IIIA Easidrive: 2050
16	27.9	23.2	10.1	1974	Avenger 1300 GL: 2078
17	27.8	23.1	10.2	1970	Avenger GL: 2069
18	27.1	22.6	10.4	1967	Minx: 2066
19	26.9	22.4	10.5	1970	Avenger GT: 2070
				1963	Hunter Husky III: 2055
20	26.8	22.3	10.5	1957	Minx Convertible: 2044
21	26.0	21.6	10.9	1952	Minx Convertible: 2038
22	25.2	21.0	11.2	1969	Hunter Mk II: 2068
23	25.1	20.9	11.3	1972	Avenger Estate: 2074
24	24.8	20.7	11.4	1960	Hunter Husky Series II: 2052
25	24.7	20.6	11.4	1964	Minx Series V Automatic: 2057
26	24.6	20.5	11.5	1964	Super Minx III: 2059
27	24.4	20.3	11.6	1963	Avenger GLS: 2077
				1965	Minx Series VI de Luxe: 2060
28	24.3	20.2	11.6	1975	Hunter Super: 2081
29	24.0	20.0	11.8	1962	Super Minx Mk II: 2054
30	23.9	19.9	11.8	1962	Super Minx: 2053
31	23.4	19.5	12.1	1971	Hunter Super: 2072
32	22.9	19.1	12.3	1970	Avenger Super: 2071
33	22.6	18.8	12.5	1969	GT: 2067
34	22.1	18.4	12.8	1974	Avenger 1600 GLS: 2079
35	21.5	17.9	13.1	1972	Hunter GLS: 2075
36	20.0	16.7	14.1	1964	Super Minx Convertible: 2058
				1966	Super Minx Estate: 2062

Holden

1	28.0	23.3	10.1	1952	Saloon: 2085
2	15.0	12.5	18.8	1969	Brougham: 2086

Honda

1	39.4	32.8	7.2	1968	N360: 2089
2	35.3	29.4	8.0	1984	Jazz: 2115
3	34.7	28.9	8.1	1987	Civic 1.4 GL 3-door: 2136
4	33.3	27.7	8.5	1987	Ballade EX: 2135
5	32.8	27.3	8.6	1963	Civic Hondamatic: 2093
6	32.3	26.9	8.7	1984	Civic CRX: 2113
7	32.1	26.7	8.8	1984	Civic DL: 2114
8	31.9	26.6	8.9	1991	Civic 1.5 VEi: 2153
9	31.8	26.5	8.9	1985	Civic Shuttle: 2122
10	30.5	25.4	9.3	1985	Civic GT: 2120
11	30.4	25.3	9.3	1979	Prelude: 2101
12	30.3	25.2	9.3	1977	Civic 1500: 2097
13	30.0	25.0	9.4	1991	Civic 1.6i VT: 2154
				1986	CRX Coupe 1.6i 16: 2128
14	29.6	24.6	9.5	1988	Civic CRX: 2140
15	29.3	24.4	9.6	1978	Civic: 2099
16	29.1	24.2	9.7	1986	Integra 1.5: 2131
17	28.1	23.4	10.1	1990	CRX 1.6i VT: 2152
18	27.5	22.9	10.3	1986	Integra EX 16: 2132
19	26.1	21.7	10.8	1990	Accord 2.0 EXi: 2150
20	25.8	21.5	10.9	1981	Quintet: 2108
21	25.7	21.4	11.0	1990	Concerto 1.6i 16: 2151
22	25.5	21.2	11.1	1977	Accord: 2096
23	24.9	20.7	11.3	1983	Prelude EX ALB: 2112
24	24.6	20.5	11.5	1967	S800: 2088
25	24.3	20.2	11.6	1985	Accord 2.0 EXi: 2117
26	23.4	19.5	12.1	1985	Accord EX Automatic: 2118
27	23.3	19.4	12.1	1989	Shuttle 1.4 GL Automatic: 2149
28	22.9	19.1	12.3	1988	Shuttle 1.6i RT4 4WD: 2144
29	21.5	17.9	13.1	1986	Legend: 2133
				1992	Legend Coupe: 2158
30	21.0	17.5	13.5	1987	Prelude 2.0i 16: 2139
31	20.3	16.9	13.9	1987	Legend Coupe: 2137
32	19.6	16.3	14.4	1991	NSX: 2156
33	19.1	15.9	14.8	1991	Legend: 2155
34	18.4	15.3	15.4	1988	Legend Saloon Automatic: 2143
35	18.3	15.2	15.4	1992	NSX Auto: 2159

Hudson

1	23.0	19.2	12.3	1956	Rambler: 2179

Humber

1	26.6	22.1	10.6	1954	Hawk Mk VI: 2201
2	25.7	21.4	11.0	1956	Hawk Estate: 2202
3	25.0	20.8	11.3	1967	Sceptre: 2214
4	24.5	20.4	11.5	1974	Sceptre Estate: 2215
5	22.8	19.0	12.4	1963	Sceptre: 2211
6	21.0	17.5	13.5	1957	Hawk: 2203
7	20.9	17.4	13.5	1966	Sceptre II Automatic: 2213
8	20.1	16.7	14.1	1958	Hawk Estate: 2204
9	19.1	15.9	14.8	1963	Hawk III: 2210
10	18.2	15.2	15.5	1958	Super Snipe: 2205
11	17.7	14.7	16.0	1961	Super Snipe Series III: 2209
12	17.5	14.6	16.1	1965	Imperial: 2212
13	16.9	14.1	16.7	1952	Pullman Limousine: 2197
				1960	Super Snipe Estate: 2207
14	16.0	13.3	17.7	1952	Super Snipe: 2198
				1953	Super Snipe Mk IV: 2200

Hyundai

1	30.8	25.6	9.2	1991	S Coupe GSi: 2227
2	30.2	25.1	9.4	1984	Stellar 1600 GSL: 2220
3	29.8	24.8	9.5	1985	Pony 1.5 GLS: 2221
4	29.5	24.6	9.6	1982	Pony 1400 TLS: 2219
5	28.0	23.3	10.1	1991	X2 1.5 GSi: 2228
6	27.1	22.6	10.4	1991	Lantra 1.6 Cdi: 2226
7	23.0	19.2	12.3	1989	Sonata 2.0i GLS: 2224
8	22.7	18.9	12.4	1990	Sonata 2.4i GLS: 2225

Iso

1	15.7	13.1	18.0	1966	Grifo GL 365: 2248
2	12.1	10.1	23.3	1964	Rivolta IR-340: 2247
3	11.7	9.7	24.1	1974	Rivolta Fidia: 2251

Isuzu

1	22.3	18.6	12.7	1987	Trooper 3-door TD: 2257

Jaguar

1	23.1	19.2	12.2	1957	2.4 Saloon: 2288
2	21.8	18.2	13.0	1967	E Type Roadster: 2312
3	21.7	18.1	13.0	1956	XK 140: 2287
4	20.7	17.2	13.6	1986	XJ6 3.6: 2348
5	20.5	17.1	13.8	1958	XK150: 2293
6	20.0	16.7	14.1	1953	Mk VII: 2278
7	19.9	16.6	14.2	1991	XJ6 3.2: 2368
8	19.3	16.1	14.6	1987	XJ6 2.9: 2353
9	19.0	15.8	14.9	1952	Mk VII: 2277
10	18.8	15.7	15.0	1991	XJS 4.0 Auto: 2371
11	18.6	15.5	15.2	1963	E Type Coupe: 2303
12	18.5	15.4	15.3	1989	4.0 Sovereign: 2358
				1956	Mk VII Auto: 2286
13	18.4	15.3	15.4	1968	240: 2314
14	18.0	15.0	15.7	1987	XJS 3.6 Automatic: 2354
15	17.9	14.9	15.8	1961	E Type Coupe: 2298
				1957	Mk VIII: 2289
16	17.6	14.7	16.1	1984	XJS 3.6: 2345
17	17.3	14.4	16.3	1963	3.8 Mk II Automatic: 2302
18	17.2	14.3	16.4	1990	XJR 4.0: 2363
19	17.1	14.2	16.5	1965	E Type 4.2: 2309
20	17.0	14.2	16.6	1959	XK150S: 2295
21	16.8	14.0	16.8	1979	XJ6 4.2: 2336
22	16.7	13.9	16.9	1975	XJ3.4: 2327
23	16.2	13.5	17.4	1953	XK120 Coupe: 2279
24	16.0	13.3	17.7	1958	3.4: 2292
				1965	4.2 litre Mk X Overdrive: 2308
				1971	XJ6 4.2: 2320
				1982	XJS HE: 2342
25	15.7	13.1	18.0	1963	3.8 Mk II: 2301
				1967	420: 2311
26	15.4	12.8	18.3	1976	XJS: 2330
27	15.2	12.7	18.6	1971	E Type V12: 2319
				1969	XJ6 4.2 Automatic: 2316
28	15.0	12.5	18.8	1977	XJ4.2: 2331
29	14.5	12.1	19.5	1964	4.2 litre Mk X: 2305
				1985	XJS HE Cabriolet: 2347
30	14.3	11.9	19.8	1981	XJS Automatic: 2341
31	14.1	11.7	20.0	1962	Mk X: 2300
32	14.0	11.7	20.2	1977	XJS Automatic: 2332
33	13.8	11.5	20.5	1975	XJ5.3C: 2328
				1988	XJS V12 Convertible: 2357
34	13.2	11.0	21.4	1978	XJ5.3 Automatic: 2335
35	12.8	10.7	22.1	1965	3.8S: 2307
36	11.4	9.5	24.8	1963	XJ12: 2324

Jeep

1	14.8	12.3	19.1	1964	Wagoneer: 2373
2	13.7	11.4	20.6	1974	CJ6: 2381
3	12.5	10.4	22.6	1978	Cherokee Chief: 2383

Jensen

1	20.0	16.7	14.1	1956	541: 2387
2	19.5	16.2	14.5	1976	GT: 2402
3	18.0	15.0	15.7	1958	541R: 2388
4	15.5	12.9	18.2	1961	541S Automatic: 2389
5	14.4	12.0	19.6	1963	CV8: 2390
6	13.6	11.3	20.8	1968	FF: 2392
				1967	Interceptor: 2391
7	13.0	10.8	21.7	1971	SP: 2397
8	12.9	10.7	21.9	1969	Interceptor: 2393
9	12.5	10.4	22.6	1974	Interceptor III Convertible: 2401
10	11.9	9.9	23.7	1970	FF II: 2394

Jensen-Healey

1	21.0	17.5	13.5	1972	2-litre: 2405

Jowett

1	21.8	18.2	13.0	1953	Jupiter Mk IA: 2411

Kaiser

1	18.0	15.0	15.7	1952	Henry J 6: 2414

Lada

1	31.1	25.9	9.1	1987	Samara 1300 SL: 2429
2	30.5	25.4	9.3	1989	Samara 1300L 5-door: 2430
3	30.1	25.1	9.4	1986	Riva 1500 Estate: 2427
4	28.3	23.6	10.0	1975	1200: 2423
5	26.8	22.3	10.5	1976	1500: 2424
6	24.1	20.1	11.7	1978	1300 ES: 2425
7	20.0	16.7	14.1	1979	Niva 1600: 2426
8	18.8	15.7	15.0	1987	Niva Cossack Cabrio: 2428

Lagonda

1	17.5	14.6	16.1	1956	3-litre Saloon: 2448

Lamborghini

1	18.7	15.6	15.1	1974	Urraco S: 2460
2	15.9	13.2	17.8	1986	Jalpa 3500: 2470
3	14.6	12.2	19.3	1982	Countach LP 500S: 2465
4	13.7	11.4	20.6	1985	Countach: 2468
5	13.4	11.2	21.1	1970	Miura P400S: 2455

Lancia

1	40.6	33.8	7.0	1986	Y10 Fire: 2545
2	32.6	27.1	8.7	1962	Appia III: 2499
3	32.3	26.9	8.7	1985	Y10 Turbo: 2540
4	29.8	24.8	9.5	1990	Y10 GTie: 2554
5	29.6	24.6	9.5	1976	Beta 1300: 2518
6	28.3	23.6	10.0	1966	Fulvia Coupe: 2506
7	27.7	23.1	10.2	1985	Coupe 2000ie: 2538
8	27.1	22.6	10.4	1986	Prisma 1600ie LX: 2543
9	26.6	22.1	10.6	1982	Delta Automatic: 2535
10	26.5	22.1	10.7	1983	Prisma 1600: 2536
11	25.9	21.6	10.9	1986	Thema 2.0ie: 2544
12	25.5	21.2	11.1	1981	Trevi 2000: 2533
13	25.4	21.1	11.1	1979	Beta HPE 1600: 2528
				1961	Flavia: 2498
14	25.3	21.1	11.2	1967	Flavia Injection: 2507
15	25.2	21.0	11.2	1975	Beta Monte Carlo: 2517
				1990	Dedra 1.8i: 2551
16	25.0	20.8	11.3	1981	Montecarlo Spyder: 2532
17	24.5	20.4	11.5	1952	Aurelia 2-litre Saloon: 2489
				1986	Delta HF Turbo ie: 2542
18	24.4	20.3	11.6	1989	Thema 2.0ie 16v: 2550
19	24.3	20.2	11.6	1963	Beta 1800: 2514
				1964	Fulvia: 2502
				1964	Fulvia 2C: 2503
20	24.1	20.1	11.7	1970	Fulvia Sedan: 2511
21	24.0	20.0	11.8	1975	Beta 1600 Coupe: 2516
				1976	Beta 2000: 2519
22	23.7	19.7	11.9	1990	Dedra 2.0ie: 2552
23	23.6	19.7	12.0	1958	Aurelia GT 2500: 2492
24	23.1	19.2	12.2	1979	Beta 2000 Automatic: 2527
25	22.9	19.1	12.3	1964	Flavia Coupe: 2501
				1969	Fulvia Coupe: 2510
26	22.4	18.7	12.6	1971	Fulvia Sedan: 2512
27	22.1	18.4	12.8	1991	Dedra 2000 Turbo: 2555
28	21.9	18.2	12.9	1985	Thema 2.0 ie LX Turbo: 2539
29	21.1	17.6	13.4	1990	Thema 2.0ie 16v SE Turbo: 2553
30	20.8	17.3	13.6	1958	Flaminia: 2493
31	20.5	17.1	13.8	1965	Flavia Zagato Sport: 2505
32	20.3	16.9	13.9	1977	Beta HPE 2000: 2523
33	20.2	16.8	14.0	1962	Flaminia Sedan: 2500
34	20.1	16.7	14.1	1972	2000: 2513
				1960	Flaminia Coupe: 2496
				1974	Fulvia Coupe S3: 2515
35	19.8	16.5	14.3	1986	Delta HF 4WD: 2541
36	19.1	15.9	14.8	1989	Delta Integrale 16v: 2549
				1978	Gamma Berlina: 2526
37	19.0	15.8	14.9	1955	Aurelia Gran Turismo 2500: 2490
38	17.6	14.7	16.1	1988	Delta HF Integrale: 2547
39	16.2	13.5	17.4	1965	Flaminia Coupe 3B: 2504
40	15.6	13.0	18.1	1988	Thema 8.32: 2548

Land-Rover

1	23.9	19.9	11.8	1990	Discovery TDi: 2563
2	21.0	17.5	13.5	1955	Station Wagon: 2556
3	18.0	15.0	15.7	1987	Ninety County Turbo Diesel: 2560
				1963	SWB: 2558
4	16.5	13.7	17.1	1991	Discovery V8i 5DR: 2565
5	14.9	12.4	19.0	1971	Series III: 2557
6	14.0	11.7	20.2	1990	Discovery V8: 2564
7	13.9	11.6	20.3	1982	County: 2559
8	13.4	11.2	21.1	1987	One Ten County V8: 2561
9	12.1	10.1	23.3	1989	Ninety County V8: 2562

Lexus

1	19.7	16.4	14.3	1990	LS400: 2570

Lloyd

1	47.3	39.4	6.0	1958	LP 600: 2588

Lotus

1	47.8	39.8	5.9	1957	11 Le Mans: 2589
2	30.0	25.0	9.4	1969	Elan S4 Drophead SE: 2603
3	27.9	23.2	10.1	1964	Elan 1600: 2599
4	27.1	22.6	10.4	1968	Elan +2: 2602
5	26.0	21.6	10.9	1967	Elan Coupe SE: 2600
6	25.6	21.3	11.0	1972	Plus 2S 130/5: 2615
7	25.5	21.2	11.1	1971	Elan Sprint: 2608
8	25.1	20.9	11.3	1971	Europa S2: 2609
9	23.5	19.6	12.0	1989	Esprit Turbo SE: 2637
10	23.3	19.4	12.1	1977	Esprit: 2620
				1972	Europa Twin Cam: 2614
				1971	Plus 2S 130: 2610
11	22.9	19.1	12.3	1961	Super 7: 2594

12	22.2	18.5	12.7	1987	Excel SA: 2634
13	20.9	17.4	13.5	1975	Elite 503: 2618
				1987	Esprit Turbo HC: 2633
14	20.7	17.2	13.6	1977	Eclat 523: 2619
15	20.4	17.0	13.8	1988	Esprit Turbo: 2635
16	20.1	16.7	14.1	1990	Elan SE: 2639
17	19.6	16.3	14.4	1986	Excel SE: 2631
18	19.5	16.2	14.5	1983	Eclat Excel: 2628
19	19.4	16.2	14.6	1979	Esprit S2: 2625
20	19.2	16.0	14.7	1970	7 Twin Cam SS: 2605
21	18.0	15.0	15.7	1981	Esprit Turbo: 2627

Marcos

1	26.0	21.6	10.9	1965	1800: 2644
2	22.3	18.6	12.7	1971	3-litre Volvo: 2646
3	21.5	17.9	13.1	1968	1600GT: 2645

Maserati

1	18.5	15.4	15.3	1987	Biturbo Spyder: 2675
2	17.9	14.9	15.8	1981	Merak SS: 2670
3	17.4	14.5	16.2	1975	Merak: 2663
4	15.3	12.7	18.5	1978	Kyalami: 2667
5	15.1	12.6	18.7	1975	Khamsin Automatic: 2662
6	14.8	12.3	19.1	1963	3500 GTI Sebring: 2655
7	14.3	11.9	19.8	1978	Khamsin: 2666
8	13.9	11.6	20.3	1971	Indy: 2659
9	11.9	9.9	23.7	1963	Bora: 2660

Matra

1	26.9	22.4	10.5	1969	M530A: 2682
2	25.7	21.4	11.0	1978	Rancho: 2683

Matra-Simca

1	31.0	25.8	9.1	1975	Bagheera: 2684

Mazda

1	31.8	26.5	8.9	1981	323 1300: 2716
2	31.4	26.1	9.0	1985	323 1.5 GLX: 2726
3	30.8	25.6	9.2	1988	121 1.3 LX Sun Top: 2741
4	30.7	25.6	9.2	1991	121 GSX: 2765
5	30.6	25.5	9.2	1983	626 1600 LX: 2722
6	30.1	25.1	9.4	1987	323 1.5 GLX: 2738
7	29.5	24.6	9.6	1986	626 2.0i 5-door: 2733
8	29.2	24.3	9.7	1979	1.4 SP: 2706
				1970	1200 de Luxe: 2687
9	28.9	24.1	9.8	1985	323 1.6i: 2727
10	28.6	23.8	9.9	1989	323 1.8 GT: 2753
11	28.5	23.7	9.9	1991	323 1.8 GT: 2766
12	27.9	23.2	10.1	1977	323: 2702
				1980	Montrose GLS Coupe: 2713
				1992	MX-3 1.6 Auto: 2772
13	27.5	22.9	10.3	1989	323 1.6i: 2752
14	26.2	21.8	10.8	1968	1500 de Luxe: 2686
15	25.7	21.4	11.0	1974	1300: 2695
16	25.0	20.8	11.3	1991	MX-3 V6: 2767
17	24.9	20.7	11.3	1979	Montrose 1600 GLS: 2709
18	24.8	20.7	11.4	1987	626 2.0 GLS Executive: 2739
19	24.5	20.4	11.5	1988	626 2.0i GT 4WS: 2745
20	22.9	19.1	12.3	1988	626 2.0 GLX Executive Estate: 2744
21	22.5	18.7	12.6	1974	929: 2696
22	22.0	18.3	12.8	1982	RX-7: 2720
23	21.3	17.7	13.3	1986	323 Turbo 4x4 Lux: 2732
24	20.7	17.2	13.6	1988	323 Turbo 4x4: 2743
25	20.4	17.0	13.8	1986	323 1.5 GLX Estate: 2729
26	18.7	15.6	15.1	1986	RX-7: 2735
27	18.2	15.2	15.5	1979	RX-7: 2710
28	17.8	14.8	15.9	1968	110S Coupe: 2685
				1972	RX-2: 2691
29	16.2	13.5	17.4	1963	RX-4: 2694
30	14.3	11.9	19.8	1989	RX-7 Turbo II: 2759

Mercedes-Benz

1	32.2	26.8	8.8	1965	190D: 2813
2	29.4	24.5	9.6	1954	180 Saloon: 2790
3	29.2	24.3	9.7	1983	190: 2872
4	28.6	23.8	9.9	1990	300D: 2911
5	28.0	23.3	10.1	1989	190: 2900
6	27.9	23.2	10.1	1983	190E: 2873
7	27.2	22.6	10.4	1966	300D: 2819
8	26.1	21.7	10.8	1991	190E 1.8 Auto: 2914
9	25.1	20.9	11.3	1958	220S: 2799
10	24.6	20.5	11.5	1963	190C Automatic: 2809
11	23.6	19.7	12.0	1986	200: 2884
12	23.5	19.6	12.0	1985	190E 2.3-16: 2879
13	23.3	19.4	12.1	1989	200E Automatic: 2904
14	23.1	19.2	12.2	1988	260E Auto: 2896
15	22.8	19.0	12.4	1959	220SE: 2801
16	22.7	18.9	12.4	1963	230/4: 2838
				1985	300E: 2881
17	22.5	18.7	12.6	1981	230TE: 2866
18	22.4	18.7	12.6	1958	190SL: 2798
				1961	220SE Coupe: 2806
19	22.3	18.6	12.7	1964	230SL: 2811
20	22.1	18.4	12.8	1978	200: 2855
21	22.0	18.3	12.8	1989	190E 2.5-16: 2901
22	21.9	18.2	12.9	1961	190: 2805
				1981	230E: 2865
23	21.5	17.9	13.1	1986	300TE: 2886
24	21.4	17.8	13.2	1987	300CE: 2892
25	21.1	17.6	13.4	1974	280E: 2844
26	21.0	17.5	13.5	1987	190E 2.6: 2891
27	20.8	17.3	13.6	1979	280CE: 2860
28	20.2	16.8	14.0	1969	220: 2826
29	20.0	16.7	14.1	1982	380SEC: 2870
30	19.3	16.1	14.6	1981	300GD: 2867
31	19.2	16.0	14.7	1991	300SL-24 5-speed Auto: 2917
32	19.0	15.8	14.9	1983	280SE: 2874
				1970	280SL: 2832
33	18.7	15.6	15.1	1977	230C: 2852
34	18.6	15.5	15.2	1988	300E 4Matic: 2898
				1986	560SEL: 2889
35	18.5	15.4	15.3	1990	300E-24: 2912
36	18.4	15.3	15.4	1955	300SL: 2793
				1986	420SE: 2887
37	18.1	15.1	15.6	1979	250T: 2859
38	17.6	14.7	16.1	1966	230 Automatic: 2817
				1963	280CE Auto: 2840
39	17.5	14.6	16.1	1970	280SE: 2830
40	17.4	14.5	16.2	1967	250SE: 2820
41	17.3	14.4	16.3	1968	250 Automatic: 2824
42	17.1	14.2	16.5	1991	G-Wagen 300 GD LWB: 2921
43	16.9	14.1	16.7	1976	280E: 2850
44	16.8	14.0	16.8	1965	220SE: 2814
				1955	300B: 2792
45	16.7	13.9	16.9	1963	280SE: 2841
46	16.5	13.7	17.1	1991	500E: 2919
47	16.2	13.5	17.4	1990	500SL: 2913
48	16.0	13.3	17.7	1972	280SE 3.5: 2835
49	15.7	13.1	18.0	1985	500SEL: 2882
50	15.3	12.7	18.5	1952	300: 2787
51	15.1	12.6	18.7	1964	300SE LWB: 2812
				1969	300SEL 6.3: 2828
52	14.7	12.2	19.2	1971	300SL: 2834
				1974	450SEL: 2845
53	14.6	12.2	19.3	1991	400SE: 2918
54	14.1	11.7	20.0	1975	450SLC: 2849
55	13.6	11.3	20.8	1979	450SEL 6.9: 2862
56	11.6	9.7	24.4	1967	600: 2821

Mercury

1	12.5	10.4	22.6	1977	Monarch: 2953

Messerschmitt (FMR)

1	43.8	36.5	6.4	1958	Tg 500: 2966

MG

1	38.8	32.3	7.3	1982	Metro 1300: 3036
2	33.4	27.8	8.5	1961	Midget: 3002
3	30.3	25.2	9.3	1983	Metro Turbo: 3037
4	29.6	24.6	9.5	1971	Midget Mk III: 3021
5	29.3	24.4	9.6	1984	Montego EFi: 3038
6	29.1	24.2	9.7	1962	1100: 3003
				1963	Midget: 3007
7	28.4	23.6	9.9	1967	Midget Mk III: 3012
8	28.0	23.3	10.1	1957	A Coupe: 2993
9	27.9	23.2	10.1	1975	Midget 1500: 3028
10	27.0	22.5	10.5	1956	A: 2992
11	26.8	22.3	10.5	1968	1300 Mk II: 3013
12	26.6	22.1	10.6	1959	Magnette Mk III: 2999
13	26.5	22.1	10.7	1952	1.25-litre Saloon: 2981
14	26.1	21.7	10.8	1975	B: 3027
15	25.7	21.4	11.0	1977	B GT: 3032
16	25.5	21.2	11.1	1970	B Automatic: 3018
17	25.4	21.1	11.1	1968	1300 Mk II Auto: 3014
18	25.3	21.1	11.2	1955	Magnette: 2991
19	25.2	21.0	11.2	1963	Magnette Mk IV: 3006
20	25.1	20.9	11.3	1958	Magnette: 2996
21	25.0	20.8	11.3	1953	Midget: 2982
22	24.1	20.1	11.7	1959	A 1600: 2998
23	23.7	19.7	11.9	1971	B GT: 3020
24	23.4	19.5	12.1	1963	B GT V8: 3025
25	23.0	19.2	12.3	1985	Montego Turbo: 3039
26	22.8	19.0	12.4	1966	B GT Coupe: 3010
27	22.3	18.6	12.7	1961	A 1600 Mk II: 3000
28	22.0	18.3	12.8	1965	B: 3008
29	21.8	18.2	13.0	1958	Twin Cam MGA: 2997
30	21.4	17.8	13.2	1962	B 1800: 3004
31	20.9	17.4	13.5	1989	Maestro Turbo: 3040
32	19.0	15.8	14.9	1968	C GT Automatic: 3016
33	18.8	15.7	15.0	1972	Costello B GT V8: 3022
34	17.5	14.6	16.1	1967	C: 3011

Mini

1	40.1	33.4	7.0	1959	Minor de Luxe: 3043
2	38.4	32.0	7.4	1960	Traveller: 3045
3	38.1	31.7	7.4	1979	850 Super de Luxe: 3060
4	37.2	31.0	7.6	1976	Clubman 1100: 3059
5	36.6	30.5	7.7	1963	Super de Luxe: 3048
6	35.6	29.6	7.9	1963	850: 3055
7	34.2	28.5	8.3	1975	1000: 3057
8	34.0	28.3	8.3	1967	Super de Luxe Mk II: 3052
9	33.1	27.6	8.5	1975	Automatic: 3058
10	32.5	27.1	8.7	1965	Cooper: 3050
11	30.8	25.6	9.2	1974	1275GT: 3056
12	30.5	25.4	9.3	1971	1275GT: 3054
13	30.2	25.1	9.4	1969	1275GT: 3053
14	29.4	24.5	9.6	1963	Cooper S: 3047
15	28.5	23.7	9.9	1964	Cooper 1275S: 3049
16	26.8	22.3	10.5	1961	Cooper: 3046

Mitsubishi

1	34.4	28.6	8.2	1979	Colt 1400 GLX: 3067
2	29.3	24.4	9.6	1968	Colt 1100F: 3061
3	29.2	24.3	9.7	1987	Colt 1500 GLX 5-door: 3091
4	29.0	24.1	9.7	1982	Colt Hatchback Turbo: 3070
5	27.8	23.1	10.2	1986	Lancer 1.5 GLX Estate: 3088
6	27.7	23.1	10.2	1984	Galant 1600 GL: 3079
7	27.2	22.6	10.4	1991	Space Runner 1800-16v GLXi: 3117
8	27.1	22.6	10.4	1985	Space Wagon 1800GLX: 3084
9	26.9	22.4	10.5	1991	Colt 1800 GTI-16v: 3112
10	26.0	21.6	10.9	1981	Colt Lancer 2000 Turbo: 3068
11	25.9	21.6	10.9	1988	Lancer GTi 16v: 3100
12	25.3	21.1	11.2	1987	Galant 2000 GLS Automatic: 3092
13	25.2	21.0	11.2	1982	Colt Cordia Turbo: 3069
14	24.9	20.7	11.3	1976	Colt Celeste 2000: 3063
15	24.8	20.7	11.4	1987	Galant Sapporo: 3093
16	24.6	20.5	11.5	1990	Lancer GLXi 4WD Liftback: 3109
17	24.4	20.3	11.6	1978	Colt Lancer Estate: 3065
				1988	Galant GTi-16v: 3099
18	24.0	20.0	11.8	1975	Colt Galant 2000: 3062
19	23.0	19.2	12.3	1984	Colt 1600 Turbo: 3077
				1977	Colt Sigma 2000: 3064
				1990	Galant 2000 GLSi Coupe: 3108
20	22.9	19.1	12.3	1990	Lancer Liftback 1800 GTi-16v: 3110
21	22.1	18.4	12.8	1982	Colt Starion Turbo: 3071
				1985	Galant Turbo: 3083
				1987	Shogun Turbo Diesel 5-door: 3094
22	21.2	17.7	13.3	1988	Galant 2000 GLSi: 3098
23	20.8	17.3	13.6	1978	Colt Sappore 2000 GSR: 3066
24	20.6	17.2	13.7	1985	Colt Starion Turbo: 3081
25	19.7	16.4	14.3	1989	Shogun V6 5-door: 3105
26	19.0	15.8	14.9	1987	Starion 2000 Turbo: 3095
27	18.8	15.7	15.0	1983	Colt Shogun: 3073
				1989	Starion 2.6 Turbo: 3106
28	18.3	15.2	15.4	1991	Sigma: 3116
29	16.1	13.4	17.5	1991	Shogun V6 LWB: 3115

Monteverdi

1	11.6	9.7	24.4	1969	375L: 3118

Morgan

1	30.0	25.0	9.4	1954	Plus 4: 3124
2	20.9	17.4	13.5	1987	Plus 8: 3134
3	20.5	17.1	13.8	1978	Plus 8: 3131
4	20.1	16.7	14.1	1991	Plus 8: 3137
5	18.3	15.2	15.4	1968	Plus 8: 3129

Morris

1	39.4	32.8	7.2	1957	Minor 1000: 3167
2	38.0	31.6	7.4	1958	Minor 1000 Traveller: 3170
3	36.2	30.1	7.8	1953	Minor Series II: 3161
4	34.7	28.9	8.1	1961	Minor 1000: 3172
5	32.7	27.2	8.6	1963	1100: 3173
6	31.2	26.0	9.1	1964	Minor 1000 de Luxe: 3174
7	29.2	24.3	9.7	1957	Oxford Series III: 3169
8	29.0	24.1	9.7	1955	Cowley: 3165
9	28.9	24.1	9.8	1971	Marina 1.3 Super Coupe: 3179
10	28.0	23.3	10.1	1977	Marina 1.3 Super Coupe: 3184
11	27.5	22.9	10.3	1978	Marina 1700HL: 3185
12	27.2	22.6	10.4	1976	Marina 1.8 HL: 3183
13	27.1	22.6	10.4	1970	1100 Mk II: 3178
				1981	Ital 2.0 HLS Automatic: 3186
14	26.2	21.8	10.8	1958	Oxford Traveller Series III: 3171
15	26.0	21.6	10.9	1954	Oxford Saloon: 3164
				1964	Oxford VI Traveller: 3175
16	25.2	21.0	11.2	1972	Marina Estate: 3182
17	23.2	19.3	12.2	1966	1800: 3176
17				1953	Oxford Travellers' Car: 3162
18	23.0	19.2	12.3	1956	Isis: 3166
19	22.3	18.6	12.7	1969	1800S: 3177
20	21.5	17.9	13.1	1971	Marina TC: 3181

Moskvich

1	24.7	20.6	11.4	1975	1500: 3188
2	23.4	19.5	12.1	1967	De Luxe: 3187

Nash

1	34.0	28.3	8.3	1955	Metropolitan: 3199
2	31.0	25.8	9.1	1958	Metropolitan 1500: 3202
3	22.5	18.7	12.6	1956	Rambler Station Wagon: 3201
4	22.0	18.3	12.8	1952	Rambler Station Wagon: 3196

Naylor

1	25.9	21.6	10.9	1985	TF 1700: 3203

Nissan

1	40.9	34.1	6.9	1987	Micra SGL 5-DR: 3225
2	32.3	26.9	8.7	1985	Cherry 1.3 SGT: 3213
				1989	Micra 1.2 GSX: 3237
3	31.6	26.3	8.9	1991	Sunny 1.6 GS 5-door: 3253
4	31.0	25.8	9.1	1986	Sunny 1.3 LX 5-door: 3221
5	29.2	24.3	9.7	1990	Primera 1.6 LS: 3242
6	28.9	24.1	9.8	1989	Sunny 1.4 LS: 3239
7	28.7	23.9	9.8	1987	Sunny 1.6 SLX Coupe: 3228
8	27.8	23.1	10.2	1992	Sunny 2.0 GTi: 3255
9	27.7	23.1	10.2	1985	Bluebird Turbo ZX: 3212
10	27.2	22.6	10.4	1991	100NX: 3244
				1987	SunnyZX Coupe: 3227
11	26.8	22.3	10.5	1991	Primera 2.0E ZX: 3251
12	26.0	21.6	10.9	1991	Primera 2.0 GSX: 3250
13	23.8	19.8	11.9	1986	Bluebird 1.8 ZX: 3217
14	23.0	19.2	12.3	1984	Silvia Turbo ZX: 3211
15	21.5	17.9	13.1	1984	300ZX Turbo: 3209
16	20.6	17.2	13.7	1989	Prairie: 3238
17	20.0	16.7	14.1	1986	Laurel 2.4 SGL Automatic: 3218
18	19.7	16.4	14.3	1992	200SX: 3254
19	19.5	16.2	14.5	1989	200SX: 3232
20	19.2	16.0	14.7	1987	300ZX Turbo: 3224
21	17.0	14.2	16.6	1990	300ZX: 3240
22	16.8	14.0	16.8	1989	Maxima: 3235

NSU

1	46.1	38.4	6.1	1959	Prinz II: 3257
2	37.4	31.1	7.6	1962	Prinz 4: 3259
				1960	Sport-Prinz: 3258
3	34.6	28.8	8.2	1968	Super Prinz: 3265
4	33.1	27.6	8.5	1965	Prinz 1000L: 3260
5	26.9	22.4	10.5	1966	Typ 110: 3263
6	26.2	21.8	10.8	1965	Wankel Spider: 3262
7	18.2	15.2	15.5	1968	Ro80: 3264
8	16.0	13.3	17.7	1974	Ro80: 3266

Ogle

1	29.4	24.5	9.6	1962	Austin Mini Cooper GT: 3268
2	28.2	23.5	10.0	1961	1.5: 3267

Oldsmobile

1	20.8	17.3	13.6	1961	F-85 Station Wagon: 3274
2	19.0	15.8	14.9	1955	Super 88: 3271
3	16.0	13.3	17.7	1958	Super 88: 3272
4	11.8	9.8	23.9	1966	Toronado: 3288

Opel

1	32.0	26.6	8.8	1974	Kadett Coupe: 3338
2	30.2	25.1	9.4	1979	Kadett 1.3S Berlina: 3345
3	29.1	24.2	9.7	1983	Manta GTE: 3349
4	28.7	23.9	9.8	1969	GT 1900: 3321
5	27.8	23.1	10.2	1983	Manta Berlinetta 1.8S: 3348
6	27.4	22.8	10.3	1967	Rekord Coupe: 3313
7	27.0	22.5	10.5	1976	Rekord 2100D: 3342
8	25.7	21.4	11.0	1975	Ascona 1900SR: 3340
9	25.3	21.1	11.2	1970	Manta Rallye 1.9: 3324
10	25.2	21.0	11.2	1963	Manta Berlinetta Auto: 3335
11	24.9	20.7	11.3	1971	Ascona Voyage: 3326
12	24.1	20.1	11.7	1972	Rekord 1900: 3329
13	23.5	19.6	12.0	1963	Ascona 1900SR: 3331
14	23.2	19.3	12.2	1978	Rekord 2.0S: 3344
15	23.0	19.2	12.3	1981	Manta Monza S3.0E: 3347
16	22.6	18.8	12.5	1976	Rekord Berlina Pacesetter: 3343
17	22.3	18.6	12.7	1981	Manta GTJ: 3346
18	20.5	17.1	13.8	1984	Manta Monza GSE: 3350
19	20.3	16.9	13.9	1969	Commodore GS Coupe: 3318
20	18.6	15.5	15.2	1970	Senator: 3325
21	18.2	15.2	15.5	1963	Commodore GS Coupe: 3332
22	18.1	15.1	15.6	1974	Commodore GSE: 3337
23	16.4	13.7	17.2	1965	Diplomat: 3310
24	14.3	11.9	19.8	1970	Diplomat: 3323

Panhard

1 34.0 28.3 8.3 1954 Dyna: 3365
2 33.3 27.7 8.5 1964 24CT Sports Coupe: 3371
3 32.1 26.7 8.8 1959 PL17: 3369
4 28.7 23.9 9.8 1962 PL17 Tiger: 3370

Panther

1 24.4 20.3 11.6 1984 Kallista 2.8: 3377
2 24.1 20.1 11.7 1983 Kallista 2.8: 3376
3 23.7 19.7 11.9 1985 Kallista 1.6L: 3378
4 21.8 18.2 13.0 1977 Lima: 3375
5 19.4 16.2 14.6 1990 Solo: 3380
6 14.3 11.9 19.8 1972 J72: 3372

Paramount

1 26.0 21.6 10.9 1956 Roadster: 3381

Peugeot

1 39.5 32.9 7.2 1989 205 1.1GL: 3450
2 38.2 31.8 7.4 1988 405 GRD: 3447
3 37.4 31.1 7.6 1983 205 GR: 3429
4 37.2 31.0 7.6 1989 205 CJ: 3451
5 36.5 30.4 7.7 1985 205 XL: 3434
6 35.5 29.6 8.0 1985 305 GRD Estate: 3435
7 35.0 29.1 8.1 1976 104: 3414
8 34.4 28.6 8.2 1991 205 D Turbo: 3464
9 33.3 27.7 8.5 1991 605 SR TD: 3465
10 32.7 27.2 8.6 1992 106 XT: 3468
11 32.6 27.1 8.7 1983 305 SR: 3430
12 32.3 26.9 8.7 1965 404 Diesel: 3392
13 32.1 26.7 8.8 1991 106 XR: 3462
1966 204: 3394
14 31.3 26.1 9.0 1989 405 GTD Turbo: 3454
15 31.2 26.0 9.1 1963 104: 3407
16 31.1 25.9 9.1 1974 504 L Diesel: 3410
17 30.9 25.7 9.1 1986 309 SR Injection: 3440
18 30.4 25.3 9.3 1990 309 Style 5-door: 3456
19 29.9 24.9 9.4 1986 205 GTi: 3438
1981 305 S: 3425
20 29.8 24.8 9.5 1986 309 1.6 GR: 3439
20 1955 403: 3385
21 29.7 24.7 9.5 1985 309 1.3 GL: 3436
22 29.5 24.6 9.6 1976 104 ZS: 3415
1984 205 GTi: 3431
23 28.3 23.6 10.0 1987 309 GTi: 3444
24 28.2 23.5 10.0 1972 204: 3404
1989 309 GLX: 3452
25 28.1 23.4 10.1 1987 205 GTi 1.9: 3443
26 27.9 23.2 10.1 1988 405 1.6 GL: 3446
27 27.7 23.1 10.2 1980 604 D Turbo: 3424
28 27.5 22.9 10.3 1968 204 Coupe: 3397
29 27.4 22.8 10.3 1984 505 GRi: 3432
30 27.3 22.7 10.3 1990 405 GR Injection Auto: 3458
31 26.9 22.4 10.5 1991 106 XSi: 3463
32 26.8 22.3 10.5 1962 404 U6 Estate Car: 3390
33 26.6 22.1 10.6 1988 405 Mi16: 3448
34 26.2 21.8 10.8 1982 505 GR Estate: 3427
35 26.1 21.7 10.8 1978 305 SR: 3418
36 26.0 21.6 10.9 1990 405 Mi16x4: 3459
37 25.9 21.6 10.9 1960 404: 3387
38 25.3 21.1 11.2 1968 504 Injection: 3399
39 25.2 21.0 11.2 1989 309 GTi: 3453
40 25.1 20.9 11.3 1965 404 KF2: 3393
41 25.0 20.8 11.3 1972 304 Estate Car: 3405
42 24.7 20.6 11.4 1962 403 B Estate Car: 3389
1990 605 SRi: 3461
43 24.4 20.3 11.6 1990 405 GLx4: 3457
44 24.1 20.1 11.7 1979 504: 3419
45 23.8 19.8 11.9 1988 405 SRi: 3449
46 23.4 19.5 12.1 1969 404 Automatic: 3400
47 22.6 18.8 12.5 1979 505 STI: 3420
48 22.2 18.5 12.7 1967 404 L Estate: 3396
49 20.9 17.4 13.5 1972 504 Family Estate: 3406
50 20.6 17.2 13.7 1986 505 GTi Family Estate: 3441
51 20.4 17.0 13.8 1991 605 SVE 24: 3467
52 19.9 16.6 14.2 1971 504 Automatic: 3403
53 19.8 16.5 14.3 1991 605 SV 3.0 Auto: 3466
54 19.6 16.3 14.4 1975 604: 3413

Plymouth

1 16.9 14.1 16.7 1967 Barracuda: 3493
2 16.4 13.7 17.2 1956 Savoy: 3473
3 16.2 13.5 17.4 1959 Fury: 3475
4 15.5 12.9 18.2 1963 Fury: 3482
5 11.7 9.7 24.1 1968 Fury III: 3500

Polonez

1 21.9 18.2 12.9 1979 1500: 3524

Polski Fiat

1 29.0 24.1 9.7 1975 125P: 3525

Pontiac

1 15.2 12.7 18.6 1962 Parisienne: 3534
2 12.7 10.6 22.2 1966 GTO: 3544
3 11.8 9.8 23.9 1959 Bonneville: 3528

Porsche

1 32.1 26.7 8.8 1958 1600: 3611
2 31.0 25.8 9.1 1956 1600: 3605
3 29.2 24.3 9.7 1960 Super 75: 3615
4 28.0 23.3 10.1 1954 356: 3602
5 27.8 23.1 10.2 1977 924: 3656
6 26.2 21.8 10.8 1982 944 Lux: 3674
7 25.0 20.8 11.3 1978 924 Lux: 3660
8 24.4 20.3 11.6 1962 Super 90 Cabriolet: 3619
9 23.6 19.7 12.0 1965 912: 3623
10 23.5 19.6 12.0 1986 944 S: 3694
11 23.2 19.3 12.2 1974 911S 2.7-litre: 3645
12 22.9 19.1 12.3 1986 944 Turbo: 3695
13 22.6 18.8 12.5 1987 924 S: 3700
14 21.4 17.8 13.2 1985 944 Lux: 3685
15 20.7 17.2 13.6 1989 944: 3728
1989 944 S2: 3729
16 20.6 17.2 13.7 1988 911 Carrera Club Sport: 3705
17 20.4 17.0 13.8 1990 911 Carrera 2: 3732
18 19.8 16.5 14.3 1979 924 Turbo: 3664
19 19.7 16.4 14.3 1981 911 SC: 3670
20 19.2 16.0 14.7 1986 911 Carrera SE: 3688
21 19.1 15.9 14.8 1988 944 Turbo SE: 3716
22 19.0 15.8 14.9 1968 911 E Sportomatic: 3627
23 18.6 15.5 15.2 1989 928 S4 SE: 3727
24 18.5 15.4 15.3 1975 Turbo 3-litre: 3648
25 18.0 15.0 15.7 1985 928 S Series II: 3684
26 17.9 14.9 15.8 1977 911 SC: 3654
1970 911 T: 3632
27 17.4 14.5 16.2 1990 Carrera 2 Cabriolet Tiptronic: 3744
28 17.1 14.2 16.5 1978 928: 3661
29 17.0 14.2 16.6 1986 928 S4 Automatic: 3692
30 16.7 13.9 16.9 1963 Carrera RS Touring: 3641
31 16.6 13.8 17.0 1989 911 3.3 Turbo: 3719
32 16.4 13.7 17.2 1983 911 Turbo: 3676
33 15.7 13.1 18.0 1966 911 S: 3624
34 15.6 13.0 18.1 1971 911 E 2.4-litre: 3635
35 15.1 12.6 18.7 1991 911 Turbo: 3750
36 14.6 12.2 19.3 1978 928 Automatic: 3662

Proton

1 28.5 23.7 9.9 1991 1.5 SE Triple Valve Aeroback: 3755
2 28.0 23.3 10.1 1989 1.5 SE Aeroback: 3754

Rambler

1 24.3 20.2 11.6 1959 American: 3761
2 19.4 16.2 14.6 1961 Estate: 3766
3 18.7 15.6 15.1 1960 Super 6 Station Wagon: 3764
4 18.3 15.2 15.4 1964 770 Six: 3767
5 17.4 14.5 16.2 1967 Rebel 6 Estate Car: 3769
6 15.5 12.9 18.2 1968 Javelin Hardtop SST: 3770
7 15.1 12.6 18.7 1966 770 V8 Convertible: 3768

Range Rover

1 21.4 17.8 13.2 1988 Vogue Turbo D: 3776
2 18.7 15.6 15.1 1989 Vogue: 3777
3 15.8 13.2 17.9 1989 Vogue SE: 3778
4 15.0 12.5 18.8 1986 Vogue: 3774
5 14.6 12.2 19.3 1990 Vogue SE: 3780
6 14.4 12.0 19.6 1970 V8: 3771
7 14.2 11.8 19.9 1978 V8: 3773
1992 Vogue SE: 3781
8 14.1 11.7 20.0 1975 V8: 3772

Reliant

1 41.5 34.6 6.8 1975 Kitten: 3789
1976 Kitten DL Estate: 3790
2 38.1 31.7 7.4 1968 Rebel 700 Estate: 3786
3 32.8 27.3 8.6 1985 Scimitar SS1 1600: 3794
4 28.8 24.0 9.8 1962 Sabre Sports: 3782
5 22.1 18.4 12.8 1967 Scimitar GT: 3785
6 21.7 18.1 13.0 1990 Scimitar SST 1800Ti: 3796
1986 Scimitar Ti: 3795
7 21.1 17.6 13.4 1977 Scimitar GTE: 3792
8 20.8 17.3 13.6 1963 Scimitar GTE: 3788
9 20.5 17.1 13.8 1981 Scimitar GTE: 3793
10 20.4 17.0 13.8 1970 Scimitar GTE Automatic: 3787
11 20.3 16.9 13.9 1964 Sabre Six GT: 3783
1976 Scimitar GTE: 3791
12 19.8 16.5 14.3 1965 Scimitar: 3784

Renault

1	50.0	41.6	5.6	1955	750: 3804
2	44.0	36.6	6.4	1953	750: 3802
3	42.1	35.1	6.7	1959	Dauphine Gordini: 3811
4	42.0	35.0	6.7	1976	5 GTL: 3854
				1957	Dauphine: 3806
5	41.3	34.4	6.8	1979	5 TL: 3866
6	41.0	34.1	6.9	1989	5 Campus: 3911
7	40.9	34.1	6.9	1959	Dauphine: 3810
8	38.3	31.9	7.4	1991	Clio 1.4RT: 3920
9	37.0	30.8	7.6	1966	4 Estate Car: 3829
10	36.8	30.6	7.7	1991	Clio 1.2 RN: 3919
11	36.4	30.3	7.8	1964	R8 1100: 3823
12	35.5	29.6	8.0	1986	5 GTL 5-door: 3896
13	35.4	29.5	8.0	1982	9 TC: 3878
14	35.3	29.4	8.0	1963	4 L Estate Car: 3819
				1960	Floride: 3813
15	34.9	29.1	8.1	1989	19 TSE: 3907
16	34.7	28.9	8.1	1962	Dauphine Gordini de Luxe: 3817
17	34.6	28.8	8.2	1966	1100 Automatic: 3827
				1974	6 TL: 3846
18	34.3	28.6	8.2	1982	9 TSE: 3879
19	34.1	28.4	8.3	1983	11 TSE: 3883
20	33.7	28.1	8.4	1962	R8: 3818
21	32.5	27.1	8.7	1977	14: 3856
22	32.4	27.0	8.7	1982	9 GLT: 3877
23	32.1	26.7	8.8	1969	6: 3834
24	31.9	26.6	8.9	1975	5 TS: 3849
25	31.8	26.5	8.9	1972	15 TL: 3842
26	31.7	26.4	8.9	1979	18 TS Estate: 3862
27	31.3	26.1	9.0	1971	6 1100: 3838
28	31.2	26.0	9.1	1963	Floride Caravelle: 3821
				1982	Fuego GTS: 3881
29	30.9	25.7	9.1	1970	10: 3835
				1976	15 GTL: 3850
				1990	19 TXE Chamade: 3913
30	30.7	25.6	9.2	1981	14 TS: 3869
31	30.4	25.3	9.3	1965	Caravelle: 3825
32	30.1	25.1	9.4	1982	5 Gordini Turbo: 3876
33	30.0	25.0	9.4	1979	5 Gordini: 3864
				1987	5 GTX 3-DR: 3902
34	29.8	24.8	9.5	1972	12 Estate: 3839
35	29.7	24.7	9.5	1986	21 GTS: 3893
36	29.5	24.6	9.6	1985	5 TSE: 3890
37	29.4	24.5	9.6	1986	9 Turbo: 3897
38	28.8	24.0	9.8	1979	18 GTS: 3861
39	28.4	23.6	9.9	1978	5 Automatic: 3860
				1987	5 GT Turbo: 3901
40	28.2	23.5	10.0	1991	19 16v: 3917
41	28.1	23.4	10.1	1982	18 GTX Estate: 3875
				1989	21 GTS Hatchback: 3909
42	28.0	23.3	10.1	1971	16 TL Automatic: 3837
43	27.9	23.2	10.1	1970	12 TL: 3836
44	27.8	23.1	10.2	1986	21 Savanna GTX: 3894
45	27.3	22.7	10.3	1987	11 Turbo: 3900
46	26.9	22.4	10.5	1966	16 GL: 3828
47	26.8	22.3	10.5	1977	12 TL: 3855
				1963	5 TL: 3845
48	26.7	22.2	10.6	1989	Espace TXE: 3912
49	26.1	21.7	10.8	1977	17 TS: 3857
				1989	19 TXE: 3908
50	26.0	21.6	10.9	1992	Cleo 16v: 3923
51	25.9	21.6	10.9	1981	18 Turbo: 3870
52	25.7	21.4	11.0	1988	21 Ti: 3904
53	25.5	21.2	11.1	1990	21 TXi: 3915
54	25.4	21.1	11.1	1976	20 TL: 3852
55	25.2	21.0	11.2	1975	17 Gordini: 3848
56	25.0	20.8	11.3	1965	8 Gordini: 3824
57	24.9	20.7	11.3	1992	19 16v Cabriolet: 3922
58	24.7	20.6	11.4	1972	16 TS: 3843
59	24.3	20.2	11.6	1985	Espace 2000 TSE: 3892
60	23.3	19.4	12.1	1969	16 TS: 3833
61	23.1	19.2	12.2	1981	20 TX: 3872
62	22.9	19.1	12.3	1977	20 TS: 3858
63	22.5	18.7	12.6	1989	25 TXi: 3910
				1967	8 Gordini 1300: 3831
64	22.1	18.4	12.8	1990	21 Turbo Quadra: 3914
65	22.0	18.3	12.8	1986	5 GT Turbo: 3895
66	21.2	17.7	13.3	1990	25 V6 2.9 Auto: 3916
67	20.8	17.3	13.6	1958	Fregate Transfluide: 3808
68	20.5	17.1	13.8	1986	GTA V6 Turbo: 3899
69	20.2	16.8	14.0	1976	30 TS: 3853
70	19.9	16.6	14.2	1984	25 V6: 3885
				1991	Espace V6: 3921
71	19.5	16.2	14.5	1979	30 TX: 3863
72	19.1	15.9	14.8	1988	GTA V6: 3906
73	18.5	15.4	15.3	1985	25 V6 Turbo: 3889
				1978	30 TS: 3859
74	18.3	15.2	15.4	1988	21 Turbo: 3905

Riley

1	32.9	27.4	8.6	1962	Elf: 3944
2	29.6	24.6	9.5	1967	Kestrel: 3945
3	27.6	23.0	10.2	1958	1.5: 3941
4	25.2	21.0	11.2	1961	1.5: 3943
5	24.0	20.0	11.8	1953	1.5: 3937
6	23.7	19.7	11.9	1956	Pathfinder: 3940
7	23.3	19.4	12.1	1960	4/68: 3942
8	21.0	17.5	13.5	1955	Pathfinder: 3939
9	20.8	17.3	13.6	1953	2.5: 3938

Rolls-Royce

1	14.2	11.8	19.9	1954	Silver Dawn: 3955
2	14.0	11.7	20.2	1981	Silver Spirit: 3969
3	13.8	11.5	20.5	1991	Silver Spirit II: 3972
4	13.6	11.3	20.8	1976	Silver Shadow: 3965
5	13.2	11.0	21.4	1978	Silver Wraith II: 3967
6	12.4	10.3	22.8	1972	Silver Shadow: 3963
7	12.3	10.2	23.0	1982	Corniche: 3970
				1963	Silver Cloud III: 3960
8	12.2	10.2	23.2	1966	Silver Shadow: 3961
9	12.0	10.0	23.5	1958	Silver Cloud: 3956
10	11.9	9.9	23.7	1974	Corniche: 3964
11	11.8	9.8	23.9	1960	Silver Cloud II: 3958

Rover

1	39.7	33.1	7.1	1989	Montego 2.0 DSL Turbo: 4034
2	36.2	30.1	7.8	1991	825 TD: 4047
3	35.3	29.4	8.0	1991	218 SD: 4045
4	33.7	28.1	8.4	1990	Metro 1.4SL: 4041
5	32.7	27.2	8.6	1990	414 Si: 4039
6	32.0	26.6	8.8	1985	216 Vitesse: 4026
7	31.6	26.3	8.9	1990	Metro GTi 16v: 4042
8	30.9	25.7	9.1	1984	213 Vanden Plas: 4025
9	30.0	25.0	9.4	1991	214S: 4043
10	29.6	24.6	9.5	1982	SD Turbo: 4023
11	29.5	24.6	9.6	1987	Montego 1.6L: 4029
12	29.0	24.1	9.7	1956	60: 3988
13	28.9	24.1	9.8	1990	214 GSi: 4037
14	28.7	23.9	9.8	1954	60: 3985
15	27.4	22.8	10.3	1992	820i: 4050
16	27.1	22.6	10.4	1991	220 GTi: 4046
17	26.6	22.1	10.6	1987	820SE: 4028
18	26.5	22.1	10.7	1991	Mini Cooper S: 4048
19	26.3	21.9	10.7	1986	825i: 4027
20	26.0	21.6	10.9	1990	216 GSi: 4038
21	25.3	21.1	11.2	1963	2000SC: 4013
22	25.1	20.9	11.3	1990	416 GTi: 4040
23	24.5	20.4	11.5	1991	216 GTi: 4044
24	24.4	20.3	11.6	1988	820 Fastback: 4031
25	24.0	20.0	11.8	1963	2000: 3999
26	23.7	19.7	11.9	1952	75: 3983
27	23.4	19.5	12.1	1956	90: 3989
28	22.8	19.0	12.4	1982	2000: 4022
29	22.4	18.7	12.6	1971	2000TC: 4011
				1977	2600: 4018
30	22.3	18.6	12.7	1954	90: 3986
31	22.1	18.4	12.8	1989	Vitesse: 4036
32	22.0	18.3	12.8	1978	2300: 4019
33	21.9	18.2	12.9	1955	75: 3987
34	21.8	18.2	13.0	1966	2000 Automatic: 4003
				1983	Vitesse: 4024
35	21.4	17.8	13.2	1958	105R de Luxe: 3991
36	21.3	17.7	13.3	1989	Sterling Catalyst: 4035
37	21.0	17.5	13.5	1987	Sterling Automatic: 4030
38	20.9	17.4	13.5	1974	2200TC: 4015
39	20.7	17.2	13.6	1981	Vanden Plas: 4021
40	20.5	17.1	13.8	1963	2200SC Automatic: 4014
				1976	3500: 4016
41	20.1	16.7	14.1	1971	3500S: 4012
42	19.9	16.6	14.2	1988	Vitesse: 4033
43	19.8	16.5	14.3	1959	80: 3993
44	19.6	16.3	14.4	1992	Sterling Automatic: 4051
45	19.5	16.2	14.5	1960	100: 3994
46	19.2	16.0	14.7	1959	3-litre: 3992
				1967	3.5-litre: 4007
47	18.5	15.4	15.3	1957	105S: 3990
48	18.2	15.2	15.5	1966	3-litre Coupe Mk III: 4005
49	18.0	15.0	15.7	1970	3500: 4009
				1976	3500 Automatic: 4017
50	17.9	14.9	15.8	1988	827 SLi Auto: 4032
51	17.6	14.7	16.1	1963	3-litre Coupe: 4000
52	15.6	13.0	18.1	1961	3-litre Automatic: 3997

Ruger

1	10.0	8.3	28.2	1970	Bentley Clone: 4052

Saab

1	35.0	29.1	8.1	1956	93: 4053
2	29.4	24.5	9.6	1967	96 V4: 4061
3	28.7	23.9	9.8	1960	96: 4056
4	28.3	23.6	10.0	1981	900GLS: 4086
5	27.8	23.1	10.2	1963	95: 4058
6	26.5	22.1	10.7	1971	99: 4070
7	25.8	21.5	10.9	1972	99CM4 2.0: 4071
8	25.7	21.4	11.0	1986	9000i: 4093
9	25.0	20.8	11.3	1972	99EA: 4073
10	24.5	20.4	11.5	1979	900GL: 4083
11	24.4	20.3	11.6	1985	900i: 4091

12	24.0	20.0	11.8	1970	99: 4067
13	23.6	19.7	12.0	1992	9000 2.3CS: 4105
14	23.2	19.3	12.2	1975	99EMS: 4078
15	22.7	18.9	12.4	1985	9000 Turbo 16v: 4090
16	22.5	18.7	12.6	1976	99GL Super Combi: 4079
17	22.2	18.5	12.7	1979	900 Turbo: 4082
				1991	9000CS Turbo S: 4103
18	22.0	18.3	12.8	1966	96: 4060
				1990	CDS 2.3: 4100
19	21.6	18.0	13.1	1989	Carlsson: 4097
20	21.4	17.8	13.2	1978	Turbo: 4081
21	20.7	17.2	13.6	1969	Sport: 4066
22	20.3	16.9	13.9	1988	9000CD: 4094
23	19.7	16.4	14.3	1991	9000 2.3 Turbo TCS: 4101
24	19.1	15.9	14.8	1989	900 Turbo S: 4095

Seat

1	37.6	31.3	7.5	1992	Toledo 1.9 CL Diesel: 4114
2	34.9	29.1	8.1	1989	Ibiza SXi: 4113
3	31.8	26.5	8.9	1992	Toledo 2.0 GTi: 4115
4	31.3	26.1	9.0	1986	Malaga 1.2L: 4112
5	30.3	25.2	9.3	1985	1.5 GLX: 4111
6	29.9	24.9	9.4	1976	1200 Sport: 4110

Simca

1	36.5	30.4	7.7	1962	1000: 4143
2	35.0	29.1	8.1	1954	Aronde: 4131
3	34.0	28.3	8.3	1955	Aronde: 4132
4	33.7	28.1	8.4	1977	1000LS: 4158
5	31.6	26.3	8.9	1963	1000 Special: 4146
6	31.4	26.1	9.0	1966	1000GLS: 4150
7	31.0	25.8	9.1	1956	Elysee: 4133
8	30.3	25.2	9.3	1970	1204 Special: 4156
9	30.0	25.0	9.4	1952	Aronde: 4130
10	29.3	24.4	9.6	1961	Aronde Montlhery: 4142
11	29.1	24.2	9.7	1963	1300GL: 4147
12	28.8	24.0	9.8	1958	Aronde Montlhery: 4136
13	28.6	23.8	9.9	1967	1301: 4152
14	28.4	23.6	9.9	1974	1100 Special: 4157
15	28.0	23.3	10.1	1968	1100GLS: 4153
16	27.8	23.1	10.2	1960	Etoile: 4139
17	27.7	23.1	10.2	1964	1500: 4148
18	24.8	20.7	11.4	1965	1500GL Estate: 4149
19	22.5	18.7	12.6	1969	1501 Special Estate: 4155
20	22.0	18.3	12.8	1958	Vedette Beaulieu: 4137

Singer

1	35.7	29.7	7.9	1969	Chamois: 4181
2	35.4	29.5	8.0	1964	Chamois: 4175
3	31.2	26.0	9.1	1958	Gazelle IIA Convertible: 4171
4	29.0	24.1	9.7	1952	SM1500 Saloon: 4166
5	28.0	23.3	10.1	1952	SM Roadster: 4165
6	27.6	23.0	10.2	1964	Gazelle Series V: 4176
7	27.0	22.5	10.5	1954	SM Roadster: 4169
8	26.2	21.8	10.8	1967	Gazelle: 4180
9	25.3	21.1	11.2	1961	Gazelle Series IIIB: 4172
10	24.1	20.1	11.7	1966	Vogue Automatic: 4179
11	23.4	19.5	12.1	1961	Vogue: 4173
12	22.9	19.1	12.3	1965	Vogue Mk III Estate: 4177
13	22.8	19.0	12.4	1963	Vogue Mk II: 4174
14	21.9	18.2	12.9	1966	Vogue: 4178
15	21.5	17.9	13.1	1955	Hunter: 4170
16	20.6	17.2	13.7	1953	SM1500 Saloon: 4168

Skoda

1	34.4	28.6	8.2	1972	S110LS: 4186
2	32.6	27.1	8.7	1970	S100L: 4185
3	31.4	26.1	9.0	1965	1000MB: 4184
4	30.6	25.5	9.2	1989	136 Rapide Coupe: 4189
5	30.4	25.3	9.3	1977	120L: 4187
6	30.1	25.1	9.4	1986	Estelle 120 LSE: 4188
7	28.3	23.6	10.0	1960	Octavia: 4182
8	25.8	21.5	10.9	1961	Felicia: 4183

Standard

1	44.0	36.6	6.4	1953	8: 4200
				1958	8: 4207
2	40.5	33.7	7.0	1958	Super 10: 4210
3	39.6	33.0	7.1	1958	Pennant: 4209
4	35.5	29.6	8.0	1955	10: 4203
5	31.2	26.0	9.1	1957	Vanguard III: 4206
6	30.8	25.6	9.2	1956	Vanguard III: 4204
7	28.2	23.5	10.0	1958	Ensign: 4208
8	27.6	23.0	10.2	1952	Vanguard: 4199
9	25.8	21.5	10.9	1956	Vanguard Sportsman: 4205
10	25.4	21.1	11.1	1958	Vanguard III Automatic: 4211
11	24.8	20.7	11.4	1962	Ensign de Luxe Estate: 4213
12	21.7	18.1	13.0	1953	Vanguard Estate: 4201
13	21.5	17.9	13.1	1953	Vanguard Phase II: 4202
14	20.0	16.7	14.1	1961	Vanguard: 4212

Subaru

1	32.9	27.4	8.6	1987	Justy: 4267
2	32.2	26.8	8.8	1978	1600 Coupe: 4252
3	31.0	25.8	9.1	1989	Justy GL II 5-door 4WD: 4273
4	28.8	24.0	9.8	1977	1600 4WD Estate: 4251
5	28.1	23.4	10.1	1981	1800 4WD Estate: 4255
6	25.8	21.5	10.9	1987	XT Turbo 4WD: 4268
7	25.2	21.0	11.2	1985	1.8 GTi: 4258
8	25.0	20.8	11.3	1990	Legacy 2.2 GX 4WD: 4276
9	22.6	18.8	12.5	1985	1.8 RX Turbo: 4259
				1986	4WD 3-door Turbo Coupe: 4265
10	21.8	18.2	13.0	1991	Legacy 2.0 4Cam Turbo Estate: 4277
11	20.0	16.7	14.1	1985	XT Turbo Coupe: 4264
12	19.9	16.6	14.2	1988	4WD Turbo Estate: 4269
				1985	Turbo 4WD Estate: 4262

Sunbeam

1	34.0	28.3	8.3	1956	Rapier: 4286
2	33.1	27.6	8.5	1966	Imp Sport: 4305
3	32.4	27.0	8.7	1967	Stiletto: 4306
4	31.5	26.2	9.0	1958	Rapier Series II: 4289
5	30.2	25.1	9.4	1958	Rapier: 4288
6	29.2	24.3	9.7	1959	Rapier III: 4291
7	26.6	22.1	10.6	1968	Rapier: 4309
8	25.8	21.5	10.9	1969	Alpine: 4310
9	25.5	21.2	11.1	1959	Alpine: 4290
				1966	Alpine Series V: 4304
10	24.9	20.7	11.3	1963	Alpine GT: 4296
11	24.6	20.5	11.5	1954	Alpine: 4283
12	24.3	20.2	11.6	1975	Rapier: 4313
13	21.9	18.2	12.9	1969	Rapier H120: 4312
14	20.9	17.4	13.5	1964	Alpine GT Series IV Automatic: 4298
15	20.8	17.3	13.6	1955	Mk III: 4285
16	20.6	17.2	13.7	1954	Alpine II: 4284
17	20.1	16.7	14.1	1962	Harrington Le Mans: 4294
18	16.9	14.1	16.7	1965	Tiger 260: 4302

Sunbeam-Talbot

1	28.1	23.4	10.1	1953	90 Mk IIA: 4319
1	40.1	33.4	7.0	1981	Alto FX: 4322
2	38.9	32.4	7.3	1980	SC 100: 4321
3	37.0	30.8	7.6	1987	Swift 1.3 GLX: 4328
4	36.0	30.0	7.8	1987	Swift 1.3 GLX Executive: 4329
5	35.7	29.7	7.9	1989	Swift 1.3 GLX: 4330
6	35.0	29.1	8.1	1986	Alto GLA: 4325
7	34.9	29.1	8.1	1983	Alto FX Automatic: 4323
8	33.3	27.7	8.5	1985	Swift 1.3GS: 4324
9	30.9	25.7	9.1	1986	Swift 1.3 GTi: 4326
10	29.2	24.3	9.7	1989	Swift 1.3 GTi: 4331
11	24.8	20.7	11.4	1987	SJ413V JX: 4327
12	24.2	20.2	11.7	1989	Vitara JLX: 4332

Swallow

1	28.0	23.3	10.1	1955	Doretti: 4334

Talbot

1	37.6	31.3	7.5	1983	Horizon 1.9LD: 4348
2	37.3	31.1	7.6	1982	Samba GL: 4347
3	35.3	29.4	8.0	1982	Samba Cabriolet: 4346
4	29.0	24.1	9.7	1981	Solara GLS: 4344
5	23.9	19.9	11.8	1981	Tagora 2.2GLS: 4345

Toyota

1	38.1	31.7	7.4	1990	Starlet GL: 4475
2	35.9	29.9	7.9	1976	1000: 4393
3	35.6	29.6	7.9	1984	Carina II 116GL: 4424
4	34.2	28.5	8.3	1983	Tercel GL: 4423
5	33.5	27.9	8.4	1985	Starlet 1.0GL: 4435
6	32.3	26.9	8.7	1968	Corolla de Luxe: 4360
7	31.2	26.0	9.1	1988	Corolla 1.3 GL: 4456
				1985	Tercel 4WD Estate: 4437
8	31.1	25.9	9.1	1975	Corolla 30: 4389
9	30.5	25.4	9.3	1987	Camry 2.0 GLi: 4445
10	30.4	25.3	9.3	1971	Corolla 1200SL: 4369
11	30.2	25.1	9.4	1983	Corolla GL: 4418
12	30.0	25.0	9.4	1989	Carina II 1.6 GL Liftback: 4462
13	29.8	24.8	9.5	1975	Celica GT: 4387
14	29.6	24.6	9.5	1987	Corolla Executive: 4448
15	29.1	24.2	9.7	1985	MR2: 4433
16	28.8	24.0	9.8	1985	Corolla GT Hatchback: 4432
17	28.7	23.9	9.8	1987	Camry 2.0 GLi Estate: 4446
				1987	Celica GT Cabriolet: 4447
18	28.6	23.8	9.9	1986	MR2 T-Bar: 4441
19	28.5	23.7	9.9	1988	Carina 1.6 GL: 4453
20	28.0	23.3	10.1	1971	Celica: 4367
				1979	Corona Liftback: 4405
21	27.6	23.0	10.2	1976	Celica Liftback: 4395
22	27.2	22.6	10.4	1990	MR2 GT: 4472
23	27.0	22.5	10.5	1976	Carina: 4394

				1984	Corolla GT Coupe: 4426
24	26.8	22.3	10.5	1966	Corona: 4353
25	26.7	22.2	10.6	1991	MR2: 4479
26	26.0	21.6	10.9	1981	Cressida DX Estate: 4410
27	25.2	21.0	11.2	1982	Celica 2.0ST: 4413
28	25.0	20.8	11.3	1986	Celica 2.0GT: 4438
29	24.5	20.4	11.5	1991	Camry 2.2 GL: 4476
30	24.4	20.3	11.6	1984	Celica 2.8i Supra: 4425
31	24.2	20.2	11.7	1974	Corona 2000 Mk II Automatic: 4384
32	23.9	19.9	11.8	1978	Celica 2000GT: 4400
33	23.8	19.8	11.9	1971	1900SL: 4366
34	23.6	19.7	12.0	1977	Corona Cressida: 4398
35	23.0	19.2	12.3	1982	Celica Supra: 4415
				1985	Space Cruiser: 4434
36	22.9	19.1	12.3	1970	Corona Mk II 1900: 4364
37	22.5	18.7	12.6	1990	Celica 2.0 GT: 4468
38	21.6	18.0	13.1	1991	Previa: 4481
39	21.3	17.7	13.3	1988	Corolla 4WD Estate: 4457
40	20.6	17.2	13.7	1989	Camry V6 GXi: 4461
41	20.2	16.8	14.0	1988	Landcruiser II TD: 4458
42	19.8	16.5	14.3	1991	Landcruiser VX: 4478
43	19.4	16.2	14.6	1986	Supra 3.0i: 4443
44	19.2	16.0	14.7	1988	Celica GT4: 4455
45	19.0	15.8	14.9	1975	Crown Super: 4391
46	18.8	15.7	15.0	1989	Supra 3.0i Turbo: 4465
47	18.5	15.4	15.3	1972	Custom Crown Estate: 4376
48	17.9	14.9	15.8	1987	Landcruiser: 4450
49	17.3	14.4	16.3	1969	Crown Toyoglide: 4362

Triumph

1	33.2	27.6	8.5	1959	Herald Coupe: 4507
2	32.4	27.0	8.7	1959	Herald Saloon: 4508
3	32.1	26.7	8.8	1962	Herald 1200 Estate: 4513
				1971	Spitfire 4: 4548
4	32.0	26.6	8.8	1954	TR2 Sports: 4501
5	31.8	26.5	8.9	1981	Acclaim HL: 4580
6	31.7	26.4	8.9	1961	Herald 1200: 4511
7	31.3	26.1	9.0	1963	Herald 12/50: 4517
8	31.2	26.0	9.1	1962	Spitfire 4: 4514
9	31.0	25.8	9.1	1955	TR2 Hardtop: 4502
10	30.3	25.2	9.3	1970	Toledo: 4545
11	29.9	24.9	9.4	1979	Dolomite 1850HL: 4573
12	29.8	24.8	9.5	1966	Spitfire Mk II: 4529
13	29.2	24.3	9.7	1975	Spitfire 1500: 4566
14	28.8	24.0	9.8	1974	Toledo: 4562
15	28.3	23.6	10.0	1968	Herald 13/60 Convertible: 4533
16	28.1	23.4	10.1	1967	Herald 1200: 4531
17	28.0	23.3	10.1	1966	1300: 4527
18	27.7	23.1	10.2	1975	Dolomite: 4564
19	27.6	23.0	10.2	1971	GT6 Mk III: 4547
				1960	Herald Convertible: 4509
20	27.1	22.6	10.4	1976	Dolomite 1500HL: 4568
21	27.0	22.5	10.5	1963	1500TC: 4554
				1972	Dolomite: 4553
22	26.6	22.1	10.6	1970	1500: 4543
23	26.4	22.0	10.7	1976	TR7: 4570
24	25.9	21.6	10.9	1963	Dolomite Automatic: 4555
25	25.8	21.5	10.9	1965	Vitesse Convertible: 4526
26	25.4	21.1	11.1	1965	TR4A IRS: 4525
27	25.2	21.0	11.2	1969	GT6 Mk II: 4540
28	24.9	20.7	11.3	1957	TR2 Hardtop: 4504
29	24.8	20.7	11.4	1975	2500S: 4563
30	24.6	20.5	11.5	1963	Vitesse 6: 4519
31	24.5	20.4	11.5	1964	2000: 4520
32	24.1	20.1	11.7	1974	2500TC: 4560
33	23.6	19.7	12.0	1975	Dolomite Sprint: 4565
34	23.5	19.6	12.0	1969	Vitesse 2-litre Mk II: 4542
35	22.5	18.7	12.6	1962	TR4: 4516
36	21.8	18.2	13.0	1966	2000 Estate Car: 4528
37	21.6	18.0	13.1	1969	2.5PI: 4537
38	20.6	17.2	13.7	1970	Stag: 4544
39	20.2	16.8	14.0	1972	2.5PI Mk II: 4552
				1967	GT6: 4530
40	20.1	16.7	14.1	1969	2000 Mk II: 4538
41	19.8	16.5	14.3	1969	TR6: 4541
42	19.6	16.3	14.4	1968	TR5 PI: 4536
43	17.2	14.3	16.4	1971	Stag Automatic: 4551

Turner

1	25.5	21.2	11.1	1960	Turner-Climax: 4582

TVR

1	27.3	22.7	10.3	1987	S Convertible: 4600
2	26.5	22.1	10.7	1969	Vixen S2: 4585
3	25.8	21.5	10.9	1961	Grantura: 4584
4	25.2	21.0	11.2	1976	1600M: 4590
5	21.4	17.8	13.2	1974	3000M: 4589
6	21.1	17.6	13.4	1977	Taimar: 4592
7	20.7	17.2	13.6	1981	Tasmin: 4596
8	20.1	16.7	14.1	1991	V8 S: 4603
9	19.6	16.3	14.4	1985	350i Series II: 4598
10	17.7	14.7	16.0	1979	Convertible Turbo: 4593
11	16.6	13.8	17.0	1987	390 SE: 4599

Vanden Plas

1	30.8	25.6	9.2	1965	Princess 1100: 4606
2	27.2	22.6	10.4	1974	1500: 4607
3	18.3	15.2	15.4	1963	Princess 3-litre Automatic: 4605
4	17.1	14.2	16.5	1960	Princess: 4604
5	14.8	12.3	19.1	1974	Princess R: 4608

Vauxhall

1	44.2	36.8	6.4	1989	Astra 1.7 DL: 4716
2	43.8	36.5	6.4	1990	Nova 1.5TD Merit: 4727
3	38.2	31.8	7.4	1982	Cavalier LD: 4693
4	37.1	30.9	7.6	1992	Cavalier 1.7 GL TD: 4733
5	36.9	30.7	7.7	1983	Nova 1.2L: 4697
6	35.6	29.6	7.9	1991	Nova 1.2 Luxe: 4730
7	35.1	29.2	8.0	1986	Nova 1.3 GL 5-door: 4705
8	34.8	29.0	8.1	1989	Cavalier 1.4L: 4717
9	34.7	28.9	8.1	1992	1.4i GLS: 4732
10	34.1	28.4	8.3	1989	Cavalier 1.6L: 4718
11	34.0	28.3	8.3	1987	Belmont 1.6 GL: 4707
12	33.4	27.8	8.5	1987	Astra GTE 2.0i: 4706
13	33.2	27.6	8.5	1974	Viva 1256 DL: 4674
14	32.9	27.4	8.6	1976	Blydenstein Chevette 1500: 4678
15	32.5	27.1	8.7	1988	Nova GTE: 4715
16	32.2	26.8	8.8	1985	Astra 1.3 GL: 4699
17	32.1	26.7	8.8	1964	Bedford Beagle: 4643
18	32.0	26.6	8.8	1986	Belmont 1.8 GLSi: 4703
19	31.9	26.6	8.9	1982	Cavalier GLS: 4692
				1976	Chevette L: 4681
20	31.4	26.1	9.0	1988	Carlton L 1.8i: 4712
				1963	Viva de Luxe: 4642
21	31.0	25.8	9.1	1988	Carlton L 2.3D: 4713
22	30.9	25.7	9.1	1977	Cavalier 1300L: 4683
23	30.7	25.6	9.2	1958	Victor Estate: 4632
24	30.3	25.2	9.3	1975	Chevette L: 4676
25	30.1	25.1	9.4	1981	Cavalier 1.6S GL: 4690
26	29.6	24.6	9.5	1983	Cavalier CD: 4696
27	29.3	24.4	9.6	1991	Calibra 2.0i: 4728
				1971	Viva de Luxe: 4664
28	29.2	24.3	9.7	1972	Viva HC Estate: 4669
29	29.1	24.2	9.7	1983	Astra GTE: 4694
30	28.6	23.8	9.9	1955	Wyvern: 4629
31	28.3	23.6	10.0	1988	Cavalier 4x4: 4714
32	28.2	23.5	10.0	1984	Astra GTE: 4698
33	28.1	23.4	10.1	1959	Victor de Luxe: 4634
				1966	Viva de Luxe: 4652
34	28.0	23.3	10.1	1962	Victor Super: 4639
35	27.8	23.1	10.2	1952	Wyvern: 4626
36	27.7	23.1	10.2	1965	Viva SL90: 4649
37	27.3	22.7	10.3	1991	Calibra 4x4: 4729
				1983	Carlton 2.0 GL: 4695
38	27.2	22.6	10.4	1976	Cavalier 1600 GL: 4679
39	27.1	22.6	10.4	1985	Cavalier SRi: 4701
40	27.0	22.5	10.5	1985	Astra 1.6 SR: 4700
				1987	Cavalier SRi 130 4-door: 4710
41	26.7	22.2	10.6	1986	Carlton CD 2.0i: 4704
42	26.5	22.1	10.7	1969	Victor: 4660
43	26.3	21.9	10.7	1975	Magnum 1800: 4677
44	26.1	21.7	10.8	1987	Cavalier 2.0i CD: 4709
45	25.9	21.6	10.9	1961	Victor Estate: 4638
46	25.8	21.5	10.9	1968	Viva SL90 Estate: 4659
47	25.7	21.4	11.0	1977	Magnum 1800: 4684
				1952	Velox: 4625
48	25.6	21.3	11.0	1978	Cavalier 2000 GLS: 4687
49	25.5	21.2	11.1	1990	Calibra 2.0i 16v: 4722
50	25.3	21.1	11.2	1989	Cavalier SRi: 4719
				1974	Magnum 2300: 4673
51	25.2	21.0	11.2	1970	Viva GT: 4662
52	25.1	20.9	11.3	1976	VX1800: 4682
53	25.0	20.8	11.3	1978	Carlton: 4686
				1990	Cavalier GSi 2000 16v: 4725
54	24.9	20.7	11.3	1987	Carlton 3000 GSi: 4708
55	24.8	20.7	11.4	1964	VX4/90: 4645
56	24.5	20.4	11.5	1954	Velox: 4627
57	24.2	20.2	11.7	1962	VX4/90: 4640
58	24.1	20.1	11.7	1955	Cresta: 4628
59	24.0	20.0	11.8	1990	Cavalier GSi 2000 16v 4x4: 4726
				1964	Victor Estate: 4644
60	23.7	19.7	11.9	1976	Cavalier GL Coupe: 4680
61	23.6	19.7	12.0	1982	Astra 1600 GL: 4691
				1967	Victor 2000: 4655
62	23.5	19.6	12.0	1958	Cresta: 4630
				1960	Cresta: 4635
63	23.3	19.4	12.1	1965	VX4/90: 4650
64	23.2	19.3	12.2	1974	VX4/90: 4675
65	23.1	19.2	12.2	1967	Victor 101 de Luxe: 4654
				1972	Viva 1800: 4668
66	22.9	19.1	12.3	1985	Senator 3.0i CD: 4702
67	22.8	19.0	12.4	1992	Frontera 2.3 TD Estate: 4734
				1977	VX2300 Estate: 4685
68	22.7	18.9	12.4	1987	Senator 3.0i CD: 4711
69	22.3	18.6	12.7	1971	Firenza: 4663
				1968	Viva GT: 4658
70	22.2	18.5	12.7	1972	Firenza Sport SL: 4665
				1989	Senator 2.5i: 4720
71	22.1	18.4	12.8	1960	Velox III: 4637
72	21.9	18.2	12.9	1959	Friary Estate Car: 4633
73	21.6	18.0	13.1	1972	Victor 2300 SL: 4667

74	21.5	17.9	13.1	1972	VX4/90: 4670
75	21.4	17.8	13.2	1991	Senator 3.0i 24v: 4731
76	21.3	17.7	13.3	1978	Chevette 2300 HS: 4688
77	21.2	17.7	13.3	1965	Victor 101 Estate: 4648
				1963	Victor Estate: 4671
78	21.0	17.5	13.5	1990	Carlton 3.0i CDX Estate: 4723
79	20.6	17.2	13.7	1970	Ventora II: 4661
80	20.2	16.8	14.0	1960	Cresta Overdrive: 4636
81	20.1	16.7	14.1	1974	Firenza: 4672
82	19.5	16.2	14.5	1990	Carlton GSi 3000 24v: 4724
83	19.3	16.1	14.6	1989	Senator 3.0i CD: 4721
				1968	Victor 2000 Estate Automatic: 4657
84	18.7	15.6	15.1	1965	Velox: 4647
85	18.4	15.3	15.4	1979	Royale Coupe: 4689
86	18.3	15.2	15.4	1967	Cresta Estate: 4653
				1963	Cresta Series PB: 4641
87	18.0	15.0	15.7	1972	Ventora: 4666
88	16.8	14.0	16.8	1968	Ventora: 4656
89	14.9	12.4	19.0	1965	Cresta de Luxe Powerglide: 4646
90	14.3	11.9	19.8	1966	Viscount Automatic: 4651

Volga

1	20.4	17.0	13.8	1960	M21K: 4737

Volkswagen

1	46.0	38.3	6.1	1978	Golf LD: 4814
2	40.7	33.9	6.9	1984	Passat CL Turbo Diesel Estate: 4845
3	39.3	32.7	7.2	1988	Jetta Turbo Diesel: 4868
4	38.4	32.0	7.4	1989	Golf CL Catalyst: 4876
5	37.8	31.5	7.5	1982	Polo C Formel E: 4834
6	37.7	31.4	7.5	1953	Export Saloon: 4739
7	37.0	30.8	7.6	1990	Passat CL TD Estate: 4880
8	35.2	29.3	8.0	1991	Polo 1.3 CL Coupe: 4886
9	35.0	29.1	8.1	1982	Polo C: 4833
10	34.9	29.1	8.1	1975	Polo: 4800
				1991	Polo GT Coupe: 4888
11	34.3	28.6	8.2	1954	De Luxe: 4740
12	34.0	28.3	8.3	1958	De Luxe Saloon: 4750
13	33.5	27.9	8.4	1977	Polo LS: 4808
14	32.2	26.8	8.8	1992	Golf 1.8 GL: 4889
15	31.7	26.4	8.9	1984	Jetta GLX: 4844
16	31.6	26.3	8.9	1960	De Luxe: 4751
17	31.2	26.0	9.1	1961	Karmann Ghia: 4754
18	31.0	25.8	9.1	1981	Golf 1300 LS: 4824
19	30.9	25.7	9.1	1962	1200 de Luxe: 4758
				1988	Polo C Saloon: 4870
20	30.7	25.6	9.2	1968	Derby LS: 4779
				1981	Passat CL Formel E: 4825
21	30.5	25.4	9.3	1979	Scirocco GLi: 4816
22	30.3	25.2	9.3	1987	Passat GT 5-door: 4865
23	30.1	25.1	9.4	1975	Golf 1100L: 4799
				1991	Polo G40: 4887
24	30.0	25.0	9.4	1987	Golf Cabriolet Clipper: 4862
25	29.9	24.9	9.4	1977	Scirocco GTi: 4811
26	29.6	24.6	9.5	1977	Passat GLS: 4807
27	29.4	24.5	9.6	1979	Scirocco GLS: 4817
28	29.2	24.3	9.7	1988	Passat GT: 4869
				1982	Scirocco GL: 4837
29	28.8	24.0	9.8	1966	1300: 4767
				1992	Golf GTi: 4890
				1987	Jetta GTi 16v: 4864
30	28.5	23.7	9.9	1982	Golf GTi 1800: 4832
				1974	Scirocco TS: 4797
31	28.2	23.5	10.0	1978	Golf GLS: 4813
32	27.9	23.2	10.1	1961	1500: 4753
				1967	1500: 4772
33	27.8	23.1	10.2	1981	Passat GL 5S Estate: 4826
				1963	Passat LS: 4790
34	27.6	23.0	10.2	1982	Santana GX5: 4836
				1976	Scirocco TS: 4804
35	27.4	22.8	10.3	1966	1500: 4769
				1989	Passat GT 16v: 4878
36	27.3	22.7	10.3	1977	Golf GTi: 4806
37	27.2	22.6	10.4	1976	Golf 1600 LS: 4803
38	27.0	22.5	10.5	1966	1600 TL: 4771
39	26.7	22.2	10.6	1985	Scirocco GTX: 4854
40	26.4	22.0	10.7	1985	Scirocco 16v: 4853
41	26.3	21.9	10.7	1964	1500S: 4764
42	25.9	21.6	10.9	1989	Corrado 16v: 4875
43	25.6	21.3	11.0	1986	Jetta GT: 4857
44	25.5	21.2	11.1	1983	Scirocco GTi: 4841
45	25.3	21.1	11.2	1986	Golf GTi 16v: 4856
46	25.2	21.0	11.2	1963	1500 Estate: 4762
47	25.1	20.9	11.3	1968	1500 Semi-automatic: 4775
48	24.1	20.1	11.7	1972	K70: 4788
49	24.0	20.0	11.8	1980	Jetta GLS: 4820
				1970	Super Beetle: 4783
50	22.5	18.7	12.6	1968	411 L: 4778
				1970	411 LE Variant: 4781
51	22.4	18.7	12.6	1968	1600 TL Automatic: 4777
52	22.3	18.6	12.7	1989	Jetta Syncro: 4877
53	22.0	18.3	12.8	1991	Corrado G60: 4882
54	21.3	17.7	13.3	1971	Porsche 914/b: 4785
55	20.7	17.2	13.6	1986	Caravelle Syncro: 4855
56	20.5	17.1	13.8	1970	Porsche 914: 4782
57	18.1	15.1	15.6	1989	Caravelle Carat Automatic: 4873

Volvo

1	33.0	27.5	8.6	1956	PV444 California: 4892
2	32.8	27.3	8.6	1957	PV444 Sports: 4894
3	29.5	24.6	9.6	1963	121 Estate: 4904
4	29.1	24.2	9.7	1986	340 GLE: 4953
5	28.8	24.0	9.8	1987	480 ES: 4954
6	28.0	23.3	10.1	1954	444: 4891
7	26.9	22.4	10.5	1990	440 GLE: 4960
8	26.8	22.3	10.5	1978	343: 4938
9	26.5	22.1	10.7	1965	131: 4907
10	26.4	22.0	10.7	1990	460 GLi: 4961
				1990	460 Turbo: 4962
11	26.0	21.6	10.9	1977	343: 4933
				1958	Amazon: 4897
12	25.3	21.1	11.2	1962	122: 4901
13	25.0	20.8	11.3	1984	740 GLT: 4948
14	24.9	20.7	11.3	1962	P1800: 4903
15	24.0	20.0	11.8	1966	1800S: 4908
16	23.9	19.9	11.8	1982	360 GLT: 4943
17	23.8	19.8	11.9	1971	144 Grand Luxe: 4918
18	23.5	19.6	12.0	1963	144 de Luxe: 4922
19	23.1	19.2	12.2	1982	240 GL: 4942
20	22.7	18.9	12.4	1967	144S: 4909
21	22.5	18.7	12.6	1989	440 Turbo: 4957
22	22.3	18.6	12.7	1969	144S: 4913
23	21.8	18.2	13.0	1987	740 Turbo: 4955
24	21.3	17.7	13.3	1975	244 GL: 4928
25	21.2	17.7	13.3	1991	940 SE Turbo: 4966
26	21.1	17.6	13.4	1990	740 GLT 16v Estate: 4963
27	20.7	17.2	13.6	1968	145S Estate: 4910
28	20.3	16.9	13.9	1982	760 GLE: 4944
29	19.8	16.5	14.3	1985	760 Turbo Estate: 4952
30	19.6	16.3	14.4	1978	265 GLE Estate: 4937
31	19.5	16.2	14.5	1987	760 GLE: 4956
32	18.9	15.7	14.9	1971	145E Estate: 4919
33	18.7	15.6	15.1	1981	265 GLE: 4941
34	18.6	15.5	15.2	1975	264 GL: 4929
35	18.5	15.4	15.3	1983	760 Turbo: 4947
36	18.4	15.3	15.4	1991	960 24v: 4968
37	17.9	14.9	15.8	1970	164 Automatic: 4915
38	17.5	14.6	16.1	1963	164E: 4924

Wartburg

1	27.7	23.1	10.2	1963	Knight: 4971
2	24.7	20.6	11.4	1967	Knight: 4970

Warwick

1	23.8	19.8	11.9	1961	GT: 4972

Westfield

1	20.0	16.7	14.1	1991	SEight: 4973

Wolseley

1	35.3	29.4	8.0	1963	Hornet: 4998
2	34.5	28.7	8.2	1958	1500: 4993
3	29.4	24.5	9.6	1957	15/50: 4991
4	27.9	23.2	10.1	1959	15/60: 4994
5	26.5	22.1	10.7	1965	1100: 4999
6	24.2	20.2	11.7	1962	16/60 Automatic: 4996
7	24.0	20.0	11.8	1953	4/44: 4989
8	23.6	19.7	12.0	1957	6/90: 4992
9	23.5	19.6	12.0	1969	18/85 Mk II: 5001
10	21.9	18.2	12.9	1967	18/85: 5000
11	21.4	17.8	13.2	1955	6/90: 4990
12	19.4	16.2	14.6	1962	6/110: 4997
13	18.1	15.1	15.6	1952	6/80: 4988
14	17.2	14.3	16.4	1959	6/99: 4995

Yugo

1	34.7	28.9	8.1	1987	45 GLS: 5003
2	31.1	25.9	9.1	1988	65A GLX: 5004
3	28.1	23.4	10.1	1990	Sana 1.4: 5005

Zastava

1	31.1	25.9	9.1	1981	1300 ZLX-E: 5006

Total:2,161

Road & Track 'normal' or 'average' figures from 1947.

Acura

	mpg	mpg US	L/ 100km		
1	32.3	26.9	8.7	1990	Integra GS: 34
2	30.0	25.0	9.4	1989	Integra LS: 32
				1988	Integra LS Special Edition: 31
3	29.4	24.5	9.6	1986	Integra RS: 28
4	27.6	23.0	10.2	1990	NSX: 36
5	27.0	22.5	10.5	1987	Integra LS: 30
6	24.6	20.5	11.5	1986	Legend: 29
7	23.4	19.5	12.1	1990	Legend Coupe: 35
				1989	Legend Coupe L: 33
8	22.8	19.0	12.4	1991	Legend LS: 37

Alfa Romeo

	mpg	mpg US	L/ 100km		
1	33.0	27.5	8.6	1977	Spider: 99
2	31.2	26.0	9.0	1982	Spider Veloce 2000: 111
3	30.6	25.5	9.2	1980	Spider: 107
4	29.4	24.5	9.6	1984	GTV6: 114
5	28.8	24.0	9.8	1976	Alfetta GT: 92
				1967	Duetto Spider: 67
6	28.6	23.8	9.9	1972	2000 GTV Injection: 80
				1985	Graduate: 121
7	28.3	23.6	10.0	1971	1750 Spider Veloce: 76
8	28.1	23.4	10.1	1991	Spider Veloce: 147
9	27.6	23.0	10.2	1990	164S: 143
10	27.0	22.5	10.5	1984	Spider: 115
				1988	Spider: 136
				1982	Spider Veloce: 110
				1979	Sport Sedan Automatic: 105
11	26.5	22.1	10.6	1991	164L: 146
12	26.3	21.9	10.7	1986	GTV6: 126
13	26.2	21.8	10.8	1986	Milano Platinum: 127
14	25.8	21.5	10.9	1969	1750 Spider: 74
15	25.2	21.0	11.2	1972	Alfasud: 81
				1987	Milano Verde 3.0: 133
				1986	Spider Quadrifoglio: 128
				1978	Sport Sedan: 103
				1979	Sprint Veloce: 106
16	24.6	20.5	11.5	1963	Alfetta: 85
17	24.5	20.4	11.5	1969	1750 Berlina: 73
18	24.0	20.0	11.8	1972	1750 Berlina: 77
				1989	Milano 3.0: 140
19	22.2	18.5	12.7	1985	GTV Callaway Twin Turbo: 122
20	6.0	5.0	47.0	1972	1750 GTV TransAm: 78

AMC

	mpg	mpg US	L/ 100km		
1	23.4	19.5	12.1	1977	Gremlin 2-litre: 204
2	23.2	19.3	12.2	1970	Hornet 3.8-litre: 196
3	21.0	17.5	13.4	1977	Pacer Wagon: 205
4	20.4	17.0	13.8	1968	Ambassador: 188
5	20.2	16.8	14.0	1970	Gremlin: 195
6	19.6	16.3	14.4	1970	Hornet 4.9-litre: 197
7	19.2	16.0	14.7	1963	Hornet Hatchback: 199
				1975	Pacer: 202
				1974	Sportabout: 201
8	16.1	13.4	17.6	1970	Javelin 390: 198
9	15.6	13.0	18.1	1980	Eagle: 206
				1974	Matador X: 200

Aston Martin

	mpg	mpg US	L/ 100km		
1	18.1	15.1	15.6	1958	Mk III: 236
2	15.6	13.0	18.1	1984	Vantage: 255
				1983	Volante: 253
3	15.0	12.5	18.8	1982	Lagonda: 251
4	14.4	12.0	19.6	1984	Lagonda: 254
5	11.4	9.5	24.8	1977	V8 Coupe: 247

Audi

	mpg	mpg US	L/ 100km		
1	36.0	30.0	7.8	1980	5000 S Diesel: 284
2	32.4	27.0	8.7	1963	Fox: 270
3	31.8	26.5	8.9	1980	4000: 283
4	30.0	25.0	9.4	1981	4000 Automatic: 286
5	29.4	24.5	9.6	1986	5000 S: 311
6	29.2	24.3	9.7	1970	100 LS: 265
				1991	90 Quattro 20v: 336
7	27.0	22.5	10.5	1981	Coupe: 288
8	26.4	22.0	10.7	1986	Coupe GT: 314
9	25.2	21.0	11.2	1984	4000 S Quattro: 298
				1983	5000 S: 294
				1989	90: 324
				1988	90 Quattro: 322
10	24.6	20.5	11.5	1984	5000 S Avant: 299
11	24.0	20.0	11.8	1963	100 LS: 268
				1978	5000: 280
				1985	5000 S Turbo Quattro: 305
				1984	Coupe GT: 302
12	23.4	19.5	12.1	1991	200 Quattro: 334
13	21.6	18.0	13.1	1984	5000 S Turbo: 300
				1990	90 Quattro: 329
14	21.0	17.5	13.4	1982	Quattro: 292
15	20.4	17.0	13.8	1981	5000 Turbo: 287
16	19.2	16.0	14.7	1991	V8 Quattro: 338

Austin

	mpg	mpg US	L/ 100km		
1	30.0	25.0	9.4	1951	A40 Sport: 365
2	28.8	24.0	9.8	1963	Marina GT: 407

Avanti

	mpg	mpg US	L/ 100km		
1	16.8	14.0	16.8	1984	II: 460

Bentley

	mpg	mpg US	L/ 100km		
1	13.8	11.5	20.5	1991	Turbo R: 483

Bitter

	mpg	mpg US	L/ 100km		
1	24.6	20.5	11.5	1984	SC: 492
2	16.8	14.0	16.8	1986	SC: 493

BMW

	mpg	mpg US	L/ 100km		
1	33.6	28.0	8.4	1986	325 ES: 578
				1984	325E: 569
2	31.2	26.0	9.0	1983	318i: 563
				1980	320i: 554
3	30.6	25.5	9.2	1986	524 TD: 581
4	30.0	25.0	9.4	1967	1600-2: 513
5	28.8	24.0	9.8	1982	528e: 560
6	28.2	23.5	10.0	1974	2002 Tii: 533
7	27.3	22.7	10.4	1972	2002 Tii: 527
8	26.4	22.0	10.7	1992	325i: 623
				1990	325i Convertible: 610
				1979	528i: 551
9	25.8	21.5	10.9	1977	320i: 542
10	25.2	21.0	11.2	1967	2000 TiLux: 514
11	24.6	20.5	11.5	1981	323i Hardy & Beck: 557
				1989	325i S: 599
				1988	325i S: 591
				1984	633 CSi: 570
				1991	M3 Sport Evolution: 621
12	24.0	20.0	11.8	1988	325i X: 592
				1978	333i Alpina: 548
				1991	525i: 617
13	23.4	19.5	12.1	1970	2002 Automatic: 520
14	22.8	19.0	12.4	1970	2800 CS: 521
				1975	525: 538
				1975	530i: 539
				1983	533i: 566
				1980	633 CSi: 555
				1978	733i: 550
15	22.2	18.5	12.7	1978	320i Alpina: 546
				1989	535i Automatic: 601
16	21.6	18.0	13.1	1977	630 CSi: 544
				1988	735i: 595
				1982	745i: 562
				1971	Bavaria: 526
17	21.0	17.5	13.4	1986	635 CSi: 583
18	20.4	17.0	13.8	1963	3.0 CS: 529
				1985	327S Hardy & Beck: 574
				1989	535i: 600
				1986	535i: 582
				1986	735i: 584
				1963	Bavaria: 532
19	19.8	16.5	14.3	1985	M635 CSi Hardy & Beck: 577
20	19.2	16.0	14.7	1988	750i L: 596
21	18.6	15.5	15.2	1991	M5: 622
22	15.6	13.0	18.1	1980	M1: 556
23	15.0	12.5	18.8	1988	M6: 597
24	4.8	4.0	58.8	1972	2002 TransAm: 528

Bricklin

	mpg	mpg US	L/ 100km		
1	19.2	16.0	14.7	1975	SV-1: 637

Buick

	mpg	mpg US	L/ 100km		
1	33.0	27.5	8.6	1976	Opel by Isuzu: 689
2	25.2	21.0	11.2	1976	Skyhawk: 690
				1975	Skylark: 688
3	24.6	20.5	11.5	1983	Century T-type: 693
				1988	Regal Custom: 696
4	22.8	19.0	12.4	1986	Electra T-type: 694
5	19.8	16.5	14.3	1988	Reatta: 695
				1991	Reatta Convertible: 698
6	18.0	15.0	15.7	1979	Riviera S-type: 692

Cadillac

1	29.1	24.2	9.7	1990	Eldorado Touring Coupe: 718
2	27.0	22.5	10.5	1985	Cimarron: 714
3	26.9	22.4	10.5	1988	Allante: 715
4	26.4	22.0	10.7	1982	Cimarron: 713
				1978	Seville Diesel: 711
5	22.2	18.5	12.7	1991	Seville Touring Sedan: 720
6	21.0	17.5	13.4	1981	Seville Diesel: 712
7	19.9	16.6	14.2	1991	Allante: 719
8	19.8	16.5	14.3	1976	Seville: 710

Chevrolet

1	52.8	44.0	5.3	1984	Sprint: 895
2	48.6	40.5	5.8	1986	Sprint: 904
3	45.0	37.5	6.3	1988	Sprint: 924
4	36.0	30.0	7.8	1986	Nova CL: 903
5	33.0	27.5	8.6	1976	Chevette Rally 1.6: 868
6	31.8	26.5	8.9	1988	Nova Twin Cam: 923
7	31.2	26.0	9.0	1963	Vega: 860
8	30.0	25.0	9.4	1991	Baretta GTZ: 946
				1988	Cavalier Z24 Convertible: 915
9	28.8	24.0	9.8	1983	Cavalier CS: 889
				1979	Citation X11: 880
10	27.0	22.5	10.5	1990	Lumina APV: 945
				1963	Vega Station Wagon: 861
11	26.4	22.0	10.7	1989	Baretta GTU: 925
				1986	Cavalier Z24: 898
12	25.8	21.5	10.9	1991	Lumina Z34: 957
13	25.3	21.1	11.1	1990	Beretta GTZ: 936
14	25.2	21.0	11.2	1988	Camaro: 911
				1980	Citation: 883
				1974	Vega: 863
15	24.6	20.5	11.5	1976	Cosworth Vega: 871
				1971	Vega: 852
16	24.0	20.0	11.8	1990	Beretta GT: 935
				1987	Beretta GT: 905
17	23.4	19.5	12.1	1983	Citation X11 HO: 890
				1989	Corvette L98: 933
18	23.2	19.3	12.2	1986	Celebrity CL Eurosport: 899
				1988	Corvette Convertible: 919
19	23.1	19.2	12.3	1990	Cavalier Z24: 939
20	22.8	19.0	12.4	1986	Corvette Z51: 902
21	22.3	18.6	12.6	1990	Camaro IROC-Z Convertible: 937
				1991	Camaro Z/28 Convertible: 947
				1971	Vega L11: 854
22	21.7	18.1	13.0	1991	Corvette ZR-1: 953
23	21.6	18.0	13.1	1992	Camaro Z28: 958
				1983	Corvette: 891
				1990	Corvette Callaway: 940
24	21.5	17.9	13.1	1989	Corvette: 930
25	21.0	17.5	13.4	1983	Camaro: 887
				1988	Corvette: 916
				1987	Corvette: 908
				1988	Corvette Z51: 922
26	20.9	17.4	13.5	1990	Corvette L98: 944
27	20.4	17.0	13.8	1987	Corvette Convertible: 910
				1992	Corvette LT1: 959
				1976	Monza 2+2 V8: 873
				1975	Monza 2+2 V8: 864
28	20.1	16.7	14.1	1987	Camaro IROC-Z: 906
29	19.2	16.0	14.7	1984	Camaro: 892
				1985	Camaro IROC-Z: 896
				1989	Camaro IROC-Z: 927
				1988	Camaro IROC-Z 5.7: 913
				1989	Camaro IROC-Z Automatic: 928
				1990	Camaro Z/28: 938
				1982	Camaro Z/28: 885
				1983	Camaro Z/28: 888
				1986	Corvette: 900
				1982	Corvette: 886
				1991	Corvette Callaway Twin Turbo: 950
30	18.6	15.5	15.2	1988	Camaro IROC-Z 5.0: 912
				1969	Corvette ZQ3: 838
31	18.1	15.1	15.6	1972	Camaro Budget: 855
32	18.0	15.0	15.7	1976	Camaro: 867
				1979	Corvette: 881
				1977	Corvette Sting Ray: 875
				1978	Malibu: 879
				1976	Monza: 872
33	17.4	14.5	16.2	1978	Camaro Z/28: 878
				1980	Corvette: 884
				1963	Corvette LT-1: 858
34	17.3	14.4	16.3	1970	Camaro: 840
35	17.2	14.3	16.4	1969	Corvette Stingray: 837
36	16.9	14.1	16.7	1969	Corvette L46: 831
37	16.8	14.0	16.8	1976	Corvette: 869
				1963	Monte Carlo: 859
38	16.3	13.6	17.3	1972	Camaro Luxury: 856
				1970	Chevelle SS396: 843
39	16.2	13.5	17.4	1974	Corvette: 862
				1965	Corvette Injection: 797
				1975	Nova LN: 865
40	15.9	13.2	17.8	1969	Corvette L36: 830
				1970	Nova SS350: 848
41	15.7	13.1	18.0	1969	Corvette L68: 832
42	15.6	13.0	18.1	1967	Camaro: 804
43	15.5	12.9	18.2	1969	Corvette L71/89: 834
44	15.4	12.8	18.4	1969	Corvette LT-1: 836
				1970	Monte Carlo: 847
45	14.8	12.3	19.1	1972	Camaro Z/28: 857
46	14.4	12.0	19.6	1979	Corvette Automatic: 882
47	14.2	11.8	19.9	1970	Camaro Z/28: 841
48	13.6	11.3	20.8	1968	Corvette L88: 820
				1969	Corvette L88: 835
49	13.2	11.0	21.4	1970	Corvette LT-1: 845
50	12.5	10.4	22.6	1969	Corvette L71: 833
51	12.0	10.0	23.5	1969	Camaro Z/28: 825
				1969	Corvette 435hp: 829
				1988	Corvette Bakeracing SCCA Escort: 917
				1988	Corvette Morrison/Baker Nelson Ledges: 921
52	10.8	9.0	26.1	1970	Corvette 454: 844
53	6.0	5.0	47.0	1976	Monza Mike Keyser: 874
54	5.4	4.5	52.3	1978	Camaro IROC: 877
55	4.8	4.0	58.8	1976	Corvette Greenwood: 870

Chrysler

1	30.6	25.5	9.2	1985	Le Baron GTS: 1004
2	27.6	23.0	10.2	1984	Laser XE: 1003
3	25.2	21.0	11.2	1986	Laser XT: 1005
4	24.6	20.5	11.5	1987	Le Baron Coupe: 1006
5	24.0	20.0	11.8	1988	Conquest TSi: 1007
				1989	TC by Maserati: 1008
6	15.5	12.9	18.2	1970	300-H: 989
7	15.0	12.5	18.8	1951	Saratoga Club Coupe: 970

Citroen

1	51.0	42.5	5.5	1985	2CV6 Charleston: 1065
2	25.2	21.0	11.2	1972	GS: 1042
3	24.0	20.0	11.8	1968	DS21 Safari: 1036
4	19.1	15.9	14.8	1972	SM: 1043

Consulier

1	21.9	18.2	12.9	1990	GTP LX: 1096

Daihatsu

1	43.8	36.5	6.4	1988	Charade CLX: 1126
2	35.4	29.5	8.0	1989	Charade CLS: 1129

Datsun

1	39.0	32.5	7.2	1976	F10: 1199
2	37.8	31.5	7.5	1979	210: 1209
3	37.2	31.0	7.6	1979	310 Coupe: 1214
4	36.6	30.5	7.7	1976	B210: 1197
5	33.6	28.0	8.4	1971	1200 Coupe: 1173
				1980	510: 1222
6	33.0	27.5	8.6	1974	B210: 1189
7	32.4	27.0	8.7	1975	B210: 1194
8	30.4	25.3	9.3	1971	510: 1177
9	30.0	25.0	9.4	1980	200SX: 1217
				1978	510: 1206
10	29.4	24.5	9.6	1983	200SX: 1228
				1963	610 1800: 1183
11	28.8	24.0	9.8	1982	280ZX: 1225
12	28.2	23.5	10.0	1977	200SX: 1201
13	27.6	23.0	10.2	1970	1600 Pickup: 1170
				1979	810 Coupe: 1215
				1977	810 Sedan: 1203
14	26.4	22.0	10.7	1979	280ZX: 1211
				1980	280ZX: 1218
				1983	280ZX: 1229
				1963	610 Station Wagon: 1184
				1974	710: 1188
15	25.2	21.0	11.2	1970	240Z: 1171
				1980	280ZX Automatic: 1219
16	24.6	20.5	11.5	1983	280ZX Turbo: 1231
17	24.0	20.0	11.8	1974	260Z: 1186
				1981	280ZX Turbo: 1223
18	23.4	19.5	12.1	1975	280Z: 1192
19	22.8	19.0	12.4	1963	240Z: 1182
				1971	240Z Automatic: 1176
				1981	810 Maxima: 1224
20	18.6	15.5	15.2	1979	280ZX Automatic: 1213
21	13.2	11.0	21.4	1978	280Z Scarab: 1205
22	10.8	9.0	26.1	1976	B210 Electramotive: 1198
23	8.4	7.0	33.6	1980	280ZX Electramotive: 1220
				1972	510 TransAm: 1180
24	7.8	6.5	36.2	1980	280ZX Sharp: 1221
25	7.2	6.0	39.2	1975	240Z Sharp: 1190
26	4.8	4.0	58.8	1983	280ZX Electramotive: 1230

De Lorean

1	23.4	19.5	12.1	1982	DMC 2.8-litre Coupe: 1233

De Tomaso

1	19.8	16.5	14.3	1969	Mangusta: 1235
2	16.6	13.8	17.0	1971	Pantera: 1236
3	14.4	12.0	19.6	1974	Pantera GTS: 1239
4	12.6	10.5	22.4	1963	Pantera: 1238
				1974	Pantera L: 1240
5	12.0	10.0	23.5	1984	Pantera GT5: 1241

Dodge

1	38.4	32.0	7.4	1979	Colt Hatchback: 1323
2	37.8	31.5	7.5	1977	Colt Lancer: 1322
3	32.4	27.0	8.7	1981	Aires Wagon: 1324
				1986	Colt Turbo: 1333
4	32.2	26.8	8.8	1971	Colt: 1316
5	31.2	26.0	9.0	1984	Colt Vista: 1329
6	30.6	25.5	9.2	1963	Colt Station Wagon: 1319
				1985	Omni GLH: 1332
7	27.6	23.0	10.2	1990	Daytona Shelby: 1344
				1988	Daytona Shelby Z: 1336
8	26.4	22.0	10.7	1984	Conquest: 1330
				1983	Shelby Charger: 1328
9	26.3	21.9	10.7	1990	Shadow ES VNT: 1345
10	25.8	21.5	10.9	1982	Challenger: 1325
				1988	Lancer Shelby: 1337
				1988	Shelby CSX: 1338
				1991	Spirit R/T: 1346
11	25.2	21.0	11.2	1982	Charger 2.2: 1326
				1986	Omni GLH: 1334
12	24.6	20.5	11.5	1990	Daytona ES: 1343
				1989	Shelby CSX: 1341
13	24.1	20.1	11.7	1989	Shelby CSX VNT: 1342
14	24.0	20.0	11.8	1974	Colt GT 2-litre: 1320
				1986	Shelby GLH-S: 1335
15	22.8	19.0	12.4	1989	Shadow ES Turbo: 1340
16	21.6	18.0	13.1	1975	Colt GT: 1321
				1991	Stealth R/T Turbo: 1347
17	20.3	16.9	13.9	1989	Daytona Shelby: 1339
18	18.6	15.5	15.2	1983	600ES: 1327
19	16.8	14.0	16.8	1971	Pickup Power Wagon: 1317
20	13.9	11.6	20.3	1970	Charger R/T: 1315
21	12.9	10.7	22.0	1970	Challenger R/T: 1314

Eagle

1	22.8	19.0	12.4	1988	Premier ES: 1354
2	19.8	16.5	14.3	1990	Talon: 1355
				1991	Talon TSi 4WD: 1357

Ferrari

1	24.0	20.0	11.8	1952	212 Touring: 1372
2	19.8	16.5	14.3	1987	328 GTS: 1431
3	19.2	16.0	14.7	1983	308 GTBi Quattrovalvole: 1419
				1991	348tb: 1449
				1989	Mondial 3.2 Cabriolet: 1440
				1988	Mondial Cabriolet: 1436
				1987	Mondial Cabriolet 3.2: 1433
4	18.6	15.5	15.2	1974	246 GTS Dino: 1401
5	18.0	15.0	15.7	1978	308 GTS: 1412
				1991	Mondial t Cabriolet: 1453
6	17.4	14.5	16.2	1963	250 GT Berlinetta Lusso: 1388
7	16.8	14.0	16.8	1980	308 GT4 Dino: 1414
8	16.2	13.5	17.4	1984	288 GTO: 1421
				1975	308 Dino GT4: 1405
				1976	308 GT4 Dino: 1408
				1984	Mondial Cabriolet Quattrovalvole: 1424
9	15.6	13.0	18.1	1977	308 GTB: 1411
				1985	365 GTB Goldsmith: 1425
				1991	F40: 1450
				1984	GTO: 1423
				1982	Mondial 8: 1418
10	15.3	12.7	18.5	1972	246 GT Dino: 1399
11	15.1	12.6	18.7	1972	365 GTC4: 1400
12	15.0	12.5	18.8	1974	308 GT4 Dino: 1402
13	14.4	12.0	19.6	1970	365 GTB/4 Daytona: 1396
				1975	512 BB: 1407
				1988	Testa Rossa: 1437
				1985	Testa Rossa: 1426
14	13.8	11.5	20.5	1981	308 GTSi: 1415
				1983	308 GTSi Targa: 1420
15	12.6	10.5	22.4	1974	365 GTB/4 Daytona: 1404
16	12.0	10.0	23.5	1969	365 GTS 2+2: 1394
				1984	512 BBi: 1422
17	10.8	9.0	26.1	1987	412: 1432
18	6.6	5.5	42.8	1974	365 GTB/4 Competitione: 1403

Fiat

1	41.6	34.6	6.8	1971	128: 1529
2	37.2	31.0	7.6	1970	850 Racer: 1524
3	36.6	30.5	7.7	1963	128 Station Wagon: 1540
				1979	X1/9 1300: 1569
4	36.0	30.0	7.8	1979	Strada: 1566
				1974	X1/9: 1543
5	34.8	29.0	8.1	1972	128 SL 1300 Coupe: 1532
6	33.6	28.0	8.4	1968	850 Idromatic: 1512
7	32.4	27.0	8.7	1982	X1/9: 1579
				1984	X1/9: 1587
8	31.2	26.0	9.0	1968	124 Station Wagon: 1511
				1982	Spider 2000: 1576
9	30.4	25.3	9.3	1985	X1/9: 1590
10	30.0	25.0	9.4	1963	124 Station Wagon: 1537
				1952	1400: 1463
				1983	Spider 2000: 1580
11	29.4	24.5	9.6	1975	124 Sport Coupe 1800: 1545
				1975	128: 1546
12	29.2	24.3	9.7	1970	124 Spider: 1522
13	28.2	23.5	10.0	1979	124 Sports Spider: 1563
				1969	Abarth 1300: 1519
				1978	Super Brava: 1561
				1988	X1/9: 1599
				1989	X1/9: 1601
14	27.9	23.2	10.1	1963	124 Spider 1600: 1535
				1971	124 Spider 1600: 1526
15	27.6	23.0	10.2	1976	124 Sport Spider: 1551
				1981	Brava: 1573
16	26.9	22.4	10.5	1970	124 Special: 1521
17	26.5	22.1	10.6	1971	124 Sport Coupe: 1527
18	26.4	22.0	10.7	1975	124 Special TC: 1544
				1976	124 Spider: 1550
				1982	Spider Turbo: 1577
19	25.8	21.5	10.9	1976	131: 1554
20	25.2	21.0	11.2	1979	124 Spider: 1562
21	14.4	12.0	19.6	1980	Brava Abarth Rally: 1571

Fiberfab

1	18.0	15.0	15.7	1969	Jamaican Buick V8: 1607

Ford

1	44.4	37.0	6.4	1987	Festiva L: 1919
2	42.0	35.0	6.7	1977	Fiesta Ghia: 1855
3	35.1	29.2	8.1	1986	Escort L: 1910
4	34.2	28.5	8.3	1985	Escort GL: 1900
5	33.6	28.0	8.4	1991	Escort GT: 1963
6	33.0	27.5	8.6	1980	Fiesta: 1869
7	32.4	27.0	8.7	1979	Fiesta Healey: 1864
8	30.6	25.5	9.2	1971	Capri 2000: 1791
9	30.0	25.0	9.4	1952	Customline 6: 1626
				1981	Escort: 1873
10	29.3	24.4	9.6	1970	Capri 1600: 1781
11	28.8	24.0	9.8	1972	Capri 2600 V6: 1803
				1984	Tempo GLX: 1899
12	28.1	23.4	10.1	1990	Probe GT: 1956
13	27.1	22.6	10.4	1971	Pinto 1600: 1799
14	27.0	22.5	10.5	1991	Crown Victoria LX: 1959
				1971	Pinto 2-litre: 1800
15	26.4	22.0	10.7	1969	Cortina 1600 GT: 1770
				1968	Cortina Station Wagon: 1755
				1971	Pinto: 1798
				1989	Taurus SHO: 1946
				1991	Taurus SHO: 1971
16	25.8	21.5	10.9	1963	Pinto Station Wagon: 1820
17	25.2	21.0	11.2	1984	Mustang SVO: 1897
				1990	Probe LX: 1957
18	24.6	20.5	11.5	1969	Maverick: 1774
				1991	Probe GT: 1969
19	24.0	20.0	11.8	1974	Capri 2800 V6: 1821
				1988	Probe GT: 1933
20	23.4	19.5	12.1	1976	Capri II 2.8 V6: 1839
				1972	Capri RS2600: 1805
				1979	Mustang Turbo: 1867
				1980	Mustang Turbo: 1870
21	22.8	19.0	12.4	1992	Mustang LX: 1975
22	22.2	18.5	12.7	1986	Aerostar XLT: 1908
				1963	Pinto Pangra: 1819
23	21.6	18.0	13.1	1980	Fairmont: 1868
24	21.0	17.5	13.4	1988	Taurus 3.8: 1935
				1992	Taurus LX: 1976
25	20.4	17.0	13.8	1976	Capri V6 Black Gold: 1840
				1982	Mustang 4.2: 1880
				1990	Mustang LX 5.0L: 1955
				1984	Sierra XR4i: 1898
				1991	Thunderbird LX: 1972
				1989	Thunderbird Super Coupe: 1947
				1987	Thunderbird Turbo Coupe: 1927
26	19.8	16.5	14.3	1974	Mustang II Mach I: 1827
27	19.7	16.4	14.3	1987	Mustang LX 5.0: 1924
28	19.2	16.0	14.7	1974	Granada GXL: 1825
				1988	Mustang GT: 1930
				1984	Mustang GT 5.0: 1896
29	18.6	15.5	15.2	1985	Mustang GT: 1905
				1982	Mustang GT 5.0: 1881
				1983	Mustang GT 5.0: 1888
				1986	Mustang Saleen: 1914
30	18.3	15.2	15.5	1956	Interceptor Coupe: 1639
31	18.0	15.0	15.7	1970	Capri Plus 50: 1782
32	17.2	14.3	16.4	1990	Mustang GT Convertible: 1954
33	16.8	14.0	16.8	1967	Mustang: 1747
				1976	Mustang II: 1847
34	15.6	13.0	18.1	1976	Mustang II V8: 1848

35	15.4	12.8	18.4	1970	Torino GT: 1788
36	15.0	12.5	18.8	1975	Granada 5-litre: 1835
37	13.0	10.8	21.8	1972	LTD: 1809
38	12.2	10.2	23.1	1969	Fairlane Cobra: 1772
39	12.0	10.0	23.5	1970	Mustang Boss 302: 1787
40	6.0	5.0	47.0	1976	Cobra II Kemp: 1841
41	4.8	4.0	58.8	1971	Mustang TransAm: 1796

Geo

1	32.4	27.0	8.7	1991	Storm GSi: 1994

GMC

1	16.8	14.0	16.8	1985	Safari Cargo Mover: 2003

Hillman

1	25.2	21.0	11.2	1951	Minx Sedan: 2037

Honda

1	51.6	43.0	5.5	1972	600 Coupe: 2091
2	43.8	36.5	6.4	1975	Civic CVCC: 2094
3	42.0	35.0	6.7	1983	CRX 1.5: 2111
				1985	CRX Si: 2124
4	39.2	32.6	7.2	1986	Civic Hatchback: 2127
5	38.4	32.0	7.4	1976	Accord: 2095
6	38.0	31.6	7.4	1970	600: 2090
7	37.8	31.5	7.5	1986	CRX Si: 2129
8	37.2	31.0	7.6	1988	CRX Si: 2141
9	36.0	30.0	7.8	1979	Accord 4-door: 2100
				1963	Civic: 2092
10	34.8	29.0	8.1	1988	CRX Si Jackson: 2142
				1981	Prelude: 2107
11	34.2	28.5	8.3	1989	Civic Si: 2145
12	33.6	28.0	8.4	1980	Civic: 2102
				1985	Civic S: 2121
				1985	Civic Wagon: 2123
				1985	Prelude: 2125
13	33.0	27.5	8.6	1978	Accord: 2098
				1980	Civic GL 1500: 2103
14	32.4	27.0	8.7	1986	CRX Si Jackson Turbo: 2130
15	31.8	26.5	8.9	1982	Accord: 2109
				1981	Civic 4-door Sedan: 2106
16	31.2	26.0	9.0	1986	Prelude 2.0 Si: 2134
17	30.6	25.5	9.2	1984	Prelude: 2116
18	29.4	24.5	9.6	1981	Accord: 2105
				1985	Accord SEi: 2119
19	28.8	24.0	9.8	1986	Accord LXi: 2126
				1991	Prelude Si: 2157
				1992	Prelude Si 4WS: 2160
20	28.2	23.5	10.0	1982	Accord LX: 2110
				1980	Prelude: 2104
21	26.4	22.0	10.7	1987	Prelude 2.0 Si: 2138
22	24.6	20.5	11.5	1989	Prelude Si 4WS: 2148

Hyundai

1	37.8	31.5	7.5	1986	Excel GLS: 2223
2	35.9	29.9	7.9	1986	Excel GL: 2222

Infiniti

1	28.8	24.0	9.8	1991	G20: 2232
2	24.0	20.0	11.8	1990	M30: 2230
3	20.7	17.2	13.7	1990	Q45: 2231

International

1	9.4	7.8	30.2	1971	Pickup 4WD 1210 Camper Special: 2237
2	9.0	7.5	31.4	1971	Travelall 1210: 2239

Iso

1	18.1	15.1	15.6	1969	Rivolta S4: 2249

Isuzu

1	45.6	38.0	6.2	1983	I-Mark LS: 2252
2	42.6	35.5	6.6	1986	I-Mark: 2254
3	34.8	29.0	8.1	1984	Impulse: 2253
				1986	Impulse Sports Coupe: 2255
4	31.2	26.0	9.0	1986	Impulse Turbo: 2256
5	30.6	25.5	9.2	1988	Impulse Turbo: 2259
6	29.9	24.9	9.4	1991	Impulse RS: 2261
7	28.8	24.0	9.8	1990	Impulse XS: 2260
8	27.6	23.0	10.2	1988	I-Mark RS Turbo: 2258

Jaguar

1	22.8	19.0	12.4	1951	XK120: 2275
2	22.5	18.7	12.6	1990	XJS: 2365
				1991	XJS Convertible: 2372
3	21.6	18.0	13.1	1990	XJ6 Vanden Plas: 2362
4	21.0	17.5	13.4	1987	XJ6: 2352
				1984	XJ6 Vanden Plas: 2344
				1979	XJ6L: 2337
5	19.1	15.9	14.8	1969	XKE Coupe: 2317
6	18.3	15.2	15.5	1972	XJ6: 2322
				1953	XK120M: 2281
7	18.0	15.0	15.7	1981	XJS: 2340
8	17.4	14.5	16.2	1972	XKE V12: 2323
9	16.8	14.0	16.8	1988	XJS: 2355
10	16.3	13.6	17.3	1970	XJ6: 2318
11	16.2	13.5	17.4	1976	XJ12C: 2329
				1980	XJ6 Series III: 2339
				1983	XJS: 2343
				1984	XJS HE: 2346
				1986	XJSC HE: 2351
12	15.9	13.2	17.8	1986	XJS: 2349
13	15.6	13.0	18.1	1978	XJ12L: 2334
				1989	XJS V12 Convertible: 2361
				1986	XJSC: 2350
14	14.4	12.0	19.6	1974	XKE V12: 2325
15	13.8	11.5	20.5	1975	XJ12L: 2326
				1979	XJS: 2338
16	12.4	10.3	22.8	1972	XJ12: 2321
17	4.8	4.0	58.8	1977	XJS Tullius: 2333

Jeep

1	19.2	16.0	14.7	1971	CJ-5: 2374
2	18.0	15.0	15.7	1972	CJ-5 V8: 2379
3	16.8	14.0	16.8	1971	Wagoneer: 2377
4	15.6	13.0	18.1	1971	Commando: 2375
5	14.7	12.2	19.3	1971	Wagoneer 1414C: 2378
6	14.4	12.0	19.6	1972	Commando: 2380
				1974	Wagoneer: 2382
7	13.2	11.0	21.4	1971	Gladiator Pickup J-2500 Townside: 2376

Jensen

1	29.4	24.5	9.6	1963	Healey: 2398
2	25.2	21.0	11.2	1977	GT: 2404
3	15.0	12.5	18.8	1976	Interceptor III Convertible: 2403
4	14.9	12.4	19.0	1970	Interceptor II: 2395
5	14.4	12.0	19.6	1971	Interceptor: 2396
6	13.8	11.5	20.5	1974	Interceptor III: 2400
7	8.4	7.0	33.6	1974	Healey Huffaker: 2399

Jowett

1	30.0	25.0	9.4	1953	Jupiter: 2410

Lamborghini

1	16.7	13.9	16.9	1970	Miura S: 2456
2	16.2	13.5	17.4	1988	Jalpa: 2471
3	15.6	13.0	18.1	1976	Urraco: 2463
4	14.4	12.0	19.6	1976	Countach: 2461
				1982	Jalpa: 2467
5	13.8	11.5	20.5	1976	Silhouette 3000: 2462
6	13.2	11.0	21.4	1979	Countach S: 2464
				1991	Diablo: 2475
7	13.1	10.9	21.6	1972	Jarama 400GT: 2457
8	13.0	10.8	21.8	1969	Espada: 2453
9	12.0	10.0	23.5	1989	Countach 25th Anniversary: 2473
				1986	Countach 5000S: 2469
9.0	7.5	31.4	1988	LM129: 2472	

Lancia

1	30.0	25.0	9.4	1979	HPE: 2529
2	28.8	24.0	9.8	1976	Beta Coupe: 2520
3	25.8	21.5	10.9	1976	Beta Sedan: 2521
4	25.2	21.0	11.2	1982	Beta Coupe: 2534
5	24.6	20.5	11.5	1980	Zagato: 2530
6	24.0	20.0	11.8	1977	Gamma: 2525
				1984	Rally: 2537
7	23.4	19.5	12.1	1977	Beta Scorpion: 2524
8	5.6	4.7	50.0	1981	Montecarlo Group 5 Turbo: 2531

Lexus

1	25.2	21.0	11.2	1992	ES300: 2572
2	24.0	20.0	11.8	1991	SC400: 2571

Lincoln

1	19.2	16.0	14.7	1989	Continental Mk VII: 2586
				1990	Continental Mk VII LSC: 2587
				1986	Continental Mk VII LSC: 2585
				1985	Continental Mk VII LSC: 2584
2	12.6	10.5	22.4	1976	Continental Limousine: 2582

Lotus

1	37.2	31.0	7.6	1970	Europa S2: 2606

2	33.0	27.5	8.6	1977	Esprit 16v: 2621
				1963	Europa Special 5-speed: 2616
3	32.7	27.2	8.6	1969	Elan S4 SE: 2604
4	31.2	26.0	9.0	1991	Elan SE: 2641
5	27.6	23.0	10.2	1980	Eclat: 2626
				1979	Elite: 2624
				1977	Sprint: 2622
6	27.3	22.7	10.4	1972	Europa: 2613
7	26.4	22.0	10.7	1972	Elan Sprint: 2612
				1975	Elite: 2617
8	25.0	20.8	11.3	1972	Elan Plus 2S 130: 2611
9	24.0	20.0	11.8	1970	Super 7 Twincam: 2607
10	21.0	17.5	13.4	1983	Esprit Turbo: 2629
11	20.4	17.0	13.8	1989	Esprit Turbo: 2636
12	19.8	16.5	14.3	1990	Esprit Turbo SE: 2640
13	18.6	15.5	15.2	1986	Esprit Turbo: 2630
14	18.0	15.0	15.7	1978	Elite V8: 2623
15	7.2	6.0	39.2	1987	Elan Autocrosser: 2632

Maserati

1	21.6	18.0	13.1	1985	Biturbo: 2672
				1985	Biturbo E: 2674
2	20.4	17.0	13.8	1989	430: 2678
				1974	Merak: 2661
3	18.6	15.5	15.2	1990	228: 2680
				1989	Spyder: 2679
4	18.0	15.0	15.7	1985	Biturbo Automatic: 2673
5	16.8	14.0	16.8	1978	Merak: 2668
6	16.2	13.5	17.4	1988	Biturbo: 2677
7	15.6	13.0	18.1	1970	Indy: 2657
8	14.2	11.8	19.9	1971	Ghibli: 2658
9	13.8	11.5	20.5	1976	Bora: 2664
				1976	Khamsin: 2665
				1979	Khamsin: 2669
10	10.8	9.0	26.1	1983	Quattroporte: 2671

Mazda

1	41.4	34.5	6.8	1977	GLC: 2703
2	39.6	33.0	7.1	1979	GLC Wagon: 2708
3	34.8	29.0	8.1	1979	626 Coupe: 2707
4	32.8	27.3	8.6	1986	323 1.6i: 2730
5	32.4	27.0	8.7	1983	626: 2721
6	31.8	26.5	8.9	1981	GLC: 2717
				1981	GLC Sport: 2718
7	31.2	26.0	9.0	1990	Protege: 2762
8	30.6	25.5	9.2	1989	MX-5 Miata: 2755
9	29.4	24.5	9.6	1986	323 LX: 2731
10	28.8	24.0	9.8	1986	626 GT: 2734
				1992	MX-3 GS: 2773
				1988	MX-6 GT: 2748
11	28.2	23.5	10.0	1980	626: 2712
12	27.7	23.1	10.2	1985	RX-7 GSL: 2728
13	26.4	22.0	10.7	1978	RX-7: 2705
				1980	RX-7: 2714
14	25.8	21.5	10.9	1988	323 GTX: 2742
15	25.2	21.0	11.2	1975	808: 2700
				1989	MPV: 2754
				1983	RX-7: 2723
				1981	RX-7 GSL: 2719
				1988	RX-7 GTU: 2750
16	24.6	20.5	11.5	1976	Cosmo: 2701
17	24.3	20.2	11.6	1971	1800: 2688
18	24.0	20.0	11.8	1988	MX-6: 2747
19	23.3	19.4	12.1	1971	RX-2: 2690
20	23.1	19.2	12.3	1986	RX-7 Turbo: 2737
				1987	RX-7 Turbo: 2740
21	22.8	19.0	12.4	1990	MX-6 GT: 2761
				1989	MX-6 GT 4WS: 2756
				1990	RX-7 Convertible: 2763
				1989	RX-7 GTUs: 2758
				1986	RX-7 GXL: 2736
				1988	RX-7 Turbo: 2751
22	22.2	18.5	12.7	1988	929: 2746
				1984	RX-7: 2724
23	21.6	18.0	13.1	1972	RX-3: 2692
				1963	RX-3 Station Wagon: 2693
				1984	RX-7 GSL SE: 2725
24	21.0	17.5	13.4	1974	RX-4 Coupe: 2698
25	20.4	17.0	13.8	1974	RX-4 Station Wagon: 2699
26	19.8	16.5	14.3	1974	Rotary Pickup: 2697
27	19.2	16.0	14.7	1988	RX-7 Convertible: 2749
				1979	RX-7 GS: 2711
				1990	RX-7 Turbo: 2764
				1991	RX-7 Turbo: 2771
28	18.0	15.0	15.7	1990	MX-5 Miata Millen: 2760
				1971	Rotary: 2689
29	17.4	14.5	16.2	1991	RX-7 Infini IV: 2769
30	7.8	6.5	36.2	1980	RX-7 Racer: 2715

Mercedes-Benz

1	32.4	27.0	8.7	1984	190E: 2876
2	30.5	25.4	9.3	1971	220D: 2833
3	30.4	25.3	9.3	1991	190E 2.3: 2915
4	30.0	25.0	9.4	1978	300SD: 2857
				1981	300TD: 2868
5	29.4	24.5	9.6	1975	300D: 2848
6	28.8	24.0	9.8	1978	300CD: 2856
7	27.6	23.0	10.2	1979	300TD: 2861
8	26.4	22.0	10.7	1985	190E 2.3: 2878
				1986	300E: 2885
				1987	300TD: 2893
9	25.2	21.0	11.2	1986	190E 2.3-16: 2883
10	24.6	20.5	11.5	1989	190E 2.6: 2902
				1985	190E BBS/Callaway Turbo: 2880
				1989	300E: 2906
11	23.4	19.5	12.1	1990	300CE: 2909
12	22.8	19.0	12.4	1983	380SL: 2875
13	21.6	18.0	13.1	1991	190E 2.5-16 Evolution II: 2916
				1981	380SEL: 2869
14	21.0	17.5	13.4	1982	380SL: 2871
15	20.4	17.0	13.8	1977	280E: 2853
16	19.8	16.5	14.3	1953	300 Sedan: 2789
				1976	450SL: 2851
				1984	500SEC: 2877
				1989	560SL: 2907
17	19.2	16.0	14.7	1970	250 Coupe: 2829
				1987	420SEL: 2894
				1980	450SL: 2864
				1991	500SL: 2920
18	19.0	15.8	14.9	1970	280SE 3.5: 2831
19	18.6	15.5	15.2	1969	280SL: 2827
				1963	450SLC: 2843
20	18.3	15.2	15.5	1972	350SL: 2837
21	18.0	15.0	15.7	1975	280S: 2847
				1979	450SL: 2863
				1986	560SL: 2890
22	17.4	14.5	16.2	1963	280: 2839
				1974	450SL: 2846
				1986	560SEC: 2888
23	15.6	13.0	18.1	1963	450SE: 2842
				1977	600SE: 2854
24	13.8	11.5	20.5	1972	280SEL: 2836
				1992	500SEL: 2922

Mercury

1	39.6	33.0	7.1	1987	Tracer: 2959
2	32.4	27.0	8.7	1991	Tracer LTS: 2962
3	30.0	25.0	9.4	1990	Capri XR-2: 2961
4	29.4	24.5	9.6	1981	Lynx Hatchback RS: 2956
5	27.6	23.0	10.2	1981	LN7: 2955
6	26.4	22.0	10.7	1977	Zephyr: 2954
7	23.8	19.8	11.9	1986	Sable LS: 2958
8	23.4	19.5	12.1	1975	Capri II 2.8 V6: 2952
9	22.2	18.5	12.7	1983	Capri: 2957
10	21.0	17.5	13.4	1975	Bobcat 2.3-litre: 2951
11	20.4	17.0	13.8	1989	Cougar XR-7: 2960
12	12.7	10.6	22.2	1970	Cougar Eliminator: 2950

Merkur

1	28.8	24.0	9.8	1988	XR4Ti: 2965
2	27.6	23.0	10.2	1985	XR4Ti: 2963
3	25.2	21.0	11.2	1987	Scorpio: 2964

MG

1	34.8	29.0	8.1	1976	Midget: 3030
2	34.2	28.5	8.3	1979	Midget: 3034
3	33.0	27.5	8.6	1976	Midget Mk IV: 3031
4	30.0	25.0	9.4	1990	B British Motor Heritage: 3041
5	28.8	24.0	9.8	1963	Midget: 3026
6	28.2	23.5	10.0	1970	B Mk II: 3019
7	26.4	22.0	10.7	1976	B: 3029
				1963	B: 3023
				1949	TC: 2978
8	22.2	18.5	12.7	1979	B: 3033
				1980	B: 3035
9	21.4	17.8	13.2	1969	C: 3017

Mitsubishi

1	35.2	29.3	8.0	1986	Mirage: 3089
2	34.8	29.0	8.1	1984	Mirage Turbo: 3080
3	32.4	27.0	8.7	1982	Cordia LS: 3072
4	30.0	25.0	9.4	1988	Mirage Turbo: 3101
5	27.6	23.0	10.2	1989	Eclipse: 3102
6	27.5	22.9	10.3	1989	Galant GS: 3104
7	26.4	22.0	10.7	1984	Cordia Turbo 1.8: 3078
				1983	Tredia Turbo: 3076
8	25.2	21.0	11.2	1988	Cordia Turbo: 3097
				1985	Galant: 3082
				1991	Galant VR-4: 3114
9	24.6	20.5	11.5	1986	Cordia Turbo: 3087
				1983	Starion: 3074
10	24.0	20.0	11.8	1989	Starion ESI-R: 3107
11	23.8	19.8	11.9	1987	Starion ESI-R: 3096
12	22.8	19.0	12.4	1991	Diamante LS: 3113
				1985	Starion ESI: 3086
13	22.2	18.5	12.7	1986	Starion ESI-R: 3090
14	21.6	18.0	13.1	1991	3000GT VR-4: 3111

				1983	Starion Turbo: 3075
15	19.8	16.5	14.3	1989	Eclipse GSX: 3103

Morgan

1	23.4	19.5	12.1	1984	4/4: 3133
				1988	Plus 8: 3135
2	19.2	16.0	14.7	1970	Plus 8: 3130
				1980	Plus 8 Turbo: 3132

Morris

1	25.2	21.0	11.2	1971	Marina 1.8TC: 3180

Nissan

1	39.6	33.0	7.1	1982	Sentra: 3204
2	36.0	30.0	7.8	1991	NX2000: 3249
3	35.9	29.9	7.9	1986	Sentra: 3219
4	34.2	28.5	8.3	1982	Stanza XE: 3205
5	32.4	27.0	8.7	1986	Sentra Sport Coupe SE: 3220
6	31.8	26.5	8.9	1983	Pulsar NX: 3206
7	30.0	25.0	9.4	1988	240SX: 3230
8	28.8	24.0	9.8	1987	Pulsar NX SE: 3226
9	28.6	23.8	9.9	1991	240SX: 3245
10	28.2	23.5	10.0	1989	300ZX: 3234
11	27.6	23.0	10.2	1984	Pulsar NX Turbo: 3210
12	25.2	21.0	11.2	1988	300ZX: 3231
13	24.6	20.5	11.5	1984	200SX Turbo: 3207
				1989	Maxima SE: 3236
14	24.0	20.0	11.8	1987	200SX SE V6: 3222
				1985	Maxima SE: 3214
15	23.8	19.8	11.9	1987	300ZX: 3223
16	23.5	19.6	12.0	1991	300ZX Twin Turbo: 3248
17	23.4	19.5	12.1	1988	200SX SE V6: 3229
18	21.6	18.0	13.1	1984	300ZX: 3208
				1986	300ZX: 3215
19	20.4	17.0	13.8	1986	300ZX Turbo: 3216
20	19.2	16.0	14.7	1991	300ZX Turbo Millen Super GTZ: 3247
				1991	Sentra SE-R: 3252

NSU

1	27.0	22.5	10.5	1965	Spider: 3261

Oldsmobile

1	32.4	27.0	8.7	1989	Calais HO Quad 4: 3303
				1989	Cutlass Calais International Series HO: 3304
2	27.6	23.0	10.2	1988	Cutlass Calais International Series: 3301
3	26.4	22.0	10.7	1976	Starfire: 3299
4	24.6	20.5	11.5	1988	Cutlass International Series: 3302
5	24.0	20.0	11.8	1980	Cutlass Diesel: 3300
6	21.4	17.8	13.2	1990	Toronado Trofeo: 3305
7	16.1	13.4	17.6	1970	Rallye 350: 3297
8	14.7	12.2	19.3	1970	4-4-2 W30: 3296
9	13.8	11.5	20.5	1963	Cutlass Salon: 3298

Opel

1	33.0	27.5	8.6	1969	GT 1.9: 3320
2	31.1	25.9	9.1	1971	GT: 3327
3	30.6	25.5	9.2	1971	Rallye 1900: 3328
4	30.0	25.0	9.4	1991	Calibra 2.0i 16v: 3351
5	29.4	24.5	9.6	1963	1900 Station Wagon: 3330
6	28.8	24.0	9.8	1963	GT: 3333
7	27.6	23.0	10.2	1968	Station Wagon 1.5: 3316
8	27.0	22.5	10.5	1963	Manta: 3334
9	22.8	19.0	12.4	1975	Manta: 3341
10	18.0	15.0	15.7	1974	Commodore GS 2.8: 3336

Panhard

1	53.8	44.8	5.3	1954	Dyna Junior Sports: 3366

Panther

1	16.2	13.5	17.4	1975	J72: 3374
2	13.2	11.0	21.4	1975	De Ville: 3373

Peugeot

1	36.5	30.4	7.7	1971	304: 3402
2	35.4	29.5	8.0	1963	504 Diesel: 3409
3	32.4	27.0	8.7	1981	505 S Turbodiesel: 3426
				1980	505 SD: 3423
4	30.0	25.0	9.4	1977	504 Diesel Automatique: 3416
5	28.8	24.0	9.8	1968	404 Station Wagon: 3398
				1987	505 STX: 3445
6	27.6	23.0	10.2	1982	505 STI: 3428
7	26.4	22.0	10.7	1989	405 Mi16: 3455
8	25.8	21.5	10.9	1970	504: 3401
9	25.2	21.0	11.2	1975	504: 3412
10	24.0	20.0	11.8	1963	504: 3408
11	22.8	19.0	12.4	1980	505 S: 3422
12	22.2	18.5	12.7	1974	504 Station Wagon: 3411
				1984	505 S Wagon: 3433
				1986	505 Turbo: 3442
				1985	505 Turbo: 3437
13	19.2	16.0	14.7	1979	604: 3421
14	18.0	15.0	15.7	1977	604 SLV-6: 3417

Pininfarina

1	30.0	25.0	9.4	1984	Spider: 3470
2	28.8	24.0	9.8	1984	Azzurra: 3469

Plymouth

1	36.6	30.5	7.7	1984	Colt GTS Turbo: 3518
2	33.6	28.0	8.4	1978	Horizon: 3514
3	32.4	27.0	8.7	1980	Champ: 3517
4	30.0	25.0	9.4	1979	Fire Arrow: 3516
5	29.5	24.6	9.6	1990	Laser RS Turbo: 3522
6	29.4	24.5	9.6	1986	Horizon America: 3520
7	28.2	23.5	10.0	1978	Sapporo: 3515
8	27.6	23.0	10.2	1976	Arrow GT: 3512
				1989	Laser RS: 3521
9	26.8	22.3	10.5	1952	Cambridge: 3471
10	26.4	22.0	10.7	1971	Cricket: 3511
11	24.0	20.0	11.8	1991	Laser RS Turbo: 3523
12	21.0	17.5	13.4	1984	Voyager: 3519
13	17.8	14.8	15.9	1970	Duster 340: 3510
14	16.7	13.9	16.9	1970	Barracuda: 3509
15	15.0	12.5	18.8	1976	Volare Station Wagon: 3513
16	14.4	12.0	19.6	1969	Road Runner: 3507

Pontiac

1	36.6	30.5	7.7	1987	Le Mans: 3583
2	31.2	26.0	9.0	1988	Sunbird GT: 3587
3	30.0	25.0	9.4	1984	Fiero SE: 3574
4	27.0	22.5	10.5	1986	Fiero GT: 3578
5	26.4	22.0	10.7	1984	Fiero: 3573
				1985	Fiero GT: 3577
				1981	J2000: 3569
				1980	Phoenix: 3568
6	25.8	21.5	10.9	1988	Grand Prix SE: 3586
7	25.2	21.0	11.2	1991	Grand Prix GTP: 3599
				1989	Grand Prix McLaren Turbo: 3592
8	24.5	20.4	11.5	1990	Grand Prix STE Turbo: 3595
9	24.0	20.0	11.8	1992	Bonneville SSEi: 3600
10	23.4	19.5	12.1	1987	Fiero GT: 3581
11	22.8	19.0	12.4	1991	Firebird TransAm Convertible: 3598
12	22.2	18.5	12.7	1987	Bonneville SE: 3579
13	21.7	18.1	13.0	1983	6000STE: 3572
14	21.6	18.0	13.1	1988	Bonneville SE: 3585
15	21.3	17.7	13.3	1991	Firebird GTA: 3596
				1990	Firebird TransAm GTA: 3594
16	20.7	17.2	13.7	1987	Fiero Formula: 3580
17	18.6	15.5	15.2	1978	Firebird TransAm: 3565
18	18.3	15.2	15.5	1987	Firebird Formula 5.0: 3582
19	17.4	14.5	16.2	1976	Firebird TransAm: 3563
				1982	Firebird TransAm: 3570
20	16.8	14.0	16.8	1989	Firebird TransAm Turbo: 3590
21	16.2	13.5	17.4	1977	Bonneville: 3564
22	15.6	13.0	18.1	1980	Firebird TransAm Turbo: 3567
23	15.0	12.5	18.8	1970	Formula 400: 3559
24	14.2	11.8	19.9	1970	GTO 455: 3561
25	13.2	11.0	21.4	1963	Grand Am: 3562
				1969	Grand Prix: 3556
26	10.8	9.0	26.1	1969	Firebird TransAm: 3555
27	10.7	8.9	26.4	1970	GTO 400: 3560
28	5.4	4.5	52.3	1982	Petty Grand National: 3571
29	4.8	4.0	58.8	1978	Firebird TransAm Silverbird: 3566

Porsche

1	42.3	35.2	6.7	1956	Continental Coupe: 3607
2	38.0	31.6	7.4	1956	Continental Speedster: 3608
3	31.8	26.5	8.9	1976	914 2.0-litre: 3652
4	30.6	25.5	9.2	1970	914: 3633
5	29.4	24.5	9.6	1963	914 2-litre: 3640
				1976	924: 3653
6	28.2	23.5	10.0	1983	911 Cabriolet: 3675
7	27.6	23.0	10.2	1976	912 E: 3651
				1980	924: 3667
				1990	944 Cabriolet: 3741
8	27.0	22.5	10.5	1988	911 Cabriolet: 3703
				1982	924 Weissach: 3672
9	26.5	22.1	10.6	1986	944: 3693
10	26.4	22.0	10.7	1986	924 S: 3690
				1988	924 S: 3711
				1982	944: 3673
11	25.8	21.5	10.9	1983	944: 3678
12	25.6	21.3	11.0	1969	911 T: 3630
				1970	914 6: 3634
13	25.2	21.0	11.2	1988	944: 3713
				1987	944 S: 3701
14	24.6	20.5	11.5	1984	911 Carrera: 3679

15	24.0	20.0	11.8	1989	911 Carrera Cabriolet: 3721
				1976	911 S: 3649
				1990	911 Speedster: 3735
				1980	924 S Turbo: 3668
16	23.8	19.8	11.9	1971	911 T Sportomatic: 3636
17	23.4	19.5	12.1	1988	944 S: 3714
				1985	944 Turbo: 3686
18	22.8	19.0	12.4	1985	911 Carrera: 3682
				1981	924 Turbo: 3671
				1988	944 Turbo: 3715
19	22.3	18.6	12.6	1986	911 Cabriolet: 3687
				1972	911 E: 3637
20	22.2	18.5	12.7	1987	911 Carrera: 3696
				1980	911 SC: 3666
				1979	924: 3663
				1990	944 S2: 3742
				1990	944 S2 Cabriolet: 3743
				1989	944 Turbo: 3730
21	22.1	18.4	12.8	1969	911 E: 3629
22	21.6	18.0	13.1	1988	911 Carrera: 3704
				1988	911 Club Sport: 3706
				1978	911 SC: 3658
				1980	928: 3669
23	21.0	17.5	13.4	1975	911 Carrera: 3646
				1990	911 Carrera 2 Tiptronic: 3733
24	20.4	17.0	13.8	1989	911 Carrera 4: 3720
				1990	911 Carrera 4: 3734
				1986	911 Turbo: 3689
				1977	911 Turbo: 3655
				1976	911 Turbo Carrera: 3650
				1985	928 S: 3683
25	19.8	16.5	14.3	1990	911 Turbo: 3736
				1988	928 S4: 3712
26	19.6	16.3	14.4	1986	928 S: 3691
27	19.2	16.0	14.7	1974	911 Carrera: 3643
				1989	911 Turbo: 3723
				1988	911 Turbo: 3708
				1978	911 Turbo: 3659
				1984	911 Turbo Cabriolet Ruf: 3680
				1983	928 S: 3677
28	18.6	15.5	15.2	1974	911 Targa: 3644
29	18.0	15.0	15.7	1991	911 Carrera Turbo: 3746
				1970	911 S 2.2-litre: 3631
				1979	928 Automatic: 3665
30	16.8	14.0	16.8	1991	911 Ruf CTR: 3748
31	15.0	12.5	18.8	1963	911 S: 3638
32	13.8	11.5	20.5	1975	Carrera RS 3-litre: 3647
33	7.2	6.0	39.2	1963	Carrera RSR: 3642
34	4.8	4.0	58.8	1977	935 Group 4 Holbert: 3657

Range Rover

1	16.2	13.5	17.4	1990	County: 3779
				1987	V8: 3775

Renault

1	45.6	38.0	6.2	1948	4CV: 3801
2	38.4	32.0	7.4	1982	Alliance DL: 3880
3	37.0	30.8	7.6	1986	Alliance 1.7L: 3898
4	36.6	30.5	7.7	1985	Encore GS: 3891
5	36.0	30.0	7.8	1979	Le Car: 3868
6	34.8	29.0	8.1	1968	16: 3832
7	33.6	28.0	8.4	1963	17: 3844
8	33.0	27.5	8.6	1982	Fuego Turbo: 3882
9	32.4	27.0	8.7	1983	Fuego Turbo: 3884
10	31.8	26.5	8.9	1981	18i: 3871
11	31.2	26.0	9.0	1976	17 Gordini: 3851
12	30.6	25.5	9.2	1987	Alliance GTA: 3903
13	30.0	25.0	9.4	1984	Fuego 2.2: 3888
14	28.6	23.8	9.9	1972	12 TL: 3840
15	28.2	23.5	10.0	1972	15 Coupe: 3841
				1984	Fuego: 3887
16	27.6	23.0	10.2	1975	12: 3847
17	24.0	20.0	11.8	1979	Gordini: 3867
18	21.6	18.0	13.1	1984	5 Turbo 2: 3886
19	18.0	15.0	15.7	1981	5 Turbo: 3873
20	13.3	11.1	21.2	1979	5 Racer: 3865
21	6.0	5.0	47.0	1981	Le Car Turbo: 3874

Rolls-Royce

1	12.6	10.5	22.4	1977	Silver Shadow: 3966
2	12.0	10.0	23.5	1982	Silver Spur: 3971
3	11.6	9.7	24.2	1969	Silver Shadow: 3962
4	11.4	9.5	24.8	1980	Silver Shadow II: 3968

Rover

1	25.6	21.3	11.0	1991	Sterling 827SL: 4049
2	24.7	20.6	11.4	1969	2000TC: 4008
3	24.6	20.5	11.5	1980	3500: 4020
4	21.0	17.5	13.4	1970	3500S: 4010
5	14.2	11.8	19.9	1966	Rover-BRM Turbine: 4006

Saab

1	31.7	26.4	8.9	1972	Sonnet III: 4074
2	31.2	26.0	9.0	1968	Station Wagon V4: 4064
3	28.8	24.0	9.8	1970	99E: 4068
				1972	99E 1.85: 4072
4	28.0	23.3	10.1	1991	9000S: 4104
				1969	99: 4065
5	27.6	23.0	10.2	1981	900 Turbo: 4085
				1991	9000 Turbo: 4102
				1970	Sonnet III: 4069
6	27.0	22.5	10.5	1985	900 Turbo: 4089
				1982	900 Turbo: 4088
				1980	900GLE: 4084
7	26.4	22.0	10.7	1982	900: 4087
				1963	99E: 4075
8	25.7	21.4	11.0	1990	900SPG: 4099
9	25.2	21.0	11.2	1986	9000: 4092
				1989	9000 Turbo: 4096
				1990	9000CD: 4098
10	24.0	20.0	11.8	1974	99LE Wagonback: 4077

Saturn

1	31.2	26.0	9.0	1991	Sports Coupe: 4107

Shelby

1	14.4	12.0	19.6	1974	Cobra 427: 4126

Siata

1	36.0	30.0	7.8	1969	Spring 850: 4128

Simca

1	34.8	29.0	8.1	1967	1000GLS: 4151
2	32.4	27.0	8.7	1969	1204: 4154

Studebaker

1	24.0	20.0	11.8	1951	Land Cruiser: 4223
2	19.0	15.8	14.9	1954	Commander Coupe: 4226

Subaru

1	50.4	42.0	5.6	1971	Hapi Van 360: 4245
2	36.0	30.0	7.8	1978	DL: 4253
3	35.9	29.9	7.9	1988	Justy 4WD GL: 4270
4	35.4	29.5	8.0	1988	Justy GL: 4271
5	34.8	29.0	8.1	1972	FF-1 1300: 4246
6	34.3	28.6	8.2	1986	Hatchback: 4266
7	33.6	28.0	8.4	1969	360: 4243
8	33.4	27.8	8.5	1969	Star: 4244
9	32.4	27.0	8.7	1963	1300 GL Coupe: 4247
10	31.8	26.5	8.9	1963	1400 DL: 4248
				1975	DL: 4249
				1980	DL-5: 4254
				1985	XT Coupe DL: 4263
11	31.2	26.0	9.0	1982	GL: 4256
12	29.3	24.4	9.6	1989	XT6: 4275
				1988	XT6 4WD: 4272
13	27.6	23.0	10.2	1985	4WD Turbo: 4260
14	25.8	21.5	10.9	1976	4WD Station Wagon: 4250
15	25.2	21.0	11.2	1985	4WD Turbo XT Coupe: 4261
16	24.0	20.0	11.8	1983	GL Turbo Traction Wagon: 4257
				1991	Legacy Sports Sedan: 4278
17	21.0	17.5	13.4	1992	SVX: 4279

Sunbeam

1	27.3	22.7	10.4	1969	Alpine GT: 4311
2	26.4	22.0	10.7	1968	Arrow Station Wagon: 4308

Suzuki

1	37.8	31.5	7.5	1990	Swift GT: 4333
2	33.6	28.0	8.4	1971	Brute: 4320

Toyota

1	44.4	37.0	6.4	1981	Starlet: 4411
2	42.0	35.0	6.7	1977	Corolla 1200: 4397
3	37.2	31.0	7.6	1984	Corolla LE: 4428
4	36.3	30.2	7.8	1971	Corolla: 4368
5	36.0	30.0	7.8	1992	Paseo: 4483
				1991	Tercel LE: 4482
6	35.5	29.6	7.9	1971	Corolla 1600: 4370
7	34.8	29.0	8.1	1983	Corolla SR5 Hardtop: 4419
8	34.2	28.5	8.3	1983	Tercel 4WD Wagon: 4422
9	33.9	28.2	8.3	1986	Tercel DX: 4444
10	33.6	28.0	8.4	1989	Corolla GTS: 4463
				1980	Corolla Tercel SR5: 4408
11	33.0	27.5	8.6	1976	Corolla Liftback: 4396
12	32.4	27.0	8.7	1980	Celica GT: 4406
13	31.6	26.3	8.9	1972	Carina: 4374

14	31.2	26.0	9.0	1978	Celica GT Liftback: 4401
				1963	Corolla: 4378
15	30.6	25.5	9.2	1987	Corolla FX-16 GTS: 4449
16	30.0	25.0	9.4	1984	Corolla GTS: 4427
				1980	Corolla Sport Coupe: 4407
				1986	MR2: 4440
				1984	Van LE: 4430
17	29.8	24.8	9.5	1990	Celica GTS: 4470
18	29.4	24.5	9.6	1982	Celica: 4412
				1974	Celica GT: 4383
				1975	Corolla: 4388
				1975	Corolla SR5: 4390
19	29.3	24.4	9.6	1970	Corona Mk II: 4363
20	28.8	24.0	9.8	1982	Celica GTA: 4414
				1990	MR2: 4471
21	27.6	23.0	10.2	1991	Celica GT Convertible: 4477
				1983	Celica GTS: 4417
				1963	Corolla SR5: 4379
				1974	Corona SR: 4385
				1989	MR2 Supercharged: 4464
22	27.0	22.5	10.5	1978	Celica: 4399
23	26.4	22.0	10.7	1963	Celica: 4377
				1989	Supra Turbo: 4466
24	25.8	21.5	10.9	1963	Corona: 4380
25	25.3	21.1	11.1	1987	MR2 Supercharged: 4451
26	25.2	21.0	11.2	1979	Corona 5-door: 4404
				1983	Supra: 4421
27	24.9	20.7	11.4	1970	Crown: 4365
28	24.6	20.5	11.5	1984	Supra: 4429
29	24.3	20.2	11.6	1986	Celica GTS: 4439
30	24.0	20.0	11.8	1988	Celica All-Trac Turbo: 4454
				1979	Celica Supra: 4403
				1978	Cressida: 4402
				1963	Mk II: 4381
				1975	Pickup SR5: 4392
				1988	Supra Turbo: 4460
31	23.4	19.5	12.1	1981	Cressida: 4409
32	22.9	19.1	12.3	1971	Corona de Luxe: 4371
33	22.8	19.0	12.4	1990	Previa LE: 4474
				1987	Supra: 4452
34	22.2	18.5	12.7	1983	Cressida: 4420
				1990	MR2 Turbo: 4473
35	21.6	18.0	13.1	1988	Supra: 4459
				1986	Supra: 4442
36	21.0	17.5	13.4	1963	Mk II 2.6: 4382
37	20.4	17.0	13.8	1974	Mk II Station Wagon: 4386
38	19.2	16.0	14.7	1972	Crown 2600: 4375
39	18.0	15.0	15.7	1971	Land Cruiser: 4372
40	14.4	12.0	19.6	1971	Land Cruiser Wagon: 4373

Trihawk

1	31.2	26.0	9.0	1982	304: 4486

Triumph

1	36.4	30.3	7.8	1971	Spitfire Mk IV: 4549
2	33.0	27.5	8.6	1979	TR7: 4575
				1977	TR7: 4571
				1975	TR7: 4567
				1982	TR7 Convertible: 4581
3	31.8	26.5	8.9	1979	Spitfire: 4574
4	30.0	25.0	9.4	1976	Spitfire: 4569
				1974	Spitfire: 4561
				1963	Spitfire 1500: 4558
5	28.8	24.0	9.8	1980	Spitfire: 4576
				1970	TR6: 4546
6	28.7	23.9	9.8	1969	GT6: 4539
7	25.2	21.0	11.2	1963	GT6: 4556
8	21.6	18.0	13.1	1963	TR6: 4559
9	21.5	17.9	13.1	1971	Stag: 4550
10	18.0	15.0	15.7	1980	TR8: 4577
11	7.8	6.5	36.2	1977	TR7 Tullius: 4572
12	3.6	3.0	78.4	1980	TR8 Group 44: 4578

TVR

1	31.2	26.0	9.0	1963	Vixen 2500M: 4588
2	30.6	25.5	9.2	1970	Vixen: 4587
3	27.6	23.0	10.2	1977	2500M: 4591
4	24.0	20.0	11.8	1980	3000S Roadster: 4595
				1979	Taimar Roadster: 4594
				1983	Tasmin Convertible: 4597
5	18.7	15.6	15.1	1970	Tuscan: 4586

Vector

1	16.2	13.5	17.4	1991	W8 Twin Turbo: 4736

Volkswagen

1	51.6	43.0	5.5	1981	Rabbit Diesel: 4829
				1977	Rabbit Diesel: 4809
2	48.6	40.5	5.8	1980	Dasher Diesel: 4818
3	36.0	30.0	7.8	1975	Rabbit: 4801
				1977	Scirocco Fi: 4810
4	35.4	29.5	8.0	1975	Scirocco: 4802
5	34.8	29.0	8.1	1968	1600 Squareback: 4776
				1982	Quantum: 4835
				1981	Rabbit: 4827
				1983	Rabbit GTi: 4839
				1983	Scirocco: 4840
6	34.5	28.7	8.2	1971	Super Beetle: 4786
7	33.6	28.0	8.4	1979	Scirocco: 4815
				1963	Type III: 4793
8	33.0	27.5	8.6	1975	Beetle: 4798
				1980	Jetta: 4819
9	32.4	27.0	8.7	1985	Golf GTi: 4850
				1981	Rabbit Convertible: 4828
				1984	Scirocco: 4846
				1963	SP-2: 4791
10	31.8	26.5	8.9	1974	Dasher: 4796
				1977	Dasher: 4805
11	31.2	26.0	9.0	1985	Golf: 4849
12	30.6	25.5	9.2	1985	Jetta GLi: 4851
13	30.0	25.0	9.4	1987	Fox GL: 4861
				1991	GTi 16v: 4884
				1984	Jetta GLi: 4843
				1990	Passat GL: 4881
				1980	Rabbit: 4821
				1988	Scirocco 16v: 4872
				1986	Scirocco 16v: 4859
14	29.4	24.5	9.6	1969	1600 Squareback: 4780
				1980	Scirocco: 4822
15	28.8	24.0	9.8	1988	GTi 16v: 4866
				1987	GTi 16v: 4863
				1991	Jetta GLi 16v: 4885
				1988	Jetta GLi 16v: 4867
16	27.6	23.0	10.2	1978	Beetle Convertible: 4812
				1963	Sports Bug: 4792
17	27.0	22.5	10.5	1971	411: 4784
18	26.4	22.0	10.7	1985	Cabriolet Wolfsburg: 4848
19	25.8	21.5	10.9	1990	Corrado G60: 4879
				1988	Quantum GLS Synchro Wagon: 4871
20	25.2	21.0	11.2	1983	Quantum GL5: 4838
21	24.6	20.5	11.5	1974	412: 4795
				1984	Scirocco 16v: 4847
22	23.4	19.5	12.1	1986	Quantum Synchro Wagon: 4858
				1983	Vanagon Wasserboxer: 4842
23	19.8	16.5	14.3	1980	Vanagon: 4823

Volvo

1	36.0	30.0	7.8	1983	760 GLE: 4946
2	32.4	27.0	8.7	1980	Diesel: 4939
3	31.8	26.5	8.9	1990	740 Turbo: 4964
4	28.8	24.0	9.8	1985	740 Turbo Wagon: 4951
5	28.5	23.7	9.9	1971	142E: 4917
6	27.0	22.5	10.5	1972	1800 ES: 4921
7	26.7	22.2	10.6	1989	740 GLE: 4958
8	26.4	22.0	10.7	1968	145S Wagon: 4911
9	25.8	21.5	10.9	1991	940 Turbo: 4967
10	25.2	21.0	11.2	1969	142S 2.0: 4912
				1976	242 GL: 4930
11	25.1	20.9	11.3	1970	1800E: 4916
12	24.6	20.5	11.5	1980	GL: 4940
				1982	GLT Turbo: 4945
13	24.0	20.0	11.8	1974	142 GL: 4925
				1978	242 GT: 4934
				1978	242 IPD: 4935
				1991	940 SE: 4965
				1992	960: 4969
14	23.4	19.5	12.1	1963	144E: 4923
15	22.8	19.0	12.4	1974	145: 4926
16	22.6	18.8	12.5	1989	740 Turbo: 4959
17	22.2	18.5	12.7	1975	242 GL: 4927
18	21.6	18.0	13.1	1984	GLT Wagon: 4950
19	21.3	17.7	13.3	1972	164E: 4920
20	21.0	17.5	13.4	1969	164: 4914
21	20.4	17.0	13.8	1984	760 GLE: 4949
22	19.8	16.5	14.3	1978	262C: 4936
23	19.2	16.0	14.7	1976	265 DL: 4931

Yugo

1	36.0	30.0	7.8	1986	GV: 5002

Total: 1,250

Engines, ABS and 4-WD

ordered by year, make and model with year and grand totals.

Multi-valve engines.

	No.of Valves	
1955	32	Mercedes-Benz 300SLR: 2795
1957	16	Ferrari TRC 2500 Testa Rossa: 1379
1958	16	Porsche RSK: 3613
1961	24	Jaguar XKE: 2299
1966	24	Jaguar XKE 4.2 2+2: 2310
1967	32	Alfa Romeo 33 2.0 Stradale: 66
1971	48	Ferrari Daytona Cannonball: 1398
1975	12	Honda Civic CVCC: 2094
	16	Lotus Elite: 2617
	16	Lotus Elite 503: 2618
	16	Triumph Dolomite Sprint: 4565
1976	16	Chevrolet Cosworth Vega: 871
	12	Honda Accord: 2095
1977	16	Lotus Esprit 16v: 2621
1978	12	Honda Accord: 2098
	16	Vauxhall Chevette 2300 HS: 4688
1979	12	Honda Accord 4-door: 2100
1980	24	BMW M1: 556
	16	Fiat Brava Abarth Rally: 1571
	12	Honda Civic: 2102
	12	Honda Civic GL 1500: 2103
	12	Honda Prelude: 2104
	16	Lotus Eclat: 2626
1981	12	Honda Accord: 2105
	12	Honda Civic 4-door Sedan: 2106
	12	Honda Prelude: 2107
	16	Lancia Montecarlo Group 5 Turbo: 2531
	16	Lotus Esprit Turbo: 2627
1982	32	Ferrari 288 GTO: 1416
	48	Ferrari 512 BB: 1417
	12	Honda Accord: 2109
	12	Honda Accord LX: 2110
1983	32	Ferrari 308 GTBi Quattrovalvole: 1419
	12	Honda CRX 1.5: 2111
	16	Lotus Eclat Excel: 2628
	16	Lotus Esprit Turbo: 2629
	24	Toyota Cressida: 4420
	24	Toyota Supra: 4421
1984	24	BMW M635 CSi: 572
	32	Ferrari 288 GTO: 1421
	48	Ferrari 512 BBi: 1422
	32	Ferrari GTO: 1423
	32	Ferrari Mondial Cabriolet Quattrovalvole: 1424
	12	Honda Civic CRX: 2113
	12	Honda Civic DL: 2114
	24	Jaguar XJS 3.6: 2345
	16	Lancia Rally: 2537
	16	Morgan 4/4: 3133
	16	Pininfarina Azzurra: 3469
	12	Rover 213 Vanden Plas: 4025
	16	Toyota Corolla GT Coupe: 4426
	16	Toyota Corolla GTS: 4427
	16	Volkswagen Scirocco 16v: 4847
Year total: 15		
1985	20	Audi Quattro Sport: 309
	24	BMW M635 CSi Hardy & Beck: 577
	48	Ferrari Testa Rossa: 1426
	12	Honda Accord 2.0 EXi: 2117
	12	Honda Accord EX Automatic: 2118
	12	Honda Civic GT: 2120
	12	Honda Civic S: 2121
	12	Honda Civic Shuttle: 2122
	12	Honda Civic Wagon: 2123
	48	Lamborghini Countach: 2468
	18	Maserati Biturbo: 2672
	16	Mercedes-Benz 190E 2.3-16: 2879
	32	Porsche 928 S: 3683
	16	Saab 900 Turbo: 4089
	16	Saab 9000 Turbo 16v: 4090
	16	Toyota Corolla GT Hatchback: 4432
	16	Toyota MR2: 4433
	12	Toyota Starlet 1.0GL: 4435
	24	Toyota Supra: 4436
	16	Volkswagen Scirocco 16v: 4853
Year total: 20		

1986 16 Acura Integra RS: 28
24 Acura Legend: 29
32 Ferrari 3.2 Mondial: 1427
32 Ferrari 328 GTB: 1428
32 Ferrari Mondial 3.2: 1429
32 Ferrari Mondial 3.2QV: 1430
16 Ford RS200: 1917
12 Honda Civic Hatchback: 2127
16 Honda CRX Coupe 1.6i 16: 2128
16 Honda CRX Si Jackson Turbo: 2130
12 Honda Integra 1.5: 2131
16 Honda Integra EX 16: 2132
24 Honda Legend: 2133
24 Jaguar XJ6 3.6: 2348
48 Lamborghini Countach 5000S: 2469
16 Lotus Esprit Turbo: 2630
16 Lotus Excel SE: 2631
16 Mazda 323 Turbo 4x4 Lux: 2732
16 Mercedes-Benz 190E 2.3-16: 2883
32 Porsche 928 S4 Automatic: 3692
16 Porsche 944 S: 3694
24 Rover 825i: 4027
16 Saab 9000: 4092
16 Saab 9000i: 4093
16 Suzuki Swift 1.3 GTi: 4326
16 Toyota Celica 2.0GT: 4438
16 Toyota Celica GTS: 4439
16 Toyota MR2: 4440
16 Toyota MR2 T-Bar: 4441
24 Toyota Supra: 4442
24 Toyota Supra 3.0i: 4443
16 Volkswagen Golf GTi 16v: 4856
16 Volkswagen Scirocco 16v: 4859
16 Volkswagen Scirocco GTX 16v: 4860
Year total: 34

1987 16 Acura Integra LS: 30
48 BMW 750i L: 589
16 BMW M3: 590
16 Citroen BX GTi 16v: 1077
12 Daihatsu Charade GT ti: 1124
32 Ferrari 328 GTS: 1431
32 Ferrari Mondial Cabriolet 3.2: 1433
12 Honda Ballade EX: 2135
16 Honda Civic 1.4 GL 3-door: 2136
24 Honda Legend Coupe: 2137
16 Honda Prelude 2.0 Si: 2138
16 Honda Prelude 2.0i 16: 2139
24 Jaguar XJ6: 2352
24 Jaguar XJS 3.6 Automatic: 2354
32 Lancia Thema 8.32: 2546
16 Lotus Elan Autocrosser: 2632
16 Lotus Esprit Turbo HC: 2633
16 Lotus Excel SA: 2634
18 Maserati Biturbo Spyder: 2675
12 Mazda 626 2.0 GLS Executive: 2739
24 Nissan 300ZX: 3223
16 Nissan Pulsar NX SE: 3226
16 Nissan Sunny ZX Coupe: 3227
16 Porsche 944 S: 3701
24 Porsche 959 S: 3702
16 Rover 820SE: 4028
24 Rover Sterling Automatic: 4030
9 Subaru Justy: 4267
16 Toyota Camry 2.0 GLi: 4445
16 Toyota Camry 2.0 GLi Estate: 4446
16 Toyota Celica GT Cabriolet: 4447
16 Toyota Corolla Executive: 4448
16 Toyota Corolla FX-16 GTS: 4449
16 Toyota MR2 Supercharged: 4451
24 Toyota Supra: 4452
16 Volkswagen GTi 16v: 4863
16 Volkswagen Jetta GTi 16v: 4864
Year total: 37

1988 16 Acura Integra LS Special Edition: 31
16 Alfa Romeo 75 Evoluzione: 135
24 BMW M6: 597
16 Chevrolet Nova Twin Cam: 923
32 Ferrari F40: 1435
32 Ferrari Mondial Cabriolet: 1436
48 Ferrari Testa Rossa: 1437
48 Ferrari Testa Rossa Straman Spyder: 1438
12 Ford Probe GT: 1933
16 Ford Sierra RS Cosworth: 1934
16 Honda Civic CRX: 2140
16 Honda CRX Si: 2141
16 Honda CRX Si Jackson: 2142
24 Honda Legend Saloon Automatic: 2143
16 Honda Shuttle 1.6i RT4 4WD: 2144
32 Isdera Imperator: 2244
48 Lamborghini LM129: 2472
32 Lancia Thema 8.32: 2548
16 Lotus Esprit Turbo: 2635
16 Mazda 323 GTX: 2742
16 Mazda 323 Turbo 4x4: 2743
12 Mazda 626 2.0 GLX Executive Estate: 2744
16 Mazda 626 2.0i GT 4WS: 2745
18 Mazda 929: 2746
12 Mazda MX-6: 2747
32 Mercedes-Benz 300E AMG Hammer: 2899
16 Mitsubishi Galant GTi-16v: 3099
16 Mitsubishi Lancer GTi 16v: 3100
12 Nissan 240SX: 3230
16 Oldsmobile Cutlass Calais International Series: 3301
16 Peugeot 405 Mi16: 3448
32 Porsche 928 S4: 3712
16 Porsche 944 S: 3714
24 Porsche 959 Comfort: 3717
24 Porsche 959 Sport: 3718
24 Rover 827 SLi Auto: 4032
24 Rover Vitesse: 4033
16 Saab 9000CD: 4094
9 Subaru Justy 4WD GL: 4270
16 Toyota Carina 1.6 GL: 4453
16 Toyota Celica All-Trac Turbo: 4454
16 Toyota Celica GT4: 4455
16 Toyota Corolla 4WD Estate: 4457
24 Toyota Supra: 4459
24 Toyota Supra Turbo: 4460
16 Volkswagen GTi 16v: 4866
16 Volkswagen Jetta GLi 16v: 4867
16 Volkswagen Scirocco 16v: 4872
Year total: 48

1989 16 Acura Integra LS: 32
24 Acura Legend Coupe L: 33
32 Aston Martin Virage: 258
20 Audi 90 Quattro 20v: 325
16 BMW M3: 603
16 BMW M3 Evolution: 604
16 BMW M3 Hor Technologie: 605
24 BMW M5: 606
24 BMW M635 CSi: 607
32 Chevrolet Corvette ZR-1: 934
16 Chrysler TC by Maserati: 1008
16 Daihatsu Charade 1.3 CX: 1128
16 Daihatsu Charade CLS: 1129
16 Daihatsu Sportrak EL: 1130
32 Ferrari Mondial 3.2 Cabriolet: 1440
32 Ferrari Mondial t: 1441
48 Ferrari Testa Rossa: 1442
48 Ferrari Testa Rossa Gemballa: 1443
48 Ferrari Testa Rossa Norwood: 1444
12 Ford Probe GT Suspension Techniques/HKS: 1943
24 Ford Taurus SHO: 1946
16 Honda Civic Si: 2145
12 Honda Civic Si HKS: 2146
12 Honda CRX Si HKS: 2147
16 Honda Prelude Si 4WS: 2148
16 Honda Shuttle 1.4 GL Automatic: 2149
24 Jaguar 4.0 Sovereign: 2358
48 Jaguar XJ220: 2359
48 Koenig Competition: 2417
48 Lamborghini Countach 25th Anniversary: 2473
16 Lancia Delta Integrale 16v: 2549
16 Lancia Thema 2.0ie 16v: 2550
16 Lotus Esprit Turbo: 2636
16 Lotus Esprit Turbo SE: 2637
18 Maserati 430: 2678
18 Maserati Spyder: 2679
16 Mazda 323 1.8 GT: 2753
18 Mazda MPV: 2754
16 Mazda MX-5 Miata: 2755
12 Mazda MX-6 GT 4WS: 2756
16 Mercedes-Benz 190E 2.5-16: 2901
16 Mitsubishi Eclipse: 3102
16 Mitsubishi Eclipse GSX: 3103
16 Mitsubishi Galant GS: 3104
12 Mitsubishi Starion 2.6 Turbo: 3106
16 Nissan 200SX: 3232
12 Nissan 240SX Turbo Tokico/Cartech: 3233
24 Nissan 300ZX: 3234
12 Nissan Sunny 1.4 LS: 3239
16 Oldsmobile Calais HO Quad 4: 3303
16 Oldsmobile Cutlass Calais International Series HO: 3304
16 Peugeot 405 Mi16: 3455
16 Plymouth Laser RS: 3521
32 Porsche 928 Cabrio Strosek: 3725
32 Porsche 928 S4 Koenig: 3726
32 Porsche 928 S4 SE: 3727
16 Porsche 944 S2: 3729
24 Porsche 959: 3731
12 Renault 25 TXi: 3910
24 Rover Sterling Catalyst: 4035
24 Rover Vitesse: 4036
16 Saab 9000 Turbo: 4096
16 Saab Carlsson: 4097
16 Subaru Legacy FIA Record: 4274
16 Suzuki Swift 1.3 GTi: 4331
24 Toyota Camry V6 GXi: 4461
16 Toyota Carina II 1.6 GL Liftback: 4462
16 Toyota Corolla GTS: 4463
16 Toyota MR2 Supercharged: 4464
24 Toyota Supra 3.0i Turbo: 4465
24 Toyota Supra Turbo: 4466

24 Toyota Supra Turbo TRD: 4467
16 Treser T1: 4485
16 Volkswagen Corrado 16v: 4875
16 Volkswagen Passat GT 16v: 4878
16 Volvo 740 GLE: 4958
Year total: 76

1990 16 Acura Integra GS: 34
24 Acura Legend Coupe: 35
24 Acura NSX: 36
16 Alfa Romeo 33 Boxer 16v: 144
20 Audi 90 Quattro: 329
20 Audi Quattro 20v: 330
32 Audi V8 Quattro: 331
32 Audi V8 Quattro Automatic: 332
24 Bitter Type 3 Cabrio: 494
16 BMW 318i S: 609
48 BMW 750i: 612
16 Caterham 7 HPC: 725
16 Chevrolet Beretta GTZ: 936
64 Cizeta Moroder V16T: 1094
16 Daihatsu Applause 16 Xi: 1131
16 Eagle Talon: 1355
32 Ferrari 348tb: 1445
32 Ferrari F40: 1446
32 Ferrari Mondial: 1447
48 Ferrari Pininfarina Mythos: 1448
12 Ford Probe GT: 1956
16 Ford Sierra Sapphire Cosworth 4x4: 1958
16 Honda Accord 2.0 EXi: 2150
16 Honda Concerto 1.6i 16: 2151
16 Honda CRX 1.6i VT: 2152
16 IAD Venus: 2229
32 Infiniti Q45: 2231
16 Isuzu Impulse XS: 2260
20 Ital Design Aztec: 2262
24 Jaguar XJ6 Vanden Plas: 2362
24 Jaguar XJR 4.0: 2363
48 Koenig Competition Evolution: 2418
48 Lamborghini Diablo: 2474
16 Lancia Thema 2.0ie 16v SE Turbo: 2553
32 Lexus LS400: 2570
16 Lotus Elan: 2638
16 Lotus Elan SE: 2639
16 Lotus Esprit Turbo SE: 2640
18 Maserati 228: 2680
32 Maserati Shamal: 2681
16 Mazda MX-5 Miata Millen: 2760
12 Mazda MX-6 GT: 2761
16 Mazda Protege: 2762
16 Mercedes-Benz 190E 2.5-16 Evolution II: 2908
24 Mercedes-Benz 300CE: 2909
32 Mercedes-Benz 300CE AMG Hammer: 2910
24 Mercedes-Benz 300E-24: 2912
32 Mercedes-Benz 500SL: 2913
16 Mercury Capri XR-2: 2961
16 Mitsubishi Lancer Liftback 1800 GTi-16v: 3110
16 Morgan Plus 4 Mk III: 3136
24 Nissan 300ZX: 3240
24 Nissan 300ZX Turbo: 3241
16 Nissan Primera 1.6 LS: 3242
24 Nissan Skyline GT-R: 3243
16 Panther Solo: 3380
16 Peugeot 405 Mi16x4: 3459
16 Peugeot 405 Turbo 16 Pike's Peak: 3460
16 Plymouth Laser RS Turbo: 3522
32 Porsche 928: 3738
32 Porsche 928 Automatic: 3739
32 Porsche 928 Gemballa: 3740
16 Porsche 944 Cabriolet: 3741
16 Porsche 944 S2: 3742
16 Porsche 944 S2 Cabriolet: 3743
24 Porsche Carrera 2 Cabriolet Tiptronic: 3744
12 Renault 21 TXi: 3915
24 Renault 25 V6 2.9 Auto: 3916
16 Rover 214 GSi: 4037
16 Rover 216 GSi: 4038
16 Rover 414 Si: 4039
16 Rover 416 GTi: 4040
16 Rover Metro GTi 16v: 4042
16 Saab 9000CD: 4098
16 Saab 900SPG: 4099
16 Saab CDS 2.3: 4100
24 Sbarro Chrono 3.5: 4108
16 Subaru Legacy 2.2 GX 4WD: 4276
16 Suzuki Swift GT: 4333
16 Toyota Celica 2.0 GT: 4468
16 Toyota Celica All-Trac Turbo: 4469
16 Toyota Celica GTS: 4470
16 Toyota MR2: 4471
16 Toyota MR2 GT: 4472
16 Toyota MR2 Turbo: 4473
16 Toyota Previa LE: 4474
12 Toyota Starlet GL: 4475
16 Vauxhall Calibra 2.0i 16v: 4722
24 Vauxhall Carlton GSi 3000 24v: 4724
16 Vauxhall Cavalier GSi 2000 16v: 4725
16 Vauxhall Cavalier GSi 2000 16v 4x4: 4726
16 Volkswagen Passat GL: 4881
16 Volvo 740 GLT 16v Estate: 4963
32 Zender Fact 4: 5008
Year total: 94

1991 24 Acura Legend LS: 37
32 Aston Martin Virage: 261
20 Audi 200 Quattro: 334
16 Audi 80 16v Sport: 335
20 Audi 90 Quattro 20v: 336
20 Audi Coupe S2: 337
32 Audi V8 Quattro: 338
16 Bertone Emotion Lotus: 489
24 BMW 325i SE: 615
24 BMW 520i: 616
24 BMW 525i: 617
24 BMW 525i SE 24v: 618
16 BMW M3 Sport Evolution: 621
24 BMW M5: 622
48 Bugatti EB110: 652
16 Chevrolet Baretta GTZ: 946
32 Chevrolet Corvette ZR-1: 953
32 Chevrolet Corvette ZR-1 Geiger: 954
32 Chevrolet Corvette ZR-1 SS: 955
24 Chevrolet Lumina Z34: 957
24 Citroen XM V6.24: 1089
16 Dodge Spirit R/T: 1346
24 Dodge Stealth R/T Turbo: 1347
16 Eagle Talon TSi 4WD: 1357
32 Ferrari 348tb: 1449
32 Ferrari F40: 1450
32 Ferrari GTO Norwood: 1451
32 Ferrari Mondial t: 1452
32 Ferrari Mondial t Cabriolet: 1453
16 Ford Escort GT: 1963
16 Ford Escort Millen: 1964
24 Ford Festiva Shogun: 1965
12 Ford Probe GT: 1969
24 Ford Scorpio 24v: 1970
24 Ford Taurus SHO: 1971
16 Geo Storm GSi: 1994
16 Honda Civic 1.5 VEi: 2153
16 Honda Civic 1.6i VT: 2154
24 Honda Legend: 2155
24 Honda NSX: 2156
16 Honda Prelude Si: 2157
16 Hyundai Lantra 1.6 Cdi: 2226
16 Infiniti G20: 2232
16 Isuzu Impulse RS: 2261
24 Jaguar XJ6 3.2: 2368
24 Jaguar XJS 4.0 Auto: 2371
48 Lamborghini Diablo: 2475
32 Lexus SC400: 2571
16 Lotus Elan SE: 2641
16 Mazda 121 GSX: 2765
16 Mazda 323 1.8 GT: 2766
24 Mazda MX-3 V6: 2767
16 Mercedes-Benz 190E 2.5-16 Evolution II: 2916
24 Mercedes-Benz 300SL-24 5-speed Auto: 2917
32 Mercedes-Benz 400SE: 2918
32 Mercedes-Benz 500E: 2919
32 Mercedes-Benz 500SL: 2920
16 Mercury Tracer LTS: 2962
24 Mitsubishi 3000GT VR-4: 3111
16 Mitsubishi Colt 1800 GTI-16v: 3112
24 Mitsubishi Diamante LS: 3113
16 Mitsubishi Galant VR-4: 3114
24 Mitsubishi Sigma: 3116
16 Mitsubishi Space Runner 1800-16v GLXi: 3117
16 Nissan 100NX: 3244
16 Nissan 240SX: 3245
24 Nissan 300ZX Motor Sports International SR-71: 3246
24 Nissan 300ZX Turbo Millen Super GTZ: 3247
24 Nissan 300ZX Twin Turbo: 3248
16 Nissan NX2000: 3249
16 Nissan Primera 2.0 GSX: 3250
16 Nissan Primera 2.0E ZX: 3251
16 Nissan Sentra SE-R: 3252
16 Nissan Sunny 1.6 GS 5-door: 3253
16 Opel Calibra 2.0i 16v: 3351
24 Opel Omega Lotus: 3352
24 Peugeot 605 SVE 24: 3467
16 Plymouth Laser RS Turbo: 3523
24 Pontiac Grand Prix GTP: 3599
32 Porsche 928: 3752
12 Proton 1.5 SE Triple Valve Aeroback: 3755
16 Renault 19 16v: 3917
16 Rover 216 GTi: 4044
16 Rover 220 GTi: 4046
24 Rover Sterling 827SL: 4049
16 Saab 9000 2.3 Turbo TCS: 4101
16 Saab 9000 Turbo: 4102
16 Saab 9000CS Turbo S: 4103
16 Saab 9000S: 4104
16 Saturn Sports Coupe: 4107
32 Subaru Legacy 2.0 4Cam Turbo Estate: 4277
16 Subaru Legacy Sports Sedan: 4278
16 Toyota Camry 2.2 GL: 4476

16 Toyota Celica GT Convertible: 4477
16 Toyota MR2: 4479
16 Toyota MR2 HKS: 4480
16 Toyota Previa: 4481
12 Toyota Tercel LE: 4482
16 Vauxhall Calibra 4x4: 4729
24 Vauxhall Senator 3.0i 24v: 4731
16 Volkswagen GTi 16v: 4884
16 Volkswagen Jetta GLi 16v: 4885
24 Volvo 960 24v: 4968
Year total: 103

1992 24 BMW 325i: 623
24 BMW 520i SE Touring: 624
12 Citroen XM Turbo SD Estate: 1093
16 Ford Escort RS2000: 1973
16 Ford Escort XR3i: 1974
24 Honda Legend Coupe: 2158
24 Honda NSX Auto: 2159
16 Honda Prelude Si 4WS: 2160
24 Lexus ES300: 2572
16 Mazda MX-3 1.6 Auto: 2772
24 Mazda MX-3 GS: 2773
48 Mercedes-Benz 600SEL: 2923
16 Nissan 200SX: 3254
16 Nissan Sunny 2.0 GTi: 3255
16 Renault 19 16v Cabriolet: 3922
16 Renault Cleo 16v: 3923
16 Rover 820i: 4050
24 Rover Sterling Automatic: 4051
16 Saab 9000 2.3CS: 4105
24 Subaru SVX: 4279
16 Toyota Paseo: 4483
24 Volvo 960: 4969
Year total: 22

Total No: 487

Turbocharged engines.

1962 Chevrolet Corvair Navarro: 764
Chevrolet Corvair Spyder: 765
Oldsmobile F-85 Jetfire Sports Coupe: 3277

1973 Ford Pinto Pangra: 1819

1974 BMW 2002 Turbo: 534

1975 Porsche Turbo 3-litre: 3648

1976 Porsche 911 Turbo Carrera: 3650

1977 Porsche 911 Turbo: 3655
Porsche 935 Group 4 Holbert: 3657

1978 Mercedes-Benz 300SD: 2857
Porsche 911 Turbo: 3659
Saab Turbo: 4081

1979 Ford Mustang Ghia Turbo: 1866
Ford Mustang Turbo: 1867
Porsche 924 Turbo: 3664
Saab 900 Turbo: 4082
TVR Convertible Turbo: 4593

1980 Ford Mustang Turbo: 1870
Morgan Plus 8 Turbo: 3132
Peugeot 604 D Turbo: 3424
Pontiac Firebird TransAm Turbo: 3567
Porsche 924 S Turbo: 3668

1981 Audi 5000 Turbo: 287
Datsun 280ZX Turbo: 1223
Lancia Montecarlo Group 5 Turbo: 2531
Lotus Esprit Turbo: 2627
Mercedes-Benz 300TD: 2868
Mitsubishi Colt Lancer 2000 Turbo: 3068
Peugeot 505 S Turbodiesel: 3426
Porsche 924 Turbo: 3671
Renault 18 Turbo: 3870
Renault 5 Turbo: 3873
Renault Le Car Turbo: 3874
Saab 900 Turbo: 4085
Year total: 12

1982 Audi 80 Turbo Diesel: 291
Audi Quattro: 292
Bentley Mulsanne Turbo: 479
BMW 745i: 562
Ferrari 288 GTO: 1416
Fiat Spider Turbo: 1577
Mitsubishi Colt Cordia Turbo: 3069
Mitsubishi Colt Hatchback Turbo: 3070
Mitsubishi Colt Starion Turbo: 3071
Renault 5 Gordini Turbo: 3876
Renault Fuego Turbo: 3882
Rover SD Turbo: 4023
Saab 900 Turbo: 4088
Volvo GLT Turbo: 4945
Year total: 14

1983 Audi 200 Turbo: 293
Datsun 280ZX Electramotive: 1230
Datsun 280ZX Turbo: 1231
Ford Thunderbird Turbo Coupe: 1891
Lotus Esprit Turbo: 2629
MG Metro Turbo: 3037
Mitsubishi Starion: 3074
Mitsubishi Starion Turbo: 3075
Mitsubishi Tredia Turbo: 3076
Porsche 911 Turbo: 3676
Renault Fuego Turbo: 3884
Subaru GL Turbo Traction Wagon: 4257
Volvo 760 GLE: 4946
Volvo 760 Turbo: 4947
Year total: 14

1984 Audi 200 Quattro Turbo: 297
Audi 5000 S Turbo: 300
Chrysler Laser XE: 1003
Citroen CX GTi Turbo: 1062
Dodge Conquest: 1330
Dodge Daytona Turbo Z: 1331
Ferrari 288 GTO: 1421
Ferrari GTO: 1423
Ford Mustang SVO: 1897
Mitsubishi Colt 1600 Turbo: 3077
Mitsubishi Cordia Turbo 1.8: 3078
Mitsubishi Mirage Turbo: 3080
Nissan 200SX Turbo: 3207
Nissan 300ZX Turbo: 3209
Nissan Pulsar NX Turbo: 3210
Nissan Silvia Turbo ZX: 3211
Plymouth Colt GTS Turbo: 3518
Porsche 911 Turbo Cabriolet Ruf: 3680
Renault 5 Turbo 2: 3886
Volkswagen Passat CL Turbo Diesel Estate: 4845
Volvo GLT Wagon: 4950
Year total: 21

1985 Alfa Romeo GTV Callaway Twin Turbo: 122
Audi 200 Avant Quattro: 304
Audi 5000 S Turbo Quattro: 305
Audi Quattro: 308
Audi Quattro Sport: 309
Bentley Mulsanne Turbo: 480
Chrysler Le Baron GTS: 1004
Fiat Uno Turbo ie: 1589
Ford Escort RS Turbo: 1901
Lancia Thema 2.0 ie LX Turbo: 2539
Lancia Y10 Turbo: 2540
Maserati Biturbo: 2672
Maserati Biturbo Automatic: 2673
Maserati Biturbo E: 2674
Mercedes-Benz 190E BBS/Callaway Turbo: 2880
Merkur XR4Ti: 2963
MG Montego Turbo: 3039
Mitsubishi Colt Starion Turbo: 3081
Mitsubishi Galant Turbo: 3083
Mitsubishi Starion: 3085
Mitsubishi Starion ESI: 3086
Nissan Bluebird Turbo ZX: 3212
Peugeot 505 Turbo: 3437
Porsche 944 Turbo: 3686
Renault 25 V6 Turbo: 3889
Saab 900 Turbo: 4089
Saab 9000 Turbo 16v: 4090
Subaru 1.8 RX Turbo: 4259
Subaru 4WD Turbo: 4260
Subaru 4WD Turbo XT Coupe: 4261
Subaru Turbo 4WD Estate: 4262
Subaru XT Turbo Coupe: 4264
Volvo 740 Turbo Wagon: 4951
Volvo 760 Turbo Estate: 4952
Year total: 34

1986 Audi 100 Turbo Diesel: 310
BMW 524 TD: 581
Chevrolet Corvette Callaway: 901
Chrysler Laser XT: 1005
Dodge Colt Turbo: 1333
Dodge Omni GLH: 1334
Dodge Shelby GLH-S: 1335
Ford Escort RS Turbo: 1911
Ford Mustang SVO: 1915
Ford RS200: 1917
Honda CRX Si Jackson Turbo: 2130
Isuzu Impulse Turbo: 2256
Lancia Delta HF Turbo ie: 2542
Lotus Esprit Turbo: 2630
Mazda 323 Turbo 4x4 Lux: 2732
Mazda 626 GT: 2734
Mazda RX-7 Turbo: 2737

Mitsubishi Cordia Turbo: 3087
Mitsubishi Starion ESI-R: 3090
Nissan 300ZX Turbo: 3216
Nissan Bluebird 1.8 ZX: 3217
Peugeot 505 Turbo: 3442
Porsche 911 Turbo: 3689
Porsche 944 Turbo: 3695
Reliant Scimitar Ti: 3795
Renault 5 GT Turbo: 3895
Renault 9 Turbo: 3897
Renault GTA V6 Turbo: 3899
Subaru 4WD 3-door Turbo Coupe: 4265
Year total: 29

1987 Bentley Turbo R: 481
Chrysler Le Baron Coupe: 1006
Citroen CX25 DTR Turbo 2: 1078
Daihatsu Charade CX Diesel Turbo: 1123
Daihatsu Charade GT ti: 1124
Daihatsu Fourtrak Estate DT EL: 1125
Ford Thunderbird Turbo Coupe: 1927
Isuzu Trooper 3-door TD: 2257
Land Rover Ninety County Turbo Diesel: 2560
Lotus Esprit Turbo HC: 2633
Maserati Biturbo Spyder: 2675
Mazda RX-7 Turbo: 2740
Mercedes-Benz 300TD: 2893
Mitsubishi Shogun Turbo Diesel 5-door: 3094
Mitsubishi Starion 2000 Turbo: 3095
Mitsubishi Starion ESI-R: 3096
MVS Venturi GT: 3190
Nissan 300ZX Turbo: 3224
Porsche 911 Turbo Gemballa Avalanche: 3697
Porsche 911 Turbo Ruf 3.4: 3698
Porsche 911 Turbo Slant-Nose: 3699
Porsche 959 S: 3702
Renault 11 Turbo: 3900
Renault 5 GT Turbo: 3901
Subaru XT Turbo 4WD: 4268
Volvo 740 Turbo: 4955
Year total: 26

1988 Alfa Romeo 75 Evoluzione: 135
Audi Quattro: 323
Chevrolet Corvette Callaway: 918
Chrysler Conquest TSi: 1007
Citroen BX DTR Turbo: 1080
Daihatsu Charade Turbo: 1127
Dodge Daytona Shelby Z: 1336
Dodge Lancer Shelby: 1337
Dodge Shelby CSX: 1338
Ferrari F40: 1435
Ford Mustang Cartech Turbo: 1928
Ford Probe GT: 1933
Ford Sierra RS Cosworth: 1934
Isuzu I-Mark RS Turbo: 2258
Isuzu Impulse Turbo: 2259
Lancia Delta HF Integrale: 2547
Lotus Esprit Turbo: 2635
Maserati 430: 2676
Maserati Biturbo: 2677
Mazda 323 GTX: 2742
Mazda 323 Turbo 4x4: 2743
Mazda MX-6: 2747
Mazda MX-6 GT: 2748
Mazda RX-7 Turbo: 2751
Merkur XR4Ti: 2965
Mitsubishi Cordia Turbo: 3097
Mitsubishi Mirage Turbo: 3101
Nissan 300ZX: 3231
Pontiac Sunbird GT: 3587
Porsche 911 Turbo: 3708
Porsche 911 Turbo Koenig RS: 3709
Porsche 911 Turbo Ruf Twin Turbo: 3710
Porsche 944 Turbo: 3715
Porsche 944 Turbo SE: 3716
Porsche 959 Comfort: 3717
Porsche 959 Sport: 3718
Range Rover Vogue Turbo D: 3776
Renault 21 Turbo: 3905
Saab 9000CD: 4094
Subaru 4WD Turbo Estate: 4269
Toyota Celica All-Trac Turbo: 4454
Toyota Celica GT4: 4455
Toyota Landcruiser II TD: 4458
Toyota Supra Turbo: 4460
Volkswagen Jetta Turbo Diesel: 4868
Year total: 45

1989 Buick Reatta Turbo Buick Engineering: 697
Chevrolet Corvette Callaway: 931
Chrysler TC by Maserati: 1008
Dodge Daytona Shelby: 1339
Dodge Shadow ES Turbo: 1340
Dodge Shelby CSX: 1341
Dodge Shelby CSX VNT: 1342
Ferrari 308 Norwood: 1439
Ferrari Testa Rossa Norwood: 1444
Ford Mustang 5.0 Cartech Turbo: 1940
Ford Probe GT Suspension Techniques/HKS: 1943
Honda Civic Si HKS: 2146
Honda CRX Si HKS: 2147
Koenig Competition: 2417
Lancia Delta Integrale 16v: 2549
Lotus Esprit Turbo: 2636
Lotus Esprit Turbo SE: 2637
Maserati 430: 2678
Maserati Spyder: 2679
Mazda MX-6 GT 4WS: 2756
Mazda RX-7 Turbo II: 2759
MG Maestro Turbo: 3040
Mitsubishi Eclipse: 3102
Mitsubishi Eclipse GSX: 3103
Mitsubishi Starion 2.6 Turbo: 3106
Mitsubishi Starion ESI-R: 3107
Nissan 200SX: 3232
Nissan 240SX Turbo Tokico/Cartech: 3233
Peugeot 405 GTD Turbo: 3454
Plymouth Laser RS: 3521
Pontiac Firebird T/A Turbo Pontiac Engineering: 3588
Pontiac Firebird TransAm 20th Anniversary: 3589
Pontiac Firebird TransAm Turbo: 3590
Pontiac Grand Am Turbo: 3591
Pontiac Grand Prix McLaren Turbo: 3592
Porsche 911 3.3 Turbo: 3719
Porsche 911 Turbo: 3723
Porsche 911 Turbo Motorsport Design: 3724
Porsche 944 Turbo: 3730
Porsche 959: 3731
Rover Montego 2.0 DSL Turbo: 4034
Saab 900 Turbo S: 4095
Saab 9000 Turbo: 4096
Saab Carlsson: 4097
Subaru Legacy FIA Record: 4274
Toyota Supra 3.0i Turbo: 4465
Toyota Supra Turbo: 4466
Toyota Supra Turbo TRD: 4467
Volvo 440 Turbo: 4957
Volvo 740 Turbo: 4959
Year total: 50

1990 Audi Quattro 20v: 330
Bentley Turbo R: 482
Bertone Zabrus: 488
Chevrolet Corvette Callaway: 940
Chevrolet Corvette Callaway Sledgehammer: 941
Citroen CX25 GTi Turbo 2 CX Auto: 1085
Consulier GTP LX: 1096
Dodge Daytona Shelby: 1344
Dodge Shadow ES VNT: 1345
Eagle Talon: 1355
Ferrari F40: 1446
Fiat Uno Turbo ie: 1605
Ford Fiesta RS Turbo: 1949
Ford Granada 2.5 GL Diesel: 1951
Ford Probe GT: 1956
Ford Sierra Sapphire Cosworth 4x4: 1958
Ital Design Aztec: 2262
Koenig Competition Evolution: 2418
Lancia Thema 2.0ie 16v SE Turbo: 2553
Land Rover Discovery TDi: 2563
Lotus Elan: 2638
Lotus Elan SE: 2639
Lotus Esprit Turbo SE: 2640
Maserati 228: 2680
Maserati Shamal: 2681
Mazda MX-5 Miata Millen: 2760
Mazda MX-6 GT: 2761
Mazda RX-7 Turbo: 2764
Mercury Capri XR-2: 2961
MVS Venturi: 3191
Nissan 300ZX: 3240
Nissan 300ZX Turbo: 3241
Nissan Skyline GT-R: 3243
Panther Solo: 3380
Peugeot 405 Turbo 16 Pike's Peak: 3460
Plymouth Laser RS Turbo: 3522
Pontiac Grand Prix STE Turbo: 3595
Porsche 911 Turbo: 3736
Porsche 911 Turbo RS Tuning: 3737
Reliant Scimitar SST 1800Ti: 3796
Renault 21 Turbo Quadra: 3914
Saab 900SPG: 4099
Toyota Celica All-Trac Turbo: 4469
Toyota MR2 Turbo: 4473
Vauxhall Nova 1.5TD Merit: 4727
Vector W2: 4735
Volkswagen Passat CL TD Estate: 4880
Volvo 460 Turbo: 4962
Volvo 740 Turbo: 4964
Zender Fact 4: 5008
Year total: 50

1991 Audi 200 Quattro: 334
Audi Coupe S2: 337
Bentley Turbo R: 483

Bertone Emotion Lotus: 489
BMW 535i Alpina B10 Bi-Turbo: 619
Bugatti EB110: 652
Chevrolet Corvette Callaway: 948
Chevrolet Corvette Callaway Speedster: 949
Chevrolet Corvette Callaway Twin Turbo: 950
Dodge Spirit R/T: 1346
Dodge Stealth R/T Turbo: 1347
Eagle Talon TSi 4WD: 1357
Ferrari F40: 1450
Ferrari GTO Norwood: 1451
Ford Escort Millen: 1964
Ford Probe GT: 1969
Isuzu Impulse RS: 2261
Koenig C62: 2419
Lancia Dedra 2000 Turbo: 2555
Lotus Elan SE: 2641
Mazda RX-7 Cartech: 2768
Mazda RX-7 Mariah Mode Six: 2770
Mazda RX-7 Turbo: 2771
Mitsubishi 3000GT VR-4: 3111
Mitsubishi Galant VR-4: 3114
Nissan 300ZX Motor Sports International SR-71: 3246
Nissan 300ZX Turbo Millen Super GTZ: 3247
Nissan 300ZX Twin Turbo: 3248
Opel Omega Lotus: 3352
Peugeot 205 D Turbo: 3464
Peugeot 605 SR TD: 3465
Plymouth Laser RS Turbo: 3523
Pontiac Firebird TDM Technologies: 3597
Porsche 911 Carrera Turbo: 3746
Porsche 911 Ruf: 3747
Porsche 911 Ruf CTR: 3748
Porsche 911 Turbo: 3750
Porsche 911 Turbo Gemballa Mirage: 3751
Renault Alpine A610 Turbo: 3918
Rover 825 TD: 4047
Saab 9000 2.3 Turbo TCS: 4101
Saab 9000 Turbo: 4102
Saab 9000CS Turbo S: 4103
Subaru Legacy 2.0 4Cam Turbo Estate: 4277
Toyota Landcruiser VX: 4478
Toyota MR2 HKS: 4480
Vector W8 Twin Turbo: 4736
Volvo 940 SE: 4965
Volvo 940 SE Turbo: 4966
Volvo 940 Turbo: 4967
Year total: 50

1992 Citroen XM Turbo SD Estate: 1093
Nissan 200SX: 3254
Vauxhall Frontera 2.3 TD Estate: 4734
Year total: 3

Total No: 384

Supercharged engines.

1929 Lea-Francis Hyper-sports: 2567
1930 Bentley 4.5-litre Supercharged: 462
HE Supercharged Six Coupe: 2018
Lagonda 2-litre Supercharged: 2433
Triumph Supercharged 7: 4488

1931 Alfa Romeo Supercharged Straight Eight: 39
MG Mk II Montlhery Supercharged: 2970

1932 Alfa Romeo 1750: 40
Alfa Romeo 8C2300: 41
Bugatti 55: 651

1935 Graham 33.8hp Supercharged Saloon: 2012
Squire X101: 4190

1936 Graham 26hp Supercharged Saloon: 2013
Mercedes-Benz Type 500 Supercharged: 2782

1937 Cord 812-S: 1101
Cord Supercharged Saloon: 1102
Lammas-Graham Drop-head Coupe: 2476

1938 Duesenberg SJ Town Car: 1353
Graham 26hp Supercharged Saloon: 2014

1953 Studebaker Commander Supercharged: 4225

1954 Hillman Minx Supercharged: 2040
MG TF Supercharged: 2989

1955 Nash Nash-Healey Roadster Supercharged: 3200
Volkswagen Sedan Supercharged: 4743

1957 Volkswagen Sedan Judson: 4748

1960 Austin-Healey Sprite Supercharged: 439

1961 Pontiac Tempest Supercharged: 3532

1963 Oldsmobile F-85 Jetfire: 3279
Studebaker Regal Wagonaire Supercharged: 4237

1964 Excalibur SS: 1363

1966 Shelby GT 350-S: 4121

1984 Lancia Rally: 2537

1987 Toyota MR2 Supercharged: 4451

1989 Ford Thunderbird Super Coupe: 1947
Ford Thunderbird Super Coupe Ford Engineering: 1948
Koenig Competition: 2417
Mercury Cougar XR-7: 2960
Porsche 928 S4 Koenig: 3726
Toyota MR2 Supercharged: 4464
Volkswagen Corrado: 4874

1990 BMW 735i Koenig: 611
Volkswagen Corrado G60: 4879

1991 Ford Mustang Holdener: 1966
Volkswagen Corrado G60: 4882
Volkswagen Corrado Neuspeed: 4883
Volkswagen Polo G40: 4887

1992 Pontiac Bonneville SSEi: 3600
Total No: 47

Fuel injected engines.

1955 Mercedes-Benz 300SL Coupe: 2794
Mercedes-Benz 300SLR: 2795

1957 Chevrolet Corvette: 739
Chevrolet Corvette Injection: 740
Chevrolet Corvette RPO 684/579E: 741
Goliath 900: 2006

1958 Mercedes-Benz 300SL Roadster: 2800

1959 Chevrolet Corvette: 743

1960 Mercedes-Benz 220SE: 2804

1961 Chevrolet Corvette 315: 753

1962 Chevrolet Chevy II Corvette: 757
Chevrolet Corvette: 766
Chevrolet Corvette Sebring: 767
Mercedes-Benz 300SE: 2808

1963 Maserati 3500 GTI Sebring: 2655

1964 Chevrolet Corvette Sting Ray: 786
Chevrolet Corvette Sting Ray Injection: 788
Mercedes-Benz 230SL: 2811
Mercedes-Benz 300SE LWB: 2812

1965 Chevrolet Corvette Injection: 797
Mercedes-Benz 190D: 2813
Mercedes-Benz 220SE: 2814
Mercedes-Benz 230SL Automatic: 2815
Mercedes-Benz 600: 2816
Peugeot 404 Diesel: 3392
Peugeot 404 KF2: 3393
Year total: 7

1966 Mercedes-Benz 300D: 2819
Rover Rover-BRM Turbine: 4006

1967 Alfa Romeo 33 2.0 Stradale: 66
Jaguar XJ13: 2313
Lancia Flavia Injection: 2507
Mercedes-Benz 250SE: 2820
Mercedes-Benz 600: 2821

1968 Mercedes-Benz 280SL: 2825
Peugeot 504 Injection: 3399
Porsche 911 E Sportomatic: 3627
Triumph TR5 PI: 4536

1969 Alfa Romeo 1750 Berlina: 73
Alfa Romeo 1750 Spider: 74
Mercedes-Benz 300SEL 6.3: 2828
Triumph 2.5PI: 4537
Triumph TR6: 4541
Volkswagen 1600 Squareback: 4780
Year total: 6

1970 Citroen DS21 EFI 139 Pallas: 1038

Mercedes-Benz 280SE: 2830
Mercedes-Benz 280SE 3.5: 2831
Mercedes-Benz 280SL: 2832
Opel Diplomat: 3323
Opel Senator: 3325
Porsche 911 S 2.2-litre: 3631
Porsche 914: 3633
Volkswagen 411 LE Variant: 4781
Volkswagen Porsche 914: 4782
Volvo 1800E: 4916
Year total: 11

1971 Alfa Romeo 1750 Spider Veloce: 76
Aston Martin DBS V8: 244
BMW 2002: 522
BMW 2002 Tii: 523
Mercedes-Benz 220D: 2833
Mercedes-Benz 300SL: 2834
Peugeot 504 Automatic: 3403
Porsche 911 E 2.4-litre: 3635
Volkswagen 411: 4784
Volvo 142E: 4917
Volvo 144 Grand Luxe: 4918
Volvo 145E Estate: 4919
Year total: 12

1972 Alfa Romeo 1750 Berlina: 77
Alfa Romeo 2000 GTV Injection: 80
Alfa Romeo Montreal: 82
BMW 2002 Tii: 527
Ford Capri RS2600: 1805
Lancia 2000: 2513
Mercedes-Benz 280SE 3.5: 2835
Mercedes-Benz 280SEL: 2836
Mercedes-Benz 350SL: 2837
Porsche 911 E: 3637
Saab 99EA: 4073
Triumph 2.5PI Mk II: 4552
Volvo 164E: 4920
Volvo 1800 ES: 4921
Year total: 14

1973 BMW 3.0 CSL: 530
BMW 520i: 531
Citroen Safari SM: 1045
Mercedes-Benz 280CE Auto: 2840
Mercedes-Benz 280SE: 2841
Mercedes-Benz 450SE: 2842
Mercedes-Benz 450SLC: 2843
Porsche 911 S: 3638
Porsche 914 2-litre: 3640
Porsche Carrera RS Touring: 3641
Porsche Carrera RSR: 3642
Renault 17: 3844
Saab 99E: 4075
Volvo 144E: 4923
Volvo 164E: 4924

Year total: 15

1974 BMW 2002 Turbo: 534
Mercedes-Benz 280E: 2844
Mercedes-Benz 450SEL: 2845
Mercedes-Benz 450SL: 2846
Opel Commodore GSE: 3337
Peugeot 504 L Diesel: 3410
Porsche 911 Carrera: 3643
Porsche 911 Targa: 3644
Porsche 911S 2.7-litre: 3645
Saab 99LE Wagonback: 4077
Year total: 10

1975 BMW 530i: 539
Jaguar XJ5.3C: 2328
Mercedes-Benz 450SLC: 2849
Opel Manta: 3341
Porsche Turbo 3-litre: 3648
Renault 17 Gordini: 3848
Saab 99EMS: 4078
Volkswagen Beetle: 4798
Volvo 242 GL: 4927
Volvo 244 GL: 4928
Volvo 264 GL: 4929
Year total: 11

1976 Alfa Romeo Alfetta GT: 92
Audi 80 GTE: 275
BMW 633 CSi: 540
Cadillac Seville: 710
Chevrolet Corvette Greenwood: 870
Ford Cobra II Kemp: 1841
Jaguar XJS: 2330
Mercedes-Benz 280E: 2850
Mercedes-Benz 450SL: 2851
Opel Rekord 2100D: 3342
Porsche 911 S: 3649
Porsche 911 Turbo Carrera: 3650
Porsche 912 E: 3651
Porsche 914 2.0-litre: 3652
Porsche 924: 3653
Renault 17 Gordini: 3851
Volvo 265 DL: 4931
Year total: 17

1977 Alfa Romeo Alfetta: 98
Audi 100 5E: 276
Audi Fox: 278
BMW 320i: 542
BMW 630 CSi: 544
BMW 733i: 545
Citroen CX 2200 Diesel: 1051
Citroen CX 2400 GTi: 1053
Datsun 810 Sedan: 1203
Jaguar XJS Automatic: 2332
Mercedes-Benz 280E: 2853
Mercedes-Benz 600SE: 2854
Porsche 911 SC: 3654
Porsche 911 Turbo: 3655
Porsche 924: 3656
Porsche 935 Group 4 Holbert: 3657
Saab 99EMS: 4080
Volkswagen Golf GTi: 4806
Volkswagen Sciroco GTi: 4811
Volvo 244 DL: 4932
Year total: 20

1978 Audi 5000: 280
BMW 323i: 547
BMW 333i Alpina: 548
BMW 528i: 549
BMW 733i: 550
Cadillac Seville Diesel: 711
Citroen CX Pallas C-Matic Injection: 1054
Ford Granada 2.1D: 1859
Ford Granada 2.8i S: 1860
Jaguar XJ5.3 Automatic: 2335
Mercedes-Benz 300CD: 2856
Mercedes-Benz 300SD: 2857
Mercedes-Benz 450SEL: 2858
Pontiac Firebird TransAm Silverbird: 3566
Porsche 924 Lux: 3660
Porsche 928: 3661
Porsche 928 Automatic: 3662
Saab Turbo: 4081
Volkswagen Golf LD: 4814
Volvo 262C: 4936
Volvo 265 GLE Estate: 4937
Year total: 21

1979 Alfa Romeo Sprint Veloce: 106
BMW 528i: 551
BMW 635 CSi: 552
BMW 732i: 553
Citroen CX 2500 Diesel Super: 1056
Datsun 240K: 1210
Datsun 280ZX: 1211
Datsun 280ZX 2+2 Automatic: 1212
Datsun 280ZX Automatic: 1213
Ford Granada 2.8i GLS Estate: 1865
Jaguar XJ6 4.2: 2336
Jaguar XJS: 2338
Mercedes-Benz 280CE: 2860
Mercedes-Benz 300TD: 2861
Mercedes-Benz 450SEL 6.9: 2862
Mercedes-Benz 450SL: 2863
Peugeot 505 STI: 3420
Porsche 924: 3663
Porsche 924 Turbo: 3664
Renault 30 TX: 3863
Renault Gordini: 3867
Saab 900 Turbo: 4082
Toyota Celica Supra: 4403
Volkswagen Scirocco: 4815
Volkswagen Sciroco GLi: 4816
Year total: 25

1980 Alfa Romeo Spider: 107
Audi 4000: 283
Audi 5000 S Diesel: 284
BMW 320i: 554
BMW 633 CSi: 555
BMW M1: 556
Datsun 200SX: 1217
Datsun 280ZX: 1218
Datsun 280ZX Automatic: 1219
Fiat Brava Abarth Rally: 1571
Jaguar XJ6 Series III: 2339
Mercedes-Benz 450SL: 2864
Oldsmobile Cutlass Diesel: 3300
Peugeot 505 S: 3422
Peugeot 505 SD: 3423
Peugeot 604 D Turbo: 3424
Porsche 911 SC: 3666
Porsche 924: 3667
Porsche 924 S Turbo: 3668
Porsche 928: 3669

Rover 3500: 4020
Saab 900GLE: 4084
Triumph TR8: 4577
Triumph TR8 Group 44: 4578
Volkswagen Dasher Diesel: 4818
Volkswagen Jetta: 4819
Volkswagen Rabbit: 4821
Volkswagen Scirocco: 4822
Volkswagen Vanagon: 4823
Volvo Diesel: 4939
Volvo GL: 4940
Year total: 31

1981 Alfa Romeo GTV6: 109
Audi 200 5E: 285
Audi 4000 Automatic: 286
Audi 5000 Turbo: 287
Audi Coupe: 288
Audi Quattro: 289
BMW 323i Hardy & Beck: 557
BMW 528i: 558
Cadillac Seville Diesel: 712
Citroen CX Pallas: 1058
Daimler Double-Six HE: 1155
Datsun 280ZX Turbo: 1223
Datsun 810 Maxima: 1224
Ferrari 308 GTSi: 1415
Fiat Brava: 1573
Ford Capri 2.8 Injection: 1871
Ford Granada 2.8i: 1877
Jaguar XJS: 2340
Jaguar XJS Automatic: 2341
Lancia Montecarlo Group 5 Turbo: 2531
Mercedes-Benz 230E: 2865
Mercedes-Benz 230TE: 2866
Mercedes-Benz 300GD: 2867
Mercedes-Benz 300TD: 2868
Mercedes-Benz 380SEL: 2869
Mitsubishi Colt Lancer 2000 Turbo: 3068
Opel Manta Monza S3.0E: 3347
Peugeot 505 S Turbodiesel: 3426
Porsche 911 SC: 3670
Porsche 924 Turbo: 3671
Renault 18i: 3871
Renault 5 Turbo: 3873
Renault Le Car Turbo: 3874
Saab 900 Turbo: 4085
Toyota Cressida: 4409
TVR Tasmin: 4596
Volkswagen Rabbit: 4827
Volkswagen Rabbit Convertible: 4828
Volkswagen Rabbit Diesel: 4829
Volkswagen Scirocco S: 4831
Volvo 265 GLE: 4941
Year total: 41

1982 Alfa Romeo Spider Veloce: 110
Alfa Romeo Spider Veloce 2000: 111
Audi 100 CD: 290
Audi 80 Turbo Diesel: 291
Audi Quattro: 292
BMW 528e: 560
BMW 635 CSi: 561
BMW 745i: 562
Datsun 280ZX: 1225
De Lorean DMC 2.8-litre Coupe: 1233
Ferrari 288 GTO: 1416
Ferrari Mondial 8: 1418
Fiat Spider 2000: 1576
Fiat Spider Turbo: 1577
Fiat X1/9: 1579
Jaguar XJS HE: 2342
Lancia Beta Coupe: 2534
Mercedes-Benz 380SEC: 2870
Mercedes-Benz 380SL: 2871
Mitsubishi Colt Starion Turbo: 3071
Peugeot 505 STI: 3428
Pontiac Firebird TransAm: 3570
Porsche 924 Weissach: 3672
Porsche 944: 3673
Porsche 944 Lux: 3674
Renault Alliance DL: 3880
Renault Fuego Turbo: 3882
Rolls-Royce Silver Spur: 3971
Rover SD Turbo: 4023
Saab 900: 4087
Saab 900 Turbo: 4088
Toyota Celica Supra: 4415
Vauxhall Cavalier LD: 4693
Volkswagen Golf GTi 1800: 4832
Volkswagen Quantum: 4835
Volvo 360 GLT: 4943
Volvo 760 GLE: 4944
Volvo GLT Turbo: 4945
Year total: 38

1983 Audi 200 Turbo: 293
Audi 5000 S: 294
Audi 80 Quattro: 295
Audi Coupe Injection: 296
BMW 318i: 563
BMW 320i: 564
BMW 525E: 565
BMW 533i: 566
BMW 735i: 567
Chevrolet Cavalier CS: 889
Chevrolet Corvette: 891
Daihatsu Charade Diesel: 1120
Datsun 200SX: 1228
Datsun 280ZX: 1229
Datsun 280ZX Electramotive: 1230
Datsun 280ZX Turbo: 1231
Ferrari 308 GTBi Quattrovalvole: 1419
Ferrari 308 GTSi Targa: 1420
Fiat Spider 2000: 1580
Ford Escort XR3i: 1885
Ford Granada 2.5 Diesel Estate: 1887
Ford Sierra XR4i: 1890
Ford Thunderbird Turbo Coupe: 1891
Isuzu I-Mark LS: 2252
Jaguar XJS: 2343
Mercedes-Benz 190E: 2873
Mercedes-Benz 280SE: 2874
Mercedes-Benz 380SL: 2875
Mitsubishi Starion: 3074
Mitsubishi Starion Turbo: 3075
Mitsubishi Tredia Turbo: 3076
Opel Manta GTE: 3349
Porsche 911 Cabriolet: 3675
Porsche 911 Turbo: 3676
Porsche 928 S: 3677
Porsche 944: 3678
Renault Fuego Turbo: 3884
Rover Vitesse: 4024
Subaru GL Turbo Traction Wagon: 4257
Talbot Horizon 1.9LD: 4348
Toyota Camry LE: 4416
Toyota Celica GTS: 4417
Toyota Cressida: 4420
Toyota Supra: 4421
TVR Tasmin Convertible: 4597
Vauxhall Astra GTE: 4694
Vauxhall Cavalier CD: 4696
Volkswagen Quantum GL5: 4838
Volkswagen Rabbit GTi: 4839
Volkswagen Scirocco: 4840
Volkswagen Scirocco GTi: 4841
Volkswagen Vanagon Wasserboxer: 4842
Volvo 760 GLE: 4946
Volvo 760 Turbo: 4947
Year total: 54

1984 Alfa Romeo Alfetta Gold Cloverleaf: 113
Alfa Romeo GTV6: 114
Alfa Romeo Spider: 115
Audi 200 Quattro Turbo: 297
Audi 4000 S Quattro: 298
Audi 5000 S Avant: 299
Audi 5000 S Turbo: 300
Audi Coupe GT: 302
Bitter SC: 492
BMW 318i: 568
BMW 325E: 569
BMW 633 CSi: 570
BMW 735i Automatic: 571
BMW M635 CSi: 572
Chrysler Laser XE: 1003
Citroen BX19 RD Diesel: 1061
Citroen CX GTi Turbo: 1062
Dodge Conquest: 1330
Ferrari 288 GTO: 1421
Ferrari 512 BBi: 1422
Ferrari GTO: 1423
Ferrari Mondial Cabriolet Quattrovalvole: 1424
Fiat X1/9: 1587
Ford Fiesta 1.6L Diesel: 1893
Ford Mustang SVO: 1897
Ford Sierra XR4i: 1898
Honda Civic CRX: 2113
Isuzu Impulse: 2253
Jaguar XJ6 Vanden Plas: 2344
Jaguar XJS 3.6: 2345
Jaguar XJS HE: 2346
Lincoln Continental Mk VII: 2583
Mazda RX-7: 2724
Mazda RX-7 GSL SE: 2725
Mercedes-Benz 190E: 2876
Mercedes-Benz 500SEC: 2877
MG Montego EFi: 3038
Mitsubishi Colt 1600 Turbo: 3077
Mitsubishi Cordia Turbo 1.8: 3078
Mitsubishi Mirage Turbo: 3080
Nissan 200SX Turbo: 3207
Nissan 300ZX: 3208
Nissan Pulsar NX Turbo: 3210
Nissan Silvia Turbo ZX: 3211

Opel Manta Monza GSE: 3350
Panther Kallista 2.8: 3377
Peugeot 205 GTi: 3431
Peugeot 505 GRi: 3432
Peugeot 505 S Wagon: 3433
Pininfarina Azzurra: 3469
Pininfarina Spider: 3470
Plymouth Colt GTS Turbo: 3518
Pontiac Fiero: 3573
Pontiac Fiero SE: 3574
Porsche 911 Carrera: 3679
Porsche 911 Turbo Cabriolet Ruf: 3680
Renault 25 V6: 3885
Renault 5 Turbo 2: 3886
Renault Fuego 2.2: 3888
Toyota Celica 2.8i Supra: 4425
Toyota Corolla GT Coupe: 4426
Toyota Corolla GTS: 4427
Toyota Supra: 4429
Toyota Van LE: 4430
Vauxhall Astra GTE: 4698
Volkswagen Jetta GLi: 4843
Volkswagen Passat CL Turbo Diesel Estate: 4845
Volkswagen Scirocco: 4846
Volkswagen Scirocco 16v: 4847
Volvo 740 GLT: 4948
Volvo 760 GLE: 4949
Volvo GLT Wagon: 4950
Year total: 72

1985 Alfa Romeo Alfa 90 2.5 Gold Cloverleaf: 118
Alfa Romeo Graduate: 121
Alfa Romeo GTV Callaway Twin Turbo: 122
Audi 100 Quattro: 303
Audi 200 Avant Quattro: 304
Audi 5000 S Turbo Quattro: 305
Audi 90 Quattro: 306
Audi Coupe GT: 307
Audi Quattro: 308
Audi Quattro Sport: 309
BMW 325i: 573
BMW 327S Hardy & Beck: 574
BMW 732i: 575
BMW M535i: 576
BMW M635 CSi Hardy & Beck: 577
Cadillac Cimarron: 714
Chevrolet Corvette: 897
Chrysler Le Baron GTS: 1004
Citroen Visa 17RD: 1069
Citroen Visa GTi: 1070
Ferrari Testa Rossa: 1426
Fiat Uno Turbo ie: 1589
Fiat X1/9: 1590
Ford Escort RS Turbo: 1901
Ford Granada Scorpio: 1903
Ford Granada Scorpio 4x4: 1904
Ford Sierra 2.0i S: 1907
Honda Accord 2.0 EXi: 2117
Honda Accord SEi: 2119
Honda Civic GT: 2120
Honda CRX Si: 2124
Jaguar XJS HE Cabriolet: 2347
Lancia Coupe 2000ie: 2538
Lancia Thema 2.0 ie LX Turbo: 2539
Lincoln Continental Mk VII LSC: 2584
Mazda 323 1.6i: 2727
Mercedes-Benz 190E 2.3: 2878
Mercedes-Benz 190E 2.3-16: 2879
Mercedes-Benz 190E BBS/Callaway Turbo: 2880
Mercedes-Benz 300E: 2881
Mercedes-Benz 500SEL: 2882
Merkur XR4Ti: 2963
Mitsubishi Colt Starion Turbo: 3081
Mitsubishi Galant: 3082
Mitsubishi Galant Turbo: 3083
Mitsubishi Starion: 3085
Mitsubishi Starion ESI: 3086
Nissan Bluebird Turbo ZX: 3212
Nissan Maxima SE: 3214
Peugeot 305 GRD Estate: 3435
Peugeot 505 Turbo: 3437
Pontiac Fiero GT: 3577
Porsche 911 Carrera: 3682
Porsche 928 S: 3683
Porsche 928 S Series II: 3684
Porsche 944 Lux: 3685
Porsche 944 Turbo: 3686
Renault 25 V6 Turbo: 3889
Renault Encore GS: 3891
Rover 216 Vitesse: 4026
Saab 900 Turbo: 4089
Saab 9000 Turbo 16v: 4090
Saab 900i: 4091
Subaru 1.8 GTi: 4258
Subaru 1.8 RX Turbo: 4259
Subaru 4WD Turbo: 4260
Subaru 4WD Turbo XT Coupe: 4261
Subaru Turbo 4WD Estate: 4262
Subaru XT Turbo Coupe: 4264
Toyota Celica GTS: 4431
Toyota Corolla GT Hatchback: 4432
Toyota MR2: 4433
Toyota Supra: 4436
TVR 350i Series II: 4598
Vauxhall Cavalier SRi: 4701
Vauxhall Senator 3.0i CD: 4702
Volkswagen Cabriolet Wolfsburg: 4848
Volkswagen Golf: 4849
Volkswagen Golf GTi: 4850
Volkswagen Jetta GLi: 4851
Volkswagen Scirocco: 4852
Volkswagen Scirocco 16v: 4853
Volkswagen Scirocco GTX: 4854
Volvo 740 Turbo Wagon: 4951
Volvo 760 Turbo Estate: 4952
Year total: 85

1986 Acura Integra RS: 28
Acura Legend: 29
Alfa Romeo Alfa 75 2.5 Green Cloverleaf: 125
Alfa Romeo GTV6: 126
Alfa Romeo Milano Platinum: 127
Alfa Romeo Spider Quadrifoglio: 128
Aston Martin Volante: 256
Audi 100 Turbo Diesel: 310
Audi 5000 S: 311
Audi 90: 313
Audi Coupe GT: 314
Audi Coupe GT 2.2: 315
Audi Coupe Quattro: 316
Austin Montego 2.0 Vanden Plas EFI: 425
Bitter SC: 493
BMW 325 ES: 578
BMW 325i Convertible: 579
BMW 520i: 580
BMW 524 TD: 581
BMW 535i: 582
BMW 635 CSi: 583
BMW 735i: 584
BMW 735i Automatic: 585
Buick Electra T-type: 694
Chevrolet Cavalier Z24: 898
Chevrolet Celebrity CL Eurosport: 899
Chevrolet Corvette: 900
Chevrolet Corvette Callaway: 901
Chevrolet Corvette Z51: 902
Chrysler Laser XT: 1005
Citroen BX19 RD Estate: 1071
Citroen CX25 Ri Familiale Auto: 1072
Citroen Visa GTi: 1073
Dodge Shelby GLH-S: 1335
Ferrari 3.2 Mondial: 1427
Ferrari 328 GTB: 1428
Ferrari Mondial 3.2: 1429
Fiat Regata DS: 1594
Ford Escort RS Turbo: 1911
Ford Escort XR3i: 1912
Ford Mustang GT 5.0: 1913
Ford Mustang SVO: 1915
Ford RS200: 1917
Ford Sierra Ghia 4x4 Estate: 1918
Honda Accord LXi: 2126
Honda CRX Coupe 1.6i 16: 2128
Honda CRX Si: 2129
Honda Integra EX 16: 2132
Honda Legend: 2133
Honda Prelude 2.0 Si: 2134
Isuzu Impulse Sports Coupe: 2255
Isuzu Impulse Turbo: 2256
Jaguar XJ6 3.6: 2348
Jaguar XJS: 2349
Jaguar XJSC: 2350
Jaguar XJSC HE: 2351
Lamborghini Countach 5000S: 2469
Lancia Delta HF 4WD: 2541
Lancia Delta HF Turbo ie: 2542
Lancia Prisma 1600ie LX: 2543
Lancia Thema 2.0ie: 2544
Lotus Esprit Turbo: 2630
Mazda 323 1.6i: 2730
Mazda 323 LX: 2731
Mazda 323 Turbo 4x4 Lux: 2732
Mazda 626 2.0i 5-door: 2733
Mazda 626 GT: 2734
Mazda RX-7: 2735
Mazda RX-7 GXL: 2736
Mazda RX-7 Turbo: 2737
Mercedes-Benz 190E 2.3-16: 2883
Mercedes-Benz 300E: 2885
Mercedes-Benz 300TE: 2886
Mercedes-Benz 420SE: 2887
Mercedes-Benz 560SEC: 2888
Mercedes-Benz 560SEL: 2889
Mercedes-Benz 560SL: 2890
Mercury Sable LS: 2958
Mitsubishi Cordia Turbo: 3087

Mitsubishi Starion ESI-R: 3090
Nissan 300ZX: 3215
Nissan 300ZX Turbo: 3216
Nissan Bluebird 1.8 ZX: 3217
Nissan Laurel 2.4 SGL Automatic: 3218
Peugeot 205 GTi: 3438
Peugeot 309 SR Injection: 3440
Peugeot 505 GTi Family Estate: 3441
Peugeot 505 Turbo: 3442
Pontiac Fiero GT: 3578
Porsche 911 Cabriolet: 3687
Porsche 911 Carrera SE: 3688
Porsche 911 Turbo: 3689
Porsche 924 S: 3690
Porsche 928 S: 3691
Porsche 928 S4 Automatic: 3692
Porsche 944: 3693
Porsche 944 S: 3694
Porsche 944 Turbo: 3695
Range Rover Vogue: 3774
Reliant Scimitar Ti: 3795
Renault 21 Savanna GTX: 3894
Renault Alliance 1.7L: 3898
Renault GTA V6 Turbo: 3899
Rover 825i: 4027
Saab 9000: 4092
Saab 9000i: 4093
Subaru 4WD 3-door Turbo Coupe: 4265
Suzuki Swift 1.3 GTi: 4326
Toyota Celica 2.0GT: 4438
Toyota Celica GTS: 4439
Toyota MR2: 4440
Toyota MR2 T-Bar: 4441
Toyota Supra: 4442
Toyota Supra 3.0i: 4443
Vauxhall Belmont 1.8 GLSi: 4703
Vauxhall Carlton CD 2.0i: 4704
Volkswagen Golf GTi 16v: 4856
Volkswagen Jetta GT: 4857
Volkswagen Quantum Synchro Wagon: 4858
Volkswagen Scirocco 16v: 4859
Volkswagen Scirocco GTX 16v: 4860
Year total: 121

1987 Acura Integra LS: 30
Alfa Romeo Alfa 75 2.0i Twin Spark: 131
Alfa Romeo Alfa 75 V6 3.0: 132
Alfa Romeo Milano Verde 3.0: 133
Audi 90 2.2E: 317
Audi 90 Quattro: 318
Bentley Turbo R: 481
BMW 318i 2-door: 586
BMW 325i Cabriolet: 587
BMW 730i SE: 588
BMW 750i L: 589
BMW M3: 590
Chevrolet Beretta GT: 905
Chevrolet Camaro IROC-Z: 906
Chevrolet Camaro IROC-Z L98: 907
Chevrolet Corvette: 908
Chevrolet Corvette ASC Geneve: 909
Chevrolet Corvette Convertible: 910
Chrysler Le Baron Coupe: 1006
Citroen BX GTi 16v: 1077
Citroen CX25 DTR Turbo 2: 1078
Daihatsu Charade CX Diesel Turbo: 1123
Daihatsu Charade GT ti: 1124
Daihatsu Fourtrak Estate DT EL: 1125
Ferrari 328 GTS: 1431
Ferrari 412: 1432
Ferrari Mondial Cabriolet 3.2: 1433
Fiat Croma ie Super: 1595
Fiat Regata 100S ie: 1596
Ford Granada 2.4i Ghia: 1921
Ford Granada Scorpio 2.9 EX: 1922
Ford Mustang GT: 1923
Ford Mustang LX 5.0: 1924
Ford Sierra Sapphire 2.0 Ghia: 1925
Ford Thunderbird Bondurant 5.0: 1926
Ford Thunderbird Turbo Coupe: 1927
Honda Legend Coupe: 2137
Honda Prelude 2.0 Si: 2138
Honda Prelude 2.0i 16: 2139
Isuzu Trooper 3-door TD: 2257
Jaguar XJ6: 2352
Jaguar XJ6 2.9: 2353
Jaguar XJS 3.6 Automatic: 2354
Lancia Thema 8.32: 2546
Land Rover Ninety County Turbo Diesel: 2560
Mercedes-Benz 190E 2.6: 2891
Mercedes-Benz 300CE: 2892
Mercedes-Benz 300TD: 2893
Mercedes-Benz 420SEL: 2894
Mercedes-Benz 560SEC Cabriolet Straman: 2895
Mercury Tracer: 2959
Merkur Scorpio: 2964
Mitsubishi Galant Sapporo: 3093
Mitsubishi Shogun Turbo Diesel 5-door: 3094
Mitsubishi Starion 2000 Turbo: 3095
Morgan Plus 8: 3134
MVS Venturi GT: 3190
Nissan 300ZX: 3223
Nissan 300ZX Turbo: 3224
Nissan Pulsar NX SE: 3226
Nissan Sunny ZX Coupe: 3227
Peugeot 205 GTi 1.9: 3443
Peugeot 309 GTi: 3444
Peugeot 505 STX: 3445
Pontiac Bonneville SE: 3579
Pontiac Fiero Formula: 3580
Pontiac Firebird Formula 5.0: 3582
Pontiac Le Mans: 3583
Porsche 911 Turbo Gemballa Avalanche: 3697
Porsche 911 Turbo Ruf 3.4: 3698
Porsche 911 Turbo Slant-Nose: 3699
Porsche 924 S: 3700
Porsche 959 S: 3702
Range Rover V8: 3775
Renault Alliance GTA: 3903
Rover 820SE: 4028
Rover Sterling Automatic: 4030
Subaru XT Turbo 4WD: 4268
Toyota Camry 2.0 GLi: 4445
Toyota Camry 2.0 GLi Estate: 4446
Toyota Celica GT Cabriolet: 4447
Toyota Corolla FX-16 GTS: 4449
Toyota Landcruiser: 4450
Toyota MR2 Supercharged: 4451
Toyota Supra: 4452
TVR 390 SE: 4599
TVR S Convertible: 4600
Vauxhall Astra GTE 2.0i: 4706
Vauxhall Carlton 3000 GSi: 4708
Vauxhall Cavalier 2.0i CD: 4709
Vauxhall Cavalier SRi 130 4-door: 4710
Vauxhall Senator 3.0i CD: 4711
Volkswagen Fox GL: 4861
Volkswagen GTi 16v: 4863
Volkswagen Jetta GTi 16v: 4864
Volvo 480 ES: 4954
Volvo 740 Turbo: 4955
Volvo 760 GLE: 4956
Year total: 98

1988 Acura Integra LS Special Edition: 31
Alfa Romeo 75 2.5 Auto: 134
Alfa Romeo 75 Evoluzione: 135
Alfa Romeo Spider: 136
Audi 100 Avant Quattro: 319
Audi 100 Sport: 320
Audi 80 1.8E: 321
Audi 90 Quattro: 322
Audi Quattro: 323
BMW 325i S: 591
BMW 325i X: 592
BMW 535i SE: 593
BMW 635 CSi: 594
BMW 735i: 595
BMW 750i L: 596
BMW M6: 597
Buick Reatta: 695
Buick Regal Custom: 696
Cadillac Allante: 715
Chevrolet Camaro: 911
Chevrolet Camaro IROC-Z 5.0: 912
Chevrolet Camaro IROC-Z 5.7: 913
Chevrolet Cavalier Z24 Convertible: 915
Chevrolet Corvette: 916
Chevrolet Corvette Bakeracing SCCA Escort: 917
Chevrolet Corvette Callaway: 918
Chevrolet Corvette Convertible: 919
Chevrolet Corvette Guldstrand Grand Sport 80: 920
Chevrolet Corvette Morrison/Baker Nelson Ledges: 921
Chevrolet Corvette Z51: 922
Chevrolet Nova Twin Cam: 923
Chrysler Conquest TSi: 1007
Citroen BX DTR Turbo: 1080
Daihatsu Charade CLX: 1126
Dodge Daytona Shelby Z: 1336
Dodge Lancer Shelby: 1337
Dodge Shelby CSX: 1338
Eagle Premier ES: 1354
Ferrari 308 Norwood Bonneville GTO: 1434
Ferrari F40: 1435
Ferrari Mondial Cabriolet: 1436
Ferrari Testa Rossa: 1437
Ferrari Testa Rossa Straman Spyder: 1438
Fiat X1/9: 1599
Ford Mustang Cartech Turbo: 1928
Ford Mustang Convertible Saleen: 1929
Ford Mustang GT: 1930
Ford Mustang JBA/Saleen: 1931
Ford Probe GT: 1933
Ford Sierra RS Cosworth: 1934
Ford Taurus 3.8: 1935
Honda Civic CRX: 2140

Pontiac Firebird T/A Turbo Pontiac Engineering: 3588
Pontiac Firebird TransAm 20th Anniversary: 3589
Pontiac Firebird TransAm Turbo: 3590
Pontiac Grand Am Turbo: 3591
Pontiac Grand Prix McLaren Turbo: 3592
Porsche 911 3.3 Turbo: 3719
Porsche 911 Carrera 4: 3720
Porsche 911 Carrera Cabriolet: 3721
Porsche 911 Club Sport: 3722
Porsche 911 Turbo: 3723
Porsche 911 Turbo Motorsport Design: 3724
Porsche 928 Cabrio Strosek: 3725
Porsche 928 S4 Koenig: 3726
Porsche 928 S4 SE: 3727
Porsche 944: 3728
Porsche 944 S2: 3729
Porsche 944 Turbo: 3730
Porsche 959: 3731
Range Rover Vogue: 3777
Range Rover Vogue SE: 3778
Renault 25 TXi: 3910
Renault Espace TXE: 3912
Rover Montego 2.0 DSL Turbo: 4034
Rover Sterling Catalyst: 4035
Rover Vitesse: 4036
Saab 900 Turbo S: 4095
Saab 9000 Turbo: 4096
Saab Carlsson: 4097
Seat Ibiza SXi: 4113
Subaru Legacy FIA Record: 4274
Subaru XT6: 4275
Suzuki Swift 1.3 GTi: 4331
Toyota Camry V6 GXi: 4461
Toyota Corolla GTS: 4463
Toyota MR2 Supercharged: 4464
Toyota Supra 3.0i Turbo: 4465
Toyota Supra Turbo: 4466
Toyota Supra Turbo TRD: 4467
Treser T1: 4485
TVR 420 SEAC: 4601
TVR S Convertible: 4602
Vauxhall Astra 1.7 DL: 4716
Vauxhall Cavalier SRi: 4719
Vauxhall Senator 2.5i: 4720
Vauxhall Senator 3.0i CD: 4721
Volkswagen Caravelle Carat Automatic: 4873
Volkswagen Corrado 16v: 4875
Volkswagen Passat GT 16v: 4878
Volvo 440 Turbo: 4957
Volvo 740 GLE: 4958
Volvo 740 Turbo: 4959
Zender Vision 3: 5007

Year total: 159

1990 Acura Integra GS: 34
Acura Legend Coupe: 35
Acura NSX: 36
Alfa Romeo 164 Twin Spark Lusso: 142
Alfa Romeo 164S: 143
Alfa Romeo 33 Boxer 16v: 144
Audi 80 2.0E: 328
Audi 90 Quattro: 329
Audi Quattro 20v: 330
Audi V8 Quattro: 331
Audi V8 Quattro Automatic: 332
Bentley Turbo R: 482
Bitter Type 3 Cabrio: 494
BMW 318i S: 609
BMW 325i Convertible: 610
BMW 735i Koenig: 611
BMW 750i: 612
BMW 750i Alpina B12: 613
Cadillac Allante: 716
Cadillac Aurora: 717
Cadillac Eldorado Touring Coupe: 718
Chevrolet Beretta GT: 935
Chevrolet Beretta GTZ: 936
Chevrolet Camaro IROC-Z Convertible: 937
Chevrolet Camaro Z/28: 938
Chevrolet Cavalier Z24: 939
Chevrolet Corvette Callaway: 940
Chevrolet Corvette Callaway Sledgehammer: 941
Chevrolet Corvette L98: 944
Chevrolet Lumina APV: 945
Citroen BX GTi 4x4: 1084
Citroen CX25 GTi Turbo 2 CX Auto: 1085
Citroen XM 2.0SEi: 1086
Cizeta Moroder V16T: 1094
Consulier GTP LX: 1096
Daihatsu Applause 16 Xi: 1131
De Tomaso Pantera GT5 S: 1244
Dodge Daytona ES: 1343
Dodge Daytona Shelby: 1344
Dodge Shadow ES VNT: 1345
Eagle Talon: 1355
Evans Series I: 1362
Ferrari 348tb: 1445
Ferrari F40: 1446
Ferrari Mondial: 1447
Ferrari Pininfarina Mythos: 1448
Fiat Uno Turbo ie: 1605
Ford Fiesta RS Turbo: 1949
Ford Fiesta XR2i: 1950
Ford Granada 2.5 GL Diesel: 1951
Ford Granada Ghia X 2.9 EFi Saloon: 1952
Ford Granada Scorpio 2.0i Auto: 1953
Ford Mustang GT Convertible: 1954
Ford Mustang LX 5.0L: 1955
Ford Probe GT: 1956
Ford Probe LX: 1957
Ford Sierra Sapphire Cosworth 4x4: 1958
Ginetta G32: 1998
Honda Accord 2.0 EXi: 2150
Honda Concerto 1.6i 16: 2151
Honda CRX 1.6i VT: 2152
Hyundai Sonata 2.4i GLS: 2225
Infiniti M30: 2230
Infiniti Q45: 2231
Isuzu Impulse XS: 2260
Ital Design Aztec: 2262
Jaguar XJ6 Vanden Plas: 2362
Jaguar XJR 4.0: 2363
Jaguar XJRS: 2364
Jaguar XJS: 2365
Jaguar XJS Lister Le Mans: 2366
Jaguar XJS Railton: 2367
Koenig Competition Evolution: 2418
Lamborghini Diablo: 2474
Lancia Dedra 1.8i: 2551
Lancia Dedra 2.0ie: 2552
Lancia Thema 2.0ie 16v SE Turbo: 2553
Lancia Y10 GTie: 2554
Land Rover Discovery TDi: 2563
Lexus LS400: 2570
Lincoln Continental Mk VII LSC: 2587
Lotus Elan: 2638
Lotus Elan SE: 2639
Lotus Esprit Turbo SE: 2640
Maserati 228: 2680
Maserati Shamal: 2681
Mazda MX-5 Miata Millen: 2760
Mazda MX-6 GT: 2761
Mazda Protege: 2762
Mazda RX-7 Turbo: 2764
Mercedes-Benz 190E 2.5-16 Evolution II: 2908
Mercedes-Benz 300CE: 2909
Mercedes-Benz 300CE AMG Hammer: 2910
Mercedes-Benz 300D: 2911
Mercedes-Benz 300E-24: 2912
Mercedes-Benz 500SL: 2913
Mercury Capri XR-2: 2961
Mitsubishi Galant 2000 GLSi Coupe: 3108
Mitsubishi Lancer GLXi 4WD Liftback: 3109
Mitsubishi Lancer Liftback 1800 GTi-16v: 3110
Morgan Plus 4 Mk III: 3136
MVS Venturi: 3191
Nissan 300ZX: 3240
Nissan 300ZX Turbo: 3241
Nissan Skyline GT-R: 3243
Oldsmobile Toronado Trofeo: 3305
Panther Solo: 3380
Peugeot 405 GR Injection Auto: 3458
Peugeot 405 Mi16x4: 3459
Peugeot 405 Turbo 16 Pike's Peak: 3460
Peugeot 605 SRi: 3461
Plymouth Laser RS Turbo: 3522
Pontiac Firebird Formula: 3593
Pontiac Firebird TransAm GTA: 3594
Pontiac Grand Prix STE Turbo: 3595
Porsche 911 Carrera 2: 3732
Porsche 911 Carrera 2 Tiptronic: 3733
Porsche 911 Carrera 4: 3734
Porsche 911 Speedster: 3735
Porsche 911 Turbo: 3736
Porsche 911 Turbo RS Tuning: 3737
Porsche 928: 3738
Porsche 928 Automatic: 3739
Porsche 928 Gemballa: 3740
Porsche 944 S2: 3742
Porsche 944 S2 Cabriolet: 3743
Porsche Carrera 2 Cabriolet Tiptronic: 3744
Porsche Panamericana: 3745
Range Rover County: 3779
Range Rover Vogue SE: 3780
Reliant Scimitar SST 1800Ti: 3796
Renault 21 Turbo Quadra: 3914
Renault 21 TXi: 3915
Renault 25 V6 2.9 Auto: 3916
Rover 214 GSi: 4037
Rover 216 GSi: 4038
Rover 414 Si: 4039
Rover 416 GTi: 4040
Rover Metro GTi 16v: 4042
Saab 9000CD: 4098
Saab 900SPG: 4099

Saab CDS 2.3: 4100
Sbarro Chrono 3.5: 4108
Subaru Legacy 2.2 GX 4WD: 4276
Suzuki Swift GT: 4333
Toyota Celica 2.0 GT: 4468
Toyota Celica All-Trac Turbo: 4469
Toyota Celica GTS: 4470
Toyota MR2 GT: 4472
Toyota MR2 Turbo: 4473
Toyota Previa LE: 4474
Vauxhall Calibra 2.0i 16v: 4722
Vauxhall Carlton 3.0i CDX Estate: 4723
Vauxhall Carlton GSi 3000 24v: 4724
Vauxhall Cavalier GSi 2000 16v: 4725
Vauxhall Cavalier GSi 2000 16v 4x4: 4726
Vauxhall Nova 1.5TD Merit: 4727
Vector W2: 4735
Volkswagen Corrado G60: 4879
Volkswagen Passat CL TD Estate: 4880
Volkswagen Passat GL: 4881
Volvo 460 GLi: 4961
Volvo 460 Turbo: 4962
Volvo 740 GLT 16v Estate: 4963
Volvo 740 Turbo: 4964
Zender Fact 4: 5008
Year total: 166

1991 Acura Legend LS: 37
Alfa Romeo 164 Cloverleaf: 145
Alfa Romeo Spider Veloce: 147
Aston Martin Virage: 261
Audi 100 2.8E Auto: 333
Audi 200 Quattro: 334
Audi 80 16v Sport: 335
Audi Coupe S2: 337
Audi V8 Quattro: 338
Bentley Turbo R: 483
Bertone Emotion Lotus: 489
BMW 318i: 614
BMW 325i SE: 615
BMW 520i: 616
BMW 525i: 617
BMW 525i SE 24v: 618
BMW 535i Alpina B10 Bi-Turbo: 619
BMW 850i: 620
BMW M3 Sport Evolution: 621
BMW M5: 622
Bugatti EB110: 652
Buick Reatta Convertible: 698
Cadillac Allante: 719
Cadillac Seville Touring Sedan: 720
Chevrolet Baretta GTZ: 946
Chevrolet Camaro Z/28 Convertible: 947
Chevrolet Corvette Callaway: 948
Chevrolet Corvette Callaway Speedster: 949
Chevrolet Corvette Callaway Twin Turbo: 950
Chevrolet Corvette Lingenfelter: 951
Chevrolet Corvette Rick Mears: 952
Chevrolet Corvette ZR-1: 953
Chevrolet Corvette ZR-1 Geiger: 954
Chevrolet Corvette ZR-1 SS: 955
Chevrolet Corvette ZR-2: 956
Chevrolet Lumina Z34: 957
Citroen XM 3.0 SEi Auto: 1088
Citroen XM V6.24: 1089
Citroen ZX Volcane: 1091
Dodge Spirit R/T: 1346
Dodge Stealth R/T Turbo: 1347
Eagle Talon TSi 4WD: 1357
Ferrari 348tb: 1449
Ferrari F40: 1450
Ferrari GTO Norwood: 1451
Ferrari Mondial t: 1452
Ferrari Mondial t Cabriolet: 1453
Ford Crown Victoria LX: 1959
Ford Escort Cabriolet: 1962
Ford Escort GT: 1963
Ford Escort Millen: 1964
Ford Festiva Shogun: 1965
Ford Mustang NOS/Saleen: 1967
Ford Orion 1.6i Ghia: 1968
Ford Probe GT: 1969
Ford Scorpio 24v: 1970
Ford Taurus SHO: 1971
Ford Thunderbird LX: 1972
Geo Storm GSi: 1994
Honda Civic 1.5 VEi: 2153
Honda Civic 1.6i VT: 2154
Honda Legend: 2155
Honda NSX: 2156
Honda Prelude Si: 2157
Hyundai Lantra 1.6 Cdi: 2226
Hyundai S Coupe GSi: 2227
Hyundai X2 1.5 GSi: 2228
Infiniti G20: 2232
Isuzu Impulse RS: 2261
Jaguar XJ6 3.2: 2368
Jaguar XJR15: 2369
Jaguar XJS: 2370
Jaguar XJS 4.0 Auto: 2371
Jaguar XJS Convertible: 2372
Koenig C62: 2419
Lamborghini Diablo: 2475
Lancia Dedra 2000 Turbo: 2555
Land Rover Discovery V8i 5DR: 2565
Lexus SC400: 2571
Lotus Elan SE: 2641
Mazda 121 GSX: 2765
Mazda 323 1.8 GT: 2766
Mazda MX-3 V6: 2767
Mazda RX-7 Cartech: 2768
Mazda RX-7 Infini IV: 2769
Mazda RX-7 Mariah Mode Six: 2770
Mazda RX-7 Turbo: 2771
Mercedes-Benz 190E 1.8 Auto: 2914
Mercedes-Benz 190E 2.5-16 Evolution II: 2916
Mercedes-Benz 300SL-24 5-speed Auto: 2917
Mercedes-Benz 400SE: 2918
Mercedes-Benz 500E: 2919
Mercedes-Benz 500SL: 2920
Mercedes-Benz G-Wagen 300 GD LWB: 2921
Mercury Tracer LTS: 2962
Mitsubishi 3000GT VR-4: 3111
Mitsubishi Colt 1800 GTI-16v: 3112
Mitsubishi Diamante LS: 3113
Mitsubishi Galant VR-4: 3114
Mitsubishi Shogun V6 LWB: 3115
Mitsubishi Sigma: 3116
Mitsubishi Space Runner 1800-16v GLXi: 3117
Morgan Plus 8: 3137
Nissan 240SX: 3245
Nissan 300ZX Motor Sports International SR-71: 3246
Nissan 300ZX Turbo Millen Super GTZ: 3247
Nissan 300ZX Twin Turbo: 3248
Nissan NX2000: 3249
Nissan Primera 2.0 GSX: 3250
Nissan Primera 2.0E ZX: 3251
Nissan Sentra SE-R: 3252
Opel Calibra 2.0i 16v: 3351
Opel Omega Lotus: 3352
Parradine V-12: 3382
Peugeot 106 XR: 3462
Peugeot 106 XSi: 3463
Peugeot 205 D Turbo: 3464
Peugeot 605 SR TD: 3465
Peugeot 605 SV 3.0 Auto: 3466
Peugeot 605 SVE 24: 3467
Plymouth Laser RS Turbo: 3523
Pontiac Firebird GTA: 3596
Pontiac Firebird TransAm Convertible: 3598
Pontiac Grand Prix GTP: 3599
Porsche 911 Carrera Turbo: 3746
Porsche 911 Ruf: 3747
Porsche 911 Ruf CTR: 3748
Porsche 911 Turbo: 3750
Porsche 911 Turbo Gemballa Mirage: 3751
Porsche 928: 3752
Renault 19 16v: 3917
Renault Alpine A610 Turbo: 3918
Renault Clio 1.2 RN: 3919
Renault Clio 1.4RT: 3920
Renault Espace V6: 3921
Rolls-Royce Silver Spirit II: 3972
Rover 216 GTi: 4044
Rover 218 SD: 4045
Rover 220 GTi: 4046
Rover 825 TD: 4047
Saab 9000 2.3 Turbo TCS: 4101
Saab 9000 Turbo: 4102
Saab 9000CS Turbo S: 4103
Saturn Sports Coupe: 4107
Subaru Legacy 2.0 4Cam Turbo Estate: 4277
Subaru Legacy Sports Sedan: 4278
Toyota Camry 2.2 GL: 4476
Toyota Celica GT Convertible: 4477
Toyota Landcruiser VX: 4478
Toyota MR2: 4479
Toyota MR2 HKS: 4480
Toyota Previa: 4481
Toyota Tercel LE: 4482
TVR V8 S: 4603
Vauxhall Calibra 2.0i: 4728
Vauxhall Calibra 4x4: 4729
Vauxhall Senator 3.0i 24v: 4731
Vector W8 Twin Turbo: 4736
Volkswagen Corrado G60: 4882
Volkswagen Corrado Neuspeed: 4883
Volkswagen GTi 16v: 4884
Volkswagen Jetta GLi 16v: 4885
Volkswagen Polo 1.3 CL Coupe: 4886
Volkswagen Polo G40: 4887
Volkswagen Polo GT Coupe: 4888
Volvo 940 SE: 4965
Volvo 940 SE Turbo: 4966
Volvo 960 24v: 4968
Year total: 168

1992 Audi 80 2.8E V6 Quattro: 339
BMW 325i: 623
BMW 520i SE Touring: 624
BMW 850i Manual: 625
Chevrolet Camaro Z28: 958
Chevrolet Corvette LT1: 959
Citroen AX GTi: 1092
Citroen XM Turbo SD Estate: 1093
Dodge Viper: 1348
Fiat Tipo 1.8ie DGT SX: 1606
Ford Escort RS2000: 1973
Ford Escort XR3i: 1974
Ford Mustang LX: 1975
Ford Taurus LX: 1976
Honda Legend Coupe: 2158
Honda NSX Auto: 2159
Honda Prelude Si 4WS: 2160
Lexus ES300: 2572
Mazda MX-3 1.6 Auto: 2772
Mazda MX-3 GS: 2773
Mercedes-Benz 500SEL: 2922
Mercedes-Benz 600SEL: 2923
Nissan 200SX: 3254
Nissan Sunny 2.0 GTi: 3255
Pontiac Bonneville SSEi: 3600
Porsche 911 Carrera RS: 3753
Range Rover Vogue SE: 3781
Renault 19 16v Cabriolet: 3922
Renault Cleo 16v: 3923
Rover 820i: 4050
Rover Sterling Automatic: 4051
Saab 9000 2.3CS: 4105
Seat Toledo 1.9 CL Diesel: 4114
Seat Toledo 2.0 GTi: 4115
Subaru SVX: 4279
Toyota Paseo: 4483
Vauxhall 1.4i GLS: 4732
Vauxhall Cavalier 1.7 GL TD: 4733
Vauxhall Frontera 2.3 TD Estate: 4734
Volkswagen Golf 1.8 GL: 4889
Volkswagen Golf GTi: 4890
Volvo 960: 4969
Year total: 42

Total No: 1,411

3 or more carburettors.

	No.	
1932	3	Alvis Speed 20 (87bhp): 156
1933	3	AC Ace Fixed-head Coupe: 3
	3	Frazer-Nash 1.5-litre: 1981
1934	3	AC Ace Sports Four-seater: 4
	3	AC Greyhound Close-coupled Saloon: 5
1935	3	AC Ace Drop-head Coupe: 6
	3	Marendaz 15/90 Special Tourer: 2647
1936	3	AC Ace: 8
1937	3	AC 2-litre Fixed-head Coupe: 9
	3	Alvis Crested Eagle 25: 159
	3	Frazer-Nash 1.5-litre: 1984
1938	3	AC 2-litre Sports: 10
	3	Alvis Speed 25: 161
	3	Talbot Figoni et Falaschi: 4343
1939	3	AC 2-litre: 11
	3	Alvis 4.3-litre: 162
	3	Frazer-Nash BMW Type 327 Cabriolet: 1991
	3	Triumph 2-litre Dolomite: 4495
1949	3	AC 2-litre Saloon: 12
1952	3	Ferrari 212 Touring: 1372
	3	Ferrari 375 Indianapolis: 1373
	3	Mercedes-Benz 300SL Carrera Panamericana: 2788
1953	3	Chevrolet Corvette: 732
1954	3	Maserati A6G/54 Frua Gran Sport: 2652
1955	3	Nardi Blue Ray 1: 3192
1956	3	Aston Martin Spyder Touring: 235
	6	Ferrari 412 MI: 1377
	3	Jaguar D Type: 2285
1957	3	AC Ace Bristol: 16
	6	Ferrari 250 Testa Rossa: 1378
1958	3	AC AC-Bristol Zagato: 17
	3	Ferrari 250 GT Cabriolet: 1380
	3	Ferrari 250 GT Coupe: 1381
	6	Ferrari 250 Testa Rossa: 1382
1959	3	Cadillac Eldorado Convertible: 701
1960	6	Ferrari 250 GT Berlinetta SWB: 1383
1961	6	Fairthorpe Zeta: 1369
1962	3	Aston Martin DB4 GT Zagato: 240
	3	Ferrari 250 GTO: 1386
	3	Jaguar Mk X: 2300
	3	Mercury S-55 406: 2930
	3	Pontiac Royal Bobcat: 3535
Year total: 5		
1963	3	Ferrari 250 GT Berlinetta Lusso: 1388
	3	Jaguar E Type Coupe: 2303
	3	Pontiac Grand Prix: 3538
1964	3	Aston Martin DB5: 241
	4	Chevrolet Corvair Sprint: 785
	3	Jaguar 4.2 litre Mk X: 2305
	3	Jaguar XKE: 2306
	3	Saab 850GT: 4059
	4	Shelby Cobra USRRC: 4118
Year total: 6		
1965	3	Ferrari 365 GTC: 1390
	4	Honda S600: 2087
	3	Jaguar 4.2 litre Mk X Overdrive: 2308
	3	Jaguar E Type 4.2: 2309
	6	Lamborghini 350GT: 2449
	3	Pontiac Tempest GTO: 3543
	3	Reliant Scimitar: 3784
	4	Shelby Cobra Daytona Coupe: 4119
Year total: 8		
1966	3	Alfa Romeo 2600 Sprint: 63
	4	Bizzarrini GT America: 496
	6	Bizzarrini P538: 497
	3	Ferrari 275 GTS: 1391
	4	Ford GT40 Super Street: 1738
	3	Jaguar XKE 4.2 2+2: 2310
	6	Lamborghini 400GT: 2450
	3	Oldsmobile Cutlass 442: 3287
	3	Pontiac GTO: 3544
Year total: 9		
1967	6	Ferrari 275 GTS/4 NART: 1392
	3	Jaguar E Type Roadster: 2312
	6	Lamborghini Miura: 2451
	3	Toyota 2000GT: 4356
1968	3	Aston Martin DBS: 243
	4	Chevrolet Corvair Monza: 815
	4	Chevrolet Corvair Sport Coupe: 816
	3	Chevrolet Corvette Convertible: 818
	3	Ferrari 330 GTS: 1393
	4	Ford GT40: 1760
	6	Lamborghini Miura: 2452
	4	Maserati Quattroporte: 2656
Year total: 8		
1969	3	Chevrolet Corvette L68: 832
	3	Chevrolet Corvette L71: 833
	3	Chevrolet Corvette L71/89: 834
	3	Dodge Super Bee Six-Pack: 1312
	3	Ferrari 365 GTS 2+2: 1394
	6	Ferrari Daytona Sportwagen: 1395
	6	Lamborghini Espada: 2453
	3	Saab Sport: 4066
Year total: 8		
1970	3	Dodge Challenger R/T: 1314
	6	Ferrari 365 GTB/4 Daytona: 1396
	6	Lamborghini Espada: 2454
	4	Lamborghini Miura P400S: 2455
	4	Lamborghini Miura S: 2456
	4	Maserati Indy: 2657
Year total: 6		
1971	3	Citroen Safari SM: 1041
	6	Ferrari Daytona: 1397
	6	Ferrari Daytona Cannonball: 1398
	4	Jaguar E Type V12: 2319
	3	Jensen SP: 2397
	4	Maserati Ghibli: 2658
	4	Maserati Indy: 2659
Year total: 7		
1972	3	Citroen SM: 1043
	3	Ferrari 246 GT Dino: 1399
	6	Ferrari 365 GTC4: 1400
	4	Jaguar XJ12: 2321
	4	Jaguar XKE V12: 2323
	6	Lamborghini Jarama 400GT: 2457
Year total: 6		

1973 4 Aston Martin V8 Automatic: 245
4 Jaguar XJ12: 2324
4 Lamborghini Bravo: 2458
6 Lamborghini Jarama 400GT: 2459
4 Maserati Bora: 2660
Year total: 5

1974 3 Ferrari 246 GTS Dino: 1401
6 Ferrari 365 GTB/4 Competitione: 1403
4 Jaguar XKE V12: 2325
4 Lamborghini Urraco S: 2460
3 Maserati Merak: 2661
Year total: 5

1975 4 Aston Martin V8: 246
3 Datsun 240Z Sharp: 1190
4 Ferrari 308 Dino GT4: 1405
6 Ferrari 365 GT4 2+2: 1406
4 Ferrari 512 BB: 1407
4 Maserati Khamsin Automatic: 2662
Year total: 6

1976 4 Chevrolet Monza Mike Keyser: 874
4 Ferrari 308 GT4 Dino: 1408
4 Ferrari 308 GTB: 1409
4 Ferrari Dino 308 GT4 2+2: 1410
6 Lamborghini Countach: 2461
4 Lamborghini Urraco: 2463
4 Maserati Khamsin: 2665
Year total: 7

1977 4 Aston Martin V8 Coupe: 247
4 Aston Martin V8 Vantage: 248
4 Ferrari 308 GTB: 1411
6 Jaguar XJS Tullius: 2333

1978 4 Aston Martin V8: 249
4 Ferrari 512 BB: 1413
4 Maserati Khamsin: 2666
4 Maserati Kyalami: 2667

1979 6 Lamborghini Countach S: 2464
4 Maserati Khamsin: 2669

1980 4 Aston Martin Lagonda: 250
3 Datsun 280ZX Electramotive: 1220
3 Datsun 280ZX Sharp: 1221
4 Ferrari 308 GT4 Dino: 1414

1981 3 Maserati Merak SS: 2670

1982 4 Aston Martin Lagonda: 251
4 Aston Martin V8: 252
4 Ferrari 512 BB: 1417
6 Lamborghini Countach LP 500S: 2465
6 Lamborghini Countach S: 2466
4 Lamborghini Jalpa: 2467
Year total: 6

1983 4 Aston Martin Volante: 253
4 Maserati Quattroporte: 2671

1984 4 Aston Martin Lagonda: 254
4 Aston Martin Vantage: 255

1985 6 Ferrari 365 GTB Goldsmith: 1425
6 Lamborghini Countach: 2468

1986 4 Lamborghini Jalpa 3500: 2470

1987 3 Lynx D Type: 2642

1988 4 Aston Martin Zagato: 257
4 Lamborghini Jalpa: 2471
6 Lamborghini LM129: 2472

1989 4 AC Cobra 427 Modified 1965: 27
4 De Tomaso Pantera Group 3: 1243
6 Lamborghini Countach 25th Anniversary: 2473

1991 4 Westfield SEight: 4973
Total No: 166

Diesel engines.

1936 Mercedes-Benz 20.8hp Diesel Saloon: 2781

1958 Mercedes-Benz 180D: 2797

1965 Mercedes-Benz 190D: 2813
Peugeot 404 Diesel: 3392

1966 Mercedes-Benz 300D: 2819

1971 Mercedes-Benz 220D: 2833

1973 Peugeot 504 Diesel: 3409

1974 Peugeot 504 L Diesel: 3410

1975 Mercedes-Benz 300D: 2848

1976 Opel Rekord 2100D: 3342

1977 Citroen CX 2200 Diesel: 1051
Peugeot 504 Diesel Automatique: 3416
Volkswagen Rabbit Diesel: 4809

1978 Cadillac Seville Diesel: 711
Ford Granada 2.1D: 1859
Mercedes-Benz 300CD: 2856
Mercedes-Benz 300SD: 2857
Volkswagen Golf LD: 4814
Year total: 5

1979 Citroen CX 2500 Diesel Super: 1056
Mercedes-Benz 300TD: 2861

1980 Audi 5000 S Diesel: 284
Oldsmobile Cutlass Diesel: 3300
Peugeot 505 SD: 3423
Peugeot 604 D Turbo: 3424
Volkswagen Dasher Diesel: 4818
Volvo Diesel: 4939
Year total: 5

1981 Cadillac Seville Diesel: 712
Mercedes-Benz 300GD: 2867
Mercedes-Benz 300TD: 2868
Peugeot 505 S Turbodiesel: 3426
Volkswagen Rabbit Diesel: 4829
Year total: 5

1982 Audi 80 Turbo Diesel: 291
Rover SD Turbo: 4023
Vauxhall Cavalier LD: 4693

1983 Daihatsu Charade Diesel: 1120
Ford Granada 2.5 Diesel Estate: 1887
Isuzu I-Mark LS: 2252
Talbot Horizon 1.9LD: 4348
Volvo 760 GLE: 4946
Year total: 5

1984 Citroen BX19 RD Diesel: 1061
Ford Fiesta 1.6L Diesel: 1893
Volkswagen Passat CL Turbo Diesel Estate: 4845

1985 Citroen Visa 17RD: 1069
Peugeot 305 GRD Estate: 3435

1986 Audi 100 Turbo Diesel: 310
BMW 524 TD: 581
Citroen BX19 RD Estate: 1071
Fiat Regata DS: 1594

1987 Citroen CX25 DTR Turbo 2: 1078
Daihatsu Charade CX Diesel Turbo: 1123
Daihatsu Fourtrak Estate DT EL: 1125
Isuzu Trooper 3-door TD: 2257
Land Rover Ninety County Turbo Diesel: 2560
Mercedes-Benz 300TD: 2893
Mitsubishi Shogun Turbo Diesel 5-door: 3094
Toyota Landcruiser: 4450
Year total: 8

1988 Citroen BX DTR Turbo: 1080
Peugeot 405 GRD: 3447
Range Rover Vogue Turbo D: 3776
Toyota Landcruiser II TD: 4458
Vauxhall Carlton L 2.3D: 4713
Volkswagen Jetta Turbo Diesel: 4868
Year total: 6

1989 Carbodies Fairway 2.7 Silver: 721
Citroen AX14 DTR: 1081
Peugeot 405 GTD Turbo: 3454
Rover Montego 2.0 DSL Turbo: 4034
Vauxhall Astra 1.7 DL: 4716
Year total: 5

1990 Ford Granada 2.5 GL Diesel: 1951
Land Rover Discovery TDi: 2563
Mercedes-Benz 300D: 2911
Vauxhall Nova 1.5TD Merit: 4727
Volkswagen Passat CL TD Estate: 4880
Year total: 5

1991 Mercedes-Benz G-Wagen 300 GD LWB: 2921
Peugeot 205 D Turbo: 3464
Peugeot 605 SR TD: 3465
Rover 218 SD: 4045
Rover 825 TD: 4047

Toyota Landcruiser VX: 4478
Year total: 6

1992 Citroen XM Turbo SD Estate: 1093
Seat Toledo 1.9 CL Diesel: 4114
Vauxhall Cavalier 1.7 GL TD: 4733
Vauxhall Frontera 2.3 TD Estate: 4734
Total No: 81

2-stroke engines.

1937 DKW 7.1hp Cabriolet: 1260

1954 DKW Sonderklasse: 1261

1955 DKW 3-6: 1262

1956 DKW 3-6: 1263
DKW Karavan: 1264
Saab 93: 4053

1957 Berkeley Sports: 484
Goliath 900: 2006
Saab 93: 4054

1958 Auto Union 1000: 449
Berkeley Sports: 485
Berkeley Sports 4: 486
BMW Isetta 300: 502
DKW 3-6 Sonderklasse Coupe: 1265
Frisky Coupe: 1993
Messerschmitt (FMR) Tg 500: 2966
Saab Gran Turismo: 4055
Year total: 8

1959 Auto Union 1000: 450
Goggomobil TS400: 2004

1960 DKW 750: 1266
Saab 96: 4056

1961 Auto Union Universal: 451
DKW Junior: 1267
Saab 96 Sedan: 4057

1962 DKW Junior de Luxe: 1268

1963 Saab 95: 4058

1964 Saab 850GT: 4059

1966 Saab 96: 4060

1967 Wartburg Knight: 4970

1969 Saab Sport: 4066
Subaru 360: 4243

1971 Subaru Hapi Van 360: 4245
Suzuki Brute: 4320

1973 Wartburg Knight: 4971

Total No: 34

Wankel Rotary engines.

1965 NSU Spider: 3261
NSU Wankel Spider: 3262

1968 Mazda 110S Coupe: 2685
NSU Ro80: 3264

1971 Mazda Rotary: 2689
Mazda RX-2: 2690

1972 Mazda RX-2: 2691
Mazda RX-3: 2692

1973 Mazda RX-3 Station Wagon: 2693
Mazda RX-4: 2694

1974 Mazda Rotary Pickup: 2697
Mazda RX-4 Coupe: 2698
Mazda RX-4 Station Wagon: 2699
NSU Ro80: 3266

1976 Mazda Cosmo: 2701

1977 Mazda RX-4: 2704

1978 Mazda RX-7: 2705

1979 Mazda RX-7: 2710
Mazda RX-7 GS: 2711

1980 Mazda RX-7: 2714
Mazda RX-7 Racer: 2715

1981 Mazda RX-7 GSL: 2719

1982 Mazda RX-7: 2720

1983 Mazda RX-7: 2723

1984 Mazda RX-7: 2724
Mazda RX-7 GSL SE: 2725

1985 Mazda RX-7 GSL: 2728

1986 Mazda RX-7: 2735
Mazda RX-7 GXL: 2736
Mazda RX-7 Turbo: 2737

1987 Mazda RX-7 Turbo: 2740

1988 Mazda RX-7 Convertible: 2749
Mazda RX-7 GTU: 2750
Mazda RX-7 Turbo: 2751

1989 Mazda RX-7 Convertible Racing Beat: 2757
Mazda RX-7 GTUs: 2758
Mazda RX-7 Turbo II: 2759

1990 Mazda RX-7 Convertible: 2763
Mazda RX-7 Turbo: 2764

1991 Mazda RX-7 Cartech: 2768
Mazda RX-7 Infini IV: 2769
Mazda RX-7 Mariah Mode Six: 2770
Mazda RX-7 Turbo: 2771
Total No: 43

Two cylinders in line.

1957 Berkeley Sports: 484
Goliath 900: 2006

1958 Berkeley Sports: 485
Fiat 500: 1477
Frisky Coupe: 1993
Lloyd LP 600: 2588
Messerschmitt (FMR) Tg 500: 2966
Year total: 5

1959 Fiat 500: 1482
Fiat 500 Nuova: 1483
Goggomobil TS400: 2004
NSU Prinz 34hp: 3256
NSU Prinz II: 3257
Year total: 5

1960 Berkeley B95: 487
NSU Sport-Prinz: 3258

1961 Fiat 500 Giardiniera: 1492
1962 NSU Prinz 4: 3259

1964 Fiat 500D: 1498

1966 Fiat 500F: 1504
Fiat Abarth 595: 1506

1968 Honda N360: 2089
NSU Super Prinz: 3265

1969 Subaru 360: 4243

1970 Honda 600: 2090

1971 Subaru Hapi Van 360: 4245
Suzuki Brute: 4320

1972 Honda 600 Coupe: 2091

1973 Fiat 126: 1539

1979 Fiat 126 de Ville: 1564

1981 Daihatsu Domino: 1117

Total No: 29

Three cylinders in line.

1954 DKW Sonderklasse: 1261

1955 DKW 3-6: 1262

1956 DKW 3-6: 1263
DKW Karavan: 1264
Saab 93: 4053

1957 Saab 93: 4054

1958 Auto Union 1000: 449
Berkeley Sports 4: 486
DKW 3-6 Sonderklasse Coupe: 1265
Saab Gran Turismo: 4055

1959 Auto Union 1000: 450

1960 DKW 750: 1266
Saab 96: 4056

1961 Auto Union Universal: 451
DKW Junior: 1267
Saab 96 Sedan: 4057

1962 DKW Junior de Luxe: 1268

1963 Saab 95: 4058

1964 Saab 850GT: 4059

1966 Saab 96: 4060

1967 Wartburg Knight: 4970

1969 Saab Sport: 4066

1973 Wartburg Knight: 4971

1979 Daihatsu Charade XTE: 1116

1981 Suzuki Alto FX: 4322

1983 Daihatsu Charade CX: 1119
Daihatsu Charade Diesel: 1120
Suzuki Alto FX Automatic: 4323

1984 Chevrolet Sprint: 895

1986 Chevrolet Sprint: 904
Daihatsu Domino: 1122
Suzuki Alto GLA: 4325

1987 Daihatsu Charade CX Diesel Turbo: 1123
Daihatsu Charade GT ti: 1124
Subaru Justy: 4267

1988 Chevrolet Sprint: 924
Daihatsu Charade CLX: 1126
Daihatsu Charade Turbo: 1127
Subaru Justy 4WD GL: 4270
Subaru Justy GL: 4271
Year total: 5

1989 Subaru Justy GL II 5-door 4WD: 4273
Total No: 41

Four cylinders in line.

1915 Ford Model T: 1608

1928 Hillman Safety Saloon: 2022
Morris Minor Saloon: 3138

1929 Aston Martin Super Sports: 222
Austin 7 Tourer: 340
Bentley 4.5-litre: 461
Lea-Francis 12/40 Saloon: 2566
Lea-Francis Hyper-sports: 2567
MG Midget: 2968
Year total: 6

1930 AJS 9hp Saloon: 38
Bentley 4.5-litre Supercharged: 462
Ford 24 Saloon: 1609
Frazer-Nash Super Sports: 1979
Lagonda 2-litre Supercharged: 2433
Morris 8 Minor: 3140
Tracta Sports Two-seater: 4484
Triumph Super 7 Saloon: 4487
Triumph Supercharged 7: 4488
Year total: 9

1931 Alvis 12/60 Sports: 154
Aston Martin Sports Four-seater: 223
Austin 7 Saloon: 341
Austin 7 Sports Two-seater: 342
Austin 7 Sunshine Saloon: 343
Frazer-Nash Boulogne II: 1980
MG Mk II Montlhery Supercharged: 2970
Year total: 7

1932 Aston Martin 1.5-litre: 224
BSA FWD Tourer: 646
Hillman Minx Sports Tourer: 2025
Year total: 3

1933 Aston Martin Le Mans: 225
Ford 8 Tudor Saloon: 1611
Frazer-Nash TT Replica: 1982
Morris 10/4: 3142
Morris Cowley Saloon: 3144
Singer 9 Sports: 4160
Year total: 6

1934 Aston Martin 1.5-litre Mk II: 226
Austin 10/4 Saloon: 344
British Salmson Closed-coupled Saloon: 642
Crossley 10hp Torquay: 1104
Fiat Balilla Pillarless Saloon: 1455
Ford 10 de Luxe Saloon: 1612
Ford Model A: 1613
Hillman Aero Minx Coupe: 2028
Humber 12 Vogue: 2183
Lagonda Rapier Four-seater Tourer: 2438
Mercedes-Benz 12hp Rear-engined Saloon: 2779
MG Midget P Type: 2973
Morris 8 Saloon: 3147
Rover 12 Saloon: 3975
Year total: 14

1935 Alvis Firebird Saloon: 157
Aston Martin 1.5-litre: 227
Austin 7 Ruby Saloon: 349
British Adler 13.67 Cabriolet: 641
Crossley 10hp Regis Sports Saloon: 1105
Fiat Balilla Sports Two-seater: 1457
Hillman Aero Minx Cresta Saloon: 2030
Humber 12 Six-light Saloon: 2184
Renault 12.1hp Airline Saloon: 3798
Riley 1.5 Kestrel Special: 3925
Singer Le Mans Special Speed Model: 4161
Squire X101: 4190
Year total: 12

1936 Aston Martin Sports Saloon: 228
Austin 7 Ruby Saloon: 351
British Salmson 12hp Four-seater Tourer: 643
Citroen Super Model Twelve: 1011
Citroen Super Modern Fifteen Saloon: 1012
Fiat 500 Convertible Saloon: 1458
Mercedes-Benz 20.8hp Diesel Saloon: 2781
MG Midget PB: 2975
MG Midget Series T: 2976
Morgan 4/4: 3120
Riley 1.5 Falcon Saloon: 3926
Triumph 14/60 Dolomite Saloon: 4491
Triumph Vitesse: 4493
Year total: 13

1937 Aston Martin 2-litre: 229
Austin 10 Cambridge: 352
Austin Big 7: 354
Bianchi 12hp Pillarless Saloon: 491
British Salmson 14hp Saloon: 645
Citroen Sports Twelve Saloon: 1013
Fiat Balilla Pillarless Saloon: 1460
Ford 10: 1615
Hillman Minx Saloon de Luxe: 2033
HRG 12hp Sports Two-seater: 2166
Morris 10 Series II: 3151
Opel Kadet Saloon: 3306
Renault 17.9hp Touring Saloon: 3800
Riley 9 Monaco: 3928
Riley Kestrel Sprite: 3929
Riley Sprite: 3930
Standard Flying 10: 4194
Triumph Gloria 12: 4494
Vauxhall 10/4 de Luxe Saloon: 4613
Year total: 19

1938 Alvis 12/70 Tourer: 160
Aston Martin Drop-head Coupe: 230
Ford Prefect: 1616
HRG 1.5-litre: 2167
Jaguar SS 1.5-litre: 2266
Lanchester 11 Saloon: 2481
Morgan 4/4: 3121
Morris 10 Series III: 3152
Morris 8 Tourer: 3153
Morris 8hp Tourer: 3154
Opel Olympia Saloon: 3307
Railton 10 Drop-head Coupe: 3760
Riley 16 2.5: 3931
Talbot 10hp Drop-head Coupe: 4341
Vauxhall 10 Saloon de Luxe: 4615
Vauxhall 12/4 de Luxe Saloon: 4616

Year total: 16

1939 Aston Martin 2-litre: 231
Austin 8 Saloon: 356
BSA Scout: 647
Ford 8: 1618
Morris 8 Series E Tourer: 3155
Morris 8hp Series E Tourer: 3156
Sunbeam-Talbot 2-litre Sports Tourer: 4314
Wolseley 12/48: 4985
Year total: 8

1940 Citroen Light Fifteen Roadster: 1014
Singer Super 10 Saloon: 4162
Vauxhall 12 Saloon: 4618

Year total: 3

1947 Austin 16 Saloon: 357
Austin 8 Saloon: 358
Cisitalia Aerodinamica Mille Miglia: 1009
Hillman Minx Saloon: 2034
Humber Hawk Saloon: 2191
MG TC Midget: 2977
Riley 1.5: 3932
Riley 2.5 Saloon: 3933
Standard 12 Saloon: 4196
Sunbeam-Talbot 10 Sports Saloon: 4315
Sunbeam-Talbot 2-litre Sports Saloon: 4316
Triumph 1800 Roadster: 4496
Triumph 1800 Saloon: 4497
Vauxhall 12 Saloon: 4619
Year total: 14

1948 Austin A40: 360
Citroen Light Fifteen: 1015
Ford Prefect: 1620
Healey 2.4-litre Roadster: 2019
HRG 1.5-litre: 2168
Lea-Francis Sports: 2569
Morris Minor: 3157
Morris Oxford: 3158
Renault 4CV: 3801
Riley 2.5 Sports: 3934
Standard 8: 4197
Standard Vanguard: 4198
Sunbeam-Talbot 90 Sports Saloon: 4317
Year total: 13

1949 Austin A70: 362
Austin A90 Atlantic: 363
Ford Anglia 10 Saloon: 1622
Ford Anglia 8 Saloon: 1623
Hillman Minx Saloon: 2035
Humber Hawk: 2192
Lanchester 10: 2484
MG TC: 2978
Riley 2.5 Saloon: 3935
Singer 9 Roadster: 4163
Singer SM1500 Saloon: 4164
Sunbeam-Talbot 80 Saloon: 4318
Triumph 2000 Saloon: 4498
Triumph Roadster: 4499
Vauxhall Wyvern: 4622
Wolseley 4/50: 4986
Year total: 16

1950 Fiat 1400 Saloon: 1461
MG TD: 2979
Morris Minor Tourer: 3159
Morris Oxford Saloon: 3160
Year total: 4

1951 Austin A40: 364
Austin A40 Sport: 365
Fiat 500C Convertible (Topolino): 1462
Ford Consul: 1624
Hillman Minx Estate: 2036
Hillman Minx Sedan: 2037
Humber Hawk: 2196
MG TD: 2980
Simca 8 Sport: 4129
Sunbeam Talbot 90: 4282
Year total: 10

1952 Austin A40 Somerset: 366
Citroen Light Fifteen: 1017
Fiat 1400: 1463
Fiat 500C Convertible: 1464
Healey Tickford Saloon: 2020
Hillman Minx Convertible: 2038
Holden Saloon: 2085
Mercedes-Benz 170S: 2786
MG 1.25-litre Saloon: 2981
Morgan Plus 4: 3123
Riley 2.5: 3936
Simca Aronde: 4130
Singer SM Roadster: 4165
Singer SM1500 Saloon: 4166
Standard Vanguard: 4199
Vauxhall Wyvern: 4626
Year total: 16

1953 Alfa Romeo 1900: 43
Austin A30: 368
Austin-Healey 100: 428
Citroen 11CV: 1018
Citroen Big Fifteen: 1020
Fiat 1100: 1465
Fiat 1900: 1466
Hillman Minx Califonian Coupe: 2039
MG Midget: 2982
MG TD: 2983
MG TDC Mk II: 2984
Morris Minor Series II: 3161
Morris Oxford Travellers' Car: 3162
Renault 750: 3802
Riley 1.5: 3937
Riley 2.5: 3938
Singer Roadster: 4167
Singer SM1500 Saloon: 4168
Standard 8: 4200
Standard Vanguard Estate: 4201
Standard Vanguard Phase II: 4202
Sunbeam-Talbot 90 Mk IIA: 4319
Wolseley 4/44: 4989
Year total: 23

1954 Alfa Romeo B.A.T.7 Scaglione: 44
Austin A30: 369
Austin A40 Somerset Coupe: 370
Fiat 1100 TV Saloon: 1467
Ford Anglia Saloon: 1630
Ford Popular: 1631
Hillman Minx Supercharged: 2040
Humber Hawk Mk VI: 2201
Mercedes-Benz 180 Saloon: 2790
MG Magnette: 2985
MG TD Laystall: 2986
MG TF: 2987
MG TF 1500: 2988
MG TF Supercharged: 2989
Moretti 750 Grand Sport Berlinetta Coupe: 3119
Morgan Plus 4: 3124
Morris Minor: 3163
Morris Oxford Saloon: 3164
Nash Metropolitan: 3197
Rover 60: 3985
Simca Aronde: 4131
Singer SM Roadster: 4169
Sunbeam Alpine: 4283
Sunbeam Alpine II: 4284
Triumph TR2: 4500
Triumph TR2 Sports: 4501
Volvo 444: 4891
Year total: 27

1955 Austin A50 Cambridge: 372
Austin-Healey 100S: 430
Borgward Isabella 1500: 630
Fiat 600: 1469
Ford Anglia: 1632
Ford Prefect: 1633
Ford Prefect 1172cc: 1634
Hillman Husky: 2041
Hillman Minx de Luxe: 2042
Land Rover Station Wagon: 2556
Mercedes-Benz 190SL: 2791
MG A: 2990
MG Magnette: 2991
Morgan Plus 4: 3125
Morris Cowley: 3165
Nash Metropolitan: 3199
Osca 1490cc Spyder: 3353
Peugeot 203: 3384
Peugeot 403: 3385
Renault 4CV: 3803
Renault 750: 3804
Riley Pathfinder: 3939
Simca Aronde: 4132
Singer Hunter: 4170
Standard 10: 4203
Sunbeam Mk III: 4285
Swallow Doretti: 4334
Triumph TR2 Hardtop: 4502
Vauxhall Wyvern: 4629
Year total: 29

1956 Alfa Romeo Giulietta Spyder: 45
Austin A30 Countryman: 375
Austin-Healey 100M: 431
Borgward Isabella TS: 631
Citroen DS19: 1023
Dellow Mk V: 1254
Ford Anglia: 1637
Ford Consul Mk II: 1638
Ford Taunus 15M: 1640

Hillman Minx de Luxe: 2043
Humber Hawk Estate: 2202
MG A: 2992
Paramount Roadster: 3381
Renault Dauphine: 3805
Riley Pathfinder: 3940
Rover 60: 3988
Simca Elysee: 4133
Simca Sports Coupe: 4134
Standard Vanguard III: 4204
Standard Vanguard Sportsman: 4205
Sunbeam Rapier: 4286
Triumph TR3: 4503
Volvo PV444 California: 4892
Year total: 23

1957 Austin A55: 376
Citroen DS19: 1024
Ferrari TRC 2500 Testa Rossa: 1379
Fiat 1100: 1470
Fiat 1100 Saloon: 1471
Fiat 600: 1472
Fiat 600 Multipla: 1473
Fiat Multipla: 1474
Hillman Minx Convertible: 2044
Humber Hawk: 2203
Lotus 11 Le Mans: 2589
Lotus Mk XI: 2590
Lotus Sports: 2591
MG A Coupe: 2993
Morgan 4/4 Modified: 3126
Morris Minor 1000: 3167
Morris Minor 1100: 3168
Morris Oxford Series III: 3169
Renault Dauphine: 3806
Standard Vanguard III: 4206
Sunbeam Rapier: 4287
Triumph TR2 Hardtop: 4504
Triumph TR3: 4505
Volvo PV444: 4893
Volvo PV444 Sports: 4894
Volvo PV444L: 4895
Wolseley 15/50: 4991
Year total: 27

1958 Abarth Zagato 750 GT: 1
Alfa Romeo 1300 SV Spider: 46
Austin A35 4-door: 379
Austin A40: 380
Austin A55: 381
Austin-Healey Sprite: 435
Borgward Isabella Coupe: 632
Borgward Isabella TS: 633
Citroen ID19: 1025
DAF 55: 1107
Datsun 1000: 1157
Elva Courier: 1358
Fiat 1200 Gran Luce: 1475
Fiat 1200 TV Spyder: 1476
Fiat 750 Abarth: 1478
Fiat Abarth 750GT Zagato: 1479
Fiat Abarth Zagato: 1480
Ford Anglia de Luxe: 1644
Ford Consul: 1645
Ford Taunus 17M: 1647
Hillman Hunter Husky: 2045
Hillman Husky: 2046
Hillman Minx Estate: 2047
Hillman Minx Series II: 2048
Hillman Minx Series III Convertible: 2049
Humber Hawk Estate: 2204
Mercedes-Benz 180D: 2797
Mercedes-Benz 190SL: 2798
MG A Judson: 2994
MG A Twin Cam: 2995
MG Magnette: 2996
MG Twin Cam MGA: 2997
Morris Minor 1000 Traveller: 3170
Morris Oxford Traveller Series III: 3171
Nash Metropolitan 1500: 3202
Opel Rekord: 3308
Renault Dauphine Ferry: 3807
Renault Fregate Transfluide: 3808
Riley 1.5: 3941
Simca Aronde Montlhery: 4136
Singer Gazelle IIA Convertible: 4171
Standard 8: 4207
Standard Ensign: 4208
Standard Pennant: 4209
Standard Super 10: 4210
Standard Vanguard III Automatic: 4211
Sunbeam Rapier: 4288
Sunbeam Rapier Series II: 4289
Toyota Toyopet Crown de Luxe: 4350
Triumph Station Wagon: 4506
Vauxhall Victor: 4631
Vauxhall Victor Estate: 4632
Volvo 4-speed: 4896
Volvo Amazon: 4897
Wolseley 1500: 4993
Year total: 55

1959 Alfa Romeo 2000 Spider: 47
Alfa Romeo Super Spider: 48
Austin A55 Cambridge Mk II: 384
Austin Gipsy: 386
Austin-Healey Sprite Hardtop: 437
Fiat 1200 Gran Luce: 1481
Ford Anglia: 1649
Ford Popular II: 1651
Ford Taunus 17M Estate: 1652
Hillman Minx Series IIIA Easidrive: 2050
MG A 1600: 2998
MG Magnette Mk III: 2999
Mini Minor de Luxe: 3043
Morgan Plus 4: 3127
Peerless GT Coupe: 3383
Renault Carvelle: 3809
Renault Dauphine: 3810
Renault Dauphine Gordini: 3811
Rover 80: 3993
Simca Elysee: 4138
Sunbeam Alpine: 4290
Sunbeam Rapier III: 4291
Triumph Herald Coupe: 4507
Triumph Herald Saloon: 4508
Vauxhall Victor de Luxe: 4634
Volvo 122S: 4898
Wolseley 15/60: 4994
Year total: 27

1960 Alfa Romeo 2000: 49
ASA 1000GT: 221
Austin A40 Countryman: 387
Austin-Healey Sebring Sprite: 438
Austin-Healey Sprite Supercharged: 439
Borgward Isabella TS: 635
Borgward Isabella TS Coupe: 636
Citroen ID Safari: 1026
Citroen ID19: 1027
Fiat 1500: 1484
Fiat 600: 1486
Fiat Abarth 850: 1487
Fiat Abarth Twin Cam: 1488
Ford Anglia: 1654
Ford Consul Mk II: 1655
Ford Taunus 17M: 1659
Hillman Easidrive: 2051
Hillman Hunter Husky Series II: 2052
Lotus Elite: 2592
Mercedes-Benz 190SL: 2802
Mini Minor: 3044
Mini Traveller: 3045
Peugeot 403: 3386
Peugeot 404: 3387
Renault Caravelle: 3812
Renault Floride: 3813
Riley 4/68: 3942
Simca Etoile: 4139
Simca Oceane: 4140
Skoda Octavia: 4182
Sunbeam Alpine: 4292
Toyota Toyopet Tiara: 4351
Triumph Herald Convertible: 4509
Triumph Herald Coupe: 4510
Turner Turner-Climax: 4582
Volga M21K: 4737
Year total: 36

1961 Alfa Romeo Giulia SS: 50
Alfa Romeo Giulietta Sprint: 51
Alfa Romeo Giulietta ti: 52
Alfa Romeo Sprint Speciale: 53
Alfa Romeo Sprint Zagato: 54
Austin A55 Countryman: 390
Austin Seven 850: 391
Austin-Healey Sprite Mk II: 441
Citroen DS: 1029
Datsun Bluebird Station Wagon: 1158
Facel Vega Facellia 1600: 1367
Fiat 1200 Spider: 1489
Fiat 1300: 1490
Fiat 1500: 1491
Fiat 600D: 1493
Ford Consul Capri: 1661
Ford Taunus 17M: 1664
Gilbern GT: 1995
International Scout: 2234
Lotus 7: 2593
Lotus Super 7: 2594
Mercedes-Benz 190: 2805
MG A 1600 Mk II: 3000
MG A Mk II: 3001
MG Midget: 3002
Mini Cooper: 3046
Morris Minor 1000: 3172

Ogle 1.5: 3267
Peugeot 404: 3388
Pontiac Tempest: 3530
Pontiac Tempest Automatic: 3531
Pontiac Tempest Supercharged: 3532
Renault Dauphine Gordini: 3814
Riley 1.5: 3943
Simca Aronde Montlhery: 4142
Singer Gazelle Series IIIB: 4172
Singer Vogue: 4173
Skoda Felicia: 4183
Sunbeam Alpine Mk II: 4293
Triumph Herald 1200: 4511
Turner Sports: 4583
TVR Grantura: 4584
Vauxhall Victor Estate: 4638
Volvo 122S: 4899
Volvo P1800: 4900
Warwick GT: 4972
Year total: 46

1962 AMC Rambler American: 174
Austin A40 Mk II: 392
Austin A60 Cambridge: 393
Chevrolet Chevy II Four Automatic: 758
Chevrolet Chevy II Four Manual: 759
Ford Anglia de Luxe Estate: 1666
Ford Anglia Super: 1667
Ford Consul Capri: 1668
Ford Consul Cortina: 1669
Ford Zephyr 4: 1681
Ford Zephyr 4 Automatic: 1682
Hillman Super Minx: 2053
Hillman Super Minx Mk II: 2054
Lotus Super 7: 2595
MG 1100: 3003
MG B 1800: 3004
Ogle Austin Mini Cooper GT: 3268
Peugeot 403 B Estate Car: 3389
Peugeot 404 U6 Estate Car: 3390
Pontiac Tempest 4: 3536
Reliant Sabre Sports: 3782
Renault Caravelle S: 3815
Renault Dauphine: 3816
Renault Dauphine Gordini de Luxe: 3817
Renault R8: 3818
Riley Elf: 3944
Simca 1000: 4143
Simca 5: 4144
Standard Ensign de Luxe Estate: 4213
Sunbeam Harrington Le Mans: 4294
Sunbeam Le Mans: 4295
Triumph Herald: 4512
Triumph Herald 1200 Estate: 4513
Triumph Spitfire 4: 4514
Triumph TR4: 4516
Vauxhall Victor Super: 4639
Vauxhall VX4/90: 4640
Volvo 122: 4901
Volvo 122S B18: 4902
Volvo P1800: 4903
Wolseley 16/60 Automatic: 4996
Year total: 41

1963 Alfa Romeo Giulia ti: 57
Austin-Healey Sprite 1100: 444
BMW 1500: 505
BMW 1800 Saloon: 506
Citroen DS: 1031
Dove GTR4: 1349
Fiat 1100: 1495
Fiat 1100D: 1496
Ford Capri GT: 1684
Ford Consul Corsair GT: 1685
Ford Consul Cortina: 1686
Ford Consul Cortina 1500: 1687
Ford Cortina Estate de Luxe: 1688
Ford Cortina Lotus: 1689
Ford Cortina Super: 1690
Hillman Hunter Husky III: 2055
Hillman Imp de Luxe: 2056
Humber Hawk III: 2210
Humber Sceptre: 2211
International 900 Pickup: 2236
Lotus Elan 1600: 2596
Lotus Elite: 2597
Mercedes-Benz 190C Automatic: 2809
MG 1100: 3005
MG Magnette Mk IV: 3006
MG Midget: 3007
Mini Cooper S: 3047
Mini Super de Luxe: 3048
Morgan 4/4: 3128
Morris 1100: 3173
Plymouth Valiant V-100: 3484
Renault 4 L Estate Car: 3819
Renault Dauphine Automatic: 3820
Renault Floride Caravelle: 3821
Renault R8: 3822
Rover 2000: 3999
Simca 1000: 4145
Simca 1000 Special: 4146
Simca 1300GL: 4147
Singer Vogue Mk II: 4174
Sunbeam Alpine GT: 4296
Sunbeam Alpine Series III: 4297
Triumph Herald 12/50: 4517
Triumph Spitfire 4: 4518
Vauxhall Viva de Luxe: 4642
Volvo 121 Estate: 4904
Volvo PV544: 4905
Wolseley Hornet: 4998
Year total: 48

1964 Alfa Romeo Giulia 1600 Spider: 58
Alfa Romeo Sprint GT: 59
Austin 1800: 394
Bond Equipe GT: 626
Datsun SPL-310: 1159
Fiat 1500L: 1497
Fiat 850 Super: 1499
Ford Consul Corsair: 1701
Ford Cortina Super: 1702
Hillman Minx Series V Automatic: 2057
Hillman Super Minx Convertible: 2058
Hillman Super Minx III: 2059
Innocenti S: 2233
Lotus Cortina: 2598
Lotus Elan 1600: 2599
Mini Cooper 1275S: 3049
Morris Minor 1000 de Luxe: 3174
Morris Oxford VI Traveller: 3175
Opel Kadett: 3309
Renault R8 1100: 3823
Rover 2000: 4002
Simca 1500: 4148
Singer Chamois: 4175
Singer Gazelle Series V: 4176
Sunbeam Alpine GT Series IV Automatic: 4298
Sunbeam Alpine Series IV: 4299
Sunbeam Imp: 4300
Toyota 1900: 4352
Triumph TR4: 4521
Vauxhall Bedford Beagle: 4643
Vauxhall Victor Estate: 4644
Vauxhall VX4/90: 4645
Year total: 32

1965 Alfa Romeo Giulia ti: 60
Alfa Romeo Giulia Veloce: 61
BMW 1800 Ti: 508
Bond Equipe GT 4S: 627
Citroen DS21 Pallas M: 1032
Citroen DSM: 1033
Daihatsu Compagno Berlina: 1115
Fiat 1500: 1500
Fiat 1500 Spider: 1501
Fiat Abarth OT 1600: 1502
Ford Anglia Estate: 1710
Ford Cortina GT: 1712
Glas 1300GT: 1999
Hillman Minx Series VI de Luxe: 2060
Hillman Super Imp: 2061
Honda S600: 2087
Marcos 1800: 2644
Mercedes-Benz 190D: 2813
MG B: 3008
Mini Cooper: 3050
Mini Cooper 1275S: 3051
NSU Prinz 1000L: 3260
Peugeot 404: 3391
Peugeot 404 Diesel: 3392
Peugeot 404 KF2: 3393
Renault 8 Gordini: 3824
Renault Caravelle: 3825
Renault R8 Rally: 3826
Simca 1500GL Estate: 4149
Singer Vogue Mk III Estate: 4177
Skoda 1000MB: 4184
Triumph Spitfire Mk II: 4523
Triumph TR4A: 4524
Triumph TR4A IRS: 4525
Vanden Plas Princess 1100: 4606
Vauxhall Victor 101 Estate: 4648
Vauxhall Viva SL90: 4649
Vauxhall VX4/90: 4650
Volvo 122 Automatic: 4906
Volvo 131: 4907
Wolseley 1100: 4999
Year total: 41

1966 Alfa Romeo 1600 Spider: 62
Alfa Romeo Giulia Sprint GTV: 64
Alfa Romeo Sprint Speciale: 65
Auto Union Audi: 452
BMW 2000: 509

BMW 2000 CS: 510
BMW 2000 Ti: 511
Bond 875: 628
Citroen DS21: 1034
Fiat 1100R: 1503
Fiat 850 Coupe: 1505
Ford Cortina 1300 de Luxe: 1731
Ford Cortina Lotus: 1732
Ford Cortina Super Estate: 1733
Glas 1700GT: 2000
Hillman Super Minx Estate: 2062
Humber Sceptre II Automatic: 2213
MG B GT: 3009
MG B GT Coupe: 3010
Morris 1800: 3176
NSU Typ 110: 3263
Opel Kadett S: 3311
Peugeot 204: 3394
Renault 1100 Automatic: 3827
Renault 16 GL: 3828
Renault 4 Estate Car: 3829
Rover 2000 Automatic: 4003
Rover 2000TC: 4004
Simca 1000GLS: 4150
Singer Vogue: 4178
Singer Vogue Automatic: 4179
Sunbeam Alpine 1.7: 4303
Sunbeam Alpine Series V: 4304
Sunbeam Imp Sport: 4305
Toyota Corona: 4353
Toyota Corona 1900: 4354
Triumph 1300: 4527
Triumph Spitfire Mk II: 4529
Vauxhall Viva de Luxe: 4652
Volvo 1800S: 4908

Year total: 40

1967 Alfa Romeo Duetto Spider: 67
Alfa Romeo Giulia 1300 ti: 68
Alfa Romeo GTV: 69
Auto Union Audi Super 90: 453
BMW 1600 Coupe: 512
BMW 1600-2: 513
BMW 2000 TiLux: 514
Datsun 1600 Sedan: 1160
Datsun 1600 Sports: 1161
Datsun 2000 Sports: 1162
Fiat 124: 1507
Fiat 125: 1508
Ford Cortina 1600E: 1742
Ford Cortina GT: 1743
Ford Cortina Lotus: 1744
Ford Cortina Super Estate: 1745
Frazer-Nash BMW 2000TI: 1992
Hillman Estate: 2063
Hillman Hunter Husky: 2064
Hillman Imp Californian: 2065
Hillman Minx: 2066
Honda S800: 2088
Humber Sceptre: 2214
Lotus Elan Coupe SE: 2600
Lotus Elan SE: 2601
MG Midget Mk III: 3012
Mini Super de Luxe Mk II: 3052
Moskvich De Luxe: 3187
Opel Kadett Rallye: 3312
Opel Rekord Coupe: 3313
Peugeot 404 Automatique: 3395
Peugeot 404 L Estate: 3396
Renault 10: 3830
Renault 8 Gordini 1300: 3831
Riley Kestrel: 3945
Simca 1000GLS: 4151
Simca 1301: 4152
Singer Gazelle: 4180
Sunbeam Stiletto: 4306
Toyota Corona Coupe: 4357
Triumph Herald 1200: 4531
Triumph Spitfire Mk III: 4532
Vauxhall Victor 101 de Luxe: 4654
Vauxhall Victor 2000: 4655
Volvo 144S: 4909
Wolseley 18/85: 5000

Year total: 46

1968 Alfa Romeo 1750 Berlina: 70
Alfa Romeo 1750 GT Veloce: 71
Alfa Romeo Giulia Super: 72
Austin 1800 Mk II: 395
Austin America: 397
Austin-Healey Sprite: 447
BMW 2000 CS: 515
BMW 2002: 516
Citroen DS21 Safari: 1036
Datsun 1600: 1163
Datsun 2000 Sports: 1164
Datsun 510: 1165
Datsun 510 Sedan: 1166
Datsun 510 Station Wagon: 1167
Fiat 124 Sport Coupe: 1509
Fiat 124 Sport Spider: 1510
Fiat 124 Station Wagon: 1511
Fiat 850 Idromatic: 1512
Fiat 850 Special: 1513
Fiat 850 Spider: 1514
Ford Cortina 1300 de Luxe: 1751
Ford Cortina GT: 1752
Ford Cortina GT Estate: 1753
Ford Cortina Station Wagon: 1755
Ford Escort: 1756
Ford Escort 1300: 1757
Ford Escort Twin Cam: 1758
Lotus Elan +2: 2602
Marcos 1600GT: 2645
Mazda 1500 de Luxe: 2686
Mercedes-Benz 220: 2822
MG 1300 Mk II: 3013
MG 1300 Mk II Auto: 3014
MG B All-Synchro: 3015
Mitsubishi Colt 1100F: 3061
Opel Kadette Rallye 1.9: 3314
Opel Station Wagon 1.1: 3315
Opel Station Wagon 1.5: 3316
Opel Station Wagon 1.9: 3317
Peugeot 204 Coupe: 3397
Peugeot 404 Station Wagon: 3398
Peugeot 504 Injection: 3399
Reliant Rebel 700 Estate: 3786
Renault 16: 3832
Simca 1100GLS: 4153
Sunbeam Arrow Station Wagon: 4308
Sunbeam Rapier: 4309
Toyota Corolla: 4359
Toyota Corolla de Luxe: 4360
Toyota Corona: 4361
Triumph Herald 13/60 Convertible: 4533
Triumph Spitfire: 4534
Vauxhall Victor 2000 Estate Automatic: 4657
Vauxhall Viva GT: 4658
Vauxhall Viva SL90 Estate: 4659
Volkswagen Derby LS: 4779
Volvo 145S Estate: 4910
Volvo 145S Wagon: 4911

Year total: 58

1969 Alfa Romeo 1750 Berlina: 73
Alfa Romeo 1750 Spider: 74
Alfa Romeo GT 1300 Junior: 75
Austin 1300 GT: 398
Austin 1300 Super: 399
Austin Maxi: 400
Auto Union 100 LS: 454
BMW 2000 Tilux: 517
BMW 2002: 518
Datsun 1000 de Luxe: 1168
Fiat 124 Coupe: 1515
Fiat 124 Estate Car: 1516
Fiat 125 Special: 1517
Fiat 850 Coupe: 1518
Fiat Abarth 1300: 1519
Ford Capri 1600 GT: 1766
Ford Cortina 1100: 1769
Ford Cortina 1600 GT: 1770
Hillman GT: 2067
Hillman Hunter Mk II: 2068
Lotus Elan S4 Drophead SE: 2603
Lotus Elan S4 SE: 2604
Mercedes-Benz 220: 2826
Mini 1275GT: 3053
Morris 1800S: 3177
Opel GT: 3319
Opel GT 1.9: 3320
Opel GT 1900: 3321
Opel Kadett Rallye 1.9: 3322
Peugeot 404 Automatic: 3400
Renault 16 TS: 3833
Renault 6: 3834
Rover 2000TC: 4008
Saab 99: 4065
Siata Spring 850: 4128
Simca 1204: 4154
Simca 1501 Special Estate: 4155
Singer Chamois: 4181
Sunbeam Alpine: 4310
Sunbeam Alpine GT: 4311
Sunbeam Rapier H120: 4312
TVR Vixen S2: 4585
Vauxhall Victor: 4660
Volvo 142S 2.0: 4912
Volvo 144S: 4913
Wolseley 18/85 Mk II: 5001

Year total: 46

1970 Audi 100 LS: 265
Austin Maxi 1750: 402
BMW 2002 Automatic: 520

Bond Bug: 629
Citroen DS21 EFI 139 Pallas: 1038
Datsun 1200: 1169
Datsun 1600 Pickup: 1170
Fiat 124 Coupe 1600: 1520
Fiat 124 Special: 1521
Fiat 124 Spider: 1522
Fiat 128 4-door: 1523
Fiat 850 Racer: 1524
Ford Capri 1300 GT: 1780
Ford Capri 1600: 1781
Ford Capri Plus 50: 1782
Ford Cortina 2000 GXL: 1783
Ford Escort 1300 Super Estate: 1784
Ford Escort 1600 RS: 1785
Hillman Avenger GL: 2069
Hillman Avenger GT: 2070
Hillman Avenger Super: 2071
Lotus 7 Twin Cam SS: 2605
Lotus Europa S2: 2606
Lotus Super 7 Twincam: 2607
Mazda 1200 de Luxe: 2687
MG B Automatic: 3018
MG B Mk II: 3019
Morris 1100 Mk II: 3178
Opel Manta Rallye 1.9: 3324
Peugeot 504: 3401
Renault 10: 3835
Renault 12 TL: 3836
Saab 99: 4067
Saab 99E: 4068
Simca 1204 Special: 4156
Skoda S100L: 4185
Toyota Corona Mk II: 4363
Toyota Corona Mk II 1900: 4364
Triumph 1500: 4543
Triumph Toledo: 4545
TVR Vixen: 4587
Vauxhall Viva GT: 4662
Volvo 1800E: 4916
Year total: 43

1971 Alfa Romeo 1750 Spider Veloce: 76
Audi 100 LS Auto: 266
Austin 1300 Mk III: 403
BMW 2002: 522
BMW 2002 Tii: 523
Chevrolet Vega: 852
Chevrolet Vega 2300: 853
Chevrolet Vega L11: 854
Chrysler 180: 991
Citroen Safari 21: 1040
Clan Crusader: 1095
DAF 55 Estate: 1112
Datsun 100A: 1172
Datsun 1200 Coupe: 1173
Datsun 1200 Estate: 1174
Datsun 510: 1177
Dodge Colt: 1316
Fiat 124 Special T: 1525
Fiat 124 Spider 1600: 1526
Fiat 124 Sport Coupe: 1527
Fiat 127: 1528
Fiat 128: 1529
Ford 1600 GT: 1789
Ford Capri 2000: 1791
Ford Escort 1300 GT: 1793
Ford Escort 1300 XL: 1794
Ford Escort Sport: 1795
Ford Pinto: 1798
Ford Pinto 1600: 1799
Ford Pinto 2-litre: 1800
Hillman Hunter Super: 2072
Hillman Imp de Luxe: 2073
Lotus Elan Sprint: 2608
Lotus Europa S2: 2609
Lotus Plus 2S 130: 2610
Mazda 1800: 2688
Mercedes-Benz 220D: 2833
MG B GT: 3020
MG Midget Mk III: 3021
Mini 1275GT: 3054
Morris Marina 1.3 Super Coupe: 3179
Morris Marina 1.8TC: 3180
Morris Marina TC: 3181
Opel Ascona Voyage: 3326
Opel GT: 3327
Opel Rallye 1900: 3328
Peugeot 304: 3402
Peugeot 504 Automatic: 3403
Plymouth Cricket: 3511
Renault 16 TL Automatic: 3837
Renault 6 1100: 3838
Rover 2000TC: 4011
Saab 99: 4070
Toyota 1900SL: 4366
Toyota Celica: 4367
Toyota Corolla: 4368
Toyota Corolla 1200SL: 4369
Toyota Corolla 1600: 4370
Toyota Corona de Luxe: 4371
Triumph Spitfire 4: 4548
Triumph Spitfire Mk IV: 4549
Vauxhall Firenza: 4663
Vauxhall Viva de Luxe: 4664
Volvo 142E: 4917
Volvo 144 Grand Luxe: 4918
Volvo 145E Estate: 4919
Year total: 66

1972 Alfa Romeo 1750 Berlina: 77
Alfa Romeo 1750 GTV TransAm: 78
Alfa Romeo 2000 GTV: 79
Alfa Romeo 2000 GTV Injection: 80
Audi 100 Coupe S: 267
Austin Maxi High Line: 405
BMW 2002 Tii: 527
BMW 2002 TransAm: 528
Datsun 180B: 1178
Datsun 510 TransAm: 1180
Fiat 124: 1530
Fiat 128 Coupe 1300: 1531
Fiat 128 SL 1300 Coupe: 1532
Ford 1600 XL Auto: 1801
Ford Capri 1600 XL: 1802
Ford Cortina 1300L: 1807
Hillman Avenger Estate: 2074
Hillman Hunter GLS: 2075
Jensen-Healey 2-litre: 2405
Lotus Elan Plus 2S 130: 2611
Lotus Elan Sprint: 2612
Lotus Europa: 2613
Lotus Europa Twin Cam: 2614
Lotus Plus 2S 130/5: 2615
Morris Marina Estate: 3182
Opel Rekord 1900: 3329
Peugeot 204: 3404
Peugeot 304 Estate Car: 3405
Peugeot 504 Family Estate: 3406
Renault 12 Estate: 3839
Renault 12 TL: 3840
Renault 15 Coupe: 3841
Renault 15 TL: 3842
Renault 16 TS: 3843
Saab 99CM4 2.0: 4071
Saab 99E 1.85: 4072
Saab 99EA: 4073
Skoda S110LS: 4186
Toyota Carina: 4374
Triumph Dolomite: 4553
Vauxhall Firenza Sport SL: 4665
Vauxhall Victor 2300 SL: 4667
Vauxhall Viva 1800: 4668
Vauxhall Viva HC Estate: 4669
Vauxhall VX4/90: 4670
Volkswagen K70: 4788
Volvo 1800 ES: 4921
Year total: 47

1973 Alfa Romeo 2000: 83
Alfa Romeo Alfetta: 85
Alfa Romeo Giulia 1600 Sprint: 86
Audi 100 LS: 268
Audi 80 LS: 269
Audi Fox: 270
Austin Allegro 1300 Super: 406
Austin Marina GT: 407
BMW 520i: 531
Chevrolet Vega: 860
Chevrolet Vega Station Wagon: 861
Chrysler 2-litre: 992
DAF 66SL: 1113
Datsun 200L: 1181
Datsun 610 1800: 1183
Datsun 610 Station Wagon: 1184
Dodge Colt Station Wagon: 1319
Fiat 124 Spider: 1534
Fiat 124 Spider 1600: 1535
Fiat 124 Sport Coupe 1800: 1536
Fiat 124 Station Wagon: 1537
Fiat 124S Automatic: 1538
Fiat 128 Station Wagon: 1540
Fiat 132 1800 Special: 1541
Ford Cortina 1600 XL: 1813
Ford Cortina 1600 XL Estate: 1814
Ford Cortina 2000 Estate: 1815
Ford Cortina 2000E: 1816
Ford Escort RS2000: 1817
Ford Pinto Pangra: 1819
Ford Pinto Station Wagon: 1820
Hillman Avenger DL: 2076
Hillman Avenger GLS: 2077
Honda Civic: 2092
Honda Civic Hondamatic: 2093
Jensen Healey: 2398
Lancia Beta 1800: 2514

Land Rover SWB: 2558
Lotus Europa Special 5-speed: 2616
Mercedes-Benz 230/4: 2838
MG B: 3023
MG B GT: 3024
MG Midget: 3026
Mini 850: 3055
Opel 1900 Station Wagon: 3330
Opel Ascona 1900SR: 3331
Opel GT: 3333
Opel Manta: 3334
Opel Manta Berlinetta Auto: 3335
Peugeot 104: 3407
Peugeot 504: 3408
Peugeot 504 Diesel: 3409
Renault 17: 3844
Renault 5 TL: 3845
Rover 2000SC: 4013
Rover 2200SC Automatic: 4014
Saab 99E: 4075
Saab Sonnet: 4076
Toyota Celica: 4377
Toyota Corolla: 4378
Toyota Corolla SR5: 4379
Toyota Corona: 4380
Triumph 1500TC: 4554
Triumph Dolomite Automatic: 4555
Triumph Spitfire: 4557
Triumph Spitfire 1500: 4558
Vauxhall Victor Estate: 4671
Volkswagen Passat LS: 4790
Volvo 144 de Luxe: 4922
Volvo 144E: 4923

Year total: 70

1974 Alfa Romeo Alfetta: 89
Audi 80 GT: 271
Austin Allegro 1500 Special Automatic: 408
Austin Allegro HL: 409
Austin Vanden Plas 1500: 410
BMW 2002 Tii: 533
BMW 2002 Turbo: 534
Chevrolet Vega: 863
DAF 66SL 1300: 1114
Datsun 120Y: 1185
Datsun 710: 1188
Datsun B210: 1189
Dodge Colt GT 2-litre: 1320
Fiat 132 GLS: 1542
Fiat X1/9: 1543
Ford Capri II 1600 GT: 1822
Ford Escort 1100L: 1823
Glas 1700: 2001
Hillman Avenger 1300 GL: 2078
Hillman Avenger 1600 GLS: 2079
Humber Sceptre Estate: 2215
Jensen Healey Huffaker: 2399
Mazda 1300: 2695
Mazda 929: 2696
Mini 1275GT: 3056
Opel Kadett Coupe: 3338
Peugeot 504 L Diesel: 3410
Peugeot 504 Station Wagon: 3411
Renault 6 TL: 3846
Rover 2200TC: 4015
Saab 99LE Wagonback: 4077
Simca 1100 Special: 4157
Toyota Celica GT: 4383
Toyota Corona 2000 Mk II Automatic: 4384
Toyota Corona SR: 4385
Triumph Spitfire: 4561
Triumph Toledo: 4562
Vanden Plas 1500: 4607
Vauxhall Firenza: 4672
Vauxhall Magnum 2300: 4673
Vauxhall Viva 1256 DL: 4674
Vauxhall VX4/90: 4675
Volkswagen Dasher: 4796
Volkswagen Sciroco TS: 4797
Volvo 142 GL: 4925
Volvo 145: 4926

Year total: 46

1975 Alfa Romeo Alfetta GT: 90
Audi 100 GL Automatic: 272
Audi 80 Estate: 273
Audi Fox: 274
Austin Allegro 1300 Estate: 412
BMW 1602L: 537
Caterham Super 7: 722
Chevrolet Vega GT: 866
Citroen CX 2000: 1047
Datsun 710: 1193
Datsun B210: 1194
Dodge Colt GT: 1321
Fiat 124 Special TC: 1544
Fiat 124 Sport Coupe 1800: 1545
Fiat 128: 1546
Fiat 128 Special: 1547
Fiat 131 1300S: 1548
Fiat 133: 1549
Ford Capri 2000S GT: 1828
Ford Consul 2000L: 1829
Ford Cortina 1300L: 1830
Ford Cortina 2000E Estate: 1831
Ford Escort 1.3 Ghia: 1832
Ford Escort RS1800: 1833
Ford Granada 2000 GL: 1834
Ford Pinto 2300: 1836
Hillman Avenger GLS: 2080
Hillman Hunter Super: 2081
Honda Civic CVCC: 2094
Lada 1200: 2423
Lancia Beta 1600 Coupe: 2516
Lancia Beta Monte Carlo: 2517
Lotus Elite: 2617
Lotus Elite 503: 2618
Matra-Simca Bagheera: 2684
Mazda 808: 2700
Mercury Bobcat 2.3-litre: 2951
MG B: 3027
MG Midget 1500: 3028
Mini 1000: 3057
Mini Automatic: 3058
Mitsubishi Colt Galant 2000: 3062
Moskvich 1500: 3188
Opel 1900: 3339
Opel Ascona 1900SR: 3340
Opel Manta: 3341
Peugeot 504: 3412
Polski Fiat 125P: 3525
Reliant Kitten: 3789
Renault 12: 3847
Renault 17 Gordini: 3848
Renault 5 TS: 3849
Saab 99EMS: 4078
Sunbeam Rapier: 4313
Toyota Celica GT: 4387
Toyota Corolla: 4388
Toyota Corolla 30: 4389
Toyota Corolla SR5: 4390
Toyota Pickup SR5: 4392
Triumph Dolomite: 4564
Triumph Dolomite Sprint: 4565
Triumph Spitfire 1500: 4566
Triumph TR7: 4567
Vauxhall Chevette L: 4676
Vauxhall Magnum 1800: 4677
Volkswagen Golf 1100L: 4799
Volkswagen Polo: 4800
Volkswagen Rabbit: 4801
Volkswagen Scirocco: 4802
Volvo 242 GL: 4927
Volvo 244 GL: 4928

Year total: 71

1976 Alfa Romeo Alfetta 1.6: 91
Alfa Romeo Alfetta GT: 92
Alfa Romeo Alfetta GTV: 93
Alfa Romeo Spider Veloce 2000: 94
Audi 80 GTE: 275
Austin Allegro 1100: 413
Buick Opel by Isuzu: 689
Chevrolet Chevette Rally 1.6: 868
Chevrolet Cosworth Vega: 871
Chrysler Alpine S: 993
Chrysler Avenger Super 1300: 994
Citroen CX 2200 Pallas: 1049
Datsun 140J Violet: 1195
Datsun B210: 1197
Datsun B210 Electramotive: 1198
Datsun F10: 1199
Fiat 124 Spider: 1550
Fiat 124 Sport Spider: 1551
Fiat 128 3P: 1552
Fiat 128 Estate: 1553
Fiat 131: 1554
Ford Capri 1300: 1837
Ford Cortina 2.0 Ghia: 1842
Ford Escort 1300 GL: 1843
Ford Escort RS2000: 1844
Ford Fiesta: 1845
Ginetta G21S: 1997
Hillman Avenger 1600 Super: 2082
Honda Accord: 2095
Jensen GT: 2402
Lada 1500: 2424
Lancia Beta 1300: 2518
Lancia Beta 2000: 2519
Lancia Beta Coupe: 2520
Lancia Beta Sedan: 2521
MG B: 3029
MG Midget: 3030
MG Midget Mk IV: 3031
Mini Clubman 1100: 3059
Mitsubishi Colt Celeste 2000: 3063

Morris Marina 1.8 HL: 3183
Oldsmobile Starfire: 3299
Opel Rekord 2100D: 3342
Opel Rekord Berlina Pacesetter: 3343
Peugeot 104: 3414
Peugeot 104 ZS: 3415
Plymouth Arrow GT: 3512
Porsche 924: 3653
Reliant Kitten DL Estate: 3790
Renault 15 GTL: 3850
Renault 17 Gordini: 3851
Renault 20 TL: 3852
Renault 5 GTL: 3854
Saab 99GL Super Combi: 4079
Seat 1200 Sport: 4110
Toyota 1000: 4393
Toyota Carina: 4394
Toyota Celica Liftback: 4395
Toyota Corolla Liftback: 4396
Triumph Dolomite 1500HL: 4568
Triumph Spitfire: 4569
Triumph TR7: 4570
TVR 1600M: 4590
Vauxhall Blydenstein Chevette 1500: 4678
Vauxhall Cavalier 1600 GL: 4679
Vauxhall Cavalier GL Coupe: 4680
Vauxhall Chevette L: 4681
Vauxhall VX1800: 4682
Volkswagen Golf 1600 LS: 4803
Volkswagen Sciroco TS: 4804
Volvo 242 GL: 4930
Year total: 71

1977 Alfa Romeo Alfetta: 98
Alfa Romeo Spider: 99
AMC Gremlin 2-litre: 204
Audi 100 GLS: 277
Audi Fox: 278
Austin Allegro 1750 HL: 415
Austin Maxi 1750: 416
BMW 320i: 542
Chrysler Alpine GL: 995
Chrysler Avenger 1600 Estate: 996
Chrysler Sunbeam 1.0LS: 997
Chrysler Sunbeam 1.6S: 998
Citroen CX 2200 Diesel: 1051
Citroen CX 2400: 1052
Citroen CX 2400 GTi: 1053
Datsun 180B Bluebird: 1200
Datsun 200SX: 1201
Datsun Cherry F11: 1204
Dodge Colt Lancer: 1322
Fiat 127 1050 CL: 1555
Fiat 131: 1556
Fiat X1/9: 1557
Ford Escort 1300 GL: 1850
Ford Escort 1600 Sport: 1851
Ford Fiesta 1000: 1852
Ford Fiesta 1100 Ghia: 1853
Ford Fiesta 1300 S: 1854
Ford Fiesta Ghia: 1855
Honda Accord: 2096
Honda Civic 1500: 2097
Jensen GT: 2404
Lancia Beta: 2522
Lancia Beta HPE 2000: 2523
Lancia Beta Scorpion: 2524
Lotus Eclat 523: 2619
Lotus Esprit: 2620
Lotus Esprit 16v: 2621
Lotus Sprint: 2622
Mazda 323: 2702
Mazda GLC: 2703
Mercedes-Benz 230C: 2852
Mercury Zephyr: 2954
MG B GT: 3032
Mitsubishi Colt Sigma 2000: 3064
Morris Marina 1.3 Super Coupe: 3184
Panther Lima: 3375
Peugeot 504 Diesel Automatique: 3416
Porsche 924: 3656
Renault 12 TL: 3855
Renault 14: 3856
Renault 17 TS: 3857
Renault 20 TS: 3858
Saab 99EMS: 4080
Simca 1000LS: 4158
Skoda 120L: 4187
Toyota Corolla 1200: 4397
Toyota Corona Cressida: 4398
Triumph TR7: 4571
Triumph TR7 Tullius: 4572
Vauxhall Cavalier 1300L: 4683
Vauxhall Magnum 1800: 4684
Vauxhall VX2300 Estate: 4685
Volkswagen Dasher: 4805
Volkswagen Golf GTi: 4806
Volkswagen Passat GLS: 4807
Volkswagen Polo LS: 4808
Volkswagen Rabbit Diesel: 4809
Volkswagen Scirocco Fi: 4810
Volkswagen Sciroco GTi: 4811
Volvo 244 DL: 4932
Volvo 343: 4933
Year total: 71

1978 Alfa Romeo Alfetta 2.0: 101
Alfa Romeo Giulietta 1.6: 102
Alfa Romeo Sport Sedan: 103
Austin Princess II 2000 HL: 417
BMW 320i Alpina: 546
Chrysler 1300 GL: 999
Chrysler Alpine GLS: 1000
Chrysler Horizon GL: 1001
Citroen CX Pallas C-Matic Injection: 1054
Datsun 510: 1206
Fiat 127 Sport: 1558
Fiat 131 Supermirafiori: 1559
Fiat 132 2000 GLS: 1560
Fiat Super Brava: 1561
Ford Capri 1600S: 1857
Ford Granada 2.0L: 1858
Ford Granada 2.1D: 1859
Honda Accord: 2098
Honda Civic: 2099
Lada 1300 ES: 2425
Matra Rancho: 2683
Mercedes-Benz 200: 2855
Mitsubishi Colt Lancer Estate: 3065
Mitsubishi Colt Sappore 2000 GSR: 3066
Morris Marina 1700HL: 3185
Opel Rekord 2.0S: 3344
Peugeot 305 SR: 3418
Plymouth Horizon: 3514
Plymouth Sapporo: 3515
Porsche 924 Lux: 3660
Renault 5 Automatic: 3860
Saab Turbo: 4081
Toyota Celica: 4399
Toyota Celica 2000GT: 4400
Toyota Celica GT Liftback: 4401
Vauxhall Carlton: 4686
Vauxhall Cavalier 2000 GLS: 4687
Vauxhall Chevette 2300 HS: 4688
Volkswagen Golf GLS: 4813
Volkswagen Golf LD: 4814
Volvo 242 GT: 4934
Volvo 242 IPD: 4935
Volvo 343: 4938
Year total: 43

1979 Alfa Romeo Sport Sedan Automatic: 105
Alfa Romeo Sprint Veloce: 106
Audi 80 GLS: 282
Chrysler Sunbeam 1600 Ti: 1002
Citroen Athena: 1055
Citroen CX 2500 Diesel Super: 1056
Datsun 210: 1209
Datsun 310 Coupe: 1214
Datsun New Sunny: 1216
Dodge Colt Hatchback: 1323
Fiat 124 Spider: 1562
Fiat 124 Sports Spider: 1563
Fiat Mirafiori Sport: 1565
Fiat Strada: 1566
Fiat Strada 65CL: 1567
Fiat Strada 75CL: 1568
Fiat X1/9 1300: 1569
Fiat X1/9 1500: 1570
Ford Capri 2000S: 1861
Ford Cortina 1600L: 1862
Ford Fiesta Healey: 1864
Ford Mustang Ghia Turbo: 1866
Ford Mustang Turbo: 1867
Honda Accord 4-door: 2100
Honda Prelude: 2101
Lada Niva 1600: 2426
Lancia Beta 2000 Automatic: 2527
Lancia Beta HPE 1600: 2528
Lancia HPE: 2529
Lotus Elite: 2624
Lotus Esprit S2: 2625
Mazda 1.4 SP: 2706
Mazda 626 Coupe: 2707
Mazda GLC Wagon: 2708
Mazda Montrose 1600 GLS: 2709
MG B: 3033
MG Midget: 3034
Mini 850 Super de Luxe: 3060
Mitsubishi Colt 1400 GLX: 3067
Opel Kadett 1.3S Berlina: 3345
Peugeot 504: 3419
Peugeot 505 STI: 3420
Plymouth Fire Arrow: 3516
Polonez 1500: 3524
Porsche 924: 3663

Porsche 924 Turbo: 3664
Renault 18 GTS: 3861
Renault 18 TS Estate: 3862
Renault 5 Gordini: 3864
Renault 5 Racer: 3865
Renault 5 TL: 3866
Renault Gordini: 3867
Renault Le Car: 3868
Saab 900 Turbo: 4082
Saab 900GL: 4083
Toyota Corona 5-door: 4404
Toyota Corona Liftback: 4405
Triumph Dolomite 1850HL: 4573
Triumph Spitfire: 4574
Triumph TR7: 4575
Volkswagen Scirocco: 4815
Volkswagen Sciroco GLi: 4816
Volkswagen Sciroco GLS: 4817
Year total: 63

1980 Alfa Romeo Spider: 107
Audi 4000: 283
BMW 320i: 554
Datsun 200SX: 1217
Datsun 510: 1222
Fiat Brava Abarth Rally: 1571
Ford Fiesta: 1869
Ford Mustang Turbo: 1870
Honda Civic: 2102
Honda Civic GL 1500: 2103
Honda Prelude: 2104
Lancia Zagato: 2530
Lotus Eclat: 2626
Mazda 626: 2712
Mazda Montrose GLS Coupe: 2713
MG B: 3035
Peugeot 505 S: 3422
Peugeot 505 SD: 3423
Peugeot 604 D Turbo: 3424
Plymouth Champ: 3517
Pontiac Phoenix: 3568
Porsche 924: 3667
Porsche 924 S Turbo: 3668
Saab 900GLE: 4084
Suzuki SC 100: 4321
Toyota Celica GT: 4406
Toyota Corolla Sport Coupe: 4407
Toyota Corolla Tercel SR5: 4408
Triumph Spitfire: 4576
Volkswagen Dasher Diesel: 4818
Volkswagen Jetta: 4819
Volkswagen Jetta GLS: 4820
Volkswagen Rabbit: 4821
Volkswagen Scirocco: 4822
Volvo GL: 4940
Year total: 35

1981 Austin Metro Automatic: 418
Austin Mini Metro: 419
Citroen CX Pallas: 1058
Datsun 280ZX Turbo: 1223
Dodge Aires Wagon: 1324
Fiat 127 1050 Super: 1572
Fiat Brava: 1573
Fiat Panda: 1574
Ford Cortina 2.0 GL: 1872
Ford Escort: 1873
Ford Escort 1.6L Estate: 1874
Ford Fiesta Popular: 1875
Ford Fiesta XR2: 1876
Honda Accord: 2105
Honda Civic 4-door Sedan: 2106
Honda Prelude: 2107
Honda Quintet: 2108
Lancia Montecarlo Group 5 Turbo: 2531
Lancia Montecarlo Spyder: 2532
Lancia Trevi 2000: 2533
Lotus Esprit Turbo: 2627
Mazda 323 1300: 2716
Mazda GLC: 2717
Mazda GLC Sport: 2718
Mercedes-Benz 230E: 2865
Mercedes-Benz 230TE: 2866
Mercury LN7: 2955
Mercury Lynx Hatchback RS: 2956
Mitsubishi Colt Lancer 2000 Turbo: 3068
Morris Ital 2.0 HLS Automatic: 3186
Opel Manta GTJ: 3346
Peugeot 305 S: 3425
Peugeot 505 S Turbodiesel: 3426
Pontiac J2000: 3569
Porsche 924 Turbo: 3671
Renault 14 TS: 3869
Renault 18 Turbo: 3870
Renault 18i: 3871
Renault 20 TX: 3872
Renault 5 Turbo: 3873
Renault Le Car Turbo: 3874
Saab 900 Turbo: 4085
Saab 900GLS: 4086
Talbot Solara GLS: 4344
Talbot Tagora 2.2GLS: 4345
Toyota Cressida DX Estate: 4410
Toyota Starlet: 4411
Triumph Acclaim HL: 4580
Vauxhall Cavalier 1.6S GL: 4690
Volkswagen Golf 1300 LS: 4824
Volkswagen Passat CL Formel E: 4825
Volkswagen Rabbit: 4827
Volkswagen Rabbit Convertible: 4828
Volkswagen Rabbit Diesel: 4829
Volkswagen Scirocco GT-3 Davey: 4830
Volkswagen Scirocco S: 4831
Zastava 1300 ZLX-E: 5006
Year total: 57

1982 Alfa Romeo Spider Veloce: 110
Alfa Romeo Spider Veloce 2000: 111
Audi 80 Turbo Diesel: 291
Austin Ambassador 2.0 HL: 420
BMW 316: 559
Cadillac Cimarron: 713
Daihatsu Charmant 1600LE: 1118
Datsun Stanza 1.6 GL: 1226
Datsun Sunny 1.5 DX: 1227
Dodge Challenger: 1325
Dodge Charger 2.2: 1326
Fiat Mirafiori 1400CL: 1575
Fiat Spider 2000: 1576
Fiat Spider Turbo: 1577
Fiat Strada Super 85: 1578
Fiat X1/9: 1579
Ford Escort 1600 GL: 1878
Ford Sierra 1.6L: 1882
Honda Accord: 2109
Honda Accord LX: 2110
Hyundai Pony 1400 TLS: 2219
Lancia Beta Coupe: 2534
Lancia Delta Automatic: 2535
MG Metro 1300: 3036
Mitsubishi Colt Cordia Turbo: 3069
Mitsubishi Colt Hatchback Turbo: 3070
Mitsubishi Colt Starion Turbo: 3071
Mitsubishi Cordia LS: 3072
Nissan Sentra: 3204
Nissan Stanza XE: 3205
Peugeot 505 GR Estate: 3427
Peugeot 505 STI: 3428
Porsche 924 Weissach: 3672
Porsche 944: 3673
Porsche 944 Lux: 3674
Renault 18 GTX Estate: 3875
Renault 5 Gordini Turbo: 3876
Renault 9 GLT: 3877
Renault 9 TC: 3878
Renault 9 TSE: 3879
Renault Alliance DL: 3880
Renault Fuego GTS: 3881
Renault Fuego Turbo: 3882
Rover 2000: 4022
Rover SD Turbo: 4023
Saab 900: 4087
Saab 900 Turbo: 4088
Talbot Samba Cabriolet: 4346
Talbot Samba GL: 4347
Toyota Celica: 4412
Toyota Celica 2.0ST: 4413
Toyota Celica GTA: 4414
Triumph TR7 Convertible: 4581
Vauxhall Astra 1600 GL: 4691
Vauxhall Cavalier GLS: 4692
Vauxhall Cavalier LD: 4693
Volkswagen Golf GTi 1800: 4832
Volkswagen Polo C: 4833
Volkswagen Polo C Formel E: 4834
Volkswagen Quantum: 4835
Volkswagen Scirocco GL: 4837
Volvo 240 GL: 4942
Volvo 360 GLT: 4943
Volvo GLT Turbo: 4945
Year total: 64

1983 Austin Maestro 1.6 HLS: 421
Austin Maestro 1600: 422
BMW 318i: 563
Chevrolet Cavalier CS: 889
Citroen BX14 RE: 1059
Citroen BX16 TRS: 1060
Datsun 200SX: 1228
Datsun Micra GL: 1232
Dodge 600ES: 1327
Dodge Shelby Charger: 1328
Fiat Spider 2000: 1580
Fiat Strada 60 Comfort ES: 1581
Fiat Uno 55 S: 1582
Fiat Uno 70 SX: 1583

Ford Escort 1.6 GL Automatic: 1884
Ford Escort XR3i: 1885
Ford Fiesta 1.1 Ghia: 1886
Ford Granada 2.5 Diesel Estate: 1887
Ford Orion 1.6 GL: 1889
Ford Thunderbird Turbo Coupe: 1891
Honda CRX 1.5: 2111
Honda Prelude EX ALB: 2112
Isuzu I-Mark LS: 2252
Lancia Prisma 1600: 2536
Lotus Eclat Excel: 2628
Lotus Esprit Turbo: 2629
Mazda 626: 2721
Mazda 626 1600 LX: 2722
Mercedes-Benz 190: 2872
Mercedes-Benz 190E: 2873
MG Metro Turbo: 3037
Mitsubishi Colt Shogun: 3073
Mitsubishi Starion: 3074
Mitsubishi Starion Turbo: 3075
Mitsubishi Tredia Turbo: 3076
Nissan Pulsar NX: 3206
Opel Manta Berlinetta 1.8S: 3348
Opel Manta GTE: 3349
Peugeot 205 GR: 3429
Peugeot 305 SR: 3430
Porsche 944: 3678
Renault 11 TSE: 3883
Renault Fuego Turbo: 3884
Talbot Horizon 1.9LD: 4348
Toyota Camry LE: 4416
Toyota Celica GTS: 4417
Toyota Corolla GL: 4418
Toyota Corolla SR5 Hardtop: 4419
Toyota Tercel 4WD Wagon: 4422
Toyota Tercel GL: 4423
Vauxhall Astra GTE: 4694
Vauxhall Carlton 2.0 GL: 4695
Vauxhall Cavalier CD: 4696
Vauxhall Nova 1.2L: 4697
Volkswagen Rabbit GTi: 4839
Volkswagen Scirocco: 4840
Volkswagen Scirocco GTi: 4841
Volvo 760 Turbo: 4947
Year total: 58

1984 Alfa Romeo Alfetta Gold Cloverleaf: 113
Alfa Romeo Spider: 115
Audi 80 GL: 301
Austin Montego 1.6L: 423
BMW 318i: 568
Chrysler Laser XE: 1003
Citroen BX19 RD Diesel: 1061
Citroen CX GTi Turbo: 1062
Citroen LNA 11RE: 1063
Citroen Visa Convertible: 1064
Dodge Colt Vista: 1329
Dodge Conquest: 1330
Dodge Daytona Turbo Z: 1331
Fiat Regata 100 S: 1584
Fiat Regata 70 ES: 1585
Fiat Strada Abarth 130TC: 1586
Fiat X1/9: 1587
Ford Fiesta 1.3L CVH: 1892
Ford Fiesta 1.6L Diesel: 1893
Ford Fiesta XR2: 1894
Ford Mustang SVO: 1897
Ford Tempo GLX: 1899
Honda Civic CRX: 2113
Honda Civic DL: 2114
Honda Jazz: 2115
Honda Prelude: 2116
Hyundai Stellar 1600 GSL: 2220
Isuzu Impulse: 2253
Lancia Rally: 2537
Mercedes-Benz 190E: 2876
MG Montego EFi: 3038
Mitsubishi Colt 1600 Turbo: 3077
Mitsubishi Cordia Turbo 1.8: 3078
Mitsubishi Galant 1600 GL: 3079
Mitsubishi Mirage Turbo: 3080
Morgan 4/4: 3133
Nissan 200SX Turbo: 3207
Nissan Pulsar NX Turbo: 3210
Nissan Silvia Turbo ZX: 3211
Peugeot 205 GTi: 3431
Peugeot 505 GRi: 3432
Peugeot 505 S Wagon: 3433
Pininfarina Azzurra: 3469
Pininfarina Spider: 3470
Plymouth Colt GTS Turbo: 3518
Plymouth Voyager: 3519
Pontiac Fiero: 3573
Pontiac Fiero SE: 3574
Porsche 944: 3681
Renault 5 Turbo 2: 3886
Renault Fuego: 3887
Renault Fuego 2.2: 3888
Rover 213 Vanden Plas: 4025
Toyota Carina II 116GL: 4424
Toyota Corolla GT Coupe: 4426
Toyota Corolla GTS: 4427
Toyota Corolla LE: 4428
Toyota Van LE: 4430
Vauxhall Astra GTE: 4698
Volkswagen Jetta GLi: 4843
Volkswagen Jetta GLX: 4844
Volkswagen Passat CL Turbo Diesel Estate: 4845
Volkswagen Scirocco: 4846
Volkswagen Scirocco 16v: 4847
Volvo 740 GLT: 4948
Volvo GLT Wagon: 4950
Year total: 66

1985 Alfa Romeo Graduate: 121
Audi 5000 S Turbo Quattro: 305
Austin Montego 2.0 HL: 424
Caterham 1700 Super Sprint: 723
Caterham 7: 724
Chrysler Le Baron GTS: 1004
Citroen BX16 TRS Automatic: 1066
Citroen CX22 TRS: 1067
Citroen Visa 14TRS: 1068
Citroen Visa 17RD: 1069
Citroen Visa GTi: 1070
Dacia Duster GLX: 1106
Daihatsu Charmant 1300LC: 1121
Dodge Omni GLH: 1332
Fiat Uno 70 SX: 1588
Fiat Uno Turbo ie: 1589
Fiat X1/9: 1590
Fiat X1/9VS: 1591
Ford Escort GL: 1900
Ford Escort RS Turbo: 1901
Ford Fiesta XR2: 1902
Ford Sierra 1.8 Ghia: 1906
Ford Sierra 2.0i S: 1907
Honda Accord 2.0 EXi: 2117
Honda Accord EX Automatic: 2118
Honda Accord SEi: 2119
Honda Civic GT: 2120
Honda Civic S: 2121
Honda Civic Shuttle: 2122
Honda Civic Wagon: 2123
Honda CRX Si: 2124
Honda Prelude: 2125
Hyundai Pony 1.5 GLS: 2221
Lancia Coupe 2000ie: 2538
Lancia Thema 2.0 ie LX Turbo: 2539
Lancia Y10 Turbo: 2540
Mazda 323 1.5 GLX: 2726
Mazda 323 1.6i: 2727
Mercedes-Benz 190E 2.3: 2878
Mercedes-Benz 190E 2.3-16: 2879
Mercedes-Benz 190E BBS/Callaway Turbo: 2880
Merkur XR4Ti: 2963
MG Montego Turbo: 3039
Mitsubishi Colt Starion Turbo: 3081
Mitsubishi Galant: 3082
Mitsubishi Galant Turbo: 3083
Mitsubishi Space Wagon 1800GLX: 3084
Mitsubishi Starion: 3085
Mitsubishi Starion ESI: 3086
Naylor TF 1700: 3203
Nissan Bluebird Turbo ZX: 3212
Nissan Cherry 1.3 SGT: 3213
Panther Kallista 1.6L: 3378
Peugeot 205 XL: 3434
Peugeot 305 GRD Estate: 3435
Peugeot 309 1.3 GL: 3436
Peugeot 505 Turbo: 3437
Porsche 944 Lux: 3685
Porsche 944 Turbo: 3686
Reliant Scimitar SS1 1600: 3794
Renault 5 TSE: 3890
Renault Encore GS: 3891
Renault Espace 2000 TSE: 3892
Rover 216 Vitesse: 4026
Saab 900 Turbo: 4089
Saab 9000 Turbo 16v: 4090
Saab 900i: 4091
Seat 1.5 GLX: 4111
Suzuki Swift 1.3GS: 4324
Toyota Celica GTS: 4431
Toyota Corolla GT Hatchback: 4432
Toyota MR2: 4433
Toyota Space Cruiser: 4434
Toyota Starlet 1.0GL: 4435
Toyota Tercel 4WD Estate: 4437
Vauxhall Astra 1.3 GL: 4699
Vauxhall Astra 1.6 SR: 4700
Vauxhall Cavalier SRi: 4701
Volkswagen Cabriolet Wolfsburg: 4848
Volkswagen Golf: 4849
Volkswagen Golf GTi: 4850
Volkswagen Jetta GLi: 4851

Volkswagen Scirocco: 4852
Volkswagen Scirocco 16v: 4853
Volkswagen Scirocco GTX: 4854
Volvo 740 Turbo Wagon: 4951
Volvo 760 Turbo Estate: 4952
Year total: 87

1986 Acura Integra RS: 28
Alfa Romeo Alfa 75 1.8: 124
Alfa Romeo Spider Quadrifoglio: 128
Audi 80 1.8S: 312
Austin Montego 2.0 Vanden Plas EFI: 425
Chevrolet Nova CL: 903
Chrysler Laser XT: 1005
Citroen BX19 RD Estate: 1071
Citroen CX25 Ri Familiale Auto: 1072
Citroen Visa GTi: 1073
Dodge Omni GLH: 1334
Dodge Shelby GLH-S: 1335
Fiat Panda 1000 S: 1592
Fiat Panda 750 L: 1593
Fiat Regata DS: 1594
Ford Escort 1.4 GL: 1909
Ford Escort L: 1910
Ford Escort RS Turbo: 1911
Ford Escort XR3i: 1912
Ford Mustang SVO: 1915
Ford Orion 1.4 GL: 1916
Ford RS200: 1917
Honda Accord LXi: 2126
Honda Civic Hatchback: 2127
Honda CRX Coupe 1.6i 16: 2128
Honda CRX Si: 2129
Honda CRX Si Jackson Turbo: 2130
Honda Integra 1.5: 2131
Honda Integra EX 16: 2132
Honda Prelude 2.0 Si: 2134
Hyundai Excel GL: 2222
Hyundai Excel GLS: 2223
Isuzu I-Mark: 2254
Isuzu Impulse Sports Coupe: 2255
Isuzu Impulse Turbo: 2256
Lada Riva 1500 Estate: 2427
Lancia Delta HF 4WD: 2541
Lancia Delta HF Turbo ie: 2542
Lancia Prisma 1600ie LX: 2543
Lancia Thema 2.0ie: 2544
Lancia Y10 Fire: 2545
Lotus Esprit Turbo: 2630
Lotus Excel SE: 2631
Mazda 323 1.5 GLX Estate: 2729
Mazda 323 1.6i: 2730
Mazda 323 LX: 2731
Mazda 323 Turbo 4x4 Lux: 2732
Mazda 626 2.0i 5-door: 2733
Mazda 626 GT: 2734
Mercedes-Benz 190E 2.3-16: 2883
Mercedes-Benz 200: 2884
Mitsubishi Cordia Turbo: 3087
Mitsubishi Lancer 1.5 GLX Estate: 3088
Mitsubishi Mirage: 3089
Mitsubishi Starion ESI-R: 3090
Nissan Bluebird 1.8 ZX: 3217
Nissan Sentra: 3219
Nissan Sentra Sport Coupe SE: 3220
Nissan Sunny 1.3 LX 5-door: 3221
Peugeot 205 GTi: 3438
Peugeot 309 1.6 GR: 3439
Peugeot 309 SR Injection: 3440
Peugeot 505 GTi Family Estate: 3441
Peugeot 505 Turbo: 3442
Plymouth Horizon America: 3520
Porsche 924 S: 3690
Porsche 944: 3693
Porsche 944 S: 3694
Porsche 944 Turbo: 3695
Reliant Scimitar Ti: 3795
Renault 21 GTS: 3893
Renault 21 Savanna GTX: 3894
Renault 5 GT Turbo: 3895
Renault 5 GTL 5-door: 3896
Renault 9 Turbo: 3897
Renault Alliance 1.7L: 3898
Saab 9000: 4092
Saab 9000i: 4093
Seat Malaga 1.2L: 4112
Skoda Estelle 120 LSE: 4188
Suzuki Swift 1.3 GTi: 4326
Toyota Celica 2.0GT: 4438
Toyota Celica GTS: 4439
Toyota MR2: 4440
Toyota MR2 T-Bar: 4441
Toyota Tercel DX: 4444
Vauxhall Belmont 1.8 GLSi: 4703
Vauxhall Carlton CD 2.0i: 4704
Vauxhall Nova 1.3 GL 5-door: 4705
Volkswagen Golf GTi 16v: 4856
Volkswagen Jetta GT: 4857
Volkswagen Scirocco 16v: 4859
Volkswagen Scirocco GTX 16v: 4860
Volvo 340 GLE: 4953
Yugo GV: 5002
Year total: 95

1987 Acura Integra LS: 30
Alfa Romeo Alfa 75 2.0i Twin Spark: 131
Austin Metro 1.3L 3-door: 426
BMW 318i 2-door: 586
BMW M3: 590
Chrysler Le Baron Coupe: 1006
Citroen AX GT: 1074
Citroen AX11 TRE: 1075
Citroen AX14 TRS: 1076
Citroen BX GTi 16v: 1077
Citroen CX25 DTR Turbo 2: 1078
Daihatsu Fourtrak Estate DT EL: 1125
Fiat Croma ie Super: 1595
Fiat Regata 100S ie: 1596
Fiat Uno Selecta: 1597
Ford Festiva L: 1919
Ford Fiesta 1.1 Ghia Auto: 1920
Ford Sierra Sapphire 2.0 Ghia: 1925
Ford Thunderbird Turbo Coupe: 1927
Honda Ballade EX: 2135
Honda Civic 1.4 GL 3-door: 2136
Honda Prelude 2.0 Si: 2138
Honda Prelude 2.0i 16: 2139
Isuzu Trooper 3-door TD: 2257
Lada Niva Cossack Cabrio: 2428
Lada Samara 1300 SL: 2429
Land Rover Ninety County Turbo Diesel: 2560
Lotus Elan Autocrosser: 2632
Lotus Esprit Turbo HC: 2633
Lotus Excel SA: 2634
Mazda 323 1.5 GLX: 2738
Mazda 626 2.0 GLS Executive: 2739
Mercury Tracer: 2959
Mitsubishi Colt 1500 GLX 5-door: 3091
Mitsubishi Galant 2000 GLS Automatic: 3092
Mitsubishi Galant Sapporo: 3093
Mitsubishi Shogun Turbo Diesel 5-door: 3094
Mitsubishi Starion 2000 Turbo: 3095
Mitsubishi Starion ESI-R: 3096
Nissan Micra SGL 5-DR: 3225
Nissan Pulsar NX SE: 3226
Nissan Sunny ZX Coupe: 3227
Nissan Sunny 1.6 SLX Coupe: 3228
Peugeot 205 GTi 1.9: 3443
Peugeot 309 GTi: 3444
Pontiac Le Mans: 3583
Porsche 924 S: 3700
Porsche 944 S: 3701
Renault 11 Turbo: 3900
Renault 5 GT Turbo: 3901
Renault 5 GTX 3-DR: 3902
Renault Alliance GTA: 3903
Rover 820SE: 4028
Rover Montego 1.6L: 4029
Suzuki SJ413V JX: 4327
Suzuki Swift 1.3 GLX: 4328
Suzuki Swift 1.3 GLX Executive: 4329
Toyota Camry 2.0 GLi: 4445
Toyota Camry 2.0 GLi Estate: 4446
Toyota Celica GT Cabriolet: 4447
Toyota Corolla Executive: 4448
Toyota Corolla FX-16 GTS: 4449
Toyota MR2 Supercharged: 4451
Vauxhall Astra GTE 2.0i: 4706
Vauxhall Belmont 1.6 GL: 4707
Vauxhall Cavalier 2.0i CD: 4709
Vauxhall Cavalier SRi 130 4-door: 4710
Volkswagen Fox GL: 4861
Volkswagen Golf Cabriolet Clipper: 4862
Volkswagen GTi 16v: 4863
Volkswagen Jetta GTi 16v: 4864
Volkswagen Passat GT 5-door: 4865
Volvo 480 ES: 4954
Volvo 740 Turbo: 4955
Yugo 45 GLS: 5003
Year total: 75

1988 Acura Integra LS Special Edition: 31
Alfa Romeo 75 Evoluzione: 135
Alfa Romeo Spider: 136
Audi 80 1.8E: 321
Chevrolet Nova Twin Cam: 923
Chrysler Conquest TSi: 1007
Citroen AX11 TRE 5DR: 1079
Citroen BX DTR Turbo: 1080
Dodge Daytona Shelby Z: 1336
Dodge Lancer Shelby: 1337
Dodge Shelby CSX: 1338
Fiat Tipo 1.4: 1598
Fiat X1/9: 1599
Ford Probe GT: 1933
Ford Sierra RS Cosworth: 1934

Honda Civic CRX: 2140
Honda CRX Si: 2141
Honda CRX Si Jackson: 2142
Honda Shuttle 1.6i RT4 4WD: 2144
Isuzu I-Mark RS Turbo: 2258
Isuzu Impulse Turbo: 2259
Lancia Delta HF Integrale: 2547
Lotus Esprit Turbo: 2635
Mazda 121 1.3 LX Sun Top: 2741
Mazda 323 GTX: 2742
Mazda 323 Turbo 4x4: 2743
Mazda 626 2.0 GLX Executive Estate: 2744
Mazda 626 2.0i GT 4WS: 2745
Mazda MX-6: 2747
Mazda MX-6 GT: 2748
Merkur XR4Ti: 2965
Mitsubishi Cordia Turbo: 3097
Mitsubishi Galant 2000 GLSi: 3098
Mitsubishi Galant GTi-16v: 3099
Mitsubishi Lancer GTi 16v: 3100
Mitsubishi Mirage Turbo: 3101
Nissan 240SX: 3230
Oldsmobile Cutlass Calais International Series: 3301
Peugeot 405 1.6 GL: 3446
Peugeot 405 GRD: 3447
Peugeot 405 Mi16: 3448
Peugeot 405 SRi: 3449
Pontiac Sunbird GT: 3587
Porsche 924 S: 3711
Porsche 944: 3713
Porsche 944 S: 3714
Porsche 944 Turbo: 3715
Porsche 944 Turbo SE: 3716
Range Rover Vogue Turbo D: 3776
Renault 21 Ti: 3904
Renault 21 Turbo: 3905
Rover 820 Fastback: 4031
Saab 9000CD: 4094
Toyota Carina 1.6 GL: 4453
Toyota Celica All-Trac Turbo: 4454
Toyota Celica GT4: 4455
Toyota Corolla 1.3 GL: 4456
Toyota Corolla 4WD Estate: 4457
Toyota Landcruiser II TD: 4458
Vauxhall Carlton L 1.8i: 4712
Vauxhall Carlton L 2.3D: 4713
Vauxhall Cavalier 4x4: 4714
Vauxhall Nova GTE: 4715
Volkswagen GTi 16v: 4866
Volkswagen Jetta GLi 16v: 4867
Volkswagen Jetta Turbo Diesel: 4868
Volkswagen Passat GT: 4869
Volkswagen Polo C Saloon: 4870
Volkswagen Scirocco 16v: 4872
Yugo 65A GLX: 5004

Year total: 70

1989 Acura Integra LS: 32
Alfa Romeo Spider Quadrifoglio: 141
Audi 90: 324
Austin Metro GTa: 427
BMW 316i 4-door: 598
BMW M3: 603
BMW M3 Evolution: 604
BMW M3 Hor Technologie: 605
Carbodies Fairway 2.7 Silver: 721
Chrysler TC by Maserati: 1008
Citroen AX14 DTR: 1081
Citroen BX14 TGE: 1082
Daihatsu Charade 1.3 CX: 1128
Daihatsu Charade CLS: 1129
Daihatsu Sportrak EL: 1130
Dodge Daytona Shelby: 1339
Dodge Shadow ES Turbo: 1340
Dodge Shelby CSX: 1341
Dodge Shelby CSX VNT: 1342
Fiat Tipo 1.6 DGT SX: 1600
Fiat X1/9: 1601
Ford Escort 1.3L 3-door: 1936
Ford Fiesta 1.1LX 5-door: 1937
Ford Fiesta 1.4 Ghia: 1938
Ford Fiesta 1.6S: 1939
Ford Probe GT Suspension Techniques/HKS: 1943
Ford Sierra Sapphire 2000E: 1944
Honda Civic Si: 2145
Honda Civic Si HKS: 2146
Honda CRX Si HKS: 2147
Honda Prelude Si 4WS: 2148
Honda Shuttle 1.4 GL Automatic: 2149
Hyundai Sonata 2.0i GLS: 2224
Lada Samara 1300L 5-door: 2430
Lancia Delta Integrale 16v: 2549
Lancia Thema 2.0ie 16v: 2550
Lotus Esprit Turbo: 2636
Lotus Esprit Turbo SE: 2637
Mazda 323 1.6i: 2752
Mazda 323 1.8 GT: 2753
Mazda MX-5 Miata: 2755
Mazda MX-6 GT 4WS: 2756
Mercedes-Benz 190: 2900
Mercedes-Benz 190E 2.5-16: 2901
Mercedes-Benz 200E Automatic: 2904
MG Maestro Turbo: 3040
Mitsubishi Eclipse: 3102
Mitsubishi Eclipse GSX: 3103
Mitsubishi Galant GS: 3104
Mitsubishi Starion 2.6 Turbo: 3106
Mitsubishi Starion ESI-R: 3107
Nissan 200SX: 3232
Nissan 240SX Turbo Tokico/Cartech: 3233
Nissan Micra 1.2 GSX: 3237
Nissan Prairie: 3238
Nissan Sunny 1.4 LS: 3239
Oldsmobile Calais HO Quad 4: 3303
Oldsmobile Cutlass Calais International Series HO: 3304
Peugeot 205 1.1GL: 3450
Peugeot 205 CJ: 3451
Peugeot 309 GLX: 3452
Peugeot 309 GTi: 3453
Peugeot 405 GTD Turbo: 3454
Peugeot 405 Mi16: 3455
Plymouth Laser RS: 3521
Pontiac Grand Am Turbo: 3591
Porsche 944: 3728
Porsche 944 S2: 3729
Porsche 944 Turbo: 3730
Proton 1.5 SE Aeroback: 3754
Renault 19 TSE: 3907
Renault 19 TXE: 3908
Renault 21 GTS Hatchback: 3909
Renault 25 TXi: 3910
Renault 5 Campus: 3911
Renault Espace TXE: 3912
Rover Montego 2.0 DSL Turbo: 4034
Saab 900 Turbo S: 4095
Saab 9000 Turbo: 4096
Saab Carlsson: 4097
Seat Ibiza SXi: 4113
Skoda 136 Rapide Coupe: 4189
Suzuki Swift 1.3 GLX: 4330
Suzuki Swift 1.3 GTi: 4331
Suzuki Vitara JLX: 4332
Toyota Carina II 1.6 GL Liftback: 4462
Toyota Corolla GTS: 4463
Toyota MR2 Supercharged: 4464
Treser T1: 4485
Vauxhall Astra 1.7 DL: 4716
Vauxhall Cavalier 1.4L: 4717
Vauxhall Cavalier 1.6L: 4718
Vauxhall Cavalier SRi: 4719
Volkswagen Corrado: 4874
Volkswagen Corrado 16v: 4875
Volkswagen Golf CL Catalyst: 4876
Volkswagen Jetta Syncro: 4877
Volkswagen Passat GT 16v: 4878
Volvo 440 Turbo: 4957
Volvo 740 GLE: 4958
Volvo 740 Turbo: 4959

Year total: 101

1990 Acura Integra GS: 34
Alfa Romeo 164 Twin Spark Lusso: 142
Audi 80 2.0E: 328
Bertone Zabrus: 488
BMW 318i S: 609
Caterham 7 HPC: 725
Chevrolet Beretta GTZ: 936
Citroen AX GT5: 1083
Citroen BX GTi 4x4: 1084
Citroen CX25 GTi Turbo 2 CX Auto: 1085
Citroen XM 2.0SEi: 1086
Consulier GTP LX: 1096
Daihatsu Applause 16 Xi: 1131
Dodge Daytona Shelby: 1344
Dodge Shadow ES VNT: 1345
Eagle Talon: 1355
Fiat Croma CHT: 1602
Fiat Tempra 1.6 SX: 1603
Fiat Uno 60S: 1604
Fiat Uno Turbo ie: 1605
Ford Fiesta RS Turbo: 1949
Ford Fiesta XR2i: 1950
Ford Granada 2.5 GL Diesel: 1951
Ford Granada Scorpio 2.0i Auto: 1953
Ford Probe GT: 1956
Ford Sierra Sapphire Cosworth 4x4: 1958
Ginetta G32: 1998
Honda Accord 2.0 EXi: 2150
Honda Concerto 1.6i 16: 2151
Honda CRX 1.6i VT: 2152
Hyundai Sonata 2.4i GLS: 2225
IAD Venus: 2229
Isuzu Impulse XS: 2260
Lancia Dedra 1.8i: 2551
Lancia Dedra 2.0ie: 2552
Lancia Thema 2.0ie 16v SE Turbo: 2553

Lancia Y10 GTie: 2554
Land Rover Discovery TDi: 2563
Lotus Elan: 2638
Lotus Elan SE: 2639
Lotus Esprit Turbo SE: 2640
Mazda MX-5 Miata Millen: 2760
Mazda MX-6 GT: 2761
Mazda Protege: 2762
Mercedes-Benz 190E 2.5-16 Evolution II: 2908
Mercury Capri XR-2: 2961
MG B British Motor Heritage: 3041
Mitsubishi Galant 2000 GLSi Coupe: 3108
Mitsubishi Lancer GLXi 4WD Liftback: 3109
Mitsubishi Lancer Liftback 1800 GTi-16v: 3110
Morgan Plus 4 Mk III: 3136
Nissan Primera 1.6 LS: 3242
Panther Kallista: 3379
Panther Solo: 3380
Peugeot 309 Style 5-door: 3456
Peugeot 405 GLx4: 3457
Peugeot 405 GR Injection Auto: 3458
Peugeot 405 Mi16x4: 3459
Peugeot 405 Turbo 16 Pike's Peak: 3460
Peugeot 605 SRi: 3461
Plymouth Laser RS Turbo: 3522
Porsche 944 Cabriolet: 3741
Porsche 944 S2: 3742
Porsche 944 S2 Cabriolet: 3743
Reliant Scimitar SST 1800Ti: 3796
Renault 19 TXE Chamade: 3913
Renault 21 Turbo Quadra: 3914
Renault 21 TXi: 3915
Rover 214 GSi: 4037
Rover 216 GSi: 4038
Rover 414 Si: 4039
Rover 416 GTi: 4040
Rover Metro 1.4SL: 4041
Rover Metro GTi 16v: 4042
Saab 9000CD: 4098
Saab 900SPG: 4099
Saab CDS 2.3: 4100
Suzuki Swift GT: 4333
Toyota Celica 2.0 GT: 4468
Toyota Celica All-Trac Turbo: 4469
Toyota Celica GTS: 4470
Toyota MR2: 4471
Toyota MR2 GT: 4472
Toyota MR2 Turbo: 4473
Toyota Previa LE: 4474
Toyota Starlet GL: 4475
Vauxhall Calibra 2.0i 16v: 4722
Vauxhall Cavalier GSi 2000 16v: 4725
Vauxhall Cavalier GSi 2000 16v 4x4: 4726
Vauxhall Nova 1.5TD Merit: 4727
Volkswagen Corrado G60: 4879
Volkswagen Passat CL TD Estate: 4880
Volkswagen Passat GL: 4881
Volvo 440 GLE: 4960
Volvo 460 GLi: 4961
Volvo 460 Turbo: 4962
Volvo 740 GLT 16v Estate: 4963
Volvo 740 Turbo: 4964
Yugo Sana 1.4: 5005
Year total: 99

1991 Alfa Romeo Spider Veloce: 147
Audi 80 16v Sport: 335
Bertone Emotion Lotus: 489
BMW 318i: 614
BMW M3 Sport Evolution: 621
Caterham Super 7: 726
Chevrolet Baretta GTZ: 946
Citroen AX11 TZX: 1087
Citroen ZX 1.4 Avantage: 1090
Citroen ZX Volcane: 1091
Dodge Spirit R/T: 1346
Eagle Talon TSi 4WD: 1357
Ford Escort 1.4LX: 1960
Ford Escort 1.6 Ghia Estate: 1961
Ford Escort Cabriolet: 1962
Ford Escort GT: 1963
Ford Escort Millen: 1964
Ford Orion 1.6i Ghia: 1968
Ford Probe GT: 1969
Geo Storm GSi: 1994
Honda Civic 1.5 VEi: 2153
Honda Civic 1.6i VT: 2154
Honda Prelude Si: 2157
Hyundai Lantra 1.6 Cdi: 2226
Hyundai S Coupe GSi: 2227
Hyundai X2 1.5 GSi: 2228
Infiniti G20: 2232
Isuzu Impulse RS: 2261
Lancia Dedra 2000 Turbo: 2555
Lotus Elan SE: 2641
Mazda 121 GSX: 2765
Mazda 323 1.8 GT: 2766
Mercedes-Benz 190E 1.8 Auto: 2914
Mercedes-Benz 190E 2.3: 2915
Mercedes-Benz 190E 2.5-16 Evolution II: 2916
Mercury Tracer LTS: 2962
Mitsubishi Colt 1800 GTI-16v: 3112
Mitsubishi Galant VR-4: 3114
Mitsubishi Space Runner 1800-16v GLXi: 3117
Nissan 100NX: 3244
Nissan 240SX: 3245
Nissan NX2000: 3249
Nissan Primera 2.0 GSX: 3250
Nissan Primera 2.0E ZX: 3251
Nissan Sentra SE-R: 3252
Nissan Sunny 1.6 GS 5-door: 3253
Opel Calibra 2.0i 16v: 3351
Peugeot 106 XR: 3462
Peugeot 106 XSi: 3463
Peugeot 205 D Turbo: 3464
Peugeot 605 SR TD: 3465
Plymouth Laser RS Turbo: 3523
Proton 1.5 SE Triple Valve Aeroback: 3755
Renault 19 16v: 3917
Renault Clio 1.2 RN: 3919
Renault Clio 1.4RT: 3920
Rover 214S: 4043
Rover 216 GTi: 4044
Rover 218 SD: 4045
Rover 220 GTi: 4046
Rover 825 TD: 4047
Rover Mini Cooper S: 4048
Saab 9000 2.3 Turbo TCS: 4101
Saab 9000 Turbo: 4102
Saab 9000CS Turbo S: 4103
Saab 9000S: 4104
Saturn Sports Coupe: 4107
Toyota Camry 2.2 GL: 4476
Toyota Celica GT Convertible: 4477
Toyota MR2: 4479
Toyota MR2 HKS: 4480
Toyota Previa: 4481
Toyota Tercel LE: 4482
Vauxhall Calibra 2.0i: 4728
Vauxhall Calibra 4x4: 4729
Vauxhall Nova 1.2 Luxe: 4730
Volkswagen Corrado G60: 4882
Volkswagen Corrado Neuspeed: 4883
Volkswagen GTi 16v: 4884
Volkswagen Jetta GLi 16v: 4885
Volkswagen Polo 1.3 CL Coupe: 4886
Volkswagen Polo G40: 4887
Volkswagen Polo GT Coupe: 4888
Volvo 940 SE: 4965
Volvo 940 SE Turbo: 4966
Volvo 940 Turbo: 4967
Year total: 86

1992 Citroen AX GTi: 1092
Citroen XM Turbo SD Estate: 1093
Fiat Tipo 1.8ie DGT SX: 1606
Ford Escort RS2000: 1973
Ford Escort XR3i: 1974
Honda Prelude Si 4WS: 2160
Mazda MX-3 1.6 Auto: 2772
Nissan 200SX: 3254
Nissan Sunny 2.0 GTi: 3255
Peugeot 106 XT: 3468
Renault 19 16v Cabriolet: 3922
Renault Cleo 16v: 3923
Rover 820i: 4050
Saab 9000 2.3CS: 4105
Seat Toledo 1.9 CL Diesel: 4114
Seat Toledo 2.0 GTi: 4115
Toyota Paseo: 4483
Vauxhall 1.4i GLS: 4732
Vauxhall Cavalier 1.7 GL TD: 4733
Vauxhall Frontera 2.3 TD Estate: 4734
Volkswagen Golf 1.8 GL: 4889
Volkswagen Golf GTi: 4890
Year total: 22

Total No: 2,343

Five cylinders in line.

1975 Mercedes-Benz 300D: 2848

1977 Audi 100 5E: 276

1978 Audi 100 L Avant: 279
Audi 5000: 280
Mercedes-Benz 300CD: 2856
Mercedes-Benz 300SD: 2857

1979 Audi 100 GL5S: 281
Mercedes-Benz 300TD: 2861

1980 Audi 5000 S Diesel: 284

1981 Audi 200 5E: 285
Audi 4000 Automatic: 286
Audi 5000 Turbo: 287
Audi Coupe: 288
Audi Quattro: 289
Mercedes-Benz 300GD: 2867
Mercedes-Benz 300TD: 2868
Volkswagen Passat GL 5S Estate: 4826
Year total: 8

1982 Audi 100 CD: 290
Audi Quattro: 292
Volkswagen Santana GX5: 4836

1983 Audi 200 Turbo: 293
Audi 5000 S: 294
Audi 80 Quattro: 295
Audi Coupe Injection: 296
Volkswagen Quantum GL5: 4838
Year total: 5

1984 Audi 200 Quattro Turbo: 297
Audi 4000 S Quattro: 298
Audi 5000 S Avant: 299
Audi 5000 S Turbo: 300
Audi Coupe GT: 302
Year total: 5

1985 Audi 100 Quattro: 303
Audi 200 Avant Quattro: 304
Audi 90 Quattro: 306
Audi Coupe GT: 307
Audi Quattro: 308
Audi Quattro Sport: 309
Year total: 6

1986 Audi 100 Turbo Diesel: 310
Audi 5000 S: 311
Audi 90: 313
Audi Coupe GT: 314
Audi Coupe GT 2.2: 315
Audi Coupe Quattro: 316
Dodge Colt Turbo: 1333
Volkswagen Quantum Synchro Wagon: 4858
Year total: 8

1987 Audi 90 2.2E: 317
Audi 90 Quattro: 318

1988 Audi 100 Avant Quattro: 319
Audi 100 Sport: 320
Audi 90 Quattro: 322
Audi Quattro: 323
Volkswagen Quantum GLS Synchro Wagon: 4871
Year total: 5

1989 Audi 90 Quattro 20v: 325
Audi Coupe 2.2E: 326
Audi Coupe Quattro: 327

1990 Audi 90 Quattro: 329
Audi Quattro 20v: 330
Ital Design Aztec: 2262

1991 Audi 200 Quattro: 334
Audi 90 Quattro 20v: 336
Audi Coupe S2: 337
Total No: 60

Six cylinders in line.

1926 Wills Sainte Claire Six: 4974

1927 Rolls-Royce Phantom I Phaeton: 3946

1928 Buick Empire Saloon: 653
Delage 21hp Weymann Saloon: 1245
Fiat 17/50 Saloon: 1454
Invicta 4.5-litre: 2241
Mercedes-Benz 36/220-S: 2774
Year total: 5

1929 Chrysler 65 Saloon: 960
Chrysler 75 Saloon: 961
Crossley 2-litre Saloon: 1103
Delaunay-Belleville 21hp Saloon: 1253
Dodge New Six Saloon: 1269
Franklin 29.4hp Saloon: 1977
Graham-Paige 21.6hp Saloon: 2015
HE 16/60 Sports Four-seater: 2017
Humber Snipe: 2180
Lagonda 3-litre Tourer: 2432
Mercedes-Benz SSKL: 2776
MG Six Sports: 2969
Morris Isis: 3139
Rolls-Royce 20 Saloon: 3947
Sunbeam Weymann Saloon: 4280
Vauxhall 20/60 Limousine: 4609
Year total: 16

1930 Bentley 8-litre Saloon: 463
Bentley Speed Six Weymann: 464
Buick 28.4hp Saloon: 654
Chrysler 77 Saloon: 962
Citroen Six Saloon: 1010
Delage 18.2hp Saloon: 1246
HE Supercharged Six Coupe: 2018
Panhard 18hp Saloon: 3364
Renault Vivasix Saloon: 3797
Studebaker Erskine Saloon: 4216
Wolseley Hornet: 4977
Year total: 11

1931 AC Acedes Magna Coupe: 2
Armstrong Siddeley 15 Saloon: 209
Invicta 4.5-litre: 2242
Jaguar SS1 Sports Tourer: 2263
Lagonda 3-litre Special Tourer: 2434
Mercedes-Benz 21/60 Coupe: 2778
Morris Major Six Saloon: 3141
Rolls-Royce 25 Saloon: 3948
Rover Light Six Speed Model: 3973
Vauxhall Cadet Saloon: 4610
Wolseley Viper Saloon: 4978
Year total: 11

1932 Alfa Romeo 1750: 40
Alvis Speed 20 (72bhp): 155
Alvis Speed 20 (87bhp): 156
Armstrong Siddeley Rally Tourer: 210
Essex Terraplane Tourer: 1360
Hillman Wizard 65 Saloon de Luxe: 2026
Humber 16/60 Saloon: 2181
Humber Pullman Limousine: 2182
Lanchester 15/18 Saloon: 2477
Rolls-Royce Phantom II: 3949
Rover Pilot: 3974
Singer 14/6 Saloon: 4159
Talbot 65 Saloon: 4335
Year total: 13

1933 AC Ace Fixed-head Coupe: 3
Armstrong Siddeley Long 15hp Saloon: 211
Daimler 15hp Saloon: 1133
Delage D6-11 Sports Saloon: 1249
Frazer-Nash 1.5-litre: 1981
Hotchkiss 3.5-litre Coupe: 2161
Lagonda 16/80 Tourer: 2435
Lea-Francis 2-litre Saloon: 2568
Morris 10/6: 3143
Morris Cowley Six: 3145
Rolls-Royce Phantom II: 3950
Standard 16 Special Saloon: 4191
Standard Avon 16 Open Four-Seater: 4192
Standard Avon Coupe: 4193
Talbot 105 Speed Model: 4336
Year total: 15

1934 AC Ace Sports Four-seater: 4
AC Greyhound Close-coupled Saloon: 5
Austin 12/6: 345
Austin 15.9hp Ascot Saloon: 346
Austin 20 Ranelagh Landaulet: 347
Bentley Sedan: 465
Frazer-Nash 14hp Sports Tourer: 1983
Hillman 20/70 Limousine: 2027
Hispano-Suiza 30/120 Saloon: 2083
Hotchkiss Paris-Nice Speed Model: 2162
Lagonda 3.5-litre Tourer: 2436
Lagonda Le Mans: 2437
MG Magna Continential Coupe: 2971
MG Magnette N Two-seater: 2972
Morris 15/6 Saloon: 3146
Riley 12 Mentone Saloon: 3924
Talbot 75 Saloon: 4337
Triumph Gloria 6 Vitesse: 4489
Vauxhall 20 Saloon: 4611
Year total: 19

1935 AC Ace Drop-head Coupe: 6
Armstrong Siddeley 17hp Sports Foursome: 212
Armstrong Siddeley 30 Special Sports Saloon: 213
Austin 16 Hertford Saloon: 348
Chevrolet 26.3hp Saloon de Luxe: 729
Fiat 1500 Saloon: 1456
Frazer-Nash BMW 12.5hp Saloon: 1987
Frazer-Nash BMW Type 55 Cabriolet: 1988
Hillman 20/27 Sports Saloon: 2029
Hotchkiss Paris-Nice Saloon: 2163
Hudson Terraplane Big Six Saloon: 2172
Humber Snipe Sports Saloon: 2185

Hupmobile 29.4hp Saloon: 2217
Lagonda Rapide Tourer: 2439
Lanchester 18 Saloon: 2478
Marendaz 15/90 Special Tourer: 2647
Mercedes-Benz Type 290 Cabriolet: 2780
MG Magnette KN Saloon: 2974
Morris 10/6 Sports Tourer: 3148
Morris 16 Series II Saloon: 3149
Morris 21 Series II Saloon: 3150
Oldsmobile 26.3hp Saloon: 3269
Packard 120 Saloon: 3360
Renault 24hp Big Six Saloon: 3799
Rolls-Royce 20/25 Touring Saloon: 3951
Rover Speed 14 Streamline Coupe: 3976
Studebaker Dictator Saloon de Luxe: 4218
Sunbeam 20 Saloon: 4281
Talbot 75 Drop-frame Sports Saloon: 4338
Triumph 2-litre Southern Cross: 4490
Vauxhall 27 Saloon: 4612
Wolseley 14 Hornet Special: 4979
Year total: 32

1936 AC 2-litre Aero Saloon: 7
AC Ace: 8
Armstrong Siddeley 17hp Touring Saloon: 214
Austin 20 Mayfair Limousine: 350
Bentley 4.25-litre: 466
British Salmson 20.8hp Sports Two-seater: 644
Chrysler 23.4hp Wimbledon Saloon: 966
Daimler 15hp Saloon: 1134
Delahaye 23.8hp Drop-head Coupe: 1252
Graham 26hp Supercharged Saloon: 2013
Hillman Hawk Sports Saloon: 2031
Hudson 22hp Six Saloon: 2173
Humber Pullman Limousine: 2186
Humber Snipe Sports Saloon: 2187
Jaguar SS 2.5-litre: 2264
Lagonda 4.5-litre Tourer: 2440
Pontiac Touring Saloon de Luxe: 3526
Studebaker De Luxe Saloon: 4220
Talbot 105 Airline Saloon: 4339
Talbot 3.5-litre Speed Saloon: 4340
Triumph Gloria 6 Vitesse: 4492
Wolseley Super 6: 4980
Year total: 22

1937 AC 2-litre Fixed-head Coupe: 9
Alvis 4.3-litre Vanden Plas Saloon: 158
Alvis Crested Eagle 25: 159
Armstrong Siddeley 25.3hp Town and Country Saloon: 215
Armstrong Siddeley Six-light Saloon: 216
Austin 14 Goodwood Saloon: 353
Bentley 4.5-litre: 467
Chevrolet Master de Luxe Sports Sedan: 730
Chrysler Richmond Touring Saloon: 967
Delage D6-70 Sports Coupe: 1250
Dodge Victory Six Touring Saloon: 1271
Fiat 1500 Pillarless Saloon: 1459
Frazer-Nash 1.5-litre: 1984
Frazer-Nash BMW Grand Prix Two-seater: 1989
Hillman 80 Limousine: 2032
Hotchkiss 28hp Cabourg Saloon: 2164
Hudson Terraplane Saloon: 2174
Humber Snipe Drop-head Foursome: 2188
Jaguar SS 100 2.5-litre: 2265
Lagonda Rapide: 2441
Lammas-Graham Drop-head Coupe: 2476
Lanchester 18: 2479
Lanchester SS 2.5-litre: 2480
Mercedes-Benz Type 230 Saloon: 2783
Rover 16 Sports Saloon: 3977
Studebaker Dictator de Luxe Saloon: 4221
Vauxhall 14 de Luxe: 4614
Wolseley Salon de Ville: 4981
Year total: 28

1938 AC 2-litre Sports: 10
Alvis Speed 25: 161
Armstrong Siddeley 16 Saloon: 217
Austin 14: 355
Bentley 4.25-litre: 468
Chevrolet Master de Luxe Saloon: 731
Chrysler Royal Saloon: 969
Daimler 18hp 2.5-litre: 1136
Daimler 24hp Limousine: 1137
Dodge De Luxe Saloon: 1272
Frazer-Nash BMW Type 326 Saloon: 1990
Graham 26hp Supercharged Saloon: 2014
Hotchkiss 3.5-litre Saloon: 2165
Hudson 22hp Six Special Saloon: 2175
Humber 16.9hp Saloon: 2189
Humber Snipe Sports Saloon: 2190
Jaguar SS 100 3.5-litre: 2267
Lagonda 4.5-litre: 2442
Lanchester Roadrider de Luxe Saloon: 2482
Mercedes-Benz Type 320 Saloon: 2784
Nash Ambassador Six Saloon: 3195
Packard 30hp Six Saloon: 3363
Rover 14: 3978
Rover 16 Saloon: 3979
Standard Flying 20: 4195
Talbot 3-litre Saloon: 4342
Talbot Figoni et Falaschi: 4343
Vauxhall 25 Saloon: 4617
Wolseley 14/56 Salon de Ville: 4982
Wolseley Drop-head Coupe: 4983
Wolseley Super 6: 4984
Year total: 31

1939 AC 2-litre: 11
Alvis 4.3-litre: 162
Bentley 4.5-litre: 469
Frazer-Nash BMW Type 327 Cabriolet: 1991
Triumph 2-litre Dolomite: 4495
Year total: 5

1940 Jaguar SS 2.5-litre: 2268
Jaguar SS1 2.5-litre: 2269
Lanchester Roadrider de Luxe Saloon: 2483

1946 Daimler Twenty-Seven Limousine: 1138

1947 Bentley 4.5-litre Mk VI Saloon: 470

1948 Armstrong Siddeley 2-litre Saloon: 218
Austin A125 Sheerline: 359
Bristol 400: 638
Jaguar 3.5-litre: 2270
Jaguar Mk IV: 2271
Vauxhall 14: 4620
Vauxhall Velox: 4621
Year total: 7

1949 AC 2-litre Saloon: 12
Austin A135 Princess: 361
Citroen Six Saloon: 1016
Frazer Saloon: 1978
Humber Imperial: 2193
Humber Imperial Saloon: 2194
Humber Super Snipe: 2195
Jaguar 3.5-litre Mk V: 2272
Lagonda 2.5-litre Saloon: 2447
Rolls-Royce Silver Wraith: 3953
Rover 75: 3980
Rover 75 Saloon: 3981
Studebaker Champion: 4222
Year total: 13

1950 Jaguar XK120: 2273
Kaiser Henry J: 2412
Kaiser Henry J de Luxe: 2413
Rover 75: 3982
Vauxhall Velox: 4623
Wolseley 6/80: 4987
Year total: 6

1951 Aston Martin DB2: 232
Jaguar C Type: 2274
Jaguar XK120: 2275
Jaguar XK140: 2276
Jensen Interceptor Cabriolet: 2386
Vauxhall Velox: 4624
Year total: 6

1952 Alvis 3-litre: 163
Austin Princess: 367
Bentley Continental: 471
Bentley Mk VI: 472
Bentley Sports Saloon: 473
Bristol 401: 639
Ford Customline 6: 1626
Hudson Hornet: 2177
Humber Pullman Limousine: 2197
Humber Super Snipe: 2198
Jaguar Mk VII: 2277
Kaiser Henry J 6: 2414
Mercedes-Benz 300: 2787
Mercedes-Benz 300SL Carrera Panamericana: 2788
Nash Rambler Station Wagon: 3196
Plymouth Cambridge: 3471
Rover 75: 3983
Vauxhall Velox: 4625
Willys Aero Wing: 4975
Wolseley 6/80: 4988
Year total: 20

1953 AC 2-litre: 13
Alvis 3-litre: 164
Armstrong Siddeley Sapphire Saloon: 219
Aston Martin DB2/4 Saloon: 233
Chevrolet Corvette: 732
Daimler Conquest: 1140
Ford Zephyr Sedan: 1628
Ford Zephyr Sedan Modified: 1629
Frazer-Nash Targa Florio Turismo: 1985
Healey Sports Convertible: 2021

Hudson Super Jet: 2178
Humber Super Snipe: 2199
Humber Super Snipe Mk IV: 2200
Jaguar Mk VII: 2278
Jaguar XK120 Coupe: 2279
Jaguar XK120C: 2280
Jaguar XK120M: 2281
Kurtis Hornet Roadster: 2420
Mercedes-Benz 300 Sedan: 2789
Rolls-Royce Silver Dawn: 3954
Year total: 20

1954 Allard Palm Beach: 152
Aston Martin DB2: 234
Austin Princess: 371
Austin-Healey 100: 429
Bentley Sports: 474
Chevrolet Corvette: 733
Citroen Six: 1021
Maserati A6G/54 Frua Gran Sport: 2652
Nash Nash-Healey Roadster: 3198
Rolls-Royce Silver Dawn: 3955
Rover 90: 3986
Vauxhall Velox: 4627
Year total: 12

1955 Austin A90 Westminster: 373
Daimler One-O-Four Ladies' Model: 1141
Daimler Regency Mk II: 1142
Ford Zodiac: 1636
Frazer-Nash Targa Florio Fast Roadster: 1986
Jaguar Mk VII: 2282
Jaguar XK140MC: 2283
Mercedes-Benz 300B: 2792
Mercedes-Benz 300SL: 2793
Mercedes-Benz 300SL Coupe: 2794
Nash Nash-Healey Roadster Supercharged: 3200
Rover 75: 3987
Vauxhall Cresta: 4628
Wolseley 6/90: 4990
Year total: 14

1956 AC Ace Roadster: 14
AC Aceca: 15
Aston Martin Spyder Touring: 235
Austin A105: 374
Bentley Continental Park Ward DH Coupe: 475
Bentley Series S: 476
Ford Zephyr: 1642
Hudson Rambler: 2179
Jaguar 2.4 Sedan: 2284
Jaguar D Type: 2285
Jaguar Mk VII Auto: 2286
Jaguar XK 140: 2287
Jensen 541: 2387
Lagonda 3-litre Saloon: 2448
Morris Isis: 3166
Nash Rambler Station Wagon: 3201
Rover 90: 3989
Year total: 17

1957 AC Ace Bristol: 16
Alvis 3-litre Graber: 165
Austin A95 Westminster: 377
Austin-Healey 100/6: 432
Daimler One-O-Four: 1143
Ford Zodiac Automatic: 1643
Jaguar 2.4 Saloon: 2288
Jaguar Mk VIII: 2289
Jaguar XK150: 2290
Jaguar XKSS: 2291
Mercedes-Benz 219: 2796
Rover 105S: 3990
Wolseley 6/90: 4992
Year total: 13

1958 AC AC-Bristol Zagato: 17
AC Aceca-Bristol Coupe: 18
AC Bristol: 19
AC Bristol D-2: 20
Aston Martin Mk III: 236
Austin A105 Automatic: 378
Austin A95 Countryman: 382
Austin-Healey 100/6: 433
Austin-Healey Mille Miglia: 434
Daimler Majestic: 1144
Ford Zephyr Estate: 1648
Humber Super Snipe: 2205
Jaguar 3.4: 2292
Jaguar XK150: 2293
Jaguar XK150S: 2294
Jensen 541R: 2388
Mercedes-Benz 220S: 2799
Mercedes-Benz 300SL Roadster: 2800
Rolls-Royce Silver Cloud: 3956
Rolls-Royce Silver Cloud "S": 3957
Rover 105R de Luxe: 3991
Vauxhall Cresta: 4630
Year total: 22

1959 Allard GT Coupe: 153
Alvis 3-litre TD21: 166
Armstrong Siddeley Star Sapphire: 220
Aston Martin DB4: 237
Austin A105 Vanden Plas: 383
Austin A99: 385
Austin-Healey 3000: 436
Daimler DK 400B: 1145
Ford Falcon: 1650
Humber Super Snipe: 2206
Jaguar XK150S: 2295
Maserati GT Coupe: 2653
Mercedes-Benz 220SE: 2801
Rambler American: 3761
Rover 3-litre: 3992
Studebaker Lark 6: 4227
Vauxhall Friary Estate Car: 4633
Wolseley 6/99: 4995
Year total: 18

1960 AC Aceca-Bristol: 21
Austin A99: 388
Austin A99 Automatic: 389
Borgward 2.3 Grosse: 634
Chrysler Valiant: 974
Fiat 2100: 1485
Ford Falcon: 1656
Ford Falcon Automatic: 1657
Ford Zephyr: 1660
Humber Super Snipe Estate: 2207
Jaguar 3.4: 2296
Jaguar 3.8 Sedan: 2297
Mercedes-Benz 220: 2803
Mercedes-Benz 220SE: 2804
Mercury Comet: 2925
Plymouth Valiant: 3476
Plymouth Valiant Automatic: 3477
Rambler Six: 3763
Rambler Super 6 Station Wagon: 3764
Rover 100: 3994
Rover 3-litre: 3995
Studebaker Lark 6: 4228
Vanden Plas Princess: 4604
Vauxhall Cresta: 4635
Vauxhall Cresta Overdrive: 4636
Vauxhall Velox III: 4637
Year total: 26

1961 AC Greyhound: 22
AMC Rambler American: 170
AMC Rambler Classic Super 6: 171
Aston Martin DB4: 238
Austin-Healey 3000: 440
Dodge Lancer: 1277
Dodge Lancer 225 Hyper-Pack: 1278
Fairthorpe Zeta: 1369
Ford Econoline: 1662
Humber 3-litre: 2208
Humber Super Snipe Series III: 2209
Jaguar E Type Coupe: 2298
Jaguar XKE: 2299
Jensen 541S Automatic: 2389
Maserati 3500GT: 2654
Mercedes-Benz 220SE Coupe: 2806
Mercedes-Benz 300SL Roadster: 2807
Mercury Comet: 2926
Mercury Comet 170: 2927
Plymouth Savoy 6: 3478
Rambler American: 3765
Rambler Estate: 3766
Rover 100: 3996
Rover 3-litre Automatic: 3997
Standard Vanguard: 4212
Studebaker Lark 6: 4231
Year total: 26

1962 AC Greyhound: 24
Alfa Romeo 2600: 55
Alvis 3-litre TD21 Series II Automatic: 167
Aston Martin DB4: 239
Aston Martin DB4 GT Zagato: 240
Austin-Healey 3000: 442
Austin-Healey 3000 Mk II: 443
Chevrolet Chevy II: 756
Chevrolet Chevy II Six Automatic: 760
Chevrolet Chevy II Six Manual: 761
Dodge Lancer Gran Turismo: 1282
Fiat 2300: 1494
Ford Falcon 144 Automatic: 1674
Ford Falcon 144 Manual: 1675
Ford Falcon 170 Automatic: 1676
Ford Falcon 170 Manual: 1677
Ford Zodiac Mk III: 1683
Jaguar Mk X: 2300
Mercedes-Benz 300SE: 2808
Rover 3-litre: 3998

Triumph Sports 6: 4515
Wolseley 6/110: 4997
Year total: 22

1963 Alfa Romeo 2600 Saloon: 56
AMC Rambler 660: 176
Chevrolet Bel Air: 770
Chevrolet C-10 Fleetside Pickup: 772
Dodge Dart 270: 1284
Dodge Dart GT 225 Smogburner: 1285
Ford Econoline: 1691
Ford Falcon Futura: 1694
Ford Zephyr 6 Estate: 1700
Jaguar 3.8 Mk II: 2301
Jaguar 3.8 Mk II Automatic: 2302
Jaguar E Type Coupe: 2303
Maserati 3500 GTI Sebring: 2655
Mercedes-Benz 230SL: 2810
Rover 3-litre Coupe: 4000
Rover Coupe: 4001
Triumph Vitesse 6: 4519
Vanden Plas Princess 3-litre Automatic: 4605
Vauxhall Cresta Series PB: 4641
Willys Wagoneer 4WD: 4976
Year total: 20

1964 AMC Rambler American 440: 177
AMC Rambler Classic Typhoon: 179
Aston Martin DB5: 241
Austin-Healey 3000 Mk III: 445
Chevrolet Chevelle 300: 780
Chevrolet Chevelle Malibu: 781
Daimler Conquest Century Saloon: 1151
Dodge Safari Super Sport: 1291
Ford Zephyr 6: 1709
Jaguar 3.8S Sedan: 2304
Jaguar 4.2 litre Mk X: 2305
Jaguar XKE: 2306
Jeep Wagoneer: 2373
Mercedes-Benz 230SL: 2811
Mercedes-Benz 300SE LWB: 2812
Rambler 770 Six: 3767
Reliant Sabre Six GT: 3783
Triumph 2000: 4520
Year total: 18

1965 Alvis 3-litre Series III: 168
Alvis TE21S: 169
AMC Rambler American 440-H: 180
Austin-Healey 3000 Mk III: 446
Chevrolet Chevelle Malibu: 791
Ford Mustang: 1716
Ford Mustang 6: 1717
Ford Zodiac Executive: 1728
Humber Imperial: 2212
Jaguar 3.8S: 2307
Jaguar 4.2 litre Mk X Overdrive: 2308
Jaguar E Type 4.2: 2309
Mercedes-Benz 220SE: 2814
Mercedes-Benz 230SL Automatic: 2815
Reliant Scimitar: 3784
Triumph 2000: 4522
Triumph Vitesse Convertible: 4526
Vauxhall Cresta de Luxe Powerglide: 4646
Vauxhall Velox: 4647
Year total: 19

1966 Alfa Romeo 2600 Sprint: 63
Aston Martin DB6: 242
Chevrolet Bel Air Six: 800
Ford Bronco: 1729
Ford Custom 500: 1734
Jaguar XKE 4.2 2+2: 2310
Mercedes-Benz 230 Automatic: 2817
Mercedes-Benz 250S: 2818
Mercedes-Benz 300D: 2819
Pontiac Le Mans OHC: 3545
Pontiac Tempest Sprint: 3547
Pontiac Tempest Sprint Automatic: 3548
Rover 3-litre Coupe Mk III: 4005
Toyota Crown Custom: 4355
Triumph 2000 Estate Car: 4528
Vauxhall Viscount Automatic: 4651
Year total: 16

1967 AMC Rambler American 220: 185
AMC Rambler Rebel 770: 186
Chevrolet Camaro Six: 806
Dodge Dart 270: 1301
Jaguar 420: 2311
Jaguar E Type Roadster: 2312
Mercedes-Benz 250SE: 2820
MG C: 3011
Plymouth Barracuda 6: 3494
Pontiac Firebird Sprint: 3550
Rambler Rebel 6 Estate Car: 3769
Toyota 2000GT: 4356
Toyota Land Cruiser: 4358
Triumph GT6: 4530
Vauxhall Cresta Estate: 4653
Year total: 15

1968 Aston Martin DBS: 243
Austin 3-litre Automatic: 396
Jaguar 240: 2314
Jaguar 420 Sedan: 2315
Mercedes-Benz 250: 2823
Mercedes-Benz 250 Automatic: 2824
Mercedes-Benz 280SL: 2825
MG C GT Automatic: 3016
Triumph TR250: 4535
Triumph TR5 PI: 4536
Vauxhall Ventora: 4656
Year total: 11

1969 BMW 2500: 519
Ford Maverick: 1774
Jaguar XJ6 4.2 Automatic: 2316
Jaguar XKE Coupe: 2317
Mercedes-Benz 280SL: 2827
MG C: 3017
Opel Commodore GS Coupe: 3318
Toyota Crown Toyoglide: 4362
Triumph 2.5PI: 4537
Triumph 2000 Mk II: 4538
Triumph GT6: 4539
Triumph GT6 Mk II: 4540
Triumph TR6: 4541
Triumph Vitesse 2-litre Mk II: 4542
Volvo 164: 4914
Year total: 15

1970 AMC Gremlin: 195
Austin 3-litre: 401
BMW 2800 CS: 521
Datsun 240Z: 1171
Ford Maverick: 1786
Jaguar XJ6: 2318
Mercedes-Benz 250 Coupe: 2829
Mercedes-Benz 280SE: 2830
Mercedes-Benz 280SL: 2832
Opel Diplomat: 3323
Opel Senator: 3325
Toyota Crown: 4365
Triumph TR6: 4546
Vauxhall Ventora II: 4661
Volvo 164 Automatic: 4915
Year total: 15

1971 BMW 3.0 CS: 524
BMW 3.0S: 525
BMW Bavaria: 526
Datsun 240Z: 1175
Datsun 240Z Automatic: 1176
Dodge Pickup Power Wagon: 1317
Ford Pickup 4WD: 1797
Jaguar XJ6 4.2: 2320
Land Rover Series III: 2557
Marcos 3-litre Volvo: 2646
Porsche 911 T Sportomatic: 3636
Toyota Land Cruiser: 4372
Toyota Land Cruiser Wagon: 4373
Triumph GT6 Mk III: 4547
Year total: 14

1972 Austin 2200: 404
Daimler Sovereign: 1153
Datsun 240C: 1179
Jaguar XJ6: 2322
Panther J72: 3372
Porsche 911 E: 3637
Toyota Crown 2600: 4375
Toyota Custom Crown Estate: 4376
Triumph 2.5PI Mk II: 4552
Vauxhall Ventora: 4666
Volvo 164E: 4920
Year total: 11

1973 BMW 3.0 CS: 529
BMW 3.0 CSL: 530
BMW Bavaria: 532
Datsun 240Z: 1182
Mercedes-Benz 280: 2839
Mercedes-Benz 280CE Auto: 2840
Mercedes-Benz 280SE: 2841
Opel Commodore GS Coupe: 3332
Toyota Mk II: 4381
Toyota Mk II 2.6: 4382
Triumph GT6: 4556
Triumph TR6: 4559
TVR Vixen 2500M: 4588
Volvo 164E: 4924
Year total: 14

1974 BMW 3.3L: 535
BMW 525: 536

Daimler Sovereign LWB Automatic: 1154
Datsun 260Z: 1186
Datsun 260Z 2+2: 1187
Ford Mustang II Ghia: 1826
Jeep CJ6: 2381
Mercedes-Benz 280E: 2844
Opel Commodore GS 2.8: 3336
Opel Commodore GSE: 3337
Toyota Mk II Station Wagon: 4386
Triumph 2500TC: 4560
Vanden Plas Princess R: 4608
Year total: 13

1975 AMC Pacer: 202
Austin 2200 HL: 411
BMW 525: 538
BMW 530i: 539
Datsun 240Z Sharp: 1190
Datsun 260C Estate: 1191
Datsun 280Z: 1192
Jaguar XJ3.4: 2327
Mercedes-Benz 280S: 2847
Panther J72: 3374
Toyota Crown Super: 4391
Triumph 2500S: 4563
Year total: 12

1976 AMC Pacer: 203
Austin Princess 2200 HLS: 414
BMW 633 CSi: 540
Datsun 200L-6: 1196
Mercedes-Benz 280E: 2850
Year total: 5

1977 AMC Pacer Wagon: 205
BMW 320: 541
BMW 528: 543
BMW 630 CSi: 544
BMW 733i: 545
Datsun 260Z: 1202
Datsun 810 Sedan: 1203
Jaguar XJ4.2: 2331
Mercedes-Benz 280E: 2853
Rover 2600: 4018
TVR 2500M: 4591
Year total: 11

1978 BMW 323i: 547
BMW 333i Alpina: 548
BMW 528i: 549
BMW 733i: 550
Datsun Laurel Six: 1207
Rover 2300: 4019
Toyota Cressida: 4402
Year total: 7

1979 BMW 528i: 551
BMW 635 CSi: 552
BMW 732i: 553
Datsun 2.4 Laurel Six: 1208
Datsun 240K: 1210
Datsun 280ZX: 1211
Datsun 280ZX 2+2 Automatic: 1212
Datsun 280ZX Automatic: 1213
Datsun 810 Coupe: 1215
Jaguar XJ6 4.2: 2336
Jaguar XJ6L: 2337
Mercedes-Benz 250T: 2859
Mercedes-Benz 280CE: 2860
Toyota Celica Supra: 4403
TVR Convertible Turbo: 4593
Vauxhall Royale Coupe: 4689
Year total: 16

1980 AMC Eagle: 206
BMW 633 CSi: 555
BMW M1: 556
Datsun 280ZX: 1218
Datsun 280ZX Automatic: 1219
Datsun 280ZX Electramotive: 1220
Datsun 280ZX Sharp: 1221
Ford Fairmont: 1868
Jaguar XJ6 Series III: 2339
Volvo Diesel: 4939
Year total: 10

1981 BMW 323i Hardy & Beck: 557
BMW 528i: 558
Datsun 810 Maxima: 1224
Opel Manta Monza S3.0E: 3347
Toyota Cressida: 4409
Volvo 265 GLE: 4941
Year total: 6

1982 BMW 528e: 560
BMW 635 CSi: 561
BMW 745i: 562
Datsun 280ZX: 1225
Toyota Celica Supra: 4415
Volvo 760 GLE: 4944
Year total: 6

1983 BMW 320i: 564
BMW 525E: 565
BMW 533i: 566
BMW 735i: 567
Datsun 280ZX: 1229
Datsun 280ZX Electramotive: 1230
Datsun 280ZX Turbo: 1231
Mercedes-Benz 280SE: 2874
Toyota Cressida: 4420
Toyota Supra: 4421
Volvo 760 GLE: 4946
Year total: 11

1984 Bitter SC: 492
BMW 325E: 569
BMW 633 CSi: 570
BMW 735i Automatic: 571
BMW M635 CSi: 572
Jaguar XJ6 Vanden Plas: 2344
Jaguar XJS 3.6: 2345
Opel Manta Monza GSE: 3350
Porsche 911 Turbo Cabriolet Ruf: 3680
Toyota Celica 2.8i Supra: 4425
Toyota Supra: 4429
Year total: 11

1985 BMW 325i: 573
BMW 327S Hardy & Beck: 574
BMW 732i: 575
BMW M535i: 576
BMW M635 CSi Hardy & Beck: 577
Mercedes-Benz 300E: 2881
Toyota Supra: 4436
Vauxhall Senator 3.0i CD: 4702
Year total: 8

1986 Bitter SC: 493
BMW 325 ES: 578
BMW 325i Convertible: 579
BMW 520i: 580
BMW 524 TD: 581
BMW 535i: 582
BMW 635 CSi: 583
BMW 735i: 584
BMW 735i Automatic: 585
Jaguar XJ6 3.6: 2348
Mercedes-Benz 300E: 2885
Mercedes-Benz 300TE: 2886
Nissan Laurel 2.4 SGL Automatic: 3218
Toyota Supra: 4442
Toyota Supra 3.0i: 4443
Year total: 15

1987 BMW 325i Cabriolet: 587
BMW 730i SE: 588
Jaguar XJ6: 2352
Jaguar XJ6 2.9: 2353
Jaguar XJS 3.6 Automatic: 2354
Lynx D Type: 2642
Mercedes-Benz 190E 2.6: 2891
Mercedes-Benz 300CE: 2892
Mercedes-Benz 300TD: 2893
Toyota Landcruiser: 4450
Toyota Supra: 4452
Vauxhall Carlton 3000 GSi: 4708
Vauxhall Senator 3.0i CD: 4711
Year total: 13

1988 BMW 325i S: 591
BMW 325i X: 592
BMW 535i SE: 593
BMW 635 CSi: 594
BMW 735i: 595
BMW M6: 597
Mercedes-Benz 260E Auto: 2896
Mercedes-Benz 300CE: 2897
Mercedes-Benz 300E 4Matic: 2898
Toyota Supra: 4459
Toyota Supra Turbo: 4460
Year total: 11

1989 BMW 325i S: 599
BMW 535i: 600
BMW 535i Automatic: 601
BMW 735i Alpina B11: 602
BMW M5: 606
BMW M635 CSi: 607
BMW Z1: 608
Irmsher GT: 2243
Jaguar 4.0 Sovereign: 2358
Mercedes-Benz 190E 2.6: 2902
Mercedes-Benz 190E AMG Baby Hammer: 2903
Mercedes-Benz 300CE Cabriolet Straman: 2905
Mercedes-Benz 300E: 2906

Toyota Supra 3.0i Turbo: 4465
Toyota Supra Turbo: 4466
Toyota Supra Turbo TRD: 4467
Vauxhall Senator 2.5i: 4720
Vauxhall Senator 3.0i CD: 4721
Year total: 18

1990 Bitter Type 3 Cabrio: 494
BMW 325i Convertible: 610
BMW 735i Koenig: 611
Jaguar XJ6 Vanden Plas: 2362
Jaguar XJR 4.0: 2363
Mercedes-Benz 300CE: 2909
Mercedes-Benz 300D: 2911
Mercedes-Benz 300E-24: 2912
Nissan Skyline GT-R: 3243
Sbarro Chrono 3.5: 4108
Vauxhall Carlton 3.0i CDX Estate: 4723
Vauxhall Carlton GSi 3000 24v: 4724
Year total: 12

1991 BMW 325i SE: 615
BMW 520i: 616
BMW 525i: 617
BMW 525i SE 24v: 618
BMW 535i Alpina B10 Bi-Turbo: 619
BMW M5: 622
Jaguar XJ6 3.2: 2368
Jaguar XJS 4.0 Auto: 2371
Mercedes-Benz 300SL-24 5-speed Auto: 2917
Mercedes-Benz G-Wagen 300 GD LWB: 2921
Opel Omega Lotus: 3352
Toyota Landcruiser VX: 4478
Vauxhall Senator 3.0i 24v: 4731
Volvo 960 24v: 4968
Year total: 14

1992 BMW 325i: 623
BMW 520i SE Touring: 624
Volvo 960: 4969
Total No: 827

Eight cylinders in line.

1926 Bugatti 50S: 648

1927 Kissel 8-65 Gold Bug: 2416

1928 Stutz Roadster: 4239

1929 Auburn 8-120 Speedster: 262
Du Pont Speedster: 1350
Graham-Paige Straight Eight: 2016
Hillman Segrave Saloon: 2023
Hillman Straight Eight Saloon: 2024
Marmon Roosevelt Saloon: 2648
Mercedes-Benz 32/90 Saloon: 2775
Packard 32.5hp Saloon: 3354
Studebaker Double-twelve Open Tourer: 4214
Stutz 36.4hp Saloon: 4240
Year total: 10

1930 Amilcar Straight Eight Saloon: 207
Bugatti 49: 649
Buick Light Eight Saloon: 655
Chrysler Eight Saloon: 963
Cord L-29: 1097
Delage Straight Eight Sports Saloon: 1247
Dodge Eight Saloon: 1270
Du Pont Town Car: 1351
Duesenberg J Coupe: 1352
Hudson Straight Eight Roadster: 2169
Hupmobile Straight Eight Limousine: 2216
Lincoln 39.2hp Town Saloon: 2573
Marmon 69 Saloon: 2649
Marmon 79 Saloon: 2650
Mercedes-Benz 32/90 Limousine: 2777
Minerva 22/28hp Limousine: 3042
Nash Straight Eight Saloon: 3194
Packard 7-34 Phaeton: 3355
Studebaker Commander Brougham: 4215
Year total: 19

1931 Alfa Romeo Supercharged Straight Eight: 39
Austro Daimler 32/100 Saloon: 448
Bianchi Straight Eight Saloon: 490
Bugatti 5-litre Saloon: 650
Chrysler Custom Imperial Le Baron: 964
Cord Front Wheel Drive Phaeton: 1098
De Soto Straight Eight Saloon: 1234
Delage Super Sports Straight Eight: 1248
Lincoln 39.2hp Saloon: 2574
Studebaker President Limousine: 4217
Stutz Straight Eight Saloon: 4241
Year total: 11

1932 Alfa Romeo 8C2300: 41
Bugatti 55: 651
Darracq Straight Eight Saloon: 1156
Graham Blue Streak Saloon: 2010
Packard Super 8 Phaeton: 3356
Stutz DV32 Sports Saloon: 4242
Year total: 6

1933 Alfa Romeo 2.3 Mille Miglia: 42
Buick Straight Eight Saloon: 656
Essex Terraplane Straight Eight: 1361
Packard Straight Eight Saloon: 3357

1934 Hudson Terraplane: 2170
Packard 32.5hp Saloon: 3358
Railton Terraplane: 3756

1935 Buick Light Eight Viceroy Saloon: 657
Chrysler Heston Airflow Saloon: 965
Graham 21.6hp Saloon: 2011
Graham 33.8hp Supercharged Saloon: 2012
Hudson Eight Saloon: 2171
Hupmobile 32.5hp Saloon: 2218
Railton Light Sports Tourer: 3757
Studebaker President Saloon: 4219
Year total: 8

1936 Auburn 38hp Saloon: 263
Auburn 8-52 Speedster: 264
Buick Century Saloon: 658
Cord Front Wheel Drive Saloon: 1099
Daimler 25.7hp Light Straight Eight Coupe: 1135
Mercedes-Benz Type 500 Supercharged: 2782
Oldsmobile 28.8hp Saloon: 3270
Packard 32.5hp Standard Eight Saloon: 3361
Railton Straight Eight Saloon: 3758
Year total: 9

1937 Chrysler Super Power Saloon: 968
Cord Supercharged Saloon: 1102
Packard 120 Saloon: 3362
Pontiac Eight Fixed-head Coupe: 3527
Railton Cobham Saloon: 3759
Riley 8/90 Adelphi Saloon: 3927
Year total: 6

1938 Buick Viceroy Saloon: 659
Delage D8-120 Super Sports: 1251
Duesenberg SJ Town Car: 1353
Mercedes-Benz Type 540: 2785

1948 Daimler Straight Eight: 1139

1949 Hudson Commodore: 2176

1955 Mercedes-Benz 300SLR: 2795

Total No: 86

Vee-2 engines.

1939 Morgan SS: 3122
Total No: 1

Vee-4 engines.

1934 Lancia Augusta Saloon: 2486

1937 Lancia Aprilia Pillarless Saloon: 2487

1938 Lancia Aprilia Saloon: 2488

1959 Lancia Appia Sedan: 2494

1962 Lancia Appia III: 2499

1964 Lancia Fulvia: 2502
Lancia Fulvia 2C: 2503

1965 Ford Corsair GT: 1711

1966 Ford Corsair GT Estate: 1730
Lancia Fulvia Coupe: 2506

1967 Ford Corsair 2000E: 1741
Lancia Fulvia 1.3 Rallye: 2508
Lancia Fulvia 1.3 Zagato: 2509
Saab 96 V4: 4061
Saab V4: 4062
Year total: 5

1968 Ford Zephyr de Luxe: 1765
Saab Sonnet V4: 4063
Saab Station Wagon V4: 4064

1969 Ford Capri 2000 GT: 1767
Lancia Fulvia Coupe: 2510
Matra M530A: 2682

1970 Lancia Fulvia Sedan: 2511
Saab Sonnet III: 4069

1971 Lancia Fulvia Sedan: 2512

1972 Ford Consul 2000L: 1806
Saab Sonnet III: 4074

1974 Lancia Fulvia Coupe S3: 2515

Total No: 27

Vee-6 engines.

1952 Lancia Aurelia 2-litre Saloon: 2489

1955 Lancia Aurelia Gran Turismo 2500: 2490
Lancia Spyder: 2491
Nardi Blue Ray 1: 3192

1958 Lancia Aurelia GT 2500: 2492
Lancia Flaminia: 2493
Nardi Blue Ray 2: 3193

1959 Lancia Flaminia: 2495

1960 Lancia Flaminia Coupe: 2496
Lancia Zagato: 2497

1962 Buick Special V6: 666
Lancia Flaminia Sedan: 2500

1964 Buick Special: 671

1965 Ford Taunus 20M: 1726
Lancia Flaminia Coupe 3B: 2504

1966 Ford Zephyr 6 Mk IV: 1740

1967 Ford Zodiac Executive: 1750
Kaiser Jeepster: 2415
Reliant Scimitar GT: 3785

1968 Ford Cortina Race-proved Savage: 1754

1969 Ford Capri 3000 GT XLR: 1768
Gilbern Invader: 1996

1970 Reliant Scimitar GTE Automatic: 3787

1971 Citroen Safari SM: 1041
Jeep CJ-5: 2374
Jeep Commando: 2375

1972 Citroen SM: 1043
Ferrari 246 GT Dino: 1399
Fiat 130 Automatic: 1533
Ford Capri 2600 V6: 1803
Ford Capri 3000E: 1804
Ford Capri RS2600: 1805
Ford Granada GXL: 1808
Year total: 7

1973 Citroen Safari SM: 1045
Ford Capri 3000 GXL: 1811
Ford Consul 3000 GT: 1812
Ford Granada Estate Auto: 1818
Reliant Scimitar GTE: 3788
Year total: 5

1974 Ferrari 246 GTS Dino: 1401
Ford Capri 2800 V6: 1821
Ford Granada Ghia Coupe: 1824
Ford Granada GXL: 1825
Ford Mustang II Mach I: 1827
Maserati Merak: 2661
TVR 3000M: 4589
Year total: 7

1975 Buick Skylark: 688
Maserati Merak: 2663
Mercury Capri II 2.8 V6: 2952
Peugeot 604: 3413
Volvo 264 GL: 4929
Year total: 5

1976 Buick Skyhawk: 690
Ford Capri 3000S: 1838
Ford Capri II 2.8 V6: 1839
Ford Capri V6 Black Gold: 1840
Ford Granada 3000 S: 1846
Reliant Scimitar GTE: 3791
Renault 30 TS: 3853
Volvo 265 DL: 4931
Year total: 8

1977 Ford Cortina 2.3 Ghia: 1849
Ford Granada 2.3 GL Auto: 1856
Peugeot 604 SLV-6: 3417
Reliant Scimitar GTE: 3792
TVR Taimar: 4592
Year total: 5

1978 Ford Granada 2.8i S: 1860
Maserati Merak: 2668
Renault 30 TS: 3859
Volvo 262C: 4936
Volvo 265 GLE Estate: 4937
Year total: 5

1979 Buick Riviera S-type: 692
Chevrolet Citation X11: 880
Ford Cortina 2.3 Ghia S: 1863
Ford Granada 2.8i GLS Estate: 1865
Peugeot 604: 3421
Renault 30 TX: 3863
TVR Taimar Roadster: 4594
Year total: 7

1980 Chevrolet Citation: 883
TVR 3000S Roadster: 4595

1981 Alfa Romeo GTV6: 109
Ford Capri 2.8 Injection: 1871
Ford Granada 2.8i: 1877
Maserati Merak SS: 2670
Reliant Scimitar GTE: 3793
TVR Tasmin: 4596
Year total: 6

1982 De Lorean DMC 2.8-litre Coupe: 1233
Ford Granada 2.3L Estate: 1879
Ford Sierra 2.3 Ghia Automatic: 1883

1983 Buick Century T-type: 693
Chevrolet Citation X11 HO: 890
Ford Sierra XR4i: 1890
Panther Kallista 2.8: 3376
Pontiac 6000STE: 3572
TVR Tasmin Convertible: 4597
Year total: 6

1984 Alfa Romeo GTV6: 114
Ford Sierra XR4i: 1898
Nissan 300ZX: 3208
Nissan 300ZX Turbo: 3209
Panther Kallista 2.8: 3377
Renault 25 V6: 3885
Volvo 760 GLE: 4949
Year total: 7

1985 Alfa Romeo Alfa 90 2.5 Gold Cloverleaf: 118
Alfa Romeo GTV Callaway Twin Turbo: 122
Cadillac Cimarron: 714
Ford Granada Scorpio: 1903
Ford Granada Scorpio 4x4: 1904
GMC Safari Cargo Mover: 2003
Maserati Biturbo: 2672
Maserati Biturbo Automatic: 2673
Maserati Biturbo E: 2674
Nissan Maxima SE: 3214
Pontiac Fiero GT: 3577
Renault 25 V6 Turbo: 3889
TVR 350i Series II: 4598
Year total: 13

1986 Acura Legend: 29
Alfa Romeo Alfa 75 2.5 Green Cloverleaf: 125
Alfa Romeo GTV6: 126
Alfa Romeo Milano Platinum: 127
Buick Electra T-type: 694
Chevrolet Cavalier Z24: 898
Chevrolet Celebrity CL Eurosport: 899
Ford Aerostar XLT: 1908
Ford Sierra Ghia 4x4 Estate: 1918
Honda Legend: 2133
Mercury Sable LS: 2958
Nissan 300ZX: 3215
Nissan 300ZX Turbo: 3216
Pontiac Fiero GT: 3578
Renault GTA V6 Turbo: 3899
Rover 825i: 4027
Year total: 16

1987 Alfa Romeo Alfa 75 V6 3.0: 132

Alfa Romeo Milano Verde 3.0: 133
Chevrolet Beretta GT: 905
Ford Granada 2.4i Ghia: 1921
Ford Granada Scorpio 2.9 EX: 1922
Honda Legend Coupe: 2137
Maserati Biturbo Spyder: 2675
Merkur Scorpio: 2964
MVS Venturi GT: 3190
Nissan 200SX SE V6: 3222
Nissan 300ZX: 3223
Nissan 300ZX Turbo: 3224
Peugeot 505 STX: 3445
Pontiac Bonneville SE: 3579
Pontiac Fiero Formula: 3580
Pontiac Fiero GT: 3581
Rover Sterling Automatic: 4030
TVR S Convertible: 4600
Volvo 760 GLE: 4956
Year total: 19

1988 Alfa Romeo 75 2.5 Auto: 134
Buick Reatta: 695
Buick Regal Custom: 696
Chevrolet Camaro: 911
Chevrolet Cavalier Z24 Convertible: 915
Eagle Premier ES: 1354
Ford Taurus 3.8: 1935
Honda Legend Saloon Automatic: 2143
Maserati 430: 2676
Maserati Biturbo: 2677
Mazda 929: 2746
Nissan 200SX SE V6: 3229
Nissan 300ZX: 3231
Oldsmobile Cutlass International Series: 3302
Pontiac 6000STE AWD: 3584
Pontiac Bonneville SE: 3585
Pontiac Grand Prix SE: 3586
Renault GTA V6: 3906
Rover 827 SLi Auto: 4032
Rover Vitesse: 4033
Year total: 20

1989 Acura Legend Coupe L: 33
Alfa Romeo 164 3.0 Lusso: 138
Alfa Romeo 164 Automatic: 139
Alfa Romeo Milano 3.0: 140
Buick Reatta Turbo Buick Engineering: 697
Chevrolet Baretta GTU: 925
Ford Sierra XR 4x4: 1945
Ford Taurus SHO: 1946
Ford Thunderbird Super Coupe: 1947
Ford Thunderbird Super Coupe Ford Engineering: 1948
Maserati 430: 2678
Maserati Spyder: 2679
Mazda MPV: 2754
Mercury Cougar XR-7: 2960
Mitsubishi Shogun V6 5-door: 3105
Nissan 300ZX: 3234
Nissan Maxima: 3235
Nissan Maxima SE: 3236
Pontiac Firebird T/A Turbo Pontiac Engineering: 3588
Pontiac Firebird TransAm 20th Anniversary: 3589
Pontiac Firebird TransAm Turbo: 3590
Pontiac Grand Prix McLaren Turbo: 3592
Rover Sterling Catalyst: 4035
Rover Vitesse: 4036
Toyota Camry V6 GXi: 4461
TVR S Convertible: 4602
Year total: 26

1990 Acura Legend Coupe: 35
Acura NSX: 36
Alfa Romeo 164S: 143
Chevrolet Beretta GT: 935
Chevrolet Cavalier Z24: 939
Chevrolet Lumina APV: 945
Dodge Daytona ES: 1343
Ford Granada Ghia X 2.9 EFi Saloon: 1952
Ford Probe LX: 1957
Infiniti M30: 2230
Maserati 228: 2680
MVS Venturi: 3191
Nissan 300ZX: 3240
Nissan 300ZX Turbo: 3241
Oldsmobile Toronado Trofeo: 3305
Pontiac Grand Prix STE Turbo: 3595
Renault 25 V6 2.9 Auto: 3916
Year total: 17

1991 Acura Legend LS: 37
Alfa Romeo 164 Cloverleaf: 145
Alfa Romeo 164L: 146
Audi 100 2.8E Auto: 333
Buick Reatta Convertible: 698
Chevrolet Lumina Z34: 957
Citroen XM 3.0 SEi Auto: 1088
Citroen XM V6.24: 1089
Dodge Stealth R/T Turbo: 1347
Ford Festiva Shogun: 1965
Ford Scorpio 24v: 1970
Ford Taurus SHO: 1971
Honda Legend: 2155
Honda NSX: 2156
Mazda MX-3 V6: 2767
Mitsubishi 3000GT VR-4: 3111
Mitsubishi Diamante LS: 3113
Mitsubishi Shogun V6 LWB: 3115
Mitsubishi Sigma: 3116
Nissan 300ZX Motor Sports International SR-71: 3246
Nissan 300ZX Turbo Millen Super GTZ: 3247
Nissan 300ZX Twin Turbo: 3248
Peugeot 605 SV 3.0 Auto: 3466
Peugeot 605 SVE 24: 3467
Pontiac Grand Prix GTP: 3599
Renault Alpine A610 Turbo: 3918
Renault Espace V6: 3921
Rover Sterling 827SL: 4049
Year total: 28

1992 Audi 80 2.8E V6 Quattro: 339
Ford Taurus LX: 1976
Honda Legend Coupe: 2158
Honda NSX Auto: 2159
Lexus ES300: 2572
Mazda MX-3 GS: 2773
Pontiac Bonneville SSEi: 3600
Rover Sterling Automatic: 4051
Year total: 8
Total No: 246

Vee-8 engines.

1930 La Salle Enclosed Drive Limousine: 2421

1932 Ford V8: 1610

1934 Lancia 27.6hp Astura Saloon: 2485

1936 Ford V8 Touring Saloon: 1614
Jensen 3.5-litre Saloon: 2384

1937 Cord 812: 1100
Cord 812-S: 1101

1938 Ford V8 30: 1617
Jensen 3.5-litre Tourer: 2385
La Salle 37-50 V8 Saloon: 2422

1947 Ford Tudor Sedan: 1619

1948 Allard Drop-head Coupe: 148
Allard V8: 149
Ford V8 Pilot: 1621

1949 Mercury Coupe: 2924

1951 Chrysler Saratoga Club Coupe: 970
Muntz Jet: 3189
Studebaker Land Cruiser: 4223

1952 Allard K2: 150
Ford Comete: 1625
Ford Customline 8: 1627

1953 Chrysler New Yorker Saloon: 971
Lincoln Cosmopolitan Sedan: 2578
Siata Spyder V8: 4127
Studebaker Commander Coupe: 4224
Studebaker Commander Supercharged: 4225
Year total: 5

1954 Allard K3 Convertible: 151
Buick Roadmaster: 660
Fiat 8V: 1468
Studebaker Commander Coupe: 4226

1955 Chevrolet 210 Coupe Club V8: 734
Chevrolet Corvette V8: 735
Chrysler Windsor de Luxe: 972
Ford Thunderbird: 1635
Oldsmobile Super 88: 3271

Year total: 5

1956 BMW 501: 498
Chevrolet 210: 736
Chevrolet Corvette: 737
Chevrolet Corvette Sebring: 738
Facel Vega Coupe: 1364
Ford Interceptor Coupe: 1639
Ford Thunderbird: 1641
Plymouth Fury: 3472

Plymouth Savoy: 3473
Year total: 9

1957 BMW 507: 500
Chevrolet Corvette: 739
Chevrolet Corvette Injection: 740
Chevrolet Corvette RPO 684/579E: 741
Simca Versailles V8: 4135
Year total: 5

1958 Chrysler 300-D: 973
Dodge Custom Royal: 1273
Facel Vega FVS: 1365
Ford Fairlane 500: 1646
Lincoln Continental Mk III: 2579
Oldsmobile Super 88: 3272
Plymouth Fury: 3474
Simca Vedette Beaulieu: 4137
Year total: 8

1959 Cadillac Eldorado Convertible: 701
Chevrolet Corvette: 743
Daimler V8 SP250: 1146
Devin Super Sports: 1257
Dodge Custom Royal: 1274
Ford Thunderbird: 1653
Lago America: 2431
Plymouth Fury: 3475
Pontiac Bonneville: 3528
Scarab Mk II: 4109
Year total: 10

1960 Bentley S2 Continental: 477
Buick Special: 661
Daimler SP250: 1147
Facel Vega HK-500: 1366
Ford Galaxie: 1658
Gordon GT: 2008
Rambler Rebel V8: 3762
Rolls-Royce Silver Cloud II: 3958
Rolls-Royce Silver Cloud II V8: 3959
Simca Vedette V8: 4141
Studebaker Lark V8: 4229
Year total: 11

1961 AMC Rambler Classic V8: 172
Bristol 407: 640
Buick Special: 662
Cadillac Coupe de Ville: 702
Cadillac Fleetwood: 703
Chevrolet Corvette: 750
Chevrolet Corvette 230: 751
Chevrolet Corvette 270: 752
Chevrolet Corvette 315: 753
Chevrolet Impala: 754
Chrysler 300-G: 975
Chrysler Enforcer: 976
Chrysler Imperial: 977
Chrysler Newport: 978
Daimler Majestic Major: 1148
Dodge Dart: 1275
Dodge Dart Phoenix: 1276
Ford Galaxie: 1663
Ford Thunderbird: 1665
Lincoln Continental: 2580
Mercury Meteor 800: 2928
Oldsmobile F-85: 3273
Oldsmobile F-85 Station Wagon: 3274
Pontiac Catalina Super Stock: 3529
Studebaker Hawk 4-speed: 4230
Studebaker Lark Cruiser: 4232
Year total: 26

1962 AC Aceca-Buick: 23
AMC Ambassador 400: 173
Buick Invicta: 663
Buick Skylark: 664
Buick Skylark Automatic: 665
Buick Wildcat: 667
Chevrolet Bel Air 409 SS/S: 755
Chevrolet Chevy II Corvette: 757
Chevrolet Corvette: 766
Chevrolet Corvette Sebring: 767
Chevrolet Impala SS 409: 768
Chevrolet Impala Station Wagon: 769
Chrysler 300: 979
Chrysler 300-H: 980
Dodge Custom 880: 1279
Dodge Dart 413: 1280
Dodge Dreamer: 1281
Facel Vega Facel II: 1368
Ford Country Sedan: 1670
Ford Fairlane 500: 1671
Ford Fairlane 500 Sports Coupe: 1672
Ford Fairlane V8: 1673
Ford Galaxie: 1678
Ford Galaxie 406: 1679
Ford Thunderbird Sports Roadster: 1680
International Travelall: 2235
Mercury Meteor: 2929
Mercury S-55 406: 2930
Oldsmobile 98 Holiday Sports Sedan: 3275
Oldsmobile Dynamic 88 Celebrity Sedan: 3276
Oldsmobile F-85 Jetfire Sports Coupe: 3277
Oldsmobile F-85 V8: 3278
Plymouth Savoy Station Wagon: 3479
Plymouth Savoy V8: 3480
Plymouth Sport Fury: 3481
Pontiac Grand Prix 421: 3533
Pontiac Parisienne: 3534
Pontiac Royal Bobcat: 3535
Shelby AC Ford Cobra: 4116
Studebaker Avanti: 4233
Studebaker Hawk Gran Turismo: 4234
Studebaker Lark Daytona: 4235
Year total: 42

1963 AMC Ambassador 990: 175
Apollo GT: 208
Avanti R2: 457
Buick Riviera: 668
Cadillac Park Avenue: 704
Chevrolet Biscayne V8: 771
Chevrolet Corvette: 775
Chevrolet Corvette Grand Sport Roadster: 776
Chevrolet Corvette Sting Ray: 777
Chevrolet Corvette Sting Ray Automatic: 778
Chevrolet Impala Super Sport 409: 779
Chrysler 300-J: 981
Daimler 2.5-litre V8 Saloon: 1149
Daimler Limousine: 1150
Dodge D-100 Sweptline Pickup: 1283
Dodge Polara: 1286
Dodge Ramcharger 426 Super/Stock: 1287
Ford F-100 Styleside Pickup: 1692
Ford Fairlane Squire Wagon: 1693
Ford Falcon Futura V8: 1695
Ford Falcon Sprint Convertible: 1696
Ford Falcon V8: 1697
Ford Fastback NASCAR: 1698
Ford Galaxie 500 XL: 1699
Iso Grifo A3L Berlinetta: 2245
Jensen CV8: 2390
Mercury Comet S-22 Sportster: 2931
Mercury Super Marauder S-55: 2932
Oldsmobile F-85 Jetfire: 3279
Oldsmobile Starfire: 3280
Plymouth Fury: 3482
Plymouth Sport Fury: 3483
Pontiac Catalina: 3537
Pontiac Grand Prix: 3538
Pontiac Tempest Le Mans V8: 3539
Rolls-Royce Silver Cloud III: 3960
Studebaker Avanti: 4236
Studebaker Regal Wagonaire Supercharged: 4237
Year total: 38

1964 AMC Rambler Classic 770: 178
Buick Electra 225: 669
Buick Skylark Sports Wagon: 670
Buick Wildcat: 672
Cadillac Coupe de Ville: 705
Cadillac Sedan de Ville: 706
Chevrolet Chevelle Super Sport: 782
Chevrolet Chevy II V8 Station Wagon: 783
Chevrolet Corvette Sting Ray: 786
Chevrolet Corvette Sting Ray Automatic: 787
Chevrolet Corvette Sting Ray Injection: 788
Chevrolet El Camino: 789
Chrysler Imperial Le Baron: 982
Dodge Dart GT: 1288
Dodge Polara: 1289
Dodge Polara 500: 1290
Excalibur SS: 1363
Ford Custom 500: 1703
Ford Falcon Sprint: 1704
Ford Galaxie 500: 1705
Ford Mustang: 1706
Ford Mustang 271hp: 1707
Ford Mustang Convertible: 1708
Iso GT: 2246
Iso Rivolta IR-340: 2247
Lincoln Continental: 2581
Mercury Comet A/FX: 2933
Mercury Comet Caliente: 2934
Mercury Comet Cyclone 4-speed: 2935
Mercury Comet Cyclone Automatic: 2936
Mercury Park Lane: 2937
Oldsmobile Cutlass 442: 3281
Oldsmobile F-85 Cutlass Holiday: 3282
Oldsmobile Jetstar I: 3283
Plymouth Barracuda: 3485
Pontiac Tempest GTO: 3540
Shelby AC Ford Cobra: 4117
Shelby Cobra USRRC: 4118
Studebaker Daytona R-4: 4238

Sunbeam Tiger: 4301
Year total: 40

1965 AC Cobra: 25
Bizzarrini 5300 Spyder: 495
Buick LeSabre 400: 673
Buick Riviera: 674
Buick Skylark: 675
Buick Skylark Gran Sport: 676
Chevrolet Caprice Custom 396: 790
Chevrolet Chevelle Malibu 396: 792
Chevrolet Corvette: 795
Chevrolet Corvette 396: 796
Chevrolet Corvette Injection: 797
Chevrolet Corvette Sting Ray 396: 798
Chevrolet Impala SS: 799
Chrysler Newport: 983
Dodge A-100 Super/Surfer: 1292
Dodge Coronet: 1293
Dodge Coronet 426-S: 1294
Dodge Coronet 440: 1295
Dodge Coronet 500: 1296
Dodge Dart GT: 1297
Ford Fairlane 500: 1713
Ford Galaxie 500 XL 427: 1714
Ford Galaxie LTD: 1715
Ford Mustang Convertible: 1718
Ford Mustang Convertible V8: 1719
Ford Mustang Coupe: 1720
Ford Mustang Coupe Automatic: 1721
Ford Mustang Fastback: 1722
Ford Mustang High Performance: 1723
Ford Mustang V8 4.2-litre: 1724
Ford Mustang V8 4.7-litre: 1725
Ford Thunderbird: 1727
Gordon Keeble GK1: 2009
Mercedes-Benz 600: 2816
Mercury Monterey: 2938
Mercury Park Lane: 2939
Oldsmobile Cutlass Holiday 442: 3284
Oldsmobile Dynamic Delta 88 Holiday: 3285
Oldsmobile Toronado: 3286
Opel Diplomat: 3310
Plymouth Barracuda S: 3486
Plymouth Belvedere Satellite: 3487
Plymouth Fury Station Wagon: 3488
Pontiac Bonneville Vista: 3541
Pontiac Catalina 2+2: 3542
Pontiac Tempest GTO: 3543
Shelby Cobra Daytona Coupe: 4119
Shelby GT 350: 4120
Sunbeam Tiger 260: 4302
Year total: 49

1966 AMC Ambassador DPL: 181
AMC Rogue V8: 182
Avanti II: 458
Bizzarrini GT America: 496
Buick Riviera Gran Sport: 677
Cadillac Calais: 707
Chevrolet Chevy II Nova SS: 801
Chevrolet Corvette: 802
Chevrolet Corvette Convertible: 803
Chrysler 300: 984
Chrysler Valiant Premium Auto: 986
Daimler 2.5-litre V8: 1152
Dodge Charger: 1298
Ford Fairlane GTA: 1735
Ford Falcon Ranchero Custom: 1736
Ford Galaxie 7-litre: 1737
Ford GT40 Super Street: 1738
Ford Thunderbird Town Landau: 1739
Iso Grifo GL 365: 2248
Mercury Comet Cyclone GT: 2940
Oldsmobile Cutlass 442: 3287
Oldsmobile Toronado: 3288
Plymouth Barracuda S: 3489
Plymouth Satellite: 3490
Plymouth Satellite Street Hemi: 3491
Plymouth VIP: 3492
Pontiac GTO: 3544
Pontiac Tempest GTO: 3546
Rambler 770 V8 Convertible: 3768
Rolls-Royce Silver Shadow: 3961
Shelby GT 350-S: 4121
Year total: 31

1967 Alfa Romeo 33 2.0 Stradale: 66
AMC Javelin SST 343: 183
AMC Marlin: 184
AMC Rambler Rebel SST: 187
Buick California GS: 678
Buick GS400: 679
Buick Wildcat: 680
Cadillac Eldorado: 708
Chevrolet Camaro: 804
Chevrolet Camaro 427 Dana: 805
Chevrolet Camaro SS350: 807
Chevrolet Corvette: 808
Chevrolet Impala SS427: 809
Chrysler Imperial Crown: 987
Dodge Charger: 1299
Dodge Coronet R/T: 1300
Dodge Monaco Wagon: 1302
Ford Fairlane Ranchero: 1746
Ford Mustang: 1747
Ford Mustang 390 Fastback: 1748
Ford Thunderbird: 1749
Jensen Interceptor: 2391
Mercedes-Benz 600: 2821
Mercury Cougar: 2941
Mercury Cougar Group 2: 2942
Mercury Cougar GT: 2943
Mercury Marquis: 2944
Oldsmobile F-85 Cutlass Cruiser: 3289
Plymouth Barracuda: 3493
Plymouth Barracuda Fastback V8: 3495
Plymouth Fury III: 3496
Plymouth GTX: 3497
Pontiac Firebird 440: 3549
Pontiac Grand Prix: 3551
Pontiac GTO Ram Air: 3552
Rover 3.5-litre: 4007
Shelby GT 500: 4122
Sunbeam Tiger II: 4307
Year total: 38

1968 AC 428 Fastback: 26
AMC Ambassador: 188
AMC AMX: 189
AMC AMX Automatic: 190
AMC Javelin: 191
AMC Javelin SST: 192
Buick GS400: 681
Buick Riviera: 682
Cadillac Coupe de Ville: 709
Checker Marathon: 727
Chevrolet Camaro SS396: 810
Chevrolet Camaro Z/28: 811
Chevrolet Chevelle Malibu: 812
Chevrolet Chevelle SS396: 813
Chevrolet Chevy II: 814
Chevrolet Corvette: 817
Chevrolet Corvette Convertible: 818
Chevrolet Corvette Coupe: 819
Chevrolet Corvette L88: 820
Chevrolet El Camino: 821
Chevrolet Impala: 822
Chevrolet Malibu 327: 823
Dodge Charger R/T: 1303
Dodge Coronet R/T: 1304
Dodge Dart GTS: 1305
Dodge Dart GTS 340: 1306
Ford Galaxie: 1759
Ford GT40: 1760
Ford Mustang 428 Cobra Jet: 1761
Ford Mustang Fastback: 1762
Ford Torino: 1763
Ford XL Fastback 428: 1764
Jensen FF: 2392
Maserati Quattroporte: 2656
Mercury Cougar: 2945
Mercury Cougar XR-7: 2946
Mercury Cyclone: 2947
Morgan Plus 8: 3129
Oldsmobile 4-4-2: 3290
Oldsmobile Delmont: 3291
Oldsmobile Toronado: 3292
Plymouth Barracuda 340-S: 3498
Plymouth Barracuda Fastback: 3499
Plymouth Fury III: 3500
Plymouth GTX: 3501
Plymouth GTX Hemi: 3502
Plymouth Road Runner: 3503
Pontiac Firebird RA400: 3553
Pontiac GTO: 3554
Rambler Javelin Hardtop SST: 3770
Shelby GT 350: 4123
Shelby GT 500-KR: 4124
Year total: 52

1969 AMC Ambassador SST Wagon: 193
AMC Rambler Scrambler: 194
Avanti II: 459
Buick Riviera: 683
Buick Skylark: 684
Buick Sportswagon: 685
Buick Wildcat: 686
Checker Marathon: 728
Chevrolet Camaro SS 396: 824
Chevrolet Camaro Z/28: 825
Chevrolet Camaro Z/28 Yenko/SC: 826
Chevrolet Caprice: 827
Chevrolet Chevelle Malibu: 828
Chevrolet Corvette 435hp: 829
Chevrolet Corvette L36: 830

Plymouth Volare Station Wagon: 3513
Pontiac Firebird TransAm: 3563
Rolls-Royce Silver Shadow: 3965
Rover 3500: 4016
Rover 3500 Automatic: 4017
Year total: 25

1977 Aston Martin V8 Coupe: 247
Aston Martin V8 Vantage: 248
Chevrolet Corvette Sting Ray: 875
Ferrari 308 GTB: 1411
Mercedes-Benz 600SE: 2854
Mercury Monarch: 2953
Pontiac Bonneville: 3564
Rolls-Royce Silver Shadow: 3966
Year total: 8

1978 Aston Martin V8: 249
Buick Century: 691
Cadillac Seville Diesel: 711
Chevrolet Blazer: 876
Chevrolet Camaro IROC: 877
Chevrolet Camaro Z/28: 878
Chevrolet Malibu: 879
Datsun 280Z Scarab: 1205
Ferrari 308 GTS: 1412
Jeep Cherokee Chief: 2383
Lotus Elite V8: 2623
Maserati Khamsin: 2666
Maserati Kyalami: 2667
Mercedes-Benz 450SEL: 2858
Morgan Plus 8: 3131
Pontiac Firebird TransAm: 3565
Pontiac Firebird TransAm Silverbird: 3566
Porsche 928: 3661
Porsche 928 Automatic: 3662
Range Rover V8: 3773
Rolls-Royce Silver Wraith II: 3967
Year total: 21

1979 Bentley T2: 478
Chevrolet Corvette: 881
Chevrolet Corvette Automatic: 882
Maserati Khamsin: 2669
Mercedes-Benz 450SEL 6.9: 2862
Mercedes-Benz 450SL: 2863
Porsche 928 Automatic: 3665
Year total: 7

1980 Aston Martin Lagonda: 250
Chevrolet Corvette: 884
Ferrari 308 GT4 Dino: 1414
Mercedes-Benz 450SL: 2864
Morgan Plus 8 Turbo: 3132
Oldsmobile Cutlass Diesel: 3300
Pontiac Firebird TransAm Turbo: 3567
Porsche 928: 3669
Rolls-Royce Silver Shadow II: 3968
Rover 3500: 4020
Triumph TR8: 4577
Triumph TR8 Group 44: 4578
Triumph TR8 Libra Rally: 4579
Year total: 13

1981 Cadillac Seville Diesel: 712
Ferrari 308 GTSi: 1415
Mercedes-Benz 380SEL: 2869
Rolls-Royce Silver Spirit: 3969
Rover Vanden Plas: 4021
Year total: 5

1982 Aston Martin Lagonda: 251
Aston Martin V8: 252
Bentley Mulsanne Turbo: 479
Chevrolet Camaro Z/28: 885
Chevrolet Corvette: 886
Ferrari 288 GTO: 1416
Ferrari Mondial 8: 1418
Ford Mustang 4.2: 1880
Ford Mustang GT 5.0: 1881
Lamborghini Jalpa: 2467
Land Rover County: 2559
Mercedes-Benz 380SEC: 2870
Mercedes-Benz 380SL: 2871
Pontiac Firebird TransAm: 3570
Pontiac Petty Grand National: 3571
Rolls-Royce Corniche: 3970
Rolls-Royce Silver Spur: 3971
Year total: 17

1983 Aston Martin Volante: 253
Chevrolet Camaro: 887
Chevrolet Camaro Z/28: 888
Chevrolet Corvette: 891
Ferrari 308 GTBi Quattrovalvole: 1419
Ferrari 308 GTSi Targa: 1420
Ford Mustang GT 5.0: 1888
Maserati Quattroporte: 2671
Mercedes-Benz 380SL: 2875
Mercury Capri: 2957
Porsche 928 S: 3677
Rover Vitesse: 4024
Year total: 12

1984 Aston Martin Lagonda: 254
Aston Martin Vantage: 255
Avanti II: 460
Chevrolet Camaro: 892
Chevrolet Camaro Z/28: 893
Chevrolet Corvette: 894
De Tomaso Pantera GT5: 1241
Ferrari 288 GTO: 1421
Ferrari GTO: 1423
Ferrari Mondial Cabriolet Quattrovalvole: 1424
Ford Mustang GT: 1895
Ford Mustang GT 5.0: 1896
Lincoln Continental Mk VII: 2583
Mercedes-Benz 500SEC: 2877
Pontiac Firebird TransAm: 3575
Pontiac Firebird TransAm HO: 3576
Year total: 16

1985 Autokraft AC Cobra Mk IV: 455
Bentley Mulsanne Turbo: 480
Chevrolet Camaro IROC-Z: 896
Chevrolet Corvette: 897
Ford Mustang GT: 1905
Lincoln Continental Mk VII LSC: 2584
Mercedes-Benz 500SEL: 2882
Porsche 928 S: 3683
Porsche 928 S Series II: 3684
Year total: 9

1986 Aston Martin Volante: 256
Chevrolet Corvette: 900
Chevrolet Corvette Callaway: 901
Chevrolet Corvette Z51: 902
De Tomaso Pantera GT5-S: 1242
Ferrari 3.2 Mondial: 1427
Ferrari 328 GTB: 1428
Ferrari Mondial 3.2: 1429
Ferrari Mondial 3.2QV: 1430
Ford Mustang GT 5.0: 1913
Ford Mustang Saleen: 1914
Lamborghini Jalpa 3500: 2470
Lincoln Continental Mk VII LSC: 2585
Mercedes-Benz 420SE: 2887
Mercedes-Benz 560SEC: 2888
Mercedes-Benz 560SEL: 2889
Mercedes-Benz 560SL: 2890
Porsche 928 S: 3691
Porsche 928 S4 Automatic: 3692
Range Rover Vogue: 3774
Year total: 20

1987 Autokraft AC Cobra Mk IV: 456
Bentley Turbo R: 481
Chevrolet Camaro IROC-Z: 906
Chevrolet Camaro IROC-Z L98: 907
Chevrolet Corvette: 908
Chevrolet Corvette ASC Geneve: 909
Chevrolet Corvette Convertible: 910
Ferrari 328 GTS: 1431
Ferrari Mondial Cabriolet 3.2: 1433
Ford Mustang GT: 1923
Ford Mustang LX 5.0: 1924
Ford Thunderbird Bondurant 5.0: 1926
Lancia Thema 8.32: 2546
Land Rover One Ten County V8: 2561
Mercedes-Benz 420SEL: 2894
Mercedes-Benz 560SEC Cabriolet Straman: 2895
Morgan Plus 8: 3134
Pontiac Firebird Formula 5.0: 3582
Range Rover V8: 3775
TVR 390 SE: 4599
Year total: 20

1988 Aston Martin Zagato: 257
Cadillac Allante: 715
Chevrolet Camaro IROC-Z 5.0: 912
Chevrolet Camaro IROC-Z 5.7: 913
Chevrolet Camaro IROC-Z 8.3-litre: 914
Chevrolet Corvette: 916
Chevrolet Corvette Bakeracing SCCA Escort: 917
Chevrolet Corvette Callaway: 918
Chevrolet Corvette Convertible: 919
Chevrolet Corvette Guldstrand Grand Sport 80: 920
Chevrolet Corvette Morrison/Baker Nelson Ledges: 921
Chevrolet Corvette Z51: 922
Ferrari 308 Norwood Bonneville GTO: 1434
Ferrari F40: 1435
Ferrari Mondial Cabriolet: 1436
Ford Mustang Cartech Turbo: 1928
Ford Mustang Convertible Saleen: 1929
Ford Mustang GT: 1930
Ford Mustang JBA/Saleen: 1931

Ford Mustang Kaufmann: 1932
Isdera Imperator: 2244
Lamborghini Jalpa: 2471
Lancia Thema 8.32: 2548
Mercedes-Benz 300E AMG Hammer: 2899
Morgan Plus 8: 3135
Porsche 928 S4: 3712
Year total: 26

1989 AC Cobra 427 Modified 1965: 27
Aston Martin Virage: 258
Aston Martin Volante: 259
Aston Martin Zagato Volante: 260
Chevrolet Camaro Gottlieb 1969: 926
Chevrolet Camaro IROC-Z: 927
Chevrolet Camaro IROC-Z Automatic: 928
Chevrolet Camaro IROC-Z Chevrolet Engineering: 929
Chevrolet Corvette: 930
Chevrolet Corvette Callaway: 931
Chevrolet Corvette Guldstrand Grand Sport 80: 932
Chevrolet Corvette L98: 933
Chevrolet Corvette ZR-1: 934
De Tomaso Pantera Group 3: 1243
Ferrari 308 Norwood: 1439
Ferrari Mondial 3.2 Cabriolet: 1440
Ferrari Mondial t: 1441
Ford Mustang 5.0 Cartech Turbo: 1940
Ford Mustang Saleen SSC: 1941
Ford Mustang SVO J Bittle American: 1942
Land Rover Ninety County V8: 2562
Lincoln Continental Mk VII: 2586
Mercedes-Benz 560SL: 2907
Porsche 928 Cabrio Strosek: 3725
Porsche 928 S4 Koenig: 3726
Porsche 928 S4 SE: 3727
Range Rover Vogue: 3777
Range Rover Vogue SE: 3778
TVR 420 SEAC: 4601
Zender Vision 3: 5007
Year total: 30

1990 Audi V8 Quattro: 331
Audi V8 Quattro Automatic: 332
Bentley Turbo R: 482
Cadillac Allante: 716
Cadillac Aurora: 717
Cadillac Eldorado Touring Coupe: 718
Chevrolet Camaro IROC-Z Convertible: 937
Chevrolet Camaro Z/28: 938
Chevrolet Corvette Callaway: 940
Chevrolet Corvette Callaway Sledgehammer: 941
Chevrolet Corvette Convertible: 942
Chevrolet Corvette Coupe: 943
Chevrolet Corvette L98: 944
De Tomaso Pantera GT5 S: 1244
Evans Series I: 1362
Ferrari 348tb: 1445
Ferrari F40: 1446
Ferrari Mondial: 1447
Ford Mustang GT Convertible: 1954
Ford Mustang LX 5.0L: 1955
Infiniti Q45: 2231
Land Rover Discovery V8: 2564
Lexus LS400: 2570
Lincoln Continental Mk VII LSC: 2587
Maserati Shamal: 2681
Mercedes-Benz 300CE AMG Hammer: 2910
Mercedes-Benz 500SL: 2913
Pontiac Firebird Formula: 3593
Pontiac Firebird TransAm GTA: 3594
Porsche 928: 3738
Porsche 928 Automatic: 3739
Porsche 928 Gemballa: 3740
Range Rover County: 3779
Range Rover Vogue SE: 3780
Vector W2: 4735
Zender Fact 4: 5008
Year total: 36

1991 Aston Martin Virage: 261
Audi V8 Quattro: 338
Bentley Turbo R: 483
Cadillac Allante: 719
Cadillac Seville Touring Sedan: 720
Chevrolet Camaro Z/28 Convertible: 947
Chevrolet Corvette Callaway: 948
Chevrolet Corvette Callaway Speedster: 949
Chevrolet Corvette Callaway Twin Turbo: 950
Chevrolet Corvette Lingenfelter: 951
Chevrolet Corvette Rick Mears: 952
Chevrolet Corvette ZR-1: 953
Chevrolet Corvette ZR-1 Geiger: 954
Chevrolet Corvette ZR-1 SS: 955
Chevrolet Corvette ZR-2: 956
Eagle GTP: 1356
Ferrari 348tb: 1449
Ferrari F40: 1450
Ferrari GTO Norwood: 1451
Ferrari Mondial t: 1452
Ferrari Mondial t Cabriolet: 1453
Ford Crown Victoria LX: 1959
Ford Mustang Holdener: 1966
Ford Mustang NOS/Saleen: 1967
Ford Thunderbird LX: 1972
Land Rover Discovery V8i 5DR: 2565
Lexus SC400: 2571
Mercedes-Benz 400SE: 2918
Mercedes-Benz 500E: 2919
Mercedes-Benz 500SL: 2920
Morgan Plus 8: 3137
Pontiac Firebird GTA: 3596
Pontiac Firebird TDM Technologies: 3597
Pontiac Firebird TransAm Convertible: 3598
Porsche 928: 3752
Rolls-Royce Silver Spirit II: 3972
Safir GT40: 4106
TVR V8 S: 4603
Vector W8 Twin Turbo: 4736
Westfield SEight: 4973
Year total: 40

1992 Chevrolet Camaro Z28: 958
Chevrolet Corvette LT1: 959
Ford Mustang LX: 1975
Mercedes-Benz 500SEL: 2922
Range Rover Vogue SE: 3781
Year total: 5
Total No: 881

Vee-10 engines.

1992 Dodge Viper: 1348
Total No: 1

Vee-12 engines.

1929 Daimler 30hp Double-six Saloon: 1132

1932 Lincoln Twelve Cylinder Town Sedan: 2575

1934 Hispano-Suiza 54/220: 2084
Packard Twelve Victoria: 3359

1936 Lincoln Zephyr Saloon: 2576
Rolls-Royce Phantom III: 3952

1938 Lagonda 4.5-litre 12 Cylinder Saloon: 2443
Lagonda Saloon de Ville: 2444
Lincoln Zephyr Saloon: 2577

1939 Lagonda Rapide: 2445

1940 Lagonda Drop-head Coupe: 2446

1948 Ferrari 166 Mille Miglia Barchetta: 1371

1952 Ferrari 212 Touring: 1372
Ferrari 375 Indianapolis: 1373

1953 Ferrari 212 Coupe: 1374
Ferrari 4.1 Coupe: 1375

1954 Ferrari 250 Mille Miglia: 1376

1956 Ferrari 412 MI: 1377

1957 Ferrari 250 Testa Rossa: 1378

1958 Ferrari 250 GT Cabriolet: 1380
Ferrari 250 GT Coupe: 1381
Ferrari 250 Testa Rossa: 1382

1960 Ferrari 250 GT Berlinetta SWB: 1383
Ferrari 250 GT Coupe: 1384
1962 Ferrari 250 GT 2+2: 1385
Ferrari 250 GTO: 1386
Ferrari 4.9: 1387

1963 Ferrari 250 GT Berlinetta Lusso: 1388
Ferrari 400 Super America: 1389

1965 Ferrari 365 GTC: 1390
Lamborghini 350GT: 2449

1966 Bizzarrini P538: 497
Ferrari 275 GTS: 1391
Lamborghini 400GT: 2450

1967 Ferrari 275 GTS/4 NART: 1392
Jaguar XJ13: 2313

	Lamborghini Miura: 2451
1968	Ferrari 330 GTS: 1393 Lamborghini Miura: 2452
1969	Ferrari 365 GTS 2+2: 1394 Ferrari Daytona Sportwagen: 1395 Lamborghini Espada: 2453
1970	Ferrari 365 GTB/4 Daytona: 1396 Lamborghini Espada: 2454 Lamborghini Miura P400S: 2455 Lamborghini Miura S: 2456
1971	Ferrari Daytona: 1397 Ferrari Daytona Cannonball: 1398 Jaguar E Type V12: 2319
1972	Ferrari 365 GTC4: 1400 Jaguar XJ12: 2321 Jaguar XKE V12: 2323 Lamborghini Jarama 400GT: 2457
1973	Jaguar XJ12: 2324 Lamborghini Jarama 400GT: 2459
1974	Ferrari 365 GTB/4 Competitione: 1403 Ferrari 365 GTB/4 Daytona: 1404 Jaguar XKE V12: 2325
1975	Ferrari 365 GT4 2+2: 1406 Jaguar XJ12L: 2326 Jaguar XJ5.3C: 2328 Panther De Ville: 3373
1976	Jaguar XJ12C: 2329 Jaguar XJS: 2330 Lamborghini Countach: 2461
1977	Jaguar XJS Automatic: 2332 Jaguar XJS Tullius: 2333
1978	Ferrari 512 BB: 1413 Jaguar XJ12L: 2334 Jaguar XJ5.3 Automatic: 2335
1979	Jaguar XJS: 2338 Lamborghini Countach S: 2464
1981	Daimler Double-Six HE: 1155 Jaguar XJS: 2340 Jaguar XJS Automatic: 2341
1982	Jaguar XJS HE: 2342 Lamborghini Countach LP 500S: 2465 Lamborghini Countach S: 2466
1983	Jaguar XJS: 2343
1984	Jaguar XJS HE: 2346
1985	Ferrari 365 GTB Goldsmith: 1425 Jaguar XJS HE Cabriolet: 2347 Lamborghini Countach: 2468
1986	Jaguar XJS: 2349 Jaguar XJSC: 2350 Jaguar XJSC HE: 2351 Lamborghini Countach 5000S: 2469
1987	BMW 750i L: 589 Ferrari 412: 1432
1988	BMW 750i L: 596 Jaguar XJS: 2355 Jaguar XJS Koenig: 2356 Jaguar XJS V12 Convertible: 2357 Lamborghini LM129: 2472 Lynx XJS Eventer: 2643
Year total: 6	
1989	Ferrari Testa Rossa Gemballa: 1443 Jaguar XJ220: 2359 Jaguar XJS Convertible: 2360 Jaguar XJS V12 Convertible: 2361 Lamborghini Countach 25th Anniversary: 2473
Year total: 5	
1990	BMW 750i: 612 BMW 750i Alpina B12: 613 Jaguar XJRS: 2364 Jaguar XJS: 2365 Jaguar XJS Lister Le Mans: 2366 Jaguar XJS Railton: 2367 Lamborghini Diablo: 2474
Year total: 7	
1991	BMW 850i: 620 Bugatti EB110: 652 Jaguar XJR15: 2369 Jaguar XJS: 2370 Jaguar XJS Convertible: 2372 Lamborghini Diablo: 2475 Parradine V-12: 3382
Year total: 7	
1992	BMW 850i Manual: 625 Mercedes-Benz 600SEL: 2923

Total No: 116

Vee-16 engines.

1930	Cadillac V16 "Madame X": 699
1931	Cadillac V16 Fleetwood Roadster: 700
1932	Marmon 16: 2651
1990	Cizeta Moroder V16T: 1094

Total No: 4

Flat-2 or Boxer engines.

1934	DKW 7.1hp Cabriolet: 1259
1935	Jowett 7hp Curlew de Luxe: 2406
1937	DKW 7.1hp Cabriolet: 1260
1939	Jowett 8hp: 2408
1953	Citroen 2CV Cabriolet: 1019
1954	Panhard Dyna: 3365 Panhard Dyna Junior Sports: 3366
1955	Citroen 2CV: 1022
1956	Panhard Dyna Sedan: 3367
1957	Deutsch-Bonnet Coupe: 1256
1958	BMW 600: 501
1959	Panhard Dyna: 3368 Panhard PL17: 3369
1960	BMW 700: 503 DAF 600 de Luxe: 1108
1961	Citroen Bijou: 1028
1962	BMW 700 Coupe: 504 Citroen Ami 6: 1030 DAF Daffodil: 1109 DAF Daffodil de Luxe Extra: 1110 Panhard PL17 Tiger: 3370
1964	BMW 700 LS: 507 Panhard 24CT Sports Coupe: 3371
1967	Citroen Ami 6 Break: 1035 DAF 44: 1111
1970	Citroen Ami 8 Club: 1037
1975	Citroen 2CV6: 1046
1979	Citroen Visa Club: 1057
1985	Citroen 2CV6 Charleston: 1065

Total No: 29

Flat-4 or Boxer engines.

1932	Tatra 12hp Drop-head Coupe: 4349
1937	Jowett De Luxe Saloon: 2407
1948	Jowett Javelin: 2409
1952	Porsche 356 4: 3601 Volkswagen Sedan de Luxe: 4738
1953	Jowett Jupiter: 2410 Jowett Jupiter Mk IA: 2411 Volkswagen Export Saloon: 4739

1954 Porsche 356: 3602
Porsche Super Coupe: 3603
Volkswagen De Luxe: 4740
Volkswagen Sedan: 4741
Volkswagen Sedan TC: 4742
Year total: 5

1955 Porsche 1500 S Speedster: 3604
Volkswagen Sedan Supercharged: 4743

1956 Porsche 1600: 3605
Porsche Carrera Coupe: 3606
Porsche Continental Coupe: 3607
Porsche Continental Speedster: 3608
Volkswagen Karmann-Ghia: 4744
Volkswagen Micro Bus: 4745
Volkswagen Sedan: 4746
Year total: 7

1957 Denzel 1300: 1255
Goliath 1100 Sedan: 2005
Porsche 1600 Coupe: 3609
Porsche 550 Spyder: 3610
Volkswagen Karmann-Ghia Okrasa: 4747
Volkswagen Sedan Judson: 4748
Year total: 6

1958 Porsche 1600: 3611
Porsche 1600 Super Speedster: 3612
Porsche RSK: 3613
Volkswagen Alken-VW: 4749
Volkswagen De Luxe Saloon: 4750
Year total: 5

1959 Goliath Tiger: 2007
Porsche 1600 Convertible D: 3614

1960 Devin VW: 1258
Porsche Super 75: 3615
Porsche Super 90 Cabriolet: 3616
Volkswagen De Luxe: 4751
Volkswagen Sedan: 4752
Year total: 5

1961 Lancia Flavia: 2498
Porsche 1600 N: 3617
Volkswagen 1500: 4753
Volkswagen Karmann Ghia: 4754
Volkswagen Sedan: 4755
Volkswagen Station Wagon: 4756
Volkswagen Van: 4757
Year total: 7

1962 Porsche Carrera 2-litre: 3618
Porsche Super 90 Cabriolet: 3619
Volkswagen 1200 de Luxe: 4758
Volkswagen 1500: 4759
Volkswagen Karmann-Ghia: 4760
Volkswagen Sedan EMPI: 4761
Year total: 6

1963 Volkswagen 1500 Estate: 4762
Volkswagen Karmann-Ghia 1500: 4763

1964 Lancia Flavia Coupe: 2501
Porsche 356 C: 3620
Porsche 904 Carrera GTS: 3621
Volkswagen 1500S: 4764

1965 Lancia Flavia Zagato Sport: 2505
Meyers Manx: 2967
Porsche 912: 3623
Volkswagen 1200: 4765
Volkswagen 1300: 4766
Year total: 5

1966 Ferguson R5: 1370
Porsche 912: 3625
Volkswagen 1300: 4767
Volkswagen 1300 de Luxe: 4768
Volkswagen 1500: 4769
Volkswagen 1600 Fastback: 4770
Volkswagen 1600 TL: 4771
Year total: 7

1967 Lancia Flavia Injection: 2507
Volkswagen 1500: 4772
Volkswagen Beetle 1500: 4773

1968 Volkswagen 1500 Automatic: 4774
Volkswagen 1500 Semi-automatic: 4775
Volkswagen 1600 Squareback: 4776
Volkswagen 1600 TL Automatic: 4777
Volkswagen 411 L: 4778
Year total: 5

1969 Subaru Star: 4244
Volkswagen 1600 Squareback: 4780

1970 Porsche 914: 3633
Volkswagen 411 LE Variant: 4781
Volkswagen Porsche 914: 4782
Volkswagen Super Beetle: 4783

1971 Citroen GS: 1039
Volkswagen 411: 4784
Volkswagen Super Beetle: 4786
Volkswagen Van: 4787

1972 Alfa Romeo Alfasud: 81
Citroen GS: 1042
Lancia 2000: 2513
Subaru FF-1 1300: 4246

1973 Alfa Romeo Alfasud: 84
Citroen GS 1220: 1044
Porsche 914 1.7-litre: 3639
Porsche 914 2-litre: 3640
Subaru 1300 GL Coupe: 4247
Subaru 1400 DL: 4248
Volkswagen Karmann-Ghia: 4789
Volkswagen SP-2: 4791
Volkswagen Sports Bug: 4792
Volkswagen Type III: 4793
Year total: 10

1974 Alfa Romeo Alfasud ti: 88
Volkswagen 181: 4794
Volkswagen 412: 4795

1975 Citroen GS Pallas: 1048
Subaru DL: 4249
Volkswagen Beetle: 4798

1976 Citroen GS X2: 1050
Porsche 912 E: 3651
Porsche 914 2.0-litre: 3652
Subaru 4WD Station Wagon: 4250

1977 Alfa Romeo Alfasud 1200ti: 95
Alfa Romeo Alfasud 1300ti: 96
Alfa Romeo Alfasud 5M: 97
Lancia Gamma: 2525
Subaru 1600 4WD Estate: 4251
Year total: 5

1978 Alfa Romeo Alfasud Sprint 1.5: 100
Lancia Gamma Berlina: 2526
Subaru 1600 Coupe: 4252
Subaru DL: 4253
Volkswagen Beetle Convertible: 4812
Year total: 5

1979 Alfa Romeo Alfasud 1.5 Sprint Veloce: 104

1980 Subaru DL-5: 4254
Volkswagen Vanagon: 4823

1981 Alfa Romeo Alfasud 1.5: 108
Subaru 1800 4WD Estate: 4255

1982 Subaru GL: 4256
Trihawk 304: 4486

1983 Alfa Romeo Alfa 33 1.5: 112
Subaru GL Turbo Traction Wagon: 4257
Volkswagen Vanagon Wasserboxer: 4842

1984 Alfa Romeo Sprint Green Cloverleaf: 116

1985 Alfa Romeo Alfa 33 1.5 4x4 Estate: 117
Alfa Romeo Arna 1.3SL: 119
Alfa Romeo Arna ti: 120
Subaru 1.8 GTi: 4258
Subaru 1.8 RX Turbo: 4259
Subaru 4WD Turbo: 4260
Subaru 4WD Turbo XT Coupe: 4261
Subaru Turbo 4WD Estate: 4262
Subaru XT Coupe DL: 4263
Subaru XT Turbo Coupe: 4264
Year total: 10

1986 Alfa Romeo Alfa 33 1.3 S: 123
Subaru 4WD 3-door Turbo Coupe: 4265
Subaru Hatchback: 4266
Volkswagen Caravelle Syncro: 4855

1987 Alfa Romeo 33 1.7 Veloce: 129
Alfa Romeo Alfa 33 1.7 Sportwagon Veloce: 130
Subaru XT Turbo 4WD: 4268

1988 Alfa Romeo Sprint 1.7 Cloverleaf: 137
Subaru 4WD Turbo Estate: 4269

1989 Subaru Legacy FIA Record: 4274
Volkswagen Caravelle Carat Automatic: 4873

1990 Alfa Romeo 33 Boxer 16v: 144
Subaru Legacy 2.2 GX 4WD: 4276

1991 Subaru Legacy 2.0 4Cam Turbo Estate: 4277
Subaru Legacy Sports Sedan: 4278
Total No: 159

Flat-6 or Boxer engines.

1959 Chevrolet Corvair: 742

1960 Chevrolet Corvair 4-speed: 744
Chevrolet Corvair Automatic: 745

1961 Chevrolet Corvair 700: 746
Chevrolet Corvair Greenbrier: 747
Chevrolet Corvair Monza: 748
Chevrolet Corvair Monza 4-speed: 749

1962 Chevrolet Corvair Monza: 762
Chevrolet Corvair Monza Coupe: 763
Chevrolet Corvair Navarro: 764
Chevrolet Corvair Spyder: 765

1963 Chevrolet Corvair Monza Convertible: 773
Chevrolet Corvair Monza EMPI: 774

1964 Chevrolet Corvair Monza: 784
Chevrolet Corvair Sprint: 785

1965 Chevrolet Corvair Corsa IECO: 793
Chevrolet Corvair Monza: 794
Porsche 911: 3622

1966 Porsche 911 S: 3624

1967 Porsche 911 S: 3626

1968 Chevrolet Corvair Monza: 815
Chevrolet Corvair Sport Coupe: 816
Porsche 911 E Sportomatic: 3627
Porsche 911 Sportomatic: 3628

1969 Porsche 911 E: 3629
Porsche 911 T: 3630

1970 Porsche 911 S 2.2-litre: 3631
Porsche 911 T: 3632
Porsche 914 6: 3634

1971 Porsche 911 E 2.4-litre: 3635
Volkswagen Porsche 914/b: 4785

1973 Porsche 911 S: 3638
Porsche Carrera RS Touring: 3641
Porsche Carrera RSR: 3642

1974 Porsche 911 Carrera: 3643
Porsche 911 Targa: 3644
Porsche 911S 2.7-litre: 3645

1975 Porsche 911 Carrera: 3646
Porsche Carrera RS 3-litre: 3647
Porsche Turbo 3-litre: 3648

1976 Porsche 911 S: 3649
Porsche 911 Turbo Carrera: 3650

1977 Porsche 911 SC: 3654
Porsche 911 Turbo: 3655
Porsche 935 Group 4 Holbert: 3657

1978 Porsche 911 SC: 3658
Porsche 911 Turbo: 3659

1980 Porsche 911 SC: 3666

1981 Porsche 911 SC: 3670

1983 Porsche 911 Cabriolet: 3675
Porsche 911 Turbo: 3676

1984 Porsche 911 Carrera: 3679

1985 Porsche 911 Carrera: 3682

1986 Porsche 911 Cabriolet: 3687
Porsche 911 Carrera SE: 3688
Porsche 911 Turbo: 3689

1987 Porsche 911 Carrera: 3696
Porsche 911 Turbo Gemballa Avalanche: 3697
Porsche 911 Turbo Ruf 3.4: 3698
Porsche 911 Turbo Slant-Nose: 3699
Porsche 959 S: 3702
Year total: 5

1988 Porsche 911 Cabriolet: 3703
Porsche 911 Carrera: 3704
Porsche 911 Carrera Club Sport: 3705
Porsche 911 Club Sport: 3706
Porsche 911 Speedster: 3707
Porsche 911 Turbo: 3708
Porsche 911 Turbo Koenig RS: 3709
Porsche 911 Turbo Ruf Twin Turbo: 3710
Porsche 959 Comfort: 3717
Porsche 959 Sport: 3718
Subaru XT6 4WD: 4272
Year total: 11

1989 Porsche 911 3.3 Turbo: 3719
Porsche 911 Carrera 4: 3720
Porsche 911 Carrera Cabriolet: 3721
Porsche 911 Club Sport: 3722
Porsche 911 Turbo: 3723
Porsche 911 Turbo Motorsport Design: 3724
Porsche 959: 3731
Subaru XT6: 4275
Year total: 8

1990 Porsche 911 Carrera 2: 3732
Porsche 911 Carrera 2 Tiptronic: 3733
Porsche 911 Carrera 4: 3734
Porsche 911 Speedster: 3735
Porsche 911 Turbo: 3736
Porsche 911 Turbo RS Tuning: 3737
Porsche Carrera 2 Cabriolet Tiptronic: 3744
Porsche Panamericana: 3745
Year total: 8

1991 Koenig C62: 2419
Porsche 911 Carrera Turbo: 3746
Porsche 911 Ruf: 3747
Porsche 911 Ruf CTR: 3748
Porsche 911 Ruf TR2: 3749
Porsche 911 Turbo: 3750
Porsche 911 Turbo Gemballa Mirage: 3751
Year total: 7

1992 Porsche 911 Carrera RS: 3753
Subaru SVX: 4279

Total No: 97

Flat-12 or Boxer engines.

1975 Ferrari 512 BB: 1407

1982 Ferrari 512 BB: 1417

1984 Ferrari 512 BBi: 1422

1985 Ferrari Testa Rossa: 1426

1988 Ferrari Testa Rossa: 1437
Ferrari Testa Rossa Straman Spyder: 1438

1989 Ferrari Testa Rossa: 1442
Ferrari Testa Rossa Norwood: 1444
Koenig Competition: 2417

1990 Ferrari Pininfarina Mythos: 1448
Koenig Competition Evolution: 2418
Total No: 11

Cars with anti-lock brakes (ABS).

1982 BMW 745i: 562

1983 Mitsubishi Starion Turbo: 3075

1985 Audi 5000 S Turbo Quattro: 305
BMW M635 CSi Hardy & Beck: 577
Ford Granada Scorpio: 1903
Lincoln Continental Mk VII LSC: 2584
Mercedes-Benz 190E 2.3: 2878
Mercedes-Benz 190E BBS/Callaway Turbo: 2880
Porsche 928 S Series II: 3684
Year total: 7

1986 Alfa Romeo Milano Platinum: 127
BMW 325 ES: 578
BMW 535i: 582
BMW 635 CSi: 583
BMW 735i: 584
BMW 735i Automatic: 585
Chevrolet Corvette: 900

Chevrolet Corvette Callaway: 901
Chevrolet Corvette Z51: 902
Ford Escort 1.4 GL: 1909
Ford Escort RS Turbo: 1911
Ford Sierra Ghia 4x4 Estate: 1918
Lincoln Continental Mk VII LSC: 2585
Mercedes-Benz 190E 2.3-16: 2883
Mercedes-Benz 300E: 2885
Mercedes-Benz 560SEC: 2888
Mercedes-Benz 560SL: 2890
Porsche 928 S: 3691
Porsche 928 S4 Automatic: 3692
Toyota Supra 3.0i: 4443
Year total: 20

1987 Alfa Romeo Milano Verde 3.0: 133
Bentley Turbo R: 481
BMW 325i Cabriolet: 587
BMW 730i SE: 588
Chevrolet Corvette: 908
Chevrolet Corvette ASC Geneve: 909
Chevrolet Corvette Convertible: 910
Citroen BX GTi 16v: 1077
Citroen CX25 DTR Turbo 2: 1078
Ferrari 412: 1432
Ford Thunderbird Bondurant 5.0: 1926
Ford Thunderbird Turbo Coupe: 1927
Honda Legend Coupe: 2137
Jaguar XJ6: 2352
Lancia Thema 8.32: 2546
Mazda RX-7 Turbo: 2740
Mercedes-Benz 300CE: 2892
Mercedes-Benz 300TD: 2893
Mercedes-Benz 420SEL: 2894
Mercedes-Benz 560SEC Cabriolet Straman: 2895
Merkur Scorpio: 2964
Mitsubishi Galant Sapporo: 3093
Mitsubishi Starion 2000 Turbo: 3095
Mitsubishi Starion ESI-R: 3096
Peugeot 505 STX: 3445
Porsche 959 S: 3702
Toyota Supra: 4452
Vauxhall Carlton 3000 GSi: 4708
Volvo 760 GLE: 4956
Year total: 29

1988 Alfa Romeo 75 Evoluzione: 135
Audi 100 Sport: 320
Audi 90 Quattro: 322
Audi Quattro: 323
BMW 325i S: 591
BMW 325i X: 592
BMW 535i SE: 593
BMW 635 CSi: 594
BMW 735i: 595
BMW 750i L: 596
BMW M6: 597
Buick Reatta: 695
Cadillac Allante: 715
Chevrolet Corvette: 916
Chevrolet Corvette Bakeracing SCCA Escort: 917
Chevrolet Corvette Callaway: 918
Chevrolet Corvette Convertible: 919
Chevrolet Corvette Guldstrand Grand Sport 80: 920
Chevrolet Corvette Morrison/Baker Nelson Ledges: 921
Chevrolet Corvette Z51: 922
Chrysler Conquest TSi: 1007
Citroen BX DTR Turbo: 1080
Ford Probe GT: 1933
Ford Sierra RS Cosworth: 1934
Honda Legend Saloon Automatic: 2143
Jaguar XJS V12 Convertible: 2357
Lancia Thema 8.32: 2548
Mazda 626 2.0i GT 4WS: 2745
Mazda 929: 2746
Mazda RX-7 Turbo: 2751
Mercedes-Benz 260E Auto: 2896
Mercedes-Benz 300CE: 2897
Mercedes-Benz 300E 4Matic: 2898
Mercedes-Benz 300E AMG Hammer: 2899
Mitsubishi Galant 2000 GLSi: 3098
Mitsubishi Galant GTi-16v: 3099
Peugeot 405 Mi16: 3448
Pontiac 6000STE AWD: 3584
Porsche 928 S4: 3712
Porsche 944 Turbo SE: 3716
Porsche 959 Comfort: 3717
Porsche 959 Sport: 3718
Renault 21 Turbo: 3905
Rover 827 SLi Auto: 4032
Rover Vitesse: 4033
Saab 9000CD: 4094
Toyota Celica All-Trac Turbo: 4454
Toyota Celica GT4: 4455
Toyota Supra Turbo: 4460
Vauxhall Carlton L 1.8i: 4712
Year total: 50

1989 Acura Legend Coupe L: 33
Alfa Romeo 164 3.0 Lusso: 138
Alfa Romeo 164 Automatic: 139
Alfa Romeo Milano 3.0: 140
Audi 90: 324
Audi 90 Quattro 20v: 325
Audi Coupe Quattro: 327
BMW 316i 4-door: 598
BMW 325i S: 599
BMW 535i: 600
BMW 535i Automatic: 601
BMW 735i Alpina B11: 602
BMW M3: 603
BMW M3 Hor Technologie: 605
BMW M5: 606
BMW Z1: 608
Buick Reatta Turbo Buick Engineering: 697
Chevrolet Corvette: 930
Chevrolet Corvette Callaway: 931
Chevrolet Corvette Guldstrand Grand Sport 80: 932
Chevrolet Corvette L98: 933
Chevrolet Corvette ZR-1: 934
Chrysler TC by Maserati: 1008
Ferrari Mondial t: 1441
Ford Fiesta 1.6S: 1939
Ford Probe GT Suspension Techniques/HKS: 1943
Ford Sierra Sapphire 2000E: 1944
Ford Thunderbird Super Coupe: 1947
Ford Thunderbird Super Coupe Ford Engineering: 1948
Irmsher GT: 2243
Jaguar 4.0 Sovereign: 2358
Jaguar XJ220: 2359
Jaguar XJS Convertible: 2360
Jaguar XJS V12 Convertible: 2361
Lancia Delta Integrale 16v: 2549
Lincoln Continental Mk VII: 2586
Mazda RX-7 Turbo II: 2759
Mercedes-Benz 190: 2900
Mercedes-Benz 190E 2.5-16: 2901
Mercedes-Benz 190E 2.6: 2902
Mercedes-Benz 190E AMG Baby Hammer: 2903
Mercedes-Benz 200E Automatic: 2904
Mercedes-Benz 300CE Cabriolet Straman: 2905
Mercedes-Benz 300E: 2906
Mercedes-Benz 560SL: 2907
Mercury Cougar XR-7: 2960
Mitsubishi Galant GS: 3104
Mitsubishi Starion ESI-R: 3107
Nissan 200SX: 3232
Nissan 300ZX: 3234
Nissan Maxima SE: 3236
Nissan Prairie: 3238
Pontiac Grand Prix McLaren Turbo: 3592
Porsche 911 Carrera 4: 3720
Porsche 928 Cabrio Strosek: 3725
Porsche 928 S4 Koenig: 3726
Porsche 928 S4 SE: 3727
Porsche 944: 3728
Porsche 944 S2: 3729
Porsche 944 Turbo: 3730
Porsche 959: 3731
Rover Sterling Catalyst: 4035
Rover Vitesse: 4036
Saab 9000 Turbo: 4096
Saab Carlsson: 4097
Toyota Camry V6 GXi: 4461
Toyota Supra 3.0i Turbo: 4465
Toyota Supra Turbo: 4466
Toyota Supra Turbo TRD: 4467
Vauxhall Cavalier SRi: 4719
Vauxhall Senator 2.5i: 4720
Vauxhall Senator 3.0i CD: 4721
Volkswagen Caravelle Carat Automatic: 4873
Volkswagen Passat GT 16v: 4878
Volvo 440 Turbo: 4957
Volvo 740 GLE: 4958
Volvo 740 Turbo: 4959
Year total: 77

1990 Acura Integra GS: 34
Acura Legend Coupe: 35
Acura NSX: 36
Alfa Romeo 164 Twin Spark Lusso: 142
Alfa Romeo 164S: 143
Audi 80 2.0E: 328
Audi 90 Quattro: 329
Audi Quattro 20v: 330
Audi V8 Quattro: 331
Audi V8 Quattro Automatic: 332
Bentley Turbo R: 482
Bitter Type 3 Cabrio: 494
BMW 318i S: 609
BMW 325i Convertible: 610
BMW 735i Koenig: 611
BMW 750i: 612
BMW 750i Alpina B12: 613
Cadillac Allante: 716

Saab 9000 Turbo: 4102
Saab 9000CS Turbo S: 4103
Saab 9000S: 4104
Saturn Sports Coupe: 4107
Subaru Legacy 2.0 4Cam Turbo Estate: 4277
Subaru Legacy Sports Sedan: 4278
Toyota Camry 2.2 GL: 4476
Vauxhall Calibra 2.0i: 4728
Vauxhall Calibra 4x4: 4729
Vauxhall Senator 3.0i 24v: 4731
Volkswagen Corrado G60: 4882
Volkswagen Jetta GLi 16v: 4885
Volvo 940 SE: 4965
Volvo 940 Turbo: 4967
Volvo 960 24v: 4968
Year total: 117

1992 BMW 325i: 623
BMW 520i SE Touring: 624
BMW 850i Manual: 625
Chevrolet Corvette LT1: 959
Citroen AX GTi: 1092
Fiat Tipo 1.8ie DGT SX: 1606
Ford Escort RS2000: 1973
Ford Taurus LX: 1976
Honda NSX Auto: 2159
Honda Prelude Si 4WS: 2160
Lexus ES300: 2572
Mercedes-Benz 500SEL: 2922
Mercedes-Benz 600SEL: 2923
Nissan 200SX: 3254
Nissan Sunny 2.0 GTi: 3255
Pontiac Bonneville SSEi: 3600
Porsche 911 Carrera RS: 3753
Renault Cleo 16v: 3923
Rover 820i: 4050
Rover Sterling Automatic: 4051
Seat Toledo 2.0 GTi: 4115
Subaru SVX: 4279
Vauxhall 1.4i GLS: 4732
Volvo 960: 4969
Year total: 24
Total No: 437

4-wheel drive and engageable.

1955 Land Rover Station Wagon: 2556
1961 International Scout: 2234

1963 Willys Wagoneer 4WD: 4976

1964 Dodge Safari Super Sport: 1291
Jeep Wagoneer: 2373
1966 Ferguson R5: 1370
Ford Bronco: 1729

1967 Kaiser Jeepster: 2415
Toyota Land Cruiser: 4358

1968 Jensen FF: 2392

1970 Jensen FF II: 2394
Range Rover V8: 3771

1971 Chevrolet Blazer: 850
Chevrolet Pickup Cheyenne Fleetside: 851
Dodge Pickup Power Wagon: 1317
Ford Bronco: 1790
Ford Pickup 4WD: 1797
International Pickup 4WD 1210 Camper Special: 2237
International Scout: 2238
International Travelall 1210: 2239
Jeep CJ-5: 2374
Jeep Commando: 2375
Jeep Gladiator Pickup J-2500 Townside: 2376
Jeep Wagoneer: 2377
Jeep Wagoneer 1414C: 2378
Land Rover Series III: 2557
Suzuki Brute: 4320
Toyota Land Cruiser: 4372
Toyota Land Cruiser Wagon: 4373
Year total 17

1972 International Scout: 2240
Jeep CJ-5 V8: 2379
Jeep Commando: 2380

1973 Land Rover SWB: 2558

1974 Jeep CJ6: 2381
Jeep Wagoneer: 2382

1975 Range Rover V8: 3772

1976 Subaru 4WD Station Wagon: 4250

1977 Subaru 1600 4WD Estate: 4251

1978 Chevrolet Blazer: 876
Jeep Cherokee Chief: 2383
Range Rover V8: 3773

1979 Lada Niva 1600: 2426

1980 AMC Eagle: 206

1981 Audi Quattro: 289
Mercedes-Benz 300GD: 2867
Subaru 1800 4WD Estate: 4255

1982 Audi Quattro: 292
Land Rover County: 2559

1983 Mitsubishi Colt Shogun: 3073
Subaru GL Turbo Traction Wagon: 4257
Toyota Tercel 4WD Wagon: 4422

1984 Audi 200 Quattro Turbo: 297
Audi 4000 S Quattro: 298

1985 Alfa Romeo Alfa 33 1.5 4x4 Estate: 117
Audi 100 Quattro: 303
Audi 200 Avant Quattro: 304
Audi 5000 S Turbo Quattro: 305
Audi 90 Quattro: 306
Audi Quattro: 308
Audi Quattro Sport: 309
Dacia Duster GLX: 1106
Ford Granada Scorpio 4x4: 1904
Subaru 1.8 RX Turbo: 4259
Subaru 4WD Turbo: 4260
Subaru 4WD Turbo XT Coupe: 4261
Subaru Turbo 4WD Estate: 4262
Subaru XT Turbo Coupe: 4264
Toyota Tercel 4WD Estate: 4437
Year total: 15

1986 Audi Coupe Quattro: 316
Ford RS200: 1917
Ford Sierra Ghia 4x4 Estate: 1918
Lancia Delta HF 4WD: 2541
Mazda 323 Turbo 4x4 Lux: 2732
Range Rover Vogue: 3774
Subaru 4WD 3-door Turbo Coupe: 4265
Volkswagen Caravelle Syncro: 4855
Volkswagen Quantum Synchro Wagon: 4858
Year total: 9

1987 Audi 90 Quattro: 318
Daihatsu Fourtrak Estate DT EL: 1125
Isuzu Trooper 3-door TD: 2257
Lada Niva Cossack Cabrio: 2428
Land Rover Ninety County Turbo Diesel: 2560
Land Rover One Ten County V8: 2561
Mitsubishi Shogun Turbo Diesel 5-door: 3094
Porsche 959 S: 3702
Range Rover V8: 3775
Subaru Justy: 4267
Subaru XT Turbo 4WD: 4268
Suzuki SJ413V JX: 4327
Toyota Landcruiser: 4450
Year total: 13

1988 Audi 100 Avant Quattro: 319
Audi 90 Quattro: 322
Audi Quattro: 323
BMW 325i X: 592
Honda Shuttle 1.6i RT4 4WD: 2144
Lamborghini LM129: 2472
Lancia Delta HF Integrale: 2547
Mazda 323 GTX: 2742
Mazda 323 Turbo 4x4: 2743
Pontiac 6000STE AWD: 3584
Porsche 959 Comfort: 3717
Porsche 959 Sport: 3718
Range Rover Vogue Turbo D: 3776
Subaru 4WD Turbo Estate: 4269
Subaru Justy 4WD GL: 4270
Subaru XT6 4WD: 4272
Toyota Celica All-Trac Turbo: 4454
Toyota Celica GT4: 4455
Toyota Corolla 4WD Estate: 4457
Toyota Landcruiser II TD: 4458
Vauxhall Cavalier 4x4: 4714
Volkswagen Quantum GLS Synchro Wagon: 4871
Year total: 22

1989 Audi 90 Quattro 20v: 325
Audi Coupe Quattro: 327
Daihatsu Sportrak EL: 1130
Ford Sierra XR 4x4: 1945
Jaguar XJ220: 2359
Lancia Delta Integrale 16v: 2549
Land Rover Ninety County V8: 2562

Mitsubishi Eclipse GSX: 3103
Mitsubishi Shogun V6 5-door: 3105
Porsche 911 Carrera 4: 3720
Porsche 959: 3731
Range Rover Vogue: 3777
Range Rover Vogue SE: 3778
Subaru Justy GL II 5-door 4WD: 4273
Subaru Legacy FIA Record: 4274
Subaru XT6: 4275
Suzuki Vitara JLX: 4332
Volkswagen Jetta Syncro: 4877

Year total: 18

1990 Audi Quattro 20v: 330
Audi V8 Quattro: 331
Audi V8 Quattro Automatic: 332
Bertone Zabrus: 488
Cadillac Aurora: 717
Citroen BX GTi 4x4: 1084
Eagle Talon: 1355
Ford Sierra Sapphire Cosworth 4x4: 1958
Ital Design Aztec: 2262
Land Rover Discovery TDi: 2563
Land Rover Discovery V8: 2564
Mitsubishi Lancer GLXi 4WD Liftback: 3109
Nissan Skyline GT-R: 3243
Panther Solo: 3380
Peugeot 405 GLx4: 3457
Peugeot 405 Mi16x4: 3459
Peugeot 405 Turbo 16 Pike's Peak: 3460
Porsche 911 Carrera 4: 3734
Porsche Panamericana: 3745
Range Rover County: 3779
Range Rover Vogue SE: 3780
Subaru Legacy 2.2 GX 4WD: 4276
Toyota Celica All-Trac Turbo: 4469
Vauxhall Cavalier GSi 2000 16v 4x4: 4726

Year total: 24

1991 Audi 200 Quattro: 334
Audi 90 Quattro 20v: 336
Audi Coupe S2: 337
Audi V8 Quattro: 338
Bugatti EB110: 652
Dodge Stealth R/T Turbo: 1347
Eagle Talon TSi 4WD: 1357
Isuzu Impulse RS: 2261
Land Rover Discovery V8i 5DR: 2565
Mercedes-Benz G-Wagen 300 GD LWB: 2921
Mitsubishi 3000GT VR-4: 3111
Mitsubishi Galant VR-4: 3114
Mitsubishi Shogun V6 LWB: 3115
Subaru Legacy 2.0 4Cam Turbo Estate: 4277
Subaru Legacy Sports Sedan: 4278
Toyota Landcruiser VX: 4478
Vauxhall Calibra 4x4: 4729

Year total: 17

1992 Audi 80 2.8E V6 Quattro: 339
Range Rover Vogue SE: 3781
Subaru SVX: 4279
Vauxhall Frontera 2.3 TD Estate: 4734

Total No: 175

Single parameter ranked lists

with upper or lower set limits.

Maximum speed - fastest. Limit set at 165mph.

	mph	kmh	
1	255.0	410.3	Chevrolet Corvette Callaway Sledgehammer: 941
2	235.0	378.1	Koenig C62: 2419
3	230.0	370.1	Koenig Competition Evolution: 2418
4	221.0	355.6	Chevrolet Corvette Greenwood: 870
5	218.0	350.8	Vector W8 Twin Turbo: 4736
6	217.0	349.2	Koenig Competition: 2417
7	216.0	347.5	Porsche 911 Turbo RS Tuning: 3737
8	214.0	344.3	Bugatti EB110: 652
9	211.0	339.5	Porsche 911 Turbo Ruf Twin Turbo: 3710
10	210.0	337.9	Ferrari Testa Rossa Norwood: 1444
11	208.0	334.7	Porsche 911 Ruf CTR: 3748
12	205.0	329.8	Ford GT40: 1760
			Porsche 911 Turbo Gemballa Mirage: 3751
13	204.0	328.2	Chevrolet Corvette Lingenfelter: 951
			Cizeta Moroder V16T: 1094
14	203.0	326.6	Chevrolet Camaro Gottlieb 1969: 926
15	202.0	325.0	Lamborghini Diablo: 2474
			Lamborghini Diablo: 2475
16	201.0	323.4	Chevrolet Corvette Callaway Speedster: 949
			Ferrari F40: 1435
			Porsche 911 Turbo Koenig RS: 3709
			Porsche 959 S: 3702
17	200.0	321.8	Eagle GTP: 1356
			Ferrari F40: 1446
			Jaguar XJ220: 2359
			Jaguar XJS Lister Le Mans: 2366
			Vector W2: 4735
18	199.0	320.2	Ferrari GTO Norwood: 1451
19	198.0	318.6	Ferrari 308 Norwood Bonneville GTO: 1434
			Porsche 959: 3731
			Porsche 959 Comfort: 3717
			Porsche 959 Sport: 3718
20	196.1	315.5	Porsche 911 Ruf TR2: 3749
21	196.0	315.4	Ferrari F40: 1450
			Porsche 911 Ruf: 3747
22	193.0	310.5	Chevrolet Camaro IROC-Z Chevrolet Engineering: 929
			Safir GT40: 4106
23	192.0	308.9	Jaguar D Type: 2285
			Lamborghini Countach: 2461
			Pontiac Firebird TDM Technologies: 3597
24	191.0	307.3	Chevrolet Corvette Callaway: 931
			Chevrolet Corvette Callaway: 918
25	190.0	305.7	Dodge Viper: 1348
			Shelby Cobra Daytona Coupe: 4119
26	189.0	304.1	Ferrari 288 GTO: 1421
27	186.0	299.3	Chevrolet Corvette ZR-1 Geiger: 954
			Ferrari 365 GTB/4 Competitione: 1403
			Ford Mustang NOS/Saleen: 1967
			Porsche 928 S4 Koenig: 3726
			Zender Fact 4: 5008
28	185.0	297.7	Chevrolet Corvette ZR-2: 956
			Ferrari Testa Rossa Gemballa: 1443
			Ford Mustang 5.0 Cartech Turbo: 1940
			Jaguar XJR15: 2369
			Mercedes-Benz 300CE AMG Hammer: 2910
29	184.0	296.1	Chevrolet Corvette Callaway: 948
			Jaguar XJ13: 2313
30	183.0	294.4	Aston Martin Zagato: 257
			Mercedes-Benz 300E AMG Hammer: 2899
			Pontiac Petty Grand National: 3571
			Porsche 911 Turbo Motorsport Design: 3724
31	182.0	292.8	Ferrari 308 Norwood: 1439
32	181.0	291.2	Ferrari Testa Rossa: 1437
			Ferrari Testa Rossa Straman Spyder: 1438
33	180.0	289.6	Bizzarrini P538: 497
			Ferrari 288 GTO: 1416
			Ferrari 375 Indianapolis: 1373
			Ferrari 400 Super America: 1389
			Ferrari GTO: 1423
			Ferrari Pininfarina Mythos: 1448
			Jaguar XJS Tullius: 2333
			Lamborghini Miura: 2451
			Mercedes-Benz 300SLR: 2795
34	179.0	288.0	BMW 535i Alpina B10 Bi-Turbo: 619
			Lamborghini Countach: 2468
			Lamborghini Countach 25th Anniversary: 2473
35	178.0	286.4	Chevrolet Corvette Callaway: 901
			Ferrari Testa Rossa: 1426
			Mazda RX-7 Cartech: 2768
			Pontiac Firebird T/A Turbo Pontiac Engineering: 3588
			Porsche Carrera RSR: 3642
36	177.0	284.8	Ferrari 365 GTB Goldsmith: 1425
			Ford Mustang Cartech Turbo: 1928
37	176.0	283.2	Isdera Imperator: 2244
38	175.0	281.6	Ferrari 250 GTO: 1386
			Ferrari 512 BB: 1407
			Ferrari Daytona: 1397
			Zender Vision 3: 5007
39	174.0	280.0	Ferrari 412 MI: 1377
			Ferrari Testa Rossa: 1442
			Ford Mustang Holdener: 1966

			Opel Omega Lotus: 3352
40	173.0	278.4	Ferrari 365 GTB/4 Daytona: 1396
			Ferrari Daytona Cannonball: 1398
			Ferrari Daytona Sportwagen: 1395
			Ford Mustang SVO J Bittle American: 1942
			Lamborghini Countach 5000S: 2469
			Lamborghini Miura P400S: 2455
41	172.0	276.7	Chevrolet Corvette Guldstrand Grand Sport 80: 920
42	171.0	275.1	BMW 750i Alpina B12: 613
			Chevrolet Corvette Guldstrand Grand Sport 80: 932
			Ferrari 348tb: 1449
			Porsche 911 Turbo: 3750
43	170.0	273.5	Aston Martin V8 Vantage: 248
			Bertone Emotion Lotus: 489
			Chevrolet Corvette Callaway: 940
			Chevrolet Corvette ZR-1: 934
			Lamborghini Bravo: 2458
			Mazda RX-7 Mariah Mode Six: 2770
			Parradine V-12: 3382
44	169.0	271.9	Chevrolet Corvette Bakeracing SCCA Escort: 917
45	168.0	270.3	Acura NSX: 36
			De Tomaso Pantera Group 3: 1243
			Ferrari 250 Testa Rossa: 1378
			Ferrari 512 BB: 1417
			Lamborghini Miura S: 2456
			Porsche 911 Carrera Turbo: 3746
46	167.0	268.7	De Tomaso Pantera GT5 S: 1244
47	166.0	267.1	Nissan 300ZX Turbo Millen Super GTZ: 3247
48	165.0	265.5	Aston Martin Zagato Volante: 260
			Bizzarrini 5300 Spyder: 495
			De Tomaso Pantera GT5-S: 1242
			Ferrari 4.9: 1387
			IAD Venus: 2229
			Lamborghini Countach LP 500S: 2465
			Lotus Esprit Turbo SE: 2640
			Porsche 911 Turbo: 3676
			Porsche 911 Turbo Gemballa Avalanche: 3697
			Porsche 928 S4: 3712
			Renault Alpine A610 Turbo: 3918
			TVR 420 SEAC: 4601

Total: 131

Maximum speed - slowest. Limit set at 65mph.

	mph	kmh	
1	37.0	59.5	Enfield 8000 Electric: 1359
2	41.0	66.0	Citroen 2CV Cabriolet: 1019
3	44.0	70.8	Ford Model T: 1608
4	47.6	76.6	Austin 7 Saloon: 341
5	48.0	77.2	Suzuki Brute: 4320
6	49.2	79.2	Citroen 2CV: 1022
7	49.7	80.0	BMW Isetta 300: 502
8	50.2	80.8	Dodge Safari Super Sport: 1291
9	50.5	81.3	Citroen Bijou: 1028
10	50.8	81.7	Austin 7 Ruby Saloon: 349
11	51.0	82.1	Austin 7 Tourer: 340
12	52.6	84.6	Austin 7 Sunshine Saloon: 343
			Fiat 500 Convertible Saloon: 1458
13	52.9	85.1	Austin 7 Ruby Saloon: 351
			Triumph Super 7 Saloon: 4487
14	53.5	86.1	DKW 7.1hp Cabriolet: 1259
15	54.0	86.9	Austin 10/4 Saloon: 344
			BMW Isetta Motocoupe: 499
			Fiat 500: 1477
16	54.5	87.7	Jowett 7hp Curlew de Luxe: 2406
17	55.0	88.5	Fiat 17/50 Saloon: 1454
			Fiat 600 Multipla: 1473
			Morris Minor Saloon: 3138
18	55.2	88.8	Morris 8 Minor: 3140
19	55.5	89.3	Mercedes-Benz 12hp Rear-engined Saloon: 2779
20	56.0	90.1	Frisky Coupe: 1993
			Hillman Safety Saloon: 2022
			Subaru 360: 4243
21	56.2	90.4	Jowett 8hp: 2408
			Mercedes-Benz 20.8hp Diesel Saloon: 2781
22	56.6	91.1	DKW 7.1hp Cabriolet: 1260
23	56.9	91.6	AJS 9hp Saloon: 38
			Austin 8 Saloon: 356
			Morris Cowley Saloon: 3144
24	57.0	91.7	DAF 600 de Luxe: 1108
			Hillman Segrave Saloon: 2023
25	57.3	92.2	Austin Big 7: 354
			Morris 10/4: 3142
26	57.5	92.5	Fiat Balilla Pillarless Saloon: 1455
27	57.6	92.7	Tatra 12hp Drop-head Coupe: 4349
28	58.0	93.3	Berkeley Sports: 485
			Morris 8 Saloon: 3147
			Morris Major Six Saloon: 3141
			Renault 12.1hp Airline Saloon: 3798
29	58.4	94.0	BSA FWD Tourer: 646
30	58.8	94.6	Fiat Multipla: 1474
			Ford 8 Tudor Saloon: 1611
31	59.0	94.9	Ford Anglia 8 Saloon: 1623
			Volkswagen Micro Bus: 4745
32	59.2	95.3	Bianchi 12hp Pillarless Saloon: 491
			Morris 10 Series II: 3151
			Morris 10/6: 3143
			Morris 8 Tourer: 3153
			Morris 8hp Tourer: 3154
			Opel Kadet Saloon: 3306
33	59.3	95.4	Morris 15/6 Saloon: 3146
34	59.5	95.7	Fiat 600: 1469
			Land Rover Station Wagon: 2556
35	60.0	96.5	Austin A40: 360
			Crossley 10hp Torquay: 1104
			Fiat 500 Giardiniera: 1492
			Lea-Francis 12/40 Saloon: 2566
			Morris Isis: 3139
			Renault 4CV: 3801
			Renault 750: 3802
			Renault Vivasix Saloon: 3797
			Volkswagen Station Wagon: 4756
			Wolseley Viper Saloon: 4978
36	60.3	97.0	Fiat 500C Convertible: 1464
			Fiat 500C Convertible (Topolino): 1462
			Fiat 600: 1472
37	60.4	97.2	Ford 8: 1618
			Vauxhall 10/4 de Luxe Saloon: 4613
38	60.7	97.7	Austin 15.9hp Ascot Saloon: 346
39	60.8	97.8	Armstrong Siddeley 15 Saloon: 209
			Austin 10 Cambridge: 352
			Austin 16 Hertford Saloon: 348
			Citroen Six Saloon: 1010
			Hillman Minx Sports Tourer: 2025
			Rover Pilot: 3974
			Singer 14/6 Saloon: 4159
40	61.0	98.1	Austin 8 Saloon: 358
			Fiat 500: 1482
			Fiat 500D: 1498
			Fiat 500F: 1504
			Ford Popular: 1631
			Ford Prefect: 1620
			Goggomobil TS400: 2004
			Morris Minor Tourer: 3159
			Standard 8: 4197
41	61.2	98.5	British Adler 13.67 Cabriolet: 641
			Morris Cowley Six: 3145
			Vauxhall Cadet Saloon: 4610
42	61.6	99.1	AC Acedes Magna Coupe: 2
			Armstrong Siddeley Long 15hp Saloon: 211
			Austin 20 Ranelagh Landaulet: 347
			Jowett De Luxe Saloon: 2407
			Standard 16 Special Saloon: 4191
43	61.9	99.6	DKW Karavan: 1264
44	62.0	99.8	Ford Model A: 1613
			Graham-Paige 21.6hp Saloon: 2015
			Morris Minor: 3157
			Morris Minor Series II: 3161
			Vauxhall Wyvern: 4622
45	62.2	100.1	Wolseley Hornet: 4977
46	62.5	100.6	Hillman Minx Saloon de Luxe: 2033
			Mercedes-Benz 21/60 Coupe: 2778
			Mercedes-Benz 32/90 Limousine: 2777
			Singer Super 10 Saloon: 4162
			Studebaker Erskine Saloon: 4216
47	62.7	100.9	Morris Minor: 3163
48	62.8	101.0	BMW 600: 501
49	62.9	101.2	Austin 14 Goodwood Saloon: 353
50	63.0	101.4	Austin A30: 369
			Austin A30: 368
			Austin A30 Countryman: 375
			Ford Anglia 10 Saloon: 1622
			Hillman Minx Saloon: 2034
			Standard 8: 4200
51	63.3	101.8	Citroen Super Model Twelve: 1011
			Lanchester 11 Saloon: 2481
			Vauxhall 10 Saloon de Luxe: 4615
			Vauxhall 12 Saloon: 4618
52	63.4	102.0	Lloyd LP 600: 2588
53	63.5	102.2	DAF Daffodil: 1109
			DAF Daffodil de Luxe Extra: 1110
54	63.8	102.7	Morris 8 Series E Tourer: 3155
			Morris 8hp Series E Tourer: 3156
			Riley 9 Monaco: 3928
			Standard Flying 10: 4194
55	64.0	103.0	Chrysler 65 Saloon: 960
			Dodge New Six Saloon: 1269
			Franklin 29.4hp Saloon: 1977
			Humber Hawk Saloon: 2191
			MG Midget: 2968
			NSU Prinz II: 3257
			Renault 750: 3804
56	64.2	103.3	Ford 24 Saloon: 1609
57	64.7	104.1	Delage 18.2hp Saloon: 1246
			Humber 16/60 Saloon: 2181
58	65.0	104.6	Austin Gipsy: 386
			Berkeley Sports: 484
			BSA Scout: 647
			Fiat 126: 1539
			Hillman Straight Eight Saloon: 2024
			Marmon Roosevelt Saloon: 2648
			Rolls-Royce 20 Saloon: 3947

		Standard 8: 4207
		Vauxhall 12 Saloon: 4619
		Vauxhall 20/60 Limousine: 4609
		Volkswagen De Luxe Saloon: 4750
		Volkswagen Sedan: 4741

Total: 152

Acceleration - fastest to 60mph. Limit set at 5 seconds.

	sec	
1	3.4	Chevrolet Corvette Lingenfelter: 951
2	3.5	AC Cobra 427 Modified 1965: 27
		Jaguar XJ220: 2359
		Koenig C62: 2419
		Koenig Competition Evolution: 2418
		Sbarro Chrono 3.5: 4108
3	3.6	Lancia Montecarlo Group 5 Turbo: 2531
		Porsche 959: 3731
		Porsche 959 Sport: 3718
4	3.7	Ferrari 308 Norwood Bonneville GTO: 1434
5	3.8	Datsun 280ZX Electramotive: 1230
		Ferrari F40: 1450
		Porsche 911 Ruf: 3747
		Porsche 911 Ruf TR2: 3749
6	3.9	Bugatti EB110: 652
		Chevrolet Corvette Callaway Sledgehammer: 941
		Porsche 911 Ruf CTR: 3748
7	4.0	Chevrolet Bel Air 409 SS/S: 755
		Koenig Competition: 2417
		Pontiac Firebird TransAm Silverbird: 3566
		Porsche 911 Turbo Koenig RS: 3709
		Porsche 911 Turbo Motorsport Design: 3724
		Porsche 911 Turbo Ruf Twin Turbo: 3710
		Porsche 959 Comfort: 3717
		Safir GT40: 4106
		Vector W2: 4735
8	4.1	Dodge Viper: 1348
		Ford Cobra II Kemp: 1841
		Pontiac Firebird TDM Technologies: 3597
		Porsche 911 Turbo Gemballa Mirage: 3751
9	4.2	Chevrolet Corvette ZR-1 SS: 955
		Dodge Ramcharger 426 Super/Stock: 1287
		Mercury Comet A/FX: 2933
		Scarab Mk II: 4109
		Shelby AC Ford Cobra: 4116
		Vector W8 Twin Turbo: 4736
10	4.3	De Tomaso Pantera Group 3: 1243
		Triumph TR8 Group 44: 4578
		Westfield SEight: 4973
		Zender Fact 4: 5008
11	4.4	Chevrolet Corvette Callaway Speedster: 949
		Jaguar XJS Lister Le Mans: 2366
12	4.5	Chevrolet Camaro IROC-Z Chevrolet Engineering: 929
		Chevrolet Corvette Bakeracing SCCA Escort: 917
		Cizeta Moroder V16T: 1094
		Ferrari 250 Testa Rossa: 1378
		Ferrari F40: 1446
		Lamborghini Diablo: 2475
		Porsche 911 Turbo Ruf 3.4: 3698
13	4.6	Chevrolet Corvette Callaway: 918
		Evans Series I: 1362
		Pontiac Catalina Super Stock: 3529
		Porsche 911 Carrera Turbo: 3746
		Porsche 911 Turbo RS Tuning: 3737
14	4.7	Chevrolet Monza Mike Keyser: 874
		Ferrari 308 Norwood: 1439
		Ferrari Testa Rossa Norwood: 1444
		Jaguar D Type: 2285
		Lamborghini Countach 25th Anniversary: 2473
		Porsche 911 Turbo: 3750
		Porsche 959 S: 3702
15	4.8	Aston Martin Zagato: 257
		Audi Quattro Sport: 309
		Chevrolet Camaro Gottlieb 1969: 926
		Ford Galaxie 500 XL 427: 1714
		Mazda RX-7 Mariah Mode Six: 2770
		Porsche 911 Turbo: 3723
		Porsche 928 S4 Koenig: 3726
		Renault Le Car Turbo: 3874
16	4.9	Chevrolet Corvette Callaway: 948
		Chevrolet Corvette Callaway: 931
		Chevrolet Corvette Callaway Twin Turbo: 950
		Chevrolet Corvette Morrison/Baker Nelson Ledges: 921
		Chevrolet Corvette ZR-1: 934
		Chevrolet Corvette ZR-1: 953
		Chevrolet Corvette ZR-1 Geiger: 954
		Chevrolet Corvette ZR-2: 956
		Ford Mustang Cartech Turbo: 1928
		Ford Mustang Holdener: 1966
		Lamborghini Countach: 2468
		Lotus Esprit Turbo SE: 2637
		Opel Omega Lotus: 3352
		Porsche 911 3.3 Turbo: 3719
		Porsche 911 Carrera 4: 3720
		Porsche 911 Carrera RS: 3753
		Porsche 911 Turbo Gemballa Avalanche: 3697
17	5.0	Autokraft AC Cobra Mk IV: 456
		Bertone Emotion Lotus: 489
		Chevrolet Corvette Callaway: 901
		Chevrolet Corvette Grand Sport Roadster: 776
		Eagle GTP: 1356
		Ferrari 288 GTO: 1416
		Ferrari 288 GTO: 1421
		Ferrari GTO: 1423
		Ford GT40: 1760
		IAD Venus: 2229
		Isdera Imperator: 2244
		Jaguar XJS Tullius: 2333
		Mercedes-Benz 300CE AMG Hammer: 2910
		Nissan 300ZX Turbo Millen Super GTZ: 3247
		Porsche 911 Turbo: 3659
		Porsche 911 Turbo: 3689
		Porsche 911 Turbo: 3708
		Porsche 911 Turbo Slant-Nose: 3699
		Porsche RSK: 3613
		TVR 420 SEAC: 4601

Total: 106

Acceleration - slowest to 60mph. Limit set at 30 seconds.

	sec	
1	62.2	Fiat 126: 1539
2	60.0	DKW Karavan: 1264
3	54.7	Citroen Ami 6 Break: 1035
4	54.4	Standard 8: 4207
5	54.0	Fiat 600: 1472
6	52.5	Morris Minor: 3163
7	52.0	DAF Daffodil: 1109
		Standard 8: 4200
8	49.7	Standard Flying 10: 4194
9	47.9	Ford 10: 1615
10	46.7	Armstrong Siddeley 17hp Touring Saloon: 214
		Morris Oxford Saloon: 3160
11	46.0	Datsun 1000: 1157
12	45.8	Morris Oxford Travellers' Car: 3162
13	45.7	Renault Dauphine: 3806
14	45.5	Renault 17.9hp Touring Saloon: 3800
15	45.4	Austin 20 Mayfair Limousine: 350
16	44.7	Lanchester 10: 2484
17	44.4	Mercedes-Benz Type 290 Cabriolet: 2780
18	44.0	Citroen Ami 6: 1030
		Saab 95: 4058
19	43.9	Renault Dauphine: 3810
20	43.2	Austin A40 Countryman: 387
21	42.8	Morris 10/6 Sports Tourer: 3148
22	42.1	Fiat 126 de Ville: 1564
23	41.5	DAF 600 de Luxe: 1108
24	41.4	Morris Oxford: 3158
25	41.3	Rover 14: 3978
26	40.7	Triumph Gloria 12: 4494
27	40.5	Renault 4 L Estate Car: 3819
28	40.2	Hillman Minx Saloon: 2035
29	40.0	Hillman Minx Sedan: 2037
30	39.9	Renault Dauphine Automatic: 3820
31	39.8	Daimler 15hp Saloon: 1134
32	39.5	Fiat Balilla Pillarless Saloon: 1460
33	39.4	Morris 21 Series II Saloon: 3150
34	39.3	Mercedes-Benz Type 230 Saloon: 2783
35	39.2	Volkswagen Sedan: 4741
36	38.9	Ford Prefect 1172cc: 1634
37	38.8	Humber 12 Six-light Saloon: 2184
38	38.7	Mercedes-Benz 190D: 2813
39	38.5	British Salmson 14hp Saloon: 645
40	38.4	Volkswagen Van: 4787
41	38.3	Berkeley Sports: 484
42	38.1	Renault 4 Estate Car: 3829
		Standard Super 10: 4210
43	38.0	Vauxhall 14 de Luxe: 4614
44	37.8	Hillman Aero Minx Cresta Saloon: 2030
45	37.7	Citroen Super Modern Fifteen Saloon: 1012
46	37.6	DKW Junior: 1267
47	37.5	Morris Cowley: 3165
48	37.2	Fiat 500 Nuova: 1483
		Volkswagen Sedan de Luxe: 4738
49	37.0	Sunbeam 20 Saloon: 4281
50	36.8	Lanchester 18: 2479
		Lanchester 18 Saloon: 2478
51	36.7	Singer SM1500 Saloon: 4164
52	36.6	Austin A40 Somerset: 366
		Fiat 1500 Pillarless Saloon: 1459
53	36.4	Alvis Firebird Saloon: 157
		Ford Anglia de Luxe Estate: 1666
		Ford Popular II: 1651
		Sunbeam-Talbot 80 Saloon: 4318
54	36.1	Citroen Sports Twelve Saloon: 1013
		Wolseley 4/50: 4986
55	36.0	Standard 12 Saloon: 4196
56	35.9	Daimler 24hp Limousine: 1137

		Hillman Hunter Husky III: 2055
		Reliant Rebel 700 Estate: 3786
57	35.7	Auto Union Universal: 451
		NSU Super Prinz: 3265
		Wolseley 14/56 Salon de Ville: 4982
58	35.6	Austin A40: 380
		Railton 10 Drop-head Coupe: 3760
59	35.4	Austin 14: 355
60	35.2	Sunbeam-Talbot 10 Sports Saloon: 4315
61	35.0	Volkswagen Sedan TC: 4742
62	34.9	Citroen Light Fifteen Roadster: 1014
		Standard Pennant: 4209
63	34.8	Singer Le Mans Special Speed Model: 4161
64	34.7	Hillman Minx Califonian Coupe: 2039
65	34.5	Peugeot 203: 3384
		Renault Dauphine: 3816
66	34.4	Humber Hawk: 2192
		Talbot 75 Drop-frame Sports Saloon: 4338
		Triumph 1800 Roadster: 4496
67	34.2	Opel Olympia Saloon: 3307
68	34.1	Morris Minor 1000 Traveller: 3170
69	33.9	Austin A40 Somerset Coupe: 370
70	33.8	Mini Traveller: 3045
		Standard 10: 4203
71	33.4	Ford 10 de Luxe Saloon: 1612
72	33.2	Armstrong Siddeley Six-light Saloon: 216
		Ford Anglia Saloon: 1630
		Lanchester Roadrider de Luxe Saloon: 2483
73	33.1	Lanchester Roadrider de Luxe Saloon: 2482
		Skoda Octavia: 4182
74	32.7	Citroen 2CV6: 1046
		Fiat 1100: 1465
75	32.6	Morris Minor 1000: 3172
		Wolseley 4/44: 4989
76	32.4	Ford Anglia de Luxe: 1644
77	32.3	Hillman Minx Convertible: 2038
		Mercedes-Benz 180D: 2797
		Riley Elf: 3944
78	32.2	Chevrolet Corvair Greenbrier: 747
		MG Midget P Type: 2973
		Triumph 14/60 Dolomite Saloon: 4491
79	32.1	Volkswagen De Luxe: 4751
80	32.0	Goliath 900: 2006
		Mercedes-Benz Type 320 Saloon: 2784
		Mini Automatic: 3058
81	31.9	Renault 4CV: 3803
82	31.8	Austin A55: 376
83	31.7	Armstrong Siddeley 25.3hp Town and Country Saloon: 215
		Citroen Ami 8 Club: 1037
		Land Rover Series III: 2557
84	31.6	Delage D6-11 Sports Saloon: 1249
		Ford Consul: 1624
		Renault 24hp Big Six Saloon: 3799
85	31.5	Renault Fregate Transfluide: 3808
		Vauxhall Wyvern: 4626
86	31.4	Hillman Hunter Husky: 2045
		Renault Dauphine Gordini: 3811
		Rolls-Royce 20/25 Touring Saloon: 3951
87	31.3	Morris Minor 1000: 3167
88	31.2	DAF 44: 1111
		Humber 16.9hp Saloon: 2189
		Morris Minor 1100: 3168
		Riley 1.5: 3932
89	31.1	Vauxhall Wyvern: 4629
90	31.0	Austin A35 4-door: 379
		British Salmson 12hp Four-seater Tourer: 643
		Daimler 18hp 2.5-litre: 1136
		Ford Prefect: 1633
91	30.8	Renault Dauphine: 3805
		Skoda 1000MB: 4184
92	30.6	Paramount Roadster: 3381
		Vauxhall Velox: 4623
93	30.4	Fiat Balilla Sports Two-seater: 1457
		MG 1.25-litre Saloon: 2981
		Triumph Herald Saloon: 4508
94	30.3	Volga M21K: 4737
95	30.0	Ford Anglia: 1637
		Hillman Hunter Husky Series II: 2052
		Volkswagen Karmann-Ghia: 4760

Total: 146

Time to 1/4 mile - fastest. Limit set at 14 seconds.

	sec	
1	10.6	Chevrolet Corvette Callaway Sledgehammer: 941
2	11.3	Lancia Montecarlo Group 5 Turbo: 2531
3	11.5	AC Cobra 427 Modified 1965: 27
		Datsun 280ZX Electramotive: 1230
4	11.6	Ferrari F40: 1446
		Porsche 911 Turbo Koenig RS: 3709
5	11.7	Porsche 911 Turbo Ruf Twin Turbo: 3710
6	11.8	Chevrolet Corvette Lingenfelter: 951
		Ferrari F40: 1450
		Ferrari GTO Norwood: 1451
		Vector W2: 4735
7	11.9	Chevrolet Camaro Z/28 Yenko/SC: 826
		Porsche 911 Ruf CTR: 3748
		Porsche 959: 3731
		Porsche 959 S: 3702
		Porsche 959 Sport: 3718
		Safir GT40: 4106
8	12.0	Ford Mustang TransAm: 1796
		Mercury Comet A/FX: 2933
		Porsche 911 Ruf: 3747
		Porsche 911 Ruf TR2: 3749
		Vector W8 Twin Turbo: 4736
9	12.1	Chevrolet Monza Mike Keyser: 874
		Ferrari Testa Rossa Norwood: 1444
		Ford Cobra II Kemp: 1841
		Rover Jet: 3984
10	12.2	Chevrolet Bel Air 409 SS/S: 755
		Chevrolet Camaro Gottlieb 1969: 926
		Scarab Mk II: 4109
11	12.3	Ferrari 308 Norwood Bonneville GTO: 1434
		Pontiac Firebird TransAm Silverbird: 3566
		Porsche 911 Turbo Gemballa Mirage: 3751
12	12.4	Porsche 911 Turbo Motorsport Design: 3724
		Porsche 959 Comfort: 3717
13	12.5	Chevrolet Corvette ZR-1 SS: 955
		Dodge Ramcharger 426 Super/Stock: 1287
		Dodge Viper: 1348
		Ford GT40: 1760
14	12.6	Jaguar XJS Lister Le Mans: 2366
15	12.7	De Tomaso Pantera Group 3: 1243
		Ferrari 308 Norwood: 1439
		Pontiac Firebird TDM Technologies: 3597
		Triumph TR8 Group 44: 4578
16	12.8	Chevrolet Camaro IROC-Z Chevrolet Engineering: 929
		Chevrolet Corvette Grand Sport Roadster: 776
17	12.9	Evans Series I: 1362
		Lamborghini Countach 25th Anniversary: 2473
		Porsche 911 Carrera Turbo: 3746
18	13.0	Chevrolet Corvette Callaway: 918
		Ferrari 250 Testa Rossa: 1378
		Lamborghini Countach: 2468
		Porsche 911 Turbo Gemballa Avalanche: 3697
		Porsche 911 Turbo Ruf 3.4: 3698
19	13.1	Chevrolet Camaro IROC-Z 8.3-litre: 914
		Porsche 911 3.3 Turbo: 3719
20	13.2	Chevrolet Corvette Bakeracing SCCA Escort: 917
		Mercedes-Benz 300CE AMG Hammer: 2910
		Porsche Carrera RSR: 3642
		Shelby Cobra USRRC: 4118
		Westfield SEight: 4973
21	13.3	Chevrolet Camaro IROC: 877
		Chevrolet Corvette Callaway: 948
		Chevrolet Corvette Callaway Twin Turbo: 950
		Chevrolet Corvette ZR-2: 956
		Ferrari Testa Rossa: 1437
		Ferrari Testa Rossa Gemballa: 1443
		Ferrari Testa Rossa Straman Spyder: 1438
		Ferrari TRC 2500 Testa Rossa: 1379
		Ford Mustang Cartech Turbo: 1928
		Ford Mustang Holdener: 1966
		Isdera Imperator: 2244
		Lamborghini Diablo: 2475
		Porsche 911 Turbo: 3750
		Renault Le Car Turbo: 3874
22	13.4	Chevrolet Corvette Callaway: 940
		Chevrolet Corvette Callaway: 931
		Chevrolet Corvette Convertible: 818
		Chevrolet Corvette ZR-1: 934
		Chevrolet Corvette ZR-1: 953
		Ford Mustang 5.0 Cartech Turbo: 1940
		Ford Mustang SVO J Bittle American: 1942
		Porsche 911 Carrera RS: 3753
		Porsche 911 Turbo: 3689
		Porsche 911 Turbo: 3708
		Porsche 911 Turbo: 3676
		Porsche 911 Turbo Slant-Nose: 3699
23	13.5	Audi Quattro Sport: 309
		Autokraft AC Cobra Mk IV: 456
		Chevrolet Corvette Guldstrand Grand Sport 80: 932
		Ferrari 512 BB: 1417
		Ferrari Testa Rossa: 1442
		Ford Mustang Kaufmann: 1932
		Lotus Esprit Turbo SE: 2637
		Nissan 300ZX Turbo Millen Super GTZ: 3247
		Opel Omega Lotus: 3352
		Pontiac Petty Grand National: 3571
		Porsche 911 Carrera 4: 3720
24	13.6	BMW 535i Alpina B10 Bi-Turbo: 619
		Caterham 7 HPC: 725
		Chevrolet Corvette Guldstrand Grand Sport 80: 920
		De Tomaso Pantera GT5-S: 1242
		Ferrari 512 BB: 1413
		Ferrari Testa Rossa: 1426
		Ford Mustang 428 Cobra Jet: 1761
		Jaguar XJS Tullius: 2333
		Lotus Esprit Turbo: 2636
		Mercedes-Benz 300E AMG Hammer: 2899
		Nissan Skyline GT-R: 3243

		Porsche 911 Carrera 2: 3732
		Porsche 911 Turbo: 3736
		Porsche 911 Turbo: 3723
25	13.7	Aston Martin V8 Vantage: 248
		Autokraft AC Cobra Mk IV: 455
		Chevrolet Corvette Callaway: 901
		Chevrolet Corvette Morrison/Baker Nelson Ledges: 921
		Datsun 280ZX Sharp: 1221
		Dodge Hemi Charger 500 Manual: 1309
		Ferrari 365 GTB Goldsmith: 1425
		Ferrari Daytona: 1397
		Jaguar D Type: 2285
		Lamborghini Countach 5000S: 2469
		Lotus Esprit Turbo: 2635
		Lotus Esprit Turbo SE: 2640
		Pontiac Catalina Super Stock: 3529
		Pontiac Firebird TransAm 20th Anniversary: 3589
		Porsche 911 Turbo: 3659
26	13.8	Dodge Super Bee Six-Pack: 1312
		Eagle GTP: 1356
		Ferrari 348tb: 1445
		Ferrari 365 GTB/4 Daytona: 1396
		Ferrari Daytona Cannonball: 1398
		Ferrari Daytona Sportwagen: 1395
		Porsche 928 S4 SE: 3727
		Shelby AC Ford Cobra: 4116
		Shelby Cobra 427: 4126
27	13.9	AC Cobra: 25
		Alfa Romeo 1750 GTV TransAm: 78
		Chevrolet Corvette Greenwood: 870
		Chevrolet Corvette L71: 833
		Dodge Hemi Charger 500 Automatic: 1308
		Ford Mustang 428 Mach I: 1775
		Ford Mustang JBA/Saleen: 1931
		Lamborghini Miura: 2451
		Lamborghini Miura S: 2456
		Lotus Elan Autocrosser: 2632
		Lynx D Type: 2642
		Mazda RX-7 Cartech: 2768
		Nissan 300ZX Motor Sports International SR-71: 3246
		Pontiac Firebird TransAm Turbo: 3590
		Porsche 911 Carrera Club Sport: 3705
		Porsche 911 Club Sport: 3722
		Porsche 928 Cabrio Strosek: 3725
		Porsche 928 S4: 3712
		Triumph TR8 Libra Rally: 4579
28	14.0	Acura NSX: 36
		Chevrolet Corvette: 766
		Chevrolet Corvette Convertible: 803
		De Tomaso Pantera GT5: 1241
		Devin Super Sports: 1257
		Ford Festiva Shogun: 1965
		Lamborghini Countach LP 500S: 2465
		Plymouth Cuda 440: 3505
		Plymouth GTX Hemi: 3502
		Porsche 911 Carrera: 3682
		Porsche Carrera RS 3-litre: 3647
		Porsche RSK: 3613
		Shelby AC Ford Cobra: 4117
		Shelby GT 350-S: 4121
		TVR V8 S: 4603

Total: 169

Time to 1/4 mile - slowest. Limit set at 24 seconds.

	sec	
1	37.6	Citroen 2CV Cabriolet: 1019
2	35.8	DKW Karavan: 1264
3	32.0	Ford Model T: 1608
4	31.9	Fiat 500: 1477
5	31.6	Citroen Bijou: 1028
6	29.8	BMW Isetta Motocoupe: 499
7	29.7	Fiat 600 Multipla: 1473
8	29.4	Citroen 2CV: 1022
9	29.3	Dodge Safari Super Sport: 1291
10	29.0	Fiat 500: 1482
11	28.5	DAF 600 de Luxe: 1108
12	28.3	Austin A30 Countryman: 375
13	27.7	BMW Isetta 300: 502
		Fiat 500 Giardiniera: 1492
14	27.5	Mercedes-Benz 170S: 2786
15	27.4	Subaru 360: 4243
16	27.3	Fiat 600: 1469
		Fiat Multipla: 1474
17	27.2	Frisky Coupe: 1993
18	27.1	Morris Minor: 3163
19	27.0	Fiat 600: 1486
		Volkswagen Micro Bus: 4745
20	26.9	Morris Minor Series II: 3161
21	26.8	Toyota Supra: 4429
22	26.7	Austin A30: 369
		Fiat 500F: 1504
		Morris Oxford Travellers' Car: 3162
23	26.6	Fiat 500D: 1498
		Renault 750: 3802
24	26.3	Ford Popular: 1631
		Hillman Husky: 2041
25	26.1	Fiat 600: 1472
26	26.0	Goggomobil TS400: 2004
		Humber Hawk: 2196
		Mercedes-Benz 180D: 2797
		Renault Dauphine Automatic: 3820
		Standard Super 10: 4210
27	25.9	Renault 750: 3804
		Standard 8: 4207
28	25.8	Berkeley Sports: 485
29	25.7	DAF Daffodil de Luxe Extra: 1110
		Morris Cowley: 3165
		Standard 8: 4200
30	25.6	Berkeley Sports: 484
		Fiat 126: 1539
		Ford Anglia de Luxe: 1644
		NSU Prinz II: 3257
		Volkswagen Station Wagon: 4756
31	25.4	Citroen Ami 6 Break: 1035
		DAF Daffodil: 1109
		Lanchester Roadrider de Luxe Saloon: 2483
		Land Rover Station Wagon: 2556
		Renault Dauphine: 3806
32	25.3	Austin A30: 368
		Vauxhall Wyvern: 4626
33	25.2	Citroen Ami 6: 1030
		Fiat 1400: 1463
		Renault Dauphine: 3810
		Renault Fregate Transfluide: 3808
		Volkswagen Sedan de Luxe: 4738
34	25.1	Mercedes-Benz 190D: 2813
35	25.0	Chevrolet Corvair Greenbrier: 747
		Datsun 1000: 1157
		Fiat 500 Nuova: 1483
		Hillman Minx Sedan: 2037
		Standard Pennant: 4209
		Toyota Camry V6 GXi: 4461
		Vauxhall Cavalier 1.6L: 4718
36	24.9	Fiat 600D: 1493
		NSU Super Prinz: 3265
		Standard Vanguard III: 4206
37	24.8	Fiat 126 de Ville: 1564
		Hillman Minx Califonian Coupe: 2039
		Hillman Minx Series V Automatic: 2057
		Saab 95: 4058
		Volkswagen Export Saloon: 4739
38	24.7	Austin Gipsy: 386
		Renault 4CV: 3803
39	24.6	Renault 4 Estate Car: 3829
		Renault Dauphine Gordini: 3811
		Volkswagen De Luxe Saloon: 4750
		Wolseley 4/44: 4989
40	24.5	Austin A40: 380
		Austin A40 Countryman: 387
		BMW 600: 501
		Citroen Ami 8 Club: 1037
		Daihatsu Compagno Berlina: 1115
		Fiat 1100: 1465
		Hillman Hunter Husky III: 2055
		Hillman Minx Series II: 2048
		International 900 Pickup: 2236
		MG 1.25-litre Saloon: 2981
		Rover 105R de Luxe: 3991
41	24.4	Austin A40: 364
		Ford Popular II: 1651
		Moskvich De Luxe: 3187
		Paramount Roadster: 3381
42	24.3	Austin A40 Somerset: 366
		Austin A40 Somerset Coupe: 370
		Ford Anglia Saloon: 1630
		Ford Prefect 1172cc: 1634
		Hillman Hunter Husky: 2045
		Mini Automatic: 3058
		Mini Traveller: 3045
		Renault 4 L Estate Car: 3819
		Triumph Herald Saloon: 4508
		Vauxhall Wyvern: 4629
43	24.2	Morris Minor 1000: 3167
		Morris Oxford Saloon: 3164
		Morris Oxford Traveller Series III: 3171
		Renault Dauphine: 3805
		Volkswagen De Luxe: 4740
		Volkswagen Sedan: 4741
44	24.1	DAF 44: 1111
		Hillman Minx Estate: 2047
		Lloyd LP 600: 2588
		Panhard PL17: 3369
		Singer SM1500 Saloon: 4166
		Standard 10: 4203
		Volga M21K: 4737
		Wolseley 15/50: 4991
45	24.0	Auto Union Universal: 451
		Datsun Bluebird Station Wagon: 1158
		DKW Junior: 1267
		Ford Anglia: 1654
		Ford Anglia: 1637
		Ford Anglia: 1632

		Morris Minor 1100: 3168
		Opel Rekord 2100D: 3342
		Renault Dauphine: 3816
		Rolls-Royce Phantom I Phaeton: 3946
		Skoda Octavia: 4182
		Wolseley 16/60 Automatic: 4996

Total: 133

Time to 1 kilometre - fastest. Limit set at 28 seconds.

	sec	
1	23.3	Lamborghini Countach: 2468
2	23.6	BMW M635 CSi: 607
3	23.8	Ferrari Testa Rossa: 1442
4	23.9	Audi Quattro Sport: 309
5	24.0	Porsche 911 Turbo: 3750
6	24.1	Porsche 911 3.3 Turbo: 3719
7	24.3	Ferrari Daytona: 1397
		Porsche 911 Carrera RS: 3753
8	24.5	Porsche 911 Turbo: 3676
9	24.6	Porsche 911 Carrera 2: 3732
10	24.9	Alfa Romeo Alfa 75 V6 3.0: 132
		Lamborghini Countach LP 500S: 2465
11	25.0	Ferrari 512 BB: 1413
		Lotus Esprit Turbo: 2635
12	25.1	Porsche 928 S4 SE: 3727
13	25.2	Aston Martin V8 Vantage: 248
		De Tomaso Pantera GT5-S: 1242
14	25.3	Ferrari 348tb: 1445
		Lotus Esprit Turbo SE: 2637
		Mercedes-Benz 500SL: 2913
		Porsche 911 Carrera Club Sport: 3705
		TVR V8 S: 4603
15	25.4	Aston Martin DB6: 242
		Porsche Carrera RS Touring: 3641
16	25.5	Honda NSX: 2156
17	25.6	Aston Martin DBS V8: 244
		Nissan 300ZX: 3240
		TVR 390 SE: 4599
18	25.7	Caterham 7 HPC: 725
19	25.8	Porsche 944 Turbo SE: 3716
20	26.0	De Tomaso Pantera: 1237
		Ferrari 365 GTC: 1390
		Porsche Turbo 3-litre: 3648
21	26.1	Lamborghini Miura P400S: 2455
		Porsche 944 S2: 3729
		Porsche Carrera 2 Cabriolet Tiptronic: 3744
22	26.2	AC 428 Fastback: 26
		Lotus Esprit Turbo HC: 2633
		Porsche 911 SC: 3670
		Porsche 928 S4 Automatic: 3692
		Volkswagen Polo G40: 4887
23	26.3	Mercedes-Benz 500E: 2919
		Monteverdi 375L: 3118
		TVR Convertible Turbo: 4593
24	26.4	Maserati Bora: 2660
		Porsche 911 Carrera SE: 3688
25	26.5	BMW M635 CSi: 572
26	26.6	Jaguar E Type V12: 2319
		Maserati Khamsin: 2666
27	26.7	Aston Martin V8 Automatic: 245
		Aston Martin Virage: 261
		Audi Coupe S2: 337
		Jensen SP: 2397
		Lotus Esprit Turbo: 2627
		Morgan Plus 8: 3134
28	26.8	Ford Sierra RS Cosworth: 1934
		Ford Sierra Sapphire Cosworth 4x4: 1958
		Lamborghini Jalpa 3500: 2470
		Lotus Plus 2S 130: 2610
29	26.9	Aston Martin V8: 252
		Audi Quattro 20v: 330
		Chevrolet Corvette: 897
		Ferrari 308 GTB: 1409
		Jaguar XJS HE: 2342
		Porsche 911 E 2.4-litre: 3635
30	27.0	Aston Martin V8: 249
		Mazda RX-7 Turbo II: 2759
		Porsche 944 Turbo: 3695
31	27.1	Iso Grifo GL 365: 2248
		Jaguar XJS Automatic: 2341
32	27.2	BMW 850i: 620
		Porsche 928 S Series II: 3684
		TVR 350i Series II: 4598
33	27.3	Audi 200 Quattro Turbo: 297
		Jaguar XJS: 2330
34	27.4	Ferrari Mondial 3.2QV: 1430
		Ford RS200: 1917
		Lotus Elan SE: 2639
		Panther Solo: 3380
		Porsche 911S 2.7-litre: 3645
		Renault GTA V6 Turbo: 3899
35	27.5	Audi Quattro: 323
		BMW 850i Manual: 625
		Ferrari 365 GT4 2+2: 1406
		Porsche 911 SC: 3654
		Porsche 924 Turbo: 3664
		Toyota MR2 GT: 4472
36	27.6	BMW M3 Evolution: 604
		Ferrari Dino 308 GT4 2+2: 1410
37	27.7	Audi Quattro: 289
		BMW 750i: 612
		Caterham 1700 Super Sprint: 723
		Chevrolet Corvette: 894
		Datsun 240Z: 1175
		Jensen Interceptor: 2393
		Lancia Thema 2.0ie 16v SE Turbo: 2553
		Pontiac GTO: 3544
		Saab 9000 2.3 Turbo TCS: 4101
38	27.8	Bentley Mulsanne Turbo: 480
		Bentley Mulsanne Turbo: 479
		Jaguar XJS Automatic: 2332
		Morgan Plus 8: 3137
		Nissan 200SX: 3254
		Porsche 944 S: 3694
39	27.9	Aston Martin V8: 246
		Lancia Delta HF Integrale: 2547
		Maserati Khamsin Automatic: 2662
		Morgan Plus 8: 3129
40	28.0	Nissan 200SX: 3232
		Toyota Supra 3.0i Turbo: 4465

Total: 110

Time to 1 kilometre - slowest. Limit set at 40 seconds.

	sec	
1	53.0	Fiat 500F: 1504
2	50.1	Fiat 126: 1539
3	49.5	Fiat 126 de Ville: 1564
4	48.8	Citroen Ami 6 Break: 1035
5	48.1	Renault 4 Estate Car: 3829
6	47.5	NSU Super Prinz: 3265
7	46.3	Citroen Ami 8 Club: 1037
8	46.2	Moskvich De Luxe: 3187
9	46.0	Citroen 2CV6: 1046
		Ford Granada 2.1D: 1859
		Reliant Rebel 700 Estate: 3786
10	45.9	Toyota Landcruiser: 4450
11	45.6	Renault 6: 3834
12	45.4	DAF 44: 1111
		Peugeot 205 CJ: 3451
13	45.3	Skoda S100L: 4185
14	45.1	Ford Cortina 1100: 1769
15	44.9	Opel Rekord 2100D: 3342
16	44.7	Honda N360: 2089
		Volkswagen Caravelle Syncro: 4855
17	44.5	Land Rover Series III: 2557
18	44.4	Daihatsu Domino: 1117
		Fiat 133: 1549
19	44.3	Mini 850: 3055
20	44.2	Land Rover SWB: 2558
21	44.0	Mini Super de Luxe Mk II: 3052
22	43.9	Singer Chamois: 4181
23	43.7	Citroen Visa Club: 1057
24	43.6	Mercedes-Benz G-Wagen 300 GD LWB: 2921
		Vauxhall Nova 1.2 Luxe: 4730
		Volkswagen 1500 Semi-automatic: 4775
25	43.5	Chrysler Sunbeam 1.0LS: 997
		Morris 1100 Mk II: 3178
		Simca 1000GLS: 4150
26	43.4	DAF 55 Estate: 1112
		Ford Cortina Super Estate: 1745
27	43.3	Hillman Hunter Husky: 2064
		Renault 1100 Automatic: 3827
		Suzuki Alto GLA: 4325
28	43.2	Isuzu Trooper 3-door TD: 2257
		Mercedes-Benz 300GD: 2867
29	43.1	Carbodies Fairway 2.7 Silver: 721
		DAF 66SL: 1113
30	43.0	DAF 55: 1107
		Volkswagen 1300: 4767
31	42.9	Ford Orion 1.4 GL: 1916
		Suzuki Alto FX Automatic: 4323
32	42.6	Bond Bug: 629
		Lada Niva 1600: 2426
		Triumph Herald 1200: 4531
33	42.4	Fiat Panda 750 L: 1593
		Ford Escort: 1756
		Peugeot 504 L Diesel: 3410
		Toyota Landcruiser II TD: 4458
		Wartburg Knight: 4970
34	42.3	Land Rover Ninety County Turbo Diesel: 2560
		Volkswagen 1600 TL Automatic: 4777
35	42.1	Vauxhall Viva de Luxe: 4664
36	42.0	Ford Cortina 1300 de Luxe: 1731
		Mini 850 Super de Luxe: 3060
		Simca 1000LS: 4158
		Volkswagen 1500: 4769
37	41.9	Yugo 45 GLS: 5003
38	41.8	Hillman Imp Californian: 2065

		Suzuki SC 100: 4321
39	41.7	Renault 6 1100: 3838
40	41.6	Ford Escort 1300: 1757
41	41.5	Simca 1301: 4152
42	41.4	Ford Escort 1300 Super Estate: 1784
43	41.3	Daihatsu Charade CX Diesel Turbo: 1123
		Daihatsu Charade Diesel: 1120
		Renault 5 TL: 3845
		Skoda Estelle 120 LSE: 4188
44	41.2	Austin Allegro 1300 Estate: 412
		Austin Mini Metro: 419
		Datsun 1000 de Luxe: 1168
		Hillman Estate: 2063
		Renault 5 Automatic: 3860
		Vauxhall Victor 101 de Luxe: 4654
45	41.0	Fiat 850 Coupe: 1505
		Fiat Uno Selecta: 1597
		Skoda S110LS: 4186
46	40.9	Ford Escort 1100L: 1823
		Reliant Kitten: 3789
		Suzuki SJ413V JX: 4327
47	40.8	Fiat 850 Special: 1513
		Ford Cortina Super Estate: 1733
		Hillman Avenger Super: 2071
		Mercedes-Benz 300D: 2819
		Volkswagen 1600 TL: 4771
48	40.7	Citroen CX 2200 Diesel: 1051
		Datsun New Sunny: 1216
		Ford Fiesta Popular: 1875
		Lada 1200: 2423
		Skoda 120L: 4187
49	40.6	DAF 66SL 1300: 1114
		Lada Niva Cossack Cabrio: 2428
		Peugeot 404 Automatic: 3400
50	40.5	Austin Metro Automatic: 418
		Ford Fiesta 1000: 1852
		Hillman Super Minx Estate: 2062
		Reliant Kitten DL Estate: 3790
		Renault 10: 3835
		Simca 1100GLS: 4153
		Singer Gazelle: 4180
		Vauxhall Viva de Luxe: 4652
51	40.4	Hillman Imp de Luxe: 2073
		Peugeot 404 L Estate: 3396
		Volkswagen Polo: 4800
52	40.3	Austin Allegro 1100: 413
		Austin Allegro 1500 Special Automatic: 408
		Datsun Cherry F11: 1204
		Ford Cortina 1300L: 1807
		Honda Civic Hondamatic: 2093
		Peugeot 104: 3414
		Simca 1501 Special Estate: 4155
53	40.2	Hillman Minx: 2066
		Triumph 1300: 4527
		Triumph Toledo: 4545
54	40.1	Daihatsu Sportrak EL: 1130
		Ford Cortina 1300 de Luxe: 1751
		Morris Marina 1.3 Super Coupe: 3184
		NSU Typ 110: 3263
		Renault 6 TL: 3846
		Vauxhall Viva SL90 Estate: 4659
		Wartburg Knight: 4971
55	40.0	Mitsubishi Shogun Turbo Diesel 5-door: 3094
		Peugeot 204 Coupe: 3397
		Renault 9 TC: 3878
		Vauxhall Victor: 4660
		Vauxhall Viva HC Estate: 4669
		Volkswagen Golf LD: 4814
		Volkswagen Super Beetle: 4783

Total: 133

Highest power. Limit set at 400bhp.

	bhp	kW	PS	
1	1600.0	1193.1	1622.2	Ferrari GTO Norwood: 1451
2	1000.0	745.7	1013.9	Koenig Competition Evolution: 2418
3	943.0	703.2	956.1	Ferrari Testa Rossa Norwood: 1444
4	880.0	656.2	892.2	Chevrolet Corvette Callaway Sledgehammer: 941
5	800.0	596.6	811.1	Koenig Competition: 2417
6	798.0	595.1	809.1	Chevrolet Camaro Gottlieb 1969: 926
7	700.0	522.0	709.7	Chevrolet Corvette Greenwood: 870
8	685.0	510.8	694.5	Pontiac Firebird TDM Technologies: 3597
9	671.0	500.4	680.3	Ferrari 308 Norwood Bonneville GTO: 1434
10	640.0	477.2	648.9	Peugeot 405 Turbo 16 Pike's Peak: 3460
11	625.0	466.1	633.7	Vector W8 Twin Turbo: 4736
12	600.0	447.4	608.3	Bugatti EB110: 652
				Porsche 959 S: 3702
				Safir GT40: 4106
				Vector W2: 4735
13	590.0	440.0	598.2	Pontiac Firebird TransAm Silverbird: 3566
				Pontiac Petty Grand National: 3571
14	588.0	438.5	596.2	Koenig C62: 2419
15	580.0	432.5	588.0	AC Cobra 427 Modified 1965: 27
				Datsun 280ZX Electramotive: 1230
				Porsche 911 Turbo RS Tuning: 3737
16	570.0	425.0	577.9	Ford Cobra II Kemp: 1841
17	560.0	417.6	567.8	Cizeta Moroder V16T: 1094
18	550.0	410.1	557.6	Chevrolet Corvette Grand Sport Roadster: 776
19	536.0	399.7	543.4	Chevrolet Monza Mike Keyser: 874
20	530.0	395.2	537.3	Chevrolet Camaro IROC-Z Chevrolet Engineering: 929
				Chevrolet Corvette Lingenfelter: 951
				Jaguar XJ220: 2359
21	520.0	387.8	527.2	Porsche 911 Turbo Koenig RS: 3709
22	510.0	380.3	517.1	Ford Mustang SVO J Bittle American: 1942
23	500.0	372.8	506.9	Sbarro Chrono 3.5: 4108
24	496.0	369.9	502.9	Chevrolet Camaro IROC-Z 8.3-litre: 914
				Jaguar XJS Lister Le Mans: 2366
25	492.0	366.9	498.8	Lamborghini Diablo: 2475
26	490.0	365.4	496.8	Porsche 911 Turbo Gemballa Mirage: 3751
27	488.0	363.9	494.8	Porsche 911 Turbo Motorsport Design: 3724
28	485.0	361.7	491.7	Lamborghini Diablo: 2474
				Porsche 935 Group 4 Holbert: 3657
29	478.0	356.4	484.6	Ferrari F40: 1450
				Ferrari F40: 1446
				Ferrari F40: 1435
30	475.0	354.2	481.6	Jaguar XJS Tullius: 2333
31	472.0	352.0	478.5	Jaguar XJ13: 2313
32	470.0	350.5	476.5	Ford Mustang 5.0 Cartech Turbo: 1940
33	469.0	349.7	475.5	Porsche 911 Ruf CTR: 3748
				Porsche 911 Turbo Ruf Twin Turbo: 3710
34	465.0	346.7	471.4	De Tomaso Pantera Group 3: 1243
35	460.0	343.0	466.4	Ford Mustang TransAm: 1796
				Nissan 300ZX Turbo Millen Super GTZ: 3247
36	455.0	339.3	461.3	Lamborghini Countach: 2468
				Lamborghini Countach 25th Anniversary: 2473
				Porsche 911 Ruf: 3747
				Porsche 911 Ruf TR2: 3749
37	450.0	335.6	456.2	Chevrolet Camaro IROC: 877
				Chevrolet Camaro Z/28 Yenko/SC: 826
				Ferrari 308 Norwood: 1439
				Ford Mustang Holdener: 1966
				Jaguar XJR15: 2369
				Porsche 959: 3731
				Porsche 959 Comfort: 3717
				Porsche 959 Sport: 3718
38	448.0	334.1	454.2	Zender Fact 4: 5008
39	435.0	324.4	441.0	Chevrolet Corvette 435hp: 829
				Chevrolet Corvette Convertible: 818
				Chevrolet Corvette L71: 833
				Chevrolet Corvette L71/89: 834
40	432.0	322.1	438.0	Aston Martin Zagato: 257
41	430.0	320.6	436.0	Chevrolet Corvette L88: 835
				Chevrolet Corvette L88: 820
				Lamborghini Miura S: 2456
				Porsche 928 S4 Koenig: 3726
				Toyota Supra Turbo TRD: 4467
42	428.0	319.2	433.9	Nissan 300ZX Motor Sports International SR-71: 3246
43	425.0	316.9	430.9	Chevrolet Camaro 427 Dana: 805
				Chevrolet Corvette: 795
				Chevrolet Corvette 396: 796
				Chevrolet Corvette Convertible: 803
				Chevrolet Corvette Sting Ray 396: 798
				Chevrolet Corvette ZR-1 SS: 955
				Dodge Charger: 1299
				Dodge Charger R/T: 1303
				Dodge Hemi Charger 500 Automatic: 1308
				Dodge Hemi Charger 500 Manual: 1309
				Dodge Ramcharger 426 Super/Stock: 1287
				Ford Galaxie 500 XL 427: 1714
				Mercury Comet A/FX: 2933
				Mercury Super Marauder S-55: 2932
				Plymouth GTX Hemi: 3502
				Plymouth Satellite Street Hemi: 3491
				Ruger Bentley Clone: 4052
				Shelby Cobra 427: 4126
44	420.0	313.2	425.8	Ferrari 400 Super America: 1389
				Lamborghini Countach 5000S: 2469
45	415.0	309.5	420.8	Ferrari 412 MI: 1377
				Lamborghini LM129: 2472
46	410.0	305.7	415.7	Chevrolet Corvette ZR-1 Geiger: 954
				Ford Fastback NASCAR: 1698
47	409.0	305.0	414.7	Chevrolet Bel Air 409 SS/S: 755
48	408.0	304.2	413.7	Mercedes-Benz 600SEL: 2923
49	405.0	302.0	410.6	Ferrari 365 GTB/4 Daytona: 1396
				Ford Galaxie 406: 1679
				Mercury S-55 406: 2930
				Pontiac Grand Prix 421: 3533
50	403.0	300.5	408.6	Chevrolet Corvette Callaway: 948
				Chevrolet Corvette Callaway Speedster: 949

				Chevrolet Corvette Callaway Twin Turbo: 950
51	402.0	299.8	407.6	Ferrari 365 GTB/4 Competitione: 1403
52	400.0	298.3	405.5	Bizzarrini GT America: 496
				Chevrolet Corvette L68: 832
				Dodge Viper: 1348
				Ferrari 288 GTO: 1421
				Ferrari 365 GTB Goldsmith: 1425
				Ferrari GTO: 1423
				Lamborghini Miura: 2452
				Lancia Montecarlo Group 5 Turbo: 2531
				Oldsmobile Toronado: 3292

Total: 116

Lowest power. Limit set at 30bhp.

	bhp	Kw	PS	
1	8.0	6.0	8.2	Enfield 8000 Electric: 1359
2	9.0	6.7	9.1	Citroen 2CV Cabriolet: 1019
3	10.5	7.8	10.6	Austin 7 Saloon: 341
				Austin 7 Sports Two-seater: 342
				Austin 7 Sunshine Saloon: 343
				Austin 7 Tourer: 340
4	12.0	8.9	12.2	Austin 7 Ruby Saloon: 349
				Austin 7 Ruby Saloon: 351
				BMW Isetta Motocoupe: 499
				Citroen 2CV: 1022
				Citroen Bijou: 1028
5	13.0	9.7	13.2	BMW Isetta 300: 502
				Fiat 500: 1477
6	16.0	11.9	16.2	Frisky Coupe: 1993
7	16.5	12.3	16.7	Fiat 500: 1482
				Fiat 500C Convertible: 1464
				Fiat 500C Convertible (Topolino): 1462
8	17.0	12.7	17.2	Jowett 8hp: 2408
9	17.5	13.0	17.7	Fiat 500 Giardiniera: 1492
				Fiat 500D: 1498
10	18.0	13.4	18.2	Fiat 500F: 1504
11	18.2	13.6	18.4	Berkeley Sports: 485
				Berkeley Sports: 484
12	19.0	14.2	19.3	Lloyd LP 600: 2588
				Renault 4CV: 3801
13	19.5	14.5	19.8	BMW 600: 501
14	20.0	14.9	20.3	Ford Model T: 1608
				Goggomobil TS400: 2004
				MG Midget: 2968
15	21.0	15.7	21.3	Renault 750: 3802
				Renault 750: 3804
				Triumph Super 7 Saloon: 4487
16	21.5	16.0	21.8	Fiat 500 Nuova: 1483
				Fiat 600: 1472
				Fiat 600: 1469
				Fiat 600 Multipla: 1473
				Fiat Multipla: 1474
17	22.0	16.4	22.3	Citroen Ami 6: 1030
				DAF 600 de Luxe: 1108
				Ford 8 Tudor Saloon: 1611
18	23.0	17.1	23.3	Austin 8 Saloon: 358
				Fiat 126: 1539
19	23.4	17.4	23.7	Ford 8: 1618
				Ford Anglia 8 Saloon: 1623
20	24.0	17.9	24.3	Austin 12/6: 345
				Austin 8 Saloon: 356
				Fiat 126 de Ville: 1564
				Messerschmitt (FMR) Tg 500: 2966
				NSU Prinz II: 3257
21	24.5	18.3	24.8	Volkswagen Export Saloon: 4739
22	25.0	18.6	25.3	Austin Big 7: 354
				Subaru 360: 4243
				Subaru Hapi Van 360: 4245
				Volkswagen Sedan de Luxe: 4738
23	26.0	19.4	26.4	Citroen Ami 6 Break: 1035
				DAF Daffodil de Luxe Extra: 1110
				Standard 8: 4200
24	26.5	19.8	26.9	Renault Dauphine: 3806
25	27.0	20.1	27.4	Daihatsu Domino: 1117
				Fiat Abarth 595: 1506
				Honda N360: 2089
				Morris Cowley Saloon: 3144
26	27.5	20.5	27.9	Morris Minor Tourer: 3159
27	28.0	20.9	28.4	Austin A30: 369
				Austin A30 Countryman: 375
				Renault 4 L Estate Car: 3819
				Renault 4CV: 3803
				Standard 8: 4197
28	28.5	21.2	28.9	Citroen 2CV6: 1046
				Fiat 600: 1486
29	29.0	21.6	29.4	Citroen 2CV6 Charleston: 1065
				Fiat 600D: 1493
				Riley 9 Monaco: 3928
30	29.5	22.0	29.9	Morris Minor: 3157
31	29.6	22.1	30.0	Morris 8 Series E Tourer: 3155
32	30.0	22.4	30.4	Austin A30: 368
				Berkeley Sports 4: 486

			DAF Daffodil: 1109
			Ford 10: 1615
			Ford Prefect: 1616
			Morris Minor: 3163
			Morris Minor Series II: 3161
			NSU Prinz 4: 3259
			NSU Sport-Prinz: 3258
			NSU Super Prinz: 3265
			Renault 4 Estate Car: 3829
			Volkswagen De Luxe: 4740
			Volkswagen Sedan: 4741
			Volkswagen Sedan TC: 4742

Total: 89

Highest torque. Limit set at 450lbft.

	lbft	Nm	
1	900.0	1219.5	Ferrari GTO Norwood: 1451
2	785.0	1063.7	Pontiac Firebird TDM Technologies: 3597
3	772.0	1046.1	Chevrolet Corvette Callaway Sledgehammer: 941
4	738.0	1000.0	Koenig Competition Evolution: 2418
5	672.0	910.6	Chevrolet Camaro IROC-Z Chevrolet Engineering: 929
6	664.0	899.7	Koenig Competition: 2417
7	638.0	864.5	Chevrolet Camaro Gottlieb 1969: 926
8	630.0	853.7	Vector W8 Twin Turbo: 4736
9	620.0	840.1	Chevrolet Corvette Greenwood: 870
10	603.0	817.1	Safir GT40: 4106
11	580.0	785.9	Vector W2: 4735
12	575.0	779.1	Chevrolet Corvette Callaway: 948
			Chevrolet Corvette Callaway Speedster: 949
			Chevrolet Corvette Callaway Twin Turbo: 950
13	570.0	772.4	Chevrolet Corvette Lingenfelter: 951
14	562.0	761.5	Chevrolet Corvette Callaway: 931
			Chevrolet Corvette Callaway: 940
15	550.0	745.3	Chevrolet Camaro IROC-Z 8.3-litre: 914
			Ford Mustang Cartech Turbo: 1928
16	545.0	738.5	Chevrolet Corvette Callaway: 918
17	542.0	734.4	Peugeot 405 Turbo 16 Pike's Peak: 3460
18	541.0	733.1	AC Cobra 427 Modified 1965: 27
19	533.0	722.2	Koenig C62: 2419
20	530.0	718.2	Ford Cobra II Kemp: 1841
21	525.0	711.4	Cadillac Coupe de Ville: 709
22	520.0	704.6	Datsun 280ZX Electramotive: 1230
23	510.0	691.1	Buick GS455 Stage 1: 687
			Oldsmobile 88 Delta Royale: 3294
24	502.0	680.2	Ferrari 308 Norwood Bonneville GTO: 1434
25	500.0	677.5	Chevrolet Corvette 454: 844
			Chevrolet Impala: 846
			Chevrolet Monte Carlo: 847
			Jaguar XJS Lister Le Mans: 2366
			Oldsmobile 4-4-2 W30: 3296
			Oldsmobile 442 Hurst: 3293
			Oldsmobile Toronado: 3292
			Pontiac GTO 455: 3561
26	495.0	670.7	Chrysler 300-G: 975
27	490.0	664.0	Dodge Challenger R/T: 1314
			Dodge Charger: 1299
			Dodge Charger R/T: 1303
			Dodge Hemi Charger 500 Automatic: 1308
			Dodge Hemi Charger 500 Manual: 1309
			Ford Thunderbird: 1653
			Jensen SP: 2397
			Lincoln Continental Mk III: 2579
			Oldsmobile Delmont: 3291
			Plymouth GTX Hemi: 3502
			Plymouth Satellite Street Hemi: 3491
			Porsche 911 Turbo Koenig RS: 3709
			Porsche 911 Turbo Motorsport Design: 3724
			Ruger Bentley Clone: 4052
28	485.0	657.2	Bentley Turbo R: 483
			Chrysler 300-J: 981
29	483.0	654.5	Porsche 911 Ruf TR2: 3749
30	482.0	653.1	Porsche 911 Ruf: 3747
31	480.0	650.4	Cadillac Calais: 707
			Cadillac Coupe de Ville: 705
			Cadillac Eldorado: 708
			Cadillac Sedan de Ville: 706
			Chrysler 300: 984
			Chrysler 300: 988
			Chrysler 300-H: 989
			Chrysler Imperial Crown: 987
			Dodge Charger R/T: 1315
			Dodge Coronet R/T: 1304
			Dodge Coronet R/T: 1300
			Dodge Monaco: 1310
			Dodge Ramcharger 426 Super/Stock: 1287
			Ford Galaxie 500 XL 427: 1714
			Ford LTD: 1773
			Ford Thunderbird: 1779
			Mercury Comet A/FX: 2933
			Mercury Marquis Brougham: 2948
			Mercury Marquis Marauder X-100: 2949
			Mercury Super Marauder S-55: 2932

			Monteverdi 375L: 3118
			Plymouth Cuda 440: 3505
			Plymouth GTX: 3497
			Plymouth GTX: 3501
			Shelby Cobra 427: 4126
32	476.0	645.0	Ford Fastback NASCAR: 1698
33	475.0	643.6	Buick Riviera: 683
			Buick Riviera: 682
			Buick Wildcat: 680
			Buick Wildcat: 686
			Oldsmobile Toronado: 3286
			Oldsmobile Toronado: 3288
34	472.0	639.6	Pontiac Grand Prix: 3556
35	470.0	636.9	Chrysler 300: 979
			Chrysler Imperial: 977
			Chrysler Imperial Le Baron: 982
			Dodge Coronet 426-S: 1294
			Dodge Polara 500: 1290
			Porsche 928 S4 Koenig: 3726
36	465.0	630.1	Buick Riviera: 674
			Buick Riviera: 668
			Buick Riviera Gran Sport: 677
			Buick Wildcat: 672
			Chevrolet Corvette Callaway: 901
			Lincoln Continental: 2580
			Porsche 911 Turbo RS Tuning: 3737
37	462.0	626.0	AC 428 Fastback: 26
			Ford Galaxie 7-litre: 1737
			Ford Thunderbird: 1749
			Ford Thunderbird Town Landau: 1739
			Ford XL Fastback 428: 1764
38	460.0	623.3	Chevrolet Camaro 427 Dana: 805
			Chevrolet Camaro Z/28 Yenko/SC: 826
			Chevrolet Caprice: 827
			Chevrolet Corvette 435hp: 829
			Chevrolet Corvette Convertible: 818
			Chevrolet Corvette Convertible: 803
			Chevrolet Corvette L36: 830
			Chevrolet Corvette L68: 832
			Chevrolet Corvette L71: 833
			Chevrolet Corvette L71/89: 834
			Chevrolet Corvette L88: 820
			Chevrolet Impala SS427: 809
			Chevrolet Kingswood Estate Wagon: 839
			Facel Vega HK-500: 1366
			Mercury Cougar XR-7: 2946
			Pontiac Firebird TransAm Silverbird: 3566
			Pontiac Royal Bobcat: 3535
39	459.0	622.0	Lincoln Continental: 2581
			Pontiac Catalina 2+2: 3542
40	457.0	619.2	Porsche 911 Turbo Ruf Twin Turbo: 3710
41	455.0	616.5	Dodge Dart 413: 1280
42	450.0	609.8	Chevrolet Corvette L88: 835
			Chrysler 300-H: 980
			Dodge Viper: 1348
			Oldsmobile Dynamic Delta 88 Holiday: 3285

Total: 132

Lowest torque. Limit set at 45lbft.

	lbft	Nm	
1	14.0	19.0	BMW Isetta 300: 502
2	16.6	22.5	Citroen 2CV Cabriolet: 1019
3	17.4	23.6	Citroen Bijou: 1028
4	18.0	24.4	Frisky Coupe: 1993
5	20.2	27.4	Fiat 500: 1477
6	20.3	27.5	Fiat 500: 1482
7	21.6	29.3	Berkeley Sports: 485
			Berkeley Sports: 484
8	21.7	29.4	Fiat 500 Giardiniera: 1492
			Fiat 500C Convertible: 1464
			Fiat 500C Convertible (Topolino): 1462
9	22.0	29.8	Fiat 500 Nuova: 1483
10	22.4	30.4	Fiat 500D: 1498
			Fiat 500F: 1504
11	23.9	32.4	Goggomobil TS400: 2004
12	24.0	32.5	Honda N360: 2089
13	24.6	33.3	Messerschmitt (FMR) Tg 500: 2966
14	25.0	33.9	BMW Isetta Motocoupe: 499
			Subaru 360: 4243
			Subaru Hapi Van 360: 4245
15	27.0	36.6	Suzuki Brute: 4320
16	28.0	37.9	Daihatsu Domino: 1117
17	28.2	38.2	Lloyd LP 600: 2588
18	28.9	39.2	BMW 600: 501
			Fiat 600: 1472
			Fiat 600: 1486
			Fiat 600: 1469
			Fiat 600 Multipla: 1473
			Fiat Multipla: 1474
19	29.0	39.3	Citroen 2CV6 Charleston: 1065
			Fiat 126: 1539
			Renault 750: 3802
20	29.6	40.1	Citroen Ami 6: 1030
21	30.0	40.7	Citroen Ami 6 Break: 1035
22	30.4	41.2	NSU Prinz 34hp: 3256
23	30.5	41.3	Citroen 2CV6: 1046
			Fiat 126 de Ville: 1564
24	31.0	42.0	Citroen Ami 8 Club: 1037
			NSU Sport-Prinz: 3258
25	32.0	43.4	Honda 600: 2090
			Honda 600 Coupe: 2091
26	32.5	44.0	NSU Prinz 4: 3259
			NSU Super Prinz: 3265
27	32.6	44.2	DAF 600 de Luxe: 1108
28	33.0	44.7	Fiat Abarth 595: 1506
29	33.2	45.0	Renault 750: 3804
30	33.5	45.4	NSU Prinz II: 3257
31	35.4	48.0	Berkeley Sports 4: 486
32	36.0	48.8	Abarth Zagato 750 GT: 1
33	36.4	49.3	Ford Anglia 8 Saloon: 1623
34	37.0	50.1	BMW 700 LS: 507
35	37.2	50.4	BMW 700: 503
36	37.5	50.8	Honda S600: 2087
37	38.0	51.5	BMW 700 Coupe: 504
			Bond Bug: 629
			Citroen Visa Club: 1057
			Reliant Rebel 700 Estate: 3786
38	39.0	52.8	Morris Minor Tourer: 3159
39	39.2	53.1	Standard 8: 4200
40	39.8	53.9	Fiat 750 Abarth: 1478
41	40.0	54.2	Austin A30: 368
			Austin A30: 369
			Austin A30 Countryman: 375
			Fiat 600D: 1493
			Fiat Abarth 750GT Zagato: 1479
			Fiat Abarth Zagato: 1480
			Morris Minor: 3163
			Morris Minor Series II: 3161
42	40.4	54.7	Hyundai Pony 1400 TLS: 2219
43	40.5	54.9	Fiat 133: 1549
			Fiat 850 Super: 1499
44	42.0	56.9	DAF Daffodil: 1109
			DAF Daffodil de Luxe Extra: 1110
			Fiat Panda 750 L: 1593
			Renault 6: 3834
45	42.5	57.6	Berkeley B95: 487
			Standard 8: 4207
46	43.0	58.3	Suzuki Alto GLA: 4325
47	43.4	58.8	Suzuki Alto FX: 4322
			Suzuki Alto FX Automatic: 4323
48	44.0	59.6	Austin Seven 850: 391
			Fiat 850 Coupe: 1505
			Fiat 850 Idromatic: 1512
			Fiat 850 Special: 1513
			Mini 850: 3055
			Mini 850 Super de Luxe: 3060
			Mini Automatic: 3058
			Mini Minor: 3044
			Mini Minor de Luxe: 3043
			Mini Super de Luxe: 3048
			Mini Traveller: 3045
			Riley Elf: 3944
			Siata Spring 850: 4128
49	45.0	61.0	Daihatsu Charade Diesel: 1120
			Renault 5 TL: 3845
			Volkswagen Polo: 4800

Total: 96

Highest rpm at peak power. Limit set at 7000rpm.

	rpm	
1	45000	Rover Jet: 3984
2	39000	Rover Rover-BRM Turbine: 4006
3	10000	Ferrari Testa Rossa Norwood: 1444
4	9200	Sbarro Chrono 3.5: 4108
5	9000	Bugatti EB110: 652
		Datsun B210 Electramotive: 1198
		Mazda RX-7 Racer: 2715
6	8800	Alfa Romeo 33 2.0 Stradale: 66
		Lancia Montecarlo Group 5 Turbo: 2531
7	8500	Honda S600: 2087
		Volkswagen Scirocco GT-3 Davey: 4830
8	8300	Ferrari 365 GTB/4 Competitione: 1403
9	8250	Datsun 240Z Sharp: 1190
10	8000	Cizeta Moroder V16T: 1094
		Ferrari 275 GTS/4 NART: 1392
		Honda N360: 2089
		Honda S800: 2088
		Lamborghini Countach: 2461
		Lotus Elan Autocrosser: 2632
		Porsche Carrera RSR: 3642
		Porsche RSK: 3613
		Renault 5 Racer: 3865
		Triumph TR8 Group 44: 4578
11	7900	Ford Mustang SVO J Bittle American: 1942
12	7850	Ferrari 308 Norwood Bonneville GTO: 1434
13	7800	Datsun 510 TransAm: 1180

		Lamborghini Bravo: 2458
14	7700	Ferrari 308 GT4 Dino: 1402
		Ferrari 308 GTB: 1409
		Ferrari Dino 308 GT4 2+2: 1410
		Lamborghini Miura P400S: 2455
15	7600	Ferrari 246 GTS Dino: 1401
		Ferrari 412 MI: 1377
		Fiat Abarth OT 1600: 1502
		Honda Civic 1.6i VT: 2154
		Honda CRX 1.6i VT: 2152
		Jaguar XJS Tullius: 2333
16	7500	Alfa Romeo 1750 GTV TransAm: 78
		Datsun 280ZX Electramotive: 1220
		Datsun 280ZX Electramotive: 1230
		Datsun 280ZX Sharp: 1221
		Ferrari 250 GT Berlinetta Lusso: 1388
		Ferrari 250 GTO: 1386
		Ferrari 365 GTB Goldsmith: 1425
		Ferrari 365 GTB/4 Daytona: 1404
		Ferrari 365 GTB/4 Daytona: 1396
		Ferrari 375 Indianapolis: 1373
		Ferrari 400 Super America: 1389
		Ferrari Daytona: 1397
		Ferrari Daytona Cannonball: 1398
		Ferrari Daytona Sportwagen: 1395
		Fiat Brava Abarth Rally: 1571
		Ford Mustang TransAm: 1796
		Lamborghini Countach S: 2466
		Lamborghini Countach S: 2464
		Lamborghini Jarama 400GT: 2457
		Lamborghini Jarama 400GT: 2459
		Lamborghini Silhouette 3000: 2462
		Lamborghini Urraco: 2463
		Lamborghini Urraco S: 2460
		Mercedes-Benz 300SLR: 2795
		Pontiac Firebird TransAm Silverbird: 3566
		Pontiac Petty Grand National: 3571
17	7350	Lamborghini Miura S: 2456
18	7250	Jaguar XJ13: 2313
19	7200	Chevrolet Monza Mike Keyser: 874
		Ferrari 212 Touring: 1372
		Ferrari 250 Mille Miglia: 1376
		Ferrari 250 Testa Rossa: 1382
		Ferrari 250 Testa Rossa: 1378
		Ferrari 348tb: 1445
		Ferrari 512 BB: 1407
		Ferrari GTO Norwood: 1451
		Ferrari Mondial t: 1452
		Ferrari Mondial t: 1441
		Mercedes-Benz 190E 2.5-16 Evolution II: 2908
		Mercedes-Benz 190E 2.5-16 Evolution II: 2916
		Porsche 904 Carrera GTS: 3621
20	7100	Acura NSX: 36
		BMW 2002 TransAm: 528
		Honda NSX: 2156
21	7000	Bizzarrini P538: 497
		BMW M3 Hor Technologie: 605
		BMW M3 Sport Evolution: 621
		Chevrolet Camaro Gottlieb 1969: 926
		Ferrari 166 Mille Miglia Barchetta: 1371
		Ferrari 246 GT Dino: 1399
		Ferrari 250 GT 2+2: 1385
		Ferrari 250 GT Berlinetta SWB: 1383
		Ferrari 250 GT Cabriolet: 1380
		Ferrari 250 GT Coupe: 1381
		Ferrari 250 GT Coupe: 1384
		Ferrari 275 GTS: 1391
		Ferrari 288 GTO: 1421
		Ferrari 288 GTO: 1416
		Ferrari 3.2 Mondial: 1427
		Ferrari 328 GTB: 1428
		Ferrari 328 GTS: 1431
		Ferrari 330 GTS: 1393
		Ferrari 348tb: 1449
		Ferrari 4.9: 1387
		Ferrari F40: 1435
		Ferrari F40: 1446
		Ferrari F40: 1450
		Ferrari GTO: 1423
		Ferrari Mondial: 1447
		Ferrari Mondial 3.2: 1429
		Ferrari Mondial 3.2 Cabriolet: 1440
		Ferrari Mondial 3.2QV: 1430
		Ferrari Mondial Cabriolet: 1436
		Ferrari Mondial Cabriolet 3.2: 1433
		Ferrari Mondial t Cabriolet: 1453
		Fiat Abarth Twin Cam: 1488
		Ford Cobra II Kemp: 1841
		Geo Storm GSi: 1994
		Jaguar XJ220: 2359
		Jensen Healey Huffaker: 2399
		Lamborghini Countach: 2468
		Lamborghini Countach 25th Anniversary: 2473
		Lamborghini Countach 5000S: 2469
		Lamborghini Countach LP 500S: 2465
		Lamborghini Diablo: 2474
		Lamborghini Espada: 2453
		Lamborghini Jalpa: 2471
		Lamborghini Jalpa: 2467
		Lamborghini Jalpa 3500: 2470
		Lamborghini Miura: 2452
		Lamborghini Miura: 2451
		Lancia Rally: 2537
		Mazda 110S Coupe: 2685
		Mazda Rotary: 2689
		Mazda RX-2: 2690
		Mazda RX-2: 2691
		Mazda RX-4: 2694
		Mazda RX-7 Convertible: 2763
		Mazda RX-7 GTUs: 2758
		Peugeot 405 Turbo 16 Pike's Peak: 3460
		Porsche 935 Group 4 Holbert: 3657
		Renault Le Car Turbo: 3874
		Triumph TR8 Libra Rally: 4579

Total: 140

Lowest rpm at peak power. Limit set at 3700rpm.

	rpm	
1	1600	Ford Model T: 1608
2	2200	Ford 24 Saloon: 1609
		Ford Model A: 1613
3	2250	Fiat Panda 750 L: 1593
4	2400	Austin 12/6: 345
		Austin 7 Saloon: 341
		Austin 7 Sports Two-seater: 342
		Austin 7 Sunshine Saloon: 343
		Austin 7 Tourer: 340
5	2750	Rolls-Royce Phantom I Phaeton: 3946
6	3000	Ford Mustang 271hp: 1707
		Rolls-Royce 20 Saloon: 3947
		Rolls-Royce Phantom II: 3949
		Wills Sainte Claire Six: 4974
7	3200	AMC Eagle: 206
		Armstrong Siddeley 30 Special Sports Saloon: 213
		Cadillac Seville Diesel: 712
		Chrysler Custom Imperial Le Baron: 964
		Du Pont Town Car: 1351
		Invicta 4.5-litre: 2242
		Invicta 4.5-litre: 2241
		Kissel 8-65 Gold Bug: 2416
		Mercedes-Benz 36/220-S: 2774
		Mercedes-Benz SSKL: 2776
		Oldsmobile Cutlass Diesel: 3300
		Packard Super 8 Phaeton: 3356
		Packard Twelve Victoria: 3359
8	3300	Armstrong Siddeley Six-light Saloon: 216
		Auburn 8-120 Speedster: 262
		Humber Snipe Sports Saloon: 2190
		Vauxhall Cadet Saloon: 4610
		Vauxhall Velox: 4621
		Volkswagen Export Saloon: 4739
		Volkswagen Sedan de Luxe: 4738
9	3400	Cadillac V16 "Madame X": 699
		Cadillac V16 Fleetwood Roadster: 700
		Ford Mustang 4.2: 1880
		Ford V8: 1610
		Ford V8 30: 1617
		Humber Hawk: 2196
		Humber Imperial: 2193
		Humber Imperial Saloon: 2194
		Humber Pullman Limousine: 2197
		Humber Snipe Drop-head Foursome: 2188
		Humber Super Snipe: 2198
		Humber Super Snipe: 2199
		Humber Super Snipe: 2195
		Lincoln Continental Mk VII: 2583
		Marmon 16: 2651
		Morris Cowley Saloon: 3144
		Packard 7-34 Phaeton: 3355
		Volkswagen De Luxe: 4740
		Volkswagen De Luxe Saloon: 4750
		Volkswagen Sedan: 4741
		Volkswagen Sedan TC: 4742
10	3500	AC Ace Fixed-head Coupe: 3
		AMC Pacer: 202
		AMC Pacer: 203
		Bentley 4.5-litre: 461
		Bentley 4.5-litre Supercharged: 462
		Bentley 8-litre Saloon: 463
		Bentley Speed Six Weymann: 464
		Citroen 2CV: 1022
		Citroen 2CV Cabriolet: 1019
		Cord 812: 1100
		Daihatsu Fourtrak Estate DT EL: 1125
		Ford Customline 6: 1626
		Ford V8 Pilot: 1621
		Jowett 8hp: 2408
		Land Rover County: 2559
		Mercedes-Benz 180D: 2797
		Pontiac Firebird TransAm: 3563
		Rolls-Royce Phantom II: 3950

		Toyota Landcruiser: 4450
		Vauxhall Velox: 4623
		Vauxhall Velox: 4624
		Volkswagen Polo C: 4833
11	3600	Alvis 4.3-litre: 162
		AMC Pacer Wagon: 205
		Bugatti 49: 649
		Cadillac Seville Diesel: 711
		Chevrolet Monza 2+2 V8: 864
		Chevrolet Monza 2+2 V8: 873
		Chrysler Turbine: 985
		Cord L-29: 1097
		Daimler Straight Eight: 1139
		Daimler Twenty-Seven Limousine: 1138
		Dodge Safari Super Sport: 1291
		Du Pont Speedster: 1350
		Ford Mustang II: 1847
		Ford Mustang II V8: 1848
		Frazer Saloon: 1978
		Humber Super Snipe Mk IV: 2200
		International Scout: 2240
		Jeep CJ6: 2381
		Jensen Interceptor III: 2400
		Lagonda Le Mans: 2437
		Lanchester 18: 2479
		Mercury Coupe: 2924
		Mercury Monarch: 2953
		Muntz Jet: 3189
		Plymouth Cambridge: 3471
		Pontiac Grand Am: 3562
		Stutz Roadster: 4239
		Sunbeam Weymann Saloon: 4280
		Toyota Landcruiser VX: 4478
		Vauxhall 12 Saloon: 4618
		Vauxhall 12 Saloon: 4619
		Vauxhall 14: 4620
		Vauxhall Wyvern: 4622
		Volkswagen 1200 de Luxe: 4758
		Wolseley Drop-head Coupe: 4983
		Wolseley Super 6: 4984
12	3700	Austin A135 Princess: 361
		Austin Princess: 367
		Citroen Six Saloon: 1016
		Devin VW: 1258
		Fiat 1900: 1466
		Jensen Interceptor Cabriolet: 2386
		Volkswagen Alken-VW: 4749
		Volkswagen Karmann-Ghia: 4744
		Volkswagen Micro Bus: 4745
		Volkswagen Sedan: 4746
		Volkswagen Sedan: 4752
		Volkswagen Sedan Supercharged: 4743

Total: 125

Highest power-to-weight ratio. Limit set at 300bhp.

	bhp/ ton	bhp/ tonne	
1	1257.5	1236.6	Ferrari GTO Norwood: 1451
2	780.5	767.5	Sbarro Chrono 3.5: 4108
3	764.6	751.8	Peugeot 405 Turbo 16 Pike's Peak: 3460
4	640.0	629.3	Koenig Competition Evolution: 2418
5	595.8	585.9	Chevrolet Camaro Gottlieb 1969: 926
6	589.4	579.6	Ferrari 308 Norwood Bonneville GTO: 1434
7	570.9	561.4	Ferrari Testa Rossa Norwood: 1444
8	564.7	555.3	Safir GT40: 4106
9	560.0	550.7	Chevrolet Corvette Grand Sport Roadster: 776
10	543.5	534.4	Chevrolet Corvette Greenwood: 870
11	543.1	534.1	Koenig C62: 2419
12	537.1	528.1	Chevrolet Corvette Callaway Sledgehammer: 941
13	520.9	512.2	Lancia Montecarlo Group 5 Turbo: 2531
14	513.5	504.9	AC Cobra 427 Modified 1965: 27
15	512.0	503.5	Koenig Competition: 2417
16	510.8	502.2	Ferrari 412 MI: 1377
17	507.9	499.4	Ferrari 375 Indianapolis: 1373
18	499.7	491.4	Datsun 280ZX Electramotive: 1230
19	483.4	475.4	Vector W2: 4735
20	480.6	472.6	Jaguar XJ13: 2313
21	476.4	468.5	Ford Cobra II Kemp: 1841
22	455.7	448.1	Pontiac Firebird TransAm Silverbird: 3566
23	454.8	447.2	Bugatti EB110: 652
24	451.0	443.5	Porsche 959 S: 3702
25	448.0	440.5	Chevrolet Monza Mike Keyser: 874
26	441.5	434.2	Ferrari F40: 1435
			Ferrari F40: 1446
27	436.4	429.1	Jaguar XJR15: 2369
28	426.2	419.1	Pontiac Firebird TDM Technologies: 3597
29	424.4	417.3	Scarab Mk II: 4109
30	421.7	414.6	Vector W8 Twin Turbo: 4736
31	416.0	409.1	Porsche 911 Turbo Koenig RS: 3709
32	415.2	408.3	Porsche 911 Turbo Ruf Twin Turbo: 3710
33	412.6	405.7	Bizzarrini P538: 497
34	411.3	404.4	Zender Fact 4: 5008
35	409.2	402.4	Porsche 935 Group 4 Holbert: 3657
36	408.9	402.1	Alfa Romeo 33 2.0 Stradale: 66
37	396.6	390.0	Westfield SEight: 4973
38	396.3	389.7	Eagle GTP: 1356
39	381.8	375.4	Ferrari 250 Testa Rossa: 1382
40	376.3	370.0	Shelby Cobra 427: 4126
41	375.0	368.7	Shelby Cobra Daytona Coupe: 4119
42	368.3	362.2	Porsche 911 Turbo Gemballa Mirage: 3751
43	367.8	361.7	Ferrari 250 GTO: 1386
44	366.8	360.7	Porsche 911 Turbo Motorsport Design: 3724
45	366.0	359.9	Ford GT40 Super Street: 1738
46	362.6	356.5	Ford Mustang Holdener: 1966
47	359.3	353.3	Ferrari F40: 1450
48	356.7	350.8	Pontiac Petty Grand National: 3571
49	355.9	349.9	Ford Mustang SVO J Bittle American: 1942
50	353.0	347.1	Renault Le Car Turbo: 3874
51	351.4	345.5	Bizzarrini GT America: 496
52	350.7	344.8	Ferrari 288 GTO: 1421
			Ferrari GTO: 1423
53	348.7	342.9	Mercedes-Benz 300SLR: 2795
54	348.4	342.6	Lamborghini 350GT: 2449
55	347.5	341.7	Shelby Cobra USRRC: 4118
56	345.6	339.8	Porsche 911 Ruf CTR: 3748
57	345.1	339.4	Jaguar XJ220: 2359
58	342.5	336.8	Ford GT40: 1760
59	341.6	335.9	Chevrolet Corvette Lingenfelter: 951
60	339.9	334.3	Jaguar XJS Tullius: 2333
61	339.4	333.7	Porsche 959 Sport: 3718
62	339.0	333.4	Porsche Carrera RSR: 3642
63	335.8	330.2	Porsche 911 Ruf: 3747
64	335.3	329.7	Porsche 911 Ruf TR2: 3749
65	334.5	328.9	Cizeta Moroder V16T: 1094
66	331.6	326.0	Lamborghini Miura S: 2456
67	328.5	323.0	Porsche 904 Carrera GTS: 3621
68	324.6	319.2	Ferrari 250 Testa Rossa: 1378
69	324.0	318.6	Iso Grifo A3L Berlinetta: 2245
70	320.9	315.5	Chevrolet Camaro IROC-Z Chevrolet Engineering: 929
71	319.7	314.4	Lamborghini Countach: 2468
72	319.0	313.7	Ford Mustang 5.0 Cartech Turbo: 1940
73	318.0	312.7	Ford Mustang TransAm: 1796
74	317.1	311.8	Isdera Imperator: 2244
75	316.0	310.7	Porsche 959: 3731
			Porsche 959 Comfort: 3717
76	315.2	309.9	De Tomaso Pantera Group 3: 1243
77	315.0	309.7	Triumph TR8 Group 44: 4578
78	314.4	309.1	Lamborghini Miura: 2452
79	311.1	305.9	Ferrari 308 Norwood: 1439
80	310.7	305.5	Lamborghini Countach 25th Anniversary: 2473
81	310.3	305.1	Ford Mustang Cartech Turbo: 1928
82	309.0	303.8	Ferrari Pininfarina Mythos: 1448
83	308.6	303.4	Mercury Comet A/FX: 2933
84	307.3	302.2	Chevrolet Camaro IROC: 877
85	306.4	301.3	Ferrari 288 GTO: 1416
86	305.4	300.4	TVR 420 SEAC: 4601
87	304.4	299.4	Lamborghini Diablo: 2475
88	304.2	299.1	Ferrari TRC 2500 Testa Rossa: 1379
89	304.1	299.1	Chevrolet Corvette ZR-1 SS: 955
90	301.3	296.3	Datsun 280ZX Sharp: 1221
91	301.1	296.1	Ferrari 275 GTS/4 NART: 1392

Total: 94

Lowest power-to-weight ratio. Limit set at 40bhp/ton.

	bhp/ ton	bhp/ tonn	
1	8.4	8.2	Enfield 8000 Electric: 1359
2	18.3	18.0	Citroen 2CV Cabriolet: 1019
3	18.7	18.4	Austin 7 Ruby Saloon: 351
4	19.5	19.2	Austin 7 Saloon: 341
5	19.8	19.5	Austin 7 Ruby Saloon: 349
6	20.2	19.9	Citroen Bijou: 1028
7	20.5	20.1	Jowett 8hp: 2408
8	21.5	21.2	Austin 7 Sunshine Saloon: 343
9	23.3	22.9	Austin 7 Tourer: 340
10	24.0	23.6	Austin 12/6: 345
			Citroen 2CV: 1022
			Morris Cowley Saloon: 3144
11	24.7	24.3	Austin 7 Sports Two-seater: 342
12	25.7	25.3	Riley 9 Monaco: 3928
13	27.1	26.7	Ford Model T: 1608
14	27.5	27.0	Fiat 500C Convertible: 1464
			Fiat 500C Convertible (Topolino): 1462
15	28.1	27.6	Fiat 500: 1477
16	28.7	28.3	Austin 8 Saloon: 358
17	29.7	29.2	Fiat 600 Multipla: 1473
18	30.4	29.9	Rover Pilot: 3974
19	30.9	30.4	Fiat Multipla: 1474
20	30.9	30.4	Ford 8: 1618
21	31.1	30.5	Ford Anglia 8 Saloon: 1623
22	31.2	30.7	Austin 8 Saloon: 356
23	31.5	30.9	Fiat 500 Giardiniera: 1492
24	32.0	31.5	Talbot 65 Saloon: 4335
25	32.4	31.9	DKW Karavan: 1264
26	33.1	32.5	DAF 600 de Luxe: 1108

27	33.2	32.6	Volkswagen Micro Bus: 4745
28	33.2	32.6	Fiat 500: 1482
			Ford 8 Tudor Saloon: 1611
29	33.2	32.7	Rolls-Royce 20 Saloon: 3947
30	33.3	32.7	Austin 10 Cambridge: 352
31	33.5	33.0	Austin Big 7: 354
32	33.6	33.0	Vauxhall Cadet Saloon: 4610
33	33.8	33.2	Renault 750: 3804
34	33.8	33.3	Sunbeam Weymann Saloon: 4280
35	33.9	33.3	BMW Isetta 300: 502
36	34.3	33.7	BMW Isetta Motocoupe: 499
37	34.5	33.9	Citroen Ami 6: 1030
38	34.6	34.0	Jowett De Luxe Saloon: 2407
39	34.6	34.1	Renault 750: 3802
40	34.9	34.3	Volkswagen Export Saloon: 4739
41	35.0	34.4	Standard 8: 4197
42	35.0	34.4	Lanchester 10: 2484
43	35.2	34.6	Lloyd LP 600: 2588
44	35.4	34.8	Fiat 500D: 1498
45	35.4	34.9	BMW 600: 501
46	35.6	35.0	Standard Flying 10: 4194
47	35.7	35.1	Fiat 500F: 1504
48	35.9	35.3	Hillman Minx Supercharged: 2040
			Volkswagen Sedan de Luxe: 4738
49	36.1	35.5	Austin A30 Countryman: 375
			Humber 12 Vogue: 2183
			Vauxhall Wyvern: 4622
50	36.2	35.6	Lea-Francis 12/40 Saloon: 2566
51	36.2	35.6	Fiat 600: 1472
52	36.4	35.8	Ford Prefect: 1616
53	36.5	35.9	Triumph Super 7 Saloon: 4487
54	36.6	36.0	Vauxhall 12 Saloon: 4618
55	36.8	36.1	Lanchester Roadrider de Luxe Saloon: 2483
56	36.9	36.2	Ford 10: 1615
57	37.0	36.4	Renault 4CV: 3801
58	37.1	36.5	Standard 8: 4200
59	37.2	36.6	Railton 10 Drop-head Coupe: 3760
60	37.3	36.6	Morris Oxford Travellers' Car: 3162
61	37.3	36.7	Ford 24 Saloon: 1609
			Vauxhall 12 Saloon: 4619
62	37.3	36.7	Vauxhall 10 Saloon de Luxe: 4615
63	37.4	36.8	Fiat 600: 1469
64	37.4	36.8	Morris Minor Tourer: 3159
65	37.4	36.8	Hillman Minx Estate: 2036
66	37.6	36.9	Citroen Ami 6 Break: 1035
			Vauxhall 10/4 de Luxe Saloon: 4613
67	37.6	37.0	Hillman Minx Saloon: 2034
68	37.6	37.0	Ford Model A: 1613
69	37.7	37.0	Morris Oxford: 3158
70	37.8	37.2	Morris Minor Series II: 3161
71	37.8	37.2	Hillman Minx Califonian Coupe: 2039
72	37.9	37.3	Morris Minor: 3157
73	38.0	37.4	DAF Daffodil de Luxe Extra: 1110
74	38.1	37.4	Singer Super 10 Saloon: 4162
75	38.2	37.6	Ford Prefect: 1620
76	38.3	37.7	Mercedes-Benz 180D: 2797
77	38.3	37.7	DKW Sonderklasse: 1261
78	38.4	37.7	Hillman Husky: 2041
79	38.5	37.9	Vauxhall Wyvern: 4626
80	38.5	37.9	BSA Scout: 647
81	38.6	38.0	Fiat 1400 Saloon: 1461
			Morris Minor: 3163
82	38.6	38.0	Sunbeam-Talbot 10 Sports Saloon: 4315
83	38.8	38.1	Lanchester 18: 2479
			Volkswagen Station Wagon: 4756
			Volkswagen Van: 4757
84	39.1	38.4	Morris Cowley: 3165
85	39.1	38.4	Mercedes-Benz 300GD: 2867
86	39.1	38.5	Standard 12 Saloon: 4196
87	39.1	38.5	Morris Oxford Saloon: 3160
88	39.2	38.5	Hillman Minx Convertible: 2038
89	39.2	38.6	Land Rover Station Wagon: 2556
90	39.4	38.8	Armstrong Siddeley Six-light Saloon: 216
91	39.5	38.8	Ford Anglia 10 Saloon: 1622
92	39.6	38.9	DKW 3-6: 1262
93	39.6	38.9	Hillman Minx Saloon: 2035
94	39.7	39.0	Datsun 1000: 1157
95	39.8	39.2	Austin A30: 369
96	39.9	39.2	Triumph Gloria 12: 4494
97	40.0	39.3	Fiat 126 de Ville: 1564
			MG Midget: 2968
			Riley Kestrel Sprite: 3929

Total: 111

Highest specific output. Limit set at 100bhp/litre.

	bhp/l	kW/l	PS/l	
1	336.0	250.5	340.6	Peugeot 405 Turbo 16 Pike's Peak: 3460
2	290.5	216.6	294.5	Mazda RX-7 Mariah Mode Six: 2770
3	280.7	209.3	284.6	Lancia Montecarlo Group 5 Turbo: 2531
4	263.0	196.1	266.6	Mazda RX-7 Cartech: 2768
5	235.6	175.7	238.9	Mazda RX-7 Racer: 2715
6	210.7	157.1	213.6	Datsun 280ZX Electramotive: 1230
7	210.6	157.0	213.5	Porsche 959 S: 3702
8	202.3	150.9	205.1	Koenig Competition Evolution: 2418
9	190.8	142.3	193.5	Ferrari Testa Rossa Norwood: 1444
10	190.7	142.2	193.3	Ferrari GTO Norwood: 1451
11	184.2	137.4	186.8	Mazda RX-7 Convertible Racing Beat: 2757
12	181.8	135.6	184.3	Renault Le Car Turbo: 3874
13	174.6	130.2	177.0	Koenig C62: 2419
14	172.2	128.4	174.6	Porsche 911 Turbo RS Tuning: 3737
15	171.5	127.9	173.9	Bugatti EB110: 652
16	164.4	122.6	166.6	Mazda RX-7 Infini IV: 2769
17	162.8	121.4	165.1	Ferrari F40: 1435
				Ferrari F40: 1450
				Ferrari F40: 1446
18	162.0	120.8	164.3	Porsche 935 Group 4 Holbert: 3657
19	161.9	120.7	164.1	Koenig Competition: 2417
20	157.9	117.8	160.1	Porsche 959: 3731
				Porsche 959 Comfort: 3717
				Porsche 959 Sport: 3718
21	155.4	115.9	157.6	Nissan 300ZX Turbo Millen Super GTZ: 3247
22	154.5	115.2	156.6	Porsche 911 Turbo Koenig RS: 3709
23	153.8	114.7	155.9	Ferrari 308 Norwood: 1439
24	153.5	114.5	155.6	Chevrolet Corvette Callaway Sledgehammer: 941
25	152.9	114.0	155.0	Mazda RX-7 Turbo: 2764
				Mazda RX-7 Turbo: 2771
				Mazda RX-7 Turbo II: 2759
26	147.9	110.3	150.0	Porsche 911 Turbo Motorsport Design: 3724
27	145.6	108.5	147.6	Toyota Supra Turbo TRD: 4467
28	145.5	108.5	147.5	Porsche 911 Turbo Gemballa Mirage: 3751
29	144.6	107.8	146.6	Nissan 300ZX Motor Sports International SR-71: 3246
30	144.0	107.4	146.0	Mazda MX-5 Miata Millen: 2760
31	143.4	106.9	145.4	Audi Quattro Sport: 309
32	142.9	106.6	144.9	Sbarro Chrono 3.5: 4108
33	140.1	104.5	142.0	Ferrari 288 GTO: 1421
				Ferrari GTO: 1423
34	139.3	103.9	141.3	Porsche 911 Turbo Ruf Twin Turbo: 3710
35	139.3	103.9	141.2	Porsche 911 Ruf CTR: 3748
36	139.1	103.8	141.1	Mazda RX-7 Turbo: 2737
				Mazda RX-7 Turbo: 2751
				Mazda RX-7 Turbo: 2740
37	138.0	102.9	139.9	Ferrari 288 GTO: 1416
38	132.4	98.7	134.3	Renault 5 Turbo 2: 3886
39	129.8	96.8	131.6	Porsche 911 Ruf: 3747
				Porsche 911 Ruf TR2: 3749
40	127.8	95.3	129.5	Ford RS200: 1917
41	126.4	94.3	128.2	Honda CRX Si Jackson Turbo: 2130
42	125.8	93.8	127.5	Zender Fact 4: 5008
43	122.6	91.4	124.3	Toyota MR2 HKS: 4480
44	122.3	91.2	124.0	Mazda RX-7 Convertible: 2763
				Mazda RX-7 GTUs: 2758
45	122.3	91.2	124.0	Honda CRX Si HKS: 2147
46	121.4	90.6	123.1	Bertone Emotion Lotus: 489
				Lotus Esprit Turbo SE: 2640
				Lotus Esprit Turbo SE: 2637
47	119.6	89.2	121.2	Ford Escort Millen: 1964
48	119.5	89.1	121.1	Pontiac Firebird TDM Technologies: 3597
49	117.8	87.9	119.5	Subaru Legacy FIA Record: 4274
50	116.5	86.9	118.1	Volkswagen Scirocco GT-3 Davey: 4830
51	116.0	86.5	117.6	NSU Spider: 3261
52	115.6	86.2	117.2	NSU Ro80: 3266
53	115.3	86.0	116.9	Alfa Romeo 33 2.0 Stradale: 66
				Fiat Brava Abarth Rally: 1571
54	114.7	85.5	116.3	Mazda RX-7: 2735
55	114.5	85.4	116.1	Renault 5 Turbo: 3873
56	114.2	85.1	115.8	Datsun B210 Electramotive: 1198
57	114.1	85.1	115.6	NSU Ro80: 3264
58	113.4	84.6	115.0	Mazda RX-2: 2690
				Mazda RX-4: 2694
59	113.3	84.5	114.8	Alfa Romeo 1750 GTV TransAm: 78
60	112.3	83.7	113.9	Ital Design Aztec: 2262
61	112.0	83.5	113.6	Mazda 110S Coupe: 2685
62	111.8	83.4	113.4	Ferrari 308 Norwood Bonneville GTO: 1434
63	111.6	83.2	113.2	Mazda RX-7 Convertible: 2749
				Mazda RX-7 GTU: 2750
				Mazda RX-7 GXL: 2736
64	111.1	82.9	112.6	Porsche 911 Turbo Ruf 3.4: 3698
65	110.4	82.3	111.9	Ford Sierra Sapphire Cosworth 4x4: 1958
66	109.4	81.6	111.0	Lamborghini Miura S: 2456
67	108.7	81.0	110.2	Renault 5 Racer: 3865
68	108.6	81.0	110.1	Datsun 280ZX Electramotive: 1220
69	107.9	80.5	109.4	Datsun 510 TransAm: 1180
70	107.5	80.1	109.0	Nissan Skyline GT-R: 3243
71	106.5	79.4	107.9	Datsun 280ZX Sharp: 1221
72	106.4	79.3	107.9	Volkswagen Corrado Neuspeed: 4883
73	105.3	78.5	106.8	Datsun 240Z Sharp: 1190
74	105.0	78.3	106.4	BMW 535i Alpina B10 Bi-Turbo: 619
75	104.9	78.2	106.3	Lotus Esprit Turbo: 2636
76	104.7	78.1	106.2	Mazda RX-2: 2691
77	104.6	78.0	106.1	Vector W8 Twin Turbo: 4736
78	103.9	77.5	105.3	Lotus Elan: 2638
				Lotus Elan SE: 2639
79	103.7	77.3	105.1	Opel Omega Lotus: 3352
80	103.2	77.0	104.6	Mazda RX-7: 2724

				Mazda RX-7 GSL SE: 2725
81	103.2	76.9	104.6	Ferrari 412 MI: 1377
82	102.8	76.6	104.2	Saab Carlsson: 4097
83	102.8	76.6	104.2	Lancia Rally: 2537
84	102.4	76.3	103.8	Ford Sierra RS Cosworth: 1934
				Panther Solo: 3380
85	102.3	76.2	103.7	Lotus Elan Autocrosser: 2632
86	102.0	76.1	103.4	Lotus Elan SE: 2641
87	101.8	75.9	103.2	Mazda Rotary: 2689
88	101.8	75.9	103.2	Lamborghini Miura: 2452
89	101.6	75.8	103.0	Dodge Spirit R/T: 1346
				Ferrari 250 Testa Rossa: 1378
				Ferrari 250 Testa Rossa: 1382
90	101.3	75.6	102.8	Nissan 300ZX Turbo: 3241
				Nissan 300ZX Twin Turbo: 3248
91	101.3	75.5	102.7	Porsche RSK: 3613
92	101.3	75.5	102.7	Mercedes-Benz 300SLR: 2795
93	101.2	75.5	102.6	Ford Mustang SVO J Bittle American: 1942
94	101.0	75.3	102.4	Maserati Shamal: 2681
95	100.9	75.3	102.3	Dodge Stealth R/T Turbo: 1347
				Mitsubishi 3000GT VR-4: 3111
96	100.8	75.2	102.2	Porsche 944 Turbo: 3730
				Porsche 944 Turbo SE: 3716
97	100.8	75.1	102.1	Isuzu Impulse RS: 2261
98	100.7	75.1	102.1	Ford Probe GT Suspension Techniques/ HKS: 1943
99	100.7	75.1	102.1	Porsche 904 Carrera GTS: 3621
100	100.4	74.9	101.8	Ferrari 275 GTS/4 NART: 1392
101	100.3	74.8	101.7	Mazda RX-7: 2720
102	100.2	74.8	101.6	Lancia Delta Integrale 16v: 2549
103	100.2	74.7	101.6	Pontiac Firebird T/A Turbo Pontiac Engineering: 3588
104	100.2	74.7	101.6	Pontiac Petty Grand National: 3571
105	100.1	74.7	101.5	Lamborghini Bravo: 2458
106	100.1	74.6	101.5	Toyota Celica All-Trac Turbo: 4469
				Toyota MR2 Turbo: 4473
107	100.0	74.6	101.4	NSU Wankel Spider: 3262
				Vector W2: 4735

Total: 134

Lowest specific output. Limit set at 26bhp/litre.

	bhp/l	kW/l	PS/l	
1	6.9	5.1	7.0	Ford Model T: 1608
2	12.2	9.1	12.3	Ford Model A: 1613
3	12.2	9.1	12.3	Ford 24 Saloon: 1609
4	13.9	10.4	14.1	Rolls-Royce Phantom I Phaeton: 3946
5	14.1	10.5	14.3	Austin 7 Saloon: 341
				Austin 7 Sports Two-seater: 342
				Austin 7 Sunshine Saloon: 343
				Austin 7 Tourer: 340
6	14.7	11.0	14.9	Wills Sainte Claire Six: 4974
7	15.6	11.7	15.9	Rolls-Royce Phantom II: 3950
8	16.0	11.9	16.2	Rolls-Royce 20 Saloon: 3947
9	16.0	12.0	16.3	Austin 12/6: 345
10	16.0	12.0	16.3	Kissel 8-65 Gold Bug: 2416
11	16.1	12.0	16.3	Austin 7 Ruby Saloon: 349
				Austin 7 Ruby Saloon: 351
12	17.4	13.0	17.7	Morris Cowley Saloon: 3144
13	17.6	13.1	17.8	Rolls-Royce Phantom II: 3949
14	17.9	13.4	18.2	Ford V8: 1610
				Ford V8 30: 1617
				Jowett 8hp: 2408
15	18.3	13.6	18.6	Oldsmobile Cutlass Diesel: 3300
16	18.3	13.7	18.6	Cadillac Seville Diesel: 712
17	18.9	14.1	19.1	Sunbeam Weymann Saloon: 4280
18	19.8	14.8	20.1	Chrysler Custom Imperial Le Baron: 964
19	20.5	15.3	20.8	Vauxhall Cadet Saloon: 4610
20	20.9	15.6	21.2	Cadillac Seville Diesel: 711
21	21.4	16.0	21.7	Packard Super 8 Phaeton: 3356
22	21.4	16.0	21.7	Packard Twelve Victoria: 3359
23	21.5	16.0	21.8	Du Pont Town Car: 1351
24	21.7	16.1	22.0	Volkswagen Export Saloon: 4739
25	21.8	16.3	22.1	Rolls-Royce Phantom III: 3952
26	22.1	16.5	22.4	Volkswagen Sedan de Luxe: 4738
27	22.2	16.5	22.5	Rover Pilot: 3974
28	22.3	16.6	22.6	Cadillac V16 "Madame X": 699
29	22.7	17.0	23.0	Bentley 4.5-litre: 461
30	23.0	17.1	23.3	Packard 7-34 Phaeton: 3355
31	23.3	17.4	23.7	Hispano-Suiza 54/220: 2084
32	23.4	17.4	23.7	Rover Light Six Speed Model: 3973
33	23.5	17.5	23.8	Allard Drop-head Coupe: 148
				Allard V8: 149
				Ford V8 Pilot: 1621
34	23.5	17.5	23.8	Stutz Roadster: 4239
35	23.6	17.6	23.9	Ford 8 Tudor Saloon: 1611
				Humber Snipe Sports Saloon: 2190
36	23.6	17.6	23.9	MG Midget: 2968
37	23.6	17.6	23.9	Cadillac V16 Fleetwood Roadster: 700
38	23.6	17.6	24.0	AMC Pacer: 202
39	24.0	17.9	24.3	Citroen 2CV Cabriolet: 1019
40	24.1	17.9	24.4	Vauxhall Velox: 4621
41	24.2	18.0	24.5	Lanchester 18: 2479
42	24.3	18.1	24.6	Vauxhall 12 Saloon: 4619
				Vauxhall 12 Saloon: 4618
				Vauxhall Wyvern: 4622
43	24.4	18.2	24.7	Standard Flying 20: 4195
44	24.5	18.2	24.8	Humber Imperial: 2193
				Humber Imperial Saloon: 2194
				Humber Pullman Limousine: 2197
				Humber Snipe Drop-head Foursome: 2188
				Humber Super Snipe: 2198
				Humber Super Snipe: 2195
45	24.5	18.3	24.8	Hispano-Suiza 30/120 Saloon: 2083
46	24.6	18.4	25.0	Invicta 4.5-litre: 2241
				Invicta 4.5-litre: 2242
47	24.9	18.5	25.2	Marmon 16: 2651
48	25.0	18.6	25.3	Armstrong Siddeley 30 Special Sports Saloon: 213
				Renault 4CV: 3801
49	25.0	18.7	25.4	Armstrong Siddeley Six-light Saloon: 216
50	25.1	18.7	25.4	Ford 8: 1618
				Ford Anglia 8 Saloon: 1623
51	25.2	18.8	25.5	Humber 12 Vogue: 2183
52	25.2	18.8	25.5	Volkswagen De Luxe: 4740
				Volkswagen Sedan: 4741
				Volkswagen Sedan TC: 4742
53	25.2	18.8	25.6	Triumph Super 7 Saloon: 4487
54	25.4	18.9	25.8	Lea-Francis 12/40 Saloon: 2566
55	25.5	19.0	25.8	International Scout: 2240
56	25.5	19.0	25.8	Ford Tudor Sedan: 1619
57	25.5	19.0	25.9	Auburn 8-120 Speedster: 262
58	25.5	19.0	25.9	Cord L-29: 1097
59	25.6	19.1	25.9	Austin 8 Saloon: 358
60	25.6	19.1	25.9	Chevrolet Monza 2+2 V8: 873
				Chevrolet Monza 2+2 V8: 864
61	25.6	19.1	25.9	Humber Hawk: 2196
62	25.6	19.1	26.0	Ford 10: 1615
				Ford Prefect: 1616
63	25.6	19.1	26.0	Mercedes-Benz 300CD: 2856
				Mercedes-Benz 300D: 2848
64	25.6	19.1	26.0	Toyota Landcruiser: 4450
				Vauxhall Velox: 4623
				Vauxhall Velox: 4624
65	25.7	19.2	26.0	Ford Anglia 10 Saloon: 1622
				Ford Popular: 1631
				Ford Prefect: 1620
				Mercedes-Benz 300TD: 2861
66	25.8	19.2	26.1	Land Rover County: 2559
67	25.9	19.3	26.3	Pontiac Grand Am: 3562

Total: 96

Highest piston speed at peak power. Limit set at 63ft/sec.

	ft/sec	m/sec	
1	89.8	27.4	Ferrari GTO Norwood: 1451
2	85.3	26.0	Ferrari Testa Rossa Norwood: 1444
3	84.6	25.8	Sbarro Chrono 3.5: 4108
4	82.6	25.2	Chevrolet Camaro Gottlieb 1969: 926
5	77.6	23.6	Ferrari 308 Norwood Bonneville GTO: 1434
6	75.7	23.1	Datsun B210 Electramotive: 1198
7	75.6	23.0	Chevrolet Corvette Greenwood: 870
8	74.4	22.7	Volkswagen Scirocco GT-3 Davey: 4830
9	73.7	22.5	Fiat Brava Abarth Rally: 1571
10	72.9	22.2	Pontiac Petty Grand National: 3571
11	72.8	22.2	Safir GT40: 4106
12	72.5	22.1	Alfa Romeo 1750 GTV TransAm: 78
13	70.4	21.5	Pontiac Firebird TransAm Silverbird: 3566
14	69.6	21.2	Chevrolet Monza Mike Keyser: 874
15	69.5	21.2	Jaguar XK120C: 2280
			Jaguar XKSS: 2291
16	68.8	21.0	Lancia Rally: 2537
17	68.9	21.0	Triumph TR8 Group 44: 4578
18	68.1	20.7	Ford Cobra II Kemp: 1841
19	67.6	20.6	Datsun 510 TransAm: 1180
20	67.3	20.5	Peugeot 405 Turbo 16 Pike's Peak: 3460
			Renault 5 Racer: 3865
21	67.2	20.5	Jaguar C Type: 2274
22	66.9	20.4	Honda Civic CRX: 2140
			Honda Concerto 1.6i 16: 2151
			Rover 216 GTi: 4044
			Rover 416 GTi: 4040
23	66.8	20.4	Chevrolet Corvette: 795
			Chevrolet Corvette 396: 796
			Chevrolet Corvette Sting Ray 396: 798
24	66.6	20.3	Jaguar D Type: 2285
			Jaguar XK 140: 2287
25	66.7	20.3	BMW M3 Sport Evolution: 621
			Jaguar XK140: 2276
			Jaguar XK140MC: 2283
26	66.5	20.3	Datsun 240Z Sharp: 1190
27	66.3	20.2	Ruger Bentley Clone: 4052
28	65.8	20.1	Ford Mustang SVO J Bittle American: 1942
29	65.2	19.9	Mercedes-Benz 190E 2.5-16 Evolution II: 2916
			Mercedes-Benz 190E 2.5-16 Evolution II: 2908
30	65.1	19.8	MG A Twin Cam: 2995

			MG Twin Cam MGA: 2997
31	65.1	19.8	Chevrolet Corvette ZR-1 SS: 955
32	65.0	19.8	Lancia Montecarlo Group 5 Turbo: 2531
33	65.0	19.8	BMW M5: 606
			BMW M5: 622
34	64.8	19.7	Datsun 280ZX Electramotive: 1230
			Datsun 280ZX Sharp: 1221
35	64.6	19.7	Jensen Interceptor III Convertible: 2403
36	64.6	19.6	Ferrari 365 GTB/4 Competitione: 1403
37	64.4	19.6	Honda Prelude 2.0 Si: 2138
			Honda Prelude Si 4WS: 2148
38	64.4	19.6	Honda Civic 1.6i VT: 2154
39	64.4	19.6	BMW M3 Hor Technologie: 605
40	64.0	19.5	Honda CRX 1.6i VT: 2152
41	63.9	19.5	Acura Integra LS: 32
			Honda CRX Coupe 1.6i 16: 2128
			Honda CRX Si Jackson: 2142
			Honda Integra EX 16: 2132
			Mercedes-Benz 300SLR: 2795
			Toyota Supra Turbo TRD: 4467
42	63.7	19.4	Allard GT Coupe: 153
			Jaguar 3.4: 2292
			Jaguar 3.8 Mk II: 2301
			Jaguar 3.8 Mk II Automatic: 2302
			Jaguar 3.8 Sedan: 2297
			Jaguar 3.8S: 2307
			Jaguar 420: 2311
			Jaguar 420 Sedan: 2315
			Jaguar E Type Coupe: 2298
			Jaguar E Type Coupe: 2303
			Jaguar Mk VII Auto: 2286
			Jaguar Mk VIII: 2289
			Jaguar Mk X: 2300
			Jaguar XJ6: 2318
			Jaguar XJ6 4.2: 2320
			Jaguar XJ6 4.2 Automatic: 2316
			Jaguar XK150: 2293
			Jaguar XK150S: 2295
			Jaguar XKE Coupe: 2317
43	63.7	19.4	Jaguar 3.4: 2296
			Jaguar 3.8S Sedan: 2304
			Jaguar Mk VII: 2282
			Jaguar XK150: 2290
			Jaguar XK150S: 2294
			Jaguar XKE: 2299
			Jaguar XKE: 2306
44	63.8	19.4	Lotus Elan Autocrosser: 2632
45	63.6	19.4	AC Cobra 427 Modified 1965: 27
46	63.3	19.3	Audi Quattro Sport: 309
47	63.2	19.3	Chevrolet Camaro IROC: 877
			De Tomaso Pantera GT5-S: 1242
48	63.2	19.2	Shelby Cobra 427: 4126
49	63.0	19.2	Chevrolet Corvette ZR-1: 934
			Mercury Comet A/FX: 2933
50	63.0	19.2	AC AC-Bristol Zagato: 17
			AC Aceca-Bristol: 21
			AC Bristol: 19
			Ford Galaxie 500 XL 427: 1714
			Mercury Super Marauder S-55: 2932

Total: 100

Lowest piston speed at peak power. Limit set at 33ft/sec.

	ft/sec	m/sec	
1	14.2	4.3	Fiat Panda 750 L: 1593
2	17.8	5.4	Ford Model T: 1608
3	19.9	6.1	Austin 7 Saloon: 341
			Austin 7 Sports Two-seater: 342
			Austin 7 Sunshine Saloon: 343
			Austin 7 Tourer: 340
4	22.2	6.8	Austin 12/6: 345
5	22.6	6.9	Volkswagen Polo C: 4833
6	23.1	7.0	Volkswagen Export Saloon: 4739
			Volkswagen Sedan de Luxe: 4738
7	23.7	7.2	Citroen 2CV: 1022
			Citroen 2CV Cabriolet: 1019
8	23.8	7.2	Volkswagen De Luxe: 4740
			Volkswagen De Luxe Saloon: 4750
			Volkswagen Sedan: 4741
			Volkswagen Sedan TC: 4742
9	23.9	7.3	Ford Mustang 271hp: 1707
10	25.2	7.7	Volkswagen 1200 de Luxe: 4758
11	25.9	7.9	Devin VW: 1258
			Volkswagen Alken-VW: 4749
			Volkswagen Karmann-Ghia: 4744
			Volkswagen Micro Bus: 4745
			Volkswagen Sedan: 4746
			Volkswagen Sedan: 4752
			Volkswagen Sedan Supercharged: 4743
12	26.0	7.9	Ford 24 Saloon: 1609
			Ford Model A: 1613
13	26.5	8.1	Ford Anglia: 1649
			Ford Anglia de Luxe Estate: 1666
			Ford Prefect: 1633
14	26.5	8.1	Ford Anglia: 1654
15	27.1	8.3	Citroen Bijou: 1028
16	27.2	8.3	Land Rover County: 2559
17	27.3	8.3	Volkswagen 1200: 4765
			Volkswagen De Luxe: 4751
			Volkswagen Karmann Ghia: 4754
			Volkswagen Karmann-Ghia: 4760
			Volkswagen Sedan: 4755
			Volkswagen Station Wagon: 4756
			Volkswagen Van: 4757
18	27.8	8.5	Ford Falcon: 1650
19	28.0	8.5	Volkswagen Sedan Judson: 4748
20	28.1	8.6	Fiat 600: 1472
			Fiat Multipla: 1474
21	28.1	8.6	Fiat 600: 1469
			Fiat 600: 1486
			Fiat 600 Multipla: 1473
22	28.4	8.6	Datsun 1000: 1157
			Ford Mustang 4.2: 1880
23	28.4	8.7	DAF 600 de Luxe: 1108
			DAF Daffodil: 1109
			DAF Daffodil de Luxe Extra: 1110
24	28.7	8.7	Volkswagen 1500: 4753
			Volkswagen 1500: 4772
25	28.7	8.8	Volkswagen Karmann-Ghia 1500: 4763
26	29.2	8.9	Ford Econoline: 1691
			Ford Econoline: 1662
			Ford Falcon: 1656
			Ford Falcon Automatic: 1657
			Mercury Comet: 2925
27	29.4	9.0	Volkswagen Karmann-Ghia Okrasa: 4747
28	29.5	9.0	Meyers Manx: 2967
29	29.8	9.1	BMW 600: 501
			Goliath 1100 Sedan: 2005
30	29.8	9.1	DKW Junior de Luxe: 1268
31	30.0	9.1	Ford Mustang II: 1847
			Ford Mustang II V8: 1848
			Mercury Monarch: 2953
32	30.1	9.2	Cadillac Seville Diesel: 712
			Oldsmobile Cutlass Diesel: 3300
33	30.2	9.2	Volkswagen 1300: 4767
			Volkswagen 1500: 4769
			Volkswagen 1500 Estate: 4762
			Volkswagen 1500 Semi-automatic: 4775
			Volkswagen 1600 TL: 4771
			Volkswagen 1600 TL Automatic: 4777
			Volkswagen 181: 4794
			Volkswagen Sports Bug: 4792
			Volkswagen Super Beetle: 4783
34	30.2	9.2	Volkswagen 1500: 4759
35	30.3	9.2	Saab 96 V4: 4061
36	30.4	9.3	Ford Fiesta Popular: 1875
37	30.5	9.3	Ford Anglia Super: 1667
			Ford Consul Cortina: 1686
			Ford Consul Cortina: 1669
			Ford Cortina Estate de Luxe: 1688
38	30.7	9.3	Fiat 500: 1482
			Fiat 500: 1477
			Goggomobil TS400: 2004
39	30.7	9.3	Volkswagen Sedan EMPI: 4761
40	31.0	9.4	Chevrolet Monza 2+2 V8: 873
			Chevrolet Monza 2+2 V8: 864
41	31.1	9.5	Bond 875: 628
42	31.2	9.5	Ford Anglia Estate: 1710
43	31.3	9.5	Ford Zephyr 6 Mk IV: 1740
			Ford Zephyr de Luxe: 1765
44	31.5	9.6	Subaru DL-5: 4254
45	31.5	9.6	Lloyd LP 600: 2588
			Subaru Hatchback: 4266
46	31.7	9.6	Ford Granada 5-litre: 1835
47	31.7	9.7	Hillman Imp de Luxe: 2073
			Volkswagen 1500 Automatic: 4774
			Volkswagen Beetle: 4798
			Volkswagen Beetle 1500: 4773
			Volkswagen Beetle Convertible: 4812
48	31.8	9.7	Chevrolet Corvair: 742
			Chevrolet Corvair 4-speed: 744
			Chevrolet Corvair 700: 746
			Chevrolet Corvair Automatic: 745
			Chevrolet Corvair Greenbrier: 747
			Chevrolet Corvair Monza: 762
			Chevrolet Corvair Monza: 748
			Chevrolet Corvair Monza Convertible: 773
			Chevrolet Corvair Monza Coupe: 763
			Chevrolet Corvair Monza EMPI: 774
			Chevrolet Corvair Spyder: 765
			Fiat 1400: 1463
			Fiat 1400 Saloon: 1461
49	31.9	9.7	DKW 750: 1266
			Ford Escort 1100L: 1823
50	32.0	9.7	DKW Junior: 1267
51	32.1	9.8	Ford Cortina 1100: 1769
			Ford Escort: 1756
52	32.2	9.8	Saab Sonnet V4: 4063
			Saab V4: 4062
53	32.3	9.8	Fiat 500C Convertible: 1464
			Fiat 500C Convertible (Topolino): 1462
			Subaru GL: 4256

54	32.3	9.9	Porsche 356: 3602
55	32.5	9.9	Volkswagen 411 L: 4778
56	32.7	9.9	Volkswagen Vanagon: 4823
57	32.8	10.0	Ford Granada 2.3L Estate: 1879
			Ford Taunus 20M: 1726
58	32.9	10.0	Ford Cortina 2.3 Ghia: 1849
			Ford Cortina 2.3 Ghia S: 1863
			Ford Granada 2.3 GL Auto: 1856
59	32.9	10.0	Chrysler Sunbeam 1.0LS: 997

Total: 137

Undersquare bore and stroke. Stroke limit set at 4.5in.

	stroke		bore		
	in	mm	in	mm	
1	5.9	150.1	3.9	98.0	Mercedes-Benz 36/220-S: 2774
					Mercedes-Benz SSKL: 2776
2	5.5	140.0	3.9	100.0	Bentley 4.5-litre: 461
					Bentley 4.5-litre Supercharged: 462
					Bentley 8-litre Saloon: 463
					Bentley Speed Six Weymann: 464
					Rolls-Royce Phantom II: 3950
3	5.5	139.7	4.2	108.0	Rolls-Royce Phantom I Phaeton: 3946
					Rolls-Royce Phantom II: 3949
					Wills Sainte Claire Six: 4974
4	5.2	133.4	3.5	88.9	Armstrong Siddeley 30 Special Sports Saloon: 213
5	5.1	130.0	3.2	81.0	Bugatti 5-litre Saloon: 650
6	5.0	127.0	2.9	73.0	Armstrong Siddeley Rally Tourer: 210
					Chrysler 77 Saloon: 962
					Chrysler Custom Imperial Le Baron: 964
					Hudson 22hp Six Saloon: 2173
					Hudson 22hp Six Special Saloon: 2175
					Hudson Terraplane Big Six Saloon: 2172
					Hudson Terraplane Saloon: 2174
					Lincoln 39.2hp Saloon: 2574
					Lincoln 39.2hp Town Saloon: 2573
					Packard 32.5hp Saloon: 3358
					Packard 32.5hp Saloon: 3354
					Packard 32.5hp Standard Eight Saloon: 3361
					Packard 7-34 Phaeton: 3355
					Packard Straight Eight Saloon: 3357
					Packard Super 8 Phaeton: 3356
7	4.9	125.4	3.3	84.1	La Salle Enclosed Drive Limousine: 2421
8	4.9	123.8	3.2	82.6	Chrysler Super Power Saloon: 968
9	4.8	121.0	2.7	67.4	Essex Terraplane Tourer: 1360
10	4.7	120.7	3.1	77.8	Auburn 38hp Saloon: 263
					Duesenberg J Coupe: 1352
					Duesenberg SJ Town Car: 1353
					Franklin 29.4hp Saloon: 1977
					Hudson Super Jet: 2178
					Hupmobile 32.5hp Saloon: 2218
					Hupmobile Straight Eight Limousine: 2216
					Invicta 4.5-litre: 2241
					Invicta 4.5-litre: 2242
					Kissel 8-65 Gold Bug: 2416
					Lagonda 4.5-litre: 2442
					Lagonda 4.5-litre Tourer: 2440
					Lagonda Rapide: 2441
					Lagonda Rapide Tourer: 2439
					Marmon 79 Saloon: 2650
11	4.7	120.1	3.1	77.7	Auburn 8-52 Speedster: 264
12	4.7	120.0	3.2	82.5	Chrysler 75 Saloon: 961
					Daimler Straight Eight: 1139
					Daimler Twenty-Seven Limousine: 1138
					Delage 21hp Weymann Saloon: 1245
					Delaunay-Belleville 21hp Saloon: 1253
					Healey 2.4-litre Roadster: 2019
					Healey Tickford Saloon: 2020
					Hillman 80 Limousine: 2032
					Hillman Hawk Sports Saloon: 2031
					Hillman Safety Saloon: 2022
					Humber 16.9hp Saloon: 2189
					Humber Imperial: 2193
					Humber Imperial Saloon: 2194
					Humber Pullman Limousine: 2197
					Humber Pullman Limousine: 2186
					Humber Snipe Drop-head Foursome: 2188
					Humber Snipe Sports Saloon: 2190
					Humber Snipe Sports Saloon: 2187
					Humber Super Snipe: 2198
					Humber Super Snipe: 2195
					Lagonda 2-litre Supercharged: 2433
					Lagonda 3-litre Special Tourer: 2434
					Lagonda 3-litre Tourer: 2432
					Lagonda 3.5-litre Tourer: 2436
					Lagonda Le Mans: 2437
					Renault 24hp Big Six Saloon: 3799
					Renault Vivasix Saloon: 3797
					Riley 16 2.5: 3931
					Riley 2.5: 3938
					Riley 2.5: 3936
					Riley 2.5 Saloon: 3935
					Riley 2.5 Saloon: 3933
					Riley 2.5 Sports: 3934
					Riley Pathfinder: 3940
					Riley Pathfinder: 3939
					Talbot 3-litre Saloon: 4342
13	4.6	117.5	3.3	84.1	Buick Empire Saloon: 653
14	4.6	117.5	3.4	87.3	Buick 28.4hp Saloon: 654
15	4.6	116.0	3.1	80.0	Humber Pullman Limousine: 2182
					Humber Snipe: 2180
					Humber Snipe Sports Saloon: 2185
16	4.5	115.0	3.1	80.0	Austro Daimler 32/100 Saloon: 448
					HE 16/60 Sports Four-seater: 2017
					Mercedes-Benz 32/90 Limousine: 2777
					Mercedes-Benz 32/90 Saloon: 2775
17	4.5	114.5	3.1	79.5	Austin 20 Mayfair Limousine: 350
					Austin 20 Ranelagh Landaulet: 347
18	4.5	114.3	3.2	82.5	Armstrong Siddeley 25.3hp Town and Country Saloon: 215
					Armstrong Siddeley Six-light Saloon: 216
					Auburn 8-120 Speedster: 262
					Bentley 4.25-litre: 468
					Bentley Continental: 471
					Bentley Continental Park Ward DH Coupe: 475
					Bentley Sedan: 465
					Bentley Series S: 476
					Chrysler Heston Airflow Saloon: 965
					Chrysler Royal Saloon: 969
					Cord L-29: 1097
					Dodge Safari Super Sport: 1291
					Du Pont Speedster: 1350
					Du Pont Town Car: 1351
					Graham-Paige 21.6hp Saloon: 2015
					Graham-Paige Straight Eight: 2016
					Hudson Commodore: 2176
					Hudson Hornet: 2177
					Hudson Straight Eight Roadster: 2169
					Kurtis Hornet Roadster: 2420
					La Salle 37-50 V8 Saloon: 2422
					Nash Straight Eight Saloon: 3194
					Packard 120 Saloon: 3360
					Rolls-Royce 20 Saloon: 3947
					Rolls-Royce 25 Saloon: 3948
					Rolls-Royce Phantom III: 3952
					Rolls-Royce Silver Cloud: 3956
					Rolls-Royce Silver Cloud "S": 3957
					Rolls-Royce Silver Dawn: 3955
					Rolls-Royce Silver Dawn: 3954
					Stutz 36.4hp Saloon: 4240
					Stutz DV32 Sports Saloon: 4242
					Stutz Roadster: 4239
					Stutz Straight Eight Saloon: 4241

Total: 127

Square bore and stroke. Limit set at 3in.

	bore		stroke		
	in	mm	in	mm	
1	4.0	101.6	4.0	101.6	Ford LTD: 1809
2	3.9	100.0	3.9	100.0	Hispano-Suiza 54/220: 2084
3	3.6	92.2	3.6	92.2	Chrysler Windsor de Luxe: 972
4	3.6	91.9	3.6	91.9	Aston Martin DB4: 237
					Aston Martin DB4: 238
					Aston Martin DB4: 239
					Aston Martin DB4 GT Zagato: 240
					Cadillac Seville Touring Sedan: 720
					Toyota Landcruiser II TD: 4458
					Volga M21K: 4737
5	3.5	90.0	3.5	90.0	Armstrong Siddeley Sapphire Saloon: 219
					Saab 9000 2.3 Turbo TCS: 4101
					Saab 9000 2.3CS: 4105
					Saab 9000 Turbo: 4102
					Saab 9000CD: 4098
					Saab 9000CS Turbo S: 4103
					Saab 9000S: 4104
					Saab CDS 2.3: 4100
6	3.5	88.0	3.5	88.0	Renault Fregate Transfluide: 3808
7	3.4	86.0	3.4	86.0	Caterham 7 HPC: 725
					Citroen XM 2.0SEi: 1086
					Ford Escort RS2000: 1973
					Ford Granada Scorpio 2.0i Auto: 1953
					Ford Sierra Sapphire 2000E: 1944
					Infiniti G20: 2232
					Mazda 626: 2721
					Mazda 626 2.0 GLS Executive: 2739
					Mazda 626 2.0 GLX Executive Estate: 2744
					Mazda 626 2.0i 5-door: 2733
					Mazda 626 2.0i GT 4WS: 2745
					Mazda 626 GT: 2734
					Nissan NX2000: 3249

					Nissan Primera 2.0 GSX: 3250
					Nissan Primera 2.0E ZX: 3251
					Nissan Sentra SE-R: 3252
					Nissan Sunny 2.0 GTi: 3255
					Opel Calibra 2.0i 16v: 3351
					Peugeot 605 SRi: 3461
					Pontiac Grand Am Turbo: 3591
					Pontiac Sunbird GT: 3587
					Toyota Camry 2.0 GLi: 4445
					Toyota Camry 2.0 GLi Estate: 4446
					Toyota Celica 2.0 GT: 4468
					Toyota Celica 2.0GT: 4438
					Toyota Celica All-Trac Turbo: 4454
					Toyota Celica All-Trac Turbo: 4469
					Toyota Celica GT Cabriolet: 4447
					Toyota Celica GT4: 4455
					Toyota Celica GTS: 4439
					Toyota MR2: 4479
					Toyota MR2 GT: 4472
					Toyota MR2 HKS: 4480
					Toyota MR2 Turbo: 4473
					Toyota Space Cruiser: 4434
					Toyota Van LE: 4430
					Vauxhall Astra GTE 2.0i: 4706
					Vauxhall Calibra 2.0i: 4728
					Vauxhall Calibra 2.0i 16v: 4722
					Vauxhall Calibra 4x4: 4729
					Vauxhall Carlton CD 2.0i: 4704
					Vauxhall Cavalier 2.0i CD: 4709
					Vauxhall Cavalier 4x4: 4714
					Vauxhall Cavalier GSi 2000 16v: 4725
					Vauxhall Cavalier GSi 2000 16v 4x4: 4726
					Vauxhall Cavalier SRi: 4719
					Vauxhall Cavalier SRi 130 4-door: 4710
8	3.4	85.6	3.4	85.6	Morgan SS: 3122
					Rover 2000: 3999
					Rover 2000: 4002
					Rover 2000 Automatic: 4003
					Rover 2000SC: 4013
					Rover 2000TC: 4011
					Rover 2000TC: 4008
					Rover 2000TC: 4004
9	3.2	82.6	3.2	82.6	Humber Super Snipe: 2206
					Humber Super Snipe: 2205
					Vauxhall Cresta Overdrive: 4636
					Vauxhall Cresta Series PB: 4641
10	3.1	80.0	3.1	80.0	Fiat 124 Coupe 1600: 1520
					Fiat 124 Spider 1600: 1526
					Fiat 124 Sport Coupe: 1527
					Fiat 125: 1508
					Fiat 125 Special: 1517
					Ford Escort 1.6 Ghia Estate: 1961
					Ford Fiesta 1.6L Diesel: 1893
					Maserati Shamal: 2681
11	3.1	79.6	3.1	79.5	Ford Escort RS Turbo: 1911
12	3.1	78.0	3.1	78.0	Fiat 1500: 1484
					Mazda 1500 de Luxe: 2686
					Mercedes-Benz 300SLR: 2795
					Osca 1490cc Spyder: 3353
					Toyota Corona: 4353
13	3.0	76.9	3.0	77.0	Renault Le Car Turbo: 3874
14	3.0	76.2	3.0	76.2	Hillman Hunter Husky: 2045
					Hillman Hunter Husky III: 2055
					Hillman Hunter Husky Series II: 2052
					Hillman Husky: 2046
					Hillman Minx Convertible: 2044
					Hillman Minx de Luxe: 2042
					Hillman Minx de Luxe: 2043
					Hillman Minx Estate: 2047
					Hillman Minx Series II: 2048
					Sunbeam Rapier: 4288
					Sunbeam Rapier: 4287
					Sunbeam Rapier: 4286

Total: 105

Oversquare bore and stroke. Bore limit set at 4in.

	bore		stroke		
	in	mm	in	mm	
1	4.5	115.0	4.0	101.0	Shelby GT 500: 4122
2	4.5	114.3	4.2	108.0	Chevrolet Camaro Gottlieb 1969: 926
					Chevrolet Camaro IROC-Z 8.3-litre: 914
					Chevrolet Camaro IROC-Z Chevrolet Engineering: 929
3	4.4	110.7	3.6	91.2	Ford LTD: 1773
					Ford Mustang Boss 429: 1777
					Ford Thunderbird: 1779
					Lincoln Continental Limousine: 2582
					Mercury Marquis Brougham: 2948
					Mercury Marquis Marauder X-100: 2949
4	4.3	110.0	3.8	95.2	Dodge Coronet R/T: 1300
5	4.3	109.7	3.8	95.3	Chrysler 300: 984
					Chrysler 300: 988
					Chrysler 300-H: 989
					Chrysler Imperial Crown: 987
					Dodge Challenger R/T: 1314
					Dodge Charger R/T: 1315
					Dodge Coronet R/T: 1304
					Dodge Monaco: 1310
					Dodge Super Bee Six-Pack: 1312
					Jensen Interceptor III: 2400
					Jensen Interceptor III Convertible: 2403
					Jensen SP: 2397
					Monteverdi 375L: 3118
					Plymouth Cuda 440: 3505
					Plymouth GTX: 3501
					Plymouth GTX: 3497
6	4.3	109.5	3.9	99.1	Buick GS455 Stage 1: 687
					Buick Riviera: 668
					Buick Riviera: 674
					Buick Riviera Gran Sport: 677
					Buick Wildcat: 672
					Chevrolet Bel Air 409 SS/S: 755
					Chevrolet Corvette Greenwood: 870
					Chevrolet Impala SS 409: 768
					Chevrolet Impala Super Sport 409: 779
7	4.3	109.2	4.1	103.1	Cadillac Coupe de Ville: 709
					Ford Thunderbird: 1653
					Ford Thunderbird: 1665
					Lincoln Continental: 2580
					Lincoln Continental: 2581
					Lincoln Continental Mk III: 2579
8	4.3	108.7	3.8	95.2	Jensen Interceptor III Convertible: 2401
9	4.3	108.1	4.0	101.2	AC Cobra 427 Modified 1965: 27
10	4.2	108.0	3.3	82.7	Avanti II: 458
					Chevrolet Camaro: 804
					Chevrolet Camaro 427 Dana: 805
					Chevrolet Camaro Z/28 Yenko/SC: 826
					Chevrolet Caprice: 827
					Chevrolet Corvette 435hp: 829
					Chevrolet Corvette 454: 844
					Chevrolet Corvette Convertible: 803
					Chevrolet Corvette Convertible: 818
					Chevrolet Corvette Grand Sport Roadster: 776
					Chevrolet Corvette L36: 830
					Chevrolet Corvette L68: 832
					Chevrolet Corvette L71: 833
					Chevrolet Corvette L71/89: 834
					Chevrolet Corvette L88: 835
					Chevrolet Corvette L88: 820
					Chevrolet Corvette ZR-2: 956
					Chevrolet Impala: 846
					Chevrolet Impala SS427: 809
					Chevrolet Kingswood Estate Wagon: 839
					Chevrolet Monte Carlo: 847
					Chevrolet Monte Carlo: 859
					Chrysler Enforcer: 976
					Chrysler Newport: 983
					Dodge Charger: 1298
					Dodge Charger: 1299
					Dodge Charger R/T: 1303
					Dodge Coronet 426-S:1294
					Dodge Coronet 500: 1296
					Dodge Coronet 500 Station Wagon: 1307
					Dodge Hemi Charger 500 Automatic: 1308
					Dodge Hemi Charger 500 Manual: 1309
					Dodge Monaco Wagon: 1302
					Dodge Polara: 1289
					Dodge Polara: 1286
					Dodge Polara 500: 1290
					Dodge Ramcharger 426 Super/Stock: 1287
					Dodge Super Bee: 1311
					Facel Vega Facel II: 1368
					Jensen FF: 2392
					Jensen FF II: 2394
					Jensen Interceptor: 2396
					Jensen Interceptor: 2393
					Jensen Interceptor: 2391
					Jensen Interceptor II: 2395
					Plymouth Belvedere Satellite: 3487
					Plymouth Fury III: 3506
					Plymouth Fury III: 3496
					Plymouth Fury III: 3500
					Plymouth Fury Station Wagon: 3488
					Plymouth GTX Hemi: 3502
					Plymouth Road Runner: 3507
					Plymouth Road Runner: 3503
					Plymouth Satellite: 3490
					Plymouth Satellite Street Hemi: 3491
					Plymouth Sport Fury: 3483
					Plymouth VIP: 3492
					Shelby Cobra 427: 4126
11	4.2	107.8	3.4	85.9	Facel Vega HK-500: 1366
					Ford Fastback NASCAR: 1698
					Mercury Comet A/FX: 2933
12	4.2	107.4	3.8	96.0	Ford Galaxie 500 XL 427: 1714
					Mercury Cougar XR-7: 2946
					Mercury Super Marauder S-55: 2932

13	4.2	107.0	3.7	95.0	Mercedes-Benz 450SEL 6.9: 2862
					Mercedes-Benz 600SE: 2854

Total: 110

Longest stroke. Limit set at 4.5in.

	in	mm	
1	5.9	150.1	Mercedes-Benz 36/220-S: 2774
			Mercedes-Benz SSKL: 2776
2	5.5	140.0	Bentley 4.5-litre: 461
			Bentley 4.5-litre Supercharged: 462
			Bentley 8-litre Saloon: 463
			Bentley Speed Six Weymann: 464
			Rolls-Royce Phantom II: 3950
3	5.5	139.7	Rolls-Royce Phantom I Phaeton: 3946
			Rolls-Royce Phantom II: 3949
			Wills Sainte Claire Six: 4974
4	5.2	133.4	Armstrong Siddeley 30 Special Sports Saloon: 213
5	5.1	130.0	Bugatti 5-litre Saloon: 650
6	5.0	127.0	Armstrong Siddeley Rally Tourer: 210
			Chrysler 77 Saloon: 962
			Chrysler Custom Imperial Le Baron: 964
			Hudson 22hp Six Saloon: 2173
			Hudson 22hp Six Special Saloon: 2175
			Hudson Terraplane Big Six Saloon: 2172
			Hudson Terraplane Saloon: 2174
			Lincoln 39.2hp Saloon: 2574
			Lincoln 39.2hp Town Saloon: 2573
			Packard 32.5hp Saloon: 3358
			Packard 32.5hp Saloon: 3354
			Packard 32.5hp Standard Eight Saloon: 3361
			Packard 7-34 Phaeton: 3355
			Packard Straight Eight Saloon: 3357
			Packard Super 8 Phaeton: 3356
7	4.9	125.4	La Salle Enclosed Drive Limousine: 2421
8	4.9	123.8	Chrysler Super Power Saloon: 968
9	4.8	121.0	Essex Terraplane Tourer: 1360
10	4.7	120.7	Auburn 38hp Saloon: 263
			Duesenberg J Coupe: 1352
			Duesenberg SJ Town Car: 1353
			Franklin 29.4hp Saloon: 1977
			Hudson Super Jet: 2178
			Hupmobile 32.5hp Saloon: 2218
			Hupmobile Straight Eight Limousine: 2216
			Invicta 4.5-litre: 2241
			Invicta 4.5-litre: 2242
			Kissel 8-65 Gold Bug: 2416
			Lagonda 4.5-litre: 2442
			Lagonda 4.5-litre Tourer: 2440
			Lagonda Rapide: 2441
			Lagonda Rapide Tourer: 2439
			Marmon 79 Saloon: 2650
11	4.7	120.1	Auburn 8-52 Speedster: 264
12	4.7	120.0	Chrysler 75 Saloon: 961
			Daimler Straight Eight: 1139
			Daimler Twenty-Seven Limousine: 1138
			Delage 21hp Weymann Saloon: 1245
			Delaunay-Belleville 21hp Saloon: 1253
			Healey 2.4-litre Roadster: 2019
			Healey Tickford Saloon: 2020
			Hillman 80 Limousine: 2032
			Hillman Hawk Sports Saloon: 2031
			Hillman Safety Saloon: 2022
			Humber 16.9hp Saloon: 2189
			Humber Imperial: 2193
			Humber Imperial Saloon: 2194
			Humber Pullman Limousine: 2197
			Humber Pullman Limousine: 2186
			Humber Snipe Drop-head Foursome: 2188
			Humber Snipe Sports Saloon: 2190
			Humber Snipe Sports Saloon: 2187
			Humber Super Snipe: 2198
			Humber Super Snipe: 2195
			Lagonda 2-litre Supercharged: 2433
			Lagonda 3-litre Special Tourer: 2434
			Lagonda 3-litre Tourer: 2432
			Lagonda 3.5-litre Tourer: 2436
			Lagonda Le Mans: 2437
			Renault 24hp Big Six Saloon: 3799
			Renault Vivasix Saloon: 3797
			Riley 16 2.5: 3931
			Riley 2.5: 3938
			Riley 2.5: 3936
			Riley 2.5 Saloon: 3935
			Riley 2.5 Saloon: 3933
			Riley 2.5 Sports: 3934
			Riley Pathfinder: 3940
			Riley Pathfinder: 3939
			Talbot 3-litre Saloon: 4342
13	4.6	117.5	Buick Empire Saloon: 653
14	4.6	117.5	Buick 28.4hp Saloon: 654
15	4.6	116.0	Humber Pullman Limousine: 2182
			Humber Snipe: 2180
			Humber Snipe Sports Saloon: 2185
16	4.5	115.0	Austro Daimler 32/100 Saloon: 448
			HE 16/60 Sports Four-seater: 2017
			Mercedes-Benz 32/90 Limousine: 2777
			Mercedes-Benz 32/90 Saloon: 2775
17	4.5	114.5	Austin 20 Mayfair Limousine: 350
			Austin 20 Ranelagh Landaulet: 347
18	4.5	114.3	Armstrong Siddeley 25.3hp Town and Country Saloon: 215
			Armstrong Siddeley Six-light Saloon: 216
			Auburn 8-120 Speedster: 262
			Bentley 4.25-litre: 468
			Bentley Continental: 471
			Bentley Continental Park Ward DH Coupe: 475
			Bentley Sedan: 465
			Bentley Series S: 476
			Chrysler Heston Airflow Saloon: 965
			Chrysler Royal Saloon: 969
			Cord L-29: 1097
			Dodge Safari Super Sport: 1291
			Du Pont Speedster: 1350
			Du Pont Town Car: 1351
			Graham-Paige 21.6hp Saloon: 2015
			Graham-Paige Straight Eight: 2016
			Hudson Commodore: 2176
			Hudson Hornet: 2177
			Hudson Straight Eight Roadster: 2169
			Kurtis Hornet Roadster: 2420
			La Salle 37-50 V8 Saloon: 2422
			Nash Straight Eight Saloon: 3194
			Packard 120 Saloon: 3360
			Rolls-Royce 20 Saloon: 3947
			Rolls-Royce 25 Saloon: 3948
			Rolls-Royce Phantom III: 3952
			Rolls-Royce Silver Cloud: 3956
			Rolls-Royce Silver Cloud "S": 3957
			Rolls-Royce Silver Dawn: 3955
			Rolls-Royce Silver Dawn: 3954
			Stutz 36.4hp Saloon: 4240
			Stutz DV32 Sports Saloon: 4242
			Stutz Roadster: 4239
			Stutz Straight Eight Saloon: 4241

Total: 127

Shortest stroke. Limit set at 2.4in.

	in	mm	
1	1.9	48.5	Ford Anglia: 1654
			Ford Anglia: 1649
			Ford Anglia de Luxe Estate: 1666
			Ford Prefect: 1633
2	2.1	52.2	Alfa Romeo 33 2.0 Stradale: 66
3	2.1	53.0	Ford Escort 1100L: 1823
			Lamborghini Urraco: 2463
			Lamborghini Urraco S: 2460
4	2.1	53.3	Ford Cortina 1100: 1769
			Ford Escort: 1756
5	2.2	55.4	Fiat Regata 70 ES: 1585
6	2.2	55.5	Fiat 128: 1529
			Fiat 128: 1546
			Fiat 128 3P: 1552
			Fiat 128 4-door: 1523
			Fiat 128 Coupe 1300: 1531
			Fiat 128 SL 1300 Coupe: 1532
			Fiat 128 Special: 1547
			Fiat Strada 60 Comfort ES: 1581
			Fiat Strada 65CL: 1567
			Fiat Uno 55 S: 1582
			Fiat Uno 70 SX: 1588
			Fiat Uno 70 SX: 1583
			Fiat Uno Selecta: 1597
			Fiat X1/9: 1557
			Fiat X1/9: 1543
			Fiat X1/9 1300: 1569
			Ford Fiesta: 1845
			Ford Fiesta 1000: 1852
			Ford Fiesta Popular: 1875
			Yugo 65A GLX: 5004
			Yugo GV: 5002
			Zastava 1300 ZLX-E: 5006
7	2.2	55.8	Ferrari 250 Testa Rossa: 1382
			Fiat 128 Estate: 1553
			Fiat 600: 1486
			Fiat 600: 1472
			Fiat 600: 1469
			Fiat 600 Multipla: 1473
			Fiat Multipla: 1474
			Goggomobil TS400: 2004
8	2.2	56.6	Bugatti EB110: 652
9	2.3	57.8	Fiat 127 1050 CL: 1555
			Fiat 127 1050 Super: 1572
			Fiat 127 Sport: 1558
			Fiat Panda 750 L: 1593
			Honda N360: 2089
			Lancia Y10 Turbo: 2540

10	2.3	58.2	Ford Anglia Estate: 1710
			Ford Anglia Super: 1667
			Ford Consul Cortina: 1669
			Ford Consul Cortina: 1686
			Ford Cortina Estate de Luxe: 1688
11	2.3	58.7	Ferrari 166 Mille Miglia Barchetta: 1371
			Ferrari 212 Coupe: 1374
			Ferrari 212 Touring: 1372
			Ferrari 250 GT 2+2: 1385
			Ferrari 250 GT Berlinetta Lusso: 1388
			Ferrari 250 GT Cabriolet: 1380
			Ferrari 250 GT Coupe: 1384
			Ferrari 250 GT Coupe: 1381
			Ferrari 250 Mille Miglia: 1376
			Ferrari 250 Testa Rossa: 1378
			Ferrari 275 GTS: 1391
			Ferrari 275 GTS/4 NART: 1392
12	2.3	59.0	Alfa Romeo Alfasud: 81
			Alfa Romeo Alfasud: 84
			Alfa Romeo Alfasud 1200ti: 95
			Alfa Romeo Alfasud 5M: 97
			Alfa Romeo Alfasud ti: 88
			Citroen GS: 1042
			Citroen GS: 1039
			Datsun 1000: 1157
			Datsun 1000 de Luxe: 1168
			Datsun 100A: 1172
			Datsun Cherry F11: 1204
			Saab 96 V4: 4061
			Saab Sonnet V4: 4063
			Saab V4: 4062
			Volkswagen Polo: 4800
			Volkswagen Polo C: 4833
			Volkswagen Polo C Saloon: 4870
13	2.4	60.0	Ferrari 246 GT Dino: 1399
			Ferrari 246 GTS Dino: 1401
			Ford Granada 2.3L Estate: 1879
			Ford Taunus 20M: 1726
			Subaru 1300 GL Coupe: 4247
			Subaru 1600 4WD Estate: 4251
			Subaru 1600 Coupe: 4252
			Subaru 360: 4243
			Subaru 4WD Station Wagon: 4250
			Subaru DL: 4249
			Subaru DL: 4253
			Subaru DL-5: 4254
			Subaru FF-1 1300: 4246
			Subaru Hapi Van 360: 4245
			Subaru Hatchback: 4266
			Subaru Star: 4244
14	2.4	60.3	Chrysler Sunbeam 1.0LS: 997
			Ford Cortina 2.3 Ghia: 1849
			Ford Cortina 2.3 Ghia S: 1863
			Ford Granada 2.3 GL Auto: 1856
			Ford Sierra 2.3 Ghia Automatic: 1883
			Ford Zephyr 6 Mk IV: 1740
			Ford Zephyr de Luxe: 1765
15	2.4	60.4	Bond 875: 628
			Clan Crusader: 1095
			Hillman Hunter Husky: 2064
			Hillman Imp Californian: 2065
			Hillman Imp de Luxe: 2073
			Hillman Imp de Luxe: 2056
			Hillman Super Imp: 2061
			Singer Chamois: 4175
			Singer Chamois: 4181
			Sunbeam Imp: 4300
			Sunbeam Imp Sport: 4305
			Sunbeam Stiletto: 4306
16	2.4	61.0	Bond Bug: 629
			Opel Kadett: 3309
			Opel Kadett Rallye: 3312
			Opel Kadett S: 3311
			Reliant Rebel 700 Estate: 3786
			Toyota 1000: 4393
			Toyota Corolla: 4359
			Toyota Corolla de Luxe: 4360
			Vauxhall Bedford Beagle: 4643
			Vauxhall Chevette L: 4681
			Vauxhall Chevette L: 4676
			Vauxhall Viva 1256 DL: 4674
			Vauxhall Viva de Luxe: 4652
			Vauxhall Viva de Luxe: 4664
			Vauxhall Viva de Luxe: 4642
			Vauxhall Viva HC Estate: 4669
			Vauxhall Viva SL90: 4649
			Vauxhall Viva SL90 Estate: 4659

Total: 135

Widest bore. Limit set at 4.2in.

	in	mm	
1	4.5	115.0	Shelby GT 500: 4122
2	4.5	114.3	Chevrolet Camaro Gottlieb 1969: 926
			Chevrolet Camaro IROC-Z 8.3-litre: 914
			Chevrolet Camaro IROC-Z Chevrolet Engineering: 929
3	4.4	110.7	Ford LTD: 1773
			Ford Mustang Boss 429: 1777
			Ford Thunderbird: 1779
			Lincoln Continental Limousine: 2582
			Mercury Marquis Brougham: 2948
			Mercury Marquis Marauder X-100: 2949
4	4.3	110.0	Bentley 8-litre Saloon: 463
			Dodge Coronet R/T: 1300
5	4.3	109.7	Chrysler 300: 988
			Chrysler 300: 984
			Chrysler 300-H: 989
			Chrysler Imperial Crown: 987
			Dodge Challenger R/T: 1314
			Dodge Charger R/T: 1315
			Dodge Coronet R/T: 1304
			Dodge Monaco: 1310
			Dodge Super Bee Six-Pack: 1312
			Jensen Interceptor III: 2400
			Jensen Interceptor III Convertible: 2403
			Jensen SP: 2397
			Monteverdi 375L: 3118
			Plymouth Cuda 440: 3505
			Plymouth GTX: 3497
			Plymouth GTX: 3501
6	4.3	109.5	Buick GS455 Stage 1: 687
			Buick Riviera: 668
			Buick Riviera: 674
			Buick Riviera Gran Sport: 677
			Buick Wildcat: 672
			Chevrolet Bel Air 409 SS/S: 755
			Chevrolet Corvette Greenwood: 870
			Chevrolet Impala SS 409: 768
			Chevrolet Impala Super Sport 409: 779
7	4.3	109.2	Cadillac Coupe de Ville: 709
			Ford Thunderbird: 1653
			Ford Thunderbird: 1665
			Lincoln Continental: 2581
			Lincoln Continental: 2580
			Lincoln Continental Mk III: 2579
8	4.3	108.7	Jensen Interceptor III Convertible: 2401
9	4.3	108.1	AC Cobra 427 Modified 1965: 27
10	4.2	108.0	Avanti II: 458
			Chevrolet Camaro: 804
			Chevrolet Camaro 427 Dana: 805
			Chevrolet Camaro Z/28 Yenko/SC: 826
			Chevrolet Caprice: 827
			Chevrolet Corvette 435hp: 829
			Chevrolet Corvette 454: 844
			Chevrolet Corvette Convertible: 818
			Chevrolet Corvette Convertible: 803
			Chevrolet Corvette Grand Sport Roadster: 776
			Chevrolet Corvette L36: 830
			Chevrolet Corvette L68: 832
			Chevrolet Corvette L71: 833
			Chevrolet Corvette L71/89: 834
			Chevrolet Corvette L88: 820
			Chevrolet Corvette L88: 835
			Chevrolet Corvette ZR-2: 956
			Chevrolet Impala: 846
			Chevrolet Impala SS427: 809
			Chevrolet Kingswood Estate Wagon: 839
			Chevrolet Monte Carlo: 859
			Chevrolet Monte Carlo: 847
			Chrysler Enforcer: 976
			Chrysler Newport: 983
			Dodge Charger: 1299
			Dodge Charger: 1298
			Dodge Charger R/T: 1303
			Dodge Coronet 426-S: 1294
			Dodge Coronet 500: 1296
			Dodge Coronet 500 Station Wagon: 1307
			Dodge Hemi Charger 500 Automatic: 1308
			Dodge Hemi Charger 500 Manual: 1309
			Dodge Monaco Wagon: 1302
			Dodge Polara: 1289
			Dodge Polara: 1286
			Dodge Polara 500: 1290
			Dodge Ramcharger 426 Super/Stock: 1287
			Dodge Super Bee: 1311
			Facel Vega Facel II: 1368
			Jensen FF: 2392
			Jensen FF II: 2394
			Jensen Interceptor: 2391
			Jensen Interceptor: 2396
			Jensen Interceptor: 2393
			Jensen Interceptor II: 2395
			Plymouth Belvedere Satellite: 3487
			Plymouth Fury III: 3500
			Plymouth Fury III: 3496
			Plymouth Fury III: 3506
			Plymouth Fury Station Wagon: 3488
			Plymouth GTX Hemi: 3502
			Plymouth Road Runner: 3507
			Plymouth Road Runner: 3503
			Plymouth Satellite: 3490

			Plymouth Satellite Street Hemi: 3491
			Plymouth Sport Fury: 3483
			Plymouth VIP: 3492
			Rolls-Royce Phantom I Phaeton: 3946
			Rolls-Royce Phantom II: 3949
			Rolls-Royce Phantom II: 3950
			Shelby Cobra 427: 4126
11	4.2	107.8	Facel Vega HK-500: 1366
			Ford Fastback NASCAR: 1698
			Mercury Comet A/FX: 2933
12	4.2	107.4	Ford Galaxie 500 XL 427: 1714
			Mercury Cougar XR-7: 2946
			Mercury Super Marauder S-55: 2932
			Safir GT40: 4106
13	4.2	107.0	Mercedes-Benz 450SEL 6.9: 2862
			Mercedes-Benz 600SE: 2854

Total: 115

Narrowest bore. Limit set at 2.4in.

	in	mm	
1	2.0	50.0	Renault 4CV: 3801
2	2.0	52.0	Fiat 500 Convertible Saloon: 1458
			Fiat 500C Convertible: 1464
			Fiat 500C Convertible (Topolino): 1462
3	2.1	53.0	MG Mk II Montlhery Supercharged: 2970
4	2.1	54.6	Honda S600: 2087
			Renault 4CV: 3803
			Renault 750: 3804
			Renault 750: 3802
5	2.2	56.0	Austin 7 Ruby Saloon: 351
			Austin 7 Ruby Saloon: 349
			Austin 7 Saloon: 341
			Austin 7 Sports Two-seater: 342
			Austin 7 Sunshine Saloon: 343
			Austin 7 Tourer: 340
			HE Supercharged Six Coupe: 2018
6	2.2	56.5	Triumph Super 7 Saloon: 4487
			Triumph Supercharged 7: 4488
7	2.2	56.6	Ford 8: 1618
			Ford 8 Tudor Saloon: 1611
			Ford Anglia 8 Saloon: 1623
			Standard 8: 4197
8	2.2	56.8	Austin 8 Saloon: 358
			Austin 8 Saloon: 356
			Austin Big 7: 354
			Frazer-Nash 1.5-litre: 1981
			Frazer-Nash 1.5-litre: 1984
			Frisky Coupe: 1993
			MG Magna Continential Coupe: 2971
			MG Magnette KN Saloon: 2974
			MG Magnette N Two-seater: 2972
			MG Midget: 2968
			MG Midget P Type: 2973
			Morris 10/6: 3143
			Morris 10/6 Sports Tourer: 3148
			Morris 8 Minor: 3140
			Morris 8 Saloon: 3147
			Morris 8 Series E Tourer: 3155
			Morris 8 Tourer: 3153
			Morris 8hp Series E Tourer: 3156
			Morris 8hp Tourer: 3154
			Morris Minor: 3157
			Morris Minor Saloon: 3138
			Morris Minor Tourer: 3159
			Riley 12 Mentone Saloon: 3924
			Wolseley Hornet: 4977
9	2.3	58.0	Austin A30: 368
			Austin A30: 369
			Austin A30 Countryman: 375
			Berkeley Sports: 485
			Berkeley Sports: 484
			Berkeley Sports 4: 486
			Frazer-Nash BMW 12.5hp Saloon: 1987
			Morris Minor: 3163
			Morris Minor Series II: 3161
			Renault 4 Estate Car: 3829
			Renault 4 L Estate Car: 3819
			Renault 6: 3834
			Renault Caravelle: 3812
			Renault Carvelle: 3809
			Renault Dauphine: 3810
			Renault Dauphine: 3806
			Renault Dauphine: 3816
			Renault Dauphine: 3805
			Renault Dauphine Automatic: 3820
			Renault Dauphine Ferry: 3807
			Renault Dauphine Gordini: 3814
			Renault Dauphine Gordini: 3811
			Renault Dauphine Gordini de Luxe: 3817
			Renault Floride: 3813
			Standard 8: 4207
			Standard 8: 4200
10	2.4	60.0	AJS 9hp Saloon: 38
			BSA FWD Tourer: 646
			Bugatti 55: 651
			Ferrari 166 Mille Miglia Barchetta: 1371
			Fiat 600: 1472
			Fiat 600: 1486
			Fiat 600: 1469
			Fiat 600 Multipla: 1473
			Fiat Multipla: 1474
			Frazer-Nash 14hp Sports Tourer: 1983
			Honda S800: 2088
			MG Midget PB: 2975
			Moretti 750 Grand Sport Berlinetta Coupe: 3119
			Singer 14/6 Saloon: 4159
			Singer 9 Roadster: 4163
			Singer 9 Sports: 4160
			Singer Le Mans Special Speed Model: 4161
11	2.4	60.3	Riley 8/90 Adelphi Saloon: 3927
			Riley 9 Monaco: 3928
12	2.4	60.4	Bond Bug: 629
			Reliant Rebel 700 Estate: 3786
13	2.4	61.0	Abarth Zagato 750 GT: 1
			Fiat 750 Abarth: 1478
			Fiat Abarth 750GT Zagato: 1479
			Fiat Abarth Twin Cam: 1488
			Fiat Abarth Zagato: 1480
			Rover Pilot: 3974
			Rover Speed 14 Streamline Coupe: 3976
			Suzuki Brute: 4320
			Talbot 65 Saloon: 4335

Total: 102

Theoretical maximum speed at peak engine power. Limit set at 150mph.

	mph	kmh	
1	228.9	368.4	Ferrari 288 GTO: 1421
			Ferrari GTO: 1423
2	210.0	337.9	Ferrari 365 GTB/4 Competitione: 1403
3	201.3	323.9	Chevrolet Corvette Greenwood: 870
4	198.0	318.6	Porsche 928 S4: 3712
5	196.0	315.4	Ferrari 250 GT 2+2: 1385
6	189.2	304.4	Porsche 928 S: 3691
7	186.4	300.0	Lamborghini Countach: 2461
			Porsche Carrera RSR: 3642
8	186.0	299.3	Ferrari 365 GTB/4 Daytona: 1396
9	184.5	296.9	Ferrari Daytona: 1397
10	184.1	296.2	Porsche 928 S Series II: 3684
11	183.7	295.7	Ferrari 400 Super America: 1389
12	182.1	293.0	Mercedes-Benz 300SL-24 5-speed Auto: 2917
13	181.4	292.0	Ferrari 512 BB: 1407
14	180.0	289.7	Ferrari 365 GTB/4 Daytona: 1404
15	180.0	289.6	Porsche 928 S: 3683
16	178.2	286.8	Porsche 928 S: 3677
17	177.9	286.2	Lamborghini Miura S: 2456
18	176.3	283.7	Vauxhall Senator 3.0i CD: 4702
19	175.6	282.5	Lamborghini Miura P400S: 2455
20	175.5	282.4	De Tomaso Pantera GT5-S: 1242
21	173.0	278.5	Vauxhall Senator 3.0i CD: 4711
22	171.7	276.4	Pontiac Petty Grand National: 3571
23	171.5	276.0	Lamborghini Countach LP 500S: 2465
24	170.9	275.1	Ferrari 308 GT4 Dino: 1402
25	170.8	274.9	Lamborghini Countach: 2468
26	170.4	274.2	Porsche 911 Turbo Ruf 3.4: 3698
27	169.4	272.6	Ferrari 4.9: 1387
28	168.7	271.6	Lamborghini Countach S: 2464
29	168.7	271.5	Jaguar XJS Tullius: 2333
			Mercedes-Benz 300E: 2885
30	168.6	271.4	Ferrari 512 BB: 1413
31	168.0	270.4	Lamborghini Miura: 2452
			Maserati Bora: 2660
			Porsche 928 S4 Automatic: 3692
32	167.9	270.1	Ferrari 308 GTB: 1409
33	167.8	270.0	Ferrari 348tb: 1445
34	167.6	269.7	Volvo 760 GLE: 4944
35	166.9	268.7	Ferrari Testa Rossa: 1442
36	166.9	268.6	BMW 750i: 612
			BMW 750i L: 589
37	166.2	267.5	Mitsubishi Galant 2000 GLS Automatic: 3092
38	165.6	266.5	Vauxhall Senator 3.0i 24v: 4731
39	165.4	266.1	BMW 850i: 620
40	164.5	264.7	Nissan 300ZX: 3240
41	164.4	264.6	De Tomaso Pantera GTS: 1239
42	163.8	263.6	BMW 533i: 566
			Lamborghini Countach 5000S: 2469
			Maserati Bora: 2664
43	163.6	263.2	Porsche 944 Lux: 3685
44	163.5	263.1	Nissan Maxima: 3235
45	163.5	263.1	Porsche Carrera 2 Cabriolet Tiptronic: 3744
46	163.3	262.8	Honda NSX: 2156
47	163.0	262.3	Audi 100 CD: 290
48	162.8	262.0	Ford Mustang GT: 1923
49	162.6	261.7	Aston Martin Virage: 261
50	162.5	261.5	Lotus Excel SA: 2634
51	162.5	261.5	Ferrari Dino 308 GT4 2+2: 1410
52	162.0	260.7	BMW 633 CSi: 570

53	161.7	260.3	BMW 735i: 567
54	161.3	259.6	BMW 735i Automatic: 585
55	161.3	259.5	Chevrolet Monza Mike Keyser: 874
			Vauxhall Senator 3.0i CD: 4721
56	160.7	258.6	BMW 735i Automatic: 571
57	160.6	258.4	BMW 732i: 575
58	160.2	257.8	Porsche 944 Turbo: 3730
59	160.2	257.7	Plymouth Horizon America: 3520
60	160.1	257.6	BMW 730i SE: 588
61	159.8	257.2	Porsche 911 Turbo: 3750
62	159.6	256.9	Ford Mustang GT: 1905
63	159.5	256.7	Allard GT Coupe: 153
			BMW M535i: 576
64	159.3	256.4	Chevrolet Kingswood Estate Wagon: 839
65	158.9	255.7	Porsche 935 Group 4 Holbert: 3657
66	158.1	254.4	BMW 850i Manual: 625
67	157.9	254.2	Mazda RX-7 Turbo II: 2759
68	157.9	254.1	Mercedes-Benz 400SE: 2918
69	157.5	253.5	Lamborghini Jarama 400GT: 2457
			Volkswagen Passat GT 16v: 4878
70	157.4	253.4	Chevrolet Cavalier CS: 889
71	157.3	253.1	Porsche 911 Turbo: 3689
			Porsche 911 Turbo: 3708
72	156.8	252.3	Ferrari 275 GTS/4 NART: 1392
73	156.6	252.0	Porsche 928 S4 SE: 3727
74	156.2	251.4	Iso Grifo GL 365: 2248
75	156.2	251.4	Aston Martin Mk III: 236
76	156.0	251.0	BMW M635 CSi: 607
			BMW M635 CSi Hardy & Beck: 577
77	155.9	250.9	Rover Vanden Plas: 4021
78	155.7	250.5	Aston Martin V8 Coupe: 247
79	155.6	250.5	Mercedes-Benz 500SL: 2913
			Reliant Scimitar GTE: 3792
80	155.6	250.4	BMW 635 CSi: 594
81	155.2	249.8	Pontiac Firebird TransAm Silverbird: 3566
82	155.2	249.8	Rover Vitesse: 4024
83	155.0	249.5	Honda NSX Auto: 2159
84	155.0	249.4	Mercedes-Benz 420SE: 2887
85	154.9	249.2	Porsche 924 S: 3711
			Porsche 944: 3713
			Porsche 944: 3693
			Porsche 944 Turbo: 3715
86	154.8	249.1	Avanti II: 460
			Ruger Bentley Clone: 4052
			Volvo 960 24v: 4968
87	154.7	249.0	BMW M635 CSi: 572
			Ferrari 330 GTS: 1393
			Lamborghini 400GT: 2450
88	154.7	248.9	TVR V8 S: 4603
89	153.9	247.7	Westfield SEight: 4973
90	153.8	247.5	Lotus Elite: 2624
			Lotus Elite: 2617
91	153.4	246.9	Porsche 911 Turbo: 3659
92	152.9	246.1	Mercedes-Benz 500SEL: 2882
93	152.8	245.9	Volkswagen Passat GL 5S Estate: 4826
94	152.8	245.9	Jaguar XJS 3.6 Automatic: 2354
95	152.6	245.6	Jaguar XJS 3.6: 2345
96	152.2	245.0	Jaguar XJR 4.0: 2363
97	152.2	244.9	Panther Kallista 2.8: 3377
98	151.9	244.4	Ferrari 365 GTC4: 1400
99	151.8	244.3	Porsche 911 Turbo: 3723
			Porsche 944 Turbo SE: 3716
			Renault GTA V6 Turbo: 3899
100	151.7	244.2	Nissan 300ZX Turbo: 3224
101	151.2	243.4	Jaguar XJ6 4.2: 2320
			Porsche 911 Turbo Cabriolet Ruf: 3680
102	151.2	243.3	Chevrolet Camaro IROC-Z: 896
			Datsun 280ZX Turbo: 1231
			Porsche Carrera RS Touring: 3641
103	150.8	242.7	Aston Martin DBS V8: 244
104	150.7	242.5	Porsche 911 3.3 Turbo: 3719
			Porsche 911 Turbo: 3676
105	150.6	242.4	Vauxhall Cavalier 2.0i CD: 4709
106	150.6	242.4	Peugeot 605 SV 3.0 Auto: 3466
107	150.5	242.2	Ferrari 365 GTC: 1390
			Ford Granada Ghia X 2.9 EFi Saloon: 1952
			Mercedes-Benz 500E: 2919
108	150.1	241.6	BMW M1: 556
			Lotus Esprit Turbo SE: 2637
			Porsche 924 S Turbo: 3668
			Rover 3500: 4016
109	150.1	241.5	Aston Martin DBS: 243
			Ferrari Testa Rossa: 1426
110	150.0	241.4	Ford Mustang TransAm: 1796
			Lamborghini Silhouette 3000: 2462
			Rover Sterling Automatic: 4030
			Shelby Cobra 427: 4126

Total: 147

Cruising speed at 3,500rpm in top gear. Limit set at 100mph.

	mph	kmh	
1	135.4	218.0	Avanti II: 460
2	129.5	208.2	Ford Mustang GT: 1923
3	127.4	205.1	Chevrolet Corvette: 900
4	126.7	203.7	Mercedes-Benz SSKL: 2776
5	124.6	200.5	Bentley Turbo R: 481
6	123.5	198.8	Chevrolet Corvette: 897
7	122.8	197.7	Mercedes-Benz 36/220-S: 2774
8	122.5	197.0	Hudson Rambler: 2179
9	121.8	196.0	Chevrolet Corvette: 894
10	121.4	195.3	Ford Mustang GT: 1905
11	119.0	191.4	Lincoln Continental Mk VII LSC: 2584
12	117.6	189.3	BMW 525E: 565
13	117.2	188.6	GMC Safari Cargo Mover: 2003
14	115.8	186.5	Chevrolet Camaro IROC-Z L98: 907
15	115.5	185.8	Porsche 928 S4: 3712
16	115.1	185.1	Porsche 928 S: 3691
17	114.8	184.8	Chevrolet Cavalier CS: 889
18	114.4	184.1	Ferrari 288 GTO: 1421
			Ferrari GTO: 1423
19	113.4	182.3	Chevrolet Corvette: 891
			Porsche 928 S: 3677
20	112.7	181.3	Mercedes-Benz 500SEL: 2882
21	112.3	180.6	BMW 750i: 612
			BMW 750i L: 589
			Oldsmobile Delmont: 3291
			Rambler American: 3765
22	111.3	179.2	BMW 850i: 620
23	110.9	178.5	Cadillac Seville Diesel: 712
24	110.6	177.8	Buick Century: 691
			Ford Mustang GT 5.0: 1881
25	110.2	177.4	Chevrolet Camaro IROC-Z: 896
			Chevrolet Impala: 846
			Oldsmobile F-85 Cutlass Cruiser: 3289
26	109.5	176.4	Porsche 928 S: 3683
27	109.2	175.7	Porsche 928 S Series II: 3684
28	108.8	175.0	BMW 735i: 567
29	108.5	174.6	Cadillac Seville Diesel: 711
			Oldsmobile Dynamic 88 Celebrity Sedan: 3276
30	108.1	173.9	BMW 735i Automatic: 571
			Vauxhall Senator 3.0i CD: 4711
31	107.8	173.6	Plymouth Horizon America: 3520
32	106.4	171.1	BMW 850i Manual: 625
			Vauxhall Senator 3.0i CD: 4702
33	106.0	170.8	BMW 325E: 569
34	105.7	170.1	Buick Skylark: 684
35	105.0	169.0	Chevrolet Corvette: 886
			Ford Mustang 4.2: 1880
			Ford Mustang GT 5.0: 1888
			Jensen 541R: 2388
			Rolls-Royce Silver Spirit II: 3972
36	104.6	168.3	Bentley Mulsanne Turbo: 479
37	104.3	167.6	AC 428 Fastback: 26
			Mercedes-Benz 420SE: 2887
38	103.9	167.3	Rover Vanden Plas: 4021
39	103.6	166.6	Chevrolet Corvette Greenwood: 870
			Mercedes-Benz 300E: 2885
			Mercury Monarch: 2953
			Pontiac Bonneville Vista: 3541
40	103.2	166.2	Carbodies Fairway 2.7 Silver: 721
			Chevrolet Kingswood Estate Wagon: 839
41	102.9	165.5	Rover Vitesse: 4024
			Volvo 760 GLE: 4944
42	102.5	164.8	Toyota Camry LE: 4416
43	102.2	164.5	BMW 732i: 575
			Ford LTD: 1809
			Ford Thunderbird: 1779
			Nissan Maxima: 3235
			Pontiac Catalina: 3537
44	101.8	163.8	Jaguar XJS 3.6 Automatic: 2354
			Jaguar XJS 4.0 Auto: 2371
45	101.5	163.4	Allard GT Coupe: 153
			BMW M535i: 576
			Cadillac Seville: 710
			Jaguar 4.0 Sovereign: 2358
			Jaguar XJR 4.0: 2363
			Lincoln Continental Mk III: 2579
46	101.1	162.7	Citroen CX25 DTR Turbo 2: 1078
			Mercedes-Benz 300SL-24 5-speed Auto: 2917
			Oldsmobile 88 Delta Royale: 3294
			Plymouth Satellite Sport: 3508
			Pontiac Grand Prix: 3551
47	100.8	162.0	BMW 635 CSi: 561
			Jaguar XJS 3.6: 2345
			Rover 825 TD: 4047
			Vauxhall Senator 3.0i CD: 4721
48	100.4	161.7	Bentley Mulsanne Turbo: 480
			Lagonda Le Mans: 2437
			Lincoln Continental: 2581
			Riley Pathfinder: 3940
			Rover Montego 2.0 DSL Turbo: 4034
49	100.1	161.0	Audi 100 CD: 290
			Chevrolet Monte Carlo: 847
			Ford Galaxie 500: 1705
			Nissan Maxima SE: 3214
			Porsche 911 Turbo: 3689
			Porsche 911 Turbo: 3708
			Rover 3500: 4016
			Rover 3500: 4020

Total: 98

Highest top gear ratios. Limit set at 28mph/1000rpm..

	mph	kmh	
1	38.7	62.3	Avanti II: 460
2	37.0	59.5	Ford Mustang GT: 1923
3	36.4	58.6	Chevrolet Corvette: 900
4	36.2	58.2	Mercedes-Benz SSKL: 2776
5	35.6	57.3	Bentley Turbo R: 481
6	35.3	56.8	Chevrolet Corvette: 897
7	35.1	56.5	Mercedes-Benz 36/220-S: 2774
8	35.0	56.3	Hudson Rambler: 2179
9	34.8	56.0	Chevrolet Corvette: 894
10	34.7	55.8	Ford Mustang GT: 1905
11	34.0	54.7	Lincoln Continental Mk VII LSC: 2584
12	33.6	54.1	BMW 525E: 565
13	33.5	53.9	GMC Safari Cargo Mover: 2003
14	33.1	53.3	Chevrolet Camaro IROC-Z L98: 907
15	33.0	53.1	Porsche 928 S4: 3712
16	32.9	52.9	Porsche 928 S: 3691
17	32.8	52.8	Chevrolet Cavalier CS: 889
18	32.7	52.6	Ferrari 288 GTO: 1421
			Ferrari GTO: 1423
19	32.4	52.1	Chevrolet Corvette: 891
			Porsche 928 S: 3677
20	32.2	51.8	Mercedes-Benz 500SEL: 2882
21	32.1	51.6	BMW 750i: 612
			BMW 750i L: 589
			Oldsmobile Delmont: 3291
			Rambler American: 3765
22	31.8	51.2	BMW 850i: 620
23	31.7	51.0	Cadillac Seville Diesel: 712
24	31.6	50.8	Buick Century: 691
			Ford Mustang GT 5.0: 1881
25	31.5	50.7	Chevrolet Camaro IROC-Z: 896
			Chevrolet Impala: 846
			Oldsmobile F-85 Cutlass Cruiser: 3289
26	31.3	50.4	Porsche 928 S: 3683
27	31.2	50.2	Porsche 928 S Series II: 3684
28	31.1	50.0	BMW 735i: 567
29	31.0	49.9	Cadillac Seville Diesel: 711
			Oldsmobile Dynamic 88 Celebrity Sedan: 3276
30	30.9	49.7	BMW 735i Automatic: 571
			Vauxhall Senator 3.0i CD: 4711
31	30.8	49.6	Plymouth Horizon America: 3520
32	30.4	48.9	BMW 850i Manual: 625
			Vauxhall Senator 3.0i CD: 4702
33	30.3	48.8	BMW 325E: 569
34	30.2	48.6	Buick Skylark: 684
35	30.0	48.3	Chevrolet Corvette: 886
			Ford Mustang 4.2: 1880
			Ford Mustang GT 5.0: 1888
			Jensen 541R: 2388
			Rolls-Royce Silver Spirit II: 3972
36	29.9	48.1	Bentley Mulsanne Turbo: 479
37	29.8	47.9	AC 428 Fastback: 26
			Mercedes-Benz 420SE: 2887
38	29.7	47.8	Rover Vanden Plas: 4021
39	29.6	47.6	Chevrolet Corvette Greenwood: 870
			Mercedes-Benz 300E: 2885
			Mercury Monarch: 2953
			Pontiac Bonneville Vista: 3541
40	29.5	47.5	Carbodies Fairway 2.7 Silver: 721
			Chevrolet Kingswood Estate Wagon: 839
41	29.4	47.3	Rover Vitesse: 4024
			Volvo 760 GLE: 4944
42	29.3	47.1	Toyota Camry LE: 4416
43	29.2	47.0	BMW 732i: 575
			Ford LTD: 1809
			Ford Thunderbird: 1779
			Nissan Maxima: 3235
			Pontiac Catalina: 3537
44	29.1	46.8	Jaguar XJS 3.6 Automatic: 2354
			Jaguar XJS 4.0 Auto: 2371
45	29.0	46.7	Allard GT Coupe: 153
			BMW M535i: 576
			Cadillac Seville: 710
			Jaguar 4.0 Sovereign: 2358
			Jaguar XJR 4.0: 2363
			Lincoln Continental Mk III: 2579
46	28.9	46.5	Citroen CX25 DTR Turbo 2: 1078
			Mercedes-Benz 300SL-24 5-speed Auto: 2917
			Oldsmobile 88 Delta Royale: 3294
			Plymouth Satellite Sport: 3508
			Pontiac Grand Prix: 3551
47	28.8	46.3	BMW 635 CSi: 561
			Jaguar XJS 3.6: 2345
			Rover 825 TD: 4047
			Vauxhall Senator 3.0i CD: 4721
48	28.7	46.2	Bentley Mulsanne Turbo: 480
			Lagonda Le Mans: 2437
			Lincoln Continental: 2581
			Riley Pathfinder: 3940
			Rover Montego 2.0 DSL Turbo: 4034
49	28.6	46.0	Audi 100 CD: 290
			Chevrolet Monte Carlo: 847
			Ford Galaxie 500: 1705
			Nissan Maxima SE: 3214
			Porsche 911 Turbo: 3708
			Porsche 911 Turbo: 3689
			Rover 3500: 4016
			Rover 3500: 4020
50	28.5	45.9	Cadillac Coupe de Ville: 709
			Chevrolet Caprice Custom 396: 790
			Kurtis Hornet Roadster: 2420
			Mercedes-Benz 380SEC: 2870
			MG B GT V8: 3025
			Plymouth Fury: 3482
			Plymouth Fury III: 3500
51	28.4	45.7	Aston Martin Mk III: 236
			Bentley Continental Park Ward DH Coupe: 475
			Chrysler Imperial Le Baron: 982
			Ford XL Fastback 428: 1764
			Mercury Marquis Brougham: 2948
			Porsche 911 Turbo Ruf 3.4: 3698
52	28.3	45.5	BMW 735i Automatic: 585
			Chevrolet C-10 Fleetside Pickup: 772
			Mercedes-Benz 500SL: 2913
			Mercury Marquis: 2944
			Reliant Scimitar GTE: 3792
53	28.2	45.4	Mercedes-Benz 560SEL: 2889
			Panther J72: 3372
			Porsche 944 Lux: 3685
54	28.1	45.2	AMC Hornet 3.8-litre: 196
			Jaguar XJ6 3.6: 2348
			Jensen 541: 2387
			Mercury Marquis Marauder X-100: 2949
			Nissan 300ZX Turbo: 3224
55	28.0	45.1	Ferrari 250 GT 2+2: 1385
			Lincoln Continental: 2580
			Maserati Bora: 2660
			Monteverdi 375L: 3118
			Plymouth Fury III: 3506
			Plymouth Sport Fury: 3481
			Porsche 928 S4 Automatic: 3692

Total: 131

Lowest top gear ratios. Limit set at 14.5mph/1000rpm.

	mph	kmh	
1	3.5	5.6	Rover Rover-BRM Turbine: 4006
2	8.8	14.2	Honda N360: 2089
3	9.9	15.9	Honda S600: 2087
4	10.9	17.5	Goggomobil TS400: 2004
5	11.0	17.7	Daihatsu Domino: 1117
			Subaru 360: 4243
6	11.7	18.8	Berkeley Sports: 484
7	11.8	19.0	Honda S800: 2088
8	12.0	19.3	Honda 600 Coupe: 2091
9	12.1	19.5	Citroen 2CV Cabriolet: 1019
			Citroen Bijou: 1028
10	12.2	19.6	NSU Prinz 4: 3259
11	12.4	20.0	BMW 600: 501
			Citroen 2CV6: 1046
12	12.5	20.1	Fiat 500: 1477
			Lloyd LP 600: 2588
13	12.6	20.3	Austin A30: 369
			Austin A30: 368
			Austin A30 Countryman: 375
			Citroen 2CV6 Charleston: 1065
14	12.7	20.4	Fiat 500 Giardiniera: 1492
			Fiat 500D: 1498
			Fiat 500F: 1504
			Fiat Abarth 595: 1506
			Fiat Abarth Twin Cam: 1488
			Honda 600: 2090
15	12.8	20.6	Fiat 500: 1482
			Fiat 600: 1486
			NSU Sport-Prinz: 3258
			Renault 5 Racer: 3865
16	12.9	20.8	BMW 700 Coupe: 504
17	13.0	20.9	Fiat 850 Idromatic: 1512
			Morris Minor Series II: 3161
			NSU Super Prinz: 3265
18	13.1	21.1	Citroen Visa Club: 1057
			Morris Minor: 3163
			NSU Prinz II: 3257
19	13.2	21.2	Berkeley Sports 4: 486
20	13.3	21.4	Citroen Ami 8 Club: 1037
			NSU Prinz 34hp: 3256
			Triumph Herald Saloon: 4508
21	13.4	21.6	Citroen Ami 6 Break: 1035
22	13.5	21.7	Datsun B210 Electramotive: 1198
			Fiat 500C Convertible: 1464
			Fiat 500C Convertible (Topolino): 1462
			Renault 750: 3802
			Saab 93: 4053
			Standard 8: 4200
			Suzuki Alto FX Automatic: 4323
23	13.6	21.9	Fiat 850 Racer: 1524

			Fiat 850 Spider: 1514
			Saab 96: 4056
			Saab 96 Sedan: 4057
			Siata Spring 850: 4128
			Suzuki Alto GLA: 4325
24	13.7	22.0	Daihatsu Compagno Berlina: 1115
			Fiat 126: 1539
			Fiat 600: 1469
			Fiat 600 Multipla: 1473
			Fiat 850 Special: 1513
			Ford Anglia 8 Saloon: 1623
25	13.8	22.2	BMW 700: 503
			BMW 700 LS: 507
			Fiat 133: 1549
			Fiat 850 Coupe: 1518
			Fiat 850 Super: 1499
26	13.9	22.4	Ford Popular: 1631
			Singer 9 Roadster: 4163
27	14.0	22.5	Fiat 126 de Ville: 1564
			Fiat 127: 1528
			Fiat 500 Nuova: 1483
			Fiat 850 Coupe: 1505
			Mitsubishi Colt 1100F: 3061
			Nash Metropolitan: 3197
			Nash Metropolitan: 3199
			Reliant Rebel 700 Estate: 3786
			Renault 750: 3804
			Triumph Herald Convertible: 4509
			Triumph Herald Coupe: 4507
28	14.1	22.7	Datsun 510 TransAm: 1180
			Fiat 600D: 1493
29	14.2	22.8	Austin A40: 380
			Austin A40 Somerset: 366
			Austin A40 Somerset Coupe: 370
			DAF 600 de Luxe: 1108
			Hillman Minx Califonian Coupe: 2039
			Hillman Minx Estate: 2047
			Hillman Minx Saloon: 2035
30	14.3	23.0	Austin A35 4-door: 379
			Citroen GS: 1039
			Citroen GS: 1042
			Datsun 1000 de Luxe: 1168
			Datsun 280ZX Electramotive: 1220
			Hillman Avenger Super: 2071
			Hillman Minx Convertible: 2038
			Hillman Minx Estate: 2036
			Moretti 750 Grand Sport Berlinetta Coupe: 3119
			Morris Cowley: 3165
			Triumph TR8 Libra Rally: 4579
31	14.4	23.2	Citroen Ami 6: 1030
			MG 1.25-litre Saloon: 2981
			MG TD: 2983
			MG TD Laystall: 2986
			Volkswagen Derby LS: 4779
32	14.5	23.3	Chrysler Sunbeam 1.0LS: 997
			Fiat 127 Sport: 1558
			MG Midget: 2982
			Renault 4 Estate Car: 3829
			Renault 4 L Estate Car: 3819
			Vauxhall Victor Estate: 4632
			Volkswagen Polo LS: 4808
			Wolseley 4/44: 4989

Total: 112

Most economical (Autocar & Motor). Limit set at 35mpg.

	mpg	US mpg	L/100 km	
1	63.2	52.6	4.5	Citroen 2CV Cabriolet: 1019
2	61.0	50.8	4.6	BMW Isetta Motocoupe: 499
3	56.5	47.0	5.0	Frisky Coupe: 1993
4	55.5	46.2	5.1	Fiat 500: 1477
5	54.7	45.5	5.2	Citroen AX14 DTR: 1081
6	53.2	44.3	5.3	Fiat 500: 1482
7	50.0	41.6	5.6	Renault 750: 3804
8	49.2	41.0	5.7	Citroen Bijou: 1028
9	49.0	40.8	5.8	Fiat 600: 1469
10	48.5	40.4	5.8	Daihatsu Charade Diesel: 1120
11	47.8	39.8	5.9	Goggomobil TS400: 2004
				Lotus 11 Le Mans: 2589
12	47.3	39.4	6.0	Lloyd LP 600: 2588
13	46.8	39.0	6.0	Fiat 500 Giardiniera: 1492
				Ford Fiesta 1.6L Diesel: 1893
14	46.1	38.4	6.1	NSU Prinz II: 3257
15	46.0	38.3	6.1	Fiat 500D: 1498
				Volkswagen Golf LD: 4814
16	45.9	38.2	6.2	Citroen 2CV6: 1046
17	45.6	38.0	6.2	BMW 600: 501
18	45.5	37.9	6.2	Daihatsu Charade CX Diesel Turbo: 1123
19	44.7	37.2	6.3	Berkeley Sports: 484
20	44.5	37.1	6.3	Citroen Ami 6: 1030
21	44.2	36.8	6.4	Vauxhall Astra 1.7 DL: 4716
22	44.0	36.6	6.4	Renault 750: 3802
				Standard 8: 4207
				Standard 8: 4200
23	43.9	36.6	6.4	Citroen Visa 17RD: 1069
24	43.8	36.5	6.4	Messerschmitt (FMR) Tg 500: 2966
				Vauxhall Nova 1.5TD Merit: 4727
25	43.7	36.4	6.5	Datsun Micra GL: 1232
26	42.8	35.6	6.6	Austin A30: 369
				Fiat 500F: 1504
27	42.6	35.5	6.6	Abarth Zagato 750 GT: 1
28	42.1	35.1	6.7	Citroen BX19 RD Diesel: 1061
				Renault Dauphine Gordini: 3811
29	42.0	35.0	6.7	Austin A30: 368
				Renault 5 GTL: 3854
				Renault Dauphine: 3806
30	41.8	34.8	6.8	Austin A35 4-door: 379
				Fiat Regata DS: 1594
31	41.5	34.6	6.8	Reliant Kitten: 3789
				Reliant Kitten DL Estate: 3790
32	41.3	34.4	6.8	Renault 5 TL: 3866
33	41.0	34.1	6.9	Fiat 500C Convertible: 1464
				Renault 5 Campus: 3911
34	40.9	34.1	6.9	Nissan Micra SGL 5-DR: 3225
				Renault Dauphine: 3810
35	40.7	33.9	6.9	Volkswagen Passat CL Turbo Diesel Estate: 4845
36	40.6	33.8	7.0	Lancia Y10 Fire: 2545
37	40.5	33.7	7.0	Standard Super 10: 4210
38	40.3	33.6	7.0	Austin-Healey Sprite Hardtop: 437
39	40.2	33.5	7.0	Austin A30 Countryman: 375
				Daihatsu Charade CX: 1119
40	40.1	33.4	7.0	Mini Minor de Luxe: 3043
				Suzuki Alto FX: 4322
41	39.7	33.1	7.1	Rover Montego 2.0 DSL Turbo: 4034
42	39.6	33.0	7.1	Standard Pennant: 4209
43	39.5	32.9	7.2	Peugeot 205 1.1GL: 3450
44	39.4	32.8	7.2	Fiat 600 Multipla: 1473
				Honda N360: 2089
				Morris Minor 1000: 3167
45	39.3	32.7	7.2	Volkswagen Jetta Turbo Diesel: 4868
46	39.1	32.6	7.2	Daihatsu Domino: 1117
47	39.0	32.5	7.2	Fiat Uno 60S: 1604
48	38.9	32.4	7.3	Citroen AX11 TRE: 1075
				Fiat Strada 60 Comfort ES: 1581
				Suzuki SC 100: 4321
49	38.8	32.3	7.3	Citroen AX11 TZX: 1087
				Fiat 600: 1486
				MG Metro 1300: 3036
50	38.7	32.2	7.3	Fiat 127 1050 Super: 1572
				Fiat Panda: 1574
51	38.4	32.0	7.4	Citroen BX19 RD Estate: 1071
				Mini Traveller: 3045
				Volkswagen Golf CL Catalyst: 4876
52	38.3	31.9	7.4	Renault Clio 1.4RT: 3920
53	38.2	31.8	7.4	Peugeot 405 GRD: 3447
				Vauxhall Cavalier LD: 4693
54	38.1	31.7	7.4	Hillman Imp de Luxe: 2056
				Mini 850 Super de Luxe: 3060
				Reliant Rebel 700 Estate: 3786
				Toyota Starlet GL: 4475
55	38.0	31.6	7.4	Austin A40: 380
				Fiat 600D: 1493
				Morris Minor 1000 Traveller: 3170
56	37.8	31.5	7.5	Austin A40 Countryman: 387
				Volkswagen Polo C Formel E: 4834
57	37.7	31.4	7.5	Volkswagen Export Saloon: 4739
58	37.6	31.3	7.5	Seat Toledo 1.9 CL Diesel: 4114
				Talbot Horizon 1.9LD: 4348
59	37.4	31.1	7.6	NSU Prinz 4: 3259
				NSU Sport-Prinz: 3258
				Peugeot 205 GR: 3429
60	37.3	31.1	7.6	Audi 80 Turbo Diesel: 291
				Talbot Samba GL: 4347
61	37.2	31.0	7.6	Daihatsu Domino: 1122
				Datsun Cherry F11: 1204
				Ford Fiesta 1.1 Ghia: 1886
				Mini Clubman 1100: 3059
				Peugeot 205 CJ: 3451
62	37.1	30.9	7.6	Fiat 126 de Ville: 1564
				Vauxhall Cavalier 1.7 GL TD: 4733
63	37.0	30.8	7.6	Renault 4 Estate Car: 3829
				Suzuki Swift 1.3 GLX: 4328
				Volkswagen Passat CL TD Estate: 4880
64	36.9	30.7	7.7	Austin Metro 1.3L 3-door: 426
				Vauxhall Nova 1.2L: 4697
65	36.8	30.6	7.7	Fiat 126: 1539
				Renault Clio 1.2 RN: 3919
66	36.7	30.6	7.7	Datsun Sunny 1.5 DX: 1227
67	36.6	30.5	7.7	Mini Super de Luxe: 3048
68	36.5	30.4	7.7	Daihatsu Charade XTE: 1116
				Peugeot 205 XL: 3434
				Simca 1000: 4143
69	36.4	30.3	7.8	Renault R8 1100: 3823
70	36.2	30.1	7.8	Citroen BX DTR Turbo: 1080
				Fiat 1100: 1465
				Morris Minor Series II: 3161
				Rover 825 TD: 4047
71	36.1	30.1	7.8	Citroen Visa Club: 1057
				Ford Anglia: 1649
				Ford Escort 1.3L 3-door: 1936
72	36.0	30.0	7.8	Fiat 133: 1549

	mpg	US mpg	L/100 km	
				Suzuki Swift 1.3 GLX Executive: 4329
73	35.9	29.9	7.9	Citroen AX GT5: 1083
				Toyota 1000: 4393
74	35.8	29.8	7.9	Fiat Uno 55 S: 1582
75	35.7	29.7	7.9	Austin A55: 381
				Fiat Uno 70 SX: 1588
				Singer Chamois: 4181
				Suzuki Swift 1.3 GLX: 4330
76	35.6	29.6	7.9	Mini 850: 3055
				Toyota Carina II 116GL: 4424
				Vauxhall Nova 1.2 Luxe: 4730
77	35.5	29.6	8.0	BMW 700 Coupe: 504
				Fiat 850 Super: 1499
				Fiat Panda 750 L: 1593
				Fiat Regata 70 ES: 1585
				Hillman Super Imp: 2061
				Peugeot 305 GRD Estate: 3435
				Renault 5 GTL 5-door: 3896
				Standard 10: 4203
78	35.4	29.5	8.0	Fiat Uno 70 SX: 1583
				Renault 9 TC: 3878
				Singer Chamois: 4175
79	35.3	29.4	8.0	Honda Jazz: 2115
				Renault 4 L Estate Car: 3819
				Renault Floride: 3813
				Rover 218 SD: 4045
				Talbot Samba Cabriolet: 4346
				Wolseley Hornet: 4998
80	35.2	29.3	8.0	Austin Mini Metro: 419
				Citroen LNA 11RE: 1063
				Ford Fiesta 1000: 1852
				Volkswagen Polo 1.3 CL Coupe: 4886
81	35.1	29.2	8.0	Vauxhall Nova 1.3 GL 5-door: 4705
82	35.0	29.1	8.1	Bond Bug: 629
				Citroen Ami 6 Break: 1035
				Ford Fiesta 1.1 Ghia Auto: 1920
				Ford Popular: 1631
				Peugeot 104: 3414
				Saab 93: 4053
				Simca Aronde: 4131
				Suzuki Alto GLA: 4325
				Volkswagen Polo C: 4833

Total: 166

Most economical (Road & Track). Limit set at 35mpg.

	mpg	US mpg	L/100 km	
1	53.8	44.8	5.3	Panhard Dyna Junior Sports: 3366
2	52.8	44.0	5.3	Chevrolet Sprint: 895
3	51.6	43.0	5.5	Honda 600 Coupe: 2091
				Volkswagen Rabbit Diesel: 4829
				Volkswagen Rabbit Diesel: 4809
4	51.0	42.5	5.5	Citroen 2CV6 Charleston: 1065
5	50.4	42.0	5.6	Subaru Hapi Van 360: 4245
6	48.6	40.5	5.8	Chevrolet Sprint: 904
				Volkswagen Dasher Diesel: 4818
7	45.6	38.0	6.2	Isuzu I-Mark LS: 2252
8	45.0	37.5	6.3	Chevrolet Sprint: 924
9	44.4	37.0	6.4	Ford Festiva L: 1919
				Toyota Starlet: 4411
10	43.8	36.5	6.4	Daihatsu Charade CLX: 1126
				Honda Civic CVCC: 2094
11	42.6	35.5	6.6	Isuzu I-Mark: 2254
12	42.3	35.2	6.7	Porsche Continental Coupe: 3607
13	42.0	35.0	6.7	Ford Fiesta Ghia: 1855
				Honda CRX 1.5: 2111
				Honda CRX Si: 2124
				Toyota Corolla 1200: 4397
14	41.6	34.6	6.8	Fiat 128: 1529
15	41.4	34.5	6.8	Mazda GLC: 2703
16	39.6	33.0	7.1	Mazda GLC Wagon: 2708
				Mercury Tracer: 2959
				Nissan Sentra: 3204
17	39.2	32.6	7.2	Honda Civic Hatchback: 2127
18	39.0	32.5	7.2	Datsun F10: 1199
19	38.4	32.0	7.4	Dodge Colt Hatchback: 1323
				Honda Accord: 2095
				Renault Alliance DL: 3880
20	38.0	31.6	7.4	Honda 600: 2090
				Porsche Continental Speedster: 3608
21	37.8	31.5	7.5	Datsun 210: 1209
				Dodge Colt Lancer: 1322
				Honda CRX Si: 2129
				Hyundai Excel GLS: 2223
				Suzuki Swift GT: 4333
22	37.2	31.0	7.6	Datsun 310 Coupe: 1214
				Fiat 850 Racer: 1524
				Honda CRX Si: 2141
				Lotus Europa S2: 2606
				Toyota Corolla LE: 4428
23	37.0	30.8	7.6	Renault Alliance 1.7L: 3898
24	36.6	30.5	7.7	Datsun B210: 1197
				Fiat 128 Station Wagon: 1540
				Fiat X1/9 1300: 1569
				Plymouth Colt GTS Turbo: 3518
				Pontiac Le Mans: 3583
				Renault Encore GS: 3891
25	36.5	30.4	7.7	Peugeot 304: 3402
26	36.4	30.3	7.8	Triumph Spitfire Mk IV: 4549
27	36.3	30.2	7.8	Toyota Corolla: 4368
28	36.0	30.0	7.8	Audi 5000 S Diesel: 284
				Chevrolet Nova CL: 903
				Fiat Strada: 1566
				Fiat X1/9: 1543
				Honda Accord 4-door: 2100
				Honda Civic: 2092
				Nissan NX2000: 3249
				Renault Le Car: 3868
				Siata Spring 850: 4128
				Subaru DL: 4253
				Toyota Paseo: 4483
				Toyota Tercel LE: 4482
				Volkswagen Rabbit: 4801
				Volkswagen Scirocco Fi: 4810
				Volvo 760 GLE: 4946
				Yugo GV: 5002
29	35.9	29.9	7.9	Hyundai Excel GL: 2222
				Nissan Sentra: 3219
				Subaru Justy 4WD GL: 4270
30	35.5	29.6	7.9	Toyota Corolla 1600: 4370
31	35.4	29.5	8.0	Daihatsu Charade CLS: 1129
				Peugeot 504 Diesel: 3409
				Subaru Justy GL: 4271
				Volkswagen Scirocco: 4802
32	35.2	29.3	8.0	Mitsubishi Mirage: 3089
33	35.1	29.2	8.1	Ford Escort L: 1910

Total: 79

Least economical (Autocar & Motor). Limit set at 15mpg.

	mpg	US mpg	L/100 km	
1	10.0	8.3	28.2	Ruger Bentley Clone: 4052
2	10.3	8.6	27.4	Chevrolet Impala: 846
3	10.4	8.7	27.2	Cadillac Coupe de Ville: 709
4	10.6	8.8	26.6	Chevrolet Blazer: 876
5	10.8	9.0	26.2	Buick Riviera: 674
6	10.9	9.1	25.9	Cadillac Coupe de Ville: 705
				Cadillac Fleetwood: 703
7	11.0	9.2	25.7	Ferrari 365 GT4 2+2: 1406
8	11.4	9.5	24.8	Jaguar XJ12: 2324
9	11.6	9.7	24.4	Mercedes-Benz 600: 2821
				Monteverdi 375L: 3118
10	11.7	9.7	24.1	Aston Martin V8: 246
				Ford Galaxie 500: 1705
				Iso Rivolta Fidia: 2251
				Plymouth Fury III: 3500
11	11.8	9.8	23.9	Oldsmobile Toronado: 3288
				Pontiac Bonneville: 3528
				Rolls-Royce Silver Cloud II: 3958
12	11.9	9.9	23.7	Ferrari 365 GTC: 1390
				Jensen FF II: 2394
				Maserati Bora: 2660
				Rolls-Royce Corniche: 3964
13	12.0	10.0	23.5	Rolls-Royce Silver Cloud: 3956
14	12.1	10.1	23.3	Bentley Mulsanne Turbo: 479
				Iso Rivolta IR-340: 2247
				Land Rover Ninety County V8: 2562
15	12.2	10.2	23.2	Aston Martin DBS V8: 244
				Rolls-Royce Silver Shadow: 3961
16	12.3	10.2	23.0	Allard K2: 150
				Bentley Sports Saloon: 473
				Daimler DK 400B: 1145
				Rolls-Royce Corniche: 3970
				Rolls-Royce Silver Cloud III: 3960
17	12.4	10.3	22.8	Aston Martin V8 Automatic: 245
				Ferrari Daytona: 1397
				Rolls-Royce Silver Shadow: 3963
18	12.5	10.4	22.6	Jeep Cherokee Chief: 2383
				Jensen Interceptor III Convertible: 2401
				Mercury Monarch: 2953
19	12.6	10.5	22.4	Aston Martin DB6: 242
20	12.7	10.6	22.2	Aston Martin DBS: 243
				Pontiac GTO: 3544
21	12.8	10.7	22.1	Ford Mustang Convertible: 1708
				Jaguar 3.8S: 2307
22	12.9	10.7	21.9	Jensen Interceptor: 2393
23	13.0	10.8	21.7	Aston Martin V8: 249
				Bentley S2 Continental: 477
				De Tomaso Pantera: 1237
				Jensen SP: 2397
24	13.1	10.9	21.6	Facel Vega Facel II: 1368
25	13.2	11.0	21.4	Jaguar XJ5.3 Automatic: 2335
				Rolls-Royce Silver Wraith II: 3967
26	13.4	11.2	21.1	Bentley Mulsanne Turbo: 480
				Lamborghini Miura P400S: 2455
				Land Rover One Ten County V8: 2561

27	13.5	11.2	20.9	Aston Martin V8 Vantage: 248
28	13.6	11.3	20.8	Bentley T2: 478
				Jensen FF: 2392
				Jensen Interceptor: 2391
				Mercedes-Benz 450SEL 6.9: 2862
				Rolls-Royce Silver Shadow: 3965
29	13.7	11.4	20.6	Aston Martin Lagonda: 250
				Ford Thunderbird: 1665
				Jeep CJ6: 2381
				Lamborghini Countach: 2468
30	13.8	11.5	20.5	Jaguar XJ5.3C: 2328
				Jaguar XJS V12 Convertible: 2357
				Rolls-Royce Silver Spirit II: 3972
31	13.9	11.6	20.3	Aston Martin DB4 GT Zagato: 240
				Land Rover County: 2559
				Maserati Indy: 2659
32	14.0	11.7	20.2	Aston Martin V8: 252
				Bentley Series S: 476
				Chrysler Charger: 990
				Jaguar XJS Automatic: 2332
				Land Rover Discovery V8: 2564
				Rolls-Royce Silver Spirit: 3969
33	14.1	11.7	20.0	Armstrong Siddeley Star Sapphire: 220
				Bristol 407: 640
				Chrysler Windsor de Luxe: 972
				Jaguar Mk X: 2300
				Mercedes-Benz 450SLC: 2849
				Range Rover V8: 3772
34	14.2	11.8	19.9	Austin Princess: 371
				Bentley Turbo R: 481
				Gordon GT: 2008
				Range Rover V8: 3773
				Range Rover Vogue SE: 3781
				Rolls-Royce Silver Dawn: 3955
35	14.3	11.9	19.8	Daimler Sovereign LWB Automatic: 1154
				Jaguar XJS Automatic: 2341
				Maserati Khamsin: 2666
				Mazda RX-7 Turbo II: 2759
				Opel Diplomat: 3323
				Panther J72: 3372
				Vauxhall Viscount Automatic: 4651
36	14.4	12.0	19.6	BMW 850i: 620
				Facel Vega FVS: 1365
				Jensen CV8: 2390
				Range Rover V8: 3771
37	14.5	12.1	19.5	Dodge Custom Royal: 1273
				Gordon Keeble GK1: 2009
				Jaguar 4.2 litre Mk X: 2305
				Jaguar XJS HE Cabriolet: 2347
38	14.6	12.2	19.3	Chevrolet Corvette Sting Ray: 786
				Lamborghini Countach LP 500S: 2465
				Mercedes-Benz 400SE: 2918
				Porsche 928 Automatic: 3662
				Range Rover Vogue SE: 3780
39	14.7	12.2	19.2	Aston Martin DB5: 241
				BMW 850i Manual: 625
				Daimler Limousine: 1150
				Mercedes-Benz 300SL: 2834
				Mercedes-Benz 450SEL: 2845
40	14.8	12.3	19.1	Daimler Majestic Major: 1148
				Jeep Wagoneer: 2373
				Maserati 3500 GTI Sebring: 2655
				Vanden Plas Princess R: 4608
41	14.9	12.4	19.0	Alfa Romeo Montreal: 82
				Austin 3-litre Automatic: 396
				Land Rover Series III: 2557
				Vauxhall Cresta de Luxe Powerglide: 4646
42	15.0	12.5	18.8	Austin Princess: 367
				Bentley Mk VI: 472
				Holden Brougham: 2086
				Jaguar XJ4.2: 2331
				Range Rover Vogue: 3774

Total: 127

Least economical (Road & Track). Limit set at 15mpg.

	mpg	US mpg	L/100 km	
1	3.6	3.0	78.4	Triumph TR8 Group 44: 4578
2	4.8	4.0	58.8	BMW 2002 TransAm: 528
				Chevrolet Corvette Greenwood: 870
				Datsun 280ZX Electramotive: 1230
				Ford Mustang TransAm: 1796
				Jaguar XJS Tullius: 2333
				Pontiac Firebird TransAm Silverbird: 3566
				Porsche 935 Group 4 Holbert: 3657
3	5.4	4.5	52.3	Chevrolet Camaro IROC: 877
				Pontiac Petty Grand National: 3571
4	5.6	4.7	50.0	Lancia Montecarlo Group 5 Turbo: 2531
5	6.0	5.0	47.0	Alfa Romeo 1750 GTV TransAm: 78
				Chevrolet Monza Mike Keyser: 874
				Ford Cobra II Kemp: 1841
				Renault Le Car Turbo: 3874
6	6.6	5.5	42.8	Ferrari 365 GTB/4 Competitione: 1403
7	7.2	6.0	39.2	Datsun 240Z Sharp: 1190
				Lotus Elan Autocrosser: 2632
				Porsche Carrera RSR: 3642
8	7.8	6.5	36.2	Datsun 280ZX Sharp: 1221
				Mazda RX-7 Racer: 2715
				Triumph TR7 Tullius: 4572
9	8.4	7.0	33.6	Datsun 280ZX Electramotive: 1220
				Datsun 510 TransAm: 1180
				Jensen Healey Huffaker: 2399
10	9.0	7.5	31.4	International Travelall 1210: 2239
				Lamborghini LM129: 2472
11	9.4	7.8	30.2	International Pickup 4WD 1210 Camper Special: 2237
12	10.7	8.9	26.4	Pontiac GTO 400: 3560
13	10.8	9.0	26.1	Chevrolet Corvette 454: 844
				Datsun B210 Electramotive: 1198
				Ferrari 412: 1432
				Maserati Quattroporte: 2671
				Pontiac Firebird TransAm: 3555
14	11.4	9.5	24.8	Aston Martin V8 Coupe: 247
				Rolls-Royce Silver Shadow II: 3968
15	11.6	9.7	24.2	Rolls-Royce Silver Shadow: 3962
16	12.0	10.0	23.5	Chevrolet Camaro Z/28: 825
				Chevrolet Corvette 435hp: 829
				Chevrolet Corvette Bakeracing SCCA Escort: 917
				Chevrolet Corvette Morrison/Baker Nelson Ledges: 921
				De Tomaso Pantera GT5: 1241
				Ferrari 365 GTS 2+2: 1394
				Ferrari 512 BBi: 1422
				Ford Mustang Boss 302: 1787
				Lamborghini Countach 25th Anniversary: 2473
				Lamborghini Countach 5000S: 2469
				Rolls-Royce Silver Spur: 3971
17	12.2	10.2	23.1	Ford Fairlane Cobra: 1772
18	12.4	10.3	22.8	Jaguar XJ12: 2321
19	12.5	10.4	22.6	Chevrolet Corvette L71: 833
20	12.6	10.5	22.4	De Tomaso Pantera: 1238
				De Tomaso Pantera L: 1240
				Ferrari 365 GTB/4 Daytona: 1404
				Lincoln Continental Limousine: 2582
				Rolls-Royce Silver Shadow: 3966
21	12.7	10.6	22.2	Mercury Cougar Eliminator: 2950
22	12.9	10.7	22.0	Dodge Challenger R/T: 1314
23	13.0	10.8	21.8	Ford LTD: 1809
				Lamborghini Espada: 2453
24	13.1	10.9	21.6	Lamborghini Jarama 400GT: 2457
25	13.2	11.0	21.4	Chevrolet Corvette LT-1: 845
				Datsun 280Z Scarab: 1205
				Jeep Gladiator Pickup J-2500 Townside: 2376
				Lamborghini Countach S: 2464
				Lamborghini Diablo: 2475
				Panther De Ville: 3373
				Pontiac Grand Am: 3562
				Pontiac Grand Prix: 3556
26	13.3	11.1	21.2	Renault 5 Racer: 3865
27	13.6	11.3	20.8	Chevrolet Corvette L88: 835
				Chevrolet Corvette L88: 820
28	13.8	11.5	20.5	Bentley Turbo R: 483
				Ferrari 308 GTSi: 1415
				Ferrari 308 GTSi Targa: 1420
				Jaguar XJ12L: 2326
				Jaguar XJS: 2338
				Jensen Interceptor III: 2400
				Lamborghini Silhouette 3000: 2462
				Maserati Bora: 2664
				Maserati Khamsin: 2665
				Maserati Khamsin: 2669
				Mercedes-Benz 280SEL: 2836
				Mercedes-Benz 500SEL: 2922
				Oldsmobile Cutlass Salon: 3298
				Porsche Carrera RS 3-litre: 3647
29	13.9	11.6	20.3	Dodge Charger R/T: 1315
30	14.2	11.8	19.9	Chevrolet Camaro Z/28: 841
				Maserati Ghibli: 2658
				Pontiac GTO 455: 3561
				Rover Rover-BRM Turbine: 4006
31	14.4	12.0	19.6	Aston Martin Lagonda: 254
				Chevrolet Corvette Automatic: 882
				De Tomaso Pantera GTS: 1239
				Ferrari 365 GTB/4 Daytona: 1396
				Ferrari 512 BB: 1407
				Ferrari Testa Rossa: 1426
				Ferrari Testa Rossa: 1437
				Fiat Brava Abarth Rally: 1571
				Jaguar XKE V12: 2325
				Jeep Commando: 2380
				Jeep Wagoneer: 2382
				Jensen Interceptor: 2396
				Lamborghini Countach: 2461
				Lamborghini Jalpa: 2467
				Plymouth Road Runner: 3507
				Shelby Cobra 427: 4126
				Toyota Land Cruiser Wagon: 4373

32	14.7	12.2	19.3	Jeep Wagoneer 1414C: 2378
				Oldsmobile 4-4-2 W30: 3296
33	14.8	12.3	19.1	Chevrolet Camaro Z/28: 857
34	14.9	12.4	19.0	Jensen Interceptor II: 2395
35	15.0	12.5	18.8	Aston Martin Lagonda: 251
				BMW M6: 597
				Ferrari 308 GT4 Dino: 1402
				Ford Granada 5-litre: 1835
				Jensen Interceptor III Convertible: 2403
				Plymouth Volare Station Wagon: 3513
				Pontiac Formula 400: 3559
				Porsche 911 S: 3638

Total: 120

Longest range on full tank (Autocar & Motor). Limit set at 400 miles.

	miles	km	
1	860.4	1384.6	Lotus 11 Le Mans: 2589
2	588.3	946.7	Peugeot 405 GRD: 3447
3	582.8	937.8	Peugeot 605 SR TD: 3465
4	569.8	917.0	Volkswagen Passat CL TD Estate: 4880
5	563.2	906.4	Citroen XM Turbo SD Estate: 1093
6	559.5	900.4	Audi 80 Turbo Diesel: 291
7	543.0	873.9	Rover 825 TD: 4047
8	537.2	864.6	Volkswagen Passat CL Turbo Diesel Estate: 4845
9	524.9	844.7	Citroen BX DTR Turbo: 1080
10	519.7	836.3	Citroen AX14 DTR: 1081
11	518.1	833.8	Vauxhall Carlton L 1.8i: 4712
12	517.4	832.7	Audi 100 CD: 290
13	515.2	829.1	Mercedes-Benz 300SL: 2793
14	511.9	823.8	Vauxhall Cavalier LD: 4693
15	511.5	823.2	Vauxhall Carlton L 2.3D: 4713
16	508.6	818.6	Audi 100 Turbo Diesel: 310
17	505.8	814.0	Fiat Regata DS: 1594
18	503.9	810.9	Vauxhall Astra 1.7 DL: 4716
19	497.1	800.1	Vauxhall Cavalier 1.7 GL TD: 4733
20	496.3	798.7	Seat Toledo 1.9 CL Diesel: 4114
21	482.2	776.1	Audi 100 Sport: 320
22	482.0	775.7	Peugeot 405 GTD Turbo: 3454
23	479.9	772.4	Citroen BX19 RD Diesel: 1061
24	478.5	770.1	Audi 80 GL: 301
25	477.0	767.6	Citroen CX 2200 Diesel: 1051
26	472.5	760.4	Citroen CX 2500 Diesel Super: 1056
27	471.6	759.0	Volkswagen Jetta Turbo Diesel: 4868
28	471.2	758.4	Ford Granada 2.5 GL Diesel: 1951
29	470.7	757.5	Fiat Strada 60 Comfort ES: 1581
			Reliant Scimitar GT: 3785
30	467.8	752.9	Mercedes-Benz 300D: 2819
31	466.3	750.5	Vauxhall Cavalier 1.4L: 4717
32	466.1	750.0	Land Rover Discovery TDi: 2563
33	460.8	741.6	Volkswagen Golf CL Catalyst: 4876
34	460.0	740.3	Volkswagen Golf LD: 4814
35	458.9	738.5	Audi 80 1.8S: 312
36	457.4	736.1	Audi 90 2.2E: 317
37	456.9	735.4	Vauxhall Cavalier 1.6L: 4718
38	454.1	730.8	Citroen XM 2.0SEi: 1086
39	451.5	726.6	Citroen CX25 DTR Turbo 2: 1078
40	449.7	723.7	Volkswagen Passat GT: 4869
41	446.6	718.7	BMW 732i: 575
			Fiat Croma ie Super: 1595
42	446.4	718.4	Mitsubishi Shogun Turbo Diesel 5-door: 3094
43	442.0	711.3	Audi 90 Quattro: 318
44	440.4	708.8	Mercedes-Benz 300D: 2911
45	439.5	707.2	Ford Granada 2.1D: 1859
46	437.8	704.5	Citroen BX19 RD Estate: 1071
47	436.8	702.9	Standard Vanguard III: 4206
48	436.7	702.8	Rover Montego 2.0 DSL Turbo: 4034
49	435.8	701.4	Fiat Croma CHT: 1602
50	435.6	701.0	Ford Sierra 1.6L: 1882
51	434.5	699.2	Peugeot 205 1.1GL: 3450
52	432.3	695.6	Peugeot 605 SRi: 3461
53	432.1	695.4	Citroen BX GTi 16v: 1077
54	431.2	693.9	BMW 735i: 567
55	430.8	693.2	Toyota Carina II 116GL: 4424
56	430.7	693.1	Renault 21 GTS: 3893
57	429.7	691.5	Peugeot 405 1.6 GL: 3446
58	429.2	690.7	Rover SD Turbo: 4023
59	429.0	690.4	Ford Escort XR3i: 1974
60	427.5	687.9	Vauxhall Cavalier GLS: 4692
61	427.1	687.4	Rover 218 SD: 4045
62	426.6	686.5	Peugeot 604 D Turbo: 3424
63	426.0	685.6	Fiat Regata 70 ES: 1585
64	424.7	683.5	Fiat Tipo 1.4: 1598
65	424.0	682.3	Austin Ambassador 2.0 HL: 420
66	422.3	679.6	Renault 19 TSE: 3907
67	422.0	679.1	Peugeot 505 GRi: 3432
			Reliant Scimitar GTE: 3792
			Volkswagen Passat GT 16v: 4878
68	420.4	676.6	Peugeot 405 GR Injection Auto: 3458
69	420.0	675.9	Audi 80 16v Sport: 335
70	418.7	673.8	Audi 80 1.8E: 321
			Audi 80 GLS: 282
71	418.2	673.0	Lancia Y10 Fire: 2545
72	417.6	672.0	Citroen DS: 1029
73	417.1	671.2	Citroen Visa 17RD: 1069
74	417.0	671.1	Aston Martin DB4 GT Zagato: 240
75	416.3	669.9	BMW 750i L: 589
76	415.8	669.2	Mercedes-Benz 420SE: 2887
			Opel Rekord 2100D: 3342
			Toyota Landcruiser VX: 4478
77	415.0	667.9	Ferrari Testa Rossa: 1442
78	414.7	667.4	Ford Escort Cabriolet: 1962
79	414.0	666.3	Standard Vanguard: 4199
80	413.6	665.6	BMW 735i Automatic: 571
			Porsche 944 S: 3694
81	411.4	662.1	Peugeot 205 GR: 3429
82	411.2	661.7	Vauxhall Carlton CD 2.0i: 4704
83	411.0	661.4	Audi Coupe GT 2.2: 315
84	410.9	661.2	Vauxhall Carlton 3000 GSi: 4708
85	410.4	660.4	Saab 900GLS: 4086
86	410.2	660.1	Vauxhall Calibra 2.0i: 4728
87	410.0	659.8	Reliant Scimitar GTE: 3793
88	409.6	659.2	Peugeot 405 Mi16: 3448
			Rover 820i: 4050
89	409.2	658.5	Matra-Simca Bagheera: 2684
			Peugeot 205 CJ: 3451
90	408.3	657.1	Porsche 911S 2.7-litre: 3645
91	408.1	656.7	Isuzu Trooper 3-door TD: 2257
92	407.5	655.7	Renault 21 GTS Hatchback: 3909
93	406.0	653.4	Reliant Scimitar GTE: 3791
94	405.8	653.1	Rambler American: 3761
95	405.7	652.9	Jaguar XJ6 3.6: 2348
96	405.6	652.7	Aston Martin Virage: 261
97	405.2	652.2	Volkswagen Passat CL Formel E: 4825
98	405.0	651.8	Audi Coupe Quattro: 327
99	403.7	649.7	Datsun Sunny 1.5 DX: 1227
100	403.5	649.3	BMW 525E: 565
101	403.3	649.1	Vauxhall Cavalier 1.6S GL: 4690
102	403.1	648.7	Renault 21 Savanna GTX: 3894
103	403.0	648.6	Porsche 944 Turbo: 3695
			Vauxhall Nova 1.5TD Merit: 4727
104	402.6	647.9	Toyota Camry 2.0 GLi: 4445
105	401.9	646.8	Audi Coupe 2.2E: 326
106	401.8	646.7	Fiat Tempra 1.6 SX: 1603
107	401.5	646.1	Alfa Romeo 164 3.0 Lusso: 138
			Peugeot 205 XL: 3434
108	401.0	645.3	Peugeot 305 SR: 3430
109	400.8	645.0	Vauxhall Frontera 2.3 TD Estate: 4734
110	400.4	644.4	BMW M3 Evolution: 604
			Panther J72: 3372
			Peugeot 405 Mi16x4: 3459
111	400.0	643.7	Toyota Landcruiser II TD: 4458
			Triumph TR2 Sports: 4501
			Volkswagen Passat GT 5-door: 4865

Total: 127

Longest range on full tank (Road & Track). Limit set at 400 miles.

	miles	km	
1	998.4	1606.7	Ferrari 212 Touring: 1372
2	646.9	1041.1	Volvo 760 GLE: 4946
3	592.9	954.2	Audi 5000 S Diesel: 284
4	541.5	871.4	Mercedes-Benz 300SD: 2857
5	522.0	840.1	BMW 323i Hardy & Beck: 557
6	519.8	836.6	Isuzu I-Mark LS: 2252
7	516.3	830.8	Audi 5000 S: 311
8	505.7	813.9	Datsun 280ZX: 1225
			Mercedes-Benz 300CD: 2856
9	505.4	813.4	Porsche 911 Cabriolet: 3703
10	492.7	792.8	Porsche 911 Cabriolet: 3675
11	492.3	792.2	Cadillac Allante: 715
12	491.3	790.6	Mercedes-Benz 300TD: 2861
13	486.1	782.3	Lotus Esprit 16v: 2621
14	485.4	781.1	Peugeot 505 S Turbodiesel: 3426
			Peugeot 505 SD: 3423
15	484.7	780.0	Porsche 912 E: 3651
16	481.1	774.3	Volkswagen Dasher Diesel: 4818
17	468.0	753.2	Volkswagen Rabbit Diesel: 4809
18	463.6	746.0	Datsun 280ZX: 1211
			Datsun 280ZX: 1229
			Datsun 280ZX: 1218
19	461.7	743.0	Mercedes-Benz 300TD: 2868
			Peugeot 504 Diesel Automatique: 3416
			Volkswagen Passat GL: 4881
20	461.2	742.2	Cadillac Seville Diesel: 711
			Toyota Corolla 1200: 4397
21	458.4	737.7	TVR Vixen: 4587
22	457.6	736.5	Volkswagen Quantum: 4835
23	455.3	732.7	Lamborghini LM129: 2472
24	455.1	732.4	Cadillac Eldorado Touring Coupe: 718
			Volkswagen Rabbit Diesel: 4829
25	449.3	723.0	Chevrolet Lumina APV: 945
			Ford Crown Victoria LX: 1959
			Jaguar XJS: 2365
			Jaguar XJS Convertible: 2372
			Porsche 911 Carrera Cabriolet: 3721
			Porsche 911 Speedster: 3735

26	444.9	715.9	Mercedes-Benz 190E: 2876
27	443.7	714.1	Jaguar XJ6L: 2337
28	442.5	712.1	Audi 5000 S: 294
			Datsun 280ZX Automatic: 1219
			Porsche 944: 3713
29	441.8	711.1	Honda Prelude: 2125
30	440.2	708.5	Mercedes-Benz 190E 2.3-16: 2883
31	438.8	706.1	Nissan 300ZX: 3234
32	437.1	703.4	Isuzu Impulse: 2253
			Isuzu Impulse Sports Coupe: 2255
33	436.5	702.4	Mercedes-Benz 220D: 2833
34	435.8	701.3	Peugeot 504 Diesel: 3409
35	435.4	700.6	Volvo 960: 4969
36	434.8	699.7	Dodge Conquest: 1330
			Nissan Sentra: 3204
37	434.3	698.9	Ferrari 250 GT Berlinetta Lusso: 1388
38	434.2	698.7	Toyota Celica GT: 4406
39	433.8	698.0	Porsche 914 2.0-litre: 3652
40	432.0	695.2	Audi 5000 S Avant: 299
			Datsun 280ZX Turbo: 1231
41	431.4	694.3	Peugeot 505 STX: 3445
42	430.4	692.7	Alfa Romeo GTV6: 114
43	429.8	691.6	Porsche 911 Carrera: 3679
44	429.3	690.9	Opel Calibra 2.0i 16v: 3351
45	427.7	688.3	Mercedes-Benz 380SEL: 2869
46	427.2	687.5	Ferrari 288 GTO: 1421
47	426.8	686.9	BMW 733i: 550
			Mercedes-Benz 380SL: 2875
48	426.1	685.7	Mazda 626: 2721
			Volvo Diesel: 4939
49	424.8	683.6	Acura NSX: 36
50	422.6	680.1	BMW 524 TD: 581
51	421.8	678.8	Aston Martin Lagonda: 251
52	421.6	678.5	Honda Accord: 2095
53	421.4	678.2	Audi 5000 S Turbo Quattro: 305
			BMW 525i: 617
			Datsun 280ZX Turbo: 1223
			Porsche 911 S: 3649
54	420.7	677.1	Mercedes-Benz 300D: 2848
55	420.6	676.8	Panther J72: 3374
56	419.7	675.4	Mazda 626 Coupe: 2707
57	419.3	674.8	Volvo 940 SE: 4965
58	418.7	673.8	Jaguar XJ6: 2322
59	418.2	673.0	Audi 4000: 283
			Honda Accord: 2109
			Volvo 740 Turbo: 4964
60	418.1	672.8	Toyota Celica GT Liftback: 4401
61	417.4	671.7	Mercedes-Benz 300TD: 2893
			Porsche 914: 3633
62	416.9	670.9	Jaguar XJ6 Vanden Plas: 2362
			Renault 5 Turbo 2: 3886
			Saab Sonnet III: 4074
63	415.8	669.2	Audi Quattro: 292
64	415.0	667.9	Datsun 210: 1209
			Dodge Colt Lancer: 1322
65	413.5	665.4	Peugeot 505 STI: 3428
66	412.4	663.7	Jaguar XJ6 Vanden Plas: 2344
67	411.8	662.8	Lotus Europa Special 5-speed: 2616
68	411.4	662.0	Ferrari F40: 1450
			Ferrari GTO: 1423
			Lexus SC400: 2571
69	411.0	661.4	Mazda MPV: 2754
70	410.9	661.3	Audi 200 Quattro: 334
			Porsche 944 S: 3714
71	409.0	658.1	Sunbeam Alpine GT: 4311
72	408.7	657.7	Ford Taurus SHO: 1946
73	408.5	657.3	Datsun 310 Coupe: 1214
			Toyota Corolla LE: 4428
74	407.0	655.0	Nissan Stanza XE: 3205
75	406.6	654.3	Lotus Eclat: 2626
76	406.3	653.9	Mercedes-Benz 300E: 2885
			Oldsmobile Starfire: 3299
			Toyota Supra Turbo: 4466
77	406.2	653.8	Renault Fuego Turbo: 3882
78	405.3	652.3	Jaguar XJ6: 2352
79	405.2	652.1	BMW 325 ES: 578
			BMW 325E: 569
			Mitsubishi Starion: 3074
			Renault 17: 3844
80	404.4	650.7	Porsche 911 Carrera: 3704
			Porsche 911 Club Sport: 3706
81	402.6	647.9	BMW 745i: 562
82	402.4	647.6	Honda Prelude: 2116
83	401.9	646.8	Cadillac Seville Diesel: 712
			Lotus Elite: 2624
84	401.0	645.4	Porsche 914 2-litre: 3640
			Porsche 924: 3653
			Triumph TR7: 4575
85	400.8	645.0	Honda Civic CVCC: 2094
86	400.4	644.3	Porsche 944 Turbo: 3715

Total: 128

Shortest range on full tank (Autocar & Motor). Limit set at 200 miles.

	miles	km	
1	114.5	184.3	Lotus Super 7: 2594
2	134.2	216.0	BMW Isetta Motocoupe: 499
3	145.2	233.7	Land Rover Ninety County V8: 2562
4	146.6	236.0	Turner Turner-Climax: 4582
5	147.4	237.2	Mini Cooper: 3046
6	153.6	247.2	Lotus 7 Twin Cam SS: 2605
7	153.8	247.5	Hillman Hunter Husky Series II: 2052
8	154.6	248.7	Fiat Abarth 595: 1506
9	156.5	251.8	Berkeley Sports: 484
10	156.8	252.3	Mini Cooper 1275S: 3049
11	161.7	260.2	Mini Cooper S: 3047
12	163.8	263.6	Ford Galaxie 500: 1705
			Ford Mustang Convertible: 1708
13	163.9	263.8	Land Rover Series III: 2557
14	165.5	266.3	Berkeley Sports 4: 486
15	166.1	267.3	Mini 1275GT: 3053
16	166.4	267.8	Ford Cortina Lotus: 1689
17	166.8	268.4	Hillman Hunter Husky III: 2055
18	167.8	270.0	Mini 1275GT: 3054
19	169.2	272.3	Chevrolet Corvair 700: 746
20	169.3	272.4	Fiat 126: 1539
21	169.8	273.3	Austin-Healey Sprite Supercharged: 439
22	170.3	274.0	Skoda Felicia: 4183
23	170.4	274.2	MG Midget Mk III: 3012
24	170.7	274.6	Fiat 126 de Ville: 1564
25	173.0	278.4	Caterham 7 HPC: 725
26	174.6	281.0	MG Midget: 3007
27	175.0	281.6	Bond Bug: 629
28	175.7	282.8	Lotus Europa S2: 2609
29	176.4	283.9	Riley 1.5: 3943
30	176.7	284.4	Jeep CJ6: 2381
31	177.6	285.8	MG Midget Mk III: 3021
32	178.4	287.1	Vauxhall Viva GT: 4658
33	178.8	287.7	Mini Cooper: 3050
34	178.9	287.9	Vauxhall Chevette 2300 HS: 4688
35	179.2	288.4	Ford Cortina Super Estate: 1745
			Jaguar 3.8S: 2307
36	179.3	288.5	Buick Riviera: 674
37	180.0	289.7	Kaiser Henry J 6: 2414
			Land Rover SWB: 2558
38	180.9	291.1	Sunbeam Harrington Le Mans: 4294
39	181.0	291.2	Daihatsu Compagno Berlina: 1115
			Fairthorpe Zeta: 1369
			Morris Minor Series II: 3161
			Riley Elf: 3944
40	182.1	293.0	Mini Automatic: 3058
41	182.2	293.2	Saab Sport: 4066
42	183.0	294.5	Ruger Bentley Clone: 4052
43	183.6	295.5	Allard Palm Beach: 152
44	184.0	296.0	Triumph Herald 13/60 Convertible: 4533
45	184.7	297.2	Mini 1000: 3057
46	185.2	298.0	Ford Falcon Sprint Convertible: 1696
47	185.4	298.4	Sunbeam Alpine II: 4284
48	186.8	300.6	Skoda Octavia: 4182
49	187.0	300.9	Mini Super de Luxe Mk II: 3052
50	187.2	301.3	Hillman Minx Convertible: 2038
			Plymouth Fury III: 3500
51	187.6	301.9	Hillman Minx Convertible: 2044
52	188.0	302.6	Caterham 1700 Super Sprint: 723
			Lada Niva Cossack Cabrio: 2428
53	188.4	303.2	Jaguar 3.8 Mk II: 2301
54	188.8	303.8	Ford Cortina GT Estate: 1753
55	189.0	304.2	Singer SM Roadster: 4169
56	189.4	304.8	Honda S800: 2088
57	190.1	306.0	Sunbeam Tiger 260: 4302
58	190.8	307.0	Cadillac Fleetwood: 703
59	191.3	307.8	Renault 8 Gordini 1300: 3831
60	191.4	308.0	Fiat 850 Special: 1513
61	192.0	309.0	Jaguar 3.4: 2292
62	192.5	309.8	Citroen Ami 6 Break: 1035
63	193.2	310.9	Riley 1.5: 3941
			Triumph Herald Convertible: 4509
64	193.5	311.4	Ford Escort 1600 RS: 1785
			Ford Escort Twin Cam: 1758
65	193.6	311.6	Saab 96: 4060
66	193.9	312.0	Austin Metro Automatic: 418
			Vauxhall Viva SL90: 4649
67	194.2	312.5	Wolseley Hornet: 4998
68	194.4	312.9	Hillman Imp de Luxe: 2073
			Sunbeam Stiletto: 4306
69	194.7	313.3	Lancia Fulvia Coupe: 2510
70	195.3	314.3	MG Midget 1500: 3028
71	195.8	315.1	Mini 850: 3055
72	196.0	315.4	Singer SM Roadster: 4165
73	196.6	316.3	Ford Mustang Ghia Turbo: 1866
74	196.7	316.5	BMW 1800 Ti: 508
			Triumph Herald 1200: 4531
75	196.9	316.8	Fiat 500F: 1504
76	197.0	317.1	BMW 700 LS: 507
			Morris Minor 1000: 3167
			Triumph GT6: 4530
77	197.1	317.2	Volkswagen 1600 TL Automatic: 4777

78	197.3	317.6	Seat 1200 Sport: 4110
79	197.4	317.7	Ogle 1.5: 3267
80	197.6	318.0	Ford Cortina Super Estate: 1733
			Vauxhall Cresta Series PB: 4641
81	197.8	318.2	Frisky Coupe: 1993
82	198.0	318.6	Lada Niva 1600: 2426
83	198.4	319.3	Ford Cortina Super: 1702
84	198.6	319.6	Sunbeam Imp Sport: 4305
85	198.8	319.9	Rover Mini Cooper S: 4048
86	199.2	320.6	Austin-Healey Sprite Mk II: 441
87	200.0	321.8	Ford Taunus 20M: 1726
			Mercury Monarch: 2953
			MG Metro Turbo: 3037
			Westfield SEight: 4973

Total: 106

Shortest range on full tank (Road & Track). Limit set at 225 miles.

	miles	km	
1	59.9	96.4	BMW 2002 TransAm: 528
2	61.1	98.4	Lotus Elan Autocrosser: 2632
3	71.9	115.8	Datsun B210 Electramotive: 1198
4	74.9	120.5	Alfa Romeo 1750 GTV TransAm: 78
5	83.8	134.9	Jensen Healey Huffaker: 2399
6	87.8	141.4	Ford Mustang TransAm: 1796
7	90.9	146.2	Triumph TR7 Tullius: 4572
8	95.3	153.3	Triumph TR8 Group 44: 4578
9	97.3	156.7	Datsun 280ZX Sharp: 1221
10	98.8	159.0	Pontiac Petty Grand National: 3571
11	104.8	168.7	Datsun 510 TransAm: 1180
12	119.8	192.8	International Travelall 1210: 2239
			Jaguar XJS Tullius: 2333
13	125.1	201.3	International Pickup 4WD 1210Camper Special: 2237
14	126.6	203.7	Datsun 280ZX Electramotive: 1230
			Porsche 935 Group 4 Holbert: 3657
15	127.8	205.6	Chevrolet Corvette Greenwood: 870
			Pontiac Firebird TransAm Silverbird: 3566
16	131.8	212.0	Datsun 240Z Sharp: 1190
17	142.8	229.7	Ferrari 365 GTB/4 Competitione: 1403
18	144.8	233.0	Renault Le Car Turbo: 3874
19	147.7	237.7	Lancia Montecarlo Group 5 Turbo: 2531
20	148.3	238.6	Chevrolet Camaro IROC: 877
21	158.2	254.6	Chevrolet Monza Mike Keyser: 874
			Ford Cobra II Kemp: 1841
22	161.8	260.4	Chevrolet Corvette 454: 844
23	166.2	267.5	Pontiac Firebird TransAm: 3555
24	173.7	279.6	Porsche Carrera RSR: 3642
25	174.6	281.1	Datsun 280Z Scarab: 1205
26	174.8	281.3	MG Midget: 3026
27	178.2	286.8	Mazda MX-5 Miata Millen: 2760
28	179.6	289.1	Fiberfab Jamaican Buick V8: 1607
29	181.8	292.5	Ford Mustang II: 1847
30	184.1	296.3	NSU Spider: 3261
31	184.5	296.9	Subaru 360: 4243
32	184.7	297.2	Chevrolet Camaro Z/28: 825
33	185.3	298.2	Fiat Abarth 1300: 1519
34	185.8	298.9	Fiat Brava Abarth Rally: 1571
35	188.2	302.9	Mazda RX-7 Racer: 2715
36	189.6	305.1	Pontiac GTO 400: 3560
37	191.8	308.6	Lotus Super 7 Twincam: 2607
38	193.2	311.0	Dodge Challenger R/T: 1314
39	194.7	313.3	Jeep Commando: 2375
40	195.6	314.7	Suzuki Brute: 4320
41	197.6	318.1	Mazda Rotary: 2689
42	197.7	318.2	Jeep Commando: 2380
			Plymouth Cricket: 3511
43	199.7	321.4	Chevrolet Corvette 435hp: 829
			Chevrolet Corvette Bakeracing SCCA Escort: 917
			Chevrolet Corvette Morrison/Baker Nelson Ledges: 921
			Ford Mustang Boss 302: 1787
44	200.5	322.6	Chevrolet Vega L11: 854
45	201.3	323.9	Dodge 600ES: 1327
46	202.7	326.2	Datsun 280ZX Electramotive: 1220
47	203.0	326.7	Ford Fairlane Cobra: 1772
48	203.1	326.9	Ford Pinto Pangra: 1819
49	204.6	329.3	Porsche 911 S: 3638
50	204.9	329.8	Pontiac Fiero Formula: 3580
51	205.4	330.6	BMW 327S Hardy & Beck: 574
52	205.9	331.4	MG Midget Mk IV: 3031
53	207.2	333.4	BMW M6: 597
54	208.0	334.7	Chevrolet Corvette L71: 833
55	210.7	339.1	De Tomaso Pantera GT5: 1241
56	210.8	339.3	Nissan Sentra SE-R: 3252
			Triumph Spitfire: 4576
57	210.9	339.5	Fiat 124 Special TC: 1544
58	212.2	341.4	Ford Mustang 4.2: 1880
59	212.4	341.8	Ferrari 308 GTSi: 1415
			Ferrari 308 GTSi Targa: 1420
60	212.7	342.3	Chevrolet Camaro Z/28: 841
61	213.4	343.4	MG Midget: 3034
			Rolls-Royce Silver Shadow II: 3968
62	214.2	344.8	Ford Mustang II Mach I: 1827
			Ford Mustang II V8: 1848
63	215.6	347.0	Ford Capri V6 Black Gold: 1840
64	215.7	347.1	Shelby Cobra 427: 4126
65	216.7	348.8	Pontiac Firebird TransAm Turbo: 3590
66	217.2	349.5	MG Midget: 3030
67	218.1	351.0	Honda 600: 2090
68	219.7	353.5	Chevrolet Corvette LT-1: 845
			Jeep Gladiator Pickup J-2500 Townside: 2376
69	219.8	353.7	Dodge Charger R/T: 1315
70	220.1	354.2	De Tomaso Pantera: 1238
			De Tomaso Pantera L: 1240
71	220.3	354.6	Ford Mustang GT Convertible: 1954
72	220.8	355.3	Fiat 850 Idromatic: 1512
73	221.2	355.9	Chevrolet Vega: 852
74	221.7	356.8	Chevrolet Camaro Z/28: 857
75	222.8	358.6	Lamborghini Espada: 2453
76	223.7	360.0	Jeep CJ-5: 2374
77	224.1	360.7	Pontiac Fiero: 3573
			Pontiac Fiero GT: 3577
78	224.7	361.6	Plymouth Volare Station Wagon: 3513

Total: 93

Biggest fuel tank. Limit set at 23 gal.

	gal	galUS	L	
1	58.2	70.0	264.9	Mercedes-Benz 300SLR: 2795
2	50.6	60.8	230.1	Lamborghini LM129: 2472
3	49.9	60.0	227.1	Bizzarrini P538: 497
4	43.6	52.4	198.3	Ferrari 375 Indianapolis: 1373
5	41.6	50.0	189.2	Ferrari 212 Touring: 1372
				Jaguar C Type: 2274
6	37.4	45.0	170.3	Mercedes-Benz 300SL Carrera Panamericana: 2788
7	35.8	43.0	162.8	Ferrari 412 MI: 1377
8	33.3	40.0	151.4	Jaguar XJ13: 2313
9	31.6	38.0	143.8	Ferrari 250 GTO: 1386
10	31.2	37.5	141.9	Chevrolet Corvette Sebring: 738
11	30.8	37.0	140.0	Ford GT40: 1760
				Ford GT40 Super Street: 1738
12	30.0	36.1	136.5	Aston Martin DB4 GT Zagato: 240
				Studebaker Double-twelve Open Tourer: 4214
13	29.1	35.0	132.5	Bizzarrini 5300 Spyder: 495
				Bizzarrini GT America: 496
14	29.0	34.9	131.9	Monteverdi 375L: 3118
15	28.7	34.5	130.6	Mercedes-Benz 300SL Coupe: 2794
16	28.3	34.0	128.7	Ferrari 250 Testa Rossa: 1382
17	28.2	33.9	128.3	Jaguar XJS Lister Le Mans: 2366
18	28.1	33.8	127.9	Aston Martin Lagonda: 251
19	28.0	33.6	127.4	Aston Martin Lagonda: 250
				Ferrari Daytona: 1397
				Hispano-Suiza 54/220: 2084
				Mercedes-Benz 300SL: 2793
				Panther J72: 3372
20	27.5	33.0	124.9	Chevrolet Camaro IROC: 877
21	26.6	32.0	121.1	Chevrolet Corvette Greenwood: 870
				Pontiac Firebird TransAm Silverbird: 3566
22	26.5	31.8	120.6	Mercedes-Benz Type 540: 2785
23	26.5	31.8	120.4	Cizeta Moroder V16T: 1094
				Triumph TR8 Group 44: 4578
24	26.4	31.7	120.1	Lamborghini Countach: 2468
				Lamborghini Countach LP 500S: 2465
25	26.4	31.7	120.0	Bugatti EB110: 652
				Chevrolet Monza Mike Keyser: 874
				Datsun 280ZX Electramotive: 1230
				Ferrari 288 GTO: 1416
				Ferrari 288 GTO: 1421
				Ferrari 512 BB: 1407
				Ferrari 512 BB: 1417
				Ferrari 512 BBi: 1422
				Ferrari F40: 1450
				Ferrari GTO: 1423
				Ford Cobra II Kemp: 1841
				Jaguar XJR15: 2369
				Lamborghini Countach: 2461
				Lamborghini Countach 25th Anniversary: 2473
				Lamborghini Countach 5000S: 2469
				Lamborghini Countach S: 2464
				Lamborghini Countach S: 2466
				Lancia Montecarlo Group 5 Turbo: 2531
				Porsche 935 Group 4 Holbert: 3657
26	26.3	31.6	119.6	Ferrari F40: 1435
27	26.0	31.3	118.3	Aston Martin Virage: 261
				Chevrolet Blazer: 876
				Ferrari 365 GT4 2+2: 1406
28	26.0	31.2	118.1	Panther De Ville: 3373
				Panther J72: 3374
29	25.8	31.0	117.3	Ferrari F40: 1446
30	25.5	30.6	115.8	BMW M1: 556
31	25.3	30.4	115.1	Ferrari Pininfarina Mythos: 1448
32	25.0	30.0	113.7	Aston Martin V8: 252
				Aston Martin V8: 249
				Aston Martin V8 Vantage: 248
				Bentley 8-litre Saloon: 463

				Bentley Speed Six Weymann: 464
				Ferrari Testa Rossa: 1442
33	25.0	30.0	113.5	Ferrari 250 GT Berlinetta Lusso: 1388
				Isdera Imperator: 2244
				Jaguar XJS Tullius: 2333
34	24.7	29.7	112.4	Mercedes-Benz 600SEL: 2923
35	24.6	29.6	112.0	Mercedes-Benz 600: 2816
36	24.6	29.6	111.9	Mercedes-Benz 600: 2821
37	24.2	29.1	110.1	Ferrari 512 BB: 1413
38	24.1	29.0	109.8	BMW 535i Alpina B10 Bi-Turbo: 619
				Datsun 280ZX Electramotive: 1220
				Ferrari 412: 1432
				Mazda RX-7 Racer: 2715
				Porsche 904 Carrera GTS: 3621
				Porsche Carrera RSR: 3642
				Renault Le Car Turbo: 3874
				Rover Rover-BRM Turbine: 4006
39	24.0	28.8	109.2	Alfa Romeo Supercharged Straight Eight: 39
				Daimler Sovereign: 1153
				Darracq Straight Eight Saloon: 1156
				Jaguar XJ6 4.2: 2320
				Mercedes-Benz 32/90 Limousine: 2777
				Mercedes-Benz 32/90 Saloon: 2775
				Mercedes-Benz Type 500 Supercharged: 2782
				Rolls-Royce Silver Shadow: 3961
40	23.8	28.6	108.3	Bentley Turbo R: 481
41	23.7	28.5	108.1	Bentley Mulsanne Turbo: 480
42	23.7	28.5	107.9	Bentley Turbo R: 483
				Bentley Turbo R: 482
				Rolls-Royce Silver Spur: 3971
43	23.7	28.5	107.8	Rolls-Royce Silver Spirit II: 3972
44	23.5	28.2	106.9	Bentley Mulsanne Turbo: 479
				Bentley T2: 478
				Rolls-Royce Corniche: 3964
				Rolls-Royce Corniche: 3970
				Rolls-Royce Silver Shadow: 3965
				Rolls-Royce Silver Shadow: 3963
				Rolls-Royce Silver Spirit: 3969
				Rolls-Royce Silver Wraith II: 3967
45	23.3	28.0	106.0	Rolls-Royce Silver Shadow: 3962
				Vector W2: 4735
				Vector W8 Twin Turbo: 4736
46	23.1	27.8	105.1	Mercedes-Benz 300SEL 6.3: 2828
47	23.0	27.7	104.8	Ferrari Testa Rossa: 1426
				Ferrari Testa Rossa: 1437
				Ferrari Testa Rossa Gemballa: 1443
				Ferrari Testa Rossa Straman Spyder: 1438
				Koenig Competition: 2417
48	23.0	27.6	104.6	Bugatti 5-litre Saloon: 650
				Jaguar XJ6 4.2 Automatic: 2316
				Lincoln 39.2hp Saloon: 2574
				Lincoln Twelve Cylinder Town Sedan: 2575

Total: 119

Smallest fuel tank. Limit set at 6 gal.

	gal	gal US	L	
1	2.2	2.6	10.0	BMW Isetta Motocoupe: 499
2	3.5	4.2	15.9	Berkeley Sports: 484
				Frisky Coupe: 1993
3	4.0	4.8	18.2	Austin 7 Tourer: 340
4	4.3	5.2	19.6	Citroen Bijou: 1028
5	4.4	5.3	20.0	Citroen 2CV Cabriolet: 1019
				Citroen 2CV6: 1046
6	4.5	5.4	20.5	Fiat 500: 1477
				Fiat 500: 1482
				MG Midget: 2968
				Triumph Super 7 Saloon: 4487
7	4.6	5.5	20.9	Fiat 126: 1539
				Fiat 126 de Ville: 1564
				Fiat 500 Giardiniera: 1492
				Fiat 500D: 1498
				Fiat 500F: 1504
				Fiat Abarth 595: 1506
8	4.7	5.7	21.6	Fiat 500 Convertible Saloon: 1458
9	5.0	6.0	22.7	Austin 7 Ruby Saloon: 349
				Austin 7 Ruby Saloon: 351
				Austin 7 Saloon: 341
				Austin 7 Sunshine Saloon: 343
				Berkeley Sports 4: 486
				BMW 600: 501
				Bond Bug: 629
				Lotus Super 7: 2594
				Morris 8 Minor: 3140
				Morris Minor: 3157
				Morris Minor 1000: 3167
				Morris Minor Series II: 3161
				Morris Minor Tourer: 3159
				Wolseley Hornet: 4977
10	5.0	6.1	23.0	Fiat 500C Convertible: 1464
				Fiat 500C Convertible (Topolino): 1462
11	5.2	6.3	23.7	Daihatsu Compagno Berlina: 1115
12	5.4	6.5	24.6	Mini 1000: 3057
				Mini Clubman 1100: 3059
13	5.4	6.5	24.6	Mini Cooper 1275S: 3051
14	5.5	6.6	25.0	Citroen 2CV6 Charleston: 1065
				Honda S600: 2087
				Subaru 360: 4243
15	5.5	6.6	25.0	Citroen Ami 6: 1030
				Citroen Ami 6 Break: 1035
				Goggomobil TS400: 2004
				Lloyd LP 600: 2588
				Mini 1275GT: 3053
				Mini 1275GT: 3054
				Mini 850: 3055
				Mini 850 Super de Luxe: 3060
				Mini Automatic: 3058
				Mini Cooper: 3050
				Mini Cooper: 3046
				Mini Cooper 1275S: 3049
				Mini Cooper S: 3047
				Mini Minor de Luxe: 3043
				Mini Super de Luxe: 3048
				Mini Super de Luxe Mk II: 3052
				Morris 8 Saloon: 3147
				Morris 8 Series E Tourer: 3155
				Morris 8 Tourer: 3153
				Morris 8hp Series E Tourer: 3156
				Morris 8hp Tourer: 3154
				Morris Minor Saloon: 3138
				NSU Prinz II: 3257
				NSU Sport-Prinz: 3258
				Riley Elf: 3944
				Tatra 12hp Drop-head Coupe: 4349
				Wolseley Hornet: 4998
16	5.7	6.8	25.9	Austin A30: 368
				Austin A30: 369
				Austin A30 Countryman: 375
				Daihatsu Domino: 1117
				Honda N360: 2089
				Suzuki SC 100: 4321
17	5.7	6.9	26.1	Honda 600: 2090
				Honda 600 Coupe: 2091
18	5.7	6.9	26.2	Austin 7 Sports Two-seater: 342
				Austin A35 4-door: 379
				Opel Kadet Saloon: 3306
				Renault 4 Estate Car: 3829
				Renault 4 L Estate Car: 3819
				Turner Turner-Climax: 4582
19	5.8	7.0	26.5	Suzuki Brute: 4320
20	5.9	7.1	26.8	Suzuki Alto FX: 4322
				Suzuki Alto FX Automatic: 4323
21	6.0	7.2	27.2	Sunbeam Imp: 4300
22	6.0	7.2	27.3	Abarth Zagato 750 GT: 1
				Austin 10 Cambridge: 352
				Austin 10/4 Saloon: 344
				Austin 8 Saloon: 356
				Austin 8 Saloon: 358
				Austin A40: 380
				Austin A40 Countryman: 387
				Austin Big 7: 354
				Austin-Healey Sprite: 435
				Austin-Healey Sprite Hardtop: 437
				Austin-Healey Sprite Mk II: 441
				Austin-Healey Sprite Supercharged: 439
				Bond 875: 628
				British Adler 13.67 Cabriolet: 641
				Clan Crusader: 1095
				DKW 7.1hp Cabriolet: 1259
				Fiat 600: 1486
				Fiat 600: 1469
				Fiat 600 Multipla: 1473
				Fiat 600D: 1493
				Hillman Hunter Husky: 2064
				Hillman Imp Californian: 2065
				Hillman Imp de Luxe: 2056
				Hillman Imp de Luxe: 2073
				Hillman Super Imp: 2061
				Jowett 7hp Curlew de Luxe: 2406
				MG Midget: 3007
				MG Midget: 3002
				MG Midget Mk III: 3012
				MG Midget Mk III: 3021
				Opel Olympia Saloon: 3307
				Reliant Kitten: 3789
				Reliant Kitten DL Estate: 3790
				Reliant Rebel 700 Estate: 3786
				Renault 750: 3802
				Renault 750: 3804
				Singer Chamois: 4175
				Singer Chamois: 4181
				Standard 8: 4197
				Sunbeam Imp Sport: 4305
				Sunbeam Stiletto: 4306
				Triumph Supercharged 7: 4488

Total: 128

Heaviest.
Limit set at 4600lb.

	lb	kg	
1	6675.0	3030.4	Lamborghini LM129: 2472
2	6400.0	2905.6	Duesenberg SJ Town Car: 1353
3	6200.0	2814.8	Cadillac V16 "Madame X": 699
4	5939.0	2696.3	Lincoln Twelve Cylinder Town Sedan: 2575
5	5908.0	2682.2	Daimler Straight Eight: 1139
6	5900.0	2678.6	Lincoln Continental Limousine: 2582
7	5850.0	2655.9	Rolls-Royce Phantom III: 3952
8	5824.0	2644.1	Daimler Twenty-Seven Limousine: 1138
9	5796.0	2631.4	Mercedes-Benz Type 540: 2785
10	5700.0	2587.8	International Travelall 1210: 2239
11	5670.0	2574.2	Cadillac Fleetwood: 703
12	5600.0	2542.4	Packard Twelve Victoria: 3359
13	5591.0	2538.3	Lincoln 39.2hp Saloon: 2574
14	5490.0	2492.5	Mercedes-Benz 600: 2816
			Rolls-Royce Phantom II: 3949
15	5488.0	2491.5	Rolls-Royce Phantom II: 3950
16	5460.0	2478.8	Mercedes-Benz Type 500 Supercharged: 2782
17	5390.0	2447.1	Bentley 8-litre Saloon: 463
18	5380.0	2442.5	Mercedes-Benz 600: 2821
19	5340.0	2424.4	Chrysler Imperial Le Baron: 982
			Dodge Dreamer: 1281
20	5325.0	2417.5	Cadillac V16 Fleetwood Roadster: 700
21	5310.0	2410.7	Lincoln Continental: 2581
22	5300.0	2406.2	Marmon 16: 2651
23	5280.0	2397.1	Lincoln Continental Mk III: 2579
24	5270.0	2392.6	Bentley Turbo R: 482
25	5256.0	2386.2	Armstrong Siddeley 30 Special Sports Saloon: 213
26	5230.0	2374.4	Chrysler Imperial Crown: 987
27	5220.0	2369.9	Lincoln Continental: 2580
28	5215.0	2367.6	Bentley Turbo R: 483
29	5210.0	2365.3	International Pickup 4WD 1210 Camper Special: 2237
30	5166.0	2345.4	La Salle Enclosed Drive Limousine: 2421
31	5150.0	2338.1	Lincoln 39.2hp Town Saloon: 2573
32	5113.0	2321.3	Packard 32.5hp Standard Eight Saloon: 3361
33	5110.0	2319.9	Chrysler Imperial: 977
34	5066.0	2300.0	Rolls-Royce Corniche: 3970
35	5060.0	2297.2	Cadillac Eldorado Convertible: 701
36	5050.7	2293.0	Mercedes-Benz G-Wagen 300 GD LWB: 2921
37	5044.0	2290.0	Rolls-Royce Silver Spirit II: 3972
38	5040.0	2288.2	Bentley Speed Six Weymann: 464
			Chevrolet Kingswood Estate Wagon: 839
			Stutz 36.4hp Saloon: 4240
39	5035.0	2285.9	Mercury Marquis Brougham: 2948
40	5006.0	2272.7	Cadillac Coupe de Ville: 705
41	5005.0	2272.3	Rolls-Royce Silver Shadow: 3966
42	5000.0	2270.0	Duesenberg J Coupe: 1352
43	4980.0	2260.9	Packard Super 8 Phaeton: 3356
44	4975.0	2258.6	Rolls-Royce Silver Spur: 3971
45	4971.4	2257.0	Toyota Landcruiser VX: 4478
46	4970.0	2256.4	Rolls-Royce Silver Shadow II: 3968
47	4965.0	2254.1	Dodge Safari Super Sport: 1291
48	4964.0	2253.7	Daimler DK 400B: 1145
49	4960.3	2252.0	Bentley Turbo R: 481
50	4952.0	2248.2	Cadillac Coupe de Ville: 709
51	4928.0	2237.3	Stutz Straight Eight Saloon: 4241
52	4926.0	2236.4	Bentley Mulsanne Turbo: 479
53	4920.0	2233.7	Chrysler 300-D: 973
54	4907.0	2227.8	Rolls-Royce Silver Spirit: 3969
55	4900.0	2224.6	Cadillac Sedan de Ville: 706
			Chevrolet Blazer: 850
			Du Pont Town Car: 1351
			Mercedes-Benz 36/220-S: 2774
56	4896.0	2222.8	Bentley Mulsanne Turbo: 480
57	4855.0	2204.2	Cadillac Park Avenue: 704
			Mercedes-Benz 500SEL: 2922
58	4840.0	2197.4	Ford Thunderbird Town Landau: 1739
59	4830.0	2192.8	Mercedes-Benz 600SEL: 2923
60	4816.0	2186.5	Humber Pullman Limousine: 2197
			Rolls-Royce Corniche: 3964
			Stutz DV32 Sports Saloon: 4242
61	4809.0	2183.3	Austin Princess: 371
			Bentley T2: 478
62	4790.0	2174.7	Cadillac Eldorado: 708
63	4780.0	2170.1	Cadillac Coupe de Ville: 702
64	4779.7	2170.0	Toyota Landcruiser: 4450
65	4775.0	2167.8	Plymouth Fury Station Wagon: 3488
66	4760.0	2161.0	Cadillac Calais: 707
67	4752.0	2157.4	Rolls-Royce Silver Shadow: 3965
68	4750.0	2156.5	Chrysler Custom Imperial Le Baron: 964
			Maserati Quattroporte: 2671
69	4732.0	2148.3	Rolls-Royce Silver Wraith: 3953
70	4730.0	2147.4	Rolls-Royce Phantom I Phaeton: 3946
71	4720.0	2142.9	Chrysler 300: 984
72	4704.0	2135.6	Mercedes-Benz 32/90 Limousine: 2777
			Mercedes-Benz 32/90 Saloon: 2775
			Packard 32.5hp Saloon: 3358
73	4700.0	2133.8	Chevrolet Pickup Cheyenne Fleetside: 851
74	4690.0	2129.3	Ford Thunderbird Sports Roadster: 1680
			Rolls-Royce Silver Shadow: 3962
75	4683.0	2126.1	Daimler Limousine: 1150
76	4680.0	2124.7	Rolls-Royce Silver Cloud II V8: 3959
77	4670.0	2120.2	Mercedes-Benz 400SE: 2918
			Rolls-Royce Silver Shadow: 3963
78	4667.0	2118.8	Lagonda Saloon de Ville: 2444
79	4660.0	2115.6	Oldsmobile Toronado: 3292
			Rolls-Royce Silver Shadow: 3961
80	4655.0	2113.4	Oldsmobile Toronado: 3286
81	4648.0	2110.2	Austro Daimler 32/100 Saloon: 448
82	4645.0	2108.8	Buick Sportswagon: 685
83	4640.0	2106.6	Dodge Monaco Wagon: 1302
84	4630.0	2102.0	Aston Martin Lagonda: 251
			Oldsmobile 98 Holiday Sports Sedan: 3275
85	4620.0	2097.5	Aston Martin Lagonda: 254
86	4615.0	2095.2	Ford Thunderbird: 1727
87	4610.0	2092.9	Buick Riviera: 683
88	4606.0	2091.1	Humber Imperial: 2193
			Humber Imperial Saloon: 2194
			Packard Straight Eight Saloon: 3357

Total: 108

Lightest.
Limit set at 1400lb.

	lb	kg	
1	700.0	317.8	Berkeley Sports: 484
2	710.0	322.3	Berkeley Sports: 485
3	756.0	343.2	Frisky Coupe: 1993
4	784.0	355.9	BMW Isetta Motocoupe: 499
5	847.0	384.5	Berkeley Sports 4: 486
			Messerschmitt (FMR) Tg 500: 2966
6	860.0	390.4	BMW Isetta 300: 502
7	868.0	394.1	Bond Bug: 629
8	896.0	406.8	Morgan SS: 3122
9	915.0	415.4	Berkeley B95: 487
10	952.0	432.2	Austin 7 Sports Two-seater: 342
11	960.0	435.8	Lotus 7: 2593
12	966.0	438.6	Lotus Super 7: 2594
13	970.0	440.4	Lotus Sports: 2591
14	980.0	444.9	Subaru 360: 4243
15	1000.0	454.0	Lotus Mk XI: 2590
16	1001.0	454.4	Goggomobil TS400: 2004
17	1008.0	457.6	Austin 7 Tourer: 340
18	1015.0	460.8	Lotus Super 7: 2595
19	1019.0	462.6	Lotus 11 Le Mans: 2589
20	1036.0	470.3	Fiat 500: 1477
21	1060.0	481.2	Fiat 500 Nuova: 1483
22	1092.0	495.8	Austin 7 Sunshine Saloon: 343
23	1100.0	499.4	Citroen 2CV Cabriolet: 1019
			NSU Prinz 34hp: 3256
24	1106.0	502.1	Fiat 500D: 1498
25	1113.0	505.3	Fiat 500: 1482
			NSU Prinz II: 3257
26	1119.0	508.0	Honda N360: 2089
27	1120.0	508.5	Citroen 2CV: 1022
			MG Midget: 2968
			Moretti 750 Grand Sport Berlinetta Coupe: 3119
28	1125.0	510.7	Caterham 7: 724
29	1130.0	513.0	Fiat 500F: 1504
			Fiat Abarth 595: 1506
30	1150.0	522.1	Renault 4CV: 3801
31	1159.0	526.2	Reliant Kitten: 3789
32	1162.0	527.5	Caterham Super 7: 722
33	1185.0	538.0	Fiat 500 Convertible Saloon: 1458
34	1188.0	539.3	Reliant Kitten DL Estate: 3790
35	1196.0	543.0	Caterham 1700 Super Sprint: 723
36	1200.0	544.8	Subaru Hapi Van 360: 4245
37	1202.0	545.7	NSU Sport-Prinz: 3258
38	1204.0	546.6	Austin 7 Saloon: 341
39	1208.0	548.4	Lloyd LP 600: 2588
40	1210.0	549.3	Lotus Super 7 Twincam: 2607
41	1232.0	559.3	Abarth Zagato 750 GT: 1
			BMW 600: 501
			NSU Prinz 4: 3259
42	1238.0	562.0	Morris 8 Minor: 3140
43	1245.0	565.2	NSU Super Prinz: 3265
44	1246.0	565.7	Fiat 500 Giardiniera: 1492
45	1250.0	567.5	Fiat Abarth 750GT Zagato: 1479
			Fiat Abarth Zagato: 1480
46	1258.0	571.1	Lotus 7 Twin Cam SS: 2605
47	1260.0	572.0	Alfa Romeo 33 2.0 Stradale: 66
			Daihatsu Domino: 1117
48	1265.0	574.3	Citroen 2CV6 Charleston: 1065
			Devin VW: 1258
49	1271.0	577.0	Fiat 126: 1539
50	1274.0	578.4	Fiat Uno Turbo ie: 1589
51	1278.0	580.2	Clan Crusader: 1095
52	1280.0	581.1	Caterham Super 7: 726
			Osca 1490cc Spyder: 3353
53	1288.0	584.7	Fiat 600: 1469
			Triumph Super 7 Saloon: 4487
54	1290.0	585.7	Turner Sports: 4583
55	1295.0	587.9	Mini 850: 3055
56	1315.0	597.0	Bond 875: 628
57	1320.0	599.3	Dellow Mk V: 1254
			Fiat 600: 1486
58	1323.0	600.6	Renault 4 L Estate Car: 3819
59	1325.0	601.5	Porsche RSK: 3613

60	1326.0	602.0	Mini 1000: 3057
			Suzuki Alto FX Automatic: 4323
61	1327.0	602.5	Citroen 2CV6: 1046
62	1330.0	603.8	Citroen Bijou: 1028
			Fiat 600: 1472
63	1337.0	607.0	Mini Minor de Luxe: 3043
64	1340.0	608.4	Austin Seven 850: 391
			Fiat Abarth Twin Cam: 1488
			Mini Minor: 3044
			Reliant Rebel 700 Estate: 3786
65	1344.0	610.2	Fiat 126 de Ville: 1564
			Fiat 500C Convertible: 1464
			Fiat 500C Convertible (Topolino): 1462
66	1345.0	610.6	Fiat Abarth 850: 1487
67	1350.0	612.9	Fiat 750 Abarth: 1478
			Porsche 904 Carrera GTS: 3621
			Renault 4CV: 3803
			Suzuki Brute: 4320
68	1351.0	613.3	Fiat 600D: 1493
			Mini 850 Super de Luxe: 3060
69	1355.0	615.2	Honda 600: 2090
			Volkswagen Alken-VW: 4749
70	1356.8	616.0	Daihatsu Domino: 1122
71	1358.0	616.5	Austin 7 Ruby Saloon: 349
			Renault 750: 3802
72	1360.0	617.4	Meyers Manx: 2967
73	1372.0	622.9	Triumph Supercharged 7: 4488
			Turner Turner-Climax: 4582
74	1375.0	624.2	Honda 600 Coupe: 2091
75	1379.0	626.1	Mini Super de Luxe Mk II: 3052
76	1380.0	626.5	Trihawk 304: 4486
77	1381.0	627.0	Mini Clubman 1100: 3059
78	1383.0	627.9	Caterham 7 HPC: 725
79	1389.0	630.6	Mini Automatic: 3058
80	1392.1	632.0	Citroen AX11 TRE: 1075
81	1393.0	632.4	Renault 4 Estate Car: 3829
			Renault 750: 3804
			Wolseley Hornet: 4998
82	1400.0	635.6	Mini Cooper: 3050
			Mini Super de Luxe: 3048

Total: 113

Longest.
Limit set at 210in.

	in	cm	
1	248.9	632.2	Lincoln Continental Limousine: 2582
2	246.0	624.8	Duesenberg SJ Town Car: 1353
3	244.8	621.8	Cadillac Fleetwood: 703
4	239.0	607.1	Dodge Dreamer: 1281
5	232.0	589.3	Cadillac V16 "Madame X": 699
6	229.0	581.7	Lincoln Continental Mk III: 2579
7	227.8	578.6	Chrysler Imperial Le Baron: 982
8	227.3	577.3	Chrysler Imperial: 977
9	226.0	574.0	Daimler Limousine: 1150
10	225.1	571.8	Chrysler 300-H: 989
11	225.0	571.5	Cadillac Eldorado Convertible: 701
			Chrysler 300: 988
12	224.7	570.7	Cadillac Coupe de Ville: 709
			Chrysler Imperial Crown: 987
13	224.0	569.0	Cadillac Calais: 707
			Mercury Marquis Brougham: 2948
14	223.5	567.7	Cadillac Coupe de Ville: 705
			Cadillac Sedan de Ville: 706
15	222.8	565.9	Buick Electra 225: 669
16	222.0	563.9	Cadillac Coupe de Ville: 702
			Daimler Straight Eight: 1139
			Rolls-Royce Phantom II: 3949
17	221.9	563.6	Chrysler 300: 984
18	221.7	563.1	Pontiac Bonneville Vista: 3541
19	221.3	562.1	Dodge Monaco Wagon: 1302
20	221.0	561.3	Cadillac Eldorado: 708
			Dodge Monaco: 1310
21	220.7	560.6	Pontiac Bonneville: 3528
22	220.5	560.1	Buick Wildcat: 680
23	220.0	558.8	Chrysler 300-G: 975
			Oldsmobile 98 Holiday Sports Sedan: 3275
24	219.0	556.3	Mercury Marquis Marauder X-100: 2949
			Oldsmobile 88 Delta Royale: 3294
25	218.8	555.8	Buick Wildcat: 672
26	218.6	555.2	Chrysler Windsor de Luxe: 972
27	218.5	555.0	Mercury Marquis: 2944
28	218.4	554.7	Ford LTD: 1809
			Mercury Monterey: 2938
			Mercury Park Lane: 2939
29	218.2	554.2	Chrysler Newport: 983
30	218.0	553.7	Buick Wildcat: 686
			Mercedes-Benz 600: 2821
			Mercedes-Benz 600: 2816
31	217.8	553.2	Oldsmobile Delmont: 3291
32	217.4	552.2	Dodge Custom Royal: 1274
33	217.0	551.2	Chrysler Custom Imperial Le Baron: 964
			Daimler DK 400B: 1145
			Pontiac Catalina Super Stock: 3529
34	216.9	550.9	Buick LeSabre 400: 673
			Oldsmobile Dynamic Delta 88 Holiday: 3285
35	216.8	550.7	Buick Roadmaster: 660
36	216.7	550.4	Chevrolet Kingswood Estate Wagon: 839
37	216.3	549.4	Lincoln Continental: 2581
38	216.1	548.9	Plymouth Fury Station Wagon: 3488
39	216.0	548.6	Chevrolet Caprice: 827
			Chrysler Enforcer: 976
40	215.9	548.4	Chevrolet Impala: 846
41	215.6	547.6	Chrysler Newport: 978
			Pontiac Grand Prix: 3551
42	215.5	547.4	Chrysler 300-J: 981
			Mercury Park Lane: 2937
43	215.3	546.9	Chrysler 300-H: 980
			Oldsmobile Jetstar I: 3283
44	215.2	546.6	Buick Riviera: 682
			Buick Riviera: 683
45	215.0	546.1	Austin Princess: 371
			Cadillac Park Avenue: 704
			Du Pont Town Car: 1351
			Mercury Super Marauder S-55: 2932
			Plymouth Fury III: 3506
46	214.9	545.8	Chrysler 300: 979
47	214.7	545.3	Chevrolet Impala: 822
48	214.6	545.1	Mercury Meteor 800: 2928
			Pontiac Catalina 2+2: 3542
49	214.5	544.8	Oldsmobile Starfire: 3280
50	214.1	543.8	Buick Invicta: 663
			Buick Sportswagon: 685
			Buick Wildcat: 667
51	214.0	543.6	Dodge D-100 Sweptline Pickup: 1283
			Ford LTD: 1773
52	213.9	543.3	Oldsmobile Dynamic 88 Celebrity Sedan: 3276
53	213.8	543.1	Pontiac Bonneville: 3564
54	213.7	542.8	Ford Galaxie: 1658
55	213.5	542.3	Daimler Twenty-Seven Limousine: 1138
			Dodge Custom 880: 1279
56	213.3	541.8	Ford Galaxie: 1759
			Ford XL Fastback 428: 1764
57	213.2	541.5	Chevrolet Bel Air Six: 800
			Chevrolet Impala SS427: 809
58	213.1	541.3	Chevrolet Caprice Custom 396: 790
			Plymouth Fury III: 3496
59	213.0	541.0	Chevrolet Impala SS: 799
			Plymouth Fury III: 3500
60	212.9	540.8	Oldsmobile Cutlass Salon: 3298
61	212.4	539.5	Ford Crown Victoria LX: 1959
			Lincoln Continental: 2580
62	212.2	539.0	Dodge Custom Royal: 1273
63	212.0	538.5	Lincoln 39.2hp Saloon: 2574
			Rolls-Royce Silver Cloud II V8: 3959
64	211.9	538.2	Humber Pullman Limousine: 2197
			Pontiac Catalina: 3537
			Pontiac Grand Prix: 3538
65	211.8	538.0	Rolls-Royce Silver Spur: 3971
66	211.7	537.7	Bentley Series S: 476
			Rolls-Royce Silver Cloud: 3956
			Rolls-Royce Silver Cloud II: 3958
67	211.6	537.5	Pontiac Grand Prix 421: 3533
			Pontiac Parisienne: 3534
			Pontiac Royal Bobcat: 3535
68	211.5	537.2	Rolls-Royce Silver Shadow: 3966
			Rolls-Royce Silver Shadow II: 3968
69	211.4	537.0	Oldsmobile Toronado: 3292
70	211.2	536.4	Buick Riviera Gran Sport: 677
71	211.0	535.9	Chrysler New Yorker Saloon: 971
			Oldsmobile Toronado: 3288
			Oldsmobile Toronado: 3286
72	210.5	534.7	Bentley Continental Park Ward DH Coupe: 475
			Bentley S2 Continental: 477
			Humber Imperial: 2193
			Humber Imperial Saloon: 2194
73	210.4	534.4	Chevrolet Bel Air: 770
			Chevrolet Biscayne V8: 771
			Chevrolet Impala Super Sport 409: 779
			Chevrolet Monte Carlo: 859
74	210.2	533.9	Pontiac Grand Prix: 3556
			Rolls-Royce Silver Cloud III: 3960
75	210.0	533.4	Buick Riviera: 674
			Ford Custom 500: 1734
			Ford Galaxie: 1663
			Ford Galaxie 500 XL 427: 1714
			Ford Galaxie 7-litre: 1737
			Ford Galaxie LTD: 1715
			Marmon 16: 2651
			Mercedes-Benz 600SE: 2854
			Minerva 22/28hp Limousine: 3042
			Packard Twelve Victoria: 3359
			Plymouth Savoy Station Wagon: 3479

Total: 137

Shortest.
Limit set at 135in.

	in	cm	
1	90.0	228.6	BMW Isetta Motocoupe: 499

2	97.0	246.4	Lotus Super 7: 2594
3	110.0	279.4	Austin 7 Tourer: 340
			Bond Bug: 629
4	111.0	281.9	Austin 7 Sunshine Saloon: 343
5	112.0	284.5	Enfield 8000 Electric: 1359
6	112.5	285.8	Frisky Coupe: 1993
7	114.0	289.6	BMW 600: 501
8	116.0	294.6	Austin 7 Saloon: 341
			Fiat 500: 1482
			Fiat 500: 1477
9	116.7	296.4	Fiat 500D: 1498
10	117.0	297.2	Fiat 500 Nuova: 1483
			Fiat 500F: 1504
			Fiat Abarth 595: 1506
11	117.9	299.5	Subaru 360: 4243
			Subaru Hapi Van 360: 4245
			Suzuki Brute: 4320
12	118.0	299.7	Honda N360: 2089
			Triumph Super 7 Saloon: 4487
13	119.5	303.5	Goggomobil TS400: 2004
14	120.0	304.8	Austin 7 Sports Two-seater: 342
			Austin Seven 850: 391
			Messerschmitt (FMR) Tg 500: 2966
			Mini Cooper: 3046
			Mini Minor: 3044
			Mini Minor de Luxe: 3043
			Morris Minor Saloon: 3138
15	120.1	305.1	Fiat 126: 1539
			Sbarro Chrono 3.5: 4108
16	120.2	305.3	Mini Automatic: 3058
			Mini Cooper: 3050
			Mini Cooper 1275S: 3049
			Mini Cooper S: 3047
			Mini Super de Luxe: 3048
			Mini Super de Luxe Mk II: 3052
17	120.3	305.6	Mini 850 Super de Luxe: 3060
18	120.5	306.1	Mini 1000: 3057
			Mini 850: 3055
19	120.8	306.8	Mini Cooper 1275S: 3051
20	122.2	310.4	Rover Mini Cooper S: 4048
21	122.8	311.9	Honda 600 Coupe: 2091
22	123.0	312.4	Berkeley B95: 487
			Berkeley Sports: 484
			Berkeley Sports 4: 486
			MG Midget: 2968
			NSU Prinz II: 3257
23	123.2	312.9	Fiat 126 de Ville: 1564
24	123.5	313.7	Meyers Manx: 2967
25	124.0	315.0	NSU Prinz 34hp: 3256
26	125.0	317.5	Honda 600: 2090
27	125.2	318.0	Fiat 500 Giardiniera: 1492
			Mini 1275GT: 3053
			Mini 1275GT: 3054
			Mini 1275GT: 3056
			Mini Clubman 1100: 3059
28	125.8	319.5	Daihatsu Domino: 1122
			Daihatsu Domino: 1117
29	126.0	320.0	Suzuki SC 100: 4321
30	126.5	321.3	Fiat 600: 1469
31	127.0	322.6	Morris 8 Minor: 3140
32	127.7	324.4	Fiat 500C Convertible: 1464
			Fiat 500C Convertible (Topolino): 1462
33	128.0	325.1	Fiat Abarth 750GT Zagato: 1479
			Fiat Abarth Zagato: 1480
34	128.8	327.2	Riley Elf: 3944
			Wolseley Hornet: 4998
35	129.0	327.7	Bond 875: 628
			Fiat 600D: 1493
			Triumph Supercharged 7: 4488
36	129.3	328.4	Fiat 600: 1486
37	129.8	329.7	Mini Traveller: 3045
38	129.9	330.0	Suzuki Alto GLA: 4325
39	130.0	330.2	Honda S600: 2087
			Suzuki Alto FX: 4322
			Suzuki Alto FX Automatic: 4323
40	130.1	330.5	Peugeot 104 ZS: 3415
41	130.5	331.5	Fiat 750 Abarth: 1478
42	131.2	333.2	Lotus Super 7: 2595
43	131.3	333.5	Honda S800: 2088
44	132.0	335.3	Fiat Abarth 850: 1487
			Lloyd LP 600: 2588
			Lotus 7: 2593
45	133.0	337.8	AJS 9hp Saloon: 38
			Caterham 7: 724
			Caterham Super 7: 722
			Caterham Super 7: 726
			Fiat Panda: 1574
			Fiat Panda 1000 S: 1592
			Fiat Panda 750 L: 1593
			Lotus 7 Twin Cam SS: 2605
			Lotus Super 7 Twincam: 2607
			Reliant Kitten: 3789
			Reliant Kitten DL Estate: 3790
			Wolseley Hornet: 4977
46	133.1	338.1	Honda Jazz: 2115
47	133.5	339.1	Caterham 1700 Super Sprint: 723
			Caterham 7 HPC: 725
			Lancia Y10 Fire: 2545
			Lancia Y10 GTie: 2554
			Lancia Y10 Turbo: 2540
48	134.0	340.4	Austin Metro 1.3L 3-door: 426
			Hillman Minx Sports Tourer: 2025
			Lotus 11 Le Mans: 2589
49	134.1	340.6	Austin Metro Automatic: 418
			Austin Metro GTa: 427
			MG Metro 1300: 3036
			MG Metro Turbo: 3037
50	135.0	342.9	Citroen LNA 11RE: 1063
			Ford Model T: 1608
			Hillman Imp Californian: 2065
			Ogle Austin Mini Cooper GT: 3268
			Sunbeam Stiletto: 4306
			Suzuki SJ413V JX: 4327

Total: 114

Widest. Limit set at 79in.

	in	cm	
1	86.4	219.5	Koenig Competition: 2417
			Koenig Competition Evolution: 2418
2	84.5	214.6	Jaguar XJS Koenig: 2356
3	82.7	210.1	Ferrari Testa Rossa Gemballa: 1443
			Porsche 911 Turbo Gemballa Mirage: 3751
4	82.6	209.8	Ferrari Pininfarina Mythos: 1448
5	82.0	208.3	Chevrolet Corvette Greenwood: 870
			Datsun 240Z Sharp: 1190
			Vector W8 Twin Turbo: 4736
6	81.7	207.5	Chrysler Imperial: 977
7	81.5	207.0	Ford Galaxie: 1658
8	81.1	206.0	Cizeta Moroder V16T: 1094
9	80.8	205.2	Koenig C62: 2419
10	80.7	205.0	Pontiac Bonneville: 3528
11	80.3	204.0	Cadillac Eldorado Convertible: 701
			Lamborghini Diablo: 2475
			Lamborghini Diablo: 2474
			Lamborghini LM129: 2472
12	80.1	203.5	Lincoln Continental Mk III: 2579
13	80.0	203.2	BMW 735i Koenig: 611
			Buick LeSabre 400: 673
			Buick Wildcat: 686
			Buick Wildcat: 680
			Cadillac Calais: 707
			Cadillac Coupe de Ville: 709
			Cadillac Fleetwood: 703
			Chevrolet Bel Air Six: 800
			Chevrolet Camaro IROC: 877
			Chevrolet Caprice: 827
			Chrysler Imperial Le Baron: 982
			Dodge D-100 Sweptline Pickup: 1283
			Ford Custom 500: 1703
			Ford Galaxie 500: 1705
			Ford LTD: 1773
			Mercury Marquis Brougham: 2948
			Mercury Marquis Marauder X-100: 2949
			Mercury Park Lane: 2937
			Mercury Super Marauder S-55: 2932
			Oldsmobile 88 Delta Royale: 3294
			Oldsmobile Dynamic Delta 88 Holiday: 3285
			Plymouth Fury III: 3506
			Plymouth Savoy 6: 3478
14	79.9	202.9	Buick Roadmaster: 660
			Cadillac Eldorado: 708
			Cadillac Park Avenue: 704
			Chevrolet Beauville: 849
			Chevrolet Impala SS427: 809
			Ford Fastback NASCAR: 1698
			Ford Galaxie: 1663
			Ford Galaxie 406: 1679
			Ford Galaxie 500 XL: 1699
			Mercury Meteor 800: 2928
			Mercury S-55 406: 2930
15	79.8	202.7	Cadillac Coupe de Ville: 702
			Chevrolet Impala: 846
			Chevrolet Kingswood Estate Wagon: 839
			Dodge Monaco Wagon: 1302
			Dodge Pickup Power Wagon: 1317
			Ford F-100 Styleside Pickup: 1692
16	79.7	202.4	Cadillac Coupe de Ville: 705
			Cadillac Sedan de Ville: 706
17	79.6	202.2	Chevrolet Blazer: 876
			Chevrolet Caprice Custom 396: 790
			Chevrolet Impala: 822
			Chevrolet Impala SS: 799
			Chrysler Imperial Crown: 987
			Lincoln Continental Limousine: 2582
			Mercury Monterey: 2938
			Pontiac Bonneville Vista: 3541
			Pontiac Catalina 2+2: 3542
18	79.5	201.9	Chrysler 300: 984
			Chrysler Newport: 983
			Ford Econoline Chateau Wagon: 1792
19	79.4	201.7	Chevrolet Bel Air: 770

			Chevrolet Biscayne V8: 771
			Chrysler 300: 979
			Chrysler 300-G: 975
			Chrysler 300-H: 980
			Chrysler Enforcer: 976
			Chrysler Newport: 978
			Ford Pickup 4WD: 1797
			Mercury Park Lane: 2939
			Pontiac Grand Prix: 3551
20	79.3	201.5	Jaguar 4.0 Sovereign: 2358
			Jaguar XJ6 3.2: 2368
			Jaguar XJR 4.0: 2363
			Oldsmobile Delmont: 3291
21	79.2	201.2	Buick Riviera: 683
			Ford Country Sedan: 1670
			Ford Galaxie: 1678
			Ford LTD: 1809
22	79.1	200.9	Chrysler Windsor de Luxe: 972
23	79.0	200.7	Bentley Turbo R: 482
			Chevrolet Bel Air 409 SS/S: 755
			Chevrolet Blazer: 850
			Chevrolet C-10 Fleetside Pickup: 772
			Chevrolet Impala SS 409: 768
			Chevrolet Impala Station Wagon: 769
			Chevrolet Impala Super Sport 409: 779
			Chevrolet Monza Mike Keyser: 874
			Chevrolet Pickup Cheyenne Fleetside: 851
			Chrysler 300: 988
			Chrysler 300-H: 989
			Chrysler 300-J: 981
			Dodge Monaco: 1310
			Eagle GTP: 1356
			Evans Series I: 1362
			Ford Custom 500: 1734
			Ford Galaxie 7-litre: 1737
			Mercedes-Benz 560SEL: 2889

Total: 110

Narrowest.
Limit set at 56in.

	in	cm	
1	46.0	116.8	Austin 7 Tourer: 340
2	47.0	119.4	Austin 7 Sports Two-seater: 342
3	49.5	125.7	Morris Minor Saloon: 3138
4	50.0	127.0	Austin 7 Sunshine Saloon: 343
			Berkeley B95: 487
			Berkeley Sports: 484
			Berkeley Sports 4: 486
			Frazer-Nash Boulogne II: 1980
			MG Midget: 2968
			Morris 8 Minor: 3140
5	50.5	128.3	Fiat 500C Convertible (Topolino): 1462
6	50.6	128.5	Fiat 500C Convertible: 1464
7	51.0	129.5	Honda 600 Coupe: 2091
			Honda N360: 2089
			Messerschmitt (FMR) Tg 500: 2966
			Subaru Hapi Van 360: 4245
			Suzuki Brute: 4320
			Triumph Super 7 Saloon: 4487
			Triumph Supercharged 7: 4488
			Wolseley Hornet: 4977
8	51.2	130.0	Subaru 360: 4243
9	52.0	132.1	Fiat 500: 1482
			Fiat 500: 1477
			Fiat 500D: 1498
			Fiat 500F: 1504
			Fiat Abarth 595: 1506
			MG Mk II Montlhery Supercharged: 2970
10	52.1	132.3	Fiat 500 Giardiniera: 1492
11	52.3	132.8	Fiat 500 Nuova: 1483
12	52.5	133.4	Honda 600: 2090
13	53.0	134.6	Abarth Zagato 750 GT: 1
			Austin 7 Saloon: 341
			Austin-Healey Sprite: 435
			Austin-Healey Sprite Hardtop: 437
			Austin-Healey Sprite Mk II: 441
			Austin-Healey Sprite Supercharged: 439
			MG Midget: 3002
			MG Midget: 3007
			MG Midget Mk III: 3012
14	53.1	134.9	Fiat Abarth Twin Cam: 1488
15	53.7	136.4	Goggomobil TS400: 2004
16	54.0	137.2	Austin-Healey Sebring Sprite: 438
			Austin-Healey Sprite 1100: 444
			BMW Isetta Motocoupe: 499
			Fiat 600: 1469
			MG Midget: 3034
			MG Midget: 3030
			MG Midget Mk IV: 3031
			Turner Turner-Climax: 4582
17	54.2	137.7	Fiat 126: 1539
18	54.3	137.9	Fiat 600: 1486
			Fiat 600D: 1493
			Fiat 750 Abarth: 1478
			Fiat Abarth 750GT Zagato: 1479
			Fiat Abarth Zagato: 1480
19	54.5	138.4	Fiat 126 de Ville: 1564
20	54.9	139.5	Daihatsu Domino: 1122
			Daihatsu Domino: 1117
			MG B: 3029
			MG Midget: 3026
			MG Midget 1500: 3028
			MG Midget Mk III: 3021
			Suzuki Alto FX: 4322
			Suzuki Alto FX Automatic: 4323
			Suzuki SC 100: 4321
21	55.0	139.7	BMW 600: 501
			Bond 875: 628
			Bond Bug: 629
			HRG 1.5-litre: 2168
			Mini Cooper: 3046
22	55.1	140.0	Honda S800: 2088
			Siata Spring 850: 4128
23	55.2	140.2	Austin A30: 369
			Austin A30: 368
			Austin A35 4-door: 379
24	55.3	140.5	Suzuki Alto GLA: 4325
25	55.5	141.0	Austin Seven 850: 391
			Frisky Coupe: 1993
			Lloyd LP 600: 2588
			Mini 1000: 3057
			Mini 1275GT: 3056
			Mini 1275GT: 3053
			Mini 1275GT: 3054
			Mini 850: 3055
			Mini 850 Super de Luxe: 3060
			Mini Automatic: 3058
			Mini Clubman 1100: 3059
			Mini Cooper: 3050
			Mini Cooper 1275S: 3049
			Mini Cooper 1275S: 3051
			Mini Cooper S: 3047
			Mini Minor: 3044
			Mini Minor de Luxe: 3043
			Mini Super de Luxe: 3048
			Mini Super de Luxe Mk II: 3052
			Mini Traveller: 3045
			Riley Elf: 3944
			Rover Mini Cooper S: 4048
			Triumph TR2 Hardtop: 4502
			Triumph TR2 Hardtop: 4504
			Triumph TR2 Sports: 4501
			Wolseley Hornet: 4998
26	55.7	141.5	Ford Taunus 17M Estate: 1652
			Singer 9 Roadster: 4163
27	55.9	142.0	Fiat Abarth 850: 1487
			Ford Anglia 8 Saloon: 1623
			NSU Prinz 34hp: 3256
28	56.0	142.2	Austin 8 Saloon: 358
			Austin A30 Countryman: 375
			Enfield 8000 Electric: 1359
			Fiat 133: 1549
			Fiat 850 Special: 1513
			Fiat 850 Super: 1499
			Lotus Elan 1600: 2596
			Lotus Elan Coupe SE: 2600
			Lotus Elan S4 Drophead SE: 2603
			Lotus Elan S4 SE: 2604
			Lotus Elan SE: 2601
			Lotus Elan Sprint: 2612
			Lotus Elan Sprint: 2608
			Lotus Super 7: 2594
			MG TC: 2978
			MG TC Midget: 2977
			Morgan 4/4: 3133
			Morgan 4/4: 3128
			Morgan Plus 4: 3127
			Morgan Plus 4: 3124
			Morgan Plus 4: 3123
			NSU Prinz II: 3257
			Reliant Kitten: 3789
			Reliant Kitten DL Estate: 3790
			Standard 8: 4197

Total: 132

Highest.
Limit set at 70in.

	in	cm	
1	80.5	204.5	Dodge Safari Super Sport: 1291
2	80.4	204.2	Chevrolet Beauville: 849
3	80.1	203.5	Land Rover One Ten County V8: 2561
4	79.0	200.7	Land Rover County: 2559
			Land Rover Series III: 2557
			Land Rover SWB: 2558
5	78.5	199.4	Ford Econoline: 1691
			Ford Econoline: 1662
6	78.3	198.9	Land Rover Ninety County Turbo Diesel: 2560
			Land Rover Ninety County V8: 2562

			Volkswagen Caravelle Carat Automatic: 4873
			Volkswagen Caravelle Syncro: 4855
7	78.2	198.6	Dodge A-100 Super/Surfer: 1292
			Dodge Super/Surver Van: 1318
8	78.1	198.4	Mercedes-Benz 300GD: 2867
9	78.0	198.1	Land Rover Station Wagon: 2556
10	77.8	197.6	Ford Econoline Chateau Wagon: 1792
			Mercedes-Benz G-Wagen 300 GD LWB: 2921
11	77.2	196.1	Volkswagen Vanagon: 4823
			Volkswagen Vanagon Wasserboxer: 4842
12	77.0	195.6	Volkswagen Van: 4787
13	76.4	194.1	Volkswagen Micro Bus: 4745
			Volkswagen Station Wagon: 4756
			Volkswagen Van: 4757
14	76.3	193.8	Ford F-100 Styleside Pickup: 1692
15	76.0	193.0	Humber Pullman Limousine: 2182
			Toyota Land Cruiser: 4372
16	75.6	191.9	Land Rover Discovery TDi: 2563
			Land Rover Discovery V8: 2564
			Land Rover Discovery V8i 5DR: 2565
17	75.4	191.5	Daihatsu Fourtrak Estate DT EL: 1125
18	75.0	190.5	De Soto Straight Eight Saloon: 1234
			Franklin 29.4hp Saloon: 1977
			La Salle Enclosed Drive Limousine: 2421
			Vauxhall 20/60 Limousine: 4609
19	74.8	190.0	DKW Karavan: 1264
			Toyota Landcruiser VX: 4478
20	74.3	188.7	Ford Pickup 4WD: 1797
21	74.2	188.5	Lincoln 39.2hp Town Saloon: 2573
22	74.0	188.0	Cadillac V16 "Madame X": 699
			Chrysler 75 Saloon: 961
			Mitsubishi Shogun Turbo Diesel 5-door: 3094
			Mitsubishi Shogun V6 5-door: 3105
			Packard 32.5hp Saloon: 3354
			Studebaker President Limousine: 4217
23	73.8	187.5	Toyota Landcruiser II TD: 4458
24	73.6	186.9	Mitsubishi Shogun V6 LWB: 3115
25	73.5	186.7	Austin Gipsy: 386
			Mercedes-Benz 32/90 Saloon: 2775
26	73.4	186.4	Toyota Land Cruiser Wagon: 4373
27	73.0	185.4	Chrysler 77 Saloon: 962
			Graham-Paige Straight Eight: 2016
			Mercedes-Benz 300 Sedan: 2789
			Renault Vivasix Saloon: 3797
			Rolls-Royce 20 Saloon: 3947
			Sunbeam Weymann Saloon: 4280
28	72.6	184.4	Ford Aerostar XLT: 1908
			Mitsubishi Colt Shogun: 3073
29	72.5	184.2	Chevrolet Pickup Cheyenne Fleetside: 851
30	72.4	183.9	Lamborghini LM129: 2472
31	72.2	183.4	Ford 24 Saloon: 1609
32	72.0	182.9	AMC Javelin: 191
			Bentley Speed Six Weymann: 464
			Buick 28.4hp Saloon: 654
			Buick Light Eight Saloon: 655
			Chevrolet Blazer: 876
			Daimler 30hp Double-six Saloon: 1132
			Daimler Straight Eight: 1139
			Daimler Twenty-Seven Limousine: 1138
			Dodge Eight Saloon: 1270
			Graham-Paige 21.6hp Saloon: 2015
			Humber 16/60 Saloon: 2181
			Hupmobile Straight Eight Limousine: 2216
			Lincoln Twelve Cylinder Town Sedan: 2575
			Minerva 22/28hp Limousine: 3042
			Nash Straight Eight Saloon: 3194
			Panhard 18hp Saloon: 3364
			Rolls-Royce 25 Saloon: 3948
			Studebaker Commander Brougham: 4215
			Stutz Roadster: 4239
33	71.8	182.4	International Pickup 4WD 1210 Camper Special: 2237
34	71.7	182.1	GMC Safari Cargo Mover: 2003
35	71.5	181.6	Bentley 8-litre Saloon: 463
			Mercedes-Benz 32/90 Limousine: 2777
36	71.4	181.4	Ford Bronco: 1729
37	71.2	180.8	Dodge Pickup Power Wagon: 1317
38	71.1	180.5	Renault Espace V6: 3921
39	71.0	180.3	Chevrolet C-10 Fleetside Pickup: 772
			Chrysler 65 Saloon: 960
			Chrysler Eight Saloon: 963
			Fiat 17/50 Saloon: 1454
			Ford Model T: 1608
			Rolls-Royce Silver Wraith: 3953
			Wolseley Viper Saloon: 4978
40	70.9	180.0	Toyota Landcruiser: 4450
41	70.8	179.8	Range Rover County: 3779
			Range Rover V8: 3775
			Toyota Space Cruiser: 4434
42	70.7	179.6	Ford Bronco: 1790
43	70.5	179.1	Hillman Wizard 65 Saloon de Luxe: 2026
			Morris Isis: 3139
			Toyota Previa: 4481
44	70.4	178.8	Marmon 69 Saloon: 2649
45	70.3	178.6	Daimler DK 400B: 1145
46	70.1	178.1	Toyota Van LE: 4430
47	70.0	177.8	Armstrong Siddeley 15 Saloon: 209
			Austin Princess: 371
			Duesenberg SJ Town Car: 1353
			Ford V8: 1610
			Graham Blue Streak Saloon: 2010
			Humber Snipe: 2180
			Lincoln 39.2hp Saloon: 2574
			Marmon 79 Saloon: 2650
			Mercedes-Benz 21/60 Coupe: 2778
			Packard Super 8 Phaeton: 3356
			Range Rover V8: 3771
			Range Rover V8: 3772
			Range Rover V8: 3773
			Range Rover Vogue: 3774
			Range Rover Vogue: 3777
			Range Rover Vogue SE: 3778
			Range Rover Vogue SE: 3781
			Range Rover Vogue SE: 3780
			Range Rover Vogue Turbo D: 3776
			Studebaker Double-twelve Open Tourer: 4214
			Studebaker Erskine Saloon: 4216
			Wills Sainte Claire Six: 4974

Total: 127

Lowest. Limit set 44in.

	in	cm	
1	28.0	71.1	Lotus Super 7: 2594
2	31.5	80.0	Lynx D Type: 2642
3	32.5	82.6	Bizzarrini P538: 497
4	34.6	87.9	Porsche RSK: 3613
5	37.0	94.0	Caterham Super 7: 722
			Lotus 11 Le Mans: 2589
			Lotus 7 Twin Cam SS: 2605
			Lotus Super 7 Twincam: 2607
6	38.0	96.5	Ferrari 212 Touring: 1372
			Tracta Sports Two-seater: 4484
7	39.0	99.1	Alfa Romeo 33 2.0 Stradale: 66
8	39.4	100.1	Sbarro Chrono 3.5: 4108
9	39.5	100.3	Ferrari 250 Testa Rossa: 1378
			Ferrari 250 Testa Rossa: 1382
			Jaguar XJ13: 2313
10	40.0	101.6	Ford GT40: 1760
			Frazer-Nash Boulogne II: 1980
			Lotus Esprit Turbo HC: 2633
11	40.5	102.9	Ford GT40 Super Street: 1738
12	41.0	104.1	Eagle GTP: 1356
			Evans Series I: 1362
			Ferrari 412 MI: 1377
			Lamborghini Bravo: 2458
			Marcos 1600GT: 2645
			Marcos 3-litre Volvo: 2646
			Safir GT40: 4106
13	41.5	105.4	Lamborghini Miura: 2452
			Lamborghini Miura S: 2456
14	41.6	105.7	De Tomaso Pantera GT5: 1241
15	41.7	105.9	Bugatti EB110: 652
16	41.9	106.4	Ferrari Pininfarina Mythos: 1448
			Porsche 904 Carrera GTS: 3621
17	42.0	106.7	Clan Crusader: 1095
			Essex Terraplane Tourer: 1360
			Ferrari 166 Mille Miglia Barchetta: 1371
			Ferrari GTO Norwood: 1451
			Lamborghini Miura P400S: 2455
			Scarab Mk II: 4109
			Westfield SEight: 4973
18	42.1	106.9	De Tomaso Mangusta: 1235
			Lamborghini Countach: 2468
			Lamborghini Countach: 2461
			Lamborghini Countach 25th Anniversary: 2473
			Lamborghini Countach 5000S: 2469
			Lamborghini Countach LP 500S: 2465
			Lamborghini Countach S: 2464
			Lamborghini Countach S: 2466
19	42.5	108.0	Berkeley Sports: 484
			Berkeley Sports 4: 486
			Caterham 1700 Super Sprint: 723
			Caterham 7 HPC: 725
			Ferrari 365 GTB Goldsmith: 1425
			Jaguar C Type: 2274
			Lotus Europa: 2613
			Lotus Europa S2: 2606
			Lotus Europa Special 5-speed: 2616
			Rover Rover-BRM Turbine: 4006
			Vector W2: 4735
			Vector W8 Twin Turbo: 4736
20	42.9	109.0	Lamborghini Miura: 2451
21	43.0	109.2	Caterham 7: 724
			Caterham Super 7: 726
			Chevrolet Corvette Sebring: 738
			De Tomaso Pantera: 1237
			De Tomaso Pantera Group 3: 1243
			Ford Cobra II Kemp: 1841
			Lotus 7: 2593
			Lotus Elan Autocrosser: 2632
			Lotus Europa S2: 2609
22	43.2	109.7	Bertone Emotion Lotus: 489

23	43.3	110.0	De Tomaso Pantera GT5 S: 1244
			De Tomaso Pantera GT5-S: 1242
			De Tomaso Pantera GTS: 1239
			Jaguar XJR15: 2369
			Lancia Montecarlo Group 5 Turbo: 2531
24	43.5	110.5	Lamborghini Diablo: 2474
			Lamborghini Diablo: 2475
25	43.6	110.7	Lamborghini Urraco: 2463
26	43.7	111.0	Bizzarrini 5300 Spyder: 495
			Bizzarrini GT America: 496
			Ferrari 375 Indianapolis: 1373
			IAD Venus: 2229
			Lamborghini Urraco S: 2460
			Lotus Esprit: 2620
			Lotus Esprit S2: 2625
			Zender Vision 3: 5007
27	43.8	111.3	Lotus Esprit 16v: 2621
28	43.9	111.5	Cizeta Moroder V16T: 1094
			Lamborghini Jalpa: 2471
			Lamborghini Jalpa: 2467
			Lamborghini Silhouette 3000: 2462
29	44.0	111.8	Alfa Romeo 2.3 Mille Miglia: 42
			Alfa Romeo Supercharged Straight Eight: 39
			Devin Super Sports: 1257
			Ferrari 308 GTB: 1409
			Ferrari 512 BB: 1417
			Ferrari 512 BB: 1413
			Fiberfab Jamaican Buick V8: 1607
			Koenig C62: 2419
			Lotus Esprit Turbo: 2627
			Pontiac Firebird TransAm Silverbird: 3566
			Trihawk 304: 4486
			TVR Convertible Turbo: 4593
			TVR S Convertible: 4602
			TVR S Convertible: 4600

Total: 105

Most ground clearance. Limit set at 8.3in.

	in	cm	
1	15.5	39.4	Dodge Safari Super Sport: 1291
2	15.0	38.1	Land Rover One Ten County V8: 2561
3	11.0	27.9	Volkswagen 181: 4794
4	10.0	25.4	Land Rover Ninety County Turbo Diesel: 2560
			Land Rover Ninety County V8: 2562
			Land Rover Series III: 2557
			Land Rover SWB: 2558
5	9.5	24.1	Allard V8: 149
			Ford Model T: 1608
			Peugeot 204: 3394
			Suzuki Brute: 4320
6	9.4	23.9	Volkswagen Station Wagon: 4756
			Volkswagen Van: 4757
7	9.3	23.5	Lada Niva Cossack Cabrio: 2428
8	9.2	23.4	Cadillac V16 "Madame X": 699
			Lada Niva 1600: 2426
9	9.0	22.9	Allard Drop-head Coupe: 148
			Allard K2: 150
			Chevrolet Blazer: 850
			Chevrolet Pickup Cheyenne Fleetside: 851
			Cord 812-S: 1101
			Cord Front Wheel Drive Saloon: 1099
			Ford Fairlane 500: 1671
			International Pickup 4WD 1210 Camper Special: 2237
			International Scout: 2234
			Lancia Flavia Injection: 2507
			Rambler Rebel 6 Estate Car: 3769
			Renault 6: 3834
			Renault 6 1100: 3838
			Renault 6 TL: 3846
			Volga M21K: 4737
10	8.9	22.6	Dacia Duster GLX: 1106
			Ford Anglia 10 Saloon: 1622
			Isuzu Trooper 3-door TD: 2257
			Suzuki SJ413V JX: 4327
11	8.8	22.4	Ford Anglia 8 Saloon: 1623
12	8.7	22.1	Alfa Romeo Alfasud 1.5 Sprint Veloce: 104
			Alfa Romeo Alfasud Sprint 1.5: 100
			British Adler 13.67 Cabriolet: 641
			Ford Popular: 1631
			Ford Prefect: 1620
			Rover 80: 3993
			Toyota Land Cruiser: 4358
13	8.6	21.8	Skoda Felicia: 4183
			Skoda Octavia: 4182
			Toyota Landcruiser VX: 4478
14	8.5	21.6	Armstrong Siddeley Star Sapphire: 220
			Aston Martin DB2: 234
			Aston Martin DB2: 232
			Chrysler New Yorker Saloon: 971
			Chrysler Saratoga Club Coupe: 970
			Fiat Brava Abarth Rally: 1571
			Ford Bronco: 1790
			Ford V8 Touring Saloon: 1614
			Graham 33.8hp Supercharged Saloon: 2012
			Holden Saloon: 2085
			International Scout: 2240
			International Travelall 1210: 2239
			Jeep CJ-5: 2374
			Jeep CJ-5 V8: 2379
			Jeep Commando: 2380
			Marendaz 15/90 Special Tourer: 2647
			Matra Rancho: 2683
			Mercedes-Benz 220S: 2799
			Mercedes-Benz 300B: 2792
			Mercedes-Benz 300GD: 2867
			Mercedes-Benz 450SLC: 2849
			Mitsubishi Shogun V6 LWB: 3115
			NSU Typ 110: 3263
			Opel Ascona 1900SR: 3340
			Rolls-Royce 20/25 Touring Saloon: 3951
			Rover 2000: 4002
			Rover 2000TC: 4008
			Stutz Roadster: 4239
			Toyota Corolla 4WD Estate: 4457
			Volkswagen Vanagon: 4823
15	8.3	21.0	Daihatsu Fourtrak Estate DT EL: 1125
			Daihatsu Sportrak EL: 1130
			International Scout: 2238
			Jeep Wagoneer: 2382
			Mitsubishi Colt Shogun: 3073
			Volkswagen Sedan de Luxe: 4738

Total: 82

Least ground clearance. Limit set at 4.3in.

	in	cm	
1	2.0	5.1	Renault 5 Racer: 3865
			Renault Le Car Turbo: 3874
2	2.4	6.1	Lancia Montecarlo Group 5 Turbo: 2531
3	2.5	6.4	Ford Mustang TransAm: 1796
			Ford Pinto Pangra: 1819
			Lotus Elan Autocrosser: 2632
4	2.6	6.6	Datsun B210 Electramotive: 1198
5	2.7	6.9	Fiat 124 Special: 1521
6	2.9	7.4	Ford Cobra II Kemp: 1841
7	3.0	7.6	Chevrolet Corvette Greenwood: 870
			Datsun 280ZX Electramotive: 1230
			Ferrari 308 GTB: 1411
			Jaguar XJS Tullius: 2333
			Lotus 7 Twin Cam SS: 2605
			Lotus Super 7 Twincam: 2607
			Mazda RX-7 Racer: 2715
			Pontiac Firebird TransAm Silverbird: 3566
			Triumph TR7 Tullius: 4572
			Triumph TR8 Group 44: 4578
			Volkswagen Scirocco GT-3 Davey: 4830
8	3.1	7.9	Porsche 935 Group 4 Holbert: 3657
9	3.3	8.4	Datsun 280ZX Sharp: 1221
10	3.4	8.6	De Tomaso Pantera GT5: 1241
11	3.5	8.9	Chevrolet Monza Mike Keyser: 874
			Elva Courier: 1358
			Triumph TR8: 4577
			Turner Sports: 4583
12	3.6	9.1	Datsun 240Z Sharp: 1190
			Datsun 280ZX Electramotive: 1220
13	3.7	9.4	BMW 630 CSi: 544
			BMW 633 CSi: 555
			BMW 635 CSi: 561
			BMW 635 CSi: 594
			BMW M635 CSi: 572
			BMW M635 CSi: 607
14	3.8	9.7	Renault R8 Rally: 3826
15	3.9	10.0	Audi 100 2.8E Auto: 333
			Fiberfab Jamaican Buick V8: 1607
			Panther Kallista 1.6L: 3378
			Panther Kallista 2.8: 3377
			Panther Kallista 2.8: 3376
16	4.0	10.2	AC Cobra: 25
			Alfa Romeo Milano Platinum: 127
			Aston Martin DB5: 241
			Aston Martin DB6: 242
			Audi V8 Quattro: 331
			Audi V8 Quattro Automatic: 332
			Avanti II: 460
			Ferrari 328 GTS: 1431
			Ferrari 365 GT4 2+2: 1406
			Ford Capri RS2600: 1805
			Jensen Healey Huffaker: 2399
			Lamborghini Jalpa 3500: 2470
			Lancia Flaminia Coupe: 2496
			Marcos 1800: 2644
			Pontiac Petty Grand National: 3571
			Triumph Spitfire 1500: 4558
			Westfield SEight: 4973
17	4.1	10.4	Chevrolet Corvette: 884
			Chevrolet Corvette: 886
			Volkswagen Passat CL TD Estate: 4880

			Volkswagen Passat GT: 4869
			Volkswagen Passat GT 16v: 4878
			Volkswagen Polo 1.3 CL Coupe: 4886
			Volkswagen Polo G40: 4887
			Volkswagen Polo GT Coupe: 4888
			Volvo 760 GLE: 4946
18	4.2	10.7	Chevrolet Corvette: 862
			Lancia Appia III: 2499
			Mercedes-Benz 220: 2822
			Mercedes-Benz 250: 2823
			Mercedes-Benz 250 Coupe: 2829
			MG B: 3029
			Pontiac Grand Am: 3562
19	4.3	10.9	Bitter SC: 493
			Buick Opel by Isuzu: 689
			Chevrolet Corvette LT-1: 858
			Citroen AX GT: 1074
			Citroen AX GT5: 1083
			Citroen AX GTi: 1092
			Citroen AX11 TRE: 1075
			Citroen AX11 TRE 5DR: 1079
			Citroen AX11 TZX: 1087
			Citroen AX14 DTR: 1081
			Citroen AX14 TRS: 1076
			Dodge Colt Hatchback: 1323
			Ferrari F40: 1450
			Lotus Europa: 2613
			Mitsubishi Tredia Turbo: 3076
			Plymouth Colt GTS Turbo: 3518
			Pontiac Grand Prix: 3556
			Sunbeam Alpine 1.7: 4303
			Volkswagen Scirocco 16v: 4853
			Volkswagen Scirocco GL: 4837
			Volkswagen Scirocco GTi: 4841
			Volkswagen Scirocco GTX: 4854
			Volvo 480 ES: 4954

Total: 97

Sets of eight ranked lists

ordered by maximum speed, acceleration to 60mph/96.5km, highest power, highest torque, highest rpm at peak power, highest power-to-weight-ratio, highest specific output and highest piston speeds at peak power.

Multivalve engines. Maximum speed. Limit set at 160mph.

	mph	kmh	
1	230.0	370.1	Koenig Competition Evolution: 2418
2	217.0	349.2	Koenig Competition: 2417
3	214.0	344.3	Bugatti EB110: 652
4	210.0	337.9	Ferrari Testa Rossa Norwood: 1444
5	204.0	328.2	Cizeta Moroder V16T: 1094
6	202.0	325.0	Lamborghini Diablo: 2474
			Lamborghini Diablo: 2475
7	201.0	323.4	Ferrari F40: 1435
			Porsche 959 S: 3702
8	200.0	321.8	Ferrari F40: 1446
			Jaguar XJ220: 2359
9	199.0	320.2	Ferrari GTO Norwood: 1451
10	198.0	318.6	Porsche 959: 3731
			Porsche 959 Comfort: 3717
			Porsche 959 Sport: 3718
11	196.0	315.4	Ferrari F40: 1450
12	189.0	304.1	Ferrari 288 GTO: 1421
13	186.0	299.3	Chevrolet Corvette ZR-1 Geiger: 954
			Porsche 928 S4 Koenig: 3726
			Zender Fact 4: 5008
14	185.0	297.7	Ferrari Testa Rossa Gemballa: 1443
			Mercedes-Benz 300CE AMG Hammer: 2910
15	183.0	294.4	Mercedes-Benz 300E AMG Hammer: 2899
16	181.0	291.2	Ferrari Testa Rossa: 1437
			Ferrari Testa Rossa Straman Spyder: 1438
17	180.0	289.6	Ferrari 288 GTO: 1416
			Ferrari GTO: 1423
			Ferrari Pininfarina Mythos: 1448
			Mercedes-Benz 300SLR: 2795
18	179.0	288.0	Lamborghini Countach: 2468
			Lamborghini Countach 25th Anniversary: 2473
19	178.0	286.4	Ferrari Testa Rossa: 1426
20	176.0	283.2	Isdera Imperator: 2244
21	174.0	280.0	Ferrari Testa Rossa: 1442
			Opel Omega Lotus: 3352
22	173.0	278.4	Ferrari Daytona Cannonball: 1398
			Lamborghini Countach 5000S: 2469
23	171.0	275.1	Ferrari 348tb: 1449
24	170.0	273.5	Bertone Emotion Lotus: 489
			Chevrolet Corvette ZR-1: 934
25	168.0	270.3	Acura NSX: 36
			Ferrari 512 BB: 1417
26	166.0	267.1	Nissan 300ZX Turbo Millen Super GTZ: 3247
27	165.0	265.5	IAD Venus: 2229
			Lotus Esprit Turbo SE: 2640
			Porsche 928 S4: 3712
28	164.0	263.9	Ferrari 348tb: 1445
29	162.0	260.7	Honda NSX: 2156
			Porsche 928 S4 SE: 3727
30	161.0	259.0	Alfa Romeo 33 2.0 Stradale: 66
			Lotus Esprit Turbo SE: 2637
			Porsche 928 S4 Automatic: 3692
			Subaru Legacy FIA Record: 4274
31	160.0	257.4	Aston Martin Virage: 261
			Maserati Shamal: 2681
			Mercedes-Benz 500SL: 29

Total: 56

Multivalve engines. Acceleration to 60mph/ 96.5km. Limit set at 5.5 seconds.

	sec	
1	3.5	Jaguar XJ220: 2359
		Koenig Competition Evolution: 2418
		Sbarro Chrono 3.5: 4108
2	3.6	Lancia Montecarlo Group 5 Turbo: 2531
		Porsche 959: 3731
		Porsche 959 Sport: 3718
3	3.8	Ferrari F40: 1450
4	3.9	Bugatti EB110: 652
5	4.0	Koenig Competition: 2417
		Porsche 959 Comfort: 3717
6	4.2	Chevrolet Corvette ZR-1 SS: 955
7	4.3	Zender Fact 4: 5008
8	4.5	Cizeta Moroder V16T: 1094
		Ferrari F40: 1446
		Lamborghini Diablo: 2475
9	4.7	Ferrari Testa Rossa Norwood: 1444
		Lamborghini Countach 25th Anniversary: 2473
		Porsche 959 S: 3702
10	4.8	Audi Quattro Sport: 309
		Porsche 928 S4 Koenig: 3726
11	4.9	Chevrolet Corvette ZR-1: 953
		Chevrolet Corvette ZR-1: 934
		Chevrolet Corvette ZR-1 Geiger: 954
		Lamborghini Countach: 2468
		Lotus Esprit Turbo SE: 2637
		Opel Omega Lotus: 3352
12	5.0	Bertone Emotion Lotus: 489

		Ferrari 288 GTO: 1416
		Ferrari 288 GTO: 1421
		Ferrari GTO: 1423
		IAD Venus: 2229
		Isdera Imperator: 2244
		Mercedes-Benz 300CE AMG Hammer: 2910
		Nissan 300ZX Turbo Millen Super GTZ: 3247
		Porsche RSK: 3613
13	5.1	Ferrari 512 BB: 1417
		Lotus Esprit Turbo SE: 2640
14	5.2	Caterham 7 HPC: 725
		Ferrari Testa Rossa: 1442
		Lamborghini Countach 5000S: 2469
		Lotus Esprit Turbo: 2636
		Mercedes-Benz 300E AMG Hammer: 2899
15	5.3	Ferrari Testa Rossa: 1437
		Ferrari Testa Rossa: 1426
		Ferrari Testa Rossa Gemballa: 1443
		Ferrari Testa Rossa Straman Spyder: 1438
		Ford Festiva Shogun: 1965
		Lotus Elan Autocrosser: 2632
16	5.4	Lotus Esprit Turbo: 2635
17	5.5	Porsche 928 Cabrio Strosek: 3725
		Porsche 928 S4: 3712
		Porsche 928 S4 SE: 3727

Total: 52

Multivalve engines. Highest power. Limit set at 350bhp.

	bhp	kW	PS	
1	1600.0	1193.1	1622.2	Ferrari GTO Norwood: 1451
2	1000.0	745.7	1013.9	Koenig Competition Evolution: 2418
3	943.0	703.2	956.1	Ferrari Testa Rossa Norwood: 1444
4	800.0	596.6	811.1	Koenig Competition: 2417
5	640.0	477.2	648.9	Peugeot 405 Turbo 16 Pike's Peak: 3460
6	600.0	447.4	608.3	Bugatti EB110: 652
				Porsche 959 S: 3702
7	560.0	417.6	567.8	Cizeta Moroder V16T: 1094
8	530.0	395.2	537.3	Jaguar XJ220: 2359
9	500.0	372.8	506.9	Sbarro Chrono 3.5: 4108
10	492.0	366.9	498.8	Lamborghini Diablo: 2475
11	485.0	361.7	491.7	Lamborghini Diablo: 2474
12	478.0	356.4	484.6	Ferrari F40: 1450
				Ferrari F40: 1435
				Ferrari F40: 1446
13	460.0	343.0	466.4	Nissan 300ZX Turbo Millen Super GTZ: 3247
14	455.0	339.3	461.3	Lamborghini Countach: 2468
				Lamborghini Countach 25th Anniversary: 2473
15	450.0	335.6	456.2	Porsche 959: 3731
				Porsche 959 Comfort: 3717
				Porsche 959 Sport: 3718
16	448.0	334.1	454.2	Zender Fact 4: 5008
17	430.0	320.6	436.0	Porsche 928 S4 Koenig: 3726
				Toyota Supra Turbo TRD: 4467
18	428.0	319.2	433.9	Nissan 300ZX Motor Sports International SR-71: 3246
19	425.0	316.9	430.9	Chevrolet Corvette ZR-1 SS: 955
20	420.0	313.2	425.8	Lamborghini Countach 5000S: 2469
21	415.0	309.5	420.8	Lamborghini LM129: 2472
22	410.0	305.7	415.7	Chevrolet Corvette ZR-1 Geiger: 954
23	408.0	304.2	413.7	Mercedes-Benz 600SEL: 2923
24	400.0	298.3	405.5	Ferrari 288 GTO: 1421
				Ferrari GTO: 1423
				Lancia Montecarlo Group 5 Turbo: 2531
25	394.0	293.8	399.5	Ferrari 288 GTO: 1416
26	390.0	290.8	395.4	Ferrari Testa Rossa: 1442
				Isdera Imperator: 2244
27	380.0	283.4	385.3	Chevrolet Corvette ZR-1: 934
				Ferrari Pininfarina Mythos: 1448
				Ferrari Testa Rossa: 1426
				Ferrari Testa Rossa: 1437
				Ferrari Testa Rossa Gemballa: 1443
				Ferrari Testa Rossa Straman Spyder: 1438
28	377.0	281.1	382.2	Opel Omega Lotus: 3352
29	375.0	279.6	380.2	Chevrolet Corvette ZR-1: 953
				Mercedes-Benz 300CE AMG Hammer: 2910
				Mercedes-Benz 300E AMG Hammer: 2899
30	360.0	268.4	365.0	Ferrari 512 BB: 1417
31	352.0	262.5	356.9	Ferrari Daytona Cannonball: 1398

Total: 48

Multivalve engines. Highest torque. Limit set at 330lbft.

	lbft	Nm	
1	900.0	1219.5	Ferrari GTO Norwood: 1451
2	738.0	1000.0	Koenig Competition Evolution: 2418
3	664.0	899.7	Koenig Competition: 2417
4	542.0	734.4	Peugeot 405 Turbo 16 Pike's Peak: 3460
5	470.0	636.9	Porsche 928 S4 Koenig: 3726
6	430.0	582.7	Nissan 300ZX Turbo Millen Super GTZ: 3247
7	428.0	579.9	Lamborghini Diablo: 2475
			Lamborghini Diablo: 2474
			Mercedes-Benz 600SEL: 2923
8	425.0	575.9	Ferrari F40: 1446
			Ferrari F40: 1450
			Ferrari F40: 1435
9	419.0	567.8	Bugatti EB110: 652
10	409.0	554.2	Opel Omega Lotus: 3352
11	407.0	551.5	Mercedes-Benz 300CE AMG Hammer: 2910
			Mercedes-Benz 300E AMG Hammer: 2899
12	406.0	550.1	Nissan 300ZX Motor Sports International SR-71: 3246
13	400.0	542.0	Chevrolet Corvette ZR-1 SS: 955
			Jaguar XJ220: 2359
14	398.0	539.3	Cizeta Moroder V16T: 1094
15	390.0	528.5	Lancia Montecarlo Group 5 Turbo: 2531
			Zender Fact 4: 5008
16	387.0	524.4	Isdera Imperator: 2244
17	382.0	517.6	Toyota Supra Turbo TRD: 4467
18	370.0	501.4	Chevrolet Corvette ZR-1: 953
			Chevrolet Corvette ZR-1: 934
			Chevrolet Corvette ZR-1 Geiger: 954
			Porsche 959: 3731
			Porsche 959 Comfort: 3717
			Porsche 959 Sport: 3718
19	369.0	500.0	Lamborghini Countach: 2468
			Porsche 959 S: 3702
20	368.0	498.6	Lamborghini Countach 25th Anniversary: 2473
21	366.0	495.9	Ferrari 288 GTO: 1421
			Ferrari 288 GTO: 1416
			Ferrari GTO: 1423
22	363.1	492.0	Ferrari Testa Rossa: 1442
23	363.0	491.9	Lamborghini LM129: 2472
24	354.0	479.7	Ferrari Pininfarina Mythos: 1448
			Ferrari Testa Rossa: 1437
			Ferrari Testa Rossa: 1426
			Ferrari Testa Rossa Gemballa: 1443
			Ferrari Testa Rossa Straman Spyder: 1438
			Mercedes-Benz 500E: 2919
25	350.0	474.3	Aston Martin Virage: 258
26	347.0	470.2	Sbarro Chrono 3.5: 4108
27	341.0	462.1	Lamborghini Countach 5000S: 2469
28	339.5	460.0	Aston Martin Virage: 261
			Mercedes-Benz 500SL: 2913
29	333.0	451.2	Ferrari 512 BB: 1417
			Ferrari 512 BBi: 1422
30	332.1	450.0	BMW 750i: 612
31	332.0	449.9	BMW 750i L: 589
			Mercedes-Benz 500SL: 2920

Total: 54

Multivalve engines. Highest rpm at peak power. Limit set at 6800rpm.

	rpm	
1	10000	Ferrari Testa Rossa Norwood: 1444
2	9200	Sbarro Chrono 3.5: 4108
3	9000	Bugatti EB110: 652
4	8800	Alfa Romeo 33 2.0 Stradale: 66
		Lancia Montecarlo Group 5 Turbo: 2531
5	8000	Cizeta Moroder V16T: 1094
		Lotus Elan Autocrosser: 2632
		Porsche RSK: 3613
6	7600	Honda Civic 1.6i VT: 2154
		Honda CRX 1.6i VT: 2152
7	7500	Ferrari Daytona Cannonball: 1398
		Fiat Brava Abarth Rally: 1571
		Mercedes-Benz 300SLR: 2795
8	7200	Ferrari 348tb: 1445
		Ferrari GTO Norwood: 1451
		Ferrari Mondial t: 1452
		Ferrari Mondial t: 1441
		Mercedes-Benz 190E 2.5-16 Evolution II: 2916
		Mercedes-Benz 190E 2.5-16 Evolution II: 2908
9	7100	Acura NSX: 36
		Honda NSX: 2156
10	7000	BMW M3 Hor Technologie: 605
		BMW M3 Sport Evolution: 621
		Ferrari 288 GTO: 1421
		Ferrari 288 GTO: 1416
		Ferrari 3.2 Mondial: 1427
		Ferrari 328 GTB: 1428
		Ferrari 328 GTS: 1431

		Ferrari 348tb: 1449
		Ferrari F40: 1446
		Ferrari F40: 1450
		Ferrari F40: 1435
		Ferrari GTO: 1423
		Ferrari Mondial: 1447
		Ferrari Mondial 3.2: 1429
		Ferrari Mondial 3.2 Cabriolet: 1440
		Ferrari Mondial 3.2QV: 1430
		Ferrari Mondial Cabriolet: 1436
		Ferrari Mondial Cabriolet 3.2: 1433
		Ferrari Mondial t Cabriolet: 1453
		Geo Storm GSi: 1994
		Jaguar XJ220: 2359
		Lamborghini Countach: 2468
		Lamborghini Countach 25th Anniversary: 2473
		Lamborghini Countach 5000S: 2469
		Lamborghini Diablo: 2474
		Lancia Rally: 2537
		Peugeot 405 Turbo 16 Pike's Peak: 3460
11	6900	BMW M5: 622
		BMW M5: 606
		Lamborghini LM129: 2472
12	6800	Ferrari 308 GTBi Quattrovalvole: 1419
		Ferrari Mondial Cabriolet Quattrovalvole: 1424
		Honda Civic CRX: 2140
		Honda Concerto 1.6i 16: 2151
		Honda NSX Auto: 2159
		Isuzu Impulse XS: 2260
		Lamborghini Diablo: 2475
		Mazda MX-3 V6: 2767
		Nissan Skyline GT-R: 3243
		Rover 216 GTi: 4044
		Rover 416 GTi: 4040

Total: 62

Multivalve engines. Highest power-to-weight ratio. Limit set at 250bhp/ton.

	bhp/ ton	bhp/ tonne	
1	1257.5	1236.6	Ferrari GTO Norwood: 1451
2	780.5	767.5	Sbarro Chrono 3.5: 4108
3	764.6	751.8	Peugeot 405 Turbo 16 Pike's Peak: 3460
4	640.0	629.3	Koenig Competition Evolution: 2418
5	570.9	561.4	Ferrari Testa Rossa Norwood: 1444
6	520.9	512.2	Lancia Montecarlo Group 5 Turbo: 2531
7	512.0	503.5	Koenig Competition: 2417
8	454.8	447.2	Bugatti EB110: 652
9	451.0	443.5	Porsche 959 S: 3702
10	441.5	434.2	Ferrari F40: 1435
			Ferrari F40: 1446
11	411.3	404.4	Zender Fact 4: 5008
12	408.9	402.1	Alfa Romeo 33 2.0 Stradale: 66
13	359.3	353.3	Ferrari F40: 1450
14	350.7	344.8	Ferrari 288 GTO: 1421
			Ferrari GTO: 1423
15	348.7	342.9	Mercedes-Benz 300SLR: 2795
16	345.1	339.4	Jaguar XJ220: 2359
17	339.4	333.7	Porsche 959 Sport: 3718
18	334.5	328.9	Cizeta Moroder V16T: 1094
19	319.7	314.4	Lamborghini Countach: 2468
20	317.1	311.8	Isdera Imperator: 2244
21	316.0	310.7	Porsche 959: 3731
			Porsche 959 Comfort: 3717
22	310.7	305.5	Lamborghini Countach 25th Anniversary: 2473
23	309.0	303.8	Ferrari Pininfarina Mythos: 1448
24	306.4	301.3	Ferrari 288 GTO: 1416
25	304.4	299.4	Lamborghini Diablo: 2475
26	304.2	299.1	Ferrari TRC 2500 Testa Rossa: 1379
27	304.1	299.1	Chevrolet Corvette ZR-1 SS: 955
28	298.5	293.5	Lamborghini Diablo: 2474
29	295.2	290.3	Nissan 300ZX Turbo Millen Super GTZ: 3247
30	287.4	282.6	Porsche RSK: 3613
31	286.4	281.6	Lamborghini Countach 5000S: 2469
32	283.4	278.7	Caterham 7 HPC: 725
33	270.1	265.6	Nissan 300ZX Motor Sports International SR-71: 3246
34	259.9	255.5	Lotus Elan Autocrosser: 2632
35	258.2	253.9	Toyota Supra Turbo TRD: 4467
36	256.3	252.1	Maserati Shamal: 2681
37	253.5	249.2	Porsche 928 S4 Koenig: 3726

Total: 40

Multivalve engines. Highest specific output. Limit set at 100bhp/litre.

	bhp/l	kW/l	PS/l	
1	336.0	250.5	340.6	Peugeot 405 Turbo 16 Pike's Peak: 3460
2	280.7	209.3	284.6	Lancia Montecarlo Group 5 Turbo: 2531
3	210.6	157.0	213.5	Porsche 959 S: 3702
4	202.3	150.9	205.1	Koenig Competition Evolution: 2418
5	190.8	142.3	193.5	Ferrari Testa Rossa Norwood: 1444
6	190.7	142.2	193.3	Ferrari GTO Norwood: 1451
7	171.5	127.9	173.9	Bugatti EB110: 652
8	162.8	121.4	165.1	Ferrari F40: 1446
				Ferrari F40: 1450
				Ferrari F40: 1435
9	161.9	120.7	164.1	Koenig Competition: 2417
10	157.9	117.8	160.1	Porsche 959: 3731
				Porsche 959 Comfort: 3717
				Porsche 959 Sport: 3718
11	155.4	115.9	157.6	Nissan 300ZX Turbo Millen Super GTZ: 3247
12	145.6	108.5	147.6	Toyota Supra Turbo TRD: 4467
13	144.6	107.8	146.6	Nissan 300ZX Motor Sports International SR-71: 3246
14	144.0	107.4	146.0	Mazda MX-5 Miata Millen: 2760
15	143.4	106.9	145.4	Audi Quattro Sport: 309
16	142.9	106.6	144.9	Sbarro Chrono 3.5: 4108
17	140.1	104.5	142.0	Ferrari 288 GTO: 1421
				Ferrari GTO: 1423
18	138.0	102.9	139.9	Ferrari 288 GTO: 1416
19	127.8	95.3	129.5	Ford RS200: 1917
20	126.4	94.3	128.2	Honda CRX Si Jackson Turbo: 2130
21	125.8	93.8	127.5	Zender Fact 4: 5008
22	122.6	91.4	124.3	Toyota MR2 HKS: 4480
23	122.3	91.2	124.0	Honda CRX Si HKS: 2147
24	121.4	90.6	123.1	Bertone Emotion Lotus: 489
				Lotus Esprit Turbo SE: 2637
				Lotus Esprit Turbo SE: 2640
25	119.6	89.2	121.2	Ford Escort Millen: 1964
26	117.8	87.9	119.5	Subaru Legacy FIA Record: 4274
27	115.3	86.0	116.9	Alfa Romeo 33 2.0 Stradale: 66
				Fiat Brava Abarth Rally: 1571
28	112.3	83.7	113.9	Ital Design Aztec: 2262
29	110.4	82.3	111.9	Ford Sierra Sapphire Cosworth 4x4: 1958
30	107.5	80.1	109.0	Nissan Skyline GT-R: 3243
31	104.9	78.2	106.3	Lotus Esprit Turbo: 2636
32	103.9	77.5	105.3	Lotus Elan: 2638
				Lotus Elan SE: 2639
33	103.7	77.3	105.1	Opel Omega Lotus: 3352
34	102.8	76.6	104.2	Saab Carlsson: 4097
35	102.8	76.6	104.2	Lancia Rally: 2537
36	102.4	76.3	103.8	Ford Sierra RS Cosworth: 1934
				Panther Solo: 3380
37	102.3	76.2	103.7	Lotus Elan Autocrosser: 2632
38	102.0	76.1	103.4	Lotus Elan SE: 2641
39	101.6	75.8	103.0	Dodge Spirit R/T: 1346
40	101.3	75.6	102.8	Nissan 300ZX Turbo: 3241
				Nissan 300ZX Twin Turbo: 3248
41	101.3	75.5	102.7	Porsche RSK: 3613
42	101.3	75.5	102.7	Mercedes-Benz 300SLR: 2795
43	101.0	75.3	102.4	Maserati Shamal: 2681
44	100.9	75.3	102.3	Dodge Stealth R/T Turbo: 1347
				Mitsubishi 3000GT VR-4: 3111
45	100.8	75.1	102.1	Isuzu Impulse RS: 2261
46	100.7	75.1	102.1	Ford Probe GT Suspension Techniques/ HKS: 1943
47	100.2	74.8	101.6	Lancia Delta Integrale 16v: 2549
48	100.1	74.6	101.5	Toyota Celica All-Trac Turbo: 4469
				Toyota MR2 Turbo: 4473

Total: 61

Multivalve engines. Highest piston speed. Limit set at 62ft/sec.

	ft/sec	m/sec	
1	89.8	27.4	Ferrari GTO Norwood: 1451
2	85.3	26.0	Ferrari Testa Rossa Norwood: 1444
3	84.6	25.8	Sbarro Chrono 3.5: 4108
4	73.7	22.5	Fiat Brava Abarth Rally: 1571
5	68.8	21.0	Lancia Rally: 2537
6	67.3	20.5	Peugeot 405 Turbo 16 Pike's Peak: 3460
7	66.9	20.4	Honda Civic CRX: 2140
			Honda Concerto 1.6i 16: 2151
			Rover 216 GTi: 4044
			Rover 416 GTi: 4040
8	66.7	20.3	BMW M3 Sport Evolution: 621
9	65.2	19.9	Mercedes-Benz 190E 2.5-16 Evolution II: 2908
			Mercedes-Benz 190E 2.5-16 Evolution II: 2916
10	65.1	19.8	Chevrolet Corvette ZR-1 SS: 955
11	65.0	19.8	Lancia Montecarlo Group 5 Turbo: 2531
12	65.0	19.8	BMW M5: 606
			BMW M5: 622
13	64.4	19.6	Honda Prelude 2.0 Si: 2138
			Honda Prelude Si 4WS: 2148
14	64.4	19.6	Honda Civic 1.6i VT: 2154
15	64.4	19.6	BMW M3 Hor Technologie: 605
16	64.0	19.5	Honda CRX 1.6i VT: 2152
17	63.9	19.5	Acura Integra LS: 32
			Honda CRX Coupe 1.6i 16: 2128
			Honda CRX Si Jackson: 2142
			Honda Integra EX 16: 2132
			Mercedes-Benz 300SLR: 2795

			Toyota Supra Turbo TRD: 4467
18	63.7	19.4	Jaguar XKE: 2299
19	63.8	19.4	Lotus Elan Autocrosser: 2632
20	63.3	19.3	Audi Quattro Sport: 309
21	63.0	19.2	Chevrolet Corvette ZR-1: 934
22	62.5	19.1	Jaguar XKE 4.2 2+2: 2310
23	62.5	19.1	Citroen BX GTi 16v: 1077
			Mitsubishi Colt 1800 GTI-16v: 3112
			Mitsubishi Galant GTi-16v: 3099
			Mitsubishi Lancer Liftback 1800 GTi-16v: 3110
			Peugeot 405 Mi16: 3448
			Peugeot 405 Mi16x4: 3459
24	62.3	19.0	Honda Prelude 2.0i 16: 2139
25	62.1	18.9	Toyota Celica 2.0 GT: 4468
			Toyota MR2 GT: 4472
26	62.1	18.9	BMW M3: 590
			BMW M3: 603
			BMW M3 Evolution: 604

Total: 45

Turbocharged engines. Maximum speed. Limit set at 165mph.

	mph	kmh	
1	255.0	410.3	Chevrolet Corvette Callaway Sledgehammer: 941
2	235.0	378.1	Koenig C62: 2419
3	230.0	370.1	Koenig Competition Evolution: 2418
4	218.0	350.8	Vector W8 Twin Turbo: 4736
5	217.0	349.2	Koenig Competition: 2417
6	216.0	347.5	Porsche 911 Turbo RS Tuning: 3737
7	214.0	344.3	Bugatti EB110: 652
8	211.0	339.5	Porsche 911 Turbo Ruf Twin Turbo: 3710
9	210.0	337.9	Ferrari Testa Rossa Norwood: 1444
10	208.0	334.7	Porsche 911 Ruf CTR: 3748
11	205.0	329.8	Porsche 911 Turbo Gemballa Mirage: 3751
12	201.0	323.4	Chevrolet Corvette Callaway Speedster: 949
			Ferrari F40: 1435
			Porsche 911 Turbo Koenig RS: 3709
			Porsche 959 S: 3702
13	200.0	321.8	Ferrari F40: 1446
			Vector W2: 4735
14	199.0	320.2	Ferrari GTO Norwood: 1451
15	198.0	318.6	Porsche 959: 3731
			Porsche 959 Comfort: 3717
			Porsche 959 Sport: 3718
16	196.0	315.4	Ferrari F40: 1450
			Porsche 911 Ruf: 3747
17	192.0	308.9	Pontiac Firebird TDM Technologies: 3597
18	191.0	307.3	Chevrolet Corvette Callaway: 918
			Chevrolet Corvette Callaway: 931
19	189.0	304.1	Ferrari 288 GTO: 1421
20	186.0	299.3	Zender Fact 4: 5008
21	185.0	297.7	Ford Mustang 5.0 Cartech Turbo: 1940
22	184.0	296.1	Chevrolet Corvette Callaway: 948
23	183.0	294.4	Porsche 911 Turbo Motorsport Design: 3724
24	182.0	292.8	Ferrari 308 Norwood: 1439
25	180.0	289.6	Ferrari 288 GTO: 1416
			Ferrari GTO: 1423
26	179.0	288.0	BMW 535i Alpina B10 Bi-Turbo: 619
27	178.0	286.4	Chevrolet Corvette Callaway: 901
			Mazda RX-7 Cartech: 2768
			Pontiac Firebird T/A Turbo Pontiac Engineering: 3588
28	177.0	284.8	Ford Mustang Cartech Turbo: 1928
29	174.0	280.0	Opel Omega Lotus: 3352
30	171.0	275.1	Porsche 911 Turbo: 3750
31	170.0	273.5	Bertone Emotion Lotus: 489
			Chevrolet Corvette Callaway: 940
			Mazda RX-7 Mariah Mode Six: 2770
32	168.0	270.3	Porsche 911 Carrera Turbo: 3746
33	166.0	267.1	Nissan 300ZX Turbo Millen Super GTZ: 3247
34	165.0	265.5	Lotus Esprit Turbo SE: 2640
			Porsche 911 Turbo: 3676
			Porsche 911 Turbo Gemballa Avalanche: 3697
			Renault Alpine A610 Turbo: 3918

Total: 50

Turbocharged engines. Acceleration to 60mph/96.5kmh. Limit set at 5 seconds.

	sec	
1	3.5	Koenig C62: 2419
		Koenig Competition Evolution: 2418
2	3.6	Lancia Montecarlo Group 5 Turbo: 2531
		Porsche 959: 3731
		Porsche 959 Sport: 3718
3	3.8	Datsun 280ZX Electramotive: 1230
		Ferrari F40: 1450
		Porsche 911 Ruf: 3747
4	3.9	Bugatti EB110: 652
		Chevrolet Corvette Callaway Sledgehammer: 941
		Porsche 911 Ruf CTR: 3748
5	4.0	Koenig Competition: 2417
		Porsche 911 Turbo Koenig RS: 3709
		Porsche 911 Turbo Motorsport Design: 3724
		Porsche 911 Turbo Ruf Twin Turbo: 3710
		Porsche 959 Comfort: 3717
		Vector W2: 4735
6	4.1	Pontiac Firebird TDM Technologies: 3597
		Porsche 911 Turbo Gemballa Mirage: 3751
7	4.2	Vector W8 Twin Turbo: 4736
8	4.3	Zender Fact 4: 5008
9	4.4	Chevrolet Corvette Callaway Speedster: 949
10	4.5	Ferrari F40: 1446
		Porsche 911 Turbo Ruf 3.4: 3698
11	4.6	Chevrolet Corvette Callaway: 918
		Porsche 911 Carrera Turbo: 3746
		Porsche 911 Turbo RS Tuning: 3737
12	4.7	Ferrari 308 Norwood: 1439
		Ferrari Testa Rossa Norwood: 1444
		Porsche 911 Turbo: 3750
		Porsche 959 S: 3702
13	4.8	Audi Quattro Sport: 309
		Mazda RX-7 Mariah Mode Six: 2770
		Porsche 911 Turbo: 3723
		Renault Le Car Turbo: 3874
14	4.9	Chevrolet Corvette Callaway: 948
		Chevrolet Corvette Callaway: 931
		Chevrolet Corvette Callaway Twin Turbo: 950
		Ford Mustang Cartech Turbo: 1928
		Lotus Esprit Turbo SE: 2637
		Opel Omega Lotus: 3352
		Porsche 911 3.3 Turbo: 3719
		Porsche 911 Turbo Gemballa Avalanche: 3697
15	5.0	Bertone Emotion Lotus: 489
		Chevrolet Corvette Callaway: 901
		Ferrari 288 GTO: 1421
		Ferrari 288 GTO: 1416
		Ferrari GTO: 1423
		Nissan 300ZX Turbo Millen Super GTZ: 3247
		Porsche 911 Turbo: 3659
		Porsche 911 Turbo: 3708
		Porsche 911 Turbo: 3689
		Porsche 911 Turbo Slant-Nose: 3699

Total: 53

Turbocharged engines. Highest power. Limit set at 350bhp.

	bhp	kW	PS	
1	1600.0	1193.1	1622.2	Ferrari GTO Norwood: 1451
2	1000.0	745.7	1013.9	Koenig Competition Evolution: 2418
3	943.0	703.2	956.1	Ferrari Testa Rossa Norwood: 1444
4	880.0	656.2	892.2	Chevrolet Corvette Callaway Sledgehammer: 941
5	800.0	596.6	811.1	Koenig Competition: 2417
6	685.0	510.8	694.5	Pontiac Firebird TDM Technologies: 3597
7	640.0	477.2	648.9	Peugeot 405 Turbo 16 Pike's Peak: 3460
8	625.0	466.1	633.7	Vector W8 Twin Turbo: 4736
9	600.0	447.4	608.3	Bugatti EB110: 652
				Porsche 959 S: 3702
				Vector W2: 4735
10	588.0	438.5	596.2	Koenig C62: 2419
11	580.0	432.5	588.0	Datsun 280ZX Electramotive: 1230
				Porsche 911 Turbo RS Tuning: 3737
12	520.0	387.8	527.2	Porsche 911 Turbo Koenig RS: 3709
13	490.0	365.4	496.8	Porsche 911 Turbo Gemballa Mirage: 3751
14	488.0	363.9	494.8	Porsche 911 Turbo Motorsport Design: 3724
15	485.0	361.7	491.7	Porsche 935 Group 4 Holbert: 3657
16	478.0	356.4	484.6	Ferrari F40: 1435
				Ferrari F40: 1446
				Ferrari F40: 1450
17	470.0	350.5	476.5	Ford Mustang 5.0 Cartech Turbo: 1940
18	469.0	349.7	475.5	Porsche 911 Ruf CTR: 3748
				Porsche 911 Turbo Ruf Twin Turbo: 3710
19	460.0	343.0	466.4	Nissan 300ZX Turbo Millen Super GTZ: 3247
20	455.0	339.3	461.3	Porsche 911 Ruf: 3747
21	450.0	335.6	456.2	Ferrari 308 Norwood: 1439
				Porsche 959: 3731
				Porsche 959 Comfort: 3717
				Porsche 959 Sport: 3718
22	448.0	334.1	454.2	Zender Fact 4: 5008
23	430.0	320.6	436.0	Toyota Supra Turbo TRD: 4467
24	428.0	319.2	433.9	Nissan 300ZX Motor Sports International SR-71: 3246
25	403.0	300.5	408.6	Chevrolet Corvette Callaway: 948
				Chevrolet Corvette Callaway Speedster: 949
				Chevrolet Corvette Callaway Twin Turbo: 950
26	400.0	298.3	405.5	Ferrari 288 GTO: 1421
				Ferrari GTO: 1423
				Lancia Montecarlo Group 5 Turbo: 2531

27	394.0	293.8	399.5	Ferrari 288 GTO: 1416
28	392.0	292.3	397.4	Ford Mustang Cartech Turbo: 1928
29	390.0	290.8	395.4	Chevrolet Corvette Callaway: 940
30	382.0	284.9	387.3	Chevrolet Corvette Callaway: 931
				Chevrolet Corvette Callaway: 918
31	380.0	283.4	385.3	Mazda RX-7 Mariah Mode Six: 2770
				Pontiac Firebird T/A Turbo Pontiac Engineering: 3588
32	377.0	281.1	382.2	Opel Omega Lotus: 3352
33	374.0	278.9	379.2	Porsche 911 Turbo Ruf 3.4: 3698
34	360.0	268.4	365.0	BMW 535i Alpina B10 Bi-Turbo: 619

Total: 49

Turbocharged engines. Highest torque. Limit set at 350lbft.

	lbft	Nm	
1	900.0	1219.5	Ferrari GTO Norwood: 1451
2	785.0	1063.7	Pontiac Firebird TDM Technologies: 3597
3	772.0	1046.1	Chevrolet Corvette Callaway Sledgehammer: 941
4	738.0	1000.0	Koenig Competition Evolution: 2418
5	664.0	899.7	Koenig Competition: 2417
6	630.0	853.7	Vector W8 Twin Turbo: 4736
7	580.0	785.9	Vector W2: 4735
8	575.0	779.1	Chevrolet Corvette Callaway: 948
			Chevrolet Corvette Callaway Speedster: 949
			Chevrolet Corvette Callaway Twin Turbo: 950
9	562.0	761.5	Chevrolet Corvette Callaway: 940
			Chevrolet Corvette Callaway: 931
10	550.0	745.3	Ford Mustang Cartech Turbo: 1928
11	545.0	738.5	Chevrolet Corvette Callaway: 918
12	542.0	734.4	Peugeot 405 Turbo 16 Pike's Peak: 3460
13	533.0	722.2	Koenig C62: 2419
14	520.0	704.6	Datsun 280ZX Electramotive: 1230
15	490.0	664.0	Porsche 911 Turbo Koenig RS: 3709
			Porsche 911 Turbo Motorsport Design: 3724
16	485.0	657.2	Bentley Turbo R: 483
17	482.0	653.1	Porsche 911 Ruf: 3747
18	465.0	630.1	Chevrolet Corvette Callaway: 901
			Porsche 911 Turbo RS Tuning: 3737
19	457.0	619.2	Porsche 911 Turbo Ruf Twin Turbo: 3710
20	445.0	603.0	Ford Mustang 5.0 Cartech Turbo: 1940
21	434.0	588.1	Porsche 935 Group 4 Holbert: 3657
22	430.0	582.7	Nissan 300ZX Turbo Millen Super GTZ: 3247
23	425.0	575.9	Ferrari F40: 1435
			Ferrari F40: 1446
			Ferrari F40: 1450
			Pontiac Firebird T/A Turbo Pontiac Engineering: 3588
24	420.0	569.1	Porsche 911 Turbo Gemballa Mirage: 3751
25	419.0	567.8	Bugatti EB110: 652
26	409.0	554.2	Opel Omega Lotus: 3352
27	408.0	552.8	Porsche 911 Ruf CTR: 3748
28	406.0	550.1	Nissan 300ZX Motor Sports International SR-71: 3246
29	390.0	528.5	Lancia Montecarlo Group 5 Turbo: 2531
			Zender Fact 4: 5008
30	382.0	517.6	BMW 535i Alpina B10 Bi-Turbo: 619
			Toyota Supra Turbo TRD: 4467
31	370.0	501.4	Porsche 959: 3731
			Porsche 959 Comfort: 3717
			Porsche 959 Sport: 3718
32	369.0	500.0	Porsche 959 S: 3702
33	366.0	495.9	Ferrari 288 GTO: 1416
			Ferrari 288 GTO: 1421
			Ferrari GTO: 1423
34	354.0	479.7	Porsche 911 Turbo Ruf 3.4: 3698

Total: 48

Turbocharged engines. Highest rpm at peak power. Limit set at 6400rpm.

	rpm	
1	10000	Ferrari Testa Rossa Norwood: 1444
2	9000	Bugatti EB110: 652
3	8800	Lancia Montecarlo Group 5 Turbo: 2531
4	7500	Datsun 280ZX Electramotive: 1230
5	7200	Ferrari GTO Norwood: 1451
6	7000	Ferrari 288 GTO: 1416
		Ferrari 288 GTO: 1421
		Ferrari F40: 1450
		Ferrari F40: 1446
		Ferrari F40: 1435
		Ferrari GTO: 1423
		Peugeot 405 Turbo 16 Pike's Peak: 3460
		Porsche 935 Group 4 Holbert: 3657
		Renault Le Car Turbo: 3874
7	6900	Porsche 911 Turbo RS Tuning: 3737
8	6800	Mazda RX-7 Mariah Mode Six: 2770
		Nissan Skyline GT-R: 3243
9	6700	Audi Quattro Sport: 309
		Ferrari 308 Norwood: 1439
		Koenig Competition Evolution: 2418
		Nissan 300ZX Motor Sports International SR-71: 3246
10	6600	Isuzu Impulse RS: 2261
		Lotus Elan: 2638
		Lotus Elan SE: 2639
		Lotus Elan SE: 2641
11	6500	Bertone Emotion Lotus: 489
		Daihatsu Charade GT ti: 1124
		Lotus Esprit Turbo: 2636
		Lotus Esprit Turbo SE: 2640
		Lotus Esprit Turbo SE: 2637
		Mazda RX-7 Cartech: 2768
		Mazda RX-7 Turbo: 2771
		Mazda RX-7 Turbo: 2740
		Mazda RX-7 Turbo: 2764
		Mazda RX-7 Turbo: 2737
		Mazda RX-7 Turbo: 2751
		Mazda RX-7 Turbo II: 2759
		Nissan 300ZX Turbo Millen Super GTZ: 3247
		Porsche 959: 3731
		Porsche 959 Comfort: 3717
		Porsche 959 S: 3702
		Porsche 959 Sport: 3718
		Toyota Supra Turbo TRD: 4467
		Zender Fact 4: 5008
12	6400	Nissan 200SX: 3254
		Nissan 200SX: 3232
		Nissan 300ZX: 3240
		Nissan 300ZX Turbo: 3241
		Nissan 300ZX Twin Turbo: 3248
		Subaru Legacy FIA Record: 4274

Total: 50

Turbocharged engines. Highest power-to-weight ratio. Limit set at 250 bhp/ton.

	bhp/ton	bhp/tonne	
1	1257.5	1236.6	Ferrari GTO Norwood: 1451
2	764.6	751.8	Peugeot 405 Turbo 16 Pike's Peak: 3460
3	640.0	629.3	Koenig Competition Evolution: 2418
4	570.9	561.4	Ferrari Testa Rossa Norwood: 1444
5	543.1	534.1	Koenig C62: 2419
6	537.1	528.1	Chevrolet Corvette Callaway Sledgehammer: 941
7	520.9	512.2	Lancia Montecarlo Group 5 Turbo: 2531
8	512.0	503.5	Koenig Competition: 2417
9	499.7	491.4	Datsun 280ZX Electramotive: 1230
10	483.4	475.4	Vector W2: 4735
11	454.8	447.2	Bugatti EB110: 652
12	451.0	443.5	Porsche 959 S: 3702
13	441.5	434.2	Ferrari F40: 1435
			Ferrari F40: 1446
14	426.2	419.1	Pontiac Firebird TDM Technologies: 3597
15	421.7	414.6	Vector W8 Twin Turbo: 4736
16	416.0	409.1	Porsche 911 Turbo Koenig RS: 3709
17	415.2	408.3	Porsche 911 Turbo Ruf Twin Turbo: 3710
18	411.3	404.4	Zender Fact 4: 5008
19	409.2	402.4	Porsche 935 Group 4 Holbert: 3657
20	368.3	362.2	Porsche 911 Turbo Gemballa Mirage: 3751
21	366.8	360.7	Porsche 911 Turbo Motorsport Design: 3724
22	359.3	353.3	Ferrari F40: 1450
23	353.0	347.1	Renault Le Car Turbo: 3874
24	350.7	344.8	Ferrari 288 GTO: 1421
			Ferrari GTO: 1423
25	345.6	339.8	Porsche 911 Ruf CTR: 3748
26	339.4	333.7	Porsche 959 Sport: 3718
27	335.8	330.2	Porsche 911 Ruf: 3747
28	319.0	313.7	Ford Mustang 5.0 Cartech Turbo: 1940
29	316.0	310.7	Porsche 959: 3731
			Porsche 959 Comfort: 3717
30	311.1	305.9	Ferrari 308 Norwood: 1439
31	310.3	305.1	Ford Mustang Cartech Turbo: 1928
32	306.4	301.3	Ferrari 288 GTO: 1416
33	299.2	294.2	Porsche 911 Turbo Ruf 3.4: 3698
34	295.2	290.3	Nissan 300ZX Turbo Millen Super GTZ: 3247
35	282.1	277.4	Chevrolet Corvette Callaway Speedster: 949
36	279.1	274.4	Mazda RX-7 Mariah Mode Six: 2770
37	270.4	265.9	Mazda RX-7 Cartech: 2768
38	270.1	265.6	Nissan 300ZX Motor Sports International SR-71: 3246
39	262.4	258.0	Chevrolet Corvette Callaway: 948
			Chevrolet Corvette Callaway Twin Turbo: 950
40	258.2	253.9	Toyota Supra Turbo TRD: 4467
41	256.9	252.7	Chevrolet Corvette Callaway: 940
42	256.3	252.1	Maserati Shamal: 2681

Total: 46

Turbocharged engines. Highest specific output. Limit set at 110bhp/litre.

	bhp/l	kW/l	PS/l	
1	336.0	250.5	340.6	Peugeot 405 Turbo 16 Pike's Peak: 3460

2	290.5	216.6	294.5	Mazda RX-7 Mariah Mode Six: 2770
3	280.7	209.3	284.6	Lancia Montecarlo Group 5 Turbo: 2531
4	263.0	196.1	266.6	Mazda RX-7 Cartech: 2768
5	210.7	157.1	213.6	Datsun 280ZX Electramotive: 1230
6	210.6	157.0	213.5	Porsche 959 S: 3702
7	202.3	150.9	205.1	Koenig Competition Evolution: 2418
8	190.8	142.3	193.5	Ferrari Testa Rossa Norwood: 1444
9	190.7	142.2	193.3	Ferrari GTO Norwood: 1451
10	181.8	135.6	184.3	Renault Le Car Turbo: 3874
11	174.6	130.2	177.0	Koenig C62: 2419
12	172.2	128.4	174.6	Porsche 911 Turbo RS Tuning: 3737
13	171.5	127.9	173.9	Bugatti EB110: 652
14	162.8	121.4	165.1	Ferrari F40: 1450
				Ferrari F40: 1446
				Ferrari F40: 1435
15	162.0	120.8	164.3	Porsche 935 Group 4 Holbert: 3657
16	161.9	120.7	164.1	Koenig Competition: 2417
17	157.9	117.8	160.1	Porsche 959: 3731
				Porsche 959 Comfort: 3717
				Porsche 959 Sport: 3718
18	155.4	115.9	157.6	Nissan 300ZX Turbo Millen Super GTZ: 3247
19	154.5	115.2	156.6	Porsche 911 Turbo Koenig RS: 3709
20	153.8	114.7	155.9	Ferrari 308 Norwood: 1439
21	153.5	114.5	155.6	Chevrolet Corvette Callaway Sledgehammer: 941
22	152.9	114.0	155.0	Mazda RX-7 Turbo: 2771
				Mazda RX-7 Turbo: 2764
				Mazda RX-7 Turbo II: 2759
23	147.9	110.3	150.0	Porsche 911 Turbo Motorsport Design: 3724
24	145.6	108.5	147.6	Toyota Supra Turbo TRD: 4467
25	145.5	108.5	147.5	Porsche 911 Turbo Gemballa Mirage: 3751
26	144.6	107.8	146.6	Nissan 300ZX Motor Sports International SR-71: 3246
27	144.0	107.4	146.0	Mazda MX-5 Miata Millen: 2760
28	143.4	106.9	145.4	Audi Quattro Sport: 309
29	140.1	104.5	142.0	Ferrari 288 GTO: 1421
				Ferrari GTO: 1423
30	139.3	103.9	141.3	Porsche 911 Turbo Ruf Twin Turbo: 3710
31	139.3	103.9	141.2	Porsche 911 Ruf CTR: 3748
32	139.1	103.8	141.1	Mazda RX-7 Turbo: 2740
				Mazda RX-7 Turbo: 2737
				Mazda RX-7 Turbo: 2751
33	138.0	102.9	139.9	Ferrari 288 GTO: 1416
34	132.4	98.7	134.3	Renault 5 Turbo 2: 3886
35	129.8	96.8	131.6	Porsche 911 Ruf: 3747
36	127.8	95.3	129.5	Ford RS200: 1917
37	126.4	94.3	128.2	Honda CRX Si Jackson Turbo: 2130
38	125.8	93.8	127.5	Zender Fact 4: 5008
39	122.6	91.4	124.3	Toyota MR2 HKS: 4480
40	122.3	91.2	124.0	Honda CRX Si HKS: 2147
41	121.4	90.6	123.1	Bertone Emotion Lotus: 489
				Lotus Esprit Turbo SE: 2640
				Lotus Esprit Turbo SE: 2637
42	119.6	89.2	121.2	Ford Escort Millen: 1964
43	119.5	89.1	121.1	Pontiac Firebird TDM Technologies: 3597
44	117.8	87.9	119.5	Subaru Legacy FIA Record: 4274
45	114.5	85.4	116.1	Renault 5 Turbo: 3873
46	112.3	83.7	113.9	Ital Design Aztec: 2262
47	111.1	82.9	112.6	Porsche 911 Turbo Ruf 3.4: 3698
48	110.4	82.3	111.9	Ford Sierra Sapphire Cosworth 4x4: 1958

Total: 59

Turbocharged engines. Highest piston speed. Limit set at 55ft/sec.

	ft/sec	m/sec	
1	89.8	27.4	Ferrari GTO Norwood: 1451
2	85.3	26.0	Ferrari Testa Rossa Norwood: 1444
3	67.3	20.5	Peugeot 405 Turbo 16 Pike's Peak: 3460
4	65.0	19.8	Lancia Montecarlo Group 5 Turbo: 2531
5	64.8	19.7	Datsun 280ZX Electramotive: 1230
6	63.9	19.5	Toyota Supra Turbo TRD: 4467
7	63.3	19.3	Audi Quattro Sport: 309
8	61.4	18.7	Zender Fact 4: 5008
9	60.9	18.5	Nissan 300ZX Motor Sports International SR-71: 3246
10	60.4	18.4	Chevrolet Corvette Callaway Sledgehammer: 941
11	60.3	18.4	Dodge Spirit R/T: 1346
12	59.0	18.0	Fiat Spider Turbo: 1577
13	59.0	18.0	Nissan 300ZX Turbo Millen Super GTZ: 3247
14	58.9	18.0	Renault Le Car Turbo: 3874
15	58.8	17.9	Nissan 200SX: 3254
16	58.6	17.9	Ital Design Aztec: 2262
17	58.5	17.8	Nissan 200SX: 3232
18	58.4	17.8	Toyota MR2 HKS: 4480
19	58.1	17.7	Nissan 300ZX: 3240
			Nissan 300ZX Turbo: 3241
			Nissan 300ZX Twin Turbo: 3248
20	57.7	17.6	Eagle Talon: 1355
			Eagle Talon TSi 4WD: 1357
			Mitsubishi Colt Starion Turbo: 3081
			Mitsubishi Eclipse: 3102
			Mitsubishi Eclipse GSX: 3103
			Mitsubishi Galant VR-4: 3114
			Mitsubishi Starion 2000 Turbo: 3095
			Plymouth Laser RS: 3521
			Plymouth Laser RS Turbo: 3523
			Plymouth Laser RS Turbo: 3522
21	57.5	17.5	Vector W2: 4735
22	57.5	17.5	Koenig Competition Evolution: 2418
23	57.5	17.5	Vector W8 Twin Turbo: 4736
24	57.0	17.4	Isuzu Impulse RS: 2261
			Lotus Elan: 2638
			Lotus Elan SE: 2639
			Lotus Elan SE: 2641
25	56.8	17.3	Honda Civic Si HKS: 2146
26	56.5	17.2	Lancia Thema 2.0 ie LX Turbo: 2539
27	56.5	17.2	Toyota Celica All-Trac Turbo: 4469
28	56.5	17.2	BMW 535i Alpina B10 Bi-Turbo: 619
			Toyota Celica All-Trac Turbo: 4454
			Toyota Celica GT4: 4455
			Toyota MR2 Turbo: 4473
29	56.3	17.2	Chrysler Laser XE: 1003
			Dodge Daytona Turbo Z: 1331
30	56.1	17.1	Alfa Romeo 75 Evoluzione: 135
			Porsche 911 Turbo RS Tuning: 3737
31	55.8	17.0	Ford Escort Millen: 1964
32	55.7	17.0	Toyota Supra 3.0i Turbo: 4465
33	55.7	17.0	Bugatti EB110: 652
34	55.7	17.0	Toyota Supra Turbo: 4460
			Toyota Supra Turbo: 4466
35	55.6	17.0	Nissan 240SX Turbo Tokico/Cartech: 3233
36	55.6	16.9	Audi Coupe S2: 337
			Audi Quattro 20v: 330
37	55.3	16.9	Chrysler TC by Maserati: 1008
38	55.2	16.8	Mazda 323 Turbo 4x4: 2743

Total: 59

Supercharged engines. Maximum speed. No limits set. All cars with figures included.

	mph	kmh	
1	217.0	349.2	Koenig Competition: 2417
2	186.0	299.3	Porsche 928 S4 Koenig: 3726
3	174.0	280.0	Ford Mustang Holdener: 1966
4	160.0	257.4	Ford Thunderbird Super Coupe Ford Engineering: 1948
5	158.0	254.2	BMW 735i Koenig: 611
6	143.0	230.1	Mercury Cougar XR-7: 2960
7	140.0	225.3	Ford Thunderbird Super Coupe: 1947
			Volkswagen Corrado: 4874
8	139.0	223.7	Volkswagen Corrado G60: 4882
9	137.0	220.4	Volkswagen Corrado G60: 4879
10	135.0	217.2	Toyota MR2 Supercharged: 4464
			Toyota MR2 Supercharged: 4451
11	128.0	206.0	Lancia Rally: 2537
			Pontiac Bonneville SSEi: 3600
12	127.0	204.3	Pontiac Tempest Supercharged: 3532
			Shelby GT 350-S: 4121
13	125.0	201.1	Excalibur SS: 1363
14	121.0	194.7	Studebaker Regal Wagonaire Supercharged: 4237
15	120.0	193.1	Volkswagen Polo G40: 4887
16	112.8	181.5	Nash Nash-Healey Roadster Supercharged: 3200
17	112.0	180.2	Cord 812-S: 1101
18	110.0	177.0	Alfa Romeo 8C2300: 41
			Bugatti 55: 651
19	107.1	172.3	Studebaker Commander Supercharged: 4225
20	106.8	171.8	Alfa Romeo Supercharged Straight Eight: 39
21	106.0	170.6	Duesenberg SJ Town Car: 1353
22	105.0	168.9	Squire X101: 4190
23	102.2	164.4	Cord Supercharged Saloon: 1102
24	100.5	161.7	Mercedes-Benz Type 500 Supercharged: 2782
25	100.0	160.9	Oldsmobile F-85 Jetfire: 3279
26	97.8	157.4	Bentley 4.5-litre Supercharged: 462
27	94.7	152.4	Lammas-Graham Drop-head Coupe: 2476
28	91.8	147.7	Graham 26hp Supercharged Saloon: 2014
			Graham 33.8hp Supercharged Saloon: 2012
29	91.0	146.4	Alfa Romeo 1750: 40
30	90.0	144.8	Austin-Healey Sprite Supercharged: 439
31	89.1	143.4	Graham 26hp Supercharged Saloon: 2013
32	88.2	141.9	Lagonda 2-litre Supercharged: 2433
33	87.8	141.3	MG Mk II Montlhery Supercharged: 2970
34	87.0	140.0	MG TF Supercharged: 2989
35	85.0	136.8	Lea-Francis Hyper-sports: 2567
36	83.8	134.8	Volkswagen Sedan Judson: 4748
37	80.0	128.7	Hillman Minx Supercharged: 2040
38	74.5	119.9	Volkswagen Sedan Supercharged: 4743
39	67.6	108.8	Triumph Supercharged 7: 4488
40	66.4	106.8	HE Supercharged Six Coupe: 2018

Total: 46

Supercharged engines. Acceleration to 60mph/96.5kmh. No limits set. All cars with figures included.

	sec	
1	4.0	Koenig Competition: 2417
2	4.8	Porsche 928 S4 Koenig: 3726
3	4.9	Ford Mustang Holdener: 1966
4	5.2	Ford Thunderbird Super Coupe Ford Engineering: 1948
5	6.0	BMW 735i Koenig: 611
6	6.2	Shelby GT 350-S: 4121
7	7.0	Excalibur SS: 1363
		Pontiac Tempest Supercharged: 3532
		Toyota MR2 Supercharged: 4451
8	7.1	Lancia Rally: 2537
9	7.4	Ford Thunderbird Super Coupe: 1947
		Mercury Cougar XR-7: 2960
		Volkswagen Corrado Neuspeed: 4883
10	7.7	Toyota MR2 Supercharged: 4464
11	7.8	Studebaker Regal Wagonaire Supercharged: 4237
		Volkswagen Corrado: 4874
12	8.4	Volkswagen Polo G40: 4887
13	8.9	Volkswagen Corrado G60: 4879
		Volkswagen Corrado G60: 4882
14	9.0	Pontiac Bonneville SSEi: 3600
15	9.8	Duesenberg SJ Town Car: 1353
		Nash Nash-Healey Roadster Supercharged: 3200
		Oldsmobile F-85 Jetfire: 3279
16	10.8	Alfa Romeo 8C2300: 41
17	10.9	Squire X101: 4190
18	11.9	Studebaker Commander Supercharged: 4225
19	13.2	Cord Supercharged Saloon: 1102
20	13.7	Cord 812-S: 1101
21	13.9	Alfa Romeo 1750: 40
22	14.5	Graham 26hp Supercharged Saloon: 2013
23	15.3	Austin-Healey Sprite Supercharged: 439
24	15.5	MG TF Supercharged: 2989
25	15.8	Graham 33.8hp Supercharged Saloon: 2012
26	16.2	Lammas-Graham Drop-head Coupe: 2476
27	16.4	Graham 26hp Supercharged Saloon: 2014
28	16.5	Mercedes-Benz Type 500 Supercharged: 2782
29	17.3	Bugatti 55: 651
30	18.0	Volkswagen Sedan Judson: 4748
31	20.2	Hillman Minx Supercharged: 2040
32	22.0	Volkswagen Sedan Supercharged: 4743

Total: 40

Supercharged engines. Highest power. No limits set. All cars with figures included.

	bhp	kW	PS	
1	800.0	596.6	811.1	Koenig Competition: 2417
2	450.0	335.6	456.2	Ford Mustang Holdener: 1966
3	430.0	320.6	436.0	Porsche 928 S4 Koenig: 3726
4	390.0	290.8	395.4	Shelby GT 350-S: 4121
5	330.0	246.1	334.6	Ford Thunderbird Super Coupe Ford Engineering: 1948
6	320.0	238.6	324.4	Duesenberg SJ Town Car: 1353
7	290.0	216.2	294.0	BMW 735i Koenig: 611
8	289.0	215.5	293.0	Excalibur SS: 1363
9	280.0	208.8	283.9	Studebaker Regal Wagonaire Supercharged: 4237
10	250.0	186.4	253.5	Pontiac Tempest Supercharged: 3532
11	215.0	160.3	218.0	Oldsmobile F-85 Jetfire: 3279
				Volkswagen Corrado Neuspeed: 4883
12	210.0	156.6	212.9	Ford Thunderbird Super Coupe: 1947
				Mercury Cougar XR-7: 2960
13	205.0	152.9	207.8	Lancia Rally: 2537
				Pontiac Bonneville SSEi: 3600
14	190.0	141.7	192.6	Cord 812-S: 1101
15	175.0	130.5	177.4	Bentley 4.5-litre Supercharged: 462
16	160.0	119.3	162.2	Volkswagen Corrado G60: 4882
17	158.0	117.8	160.2	Volkswagen Corrado: 4874
				Volkswagen Corrado G60: 4879
18	150.0	111.9	152.1	Alfa Romeo 8C2300: 41
19	145.0	108.1	147.0	Toyota MR2 Supercharged: 4464
				Toyota MR2 Supercharged: 4451
20	140.0	104.4	141.9	Nash Nash-Healey Roadster Supercharged: 3200
21	135.0	100.7	136.9	Bugatti 55: 651
22	128.0	95.4	129.8	Lammas-Graham Drop-head Coupe: 2476
23	113.0	84.3	114.6	Volkswagen Polo G40: 4887
24	110.0	82.0	111.5	Squire X101: 4190
25	85.0	63.4	86.2	Alfa Romeo 1750: 40
26	68.0	50.7	68.9	Austin-Healey Sprite Supercharged: 439
27	57.5	42.9	58.3	MG TF Supercharged: 2989
28	50.0	37.3	50.7	Volkswagen Sedan Judson: 4748
29	37.5	28.0	38.0	Hillman Minx Supercharged: 2040
30	36.0	26.8	36.5	Volkswagen Sedan Supercharged: 4743

Total: 35

Supercharged engines. Highest torque. No limits set. All cars with figures included.

	lbft	Nm	
1	664.0	899.7	Koenig Competition: 2417
2	470.0	636.9	Porsche 928 S4 Koenig: 3726
3	425.0	575.9	Duesenberg SJ Town Car: 1353
4	420.0	569.1	Ford Mustang Holdener: 1966
5	403.0	546.1	Ford Thunderbird Super Coupe Ford Engineering: 1948
6	330.0	447.2	Studebaker Regal Wagonaire Supercharged: 4237
7	329.0	445.8	Shelby GT 350-S: 4121
8	315.0	426.8	Ford Thunderbird Super Coupe: 1947
			Mercury Cougar XR-7: 2960
9	300.0	406.5	Oldsmobile F-85 Jetfire: 3279
10	299.0	405.1	BMW 735i Koenig: 611
11	272.0	368.6	Cord 812-S: 1101
12	260.0	352.3	Pontiac Bonneville SSEi: 3600
13	255.0	345.5	Pontiac Tempest Supercharged: 3532
14	230.0	311.7	Nash Nash-Healey Roadster Supercharged: 3200
15	205.0	277.8	Volkswagen Corrado Neuspeed: 4883
16	167.0	226.3	Lancia Rally: 2537
17	166.1	225.0	Volkswagen Corrado G60: 4882
18	166.0	224.9	Volkswagen Corrado: 4874
			Volkswagen Corrado G60: 4879
19	140.0	189.7	Toyota MR2 Supercharged: 4464
			Toyota MR2 Supercharged: 4451
20	110.7	150.0	Volkswagen Polo G40: 4887
21	105.0	142.3	Alfa Romeo 1750: 40
22	70.0	94.9	Volkswagen Sedan Judson: 4748
23	65.0	88.1	Austin-Healey Sprite Supercharged: 439

Total: 26

Supercharged engines. Highest rpm at peak power. No limits set. All cars with figures included.

	rpm	
1	7000	Lancia Rally: 2537
2	6400	Toyota MR2 Supercharged: 4451
		Toyota MR2 Supercharged: 4464
3	6250	Koenig Competition: 2417
4	6000	Porsche 928 S4 Koenig: 3726
		Shelby GT 350-S: 4121
		Volkswagen Polo G40: 4887
5	5700	Austin-Healey Sprite Supercharged: 439
6	5600	Ford Mustang Holdener: 1966
		Pontiac Tempest Supercharged: 3532
		Volkswagen Corrado: 4874
		Volkswagen Corrado G60: 4882
		Volkswagen Corrado G60: 4879
7	5500	Bugatti 55: 651
		Ford Thunderbird Super Coupe Ford Engineering: 1948
		MG TF Supercharged: 2989
		Volkswagen Corrado Neuspeed: 4883
8	5200	Alfa Romeo 8C2300: 41
		BMW 735i Koenig: 611
		Studebaker Regal Wagonaire Supercharged: 4237
9	5000	Squire X101: 4190
10	4800	Excalibur SS: 1363
11	4600	Oldsmobile F-85 Jetfire: 3279
		Pontiac Bonneville SSEi: 3600
12	4500	Alfa Romeo 1750: 40
13	4400	Lammas-Graham Drop-head Coupe: 2476
14	4200	Cord 812-S: 1101
		Duesenberg SJ Town Car: 1353
		Hillman Minx Supercharged: 2040
15	4000	Ford Thunderbird Super Coupe: 1947
		Mercury Cougar XR-7: 2960
		Nash Nash-Healey Roadster Supercharged: 3200
		Volkswagen Sedan Judson: 4748
16	3700	Volkswagen Sedan Supercharged: 4743
17	3500	Bentley 4.5-litre Supercharged: 462

Total: 35

Supercharged engines. Highest power-to-weight ratio.No limits set. All cars with figures included.

	bhp/ ton	bhp/ tonne	
1	512.0	503.5	Koenig Competition: 2417
2	362.6	356.5	Ford Mustang Holdener: 1966
3	296.1	291.2	Shelby GT 350-S: 4121
4	257.9	253.6	Excalibur SS: 1363
5	253.5	249.2	Porsche 928 S4 Koenig: 3726
6	201.6	198.2	Ford Thunderbird Super Coupe Ford Engineering: 1948

7	187.9	184.8	Pontiac Tempest Supercharged: 3532
8	180.8	177.8	Lancia Rally: 2537
9	175.1	172.2	Volkswagen Corrado Neuspeed: 4883
10	164.5	161.7	BMW 735i Koenig: 611
11	164.4	161.6	Oldsmobile F-85 Jetfire: 3279
12	157.0	154.4	Studebaker Regal Wagonaire Supercharged: 4237
13	143.9	141.5	Volkswagen Corrado: 4874
14	141.5	139.1	Volkswagen Corrado G60: 4882
15	136.0	133.7	Volkswagen Polo G40: 4887
16	134.4	132.2	Alfa Romeo 8C2300: 41
17	131.3	129.1	Volkswagen Corrado G60: 4879
18	127.7	125.6	Pontiac Bonneville SSEi: 3600
19	126.8	124.7	Mercury Cougar XR-7: 2960
20	124.8	122.7	Ford Thunderbird Super Coupe: 1947
21	124.0	121.9	Toyota MR2 Supercharged: 4451
			Toyota MR2 Supercharged: 4464
22	114.3	112.4	Bugatti 55: 651
23	112.0	110.1	Duesenberg SJ Town Car: 1353
24	107.1	105.3	Squire X101: 4190
25	106.3	104.5	Nash Nash-Healey Roadster Supercharged: 3200
26	103.4	101.7	Cord 812-S: 1101
27	102.2	100.5	Austin-Healey Sprite Supercharged: 439
28	94.6	93.0	Bentley 4.5-litre Supercharged: 462
29	81.0	79.7	Alfa Romeo 1750: 40
30	79.0	77.7	Lammas-Graham Drop-head Coupe: 2476
31	67.5	66.3	Volkswagen Sedan Judson: 4748
32	62.8	61.8	MG TF Supercharged: 2989
33	47.2	46.4	Volkswagen Sedan Supercharged: 4743
34	35.9	35.3	Hillman Minx Supercharged: 2040

Total: 35

Supercharged engines. Highest specific output. No limits set. All cars with figures included.

	bhp/l	kW/l	PS/l	
1	161.9	120.7	164.1	Koenig Competition: 2417
2	106.4	79.3	107.9	Volkswagen Corrado Neuspeed: 4883
3	102.8	76.6	104.2	Lancia Rally: 2537
4	91.4	68.1	92.6	Toyota MR2 Supercharged: 4451
				Toyota MR2 Supercharged: 4464
5	91.1	67.9	92.3	Ford Mustang Holdener: 1966
6	89.8	67.0	91.1	Volkswagen Corrado G60: 4882
7	88.8	66.2	90.1	Volkswagen Polo G40: 4887
8	88.7	66.1	89.9	Volkswagen Corrado: 4874
				Volkswagen Corrado G60: 4879
9	86.9	64.8	88.1	Ford Thunderbird Super Coupe Ford Engineering: 1948
10	86.7	64.7	87.9	Porsche 928 S4 Koenig: 3726
11	84.5	63.0	85.7	BMW 735i Koenig: 611
12	82.3	61.4	83.5	Shelby GT 350-S: 4121
13	78.4	58.5	79.5	Pontiac Tempest Supercharged: 3532
14	73.5	54.8	74.5	Squire X101: 4190
15	71.7	53.5	72.7	Austin-Healey Sprite Supercharged: 439
16	64.2	47.9	65.1	Alfa Romeo 8C2300: 41
17	61.0	45.5	61.8	Excalibur SS: 1363
18	60.9	45.4	61.7	Oldsmobile F-85 Jetfire: 3279
19	59.7	44.5	60.5	Bugatti 55: 651
20	59.1	44.1	59.9	Studebaker Regal Wagonaire Supercharged: 4237
21	55.3	41.2	56.1	Ford Thunderbird Super Coupe: 1947
				Mercury Cougar XR-7: 2960
22	54.1	40.3	54.8	Pontiac Bonneville SSEi: 3600
23	48.5	36.2	49.2	Alfa Romeo 1750: 40
24	46.5	34.7	47.1	Duesenberg SJ Town Car: 1353
25	46.0	34.3	46.6	MG TF Supercharged: 2989
26	41.9	31.3	42.5	Volkswagen Sedan Judson: 4748
27	40.1	29.9	40.7	Cord 812-S: 1101
28	39.8	29.7	40.3	Bentley 4.5-litre Supercharged: 462
29	35.9	26.8	36.4	Lammas-Graham Drop-head Coupe: 2476
30	33.8	25.2	34.3	Nash Nash-Healey Roadster Supercharged: 3200
31	30.2	22.5	30.6	Volkswagen Sedan Supercharged: 4743
32	29.6	22.1	30.1	Hillman Minx Supercharged: 2040

Total: 35

Supercharged engines. Highest piston speed. No limits set. All cars with figures included.

	ft/sec	m/sec	
1	68.8	21.0	Lancia Rally: 2537
2	60.2	18.3	Bugatti 55: 651
3	58.3	17.8	Pontiac Tempest Supercharged: 3532
4	56.8	17.3	Volkswagen Corrado Neuspeed: 4883
5	55.4	16.9	Duesenberg SJ Town Car: 1353
6	54.7	16.7	Squire X101: 4190
7	54.1	16.5	MG TF Supercharged: 2989
8	53.9	16.4	Toyota MR2 Supercharged: 4464
			Toyota MR2 Supercharged: 4451
9	53.6	16.3	Bentley 4.5-litre Supercharged: 462
10	53.4	16.3	Lammas-Graham Drop-head Coupe: 2476
11	53.3	16.2	Koenig Competition: 2417
12	52.9	16.1	Volkswagen Corrado: 4874
			Volkswagen Corrado G60: 4882
			Volkswagen Corrado G60: 4879
13	51.8	15.8	Porsche 928 S4 Koenig: 3726
14	51.8	15.8	Ford Thunderbird Super Coupe Ford Engineering: 1948
15	50.6	15.4	Studebaker Regal Wagonaire Supercharged: 4237
16	50.0	15.2	Alfa Romeo 8C2300: 41
17	49.0	14.9	BMW 735i Koenig: 611
18	48.7	14.8	Nash Nash-Healey Roadster Supercharged: 3200
19	48.4	14.7	Excalibur SS: 1363
20	47.8	14.6	Shelby GT 350-S: 4121
21	47.5	14.5	Austin-Healey Sprite Supercharged: 439
22	47.2	14.4	Volkswagen Polo G40: 4887
23	46.7	14.2	Ford Mustang Holdener: 1966
24	43.8	13.3	Cord 812-S: 1101
25	43.6	13.3	Hillman Minx Supercharged: 2040
26	43.4	13.2	Pontiac Bonneville SSEi: 3600
27	43.2	13.2	Alfa Romeo 1750: 40
28	37.7	11.5	Ford Thunderbird Super Coupe: 1947
			Mercury Cougar XR-7: 2960
29	35.8	10.9	Oldsmobile F-85 Jetfire: 3279
30	28.0	8.5	Volkswagen Sedan Judson: 4748
31	25.9	7.9	Volkswagen Sedan Supercharged: 4743

Total: 35

Multi-cylinder in-line (5 or more cylinders). Maximum speed. Limit set at 145mph.

	mph	kmh	
1	192.0	308.9	Jaguar D Type: 2285
2	180.0	289.6	Mercedes-Benz 300SLR: 2795
3	179.0	288.0	BMW 535i Alpina B10 Bi-Turbo: 619
4	174.0	280.0	Opel Omega Lotus: 3352
5	160.0	257.4	Porsche 911 Turbo Cabriolet Ruf: 3680
6	158.0	254.2	BMW 735i Koenig: 611
			BMW M635 CSi: 572
7	156.0	251.0	BMW M1: 556
			Jaguar E Type 4.2: 2309
			Nissan Skyline GT-R: 3243
8	155.0	249.4	Audi Quattro Sport: 309
			BMW M5: 606
			BMW M5: 622
			Jaguar E Type Coupe: 2303
9	154.0	247.8	BMW 735i Alpina B11: 602
10	153.5	247.0	Aston Martin DB4 GT Zagato: 240
11	153.0	246.2	Audi Coupe S2: 337
12	151.7	244.1	Jaguar E Type Coupe: 2298
13	151.0	243.0	Jaguar C Type: 2274
			Mercedes-Benz 300CE: 2909
14	150.0	241.4	Audi 200 Quattro: 334
			BMW M635 CSi: 607
			Irmsher GT: 2243
			Ital Design Aztec: 2262
			Jaguar XKE: 2299
			Jaguar XKE: 2306
			Lynx D Type: 2642
			Mercedes-Benz 300SL Carrera Panamericana: 2788
15	149.0	239.7	Jaguar XKSS: 2291
16	148.0	238.1	Aston Martin DB4: 239
			Aston Martin DB6: 242
			Mercedes-Benz 300E-24: 2912
			Vauxhall Carlton GSi 3000 24v: 4724
17	147.0	236.5	BMW 735i Automatic: 585
			BMW M6: 597
			Datsun 240Z Sharp: 1190
18	146.0	234.9	BMW M535i: 576
			Mercedes-Benz 300SL Coupe: 2794
			Toyota Supra 3.0i Turbo: 4465
19	145.0	233.3	Audi 200 Quattro Turbo: 297
			BMW 535i SE: 593
			BMW M635 CSi Hardy & Beck: 577
			Datsun 280ZX Electramotive: 1230

Total: 43

Multi-cylinder in-line (5 or more cylinders). Acceleration to 60mph/96.5kmh. Limit set at 7.5 seconds.

	sec	
1	3.5	Sbarro Chrono 3.5: 4108
2	3.8	Datsun 280ZX Electramotive: 1230
3	4.7	Jaguar D Type: 2285
4	4.8	Audi Quattro Sport: 309

5	4.9	Opel Omega Lotus: 3352
6	5.1	BMW 535i Alpina B10 Bi-Turbo: 619
7	5.2	Jaguar XKSS: 2291
8	5.3	Lynx D Type: 2642
		Porsche 911 Turbo Cabriolet Ruf: 3680
9	5.6	Datsun 280ZX Sharp: 1221
		Nissan Skyline GT-R: 3243
10	5.7	Datsun 280ZX Electramotive: 1220
11	5.8	Toyota Supra Turbo TRD: 4467
		TVR Convertible Turbo: 4593
12	5.9	Audi Coupe S2: 337
13	6.0	BMW 735i Koenig: 611
		BMW M635 CSi: 607
14	6.1	Aston Martin DB4 GT Zagato: 240
		BMW M635 CSi: 572
15	6.2	BMW M1: 556
16	6.3	Audi Quattro: 323
		Audi Quattro 20v: 330
		BMW M5: 606
17	6.4	BMW M5: 622
		BMW M635 CSi Hardy & Beck: 577
		Panther J72: 3372
18	6.5	Aston Martin DB6: 242
19	6.6	Jaguar C Type: 2274
		Jaguar XK120C: 2280
		Porsche 911 E: 3637
		Toyota Supra Turbo: 4466
20	6.9	BMW 327S Hardy & Beck: 574
		Jaguar E Type Coupe: 2298
		Toyota Supra 3.0i Turbo: 4465
21	7.0	BMW 333i Alpina: 548
		Datsun 240Z Sharp: 1190
		Mercedes-Benz 190E AMG Baby Hammer: 2903
		Mercedes-Benz 300SL Roadster: 2800
		Toyota Supra: 4442
		Toyota Supra Turbo: 4460
		Vauxhall Carlton GSi 3000 24v: 4724
22	7.2	Audi 200 Quattro: 334
		BMW M6: 597
		Jaguar E Type Coupe: 2303
23	7.3	Audi 200 Avant Quattro: 304
		Audi Quattro: 289
		BMW 3.0 CSL: 530
		BMW 325i SE: 615
		BMW 635 CSi: 561
		Jaguar XK150S: 2294
24	7.4	Audi 200 Quattro Turbo: 297
		BMW 325i: 573
		BMW 535i SE: 593
		BMW 735i Alpina B11: 602
		BMW M535i: 576
		Jaguar E Type Roadster: 2312
		Jaguar XJ6L: 2337
		Jaguar XJS 3.6: 2345
		Jaguar XKE: 2299
		Jaguar XKE: 2306
25	7.5	Aston Martin DB4: 237
		BMW 325i Cabriolet: 587
		BMW 325i Convertible: 610
		BMW 325i S: 591
		BMW 325i S: 599
		Marcos 3-litre Volvo: 2646
		Maserati GT Coupe: 2653
		Mercedes-Benz 300CE: 2892
		Mercedes-Benz 300E: 2885
		Toyota Supra: 4459

Total: 70

Multi cylinder in line (5 or more cylinders) Highest power. Limit set at 250bhp.

	bhp	kW	PS	
1	580.0	432.5	588.0	Datsun 280ZX Electramotive: 1230
2	500.0	372.8	506.9	Sbarro Chrono 3.5: 4108
3	430.0	320.6	436.0	Toyota Supra Turbo TRD: 4467
4	377.0	281.1	382.2	Opel Omega Lotus: 3352
5	360.0	268.4	365.0	BMW 535i Alpina B10 Bi-Turbo: 619
6	325.0	242.3	329.5	Aston Martin DB6: 242
9	314.0	234.1	318.4	Aston Martin DB4 GT Zagato: 240
10	310.0	231.2	314.3	BMW M5: 622
11	306.0	228.2	310.2	Audi Quattro Sport: 309
12	302.0	225.2	306.2	Mercedes-Benz 300SLR: 2795
13	300.0	223.7	304.2	Datsun 280ZX Sharp: 1221
				Porsche 911 Turbo Cabriolet Ruf: 3680
14	290.0	216.2	294.0	BMW 735i Koenig: 611
15	286.0	213.3	290.0	BMW M635 CSi: 607
				BMW M635 CSi: 572
16	285.0	212.5	288.9	Jaguar D Type: 2285
				Lynx D Type: 2642
17	282.0	210.3	285.9	Aston Martin DB5: 241
18	281.0	209.5	284.9	BMW M635 CSi Hardy & Beck: 577
19	276.0	205.8	279.8	Nissan Skyline GT-R: 3243
20	270.0	201.3	273.7	Datsun 280ZX Electramotive: 1220
21	265.0	197.6	268.7	Duesenberg J Coupe: 1352
				Jaguar 4.2 litre Mk X: 2305
				Jaguar 4.2 litre Mk X Overdrive: 2308
				Jaguar E Type 4.2: 2309
				Jaguar E Type Coupe: 2298
				Jaguar E Type Coupe: 2303
				Jaguar E Type Roadster: 2312
				Jaguar XKE: 2299
				Jaguar XKE: 2306
				Jaguar XKE 4.2 2+2: 2310
22	263.0	196.1	266.6	Aston Martin DB4: 239
				Aston Martin DB4: 237
23	260.0	193.9	263.6	Jaguar XKSS: 2291
24	258.0	192.4	261.6	Datsun 240Z Sharp: 1190
25	256.0	190.9	259.5	BMW M6: 597
26	252.0	187.9	255.5	BMW 745i: 562
27	251.0	187.2	254.5	Jaguar XJR 4.0: 2363
28	250.0	186.4	253.5	BMW 735i Alpina B11: 602
				Bugatti 50S: 648
				Ital Design Aztec: 2262
				Jaguar Mk X: 2300
				Jaguar XK150S: 2294
				Jaguar XK150S: 2295
				Mercedes-Benz 300SL Roadster: 2807
				Mercedes-Benz 300SL Roadster: 2800
				Mercedes-Benz SSKL: 2776

Total: 50

Multi-cylinder in-line (5 or more cylinders). Highest torque. Limit set at 250lbft.

	lbft	Nm	
1	520.0	704.6	Datsun 280ZX Electramotive: 1230
2	425.0	575.9	Duesenberg SJ Town Car: 1353
3	420.0	569.1	Mercedes-Benz SSKL: 2776
4	409.0	554.2	Opel Omega Lotus: 3352
5	390.0	528.5	Mercedes-Benz 36/220-S: 2774
6	382.0	517.6	BMW 535i Alpina B10 Bi-Turbo: 619
			Toyota Supra Turbo TRD: 4467
7	374.0	506.8	Duesenberg J Coupe: 1352
8	347.0	470.2	Sbarro Chrono 3.5: 4108
9	340.0	460.7	Rolls-Royce Phantom II: 3949
10	320.0	433.6	Rolls-Royce Phantom I Phaeton: 3946
11	310.0	420.1	Bugatti 50S: 648
12	304.0	411.9	Porsche 911 Turbo Cabriolet Ruf: 3680
13	299.0	405.1	BMW 735i Koenig: 611
14	290.0	393.0	Aston Martin DB6: 242
			Aston Martin DBS: 243
			Chrysler Custom Imperial Le Baron: 964
			Packard 7-34 Phaeton: 3355
			Packard Super 8 Phaeton: 3356
15	285.6	387.0	Jaguar 4.0 Sovereign: 2358
16	283.0	383.5	Jaguar 4.2 litre Mk X: 2305
			Jaguar 4.2 litre Mk X Overdrive: 2308
			Jaguar 420: 2311
			Jaguar E Type 4.2: 2309
			Jaguar E Type Roadster: 2312
			Jaguar XJ6: 2318
			Jaguar XJ6 4.2: 2320
			Jaguar XJ6 4.2 Automatic: 2316
			Jaguar XKE 4.2 2+2: 2310
17	282.0	382.1	Jaguar 420 Sedan: 2315
18	280.0	379.4	Aston Martin DB5: 241
			BMW 745i: 562
			Rolls-Royce Silver Cloud "S": 3957
19	278.2	377.0	Jaguar XJR 4.0: 2363
			Jaguar XJS 4.0 Auto: 2371
20	278.0	376.7	Aston Martin DB4 GT Zagato: 240
			Jaguar XJ6 Vanden Plas: 2362
21	273.0	369.9	TVR Convertible Turbo: 4593
22	266.0	360.4	BMW M5: 606
23	265.0	359.1	BMW M5: 622
24	263.0	356.4	Jaguar XKE Coupe: 2317
25	260.0	352.3	Armstrong Siddeley Star Sapphire: 220
			Daimler DK 400B: 1145
			Du Pont Speedster: 1350
			Jaguar E Type Coupe: 2298
			Jaguar E Type Coupe: 2303
			Jaguar XKE: 2306
			Jaguar XKE: 2299
			Jaguar XKSS: 2291
			Nissan Skyline GT-R: 3243
26	259.0	350.9	Audi 200 Quattro Turbo: 297
			Audi 200 Turbo: 293
27	258.0	349.6	Audi Quattro Sport: 309
28	257.0	348.2	Hudson Hornet: 2177
			Kurtis Hornet Roadster: 2420
29	254.6	345.0	Toyota Supra 3.0i Turbo: 4465
30	254.0	344.2	Toyota Supra Turbo: 4466
31	251.0	340.1	BMW M635 CSi: 572
			BMW M635 CSi Hardy & Beck: 577
32	250.9	340.0	BMW M635 CSi: 607
33	250.0	338.8	Delage D8-120 Super Sports: 1251
			Jaguar Mk X: 2300

Total: 62

Multi-cylinder in-line (5 or more cylinders). Highest rpm at peak power. Limit set at 6000rpm.

	rpm	
1	9200	Sbarro Chrono 3.5: 4108
2	8250	Datsun 240Z Sharp: 1190
3	7500	Datsun 280ZX Electramotive: 1230
		Datsun 280ZX Electramotive: 1220
		Datsun 280ZX Sharp: 1221
		Mercedes-Benz 300SLR: 2795
4	6900	BMW M5: 606
		BMW M5: 622
5	6800	Nissan Skyline GT-R: 3243
6	6700	Audi Quattro Sport: 309
7	6600	Toyota 2000GT: 4356
8	6500	BMW M1: 556
		BMW M6: 597
		BMW M635 CSi: 607
		BMW M635 CSi: 572
		BMW M635 CSi Hardy & Beck: 577
		Toyota Supra Turbo TRD: 4467
9	6400	Mercedes-Benz 300CE: 2909
10	6300	Mercedes-Benz 300E-24: 2912
		Mercedes-Benz 300SL-24 5-speed Auto: 2917
11	6200	Ital Design Aztec: 2262
		Mercedes-Benz 300SL Roadster: 2807
		Mercedes-Benz 300SL Roadster: 2800
		Porsche 911 E: 3637
12	6100	Mercedes-Benz 300SL: 2793
		Mercedes-Benz 300SL Coupe: 2794
13	6000	AC AC-Bristol Zagato: 17
		AC Aceca-Bristol: 21
		AC Bristol: 19
		Aston Martin DB4 GT Zagato: 240
		Audi 90 Quattro: 329
		Audi 90 Quattro 20v: 336
		Audi 90 Quattro 20v: 325
		BMW 2500: 519
		BMW 2800 CS: 521
		BMW 3.0 CS: 524
		BMW 3.0S: 525
		BMW 320: 541
		BMW 323i: 547
		BMW 327S Hardy & Beck: 574
		BMW 333i Alpina: 548
		BMW 525: 538
		BMW 525: 536
		BMW 533i: 566
		BMW 535i Alpina B10 Bi-Turbo: 619
		BMW 633 CSi: 570
		BMW Bavaria: 526
		Datsun 240Z: 1182
		Datsun 240Z: 1171
		Datsun 240Z Automatic: 1176
		Jaguar XK120C: 2280
		Jaguar XKSS: 2291
		Maserati A6G/54 Frua Gran Sport: 2652
		Mercedes-Benz 280CE Auto: 2840
		Mercedes-Benz 280E: 2844
		Mercedes-Benz 280E: 2850
		Mercedes-Benz 280SE: 2841
		Toyota Supra: 4452
		Toyota Supra: 4442
		Toyota Supra: 4459
		Toyota Supra 3.0i: 4443
		Vauxhall Carlton GSi 3000 24v: 4724
		Vauxhall Senator 3.0i 24v: 4731
		Volvo 960: 4969
		Volvo 960 24v: 4968

Total: 65

Multi-cylinder in-line (5 or more cylinders) Highest power-to-weight ratio. Limit set at 180bhp/ton.

	bhp/ ton	bhp/ tonne	
1	780.5	767.5	Sbarro Chrono 3.5: 4108
2	499.7	491.4	Datsun 280ZX Electramotive: 1230
3	348.7	342.9	Mercedes-Benz 300SLR: 2795
4	301.3	296.3	Datsun 280ZX Sharp: 1221
5	299.7	294.7	Lynx D Type: 2642
6	298.3	293.3	Jaguar D Type: 2285
7	262.7	258.3	Datsun 240Z Sharp: 1190
8	261.2	256.8	Jaguar XKSS: 2291
9	258.2	253.9	Toyota Supra Turbo TRD: 4467
10	254.4	250.1	Aston Martin DB4 GT Zagato: 240
11	248.9	244.7	Datsun 280ZX Electramotive: 1220
12	244.2	240.1	Audi Quattro Sport: 309
13	227.0	223.2	Opel Omega Lotus: 3352
14	225.5	221.7	Porsche 911 Turbo Cabriolet Ruf: 3680
15	219.7	216.0	Jaguar E Type Coupe: 2298
16	218.2	214.6	Jaguar XKE: 2299
17	216.2	212.6	BMW 535i Alpina B10 Bi-Turbo: 619
18	213.1	209.6	Aston Martin DB6: 242
19	212.0	208.5	Jaguar E Type Coupe: 2303
20	211.5	208.0	TVR Convertible Turbo: 4593
21	210.0	206.5	Jaguar XK120C: 2280
22	209.8	206.3	Aston Martin Spyder Touring: 235
23	208.4	204.9	Jaguar E Type Roadster: 2312
24	205.3	201.8	Jaguar E Type 4.2: 2309
25	204.7	201.3	Jaguar XKE: 2306
26	204.3	200.9	Aston Martin DB4: 237
27	202.5	199.1	Mercedes-Benz 300SL Carrera Panamericana: 2788
28	200.0	196.7	Jaguar C Type: 2274
29	196.3	193.0	Nissan Skyline GT-R: 3243
30	194.9	191.7	Mercedes-Benz 300SL: 2793
31	193.7	190.4	Aston Martin DBS: 243
32	193.1	189.9	Aston Martin DB4: 239
33	192.8	189.6	BMW M635 CSi: 572
34	192.1	188.9	Jaguar XKE 4.2 2+2: 2310
35	190.8	187.7	Aston Martin DB5: 241
36	187.9	184.8	BMW M635 CSi Hardy & Beck: 577
37	185.3	182.2	BMW M635 CSi: 607
38	184.9	181.8	Mercedes-Benz 190E AMG Baby Hammer: 2903
39	184.7	181.6	BMW M5: 606
40	183.9	180.8	Mercedes-Benz 300SL Coupe: 2794
41	183.6	180.5	Mercedes-Benz 300SL Roadster: 2807
42	182.6	179.5	Jaguar XKE Coupe: 2317
43	182.1	179.1	Mercedes-Benz 300SL Roadster: 2800
44	181.4	178.4	Maserati A6G/54 Frua Gran Sport: 2652
45	180.1	177.1	Bitter Type 3 Cabrio: 494

Total: 45

Multi-cylinder in-line (5 or more cylinders) Highest specific output. Limit set at 75bhp/litre.

	bhp/l	kW/l	PS/l	
1	210.7	157.1	213.6	Datsun 280ZX Electramotive: 1230
2	145.6	108.5	147.6	Toyota Supra Turbo TRD: 4467
3	143.4	106.9	145.4	Audi Quattro Sport: 309
4	142.9	106.6	144.9	Sbarro Chrono 3.5: 4108
5	112.3	83.7	113.9	Ital Design Aztec: 2262
6	108.6	81.0	110.1	Datsun 280ZX Electramotive: 1220
7	107.5	80.1	109.0	Nissan Skyline GT-R: 3243
8	106.5	79.4	107.9	Datsun 280ZX Sharp: 1221
9	105.3	78.5	106.8	Datsun 240Z Sharp: 1190
10	105.0	78.3	106.4	BMW 535i Alpina B10 Bi-Turbo: 619
11	103.7	77.3	105.1	Opel Omega Lotus: 3352
12	101.3	75.5	102.7	Mercedes-Benz 300SLR: 2795
13	98.8	73.7	100.2	Audi Coupe S2: 337
				Audi Quattro 20v: 330
14	97.5	72.7	98.8	Audi 200 Quattro: 334
15	91.0	67.8	92.2	Porsche 911 Turbo Cabriolet Ruf: 3680
16	90.3	67.4	91.6	Audi Quattro: 289
17	89.8	67.0	91.1	Audi Quattro: 323
18	89.1	66.4	90.3	BMW M5: 606
19	87.7	65.4	88.9	BMW M5: 622
20	85.6	63.8	86.7	Aston Martin DB4 GT Zagato: 240
21	84.9	63.3	86.1	Audi 200 Avant Quattro: 304
				Audi 200 Quattro Turbo: 297
				Audi 200 Turbo: 293
22	84.5	63.0	85.7	BMW 735i Koenig: 611
23	83.4	62.2	84.6	Mercedes-Benz 300SL Roadster: 2800
				Mercedes-Benz 300SL Roadster: 2807
24	82.8	61.8	84.0	BMW M635 CSi: 607
				BMW M635 CSi: 572
25	81.4	60.7	82.5	BMW M635 CSi Hardy & Beck: 577
26	81.3	60.7	82.5	Aston Martin DB6: 242
				Aston Martin DBS: 243
27	81.1	60.5	82.2	Mercedes-Benz 300SL Coupe: 2794
28	80.8	60.3	82.0	Bitter Type 3 Cabrio: 494
29	80.1	59.7	81.2	Mercedes-Benz 300SL: 2793
30	78.9	58.8	80.0	Toyota Supra Turbo: 4466
31	78.5	58.6	79.6	Toyota Supra 3.0i Turbo: 4465
32	78.5	58.5	79.6	BMW 745i: 562
33	78.0	58.2	79.1	Mercedes-Benz 300SL-24 5-speed Auto: 2917
34	78.0	58.2	79.1	Mercedes-Benz 300E-24: 2912
35	77.9	58.1	78.9	Toyota Supra Turbo: 4460
36	77.0	57.4	78.0	BMW 520i SE Touring: 624
				BMW 525i SE 24v: 618
37	76.8	57.3	77.9	TVR Convertible Turbo: 4593
38	75.8	56.5	76.8	BMW 325i: 623
				BMW 325i SE: 615
				BMW 525i: 617
39	75.5	56.3	76.6	Jaguar XKSS: 2291
40	75.5	56.3	76.6	Maserati A6G/54 Frua Gran Sport: 2652
41	75.4	56.3	76.5	Toyota 2000GT: 4356
42	75.4	56.2	76.4	Jaguar D Type: 2285
				Lynx D Type: 2642
43	75.3	56.2	76.4	BMW 520i: 616

Total: 53

Multi-cylinder in-line (5 or more cylinders). Highest piston speed. Limit set at 60ft/sec.

	ft/sec	m/sec	
1	84.6	25.8	Sbarro Chrono 3.5: 4108
2	69.5	21.2	Jaguar XK120C: 2280
			Jaguar XKSS: 2291
3	67.2	20.5	Jaguar C Type: 2274
4	66.6	20.3	Jaguar D Type: 2285
			Jaguar XK 140: 2287
5	66.6	20.3	Jaguar XK140: 2276
			Jaguar XK140MC: 2283
6	66.5	20.3	Datsun 240Z Sharp: 1190
7	65.0	19.8	BMW M5: 606
			BMW M5: 622
8	64.8	19.7	Datsun 280ZX Electramotive: 1230
			Datsun 280ZX Sharp: 1221
9	64.0	19.5	Mercedes-Benz 300SLR: 2795
			Toyota Supra Turbo TRD: 4467
10	63.7	19.4	Allard GT Coupe: 153
			Jaguar 3.4: 2292
			Jaguar 3.8 Mk II: 2301
			Jaguar 3.8 Mk II Automatic: 2302
			Jaguar 3.8 Sedan: 2297
			Jaguar 3.8S: 2307
			Jaguar 420: 2311
			Jaguar 420 Sedan: 2315
			Jaguar E Type Coupe: 2303
			Jaguar E Type Coupe: 2298
			Jaguar Mk VII Auto: 2286
			Jaguar Mk VIII: 2289
			Jaguar Mk X: 2300
			Jaguar XJ6: 2318
			Jaguar XJ6 4.2: 2320
			Jaguar XJ6 4.2 Automatic: 2316
			Jaguar XK150: 2293
			Jaguar XK150S: 2295
			Jaguar XKE Coupe: 2317
11	63.7	19.4	Jaguar 3.4: 2296
			Jaguar 3.8S Sedan: 2304
			Jaguar Mk VII: 2282
			Jaguar XK150: 2290
			Jaguar XK150S: 2294
			Jaguar XKE: 2306
			Jaguar XKE: 2299
12	63.3	19.3	Audi Quattro Sport: 309
13	63.0	19.2	AC AC-Bristol Zagato: 17
			AC Aceca-Bristol: 21
			AC Bristol: 19
14	62.5	19.1	Jaguar 4.2 litre Mk X: 2305
			Jaguar 4.2 litre Mk X Overdrive: 2308
			Jaguar E Type 4.2: 2309
			Jaguar E Type Roadster: 2312
			Jaguar XK120: 2275
			Jaguar XKE 4.2 2+2: 2310
15	61.4	18.7	Jaguar XK120 Coupe: 2279
			Jaguar XK120M: 2281
			Lynx D Type: 2642
16	60.4	18.4	Datsun 280ZX Electramotive: 1220
17	60.4	18.4	AC Ace Bristol: 16
			AC Bristol D-2: 20
			AC Greyhound: 22
			Aston Martin DB4 GT Zagato: 240
18	60.2	18.4	Jaguar Mk VII: 2278
			Jaguar Mk VII: 2277
19	60.2	18.3	Maserati 3500GT: 2654
			Maserati GT Coupe: 2653
20	60.2	18.3	Bugatti 55: 651
			Maserati 3500 GTI Sebring: 2655

Total: 65

Vee cylinder configuration. Maximum speed. Limit set at 175mph.

	mph	kmh	
1	255.0	410.3	Chevrolet Corvette Callaway Sledgehammer: 941
2	221.0	355.6	Chevrolet Corvette Greenwood: 870
3	218.0	350.8	Vector W8 Twin Turbo: 4736
4	214.0	344.3	Bugatti EB110: 652
5	205.0	329.8	Ford GT40: 1760
6	204.0	328.2	Chevrolet Corvette Lingenfelter: 951
			Cizeta Moroder V16T: 1094
7	203.0	326.6	Chevrolet Camaro Gottlieb 1969: 926
8	202.0	325.0	Lamborghini Diablo: 2475
			Lamborghini Diablo: 2474
9	201.0	323.4	Chevrolet Corvette Callaway Speedster: 949
			Ferrari F40: 1435
10	200.0	321.8	Eagle GTP: 1356
			Ferrari F40: 1446
			Jaguar XJ220: 2359
			Jaguar XJS Lister Le Mans: 2366
			Vector W2: 4735
11	199.0	320.2	Ferrari GTO Norwood: 1451
12	198.0	318.6	Ferrari 308 Norwood Bonneville GTO: 1434
13	196.0	315.4	Ferrari F40: 1450
14	193.0	310.5	Chevrolet Camaro IROC-Z Chevrolet Engineering: 929
			Safir GT40: 4106
15	192.0	308.9	Lamborghini Countach: 2461
			Pontiac Firebird TDM Technologies: 3597
16	191.0	307.3	Chevrolet Corvette Callaway: 918
			Chevrolet Corvette Callaway: 931
17	190.0	305.7	Dodge Viper: 1348
			Shelby Cobra Daytona Coupe: 4119
18	189.0	304.1	Ferrari 288 GTO: 1421
19	186.0	299.3	Chevrolet Corvette ZR-1 Geiger: 954
			Ferrari 365 GTB/4 Competitione: 1403
			Ford Mustang NOS/Saleen: 1967
			Porsche 928 S4 Koenig: 3726
			Zender Fact 4: 5008
20	185.0	297.7	Chevrolet Corvette ZR-2: 956
			Ferrari Testa Rossa Gemballa: 1443
			Ford Mustang 5.0 Cartech Turbo: 1940
			Jaguar XJR15: 2369
			Mercedes-Benz 300CE AMG Hammer: 2910
21	184.0	296.1	Chevrolet Corvette Callaway: 948
			Jaguar XJ13: 2313
22	183.0	294.4	Aston Martin Zagato: 257
			Mercedes-Benz 300E AMG Hammer: 2899
			Pontiac Petty Grand National: 3571
23	182.0	292.8	Ferrari 308 Norwood: 1439
24	180.0	289.6	Bizzarrini P538: 497
			Ferrari 288 GTO: 1416
			Ferrari 375 Indianapolis: 1373
			Ferrari 400 Super America: 1389
			Ferrari GTO: 1423
			Jaguar XJS Tullius: 2333
			Lamborghini Miura: 2451
25	179.0	288.0	Lamborghini Countach: 2468
			Lamborghini Countach 25th Anniversary: 2473
26	178.0	286.4	Chevrolet Corvette Callaway: 901
			Pontiac Firebird T/A Turbo Pontiac Engineering: 3588
27	177.0	284.8	Ferrari 365 GTB Goldsmith: 1425
			Ford Mustang Cartech Turbo: 1928
28	176.0	283.2	Isdera Imperator: 2244
29	175.0	281.6	Ferrari 250 GTO: 1386
			Ferrari Daytona: 1397
			Zender Vision 3: 5007

Total: 62

Vee cylinder configuration. Acceleration to 60mph/96.5kmh. Limit set at 5 seconds.

	sec	
1	3.4	Chevrolet Corvette Lingenfelter: 951
2	3.5	AC Cobra 427 Modified 1965: 27
		Jaguar XJ220: 2359
3	3.7	Ferrari 308 Norwood Bonneville GTO: 1434
4	3.8	Ferrari F40: 1450
5	3.9	Bugatti EB110: 652
		Chevrolet Corvette Callaway Sledgehammer: 941
6	4.0	Chevrolet Bel Air 409 SS/S: 755
		Pontiac Firebird TransAm Silverbird: 3566
		Safir GT40: 4106
		Vector W2: 4735
7	4.1	Dodge Viper: 1348
		Ford Cobra II Kemp: 1841
		Pontiac Firebird TDM Technologies: 3597
8	4.2	Chevrolet Corvette ZR-1 SS: 955
		Dodge Ramcharger 426 Super/Stock: 1287
		Mercury Comet A/FX: 2933
		Scarab Mk II: 4109
		Shelby AC Ford Cobra: 4116
		Vector W8 Twin Turbo: 4736
9	4.3	De Tomaso Pantera Group 3: 1243
		Triumph TR8 Group 44: 4578
		Westfield SEight: 4973
		Zender Fact 4: 5008
10	4.4	Chevrolet Corvette Callaway Speedster: 949
		Jaguar XJS Lister Le Mans: 2366
11	4.5	Chevrolet Camaro IROC-Z Chevrolet Engineering: 929
		Chevrolet Corvette Bakeracing SCCA Escort: 917
		Cizeta Moroder V16T: 1094
		Ferrari 250 Testa Rossa: 1378
		Ferrari F40: 1446
		Lamborghini Diablo: 2475
12	4.6	Chevrolet Corvette Callaway: 918
		Evans Series I: 1362
		Pontiac Catalina Super Stock: 3529
13	4.7	Chevrolet Monza Mike Keyser: 874
		Ferrari 308 Norwood: 1439
		Lamborghini Countach 25th Anniversary: 2473
14	4.8	Aston Martin Zagato: 257
		Chevrolet Camaro Gottlieb 1969: 926
		Ford Galaxie 500 XL 427: 1714
		Porsche 928 S4 Koenig: 3726
15	4.9	Chevrolet Corvette Callaway: 931
		Chevrolet Corvette Callaway: 948
		Chevrolet Corvette Callaway Twin Turbo: 950

		Chevrolet Corvette Morrison/Baker Nelson Ledges: 921
		Chevrolet Corvette ZR-1: 953
		Chevrolet Corvette ZR-1: 934
		Chevrolet Corvette ZR-1 Geiger: 954
		Chevrolet Corvette ZR-2: 956
		Ford Mustang Cartech Turbo: 1928
		Ford Mustang Holdener: 1966
		Lamborghini Countach: 2468
16	5.0	Autokraft AC Cobra Mk IV: 456
		Chevrolet Corvette Callaway: 901
		Chevrolet Corvette Grand Sport Roadster: 776
		Eagle GTP: 1356
		Ferrari 288 GTO: 1421
		Ferrari 288 GTO: 1416
		Ferrari GTO: 1423
		Ford GT40: 1760
		Isdera Imperator: 2244
		Jaguar XJS Tullius: 2333
		Mercedes-Benz 300CE AMG Hammer: 2910
		Nissan 300ZX Turbo Millen Super GTZ: 3247
		TVR 420 SEAC: 4601

Total: 66

Vee cylinder configuration. Highest power. Limit set at 425bhp.

	bhp	kW	PS	
1	1600.0	1193.1	1622.2	Ferrari GTO Norwood: 1451
2	880.0	656.2	892.2	Chevrolet Corvette Callaway Sledgehammer: 941
3	798.0	595.1	809.1	Chevrolet Camaro Gottlieb 1969: 926
4	700.0	522.0	709.7	Chevrolet Corvette Greenwood: 870
5	685.0	510.8	694.5	Pontiac Firebird TDM Technologies: 3597
6	671.0	500.4	680.3	Ferrari 308 Norwood Bonneville GTO: 1434
7	625.0	466.1	633.7	Vector W8 Twin Turbo: 4736
8	600.0	447.4	608.3	Bugatti EB110: 652
				Safir GT40: 4106
				Vector W2: 4735
9	590.0	440.0	598.2	Pontiac Firebird TransAm Silverbird: 3566
				Pontiac Petty Grand National: 3571
10	580.0	432.5	588.0	AC Cobra 427 Modified 1965: 27
11	570.0	425.0	577.9	Ford Cobra II Kemp: 1841
12	560.0	417.6	567.8	Cizeta Moroder V16T: 1094
13	550.0	410.1	557.6	Chevrolet Corvette Grand Sport Roadster: 776
14	536.0	399.7	543.4	Chevrolet Monza Mike Keyser: 874
15	530.0	395.2	537.3	Chevrolet Camaro IROC-Z Chevrolet Engineering: 929
				Chevrolet Corvette Lingenfelter: 951
				Jaguar XJ220: 2359
16	510.0	380.3	517.1	Ford Mustang SVO J Bittle American: 1942
17	496.0	369.9	502.9	Chevrolet Camaro IROC-Z 8.3-litre: 914
				Jaguar XJS Lister Le Mans: 2366
18	492.0	366.9	498.8	Lamborghini Diablo: 2475
19	485.0	361.7	491.7	Lamborghini Diablo: 2474
20	478.0	356.4	484.6	Ferrari F40: 1435
				Ferrari F40: 1450
				Ferrari F40: 1446
21	475.0	354.2	481.6	Jaguar XJS Tullius: 2333
22	472.0	352.0	478.5	Jaguar XJ13: 2313
23	470.0	350.5	476.5	Ford Mustang 5.0 Cartech Turbo: 1940
24	465.0	346.7	471.4	De Tomaso Pantera Group 3: 1243
25	460.0	343.0	466.4	Ford Mustang TransAm: 1796
				Nissan 300ZX Turbo Millen Super GTZ: 3247
26	455.0	339.3	461.3	Lamborghini Countach: 2468
				Lamborghini Countach 25th Anniversary: 2473
27	450.0	335.6	456.2	Chevrolet Camaro IROC: 877
				Chevrolet Camaro Z/28 Yenko/SC: 826
				Ferrari 308 Norwood: 1439
				Ford Mustang Holdener: 1966
				Jaguar XJR15: 2369
28	448.0	334.1	454.2	Zender Fact 4: 5008
29	435.0	324.4	441.0	Chevrolet Corvette 435hp: 829
				Chevrolet Corvette Convertible: 818
				Chevrolet Corvette L71: 833
				Chevrolet Corvette L71/89: 834
30	432.0	322.1	438.0	Aston Martin Zagato: 257
31	430.0	320.6	436.0	Chevrolet Corvette L88: 835
				Chevrolet Corvette L88: 820
				Lamborghini Miura S: 2456
				Porsche 928 S4 Koenig: 3726
32	428.0	319.2	433.9	Nissan 300ZX Motor Sports International SR-71: 3246
33	425.0	316.9	430.9	Chevrolet Camaro 427 Dana: 805
				Chevrolet Corvette: 795
				Chevrolet Corvette 396: 796
				Chevrolet Corvette Convertible: 803
				Chevrolet Corvette Sting Ray 396: 798
				Chevrolet Corvette ZR-1 SS: 955
				Dodge Charger: 1299
				Dodge Charger R/T: 1303
				Dodge Hemi Charger 500 Automatic: 1308
				Dodge Hemi Charger 500 Manual: 1309
				Dodge Ramcharger 426 Super/Stock: 1287
				Ford Galaxie 500 XL 427: 1714
				Mercury Comet A/FX: 2933
				Mercury Super Marauder S-55: 2932
				Plymouth GTX Hemi: 3502
				Plymouth Satellite Street Hemi: 3491
				Ruger Bentley Clone: 4052
				Shelby Cobra 427: 4126

Total: 70

Vee cylinder configuration. Highest torque. Limit set at 475lbft.

	lbft	Nm	
1	900.0	1219.5	Ferrari GTO Norwood: 1451
2	785.0	1063.7	Pontiac Firebird TDM Technologies: 3597
3	772.0	1046.1	Chevrolet Corvette Callaway Sledgehammer: 941
4	672.0	910.6	Chevrolet Camaro IROC-Z Chevrolet Engineering: 929
5	638.0	864.5	Chevrolet Camaro Gottlieb 1969: 926
6	630.0	853.7	Vector W8 Twin Turbo: 4736
7	620.0	840.1	Chevrolet Corvette Greenwood: 870
8	603.0	817.1	Safir GT40: 4106
9	580.0	785.9	Vector W2: 4735
10	575.0	779.1	Chevrolet Corvette Callaway: 948
			Chevrolet Corvette Callaway Speedster: 949
			Chevrolet Corvette Callaway Twin Turbo: 950
11	570.0	772.4	Chevrolet Corvette Lingenfelter: 951
12	562.0	761.5	Chevrolet Corvette Callaway: 940
			Chevrolet Corvette Callaway: 931
13	550.0	745.3	Chevrolet Camaro IROC-Z 8.3-litre: 914
			Ford Mustang Cartech Turbo: 1928
14	545.0	738.5	Chevrolet Corvette Callaway: 918
15	541.0	733.1	AC Cobra 427 Modified 1965: 27
16	530.0	718.2	Ford Cobra II Kemp: 1841
17	525.0	711.4	Cadillac Coupe de Ville: 709
18	510.0	691.1	Buick GS455 Stage 1: 687
			Oldsmobile 88 Delta Royale: 3294
19	502.0	680.2	Ferrari 308 Norwood Bonneville GTO: 1434
20	500.0	677.5	Chevrolet Corvette 454: 844
			Chevrolet Impala: 846
			Chevrolet Monte Carlo: 847
			Jaguar XJS Lister Le Mans: 2366
			Oldsmobile 4-4-2 W30: 3296
			Oldsmobile 442 Hurst: 3293
			Oldsmobile Toronado: 3292
			Pontiac GTO 455: 3561
21	495.0	670.7	Chrysler 300-G: 975
22	490.0	664.0	Dodge Challenger R/T: 1314
			Dodge Charger: 1299
			Dodge Charger R/T: 1303
			Dodge Hemi Charger 500 Automatic: 1308
			Dodge Hemi Charger 500 Manual: 1309
			Ford Thunderbird: 1653
			Jensen SP: 2397
			Lincoln Continental Mk III: 2579
			Oldsmobile Delmont: 3291
			Plymouth GTX Hemi: 3502
			Plymouth Satellite Street Hemi: 3491
			Ruger Bentley Clone: 4052
23	485.0	657.2	Bentley Turbo R: 483
			Chrysler 300-J: 981
24	480.0	650.4	Cadillac Calais: 707
			Cadillac Coupe de Ville: 705
			Cadillac Eldorado: 708
			Cadillac Sedan de Ville: 706
			Chrysler 300: 988
			Chrysler 300: 984
			Chrysler 300-H: 989
			Chrysler Imperial Crown: 987
			Dodge Charger R/T: 1315
			Dodge Coronet R/T: 1304
			Dodge Coronet R/T: 1300
			Dodge Monaco: 1310
			Dodge Ramcharger 426 Super/Stock: 1287
			Ford Galaxie 500 XL 427: 1714
			Ford LTD: 1773
			Ford Thunderbird: 1779
			Mercury Comet A/FX: 2933
			Mercury Marquis Brougham: 2948
			Mercury Marquis Marauder X-100: 2949
			Mercury Super Marauder S-55: 2932
			Monteverdi 375L: 3118
			Plymouth Cuda 440: 3505
			Plymouth GTX: 3501
			Plymouth GTX: 3497
			Shelby Cobra 427: 4126
25	476.0	645.0	Ford Fastback NASCAR: 1698
26	475.0	643.6	Buick Riviera: 682
			Buick Riviera: 683

		Buick Wildcat: 680
		Buick Wildcat: 686
		Oldsmobile Toronado: 3286
		Oldsmobile Toronado: 3288

Total: 79

Vee cylinder configuration. Highest rpm at peak power. Limit set at 7200rpm.

	rpm	
1	9000	Bugatti EB110: 652
2	8800	Alfa Romeo 33 2.0 Stradale: 66
3	8300	Ferrari 365 GTB/4 Competitione: 1403
4	8000	Cizeta Moroder V16T: 1094
		Ferrari 275 GTS/4 NART: 1392
		Lamborghini Countach: 2461
		Triumph TR8 Group 44: 4578
5	7900	Ford Mustang SVO J Bittle American: 1942
6	7850	Ferrari 308 Norwood Bonneville GTO: 1434
7	7800	Lamborghini Bravo: 2458
8	7700	Ferrari 308 GT4 Dino: 1402
		Ferrari 308 GTB: 1409
		Ferrari Dino 308 GT4 2+2: 1410
		Lamborghini Miura P400S: 2455
9	7600	Ferrari 246 GTS Dino: 1401
		Ferrari 412 MI: 1377
		Jaguar XJS Tullius: 2333
10	7500	Ferrari 250 GT Berlinetta Lusso: 1388
		Ferrari 250 GTO: 1386
		Ferrari 365 GTB Goldsmith: 1425
		Ferrari 365 GTB/4 Daytona: 1396
		Ferrari 365 GTB/4 Daytona: 1404
		Ferrari 375 Indianapolis: 1373
		Ferrari 400 Super America: 1389
		Ferrari Daytona: 1397
		Ferrari Daytona Cannonball: 1398
		Ferrari Daytona Sportwagen: 1395
		Ford Mustang TransAm: 1796
		Lamborghini Countach S: 2464
		Lamborghini Countach S: 2466
		Lamborghini Jarama 400GT: 2457
		Lamborghini Jarama 400GT: 2459
		Lamborghini Silhouette 3000: 2462
		Lamborghini Urraco: 2463
		Lamborghini Urraco S: 2460
		Pontiac Firebird TransAm Silverbird: 3566
		Pontiac Petty Grand National: 3571
11	7350	Lamborghini Miura S: 2456
12	7250	Jaguar XJ13: 2313
13	7200	Chevrolet Monza Mike Keyser: 874
		Ferrari 212 Touring: 1372
		Ferrari 250 Mille Miglia: 1376
		Ferrari 250 Testa Rossa: 1378
		Ferrari 250 Testa Rossa: 1382
		Ferrari 348tb: 1445
		Ferrari GTO Norwood: 1451
		Ferrari Mondial t: 1441
		Ferrari Mondial t: 1452

Total: 48

Vee cylinder configuration. Highest power-to-weight ratio. Limit set at 300bhp/ton.

	bhp/ ton	bhp/ tonne	
1	1257.5	1236.6	Ferrari GTO Norwood: 1451
2	595.8	585.9	Chevrolet Camaro Gottlieb 1969: 926
3	589.4	579.6	Ferrari 308 Norwood Bonneville GTO: 1434
4	564.7	555.3	Safir GT40: 4106
5	560.0	550.7	Chevrolet Corvette Grand Sport Roadster: 776
6	543.5	534.4	Chevrolet Corvette Greenwood: 870
7	537.1	528.1	Chevrolet Corvette Callaway Sledgehammer: 941
8	513.5	504.9	AC Cobra 427 Modified 1965: 27
9	510.8	502.2	Ferrari 412 MI: 1377
10	507.9	499.4	Ferrari 375 Indianapolis: 1373
11	483.4	475.4	Vector W2: 4735
12	480.6	472.6	Jaguar XJ13: 2313
13	476.4	468.5	Ford Cobra II Kemp: 1841
14	455.7	448.1	Pontiac Firebird TransAm Silverbird: 3566
15	454.8	447.2	Bugatti EB110: 652
16	448.0	440.5	Chevrolet Monza Mike Keyser: 874
17	441.5	434.2	Ferrari F40: 1446
			Ferrari F40: 1435
18	436.4	429.1	Jaguar XJR15: 2369
19	426.2	419.1	Pontiac Firebird TDM Technologies: 3597
20	424.4	417.3	Scarab Mk II: 4109
21	421.7	414.6	Vector W8 Twin Turbo: 4736
22	412.6	405.7	Bizzarrini P538: 497
23	411.3	404.4	Zender Fact 4: 5008
24	408.9	402.1	Alfa Romeo 33 2.0 Stradale: 66
25	396.6	390.0	Westfield SEight: 4973
26	396.3	389.7	Eagle GTP: 1356
27	381.8	375.4	Ferrari 250 Testa Rossa: 1382
28	376.3	370.0	Shelby Cobra 427: 4126
29	375.0	368.7	Shelby Cobra Daytona Coupe: 4119
30	367.8	361.7	Ferrari 250 GTO: 1386
31	366.0	359.9	Ford GT40 Super Street: 1738
32	362.6	356.5	Ford Mustang Holdener: 1966
33	359.3	353.3	Ferrari F40: 1450
34	356.7	350.8	Pontiac Petty Grand National: 3571
35	355.9	349.9	Ford Mustang SVO J Bittle American: 1942
36	351.4	345.5	Bizzarrini GT America: 496
37	350.7	344.8	Ferrari 288 GTO: 1421
			Ferrari GTO: 1423
38	348.4	342.6	Lamborghini 350GT: 2449
39	347.5	341.7	Shelby Cobra USRRC: 4118
40	345.1	339.4	Jaguar XJ220: 2359
41	342.5	336.8	Ford GT40: 1760
42	341.6	335.9	Chevrolet Corvette Lingenfelter: 951
43	339.9	334.3	Jaguar XJS Tullius: 2333
44	334.5	328.9	Cizeta Moroder V16T: 1094
45	331.6	326.0	Lamborghini Miura S: 2456
46	324.6	319.2	Ferrari 250 Testa Rossa: 1378
47	324.0	318.6	Iso Grifo A3L Berlinetta: 2245
48	320.9	315.5	Chevrolet Camaro IROC-Z Chevrolet Engineering: 929
49	319.7	314.4	Lamborghini Countach: 2468
50	319.0	313.7	Ford Mustang 5.0 Cartech Turbo: 1940
51	318.0	312.7	Ford Mustang TransAm: 1796
52	317.1	311.8	Isdera Imperator: 2244
53	315.2	309.9	De Tomaso Pantera Group 3: 1243
54	315.0	309.7	Triumph TR8 Group 44: 4578
55	314.4	309.1	Lamborghini Miura: 2452
56	311.1	305.9	Ferrari 308 Norwood: 1439
57	310.7	305.5	Lamborghini Countach 25th Anniversary: 2473
58	310.3	305.1	Ford Mustang Cartech Turbo: 1928
59	308.6	303.4	Mercury Comet A/FX: 2933
60	307.3	302.2	Chevrolet Camaro IROC: 877
61	306.4	301.3	Ferrari 288 GTO: 1416
62	305.4	300.4	TVR 420 SEAC: 4601
63	304.4	299.4	Lamborghini Diablo: 2475
64	304.1	299.1	Chevrolet Corvette ZR-1 SS: 955
65	301.1	296.1	Ferrari 275 GTS/4 NART: 1392

Total: 67

Vee cylinder configuration. Highest specific output. Limit set at 95bhp/litre.

	bhp/L	kW/L	PS/L	
1	190.7	142.2	193.3	Ferrari GTO Norwood: 1451
2	171.5	127.9	173.9	Bugatti EB110: 652
3	162.8	121.4	165.1	Ferrari F40: 1435
				Ferrari F40: 1446
				Ferrari F40: 1450
4	155.4	115.9	157.6	Nissan 300ZX Turbo Millen Super GTZ: 3247
5	153.8	114.7	155.9	Ferrari 308 Norwood: 1439
6	153.5	114.5	155.6	Chevrolet Corvette Callaway Sledgehammer: 941
7	144.6	107.8	146.6	Nissan 300ZX Motor Sports International SR-71: 3246
8	140.1	104.5	142.0	Ferrari 288 GTO: 1421
				Ferrari GTO: 1423
9	138.0	102.9	139.9	Ferrari 288 GTO: 1416
10	125.8	93.8	127.5	Zender Fact 4: 5008
11	119.5	89.1	121.1	Pontiac Firebird TDM Technologies: 3597
12	115.3	86.0	116.9	Alfa Romeo 33 2.0 Stradale: 66
13	111.8	83.4	113.4	Ferrari 308 Norwood Bonneville GTO: 1434
14	109.4	81.6	111.0	Lamborghini Miura S: 2456
15	104.6	78.0	106.1	Vector W8 Twin Turbo: 4736
16	103.2	76.9	104.6	Ferrari 412 MI: 1377
17	101.8	75.9	103.2	Lamborghini Miura: 2452
18	101.6	75.8	103.0	Ferrari 250 Testa Rossa: 1378
				Ferrari 250 Testa Rossa: 1382
19	101.3	75.6	102.8	Nissan 300ZX Turbo: 3241
				Nissan 300ZX Twin Turbo: 3248
20	101.2	75.5	102.6	Ford Mustang SVO J Bittle American: 1942
21	101.0	75.3	102.4	Maserati Shamal: 2681
22	100.9	75.3	102.3	Dodge Stealth R/T Turbo: 1347
				Mitsubishi 3000GT VR-4: 3111
23	100.4	74.9	101.8	Ferrari 275 GTS/4 NART: 1392
24	100.2	74.7	101.6	Pontiac Firebird T/A Turbo Pontiac Engineering: 3588
25	100.2	74.7	101.6	Pontiac Petty Grand National: 3571
26	100.1	74.7	101.5	Lamborghini Bravo: 2458
27	100.0	74.6	101.4	Vector W2: 4735
28	99.3	74.0	100.6	Lamborghini Espada: 2453
29	99.1	73.9	100.4	Ford Cobra II Kemp: 1841
30	98.4	73.3	99.7	Pontiac Firebird TransAm Silverbird: 3566
31	98.3	73.3	99.7	Ferrari 250 GTO: 1386
32	98.2	73.2	99.6	Ferrari 250 GT Berlinetta Lusso: 1388
33	97.0	72.3	98.3	Lamborghini 350GT: 2449
34	95.4	71.2	96.8	Lamborghini Countach: 2461
35	95.1	70.9	96.4	Ford Mustang 5.0 Cartech Turbo: 1940

Total: 41

Vee cylinder configuration. Highest piston speed. Limit set at 60ft/sec.

	ft/sec	m/sec	
1	89.8	27.4	Ferrari GTO Norwood: 1451
2	82.6	25.2	Chevrolet Camaro Gottlieb 1969: 926
3	77.6	23.6	Ferrari 308 Norwood Bonneville GTO: 1434
4	75.6	23.0	Chevrolet Corvette Greenwood: 870
5	72.9	22.2	Pontiac Petty Grand National: 3571
6	72.8	22.2	Safir GT40: 4106
7	70.4	21.5	Pontiac Firebird TransAm Silverbird: 3566
8	69.6	21.2	Chevrolet Monza Mike Keyser: 874
9	68.9	21.0	Triumph TR8 Group 44: 4578
10	68.1	20.7	Ford Cobra II Kemp: 1841
11	66.8	20.4	Chevrolet Corvette: 795
			Chevrolet Corvette 396: 796
			Chevrolet Corvette Sting Ray 396: 798
12	66.3	20.2	Ruger Bentley Clone: 4052
13	65.8	20.1	Ford Mustang SVO J Bittle American: 1942
14	65.1	19.8	Chevrolet Corvette ZR-1 SS: 955
15	64.6	19.7	Jensen Interceptor III Convertible: 2403
16	64.6	19.6	Ferrari 365 GTB/4 Competitione: 1403
17	63.6	19.4	AC Cobra 427 Modified 1965: 27
18	63.2	19.3	Chevrolet Camaro IROC: 877
			De Tomaso Pantera GT5-S: 1242
19	63.2	19.2	Shelby Cobra 427: 4126
20	63.0	19.2	Chevrolet Corvette ZR-1: 934
			Mercury Comet A/FX: 2933
21	63.0	19.2	Ford Galaxie 500 XL 427: 1714
			Mercury Super Marauder S-55: 2932
22	62.5	19.0	Ford Mustang TransAm: 1796
23	62.5	19.0	Chevrolet Corvette Grand Sport Roadster: 776
24	62.2	19.0	Pontiac Grand Prix 421: 3533
25	61.9	18.9	Mercury Cyclone: 2947
26	61.4	18.7	Oldsmobile 4-4-2 W30: 3296
			Zender Fact 4: 5008
27	61.2	18.7	Lamborghini Diablo: 2474
28	61.0	18.6	Ferrari 375 Indianapolis: 1373
29	60.9	18.6	Ford Galaxie 406: 1679
			Mercury S-55 406: 2930
30	60.9	18.5	Nissan 300ZX Motor Sports International SR-71: 3246
31	60.5	18.5	Acura NSX: 36
			Chevrolet Corvette Convertible: 818
			Chevrolet Corvette L71: 833
			Chevrolet Corvette L71/89: 834
			Honda NSX: 2156
32	60.4	18.4	Chevrolet Corvette Callaway Sledgehammer: 941
			De Tomaso Pantera Group 3: 1243
33	60.4	18.4	Chevrolet Corvette 435hp: 829
			Chevrolet Corvette L88: 820

Total: 46

Flat or Boxer cylinder configuration. Maximum speed. Limit set at 150mph.

	mph	kmh	
1	235.0	378.1	Koenig C62: 2419
2	230.0	370.1	Koenig Competition Evolution: 2418
3	217.0	349.2	Koenig Competition: 2417
4	216.0	347.5	Porsche 911 Turbo RS Tuning: 3737
5	211.0	339.5	Porsche 911 Turbo Ruf Twin Turbo: 3710
6	210.0	337.9	Ferrari Testa Rossa Norwood: 1444
7	208.0	334.7	Porsche 911 Ruf CTR: 3748
8	205.0	329.8	Porsche 911 Turbo Gemballa Mirage: 3751
9	201.0	323.4	Porsche 911 Turbo Koenig RS: 3709
			Porsche 959 S: 3702
10	198.0	318.6	Porsche 959: 3731
			Porsche 959 Comfort: 3717
			Porsche 959 Sport: 3718
11	196.1	315.5	Porsche 911 Ruf TR2: 3749
12	196.0	315.4	Porsche 911 Ruf: 3747
13	183.0	294.4	Porsche 911 Turbo Motorsport Design: 3724
14	181.0	291.2	Ferrari Testa Rossa: 1437
			Ferrari Testa Rossa Straman Spyder: 1438
15	180.0	289.6	Ferrari Pininfarina Mythos: 1448
16	178.0	286.4	Ferrari Testa Rossa: 1426
			Porsche Carrera RSR: 3642
17	175.0	281.6	Ferrari 512 BB: 1407
18	174.0	280.0	Ferrari Testa Rossa: 1442
19	171.0	275.1	Porsche 911 Turbo: 3750
20	168.0	270.3	Ferrari 512 BB: 1417
			Porsche 911 Carrera Turbo: 3746
21	165.0	265.5	Porsche 911 Turbo: 3676
			Porsche 911 Turbo Gemballa Avalanche: 3697
22	163.0	262.3	Porsche 935 Group 4 Holbert: 3657
23	161.0	259.0	Porsche 911 Carrera 4: 3734
			Porsche 911 Carrera 4: 3720
			Porsche 911 Carrera RS: 3753
			Subaru Legacy FIA Record: 4274
24	160.0	257.4	Porsche 911 Carrera 2: 3732
25	159.0	255.8	Porsche 911 Carrera 2 Tiptronic: 3733
			Porsche 911 Turbo: 3723
			Porsche 911 Turbo: 3736
			Porsche Carrera 2 Cabriolet Tiptronic: 3744
26	158.0	254.2	Porsche 911 3.3 Turbo: 3719
			Porsche 911 Turbo Ruf 3.4: 3698
27	157.0	252.6	Porsche 911 Turbo Slant-Nose: 3699
28	156.0	251.0	Porsche 911 Turbo: 3659
			Porsche 911 Turbo Carrera: 3650
29	155.0	249.4	Porsche 911 Speedster: 3707
			Porsche 911 Turbo: 3708
			Porsche RSK: 3613
30	154.0	247.8	Porsche 911 Club Sport: 3722
31	153.0	246.2	Porsche 911 Turbo: 3689
			Porsche Turbo 3-litre: 3648
32	152.0	244.6	Porsche 911 Carrera Club Sport: 3705
33	151.0	243.0	Porsche 911 Carrera: 3682
34	150.0	241.4	Porsche 904 Carrera GTS: 3621

Total: 52

Flat or Boxer cylinder configuration. Acceleration to 60mph/96.5kmh. Limit set at 6 seconds.

	sec	
1	3.5	Koenig C62: 2419
		Koenig Competition Evolution: 2418
2	3.6	Porsche 959: 3731
		Porsche 959 Sport: 3718
3	3.8	Porsche 911 Ruf: 3747
		Porsche 911 Ruf TR2: 3749
4	3.9	Porsche 911 Ruf CTR: 3748
5	4.0	Koenig Competition: 2417
		Porsche 911 Turbo Koenig RS: 3709
		Porsche 911 Turbo Motorsport Design: 3724
		Porsche 911 Turbo Ruf Twin Turbo: 3710
		Porsche 959 Comfort: 3717
6	4.1	Porsche 911 Turbo Gemballa Mirage: 3751
7	4.5	Porsche 911 Turbo Ruf 3.4: 3698
8	4.6	Porsche 911 Carrera Turbo: 3746
		Porsche 911 Turbo RS Tuning: 3737
9	4.7	Ferrari Testa Rossa Norwood: 1444
		Porsche 911 Turbo: 3750
		Porsche 959 S: 3702
10	4.8	Porsche 911 Turbo: 3723
11	4.9	Porsche 911 3.3 Turbo: 3719
		Porsche 911 Carrera 4: 3720
		Porsche 911 Carrera RS: 3753
		Porsche 911 Turbo Gemballa Avalanche: 3697
12	5.0	Porsche 911 Turbo: 3659
		Porsche 911 Turbo: 3708
		Porsche 911 Turbo: 3689
		Porsche 911 Turbo Slant-Nose: 3699
		Porsche RSK: 3613
13	5.1	Ferrari 512 BB: 1417
		Porsche 911 Carrera 2: 3732
		Porsche 911 Turbo: 3736
		Porsche 911 Turbo: 3676
14	5.2	Ferrari Testa Rossa: 1442
		Porsche 911 Carrera Club Sport: 3705
		Porsche Carrera RS 3-litre: 3647
15	5.3	Ferrari Testa Rossa: 1437
		Ferrari Testa Rossa: 1426
		Ferrari Testa Rossa Straman Spyder: 1438
		Porsche 911 Club Sport: 3722
16	5.5	Porsche 911 Carrera: 3682
		Porsche Carrera RS Touring: 3641
17	5.6	Porsche 911 Carrera SE: 3688
		Porsche Carrera RSR: 3642
18	5.7	Porsche 911 Cabriolet: 3687
		Porsche 911 Carrera: 3696
		Porsche 911 Club Sport: 3706
19	5.8	Porsche 911 Carrera 4: 3734
		Porsche 911 SC: 3670
		Porsche 935 Group 4 Holbert: 3657
		Porsche Panamericana: 3745
20	6.0	Ferrari 512 BBi: 1422
		Porsche 911 Speedster: 3735

Total: 53

Flat or Boxer cylinder configuration. Highest power. Limit set at 250bhp.

	bhp	kW	PS	
1	1000.0	745.7	1013.9	Koenig Competition Evolution: 2418
2	943.0	703.2	956.1	Ferrari Testa Rossa Norwood: 1444
3	800.0	596.6	811.1	Koenig Competition: 2417
4	600.0	447.4	608.3	Porsche 959 S: 3702
5	588.0	438.5	596.2	Koenig C62: 2419
6	580.0	432.5	588.0	Porsche 911 Turbo RS Tuning: 3737
7	520.0	387.8	527.2	Porsche 911 Turbo Koenig RS: 3709
8	490.0	365.4	496.8	Porsche 911 Turbo Gemballa Mirage: 3751

9	488.0	363.9	494.8	Porsche 911 Turbo Motorsport Design: 3724
10	485.0	361.7	491.7	Porsche 935 Group 4 Holbert: 3657
11	469.0	349.7	475.5	Porsche 911 Ruf CTR: 3748
				Porsche 911 Turbo Ruf Twin Turbo: 3710
12	455.0	339.3	461.3	Porsche 911 Ruf: 3747
				Porsche 911 Ruf TR2: 3749
13	450.0	335.6	456.2	Porsche 959: 3731
				Porsche 959 Comfort: 3717
				Porsche 959 Sport: 3718
14	390.0	290.8	395.4	Ferrari Testa Rossa: 1442
15	380.0	283.4	385.3	Ferrari Pininfarina Mythos: 1448
				Ferrari Testa Rossa: 1426
				Ferrari Testa Rossa: 1437
				Ferrari Testa Rossa Straman Spyder: 1438
16	374.0	278.9	379.2	Porsche 911 Turbo Ruf 3.4: 3698
17	360.0	268.4	365.0	Ferrari 512 BB: 1417
18	344.0	256.5	348.8	Ferrari 512 BB: 1407
19	340.0	253.5	344.7	Ferrari 512 BBi: 1422
20	320.0	238.6	324.4	Porsche 911 Carrera Turbo: 3746
				Porsche 911 Turbo: 3750
21	300.0	223.7	304.2	Porsche 911 3.3 Turbo: 3719
				Porsche 911 Turbo: 3736
				Porsche 911 Turbo: 3676
22	282.0	210.3	285.9	Porsche 911 Turbo: 3708
				Porsche 911 Turbo: 3723
				Porsche 911 Turbo: 3689
				Porsche 911 Turbo Gemballa Avalanche: 3697
				Porsche 911 Turbo Slant-Nose: 3699
23	280.0	208.8	283.9	Porsche Carrera RSR: 3642
24	260.0	193.9	263.6	Porsche 911 Carrera RS: 3753
				Porsche Turbo 3-litre: 3648
25	253.0	188.7	256.5	Porsche 911 Turbo: 3659
26	250.0	186.4	253.5	Porsche 911 Carrera 2: 3732
				Porsche 911 Carrera 4: 3734
				Porsche 911 Carrera 4: 3720
				Porsche Carrera 2 Cabriolet Tiptronic: 3744
				Porsche Panamericana: 3745

Total: 45

Flat or Boxer cylinder configuration. Highest torque. Limit set at 225lbft.

	lbft	Nm	
1	738.0	1000.0	Koenig Competition Evolution: 2418
2	664.0	899.7	Koenig Competition: 2417
3	533.0	722.2	Koenig C62: 2419
4	490.0	664.0	Porsche 911 Turbo Koenig RS: 3709
			Porsche 911 Turbo Motorsport Design: 3724
5	483.0	654.5	Porsche 911 Ruf TR2: 3749
6	482.0	653.1	Porsche 911 Ruf: 3747
7	465.0	630.1	Porsche 911 Turbo RS Tuning: 3737
8	457.0	619.2	Porsche 911 Turbo Ruf Twin Turbo: 3710
9	434.0	588.1	Porsche 935 Group 4 Holbert: 3657
10	420.0	569.1	Porsche 911 Turbo Gemballa Mirage: 3751
11	408.0	552.8	Porsche 911 Ruf CTR: 3748
12	370.0	501.4	Porsche 959: 3731
			Porsche 959 Comfort: 3717
			Porsche 959 Sport: 3718
13	369.0	500.0	Porsche 959 S: 3702
14	363.1	492.0	Ferrari Testa Rossa: 1442
15	354.0	479.7	Ferrari Pininfarina Mythos: 1448
			Ferrari Testa Rossa: 1426
			Ferrari Testa Rossa: 1437
			Ferrari Testa Rossa Straman Spyder: 1438
			Porsche 911 Turbo Ruf 3.4: 3698
16	333.0	451.2	Ferrari 512 BB: 1417
			Ferrari 512 BBi: 1422
17	332.1	450.0	Porsche 911 Turbo: 3750
18	332.0	449.9	Porsche 911 Carrera Turbo: 3746
19	318.0	430.9	Porsche 911 Turbo: 3676
20	317.3	430.0	Porsche 911 3.3 Turbo: 3719
21	317.0	429.5	Porsche 911 Turbo: 3736
22	302.0	409.2	Ferrari 512 BB: 1407
23	288.0	390.2	Porsche 911 Turbo: 3723
24	282.0	382.1	Porsche 911 Turbo: 3659
25	278.0	376.7	Porsche 911 Turbo: 3708
			Porsche 911 Turbo: 3689
			Porsche 911 Turbo Gemballa Avalanche: 3697
			Porsche 911 Turbo Slant-Nose: 3699
26	253.0	342.8	Porsche Turbo 3-litre: 3648
27	246.0	333.3	Porsche 911 Turbo: 3655
			Porsche 911 Turbo Carrera: 3650
28	239.9	325.0	Porsche 911 Carrera RS: 3753
29	229.0	310.3	Porsche 911 Carrera 4: 3720
			Porsche 911 Carrera 4: 3734
			Porsche Panamericana: 3745
30	228.8	310.0	Porsche 911 Carrera 2: 3732
			Porsche Carrera 2 Cabriolet Tiptronic: 3744
31	228.0	308.9	Porsche 911 Carrera 2 Tiptronic: 3733

Total: 46

Flat or Boxer cylinder configuration. Highest rpm at peak power. Limit set at 6000rpm.

	rpm	
1	10000	Ferrari Testa Rossa Norwood: 1444
2	8000	Porsche Carrera RSR: 3642
		Porsche RSK: 3613
3	7200	Ferrari 512 BB: 1407
		Porsche 904 Carrera GTS: 3621
4	7000	Porsche 935 Group 4 Holbert: 3657
5	6900	Porsche 911 Turbo RS Tuning: 3737
6	6700	Koenig Competition Evolution: 2418
7	6600	Porsche 911 S: 3626
		Porsche 911 S: 3624
8	6500	Alfa Romeo 33 Boxer 16v: 144
		Citroen GS: 1039
		Citroen GS: 1042
		Citroen GS 1220: 1044
		Porsche 911 E: 3629
		Porsche 911 E Sportomatic: 3627
		Porsche 911 S: 3638
		Porsche 911 S 2.2-litre: 3631
		Porsche 959: 3731
		Porsche 959 Comfort: 3717
		Porsche 959 S: 3702
		Porsche 959 Sport: 3718
9	6400	Subaru 1300 GL Coupe: 4247
		Subaru DL: 4249
		Subaru FF-1 1300: 4246
		Subaru Legacy FIA Record: 4274
10	6300	Ferrari Testa Rossa: 1442
		Koenig C62: 2419
		Porsche 911 Turbo Koenig RS: 3709
		Porsche Carrera RS Touring: 3641
11	6250	Koenig Competition: 2417
		Porsche 911 Turbo Motorsport Design: 3724
12	6200	Ferrari 512 BB: 1417
		Porsche 550 Spyder: 3610
		Porsche 911 E 2.4-litre: 3635
		Porsche Carrera 2-litre: 3618
		Porsche Carrera Coupe: 3606
		Porsche Carrera RS 3-litre: 3647
13	6100	Porsche 911: 3622
		Porsche 911 Carrera 2: 3732
		Porsche 911 Carrera 2 Tiptronic: 3733
		Porsche 911 Carrera 4: 3734
		Porsche 911 Carrera 4: 3720
		Porsche 911 Carrera RS: 3753
		Porsche 911 Sportomatic: 3628
		Porsche Carrera 2 Cabriolet Tiptronic: 3744
		Porsche Panamericana: 3745
14	6000	Alfa Romeo 33 1.7 Veloce: 129
		Alfa Romeo Alfa 33 1.7 Sportwagon Veloce: 130
		Alfa Romeo Alfasud: 84
		Alfa Romeo Alfasud: 81
		Alfa Romeo Alfasud 1200ti: 95
		Alfa Romeo Alfasud 1300ti: 96
		Alfa Romeo Alfasud 5M: 97
		Alfa Romeo Alfasud ti: 88
		Alfa Romeo Sprint Green Cloverleaf: 116
		Ferrari 512 BBi: 1422
		Panhard 24CT Sports Coupe: 3371
		Porsche 911 Turbo Ruf 3.4: 3698
		Subaru 1.8 GTi: 4258
		Subaru Legacy 2.0 4Cam Turbo Estate: 4277
		Subaru Legacy 2.2 GX 4WD: 4276
		Subaru Star: 4244

Total: 63

Flat or Boxer cylinder configuration. Highest power-to-weight ratio. Limit set at 200bhp/ton.

	bhp/ ton	bhp/ tonne	
1	640.0	629.3	Koenig Competition Evolution: 2418
2	570.9	561.4	Ferrari Testa Rossa Norwood: 1444
3	543.1	534.1	Koenig C62: 2419
4	512.0	503.5	Koenig Competition: 2417
5	451.0	443.5	Porsche 959 S: 3702
6	416.0	409.1	Porsche 911 Turbo Koenig RS: 3709
7	415.2	408.3	Porsche 911 Turbo Ruf Twin Turbo: 3710
8	409.2	402.4	Porsche 935 Group 4 Holbert: 3657
9	368.3	362.2	Porsche 911 Turbo Gemballa Mirage: 3751
10	366.8	360.7	Porsche 911 Turbo Motorsport Design: 3724
11	345.6	339.8	Porsche 911 Ruf CTR: 3748
12	339.4	333.7	Porsche 959 Sport: 3718
13	339.0	333.4	Porsche Carrera RSR: 3642
14	335.8	330.2	Porsche 911 Ruf: 3747
15	335.3	329.7	Porsche 911 Ruf TR2: 3749
16	328.5	323.0	Porsche 904 Carrera GTS: 3621

17	316.0	310.7	Porsche 959: 3731
			Porsche 959 Comfort: 3717
18	309.0	303.8	Ferrari Pininfarina Mythos: 1448
19	299.2	294.2	Porsche 911 Turbo Ruf 3.4: 3698
20	287.4	282.6	Porsche RSK: 3613
21	237.6	233.7	Ferrari Testa Rossa: 1442
22	232.6	228.7	Ferrari Testa Rossa: 1437
			Ferrari Testa Rossa: 1426
23	232.4	228.5	Ferrari 512 BB: 1417
24	226.4	222.6	Porsche 911 Turbo: 3676
25	225.3	221.5	Ferrari 512 BB: 1407
26	225.0	221.2	Ferrari 512 BBi: 1422
27	222.9	219.2	Porsche 911 Turbo: 3750
28	221.7	218.0	Ferrari Testa Rossa Straman Spyder: 1438
29	221.3	217.6	Porsche 911 Carrera RS: 3753
30	220.3	216.6	Porsche 911 3.3 Turbo: 3719
31	220.0	216.3	Porsche 911 Turbo: 3736
32	218.9	215.2	Porsche 911 Carrera Turbo: 3746
33	215.5	211.9	Porsche Turbo 3-litre: 3648
34	212.3	208.8	Porsche 911 Turbo Slant-Nose: 3699
35	211.9	208.3	Porsche Carrera 2 Cabriolet Tiptronic: 3744
36	206.8	203.3	Porsche 911 Turbo: 3723
			Porsche 911 Turbo: 3708
37	206.4	203.0	Porsche 911 Turbo: 3689
38	204.5	201.1	Porsche Carrera RS 3-litre: 3647
39	203.2	199.8	Porsche 550 Spyder: 3610
40	200.6	197.2	Porsche 911 Speedster: 3707

Total: 43

Flat or Boxer cylinder configuration. Highest specific output. Limit set at 75bhp/litre.

	bhp/L	kW/L	PS/L	
1	210.6	157.0	213.5	Porsche 959 S: 3702
2	202.3	150.9	205.1	Koenig Competition Evolution: 2418
3	190.8	142.3	193.5	Ferrari Testa Rossa Norwood: 1444
4	174.6	130.2	177.0	Koenig C62: 2419
5	172.2	128.4	174.6	Porsche 911 Turbo RS Tuning: 3737
6	162.0	120.8	164.3	Porsche 935 Group 4 Holbert: 3657
7	161.9	120.7	164.1	Koenig Competition: 2417
8	157.9	117.8	160.1	Porsche 959: 3731
				Porsche 959 Comfort: 3717
				Porsche 959 Sport: 3718
9	154.5	115.2	156.6	Porsche 911 Turbo Koenig RS: 3709
10	147.9	110.3	150.0	Porsche 911 Turbo Motorsport Design: 3724
11	145.5	108.5	147.5	Porsche 911 Turbo Gemballa Mirage: 3751
12	139.3	103.9	141.3	Porsche 911 Turbo Ruf Twin Turbo: 3710
13	139.3	103.9	141.2	Porsche 911 Ruf CTR: 3748
14	129.8	96.8	131.6	Porsche 911 Ruf: 3747
				Porsche 911 Ruf TR2: 3749
15	117.8	87.9	119.5	Subaru Legacy FIA Record: 4274
16	111.1	82.9	112.6	Porsche 911 Turbo Ruf 3.4: 3698
17	101.3	75.5	102.7	Porsche RSK: 3613
18	100.7	75.1	102.1	Porsche 904 Carrera GTS: 3621
19	99.8	74.4	101.2	Porsche Carrera RSR: 3642
20	98.8	73.7	100.2	Subaru Legacy 2.0 4Cam Turbo Estate: 4277
21	97.0	72.3	98.3	Porsche 911 Carrera Turbo: 3746
				Porsche 911 Turbo: 3750
22	91.5	68.2	92.7	Porsche 550 Spyder: 3610
23	91.1	67.9	92.4	Porsche 911 S 2.2-litre: 3631
24	90.9	67.8	92.2	Porsche 911 3.3 Turbo: 3719
				Porsche 911 Turbo: 3736
				Porsche 911 Turbo: 3676
25	90.4	67.4	91.7	Porsche 911 S: 3626
26	86.8	64.8	88.0	Porsche Turbo 3-litre: 3648
27	85.5	63.7	86.7	Porsche 911 Turbo: 3689
				Porsche 911 Turbo: 3708
				Porsche 911 Turbo: 3723
				Porsche 911 Turbo Gemballa Avalanche: 3697
				Porsche 911 Turbo Slant-Nose: 3699
28	80.4	59.9	81.5	Porsche 911 E: 3629
				Porsche 911 S: 3624
29	80.0	59.7	81.1	Alfa Romeo 33 Boxer 16v: 144
30	78.9	58.8	80.0	Ferrari Testa Rossa: 1442
31	78.4	58.4	79.4	Ferrari 512 BB: 1407
32	78.2	58.3	79.3	Porsche 911 Turbo: 3655
				Porsche 911 Turbo Carrera: 3650
33	78.1	58.3	79.2	Porsche Carrera RS Touring: 3641
34	77.3	57.6	78.4	Porsche 911 S: 3638
35	77.3	57.7	78.4	Porsche Carrera 2-litre: 3618
36	76.9	57.3	78.0	Ferrari Pininfarina Mythos: 1448
				Ferrari Testa Rossa: 1426
				Ferrari Testa Rossa: 1437
				Ferrari Testa Rossa Straman Spyder: 1438
37	76.7	57.2	77.7	Porsche 911 Turbo: 3659
38	75.2	56.1	76.3	Subaru 1.8 RX Turbo: 4259
				Subaru 4WD 3-door Turbo Coupe: 4265
				Subaru 4WD Turbo Estate: 4269
				Subaru Turbo 4WD Estate: 4262
				Subaru XT Turbo 4WD: 4268
				Subaru XT Turbo Coupe: 4264

Total: 58

Flat or Boxer cylinder configuration. Highest piston speed. Limit set at 47ft/sec.

	ft/sec	m/sec	
1	85.3	26.0	Ferrari Testa Rossa Norwood: 1444
2	61.6	18.8	Porsche Carrera RSR: 3642
3	58.2	17.7	Porsche 904 Carrera GTS: 3621
4	57.8	17.6	Porsche RSK: 3613
5	57.5	17.5	Koenig Competition Evolution: 2418
6	56.2	17.1	Porsche 911 Turbo RS Tuning: 3737
7	56.0	17.0	Ferrari 512 BB: 1407
8	53.9	16.4	Porsche 935 Group 4 Holbert: 3657
9	53.7	16.4	Ferrari Testa Rossa: 1442
10	53.3	16.2	Koenig Competition: 2417
11	52.9	16.1	Ferrari 512 BB: 1417
12	52.4	16.0	Subaru Legacy FIA Record: 4274
13	51.3	15.6	Porsche 911 Turbo Koenig RS: 3709
14	51.1	15.6	Alfa Romeo 33 Boxer 16v: 144
15	51.0	15.6	Porsche 911 Carrera 2 Tiptronic: 3733
16	51.0	15.5	Porsche 911 Carrera 2: 3732
			Porsche 911 Carrera 4: 3720
			Porsche 911 Carrera 4: 3734
			Porsche 911 Carrera RS: 3753
			Porsche Carrera 2 Cabriolet Tiptronic: 3744
			Porsche Panamericana: 3745
17	50.9	15.5	Porsche 911 Turbo Motorsport Design: 3724
18	50.7	15.5	Lancia 2000: 2513
19	50.1	15.3	Porsche Carrera 2-litre: 3618
20	50.0	15.2	Porsche 911 S: 3638
21	49.2	15.0	Panhard 24CT Sports Coupe: 3371
			Subaru Legacy 2.0 4Cam Turbo Estate: 4277
			Subaru Legacy 2.2 GX 4WD: 4276
22	49.0	14.9	Ferrari Pininfarina Mythos: 1448
			Ferrari Testa Rossa: 1437
			Ferrari Testa Rossa: 1426
			Ferrari Testa Rossa Straman Spyder: 1438
23	48.5	14.8	Porsche Carrera RS Touring: 3641
24	48.4	14.8	Porsche 911 Ruf CTR: 3748
			Porsche 911 Turbo Ruf Twin Turbo: 3710
25	48.3	14.7	Porsche 911 Speedster: 3735
26	48.0	14.6	Porsche 911 Cabriolet: 3703
			Porsche 911 Cabriolet: 3687
			Porsche 911 Carrera: 3704
			Porsche 911 Carrera: 3682
			Porsche 911 Carrera: 3679
			Porsche 911 Carrera Cabriolet: 3721
			Porsche 911 Carrera Club Sport: 3705
			Porsche 911 Carrera SE: 3688
			Porsche 911 Club Sport: 3706
			Porsche 911 Club Sport: 3722
			Porsche 911 SC: 3670
			Porsche 911 Speedster: 3707
			Porsche 911 Turbo Gemballa Mirage: 3751
27	47.7	14.5	Porsche 911 E 2.4-litre: 3635
			Porsche Carrera RS 3-litre: 3647
28	47.7	14.5	Porsche 911 S: 3624
			Porsche 911 S: 3626
			Porsche 959: 3731
			Porsche 959 Comfort: 3717
			Porsche 959 S: 3702
			Porsche 959 Sport: 3718
29	47.5	14.5	Panhard PL17 Tiger: 3370
30	47.3	14.4	Alfa Romeo 33 1.7 Veloce: 129
			Alfa Romeo Alfa 33 1.7 Sportwagon Veloce: 130
31	47.2	14.4	Porsche 911 Ruf: 3747

Total: 61

Diesel engines. Maximum speed. Limit set at 90mph.

	mph	kmh	
1	117.0	188.3	Rover 825 TD: 4047
2	116.0	186.6	Peugeot 605 SR TD: 3465
3	115.0	185.0	Mercedes-Benz 300D: 2911
			Mercedes-Benz 300TD: 2893
4	113.0	181.8	Audi 100 Turbo Diesel: 310
			Citroen CX25 DTR Turbo 2: 1078
5	112.0	180.2	Citroen XM Turbo SD Estate: 1093
6	111.0	178.6	Vauxhall Cavalier 1.7 GL TD: 4733
7	110.0	177.0	Mercedes-Benz 300SD: 2857
8	109.0	175.4	Peugeot 405 GTD Turbo: 3454
9	107.0	172.2	Ford Granada 2.5 GL Diesel: 1951
10	106.0	170.6	Citroen BX DTR Turbo: 1080
			Rover SD Turbo: 4023
11	105.0	168.9	Vauxhall Carlton L 2.3D: 4713
			Volvo 760 GLE: 4946
12	104.0	167.3	Toyota Landcruiser VX: 4478

			Volkswagen Jetta Turbo Diesel: 4868
			Volkswagen Passat CL Turbo Diesel Estate: 4845
13	103.0	165.7	Audi 80 Turbo Diesel: 291
			Peugeot 205 D Turbo: 3464
			Seat Toledo 1.9 CL Diesel: 4114
			Volkswagen Passat CL TD Estate: 4880
14	102.0	164.1	BMW 524 TD: 581
			Mercedes-Benz 300TD: 2868
			Peugeot 405 GRD: 3447
			Rover Montego 2.0 DSL Turbo: 4034
			Vauxhall Nova 1.5TD Merit: 4727
15	100.0	160.9	Citroen BX19 RD Diesel: 1061
16	99.0	159.3	Citroen CX 2500 Diesel Super: 1056
17	98.0	157.7	Talbot Horizon 1.9LD: 4348
18	97.0	156.1	Mercedes-Benz 300TD: 2861
			Rover 218 SD: 4045
19	96.0	154.5	Fiat Regata DS: 1594
			Peugeot 604 D Turbo: 3424
			Vauxhall Astra 1.7 DL: 4716
20	95.0	152.9	Cadillac Seville Diesel: 712
			Cadillac Seville Diesel: 711
			Mercedes-Benz 300CD: 2856
21	94.0	151.2	Citroen BX19 RD Estate: 1071
			Volkswagen Dasher Diesel: 4818
22	93.0	149.6	Citroen Visa 17RD: 1069
			Peugeot 305 GRD Estate: 3435
			Range Rover Vogue Turbo D: 3776
			Vauxhall Cavalier LD: 4693
23	92.0	148.0	Citroen AX14 DTR: 1081
			Ford Fiesta 1.6L Diesel: 1893
			Land Rover Discovery TDi: 2563
24	91.0	146.4	Mercedes-Benz 300D: 2819
25	90.0	144.8	Citroen CX 2200 Diesel: 1051
			Peugeot 505 S Turbodiesel: 3426
			Volkswagen Rabbit Diesel: 4809

Total: 51

Diesel engines. Acceleration to 60mph/ 96.5kmh. Limit set at 20 seconds.

	sec	
1	10.1	Citroen CX25 DTR Turbo 2: 1078
2	10.3	Mercedes-Benz 300TD: 2893
3	11.0	BMW 524 TD: 581
4	11.7	Rover 825 TD: 4047
5	11.9	Citroen BX DTR Turbo: 1080
6	12.2	Peugeot 405 GTD Turbo: 3454
		Vauxhall Nova 1.5TD Merit: 4727
7	12.3	Peugeot 205 D Turbo: 3464
		Volvo 760 GLE: 4946
8	12.6	Audi 100 Turbo Diesel: 310
		Toyota Landcruiser VX: 4478
9	12.7	Mercedes-Benz 300SD: 2857
10	12.8	Audi 80 Turbo Diesel: 291
		Peugeot 605 SR TD: 3465
		Vauxhall Cavalier 1.7 GL TD: 4733
11	12.9	Volkswagen Jetta Turbo Diesel: 4868
12	13.1	Citroen XM Turbo SD Estate: 1093
13	13.2	Mercedes-Benz 300TD: 2868
		Rover Montego 2.0 DSL Turbo: 4034
14	13.4	Ford Granada 2.5 GL Diesel: 1951
15	13.6	Volkswagen Passat CL Turbo Diesel Estate: 4845
16	13.8	Talbot Horizon 1.9LD: 4348
17	14.3	Rover SD Turbo: 4023
18	15.1	Vauxhall Astra 1.7 DL: 4716
19	15.4	Peugeot 405 GRD: 3447
20	15.5	Mercedes-Benz 300D: 2911
21	15.6	Citroen BX19 RD Diesel: 1061
		Fiat Regata DS: 1594
		Seat Toledo 1.9 CL Diesel: 4114
		Volkswagen Passat CL TD Estate: 4880
22	15.7	Cadillac Seville Diesel: 711
23	15.8	Ford Fiesta 1.6L Diesel: 1893
		Volkswagen Rabbit Diesel: 4809
24	16.2	Citroen AX14 DTR: 1081
		Vauxhall Carlton L 2.3D: 4713
25	16.5	Range Rover Vogue Turbo D: 3776
26	16.8	Peugeot 305 GRD Estate: 3435
27	16.9	Rover 218 SD: 4045
28	17.0	Citroen CX 2500 Diesel Super: 1056
		Peugeot 604 D Turbo: 3424
29	17.1	Land Rover Discovery TDi: 2563
		Mercedes-Benz 300CD: 2856
30	17.5	Ford Granada 2.5 Diesel Estate: 1887
31	17.6	Peugeot 505 S Turbodiesel: 3426
32	17.8	Mitsubishi Shogun Turbo Diesel 5-door: 3094
		Vauxhall Cavalier LD: 4693
33	17.9	Citroen BX19 RD Estate: 1071
		Daihatsu Fourtrak Estate DT EL: 1125
34	18.1	Mercedes-Benz 300TD: 2861
		Vauxhall Frontera 2.3 TD Estate: 4734
35	18.2	Oldsmobile Cutlass Diesel: 3300
		Volkswagen Golf LD: 4814
36	18.5	Volvo Diesel: 4939
37	19.1	Citroen Visa 17RD: 1069
38	19.4	Volkswagen Dasher Diesel: 4818
39	19.9	Isuzu I-Mark LS: 2252

Total: 56

Diesel engines. Highest power. Limit set at 70bhp.

	bhp	kW	PS	
1	165.0	123.0	167.3	Toyota Landcruiser VX: 4478
2	143.0	106.6	145.0	Mercedes-Benz 300TD: 2893
3	120.0	89.5	121.7	Cadillac Seville Diesel: 711
				Citroen CX25 DTR Turbo 2: 1078
				Mercedes-Benz 300TD: 2868
4	118.0	88.0	119.6	Rover 825 TD: 4047
5	114.0	85.0	115.6	BMW 524 TD: 581
6	113.0	84.3	114.6	Mercedes-Benz G-Wagen 300 GD LWB: 2921
7	112.0	83.5	113.5	Range Rover Vogue Turbo D: 3776
8	111.0	82.8	112.5	Land Rover Discovery TDi: 2563
9	110.0	82.0	111.5	Citroen XM Turbo SD Estate: 1093
				Mercedes-Benz 300SD: 2857
				Peugeot 605 SR TD: 3465
10	109.0	81.3	110.5	Mercedes-Benz 300D: 2911
11	105.0	78.3	106.5	Cadillac Seville Diesel: 712
				Oldsmobile Cutlass Diesel: 3300
12	103.0	76.8	104.4	Volvo 760 GLE: 4946
13	102.0	76.1	103.4	Toyota Landcruiser: 4450
14	100.0	74.6	101.4	Vauxhall Frontera 2.3 TD Estate: 4734
15	92.0	68.6	93.3	Ford Granada 2.5 GL Diesel: 1951
				Peugeot 405 GTD Turbo: 3454
16	90.0	67.1	91.2	Citroen BX DTR Turbo: 1080
				Rover SD Turbo: 4023
17	87.0	64.9	88.2	Audi 100 Turbo Diesel: 310
				Daihatsu Fourtrak Estate DT EL: 1125
18	85.0	63.4	86.2	Land Rover Ninety County Turbo Diesel: 2560
19	84.0	62.6	85.2	Mitsubishi Shogun Turbo Diesel 5-door: 3094
				Toyota Landcruiser II TD: 4458
20	82.0	61.1	83.1	Vauxhall Cavalier 1.7 GL TD: 4733
21	81.0	60.4	82.1	Rover Montego 2.0 DSL Turbo: 4034
22	80.0	59.7	81.1	Mercedes-Benz 300D: 2819
				Mercedes-Benz 300GD: 2867
				Peugeot 505 S Turbodiesel: 3426
				Peugeot 604 D Turbo: 3424
				Volkswagen Passat CL TD Estate: 4880
23	78.0	58.2	79.1	Carbodies Fairway 2.7 Silver: 721
				Peugeot 205 D Turbo: 3464
				Volvo Diesel: 4939
24	77.0	57.4	78.1	Mercedes-Benz 300CD: 2856
				Mercedes-Benz 300D: 2848
				Mercedes-Benz 300TD: 2861
25	75.0	55.9	76.0	Citroen CX 2500 Diesel Super: 1056
26	74.0	55.2	75.0	Isuzu Trooper 3-door TD: 2257
27	73.0	54.4	74.0	Vauxhall Carlton L 2.3D: 4713
28	71.0	52.9	72.0	Peugeot 504 Diesel Automatique: 3416
				Peugeot 505 SD: 3423
29	70.0	52.2	71.0	Audi 80 Turbo Diesel: 291
				Peugeot 405 GRD: 3447
				Volkswagen Jetta Turbo Diesel: 4868
				Volkswagen Passat CL Turbo Diesel Estate: 4845

Total: 50

Diesel engines. Highest torque. Limit set at 100lbft.

	lbft	Nm	
1	220.0	298.1	Cadillac Seville Diesel: 711
2	205.0	277.8	Cadillac Seville Diesel: 712
			Oldsmobile Cutlass Diesel: 3300
3	197.8	268.0	Rover 825 TD: 4047
4	195.6	265.0	Land Rover Discovery TDi: 2563
5	195.0	264.2	Mercedes-Benz 300TD: 2893
6	188.0	254.7	Citroen CX25 DTR Turbo 2: 1078
7	183.0	248.0	Citroen XM Turbo SD Estate: 1093
			Peugeot 605 SR TD: 3465
			Range Rover Vogue Turbo D: 3776
8	178.0	241.2	Toyota Landcruiser: 4450
9	170.0	230.4	Mercedes-Benz 300TD: 2868
10	168.0	227.6	Mercedes-Benz 300SD: 2857
11	158.7	215.0	Vauxhall Frontera 2.3 TD Estate: 4734
12	155.0	210.0	BMW 524 TD: 581
			Daihatsu Fourtrak Estate DT EL: 1125
13	150.6	204.0	Ford Granada 2.5 GL Diesel: 1951
14	150.0	203.3	Land Rover Ninety County Turbo Diesel: 2560
15	148.0	200.5	Mitsubishi Shogun Turbo Diesel 5-door: 3094
16	143.9	195.0	Toyota Landcruiser VX: 4478
17	142.0	192.4	Rover SD Turbo: 4023
18	141.0	191.0	Mercedes-Benz G-Wagen 300 GD LWB: 2921
19	139.0	188.3	Volvo 760 GLE: 4946
20	138.0	187.0	Toyota Landcruiser II TD: 4458

21	136.5	185.0	Mercedes-Benz 300D: 2911
22	136.0	184.3	Peugeot 505 S Turbodiesel: 3426
			Peugeot 604 D Turbo: 3424
23	134.3	182.0	Citroen BX DTR Turbo: 1080
24	132.8	180.0	Peugeot 405 GTD Turbo: 3454
25	127.7	173.0	Carbodies Fairway 2.7 Silver: 721
26	126.6	171.5	Mercedes-Benz 300D: 2819
27	126.5	171.4	Mercedes-Benz 300GD: 2867
28	126.0	170.7	Audi 100 Turbo Diesel: 310
29	124.0	168.0	Vauxhall Cavalier 1.7 GL TD: 4733
30	116.6	158.0	Rover Montego 2.0 DSL Turbo: 4034
31	115.9	157.0	Peugeot 205 D Turbo: 3464
32	115.0	155.8	Mercedes-Benz 300CD: 2856
			Mercedes-Benz 300D: 2848
			Mercedes-Benz 300TD: 2861
33	114.4	155.0	Volkswagen Passat CL TD Estate: 4880
34	114.2	154.7	Isuzu Trooper 3-door TD: 2257
35	111.0	150.4	Citroen CX 2500 Diesel Super: 1056
36	109.0	147.7	Ford Granada 2.5 Diesel Estate: 1887
37	102.0	138.2	Volvo Diesel: 4939
38	101.8	138.0	Vauxhall Carlton L 2.3D: 4713

Total: 45

Diesel engines. Highest rpm at peak power. Limit set at 4300rpm.

	rpm	
1	5000	Citroen AX14 DTR: 1081
		Isuzu I-Mark LS: 2252
		Volkswagen Dasher Diesel: 4818
		Volkswagen Golf LD: 4814
		Volkswagen Rabbit Diesel: 4829
		Volkswagen Rabbit Diesel: 4809
2	4800	Audi 5000 S Diesel: 284
		BMW 524 TD: 581
		Daihatsu Charade CX Diesel Turbo: 1123
		Ford Fiesta 1.6L Diesel: 1893
		Volvo 760 GLE: 4946
		Volvo Diesel: 4939
3	4600	Citroen BX19 RD Diesel: 1061
		Citroen BX19 RD Estate: 1071
		Citroen Visa 17RD: 1069
		Daihatsu Charade Diesel: 1120
		Fiat Regata DS: 1594
		Mercedes-Benz 300D: 2911
		Mercedes-Benz 300TD: 2893
		Mercedes-Benz G-Wagen 300 GD LWB: 2921
		Peugeot 305 GRD Estate: 3435
		Peugeot 405 GRD: 3447
		Rover 218 SD: 4045
		Talbot Horizon 1.9LD: 4348
		Vauxhall Astra 1.7 DL: 4716
		Vauxhall Cavalier LD: 4693
		Vauxhall Nova 1.5TD Merit: 4727
4	4500	Audi 100 Turbo Diesel: 310
		Audi 80 Turbo Diesel: 291
		Citroen CX 2200 Diesel: 1051
		Ford Granada 2.1D: 1859
		Peugeot 404 Diesel: 3392
		Peugeot 504 Diesel: 3409
		Peugeot 504 Diesel Automatique: 3416
		Peugeot 504 L Diesel: 3410
		Peugeot 505 SD: 3423
		Rover Montego 2.0 DSL Turbo: 4034
		Volkswagen Jetta Turbo Diesel: 4868
		Volkswagen Passat CL TD Estate: 4880
		Volkswagen Passat CL Turbo Diesel Estate: 4845
5	4400	Opel Rekord 2100D: 3342
		Seat Toledo 1.9 CL Diesel: 4114
		Vauxhall Carlton L 2.3D: 4713
		Vauxhall Cavalier 1.7 GL TD: 4733
6	4350	Mercedes-Benz 300TD: 2868
7	4300	Carbodies Fairway 2.7 Silver: 721
		Citroen BX DTR Turbo: 1080
		Citroen XM Turbo SD Estate: 1093
		Peugeot 205 D Turbo: 3464
		Peugeot 405 GTD Turbo: 3454
		Peugeot 605 SR TD: 3465

Total: 51

Diesel engines. Highest power-to-weight ratio. Limit set at 55bhp/ton.

	bhp/ ton	bhp/ tonne	
1	90.3	88.8	Citroen CX25 DTR Turbo 2: 1078
2	86.2	84.8	Mercedes-Benz 300TD: 2893
3	85.9	84.5	Citroen BX DTR Turbo: 1080
4	83.5	82.1	Peugeot 205 D Turbo: 3464
5	83.1	81.7	Vauxhall Nova 1.5TD Merit: 4727
6	82.7	81.3	Peugeot 405 GTD Turbo: 3454
7	82.5	81.1	Rover 825 TD: 4047
8	78.7	77.4	BMW 524 TD: 581
9	74.9	73.6	Rover Montego 2.0 DSL Turbo: 4034
10	74.8	73.6	Peugeot 605 SR TD: 3465
11	74.3	73.1	Toyota Landcruiser VX: 4478
12	74.1	72.9	Mercedes-Benz 300D: 2911
13	73.8	72.6	Citroen AX14 DTR: 1081
14	73.7	72.5	Volvo 760 GLE: 4946
15	72.3	71.0	Audi 80 Turbo Diesel: 291
16	71.1	69.9	Volkswagen Jetta Turbo Diesel: 4868
17	71.0	69.8	Vauxhall Cavalier 1.7 GL TD: 4733
18	70.6	69.5	Mercedes-Benz 300TD: 2868
19	70.5	69.3	Audi 100 Turbo Diesel: 310
20	67.7	66.6	Citroen Visa 17RD: 1069
21	67.3	66.2	Ford Granada 2.5 GL Diesel: 1951
22	65.6	64.5	Volkswagen Passat CL Turbo Diesel Estate: 4845
23	65.4	64.3	Seat Toledo 1.9 CL Diesel: 4114
24	65.3	64.3	Volkswagen Passat CL TD Estate: 4880
25	65.1	64.1	Citroen XM Turbo SD Estate: 1093
26	65.0	63.9	Talbot Horizon 1.9LD: 4348
27	64.4	63.3	Citroen BX19 RD Diesel: 1061
28	63.9	62.8	Fiat Regata DS: 1594
29	63.4	62.4	Mercedes-Benz 300SD: 2857
30	63.3	62.2	Peugeot 405 GRD: 3447
31	63.1	62.0	Ford Fiesta 1.6L Diesel: 1893
32	62.5	61.4	Oldsmobile Cutlass Diesel: 3300
33	62.2	61.2	Rover SD Turbo: 4023
34	62.1	61.0	Citroen BX19 RD Estate: 1071
35	60.7	59.7	Cadillac Seville Diesel: 711
36	60.6	59.6	Peugeot 305 GRD Estate: 3435
37	58.4	57.4	Volkswagen Golf LD: 4814
38	58.3	57.3	Vauxhall Astra 1.7 DL: 4716
39	58.1	57.2	Daihatsu Charade CX Diesel Turbo: 1123
40	57.7	56.7	Vauxhall Carlton L 2.3D: 4713
41	56.8	55.8	Citroen CX 2500 Diesel Super: 1056
42	56.5	55.6	Range Rover Vogue Turbo D: 3776
43	56.1	55.2	Land Rover Discovery TDi: 2563
44	55.9	55.0	Rover 218 SD: 4045
45	55.5	54.6	Volvo Diesel: 4939
46	55.3	54.4	Peugeot 505 S Turbodiesel: 3426
47	55.3	54.3	Cadillac Seville Diesel: 712

Total: 47

Diesel engines. Highest specific output. Limit set at 30bhp/litre.

	bhp/L	kW/L	PS/L	
1	52.7	39.3	53.4	Citroen XM Turbo SD Estate: 1093
				Peugeot 605 SR TD: 3465
2	52.0	38.8	52.7	Peugeot 405 GTD Turbo: 3454
3	50.9	37.9	51.6	Citroen BX DTR Turbo: 1080
4	50.4	37.6	51.1	Volkswagen Passat CL TD Estate: 4880
5	48.6	36.3	49.3	Vauxhall Cavalier 1.7 GL TD: 4733
6	48.5	36.2	49.2	Citroen CX25 DTR Turbo 2: 1078
7	47.7	35.6	48.4	Mercedes-Benz 300TD: 2893
8	47.3	35.3	48.0	Daihatsu Charade CX Diesel Turbo: 1123
9	47.2	35.2	47.9	Rover 825 TD: 4047
10	46.8	34.9	47.5	Range Rover Vogue Turbo D: 3776
11	46.7	34.8	47.3	BMW 524 TD: 581
12	45.0	33.6	45.6	Vauxhall Nova 1.5TD Merit: 4727
13	44.5	33.2	45.1	Land Rover Discovery TDi: 2563
14	44.2	33.0	44.9	Vauxhall Frontera 2.3 TD Estate: 4734
15	44.1	32.9	44.7	Peugeot 205 D Turbo: 3464
16	44.1	32.9	44.7	Audi 80 Turbo Diesel: 291
				Volkswagen Jetta Turbo Diesel: 4868
				Volkswagen Passat CL Turbo Diesel Estate: 4845
17	43.8	32.7	44.4	Audi 100 Turbo Diesel: 310
18	43.2	32.2	43.8	Volvo 760 GLE: 4946
19	40.6	30.3	41.2	Rover Montego 2.0 DSL Turbo: 4034
20	40.0	29.8	40.6	Mercedes-Benz 300TD: 2868
21	39.6	29.5	40.2	Toyota Landcruiser VX: 4478
22	39.5	29.4	40.0	Citroen AX14 DTR: 1081
23	37.7	28.1	38.2	Mercedes-Benz G-Wagen 300 GD LWB: 2921
24	37.6	28.0	38.1	Rover SD Turbo: 4023
25	37.3	27.8	37.8	Daihatsu Charade Diesel: 1120
26	36.8	27.5	37.3	Ford Granada 2.5 GL Diesel: 1951
27	36.8	27.4	37.3	Mercedes-Benz 300D: 2911
28	36.7	27.4	37.2	Peugeot 405 GRD: 3447
29	36.7	27.4	37.2	Mercedes-Benz 300SD: 2857
30	35.9	26.7	36.4	Seat Toledo 1.9 CL Diesel: 4114
31	34.7	25.9	35.2	Peugeot 505 S Turbodiesel: 3426
				Peugeot 604 D Turbo: 3424
32	34.6	25.8	35.1	Rover 218 SD: 4045
33	34.3	25.6	34.8	Toyota Landcruiser II TD: 4458
34	34.1	25.4	34.6	Citroen BX19 RD Diesel: 1061
				Citroen BX19 RD Estate: 1071
				Peugeot 305 GRD Estate: 3435
35	34.1	25.4	34.5	Land Rover Ninety County Turbo Diesel: 2560
36	34.0	25.3	34.5	Volkswagen Golf LD: 4814
37	33.9	25.3	34.4	Citroen Visa 17RD: 1069
38	33.9	25.3	34.4	Mitsubishi Shogun Turbo Diesel 5-door: 3094
39	33.8	25.2	34.3	Vauxhall Cavalier LD: 4693
40	33.7	25.2	34.2	Audi 5000 S Diesel: 284

41	33.7	25.1	34.2	Fiat Regata DS: 1594
42	33.6	25.0	34.1	Talbot Horizon 1.9LD: 4348
43	33.6	25.0	34.0	Ford Fiesta 1.6L Diesel: 1893
44	33.5	25.0	34.0	Vauxhall Astra 1.7 DL: 4716
45	33.1	24.7	33.5	Isuzu Trooper 3-door TD: 2257
46	32.7	24.4	33.2	Volvo Diesel: 4939
47	32.6	24.3	33.1	Volkswagen Dasher Diesel: 4818
				Volkswagen Rabbit Diesel: 4829
				Volkswagen Rabbit Diesel: 4809
48	32.3	24.1	32.7	Vauxhall Carlton L 2.3D: 4713
49	31.5	23.5	31.9	Daihatsu Fourtrak Estate DT EL: 1125
50	30.8	23.0	31.2	Peugeot 504 Diesel Automatique: 3416
				Peugeot 505 SD: 3423
51	30.3	22.6	30.8	Citroen CX 2200 Diesel: 1051
52	30.2	22.5	30.6	Mercedes-Benz 190D: 2813
53	30.0	22.4	30.4	Citroen CX 2500 Diesel Super: 1056

Total: 62

Diesel engines. Highest piston speed. Limit set at 40ft/sec.

	ft/sec	m/sec	
1	46.0	14.0	Seat Toledo 1.9 CL Diesel: 4114
2	45.3	13.8	Audi 5000 S Diesel: 284
			Volvo 760 GLE: 4946
			Volvo Diesel: 4939
3	45.2	13.8	Fiat Regata DS: 1594
4	44.9	13.7	Isuzu I-Mark LS: 2252
5	44.2	13.5	Citroen BX19 RD Diesel: 1061
			Citroen BX19 RD Estate: 1071
			Citroen Visa 17RD: 1069
			Peugeot 305 GRD Estate: 3435
			Peugeot 405 GRD: 3447
			Rover 218 SD: 4045
			Talbot Horizon 1.9LD: 4348
6	44.0	13.4	Mercedes-Benz 300TD: 2868
7	43.8	13.3	Rover Montego 2.0 DSL Turbo: 4034
8	43.8	13.3	Volkswagen Dasher Diesel: 4818
			Volkswagen Rabbit Diesel: 4829
			Volkswagen Rabbit Diesel: 4809
9	43.6	13.3	Mitsubishi Shogun Turbo Diesel 5-door: 3094
10	43.2	13.2	Carbodies Fairway 2.7 Silver: 721
			Citroen XM Turbo SD Estate: 1093
			Peugeot 605 SR TD: 3465
11	43.2	13.2	Ford Granada 2.5 Diesel Estate: 1887
			Rover 825 TD: 4047
12	42.7	13.0	Citroen CX 2500 Diesel Super: 1056
13	42.5	13.0	Audi 100 Turbo Diesel: 310
			Audi 80 Turbo Diesel: 291
			BMW 524 TD: 581
			Volkswagen Jetta Turbo Diesel: 4868
			Volkswagen Passat CL TD Estate: 4880
			Volkswagen Passat CL Turbo Diesel Estate: 4845
14	42.5	12.9	Mercedes-Benz 220D: 2833
			Mercedes-Benz 300SD: 2857
15	42.4	12.9	Land Rover Discovery TDi: 2563
			Land Rover Ninety County Turbo Diesel: 2560
16	42.3	12.9	Mercedes-Benz 300D: 2911
			Mercedes-Benz 300TD: 2893
			Mercedes-Benz G-Wagen 300 GD LWB: 2921
17	42.1	12.8	Rover SD Turbo: 4023
18	42.1	12.8	Citroen AX14 DTR: 1081
			Citroen CX 2200 Diesel: 1051
19	42.0	12.8	Ford Fiesta 1.6L Diesel: 1893
20	41.8	12.7	Volkswagen Golf LD: 4814
21	41.3	12.6	Citroen BX DTR Turbo: 1080
			Peugeot 205 D Turbo: 3464
			Peugeot 405 GTD Turbo: 3454
			Vauxhall Cavalier 1.7 GL TD: 4733
22	41.3	12.6	Range Rover Vogue Turbo D: 3776
23	41.3	12.6	Vauxhall Nova 1.5TD Merit: 4727
24	40.9	12.5	Opel Rekord 2100D: 3342
			Vauxhall Carlton L 2.3D: 4713
25	40.9	12.4	Ford Granada 2.1D: 1859
			Ford Granada 2.5 GL Diesel: 1951
			Peugeot 504 Diesel: 3409
26	40.7	12.4	Peugeot 504 Diesel Automatique: 3416
			Peugeot 505 SD: 3423
27	40.4	12.3	Mercedes-Benz 300D: 2848
28	40.4	12.3	Mercedes-Benz 300CD: 2856
			Mercedes-Benz 300D: 2819
			Mercedes-Benz 300GD: 2867
			Mercedes-Benz 300TD: 2861
29	40.2	12.3	Isuzu Trooper 3-door TD: 2257
			Toyota Landcruiser II TD: 4458

Total: 63

Up to 500cc. Maximum speed. No limit set. All cars with figures included.

	mph	kmh	
1	98.0	157.7	NSU Wankel Spider: 3262
2	96.0	154.5	NSU Spider: 3261
3	83.0	133.5	Berkeley Sports 4: 486
4	74.0	119.1	Honda N360: 2089
5	68.0	109.4	Messerschmitt (FMR) Tg 500: 2966
6	66.6	107.2	Fiat 500 Nuova: 1483
7	65.0	104.6	Berkeley Sports: 484
8	61.0	98.1	Fiat 500: 1482
			Fiat 500D: 1498
			Fiat 500F: 1504
			Goggomobil TS400: 2004
9	60.0	96.5	Fiat 500 Giardiniera: 1492
10	58.0	93.3	Berkeley Sports: 485
11	56.0	90.1	Frisky Coupe: 1993
			Subaru 360: 4243
12	54.0	86.9	BMW Isetta Motocoupe: 499
			Fiat 500: 1477
13	50.5	81.3	Citroen Bijou: 1028
14	49.7	80.0	BMW Isetta 300: 502
15	49.2	79.2	Citroen 2CV: 1022
16	48.0	77.2	Suzuki Brute: 4320
17	41.0	66.0	Citroen 2CV Cabriolet: 1019

Total: 22

Up to 500cc. Acceleration to 60mph/96.5kmh. No limit set. All cars with figures included.

	sec	
1	14.2	NSU Spider: 3261
2	16.7	NSU Wankel Spider: 3262
3	21.8	Berkeley Sports 4: 486
4	27.8	Messerschmitt (FMR) Tg 500: 2966
5	29.3	Honda N360: 2089
6	37.2	Fiat 500 Nuova: 1483
7	38.3	Berkeley Sports: 484

Total: 7

Up to 500cc. Highest power. No limit set. All cars with figures included.

	bhp	kW	PS	
1	58.0	43.2	58.8	NSU Spider: 3261
2	50.0	37.3	50.7	NSU Wankel Spider: 3262
3	32.0	23.9	32.4	Suzuki Brute: 4320
4	30.0	22.4	30.4	Berkeley Sports 4: 486
5	27.0	20.1	27.4	Honda N360: 2089
6	25.0	18.6	25.3	Subaru 360: 4243
				Subaru Hapi Van 360: 4245
7	24.0	17.9	24.3	Messerschmitt (FMR) Tg 500: 2966
8	21.5	16.0	21.8	Fiat 500 Nuova: 1483
9	20.0	14.9	20.3	Goggomobil TS400: 2004
10	18.2	13.6	18.4	Berkeley Sports: 485
				Berkeley Sports: 484
11	18.0	13.4	18.2	Fiat 500F: 1504
12	17.5	13.0	17.7	Fiat 500 Giardiniera: 1492
				Fiat 500D: 1498
13	16.5	12.3	16.7	Fiat 500: 1482
14	16.0	11.9	16.2	Frisky Coupe: 1993
15	13.0	9.7	13.2	BMW Isetta 300: 502
				Fiat 500: 1477
16	12.0	8.9	12.2	BMW Isetta Motocoupe: 499
				Citroen 2CV: 1022
				Citroen Bijou: 1028
17	9.0	6.7	9.1	Citroen 2CV Cabriolet: 1019

Total: 23

Up to 500cc. Highest torque. No limit set. All cars with figures included.

	lbft	Nm	
1	52.0	70.5	NSU Spider: 3261
			NSU Wankel Spider: 3262
2	35.4	48.0	Berkeley Sports 4: 486
3	27.0	36.6	Suzuki Brute: 4320
4	25.0	33.9	BMW Isetta Motocoupe: 499
			Subaru 360: 4243
			Subaru Hapi Van 360: 4245
5	24.6	33.3	Messerschmitt (FMR) Tg 500: 2966
6	24.0	32.5	Honda N360: 2089
7	23.9	32.4	Goggomobil TS400: 2004
8	22.4	30.4	Fiat 500D: 1498
			Fiat 500F: 1504
9	22.0	29.8	Fiat 500 Nuova: 1483
10	21.7	29.4	Fiat 500 Giardiniera: 1492
11	21.6	29.3	Berkeley Sports: 484
			Berkeley Sports: 485
12	20.3	27.5	Fiat 500: 1482
13	20.2	27.4	Fiat 500: 1477
14	18.0	24.4	Frisky Coupe: 1993

15	17.4	23.6	Citroen Bijou: 1028
16	16.6	22.5	Citroen 2CV Cabriolet: 1019
17	14.0	19.0	BMW Isetta 300: 502

Total: 22

Up to 500cc. Highest rpm at peak power. No limit set. All cars with figures included.

	rpm	
1	8000	Honda N360: 2089
2	6000	Suzuki Brute: 4320
3	5800	BMW Isetta 300: 502
		BMW Isetta Motocoupe: 499
4	5500	Frisky Coupe: 1993
		Subaru 360: 4243
		Subaru Hapi Van 360: 4245
5	5250	Berkeley Sports: 484
		Berkeley Sports: 485
6	5000	Berkeley Sports 4: 486
		Goggomobil TS400: 2004
		Messerschmitt (FMR) Tg 500: 2966
		NSU Spider: 3261
		NSU Wankel Spider: 3262
7	4600	Fiat 500 Giardiniera: 1492
		Fiat 500F: 1504
8	4500	Fiat 500 Nuova: 1483
9	4400	Fiat 500D: 1498
10	4000	Citroen Bijou: 1028
		Fiat 500: 1477
		Fiat 500: 1482
11	3500	Citroen 2CV: 1022
		Citroen 2CV Cabriolet: 1019

Total: 23

Up to 500cc. Highest power-to-weight ratio. No limits set. All cars with figures included.

	bhp/ ton	bhp/ tonne	
1	83.8	82.4	NSU Spider: 3261
2	79.3	78.0	Berkeley Sports 4: 486
3	72.7	71.5	NSU Wankel Spider: 3262
4	63.5	62.4	Messerschmitt (FMR) Tg 500: 2966
5	58.2	57.3	Berkeley Sports: 484
6	57.4	56.5	Berkeley Sports: 485
7	57.1	56.2	Subaru 360: 4243
8	54.0	53.1	Honda N360: 2089
9	53.1	52.2	Suzuki Brute: 4320
10	47.4	46.6	Frisky Coupe: 1993
11	46.7	45.9	Subaru Hapi Van 360: 4245
12	45.4	44.7	Fiat 500 Nuova: 1483
13	44.8	44.0	Goggomobil TS400: 2004
14	35.7	35.1	Fiat 500F: 1504
15	35.4	34.8	Fiat 500D: 1498
16	34.3	33.7	BMW Isetta Motocoupe: 499
17	33.9	33.3	BMW Isetta 300: 502
18	33.2	32.6	Fiat 500: 1482
19	31.5	30.9	Fiat 500 Giardiniera: 1492
20	28.1	27.6	Fiat 500: 1477
21	24.0	23.6	Citroen 2CV: 1022
22	20.2	19.9	Citroen Bijou: 1028
23	18.3	18.0	Citroen 2CV Cabriolet: 1019

Total: 23

Up to 500cc. Highest specific output. No limit set. All cars with figures included.

	bhp/L	kW/L	PS/L	
1	116.0	86.5	117.6	NSU Spider: 3261
2	100.0	74.6	101.4	NSU Wankel Spider: 3262
3	88.9	66.3	90.1	Suzuki Brute: 4320
4	76.3	56.9	77.3	Honda N360: 2089
5	70.2	52.4	71.2	Subaru 360: 4243
				Subaru Hapi Van 360: 4245
6	61.0	45.5	61.8	Berkeley Sports 4: 486
7	55.5	41.4	56.3	Berkeley Sports: 484
				Berkeley Sports: 485
8	51.0	38.0	51.7	Goggomobil TS400: 2004
9	49.4	36.8	50.1	Frisky Coupe: 1993
10	49.0	36.5	49.7	BMW Isetta Motocoupe: 499
				Messerschmitt (FMR) Tg 500: 2966
11	44.9	33.5	45.5	Fiat 500 Nuova: 1483
12	43.8	32.6	44.4	BMW Isetta 300: 502
13	36.1	26.9	36.6	Fiat 500F: 1504
14	35.1	26.1	35.5	Fiat 500 Giardiniera: 1492
				Fiat 500D: 1498
15	34.4	25.7	34.9	Fiat 500: 1482
16	28.2	21.1	28.6	Citroen 2CV: 1022
				Citroen Bijou: 1028
17	27.1	20.2	27.5	Fiat 500: 1477
18	24.0	17.9	24.3	Citroen 2CV Cabriolet: 1019

Total: 23

Up to 500cc. Highest piston speed. No limit set. All cars with figures included.

	ft/sec	m/sec	
1	50.7	15.4	Honda N360: 2089
2	46.2	14.1	BMW Isetta 300: 502
3	43.2	13.1	BMW Isetta Motocoupe: 499
4	40.3	12.3	Suzuki Brute: 4320
5	38.3	11.7	Messerschmitt (FMR) Tg 500: 2966
6	38.2	11.6	Frisky Coupe: 1993
7	36.1	11.0	Subaru 360: 4243
8	36.1	11.0	Subaru Hapi Van 360: 4245
9	35.6	10.8	Berkeley Sports: 484
			Berkeley Sports: 485
10	35.3	10.7	Fiat 500 Giardiniera: 1492
			Fiat 500F: 1504
11	34.5	10.5	Fiat 500 Nuova: 1483
12	33.9	10.3	Berkeley Sports 4: 486
13	33.7	10.3	Fiat 500D: 1498
14	30.7	9.3	Fiat 500: 1482
			Fiat 500: 1477
			Goggomobil TS400: 2004
15	27.1	8.3	Citroen Bijou: 1028
16	23.7	7.2	Citroen 2CV: 1022
			Citroen 2CV Cabriolet: 1019

Total: 21

501 - 1000cc. Maximum speed. Limit set at 85mph.

	mph	kmh	
1	118.0	189.9	Mazda 110S Coupe: 2685
2	116.0	186.6	Daihatsu Charade GT ti: 1124
3	112.0	180.2	NSU Ro80: 3266
4	108.0	173.8	NSU Ro80: 3264
5	102.0	164.1	Clan Crusader: 1095
			Fiat Abarth Twin Cam: 1488
6	100.0	160.9	Fiat Abarth 850: 1487
			Moretti 750 Grand Sport Berlinetta Coupe: 3119
7	99.0	159.3	Ogle Austin Mini Cooper GT: 3268
8	96.5	155.3	Abarth Zagato 750 GT: 1
9	96.0	154.5	Daihatsu Charade Turbo: 1127
			Honda S800: 2088
10	95.0	152.9	Fiat 850 Coupe: 1518
11	94.0	151.2	Lancia Y10 Fire: 2545
			Mazda Rotary: 2689
12	92.0	148.0	Panhard 24CT Sports Coupe: 3371
13	91.0	146.4	Ford Fiesta: 1845
			Gilbern GT: 1995
			Toyota Starlet GL: 4475
14	90.0	144.8	Austin-Healey Sprite Supercharged: 439
			Fiat 850 Coupe: 1505
			Honda S600: 2087
			Mini Cooper: 3050
			Sunbeam Imp Sport: 4305
15	89.0	143.2	Fiat Panda: 1574
			Fiat Panda 1000 S: 1592
			Nissan Micra SGL 5-DR: 3225
			Sunbeam Stiletto: 4306
16	88.0	141.6	Daihatsu Charade CX: 1119
			Daihatsu Domino: 1122
			Datsun Micra GL: 1232
			Deutsch-Bonnet Coupe: 1256
			Saab Gran Turismo: 4055
			Saab Sport: 4066
			Toyota 1000: 4393
			Toyota Starlet 1.0GL: 4435
17	87.8	141.3	MG Mk II Montlhery Supercharged: 2970
18	87.4	140.6	Austin-Healey Sebring Sprite: 438
			Mini Cooper: 3046
19	87.1	140.1	Fiat Abarth 750GT Zagato: 1479
			Fiat Abarth Zagato: 1480
20	87.0	140.0	Austin Mini Metro: 419
			Chevrolet Sprint: 895
			Datsun 100A: 1172
			Renault 5 TL: 3845
			Saab 850GT: 4059
			Wartburg Knight: 4971
21	86.0	138.4	Austin-Healey Sprite Hardtop: 437
			MG Midget: 3002
			Peugeot 104: 3407
22	85.5	137.6	Austin-Healey Sprite Mk II: 441
23	85.0	136.8	Daihatsu Charade XTE: 1116
			Datsun Cherry F11: 1204
			Fiat 127: 1528
			Lotus 7: 2593
			Morgan SS: 3122
			Peugeot 104: 3414
			Renault Caravelle S: 3815

Total: 58

501 - 1000cc. Acceleration to 60mph/ 96.5kmh. Limit set at 20 seconds.

	sec	
1	7.9	Daihatsu Charade GT ti: 1124
2	10.2	Mazda 110S Coupe: 2685
3	11.2	Fiat Abarth Twin Cam: 1488
4	11.3	Daihatsu Charade Turbo: 1127
5	12.5	Clan Crusader: 1095
6	13.1	NSU Ro80: 3266
7	13.4	Chevrolet Sprint: 904
		Honda S800: 2088
8	13.5	Mazda Rotary: 2689
9	13.9	NSU Ro80: 3264
10	14.0	Morgan SS: 3122
11	14.2	Austin-Healey Sebring Sprite: 438
12	14.3	Lotus 7: 2593
13	14.5	Chevrolet Sprint: 895
		Nissan Micra SGL 5-DR: 3225
14	14.6	Chevrolet Sprint: 924
15	14.7	Daihatsu Domino: 1122
		Toyota Starlet GL: 4475
16	14.8	Toyota Starlet 1.0GL: 4435
17	15.0	Datsun Micra GL: 1232
18	15.2	Daihatsu Charade CLX: 1126
		Saab Gran Turismo: 4055
19	15.3	Austin-Healey Sprite Supercharged: 439
20	15.5	Moretti 750 Grand Sport Berlinetta Coupe: 3119
21	15.6	Daihatsu Charade CX: 1119
		Fiat 850 Coupe: 1518
22	15.8	Abarth Zagato 750 GT: 1
		Suzuki Alto FX: 4322
23	16.0	Fiat Panda 1000 S: 1592
24	16.1	Daihatsu Charade XTE: 1116
25	16.2	Fiat Panda: 1574
		Ogle Austin Mini Cooper GT: 3268
26	16.3	Sunbeam Imp Sport: 4305
27	16.7	Lancia Y10 Fire: 2545
28	16.8	Datsun 100A: 1172
		Mini Cooper: 3050
29	16.9	Toyota 1000: 4393
30	17.2	Berkeley B95: 487
31	17.3	Fiat Abarth 750GT Zagato: 1479
		Fiat Abarth Zagato: 1480
32	17.4	Bond 875: 628
		Fiat 127: 1528
		Gilbern GT: 1995
33	17.6	Fiat Abarth 850: 1487
		Sunbeam Stiletto: 4306
34	17.8	Honda S600: 2087
35	17.9	Fiat 850 Racer: 1524
36	18.0	Mini Cooper: 3046
		Volkswagen Polo: 4800
37	18.2	Fiat 850 Coupe: 1505
38	18.5	Peugeot 104: 3407
39	18.7	Mini 1000: 3057
		Wartburg Knight: 4971
40	18.9	Austin Mini Metro: 419
41	19.0	Fiat 850 Special: 1513
		Ford Fiesta 1000: 1852
		Peugeot 104: 3414
42	19.1	Saab Sport: 4066
43	19.4	Renault Caravelle S: 3815
44	19.6	Fiat 750 Abarth: 1478
		Ford Fiesta: 1845
		Ford Fiesta Popular: 1875
		Reliant Kitten: 3789
45	19.8	Austin-Healey Sprite Mk II: 441
46	20.0	Fiat 850 Spider: 1514

Total: 65

501 - 1000cc. Highest power. Limit set at 50bhp.

	bhp	kW	PS	
1	115.0	85.8	116.6	NSU Ro80: 3266
2	113.5	84.6	115.1	NSU Ro80: 3264
3	110.0	82.0	111.5	Mazda 110S Coupe: 2685
4	100.0	74.6	101.4	Mazda Rotary: 2689
5	99.0	73.8	100.4	Daihatsu Charade GT ti: 1124
6	70.0	52.2	71.0	Honda S800: 2088
7	68.0	50.7	68.9	Austin-Healey Sprite Supercharged: 439
				Gilbern GT: 1995
				Ogle Austin Mini Cooper GT: 3268
8	67.0	50.0	67.9	Daihatsu Charade Turbo: 1127
9	62.0	46.2	62.9	Datsun 1000 de Luxe: 1168
10	61.0	45.5	61.8	Fiat Abarth Twin Cam: 1488
11	60.0	44.7	60.8	Panhard 24CT Sports Coupe: 3371
12	59.0	44.0	59.8	Datsun 100A: 1172
13	58.0	43.2	58.8	Fiat 850 Racer: 1524
14	57.0	42.5	57.8	Honda S600: 2087
				Saab 850GT: 4059
15	55.0	41.0	55.8	Austin-Healey Sebring Sprite: 438
				Datsun Micra GL: 1232
				Mini Cooper: 3046
				Mini Cooper: 3050
				Nissan Micra SGL 5-DR: 3225
				Saab Sport: 4066
16	54.0	40.3	54.7	Toyota Starlet 1.0GL: 4435
				Toyota Starlet GL: 4475
17	53.0	39.5	53.7	Daihatsu Charade CLX: 1126
18	52.0	38.8	52.7	Fiat 850 Coupe: 1518
				Fiat 850 Spider: 1514
				Fiat Abarth 850: 1487
				Simca 1000GLS: 4150
				Simca 1000GLS: 4151
19	51.0	38.0	51.7	Clan Crusader: 1095
				Daihatsu Charade CX: 1119
				Deutsch-Bonnet Coupe: 1256
				Moretti 750 Grand Sport Berlinetta Coupe: 3119
				Renault Caravelle S: 3815
				Sunbeam Imp Sport: 4305
				Sunbeam Stiletto: 4306
20	50.5	37.7	51.2	Triumph Herald Coupe: 4510
21	50.0	37.3	50.7	Austin-Healey Sprite: 435
				Auto Union 1000: 449
				Daihatsu Charade XTE: 1116
				Panhard Dyna Sedan: 3367
				Panhard PL17 Tiger: 3370
				Peugeot 104: 3407
				Saab Gran Turismo: 4055
				Simca 1000 Special: 4146
				Wartburg Knight: 4971

Total: 48

501 - 1000cc. Highest torque. Limit set at 52lbft.

	lbft	Nm	
1	121.0	164.0	NSU Ro80: 3266
2	117.2	158.8	NSU Ro80: 3264
3	96.0	130.1	Mazda 110S Coupe: 2685
4	95.8	129.8	Daihatsu Charade GT ti: 1124
5	92.0	124.7	Mazda Rotary: 2689
6	78.2	106.0	Daihatsu Charade Turbo: 1127
7	69.0	93.5	Wartburg Knight: 4971
8	68.0	92.1	Saab 850GT: 4059
9	67.0	90.8	Saab Sport: 4066
			Wartburg Knight: 4970
10	65.0	88.1	Austin-Healey Sprite Supercharged: 439
11	64.8	87.8	Gilbern GT: 1995
12	63.0	85.4	Daihatsu Charade CX Diesel Turbo: 1123
13	62.0	84.0	Auto Union 1000: 450
14	61.5	83.3	Auto Union 1000: 449
			Datsun 1000 de Luxe: 1168
15	61.0	82.7	Auto Union Universal: 451
			Suzuki SC 100: 4321
16	60.0	81.3	Datsun 100A: 1172
			Saab 96: 4060
17	59.0	79.9	Austin-Healey Sebring Sprite: 438
			Fiat Panda 1000 S: 1592
			Lancia Y10 Fire: 2545
			Saab 95: 4058
			Saab 96: 4056
			Saab 96 Sedan: 4057
18	58.0	78.6	Daihatsu Charade CLX: 1126
19	57.0	77.2	Chevrolet Sprint: 904
			Chevrolet Sprint: 924
			Chevrolet Sprint: 895
			Mini Cooper: 3050
20	56.0	75.9	Datsun Micra GL: 1232
			Nissan Micra SGL 5-DR: 3225
			Saab Gran Turismo: 4055
21	55.7	75.5	Datsun Cherry F11: 1204
			DKW Junior de Luxe: 1268
22	55.6	75.3	Daihatsu Charade CX: 1119
23	55.5	75.2	Ford Anglia de Luxe Estate: 1666
24	55.4	75.0	Toyota Starlet GL: 4475
25	55.0	74.5	Renault Dauphine Ferry: 3807
			Renault R8: 3822
			Simca 1000GLS: 4151
			Simca 1000GLS: 4150
			Toyota Starlet 1.0GL: 4435
26	54.5	73.8	Mini Cooper: 3046
			Ogle Austin Mini Cooper GT: 3268
27	54.2	73.4	DKW 3-6: 1263
			DKW Karavan: 1264
			Simca 1000: 4143
			Simca 1000 Special: 4146
28	54.0	73.2	Goliath 900: 2006
			Opel Kadett: 3309
			Panhard 24CT Sports Coupe: 3371
			Peugeot 104: 3407
			Renault Caravelle S: 3815
			Renault Floride Caravelle: 3821
			Skoda S100L: 4185
29	53.5	72.5	Daihatsu Charade XTE: 1116
30	53.3	72.2	Renault R8: 3818
31	53.0	71.8	Austin-Healey Sprite Mk II: 441
			MG Midget: 3002

			NSU Prinz 1000L: 3260
32	52.8	71.5	Ford Prefect: 1633
33	52.5	71.1	Ford Anglia: 1649
			Ford Anglia: 1654
34	52.1	70.6	Saab 93: 4053
35	52.0	70.5	Austin-Healey Sprite: 435
			Austin-Healey Sprite Hardtop: 437
			Clan Crusader: 1095
			Hillman Hunter Husky: 2064
			Hillman Imp Californian: 2065
			Hillman Imp de Luxe: 2056
			Hillman Super Imp: 2061
			Mini Super de Luxe Mk II: 3052
			Saab 93: 4054
			Singer Chamois: 4175
			Singer Chamois: 4181
			Sunbeam Imp: 4300
			Sunbeam Imp Sport: 4305
			Sunbeam Stiletto: 4306
			Wolseley Hornet: 4998

Total: 81

501 - 1000cc. Highest rpm at peak power. Limit set at 5700rpm.

	rpm	
1	8500	Honda S600: 2087
2	8000	Honda S800: 2088
3	7000	Fiat Abarth Twin Cam: 1488
		Mazda 110S Coupe: 2685
		Mazda Rotary: 2689
4	6500	Daihatsu Charade GT ti: 1124
		Fiat 850 Coupe: 1518
5	6400	Fiat 850 Racer: 1524
6	6250	Peugeot 104: 3407
7	6200	Fiat 127: 1528
		Fiat 850 Coupe: 1505
		Fiat 850 Special: 1513
		Fiat 850 Spider: 1514
8	6100	Clan Crusader: 1095
		Sunbeam Imp Sport: 4305
		Sunbeam Stiletto: 4306
9	6000	Abarth Zagato 750 GT: 1
		Daihatsu Domino: 1117
		Datsun 1000 de Luxe: 1168
		Datsun 100A: 1172
		Datsun Micra GL: 1232
		Fiat Abarth 850: 1487
		Ford Fiesta: 1845
		Honda 600: 2090
		Honda 600 Coupe: 2091
		Mini Cooper: 3046
		Moretti 750 Grand Sport Berlinetta Coupe: 3119
		Nissan Micra SGL 5-DR: 3225
		Ogle Austin Mini Cooper GT: 3268
		Panhard 24CT Sports Coupe: 3371
		Peugeot 104: 3414
		Toyota Starlet 1.0GL: 4435
		Toyota Starlet GL: 4475
		Triumph Herald Coupe: 4510
10	5900	Volkswagen Polo: 4800
11	5800	Austin-Healey Sebring Sprite: 438
		BMW 700 Coupe: 504
		Fiat Abarth 750GT Zagato: 1479
		Fiat Abarth Zagato: 1480
		Mini Cooper: 3050
		NSU Prinz 34hp: 3256
		Panhard PL17 Tiger: 3370
		Simca 1000LS: 4158
		Toyota 1000: 4393
		Triumph Herald Convertible: 4509
		Yugo 45 GLS: 5003
12	5750	Citroen 2CV6: 1046
		Citroen 2CV6 Charleston: 1065
		Citroen Ami 8 Club: 1037
13	5700	Austin-Healey Sprite Supercharged: 439
		Deutsch-Bonnet Coupe: 1256
		Gilbern GT: 1995

Total: 52

501 - 1000cc. Highest power-to-weight ratio. Limit set at 70bhp/ton.

	bhp/ ton	bhp/to tonne	
1	123.1	121.0	Daihatsu Charade GT ti: 1124
2	116.7	114.8	Mazda 110S Coupe: 2685
3	111.4	109.6	Mazda Rotary: 2689
4	102.2	100.5	Austin-Healey Sprite Supercharged: 439
5	102.0	100.3	Moretti 750 Grand Sport Berlinetta Coupe: 3119
6	102.0	100.3	Fiat Abarth Twin Cam: 1488
7	101.1	99.4	Ogle Austin Mini Cooper GT: 3268
8	97.9	96.3	Berkeley B95: 487
9	97.5	95.9	Morgan SS: 3122
10	96.3	94.7	Gilbern GT: 1995
11	95.8	94.2	NSU Ro80: 3266
12	95.3	93.7	NSU Ro80: 3264
13	93.3	91.8	Lotus 7: 2593
14	92.6	91.0	Honda S800: 2088
15	91.5	89.9	Datsun 100A: 1172
16	89.4	87.9	Clan Crusader: 1095
17	88.6	87.1	Datsun 1000 de Luxe: 1168
18	88.0	86.5	Mini Cooper: 3050
19	86.6	85.2	Fiat Abarth 850: 1487
20	85.8	84.4	Mini Cooper: 3046
21	85.7	84.3	Daihatsu Charade Turbo: 1127
22	84.1	82.7	Datsun Micra GL: 1232
23	83.5	82.1	Austin-Healey Sebring Sprite: 438
24	80.5	79.1	Nissan Micra SGL 5-DR: 3225
25	80.0	78.7	Abarth Zagato 750 GT: 1
			Bond Bug: 629
26	77.8	76.6	Honda S600: 2087
27	77.7	76.4	Deutsch-Bonnet Coupe: 1256
28	77.3	76.0	Reliant Kitten: 3789
29	77.1	75.8	Fiat Abarth 750GT Zagato: 1479
			Fiat Abarth Zagato: 1480
30	76.9	75.6	Fiat 850 Racer: 1524
31	76.6	75.3	Austin-Healey Sprite: 435
32	75.4	74.2	Reliant Kitten DL Estate: 3790
33	74.7	73.4	Turner Sports: 4583
34	74.5	73.2	Toyota Starlet 1.0GL: 4435
35	73.8	72.6	Daihatsu Charade XTE: 1116
36	73.3	72.1	Panhard 24CT Sports Coupe: 3371
37	72.6	71.4	Daihatsu Domino: 1122
38	72.4	71.2	Fiat 850 Coupe: 1518
39	71.8	70.6	Suzuki SC 100: 4321
40	71.0	69.8	Fiat 850 Spider: 1514
41	70.6	69.4	Simca 1000GLS: 4151
42	70.5	69.3	Renault Dauphine Ferry: 3807
43	70.4	69.2	Toyota Starlet GL: 4475
44	70.2	69.0	Simca 1000GLS: 4150

Total: 46

501 - 1000cc. Highest specific output. Limit set at 55bhp/litre.

	bhp/L	kW/L	PS/L	
1	115.6	86.2	117.2	NSU Ro80: 3266
2	114.1	85.1	115.6	NSU Ro80: 3264
3	112.0	83.5	113.6	Mazda 110S Coupe: 2685
4	101.8	75.9	103.2	Mazda Rotary: 2689
5	99.7	74.3	101.1	Daihatsu Charade GT ti: 1124
6	94.1	70.1	95.4	Honda S600: 2087
7	88.5	66.0	89.7	Honda S800: 2088
8	81.7	60.9	82.8	Fiat Abarth Twin Cam: 1488
9	71.7	53.5	72.7	Austin-Healey Sprite Supercharged: 439
				Gilbern GT: 1995
10	70.7	52.8	71.7	Panhard 24CT Sports Coupe: 3371
11	68.2	50.9	69.1	Ogle Austin Mini Cooper GT: 3268
12	68.2	50.8	69.1	Moretti 750 Grand Sport Berlinetta Coupe: 3119
13	67.8	50.5	68.7	Saab 850GT: 4059
14	67.5	50.3	68.4	Daihatsu Charade Turbo: 1127
15	66.8	49.8	67.8	Saab Gran Turismo: 4055
16	65.4	48.8	66.3	Saab Sport: 4066
17	64.2	47.9	65.1	Fiat 850 Racer: 1524
18	63.6	47.5	64.5	Fiat 850 Spider: 1514
19	62.7	46.8	63.6	Datsun 1000 de Luxe: 1168
20	62.4	46.5	63.3	Fiat Abarth 850: 1487
21	60.2	44.9	61.0	Honda 600: 2090
22	59.9	44.7	60.8	Deutsch-Bonnet Coupe: 1256
23	59.7	44.5	60.5	Datsun 100A: 1172
24	59.0	44.0	59.8	Panhard PL17 Tiger: 3370
25	58.9	43.9	59.7	Abarth Zagato 750 GT: 1
26	58.8	43.9	59.6	Panhard Dyna Sedan: 3367
27	58.3	43.5	59.1	NSU Prinz 34hp: 3256
28	58.3	43.5	59.1	Clan Crusader: 1095
				Sunbeam Imp Sport: 4305
				Sunbeam Stiletto: 4306
29	58.0	43.3	58.8	Austin-Healey Sebring Sprite: 438
30	57.8	43.1	58.6	Berkeley B95: 487
31	57.6	42.9	58.4	Fiat 850 Coupe: 1518
32	57.6	42.9	58.4	Fiat Abarth 750GT Zagato: 1479
				Fiat Abarth Zagato: 1480
33	57.4	42.8	58.2	BMW 700 Coupe: 504
34	55.7	41.6	56.5	Fiat 850 Coupe: 1505
				Fiat 850 Special: 1513
35	55.7	41.5	56.4	Nissan Micra SGL 5-DR: 3225
36	55.6	41.4	56.3	Fiat 750 Abarth: 1478
37	55.2	41.2	56.0	Citroen Visa Club: 1057
38	55.2	41.1	55.9	Mini Cooper: 3046
39	55.1	41.1	55.9	Datsun Micra GL: 1232
				Mini Cooper: 3050
40	55.1	41.1	55.8	Simca 1000GLS: 4151
				Simca 1000GLS: 4150

Total: 47

501 - 1000cc. Highest piston speed. Limit set at 43ft/sec.

	ft/sec	m/sec	
1	61.3	18.7	Honda S800: 2088
2	60.4	18.4	Honda S600: 2087
3	54.1	16.5	Berkeley B95: 487
4	53.3	16.3	Ogle Austin Mini Cooper GT: 3268
5	53.3	16.2	Mini Cooper: 3046
6	51.8	15.8	Daihatsu Charade GT ti: 1124
7	50.0	15.2	MG Midget P Type: 2973
			MG Midget PB: 2975
8	49.2	15.0	Panhard 24CT Sports Coupe: 3371
9	49.0	14.9	Fiat Abarth Twin Cam: 1488
10	48.7	14.8	Daihatsu Domino: 1122
11	48.3	14.7	Triumph Herald Coupe: 4510
12	48.3	14.7	Austin-Healey Sebring Sprite: 438
			Fiat 850 Coupe: 1518
			Mini Cooper: 3050
13	48.2	14.7	Triumph Herald Convertible: 4509
14	47.6	14.5	Fiat 850 Racer: 1524
15	47.5	14.5	Panhard PL17 Tiger: 3370
16	47.5	14.5	Austin-Healey Sprite Supercharged: 439
			Gilbern GT: 1995
17	46.7	14.2	Deutsch-Bonnet Coupe: 1256
18	46.2	14.1	BMW 700 Coupe: 504
19	46.2	14.0	Fiat 127: 1528
20	45.8	14.0	Austin-Healey Sprite: 435
			Austin-Healey Sprite Hardtop: 437
			Austin-Healey Sprite Mk II: 441
			MG Midget: 3002
21	45.7	13.9	Triumph Herald Coupe: 4507
22	45.7	13.9	Honda 600: 2090
			Honda 600 Coupe: 2091
23	45.3	13.8	Fiat Abarth 850: 1487
24	45.0	13.7	Austin Mini Metro: 419
25	44.6	13.6	Daihatsu Charade CX: 1119
26	44.7	13.6	Daihatsu Domino: 1117
			Datsun Micra GL: 1232
			Nissan Micra SGL 5-DR: 3225
27	44.1	13.4	Citroen 2CV6: 1046
			Citroen 2CV6 Charleston: 1065
			Citroen Ami 8 Club: 1037
28	43.8	13.4	Daihatsu Charade Turbo: 1127
			Daihatsu Charade XTE: 1116
29	43.8	13.3	Mini Super de Luxe Mk II: 3052
			Wolseley Hornet: 4998
30	43.8	13.3	Renault 6: 3834
			Renault 750: 3802
			Renault Caravelle: 3812
			Renault Carvelle: 3809
			Renault Dauphine Ferry: 3807
			Renault Dauphine Gordini: 3814
			Renault Dauphine Gordini: 3811
			Renault Dauphine Gordini de Luxe: 3817
			Renault Floride: 3813
31	43.4	13.2	Panhard PL17: 3369
32	43.4	13.2	Renault Caravelle S: 3815
33	43.3	13.2	Moretti 750 Grand Sport Berlinetta Coupe: 3119
			Morris 8 Series E Tourer: 3155
			Morris Minor: 3157
			Morris Minor Tourer: 3159
			Renault 5 TL: 3845
			Renault Floride Caravelle: 3821
			Suzuki Alto FX: 4322
			Suzuki Alto FX Automatic: 4323
			Suzuki Alto GLA: 4325
34	43.2	13.1	Yugo 45 GLS: 5003
35	43.1	13.1	Fiat 850 Coupe: 1505
			Fiat 850 Special: 1513
			Fiat 850 Spider: 1514

Total: 67

1001 - 1500cc. Maximum speed. Limit set at 115mph.

	mph	kmh	
1	178.0	286.4	Mazda RX-7 Cartech: 2768
2	170.0	273.5	Mazda RX-7 Mariah Mode Six: 2770
3	158.0	254.2	Renault Le Car Turbo: 3874
4	150.0	241.4	Mazda RX-7 Turbo: 2737
			Mazda RX-7 Turbo II: 2759
5	149.0	239.7	Mazda RX-7 Turbo: 2771
6	140.0	225.3	Lancia Montecarlo Group 5 Turbo: 2531
			Mazda RX-7 Turbo: 2751
			Mazda RX-7 Turbo: 2764
7	135.0	217.2	Mazda RX-7: 2735
8	133.0	214.0	Mazda RX-7 Racer: 2715
9	130.0	209.2	Mazda RX-7 GTUs: 2758
10	128.0	206.0	Fiat Uno Turbo ie: 1605
			Mazda RX-7 GTU: 2750
			Mazda RX-7 GXL: 2736
11	126.0	202.7	Mazda RX-7: 2720
			Mazda RX-7: 2724
			Renault 5 GT Turbo: 3895
			Renault 5 Turbo 2: 3886
12	125.0	201.1	Cisiyalia Aerodinamica Mille Miglia: 1009
			Mazda RX-7 Convertible: 2749
			Toyota Paseo: 4483
13	124.0	199.5	Datsun B210 Electramotive: 1198
14	123.0	197.9	Renault 11 Turbo: 3900
15	122.0	196.3	Fiat Uno Turbo ie: 1589
			Mazda RX-7: 2714
			Mazda RX-7: 2705
			Renault 5 GT Turbo: 3901
			Renault 5 Turbo: 3873
16	121.6	195.7	Porsche 550 Spyder: 3610
17	120.0	193.1	Alfa Romeo Sprint Speciale: 53
			Alfa Romeo Sprint Zagato: 54
			Mazda RX-7 GSL: 2728
			Porsche Carrera Coupe: 3606
			Volkswagen Polo G40: 4887
18	119.0	191.5	Mazda RX-2: 2690
19	118.0	189.9	Mazda RX-7: 2723
			Mazda RX-7 GSL: 2719
			Peugeot 106 XSi: 3463
20	117.0	188.3	Fiat X1/9VS: 1591
			Mazda RX-4 Coupe: 2698
21	116.0	186.6	Honda CRX Si: 2129
			Lancia Fulvia Coupe S3: 2515
			Mazda RX-2: 2691
			Renault 9 Turbo: 3897
			Suzuki Swift 1.3 GTi: 4331
22	115.0	185.0	ASA 1000GT: 221
			Citroen AX GTi: 1092
			Honda Civic CRX: 2113
			Honda CRX Si: 2124
			Lotus Elite: 2597
			Lotus Elite: 2592
			Mazda RX-7: 2710
			Renault 5 Gordini Turbo: 3876
			Rover Metro GTi 16v: 4042

Total: 55

1001 -1500cc. Acceleration to 60mph/ 96.5kmh. Limit set at 10sec.

	sec	
1	3.6	Lancia Montecarlo Group 5 Turbo: 2531
2	4.8	Mazda RX-7 Mariah Mode Six: 2770
		Renault Le Car Turbo: 3874
3	5.3	Mazda RX-7 Racer: 2715
4	5.5	Mazda RX-7 Cartech: 2768
5	5.8	Mazda RX-7 Convertible Racing Beat: 2757
6	6.4	Mazda RX-7 Turbo: 2771
		Mazda RX-7 Turbo: 2764
7	6.6	Mazda RX-7 Turbo: 2740
		Mazda RX-7 Turbo: 2751
		Mazda RX-7 Turbo: 2737
8	6.7	Datsun B210 Electramotive: 1198
		Mazda RX-7 Turbo II: 2759
		Renault 5 Turbo 2: 3886
9	7.0	Mazda RX-7 Infini IV: 2769
		Osca 1490cc Spyder: 3353
10	7.1	Renault 5 GT Turbo: 3895
11	7.3	Renault 5 GT Turbo: 3901
12	7.4	Honda CRX Si HKS: 2147
		Renault 5 Racer: 3865
13	7.6	Lotus Super 7: 2594
14	7.7	Renault 5 Turbo: 3873
15	7.9	Mazda RX-7 GXL: 2736
		Renault 11 Turbo: 3900
16	8.0	Honda Civic Si HKS: 2146
17	8.2	Porsche 550 Spyder: 3610
18	8.3	Fiat Uno Turbo ie: 1605
19	8.4	Volkswagen Polo G40: 4887
20	8.5	Honda Civic CRX: 2113
		Mazda RX-7: 2724
		Mazda RX-7: 2735
		Mazda RX-7 GSL SE: 2725
		Mazda RX-7 GTU: 2750
21	8.6	Mazda RX-7: 2720
		Mazda RX-7 GTUs: 2758
22	8.7	Honda CRX Si: 2124
		Suzuki Swift 1.3 GTi: 4331
23	8.9	Honda CRX Si: 2129
		Isuzu I-Mark RS Turbo: 2258
24	9.0	Citroen AX GT: 1074
		Lotus Mk XI: 2590
		Renault 9 Turbo: 3897
25	9.1	Fiat Uno Turbo ie: 1589
		Mazda RX-7 Convertible: 2763
		Suzuki Swift 1.3 GTi: 4326
26	9.2	Mazda RX-7: 2705
		Mazda RX-7: 2714
27	9.3	Citroen AX GTi: 1092
28	9.4	MG Metro Turbo: 3037
29	9.5	Suzuki Swift GT: 4333

30	9.7	Honda Civic 1.4 GL 3-door: 2136
		Mazda RX-4 Coupe: 2698
		Mazda RX-7: 2723
		Mazda RX-7 Convertible: 2749
		Mazda RX-7 GS: 2711
		Mazda RX-7 GSL: 2719
		Peugeot 106 XSi: 3463
31	9.8	Renault 5 Gordini Turbo: 3876
		Rover Metro GTi 16v: 4042
32	9.9	Honda Civic GT: 2120
		Lotus Super 7: 2595
		Mazda RX-7 GSL: 2728
		Mitsubishi Colt Hatchback Turbo: 3070
33	10.0	Mazda RX-2: 2690

Total: 64

1001 - 1500cc. Highest power. Limit set at 110bhp.

	bhp	kW	PS	
1	400.0	298.3	405.5	Lancia Montecarlo Group 5 Turbo: 2531
2	380.0	283.4	385.3	Mazda RX-7 Mariah Mode Six: 2770
3	344.0	256.5	348.8	Mazda RX-7 Cartech: 2768
4	270.0	201.3	273.7	Mazda RX-7 Racer: 2715
5	260.0	193.9	263.6	Renault Le Car Turbo: 3874
6	241.0	179.7	244.3	Mazda RX-7 Convertible Racing Beat: 2757
7	215.0	160.3	218.0	Mazda RX-7 Infini IV: 2769
8	200.0	149.1	202.8	Mazda RX-7 Turbo: 2764
				Mazda RX-7 Turbo: 2771
				Mazda RX-7 Turbo II: 2759
9	185.0	137.9	187.6	Renault 5 Turbo 2: 3886
10	182.0	135.7	184.5	Honda CRX Si HKS: 2147
				Mazda RX-7 Turbo: 2737
				Mazda RX-7 Turbo: 2740
				Mazda RX-7 Turbo: 2751
11	160.0	119.3	162.2	Mazda RX-7 Convertible: 2763
				Mazda RX-7 GTUs: 2758
				Renault 5 Turbo: 3873
12	150.0	111.9	152.1	Mazda RX-7: 2735
13	148.0	110.4	150.0	Datsun B210 Electramotive: 1198
14	146.0	108.9	148.0	Mazda RX-7 Convertible: 2749
				Mazda RX-7 GTU: 2750
				Mazda RX-7 GXL: 2736
15	143.0	106.6	145.0	Renault 5 Racer: 3865
16	137.0	102.2	138.9	Porsche 550 Spyder: 3610
17	135.0	100.7	136.9	Honda Civic Si HKS: 2146
				Mazda RX-7: 2724
				Mazda RX-7 GSL SE: 2725
18	130.0	96.9	131.8	Mazda RX-2: 2690
				Mazda RX-4: 2694
19	120.0	89.5	121.7	Mazda RX-2: 2691
				Renault 5 GT Turbo: 3901
20	118.0	88.0	119.6	Fiat Uno Turbo ie: 1605
21	116.0	86.5	117.6	Alfa Romeo Sprint Speciale: 53
				Alfa Romeo Sprint Zagato: 54
22	115.0	85.8	116.6	Mazda RX-7: 2720
				Renault 11 Turbo: 3900
				Renault 5 GT Turbo: 3895
23	113.0	84.3	114.6	Volkswagen Polo G40: 4887
24	110.0	82.0	111.5	Isuzu I-Mark RS Turbo: 2258
				Mazda Cosmo: 2701
				Mazda Rotary Pickup: 2697
				Mazda RX-4: 2704
				Mazda RX-4 Coupe: 2698
				Mazda RX-4 Station Wagon: 2699
				Osca 1490cc Spyder: 3353
				Porsche Carrera Coupe: 3606
				Renault 5 Gordini Turbo: 3876
				Squire X101: 4190

Total: 49

1001 - 1500cc. Highest torque. Limit set at 100lbft.

	lbft	Nm	
1	390.0	528.5	Lancia Montecarlo Group 5 Turbo: 2531
2	330.0	447.2	Mazda RX-7 Mariah Mode Six: 2770
3	285.0	386.2	Mazda RX-7 Cartech: 2768
4	238.0	322.5	Mazda RX-7 Convertible Racing Beat: 2757
5	220.0	298.1	Renault Le Car Turbo: 3874
6	206.0	279.1	Mazda RX-7 Infini IV: 2769
7	196.0	265.6	Mazda RX-7 Turbo: 2764
			Mazda RX-7 Turbo: 2771
8	195.6	265.0	Mazda RX-7 Turbo II: 2759
9	183.0	248.0	Mazda RX-7 Turbo: 2751
			Mazda RX-7 Turbo: 2740
			Mazda RX-7 Turbo: 2737
10	166.0	224.9	Mazda RX-7 Racer: 2715
11	159.0	215.4	Renault 5 Turbo 2: 3886
12	158.0	214.1	Honda CRX Si HKS: 2147
13	155.0	210.0	Renault 5 Turbo: 3873
14	140.0	189.7	Mazda RX-7 Convertible: 2763
			Mazda RX-7 GTUs: 2758
15	138.0	187.0	Mazda RX-7 Convertible: 2749
			Mazda RX-7 GTU: 2750
			Mazda RX-7 GXL: 2736
16	134.5	182.2	Mazda RX-7: 2735
17	133.0	180.2	Mazda RX-7: 2724
			Mazda RX-7 GSL SE: 2725
18	121.0	164.0	Renault 11 Turbo: 3900
			Renault 5 GT Turbo: 3895
			Renault 5 GT Turbo: 3901
19	120.0	162.6	Isuzu I-Mark RS Turbo: 2258
			Mazda Cosmo: 2701
			Mazda RX-4: 2704
20	119.0	161.2	Renault 9 Turbo: 3897
21	118.8	161.0	Fiat Uno Turbo ie: 1605
22	117.0	158.5	Mazda Rotary Pickup: 2697
			Mazda RX-4 Coupe: 2698
			Mazda RX-4 Station Wagon: 2699
23	116.0	157.2	Mazda RX-2: 2690
24	115.0	155.8	Mazda RX-4: 2694
25	114.0	154.5	Mitsubishi Colt Hatchback Turbo: 3070
26	112.0	151.8	Mazda RX-7: 2720
			Nissan Pulsar NX Turbo: 3210
27	110.7	150.0	Volkswagen Polo G40: 4887
28	108.5	147.0	Renault 5 Gordini Turbo: 3876
29	108.0	146.3	Fiat Uno Turbo ie: 1589
			Honda Civic Si HKS: 2146
30	107.0	145.0	Mazda RX-7 GSL: 2728
31	106.0	143.6	Mazda RX-7: 2710
32	105.0	142.3	Datsun B210 Electramotive: 1198
			Mazda RX-7: 2714
			Mazda RX-7: 2723
			Mazda RX-7: 2705
			Mazda RX-7 GS: 2711
			Mazda RX-7 GSL: 2719
33	103.0	139.6	Renault 5 Racer: 3865
34	101.0	136.9	Alfa Romeo GT 1300 Junior: 75
35	100.0	135.5	Mazda RX-2: 2691

Total: 55

1001 - 1500cc. Highest rpm at peak power. Limit set at 6300rpm.

	rpm	
1	9000	Datsun B210 Electramotive: 1198
		Mazda RX-7 Racer: 2715
2	8800	Lancia Montecarlo Group 5 Turbo: 2531
3	8000	Renault 5 Racer: 3865
4	7000	Mazda RX-2: 2690
		Mazda RX-2: 2691
		Mazda RX-4: 2694
		Mazda RX-7 Convertible: 2763
		Mazda RX-7 GTUs: 2758
		Renault Le Car Turbo: 3874
5	6800	ASA 1000GT: 221
		Citroen AX GTi: 1092
		Lotus 11 Le Mans: 2589
		Lotus Mk XI: 2590
		Mazda RX-7 Mariah Mode Six: 2770
		Peugeot 106 XSi: 3463
6	6750	Renault 8 Gordini 1300: 3831
7	6600	Fiat 128 Coupe 1300: 1531
		Suzuki Swift 1.3 GTi: 4326
		Toyota Corolla 1200SL: 4369
8	6500	Alfa Romeo Sprint Speciale: 53
		Alfa Romeo Sprint Zagato: 54
		Citroen GS: 1039
		Citroen GS: 1042
		Citroen GS 1220: 1044
		Daihatsu Charade 1.3 CX: 1128
		Fiat 124 Coupe: 1515
		Fiat 124 Spider: 1522
		Fiat 124 Sport Coupe: 1509
		Fiat 124 Sport Spider: 1510
		Fiat 127 Sport: 1558
		Lotus Europa S2: 2606
		Mazda RX-7: 2735
		Mazda RX-7 Cartech: 2768
		Mazda RX-7 Convertible: 2749
		Mazda RX-7 GTU: 2750
		Mazda RX-7 GXL: 2736
		Mazda RX-7 Infini IV: 2769
		Mazda RX-7 Turbo: 2751
		Mazda RX-7 Turbo: 2740
		Mazda RX-7 Turbo: 2764
		Mazda RX-7 Turbo: 2771
		Mazda RX-7 Turbo: 2737
		Mazda RX-7 Turbo II: 2759
		Renault 8 Gordini: 3824
		Renault R8 Rally: 3826
		Suzuki Swift GT: 4333
9	6450	Suzuki Swift 1.3 GTi: 4331
10	6400	Citroen AX GT: 1074
		Citroen AX GT5: 1083

		Renault 5 Gordini: 3864
		Subaru 1300 GL Coupe: 4247
		Subaru DL: 4249
		Subaru FF-1 1300: 4246
		Toyota Paseo: 4483
11	6300	Honda Civic 1.4 GL 3-door: 2136
		Honda Shuttle 1.4 GL Automatic: 2149
		Hyundai Pony 1400 TLS: 2219
		TVR Grantura: 4584

Total: 59

1001 - 1500cc. Highest power-to-weight ratio. Limit set at 120bhp/ton.

	bhp/ ton	bhp/ tonne	
1	520.9	512.2	Lancia Montecarlo Group 5 Turbo: 2531
2	353.0	347.1	Renault Le Car Turbo: 3874
3	279.1	274.4	Mazda RX-7 Mariah Mode Six: 2770
4	271.8	267.3	Mazda RX-7 Racer: 2715
5	270.4	265.9	Mazda RX-7 Cartech: 2768
6	211.7	208.2	Mazda RX-7 Convertible Racing Beat: 2757
7	204.0	200.6	Datsun B210 Electramotive: 1198
8	203.2	199.8	Porsche 550 Spyder: 3610
9	198.6	195.3	Lotus Super 7: 2595
10	197.1	193.8	Lotus Super 7: 2594
11	192.5	189.3	Osca 1490cc Spyder: 3353
12	192.3	189.1	Honda CRX Si HKS: 2147
13	190.1	186.9	Renault 5 Racer: 3865
14	185.9	182.8	Lotus Mk XI: 2590
15	185.8	182.7	Renault 5 Turbo 2: 3886
16	184.6	181.5	Fiat Uno Turbo ie: 1589
17	182.4	179.4	Lotus 11 Le Mans: 2589
18	173.9	171.0	Mazda RX-7 Infini IV: 2769
19	164.4	161.7	Renault 5 Turbo: 3873
20	152.9	150.4	Mazda RX-7 Turbo II: 2759
21	150.1	147.6	Mazda RX-7 Turbo: 2764
22	149.8	147.3	Mazda RX-7 Turbo: 2771
23	147.3	144.8	Renault 5 GT Turbo: 3895
24	144.1	141.6	Mazda RX-7 Turbo: 2737
			Mazda RX-7 Turbo: 2740
25	143.0	140.7	Mazda RX-7 Turbo: 2751
26	142.7	140.3	Renault 5 GT Turbo: 3901
27	139.3	137.0	Honda Civic Si HKS: 2146
28	137.5	135.2	Alfa Romeo Sprint Zagato: 54
29	136.0	133.7	Volkswagen Polo G40: 4887
30	134.3	132.0	Suzuki Swift 1.3 GTi: 4326
31	131.3	129.1	Renault 5 Gordini Turbo: 3876
32	129.1	127.0	Mazda RX-7 GTUs: 2758
33	127.1	125.0	Fiat Uno Turbo ie: 1605
34	126.8	124.7	Suzuki Swift 1.3 GTi: 4331
35	125.8	123.7	Lotus Europa S2: 2606
36	125.8	123.7	Mazda RX-2: 2690
37	124.9	122.8	Mazda RX-7: 2735
38	124.7	122.6	Renault 11 Turbo: 3900
39	124.0	121.9	Citroen AX GTi: 1092
40	124.0	121.9	Renault 8 Gordini: 3824
41	123.6	121.5	Mazda RX-4: 2694
42	123.3	121.3	Mitsubishi Colt Hatchback Turbo: 3070
43	123.2	121.1	Mazda RX-2: 2691
44	123.1	121.1	Alfa Romeo Sprint Speciale: 53
45	122.7	120.7	Lotus Elite: 2597
46	122.7	120.6	Renault 8 Gordini 1300: 3831
47	122.4	120.4	Turner Turner-Climax: 4582
48	121.3	119.3	Citroen AX GT: 1074
49	121.1	119.1	Mazda RX-7 GXL: 2736
50	121.1	119.1	Porsche Carrera Coupe: 3606
51	120.7	118.7	TVR Grantura: 4584

Total: 52

1001 - 1500cc. Highest specific output. Limit set at 80bhp/litre.

	bhp/L	kW/L	PS/L	
1	290.5	216.6	294.5	Mazda RX-7 Mariah Mode Six: 2770
2	280.7	209.3	284.6	Lancia Montecarlo Group 5 Turbo: 2531
3	263.0	196.1	266.6	Mazda RX-7 Cartech: 2768
4	235.6	175.7	238.9	Mazda RX-7 Racer: 2715
5	184.2	137.4	186.8	Mazda RX-7 Convertible Racing Beat: 2757
6	181.8	135.6	184.3	Renault Le Car Turbo: 3874
7	164.4	122.6	166.6	Mazda RX-7 Infini IV: 2769
8	152.9	114.0	155.0	Mazda RX-7 Turbo: 2771
				Mazda RX-7 Turbo: 2764
				Mazda RX-7 Turbo II: 2759
9	139.1	103.8	141.1	Mazda RX-7 Turbo: 2751
				Mazda RX-7 Turbo: 2740
				Mazda RX-7 Turbo: 2737
10	132.4	98.7	134.3	Renault 5 Turbo 2: 3886
11	122.3	91.2	124.0	Mazda RX-7 Convertible: 2763
				Mazda RX-7 GTUs: 2758
12	122.3	91.2	124.0	Honda CRX Si HKS: 2147
13	114.7	85.5	116.3	Mazda RX-7: 2735
14	114.5	85.4	116.1	Renault 5 Turbo: 3873
15	114.2	85.1	115.8	Datsun B210 Electramotive: 1198
16	113.4	84.6	115.0	Mazda RX-2: 2690
				Mazda RX-4: 2694
17	111.6	83.2	113.2	Mazda RX-7 Convertible: 2749
				Mazda RX-7 GTU: 2750
				Mazda RX-7 GXL: 2736
18	108.7	81.0	110.2	Renault 5 Racer: 3865
19	104.7	78.1	106.2	Mazda RX-2: 2691
20	103.2	77.0	104.6	Mazda RX-7: 2724
				Mazda RX-7 GSL SE: 2725
21	100.3	74.8	101.7	Mazda RX-7: 2720
22	91.6	68.3	92.9	Mazda RX-7: 2710
23	91.5	68.2	92.7	Porsche 550 Spyder: 3610
24	90.7	67.6	92.0	Honda Civic Si HKS: 2146
25	89.9	67.0	91.2	Alfa Romeo Sprint Speciale: 53
				Alfa Romeo Sprint Zagato: 54
26	88.8	66.2	90.1	Volkswagen Polo G40: 4887
27	88.2	65.8	89.4	ASA 1000GT: 221
28	87.3	65.1	88.5	Mazda RX-7: 2714
				Mazda RX-7: 2723
				Mazda RX-7: 2705
				Mazda RX-7 GS: 2711
				Mazda RX-7 GSL: 2719
				Mazda RX-7 GSL: 2728
29	86.0	64.1	87.2	Fiat Uno Turbo ie: 1605
30	85.9	64.0	87.1	Renault 5 GT Turbo: 3901
31	85.7	63.9	86.9	Renault 8 Gordini: 3824
				Renault R8 Rally: 3826
32	84.1	62.7	85.3	Mazda Cosmo: 2701
				Mazda Rotary Pickup: 2697
				Mazda RX-4: 2704
				Mazda RX-4 Coupe: 2698
				Mazda RX-4 Station Wagon: 2699
33	82.3	61.4	83.5	Renault 11 Turbo: 3900
				Renault 5 GT Turbo: 3895
34	82.1	61.2	83.2	Renault 8 Gordini 1300: 3831
35	81.0	60.4	82.1	Lancia Y10 Turbo: 2540
36	80.8	60.3	82.0	Fiat Uno Turbo ie: 1589

Total: 57

1001 - 1500cc. Highest piston speed. Limit set at 53ft/sec.

	ft/sec	m/sec	
1	75.7	23.1	Datsun B210 Electramotive: 1198
2	67.3	20.5	Renault 5 Racer: 3865
3	65.0	19.8	Lancia Montecarlo Group 5 Turbo: 2531
4	61.0	18.6	Toyota Paseo: 4483
5	60.2	18.3	Riley Sprite: 3930
6	59.3	18.1	Hyundai Pony 1400 TLS: 2219
7	58.9	18.0	Renault Le Car Turbo: 3874
8	57.6	17.5	Lotus Europa S2: 2606
9	57.2	17.4	Citroen AX GTi: 1092
			Peugeot 106 XSi: 3463
10	57.2	17.4	Toyota Tercel DX: 4444
11	56.8	17.3	Honda Ballade EX: 2135
			Honda Civic S: 2121
			Honda Civic Shuttle: 2122
			Honda Civic Si HKS: 2146
			Honda Civic Wagon: 2123
			Honda CRX 1.5: 2111
			Honda Integra 1.5: 2131
12	55.5	16.9	Nissan Sunny 1.4 LS: 3239
13	54.8	16.7	Mazda 121 GSX: 2765
14	54.7	16.7	Squire X101: 4190
			Triumph Gloria 12: 4494
15	54.5	16.6	MG Metro Turbo: 3037
			Suzuki Swift 1.3 GTi: 4326
16	54.4	16.6	Honda Civic 1.4 GL 3-door: 2136
			Honda Shuttle 1.4 GL Automatic: 2149
17	54.5	16.6	Honda Civic CRX: 2113
			Honda Civic GT: 2120
18	54.1	16.5	MG TDC Mk II: 2984
19	54.1	16.5	HRG 1.5-litre: 2168
			MG TF: 2987
			MG TF 1500: 2988
			MG TF Supercharged: 2989
20	54.0	16.5	Rover 214 GSi: 4037
			Rover 414 Si: 4039
			Rover Metro GTi 16v: 4042
21	53.9	16.4	Citroen AX GT: 1074
			Citroen AX GT5: 1083
			Renault 5 Gordini: 3864
22	53.8	16.4	Proton 1.5 SE Triple Valve Aeroback: 3755
23	53.6	16.4	Suzuki Swift GT: 4333
24	53.5	16.3	MG A: 2992
25	53.5	16.3	MG A: 2990
			MG A Coupe: 2993
			MG A Judson: 2994
26	53.3	16.3	Austin 1300 GT: 398
			Austin Metro GTa: 427
			Austin-Healey Sprite: 447
			MG 1300 Mk II: 3013

			MG 1300 Mk II Auto: 3014
			MG Metro 1300: 3036
			MG Midget Mk III: 3012
			Rover Mini Cooper S: 4048
27	53.3	16.2	Alfa Romeo Sprint Speciale: 53
			Alfa Romeo Sprint Zagato: 54
			Suzuki Swift 1.3 GTi: 4331
28	53.2	16.2	Lotus Europa S2: 2609
			Renault 8 Gordini 1300: 3831
29	53.2	16.2	Austin Vanden Plas 1500: 410

Total: 59

1501 - 2000cc. Maximum speed. Limit set at 130mph.

	mph	kmh	
1	161.0	259.0	Alfa Romeo 33 2.0 Stradale: 66
			Subaru Legacy FIA Record: 4274
2	155.0	249.4	Porsche RSK: 3613
3	150.0	241.4	Porsche 904 Carrera GTS: 3621
4	148.0	238.1	Saab Carlsson: 4097
5	146.0	234.9	Ford Sierra Sapphire Cosworth 4x4: 1958
			Panther Solo: 3380
6	145.0	233.3	Toyota MR2 Turbo: 4473
7	144.0	231.7	Porsche 924 Turbo: 3664
8	143.0	230.1	Eagle Talon: 1355
			Eagle Talon TSi 4WD: 1357
			Ford Sierra RS Cosworth: 1934
			Lancia Thema 2.0ie 16v SE Turbo: 2553
			Mitsubishi Eclipse: 3102
			Plymouth Laser RS: 3521
			Plymouth Laser RS Turbo: 3522
9	142.0	228.5	Rover Rover-BRM Turbine: 4006
10	141.0	226.9	Nissan 200SX: 3232
			Porsche 911 S: 3626
11	140.0	225.3	Ford RS200: 1917
			Lancia Thema 2.0 ie LX Turbo: 2539
			Mitsubishi Colt Starion Turbo: 3081
			Nissan 200SX: 3254
			Renault 21 Turbo Quadra: 3914
			Saab 9000CD: 4094
			Volkswagen Corrado: 4874
12	139.0	223.7	Renault 21 Turbo: 3905
			Saab 9000 Turbo 16v: 4090
			Toyota MR2 GT: 4472
			Vauxhall Calibra 2.0i 16v: 4722
			Volkswagen Corrado G60: 4882
13	137.0	220.4	Lotus Elan: 2638
			Lotus Elan SE: 2639
			Lotus Elan SE: 2641
			Opel Calibra 2.0i 16v: 3351
			Porsche 911 S: 3624
			Toyota Celica GT4: 4455
			Volkswagen Corrado G60: 4879
14	136.0	218.8	Fiat Abarth OT 1600: 1502
			Mitsubishi Starion 2000 Turbo: 3095
15	135.0	217.2	Lotus Esprit S2: 2625
			Saab 9000 Turbo: 4096
			Toyota MR2 Supercharged: 4451
			Toyota MR2 Supercharged: 4464
16	134.0	215.6	Jensen Healey Huffaker: 2399
			Mitsubishi Colt Starion Turbo: 3071
			Peugeot 405 Mi16: 3448
			Porsche 911 E Sportomatic: 3627
			Subaru Legacy 2.0 4Cam Turbo Estate: 4277
			Toyota Celica 2.0 GT: 4468
			Toyota Celica All-Trac Turbo: 4454
			Vauxhall Cavalier GSi 2000 16v: 4725
17	133.0	214.0	Alfa Romeo 75 Evoluzione: 135
			Citroen BX GTi 16v: 1077
			Lancia Dedra 2000 Turbo: 2555
			Toyota Celica 2.0GT: 4438
18	132.0	212.4	Audi 80 16v Sport: 335
			Ford Fiesta RS Turbo: 1949
			Honda CRX 1.6i VT: 2152
			Mitsubishi Colt Lancer 2000 Turbo: 3068
			Nissan Primera 2.0E ZX: 3251
			Nissan Sunny 2.0 GTi: 3255
			Porsche 911: 3622
			Reliant Scimitar SST 1800Ti: 3796
			Vauxhall Calibra 4x4: 4729
			Volkswagen Corrado 16v: 4875
19	131.1	211.0	Ford Escort RS2000: 1973
20	131.0	210.8	MG Maestro Turbo: 3040
			Volkswagen Scirocco 16v: 4853
21	130.0	209.2	Acura Integra GS: 34
			BMW 2002 Turbo: 534
			BMW 520i: 616
			Infiniti G20: 2232
			Isuzu Impulse Turbo: 2256
			Lancia Delta HF 4WD: 2541
			Lancia Delta HF Integrale: 2547
			Mazda Protege: 2762
			Mitsubishi Galant VR-4: 3114
			Nissan NX2000: 3249
			Peugeot 405 Mi16: 3455
			Porsche 911 E: 3629
			Renault 19 16v: 3917
			Treser T1: 4485
			Volkswagen Jetta GTi 16v: 4864

Total: 84

1501 - 2000cc. Acceleration to 60mph/ 96.5kmh. Limit set at 7.5 seconds.

	sec	
1	5.0	Porsche RSK: 3613
2	5.2	Caterham 7 HPC: 725
3	5.3	Lotus Elan Autocrosser: 2632
4	5.6	Caterham 1700 Super Sprint: 723
		Caterham Super 7: 726
5	5.7	Honda CRX Si Jackson Turbo: 2130
6	5.8	Ford Sierra RS Cosworth: 1934
		Toyota MR2 HKS: 4480
7	6.1	Ford RS200: 1917
8	6.2	Caterham Super 7: 722
		Ford Escort Millen: 1964
		Peugeot 405 Turbo 16 Pike's Peak: 3460
		Subaru Legacy FIA Record: 4274
		Toyota MR2 Turbo: 4473
9	6.3	Lancia Delta Integrale 16v: 2549
10	6.4	Lancia Delta HF Integrale: 2547
		Mazda MX-5 Miata Millen: 2760
		Porsche 904 Carrera GTS: 3621
11	6.5	Lotus Elan SE: 2639
12	6.6	Ford Sierra Sapphire Cosworth 4x4: 1958
		Lancia Delta HF 4WD: 2541
		Lotus Elan SE: 2641
		Mitsubishi Colt Starion Turbo: 3081
13	6.7	Lotus Elan: 2638
		Toyota MR2 GT: 4472
		Volkswagen Scirocco GT-3 Davey: 4830
14	6.8	Eagle Talon: 1355
		Eagle Talon TSi 4WD: 1357
		Lancia Thema 2.0ie 16v SE Turbo: 2553
		Mitsubishi Eclipse GSX: 3103
		Nissan 200SX: 3254
		Panther Solo: 3380
15	6.9	Fiat Brava Abarth Rally: 1571
		MG Maestro Turbo: 3040
		Mitsubishi Starion 2000 Turbo: 3095
		Plymouth Laser RS Turbo: 3522
		Porsche 924 Turbo: 3664
		Saab 9000CD: 4094
16	7.0	Alfa Romeo 1750 GTV TransAm: 78
		Datsun 510 TransAm: 1180
		Lotus Elan Sprint: 2608
		Lotus Europa Twin Cam: 2614
		Reliant Scimitar SST 1800Ti: 3796
		Subaru Legacy 2.0 4Cam Turbo Estate: 4277
		Toyota MR2 Supercharged: 4451
17	7.1	Lancia Rally: 2537
		Lotus 7 Twin Cam SS: 2605
		Volkswagen Jetta GTi 16v: 4864
18	7.2	Jensen Healey Huffaker: 2399
		Mitsubishi Eclipse: 3102
		Nissan 200SX: 3232
		Plymouth Laser RS: 3521
		Reliant Scimitar Ti: 3795
19	7.3	BMW 2002 Turbo: 534
		Fiat Abarth OT 1600: 1502
		Saab Carlsson: 4097
20	7.4	Lancia Dedra 2000 Turbo: 2555
		Lotus Plus 2S 130: 2610
21	7.5	Alfa Romeo 75 Evoluzione: 135
		Lotus Plus 2S 130/5: 2615
		MG Montego Turbo: 3039
		Mitsubishi Colt Starion Turbo: 3071
		Nissan Sunny 2.0 GTi: 3255

Total: 63

1501 - 2000cc. Highest power. Limit set at 165bhp.

	bhp	kW	PS	
1	640.0	477.2	648.9	Peugeot 405 Turbo 16 Pike's Peak: 3460
2	245.0	182.7	248.4	Toyota MR2 HKS: 4480
3	235.0	175.2	238.3	Subaru Legacy FIA Record: 4274
4	230.0	171.5	233.2	Alfa Romeo 33 2.0 Stradale: 66
				Fiat Brava Abarth Rally: 1571
				Ford RS200: 1917
				Mazda MX-5 Miata Millen: 2760
5	220.0	164.0	223.0	Ford Escort Millen: 1964
				Ford Sierra Sapphire Cosworth 4x4: 1958
6	205.0	152.9	207.8	Alfa Romeo 1750 GTV TransAm: 78
				Lancia Rally: 2537
7	204.0	152.1	206.8	Ford Sierra RS Cosworth: 1934

				Panther Solo: 3380
				Saab Carlsson: 4097
8	201.0	149.9	203.8	Honda CRX Si Jackson Turbo: 2130
9	200.0	149.1	202.8	Lancia Delta Integrale 16v: 2549
				Toyota Celica All-Trac Turbo: 4469
				Toyota MR2 Turbo: 4473
10	198.0	147.6	200.7	Porsche 904 Carrera GTS: 3621
11	197.0	146.9	199.7	Subaru Legacy 2.0 4Cam Turbo Estate: 4277
12	196.0	146.2	198.7	Jensen Healey Huffaker: 2399
13	195.0	145.4	197.7	Eagle Talon: 1355
				Eagle Talon TSi 4WD: 1357
				Mitsubishi Eclipse GSX: 3103
				Mitsubishi Galant VR-4: 3114
14	190.0	141.7	192.6	Mitsubishi Eclipse: 3102
				Plymouth Laser RS: 3521
				Plymouth Laser RS Turbo: 3522
				Plymouth Laser RS Turbo: 3523
				Toyota Celica All-Trac Turbo: 4454
15	185.0	137.9	187.6	Lancia Delta HF Integrale: 2547
				Lancia Thema 2.0ie 16v SE Turbo: 2553
				Volkswagen Scirocco GT-3 Davey: 4830
16	182.0	135.7	184.5	Toyota Celica GT4: 4455
17	180.0	134.2	182.5	Porsche 911 S: 3626
18	177.0	132.0	179.4	Mitsubishi Colt Starion Turbo: 3081
				Mitsubishi Starion 2000 Turbo: 3095
19	175.0	130.5	177.4	Caterham 7 HPC: 725
				Datsun 510 TransAm: 1180
				Ford Pinto Pangra: 1819
				Renault 21 Turbo: 3905
				Renault 21 Turbo Quadra: 3914
				Saab 9000 Turbo 16v: 4090
				Saab 9000CD: 4094
				Saab 900SPG: 4099
20	171.0	127.5	173.4	Nissan 200SX: 3232
21	170.0	126.8	172.4	BMW 2002 Turbo: 534
				Porsche 924 Turbo: 3664
				Porsche RSK: 3613
22	168.0	125.3	170.3	Mitsubishi Colt Lancer 2000 Turbo: 3068
				Mitsubishi Colt Starion Turbo: 3071
23	165.0	123.0	167.3	Lancia Dedra 2000 Turbo: 2555
				Lancia Delta HF 4WD: 2541
				Lancia Thema 2.0 ie LX Turbo: 2539
				Lotus Elan: 2638
				Lotus Elan SE: 2639
				Pontiac Grand Am Turbo: 3591

Total: 57

1501 - 2000cc. Highest torque. Limit set at 180lbft.

	lbft	Nm	
1	542.0	734.4	Peugeot 405 Turbo 16 Pike's Peak: 3460
2	280.0	379.4	Ford RS200: 1917
3	267.0	361.8	Rover Rover-BRM Turbine: 4006
4	251.0	340.1	Toyota MR2 HKS: 4480
5	245.0	332.0	Ford Escort Millen: 1964
6	236.2	320.0	Lancia Thema 2.0ie 16v SE Turbo: 2553
7	235.0	318.4	Mazda MX-5 Miata Millen: 2760
8	223.6	303.0	Lancia Delta HF Integrale: 2547
9	220.0	298.1	Ford Pinto Pangra: 1819
10	219.9	298.0	Lancia Delta Integrale 16v: 2549
11	214.0	290.0	Ford Sierra Sapphire Cosworth 4x4: 1958
			Mitsubishi Colt Starion Turbo: 3081
			Mitsubishi Starion 2000 Turbo: 3095
			Saab Carlsson: 4097
12	208.0	281.8	Lancia Thema 2.0 ie LX Turbo: 2539
13	205.0	277.8	Ford Sierra RS Cosworth: 1934
14	203.7	276.0	Panther Solo: 3380
15	203.0	275.1	Eagle Talon: 1355
			Eagle Talon TSi 4WD: 1357
			Mitsubishi Eclipse: 3102
			Mitsubishi Eclipse GSX: 3103
			Mitsubishi Galant VR-4: 3114
			Plymouth Laser RS: 3521
			Plymouth Laser RS Turbo: 3523
			Plymouth Laser RS Turbo: 3522
16	201.5	273.0	Saab 9000CD: 4094
17	201.0	272.4	Saab 9000 Turbo 16v: 4090
18	200.0	271.0	Toyota Celica All-Trac Turbo: 4469
			Toyota MR2 Turbo: 4473
19	199.3	270.0	Renault 21 Turbo: 3905
20	199.0	269.6	Renault 21 Turbo Quadra: 3914
21	195.0	264.2	Saab 900SPG: 4099
22	193.4	262.0	Subaru Legacy 2.0 4Cam Turbo Estate: 4277
23	191.0	258.8	Nissan Silvia Turbo ZX: 3211
24	190.0	257.5	Toyota Celica All-Trac Turbo: 4454
25	188.0	254.7	Lancia Delta HF 4WD: 2541
			Saab 900 Turbo: 4089
			Saab 9000: 4092
			Saab 9000 Turbo: 4096
26	184.5	250.0	Toyota Celica GT4: 4455
27	182.3	247.0	Lancia Dedra 2000 Turbo: 2555
28	181.0	245.3	Mitsubishi Colt Lancer 2000 Turbo: 3068
			Mitsubishi Colt Starion Turbo: 3071
			Porsche 924 Turbo: 3664
29	180.0	243.9	Mitsubishi Galant Turbo: 3083

Total: 45

1501 - 2000cc. Highest rpm at peak power. Limit set at 6600rpm.

	rpm	
1	39000	Rover Rover-BRM Turbine: 4006
2	8800	Alfa Romeo 33 2.0 Stradale: 66
3	8500	Volkswagen Scirocco GT-3 Davey: 4830
4	8000	Lotus Elan Autocrosser: 2632
		Porsche RSK: 3613
5	7800	Datsun 510 TransAm: 1180
6	7600	Fiat Abarth OT 1600: 1502
		Honda Civic 1.6i VT: 2154
		Honda CRX 1.6i VT: 2152
7	7500	Alfa Romeo 1750 GTV TransAm: 78
		Fiat Brava Abarth Rally: 1571
8	7200	Porsche 904 Carrera GTS: 3621
9	7000	Ferrari 166 Mille Miglia Barchetta: 1371
		Geo Storm GSi: 1994
		Jensen Healey Huffaker: 2399
		Lancia Rally: 2537
		Peugeot 405 Turbo 16 Pike's Peak: 3460
10	6800	Honda Civic CRX: 2140
		Honda Concerto 1.6i 16: 2151
		Isuzu Impulse XS: 2260
		Mazda MX-3 V6: 2767
		Rover 216 GTi: 4044
		Rover 416 GTi: 4040
11	6700	MG A Twin Cam: 2995
		MG Twin Cam MGA: 2997
12	6600	Chevrolet Nova Twin Cam: 923
		Fiat 124 Spider 1600: 1535
		Isuzu Impulse RS: 2261
		Lotus Elan: 2638
		Lotus Elan SE: 2641
		Lotus Elan SE: 2639
		Lotus Elite: 2624
		Lotus Elite: 2617
		Nissan Sunny ZX Coupe: 3227
		Porsche 911 S: 3626
		Porsche 911 S: 3624
		Toyota 2000GT: 4356
		Toyota Celica 2.0 GT: 4468
		Toyota Corolla FX-16 GTS: 4449
		Toyota Corolla GT Coupe: 4426
		Toyota Corolla GT Hatchback: 4432
		Toyota Corolla GTS: 4427
		Toyota Corolla GTS: 4463
		Toyota MR2: 4440
		Toyota MR2: 4433
		Toyota MR2 GT: 4472
		Toyota MR2 T-Bar: 4441

Total: 47

1501 - 2000cc. Highest power-to-weight ratio. Limit set at 155bhp/ton.

	bhp/ ton	bhp/ tonne	
1	764.6	751.8	Peugeot 405 Turbo 16 Pike's Peak: 3460
2	408.9	402.1	Alfa Romeo 33 2.0 Stradale: 66
3	328.5	323.0	Porsche 904 Carrera GTS: 3621
4	287.4	282.6	Porsche RSK: 3613
5	283.4	278.7	Caterham 7 HPC: 725
6	259.9	255.5	Lotus Elan Autocrosser: 2632
7	252.8	248.6	Caterham 1700 Super Sprint: 723
8	245.3	241.2	Fiat Brava Abarth Rally: 1571
9	242.9	238.8	Caterham Super 7: 722
10	236.2	232.3	Caterham Super 7: 726
11	231.4	227.5	Lotus Super 7 Twincam: 2607
12	230.0	226.2	Mazda MX-5 Miata Millen: 2760
13	222.6	218.9	Lotus 7 Twin Cam SS: 2605
14	221.8	218.1	Honda CRX Si Jackson Turbo: 2130
15	219.5	215.9	Jensen Healey Huffaker: 2399
16	212.5	209.0	Volkswagen Scirocco GT-3 Davey: 4830
17	204.5	201.1	Alfa Romeo 1750 GTV TransAm: 78
18	197.8	194.5	Datsun 510 TransAm: 1180
19	194.3	191.0	Toyota MR2 HKS: 4480
20	193.1	189.9	Fiat Abarth OT 1600: 1502
21	190.4	187.2	Subaru Legacy FIA Record: 4274
22	189.9	186.7	Ford Escort Millen: 1964
23	189.1	185.9	Ferrari 166 Mille Miglia Barchetta: 1371
24	181.9	178.8	Ford RS200: 1917
25	181.4	178.4	Maserati A6G/54 Frua Gran Sport: 2652
26	180.8	177.8	Lancia Rally: 2537
27	178.6	175.6	Lotus Elan Sprint: 2608
28	171.8	168.9	Ford Sierra RS Cosworth: 1934
29	171.4	168.6	Ford Sierra Sapphire Cosworth 4x4: 1958
30	170.5	167.6	Porsche 911 S: 3626

31	169.3	166.5	Ford Pinto Pangra: 1819
32	169.0	166.2	Rover Rover-BRM Turbine: 4006
33	168.7	165.9	Lancia Coupe 2000ie: 2538
34	167.2	164.5	Caterham 7: 724
35	166.7	163.9	Lotus Elan S4 Drophead SE: 2603
36	164.3	161.5	Lotus Elan: 2638
37	164.0	161.3	Lotus Elan SE: 2639
38	163.7	160.9	Lotus Elan Coupe SE: 2600
39	163.0	160.3	Lotus Elan SE: 2601
40	162.8	160.1	Lotus Europa: 2613
41	161.1	158.4	Mitsubishi Colt Lancer 2000 Turbo: 3068
42	158.6	155.9	Toyota MR2 Turbo: 4473
43	157.5	154.9	Lotus Esprit: 2620
44	157.4	154.8	Lancia Delta Integrale 16v: 2549
45	156.8	154.2	Lotus Elan 1600: 2596
46	156.8	154.2	BMW 2002 Turbo: 534
47	155.7	153.1	Morgan Plus 4 Mk III: 3136
48	155.1	152.6	Lotus Elan 1600: 2599

Total: 48

1501 - 2000cc. Highest specific output. Limit set at 85bhp/litre.

	bhp/L	kW/L	PS/L	
1	336.0	250.5	340.6	Peugeot 405 Turbo 16 Pike's Peak: 3460
2	144.0	107.4	146.0	Mazda MX-5 Miata Millen: 2760
3	127.8	95.3	129.5	Ford RS200: 1917
4	126.4	94.3	128.2	Honda CRX Si Jackson Turbo: 2130
5	122.6	91.4	124.3	Toyota MR2 HKS: 4480
6	119.6	89.2	121.2	Ford Escort Millen: 1964
7	117.8	87.9	119.5	Subaru Legacy FIA Record: 4274
8	116.5	86.9	118.1	Volkswagen Scirocco GT-3 Davey: 4830
9	115.3	86.0	116.9	Alfa Romeo 33 2.0 Stradale: 66
				Fiat Brava Abarth Rally: 1571
10	113.3	84.5	114.8	Alfa Romeo 1750 GTV TransAm: 78
11	110.4	82.3	111.9	Ford Sierra Sapphire Cosworth 4x4: 1958
12	107.9	80.5	109.4	Datsun 510 TransAm: 1180
13	103.9	77.5	105.3	Lotus Elan: 2638
				Lotus Elan SE: 2639
14	102.8	76.6	104.2	Saab Carlsson: 4097
15	102.8	76.6	104.2	Lancia Rally: 2537
16	102.4	76.3	103.8	Ford Sierra RS Cosworth: 1934
				Panther Solo: 3380
17	102.3	76.2	103.7	Lotus Elan Autocrosser: 2632
18	102.0	76.1	103.4	Lotus Elan SE: 2641
19	101.3	75.5	102.7	Porsche RSK: 3613
20	100.8	75.1	102.1	Isuzu Impulse RS: 2261
21	100.7	75.1	102.1	Porsche 904 Carrera GTS: 3621
22	100.2	74.8	101.6	Lancia Delta Integrale 16v: 2549
23	100.1	74.6	101.5	Toyota Celica All-Trac Turbo: 4469
				Toyota MR2 Turbo: 4473
24	99.3	74.1	100.7	Jensen Healey Huffaker: 2399
25	98.8	73.7	100.2	Subaru Legacy 2.0 4Cam Turbo Estate: 4277
26	97.6	72.8	99.0	Eagle Talon: 1355
				Eagle Talon TSi 4WD: 1357
				Mitsubishi Eclipse GSX: 3103
				Mitsubishi Galant VR-4: 3114
27	96.7	72.1	98.1	Fiat Abarth OT 1600: 1502
28	96.1	71.7	97.4	Mitsubishi Eclipse: 3102
				Plymouth Laser RS: 3521
29	95.1	70.9	96.5	Plymouth Laser RS Turbo: 3523
				Plymouth Laser RS Turbo: 3522
30	95.1	70.9	96.4	Toyota Celica All-Trac Turbo: 4454
31	94.5	70.5	95.8	Nissan 200SX: 3232
32	94.0	70.1	95.3	Honda Civic 1.6i VT: 2154
				Honda CRX 1.6i VT: 2152
33	92.7	69.1	94.0	Lancia Delta HF Integrale: 2547
				Lancia Thema 2.0ie 16v SE Turbo: 2553
34	92.7	69.1	94.0	Mazda 323 Turbo 4x4: 2743
				Mazda 323 Turbo 4x4 Lux: 2732
35	91.4	68.1	92.6	Toyota MR2 Supercharged: 4464
				Toyota MR2 Supercharged: 4451
36	91.1	67.9	92.3	Toyota Celica GT4: 4455
37	90.7	67.6	91.9	Nissan 200SX: 3254
38	90.4	67.4	91.7	Porsche 911 S: 3626
39	89.8	67.0	91.1	Volkswagen Corrado G60: 4882
40	88.7	66.1	89.9	Volkswagen Corrado: 4874
				Volkswagen Corrado G60: 4879
41	88.6	66.1	89.9	Mitsubishi Colt Starion Turbo: 3081
				Mitsubishi Starion 2000 Turbo: 3095
42	88.3	65.9	89.5	Lancia Delta HF Turbo ie: 2542
43	88.2	65.7	89.4	Saab 9000 Turbo 16v: 4090
				Saab 900SPG: 4099
44	87.8	65.5	89.0	Ford Pinto Pangra: 1819
45	87.7	65.4	88.9	Renault 21 Turbo: 3905
				Renault 21 Turbo Quadra: 3914
				Saab 9000CD: 4094
46	87.6	65.3	88.8	Caterham 7 HPC: 725
47	87.1	65.0	88.3	Alfa Romeo 75 Evoluzione: 135
48	85.7	63.9	86.9	Porsche 924 Turbo: 3664
49	85.4	63.7	86.6	BMW 2002 Turbo: 534

Total: 67

1501 - 2000cc. Highest piston speed. Limit set at 60ft/sec.

	ft/sec	m/sec	
1	74.4	22.7	Volkswagen Scirocco GT-3 Davey: 4830
2	73.7	22.5	Fiat Brava Abarth Rally: 1571
3	72.5	22.1	Alfa Romeo 1750 GTV TransAm: 78
4	68.8	21.0	Lancia Rally: 2537
5	67.6	20.6	Datsun 510 TransAm: 1180
6	67.3	20.5	Peugeot 405 Turbo 16 Pike's Peak: 3460
7	66.9	20.4	Honda Civic CRX: 2140
			Honda Concerto 1.6i 16: 2151
			Rover 216 GTi: 4044
			Rover 416 GTi: 4040
8	65.1	19.8	MG A Twin Cam: 2995
			MG Twin Cam MGA: 2997
9	64.4	19.6	Honda Prelude 2.0 Si: 2138
			Honda Prelude Si 4WS: 2148
10	64.4	19.6	Honda Civic 1.6i VT: 2154
11	64.0	19.5	Honda CRX 1.6i VT: 2152
12	63.9	19.5	Acura Integra LS: 32
			Honda CRX Coupe 1.6i 16: 2128
			Honda CRX Si Jackson: 2142
			Honda Integra EX 16: 2132
13	63.8	19.4	Lotus Elan Autocrosser: 2632
14	63.0	19.2	AC AC-Bristol Zagato: 17
			AC Aceca-Bristol: 21
			AC Bristol: 19
15	62.5	19.1	Citroen BX GTi 16v: 1077
			Mitsubishi Colt 1800 GTI-16v: 3112
			Mitsubishi Galant GTi-16v: 3099
			Mitsubishi Lancer Liftback 1800 GTi-16v: 3110
			Peugeot 405 Mi16: 3448
			Peugeot 405 Mi16x4: 3459
16	62.3	19.0	Honda Prelude 2.0i 16: 2139
17	62.1	18.9	Toyota Celica 2.0 GT: 4468
			Toyota MR2 GT: 4472
18	61.9	18.9	Honda Shuttle 1.6i RT4 4WD: 2144
			Rover 216 GSi: 4038
19	61.5	18.8	Peugeot 405 Mi16: 3455
20	61.5	18.8	Acura Integra LS: 30
			Acura Integra LS Special Edition: 31
			Acura Integra RS: 28
21	61.4	18.7	Aston Martin 2-litre: 231
			Aston Martin Drop-head Coupe: 230
22	60.5	18.4	Geo Storm GSi: 1994
23	60.5	18.4	Ford Escort GT: 1963
			Mazda 323 1.8 GT: 2766
			Mazda 323 1.8 GT: 2753
			Mazda Protege: 2762
			Mercury Tracer LTS: 2962
24	60.4	18.4	AC Ace Bristol: 16
			AC Bristol D-2: 20
			AC Greyhound: 22
25	60.3	18.4	Nissan Sunny ZX Coupe: 3227
26	60.3	18.3	Infiniti G20: 2232
			Nissan NX2000: 3249
			Nissan Primera 2.0E ZX: 3251
			Nissan Sentra SE-R: 3252
			Nissan Sunny 2.0 GTi: 3255
			Toyota Celica 2.0GT: 4438
			Toyota Celica GT Cabriolet: 4447
27	60.1	18.3	Ford Escort XR3i: 1974

Total: 59

2001 - 2500cc. Maximum speed. Limit set at 140mph.

	mph	kmh	
1	170.0	273.5	Bertone Emotion Lotus: 489
2	165.0	265.5	IAD Venus: 2229
			Lotus Esprit Turbo SE: 2640
3	163.0	262.3	Mitsubishi Galant: 3082
4	162.0	260.7	Porsche 944 Turbo: 3730
5	161.0	259.0	Lotus Esprit Turbo SE: 2637
6	158.0	254.2	Porsche 944 Turbo: 3695
7	156.0	251.0	Lotus Esprit Turbo: 2636
8	155.0	249.4	Audi Quattro Sport: 309
			Mercedes-Benz 190E 2.5-16 Evolution II: 2908
			Porsche 944 Turbo: 3715
9	154.0	247.8	Porsche 944 Turbo SE: 3716
10	153.0	246.2	Audi Coupe S2: 337
			Lotus Esprit Turbo: 2635
			MVS Venturi GT: 3190
			Porsche 944 Turbo: 3686
11	152.0	244.6	Lotus Esprit Turbo: 2630
			Renault GTA V6 Turbo: 3899
12	150.0	241.4	Audi 200 Quattro: 334
			Ital Design Aztec: 2262
13	149.0	239.7	Lotus Esprit Turbo: 2627
14	148.0	238.1	BMW M3 Evolution: 604
			Lotus Esprit Turbo: 2629
15	147.0	236.5	Datsun 240Z Sharp: 1190
16	146.0	234.9	Lotus Esprit Turbo HC: 2633

17	145.0	233.3	Audi 200 Quattro Turbo: 297
			Mercedes-Benz 190E 2.3-16: 2879
18	144.0	231.7	Lamborghini Urraco S: 2460
			Mercedes-Benz 190E 2.5-16: 2901
			Porsche 911 S 2.2-litre: 3631
19	143.0	230.1	BMW 325i SE: 615
			BMW M3: 603
20	142.0	228.5	Audi 200 Turbo: 293
			Audi Quattro 20v: 330
			Porsche 911 S: 3638
			Saab 9000 2.3 Turbo TCS: 4101
21	141.0	226.9	BMW 525i SE 24v: 618
			Ferrari 246 GT Dino: 1399
			Ferrari 246 GTS Dino: 1401
			Porsche 944 S: 3694
22	140.0	225.3	Audi 200 Avant Quattro: 304
			BMW M3: 590
			Consulier GTP LX: 1096
			Dodge Shelby CSX: 1341
			Dodge Spirit R/T: 1346
			Nardi Blue Ray 1: 3192
			Porsche 911 E 2.4-litre: 3635
			Porsche 944 S: 3714

Total: 48

2001 - 2500cc. Acceleration to 60mph/ 96.5kmh. Limit set at 7 seconds.

	sec	
1	4.8	Audi Quattro Sport: 309
2	4.9	Lotus Esprit Turbo SE: 2637
3	5.0	Bertone Emotion Lotus: 489
		IAD Venus: 2229
4	5.1	Lotus Esprit Turbo SE: 2640
5	5.2	Lotus Esprit Turbo: 2636
6	5.4	Lotus Esprit Turbo: 2635
7	5.5	Porsche 944 Turbo: 3730
8	5.6	Lotus Esprit Turbo: 2630
		Lotus Esprit Turbo HC: 2633
9	5.7	Consulier GTP LX: 1096
		Datsun 280ZX Electramotive: 1220
		Porsche 944 Turbo SE: 3716
10	5.8	Ferrari TRC 2500 Testa Rossa: 1379
11	5.9	Audi Coupe S2: 337
12	6.0	MVS Venturi GT: 3190
		Porsche 944 Turbo: 3715
		Porsche 944 Turbo: 3695
13	6.1	Lotus Esprit Turbo: 2627
14	6.2	Alfa Romeo GTV Callaway Twin Turbo: 122
15	6.3	Audi Quattro: 323
		Audi Quattro 20v: 330
		Maserati Biturbo E: 2674
		Nissan 240SX Turbo Tokico/Cartech: 3233
		Porsche 944 Turbo: 3686
		Renault GTA V6 Turbo: 3899
16	6.4	Porsche 911 E 2.4-litre: 3635
17	6.5	BMW M3 Sport Evolution: 621
		Dodge Spirit R/T: 1346
		MVS Venturi: 3191
18	6.6	BMW M3 Evolution: 604
		Lotus Esprit Turbo: 2629
		Porsche 911 E: 3637
19	6.7	Dodge Shelby GLH-S: 1335
		Ford Probe GT Suspension Techniques/HKS: 1943
		Panther Lima: 3375
		Porsche 944 S: 3694
20	6.8	Lotus Excel SE: 2631
		Saab 9000 Turbo: 4102
21	6.9	Chrysler TC by Maserati: 1008
		Dodge Shelby CSX: 1338
		Maserati Biturbo: 2677
		Mercedes-Benz 190E 2.5-16 Evolution II: 2916
		Triumph TR7 Tullius: 4572
22	7.0	Datsun 240Z Sharp: 1190

Total: 45

2001 - 2500cc. Highest power. Limit set at 175bhp.

	bhp	kW	PS	
1	270.0	201.3	273.7	Datsun 280ZX Electramotive: 1220
2	258.0	192.4	261.6	Datsun 240Z Sharp: 1190
3	250.0	186.4	253.5	Ital Design Aztec: 2262
				Porsche 944 Turbo: 3730
				Porsche 944 Turbo SE: 3716
4	238.0	177.5	241.3	BMW M3 Sport Evolution: 621
5	235.0	175.2	238.3	Mercedes-Benz 190E 2.5-16 Evolution II: 2908
6	232.0	173.0	235.2	Mercedes-Benz 190E 2.5-16 Evolution II: 2916
7	230.0	171.5	233.2	Alfa Romeo GTV Callaway Twin Turbo: 122
8	224.0	167.0	227.1	Dodge Spirit R/T: 1346
9	220.0	164.0	223.0	Audi Coupe S2: 337
				Audi Quattro 20v: 330
				BMW M3 Evolution: 604
				BMW M3 Hor Technologie: 605
				Ferrari TRC 2500 Testa Rossa: 1379
				Lamborghini Urraco S: 2460
				Porsche 944 Turbo: 3686
				Porsche 944 Turbo: 3695
10	217.0	161.8	220.0	Audi 200 Quattro: 334
				Porsche 944 Turbo: 3715
11	205.0	152.9	207.8	Maserati Biturbo E: 2674
12	200.0	149.1	202.8	Audi Quattro: 323
				Audi Quattro: 289
				BMW M3: 590
				Chrysler TC by Maserati: 1008
				Ford Mustang SVO: 1915
				MVS Venturi: 3191
				MVS Venturi GT: 3190
				Nissan 240SX Turbo Tokico/Cartech: 3233
				Renault GTA V6 Turbo: 3899
				Saab 9000 2.3 Turbo TCS: 4101
				Saab 9000 Turbo: 4102
				Saab 9000CS Turbo S: 4103
13	197.0	146.9	199.7	Mercedes-Benz 190E 2.5-16: 2901
14	195.0	145.4	197.7	Ferrari 246 GTS Dino: 1401
15	192.0	143.2	194.7	BMW 520i SE Touring: 624
				BMW 525i SE 24v: 618
				BMW M3: 603
				Maserati Biturbo Spyder: 2675
16	190.0	141.7	192.6	Ford Thunderbird Turbo Coupe: 1927
				Mercedes-Benz 190E BBS/Callaway Turbo: 2880
				Nardi Blue Ray 1: 3192
				Porsche 944 S: 3694
17	189.0	140.9	191.6	BMW 325i: 623
				BMW 325i SE: 615
				BMW 525i: 617
18	188.0	140.2	190.6	Porsche 944 S: 3701
				Porsche 944 S: 3714
19	187.0	139.4	189.6	Maserati Biturbo: 2677
20	185.0	137.9	187.6	Maserati Biturbo: 2672
				Maserati Biturbo Automatic: 2673
				Mercedes-Benz 190E 2.3-16: 2879
21	182.0	135.7	184.5	Renault 25 V6 Turbo: 3889
				Volvo 740 Turbo: 4955
22	181.0	135.0	183.5	Porsche 911 S: 3638
23	180.0	134.2	182.5	Chevrolet Baretta GTZ: 946
				Chevrolet Beretta GTZ: 936
				Oldsmobile Calais HO Quad 4: 3303
				Oldsmobile Cutlass Calais International Series HO: 3304
				Volvo 760 Turbo Estate: 4952
24	175.0	130.5	177.4	Dodge Shelby CSX: 1338
				Dodge Shelby CSX: 1341
				Dodge Shelby CSX VNT: 1342
				Dodge Shelby GLH-S: 1335
				Ferrari 246 GT Dino: 1399
				Ford Mustang SVO: 1897
				Lamborghini Urraco: 2463

Total: 67

2001 - 2500cc. Highest rpm at peak power. Limit set at 6000rpm.

	rpm	
1	8250	Datsun 240Z Sharp: 1190
2	7600	Ferrari 246 GTS Dino: 1401
3	7500	Datsun 280ZX Electramotive: 1220
		Lamborghini Urraco: 2463
		Lamborghini Urraco S: 2460
4	7200	Mercedes-Benz 190E 2.5-16 Evolution II: 2908
		Mercedes-Benz 190E 2.5-16 Evolution II: 2916
5	7100	BMW 2002 TransAm: 528
6	7000	BMW M3 Hor Technologie: 605
		BMW M3 Sport Evolution: 621
		Ferrari 246 GT Dino: 1399
7	6800	Triumph TR7 Tullius: 4572
8	6750	BMW M3: 590
		BMW M3: 603
		BMW M3 Evolution: 604
9	6700	Audi Quattro Sport: 309
10	6500	Bertone Emotion Lotus: 489
		Ferrari TRC 2500 Testa Rossa: 1379
		Lotus Eclat Excel: 2628
		Lotus Esprit Turbo: 2636
		Lotus Esprit Turbo SE: 2637
		Lotus Esprit Turbo SE: 2640
		Lotus Excel SA: 2634
		Lotus Excel SE: 2631
		Porsche 911 S: 3638
		Porsche 911 S 2.2-litre: 3631
11	6250	Lotus Esprit Turbo: 2630
12	6200	Chevrolet Baretta GTZ: 946

		Chevrolet Beretta GTZ: 936
		Ital Design Aztec: 2262
		Mercedes-Benz 190E 2.3-16: 2879
		Mercedes-Benz 190E 2.5-16: 2901
		Oldsmobile Calais HO Quad 4: 3303
		Oldsmobile Cutlass Calais International Series HO: 3304
		Porsche 911 E: 3637
		Porsche 911 E 2.4-litre: 3635
13	6000	Audi 90 Quattro: 329
		Audi 90 Quattro 20v: 336
		Audi 90 Quattro 20v: 325
		BMW 2500: 519
		BMW 323i: 547
		BMW 525: 538
		BMW 525: 536
		Datsun 240Z: 1171
		Datsun 240Z: 1182
		Datsun 240Z Automatic: 1176
		Dodge Spirit R/T: 1346
		Honda Legend: 2133
		IAD Venus: 2229
		Lotus Esprit Turbo: 2629
		Lotus Esprit Turbo: 2627
		Lotus Esprit Turbo: 2635
		Lotus Esprit Turbo HC: 2633
		Porsche 944 S: 3701
		Porsche 944 S: 3694
		Porsche 944 S: 3714
		Porsche 944 Turbo: 3730
		Porsche 944 Turbo SE: 3716
		Rover 825i: 4027
		Rover Sterling Automatic: 4030
		Subaru Legacy 2.2 GX 4WD: 4276

Total: 61

2001 - 2500cc. Highest power-to-weight ratio. Limit set at 155bhp/ton.

	bhp/ ton	bhp/ tonne	
1	304.2	299.1	Ferrari TRC 2500 Testa Rossa: 1379
2	262.7	258.3	Datsun 240Z Sharp: 1190
3	248.9	244.7	Datsun 280ZX Electramotive: 1220
4	244.2	240.1	Audi Quattro Sport: 309
5	224.0	220.3	Nardi Blue Ray 1: 3192
6	208.2	204.7	Porsche 944 Turbo SE: 3716
7	206.4	203.0	Lotus Esprit Turbo SE: 2640
8	201.9	198.5	Lotus Esprit Turbo SE: 2637
9	201.2	197.8	BMW M3 Sport Evolution: 621
10	199.0	195.7	Triumph TR7 Tullius: 4572
11	190.6	187.4	Lotus Esprit Turbo HC: 2633
12	187.4	184.3	Porsche 911 S 2.2-litre: 3631
13	183.6	180.5	BMW 2002 TransAm: 528
14	179.5	176.5	Lotus Esprit Turbo: 2636
15	178.3	175.3	Alfa Romeo GTV Callaway Twin Turbo: 122
16	178.1	175.2	Mercedes-Benz 190E 2.5-16 Evolution II: 2908
17	177.3	174.3	Lotus Esprit Turbo: 2627
18	175.9	172.9	Mercedes-Benz 190E 2.5-16 Evolution II: 2916
19	175.6	172.7	BMW M3 Evolution: 604
20	175.3	172.3	Porsche 944 Turbo: 3730
21	175.1	172.2	Lotus Esprit Turbo: 2630
			Volkswagen Corrado Neuspeed: 4883
22	174.7	171.8	Porsche 944 Turbo: 3686
23	174.5	171.6	Maserati Biturbo: 2672
24	172.6	169.8	MVS Venturi GT: 3190
25	171.4	168.5	BMW M3 Hor Technologie: 605
26	171.3	168.5	Renault GTA V6 Turbo: 3899
27	170.9	168.0	Lamborghini Urraco S: 2460
28	169.4	166.6	Lotus Esprit Turbo: 2629
29	167.0	164.3	Ford Probe GT Suspension Techniques/HKS: 1943
30	166.6	163.8	Consulier GTP LX: 1096
31	165.6	162.9	Porsche 944 Turbo: 3695
32	165.5	162.7	Maserati Biturbo E: 2674
33	165.4	162.6	BMW 325i: 573
34	162.4	159.7	BMW M3: 590
35	160.8	158.1	Audi Quattro: 289
36	160.6	157.9	Dodge Spirit R/T: 1346
37	160.4	157.7	Audi Quattro 20v: 330
38	158.9	156.2	MVS Venturi: 3191
39	157.8	155.2	Lotus Esprit Turbo: 2635
40	157.8	155.1	Maserati Biturbo: 2677
41	157.8	155.1	Porsche 911 S: 3638
42	156.8	154.2	Maserati Biturbo Spyder: 2675
43	156.2	153.6	Lotus Excel SE: 2631
44	156.0	153.4	Porsche 944 Turbo: 3715
45	155.6	153.0	Dodge Shelby CSX: 1338
			Nissan 240SX Turbo Tokico/Cartech: 3233
46	155.5	152.9	Lotus Excel SA: 2634

Total: 48

2001 - 2500cc. Highest specific output. Limit set at 80bhp/litre.

	bhp/L	kW/L	PS/L	
1	143.4	106.9	145.4	Audi Quattro Sport: 309
2	121.4	90.6	123.1	Bertone Emotion Lotus: 489
				Lotus Esprit Turbo SE: 2640
				Lotus Esprit Turbo SE: 2637
3	112.3	83.7	113.9	Ital Design Aztec: 2262
4	108.6	81.0	110.1	Datsun 280ZX Electramotive: 1220
5	106.4	79.3	107.9	Volkswagen Corrado Neuspeed: 4883
6	105.3	78.5	106.8	Datsun 240Z Sharp: 1190
7	104.9	78.2	106.3	Lotus Esprit Turbo: 2636
8	101.6	75.8	103.0	Dodge Spirit R/T: 1346
9	100.8	75.2	102.2	Porsche 944 Turbo: 3730
				Porsche 944 Turbo SE: 3716
10	100.7	75.1	102.1	Ford Probe GT Suspension Techniques/ HKS: 1943
11	98.9	73.7	100.3	Lotus Esprit Turbo: 2630
				Lotus Esprit Turbo: 2635
				Lotus Esprit Turbo HC: 2633
12	98.8	73.7	100.2	Audi Coupe S2: 337
				Audi Quattro 20v: 330
13	98.4	73.4	99.8	BMW 2002 TransAm: 528
14	97.5	72.7	98.8	Audi 200 Quattro: 334
15	96.6	72.0	97.9	Lotus Esprit Turbo: 2627
16	96.5	71.9	97.8	BMW M3 Sport Evolution: 621
17	95.6	71.3	96.9	BMW M3 Evolution: 604
				BMW M3 Hor Technologie: 605
18	95.4	71.1	96.7	Mercedes-Benz 190E 2.5-16 Evolution II: 2908
19	94.3	70.3	95.6	Lotus Esprit Turbo: 2629
20	94.2	70.2	95.5	Mercedes-Benz 190E 2.5-16 Evolution II: 2916
21	93.4	69.7	94.7	Bertone Zabrus: 488
22	92.3	68.8	93.6	Alfa Romeo GTV Callaway Twin Turbo: 122
23	91.1	67.9	92.4	Porsche 911 S 2.2-litre: 3631
24	90.4	67.4	91.6	Chrysler TC by Maserati: 1008
25	90.3	67.4	91.6	Audi Quattro: 289
26	89.8	67.0	91.1	Audi Quattro: 323
27	89.3	66.6	90.6	Lamborghini Urraco S: 2460
28	88.7	66.2	90.0	Porsche 944 Turbo: 3686
				Porsche 944 Turbo: 3695
29	88.1	65.7	89.3	Ferrari TRC 2500 Testa Rossa: 1379
30	87.5	65.3	88.7	Porsche 944 Turbo: 3715
31	87.3	65.1	88.5	Saab 9000 2.3 Turbo TCS: 4101
				Saab 9000 Turbo: 4102
				Saab 9000CS Turbo S: 4103
32	87.0	64.8	88.2	Ford Mustang SVO: 1915
33	86.9	64.8	88.1	BMW M3: 590
34	85.5	63.7	86.7	Triumph TR7 Tullius: 4572
35	84.9	63.3	86.1	Audi 200 Avant Quattro: 304
				Audi 200 Quattro Turbo: 297
				Audi 200 Turbo: 293
36	83.7	62.4	84.9	Nissan 240SX Turbo Tokico/Cartech: 3233
37	83.4	62.2	84.6	BMW M3: 603
38	82.8	61.7	83.9	Lotus Excel SA: 2634
				Lotus Excel SE: 2631
39	82.8	61.7	83.9	Ford Thunderbird Turbo Coupe: 1927
40	82.6	61.6	83.8	Mercedes-Benz 190E BBS/Callaway Turbo: 2880
41	82.3	61.4	83.4	Maserati Biturbo E: 2674
42	82.3	61.4	83.4	Pontiac Sunbird GT: 3587
43	82.3	61.3	83.4	Volvo 242 IPD: 4935
44	81.4	60.7	82.5	MVS Venturi: 3191
				MVS Venturi GT: 3190
				Renault GTA V6 Turbo: 3899
45	80.6	60.1	81.8	Ferrari 246 GTS Dino: 1401
46	80.5	60.0	81.6	Mercedes-Benz 190E 2.3-16: 2879

Total: 61

2001 - 2500cc. Highest piston speed. Limit set at 55ft/sec.

	ft/sec	m/sec	
1	66.7	20.3	BMW M3 Sport Evolution: 621
2	66.5	20.3	Datsun 240Z Sharp: 1190
3	65.2	19.9	Mercedes-Benz 190E 2.5-16 Evolution II: 2916
			Mercedes-Benz 190E 2.5-16 Evolution II: 2908
4	64.4	19.6	BMW M3 Hor Technologie: 605
5	63.3	19.3	Audi Quattro Sport: 309
6	62.9	19.2	Healey Tickford Saloon: 2020
7	62.1	18.9	BMW 2002 TransAm: 528
8	62.1	18.9	BMW M3: 603
			BMW M3: 590
			BMW M3 Evolution: 604
9	61.4	18.7	Ferrari TRC 2500 Testa Rossa: 1379
10	60.4	18.4	Datsun 280ZX Electramotive: 1220
11	60.3	18.4	Dodge Spirit R/T: 1346
12	60.3	18.4	Honda Prelude Si: 2157
			Honda Prelude Si 4WS: 2160
13	60.2	18.3	Bugatti 55: 651
14	59.2	18.0	Triumph TR6: 4541

15	59.2	18.0	Mercedes-Benz 190E 2.5-16: 2901
16	59.0	18.0	Healey 2.4-litre Roadster: 2019
			Riley 2.5: 3936
			Riley 2.5 Sports: 3934
17	58.8	17.9	Nissan 240SX: 3245
			Nissan 240SX: 3230
18	58.6	17.9	Ital Design Aztec: 2262
19	58.0	17.7	Triumph TR7 Tullius: 4572
20	57.7	17.6	Riley 2.5: 3938
			Riley 2.5 Saloon: 3935
			Riley Pathfinder: 3939
			Riley Pathfinder: 3940
21	57.7	17.6	Chevrolet Beretta GTZ: 936
22	57.7	17.6	Chevrolet Baretta GTZ: 946
			Oldsmobile Calais HO Quad 4: 3303
			Oldsmobile Cutlass Calais International Series HO: 3304
23	57.1	17.4	Triumph TR5 PI: 4536
24	56.8	17.3	Volkswagen Corrado Neuspeed: 4883
25	56.7	17.3	Audi 90 Quattro: 329
			Audi 90 Quattro 20v: 325
			Audi 90 Quattro 20v: 336
26	56.6	17.3	Triumph 2.5PI: 4537
			Triumph 2.5PI Mk II: 4552
27	56.4	17.2	Riley 16 2.5: 3931
			Riley 2.5 Saloon: 3933
28	56.3	17.2	Chrysler Laser XE: 1003
			Datsun 200SX: 1228
			Dodge Daytona Turbo Z: 1331
			Dodge Omni GLH: 1332
			Dodge Shelby Charger: 1328
29	55.9	17.1	Peugeot 505 GRi: 3432
			Peugeot 505 GTi Family Estate: 3441
30	55.7	17.0	Audi 80 Quattro: 295
			Audi Coupe Injection: 296
31	55.6	17.0	Nissan 240SX Turbo Tokico/Cartech: 3233
32	55.6	16.9	Audi Coupe S2: 337
			Audi Quattro 20v: 330
33	55.3	16.9	Chrysler TC by Maserati: 1008

Total: 56

2501 - 3000cc. Maximum speed. Limit set at 145mph.

	mph	kmh	
1	201.0	323.4	Ferrari F40: 1435
			Porsche 959 S: 3702
2	200.0	321.8	Ferrari F40: 1446
3	198.0	318.6	Porsche 959: 3731
			Porsche 959 Comfort: 3717
			Porsche 959 Sport: 3718
4	196.0	315.4	Ferrari F40: 1450
5	189.0	304.1	Ferrari 288 GTO: 1421
6	182.0	292.8	Ferrari 308 Norwood: 1439
7	180.0	289.6	Ferrari 288 GTO: 1416
			Ferrari GTO: 1423
			Mercedes-Benz 300SLR: 2795
8	178.0	286.4	Porsche Carrera RSR: 3642
9	170.0	273.5	Lamborghini Bravo: 2458
10	168.0	270.3	Acura NSX: 36
			Ferrari 250 Testa Rossa: 1378
11	166.0	267.1	Nissan 300ZX Turbo Millen Super GTZ: 3247
12	165.0	265.5	Renault Alpine A610 Turbo: 3918
13	163.0	262.3	Porsche 935 Group 4 Holbert: 3657
14	162.0	260.7	Honda NSX: 2156
15	159.0	255.8	Dodge Stealth R/T Turbo: 1347
			Mitsubishi 3000GT VR-4: 3111
16	158.0	254.2	Honda NSX Auto: 2159
			Nissan 300ZX: 3240
17	156.0	251.0	Nissan Skyline GT-R: 3243
			Porsche 911 Turbo Carrera: 3650
18	155.0	249.4	Nissan 300ZX Turbo: 3241
			Nissan 300ZX Twin Turbo: 3248
19	154.0	247.8	Ferrari 308 GTB: 1409
			Ferrari Dino 308 GT4 2+2: 1410
20	153.0	246.2	Porsche Turbo 3-litre: 3648
21	152.0	244.6	Ferrari 308 GT4 Dino: 1402
22	151.0	243.0	Mercedes-Benz 300CE: 2909
23	150.0	241.4	Ferrari 250 GT 2+2: 1385
			Ferrari 250 GT Berlinetta Lusso: 1388
			Mercedes-Benz 300SL Carrera Panamericana: 2788
24	149.0	239.7	Lancia Thema 8.32: 2546
			Porsche 944 S2: 3742
			Porsche 944 S2 Cabriolet: 3743
			Porsche Carrera RS 3-litre: 3647
			Porsche Carrera RS Touring: 3641
25	148.0	238.1	Mercedes-Benz 300E-24: 2912
			Nissan 300ZX: 3234
			Vauxhall Carlton GSi 3000 24v: 4724
26	147.0	236.5	Ferrari 308 GTSi: 1415
			Lamborghini Silhouette 3000: 2462
			Maserati Merak SS: 2670
			Porsche 944 S2: 3729
27	146.0	234.9	Mercedes-Benz 300SL Coupe: 2794
			Porsche 911 SC: 3670
			Toyota Supra 3.0i Turbo: 4465
28	145.0	233.3	Citroen XM V6.24: 1089
			Datsun 280ZX Electramotive: 1230
			Ferrari 308 GTS: 1412
			Maserati 430: 2678

Total: 55

2501 - 3000cc. Acceleration to 60mph/ 96.5kmh. Limit set at 6.5sec.

	sec	
1	3.6	Porsche 959: 3731
		Porsche 959 Sport: 3718
2	3.8	Datsun 280ZX Electramotive: 1230
		Ferrari F40: 1450
3	4.0	Porsche 959 Comfort: 3717
4	4.5	Ferrari 250 Testa Rossa: 1378
		Ferrari F40: 1446
5	4.7	Ferrari 308 Norwood: 1439
		Porsche 959 S: 3702
6	5.0	Ferrari 288 GTO: 1421
		Ferrari 288 GTO: 1416
		Ferrari GTO: 1423
		Nissan 300ZX Turbo Millen Super GTZ: 3247
7	5.1	Ferrari 250 Mille Miglia: 1376
8	5.2	Porsche Carrera RS 3-litre: 3647
9	5.3	Ford Festiva Shogun: 1965
10	5.5	Porsche Carrera RS Touring: 3641
11	5.6	Datsun 280ZX Sharp: 1221
		Nissan 300ZX: 3240
		Nissan 300ZX Motor Sports International SR-71: 3246
		Nissan Skyline GT-R: 3243
		Porsche Carrera RSR: 3642
12	5.7	Acura NSX: 36
		Renault Alpine A610 Turbo: 3918
13	5.8	Honda NSX: 2156
		Porsche 911 SC: 3670
		Porsche 935 Group 4 Holbert: 3657
		Toyota Supra Turbo TRD: 4467
		TVR Convertible Turbo: 4593
14	6.0	Ferrari 250 Testa Rossa: 1382
		Porsche 944 S2: 3729
15	6.1	Porsche 911S 2.7-litre: 3645
		Porsche Turbo 3-litre: 3648
16	6.3	Dodge Stealth R/T Turbo: 1347
		Ferrari 250 GT Berlinetta SWB: 1383
		Maserati 430: 2678
		Mitsubishi 3000GT VR-4: 3111
		Porsche 911 SC: 3658
17	6.4	Ferrari 308 GT4 Dino: 1402
18	6.5	Ferrari 308 GTB: 1409
		Maserati 430: 2676
		Nissan 300ZX Turbo: 3241
		Nissan 300ZX Twin Turbo: 3248
		Porsche 911 SC: 3654

Total: 44

2501 - 3000cc. Highest power. Limit set at 225bhp.

	bhp	kW	PS	
1	600.0	447.4	608.3	Porsche 959 S: 3702
2	580.0	432.5	588.0	Datsun 280ZX Electramotive: 1230
3	485.0	361.7	491.7	Porsche 935 Group 4 Holbert: 3657
4	478.0	356.4	484.6	Ferrari F40: 1435
				Ferrari F40: 1450
				Ferrari F40: 1446
5	460.0	343.0	466.4	Nissan 300ZX Turbo Millen Super GTZ: 3247
6	450.0	335.6	456.2	Ferrari 308 Norwood: 1439
				Porsche 959: 3731
				Porsche 959 Comfort: 3717
				Porsche 959 Sport: 3718
7	430.0	320.6	436.0	Toyota Supra Turbo TRD: 4467
8	428.0	319.2	433.9	Nissan 300ZX Motor Sports International SR-71: 3246
9	400.0	298.3	405.5	Ferrari 288 GTO: 1421
				Ferrari GTO: 1423
10	394.0	293.8	399.5	Ferrari 288 GTO: 1416
11	302.0	225.2	306.2	Mercedes-Benz 300SLR: 2795
12	300.0	223.7	304.2	Datsun 280ZX Sharp: 1221
				Dodge Stealth R/T Turbo: 1347
				Ferrari 250 Testa Rossa: 1382
				Ferrari 250 Testa Rossa: 1378
				Lamborghini Bravo: 2458
				Mitsubishi 3000GT VR-4: 3111
				Nissan 300ZX Turbo: 3241
				Nissan 300ZX Twin Turbo: 3248
13	290.0	216.2	294.0	Ferrari 250 GT Berlinetta Lusso: 1388
14	280.0	208.8	283.9	Nissan 300ZX: 3240
				Porsche Carrera RSR: 3642
15	276.0	205.8	279.8	Nissan Skyline GT-R: 3243
16	270.0	201.3	273.7	Acura NSX: 36

				Honda NSX: 2156
17	260.0	193.9	263.6	Ferrari 250 GT Coupe: 1381
				Lamborghini Silhouette 3000: 2462
				Porsche Turbo 3-litre: 3648
18	255.0	190.1	258.5	Ferrari 308 GTB: 1409
				Honda NSX Auto: 2159
19	250.0	186.4	253.5	Ferrari Dino 308 GT4 2+2: 1410
				Mercedes-Benz 300SL Roadster: 2807
				Mercedes-Benz 300SL Roadster: 2800
				Renault Alpine A610 Turbo: 3918
20	243.0	181.2	246.4	Mercedes-Benz 300SL Coupe: 2794
21	242.0	180.5	245.4	Ferrari 308 GT4 Dino: 1402
22	241.0	179.7	244.3	Ferrari 250 GT Berlinetta SWB: 1383
23	240.0	179.0	243.3	Bitter Type 3 Cabrio: 494
				Ferrari 250 GT 2+2: 1385
				Ferrari 250 GT Cabriolet: 1380
				Ferrari 250 GT Coupe: 1384
				Ferrari 250 Mille Miglia: 1376
				Ferrari 308 Dino GT4: 1405
				Ferrari 308 GT4 Dino: 1408
				Ferrari 308 GTB: 1411
				Mercedes-Benz 300SL: 2793
24	234.0	174.5	237.2	Porsche 911 Turbo: 3655
				Porsche 911 Turbo Carrera: 3650
25	233.0	173.7	236.2	Toyota Supra Turbo: 4466
26	232.0	173.0	235.2	Toyota Supra 3.0i Turbo: 4465
27	231.0	172.3	234.2	Mercedes-Benz 300E-24: 2912
				Mercedes-Benz 300SL-24 5-speed Auto: 2917
28	230.0	171.5	233.2	Ferrari 308 GTBi Quattrovalvole: 1419
				Ferrari Mondial Cabriolet Quattrovalvole: 1424
				Toyota Supra Turbo: 4460
				TVR Convertible Turbo: 4593
29	228.0	170.0	231.2	Nissan 300ZX Turbo: 3209
30	225.0	167.8	228.1	Maserati 228: 2680
				Maserati 430: 2678
				Maserati 430: 2676
				Maserati Spyder: 2679
				Nissan 300ZX Turbo: 3224

Total: 68

2501 - 3000cc. Highest torque. Limit set at 225lbft.

	lbft	Nm	
1	520.0	704.6	Datsun 280ZX Electramotive: 1230
2	434.0	588.1	Porsche 935 Group 4 Holbert: 3657
3	430.0	582.7	Nissan 300ZX Turbo Millen Super GTZ: 3247
4	425.0	575.9	Ferrari F40: 1450
			Ferrari F40: 1435
			Ferrari F40: 1446
5	406.0	550.1	Nissan 300ZX Motor Sports International SR-71: 3246
6	382.0	517.6	Toyota Supra Turbo TRD: 4467
7	370.0	501.4	Porsche 959: 3731
			Porsche 959 Comfort: 3717
			Porsche 959 Sport: 3718
8	369.0	500.0	Porsche 959 S: 3702
9	366.0	495.9	Ferrari 288 GTO: 1416
			Ferrari 288 GTO: 1421
			Ferrari GTO: 1423
10	307.0	416.0	Dodge Stealth R/T Turbo: 1347
			Mitsubishi 3000GT VR-4: 3111
11	283.0	383.5	Nissan 300ZX Turbo: 3241
			Nissan 300ZX Twin Turbo: 3248
12	274.5	372.0	Nissan 300ZX: 3240
13	273.0	369.9	TVR Convertible Turbo: 4593
14	266.0	360.4	Maserati 430: 2676
15	260.0	352.3	Nissan Skyline GT-R: 3243
16	258.0	349.6	Renault Alpine A610 Turbo: 3918
17	254.6	345.0	Toyota Supra 3.0i Turbo: 4465
18	254.0	344.2	Toyota Supra Turbo: 4466
19	253.0	342.8	Porsche Turbo 3-litre: 3648
20	246.0	333.3	Maserati 228: 2680
			Maserati 430: 2678
			Maserati Spyder: 2679
			Porsche 911 Turbo: 3655
			Porsche 911 Turbo Carrera: 3650
			Toyota Supra Turbo: 4460
21	245.0	332.0	Datsun 280ZX Sharp: 1221
22	242.0	327.9	Nissan 300ZX Turbo: 3209
23	240.0	325.2	Mercedes-Benz 280SE: 2874
			Nissan 300ZX Turbo: 3224
24	237.0	321.1	Lamborghini Bravo: 2458
25	235.0	318.4	Bitter Type 3 Cabrio: 494
26	234.0	317.1	Chrysler Conquest TSi: 1007
			Mitsubishi Starion ESI-R: 3107
27	228.0	308.9	Mercedes-Benz 300SL Roadster: 2807
			Mercedes-Benz 300SL Roadster: 2800
28	227.0	307.6	Nissan 300ZX: 3231
			Nissan 300ZX Turbo: 3216

Total: 45

2501 - 3000cc. Highest rpm at peak power. Limit set at 6600rpm.

	rpm	
1	8000	Porsche Carrera RSR: 3642
2	7800	Lamborghini Bravo: 2458
3	7700	Ferrari 308 GT4 Dino: 1402
		Ferrari 308 GTB: 1409
		Ferrari Dino 308 GT4 2+2: 1410
4	7500	Datsun 280ZX Electramotive: 1230
		Datsun 280ZX Sharp: 1221
		Ferrari 250 GT Berlinetta Lusso: 1388
		Lamborghini Silhouette 3000: 2462
		Mercedes-Benz 300SLR: 2795
5	7200	Ferrari 212 Touring: 1372
		Ferrari 250 Mille Miglia: 1376
		Ferrari 250 Testa Rossa: 1382
		Ferrari 250 Testa Rossa: 1378
6	7100	Acura NSX: 36
		Honda NSX: 2156
7	7000	Ferrari 250 GT 2+2: 1385
		Ferrari 250 GT Berlinetta SWB: 1383
		Ferrari 250 GT Cabriolet: 1380
		Ferrari 250 GT Coupe: 1384
		Ferrari 250 GT Coupe: 1381
		Ferrari 288 GTO: 1416
		Ferrari 288 GTO: 1421
		Ferrari F40: 1450
		Ferrari F40: 1446
		Ferrari F40: 1435
		Ferrari GTO: 1423
		Porsche 935 Group 4 Holbert: 3657
8	6800	Ferrari 308 GTBi Quattrovalvole: 1419
		Ferrari Mondial Cabriolet Quattrovalvole: 1424
		Honda NSX Auto: 2159
		Nissan Skyline GT-R: 3243
9	6750	Lancia Thema 8.32: 2546
		Lancia Thema 8.32: 2548
10	6700	Ferrari 308 Norwood: 1439
		Nissan 300ZX Motor Sports International SR-71: 3246
11	6600	Ferrari 308 Dino GT4: 1405
		Ferrari 308 GT4 Dino: 1414
		Ferrari 308 GT4 Dino: 1408
		Ferrari 308 GTB: 1411
		Ferrari 308 GTS: 1412
		Ferrari 308 GTSi: 1415
		Ferrari 308 GTSi Targa: 1420
		Ferrari Mondial 8: 1418

Total: 44

2501 - 3000cc. Highest power-to-weight ratio. Limit set at 190bhp/ton.

	bhp/ ton	bhp/ tonne	
1	499.7	491.4	Datsun 280ZX Electramotive: 1230
2	451.0	443.5	Porsche 959 S: 3702
3	441.5	434.2	Ferrari F40: 1446
			Ferrari F40: 1435
4	409.2	402.4	Porsche 935 Group 4 Holbert: 3657
5	381.8	375.4	Ferrari 250 Testa Rossa: 1382
6	359.3	353.3	Ferrari F40: 1450
7	350.7	344.8	Ferrari 288 GTO: 1421
			Ferrari GTO: 1423
8	348.7	342.9	Mercedes-Benz 300SLR: 2795
9	339.4	333.7	Porsche 959 Sport: 3718
10	339.0	333.4	Porsche Carrera RSR: 3642
11	324.6	319.2	Ferrari 250 Testa Rossa: 1378
12	316.0	310.7	Porsche 959: 3731
			Porsche 959 Comfort: 3717
13	311.1	305.9	Ferrari 308 Norwood: 1439
14	306.4	301.3	Ferrari 288 GTO: 1416
15	301.3	296.3	Datsun 280ZX Sharp: 1221
16	295.2	290.3	Nissan 300ZX Turbo Millen Super GTZ: 3247
17	281.2	276.5	Lamborghini Bravo: 2458
18	270.1	265.6	Nissan 300ZX Motor Sports International SR-71: 3246
19	262.2	257.9	Ferrari 250 Mille Miglia: 1376
20	258.2	253.9	Toyota Supra Turbo TRD: 4467
21	226.8	223.0	Ferrari 250 GT Berlinetta SWB: 1383
22	216.9	213.3	Ferrari 250 GT Berlinetta Lusso: 1388
23	215.5	211.9	Porsche Turbo 3-litre: 3648
24	211.8	208.2	Lamborghini Silhouette 3000: 2462
25	211.5	208.0	TVR Convertible Turbo: 4593
26	209.8	206.3	Aston Martin Spyder Touring: 235
27	204.9	201.5	Honda NSX: 2156
28	204.5	201.1	Porsche Carrera RS 3-litre: 3647
29	202.6	199.2	Acura NSX: 36
30	202.5	199.1	Mercedes-Benz 300SL Carrera Panamericana: 2788
31	200.8	197.5	Ferrari 250 GT Coupe: 1381
32	199.1	195.8	Ferrari 250 GT Cabriolet: 1380
			Ferrari 250 GT Coupe: 1384
33	199.0	195.7	Ferrari 308 GTB: 1409
34	196.3	193.0	Nissan Skyline GT-R: 3243
35	196.2	192.9	Porsche Carrera RS Touring: 3641

36	194.9	191.7	Mercedes-Benz 300SL: 2793
37	193.4	190.2	Nissan 300ZX Twin Turbo: 3248
38	193.1	189.9	Nissan 300ZX Turbo: 3241
39	192.8	189.6	Ferrari 212 Touring: 1372
40	192.4	189.2	Maserati 430: 2676
41	191.7	188.5	Ford Festiva Shogun: 1965
42	191.6	188.4	Ferrari Dino 308 GT4 2+2: 1410

Total: 46

2501 - 3000cc. Highest specific output. Limit set at 80bhp/litre.

	bhp/L	kW/L	PS/L	
1	210.7	157.1	213.6	Datsun 280ZX Electramotive: 1230
2	210.6	157.0	213.5	Porsche 959 S: 3702
3	162.8	121.4	165.1	Ferrari F40: 1446
				Ferrari F40: 1435
				Ferrari F40: 1450
4	162.0	120.8	164.3	Porsche 935 Group 4 Holbert: 3657
5	157.9	117.8	160.1	Porsche 959: 3731
				Porsche 959 Comfort: 3717
				Porsche 959 Sport: 3718
6	155.4	115.9	157.6	Nissan 300ZX Turbo Millen Super GTZ: 3247
7	153.8	114.7	155.9	Ferrari 308 Norwood: 1439
8	145.6	108.5	147.6	Toyota Supra Turbo TRD: 4467
9	144.6	107.8	146.6	Nissan 300ZX Motor Sports International SR-71: 3246
10	140.1	104.5	142.0	Ferrari 288 GTO: 1421
				Ferrari GTO: 1423
11	138.0	102.9	139.9	Ferrari 288 GTO: 1416
12	107.5	80.1	109.0	Nissan Skyline GT-R: 3243
13	106.5	79.4	107.9	Datsun 280ZX Sharp: 1221
14	101.6	75.8	103.0	Ferrari 250 Testa Rossa: 1382
				Ferrari 250 Testa Rossa: 1378
15	101.3	75.6	102.8	Nissan 300ZX Turbo: 3241
				Nissan 300ZX Twin Turbo: 3248
16	101.3	75.5	102.7	Mercedes-Benz 300SLR: 2795
17	100.9	75.3	102.3	Dodge Stealth R/T Turbo: 1347
				Mitsubishi 3000GT VR-4: 3111
18	100.1	74.7	101.5	Lamborghini Bravo: 2458
19	99.8	74.4	101.2	Porsche Carrera RSR: 3642
20	98.2	73.2	99.6	Ferrari 250 GT Berlinetta Lusso: 1388
21	94.6	70.5	95.9	Nissan 300ZX: 3240
22	90.7	67.6	91.9	Acura NSX: 36
				Honda NSX: 2156
23	88.0	65.7	89.3	Ferrari 250 GT Coupe: 1381
24	87.1	65.0	88.3	Ferrari 308 GTB: 1409
25	86.8	64.8	88.0	Porsche Turbo 3-litre: 3648
26	86.8	64.7	88.0	Lamborghini Silhouette 3000: 2462
27	85.7	63.9	86.8	Honda NSX Auto: 2159
28	85.4	63.7	86.6	Ferrari Dino 308 GT4 2+2: 1410
29	84.0	62.7	85.2	Renault Alpine A610 Turbo: 3918
30	83.4	62.2	84.6	Mercedes-Benz 300SL Roadster: 2800
				Mercedes-Benz 300SL Roadster: 2807
31	82.7	61.7	83.9	Ferrari 308 GT4 Dino: 1402
32	82.0	61.2	83.2	Ferrari 308 Dino GT4: 1405
				Ferrari 308 GT4 Dino: 1408
				Ferrari 308 GTB: 1411
33	81.6	60.9	82.7	Ferrari 250 GT Berlinetta SWB: 1383
34	81.3	60.6	82.4	Ferrari 250 GT 2+2: 1385
				Ferrari 250 GT Cabriolet: 1380
				Ferrari 250 GT Coupe: 1384
				Ferrari 250 Mille Miglia: 1376
35	81.1	60.5	82.2	Mercedes-Benz 300SL Coupe: 2794
36	80.8	60.3	82.0	Bitter Type 3 Cabrio: 494
37	80.6	60.1	81.8	Maserati 228: 2680
				Maserati 430: 2676
				Maserati 430: 2678
				Maserati Spyder: 2679
38	80.1	59.7	81.2	Mercedes-Benz 300SL: 2793

Total: 56

2501 and 3000cc. Highest piston speed. Limit set at 53ft/sec.

	ft/sec	m/sec	
1	64.8	19.7	Datsun 280ZX Electramotive: 1230
			Datsun 280ZX Sharp: 1221
2	64.0	19.5	Mercedes-Benz 300SLR: 2795
			Toyota Supra Turbo TRD: 4467
3	61.6	18.8	Porsche Carrera RSR: 3642
4	60.9	18.5	Nissan 300ZX Motor Sports International SR-71: 3246
5	60.5	18.5	Acura NSX: 36
			Honda NSX: 2156
6	59.9	18.2	Ferrari 308 GT4 Dino: 1402
			Ferrari 308 GTB: 1409
			Ferrari Dino 308 GT4 2+2: 1410
7	59.7	18.2	Toyota Supra: 4452
			Toyota Supra: 4459
			Toyota Supra: 4442
			Toyota Supra 3.0i: 4443
8	59.6	18.2	Mercedes-Benz 300SL Roadster: 2800
			Mercedes-Benz 300SL Roadster: 2807
9	59.0	18.0	Volvo 960: 4969
			Volvo 960 24v: 4968
10	59.0	18.0	Nissan 300ZX Turbo Millen Super GTZ: 3247
11	58.6	17.9	Mercedes-Benz 300SL: 2793
			Mercedes-Benz 300SL Coupe: 2794
12	58.1	17.7	Nissan 300ZX: 3234
			Nissan 300ZX: 3240
			Nissan 300ZX Turbo: 3241
			Nissan 300ZX Twin Turbo: 3248
13	58.0	17.7	Honda NSX Auto: 2159
14	57.4	17.5	Rover 3-litre Coupe: 4000
15	57.4	17.5	Rover Coupe: 4001
16	57.2	17.4	Austin-Healey 100S: 430
17	56.2	17.1	Mercedes-Benz 300CE: 2909
18	55.7	17.0	Porsche 944 Cabriolet: 3741
			Porsche 944 S2: 3742
			Porsche 944 S2: 3729
			Porsche 944 S2 Cabriolet: 3743
19	55.7	17.0	Toyota Supra 3.0i Turbo: 4465
20	55.7	17.0	Toyota Supra Turbo: 4460
			Toyota Supra Turbo: 4466
21	55.3	16.8	Mercedes-Benz 300E-24: 2912
22	55.1	16.8	Mercedes-Benz 300SL-24 5-speed Auto: 2917
			Rover 3-litre Coupe Mk III: 4005
			Talbot 105 Speed Model: 4336
23	55.0	16.8	Lamborghini Bravo: 2458
24	54.8	16.7	Nissan Skyline GT-R: 3243
25	54.7	16.7	Austin-Healey 100M: 431
26	54.5	16.6	Dodge Shadow ES Turbo: 1340
27	54.4	16.6	Ferrari 288 GTO: 1416
			Ferrari 288 GTO: 1421
			Ferrari GTO: 1423
28	54.2	16.5	Ford Taurus SHO: 1971
29	54.1	16.5	Aston Martin Mk III: 236
			Aston Martin Spyder Touring: 235
30	53.9	16.4	Porsche 935 Group 4 Holbert: 3657
31	53.6	16.3	Chrysler Conquest TSi: 1007
			Dodge Challenger: 1325
			Mitsubishi Starion: 3074
			Mitsubishi Starion 2.6 Turbo: 3106
			Mitsubishi Starion ESI: 3086
			Mitsubishi Starion ESI-R: 3090
			Mitsubishi Starion ESI-R: 3107
			Mitsubishi Starion Turbo: 3075
			Plymouth Fire Arrow: 3516
			Plymouth Sapporo: 3515
32	53.3	16.2	Ferrari F40: 1435
			Ferrari F40: 1450
			Ferrari F40: 1446
33	53.2	16.2	BMW 327S Hardy & Beck: 574

Total: 67

3001 - 3500cc. Maximum speed. Limit set at 145mph.

	mph	kmh	
1	235.0	378.1	Koenig C62: 2419
2	216.0	347.5	Porsche 911 Turbo RS Tuning: 3737
3	214.0	344.3	Bugatti EB110: 652
4	211.0	339.5	Porsche 911 Turbo Ruf Twin Turbo: 3710
5	208.0	334.7	Porsche 911 Ruf CTR: 3748
6	205.0	329.8	Porsche 911 Turbo Gemballa Mirage: 3751
7	201.0	323.4	Porsche 911 Turbo Koenig RS: 3709
8	183.0	294.4	Porsche 911 Turbo Motorsport Design: 3724
9	179.0	288.0	BMW 535i Alpina B10 Bi-Turbo: 619
10	171.0	275.1	Ferrari 348tb: 1449
			Porsche 911 Turbo: 3750
11	168.0	270.3	Porsche 911 Carrera Turbo: 3746
12	165.0	265.5	Porsche 911 Turbo: 3676
			Porsche 911 Turbo Gemballa Avalanche: 3697
13	164.0	263.9	Ferrari 348tb: 1445
14	160.0	257.4	Maserati Shamal: 2681
			Porsche 911 Turbo Cabriolet Ruf: 3680
15	159.0	255.8	Porsche 911 Turbo: 3736
			Porsche 911 Turbo: 3723
16	158.0	254.2	BMW 735i Koenig: 611
			BMW M635 CSi: 572
			Porsche 911 3.3 Turbo: 3719
			Porsche 911 Turbo Ruf 3.4: 3698
17	157.0	252.6	Porsche 911 Turbo Slant-Nose: 3699
18	156.0	251.0	BMW M1: 556
			Porsche 911 Turbo: 3659
19	155.0	249.4	Ferrari 275 GTS/4 NART: 1392
			Ferrari 328 GTB: 1428
			Porsche 911 Speedster: 3707
			Porsche 911 Turbo: 3708
20	154.0	247.8	BMW 735i Alpina B11: 602
			Ferrari Mondial: 1447
			Ferrari Mondial t: 1452
			Ferrari Mondial t Cabriolet: 1453
			Lamborghini Jalpa: 2471
			Porsche 911 Club Sport: 3722
21	153.0	246.2	Porsche 911 Turbo: 3689

22	152.0	244.6	Lamborghini 350GT: 2449
			Porsche 911 Carrera Club Sport: 3705
23	151.0	243.0	Jaguar C Type: 2274
			Porsche 911 Carrera: 3682
24	150.0	241.4	BMW M635 CSi: 607
25	149.0	239.7	Ferrari 328 GTS: 1431
			Ferrari Mondial 3.2: 1429
			Jaguar XKSS: 2291
			Porsche 911 Cabriolet: 3703
			Porsche 911 Carrera: 3704
			Porsche 911 Carrera Cabriolet: 3721
			Porsche 911 Carrera SE: 3688
			Porsche 911 Club Sport: 3706
			Porsche 911 Speedster: 3735
26	147.0	236.5	BMW 735i Automatic: 585
			BMW M6: 597
27	146.0	234.9	BMW M535i: 576
			Porsche 911 Carrera: 3679
28	145.0	233.3	BMW 535i SE: 593
			BMW M635 CSi Hardy & Beck: 577
			Ferrari 275 GTS: 1391
			Ferrari 3.2 Mondial: 1427
			Ferrari Mondial 3.2 Cabriolet: 1440
			Ferrari Mondial Cabriolet: 1436
			Ferrari Mondial Cabriolet 3.2: 1433
			Lamborghini Jalpa 3500: 2470

Total: 63

3001 - 3500cc. Acceleration to 60mph/ 96.5kmh. Limit set at 6.5sec.

	sec	
1	3.5	Koenig C62: 2419
		Sbarro Chrono 3.5: 4108
2	3.9	Bugatti EB110: 652
		Porsche 911 Ruf CTR: 3748
3	4.0	Porsche 911 Turbo Koenig RS: 3709
		Porsche 911 Turbo Motorsport Design: 3724
		Porsche 911 Turbo Ruf Twin Turbo: 3710
4	4.1	Porsche 911 Turbo Gemballa Mirage: 3751
5	4.5	Porsche 911 Turbo Ruf 3.4: 3698
6	4.6	Porsche 911 Carrera Turbo: 3746
		Porsche 911 Turbo RS Tuning: 3737
7	4.7	Porsche 911 Turbo: 3750
8	4.8	Porsche 911 Turbo: 3723
9	4.9	Porsche 911 3.3 Turbo: 3719
		Porsche 911 Turbo Gemballa Avalanche: 3697
10	5.0	Porsche 911 Turbo: 3689
		Porsche 911 Turbo: 3659
		Porsche 911 Turbo: 3708
		Porsche 911 Turbo Slant-Nose: 3699
11	5.1	BMW 535i Alpina B10 Bi-Turbo: 619
		Porsche 911 Turbo: 3736
		Porsche 911 Turbo: 3676
12	5.2	Jaguar XKSS: 2291
		Porsche 911 Carrera Club Sport: 3705
13	5.3	Porsche 911 Club Sport: 3722
		Porsche 911 Turbo Cabriolet Ruf: 3680
14	5.5	Porsche 911 Carrera: 3682
15	5.6	Ferrari 348tb: 1445
		Porsche 911 Carrera SE: 3688
16	5.7	Porsche 911 Cabriolet: 3687
		Porsche 911 Carrera: 3696
		Porsche 911 Club Sport: 3706
17	5.9	Ferrari 328 GTS: 1431
		Ferrari Mondial t: 1441
18	6.0	BMW 735i Koenig: 611
		BMW M635 CSi: 607
		Ferrari 348tb: 1449
		Porsche 911 Speedster: 3735
19	6.1	BMW M635 CSi: 572
		Porsche 911 Carrera Cabriolet: 3721
20	6.2	BMW M1: 556
		Lamborghini Jalpa 3500: 2470
		Porsche 911 Carrera: 3679
21	6.4	BMW M635 CSi Hardy & Beck: 577
22	6.5	Porsche 911 Cabriolet: 3703
		Porsche 911 Speedster: 3707

Total: 46

3001 - 3500cc. Highest power. Limit set at 250bhp.

	bhp	kW	PS	
1	600.0	447.4	608.3	Bugatti EB110: 652
2	588.0	438.5	596.2	Koenig C62: 2419
3	580.0	432.5	588.0	Porsche 911 Turbo RS Tuning: 3737
4	520.0	387.8	527.2	Porsche 911 Turbo Koenig RS: 3709
5	500.0	372.8	506.9	Sbarro Chrono 3.5: 4108
6	490.0	365.4	496.8	Porsche 911 Turbo Gemballa Mirage: 3751
7	488.0	363.9	494.8	Porsche 911 Turbo Motorsport Design: 3724
8	469.0	349.7	475.5	Porsche 911 Ruf CTR: 3748
				Porsche 911 Turbo Ruf Twin Turbo: 3710
9	374.0	278.9	379.2	Porsche 911 Turbo Ruf 3.4: 3698
10	360.0	268.4	365.0	BMW 535i Alpina B10 Bi-Turbo: 619
11	336.0	250.6	340.7	Lamborghini 350GT: 2449
12	330.0	246.1	334.6	Ferrari 275 GTS/4 NART: 1392
13	325.0	242.3	329.5	Maserati Shamal: 2681
14	320.0	238.6	324.4	Porsche 911 Carrera Turbo: 3746
				Porsche 911 Turbo: 3750
15	300.0	223.7	304.2	Ferrari 348tb: 1445
				Ferrari 348tb: 1449
				Ferrari Mondial: 1447
				Ferrari Mondial t: 1452
				Ferrari Mondial t Cabriolet: 1453
				Porsche 911 3.3 Turbo: 3719
				Porsche 911 Turbo: 3736
				Porsche 911 Turbo: 3676
				Porsche 911 Turbo Cabriolet Ruf: 3680
16	296.0	220.7	300.1	Ferrari Mondial t: 1441
17	290.0	216.2	294.0	BMW 735i Koenig: 611
18	286.0	213.3	290.0	BMW M635 CSi: 607
				BMW M635 CSi: 572
19	282.0	210.3	285.9	Porsche 911 Turbo: 3723
				Porsche 911 Turbo: 3689
				Porsche 911 Turbo: 3708
				Porsche 911 Turbo Gemballa Avalanche: 3697
				Porsche 911 Turbo Slant-Nose: 3699
20	281.0	209.5	284.9	BMW M635 CSi Hardy & Beck: 577
21	270.0	201.3	273.7	Ferrari Mondial 3.2QV: 1430
22	260.0	193.9	263.6	Ferrari 275 GTS: 1391
				Ferrari 3.2 Mondial: 1427
				Ferrari 328 GTB: 1428
				Ferrari 328 GTS: 1431
				Ferrari Mondial 3.2: 1429
				Ferrari Mondial 3.2 Cabriolet: 1440
				Ferrari Mondial Cabriolet: 1436
				Ferrari Mondial Cabriolet 3.2: 1433
				Jaguar XKSS: 2291
23	256.0	190.9	259.5	BMW M6: 597
24	255.0	190.1	258.5	Lamborghini Jalpa 3500: 2470
25	253.0	188.7	256.5	Porsche 911 Turbo: 3659
26	252.0	187.9	255.5	BMW 745i: 562
27	250.0	186.4	253.5	BMW 735i Alpina B11: 602
				Jaguar XK150S: 2294
				Jaguar XK150S: 2295
				Lamborghini Jalpa: 2467
				Pontiac Tempest Supercharged: 3532

Total: 54

3001 - 3500cc. Highest torque. Limit set at 225lbft.

	lbft	Nm	
1	533.0	722.2	Koenig C62: 2419
2	490.0	664.0	Porsche 911 Turbo Koenig RS: 3709
			Porsche 911 Turbo Motorsport Design: 3724
3	465.0	630.1	Porsche 911 Turbo RS Tuning: 3737
4	457.0	619.2	Porsche 911 Turbo Ruf Twin Turbo: 3710
5	420.0	569.1	Porsche 911 Turbo Gemballa Mirage: 3751
6	419.0	567.8	Bugatti EB110: 652
7	408.0	552.8	Porsche 911 Ruf CTR: 3748
8	382.0	517.6	BMW 535i Alpina B10 Bi-Turbo: 619
9	354.0	479.7	Porsche 911 Turbo Ruf 3.4: 3698
10	347.0	470.2	Sbarro Chrono 3.5: 4108
11	332.1	450.0	Porsche 911 Turbo: 3750
12	332.0	449.9	Porsche 911 Carrera Turbo: 3746
13	320.0	433.6	Maserati Shamal: 2681
14	318.0	430.9	Porsche 911 Turbo: 3676
15	317.3	430.0	Porsche 911 3.3 Turbo: 3719
16	317.0	429.5	Porsche 911 Turbo: 3736
17	304.0	411.9	Porsche 911 Turbo Cabriolet Ruf: 3680
18	299.0	405.1	BMW 735i Koenig: 611
19	288.0	390.2	Porsche 911 Turbo: 3723
20	282.0	382.1	Porsche 911 Turbo: 3659
21	280.0	379.4	BMW 745i: 562
22	278.0	376.7	Porsche 911 Turbo: 3689
			Porsche 911 Turbo: 3708
			Porsche 911 Turbo Gemballa Avalanche: 3697
			Porsche 911 Turbo Slant-Nose: 3699
23	260.0	352.3	Jaguar XKSS: 2291
			Lamborghini Jalpa: 2471
24	255.0	345.5	Pontiac Tempest Supercharged: 3532
25	254.0	344.2	Lamborghini 350GT: 2449
26	251.0	340.1	BMW M635 CSi: 572
			BMW M635 CSi Hardy & Beck: 577
27	250.9	340.0	BMW M635 CSi: 607
28	243.0	329.3	BMW 735i Alpina B11: 602
			BMW M1: 556
			BMW M6: 597
29	240.0	325.2	Ferrari 275 GTS/4 NART: 1392
			Jaguar XK150S: 2294
			Jaguar XK150S: 2295
30	238.4	323.0	Ferrari 348tb: 1445

31	238.0	322.5	Ferrari Mondial t: 1441
32	237.0	321.1	Ferrari Mondial t: 1452
33	235.0	318.4	Lamborghini Jalpa: 2467
34	234.0	317.1	Mercedes-Benz 190E AMG Baby Hammer: 2903
35	232.5	315.0	BMW 635 CSi: 594
36	232.0	314.4	BMW 735i Automatic: 585
			Maserati 3500 GTI Sebring: 2655
37	231.0	313.0	Lamborghini Jalpa 3500: 2470
			Mercedes-Benz 280SE 3.5: 2831
38	229.0	310.3	BMW 735i Automatic: 571
			BMW M535i: 576
			Ferrari 348tb: 1449
			Ferrari Mondial: 1447
			Ferrari Mondial t Cabriolet: 1453
39	228.0	308.9	BMW 333i Alpina: 548
			BMW 735i: 567
40	225.1	305.0	BMW 535i SE: 593
41	225.0	304.9	BMW 535i: 600
			BMW 535i Automatic: 601
			BMW 735i: 595
			Pontiac Grand Prix McLaren Turbo: 3592

Total: 61

3001 - 3500cc. Highest rpm at peak power. Limit set at 6000rpm.

	rpm	
1	9200	Sbarro Chrono 3.5: 4108
2	9000	Bugatti EB110: 652
3	8000	Ferrari 275 GTS/4 NART: 1392
4	7200	Ferrari 348tb: 1445
		Ferrari Mondial t: 1441
		Ferrari Mondial t: 1452
5	7000	Ferrari 275 GTS: 1391
		Ferrari 3.2 Mondial: 1427
		Ferrari 328 GTB: 1428
		Ferrari 328 GTS: 1431
		Ferrari 348tb: 1449
		Ferrari Mondial: 1447
		Ferrari Mondial 3.2: 1429
		Ferrari Mondial 3.2 Cabriolet: 1440
		Ferrari Mondial 3.2QV: 1430
		Ferrari Mondial Cabriolet: 1436
		Ferrari Mondial Cabriolet 3.2: 1433
		Ferrari Mondial t Cabriolet: 1453
		Lamborghini Jalpa: 2471
		Lamborghini Jalpa: 2467
		Lamborghini Jalpa 3500: 2470
6	6900	Porsche 911 Turbo RS Tuning: 3737
7	6500	BMW M1: 556
		BMW M6: 597
		BMW M635 CSi: 607
		BMW M635 CSi: 572
		BMW M635 CSi Hardy & Beck: 577
		Lamborghini 350GT: 2449
8	6300	Koenig C62: 2419
		Porsche 911 Turbo Koenig RS: 3709
9	6250	Porsche 911 Turbo Motorsport Design: 3724
10	6050	Mercedes-Benz 280SE 3.5: 2831
11	6000	BMW 333i Alpina: 548
		BMW 533i: 566
		BMW 535i Alpina B10 Bi-Turbo: 619
		BMW 633 CSi: 570
		Jaguar XK120C: 2280
		Jaguar XKSS: 2291
		Maserati Shamal: 2681
		Porsche 911 Turbo Ruf 3.4: 3698

Total: 40

3001 - 3500cc. Highest power-to-weight ratio. Limit set at180bhp/ton.

	bhp/ ton	bhp/ tonne	
1	780.5	767.5	Sbarro Chrono 3.5: 4108
2	543.1	534.1	Koenig C62: 2419
3	454.8	447.2	Bugatti EB110: 652
4	416.0	409.1	Porsche 911 Turbo Koenig RS: 3709
5	415.2	408.3	Porsche 911 Turbo Ruf Twin Turbo: 3710
6	368.3	362.2	Porsche 911 Turbo Gemballa Mirage: 3751
7	366.8	360.7	Porsche 911 Turbo Motorsport Design: 3724
8	348.4	342.6	Lamborghini 350GT: 2449
9	345.6	339.8	Porsche 911 Ruf CTR: 3748
10	301.1	296.1	Ferrari 275 GTS/4 NART: 1392
11	299.2	294.2	Porsche 911 Turbo Ruf 3.4: 3698
12	261.2	256.8	Jaguar XKSS: 2291
13	256.3	252.1	Maserati Shamal: 2681
14	226.4	222.6	Porsche 911 Turbo: 3676
15	225.5	221.7	Porsche 911 Turbo Cabriolet Ruf: 3680
16	222.9	219.2	Porsche 911 Turbo: 3750
17	220.3	216.6	Porsche 911 3.3 Turbo: 3719
18	220.0	216.3	Porsche 911 Turbo: 3736
19	218.9	215.2	Porsche 911 Carrera Turbo: 3746
20	216.2	212.6	BMW 535i Alpina B10 Bi-Turbo: 619
21	212.3	208.8	Porsche 911 Turbo Slant-Nose: 3699
22	210.0	206.5	Jaguar XK120C: 2280
23	208.2	204.8	Ferrari 348tb: 1445
24	207.7	204.3	Ferrari Mondial t: 1452
25	206.8	203.3	Porsche 911 Turbo: 3723
			Porsche 911 Turbo: 3708
26	206.4	203.0	Porsche 911 Turbo: 3689
27	205.5	202.1	Ferrari 348tb: 1449
28	200.6	197.2	Porsche 911 Speedster: 3707
29	200.0	196.7	Jaguar C Type: 2274
30	198.4	195.1	Porsche 911 Carrera Club Sport: 3705
31	196.8	193.5	Ferrari 275 GTS: 1391
32	194.2	191.0	Ferrari Mondial: 1447
33	193.8	190.6	Porsche 911 Carrera: 3682
34	192.8	189.6	BMW M635 CSi: 572
35	191.5	188.3	Porsche 911 Turbo: 3659
36	191.1	187.9	Porsche 911 Turbo Gemballa Avalanche: 3697
37	187.9	184.8	Pontiac Tempest Supercharged: 3532
38	187.9	184.8	BMW M635 CSi Hardy & Beck: 577
39	186.1	183.0	Porsche 911 Carrera SE: 3688
40	185.9	182.8	Ferrari Mondial 3.2QV: 1430
41	185.5	182.4	Ferrari 328 GTB: 1428
42	185.3	182.2	BMW M635 CSi: 607
43	184.9	181.8	Mercedes-Benz 190E AMG Baby Hammer: 2903
44	184.6	181.5	Ferrari Mondial t Cabriolet: 1453
45	184.4	181.3	Porsche 911 Club Sport: 3706
			Porsche 911 Club Sport: 3722
46	184.3	181.2	Lamborghini Jalpa 3500: 2470
47	183.7	180.7	Ferrari 328 GTS: 1431

Total: 49

3001 - 3500cc. Highest specific output. Limit set at 75bhp/litre.

	bhp/L	kW/L	PS/L	
1	174.6	130.2	177.0	Koenig C62: 2419
2	172.2	128.4	174.6	Porsche 911 Turbo RS Tuning: 3737
3	171.5	127.9	173.9	Bugatti EB110: 652
4	154.5	115.2	156.6	Porsche 911 Turbo Koenig RS: 3709
5	147.9	110.3	150.0	Porsche 911 Turbo Motorsport Design: 3724
6	145.5	108.5	147.5	Porsche 911 Turbo Gemballa Mirage: 3751
7	142.9	106.6	144.9	Sbarro Chrono 3.5: 4108
8	139.3	103.9	141.3	Porsche 911 Turbo Ruf Twin Turbo: 3710
9	139.3	103.9	141.2	Porsche 911 Ruf CTR: 3748
10	111.1	82.9	112.6	Porsche 911 Turbo Ruf 3.4: 3698
11	105.0	78.3	106.4	BMW 535i Alpina B10 Bi-Turbo: 619
12	101.0	75.3	102.4	Maserati Shamal: 2681
13	100.4	74.9	101.8	Ferrari 275 GTS/4 NART: 1392
14	97.0	72.3	98.3	Lamborghini 350GT: 2449
				Porsche 911 Carrera Turbo: 3746
				Porsche 911 Turbo: 3750
15	91.0	67.8	92.2	Porsche 911 Turbo Cabriolet Ruf: 3680
16	90.9	67.8	92.2	Porsche 911 3.3 Turbo: 3719
				Porsche 911 Turbo: 3676
				Porsche 911 Turbo: 3736
17	88.1	65.7	89.3	Ferrari 348tb: 1445
				Ferrari 348tb: 1449
				Ferrari Mondial: 1447
				Ferrari Mondial t: 1452
				Ferrari Mondial t Cabriolet: 1453
18	86.9	64.8	88.1	Ferrari Mondial t: 1441
19	85.5	63.7	86.7	Porsche 911 Turbo: 3689
				Porsche 911 Turbo: 3708
				Porsche 911 Turbo: 3723
				Porsche 911 Turbo Gemballa Avalanche: 3697
				Porsche 911 Turbo Slant-Nose: 3699
20	84.7	63.2	85.9	Ferrari Mondial 3.2QV: 1430
21	84.5	63.0	85.7	BMW 735i Koenig: 611
22	82.8	61.8	84.0	BMW M635 CSi: 572
				BMW M635 CSi: 607
23	81.6	60.9	82.8	Ferrari 3.2 Mondial: 1427
				Ferrari 328 GTB: 1428
				Ferrari 328 GTS: 1431
				Ferrari Mondial 3.2: 1429
				Ferrari Mondial 3.2 Cabriolet: 1440
				Ferrari Mondial Cabriolet: 1436
				Ferrari Mondial Cabriolet 3.2: 1433
24	81.4	60.7	82.5	BMW M635 CSi Hardy & Beck: 577
25	79.1	59.0	80.2	Ferrari 275 GTS: 1391
26	78.5	58.5	79.6	BMW 745i: 562
27	78.4	58.5	79.5	Pontiac Tempest Supercharged: 3532
28	76.7	57.2	77.7	Porsche 911 Turbo: 3659
29	75.5	56.3	76.6	Jaguar XKSS: 2291

Total: 48

3001 - 3500cc. Highest piston speed. Limit set at 55ft/sec.

	ft/sec	m/sec	
1	84.6	25.8	Sbarro Chrono 3.5: 4108
2	69.5	21.2	Jaguar XK120C: 2280
			Jaguar XKSS: 2291
3	67.2	20.5	Jaguar C Type: 2274
4	66.6	20.3	Jaguar XK 140: 2287
5	66.6	20.3	Jaguar XK140: 2276
			Jaguar XK140MC: 2283
6	63.7	19.4	Allard GT Coupe: 153
			Jaguar 3.4: 2292
			Jaguar Mk VII Auto: 2286
			Jaguar Mk VIII: 2289
			Jaguar XK150: 2293
			Jaguar XK150S: 2295
7	63.7	19.4	Jaguar 3.4: 2296
			Jaguar Mk VII: 2282
			Jaguar XK150: 2290
			Jaguar XK150S: 2294
8	62.5	19.1	Jaguar XK120: 2275
9	61.4	18.7	Jaguar XK120 Coupe: 2279
			Jaguar XK120M: 2281
10	60.2	18.4	Jaguar Mk VII: 2277
			Jaguar Mk VII: 2278
11	60.2	18.3	Maserati 3500GT: 2654
			Maserati GT Coupe: 2653
12	60.2	18.3	Maserati 3500 GTI Sebring: 2655
13	59.8	18.2	BMW M1: 556
			BMW M6: 597
			BMW M635 CSi: 607
			BMW M635 CSi: 572
			BMW M635 CSi Hardy & Beck: 577
14	59.1	18.0	Jaguar XK120: 2273
15	59.0	18.0	Ferrari 348tb: 1445
			Ferrari Mondial t: 1441
			Ferrari Mondial t: 1452
16	58.3	17.8	Pontiac Tempest Supercharged: 3532
17	57.9	17.7	Jaguar XJ3.4: 2327
18	57.4	17.5	Ferrari 348tb: 1449
			Ferrari Mondial: 1447
			Ferrari Mondial t Cabriolet: 1453
			Lamborghini Jalpa: 2471
			Lamborghini Jalpa: 2467
			Lamborghini Jalpa 3500: 2470
19	56.5	17.2	BMW 333i Alpina: 548
			BMW 533i: 566
			BMW 535i Alpina B10 Bi-Turbo: 619
			BMW 633 CSi: 570
20	56.4	17.2	Ferrari 3.2 Mondial: 1427
			Ferrari 328 GTS: 1431
			Ferrari Mondial 3.2 Cabriolet: 1440
			Ferrari Mondial 3.2QV: 1430
			Ferrari Mondial Cabriolet: 1436
			Ferrari Mondial Cabriolet 3.2: 1433
21	56.2	17.1	Porsche 911 Turbo RS Tuning: 3737
22	55.7	17.0	Bugatti EB110: 652
23	55.1	16.8	Talbot 3.5-litre Speed Saloon: 4340

Total: 55

3501 - 4000cc. Maximum speed. Limit set at 140mph.

	mph	kmh	
1	196.1	315.5	Porsche 911 Ruf TR2: 3749
2	196.0	315.4	Porsche 911 Ruf: 3747
3	192.0	308.9	Jaguar D Type: 2285
			Lamborghini Countach: 2461
4	186.0	299.3	Zender Fact 4: 5008
5	180.0	289.6	Bizzarrini P538: 497
			Lamborghini Miura: 2451
6	178.0	286.4	Pontiac Firebird T/A Turbo Pontiac Engineering: 3588
7	175.0	281.6	Ferrari 250 GTO: 1386
8	174.0	280.0	Opel Omega Lotus: 3352
9	173.0	278.4	Lamborghini Miura P400S: 2455
10	168.0	270.3	Lamborghini Miura S: 2456
11	164.0	263.9	Lamborghini Countach S: 2464
12	163.0	262.3	Lamborghini Miura: 2452
13	161.0	259.0	Porsche 911 Carrera 4: 3734
			Porsche 911 Carrera 4: 3720
			Porsche 911 Carrera RS: 3753
14	160.0	257.4	Ford Thunderbird Super Coupe Ford Engineering: 1948
			Porsche 911 Carrera 2: 3732
15	159.0	255.8	Porsche 911 Carrera 2 Tiptronic: 3733
			Porsche Carrera 2 Cabriolet Tiptronic: 3744
16	158.0	254.2	Lamborghini Espada: 2453
17	156.0	251.0	Lamborghini 400GT: 2450
18	155.0	249.4	BMW M5: 606
			BMW M5: 622
			Jaguar E Type Coupe: 2303
			Pontiac Firebird TransAm 20th Anniversary: 3589
19	153.5	247.0	Aston Martin DB4 GT Zagato: 240
20	152.0	244.6	Audi V8 Quattro: 338
			Lamborghini Jarama 400GT: 2459
			Lamborghini Jarama 400GT: 2457
21	151.7	244.1	Jaguar E Type Coupe: 2298
22	150.0	241.4	Irmsher GT: 2243
			Jaguar XKE: 2299
			Jaguar XKE: 2306
			Lamborghini Countach S: 2466
			Lamborghini Espada: 2454
			Lexus SC400: 2571
			Lynx D Type: 2642
			Pontiac Firebird TransAm Turbo: 3590
			Triumph TR8 Group 44: 4578
			TVR V8 S: 4603
23	148.0	238.1	Aston Martin DB4: 239
			Aston Martin DB6: 242
			Lexus LS400: 2570
			Lotus Elite V8: 2623
24	146.0	234.9	Ferrari 330 GTS: 1393
25	144.0	231.7	Audi V8 Quattro: 331
			Audi V8 Quattro Automatic: 332
			TVR 390 SE: 4599
26	143.0	230.1	Aston Martin DBS: 243
			Jaguar XJR 4.0: 2363
			Mercury Cougar XR-7: 2960
27	142.6	229.4	Aston Martin DB5: 241
28	142.0	228.5	Jaguar XJS 3.6: 2345
29	141.0	226.9	Aston Martin DB4: 238
			Jaguar 4.0 Sovereign: 2358
30	140.2	225.6	Aston Martin DB4: 237
31	140.0	225.3	Ford Thunderbird Super Coupe: 1947
			Jaguar XJ6 3.6: 2348
			Westfield SEight: 4973

Total: 61

3501 - 4000cc. Acceleration to 60mph/96.5kmh. Limit set at 7.5sec.

	sec	
1	3.8	Porsche 911 Ruf: 3747
		Porsche 911 Ruf TR2: 3749
2	4.3	Triumph TR8 Group 44: 4578
		Westfield SEight: 4973
		Zender Fact 4: 5008
3	4.7	Jaguar D Type: 2285
4	4.9	Opel Omega Lotus: 3352
		Porsche 911 Carrera 4: 3720
		Porsche 911 Carrera RS: 3753
5	5.1	Pontiac Firebird TransAm 20th Anniversary: 3589
		Porsche 911 Carrera 2: 3732
6	5.2	Ford Thunderbird Super Coupe Ford Engineering: 1948
		TVR V8 S: 4603
7	5.3	Lynx D Type: 2642
		Pontiac Firebird TransAm Turbo: 3590
		Triumph TR8 Libra Rally: 4579
8	5.5	Lamborghini Miura: 2451
		Lamborghini Miura S: 2456
9	5.6	Morgan Plus 8: 3134
10	5.7	Lamborghini Countach S: 2466
		TVR 390 SE: 4599
11	5.8	Porsche 911 Carrera 4: 3734
		Porsche Panamericana: 3745
12	5.9	Ferrari 250 GTO: 1386
		Lamborghini Countach S: 2464
13	6.1	Aston Martin DB4 GT Zagato: 240
		Morgan Plus 8: 3137
14	6.2	Porsche Carrera 2 Cabriolet Tiptronic: 3744
15	6.3	BMW M5: 606
		Lamborghini Miura: 2452
16	6.4	BMW M5: 622
		Panther J72: 3372
17	6.5	Aston Martin DB6: 242
		Lamborghini Espada: 2453
		Morgan Plus 8: 3131
		Pontiac Firebird T/A Turbo Pontiac Engineering: 3588
18	6.6	TVR 350i Series II: 4598
19	6.7	Lamborghini Miura P400S: 2455
		Morgan Plus 8: 3129
20	6.8	Buick Reatta Turbo Buick Engineering: 697
		Lamborghini Countach: 2461
		Morgan Plus 8 Turbo: 3132
21	6.9	Ferrari 330 GTS: 1393
		Jaguar E Type Coupe: 2298
		Lexus SC400: 2571
		Porsche 911 Carrera 2 Tiptronic: 3733
22	7.2	Jaguar E Type Coupe: 2303
		Lamborghini Jarama 400GT: 2457
		Lamborghini Jarama 400GT: 2459
23	7.4	Ford Thunderbird Super Coupe: 1947
		Jaguar XJS 3.6: 2345
		Jaguar XKE: 2306
		Jaguar XKE: 2299
		Mercury Cougar XR-7: 2960
		Morgan Plus 8: 3135

24	7.5	Aston Martin DB4: 237
		Audi V8 Quattro: 338
		Lamborghini 400GT: 2450

Total: 58

3501 - 4000cc. Highest power. Limit set at 250bhp.

	bhp	kW	PS	
1	455.0	339.3	461.3	Porsche 911 Ruf: 3747
				Porsche 911 Ruf TR2: 3749
2	448.0	334.1	454.2	Zender Fact 4: 5008
3	430.0	320.6	436.0	Lamborghini Miura S: 2456
4	400.0	298.3	405.5	Lamborghini Miura: 2452
5	390.0	290.8	395.4	Ferrari 250 GTO: 1386
				Lamborghini Espada: 2453
6	380.0	283.4	385.3	Pontiac Firebird T/A Turbo Pontiac Engineering: 3588
7	377.0	281.1	382.2	Opel Omega Lotus: 3352
8	375.0	279.6	380.2	Lamborghini Countach: 2461
9	370.0	275.9	375.1	Lamborghini Miura P400S: 2455
10	360.0	268.4	365.0	Lamborghini 400GT: 2450
				Triumph TR8 Group 44: 4578
11	350.0	261.0	354.8	Bizzarrini P538: 497
				Lamborghini Jarama 400GT: 2457
				Lamborghini Jarama 400GT: 2459
12	345.0	257.3	349.8	Ferrari 330 GTS: 1393
13	330.0	246.1	334.6	Ford Thunderbird Super Coupe Ford Engineering: 1948
14	325.0	242.3	329.5	Aston Martin DB6: 242
				Aston Martin DBS: 243
				Lamborghini Countach S: 2466
				Lamborghini Countach S: 2464
				Lamborghini Espada: 2454
				Lamborghini Miura: 2451
15	315.0	234.9	319.4	BMW M5: 606
16	314.0	234.1	318.4	Aston Martin DB4 GT Zagato: 240
17	310.0	231.2	314.3	BMW M5: 622
18	285.0	212.5	288.9	Jaguar D Type: 2285
				Lynx D Type: 2642
19	282.0	210.3	285.9	Aston Martin DB5: 241
20	280.0	208.8	283.9	Triumph TR8 Libra Rally: 4579
21	275.0	205.1	278.8	TVR 390 SE: 4599
22	273.0	203.6	276.8	Westfield SEight: 4973
23	265.0	197.6	268.7	Jaguar E Type Coupe: 2303
				Jaguar E Type Coupe: 2298
				Jaguar XKE: 2299
				Jaguar XKE: 2306
24	263.0	196.1	266.6	Aston Martin DB4: 239
				Aston Martin DB4: 237
25	260.0	193.9	263.6	Porsche 911 Carrera RS: 3753
26	251.0	187.2	254.5	Jaguar XJR 4.0: 2363
27	250.0	186.4	253.5	Audi V8 Quattro: 331
				Audi V8 Quattro Automatic: 332
				Jaguar Mk X: 2300
				Lexus SC400: 2571
				Pontiac Firebird TransAm 20th Anniversary: 3589
				Pontiac Firebird TransAm Turbo: 3590
				Porsche 911 Carrera 2: 3732
				Porsche 911 Carrera 4: 3734
				Porsche 911 Carrera 4: 3720
				Porsche Carrera 2 Cabriolet Tiptronic: 3744
				Porsche Panamericana: 3745

Total: 52

3501 - 4000cc. Highest torque. Limit set at 250lbft.

	lbft	Nm	
1	483.0	654.5	Porsche 911 Ruf TR2: 3749
2	482.0	653.1	Porsche 911 Ruf: 3747
3	425.0	575.9	Pontiac Firebird T/A Turbo Pontiac Engineering: 3588
4	409.0	554.2	Opel Omega Lotus: 3352
5	403.0	546.1	Ford Thunderbird Super Coupe Ford Engineering: 1948
6	390.0	528.5	Zender Fact 4: 5008
7	340.0	460.7	Pontiac Firebird TransAm 20th Anniversary: 3589
			Pontiac Firebird TransAm Turbo: 3590
8	330.0	447.2	Lamborghini Miura S: 2456
9	320.0	433.6	Lamborghini Espada: 2453
10	315.0	426.8	Ford Thunderbird Super Coupe: 1947
			Mercury Cougar XR-7: 2960
11	310.0	420.1	Triumph TR8 Group 44: 4578
12	300.0	406.5	Lamborghini Miura: 2452
			Oldsmobile F-85 Jetfire: 3279
			Oldsmobile F-85 Jetfire Sports Coupe: 3277
13	290.0	393.0	Aston Martin DB6: 242
			Aston Martin DBS: 243
			Lamborghini 400GT: 2450
14	289.0	391.6	Lamborghini Jarama 400GT: 2457
			Lamborghini Jarama 400GT: 2459
15	286.0	387.5	Lamborghini Miura: 2451
			Lamborghini Miura P400S: 2455
16	285.6	387.0	Jaguar 4.0 Sovereign: 2358
17	280.0	379.4	Aston Martin DB5: 241
			Buick Riviera S-type: 692
18	278.2	377.0	Jaguar XJR 4.0: 2363
			Jaguar XJS 4.0 Auto: 2371
19	278.0	376.7	Aston Martin DB4 GT Zagato: 240
			Jaguar XJ6 Vanden Plas: 2362
20	277.0	375.3	Ferrari 330 GTS: 1393
21	275.3	373.0	TVR V8 S: 4603
22	275.0	372.6	Lamborghini Espada: 2454
23	270.0	365.9	TVR 390 SE: 4599
24	266.0	360.4	BMW M5: 606
			Lamborghini Countach: 2461
25	265.0	359.1	BMW M5: 622
26	260.0	352.3	Armstrong Siddeley Star Sapphire: 220
			Buick Reatta Turbo Buick Engineering: 697
			Jaguar E Type Coupe: 2303
			Jaguar E Type Coupe: 2298
			Jaguar XKE: 2306
			Jaguar XKE: 2299
			Lamborghini Countach S: 2466
			Lamborghini Countach S: 2464
			Lexus SC400: 2571
			Pontiac Bonneville SSEi: 3600
			Westfield SEight: 4973
27	258.3	350.0	Lexus LS400: 2570
28	250.9	340.0	Audi V8 Quattro Automatic: 332
29	250.0	338.8	Jaguar Mk X: 2300

Total: 51

3501 - 4000cc. Highest rpm at peak power. Limit set at 5500rpm.

	rpm	
1	8000	Lamborghini Countach: 2461
		Triumph TR8 Group 44: 4578
2	7700	Lamborghini Miura P400S: 2455
3	7500	Ferrari 250 GTO: 1386
		Lamborghini Countach S: 2464
		Lamborghini Countach S: 2466
		Lamborghini Jarama 400GT: 2459
		Lamborghini Jarama 400GT: 2457
4	7350	Lamborghini Miura S: 2456
5	7000	Bizzarrini P538: 497
		Ferrari 330 GTS: 1393
		Lamborghini Espada: 2453
		Lamborghini Miura: 2452
		Lamborghini Miura: 2451
		Triumph TR8 Libra Rally: 4579
6	6900	BMW M5: 606
		BMW M5: 622
7	6500	Lamborghini 400GT: 2450
		Lamborghini Espada: 2454
		Zender Fact 4: 5008
8	6100	Porsche 911 Carrera 2: 3732
		Porsche 911 Carrera 2 Tiptronic: 3733
		Porsche 911 Carrera 4: 3720
		Porsche 911 Carrera 4: 3734
		Porsche 911 Carrera RS: 3753
		Porsche Carrera 2 Cabriolet Tiptronic: 3744
		Porsche Panamericana: 3745
9	6000	Aston Martin DB4 GT Zagato: 240
10	5800	Audi V8 Quattro: 331
		Audi V8 Quattro: 338
		Audi V8 Quattro Automatic: 332
		Porsche 911 Ruf: 3747
		Porsche 911 Ruf TR2: 3749
11	5750	Aston Martin DB6: 242
		Aston Martin DBS: 243
		Jaguar D Type: 2285
		TVR V8 S: 4603
12	5700	Aston Martin DB4: 237
		Aston Martin DB4: 239
		Lotus Elite V8: 2623
		Westfield SEight: 4973
13	5600	Lexus SC400: 2571
14	5500	Aston Martin DB4: 238
		Aston Martin DB5: 241
		Ford Thunderbird Super Coupe Ford Engineering: 1948
		Jaguar 3.8 Mk II: 2301
		Jaguar 3.8 Mk II Automatic: 2302
		Jaguar 3.8 Sedan: 2297
		Jaguar 3.8S: 2307
		Jaguar 3.8S Sedan: 2304
		Jaguar E Type Coupe: 2303
		Jaguar E Type Coupe: 2298
		Jaguar Mk X: 2300
		Jaguar XKE: 2299
		Jaguar XKE: 2306
		TVR 390 SE: 4599

Total: 56

3501 - 4000cc. Highest power-to-weight ratio. Limit set at 190bhp/ton.

	bhp/ ton	bhp/ tonne	
1	412.6	405.7	Bizzarrini P538: 497
2	411.3	404.4	Zender Fact 4: 5008
3	396.6	390.0	Westfield SEight: 4973
4	367.8	361.7	Ferrari 250 GTO: 1386
5	335.8	330.2	Porsche 911 Ruf: 3747
6	335.3	329.7	Porsche 911 Ruf TR2: 3749
7	331.6	326.0	Lamborghini Miura S: 2456
8	315.0	309.7	Triumph TR8 Group 44: 4578
9	314.4	309.1	Lamborghini Miura: 2452
10	299.7	294.7	Lynx D Type: 2642
11	298.3	293.3	Jaguar D Type: 2285
12	289.6	284.8	Lamborghini Miura P400S: 2455
13	278.1	273.5	Lamborghini Countach: 2461
14	262.4	258.0	Triumph TR8 Libra Rally: 4579
15	256.3	252.1	Lamborghini Miura: 2451
16	254.4	250.1	Aston Martin DB4 GT Zagato: 240
17	252.0	247.8	Lamborghini 400GT: 2450
18	248.9	244.7	Ferrari 330 GTS: 1393
19	239.3	235.3	TVR V8 S: 4603
20	238.1	234.1	Pontiac Firebird T/A Turbo Pontiac Engineering: 3588
21	237.7	233.7	Lamborghini Espada: 2453
22	230.7	226.9	TVR 390 SE: 4599
23	229.6	225.8	Lamborghini Countach S: 2466
			Lamborghini Countach S: 2464
24	227.0	223.2	Opel Omega Lotus: 3352
25	223.3	219.6	Lamborghini Espada: 2454
26	221.3	217.6	Porsche 911 Carrera RS: 3753
27	220.6	216.9	Morgan Plus 8 Turbo: 3132
28	219.7	216.0	Jaguar E Type Coupe: 2298
29	218.2	214.6	Jaguar XKE: 2299
30	217.8	214.1	Lamborghini Jarama 400GT: 2457
			Lamborghini Jarama 400GT: 2459
31	213.1	209.6	Aston Martin DB6: 242
32	212.0	208.5	Jaguar E Type Coupe: 2303
33	211.9	208.3	Porsche Carrera 2 Cabriolet Tiptronic: 3744
34	211.2	207.6	Morgan Plus 8: 3134
35	206.7	203.2	Morgan Plus 8: 3137
36	205.6	202.1	Morgan Plus 8: 3130
37	204.7	201.3	Jaguar XKE: 2306
38	204.3	200.9	Aston Martin DB4: 237
39	201.6	198.2	Ford Thunderbird Super Coupe Ford Engineering: 1948
40	198.9	195.6	Morgan Plus 8: 3135
41	197.3	194.0	AC Aceca-Buick: 23
42	193.7	190.4	Aston Martin DBS: 243
43	193.1	189.9	Aston Martin DB4: 239
44	190.8	187.7	Aston Martin DB5: 241
45	190.6	187.5	Lotus Elite V8: 2623

Total: 47

3501 - 4000cc. Highest specific output. Limit set at 70bhp/litre.

	bhp/L	kW/L	PS/L	
1	129.8	96.8	131.6	Porsche 911 Ruf: 3747
				Porsche 911 Ruf TR2: 3749
2	125.8	93.8	127.5	Zender Fact 4: 5008
3	109.4	81.6	111.0	Lamborghini Miura S: 2456
4	103.7	77.3	105.1	Opel Omega Lotus: 3352
5	101.8	75.9	103.2	Lamborghini Miura: 2452
6	100.2	74.7	101.6	Pontiac Firebird T/A Turbo Pontiac Engineering: 3588
7	99.3	74.0	100.6	Lamborghini Espada: 2453
8	98.3	73.3	99.7	Ferrari 250 GTO: 1386
9	95.4	71.2	96.8	Lamborghini Countach: 2461
10	94.2	70.2	95.5	Lamborghini Miura P400S: 2455
11	91.6	68.3	92.9	Lamborghini 400GT: 2450
12	90.2	67.3	91.5	Triumph TR8 Group 44: 4578
13	89.1	66.4	90.3	BMW M5: 606
14	89.1	66.4	90.3	Bizzarrini P538: 497
				Lamborghini Jarama 400GT: 2457
				Lamborghini Jarama 400GT: 2459
15	87.7	65.4	88.9	BMW M5: 622
16	87.0	64.8	88.2	Ferrari 330 GTS: 1393
17	86.9	64.8	88.1	Ford Thunderbird Super Coupe Ford Engineering: 1948
18	85.6	63.8	86.7	Aston Martin DB4 GT Zagato: 240
19	82.7	61.7	83.9	Lamborghini Countach S: 2466
				Lamborghini Countach S: 2464
				Lamborghini Espada: 2454
				Lamborghini Miura: 2451
20	81.3	60.7	82.5	Aston Martin DB6: 242
				Aston Martin DBS: 243
21	79.4	59.2	80.5	Triumph TR8 Libra Rally: 4579
22	75.4	56.2	76.4	Jaguar D Type: 2285
				Lynx D Type: 2642
23	72.2	53.9	73.2	Porsche 911 Carrera RS: 3753
24	71.7	53.4	72.7	Aston Martin DB4: 237
				Aston Martin DB4: 239
25	70.6	52.6	71.6	Aston Martin DB5: 241
26	70.4	52.5	71.4	TVR 390 SE: 4599
27	70.2	52.3	71.2	Audi V8 Quattro: 331
				Audi V8 Quattro Automatic: 332
28	70.1	52.3	71.1	Jaguar E Type Coupe: 2303
				Jaguar E Type Coupe: 2298
				Jaguar XKE: 2306
				Jaguar XKE: 2299

Total: 41

3501 - 4000cc. Highest piston speed. Limit set at 50ft/sec.

	ft/sec	m/sec	
1	68.9	21.0	Triumph TR8 Group 44: 4578
2	66.6	20.3	Jaguar D Type: 2285
3	65.0	19.8	BMW M5: 622
			BMW M5: 606
4	63.7	19.4	Jaguar 3.8 Mk II: 2301
			Jaguar 3.8 Mk II Automatic: 2302
			Jaguar 3.8 Sedan: 2297
			Jaguar 3.8S: 2307
			Jaguar E Type Coupe: 2303
			Jaguar E Type Coupe: 2298
			Jaguar Mk X: 2300
5	63.7	19.4	Jaguar 3.8S Sedan: 2304
			Jaguar XKE: 2306
			Jaguar XKE: 2299
6	61.4	18.7	Lynx D Type: 2642
7	61.4	18.7	Zender Fact 4: 5008
8	60.3	18.4	Aston Martin DB4 GT Zagato: 240
9	59.7	18.2	Dodge Lancer 225 Hyper-Pack: 1278
10	58.6	17.8	Jaguar XJR 4.0: 2363
11	58.3	17.7	Ferrari 250 GTO: 1386
12	57.9	17.7	Panther J72: 3372
13	57.8	17.6	Aston Martin DB6: 242
			Aston Martin DBS: 243
14	57.3	17.5	Aston Martin DB4: 239
			Aston Martin DB4: 237
15	55.3	16.9	Aston Martin DB4: 238
			Aston Martin DB5: 241
16	54.8	16.7	Audi V8 Quattro: 331
			Audi V8 Quattro: 338
			Audi V8 Quattro Automatic: 332
17	54.4	16.6	Triumph TR8 Libra Rally: 4579
18	54.4	16.6	Ferrari 330 GTS: 1393
19	54.2	16.5	Lamborghini Countach: 2461
20	53.4	16.3	Lammas-Graham Drop-head Coupe: 2476
21	53.3	16.2	Jaguar XJS 3.6: 2345
22	53.0	16.1	Jaguar 4.0 Sovereign: 2358
			Jaguar XJ6 Vanden Plas: 2362
			Jaguar XJS 4.0 Auto: 2371
23	52.8	16.1	Jaguar XJ6 3.6: 2348
			Jaguar XJS 3.6 Automatic: 2354
24	52.2	15.9	Lamborghini Miura P400S: 2455
25	51.9	15.8	Daimler Majestic: 1144
26	51.8	15.8	Ford Thunderbird Super Coupe Ford Engineering: 1948
27	51.0	15.6	Porsche 911 Carrera 2 Tiptronic: 3733
28	51.0	15.5	Jeep CJ-5: 2374
			Jeep Commando: 2375
29	51.0	15.5	Porsche 911 Carrera 2: 3732
			Porsche 911 Carrera 4: 3720
			Porsche 911 Carrera 4: 3734
			Porsche 911 Carrera RS: 3753
			Porsche Carrera 2 Cabriolet Tiptronic: 3744
			Porsche Panamericana: 3745
30	50.8	15.5	Lamborghini Countach S: 2466
			Lamborghini Countach S: 2464
			Lamborghini Jarama 400GT: 2457
			Lamborghini Jarama 400GT: 2459
31	50.6	15.4	Lexus SC400: 2571
32	50.4	15.4	Bitter SC: 493

Total: 58

4001 - 4500cc. Maximum speed. Limit set at 115mph.

	mph	kmh	
1	186.0	299.3	Ferrari 365 GTB/4 Competitione: 1403
2	180.0	289.6	Ferrari 375 Indianapolis: 1373
3	177.0	284.8	Ferrari 365 GTB Goldsmith: 1425
4	175.0	281.6	Ferrari 512 BB: 1407
			Ferrari Daytona: 1397
5	174.0	280.0	Ferrari 412 MI: 1377
6	173.0	278.4	Ferrari 365 GTB/4 Daytona: 1396
			Ferrari Daytona Cannonball: 1398
			Ferrari Daytona Sportwagen: 1395
7	165.0	265.5	TVR 420 SEAC: 4601
8	156.0	251.0	Jaguar E Type 4.2: 2309
9	153.0	246.2	Shelby AC Ford Cobra: 4116
10	152.0	244.6	Ferrari 365 GTC4: 1400

			Ferrari 365 GTS 2+2: 1394
11	151.0	243.0	Ferrari 365 GTC: 1390
12	150.0	241.4	Ferrari 365 GT4 2+2: 1406
			Ferrari 4.1 Coupe: 1375
			Infiniti Q45: 2231
13	148.0	238.1	Chevrolet Corvette Sebring: 738
14	147.0	236.5	Maserati Kyalami: 2667
15	146.0	234.9	Mercedes-Benz 400SE: 2918
16	143.0	230.1	Porsche 928: 3661
17	141.0	226.9	Jaguar E Type Roadster: 2312
18	140.0	225.3	Porsche 928: 3669
19	138.0	222.0	Mercedes-Benz 420SE: 2887
			Porsche 928 Automatic: 3662
20	133.0	214.0	Porsche 928 Automatic: 3665
21	131.0	210.8	Mercedes-Benz 420SEL: 2894
22	130.0	209.2	Cadillac Allante: 716
			Cadillac Allante: 719
			Jaguar XJ6 4.2: 2336
			Maserati Quattroporte: 2656
23	129.1	207.7	Chevrolet Corvette: 737
24	128.0	206.0	Jaguar XKE 4.2 2+2: 2310
25	126.0	202.7	Jaguar 420: 2311
26	125.0	201.1	Cadillac Eldorado Touring Coupe: 718
27	124.0	199.5	Jaguar 4.2 litre Mk X Overdrive: 2308
28	123.0	197.9	Ford Falcon Futura V8: 1695
			Ford Falcon V8: 1697
			Jaguar 4.2 litre Mk X: 2305
			Jaguar XJ6 4.2: 2320
29	120.0	193.1	Daimler Sovereign: 1153
			Daimler Sovereign LWB Automatic: 1154
			Jaguar 420 Sedan: 2315
			Jaguar XJ6: 2318
			Jaguar XJ6 4.2 Automatic: 2316
30	119.0	191.5	Cadillac Allante: 715
			Jaguar XJ4.2: 2331
			Jaguar XKE Coupe: 2317
31	118.0	189.9	Plymouth Barracuda Fastback V8: 3495
			Plymouth Barracuda S: 3486
			Sunbeam Tiger: 4301
			Sunbeam Tiger 260: 4302
32	117.0	188.3	Jaguar XJ6 Series III: 2339
			Jaguar XJ6 Vanden Plas: 2344
			Studebaker Avanti: 4233
33	116.9	188.1	Chevrolet Corvette V8: 735
34	116.0	186.6	Jaguar XJ6L: 2337
35	115.0	185.0	Dodge Dart GT: 1297
			Jaguar XJ6: 2322
			Plymouth Barracuda S: 3489

Total: 61

4001 - 4500cc. Acceleration to 60mph/ 96.5kmh. Limit set at 10sec.

	sec	
1	4.2	Shelby AC Ford Cobra: 4116
2	5.0	TVR 420 SEAC: 4601
3	5.1	Ferrari 365 GTB Goldsmith: 1425
4	5.2	Ferrari 412 MI: 1377
5	5.4	Ferrari Daytona: 1397
6	5.6	
		Ferrari Daytona Cannonball: 1398
7	5.8	Ferrari 365 GTB/4 Competitione: 1403
		Ferrari 375 Indianapolis: 1373
8	5.9	Ferrari 365 GTB/4 Daytona: 1396
		Ferrari Daytona Sportwagen: 1395
9	6.1	Ferrari 4.1 Coupe: 1375
10	6.3	Chevrolet Corvette Sebring: 738
		Ferrari 365 GTC: 1390
11	6.9	Infiniti Q45: 2231
12	7.1	Ferrari 365 GT4 2+2: 1406
		Ferrari 365 GTS 2+2: 1394
13	7.2	Ferrari 365 GTB/4 Daytona: 1404
		Ferrari 512 BB: 1407
14	7.3	Chevrolet Corvette: 737
		Ferrari 365 GTC4: 1400
		Studebaker Avanti: 4233
15	7.4	Jaguar E Type Roadster: 2312
		Jaguar XJ6L: 2337
16	7.5	Porsche 928: 3661
17	7.6	Jaguar E Type 4.2: 2309
		Maserati Kyalami: 2667
		Mercedes-Benz 420SE: 2887
18	7.8	Sunbeam Tiger: 4301
19	8.0	Jaguar XKE Coupe: 2317
		Porsche 928 Automatic: 3662
20	8.1	Porsche 928: 3669
21	8.2	Plymouth Barracuda S: 3486
22	8.3	Cadillac Allante: 719
		Cadillac Allante: 716
		Jaguar XKE 4.2 2+2: 2310
		Maserati Quattroporte: 2656
		Porsche 928 Automatic: 3665
23	8.4	Mercedes-Benz 400SE: 2918
24	8.5	Cadillac Eldorado Touring Coupe: 718
		Ford Falcon V8: 1697
25	8.7	Chevrolet Corvette V8: 735
		Jaguar XJ6 4.2: 2320
		Mercedes-Benz 420SEL: 2894
26	9.0	Chevrolet 210: 736
27	9.2	Plymouth Barracuda Fastback V8: 3495
		Railton Terraplane: 3756
28	9.3	Cadillac Allante: 715
		Dodge Dart GT: 1297
		Ford Falcon Futura V8: 1695
29	9.5	Sunbeam Tiger 260: 4302
30	9.7	Chevrolet 210 Coupe Club V8: 734
31	9.8	Nash Nash-Healey Roadster Supercharged: 3200
		Railton Light Sports Tourer: 3757
32	9.9	Jaguar 4.2 litre Mk X: 2305
		Jaguar 420: 2311
33	10.0	Cadillac Aurora: 717
		Jaguar XJ6 4.2: 2336

Total: 57

4001 - 4500cc. Highest power. Limit set at 200bhp.

	bhp	kW	PS	
1	415.0	309.5	420.8	Ferrari 412 MI: 1377
2	405.0	302.0	410.6	Ferrari 365 GTB/4 Daytona: 1396
3	402.0	299.8	407.6	Ferrari 365 GTB/4 Competitione: 1403
4	400.0	298.3	405.5	Ferrari 365 GTB Goldsmith: 1425
5	390.0	290.8	395.4	Ferrari 375 Indianapolis: 1373
6	368.0	274.4	373.1	Ferrari 365 GTS 2+2: 1394
7	352.0	262.5	356.9	Ferrari 365 GTB/4 Daytona: 1404
				Ferrari Daytona: 1397
				Ferrari Daytona Cannonball: 1398
				Ferrari Daytona Sportwagen: 1395
8	344.0	256.5	348.8	Ferrari 512 BB: 1407
9	320.0	238.6	324.4	Ferrari 365 GT4 2+2: 1406
				Ferrari 365 GTC: 1390
				Ferrari 365 GTC4: 1400
10	300.0	223.7	304.2	TVR 420 SEAC: 4601
11	290.0	216.2	294.0	Maserati Quattroporte: 2656
12	286.0	213.3	290.0	Mercedes-Benz 400SE: 2918
13	278.0	207.3	281.9	Infiniti Q45: 2231
14	275.0	205.1	278.8	Studebaker Avanti: 4233
15	270.0	201.3	273.7	Maserati Kyalami: 2667
16	265.0	197.6	268.7	Jaguar 4.2 litre Mk X: 2305
				Jaguar 4.2 litre Mk X Overdrive: 2308
				Jaguar E Type 4.2: 2309
				Jaguar E Type Roadster: 2312
				Jaguar XKE 4.2 2+2: 2310
17	260.0	193.9	263.6	Ferrari 4.1 Coupe: 1375
				Ford Falcon Futura V8: 1695
				Ford Falcon V8: 1697
				Shelby AC Ford Cobra: 4116
18	246.0	183.4	249.4	Jaguar XKE Coupe: 2317
19	245.0	182.7	248.4	Jaguar 420: 2311
				Jaguar 420 Sedan: 2315
				Jaguar XJ6: 2318
				Jaguar XJ6 4.2: 2320
				Jaguar XJ6 4.2 Automatic: 2316
20	240.0	179.0	243.3	Porsche 928: 3661
				Porsche 928 Automatic: 3662
21	235.0	175.2	238.3	Dodge Dart GT: 1297
				Plymouth Barracuda Fastback V8: 3495
				Plymouth Barracuda S: 3489
				Plymouth Barracuda S: 3486
22	225.0	167.8	228.1	Chevrolet Corvette: 737
				Chevrolet Corvette Sebring: 738
23	220.0	164.0	223.0	Porsche 928: 3669
24	219.0	163.3	222.0	Porsche 928 Automatic: 3665
25	218.0	162.6	221.0	Mercedes-Benz 420SE: 2887
26	205.0	152.9	207.8	Chevrolet 210: 736
				Jaguar XJ6 4.2: 2336
27	201.0	149.9	203.8	Mercedes-Benz 420SEL: 2894
28	200.0	149.1	202.8	AMC Rambler Classic V8: 172
				Cadillac Allante: 716
				Cadillac Allante: 719
				Cadillac Aurora: 717
				Rambler Rebel V8: 3762

Total: 54

4001 - 4500cc. Highest torque. Limit set at 250lbft.

	lbft	Nm	
1	440.0	596.2	Ferrari 365 GTB Goldsmith: 1425
2	365.0	494.6	Ferrari 365 GTB/4 Daytona: 1396
3	330.0	447.2	Studebaker Avanti: 4233
4	320.0	433.6	Ferrari Daytona Cannonball: 1398
5	319.0	432.2	Ferrari 365 GTB/4 Daytona: 1404
6	318.0	430.9	Ferrari 365 GT4 2+2: 1406
			Ferrari 365 GTC4: 1400
			Ferrari Daytona: 1397
7	315.0	426.8	Ferrari Daytona Sportwagen: 1395
8	308.0	417.3	Ferrari 365 GTS 2+2: 1394

9	302.0	409.2	Ferrari 512 BB: 1407
			Mercedes-Benz 400SE: 2918
10	292.0	395.7	Infiniti Q45: 2231
11	290.0	393.0	TVR 420 SEAC: 4601
12	289.0	391.6	Maserati Kyalami: 2667
13	283.0	383.5	Jaguar 4.2 litre Mk X: 2305
			Jaguar 4.2 litre Mk X Overdrive: 2308
			Jaguar 420: 2311
			Jaguar E Type 4.2: 2309
			Jaguar E Type Roadster: 2312
			Jaguar XJ6: 2318
			Jaguar XJ6 4.2: 2320
			Jaguar XJ6 4.2 Automatic: 2316
			Jaguar XKE 4.2 2+2: 2310
14	282.0	382.1	Jaguar 420 Sedan: 2315
15	280.0	379.4	Dodge Dart GT: 1297
			Plymouth Barracuda Fastback V8: 3495
			Plymouth Barracuda S: 3486
			Plymouth Barracuda S: 3489
16	270.0	365.9	Cadillac Allante: 716
			Cadillac Allante: 719
			Cadillac Aurora: 717
			Chevrolet Corvette: 737
			Chevrolet Corvette Sebring: 738
17	269.0	364.5	Ford Falcon Futura V8: 1695
			Ford Falcon V8: 1697
			Shelby AC Ford Cobra: 4116
18	268.0	363.1	Chevrolet 210: 736
			Ferrari 365 GTC: 1390
19	265.0	359.1	Plymouth Savoy: 3473
			Porsche 928: 3669
20	264.0	357.7	Ford Fairlane 500: 1646
21	263.0	356.4	Jaguar XKE Coupe: 2317
22	260.0	352.3	Chevrolet 210 Coupe Club V8: 734
			Chevrolet Corvette V8: 735
			Chrysler Valiant Premium Auto: 986
			Dodge Coronet: 1293
			Dodge Dart GT: 1288
			Maserati Quattroporte: 2656
			Plymouth Barracuda: 3493
			Plymouth Barracuda: 3485
			Studebaker Lark Daytona: 4235
			Studebaker Lark V8: 4229
23	258.0	349.6	Ford Fairlane 500 Sports Coupe: 1672
			Ford Fairlane Squire Wagon: 1693
			Ford Falcon Sprint: 1704
			Ford Falcon Sprint Convertible: 1696
			Ford Mustang Convertible: 1718
			Ford Mustang V8 4.2-litre: 1724
			Mercury Comet S-22 Sportster: 2931
			Sunbeam Tiger: 4301
			Sunbeam Tiger 260: 4302
24	257.0	348.2	Porsche 928: 3661
			Porsche 928 Automatic: 3662
25	254.0	344.2	Porsche 928 Automatic: 3665

Total: 65

4001 - 4500cc. Highest rpm at peak power. Limit set at 5000rpm.

	rpm	
1	8300	Ferrari 365 GTB/4 Competitione: 1403
2	7600	Ferrari 412 MI: 1377
3	7500	Ferrari 365 GTB Goldsmith: 1425
		Ferrari 365 GTB/4 Daytona: 1404
		Ferrari 365 GTB/4 Daytona: 1396
		Ferrari 375 Indianapolis: 1373
		Ferrari Daytona: 1397
		Ferrari Daytona Cannonball: 1398
		Ferrari Daytona Sportwagen: 1395
4	7200	Ferrari 512 BB: 1407
5	6600	Ferrari 365 GTC: 1390
		Ferrari 365 GTS 2+2: 1394
6	6500	Ferrari 4.1 Coupe: 1375
7	6200	Ferrari 365 GT4 2+2: 1406
		Ferrari 365 GTC4: 1400
8	6000	Infiniti Q45: 2231
		Maserati Kyalami: 2667
9	5800	Ford Falcon Futura V8: 1695
		Ford Falcon V8: 1697
		Shelby AC Ford Cobra: 4116
10	5700	Mercedes-Benz 400SE: 2918
11	5500	Jaguar 420: 2311
		Jaguar 420 Sedan: 2315
		Jaguar XJ6: 2318
		Jaguar XJ6 4.2: 2320
		Jaguar XJ6 4.2 Automatic: 2316
		Jaguar XKE Coupe: 2317
		Lagonda Drop-head Coupe: 2446
		Lagonda Rapide: 2445
		Lagonda Saloon de Ville: 2444
		Porsche 928: 3669
		Porsche 928: 3661
		Porsche 928 Automatic: 3662
		TVR 420 SEAC: 4601
12	5400	Jaguar 4.2 litre Mk X: 2305
		Jaguar 4.2 litre Mk X Overdrive: 2308
		Jaguar E Type 4.2: 2309
		Jaguar E Type Roadster: 2312
		Jaguar XKE 4.2 2+2: 2310
13	5250	Porsche 928 Automatic: 3665
14	5200	Chevrolet Corvette: 737
		Chevrolet Corvette Sebring: 738
		Dodge Dart GT: 1297
		Maserati Quattroporte: 2656
		Mercedes-Benz 420SE: 2887
		Mercedes-Benz 420SEL: 2894
		Plymouth Barracuda Fastback V8: 3495
		Plymouth Barracuda S: 3489
		Plymouth Barracuda S: 3486
		Studebaker Avanti: 4233
15	5000	Jaguar XJ6 4.2: 2336

Total: 51

4001 - 4500cc. Highest power-to-weight ratio. Limit set at 140bhp/ton.

	bhp/ ton	bhp/ tonne	
1	510.8	502.2	Ferrari 412 MI: 1377
2	507.9	499.4	Ferrari 375 Indianapolis: 1373
3	305.4	300.4	TVR 420 SEAC: 4601
4	288.3	283.5	Shelby AC Ford Cobra: 4116
5	285.3	280.6	Ferrari 365 GTB Goldsmith: 1425
6	284.1	279.4	Ferrari 4.1 Coupe: 1375
7	282.3	277.6	Ferrari 365 GTB/4 Competitione: 1403
8	252.0	247.8	Ferrari 365 GTB/4 Daytona: 1396
9	225.3	221.5	Ferrari 512 BB: 1407
10	224.1	220.4	Ferrari 365 GTC: 1390
11	223.4	219.6	Ferrari Daytona: 1397
12	219.8	216.1	Ford Falcon V8: 1697
13	219.0	215.4	Ferrari Daytona Cannonball: 1398
14	218.1	214.5	Ferrari 365 GTB/4 Daytona: 1404
15	213.5	209.9	Ford Falcon Futura V8: 1695
16	213.1	209.5	Ferrari Daytona Sportwagen: 1395
17	208.4	204.9	Jaguar E Type Roadster: 2312
18	205.3	201.8	Jaguar E Type 4.2: 2309
19	205.0	201.6	Ferrari 365 GTS 2+2: 1394
20	192.1	188.9	Jaguar XKE 4.2 2+2: 2310
21	187.4	184.3	Ferrari 365 GTC4: 1400
22	186.7	183.5	Chevrolet Corvette Sebring: 738
23	182.6	179.5	Jaguar XKE Coupe: 2317
24	181.2	178.1	Studebaker Avanti: 4233
25	180.9	177.9	Ferrari 365 GT4 2+2: 1406
26	169.1	166.3	Chevrolet Corvette: 737
27	167.8	165.0	Maserati Quattroporte: 2656
28	164.5	161.8	Plymouth Barracuda S: 3486
29	164.0	161.2	Dodge Dart GT: 1297
30	160.6	157.9	Porsche 928 Automatic: 3662
31	160.5	157.8	Plymouth Barracuda S: 3489
32	160.5	157.8	Porsche 928: 3661
33	159.0	156.4	Plymouth Barracuda Fastback V8: 3495
34	157.7	155.0	Maserati Kyalami: 2667
35	155.1	152.5	Infiniti Q45: 2231
36	151.7	149.1	Chevrolet Corvette V8: 735
37	151.3	148.8	Jaguar XJ6 4.2 Automatic: 2316
38	150.4	147.9	Jaguar XJ6 4.2: 2320
39	149.2	146.7	Jaguar 420: 2311
40	147.5	145.1	Jaguar XJ6: 2318
41	146.8	144.3	Jaguar 4.2 litre Mk X Overdrive: 2308
42	146.2	143.8	Porsche 928: 3669
43	144.8	142.4	Jaguar 420 Sedan: 2315
44	143.2	140.8	Sunbeam Tiger: 4301
45	143.0	140.6	Jaguar 4.2 litre Mk X: 2305
46	140.8	138.4	Panther J72: 3374

Total: 46

4001 - 4500cc. Highest specific output. Limit set at 50bhp/litre.

	bhp/L	kW/L	PS/L	
1	103.2	76.9	104.6	Ferrari 412 MI: 1377
2	92.3	68.8	93.5	Ferrari 365 GTB/4 Daytona: 1396
3	91.6	68.3	92.8	Ferrari 365 GTB/4 Competitione: 1403
4	91.1	68.0	92.4	Ferrari 365 GTB Goldsmith: 1425
5	86.8	64.7	88.0	Ferrari 375 Indianapolis: 1373
6	83.8	62.5	85.0	Ferrari 365 GTS 2+2: 1394
7	80.2	59.8	81.3	Ferrari 365 GTB/4 Daytona: 1404
				Ferrari Daytona: 1397
				Ferrari Daytona Cannonball: 1398
				Ferrari Daytona Sportwagen: 1395
8	78.4	58.4	79.4	Ferrari 512 BB: 1407
9	72.9	54.4	73.9	Ferrari 365 GT4 2+2: 1406
				Ferrari 365 GTC: 1390
				Ferrari 365 GTC4: 1400
10	71.0	52.9	71.9	TVR 420 SEAC: 4601
11	70.1	52.3	71.1	Maserati Quattroporte: 2656

12	68.2	50.8	69.1	Mercedes-Benz 400SE: 2918
13	65.3	48.7	66.2	Maserati Kyalami: 2667
14	64.7	48.3	65.6	Studebaker Avanti: 4233
15	63.4	47.3	64.3	Ferrari 4.1 Coupe: 1375
16	62.6	46.7	63.4	Jaguar 4.2 litre Mk X: 2305
				Jaguar 4.2 litre Mk X Overdrive: 2308
				Jaguar E Type 4.2: 2309
				Jaguar E Type Roadster: 2312
				Jaguar XKE 4.2 2+2: 2310
17	61.9	46.1	62.7	Infiniti Q45: 2231
18	61.0	45.5	61.9	Ford Falcon Futura V8: 1695
				Ford Falcon V8: 1697
				Shelby AC Ford Cobra: 4116
19	58.1	43.3	58.9	Jaguar XKE Coupe: 2317
20	57.8	43.1	58.6	Jaguar 420: 2311
				Jaguar 420 Sedan: 2315
				Jaguar XJ6: 2318
				Jaguar XJ6 4.2: 2320
				Jaguar XJ6 4.2 Automatic: 2316
21	53.6	40.0	54.4	Porsche 928: 3661
				Porsche 928 Automatic: 3662
22	52.5	39.2	53.2	Plymouth Barracuda S: 3486
				Plymouth Barracuda S: 3489
23	52.4	39.1	53.2	Dodge Dart GT: 1297
24	52.4	39.0	53.1	Plymouth Barracuda Fastback V8: 3495
25	51.9	38.7	52.7	Mercedes-Benz 420SE: 2887
26	51.8	38.6	52.5	Chevrolet Corvette Sebring: 738
27	51.8	38.6	52.5	Chevrolet Corvette: 737

Total: 44

4001 - 4500cc. Highest piston speed. Limit set at 45ft/sec.

	ft/sec	m/sec	
1	64.6	19.6	Ferrari 365 GTB/4 Competitione: 1403
2	63.7	19.4	Jaguar 420: 2311
			Jaguar 420 Sedan: 2315
			Jaguar XJ6: 2318
			Jaguar XJ6 4.2: 2320
			Jaguar XJ6 4.2 Automatic: 2316
			Jaguar XKE Coupe: 2317
3	62.5	19.1	Jaguar 4.2 litre Mk X: 2305
			Jaguar 4.2 litre Mk X Overdrive: 2308
			Jaguar E Type 4.2: 2309
			Jaguar E Type Roadster: 2312
			Jaguar XKE 4.2 2+2: 2310
4	61.0	18.6	Ferrari 375 Indianapolis: 1373
5	59.7	18.2	Ferrari 412 MI: 1377
6	58.3	17.7	Ferrari 365 GTB Goldsmith: 1425
			Ferrari 365 GTB/4 Daytona: 1404
			Ferrari 365 GTB/4 Daytona: 1396
			Ferrari Daytona: 1397
			Ferrari Daytona Cannonball: 1398
			Ferrari Daytona Sportwagen: 1395
7	57.9	17.7	Jaguar XJ6 4.2: 2336
8	56.0	17.0	Ferrari 512 BB: 1407
9	55.8	17.0	Maserati Kyalami: 2667
10	55.0	16.8	Jaguar XJ6 Series III: 2339
			Jaguar XJ6 Vanden Plas: 2344
11	55.0	16.8	Jaguar XJ6L: 2337
12	54.3	16.5	Infiniti Q45: 2231
13	53.6	16.3	Bentley 4.5-litre: 461
			Bentley 4.5-litre Supercharged: 462
14	52.8	16.1	Lagonda Rapide: 2441
15	52.5	16.0	Hudson Commodore: 2176
16	52.4	16.0	Railton Cobham Saloon: 3759
			Railton Straight Eight Saloon: 3758
17	52.1	15.9	Daimler Sovereign: 1153
			Daimler Sovereign LWB Automatic: 1154
			Jaguar XJ4.2: 2331
			Panther J72: 3374
18	52.1	15.9	Jaguar XJ6: 2322
19	51.3	15.6	Ferrari 365 GTC: 1390
			Ferrari 365 GTS 2+2: 1394
20	50.9	15.5	Lagonda Rapide: 2445
21	50.9	15.5	Lagonda Drop-head Coupe: 2446
			Lagonda Saloon de Ville: 2444
22	49.2	15.0	Mercedes-Benz 400SE: 2918
23	48.7	14.8	Nash Nash-Healey Roadster: 3198
			Nash Nash-Healey Roadster Supercharged: 3200
24	48.4	14.8	Ferrari 4.1 Coupe: 1375
25	48.4	14.7	Maserati Quattroporte: 2656
26	48.2	14.7	Ferrari 365 GT4 2+2: 1406
			Ferrari 365 GTC4: 1400
27	47.8	14.6	Dodge Dart GT: 1297
			Plymouth Barracuda Fastback V8: 3495
			Plymouth Barracuda S: 3489
			Plymouth Barracuda S: 3486
28	47.5	14.5	Bentley 4.25-litre: 468
29	47.5	14.5	Porsche 928: 3669
			Porsche 928: 3661
			Porsche 928 Automatic: 3662
30	47.4	14.4	Railton Light Sports Tourer: 3757
			Railton Terraplane: 3756
31	47.2	14.4	Daimler Twenty-Seven Limousine: 1138
32	47.2	14.4	Lagonda Le Mans: 2437
33	46.9	14.3	Studebaker Avanti: 4233
34	46.3	14.1	TVR 420 SEAC: 4601
35	46.2	14.1	Ford Falcon Futura V8: 1695
			Shelby AC Ford Cobra: 4116
36	45.9	14.0	Ford Falcon V8: 1697
37	45.8	14.0	Wills Sainte Claire Six: 4974
38	45.3	13.8	Porsche 928 Automatic: 3665
39	45.0	13.7	Dodge Safari Super Sport: 1291

Total: 70

4501 - 5000cc. Maximum speed. Limit set at 150mph.

	mph	kmh	
1	230.0	370.1	Koenig Competition Evolution: 2418
2	217.0	349.2	Koenig Competition: 2417
3	210.0	337.9	Ferrari Testa Rossa Norwood: 1444
4	205.0	329.8	Ford GT40: 1760
5	190.0	305.7	Shelby Cobra Daytona Coupe: 4119
6	186.0	299.3	Ford Mustang NOS/Saleen: 1967
			Porsche 928 S4 Koenig: 3726
7	185.0	297.7	Ferrari Testa Rossa Gemballa: 1443
			Ford Mustang 5.0 Cartech Turbo: 1940
8	184.0	296.1	Jaguar XJ13: 2313
9	181.0	291.2	Ferrari Testa Rossa: 1437
			Ferrari Testa Rossa Straman Spyder: 1438
10	180.0	289.6	Ferrari 400 Super America: 1389
			Ferrari Pininfarina Mythos: 1448
11	178.0	286.4	Ferrari Testa Rossa: 1426
12	177.0	284.8	Ford Mustang Cartech Turbo: 1928
13	174.0	280.0	Ferrari Testa Rossa: 1442
			Ford Mustang Holdener: 1966
14	171.0	275.1	BMW 750i Alpina B12: 613
15	168.0	270.3	Ferrari 512 BB: 1417
16	167.0	268.7	De Tomaso Pantera GT5 S: 1244
17	165.0	265.5	Ferrari 4.9: 1387
			Lamborghini Countach LP 500S: 2465
			Porsche 928 S4: 3712
18	164.0	263.9	Ford GT40 Super Street: 1738
19	163.0	262.3	Ferrari 512 BB: 1413
			Maserati Bora: 2664
20	162.0	260.7	Maserati Bora: 2660
			Porsche 928 S4 SE: 3727
21	161.0	259.0	BMW 850i: 620
			Porsche 928 S4 Automatic: 3692
22	160.0	257.4	BMW 850i Manual: 625
			Maserati Khamsin: 2666
			Mercedes-Benz 500SL: 2913
23	159.0	255.8	Mercedes-Benz 500E: 2919
24	158.0	254.2	BMW 750i L: 589
25	157.0	252.6	Maserati Indy: 2659
26	155.0	249.4	BMW 750i L: 596
			Mercedes-Benz 500SEL: 2922
			Mercedes-Benz 500SL: 2920
			Porsche 928 Cabrio Strosek: 3725
27	154.0	247.8	Maserati Ghibli: 2658
28	153.0	246.2	BMW 750i: 612
29	152.0	244.6	Porsche 928 S: 3691
30	151.0	243.0	Ford Mustang TransAm: 1796
			Porsche 928 S Series II: 3684
31	150.0	241.4	Chevrolet Camaro IROC-Z: 906

Total: 47

4501 - 5000cc. Acceleration to 60mph/ 96.5kmh. Limit set at 7 seconds.

	sec	
1	3.5	Koenig Competition Evolution: 2418
2	4.0	Koenig Competition: 2417
3	4.7	Ferrari Testa Rossa Norwood: 1444
4	4.8	Porsche 928 S4 Koenig: 3726
5	4.9	Ford Mustang Cartech Turbo: 1928
		Ford Mustang Holdener: 1966
6	5.0	Ford GT40: 1760
7	5.1	Ferrari 512 BB: 1417
		Shelby Cobra USRRC: 4118
8	5.2	Ferrari Testa Rossa: 1442
9	5.3	Ferrari Testa Rossa: 1426
		Ferrari Testa Rossa: 1437
		Ferrari Testa Rossa Gemballa: 1443
		Ferrari Testa Rossa Straman Spyder: 1438
		Ford GT40 Super Street: 1738
10	5.4	Ford Mustang 5.0 Cartech Turbo: 1940
11	5.5	AC Cobra: 25
		Chevrolet Corvette 315: 753
		Ford Mustang TransAm: 1796
		Porsche 928 Cabrio Strosek: 3725
		Porsche 928 S4: 3712
		Porsche 928 S4 SE: 3727
12	5.6	Lamborghini Countach LP 500S: 2465
13	5.7	Chevrolet Corvette: 739

		Chevrolet Corvette Injection: 740
		Chevrolet Corvette RPO 684/579E: 741
		Devin Super Sports: 1257
		Ford Mustang NOS/Saleen: 1967
14	5.8	Ford Mustang Boss 302: 1787
15	5.9	Chevrolet Corvette 270: 752
		Mercedes-Benz 500SL: 2913
		Porsche 928 S: 3683
16	6.0	Ferrari 512 BBi: 1422
		Ford Mustang Convertible Saleen: 1929
		Ford Mustang GT: 1930
		Ford Mustang LX 5.0: 1924
17	6.1	Porsche 928: 3738
		Porsche 928 Gemballa: 3740
18	6.2	Ferrari 512 BB: 1413
		Ferrari Pininfarina Mythos: 1448
		Porsche 928 S4 Automatic: 3692
		Shelby GT 350-S: 4121
19	6.3	Ford Mustang Saleen SSC: 1941
		Mercedes-Benz 500E: 2919
		Porsche 928: 3752
		Porsche 928 Automatic: 3739
		Porsche 928 S: 3691
		Shelby GT 350: 4123
20	6.4	Mercedes-Benz 500SL: 2920
21	6.5	Maserati Bora: 2660
		Maserati Khamsin: 2666
22	6.6	Chevrolet Camaro IROC-Z: 906
		Chevrolet Corvette: 743
		Chevrolet Corvette: 750
		Ferrari 4.9: 1387
		Ford Mustang LX 5.0L: 1955
		Shelby AC Ford Cobra: 4117
23	6.7	Ferrari 412: 1432
		Ford Mustang GT: 1923
		Porsche 928 S Series II: 3684
24	6.8	Ford Thunderbird Bondurant 5.0: 1926
		Shelby GT 350: 4120
25	6.9	BMW 750i Alpina B12: 613
		BMW 750i L: 596
		Ford Mustang Boss 302: 1776
		Ford Mustang GT 5.0: 1913
26	7.0	De Tomaso Mangusta: 1235
		Excalibur SS: 1363
		Ford Mustang GT 5.0: 1896
		Ford Mustang Saleen: 1914
		Porsche 928 S: 3677

Total: 71

4501 - 5000cc. Highest power. Limit set at 300bhp.

	bhp	kW	PS	
1	1000.0	745.7	1013.9	Koenig Competition Evolution: 2418
2	943.0	703.2	956.1	Ferrari Testa Rossa Norwood: 1444
3	800.0	596.6	811.1	Koenig Competition: 2417
4	472.0	352.0	478.5	Jaguar XJ13: 2313
5	470.0	350.5	476.5	Ford Mustang 5.0 Cartech Turbo: 1940
6	460.0	343.0	466.4	Ford Mustang TransAm: 1796
7	450.0	335.6	456.2	Ford Mustang Holdener: 1966
8	430.0	320.6	436.0	Porsche 928 S4 Koenig: 3726
9	420.0	313.2	425.8	Ferrari 400 Super America: 1389
10	392.0	292.3	397.4	Ford Mustang Cartech Turbo: 1928
11	390.0	290.8	395.4	Ferrari Testa Rossa: 1442
				Shelby GT 350-S: 4121
12	385.0	287.1	390.3	Shelby Cobra Daytona Coupe: 4119
13	380.0	283.4	385.3	Ferrari Pininfarina Mythos: 1448
				Ferrari Testa Rossa: 1437
				Ferrari Testa Rossa: 1426
				Ferrari Testa Rossa Gemballa: 1443
				Ferrari Testa Rossa Straman Spyder: 1438
				Ford GT40: 1760
14	375.0	279.6	380.2	Lamborghini Countach LP 500S: 2465
15	360.0	268.4	365.0	Ferrari 4.9: 1387
				Ferrari 512 BB: 1417
				Ferrari 512 BB: 1413
16	350.0	261.0	354.8	BMW 750i Alpina B12: 613
17	341.0	254.3	345.7	Mercury Cougar Group 2: 2942
18	340.0	253.5	344.7	Ferrari 412: 1432
				Ferrari 512 BBi: 1422
				Maserati Ghibli: 2658
19	335.0	249.8	339.6	Ford GT40 Super Street: 1738
20	330.0	246.1	334.6	Maserati Indy: 2657
21	326.0	243.1	330.5	Mercedes-Benz 500E: 2919
				Mercedes-Benz 500SL: 2913
				Porsche 928: 3752
				Porsche 928: 3738
				Porsche 928 Gemballa: 3740
22	325.0	242.3	329.5	Porsche 928 Cabrio Strosek: 3725
23	322.0	240.1	326.5	Mercedes-Benz 500SEL: 2922
				Mercedes-Benz 500SL: 2920
24	320.0	238.6	324.4	Maserati Khamsin: 2666
				Maserati Khamsin Automatic: 2662
				Porsche 928 S4 Automatic: 3692
				Porsche 928 S4 SE: 3727
25	318.0	237.1	322.4	Shelby Cobra USRRC: 4118
26	316.0	235.6	320.4	Porsche 928 Automatic: 3739
				Porsche 928 S4: 3712
27	315.0	234.9	319.4	Chevrolet Corvette: 750
				Chevrolet Corvette 315: 753
				Maserati Khamsin: 2669
				Maserati Khamsin: 2665
				Shelby GT 350: 4123
28	310.0	231.2	314.3	Ford Mustang NOS/Saleen: 1967
				Maserati Bora: 2660
				Porsche 928 S Series II: 3684
29	306.0	228.2	310.2	Shelby GT 350: 4120
30	305.0	227.4	309.2	De Tomaso Pantera GT5 S: 1244
31	300.0	223.7	304.2	AC Cobra: 25
				BMW 750i: 612
				BMW 750i L: 596
				BMW 750i L: 589
				BMW 850i: 620
				BMW 850i Manual: 625
				Maserati Bora: 2664

Total: 62

4501 - 5000cc. Highest torque. Limit set at 325lbft.

	lbft	Nm	
1	738.0	1000.0	Koenig Competition Evolution: 2418
2	664.0	899.7	Koenig Competition: 2417
3	550.0	745.3	Ford Mustang Cartech Turbo: 1928
4	470.0	636.9	Porsche 928 S4 Koenig: 3726
5	445.0	603.0	Ford Mustang 5.0 Cartech Turbo: 1940
6	420.0	569.1	Ford Mustang Holdener: 1966
7	381.0	516.3	Jaguar XJ13: 2313
8	363.1	492.0	Ferrari Testa Rossa: 1442
9	360.0	487.8	Ford Mustang TransAm: 1796
10	354.0	479.7	Ferrari Pininfarina Mythos: 1448
			Ferrari Testa Rossa: 1426
			Ferrari Testa Rossa: 1437
			Ferrari Testa Rossa Gemballa: 1443
			Ferrari Testa Rossa Straman Spyder: 1438
			Maserati Khamsin: 2666
			Maserati Khamsin Automatic: 2662
			Mercedes-Benz 500E: 2919
			Mercedes-Benz 500SEL: 2922
11	347.0	470.2	BMW 750i Alpina B12: 613
12	345.0	467.5	Pontiac Firebird TransAm Turbo: 3567
13	340.0	460.7	Maserati Bora: 2660
			Shelby Cobra Daytona Coupe: 4119
14	339.5	460.0	Mercedes-Benz 500SL: 2913
15	335.0	453.9	Buick LeSabre 400: 673
			Buick Skylark: 675
			Buick Skylark Sports Wagon: 670
16	333.0	451.2	De Tomaso Pantera GT5 S: 1244
			Ferrari 412: 1432
			Ferrari 512 BB: 1417
			Ferrari 512 BBi: 1422
			Shelby GT 350: 4123
17	332.1	450.0	BMW 750i: 612
			BMW 850i Manual: 625
18	332.0	449.9	BMW 750i L: 589
			BMW 750i L: 596
			BMW 850i: 620
			Ferrari 512 BB: 1413
			Mercedes-Benz 500SL: 2920
19	330.0	447.2	Ford GT40: 1760
			Ford Mustang JBA/Saleen: 1931
			Studebaker Regal Wagonaire Supercharged: 4237
20	329.0	445.8	Ford GT40 Super Street: 1738
			Shelby GT 350: 4120
			Shelby GT 350-S: 4121
21	327.0	443.1	Ford Mustang Saleen SSC: 1941
22	326.0	441.7	Maserati Ghibli: 2658
23	325.0	440.4	Maserati Bora: 2664
			Maserati Indy: 2657

Total: 48

4501 - 5000cc. Highest rpm at peak power. Limit set at 5600rpm.

	rpm	
1	10000	Ferrari Testa Rossa Norwood: 1444
2	7500	Ferrari 400 Super America: 1389
		Ford Mustang TransAm: 1796
3	7250	Jaguar XJ13: 2313
4	7000	Ferrari 4.9: 1387
		Lamborghini Countach LP 500S: 2465
5	6750	Shelby Cobra Daytona Coupe: 4119
6	6700	Koenig Competition Evolution: 2418
7	6500	Ford GT40: 1760
8	6300	Ferrari Testa Rossa: 1442
9	6250	Ford GT40 Super Street: 1738

		Gordon GT: 2008
		Koenig Competition: 2417
10	6200	Chevrolet Corvette: 750
		Chevrolet Corvette: 739
		Chevrolet Corvette: 743
		Chevrolet Corvette 315: 753
		Chevrolet Corvette Injection: 740
		Chevrolet Corvette RPO 684/579E: 741
		Ferrari 512 BB: 1413
		Ferrari 512 BB: 1417
		Porsche 928: 3738
		Porsche 928: 3752
		Porsche 928 Gemballa: 3740
11	6000	Chevrolet Corvette 270: 752
		Ferrari 412: 1432
		Ferrari 512 BBi: 1422
		Ford Mustang Convertible: 1708
		Ford Mustang Fastback: 1722
		Ford Mustang High Performance: 1723
		Ford Mustang NOS/Saleen: 1967
		Maserati Bora: 2660
		Maserati Bora: 2664
		Porsche 928 Automatic: 3739
		Porsche 928 Cabrio Strosek: 3725
		Porsche 928 S4: 3712
		Porsche 928 S4 Automatic: 3692
		Porsche 928 S4 Koenig: 3726
		Porsche 928 S4 SE: 3727
		Shelby AC Ford Cobra: 4117
		Shelby Cobra USRRC: 4118
		Shelby GT 350: 4120
		Shelby GT 350-S: 4121
12	5900	Porsche 928 S Series II: 3684
13	5800	Chevrolet Camaro Z/28: 825
		Chevrolet Camaro Z/28: 811
		De Tomaso Pantera GT5 S: 1244
		Ford Mustang Boss 302: 1776
		Ford Mustang Boss 302: 1787
		Mercury Cougar Eliminator: 2950
		Mercury Cougar Group 2: 2942
14	5750	AC Cobra: 25
		Ferrari Pininfarina Mythos: 1448
		Ferrari Testa Rossa: 1426
		Ferrari Testa Rossa: 1437
		Ferrari Testa Rossa Gemballa: 1443
		Ferrari Testa Rossa Straman Spyder: 1438
		Porsche 928 S: 3691
		Porsche 928 S: 3683
15	5700	Mercedes-Benz 500E: 2919
		Mercedes-Benz 500SEL: 2922
16	5600	Ford Mustang Holdener: 1966
		Maserati Quattroporte: 2671

Total: 63

4501 - 5000cc. Highest power-to-weight ratio. Limit set at 200bhp/ton.

	bhp/ ton	bhp/ tonne	
1	640.0	629.3	Koenig Competition Evolution: 2418
2	570.9	561.4	Ferrari Testa Rossa Norwood: 1444
3	512.0	503.5	Koenig Competition: 2417
4	480.6	472.6	Jaguar XJ13: 2313
5	375.0	368.7	Shelby Cobra Daytona Coupe: 4119
6	366.0	359.9	Ford GT40 Super Street: 1738
7	362.6	356.5	Ford Mustang Holdener: 1966
8	347.5	341.7	Shelby Cobra USRRC: 4118
9	342.5	336.8	Ford GT40: 1760
10	319.0	313.7	Ford Mustang 5.0 Cartech Turbo: 1940
11	318.0	312.7	Ford Mustang TransAm: 1796
12	310.3	305.1	Ford Mustang Cartech Turbo: 1928
13	309.0	303.8	Ferrari Pininfarina Mythos: 1448
14	296.1	291.2	Shelby GT 350-S: 4121
15	290.3	285.4	AC Cobra: 25
16	288.4	283.5	Lamborghini Countach LP 500S: 2465
17	281.7	277.0	Ferrari 400 Super America: 1389
18	279.7	275.1	Shelby AC Ford Cobra: 4117
19	257.9	253.6	Excalibur SS: 1363
20	253.5	249.2	Porsche 928 S4 Koenig: 3726
21	245.7	241.6	Shelby GT 350: 4120
22	237.6	233.7	Ferrari Testa Rossa: 1442
23	237.0	233.0	Mercury Cougar Group 2: 2942
24	235.4	231.5	Ferrari 512 BB: 1413
25	232.6	228.7	Ferrari Testa Rossa: 1426
			Ferrari Testa Rossa: 1437
26	232.4	228.5	Ferrari 512 BB: 1417
27	232.1	228.2	Chevrolet Corvette 315: 753
28	231.8	228.0	Ford Mustang NOS/Saleen: 1967
29	231.3	227.4	Ferrari Testa Rossa Gemballa: 1443
30	229.1	225.3	Chevrolet Corvette: 750
31	227.1	223.4	Ferrari 4.9: 1387
32	227.1	223.3	Devin Super Sports: 1257
33	225.0	221.2	Ferrari 512 BBi: 1422
34	221.7	218.0	Ferrari Testa Rossa Straman Spyder: 1438
35	220.1	216.4	Chevrolet Corvette: 739
			Chevrolet Corvette Injection: 740
			Chevrolet Corvette RPO 684/579E: 741
36	220.0	216.3	TVR Tuscan: 4586
37	215.1	211.5	Chevrolet Corvette: 743
38	213.3	209.8	Maserati Indy: 2657
39	211.6	208.0	Shelby GT 350: 4123
40	208.9	205.4	De Tomaso Pantera GT5 S: 1244
41	208.3	204.9	Porsche 928: 3752
42	206.9	203.4	Porsche 928: 3738
43	206.5	203.1	Porsche 928 Cabrio Strosek: 3725
44	206.2	202.8	Gordon GT: 2008
45	206.0	202.5	Porsche 928 S4 SE: 3727
46	205.2	201.8	Porsche 928 S4 Automatic: 3692
47	205.0	201.6	Chevrolet Corvette 270: 752
48	203.4	200.0	Maserati Ghibli: 2658
49	200.8	197.5	Porsche 928 S4: 3712
50	200.5	197.2	Porsche 928 Automatic: 3739

Total: 53

4501 - 5000cc. Highest specific output. Limit set at 60bhp/litre.

	bhp/L	kW/L	PS/L	
1	202.3	150.9	205.1	Koenig Competition Evolution: 2418
2	190.8	142.3	193.5	Ferrari Testa Rossa Norwood: 1444
3	161.9	120.7	164.1	Koenig Competition: 2417
4	95.1	70.9	96.4	Ford Mustang 5.0 Cartech Turbo: 1940
5	94.6	70.5	95.9	Jaguar XJ13: 2313
6	93.1	69.4	94.4	Ford Mustang TransAm: 1796
7	91.5	68.2	92.8	Ferrari 400 Super America: 1389
8	91.1	67.9	92.3	Ford Mustang Holdener: 1966
9	86.7	64.7	87.9	Porsche 928 S4 Koenig: 3726
10	82.3	61.4	83.5	Shelby GT 350-S: 4121
11	81.4	60.7	82.6	Shelby Cobra Daytona Coupe: 4119
12	80.2	59.8	81.3	Ford GT40: 1760
13	79.3	59.1	80.4	Ford Mustang Cartech Turbo: 1928
14	78.9	58.8	80.0	Ferrari Testa Rossa: 1442
15	78.9	58.8	80.0	Lamborghini Countach LP 500S: 2465
16	76.9	57.3	78.0	Ferrari Pininfarina Mythos: 1448
				Ferrari Testa Rossa: 1437
				Ferrari Testa Rossa: 1426
				Ferrari Testa Rossa Gemballa: 1443
				Ferrari Testa Rossa Straman Spyder: 1438
17	72.8	54.3	73.8	Ferrari 512 BB: 1417
				Ferrari 512 BB: 1413
18	72.5	54.1	73.6	Ferrari 4.9: 1387
19	72.0	53.7	73.0	Maserati Ghibli: 2658
20	72.0	53.7	73.0	Mercury Cougar Group 2: 2942
21	70.7	52.7	71.7	Ford GT40 Super Street: 1738
22	70.2	52.3	71.1	BMW 750i Alpina B12: 613
23	69.9	52.1	70.9	Maserati Indy: 2657
24	68.8	51.3	69.7	Ferrari 412: 1432
25	68.8	51.3	69.7	Ferrari 512 BBi: 1422
26	67.9	50.6	68.8	Chevrolet Corvette: 750
				Chevrolet Corvette 315: 753
27	67.2	50.1	68.1	Shelby Cobra USRRC: 4118
28	66.5	49.6	67.4	Porsche 928 S Series II: 3684
29	65.7	49.0	66.6	Maserati Bora: 2660
30	65.6	48.9	66.5	Porsche 928 Cabrio Strosek: 3725
31	65.5	48.9	66.5	Mercedes-Benz 500E: 2919
				Mercedes-Benz 500SL: 2913
32	65.5	48.9	66.4	Porsche 928: 3738
				Porsche 928: 3752
				Porsche 928 Gemballa: 3740
33	64.9	48.4	65.8	Maserati Khamsin: 2666
				Maserati Khamsin Automatic: 2662
34	64.7	48.3	65.6	Mercedes-Benz 500SEL: 2922
				Mercedes-Benz 500SL: 2920
35	64.6	48.2	65.5	Shelby GT 350: 4120
36	64.6	48.1	65.4	Porsche 928 S4 Automatic: 3692
				Porsche 928 S4 SE: 3727
37	63.9	47.6	64.8	Maserati Khamsin: 2669
				Maserati Khamsin: 2665
38	63.7	47.5	64.6	Porsche 928 S4: 3712
39	63.6	47.5	64.5	Shelby GT 350: 4123
40	63.6	47.4	64.4	Maserati Bora: 2664
41	63.5	47.4	64.4	Porsche 928 Automatic: 3739
42	63.5	47.3	64.3	AC Cobra: 25
43	62.7	46.8	63.6	Ford Mustang NOS/Saleen: 1967
44	62.5	46.6	63.4	Chevrolet Corvette: 743
				Gordon GT: 2008
45	61.7	46.0	62.6	De Tomaso Pantera GT5 S: 1244
46	61.4	45.8	62.3	Maserati Indy: 2659
47	61.0	45.5	61.9	Chevrolet Corvette RPO 684/579E: 741
				Ford Interceptor Coupe: 1639
48	61.0	45.5	61.8	Chevrolet Corvette: 739
				Chevrolet Corvette Injection: 740
				Excalibur SS: 1363
49	60.1	44.8	61.0	BMW 750i: 612
				BMW 750i L: 589
				BMW 750i L: 596
				BMW 850i: 620
				BMW 850i Manual: 625

Total: 70

4501 - 5000cc. Highest piston speed. Limit set at 50ft/sec.

	ft/sec	m/sec	
1	85.3	26.0	Ferrari Testa Rossa Norwood: 1444
2	62.5	19.0	Ford Mustang TransAm: 1796
3	58.3	17.8	Ferrari 400 Super America: 1389
4	57.5	17.5	Koenig Competition Evolution: 2418
5	55.8	17.0	Maserati Bora: 2660
			Maserati Bora: 2664
6	55.6	16.9	Jaguar XJ13: 2313
7	54.4	16.6	Maserati Quattroporte: 2671
8	53.8	16.4	Shelby Cobra Daytona Coupe: 4119
9	53.7	16.4	Ferrari Testa Rossa: 1442
10	53.6	16.3	Porsche 928: 3738
			Porsche 928: 3752
			Porsche 928 Gemballa: 3740
11	53.5	16.3	Maserati Khamsin: 2666
			Maserati Khamsin Automatic: 2662
12	53.3	16.2	Koenig Competition: 2417
13	53.0	16.1	Mercedes-Benz 500E: 2919
14	52.9	16.1	Ferrari 512 BB: 1417
			Ferrari 512 BB: 1413
15	52.9	16.1	Lamborghini Countach LP 500S: 2465
16	52.6	16.0	Bugatti 50S: 648
17	52.6	16.0	Auburn 8-52 Speedster: 264
18	52.1	15.9	Ferrari 4.9: 1387
19	52.1	15.9	Gordon GT: 2008
20	51.8	15.8	Ford GT40: 1760
			Porsche 928 Automatic: 3739
21	51.8	15.8	Porsche 928 Cabrio Strosek: 3725
			Porsche 928 S4: 3712
			Porsche 928 S4 Automatic: 3692
			Porsche 928 S4 Koenig: 3726
			Porsche 928 S4 SE: 3727
22	51.7	15.7	Chevrolet Corvette: 743
			Chevrolet Corvette: 739
			Chevrolet Corvette: 750
			Chevrolet Corvette 315: 753
			Chevrolet Corvette Injection: 740
			Chevrolet Corvette RPO 684/579E: 741
23	51.2	15.6	Ferrari 412: 1432
24	51.2	15.6	Maserati Ghibli: 2658
			Maserati Indy: 2659
			Mercedes-Benz 500SL: 2920
			Mercedes-Benz 500SL: 2913
25	50.8	15.5	Porsche 928 S Series II: 3684
26	50.6	15.4	Studebaker Regal Wagonaire Supercharged: 4237
27	50.4	15.3	Studebaker Daytona R-4: 4238
28	50.0	15.2	Chevrolet Corvette 270: 752
			Ford Mustang NOS/Saleen: 1967
			Rolls-Royce Silver Cloud "S": 3957

Total: 48

5001 - 5500cc. Maximum speed. Limit set at 130mph.

	mph	kmh	
1	183.0	294.4	Aston Martin Zagato: 257
2	180.0	289.6	Jaguar XJS Tullius: 2333
3	179.0	288.0	Lamborghini Countach: 2468
			Lamborghini Countach 25th Anniversary: 2473
4	173.0	278.4	Ford Mustang SVO J Bittle American: 1942
			Lamborghini Countach 5000S: 2469
5	170.0	273.5	Aston Martin V8 Vantage: 248
			Parradine V-12: 3382
6	165.0	265.5	Aston Martin Zagato Volante: 260
			Bizzarrini 5300 Spyder: 495
7	163.0	262.3	Iso Grifo GL 365: 2248
8	162.0	260.7	Aston Martin DBS V8: 244
9	160.0	257.4	Aston Martin Virage: 261
10	157.0	252.6	Iso Grifo GL: 2250
			Jaguar XJS HE: 2342
11	155.0	249.4	Aston Martin Virage: 258
12	154.0	247.8	Jaguar XJS: 2330
			Jaguar XJS Automatic: 2341
13	153.0	246.2	Iso Grifo A3L Berlinetta: 2245
14	151.0	243.0	Daimler Double-Six HE: 1155
			Lynx XJS Eventer: 2643
15	150.0	241.4	Jaguar XJRS: 2364
			Jaguar XJS Convertible: 2360
			Jaguar XJS Koenig: 2356
			Jaguar XJSC HE: 2351
16	148.0	238.1	Aston Martin V8: 252
			Chevrolet Corvette Sting Ray: 786
			Jaguar XJ12: 2324
			Jaguar XJ5.3 Automatic: 2335
			Jaguar XJ5.3C: 2328
17	147.0	236.5	Aston Martin V8: 246
			Aston Martin V8: 249
			Aston Martin V8 Automatic: 245
			Jaguar XJS: 2370
18	146.0	234.9	Jaguar XJS HE Cabriolet: 2347
			Jaguar XJS V12 Convertible: 2357
19	145.0	233.3	Aston Martin Volante: 256
			Bizzarrini GT America: 496
			Chevrolet Camaro IROC-Z: 927
20	144.0	231.7	Aston Martin Lagonda: 250
21	143.0	230.1	Jaguar E Type V12: 2319
			Jaguar XJS Automatic: 2332
22	142.0	228.5	Aston Martin Volante: 253
			Chevrolet Corvette: 775
			Chevrolet Corvette Sting Ray: 777
			Iso Rivolta IR-340: 2247
			Jaguar XJ12: 2321
23	141.0	226.9	Jaguar XJS V12 Convertible: 2361
			Jaguar XJSC: 2350
24	140.0	225.3	Aston Martin Lagonda: 251
			Aston Martin V8 Coupe: 247
			Chevrolet Camaro Z28: 958
			Jaguar XJS: 2343
			Jaguar XJS: 2355
			Jaguar XJS HE: 2346
25	139.0	223.7	Jaguar XJ12C: 2329
			Jaguar XJS: 2340
26	138.0	222.0	Chevrolet Corvette Sting Ray Injection: 788
			Jaguar XKE V12: 2325
27	137.0	220.4	Gordon Keeble GK1: 2009
			Jaguar XJS: 2338
28	135.0	217.2	Aston Martin Volante: 259
			Chevrolet Camaro IROC-Z: 896
			Iso GT: 2246
			Jaguar XJS: 2365
			Jaguar XJS Convertible: 2372
			Jaguar XJS Railton: 2367
			Jaguar XKE V12: 2323
			Pontiac Firebird Formula: 3593
29	132.0	212.4	Jaguar XJS: 2349
30	131.0	210.8	Chevrolet Chevy II Corvette: 757
			Jaguar XJ12L: 2326
31	130.0	209.2	Avanti II: 460
			Chevrolet Corvette Sting Ray Automatic: 778
			Chevrolet Corvette Sting Ray Automatic: 787
			Datsun 280Z Scarab: 1205
			Pontiac Firebird TransAm Convertible: 3598

Total: 77

5001 - 5500cc. Acceleration to 60mph/96.5kmh. Limit set at 8sec.

	sec	
1	4.7	Lamborghini Countach 25th Anniversary: 2473
2	4.8	Aston Martin Zagato: 257
3	4.9	Lamborghini Countach: 2468
4	5.0	Jaguar XJS Tullius: 2333
5	5.2	Ford Mustang SVO J Bittle American: 1942
		Lamborghini Countach 5000S: 2469
6	5.3	Chevrolet Corvette Sebring: 767
7	5.4	Aston Martin V8 Vantage: 248
		Parradine V-12: 3382
8	5.6	Aston Martin Zagato Volante: 260
9	5.9	Chevrolet Corvette: 766
		Chevrolet Corvette: 775
		Chevrolet Corvette Sting Ray: 777
10	6.0	Aston Martin DBS V8: 244
		Aston Martin Virage: 258
11	6.2	Aston Martin V8 Automatic: 245
		Datsun 280Z Scarab: 1205
		Iso Grifo A3L Berlinetta: 2245
12	6.3	Chevrolet Corvette Injection: 797
		Chevrolet Corvette Sting Ray Injection: 788
		Pontiac Firebird Formula 5.0: 3582
13	6.4	Bizzarrini 5300 Spyder: 495
		Bizzarrini GT America: 496
14	6.5	Chevrolet Corvette Sting Ray: 786
		Jaguar XJS HE: 2342
15	6.6	Aston Martin V8: 252
		Chevrolet Camaro IROC-Z: 927
		Jaguar XJS Automatic: 2341
		Pontiac Firebird Formula: 3593
16	6.7	Chevrolet Camaro Z28: 958
17	6.8	Aston Martin Virage: 261
		Jaguar E Type V12: 2319
18	6.9	Chevrolet Camaro IROC-Z 5.0: 912
		Jaguar XJS: 2330
19	7.2	Aston Martin V8: 249
		Chevrolet Chevy II Nova SS: 801
		Chevrolet Corvette Sting Ray Automatic: 778
		Iso Grifo GL: 2250
		Jaguar XJSC HE: 2351
20	7.3	Chevrolet Chevy II Corvette: 757
21	7.4	Aston Martin V8 Coupe: 247
		Iso Grifo GL 365: 2248
		Jaguar XJ12: 2324
		Jaguar XKE V12: 2323
		Oldsmobile Cutlass 442: 3281
22	7.5	Aston Martin V8: 246
		Gordon Keeble GK1: 2009
		Jaguar XJS Automatic: 2332

		Jaguar XJS Koenig: 2356
23	7.6	Lynx XJS Eventer: 2643
24	7.7	Chevrolet Corvette: 817
		Jaguar XJRS: 2364
		Jaguar XJS HE Cabriolet: 2347
		Kurtis Hornet Roadster: 2420
25	7.8	Aston Martin Volante: 259
		Chevrolet Corvette: 808
		Iso Rivolta S4: 2249
		Jaguar XJ5.3 Automatic: 2335
		Jaguar XJS: 2370
		Jaguar XJS: 2340
		Lamborghini LM129: 2472
		Pontiac Firebird TransAm Convertible: 3598
26	7.9	Pontiac Firebird TransAm HO: 3576
27	8.0	Chevrolet Corvette Sting Ray Automatic: 787
		Iso Rivolta IR-340: 2247
		Jaguar XJS V12 Convertible: 2357
		Jaguar XKE V12: 2325

Total: 67

5001 and 5500cc. Highest power. Limit set at 275bhp.

	bhp	kW	PS	
1	510.0	380.3	517.1	Ford Mustang SVO J Bittle American: 1942
2	475.0	354.2	481.6	Jaguar XJS Tullius: 2333
3	455.0	339.3	461.3	Lamborghini Countach: 2468
				Lamborghini Countach 25th Anniversary: 2473
4	432.0	322.1	438.0	Aston Martin Zagato: 257
5	420.0	313.2	425.8	Lamborghini Countach 5000S: 2469
6	415.0	309.5	420.8	Lamborghini LM129: 2472
7	400.0	298.3	405.5	Bizzarrini GT America: 496
8	375.0	279.6	380.2	Chevrolet Corvette Injection: 797
				Chevrolet Corvette Sting Ray Injection: 788
9	365.0	272.2	370.1	Iso Grifo GL 365: 2248
10	360.0	268.4	365.0	Chevrolet Chevy II Corvette: 757
				Chevrolet Corvette: 766
				Chevrolet Corvette: 775
				Chevrolet Corvette Sting Ray: 777
				Chevrolet Corvette Sting Ray: 786
11	350.0	261.0	354.8	Aston Martin Volante: 256
				Bizzarrini 5300 Spyder: 495
				Chevrolet Chevy II Nova SS: 801
				Chevrolet Corvette: 817
				Datsun 280Z Scarab: 1205
				Iso Grifo A3L Berlinetta: 2245
				Iso Grifo GL: 2250
12	340.0	253.5	344.7	Aston Martin V8 Coupe: 247
				Iso Rivolta IR-340: 2247
13	330.0	246.1	334.6	Aston Martin Virage: 261
				Aston Martin Virage: 258
14	325.0	242.3	329.5	Aston Martin Lagonda: 251
				Chevrolet Chevy II: 814
15	310.0	231.2	314.3	Chevrolet Corvette Sebring: 767
				Oldsmobile Cutlass 442: 3281
16	305.0	227.4	309.2	Aston Martin Zagato Volante: 260
17	300.0	223.7	304.2	Aston Martin Lagonda: 254
				Aston Martin Vantage: 255
				Aston Martin Volante: 253
				Avanti II: 458
				Chevrolet Corvette: 808
				Chevrolet Corvette: 802
				Chevrolet Corvette Coupe: 819
				Chevrolet Corvette Sting Ray Automatic: 787
				Chevrolet Corvette Sting Ray Automatic: 778
				Gordon Keeble GK1: 2009
				Iso GT: 2246
				Iso Rivolta S4: 2249
18	299.0	223.0	303.1	Daimler Double-Six HE: 1155
				Jaguar XJS HE: 2342
19	296.0	220.7	300.1	Jaguar XJS Automatic: 2341
20	295.0	220.0	299.1	Jaguar XJS HE Cabriolet: 2347
				Jaguar XJSC HE: 2351
				Lynx XJS Eventer: 2643
21	291.0	217.0	295.0	Jaguar XJS V12 Convertible: 2357
22	290.0	216.2	294.0	Oldsmobile F-85 Cutlass Holiday: 3282
23	286.0	213.3	290.0	Jaguar XJRS: 2364
				Jaguar XJS Railton: 2367
24	285.0	212.5	288.9	Jaguar XJ5.3 Automatic: 2335
				Jaguar XJ5.3C: 2328
				Jaguar XJS: 2330
				Jaguar XJS Automatic: 2332
25	280.0	208.8	283.9	Jaguar XJS: 2370
				Jaguar XJS Koenig: 2356
26	277.0	206.6	280.8	Parradine V-12: 3382
27	275.0	205.1	278.8	Checker Marathon: 728
				Chevrolet Camaro: 804
				Chevrolet Chevelle Malibu: 812
				Chevrolet Malibu 327: 823

Total: 65

5001 and 5500cc. Highest torque. Limit set at 350lbft.

	lbft	Nm	
1	400.0	542.0	Aston Martin V8 Coupe: 247
			Aston Martin Volante: 256
2	397.0	537.9	Parradine V-12: 3382
3	395.0	535.2	Aston Martin Zagato: 257
4	375.0	508.1	Aston Martin Lagonda: 251
			Bizzarrini 5300 Spyder: 495
			Bizzarrini GT America: 496
5	369.0	500.0	Lamborghini Countach: 2468
6	368.0	498.6	Ford Mustang SVO J Bittle American: 1942
			Lamborghini Countach 25th Anniversary: 2473
7	363.0	491.9	Lamborghini LM129: 2472
8	361.0	489.2	Iso Rivolta S4: 2249
9	360.0	487.8	AMC Ambassador 990: 175
			AMC Ambassador DPL: 181
			Avanti II: 458
			Chevrolet Chevy II Nova SS: 801
			Chevrolet Corvette: 802
			Chevrolet Corvette: 817
			Chevrolet Corvette: 808
			Chevrolet Corvette Coupe: 819
			Chevrolet Corvette Injection: 797
			Chevrolet Corvette Sting Ray Automatic: 778
			Chevrolet Corvette Sting Ray Automatic: 787
			Chevrolet Corvette Sting Ray Injection: 788
			Datsun 280Z Scarab: 1205
			Gordon Keeble GK1: 2009
			Iso Grifo A3L Berlinetta: 2245
			Iso Grifo GL: 2250
			Iso Grifo GL 365: 2248
			Iso GT: 2246
			Jaguar XJS Tullius: 2333
10	355.0	481.0	Checker Marathon: 728
			Chevrolet Camaro: 804
			Chevrolet Chevelle Malibu: 812
			Chevrolet Chevy II: 814
			Chevrolet Malibu 327: 823
			Oldsmobile Cutlass 442: 3281
			Oldsmobile F-85 Cutlass Holiday: 3282
11	352.0	477.0	Chevrolet Chevy II Corvette: 757
			Chevrolet Corvette: 775
			Chevrolet Corvette: 766
			Chevrolet Corvette Sting Ray: 786
			Chevrolet Corvette Sting Ray: 777
			Pontiac Tempest Le Mans V8: 3539
12	350.0	474.3	Aston Martin Lagonda: 254
			Aston Martin Vantage: 255
			Aston Martin Virage: 258
			Aston Martin Volante: 253
			Chevrolet Impala SS: 799
			Chevrolet Impala Station Wagon: 769
			Facel Vega Coupe: 1364

Total: 51

5001 - 5500cc. Highest rpm at peak power. Limit set at 5500rpm.

	rpm	
1	7900	Ford Mustang SVO J Bittle American: 1942
2	7600	Jaguar XJS Tullius: 2333
3	7000	Lamborghini Countach: 2468
		Lamborghini Countach 25th Anniversary: 2473
		Lamborghini Countach 5000S: 2469
4	6900	Lamborghini LM129: 2472
5	6200	Aston Martin Zagato: 257
		Chevrolet Corvette Injection: 797
		Chevrolet Corvette Sebring: 767
		Chevrolet Corvette Sting Ray Injection: 788
		Iso Grifo GL 365: 2248
6	6000	Aston Martin Virage: 258
		Aston Martin Virage: 261
		Bizzarrini GT America: 496
		Chevrolet Chevy II Corvette: 757
		Chevrolet Corvette: 775
		Chevrolet Corvette: 766
		Chevrolet Corvette Sting Ray: 786
		Chevrolet Corvette Sting Ray: 777
		Iso Rivolta IR-340: 2247
		Jaguar XJ12: 2321
		Jaguar XJ12: 2324
		Jaguar XKE V12: 2323
7	5850	Jaguar E Type V12: 2319
8	5800	Aston Martin DBS V8: 244
		Chevrolet Chevy II Nova SS: 801
		Chevrolet Corvette: 817
		Datsun 280Z Scarab: 1205
		Iso Grifo A3L Berlinetta: 2245
		Iso Grifo GL: 2250
9	5750	Jaguar XJ12L: 2326
		Jaguar XJ5.3 Automatic: 2335
		Jaguar XJ5.3C: 2328

		Jaguar XKE V12: 2325
		Panther De Ville: 3373
10	5600	Aston Martin Lagonda: 254
		Aston Martin Lagonda: 251
		Aston Martin V8 Coupe: 247
		Aston Martin Vantage: 255
		Aston Martin Volante: 253
		Chevrolet Chevy II: 814
11	5550	Jaguar XJS: 2370
12	5500	Aston Martin Volante: 256
		Aston Martin Volante: 259
		Aston Martin Zagato Volante: 260
		Daimler Double-Six HE: 1155
		Jaguar XJS: 2330
		Jaguar XJS Automatic: 2332
		Jaguar XJS HE: 2342
		Jaguar XJS HE Cabriolet: 2347
		Jaguar XJS V12 Convertible: 2357
		Jaguar XJSC HE: 2351
		Lynx XJS Eventer: 2643

Total: 53

5001 - 5500cc. Highest power-to-weight ratio. Limit set at 180bhp/ton.

	bhp/ ton	bhp/ tonne	
1	355.9	349.9	Ford Mustang SVO J Bittle American: 1942
2	351.4	345.5	Bizzarrini GT America: 496
3	339.9	334.3	Jaguar XJS Tullius: 2333
4	324.0	318.6	Iso Grifo A3L Berlinetta: 2245
5	319.7	314.4	Lamborghini Countach: 2468
6	310.7	305.5	Lamborghini Countach 25th Anniversary: 2473
7	286.4	281.6	Lamborghini Countach 5000S: 2469
8	284.6	279.8	Bizzarrini 5300 Spyder: 495
9	275.4	270.8	Chevrolet Corvette Sting Ray Injection: 788
10	269.7	265.2	Chevrolet Chevy II Corvette: 757
11	266.6	262.1	Aston Martin Zagato: 257
12	266.2	261.8	Datsun 280Z Scarab: 1205
13	266.1	261.7	Chevrolet Corvette: 775
			Chevrolet Corvette Sting Ray: 777
14	261.8	257.4	Chevrolet Corvette: 766
15	260.1	255.7	Chevrolet Corvette Injection: 797
16	257.3	253.1	Iso Grifo GL 365: 2248
17	249.7	245.5	Chevrolet Chevy II Nova SS: 801
18	248.3	244.1	Chevrolet Corvette Sting Ray: 786
19	240.5	236.5	Chevrolet Corvette: 817
20	225.6	221.9	Parradine V-12: 3382
21	223.0	219.3	Iso Grifo GL: 2250
22	222.5	218.8	Iso Rivolta IR-340: 2247
23	220.5	216.8	Chevrolet Corvette Sting Ray Automatic: 778
24	220.3	216.6	Chevrolet Corvette Sting Ray Automatic: 787
25	217.0	213.4	Chevrolet Corvette Sebring: 767
26	214.1	210.5	Chevrolet Chevy II: 814
27	212.7	209.1	Chevrolet Corvette: 808
28	212.4	208.8	Gordon Keeble GK1: 2009
29	209.3	205.8	Chevrolet Corvette: 802
30	199.1	195.8	Chevrolet Corvette Coupe: 819
31	197.4	194.1	Iso GT: 2246
32	196.9	193.6	Oldsmobile F-85 Cutlass Holiday: 3282
33	195.5	192.2	Aston Martin Volante: 256
34	193.1	189.9	Avanti II: 458
35	190.1	186.9	Chevrolet Camaro: 804
36	187.6	184.5	Aston Martin Virage: 258
37	184.4	181.3	Aston Martin V8 Coupe: 247
38	184.4	181.3	Aston Martin Zagato Volante: 260
39	184.1	181.1	Jaguar E Type V12: 2319
40	181.6	178.6	Iso Rivolta S4: 2249

Total: 41

5001 - 5500cc. Highest specific output. Limit set at 55bhp/litre.

	bhp/L	kW/L	PS/L	
1	101.2	75.5	102.6	Ford Mustang SVO J Bittle American: 1942
2	88.9	66.3	90.1	Jaguar XJS Tullius: 2333
3	88.1	65.7	89.3	Lamborghini Countach: 2468
				Lamborghini Countach 25th Anniversary: 2473
4	81.3	60.6	82.4	Lamborghini Countach 5000S: 2469
5	80.9	60.3	82.0	Aston Martin Zagato: 257
6	80.3	59.9	81.4	Lamborghini LM129: 2472
7	74.7	55.7	75.7	Bizzarrini GT America: 496
8	70.0	52.2	71.0	Chevrolet Corvette Injection: 797
				Chevrolet Corvette Sting Ray Injection: 788
9	68.1	50.8	69.0	Iso Grifo GL 365: 2248
10	67.4	50.3	68.3	Chevrolet Corvette: 775
				Chevrolet Corvette Sting Ray: 777
11	67.2	50.1	68.1	Chevrolet Chevy II Corvette: 757
				Chevrolet Corvette: 766
12	67.1	50.1	68.1	Chevrolet Corvette Sting Ray: 786
13	65.5	48.9	66.4	Aston Martin Volante: 256
14	65.4	48.7	66.3	Bizzarrini 5300 Spyder: 495
				Iso Grifo GL: 2250
15	65.3	48.7	66.2	Chevrolet Corvette: 817
16	65.3	48.7	66.2	Chevrolet Chevy II Nova SS: 801
				Datsun 280Z Scarab: 1205
				Iso Grifo A3L Berlinetta: 2245
17	63.7	47.5	64.5	Aston Martin V8 Coupe: 247
18	63.4	47.3	64.3	Iso Rivolta IR-340: 2247
19	61.8	46.1	62.7	Aston Martin Virage: 258
				Aston Martin Virage: 261
20	60.9	45.4	61.7	Aston Martin Lagonda: 251
21	60.6	45.2	61.5	Chevrolet Chevy II: 814
22	57.8	43.1	58.6	Chevrolet Corvette Sebring: 767
23	57.3	42.7	58.1	Oldsmobile Cutlass 442: 3281
24	57.1	42.6	57.9	Aston Martin Zagato Volante: 260
25	56.2	41.9	57.0	Aston Martin Lagonda: 254
				Aston Martin Vantage: 255
				Aston Martin Volante: 253
26	56.0	41.8	56.8	Chevrolet Corvette Sting Ray Automatic: 778
27	56.0	41.8	56.8	Gordon Keeble GK1: 2009
28	56.0	41.8	56.8	Chevrolet Corvette: 808
				Chevrolet Corvette Sting Ray Automatic: 787
				Iso GT: 2246
				Iso Rivolta S4: 2249
29	56.0	41.7	56.8	Chevrolet Corvette: 802
				Chevrolet Corvette Coupe: 819
30	55.9	41.7	56.7	Daimler Double-Six HE: 1155
				Jaguar XJS HE: 2342
31	55.9	41.7	56.7	Avanti II: 458
32	55.4	41.3	56.2	Jaguar XJS Automatic: 2341
33	55.2	41.2	56.0	Jaguar XJSC HE: 2351
34	55.2	41.2	56.0	Jaguar XJS HE Cabriolet: 2347
				Lynx XJS Eventer: 2643

Total: 50

5001 - 5500cc. Highest piston speed. Limit set at 45ft/sec.

	ft/sec	m/sec	
1	65.8	20.1	Ford Mustang SVO J Bittle American: 1942
2	58.3	17.7	Jaguar XJS Tullius: 2333
3	57.7	17.6	Aston Martin Zagato: 257
4	57.4	17.5	Lamborghini Countach: 2468
			Lamborghini Countach 25th Anniversary: 2473
			Lamborghini Countach 5000S: 2469
5	56.5	17.2	Lamborghini LM129: 2472
6	56.0	17.1	Chevrolet Corvette Injection: 797
			Iso Grifo GL 365: 2248
7	55.8	17.0	Chevrolet Corvette Sting Ray Injection: 788
8	55.8	17.0	Aston Martin Virage: 261
9	54.8	16.7	Chevrolet Corvette Sting Ray: 786
10	54.2	16.5	Bizzarrini GT America: 496
			Chevrolet Chevy II Corvette: 757
			Chevrolet Corvette: 766
			Chevrolet Corvette: 775
			Chevrolet Corvette Sting Ray: 777
			Iso Rivolta IR-340: 2247
11	54.0	16.4	Aston Martin DBS V8: 244
12	52.7	16.0	Datsun 280Z Scarab: 1205
13	52.4	16.0	Chevrolet Chevy II Nova SS: 801
			Chevrolet Corvette: 817
			Iso Grifo A3L Berlinetta: 2245
			Iso Grifo GL: 2250
14	52.1	15.9	Aston Martin Lagonda: 254
			Aston Martin Lagonda: 251
			Aston Martin V8 Coupe: 247
			Aston Martin Volante: 253
15	51.2	15.6	Aston Martin Volante: 259
			Aston Martin Zagato Volante: 260
16	50.6	15.4	Chevrolet Chevy II: 814
17	50.0	15.2	Pontiac Tempest Le Mans V8: 3539
18	50.0	15.2	Kurtis Hornet Roadster: 2420
19	48.7	14.9	Bizzarrini 5300 Spyder: 495
20	47.5	14.5	Hudson Hornet: 2177
21	47.2	14.4	Daimler Straight Eight: 1139
22	46.4	14.1	Dodge Custom Royal: 1273
			Facel Vega Coupe: 1364
23	46.4	14.1	Chevrolet Camaro IROC-Z: 896
			Pontiac Firebird TransAm HO: 3576
24	46.0	14.0	Jaguar XJ12: 2321
			Jaguar XJ12: 2324
			Jaguar XKE V12: 2323
25	45.3	13.8	Avanti II: 458
26	45.1	13.8	Chevrolet Corvette: 808
			Chevrolet Corvette: 802
			Chevrolet Corvette Coupe: 819
			Chevrolet Corvette Sting Ray Automatic: 778
			Iso GT: 2246
			Iso Rivolta S4: 2249
27	45.2	13.8	Oldsmobile F-85 Cutlass Holiday: 3282
28	45.1	13.7	Gordon Keeble GK1: 2009

29	45.0	13.7	Du Pont Speedster: 1350
30	45.0	13.7	Chevrolet Corvette Sting Ray Automatic: 787

Total: 54

5501 - 6000cc. Maximum speed. Limit set at 145mph.

	mph	kmh	
1	255.0	410.3	Chevrolet Corvette Callaway Sledgehammer: 941
2	218.0	350.8	Vector W8 Twin Turbo: 4736
3	204.0	328.2	Cizeta Moroder V16T: 1094
4	202.0	325.0	Lamborghini Diablo: 2474
			Lamborghini Diablo: 2475
5	201.0	323.4	Chevrolet Corvette Callaway Speedster: 949
6	200.0	321.8	Eagle GTP: 1356
			Vector W2: 4735
7	198.0	318.6	Ferrari 308 Norwood Bonneville GTO: 1434
8	192.0	308.9	Pontiac Firebird TDM Technologies: 3597
9	191.0	307.3	Chevrolet Corvette Callaway: 931
			Chevrolet Corvette Callaway: 918
10	186.0	299.3	Chevrolet Corvette ZR-1 Geiger: 954
11	185.0	297.7	Jaguar XJR15: 2369
			Mercedes-Benz 300CE AMG Hammer: 2910
12	184.0	296.1	Chevrolet Corvette Callaway: 948
13	183.0	294.4	Mercedes-Benz 300E AMG Hammer: 2899
			Pontiac Petty Grand National: 3571
14	178.0	286.4	Chevrolet Corvette Callaway: 901
15	176.0	283.2	Isdera Imperator: 2244
16	175.0	281.6	Zender Vision 3: 5007
17	170.0	273.5	Chevrolet Corvette Callaway: 940
			Chevrolet Corvette ZR-1: 934
18	169.0	271.9	Chevrolet Corvette Bakeracing SCCA Escort: 917
19	165.0	265.5	De Tomaso Pantera GT5-S: 1242
20	163.0	262.3	Chevrolet Corvette LT1: 959
21	161.0	259.0	Scarab Mk II: 4109
22	159.0	255.8	De Tomaso Pantera: 1237
			De Tomaso Pantera GTS: 1239
23	158.0	254.2	Chevrolet Corvette Convertible: 919
			Chevrolet Corvette Z51: 922
24	155.0	249.4	Chevrolet Corvette: 916
			Chevrolet Corvette L98: 933
			Mercedes-Benz 600SEL: 2923
25	154.0	247.8	Chevrolet Corvette: 900
			Chevrolet Corvette: 908
			Chevrolet Corvette ASC Geneve: 909
			Chevrolet Corvette Z51: 902
			Chevrolet Corvette ZR-1: 953
			Chevrolet Monza Mike Keyser: 874
26	153.0	246.2	Ford Cobra II Kemp: 1841
27	152.0	244.6	Chevrolet Camaro IROC: 877
			Chevrolet Corvette: 897
28	151.0	243.0	Mercedes-Benz 560SEL: 2889
29	150.0	241.4	Chevrolet Corvette Convertible: 910
			Pontiac Firebird GTA: 3596
30	149.0	239.7	Chevrolet Camaro IROC-Z L98: 907
			Chevrolet Corvette: 930
			Chevrolet Corvette L98: 944
31	147.0	236.5	Chevrolet Corvette Rick Mears: 952
32	146.0	234.9	Mercedes-Benz 560SEC Cabriolet Straman: 2895
33	145.0	233.3	Chevrolet Camaro IROC-Z Automatic: 928
			Chevrolet Camaro Z/28: 938
			Chevrolet Corvette: 894
			Mercedes-Benz 560SEC: 2888

Total: 55

5501 - 6000cc. Acceleration to 60mph/ 96.5kmh. Limit set at 6.5sec.

	sec	
1	3.7	Ferrari 308 Norwood Bonneville GTO: 1434
2	3.9	Chevrolet Corvette Callaway Sledgehammer: 941
3	4.0	Pontiac Firebird TransAm Silverbird: 3566
		Vector W2: 4735
4	4.1	Ford Cobra II Kemp: 1841
		Pontiac Firebird TDM Technologies: 3597
5	4.2	Chevrolet Corvette ZR-1 SS: 955
		Scarab Mk II: 4109
		Vector W8 Twin Turbo: 4736
6	4.4	Chevrolet Corvette Callaway Speedster: 949
7	4.5	Chevrolet Corvette Bakeracing SCCA Escort: 917
		Cizeta Moroder V16T: 1094
		Lamborghini Diablo: 2475
8	4.6	Chevrolet Corvette Callaway: 918
		Evans Series I: 1362
9	4.7	Chevrolet Monza Mike Keyser: 874
10	4.9	Chevrolet Corvette Callaway: 931
		Chevrolet Corvette Callaway: 948
		Chevrolet Corvette Callaway Twin Turbo: 950
		Chevrolet Corvette Morrison/Baker Nelson Ledges: 921
		Chevrolet Corvette ZR-1: 934
		Chevrolet Corvette ZR-1: 953
		Chevrolet Corvette ZR-1 Geiger: 954
11	5.0	Autokraft AC Cobra Mk IV: 456
		Chevrolet Corvette Callaway: 901
		Eagle GTP: 1356
		Isdera Imperator: 2244
		Mercedes-Benz 300CE AMG Hammer: 2910
12	5.1	Chevrolet Corvette Callaway: 940
13	5.2	Autokraft AC Cobra Mk IV: 455
		Chevrolet Camaro IROC: 877
		Mercedes-Benz 300E AMG Hammer: 2899
		Pontiac Petty Grand National: 3571
14	5.4	De Tomaso Pantera GT5-S: 1242
15	5.5	De Tomaso Pantera GT5: 1241
16	5.7	Chevrolet Corvette LT-1: 845
		Chevrolet Corvette LT1: 959
17	5.8	Chevrolet Camaro Z/28 RS: 842
		Chevrolet Corvette: 900
		Chevrolet Corvette ASC Geneve: 909
		Chevrolet Corvette Z51: 902
18	5.9	Chevrolet Corvette: 908
19	6.0	Chevrolet Corvette: 916
		Chevrolet Corvette: 897
		Chevrolet Corvette Convertible: 919
		Chevrolet Corvette Z51: 922
		Zender Vision 3: 5007
20	6.1	Mercedes-Benz 600SEL: 2923
21	6.2	Chevrolet Corvette: 930
		Chevrolet Corvette Coupe: 943
		De Tomaso Pantera: 1237
		Plymouth Duster 340: 3510
22	6.3	Chevrolet Corvette Convertible: 910
		Chevrolet Corvette Convertible: 942
		Chevrolet Corvette L98: 944
		Chevrolet Corvette Rick Mears: 952
		Dodge Dart GTS: 1305
		Dodge Dart GTS 340: 1306
23	6.4	Chevrolet Corvette L46: 831
24	6.5	Chevrolet Camaro Z/28: 841
		Chevrolet Corvette: 881
		De Tomaso Pantera GTS: 1239

Total: 62

5501 - 6000cc. Highest power. Limit set at 300bhp.

	bhp	kW	PS	
1	880.0	656.2	892.2	Chevrolet Corvette Callaway Sledgehammer: 941
2	685.0	510.8	694.5	Pontiac Firebird TDM Technologies: 3597
3	671.0	500.4	680.3	Ferrari 308 Norwood Bonneville GTO: 1434
4	625.0	466.1	633.7	Vector W8 Twin Turbo: 4736
5	600.0	447.4	608.3	Vector W2: 4735
6	590.0	440.0	598.2	Pontiac Firebird TransAm Silverbird: 3566
				Pontiac Petty Grand National: 3571
7	570.0	425.0	577.9	Ford Cobra II Kemp: 1841
8	560.0	417.6	567.8	Cizeta Moroder V16T: 1094
9	536.0	399.7	543.4	Chevrolet Monza Mike Keyser: 874
10	492.0	366.9	498.8	Lamborghini Diablo: 2475
11	485.0	361.7	491.7	Lamborghini Diablo: 2474
12	450.0	335.6	456.2	Chevrolet Camaro IROC: 877
				Jaguar XJR15: 2369
13	425.0	316.9	430.9	Chevrolet Corvette ZR-1 SS: 955
14	410.0	305.7	415.7	Chevrolet Corvette ZR-1 Geiger: 954
15	408.0	304.2	413.7	Mercedes-Benz 600SEL: 2923
16	403.0	300.5	408.6	Chevrolet Corvette Callaway: 948
				Chevrolet Corvette Callaway Speedster: 949
				Chevrolet Corvette Callaway Twin Turbo: 950
17	390.0	290.8	395.4	Chevrolet Corvette Callaway: 940
				Isdera Imperator: 2244
18	382.0	284.9	387.3	Chevrolet Corvette Callaway: 931
				Chevrolet Corvette Callaway: 918
19	380.0	283.4	385.3	Chevrolet Corvette ZR-1: 934
20	375.0	279.6	380.2	Chevrolet Corvette ZR-1: 953
				Mercedes-Benz 300CE AMG Hammer: 2910
				Mercedes-Benz 300E AMG Hammer: 2899
21	370.0	275.9	375.1	Chevrolet Corvette LT-1: 845
				Chevrolet Corvette LT-1: 836
22	360.0	268.4	365.0	Chevrolet Camaro Z/28: 841
				Chevrolet Camaro Z/28 RS: 842
				Chevrolet Corvette Morrison/Baker Nelson Ledges: 921
				Scarab Mk II: 4109
23	350.0	261.0	354.8	Chevrolet Corvette L46: 831
				De Tomaso Pantera GT5: 1241
				Ford Mustang Kaufmann: 1932
24	345.0	257.3	349.8	Chevrolet Corvette Callaway: 901
				Eagle GTP: 1356
25	335.0	249.8	339.6	De Tomaso Pantera GTS: 1239
26	330.0	246.1	334.6	De Tomaso Pantera: 1237
27	325.0	242.3	329.5	Chevrolet Corvette Bakeracing SCCA Escort: 917

				Facel Vega FVS: 1365
				Iso Rivolta Fidia: 2251
				Oldsmobile Cutlass W-31: 3295
28	310.0	231.2	314.3	De Tomaso Pantera: 1236
				Oldsmobile Rallye 350: 3297
29	305.0	227.4	309.2	Jensen CV8: 2390
				Plymouth Fury: 3474
				Plymouth Sport Fury: 3481
30	300.0	223.7	304.2	Autokraft AC Cobra Mk IV: 455
				Autokraft AC Cobra Mk IV: 456
				Avanti II: 459
				Chevrolet Camaro: 840
				Chevrolet Chevelle Malibu: 828
				Chevrolet Corvette LT1: 959
				Chevrolet Corvette Stingray: 837
				Chevrolet Corvette ZQ3: 838
				Chevrolet Nova SS350: 848
				De Tomaso Pantera GT5-S: 1242
				Evans Series I: 1362
				Ford Torino GT: 1788
				Zender Vision 3: 5007

Total: 63

5501 - 6000cc. Highest torque. Limit set at 370lbft.

	lbft	Nm	
1	785.0	1063.7	Pontiac Firebird TDM Technologies: 3597
2	772.0	1046.1	Chevrolet Corvette Callaway Sledgehammer: 941
3	630.0	853.7	Vector W8 Twin Turbo: 4736
4	580.0	785.9	Vector W2: 4735
5	575.0	779.1	Chevrolet Corvette Callaway: 948
			Chevrolet Corvette Callaway Speedster: 949
			Chevrolet Corvette Callaway Twin Turbo: 950
6	562.0	761.5	Chevrolet Corvette Callaway: 931
			Chevrolet Corvette Callaway: 940
7	545.0	738.5	Chevrolet Corvette Callaway: 918
8	530.0	718.2	Ford Cobra II Kemp: 1841
9	502.0	680.2	Ferrari 308 Norwood Bonneville GTO: 1434
10	465.0	630.1	Chevrolet Corvette Callaway: 901
11	460.0	623.3	Pontiac Firebird TransAm Silverbird: 3566
12	440.0	596.2	Chevrolet Monza Mike Keyser: 874
13	437.0	592.1	Chevrolet Corvette Morrison/Baker Nelson Ledges: 921
14	430.0	582.7	Facel Vega FVS: 1365
15	428.0	579.9	Lamborghini Diablo: 2475
			Lamborghini Diablo: 2474
			Mercedes-Benz 600SEL: 2923
16	420.0	569.1	Jaguar XJR15: 2369
17	410.0	555.6	Chevrolet Corvette Bakeracing SCCA Escort: 917
			Ford Mustang Kaufmann: 1932
18	407.0	551.5	Mercedes-Benz 300CE AMG Hammer: 2910
			Mercedes-Benz 300E AMG Hammer: 2899
19	400.0	542.0	Chevrolet Corvette ZR-1 SS: 955
20	398.0	539.3	Cizeta Moroder V16T: 1094
21	396.0	536.6	Chevrolet Camaro IROC: 877
22	395.0	535.2	Jensen CV8: 2390
			Plymouth Sport Fury: 3481
23	390.0	528.5	Dodge Custom Royal: 1274
			Oldsmobile Rallye 350: 3297
24	387.0	524.4	Isdera Imperator: 2244
25	385.0	521.7	Ford Mustang Grande: 1778
26	380.0	514.9	Avanti II: 459
			Chevrolet Camaro: 840
			Chevrolet Camaro SS350: 807
			Chevrolet Camaro Z/28: 841
			Chevrolet Camaro Z/28 RS: 842
			Chevrolet Chevelle Malibu: 828
			Chevrolet Corvette L46: 831
			Chevrolet Corvette LT-1: 845
			Chevrolet Corvette ZQ3: 838
			Chevrolet Nova SS350: 848
			Chrysler Newport: 978
			De Tomaso Pantera: 1236
			Dodge Coronet 440: 1295
			Dodge Custom 880: 1279
			Ford Torino GT: 1788
			Scarab Mk II: 4109
27	370.0	501.4	Chevrolet Corvette LT-1: 836
			Chevrolet Corvette ZR-1: 953
			Chevrolet Corvette ZR-1: 934
			Chevrolet Corvette ZR-1 Geiger: 954
			Plymouth Fury: 3474

Total: 55

5501 - 6000cc. Highest rpm at maximum power. Limit set at 5000rpm.

	rpm	
1	8000	Cizeta Moroder V16T: 1094
2	7850	Ferrari 308 Norwood Bonneville GTO: 1434
3	7500	Pontiac Firebird TransAm Silverbird: 3566
		Pontiac Petty Grand National: 3571
4	7200	Chevrolet Monza Mike Keyser: 874
5	7000	Ford Cobra II Kemp: 1841
		Lamborghini Diablo: 2474
6	6800	Lamborghini Diablo: 2475
7	6500	Chevrolet Camaro IROC: 877
		De Tomaso Pantera GT5-S: 1242
8	6400	Chevrolet Corvette ZR-1 SS: 955
9	6250	Chevrolet Corvette Callaway Sledgehammer: 941
		Jaguar XJR15: 2369
10	6200	Chevrolet Corvette ZR-1: 934
11	6000	Autokraft AC Cobra Mk IV: 455
		Autokraft AC Cobra Mk IV: 456
		Chevrolet Camaro Z/28: 841
		Chevrolet Camaro Z/28 RS: 842
		Chevrolet Corvette LT-1: 845
		De Tomaso Pantera GT5: 1241
		De Tomaso Pantera GTS: 1239
		Scarab Mk II: 4109
12	5800	Chevrolet Corvette LT-1: 836
		Chevrolet Corvette ZR-1: 953
		Chevrolet Corvette ZR-1 Geiger: 954
		Iso Rivolta Fidia: 2251
13	5700	Vector W2: 4735
		Vector W8 Twin Turbo: 4736
14	5600	Chevrolet Camaro Z/28: 857
		Chevrolet Corvette L46: 831
		Eagle GTP: 1356
15	5500	Isdera Imperator: 2244
		Mercedes-Benz 300CE AMG Hammer: 2910
		Mercedes-Benz 300E AMG Hammer: 2899
16	5400	De Tomaso Pantera: 1237
		De Tomaso Pantera: 1236
		De Tomaso Pantera: 1238
		De Tomaso Pantera L: 1240
		Ford Mustang Kaufmann: 1932
		Ford Torino GT: 1788
		Oldsmobile Cutlass W-31: 3295
17	5200	Chevrolet Corvette: 881
		Chevrolet Corvette: 869
		Chevrolet Corvette: 862
		Chevrolet Corvette Automatic: 882
		Chevrolet Corvette LT-1: 858
		Chevrolet Corvette Sting Ray: 875
		Mercedes-Benz 560SEC: 2888
		Mercedes-Benz 600SEL: 2923
18	5000	Chevrolet Corvette LT1: 959
		Chevrolet Corvette Morrison/Baker Nelson Ledges: 921
		Dodge Dart GTS: 1305
		Dodge Dart GTS 340: 1306
		Dodge Swinger: 1313
		Mercedes-Benz 560SEL: 2889
		Plymouth Barracuda: 3509
		Plymouth Barracuda 340-S: 3498
		Plymouth Cuda 340: 3504
		Plymouth Duster 340: 3510
		Plymouth Fury: 3474
		Zender Vision 3: 5007

Total: 61

5501 - 6000cc. Highest power-to-weight ratio. Limit set at 200bhp/ton.

	bhp/ ton	bhp/ tonne	
1	589.4	579.6	Ferrari 308 Norwood Bonneville GTO: 1434
2	537.1	528.1	Chevrolet Corvette Callaway Sledgehammer: 941
3	483.4	475.4	Vector W2: 4735
4	476.4	468.5	Ford Cobra II Kemp: 1841
5	455.7	448.1	Pontiac Firebird TransAm Silverbird: 3566
6	448.0	440.5	Chevrolet Monza Mike Keyser: 874
7	436.4	429.1	Jaguar XJR15: 2369
8	426.2	419.1	Pontiac Firebird TDM Technologies: 3597
9	424.4	417.3	Scarab Mk II: 4109
10	421.7	414.6	Vector W8 Twin Turbo: 4736
11	396.3	389.7	Eagle GTP: 1356
12	356.7	350.8	Pontiac Petty Grand National: 3571
13	334.5	328.9	Cizeta Moroder V16T: 1094
14	317.1	311.8	Isdera Imperator: 2244
15	307.3	302.2	Chevrolet Camaro IROC: 877
16	304.4	299.4	Lamborghini Diablo: 2475
17	304.1	299.1	Chevrolet Corvette ZR-1 SS: 955
18	298.5	293.5	Lamborghini Diablo: 2474
19	293.4	288.6	Evans Series I: 1362
20	282.1	277.4	Chevrolet Corvette Callaway Speedster: 949
21	274.3	269.7	Autokraft AC Cobra Mk IV: 455
			Autokraft AC Cobra Mk IV: 456
22	262.4	258.0	Chevrolet Corvette Callaway: 948
			Chevrolet Corvette Callaway Twin Turbo: 950
23	256.9	252.7	Chevrolet Corvette Callaway: 940
24	255.8	251.5	Chevrolet Corvette LT-1: 836
25	253.2	249.0	Chevrolet Camaro Z/28 RS: 842
26	252.0	247.8	Chevrolet Corvette Morrison/Baker Nelson Ledges: 921
27	248.5	244.4	Chevrolet Corvette LT-1: 845

28	248.5	244.3	De Tomaso Pantera GTS: 1239
29	248.0	243.9	Chevrolet Corvette Callaway: 918
30	244.5	240.4	Chevrolet Corvette Callaway: 931
31	242.4	238.4	Chevrolet Corvette ZR-1: 953
32	241.2	237.2	De Tomaso Pantera GT5: 1241
33	241.1	237.1	Chevrolet Corvette ZR-1: 934
34	237.9	234.0	Chevrolet Corvette L46: 831
35	237.5	233.6	De Tomaso Pantera: 1237
36	231.1	227.2	Mercedes-Benz 300E AMG Hammer: 2899
37	227.5	223.7	Chevrolet Corvette Bakeracing SCCA Escort: 917
38	226.4	222.6	Mercedes-Benz 300CE AMG Hammer: 2910
39	225.9	222.1	Zender Vision 3: 5007
40	225.3	221.5	Chevrolet Corvette Callaway: 901
41	225.2	221.5	Chevrolet Camaro Z/28: 841
42	220.1	216.4	De Tomaso Pantera: 1236
43	209.0	205.5	De Tomaso Pantera GT5-S: 1242
44	207.9	204.4	Ford Mustang Grande: 1778
45	205.9	202.4	Chevrolet Camaro SS350: 807
46	201.8	198.4	Chevrolet Corvette LT1: 959
47	200.6	197.2	Avanti II: 459
48	200.0	196.7	Oldsmobile Cutlass W-31: 3295

Total: 50

5501 - 6000cc. Highest specific output. Limit set at 55bhp/litre.

	bhp/L	kW/L	PS/L	
1	153.5	114.5	155.6	Chevrolet Corvette Callaway Sledgehammer: 941
2	119.5	89.1	121.1	Pontiac Firebird TDM Technologies: 3597
3	111.8	83.4	113.4	Ferrari 308 Norwood Bonneville GTO: 1434
4	104.6	78.0	106.1	Vector W8 Twin Turbo: 4736
5	100.2	74.7	101.6	Pontiac Petty Grand National: 3571
6	100.0	74.6	101.4	Vector W2: 4735
7	99.1	73.9	100.4	Ford Cobra II Kemp: 1841
8	98.4	73.3	99.7	Pontiac Firebird TransAm Silverbird: 3566
9	93.5	69.7	94.8	Chevrolet Monza Mike Keyser: 874
10	93.4	69.7	94.7	Cizeta Moroder V16T: 1094
11	86.2	64.3	87.4	Lamborghini Diablo: 2475
12	85.0	63.4	86.2	Lamborghini Diablo: 2474
13	78.4	58.5	79.5	Chevrolet Camaro IROC: 877
14	75.1	56.0	76.1	Jaguar XJR15: 2369
15	74.2	55.3	75.2	Chevrolet Corvette ZR-1 SS: 955
16	71.6	53.4	72.6	Chevrolet Corvette ZR-1 Geiger: 954
17	70.3	52.4	71.3	Isdera Imperator: 2244
18	70.3	52.4	71.2	Chevrolet Corvette Callaway: 948
				Chevrolet Corvette Callaway Speedster: 949
				Chevrolet Corvette Callaway Twin Turbo: 950
19	68.1	50.8	69.1	Mercedes-Benz 600SEL: 2923
20	68.0	50.7	68.9	Chevrolet Corvette Callaway: 940
21	66.6	49.7	67.6	Chevrolet Corvette Callaway: 931
22	66.5	49.6	67.4	Chevrolet Corvette Callaway: 918
23	66.3	49.5	67.3	Chevrolet Corvette ZR-1: 934
24	65.5	48.8	66.4	Chevrolet Corvette ZR-1: 953
25	64.7	48.3	65.6	Scarab Mk II: 4109
26	64.5	48.1	65.4	Chevrolet Corvette LT-1: 836
				Chevrolet Corvette LT-1: 845
27	63.0	47.0	63.9	Mercedes-Benz 300CE AMG Hammer: 2910
				Mercedes-Benz 300E AMG Hammer: 2899
28	62.8	46.8	63.6	Chevrolet Camaro Z/28 RS: 842
29	62.8	46.8	63.6	Chevrolet Camaro Z/28: 841
30	61.0	45.5	61.9	Chevrolet Corvette L46: 831
31	60.9	45.4	61.8	Chevrolet Corvette Morrison/Baker Nelson Ledges: 921
32	60.9	45.4	61.7	Ford Mustang Kaufmann: 1932
33	60.7	45.3	61.6	De Tomaso Pantera GT5: 1241
34	60.2	44.9	61.0	Chevrolet Corvette Callaway: 901
				Eagle GTP: 1356
35	58.1	43.3	58.9	De Tomaso Pantera GTS: 1239
36	57.3	42.7	58.1	De Tomaso Pantera: 1237
37	56.7	42.3	57.5	Oldsmobile Cutlass W-31: 3295
38	56.6	42.2	57.4	Chevrolet Corvette Bakeracing SCCA Escort: 917
39	56.3	42.0	57.1	Iso Rivolta Fidia: 2251
40	56.0	41.8	56.8	Facel Vega FVS: 1365

Total: 45

5501 - 6000cc. Highest piston speed. Limit set at 50ft/sec.

	ft/sec	m/sec	
1	77.6	23.6	Ferrari 308 Norwood Bonneville GTO: 1434
2	72.9	22.2	Pontiac Petty Grand National: 3571
3	70.4	21.5	Pontiac Firebird TransAm Silverbird: 3566
4	69.6	21.2	Chevrolet Monza Mike Keyser: 874
5	68.1	20.7	Ford Cobra II Kemp: 1841
6	65.1	19.8	Chevrolet Corvette ZR-1 SS: 955
7	63.2	19.3	Chevrolet Camaro IROC: 877
			De Tomaso Pantera GT5-S: 1242
8	63.0	19.2	Chevrolet Corvette ZR-1: 934
9	61.2	18.7	Lamborghini Diablo: 2474
10	60.4	18.4	Chevrolet Corvette Callaway Sledgehammer: 941
11	59.5	18.1	Lamborghini Diablo: 2475
12	59.0	18.0	Chevrolet Corvette ZR-1: 953
			Chevrolet Corvette ZR-1 Geiger: 954
13	58.3	17.8	De Tomaso Pantera GT5: 1241
			De Tomaso Pantera GTS: 1239
14	58.0	17.7	Chevrolet Camaro Z/28: 841
			Chevrolet Camaro Z/28 RS: 842
			Chevrolet Corvette LT-1: 845
15	57.5	17.5	Vector W2: 4735
16	57.5	17.5	Vector W8 Twin Turbo: 4736
17	57.0	17.4	Isdera Imperator: 2244
			Mercedes-Benz 300E AMG Hammer: 2899
18	57.0	17.4	Mercedes-Benz 300CE AMG Hammer: 2910
19	56.4	17.2	Cizeta Moroder V16T: 1094
20	56.4	17.2	Iso Rivolta Fidia: 2251
21	56.3	17.2	Scarab Mk II: 4109
22	56.1	17.1	Chevrolet Corvette LT-1: 836
23	54.1	16.5	Chevrolet Camaro Z/28: 857
			Chevrolet Corvette L46: 831
			Eagle GTP: 1356
24	53.9	16.4	Mercedes-Benz 560SEC: 2888
25	53.6	16.3	Jaguar XJR15: 2369
26	52.5	16.0	De Tomaso Pantera: 1238
			De Tomaso Pantera: 1236
			De Tomaso Pantera L: 1240
27	52.5	16.0	De Tomaso Pantera: 1237
			Ford Mustang Kaufmann: 1932
			Ford Torino GT: 1788
28	51.8	15.8	Mercedes-Benz 560SEL: 2889
			Zender Vision 3: 5007
29	50.8	15.5	Oldsmobile Cutlass W-31: 3295
30	50.3	15.3	Chevrolet Corvette: 869
			Chevrolet Corvette: 862
			Chevrolet Corvette: 881
			Chevrolet Corvette Automatic: 882
			Chevrolet Corvette LT-1: 858
			Chevrolet Corvette Sting Ray: 875

Total: 48

6001 - 6500cc. Maximum speed. Limit set at 115mph.

	mph	kmh	
1	200.0	321.8	Jaguar XJ220: 2359
2	172.0	276.7	Chevrolet Corvette Guldstrand Grand Sport 80: 920
3	171.0	275.1	Chevrolet Corvette Guldstrand Grand Sport 80: 932
4	168.0	270.3	De Tomaso Pantera Group 3: 1243
5	141.0	226.9	Jensen FF II: 2394
6	138.0	222.0	Chevrolet Corvette Sting Ray 396: 798
7	137.0	220.4	Jensen Interceptor: 2393
8	136.0	218.8	Chevrolet Corvette: 795
			Chevrolet Corvette 396: 796
			Jensen Interceptor: 2396
9	135.0	217.2	Chrysler 300-D: 973
10	134.0	215.6	Mercedes-Benz 300SEL 6.3: 2828
11	133.0	214.0	Facel Vega Facel II: 1368
			Jensen Interceptor: 2391
12	132.0	212.4	Chevrolet El Camino: 821
			Mercedes-Benz 600: 2821
13	130.0	209.2	Chevrolet Chevelle Malibu 396: 792
			Chrysler Enforcer: 976
			Facel Vega HK-500: 1366
			Jensen FF: 2392
14	126.0	202.7	Chevrolet Camaro SS 396: 824
			Dodge Coronet 500 Station Wagon: 1307
15	125.0	201.1	Pontiac Tempest GTO: 3546
16	122.0	196.3	Ford Galaxie: 1663
			Jensen Interceptor II: 2395
			Oldsmobile 98 Holiday Sports Sedan: 3275
			Plymouth Road Runner: 3503
			Pontiac Tempest GTO: 3540
17	121.0	194.7	AMC Ambassador SST Wagon: 193
			Chevrolet Camaro SS396: 810
			Pontiac GTO: 3544
18	120.0	193.1	AMC Javelin 390: 198
			Cadillac Fleetwood: 703
			Chevrolet Chevelle SS396: 813
			Dodge Charger: 1298
			Ford Galaxie 500: 1705
			Ford Thunderbird: 1665
			Mercury Comet Cyclone GT: 2940
			Plymouth Satellite: 3490
19	119.0	191.5	Ford Thunderbird Sports Roadster: 1680
			Plymouth Sport Fury: 3483
			Pontiac Bonneville Vista: 3541
20	118.0	189.9	Dodge Polara: 1289
			Rolls-Royce Silver Shadow: 3961
21	117.0	188.3	Oldsmobile Jetstar I: 3283
			Pontiac Catalina: 3537
			Pontiac Royal Bobcat: 3535

			Rolls-Royce Silver Cloud III: 3960
22	116.0	186.6	Ford Galaxie LTD: 1715
			Mercury Park Lane: 2937
23	115.0	185.0	Cadillac Coupe de Ville: 702
			Cadillac Eldorado Convertible: 701
			Dodge Coronet 500: 1296
			Dodge Polara: 1286
			Ford Fairlane GTA: 1735
			Ford Galaxie: 1678
			Ford Thunderbird: 1727
			Mercedes-Benz 600: 2816
			Mercury Cougar GT: 2943
			Mercury Park Lane: 2939
			Oldsmobile Dynamic 88 Celebrity Sedan: 3276
			Oldsmobile Super 88: 3272
			Plymouth Belvedere Satellite: 3487
			Plymouth Fury III: 3506
			Plymouth Fury III: 3496
			Rolls-Royce Silver Cloud II: 3958

Total: 66

6001 - 6500cc. Acceleration to 60mph/ 96.5kmh. Limit set at 8.5sec.

	sec	
1	3.5	Jaguar XJ220: 2359
2	4.3	De Tomaso Pantera Group 3: 1243
3	4.6	Pontiac Catalina Super Stock: 3529
4	5.1	Chevrolet Corvette Guldstrand Grand Sport 80: 932
		Plymouth Road Runner: 3507
5	5.2	Chevrolet Corvette Guldstrand Grand Sport 80: 920
6	5.7	Chevrolet Corvette: 795
		Chevrolet Corvette 396: 796
7	5.8	Pontiac Tempest GTO: 3543
8	6.0	Chevrolet Corvette Sting Ray 396: 798
9	6.3	AMC Rambler Scrambler: 194
10	6.4	Jensen Interceptor: 2393
11	6.5	Chevrolet Chevelle Malibu 396: 792
		Dodge Coronet 500 Station Wagon: 1307
		Pontiac Royal Bobcat: 3535
12	6.6	Chevrolet Chevelle SS396: 813
		Dodge Super Bee: 1311
		Mercury Comet Cyclone GT: 2940
13	6.8	Chevrolet Camaro SS 396: 824
		Chevrolet El Camino: 821
		Pontiac Tempest GTO: 3546
14	6.9	Pontiac Tempest GTO: 3540
15	7.0	AMC Javelin: 191
16	7.1	Jensen Interceptor II: 2395
		Mercedes-Benz 300SEL 6.3: 2828
		Plymouth Satellite: 3490
17	7.2	AMC AMX: 189
		AMC AMX Automatic: 190
		Dodge Charger: 1298
18	7.3	Jensen Interceptor: 2391
		Plymouth Road Runner: 3503
19	7.4	Jensen Interceptor: 2396
20	7.5	Oldsmobile Jetstar I: 3283
21	7.6	AMC Javelin 390: 198
		Chevrolet Camaro SS396: 810
22	7.7	Ford Torino: 1763
		Mercury Cougar GT: 2943
23	7.8	Facel Vega Facel II: 1368
		Ford Mustang 390 Fastback: 1748
24	7.9	Pontiac GTO: 3544
25	8.0	Dodge Coronet 500: 1296
		Plymouth Sport Fury: 3483
26	8.1	Jensen FF II: 2394
27	8.2	AMC Ambassador SST Wagon: 193
28	8.3	Chrysler Enforcer: 976
29	8.4	Chevrolet Caprice Custom 396: 790
		Chrysler 300-D: 973
		Dodge Polara: 1289
		Jensen FF: 2392
30	8.5	Oldsmobile Starfire: 3280

Total: 50

6001 - 6500cc. Highest power. Limit set at 325bhp.

	bhp	kW	PS	
1	530.0	395.2	537.3	Jaguar XJ220: 2359
2	465.0	346.7	471.4	De Tomaso Pantera Group 3: 1243
3	425.0	316.9	430.9	Chevrolet Corvette: 795
				Chevrolet Corvette 396: 796
				Chevrolet Corvette Sting Ray 396: 798
4	380.0	283.4	385.3	Chrysler 300-D: 973
5	375.0	279.6	380.2	Chevrolet Camaro SS 396: 824
				Chevrolet Chevelle Malibu 396: 792
				Chevrolet Chevelle SS396: 813
6	374.0	278.9	379.2	Chevrolet Corvette Guldstrand Grand Sport 80: 920
7	370.0	275.9	375.1	Pontiac Royal Bobcat: 3535
8	365.0	272.2	370.1	Pontiac GTO: 3544
9	360.0	268.4	365.0	Pontiac Tempest GTO: 3543
10	355.0	264.7	359.9	Chevrolet Corvette Guldstrand Grand Sport 80: 932
				Facel Vega Facel II: 1368
11	350.0	261.0	354.8	Chevrolet El Camino: 821
12	348.0	259.5	352.8	Pontiac Catalina Super Stock: 3529
13	345.0	257.3	349.8	Cadillac Eldorado Convertible: 701
				Oldsmobile Jetstar I: 3283
				Oldsmobile Starfire: 3280
14	335.0	249.8	339.6	Dodge Super Bee: 1311
				Ford Fairlane GTA: 1735
				Ford Mustang 390 Fastback: 1748
				Mercury Comet Cyclone GT: 2940
				Plymouth Road Runner: 3507
				Plymouth Road Runner: 3503
				Pontiac Tempest GTO: 3546
15	330.0	246.1	334.6	Dodge Coronet 500: 1296
				Dodge Coronet 500 Station Wagon: 1307
				Dodge Polara: 1289
				Facel Vega HK-500: 1366
				Jensen FF II: 2394
				Jensen Interceptor: 2396
				Jensen Interceptor: 2393
				Jensen Interceptor II: 2395
				Oldsmobile 98 Holiday Sports Sedan: 3275
				Plymouth Belvedere Satellite: 3487
				Plymouth Fury Station Wagon: 3488
				Plymouth Sport Fury: 3483
16	325.0	242.3	329.5	AMC Javelin 390: 198
				Cadillac Coupe de Ville: 702
				Cadillac Fleetwood: 703
				Cadillac Park Avenue: 704
				Chevrolet Camaro SS396: 810
				Chevrolet Caprice Custom 396: 790
				Chrysler Enforcer: 976
				Dodge Charger: 1298
				Dodge Monaco Wagon: 1302
				Jensen FF: 2392
				Jensen Interceptor: 2391
				Plymouth Fury III: 3496
				Plymouth Satellite: 3490
				Plymouth VIP: 3492
				Pontiac Bonneville Vista: 3541
				Pontiac Tempest GTO: 3540

Total: 55

6001 - 6500cc. Highest torque. Limit set at 425lbft.

	lbft	Nm	
1	460.0	623.3	Facel Vega HK-500: 1366
			Pontiac Royal Bobcat: 3535
2	442.0	598.9	Chevrolet Corvette Guldstrand Grand Sport 80: 920
3	440.0	596.2	De Tomaso Pantera Group 3: 1243
			Oldsmobile 98 Holiday Sports Sedan: 3275
			Oldsmobile Jetstar I: 3283
			Oldsmobile Starfire: 3280
4	435.0	589.4	Cadillac Eldorado Convertible: 701
			Chrysler 300-D: 973
5	434.0	588.1	Mercedes-Benz 600: 2816
6	431.0	584.0	Pontiac Tempest GTO: 3546
7	430.0	582.7	Cadillac Coupe de Ville: 702
			Cadillac Fleetwood: 703
			Cadillac Park Avenue: 704
			Oldsmobile Dynamic 88 Celebrity Sedan: 3276
			Pontiac Catalina Super Stock: 3529
			Pontiac Grand Prix: 3538
8	429.0	581.3	Pontiac Bonneville Vista: 3541
9	428.0	579.9	Pontiac Tempest GTO: 3540
10	427.0	578.6	Ford Fairlane GTA: 1735
			Ford Fairlane Ranchero: 1746
			Ford Galaxie: 1678
			Ford Galaxie: 1663
			Ford Galaxie 500: 1705
			Ford Galaxie LTD: 1715
			Ford Mustang 390 Fastback: 1748
			Ford Thunderbird: 1665
			Ford Thunderbird: 1727
			Ford Thunderbird Sports Roadster: 1680
			Ford Torino: 1763
			Mercury Comet Cyclone GT: 2940
			Mercury Cougar GT: 2943
			Mercury Park Lane: 2937
			Mercury Park Lane: 2939
11	425.0	575.9	AMC Ambassador SST Wagon: 193
			AMC AMX: 189
			AMC AMX Automatic: 190
			AMC Javelin: 191
			AMC Rambler Scrambler: 194
			Chevrolet Corvette Guldstrand Grand Sport 80: 932
			Chrysler Enforcer: 976
			Dodge Charger: 1298

Dodge Coronet 500: 1296
Dodge Coronet 500 Station Wagon: 1307
Dodge Monaco Wagon: 1302
Dodge Polara: 1289
Dodge Super Bee: 1311
Jensen FF: 2392
Jensen FF II: 2394
Jensen Interceptor: 2393
Jensen Interceptor: 2391
Jensen Interceptor: 2396
Jensen Interceptor II: 2395
Plymouth Belvedere Satellite: 3487
Plymouth Fury III: 3496
Plymouth Fury Station Wagon: 3488
Plymouth Road Runner: 3503
Plymouth Road Runner: 3507
Plymouth Satellite: 3490
Plymouth Sport Fury: 3483
Plymouth VIP: 3492

Total: 61

6001 - 6500cc. Highest rpm at peak power. Limit set at 4600rpm.

	rpm	
1	7000	Jaguar XJ220: 2359
2	6400	Chevrolet Corvette: 795
		Chevrolet Corvette 396: 796
		Chevrolet Corvette Sting Ray 396: 798
3	5800	De Tomaso Pantera Group 3: 1243
4	5600	Chevrolet Camaro SS 396: 824
		Chevrolet Chevelle Malibu 396: 792
		Chevrolet Chevelle SS396: 813
		Chevrolet Corvette Guldstrand Grand Sport 80: 920
5	5200	Chevrolet Corvette Guldstrand Grand Sport 80: 932
		Chevrolet El Camino: 821
		Chrysler 300-D: 973
		Dodge Super Bee: 1311
		Plymouth Road Runner: 3503
		Plymouth Road Runner: 3507
		Pontiac GTO: 3544
		Pontiac Tempest GTO: 3543
6	5000	AMC Javelin 390: 198
		Dodge Coronet 500 Station Wagon: 1307
		Jensen FF II: 2394
		Jensen Interceptor: 2396
		Pontiac Tempest GTO: 3546
7	4800	Cadillac Coupe de Ville: 702
		Cadillac Eldorado Convertible: 701
		Cadillac Fleetwood: 703
		Cadillac Park Avenue: 704
		Chevrolet Camaro SS396: 810
		Chevrolet Caprice Custom 396: 790
		Dodge Charger: 1298
		Dodge Monaco Wagon: 1302
		Facel Vega Facel II: 1368
		Ford Fairlane GTA: 1735
		Ford Mustang 390 Fastback: 1748
		Mercury Comet Cyclone GT: 2940
		Mercury Cougar GT: 2943
		Oldsmobile Jetstar I: 3283
		Oldsmobile Starfire: 3280
		Plymouth Fury III: 3496
		Plymouth Satellite: 3490
		Plymouth VIP: 3492
		Pontiac Bonneville Vista: 3541
		Pontiac Catalina Super Stock: 3529
		Pontiac Royal Bobcat: 3535
		Pontiac Tempest GTO: 3540
8	4600	AMC Ambassador SST Wagon: 193
		AMC AMX: 189
		AMC AMX Automatic: 190
		AMC Javelin: 191
		AMC Rambler Scrambler: 194
		Chrysler Enforcer: 976
		Dodge Coronet 500: 1296
		Dodge Polara: 1286
		Dodge Polara: 1289
		Facel Vega HK-500: 1366
		Ford Fairlane Ranchero: 1746
		Ford Galaxie: 1678
		Ford Galaxie: 1663
		Ford Galaxie 500: 1705
		Ford Galaxie LTD: 1715
		Ford Thunderbird: 1665
		Ford Thunderbird: 1727
		Ford Thunderbird Sports Roadster: 1680
		Ford Torino: 1763
		Jensen FF: 2392
		Jensen Interceptor: 2393
		Jensen Interceptor: 2391
		Jensen Interceptor II: 2395
		Mercury Park Lane: 2937
		Mercury Park Lane: 2939
		Oldsmobile 98 Holiday Sports Sedan: 3275
		Oldsmobile Super 88: 3272
		Plymouth Belvedere Satellite: 3487
		Plymouth Fury Station Wagon: 3488
		Plymouth Sport Fury: 3483
		Pontiac Bonneville: 3528
		Pontiac Grand Prix: 3538

Total: 76

6001 - 6500cc. Highest power-to-weight ratio. Limit set at 180bhp/ton.

	bhp/ton	bhp/tonne	
1	345.1	339.4	Jaguar XJ220: 2359
2	315.2	309.9	De Tomaso Pantera Group 3: 1243
3	292.0	287.1	Chevrolet Corvette: 795
			Chevrolet Corvette 396: 796
			Chevrolet Corvette Sting Ray 396: 798
4	254.2	250.0	Chevrolet Corvette Guldstrand Grand Sport 80: 920
5	240.7	236.7	Chevrolet Camaro SS 396: 824
6	238.8	234.8	Chevrolet Corvette Guldstrand Grand Sport 80: 932
7	230.1	226.3	Chevrolet Chevelle Malibu 396: 792
8	224.6	220.9	Pontiac GTO: 3544
			Pontiac Tempest GTO: 3543
9	224.0	220.3	AMC Rambler Scrambler: 194
10	220.7	217.0	Ford Mustang 390 Fastback: 1748
11	215.7	212.1	AMC Javelin 390: 198
12	214.4	210.8	Ford Fairlane GTA: 1735
13	214.1	210.5	Pontiac Tempest GTO: 3540
14	211.3	207.7	AMC AMX: 189
15	211.1	207.6	Dodge Super Bee: 1311
16	210.6	207.1	AMC AMX Automatic: 190
17	209.6	206.1	Mercury Comet Cyclone GT: 2940
18	209.3	205.8	Pontiac Royal Bobcat: 3535
19	208.5	205.0	Chevrolet El Camino: 821
20	208.4	205.0	AMC Javelin: 191
21	207.3	203.8	Pontiac Tempest GTO: 3546
22	205.9	202.4	Plymouth Road Runner: 3507
23	205.6	202.2	Plymouth Road Runner: 3503
24	203.1	199.7	Mercury Cougar GT: 2943
25	202.5	199.1	Plymouth Sport Fury: 3483
26	201.9	198.6	Chevrolet Chevelle SS396: 813
27	200.9	197.6	Pontiac Catalina Super Stock: 3529
28	200.0	196.7	Jensen Interceptor: 2393
			Jensen Interceptor II: 2395
29	198.8	195.4	Ford Fairlane Ranchero: 1746
30	198.7	195.4	Dodge Polara: 1289
			Plymouth Belvedere Satellite: 3487
31	197.6	194.3	Dodge Coronet 500: 1296
32	196.9	193.6	Jensen Interceptor: 2391
33	195.9	192.6	Facel Vega Facel II: 1368
34	192.6	189.4	Plymouth Satellite: 3490
35	189.3	186.1	Jensen Interceptor: 2396
36	188.8	185.7	Chevrolet Camaro SS396: 810
37	187.7	184.5	Ford Torino: 1763
38	182.9	179.8	Jensen FF: 2392
39	182.5	179.4	Dodge Charger: 1298
40	181.2	178.2	Dodge Polara: 1286

Total: 45

6001 - 6500cc. Highest specific output. Limit set at 50bhp/litre.

	bhp/L	kW/L	PS/L	
1	85.2	63.5	86.4	Jaguar XJ220: 2359
2	73.9	55.1	74.9	De Tomaso Pantera Group 3: 1243
3	65.5	48.8	66.4	Chevrolet Corvette: 795
				Chevrolet Corvette 396: 796
				Chevrolet Corvette Sting Ray 396: 798
4	61.3	45.7	62.2	Chevrolet Corvette Guldstrand Grand Sport 80: 920
5	59.1	44.1	59.9	Chrysler 300-D: 973
6	58.2	43.4	59.0	Chevrolet Corvette Guldstrand Grand Sport 80: 932
7	58.0	43.3	58.8	Pontiac Royal Bobcat: 3535
8	57.8	43.1	58.6	Chevrolet Camaro SS 396: 824
				Chevrolet Chevelle Malibu 396: 792
				Chevrolet Chevelle SS396: 813
9	57.2	42.7	58.0	Pontiac GTO: 3544
10	56.5	42.1	57.3	Facel Vega Facel II: 1368
				Pontiac Tempest GTO: 3543
11	54.6	40.7	55.3	Pontiac Catalina Super Stock: 3529
12	54.1	40.3	54.8	Cadillac Eldorado Convertible: 701
13	53.9	40.2	54.7	Chevrolet El Camino: 821
14	53.4	39.8	54.2	Oldsmobile Jetstar I: 3283
				Oldsmobile Starfire: 3280
15	53.4	39.8	54.1	Dodge Super Bee: 1311
				Plymouth Road Runner: 3503
				Plymouth Road Runner: 3507
16	52.6	39.2	53.3	Dodge Coronet 500: 1296
				Dodge Coronet 500 Station Wagon: 1307
				Dodge Polara: 1289

				Jensen FF II: 2394
				Jensen Interceptor: 2396
				Jensen Interceptor: 2393
				Jensen Interceptor II: 2395
				Plymouth Belvedere Satellite: 3487
				Plymouth Fury Station Wagon: 3488
				Plymouth Sport Fury: 3483
17	52.6	39.2	53.3	Facel Vega HK-500: 1366
18	52.5	39.2	53.3	Pontiac Tempest GTO: 3546
19	52.5	39.1	53.2	Ford Mustang 390 Fastback: 1748
20	52.4	39.1	53.1	Ford Fairlane GTA: 1735
				Mercury Comet Cyclone GT: 2940
21	51.8	38.6	52.5	Dodge Charger: 1298
				Jensen FF: 2392
				Jensen Interceptor: 2391
				Plymouth Satellite: 3490
				Plymouth VIP: 3492
22	51.8	38.6	52.5	Chrysler Enforcer: 976
23	51.7	38.5	52.4	Dodge Monaco Wagon: 1302
				Plymouth Fury III: 3496
24	51.1	38.1	51.8	Oldsmobile 98 Holiday Sports Sedan: 3275
25	51.0	38.0	51.7	Pontiac Bonneville Vista: 3541
26	51.0	38.0	51.7	Pontiac Tempest GTO: 3540
27	50.9	38.0	51.6	Cadillac Fleetwood: 703
28	50.8	37.9	51.6	AMC Javelin 390: 198
				Cadillac Park Avenue: 704
29	50.8	37.9	51.5	Cadillac Coupe de Ville: 702
30	50.2	37.4	50.9	Chrysler Newport: 983
				Oldsmobile Super 88: 3272
31	50.1	37.4	50.8	Mercury Cougar GT: 2943
32	50.1	37.3	50.8	Chevrolet Camaro SS396: 810
				Chevrolet Caprice Custom 396: 790

Total: 58

6001 - 6500cc. Highest piston speed. Limit set at 45ft/sec.

	ft/sec	m/sec	
1	66.8	20.4	Chevrolet Corvette: 795
			Chevrolet Corvette 396: 796
			Chevrolet Corvette Sting Ray 396: 798
2	60.4	18.4	De Tomaso Pantera Group 3: 1243
3	59.7	18.2	Jaguar XJ220: 2359
4	58.5	17.8	Chevrolet Camaro SS 396: 824
			Chevrolet Chevelle Malibu 396: 792
			Chevrolet Chevelle SS396: 813
5	56.3	17.2	Chrysler 300-D: 973
6	54.3	16.5	Chevrolet El Camino: 821
7	54.2	16.5	Pontiac GTO: 3544
			Pontiac Tempest GTO: 3543
8	54.1	16.5	Chevrolet Corvette Guldstrand Grand Sport 80: 920
9	52.1	15.9	Pontiac Tempest GTO: 3546
10	51.6	15.7	Cadillac Eldorado Convertible: 701
			Cadillac Fleetwood: 703
			Cadillac Park Avenue: 704
11	51.6	15.7	Cadillac Coupe de Ville: 702
12	50.4	15.4	Ford Fairlane GTA: 1735
			Ford Mustang 390 Fastback: 1748
			Mercury Comet Cyclone GT: 2940
			Mercury Cougar GT: 2943
13	50.3	15.3	Facel Vega Facel II: 1368
14	50.3	15.3	Chevrolet Corvette Guldstrand Grand Sport 80: 932
15	50.1	15.3	Chevrolet Camaro SS396: 810
			Chevrolet Caprice Custom 396: 790
16	50.0	15.2	Pontiac Bonneville Vista: 3541
			Pontiac Catalina Super Stock: 3529
			Pontiac Royal Bobcat: 3535
17	50.0	15.2	Pontiac Tempest GTO: 3540
18	49.6	15.1	AMC Javelin 390: 198
19	49.2	15.0	Oldsmobile Jetstar I: 3283
			Oldsmobile Starfire: 3280
20	48.8	14.9	Dodge Super Bee: 1311
			Plymouth Road Runner: 3507
			Plymouth Road Runner: 3503
21	48.3	14.7	Ford Fairlane Ranchero: 1746
			Ford Galaxie: 1663
			Ford Galaxie: 1678
			Ford Galaxie 500: 1705
			Ford Galaxie LTD: 1715
			Ford Thunderbird: 1665
			Ford Thunderbird: 1727
			Ford Thunderbird Sports Roadster: 1680
			Ford Torino: 1763
			Mercury Park Lane: 2937
			Mercury Park Lane: 2939
22	47.9	14.6	Pontiac Grand Prix: 3538
23	47.9	14.6	Pontiac Bonneville: 3528
24	47.2	14.4	Packard 7-34 Phaeton: 3355
25	47.1	14.4	Oldsmobile 98 Holiday Sports Sedan: 3275
			Oldsmobile Super 88: 3272
26	47.1	14.3	Jensen FF II: 2394
			Jensen Interceptor: 2396
27	46.9	14.3	Dodge Coronet 500 Station Wagon: 1307
28	46.2	14.1	Mercury Monterey: 2938
29	45.6	13.9	AMC Ambassador SST Wagon: 193
30	45.6	13.9	AMC AMX: 189
			AMC AMX Automatic: 190
			AMC Javelin: 191
			AMC Rambler Scrambler: 194
31	45.1	13.7	Dodge Charger: 1298
			Dodge Monaco Wagon: 1302
			Oldsmobile Dynamic 88 Celebrity Sedan: 3276
			Plymouth Fury III: 3496
			Plymouth Satellite: 3490
			Plymouth VIP: 3492

Total: 67

6501 - 7000cc. Maximum speed. Limit set at 120mph.

	mph	kmh	
1	204.0	328.2	Chevrolet Corvette Lingenfelter: 951
2	200.0	321.8	Jaguar XJS Lister Le Mans: 2366
3	162.0	260.7	Shelby Cobra 427: 4126
4	155.0	249.4	Ford Fastback NASCAR: 1698
5	151.0	243.0	Chevrolet Corvette L88: 835
			Chevrolet Corvette L88: 820
6	150.0	241.4	Chevrolet Corvette Grand Sport Roadster: 776
7	146.0	234.9	Bentley Turbo R: 481
8	145.0	233.3	Bentley Turbo R: 482
9	144.0	231.7	Plymouth GTX Hemi: 3502
10	142.0	228.5	Chevrolet Corvette Convertible: 818
11	141.0	226.9	Chevrolet Corvette L71/89: 834
12	140.0	225.3	Mercedes-Benz 450SEL 6.9: 2862
13	137.0	220.4	Chevrolet Corvette L68: 832
			Mercedes-Benz 600SE: 2854
14	136.0	218.8	Dodge Hemi Charger 500 Automatic: 1308
			Ford Galaxie 500 XL 427: 1714
15	135.0	217.2	Bentley Mulsanne Turbo: 479
			Pontiac Grand Prix 421: 3533
16	134.0	215.6	Bentley Mulsanne Turbo: 480
			Chevrolet Corvette L36: 830
			Dodge Charger: 1299
			Dodge Hemi Charger 500 Manual: 1309
17	133.0	214.0	Chrysler 300-H: 980
			Mercury Comet A/FX: 2933
18	132.0	212.4	Dodge Charger R/T: 1303
19	131.0	210.8	Chrysler 300-G: 975
20	130.0	209.2	Chevrolet Camaro 427 Dana: 805
			Chevrolet Corvette Convertible: 803
			Chrysler 300-J: 981
			Ford Galaxie 406: 1679
			Mercury S-55 406: 2930
			Oldsmobile F-85 Cutlass Cruiser: 3289
			Plymouth Satellite Street Hemi: 3491
21	129.0	207.6	Rolls-Royce Corniche: 3970
22	128.0	206.0	Bentley Turbo R: 483
			Rolls-Royce Silver Spirit II: 3972
23	127.0	204.3	Oldsmobile Toronado: 3288
24	126.0	202.7	Chevrolet Caprice: 827
25	125.0	201.1	Chevrolet Impala SS 409: 768
			Chevrolet Impala SS427: 809
			Dodge Polara 500: 1290
26	124.0	199.5	Chevrolet Chevelle SS396: 843
			Chevrolet Impala Super Sport 409: 779
			Chevrolet Kingswood Estate Wagon: 839
			Oldsmobile Toronado: 3286
			Pontiac GTO Judge: 3557
27	123.0	197.9	Buick Riviera: 668
			Ford XL Fastback 428: 1764
			Pontiac Formula 400: 3559
28	122.0	196.3	Buick Riviera: 674
			Chevrolet Corvette 435hp: 829
			Mercury Cougar XR-7: 2946
			Rolls-Royce Corniche: 3964
29	121.0	194.7	Buick Skylark Gran Sport: 676
			Chrysler Imperial Le Baron: 982
			Oldsmobile Cutlass 442: 3287
			Pontiac GTO 400: 3560
30	120.0	193.1	Bentley T2: 478
			Buick Electra 225: 669
			Buick Riviera Gran Sport: 677
			Chrysler 300: 979
			Chrysler Imperial: 977
			Dodge Coronet 426-S: 1294
			Ford Thunderbird: 1749
			Mercury Marquis: 2944
			Pontiac Catalina 2+2: 3542
			Rolls-Royce Silver Shadow: 3965
			Rolls-Royce Silver Wraith II: 3967

Total: 69

6501 - 7000cc. Acceleration to 60mph/ 96.5kmh. Limit set at 7.5sec.

	sec	
1	3.4	Chevrolet Corvette Lingenfelter: 951
2	4.0	Chevrolet Bel Air 409 SS/S: 755
3	4.2	Dodge Ramcharger 426 Super/Stock: 1287
		Mercury Comet A/FX: 2933
4	4.4	Jaguar XJS Lister Le Mans: 2366
5	4.8	Ford Galaxie 500 XL 427: 1714
6	5.0	Chevrolet Corvette Grand Sport Roadster: 776
7	5.3	Shelby Cobra 427: 4126
8	5.7	Chevrolet Corvette Convertible: 803
		Dodge Hemi Charger 500 Automatic: 1308
		Dodge Hemi Charger 500 Manual: 1309
9	5.8	Pontiac Firebird TransAm: 3555
10	6.0	Buick GS400: 679
		Pontiac Grand Prix 421: 3533
		Pontiac GTO 400: 3560
11	6.1	Buick GS400: 681
		Chevrolet Corvette 435hp: 829
		Pontiac GTO Ram Air: 3552
12	6.2	Pontiac GTO Judge: 3557
13	6.3	Chevrolet Camaro 427 Dana: 805
		Ford Fastback NASCAR: 1698
		Oldsmobile Cutlass 442: 3287
		Plymouth GTX Hemi: 3502
14	6.4	Dodge Charger: 1299
		Pontiac Formula 400: 3559
15	6.5	Chevrolet Corvette Convertible: 818
		Pontiac Firebird 440: 3549
		Pontiac Firebird TransAm: 3565
16	6.6	Chevrolet Corvette L71/89: 834
		Chevrolet Impala Super Sport 409: 779
		Pontiac GTO: 3554
17	6.7	Bentley Turbo R: 482
		Pontiac Firebird RA400: 3553
18	6.8	Chevrolet Corvette L88: 835
		Chevrolet Corvette L88: 820
19	6.9	Bentley Mulsanne Turbo: 480
20	7.0	Bentley Mulsanne Turbo: 479
		Bentley Turbo R: 481
		Chevrolet Corvette L71: 833
		Ford Galaxie 406: 1679
		Mercury Super Marauder S-55: 2932
		Oldsmobile 4-4-2: 3290
21	7.1	Bentley Turbo R: 483
		Mercury Cougar XR-7: 2946
		Plymouth Satellite Street Hemi: 3491
22	7.2	Dodge Polara 500: 1290
23	7.3	Chevrolet Corvette L68: 832
		Chevrolet Impala SS 409: 768
		Mercedes-Benz 450SEL 6.9: 2862
24	7.4	Buick Riviera: 674
		Buick Skylark Gran Sport: 676
		Dodge Dart 413: 1280
		Pontiac Catalina 2+2: 3542

Total: 53

6501 - 7000cc. Highest power. Limit set at 350bhp.

	bhp	kW	PS	
1	550.0	410.1	557.6	Chevrolet Corvette Grand Sport Roadster: 776
2	530.0	395.2	537.3	Chevrolet Corvette Lingenfelter: 951
3	496.0	369.9	502.9	Jaguar XJS Lister Le Mans: 2366
4	450.0	335.6	456.2	Chevrolet Camaro Z/28 Yenko/SC: 826
5	435.0	324.4	441.0	Chevrolet Corvette 435hp: 829
				Chevrolet Corvette Convertible: 818
				Chevrolet Corvette L71: 833
				Chevrolet Corvette L71/89: 834
6	430.0	320.6	436.0	Chevrolet Corvette L88: 820
				Chevrolet Corvette L88: 835
7	425.0	316.9	430.9	Chevrolet Camaro 427 Dana: 805
				Chevrolet Corvette Convertible: 803
				Dodge Charger: 1299
				Dodge Charger R/T: 1303
				Dodge Hemi Charger 500 Automatic: 1308
				Dodge Hemi Charger 500 Manual: 1309
				Dodge Ramcharger 426 Super/Stock: 1287
				Ford Galaxie 500 XL 427: 1714
				Mercury Comet A/FX: 2933
				Mercury Super Marauder S-55: 2932
				Plymouth GTX Hemi: 3502
				Plymouth Satellite Street Hemi: 3491
				Ruger Bentley Clone: 4052
				Shelby Cobra 427: 4126
8	410.0	305.7	415.7	Ford Fastback NASCAR: 1698
9	409.0	305.0	414.7	Chevrolet Bel Air 409 SS/S: 755
10	405.0	302.0	410.6	Ford Galaxie 406: 1679
				Mercury S-55 406: 2930
				Pontiac Grand Prix 421: 3533
11	400.0	298.3	405.5	Chevrolet Corvette L68: 832
12	390.0	290.8	395.4	Chevrolet Caprice: 827
				Chevrolet Corvette L36: 830
				Chevrolet Kingswood Estate Wagon: 839
				Chrysler 300-J: 981
				Mercury Cougar XR-7: 2946
13	385.0	287.1	390.3	Chevrolet Impala SS427: 809
				Dodge Dart 413: 1280
				Oldsmobile Toronado: 3286
				Oldsmobile Toronado: 3288
14	380.0	283.4	385.3	Chevrolet Impala SS 409: 768
				Chrysler 300-H: 980
15	375.0	279.6	380.2	Chrysler 300-G: 975
16	370.0	275.9	375.1	Pontiac GTO Judge: 3557
17	366.0	272.9	371.1	Pontiac GTO 400: 3560
18	365.0	272.2	370.1	Dodge Coronet 426-S: 1294
				Dodge Polara 500: 1290
19	360.0	268.4	365.0	Buick Riviera: 674
				Buick Riviera Gran Sport: 677
				Buick Wildcat: 672
				Oldsmobile Cutlass 442: 3287
				Pontiac GTO: 3554
				Pontiac GTO Ram Air: 3552
20	350.0	261.0	354.8	Chevrolet Chevelle SS396: 843
				Chrysler Imperial: 977
				Oldsmobile 4-4-2: 3290
				Pontiac Grand Prix: 3551

Total: 56

6501 - 7000cc. Highest torque. Limit set at 450lbft.

	lbft	Nm	
1	570.0	772.4	Chevrolet Corvette Lingenfelter: 951
2	500.0	677.5	Jaguar XJS Lister Le Mans: 2366
3	495.0	670.7	Chrysler 300-G: 975
4	490.0	664.0	Dodge Charger: 1299
			Dodge Charger R/T: 1303
			Dodge Hemi Charger 500 Automatic: 1308
			Dodge Hemi Charger 500 Manual: 1309
			Plymouth GTX Hemi: 3502
			Plymouth Satellite Street Hemi: 3491
			Ruger Bentley Clone: 4052
5	485.0	657.2	Bentley Turbo R: 483
			Chrysler 300-J: 981
6	480.0	650.4	Dodge Ramcharger 426 Super/Stock: 1287
			Ford Galaxie 500 XL 427: 1714
			Mercury Comet A/FX: 2933
			Mercury Super Marauder S-55: 2932
			Shelby Cobra 427: 4126
7	476.0	645.0	Ford Fastback NASCAR: 1698
8	475.0	643.6	Oldsmobile Toronado: 3288
			Oldsmobile Toronado: 3286
9	470.0	636.9	Chrysler 300: 979
			Chrysler Imperial: 977
			Chrysler Imperial Le Baron: 982
			Dodge Coronet 426-S: 1294
			Dodge Polara 500: 1290
10	465.0	630.1	Buick Riviera: 674
			Buick Riviera: 668
			Buick Riviera Gran Sport: 677
			Buick Wildcat: 672
11	462.0	626.0	Ford Thunderbird: 1749
			Ford XL Fastback 428: 1764
12	460.0	623.3	Chevrolet Camaro 427 Dana: 805
			Chevrolet Camaro Z/28 Yenko/SC: 826
			Chevrolet Caprice: 827
			Chevrolet Corvette 435hp: 829
			Chevrolet Corvette Convertible: 803
			Chevrolet Corvette Convertible: 818
			Chevrolet Corvette L36: 830
			Chevrolet Corvette L68: 832
			Chevrolet Corvette L71: 833
			Chevrolet Corvette L71/89: 834
			Chevrolet Corvette L88: 820
			Chevrolet Impala SS427: 809
			Chevrolet Kingswood Estate Wagon: 839
			Mercury Cougar XR-7: 2946
13	459.0	622.0	Pontiac Catalina 2+2: 3542
14	455.0	616.5	Dodge Dart 413: 1280
15	450.0	609.8	Chevrolet Corvette L88: 835
			Chrysler 300-H: 980
			Oldsmobile Dynamic Delta 88 Holiday: 3285

Total: 50

6501 and 7000cc. Highest rpm at peak power. Limit set at 4600rpm.

	rpm	
1	6200	Jaguar XJS Lister Le Mans: 2366
2	6000	Chevrolet Bel Air 409 SS/S: 755

		Chevrolet Corvette Grand Sport Roadster: 776
		Ford Galaxie 500 XL 427: 1714
		Mercury Comet A/FX: 2933
		Mercury Super Marauder S-55: 2932
		Ruger Bentley Clone: 4052
		Shelby Cobra 427: 4126
3	5800	Chevrolet Corvette 435hp: 829
		Chevrolet Corvette Convertible: 818
		Chevrolet Corvette L71: 833
		Chevrolet Corvette L71/89: 834
		Chevrolet Corvette L88: 820
		Chevrolet Impala SS 409: 768
		Ford Galaxie 406: 1679
		Mercury S-55 406: 2930
4	5600	Chevrolet Camaro 427 Dana: 805
		Chevrolet Corvette Convertible: 803
		Dodge Ramcharger 426 Super/Stock: 1287
		Ford Fastback NASCAR: 1698
		Mercury Cougar XR-7: 2946
		Pontiac Grand Prix 421: 3533
5	5500	Chevrolet Corvette Lingenfelter: 951
		Pontiac GTO Judge: 3557
6	5400	Chevrolet Caprice: 827
		Chevrolet Corvette L36: 830
		Chevrolet Corvette L68: 832
		Chevrolet Kingswood Estate Wagon: 839
		Pontiac GTO: 3554
		Pontiac GTO Ram Air: 3552
7	5300	Pontiac Firebird RA400: 3553
8	5200	Chevrolet Chevelle SS396: 843
		Chevrolet Corvette L88: 835
		Chevrolet Impala SS427: 809
		Chrysler 300-H: 980
		Dodge Dart 413: 1280
9	5100	Pontiac GTO 400: 3560
10	5000	Buick GS400: 679
		Buick Sportswagon: 685
		Chevrolet Camaro Z/28 Yenko/SC: 826
		Chevrolet Impala Super Sport 409: 779
		Chrysler 300-G: 975
		Dodge Charger: 1299
		Dodge Charger R/T: 1303
		Dodge Hemi Charger 500 Automatic: 1308
		Dodge Hemi Charger 500 Manual: 1309
		Oldsmobile Cutlass 442: 3287
		Plymouth GTX Hemi: 3502
		Plymouth Satellite Street Hemi: 3491
		Pontiac Firebird TransAm: 3555
		Pontiac Grand Prix: 3551
11	4800	Buick GS400: 681
		Chrysler 300-J: 981
		Dodge Coronet 426-S: 1294
		Dodge Polara 500: 1290
		Oldsmobile 4-4-2: 3290
		Oldsmobile Cutlass Holiday 442: 3284
		Oldsmobile Toronado: 3288
		Oldsmobile Toronado: 3286
		Pontiac Firebird 440: 3549
		Pontiac Formula 400: 3559
12	4600	Chrysler 300: 979
		Chrysler Imperial: 977
		Chrysler Imperial Le Baron: 982
		Ford Thunderbird: 1749
		Ford XL Fastback 428: 1764
		Mercury Marquis: 2944
		Oldsmobile F-85 Cutlass Cruiser: 3289
		Pontiac Catalina 2+2: 3542

Total: 69

6501 - 7000cc. Highest power-to-weight ratio. Limit set at 200bhp/ton.

	bhp/ ton	bhp/ tonne	
1	560.0	550.7	Chevrolet Corvette Grand Sport Roadster: 776
2	376.3	370.0	Shelby Cobra 427: 4126
3	341.6	335.9	Chevrolet Corvette Lingenfelter: 951
4	308.6	303.4	Mercury Comet A/FX: 2933
5	296.6	291.7	Chevrolet Corvette Convertible: 818
6	296.5	291.5	Chevrolet Camaro Z/28 Yenko/SC: 826
7	295.8	290.9	Dodge Ramcharger 426 Super/Stock: 1287
8	291.1	286.3	Chevrolet Corvette Convertible: 803
9	282.7	277.9	Chevrolet Camaro 427 Dana: 805
10	282.5	277.7	Chevrolet Corvette L88: 820
			Chevrolet Corvette L88: 835
11	279.9	275.2	Jaguar XJS Lister Le Mans: 2366
12	278.0	273.4	Chevrolet Corvette L71/89: 834
13	273.7	269.1	Chevrolet Corvette L71: 833
14	273.5	269.0	Chevrolet Corvette 435hp: 829
15	269.4	264.9	Ruger Bentley Clone: 4052
16	261.8	257.4	Chevrolet Bel Air 409 SS/S: 755
17	254.2	249.9	Chevrolet Corvette L68: 832
18	247.2	243.1	Ford Fastback NASCAR: 1698
19	244.7	240.6	Chevrolet Corvette L36: 830
20	243.6	239.5	Dodge Dart 413: 1280
21	241.6	237.6	Dodge Charger R/T: 1303
			Plymouth Satellite Street Hemi: 3491
22	241.0	237.0	Dodge Hemi Charger 500 Automatic: 1308
			Plymouth GTX Hemi: 3502
23	238.6	234.6	Mercury Cougar XR-7: 2946
24	236.5	232.6	Dodge Hemi Charger 500 Manual: 1309
25	233.8	229.9	Ford Galaxie 406: 1679
26	232.4	228.5	Ford Galaxie 500 XL 427: 1714
27	229.1	225.3	Mercury Super Marauder S-55: 2932
28	228.8	225.0	Dodge Charger: 1299
29	228.2	224.4	Chevrolet Impala SS 409: 768
30	227.4	223.6	Pontiac Grand Prix 421: 3533
31	224.9	221.1	Chevrolet Impala SS427: 809
32	222.8	219.0	Oldsmobile Cutlass 442: 3287
33	221.9	218.2	Pontiac GTO Judge: 3557
34	217.5	213.9	Pontiac Firebird RA400: 3553
35	217.1	213.5	Oldsmobile Cutlass Holiday 442: 3284
36	214.7	211.2	Pontiac GTO: 3554
37	214.1	210.5	Pontiac GTO 400: 3560
38	213.3	209.8	Pontiac GTO Ram Air: 3552
39	212.0	208.4	Mercury S-55 406: 2930
40	211.8	208.3	Buick GS400: 681
41	210.7	207.2	Oldsmobile 4-4-2: 3290
42	210.5	207.0	Dodge Coronet 426-S: 1294
43	203.3	200.0	Pontiac Firebird 440: 3549
44	202.4	199.0	Dodge Polara 500: 1290
45	202.3	198.9	Buick GS400: 679
46	201.7	198.3	Chrysler 300-H: 980

Total: 49

6501 - 7000cc. Highest specific output. Limit set at 55bhp/litre.

	bhp/L	kW/L	PS/L	
1	79.7	59.4	80.8	Chevrolet Corvette Lingenfelter: 951
2	78.6	58.6	79.7	Chevrolet Corvette Grand Sport Roadster: 776
3	70.9	52.9	71.9	Jaguar XJS Lister Le Mans: 2366
4	64.3	47.9	65.2	Chevrolet Camaro Z/28 Yenko/SC: 826
5	62.2	46.4	63.0	Chevrolet Corvette 435hp: 829
				Chevrolet Corvette Convertible: 818
				Chevrolet Corvette L71: 833
				Chevrolet Corvette L71/89: 834
6	61.4	45.8	62.3	Chevrolet Corvette L88: 820
				Chevrolet Corvette L88: 835
7	61.0	45.5	61.9	Chevrolet Bel Air 409 SS/S: 755
8	61.0	45.5	61.8	Dodge Charger: 1299
9	60.9	45.4	61.8	Dodge Charger R/T: 1303
				Plymouth GTX Hemi: 3502
10	60.9	45.4	61.7	Dodge Hemi Charger 500 Automatic: 1308
				Dodge Hemi Charger 500 Manual: 1309
				Dodge Ramcharger 426 Super/Stock: 1287
				Plymouth Satellite Street Hemi: 3491
11	60.9	45.4	61.7	Ford Galaxie 406: 1679
				Mercury S-55 406: 2930
12	60.8	45.3	61.6	Chevrolet Camaro 427 Dana: 805
				Ruger Bentley Clone: 4052
13	60.7	45.3	61.6	Chevrolet Corvette Convertible: 803
				Ford Galaxie 500 XL 427: 1714
				Mercury Comet A/FX: 2933
				Mercury Super Marauder S-55: 2932
14	60.7	45.3	61.6	Shelby Cobra 427: 4126
15	58.7	43.8	59.5	Pontiac Grand Prix 421: 3533
16	58.6	43.7	59.4	Ford Fastback NASCAR: 1698
17	57.6	43.0	58.4	Chrysler 300-J: 981
18	57.2	42.6	58.0	Chevrolet Corvette L68: 832
19	56.9	42.4	57.7	Dodge Dart 413: 1280
20	56.7	42.3	57.5	Chevrolet Impala SS 409: 768
21	56.4	42.1	57.2	Pontiac GTO Judge: 3557
22	56.1	41.9	56.9	Chrysler 300-H: 980
23	55.8	41.6	56.6	Pontiac GTO 400: 3560
24	55.7	41.6	56.5	Chevrolet Caprice: 827
				Chevrolet Corvette L36: 830
				Chevrolet Kingswood Estate Wagon: 839
				Mercury Cougar XR-7: 2946
25	55.4	41.3	56.2	Chrysler 300-G: 975
26	55.3	41.2	56.0	Oldsmobile Toronado: 3286
				Oldsmobile Toronado: 3288
27	55.0	41.0	55.8	Chevrolet Impala SS427: 809

Total: 44

6501 - 7000cc. Highest piston speed. Limit set at 52ft/sec.

	ft/sec	m/sec	
1	66.3	20.2	Ruger Bentley Clone: 4052
2	63.2	19.2	Shelby Cobra 427: 4126
3	63.0	19.2	Mercury Comet A/FX: 2933
4	63.0	19.2	Ford Galaxie 500 XL 427: 1714
			Mercury Super Marauder S-55: 2932

5	62.5	19.0	Chevrolet Corvette Grand Sport Roadster: 776
6	62.2	19.0	Pontiac Grand Prix 421: 3533
7	60.9	18.6	Ford Galaxie 406: 1679
			Mercury S-55 406: 2930
8	60.6	18.5	Chevrolet Corvette Convertible: 818
			Chevrolet Corvette L71: 833
			Chevrolet Corvette L71/89: 834
9	60.4	18.4	Chevrolet Corvette 435hp: 829
			Chevrolet Corvette L88: 820
10	58.8	17.9	Ford Fastback NASCAR: 1698
11	58.8	17.9	Mercury Cougar XR-7: 2946
12	58.5	17.8	Chevrolet Camaro 427 Dana: 805
			Chevrolet Corvette Convertible: 803
13	58.3	17.8	Dodge Ramcharger 426 Super/Stock: 1287
14	58.3	17.8	Chevrolet Bel Air 409 SS/S: 755
15	57.3	17.5	Chevrolet Corvette Lingenfelter: 951
			Pontiac GTO Judge: 3557
16	57.0	17.4	Jaguar XJS Lister Le Mans: 2366
17	56.7	17.3	Oldsmobile 4-4-2: 3290
18	56.4	17.2	Chevrolet Caprice: 827
			Chevrolet Corvette L36: 830
			Chevrolet Corvette L68: 832
			Chevrolet Impala SS 409: 768
			Chevrolet Kingswood Estate Wagon: 839
19	56.3	17.1	Pontiac GTO: 3554
			Pontiac GTO Ram Air: 3552
20	55.4	16.9	Duesenberg J Coupe: 1352
			Duesenberg SJ Town Car: 1353
21	55.2	16.8	Pontiac Firebird RA400: 3553
22	55.3	16.8	Oldsmobile Cutlass 442: 3287
23	54.3	16.5	Chevrolet Chevelle SS396: 843
			Chevrolet Corvette L88: 835
			Chevrolet Impala SS427: 809
24	54.2	16.5	Buick GS400: 679
			Buick Sportswagon: 685
			Chrysler 300-H: 980
			Dodge Dart 413: 1280
25	53.6	16.3	Bentley Speed Six Weymann: 464
26	53.0	16.2	Pontiac GTO 400: 3560
27	53.1	16.2	Oldsmobile Cutlass Holiday 442: 3284
			Oldsmobile Toronado: 3286
			Oldsmobile Toronado: 3288
28	52.5	16.0	Mercedes-Benz 36/220-S: 2774
29	52.2	15.9	Chevrolet Camaro Z/28 Yenko/SC: 826
30	52.1	15.9	Chrysler 300-G: 975
			Dodge Charger: 1299
			Dodge Charger R/T: 1303
			Dodge Hemi Charger 500 Automatic: 1308
			Dodge Hemi Charger 500 Manual: 1309
			Plymouth GTX Hemi: 3502
			Plymouth Satellite Street Hemi: 3491
			Pontiac Grand Prix: 3551
31	52.0	15.9	Buick GS400: 681

Total: 58

7001cc - . Maximum speed. Limit set at 115mph.

	mph	kmh	
1	221.0	355.6	Chevrolet Corvette Greenwood: 870
2	203.0	326.6	Chevrolet Camaro Gottlieb 1969: 926
3	199.0	320.2	Ferrari GTO Norwood: 1451
4	193.0	310.5	Chevrolet Camaro IROC-Z Chevrolet Engineering: 929
			Safir GT40: 4106
5	190.0	305.7	Dodge Viper: 1348
6	185.0	297.7	Chevrolet Corvette ZR-2: 956
7	152.0	244.6	Monteverdi 375L: 3118
8	145.0	233.3	Jensen SP: 2397
9	144.0	231.7	Chevrolet Corvette 454: 844
10	143.0	230.1	AC 428 Fastback: 26
11	133.0	214.0	Jensen Interceptor III: 2400
12	132.0	212.4	Chevrolet Monte Carlo: 847
			Oldsmobile 442 Hurst: 3293
			Shelby GT 500: 4122
13	130.0	209.2	Shelby GT 500: 4125
			Shelby GT 500-KR: 4124
14	129.5	208.4	Buick GS455 Stage 1: 687
15	129.0	207.6	Pontiac Grand Prix: 3556
16	128.0	206.0	Dodge Challenger R/T: 1314
17	127.0	204.3	Chrysler 300-H: 989
			Dodge Monaco: 1310
18	126.0	202.7	Ford Thunderbird: 1779
			Jensen Interceptor III Convertible: 2401
			Mercury Marquis Marauder X-100: 2949
19	125.5	201.9	Ford Fairlane Cobra: 1772
20	125.0	201.1	Buick Wildcat: 680
21	124.0	199.5	Buick Riviera: 683
22	123.0	197.9	Cadillac Coupe de Ville: 705
			Dodge Coronet R/T: 1304
			Ford LTD: 1773
			Oldsmobile Toronado: 3292
23	122.0	196.3	Buick Wildcat: 686
24	121.0	194.7	Cadillac Sedan de Ville: 706
			Ford Mustang 428 Mach I: 1775
			Lincoln Continental: 2581
			Plymouth GTX: 3501
25	120.0	193.1	Cadillac Coupe de Ville: 709
			Cadillac Eldorado: 708
			Chrysler 300: 984
			Ford Thunderbird: 1653
			Jensen Interceptor III Convertible: 2403
			Mercedes-Benz SSKL: 2776
			Oldsmobile Delmont: 3291
			Plymouth GTX: 3497
26	119.0	191.5	Chrysler 300: 988
27	118.0	189.9	Buick Riviera: 682
			Chevrolet Impala: 846
			Ford Mustang Boss 429: 1777
			Oldsmobile 88 Delta Royale: 3294
			Plymouth Cuda 440: 3505
			Pontiac GTO 455: 3561
28	117.0	188.3	Chevrolet Monte Carlo: 859
			Chrysler Imperial Crown: 987
			Dodge Super Bee Six-Pack: 1312
			Ford Thunderbird Town Landau: 1739
			Lincoln Continental: 2580
			Mercury Cyclone: 2947
29	116.0	186.6	Ford Galaxie 7-litre: 1737
			Lincoln Continental Mk III: 2579
			Oldsmobile 4-4-2 W30: 3296
30	115.0	185.0	Cadillac Calais: 707
			Dodge Charger R/T: 1315

Total: 63

7001cc - . Acceleration to 60mph/96.5kmh. Limit set at 8.5sec.

	sec	
1	3.5	AC Cobra 427 Modified 1965: 27
2	4.0	Safir GT40: 4106
3	4.1	Dodge Viper: 1348
4	4.5	Chevrolet Camaro IROC-Z Chevrolet Engineering: 929
5	4.8	Chevrolet Camaro Gottlieb 1969: 926
6	4.9	Chevrolet Corvette ZR-2: 956
7	5.5	Ford Mustang 428 Mach I: 1775
8	5.6	Plymouth Cuda 440: 3505
9	5.7	Oldsmobile 4-4-2 W30: 3296
10	5.9	Ford Mustang 428 Cobra Jet: 1761
11	6.2	AC 428 Fastback: 26
		Chevrolet Corvette Greenwood: 870
		Mercury Cyclone: 2947
		Oldsmobile 442 Hurst: 3293
12	6.3	Dodge Super Bee Six-Pack: 1312
		Monteverdi 375L: 3118
13	6.5	Buick GS455 Stage 1: 687
14	6.6	Dodge Coronet R/T: 1304
		Plymouth GTX: 3497
		Pontiac GTO 455: 3561
15	6.8	Plymouth GTX: 3501
		Pontiac Grand Prix: 3556
16	6.9	Jensen SP: 2397
		Shelby GT 500: 4125
		Shelby GT 500-KR: 4124
17	7.0	Chevrolet Corvette 454: 844
18	7.1	Dodge Challenger R/T: 1314
		Ford Mustang Boss 429: 1777
19	7.2	Dodge Charger R/T: 1315
		Shelby GT 500: 4122
20	7.3	Ford Fairlane Cobra: 1772
21	7.5	Mercury Marquis Marauder X-100: 2949
22	7.6	Dodge Monaco: 1310
		Jensen Interceptor III Convertible: 2401
23	7.7	Chevrolet Monte Carlo: 847
		Chrysler 300: 984
24	8.0	Ford Galaxie 7-litre: 1737
		Oldsmobile Toronado: 3292
25	8.2	Ford Thunderbird: 1653
		Mercury Marquis Brougham: 2948
26	8.4	Buick Wildcat: 680
		Pontiac Firebird TransAm: 3563
27	8.5	Cadillac Sedan de Ville: 706
		Chrysler 300: 988

Total: 45

7001cc - . Highest power. Limit set at 350bhp.

	bhp	kW	PS	
1	1600.0	1193.1	1622.2	Ferrari GTO Norwood: 1451
2	798.0	595.1	809.1	Chevrolet Camaro Gottlieb 1969: 926
3	700.0	522.0	709.7	Chevrolet Corvette Greenwood: 870
4	600.0	447.4	608.3	Safir GT40: 4106
5	580.0	432.5	588.0	AC Cobra 427 Modified 1965: 27
6	530.0	395.2	537.3	Chevrolet Camaro IROC-Z Chevrolet Engineering: 929
7	496.0	369.9	502.9	Chevrolet Camaro IROC-Z 8.3-litre: 914

8	400.0	298.3	405.5	Dodge Viper: 1348
				Oldsmobile Toronado: 3292
9	390.0	290.8	395.4	Chevrolet Corvette 454: 844
				Dodge Challenger R/T: 1314
				Dodge Super Bee Six-Pack: 1312
				Pontiac Grand Prix: 3556
10	385.0	287.1	390.3	Chevrolet Corvette ZR-2: 956
11	380.0	283.4	385.3	Monteverdi 375L: 3118
				Oldsmobile 442 Hurst: 3293
12	375.0	279.6	380.2	Cadillac Coupe de Ville: 709
				Chrysler 300-H: 989
				Dodge Charger R/T: 1315
				Dodge Coronet R/T: 1300
				Dodge Coronet R/T: 1304
				Dodge Monaco: 1310
				Ford Mustang Boss 429: 1777
				Lincoln Continental Mk III: 2579
				Plymouth Cuda 440: 3505
				Plymouth GTX: 3497
				Plymouth GTX: 3501
13	370.0	275.9	375.1	Oldsmobile 4-4-2 W30: 3296
14	365.0	272.2	370.1	Chrysler 300: 984
				Oldsmobile 88 Delta Royale: 3294
15	360.0	268.4	365.0	Buick GS455 Stage 1: 687
				Buick Riviera: 682
				Buick Riviera: 683
				Buick Wildcat: 686
				Buick Wildcat: 680
				Chevrolet Monte Carlo: 847
				Ford LTD: 1773
				Ford Thunderbird: 1779
				Mercury Marquis Brougham: 2948
				Mercury Marquis Marauder X-100: 2949
				Pontiac GTO 455: 3561
16	355.0	264.7	359.9	Shelby GT 500: 4122
17	350.0	261.0	354.8	Chrysler 300: 988
				Chrysler Imperial Crown: 987
				Ford Thunderbird: 1653

Total: 45

7001cc - . Highest torque. Limit set at 450lbft.

	lbft	Nm	
1	900.0	1219.5	Ferrari GTO Norwood: 1451
2	672.0	910.6	Chevrolet Camaro IROC-Z Chevrolet Engineering: 929
3	638.0	864.5	Chevrolet Camaro Gottlieb 1969: 926
4	620.0	840.1	Chevrolet Corvette Greenwood: 870
5	603.0	817.1	Safir GT40: 4106
6	550.0	745.3	Chevrolet Camaro IROC-Z 8.3-litre: 914
7	541.0	733.1	AC Cobra 427 Modified 1965: 27
8	525.0	711.4	Cadillac Coupe de Ville: 709
9	510.0	691.1	Buick GS455 Stage 1: 687
			Oldsmobile 88 Delta Royale: 3294
10	500.0	677.5	Chevrolet Corvette 454: 844
			Chevrolet Impala: 846
			Chevrolet Monte Carlo: 847
			Oldsmobile 4-4-2 W30: 3296
			Oldsmobile 442 Hurst: 3293
			Oldsmobile Toronado: 3292
			Pontiac GTO 455: 3561
11	490.0	664.0	Dodge Challenger R/T: 1314
			Ford Thunderbird: 1653
			Jensen SP: 2397
			Lincoln Continental Mk III: 2579
			Oldsmobile Delmont: 3291
12	480.0	650.4	Cadillac Calais: 707
			Cadillac Coupe de Ville: 705
			Cadillac Eldorado: 708
			Cadillac Sedan de Ville: 706
			Chrysler 300: 984
			Chrysler 300: 988
			Chrysler 300-H: 989
			Chrysler Imperial Crown: 987
			Dodge Charger R/T: 1315
			Dodge Coronet R/T: 1300
			Dodge Coronet R/T: 1304
			Dodge Monaco: 1310
			Ford LTD: 1773
			Ford Thunderbird: 1779
			Mercury Marquis Brougham: 2948
			Mercury Marquis Marauder X-100: 2949
			Monteverdi 375L: 3118
			Plymouth Cuda 440: 3505
			Plymouth GTX: 3501
			Plymouth GTX: 3497
13	475.0	643.6	Buick Riviera: 683
			Buick Riviera: 682
			Buick Wildcat: 686
			Buick Wildcat: 680
14	472.0	639.6	Pontiac Grand Prix: 3556
15	465.0	630.1	Lincoln Continental: 2580
16	462.0	626.0	AC 428 Fastback: 26
			Ford Galaxie 7-litre: 1737
			Ford Thunderbird Town Landau: 1739
17	459.0	622.0	Lincoln Continental: 2581
18	450.0	609.8	Dodge Viper: 1348

Total: 53

7001cc - . Highest rpm at peak power. Limit set at 4600rpm.

	rpm	
1	7200	Ferrari GTO Norwood: 1451
2	7000	Chevrolet Camaro Gottlieb 1969: 926
3	6800	Chevrolet Corvette Greenwood: 870
4	6200	Jensen Interceptor III Convertible: 2403
5	6000	Safir GT40: 4106
6	5750	AC Cobra 427 Modified 1965: 27
7	5600	Mercury Cyclone: 2947
8	5500	Dodge Viper: 1348
9	5400	Ford Mustang 428 Cobra Jet: 1761
		Shelby GT 500: 4122
10	5200	Chevrolet Camaro IROC-Z 8.3-litre: 914
		Chevrolet Corvette ZR-2: 956
		Dodge Challenger R/T: 1314
		Ford Fairlane Cobra: 1772
		Ford Mustang 428 Mach I: 1775
		Ford Mustang Boss 429: 1777
		Oldsmobile 4-4-2 W30: 3296
		Pontiac Grand Prix: 3556
		Shelby GT 500: 4125
		Shelby GT 500-KR: 4124
11	5000	Buick Riviera: 683
		Buick Riviera: 682
		Buick Wildcat: 680
		Buick Wildcat: 686
		Chevrolet Camaro IROC-Z Chevrolet Engineering: 929
		Oldsmobile 442 Hurst: 3293
12	4800	Chevrolet Corvette 454: 844
		Ford Thunderbird: 1653
		Jensen Interceptor III Convertible: 2401
		Lincoln Continental Mk III: 2579
		Oldsmobile Toronado: 3292
13	4700	Dodge Super Bee Six-Pack: 1312
		Jensen SP: 2397
14	4600	AC 428 Fastback: 26
		Buick GS455 Stage 1: 687
		Cadillac Calais: 707
		Cadillac Coupe de Ville: 705
		Cadillac Eldorado: 708
		Cadillac Sedan de Ville: 706
		Chrysler 300: 984
		Chrysler 300-H: 989
		Dodge Charger R/T: 1315
		Dodge Coronet R/T: 1300
		Dodge Coronet R/T: 1304
		Dodge Monaco: 1310
		Ford Galaxie 7-litre: 1737
		Ford LTD: 1773
		Ford Thunderbird: 1779
		Ford Thunderbird Town Landau: 1739
		Lincoln Continental: 2581
		Mercury Marquis Brougham: 2948
		Mercury Marquis Marauder X-100: 2949
		Monteverdi 375L: 3118
		Oldsmobile 88 Delta Royale: 3294
		Plymouth Cuda 440: 3505
		Plymouth GTX: 3501
		Plymouth GTX: 3497

Total: 57

7001cc - . Highest power-to-weight ratio. Limit set at 150bhp/ton.

	bhp/ ton	bhp/ tonne	
1	1257.5	1236.6	Ferrari GTO Norwood: 1451
2	595.8	585.9	Chevrolet Camaro Gottlieb 1969: 926
3	564.7	555.3	Safir GT40: 4106
4	543.5	534.4	Chevrolet Corvette Greenwood: 870
5	513.5	504.9	AC Cobra 427 Modified 1965: 27
6	320.9	315.5	Chevrolet Camaro IROC-Z Chevrolet Engineering: 929
7	299.7	294.7	Dodge Viper: 1348
8	246.7	242.6	Plymouth Cuda 440: 3505
9	244.3	240.2	Chevrolet Corvette ZR-2: 956
10	236.5	232.6	AC 428 Fastback: 26
11	236.0	232.0	Ford Mustang Boss 429: 1777
12	233.6	229.7	Chevrolet Corvette 454: 844
13	227.2	223.4	Dodge Super Bee Six-Pack: 1312
14	225.9	222.1	Shelby GT 500: 4122
15	224.7	220.9	Ford Mustang 428 Cobra Jet: 1761
16	224.0	220.3	Dodge Challenger R/T: 1314
17	220.7	217.0	Oldsmobile 4-4-2 W30: 3296
18	219.4	215.8	Ford Mustang 428 Mach I: 1775
19	219.3	215.7	Dodge Coronet R/T: 1300

			Plymouth GTX: 3497
20	219.1	215.4	Oldsmobile 442 Hurst: 3293
21	218.5	214.8	Dodge Coronet R/T: 1304
22	217.0	213.4	Plymouth GTX: 3501
23	216.0	212.4	Monteverdi 375L: 3118
24	215.6	212.0	Pontiac Grand Prix: 3556
25	214.4	210.8	Shelby GT 500-KR: 4124
26	204.1	200.7	Buick GS455 Stage 1: 687
27	201.4	198.1	Dodge Charger R/T: 1315
28	200.6	197.3	Mercury Cyclone: 2947
29	198.9	195.5	Pontiac GTO 455: 3561
30	195.2	191.9	Ford Fairlane Cobra: 1772
31	194.9	191.7	Shelby GT 500: 4125
32	194.8	191.5	Chevrolet Monte Carlo: 847
33	193.4	190.2	Buick Wildcat: 686
34	192.3	189.1	Oldsmobile Toronado: 3292
35	189.2	186.0	Chrysler 300-H: 989
			Dodge Monaco: 1310
36	188.0	184.8	Mercury Marquis Marauder X-100: 2949
37	187.9	184.8	Jensen SP: 2397
38	187.7	184.5	Ford Galaxie 7-litre: 1737
39	187.1	184.0	Oldsmobile 88 Delta Royale: 3294
40	179.6	176.6	Buick Wildcat: 680
41	179.0	176.0	Ford Thunderbird: 1653
42	177.5	174.5	Ford Thunderbird: 1779
43	177.2	174.3	Buick Riviera: 682
44	176.6	173.7	Ford LTD: 1773
45	176.2	173.2	Chrysler 300: 988
46	175.6	172.7	Chevrolet Impala: 846
47	174.9	172.0	Buick Riviera: 683
48	173.2	170.3	Chrysler 300: 984
49	169.6	166.8	Cadillac Coupe de Ville: 709
50	167.1	164.3	Oldsmobile Delmont: 3291
51	160.2	157.5	Mercury Marquis Brougham: 2948
52	160.0	157.3	Cadillac Calais: 707
			Mercedes-Benz SSKL: 2776
53	159.7	157.0	Ford Thunderbird Town Landau: 1739
54	159.1	156.4	Lincoln Continental Mk III: 2579
55	159.0	156.3	Cadillac Eldorado: 708
56	156.9	154.3	Jensen Interceptor III Convertible: 2401
57	155.4	152.8	Cadillac Sedan de Ville: 706
58	152.1	149.6	Cadillac Coupe de Ville: 705

Total: 61

7001cc - . Highest specific output. Limit set at 45bhp/litre.

	bhp/L	kW/L	PS/L	
1	190.7	142.2	193.3	Ferrari GTO Norwood: 1451
2	91.5	68.2	92.7	Chevrolet Corvette Greenwood: 870
3	90.0	67.1	91.3	Chevrolet Camaro Gottlieb 1969: 926
4	78.1	58.2	79.1	AC Cobra 427 Modified 1965: 27
5	74.3	55.4	75.4	Safir GT40: 4106
6	63.9	47.7	64.8	Chevrolet Camaro IROC-Z Chevrolet Engineering: 929
7	59.8	44.6	60.6	Chevrolet Camaro IROC-Z 8.3-litre: 914
8	55.6	41.5	56.4	Pontiac Grand Prix: 3556
9	54.1	40.3	54.8	Dodge Challenger R/T: 1314
				Dodge Super Bee Six-Pack: 1312
10	53.6	40.0	54.4	Oldsmobile Toronado: 3292
11	53.3	39.8	54.1	Ford Mustang Boss 429: 1777
12	53.2	39.7	53.9	Lincoln Continental Mk III: 2579
13	52.7	39.3	53.5	Monteverdi 375L: 3118
14	52.4	39.1	53.1	Chevrolet Corvette 454: 844
15	52.1	38.8	52.8	Plymouth GTX: 3497
16	52.0	38.8	52.8	Dodge Coronet R/T: 1300
				Plymouth GTX: 3501
17	52.0	38.8	52.7	Chrysler 300-H: 989
				Dodge Charger R/T: 1315
				Dodge Coronet R/T: 1304
				Dodge Monaco: 1310
				Plymouth Cuda 440: 3505
18	51.7	38.6	52.5	Chevrolet Corvette ZR-2: 956
19	51.2	38.2	51.9	Ford LTD: 1773
				Ford Thunderbird: 1779
				Mercury Marquis Brougham: 2948
				Mercury Marquis Marauder X-100: 2949
20	51.1	38.1	51.8	Buick Riviera: 682
				Buick Wildcat: 680
21	51.1	38.1	51.8	Buick Riviera: 683
				Buick Wildcat: 686
22	51.0	38.0	51.7	Oldsmobile 442 Hurst: 3293
23	50.6	37.7	51.3	Chrysler 300: 984
24	50.6	37.7	51.3	Shelby GT 500: 4122
25	50.1	37.3	50.8	Dodge Viper: 1348
26	49.6	37.0	50.3	Ford Thunderbird: 1653
27	49.6	37.0	50.3	Oldsmobile 4-4-2 W30: 3296
28	49.2	36.7	49.9	AC 428 Fastback: 26
				Ford Galaxie 7-litre: 1737
				Ford Thunderbird Town Landau: 1739
29	48.9	36.5	49.6	Oldsmobile 88 Delta Royale: 3294
30	48.6	36.2	49.3	Chrysler Imperial Crown: 987
31	48.5	36.2	49.2	Chrysler 300: 988
32	48.5	36.2	49.2	Cadillac Coupe de Ville: 709
33	48.4	36.1	49.1	Cadillac Eldorado: 708
34	48.4	36.1	49.1	Chevrolet Monte Carlo: 847
35	48.4	36.1	49.0	Cadillac Calais: 707
				Cadillac Coupe de Ville: 705
				Cadillac Sedan de Ville: 706
36	48.3	36.0	48.9	Buick GS455 Stage 1: 687
				Pontiac GTO 455: 3561
37	47.8	35.6	48.4	Ford Fairlane Cobra: 1772
				Ford Mustang 428 Mach I: 1775
				Mercury Cyclone: 2947
				Shelby GT 500-KR: 4124
38	47.7	35.6	48.4	Shelby GT 500: 4125
39	47.7	35.6	48.4	Ford Mustang 428 Cobra Jet: 1761
40	46.4	34.6	47.0	Chevrolet Impala: 846
41	45.8	34.1	46.4	Jensen SP: 2397
42	45.4	33.9	46.0	Lincoln Continental: 2581

Total: 61

7001cc - . Highest piston speed. Limit set at 48ft/sec.

	ft/sec	m/sec	
1	89.8	27.4	Ferrari GTO Norwood: 1451
2	82.6	25.2	Chevrolet Camaro Gottlieb 1969: 926
3	75.6	23.0	Chevrolet Corvette Greenwood: 870
4	72.8	22.2	Safir GT40: 4106
5	64.6	19.7	Jensen Interceptor III Convertible: 2403
6	63.6	19.4	AC Cobra 427 Modified 1965: 27
7	61.9	18.9	Mercury Cyclone: 2947
8	61.4	18.7	Oldsmobile 4-4-2 W30: 3296
9	59.7	18.2	Ford Mustang 428 Cobra Jet: 1761
10	59.7	18.2	Shelby GT 500: 4122
11	59.3	18.1	Dodge Viper: 1348
12	59.0	18.0	Oldsmobile 442 Hurst: 3293
13	57.8	17.6	Chevrolet Camaro IROC-Z 8.3-litre: 914
			Chevrolet Corvette ZR-2: 956
14	57.5	17.5	Ford Fairlane Cobra: 1772
15	57.5	17.5	Ford Mustang 428 Mach I: 1775
			Shelby GT 500: 4125
			Shelby GT 500-KR: 4124
16	56.7	17.3	Oldsmobile Toronado: 3292
17	55.6	16.9	Chevrolet Camaro IROC-Z Chevrolet Engineering: 929
18	54.3	16.6	Oldsmobile 88 Delta Royale: 3294
19	54.2	16.5	Buick Riviera: 682
			Buick Wildcat: 680
			Buick Wildcat: 686
			Dodge Challenger R/T: 1314
			Pontiac Grand Prix: 3556
20	54.2	16.5	Buick Riviera: 683
21	53.6	16.3	Bentley 8-litre Saloon: 463
			Rolls-Royce Phantom II: 3950
22	53.3	16.2	Chevrolet Corvette 454: 844
23	52.5	16.0	Mercedes-Benz SSKL: 2776
24	51.9	15.8	Ford Mustang Boss 429: 1777
25	51.1	15.6	Cadillac Calais: 707
			Cadillac Coupe de Ville: 705
			Cadillac Eldorado: 708
			Cadillac Sedan de Ville: 706
26	50.9	15.5	AC 428 Fastback: 26
			Ford Thunderbird Town Landau: 1739
27	50.9	15.5	Ford Galaxie 7-litre: 1737
28	50.3	15.3	Pontiac GTO 455: 3561
29	50.0	15.2	Jensen Interceptor III Convertible: 2401
			Rolls-Royce Phantom III: 3952
30	49.8	15.2	Buick GS455 Stage 1: 687
31	49.6	15.1	Cadillac Coupe de Ville: 709
			Oldsmobile Delmont: 3291
32	49.3	15.0	Ford Thunderbird: 1653
			Lincoln Continental Mk III: 2579
33	49.1	15.0	Jensen SP: 2397
34	49.0	14.9	Dodge Super Bee Six-Pack: 1312
35	48.9	14.9	Chevrolet Monte Carlo: 847
36	48.6	14.8	Chevrolet Impala: 846

Total: 51

Sets of eight ranked lists over time. Up to and including 1940. Maximum speed. Limit set at 90mph.

	mph	kmh	
1	121.0	194.7	Bugatti 50S: 648
2	120.0	193.1	Mercedes-Benz SSKL: 2776
3	115.0	185.0	Duesenberg J Coupe: 1352
			Talbot Figoni et Falaschi: 4343
4	112.0	180.2	Cord 812-S: 1101
5	110.1	177.2	Lagonda Rapide: 2445
6	110.0	177.0	Alfa Romeo 8C2300: 41
			Bugatti 55: 651
			Lagonda Le Mans: 2437
7	108.0	173.8	Alfa Romeo 2.3 Mille Miglia: 42
			Mercedes-Benz 36/220-S: 2774
8	106.8	171.8	Alfa Romeo Supercharged Straight Eight: 39

9	106.0	170.6	Duesenberg SJ Town Car: 1353
10	105.0	168.9	Marmon 16: 2651
			Squire X101: 4190
11	104.6	168.3	Mercedes-Benz Type 540: 2785
12	104.2	167.7	Lagonda Rapide: 2441
13	104.0	167.3	Auburn 8-52 Speedster: 264
14	103.4	166.4	Frazer-Nash BMW Grand Prix Two-seater: 1989
			Lagonda 4.5-litre 12 Cylinder Saloon: 2443
15	102.3	164.6	Cord 812: 1100
16	102.2	164.4	Cord Supercharged Saloon: 1102
17	101.1	162.7	Bentley 8-litre Saloon: 463
			Jaguar SS 100 3.5-litre: 2267
18	100.5	161.7	Lagonda Rapide Tourer: 2439
			Mercedes-Benz Type 500 Supercharged: 2782
			Railton Light Sports Tourer: 3757
19	100.0	160.9	Alvis 4.3-litre: 162
			Hispano-Suiza 54/220: 2084
			Lagonda Saloon de Ville: 2444
20	98.9	159.1	Delage Super Sports Straight Eight: 1248
			Delahaye 23.8hp Drop-head Coupe: 1252
21	97.8	157.4	Aston Martin 2-litre: 231
			Bentley 4.5-litre Supercharged: 462
22	97.0	156.1	Du Pont Speedster: 1350
23	96.7	155.6	Alvis Speed 25: 161
			Frazer-Nash BMW Type 327 Cabriolet: 1991
			Lagonda 4.5-litre Tourer: 2440
24	96.5	155.3	Delage D8-120 Super Sports: 1251
25	96.0	154.5	Bentley 4.25-litre: 468
			Chrysler Custom Imperial Le Baron: 964
26	95.7	154.0	Hotchkiss Paris-Nice Saloon: 2163
			Lagonda 4.5-litre: 2442
			Lincoln Twelve Cylinder Town Sedan: 2575
27	94.7	152.4	Bentley 4.25-litre: 466
			Chrysler Super Power Saloon: 968
			Hotchkiss 3.5-litre Saloon: 2165
			Jaguar SS 100 2.5-litre: 2265
			Lagonda Drop-head Coupe: 2446
			Lammas-Graham Drop-head Coupe: 2476
28	93.2	150.0	Hotchkiss Paris-Nice Speed Model: 2162
29	92.7	149.2	Bentley 4.5-litre: 469
			Talbot 3.5-litre Speed Saloon: 4340
30	92.5	148.8	Packard 7-34 Phaeton: 3355
			Rolls-Royce Phantom III: 3952
31	92.4	148.7	Cord Front Wheel Drive Saloon: 1099
32	92.3	148.5	Rolls-Royce Phantom II: 3950
33	92.0	148.0	Bentley 4.5-litre: 461
			Invicta 4.5-litre: 2242
34	91.8	147.7	Alvis 4.3-litre Vanden Plas Saloon: 158
			Bentley 4.5-litre: 467
			Graham 26hp Supercharged Saloon: 2014
			Graham 33.8hp Supercharged Saloon: 2012
			Railton Straight Eight Saloon: 3758
35	91.0	146.4	Alfa Romeo 1750: 40
			Bentley Sedan: 465
			Studebaker Double-twelve Open Tourer: 4214
36	90.9	146.3	Lincoln Zephyr Saloon: 2576
37	90.0	144.8	AC 2-litre Sports: 10
			Auburn 8-120 Speedster: 262
			Daimler 25.7hp Light Straight Eight Coupe: 1135
			Jaguar SS 2.5-litre: 2268
			Lincoln Zephyr Saloon: 2577
			Stutz DV32 Sports Saloon: 4242
			Wolseley Drop-head Coupe: 4983

Averages for period:
98.7 158.7
Total: 75

Up to and including 1940. Acceleration to 60mph/96.5kmh. Limit set at 18 seconds.

	sec	
1	8.0	Bugatti 50S: 648
2	8.6	Duesenberg J Coupe: 1352
3	9.2	Railton Terraplane: 3756
4	9.4	Alfa Romeo 2.3 Mille Miglia: 42
5	9.5	Frazer-Nash BMW Grand Prix Two-seater: 1989
		Mercedes-Benz SSKL: 2776
6	9.8	Duesenberg SJ Town Car: 1353
		Railton Light Sports Tourer: 3757
7	10.4	Jaguar SS 100 3.5-litre: 2267
8	10.8	Alfa Romeo 8C2300: 41
9	10.9	Squire X101: 4190
10	11.2	Railton Straight Eight Saloon: 3758
11	12.0	Hispano-Suiza 54/220: 2084
12	12.5	Lagonda Rapide: 2445
13	12.9	Lagonda 4.5-litre 12 Cylinder Saloon: 2443
14	13.1	Alvis 4.3-litre: 162
		Lagonda Drop-head Coupe: 2446
		Lagonda Rapide: 2441
15	13.2	Cord Supercharged Saloon: 1102
16	13.5	Cord 812: 1100
17	13.7	Cord 812-S: 1101
		Delahaye 23.8hp Drop-head Coupe: 1252
		Hotchkiss 3.5-litre Saloon: 2165
18	13.8	Frazer-Nash 1.5-litre: 1984
		Hotchkiss Paris-Nice Saloon: 2163
19	13.9	Alfa Romeo 1750: 40
20	14.0	Frazer-Nash 14hp Sports Tourer: 1983
		Hotchkiss Paris-Nice Speed Model: 2162
		Marmon 16: 2651
		Mercedes-Benz 36/220-S: 2774
		Morgan SS: 3122
21	14.2	Bentley 4.25-litre: 468
22	14.3	HRG 12hp Sports Two-seater: 2166
23	14.5	Graham 26hp Supercharged Saloon: 2013
24	14.6	Lagonda Rapide Tourer: 2439
25	14.8	Invicta 4.5-litre: 2242
		Lagonda Saloon de Ville: 2444
26	15.0	Alvis Speed 25: 161
		Auburn 8-52 Speedster: 264
27	15.2	Frazer-Nash BMW Type 327 Cabriolet: 1991
28	15.3	Alvis 4.3-litre Vanden Plas Saloon: 158
29	15.4	Aston Martin 2-litre: 231
30	15.5	Bentley 4.25-litre: 466
		Lagonda Le Mans: 2437
		Lincoln Zephyr Saloon: 2577
31	15.6	Railton Cobham Saloon: 3759
32	15.8	Graham 33.8hp Supercharged Saloon: 2012
		Marendaz 15/90 Special Tourer: 2647
33	16.0	Essex Terraplane Straight Eight: 1361
		Frazer-Nash 1.5-litre: 1981
		Lincoln Zephyr Saloon: 2576
34	16.1	Bentley 4.5-litre: 469
35	16.2	Du Pont Speedster: 1350
		HRG 1.5-litre: 2167
		Lammas-Graham Drop-head Coupe: 2476
36	16.4	Buick Century Saloon: 658
		Graham 26hp Supercharged Saloon: 2014
		Lagonda 4.5-litre: 2442
		Mercedes-Benz Type 540: 2785
37	16.5	Auburn 8-120 Speedster: 262
		Lanchester SS 2.5-litre: 2480
		Mercedes-Benz Type 500 Supercharged: 2782
		Rolls-Royce Phantom III: 3952
38	16.6	Hupmobile 29.4hp Saloon: 2217
39	16.8	Talbot 3.5-litre Speed Saloon: 4340
40	16.9	Chrysler Super Power Saloon: 968
41	17.0	Hudson Terraplane: 2170
42	17.1	Bentley 4.5-litre: 467
43	17.2	Lagonda 4.5-litre Tourer: 2440
		Packard 7-34 Phaeton: 3355
44	17.3	Bugatti 55: 651
		Buick Viceroy Saloon: 659
45	17.4	Ford V8 30: 1617
		Jaguar SS 2.5-litre: 2264
46	17.5	Ford V8 Touring Saloon: 1614
47	17.6	Delage D8-120 Super Sports: 1251
		Frazer-Nash BMW Type 55 Cabriolet: 1988
		Hudson Eight Saloon: 2171
48	18.0	Frazer-Nash TT Replica: 1982

Average for period:
14.6
Total: 79

Up to and including 1940. Highest power. Limit set at 100bhp.

	bhp	kW	PS	
1	320.0	238.6	324.4	Duesenberg SJ Town Car: 1353
2	265.0	197.6	268.7	Duesenberg J Coupe: 1352
3	250.0	186.4	253.5	Bugatti 50S: 648
				Mercedes-Benz SSKL: 2776
4	220.0	164.0	223.0	Bentley 8-litre Saloon: 463
				Hispano-Suiza 54/220: 2084
5	200.0	149.1	202.8	Marmon 16: 2651
6	190.0	141.7	192.6	Cord 812-S: 1101
7	180.0	134.2	182.5	Bentley Speed Six Weymann: 464
				Lagonda Rapide: 2445
				Mercedes-Benz 36/220-S: 2774
8	175.0	130.5	177.4	Bentley 4.5-litre Supercharged: 462
				Cadillac V16 Fleetwood Roadster: 700
				Lagonda Drop-head Coupe: 2446
				Lagonda Saloon de Ville: 2444
9	170.0	126.8	172.4	Cord 812: 1100
10	165.0	123.0	167.3	Cadillac V16 "Madame X": 699
11	160.0	119.3	162.2	Packard Twelve Victoria: 3359
				Rolls-Royce Phantom III: 3952
12	150.0	111.9	152.1	Alfa Romeo 8C2300: 41
				Auburn 8-52 Speedster: 264
				Lagonda 4.5-litre: 2442
				Lagonda Rapide: 2441
				Lagonda Rapide Tourer: 2439
13	145.0	108.1	147.0	Packard 7-34 Phaeton: 3355
14	142.0	105.9	144.0	Delage D8-120 Super Sports: 1251
15	140.0	104.4	141.9	Alfa Romeo 2.3 Mille Miglia: 42
				Du Pont Speedster: 1350
				Talbot Figoni et Falaschi: 4343
16	137.0	102.2	138.9	Alvis 4.3-litre: 162
17	135.0	100.7	136.9	Bugatti 55: 651
				Packard Super 8 Phaeton: 3356

				Rolls-Royce Phantom II: 3949
18	128.0	95.4	129.8	Lammas-Graham Drop-head Coupe: 2476
19	125.0	93.2	126.7	Auburn 8-120 Speedster: 262
				Bentley 4.25-litre: 468
				Chrysler Custom Imperial Le Baron: 964
				Cord L-29: 1097
				Jaguar SS 100 3.5-litre: 2267
20	124.0	92.5	125.7	Armstrong Siddeley 30 Special Sports Saloon: 213
				Railton Cobham Saloon: 3759
				Railton Straight Eight Saloon: 3758
21	123.0	91.7	124.7	Talbot 3.5-litre Speed Saloon: 4340
22	122.0	91.0	123.7	Lagonda Le Mans: 2437
23	120.0	89.5	121.7	Hispano-Suiza 30/120 Saloon: 2083
				Rolls-Royce Phantom II: 3950
24	115.0	85.8	116.6	Stutz Roadster: 4239
25	114.0	85.0	115.6	Du Pont Town Car: 1351
26	113.0	84.3	114.6	Railton Light Sports Tourer: 3757
				Railton Terraplane: 3756
27	110.0	82.0	111.5	Aston Martin 2-litre: 231
				Aston Martin Drop-head Coupe: 230
				Invicta 4.5-litre: 2242
				Invicta 4.5-litre: 2241
				Squire X101: 4190
28	108.0	80.5	109.5	Wolseley Drop-head Coupe: 4983
				Wolseley Super 6: 4984
29	107.0	79.8	108.5	Rolls-Royce Phantom I Phaeton: 3946
30	106.0	79.0	107.5	Alvis Crested Eagle 25: 159
				Alvis Speed 25: 161
31	104.0	77.5	105.4	Bentley Sedan: 465
				Jaguar SS 2.5-litre: 2268
				Lanchester SS 2.5-litre: 2480
32	100.0	74.6	101.4	Bentley 4.5-litre: 461
				Humber Snipe Drop-head Foursome: 2188
				Talbot 105 Speed Model: 4336

Averages for period:
145.0 108.1 147.0
Total: 66

Up to and including 1940. Highest torque. No limit set. All cars with figures included.

	lbft	Nm	
1	425.0	575.9	Duesenberg SJ Town Car: 1353
2	420.0	569.1	Mercedes-Benz SSKL: 2776
3	390.0	528.5	Marmon 16: 2651
			Mercedes-Benz 36/220-S: 2774
4	374.0	506.8	Duesenberg J Coupe: 1352
5	360.0	487.8	Cadillac V16 Fleetwood Roadster: 700
6	350.0	474.3	Rolls Royce Phantom III: 3952
7	340.0	460.7	Rolls-Royce Phantom II: 3949
8	320.0	433.6	Cadillac V16 "Madame X": 699
			Rolls-Royce Phantom I Phaeton: 3946
9	310.0	420.1	Bugatti 50S: 648
			Packard Twelve Victoria: 3359
10	290.0	393.0	Chrysler Custom Imperial Le Baron: 964
			Packard 7-34 Phaeton: 3355
			Packard Super 8 Phaeton: 3356
11	272.0	368.6	Cord 812-S: 1101
12	260.0	352.3	Cord 812: 1100
			Du Pont Speedster: 1350
13	250.0	338.8	Delage D8-120 Super Sports: 1251
14	245.0	332.0	Du Pont Town Car: 1351
15	230.0	311.7	Auburn 8-52 Speedster: 264
16	220.0	298.1	Auburn 8-120 Speedster: 262
			Cord L-29: 1097
			Lagonda Rapide: 2445
17	210.0	284.6	Lagonda Le Mans: 2437
			Lagonda Rapide: 2441
			Stutz Roadster: 4239
18	205.0	277.8	Bentley 4.25-litre: 468
19	200.0	271.0	Invicta 4.5-litre: 2242
20	190.0	257.5	Alfa Romeo 2.3 Mille Miglia: 42
21	185.0	250.7	Wills Sainte Claire Six: 4974
22	175.0	237.1	Kissel 8-65 Gold Bug: 2416
23	167.0	226.3	Bentley Sedan: 465
24	160.0	216.8	Bugatti 49: 649
25	125.0	169.4	Alvis Speed 20 (72bhp): 155
			Jaguar SS1 Sports Tourer: 2263
26	114.0	154.5	Ford Model A: 1613
27	105.0	142.3	Alfa Romeo 1750: 40
28	82.0	111.1	Ford Model T: 1608
29	50.0	67.8	Morgan SS: 3122

Averages for period:
246.7 334.3
Total: 40

Up to and including 1940. Highest rpm at peak power. Limit set at 4200rpm.

	rpm	
1	5500	Aston Martin 2-litre: 231
		Aston Martin Drop-head Coupe: 230
		Bugatti 55: 651
		Lagonda Drop-head Coupe: 2446
		Lagonda Rapide: 2445
		Lagonda Saloon de Ville: 2444
		MG Magna Continential Coupe: 2971
		MG Midget P Type: 2973
		MG Midget PB: 2975
		Riley Sprite: 3930
2	5200	Alfa Romeo 2.3 Mille Miglia: 42
		Alfa Romeo 8C2300: 41
3	5000	Singer Super 10 Saloon: 4162
		Squire X101: 4190
		Triumph Gloria 12: 4494
		Wolseley Hornet: 4977
4	4800	Riley Kestrel Sprite: 3929
5	4750	Aston Martin Le Mans: 225
		Aston Martin Sports Saloon: 228
		Triumph 2-litre Dolomite: 4495
		Triumph 2-litre Southern Cross: 4490
6	4500	Alfa Romeo 1750: 40
		Alvis 12/60 Sports: 154
		British Salmson 14hp Saloon: 645
		British Salmson Closed-coupled Saloon: 642
		Bugatti 50S: 648
		Frazer-Nash BMW Type 327 Cabriolet: 1991
		Jaguar SS 1.5-litre: 2266
		Jaguar SS 2.5-litre: 2268
		Jaguar SS1 Sports Tourer: 2263
		Lagonda 16/80 Tourer: 2435
		Lanchester SS 2.5-litre: 2480
		MG Midget Series T: 2976
		Morgan 4/4: 3121
		Morgan 4/4: 3120
		Riley 9 Monaco: 3928
		Singer 9 Sports: 4160
		Singer Le Mans Special Speed Model: 4161
		Talbot 105 Speed Model: 4336
		Talbot 3.5-litre Speed Saloon: 4340
		Talbot 65 Saloon: 4335
		Triumph Gloria 6 Vitesse: 4492
		Triumph Gloria 6 Vitesse: 4489
7	4400	Austin 8 Saloon: 356
		Lammas-Graham Drop-head Coupe: 2476
		Morris 8 Series E Tourer: 3155
8	4300	Riley 16 2.5: 3931
9	4250	AC Acedes Magna Coupe: 2
		Aston Martin 1.5-litre: 224
		Aston Martin Sports Four-seater: 223
		Aston Martin Super Sports: 222
		BSA Scout: 647
		Jaguar SS 100 3.5-litre: 2267
10	4200	Alvis Speed 20 (72bhp): 155
		Armstrong Siddeley 16 Saloon: 217
		Austin 14: 355
		Austin 14 Goodwood Saloon: 353
		Cord 812-S: 1101
		Daimler 18hp 2.5-litre: 1136
		Duesenberg J Coupe: 1352
		Duesenberg SJ Town Car: 1353
		HRG 1.5-litre: 2167
		Lanchester Roadrider de Luxe Saloon: 2483
		Morgan SS: 3122
		Railton Cobham Saloon: 3759
		Railton Straight Eight Saloon: 3758
		Wolseley 12/48: 4985

Average for period:
4627
Total: 67

Up to and including 1940. Highest power-to-weight ratio. Limit set at 70bhp/ton.

	bhp/ ton	bhp/ tonne	
1	169.7	166.9	Bugatti 50S: 648
2	160.0	157.3	Mercedes-Benz SSKL: 2776
3	134.4	132.2	Alfa Romeo 8C2300: 41
4	120.6	118.6	Alfa Romeo 2.3 Mille Miglia: 42
5	118.7	116.7	Duesenberg J Coupe: 1352
6	114.9	113.0	Railton Light Sports Tourer: 3757
7	114.3	112.4	Bugatti 55: 651
8	112.8	110.9	Hispano-Suiza 54/220: 2084
9	112.0	110.1	Duesenberg SJ Town Car: 1353
10	107.1	105.3	Squire X101: 4190
11	104.3	102.6	Railton Terraplane: 3756
12	104.2	102.5	Jaguar SS 100 3.5-litre: 2267
13	103.4	101.7	Cord 812-S: 1101
14	102.9	101.2	Railton Straight Eight Saloon: 3758

15	97.5	95.9	Morgan SS: 3122
16	96.0	94.4	Aston Martin 2-litre: 231
17	95.2	93.6	Cord 812: 1100
18	95.0	93.4	Talbot Figoni et Falaschi: 4343
19	94.9	93.3	Lagonda Rapide: 2445
20	94.6	93.0	Bentley 4.5-litre Supercharged: 462
21	94.5	92.9	Lagonda Rapide: 2441
22	91.4	89.9	Bentley 8-litre Saloon: 463
23	90.7	89.2	Railton Cobham Saloon: 3759
24	90.4	88.9	Lagonda Rapide Tourer: 2439
25	89.7	88.2	Auburn 8-52 Speedster: 264
26	89.5	88.0	Lagonda Drop-head Coupe: 2446
27	86.9	85.5	Aston Martin Drop-head Coupe: 230
28	84.5	83.1	Marmon 16: 2651
29	84.0	82.6	Lagonda Saloon de Ville: 2444
30	82.5	81.1	Du Pont Speedster: 1350
31	82.3	80.9	Mercedes-Benz 36/220-S: 2774
32	81.0	79.7	Alfa Romeo 1750: 40
33	80.0	78.7	Bentley Speed Six Weymann: 464
34	79.0	77.7	Lammas-Graham Drop-head Coupe: 2476
35	78.9	77.6	Bentley 4.25-litre: 468
36	78.2	76.9	HRG 1.5-litre: 2167
37	77.4	76.1	Lagonda 4.5-litre: 2442
38	76.9	75.6	Frazer-Nash BMW Type 327 Cabriolet: 1991
39	75.9	74.6	Invicta 4.5-litre: 2241
40	75.8	74.5	Invicta 4.5-litre: 2242
41	75.7	74.4	Auburn 8-120 Speedster: 262
42	75.5	74.3	Packard 7-34 Phaeton: 3355
43	74.5	73.2	Delage D8-120 Super Sports: 1251
44	73.7	72.5	Aston Martin Le Mans: 225
45	73.6	72.4	Cadillac V16 Fleetwood Roadster: 700
46	73.4	72.1	Lagonda Le Mans: 2437
47	72.3	71.1	Alvis 4.3-litre: 162

Averages for period:
94.5 92.9
Total: 47

Up to and including 1940. Highest specific output. Limit set at 35bhp/litre.

	bhp/L	kW/L	PS/L	
1	73.5	54.8	74.5	Squire X101: 4190
2	64.2	47.9	65.1	Alfa Romeo 8C2300: 41
3	59.9	44.7	60.8	Alfa Romeo 2.3 Mille Miglia: 42
4	59.7	44.5	60.5	Bugatti 55: 651
5	56.9	42.4	57.6	Aston Martin Sports Saloon: 228
6	56.4	42.1	57.2	Aston Martin 2-litre: 231
				Aston Martin Drop-head Coupe: 230
7	51.6	38.5	52.4	Bugatti 50S: 648
8	51.2	38.2	52.0	MG Midget PB: 2975
9	48.5	36.2	49.2	Alfa Romeo 1750: 40
10	46.9	35.0	47.5	Aston Martin Le Mans: 225
11	46.5	34.7	47.1	Duesenberg SJ Town Car: 1353
12	43.1	32.2	43.7	Frazer-Nash BMW Type 327 Cabriolet: 1991
13	42.5	31.7	43.1	MG Midget P Type: 2973
14	40.8	30.4	41.3	Riley Sprite: 3930
15	40.7	30.4	41.3	British Salmson 14hp Saloon: 645
16	40.2	30.0	40.7	Lagonda Rapide: 2445
17	40.1	29.9	40.7	Cord 812-S: 1101
18	39.8	29.7	40.3	Bentley 4.5-litre Supercharged: 462
19	39.4	29.4	39.9	Morgan SS: 3122
20	39.1	29.1	39.6	Lagonda Drop-head Coupe: 2446
				Lagonda Saloon de Ville: 2444
21	39.0	29.1	39.6	Jaguar SS 2.5-litre: 2268
				Lanchester SS 2.5-litre: 2480
22	38.8	28.9	39.3	HRG 1.5-litre: 2167
23	38.7	28.9	39.2	MG Midget Series T: 2976
24	38.5	28.7	39.0	Duesenberg J Coupe: 1352
25	37.8	28.2	38.3	Aston Martin Super Sports: 222
26	37.7	28.1	38.2	MG Magna Continential Coupe: 2971
27	37.5	28.0	38.0	Aston Martin 1.5-litre: 224
				Aston Martin Sports Four-seater: 223
28	37.4	27.9	37.9	British Salmson Closed-coupled Saloon: 642
29	37.0	27.6	37.5	Wolseley Hornet: 4977
30	36.6	27.3	37.1	Jaguar SS 1.5-litre: 2266
31	36.4	27.2	36.9	Talbot 3.5-litre Speed Saloon: 4340
32	36.0	26.8	36.5	Singer 9 Sports: 4160
				Singer Le Mans Special Speed Model: 4161
33	35.9	26.8	36.4	Cord 812: 1100
				Lammas-Graham Drop-head Coupe: 2476
34	35.9	26.7	36.3	Jaguar SS 100 3.5-litre: 2267
35	35.5	26.5	36.0	Wolseley 12/48: 4985
36	35.4	26.4	35.9	Mercedes-Benz SSKL: 2776
37	35.2	26.2	35.7	Armstrong Siddeley 16 Saloon: 217
38	35.2	26.2	35.6	AC 2-litre: 11
				AC 2-litre Fixed-head Coupe: 9
				AC 2-litre Sports: 10
				AC Ace: 8
39	35.1	26.2	35.6	Talbot Figoni et Falaschi: 4343

Averages for period:
42.3 31.5 42.9
Total: 48

Up to and including 1940. Highest piston speed. Limit set at 46ft/sec.

	ft/sec	m/sec	
1	61.4	18.7	Aston Martin 2-litre: 231
			Aston Martin Drop-head Coupe: 230
2	60.2	18.3	Bugatti 55: 651
			Riley Sprite: 3930
3	56.4	17.2	Riley 16 2.5: 3931
4	55.4	16.9	Duesenberg J Coupe: 1352
			Duesenberg SJ Town Car: 1353
5	55.1	16.8	Talbot 105 Speed Model: 4336
			Talbot 3.5-litre Speed Saloon: 4340
6	54.7	16.7	Squire X101: 4190
			Triumph Gloria 12: 4494
7	54.1	16.5	Alvis 12/60 Sports: 154
8	53.6	16.3	Bentley 4.5-litre: 461
			Bentley 4.5-litre Supercharged: 462
			Bentley 8-litre Saloon: 463
			Bentley Speed Six Weymann: 464
			Rolls-Royce Phantom II: 3950
9	53.4	16.3	Lammas-Graham Drop-head Coupe: 2476
10	52.8	16.1	Lagonda Rapide: 2441
11	52.6	16.0	Bugatti 50S: 648
12	52.6	16.0	Auburn 8-52 Speedster: 264
			Mercedes-Benz 36/220-S: 2774
			Mercedes-Benz SSKL: 2776
13	52.5	16.0	Riley Kestrel Sprite: 3929
14	52.4	16.0	Railton Cobham Saloon: 3759
			Railton Straight Eight Saloon: 3758
15	52.1	15.9	Jaguar SS 1.5-litre: 2266
			Jaguar SS 2.5-litre: 2268
			Lanchester SS 2.5-litre: 2480
16	52.1	15.9	Jaguar SS1 Sports Tourer: 2263
17	51.9	15.8	Singer Super 10 Saloon: 4162
			Triumph 2-litre Dolomite: 4495
			Triumph 2-litre Southern Cross: 4490
18	51.5	15.7	Aston Martin Le Mans: 225
			Aston Martin Sports Saloon: 228
19	51.1	15.6	Jaguar SS 100 3.5-litre: 2267
20	50.9	15.5	Lagonda Rapide: 2445
21	50.9	15.5	Lagonda Drop-head Coupe: 2446
			Lagonda Saloon de Ville: 2444
22	50.7	15.5	Daimler 18hp 2.5-litre: 1136
23	50.2	15.3	MG Midget Series T: 2976
24	50.1	15.3	Alfa Romeo 2.3 Mille Miglia: 42
25	50.0	15.2	Alfa Romeo 8C2300: 41
26	50.0	15.2	Rolls-Royce Phantom III: 3952
27	50.0	15.2	MG Midget P Type: 2973
			MG Midget PB: 2975
28	49.2	15.0	Lagonda 16/80 Tourer: 2435
			Triumph Gloria 6 Vitesse: 4492
			Triumph Gloria 6 Vitesse: 4489
29	48.2	14.7	British Salmson 14hp Saloon: 645
			British Salmson Closed-coupled Saloon: 642
30	47.5	14.5	Bentley 4.25-litre: 468
			Bentley Sedan: 465
31	47.4	14.4	Railton Light Sports Tourer: 3757
			Railton Terraplane: 3756
32	47.2	14.4	Frazer-Nash BMW Type 327 Cabriolet: 1991
33	47.2	14.4	Lagonda Le Mans: 2437
			Packard 7-34 Phaeton: 3355
34	46.9	14.3	Riley 9 Monaco: 3928
			Wolseley 12/48: 4985
35	46.8	14.2	Delage D8-120 Super Sports: 1251
			Talbot 65 Saloon: 4335
36	46.7	14.2	Armstrong Siddeley 30 Special Sports Saloon: 213
37	46.7	14.2	Lanchester Roadrider de Luxe Saloon: 2483
38	46.5	14.2	AC Acedes Magna Coupe: 2
39	46.0	14.0	Aston Martin 1.5-litre: 224
			Aston Martin Sports Four-seater: 223
			Aston Martin Super Sports: 222

Averages for period:
51.3 15.6
Total: 68

Decade 1941 - 1950. Maximum speed. Limit set at 75mph.

	mph	kmh	
1	126.0	202.7	Jaguar XK120: 2273
2	125.0	201.1	Cisitalia Aerodinamica Mille Miglia: 1009
			Ferrari 166 Mille Miglia Barchetta: 1371
3	102.0	164.1	Healey 2.4-litre Roadster: 2019
4	95.7	154.0	Austin A90 Atlantic: 363
5	94.0	151.2	Bentley 4.5-litre Mk VI Saloon: 470
6	92.0	148.0	Bristol 400: 638
			Riley 2.5 Saloon: 3935
7	91.0	146.4	Hudson Commodore: 2176
			Jaguar 3.5-litre: 2270
			Jaguar 3.5-litre Mk V: 2272
			Jaguar Mk IV: 2271
			Lagonda 2.5-litre Saloon: 2447
8	90.0	144.8	Allard Drop-head Coupe: 148

	mph	kmh	
			Riley 2.5 Saloon: 3933
			Riley 2.5 Sports: 3934
9	89.0	143.2	Austin A135 Princess: 361
10	87.0	140.0	Lea-Francis Sports: 2569
11	86.5	139.2	Mercury Coupe: 2924
12	86.0	138.4	Allard V8: 149
13	85.0	136.8	Daimler Straight Eight: 1139
14	83.0	133.5	AC 2-litre Saloon: 12
			Austin A125 Sheerline: 359
			Citroen Six Saloon: 1016
			Frazer Saloon: 1978
			HRG 1.5-litre: 2168
15	82.5	132.7	Ford V8 Pilot: 1621
16	82.0	131.9	Rover 75: 3982
17	81.3	130.8	Ford Tudor Sedan: 1619
18	81.0	130.3	Daimler Twenty-Seven Limousine: 1138
			Riley 1.5: 3932
19	80.5	129.5	Humber Super Snipe: 2195
20	80.0	128.7	Austin A70: 362
			Sunbeam-Talbot 90 Sports Saloon: 4317
			Triumph 1800 Roadster: 4496
21	79.0	127.1	Humber Imperial: 2193
			Humber Imperial Saloon: 2194
22	78.9	127.0	MG TD: 2979
23	78.5	126.3	Wolseley 6/80: 4987
24	78.0	125.5	MG TC Midget: 2977
			Standard Vanguard: 4198
25	77.5	124.7	Studebaker Champion: 4222
26	77.0	123.9	Triumph Roadster: 4499
27	76.9	123.7	Fiat 1400 Saloon: 1461
28	76.0	122.3	Citroen Light Fifteen: 1015
			Jowett Javelin: 2409
			Vauxhall Velox: 4621
29	75.0	120.7	Austin 16 Saloon: 357
			Rover 75: 3980
			Rover 75 Saloon: 3981
			Triumph 1800 Saloon: 4497
			Triumph 2000 Saloon: 4498
			Vauxhall Velox: 4623

Averages for decade:
85.6 137.6
Total: 53

Decade 1941 - 1950. Acceleration to 60mph/ 96.5kmh. Limit set at 30 secconds.

	sec	
1	10.0	Ferrari 166 Mille Miglia Barchetta: 1371
2	12.0	Jaguar XK120: 2273
3	13.6	Allard V8: 149
4	14.7	Healey 2.4-litre Roadster: 2019
5	16.8	Jaguar 3.5-litre: 2270
		Jaguar Mk IV: 2271
6	17.1	Allard Drop-head Coupe: 148
7	18.1	HRG 1.5-litre: 2168
8	18.2	Lagonda 2.5-litre Saloon: 2447
9	18.4	Austin A90 Atlantic: 363
		Hudson Commodore: 2176
		Riley 2.5 Saloon: 3935
10	18.8	Riley 2.5 Saloon: 3933
11	18.9	Jaguar 3.5-litre Mk V: 2272
12	19.0	Riley 2.5 Sports: 3934
13	19.1	Bristol 400: 638
14	19.2	Lea-Francis Sports: 2569
		Mercury Coupe: 2924
15	19.4	MG TD: 2979
16	20.0	Austin A135 Princess: 361
17	20.5	Ford V8 Pilot: 1621
18	20.6	Austin A125 Sheerline: 359
		Citroen Light Fifteen: 1015
19	21.0	Ford Tudor Sedan: 1619
20	21.2	MG TC: 2978
21	21.8	Frazer Saloon: 1978
22	21.9	Citroen Six Saloon: 1016
23	22.6	AC 2-litre Saloon: 12
24	22.7	Humber Super Snipe: 2195
		MG TC Midget: 2977
25	22.9	Austin A70: 362
26	23.1	Rover 75: 3982
27	23.3	Vauxhall Velox: 4621
28	24.0	Rolls-Royce Silver Wraith: 3953
29	24.4	Wolseley 6/80: 4987
30	24.8	Standard Vanguard: 4198
31	25.4	Jowett Javelin: 2409
32	25.8	Bentley 4.5-litre Mk VI Saloon: 470
33	25.9	Studebaker Champion: 4222
34	26.0	Daimler Straight Eight: 1139
35	26.5	Humber Imperial: 2193
		Humber Imperial Saloon: 2194
36	26.8	Sunbeam-Talbot 90 Sports Saloon: 4317
37	27.5	Fiat 1400 Saloon: 1461
38	27.9	Triumph Roadster: 4499
39	28.4	Triumph 2000 Saloon: 4498
40	28.7	Daimler Twenty-Seven Limousine: 1138
41	29.1	Triumph 1800 Saloon: 4497
42	29.3	Austin 16 Saloon: 357
43	29.4	Rover 75: 3980
		Rover 75 Saloon: 3981
44	29.7	Armstrong Siddeley 2-litre Saloon: 218

Average for decade:
22.0
Total: 52

Decade 1941 - 1950. Highest power. Limit set at 50bhp.

	bhp	kW	PS	
1	160.0	119.3	162.2	Jaguar XK120: 2273
2	150.0	111.9	152.1	Daimler Straight Eight: 1139
3	130.0	96.9	131.8	Austin A135 Princess: 361
				Ferrari 166 Mille Miglia Barchetta: 1371
4	128.0	95.4	129.8	Hudson Commodore: 2176
5	125.0	93.2	126.7	Jaguar 3.5-litre: 2270
				Jaguar Mk IV: 2271
6	120.0	89.5	121.7	Jaguar 3.5-litre Mk V: 2272
7	112.0	83.5	113.5	Frazer Saloon: 1978
8	110.0	82.0	111.5	Daimler Twenty-Seven Limousine: 1138
				Mercury Coupe: 2924
9	105.0	78.3	106.5	Lagonda 2.5-litre Saloon: 2447
10	104.0	77.5	105.4	Healey 2.4-litre Roadster: 2019
11	100.0	74.6	101.4	Ford Tudor Sedan: 1619
				Humber Imperial: 2193
				Humber Imperial Saloon: 2194
				Humber Super Snipe: 2195
				Riley 2.5 Saloon: 3935
				Riley 2.5 Sports: 3934
12	90.0	67.1	91.2	Riley 2.5 Saloon: 3933
13	88.0	65.6	89.2	Austin A90 Atlantic: 363
14	85.0	63.4	86.2	Allard Drop-head Coupe: 148
				Allard V8: 149
				Ford V8 Pilot: 1621
				Studebaker Champion: 4222
15	80.0	59.7	81.1	Bristol 400: 638
				Kaiser Henry J de Luxe: 2413
16	77.0	57.4	78.1	Lea-Francis Sports: 2569
17	76.0	56.7	77.0	Citroen Six Saloon: 1016
18	75.0	55.9	76.0	Cisitalia Aerodinamica Mille Miglia: 1009
				Rover 75: 3982
19	74.0	55.2	75.0	AC 2-litre Saloon: 12
20	72.0	53.7	73.0	Rover 75: 3980
				Rover 75 Saloon: 3981
				Wolseley 6/80: 4987
21	70.0	52.2	71.0	Armstrong Siddeley 2-litre Saloon: 218
22	68.0	50.7	68.9	Kaiser Henry J: 2412
				Standard Vanguard: 4198
				Triumph 2000 Saloon: 4498
				Triumph Roadster: 4499
23	67.0	50.0	67.9	Austin A70: 362
24	65.0	48.5	65.9	Triumph 1800 Roadster: 4496
				Triumph 1800 Saloon: 4497
25	64.0	47.7	64.9	Austin 16 Saloon: 357
				Sunbeam-Talbot 90 Sports Saloon: 4317
26	61.0	45.5	61.8	HRG 1.5-litre: 2168
27	58.3	43.5	59.1	Vauxhall Velox: 4623
28	56.0	41.8	56.8	Humber Hawk: 2192
				Humber Hawk Saloon: 2191
				Sunbeam-Talbot 2-litre Sports Saloon: 4316
29	55.9	41.7	56.7	Citroen Light Fifteen: 1015
30	55.0	41.0	55.8	Riley 1.5: 3932
31	54.7	40.8	55.5	Vauxhall Velox: 4621
32	54.4	40.6	55.1	MG TC: 2978
				MG TC Midget: 2977
33	54.0	40.3	54.7	MG TD: 2979
34	50.0	37.3	50.7	Jowett Javelin: 2409
				Singer SM1500 Saloon: 4164
				Wolseley 4/50: 4986

Averages for decade:
83.3 62.1 84.4
Total: 59

Decade 1941 - 1950. Highest torque. Limit set at 35lbft.

	lbft	Nm	
1	212.0	287.3	Austin A135 Princess: 361
2	200.0	271.0	Mercury Coupe: 2924
3	198.0	268.3	Hudson Commodore: 2176
4	197.5	267.6	Humber Imperial: 2193
			Humber Imperial Saloon: 2194
5	195.0	264.2	Jaguar XK120: 2273
6	184.0	249.3	Jaguar Mk IV: 2271
7	180.0	243.9	Jaguar 3.5-litre Mk V: 2272
8	140.0	189.7	Austin A90 Atlantic: 363
9	138.0	187.0	Studebaker Champion: 4222
10	137.8	186.7	Citroen Six Saloon: 1016
11	133.0	180.2	Kaiser Henry J de Luxe: 2413

12	125.0	169.4	Lagonda 2.5-litre Saloon: 2447
13	117.0	158.5	Ferrari 166 Mille Miglia Barchetta: 1371
14	111.0	150.4	Rover 75: 3982
15	109.0	147.7	Kaiser Henry J: 2412
16	108.3	146.7	Triumph 2000 Saloon: 4498
17	106.5	144.3	Vauxhall Velox: 4623
18	101.8	137.9	Wolseley 6/80: 4987
19	96.7	131.0	Humber Hawk: 2192
20	95.0	128.7	AC 2-litre Saloon: 12
21	79.0	107.0	Singer SM1500 Saloon: 4164
22	71.7	97.2	Wolseley 4/50: 4986
23	65.0	88.1	Morris Oxford Saloon: 3160
24	64.2	87.0	Fiat 1400 Saloon: 1461
25	64.0	86.7	MG TC: 2978
26	63.8	86.4	MG TD: 2979
27	58.3	79.0	Hillman Minx Saloon: 2035
28	47.0	63.7	Singer 9 Roadster: 4163
29	39.0	52.8	Morris Minor Tourer: 3159
30	36.4	49.3	Ford Anglia 8 Saloon: 1623

Averages for decade:
118.4 160.5
Total: 31

Decade 1941 - 1950. Highest rpm at peak power. Limit set at 4000rpm.

	rpm	
1	7000	Ferrari 166 Mille Miglia Barchetta: 1371
2	5500	Cisitalia Aerodinamica Mille Miglia: 1009
3	5200	MG TC: 2978
		MG TC Midget: 2977
		MG TD: 2979
4	5100	Jaguar XK120: 2273
		Lea-Francis Sports: 2569
5	5000	Lagonda 2.5-litre Saloon: 2447
		Singer 9 Roadster: 4163
6	4800	HRG 1.5-litre: 2168
		Sunbeam-Talbot 80 Saloon: 4318
7	4600	Wolseley 6/80: 4987
8	4500	AC 2-litre Saloon: 12
		Healey 2.4-litre Roadster: 2019
		Jaguar 3.5-litre Mk V: 2272
		Riley 1.5: 3932
		Riley 2.5 Sports: 3934
		Singer SM1500 Saloon: 4164
		Triumph 1800 Roadster: 4496
		Triumph 1800 Saloon: 4497
9	4400	Fiat 1400 Saloon: 1461
		Morris Minor: 3157
		Morris Minor Tourer: 3159
		Riley 2.5 Saloon: 3935
		Sunbeam-Talbot 10 Sports Saloon: 4315
10	4300	Austin A40: 360
		Riley 2.5 Saloon: 3933
11	4250	Citroen Light Fifteen: 1015
		Jaguar 3.5-litre: 2270
		Jaguar Mk IV: 2271
12	4200	Armstrong Siddeley 2-litre Saloon: 218
		Bristol 400: 638
		Hillman Minx Saloon: 2035
		Hudson Commodore: 2176
		Lanchester 10: 2484
		Morris Oxford: 3158
		Rover 75: 3982
		Standard Vanguard: 4198
		Triumph 2000 Saloon: 4498
		Triumph Roadster: 4499
13	4100	Hillman Minx Saloon: 2034
		Jowett Javelin: 2409
		Sunbeam-Talbot 90 Sports Saloon: 4317
14	4000	Austin 8 Saloon: 358
		Austin A90 Atlantic: 363
		Ford Anglia 10 Saloon: 1622
		Ford Anglia 8 Saloon: 1623
		Ford Prefect: 1620
		Kaiser Henry J: 2412
		Morris Oxford Saloon: 3160
		Renault 4CV: 3801
		Rover 75: 3980
		Rover 75 Saloon: 3981
		Standard 12 Saloon: 4196
		Standard 8: 4197
		Studebaker Champion: 4222
		Wolseley 4/50: 4986

Average for decade:
4424
Total: 57

Decade 1941 - 1950. Highest power-to-weight ratio. Limit set at 50bhp/ton.

	bhp/ ton	bhp/ tonne	
1	189.1	185.9	Ferrari 166 Mille Miglia Barchetta: 1371
2	122.8	120.7	Jaguar XK120: 2273
3	115.1	113.1	Cisitalia Aerodinamica Mille Miglia: 1009
4	89.9	88.4	Healey 2.4-litre Roadster: 2019
5	78.1	76.8	HRG 1.5-litre: 2168
6	77.5	76.2	Allard V8: 149
7	76.9	75.6	Jaguar 3.5-litre: 2270
			Jaguar Mk IV: 2271
8	76.5	75.3	Kaiser Henry J de Luxe: 2413
9	74.5	73.2	Hudson Commodore: 2176
10	72.7	71.5	Riley 2.5 Sports: 3934
11	72.3	71.1	Jaguar 3.5-litre Mk V: 2272
12	70.3	69.1	Lagonda 2.5-litre Saloon: 2447
13	70.2	69.0	Ford Tudor Sedan: 1619
14	70.0	68.8	Riley 2.5 Saloon: 3935
15	69.7	68.5	Mercury Coupe: 2924
16	69.1	67.9	Frazer Saloon: 1978
17	67.3	66.2	MG TC Midget: 2977
18	66.0	64.9	MG TC: 2978
19	65.8	64.7	Austin A90 Atlantic: 363
20	65.4	64.3	Austin A135 Princess: 361
21	65.1	64.0	Kaiser Henry J: 2412
22	64.1	63.1	Allard Drop-head Coupe: 148
23	63.4	62.3	Studebaker Champion: 4222
24	63.3	62.3	Bristol 400: 638
25	62.1	61.0	Riley 2.5 Saloon: 3933
26	61.9	60.9	Triumph Roadster: 4499
27	61.7	60.7	Lea-Francis Sports: 2569
28	60.3	59.3	MG TD: 2979
29	59.0	58.1	Humber Super Snipe: 2195
30	57.3	56.3	Triumph 1800 Roadster: 4496
31	56.9	55.9	Daimler Straight Eight: 1139
32	56.8	55.9	Standard Vanguard: 4198
33	56.0	55.0	AC 2-litre Saloon: 12
34	55.6	54.7	Ford V8 Pilot: 1621
35	55.6	54.7	Wolseley 6/80: 4987
36	55.2	54.3	Citroen Six Saloon: 1016
37	54.0	53.1	Triumph 2000 Saloon: 4498
38	52.9	52.0	Vauxhall Velox: 4623
39	52.5	51.7	Austin A70: 362
40	52.5	51.7	Rover 75: 3982
41	52.3	51.4	Rover 75: 3980
			Rover 75 Saloon: 3981
42	51.8	51.0	Armstrong Siddeley 2-litre Saloon: 218
43	51.5	50.7	Vauxhall Velox: 4621
44	51.5	50.6	Triumph 1800 Saloon: 4497
45	51.0	50.1	Citroen Light Fifteen: 1015
46	50.7	49.8	Sunbeam-Talbot 90 Sports Saloon: 4317

Averages for decade:
68.0 66.9
Total: 48

Decade 1941 - 1950. Highest specific output. Limit set at 30 bhp/litre.

	bhp/L	kW/L	PS/L	
1	68.9	51.4	69.8	Cisitalia Aerodinamica Mille Miglia: 1009
2	65.2	48.6	66.1	Ferrari 166 Mille Miglia Barchetta: 1371
3	46.5	34.7	47.1	Jaguar XK120: 2273
4	43.6	32.5	44.2	Lea-Francis Sports: 2569
5	43.5	32.5	44.1	MG TC: 2978
				MG TC Midget: 2977
6	43.2	32.2	43.8	MG TD: 2979
7	42.6	31.7	43.2	Healey 2.4-litre Roadster: 2019
8	40.9	30.5	41.5	Riley 2.5 Saloon: 3935
				Riley 2.5 Sports: 3934
9	40.8	30.4	41.3	HRG 1.5-litre: 2168
10	40.7	30.3	41.3	Lagonda 2.5-litre Saloon: 2447
11	40.6	30.3	41.1	Bristol 400: 638
12	39.7	29.6	40.2	Sunbeam-Talbot 80 Saloon: 4318
13	37.2	27.7	37.7	AC 2-litre Saloon: 12
14	36.8	27.5	37.3	Riley 2.5 Saloon: 3933
15	36.8	27.4	37.3	Riley 1.5: 3932
16	36.6	27.3	37.1	Triumph 1800 Roadster: 4496
				Triumph 1800 Saloon: 4497
17	35.9	26.7	36.4	Jaguar 3.5-litre: 2270
				Jaguar Mk IV: 2271
18	35.7	26.6	36.2	Rover 75: 3982
19	35.2	26.2	35.6	Armstrong Siddeley 2-litre Saloon: 218
20	34.4	25.7	34.9	Jaguar 3.5-litre Mk V: 2272
21	34.3	25.6	34.8	Rover 75: 3980
				Rover 75 Saloon: 3981
22	33.9	25.3	34.3	Wolseley 4/50: 4986
23	33.6	25.1	34.1	Jowett Javelin: 2409
24	33.5	25.0	34.0	Singer 9 Roadster: 4163
25	33.3	24.9	33.8	Austin A40: 360
26	33.2	24.8	33.7	Singer SM1500 Saloon: 4164
27	33.1	24.7	33.5	Austin A90 Atlantic: 363
28	32.9	24.6	33.4	Sunbeam-Talbot 10 Sports Saloon: 4315

29	32.9	24.5	33.4	Sunbeam-Talbot 90 Sports Saloon: 4317
30	32.6	24.3	33.0	Standard Vanguard: 4198
				Triumph 2000 Saloon: 4498
				Triumph Roadster: 4499
31	32.5	24.3	33.0	Austin A135 Princess: 361
32	32.5	24.2	33.0	Wolseley 6/80: 4987
33	32.1	24.0	32.6	Morris Minor: 3157
34	31.5	23.5	32.0	Fiat 1400 Saloon: 1461
35	31.1	23.2	31.5	Lanchester 10: 2484
36	30.9	23.1	31.3	Kaiser Henry J: 2412
37	30.7	22.9	31.1	Hudson Commodore: 2176
38	30.6	22.8	31.0	Studebaker Champion: 4222
39	30.5	22.7	30.9	Austin A70: 362
40	30.3	22.6	30.7	Kaiser Henry J de Luxe: 2413
41	30.2	22.5	30.6	Frazer Saloon: 1978

Averages for decade:

37.0	27.6	37.5

Total: 48

Decade 1941 - 1950. Highest piston speed. Limit set at 40ft/sec.

	ft/sec	m/sec	
1	59.1	18.0	Jaguar XK120: 2273
2	59.0	18.0	Healey 2.4-litre Roadster: 2019
			Riley 2.5 Sports: 3934
3	57.7	17.6	Riley 2.5 Saloon: 3935
4	56.4	17.2	Riley 2.5 Saloon: 3933
5	55.8	17.0	Lea-Francis Sports: 2569
6	54.1	16.5	Jaguar 3.5-litre Mk V: 2272
7	54.1	16.5	HRG 1.5-litre: 2168
8	52.5	16.0	Hudson Commodore: 2176
9	52.1	15.9	Triumph 1800 Roadster: 4496
			Triumph 1800 Saloon: 4497
10	51.9	15.8	Singer 9 Roadster: 4163
11	51.1	15.6	MG TC: 2978
			MG TC Midget: 2977
12	51.1	15.6	Jaguar 3.5-litre: 2270
			Jaguar Mk IV: 2271
			MG TD: 2979
13	49.9	15.2	Sunbeam-Talbot 80 Saloon: 4318
14	49.3	15.0	Sunbeam-Talbot 90 Sports Saloon: 4317
15	49.2	15.0	AC 2-litre Saloon: 12
			Lagonda 2.5-litre Saloon: 2447
			Riley 1.5: 3932
16	48.6	14.8	Austin A90 Atlantic: 363
			Kaiser Henry J: 2412
17	48.2	14.7	Rover 75: 3982
18	47.2	14.4	Daimler Straight Eight: 1139
			Daimler Twenty-Seven Limousine: 1138
19	46.7	14.2	Lanchester 10: 2484
20	46.5	14.2	Citroen Light Fifteen: 1015
21	46.3	14.1	Standard 12 Saloon: 4196
22	46.1	14.1	Austin A70: 362
23	46.1	14.1	Austin 16 Saloon: 357
24	46.0	14.0	Armstrong Siddeley 2-litre Saloon: 218
			Rover 75: 3980
			Rover 75 Saloon: 3981
25	45.7	13.9	Humber Hawk: 2192
			Humber Hawk Saloon: 2191
			Sunbeam-Talbot 10 Sports Saloon: 4315
			Sunbeam-Talbot 2-litre Sports Saloon: 4316
26	45.1	13.7	Cisitalia Aerodinamica Mille Miglia: 1009
27	44.9	13.7	Ferrari 166 Mille Miglia Barchetta: 1371
28	44.9	13.7	Austin A135 Princess: 361
29	44.6	13.6	Humber Imperial: 2193
			Humber Imperial Saloon: 2194
			Humber Super Snipe: 2195
30	44.4	13.5	Studebaker Champion: 4222
31	44.2	13.5	Singer SM1500 Saloon: 4164
32	44.1	13.4	Bristol 400: 638
33	43.8	13.3	Wolseley 6/80: 4987
34	43.7	13.3	Frazer Saloon: 1978
			Standard 8: 4197
35	43.6	13.3	Hillman Minx Saloon: 2035
36	43.3	13.2	Morris Minor: 3157
			Morris Minor Tourer: 3159
37	42.6	13.0	Hillman Minx Saloon: 2034
38	42.2	12.9	Standard Vanguard: 4198
			Triumph 2000 Saloon: 4498
			Triumph Roadster: 4499
39	41.8	12.8	Austin A40: 360
40	40.5	12.3	Citroen Six Saloon: 1016
			Ford Anglia 10 Saloon: 1622
			Ford Anglia 8 Saloon: 1623
			Ford Prefect: 1620
41	40.3	12.3	Jowett Javelin: 2409
42	40.0	12.2	Mercury Coupe: 2924
43	40.0	12.2	Morris Oxford: 3158

Averages for decade:

47.2	14.4

Total: 66

Decade 1951 - 1960. Maximum speed. Limit set at 125mph.

	mph	kmh	
1	192.0	308.9	Jaguar D Type: 2285
2	180.0	289.6	Ferrari 375 Indianapolis: 1373
			Mercedes-Benz 300SLR: 2795
3	174.0	280.0	Ferrari 412 MI: 1377
4	168.0	270.3	Ferrari 250 Testa Rossa: 1378
5	161.0	259.0	Scarab Mk II: 4109
6	155.0	249.4	Porsche RSK: 3613
7	151.0	243.0	Jaguar C Type: 2274
			Rover Jet: 3984
8	150.0	241.4	Ferrari 4.1 Coupe: 1375
			Mercedes-Benz 300SL Carrera Panamericana: 2788
9	149.0	239.7	Jaguar XKSS: 2291
10	148.0	238.1	Chevrolet Corvette Sebring: 738
11	146.0	234.9	Mercedes-Benz 300SL Coupe: 2794
12	142.0	228.5	Gordon GT: 2008
13	141.0	226.9	Jaguar XK120C: 2280
14	140.2	225.6	Aston Martin DB4: 237
15	140.0	225.3	Ferrari 250 Testa Rossa: 1382
			Nardi Blue Ray 1: 3192
16	136.0	218.8	Jaguar XK150S: 2294
			Jaguar XK150S: 2295
17	135.5	218.0	Facel Vega FVS: 1365
18	135.0	217.2	Chrysler 300-D: 973
			Ferrari 250 Mille Miglia: 1376
			Mercedes-Benz 300SL: 2793
19	132.0	212.4	Aston Martin Spyder Touring: 235
			Chevrolet Corvette: 739
			Chevrolet Corvette Injection: 740
			Chevrolet Corvette RPO 684/579E: 741
20	131.0	210.8	Devin Super Sports: 1257
21	130.0	209.2	Facel Vega HK-500: 1366
			Ferrari TRC 2500 Testa Rossa: 1379
			Mercedes-Benz 300SL Roadster: 2800
22	129.5	208.4	Jaguar XK 140: 2287
23	129.1	207.7	Chevrolet Corvette: 737
24	129.0	207.6	Maserati GT Coupe: 2653
25	128.0	206.0	Chevrolet Corvette: 743
			Ferrari 212 Coupe: 1374
26	127.5	205.1	Jensen 541R: 2388
27	127.0	204.3	Daimler SP250: 1147
28	126.0	202.7	Ferrari 250 GT Cabriolet: 1380
			Ferrari 250 GT Coupe: 1384
			Ferrari 250 GT Coupe: 1381
29	125.5	201.9	Jaguar XK150: 2293
30	125.0	201.1	Jaguar 3.8 Sedan: 2297
			Jaguar XK140: 2276
			Maserati A6G/54 Frua Gran Sport: 2652
			Nardi Blue Ray 2: 3193

Averages for decade:

140.0	225.3

Total: 48

Decade 1951 - 1960. Acceleration to 60mph/ 96.5kmh. Limit set at 9 seconds.

	sec	
1	4.2	Scarab Mk II: 4109
2	4.5	Ferrari 250 Testa Rossa: 1378
3	4.7	Jaguar D Type: 2285
4	5.0	Porsche RSK: 3613
5	5.1	Ferrari 250 Mille Miglia: 1376
6	5.2	Ferrari 412 MI: 1377
		Jaguar XKSS: 2291
7	5.7	Chevrolet Corvette: 739
		Chevrolet Corvette Injection: 740
		Chevrolet Corvette RPO 684/579E: 741
		Devin Super Sports: 1257
8	5.8	Ferrari 375 Indianapolis: 1373
		Ferrari TRC 2500 Testa Rossa: 1379
9	6.0	Ferrari 250 Testa Rossa: 1382
10	6.1	Ferrari 4.1 Coupe: 1375
11	6.3	Chevrolet Corvette Sebring: 738
		Ferrari 250 GT Berlinetta SWB: 1383
12	6.5	Rover Jet: 3984
13	6.6	Chevrolet Corvette: 743
		Jaguar C Type: 2274
		Jaguar XK120C: 2280
14	7.0	Mercedes-Benz 300SL Roadster: 2800
		Osca 1490cc Spyder: 3353
15	7.1	Ferrari 212 Touring: 1372
		Ferrari 250 GT Cabriolet: 1380
		Ferrari 250 GT Coupe: 1381
		Ferrari 250 GT Coupe: 1384
16	7.3	Chevrolet Corvette: 737
		Jaguar XK150S: 2294
17	7.5	Aston Martin DB4: 237
		Maserati GT Coupe: 2653
18	7.7	Gordon GT: 2008
		Kurtis Hornet Roadster: 2420
19	7.8	AC Bristol D-2: 20

		Austin-Healey 100S: 430
		Mercedes-Benz 300SL Carrera Panamericana: 2788
20	8.0	Plymouth Fury: 3474
21	8.2	AC Ace Bristol: 16
		Ferrari 212 Coupe: 1374
		Ford Thunderbird: 1653
		Mercedes-Benz 300SL Coupe: 2794
		Porsche 550 Spyder: 3610
22	8.4	Chrysler 300-D: 973
		Jaguar XK140: 2276
		Jaguar XK140MC: 2283
23	8.5	Jaguar XK120M: 2281
		Jaguar XK150: 2293
24	8.6	Allard K3 Convertible: 151
25	8.7	Chevrolet Corvette V8: 735
		Lincoln Continental Mk III: 2579
26	8.8	BMW 507: 500
		Ford Interceptor Coupe: 1639
		Mercedes-Benz 300SL: 2793
27	8.9	Jaguar XK150S: 2295
28	9.0	AC AC-Bristol Zagato: 17
		Chevrolet 210: 736
		Lotus Mk XI: 2590
		Plymouth Fury: 3472

Average for decade:
7.2
Total: 58

Decade 1951 - 1960. Highest power. Limit set at 200bhp.

	bhp	kW	PS	
1	415.0	309.5	420.8	Ferrari 412 MI: 1377
2	390.0	290.8	395.4	Ferrari 375 Indianapolis: 1373
3	380.0	283.4	385.3	Chrysler 300-D: 973
4	375.0	279.6	380.2	Lincoln Continental Mk III: 2579
5	360.0	268.4	365.0	Scarab Mk II: 4109
6	350.0	261.0	354.8	Ford Thunderbird: 1653
7	345.0	257.3	349.8	Cadillac Eldorado Convertible: 701
8	330.0	246.1	334.6	Facel Vega HK-500: 1366
9	325.0	242.3	329.5	Facel Vega FVS: 1365
10	305.0	227.4	309.2	Oldsmobile Super 88: 3272
				Plymouth Fury: 3474
11	302.0	225.2	306.2	Mercedes-Benz 300SLR: 2795
12	300.0	223.7	304.2	Ferrari 250 Testa Rossa: 1378
				Ferrari 250 Testa Rossa: 1382
				Pontiac Bonneville: 3528
13	295.0	220.0	299.1	Dodge Custom Royal: 1274
14	292.0	217.7	296.0	Ford Interceptor Coupe: 1639
15	290.0	216.2	294.0	Chevrolet Corvette: 743
				Gordon GT: 2008
16	285.0	212.5	288.9	Jaguar D Type: 2285
17	283.0	211.0	286.9	Chevrolet Corvette: 739
				Chevrolet Corvette Injection: 740
				Chevrolet Corvette RPO 684/579E: 741
18	263.0	196.1	266.6	Aston Martin DB4: 237
19	260.0	193.9	263.6	Ferrari 250 GT Coupe: 1381
				Ferrari 4.1 Coupe: 1375
				Jaguar XKSS: 2291
20	255.0	190.1	258.5	Facel Vega Coupe: 1364
21	250.0	186.4	253.5	Jaguar XK150S: 2295
				Jaguar XK150S: 2294
				Mercedes-Benz 300SL Roadster: 2800
22	245.0	182.7	248.4	Dodge Custom Royal: 1273
23	243.0	181.2	246.4	Mercedes-Benz 300SL Coupe: 2794
24	241.0	179.7	244.3	Ferrari 250 GT Berlinetta SWB: 1383
25	240.0	179.0	243.3	Ferrari 250 GT Cabriolet: 1380
				Ferrari 250 GT Coupe: 1384
				Ferrari 250 Mille Miglia: 1376
				Mercedes-Benz 300SL: 2793
				Plymouth Fury: 3472
				Rover Jet: 3984
26	230.0	171.5	233.2	Maserati GT Coupe: 2653
27	225.0	167.8	228.1	Chevrolet Corvette: 737
				Chevrolet Corvette Sebring: 738
				Ford Galaxie: 1658
				Ford Thunderbird: 1641
				Plymouth Fury: 3475
28	220.0	164.0	223.0	Devin Super Sports: 1257
				Ferrari TRC 2500 Testa Rossa: 1379
				Jaguar 3.8 Sedan: 2297
				Rolls-Royce Silver Cloud II V8: 3959
29	210.0	156.6	212.9	Allard GT Coupe: 153
				Jaguar 3.4: 2292
				Jaguar 3.4: 2296
				Jaguar XK 140: 2287
				Jaguar XK120C: 2280
				Jaguar XK140: 2276
				Jaguar XK140MC: 2283
				Jaguar XK150: 2290
				Jaguar XK150: 2293
30	205.0	152.9	207.8	Chevrolet 210: 736
				Lincoln Cosmopolitan Sedan: 2578
31	202.0	150.6	204.8	Oldsmobile Super 88: 3271
32	200.0	149.1	202.8	Buick Roadmaster: 660
				Jaguar C Type: 2274
				Rambler Rebel V8: 3762

Averages for decade:
260.6 194.3 264.2
Total: 65

Decade 1951 - 1960. Highest torque. Limit set at 250lbft.

	lbft	Nm	
1	490.0	664.0	Ford Thunderbird: 1653
			Lincoln Continental Mk III: 2579
2	460.0	623.3	Facel Vega HK-500: 1366
3	435.0	589.4	Cadillac Eldorado Convertible: 701
			Chrysler 300-D: 973
4	430.0	582.7	Facel Vega FVS: 1365
5	420.0	569.1	Pontiac Bonneville: 3528
6	410.0	555.6	Oldsmobile Super 88: 3272
7	390.0	528.5	Dodge Custom Royal: 1274
8	380.0	514.9	Scarab Mk II: 4109
9	370.0	501.4	Plymouth Fury: 3474
10	350.0	474.3	Facel Vega Coupe: 1364
11	340.0	460.7	Plymouth Fury: 3475
			Rolls-Royce Silver Cloud II V8: 3959
12	332.0	449.9	Oldsmobile Super 88: 3271
13	324.0	439.0	Ford Galaxie: 1658
			Ford Thunderbird: 1641
14	320.0	433.6	Dodge Custom Royal: 1273
15	312.0	422.8	Allard K3 Convertible: 151
			Chrysler New Yorker Saloon: 971
			Chrysler Saratoga Club Coupe: 970
16	310.0	420.1	Plymouth Fury: 3472
17	309.0	418.7	Buick Roadmaster: 660
18	308.0	417.3	Lincoln Cosmopolitan Sedan: 2578
19	300.0	406.5	Devin Super Sports: 1257
			Gordon GT: 2008
20	290.0	393.0	Chevrolet Corvette: 743
			Chevrolet Corvette: 739
			Chevrolet Corvette Injection: 740
			Chevrolet Corvette RPO 684/579E: 741
21	289.0	391.6	Ford Interceptor Coupe: 1639
22	286.0	387.5	Ford Thunderbird: 1635
23	280.0	379.4	Rolls-Royce Silver Cloud "S": 3957
24	275.0	372.6	Chrysler Windsor de Luxe: 972
25	270.0	365.9	Chevrolet Corvette: 737
			Chevrolet Corvette Sebring: 738
26	268.0	363.1	Chevrolet 210: 736
27	265.0	359.1	Plymouth Savoy: 3473
28	264.0	357.7	Ford Fairlane 500: 1646
29	260.0	352.3	Armstrong Siddeley Star Sapphire: 220
			Chevrolet 210 Coupe Club V8: 734
			Chevrolet Corvette V8: 735
			Daimler DK 400B: 1145
			Jaguar XKSS: 2291
			Studebaker Lark V8: 4229
30	257.0	348.2	Hudson Hornet: 2177
			Kurtis Hornet Roadster: 2420

Averages for decade:
323.5 438.3
Total: 47

Decade 1951 -1960. Highest rpm at peak power. Limit set at 6000rpm.

	rpm	
1	45000	Rover Jet: 3984
2	8000	Porsche RSK: 3613
3	7600	Ferrari 412 MI: 1377
4	7500	Ferrari 375 Indianapolis: 1373
		Mercedes-Benz 300SLR: 2795
5	7200	Ferrari 212 Touring: 1372
		Ferrari 250 Mille Miglia: 1376
		Ferrari 250 Testa Rossa: 1378
		Ferrari 250 Testa Rossa: 1382
6	7000	Ferrari 250 GT Berlinetta SWB: 1383
		Ferrari 250 GT Cabriolet: 1380
		Ferrari 250 GT Coupe: 1384
		Ferrari 250 GT Coupe: 1381
		Fiat Abarth Twin Cam: 1488
7	6800	ASA 1000GT: 221
		Lotus 11 Le Mans: 2589
		Lotus Mk XI: 2590
8	6700	MG A Twin Cam: 2995
		MG Twin Cam MGA: 2997
9	6500	Ferrari 212 Coupe: 1374
		Ferrari 4.1 Coupe: 1375
		Ferrari TRC 2500 Testa Rossa: 1379
10	6250	Gordon GT: 2008
11	6200	Chevrolet Corvette: 739
		Chevrolet Corvette: 743
		Chevrolet Corvette Injection: 740
		Chevrolet Corvette RPO 684/579E: 741
		Mercedes-Benz 300SL Roadster: 2800
		Osca 1490cc Spyder: 3353
		Porsche 550 Spyder: 3610
		Porsche Carrera Coupe: 3606

12	6100	Lotus Elite: 2592
		Mercedes-Benz 300SL: 2793
		Mercedes-Benz 300SL Coupe: 2794
13	6000	Abarth Zagato 750 GT: 1
		AC AC-Bristol Zagato: 17
		AC Aceca-Bristol: 21
		AC Bristol: 19
		Alfa Romeo 1300 SV Spider: 46
		Alfa Romeo Super Spider: 48
		Fiat 8V: 1468
		Fiat Abarth 850: 1487
		Jaguar XK120C: 2280
		Jaguar XKSS: 2291
		Maserati A6G/54 Frua Gran Sport: 2652
		Moretti 750 Grand Sport Berlinetta Coupe: 3119
		Scarab Mk II: 4109
		Triumph Herald Coupe: 4510
		Turner Turner-Climax: 4582

Average for decade:
7283
Total: 49

Decade 1951 - 1960. Highest power-to-weight ratio. Limit set at 150bhp/ton.

	bhp/ ton	bhp/ tonne	
1	510.8	502.2	Ferrari 412 MI: 1377
2	507.9	499.4	Ferrari 375 Indianapolis: 1373
3	424.4	417.3	Scarab Mk II: 4109
4	381.8	375.4	Ferrari 250 Testa Rossa: 1382
5	348.7	342.9	Mercedes-Benz 300SLR: 2795
6	324.6	319.2	Ferrari 250 Testa Rossa: 1378
7	304.2	299.1	Ferrari TRC 2500 Testa Rossa: 1379
8	298.3	293.3	Jaguar D Type: 2285
9	287.4	282.6	Porsche RSK: 3613
10	284.1	279.4	Ferrari 4.1 Coupe: 1375
11	262.2	257.9	Ferrari 250 Mille Miglia: 1376
12	261.2	256.8	Jaguar XKSS: 2291
13	227.1	223.3	Devin Super Sports: 1257
14	226.8	223.0	Ferrari 250 GT Berlinetta SWB: 1383
15	224.0	220.3	Nardi Blue Ray 1: 3192
16	220.1	216.4	Chevrolet Corvette: 739
			Chevrolet Corvette Injection: 740
			Chevrolet Corvette RPO 684/579E: 741
17	215.1	211.5	Chevrolet Corvette: 743
18	210.0	206.5	Jaguar XK120C: 2280
19	209.8	206.3	Aston Martin Spyder Touring: 235
20	206.2	202.8	Gordon GT: 2008
21	204.3	200.9	Aston Martin DB4: 237
22	203.2	199.8	Porsche 550 Spyder: 3610
23	202.5	199.1	Mercedes-Benz 300SL Carrera Panamericana: 2788
24	200.8	197.5	Ferrari 250 GT Coupe: 1381
25	200.0	196.7	Jaguar C Type: 2274
26	199.1	195.8	Ferrari 250 GT Cabriolet: 1380
			Ferrari 250 GT Coupe: 1384
27	194.9	191.7	Mercedes-Benz 300SL: 2793
28	192.8	189.6	Ferrari 212 Touring: 1372
29	192.5	189.3	Osca 1490cc Spyder: 3353
30	192.0	188.8	Rover Jet: 3984
31	191.0	187.8	Ford Interceptor Coupe: 1639
32	186.7	183.5	Chevrolet Corvette Sebring: 738
33	185.9	182.8	Lotus Mk XI: 2590
34	183.9	180.8	Mercedes-Benz 300SL Coupe: 2794
35	182.4	179.4	Lotus 11 Le Mans: 2589
36	182.2	179.2	Ferrari 212 Coupe: 1374
37	182.1	179.1	Mercedes-Benz 300SL Roadster: 2800
38	181.4	178.4	Maserati A6G/54 Frua Gran Sport: 2652
39	179.0	176.0	Ford Thunderbird: 1653
40	177.3	174.3	Facel Vega HK-500: 1366
41	177.3	174.3	Facel Vega FVS: 1365
42	177.2	174.3	Jaguar XK150S: 2294
43	174.5	171.6	Plymouth Fury: 3474
44	173.0	170.1	Chrysler 300-D: 973
45	172.4	169.5	Jaguar XK150S: 2295
46	169.1	166.3	Chevrolet Corvette: 737
47	165.2	162.5	Dodge Custom Royal: 1274
48	164.7	162.0	Allard GT Coupe: 153
49	162.0	159.3	Maserati GT Coupe: 2653
50	159.1	156.4	Lincoln Continental Mk III: 2579
51	158.2	155.6	Kurtis Hornet Roadster: 2420
52	153.8	151.3	Pontiac Bonneville: 3528
53	152.7	150.2	Cadillac Eldorado Convertible: 701
54	152.4	149.9	Oldsmobile Super 88: 3272
55	152.2	149.7	Jaguar XK150: 2290
56	151.8	149.2	AC Bristol: 19
57	151.7	149.1	AC Bristol D-2: 20
			Chevrolet Corvette V8: 735
58	150.0	147.5	Jaguar XK140: 2276
			Jaguar XK140MC: 2283
59	150.0	147.5	Jaguar XK 140: 2287

Averages for decade:
215.0 211.4
Total: 64

Decade 1951 - 1960. Highest specific output. Limit set at 63bhp/litre.

	bhp/L	kW/L	PS/L	
1	103.2	76.9	104.6	Ferrari 412 MI: 1377
2	101.6	75.8	103.0	Ferrari 250 Testa Rossa: 1382
				Ferrari 250 Testa Rossa: 1378
3	101.3	75.5	102.7	Porsche RSK: 3613
4	101.3	75.5	102.7	Mercedes-Benz 300SLR: 2795
5	91.5	68.2	92.7	Porsche 550 Spyder: 3610
6	88.2	65.8	89.4	ASA 1000GT: 221
7	88.1	65.7	89.3	Ferrari TRC 2500 Testa Rossa: 1379
8	88.0	65.7	89.3	Ferrari 250 GT Coupe: 1381
9	86.8	64.7	88.0	Ferrari 375 Indianapolis: 1373
10	83.4	62.2	84.6	Mercedes-Benz 300SL Roadster: 2800
11	81.7	60.9	82.8	Fiat Abarth Twin Cam: 1488
12	81.6	60.9	82.7	Ferrari 250 GT Berlinetta SWB: 1383
13	81.3	60.6	82.4	Ferrari 250 GT Cabriolet: 1380
				Ferrari 250 GT Coupe: 1384
				Ferrari 250 Mille Miglia: 1376
14	81.1	60.5	82.2	Mercedes-Benz 300SL Coupe: 2794
15	80.1	59.7	81.2	Mercedes-Benz 300SL: 2793
16	79.8	59.5	80.9	Alfa Romeo Super Spider: 48
17	76.0	56.7	77.1	Nardi Blue Ray 1: 3192
18	75.6	56.4	76.6	Lotus 11 Le Mans: 2589
				Lotus Mk XI: 2590
19	75.5	56.3	76.6	Jaguar XKSS: 2291
20	75.5	56.3	76.6	Maserati A6G/54 Frua Gran Sport: 2652
21	75.4	56.2	76.4	Jaguar D Type: 2285
22	73.8	55.0	74.8	Osca 1490cc Spyder: 3353
23	73.4	54.8	74.4	Porsche Carrera Coupe: 3606
24	72.6	54.2	73.6	Jaguar XK150S: 2295
				Jaguar XK150S: 2294
25	71.7	53.5	72.7	Austin-Healey Sprite Supercharged: 439
26	71.7	53.4	72.7	Aston Martin DB4: 237
27	69.8	52.0	70.7	Alfa Romeo 1300 SV Spider: 46
28	68.3	50.9	69.2	Turner Turner-Climax: 4582
29	68.2	50.8	69.1	Moretti 750 Grand Sport Berlinetta Coupe: 3119
30	68.0	50.7	68.9	MG A Twin Cam: 2995
				MG Twin Cam MGA: 2997
31	66.8	49.8	67.8	Saab Gran Turismo: 4055
32	66.3	49.5	67.3	Ferrari 212 Coupe: 1374
				Ferrari 212 Touring: 1372
33	66.0	49.2	66.9	Maserati GT Coupe: 2653
34	66.0	49.2	66.9	AC Bristol D-2: 20
35	64.7	48.3	65.6	Scarab Mk II: 4109
36	64.5	48.1	65.4	Porsche Super 90 Cabriolet: 3616
37	63.4	47.3	64.3	AC AC-Bristol Zagato: 17
				AC Ace Bristol: 16
				AC Aceca-Bristol: 21
				AC Bristol: 19
38	63.4	47.3	64.3	Ferrari 4.1 Coupe: 1375
39	63.3	47.2	64.1	Mercedes-Benz 190SL: 2798
				Mercedes-Benz 190SL: 2791
				Mercedes-Benz 190SL: 2802

Averages for decade:
76.13 56.8 77.2
Total: 51

Decade 1951 - 1960. Highest piston speed. Limit set at 55ft/sec.

	ft/sec	m/sec	
1	69.5	21.2	Jaguar XK120C: 2280
			Jaguar XKSS: 2291
2	67.2	20.5	Jaguar C Type: 2274
3	66.6	20.3	Jaguar D Type: 2285
			Jaguar XK 140: 2287
4	66.6	20.3	Jaguar XK140: 2276
			Jaguar XK140MC: 2283
5	65.1	19.8	MG A Twin Cam: 2995
			MG Twin Cam MGA: 2997
6	64.0	19.5	Mercedes-Benz 300SLR: 2795
7	63.7	19.4	Allard GT Coupe: 153
			Jaguar 3.4: 2292
			Jaguar 3.8 Sedan: 2297
			Jaguar Mk VII Auto: 2286
			Jaguar Mk VIII: 2289
			Jaguar XK150: 2293
			Jaguar XK150S: 2295
8	63.7	19.4	Jaguar 3.4: 2296
			Jaguar Mk VII: 2282
			Jaguar XK150: 2290
			Jaguar XK150S: 2294
9	63.0	19.2	AC AC-Bristol Zagato: 17
			AC Aceca-Bristol: 21
			AC Bristol: 19
			Healey Tickford Saloon: 2020
10	62.5	19.1	Jaguar XK120: 2275
11	61.4	18.7	Jaguar XK120 Coupe: 2279
			Jaguar XK120M: 2281
12	61.4	18.7	Ferrari TRC 2500 Testa Rossa: 1379
13	61.0	18.6	Ferrari 375 Indianapolis: 1373

14	60.4	18.4	AC Ace Bristol: 16
			AC Bristol D-2: 20
15	60.2	18.4	Jaguar Mk VII: 2277
			Jaguar Mk VII: 2278
16	60.2	18.3	Maserati GT Coupe: 2653
17	59.7	18.2	Ferrari 412 MI: 1377
18	59.6	18.2	Mercedes-Benz 300SL Roadster: 2800
19	59.0	18.0	Riley 2.5: 3936
20	58.6	17.9	Mercedes-Benz 300SL: 2793
			Mercedes-Benz 300SL Coupe: 2794
21	57.8	17.6	Porsche RSK: 3613
			Riley 2.5: 3938
			Riley Pathfinder: 3939
			Riley Pathfinder: 3940
22	57.3	17.5	Aston Martin DB4: 237
23	57.2	17.4	Austin-Healey 100S: 430
24	56.3	17.2	Chrysler 300-D: 973
			Scarab Mk II: 4109
25	55.3	16.8	Morgan Plus 4: 3127
26	55.1	16.8	Frazer-Nash Targa Florio Turismo: 1985

Averages for decade:
61.9 18.9
Total: 50

Decade 1961 - 1970 Maximum speed. Limit set at 145mph.

	mph	kmh	
1	205.0	329.8	Ford GT40: 1760
2	190.0	305.7	Shelby Cobra Daytona Coupe: 4119
3	184.0	296.1	Jaguar XJ13: 2313
4	180.0	289.6	Bizzarrini P538: 497
			Ferrari 400 Super America: 1389
			Lamborghini Miura: 2451
5	175.0	281.6	Ferrari 250 GTO: 1386
6	173.0	278.4	Ferrari 365 GTB/4 Daytona: 1396
			Ferrari Daytona Sportwagen: 1395
			Lamborghini Miura P400S: 2455
7	168.0	270.3	Lamborghini Miura S: 2456
8	165.0	265.5	Bizzarrini 5300 Spyder: 495
			Ferrari 4.9: 1387
9	164.0	263.9	Ford GT40 Super Street: 1738
10	163.0	262.3	Iso Grifo GL 365: 2248
			Lamborghini Miura: 2452
11	161.0	259.0	Alfa Romeo 33 2.0 Stradale: 66
12	158.0	254.2	Lamborghini Espada: 2453
13	156.0	251.0	Jaguar E Type 4.2: 2309
			Lamborghini 400GT: 2450
14	155.0	249.4	Ferrari 275 GTS/4 NART: 1392
			Ford Fastback NASCAR: 1698
			Jaguar E Type Coupe: 2303
15	153.5	247.0	Aston Martin DB4 GT Zagato: 240
16	153.0	246.2	Iso Grifo A3L Berlinetta: 2245
			Shelby AC Ford Cobra: 4116
17	152.0	244.6	Ferrari 365 GTS 2+2: 1394
			Lamborghini 350GT: 2449
			Monteverdi 375L: 3118
18	151.7	244.1	Jaguar E Type Coupe: 2298
19	151.0	243.0	Chevrolet Corvette L88: 820
			Chevrolet Corvette L88: 835
			Ferrari 365 GTC: 1390
20	150.0	241.4	Chevrolet Corvette Grand Sport Roadster: 776
			Ferrari 250 GT 2+2: 1385
			Ferrari 250 GT Berlinetta Lusso: 1388
			Jaguar XKE: 2306
			Jaguar XKE: 2299
			Lamborghini Espada: 2454
			Porsche 904 Carrera GTS: 3621
21	148.0	238.1	Aston Martin DB4: 239
			Aston Martin DB6: 242
			Chevrolet Corvette Sting Ray: 786
22	146.0	234.9	Ferrari 330 GTS: 1393
23	145.0	233.3	Bizzarrini GT America: 496
			Ferrari 275 GTS: 1391

Averages for decade:
159.7 257.0
Total: 46

Decade 1961 - 1970. Acceleration to 60mph/ 96.5kmh. Limit set at 6.5 seconds.

	sec	
1	4.0	Chevrolet Bel Air 409 SS/S: 755
2	4.2	Dodge Ramcharger 426 Super/Stock: 1287
		Mercury Comet A/FX: 2933
		Shelby AC Ford Cobra: 4116
3	4.6	Pontiac Catalina Super Stock: 3529
4	4.8	Ford Galaxie 500 XL 427: 1714
5	5.0	Chevrolet Corvette Grand Sport Roadster: 776
		Ford GT40: 1760
6	5.1	Plymouth Road Runner: 3507
		Shelby Cobra USRRC: 4118
7	5.3	Chevrolet Corvette Sebring: 767
		Ford GT40 Super Street: 1738
8	5.5	AC Cobra: 25
		Chevrolet Corvette 315: 753
		Ford Mustang 428 Mach I: 1775
		Lamborghini Miura: 2451
		Lamborghini Miura S: 2456
9	5.6	Plymouth Cuda 440: 3505
10	5.7	Chevrolet Corvette: 795
		Chevrolet Corvette 396: 796
		Chevrolet Corvette Convertible: 803
		Chevrolet Corvette LT-1: 845
		Dodge Hemi Charger 500 Automatic: 1308
		Dodge Hemi Charger 500 Manual: 1309
		Oldsmobile 4-4-2 W30: 3296
11	5.8	Chevrolet Camaro Z/28 RS: 842
		Ford Mustang Boss 302: 1787
		Pontiac Firebird TransAm: 3555
		Pontiac Tempest GTO: 3543
12	5.9	Chevrolet Corvette: 766
		Chevrolet Corvette: 775
		Chevrolet Corvette 270: 752
		Chevrolet Corvette Sting Ray: 777
		Ferrari 250 GTO: 1386
		Ferrari 365 GTB/4 Daytona: 1396
		Ferrari Daytona Sportwagen: 1395
		Ford Mustang 428 Cobra Jet: 1761
13	6.0	Buick GS400: 679
		Chevrolet Corvette Sting Ray 396: 798
		Pontiac Grand Prix 421: 3533
		Pontiac GTO 400: 3560
14	6.1	Aston Martin DB4 GT Zagato: 240
		Buick GS400: 681
		Chevrolet Corvette 435hp: 829
		Pontiac GTO Ram Air: 3552
15	6.2	AC 428 Fastback: 26
		Iso Grifo A3L Berlinetta: 2245
		Mercury Cyclone: 2947
		Oldsmobile 442 Hurst: 3293
		Plymouth Duster 340: 3510
		Pontiac GTO Judge: 3557
		Shelby GT 350-S: 4121
16	6.3	AMC Rambler Scrambler: 194
		Chevrolet Camaro 427 Dana: 805
		Chevrolet Corvette Injection: 797
		Chevrolet Corvette Sting Ray Injection: 788
		Dodge Dart GTS: 1305
		Dodge Dart GTS 340: 1306
		Dodge Super Bee Six-Pack: 1312
		Ferrari 365 GTC: 1390
		Ford Fastback NASCAR: 1698
		Lamborghini Miura: 2452
		Monteverdi 375L: 3118
		Oldsmobile Cutlass 442: 3287
		Plymouth GTX Hemi: 3502
		Shelby GT 350: 4123
17	6.4	Bizzarrini 5300 Spyder: 495
		Bizzarrini GT America: 496
		Chevrolet Corvette L46: 831
		Dodge Charger: 1299
		Jensen Interceptor: 2393
		Pontiac Formula 400: 3559
		Porsche 904 Carrera GTS: 3621
18	6.5	Aston Martin DB6: 242
		Buick GS455 Stage 1: 687
		Chevrolet Camaro Z/28: 841
		Chevrolet Chevelle Malibu 396: 792
		Chevrolet Corvette Convertible: 818
		Chevrolet Corvette Sting Ray: 786
		Dodge Coronet 500 Station Wagon: 1307
		Lamborghini Espada: 2453
		Pontiac Firebird 440: 3549
		Pontiac Royal Bobcat: 3535

Average for decade:
5.9
Total: 83

Decade 1961 - 1970. Highest power. Limit set at 390bhp.

	bhp	kW	PS	
1	550.0	410.1	557.6	Chevrolet Corvette Grand Sport Roadster: 776
2	472.0	352.0	478.5	Jaguar XJ13: 2313
3	450.0	335.6	456.2	Chevrolet Camaro Z/28 Yenko/SC: 826
4	435.0	324.4	440.5	Chevrolet Corvette 435hp: 829
				Chevrolet Corvette Convertible: 818
				Chevrolet Corvette L71: 833
				Chevrolet Corvette L71/89: 834
5	430.0	320.6	436.0	Chevrolet Corvette L88: 835
				Chevrolet Corvette L88: 820
				Lamborghini Miura S: 2456
6	425.0	316.9	430.9	Chevrolet Camaro 427 Dana: 805
				Chevrolet Corvette: 795
				Chevrolet Corvette 396: 796

				Chevrolet Corvette Convertible: 803
				Chevrolet Corvette Sting Ray 396: 798
				Dodge Charger: 1299
				Dodge Charger R/T: 1303
				Dodge Hemi Charger 500 Automatic: 1308
				Dodge Hemi Charger 500 Manual: 1309
				Dodge Ramcharger 426 Super/Stock: 1287
				Ford Galaxie 500 XL 427: 1714
				Mercury Comet A/FX: 2933
				Mercury Super Marauder S-55: 2932
				Plymouth GTX Hemi: 3502
				Plymouth Satellite Street Hemi: 3491
				Ruger Bentley Clone: 4052
7	420.0	313.2	425.8	Ferrari 400 Super America: 1389
8	410.0	305.7	415.7	Ford Fastback NASCAR: 1698
9	409.0	305.0	414.7	Chevrolet Bel Air 409 SS/S: 755
10	405.0	302.0	410.6	Ferrari 365 GTB/4 Daytona: 1396
				Ford Galaxie 406: 1679
				Mercury S-55 406: 2930
				Pontiac Grand Prix 421: 3533
11	400.0	298.3	405.5	Bizzarrini GT America: 496
				Chevrolet Corvette L68: 832
				Lamborghini Miura: 2452
				Oldsmobile Toronado: 3292
12	390.0	290.8	395.4	Chevrolet Caprice: 827
				Chevrolet Corvette 454: 844
				Chevrolet Corvette L36: 830
				Chevrolet Kingswood Estate Wagon: 839
				Chrysler 300-J: 981
				Dodge Challenger R/T: 1314
				Dodge Super Bee Six-Pack: 1312
				Ferrari 250 GTO: 1386
				Lamborghini Espada: 2453
				Mercury Cougar XR-7: 2946
				Pontiac Grand Prix: 3556
				Shelby GT 350-S: 4121

Averages for decade:
417.2 311.1 422.9
Total: 49

Decade 1961 - 1970. Highest torque. Limit set at 465lbft.

	lbft	Nm	
1	525.0	711.4	Cadillac Coupe de Ville: 709
2	510.0	691.1	Buick GS455 Stage 1: 687
			Oldsmobile 88 Delta Royale: 3294
3	500.0	677.5	Chevrolet Corvette 454: 844
			Chevrolet Impala: 846
			Chevrolet Monte Carlo: 847
			Oldsmobile 4-4-2 W30: 3296
			Oldsmobile 442 Hurst: 3293
			Oldsmobile Toronado: 3292
			Pontiac GTO 455: 3561
4	495.0	670.7	Chrysler 300-G: 975
5	490.0	664.0	Dodge Challenger R/T: 1314
			Dodge Charger: 1299
			Dodge Charger R/T: 1303
			Dodge Hemi Charger 500 Automatic: 1308
			Dodge Hemi Charger 500 Manual: 1309
			Oldsmobile Delmont: 3291
			Plymouth GTX Hemi: 3502
			Plymouth Satellite Street Hemi: 3491
			Ruger Bentley Clone: 4052
6	485.0	657.2	Chrysler 300-J: 981
7	480.0	650.4	Cadillac Calais: 707
			Cadillac Coupe de Ville: 705
			Cadillac Eldorado: 708
			Cadillac Sedan de Ville: 706
			Chrysler 300: 988
			Chrysler 300: 984
			Chrysler 300-H: 989
			Chrysler Imperial Crown: 987
			Dodge Charger R/T: 1315
			Dodge Coronet R/T: 1300
			Dodge Coronet R/T: 1304
			Dodge Monaco: 1310
			Dodge Ramcharger 426 Super/Stock: 1287
			Ford Galaxie 500 XL 427: 1714
			Ford LTD: 1773
			Ford Thunderbird: 1779
			Mercury Comet A/FX: 2933
			Mercury Marquis Brougham: 2948
			Mercury Marquis Marauder X-100: 2949
			Mercury Super Marauder S-55: 2932
			Monteverdi 375L: 3118
			Plymouth Cuda 440: 3505
			Plymouth GTX: 3497
			Plymouth GTX: 3501
8	476.0	645.0	Ford Fastback NASCAR: 1698
9	475.0	643.6	Buick Riviera: 682
			Buick Riviera: 683
			Buick Wildcat: 680
			Buick Wildcat: 686
			Oldsmobile Toronado: 3288
			Oldsmobile Toronado: 3286
10	472.0	639.6	Pontiac Grand Prix: 3556
11	470.0	636.9	Chrysler 300: 979
			Chrysler Imperial: 977
			Chrysler Imperial Le Baron: 982
			Dodge Coronet 426-S: 1294
			Dodge Polara 500: 1290
12	465.0	630.1	Buick Riviera: 668
			Buick Riviera: 674
			Buick Riviera Gran Sport: 677
			Buick Wildcat: 672
			Lincoln Continental: 2580

Averages for decade:
483.0 654.5
Total: 63

Decade 1961 - 1970. Hihjest rpm at peak power. Limit set at 6500rpm.

	rpm	
1.	39000	Rover Rover-BRM Turbine: 4006
2.	8800	Alfa Romeo 33 2.0 Stradale: 66
3.	8500	Honda S600: 2087
4.	8000	Ferrari 275 GTS/4 NART: 1392
		Honda N360: 2089
		Honda S800: 2088
5.	7700	Lamborghini Miura P400S: 2455
6.	7600	Fiat Abarth OT 1600: 1502
7.	7500	Ferrari 250 GT Berlinetta Lusso: 1388
		Ferrari 250 GTO: 1386
		Ferrari 365 GTB/4 Daytona: 1396
		Ferrari 400 Super America: 1389
		Ferrari Daytona Sportwagen: 1395
8.	7350	Lamborghini Miura S: 2456
9.	7250	Jaguar XJ13: 2313
10.	7200	Porsche 904 Carrera GTS: 3621
11.	7000	Bizzarrini P538: 497
		Ferrari 250 GT 2+2: 1385
		Ferrari 275 GTS: 1391
		Ferrari 330 GTS: 1393
		Ferrari 4.9: 1387
		Lamborghini Espada: 2453
		Lamborghini Miura: 2451
		Lamborghini Miura: 2452
		Mazda 110S Coupe: 2685
12.	6750	Renault 8 Gordini 1300: 3831
		Shelby Cobra Daytona Coupe: 4119
13.	6600	Ferrari 365 GTC: 1390
		Ferrari 365 GTS 2+2: 1394
		Porsche 911 S: 3624
		Porsche 911 S: 3626
		Toyota 2000GT: 4356
14.	6500	Alfa Romeo Giulia SS: 50
		Alfa Romeo Giulia Veloce: 61
		Alfa Romeo Sprint Speciale: 53
		Alfa Romeo Sprint Speciale: 65
		Alfa Romeo Sprint Zagato: 54
		Fiat 124 Coupe: 1515
		Fiat 124 Spider: 1522
		Fiat 124 Sport Coupe: 1509
		Fiat 124 Sport Spider: 1510
		Fiat 850 Coupe: 1518
		Ford Escort 1600 RS: 1785
		Ford GT40: 1760
		Lamborghini 350GT: 2449
		Lamborghini 400GT: 2450
		Lamborghini Espada: 2454
		Lotus Europa S2: 2606
		Porsche 911 E: 3629
		Porsche 911 E Sportomatic: 3627
		Porsche 911 S 2.2-litre: 3631
		Renault 8 Gordini: 3824
		Renault R8 Rally: 3826

Average for decad:
7564Total: 53

Decade 1961 -1970. Highest power-to-weight ratio. Limit set at 250bhp/ton.

	bhp/ ton	bhp/ tonne	
1	560.0	550.7	Chevrolet Corvette Grand Sport Roadster: 776
2	480.6	472.6	Jaguar XJ13: 2313
3	412.6	405.7	Bizzarrini P538: 497
4	408.9	402.1	Alfa Romeo 33 2.0 Stradale: 66
5	375.0	368.7	Shelby Cobra Daytona Coupe: 4119
6	367.8	361.7	Ferrari 250 GTO: 1386
7	366.0	359.9	Ford GT40 Super Street: 1738
8	351.4	345.5	Bizzarrini GT America: 496
9	348.4	342.6	Lamborghini 350GT: 2449
10	347.5	341.7	Shelby Cobra USRRC: 4118

11	342.5	336.8	Ford GT40: 1760
12	331.6	326.0	Lamborghini Miura S: 2456
13	328.5	323.0	Porsche 904 Carrera GTS: 3621
14	324.0	318.6	Iso Grifo A3L Berlinetta: 2245
15	314.4	309.1	Lamborghini Miura: 2452
16	308.6	303.4	Mercury Comet A/FX: 2933
17	301.1	296.1	Ferrari 275 GTS/4 NART: 1392
18	296.6	291.7	Chevrolet Corvette Convertible: 818
19	296.5	291.5	Chevrolet Camaro Z/28 Yenko/SC: 826
20	296.1	291.2	Shelby GT 350-S: 4121
21	295.8	290.9	Dodge Ramcharger 426 Super/Stock: 1287
22	292.0	287.1	Chevrolet Corvette: 795
			Chevrolet Corvette 396: 796
			Chevrolet Corvette Sting Ray 396: 798
23	291.1	286.3	Chevrolet Corvette Convertible: 803
24	290.3	285.4	AC Cobra: 25
25	289.6	284.8	Lamborghini Miura P400S: 2455
26	288.3	283.5	Shelby AC Ford Cobra: 4116
27	284.6	279.8	Bizzarrini 5300 Spyder: 495
28	282.7	277.9	Chevrolet Camaro 427 Dana: 805
29	282.5	277.7	Chevrolet Corvette L88: 820
			Chevrolet Corvette L88: 835
30	281.7	277.0	Ferrari 400 Super America: 1389
31	279.7	275.1	Shelby AC Ford Cobra: 4117
32	278.0	273.4	Chevrolet Corvette L71/89: 834
33	275.4	270.8	Chevrolet Corvette Sting Ray Injection: 788
34	273.7	269.1	Chevrolet Corvette L71: 833
35	273.5	269.0	Chevrolet Corvette 435hp: 829
36	269.7	265.2	Chevrolet Chevy II Corvette: 757
37	269.4	264.9	Ruger Bentley Clone: 4052
38	266.1	261.7	Chevrolet Corvette: 775
			Chevrolet Corvette Sting Ray: 777
39	261.8	257.4	Chevrolet Corvette: 766
40	261.8	257.4	Chevrolet Bel Air 409 SS/S: 755
41	260.1	255.7	Chevrolet Corvette Injection: 797
42	257.9	253.6	Excalibur SS: 1363
43	257.3	253.1	Iso Grifo GL 365: 2248
44	256.3	252.1	Lamborghini Miura: 2451
45	255.8	251.5	Chevrolet Corvette LT-1: 836
46	254.4	250.1	Aston Martin DB4 GT Zagato: 240
47	254.2	249.9	Chevrolet Corvette L68: 832
48	253.2	249.0	Chevrolet Camaro Z/28 RS: 842
49	252.0	247.8	Ferrari 365 GTB/4 Daytona: 1396
			Lamborghini 400GT: 2450

Averages for decade:
304.3 299.2
Total: 54

Decade 1961 - 1970. Highest specific output. Limit set at 80bhp/litre.

	bhp/L	kW/L	PS/L	
1	116.0	86.5	117.6	NSU Spider: 3261
2	115.3	86.0	116.9	Alfa Romeo 33 2.0 Stradale: 66
3	114.1	85.1	115.6	NSU Ro80: 3264
4	112.0	83.5	113.6	Mazda 110S Coupe: 2685
5	109.4	81.6	111.0	Lamborghini Miura S: 2456
6	101.8	75.9	103.2	Lamborghini Miura: 2452
7	100.7	75.1	102.1	Porsche 904 Carrera GTS: 3621
8	100.4	74.9	101.8	Ferrari 275 GTS/4 NART: 1392
9	100.0	74.6	101.4	NSU Wankel Spider: 3262
10	99.3	74.0	100.6	Lamborghini Espada: 2453
11	98.3	73.3	99.7	Ferrari 250 GTO: 1386
12	98.2	73.2	99.6	Ferrari 250 GT Berlinetta Lusso: 1388
13	97.0	72.3	98.3	Lamborghini 350GT: 2449
14	96.7	72.1	98.1	Fiat Abarth OT 1600: 1502
15	94.6	70.5	95.9	Jaguar XJ13: 2313
16	94.2	70.2	95.5	Lamborghini Miura P400S: 2455
17	94.1	70.1	95.4	Honda S600: 2087
18	92.3	68.8	93.5	Ferrari 365 GTB/4 Daytona: 1396
19	91.6	68.3	92.9	Lamborghini 400GT: 2450
20	91.5	68.2	92.8	Ferrari 400 Super America: 1389
21	91.1	67.9	92.4	Porsche 911 S 2.2-litre: 3631
22	90.4	67.4	91.7	Porsche 911 S: 3626
23	89.9	67.0	91.2	Alfa Romeo Sprint Speciale: 53
				Alfa Romeo Sprint Zagato: 54
24	89.1	66.4	90.3	Bizzarrini P538: 497
25	88.5	66.0	89.7	Honda S800: 2088
26	87.0	64.8	88.2	Ferrari 330 GTS: 1393
27	85.7	63.9	86.9	Renault 8 Gordini: 3824
				Renault R8 Rally: 3826
28	85.6	63.8	86.7	Aston Martin DB4 GT Zagato: 240
29	83.8	62.5	85.0	Ferrari 365 GTS 2+2: 1394
30	83.4	62.2	84.6	Mercedes-Benz 300SL Roadster: 2807
31	82.7	61.7	83.9	Lamborghini Espada: 2454
				Lamborghini Miura: 2451
32	82.3	61.4	83.5	Shelby GT 350-S: 4121
33	82.2	61.3	83.3	Alfa Romeo Giulia SS: 50
				Alfa Romeo Giulia Veloce: 61
				Alfa Romeo Sprint Speciale: 65
34	82.1	61.2	83.2	Renault 8 Gordini 1300: 3831
35	81.4	60.7	82.6	Shelby Cobra Daytona Coupe: 4119
36	81.3	60.7	82.5	Aston Martin DB6: 242
				Aston Martin DBS: 243
37	81.3	60.6	82.4	Ferrari 250 GT 2+2: 1385
38	80.4	59.9	81.5	Porsche 911 E: 3629
				Porsche 911 S: 3624
39	80.2	59.8	81.3	Ford GT40: 1760
40	80.2	59.8	81.3	Lotus 7 Twin Cam SS: 2605
				Lotus Super 7 Twincam: 2607
41	80.2	59.8	81.3	Ferrari Daytona Sportwagen: 1395

Averages for decade:
90.8 67.7 92.1
Total: 49

Decade 1961 - 1970. Highest piston speed. Limit set at 60ft/sec.

	ft/sec	m/sec	
1	66.8	20.4	Chevrolet Corvette: 795
			Chevrolet Corvette 396: 796
			Chevrolet Corvette Sting Ray 396: 798
2	66.3	20.2	Ruger Bentley Clone: 4052
3	63.7	19.4	Jaguar 3.8 Mk II: 2301
			Jaguar 3.8 Mk II Automatic: 2302
			Jaguar 3.8S: 2307
			Jaguar 420: 2311
			Jaguar 420 Sedan: 2315
			Jaguar E Type Coupe: 2298
			Jaguar E Type Coupe: 2303
			Jaguar Mk X: 2300
			Jaguar XJ6: 2318
			Jaguar XJ6 4.2 Automatic: 2316
			Jaguar XKE Coupe: 2317
4	63.7	19.4	Jaguar 3.8S Sedan: 2304
			Jaguar XKE: 2306
			Jaguar XKE: 2299
5	63.0	19.2	Mercury Comet A/FX: 2933
6	63.0	19.2	Ford Galaxie 500 XL 427: 1714
			Mercury Super Marauder S-55: 2932
7	62.5	19.1	Jaguar 4.2 litre Mk X: 2305
			Jaguar 4.2 litre Mk X Overdrive: 2308
			Jaguar E Type 4.2: 2309
			Jaguar E Type Roadster: 2312
			Jaguar XKE 4.2 2+2: 2310
8	62.5	19.0	Chevrolet Corvette Grand Sport Roadster: 776
9	62.2	19.0	Pontiac Grand Prix 421: 3533
10	61.9	18.9	Mercury Cyclone: 2947
11	61.4	18.7	Oldsmobile 4-4-2 W30: 3296
12	61.3	18.7	Honda S800: 2088
13	60.9	18.6	Ford Galaxie 406: 1679
			Mercury S-55 406: 2930
14	60.6	18.5	Chevrolet Corvette Convertible: 818
			Chevrolet Corvette L71: 833
			Chevrolet Corvette L71/89: 834
15	60.4	18.4	Honda S600: 2087
16	60.4	18.4	Chevrolet Corvette 435hp: 829
			Chevrolet Corvette L88: 820
17	60.4	18.4	AC Greyhound: 22
			Aston Martin DB4 GT Zagato: 240
18	60.2	18.3	Maserati 3500GT: 2654
19	60.2	18.3	Maserati 3500 GTI Sebring: 2655

Averages for decade:
62.7 19.1
Total: 43

Decade 1971 - 1980. Maximum speed. Limit set at 145mph.

	mph	kmh	
1	221.0	355.6	Chevrolet Corvette Greenwood: 870
2	192.0	308.9	Lamborghini Countach: 2461
3	186.0	299.3	Ferrari 365 GTB/4 Competitione: 1403
4	180.0	289.6	Jaguar XJS Tullius: 2333
5	178.0	286.4	Porsche Carrera RSR: 3642
6	175.0	281.6	Ferrari 512 BB: 1407
			Ferrari Daytona: 1397
7	173.0	278.4	Ferrari Daytona Cannonball: 1398
8	170.0	273.5	Aston Martin V8 Vantage: 248
			Lamborghini Bravo: 2458
9	164.0	263.9	Lamborghini Countach S: 2464
10	163.0	262.3	Ferrari 512 BB: 1413
			Maserati Bora: 2664
			Porsche 935 Group 4 Holbert: 3657
11	162.0	260.7	Aston Martin DBS V8: 244
			Maserati Bora: 2660
			Shelby Cobra 427: 4126
12	160.0	257.4	Maserati Khamsin: 2666
13	159.0	255.8	De Tomaso Pantera: 1237
			De Tomaso Pantera GTS: 1239
14	157.0	252.6	Iso Grifo GL: 2250
			Maserati Indy: 2659
15	156.0	251.0	BMW M1: 556
			Porsche 911 Turbo: 3659
			Porsche 911 Turbo Carrera: 3650
16	154.0	247.8	Chevrolet Monza Mike Keyser: 874
			Ferrari 308 GTB: 1409
			Ferrari Dino 308 GT4 2+2: 1410

			Jaguar XJS: 2330
			Maserati Ghibli: 2658
17	153.0	246.2	Ford Cobra II Kemp: 1841
			Porsche Turbo 3-litre: 3648
18	152.0	244.6	Chevrolet Camaro IROC: 877
			Ferrari 308 GT4 Dino: 1402
			Ferrari 365 GTC4: 1400
			Lamborghini Jarama 400GT: 2459
			Lamborghini Jarama 400GT: 2457
19	151.0	243.0	Ford Mustang TransAm: 1796
20	150.0	241.4	Ferrari 365 GT4 2+2: 1406
			Triumph TR8 Group 44: 4578
21	149.0	239.7	Porsche Carrera RS 3-litre: 3647
			Porsche Carrera RS Touring: 3641
22	148.0	238.1	Jaguar XJ12: 2324
			Jaguar XJ5.3 Automatic: 2335
			Jaguar XJ5.3C: 2328
			Lotus Elite V8: 2623
23	147.0	236.5	Aston Martin V8: 246
			Aston Martin V8: 249
			Aston Martin V8 Automatic: 245
			Datsun 240Z Sharp: 1190
			Lamborghini Silhouette 3000: 2462
			Maserati Kyalami: 2667
24	145.0	233.3	Ferrari 308 GTS: 1412
			Jensen SP: 2397

Averages for decade:
158.7 255.3
Total: 54

Decade 1971 - 1980. Acceleration to 60mph/ 96.5kmh. Limit set at 6.5 seconds.

	sec	
1	4.0	Pontiac Firebird TransAm Silverbird: 3566
2	4.1	Ford Cobra II Kemp: 1841
3	4.3	Triumph TR8 Group 44: 4578
4	4.7	Chevrolet Monza Mike Keyser: 874
5	5.0	Jaguar XJS Tullius: 2333
		Porsche 911 Turbo: 3659
6	5.2	Chevrolet Camaro IROC: 877
		Porsche Carrera RS 3-litre: 3647
7	5.3	Mazda RX-7 Racer: 2715
		Shelby Cobra 427: 4126
		Triumph TR8 Libra Rally: 4579
8	5.4	Aston Martin V8 Vantage: 248
		Ferrari Daytona: 1397
9	5.5	Ford Mustang TransAm: 1796
		Porsche Carrera RS Touring: 3641
10	5.6	Datsun 280ZX Sharp: 1221
		Ferrari Daytona Cannonball: 1398
		Porsche Carrera RSR: 3642
11	5.7	Datsun 280ZX Electramotive: 1220
12	5.8	Ferrari 365 GTB/4 Competitione: 1403
		Porsche 935 Group 4 Holbert: 3657
		TVR Convertible Turbo: 4593
13	5.9	Lamborghini Countach S: 2464
14	6.0	Aston Martin DBS V8: 244
15	6.1	Porsche 911S 2.7-litre: 3645
		Porsche Turbo 3-litre: 3648
16	6.2	Aston Martin V8 Automatic: 245
		BMW M1: 556
		Caterham Super 7: 722
		Chevrolet Corvette Greenwood: 870
		Datsun 280Z Scarab: 1205
		De Tomaso Pantera: 1237
		Ferrari 512 BB: 1413
17	6.3	Porsche 911 SC: 3658
18	6.4	Ferrari 308 GT4 Dino: 1402
		Panther J72: 3372
		Porsche 911 E 2.4-litre: 3635
19	6.5	Chevrolet Corvette: 881
		De Tomaso Pantera GTS: 1239
		Ferrari 308 GTB: 1409
		Maserati Bora: 2660
		Maserati Khamsin: 2666
		Morgan Plus 8: 3131
		Pontiac Firebird TransAm: 3565
		Porsche 911 SC: 3654

Average for decade:
5.8
Total: 45

Decade 1971 - 1980. Highest power. Limit set at 280bhp.

	bhp	kW	PS	
1	700.0	522.0	709.7	Chevrolet Corvette Greenwood: 870
2	590.0	440.0	598.2	Pontiac Firebird TransAm Silverbird: 3566
3	570.0	425.0	577.9	Ford Cobra II Kemp: 1841
4	536.0	399.7	543.4	Chevrolet Monza Mike Keyser: 874
5	485.0	361.7	491.7	Porsche 935 Group 4 Holbert: 3657
6	475.0	354.2	481.6	Jaguar XJS Tullius: 2333
7	460.0	343.0	466.4	Ford Mustang TransAm: 1796
8	450.0	335.6	456.2	Chevrolet Camaro IROC: 877
9	425.0	316.9	430.9	Shelby Cobra 427: 4126
10	402.0	299.8	407.6	Ferrari 365 GTB/4 Competitione: 1403
11	375.0	279.6	380.2	Lamborghini Countach: 2461
12	360.0	268.4	365.0	Ferrari 512 BB: 1413
				Triumph TR8 Group 44: 4578
13	352.0	262.5	356.9	Ferrari 365 GTB/4 Daytona: 1404
				Ferrari Daytona: 1397
				Ferrari Daytona Cannonball: 1398
14	350.0	261.0	354.8	Datsun 280Z Scarab: 1205
				Iso Grifo GL: 2250
				Lamborghini Jarama 400GT: 2459
				Lamborghini Jarama 400GT: 2457
15	344.0	256.5	348.8	Ferrari 512 BB: 1407
16	340.0	253.5	344.7	Aston Martin V8 Coupe: 247
				Maserati Ghibli: 2658
17	335.0	249.8	339.6	De Tomaso Pantera GTS: 1239
18	330.0	246.1	334.6	De Tomaso Pantera: 1237
				Jensen Interceptor: 2396
				Jensen SP: 2397
19	325.0	242.3	329.5	Iso Rivolta Fidia: 2251
				Lamborghini Countach S: 2464
20	320.0	238.6	324.4	Ferrari 365 GT4 2+2: 1406
				Ferrari 365 GTC4: 1400
				Maserati Khamsin: 2666
				Maserati Khamsin Automatic: 2662
21	315.0	234.9	319.4	Maserati Khamsin: 2665
				Maserati Khamsin: 2669
22	310.0	231.2	314.3	De Tomaso Pantera: 1236
				Maserati Bora: 2660
23	300.0	223.7	304.2	Datsun 280ZX Sharp: 1221
				Lamborghini Bravo: 2458
				Maserati Bora: 2664
24	290.0	216.2	294.0	Maserati Indy: 2659
25	286.0	213.3	290.0	Mercedes-Benz 450SEL 6.9: 2862
26	285.0	212.5	288.9	Jaguar XJ5.3 Automatic: 2335
				Jaguar XJ5.3C: 2328
				Jaguar XJS: 2330
				Jaguar XJS Automatic: 2332
27	280.0	208.8	283.9	Jensen Interceptor III Convertible: 2401
				Porsche Carrera RSR: 3642
				Triumph TR8 Libra Rally: 4579

Averages for decade:
359.8 268.3 364.8
Total: 49

Decade 1971 - 1980. Highest torque. Limit set at 325lbft.

	lbft	Nm	
1	620.0	840.1	Chevrolet Corvette Greenwood: 870
2	530.0	718.2	Ford Cobra II Kemp: 1841
3	490.0	664.0	Jensen SP: 2397
4	480.0	650.4	Shelby Cobra 427: 4126
5	460.0	623.3	Pontiac Firebird TransAm Silverbird: 3566
6	440.0	596.2	Chevrolet Monza Mike Keyser: 874
7	434.0	588.1	Porsche 935 Group 4 Holbert: 3657
8	425.0	575.9	Jensen Interceptor: 2396
9	405.0	548.8	Mercedes-Benz 450SEL 6.9: 2862
10	400.0	542.0	Aston Martin V8 Coupe: 247
11	396.0	536.6	Chevrolet Camaro IROC: 877
12	381.0	516.3	International Pickup 4WD 1210 Camper Special: 2237
			International Travelall 1210: 2239
13	380.0	514.9	De Tomaso Pantera: 1236
			Jensen Interceptor III Convertible: 2401
14	375.0	508.1	Chevrolet Monte Carlo: 859
15	365.0	494.6	Jeep Gladiator Pickup J-2500 Townside: 2376
			Jeep Wagoneer 1414C: 2378
16	360.0	487.8	Datsun 280Z Scarab: 1205
			Ford Mustang TransAm: 1796
			Iso Grifo GL: 2250
			Iso Rivolta Fidia: 2251
			Jaguar XJS Tullius: 2333
			Mercedes-Benz 600SE: 2854
17	354.0	479.7	Maserati Khamsin: 2666
			Maserati Khamsin Automatic: 2662
18	350.0	474.3	Chevrolet Beauville: 849
			Chevrolet Pickup Cheyenne Fleetside: 851
			Jeep Wagoneer: 2377
			Jensen Interceptor III: 2400
19	345.0	467.5	De Tomaso Pantera GTS: 1239
			Pontiac Firebird TransAm Turbo: 3567
20	340.0	460.7	Maserati Bora: 2660
21	338.0	458.0	Lincoln Continental Limousine: 2582
22	332.0	449.9	Ferrari 512 BB: 1413
23	331.0	448.5	Jaguar XJ12L: 2326
			Panther De Ville: 3373
24	330.0	447.2	Jensen Interceptor III Convertible: 2403
			Pontiac Firebird TransAm: 3563
25	326.0	441.7	Maserati Ghibli: 2658
26	325.0	440.4	De Tomaso Pantera: 1237
			Maserati Bora: 2664

Averages for decade:
380.3 515.3
Total: 42

Decade 1971 -1980. Highest rpm at peak power. Limit set at 6800rpm.

	rpm	
1	9000	Datsun B210 Electramotive: 1198
		Mazda RX-7 Racer: 2715
2	8300	Ferrari 365 GTB/4 Competitione: 1403
3	8250	Datsun 240Z Sharp: 1190
4	8000	Lamborghini Countach: 2461
		Porsche Carrera RSR: 3642
		Renault 5 Racer: 3865
		Triumph TR8 Group 44: 4578
5	7800	Datsun 510 TransAm: 1180
		Lamborghini Bravo: 2458
6	7700	Ferrari 308 GT4 Dino: 1402
		Ferrari 308 GTB: 1409
		Ferrari Dino 308 GT4 2+2: 1410
7	7600	Ferrari 246 GTS Dino: 1401
		Jaguar XJS Tullius: 2333
8	7500	Alfa Romeo 1750 GTV TransAm: 78
		Datsun 280ZX Electramotive: 1220
		Datsun 280ZX Sharp: 1221
		Ferrari 365 GTB/4 Daytona: 1404
		Ferrari Daytona: 1397
		Ferrari Daytona Cannonball: 1398
		Fiat Brava Abarth Rally: 1571
		Ford Mustang TransAm: 1796
		Lamborghini Countach S: 2464
		Lamborghini Jarama 400GT: 2457
		Lamborghini Jarama 400GT: 2459
		Lamborghini Silhouette 3000: 2462
		Lamborghini Urraco: 2463
		Lamborghini Urraco S: 2460
		Pontiac Firebird TransAm Silverbird: 3566
9	7200	Chevrolet Monza Mike Keyser: 874
		Ferrari 512 BB: 1407
10	7100	BMW 2002 TransAm: 528
11	7000	Ferrari 246 GT Dino: 1399
		Ford Cobra II Kemp: 1841
		Jensen Healey Huffaker: 2399
		Mazda Rotary: 2689
		Mazda RX-2: 2691
		Mazda RX-2: 2690
		Mazda RX-4: 2694
		Porsche 935 Group 4 Holbert: 3657
		Triumph TR8 Libra Rally: 4579
12	6800	Chevrolet Corvette Greenwood: 870
		Triumph TR7 Tullius: 4572

Average for decade:
7524
Total: 44

Decade 1971 - 1980. Highest power-to-weight ratio. Limit set at 190bhp/ton.

	bhp/ ton	bhp/ tonne	
1	543.5	534.4	Chevrolet Corvette Greenwood: 870
2	476.4	468.5	Ford Cobra II Kemp: 1841
3	455.7	448.1	Pontiac Firebird TransAm Silverbird: 3566
4	448.0	440.5	Chevrolet Monza Mike Keyser: 874
5	409.2	402.4	Porsche 935 Group 4 Holbert: 3657
6	376.3	370.0	Shelby Cobra 427: 4126
7	339.9	334.3	Jaguar XJS Tullius: 2333
8	339.0	333.4	Porsche Carrera RSR: 3642
9	318.0	312.7	Ford Mustang TransAm: 1796
10	315.0	309.7	Triumph TR8 Group 44: 4578
11	307.3	302.2	Chevrolet Camaro IROC: 877
12	301.3	296.3	Datsun 280ZX Sharp: 1221
13	282.3	277.6	Ferrari 365 GTB/4 Competitione: 1403
14	281.2	276.5	Lamborghini Bravo: 2458
15	278.1	273.5	Lamborghini Countach: 2461
16	271.8	267.3	Mazda RX-7 Racer: 2715
17	266.2	261.8	Datsun 280Z Scarab: 1205
18	262.7	258.3	Datsun 240Z Sharp: 1190
19	262.4	258.0	Triumph TR8 Libra Rally: 4579
20	248.9	244.7	Datsun 280ZX Electramotive: 1220
21	248.5	244.3	De Tomaso Pantera GTS: 1239
22	245.3	241.2	Fiat Brava Abarth Rally: 1571
23	242.9	238.8	Caterham Super 7: 722
24	237.5	233.6	De Tomaso Pantera: 1237
25	235.4	231.5	Ferrari 512 BB: 1413
26	229.6	225.8	Lamborghini Countach S: 2464
27	225.3	221.5	Ferrari 512 BB: 1407
28	223.4	219.6	Ferrari Daytona: 1397
29	223.0	219.3	Iso Grifo GL: 2250
30	220.6	216.9	Morgan Plus 8 Turbo: 3132
31	220.1	216.4	De Tomaso Pantera: 1236
32	219.5	215.9	Jensen Healey Huffaker: 2399
33	219.0	215.4	Ferrari Daytona Cannonball: 1398
34	218.1	214.5	Ferrari 365 GTB/4 Daytona: 1404
35	217.8	214.1	Lamborghini Jarama 400GT: 2459
			Lamborghini Jarama 400GT: 2457
36	215.5	211.9	Porsche Turbo 3-litre: 3648
37	211.8	208.2	Lamborghini Silhouette 3000: 2462
38	211.5	208.0	TVR Convertible Turbo: 4593
39	204.5	201.1	Alfa Romeo 1750 GTV TransAm: 78
40	204.5	201.1	Porsche Carrera RS 3-litre: 3647
41	204.0	200.6	Datsun B210 Electramotive: 1198
42	203.4	200.0	Maserati Ghibli: 2658
43	199.0	195.7	Ferrari 308 GTB: 1409
44	199.0	195.7	Triumph TR7 Tullius: 4572
45	198.1	194.8	Maserati Khamsin Automatic: 2662
46	198.1	194.8	Maserati Bora: 2660
47	197.8	194.5	Datsun 510 TransAm: 1180
48	196.2	192.9	Porsche Carrera RS Touring: 3641
49	192.5	189.3	Maserati Khamsin: 2666
50	191.6	188.4	Ferrari Dino 308 GT4 2+2: 1410
51	191.5	188.3	Porsche 911 Turbo: 3659
52	190.6	187.5	Lotus Elite V8: 2623
53	190.1	186.9	Renault 5 Racer: 3865

Averages for decade:
259.8 255.4
Total: 54

Decade 1971 - 1980. Highest specific output. Limit set at 85bhp/litre.

	bhp/L	kW/L	PS/L	
1	235.6	175.7	238.9	Mazda RX-7 Racer: 2715
2	162.0	120.8	164.3	Porsche 935 Group 4 Holbert: 3657
3	115.6	86.2	117.2	NSU Ro80: 3266
4	115.3	86.0	116.9	Fiat Brava Abarth Rally: 1571
5	114.2	85.1	115.8	Datsun B210 Electramotive: 1198
6	113.4	84.6	115.0	Mazda RX-2: 2690
				Mazda RX-4: 2694
7	113.3	84.5	114.8	Alfa Romeo 1750 GTV TransAm: 78
8	108.7	81.0	110.2	Renault 5 Racer: 3865
9	108.6	81.0	110.1	Datsun 280ZX Electramotive: 1220
10	107.9	80.5	109.4	Datsun 510 TransAm: 1180
11	106.5	79.4	107.9	Datsun 280ZX Sharp: 1221
12	105.3	78.5	106.8	Datsun 240Z Sharp: 1190
13	104.7	78.1	106.2	Mazda RX-2: 2691
14	101.8	75.9	103.2	Mazda Rotary: 2689
15	100.1	74.7	101.5	Lamborghini Bravo: 2458
16	99.8	74.4	101.2	Porsche Carrera RSR: 3642
17	99.3	74.1	100.7	Jensen Healey Huffaker: 2399
18	99.1	73.9	100.4	Ford Cobra II Kemp: 1841
19	98.4	73.4	99.8	BMW 2002 TransAm: 528
20	98.4	73.3	99.7	Pontiac Firebird TransAm Silverbird: 3566
21	95.4	71.2	96.8	Lamborghini Countach: 2461
22	93.5	69.7	94.8	Chevrolet Monza Mike Keyser: 874
23	93.1	69.4	94.4	Ford Mustang TransAm: 1796
24	91.6	68.3	92.9	Mazda RX-7: 2710
25	91.6	68.3	92.8	Ferrari 365 GTB/4 Competitione: 1403
26	91.5	68.2	92.7	Chevrolet Corvette Greenwood: 870
27	90.2	67.3	91.5	Triumph TR8 Group 44: 4578
28	89.3	66.6	90.6	Lamborghini Urraco S: 2460
29	89.1	66.4	90.3	Lamborghini Jarama 400GT: 2459
				Lamborghini Jarama 400GT: 2457
30	88.9	66.3	90.1	Jaguar XJS Tullius: 2333
31	88.9	66.3	90.1	Suzuki Brute: 4320
32	87.8	65.5	89.0	Ford Pinto Pangra: 1819
33	87.3	65.1	88.5	Mazda RX-7: 2705
				Mazda RX-7: 2714
				Mazda RX-7 GS: 2711
34	87.1	65.0	88.3	Ferrari 308 GTB: 1409
35	86.8	64.8	88.0	Porsche Turbo 3-litre: 3648
36	86.8	64.7	88.0	Lamborghini Silhouette 3000: 2462
37	85.7	63.9	86.9	Porsche 924 Turbo: 3664
38	85.5	63.7	86.7	Triumph TR7 Tullius: 4572
39	85.4	63.7	86.6	BMW 2002 Turbo: 534
40	85.4	63.7	86.6	Ferrari Dino 308 GT4 2+2: 1410

Averages for decade:
101.5 75.7 102.9
Total: 44

Decade 1971 - 1980. Highest piston speed. Limit set at 55ft/sec.

	ft/sec	m/sec	
1	75.7	23.1	Datsun B210 Electramotive: 1198
2	75.6	23.0	Chevrolet Corvette Greenwood: 870
3	73.7	22.5	Fiat Brava Abarth Rally: 1571
4	72.5	22.1	Alfa Romeo 1750 GTV TransAm: 78
5	70.4	21.5	Pontiac Firebird TransAm Silverbird: 3566
6	69.6	21.2	Chevrolet Monza Mike Keyser: 874
7	68.9	21.0	Triumph TR8 Group 44: 4578
8	68.1	20.7	Ford Cobra II Kemp: 1841
9	67.6	20.6	Datsun 510 TransAm: 1180
10	67.3	20.5	Renault 5 Racer: 3865
11	66.5	20.3	Datsun 240Z Sharp: 1190
12	64.8	19.7	Datsun 280ZX Sharp: 1221
13	64.6	19.7	Jensen Interceptor III Convertible: 2403
14	64.6	19.6	Ferrari 365 GTB/4 Competitione: 1403
15	63.7	19.4	Jaguar XJ6 4.2: 2320

16	63.2	19.3	Chevrolet Camaro IROC: 877
17	63.2	19.2	Shelby Cobra 427: 4126
18	62.5	19.0	Ford Mustang TransAm: 1796
19	62.1	18.9	BMW 2002 TransAm: 528
20	61.6	18.8	Porsche Carrera RSR: 3642
21	60.4	18.4	Datsun 280ZX Electramotive: 1220
22	59.9	18.2	Ferrari 308 GT4 Dino: 1402
			Ferrari 308 GTB: 1409
			Ferrari Dino 308 GT4 2+2: 1410
23	59.8	18.2	BMW M1: 556
24	59.0	18.0	Lancia Beta Monte Carlo: 2517
			Mitsubishi Colt Celeste 2000: 3063
			Mitsubishi Colt Galant 2000: 3062
			Mitsubishi Colt Sigma 2000: 3064
25	58.3	17.8	De Tomaso Pantera GTS: 1239
26	58.3	17.7	Ferrari 365 GTB/4 Daytona: 1404
			Ferrari Daytona: 1397
			Ferrari Daytona Cannonball: 1398
27	58.3	17.7	Jaguar XJS Tullius: 2333
28	58.0	17.7	Triumph TR7 Tullius: 4572
29	57.9	17.7	Jaguar XJ3.4: 2327
			Jaguar XJ6 4.2: 2336
			Panther J72: 3372
30	57.5	17.5	Renault 17 Gordini: 3851
			Renault Gordini: 3867
31	57.0	17.4	Fiat Mirafiori Sport: 1565
32	57.0	17.4	Fiat 124 Spider 1600: 1535
33	56.6	17.3	Triumph 2.5PI Mk II: 4552
34	56.5	17.2	Mazda 1800: 2688
35	56.5	17.2	BMW 333i Alpina: 548
36	56.4	17.2	Austin Allegro 1750 HL: 415
			Austin Allegro HL: 409
			Iso Rivolta Fidia: 2251
37	56.1	17.1	Alfa Romeo 2000 GTV Injection: 80
38	56.0	17.1	Austin Maxi High Line: 405
39	56.0	17.1	BMW 320i Alpina: 546
40	56.0	17.0	Ferrari 512 BB: 1407
41	55.8	17.0	Maserati Bora: 2664
			Maserati Bora: 2660
			Maserati Kyalami: 2667
42	55.6	16.9	Alfa Romeo Giulia 1600 Sprint: 86
43	55.1	16.8	Fiat 132 2000 GLS: 1560
			Renault 17: 3844
			Renault 17 Gordini: 3848
44	55.0	16.8	Jaguar XJ6 Series III: 2339
45	55.0	16.8	Jaguar XJ6L: 2337
			Lamborghini Bravo: 2458

Averages for decade:
60.5 18.4
Total: 62

1981 - 1992. Maximum speed. Limit set at 180mph.

	mph	kmh	
1	255.0	410.3	Chevrolet Corvette Callaway Sledgehammer: 941
2	235.0	378.1	Koenig C62: 2419
3	230.0	370.1	Koenig Competition Evolution: 2418
4	218.0	350.8	Vector W8 Twin Turbo: 4736
5	217.0	349.2	Koenig Competition: 2417
6	216.0	347.5	Porsche 911 Turbo RS Tuning: 3737
7	214.0	344.3	Bugatti EB110: 652
8	211.0	339.5	Porsche 911 Turbo Ruf Twin Turbo: 3710
9	210.0	337.9	Ferrari Testa Rossa Norwood: 1444
10	208.0	334.7	Porsche 911 Ruf CTR: 3748
11	205.0	329.8	Porsche 911 Turbo Gemballa Mirage: 3751
12	204.0	328.2	Chevrolet Corvette Lingenfelter: 951
			Cizeta Moroder V16T: 1094
13	203.0	326.6	Chevrolet Camaro Gottlieb 1969: 926
14	202.0	325.0	Lamborghini Diablo: 2474
			Lamborghini Diablo: 2475
15	201.0	323.4	Chevrolet Corvette Callaway Speedster: 949
			Ferrari F40: 1435
			Porsche 911 Turbo Koenig RS: 3709
			Porsche 959 S: 3702
16	200.0	321.8	Eagle GTP: 1356
			Ferrari F40: 1446
			Jaguar XJ220: 2359
			Jaguar XJS Lister Le Mans: 2366
			Vector W2: 4735
17	199.0	320.2	Ferrari GTO Norwood: 1451
18	198.0	318.6	Ferrari 308 Norwood Bonneville GTO: 1434
			Porsche 959: 3731
			Porsche 959 Comfort: 3717
			Porsche 959 Sport: 3718
19	196.1	315.5	Porsche 911 Ruf TR2: 3749
20	196.0	315.4	Ferrari F40: 1450
			Porsche 911 Ruf: 3747
21	193.0	310.5	Chevrolet Camaro IROC-Z Chevrolet Engineering: 929
			Safir GT40: 4106
22	192.0	308.9	Pontiac Firebird TDM Technologies: 3597
23	191.0	307.3	Chevrolet Corvette Callaway: 931
			Chevrolet Corvette Callaway: 918
24	190.0	305.7	Dodge Viper: 1348
25	189.0	304.1	Ferrari 288 GTO: 1421
26	186.0	299.3	Chevrolet Corvette ZR-1 Geiger: 954
			Ford Mustang NOS/Saleen: 1967
			Porsche 928 S4 Koenig: 3726
			Zender Fact 4: 5008
27	185.0	297.7	Chevrolet Corvette ZR-2: 956
			Ferrari Testa Rossa Gemballa: 1443
			Ford Mustang 5.0 Cartech Turbo: 1940
			Jaguar XJR15: 2369
			Mercedes-Benz 300CE AMG Hammer: 2910
28	184.0	296.1	Chevrolet Corvette Callaway: 948
29	183.0	294.4	Aston Martin Zagato: 257
			Mercedes-Benz 300E AMG Hammer: 2899
			Pontiac Petty Grand National: 3571
			Porsche 911 Turbo Motorsport Design: 3724
30	182.0	292.8	Ferrari 308 Norwood: 1439
31	181.0	291.2	Ferrari Testa Rossa: 1437
			Ferrari Testa Rossa Straman Spyder: 1438
32	180.0	289.6	Ferrari 288 GTO: 1416
			Ferrari GTO: 1423
			Ferrari Pininfarina Mythos: 1448

Averages for period:
197.1 317.1
Total: 60

1981 - 1992. Acceleration to 60mph/96.5kmh. Limit set at 5 seconds.

	sec	
1	3.4	Chevrolet Corvette Lingenfelter: 951
2	3.5	AC Cobra 427 Modified 1965: 27
		Jaguar XJ220: 2359
		Koenig C62: 2419
		Koenig Competition Evolution: 2418
		Sbarro Chrono 3.5: 4108
3	3.6	Lancia Montecarlo Group 5 Turbo: 2531
		Porsche 959: 3731
		Porsche 959 Sport: 3718
4	3.7	Ferrari 308 Norwood Bonneville GTO: 1434
5	3.8	Datsun 280ZX Electramotive: 1230
		Ferrari F40: 1450
		Porsche 911 Ruf: 3747
		Porsche 911 Ruf TR2: 3749
6	3.9	Bugatti EB110: 652
		Chevrolet Corvette Callaway Sledgehammer: 941
		Porsche 911 Ruf CTR: 3748
7	4.0	Koenig Competition: 2417
		Porsche 911 Turbo Koenig RS: 3709
		Porsche 911 Turbo Motorsport Design: 3724
		Porsche 911 Turbo Ruf Twin Turbo: 3710
		Porsche 959 Comfort: 3717
		Safir GT40: 4106
		Vector W2: 4735
8	4.1	Dodge Viper: 1348
		Pontiac Firebird TDM Technologies: 3597
		Porsche 911 Turbo Gemballa Mirage: 3751
9	4.2	Chevrolet Corvette ZR-1 SS: 955
		Vector W8 Twin Turbo: 4736
10	4.3	De Tomaso Pantera Group 3: 1243
		Westfield SEight: 4973
		Zender Fact 4: 5008
11	4.4	Chevrolet Corvette Callaway Speedster: 949
		Jaguar XJS Lister Le Mans: 2366
12	4.5	Chevrolet Camaro IROC-Z Chevrolet Engineering: 929
		Chevrolet Corvette Bakeracing SCCA Escort: 917
		Cizeta Moroder V16T: 1094
		Ferrari F40: 1446
		Lamborghini Diablo: 2475
		Porsche 911 Turbo Ruf 3.4: 3698
13	4.6	Chevrolet Corvette Callaway: 918
		Evans Series I: 1362
		Porsche 911 Carrera Turbo: 3746
		Porsche 911 Turbo RS Tuning: 3737
14	4.7	Ferrari 308 Norwood: 1439
		Ferrari Testa Rossa Norwood: 1444
		Lamborghini Countach 25th Anniversary: 2473
		Porsche 911 Turbo: 3750
		Porsche 959 S: 3702
15	4.8	Aston Martin Zagato: 257
		Audi Quattro Sport: 309
		Chevrolet Camaro Gottlieb 1969: 926
		Mazda RX-7 Mariah Mode Six: 2770
		Porsche 911 Turbo: 3723
		Porsche 928 S4 Koenig: 3726
		Renault Le Car Turbo: 3874
16	4.9	Chevrolet Corvette Callaway: 931
		Chevrolet Corvette Callaway: 948
		Chevrolet Corvette Callaway Twin Turbo: 950
		Chevrolet Corvette Morrison/Baker Nelson Ledges: 921
		Chevrolet Corvette ZR-1: 934
		Chevrolet Corvette ZR-1: 953
		Chevrolet Corvette ZR-1 Geiger: 954
		Chevrolet Corvette ZR-2: 956
		Ford Mustang Cartech Turbo: 1928
		Ford Mustang Holdener: 1966

		Lamborghini Countach: 2468
		Lotus Esprit Turbo SE: 2637
		Opel Omega Lotus: 3352
		Porsche 911 3.3 Turbo: 3719
		Porsche 911 Carrera 4: 3720
		Porsche 911 Carrera RS: 3753
		Porsche 911 Turbo Gemballa Avalanche: 3697
17	5.0	Autokraft AC Cobra Mk IV: 456
		Bertone Emotion Lotus: 489
		Chevrolet Corvette Callaway: 901
		Eagle GTP: 1356
		Ferrari 288 GTO: 1416
		Ferrari 288 GTO: 1421
		Ferrari GTO: 1423
		IAD Venus: 2229
		Isdera Imperator: 2244
		Mercedes-Benz 300CE AMG Hammer: 2910
		Nissan 300ZX Turbo Millen Super GTZ: 3247
		Porsche 911 Turbo: 3689
		Porsche 911 Turbo: 3708
		Porsche 911 Turbo Slant-Nose: 3699
		TVR 420 SEAC: 4601

Average for period:
4.5
Total: 88

1981 - 1992. Highest power. Limit set at 425bhp.

	bhp	kW	PS	
1	1600.0	1193.1	1622.2	Ferrari GTO Norwood: 1451
2	1000.0	745.7	1013.9	Koenig Competition Evolution: 2418
3	943.0	703.2	956.1	Ferrari Testa Rossa Norwood: 1444
4	880.0	656.2	892.2	Chevrolet Corvette Callaway Sledgehammer: 941
5	800.0	596.6	811.1	Koenig Competition: 2417
6	798.0	595.1	809.1	Chevrolet Camaro Gottlieb 1969: 926
7	685.0	510.8	694.5	Pontiac Firebird TDM Technologies: 3597
8	671.0	500.4	680.3	Ferrari 308 Norwood Bonneville GTO: 1434
9	640.0	477.2	648.9	Peugeot 405 Turbo 16 Pike's Peak: 3460
10	625.0	466.1	633.7	Vector W8 Twin Turbo: 4736
11	600.0	447.4	608.3	Bugatti EB110: 652
				Porsche 959 S: 3702
				Safir GT40: 4106
				Vector W2: 4735
12	590.0	440.0	598.2	Pontiac Petty Grand National: 3571
13	588.0	438.5	596.2	Koenig C62: 2419
14	580.0	432.5	588.0	AC Cobra 427 Modified 1965: 27
				Datsun 280ZX Electramotive: 1230
				Porsche 911 Turbo RS Tuning: 3737
15	560.0	417.6	567.8	Cizeta Moroder V16T: 1094
16	530.0	395.2	537.3	Chevrolet Camaro IROC-Z Chevrolet Engineering: 929
				Chevrolet Corvette Lingenfelter: 951
				Jaguar XJ220: 2359
17	520.0	387.8	527.2	Porsche 911 Turbo Koenig RS: 3709
18	510.0	380.3	517.1	Ford Mustang SVO J Bittle American: 1942
19	500.0	372.8	506.9	Sbarro Chrono 3.5: 4108
20	496.0	369.9	502.9	Chevrolet Camaro IROC-Z 8.3-litre: 914
				Jaguar XJS Lister Le Mans: 2366
21	492.0	366.9	498.8	Lamborghini Diablo: 2475
22	490.0	365.4	496.8	Porsche 911 Turbo Gemballa Mirage: 3751
23	488.0	363.9	494.8	Porsche 911 Turbo Motorsport Design: 3724
24	485.0	361.7	491.7	Lamborghini Diablo: 2474
25	478.0	356.4	484.6	Ferrari F40: 1435
				Ferrari F40: 1446
				Ferrari F40: 1450
26	470.0	350.5	476.5	Ford Mustang 5.0 Cartech Turbo: 1940
27	469.0	349.7	475.5	Porsche 911 Ruf CTR: 3748
				Porsche 911 Turbo Ruf Twin Turbo: 3710
28	465.0	346.7	471.4	De Tomaso Pantera Group 3: 1243
29	460.0	343.0	466.4	Nissan 300ZX Turbo Millen Super GTZ: 3247
30	455.0	339.3	461.3	Lamborghini Countach: 2468
				Lamborghini Countach 25th Anniversary: 2473
				Porsche 911 Ruf: 3747
				Porsche 911 Ruf TR2: 3749
31	450.0	335.6	456.2	Ferrari 308 Norwood: 1439
				Ford Mustang Holdener: 1966
				Jaguar XJR15: 2369
				Porsche 959: 3731
				Porsche 959 Comfort: 3717
				Porsche 959 Sport: 3718
32	448.0	334.1	454.2	Zender Fact 4: 5008
33	432.0	322.1	438.0	Aston Martin Zagato: 257
34	430.0	320.6	436.0	Porsche 928 S4 Koenig: 3726
				Toyota Supra Turbo TRD: 4467
35	428.0	319.2	433.9	Nissan 300ZX Motor Sports International SR-71: 3246
36	425.0	316.9	430.9	Chevrolet Corvette ZR-1 SS: 955

Averages for period:
561.9 419.0 569.7
Total: 56

1981 - 1992. Highest torque. Limit set at 400lbft.

	lbft	Nm	
1	900.0	1219.5	Ferrari GTO Norwood: 1451
2	785.0	1063.7	Pontiac Firebird TDM Technologies: 3597
3	772.0	1046.1	Chevrolet Corvette Callaway Sledgehammer: 941
4	738.0	1000.0	Koenig Competition Evolution: 2418
5	672.0	910.6	Chevrolet Camaro IROC-Z Chevrolet Engineering: 929
6	664.0	899.7	Koenig Competition: 2417
7	638.0	864.5	Chevrolet Camaro Gottlieb 1969: 926
8	630.0	853.7	Vector W8 Twin Turbo: 4736
9	603.0	817.1	Safir GT40: 4106
10	580.0	785.9	Vector W2: 4735
11	575.0	779.1	Chevrolet Corvette Callaway: 948
			Chevrolet Corvette Callaway Speedster: 949
			Chevrolet Corvette Callaway Twin Turbo: 950
12	570.0	772.4	Chevrolet Corvette Lingenfelter: 951
13	562.0	761.5	Chevrolet Corvette Callaway: 940
			Chevrolet Corvette Callaway: 931
14	550.0	745.3	Chevrolet Camaro IROC-Z 8.3-litre: 914
			Ford Mustang Cartech Turbo: 1928
15	545.0	738.5	Chevrolet Corvette Callaway: 918
16	542.0	734.4	Peugeot 405 Turbo 16 Pike's Peak: 3460
17	541.0	733.1	AC Cobra 427 Modified 1965: 27
18	533.0	722.2	Koenig C62: 2419
19	520.0	704.6	Datsun 280ZX Electramotive: 1230
20	502.0	680.2	Ferrari 308 Norwood Bonneville GTO: 1434
21	500.0	677.5	Jaguar XJS Lister Le Mans: 2366
22	490.0	664.0	Porsche 911 Turbo Koenig RS: 3709
			Porsche 911 Turbo Motorsport Design: 3724
23	485.0	657.2	Bentley Turbo R: 483
24	483.0	654.5	Porsche 911 Ruf TR2: 3749
25	482.0	653.1	Porsche 911 Ruf: 3747
26	470.0	636.9	Porsche 928 S4 Koenig: 3726
27	465.0	630.1	Chevrolet Corvette Callaway: 901
			Porsche 911 Turbo RS Tuning: 3737
28	457.0	619.2	Porsche 911 Turbo Ruf Twin Turbo: 3710
29	450.0	609.8	Dodge Viper: 1348
30	445.0	603.0	Chevrolet Corvette ZR-2: 956
			Ford Mustang 5.0 Cartech Turbo: 1940
31	442.0	598.9	Chevrolet Corvette Guldstrand Grand Sport 80: 920
32	440.0	596.2	De Tomaso Pantera Group 3: 1243
			Ferrari 365 GTB Goldsmith: 1425
33	437.0	592.1	Chevrolet Corvette Morrison/Baker Nelson Ledges: 921
34	430.0	582.7	Nissan 300ZX Turbo Millen Super GTZ: 3247
35	428.0	579.9	Lamborghini Diablo: 2474
			Lamborghini Diablo: 2475
			Mercedes-Benz 600SEL: 2923
36	425.0	575.9	Chevrolet Corvette Guldstrand Grand Sport 80: 932
			Ferrari F40: 1450
			Ferrari F40: 1446
			Ferrari F40: 1435
			Pontiac Firebird T/A Turbo Pontiac Engineering: 3588
37	420.0	569.1	Ford Mustang Holdener: 1966
			Jaguar XJR15: 2369
			Porsche 911 Turbo Gemballa Mirage: 3751
38	419.0	567.8	Bugatti EB110: 652
39	410.0	555.6	Chevrolet Corvette Bakeracing SCCA Escort: 917
			Ford Mustang Kaufmann: 1932
40	409.0	554.2	Opel Omega Lotus: 3352
41	408.0	552.8	Porsche 911 Ruf CTR: 3748
42	407.0	551.5	Mercedes-Benz 300CE AMG Hammer: 2910
			Mercedes-Benz 300E AMG Hammer: 2899
43	406.0	550.1	Nissan 300ZX Motor Sports International SR-71: 3246
44	403.0	546.1	Ford Thunderbird Super Coupe Ford Engineering: 1948
45	400.0	542.0	Aston Martin Volante: 256
			Chevrolet Corvette ZR-1 SS: 955
			Jaguar XJ220: 2359

Averages for period:
500.7 678.5
Total: 65

1981 -1992. Highest rpm at peak power. Limit set at 7000rpm.

	rpm	
1	10000	Ferrari Testa Rossa Norwood: 1444
2	9200	Sbarro Chrono 3.5: 4108
3	9000	Bugatti EB110: 652
4	8800	Lancia Montecarlo Group 5 Turbo: 2531
5	8500	Volkswagen Scirocco GT-3 Davey: 4830
6	8000	Cizeta Moroder V16T: 1094
		Lotus Elan Autocrosser: 2632
7	7900	Ford Mustang SVO J Bittle American: 1942

8	7850	Ferrari 308 Norwood Bonneville GTO: 1434
9	7600	Honda Civic 1.6i VT: 2154
		Honda CRX 1.6i VT: 2152
10	7500	Datsun 280ZX Electramotive: 1230
		Ferrari 365 GTB Goldsmith: 1425
		Lamborghini Countach S: 2466
		Pontiac Petty Grand National: 3571
11	7200	Ferrari 348tb: 1445
		Ferrari GTO Norwood: 1451
		Ferrari Mondial t: 1452
		Ferrari Mondial t: 1441
		Mercedes-Benz 190E 2.5-16 Evolution II: 2916
		Mercedes-Benz 190E 2.5-16 Evolution II: 2908
12	7100	Acura NSX: 36
		Honda NSX: 2156
13	7000	BMW M3 Hor Technologie: 605
		BMW M3 Sport Evolution: 621
		Chevrolet Camaro Gottlieb 1969: 926
		Ferrari 288 GTO: 1416
		Ferrari 288 GTO: 1421
		Ferrari 3.2 Mondial: 1427
		Ferrari 328 GTB: 1428
		Ferrari 328 GTS: 1431
		Ferrari 348tb: 1449
		Ferrari F40: 1435
		Ferrari F40: 1446
		Ferrari F40: 1450
		Ferrari GTO: 1423
		Ferrari Mondial: 1447
		Ferrari Mondial 3.2: 1429
		Ferrari Mondial 3.2 Cabriolet: 1440
		Ferrari Mondial 3.2QV: 1430
		Ferrari Mondial Cabriolet: 1436
		Ferrari Mondial Cabriolet 3.2: 1433
		Ferrari Mondial t Cabriolet: 1453
		Geo Storm GSi: 1994
		Jaguar XJ220: 2359
		Lamborghini Countach: 2468
		Lamborghini Countach 25th Anniversary: 2473
		Lamborghini Countach 5000S: 2469
		Lamborghini Countach LP 500S: 2465
		Lamborghini Diablo: 2474
		Lamborghini Jalpa: 2471
		Lamborghini Jalpa: 2467
		Lamborghini Jalpa 3500: 2470
		Lancia Rally: 2537
		Mazda RX-7 Convertible: 2763
		Mazda RX-7 GTUs: 2758
		Peugeot 405 Turbo 16 Pike's Peak: 3460
		Renault Le Car Turbo: 3874

Average for period:
7325
Total: 58

1981 -1992. Highest power-to-weight ratio. Limit set at 325bhp/ton.

	bhp/ ton	bhp/ tonne	
1	1257.5	1236.6	Ferrari GTO Norwood: 1451
2	780.5	767.5	Sbarro Chrono 3.5: 4108
3	764.6	751.8	Peugeot 405 Turbo 16 Pike's Peak: 3460
4	640.0	629.3	Koenig Competition Evolution: 2418
5	595.8	585.9	Chevrolet Camaro Gottlieb 1969: 926
6	589.4	579.6	Ferrari 308 Norwood Bonneville GTO: 1434
7	570.9	561.4	Ferrari Testa Rossa Norwood: 1444
8	564.7	555.3	Safir GT40: 4106
9	543.1	534.1	Koenig C62: 2419
10	537.1	528.1	Chevrolet Corvette Callaway Sledgehammer: 941
11	520.9	512.2	Lancia Montecarlo Group 5 Turbo: 2531
12	513.5	504.9	AC Cobra 427 Modified 1965: 27
13	512.0	503.5	Koenig Competition: 2417
14	499.7	491.4	Datsun 280ZX Electramotive: 1230
15	483.4	475.4	Vector W2: 4735
16	454.8	447.2	Bugatti EB110: 652
17	451.0	443.5	Porsche 959 S: 3702
18	441.5	434.2	Ferrari F40: 1446
			Ferrari F40: 1435
19	436.4	429.1	Jaguar XJR15: 2369
20	426.2	419.1	Pontiac Firebird TDM Technologies: 3597
21	421.7	414.6	Vector W8 Twin Turbo: 4736
22	416.0	409.1	Porsche 911 Turbo Koenig RS: 3709
23	415.2	408.3	Porsche 911 Turbo Ruf Twin Turbo: 3710
24	411.3	404.4	Zender Fact 4: 5008
25	396.6	390.0	Westfield SEight: 4973
26	396.3	389.7	Eagle GTP: 1356
27	368.3	362.2	Porsche 911 Turbo Gemballa Mirage: 3751
28	366.8	360.7	Porsche 911 Turbo Motorsport Design: 3724
29	362.6	356.5	Ford Mustang Holdener: 1966
30	359.3	353.3	Ferrari F40: 1450
31	356.7	350.8	Pontiac Petty Grand National: 3571
32	355.9	349.9	Ford Mustang SVO J Bittle American: 1942
33	353.0	347.1	Renault Le Car Turbo: 3874
34	350.7	344.8	Ferrari 288 GTO: 1421
			Ferrari GTO: 1423
35	345.6	339.8	Porsche 911 Ruf CTR: 3748
36	345.1	339.4	Jaguar XJ220: 2359
37	341.6	335.9	Chevrolet Corvette Lingenfelter: 951
38	339.4	333.7	Porsche 959 Sport: 3718
39	335.8	330.2	Porsche 911 Ruf: 3747
40	335.3	329.7	Porsche 911 Ruf TR2: 3749
41	334.5	328.9	Cizeta Moroder V16T: 1094

Averages for period:
467.1 459.3
Total: 43

1981 - 1992. Highest specific output. Limit set at 130bhp/litre.

	bhp/L	kW/L	PS/L	
1	336.0	250.5	340.6	Peugeot 405 Turbo 16 Pike's Peak: 3460
2	290.5	216.6	294.5	Mazda RX-7 Mariah Mode Six: 2770
3	280.7	209.3	284.6	Lancia Montecarlo Group 5 Turbo: 2531
4	263.0	196.1	266.6	Mazda RX-7 Cartech: 2768
5	210.7	157.1	213.6	Datsun 280ZX Electramotive: 1230
6	210.6	157.0	213.5	Porsche 959 S: 3702
7	202.3	150.9	205.1	Koenig Competition Evolution: 2418
8	190.8	142.3	193.5	Ferrari Testa Rossa Norwood: 1444
9	190.7	142.2	193.3	Ferrari GTO Norwood: 1451
10	184.2	137.4	186.8	Mazda RX-7 Convertible Racing Beat: 2757
11	181.8	135.6	184.3	Renault Le Car Turbo: 3874
12	174.6	130.2	177.0	Koenig C62: 2419
13	172.2	128.4	174.6	Porsche 911 Turbo RS Tuning: 3737
14	171.5	127.9	173.9	Bugatti EB110: 652
15	164.4	122.6	166.6	Mazda RX-7 Infini IV: 2769
16	162.8	121.4	165.1	Ferrari F40: 1450
				Ferrari F40: 1446
				Ferrari F40: 1435
17	161.9	120.7	164.1	Koenig Competition: 2417
18	157.9	117.8	160.1	Porsche 959: 3731
				Porsche 959 Comfort: 3717
				Porsche 959 Sport: 3718
19	155.4	115.9	157.6	Nissan 300ZX Turbo Millen Super GTZ: 3247
20	154.5	115.2	156.6	Porsche 911 Turbo Koenig RS: 3709
21	153.8	114.7	155.9	Ferrari 308 Norwood: 1439
22	153.5	114.5	155.6	Chevrolet Corvette Callaway Sledgehammer: 941
23	152.9	114.0	155.0	Mazda RX-7 Turbo: 2764
				Mazda RX-7 Turbo: 2771
				Mazda RX-7 Turbo II: 2759
24	147.9	110.3	150.0	Porsche 911 Turbo Motorsport Design: 3724
25	145.6	108.5	147.6	Toyota Supra Turbo TRD: 4467
26	145.5	108.5	147.5	Porsche 911 Turbo Gemballa Mirage: 3751
27	144.6	107.8	146.6	Nissan 300ZX Motor Sports International SR-71: 3246
28	144.0	107.4	146.0	Mazda MX-5 Miata Millen: 2760
29	143.4	106.9	145.4	Audi Quattro Sport: 309
30	142.9	106.6	144.9	Sbarro Chrono 3.5: 4108
31	140.1	104.5	142.0	Ferrari 288 GTO: 1421
				Ferrari GTO: 1423
32	139.3	103.9	141.3	Porsche 911 Turbo Ruf Twin Turbo: 3710
33	139.3	103.9	141.2	Porsche 911 Ruf CTR: 3748
34	139.1	103.8	141.1	Mazda RX-7 Turbo: 2751
				Mazda RX-7 Turbo: 2737
				Mazda RX-7 Turbo: 2740
35	138.0	102.9	139.9	Ferrari 288 GTO: 1416
36	132.4	98.7	134.3	Renault 5 Turbo 2: 3886

Averages for period:
170.8 127.3 173.1
Total: 45

1981 - 1992. Highest piston speed. Limit set at 63ft/sec.

	ft/sec	m/sec	
1	89.8	27.4	Ferrari GTO Norwood: 1451
2	85.3	26.0	Ferrari Testa Rossa Norwood: 1444
3	84.6	25.8	Sbarro Chrono 3.5: 4108
4	82.6	25.2	Chevrolet Camaro Gottlieb 1969: 926
5	77.6	23.6	Ferrari 308 Norwood Bonneville GTO: 1434
6	74.4	22.7	Volkswagen Scirocco GT-3 Davey: 4830
7	72.9	22.2	Pontiac Petty Grand National: 3571
8	72.8	22.2	Safir GT40: 4106
9	68.8	21.0	Lancia Rally: 2537
10	67.3	20.5	Peugeot 405 Turbo 16 Pike's Peak: 3460
11	66.9	20.4	Honda Civic CRX: 2140
			Honda Concerto 1.6i 16: 2151
			Rover 216 GTi: 4044
			Rover 416 GTi: 4040
12	66.7	20.3	BMW M3 Sport Evolution: 621
13	65.8	20.1	Ford Mustang SVO J Bittle American: 1942
14	65.2	19.9	Mercedes-Benz 190E 2.5-16 Evolution II: 2908
			Mercedes-Benz 190E 2.5-16 Evolution II: 2916

15	65.1	19.8	Chevrolet Corvette ZR-1 SS: 955
16	65.0	19.8	Lancia Montecarlo Group 5 Turbo: 2531
17	65.0	19.8	BMW M5: 606
			BMW M5: 622
18	64.8	19.7	Datsun 280ZX Electramotive: 1230
19	64.4	19.6	Honda Prelude 2.0 Si: 2138
			Honda Prelude Si 4WS: 2148
20	64.4	19.6	Honda Civic 1.6i VT: 2154
21	64.4	19.6	BMW M3 Hor Technologie: 605
22	64.0	19.5	Honda CRX 1.6i VT: 2152
23	63.9	19.5	Acura Integra LS: 32
			Honda CRX Coupe 1.6i 16: 2128
			Honda CRX Si Jackson: 2142
			Honda Integra EX 16: 2132
			Toyota Supra Turbo TRD: 4467
24	63.8	19.4	Lotus Elan Autocrosser: 2632
25	63.6	19.4	AC Cobra 427 Modified 1965: 27
26	63.3	19.3	Audi Quattro Sport: 309
27	63.2	19.3	De Tomaso Pantera GT5-S: 1242
28	63.0	19.2	Chevrolet Corvette ZR-1: 934
Averages for period:			
	68.1	20.8	
Total: 38			

A–Z
OF
SPECIFICATIONS

1 Abarth
Zagato 750 GT
1958 Italy
96.5mph 155.3kmh
0-50mph 80.5kmh: 11.0secs
0-60mph 96.5kmh: 15.8secs
0-1/4 mile: 20.0secs
44.0bhp 32.8kW 44.6PS
@ 6000rpm
36.0lbft 48.8Nm @ 3500rpm
80.0bhp/ton 78.7bhp/tonne
58.9bhp/L 43.9kW/L 59.7PS/L
42.0ft/sec 12.8m/sec
15.6mph 25.1kmh/1000rpm
42.6mpg 35.5mpgUS 6.6L/100km
Petrol 4-stroke piston
747cc 45.6cu in
In-line 4
Compression ratio: 9.8:1
Bore: 61.0mm 2.4in
Stroke: 64.0mm 2.5in
Valve type/No: Overhead 8
Transmission: Manual
No. of forward speeds: 4
Wheels driven: Rear
Springs F/R: Leaf/Coil
Brakes F/R: Drum/Drum
Wheelbase: 199.9cm 78.7in
Track F: 115.3cm 45.4in
Track R: 115.6cm 45.5in
Length: 346.7cm 136.5in
Width: 134.6cm 53.0in
Height: 119.4cm 47.0in
Ground clearance: 16.0cm 6.3in
Kerb weight: 559.3kg 1232.0lb
Fuel: 27.3L 6.0gal 7.2galUS

2 AC
Acedes Magna Coupe
1931 UK
61.6mph 99.1kmh
65.0bhp 48.5kW 65.9PS
@ 4250rpm
61.9bhp/ton 60.9bhp/tonne
32.6bhp/L 24.3kW/L 33.1PS/L
46.5ft/sec 14.2m/sec
22.0mpg 18.3mpgUS 12.8L/100km
Petrol 4-stroke piston
1991cc 121.5cu in
In-line 6 1 Carburettor
Bore: 65.0mm 2.6in
Stroke: 100.0mm 3.9in
Valve type/No: Overhead 12
Transmission: Manual
No. of forward speeds: 3
Wheels driven: Rear
Brakes F/R: Drum/Drum
Wheelbase: 302.3cm 119.0in
Track F: 127.0cm 50.0in
Track R: 127.0cm 50.0in
Length: 414.0cm 163.0in
Width: 165.1cm 65.0in
Height: 167.6cm 66.0in
Kerb weight: 1067.8kg 2352.0lb
Fuel: 45.5L 10.0gal 12.0galUS

3 AC
Ace Fixed-head Coupe
1933 UK
72.5mph 116.7kmh
0-50mph 80.5kmh: 18.6secs
0-60mph 96.5kmh: 28.8secs
56.0bhp 41.8kW 56.8PS
@ 3500rpm
50.9bhp/ton 50.1bhp/tonne
28.1bhp/L 21.0kW/L 28.5PS/L
38.3ft/sec 11.7m/sec
22.0mpg 18.3mpgUS 12.8L/100km
Petrol 4-stroke piston
1991cc 121.5cu in
In-line 6 3 Carburettor
Compression ratio: 6.2:1
Bore: 65.0mm 2.6in
Stroke: 100.0mm 3.9in
Valve type/No: Overhead 12
Transmission: Manual
No. of forward speeds: 4
Wheels driven: Rear
Brakes F/R: Drum/Drum
Kerb weight: 1118.7kg 2464.0lb
Fuel: 45.5L 10.0gal 12.0galUS

4 AC
Ace Sports Four-seater
1934 UK
80.0mph 128.7kmh
0-50mph 80.5kmh: 14.8secs
0-60mph 96.5kmh: 19.4secs
22.0mpg 18.3mpgUS 12.8L/100km
Petrol 4-stroke piston
1991cc 121.5cu in
In-line 6 3 Carburettor
Bore: 65.0mm 2.6in
Stroke: 100.0mm 3.9in
Transmission: Manual
No. of forward speeds: 4
Wheels driven: Rear
Brakes F/R: Drum/Drum
Kerb weight: 1055.1kg 2324.0lb
Fuel: 45.5L 10.0gal 12.0galUS

5 AC
Greyhound Close-coupled Saloon
1934 UK
77.5mph 124.7kmh
0-50mph 80.5kmh: 14.4secs
0-60mph 96.5kmh: 21.8secs
22.0mpg 18.3mpgUS 12.8L/100km
Petrol 4-stroke piston
1991cc 121.5cu in
In-line 6 3 Carburettor
Bore: 65.0mm 2.6in
Stroke: 100.0mm 3.9in
Transmission: Pre-selector
No. of forward speeds: 4
Wheels driven: Rear
Brakes F/R: Drum/Drum
Kerb weight: 1156.8kg 2548.0lb
Fuel: 45.5L 10.0gal 12.0galUS

6 AC
Ace Drop-head Coupe
1935 UK
72.5mph 116.7kmh
0-50mph 80.5kmh: 16.6secs
0-60mph 96.5kmh: 28.0secs
22.0mpg 18.3mpgUS 12.8L/100km
Petrol 4-stroke piston
1991cc 121.5cu in
In-line 6 3 Carburettor
Bore: 65.0mm 2.6in
Stroke: 100.0mm 3.9in
Valve type/No: Overhead 12
Transmission: Manual
No. of forward speeds: 4
Wheels driven: Rear
Brakes F/R: Drum/Drum
Kerb weight: 1203.1kg 2650.0lb
Fuel: 45.5L 10.0gal 12.0galUS

7 AC
2-litre Aero Saloon
1936 UK
81.0mph 130.3kmh
0-50mph 80.5kmh: 15.5secs
0-60mph 96.5kmh: 23.2secs
22.0mpg 18.3mpgUS 12.8L/100km
Petrol 4-stroke piston
1991cc 121.5cu in
In-line 6
Bore: 65.0mm 2.6in
Stroke: 100.0mm 3.9in
Valve type/No: Overhead 12
Transmission: Manual
No. of forward speeds: 4
Wheels driven: Rear
Brakes F/R: Drum/Drum
Kerb weight: 1230.8kg 2711.0lb
Fuel: 45.5L 10.0gal 12.0galUS

8 AC
Ace
1936 UK
85.7mph 137.9kmh
0-50mph 80.5kmh: 12.2secs
0-60mph 96.5kmh: 18.1secs
70.0bhp 52.2kW 71.0PS
@ 4000rpm
68.2bhp/ton 67.1bhp/tonne
35.2bhp/L 26.2kW/L 35.6PS/L
43.8ft/sec 13.3m/sec
20.0mpg 16.7mpgUS 14.1L/100km
Petrol 4-stroke piston
1991cc 121.5cu in
In-line 6 3 Carburettor
Compression ratio: 6.5:1
Bore: 65.0mm 2.6in
Stroke: 100.0mm 3.9in
Valve type/No: Overhead 12
Transmission: Manual
No. of forward speeds: 4
Wheels driven: Rear
Brakes F/R: Drum/Drum
Kerb weight: 1043.3kg 2298.0lb
Fuel: 91.0L 20.0gal 24.0galUS

9 AC
2-litre Fixed-head Coupe
1937 UK
79.6mph 128.1kmh
0-50mph 80.5kmh: 14.8secs
0-60mph 96.5kmh: 20.6secs
70.0bhp 52.2kW 71.0PS
@ 4000rpm
56.3bhp/ton 55.4bhp/tonne
35.2bhp/L 26.2kW/L 35.6PS/L
43.8ft/sec 13.3m/sec
19.0mpg 15.8mpgUS 14.9L/100km
Petrol 4-stroke piston
1991cc 121.5cu in
In-line 6 3 Carburettor
Compression ratio: 6.5:1
Bore: 65.0mm 2.6in
Stroke: 100.0mm 3.9in
Valve type/No: Overhead 12
Transmission: Manual
No. of forward speeds: 4
Wheels driven: Rear
Brakes F/R: Drum/Drum
Kerb weight: 1263.9kg 2784.0lb
Fuel: 45.5L 10.0gal 12.0galUS

10 AC
2-litre Sports
1938 UK
90.0mph 144.8kmh
0-50mph 80.5kmh: 12.8secs
0-60mph 96.5kmh: 18.3secs
70.0bhp 52.2kW 71.0PS
@ 4000rpm
65.7bhp/ton 64.6bhp/tonne
35.2bhp/L 26.2kW/L 35.6PS/L
43.8ft/sec 13.3m/sec
22.0mpg 18.3mpgUS 12.8L/100km
Petrol 4-stroke piston
1991cc 121.5cu in
In-line 6 3 Carburettor
Compression ratio: 6.5:1
Bore: 65.0mm 2.6in
Stroke: 100.0mm 3.9in
Valve type/No: Overhead 12
Transmission: Manual
No. of forward speeds: 4
Wheels driven: Rear
Brakes F/R: Drum/Drum
Kerb weight: 1084.1kg 2388.0lb
Fuel: 77.3L 17.0gal 20.4galUS

11 AC
2-litre
1939 UK
84.0mph 135.2kmh
0-50mph 80.5kmh: 16.2secs
70.0bhp 52.2kW 71.0PS
@ 4000rpm
56.1bhp/ton 55.2bhp/tonne
35.2bhp/L 26.2kW/L 35.6PS/L
43.8ft/sec 13.3m/sec
28.0mpg 23.3mpgUS 10.1L/100km
Petrol 4-stroke piston
1991cc 121.5cu in
In-line 6 3 Carburettor
Compression ratio: 6.5:1
Bore: 65.0mm 2.6in
Stroke: 100.0mm 3.9in
Valve type/No: Overhead 12
Transmission: Manual
No. of forward speeds: 4
Wheels driven: Rear
Brakes F/R: Drum/Drum
Kerb weight: 1268.5kg 2794.0lb
Fuel: 45.5L 10.0gal 12.0galUS

12 AC
2-litre Saloon
1949 UK
83.0mph 133.5kmh
0-50mph 80.5kmh: 16.0secs
0-60mph 96.5kmh: 22.6secs
74.0bhp 55.2kW 75.0PS
@ 4500rpm
95.0lbft 128.7Nm @ 2500rpm
56.0bhp/ton 55.0bhp/tonne
37.2bhp/L 27.7kW/L 37.7PS/L
49.2ft/sec 15.0m/sec
18.0mph 29.0kmh/1000rpm
22.0mpg 18.3mpgUS 12.8L/100km
Petrol 4-stroke piston
1991cc 121.0cu in
In-line 6 3 Carburettor
Compression ratio: 6.5:1
Bore: 65.0mm 2.6in
Stroke: 100.0mm 3.9in
Valve type/No: Overhead 12
Transmission: Manual
No. of forward speeds: 4
Wheels driven: Rear
Springs F/R: Leaf/Leaf
Brakes F/R: Drum/Drum
Wheelbase: 297.2cm 117.0in
Track F: 139.7cm 55.0in
Track R: 142.2cm 56.0in
Length: 467.4cm 184.0in
Width: 170.2cm 67.0in
Height: 154.9cm 61.0in
Ground clearance: 17.8cm 7.0in
Kerb weight: 1344.3kg 2961.0lb
Fuel: 52.3L 11.5gal 13.8galUS

13 AC
2-litre
1953 UK
84.0mph 135.2kmh
0-50mph 80.5kmh: 14.4secs
0-60mph 96.5kmh: 21.0secs
0-1/4 mile: 22.2secs
74.0bhp 55.2kW 75.0PS
@ 4500rpm
105.0lbft 142.3Nm @ 2750rpm
56.9bhp/ton 56.0bhp/tonne
37.2bhp/L 27.7kW/L 37.7PS/L
49.2ft/sec 15.0m/sec
18.0mph 29.0kmh/1000rpm
19.1mpg 15.9mpgUS 14.8L/100km
Petrol 4-stroke piston
1991cc 121.0cu in
In-line 6
Compression ratio: 6.7:1
Bore: 65.0mm 2.6in
Stroke: 100.0mm 3.9in
Valve type/No: Overhead 12
Transmission: Manual
No. of forward speeds: 4
Wheels driven: Rear
Springs F/R: Leaf/Leaf
Brakes F/R: Drum/Drum
Wheelbase: 297.2cm 117.0in
Track F: 139.7cm 55.0in
Track R: 142.2cm 56.0in
Length: 467.4cm 184.0in
Width: 170.2cm 67.0in
Height: 154.9cm 61.0in
Ground clearance: 17.8cm 7.0in
Kerb weight: 1322.0kg 2912.0lb
Fuel: 52.3L 11.5gal 13.8galUS

14 AC
Ace Roadster
1956 UK
101.9mph 164.0kmh
0-50mph 80.5kmh: 7.7secs
0-60mph 96.5kmh: 11.0secs
0-1/4 mile: 17.8secs
90.0bhp 67.1kW 91.2PS
@ 4500rpm
110.0lbft 149.1Nm @ 2500rpm
105.0bhp/ton 103.2bhp/tonne
45.2bhp/L 33.7kW/L 45.8PS/L
49.2ft/sec 15.0m/sec
Petrol 4-stroke piston
1991cc 121.5cu in
In-line 6
Compression ratio: 8.0:1
Bore: 65.0mm 2.6in
Stroke: 100.1mm 3.9in
Valve type/No: Overhead 12
Transmission: Manual
No. of forward speeds: 4
Wheels driven: Rear
Wheelbase: 228.6cm 90.0in
Track F: 127.0cm 50.0in
Track R: 127.0cm 50.0in
Kerb weight: 871.7kg 1920.0lb

15 AC
Aceca
1956 UK
104.0mph 167.3kmh
0-50mph 80.5kmh: 9.7secs

0-60mph 96.5kmh: 13.4secs
0-1/4 mile: 19.1secs
90.0bhp 67.1kW 91.2PS
@ 4500rpm
110.0lbft 149.1Nm @ 2500rpm
93.5bhp/ton 91.9bhp/tonne
45.2bhp/L 33.7kW/L 45.8PS/L
49.2ft/sec 15.0m/sec
25.0mph 40.2kmh/1000rpm
20.5mpg 17.1mpgUS 13.8L/100km
Petrol 4-stroke piston
1991cc 121.5cu in
In-line 6 1 Carburettor
Compression ratio: 8.0:1
Bore: 65.0mm 2.6in
Stroke: 100.0mm 3.9in
Valve type/No: Overhead 12
Transmission: Manual with overdrive
No. of forward speeds: 7
Wheels driven: Rear
Springs F/R: Leaf/Leaf
Brakes F/R: Drum/Drum
Wheelbase: 228.6cm 90.0in
Track F: 127.0cm 50.0in
Track R: 127.0cm 50.0in
Length: 406.4cm 160.0in
Width: 154.9cm 61.0in
Height: 132.1cm 52.0in
Ground clearance: 15.2cm 6.0in
Kerb weight: 978.8kg 2156.0lb
Fuel: 59.1L 13.0gal 15.6galUS

16 AC
Ace Bristol
1957 UK
115.2mph 185.4kmh
0-50mph 80.5kmh: 6.0secs
0-60mph 96.5kmh: 8.2secs
0-1/4 mile: 16.6secs
125.0bhp 93.2kW 126.7PS
@ 5750rpm
128.0lbft 173.4Nm @ 5000rpm
145.8bhp/ton 143.4bhp/tonne
63.4bhp/L 47.3kW/L 64.3PS/L
60.4ft/sec 18.4m/sec
Petrol 4-stroke piston
1971cc 120.3cu in
In-line 6 3 Carburettor
Compression ratio: 8.5:1
Bore: 66.0mm 2.6in
Stroke: 96.0mm 3.8in
Valve type/No: Overhead 12
Transmission: Manual
No. of forward speeds: 4
Wheels driven: Rear
Wheelbase: 228.6cm 90.0in
Track F: 127.0cm 50.0in
Track R: 127.0cm 50.0in
Kerb weight: 871.7kg 1920.0lb

17 AC
AC-Bristol Zagato
1958 UK
121.0mph 194.7kmh
0-60mph 96.5kmh: 9.0secs
0-1/4 mile: 16.8secs
125.0bhp 93.2kW 126.7PS
@ 6000rpm
141.8bhp/ton 139.4bhp/tonne
63.4bhp/L 47.3kW/L 64.3PS/L
63.0ft/sec 19.2m/sec
Petrol 4-stroke piston
1971cc 120.3cu in
In-line 6 3 Carburettor
Compression ratio: 9.0:1
Bore: 66.0mm 2.6in
Stroke: 96.0mm 3.8in
Valve type/No: Overhead 12
Transmission: Manual
No. of forward speeds: 4
Wheels driven: Rear
Springs F/R: Leaf/Leaf
Brakes F/R: Disc/Drum
Steering: Cam & peg
Wheelbase: 228.6cm 90.0in
Track F: 127.0cm 50.0in
Track R: 127.0cm 50.0in
Length: 400.1cm 157.5in
Width: 153.7cm 60.5in
Height: 126.2cm 49.7in
Kerb weight: 896.6kg 1975.0lb
Fuel: 59.0L 13.0gal 15.6galUS

18 AC
Aceca-Bristol Coupe
1958 UK
103.8mph 167.0kmh
0-50mph 80.5kmh: 6.8secs
0-60mph 96.5kmh: 9.4secs
0-1/4 mile: 17.1secs
105.0bhp 78.3kW 106.5PS
@ 4750rpm
123.0lbft 166.7Nm @ 3750rpm
110.9bhp/ton 109.1bhp/tonne
53.3bhp/L 39.7kW/L 54.0PS/L
49.9ft/sec 15.2m/sec
Petrol 4-stroke piston
1971cc 120.3cu in
In-line 6
Compression ratio: 8.5:1
Bore: 66.0mm 2.6in
Stroke: 96.0mm 3.8in
Valve type/No: Overhead 12
Transmission: Manual
No. of forward speeds: 4
Wheels driven: Rear
Wheelbase: 228.6cm 90.0in
Track F: 127.0cm 50.0in
Track R: 127.0cm 50.0in
Kerb weight: 962.5kg 2120.0lb

19 AC
Bristol
1958 UK
118.0mph 189.9kmh
0-50mph 80.5kmh: 6.8secs
0-60mph 96.5kmh: 9.1secs
0-1/4 mile: 16.5secs
125.0bhp 93.2kW 126.7PS
@ 6000rpm
122.0lbft 165.3Nm @ 4500rpm
151.8bhp/ton 149.2bhp/tonne
63.4bhp/L 47.3kW/L 64.3PS/L
63.0ft/sec 19.2m/sec
20.1mph 32.3kmh/1000rpm
21.6mpg 18.0mpgUS 13.1L/100km
Petrol 4-stroke piston
1971cc 120.3cu in
In-line 6
Compression ratio: 9.0:1
Bore: 66.0mm 2.6in
Stroke: 96.0mm 3.8in
Valve type/No: Overhead 12
Transmission: Manual
No. of forward speeds: 4
Wheels driven: Rear
Springs F/R: Leaf/Leaf
Brakes F/R: Disc/Drum
Wheelbase: 228.6cm 90.0in
Track F: 127.0cm 50.0in
Track R: 127.0cm 50.0in
Length: 386.1cm 152.0in
Width: 149.9cm 59.0in
Height: 124.5cm 49.0in
Ground clearance: 15.2cm 6.0in
Kerb weight: 837.6kg 1845.0lb
Fuel: 59.1L 13.0gal 15.6galUS

20 AC
Bristol D-2
1958 UK
115.0mph 185.0kmh
0-50mph 80.5kmh: 6.0secs
0-60mph 96.5kmh: 7.8secs
0-1/4 mile: 16.0secs
130.0bhp 96.9kW 131.8PS
@ 5750rpm
128.0lbft 173.4Nm @ 4500rpm
151.7bhp/ton 149.1bhp/tonne
66.0bhp/L 49.2kW/L 66.9PS/L
60.4ft/sec 18.4m/sec
20.2mph 32.5kmh/1000rpm
Petrol 4-stroke piston
1971cc 120.3cu in
In-line 6
Compression ratio: 9.0:1
Bore: 66.0mm 2.6in
Stroke: 96.0mm 3.8in
Valve type/No: Overhead 12
Transmission: Manual
No. of forward speeds: 4
Wheels driven: Rear
Wheelbase: 228.6cm 90.0in
Track F: 127.0cm 50.0in
Track R: 127.0cm 50.0in
Length: 386.1cm 152.0in
Width: 151.1cm 59.5in
Height: 124.0cm 48.8in
Kerb weight: 871.7kg 1920.0lb

21 AC
Aceca-Bristol
1960 UK
116.0mph 186.6kmh
0-50mph 80.5kmh: 8.0secs
0-60mph 96.5kmh: 10.3secs
0-1/4 mile: 17.8secs
125.0bhp 93.2kW 126.7PS
@ 6000rpm
122.0lbft 165.3Nm @ 4500rpm
128.2bhp/ton 126.1bhp/tonne
63.4bhp/L 47.3kW/L 64.3PS/L
63.0ft/sec 19.2m/sec
20.2mph 32.5kmh/1000rpm
20.5mpg 17.1mpgUS 13.8L/100km
Petrol 4-stroke piston
1971cc 120.3cu in
In-line 6
Compression ratio: 9.0:1
Bore: 66.0mm 2.6in
Stroke: 96.0mm 3.8in
Valve type/No: Overhead 12
Transmission: Manual
No. of forward speeds: 4
Wheels driven: Rear
Springs F/R: Leaf/Leaf
Brakes F/R: Disc/Drum
Wheelbase: 228.6cm 90.0in
Track F: 127.0cm 50.0in
Track R: 127.0cm 50.0in
Length: 406.4cm 160.0in
Width: 154.9cm 61.0in
Height: 132.1cm 52.0in
Ground clearance: 15.2cm 6.0in
Kerb weight: 991.5kg 2184.0lb
Fuel: 59.1L 13.0gal 15.6galUS

22 AC
Greyhound
1961 UK
107.0mph 172.2kmh
0-50mph 80.5kmh: 9.5secs
0-60mph 96.5kmh: 12.7secs
0-1/4 mile: 19.1secs
125.0bhp 93.2kW 126.7PS
@ 5750rpm
122.0lbft 165.3Nm @ 4500rpm
114.9bhp/ton 113.0bhp/tonne
63.4bhp/L 47.3kW/L 64.3PS/L
60.4ft/sec 18.4m/sec
18.9mph 30.4kmh/1000rpm
18.5mpg 15.4mpgUS 15.3L/100km
Petrol 4-stroke piston
1971cc 120.3cu in
In-line 6
Compression ratio: 9.0:1
Bore: 66.0mm 2.6in
Stroke: 96.0mm 3.8in
Valve type/No: Overhead 12
Transmission: Manual
No. of forward speeds: 4
Wheels driven: Rear
Springs F/R: Coil/Coil
Brakes F/R: Disc/Drum
Wheelbase: 254.0cm 100.0in
Track F: 137.2cm 54.0in
Track R: 137.2cm 54.0in
Length: 444.5cm 175.0in
Width: 166.4cm 65.5in
Height: 133.4cm 52.5in
Ground clearance: 17.8cm 7.0in
Kerb weight: 1105.9kg 2436.0lb
Fuel: 63.7L 14.0gal 16.8galUS

23 AC
Aceca-Buick
1962 UK
115.0mph 185.0kmh
0-50mph 80.5kmh: 6.0secs
0-60mph 96.5kmh: 7.7secs
0-1/4 mile: 15.3secs
185.0bhp 137.9kW 187.6PS
@ 4800rpm
230.0lbft 311.7Nm @ 2800rpm
197.3bhp/ton 194.0bhp/tonne
52.5bhp/L 39.1kW/L 53.2PS/L
37.3ft/sec 11.4m/sec
21.8mph 35.1kmh/1000rpm
Petrol 4-stroke piston
3524cc 215.0cu in
Vee 8
Compression ratio: 10.3:1
Bore: 88.9mm 3.5in
Stroke: 71.1mm 2.8in
Valve type/No: Overhead 16
Transmission: Automatic
No. of forward speeds: 2
Wheels driven: Rear
Wheelbase: 228.6cm 90.0in
Track F: 127.0cm 50.0in
Track R: 127.0cm 50.0in
Length: 406.4cm 160.0in
Width: 154.9cm 61.0in
Height: 132.1cm 52.0in
Ground clearance: 15.2cm 6.0in
Kerb weight: 953.4kg 2100.0lb

24 AC
Greyhound
1962 UK
105.0mph 168.9kmh
0-50mph 80.5kmh: 9.7secs
0-60mph 96.5kmh: 13.5secs
0-1/4 mile: 19.0secs
105.0bhp 78.3kW 106.5PS
@ 4700rpm
129.0lbft 174.8Nm @ 3000rpm
97.6bhp/ton 96.0bhp/tonne
47.4bhp/L 35.3kW/L 48.0PS/L
51.2ft/sec 15.6m/sec
24.6mph 39.6kmh/1000rpm
Petrol 4-stroke piston
2216cc 135.2cu in
In-line 6
Compression ratio: 8.5:1
Bore: 68.6mm 2.7in
Stroke: 99.6mm 3.9in
Valve type/No: Overhead 12
Transmission: Manual with overdrive
Wheels driven: Rear
Wheelbase: 254.0cm 100.0in
Track F: 132.1cm 52.0in
Track R: 131.3cm 51.7in
Length: 444.5cm 175.0in
Width: 166.4cm 65.5in
Height: 135.1cm 53.2in
Ground clearance: 13.2cm 5.2in
Kerb weight: 1094.1kg 2410.0lb

25 AC
Cobra
1965 UK
140.0mph 225.3kmh
0-50mph 80.5kmh: 4.2secs
0-60mph 96.5kmh: 5.5secs
0-1/4 mile: 13.9secs
300.0bhp 223.7kW 304.2PS
@ 5750rpm
285.0lbft 386.2Nm @ 4500rpm
290.3bhp/ton 285.4bhp/tonne
63.5bhp/L 47.3kW/L 64.3PS/L
45.8ft/sec 14.0m/sec
21.3mph 34.3kmh/1000rpm
15.1mpg 12.6mpgUS 18.7L/100km
Petrol 4-stroke piston
4727cc 288.4cu in
Vee 8 1 Carburettor
Compression ratio: 11.0:1
Bore: 101.6mm 4.0in
Stroke: 72.9mm 2.9in
Valve type/No: Overhead 16
Transmission: Manual
No. of forward speeds: 4
Wheels driven: Rear
Springs F/R: Leaf/Leaf
Brakes F/R: Disc/Disc
Steering: Rack & pinion
Wheelbase: 228.6cm 90.0in
Track F: 135.9cm 53.5in
Track R: 136.4cm 53.7in
Length: 401.3cm 158.0in
Width: 160.0cm 63.0in
Height: 121.9cm 48.0in
Ground clearance: 10.2cm 4.0in
Kerb weight: 1051.0kg 2315.0lb
Fuel: 68.2L 15.0gal 18.0galUS

26 AC
428 Fastback
1968 UK
143.0mph 230.1kmh
0-50mph 80.5kmh: 4.6secs
0-60mph 96.5kmh: 6.2secs
0-1/4 mile: 14.2secs
0-1km: 26.2secs
345.0bhp 257.3kW 349.8PS
@ 4600rpm
462.0lbft 626.0Nm @ 2800rpm
236.5bhp/ton 232.6bhp/tonne
49.2bhp/L 36.7kW/L 49.9PS/L
50.9ft/sec 15.5m/sec
29.8mph 47.9kmh/1000rpm
17.0mpg 14.2mpgUS 16.6L/100km
Petrol 4-stroke piston
7014cc 427.9cu in

Vee 8 1 Carburettor
Compression ratio: 10.5:1
Bore: 104.9mm 4.1in
Stroke: 101.2mm 4.0in
Valve type/No: Overhead 16
Transmission: Automatic
No. of forward speeds: 3
Wheels driven: Rear
Springs F/R: Coil/Coil
Brake system: PA
Brakes F/R: Disc/Disc
Steering: Rack & pinion
Wheelbase: 243.8cm 96.0in
Track F: 139.7cm 55.0in
Track R: 142.2cm 56.0in
Length: 450.9cm 177.5in
Width: 170.2cm 67.0in
Height: 127.0cm 50.0in
Ground clearance: 17.8cm 7.0in
Kerb weight: 1483.2kg 3267.0lb
Fuel: 81.9L 18.0gal 21.6galUS

27 AC
Cobra 427 Modified 1965
1989 USA
0-50mph 80.5kmh: 2.7secs
0-60mph 96.5kmh: 3.5secs
0-1/4 mile: 11.5secs
580.0bhp 432.5kW 588.0PS
@ 5750rpm
541.0lbft 733.1Nm @ 3750rpm
513.5bhp/ton 504.9bhp/tonne
78.1bhp/L 58.2kW/L 79.1PS/L
63.6ft/sec 19.4m/sec
Petrol 4-stroke piston
7430cc 453.3cu in
Vee 8 4 Carburettor
Compression ratio: 11.5:1
Bore: 108.1mm 4.3in
Stroke: 101.2mm 4.0in
Valve type/No: Overhead 16
Transmission: Manual
No. of forward speeds: 4
Wheels driven: Rear
Springs F/R: Coil/Coil
Brakes F/R: Disc/Disc
Steering: Rack & pinion
Wheelbase: 228.6cm 90.0in
Track F: 142.2cm 56.0in
Track R: 142.2cm 56.0in
Length: 396.2cm 156.0in
Width: 172.7cm 68.0in
Height: 124.5cm 49.0in
Kerb weight: 1148.6kg 2530.0lb

28 Acura
Integra RS
1986 Japan
120.0mph 193.1kmh
0-60mph 96.5kmh: 9.3secs
0-1/4 mile: 17.0secs
113.0bhp 84.3kW 114.6PS
@ 6250rpm
99.0lbft 134.1Nm @ 5500rpm
102.3bhp/ton 100.6bhp/tonne
71.1bhp/L 53.0kW/L 72.1PS/L
61.5ft/sec 18.8m/sec
29.4mpg 24.5mpgUS 9.6L/100km
Petrol 4-stroke piston
1590cc 97.0cu in
In-line 4 fuel injection
Compression ratio: 9.3:1
Bore: 75.0mm 2.9in
Stroke: 90.0mm 3.5in
Valve type/No: Overhead 16
Transmission: Manual
No. of forward speeds: 5
Wheels driven: Front
Springs F/R: Torsion bar/Coil
Brake system: PA
Brakes F/R: Disc/Disc
Steering: Rack & pinion PA
Wheelbase: 252.0cm 99.2in
Track F: 142.0cm 55.9in
Track R: 143.5cm 56.5in
Length: 435.1cm 171.3in
Width: 166.6cm 65.6in
Height: 134.6cm 53.0in
Ground clearance: 16.0cm 6.3in
Kerb weight: 1123.6kg 2475.0lb
Fuel: 50.0L 11.0gal 13.2galUS

29 Acura
Legend
1986 Japan
129.0mph 207.6kmh
0-60mph 96.5kmh: 8.1secs
0-1/4 mile: 16.4secs
151.0bhp 112.6kW 153.1PS
@ 5800rpm
154.0lbft 208.7Nm @ 4500rpm
107.2bhp/ton 105.4bhp/tonne
60.5bhp/L 45.1kW/L 61.4PS/L
47.5ft/sec 14.5m/sec
24.6mpg 20.5mpgUS 11.5L/100km
Petrol 4-stroke piston
2494cc 152.2cu in
Vee 6 fuel injection
Compression ratio: 9.0:1
Bore: 84.0mm 3.3in
Stroke: 75.0mm 2.9in
Valve type/No: Overhead 24
Transmission: Manual
No. of forward speeds: 5
Wheels driven: Front
Springs F/R: Coil/Coil
Brake system: PA
Brakes F/R: Disc/Disc
Steering: Rack & pinion PA
Wheelbase: 275.8cm 108.6in
Track F: 149.9cm 59.0in
Track R: 146.1cm 57.5in
Length: 503.9cm 198.4in
Width: 173.5cm 68.3in
Height: 138.9cm 54.7in
Ground clearance: 15.0cm 5.9in
Kerb weight: 1432.4kg 3155.0lb
Fuel: 68.1L 15.0gal 18.0galUS

30 Acura
Integra LS
1987 Japan
110.0mph 177.0kmh
0-60mph 96.5kmh: 9.3secs
0-1/4 mile: 17.0secs
113.0bhp 84.3kW 114.6PS
@ 6250rpm
99.0lbft 134.1Nm @ 5500rpm
102.3bhp/ton 100.6bhp/tonne
71.1bhp/L 53.0kW/L 72.1PS/L
61.5ft/sec 18.8m/sec
27.0mpg 22.5mpgUS 10.5L/100km
Petrol 4-stroke piston
1590cc 97.0cu in
In-line 4 fuel injection
Compression ratio: 9.3:1
Bore: 75.0mm 2.9in
Stroke: 90.0mm 3.5in
Valve type/No: Overhead 16
Transmission: Manual
No. of forward speeds: 5
Wheels driven: Front
Springs F/R: Torsion bar/Coil
Brake system: PA
Brakes F/R: Disc/Disc
Steering: Rack & pinion PA
Wheelbase: 252.0cm 99.2in
Track F: 142.0cm 55.9in
Track R: 143.5cm 56.5in
Length: 435.1cm 171.3in
Width: 166.6cm 65.6in
Height: 134.6cm 53.0in
Kerb weight: 1123.6kg 2475.0lb
Fuel: 50.0L 11.0gal 13.2galUS

31 Acura
Integra LS Special Edition
1988 Japan
112.0mph 180.2kmh
0-50mph 80.5kmh: 6.4secs
0-60mph 96.5kmh: 9.1secs
0-1/4 mile: 16.8secs
113.0bhp 84.3kW 114.6PS
@ 6250rpm
99.0lbft 134.1Nm @ 5500rpm
104.4bhp/ton 102.6bhp/tonne
71.1bhp/L 53.0kW/L 72.1PS/L
61.5ft/sec 18.8m/sec
30.0mpg 25.0mpgUS 9.4L/100km
Petrol 4-stroke piston
1590cc 97.0cu in
In-line 4 fuel injection
Compression ratio: 9.3:1
Bore: 75.0mm 2.9in
Stroke: 90.0mm 3.5in
Valve type/No: Overhead 16
Transmission: Manual
No. of forward speeds: 5
Wheels driven: Front
Springs F/R: Torsion bar/Coil
Brake system: PA
Brakes F/R: Disc/Disc
Steering: Rack & pinion PA
Wheelbase: 245.1cm 96.5in
Track F: 142.0cm 55.9in
Track R: 143.5cm 56.5in
Length: 428.0cm 168.5in
Width: 164.8cm 64.9in
Height: 134.4cm 52.9in
Kerb weight: 1100.9kg 2425.0lb
Fuel: 50.0L 11.0gal 13.2galUS

32 Acura
Integra LS
1989 Japan
112.0mph 180.2kmh
0-50mph 80.5kmh: 6.9secs
0-60mph 96.5kmh: 9.7secs
0-1/4 mile: 17.3secs
118.0bhp 88.0kW 119.6PS
@ 6500rpm
103.0lbft 139.6Nm @ 5500rpm
108.5bhp/ton 106.7bhp/tonne
74.2bhp/L 55.3kW/L 75.2PS/L
63.9ft/sec 19.5m/sec
30.0mpg 25.0mpgUS 9.4L/100km
Petrol 4-stroke piston
1590cc 97.0cu in
In-line 4 fuel injection
Compression ratio: 9.5:1
Bore: 75.0mm 2.9in
Stroke: 90.0mm 3.5in
Valve type/No: Overhead 16
Transmission: Manual
No. of forward speeds: 5
Wheels driven: Front
Springs F/R: Torsion bar/Coil
Brake system: PA
Brakes F/R: Disc/Disc
Steering: Rack & pinion PA
Wheelbase: 245.1cm 96.5in
Track F: 142.0cm 55.9in
Track R: 143.5cm 56.5in
Length: 428.0cm 168.5in
Width: 163.8cm 64.5in
Height: 134.4cm 52.9in
Kerb weight: 1105.5kg 2435.0lb
Fuel: 50.0L 11.0gal 13.2galUS

33 Acura
Legend Coupe L
1989 Japan
130.0mph 209.2kmh
0-50mph 80.5kmh: 5.9secs
0-60mph 96.5kmh: 8.0secs
0-1/4 mile: 16.2secs
161.0bhp 120.1kW 163.2PS
@ 5900rpm
162.0lbft 219.5Nm @ 4500rpm
112.0bhp/ton 110.1bhp/tonne
60.2bhp/L 44.9kW/L 61.0PS/L
48.3ft/sec 14.7m/sec
23.4mpg 19.5mpgUS 12.1L/100km
Petrol 4-stroke piston
2675cc 163.2cu in
Vee 6 fuel injection
Compression ratio: 9.0:1
Bore: 87.0mm 3.4in
Stroke: 75.0mm 2.9in
Valve type/No: Overhead 24
Transmission: Manual
No. of forward speeds: 5
Wheels driven: Front
Springs F/R: Coil/Coil
Brake system: PA ABS
Brakes F/R: Disc/Disc
Steering: Rack & pinion PA
Wheelbase: 270.5cm 106.5in
Track F: 150.1cm 59.1in
Track R: 150.1cm 59.1in
Length: 477.5cm 188.0in
Width: 174.5cm 68.7in
Height: 136.9cm 53.9in
Ground clearance: 17.3cm 6.8in
Kerb weight: 1461.9kg 3220.0lb
Fuel: 68.1L 15.0gal 18.0galUS

34 Acura
Integra GS
1990 Japan
130.0mph 209.2kmh
0-50mph 80.5kmh: 6.6secs
0-60mph 96.5kmh: 9.4secs
0-1/4 mile: 16.6secs
130.0bhp 96.9kW 131.8PS
@ 6000rpm
121.0lbft 164.0Nm @ 5000rpm
108.2bhp/ton 106.4bhp/tonne
70.9bhp/L 52.9kW/L 71.9PS/L
58.3ft/sec 17.8m/sec
32.3mpg 26.9mpgUS 8.7L/100km
Petrol 4-stroke piston
1834cc 111.9cu in
In-line 4 fuel injection
Compression ratio: 9.2:1
Bore: 81.0mm 3.2in
Stroke: 89.0mm 3.5in
Valve type/No: Overhead 16
Transmission: Manual
No. of forward speeds: 5
Wheels driven: Front
Springs F/R: Coil/Coil
Brake system: PA ABS
Brakes F/R: Disc/Disc
Steering: Rack & pinion PA
Wheelbase: 255.0cm 100.4in
Track F: 147.6cm 58.1in
Track R: 147.6cm 58.1in
Length: 439.2cm 172.9in
Width: 171.2cm 67.4in
Height: 132.6cm 52.2in
Ground clearance: 15.0cm 5.9in
Kerb weight: 1221.3kg 2690.0lb
Fuel: 50.0L 11.0gal 13.2galUS

35 Acura
Legend Coupe
1990 Japan
130.0mph 209.2kmh
0-50mph 80.5kmh: 5.9secs
0-60mph 96.5kmh: 8.0secs
0-1/4 mile: 16.2secs
161.0bhp 120.1kW 163.2PS
@ 5900rpm
162.0lbft 219.5Nm @ 4500rpm
112.0bhp/ton 110.1bhp/tonne
60.2bhp/L 44.9kW/L 61.0PS/L
48.3ft/sec 14.7m/sec
23.4mpg 19.5mpgUS 12.1L/100km
Petrol 4-stroke piston
2675cc 163.2cu in
Vee 6 fuel injection
Compression ratio: 9.0:1
Bore: 87.0mm 3.4in
Stroke: 75.0mm 2.9in
Valve type/No: Overhead 24
Transmission: Manual
No. of forward speeds: 5
Wheels driven: Front
Springs F/R: Coil/Coil
Brake system: PA ABS
Brakes F/R: Disc/Disc
Steering: Rack & pinion PA
Wheelbase: 270.5cm 106.5in
Track F: 150.1cm 59.1in
Track R: 150.1cm 59.1in
Length: 477.5cm 188.0in
Width: 174.5cm 68.7in
Height: 136.9cm 53.9in
Kerb weight: 1461.9kg 3220.0lb
Fuel: 68.1L 15.0gal 18.0galUS

36 Acura
NSX
1990 Japan
168.0mph 270.3kmh
0-50mph 80.5kmh: 4.4secs
0-60mph 96.5kmh: 5.7secs
0-1/4 mile: 14.0secs
270.0bhp 201.3kW 273.7PS
@ 7100rpm
210.0lbft 284.6Nm @ 5300rpm
202.6bhp/ton 199.2bhp/tonne
90.7bhp/L 67.6kW/L 91.9PS/L
60.5ft/sec 18.5m/sec
27.6mpg 23.0mpgUS 10.2L/100km
Petrol 4-stroke piston
2977cc 181.6cu in
Vee 6 fuel injection
Compression ratio: 10.2:1
Bore: 90.0mm 3.5in
Stroke: 78.0mm 3.1in
Valve type/No: Overhead 24
Transmission: Manual
No. of forward speeds: 5
Wheels driven: Rear
Springs F/R: Coil/Coil
Brake system: PA ABS
Brakes F/R: Disc/Disc
Steering: Rack & pinion PA
Wheelbase: 253.0cm 99.6in
Track F: 150.9cm 59.4in
Track R: 152.9cm 60.2in
Length: 440.4cm 173.4in
Width: 181.1cm 71.3in
Height: 117.1cm 46.1in

Ground clearance: 13.5cm 5.3in
Kerb weight: 1355.2kg 2985.0lb
Fuel: 70.0L 15.4gal 18.5galUS

37 Acura
Legend LS
1991 Japan
135.0mph 217.2kmh
0-50mph 80.5kmh: 6.0secs
0-60mph 96.5kmh: 7.9secs
0-1/4 mile: 16.1secs
200.0bhp 149.1kW 202.8PS
@ 5500rpm
210.0lbft 284.6Nm @ 4500rpm
128.0bhp/ton 125.9bhp/tonne
62.4bhp/L 46.5kW/L 63.2PS/L
50.6ft/sec 15.4m/sec
22.8mpg 19.0mpgUS 12.4L/100km
Petrol 4-stroke piston
3206cc 195.6cu in
Vee 6 fuel injection
Compression ratio: 9.6:1
Bore: 90.0mm 3.5in
Stroke: 84.0mm 3.3in
Valve type/No: Overhead 24
Transmission: Automatic
No. of forward speeds: 4
Wheels driven: Front
Springs F/R: Coil/Coil
Brake system: PA ABS
Brakes F/R: Disc/Disc
Steering: Rack & pinion PA
Wheelbase: 291.1cm 114.6in
Track F: 154.9cm 61.0in
Track R: 153.9cm 60.6in
Length: 495.0cm 194.9in
Width: 181.1cm 71.3in
Height: 140.0cm 55.1in
Ground clearance: 15.2cm 6.0in
Kerb weight: 1589.0kg 3500.0lb
Fuel: 68.1L 15.0gal 18.0galUS

38 AJS
9hp Saloon
1930 UK
56.9mph 91.6kmh
40.0mpg 33.3mpgUS 7.1L/100km
Petrol 4-stroke piston
1018cc 62.1cu in
In-line 4
Bore: 60.0mm 2.4in
Stroke: 90.0mm 3.5in
Transmission: Manual
No. of forward speeds: 3
Wheels driven: Rear
Brakes F/R: Drum/Drum
Wheelbase: 232.4cm 91.5in
Track F: 114.3cm 45.0in
Track R: 114.3cm 45.0in
Length: 337.8cm 133.0in
Width: 149.9cm 59.0in
Height: 170.2cm 67.0in
Kerb weight: 813.6kg 1792.0lb
Fuel: 36.4L 8.0gal 9.6galUS

39 Alfa Romeo
Supercharged Straight Eight
1931 Italy
106.8mph 171.8kmh
14.0mpg 11.7mpgUS 20.2L/100km
Petrol 4-stroke piston
2336cc 142.5cu in supercharged
In-line 8
Bore: 65.0mm 2.6in
Stroke: 88.0mm 3.5in
Transmission: Manual
No. of forward speeds: 4
Wheels driven: Rear
Brakes F/R: Drum/Drum
Wheelbase: 276.9cm 109.0in
Track F: 137.2cm 54.0in
Track R: 137.2cm 54.0in
Length: 396.2cm 156.0in
Width: 165.1cm 65.0in
Height: 111.8cm 44.0in
Kerb weight: 1118.7kg 2464.0lb
Fuel: 109.2L 24.0gal 28.8galUS

40 Alfa Romeo
1750
1932 Italy
91.0mph 146.4kmh
0-50mph 80.5kmh: 9.2secs
0-60mph 96.5kmh: 13.9secs
0-1/4 mile: 19.3secs
85.0bhp 63.4kW 86.2PS
@ 4500rpm
105.0lbft 142.3Nm
81.0bhp/ton 79.7bhp/tonne
48.5bhp/L 36.2kW/L 49.2PS/L
43.2ft/sec 13.2m/sec
Petrol 4-stroke piston
1752cc 106.9cu in supercharged
In-line 6
Compression ratio: 5.0:1
Bore: 65.0mm 2.6in
Stroke: 87.9mm 3.5in
Valve type/No: Overhead 12
Transmission: Manual
No. of forward speeds: 4
Wheels driven: Rear
Wheelbase: 274.3cm 108.0in
Track F: 137.9cm 54.3in
Track R: 137.9cm 54.3in
Kerb weight: 1066.9kg 2350.0lb

41 Alfa Romeo
8C2300
1932 Italy
110.0mph 177.0kmh
0-60mph 96.5kmh: 10.8secs
150.0bhp 111.9kW 152.1PS
@ 5200rpm
134.4bhp/ton 132.2bhp/tonne
64.2bhp/L 47.9kW/L 65.1PS/L
50.0ft/sec 15.2m/sec
Petrol 4-stroke piston
2336cc 142.5cu in supercharged
In-line 8 1 Carburettor
Bore: 65.0mm 2.6in
Stroke: 88.0mm 3.5in
Valve type/No: Overhead 16
Transmission: Manual
No. of forward speeds: 4
Wheels driven: Rear
Springs F/R: Leaf/Leaf
Brakes F/R: Drum/Drum
Steering: Worm & sector
Wheelbase: 274.3cm 108.0in
Track F: 137.2cm 54.0in
Track R: 137.2cm 54.0in
Kerb weight: 1135.0kg 2500.0lb

42 Alfa Romeo
2.3 Mille Miglia
1933 Italy
108.0mph 173.8kmh
0-50mph 80.5kmh: 6.5secs
0-60mph 96.5kmh: 9.4secs
0-1/4 mile: 17.0secs
140.0bhp 104.4kW 141.9PS
@ 5200rpm
190.0lbft 257.5Nm @ 3000rpm
120.6bhp/ton 118.6bhp/tonne
59.9bhp/L 44.7kW/L 60.8PS/L
50.1ft/sec 15.3m/sec
20.9mph 33.6kmh/1000rpm
Petrol 4-stroke piston
2336cc 142.5cu in
In-line 8
Compression ratio: 5.8:1
Bore: 65.0mm 2.6in
Stroke: 88.1mm 3.5in
Valve type/No: Overhead 16
Transmission: Manual
No. of forward speeds: 4
Wheels driven: Rear
Wheelbase: 274.3cm 108.0in
Track F: 142.2cm 56.0in
Track R: 142.2cm 56.0in
Length: 393.7cm 155.0in
Width: 170.2cm 67.0in
Height: 111.8cm 44.0in
Kerb weight: 1180.4kg 2600.0lb

43 Alfa Romeo
1900
1953 Italy
105.5mph 169.7kmh
0-50mph 80.5kmh: 12.8secs
0-60mph 96.5kmh: 17.1secs
0-1/4 mile: 21.1secs
93.0bhp 69.3kW 94.3PS
@ 5400rpm
96.0lbft 130.1Nm @ 3000rpm
80.8bhp/ton 79.5bhp/tonne
49.4bhp/L 36.8kW/L 50.0PS/L
51.9ft/sec 15.8m/sec
18.6mph 29.9kmh/1000rpm
24.6mpg 20.5mpgUS 11.5L/100km
Petrol 4-stroke piston
1884cc 114.9cu in
In-line 4
Compression ratio: 7.5:1
Bore: 82.5mm 3.2in
Stroke: 88.0mm 3.5in
Valve type/No: Overhead 8
Transmission: Manual
No. of forward speeds: 4
Wheels driven: Rear
Springs F/R: Coil/Coil
Brakes F/R: Drum/Drum
Wheelbase: 262.9cm 103.5in
Track F: 132.1cm 52.0in
Track R: 132.1cm 52.0in
Length: 442.0cm 174.0in
Width: 160.0cm 63.0in
Height: 148.6cm 58.5in
Ground clearance: 17.0cm 6.7in
Kerb weight: 1170.4kg 2578.0lb
Fuel: 52.3L 11.5gal 13.8galUS

44 Alfa Romeo
B.A.T.7 Scaglione
1954 Italy
115.0mph 185.0kmh
115.0bhp 85.8kW 116.6PS
@ 5500rpm
117.1bhp/ton 115.1bhp/tonne
58.2bhp/L 43.4kW/L 59.0PS/L
52.9ft/sec 16.1m/sec
Petrol 4-stroke piston
1975cc 120.5cu in
In-line 4 2 Carburettor
Compression ratio: 8.0:1
Bore: 84.5mm 3.3in
Stroke: 88.0mm 3.5in
Valve type/No: Overhead 8
Transmission: Manual
No. of forward speeds: 5
Wheels driven: Rear
Springs F/R: Coil/Coil
Brakes F/R: Drum/Drum
Steering: Worm & roller
Wheelbase: 249.9cm 98.4in
Track F: 131.8cm 51.9in
Track R: 132.6cm 52.2in
Length: 454.2cm 178.8in
Width: 189.2cm 74.5in
Height: 129.0cm 50.8in
Kerb weight: 998.8kg 2200.0lb
Fuel: 79.9L 17.6gal 21.1galUS

45 Alfa Romeo
Giulietta Spyder
1956 Italy
100.0mph 160.9kmh
0-50mph 80.5kmh: 10.0secs
0-60mph 96.5kmh: 14.8secs
0-1/4 mile: 20.0secs
65.0bhp 48.5kW 65.9PS
@ 5500rpm
79.5lbft 107.7Nm @ 4000rpm
75.0bhp/ton 73.8bhp/tonne
50.4bhp/L 37.6kW/L 51.1PS/L
45.1ft/sec 13.7m/sec
15.0mph 24.1kmh/1000rpm
Petrol 4-stroke piston
1290cc 78.7cu in
In-line 4
Compression ratio: 8.0:1
Bore: 73.9mm 2.9in
Stroke: 74.9mm 2.9in
Valve type/No: Overhead 8
Transmission: Manual
No. of forward speeds: 4
Wheels driven: Rear
Wheelbase: 221.0cm 87.0in
Track F: 127.0cm 50.0in
Track R: 127.0cm 50.0in
Kerb weight: 880.8kg 1940.0lb

46 Alfa Romeo
1300 SV Spider
1958 Italy
104.6mph 168.3kmh
0-50mph 80.5kmh: 9.7secs
0-60mph 96.5kmh: 14.1secs
0-1/4 mile: 17.6secs
90.0bhp 67.1kW 91.2PS
@ 6000rpm
86.8lbft 117.6Nm @ 4500rpm
98.3bhp/ton 96.7bhp/tonne
69.8bhp/L 52.0kW/L 70.7PS/L
49.2ft/sec 15.0m/sec
Petrol 4-stroke piston
1290cc 78.7cu in
In-line 4
Compression ratio: 9.5:1
Bore: 73.9mm 2.9in
Stroke: 74.9mm 2.9in
Valve type/No: Overhead 8
Transmission: Manual
No. of forward speeds: 4
Wheels driven: Rear
Wheelbase: 220.0cm 86.6in
Track F: 127.0cm 50.0in
Track R: 127.0cm 50.0in
Kerb weight: 930.7kg 2050.0lb

47 Alfa Romeo
2000 Spider
1959 Italy
111.3mph 179.1kmh
0-50mph 80.5kmh: 10.9secs
0-60mph 96.5kmh: 14.2secs
0-1/4 mile: 19.5secs
115.0bhp 85.8kW 116.6PS
@ 5500rpm
115.0lbft 155.8Nm @ 3700rpm
93.0bhp/ton 91.4bhp/tonne
58.2bhp/L 43.4kW/L 59.0PS/L
52.9ft/sec 16.1m/sec
18.8mph 30.2kmh/1000rpm
Petrol 4-stroke piston
1975cc 120.5cu in
In-line 4
Compression ratio: 8.5:1
Bore: 84.6mm 3.3in
Stroke: 87.9mm 3.5in
Valve type/No: Overhead 8
Transmission: Manual
No. of forward speeds: 5
Wheels driven: Rear
Wheelbase: 250.2cm 98.5in
Track F: 140.2cm 55.2in
Track R: 136.9cm 53.9in
Length: 449.6cm 177.0in
Width: 166.1cm 65.4in
Height: 135.9cm 53.5in
Kerb weight: 1257.6kg 2770.0lb

48 Alfa Romeo
Super Spider
1959 Italy
0-50mph 80.5kmh: 7.3secs
0-60mph 96.5kmh: 11.0secs
0-1/4 mile: 17.1secs
103.0bhp 76.8kW 104.4PS
@ 6000rpm
86.8lbft 117.6Nm @ 4500rpm
113.1bhp/ton 111.2bhp/tonne
79.8bhp/L 59.5kW/L 80.9PS/L
49.2ft/sec 15.0m/sec
18.6mph 29.9kmh/1000rpm
Petrol 4-stroke piston
1290cc 78.7cu in
In-line 4
Compression ratio: 9.5:1
Bore: 73.9mm 2.9in
Stroke: 74.9mm 2.9in
Valve type/No: Overhead 8
Transmission: Manual
No. of forward speeds: 4
Wheels driven: Rear
Wheelbase: 220.0cm 86.6in
Track F: 128.5cm 50.6in
Track R: 127.0cm 50.0in
Length: 386.1cm 152.0in
Width: 157.5cm 62.0in
Height: 132.1cm 52.0in
Kerb weight: 926.2kg 2040.0lb

49 Alfa Romeo
2000
1960 Italy
100.0mph 160.9kmh
0-50mph 80.5kmh: 11.5secs
0-60mph 96.5kmh: 15.2secs
0-1/4 mile: 19.8secs
105.0bhp 78.3kW 106.5PS
@ 5300rpm
112.0lbft 151.8Nm @ 3500rpm
79.7bhp/ton 78.4bhp/tonne
53.2bhp/L 39.6kW/L 53.9PS/L
50.9ft/sec 15.5m/sec
18.8mph 30.2kmh/1000rpm
Petrol 4-stroke piston
1975cc 120.5cu in
In-line 4 1 Carburettor
Compression ratio: 8.3:1
Bore: 84.6mm 3.3in

Stroke: 87.9mm 3.5in
Valve type/No: Overhead 8
Transmission: Manual
No. of forward speeds: 5
Wheels driven: Rear
Wheelbase: 271.8cm 107.0in
Track F: 140.0cm 55.1in
Track R: 137.2cm 54.0in
Length: 472.4cm 186.0in
Width: 170.2cm 67.0in
Height: 142.5cm 56.1in
Kerb weight: 1339.3kg 2950.0lb

50 Alfa Romeo

Giulia SS
1961 Italy
112.0mph 180.2kmh
0-60mph 96.5kmh: 12.0secs
0-1/4 mile: 18.0secs
129.0bhp 96.2kW 130.8PS
@ 6500rpm
96.0lbft 130.1Nm @ 4500rpm
127.1bhp/ton 124.9bhp/tonne
82.2bhp/L 61.3kW/L 83.3PS/L
58.3ft/sec 17.8m/sec
Petrol 4-stroke piston
1570cc 95.8cu in
In-line 4 2 Carburettor
Compression ratio: 9.7:1
Bore: 78.0mm 3.1in
Stroke: 82.0mm 3.2in
Valve type/No: Overhead 8
Transmission: Manual
No. of forward speeds: 5
Wheels driven: Rear
Springs F/R: Coil/Coil
Brake system: PA
Brakes F/R: Disc/Drum
Steering: Worm & roller
Wheelbase: 225.0cm 88.6in
Track F: 129.0cm 50.8in
Track R: 126.7cm 49.9in
Length: 412.0cm 162.2in
Width: 155.4cm 61.2in
Height: 127.5cm 50.2in
Kerb weight: 1032.4kg 2274.0lb
Fuel: 79.9L 17.6gal 21.1galUS

51 Alfa Romeo

Giulietta Sprint
1961 Italy
103.0mph 165.7kmh
0-50mph 80.5kmh: 9.1secs
0-60mph 96.5kmh: 13.2secs
0-1/4 mile: 19.2secs
92.0bhp 68.6kW 93.3PS
@ 6000rpm
79.6lbft 107.9Nm @ 4000rpm
98.6bhp/ton 97.0bhp/tonne
71.3bhp/L 53.2kW/L 72.3PS/L
49.2ft/sec 15.0m/sec
16.7mph 26.9kmh/1000rpm
Petrol 4-stroke piston
1290cc 78.7cu in
In-line 4 1 Carburettor
Compression ratio: 8.5:1
Bore: 73.9mm 2.9in
Stroke: 74.9mm 2.9in
Valve type/No: Overhead 8
Transmission: Manual
No. of forward speeds: 4
Wheels driven: Rear
Wheelbase: 238.0cm 93.7in
Track F: 128.5cm 50.6in
Track R: 127.0cm 50.0in
Length: 398.0cm 156.7in
Width: 153.4cm 60.4in
Height: 131.8cm 51.9in
Ground clearance: 17.8cm 7.0in
Kerb weight: 948.9kg 2090.0lb

52 Alfa Romeo

Giulietta ti
1961 Italy
97.0mph 156.1kmh
0-50mph 80.5kmh: 12.1secs
0-60mph 96.5kmh: 17.6secs
0-1/4 mile: 20.8secs
65.0bhp 48.5kW 65.9PS
@ 5500rpm
69.0lbft 93.5Nm @ 3500rpm
70.0bhp/ton 68.9bhp/tonne
50.4bhp/L 37.6kW/L 51.1PS/L
45.1ft/sec 13.7m/sec
15.7mph 25.3kmh/1000rpm
28.8mpg 24.0mpgUS 9.8L/100km
Petrol 4-stroke piston
1290cc 78.7cu in
In-line 4
Compression ratio: 8.5:1
Bore: 74.0mm 2.9in
Stroke: 75.0mm 2.9in
Valve type/No: Overhead 8
Transmission: Manual
No. of forward speeds: 4
Wheels driven: Rear
Springs F/R: Coil/Coil
Brakes F/R: Drum/Drum
Wheelbase: 238.8cm 94.0in
Track F: 127.0cm 50.0in
Track R: 128.3cm 50.5in
Length: 400.1cm 157.5in
Width: 156.2cm 61.5in
Height: 142.2cm 56.0in
Ground clearance: 14.0cm 5.5in
Kerb weight: 943.9kg 2079.0lb
Fuel: 40.0L 8.8gal 10.6galUS

53 Alfa Romeo

Sprint Speciale
1961 Italy
120.0mph 193.1kmh
0-50mph 80.5kmh: 8.2secs
0-60mph 96.5kmh: 12.3secs
0-1/4 mile: 18.4secs
116.0bhp 86.5kW 117.6PS
@ 6500rpm
96.2lbft 130.4Nm @ 4500rpm
123.1bhp/ton 121.1bhp/tonne
89.9bhp/L 67.0kW/L 91.2PS/L
53.3ft/sec 16.2m/sec
18.3mph 29.4kmh/1000rpm
Petrol 4-stroke piston
1290cc 78.7cu in
In-line 4 1 Carburettor
Compression ratio: 9.5:1
Bore: 73.9mm 2.9in
Stroke: 74.9mm 2.9in
Valve type/No: Overhead 8
Transmission: Manual
No. of forward speeds: 5
Wheels driven: Rear
Wheelbase: 225.0cm 88.6in
Track F: 129.3cm 50.9in
Track R: 127.0cm 50.0in
Length: 424.2cm 167.0in
Width: 165.9cm 65.3in
Height: 124.0cm 48.8in
Ground clearance: 17.8cm 7.0in
Kerb weight: 957.9kg 2110.0lb

54 Alfa Romeo

Sprint Zagato
1961 Italy
120.0mph 193.1kmh
0-50mph 80.5kmh: 8.1secs
0-60mph 96.5kmh: 11.2secs
0-1/4 mile: 17.8secs
116.0bhp 86.5kW 117.6PS
@ 6500rpm
96.0lbft 130.1Nm @ 4500rpm
137.5bhp/ton 135.2bhp/tonne
89.9bhp/L 67.0kW/L 91.2PS/L
53.3ft/sec 16.2m/sec
18.2mph 29.3kmh/1000rpm
Petrol 4-stroke piston
1290cc 78.7cu in
In-line 4 1 Carburettor
Compression ratio: 9.7:1
Bore: 73.9mm 2.9in
Stroke: 74.9mm 2.9in
Valve type/No: Overhead 8
Transmission: Manual
No. of forward speeds: 5
Wheels driven: Rear
Wheelbase: 224.8cm 88.5in
Track F: 129.0cm 50.8in
Track R: 127.0cm 50.0in
Length: 384.8cm 151.5in
Width: 152.9cm 60.2in
Height: 123.2cm 48.5in
Ground clearance: 13.0cm 5.1in
Kerb weight: 858.1kg 1890.0lb

55 Alfa Romeo

2600
1962 Italy
124.0mph 199.5kmh
0-50mph 80.5kmh: 7.7secs
0-60mph 96.5kmh: 11.1secs
0-1/4 mile: 17.6secs
145.0bhp 108.1kW 147.0PS
@ 5900rpm
140.0lbft 189.7Nm @ 4000rpm
109.9bhp/ton 108.1bhp/tonne
56.1bhp/L 41.8kW/L 56.9PS/L
51.3ft/sec 15.6m/sec
19.5mph 31.4kmh/1000rpm
Petrol 4-stroke piston
2584cc 157.7cu in
In-line 6
Compression ratio: 9.0:1
Bore: 83.1mm 3.3in
Stroke: 79.5mm 3.1in
Valve type/No: Overhead 12
Transmission: Manual
No. of forward speeds: 5
Wheels driven: Rear
Wheelbase: 249.9cm 98.4in
Track F: 140.0cm 55.1in
Track R: 136.9cm 53.9in
Length: 450.1cm 177.2in
Width: 160.0cm 63.0in
Height: 133.1cm 52.4in
Ground clearance: 15.2cm 6.0in
Kerb weight: 1341.6kg 2955.0lb

56 Alfa Romeo

2600 Saloon
1963 Italy
109.0mph 175.4kmh
0-50mph 80.5kmh: 9.4secs
0-60mph 96.5kmh: 13.0secs
0-1/4 mile: 18.5secs
130.0bhp 96.9kW 131.8PS
@ 5900rpm
148.0lbft 200.5Nm @ 3400rpm
93.9bhp/ton 92.4bhp/tonne
50.3bhp/L 37.5kW/L 51.0PS/L
51.3ft/sec 15.6m/sec
18.0mph 29.0kmh/1000rpm
19.3mpg 16.1mpgUS 14.6L/100km
Petrol 4-stroke piston
2582cc 157.5cu in
In-line 6 2 Carburettor
Compression ratio: 8.5:1
Bore: 83.0mm 3.3in
Stroke: 79.6mm 3.1in
Valve type/No: Overhead 12
Transmission: Manual
No. of forward speeds: 5
Wheels driven: Rear
Springs F/R: Coil/Coil
Brake system: PA
Brakes F/R: Disc/Drum
Steering: Worm & roller
Wheelbase: 271.8cm 107.0in
Track F: 139.7cm 55.0in
Track R: 137.2cm 54.0in
Length: 472.4cm 186.0in
Width: 170.2cm 67.0in
Height: 148.6cm 58.5in
Ground clearance: 20.3cm 8.0in
Kerb weight: 1407.4kg 3100.0lb
Fuel: 60.1L 13.2gal 15.9galUS

57 Alfa Romeo

Giulia ti
1963 Italy
107.5mph 173.0kmh
0-50mph 80.5kmh: 9.8secs
0-60mph 96.5kmh: 13.1secs
0-1/4 mile: 18.9secs
92.0bhp 68.6kW 93.3PS
@ 6000rpm
92.0bhp/ton 90.5bhp/tonne
58.6bhp/L 43.7kW/L 59.4PS/L
53.8ft/sec 16.4m/sec
16.9mph 27.2kmh/1000rpm
26.6mpg 22.1mpgUS 10.6L/100km
Petrol 4-stroke piston
1570cc 95.8cu in
In-line 4 1 Carburettor
Compression ratio: 9.0:1
Bore: 78.0mm 3.1in
Stroke: 82.0mm 3.2in
Valve type/No: Overhead 8
Transmission: Manual
No. of forward speeds: 5
Wheels driven: Rear
Springs F/R: Coil/Coil
Brake system: PA
Brakes F/R: Disc/Disc
Steering: Recirculating ball
Wheelbase: 250.2cm 98.5in
Track F: 132.1cm 52.0in
Track R: 127.0cm 50.0in
Length: 414.0cm 163.0in
Width: 157.5cm 62.0in
Height: 147.3cm 58.0in
Ground clearance: 16.5cm 6.5in
Kerb weight: 1017.0kg 2240.0lb
Fuel: 45.5L 10.0gal 12.0galUS

58 Alfa Romeo

Giulia 1600 Spider
1964 Italy
108.0mph 173.8kmh
0-50mph 80.5kmh: 9.4secs
0-60mph 96.5kmh: 12.9secs
0-1/4 mile: 18.8secs
92.0bhp 68.6kW 93.3PS
@ 6200rpm
108.0lbft 146.3Nm @ 3700rpm
99.8bhp/ton 98.1bhp/tonne
58.6bhp/L 43.7kW/L 59.4PS/L
55.6ft/sec 16.9m/sec
16.9mph 27.2kmh/1000rpm
28.5mpg 23.7mpgUS 9.9L/100km
Petrol 4-stroke piston
1570cc 95.8cu in
In-line 4 1 Carburettor
Compression ratio: 9.0:1
Bore: 78.0mm 3.1in
Stroke: 82.0mm 3.2in
Valve type/No: Overhead 8
Transmission: Manual
No. of forward speeds: 5
Wheels driven: Rear
Springs F/R: Coil/Coil
Brakes F/R: Drum/Drum
Steering: Worm & roller
Wheelbase: 226.1cm 89.0in
Track F: 129.5cm 51.0in
Track R: 127.0cm 50.0in
Length: 396.2cm 156.0in
Width: 154.9cm 61.0in
Height: 129.5cm 51.0in
Ground clearance: 14.0cm 5.5in
Kerb weight: 937.5kg 2065.0lb
Fuel: 53.2L 11.7gal 14.1galUS

59 Alfa Romeo

Sprint GT
1964 Italy
112.0mph 180.2kmh
0-50mph 80.5kmh: 8.2secs
0-60mph 96.5kmh: 10.6secs
0-1/4 mile: 18.5secs
122.0bhp 91.0kW 123.7PS
@ 6000rpm
103.0lbft 139.6Nm @ 3000rpm
124.2bhp/ton 122.1bhp/tonne
77.7bhp/L 57.9kW/L 78.8PS/L
53.8ft/sec 16.4m/sec
19.6mph 31.5kmh/1000rpm
Petrol 4-stroke piston
1570cc 95.8cu in
In-line 4 2 Carburettor
Compression ratio: 9.0:1
Bore: 77.8mm 3.1in
Stroke: 82.0mm 3.2in
Valve type/No: Overhead 8
Transmission: Manual
No. of forward speeds: 5
Wheels driven: Rear
Springs F/R: Coil/Coil
Brakes F/R: Disc/Disc
Steering: Worm & sector
Wheelbase: 236.2cm 93.0in
Track F: 130.8cm 51.5in
Track R: 127.0cm 50.0in
Length: 408.9cm 161.0in
Width: 157.5cm 62.0in
Height: 132.1cm 52.0in
Ground clearance: 12.7cm 5.0in
Kerb weight: 998.8kg 2200.0lb
Fuel: 46.2L 10.1gal 12.2galUS

60 Alfa Romeo

Giulia ti
1965 Italy
102.0mph 164.1kmh
0-50mph 80.5kmh: 9.7secs
0-60mph 96.5kmh: 13.2secs
0-1/4 mile: 18.8secs
108.0bhp 80.5kW 109.5PS
@ 6200rpm
87.0lbft 117.9Nm @ 6200rpm
105.2bhp/ton 103.4bhp/tonne
68.8bhp/L 51.3kW/L 69.7PS/L
55.6ft/sec 16.9m/sec
17.8mph 28.6kmh/1000rpm
Petrol 4-stroke piston
1570cc 95.8cu in

In-line 4 1 Carburettor
Compression ratio: 9.0:1
Bore: 78.0mm 3.1in
Stroke: 82.0mm 3.2in
Valve type/No: Overhead 8
Transmission: Manual
No. of forward speeds: 5
Wheels driven: Rear
Springs F/R: Coil/Coil
Brakes F/R: Disc/Disc
Steering: Recirculating ball
Wheelbase: 251.0cm 98.8in
Track F: 131.1cm 51.6in
Track R: 127.0cm 50.0in
Length: 414.0cm 163.0in
Width: 156.0cm 61.4in
Height: 143.0cm 56.3in
Ground clearance: 14.7cm 5.8in
Kerb weight: 1044.2kg 2300.0lb
Fuel: 45.8L 10.1gal 12.1galUS

61 Alfa Romeo

Giulia Veloce
1965 Italy
109.0mph 175.4kmh
0-50mph 80.5kmh: 8.1secs
0-60mph 96.5kmh: 10.5secs
0-1/4 mile: 17.4secs
129.0bhp 96.2kW 130.8PS
@ 6500rpm
96.0lbft 130.1Nm @ 4500rpm
134.4bhp/ton 132.2bhp/tonne
82.2bhp/L 61.3kW/L 83.3PS/L
59.4ft/sec 18.1m/sec
20.2mph 32.5kmh/1000rpm
Petrol 4-stroke piston
1570cc 95.8cu in
In-line 4 2 Carburettor
Compression ratio: 9.7:1
Bore: 78.0mm 3.1in
Stroke: 83.6mm 3.3in
Valve type/No: Overhead 8
Transmission: Manual
No. of forward speeds: 5
Wheels driven: Rear
Springs F/R: Coil/Coil
Brakes F/R: Disc/Drum
Steering: Worm & roller
Wheelbase: 225.0cm 88.6in
Track F: 129.0cm 50.8in
Track R: 127.0cm 50.0in
Length: 390.1cm 153.6in
Width: 157.5cm 62.0in
Height: 133.6cm 52.6in
Ground clearance: 14.7cm 5.8in
Kerb weight: 976.1kg 2150.0lb
Fuel: 52.2L 11.5gal 13.8galUS

62 Alfa Romeo

1600 Spider
1966 Italy
113.0mph 181.8kmh
0-50mph 80.5kmh: 8.3secs
0-60mph 96.5kmh: 11.3secs
0-1/4 mile: 18.5secs
125.0bhp 93.2kW 126.7PS
@ 6000rpm
115.0lbft 155.8Nm @ 2800rpm
127.6bhp/ton 125.4bhp/tonne
79.6bhp/L 59.4kW/L 80.7PS/L
53.8ft/sec 16.4m/sec
19.3mph 31.1kmh/1000rpm
Petrol 4-stroke piston
1570cc 95.8cu in
In-line 4 2 Carburettor
Compression ratio: 9.1:1
Bore: 78.0mm 3.1in
Stroke: 82.0mm 3.2in
Valve type/No: Overhead 8
Transmission: Manual
No. of forward speeds: 5
Wheels driven: Rear
Springs F/R: Coil/Coil
Brakes F/R: Disc/Disc
Steering: Worm & sector
Wheelbase: 225.0cm 88.6in
Track F: 131.1cm 51.6in
Track R: 127.0cm 50.0in
Length: 424.9cm 167.3in
Width: 163.1cm 64.2in
Height: 129.0cm 50.8in
Ground clearance: 14.7cm 5.8in
Kerb weight: 996.5kg 2195.0lb
Fuel: 46.2L 10.1gal 12.2galUS

63 Alfa Romeo

2600 Sprint
1966 Italy
119.0mph 191.5kmh
0-50mph 80.5kmh: 8.5secs
0-60mph 96.5kmh: 11.7secs
0-1/4 mile: 18.0secs
0-1km: 33.0secs
145.0bhp 108.1kW 147.0PS
@ 5900rpm
156.0lbft 211.4Nm @ 4000rpm
108.3bhp/ton 106.5bhp/tonne
56.2bhp/L 41.9kW/L 56.9PS/L
51.3ft/sec 15.6m/sec
20.4mph 32.8kmh/1000rpm
17.7mpg 14.7mpgUS 16.0L/100km
Petrol 4-stroke piston
2582cc 157.5cu in
In-line 6 3 Carburettor
Compression ratio: 9.0:1
Bore: 83.0mm 3.3in
Stroke: 79.6mm 3.1in
Valve type/No: Overhead 12
Transmission: Manual
No. of forward speeds: 5
Wheels driven: Rear
Springs F/R: Coil/Coil
Brake system: PA
Brakes F/R: Disc/Disc
Steering: Worm & roller
Wheelbase: 256.5cm 101.0in
Track F: 139.7cm 55.0in
Track R: 137.2cm 54.0in
Length: 457.2cm 180.0in
Width: 170.2cm 67.0in
Height: 139.7cm 55.0in
Ground clearance: 16.5cm 6.5in
Kerb weight: 1362.0kg 3000.0lb
Fuel: 60.1L 13.2gal 15.9galUS

64 Alfa Romeo

Giulia Sprint GTV
1966 Italy
115.0mph 185.0kmh
0-50mph 80.5kmh: 7.8secs
0-60mph 96.5kmh: 11.1secs
0-1/4 mile: 17.7secs
0-1km: 32.7secs
109.0bhp 81.3kW 110.5PS
@ 6000rpm
105.0lbft 142.3Nm @ 2800rpm
106.8bhp/ton 105.0bhp/tonne
69.4bhp/L 51.8kW/L 70.4PS/L
53.8ft/sec 16.4m/sec
19.6mph 31.5kmh/1000rpm
21.9mpg 18.2mpgUS 12.9L/100km
Petrol 4-stroke piston
1570cc 95.8cu in
In-line 4 2 Carburettor
Compression ratio: 9.0:1
Bore: 78.0mm 3.1in
Stroke: 82.0mm 3.2in
Valve type/No: Overhead 8
Transmission: Manual
No. of forward speeds: 5
Wheels driven: Rear
Springs F/R: Coil/Coil
Brake system: PA
Brakes F/R: Disc/Disc
Steering: Worm & roller
Wheelbase: 261.6cm 103.0in
Track F: 127.0cm 50.0in
Track R: 131.1cm 51.6in
Length: 408.9cm 161.0in
Width: 158.0cm 62.2in
Height: 131.6cm 51.8in
Ground clearance: 14.0cm 5.5in
Kerb weight: 1037.8kg 2286.0lb
Fuel: 47.8L 10.5gal 12.6galUS

65 Alfa Romeo

Sprint Speciale
1966 Italy
112.0mph 180.2kmh
0-50mph 80.5kmh: 8.5secs
0-60mph 96.5kmh: 12.0secs
0-1/4 mile: 18.0secs
129.0bhp 96.2kW 130.8PS
@ 6500rpm
96.0lbft 130.1Nm @ 4500rpm
127.1bhp/ton 125.0bhp/tonne
82.2bhp/L 61.3kW/L 83.3PS/L
58.3ft/sec 17.8m/sec
18.8mph 30.2kmh/1000rpm
Petrol 4-stroke piston
1570cc 95.8cu in
In-line 4 2 Carburettor
Compression ratio: 9.7:1
Bore: 78.0mm 3.1in
Stroke: 82.0mm 3.2in
Valve type/No: Overhead 8
Transmission: Manual
No. of forward speeds: 5
Wheels driven: Rear
Springs F/R: Coil/Coil
Brakes F/R: Disc/Drum
Steering: Worm & roller
Wheelbase: 225.0cm 88.6in
Track F: 129.0cm 50.8in
Track R: 126.7cm 49.9in
Length: 412.0cm 162.2in
Width: 155.4cm 61.2in
Height: 127.5cm 50.2in
Ground clearance: 15.0cm 5.9in
Kerb weight: 1031.9kg 2273.0lb
Fuel: 79.9L 17.6gal 21.1galUS

66 Alfa Romeo

33 2.0 Stradale
1967 Italy
161.0mph 259.0kmh
230.0bhp 171.5kW 233.2PS
@ 8800rpm
135.0lbft 182.9Nm @ 7000rpm
408.9bhp/ton 402.1bhp/tonne
115.3bhp/L 86.0kW/L 116.9PS/L
50.4ft/sec 15.3m/sec
Petrol 4-stroke piston
1995cc 121.7cu in
Vee 8 fuel injection
Compression ratio: 10.0:1
Bore: 78.0mm 3.1in
Stroke: 52.2mm 2.1in
Valve type/No: Overhead 32
Transmission: Manual
No. of forward speeds: 6
Wheels driven: Rear
Springs F/R: Coil/Coil
Brakes F/R: Disc/Disc
Steering: Rack & pinion
Wheelbase: 235.0cm 92.5in
Track F: 134.9cm 53.1in
Track R: 144.5cm 56.9in
Length: 397.0cm 156.3in
Width: 170.9cm 67.3in
Height: 99.1cm 39.0in
Kerb weight: 572.0kg 1260.0lb
Fuel: 57.9L 12.7gal 15.3galUS

67 Alfa Romeo

Duetto Spider
1967 Italy
113.0mph 181.8kmh
0-60mph 96.5kmh: 11.3secs
0-1/4 mile: 18.5secs
125.0bhp 93.2kW 126.7PS
@ 6000rpm
115.0lbft 155.8Nm @ 2800rpm
127.6bhp/ton 125.4bhp/tonne
79.8bhp/L 59.5kW/L 80.9PS/L
53.8ft/sec 16.4m/sec
28.8mpg 24.0mpgUS 9.8L/100km
Petrol 4-stroke piston
1567cc 95.6cu in
In-line 4 2 Carburettor
Compression ratio: 9.1:1
Bore: 78.0mm 3.1in
Stroke: 82.0mm 3.2in
Valve type/No: Overhead 8
Transmission: Manual
No. of forward speeds: 5
Wheels driven: Rear
Springs F/R: Coil/Coil
Brake system: PA
Brakes F/R: Disc/Disc
Steering: Worm & sector
Wheelbase: 225.0cm 88.6in
Track F: 131.1cm 51.6in
Track R: 127.0cm 50.0in
Length: 424.9cm 167.3in
Width: 163.1cm 64.2in
Height: 129.0cm 50.8in
Kerb weight: 996.5kg 2195.0lb
Fuel: 46.2L 10.1gal 12.2galUS

68 Alfa Romeo

Giulia 1300 ti
1967 Italy
101.0mph 162.5kmh
0-50mph 80.5kmh: 11.1secs
0-60mph 96.5kmh: 15.3secs
0-1/4 mile: 19.8secs
0-1km: 36.6secs
82.0bhp 61.1kW 83.1PS
@ 6000rpm
76.6lbft 103.8Nm @ 4900rpm
85.3bhp/ton 83.9bhp/tonne
63.6bhp/L 47.4kW/L 64.4PS/L
49.2ft/sec 15.0m/sec
17.4mph 28.0kmh/1000rpm
21.3mpg 17.7mpgUS 13.3L/100km
Petrol 4-stroke piston
1290cc 78.7cu in
In-line 4 1 Carburettor
Compression ratio: 9.0:1
Bore: 74.0mm 2.9in
Stroke: 75.0mm 2.9in
Valve type/No: Overhead 8
Transmission: Manual
No. of forward speeds: 5
Wheels driven: Rear
Springs F/R: Coil/Coil
Brakes F/R: Disc/Disc
Steering: Recirculating ball
Wheelbase: 250.2cm 98.5in
Track F: 132.1cm 52.0in
Track R: 132.1cm 52.0in
Length: 414.0cm 163.0in
Width: 157.5cm 62.0in
Height: 147.3cm 58.0in
Ground clearance: 16.5cm 6.5in
Kerb weight: 977.0kg 2152.0lb
Fuel: 46.0L 10.1gal 12.1galUS

69 Alfa Romeo

GTV
1967 Italy
112.0mph 180.2kmh
0-50mph 80.5kmh: 7.2secs
0-60mph 96.5kmh: 10.5secs
0-1/4 mile: 17.6secs
125.0bhp 93.2kW 126.7PS
@ 6000rpm
115.0lbft 155.8Nm @ 2800rpm
125.6bhp/ton 123.5bhp/tonne
79.6bhp/L 59.4kW/L 80.7PS/L
53.8ft/sec 16.4m/sec
19.6mph 31.5kmh/1000rpm
Petrol 4-stroke piston
1570cc 95.8cu in
In-line 4 2 Carburettor
Compression ratio: 9.0:1
Bore: 78.0mm 3.1in
Stroke: 82.0mm 3.2in
Valve type/No: Overhead 8
Transmission: Manual
No. of forward speeds: 5
Wheels driven: Rear
Springs F/R: Coil/Coil
Brake system: PA
Brakes F/R: Disc/Disc
Steering: Worm & sector
Wheelbase: 236.2cm 93.0in
Track F: 130.8cm 51.5in
Track R: 127.0cm 50.0in
Length: 408.9cm 161.0in
Width: 157.5cm 62.0in
Height: 132.1cm 52.0in
Ground clearance: 12.7cm 5.0in
Kerb weight: 1012.4kg 2230.0lb
Fuel: 53.0L 11.6gal 14.0galUS

70 Alfa Romeo

1750 Berlina
1968 Italy
117.0mph 188.3kmh
0-50mph 80.5kmh: 7.8secs
0-60mph 96.5kmh: 10.8secs
0-1/4 mile: 17.5secs
0-1km: 32.6secs
122.0bhp 91.0kW 123.7PS
@ 5500rpm
137.0lbft 185.6Nm @ 3000rpm
110.3bhp/ton 108.5bhp/tonne
68.6bhp/L 51.1kW/L 69.5PS/L
53.2ft/sec 16.2m/sec
20.8mph 33.5kmh/1000rpm
23.1mpg 19.2mpgUS 12.2L/100km
Petrol 4-stroke piston
1779cc 108.5cu in
In-line 4 2 Carburettor
Compression ratio: 9.5:1
Bore: 80.0mm 3.1in
Stroke: 88.5mm 3.5in
Valve type/No: Overhead 8
Transmission: Manual
No. of forward speeds: 5
Wheels driven: Rear
Springs F/R: Coil/Coil
Brake system: PA

Brakes F/R: Disc/Disc
Steering: Recirculating ball
Wheelbase: 256.5cm 101.0in
Track F: 132.3cm 52.1in
Track R: 127.3cm 50.1in
Length: 439.4cm 173.0in
Width: 156.7cm 61.7in
Height: 143.0cm 56.3in
Ground clearance: 15.2cm 6.0in
Kerb weight: 1124.6kg 2477.0lb
Fuel: 46.0L 10.1gal 12.1galUS

71 Alfa Romeo

1750 GT Veloce
1968 Italy
118.0mph 189.9kmh
0-50mph 80.5kmh: 7.9secs
0-60mph 96.5kmh: 11.2secs
0-1/4 mile: 18.0secs
0-1km: 33.0secs
122.0bhp 91.0kW 123.7PS
@ 5500rpm
137.0lbft 185.6Nm @ 3000rpm
122.0bhp/ton 120.0bhp/tonne
68.6bhp/L 51.1kW/L 69.5PS/L
53.2ft/sec 16.2m/sec
21.9mph 35.2kmh/1000rpm
23.9mpg 19.9mpgUS 11.8L/100km
Petrol 4-stroke piston
1779cc 108.5cu in
In-line 4 2 Carburettor
Compression ratio: 9.5:1
Bore: 80.0mm 3.1in
Stroke: 88.5mm 3.5in
Valve type/No: Overhead 8
Transmission: Manual
No. of forward speeds: 5
Wheels driven: Rear
Springs F/R: Coil/Coil
Brake system: PA
Brakes F/R: Disc/Disc
Steering: Recirculating ball
Wheelbase: 235.0cm 92.5in
Track F: 127.0cm 50.0in
Track R: 131.1cm 51.6in
Length: 408.9cm 161.0in
Width: 158.0cm 62.2in
Height: 131.6cm 51.8in
Ground clearance: 14.0cm 5.5in
Kerb weight: 1017.0kg 2240.0lb
Fuel: 46.0L 10.1gal 12.1galUS

72 Alfa Romeo

Giulia Super
1968 Italy
108.0mph 173.8kmh
0-50mph 80.5kmh: 8.3secs
0-60mph 96.5kmh: 11.5secs
0-1/4 mile: 18.4secs
112.0bhp 83.5kW 113.5PS
@ 5500rpm
110.0lbft 149.1Nm @ 2900rpm
108.1bhp/ton 106.3bhp/tonne
71.3bhp/L 53.2kW/L 72.3PS/L
49.3ft/sec 15.0m/sec
19.5mph 31.4kmh/1000rpm
Petrol 4-stroke piston
1570cc 95.8cu in
In-line 4
Compression ratio: 9.0:1
Bore: 78.0mm 3.1in
Stroke: 82.0mm 3.2in
Valve type/No: Overhead 8
Transmission: Manual
No. of forward speeds: 5
Wheels driven: Rear
Brake system: PA
Brakes F/R: Disc/Disc
Steering: Recirculating ball
Wheelbase: 251.0cm 98.8in
Track F: 131.1cm 51.6in
Track R: 127.0cm 50.0in
Length: 414.0cm 163.0in
Width: 156.0cm 61.4in
Height: 143.0cm 56.3in
Kerb weight: 1053.3kg 2320.0lb
Fuel: 45.8L 10.1gal 12.1galUS

73 Alfa Romeo

1750 Berlina
1969 Italy
110.0mph 177.0kmh
0-50mph 80.5kmh: 8.0secs
0-60mph 96.5kmh: 11.0secs
0-1/4 mile: 17.9secs
132.0bhp 98.4kW 133.8PS
@ 5500rpm
137.0lbft 185.6Nm @ 2900rpm
119.0bhp/ton 117.0bhp/tonne
74.2bhp/L 55.3kW/L 75.2PS/L
53.2ft/sec 16.2m/sec
18.6mph 29.9kmh/1000rpm
24.5mpg 20.4mpgUS 11.5L/100km
Petrol 4-stroke piston
1779cc 108.5cu in
In-line 4 fuel injection
Compression ratio: 9.5:1
Bore: 80.0mm 3.1in
Stroke: 88.5mm 3.5in
Valve type/No: Overhead 8
Transmission: Manual
No. of forward speeds: 5
Wheels driven: Rear
Springs F/R: Coil/Coil
Brake system: PA
Brakes F/R: Disc/Disc
Steering: Worm & sector
Wheelbase: 257.0cm 101.2in
Track F: 132.1cm 52.0in
Track R: 127.0cm 50.0in
Length: 438.7cm 172.7in
Width: 156.5cm 61.6in
Height: 142.0cm 55.9in
Ground clearance: 11.9cm 4.7in
Kerb weight: 1127.7kg 2484.0lb
Fuel: 46.2L 10.1gal 12.2galUS

74 Alfa Romeo

1750 Spider
1969 Italy
115.0mph 185.0kmh
0-50mph 80.5kmh: 7.5secs
0-60mph 96.5kmh: 9.9secs
0-1/4 mile: 17.3secs
132.0bhp 98.4kW 133.8PS
@ 5500rpm
137.0lbft 185.6Nm @ 2900rpm
126.0bhp/ton 123.9bhp/tonne
74.2bhp/L 55.3kW/L 75.2PS/L
53.2ft/sec 16.2m/sec
18.6mph 29.9kmh/1000rpm
25.8mpg 21.5mpgUS 10.9L/100km
Petrol 4-stroke piston
1779cc 108.5cu in
In-line 4 fuel injection
Compression ratio: 9.5:1
Bore: 80.0mm 3.1in
Stroke: 88.5mm 3.5in
Valve type/No: Overhead 8
Transmission: Manual
No. of forward speeds: 5
Wheels driven: Rear
Springs F/R: Coil/Coil
Brake system: PA
Brakes F/R: Disc/Disc
Steering: Worm & sector
Wheelbase: 225.0cm 88.6in
Track F: 131.1cm 51.6in
Track R: 127.0cm 50.0in
Length: 426.5cm 167.9in
Width: 163.1cm 64.2in
Height: 129.0cm 50.8in
Ground clearance: 14.7cm 5.8in
Kerb weight: 1065.1kg 2346.0lb
Fuel: 46.2L 10.1gal 12.2galUS

75 Alfa Romeo

GT 1300 Junior
1969 Italy
104.0mph 167.3kmh
0-50mph 80.5kmh: 9.3secs
0-60mph 96.5kmh: 13.2secs
0-1/4 mile: 19.1secs
0-1km: 35.7secs
103.0bhp 76.8kW 104.4PS
@ 6000rpm
101.0lbft 136.9Nm @ 3200rpm
103.7bhp/ton 102.0bhp/tonne
79.8bhp/L 59.5kW/L 80.9PS/L
49.2ft/sec 15.0m/sec
18.2mph 29.3kmh/1000rpm
24.4mpg 20.3mpgUS 11.6L/100km
Petrol 4-stroke piston
1290cc 78.7cu in
In-line 4 2 Carburettor
Compression ratio: 9.0:1
Bore: 74.0mm 2.9in
Stroke: 75.0mm 2.9in
Valve type/No: Overhead 8
Transmission: Manual
No. of forward speeds: 5
Wheels driven: Rear
Springs F/R: Coil/Coil
Brake system: PA
Brakes F/R: Disc/Disc
Steering: Recirculating ball
Wheelbase: 235.0cm 92.5in
Track F: 127.0cm 50.0in
Track R: 131.1cm 51.6in
Length: 408.9cm 161.0in
Width: 158.0cm 62.2in
Height: 131.6cm 51.8in
Ground clearance: 14.0cm 5.5in
Kerb weight: 1009.7kg 2224.0lb
Fuel: 46.0L 10.1gal 12.1galUS

76 Alfa Romeo

1750 Spider Veloce
1971 Italy
114.0mph 183.4kmh
0-50mph 80.5kmh: 7.1secs
0-60mph 96.5kmh: 9.9secs
0-1/4 mile: 17.5secs
135.0bhp 100.7kW 136.9PS
@ 5500rpm
137.0lbft 185.6Nm @ 2900rpm
130.6bhp/ton 128.4bhp/tonne
75.9bhp/L 56.6kW/L 76.9PS/L
53.2ft/sec 16.2m/sec
18.4mph 29.6kmh/1000rpm
28.3mpg 23.6mpgUS 10.0L/100km
Petrol 4-stroke piston
1779cc 108.5cu in
In-line 4 fuel injection
Compression ratio: 9.0:1
Bore: 80.0mm 3.1in
Stroke: 88.5mm 3.5in
Valve type/No: Overhead 8
Transmission: Manual
No. of forward speeds: 5
Wheels driven: Rear
Springs F/R: Coil/Coil
Brake system: PA
Brakes F/R: Disc/Disc
Steering: Worm & sector
Wheelbase: 225.0cm 88.6in
Track F: 132.6cm 52.2in
Track R: 127.5cm 50.2in
Length: 409.4cm 161.2in
Width: 163.1cm 64.2in
Height: 129.0cm 50.8in
Ground clearance: 14.7cm 5.8in
Kerb weight: 1051.0kg 2315.0lb
Fuel: 45.4L 10.0gal 12.0galUS

77 Alfa Romeo

1750 Berlina
1972 Italy
108.0mph 173.8kmh
0-60mph 96.5kmh: 11.0secs
0-1/4 mile: 17.9secs
115.0bhp 85.8kW 116.6PS
@ 5300rpm
120.0lbft 162.6Nm @ 2900rpm
103.7bhp/ton 101.9bhp/tonne
64.6bhp/L 48.2kW/L 65.5PS/L
51.2ft/sec 15.6m/sec
24.0mpg 20.0mpgUS 11.8L/100km
Petrol 4-stroke piston
1779cc 108.5cu in
In-line 4 fuel injection
Compression ratio: 9.5:1
Bore: 80.0mm 3.1in
Stroke: 88.5mm 3.5in
Valve type/No: Overhead 8
Transmission: Manual
No. of forward speeds: 5
Wheels driven: Rear
Springs F/R: Coil/Coil
Brake system: PA
Brakes F/R: Disc/Disc
Steering: Worm & gear
Wheelbase: 257.0cm 101.2in
Track F: 132.1cm 52.0in
Track R: 127.0cm 50.0in
Length: 438.7cm 172.7in
Width: 156.5cm 61.6in
Height: 142.0cm 55.9in
Ground clearance: 11.9cm 4.7in
Kerb weight: 1128.2kg 2485.0lb
Fuel: 46.2L 10.1gal 12.2galUS

78 Alfa Romeo

1750 GTV TransAm
1972 Italy
121.0mph 194.7kmh
0-50mph 80.5kmh: 5.1secs
0-60mph 96.5kmh: 7.0secs
0-1/4 mile: 13.9secs
205.0bhp 152.9kW 207.8PS
@ 7500rpm
204.5bhp/ton 201.1bhp/tonne
113.3bhp/L 84.5kW/L 114.8PS/L
72.5ft/sec 22.1m/sec
15.1mph 24.3kmh/1000rpm
6.0mpg 5.0mpgUS 47.0L/100km
Petrol 4-stroke piston
1810cc 110.4cu in
In-line 4
Compression ratio: 12.0:1
Bore: 81.0mm 3.2in
Stroke: 88.5mm 3.5in
Valve type/No: Overhead 8
Transmission: Manual
No. of forward speeds: 5
Wheels driven: Rear
Brake system: PA
Brakes F/R: Disc/Disc
Steering: Worm & roller
Wheelbase: 235.0cm 92.5in
Track F: 135.9cm 53.5in
Track R: 131.3cm 51.7in
Length: 407.9cm 160.6in
Width: 170.7cm 67.2in
Height: 121.9cm 48.0in
Kerb weight: 1019.2kg 2245.0lb
Fuel: 56.8L 12.5gal 15.0galUS

79 Alfa Romeo

2000 GTV
1972 Italy
122.0mph 196.3kmh
0-50mph 80.5kmh: 6.7secs
0-60mph 96.5kmh: 9.2secs
0-1/4 mile: 16.4secs
0-1km: 30.2secs
131.0bhp 97.7kW 132.8PS
@ 5500rpm
134.0lbft 181.6Nm @ 3000rpm
127.5bhp/ton 125.4bhp/tonne
66.8bhp/L 49.8kW/L 67.7PS/L
53.2ft/sec 16.2m/sec
21.9mph 35.2kmh/1000rpm
21.1mpg 17.6mpgUS 13.4L/100km
Petrol 4-stroke piston
1962cc 119.7cu in
In-line 4 2 Carburettor
Compression ratio: 9.5:1
Bore: 84.0mm 3.3in
Stroke: 88.5mm 3.5in
Valve type/No: Overhead 8
Transmission: Manual
No. of forward speeds: 5
Wheels driven: Rear
Springs F/R: Coil/Coil
Brake system: PA
Brakes F/R: Disc/Disc
Steering: Recirculating ball
Wheelbase: 235.0cm 92.5in
Track F: 127.0cm 50.0in
Track R: 131.1cm 51.6in
Length: 408.9cm 161.0in
Width: 158.0cm 62.2in
Height: 131.6cm 51.8in
Ground clearance: 14.0cm 5.5in
Kerb weight: 1044.6kg 2301.0lb
Fuel: 52.8L 11.6gal 13.9galUS

80 Alfa Romeo

2000 GTV Injection
1972 Italy
110.0mph 177.0kmh
0-50mph 80.5kmh: 6.8secs
0-60mph 96.5kmh: 9.6secs
0-1/4 mile: 17.6secs
129.0bhp 96.2kW 130.8PS
@ 5800rpm
132.0lbft 178.9Nm @ 3500rpm
124.3bhp/ton 122.2bhp/tonne
65.7bhp/L 49.0kW/L 66.7PS/L
56.1ft/sec 17.1m/sec
19.0mph 30.6kmh/1000rpm
28.6mpg 23.8mpgUS 9.9L/100km
Petrol 4-stroke piston
1962cc 119.7cu in
In-line 4 fuel injection
Compression ratio: 9.0:1
Bore: 84.0mm 3.3in
Stroke: 88.5mm 3.5in
Valve type/No: Overhead 8
Transmission: Manual
No. of forward speeds: 5
Wheels driven: Rear
Springs F/R: Coil/Coil
Brake system: PA
Brakes F/R: Disc/Disc

Steering: Recirculating ball
Wheelbase: 235.0cm 92.5in
Track F: 132.3cm 52.1in
Track R: 127.3cm 50.1in
Length: 410.0cm 161.4in
Width: 158.0cm 62.2in
Height: 131.6cm 51.8in
Ground clearance: 12.7cm 5.0in
Kerb weight: 1055.5kg 2325.0lb
Fuel: 53.0L 11.6gal 14.0galUS

81 Alfa Romeo

Alfasud
1972 Italy
96.0mph 154.5kmh
0-50mph 80.5kmh: 9.4secs
0-60mph 96.5kmh: 13.5secs
0-1/4 mile: 19.6secs
63.0bhp 47.0kW 63.9PS
@ 6000rpm
62.0lbft 84.0Nm @ 3500rpm
77.3bhp/ton 76.0bhp/tonne
53.1bhp/L 39.6kW/L 53.8PS/L
38.7ft/sec 11.8m/sec
25.2mpg 21.0mpgUS 11.2L/100km
Petrol 4-stroke piston
1186cc 72.4cu in
Flat 4
Compression ratio: 8.8:1
Bore: 80.0mm 3.1in
Stroke: 59.0mm 2.3in
Valve type/No: Overhead 8
Transmission: Manual
No. of forward speeds: 4
Wheels driven: Front
Brakes F/R: Disc/Disc
Steering: Rack & pinion
Wheelbase: 245.6cm 96.7in
Track F: 138.4cm 54.5in
Track R: 137.7cm 54.2in
Length: 389.1cm 153.2in
Width: 159.0cm 62.6in
Height: 136.9cm 53.9in
Kerb weight: 828.5kg 1825.0lb
Fuel: 50.0L 11.0gal 13.2galUS

82 Alfa Romeo

Montreal
1972 Italy
140.0mph 225.3kmh
0-50mph 80.5kmh: 5.9secs
0-60mph 96.5kmh: 7.6secs
0-1/4 mile: 15.4secs
0-1km: 28.1secs
200.0bhp 149.1kW 202.8PS
@ 6500rpm
173.0lbft 234.4Nm @ 4750rpm
158.4bhp/ton 155.7bhp/tonne
77.1bhp/L 57.5kW/L 78.2PS/L
45.9ft/sec 14.0m/sec
20.2mph 32.5kmh/1000rpm
14.9mpg 12.4mpgUS 19.0L/100km
Petrol 4-stroke piston
2593cc 158.2cu in
Vee 8 fuel injection
Compression ratio: 9.0:1
Bore: 80.0mm 3.1in
Stroke: 64.5mm 2.5in
Valve type/No: Overhead 16
Transmission: Manual
No. of forward speeds: 5
Wheels driven: Rear
Springs F/R: Coil/Coil
Brake system: PA
Brakes F/R: Disc/Disc
Steering: Recirculating ball
Wheelbase: 235.0cm 92.5in
Track F: 137.2cm 54.0in
Track R: 130.8cm 51.5in
Length: 421.6cm 166.0in
Width: 167.6cm 66.0in
Height: 123.7cm 48.7in
Ground clearance: 11.9cm 4.7in
Kerb weight: 1284.4kg 2829.0lb
Fuel: 63.7L 14.0gal 16.8galUS

83 Alfa Romeo

2000
1973 Italy
118.0mph 189.9kmh
0-50mph 80.5kmh: 6.8secs
0-60mph 96.5kmh: 9.9secs
0-1/4 mile: 17.4secs
0-1km: 32.2secs
131.0bhp 97.7kW 132.8PS
@ 5500rpm
134.0lbft 181.6Nm @ 3000rpm
117.9bhp/ton 115.9bhp/tonne
66.8bhp/L 49.8kW/L 67.7PS/L
53.2ft/sec 16.2m/sec
20.9mph 33.6kmh/1000rpm
21.8mpg 18.2mpgUS 13.0L/100km
Petrol 4-stroke piston
1962cc 119.7cu in
In-line 4 2 Carburettor
Compression ratio: 9.5:1
Bore: 84.0mm 3.3in
Stroke: 88.5mm 3.5in
Valve type/No: Overhead 8
Transmission: Manual
No. of forward speeds: 5
Wheels driven: Rear
Springs F/R: Coil/Coil
Brake system: PA
Brakes F/R: Disc/Drum
Steering: Worm & roller
Wheelbase: 256.5cm 101.0in
Track F: 132.3cm 52.1in
Track R: 127.3cm 50.1in
Length: 439.4cm 173.0in
Width: 156.7cm 61.7in
Height: 145.5cm 57.3in
Ground clearance: 15.2cm 6.0in
Kerb weight: 1130.0kg 2489.0lb
Fuel: 52.8L 11.6gal 13.9galUS

84 Alfa Romeo

Alfasud
1973 Italy
94.0mph 151.2kmh
0-50mph 80.5kmh: 10.4secs
0-60mph 96.5kmh: 15.1secs
0-1/4 mile: 20.3secs
0-1km: 37.7secs
63.0bhp 47.0kW 63.9PS
@ 6000rpm
63.0lbft 85.4Nm @ 3500rpm
74.8bhp/ton 73.6bhp/tonne
53.1bhp/L 39.6kW/L 53.8PS/L
38.7ft/sec 11.8m/sec
16.4mph 26.4kmh/1000rpm
27.4mpg 22.8mpgUS 10.3L/100km
Petrol 4-stroke piston
1186cc 72.4cu in
Flat 4 1 Carburettor
Compression ratio: 8.8:1
Bore: 80.0mm 3.1in
Stroke: 59.0mm 2.3in
Valve type/No: Overhead 8
Transmission: Manual
No. of forward speeds: 4
Wheels driven: Front
Springs F/R: Coil/Coil
Brakes F/R: Disc/Disc
Steering: Rack & pinion
Wheelbase: 246.4cm 97.0in
Track F: 138.2cm 54.4in
Track R: 137.4cm 54.1in
Length: 388.9cm 153.1in
Width: 158.8cm 62.5in
Height: 136.9cm 53.9in
Ground clearance: 16.5cm 6.5in
Kerb weight: 856.2kg 1886.0lb
Fuel: 50.0L 11.0gal 13.2galUS

85 Alfa Romeo

Alfetta
1973 Italy
112.0mph 180.2kmh
0-60mph 96.5kmh: 8.6secs
0-1/4 mile: 17.2secs
122.0bhp 91.0kW 123.7PS
@ 5500rpm
123.0lbft 166.7Nm @ 4400rpm
116.8bhp/ton 114.8bhp/tonne
68.6bhp/L 51.1kW/L 69.5PS/L
53.2ft/sec 16.2m/sec
19.7mph 31.7kmh/1000rpm
24.6mpg 20.5mpgUS 11.5L/100km
Petrol 4-stroke piston
1779cc 108.5cu in
In-line 4
Compression ratio: 9.5:1
Bore: 80.0mm 3.1in
Stroke: 88.5mm 3.5in
Valve type/No: Overhead 8
Transmission: Manual
No. of forward speeds: 5
Wheels driven: Rear
Springs F/R: Torsion bar/Coil
Brake system: PA
Brakes F/R: Disc/Disc
Steering: Rack & pinion
Wheelbase: 251.0cm 98.8in
Track F: 135.9cm 53.5in
Track R: 135.1cm 53.2in
Length: 426.7cm 168.0in
Width: 167.1cm 65.8in
Height: 143.5cm 56.5in
Kerb weight: 1062.4kg 2340.0lb
Fuel: 48.8L 10.7gal 12.9galUS

86 Alfa Romeo

Giulia 1600 Sprint
1973 Italy
112.0mph 180.2kmh
0-50mph 80.5kmh: 9.9secs
0-60mph 96.5kmh: 13.2secs
0-1/4 mile: 18.8secs
92.0bhp 68.6kW 93.3PS
@ 6200rpm
108.0lbft 146.3Nm @ 3700rpm
96.2bhp/ton 94.6bhp/tonne
58.6bhp/L 43.7kW/L 59.4PS/L
55.6ft/sec 16.9m/sec
16.9mph 27.2kmh/1000rpm
26.7mpg 22.2mpgUS 10.6L/100km
Petrol 4-stroke piston
1570cc 95.8cu in
In-line 4 1 Carburettor
Compression ratio: 9.0:1
Bore: 78.0mm 3.1in
Stroke: 82.0mm 3.2in
Valve type/No: Overhead 8
Transmission: Manual
No. of forward speeds: 5
Wheels driven: Rear
Springs F/R: Coil/Coil
Brakes F/R: Drum/Drum
Wheelbase: 237.5cm 93.5in
Track F: 128.8cm 50.7in
Track R: 127.0cm 50.0in
Length: 401.3cm 158.0in
Width: 152.4cm 60.0in
Height: 131.8cm 51.9in
Ground clearance: 12.7cm 5.0in
Kerb weight: 972.5kg 2142.0lb
Fuel: 53.2L 11.7gal 14.1galUS

87 Alfa Romeo

Montreal
1973 Italy
132.0mph 212.4kmh
0-50mph 80.5kmh: 5.9secs
0-60mph 96.5kmh: 8.0secs
0-1/4 mile: 16.6secs
200.0bhp 149.1kW 202.8PS
@ 6500rpm
174.0lbft 235.8Nm @ 4750rpm
159.4bhp/ton 156.8bhp/tonne
77.1bhp/L 57.5kW/L 78.2PS/L
45.9ft/sec 14.0m/sec
21.0mph 33.8kmh/1000rpm
Petrol 4-stroke piston
2593cc 158.2cu in
Vee 8
Compression ratio: 9.0:1
Bore: 80.0mm 3.1in
Stroke: 64.5mm 2.5in
Valve type/No: Overhead 16
Transmission: Manual
No. of forward speeds: 5
Wheels driven: Rear
Springs F/R: Coil
Brake system: PA
Brakes F/R: Disc/Disc
Steering: Recirculating ball
Wheelbase: 235.0cm 92.5in
Track F: 137.9cm 54.3in
Track R: 134.1cm 52.8in
Length: 421.6cm 166.0in
Width: 167.1cm 65.8in
Height: 124.0cm 48.8in
Kerb weight: 1275.7kg 2810.0lb
Fuel: 63.6L 14.0gal 16.8galUS

88 Alfa Romeo

Alfasud ti
1974 Italy
102.0mph 164.1kmh
0-50mph 80.5kmh: 9.4secs
0-60mph 96.5kmh: 14.0secs
0-1/4 mile: 19.5secs
0-1km: 36.4secs
68.0bhp 50.7kW 68.9PS
@ 6000rpm
66.5lbft 90.1Nm @ 3200rpm
81.4bhp/ton 80.1bhp/tonne
36.1bhp/L 26.9kW/L 36.5PS/L
38.7ft/sec 11.8m/sec
17.4mph 28.0kmh/1000rpm
26.2mpg 21.8mpgUS 10.8L/100km
Petrol 4-stroke piston
1886cc 115.1cu in
Flat 4 1 Carburettor
Compression ratio: 9.0:1
Bore: 80.0mm 3.1in
Stroke: 59.0mm 2.3in
Valve type/No: Overhead 8
Transmission: Manual
No. of forward speeds: 5
Wheels driven: Front
Springs F/R: Coil/Coil
Brakes F/R: Disc/Disc
Steering: Rack & pinion
Wheelbase: 246.4cm 97.0in
Track F: 138.4cm 54.5in
Track R: 134.9cm 53.1in
Length: 389.1cm 153.2in
Width: 158.8cm 62.5in
Height: 136.9cm 53.9in
Ground clearance: 16.5cm 6.5in
Kerb weight: 849.0kg 1870.0lb
Fuel: 50.0L 11.0gal 13.2galUS

89 Alfa Romeo

Alfetta
1974 Italy
113.0mph 181.8kmh
0-50mph 80.5kmh: 7.6secs
0-60mph 96.5kmh: 10.8secs
0-1/4 mile: 17.7secs
122.0bhp 91.0kW 123.7PS
@ 5500rpm
123.0lbft 166.7Nm @ 4000rpm
112.2bhp/ton 110.3bhp/tonne
68.6bhp/L 51.1kW/L 69.5PS/L
53.2ft/sec 16.2m/sec
20.8mph 33.5kmh/1000rpm
23.5mpg 19.6mpgUS 12.0L/100km
Petrol 4-stroke piston
1779cc 108.5cu in
In-line 4 2 Carburettor
Compression ratio: 9.5:1
Bore: 80.0mm 3.1in
Stroke: 88.5mm 3.5in
Valve type/No: Overhead 8
Transmission: Manual
No. of forward speeds: 5
Wheels driven: Rear
Springs F/R: Torsion bar/Coil
Brake system: PA
Brakes F/R: Disc/Disc
Steering: Rack & pinion
Wheelbase: 254.0cm 100.0in
Track F: 134.6cm 53.0in
Track R: 134.6cm 53.0in
Length: 434.3cm 171.0in
Width: 167.6cm 66.0in
Height: 142.2cm 56.0in
Ground clearance: 20.3cm 8.0in
Kerb weight: 1105.9kg 2436.0lb
Fuel: 48.7L 10.7gal 12.9galUS

90 Alfa Romeo

Alfetta GT
1975 Italy
122.0mph 196.3kmh
0-50mph 80.5kmh: 6.7secs
0-60mph 96.5kmh: 9.4secs
0-1/4 mile: 17.0secs
0-1km: 31.9secs
122.0bhp 91.0kW 123.7PS
@ 5500rpm
123.0lbft 166.7Nm @ 4400rpm
114.2bhp/ton 112.3bhp/tonne
68.6bhp/L 51.1kW/L 69.5PS/L
53.2ft/sec 16.2m/sec
20.7mph 33.3kmh/1000rpm
23.7mpg 19.7mpgUS 11.9L/100km
Petrol 4-stroke piston
1779cc 108.5cu in
In-line 4 2 Carburettor
Compression ratio: 9.5:1
Bore: 80.0mm 3.1in
Stroke: 88.5mm 3.5in
Valve type/No: Overhead 8
Transmission: Manual
No. of forward speeds: 5
Wheels driven: Rear
Springs F/R: Torsion bar/Coil
Brake system: PA
Brakes F/R: Disc/Disc
Steering: Rack & pinion
Wheelbase: 241.3cm 95.0in
Track F: 136.1cm 53.6in

Track R: 135.9cm 53.5in
Length: 419.1cm 165.0in
Width: 165.1cm 65.0in
Height: 133.1cm 52.4in
Ground clearance: 17.8cm 7.0in
Kerb weight: 1086.4kg 2393.0lb
Fuel: 54.1L 11.9gal 14.3galUS

91 Alfa Romeo

Alfetta 1.6
1976 Italy
105.0mph 168.9kmh
0-50mph 80.5kmh: 8.0secs
0-60mph 96.5kmh: 11.5secs
0-1/4 mile: 18.0secs
0-1km: 34.0secs
108.0bhp 80.5kW 109.5PS
@ 5600rpm
121.0lbft 164.0Nm @ 4300rpm
99.8bhp/ton 98.1bhp/tonne
68.8bhp/L 51.3kW/L 69.7PS/L
50.2ft/sec 15.3m/sec
19.7mph 31.7kmh/1000rpm
24.6mpg 20.5mpgUS 11.5L/100km
Petrol 4-stroke piston
1570cc 95.8cu in
In-line 4 2 Carburettor
Compression ratio: 9.0:1
Bore: 78.0mm 3.1in
Stroke: 82.0mm 3.2in
Valve type/No: Overhead 8
Transmission: Manual
No. of forward speeds: 5
Wheels driven: Rear
Springs F/R: Torsion bar/Coil
Brake system: PA
Brakes F/R: Disc/Disc
Steering: Rack & pinion
Wheelbase: 254.0cm 100.0in
Track F: 134.6cm 53.0in
Track R: 134.6cm 53.0in
Length: 434.3cm 171.0in
Width: 167.6cm 66.0in
Height: 142.2cm 56.0in
Ground clearance: 20.3cm 8.0in
Kerb weight: 1100.9kg 2425.0lb
Fuel: 48.7L 10.7gal 12.9galUS

92 Alfa Romeo

Alfetta GT
1976 Italy
112.0mph 180.2kmh
0-50mph 80.5kmh: 8.5secs
0-60mph 96.5kmh: 12.0secs
0-1/4 mile: 18.4secs
111.0bhp 82.8kW 112.5PS
@ 5500rpm
110.0lbft 149.1Nm @ 4500rpm
94.9bhp/ton 93.3bhp/tonne
56.6bhp/L 42.2kW/L 57.4PS/L
53.2ft/sec 16.2m/sec
20.4mph 32.8kmh/1000rpm
28.8mpg 24.0mpgUS 9.8L/100km
Petrol 4-stroke piston
1962cc 119.7cu in
In-line 4 fuel injection
Compression ratio: 9.0:1
Bore: 84.0mm 3.3in
Stroke: 88.5mm 3.5in
Valve type/No: Overhead 8
Transmission: Manual
No. of forward speeds: 5
Wheels driven: Rear
Springs F/R: Torsion bar/Coil
Brake system: PA
Brakes F/R: Disc/Disc
Steering: Rack & pinion
Wheelbase: 240.0cm 94.5in
Track F: 135.9cm 53.5in
Track R: 135.9cm 53.5in
Length: 434.3cm 171.0in
Width: 166.4cm 65.5in
Height: 133.4cm 52.5in
Ground clearance: 15.2cm 6.0in
Kerb weight: 1189.5kg 2620.0lb
Fuel: 50.0L 11.0gal 13.2galUS

93 Alfa Romeo

Alfetta GTV
1976 Italy
120.0mph 193.1kmh
0-50mph 80.5kmh: 6.2secs
0-60mph 96.5kmh: 8.9secs
0-1/4 mile: 16.9secs
0-1km: 30.9secs
122.0bhp 91.0kW 123.7PS
@ 5300rpm
129.0lbft 174.8Nm @ 4400rpm
112.8bhp/ton 110.9bhp/tonne
62.2bhp/L 46.4kW/L 63.0PS/L
50.9ft/sec 15.5m/sec
20.7mph 33.3kmh/1000rpm
23.3mpg 19.4mpgUS 12.1L/100km
Petrol 4-stroke piston
1962cc 119.7cu in
In-line 4 2 Carburettor
Compression ratio: 9.0:1
Bore: 84.0mm 3.3in
Stroke: 88.0mm 3.5in
Valve type/No: Overhead 8
Transmission: Manual
No. of forward speeds: 5
Wheels driven: Rear
Springs F/R: Torsion bar/Coil
Brake system: PA
Brakes F/R: Disc/Disc
Steering: Rack & pinion
Wheelbase: 241.3cm 95.0in
Track F: 136.1cm 53.6in
Track R: 135.9cm 53.5in
Length: 419.1cm 165.0in
Width: 165.1cm 65.0in
Height: 133.1cm 52.4in
Ground clearance: 17.8cm 7.0in
Kerb weight: 1100.0kg 2423.0lb
Fuel: 54.1L 11.9gal 14.3galUS

94 Alfa Romeo

Spider Veloce 2000
1976 Italy
119.0mph 191.5kmh
0-50mph 80.5kmh: 7.5secs
0-60mph 96.5kmh: 9.8secs
0-1/4 mile: 17.1secs
0-1km: 31.8secs
133.0bhp 99.2kW 134.8PS
@ 5500rpm
132.0lbft 178.9Nm @ 3500rpm
132.7bhp/ton 130.5bhp/tonne
67.8bhp/L 50.5kW/L 68.7PS/L
53.2ft/sec 16.2m/sec
21.2mph 34.1kmh/1000rpm
24.8mpg 20.7mpgUS 11.4L/100km
Petrol 4-stroke piston
1962cc 119.7cu in
In-line 4 2 Carburettor
Compression ratio: 9.5:1
Bore: 84.0mm 3.3in
Stroke: 88.5mm 3.5in
Valve type/No: Overhead 8
Transmission: Manual
No. of forward speeds: 5
Wheels driven: Rear
Springs F/R: Coil/Coil
Brake system: PA
Brakes F/R: Disc/Disc
Steering: Recirculating ball
Wheelbase: 225.0cm 88.6in
Track F: 132.3cm 52.1in
Track R: 127.3cm 50.1in
Length: 412.0cm 162.2in
Width: 163.1cm 64.2in
Height: 129.0cm 50.8in
Ground clearance: 17.8cm 7.0in
Kerb weight: 1019.2kg 2245.0lb
Fuel: 51.0L 11.2gal 13.5galUS

95 Alfa Romeo

Alfasud 1200ti
1977 Italy
106.0mph 170.6kmh
0-50mph 80.5kmh: 9.1secs
0-60mph 96.5kmh: 13.8secs
0-1/4 mile: 19.1secs
0-1km: 36.2secs
68.0bhp 50.7kW 68.9PS
@ 6000rpm
66.5lbft 90.1Nm @ 3200rpm
85.5bhp/ton 84.0bhp/tonne
57.3bhp/L 42.8kW/L 58.1PS/L
38.7ft/sec 11.8m/sec
17.4mph 28.0kmh/1000rpm
29.0mpg 24.1mpgUS 9.7L/100km
Petrol 4-stroke piston
1186cc 72.4cu in
Flat 4 1 Carburettor
Compression ratio: 9.0:1
Bore: 80.0mm 3.1in
Stroke: 59.0mm 2.3in
Valve type/No: Overhead 8
Transmission: Manual
No. of forward speeds: 5
Wheels driven: Front
Springs F/R: Coil/Coil
Brake system: PA
Brakes F/R: Disc/Disc
Steering: Rack & pinion
Wheelbase: 245.0cm 96.5in
Track F: 138.4cm 54.5in
Track R: 135.1cm 53.2in
Length: 389.0cm 153.1in
Width: 159.0cm 62.6in
Height: 137.0cm 53.9in
Kerb weight: 809.0kg 1782.0lb
Fuel: 50.0L 11.0gal 13.2galUS

96 Alfa Romeo

Alfasud 1300ti
1977 Italy
103.0mph 165.7kmh
0-50mph 80.5kmh: 7.9secs
0-60mph 96.5kmh: 11.8secs
0-1/4 mile: 18.4secs
0-1km: 34.8secs
76.0bhp 56.7kW 77.0PS
@ 6000rpm
76.0lbft 103.0Nm @ 3500rpm
90.2bhp/ton 88.7bhp/tonne
59.1bhp/L 44.1kW/L 59.9PS/L
42.0ft/sec 12.8m/sec
16.6mph 26.7kmh/1000rpm
29.6mpg 24.6mpgUS 9.5L/100km
Petrol 4-stroke piston
1286cc 78.5cu in
Flat 4 1 Carburettor
Compression ratio: 9.0:1
Bore: 80.0mm 3.1in
Stroke: 64.0mm 2.5in
Valve type/No: Overhead 8
Transmission: Manual
No. of forward speeds: 5
Wheels driven: Front
Springs F/R: Coil/Coil
Brake system: PA
Brakes F/R: Disc/Disc
Steering: Rack & pinion
Wheelbase: 246.4cm 97.0in
Track F: 138.2cm 54.4in
Track R: 134.9cm 53.1in
Length: 389.1cm 153.2in
Width: 159.0cm 62.6in
Height: 136.9cm 53.9in
Ground clearance: 16.5cm 6.5in
Kerb weight: 857.1kg 1888.0lb
Fuel: 50.0L 11.0gal 13.2galUS

97 Alfa Romeo

Alfasud 5M
1977 Italy
94.0mph 151.2kmh
0-50mph 80.5kmh: 11.0secs
0-60mph 96.5kmh: 16.6secs
0-1/4 mile: 20.4secs
0-1km: 38.3secs
63.0bhp 47.0kW 63.9PS
@ 6000rpm
63.0lbft 85.4Nm @ 3200rpm
79.0bhp/ton 77.7bhp/tonne
53.1bhp/L 39.6kW/L 53.8PS/L
38.7ft/sec 11.8m/sec
17.4mph 28.0kmh/1000rpm
30.5mpg 25.4mpgUS 9.3L/100km
Petrol 4-stroke piston
1186cc 72.4cu in
Flat 4 1 Carburettor
Compression ratio: 8.8:1
Bore: 80.0mm 3.1in
Stroke: 59.0mm 2.3in
Valve type/No: Overhead 8
Transmission: Manual
No. of forward speeds: 5
Wheels driven: Front
Springs F/R: Coil/Coil
Brake system: PA
Brakes F/R: Disc/Disc
Steering: Rack & pinion
Wheelbase: 246.0cm 96.9in
Track F: 138.0cm 54.3in
Track R: 135.0cm 53.1in
Length: 389.0cm 153.1in
Width: 159.0cm 62.6in
Height: 137.0cm 53.9in
Kerb weight: 810.8kg 1786.0lb
Fuel: 50.0L 11.0gal 13.2galUS

98 Alfa Romeo

Alfetta
1977 Italy
97.0mph 156.1kmh
0-60mph 96.5kmh: 14.4secs
0-1/4 mile: 19.8secs
110.0bhp 82.0kW 111.5PS
@ 5500rpm
110.0lbft 149.1Nm @ 4500rpm
94.9bhp/ton 93.4bhp/tonne
56.1bhp/L 41.8kW/L 56.8PS/L
53.2ft/sec 16.2m/sec
Petrol 4-stroke piston
1962cc 119.7cu in
In-line 4 fuel injection
Compression ratio: 9.0:1
Bore: 84.0mm 3.3in
Stroke: 88.5mm 3.5in
Valve type/No: Overhead 8
Transmission: Manual
No. of forward speeds: 5
Wheels driven: Rear
Brakes F/R: Disc/Disc
Wheelbase: 251.0cm 98.8in
Track F: 135.9cm 53.5in
Track R: 135.6cm 53.4in
Length: 437.9cm 172.4in
Width: 161.8cm 63.7in
Height: 143.0cm 56.3in
Kerb weight: 1178.1kg 2595.0lb
Fuel: 50.0L 11.0gal 13.2galUS

99 Alfa Romeo

Spider
1977 Italy
104.0mph 167.3kmh
0-50mph 80.5kmh: 7.2secs
0-60mph 96.5kmh: 10.0secs
0-1/4 mile: 17.6secs
111.0bhp 82.8kW 112.5PS
@ 5000rpm
122.0lbft 165.3Nm @ 4000rpm
102.3bhp/ton 100.6bhp/tonne
56.6bhp/L 42.2kW/L 57.4PS/L
48.3ft/sec 14.7m/sec
18.5mph 29.8kmh/1000rpm
33.0mpg 27.5mpgUS 8.6L/100km
Petrol 4-stroke piston
1962cc 119.7cu in
In-line 4
Compression ratio: 9.0:1
Bore: 84.0mm 3.3in
Stroke: 88.5mm 3.5in
Valve type/No: Overhead 8
Transmission: Manual
No. of forward speeds: 5
Wheels driven: Rear
Springs F/R: Coil/Coil
Brake system: PA
Brakes F/R: Disc/Disc
Steering: Worm & roller
Wheelbase: 225.0cm 88.6in
Track F: 132.3cm 52.1in
Track R: 127.3cm 50.1in
Length: 428.8cm 168.8in
Width: 162.8cm 64.1in
Height: 124.0cm 48.8in
Kerb weight: 1103.2kg 2430.0lb
Fuel: 45.4L 10.0gal 12.0galUS

100 Alfa Romeo

Alfasud Sprint 1.5
1978 Italy
104.0mph 167.3kmh
0-50mph 80.5kmh: 7.7secs
0-60mph 96.5kmh: 11.2secs
0-1/4 mile: 18.6secs
0-1km: 34.9secs
85.0bhp 63.4kW 86.2PS
@ 5800rpm
89.0lbft 120.6Nm @ 3500rpm
93.3bhp/ton 91.8bhp/tonne
57.0bhp/L 42.5kW/L 57.8PS/L
39.3ft/sec 12.0m/sec
17.5mph 28.2kmh/1000rpm
25.1mpg 20.9mpgUS 11.3L/100km
Petrol 4-stroke piston
1490cc 90.9cu in
Flat 4 1 Carburettor
Compression ratio: 9.0:1
Bore: 84.0mm 3.3in
Stroke: 62.0mm 2.4in
Valve type/No: Overhead 8
Transmission: Manual
No. of forward speeds: 5
Wheels driven: Front
Springs F/R: Coil/Coil
Brake system: PA
Brakes F/R: Disc/Disc
Steering: Rack & pinion
Wheelbase: 245.0cm 96.5in

Track F: 138.0cm 54.3in
Track R: 135.0cm 53.1in
Length: 402.0cm 158.3in
Width: 161.0cm 63.4in
Height: 126.0cm 49.6in
Ground clearance: 22.0cm 8.7in
Kerb weight: 926.2kg 2040.0lb
Fuel: 50.0L 11.0gal 13.2galUS

101 Alfa Romeo

Alfetta 2.0
1978 Italy
114.0mph 183.4kmh
0-50mph 80.5kmh: 7.2secs
0-60mph 96.5kmh: 10.1secs
0-1/4 mile: 17.6secs
0-1km: 32.8secs
122.0bhp 91.0kW 123.7PS
@ 5300rpm
129.0lbft 174.8Nm @ 4000rpm
108.8bhp/ton 107.0bhp/tonne
62.2bhp/L 46.4kW/L 63.0PS/L
51.2ft/sec 15.6m/sec
20.8mph 33.5kmh/1000rpm
23.4mpg 19.5mpgUS 12.1L/100km
Petrol 4-stroke piston
1962cc 119.7cu in
In-line 4 2 Carburettor
Compression ratio: 9.0:1
Bore: 84.0mm 3.3in
Stroke: 88.5mm 3.5in
Valve type/No: Overhead 8
Transmission: Manual
No. of forward speeds: 5
Wheels driven: Rear
Springs F/R: Torsion bar/Coil
Brake system: PA
Brakes F/R: Disc/Disc
Steering: Rack & pinion
Wheelbase: 251.0cm 98.8in
Track F: 135.9cm 53.5in
Track R: 135.9cm 53.5in
Length: 437.9cm 172.4in
Width: 163.8cm 64.5in
Height: 143.0cm 56.3in
Ground clearance: 20.3cm 8.0in
Kerb weight: 1140.4kg 2512.0lb
Fuel: 48.7L 10.7gal 12.9galUS

102 Alfa Romeo

Giulietta 1.6
1978 Italy
108.0mph 173.8kmh
0-50mph 80.5kmh: 8.9secs
0-60mph 96.5kmh: 12.2secs
0-1/4 mile: 18.1secs
0-1km: 34.1secs
109.0bhp 81.3kW 110.5PS
@ 5600rpm
105.0lbft 142.3Nm @ 4300rpm
98.6bhp/ton 97.0bhp/tonne
69.4bhp/L 51.8kW/L 70.4PS/L
50.2ft/sec 15.3m/sec
18.8mph 30.2kmh/1000rpm
21.9mpg 18.2mpgUS 12.9L/100km
Petrol 4-stroke piston
1570cc 95.8cu in
In-line 4 2 Carburettor
Compression ratio: 9.0:1
Bore: 78.0mm 3.1in
Stroke: 82.0mm 3.2in
Valve type/No: Overhead 8
Transmission: Manual
No. of forward speeds: 5
Wheels driven: Rear
Springs F/R: Torsion bar/Coil
Brake system: PA
Brakes F/R: Disc/Disc
Steering: Rack & pinion
Wheelbase: 251.0cm 98.8in
Track F: 136.0cm 53.5in
Track R: 136.0cm 53.5in
Length: 421.0cm 165.7in
Width: 165.0cm 65.0in
Height: 140.0cm 55.1in
Ground clearance: 12.0cm 4.7in
Kerb weight: 1124.1kg 2476.0lb
Fuel: 50.0L 11.0gal 13.2galUS

103 Alfa Romeo

Sport Sedan
1978 Italy
116.0mph 186.6kmh
0-50mph 80.5kmh: 7.2secs
0-60mph 96.5kmh: 10.1secs
0-1/4 mile: 17.8secs
111.0bhp 82.8kW 112.5PS
@ 5000rpm
122.0lbft 165.3Nm @ 4000rpm
93.5bhp/ton 91.9bhp/tonne
56.6bhp/L 42.2kW/L 57.4PS/L
48.3ft/sec 14.7m/sec
21.1mph 33.9kmh/1000rpm
25.2mpg 21.0mpgUS 11.2L/100km
Petrol 4-stroke piston
1962cc 119.7cu in
In-line 4
Compression ratio: 9.0:1
Bore: 84.0mm 3.3in
Stroke: 88.5mm 3.5in
Valve type/No: Overhead 8
Transmission: Manual
No. of forward speeds: 5
Wheels driven: Rear
Springs F/R: Torsion bar/Coil
Brake system: PA
Brakes F/R: Disc/Disc
Steering: Rack & pinion
Wheelbase: 240.0cm 94.5in
Track F: 135.9cm 53.5in
Track R: 135.9cm 53.5in
Length: 434.3cm 171.0in
Width: 166.4cm 65.5in
Height: 133.4cm 52.5in
Kerb weight: 1207.6kg 2660.0lb
Fuel: 50.0L 11.0gal 13.2galUS

104 Alfa Romeo

Alfasud 1.5 Sprint Veloce
1979 Italy
106.0mph 170.6kmh
0-50mph 80.5kmh: 7.7secs
0-60mph 96.5kmh: 10.9secs
0-1/4 mile: 17.6secs
0-1km: 33.0secs
95.0bhp 70.8kW 96.3PS
@ 5800rpm
96.0lbft 130.1Nm @ 4000rpm
104.3bhp/ton 102.6bhp/tonne
63.8bhp/L 47.5kW/L 64.6PS/L
42.5ft/sec 12.9m/sec
17.9mph 28.8kmh/1000rpm
25.7mpg 21.4mpgUS 11.0L/100km
Petrol 4-stroke piston
1490cc 90.9cu in
Flat 4 2 Carburettor
Compression ratio: 9.5:1
Bore: 84.0mm 3.3in
Stroke: 67.0mm 2.6in
Valve type/No: Overhead 8
Transmission: Manual
No. of forward speeds: 5
Wheels driven: Front
Springs F/R: Coil/Coil
Brake system: PA
Brakes F/R: Disc/Disc
Steering: Rack & pinion
Wheelbase: 245.1cm 96.5in
Track F: 137.9cm 54.3in
Track R: 134.9cm 53.1in
Length: 401.8cm 158.2in
Width: 160.8cm 63.3in
Height: 126.0cm 49.6in
Ground clearance: 22.1cm 8.7in
Kerb weight: 926.2kg 2040.0lb
Fuel: 50.0L 11.0gal 13.2galUS

105 Alfa Romeo

Sport Sedan Automatic
1979 Italy
110.0mph 177.0kmh
0-50mph 80.5kmh: 9.6secs
0-60mph 96.5kmh: 13.3secs
0-1/4 mile: 19.8secs
111.0bhp 82.8kW 112.5PS
@ 5000rpm
122.0lbft 165.3Nm @ 4000rpm
88.3bhp/ton 86.8bhp/tonne
56.6bhp/L 42.2kW/L 57.4PS/L
48.3ft/sec 14.7m/sec
19.4mph 31.2kmh/1000rpm
27.0mpg 22.5mpgUS 10.5L/100km
Petrol 4-stroke piston
1962cc 119.7cu in
In-line 4
Compression ratio: 9.0:1
Bore: 84.0mm 3.3in
Stroke: 88.5mm 3.5in
Valve type/No: Overhead 8
Transmission: Automatic
No. of forward speeds: 3
Wheels driven: Rear
Springs F/R: Torsion bar/Coil
Brake system: PA
Brakes F/R: Disc/Disc
Steering: Rack & pinion
Wheelbase: 251.0cm 98.8in
Track F: 135.9cm 53.5in
Track R: 135.6cm 53.4in
Length: 437.9cm 172.4in
Width: 161.8cm 63.7in
Height: 143.0cm 56.3in
Kerb weight: 1278.0kg 2815.0lb
Fuel: 50.0L 11.0gal 13.2galUS

106 Alfa Romeo

Sprint Veloce
1979 Italy
116.0mph 186.6kmh
0-50mph 80.5kmh: 7.2secs
0-60mph 96.5kmh: 10.1secs
0-1/4 mile: 17.8secs
111.0bhp 82.8kW 112.5PS
@ 5000rpm
122.0lbft 165.3Nm @ 4000rpm
93.5bhp/ton 91.9bhp/tonne
56.6bhp/L 42.2kW/L 57.4PS/L
48.3ft/sec 14.7m/sec
25.2mpg 21.0mpgUS 11.2L/100km
Petrol 4-stroke piston
1962cc 119.7cu in
In-line 4 fuel injection
Compression ratio: 9.0:1
Bore: 84.0mm 3.3in
Stroke: 88.5mm 3.5in
Valve type/No: Overhead 8
Transmission: Manual
No. of forward speeds: 5
Wheels driven: Rear
Springs F/R: Torsion bar/Coil
Brake system: PA
Brakes F/R: Disc/Disc
Steering: Rack & pinion
Wheelbase: 240.0cm 94.5in
Track F: 135.9cm 53.5in
Track R: 135.9cm 53.5in
Length: 434.3cm 171.0in
Width: 166.4cm 65.5in
Height: 133.4cm 52.5in
Ground clearance: 15.2cm 6.0in
Kerb weight: 1207.6kg 2660.0lb
Fuel: 50.0L 11.0gal 13.2galUS

107 Alfa Romeo

Spider
1980 Italy
110.0mph 177.0kmh
0-60mph 96.5kmh: 10.7secs
0-1/4 mile: 18.6secs
111.0bhp 82.8kW 112.5PS
@ 5000rpm
116.0lbft 157.2Nm @ 2500rpm
97.9bhp/ton 96.3bhp/tonne
56.6bhp/L 42.2kW/L 57.4PS/L
48.3ft/sec 14.7m/sec
22.1mph 35.6kmh/1000rpm
30.6mpg 25.5mpgUS 9.2L/100km
Petrol 4-stroke piston
1962cc 119.7cu in
In-line 4 fuel injection
Compression ratio: 9.0:1
Bore: 84.0mm 3.3in
Stroke: 88.5mm 3.5in
Valve type/No: Overhead 8
Transmission: Manual
No. of forward speeds: 5
Wheels driven: Rear
Springs F/R: Coil/Coil
Brake system: PA
Brakes F/R: Disc/Disc
Steering: Worm & roller
Wheelbase: 225.0cm 88.6in
Track F: 132.3cm 52.1in
Track R: 127.3cm 50.1in
Length: 428.8cm 168.8in
Width: 162.8cm 64.1in
Height: 124.0cm 48.8in
Ground clearance: 14.7cm 5.8in
Kerb weight: 1153.2kg 2540.0lb
Fuel: 45.4L 10.0gal 12.0galUS

108 Alfa Romeo

Alfasud 1.5
1981 Italy
106.0mph 170.6kmh
0-50mph 80.5kmh: 8.0secs
0-60mph 96.5kmh: 11.6secs
0-1/4 mile: 18.5secs
0-1km: 34.8secs
84.0bhp 62.6kW 85.2PS
@ 5800rpm
89.0lbft 120.6Nm @ 3500rpm
94.2bhp/ton 92.6bhp/tonne
56.4bhp/L 42.0kW/L 57.2PS/L
42.7ft/sec 13.0m/sec
18.1mph 29.1kmh/1000rpm
28.2mpg 23.5mpgUS 10.0L/100km
Petrol 4-stroke piston
1490cc 90.9cu in
Flat 4 1 Carburettor
Compression ratio: 9.0:1
Bore: 84.0mm 3.3in
Stroke: 67.2mm 2.6in
Valve type/No: Overhead 8
Transmission: Manual
No. of forward speeds: 5
Wheels driven: Front
Springs F/R: Coil/Coil
Brake system: PA
Brakes F/R: Disc/Disc
Steering: Rack & pinion
Wheelbase: 245.6cm 96.7in
Track F: 139.2cm 54.8in
Track R: 135.9cm 53.5in
Length: 397.8cm 156.6in
Width: 161.5cm 63.6in
Height: 136.9cm 53.9in
Ground clearance: 16.5cm 6.5in
Kerb weight: 907.1kg 1998.0lb
Fuel: 50.0L 11.0gal 13.2galUS

109 Alfa Romeo

GTV6
1981 Italy
132.0mph 212.4kmh
0-50mph 80.5kmh: 6.3secs
0-60mph 96.5kmh: 8.8secs
0-1/4 mile: 16.7secs
0-1km: 30.6secs
160.0bhp 119.3kW 162.2PS
@ 5600rpm
157.0lbft 212.7Nm @ 4000rpm
132.6bhp/ton 130.4bhp/tonne
64.2bhp/L 47.9kW/L 65.1PS/L
41.8ft/sec 12.7m/sec
22.0mph 35.4kmh/1000rpm
23.2mpg 19.3mpgUS 12.2L/100km
Petrol 4-stroke piston
2492cc 152.0cu in
Vee 6 fuel injection
Compression ratio: 9.0:1
Bore: 88.0mm 3.5in
Stroke: 68.3mm 2.7in
Valve type/No: Overhead 12
Transmission: Manual
No. of forward speeds: 5
Wheels driven: Rear
Springs F/R: Torsion bar/Coil
Brake system: PA
Brakes F/R: Disc/Disc
Steering: Rack & pinion
Wheelbase: 240.0cm 94.5in
Track F: 137.4cm 54.1in
Track R: 135.1cm 53.2in
Length: 426.0cm 167.7in
Width: 166.4cm 65.5in
Height: 133.1cm 52.4in
Ground clearance: 17.8cm 7.0in
Kerb weight: 1226.7kg 2702.0lb
Fuel: 75.1L 16.5gal 19.8galUS

110 Alfa Romeo

Spider Veloce
1982 Italy
110.0mph 177.0kmh
0-50mph 80.5kmh: 8.3secs
0-60mph 96.5kmh: 11.7secs
0-1/4 mile: 18.3secs
115.0bhp 85.8kW 116.6PS
@ 5500rpm
119.0lbft 161.2Nm @ 2750rpm
103.2bhp/ton 101.5bhp/tonne
58.6bhp/L 43.7kW/L 59.4PS/L
53.2ft/sec 16.2m/sec
21.5mph 34.6kmh/1000rpm
27.0mpg 22.5mpgUS 10.5L/100km
Petrol 4-stroke piston
1962cc 119.7cu in
In-line 4 fuel injection
Compression ratio: 9.0:1
Bore: 84.0mm 3.3in
Stroke: 88.5mm 3.5in
Valve type/No: Overhead 8
Transmission: Manual
No. of forward speeds: 5
Wheels driven: Rear

Springs F/R: Coil/Coil
Brake system: PA
Brakes F/R: Disc/Disc
Steering: Worm & roller
Wheelbase: 225.0cm 88.6in
Track F: 132.3cm 52.1in
Track R: 127.3cm 50.1in
Length: 428.8cm 168.8in
Width: 162.8cm 64.1in
Height: 124.0cm 48.8in
Kerb weight: 1132.7kg 2495.0lb
Fuel: 46.2L 10.1gal 12.2galUS

111 Alfa Romeo

Spider Veloce 2000
1982 Italy
108.0mph 173.8kmh
0-60mph 96.5kmh: 13.2secs
0-1/4 mile: 19.5secs
111.0bhp 82.8kW 112.5PS
@ 5000rpm
116.0lbft 157.2Nm @ 2500rpm
97.9bhp/ton 96.3bhp/tonne
56.6bhp/L 42.2kW/L 57.4PS/L
48.3ft/sec 14.7m/sec
21.8mph 35.1kmh/1000rpm
31.2mpg 26.0mpgUS 9.0L/100km
Petrol 4-stroke piston
1962cc 119.7cu in
In-line 4 fuel injection
Compression ratio: 9.0:1
Bore: 84.0mm 3.3in
Stroke: 88.5mm 3.5in
Valve type/No: Overhead 8
Transmission: Manual
No. of forward speeds: 5
Wheels driven: Rear
Springs F/R: Coil/Coil
Brake system: PA
Brakes F/R: Disc/Disc
Steering: Worm & roller
Wheelbase: 225.0cm 88.6in
Track F: 132.3cm 52.1in
Track R: 127.3cm 50.1in
Length: 428.8cm 168.8in
Width: 162.8cm 64.1in
Height: 124.0cm 48.8in
Ground clearance: 14.7cm 5.8in
Kerb weight: 1153.2kg 2540.0lb
Fuel: 46.2L 10.1gal 12.2galUS

112 Alfa Romeo

Alfa 33 1.5
1983 Italy
105.0mph 168.9kmh
0-50mph 80.5kmh: 8.0secs
0-60mph 96.5kmh: 10.8secs
0-1/4 mile: 18.1secs
0-1km: 33.6secs
85.0bhp 63.4kW 86.2PS
@ 5800rpm
69.0lbft 93.5Nm @ 3500rpm
94.8bhp/ton 93.2bhp/tonne
57.0bhp/L 42.5kW/L 57.8PS/L
42.7ft/sec 13.0m/sec
22.1mph 35.6kmh/1000rpm
29.4mpg 24.5mpgUS 9.6L/100km
Petrol 4-stroke piston
1490cc 90.9cu in
Flat 4 1 Carburettor
Compression ratio: 9.0:1
Bore: 84.0mm 3.3in
Stroke: 67.2mm 2.6in
Valve type/No: Overhead 8
Transmission: Manual
No. of forward speeds: 5
Wheels driven: Front
Springs F/R: Coil/Coil
Brake system: PA
Brakes F/R: Disc/Drum
Steering: Rack & pinion
Wheelbase: 245.6cm 96.7in
Track F: 139.2cm 54.8in
Track R: 135.9cm 53.5in
Length: 401.3cm 158.0in
Width: 161.3cm 63.5in
Height: 130.6cm 51.4in
Ground clearance: 15.0cm 5.9in
Kerb weight: 911.6kg 2008.0lb
Fuel: 50.0L 11.0gal 13.2galUS

113 Alfa Romeo

Alfetta Gold Cloverleaf
1984 Italy
112.0mph 180.2kmh
0-50mph 80.5kmh: 6.8secs
0-60mph 96.5kmh: 9.8secs
0-1/4 mile: 17.1secs
0-1km: 31.8secs
130.0bhp 96.9kW 131.8PS
@ 5400rpm
134.0lbft 181.6Nm @ 4000rpm
111.3bhp/ton 109.4bhp/tonne
66.3bhp/L 49.4kW/L 67.2PS/L
52.2ft/sec 15.9m/sec
23.8mph 38.3kmh/1000rpm
25.0mpg 20.8mpgUS 11.3L/100km
Petrol 4-stroke piston
1962cc 119.7cu in
In-line 4 fuel injection
Compression ratio: 10.0:1
Bore: 84.0mm 3.3in
Stroke: 88.5mm 3.5in
Valve type/No: Overhead 8
Transmission: Manual
No. of forward speeds: 5
Wheels driven: Rear
Springs F/R: Torsion bar/Coil
Brake system: PA
Brakes F/R: Disc/Disc
Steering: Rack & pinion
Wheelbase: 251.0cm 98.8in
Track F: 135.9cm 53.5in
Track R: 135.9cm 53.5in
Length: 438.4cm 172.6in
Width: 164.1cm 64.6in
Height: 143.0cm 56.3in
Ground clearance: 20.3cm 8.0in
Kerb weight: 1188.1kg 2617.0lb
Fuel: 50.0L 11.0gal 13.2galUS

114 Alfa Romeo

GTV6
1984 Italy
130.0mph 209.2kmh
0-50mph 80.5kmh: 7.4secs
0-60mph 96.5kmh: 9.1secs
0-1/4 mile: 17.0secs
154.0bhp 114.8kW 156.1PS
@ 5500rpm
155.0lbft 210.0Nm @ 3200rpm
121.5bhp/ton 119.4bhp/tonne
61.8bhp/L 46.1kW/L 62.7PS/L
41.1ft/sec 12.5m/sec
25.9mph 41.7kmh/1000rpm
29.4mpg 24.5mpgUS 9.6L/100km
Petrol 4-stroke piston
2492cc 152.0cu in
Vee 6 fuel injection
Compression ratio: 9.0:1
Bore: 88.0mm 3.5in
Stroke: 68.3mm 2.7in
Valve type/No: Overhead 12
Transmission: Manual
No. of forward speeds: 5
Wheels driven: Rear
Springs F/R: Torsion bar/Coil
Brake system: PA
Brakes F/R: Disc/Disc
Steering: Rack & pinion
Wheelbase: 240.0cm 94.5in
Track F: 137.2cm 54.0in
Track R: 135.1cm 53.2in
Length: 426.0cm 167.7in
Width: 166.4cm 65.5in
Height: 133.1cm 52.4in
Kerb weight: 1289.4kg 2840.0lb
Fuel: 66.6L 14.6gal 17.6galUS

115 Alfa Romeo

Spider
1984 Italy
110.0mph 177.0kmh
0-50mph 80.5kmh: 8.3secs
0-60mph 96.5kmh: 11.7secs
0-1/4 mile: 18.3secs
115.0bhp 85.8kW 116.6PS
@ 5500rpm
119.0lbft 161.2Nm @ 2750rpm
103.2bhp/ton 101.5bhp/tonne
58.6bhp/L 43.7kW/L 59.4PS/L
53.2ft/sec 16.2m/sec
21.5mph 34.6kmh/1000rpm
27.0mpg 22.5mpgUS 10.5L/100km
Petrol 4-stroke piston
1962cc 119.7cu in
In-line 4 fuel injection
Compression ratio: 9.0:1
Bore: 84.0mm 3.3in
Stroke: 88.5mm 3.5in
Valve type/No: Overhead 8
Transmission: Manual
No. of forward speeds: 5
Wheels driven: Rear
Springs F/R: Coil/Coil
Brake system: PA
Brakes F/R: Disc/Disc
Steering: Worm & roller
Wheelbase: 225.0cm 88.6in
Track F: 132.3cm 52.1in
Track R: 127.3cm 50.1in
Length: 428.8cm 168.8in
Width: 162.8cm 64.1in
Height: 124.0cm 48.8in
Kerb weight: 1132.7kg 2495.0lb
Fuel: 46.2L 10.1gal 12.2galUS

116 Alfa Romeo

Sprint Green Cloverleaf
1984 Italy
111.0mph 178.6kmh
0-50mph 80.5kmh: 7.6secs
0-60mph 96.5kmh: 10.8secs
0-1/4 mile: 18.0secs
0-1km: 33.5secs
105.0bhp 78.3kW 106.5PS
@ 6000rpm
98.0lbft 132.8Nm @ 4000rpm
109.5bhp/ton 107.7bhp/tonne
70.5bhp/L 52.5kW/L 71.4PS/L
44.2ft/sec 13.4m/sec
18.7mph 30.1kmh/1000rpm
23.9mpg 19.9mpgUS 11.8L/100km
Petrol 4-stroke piston
1490cc 90.9cu in
Flat 4 2 Carburettor
Compression ratio: 9.5:1
Bore: 84.0mm 3.3in
Stroke: 67.2mm 2.6in
Valve type/No: Overhead 8
Transmission: Manual
No. of forward speeds: 5
Wheels driven: Front
Springs F/R: Coil/Coil
Brake system: PA
Brakes F/R: Disc/Disc
Steering: Rack & pinion
Wheelbase: 245.6cm 96.7in
Track F: 139.7cm 55.0in
Track R: 136.4cm 53.7in
Length: 402.3cm 158.4in
Width: 162.1cm 63.8in
Height: 130.6cm 51.4in
Ground clearance: 16.5cm 6.5in
Kerb weight: 975.2kg 2148.0lb
Fuel: 50.0L 11.0gal 13.2galUS

117 Alfa Romeo

Alfa 33 1.5 4x4 Estate
1985 Italy
112.0mph 180.2kmh
0-50mph 80.5kmh: 7.8secs
0-60mph 96.5kmh: 10.9secs
0-1/4 mile: 18.0secs
0-1km: 33.1secs
85.0bhp 63.4kW 86.2PS
@ 5800rpm
96.0lbft 130.1Nm @ 4000rpm
89.2bhp/ton 87.7bhp/tonne
57.0bhp/L 42.5kW/L 57.8PS/L
42.7ft/sec 13.0m/sec
19.3mph 31.1kmh/1000rpm
28.6mpg 23.8mpgUS 9.9L/100km
Petrol 4-stroke piston
1490cc 90.9cu in
Flat 4 2 Carburettor
Compression ratio: 9.5:1
Bore: 84.0mm 3.3in
Stroke: 67.2mm 2.6in
Valve type/No: Overhead 8
Transmission: Manual
No. of forward speeds: 5
Wheels driven: 4-wheel drive
Springs F/R: Coil/Coil
Brake system: PA
Brakes F/R: Disc/Drum
Steering: Rack & pinion
Wheelbase: 245.6cm 96.7in
Track F: 139.7cm 55.0in
Track R: 137.4cm 54.1in
Length: 414.0cm 163.0in
Width: 161.0cm 63.4in
Height: 132.3cm 52.1in
Ground clearance: 13.0cm 5.1in
Kerb weight: 969.3kg 2135.0lb
Fuel: 50.0L 11.0gal 13.2galUS

118 Alfa Romeo

Alfa 90 2.5 Gold Cloverleaf
1985 Italy
128.0mph 206.0kmh
0-50mph 80.5kmh: 6.7secs
0-60mph 96.5kmh: 9.0secs
0-1/4 mile: 16.8secs
0-1km: 30.9secs
156.0bhp 116.3kW 158.2PS
@ 5600rpm
156.8lbft 212.5Nm @ 4000rpm
127.3bhp/ton 125.2bhp/tonne
62.6bhp/L 46.7kW/L 63.5PS/L
41.8ft/sec 12.7m/sec
25.5mph 41.0kmh/1000rpm
22.2mpg 18.5mpgUS 12.7L/100km
Petrol 4-stroke piston
2492cc 152.0cu in
Vee 6 fuel injection
Compression ratio: 9.0:1
Bore: 88.0mm 3.5in
Stroke: 68.3mm 2.7in
Valve type/No: Overhead 12
Transmission: Manual
No. of forward speeds: 5
Wheels driven: Rear
Springs F/R: Torsion bar/Coil
Brake system: PA
Brakes F/R: Disc/Disc
Steering: Rack & pinion PA
Wheelbase: 251.0cm 98.8in
Track F: 136.7cm 53.8in
Track R: 135.9cm 53.5in
Length: 439.2cm 172.9in
Width: 163.8cm 64.5in
Height: 152.4cm 60.0in
Ground clearance: 16.5cm 6.5in
Kerb weight: 1246.2kg 2745.0lb
Fuel: 49.1L 10.8gal 13.0galUS

119 Alfa Romeo

Arna 1.3SL
1985 Italy
101.0mph 162.5kmh
0-50mph 80.5kmh: 9.1secs
0-60mph 96.5kmh: 13.1secs
0-1/4 mile: 19.3secs
0-1km: 37.0secs
71.0bhp 52.9kW 72.0PS
@ 5800rpm
77.4lbft 104.9Nm @ 3000rpm
84.9bhp/ton 83.4bhp/tonne
52.5bhp/L 39.2kW/L 53.3PS/L
42.7ft/sec 13.0m/sec
20.1mph 32.3kmh/1000rpm
29.4mpg 24.5mpgUS 9.6L/100km
Petrol 4-stroke piston
1351cc 82.4cu in
Flat 4 1 Carburettor
Compression ratio: 9.0:1
Bore: 80.0mm 3.1in
Stroke: 67.2mm 2.6in
Valve type/No: Overhead 8
Transmission: Manual
No. of forward speeds: 5
Wheels driven: Rear
Springs F/R: Coil/Coil
Brake system: PA
Brakes F/R: Disc/Drum
Steering: Rack & pinion
Wheelbase: 241.6cm 95.1in
Track F: 139.4cm 54.9in
Track R: 138.4cm 54.5in
Length: 399.5cm 157.3in
Width: 162.1cm 63.8in
Height: 138.4cm 54.5in
Ground clearance: 16.5cm 6.5in
Kerb weight: 850.8kg 1874.0lb
Fuel: 50.0L 11.0gal 13.2galUS

120 Alfa Romeo

Arna ti
1985 Italy
109.0mph 175.4kmh
0-50mph 80.5kmh: 7.2secs
0-60mph 96.5kmh: 10.2secs
0-1/4 mile: 17.4secs
0-1km: 32.5secs
95.0bhp 70.8kW 96.3PS
@ 5800rpm
96.1lbft 130.2Nm @ 4000rpm
114.2bhp/ton 112.3bhp/tonne
63.8bhp/L 47.5kW/L 64.6PS/L
42.7ft/sec 13.0m/sec
21.9mph 35.2kmh/1000rpm
24.3mpg 20.2mpgUS 11.6L/100km
Petrol 4-stroke piston
1490cc 90.9cu in
Flat 4 2 Carburettor

Compression ratio: 9.5:1
Bore: 84.0mm 3.3in
Stroke: 67.2mm 2.6in
Valve type/No: Overhead 8
Transmission: Manual
No. of forward speeds: 5
Wheels driven: Rear
Springs F/R: Coil/Coil
Brake system: PA
Brakes F/R: Disc/Drum
Steering: Rack & pinion
Wheelbase: 241.6cm 95.1in
Track F: 139.4cm 54.9in
Track R: 138.4cm 54.5in
Length: 399.5cm 157.3in
Width: 162.1cm 63.8in
Height: 138.4cm 54.5in
Ground clearance: 16.5cm 6.5in
Kerb weight: 845.8kg 1863.0lb
Fuel: 50.0L 11.0gal 13.2galUS

121 Alfa Romeo

Graduate
1985 Italy
103.0mph 165.7kmh
0-60mph 96.5kmh: 10.4secs
0-1/4 mile: 17.6secs
115.0bhp 85.8kW 116.6PS
@ 5500rpm
119.0lbft 161.2Nm @ 2750rpm
103.2bhp/ton 101.5bhp/tonne
58.6bhp/L 43.7kW/L 59.4PS/L
53.2ft/sec 16.2m/sec
21.5mph 34.6kmh/1000rpm
28.6mpg 23.8mpgUS 9.9L/100km
Petrol 4-stroke piston
1962cc 119.7cu in
In-line 4 fuel injection
Bore: 84.0mm 3.3in
Stroke: 88.5mm 3.5in
Valve type/No: Overhead 8
Transmission: Manual
No. of forward speeds: 5
Wheels driven: Rear
Springs F/R: Coil/Coil
Brakes F/R: Disc/Disc
Steering: Worm & roller
Wheelbase: 225.0cm 88.6in
Track F: 132.3cm 52.1in
Track R: 127.3cm 50.1in
Length: 428.8cm 168.8in
Width: 162.8cm 64.1in
Height: 124.0cm 48.8in
Kerb weight: 1132.7kg 2495.0lb
Fuel: 46.2L 10.1gal 12.2galUS

122 Alfa Romeo

GTV Callaway Twin Turbo
1985 Italy
137.0mph 220.4kmh
0-50mph 80.5kmh: 4.7secs
0-60mph 96.5kmh: 6.2secs
0-1/4 mile: 14.5secs
230.0bhp 171.5kW 233.2PS
@ 5500rpm
245.0lbft 332.0Nm @ 2500rpm
178.3bhp/ton 175.3bhp/tonne
92.3bhp/L 68.8kW/L 93.6PS/L
41.1ft/sec 12.5m/sec
21.8mph 35.1kmh/1000rpm
22.2mpg 18.5mpgUS 12.7L/100km
Petrol 4-stroke piston
2492cc 152.0cu in turbocharged
Vee 6 fuel injection
Compression ratio: 7.5:1
Bore: 88.0mm 3.5in
Stroke: 68.3mm 2.7in
Valve type/No: Overhead 12
Transmission: Manual
No. of forward speeds: 5
Wheels driven: Rear
Springs F/R: Torsion bar/Coil
Brake system: PA
Brakes F/R: Disc/Disc
Steering: Rack & pinion
Wheelbase: 240.0cm 94.5in
Track F: 137.2cm 54.0in
Track R: 135.1cm 53.2in
Length: 426.0cm 167.7in
Width: 166.4cm 65.5in
Height: 133.1cm 52.4in
Kerb weight: 1312.1kg 2890.0lb
Fuel: 66.6L 14.6gal 17.6galUS

123 Alfa Romeo

Alfa 33 1.3 S
1986 Italy
109.0mph 175.4kmh
0-50mph 80.5kmh: 7.9secs
0-60mph 96.5kmh: 11.7secs
0-1/4 mile: 18.0secs
0-1km: 33.8secs
85.0bhp 63.4kW 86.2PS
@ 5800rpm
88.0lbft 119.2Nm @ 4000rpm
95.3bhp/ton 93.7bhp/tonne
62.9bhp/L 46.9kW/L 63.8PS/L
42.7ft/sec 13.0m/sec
21.8mph 35.1kmh/1000rpm
27.2mpg 22.6mpgUS 10.4L/100km
Petrol 4-stroke piston
1351cc 82.0cu in
Flat 4 2 Carburettor
Compression ratio: 9.5:1
Bore: 80.0mm 3.1in
Stroke: 67.2mm 2.6in
Valve type/No: Overhead 8
Transmission: Manual
No. of forward speeds: 5
Wheels driven: Front
Springs F/R: Coil/Coil
Brake system: PA
Brakes F/R: Disc/Drum
Steering: Rack & pinion
Wheelbase: 245.5cm 96.7in
Track F: 139.2cm 54.8in
Track R: 135.9cm 53.5in
Length: 401.5cm 158.1in
Width: 161.2cm 63.5in
Height: 134.0cm 52.8in
Ground clearance: 15.0cm 5.9in
Kerb weight: 907.0kg 1997.8lb
Fuel: 50.0L 11.0gal 13.2galUS

124 Alfa Romeo

Alfa 75 1.8
1986 Italy
120.0mph 193.1kmh
0-50mph 80.5kmh: 7.4secs
0-60mph 96.5kmh: 10.3secs
0-1/4 mile: 17.5secs
0-1km: 32.4secs
120.0bhp 89.5kW 121.7PS
@ 5300rpm
123.0lbft 166.7Nm @ 4000rpm
107.0bhp/ton 105.3bhp/tonne
67.4bhp/L 50.3kW/L 68.4PS/L
51.2ft/sec 15.6m/sec
20.1mph 32.3kmh/1000rpm
24.5mpg 20.4mpgUS 11.5L/100km
Petrol 4-stroke piston
1779cc 109.0cu in
In-line 4 2 Carburettor
Compression ratio: 9.5:1
Bore: 80.0mm 3.1in
Stroke: 88.5mm 3.5in
Valve type/No: Overhead 8
Transmission: Manual
No. of forward speeds: 5
Wheels driven: Rear
Springs F/R: Torsion bar/Coil
Brake system: PA
Brakes F/R: Disc/Disc
Steering: Rack & pinion
Wheelbase: 251.0cm 98.8in
Track F: 136.8cm 53.9in
Track R: 135.8cm 53.5in
Length: 433.0cm 170.5in
Width: 163.0cm 64.2in
Height: 135.0cm 53.1in
Ground clearance: 20.3cm 8.0in
Kerb weight: 1140.0kg 2511.0lb
Fuel: 49.1L 10.8gal 13.0galUS

125 Alfa Romeo

Alfa 75 2.5 Green Cloverleaf
1986 Italy
130.0mph 209.2kmh
0-50mph 80.5kmh: 6.4secs
0-60mph 96.5kmh: 8.9secs
0-1/4 mile: 16.7secs
0-1km: 30.4secs
156.0bhp 116.3kW 158.2PS
@ 5600rpm
155.0lbft 210.0Nm @ 4000rpm
130.0bhp/ton 127.9bhp/tonne
62.6bhp/L 46.7kW/L 63.5PS/L
41.8ft/sec 12.7m/sec
20.8mph 33.5kmh/1000rpm
22.8mpg 19.0mpgUS 12.4L/100km
Petrol 4-stroke piston
2492cc 152.0cu in
Vee 6 fuel injection
Compression ratio: 9.5:1
Bore: 88.0mm 3.5in
Stroke: 68.3mm 2.7in
Valve type/No: Overhead 12
Transmission: Manual
No. of forward speeds: 5
Wheels driven: Rear
Springs F/R: Torsion bar/Coil
Brake system: PA
Brakes F/R: Disc/Disc
Steering: Rack & pinion PA
Wheelbase: 251.0cm 98.8in
Track F: 136.8cm 53.9in
Track R: 135.8cm 53.5in
Length: 433.0cm 170.5in
Width: 163.0cm 64.2in
Height: 135.0cm 53.1in
Ground clearance: 20.3cm 8.0in
Kerb weight: 1220.0kg 2687.2lb
Fuel: 56.9L 12.5gal 15.0galUS

126 Alfa Romeo

GTV6
1986 Italy
133.0mph 214.0kmh
0-60mph 96.5kmh: 8.2secs
0-1/4 mile: 16.2secs
160.0bhp 119.3kW 162.2PS
@ 5800rpm
157.0lbft 212.7Nm @ 4000rpm
134.2bhp/ton 132.0bhp/tonne
64.2bhp/L 47.9kW/L 65.1PS/L
43.3ft/sec 13.2m/sec
21.8mph 35.1kmh/1000rpm
26.3mpg 21.9mpgUS 10.7L/100km
Petrol 4-stroke piston
2492cc 152.0cu in
Vee 6 fuel injection
Compression ratio: 9.0:1
Bore: 88.0mm 3.5in
Stroke: 68.3mm 2.7in
Valve type/No: Overhead 12
Transmission: Manual
No. of forward speeds: 5
Wheels driven: Rear
Springs F/R: Torsion bar/Coil
Brakes F/R: Disc/Disc
Steering: Rack & pinion
Wheelbase: 240.0cm 94.5in
Track F: 137.4cm 54.1in
Track R: 135.1cm 53.2in
Length: 426.0cm 167.7in
Width: 166.4cm 65.5in
Height: 130.0cm 51.2in
Kerb weight: 1212.2kg 2670.0lb

127 Alfa Romeo

Milano Platinum
1986 Italy
129.0mph 207.6kmh
0-50mph 80.5kmh: 6.7secs
0-60mph 96.5kmh: 9.0secs
0-1/4 mile: 16.8secs
154.0bhp 114.8kW 156.1PS
@ 5600rpm
152.0lbft 206.0Nm @ 3200rpm
115.6bhp/ton 113.6bhp/tonne
61.8bhp/L 46.1kW/L 62.7PS/L
41.8ft/sec 12.7m/sec
26.2mpg 21.8mpgUS 10.8L/100km
Petrol 4-stroke piston
2492cc 152.0cu in
Vee 6 fuel injection
Compression ratio: 9.0:1
Bore: 88.0mm 3.5in
Stroke: 68.3mm 2.7in
Valve type/No: Overhead 12
Transmission: Manual
No. of forward speeds: 5
Wheels driven: Rear
Springs F/R: Gas/Coil
Brake system: PA ABS
Brakes F/R: Disc/Disc
Steering: Rack & pinion PA
Wheelbase: 251.0cm 98.8in
Track F: 137.9cm 54.3in
Track R: 136.9cm 53.9in
Length: 433.1cm 170.5in
Width: 163.1cm 64.2in
Height: 134.9cm 53.1in
Ground clearance: 10.2cm 4.0in
Kerb weight: 1355.2kg 2985.0lb
Fuel: 66.6L 14.6gal 17.6galUS

128 Alfa Romeo

Spider Quadrifoglio
1986 Italy
110.0mph 177.0kmh
0-50mph 80.5kmh: 7.5secs
0-60mph 96.5kmh: 11.0secs
0-1/4 mile: 17.5secs
115.0bhp 85.8kW 116.6PS
@ 5500rpm
119.0lbft 161.2Nm @ 2750rpm
99.5bhp/ton 97.8bhp/tonne
58.6bhp/L 43.7kW/L 59.4PS/L
53.2ft/sec 16.2m/sec
25.2mpg 21.0mpgUS 11.2L/100km
Petrol 4-stroke piston
1962cc 119.7cu in
In-line 4 fuel injection
Compression ratio: 9.0:1
Bore: 84.0mm 3.3in
Stroke: 88.5mm 3.5in
Valve type/No: Overhead 8
Transmission: Manual
No. of forward speeds: 5
Wheels driven: Rear
Springs F/R: Coil/Coil
Brake system: PA
Brakes F/R: Disc/Disc
Steering: Worm & roller
Wheelbase: 225.0cm 88.6in
Track F: 132.3cm 52.1in
Track R: 127.3cm 50.1in
Length: 428.8cm 168.8in
Width: 162.8cm 64.1in
Height: 124.0cm 48.8in
Kerb weight: 1175.9kg 2590.0lb
Fuel: 46.2L 10.1gal 12.2galUS

129 Alfa Romeo

33 1.7 Veloce
1987 Italy
118.0mph 189.9kmh
0-50mph 80.5kmh: 6.8secs
0-60mph 96.5kmh: 9.1secs
0-1/4 mile: 16.5secs
0-1km: 31.2secs
118.0bhp 88.0kW 119.6PS
@ 6000rpm
108.5lbft 147.0Nm @ 3500rpm
128.8bhp/ton 126.6bhp/tonne
68.9bhp/L 51.4kW/L 69.9PS/L
47.3ft/sec 14.4m/sec
20.7mph 33.3kmh/1000rpm
26.2mpg 21.8mpgUS 10.8L/100km
Petrol 4-stroke piston
1712cc 104.0cu in
Flat 4 2 Carburettor
Compression ratio: 9.5:1
Bore: 87.0mm 3.4in
Stroke: 72.2mm 2.8in
Valve type/No: Overhead 8
Transmission: Manual
No. of forward speeds: 5
Wheels driven: Front
Springs F/R: Coil/Coil
Brake system: PA
Brakes F/R: Disc/Drum
Steering: Rack & pinion
Wheelbase: 245.5cm 96.7in
Track F: 139.2cm 54.8in
Track R: 135.9cm 53.5in
Length: 401.5cm 158.1in
Width: 161.2cm 63.5in
Height: 134.0cm 52.8in
Ground clearance: 15.0cm 5.9in
Kerb weight: 932.0kg 2052.9lb
Fuel: 50.0L 11.0gal 13.2galUS

130 Alfa Romeo

Alfa 33 1.7 Sportwagon Veloce
1987 Italy
118.0mph 189.9kmh
0-50mph 80.5kmh: 7.0secs
0-60mph 96.5kmh: 9.5secs
0-1/4 mile: 17.5secs
0-1km: 31.9secs
118.0bhp 88.0kW 119.6PS
@ 6000rpm
109.0lbft 147.7Nm @ 3900rpm
123.1bhp/ton 121.0bhp/tonne
68.9bhp/L 51.4kW/L 69.9PS/L
47.3ft/sec 14.4m/sec
20.7mph 33.3kmh/1000rpm
25.8mpg 21.5mpgUS 10.9L/100km
Petrol 4-stroke piston
1712cc 104.0cu in
Flat 4 2 Carburettor
Compression ratio: 9.5:1
Bore: 87.0mm 3.4in
Stroke: 72.2mm 2.8in

Valve type/No: Overhead 8
Transmission: Manual
No. of forward speeds: 5
Wheels driven: Front
Springs F/R: Coil/Coil
Brake system: PA
Brakes F/R: Disc/Drum
Steering: Rack & pinion
Wheelbase: 245.5cm 96.7in
Track F: 139.7cm 55.0in
Track R: 137.5cm 54.1in
Length: 414.0cm 163.0in
Width: 161.2cm 63.5in
Height: 132.5cm 52.2in
Ground clearance: 13.1cm 5.2in
Kerb weight: 975.0kg 2147.6lb
Fuel: 50.0L 11.0gal 13.2galUS

131 Alfa Romeo

Alfa 75 2.0i Twin Spark
1987 Italy
128.0mph 206.0kmh
0-50mph 80.5kmh: 6.7secs
0-60mph 96.5kmh: 9.3secs
0-1/4 mile: 16.3secs
0-1km: 30.5secs
148.0bhp 110.4kW 150.0PS
@ 5800rpm
137.0lbft 185.6Nm @ 4700rpm
131.2bhp/ton 129.0bhp/tonne
75.4bhp/L 56.3kW/L 76.5PS/L
56.1ft/sec 17.1m/sec
20.8mph 33.5kmh/1000rpm
25.6mpg 21.3mpgUS 11.0L/100km
Petrol 4-stroke piston
1962cc 120.0cu in
In-line 4 fuel injection
Compression ratio: 10.0:1
Bore: 84.0mm 3.3in
Stroke: 88.5mm 3.5in
Valve type/No: Overhead 8
Transmission: Manual
No. of forward speeds: 5
Wheels driven: Rear
Springs F/R: Coil/Coil
Brake system: PA
Brakes F/R: Disc/Disc
Steering: Rack & pinion PA
Wheelbase: 251.0cm 98.8in
Track F: 136.8cm 53.9in
Track R: 135.8cm 53.5in
Length: 433.0cm 170.5in
Width: 163.0cm 64.2in
Height: 135.0cm 53.1in
Ground clearance: 20.3cm 8.0in
Kerb weight: 1147.0kg 2526.4lb
Fuel: 49.1L 10.8gal 13.0galUS

132 Alfa Romeo

Alfa 75 V6 3.0
1987 Italy
138.0mph 222.0kmh
0-50mph 80.5kmh: 5.7secs
0-60mph 96.5kmh: 7.5secs
0-1/4 mile: 16.1secs
0-1km: 24.9secs
188.0bhp 140.2kW 190.6PS
@ 5800rpm
180.0lbft 243.9Nm @ 4000rpm
158.0bhp/ton 155.4bhp/tonne
63.5bhp/L 47.4kW/L 64.4PS/L
45.6ft/sec 13.9m/sec
24.2mph 38.9kmh/1000rpm
20.5mpg 17.1mpgUS 13.8L/100km
Petrol 4-stroke piston
2959cc 181.0cu in
Vee 6 fuel injection
Compression ratio: 9.5:1
Bore: 93.0mm 3.7in
Stroke: 72.0mm 2.8in
Valve type/No: Overhead 12
Transmission: Manual
No. of forward speeds: 5
Wheels driven: Rear
Springs F/R: Coil/Coil
Brake system: PA
Brakes F/R: Disc/Disc
Steering: Rack & pinion PA
Wheelbase: 251.0cm 98.8in
Track F: 136.8cm 53.9in
Track R: 135.8cm 53.5in
Length: 433.0cm 170.5in
Width: 163.0cm 64.2in
Height: 135.0cm 53.1in
Ground clearance: 20.3cm 8.0in
Kerb weight: 1210.0kg 2665.2lb
Fuel: 68.2L 15.0gal 18.0galUS

133 Alfa Romeo

Milano Verde 3.0
1987 Italy
136.0mph 218.8kmh
0-50mph 80.5kmh: 5.7secs
0-60mph 96.5kmh: 7.5secs
0-1/4 mile: 15.8secs
183.0bhp 136.5kW 185.5PS
@ 5800rpm
181.0lbft 245.3Nm @ 3000rpm
136.0bhp/ton 133.7bhp/tonne
61.8bhp/L 46.1kW/L 62.7PS/L
46.1ft/sec 14.0m/sec
25.2mpg 21.0mpgUS 11.2L/100km
Petrol 4-stroke piston
2959cc 180.5cu in
Vee 6 fuel injection
Compression ratio: 9.0:1
Bore: 93.0mm 3.7in
Stroke: 72.6mm 2.9in
Valve type/No: Overhead 12
Transmission: Manual
No. of forward speeds: 5
Wheels driven: Rear
Springs F/R: Torsion bar/Coil
Brake system: PA ABS
Brakes F/R: Disc/Disc
Steering: Rack & pinion PA
Wheelbase: 251.0cm 98.8in
Track F: 137.9cm 54.3in
Track R: 137.4cm 54.1in
Length: 433.1cm 170.5in
Width: 163.1cm 64.2in
Height: 134.9cm 53.1in
Kerb weight: 1368.8kg 3015.0lb
Fuel: 66.6L 14.6gal 17.6galUS

134 Alfa Romeo

75 2.5 Auto
1988 Italy
126.0mph 202.7kmh
0-50mph 80.5kmh: 7.4secs
0-60mph 96.5kmh: 9.8secs
0-1/4 mile: 17.7secs
0-1km: 32.0secs
156.0bhp 116.3kW 158.2PS
@ 5600rpm
155.0lbft 210.0Nm @ 4000rpm
122.9bhp/ton 120.9bhp/tonne
62.6bhp/L 46.7kW/L 63.5PS/L
41.8ft/sec 12.7m/sec
21.6mph 34.8kmh/1000rpm
22.4mpg 18.7mpgUS 12.6L/100km
Petrol 4-stroke piston
2492cc 152.0cu in
Vee 6 fuel injection
Compression ratio: 9.5:1
Bore: 88.0mm 3.5in
Stroke: 68.3mm 2.7in
Valve type/No: Overhead 12
Transmission: Automatic
No. of forward speeds: 3
Wheels driven: Rear
Springs F/R: Torsion bar/Coil
Brake system: PA
Brakes F/R: Disc/Disc
Steering: Rack & pinion PA
Wheelbase: 251.0cm 98.8in
Track F: 136.7cm 53.8in
Track R: 135.6cm 53.4in
Length: 432.8cm 170.4in
Width: 162.8cm 64.1in
Height: 134.9cm 53.1in
Ground clearance: 20.3cm 8.0in
Kerb weight: 1290.7kg 2843.0lb
Fuel: 49.1L 10.8gal 13.0galUS

135 Alfa Romeo

75 Evoluzione
1988 Italy
133.0mph 214.0kmh
0-60mph 96.5kmh: 7.5secs
155.0bhp 115.6kW 157.1PS
@ 5800rpm
166.0lbft 224.9Nm @ 2600rpm
139.7bhp/ton 137.4bhp/tonne
87.1bhp/L 65.0kW/L 88.3PS/L
56.1ft/sec 17.1m/sec
Petrol 4-stroke piston
1779cc 108.5cu in turbocharged
In-line 4 fuel injection
Compression ratio: 7.5:1
Bore: 80.0mm 3.1in
Stroke: 88.5mm 3.5in
Valve type/No: Overhead 16
Transmission: Manual
No. of forward speeds: 5
Wheels driven: Rear
Springs F/R: Torsion bar/Coil
Brake system: PA ABS
Brakes F/R: Disc/Disc
Steering: Rack & pinion PA
Wheelbase: 251.0cm 98.8in
Track F: 139.7cm 55.0in
Track R: 138.7cm 54.6in
Length: 433.1cm 170.5in
Width: 163.1cm 64.2in
Height: 134.9cm 53.1in
Kerb weight: 1128.2kg 2485.0lb
Fuel: 48.8L 10.7gal 12.9galUS

136 Alfa Romeo

Spider
1988 Italy
103.0mph 165.7kmh
0-50mph 80.5kmh: 7.3secs
0-60mph 96.5kmh: 10.4secs
0-1/4 mile: 17.6secs
125.0bhp 93.2kW 126.7PS
@ 5500rpm
119.0lbft 161.2Nm @ 2750rpm
109.4bhp/ton 107.5bhp/tonne
63.7bhp/L 47.5kW/L 64.6PS/L
53.2ft/sec 16.2m/sec
27.0mpg 22.5mpgUS 10.5L/100km
Petrol 4-stroke piston
1962cc 119.7cu in
In-line 4 fuel injection
Compression ratio: 9.0:1
Bore: 84.0mm 3.3in
Stroke: 88.5mm 3.5in
Valve type/No: Overhead 8
Transmission: Manual
No. of forward speeds: 5
Wheels driven: Rear
Springs F/R: Coil/Coil
Brake system: PA
Brakes F/R: Disc/Disc
Steering: Worm & sector
Wheelbase: 225.0cm 88.6in
Track F: 134.1cm 52.8in
Track R: 129.0cm 50.8in
Length: 426.7cm 168.0in
Width: 163.1cm 64.2in
Height: 129.0cm 50.8in
Kerb weight: 1162.2kg 2560.0lb
Fuel: 46.2L 10.1gal 12.2galUS

137 Alfa Romeo

Sprint 1.7 Cloverleaf
1988 Italy
116.0mph 186.6kmh
0-50mph 80.5kmh: 7.2secs
0-60mph 96.5kmh: 9.5secs
0-1/4 mile: 17.6secs
0-1km: 33.5secs
118.0bhp 88.0kW 119.6PS
@ 5800rpm
109.0lbft 147.7Nm @ 3500rpm
123.0bhp/ton 121.0bhp/tonne
68.9bhp/L 51.4kW/L 69.9PS/L
45.8ft/sec 14.0m/sec
20.7mph 33.3kmh/1000rpm
25.7mpg 21.4mpgUS 11.0L/100km
Petrol 4-stroke piston
1712cc 104.4cu in
Flat 4 2 Carburettor
Compression ratio: 9.5:1
Bore: 87.0mm 3.4in
Stroke: 72.2mm 2.8in
Valve type/No: Overhead 8
Transmission: Manual
No. of forward speeds: 5
Wheels driven: Front
Springs F/R: Coil/Coil
Brake system: PA
Brakes F/R: Disc/Drum
Steering: Rack & pinion
Wheelbase: 245.6cm 96.7in
Track F: 139.7cm 55.0in
Track R: 136.4cm 53.7in
Length: 402.3cm 158.4in
Width: 162.1cm 63.8in
Height: 130.6cm 51.4in
Ground clearance: 16.5cm 6.5in
Kerb weight: 975.2kg 2148.0lb
Fuel: 50.0L 11.0gal 13.2galUS

138 Alfa Romeo

164 3.0 Lusso
1989 Italy
140.0mph 225.3kmh
0-50mph 80.5kmh: 6.1secs
0-60mph 96.5kmh: 7.9secs
0-1/4 mile: 16.2secs
0-1km: 29.3secs
192.0bhp 143.2kW 194.7PS
@ 5600rpm
181.5lbft 246.0Nm @ 3000rpm
143.0bhp/ton 140.7bhp/tonne
64.9bhp/L 48.4kW/L 65.8PS/L
44.5ft/sec 13.5m/sec
25.8mph 41.5kmh/1000rpm
25.9mpg 21.6mpgUS 10.9L/100km
Petrol 4-stroke piston
2959cc 181.0cu in
Vee 6 fuel injection
Compression ratio: 9.5:1
Bore: 93.0mm 3.7in
Stroke: 72.6mm 2.9in
Valve type/No: Overhead 12
Transmission: Manual
No. of forward speeds: 5
Wheels driven: Front
Springs F/R: Coil/Coil
Brake system: PA ABS
Brakes F/R: Disc/Disc
Steering: Rack & pinion PA
Wheelbase: 266.0cm 104.7in
Track F: 151.5cm 59.6in
Track R: 148.8cm 58.6in
Length: 455.5cm 179.3in
Width: 176.0cm 69.3in
Height: 140.0cm 55.1in
Ground clearance: 16.0cm 6.3in
Kerb weight: 1365.0kg 3006.6lb
Fuel: 70.5L 15.5gal 18.6galUS

139 Alfa Romeo

164 Automatic
1989 Italy
137.0mph 220.4kmh
0-50mph 80.5kmh: 6.8secs
0-60mph 96.5kmh: 9.0secs
0-1/4 mile: 17.3secs
0-1km: 30.6secs
185.0bhp 137.9kW 187.6PS
@ 5600rpm
191.1lbft 259.0Nm @ 4400rpm
132.5bhp/ton 130.3bhp/tonne
62.5bhp/L 46.6kW/L 63.4PS/L
44.6ft/sec 13.6m/sec
24.2mph 38.9kmh/1000rpm
22.8mpg 19.0mpgUS 12.4L/100km
Petrol 4-stroke piston
2959cc 181.0cu in
Vee 6 fuel injection
Compression ratio: 9.5:1
Bore: 93.0mm 3.7in
Stroke: 73.0mm 2.9in
Valve type/No: Overhead 12
Transmission: Automatic
No. of forward speeds: 4
Wheels driven: Front
Springs F/R: Coil/Coil
Brake system: PA ABS
Brakes F/R: Disc/Disc
Steering: Rack & pinion PA
Wheelbase: 266.0cm 104.7in
Track F: 151.5cm 59.6in
Track R: 148.8cm 58.6in
Length: 455.5cm 179.3in
Width: 176.0cm 69.3in
Height: 140.0cm 55.1in
Ground clearance: 16.0cm 6.3in
Kerb weight: 1420.0kg 3127.7lb
Fuel: 70.5L 15.5gal 18.6galUS

140 Alfa Romeo

Milano 3.0
1989 Italy
125.0mph 201.1kmh
0-50mph 80.5kmh: 5.9secs
0-60mph 96.5kmh: 7.9secs
0-1/4 mile: 16.0secs
183.0bhp 136.5kW 185.5PS
@ 5800rpm
181.0lbft 245.3Nm @ 3000rpm
136.0bhp/ton 133.7bhp/tonne
61.8bhp/L 46.1kW/L 62.7PS/L
46.1ft/sec 14.0m/sec
24.0mpg 20.0mpgUS 11.8L/100km
Petrol 4-stroke piston
2959cc 180.5cu in
Vee 6 fuel injection
Compression ratio: 9.0:1
Bore: 93.0mm 3.7in
Stroke: 72.6mm 2.9in
Valve type/No: Overhead 12
Transmission: Manual

No. of forward speeds: 5
Wheels driven: Rear
Springs F/R: Torsion bar/Coil
Brake system: PA ABS
Brakes F/R: Disc/Disc
Steering: Rack & pinion PA
Wheelbase: 251.0cm 98.8in
Track F: 137.9cm 54.3in
Track R: 137.4cm 54.1in
Length: 433.1cm 170.5in
Width: 163.1cm 64.2in
Height: 134.9cm 53.1in
Kerb weight: 1368.8kg 3015.0lb
Fuel: 66.6L 14.6gal 17.6galUS

141 Alfa Romeo

Spider Quadrifoglio
1989 Italy
103.0mph 165.7kmh
0-50mph 80.5kmh: 7.7secs
0-60mph 96.5kmh: 10.8secs
0-1/4 mile: 17.8secs
120.0bhp 89.5kW 121.7PS
@ 5800rpm
117.0lbft 158.5Nm @ 2600rpm
106.0bhp/ton 104.3bhp/tonne
61.2bhp/L 45.6kW/L 62.0PS/L
56.1ft/sec 17.1m/sec
Petrol 4-stroke piston
1962cc 119.7cu in
In-line 4 fuel injection
Compression ratio: 9.0:1
Bore: 84.0mm 3.3in
Stroke: 88.5mm 3.5in
Valve type/No: Overhead 8
Transmission: Manual
No. of forward speeds: 5
Wheels driven: Rear
Springs F/R: Coil/Coil
Brake system: PA
Brakes F/R: Disc/Disc
Steering: Worm & sector
Wheelbase: 225.0cm 88.6in
Track F: 132.3cm 52.1in
Track R: 127.5cm 50.2in
Length: 424.9cm 167.3in
Width: 163.1cm 64.2in
Height: 142.0cm 55.9in
Kerb weight: 1150.9kg 2535.0lb
Fuel: 46.2L 10.1gal 12.2galUS

142 Alfa Romeo

164 Twin Spark Lusso
1990 Italy
127.0mph 204.3kmh
0-50mph 80.5kmh: 7.2secs
0-60mph 96.5kmh: 9.5secs
0-1/4 mile: 17.7secs
0-1km: 31.4secs
148.0bhp 110.4kW 150.0PS
@ 5800rpm
137.3lbft 186.0Nm @ 4000rpm
112.7bhp/ton 110.9bhp/tonne
75.4bhp/L 56.3kW/L 76.5PS/L
56.1ft/sec 17.1m/sec
23.8mph 38.3kmh/1000rpm
23.4mpg 19.5mpgUS 12.1L/100km
Petrol 4-stroke piston
1962cc 120.0cu in
In-line 4 fuel injection
Compression ratio: 10.0:1
Bore: 84.0mm 3.3in
Stroke: 88.5mm 3.5in
Valve type/No: Overhead 8
Transmission: Manual
No. of forward speeds: 5
Wheels driven: Front
Springs F/R: Coil/Coil
Brake system: PA ABS
Brakes F/R: Disc/Disc
Steering: Rack & pinion PA
Wheelbase: 265.9cm 104.7in
Track F: 141.2cm 55.6in
Track R: 148.6cm 58.5in
Length: 455.4cm 179.3in
Width: 175.8cm 69.2in
Height: 140.0cm 55.1in
Ground clearance: 16.0cm 6.3in
Kerb weight: 1335.0kg 2940.5lb
Fuel: 70.5L 15.5gal 18.6galUS

143 Alfa Romeo

164S
1990 Italy
140.0mph 225.3kmh
0-50mph 80.5kmh: 5.7secs
0-60mph 96.5kmh: 7.6secs
0-1/4 mile: 15.8secs
200.0bhp 149.1kW 202.8PS
@ 6000rpm
189.0lbft 256.1Nm @ 4400rpm
134.3bhp/ton 132.1bhp/tonne
67.6bhp/L 50.4kW/L 68.5PS/L
47.7ft/sec 14.5m/sec
27.6mpg 23.0mpgUS 10.2L/100km
Petrol 4-stroke piston
2959cc 180.5cu in
Vee 6 fuel injection
Compression ratio: 10.0:1
Bore: 93.0mm 3.7in
Stroke: 72.6mm 2.9in
Valve type/No: Overhead 12
Transmission: Manual
No. of forward speeds: 5
Wheels driven: Front
Springs F/R: Coil/Coil
Brake system: PA ABS
Brakes F/R: Disc/Disc
Steering: Rack & pinion PA
Wheelbase: 265.9cm 104.7in
Track F: 151.4cm 59.6in
Track R: 148.8cm 58.6in
Length: 455.7cm 179.4in
Width: 176.0cm 69.3in
Height: 139.2cm 54.8in
Ground clearance: 15.7cm 6.2in
Kerb weight: 1514.1kg 3335.0lb
Fuel: 65.1L 14.3gal 17.2galUS

144 Alfa Romeo

33 Boxer 16v
1990 Italy
129.0mph 207.6kmh
0-50mph 80.5kmh: 6.8secs
0-60mph 96.5kmh: 8.9secs
0-1/4 mile: 16.7secs
0-1km: 29.9secs
137.0bhp 102.2kW 138.9PS
@ 6500rpm
118.8lbft 161.0Nm @ 4600rpm
137.9bhp/ton 135.6bhp/tonne
80.0bhp/L 59.7kW/L 81.1PS/L
51.1ft/sec 15.6m/sec
19.9mph 32.0kmh/1000rpm
29.7mpg 24.7mpgUS 9.5L/100km
Petrol 4-stroke piston
1712cc 104.0cu in
Flat 4 fuel injection
Compression ratio: 9.5:1
Bore: 87.0mm 3.4in
Stroke: 72.0mm 2.8in
Valve type/No: Overhead 16
Transmission: Manual
No. of forward speeds: 5
Wheels driven: Front
Springs F/R: Coil/Coil
Brake system: PA
Brakes F/R: Disc/Drum
Steering: Rack & pinion PA
Wheelbase: 247.4cm 97.4in
Track F: 136.4cm 53.7in
Track R: 136.4cm 53.7in
Length: 407.4cm 160.4in
Width: 161.3cm 63.5in
Height: 134.9cm 53.1in
Kerb weight: 1010.0kg 2224.7lb
Fuel: 49.6L 10.9gal 13.1galUS

145 Alfa Romeo

164 Cloverleaf
1991 Italy
144.0mph 231.7kmh
0-50mph 80.5kmh: 6.2secs
0-60mph 96.5kmh: 7.8secs
0-1/4 mile: 16.4secs
0-1km: 29.0secs
200.0bhp 149.1kW 202.8PS
@ 5800rpm
198.0lbft 268.3Nm @ 4400rpm
140.8bhp/ton 138.5bhp/tonne
67.6bhp/L 50.4kW/L 68.5PS/L
46.1ft/sec 14.0m/sec
22.9mph 36.8kmh/1000rpm
21.4mpg 17.8mpgUS 13.2L/100km
Petrol 4-stroke piston
2959cc 180.5cu in
Vee 6 fuel injection
Compression ratio: 10.0:1
Bore: 93.0mm 3.7in
Stroke: 72.6mm 2.9in
Valve type/No: Overhead 12
Transmission: Manual
No. of forward speeds: 5
Wheels driven: Front
Springs F/R: Coil/Coil
Brake system: PA ABS
Brakes F/R: Disc/Disc
Steering: Rack & pinion PA
Wheelbase: 266.0cm 104.7in
Track F: 151.5cm 59.6in
Track R: 148.8cm 58.6in
Length: 455.5cm 179.3in
Width: 176.0cm 69.3in
Height: 140.0cm 55.1in
Ground clearance: 16.0cm 6.3in
Kerb weight: 1444.2kg 3181.0lb
Fuel: 70.5L 15.5gal 18.6galUS

146 Alfa Romeo

164L
1991 Italy
0-60mph 96.5kmh: 8.3secs
0-1/4 mile: 16.6secs
183.0bhp 136.5kW 185.5PS
@ 5800rpm
185.0lbft 250.7Nm @ 4400rpm
123.3bhp/ton 121.2bhp/tonne
61.8bhp/L 46.1kW/L 62.7PS/L
46.1ft/sec 14.0m/sec
26.5mpg 22.1mpgUS 10.6L/100km
Petrol 4-stroke piston
2959cc 180.5cu in
Vee 6
Bore: 93.0mm 3.7in
Stroke: 72.6mm 2.9in
Valve type/No: Overhead 12
Transmission: Manual
No. of forward speeds: 5
Wheels driven: Front
Springs F/R: Coil/Coil
Brake system: ABS
Brakes F/R: Disc/Disc
Steering: Rack & pinion PA
Wheelbase: 265.9cm 104.7in
Track F: 151.4cm 59.6in
Track R: 148.8cm 58.6in
Length: 455.7cm 179.4in
Width: 176.0cm 69.3in
Height: 139.2cm 54.8in
Kerb weight: 1509.5kg 3325.0lb

147 Alfa Romeo

Spider Veloce
1991 Italy
103.0mph 165.7kmh
0-50mph 80.5kmh: 7.7secs
0-60mph 96.5kmh: 10.8secs
0-1/4 mile: 17.8secs
120.0bhp 89.5kW 121.7PS
@ 5800rpm
117.0lbft 158.5Nm @ 2700rpm
105.4bhp/ton 103.6bhp/tonne
61.2bhp/L 45.6kW/L 62.0PS/L
56.1ft/sec 17.1m/sec
28.1mpg 23.4mpgUS 10.1L/100km
Petrol 4-stroke piston
1962cc 119.7cu in
In-line 4 fuel injection
Compression ratio: 9.0:1
Bore: 84.0mm 3.3in
Stroke: 88.5mm 3.5in
Valve type/No: Overhead 8
Transmission: Manual
No. of forward speeds: 5
Wheels driven: Rear
Springs F/R: Coil/Coil
Brake system: PA
Brakes F/R: Disc/Disc
Steering: Worm & sector PA
Wheelbase: 225.0cm 88.6in
Track F: 132.3cm 52.1in
Track R: 127.3cm 50.1in
Length: 426.0cm 167.7in
Width: 162.3cm 63.9in
Height: 126.2cm 49.7in
Kerb weight: 1157.7kg 2550.0lb
Fuel: 46.2L 10.1gal 12.2galUS

148 Allard

Drop-head Coupe
1948 UK
90.0mph 144.8kmh
0-50mph 80.5kmh: 11.4secs
0-60mph 96.5kmh: 17.1secs
85.0bhp 63.4kW 86.2PS
@ 3800rpm
64.1bhp/ton 63.1bhp/tonne
23.5bhp/L 17.5kW/L 23.8PS/L
39.6ft/sec 12.1m/sec
18.0mpg 15.0mpgUS 15.7L/100km
Petrol 4-stroke piston
3622cc 221.0cu in
Vee 8
Compression ratio: 6.1:1
Bore: 78.0mm 3.1in
Stroke: 95.2mm 3.8in
Valve type/No: Side 16
Transmission: Manual
No. of forward speeds: 3
Wheels driven: Rear
Brakes F/R: Drum/Drum
Wheelbase: 284.5cm 112.0in
Track F: 142.2cm 56.0in
Track R: 148.6cm 58.5in
Length: 464.8cm 183.0in
Width: 180.3cm 71.0in
Height: 157.5cm 62.0in
Ground clearance: 22.9cm 9.0in
Kerb weight: 1347.5kg 2968.0lb
Fuel: 77.3L 17.0gal 20.4galUS

149 Allard

V8
1948 UK
86.0mph 138.4kmh
0-50mph 80.5kmh: 9.2secs
0-60mph 96.5kmh: 13.6secs
85.0bhp 63.4kW 86.2PS
@ 3800rpm
77.5bhp/ton 76.2bhp/tonne
23.5bhp/L 17.5kW/L 23.8PS/L
39.6ft/sec 12.1m/sec
17.0mpg 14.2mpgUS 16.6L/100km
Petrol 4-stroke piston
3622cc 221.0cu in
Vee 8
Compression ratio: 6.1:1
Bore: 78.0mm 3.1in
Stroke: 95.2mm 3.8in
Valve type/No: Side 16
Transmission: Manual
No. of forward speeds: 3
Wheels driven: Rear
Brakes F/R: Drum/Drum
Wheelbase: 269.2cm 106.0in
Track F: 142.2cm 56.0in
Track R: 132.1cm 52.0in
Length: 426.7cm 168.0in
Width: 180.3cm 71.0in
Height: 151.1cm 59.5in
Ground clearance: 24.1cm 9.5in
Kerb weight: 1115.5kg 2457.0lb
Fuel: 91.0L 20.0gal 24.0galUS

150 Allard

K2
1952 UK
102.0mph 164.1kmh
0-50mph 80.5kmh: 8.5secs
0-60mph 96.5kmh: 11.6secs
0-1/4 mile: 18.1secs
140.0bhp 104.4kW 141.9PS
@ 4000rpm
225.0lbft 304.9Nm @ 2500rpm
116.6bhp/ton 114.7bhp/tonne
35.7bhp/L 26.6kW/L 36.2PS/L
43.1ft/sec 13.1m/sec
21.4mph 34.4kmh/1000rpm
12.3mpg 10.2mpgUS 23.0L/100km
Petrol 4-stroke piston
3917cc 239.0cu in
Vee 8
Compression ratio: 7.5:1
Bore: 81.0mm 3.2in
Stroke: 98.4mm 3.9in
Valve type/No: Overhead 16
Transmission: Manual
No. of forward speeds: 3
Wheels driven: Rear
Springs F/R: Coil/Leaf
Brakes F/R: Drum/Drum
Wheelbase: 269.2cm 106.0in
Track F: 143.5cm 56.5in
Track R: 133.4cm 52.5in
Length: 426.7cm 168.0in
Width: 180.3cm 71.0in
Height: 142.2cm 56.0in
Ground clearance: 22.9cm 9.0in
Kerb weight: 1220.8kg 2689.0lb
Fuel: 77.3L 17.0gal 20.4galUS

151 Allard

K3 Convertible
1954 UK
115.0mph 185.0kmh

0-50mph 80.5kmh: 6.4secs
0-60mph 96.5kmh: 8.6secs
0-1/4 mile: 16.9secs
180.0bhp 134.2kW 182.5PS
@ 4000rpm
312.0lbft 422.8Nm @ 2000rpm
128.0bhp/ton 125.9bhp/tonne
33.2bhp/L 24.7kW/L 33.6PS/L
40.2ft/sec 12.2m/sec
22.2mph 35.7kmh/1000rpm
Petrol 4-stroke piston
5428cc 331.2cu in
Vee 8
Compression ratio: 7.5:1
Bore: 96.8mm 3.8in
Stroke: 91.9mm 3.6in
Valve type/No: Overhead 16
Transmission: Manual
No. of forward speeds: 3
Wheels driven: Rear
Wheelbase: 254.0cm 100.0in
Track F: 143.5cm 56.5in
Track R: 148.6cm 58.5in
Kerb weight: 1430.1kg 3150.0lb

152 Allard

Palm Beach
1954 UK
87.0mph 140.0kmh
0-50mph 80.5kmh: 10.9secs
0-60mph 96.5kmh: 16.9secs
0-1/4 mile: 20.3secs
68.0bhp 50.7kW 68.9PS
@ 4000rpm
112.0lbft 151.8Nm @ 2000rpm
70.6bhp/ton 69.5bhp/tonne
30.1bhp/L 22.4kW/L 30.5PS/L
33.3ft/sec 10.2m/sec
18.1mph 29.1kmh/1000rpm
21.6mpg 18.0mpgUS 13.1L/100km
Petrol 4-stroke piston
2262cc 138.0cu in
In-line 6
Compression ratio: 6.8:1
Bore: 79.4mm 3.1in
Stroke: 76.2mm 3.0in
Valve type/No: Overhead 12
Transmission: Manual
No. of forward speeds: 3
Wheels driven: Rear
Springs F/R: Coil/Coil
Brakes F/R: Drum/Drum
Wheelbase: 243.8cm 96.0in
Track F: 129.5cm 51.0in
Track R: 127.0cm 50.0in
Length: 400.1cm 157.5in
Width: 149.9cm 59.0in
Height: 137.2cm 54.0in
Ground clearance: 12.7cm 5.0in
Kerb weight: 978.8kg 2156.0lb
Fuel: 38.7L 8.5gal 10.2galUS

153 Allard

GT Coupe
1959 UK
120.0mph 193.1kmh
0-50mph 80.5kmh: 7.4secs
0-60mph 96.5kmh: 9.6secs
0-1/4 mile: 17.1secs
210.0bhp 156.6kW 212.9PS
@ 5500rpm
213.0lbft 288.6Nm @ 4000rpm
164.7bhp/ton 162.0bhp/tonne
61.0bhp/L 45.5kW/L 61.9PS/L
63.7ft/sec 19.4m/sec
29.0mph 46.7kmh/1000rpm
16.3mpg 13.6mpgUS 17.3L/100km
Petrol 4-stroke piston
3442cc 210.0cu in
In-line 6
Compression ratio: 8.0:1
Bore: 83.0mm 3.3in
Stroke: 106.0mm 4.2in
Valve type/No: Overhead 12
Transmission: Manual with overdrive
No. of forward speeds: 5
Wheels driven: Rear
Springs F/R: Torsion bar/Coil
Brakes F/R: Disc/Drum
Wheelbase: 243.8cm 96.0in
Track F: 132.1cm 52.0in
Track R: 134.6cm 53.0in
Length: 411.5cm 162.0in
Width: 160.0cm 63.0in
Height: 137.2cm 54.0in
Ground clearance: 15.2cm 6.0in
Kerb weight: 1296.6kg 2856.0lb
Fuel: 79.6L 17.5gal 21.0galUS

154 Alvis

12/60 Sports
1931 UK
71.4mph 114.9kmh
52.0bhp 38.8kW 52.7PS
@ 4500rpm
48.9bhp/ton 48.1bhp/tonne
31.6bhp/L 23.6kW/L 32.0PS/L
54.1ft/sec 16.5m/sec
28.0mpg 23.3mpgUS 10.1L/100km
Petrol 4-stroke piston
1645cc 100.4cu in
In-line 4 2 Carburettor
Compression ratio: 5.8:1
Bore: 69.0mm 2.7in
Stroke: 110.0mm 4.3in
Valve type/No: Overhead 8
Transmission: Manual
No. of forward speeds: 4
Wheels driven: Rear
Brakes F/R: Drum/Drum
Wheelbase: 284.5cm 112.0in
Track F: 127.0cm 50.0in
Track R: 127.0cm 50.0in
Length: 388.6cm 153.0in
Width: 151.1cm 59.5in
Height: 146.6cm 57.7in
Kerb weight: 1080.5kg 2380.0lb
Fuel: 45.5L 10.0gal 12.0galUS

155 Alvis

Speed 20 (72bhp)
1932 UK
80.0mph 128.7kmh
0-50mph 80.5kmh: 13.1secs
0-60mph 96.5kmh: 22.0secs
0-1/4 mile: 22.0secs
72.0bhp 53.7kW 73.0PS
@ 4200rpm
125.0lbft 169.4Nm @ 2400rpm
48.3bhp/ton 47.5bhp/tonne
28.7bhp/L 21.4kW/L 29.1PS/L
46.0ft/sec 14.0m/sec
18.6mph 29.9kmh/1000rpm
Petrol 4-stroke piston
2511cc 153.2cu in
In-line 6
Compression ratio: 5.6:1
Bore: 72.9mm 2.9in
Stroke: 100.1mm 3.9in
Valve type/No: Overhead 12
Transmission: Manual
No. of forward speeds: 4
Wheels driven: Rear
Wheelbase: 312.4cm 123.0in
Track F: 142.2cm 56.0in
Track R: 142.2cm 56.0in
Length: 462.3cm 182.0in
Width: 167.6cm 66.0in
Height: 157.5cm 62.0in
Kerb weight: 1516.4kg 3340.0lb

156 Alvis

Speed 20 (87bhp)
1932 UK
89.1mph 143.4kmh
87.0bhp 64.9kW 88.2PS
@ 4000rpm
69.6bhp/ton 68.4bhp/tonne
34.6bhp/L 25.8kW/L 35.1PS/L
43.8ft/sec 13.3m/sec
18.0mpg 15.0mpgUS 15.7L/100km
Petrol 4-stroke piston
2511cc 153.2cu in
In-line 6 3 Carburettor
Compression ratio: 6.3:1
Bore: 73.0mm 2.9in
Stroke: 100.0mm 3.9in
Valve type/No: Overhead 12
Transmission: Manual
No. of forward speeds: 4
Wheels driven: Rear
Brakes F/R: Drum/Drum
Wheelbase: 312.4cm 123.0in
Track F: 142.2cm 56.0in
Track R: 142.2cm 56.0in
Length: 422.9cm 166.5in
Width: 165.1cm 65.0in
Height: 135.9cm 53.5in
Kerb weight: 1271.2kg 2800.0lb
Fuel: 66.0L 14.5gal 17.4galUS

157 Alvis

Firebird Saloon
1935 UK
70.8mph 113.9kmh
0-50mph 80.5kmh: 23.0secs
0-60mph 96.5kmh: 36.4secs
24.0mpg 20.0mpgUS 11.8L/100km
Petrol 4-stroke piston
1842cc 112.4cu in
In-line 4
Bore: 73.0mm 2.9in
Stroke: 110.0mm 4.3in
Valve type/No: Overhead 8
Transmission: Manual
No. of forward speeds: 4
Wheels driven: Rear
Brakes F/R: Drum/Drum
Kerb weight: 1411.0kg 3108.0lb
Fuel: 66.0L 14.5gal 17.4galUS

158 Alvis

4.3-litre Vanden Plas Saloon
1937 UK
91.8mph 147.7kmh
0-50mph 80.5kmh: 10.9secs
0-60mph 96.5kmh: 15.3secs
13.0mpg 10.8mpgUS 21.7L/100km
Petrol 4-stroke piston
4387cc 267.7cu in
In-line 6
Bore: 92.0mm 3.6in
Stroke: 110.0mm 4.3in
Valve type/No: Overhead 12
Transmission: Manual
No. of forward speeds: 4
Wheels driven: Rear
Brakes F/R: Drum/Drum
Kerb weight: 1761.1kg 3879.0lb
Fuel: 77.3L 17.0gal 20.4galUS

159 Alvis

Crested Eagle 25
1937 UK
84.1mph 135.3kmh
0-50mph 80.5kmh: 12.9secs
0-60mph 96.5kmh: 19.4secs
106.0bhp 79.0kW 107.5PS
@ 3800rpm
56.9bhp/ton 55.9bhp/tonne
29.7bhp/L 22.1kW/L 30.1PS/L
45.7ft/sec 13.9m/sec
15.0mpg 12.5mpgUS 18.8L/100km
Petrol 4-stroke piston
3571cc 217.9cu in
In-line 6 3 Carburettor
Compression ratio: 6.3:1
Bore: 83.0mm 3.3in
Stroke: 110.0mm 4.3in
Valve type/No: Overhead 12
Transmission: Manual
No. of forward speeds: 4
Wheels driven: Rear
Brakes F/R: Drum/Drum
Kerb weight: 1894.5kg 4173.0lb
Fuel: 91.0L 20.0gal 24.0galUS

160 Alvis

12/70 Tourer
1938 UK
81.8mph 131.6kmh
0-50mph 80.5kmh: 13.9secs
0-60mph 96.5kmh: 20.3secs
23.0mpg 19.2mpgUS 12.3L/100km
Petrol 4-stroke piston
1842cc 112.4cu in
In-line 4
Bore: 73.0mm 2.9in
Stroke: 110.0mm 4.3in
Valve type/No: Overhead 8
Transmission: Manual
No. of forward speeds: 4
Wheels driven: Rear
Brakes F/R: Drum/Drum
Kerb weight: 1202.6kg 2649.0lb
Fuel: 51.0L 11.2gal 13.5galUS

161 Alvis

Speed 25
1938 UK
96.7mph 155.6kmh
0-50mph 80.5kmh: 11.1secs
0-60mph 96.5kmh: 15.0secs
106.0bhp 79.0kW 107.5PS
@ 3800rpm
58.1bhp/ton 57.2bhp/tonne
29.7bhp/L 22.1kW/L 30.1PS/L
45.7ft/sec 13.9m/sec
16.0mpg 13.3mpgUS 17.7L/100km
Petrol 4-stroke piston
3571cc 217.9cu in
In-line 6 3 Carburettor
Compression ratio: 6.3:1
Bore: 83.0mm 3.3in
Stroke: 110.0mm 4.3in
Valve type/No: Overhead 12
Transmission: Manual
No. of forward speeds: 4
Wheels driven: Rear
Brakes F/R: Drum/Drum
Kerb weight: 1854.1kg 4084.0lb
Fuel: 77.3L 17.0gal 20.4galUS

162 Alvis

4.3-litre
1939 UK
100.0mph 160.9kmh
0-50mph 80.5kmh: 9.5secs
0-60mph 96.5kmh: 13.1secs
137.0bhp 102.2kW 138.9PS
@ 3600rpm
72.3bhp/ton 71.1bhp/tonne
31.2bhp/L 23.3kW/L 31.7PS/L
43.3ft/sec 13.2m/sec
15.0mpg 12.5mpgUS 18.8L/100km
Petrol 4-stroke piston
4387cc 267.7cu in
In-line 6 3 Carburettor
Bore: 92.0mm 3.6in
Stroke: 110.0mm 4.3in
Valve type/No: Overhead 12
Transmission: Manual
No. of forward speeds: 4
Wheels driven: Rear
Brakes F/R: Drum/Drum
Kerb weight: 1927.7kg 4246.0lb
Fuel: 86.4L 19.0gal 22.8galUS

163 Alvis

3-litre
1952 UK
86.0mph 138.4kmh
0-50mph 80.5kmh: 14.1secs
0-60mph 96.5kmh: 19.8secs
0-1/4 mile: 21.6secs
90.0bhp 67.1kW 91.2PS
@ 4000rpm
150.0lbft 203.3Nm @ 2000rpm
57.0bhp/ton 56.0bhp/tonne
30.1bhp/L 22.4kW/L 30.5PS/L
39.3ft/sec 12.0m/sec
18.9mph 30.4kmh/1000rpm
19.0mpg 15.8mpgUS 14.9L/100km
Petrol 4-stroke piston
2993cc 182.6cu in
In-line 6
Compression ratio: 7.0:1
Bore: 84.0mm 3.3in
Stroke: 90.0mm 3.5in
Valve type/No: Overhead 12
Transmission: Manual
No. of forward speeds: 4
Wheels driven: Rear
Springs F/R: Coil/Leaf
Brakes F/R: Drum/Drum
Wheelbase: 283.2cm 111.5in
Track F: 138.7cm 54.6in
Track R: 137.4cm 54.1in
Length: 462.8cm 182.2in
Width: 167.6cm 66.0in
Height: 158.8cm 62.5in
Ground clearance: 19.1cm 7.5in
Kerb weight: 1606.2kg 3538.0lb
Fuel: 65.1L 14.3gal 17.2galUS

164 Alvis

3-litre
1953 UK
101.1mph 162.7kmh
0-50mph 80.5kmh: 10.9secs
0-60mph 96.5kmh: 16.5secs
0-1/4 mile: 20.5secs
100.0bhp 74.6kW 101.4PS
@ 4000rpm
163.0lbft 220.9Nm @ 2000rpm
66.9bhp/ton 65.8bhp/tonne
33.4bhp/L 24.9kW/L 33.9PS/L
39.3ft/sec 12.0m/sec
20.5mph 33.0kmh/1000rpm
18.0mpg 15.0mpgUS 15.7L/100km

Petrol 4-stroke piston
2993cc 182.6cu in
In-line 6
Compression ratio: 8.0:1
Bore: 84.0mm 3.3in
Stroke: 90.0mm 3.5in
Valve type/No: Overhead 12
Transmission: Manual
No. of forward speeds: 4
Wheels driven: Rear
Springs F/R: Coil/Leaf
Brakes F/R: Drum/Drum
Wheelbase: 283.2cm 111.5in
Track F: 138.7cm 54.6in
Track R: 137.4cm 54.1in
Length: 463.6cm 182.5in
Width: 167.6cm 66.0in
Height: 158.8cm 62.5in
Ground clearance: 19.1cm 7.5in
Kerb weight: 1519.1kg 3346.0lb
Fuel: 65.1L 14.3gal 17.2galUS

165 Alvis

3-litre Graber
1957 UK
103.0mph 165.7kmh
0-50mph 80.5kmh: 9.8secs
0-60mph 96.5kmh: 13.5secs
0-1/4 mile: 19.8secs
104.0bhp 77.5kW 105.4PS
@ 4000rpm
163.0lbft 220.9Nm @ 2500rpm
71.0bhp/ton 69.8bhp/tonne
34.7bhp/L 25.9kW/L 35.2PS/L
39.3ft/sec 12.0m/sec
20.5mph 33.0kmh/1000rpm
18.0mpg 15.0mpgUS 15.7L/100km
Petrol 4-stroke piston
2993cc 182.6cu in
In-line 6
Compression ratio: 8.0:1
Bore: 84.0mm 3.3in
Stroke: 90.0mm 3.5in
Valve type/No: Overhead 12
Transmission: Manual
No. of forward speeds: 4
Wheels driven: Rear
Springs F/R: Coil/Leaf
Brakes F/R: Drum/Drum
Wheelbase: 283.2cm 111.5in
Track F: 138.7cm 54.6in
Track R: 137.7cm 54.2in
Length: 480.1cm 189.0in
Width: 167.6cm 66.0in
Height: 144.0cm 56.7in
Ground clearance: 17.8cm 7.0in
Kerb weight: 1490.5kg 3283.0lb
Fuel: 65.1L 14.3gal 17.2galUS

166 Alvis

3-litre TD21
1959 UK
106.0mph 170.6kmh
0-50mph 80.5kmh: 9.8secs
0-60mph 96.5kmh: 13.9secs
0-1/4 mile: 19.6secs
115.0bhp 85.8kW 116.6PS
@ 4000rpm
152.3lbft 206.4Nm @ 2500rpm
75.3bhp/ton 74.0bhp/tonne
38.4bhp/L 28.6kW/L 39.0PS/L
39.3ft/sec 12.0m/sec
20.5mph 33.0kmh/1000rpm
18.3mpg 15.2mpgUS 15.4L/100km
Petrol 4-stroke piston
2993cc 182.6cu in
In-line 6
Compression ratio: 8.5:1
Bore: 84.0mm 3.3in
Stroke: 90.0mm 3.5in
Valve type/No: Overhead 12
Transmission: Manual
No. of forward speeds: 4
Wheels driven: Rear
Springs F/R: Coil/Leaf
Brake system: PA
Brakes F/R: Disc/Drum
Wheelbase: 283.2cm 111.5in
Track F: 138.7cm 54.6in
Track R: 137.4cm 54.1in
Length: 478.8cm 188.5in
Width: 167.6cm 66.0in
Height: 152.4cm 60.0in
Ground clearance: 17.8cm 7.0in
Kerb weight: 1554.0kg 3423.0lb
Fuel: 65.1L 14.3gal 17.2galUS

167 Alvis

3-litre TD21 Series II Automatic
1962 UK
103.0mph 165.7kmh
0-50mph 80.5kmh: 12.2secs
0-60mph 96.5kmh: 16.6secs
0-1/4 mile: 21.0secs
115.0bhp 85.8kW 116.6PS
@ 4000rpm
152.3lbft 206.4Nm @ 2500rpm
73.6bhp/ton 72.4bhp/tonne
38.4bhp/L 28.6kW/L 39.0PS/L
39.3ft/sec 12.0m/sec
21.9mph 35.2kmh/1000rpm
18.5mpg 15.4mpgUS 15.3L/100km
Petrol 4-stroke piston
2993cc 182.6cu in
In-line 6 2 Carburettor
Compression ratio: 8.5:1
Bore: 84.0mm 3.3in
Stroke: 90.0mm 3.5in
Valve type/No: Overhead 12
Transmission: Automatic
No. of forward speeds: 3
Wheels driven: Rear
Springs F/R: Coil/Leaf
Brake system: PA
Brakes F/R: Disc/Disc
Wheelbase: 283.2cm 111.5in
Track F: 141.5cm 55.7in
Track R: 137.9cm 54.3in
Length: 480.1cm 189.0in
Width: 167.6cm 66.0in
Height: 147.3cm 58.0in
Ground clearance: 17.8cm 7.0in
Kerb weight: 1589.0kg 3500.0lb
Fuel: 65.1L 14.3gal 17.2galUS

168 Alvis

3-litre Series III
1965 UK
108.0mph 173.8kmh
0-50mph 80.5kmh: 8.7secs
0-60mph 96.5kmh: 12.5secs
0-1/4 mile: 18.8secs
130.0bhp 96.9kW 131.8PS
@ 5000rpm
172.0lbft 233.1Nm @ 3250rpm
83.2bhp/ton 81.8bhp/tonne
43.4bhp/L 32.4kW/L 44.0PS/L
49.2ft/sec 15.0m/sec
24.9mph 40.1kmh/1000rpm
15.9mpg 13.2mpgUS 17.8L/100km
Petrol 4-stroke piston
2993cc 182.6cu in
In-line 6
Compression ratio: 8.5:1
Bore: 84.0mm 3.3in
Stroke: 90.0mm 3.5in
Valve type/No: Overhead 12
Transmission: Manual
No. of forward speeds: 5
Wheels driven: Rear
Springs F/R: Coil/Leaf
Brake system: PA
Brakes F/R: Disc/Disc
Steering: Recirculating ball PA
Kerb weight: 1589.0kg 3500.0lb
Fuel: 65.1L 14.3gal 17.2galUS

169 Alvis

TE21S
1965 UK
108.0mph 173.8kmh
0-50mph 80.5kmh: 8.7secs
0-60mph 96.5kmh: 12.5secs
0-1/4 mile: 18.8secs
130.0bhp 96.9kW 131.8PS
@ 5000rpm
172.0lbft 233.1Nm @ 3250rpm
83.2bhp/ton 81.8bhp/tonne
43.4bhp/L 32.4kW/L 44.0PS/L
49.2ft/sec 15.0m/sec
24.9mph 40.1kmh/1000rpm
15.9mpg 13.2mpgUS 17.8L/100km
Petrol 4-stroke piston
2993cc 182.6cu in
In-line 6 2 Carburettor
Compression ratio: 8.5:1
Bore: 84.0mm 3.3in
Stroke: 90.0mm 3.5in
Valve type/No: Overhead 12
Transmission: Manual
No. of forward speeds: 5
Wheels driven: Rear
Springs F/R: Coil/Leaf
Brake system: PA
Brakes F/R: Disc/Disc
Steering: Recirculating ball PA
Kerb weight: 1589.0kg 3500.0lb
Fuel: 65.1L 14.3gal 17.2galUS

170 AMC

Rambler American
1961 USA
90.0mph 144.8kmh
0-50mph 80.5kmh: 13.2secs
0-60mph 96.5kmh: 18.7secs
0-1/4 mile: 20.9secs
125.0bhp 93.2kW 126.7PS
@ 4200rpm
180.0lbft 243.9Nm @ 1600rpm
102.0bhp/ton 100.3bhp/tonne
39.0bhp/L 29.1kW/L 39.5PS/L
49.6ft/sec 15.1m/sec
27.6mph 44.4kmh/1000rpm
Petrol 4-stroke piston
3206cc 195.6cu in
In-line 6 1 Carburettor
Compression ratio: 8.7:1
Bore: 79.4mm 3.1in
Stroke: 108.0mm 4.2in
Valve type/No: Overhead 12
Transmission: Automatic
No. of forward speeds: 3
Wheels driven: Rear
Brakes F/R: Drum/Drum
Wheelbase: 254.0cm 100.0in
Track F: 138.7cm 54.6in
Track R: 139.7cm 55.0in
Length: 439.7cm 173.1in
Width: 177.8cm 70.0in
Height: 142.7cm 56.2in
Ground clearance: 16.5cm 6.5in
Kerb weight: 1246.2kg 2745.0lb

171 AMC

Rambler Classic Super 6
1961 USA
90.0mph 144.8kmh
0-50mph 80.5kmh: 12.1secs
0-60mph 96.5kmh: 18.5secs
0-1/4 mile: 21.3secs
127.0bhp 94.7kW 128.8PS
@ 4200rpm
180.0lbft 243.9Nm @ 1600rpm
92.7bhp/ton 91.1bhp/tonne
39.6bhp/L 29.5kW/L 40.2PS/L
49.6ft/sec 15.1m/sec
24.4mph 39.3kmh/1000rpm
Petrol 4-stroke piston
3206cc 195.6cu in
In-line 6 1 Carburettor
Compression ratio: 8.7:1
Bore: 79.4mm 3.1in
Stroke: 108.0mm 4.2in
Valve type/No: Overhead 12
Transmission: Automatic
No. of forward speeds: 3
Wheels driven: Rear
Brake system: PA
Brakes F/R: Drum/Drum
Wheelbase: 274.3cm 108.0in
Track F: 149.1cm 58.7in
Track R: 150.1cm 59.1in
Length: 482.1cm 189.8in
Width: 183.9cm 72.4in
Height: 145.0cm 57.1in
Ground clearance: 16.5cm 6.5in
Kerb weight: 1393.8kg 3070.0lb

172 AMC

Rambler Classic V8
1961 USA
100.0mph 160.9kmh
0-50mph 80.5kmh: 10.7secs
0-60mph 96.5kmh: 15.8secs
0-1/4 mile: 19.1secs
200.0bhp 149.1kW 202.8PS
@ 4900rpm
245.0lbft 332.0Nm @ 2500rpm
129.9bhp/ton 127.7bhp/tonne
48.8bhp/L 36.4kW/L 49.5PS/L
44.2ft/sec 13.5m/sec
21.7mph 34.9kmh/1000rpm
Petrol 4-stroke piston
4098cc 250.0cu in
Vee 8 1 Carburettor
Compression ratio: 8.7:1
Bore: 88.9mm 3.5in
Stroke: 82.6mm 3.2in
Valve type/No: Overhead 16
Transmission: Automatic
No. of forward speeds: 3
Wheels driven: Rear
Brake system: PA
Brakes F/R: Drum/Drum
Steering: PA
Wheelbase: 274.3cm 108.0in
Track F: 149.1cm 58.7in
Track R: 150.1cm 59.1in
Length: 482.1cm 189.8in
Width: 183.9cm 72.4in
Height: 145.0cm 57.1in
Ground clearance: 16.5cm 6.5in
Kerb weight: 1566.3kg 3450.0lb

173 AMC

Ambassador 400
1962 USA
105.0mph 168.9kmh
0-50mph 80.5kmh: 10.2secs
0-60mph 96.5kmh: 14.0secs
0-1/4 mile: 18.8secs
250.0bhp 186.4kW 253.5PS
@ 4700rpm
340.0lbft 460.7Nm @ 2600rpm
152.2bhp/ton 149.6bhp/tonne
46.6bhp/L 34.8kW/L 47.3PS/L
42.4ft/sec 12.9m/sec
26.7mph 43.0kmh/1000rpm
Petrol 4-stroke piston
5359cc 327.0cu in
Vee 8 1 Carburettor
Compression ratio: 8.7:1
Bore: 101.6mm 4.0in
Stroke: 82.6mm 3.2in
Valve type/No: Overhead 16
Transmission: Automatic
No. of forward speeds: 3
Wheels driven: Rear
Brake system: PA
Steering: PA
Wheelbase: 274.3cm 108.0in
Track F: 148.8cm 58.6in
Track R: 150.1cm 59.1in
Length: 482.6cm 190.0in
Width: 183.9cm 72.4in
Height: 146.3cm 57.6in
Ground clearance: 17.8cm 7.0in
Kerb weight: 1670.7kg 3680.0lb
Fuel: 75.7L 16.6gal 20.0galUS

174 AMC

Rambler American
1962 USA
88.0mph 141.6kmh
0-50mph 80.5kmh: 12.0secs
0-60mph 96.5kmh: 18.2secs
0-1/4 mile: 20.5secs
90.0bhp 67.1kW 91.2PS
@ 3800rpm
160.0lbft 216.8Nm @ 1600rpm
78.4bhp/ton 77.1bhp/tonne
28.1bhp/L 20.9kW/L 28.5PS/L
44.9ft/sec 13.7m/sec
22.2mph 35.7kmh/1000rpm
Petrol 4-stroke piston
3205cc 195.5cu in
In-line 4
Compression ratio: 8.0:1
Bore: 79.4mm 3.1in
Stroke: 108.0mm 4.2in
Valve type/No: Side 8
No. of forward speeds: 3
Wheels driven: Rear
Wheelbase: 254.0cm 100.0in
Track F: 138.7cm 54.6in
Track R: 139.7cm 55.0in
Length: 439.7cm 173.1in
Width: 177.8cm 70.0in
Height: 142.5cm 56.1in
Ground clearance: 16.3cm 6.4in
Kerb weight: 1166.8kg 2570.0lb

175 AMC

Ambassador 990
1963 USA
114.0mph 183.4kmh
0-50mph 80.5kmh: 7.9secs
0-60mph 96.5kmh: 10.6secs
0-1/4 mile: 17.6secs
270.0bhp 201.3kW 273.7PS
@ 4700rpm
360.0lbft 487.8Nm @ 2600rpm
177.4bhp/ton 174.4bhp/tonne
50.4bhp/L 37.6kW/L 51.1PS/L
42.4ft/sec 12.9m/sec
24.3mph 39.1kmh/1000rpm

Petrol 4-stroke piston
5359cc 327.0cu in
Vee 8 1 Carburettor
Compression ratio: 9.7:1
Bore: 101.6mm 4.0in
Stroke: 82.6mm 3.2in
Valve type/No: Overhead 16
Transmission: Automatic
No. of forward speeds: 3
Wheels driven: Rear
Steering: PA
Wheelbase: 284.5cm 112.0in
Track F: 148.8cm 58.6in
Track R: 146.1cm 57.5in
Length: 479.6cm 188.8in
Width: 181.1cm 71.3in
Height: 140.5cm 55.3in
Ground clearance: 15.2cm 6.0in
Kerb weight: 1548.1kg 3410.0lb
Fuel: 71.9L 15.8gal 19.0galUS

176 AMC

Rambler 660
1963 USA
92.0mph 148.0kmh
0-50mph 80.5kmh: 13.2secs
0-60mph 96.5kmh: 19.8secs
0-1/4 mile: 20.3secs
127.0bhp 94.7kW 128.8PS
@ 4200rpm
180.0lbft 243.9Nm @ 1600rpm
98.1bhp/ton 96.5bhp/tonne
39.6bhp/L 29.5kW/L 40.2PS/L
49.6ft/sec 15.1m/sec
21.8mph 35.1kmh/1000rpm
Petrol 4-stroke piston
3205cc 195.5cu in
In-line 6 1 Carburettor
Compression ratio: 8.7:1
Bore: 79.2mm 3.1in
Stroke: 108.0mm 4.2in
Valve type/No: Overhead 12
No. of forward speeds: 3
Wheels driven: Rear
Wheelbase: 284.5cm 112.0in
Track F: 147.8cm 58.2in
Track R: 145.8cm 57.4in
Length: 479.6cm 188.8in
Width: 181.1cm 71.3in
Height: 138.7cm 54.6in
Ground clearance: 15.2cm 6.0in
Kerb weight: 1316.6kg 2900.0lb
Fuel: 71.9L 15.8gal 19.0galUS

177 AMC

Rambler American 440
1964 USA
95.0mph 152.9kmh
0-50mph 80.5kmh: 11.2secs
0-60mph 96.5kmh: 15.3secs
0-1/4 mile: 20.2secs
138.0bhp 102.9kW 139.9PS
@ 4500rpm
185.0lbft 250.7Nm @ 1800rpm
117.5bhp/ton 115.6bhp/tonne
43.1bhp/L 32.1kW/L 43.6PS/L
53.1ft/sec 16.2m/sec
26.9mph 43.3kmh/1000rpm
Petrol 4-stroke piston
3205cc 195.5cu in
In-line 6 1 Carburettor
Compression ratio: 8.7:1
Bore: 79.4mm 3.1in
Stroke: 108.0mm 4.2in
Valve type/No: Overhead 12
Transmission: Manual
No. of forward speeds: 3
Wheels driven: Rear
Wheelbase: 269.2cm 106.0in
Track F: 142.2cm 56.0in
Track R: 139.7cm 55.0in
Length: 450.3cm 177.3in
Width: 174.2cm 68.6in
Height: 138.4cm 54.5in
Ground clearance: 15.2cm 6.0in
Kerb weight: 1194.0kg 2630.0lb
Fuel: 60.6L 13.3gal 16.0galUS

178 AMC

Rambler Classic 770
1964 USA
100.0mph 160.9kmh
0-50mph 80.5kmh: 8.8secs
0-60mph 96.5kmh: 11.6secs
0-1/4 mile: 18.8secs
198.0bhp 147.6kW 200.7PS
@ 4700rpm
280.0lbft 379.4Nm @ 2600rpm
129.3bhp/ton 127.1bhp/tonne
42.1bhp/L 31.4kW/L 42.7PS/L
42.4ft/sec 12.9m/sec
26.5mph 42.6kmh/1000rpm
Petrol 4-stroke piston
4703cc 286.9cu in
Vee 8 1 Carburettor
Compression ratio: 8.7:1
Bore: 95.3mm 3.8in
Stroke: 82.6mm 3.2in
Valve type/No: Overhead 16
Transmission: Automatic
No. of forward speeds: 3
Wheels driven: Rear
Brake system: PA
Steering: PA
Wheelbase: 284.5cm 112.0in
Track F: 148.8cm 58.6in
Track R: 146.1cm 57.5in
Length: 482.6cm 190.0in
Width: 181.1cm 71.3in
Height: 137.7cm 54.2in
Ground clearance: 15.2cm 6.0in
Kerb weight: 1557.2kg 3430.0lb
Fuel: 71.9L 15.8gal 19.0galUS

179 AMC

Rambler Classic Typhoon
1964 USA
95.0mph 152.9kmh
0-50mph 80.5kmh: 9.3secs
0-60mph 96.5kmh: 12.6secs
0-1/4 mile: 19.3secs
145.0bhp 108.1kW 147.0PS
@ 4300rpm
215.0lbft 291.3Nm @ 1600rpm
106.0bhp/ton 104.2bhp/tonne
38.1bhp/L 28.4kW/L 38.7PS/L
41.8ft/sec 12.7m/sec
23.3mph 37.5kmh/1000rpm
Petrol 4-stroke piston
3802cc 232.0cu in
In-line 6 1 Carburettor
Compression ratio: 8.5:1
Bore: 95.3mm 3.8in
Stroke: 88.9mm 3.5in
Valve type/No: Overhead 12
Transmission: Automatic
No. of forward speeds: 3
Wheels driven: Rear
Wheelbase: 284.5cm 112.0in
Track F: 147.8cm 58.2in
Track R: 148.8cm 58.6in
Length: 482.6cm 190.0in
Width: 181.1cm 71.3in
Height: 135.9cm 53.5in
Ground clearance: 15.2cm 6.0in
Kerb weight: 1391.5kg 3065.0lb
Fuel: 71.9L 15.8gal 19.0galUS

180 AMC

Rambler American 440-H
1965 USA
90.0mph 144.8kmh
0-50mph 80.5kmh: 7.8secs
0-60mph 96.5kmh: 10.9secs
0-1/4 mile: 18.3secs
155.0bhp 115.6kW 157.1PS
@ 4400rpm
222.0lbft 300.8Nm @ 1600rpm
121.9bhp/ton 119.9bhp/tonne
40.8bhp/L 30.4kW/L 41.3PS/L
42.8ft/sec 13.0m/sec
21.0mph 33.8kmh/1000rpm
Petrol 4-stroke piston
3802cc 232.0cu in
In-line 6 1 Carburettor
Compression ratio: 8.5:1
Bore: 95.3mm 3.8in
Stroke: 88.9mm 3.5in
Valve type/No: Overhead 12
Transmission: Automatic
No. of forward speeds: 3
Wheels driven: Rear
Brake system: PA
Brakes F/R: Drum/Drum
Steering: PA
Wheelbase: 269.2cm 106.0in
Track F: 142.2cm 56.0in
Track R: 139.7cm 55.0in
Length: 450.3cm 177.3in
Width: 174.2cm 68.6in
Height: 135.6cm 53.4in
Ground clearance: 15.2cm 6.0in
Kerb weight: 1293.0kg 2848.0lb
Fuel: 60.6L 13.3gal 16.0galUS

181 AMC

Ambassador DPL
1966 USA
102.0mph 164.1kmh
0-50mph 80.5kmh: 9.7secs
0-60mph 96.5kmh: 12.3secs
0-1/4 mile: 18.6secs
270.0bhp 201.3kW 273.7PS
@ 4700rpm
360.0lbft 487.8Nm @ 2600rpm
166.1bhp/ton 163.4bhp/tonne
50.4bhp/L 37.6kW/L 51.1PS/L
42.4ft/sec 12.9m/sec
24.8mph 39.9kmh/1000rpm
Petrol 4-stroke piston
5359cc 327.0cu in
Vee 8 1 Carburettor
Compression ratio: 9.7:1
Bore: 101.6mm 4.0in
Stroke: 82.6mm 3.2in
Valve type/No: Overhead 16
Transmission: Automatic
No. of forward speeds: 3
Wheels driven: Rear
Springs F/R: Coil/Coil
Brake system: PA
Brakes F/R: Disc/Drum
Steering: Recirculating ball PA
Wheelbase: 294.6cm 116.0in
Track F: 148.8cm 58.6in
Track R: 146.1cm 57.5in
Length: 508.0cm 200.0in
Width: 189.2cm 74.5in
Height: 138.4cm 54.5in
Ground clearance: 16.0cm 6.3in
Kerb weight: 1652.6kg 3640.0lb
Fuel: 71.9L 15.8gal 19.0galUS

182 AMC

Rogue V8
1966 USA
106.0mph 170.6kmh
0-50mph 80.5kmh: 7.2secs
0-60mph 96.5kmh: 9.9secs
0-1/4 mile: 17.6secs
200.0bhp 149.1kW 202.8PS
@ 4600rpm
285.0lbft 386.2Nm @ 2800rpm
148.8bhp/ton 146.4bhp/tonne
42.1bhp/L 31.4kW/L 42.7PS/L
41.9ft/sec 12.8m/sec
23.0mph 37.0kmh/1000rpm
Petrol 4-stroke piston
4752cc 289.9cu in
Vee 8 1 Carburettor
Compression ratio: 9.0:1
Bore: 95.3mm 3.8in
Stroke: 83.3mm 3.3in
Valve type/No: Overhead 16
Transmission: Manual
No. of forward speeds: 4
Wheels driven: Rear
Springs F/R: Coil/Leaf
Brake system: PA
Brakes F/R: Disc/Drum
Steering: Recirculating ball PA
Wheelbase: 269.2cm 106.0in
Track F: 142.2cm 56.0in
Track R: 139.7cm 55.0in
Length: 459.7cm 181.0in
Width: 176.5cm 69.5in
Height: 136.4cm 53.7in
Ground clearance: 19.1cm 7.5in
Kerb weight: 1366.5kg 3010.0lb
Fuel: 60.6L 13.3gal 16.0galUS

183 AMC

Javelin SST 343
1967 USA
111.0mph 178.6kmh
0-50mph 80.5kmh: 6.3secs
0-60mph 96.5kmh: 7.9secs
0-1/4 mile: 15.5secs
280.0bhp 208.8kW 283.9PS
@ 4800rpm
365.0lbft 494.6Nm @ 3000rpm
186.1bhp/ton 183.0bhp/tonne
49.8bhp/L 37.1kW/L 50.5PS/L
43.7ft/sec 13.3m/sec
21.5mph 34.6kmh/1000rpm
Petrol 4-stroke piston
5622cc 343.0cu in
Vee 8
Compression ratio: 10.2:1
Bore: 103.6mm 4.1in
Stroke: 83.3mm 3.3in
Valve type/No: Overhead 16
Transmission: Manual
No. of forward speeds: 4
Wheels driven: Rear
Brake system: PA
Brakes F/R: Disc/Drum
Steering: Recirculating ball
Wheelbase: 276.9cm 109.0in
Track F: 148.3cm 58.4in
Track R: 144.8cm 57.0in
Length: 480.6cm 189.2in
Width: 182.6cm 71.9in
Height: 131.6cm 51.8in
Kerb weight: 1530.0kg 3370.0lb
Fuel: 71.9L 15.8gal 19.0galUS

184 AMC

Marlin
1967 USA
116.0mph 186.6kmh
0-50mph 80.5kmh: 6.8secs
0-60mph 96.5kmh: 9.3secs
0-1/4 mile: 17.3secs
280.0bhp 208.8kW 283.9PS
@ 4800rpm
365.0lbft 494.6Nm @ 3000rpm
165.5bhp/ton 162.7bhp/tonne
49.8bhp/L 37.2kW/L 50.5PS/L
43.7ft/sec 13.3m/sec
24.1mph 38.8kmh/1000rpm
Petrol 4-stroke piston
5619cc 342.8cu in
Vee 8 1 Carburettor
Compression ratio: 10.2:1
Bore: 103.6mm 4.1in
Stroke: 83.3mm 3.3in
Valve type/No: Overhead 16
Transmission: Automatic
No. of forward speeds: 3
Wheels driven: Rear
Springs F/R: Coil/Coil
Brake system: PA
Brakes F/R: Disc/Drum
Steering: Recirculating ball PA
Wheelbase: 299.7cm 118.0in
Track F: 148.8cm 58.6in
Track R: 148.6cm 58.5in
Length: 511.8cm 201.5in
Width: 199.1cm 78.4in
Height: 136.7cm 53.8in
Ground clearance: 17.5cm 6.9in
Kerb weight: 1720.7kg 3790.0lb
Fuel: 81.4L 17.9gal 21.5galUS

185 AMC

Rambler American 220
1967 USA
98.0mph 157.7kmh
0-50mph 80.5kmh: 9.7secs
0-60mph 96.5kmh: 13.8secs
0-1/4 mile: 19.5secs
128.0bhp 95.4kW 129.8PS
@ 4400rpm
182.0lbft 246.6Nm @ 1600rpm
105.4bhp/ton 103.6bhp/tonne
39.3bhp/L 29.3kW/L 39.8PS/L
36.7ft/sec 11.2m/sec
23.3mph 37.5kmh/1000rpm
Petrol 4-stroke piston
3257cc 198.7cu in
In-line 6
Compression ratio: 8.5:1
Bore: 95.3mm 3.8in
Stroke: 76.2mm 3.0in
Valve type/No: Overhead 12
Transmission: Manual
No. of forward speeds: 3
Wheels driven: Rear
Brakes F/R: Drum/Drum
Steering: Worm & roller
Wheelbase: 269.2cm 106.0in
Track F: 142.2cm 56.0in
Track R: 139.7cm 55.0in
Length: 459.7cm 181.0in
Width: 179.8cm 70.8in
Height: 138.4cm 54.5in
Kerb weight: 1234.9kg 2720.0lb
Fuel: 60.6L 13.3gal 16.0galUS

186 AMC

Rambler Rebel 770
1967 USA
94.0mph 151.2kmh
0-50mph 80.5kmh: 13.0secs

0-60mph 96.5kmh: 17.3secs
0-1/4 mile: 21.0secs
145.0bhp 108.1kW 147.0PS
@ 4300rpm
215.0lbft 291.3Nm @ 1600rpm
102.0bhp/ton 100.3bhp/tonne
38.2bhp/L 28.5kW/L 38.7PS/L
41.8ft/sec 12.7m/sec
23.1mph 37.2kmh/1000rpm
Petrol 4-stroke piston
3799cc 231.8cu in
In-line 6 1 Carburettor
Compression ratio: 8.5:1
Bore: 95.3mm 3.8in
Stroke: 88.9mm 3.5in
Valve type/No: Overhead 12
Transmission: Automatic
No. of forward speeds: 3
Wheels driven: Rear
Springs F/R: Coil/Coil
Brakes F/R: Drum/Drum
Steering: Recirculating ball PA
Wheelbase: 289.6cm 114.0in
Track F: 147.8cm 58.2in
Track R: 148.6cm 58.5in
Length: 500.4cm 197.0in
Width: 199.1cm 78.4in
Height: 135.9cm 53.5in
Ground clearance: 15.2cm 6.0in
Kerb weight: 1446.0kg 3185.0lb
Fuel: 81.4L 17.9gal 21.5galUS

187 AMC
Rambler Rebel SST
1967 USA
110.0mph 177.0kmh
0-50mph 80.5kmh: 6.8secs
0-60mph 96.5kmh: 9.0secs
0-1/4 mile: 16.9secs
280.0bhp 208.8kW 283.9PS
@ 4800rpm
365.0lbft 494.6Nm @ 3000rpm
176.2bhp/ton 173.2bhp/tonne
49.8bhp/L 37.2kW/L 50.5PS/L
43.7ft/sec 13.3m/sec
24.8mph 39.9kmh/1000rpm
Petrol 4-stroke piston
5619cc 342.8cu in
Vee 8 1 Carburettor
Compression ratio: 10.2:1
Bore: 103.6mm 4.1in
Stroke: 83.3mm 3.3in
Valve type/No: Overhead 16
Transmission: Automatic
No. of forward speeds: 3
Wheels driven: Rear
Springs F/R: Coil/Coil
Brake system: PA
Brakes F/R: Disc/Drum
Steering: Recirculating ball PA
Wheelbase: 289.6cm 114.0in
Track F: 148.8cm 58.6in
Track R: 148.6cm 58.5in
Length: 500.4cm 197.0in
Width: 199.1cm 78.4in
Height: 135.9cm 53.5in
Ground clearance: 17.0cm 6.7in
Kerb weight: 1616.2kg 3560.0lb
Fuel: 81.4L 17.9gal 21.5galUS

188 AMC
Ambassador
1968 USA
98.0mph 157.7kmh
0-50mph 80.5kmh: 8.7secs
0-60mph 96.5kmh: 12.0secs
0-1/4 mile: 18.5secs
200.0bhp 149.1kW 202.8PS
@ 4600rpm
285.0lbft 386.2Nm @ 2800rpm
126.2bhp/ton 124.1bhp/tonne
42.1bhp/L 31.4kW/L 42.7PS/L
41.9ft/sec 12.8m/sec
24.8mph 39.9kmh/1000rpm
20.4mpg 17.0mpgUS 13.8L/100km
Petrol 4-stroke piston
4752cc 290.0cu in
Vee 8 1 Carburettor
Compression ratio: 9.0:1
Bore: 95.3mm 3.8in
Stroke: 83.3mm 3.3in
Valve type/No: Overhead 16
Transmission: Automatic
No. of forward speeds: 3
Wheels driven: Rear
Springs F/R: Coil/Coil
Brake system: PA
Brakes F/R: Disc/Drum
Steering: Recirculating ball PA
Wheelbase: 299.7cm 118.0in
Track F: 148.8cm 58.6in
Track R: 148.6cm 58.5in
Length: 514.4cm 202.5in
Width: 196.1cm 77.2in
Height: 140.7cm 55.4in
Kerb weight: 1611.7kg 3550.0lb
Fuel: 81.4L 17.9gal 21.5galUS

189 AMC
AMX
1968 USA
110.0mph 177.0kmh
0-50mph 80.5kmh: 5.4secs
0-60mph 96.5kmh: 7.2secs
0-1/4 mile: 15.2secs
315.0bhp 234.9kW 319.4PS
@ 4600rpm
425.0lbft 575.9Nm @ 3200rpm
211.3bhp/ton 207.7bhp/tonne
49.3bhp/L 36.7kW/L 50.0PS/L
45.6ft/sec 13.9m/sec
21.4mph 34.4kmh/1000rpm
Petrol 4-stroke piston
6392cc 390.0cu in
Vee 8 1 Carburettor
Compression ratio: 10.2:1
Bore: 103.0mm 4.1in
Stroke: 90.7mm 3.6in
Valve type/No: Overhead 16
Transmission: Manual
No. of forward speeds: 4
Wheels driven: Rear
Springs F/R: Coil/Leaf
Brake system: PA
Brakes F/R: Disc/Drum
Steering: Recirculating ball PA
Wheelbase: 246.4cm 97.0in
Track F: 148.3cm 58.4in
Track R: 144.8cm 57.0in
Length: 450.1cm 177.2in
Width: 181.9cm 71.6in
Height: 131.3cm 51.7in
Ground clearance: 15.7cm 6.2in
Kerb weight: 1516.4kg 3340.0lb
Fuel: 71.9L 15.8gal 19.0galUS

190 AMC
AMX Automatic
1968 USA
107.0mph 172.2kmh
0-50mph 80.5kmh: 5.7secs
0-60mph 96.5kmh: 7.2secs
0-1/4 mile: 14.6secs
315.0bhp 234.9kW 319.4PS
@ 4600rpm
425.0lbft 575.9Nm @ 3200rpm
210.6bhp/ton 207.1bhp/tonne
49.3bhp/L 36.7kW/L 50.0PS/L
45.6ft/sec 13.9m/sec
21.3mph 34.3kmh/1000rpm
Petrol 4-stroke piston
6391cc 389.9cu in
Vee 8 1 Carburettor
Compression ratio: 10.2:1
Bore: 105.9mm 4.2in
Stroke: 90.7mm 3.6in
Valve type/No: Overhead 16
Transmission: Automatic
No. of forward speeds: 3
Wheels driven: Rear
Springs F/R: Coil/Leaf
Brake system: PA
Brakes F/R: Disc/Drum
Steering: Recirculating ball PA
Wheelbase: 246.4cm 97.0in
Track F: 148.3cm 58.4in
Track R: 144.8cm 57.0in
Length: 450.1cm 177.2in
Width: 181.9cm 71.6in
Height: 131.3cm 51.7in
Ground clearance: 15.5cm 6.1in
Kerb weight: 1520.9kg 3350.0lb
Fuel: 71.9L 15.8gal 19.0galUS

191 AMC
Javelin
1968 USA
108.0mph 173.8kmh
0-50mph 80.5kmh: 5.5secs
0-60mph 96.5kmh: 7.0secs
0-1/4 mile: 15.0secs
315.0bhp 234.9kW 319.4PS
@ 4600rpm
425.0lbft 575.9Nm @ 3200rpm
208.4bhp/ton 205.0bhp/tonne
49.3bhp/L 36.7kW/L 50.0PS/L
45.6ft/sec 13.9m/sec
20.8mph 33.5kmh/1000rpm
Petrol 4-stroke piston
6391cc 389.9cu in
Vee 8 1 Carburettor
Compression ratio: 10.2:1
Bore: 105.9mm 4.2in
Stroke: 90.7mm 3.6in
Valve type/No: Overhead 16
Transmission: Manual
No. of forward speeds: 4
Wheels driven: Rear
Springs F/R: Coil/Leaf
Brake system: PA
Brakes F/R: Disc/Drum
Steering: Recirculating ball PA
Wheelbase: 276.9cm 109.0in
Track F: 148.3cm 58.4in
Track R: 144.8cm 57.0in
Length: 480.6cm 189.2in
Width: 182.6cm 71.9in
Height: 182.9cm 72.0in
Kerb weight: 1536.8kg 3385.0lb
Fuel: 71.9L 15.8gal 19.0galUS

192 AMC
Javelin SST
1968 USA
114.0mph 183.4kmh
0-50mph 80.5kmh: 6.5secs
0-60mph 96.5kmh: 8.1secs
0-1/4 mile: 15.4secs
280.0bhp 208.8kW 283.9PS
@ 4800rpm
365.0lbft 494.6Nm @ 3000rpm
186.1bhp/ton 183.0bhp/tonne
49.8bhp/L 37.1kW/L 50.5PS/L
43.7ft/sec 13.3m/sec
21.3mph 34.3kmh/1000rpm
Petrol 4-stroke piston
5622cc 343.0cu in
Vee 8 1 Carburettor
Compression ratio: 10.2:1
Bore: 103.6mm 4.1in
Stroke: 83.3mm 3.3in
Valve type/No: Overhead 16
Transmission: Manual
No. of forward speeds: 4
Wheels driven: Rear
Springs F/R: Coil/Leaf
Brake system: PA
Brakes F/R: Disc/Drum
Steering: Recirculating ball
Wheelbase: 276.9cm 109.0in
Track F: 148.3cm 58.4in
Track R: 144.8cm 57.0in
Length: 480.6cm 189.2in
Width: 182.6cm 71.9in
Height: 132.1cm 52.0in
Ground clearance: 15.7cm 6.2in
Kerb weight: 1530.0kg 3370.0lb
Fuel: 71.9L 15.8gal 19.0galUS

193 AMC
Ambassador SST Wagon
1969 USA
121.0mph 194.7kmh
0-50mph 80.5kmh: 6.3secs
0-60mph 96.5kmh: 8.2secs
0-1/4 mile: 16.2secs
315.0bhp 234.9kW 319.4PS
@ 4600rpm
425.0lbft 575.9Nm @ 3200rpm
174.2bhp/ton 171.3bhp/tonne
49.3bhp/L 36.7kW/L 50.0PS/L
45.6ft/sec 13.9m/sec
26.8mph 43.1kmh/1000rpm
Petrol 4-stroke piston
6391cc 389.9cu in
Vee 8 1 Carburettor
Compression ratio: 10.7:1
Bore: 105.8mm 4.2in
Stroke: 90.8mm 3.6in
Valve type/No: Overhead 16
Transmission: Automatic
No. of forward speeds: 3
Wheels driven: Rear
Springs F/R: Coil/Coil
Brake system: PA
Brakes F/R: Disc/Drum
Steering: Recirculating ball PA
Wheelbase: 309.9cm 122.0in
Track F: 152.4cm 60.0in
Track R: 152.4cm 60.0in
Length: 525.8cm 207.0in
Width: 196.6cm 77.4in
Height: 143.5cm 56.5in
Kerb weight: 1838.7kg 4050.0lb
Fuel: 71.9L 15.8gal 19.0galUS

194 AMC
Rambler Scrambler
1969 USA
108.0mph 173.8kmh
0-50mph 80.5kmh: 4.6secs
0-60mph 96.5kmh: 6.3secs
0-1/4 mile: 14.2secs
315.0bhp 234.9kW 319.4PS
@ 4600rpm
425.0lbft 575.9Nm @ 3200rpm
224.0bhp/ton 220.3bhp/tonne
49.3bhp/L 36.7kW/L 50.0PS/L
45.6ft/sec 13.9m/sec
21.2mph 34.1kmh/1000rpm
Petrol 4-stroke piston
6391cc 389.9cu in
Vee 8 1 Carburettor
Compression ratio: 10.2:1
Bore: 105.9mm 4.2in
Stroke: 90.7mm 3.6in
Valve type/No: Overhead 16
Transmission: Manual
No. of forward speeds: 4
Wheels driven: Rear
Springs F/R: Coil/Leaf
Brake system: PA
Brakes F/R: Disc/Drum
Steering: Recirculating ball
Wheelbase: 269.2cm 106.0in
Track F: 142.2cm 56.0in
Track R: 139.7cm 55.0in
Length: 459.7cm 181.0in
Width: 180.3cm 71.0in
Height: 134.6cm 53.0in
Kerb weight: 1430.1kg 3150.0lb
Fuel: 60.6L 13.3gal 16.0galUS

195 AMC
Gremlin
1970 USA
95.0mph 152.9kmh
0-50mph 80.5kmh: 9.2secs
0-60mph 96.5kmh: 12.5secs
0-1/4 mile: 18.6secs
145.0bhp 108.1kW 147.0PS
@ 4300rpm
215.0lbft 291.3Nm @ 1600rpm
115.0bhp/ton 113.1bhp/tonne
38.1bhp/L 28.4kW/L 38.7PS/L
41.8ft/sec 12.7m/sec
26.1mph 42.0kmh/1000rpm
20.2mpg 16.8mpgUS 14.0L/100km
Petrol 4-stroke piston
3802cc 232.0cu in
In-line 6 1 Carburettor
Compression ratio: 8.5:1
Bore: 95.3mm 3.8in
Stroke: 88.9mm 3.5in
Valve type/No: Overhead 12
Transmission: Automatic
No. of forward speeds: 3
Wheels driven: Rear
Springs F/R: Coil/Leaf
Brakes F/R: Drum/Drum
Steering: Recirculating ball PA
Wheelbase: 243.8cm 96.0in
Track F: 146.1cm 57.5in
Track R: 144.8cm 57.0in
Length: 409.7cm 161.3in
Width: 179.3cm 70.6in
Height: 131.6cm 51.8in
Kerb weight: 1282.5kg 2825.0lb
Fuel: 79.5L 17.5gal 21.0galUS

196 AMC
Hornet 3.8-litre
1970 USA
101.0mph 162.5kmh
0-50mph 80.5kmh: 11.3secs
0-60mph 96.5kmh: 15.7secs
0-1/4 mile: 20.0secs
145.0bhp 108.1kW 147.0PS
@ 4300rpm
215.0lbft 291.3Nm @ 1600rpm
115.2bhp/ton 113.3bhp/tonne
38.1bhp/L 28.4kW/L 38.7PS/L
41.8ft/sec 12.7m/sec
28.1mph 45.2kmh/1000rpm
23.2mpg 19.3mpgUS 12.2L/100km
Petrol 4-stroke piston

3802cc 232.0cu in
Vee 8 1 Carburettor
Compression ratio: 8.5:1
Bore: 95.2mm 3.8in
Stroke: 88.9mm 3.5in
Valve type/No: Overhead 16
Transmission: Automatic
No. of forward speeds: 3
Wheels driven: Rear
Springs F/R: Coil
Brakes F/R: Drum/Drum
Steering: Recirculating ball
Wheelbase: 274.3cm 108.0in
Track F: 146.1cm 57.5in
Track R: 144.8cm 57.0in
Length: 455.4cm 179.3in
Width: 180.6cm 71.1in
Height: 133.9cm 52.7in
Ground clearance: 13.2cm 5.2in
Kerb weight: 1280.3kg 2820.0lb
Fuel: 71.9L 15.8gal 19.0galUS

197 AMC

Hornet 4.9-litre
1970 USA
112.0mph 180.2kmh
0-50mph 80.5kmh: 7.6secs
0-60mph 96.5kmh: 10.1secs
0-1/4 mile: 17.5secs
210.0bhp 156.6kW 212.9PS
@ 4400rpm
305.0lbft 413.3Nm @ 2800rpm
150.8bhp/ton 148.2bhp/tonne
42.1bhp/L 31.4kW/L 42.7PS/L
42.0ft/sec 12.8m/sec
25.4mph 40.9kmh/1000rpm
19.6mpg 16.3mpgUS 14.4L/100km
Petrol 4-stroke piston
4982cc 304.0cu in
Vee 8 1 Carburettor
Compression ratio: 9.0:1
Bore: 95.3mm 3.8in
Stroke: 87.4mm 3.4in
Valve type/No: Overhead 16
Transmission: Automatic
No. of forward speeds: 3
Wheels driven: Rear
Springs F/R: Coil/Leaf
Brakes F/R: Drum/Drum
Steering: Recirculating ball PA
Wheelbase: 274.3cm 108.0in
Track F: 145.3cm 57.2in
Track R: 144.8cm 57.0in
Length: 455.4cm 179.3in
Width: 180.6cm 71.1in
Height: 133.9cm 52.7in
Kerb weight: 1416.5kg 3120.0lb
Fuel: 71.9L 15.8gal 19.0galUS

198 AMC

Javelin 390
1970 USA
120.0mph 193.1kmh
0-50mph 80.5kmh: 6.2secs
0-60mph 96.5kmh: 7.6secs
0-1/4 mile: 15.1secs
325.0bhp 242.3kW 329.5PS
@ 5000rpm
420.0lbft 569.1Nm @ 3200rpm
215.7bhp/ton 212.1bhp/tonne
50.8bhp/L 37.9kW/L 51.6PS/L
49.6ft/sec 15.1m/sec
23.6mph 38.0kmh/1000rpm
16.1mpg 13.4mpgUS 17.6L/100km
Petrol 4-stroke piston
6391cc 389.9cu in
Vee 8 1 Carburettor
Compression ratio: 10.0:1
Bore: 105.9mm 4.2in
Stroke: 90.7mm 3.6in
Valve type/No: Overhead 16
Transmission: Automatic
No. of forward speeds: 3
Wheels driven: Rear
Springs F/R: Coil/Leaf
Brake system: PA
Brakes F/R: Disc/Drum
Steering: Recirculating ball PA
Wheelbase: 279.1cm 109.9in
Track F: 150.1cm 59.1in
Track R: 143.8cm 56.6in
Length: 485.1cm 191.0in
Width: 182.6cm 71.9in
Height: 131.1cm 51.6in
Kerb weight: 1532.2kg 3375.0lb
Fuel: 64.3L 14.1gal 17.0galUS

199 AMC

Hornet Hatchback
1973 USA
108.0mph 173.8kmh
0-50mph 80.5kmh: 6.8secs
0-60mph 96.5kmh: 9.1secs
0-1/4 mile: 16.8secs
175.0bhp 130.5kW 177.4PS
@ 4000rpm
285.0lbft 386.2Nm @ 2400rpm
116.5bhp/ton 114.5bhp/tonne
29.7bhp/L 22.1kW/L 30.1PS/L
38.2ft/sec 11.6m/sec
22.0mph 35.4kmh/1000rpm
19.2mpg 16.0mpgUS 14.7L/100km
Petrol 4-stroke piston
5900cc 360.0cu in
Vee 8 1 Carburettor
Compression ratio: 8.5:1
Bore: 103.6mm 4.1in
Stroke: 87.4mm 3.4in
Valve type/No: Overhead 16
Transmission: Automatic
No. of forward speeds: 3
Wheels driven: Rear
Springs F/R: Coil/Leaf
Brake system: PA
Brakes F/R: Disc/Drum
Steering: Recirculating ball PA
Wheelbase: 274.3cm 108.0in
Track F: 143.3cm 56.4in
Track R: 145.0cm 57.1in
Length: 469.6cm 184.9in
Width: 180.3cm 71.0in
Height: 135.4cm 53.3in
Ground clearance: 14.2cm 5.6in
Kerb weight: 1527.7kg 3365.0lb
Fuel: 60.6L 13.3gal 16.0galUS

200 AMC

Matador X
1974 USA
116.0mph 186.6kmh
0-50mph 80.5kmh: 6.7secs
0-60mph 96.5kmh: 8.9secs
0-1/4 mile: 17.1secs
220.0bhp 164.0kW 223.0PS
@ 4400rpm
315.0lbft 426.8Nm @ 3100rpm
124.8bhp/ton 122.7bhp/tonne
37.3bhp/L 27.8kW/L 37.8PS/L
42.0ft/sec 12.8m/sec
24.0mph 38.6kmh/1000rpm
15.6mpg 13.0mpgUS 18.1L/100km
Petrol 4-stroke piston
5896cc 359.7cu in
Vee 8 1 Carburettor
Compression ratio: 8.3:1
Bore: 103.6mm 4.1in
Stroke: 87.4mm 3.4in
Valve type/No: Overhead 16
Transmission: Automatic
No. of forward speeds: 3
Wheels driven: Rear
Springs F/R: Coil/Coil
Brake system: PA
Brakes F/R: Disc/Drum
Steering: Recirculating ball PA
Wheelbase: 289.6cm 114.0in
Track F: 151.6cm 59.7in
Track R: 152.4cm 60.0in
Length: 531.6cm 209.3in
Width: 196.6cm 77.4in
Height: 131.6cm 51.8in
Ground clearance: 13.7cm 5.4in
Kerb weight: 1793.3kg 3950.0lb
Fuel: 92.7L 20.4gal 24.5galUS

201 AMC

Sportabout
1974 USA
0-60mph 96.5kmh: 9.7secs
0-1/4 mile: 17.2secs
175.0bhp 130.5kW 177.4PS
@ 4000rpm
285.0lbft 386.2Nm @ 2400rpm
110.4bhp/ton 108.6bhp/tonne
29.7bhp/L 22.1kW/L 30.1PS/L
19.2mpg 16.0mpgUS 14.7L/100km
Petrol 4-stroke piston
5896cc 359.7cu in
Vee 8
Valve type/No: Overhead 16
Transmission: Automatic
No. of forward speeds: 3
Wheels driven: Rear
Brakes F/R: Disc/Drum
Wheelbase: 274.3cm 108.0in
Length: 474.7cm 186.9in
Width: 180.3cm 71.0in
Height: 132.6cm 52.2in
Kerb weight: 1611.7kg 3550.0lb

202 AMC

Pacer
1975 USA
88.0mph 141.6kmh
0-50mph 80.5kmh: 10.8secs
0-60mph 96.5kmh: 15.8secs
0-1/4 mile: 20.3secs
100.0bhp 74.6kW 101.4PS
@ 3500rpm
185.0lbft 250.7Nm @ 1800rpm
65.4bhp/ton 64.3bhp/tonne
23.6bhp/L 17.6kW/L 24.0PS/L
37.8ft/sec 11.5m/sec
22.8mph 36.7kmh/1000rpm
19.2mpg 16.0mpgUS 14.7L/100km
Petrol 4-stroke piston
4229cc 258.0cu in
In-line 6 1 Carburettor
Compression ratio: 8.0:1
Bore: 95.3mm 3.8in
Stroke: 98.9mm 3.9in
Valve type/No: Overhead 12
Transmission: Automatic
No. of forward speeds: 3
Wheels driven: Rear
Springs F/R: Coil/Leaf
Brake system: PA
Brakes F/R: Disc/Drum
Steering: Rack & pinion PA
Wheelbase: 254.0cm 100.0in
Track F: 155.4cm 61.2in
Track R: 152.9cm 60.2in
Length: 435.6cm 171.5in
Width: 195.6cm 77.0in
Height: 136.1cm 53.6in
Ground clearance: 12.7cm 5.0in
Kerb weight: 1554.9kg 3425.0lb
Fuel: 83.3L 18.3gal 22.0galUS

203 AMC

Pacer
1976 USA
97.0mph 156.1kmh
0-50mph 80.5kmh: 10.4secs
0-60mph 96.5kmh: 14.8secs
0-1/4 mile: 19.8secs
0-1km: 37.1secs
110.0bhp 82.0kW 111.5PS
@ 3500rpm
195.0lbft 264.2Nm @ 2000rpm
71.3bhp/ton 70.1bhp/tonne
26.0bhp/L 19.4kW/L 26.4PS/L
37.9ft/sec 11.5m/sec
23.7mph 38.1kmh/1000rpm
15.8mpg 13.2mpgUS 17.9L/100km
Petrol 4-stroke piston
4229cc 258.0cu in
In-line 6 1 Carburettor
Compression ratio: 8.0:1
Bore: 92.2mm 3.6in
Stroke: 99.0mm 3.9in
Valve type/No: Overhead 12
Transmission: Automatic
No. of forward speeds: 3
Wheels driven: Rear
Springs F/R: Coil/Leaf
Brake system: PA
Brakes F/R: Disc/Drum
Steering: Rack & pinion PA
Wheelbase: 256.5cm 101.0in
Track F: 156.7cm 61.7in
Track R: 155.4cm 61.2in
Length: 436.9cm 172.0in
Width: 183.4cm 72.2in
Height: 146.1cm 57.5in
Ground clearance: 16.5cm 6.5in
Kerb weight: 1568.6kg 3455.0lb
Fuel: 83.3L 18.3gal 22.0galUS

204 AMC

Gremlin 2-litre
1977 USA
97.0mph 156.1kmh
0-50mph 80.5kmh: 11.2secs
0-60mph 96.5kmh: 15.7secs
0-1/4 mile: 20.6secs
80.0bhp 59.7kW 81.1PS
@ 5000rpm
105.0lbft 142.3Nm @ 2800rpm
65.3bhp/ton 64.2bhp/tonne
40.3bhp/L 30.1kW/L 40.9PS/L
46.1ft/sec 14.1m/sec
22.4mph 36.0kmh/1000rpm
23.4mpg 19.5mpgUS 12.1L/100km
Petrol 4-stroke piston
1984cc 121.0cu in
In-line 4 1 Carburettor
Compression ratio: 8.1:1
Bore: 86.5mm 3.4in
Stroke: 84.4mm 3.3in
Valve type/No: Overhead 8
Transmission: Manual
No. of forward speeds: 4
Wheels driven: Rear
Springs F/R: Coil/Leaf
Brake system: PA
Brakes F/R: Disc/Drum
Steering: Recirculating ball
Wheelbase: 243.8cm 96.0in
Track F: 146.1cm 57.5in
Track R: 145.0cm 57.1in
Length: 422.7cm 166.4in
Width: 179.3cm 70.6in
Height: 132.8cm 52.3in
Ground clearance: 13.0cm 5.1in
Kerb weight: 1246.2kg 2745.0lb
Fuel: 56.8L 12.5gal 15.0galUS

205 AMC

Pacer Wagon
1977 USA
105.0mph 168.9kmh
0-50mph 80.5kmh: 9.7secs
0-60mph 96.5kmh: 13.7secs
0-1/4 mile: 19.8secs
120.0bhp 89.5kW 121.7PS
@ 3600rpm
200.0lbft 271.0Nm @ 2000rpm
78.2bhp/ton 76.9bhp/tonne
28.4bhp/L 21.2kW/L 28.8PS/L
38.9ft/sec 11.9m/sec
27.6mph 44.4kmh/1000rpm
21.0mpg 17.5mpgUS 13.4L/100km
Petrol 4-stroke piston
4229cc 258.0cu in
In-line 6
Compression ratio: 8.0:1
Bore: 95.3mm 3.8in
Stroke: 98.9mm 3.9in
Valve type/No: Overhead 12
Transmission: Manual
No. of forward speeds: 4
Wheels driven: Rear
Springs F/R: Coil/Leaf
Brake system: PA
Brakes F/R: Disc/Drum
Steering: Rack & pinion PA
Wheelbase: 254.0cm 100.0in
Track F: 155.4cm 61.2in
Track R: 152.9cm 60.2in
Length: 442.0cm 174.0in
Width: 195.6cm 77.0in
Height: 134.6cm 53.0in
Kerb weight: 1559.5kg 3435.0lb
Fuel: 83.3L 18.3gal 22.0galUS

206 AMC

Eagle
1980 USA
92.0mph 148.0kmh
0-50mph 80.5kmh: 10.8secs
0-60mph 96.5kmh: 15.4secs
0-1/4 mile: 20.2secs
114.0bhp 85.0kW 115.6PS
@ 3200rpm
210.0lbft 284.6Nm @ 1800rpm
71.5bhp/ton 70.3bhp/tonne
26.9bhp/L 20.1kW/L 27.3PS/L
34.7ft/sec 10.6m/sec
24.8mph 39.9kmh/1000rpm
15.6mpg 13.0mpgUS 18.1L/100km
Petrol 4-stroke piston
4230cc 258.1cu in
In-line 6 1 Carburettor
Compression ratio: 8.3:1
Bore: 95.3mm 3.8in
Stroke: 99.1mm 3.9in
Valve type/No: Overhead 12
Transmission: Automatic
No. of forward speeds: 3
Wheels driven: 4-wheel drive
Springs F/R: Coil/Leaf
Brake system: PA
Brakes F/R: Disc/Drum
Steering: Recirculating ball PA
Wheelbase: 277.6cm 109.3in
Track F: 151.4cm 59.6in

Track R: 146.3cm 57.6in
Length: 467.4cm 184.0in
Width: 180.3cm 71.0in
Height: 141.7cm 55.8in
Ground clearance: 17.8cm 7.0in
Kerb weight: 1620.8kg 3570.0lb
Fuel: 83.3L 18.3gal 22.0galUS

207 Amilcar

Straight Eight Saloon
1930 France
73.7mph 118.6kmh
19.0mpg 15.8mpgUS 14.9L/100km
Petrol 4-stroke piston
1980cc 120.8cu in
In-line 8
Bore: 63.0mm 2.5in
Stroke: 80.0mm 3.1in
Transmission: Manual
No. of forward speeds: 4
Wheels driven: Rear
Brakes F/R: Drum/Drum
Wheelbase: 304.8cm 120.0in
Track F: 142.2cm 56.0in
Track R: 142.2cm 56.0in
Length: 464.8cm 183.0in
Width: 170.2cm 67.0in
Height: 165.1cm 65.0in
Kerb weight: 1372.9kg 3024.0lb
Fuel: 54.6L 12.0gal 14.4galUS

208 Apollo

GT
1963 USA
104.0mph 167.3kmh
0-50mph 80.5kmh: 5.8secs
0-60mph 96.5kmh: 8.4secs
0-1/4 mile: 16.0secs
200.0bhp 149.1kW 202.8PS
@ 5000rpm
240.0lbft 325.2Nm @ 3200rpm
180.3bhp/ton 177.3bhp/tonne
56.7bhp/L 42.3kW/L 57.5PS/L
38.9ft/sec 11.8m/sec
18.9mph 30.4kmh/1000rpm
Petrol 4-stroke piston
3524cc 215.0cu in
Vee 8 1 Carburettor
Compression ratio: 11.0:1
Bore: 88.9mm 3.5in
Stroke: 71.1mm 2.8in
Valve type/No: Overhead 16
Transmission: Manual
No. of forward speeds: 4
Wheels driven: Rear
Wheelbase: 248.9cm 98.0in
Track F: 142.2cm 56.0in
Track R: 142.2cm 56.0in
Length: 452.1cm 178.0in
Width: 167.6cm 66.0in
Height: 127.0cm 50.0in
Ground clearance: 12.7cm 5.0in
Kerb weight: 1128.2kg 2485.0lb

209 Armstrong Siddeley

15 Saloon
1931 UK
60.8mph 97.8kmh
23.0mpg 19.2mpgUS 12.3L/100km
Petrol 4-stroke piston
1928cc 117.6cu in
In-line 6 1 Carburettor
Bore: 63.5mm 2.5in
Stroke: 101.6mm 4.0in
Valve type/No: Side 12
Transmission: Pre-selector
No. of forward speeds: 3
Wheels driven: Rear
Brakes F/R: Drum/Drum
Wheelbase: 276.9cm 109.0in
Track F: 142.2cm 56.0in
Track R: 142.2cm 56.0in
Length: 383.5cm 151.0in
Width: 172.7cm 68.0in
Height: 177.8cm 70.0in
Kerb weight: 1322.0kg 2912.0lb
Fuel: 54.6L 12.0gal 14.4galUS

210 Armstrong Siddeley

Rally Tourer
1932 UK
70.8mph 113.9kmh
17.0mpg 14.2mpgUS 16.6L/100km
Petrol 4-stroke piston
3190cc 194.6cu in
In-line 6 1 Carburettor
Bore: 73.0mm 2.9in
Stroke: 127.0mm 5.0in
Valve type/No: Overhead 12
Transmission: Pre-selector
No. of forward speeds: 4
Wheels driven: Rear
Brakes F/R: Drum/Drum
Wheelbase: 311.2cm 122.5in
Track F: 142.2cm 56.0in
Track R: 142.2cm 56.0in
Length: 442.0cm 174.0in
Width: 172.7cm 68.0in
Height: 176.5cm 69.5in
Kerb weight: 1678.0kg 3696.0lb
Fuel: 54.6L 12.0gal 14.4galUS

211 Armstrong Siddeley

Long 15hp Saloon
1933 UK
61.6mph 99.1kmh
0-50mph 80.5kmh: 24.0secs
20.0mpg 16.7mpgUS 14.1L/100km
Petrol 4-stroke piston
2169cc 132.3cu in
In-line 6
Bore: 63.5mm 2.5in
Stroke: 114.0mm 4.5in
Transmission: Pre-selector
No. of forward speeds: 4
Wheels driven: Rear
Brakes F/R: Drum/Drum
Kerb weight: 1538.1kg 3388.0lb
Fuel: 54.6L 12.0gal 14.4galUS

212 Armstrong Siddeley

17hp Sports Foursome
1935 UK
72.5mph 116.7kmh
0-50mph 80.5kmh: 17.8secs
0-60mph 96.5kmh: 28.2secs
21.0mpg 17.5mpgUS 13.5L/100km
Petrol 4-stroke piston
2394cc 146.1cu in
In-line 6
Bore: 66.7mm 2.6in
Stroke: 114.0mm 4.5in
Valve type/No: Overhead 12
Transmission: Pre-selector
No. of forward speeds: 4
Wheels driven: Rear
Brakes F/R: Drum/Drum
Kerb weight: 1450.5kg 3195.0lb
Fuel: 54.6L 12.0gal 14.4galUS

213 Armstrong Siddeley

30 Special Sports Saloon
1935 UK
85.7mph 137.9kmh
0-50mph 80.5kmh: 13.8secs
0-60mph 96.5kmh: 19.8secs
124.0bhp 92.5kW 125.7PS
@ 3200rpm
52.8bhp/ton 52.0bhp/tonne
25.0bhp/L 18.6kW/L 25.3PS/L
46.7ft/sec 14.2m/sec
12.0mpg 10.0mpgUS 23.5L/100km
Petrol 4-stroke piston
4960cc 302.6cu in
In-line 6 2 Carburettor
Compression ratio: 5.2:1
Bore: 88.9mm 3.5in
Stroke: 133.4mm 5.2in
Valve type/No: Overhead 12
Transmission: Manual
No. of forward speeds: 4
Wheels driven: Rear
Brakes F/R: Drum/Drum
Ground clearance: 15.2cm 6.0in
Kerb weight: 2386.2kg 5256.0lb
Fuel: 91.0L 20.0gal 24.0galUS

214 Armstrong Siddeley

17hp Touring Saloon
1936 UK
67.1mph 108.0kmh
0-50mph 80.5kmh: 25.1secs
0-60mph 96.5kmh: 46.7secs
18.0mpg 15.0mpgUS 15.7L/100km
Petrol 4-stroke piston
2394cc 146.1cu in
In-line 6
Bore: 66.7mm 2.6in
Stroke: 114.0mm 4.5in
Valve type/No: Overhead 12
Transmission: Pre-selector
No. of forward speeds: 4
Wheels driven: Rear
Brakes F/R: Drum/Drum
Kerb weight: 1582.2kg 3485.0lb
Fuel: 63.7L 14.0gal 16.8galUS

215 Armstrong Siddeley

25.3hp Town and Country Saloon
1937 UK
76.2mph 122.6kmh
0-50mph 80.5kmh: 18.8secs
0-60mph 96.5kmh: 31.7secs
15.0mpg 12.5mpgUS 18.8L/100km
Petrol 4-stroke piston
3670cc 223.9cu in
In-line 6
Bore: 82.5mm 3.2in
Stroke: 114.3mm 4.5in
Valve type/No: Overhead 12
Transmission: Manual
No. of forward speeds: 4
Wheels driven: Rear
Brakes F/R: Drum/Drum
Kerb weight: 1986.7kg 4376.0lb
Fuel: 63.7L 14.0gal 16.8galUS

216 Armstrong Siddeley

Six-light Saloon
1937 UK
70.8mph 113.9kmh
0-50mph 80.5kmh: 21.2secs
0-60mph 96.5kmh: 33.2secs
60.0bhp 44.7kW 60.8PS
@ 3300rpm
39.4bhp/ton 38.8bhp/tonne
25.0bhp/L 18.7kW/L 25.4PS/L
41.2ft/sec 12.6m/sec
18.0mpg 15.0mpgUS 15.7L/100km
Petrol 4-stroke piston
2396cc 146.2cu in
In-line 6
Bore: 66.7mm 2.6in
Stroke: 114.4mm 4.5in
Valve type/No: Overhead 12
Transmission: Manual
No. of forward speeds: 4
Wheels driven: Rear
Brakes F/R: Drum/Drum
Kerb weight: 1547.2kg 3408.0lb
Fuel: 45.5L 10.0gal 12.0galUS

217 Armstrong Siddeley

16 Saloon
1938 UK
73.7mph 118.6kmh
0-50mph 80.5kmh: 17.4secs
0-60mph 96.5kmh: 26.9secs
70.0bhp 52.2kW 71.0PS
@ 4200rpm
50.1bhp/ton 49.3bhp/tonne
35.2bhp/L 26.2kW/L 35.7PS/L
46.0ft/sec 14.0m/sec
23.0mpg 19.2mpgUS 12.3L/100km
Petrol 4-stroke piston
1990cc 121.4cu in
In-line 6 1 Carburettor
Compression ratio: 7.0:1
Bore: 65.0mm 2.6in
Stroke: 100.0mm 3.9in
Valve type/No: Overhead 12
Transmission: Manual
No. of forward speeds: 4
Wheels driven: Rear
Brakes F/R: Drum/Drum
Kerb weight: 1420.6kg 3129.0lb
Fuel: 50.0L 11.0gal 13.2galUS

218 Armstrong Siddeley

2-litre Saloon
1948 UK
70.0mph 112.6kmh
0-50mph 80.5kmh: 19.5secs
0-60mph 96.5kmh: 29.7secs
70.0bhp 52.2kW 71.0PS
@ 4200rpm
51.8bhp/ton 51.0bhp/tonne
35.2bhp/L 26.2kW/L 35.6PS/L
46.0ft/sec 14.0m/sec
18.0mpg 15.0mpgUS 15.7L/100km
Petrol 4-stroke piston
1991cc 121.5cu in
In-line 6
Compression ratio: 7.0:1
Bore: 65.0mm 2.6in
Stroke: 100.0mm 3.9in
Valve type/No: Overhead 12
Transmission: Manual
No. of forward speeds: 4
Wheels driven: Rear
Brakes F/R: Drum/Drum
Wheelbase: 292.1cm 115.0in
Track F: 137.2cm 54.0in
Track R: 138.4cm 54.5in
Length: 462.3cm 182.0in
Width: 172.7cm 68.0in
Height: 157.5cm 62.0in
Ground clearance: 16.5cm 6.5in
Kerb weight: 1372.9kg 3024.0lb
Fuel: 54.6L 12.0gal 14.4galUS

219 Armstrong Siddeley

Sapphire Saloon
1953 UK
91.5mph 147.2kmh
0-50mph 80.5kmh: 10.1secs
0-60mph 96.5kmh: 15.5secs
0-1/4 mile: 20.0secs
125.0bhp 93.2kW 126.7PS
@ 4400rpm
176.5lbft 239.2Nm @ 1000rpm
78.1bhp/ton 76.8bhp/tonne
36.4bhp/L 27.1kW/L 36.9PS/L
43.3ft/sec 13.2m/sec
20.2mph 32.5kmh/1000rpm
18.0mpg 15.0mpgUS 15.7L/100km
Petrol 4-stroke piston
3435cc 209.6cu in
In-line 6
Compression ratio: 7.0:1
Bore: 90.0mm 3.5in
Stroke: 90.0mm 3.5in
Valve type/No: Overhead 12
Transmission: Manual
No. of forward speeds: 4
Wheels driven: Rear
Springs F/R: Coil/Leaf
Brakes F/R: Drum/Drum
Wheelbase: 289.6cm 114.0in
Track F: 143.8cm 56.6in
Track R: 146.1cm 57.5in
Length: 490.2cm 193.0in
Width: 182.9cm 72.0in
Height: 129.5cm 51.0in
Ground clearance: 20.3cm 8.0in
Kerb weight: 1627.1kg 3584.0lb
Fuel: 72.8L 16.0gal 19.2galUS

220 Armstrong Siddeley

Star Sapphire
1959 UK
102.2mph 164.4kmh
0-50mph 80.5kmh: 10.1secs
0-60mph 96.5kmh: 14.2secs
0-1/4 mile: 19.2secs
165.0bhp 123.0kW 167.3PS
@ 4250rpm
260.0lbft 352.3Nm @ 2000rpm
94.1bhp/ton 92.5bhp/tonne
41.3bhp/L 30.8kW/L 41.9PS/L
41.8ft/sec 12.7m/sec
21.8mph 35.1kmh/1000rpm
14.1mpg 11.7mpgUS 20.0L/100km
Petrol 4-stroke piston
3990cc 243.4cu in
In-line 6

Compression ratio: 7.5:1
Bore: 97.0mm 3.8in
Stroke: 90.0mm 3.5in
Valve type/No: Overhead 12
Transmission: Automatic
No. of forward speeds: 3
Wheels driven: Rear
Springs F/R: Coil/Leaf
Brake system: PA
Brakes F/R: Disc/Drum
Wheelbase: 289.6cm 114.0in
Track F: 146.8cm 57.8in
Track R: 146.1cm 57.5in
Length: 492.8cm 194.0in
Width: 188.0cm 74.0in
Height: 161.3cm 63.5in
Ground clearance: 21.6cm 8.5in
Kerb weight: 1782.9kg 3927.0lb
Fuel: 72.8L 16.0gal 19.2galUS

221 ASA

1000GT
1960 Italy
115.0mph 185.0kmh
91.0bhp 67.9kW 92.3PS
@ 6800rpm
101.7bhp/ton 100.0bhp/tonne
88.2bhp/L 65.8kW/L 89.4PS/L
51.4ft/sec 15.6m/sec
Petrol 4-stroke piston
1032cc 63.0cu in
In-line 4 2 Carburettor
Compression ratio: 9.1:1
Bore: 69.0mm 2.7in
Stroke: 69.0mm 2.7in
Valve type/No: Overhead 8
Transmission: Manual with overdrive
Wheels driven: Rear
Springs F/R: Coil/Coil
Brakes F/R: Disc/Disc
Steering: Rack & pinion
Wheelbase: 224.8cm 88.5in
Track F: 124.0cm 48.8in
Track R: 122.7cm 48.3in
Length: 389.9cm 153.5in
Width: 154.9cm 61.0in
Height: 119.4cm 47.0in
Kerb weight: 910.3kg 2005.0lb
Fuel: 49.2L 10.8gal 13.0galUS

222 Aston Martin

Super Sports
1929 UK
81.0mph 130.3kmh
56.0bhp 41.8kW 56.8PS
@ 4250rpm
55.0bhp/ton 54.0bhp/tonne
37.8bhp/L 28.2kW/L 38.3PS/L
46.0ft/sec 14.0m/sec
28.0mpg 23.3mpgUS 10.1L/100km
Petrol 4-stroke piston
1481cc 90.4cu in
In-line 4 2 Carburettor
Compression ratio: 6.0:1
Bore: 69.0mm 2.7in
Stroke: 99.0mm 3.9in
Valve type/No: Overhead 8
Transmission: Manual
No. of forward speeds: 4
Wheels driven: Rear
Brakes F/R: Drum/Drum
Wheelbase: 259.1cm 102.0in
Track F: 132.1cm 52.0in
Track R: 132.1cm 52.0in
Length: 373.4cm 147.0in
Width: 157.5cm 62.0in
Height: 132.1cm 52.0in
Kerb weight: 1036.0kg 2282.0lb
Fuel: 54.6L 12.0gal 14.4galUS

223 Aston Martin

Sports Four-seater
1931 UK
75.0mph 120.7kmh
56.0bhp 41.8kW 56.8PS
@ 4250rpm
57.4bhp/ton 56.4bhp/tonne
37.5bhp/L 28.0kW/L 38.0PS/L
46.0ft/sec 14.0m/sec
26.0mpg 21.6mpgUS 10.9L/100km
Petrol 4-stroke piston
1493cc 91.1cu in
In-line 4 2 Carburettor
Compression ratio: 6.0:1
Bore: 69.0mm 2.7in
Stroke: 99.0mm 3.9in
Valve type/No: Overhead 8
Transmission: Manual
No. of forward speeds: 4
Wheels driven: Rear
Brakes F/R: Drum/Drum
Wheelbase: 259.1cm 102.0in
Track F: 132.1cm 52.0in
Track R: 132.1cm 52.0in
Length: 368.3cm 145.0in
Width: 160.0cm 63.0in
Height: 137.2cm 54.0in
Kerb weight: 992.0kg 2185.0lb
Fuel: 45.5L 10.0gal 12.0galUS

224 Aston Martin

1.5-litre
1932 UK
74.3mph 119.5kmh
56.0bhp 41.8kW 56.8PS
@ 4250rpm
50.9bhp/ton 50.1bhp/tonne
37.5bhp/L 28.0kW/L 38.0PS/L
46.0ft/sec 14.0m/sec
27.0mpg 22.5mpgUS 10.5L/100km
Petrol 4-stroke piston
1493cc 91.1cu in
In-line 4 2 Carburettor
Compression ratio: 6.0:1
Bore: 69.0mm 2.7in
Stroke: 99.0mm 3.9in
Valve type/No: Overhead 8
Transmission: Manual
No. of forward speeds: 4
Wheels driven: Rear
Brakes F/R: Drum/Drum
Wheelbase: 299.7cm 118.0in
Track F: 132.1cm 52.0in
Track R: 132.1cm 52.0in
Length: 426.7cm 168.0in
Width: 160.0cm 63.0in
Height: 157.5cm 62.0in
Kerb weight: 1118.7kg 2464.0lb
Fuel: 45.5L 10.0gal 12.0galUS

225 Aston Martin

Le Mans
1933 UK
84.9mph 136.6kmh
0-50mph 80.5kmh: 18.2secs
0-60mph 96.5kmh: 24.6secs
70.0bhp 52.2kW 71.0PS
@ 4750rpm
73.7bhp/ton 72.5bhp/tonne
46.9bhp/L 35.0kW/L 47.5PS/L
51.5ft/sec 15.7m/sec
27.0mpg 22.5mpgUS 10.5L/100km
Petrol 4-stroke piston
1493cc 91.1cu in
In-line 4 2 Carburettor
Compression ratio: 7.5:1
Bore: 69.0mm 2.7in
Stroke: 99.0mm 3.9in
Valve type/No: Overhead 8
Transmission: Manual
No. of forward speeds: 4
Wheels driven: Rear
Brakes F/R: Drum/Drum
Kerb weight: 966.1kg 2128.0lb
Fuel: 86.4L 19.0gal 22.8galUS

226 Aston Martin

1.5-litre Mk II
1934 UK
84.9mph 136.6kmh
0-50mph 80.5kmh: 14.6secs
0-60mph 96.5kmh: 21.8secs
22.0mpg 18.3mpgUS 12.8L/100km
Petrol 4-stroke piston
1496cc 91.3cu in
In-line 4
Bore: 69.3mm 2.7in
Stroke: 99.1mm 3.9in
Transmission: Manual
No. of forward speeds: 4
Wheels driven: Rear
Brakes F/R: Drum/Drum
Kerb weight: 966.1kg 2128.0lb
Fuel: 59.1L 13.0gal 15.6galUS

227 Aston Martin

1.5-litre
1935 UK
82.5mph 132.7kmh
0-50mph 80.5kmh: 17.6secs
0-60mph 96.5kmh: 25.6secs
26.0mpg 21.6mpgUS 10.9L/100km
Petrol 4-stroke piston
1495cc 91.2cu in
In-line 4
Bore: 69.0mm 2.7in
Stroke: 99.0mm 3.9in
Valve type/No: Overhead 8
Transmission: Manual
No. of forward speeds: 4
Wheels driven: Rear
Brakes F/R: Drum/Drum
Kerb weight: 1146.8kg 2526.0lb
Fuel: 50.0L 11.0gal 13.2galUS

228 Aston Martin

Sports Saloon
1936 UK
78.9mph 127.0kmh
0-50mph 80.5kmh: 20.0secs
0-60mph 96.5kmh: 28.4secs
85.0bhp 63.4kW 86.2PS
@ 4750rpm
67.6bhp/ton 66.5bhp/tonne
56.9bhp/L 42.4kW/L 57.6PS/L
51.5ft/sec 15.7m/sec
26.0mpg 21.6mpgUS 10.9L/100km
Petrol 4-stroke piston
1495cc 91.2cu in
In-line 4 2 Carburettor
Compression ratio: 9.0:1
Bore: 69.0mm 2.7in
Stroke: 99.0mm 3.9in
Valve type/No: Overhead 8
Transmission: Manual
No. of forward speeds: 4
Wheels driven: Rear
Brakes F/R: Drum/Drum
Kerb weight: 1278.0kg 2815.0lb
Fuel: 54.6L 12.0gal 14.4galUS

229 Aston Martin

2-litre
1937 UK
84.1mph 135.3kmh
0-50mph 80.5kmh: 13.5secs
0-60mph 96.5kmh: 19.6secs
18.0mpg 15.0mpgUS 15.7L/100km
Petrol 4-stroke piston
1950cc 119.0cu in
In-line 4
Bore: 78.0mm 3.1in
Stroke: 102.0mm 4.0in
Valve type/No: Overhead 8
Transmission: Manual
No. of forward speeds: 4
Wheels driven: Rear
Brakes F/R: Drum/Drum
Kerb weight: 1179.5kg 2598.0lb
Fuel: 63.7L 14.0gal 16.8galUS

230 Aston Martin

Drop-head Coupe
1938 UK
84.9mph 136.6kmh
0-50mph 80.5kmh: 14.2secs
0-60mph 96.5kmh: 19.8secs
110.0bhp 82.0kW 111.5PS
@ 5500rpm
86.9bhp/ton 85.5bhp/tonne
56.4bhp/L 42.1kW/L 57.2PS/L
61.4ft/sec 18.7m/sec
20.0mpg 16.7mpgUS 14.1L/100km
Petrol 4-stroke piston
1950cc 119.0cu in
In-line 4 2 Carburettor
Compression ratio: 8.3:1
Bore: 78.0mm 3.1in
Stroke: 102.0mm 4.0in
Valve type/No: Overhead 8
Transmission: Manual
No. of forward speeds: 4
Wheels driven: Rear
Brakes F/R: Drum/Drum
Kerb weight: 1287.1kg 2835.0lb
Fuel: 63.7L 14.0gal 16.8galUS

231 Aston Martin

2-litre
1939 UK
97.8mph 157.4kmh
0-50mph 80.5kmh: 11.1secs
0-60mph 96.5kmh: 15.4secs
110.0bhp 82.0kW 111.5PS
@ 5500rpm
96.0bhp/ton 94.4bhp/tonne
56.4bhp/L 42.1kW/L 57.2PS/L
61.4ft/sec 18.7m/sec
20.0mpg 16.7mpgUS 14.1L/100km
Petrol 4-stroke piston
1950cc 119.0cu in
In-line 4 2 Carburettor
Compression ratio: 8.3:1
Bore: 78.0mm 3.1in
Stroke: 102.0mm 4.0in
Valve type/No: Overhead 8
Transmission: Manual
No. of forward speeds: 4
Wheels driven: Rear
Brakes F/R: Drum/Drum
Kerb weight: 1165.0kg 2566.0lb
Fuel: 77.3L 17.0gal 20.4galUS

232 Aston Martin

DB2
1951 UK
106.0mph 170.6kmh
0-1/4 mile: 18.7secs
107.0bhp 79.8kW 108.5PS
@ 5000rpm
95.9bhp/ton 94.3bhp/tonne
41.5bhp/L 30.9kW/L 42.0PS/L
49.2ft/sec 15.0m/sec
Petrol 4-stroke piston
2580cc 157.4cu in
In-line 6
Compression ratio: 6.5:1
Bore: 78.0mm 3.1in
Stroke: 90.0mm 3.5in
Valve type/No: Overhead 12
Transmission: Manual
No. of forward speeds: 4
Wheels driven: Rear
Wheelbase: 251.5cm 99.0in
Track F: 137.2cm 54.0in
Track R: 137.2cm 54.0in
Length: 410.2cm 161.5in
Width: 165.1cm 65.0in
Height: 135.9cm 53.5in
Ground clearance: 21.6cm 8.5in
Kerb weight: 1135.0kg 2500.0lb

233 Aston Martin

DB2/4 Saloon
1953 UK
120.0mph 193.1kmh
0-50mph 80.5kmh: 8.9secs
0-60mph 96.5kmh: 12.6secs
0-1/4 mile: 18.9secs
125.0bhp 93.2kW 126.7PS
@ 5000rpm
144.0lbft 195.1Nm @ 2400rpm
101.0bhp/ton 99.3bhp/tonne
48.4bhp/L 36.1kW/L 49.1PS/L
49.2ft/sec 15.0m/sec
21.5mph 34.6kmh/1000rpm
20.3mpg 16.9mpgUS 13.9L/100km
Petrol 4-stroke piston
2580cc 157.4cu in
In-line 6
Compression ratio: 8.1:1
Bore: 78.0mm 3.1in
Stroke: 90.0mm 3.5in
Valve type/No: Overhead 12
Transmission: Manual
No. of forward speeds: 4
Wheels driven: Rear
Springs F/R: Coil/Coil
Brakes F/R: Drum/Drum
Wheelbase: 251.5cm 99.0in
Track F: 137.2cm 54.0in
Track R: 137.2cm 54.0in
Length: 430.5cm 169.5in
Width: 165.1cm 65.0in
Height: 135.9cm 53.5in
Ground clearance: 17.8cm 7.0in
Kerb weight: 1258.5kg 2772.0lb
Fuel: 77.3L 17.0gal 20.4galUS

234 Aston Martin

DB2
1954 UK
110.0mph 177.0kmh
0-50mph 80.5kmh: 9.9secs
0-60mph 96.5kmh: 12.4secs
105.0bhp 78.3kW 106.5PS
@ 5000rpm
125.0lbft 169.4Nm @ 3100rpm
88.3bhp/ton 86.9bhp/tonne
40.7bhp/L 30.3kW/L 41.3PS/L

49.2ft/sec 15.0m/sec
18.0mpg 15.0mpgUS 15.7L/100km
Petrol 4-stroke piston
2580cc 157.4cu in
In-line 6
Compression ratio: 6.5:1
Bore: 78.0mm 3.1in
Stroke: 90.0mm 3.5in
Valve type/No: Overhead 12
Transmission: Manual
No. of forward speeds: 4
Wheels driven: Rear
Brakes F/R: Drum/Drum
Wheelbase: 251.5cm 99.0in
Track F: 137.2cm 54.0in
Track R: 137.2cm 54.0in
Length: 412.8cm 162.5in
Width: 165.1cm 65.0in
Height: 135.9cm 53.5in
Ground clearance: 21.6cm 8.5in
Kerb weight: 1208.5kg 2662.0lb
Fuel: 86.4L 19.0gal 22.8galUS

235 Aston Martin

Spyder Touring
1956 UK
132.0mph 212.4kmh
178.0bhp 132.7kW 180.5PS
@ 5500rpm
178.0lbft 241.2Nm @ 3100rpm
209.8bhp/ton 206.3bhp/tonne
59.5bhp/L 44.4kW/L 60.3PS/L
54.1ft/sec 16.5m/sec
Petrol 4-stroke piston
2992cc 182.5cu in
In-line 6 3 Carburettor
Compression ratio: 8.2:1
Bore: 83.0mm 3.3in
Stroke: 90.0mm 3.5in
Valve type/No: Overhead 12
Transmission: Manual
No. of forward speeds: 4
Wheels driven: Rear
Brakes F/R: Drum/Drum
Wheelbase: 251.5cm 99.0in
Track F: 137.2cm 54.0in
Track R: 137.2cm 54.0in
Length: 426.7cm 168.0in
Width: 165.1cm 65.0in
Height: 119.4cm 47.0in
Kerb weight: 862.6kg 1900.0lb
Fuel: 71.9L 15.8gal 19.0galUS

236 Aston Martin

Mk III
1958 UK
120.0mph 193.1kmh
0-50mph 80.5kmh: 7.1secs
0-60mph 96.5kmh: 9.3secs
0-1/4 mile: 17.4secs
162.0bhp 120.8kW 164.2PS
@ 5500rpm
180.0lbft 243.9Nm @ 4000rpm
123.1bhp/ton 121.1bhp/tonne
55.4bhp/L 41.3kW/L 56.2PS/L
54.1ft/sec 16.5m/sec
28.4mph 45.7kmh/1000rpm
18.1mpg 15.1mpgUS 15.6L/100km
Petrol 4-stroke piston
2922cc 178.3cu in
In-line 6
Compression ratio: 8.2:1
Bore: 83.0mm 3.3in
Stroke: 90.0mm 3.5in
Valve type/No: Overhead 12
Transmission: Manual with overdrive
Wheels driven: Rear
Springs F/R: Coil/Coil
Brakes F/R: Disc/Drum
Wheelbase: 251.5cm 99.0in
Track F: 137.2cm 54.0in
Track R: 137.2cm 54.0in
Length: 435.6cm 171.5in
Width: 165.1cm 65.0in
Height: 135.9cm 53.5in
Ground clearance: 13.7cm 5.4in
Kerb weight: 1337.9kg 2947.0lb
Fuel: 70.5L 15.5gal 18.6galUS

237 Aston Martin

DB4
1959 UK
140.2mph 225.6kmh
0-50mph 80.5kmh: 5.9secs
0-60mph 96.5kmh: 7.5secs
0-1/4 mile: 15.8secs
263.0bhp 196.1kW 266.6PS
@ 5700rpm
245.0lbft 332.0Nm @ 4000rpm
204.3bhp/ton 200.9bhp/tonne
71.7bhp/L 53.4kW/L 72.7PS/L
57.3ft/sec 17.5m/sec
22.8mph 36.7kmh/1000rpm
Petrol 4-stroke piston
3670cc 223.9cu in
In-line 6
Compression ratio: 8.3:1
Bore: 91.9mm 3.6in
Stroke: 91.9mm 3.6in
Valve type/No: Overhead 12
Transmission: Manual
No. of forward speeds: 4
Wheels driven: Rear
Wheelbase: 248.9cm 98.0in
Track F: 137.2cm 54.0in
Track R: 135.9cm 53.5in
Length: 449.6cm 177.0in
Width: 167.6cm 66.0in
Height: 132.1cm 52.0in
Kerb weight: 1309.3kg 2884.0lb

238 Aston Martin

DB4
1961 UK
141.0mph 226.9kmh
0-50mph 80.5kmh: 6.7secs
0-60mph 96.5kmh: 8.5secs
0-1/4 mile: 16.1secs
240.0bhp 179.0kW 243.3PS
@ 5500rpm
240.0lbft 325.2Nm @ 4250rpm
175.1bhp/ton 172.2bhp/tonne
65.4bhp/L 48.8kW/L 66.3PS/L
55.3ft/sec 16.9m/sec
24.2mph 38.9kmh/1000rpm
16.4mpg 13.7mpgUS 17.2L/100km
Petrol 4-stroke piston
3670cc 223.9cu in
In-line 6
Compression ratio: 8.2:1
Bore: 92.0mm 3.6in
Stroke: 92.0mm 3.6in
Valve type/No: Overhead 12
Transmission: Manual
No. of forward speeds: 4
Wheels driven: Rear
Springs F/R: Coil/Coil
Brake system: PA
Brakes F/R: Disc/Disc
Wheelbase: 248.9cm 98.0in
Track F: 137.2cm 54.0in
Track R: 135.9cm 53.5in
Length: 448.8cm 176.7in
Width: 167.6cm 66.0in
Height: 132.1cm 52.0in
Ground clearance: 15.7cm 6.2in
Kerb weight: 1393.8kg 3070.0lb
Fuel: 86.4L 19.0gal 22.8galUS

239 Aston Martin

DB4
1962 UK
148.0mph 238.1kmh
0-50mph 80.5kmh: 6.5secs
0-60mph 96.5kmh: 8.4secs
0-1/4 mile: 16.0secs
263.0bhp 196.1kW 266.6PS
@ 5700rpm
240.0lbft 325.2Nm @ 4250rpm
193.1bhp/ton 189.9bhp/tonne
71.7bhp/L 53.4kW/L 72.7PS/L
57.3ft/sec 17.5m/sec
21.3mph 34.3kmh/1000rpm
Petrol 4-stroke piston
3670cc 223.9cu in
In-line 6
Compression ratio: 8.3:1
Bore: 91.9mm 3.6in
Stroke: 91.9mm 3.6in
Valve type/No: Overhead 12
Transmission: Manual with overdrive
Wheels driven: Rear
Wheelbase: 248.9cm 98.0in
Track F: 137.2cm 54.0in
Track R: 135.9cm 53.5in
Length: 447.8cm 176.3in
Width: 167.6cm 66.0in
Height: 132.1cm 52.0in
Ground clearance: 15.7cm 6.2in
Kerb weight: 1384.7kg 3050.0lb

240 Aston Martin

DB4 GT Zagato
1962 UK
153.5mph 247.0kmh
0-50mph 80.5kmh: 4.8secs
0-60mph 96.5kmh: 6.1secs
0-1/4 mile: 14.5secs
314.0bhp 234.1kW 318.4PS
@ 6000rpm
278.0lbft 376.7Nm @ 5400rpm
254.4bhp/ton 250.1bhp/tonne
85.6bhp/L 63.8kW/L 86.7PS/L
60.3ft/sec 18.4m/sec
24.2mph 38.9kmh/1000rpm
13.9mpg 11.6mpgUS 20.3L/100km
Petrol 4-stroke piston
3670cc 223.9cu in
In-line 6 3 Carburettor
Compression ratio: 9.7:1
Bore: 92.0mm 3.6in
Stroke: 92.0mm 3.6in
Valve type/No: Overhead 12
Transmission: Manual
No. of forward speeds: 4
Wheels driven: Rear
Springs F/R: Coil/Coil
Brakes F/R: Disc/Disc
Steering: Rack & pinion
Wheelbase: 236.2cm 93.0in
Track F: 137.2cm 54.0in
Track R: 135.9cm 53.5in
Length: 426.7cm 168.0in
Width: 165.6cm 65.2in
Height: 127.0cm 50.0in
Ground clearance: 15.7cm 6.2in
Kerb weight: 1255.3kg 2765.0lb
Fuel: 136.5L 30.0gal 36.1galUS

241 Aston Martin

DB5
1964 UK
142.6mph 229.4kmh
0-50mph 80.5kmh: 6.4secs
0-60mph 96.5kmh: 8.1secs
0-1/4 mile: 16.0secs
282.0bhp 210.3kW 285.9PS
@ 5500rpm
280.0lbft 379.4Nm @ 4500rpm
190.8bhp/ton 187.7bhp/tonne
70.6bhp/L 52.6kW/L 71.6PS/L
55.3ft/sec 16.9m/sec
25.0mph 40.2kmh/1000rpm
14.7mpg 12.2mpgUS 19.2L/100km
Petrol 4-stroke piston
3995cc 243.7cu in
In-line 6 3 Carburettor
Compression ratio: 8.9:1
Bore: 96.0mm 3.8in
Stroke: 92.0mm 3.6in
Valve type/No: Overhead 12
Transmission: Manual
No. of forward speeds: 5
Wheels driven: Rear
Springs F/R: Coil/Coil
Brake system: PA
Brakes F/R: Disc/Disc
Steering: Rack & pinion
Wheelbase: 248.9cm 98.0in
Track F: 137.2cm 54.0in
Track R: 135.9cm 53.5in
Length: 461.0cm 181.5in
Width: 167.6cm 66.0in
Height: 133.4cm 52.5in
Ground clearance: 10.2cm 4.0in
Kerb weight: 1502.7kg 3310.0lb
Fuel: 100.1L 22.0gal 26.4galUS

242 Aston Martin

DB6
1966 UK
148.0mph 238.1kmh
0-50mph 80.5kmh: 5.1secs
0-60mph 96.5kmh: 6.5secs
0-1/4 mile: 14.5secs
0-1km: 25.4secs
325.0bhp 242.3kW 329.5PS
@ 5750rpm
290.0lbft 393.0Nm @ 4500rpm
213.1bhp/ton 209.6bhp/tonne
81.3bhp/L 60.7kW/L 82.5PS/L
57.8ft/sec 17.6m/sec
25.3mph 40.7kmh/1000rpm
12.6mpg 10.5mpgUS 22.4L/100km
Petrol 4-stroke piston
3995cc 243.7cu in
In-line 6 2 Carburettor
Compression ratio: 8.9:1
Bore: 96.0mm 3.8in
Stroke: 92.0mm 3.6in
Valve type/No: Overhead 12
Transmission: Manual
No. of forward speeds: 5
Wheels driven: Rear
Springs F/R: Coil/Coil
Brake system: PA
Brakes F/R: Disc/Disc
Steering: Rack & pinion
Wheelbase: 256.5cm 101.0in
Track F: 137.2cm 54.0in
Track R: 135.9cm 53.5in
Length: 462.3cm 182.0in
Width: 167.6cm 66.0in
Height: 137.2cm 54.0in
Ground clearance: 10.2cm 4.0in
Kerb weight: 1550.9kg 3416.0lb
Fuel: 100.1L 22.0gal 26.4galUS

243 Aston Martin

DBS
1968 UK
143.0mph 230.1kmh
0-50mph 80.5kmh: 6.7secs
0-60mph 96.5kmh: 8.6secs
0-1/4 mile: 16.3secs
0-1km: 29.0secs
325.0bhp 242.3kW 329.5PS
@ 5750rpm
290.0lbft 393.0Nm @ 4500rpm
193.7bhp/ton 190.4bhp/tonne
81.3bhp/L 60.7kW/L 82.5PS/L
57.8ft/sec 17.6m/sec
26.1mph 42.0kmh/1000rpm
12.7mpg 10.6mpgUS 22.2L/100km
Petrol 4-stroke piston
3995cc 243.7cu in
In-line 6 3 Carburettor
Compression ratio: 9.4:1
Bore: 96.0mm 3.8in
Stroke: 92.0mm 3.6in
Valve type/No: Overhead 12
Transmission: Manual
No. of forward speeds: 5
Wheels driven: Rear
Springs F/R: Coil/Coil
Brake system: PA
Brakes F/R: Disc/Disc
Steering: Rack & pinion
Wheelbase: 260.9cm 102.7in
Track F: 149.9cm 59.0in
Track R: 149.9cm 59.0in
Length: 458.5cm 180.5in
Width: 182.9cm 72.0in
Height: 134.6cm 53.0in
Ground clearance: 14.0cm 5.5in
Kerb weight: 1706.6kg 3759.0lb
Fuel: 95.5L 21.0gal 25.2galUS

244 Aston Martin

DBS V8
1971 UK
162.0mph 260.7kmh
0-50mph 80.5kmh: 4.1secs
0-60mph 96.5kmh: 6.0secs
0-1/4 mile: 14.1secs
0-1km: 25.6secs
54.0ft/sec 16.4m/sec
26.0mph 41.8kmh/1000rpm
12.2mpg 10.2mpgUS 23.2L/100km
Petrol 4-stroke piston
5340cc 325.8cu in
Vee 8 fuel injection
Compression ratio: 9.0:1
Bore: 100.0mm 3.9in
Stroke: 85.0mm 3.3in
Valve type/No: Overhead 16
Transmission: Manual
No. of forward speeds: 5
Wheels driven: Rear
Springs F/R: Coil/Coil
Brake system: PA
Brakes F/R: Disc/Disc
Steering: Rack & pinion PA
Wheelbase: 260.9cm 102.7in
Track F: 149.9cm 59.0in
Track R: 149.9cm 59.0in
Length: 458.5cm 180.5in
Width: 182.9cm 72.0in
Height: 134.6cm 53.0in
Ground clearance: 14.0cm 5.5in
Kerb weight: 1820.0kg 4008.8lb
Fuel: 95.5L 21.0gal 25.2galUS

245 Aston Martin

V8 Automatic
1973 UK
147.0mph 236.5kmh
0-50mph 80.5kmh: 4.8secs
0-60mph 96.5kmh: 6.2secs
0-1/4 mile: 14.7secs
0-1km: 26.7secs
26.2mph 42.2kmh/1000rpm
12.4mpg 10.3mpgUS 22.8L/100km
Petrol 4-stroke piston
5340cc 325.8cu in
Vee 8 4 Carburettor
Compression ratio: 9.0:1
Bore: 100.0mm 3.9in
Stroke: 85.0mm 3.3in
Valve type/No: Overhead 16
Transmission: Automatic
No. of forward speeds: 3
Wheels driven: Rear
Springs F/R: Coil/Coil
Brake system: PA
Brakes F/R: Disc/Disc
Steering: Rack & pinion PA
Wheelbase: 260.9cm 102.7in
Track F: 149.9cm 59.0in
Track R: 149.9cm 59.0in
Length: 464.8cm 183.0in
Width: 182.9cm 72.0in
Height: 132.6cm 52.2in
Ground clearance: 14.0cm 5.5in
Kerb weight: 1784.2kg 3930.0lb
Fuel: 95.5L 21.0gal 25.2galUS

246 Aston Martin

V8
1975 UK
147.0mph 236.5kmh
0-50mph 80.5kmh: 5.9secs
0-60mph 96.5kmh: 7.5secs
0-1/4 mile: 15.2secs
0-1km: 27.9secs
26.9mph 43.3kmh/1000rpm
11.7mpg 9.7mpgUS 24.1L/100km
Petrol 4-stroke piston
5340cc 325.8cu in
Vee 8 4 Carburettor
Compression ratio: 8.3:1
Bore: 100.0mm 3.9in
Stroke: 85.0mm 3.3in
Valve type/No: Overhead 16
Transmission: Manual
No. of forward speeds: 5
Wheels driven: Rear
Springs F/R: Coil/Coil
Brake system: PA
Brakes F/R: Disc/Disc
Steering: Rack & pinion PA
Wheelbase: 260.9cm 102.7in
Track F: 149.9cm 59.0in
Track R: 149.9cm 59.0in
Length: 486.9cm 191.7in
Width: 182.9cm 72.0in
Height: 133.4cm 52.5in
Ground clearance: 14.0cm 5.5in
Kerb weight: 1811.5kg 3990.0lb
Fuel: 95.5L 21.0gal 25.2galUS

247 Aston Martin

V8 Coupe
1977 UK
140.0mph 225.3kmh
0-50mph 80.5kmh: 5.4secs
0-60mph 96.5kmh: 7.4secs
0-1/4 mile: 15.7secs
340.0bhp 253.5kW 344.7PS
@ 5600rpm
400.0lbft 542.0Nm @ 4500rpm
184.4bhp/ton 181.3bhp/tonne
63.7bhp/L 47.5kW/L 64.5PS/L
52.1ft/sec 15.9m/sec
27.8mph 44.7kmh/1000rpm
11.4mpg 9.5mpgUS 24.8L/100km
Petrol 4-stroke piston
5340cc 325.8cu in
Vee 8 4 Carburettor
Compression ratio: 8.3:1
Bore: 100.0mm 3.9in
Stroke: 85.0mm 3.3in
Valve type/No: Overhead 16
Transmission: Manual
No. of forward speeds: 5
Wheels driven: Rear
Springs F/R: Coil/Coil
Brake system: PA
Brakes F/R: Disc/Disc
Steering: Rack & pinion PA
Wheelbase: 261.1cm 102.8in
Track F: 149.9cm 59.0in
Track R: 149.9cm 59.0in
Length: 464.8cm 183.0in
Width: 182.9cm 72.0in
Height: 132.8cm 52.3in
Ground clearance: 14.0cm 5.5in
Kerb weight: 1875.0kg 4130.0lb
Fuel: 95.4L 21.0gal 25.2galUS

248 Aston Martin

V8 Vantage
1977 UK
170.0mph 273.5kmh
0-50mph 80.5kmh: 3.8secs
0-60mph 96.5kmh: 5.4secs
0-1/4 mile: 13.7secs
0-1km: 25.2secs
26.2mph 42.2kmh/1000rpm
13.5mpg 11.2mpgUS 20.9L/100km
Petrol 4-stroke piston
5341cc 325.9cu in
Vee 8 4 Carburettor
Compression ratio: 9.0:1
Bore: 100.0mm 3.9in
Stroke: 85.0mm 3.3in
Valve type/No: Overhead 16
Transmission: Manual
No. of forward speeds: 5
Wheels driven: Rear
Springs F/R: Coil/Coil
Brake system: PA
Brakes F/R: Disc/Disc
Steering: Rack & pinion PA
Wheelbase: 260.9cm 102.7in
Track F: 149.9cm 59.0in
Track R: 149.9cm 59.0in
Length: 458.5cm 180.5in
Width: 182.9cm 72.0in
Height: 134.6cm 53.0in
Ground clearance: 14.0cm 5.5in
Kerb weight: 1816.4kg 4001.0lb
Fuel: 113.7L 25.0gal 30.0galUS

249 Aston Martin

V8
1978 UK
147.0mph 236.5kmh
0-50mph 80.5kmh: 5.7secs
0-60mph 96.5kmh: 7.2secs
0-1/4 mile: 15.3secs
0-1km: 27.0secs
26.4mph 42.5kmh/1000rpm
13.0mpg 10.8mpgUS 21.7L/100km
Petrol 4-stroke piston
5340cc 325.8cu in
Vee 8 4 Carburettor
Compression ratio: 9.0:1
Bore: 100.0mm 3.9in
Stroke: 85.0mm 3.3in
Valve type/No: Overhead 16
Transmission: Automatic
No. of forward speeds: 3
Wheels driven: Rear
Springs F/R: Coil/Coil
Brake system: PA
Brakes F/R: Disc/Disc
Steering: Rack & pinion PA
Wheelbase: 265.9cm 104.7in
Track F: 149.9cm 59.0in
Track R: 149.9cm 59.0in
Length: 466.6cm 183.7in
Width: 182.9cm 72.0in
Height: 134.6cm 53.0in
Ground clearance: 14.0cm 5.5in
Kerb weight: 1802.4kg 3970.0lb
Fuel: 113.7L 25.0gal 30.0galUS

250 Aston Martin

Lagonda
1980 UK
144.0mph 231.7kmh
0-50mph 80.5kmh: 7.2secs
0-60mph 96.5kmh: 8.8secs
0-1/4 mile: 16.4secs
0-1km: 29.2secs
25.8mph 41.5kmh/1000rpm
13.7mpg 11.4mpgUS 20.6L/100km
Petrol 4-stroke piston
5340cc 325.8cu in
Vee 8 4 Carburettor
Compression ratio: 9.5:1
Bore: 100.0mm 3.9in
Stroke: 85.0mm 3.3in
Valve type/No: Overhead 16
Transmission: Automatic
No. of forward speeds: 3
Wheels driven: Rear
Springs F/R: Coil/Coil
Brake system: PA
Brakes F/R: Disc/Disc
Steering: Rack & pinion PA
Wheelbase: 292.1cm 115.0in
Track F: 149.9cm 59.0in
Track R: 149.9cm 59.0in
Length: 528.1cm 207.9in
Width: 179.1cm 70.5in
Height: 130.0cm 51.2in
Ground clearance: 14.0cm 5.5in
Kerb weight: 2024.4kg 4459.0lb
Fuel: 127.4L 28.0gal 33.6galUS

251 Aston Martin

Lagonda
1982 UK
140.0mph 225.3kmh
0-60mph 96.5kmh: 8.9secs
0-1/4 mile: 16.9secs
325.0bhp 242.3kW 329.5PS
@ 5600rpm
375.0lbft 508.1Nm @ 4500rpm
157.2bhp/ton 154.6bhp/tonne
60.9bhp/L 45.4kW/L 61.7PS/L
52.1ft/sec 15.9m/sec
24.6mph 39.6kmh/1000rpm
15.0mpg 12.5mpgUS 18.8L/100km
Petrol 4-stroke piston
5340cc 325.8cu in
Vee 8 4 Carburettor
Compression ratio: 9.5:1
Bore: 100.0mm 3.9in
Stroke: 85.0mm 3.3in
Valve type/No: Overhead 16
Transmission: Automatic
No. of forward speeds: 3
Wheels driven: Rear
Springs F/R: Coil/Coil
Brake system: PA
Brakes F/R: Disc/Disc
Steering: Rack & pinion PA
Wheelbase: 291.6cm 114.8in
Track F: 149.9cm 59.0in
Track R: 149.9cm 59.0in
Length: 528.3cm 208.0in
Width: 181.6cm 71.5in
Height: 130.3cm 51.3in
Ground clearance: 14.0cm 5.5in
Kerb weight: 2102.0kg 4630.0lb
Fuel: 127.9L 28.1gal 33.8galUS

252 Aston Martin

V8
1982 UK
148.0mph 238.1kmh
0-50mph 80.5kmh: 5.1secs
0-60mph 96.5kmh: 6.6secs
0-1/4 mile: 14.8secs
0-1km: 26.9secs
26.4mph 42.5kmh/1000rpm
14.0mpg 11.7mpgUS 20.2L/100km
Petrol 4-stroke piston
5340cc 325.8cu in
Vee 8 4 Carburettor
Compression ratio: 9.3:1
Bore: 100.0mm 3.9in
Stroke: 85.0mm 3.3in
Valve type/No: Overhead 16
Transmission: Automatic
No. of forward speeds: 3
Wheels driven: Rear
Springs F/R: Coil/Coil
Brake system: PA
Brakes F/R: Disc/Disc
Steering: Rack & pinion PA
Wheelbase: 265.9cm 104.7in
Track F: 149.9cm 59.0in
Track R: 149.9cm 59.0in
Length: 466.6cm 183.7in
Width: 182.9cm 72.0in
Height: 134.6cm 53.0in
Ground clearance: 14.0cm 5.5in
Kerb weight: 1801.9kg 3969.0lb
Fuel: 113.7L 25.0gal 30.0galUS

253 Aston Martin

Volante
1983 UK
142.0mph 228.5kmh
0-50mph 80.5kmh: 6.9secs
0-60mph 96.5kmh: 8.9secs
0-1/4 mile: 16.8secs
300.0bhp 223.7kW 304.2PS
@ 5600rpm
350.0lbft 474.3Nm @ 4500rpm
155.2bhp/ton 152.6bhp/tonne
56.2bhp/L 41.9kW/L 57.0PS/L
52.1ft/sec 15.9m/sec
26.5mph 42.6kmh/1000rpm
15.6mpg 13.0mpgUS 18.1L/100km
Petrol 4-stroke piston
5340cc 325.8cu in
Vee 8 4 Carburettor
Compression ratio: 8.0:1
Bore: 100.0mm 3.9in
Stroke: 85.0mm 3.3in
Valve type/No: Overhead 16
Transmission: Manual
No. of forward speeds: 5
Wheels driven: Rear
Springs F/R: Coil/Coil
Brake system: PA
Brakes F/R: Disc/Disc
Steering: Rack & pinion PA
Wheelbase: 261.1cm 102.8in
Track F: 149.9cm 59.0in
Track R: 149.9cm 59.0in
Length: 481.3cm 189.5in
Width: 182.9cm 72.0in
Height: 137.2cm 54.0in
Kerb weight: 1965.8kg 4330.0lb
Fuel: 104.1L 22.9gal 27.5galUS

254 Aston Martin

Lagonda
1984 UK
126.0mph 202.7kmh
0-60mph 96.5kmh: 10.1secs
0-1/4 mile: 17.5secs
300.0bhp 223.7kW 304.2PS
@ 5600rpm
350.0lbft 474.3Nm @ 4500rpm
145.4bhp/ton 143.0bhp/tonne
56.2bhp/L 41.9kW/L 57.0PS/L
52.1ft/sec 15.9m/sec
20.7mph 33.3kmh/1000rpm
14.4mpg 12.0mpgUS 19.6L/100km
Petrol 4-stroke piston
5340cc 325.8cu in
Vee 8 4 Carburettor
Compression ratio: 8.0:1
Bore: 100.0mm 3.9in
Stroke: 85.0mm 3.3in
Valve type/No: Overhead 16
Transmission: Automatic
No. of forward speeds: 3
Wheels driven: Rear
Springs F/R: Coil/Coil
Brake system: PA
Brakes F/R: Disc/Disc
Steering: Rack & pinion PA
Wheelbase: 291.6cm 114.8in
Track F: 149.9cm 59.0in
Track R: 149.9cm 59.0in
Length: 528.3cm 208.0in
Width: 181.6cm 71.5in
Height: 130.3cm 51.3in
Kerb weight: 2097.5kg 4620.0lb
Fuel: 104.5L 23.0gal 27.6galUS

255 Aston Martin

Vantage
1984 UK
0-60mph 96.5kmh: 8.9secs
300.0bhp 223.7kW 304.2PS
@ 5600rpm
350.0lbft 474.3Nm @ 4500rpm
155.2bhp/ton 152.6bhp/tonne
56.2bhp/L 41.9kW/L 57.0PS/L
15.6mpg 13.0mpgUS 18.1L/100km
Petrol 4-stroke piston
5340cc 325.8cu in
Vee 8 4 Carburettor
Valve type/No: Overhead 16
Transmission: Manual
No. of forward speeds: 5
Wheels driven: Rear
Springs F/R: Coil/Coil
Brakes F/R: Disc/Disc
Steering: Rack & pinion PA
Wheelbase: 261.1cm 102.8in
Length: 481.3cm 189.5in
Width: 182.9cm 72.0in
Height: 137.2cm 54.0in
Kerb weight: 1965.8kg 4330.0lb
Fuel: 104.1L 22.9gal 27.5galUS

256 Aston Martin

Volante

1986 UK
145.0mph 233.3kmh
0-60mph 96.5kmh: 8.2secs
0-1/4 mile: 16.3secs
350.0bhp 261.0kW 354.8PS
@ 5500rpm
400.0lbft 542.0Nm @ 4250rpm
195.5bhp/ton 192.2bhp/tonne
65.5bhp/L 48.9kW/L 66.4PS/L
Petrol 4-stroke piston
5340cc 325.8cu in
Vee 8 fuel injection
Valve type/No: Overhead 16
Transmission: Automatic
No. of forward speeds: 3
Wheels driven: Rear
Springs F/R: Coil/Coil
Brakes F/R: Disc/Disc
Steering: Rack & pinion PA
Wheelbase: 261.1cm 102.8in
Length: 467.4cm 184.0in
Width: 182.9cm 72.0in
Height: 137.2cm 54.0in
Kerb weight: 1820.5kg 4010.0lb
Fuel: 97.6L 21.5gal 25.8galUS

257 Aston Martin

Zagato
1988 UK
183.0mph 294.4kmh
0-60mph 96.5kmh: 4.8secs
432.0bhp 322.1kW 438.0PS
@ 6200rpm
395.0lbft 535.2Nm @ 5100rpm
266.6bhp/ton 262.1bhp/tonne
80.9bhp/L 60.3kW/L 82.0PS/L
57.7ft/sec 17.6m/sec
Petrol 4-stroke piston
5340cc 325.8cu in
Vee 8 4 Carburettor
Compression ratio: 10.2:1
Bore: 100.0mm 3.9in
Stroke: 85.0mm 3.3in
Valve type/No: Overhead 16
Transmission: Manual
No. of forward speeds: 5
Wheels driven: Rear
Springs F/R: Coil/Coil
Brake system: PA
Brakes F/R: Disc/Disc
Steering: Rack & pinion PA
Wheelbase: 262.1cm 103.2in
Track F: 152.7cm 60.1in
Track R: 154.4cm 60.8in
Length: 440.7cm 173.5in
Width: 186.7cm 73.5in
Height: 129.8cm 51.1in
Kerb weight: 1648.0kg 3630.0lb
Fuel: 97.6L 21.5gal 25.8galUS

258 Aston Martin

Virage
1989 UK
155.0mph 249.4kmh
0-60mph 96.5kmh: 6.0secs
330.0bhp 246.1kW 334.6PS
@ 6000rpm
350.0lbft 474.3Nm @ 4000rpm
187.6bhp/ton 184.5bhp/tonne
61.8bhp/L 46.1kW/L 62.7PS/L
Petrol 4-stroke piston
5340cc 325.8cu in
Vee 8 fuel injection
Compression ratio: 9.5:1
Valve type/No: Overhead 32
Transmission: Manual
No. of forward speeds: 5
Wheels driven: Rear
Springs F/R: Coil/Coil
Brake system: PA
Brakes F/R: Disc/Disc
Wheelbase: 261.1cm 102.8in
Length: 473.7cm 186.5in
Width: 185.4cm 73.0in
Height: 132.1cm 52.0in
Kerb weight: 1788.8kg 3940.0lb
Fuel: 90.5L 19.9gal 23.9galUS

259 Aston Martin

Volante
1989 UK
135.0mph 217.2kmh
0-60mph 96.5kmh: 7.8secs
240.0bhp 179.0kW 243.3PS
@ 5500rpm
288.0lbft 390.2Nm @ 5500rpm
134.1bhp/ton 131.8bhp/tonne
44.9bhp/L 33.5kW/L 45.6PS/L
51.2ft/sec 15.6m/sec
Petrol 4-stroke piston
5340cc 325.8cu in
Vee 8 fuel injection
Compression ratio: 8.0:1
Bore: 100.0mm 3.9in
Stroke: 85.0mm 3.3in
Valve type/No: Overhead 16
Transmission: Automatic
No. of forward speeds: 3
Wheels driven: Rear
Springs F/R: Coil/Coil
Brake system: PA
Brakes F/R: Disc/Disc
Steering: Rack & pinion PA
Wheelbase: 261.1cm 102.8in
Track F: 155.2cm 61.1in
Track R: 158.5cm 62.4in
Length: 467.1cm 183.9in
Width: 191.5cm 75.4in
Height: 136.9cm 53.9in
Kerb weight: 1820.5kg 4010.0lb
Fuel: 81.4L 17.9gal 21.5galUS

260 Aston Martin

Zagato Volante
1989 UK
165.0mph 265.5kmh
0-60mph 96.5kmh: 5.6secs
305.0bhp 227.4kW 309.2PS
@ 5500rpm
330.0lbft 447.2Nm @ 4750rpm
184.4bhp/ton 181.3bhp/tonne
57.1bhp/L 42.6kW/L 57.9PS/L
51.2ft/sec 15.6m/sec
Petrol 4-stroke piston
5340cc 325.8cu in
Vee 8 fuel injection
Compression ratio: 10.2:1
Bore: 100.0mm 3.9in
Stroke: 85.0mm 3.3in
Valve type/No: Overhead 16
Transmission: Manual
No. of forward speeds: 5
Wheels driven: Rear
Springs F/R: Coil/Coil
Brake system: PA
Brakes F/R: Disc/Disc
Steering: Rack & pinion PA
Wheelbase: 262.1cm 103.2in
Track F: 152.7cm 60.1in
Track R: 154.4cm 60.8in
Length: 440.7cm 173.5in
Width: 186.7cm 73.5in
Kerb weight: 1682.1kg 3705.0lb
Fuel: 97.6L 21.5gal 25.8galUS

261 Aston Martin

Virage
1991 UK
160.0mph 257.4kmh
0-50mph 80.5kmh: 5.2secs
0-60mph 96.5kmh: 6.8secs
0-1/4 mile: 14.7secs
0-1km: 26.7secs
330.0bhp 246.1kW 334.6PS
@ 6000rpm
339.5lbft 460.0Nm @ 3700rpm
172.1bhp/ton 169.2bhp/tonne
61.8bhp/L 46.1kW/L 62.7PS/L
55.8ft/sec 17.0m/sec
27.1mph 43.6kmh/1000rpm
15.6mpg 13.0mpgUS 18.1L/100km
Petrol 4-stroke piston
5340cc 326.0cu in
Vee 8 fuel injection
Compression ratio: 9.5:1
Bore: 100.0mm 3.9in
Stroke: 85.0mm 3.3in
Valve type/No: Overhead 32
Transmission: Manual
No. of forward speeds: 5
Wheels driven: Rear
Springs F/R: Coil/Coil
Brake system: PA
Brakes F/R: Disc/Disc
Steering: Rack & pinion PA
Wheelbase: 261.1cm 102.8in
Track F: 151.0cm 59.4in
Track R: 152.2cm 59.9in
Length: 474.5cm 186.8in
Width: 185.6cm 73.1in
Height: 132.0cm 52.0in
Kerb weight: 1950.0kg 4295.1lb
Fuel: 118.3L 26.0gal 31.3galUS

262 Auburn

8-120 Speedster
1929 USA
90.0mph 144.8kmh
0-50mph 80.5kmh: 11.3secs
0-60mph 96.5kmh: 16.5secs
0-1/4 mile: 20.5secs
125.0bhp 93.2kW 126.7PS
@ 3300rpm
220.0lbft 298.1Nm @ 1800rpm
75.7bhp/ton 74.4bhp/tonne
25.5bhp/L 19.0kW/L 25.9PS/L
41.2ft/sec 12.6m/sec
22.7mph 36.5kmh/1000rpm
Petrol 4-stroke piston
4896cc 298.7cu in
In-line 8 1 Carburettor
Compression ratio: 6.0:1
Bore: 82.6mm 3.2in
Stroke: 114.3mm 4.5in
Valve type/No: Side 16
Transmission: Manual
No. of forward speeds: 3
Wheels driven: Rear
Brakes F/R: Drum/Drum
Wheelbase: 330.2cm 130.0in
Track F: 142.2cm 56.0in
Track R: 142.2cm 56.0in
Length: 457.2cm 180.0in
Width: 180.3cm 71.0in
Height: 142.2cm 56.0in
Ground clearance: 20.3cm 8.0in
Kerb weight: 1679.8kg 3700.0lb

263 Auburn

38hp Saloon
1936 USA
86.5mph 139.2kmh
0-50mph 80.5kmh: 13.6secs
0-60mph 96.5kmh: 20.4secs
16.0mpg 13.3mpgUS 17.7L/100km
Petrol 4-stroke piston
4596cc 280.4cu in
In-line 8
Bore: 77.8mm 3.1in
Stroke: 120.7mm 4.7in
Valve type/No: Side 16
Transmission: Manual
No. of forward speeds: 3
Wheels driven: Rear
Brakes F/R: Drum/Drum
Kerb weight: 1815.5kg 3999.0lb
Fuel: 73.9L 16.2gal 19.5galUS

264 Auburn

8-52 Speedster
1936 USA
104.0mph 167.3kmh
0-50mph 80.5kmh: 11.6secs
0-60mph 96.5kmh: 15.0secs
0-1/4 mile: 19.5secs
150.0bhp 111.9kW 152.1PS
@ 4000rpm
230.0lbft 311.7Nm @ 2750rpm
89.7bhp/ton 88.2bhp/tonne
32.7bhp/L 24.4kW/L 33.1PS/L
52.6ft/sec 16.0m/sec
25.0mph 40.2kmh/1000rpm
Petrol 4-stroke piston
4589cc 280.0cu in
In-line 8 1 Carburettor
Compression ratio: 6.5:1
Bore: 77.7mm 3.1in
Stroke: 120.1mm 4.7in
Valve type/No: Overhead 16
Transmission: Manual
No. of forward speeds: 3
Wheels driven: Rear
Wheelbase: 322.6cm 127.0in
Track F: 149.9cm 59.0in
Track R: 157.5cm 62.0in
Length: 520.7cm 205.0in
Width: 198.1cm 78.0in
Height: 147.3cm 58.0in
Ground clearance: 19.1cm 7.5in
Kerb weight: 1700.2kg 3745.0lb

265 Audi

100 LS
1970 Germany
103.0mph 165.7kmh
0-50mph 80.5kmh: 9.5secs
0-60mph 96.5kmh: 13.6secs
0-1/4 mile: 19.2secs
115.0bhp 85.8kW 116.6PS
@ 5600rpm
119.0lbft 161.2Nm @ 3200rpm
105.8bhp/ton 104.0bhp/tonne
65.3bhp/L 48.7kW/L 66.2PS/L
51.6ft/sec 15.7m/sec
18.0mph 29.0kmh/1000rpm
29.2mpg 24.3mpgUS 9.7L/100km
Petrol 4-stroke piston
1760cc 107.4cu in
In-line 4 1 Carburettor
Compression ratio: 10.2:1
Bore: 81.5mm 3.2in
Stroke: 84.4mm 3.3in
Valve type/No: Overhead 8
Transmission: Manual
No. of forward speeds: 4
Wheels driven: Front
Springs F/R: Coil/Torsion bar
Brakes F/R: Disc/Drum
Steering: Rack & pinion
Wheelbase: 267.5cm 105.3in
Track F: 142.2cm 56.0in
Track R: 142.5cm 56.1in
Length: 463.8cm 182.6in
Width: 173.0cm 68.1in
Height: 142.5cm 56.1in
Ground clearance: 15.7cm 6.2in
Kerb weight: 1105.5kg 2435.0lb
Fuel: 57.9L 12.7gal 15.3galUS

266 Audi

100 LS Auto
1971 Germany
107.0mph 172.2kmh
0-50mph 80.5kmh: 8.9secs
0-60mph 96.5kmh: 11.8secs
0-1/4 mile: 18.7secs
0-1km: 34.5secs
100.0bhp 74.6kW 101.4PS
@ 5500rpm
111.0lbft 150.4Nm @ 3200rpm
92.8bhp/ton 91.3bhp/tonne
56.8bhp/L 42.4kW/L 57.6PS/L
50.7ft/sec 15.5m/sec
18.4mph 29.6kmh/1000rpm
23.2mpg 19.3mpgUS 12.2L/100km
Petrol 4-stroke piston
1760cc 107.4cu in
In-line 4 1 Carburettor
Compression ratio: 10.2:1
Bore: 81.5mm 3.2in
Stroke: 84.4mm 3.3in
Valve type/No: Overhead 8
Transmission: Automatic
No. of forward speeds: 3
Wheels driven: Front
Springs F/R: Coil/Torsion bar
Brake system: PA
Brakes F/R: Disc/Drum
Steering: Rack & pinion
Wheelbase: 267.5cm 105.3in
Track F: 142.0cm 55.9in
Track R: 142.5cm 56.1in
Length: 462.3cm 182.0in
Width: 172.7cm 68.0in
Height: 141.7cm 55.8in
Ground clearance: 19.6cm 7.7in
Kerb weight: 1095.5kg 2413.0lb
Fuel: 58.2L 12.8gal 15.4galUS

267 Audi

100 Coupe S
1972 Germany
114.0mph 183.4kmh
0-50mph 80.5kmh: 7.9secs
0-60mph 96.5kmh: 10.6secs
0-1/4 mile: 17.7secs
0-1km: 32.4secs
112.0bhp 83.5kW 113.5PS
@ 5600rpm
118.0lbft 159.9Nm @ 3500rpm
104.5bhp/ton 102.7bhp/tonne
59.9bhp/L 44.6kW/L 60.7PS/L
51.6ft/sec 15.7m/sec
19.7mph 31.7kmh/1000rpm
23.6mpg 19.7mpgUS 12.0L/100km
Petrol 4-stroke piston
1871cc 114.1cu in
In-line 4 1 Carburettor
Compression ratio: 10.2:1
Bore: 84.0mm 3.3in
Stroke: 84.4mm 3.3in
Valve type/No: Overhead 8
Transmission: Manual
No. of forward speeds: 4
Wheels driven: Front
Springs F/R: Coil/Torsion bar

Brake system: PA
Brakes F/R: Disc/Drum
Steering: Rack & pinion
Wheelbase: 267.5cm 105.3in
Track F: 142.0cm 55.9in
Track R: 142.5cm 56.1in
Length: 439.9cm 173.2in
Width: 167.6cm 66.0in
Height: 141.7cm 55.8in
Ground clearance: 17.8cm 7.0in
Kerb weight: 1090.0kg 2401.0lb
Fuel: 58.2L 12.8gal 15.4galUS

268 Audi

100 LS
1973 Germany
0-60mph 96.5kmh: 13.7secs
0-1/4 mile: 19.5secs
91.0bhp 67.9kW 92.3PS
@ 5200rpm
111.0lbft 150.4Nm @ 3500rpm
82.2bhp/ton 80.8bhp/tonne
48.5bhp/L 36.2kW/L 49.2PS/L
48.0ft/sec 14.6m/sec
24.0mpg 20.0mpgUS 11.8L/100km
Petrol 4-stroke piston
1875cc 114.4cu in
In-line 4 1 Carburettor
Compression ratio: 8.2:1
Bore: 84.0mm 3.3in
Stroke: 84.4mm 3.3in
Valve type/No: Overhead 8
Transmission: Automatic
No. of forward speeds: 3
Wheels driven: Front
Brakes F/R: Disc/Disc
Wheelbase: 267.5cm 105.3in
Length: 463.8cm 182.6in
Width: 173.0cm 68.1in
Height: 142.5cm 56.1in
Ground clearance: 15.7cm 6.2in
Kerb weight: 1125.9kg 2480.0lb
Fuel: 57.9L 12.7gal 15.3galUS

269 Audi

80 LS
1973 Germany
96.0mph 154.5kmh
0-50mph 80.5kmh: 9.1secs
0-60mph 96.5kmh: 13.2secs
0-1/4 mile: 19.0secs
0-1km: 35.6secs
75.0bhp 55.9kW 76.0PS
@ 5800rpm
83.0lbft 112.5Nm @ 3500rpm
88.2bhp/ton 86.8bhp/tonne
51.0bhp/L 38.0kW/L 51.7PS/L
50.7ft/sec 15.5m/sec
16.5mph 26.5kmh/1000rpm
30.4mpg 25.3mpgUS 9.3L/100km
Petrol 4-stroke piston
1470cc 89.7cu in
In-line 4 1 Carburettor
Compression ratio: 9.7:1
Bore: 76.5mm 3.0in
Stroke: 80.0mm 3.1in
Valve type/No: Overhead 8
Transmission: Manual
No. of forward speeds: 4
Wheels driven: Front
Springs F/R: Coil/Coil
Brake system: PA
Brakes F/R: Disc/Drum
Steering: Rack & pinion
Wheelbase: 248.9cm 98.0in
Track F: 133.9cm 52.7in
Track R: 133.4cm 52.5in
Length: 419.1cm 165.0in
Width: 160.0cm 63.0in
Height: 134.6cm 53.0in
Ground clearance: 14.0cm 5.5in
Kerb weight: 864.4kg 1904.0lb
Fuel: 45.5L 10.0gal 12.0galUS

270 Audi

Fox
1973 Germany
100.0mph 160.9kmh
0-50mph 80.5kmh: 9.3secs
0-60mph 96.5kmh: 12.7secs
0-1/4 mile: 19.0secs
75.0bhp 55.9kW 76.0PS
@ 5800rpm
81.5lbft 110.4Nm @ 4000rpm
83.8bhp/ton 82.4bhp/tonne
51.0bhp/L 38.0kW/L 51.7PS/L
50.7ft/sec 15.5m/sec
17.1mph 27.5kmh/1000rpm
32.4mpg 27.0mpgUS 8.7L/100km
Petrol 4-stroke piston
1471cc 89.7cu in
In-line 4 1 Carburettor
Compression ratio: 8.2:1
Bore: 76.5mm 3.0in
Stroke: 80.0mm 3.1in
Valve type/No: Overhead 8
Transmission: Manual
No. of forward speeds: 4
Wheels driven: Front
Springs F/R: Coil/Coil
Brake system: PA
Brakes F/R: Disc/Drum
Steering: Rack & pinion
Wheelbase: 246.9cm 97.2in
Track F: 133.9cm 52.7in
Track R: 133.6cm 52.6in
Length: 436.6cm 171.9in
Width: 160.0cm 63.0in
Height: 136.9cm 53.9in
Ground clearance: 14.7cm 5.8in
Kerb weight: 910.3kg 2005.0lb
Fuel: 45.4L 10.0gal 12.0galUS

271 Audi

80 GT
1974 Germany
107.0mph 172.2kmh
0-50mph 80.5kmh: 6.8secs
0-60mph 96.5kmh: 9.5secs
0-1/4 mile: 17.2secs
0-1km: 32.3secs
100.0bhp 74.6kW 101.4PS
@ 6000rpm
97.0lbft 131.4Nm @ 4000rpm
118.0bhp/ton 116.0bhp/tonne
63.0bhp/L 47.0kW/L 63.8PS/L
52.5ft/sec 16.0m/sec
17.3mph 27.8kmh/1000rpm
29.5mpg 24.6mpgUS 9.6L/100km
Petrol 4-stroke piston
1588cc 96.9cu in
In-line 4 1 Carburettor
Compression ratio: 9.8:1
Bore: 79.5mm 3.1in
Stroke: 80.0mm 3.1in
Valve type/No: Overhead 8
Transmission: Manual
No. of forward speeds: 4
Wheels driven: Front
Springs F/R: Coil/Coil
Brake system: PA
Brakes F/R: Disc/Disc
Steering: Rack & pinion
Wheelbase: 248.9cm 98.0in
Track F: 133.9cm 52.7in
Track R: 133.4cm 52.5in
Length: 419.1cm 165.0in
Width: 160.0cm 63.0in
Height: 134.6cm 53.0in
Ground clearance: 14.0cm 5.5in
Kerb weight: 862.1kg 1899.0lb
Fuel: 44.6L 9.8gal 11.8galUS

272 Audi

100 GL Automatic
1975 Germany
107.0mph 172.2kmh
0-50mph 80.5kmh: 8.4secs
0-60mph 96.5kmh: 11.9secs
0-1/4 mile: 18.7secs
0-1km: 34.8secs
112.0bhp 83.5kW 113.5PS
@ 5600rpm
118.0lbft 159.9Nm @ 3500rpm
102.4bhp/ton 100.7bhp/tonne
59.9bhp/L 44.6kW/L 60.7PS/L
51.6ft/sec 15.7m/sec
18.5mph 29.8kmh/1000rpm
23.4mpg 19.5mpgUS 12.1L/100km
Petrol 4-stroke piston
1871cc 114.1cu in
In-line 4 1 Carburettor
Compression ratio: 9.7:1
Bore: 85.0mm 3.3in
Stroke: 84.4mm 3.3in
Valve type/No: Overhead 8
Transmission: Automatic
No. of forward speeds: 3
Wheels driven: Front
Springs F/R: Coil/Torsion bar
Brake system: PA
Brakes F/R: Disc/Drum
Steering: Rack & pinion
Wheelbase: 267.5cm 105.3in
Track F: 142.0cm 55.9in
Track R: 142.5cm 56.1in
Length: 462.3cm 182.0in
Width: 172.7cm 68.0in
Height: 141.7cm 55.8in
Kerb weight: 1112.3kg 2450.0lb
Fuel: 58.2L 12.8gal 15.4galUS

273 Audi

80 Estate
1975 Germany
105.0mph 168.9kmh
0-50mph 80.5kmh: 8.6secs
0-60mph 96.5kmh: 12.2secs
0-1/4 mile: 18.7secs
0-1km: 35.0secs
85.0bhp 63.4kW 86.2PS
@ 5800rpm
80.0lbft 108.4Nm @ 4000rpm
94.9bhp/ton 93.3bhp/tonne
57.8bhp/L 43.1kW/L 58.6PS/L
50.7ft/sec 15.5m/sec
31.0mpg 25.8mpgUS 9.1L/100km
Petrol 4-stroke piston
1470cc 89.7cu in
In-line 4 1 Carburettor
Compression ratio: 9.7:1
Bore: 76.5mm 3.0in
Stroke: 80.0mm 3.1in
Valve type/No: Overhead 8
Transmission: Manual
No. of forward speeds: 4
Wheels driven: Front
Springs F/R: Coil/Coil
Brake system: PA
Brakes F/R: Disc/Drum
Steering: Rack & pinion
Wheelbase: 246.9cm 97.2in
Track F: 133.9cm 52.7in
Track R: 133.4cm 52.5in
Length: 419.1cm 165.0in
Width: 160.0cm 63.0in
Height: 135.9cm 53.5in
Kerb weight: 911.2kg 2007.0lb
Fuel: 45.5L 10.0gal 12.0galUS

274 Audi

Fox
1975 Germany
94.0mph 151.2kmh
0-50mph 80.5kmh: 9.2secs
0-60mph 96.5kmh: 13.1secs
0-1/4 mile: 18.9secs
81.0bhp 60.4kW 82.1PS
@ 5800rpm
90.0lbft 122.0Nm @ 3300rpm
81.7bhp/ton 80.4bhp/tonne
51.0bhp/L 38.0kW/L 51.7PS/L
Petrol 4-stroke piston
1588cc 96.9cu in
In-line 4
Transmission: Manual
No. of forward speeds: 4
Wheels driven: Front
Springs F/R: Coil/Coil
Brakes F/R: Disc/Drum
Wheelbase: 246.9cm 97.2in
Track F: 134.1cm 52.8in
Track R: 133.6cm 52.6in
Length: 436.9cm 172.0in
Width: 164.3cm 64.7in
Height: 136.1cm 53.6in
Kerb weight: 1007.9kg 2220.0lb

275 Audi

80 GTE
1976 Germany
113.0mph 181.8kmh
0-50mph 80.5kmh: 6.7secs
0-60mph 96.5kmh: 9.6secs
0-1/4 mile: 17.4secs
0-1km: 32.6secs
110.0bhp 82.0kW 111.5PS
@ 6000rpm
140.0lbft 189.7Nm @ 5000rpm
129.5bhp/ton 127.3bhp/tonne
69.3bhp/L 51.7kW/L 70.2PS/L
52.5ft/sec 16.0m/sec
18.0mph 29.0kmh/1000rpm
29.1mpg 24.2mpgUS 9.7L/100km
Petrol 4-stroke piston
1588cc 96.9cu in
In-line 4 fuel injection
Compression ratio: 9.5:1
Bore: 79.5mm 3.1in
Stroke: 80.0mm 3.1in
Valve type/No: Overhead 8
Transmission: Manual
No. of forward speeds: 4
Wheels driven: Front
Springs F/R: Coil/Coil
Brake system: PA
Brakes F/R: Disc/Drum
Steering: Rack & pinion
Wheelbase: 248.9cm 98.0in
Track F: 133.9cm 52.7in
Track R: 133.4cm 52.5in
Length: 420.6cm 165.6in
Width: 160.0cm 63.0in
Height: 134.6cm 53.0in
Ground clearance: 14.0cm 5.5in
Kerb weight: 864.0kg 1903.0lb
Fuel: 45.5L 10.0gal 12.0galUS

276 Audi

100 5E
1977 Germany
112.0mph 180.2kmh
0-50mph 80.5kmh: 8.5secs
0-60mph 96.5kmh: 11.8secs
0-1/4 mile: 18.7secs
0-1km: 33.9secs
136.0bhp 101.4kW 137.9PS
@ 5700rpm
134.0lbft 181.6Nm @ 4200rpm
115.7bhp/ton 113.8bhp/tonne
63.4bhp/L 47.3kW/L 64.3PS/L
53.8ft/sec 16.4m/sec
18.5mph 29.8kmh/1000rpm
23.3mpg 19.4mpgUS 12.1L/100km
Petrol 4-stroke piston
2144cc 130.8cu in
In-line 5 fuel injection
Compression ratio: 9.3:1
Bore: 79.5mm 3.1in
Stroke: 86.4mm 3.4in
Valve type/No: Overhead 10
Transmission: Automatic
No. of forward speeds: 3
Wheels driven: Front
Springs F/R: Coil/Coil
Brake system: PA
Brakes F/R: Disc/Drum
Steering: Rack & pinion
Wheelbase: 267.5cm 105.3in
Track F: 146.8cm 57.8in
Track R: 144.3cm 56.8in
Length: 467.9cm 184.2in
Width: 176.8cm 69.6in
Height: 139.2cm 54.8in
Ground clearance: 12.7cm 5.0in
Kerb weight: 1194.9kg 2632.0lb
Fuel: 60.1L 13.2gal 15.9galUS

277 Audi

100 GLS
1977 Germany
110.0mph 177.0kmh
0-50mph 80.5kmh: 7.6secs
0-60mph 96.5kmh: 10.9secs
0-1/4 mile: 17.7secs
0-1km: 33.0secs
115.0bhp 85.8kW 116.6PS
@ 5500rpm
116.0lbft 157.2Nm @ 3500rpm
101.7bhp/ton 100.0bhp/tonne
58.0bhp/L 43.2kW/L 58.8PS/L
50.7ft/sec 15.5m/sec
18.9mph 30.4kmh/1000rpm
21.4mpg 17.8mpgUS 13.2L/100km
Petrol 4-stroke piston
1984cc 121.0cu in
In-line 4 1 Carburettor
Compression ratio: 9.3:1
Bore: 86.5mm 3.4in
Stroke: 84.4mm 3.3in
Valve type/No: Overhead 8
Transmission: Manual
No. of forward speeds: 4
Wheels driven: Front
Springs F/R: Coil/Coil
Brake system: PA
Brakes F/R: Disc/Drum
Steering: Rack & pinion
Wheelbase: 267.5cm 105.3in
Track F: 146.8cm 57.8in
Track R: 144.3cm 56.8in
Length: 469.1cm 184.7in
Width: 176.8cm 69.6in
Height: 139.2cm 54.8in
Ground clearance: 12.7cm 5.0in
Kerb weight: 1149.5kg 2532.0lb
Fuel: 60.1L 13.2gal 15.9galUS

278 Audi
Fox
1977 Germany
97.0mph 156.1kmh
0-60mph 96.5kmh: 12.8secs
0-1/4 mile: 19.2secs
76.0bhp 56.7kW 77.0PS
@ 5500rpm
83.0lbft 112.5Nm @ 3200rpm
80.5bhp/ton 79.1bhp/tonne
47.9bhp/L 35.7kW/L 48.5PS/L
48.1ft/sec 14.7m/sec
Petrol 4-stroke piston
1588cc 96.9cu in
In-line 4 fuel injection
Compression ratio: 8.2:1
Bore: 79.5mm 3.1in
Stroke: 80.0mm 3.1in
Valve type/No: Overhead 8
Transmission: Manual
No. of forward speeds: 4
Wheels driven: Front
Brakes F/R: Disc/Drum
Wheelbase: 246.9cm 97.2in
Track F: 133.9cm 52.7in
Track R: 133.4cm 52.5in
Length: 441.5cm 173.8in
Width: 164.6cm 64.8in
Height: 136.1cm 53.6in
Kerb weight: 960.2kg 2115.0lb
Fuel: 45.0L 9.9gal 11.9galUS

279 Audi
100 L Avant
1978 Germany
101.0mph 162.5kmh
0-50mph 80.5kmh: 8.7secs
0-60mph 96.5kmh: 12.6secs
0-1/4 mile: 18.8secs
0-1km: 34.9secs
87.0bhp 64.9kW 88.2PS
@ 5600rpm
87.0lbft 117.9Nm @ 3200rpm
80.0bhp/ton 78.7bhp/tonne
54.8bhp/L 40.9kW/L 55.5PS/L
49.0ft/sec 14.9m/sec
18.0mph 29.0kmh/1000rpm
26.9mpg 22.4mpgUS 10.5L/100km
Petrol 4-stroke piston
1588cc 96.9cu in
In-line 5 1 Carburettor
Compression ratio: 8.2:1
Bore: 79.5mm 3.1in
Stroke: 80.0mm 3.1in
Valve type/No: Overhead 10
Transmission: Manual
No. of forward speeds: 4
Wheels driven: Front
Springs F/R: Coil/Coil
Brake system: PA
Brakes F/R: Disc/Drum
Steering: Rack & pinion
Wheelbase: 267.5cm 105.3in
Track F: 146.8cm 57.8in
Track R: 144.3cm 56.8in
Length: 458.7cm 180.6in
Width: 176.8cm 69.6in
Height: 139.2cm 54.8in
Ground clearance: 12.7cm 5.0in
Kerb weight: 1105.9kg 2436.0lb
Fuel: 60.1L 13.2gal 15.9galUS

280 Audi
5000
1978 Germany
100.0mph 160.9kmh
0-50mph 80.5kmh: 9.4secs
0-60mph 96.5kmh: 12.9secs
0-1/4 mile: 19.5secs
103.0bhp 76.8kW 104.4PS
@ 5500rpm
110.0lbft 149.1Nm @ 4000rpm
80.7bhp/ton 79.3bhp/tonne
48.0bhp/L 35.8kW/L 48.7PS/L
51.9ft/sec 15.8m/sec
17.2mph 27.7kmh/1000rpm
24.0mpg 20.0mpgUS 11.8L/100km
Petrol 4-stroke piston
2144cc 130.8cu in
In-line 5 fuel injection
Compression ratio: 8.0:1
Bore: 79.5mm 3.1in
Stroke: 86.4mm 3.4in
Valve type/No: Overhead 10
Transmission: Automatic
No. of forward speeds: 3
Wheels driven: Front
Springs F/R: Coil/Coil
Brake system: PA
Brakes F/R: Disc/Drum
Steering: Rack & pinion PA
Wheelbase: 268.5cm 105.7in
Track F: 147.1cm 57.9in
Track R: 144.5cm 56.9in
Length: 481.1cm 189.4in
Width: 176.3cm 69.4in
Height: 139.2cm 54.8in
Ground clearance: 11.2cm 4.4in
Kerb weight: 1298.4kg 2860.0lb
Fuel: 59.8L 13.1gal 15.8galUS

281 Audi
100 GL5S
1979 Germany
110.0mph 177.0kmh
0-50mph 80.5kmh: 7.2secs
0-60mph 96.5kmh: 10.7secs
0-1/4 mile: 18.0secs
0-1km: 33.5secs
115.0bhp 85.8kW 116.6PS
@ 5500rpm
122.0lbft 165.3Nm @ 4000rpm
109.1bhp/ton 107.3bhp/tonne
53.6bhp/L 40.0kW/L 54.4PS/L
51.9ft/sec 15.8m/sec
18.8mph 30.2kmh/1000rpm
21.4mpg 17.8mpgUS 13.2L/100km
Petrol 4-stroke piston
2144cc 130.8cu in
In-line 5 1 Carburettor
Compression ratio: 8.2:1
Bore: 79.5mm 3.1in
Stroke: 86.4mm 3.4in
Valve type/No: Overhead 10
Transmission: Manual
No. of forward speeds: 4
Wheels driven: Front
Springs F/R: Coil/Coil
Brake system: PA
Brakes F/R: Disc/Drum
Steering: Rack & pinion
Wheelbase: 267.5cm 105.3in
Track F: 146.8cm 57.8in
Track R: 144.3cm 56.8in
Length: 467.9cm 184.2in
Width: 176.8cm 69.6in
Height: 139.2cm 54.8in
Ground clearance: 12.7cm 5.0in
Kerb weight: 1071.4kg 2360.0lb
Fuel: 60.1L 13.2gal 15.9galUS

282 Audi
80 GLS
1979 Germany
100.0mph 160.9kmh
0-50mph 80.5kmh: 8.5secs
0-60mph 96.5kmh: 12.1secs
0-1/4 mile: 18.5secs
0-1km: 34.3secs
85.0bhp 63.4kW 86.2PS
@ 5600rpm
87.5lbft 118.6Nm @ 3200rpm
92.9bhp/ton 91.3bhp/tonne
53.5bhp/L 39.9kW/L 54.3PS/L
49.0ft/sec 14.9m/sec
16.8mph 27.0kmh/1000rpm
28.1mpg 23.4mpgUS 10.1L/100km
Petrol 4-stroke piston
1588cc 96.9cu in
In-line 4 1 Carburettor
Compression ratio: 8.2:1
Bore: 79.5mm 3.1in
Stroke: 80.0mm 3.1in
Valve type/No: Overhead 8
Transmission: Manual
No. of forward speeds: 4
Wheels driven: Front
Springs F/R: Coil/Coil
Brake system: PA
Brakes F/R: Disc/Drum
Steering: Rack & pinion
Wheelbase: 254.0cm 100.0in
Track F: 140.0cm 55.1in
Track R: 142.0cm 55.9in
Length: 439.2cm 172.9in
Width: 168.1cm 66.2in
Height: 136.4cm 53.7in
Ground clearance: 19.1cm 7.5in
Kerb weight: 930.7kg 2050.0lb
Fuel: 67.8L 14.9gal 17.9galUS

283 Audi
4000
1980 Germany
104.0mph 167.3kmh
0-60mph 96.5kmh: 11.5secs
0-1/4 mile: 18.6secs
76.0bhp 56.7kW 77.0PS
@ 5500rpm
83.0lbft 112.5Nm @ 3200rpm
73.9bhp/ton 72.6bhp/tonne
47.9bhp/L 35.7kW/L 48.5PS/L
48.1ft/sec 14.7m/sec
17.6mph 28.3kmh/1000rpm
31.8mpg 26.5mpgUS 8.9L/100km
Petrol 4-stroke piston
1588cc 96.9cu in
In-line 4 fuel injection
Compression ratio: 8.0:1
Bore: 79.5mm 3.1in
Stroke: 80.0mm 3.1in
Valve type/No: Overhead 8
Transmission: Manual
No. of forward speeds: 4
Wheels driven: Front
Springs F/R: Coil/Coil
Brake system: PA
Brakes F/R: Disc/Drum
Steering: Rack & pinion
Wheelbase: 252.7cm 99.5in
Track F: 140.0cm 55.1in
Track R: 142.0cm 55.9in
Length: 448.8cm 176.7in
Width: 168.1cm 66.2in
Height: 136.4cm 53.7in
Ground clearance: 11.7cm 4.6in
Kerb weight: 1046.5kg 2305.0lb
Fuel: 59.8L 13.1gal 15.8galUS

284 Audi
5000 S Diesel
1980 Germany
0-60mph 96.5kmh: 20.5secs
0-1/4 mile: 22.0secs
67.0bhp 50.0kW 67.9PS
@ 4800rpm
85.0lbft 115.2Nm @ 3000rpm
50.4bhp/ton 49.6bhp/tonne
33.7bhp/L 25.2kW/L 34.2PS/L
45.3ft/sec 13.8m/sec
36.0mpg 30.0mpgUS 7.8L/100km
Diesel 4-stroke piston
1986cc 121.2cu in
In-line 5 fuel injection
Compression ratio: 23.0:1
Bore: 76.5mm 3.0in
Stroke: 86.4mm 3.4in
Valve type/No: Overhead 10
Transmission: Manual
No. of forward speeds: 5
Wheels driven: Front
Brakes F/R: Disc/Drum
Wheelbase: 268.0cm 105.5in
Track F: 147.6cm 58.1in
Track R: 145.3cm 57.2in
Length: 479.8cm 188.9in
Width: 176.8cm 69.6in
Height: 138.9cm 54.7in
Kerb weight: 1350.6kg 2975.0lb
Fuel: 74.9L 16.5gal 19.8galUS

285 Audi
200 5E
1981 Germany
113.0mph 181.8kmh
0-50mph 80.5kmh: 7.6secs
0-60mph 96.5kmh: 10.5secs
0-1/4 mile: 17.9secs
0-1km: 33.3secs
136.0bhp 101.4kW 137.9PS
@ 5700rpm
127.0lbft 172.1Nm @ 4200rpm
107.7bhp/ton 105.9bhp/tonne
63.4bhp/L 47.3kW/L 64.3PS/L
53.8ft/sec 16.4m/sec
21.1mph 33.9kmh/1000rpm
20.7mpg 17.2mpgUS 13.6L/100km
Petrol 4-stroke piston
2144cc 130.8cu in
In-line 5 fuel injection
Compression ratio: 9.3:1
Bore: 79.5mm 3.1in
Stroke: 86.4mm 3.4in
Valve type/No: Overhead 10
Transmission: Automatic
No. of forward speeds: 3
Wheels driven: Front
Springs F/R: Coil/Coil
Brake system: PA
Brakes F/R: Disc/Disc
Steering: Rack & pinion PA
Wheelbase: 267.7cm 105.4in
Track F: 147.1cm 57.9in
Track R: 144.5cm 56.9in
Length: 467.9cm 184.2in
Width: 176.8cm 69.6in
Height: 139.2cm 54.8in
Ground clearance: 12.7cm 5.0in
Kerb weight: 1283.9kg 2828.0lb
Fuel: 75.1L 16.5gal 19.8galUS

286 Audi
4000 Automatic
1981 Germany
105.0mph 168.9kmh
0-50mph 80.5kmh: 9.2secs
0-60mph 96.5kmh: 12.9secs
0-1/4 mile: 19.0secs
100.0bhp 74.6kW 101.4PS
@ 5100rpm
100.0lbft 135.5Nm @ 3000rpm
90.5bhp/ton 89.0bhp/tonne
46.6bhp/L 34.8kW/L 47.3PS/L
48.2ft/sec 14.7m/sec
18.2mph 29.3kmh/1000rpm
30.0mpg 25.0mpgUS 9.4L/100km
Petrol 4-stroke piston
2144cc 130.8cu in
In-line 5 fuel injection
Compression ratio: 8.0:1
Bore: 79.5mm 3.1in
Stroke: 86.4mm 3.4in
Valve type/No: Overhead 10
Transmission: Automatic
No. of forward speeds: 3
Wheels driven: Front
Springs F/R: Coil/Coil
Brake system: PA
Brakes F/R: Disc/Drum
Steering: Rack & pinion PA
Wheelbase: 254.0cm 100.0in
Track F: 140.0cm 55.1in
Track R: 142.0cm 55.9in
Length: 448.8cm 176.7in
Width: 168.1cm 66.2in
Height: 136.4cm 53.7in
Kerb weight: 1123.6kg 2475.0lb
Fuel: 60.2L 13.2gal 15.9galUS

287 Audi
5000 Turbo
1981 Germany
113.0mph 181.8kmh
0-50mph 80.5kmh: 6.7secs
0-60mph 96.5kmh: 9.4secs
0-1/4 mile: 17.1secs
130.0bhp 96.9kW 131.8PS
@ 5400rpm
142.0lbft 192.4Nm @ 3000rpm
89.6bhp/ton 88.1bhp/tonne
60.6bhp/L 45.2kW/L 61.5PS/L
51.0ft/sec 15.5m/sec
17.9mph 28.8kmh/1000rpm
20.4mpg 17.0mpgUS 13.8L/100km
Petrol 4-stroke piston
2144cc 130.8cu in turbocharged
In-line 5 fuel injection
Compression ratio: 7.0:1
Bore: 79.5mm 3.1in
Stroke: 86.4mm 3.4in
Valve type/No: Overhead 10
Transmission: Automatic
No. of forward speeds: 3
Wheels driven: Front
Springs F/R: Coil/Coil
Brake system: PA
Brakes F/R: Disc/Disc
Steering: Rack & pinion PA
Wheelbase: 268.0cm 105.5in
Track F: 147.6cm 58.1in
Track R: 145.3cm 57.2in
Length: 479.8cm 188.9in
Width: 176.8cm 69.6in
Height: 138.9cm 54.7in
Kerb weight: 1475.5kg 3250.0lb
Fuel: 74.9L 16.5gal 19.8galUS

288 Audi
Coupe
1981 Germany
111.0mph 178.6kmh
0-50mph 80.5kmh: 7.8secs
0-60mph 96.5kmh: 11.2secs
0-1/4 mile: 18.1secs

100.0bhp 74.6kW 101.4PS
@ 5100rpm
112.0lbft 151.8Nm @ 3000rpm
89.2bhp/ton 87.7bhp/tonne
46.6bhp/L 34.8kW/L 47.3PS/L
48.2ft/sec 14.7m/sec
26.7mph 43.0kmh/1000rpm
27.0mpg 22.5mpgUS 10.5L/100km
Petrol 4-stroke piston
2144cc 130.8cu in
In-line 5 fuel injection
Compression ratio: 8.2:1
Bore: 79.5mm 3.1in
Stroke: 86.4mm 3.4in
Valve type/No: Overhead 10
Transmission: Manual
No. of forward speeds: 5
Wheels driven: Front
Springs F/R: Coil/Coil
Brake system: PA
Brakes F/R: Disc/Drum
Steering: Rack & pinion PA
Wheelbase: 253.5cm 99.8in
Track F: 140.0cm 55.1in
Track R: 142.0cm 55.9in
Length: 449.6cm 177.0in
Width: 168.4cm 66.3in
Height: 134.9cm 53.1in
Kerb weight: 1139.5kg 2510.0lb
Fuel: 59.8L 13.1gal 15.8galUS

289 Audi

Quattro
1981 Germany
137.0mph 220.4kmh
0-50mph 80.5kmh: 4.7secs
0-60mph 96.5kmh: 7.3secs
0-1/4 mile: 15.2secs
0-1km: 27.7secs
200.0bhp 149.1kW 202.8PS
@ 5500rpm
210.0lbft 284.6Nm @ 3500rpm
160.8bhp/ton 158.1bhp/tonne
90.3bhp/L 67.4kW/L 91.6PS/L
51.9ft/sec 15.8m/sec
23.5mph 37.8kmh/1000rpm
19.1mpg 15.9mpgUS 14.8L/100km
Petrol 4-stroke piston
2214cc 135.1cu in
In-line 5 fuel injection
Compression ratio: 7.0:1
Bore: 79.5mm 3.1in
Stroke: 86.4mm 3.4in
Valve type/No: Overhead 10
Transmission: Manual
No. of forward speeds: 5
Wheels driven: 4-wheel drive
Springs F/R: Coil/Coil
Brake system: PA
Brakes F/R: Disc/Disc
Steering: Rack & pinion PA
Wheelbase: 252.5cm 99.4in
Track F: 142.0cm 55.9in
Track R: 145.8cm 57.4in
Length: 440.4cm 173.4in
Width: 172.2cm 67.8in
Height: 134.4cm 52.9in
Ground clearance: 16.5cm 6.5in
Kerb weight: 1264.8kg 2786.0lb
Fuel: 91.9L 20.2gal 24.3galUS

290 Audi

100 CD
1982 Germany
129.0mph 207.6kmh
0-50mph 80.5kmh: 7.1secs
0-60mph 96.5kmh: 9.5secs
0-1/4 mile: 17.4secs
0-1km: 31.9secs
136.0bhp 101.4kW 137.9PS
@ 5700rpm
133.0lbft 180.2Nm @ 4800rpm
113.9bhp/ton 112.0bhp/tonne
63.4bhp/L 47.3kW/L 64.3PS/L
53.8ft/sec 16.4m/sec
28.6mph 46.0kmh/1000rpm
29.4mpg 24.5mpgUS 9.6L/100km
Petrol 4-stroke piston
2144cc 130.8cu in
In-line 5 fuel injection
Compression ratio: 9.3:1
Bore: 79.5mm 3.1in
Stroke: 86.4mm 3.4in
Valve type/No: Overhead 10
Transmission: Manual
No. of forward speeds: 5
Wheels driven: Front
Springs F/R: Coil/Coil
Brake system: PA
Brakes F/R: Disc/Disc
Steering: Rack & pinion PA
Wheelbase: 268.7cm 105.8in
Track F: 147.6cm 58.1in
Track R: 145.8cm 57.4in
Length: 479.3cm 188.7in
Width: 181.4cm 71.4in
Height: 142.2cm 56.0in
Ground clearance: 13.7cm 5.4in
Kerb weight: 1214.4kg 2675.0lb
Fuel: 80.1L 17.6gal 21.1galUS

291 Audi

80 Turbo Diesel
1982 Germany
103.0mph 165.7kmh
0-50mph 80.5kmh: 9.3secs
0-60mph 96.5kmh: 12.8secs
0-1/4 mile: 19.5secs
0-1km: 35.8secs
70.0bhp 52.2kW 71.0PS
@ 4500rpm
98.0lbft 132.8Nm @ 2600rpm
72.3bhp/ton 71.0bhp/tonne
44.1bhp/L 32.9kW/L 44.7PS/L
42.5ft/sec 13.0m/sec
24.0mph 38.6kmh/1000rpm
37.3mpg 31.1mpgUS 7.6L/100km
Diesel 4-stroke piston
1588cc 96.9cu in turbocharged
In-line 4 fuel injection
Compression ratio: 23.0:1
Bore: 76.5mm 3.0in
Stroke: 86.4mm 3.4in
Valve type/No: Overhead 8
Transmission: Manual
No. of forward speeds: 5
Wheels driven: Front
Springs F/R: Coil/Coil
Brake system: PA
Brakes F/R: Disc/Drum
Steering: Rack & pinion
Wheelbase: 254.0cm 100.0in
Track F: 140.0cm 55.1in
Track R: 142.0cm 55.9in
Length: 439.2cm 172.9in
Width: 169.2cm 66.6in
Height: 136.4cm 53.7in
Ground clearance: 19.1cm 7.5in
Kerb weight: 985.2kg 2170.0lb
Fuel: 68.2L 15.0gal 18.0galUS

292 Audi

Quattro
1982 Germany
128.0mph 206.0kmh
0-60mph 96.5kmh: 8.2secs
0-1/4 mile: 16.2secs
160.0bhp 119.3kW 162.2PS
@ 5500rpm
170.0lbft 230.4Nm @ 3000rpm
115.1bhp/ton 113.1bhp/tonne
74.6bhp/L 55.6kW/L 75.7PS/L
51.9ft/sec 15.8m/sec
23.1mph 37.2kmh/1000rpm
21.0mpg 17.5mpgUS 13.4L/100km
Petrol 4-stroke piston
2144cc 130.8cu in turbocharged
In-line 5 fuel injection
Compression ratio: 7.0:1
Bore: 79.5mm 3.1in
Stroke: 86.4mm 3.4in
Valve type/No: Overhead 10
Transmission: Manual
No. of forward speeds: 5
Wheels driven: 4-wheel drive
Springs F/R: Coil/Coil
Brake system: PA
Brakes F/R: Disc/Disc
Steering: Rack & pinion PA
Wheelbase: 252.5cm 99.4in
Track F: 142.0cm 55.9in
Track R: 145.8cm 57.4in
Length: 452.6cm 178.2in
Width: 172.5cm 67.9in
Height: 132.1cm 52.0in
Ground clearance: 13.5cm 5.3in
Kerb weight: 1414.2kg 3115.0lb
Fuel: 90.1L 19.8gal 23.8galUS

293 Audi

200 Turbo
1983 Germany
142.0mph 228.5kmh
0-50mph 80.5kmh: 5.9secs
0-60mph 96.5kmh: 8.4secs
0-1/4 mile: 16.2secs
0-1km: 29.5secs
182.0bhp 135.7kW 184.5PS
@ 5700rpm
259.0lbft 350.9Nm @ 3600rpm
143.3bhp/ton 141.0bhp/tonne
84.9bhp/L 63.3kW/L 86.1PS/L
53.8ft/sec 16.4m/sec
23.5mph 37.8kmh/1000rpm
21.5mpg 17.9mpgUS 13.1L/100km
Petrol 4-stroke piston
2144cc 130.8cu in turbocharged
In-line 5 fuel injection
Compression ratio: 8.8:1
Bore: 79.5mm 3.1in
Stroke: 86.4mm 3.4in
Valve type/No: Overhead 10
Transmission: Manual
No. of forward speeds: 5
Wheels driven: Front
Springs F/R: Coil/Coil
Brake system: PA
Brakes F/R: Disc/Disc
Steering: Rack & pinion PA
Wheelbase: 268.7cm 105.8in
Track F: 147.6cm 58.1in
Track R: 145.8cm 57.4in
Length: 479.3cm 188.7in
Width: 181.4cm 71.4in
Height: 142.2cm 56.0in
Ground clearance: 13.7cm 5.4in
Kerb weight: 1291.2kg 2844.0lb
Fuel: 80.1L 17.6gal 21.1galUS

294 Audi

5000 S
1983 Germany
110.0mph 177.0kmh
0-50mph 80.5kmh: 8.2secs
0-60mph 96.5kmh: 11.8secs
0-1/4 mile: 18.2secs
100.0bhp 74.6kW 101.4PS
@ 5500rpm
107.0lbft 145.0Nm @ 3000rpm
75.5bhp/ton 74.3bhp/tonne
46.6bhp/L 34.8kW/L 47.3PS/L
51.9ft/sec 15.8m/sec
23.1mph 37.2kmh/1000rpm
25.2mpg 21.0mpgUS 11.2L/100km
Petrol 4-stroke piston
2144cc 130.8cu in
In-line 5 fuel injection
Compression ratio: 8.2:1
Bore: 79.5mm 3.1in
Stroke: 86.4mm 3.4in
Valve type/No: Overhead 10
Transmission: Manual
No. of forward speeds: 5
Wheels driven: Front
Springs F/R: Coil/Coil
Brakes F/R: Disc/Drum
Steering: Rack & pinion PA
Wheelbase: 268.7cm 105.8in
Track F: 147.6cm 58.1in
Track R: 145.8cm 57.4in
Length: 489.5cm 192.7in
Width: 181.4cm 71.4in
Height: 138.9cm 54.7in
Ground clearance: 12.4cm 4.9in
Kerb weight: 1346.1kg 2965.0lb
Fuel: 79.9L 17.6gal 21.1galUS

295 Audi

80 Quattro
1983 Germany
121.0mph 194.7kmh
0-50mph 80.5kmh: 5.8secs
0-60mph 96.5kmh: 8.8secs
0-1/4 mile: 16.6secs
0-1km: 30.8secs
134.0bhp 99.9kW 135.9PS
@ 5900rpm
130.0lbft 176.2Nm @ 4500rpm
115.1bhp/ton 113.2bhp/tonne
62.5bhp/L 46.6kW/L 63.4PS/L
55.7ft/sec 17.0m/sec
20.1mph 32.3kmh/1000rpm
25.5mpg 21.2mpgUS 11.1L/100km
Petrol 4-stroke piston
2144cc 130.8cu in
In-line 5 fuel injection
Compression ratio: 9.3:1
Bore: 79.5mm 3.1in
Stroke: 86.4mm 3.4in
Valve type/No: Overhead 10
Transmission: Manual
No. of forward speeds: 5
Wheels driven: Front
Springs F/R: Coil/Coil
Brake system: PA
Brakes F/R: Disc/Disc
Steering: Rack & pinion PA
Wheelbase: 252.5cm 99.4in
Track F: 140.2cm 55.2in
Track R: 140.7cm 55.4in
Length: 438.4cm 172.6in
Width: 168.1cm 66.2in
Height: 137.7cm 54.2in
Ground clearance: 11.9cm 4.7in
Kerb weight: 1183.6kg 2607.0lb
Fuel: 70.1L 15.4gal 18.5galUS

296 Audi

Coupe Injection
1983 Germany
121.0mph 194.7kmh
0-50mph 80.5kmh: 6.3secs
0-60mph 96.5kmh: 8.8secs
0-1/4 mile: 16.9secs
0-1km: 30.8secs
130.0bhp 96.9kW 131.8PS
@ 5900rpm
126.0lbft 170.7Nm @ 4800rpm
123.1bhp/ton 121.0bhp/tonne
60.6bhp/L 45.2kW/L 61.5PS/L
55.7ft/sec 17.0m/sec
20.7mph 33.3kmh/1000rpm
25.5mpg 21.2mpgUS 11.1L/100km
Petrol 4-stroke piston
2144cc 130.8cu in
In-line 5 fuel injection
Compression ratio: 9.3:1
Bore: 79.5mm 3.1in
Stroke: 86.4mm 3.4in
Valve type/No: Overhead 10
Transmission: Manual
No. of forward speeds: 5
Wheels driven: Front
Springs F/R: Coil/Coil
Brake system: PA
Brakes F/R: Disc/Disc
Steering: Rack & pinion PA
Wheelbase: 254.0cm 100.0in
Track F: 140.0cm 55.1in
Track R: 142.0cm 55.9in
Length: 434.8cm 171.2in
Width: 168.1cm 66.2in
Height: 134.9cm 53.1in
Ground clearance: 11.9cm 4.7in
Kerb weight: 1074.2kg 2366.0lb
Fuel: 68.2L 15.0gal 18.0galUS

297 Audi

200 Quattro Turbo
1984 Germany
145.0mph 233.3kmh
0-50mph 80.5kmh: 5.3secs
0-60mph 96.5kmh: 7.4secs
0-1/4 mile: 15.6secs
0-1km: 27.3secs
182.0bhp 135.7kW 184.5PS
@ 5700rpm
259.0lbft 350.9Nm @ 3600rpm
133.8bhp/ton 131.6bhp/tonne
84.9bhp/L 63.3kW/L 86.1PS/L
53.8ft/sec 16.4m/sec
24.6mph 39.6kmh/1000rpm
19.8mpg 16.5mpgUS 14.3L/100km
Petrol 4-stroke piston
2144cc 130.8cu in turbocharged
In-line 5 fuel injection
Compression ratio: 8.8:1
Bore: 79.5mm 3.1in
Stroke: 86.4mm 3.4in
Valve type/No: Overhead 10
Transmission: Manual
No. of forward speeds: 5
Wheels driven: 4-wheel drive
Springs F/R: Coil/Coil
Brake system: PA
Brakes F/R: Disc/Disc
Steering: Rack & pinion PA
Wheelbase: 268.7cm 105.8in
Track F: 146.8cm 57.8in
Track R: 146.8cm 57.8in
Length: 480.6cm 189.2in
Width: 181.4cm 71.4in
Height: 142.2cm 56.0in
Ground clearance: 13.7cm 5.4in
Kerb weight: 1382.9kg 3046.0lb
Fuel: 80.1L 17.6gal 21.1galUS

298 Audi
4000 S Quattro
1984 Germany
116.0mph 186.6kmh
0-50mph 80.5kmh: 7.3secs
0-60mph 96.5kmh: 10.2secs
0-1/4 mile: 17.3secs
115.0bhp 85.8kW 116.6PS
@ 5500rpm
126.0lbft 170.7Nm @ 3000rpm
91.3bhp/ton 89.8bhp/tonne
51.7bhp/L 38.5kW/L 52.4PS/L
51.9ft/sec 15.8m/sec
20.0mph 32.2kmh/1000rpm
25.2mpg 21.0mpgUS 11.2L/100km
Petrol 4-stroke piston
2226cc 135.8cu in
In-line 5 fuel injection
Compression ratio: 8.5:1
Bore: 81.0mm 3.2in
Stroke: 86.4mm 3.4in
Valve type/No: Overhead 10
Transmission: Manual
No. of forward speeds: 5
Wheels driven: 4-wheel drive
Springs F/R: Coil/Coil
Brakes F/R: Disc/Disc
Steering: Rack & pinion PA
Wheelbase: 252.5cm 99.4in
Track F: 140.7cm 55.4in
Track R: 141.7cm 55.8in
Length: 448.6cm 176.6in
Width: 168.7cm 66.4in
Height: 136.7cm 53.8in
Ground clearance: 12.4cm 4.9in
Kerb weight: 1280.3kg 2820.0lb
Fuel: 70.0L 15.4gal 18.5galUS

299 Audi
5000 S Avant
1984 Germany
114.0mph 183.4kmh
0-60mph 96.5kmh: 11.2secs
0-1/4 mile: 18.0secs
100.0bhp 74.6kW 101.4PS
@ 5100rpm
112.0lbft 151.8Nm @ 3000rpm
77.9bhp/ton 76.6bhp/tonne
46.6bhp/L 34.8kW/L 47.3PS/L
48.2ft/sec 14.7m/sec
24.6mpg 20.5mpgUS 11.5L/100km
Petrol 4-stroke piston
2144cc 130.8cu in
In-line 5 fuel injection
Compression ratio: 8.2:1
Bore: 79.5mm 3.1in
Stroke: 86.4mm 3.4in
Valve type/No: Overhead 10
Transmission: Manual
No. of forward speeds: 5
Wheels driven: Front
Springs F/R: Coil/Coil
Brakes F/R: Disc/Drum
Steering: Rack & pinion PA
Wheelbase: 268.7cm 105.8in
Track F: 147.6cm 58.1in
Track R: 145.8cm 57.4in
Length: 489.5cm 192.7in
Width: 181.4cm 71.4in
Height: 138.9cm 54.7in
Kerb weight: 1305.2kg 2875.0lb
Fuel: 79.9L 17.6gal 21.1galUS

300 Audi
5000 S Turbo
1984 Germany
124.0mph 199.5kmh
0-50mph 80.5kmh: 7.6secs
0-60mph 96.5kmh: 10.6secs
0-1/4 mile: 17.8secs
140.0bhp 104.4kW 141.9PS
@ 5500rpm
149.0lbft 201.9Nm @ 2500rpm
101.5bhp/ton 99.8bhp/tonne
65.3bhp/L 48.7kW/L 66.2PS/L
51.9ft/sec 15.8m/sec
21.4mph 34.4kmh/1000rpm
21.6mpg 18.0mpgUS 13.1L/100km
Petrol 4-stroke piston
2144cc 130.8cu in turbocharged
In-line 5 fuel injection
Compression ratio: 8.3:1
Bore: 79.5mm 3.1in
Stroke: 86.4mm 3.4in
Valve type/No: Overhead 10
Transmission: Automatic
No. of forward speeds: 3
Wheels driven: Front
Springs F/R: Coil/Coil
Brakes F/R: Disc/Disc
Steering: Rack & pinion PA
Wheelbase: 268.7cm 105.8in
Track F: 146.8cm 57.8in
Track R: 146.8cm 57.8in
Length: 489.5cm 192.7in
Width: 181.4cm 71.4in
Height: 138.9cm 54.7in
Kerb weight: 1402.9kg 3090.0lb
Fuel: 79.9L 17.6gal 21.1galUS

301 Audi
80 GL
1984 Germany
106.0mph 170.6kmh
0-50mph 80.5kmh: 7.6secs
0-60mph 96.5kmh: 10.8secs
0-1/4 mile: 17.9secs
0-1km: 33.3secs
90.0bhp 67.1kW 91.2PS
@ 5200rpm
107.0lbft 145.0Nm @ 3300rpm
90.1bhp/ton 88.6bhp/tonne
50.5bhp/L 37.7kW/L 51.2PS/L
49.1ft/sec 15.0m/sec
24.0mph 38.6kmh/1000rpm
31.9mpg 26.6mpgUS 8.9L/100km
Petrol 4-stroke piston
1781cc 108.7cu in
In-line 4 1 Carburettor
Compression ratio: 10.0:1
Bore: 81.0mm 3.2in
Stroke: 86.4mm 3.4in
Valve type/No: Overhead 8
Transmission: Manual
No. of forward speeds: 5
Wheels driven: Front
Springs F/R: Coil/Coil
Brake system: PA
Brakes F/R: Disc/Drum
Steering: Rack & pinion
Wheelbase: 252.5cm 99.4in
Track F: 140.2cm 55.2in
Track R: 140.7cm 55.4in
Length: 438.4cm 172.6in
Width: 168.1cm 66.2in
Height: 137.7cm 54.2in
Ground clearance: 11.9cm 4.7in
Kerb weight: 1016.0kg 2238.0lb
Fuel: 68.2L 15.0gal 18.0galUS

302 Audi
Coupe GT
1984 Germany
112.0mph 180.2kmh
0-50mph 80.5kmh: 7.4secs
0-60mph 96.5kmh: 10.5secs
0-1/4 mile: 17.7secs
100.0bhp 74.6kW 101.4PS
@ 5100rpm
112.0lbft 151.8Nm @ 3000rpm
84.8bhp/ton 83.4bhp/tonne
46.6bhp/L 34.8kW/L 47.3PS/L
48.2ft/sec 14.7m/sec
22.3mph 35.9kmh/1000rpm
24.0mpg 20.0mpgUS 11.8L/100km
Petrol 4-stroke piston
2144cc 130.8cu in
In-line 5 fuel injection
Compression ratio: 8.2:1
Bore: 79.5mm 3.1in
Stroke: 86.4mm 3.4in
Valve type/No: Overhead 10
Transmission: Manual
No. of forward speeds: 5
Wheels driven: Front
Springs F/R: Coil/Coil
Brake system: PA
Brakes F/R: Disc/Drum
Steering: Rack & pinion PA
Wheelbase: 253.5cm 99.8in
Track F: 140.0cm 55.1in
Track R: 142.0cm 55.9in
Length: 449.6cm 177.0in
Width: 168.4cm 66.3in
Height: 134.9cm 53.1in
Kerb weight: 1198.6kg 2640.0lb
Fuel: 60.2L 13.2gal 15.9galUS

303 Audi
100 Quattro
1985 Germany
119.0mph 191.5kmh
0-50mph 80.5kmh: 6.6secs
0-60mph 96.5kmh: 9.3secs
0-1/4 mile: 17.0secs
0-1km: 31.4secs
138.0bhp 102.9kW 139.9PS
@ 5700rpm
139.0lbft 188.3Nm @ 3500rpm
104.6bhp/ton 102.9bhp/tonne
62.0bhp/L 46.2kW/L 62.8PS/L
53.8ft/sec 16.4m/sec
21.2mph 34.1kmh/1000rpm
22.7mpg 18.9mpgUS 12.4L/100km
Petrol 4-stroke piston
2226cc 135.8cu in
In-line 5 fuel injection
Compression ratio: 10.0:1
Bore: 81.0mm 3.2in
Stroke: 86.4mm 3.4in
Valve type/No: Overhead 10
Transmission: Manual
No. of forward speeds: 5
Wheels driven: 4-wheel drive
Springs F/R: Coil/Coil
Brake system: PA
Brakes F/R: Disc/Disc
Steering: Rack & pinion PA
Wheelbase: 268.7cm 105.8in
Track F: 146.8cm 57.8in
Track R: 146.6cm 57.7in
Length: 479.3cm 188.7in
Width: 181.4cm 71.4in
Height: 142.2cm 56.0in
Ground clearance: 13.7cm 5.4in
Kerb weight: 1341.1kg 2954.0lb
Fuel: 79.6L 17.5gal 21.0galUS

304 Audi
200 Avant Quattro
1985 Germany
140.0mph 225.3kmh
0-50mph 80.5kmh: 4.8secs
0-60mph 96.5kmh: 7.3secs
0-1/4 mile: 15.3secs
0-1km: 28.6secs
182.0bhp 135.7kW 184.5PS
@ 5700rpm
186.0lbft 252.0Nm @ 3600rpm
120.4bhp/ton 118.4bhp/tonne
84.9bhp/L 63.3kW/L 86.1PS/L
53.8ft/sec 16.4m/sec
23.3mph 37.5kmh/1000rpm
19.0mpg 15.8mpgUS 14.9L/100km
Petrol 4-stroke piston
2144cc 130.8cu in turbocharged
In-line 5 fuel injection
Compression ratio: 8.8:1
Bore: 79.5mm 3.1in
Stroke: 86.4mm 3.4in
Valve type/No: Overhead 10
Transmission: Manual
No. of forward speeds: 5
Wheels driven: 4-wheel drive
Springs F/R: Coil/Coil
Brake system: PA
Brakes F/R: Disc/Disc
Steering: Rack & pinion PA
Wheelbase: 268.7cm 105.8in
Track F: 146.8cm 57.8in
Track R: 146.6cm 57.7in
Length: 479.3cm 188.7in
Width: 181.4cm 71.4in
Height: 142.2cm 56.0in
Ground clearance: 13.7cm 5.4in
Kerb weight: 1537.7kg 3387.0lb
Fuel: 80.1L 17.6gal 21.1galUS

305 Audi
5000 S Turbo Quattro
1985 Germany
132.0mph 212.4kmh
0-50mph 80.5kmh: 5.9secs
0-60mph 96.5kmh: 8.3secs
0-1/4 mile: 16.4secs
158.0bhp 117.8kW 160.2PS
@ 5500rpm
166.0lbft 224.9Nm @ 3000rpm
105.6bhp/ton 103.9bhp/tonne
71.0bhp/L 52.9kW/L 72.0PS/L
51.9ft/sec 15.8m/sec
24.8mph 39.9kmh/1000rpm
24.0mpg 20.0mpgUS 11.8L/100km
Petrol 4-stroke piston
2226cc 135.8cu in turbocharged
In-line 4 fuel injection
Compression ratio: 7.8:1
Bore: 81.0mm 3.2in
Stroke: 86.4mm 3.4in
Valve type/No: Overhead 8
Transmission: Manual
No. of forward speeds: 5
Wheels driven: 4-wheel drive
Springs F/R: Coil/Coil
Brake system: ABS
Brakes F/R: Disc/Disc
Steering: Rack & pinion PA
Wheelbase: 268.7cm 105.8in
Track F: 146.8cm 57.8in
Track R: 146.8cm 57.8in
Length: 489.5cm 192.7in
Width: 181.4cm 71.4in
Height: 142.0cm 55.9in
Kerb weight: 1520.9kg 3350.0lb
Fuel: 79.9L 17.6gal 21.1galUS

306 Audi
90 Quattro
1985 Germany
120.0mph 193.1kmh
0-50mph 80.5kmh: 6.5secs
0-60mph 96.5kmh: 9.0secs
0-1/4 mile: 16.7secs
0-1km: 31.3secs
136.0bhp 101.4kW 137.9PS
@ 5700rpm
136.0lbft 184.3Nm @ 3500rpm
115.1bhp/ton 113.2bhp/tonne
61.1bhp/L 45.6kW/L 61.9PS/L
53.8ft/sec 16.4m/sec
20.5mph 33.0kmh/1000rpm
23.9mpg 19.9mpgUS 11.8L/100km
Petrol 4-stroke piston
2226cc 135.8cu in
In-line 5 fuel injection
Compression ratio: 10.0:1
Bore: 81.0mm 3.2in
Stroke: 86.4mm 3.4in
Valve type/No: Overhead 10
Transmission: Manual
No. of forward speeds: 5
Wheels driven: 4-wheel drive
Springs F/R: Coil/Coil
Brake system: PA
Brakes F/R: Disc/Disc
Steering: Rack & pinion PA
Wheelbase: 253.7cm 99.9in
Track F: 140.0cm 55.1in
Track R: 142.0cm 55.9in
Length: 440.7cm 173.5in
Width: 168.1cm 66.2in
Height: 138.9cm 54.7in
Ground clearance: 11.9cm 4.7in
Kerb weight: 1201.3kg 2646.0lb
Fuel: 68.2L 15.0gal 18.0galUS

307 Audi
Coupe GT
1985 Germany
120.0mph 193.1kmh
0-50mph 80.5kmh: 6.4secs
0-60mph 96.5kmh: 8.9secs
0-1/4 mile: 17.2secs
0-1km: 31.7secs
115.0bhp 85.8kW 116.6PS
@ 5400rpm
121.0lbft 164.0Nm @ 3200rpm
104.5bhp/ton 102.8bhp/tonne
57.7bhp/L 43.0kW/L 58.5PS/L
45.7ft/sec 13.9m/sec
22.2mph 35.7kmh/1000rpm
24.7mpg 20.6mpgUS 11.4L/100km
Petrol 4-stroke piston
1994cc 121.7cu in
In-line 5 fuel injection
Compression ratio: 10.0:1
Bore: 81.0mm 3.2in
Stroke: 77.4mm 3.0in
Valve type/No: Overhead 10
Transmission: Manual
No. of forward speeds: 5
Wheels driven: Front
Springs F/R: Coil/Coil
Brake system: PA
Brakes F/R: Disc/Drum
Steering: Rack & pinion PA
Wheelbase: 254.0cm 100.0in
Track F: 140.0cm 55.1in
Track R: 142.0cm 55.9in
Length: 434.8cm 171.2in
Width: 168.1cm 66.2in
Height: 134.9cm 53.1in
Ground clearance: 11.9cm 4.7in
Kerb weight: 1118.7kg 2464.0lb
Fuel: 68.2L 15.0gal 18.0galUS

308 Audi
Quattro
1985 Germany
128.0mph 206.0kmh
0-60mph 96.5kmh: 8.2secs
0-1/4 mile: 16.2secs
160.0bhp 119.3kW 162.2PS
@ 5500rpm
170.0lbft 230.4Nm @ 3000rpm
120.5bhp/ton 118.5bhp/tonne
74.6bhp/L 55.6kW/L 75.7PS/L
Petrol 4-stroke piston
2144cc 130.8cu in turbocharged
In-line 5 fuel injection
Valve type/No: Overhead 10
Transmission: Manual
No. of forward speeds: 5
Wheels driven: 4-wheel drive
Springs F/R: Coil/Coil
Brakes F/R: Disc/Disc
Steering: Rack & pinion PA
Wheelbase: 252.5cm 99.4in
Length: 452.6cm 178.2in
Width: 172.5cm 67.9in
Height: 132.1cm 52.0in
Kerb weight: 1350.6kg 2975.0lb
Fuel: 90.1L 19.8gal 23.8galUS

309 Audi
Quattro Sport
1985 Germany
155.0mph 249.4kmh
0-50mph 80.5kmh: 3.7secs
0-60mph 96.5kmh: 4.8secs
0-1/4 mile: 13.5secs
0-1km: 23.9secs
306.0bhp 228.2kW 310.2PS
@ 6700rpm
258.0lbft 349.6Nm @ 3700rpm
244.2bhp/ton 240.1bhp/tonne
143.4bhp/L 106.9kW/L 145.4PS/L
63.3ft/sec 19.3m/sec
21.7mph 34.9kmh/1000rpm
15.3mpg 12.7mpgUS 18.5L/100km
Petrol 4-stroke piston
2134cc 130.2cu in turbocharged
In-line 5 fuel injection
Compression ratio: 8.0:1
Bore: 79.3mm 3.1in
Stroke: 86.4mm 3.4in
Valve type/No: Overhead 20
Transmission: Manual
No. of forward speeds: 5
Wheels driven: 4-wheel drive
Springs F/R: Coil/Coil
Brake system: PA
Brakes F/R: Disc/Disc
Steering: Rack & pinion PA
Wheelbase: 222.3cm 87.5in
Track F: 148.6cm 58.5in
Track R: 148.3cm 58.4in
Length: 416.1cm 163.8in
Width: 178.1cm 70.1in
Height: 134.4cm 52.9in
Ground clearance: 15.2cm 6.0in
Kerb weight: 1274.4kg 2807.0lb
Fuel: 90.1L 19.8gal 23.8galUS

310 Audi
100 Turbo Diesel
1986 Germany
113.0mph 181.8kmh
0-50mph 80.5kmh: 9.2secs
0-60mph 96.5kmh: 12.6secs
0-1/4 mile: 18.6secs
0-1km: 34.7secs
87.0bhp 64.9kW 88.2PS
@ 4500rpm
126.0lbft 170.7Nm @ 2750rpm
70.5bhp/ton 69.3bhp/tonne
43.8bhp/L 32.7kW/L 44.4PS/L
42.5ft/sec 13.0m/sec
26.6mph 42.8kmh/1000rpm
28.9mpg 24.1mpgUS 9.8L/100km
Diesel 4-stroke piston
1986cc 121.2cu in turbocharged
In-line 5 fuel injection
Compression ratio: 23.0:1
Bore: 76.4mm 3.0in
Stroke: 86.4mm 3.4in
Valve type/No: Overhead 10
Transmission: Manual
No. of forward speeds: 5
Wheels driven: Front
Springs F/R: Coil/Coil
Brake system: PA
Brakes F/R: Disc/Drum
Steering: Rack & pinion PA
Wheelbase: 268.7cm 105.8in
Track F: 146.8cm 57.8in
Track R: 146.6cm 57.7in
Length: 479.3cm 188.7in
Width: 181.4cm 71.4in
Height: 142.2cm 56.0in
Ground clearance: 13.7cm 5.4in
Kerb weight: 1254.9kg 2764.0lb
Fuel: 80.1L 17.6gal 21.1galUS

311 Audi
5000 S
1986 Germany
113.0mph 181.8kmh
0-60mph 96.5kmh: 11.6secs
0-1/4 mile: 18.4secs
110.0bhp 82.0kW 111.5PS
@ 5500rpm
122.0lbft 165.3Nm @ 2500rpm
85.8bhp/ton 84.4bhp/tonne
49.4bhp/L 36.8kW/L 50.1PS/L
51.9ft/sec 15.8m/sec
29.4mpg 24.5mpgUS 9.6L/100km
Petrol 4-stroke piston
2226cc 135.8cu in
In-line 5 fuel injection
Compression ratio: 8.5:1
Bore: 81.0mm 3.2in
Stroke: 86.4mm 3.4in
Valve type/No: Overhead 10
Transmission: Automatic
No. of forward speeds: 3
Wheels driven: Front
Springs F/R: Coil/Coil
Brakes F/R: Disc/Drum
Steering: Rack & pinion PA
Wheelbase: 268.7cm 105.8in
Track F: 146.8cm 57.8in
Track R: 146.8cm 57.8in
Length: 489.5cm 192.7in
Width: 181.4cm 71.4in
Height: 141.5cm 55.7in
Kerb weight: 1303.0kg 2870.0lb
Fuel: 79.9L 17.6gal 21.1galUS

312 Audi
80 1.8S
1986 Germany
114.0mph 183.4kmh
0-50mph 80.5kmh: 7.8secs
0-60mph 96.5kmh: 11.1secs
0-1/4 mile: 18.2secs
0-1km: 33.2secs
90.0bhp 67.1kW 91.2PS
@ 5200rpm
150.0lbft 203.3Nm @ 3300rpm
86.5bhp/ton 85.1bhp/tonne
50.5bhp/L 37.7kW/L 51.2PS/L
49.1ft/sec 15.0m/sec
24.2mph 38.9kmh/1000rpm
30.8mpg 25.6mpgUS 9.2L/100km
Petrol 4-stroke piston
1781cc 109.0cu in
In-line 4 1 Carburettor
Compression ratio: 10.0:1
Bore: 81.0mm 3.2in
Stroke: 86.4mm 3.4in
Valve type/No: Overhead 8
Transmission: Manual
No. of forward speeds: 5
Wheels driven: Front
Springs F/R: Coil/Coil
Brake system: PA
Brakes F/R: Disc/Drum
Steering: Rack & pinion
Wheelbase: 254.6cm 100.2in
Track F: 141.1cm 55.6in
Track R: 143.1cm 56.3in
Length: 439.3cm 173.0in
Width: 169.5cm 66.7in
Height: 139.7cm 55.0in
Ground clearance: 12.0cm 4.7in
Kerb weight: 1058.0kg 2330.4lb
Fuel: 67.8L 14.9gal 17.9galUS

313 Audi
90
1986 Germany
115.0mph 185.0kmh
0-50mph 80.5kmh: 6.9secs
0-60mph 96.5kmh: 9.6secs
0-1/4 mile: 17.2secs
0-1km: 32.0secs
115.0bhp 85.8kW 116.6PS
@ 5400rpm
121.0lbft 164.0Nm @ 3200rpm
106.0bhp/ton 104.3bhp/tonne
57.7bhp/L 43.0kW/L 58.5PS/L
45.7ft/sec 13.9m/sec
20.9mph 33.6kmh/1000rpm
25.2mpg 21.0mpgUS 11.2L/100km
Petrol 4-stroke piston
1994cc 121.7cu in
In-line 5 fuel injection
Compression ratio: 10.0:1
Bore: 81.0mm 3.2in
Stroke: 77.4mm 3.0in
Valve type/No: Overhead 10
Transmission: Manual
No. of forward speeds: 5
Wheels driven: Front
Springs F/R: Coil/Coil
Brake system: PA
Brakes F/R: Disc/Drum
Steering: Rack & pinion PA
Wheelbase: 253.7cm 99.9in
Track F: 140.0cm 55.1in
Track R: 142.0cm 55.9in
Length: 440.7cm 173.5in
Width: 168.1cm 66.2in
Height: 138.9cm 54.7in
Ground clearance: 11.9cm 4.7in
Kerb weight: 1102.8kg 2429.0lb
Fuel: 68.2L 15.0gal 18.0galUS

314 Audi
Coupe GT
1986 Germany
115.0mph 185.0kmh
0-50mph 80.5kmh: 6.9secs
0-60mph 96.5kmh: 9.6secs
0-1/4 mile: 17.2secs
110.0bhp 82.0kW 111.5PS
@ 5500rpm
122.0lbft 165.3Nm @ 2500rpm
98.2bhp/ton 96.5bhp/tonne
49.4bhp/L 36.8kW/L 50.1PS/L
51.9ft/sec 15.8m/sec
26.4mpg 22.0mpgUS 10.7L/100km
Petrol 4-stroke piston
2226cc 135.8cu in
In-line 5 fuel injection
Compression ratio: 8.5:1
Bore: 81.0mm 3.2in
Stroke: 86.4mm 3.4in
Valve type/No: Overhead 10
Transmission: Manual
No. of forward speeds: 5
Wheels driven: Front
Springs F/R: Coil/Coil
Brake system: PA
Brakes F/R: Disc/Drum
Steering: Rack & pinion PA
Wheelbase: 253.5cm 99.8in
Track F: 140.2cm 55.2in
Track R: 142.0cm 55.9in
Length: 450.3cm 177.3in
Width: 168.4cm 66.3in
Height: 134.9cm 53.1in
Kerb weight: 1139.5kg 2510.0lb
Fuel: 60.2L 13.2gal 15.9galUS

315 Audi
Coupe GT 2.2
1986 Germany
126.0mph 202.7kmh
0-50mph 80.5kmh: 6.4secs
0-60mph 96.5kmh: 8.8secs
0-1/4 mile: 16.5secs
0-1km: 30.8secs
136.0bhp 101.4kW 137.9PS
@ 5700rpm
137.0lbft 185.6Nm @ 3500rpm
133.6bhp/ton 131.4bhp/tonne
61.1bhp/L 45.6kW/L 61.9PS/L
53.8ft/sec 16.4m/sec
21.8mph 35.1kmh/1000rpm
27.4mpg 22.8mpgUS 10.3L/100km
Petrol 4-stroke piston
2226cc 136.0cu in
In-line 5 fuel injection
Compression ratio: 10.0:1
Bore: 81.0mm 3.2in
Stroke: 86.4mm 3.4in
Valve type/No: Overhead 10
Transmission: Manual
No. of forward speeds: 5
Wheels driven: Front
Springs F/R: Coil/Coil
Brake system: PA
Brakes F/R: Disc/Disc
Steering: Rack & pinion PA
Wheelbase: 253.8cm 99.9in
Track F: 140.0cm 55.1in
Track R: 142.0cm 55.9in
Length: 442.1cm 174.1in
Width: 168.2cm 66.2in
Height: 135.0cm 53.1in
Ground clearance: 12.0cm 4.7in
Kerb weight: 1035.0kg 2279.7lb
Fuel: 68.2L 15.0gal 18.0galUS

316 Audi
Coupe Quattro
1986 Germany
122.0mph 196.3kmh
0-50mph 80.5kmh: 6.2secs
0-60mph 96.5kmh: 8.6secs
0-1/4 mile: 16.9secs
0-1km: 31.9secs
136.0bhp 101.4kW 137.9PS
@ 5700rpm
137.0lbft 185.6Nm @ 3500rpm
113.9bhp/ton 112.0bhp/tonne
61.1bhp/L 45.6kW/L 61.9PS/L
53.8ft/sec 16.4m/sec
19.6mph 31.5kmh/1000rpm
24.2mpg 20.2mpgUS 11.7L/100km
Petrol 4-stroke piston
2226cc 135.8cu in
In-line 5 fuel injection
Compression ratio: 10.0:1
Bore: 81.0mm 3.2in
Stroke: 86.4mm 3.4in
Valve type/No: Overhead 10
Transmission: Manual
No. of forward speeds: 5
Wheels driven: 4-wheel drive
Springs F/R: Coil/Coil
Brake system: PA
Brakes F/R: Disc/Disc
Steering: Rack & pinion PA
Wheelbase: 254.0cm 100.0in
Track F: 140.0cm 55.1in
Track R: 142.0cm 55.9in
Length: 434.8cm 171.2in
Width: 168.1cm 66.2in
Height: 134.9cm 53.1in
Ground clearance: 11.9cm 4.7in
Kerb weight: 1214.0kg 2674.0lb
Fuel: 70.1L 15.4gal 18.5galUS

317 Audi
90 2.2E
1987 Germany
127.0mph 204.3kmh
0-50mph 80.5kmh: 6.7secs
0-60mph 96.5kmh: 9.5secs
0-1/4 mile: 17.2secs
0-1km: 31.6secs
136.0bhp 101.4kW 137.9PS
@ 5700rpm
137.0lbft 185.6Nm @ 3500rpm
122.2bhp/ton 120.1bhp/tonne
61.1bhp/L 45.6kW/L 61.9PS/L
53.8ft/sec 16.4m/sec
21.9mph 35.2kmh/1000rpm
29.7mpg 24.7mpgUS 9.5L/100km
Petrol 4-stroke piston
2226cc 136.0cu in
In-line 5 fuel injection
Compression ratio: 10.0:1
Bore: 81.0mm 3.2in
Stroke: 86.4mm 3.4in
Valve type/No: Overhead 10
Transmission: Manual
No. of forward speeds: 5
Wheels driven: Front
Springs F/R: Coil/Coil
Brake system: PA
Brakes F/R: Disc/Disc
Steering: Rack & pinion PA
Wheelbase: 254.6cm 100.2in
Track F: 141.1cm 55.6in
Track R: 143.2cm 56.4in
Length: 439.3cm 173.0in
Width: 169.5cm 66.7in
Height: 139.7cm 55.0in
Ground clearance: 12.0cm 4.7in
Kerb weight: 1132.0kg 2493.4lb
Fuel: 70.1L 15.4gal 18.5galUS

318 Audi
90 Quattro
1987 Germany
127.0mph 204.3kmh
0-50mph 80.5kmh: 6.6secs
0-60mph 96.5kmh: 9.5secs

0-1/4 mile: 16.7secs
0-1km: 31.6secs
136.0bhp 101.4kW 137.9PS
@ 5700rpm
137.0lbft 185.6Nm @ 3500rpm
108.6bhp/ton 106.8bhp/tonne
61.1bhp/L 45.6kW/L 61.9PS/L
53.8ft/sec 16.4m/sec
21.2mph 34.1kmh/1000rpm
28.7mpg 23.9mpgUS 9.8L/100km
Petrol 4-stroke piston
2226cc 136.0cu in
In-line 5 fuel injection
Compression ratio: 10.0:1
Bore: 81.0mm 3.2in
Stroke: 86.4mm 3.4in
Valve type/No: Overhead 10
Transmission: Manual
No. of forward speeds: 5
Wheels driven: 4-wheel drive
Springs F/R: Coil/Coil
Brake system: PA
Brakes F/R: Disc/Disc
Steering: Rack & pinion PA
Wheelbase: 254.6cm 100.2in
Track F: 141.1cm 55.6in
Track R: 143.1cm 56.3in
Length: 439.3cm 173.0in
Width: 169.5cm 66.7in
Height: 139.7cm 55.0in
Ground clearance: 12.0cm 4.7in
Kerb weight: 1273.0kg 2804.0lb
Fuel: 70.1L 15.4gal 18.5galUS

319 Audi
100 Avant Quattro
1988 Germany
123.0mph 197.9kmh
0-50mph 80.5kmh: 7.6secs
0-60mph 96.5kmh: 10.6secs
0-1/4 mile: 17.2secs
0-1km: 31.9secs
138.0bhp 102.9kW 139.9PS
@ 5700rpm
138.0lbft 187.0Nm @ 3500rpm
96.9bhp/ton 95.3bhp/tonne
62.0bhp/L 46.2kW/L 62.8PS/L
53.8ft/sec 16.4m/sec
21.3mph 34.3kmh/1000rpm
21.4mpg 17.8mpgUS 13.2L/100km
Petrol 4-stroke piston
2226cc 136.0cu in
In-line 5 fuel injection
Compression ratio: 10.0:1
Bore: 81.0mm 3.2in
Stroke: 86.4mm 3.4in
Valve type/No: Overhead 10
Transmission: Manual
No. of forward speeds: 5
Wheels driven: 4-wheel drive
Springs F/R: Coil/Coil
Brake system: PA
Brakes F/R: Disc/Disc
Steering: Rack & pinion PA
Wheelbase: 268.7cm 105.8in
Track F: 146.8cm 57.8in
Track R: 146.9cm 57.8in
Length: 480.8cm 189.3in
Width: 181.4cm 71.4in
Height: 142.2cm 56.0in
Ground clearance: 13.6cm 5.4in
Kerb weight: 1448.0kg 3189.4lb
Fuel: 80.1L 17.6gal 21.1galUS

320 Audi
100 Sport
1988 Germany
122.0mph 196.3kmh
0-50mph 80.5kmh: 7.2secs
0-60mph 96.5kmh: 10.0secs
0-1/4 mile: 17.5secs
0-1km: 32.5secs
138.0bhp 102.9kW 139.9PS
@ 5700rpm
138.0lbft 187.0Nm @ 3500rpm
110.6bhp/ton 108.7bhp/tonne
62.0bhp/L 46.2kW/L 62.8PS/L
53.8ft/sec 16.4m/sec
21.5mph 34.6kmh/1000rpm
27.4mpg 22.8mpgUS 10.3L/100km
Petrol 4-stroke piston
2226cc 136.0cu in
In-line 5 fuel injection
Compression ratio: 10.0:1
Bore: 81.0mm 3.2in
Stroke: 86.4mm 3.4in
Valve type/No: Overhead 10
Transmission: Manual
No. of forward speeds: 5
Wheels driven: Front
Springs F/R: Coil/Coil
Brake system: PA ABS
Brakes F/R: Disc/Disc
Steering: Rack & pinion PA
Wheelbase: 268.7cm 105.8in
Track F: 146.8cm 57.8in
Track R: 146.9cm 57.8in
Length: 480.7cm 189.3in
Width: 181.4cm 71.4in
Height: 142.2cm 56.0in
Ground clearance: 13.6cm 5.4in
Kerb weight: 1269.0kg 2795.1lb
Fuel: 80.1L 17.6gal 21.1galUS

321 Audi
80 1.8E
1988 Germany
122.0mph 196.3kmh
0-50mph 80.5kmh: 6.9secs
0-60mph 96.5kmh: 9.8secs
0-1/4 mile: 17.7secs
0-1km: 32.4secs
112.0bhp 83.5kW 113.5PS
@ 5800rpm
118.1lbft 160.0Nm @ 3400rpm
103.1bhp/ton 101.4bhp/tonne
62.9bhp/L 46.9kW/L 63.8PS/L
54.6ft/sec 16.6m/sec
20.6mph 33.1kmh/1000rpm
28.1mpg 23.4mpgUS 10.1L/100km
Petrol 4-stroke piston
1781cc 109.0cu in
In-line 4 fuel injection
Compression ratio: 10.0:1
Bore: 81.0mm 3.2in
Stroke: 86.0mm 3.4in
Valve type/No: Overhead 8
Transmission: Manual
No. of forward speeds: 5
Wheels driven: Front
Springs F/R: Coil/Torsion bar
Brake system: PA
Brakes F/R: Disc/Disc
Steering: Rack & pinion PA
Wheelbase: 254.6cm 100.2in
Track F: 141.1cm 55.6in
Track R: 143.2cm 56.4in
Length: 439.3cm 173.0in
Width: 169.5cm 66.7in
Height: 139.7cm 55.0in
Ground clearance: 12.0cm 4.7in
Kerb weight: 1105.0kg 2433.9lb
Fuel: 67.8L 14.9gal 17.9galUS

322 Audi
90 Quattro
1988 Germany
128.0mph 206.0kmh
0-50mph 80.5kmh: 6.9secs
0-60mph 96.5kmh: 9.5secs
0-1/4 mile: 17.0secs
130.0bhp 96.9kW 131.8PS
@ 5700rpm
140.0lbft 189.7Nm @ 4500rpm
97.1bhp/ton 95.4bhp/tonne
56.3bhp/L 42.0kW/L 57.1PS/L
53.8ft/sec 16.4m/sec
25.2mpg 21.0mpgUS 11.2L/100km
Petrol 4-stroke piston
2309cc 140.9cu in
In-line 5 fuel injection
Compression ratio: 10.0:1
Bore: 82.5mm 3.2in
Stroke: 86.4mm 3.4in
Valve type/No: Overhead 10
Transmission: Manual
No. of forward speeds: 5
Wheels driven: 4-wheel drive
Springs F/R: Coil/Coil
Brake system: PA ABS
Brakes F/R: Disc/Disc
Steering: Rack & pinion PA
Wheelbase: 253.7cm 99.9in
Track F: 141.2cm 55.6in
Track R: 143.0cm 56.3in
Length: 447.8cm 176.3in
Width: 169.4cm 66.7in
Height: 139.2cm 54.8in
Ground clearance: 15.2cm 6.0in
Kerb weight: 1362.0kg 3000.0lb
Fuel: 70.0L 15.4gal 18.5galUS

323 Audi
Quattro
1988 Germany
136.0mph 218.8kmh
0-50mph 80.5kmh: 4.4secs
0-60mph 96.5kmh: 6.3secs
0-1/4 mile: 14.7secs
0-1km: 27.5secs
200.0bhp 149.1kW 202.8PS
@ 5500rpm
199.3lbft 270.0Nm @ 3500rpm
152.8bhp/ton 150.3bhp/tonne
89.8bhp/L 67.0kW/L 91.1PS/L
51.9ft/sec 15.8m/sec
22.3mph 35.9kmh/1000rpm
19.7mpg 16.4mpgUS 14.3L/100km
Petrol 4-stroke piston
2226cc 136.0cu in turbocharged
In-line 5 fuel injection
Compression ratio: 8.6:1
Bore: 81.0mm 3.2in
Stroke: 86.4mm 3.4in
Valve type/No: Overhead 10
Transmission: Manual
No. of forward speeds: 5
Wheels driven: 4-wheel drive
Springs F/R: Coil/Coil
Brake system: PA ABS
Brakes F/R: Disc/Disc
Steering: Rack & pinion PA
Wheelbase: 252.4cm 99.4in
Track F: 146.1cm 57.5in
Track R: 149.4cm 58.8in
Length: 440.4cm 173.4in
Width: 172.3cm 67.8in
Height: 134.4cm 52.9in
Ground clearance: 15.3cm 6.0in
Kerb weight: 1331.0kg 2931.7lb
Fuel: 90.1L 19.8gal 23.8galUS

324 Audi
90
1989 Germany
120.0mph 193.1kmh
0-50mph 80.5kmh: 6.6secs
0-60mph 96.5kmh: 9.3secs
0-1/4 mile: 17.0secs
130.0bhp 96.9kW 131.8PS
@ 5700rpm
140.0lbft 189.7Nm @ 4500rpm
104.6bhp/ton 102.8bhp/tonne
56.3bhp/L 42.0kW/L 57.1PS/L
53.8ft/sec 16.4m/sec
25.2mpg 21.0mpgUS 11.2L/100km
Petrol 4-stroke piston
2309cc 140.9cu in
In-line 4 fuel injection
Compression ratio: 10.0:1
Bore: 82.5mm 3.2in
Stroke: 86.4mm 3.4in
Valve type/No: Overhead 8
Transmission: Manual
No. of forward speeds: 5
Wheels driven: Front
Springs F/R: Coil/Coil
Brake system: PA ABS
Brakes F/R: Disc/Disc
Steering: Rack & pinion PA
Wheelbase: 254.5cm 100.2in
Track F: 141.2cm 55.6in
Track R: 143.0cm 56.3in
Length: 447.8cm 176.3in
Width: 169.4cm 66.7in
Height: 139.2cm 54.8in
Kerb weight: 1264.4kg 2785.0lb
Fuel: 67.7L 14.9gal 17.9galUS

325 Audi
90 Quattro 20v
1989 Germany
138.9mph 223.5kmh
0-50mph 80.5kmh: 6.1secs
0-60mph 96.5kmh: 8.5secs
0-1/4 mile: 16.9secs
0-1km: 29.8secs
170.0bhp 126.8kW 172.4PS
@ 6000rpm
162.4lbft 220.0Nm @ 4500rpm
125.6bhp/ton 123.5bhp/tonne
73.6bhp/L 54.9kW/L 74.6PS/L
56.7ft/sec 17.3m/sec
22.1mph 35.6kmh/1000rpm
22.2mpg 18.5mpgUS 12.7L/100km
Petrol 4-stroke piston
2309cc 141.0cu in
In-line 5 fuel injection
Compression ratio: 10.3:1
Bore: 82.5mm 3.2in
Stroke: 86.4mm 3.4in
Valve type/No: Overhead 20
Transmission: Manual
No. of forward speeds: 5
Wheels driven: 4-wheel drive
Springs F/R: Coil/Coil
Brake system: PA ABS
Brakes F/R: Disc/Disc
Steering: Rack & pinion PA
Wheelbase: 254.6cm 100.2in
Track F: 141.1cm 55.6in
Track R: 143.2cm 56.4in
Length: 439.3cm 173.0in
Width: 169.5cm 66.7in
Height: 139.7cm 55.0in
Ground clearance: 12.0cm 4.7in
Kerb weight: 1376.0kg 3030.8lb
Fuel: 68.2L 15.0gal 18.0galUS

326 Audi
Coupe 2.2E
1989 Germany
132.0mph 212.4kmh
0-50mph 80.5kmh: 7.1secs
0-60mph 96.5kmh: 9.7secs
0-1/4 mile: 17.3secs
0-1km: 31.6secs
136.0bhp 101.4kW 137.9PS
@ 5700rpm
137.3lbft 186.0Nm @ 3500rpm
114.1bhp/ton 112.2bhp/tonne
61.1bhp/L 45.6kW/L 61.9PS/L
53.8ft/sec 16.4m/sec
21.6mph 34.8kmh/1000rpm
26.1mpg 21.7mpgUS 10.8L/100km
Petrol 4-stroke piston
2226cc 136.0cu in
In-line 5 fuel injection
Compression ratio: 10.0:1
Bore: 81.0mm 3.2in
Stroke: 86.4mm 3.4in
Valve type/No: Overhead 10
Transmission: Manual
No. of forward speeds: 5
Wheels driven: Front
Springs F/R: Coil/Coil
Brake system: PA
Brakes F/R: Disc/Disc
Steering: Rack & pinion PA
Wheelbase: 254.8cm 100.3in
Track F: 145.3cm 57.2in
Track R: 143.7cm 56.6in
Length: 436.6cm 171.9in
Width: 171.6cm 67.6in
Height: 136.5cm 53.7in
Ground clearance: 12.9cm 5.1in
Kerb weight: 1212.0kg 2669.6lb
Fuel: 70.1L 15.4gal 18.5galUS

327 Audi
Coupe Quattro
1989 Germany
123.9mph 199.4kmh
0-50mph 80.5kmh: 6.6secs
0-60mph 96.5kmh: 9.5secs
0-1/4 mile: 17.0secs
0-1km: 31.7secs
136.0bhp 101.4kW 137.9PS
@ 5700rpm
137.3lbft 186.0Nm @ 3500rpm
103.8bhp/ton 102.1bhp/tonne
61.1bhp/L 45.6kW/L 61.9PS/L
53.8ft/sec 16.4m/sec
20.5mph 33.0kmh/1000rpm
27.0mpg 22.5mpgUS 10.5L/100km
Petrol 4-stroke piston
2226cc 136.0cu in
In-line 5 fuel injection
Compression ratio: 10.0:1
Bore: 81.0mm 3.2in
Stroke: 86.4mm 3.4in
Valve type/No: Overhead 10
Transmission: Manual
No. of forward speeds: 5
Wheels driven: 4-wheel drive
Springs F/R: Coil/Coil
Brake system: PA ABS
Brakes F/R: Disc/Disc
Steering: Rack & pinion PA
Wheelbase: 254.8cm 100.3in
Track F: 145.3cm 57.2in
Track R: 143.7cm 56.6in
Length: 436.6cm 171.9in
Width: 171.6cm 67.6in
Height: 136.5cm 53.7in
Ground clearance: 12.9cm 5.1in
Kerb weight: 1332.0kg 2933.9lb
Fuel: 68.2L 15.0gal 18.0galUS

328 Audi
80 2.0E
1990 Germany
121.0mph 194.7kmh
0-50mph 80.5kmh: 7.7secs
0-60mph 96.5kmh: 10.6secs
0-1/4 mile: 18.4secs
0-1km: 33.6secs
113.0bhp 84.3kW 114.6PS
@ 5300rpm
125.5lbft 170.0Nm @ 3250rpm
100.4bhp/ton 98.7bhp/tonne
57.0bhp/L 42.5kW/L 57.7PS/L
53.7ft/sec 16.4m/sec
21.1mph 33.9kmh/1000rpm
25.4mpg 21.1mpgUS 11.1L/100km
Petrol 4-stroke piston
1984cc 121.0cu in
In-line 4 fuel injection
Compression ratio: 10.5:1
Bore: 82.5mm 3.2in
Stroke: 92.8mm 3.6in
Valve type/No: Overhead 8
Transmission: Manual
No. of forward speeds: 5
Wheels driven: Front
Springs F/R: Coil/Coil
Brake system: PA ABS
Brakes F/R: Disc/Disc
Steering: Rack & pinion PA
Wheelbase: 254.5cm 100.2in
Track F: 141.0cm 55.5in
Track R: 143.0cm 56.3in
Length: 439.2cm 172.9in
Width: 169.4cm 66.7in
Height: 139.7cm 55.0in
Ground clearance: 11.9cm 4.7in
Kerb weight: 1145.0kg 2522.0lb
Fuel: 68.2L 15.0gal 18.0galUS

329 Audi
90 Quattro
1990 Germany
130.0mph 209.2kmh
0-50mph 80.5kmh: 6.4secs
0-60mph 96.5kmh: 9.0secs
0-1/4 mile: 16.6secs
164.0bhp 122.3kW 166.3PS
@ 6000rpm
157.0lbft 212.7Nm @ 4500rpm
115.5bhp/ton 113.6bhp/tonne
71.0bhp/L 53.0kW/L 72.0PS/L
56.7ft/sec 17.3m/sec
21.6mpg 18.0mpgUS 13.1L/100km
Petrol 4-stroke piston
2309cc 140.9cu in
In-line 5 fuel injection
Compression ratio: 10.3:1
Bore: 82.5mm 3.2in
Stroke: 86.4mm 3.4in
Valve type/No: Overhead 20
Transmission: Manual
No. of forward speeds: 5
Wheels driven: Front
Springs F/R: Coil/Coil
Brake system: PA ABS
Brakes F/R: Disc/Disc
Steering: Rack & pinion PA
Wheelbase: 254.0cm 100.0in
Track F: 141.2cm 55.6in
Track R: 143.0cm 56.3in
Length: 447.8cm 176.3in
Width: 169.4cm 66.7in
Height: 139.2cm 54.8in
Kerb weight: 1443.7kg 3180.0lb
Fuel: 70.0L 15.4gal 18.5galUS

330 Audi
Quattro 20v
1990 Germany
142.0mph 228.5kmh
0-50mph 80.5kmh: 4.3secs
0-60mph 96.5kmh: 6.3secs
0-1/4 mile: 14.5secs
0-1km: 26.9secs
220.0bhp 164.0kW 223.0PS
@ 5900rpm
228.0lbft 309.0Nm @ 1950rpm
160.4bhp/ton 157.7bhp/tonne
98.8bhp/L 73.7kW/L 100.2PS/L
55.6ft/sec 16.9m/sec
22.1mph 35.6kmh/1000rpm
19.1mpg 15.9mpgUS 14.8L/100km
Petrol 4-stroke piston
2226cc 136.0cu in turbocharged
In-line 5 fuel injection
Compression ratio: 9.3:1
Bore: 81.0mm 3.2in
Stroke: 86.0mm 3.4in
Valve type/No: Overhead 20
Transmission: Manual
No. of forward speeds: 5
Wheels driven: 4-wheel drive
Springs F/R: Coil/Coil
Brake system: PA ABS
Brakes F/R: Disc/Disc
Steering: Rack & pinion PA
Wheelbase: 252.4cm 99.4in
Track F: 146.1cm 57.5in
Track R: 149.4cm 58.8in
Length: 440.4cm 173.4in
Width: 172.3cm 67.8in
Height: 134.4cm 52.9in
Ground clearance: 15.3cm 6.0in
Kerb weight: 1395.0kg 3072.7lb
Fuel: 90.1L 19.8gal 23.8galUS

331 Audi
V8 Quattro
1990 Germany
144.0mph 231.7kmh
0-50mph 80.5kmh: 6.8secs
0-60mph 96.5kmh: 9.0secs
0-1/4 mile: 16.8secs
250.0bhp 186.4kW 253.5PS
@ 5800rpm
215.0lbft 291.3Nm @ 4000rpm
139.7bhp/ton 137.4bhp/tonne
70.2bhp/L 52.3kW/L 71.2PS/L
54.8ft/sec 16.7m/sec
24.5mph 39.4kmh/1000rpm
15.3mpg 12.7mpgUS 18.5L/100km
Petrol 4-stroke piston
3562cc 217.3cu in
Vee 8 fuel injection
Compression ratio: 10.6:1
Bore: 81.0mm 3.2in
Stroke: 86.4mm 3.4in
Valve type/No: Overhead 32
Transmission: Automatic
No. of forward speeds: 4
Wheels driven: 4-wheel drive
Springs F/R: Coil/Coil
Brake system: PA ABS
Brakes F/R: Disc/Disc
Steering: Rack & pinion PA
Wheelbase: 269.2cm 106.0in
Track F: 151.4cm 59.6in
Track R: 152.9cm 60.2in
Length: 487.2cm 191.8in
Width: 181.4cm 71.4in
Height: 142.0cm 55.9in
Ground clearance: 10.2cm 4.0in
Kerb weight: 1820.1kg 4009.0lb
Fuel: 80.1L 17.6gal 21.1galUS

332 Audi
V8 Quattro Automatic
1990 Germany
144.0mph 231.7kmh
0-50mph 80.5kmh: 6.8secs
0-60mph 96.5kmh: 9.0secs
0-1/4 mile: 16.8secs
0-1km: 29.9secs
250.0bhp 186.4kW 253.5PS
@ 5800rpm
250.9lbft 340.0Nm @ 4000rpm
139.7bhp/ton 137.4bhp/tonne
70.2bhp/L 52.3kW/L 71.2PS/L
54.8ft/sec 16.7m/sec
24.5mph 39.4kmh/1000rpm
15.3mpg 12.7mpgUS 18.5L/100km
Petrol 4-stroke piston
3562cc 217.0cu in
Vee 8 fuel injection
Compression ratio: 10.6:1
Bore: 81.0mm 3.2in
Stroke: 86.4mm 3.4in
Valve type/No: Overhead 32
Transmission: Automatic
No. of forward speeds: 4
Wheels driven: 4-wheel drive
Springs F/R: Coil/Coil
Brake system: PA ABS
Brakes F/R: Disc/Disc
Steering: Rack & pinion PA
Wheelbase: 270.2cm 106.4in
Track F: 151.4cm 59.6in
Track R: 153.1cm 60.3in
Length: 487.4cm 191.9in
Width: 181.4cm 71.4in
Height: 142.0cm 55.9in
Ground clearance: 10.2cm 4.0in
Kerb weight: 1820.0kg 4008.8lb
Fuel: 80.1L 17.6gal 21.1galUS

333 Audi
100 2.8E Auto
1991 Germany
136.0mph 218.8kmh
0-50mph 80.5kmh: 7.0secs
0-60mph 96.5kmh: 9.3secs
0-1/4 mile: 17.2secs
0-1km: 31.1secs
174.0bhp 129.7kW 176.4PS
@ 5500rpm
184.5lbft 250.0Nm @ 4000rpm
117.6bhp/ton 115.6bhp/tonne
62.8bhp/L 46.8kW/L 63.7PS/L
51.9ft/sec 15.8m/sec
24.8mph 39.9kmh/1000rpm
19.0mpg 15.8mpgUS 14.9L/100km
Petrol 4-stroke piston
2771cc 169.0cu in
Vee 6 fuel injection
Compression ratio: 10.0:1
Bore: 82.5mm 3.2in
Stroke: 86.4mm 3.4in
Valve type/No: Overhead 12
Transmission: Automatic
No. of forward speeds: 4
Wheels driven: Front
Springs F/R: Coil/Coil
Brake system: PA ABS
Brakes F/R: Disc/Disc
Steering: Rack & pinion PA
Wheelbase: 268.7cm 105.8in
Track F: 152.8cm 60.2in
Track R: 152.4cm 60.0in
Length: 479.0cm 188.6in
Width: 177.7cm 70.0in
Height: 142.0cm 55.9in
Ground clearance: 10.0cm 3.9in
Kerb weight: 1505.0kg 3315.0lb
Fuel: 80.0L 17.6gal 21.1galUS

334 Audi
200 Quattro
1991 Germany
150.0mph 241.4kmh
0-60mph 96.5kmh: 7.2secs
0-1/4 mile: 15.4secs
217.0bhp 161.8kW 220.0PS
@ 5700rpm
228.0lbft 308.9Nm @ 1950rpm
133.4bhp/ton 131.1bhp/tonne
97.5bhp/L 72.7kW/L 98.8PS/L
53.8ft/sec 16.4m/sec
23.4mpg 19.5mpgUS 12.1L/100km
Petrol 4-stroke piston
2226cc 135.8cu in turbocharged
In-line 5 fuel injection
Compression ratio: 9.3:1
Bore: 81.0mm 3.2in
Stroke: 86.4mm 3.4in
Valve type/No: Overhead 20
Transmission: Manual
No. of forward speeds: 5
Wheels driven: 4-wheel drive
Springs F/R: Coil/Coil
Brake system: PA ABS
Brakes F/R: Disc/Disc
Steering: Rack & pinion PA
Wheelbase: 269.5cm 106.1in
Track F: 151.4cm 59.6in
Track R: 151.1cm 59.5in
Length: 491.2cm 193.4in
Width: 181.4cm 71.4in
Height: 142.5cm 56.1in
Kerb weight: 1654.8kg 3645.0lb
Fuel: 79.9L 17.6gal 21.1galUS

335 Audi
80 16v Sport
1991 Germany
132.0mph 212.4kmh
0-50mph 80.5kmh: 6.3secs
0-60mph 96.5kmh: 8.7secs
0-1/4 mile: 16.7secs
0-1km: 30.2secs
137.0bhp 102.2kW 138.9PS
@ 5800rpm
132.8lbft 180.0Nm @ 4500rpm
115.1bhp/ton 113.2bhp/tonne
69.0bhp/L 51.5kW/L 70.0PS/L
59.0ft/sec 18.0m/sec
21.1mph 33.9kmh/1000rpm
28.0mpg 23.3mpgUS 10.1L/100km
Petrol 4-stroke piston
1984cc 121.0cu in
In-line 4 fuel injection
Compression ratio: 10.8:1
Bore: 83.0mm 3.3in
Stroke: 93.0mm 3.7in
Valve type/No: Overhead 16
Transmission: Manual
No. of forward speeds: 5
Wheels driven: Front
Springs F/R: Coil/Coil
Brake system: PA ABS
Brakes F/R: Disc/Disc
Steering: Rack & pinion PA
Wheelbase: 254.5cm 100.2in
Track F: 141.0cm 55.5in
Track R: 143.0cm 56.3in
Length: 439.2cm 172.9in
Width: 169.4cm 66.7in
Height: 139.7cm 55.0in
Ground clearance: 11.9cm 4.7in
Kerb weight: 1210.0kg 2665.2lb
Fuel: 68.2L 15.0gal 18.0galUS

336 Audi
90 Quattro 20v
1991 Germany
0-60mph 96.5kmh: 9.4secs
0-1/4 mile: 16.9secs
164.0bhp 122.3kW 166.3PS
@ 6000rpm
157.0lbft 212.7Nm @ 4500rpm
115.0bhp/ton 113.1bhp/tonne
71.0bhp/L 53.0kW/L 72.0PS/L
56.7ft/sec 17.3m/sec
29.2mpg 24.3mpgUS 9.7L/100km
Petrol 4-stroke piston
2309cc 140.9cu in
In-line 5
Bore: 82.5mm 3.2in
Stroke: 86.4mm 3.4in
Valve type/No: Overhead 20
Transmission: Manual
No. of forward speeds: 5
Wheels driven: 4-wheel drive
Springs F/R: Coil/Coil
Brake system: ABS
Brakes F/R: Disc/Disc
Steering: Rack & pinion PA
Wheelbase: 253.7cm 99.9in
Track F: 141.2cm 55.6in
Track R: 143.0cm 56.3in
Length: 447.8cm 176.3in
Width: 169.4cm 66.7in
Height: 139.2cm 54.8in
Kerb weight: 1450.5kg 3195.0lb

337 Audi
Coupe S2
1991 Germany
153.0mph 246.2kmh
0-50mph 80.5kmh: 4.6secs
0-60mph 96.5kmh: 5.9secs
0-1/4 mile: 14.5secs
0-1km: 26.7secs
220.0bhp 164.0kW 223.0PS
@ 5900rpm
228.0lbft 309.0Nm @ 1950rpm
151.7bhp/ton 149.1bhp/tonne
98.8bhp/L 73.7kW/L 100.2PS/L
55.6ft/sec 16.9m/sec
24.7mph 39.7kmh/1000rpm
18.2mpg 15.2mpgUS 15.5L/100km
Petrol 4-stroke piston
2226cc 136.0cu in turbocharged
In-line 5 fuel injection
Compression ratio: 9.3:1
Bore: 81.0mm 3.2in
Stroke: 86.0mm 3.4in
Valve type/No: Overhead 20
Transmission: Manual
No. of forward speeds: 5
Wheels driven: 4-wheel drive
Springs F/R: Coil/Coil
Brake system: PA ABS
Brakes F/R: Disc/Disc
Steering: Rack & pinion PA
Wheelbase: 252.5cm 99.4in
Track F: 146.3cm 57.6in
Track R: 142.7cm 56.2in
Length: 436.6cm 171.9in
Width: 171.7cm 67.6in
Height: 127.0cm 50.0in
Ground clearance: 12.7cm 5.0in
Kerb weight: 1475.0kg 3248.9lb
Fuel: 54.6L 12.0gal 14.4galUS

338 Audi
V8 Quattro

1991 Germany
152.0mph 244.6kmh
0-50mph 80.5kmh: 5.8secs
0-60mph 96.5kmh: 7.5secs
0-1/4 mile: 15.6secs
240.0bhp 179.0kW 243.3PS
@ 5800rpm
245.0lbft 332.0Nm @ 4000rpm
137.7bhp/ton 135.4bhp/tonne
67.4bhp/L 50.2kW/L 68.3PS/L
54.8ft/sec 16.7m/sec
19.2mpg 16.0mpgUS 14.7L/100km
Petrol 4-stroke piston
3562cc 217.3cu in
Vee 8 fuel injection
Compression ratio: 10.6:1
Bore: 81.0mm 3.2in
Stroke: 86.4mm 3.4in
Valve type/No: Overhead 32
Transmission: Manual
No. of forward speeds: 5
Wheels driven: 4-wheel drive
Springs F/R: Coil/Coil
Brake system: ABS
Brakes F/R: Disc/Disc
Steering: Rack & pinion PA
Wheelbase: 270.3cm 106.4in
Track F: 151.4cm 59.6in
Track R: 153.2cm 60.3in
Length: 487.4cm 191.9in
Width: 181.4cm 71.4in
Height: 142.0cm 55.9in
Kerb weight: 1772.9kg 3905.0lb
Fuel: 79.9L 17.6gal 21.1galUS

339 Audi

80 2.8E V6 Quattro
1992 Germany
134.0mph 215.6kmh
0-50mph 80.5kmh: 6.2secs
0-60mph 96.5kmh: 8.3secs
0-1/4 mile: 16.5secs
0-1km: 30.2secs
174.0bhp 129.7kW 176.4PS
@ 5500rpm
184.0lbft 249.3Nm @ 3000rpm
121.6bhp/ton 119.6bhp/tonne
62.8bhp/L 46.8kW/L 63.7PS/L
51.9ft/sec 15.8m/sec
22.7mph 36.5kmh/1000rpm
20.0mpg 16.7mpgUS 14.1L/100km
Petrol 4-stroke piston
2771cc 169.1cu in
Vee 6 fuel injection
Compression ratio: 10.0:1
Bore: 82.5mm 3.2in
Stroke: 86.4mm 3.4in
Valve type/No: Overhead 12
Transmission: Manual
No. of forward speeds: 5
Wheels driven: 4-wheel drive
Springs F/R: Coil/Coil
Brake system: PA
Brakes F/R: Disc/Disc
Steering: Rack & pinion PA
Wheelbase: 261.4cm 102.9in
Track F: 144.8cm 57.0in
Track R: 147.3cm 58.0in
Length: 448.3cm 176.5in
Width: 193.8cm 76.3in
Height: 140.7cm 55.4in
Ground clearance: 13.5cm 5.3in
Kerb weight: 1455.1kg 3205.0lb
Fuel: 64.2L 14.1gal 16.9galUS

340 Austin

7 Tourer
1929 UK
51.0mph 82.1kmh
10.5bhp 7.8kW 10.6PS
@ 2400rpm
23.3bhp/ton 22.9bhp/tonne
14.1bhp/L 10.5kW/L 14.3PS/L
19.9ft/sec 6.1m/sec
38.0mpg 31.6mpgUS 7.4L/100km
Petrol 4-stroke piston
747cc 45.6cu in
In-line 4 1 Carburettor
Compression ratio: 5.1:1
Bore: 56.0mm 2.2in
Stroke: 76.0mm 3.0in
Valve type/No: Side 8
Transmission: Manual
No. of forward speeds: 3
Wheels driven: Rear
Brakes F/R: Drum/Drum
Wheelbase: 190.5cm 75.0in
Track F: 101.6cm 40.0in
Track R: 101.6cm 40.0in
Length: 279.4cm 110.0in
Width: 116.8cm 46.0in
Kerb weight: 457.6kg 1008.0lb
Fuel: 18.2L 4.0gal 4.8galUS

341 Austin

7 Saloon
1931 UK
47.6mph 76.6kmh
10.5bhp 7.8kW 10.6PS
@ 2400rpm
19.5bhp/ton 19.2bhp/tonne
14.1bhp/L 10.5kW/L 14.3PS/L
19.9ft/sec 6.1m/sec
45.0mpg 37.5mpgUS 6.3L/100km
Petrol 4-stroke piston
747cc 45.6cu in
In-line 4 1 Carburettor
Compression ratio: 5.1:1
Bore: 56.0mm 2.2in
Stroke: 76.0mm 3.0in
Valve type/No: Side 8
Transmission: Manual
No. of forward speeds: 3
Wheels driven: Rear
Brakes F/R: Drum/Drum
Wheelbase: 205.7cm 81.0in
Track F: 101.6cm 40.0in
Track R: 109.2cm 43.0in
Length: 294.6cm 116.0in
Width: 134.6cm 53.0in
Height: 158.8cm 62.5in
Kerb weight: 546.6kg 1204.0lb
Fuel: 22.7L 5.0gal 6.0galUS

342 Austin

7 Sports Two-seater
1931 UK
65.6mph 105.6kmh
10.5bhp 7.8kW 10.6PS
@ 2400rpm
24.7bhp/ton 24.3bhp/tonne
14.1bhp/L 10.5kW/L 14.3PS/L
19.9ft/sec 6.1m/sec
35.0mpg 29.1mpgUS 8.1L/100km
Petrol 4-stroke piston
747cc 45.6cu in
In-line 4 1 Carburettor
Compression ratio: 5.0:1
Bore: 56.0mm 2.2in
Stroke: 76.0mm 3.0in
Valve type/No: Side 8
Transmission: Manual
No. of forward speeds: 3
Wheels driven: Rear
Brakes F/R: Drum/Drum
Wheelbase: 190.5cm 75.0in
Track F: 101.6cm 40.0in
Track R: 101.6cm 40.0in
Length: 304.8cm 120.0in
Width: 119.4cm 47.0in
Height: 140.2cm 55.2in
Kerb weight: 432.2kg 952.0lb
Fuel: 26.2L 5.7gal 6.9galUS

343 Austin

7 Sunshine Saloon
1931 UK
52.6mph 84.6kmh
10.5bhp 7.8kW 10.6PS
@ 2400rpm
21.5bhp/ton 21.2bhp/tonne
14.1bhp/L 10.5kW/L 14.3PS/L
19.9ft/sec 6.1m/sec
40.0mpg 33.3mpgUS 7.1L/100km
Petrol 4-stroke piston
747cc 45.6cu in
In-line 4 1 Carburettor
Compression ratio: 5.0:1
Bore: 56.0mm 2.2in
Stroke: 76.0mm 3.0in
Valve type/No: Side 8
Transmission: Manual
No. of forward speeds: 3
Wheels driven: Rear
Brakes F/R: Drum/Drum
Wheelbase: 190.5cm 75.0in
Track F: 101.6cm 40.0in
Track R: 101.6cm 40.0in
Length: 281.9cm 111.0in
Width: 127.0cm 50.0in
Height: 158.8cm 62.5in
Kerb weight: 495.8kg 1092.0lb
Fuel: 22.7L 5.0gal 6.0galUS

344 Austin

10/4 Saloon
1934 UK
54.0mph 86.9kmh
0-50mph 80.5kmh: 40.0secs
34.0mpg 28.3mpgUS 8.3L/100km
Petrol 4-stroke piston
1125cc 68.6cu in
In-line 4
Bore: 63.5mm 2.5in
Stroke: 89.0mm 3.5in
Transmission: Manual
No. of forward speeds: 4
Wheels driven: Rear
Brakes F/R: Drum/Drum
Kerb weight: 864.4kg 1904.0lb
Fuel: 27.3L 6.0gal 7.2galUS

345 Austin

12/6
1934 UK
68.1mph 109.6kmh
0-50mph 80.5kmh: 17.2secs
24.0bhp 17.9kW 24.3PS
@ 2400rpm
24.0bhp/ton 23.6bhp/tonne
16.0bhp/L 12.0kW/L 16.3PS/L
22.2ft/sec 6.8m/sec
24.0mpg 20.0mpgUS 11.8L/100km
Petrol 4-stroke piston
1496cc 91.3cu in
In-line 6 1 Carburettor
Bore: 61.2mm 2.4in
Stroke: 84.6mm 3.3in
Valve type/No: Side 12
Transmission: Manual
No. of forward speeds: 4
Wheels driven: Rear
Brakes F/R: Drum/Drum
Kerb weight: 1017.0kg 2240.0lb
Fuel: 36.4L 8.0gal 9.6galUS

346 Austin

15.9hp Ascot Saloon
1934 UK
60.7mph 97.7kmh
0-50mph 80.5kmh: 28.6secs
24.0mpg 20.0mpgUS 11.8L/100km
Petrol 4-stroke piston
1711cc 104.4cu in
In-line 6
Bore: 65.5mm 2.6in
Stroke: 84.6mm 3.3in
Transmission: Manual
No. of forward speeds: 4
Wheels driven: Rear
Brakes F/R: Drum/Drum
Kerb weight: 1156.8kg 2548.0lb
Fuel: 36.4L 8.0gal 9.6galUS

347 Austin

20 Ranelagh Landaulet
1934 UK
61.6mph 99.1kmh
0-50mph 80.5kmh: 27.6secs
17.0mpg 14.2mpgUS 16.6L/100km
Petrol 4-stroke piston
3400cc 207.4cu in
In-line 6 1 Carburettor
Bore: 79.5mm 3.1in
Stroke: 114.5mm 4.5in
Valve type/No: Side 12
Transmission: Manual
No. of forward speeds: 4
Wheels driven: Rear
Brakes F/R: Drum/Drum
Kerb weight: 1932.2kg 4256.0lb
Fuel: 72.8L 16.0gal 19.2galUS

348 Austin

16 Hertford Saloon
1935 UK
60.8mph 97.8kmh
0-50mph 80.5kmh: 29.4secs
22.0mpg 18.3mpgUS 12.8L/100km
Petrol 4-stroke piston
2249cc 137.2cu in
In-line 6
Bore: 65.5mm 2.6in
Stroke: 111.0mm 4.4in
Valve type/No: Side 12
Transmission: Manual
No. of forward speeds: 4
Wheels driven: Rear
Brakes F/R: Drum/Drum
Kerb weight: 1487.3kg 3276.0lb
Fuel: 45.5L 10.0gal 12.0galUS

349 Austin

7 Ruby Saloon
1935 UK
50.8mph 81.7kmh
12.0bhp 8.9kW 12.2PS
19.8bhp/ton 19.5bhp/tonne
16.1bhp/L 12.0kW/L 16.3PS/L
45.0mpg 37.5mpgUS 6.3L/100km
Petrol 4-stroke piston
747cc 45.6cu in
In-line 4 1 Carburettor
Bore: 56.0mm 2.2in
Stroke: 76.0mm 3.0in
Valve type/No: Side 8
Transmission: Manual
No. of forward speeds: 4
Wheels driven: Rear
Brakes F/R: Drum/Drum
Ground clearance: 16.8cm 6.6in
Kerb weight: 616.5kg 1358.0lb
Fuel: 22.7L 5.0gal 6.0galUS

350 Austin

20 Mayfair Limousine
1936 UK
67.1mph 108.0kmh
0-50mph 80.5kmh: 25.2secs
0-60mph 96.5kmh: 45.4secs
17.0mpg 14.2mpgUS 16.6L/100km
Petrol 4-stroke piston
3400cc 207.4cu in
In-line 6 1 Carburettor
Bore: 79.5mm 3.1in
Stroke: 114.5mm 4.5in
Valve type/No: Side 12
Transmission: Manual
No. of forward speeds: 4
Wheels driven: Rear
Brakes F/R: Drum/Drum
Kerb weight: 2056.6kg 4530.0lb
Fuel: 72.8L 16.0gal 19.2galUS

351 Austin

7 Ruby Saloon
1936 UK
52.9mph 85.1kmh
0-50mph 80.5kmh: 58.0secs
12.0bhp 8.9kW 12.2PS
18.7bhp/ton 18.4bhp/tonne
16.1bhp/L 12.0kW/L 16.3PS/L
42.0mpg 35.0mpgUS 6.7L/100km
Petrol 4-stroke piston
747cc 45.6cu in
In-line 4 1 Carburettor
Bore: 56.0mm 2.2in
Stroke: 76.0mm 3.0in
Valve type/No: Side 8
Transmission: Manual
No. of forward speeds: 4
Wheels driven: Rear
Brakes F/R: Drum/Drum
Kerb weight: 653.8kg 1440.0lb
Fuel: 22.7L 5.0gal 6.0galUS

352 Austin

10 Cambridge
1937 UK
60.8mph 97.8kmh
0-50mph 80.5kmh: 36.5secs
32.0bhp 23.9kW 32.4PS
33.3bhp/ton 32.7bhp/tonne
28.4bhp/L 21.2kW/L 28.8PS/L
28.0mpg 23.3mpgUS 10.1L/100km
Petrol 4-stroke piston
1125cc 68.6cu in
In-line 4 1 Carburettor
Compression ratio: 6.5:1
Bore: 63.5mm 2.5in
Stroke: 89.0mm 3.5in
Valve type/No: Side 8
Transmission: Manual
No. of forward speeds: 4
Wheels driven: Rear
Brakes F/R: Drum/Drum
Kerb weight: 977.0kg 2152.0lb
Fuel: 27.3L 6.0gal 7.2galUS

353 Austin
14 Goodwood Saloon
1937 UK
62.9mph 101.2kmh
0-50mph 80.5kmh: 29.3secs
52.0bhp 38.8kW 52.7PS
@ 4200rpm
42.9bhp/ton 42.2bhp/tonne
30.4bhp/L 22.7kW/L 30.8PS/L
38.8ft/sec 11.8m/sec
22.0mpg 18.3mpgUS 12.8L/100km
Petrol 4-stroke piston
1711cc 104.4cu in
In-line 6
Bore: 65.6mm 2.6in
Stroke: 84.6mm 3.3in
Valve type/No: Side 12
Transmission: Manual
No. of forward speeds: 4
Wheels driven: Rear
Brakes F/R: Drum/Drum
Kerb weight: 1232.2kg 2714.0lb
Fuel: 36.4L 8.0gal 9.6galUS

354 Austin
Big 7
1937 UK
57.3mph 92.2kmh
0-50mph 80.5kmh: 37.9secs
25.0bhp 18.6kW 25.3PS
33.5bhp/ton 33.0bhp/tonne
27.8bhp/L 20.7kW/L 28.2PS/L
35.0mpg 29.1mpgUS 8.1L/100km
Petrol 4-stroke piston
900cc 54.9cu in
In-line 4
Bore: 56.8mm 2.2in
Stroke: 89.0mm 3.5in
Valve type/No: Side 8
Transmission: Manual
No. of forward speeds: 4
Wheels driven: Rear
Brakes F/R: Drum/Drum
Kerb weight: 757.7kg 1669.0lb
Fuel: 27.3L 6.0gal 7.2galUS

355 Austin
14
1938 UK
68.4mph 110.1kmh
0-50mph 80.5kmh: 23.4secs
0-60mph 96.5kmh: 35.4secs
52.0bhp 38.8kW 52.7PS
@ 4200rpm
43.2bhp/ton 42.5bhp/tonne
30.4bhp/L 22.7kW/L 30.8PS/L
38.8ft/sec 11.8m/sec
22.0mpg 18.3mpgUS 12.8L/100km
Petrol 4-stroke piston
1711cc 104.4cu in
In-line 6
Bore: 65.5mm 2.6in
Stroke: 84.6mm 3.3in
Valve type/No: Side 12
Transmission: Manual
No. of forward speeds: 4
Wheels driven: Rear
Brakes F/R: Drum/Drum
Kerb weight: 1223.1kg 2694.0lb
Fuel: 36.4L 8.0gal 9.6galUS

356 Austin
8 Saloon
1939 UK
56.9mph 91.6kmh
0-50mph 80.5kmh: 38.9secs
24.0bhp 17.9kW 24.3PS
@ 4400rpm
31.2bhp/ton 30.7bhp/tonne
26.7bhp/L 19.9kW/L 27.0PS/L
42.8ft/sec 13.0m/sec
38.0mpg 31.6mpgUS 7.4L/100km
Petrol 4-stroke piston
900cc 54.9cu in
In-line 4 1 Carburettor
Compression ratio: 6.8:1
Bore: 56.8mm 2.2in
Stroke: 89.0mm 3.5in
Valve type/No: Side 8
Transmission: Manual
No. of forward speeds: 4
Wheels driven: Rear
Brakes F/R: Drum/Drum
Kerb weight: 781.8kg 1722.0lb
Fuel: 27.3L 6.0gal 7.2galUS

357 Austin
16 Saloon
1947 UK
75.0mph 120.7kmh
0-50mph 80.5kmh: 18.3secs
0-60mph 96.5kmh: 29.3secs
64.0bhp 47.7kW 64.9PS
@ 3800rpm
47.4bhp/ton 46.7bhp/tonne
29.1bhp/L 21.7kW/L 29.5PS/L
46.1ft/sec 14.1m/sec
20.0mpg 16.7mpgUS 14.1L/100km
Petrol 4-stroke piston
2199cc 134.2cu in
In-line 4
Compression ratio: 6.8:1
Bore: 79.3mm 3.1in
Stroke: 111.0mm 4.4in
Valve type/No: Overhead 8
Transmission: Manual
No. of forward speeds: 4
Wheels driven: Rear
Brakes F/R: Drum/Drum
Wheelbase: 265.4cm 104.5in
Track F: 135.9cm 53.5in
Track R: 142.2cm 56.0in
Length: 434.3cm 171.0in
Width: 170.2cm 67.0in
Height: 167.6cm 66.0in
Ground clearance: 17.0cm 6.7in
Kerb weight: 1371.5kg 3021.0lb
Fuel: 63.7L 14.0gal 16.8galUS

358 Austin
8 Saloon
1947 UK
61.0mph 98.1kmh
0-50mph 80.5kmh: 35.3secs
23.0bhp 17.1kW 23.3PS
@ 4000rpm
28.7bhp/ton 28.3bhp/tonne
25.6bhp/L 19.1kW/L 25.9PS/L
38.9ft/sec 11.9m/sec
37.0mpg 30.8mpgUS 7.6L/100km
Petrol 4-stroke piston
900cc 54.9cu in
In-line 4
Compression ratio: 6.8:1
Bore: 56.8mm 2.2in
Stroke: 89.0mm 3.5in
Valve type/No: Side 8
Transmission: Manual
No. of forward speeds: 4
Wheels driven: Rear
Brakes F/R: Drum/Drum
Wheelbase: 224.8cm 88.5in
Track F: 111.8cm 44.0in
Track R: 114.3cm 45.0in
Length: 378.5cm 149.0in
Width: 142.2cm 56.0in
Height: 160.0cm 63.0in
Ground clearance: 16.5cm 6.5in
Kerb weight: 813.6kg 1792.0lb
Fuel: 27.3L 6.0gal 7.2galUS

359 Austin
A125 Sheerline
1948 UK
83.0mph 133.5kmh
0-50mph 80.5kmh: 13.8secs
0-60mph 96.5kmh: 20.6secs
15.0mpg 12.5mpgUS 18.8L/100km
Petrol 4-stroke piston
3992cc 243.6cu in
In-line 6
Compression ratio: 6.8:1
Bore: 87.0mm 3.4in
Stroke: 111.0mm 4.4in
Valve type/No: Overhead 12
Transmission: Manual
No. of forward speeds: 4
Wheels driven: Front
Brakes F/R: Drum/Drum
Wheelbase: 302.3cm 119.0in
Track F: 147.3cm 58.0in
Track R: 152.4cm 60.0in
Length: 487.7cm 192.0in
Width: 185.4cm 73.0in
Height: 170.2cm 67.0in
Ground clearance: 16.5cm 6.5in
Kerb weight: 1973.5kg 4347.0lb
Fuel: 72.8L 16.0gal 19.2galUS

360 Austin
A40
1948 UK
60.0mph 96.5kmh
0-50mph 80.5kmh: 24.5secs
40.0bhp 29.8kW 40.5PS
@ 4300rpm
40.2bhp/ton 39.6bhp/tonne
33.3bhp/L 24.9kW/L 33.8PS/L
41.8ft/sec 12.8m/sec
35.0mpg 29.1mpgUS 8.1L/100km
Petrol 4-stroke piston
1200cc 73.2cu in
In-line 4
Compression ratio: 7.2:1
Bore: 65.5mm 2.6in
Stroke: 89.0mm 3.5in
Valve type/No: Overhead 8
Transmission: Manual
No. of forward speeds: 4
Wheels driven: Rear
Brakes F/R: Drum/Drum
Wheelbase: 235.0cm 92.5in
Track F: 123.2cm 48.5in
Track R: 125.7cm 49.5in
Length: 388.6cm 153.0in
Width: 154.9cm 61.0in
Height: 158.8cm 62.5in
Ground clearance: 17.0cm 6.7in
Kerb weight: 1010.6kg 2226.0lb
Fuel: 39.6L 8.7gal 10.5galUS

361 Austin
A135 Princess
1949 UK
89.0mph 143.2kmh
0-50mph 80.5kmh: 13.6secs
0-60mph 96.5kmh: 20.0secs
130.0bhp 96.9kW 131.8PS
@ 3700rpm
212.0lbft 287.3Nm @ 2200rpm
65.4bhp/ton 64.3bhp/tonne
32.5bhp/L 24.3kW/L 33.0PS/L
44.9ft/sec 13.7m/sec
20.2mph 32.5kmh/1000rpm
12.0mpg 10.0mpgUS 23.5L/100km
Petrol 4-stroke piston
3995cc 243.7cu in
In-line 6
Compression ratio: 6.8:1
Bore: 87.0mm 3.4in
Stroke: 111.0mm 4.4in
Valve type/No: Overhead 12
Transmission: Manual
No. of forward speeds: 4
Wheels driven: Rear
Brakes F/R: Drum/Drum
Wheelbase: 303.5cm 119.5in
Track F: 147.3cm 58.0in
Track R: 152.4cm 60.0in
Length: 491.5cm 193.5in
Width: 185.4cm 73.0in
Height: 167.6cm 66.0in
Ground clearance: 16.5cm 6.5in
Kerb weight: 2021.2kg 4452.0lb
Fuel: 72.8L 16.0gal 19.2galUS

362 Austin
A70
1949 UK
80.0mph 128.7kmh
0-50mph 80.5kmh: 14.9secs
0-60mph 96.5kmh: 22.9secs
67.0bhp 50.0kW 67.9PS
@ 3800rpm
52.5bhp/ton 51.7bhp/tonne
30.5bhp/L 22.7kW/L 30.9PS/L
46.1ft/sec 14.1m/sec
23.0mpg 19.2mpgUS 12.3L/100km
Petrol 4-stroke piston
2199cc 134.2cu in
In-line 4
Compression ratio: 6.8:1
Bore: 79.4mm 3.1in
Stroke: 111.1mm 4.4in
Valve type/No: Overhead 8
Transmission: Manual
No. of forward speeds: 4
Wheels driven: Rear
Brakes F/R: Drum/Drum
Wheelbase: 243.8cm 96.0in
Track F: 135.9cm 53.5in
Track R: 141.0cm 55.5in
Length: 414.5cm 163.2in
Width: 168.7cm 66.4in
Height: 165.1cm 65.0in
Ground clearance: 16.5cm 6.5in
Kerb weight: 1296.6kg 2856.0lb
Fuel: 56.9L 12.5gal 15.0galUS

363 Austin
A90 Atlantic
1949 UK
95.7mph 154.0kmh
0-50mph 80.5kmh: 13.7secs
0-60mph 96.5kmh: 18.4secs
88.0bhp 65.6kW 89.2PS
@ 4000rpm
140.0lbft 189.7Nm @ 2500rpm
65.8bhp/ton 64.7bhp/tonne
33.1bhp/L 24.7kW/L 33.5PS/L
48.6ft/sec 14.8m/sec
20.9mph 33.6kmh/1000rpm
22.0mpg 18.3mpgUS 12.8L/100km
Petrol 4-stroke piston
2660cc 162.3cu in
In-line 4 2 Carburettor
Compression ratio: 7.5:1
Bore: 87.3mm 3.4in
Stroke: 111.1mm 4.4in
Valve type/No: Overhead 8
Transmission: Manual
No. of forward speeds: 4
Wheels driven: Rear
Springs F/R: Coil/Leaf
Brakes F/R: Drum/Drum
Steering: Worm & peg
Wheelbase: 243.8cm 96.0in
Track F: 134.9cm 53.1in
Track R: 141.0cm 55.5in
Length: 449.8cm 177.1in
Width: 177.8cm 70.0in
Height: 152.4cm 60.0in
Ground clearance: 16.5cm 6.5in
Kerb weight: 1360.2kg 2996.0lb
Fuel: 56.9L 12.5gal 15.0galUS

364 Austin
A40
1951 UK
0-50mph 80.5kmh: 21.9secs
0-60mph 96.5kmh: 29.4secs
0-1/4 mile: 24.4secs
40.0bhp 29.8kW 40.5PS
@ 4300rpm
41.6bhp/ton 40.9bhp/tonne
33.3bhp/L 24.9kW/L 33.8PS/L
41.8ft/sec 12.7m/sec
Petrol 4-stroke piston
1200cc 73.2cu in
In-line 4
Bore: 65.5mm 2.6in
Stroke: 88.9mm 3.5in
Transmission: Manual
No. of forward speeds: 4
Wheels driven: Rear
Wheelbase: 235.0cm 92.5in
Track F: 123.2cm 48.5in
Track R: 125.7cm 49.5in
Length: 388.6cm 153.0in
Width: 154.9cm 61.0in
Height: 162.1cm 63.8in
Ground clearance: 19.1cm 7.5in
Kerb weight: 978.8kg 2156.0lb

365 Austin
A40 Sport
1951 UK
50.0bhp 37.3kW 50.7PS
@ 5000rpm
52.6bhp/ton 51.7bhp/tonne
41.7bhp/L 31.1kW/L 42.2PS/L
48.6ft/sec 14.8m/sec
30.0mpg 25.0mpgUS 9.4L/100km
Petrol 4-stroke piston
1200cc 73.2cu in
In-line 4 2 Carburettor
Bore: 65.5mm 2.6in
Stroke: 89.0mm 3.5in
Wheels driven: Rear
Wheelbase: 235.0cm 92.5in
Track F: 122.4cm 48.2in
Track R: 126.2cm 49.7in
Length: 403.9cm 159.0in
Width: 154.9cm 61.0in
Height: 146.1cm 57.5in
Ground clearance: 19.1cm 7.5in
Kerb weight: 966.1kg 2128.0lb

366 Austin
A40 Somerset
1952 UK
71.0mph 114.2kmh
0-50mph 80.5kmh: 19.8secs
0-60mph 96.5kmh: 36.6secs

0-1/4 mile: 24.3secs
42.0bhp 31.3kW 42.6PS
@ 4300rpm
62.0lbft 84.0Nm @ 2200rpm
41.5bhp/ton 40.8bhp/tonne
35.0bhp/L 26.1kW/L 35.5PS/L
41.8ft/sec 12.8m/sec
14.2mph 22.8kmh/1000rpm
28.5mpg 23.7mpgUS 9.9L/100km
Petrol 4-stroke piston
1200cc 73.2cu in
In-line 4 1 Carburettor
Compression ratio: 7.2:1
Bore: 65.4mm 2.6in
Stroke: 89.0mm 3.5in
Valve type/No: Overhead 8
Transmission: Manual
No. of forward speeds: 4
Wheels driven: Rear
Springs F/R: Coil/Leaf
Brakes F/R: Drum/Drum
Wheelbase: 235.0cm 92.5in
Track F: 122.2cm 48.1in
Track R: 127.0cm 50.0in
Length: 405.1cm 159.5in
Width: 160.0cm 63.0in
Height: 162.6cm 64.0in
Ground clearance: 19.1cm 7.5in
Kerb weight: 1029.7kg 2268.0lb
Fuel: 39.8L 8.8gal 10.5galUS

367 Austin

Princess
1952 UK
86.0mph 138.4kmh
0-50mph 80.5kmh: 13.1secs
0-60mph 96.5kmh: 19.5secs
130.0bhp 96.9kW 131.8PS
@ 3700rpm
212.0lbft 287.3Nm @ 2200rpm
66.7bhp/ton 65.5bhp/tonne
32.6bhp/L 24.3kW/L 33.0PS/L
44.9ft/sec 13.7m/sec
20.2mph 32.5kmh/1000rpm
15.0mpg 12.5mpgUS 18.8L/100km
Petrol 4-stroke piston
3993cc 243.6cu in
In-line 6
Compression ratio: 6.8:1
Bore: 87.3mm 3.4in
Stroke: 111.1mm 4.4in
Valve type/No: Overhead 12
Transmission: Manual
No. of forward speeds: 4
Wheels driven: Rear
Springs F/R: Coil/Leaf
Brakes F/R: Drum/Drum
Wheelbase: 302.8cm 119.2in
Track F: 147.3cm 58.0in
Track R: 152.4cm 60.0in
Length: 489.0cm 192.5in
Width: 183.4cm 72.2in
Height: 167.6cm 66.0in
Ground clearance: 16.5cm 6.5in
Kerb weight: 1983.1kg 4368.0lb
Fuel: 72.8L 16.0gal 19.2galUS

368 Austin

A30
1953 UK
63.0mph 101.4kmh
0-50mph 80.5kmh: 23.2secs
0-1/4 mile: 25.3secs
30.0bhp 22.4kW 30.4PS
@ 4800rpm
40.0lbft 54.2Nm @ 2400rpm
44.0bhp/ton 43.3bhp/tonne
37.5bhp/L 28.0kW/L 38.0PS/L
39.9ft/sec 12.2m/sec
12.6mph 20.3kmh/1000rpm
42.0mpg 35.0mpgUS 6.7L/100km
Petrol 4-stroke piston
800cc 48.8cu in
In-line 4 1 Carburettor
Compression ratio: 7.2:1
Bore: 58.0mm 2.3in
Stroke: 76.0mm 3.0in
Valve type/No: Overhead 8
Transmission: Manual
No. of forward speeds: 4
Wheels driven: Rear
Springs F/R: Coil/Leaf
Brakes F/R: Drum/Drum
Wheelbase: 201.9cm 79.5in
Track F: 114.8cm 45.2in
Track R: 113.5cm 44.7in
Length: 346.5cm 136.4in
Width: 140.2cm 55.2in
Height: 147.8cm 58.2in
Ground clearance: 16.3cm 6.4in
Kerb weight: 692.8kg 1526.0lb
Fuel: 25.9L 5.7gal 6.8galUS

369 Austin

A30
1954 UK
63.0mph 101.4kmh
0-50mph 80.5kmh: 18.0secs
0-1/4 mile: 26.7secs
28.0bhp 20.9kW 28.4PS
@ 4800rpm
40.0lbft 54.2Nm @ 2200rpm
39.8bhp/ton 39.2bhp/tonne
35.0bhp/L 26.1kW/L 35.5PS/L
39.9ft/sec 12.2m/sec
12.6mph 20.3kmh/1000rpm
42.8mpg 35.6mpgUS 6.6L/100km
Petrol 4-stroke piston
800cc 48.8cu in
In-line 4 1 Carburettor
Compression ratio: 7.2:1
Bore: 58.0mm 2.3in
Stroke: 76.0mm 3.0in
Valve type/No: Overhead 8
Transmission: Manual
No. of forward speeds: 4
Wheels driven: Rear
Springs F/R: Coil/Leaf
Brakes F/R: Drum/Drum
Wheelbase: 201.9cm 79.5in
Track F: 114.8cm 45.2in
Track R: 113.5cm 44.7in
Length: 346.5cm 136.4in
Width: 140.2cm 55.2in
Height: 147.8cm 58.2in
Ground clearance: 16.3cm 6.4in
Kerb weight: 715.0kg 1575.0lb
Fuel: 25.9L 5.7gal 6.8galUS

370 Austin

A40 Somerset Coupe
1954 UK
75.0mph 120.7kmh
0-50mph 80.5kmh: 19.8secs
0-60mph 96.5kmh: 33.9secs
0-1/4 mile: 24.3secs
42.0bhp 31.3kW 42.6PS
@ 4500rpm
58.0lbft 78.6Nm @ 2400rpm
41.3bhp/ton 40.7bhp/tonne
35.0bhp/L 26.1kW/L 35.5PS/L
43.8ft/sec 13.3m/sec
14.2mph 22.8kmh/1000rpm
30.1mpg 25.1mpgUS 9.4L/100km
Petrol 4-stroke piston
1200cc 73.2cu in
In-line 4
Compression ratio: 7.2:1
Bore: 65.5mm 2.6in
Stroke: 89.0mm 3.5in
Valve type/No: Overhead 8
Transmission: Manual
No. of forward speeds: 4
Wheels driven: Rear
Springs F/R: Coil/Leaf
Brakes F/R: Drum/Drum
Wheelbase: 235.0cm 92.5in
Track F: 122.2cm 48.1in
Track R: 127.0cm 50.0in
Length: 405.1cm 159.5in
Width: 160.0cm 63.0in
Height: 158.8cm 62.5in
Ground clearance: 19.1cm 7.5in
Kerb weight: 1032.8kg 2275.0lb
Fuel: 39.8L 8.8gal 10.5galUS

371 Austin

Princess
1954 UK
76.0mph 122.3kmh
0-50mph 80.5kmh: 16.9secs
0-60mph 96.5kmh: 26.0secs
0-1/4 mile: 23.1secs
19.1mph 30.7kmh/1000rpm
14.2mpg 11.8mpgUS 19.9L/100km
Petrol 4-stroke piston
3995cc 243.7cu in
In-line 6
Compression ratio: 6.8:1
Bore: 87.0mm 3.4in
Stroke: 111.0mm 4.4in
Valve type/No: Overhead 12
Transmission: Manual
No. of forward speeds: 4
Wheels driven: Rear
Springs F/R: Coil/Leaf
Brakes F/R: Drum/Drum
Wheelbase: 335.3cm 132.0in
Track F: 148.6cm 58.5in
Track R: 158.8cm 62.5in
Length: 546.1cm 215.0in
Width: 189.2cm 74.5in
Height: 177.8cm 70.0in
Ground clearance: 16.5cm 6.5in
Kerb weight: 2183.3kg 4809.0lb
Fuel: 72.8L 16.0gal 19.2galUS

372 Austin

A50 Cambridge
1955 UK
75.0mph 120.7kmh
0-50mph 80.5kmh: 16.7secs
0-60mph 96.5kmh: 26.0secs
0-1/4 mile: 23.5secs
50.0bhp 37.3kW 50.7PS
@ 4400rpm
70.0lbft 94.9Nm @ 2100rpm
48.9bhp/ton 48.1bhp/tonne
33.3bhp/L 24.9kW/L 33.8PS/L
42.8ft/sec 13.0m/sec
15.0mph 24.1kmh/1000rpm
28.4mpg 23.6mpgUS 9.9L/100km
Petrol 4-stroke piston
1500cc 91.5cu in
In-line 4
Compression ratio: 7.2:1
Bore: 73.0mm 2.9in
Stroke: 89.0mm 3.5in
Valve type/No: Overhead 8
Transmission: Manual
No. of forward speeds: 4
Wheels driven: Rear
Springs F/R: Coil/Leaf
Brakes F/R: Drum/Drum
Wheelbase: 252.0cm 99.2in
Track F: 121.9cm 48.0in
Track R: 124.5cm 49.0in
Length: 412.0cm 162.2in
Width: 156.2cm 61.5in
Height: 156.2cm 61.5in
Ground clearance: 17.8cm 7.0in
Kerb weight: 1039.2kg 2289.0lb
Fuel: 39.8L 8.8gal 10.5galUS

373 Austin

A90 Westminster
1955 UK
91.0mph 146.4kmh
0-50mph 80.5kmh: 12.9secs
0-60mph 96.5kmh: 18.1secs
0-1/4 mile: 20.7secs
85.0bhp 63.4kW 86.2PS
@ 4000rpm
130.0lbft 176.2Nm @ 2000rpm
64.5bhp/ton 63.5bhp/tonne
32.2bhp/L 24.0kW/L 32.7PS/L
38.9ft/sec 11.9m/sec
19.8mph 31.9kmh/1000rpm
22.0mpg 18.3mpgUS 12.8L/100km
Petrol 4-stroke piston
2639cc 161.0cu in
In-line 6
Compression ratio: 7.3:1
Bore: 79.4mm 3.1in
Stroke: 89.0mm 3.5in
Valve type/No: Overhead 12
Transmission: Manual
No. of forward speeds: 4
Wheels driven: Rear
Springs F/R: Coil/Leaf
Brakes F/R: Drum/Drum
Wheelbase: 263.4cm 103.7in
Track F: 130.8cm 51.5in
Track R: 130.8cm 51.5in
Length: 432.3cm 170.2in
Width: 162.6cm 64.0in
Height: 161.8cm 63.7in
Ground clearance: 18.8cm 7.4in
Kerb weight: 1339.3kg 2950.0lb
Fuel: 56.9L 12.5gal 15.0galUS

374 Austin

A105
1956 UK
95.0mph 152.9kmh
0-50mph 80.5kmh: 10.9secs
0-60mph 96.5kmh: 15.6secs
0-1/4 mile: 19.9secs
102.0bhp 76.1kW 103.4PS
@ 4600rpm
141.0lbft 191.1Nm @ 2600rpm
72.5bhp/ton 71.3bhp/tonne
38.6bhp/L 28.8kW/L 39.2PS/L
44.7ft/sec 13.6m/sec
26.9mph 43.3kmh/1000rpm
22.5mpg 18.7mpgUS 12.6L/100km
Petrol 4-stroke piston
2639cc 161.0cu in
In-line 6
Compression ratio: 8.2:1
Bore: 79.4mm 3.1in
Stroke: 89.0mm 3.5in
Valve type/No: Overhead 12
Transmission: Manual with overdrive
No. of forward speeds: 7
Wheels driven: Rear
Springs F/R: Coil/Leaf
Brakes F/R: Drum/Drum
Wheelbase: 263.4cm 103.7in
Track F: 130.8cm 51.5in
Track R: 130.8cm 51.5in
Length: 432.3cm 170.2in
Width: 162.6cm 64.0in
Height: 157.5cm 62.0in
Ground clearance: 18.8cm 7.4in
Kerb weight: 1431.0kg 3152.0lb
Fuel: 56.9L 12.5gal 15.0galUS

375 Austin

A30 Countryman
1956 UK
63.0mph 101.4kmh
0-1/4 mile: 28.3secs
28.0bhp 20.9kW 28.4PS
@ 4800rpm
40.0lbft 54.2Nm @ 2200rpm
36.1bhp/ton 35.5bhp/tonne
34.9bhp/L 26.0kW/L 35.3PS/L
39.9ft/sec 12.2m/sec
12.6mph 20.3kmh/1000rpm
40.2mpg 33.5mpgUS 7.0L/100km
Petrol 4-stroke piston
803cc 49.0cu in
In-line 4
Compression ratio: 7.2:1
Bore: 58.0mm 2.3in
Stroke: 76.0mm 3.0in
Valve type/No: Overhead 8
Transmission: Manual
No. of forward speeds: 4
Wheels driven: Rear
Springs F/R: Coil/Leaf
Brakes F/R: Drum/Drum
Wheelbase: 201.9cm 79.5in
Track F: 114.8cm 45.2in
Track R: 113.5cm 44.7in
Length: 350.0cm 137.8in
Width: 142.2cm 56.0in
Height: 160.0cm 63.0in
Ground clearance: 17.8cm 7.0in
Kerb weight: 788.1kg 1736.0lb
Fuel: 25.9L 5.7gal 6.8galUS

376 Austin

A55
1957 UK
76.5mph 123.1kmh
0-50mph 80.5kmh: 18.4secs
0-60mph 96.5kmh: 31.8secs
0-1/4 mile: 23.3secs
51.0bhp 38.0kW 51.7PS
@ 4250rpm
81.0lbft 109.8Nm @ 2000rpm
48.6bhp/ton 47.8bhp/tonne
34.2bhp/L 25.5kW/L 34.7PS/L
41.3ft/sec 12.6m/sec
15.8mph 25.4kmh/1000rpm
33.6mpg 28.0mpgUS 8.4L/100km
Petrol 4-stroke piston
1489cc 90.8cu in
In-line 4 1 Carburettor
Compression ratio: 8.3:1
Bore: 73.0mm 2.9in
Stroke: 89.0mm 3.5in
Valve type/No: Overhead 8
Transmission: Manual
No. of forward speeds: 4
Wheels driven: Rear
Springs F/R: Coil/Leaf
Brakes F/R: Drum/Drum
Wheelbase: 252.0cm 99.2in
Track F: 123.2cm 48.5in
Track R: 124.5cm 49.0in
Length: 423.7cm 166.8in
Width: 156.2cm 61.5in

Height: 153.7cm 60.5in
Ground clearance: 16.3cm 6.4in
Kerb weight: 1067.8kg 2352.0lb
Fuel: 39.8L 8.8gal 10.5galUS

377 Austin

A95 Westminster
1957 UK
91.0mph 146.4kmh
0-50mph 80.5kmh: 13.9secs
0-60mph 96.5kmh: 19.8secs
0-1/4 mile: 21.8secs
92.0bhp 68.6kW 93.3PS
@ 4500rpm
130.0lbft 176.2Nm @ 2000rpm
69.3bhp/ton 68.1bhp/tonne
34.9bhp/L 26.0kW/L 35.3PS/L
43.8ft/sec 13.3m/sec
26.9mph 43.3kmh/1000rpm
20.4mpg 17.0mpgUS 13.8L/100km
Petrol 4-stroke piston
2639cc 161.0cu in
In-line 6
Compression ratio: 8.2:1
Bore: 79.4mm 3.1in
Stroke: 89.0mm 3.5in
Valve type/No: Overhead 12
Transmission: Manual with overdrive
No. of forward speeds: 6
Wheels driven: Rear
Springs F/R: Coil/Leaf
Brakes F/R: Drum/Drum
Wheelbase: 268.5cm 105.7in
Track F: 130.8cm 51.5in
Track R: 130.0cm 51.2in
Length: 459.0cm 180.7in
Width: 162.6cm 64.0in
Height: 157.5cm 62.0in
Ground clearance: 19.6cm 7.7in
Kerb weight: 1350.6kg 2975.0lb
Fuel: 72.8L 16.0gal 19.2galUS

378 Austin

A105 Automatic
1958 UK
96.0mph 154.5kmh
0-50mph 80.5kmh: 13.5secs
0-60mph 96.5kmh: 18.3secs
0-1/4 mile: 22.0secs
102.0bhp 76.1kW 103.4PS
@ 4600rpm
142.0lbft 192.4Nm @ 2400rpm
74.3bhp/ton 73.1bhp/tonne
38.6bhp/L 28.8kW/L 39.2PS/L
44.7ft/sec 13.6m/sec
19.8mph 31.9kmh/1000rpm
20.8mpg 17.3mpgUS 13.6L/100km
Petrol 4-stroke piston
2639cc 161.0cu in
In-line 6 1 Carburettor
Compression ratio: 8.2:1
Bore: 79.4mm 3.1in
Stroke: 89.0mm 3.5in
Valve type/No: Overhead 12
Transmission: Automatic
No. of forward speeds: 3
Wheels driven: Rear
Springs F/R: Coil/Leaf
Brakes F/R: Drum/Drum
Wheelbase: 268.5cm 105.7in
Track F: 130.8cm 51.5in
Track R: 130.0cm 51.2in
Length: 459.0cm 180.7in
Width: 157.5cm 62.0in
Height: 162.6cm 64.0in
Ground clearance: 19.6cm 7.7in
Kerb weight: 1395.1kg 3073.0lb
Fuel: 72.8L 16.0gal 19.2galUS

379 Austin

A35 4-door
1958 UK
75.0mph 120.7kmh
0-50mph 80.5kmh: 19.1secs
0-60mph 96.5kmh: 31.0secs
0-1/4 mile: 23.7secs
34.0bhp 25.3kW 34.5PS
@ 4750rpm
50.0lbft 67.8Nm @ 2000rpm
48.4bhp/ton 47.5bhp/tonne
35.9bhp/L 26.7kW/L 36.4PS/L
39.6ft/sec 12.1m/sec
14.3mph 23.0kmh/1000rpm
41.8mpg 34.8mpgUS 6.8L/100km
Petrol 4-stroke piston
948cc 57.8cu in
In-line 4 1 Carburettor
Compression ratio: 8.3:1
Bore: 62.9mm 2.5in
Stroke: 76.2mm 3.0in
Valve type/No: Overhead 8
Transmission: Manual
No. of forward speeds: 4
Wheels driven: Rear
Springs F/R: Coil/Leaf
Brakes F/R: Drum/Drum
Wheelbase: 201.9cm 79.5in
Track F: 114.8cm 45.2in
Track R: 113.5cm 44.7in
Length: 346.7cm 136.5in
Width: 140.2cm 55.2in
Height: 150.4cm 59.2in
Ground clearance: 16.3cm 6.4in
Kerb weight: 715.0kg 1575.0lb
Fuel: 26.2L 5.7gal 6.9galUS

380 Austin

A40
1958 UK
73.0mph 117.5kmh
0-50mph 80.5kmh: 21.4secs
0-60mph 96.5kmh: 35.6secs
0-1/4 mile: 24.5secs
34.0bhp 25.3kW 34.5PS
@ 4750rpm
50.0lbft 67.8Nm @ 2000rpm
45.3bhp/ton 44.6bhp/tonne
35.9bhp/L 26.7kW/L 36.4PS/L
39.6ft/sec 12.1m/sec
14.2mph 22.8kmh/1000rpm
38.0mpg 31.6mpgUS 7.4L/100km
Petrol 4-stroke piston
948cc 57.8cu in
In-line 4 1 Carburettor
Compression ratio: 8.3:1
Bore: 62.9mm 2.5in
Stroke: 76.2mm 3.0in
Valve type/No: Overhead 8
Transmission: Manual
No. of forward speeds: 4
Wheels driven: Rear
Springs F/R: Coil/Leaf
Brakes F/R: Drum/Drum
Wheelbase: 212.1cm 83.5in
Track F: 120.7cm 47.5in
Track R: 119.4cm 47.0in
Length: 366.3cm 144.2in
Width: 150.6cm 59.3in
Height: 144.0cm 56.7in
Ground clearance: 15.7cm 6.2in
Kerb weight: 762.7kg 1680.0lb
Fuel: 27.3L 6.0gal 7.2galUS

381 Austin

A55
1958 UK
76.0mph 122.3kmh
0-50mph 80.5kmh: 18.7secs
0-60mph 96.5kmh: 29.3secs
0-1/4 mile: 23.7secs
51.0bhp 38.0kW 51.7PS
@ 4250rpm
81.0lbft 109.8Nm @ 2000rpm
48.2bhp/ton 47.4bhp/tonne
34.2bhp/L 25.5kW/L 34.7PS/L
41.3ft/sec 12.6m/sec
19.9mph 32.0kmh/1000rpm
35.7mpg 29.7mpgUS 7.9L/100km
Petrol 4-stroke piston
1489cc 90.8cu in
In-line 4 1 Carburettor
Compression ratio: 8.3:1
Bore: 73.0mm 2.9in
Stroke: 89.0mm 3.5in
Valve type/No: Overhead 8
Transmission: Manual with overdrive
No. of forward speeds: 6
Wheels driven: Rear
Springs F/R: Coil/Leaf
Brakes F/R: Drum/Drum
Wheelbase: 252.0cm 99.2in
Track F: 121.9cm 48.0in
Track R: 124.5cm 49.0in
Length: 423.7cm 166.8in
Width: 156.2cm 61.5in
Height: 153.7cm 60.5in
Ground clearance: 16.3cm 6.4in
Kerb weight: 1076.9kg 2372.0lb
Fuel: 39.8L 8.8gal 10.5galUS

382 Austin

A95 Countryman
1958 UK
92.8mph 149.3kmh
0-50mph 80.5kmh: 13.7secs
0-60mph 96.5kmh: 19.1secs
0-1/4 mile: 21.7secs
92.0bhp 68.6kW 93.3PS
@ 4500rpm
130.0lbft 176.2Nm @ 2000rpm
65.3bhp/ton 64.2bhp/tonne
34.9bhp/L 26.0kW/L 35.3PS/L
43.8ft/sec 13.3m/sec
19.3mph 31.1kmh/1000rpm
21.2mpg 17.7mpgUS 13.3L/100km
Petrol 4-stroke piston
2639cc 161.0cu in
In-line 6
Compression ratio: 8.2:1
Bore: 79.4mm 3.1in
Stroke: 89.0mm 3.5in
Valve type/No: Overhead 12
Transmission: Manual
No. of forward speeds: 4
Wheels driven: Rear
Springs F/R: Coil/Leaf
Brakes F/R: Drum/Drum
Wheelbase: 268.5cm 105.7in
Track F: 130.8cm 51.5in
Track R: 130.0cm 51.2in
Length: 459.0cm 180.7in
Width: 162.6cm 64.0in
Height: 157.5cm 62.0in
Ground clearance: 18.8cm 7.4in
Kerb weight: 1431.9kg 3154.0lb
Fuel: 66.0L 14.5gal 17.4galUS

383 Austin

A105 Vanden Plas
1959 UK
97.0mph 156.1kmh
0-50mph 80.5kmh: 12.7secs
0-60mph 96.5kmh: 17.8secs
0-1/4 mile: 21.2secs
102.0bhp 76.1kW 103.4PS
@ 4600rpm
142.0lbft 192.4Nm @ 2400rpm
73.5bhp/ton 72.3bhp/tonne
38.6bhp/L 28.8kW/L 39.2PS/L
44.7ft/sec 13.6m/sec
20.8mph 33.5kmh/1000rpm
20.3mpg 16.9mpgUS 13.9L/100km
Petrol 4-stroke piston
2639cc 161.0cu in
In-line 6
Compression ratio: 8.2:1
Bore: 79.4mm 3.1in
Stroke: 89.0mm 3.5in
Valve type/No: Overhead 12
Transmission: Automatic
No. of forward speeds: 3
Wheels driven: Rear
Springs F/R: Coil/Leaf
Brakes F/R: Drum/Drum
Wheelbase: 268.5cm 105.7in
Track F: 130.8cm 51.5in
Track R: 130.0cm 51.2in
Length: 459.0cm 180.7in
Width: 162.6cm 64.0in
Height: 157.5cm 62.0in
Ground clearance: 17.8cm 7.0in
Kerb weight: 1411.0kg 3108.0lb
Fuel: 72.8L 16.0gal 19.2galUS

384 Austin

A55 Cambridge Mk II
1959 UK
81.0mph 130.3kmh
0-50mph 80.5kmh: 15.3secs
0-60mph 96.5kmh: 23.6secs
0-1/4 mile: 22.5secs
53.0bhp 39.5kW 53.7PS
@ 4350rpm
82.5lbft 111.8Nm @ 2100rpm
49.0bhp/ton 48.2bhp/tonne
35.6bhp/L 26.5kW/L 36.1PS/L
42.3ft/sec 12.9m/sec
15.6mph 25.1kmh/1000rpm
27.0mpg 22.5mpgUS 10.5L/100km
Petrol 4-stroke piston
1489cc 90.8cu in
In-line 4 1 Carburettor
Compression ratio: 8.3:1
Bore: 73.0mm 2.9in
Stroke: 88.9mm 3.5in
Valve type/No: Overhead 8
Transmission: Manual
No. of forward speeds: 4
Wheels driven: Rear
Springs F/R: Coil/Leaf
Brakes F/R: Drum/Drum
Wheelbase: 252.0cm 99.2in
Track F: 124.0cm 48.8in
Track R: 126.5cm 49.8in
Length: 452.4cm 178.1in
Width: 161.3cm 63.5in
Height: 151.6cm 59.7in
Ground clearance: 16.5cm 6.5in
Kerb weight: 1099.6kg 2422.0lb
Fuel: 45.5L 10.0gal 12.0galUS

385 Austin

A99
1959 UK
98.0mph 157.7kmh
0-50mph 80.5kmh: 12.1secs
0-60mph 96.5kmh: 15.8secs
0-1/4 mile: 20.8secs
102.5bhp 76.4kW 103.9PS
@ 4500rpm
158.0lbft 214.1Nm @ 2000rpm
68.0bhp/ton 66.9bhp/tonne
35.2bhp/L 26.2kW/L 35.7PS/L
43.8ft/sec 13.3m/sec
27.1mph 43.6kmh/1000rpm
17.3mpg 14.4mpgUS 16.3L/100km
Petrol 4-stroke piston
2912cc 177.7cu in
In-line 6
Compression ratio: 8.3:1
Bore: 83.3mm 3.3in
Stroke: 88.9mm 3.5in
Valve type/No: Overhead 12
Transmission: Manual
No. of forward speeds: 5
Wheels driven: Rear
Springs F/R: Coil/Leaf
Brake system: PA
Brakes F/R: Disc/Drum
Wheelbase: 274.3cm 108.0in
Track F: 136.7cm 53.8in
Track R: 135.1cm 53.2in
Length: 477.5cm 188.0in
Width: 174.0cm 68.5in
Height: 152.4cm 60.0in
Ground clearance: 16.3cm 6.4in
Kerb weight: 1531.8kg 3374.0lb
Fuel: 72.8L 16.0gal 19.2galUS

386 Austin

Gipsy
1959 UK
65.0mph 104.6kmh
0-50mph 80.5kmh: 21.8secs
0-1/4 mile: 24.7secs
62.0bhp 46.2kW 62.9PS
@ 4100rpm
110.0lbft 149.1Nm @ 1500rpm
45.3bhp/ton 44.5bhp/tonne
28.2bhp/L 21.0kW/L 28.6PS/L
49.8ft/sec 15.2m/sec
15.9mph 25.6kmh/1000rpm
17.8mpg 14.8mpgUS 15.9L/100km
Petrol 4-stroke piston
2199cc 134.2cu in
In-line 4 1 Carburettor
Compression ratio: 6.8:1
Bore: 79.4mm 3.1in
Stroke: 111.0mm 4.4in
Valve type/No: Overhead 8
Transmission: Manual
No. of forward speeds: 4
Wheels driven: Rear
Brakes F/R: Drum/Drum
Wheelbase: 228.6cm 90.0in
Track F: 138.9cm 54.7in
Track R: 132.1cm 52.0in
Length: 353.1cm 139.0in
Width: 169.4cm 66.7in
Height: 186.7cm 73.5in
Ground clearance: 20.8cm 8.2in
Kerb weight: 1392.0kg 3066.0lb
Fuel: 59.1L 13.0gal 15.6galUS

387 Austin

A40 Countryman
1960 UK
73.0mph 117.5kmh
0-50mph 80.5kmh: 22.6secs
0-60mph 96.5kmh: 43.2secs
0-1/4 mile: 24.5secs
34.0bhp 25.3kW 34.5PS
@ 4750rpm
50.0lbft 67.8Nm @ 2000rpm
43.3bhp/ton 42.6bhp/tonne

35.9bhp/L 26.7kW/L 36.4PS/L
39.6ft/sec 12.1m/sec
14.7mph 23.7kmh/1000rpm
37.8mpg 31.5mpgUS 7.5L/100km
Petrol 4-stroke piston
948cc 57.8cu in
In-line 4 1 Carburettor
Compression ratio: 8.3:1
Bore: 62.9mm 2.5in
Stroke: 76.2mm 3.0in
Valve type/No: Overhead 8
Transmission: Manual
No. of forward speeds: 4
Wheels driven: Rear
Springs F/R: Coil/Leaf
Brakes F/R: Drum/Drum
Wheelbase: 212.1cm 83.5in
Track F: 120.7cm 47.5in
Track R: 119.4cm 47.0in
Length: 370.8cm 146.0in
Width: 150.9cm 59.4in
Height: 145.5cm 57.3in
Ground clearance: 17.3cm 6.8in
Kerb weight: 797.7kg 1757.0lb
Fuel: 27.3L 6.0gal 7.2galUS

388 Austin

A99
1960 UK
100.0mph 160.9kmh
0-50mph 80.5kmh: 11.2secs
0-60mph 96.5kmh: 15.0secs
0-1/4 mile: 20.6secs
112.0bhp 83.5kW 113.5PS
@ 4750rpm
158.0lbft 214.1Nm @ 2000rpm
72.7bhp/ton 71.5bhp/tonne
38.5bhp/L 28.7kW/L 39.0PS/L
46.2ft/sec 14.1m/sec
27.0mph 43.4kmh/1000rpm
Petrol 4-stroke piston
2912cc 177.7cu in
In-line 6 1 Carburettor
Compression ratio: 8.3:1
Bore: 83.1mm 3.3in
Stroke: 88.9mm 3.5in
Valve type/No: Overhead 12
Transmission: Manual
No. of forward speeds: 3
Wheels driven: Rear
Wheelbase: 274.3cm 108.0in
Track F: 136.7cm 53.8in
Track R: 135.4cm 53.3in
Length: 477.5cm 188.0in
Width: 174.0cm 68.5in
Height: 152.4cm 60.0in
Kerb weight: 1566.3kg 3450.0lb

389 Austin

A99 Automatic
1960 UK
97.5mph 156.9kmh
0-50mph 80.5kmh: 11.6secs
0-60mph 96.5kmh: 15.1secs
0-1/4 mile: 20.5secs
112.0bhp 83.5kW 113.5PS
@ 4750rpm
158.0lbft 214.1Nm @ 2000rpm
74.9bhp/ton 73.6bhp/tonne
38.5bhp/L 28.7kW/L 39.0PS/L
46.2ft/sec 14.1m/sec
20.8mph 33.5kmh/1000rpm
Petrol 4-stroke piston
2912cc 177.7cu in
In-line 6 1 Carburettor
Compression ratio: 8.2:1
Bore: 83.3mm 3.3in
Stroke: 88.9mm 3.5in
Valve type/No: Overhead 12
Transmission: Automatic
No. of forward speeds: 3
Wheels driven: Rear
Wheelbase: 274.3cm 108.0in
Track F: 136.7cm 53.8in
Track R: 135.1cm 53.2in
Length: 475.0cm 187.0in
Width: 174.0cm 68.5in
Height: 153.7cm 60.5in
Kerb weight: 1520.9kg 3350.0lb

390 Austin

A55 Countryman
1961 UK
78.0mph 125.5kmh
0-50mph 80.5kmh: 16.1secs
0-60mph 96.5kmh: 25.5secs
0-1/4 mile: 22.9secs
55.0bhp 41.0kW 55.8PS
@ 4350rpm
82.5lbft 111.8Nm @ 2100rpm
47.7bhp/ton 46.9bhp/tonne
36.9bhp/L 27.5kW/L 37.4PS/L
42.3ft/sec 12.9m/sec
15.0mph 24.1kmh/1000rpm
23.0mpg 19.2mpgUS 12.3L/100km
Petrol 4-stroke piston
1489cc 90.8cu in
In-line 4 1 Carburettor
Compression ratio: 8.3:1
Bore: 73.0mm 2.9in
Stroke: 88.9mm 3.5in
Valve type/No: Overhead 8
Transmission: Manual
No. of forward speeds: 4
Wheels driven: Rear
Springs F/R: Coil/Leaf
Brakes F/R: Drum/Drum
Wheelbase: 252.0cm 99.2in
Track F: 124.2cm 48.9in
Track R: 126.7cm 49.9in
Length: 452.1cm 178.0in
Width: 161.3cm 63.5in
Height: 152.4cm 60.0in
Ground clearance: 17.5cm 6.9in
Kerb weight: 1172.7kg 2583.0lb
Fuel: 45.5L 10.0gal 12.0galUS

391 Austin

Seven 850
1961 UK
75.0mph 120.7kmh
0-50mph 80.5kmh: 18.7secs
0-60mph 96.5kmh: 29.6secs
0-1/4 mile: 23.6secs
37.0bhp 27.6kW 37.5PS
@ 5500rpm
44.0lbft 59.6Nm @ 2900rpm
61.8bhp/ton 60.8bhp/tonne
43.6bhp/L 32.5kW/L 44.2PS/L
41.1ft/sec 12.5m/sec
15.0mph 24.1kmh/1000rpm
Petrol 4-stroke piston
848cc 51.7cu in
In-line 4 1 Carburettor
Compression ratio: 8.3:1
Bore: 63.0mm 2.5in
Stroke: 68.3mm 2.7in
Valve type/No: Overhead 8
Transmission: Manual
No. of forward speeds: 4
Wheels driven: Front
Wheelbase: 203.2cm 80.0in
Track F: 122.4cm 48.2in
Track R: 117.3cm 46.2in
Length: 304.8cm 120.0in
Width: 141.0cm 55.5in
Height: 134.6cm 53.0in
Ground clearance: 15.2cm 6.0in
Kerb weight: 608.4kg 1340.0lb

392 Austin

A40 Mk II
1962 UK
82.5mph 132.7kmh
0-50mph 80.5kmh: 15.7secs
0-60mph 96.5kmh: 23.9secs
0-1/4 mile: 22.9secs
48.0bhp 35.8kW 48.7PS
@ 5100rpm
60.0lbft 81.3Nm @ 2500rpm
60.0bhp/ton 59.0bhp/tonne
43.7bhp/L 32.6kW/L 44.3PS/L
47.2ft/sec 14.4m/sec
15.3mph 24.6kmh/1000rpm
30.5mpg 25.4mpgUS 9.3L/100km
Petrol 4-stroke piston
1098cc 67.0cu in
In-line 4 1 Carburettor
Compression ratio: 8.5:1
Bore: 64.6mm 2.5in
Stroke: 84.7mm 3.3in
Valve type/No: Overhead 8
Transmission: Manual
No. of forward speeds: 4
Wheels driven: Rear
Springs F/R: Coil/Leaf
Brakes F/R: Drum/Drum
Steering: Cam & peg
Wheelbase: 221.0cm 87.0in
Track F: 119.6cm 47.1in
Track R: 119.4cm 47.0in
Length: 368.3cm 145.0in
Width: 150.6cm 59.3in
Height: 143.5cm 56.5in
Ground clearance: 16.3cm 6.4in
Kerb weight: 813.6kg 1792.0lb
Fuel: 31.8L 7.0gal 8.4galUS

393 Austin

A60 Cambridge
1962 UK
84.0mph 135.2kmh
0-50mph 80.5kmh: 14.6secs
0-60mph 96.5kmh: 21.4secs
0-1/4 mile: 21.8secs
61.0bhp 45.5kW 61.8PS
@ 4500rpm
90.0lbft 122.0Nm @ 2100rpm
56.4bhp/ton 55.5bhp/tonne
37.6bhp/L 28.0kW/L 38.1PS/L
43.8ft/sec 13.3m/sec
16.6mph 26.7kmh/1000rpm
26.2mpg 21.8mpgUS 10.8L/100km
Petrol 4-stroke piston
1622cc 99.0cu in
In-line 4 1 Carburettor
Compression ratio: 8.3:1
Bore: 76.2mm 3.0in
Stroke: 88.9mm 3.5in
Valve type/No: Overhead 8
Transmission: Manual
No. of forward speeds: 4
Wheels driven: Rear
Springs F/R: Coil/Leaf
Brakes F/R: Drum/Drum
Steering: Cam & lever
Wheelbase: 254.5cm 100.2in
Track F: 128.5cm 50.6in
Track R: 130.6cm 51.4in
Length: 443.2cm 174.5in
Width: 161.3cm 63.5in
Height: 149.6cm 58.9in
Ground clearance: 15.0cm 5.9in
Kerb weight: 1099.6kg 2422.0lb
Fuel: 45.5L 10.0gal 12.0galUS

394 Austin

1800
1964 UK
90.0mph 144.8kmh
0-50mph 80.5kmh: 11.9secs
0-60mph 96.5kmh: 17.1secs
0-1/4 mile: 20.5secs
84.0bhp 62.6kW 85.2PS
@ 5300rpm
99.0lbft 134.1Nm @ 2100rpm
73.2bhp/ton 71.9bhp/tonne
46.7bhp/L 34.8kW/L 47.4PS/L
51.5ft/sec 15.7m/sec
16.4mph 26.4kmh/1000rpm
23.5mpg 19.6mpgUS 12.0L/100km
Petrol 4-stroke piston
1798cc 109.7cu in
In-line 4 1 Carburettor
Compression ratio: 8.2:1
Bore: 80.2mm 3.2in
Stroke: 88.9mm 3.5in
Valve type/No: Overhead 8
Transmission: Manual
No. of forward speeds: 4
Wheels driven: Front
Springs F/R: Gas/Gas
Brake system: PA
Brakes F/R: Disc/Drum
Steering: Rack & pinion
Wheelbase: 269.2cm 106.0in
Track F: 142.5cm 56.1in
Track R: 141.0cm 55.5in
Length: 418.3cm 164.7in
Width: 170.2cm 67.0in
Height: 141.0cm 55.5in
Ground clearance: 16.5cm 6.5in
Kerb weight: 1167.7kg 2572.0lb
Fuel: 48.9L 10.7gal 12.9galUS

395 Austin

1800 Mk II
1968 UK
96.0mph 154.5kmh
0-50mph 80.5kmh: 10.8secs
0-60mph 96.5kmh: 16.3secs
0-1/4 mile: 19.9secs
0-1km: 36.8secs
86.0bhp 64.1kW 87.2PS
@ 5300rpm
101.0lbft 136.9Nm @ 3000rpm
74.9bhp/ton 73.6bhp/tonne
47.8bhp/L 35.7kW/L 48.5PS/L
51.5ft/sec 15.7m/sec
18.1mph 29.1kmh/1000rpm
26.9mpg 22.4mpgUS 10.5L/100km
Petrol 4-stroke piston
1798cc 109.7cu in
In-line 4 1 Carburettor
Compression ratio: 9.0:1
Bore: 80.2mm 3.2in
Stroke: 88.9mm 3.5in
Valve type/No: Overhead 8
Transmission: Manual
No. of forward speeds: 4
Wheels driven: Front
Springs F/R: Gas/Gas
Brake system: PA
Brakes F/R: Disc/Drum
Steering: Rack & pinion PA
Wheelbase: 269.2cm 106.0in
Track F: 142.5cm 56.1in
Track R: 141.0cm 55.5in
Length: 423.4cm 166.7in
Width: 167.6cm 66.0in
Height: 141.0cm 55.5in
Ground clearance: 16.5cm 6.5in
Kerb weight: 1168.1kg 2573.0lb
Fuel: 47.8L 10.5gal 12.6galUS

396 Austin

3-litre Automatic
1968 UK
101.0mph 162.5kmh
0-50mph 80.5kmh: 10.8secs
0-60mph 96.5kmh: 14.8secs
0-1/4 mile: 20.3secs
0-1km: 37.1secs
123.6bhp 92.2kW 125.3PS
@ 4500rpm
161.0lbft 218.2Nm @ 3000rpm
82.2bhp/ton 80.8bhp/tonne
42.4bhp/L 31.6kW/L 43.0PS/L
43.8ft/sec 13.3m/sec
20.0mph 32.2kmh/1000rpm
14.9mpg 12.4mpgUS 19.0L/100km
Petrol 4-stroke piston
2912cc 177.7cu in
In-line 6 2 Carburettor
Compression ratio: 9.0:1
Bore: 83.3mm 3.3in
Stroke: 88.9mm 3.5in
Valve type/No: Overhead 12
Transmission: Automatic
No. of forward speeds: 3
Wheels driven: Rear
Springs F/R: Gas/Gas
Brake system: PA
Brakes F/R: Disc/Drum
Steering: Rack & pinion PA
Wheelbase: 293.4cm 115.5in
Track F: 144.3cm 56.8in
Track R: 142.2cm 56.0in
Length: 471.7cm 185.7in
Width: 169.4cm 66.7in
Height: 142.2cm 56.0in
Ground clearance: 16.5cm 6.5in
Kerb weight: 1529.5kg 3369.0lb
Fuel: 66.0L 14.5gal 17.4galUS

397 Austin

America
1968 UK
81.0mph 130.3kmh
0-50mph 80.5kmh: 12.5secs
0-60mph 96.5kmh: 18.0secs
0-1/4 mile: 21.7secs
58.0bhp 43.2kW 58.8PS
@ 5250rpm
69.0lbft 93.5Nm @ 3500rpm
69.8bhp/ton 68.7bhp/tonne
45.5bhp/L 33.9kW/L 46.1PS/L
46.7ft/sec 14.2m/sec
17.1mph 27.5kmh/1000rpm
Petrol 4-stroke piston
1275cc 77.8cu in
In-line 4 1 Carburettor
Compression ratio: 8.8:1
Bore: 70.6mm 2.8in
Stroke: 81.3mm 3.2in
Valve type/No: Overhead 8
Transmission: Automatic
No. of forward speeds: 4
Wheels driven: Front
Springs F/R: Gas/Gas
Brakes F/R: Disc/Drum
Steering: Rack & pinion
Wheelbase: 237.5cm 93.5in
Track F: 130.8cm 51.5in
Track R: 129.3cm 50.9in
Length: 372.9cm 146.8in

Width: 153.4cm 60.4in
Height: 134.6cm 53.0in
Ground clearance: 13.5cm 5.3in
Kerb weight: 844.4kg 1860.0lb
Fuel: 37.8L 8.3gal 10.0galUS

398 Austin

1300 GT
1969 UK
96.0mph 154.5kmh
0-50mph 80.5kmh: 10.3secs
0-60mph 96.5kmh: 15.6secs
0-1/4 mile: 20.0secs
0-1km: 37.3secs
70.0bhp 52.2kW 71.0PS
@ 6000rpm
74.0lbft 100.3Nm @ 3250rpm
82.5bhp/ton 81.1bhp/tonne
54.9bhp/L 40.9kW/L 55.7PS/L
53.3ft/sec 16.3m/sec
16.8mph 27.0kmh/1000rpm
27.0mpg 22.5mpgUS 10.5L/100km
Petrol 4-stroke piston
1275cc 77.8cu in
In-line 4 2 Carburettor
Compression ratio: 9.7:1
Bore: 70.6mm 2.8in
Stroke: 81.3mm 3.2in
Valve type/No: Overhead 8
Transmission: Manual
No. of forward speeds: 4
Wheels driven: Front
Springs F/R: Gas/Gas
Brake system: PA
Brakes F/R: Disc/Drum
Steering: Rack & pinion
Wheelbase: 237.5cm 93.5in
Track F: 130.8cm 51.5in
Track R: 129.3cm 50.9in
Length: 372.6cm 146.7in
Width: 162.6cm 64.0in
Height: 133.9cm 52.7in
Ground clearance: 15.2cm 6.0in
Kerb weight: 862.6kg 1900.0lb
Fuel: 36.4L 8.0gal 9.6galUS

399 Austin

1300 Super
1969 UK
92.0mph 148.0kmh
0-50mph 80.5kmh: 10.6secs
0-60mph 96.5kmh: 16.4secs
0-1/4 mile: 20.6secs
0-1km: 38.8secs
60.0bhp 44.7kW 60.8PS
@ 5250rpm
67.0lbft 90.8Nm @ 2500rpm
72.3bhp/ton 71.0bhp/tonne
47.1bhp/L 35.1kW/L 47.7PS/L
46.7ft/sec 14.2m/sec
17.1mph 27.5kmh/1000rpm
30.2mpg 25.1mpgUS 9.4L/100km
Petrol 4-stroke piston
1275cc 77.8cu in
In-line 4 1 Carburettor
Compression ratio: 8.8:1
Bore: 70.6mm 2.8in
Stroke: 81.3mm 3.2in
Valve type/No: Overhead 8
Transmission: Manual
No. of forward speeds: 4
Wheels driven: Front
Springs F/R: Gas/Gas
Brakes F/R: Disc/Drum
Steering: Rack & pinion
Wheelbase: 237.5cm 93.5in
Track F: 130.8cm 51.5in
Track R: 129.3cm 50.9in
Length: 372.6cm 146.7in
Width: 162.6cm 64.0in
Height: 133.9cm 52.7in
Ground clearance: 15.2cm 6.0in
Kerb weight: 844.4kg 1860.0lb
Fuel: 36.4L 8.0gal 9.6galUS

400 Austin

Maxi
1969 UK
88.0mph 141.6kmh
0-50mph 80.5kmh: 11.0secs
0-60mph 96.5kmh: 16.6secs
0-1/4 mile: 20.6secs
0-1km: 37.6secs
74.0bhp 55.2kW 75.0PS
@ 5500rpm
84.0lbft 113.8Nm @ 3500rpm
77.5bhp/ton 76.2bhp/tonne
49.8bhp/L 37.2kW/L 50.5PS/L
48.9ft/sec 14.9m/sec
19.6mph 31.5kmh/1000rpm
24.0mpg 20.0mpgUS 11.8L/100km
Petrol 4-stroke piston
1485cc 90.6cu in
In-line 4 1 Carburettor
Compression ratio: 9.0:1
Bore: 76.2mm 3.0in
Stroke: 81.3mm 3.2in
Valve type/No: Overhead 8
Transmission: Manual
No. of forward speeds: 5
Wheels driven: Front
Springs F/R: Gas/Gas
Brake system: PA
Brakes F/R: Disc/Drum
Steering: Rack & pinion
Wheelbase: 266.2cm 104.8in
Track F: 136.7cm 53.8in
Track R: 135.1cm 53.2in
Length: 403.9cm 159.0in
Width: 162.6cm 64.0in
Height: 138.4cm 54.5in
Ground clearance: 15.2cm 6.0in
Kerb weight: 971.1kg 2139.0lb
Fuel: 45.5L 10.0gal 12.0galUS

401 Austin

3-litre
1970 UK
101.0mph 162.5kmh
0-50mph 80.5kmh: 10.8secs
0-60mph 96.5kmh: 15.7secs
0-1/4 mile: 20.1secs
0-1km: 37.2secs
124.0bhp 92.5kW 125.7PS
@ 4500rpm
161.0lbft 218.2Nm @ 3000rpm
82.7bhp/ton 81.3bhp/tonne
42.6bhp/L 31.7kW/L 43.2PS/L
43.8ft/sec 13.3m/sec
20.0mph 32.2kmh/1000rpm
15.8mpg 13.2mpgUS 17.9L/100km
Petrol 4-stroke piston
2912cc 177.7cu in
In-line 6 2 Carburettor
Compression ratio: 9.0:1
Bore: 83.3mm 3.3in
Stroke: 88.9mm 3.5in
Valve type/No: Overhead 12
Transmission: Manual
No. of forward speeds: 4
Wheels driven: Rear
Springs F/R: Gas/Gas
Brake system: PA
Brakes F/R: Disc/Drum
Steering: Rack & pinion PA
Wheelbase: 293.4cm 115.5in
Track F: 144.3cm 56.8in
Track R: 142.2cm 56.0in
Length: 471.7cm 185.7in
Width: 169.4cm 66.7in
Height: 142.2cm 56.0in
Ground clearance: 16.5cm 6.5in
Kerb weight: 1524.5kg 3358.0lb
Fuel: 66.0L 14.5gal 17.4galUS

402 Austin

Maxi 1750
1970 UK
92.0mph 148.0kmh
0-50mph 80.5kmh: 10.7secs
0-60mph 96.5kmh: 15.8secs
0-1/4 mile: 20.2secs
0-1km: 38.4secs
84.0bhp 62.6kW 85.2PS
@ 5000rpm
105.0lbft 142.3Nm @ 3000rpm
87.0bhp/ton 85.6bhp/tonne
48.0bhp/L 35.8kW/L 48.7PS/L
52.4ft/sec 16.0m/sec
19.4mph 31.2kmh/1000rpm
24.5mpg 20.4mpgUS 11.5L/100km
Petrol 4-stroke piston
1748cc 106.6cu in
In-line 4 1 Carburettor
Compression ratio: 8.7:1
Bore: 76.2mm 3.0in
Stroke: 95.7mm 3.8in
Valve type/No: Overhead 8
Transmission: Manual
No. of forward speeds: 5
Wheels driven: Front
Springs F/R: Gas/Gas
Brake system: PA
Brakes F/R: Disc/Drum
Steering: Rack & pinion
Wheelbase: 266.2cm 104.8in
Track F: 136.7cm 53.8in
Track R: 135.1cm 53.2in
Length: 403.9cm 159.0in
Width: 162.6cm 64.0in
Height: 138.4cm 54.5in
Ground clearance: 15.2cm 6.0in
Kerb weight: 981.5kg 2162.0lb
Fuel: 40.9L 9.0gal 10.8galUS

403 Austin

1300 Mk III
1971 UK
93.0mph 149.6kmh
0-50mph 80.5kmh: 11.1secs
0-60mph 96.5kmh: 16.2secs
0-1/4 mile: 20.2secs
0-1km: 38.1secs
60.0bhp 44.7kW 60.8PS
@ 5250rpm
67.0lbft 90.8Nm @ 2500rpm
75.0bhp/ton 73.7bhp/tonne
47.1bhp/L 35.1kW/L 47.7PS/L
46.7ft/sec 14.2m/sec
16.8mph 27.0kmh/1000rpm
34.4mpg 28.6mpgUS 8.2L/100km
Petrol 4-stroke piston
1275cc 77.8cu in
In-line 4 1 Carburettor
Compression ratio: 8.8:1
Bore: 70.6mm 2.8in
Stroke: 81.3mm 3.2in
Valve type/No: Overhead 8
Transmission: Manual
No. of forward speeds: 4
Wheels driven: Front
Springs F/R: Gas/Gas
Brakes F/R: Disc/Drum
Steering: Rack & pinion
Wheelbase: 237.5cm 93.5in
Track F: 130.8cm 51.5in
Track R: 129.3cm 50.9in
Length: 372.6cm 146.7in
Width: 162.6cm 64.0in
Height: 133.9cm 52.7in
Ground clearance: 15.2cm 6.0in
Kerb weight: 813.6kg 1792.0lb
Fuel: 36.4L 8.0gal 9.6galUS

404 Austin

2200
1972 UK
108.0mph 173.8kmh
0-50mph 80.5kmh: 9.0secs
0-60mph 96.5kmh: 13.1secs
0-1/4 mile: 18.7secs
0-1km: 34.8secs
110.0bhp 82.0kW 111.5PS
@ 5250rpm
125.6lbft 170.2Nm @ 3500rpm
94.0bhp/ton 92.5bhp/tonne
49.4bhp/L 36.8kW/L 50.1PS/L
46.7ft/sec 14.2m/sec
18.1mph 29.1kmh/1000rpm
22.3mpg 18.6mpgUS 12.7L/100km
Petrol 4-stroke piston
2227cc 135.9cu in
In-line 6 2 Carburettor
Compression ratio: 9.0:1
Bore: 76.2mm 3.0in
Stroke: 81.3mm 3.2in
Valve type/No: Overhead 12
Transmission: Manual
No. of forward speeds: 4
Wheels driven: Rear
Springs F/R: Gas/Gas
Brake system: PA
Brakes F/R: Disc/Drum
Steering: Rack & pinion PA
Wheelbase: 269.2cm 106.0in
Track F: 142.5cm 56.1in
Track R: 141.0cm 55.5in
Length: 423.4cm 166.7in
Width: 170.2cm 67.0in
Height: 141.0cm 55.5in
Ground clearance: 16.5cm 6.5in
Kerb weight: 1189.5kg 2620.0lb
Fuel: 56.9L 12.5gal 15.0galUS

405 Austin

Maxi High Line
1972 UK
101.0mph 162.5kmh
0-50mph 80.5kmh: 8.5secs
0-60mph 96.5kmh: 13.2secs
0-1/4 mile: 19.4secs
0-1km: 35.9secs
95.0bhp 70.8kW 96.3PS
@ 5350rpm
107.0lbft 145.0Nm @ 3500rpm
96.7bhp/ton 95.1bhp/tonne
54.3bhp/L 40.5kW/L 55.1PS/L
56.0ft/sec 17.1m/sec
19.9mph 32.0kmh/1000rpm
24.8mpg 20.7mpgUS 11.4L/100km
Petrol 4-stroke piston
1748cc 106.6cu in
In-line 4 2 Carburettor
Compression ratio: 9.5:1
Bore: 76.2mm 3.0in
Stroke: 95.7mm 3.8in
Valve type/No: Overhead 8
Transmission: Manual
No. of forward speeds: 5
Wheels driven: Front
Springs F/R: Gas/Gas
Brake system: PA
Brakes F/R: Disc/Drum
Steering: Rack & pinion
Wheelbase: 266.2cm 104.8in
Track F: 136.7cm 53.8in
Track R: 135.1cm 53.2in
Length: 403.9cm 159.0in
Width: 162.6cm 64.0in
Height: 138.4cm 54.5in
Ground clearance: 15.2cm 6.0in
Kerb weight: 998.8kg 2200.0lb
Fuel: 40.9L 9.0gal 10.8galUS

406 Austin

Allegro 1300 Super
1973 UK
84.0mph 135.2kmh
0-50mph 80.5kmh: 12.7secs
0-60mph 96.5kmh: 18.4secs
0-1/4 mile: 20.9secs
0-1km: 39.7secs
58.7bhp 43.8kW 59.5PS
@ 5300rpm
68.5lbft 92.8Nm @ 3000rpm
72.2bhp/ton 71.0bhp/tonne
46.0bhp/L 34.3kW/L 46.7PS/L
47.1ft/sec 14.4m/sec
16.4mph 26.4kmh/1000rpm
30.8mpg 25.6mpgUS 9.2L/100km
Petrol 4-stroke piston
1275cc 77.8cu in
In-line 4 1 Carburettor
Compression ratio: 8.8:1
Bore: 70.6mm 2.8in
Stroke: 81.3mm 3.2in
Valve type/No: Overhead 8
Transmission: Manual
No. of forward speeds: 4
Wheels driven: Front
Springs F/R: Gas/Gas
Brake system: PA
Brakes F/R: Disc/Drum
Steering: Rack & pinion
Wheelbase: 244.1cm 96.1in
Track F: 136.1cm 53.6in
Track R: 136.4cm 53.7in
Length: 385.1cm 151.6in
Width: 161.3cm 63.5in
Height: 140.7cm 55.4in
Ground clearance: 17.8cm 7.0in
Kerb weight: 827.2kg 1822.0lb
Fuel: 47.8L 10.5gal 12.6galUS

407 Austin

Marina GT
1973 UK
96.0mph 154.5kmh
0-50mph 80.5kmh: 10.5secs
0-60mph 96.5kmh: 15.5secs
0-1/4 mile: 20.3secs
68.5bhp 51.1kW 69.4PS
@ 5000rpm
87.0lbft 117.9Nm @ 2750rpm
70.1bhp/ton 68.9bhp/tonne
38.1bhp/L 28.4kW/L 38.6PS/L
48.6ft/sec 14.8m/sec
18.2mph 29.3kmh/1000rpm
28.8mpg 24.0mpgUS 9.8L/100km
Petrol 4-stroke piston
1798cc 109.7cu in
In-line 4 1 Carburettor
Compression ratio: 8.0:1
Bore: 80.2mm 3.2in
Stroke: 88.9mm 3.5in
Valve type/No: Overhead 8

Transmission: Manual
No. of forward speeds: 4
Wheels driven: Rear
Springs F/R: Torsion bar/Leaf
Brake system: PA
Brakes F/R: Disc/Drum
Steering: Rack & pinion
Wheelbase: 243.8cm 96.0in
Track F: 132.1cm 52.0in
Track R: 132.1cm 52.0in
Length: 429.5cm 169.1in
Width: 164.6cm 64.8in
Height: 142.2cm 56.0in
Ground clearance: 12.7cm 5.0in
Kerb weight: 994.3kg 2190.0lb
Fuel: 41.6L 9.1gal 11.0galUS

408 Austin

Allegro 1500 Special Automatic
1974 UK
85.0mph 136.8kmh
0-50mph 80.5kmh: 12.1secs
0-60mph 96.5kmh: 17.3secs
0-1/4 mile: 21.4secs
0-1km: 40.3secs
69.0bhp 51.4kW 70.0PS
@ 5600rpm
69.5lbft 94.2Nm @ 3100rpm
78.5bhp/ton 77.1bhp/tonne
46.5bhp/L 34.6kW/L 47.1PS/L
49.8ft/sec 15.2m/sec
16.9mph 27.2kmh/1000rpm
23.4mpg 19.5mpgUS 12.1L/100km
Petrol 4-stroke piston
1485cc 90.6cu in
In-line 4 1 Carburettor
Compression ratio: 9.0:1
Bore: 76.2mm 3.0in
Stroke: 81.3mm 3.2in
Valve type/No: Overhead 8
Transmission: Automatic
No. of forward speeds: 4
Wheels driven: Front
Springs F/R: Gas/Gas
Brake system: PA
Brakes F/R: Disc/Drum
Steering: Rack & pinion
Wheelbase: 244.1cm 96.1in
Track F: 136.1cm 53.6in
Track R: 136.4cm 53.7in
Length: 385.1cm 151.6in
Width: 161.3cm 63.5in
Height: 140.7cm 55.4in
Ground clearance: 17.8cm 7.0in
Kerb weight: 894.4kg 1970.0lb
Fuel: 47.8L 10.5gal 12.6galUS

409 Austin

Allegro HL
1974 UK
104.0mph 167.3kmh
0-50mph 80.5kmh: 7.2secs
0-60mph 96.5kmh: 11.0secs
0-1/4 mile: 17.9secs
0-1km: 33.7secs
90.0bhp 67.1kW 91.2PS
@ 5500rpm
103.0lbft 139.6Nm @ 3100rpm
105.9bhp/ton 104.1bhp/tonne
51.5bhp/L 38.4kW/L 52.2PS/L
56.4ft/sec 17.2m/sec
19.4mph 31.2kmh/1000rpm
26.0mpg 21.6mpgUS 10.9L/100km
Petrol 4-stroke piston
1748cc 106.6cu in
In-line 4 2 Carburettor
Compression ratio: 9.5:1
Bore: 76.2mm 3.0in
Stroke: 93.8mm 3.7in
Valve type/No: Overhead 8
Transmission: Manual
No. of forward speeds: 5
Wheels driven: Front
Springs F/R: Gas/Gas
Brake system: PA
Brakes F/R: Disc/Drum
Steering: Rack & pinion
Wheelbase: 244.1cm 96.1in
Track F: 136.1cm 53.6in
Track R: 136.4cm 53.7in
Length: 385.1cm 151.6in
Width: 161.3cm 63.5in
Height: 140.7cm 55.4in
Ground clearance: 17.8cm 7.0in
Kerb weight: 864.4kg 1904.0lb
Fuel: 47.8L 10.5gal 12.6galUS

410 Austin

Vanden Plas 1500
1974 UK
91.0mph 146.4kmh
0-50mph 80.5kmh: 11.0secs
0-60mph 96.5kmh: 16.7secs
0-1/4 mile: 20.9secs
0-1km: 39.3secs
68.0bhp 50.7kW 68.9PS
@ 5500rpm
80.0lbft 108.4Nm @ 2900rpm
76.2bhp/ton 74.9bhp/tonne
45.8bhp/L 34.1kW/L 46.4PS/L
53.2ft/sec 16.2m/sec
19.4mph 31.2kmh/1000rpm
27.2mpg 22.6mpgUS 10.4L/100km
Petrol 4-stroke piston
1485cc 90.6cu in
In-line 4 1 Carburettor
Compression ratio: 9.0:1
Bore: 76.2mm 3.0in
Stroke: 88.3mm 3.5in
Valve type/No: Overhead 8
Transmission: Manual
No. of forward speeds: 5
Wheels driven: Front
Springs F/R: Gas/Gas
Brake system: PA
Brakes F/R: Disc/Drum
Steering: Rack & pinion
Wheelbase: 244.0cm 96.1in
Track F: 136.0cm 53.5in
Track R: 136.0cm 53.5in
Length: 385.0cm 151.6in
Width: 161.0cm 63.4in
Height: 140.0cm 55.1in
Kerb weight: 908.0kg 2000.0lb
Fuel: 47.8L 10.5gal 12.6galUS

411 Austin

2200 HL
1975 UK
105.0mph 168.9kmh
0-50mph 80.5kmh: 8.9secs
0-60mph 96.5kmh: 13.5secs
0-1/4 mile: 19.2secs
0-1km: 35.4secs
110.0bhp 82.0kW 111.5PS
@ 5250rpm
125.0lbft 169.4Nm @ 3250rpm
94.8bhp/ton 93.2bhp/tonne
49.4bhp/L 36.8kW/L 50.1PS/L
46.7ft/sec 14.2m/sec
18.8mph 30.2kmh/1000rpm
20.7mpg 17.2mpgUS 13.6L/100km
Petrol 4-stroke piston
2227cc 135.9cu in
In-line 6 2 Carburettor
Compression ratio: 9.0:1
Bore: 76.2mm 3.0in
Stroke: 81.3mm 3.2in
Valve type/No: Overhead 12
Transmission: Manual
No. of forward speeds: 4
Wheels driven: Rear
Springs F/R: Gas/Gas
Brake system: PA
Brakes F/R: Disc/Drum
Steering: Rack & pinion PA
Wheelbase: 266.7cm 105.0in
Track F: 148.6cm 58.5in
Track R: 147.3cm 58.0in
Length: 445.5cm 175.4in
Width: 173.0cm 68.1in
Height: 140.7cm 55.4in
Ground clearance: 19.1cm 7.5in
Kerb weight: 1180.4kg 2600.0lb
Fuel: 72.8L 16.0gal 19.2galUS

412 Austin

Allegro 1300 Estate
1975 UK
89.0mph 143.2kmh
0-50mph 80.5kmh: 11.4secs
0-60mph 96.5kmh: 16.5secs
0-1/4 mile: 20.4secs
0-1km: 41.2secs
54.0bhp 40.3kW 54.7PS
@ 5250rpm
64.8lbft 87.8Nm @ 3000rpm
67.0bhp/ton 65.9bhp/tonne
42.3bhp/L 31.6kW/L 42.9PS/L
46.7ft/sec 14.2m/sec
16.3mph 26.2kmh/1000rpm
31.2mpg 26.0mpgUS 9.1L/100km
Petrol 4-stroke piston
1275cc 77.8cu in
In-line 4 1 Carburettor
Compression ratio: 8.8:1
Bore: 70.6mm 2.8in
Stroke: 81.3mm 3.2in
Valve type/No: Overhead 8
Transmission: Manual
No. of forward speeds: 4
Wheels driven: Front
Springs F/R: Gas/Gas
Brake system: PA
Brakes F/R: Disc/Drum
Steering: Rack & pinion
Wheelbase: 244.1cm 96.1in
Track F: 136.1cm 53.6in
Track R: 136.4cm 53.7in
Length: 394.2cm 155.2in
Width: 160.0cm 63.0in
Height: 140.7cm 55.4in
Ground clearance: 17.8cm 7.0in
Kerb weight: 819.5kg 1805.0lb
Fuel: 47.8L 10.5gal 12.6galUS

413 Austin

Allegro 1100
1976 UK
88.0mph 141.6kmh
0-50mph 80.5kmh: 13.3secs
0-60mph 96.5kmh: 19.4secs
0-1/4 mile: 20.9secs
0-1km: 40.3secs
45.0bhp 33.6kW 45.6PS
@ 5250rpm
55.0lbft 74.5Nm @ 2900rpm
54.5bhp/ton 53.6bhp/tonne
41.0bhp/L 30.6kW/L 41.5PS/L
48.1ft/sec 14.6m/sec
15.5mph 24.9kmh/1000rpm
32.5mpg 27.1mpgUS 8.7L/100km
Petrol 4-stroke piston
1098cc 67.0cu in
In-line 4 1 Carburettor
Compression ratio: 8.5:1
Bore: 64.6mm 2.5in
Stroke: 83.7mm 3.3in
Valve type/No: Overhead 8
Transmission: Manual
No. of forward speeds: 4
Wheels driven: Front
Springs F/R: Gas/Gas
Brake system: PA
Brakes F/R: Disc/Drum
Steering: Rack & pinion
Wheelbase: 245.1cm 96.5in
Track F: 136.1cm 53.6in
Track R: 136.4cm 53.7in
Length: 385.3cm 151.7in
Width: 161.3cm 63.5in
Height: 138.9cm 54.7in
Ground clearance: 17.8cm 7.0in
Kerb weight: 839.9kg 1850.0lb
Fuel: 47.8L 10.5gal 12.6galUS

414 Austin

Princess 2200 HLS
1976 UK
98.0mph 157.7kmh
0-50mph 80.5kmh: 10.3secs
0-60mph 96.5kmh: 14.2secs
0-1/4 mile: 19.6secs
0-1km: 36.9secs
110.0bhp 82.0kW 111.5PS
@ 5250rpm
125.0lbft 169.4Nm @ 3250rpm
90.9bhp/ton 89.3bhp/tonne
49.4bhp/L 36.8kW/L 50.1PS/L
46.7ft/sec 14.2m/sec
18.3mph 29.4kmh/1000rpm
21.8mpg 18.2mpgUS 13.0L/100km
Petrol 4-stroke piston
2227cc 135.9cu in
In-line 6 2 Carburettor
Compression ratio: 9.0:1
Bore: 76.2mm 3.0in
Stroke: 81.3mm 3.2in
Valve type/No: Overhead 12
Transmission: Automatic
No. of forward speeds: 3
Wheels driven: Front
Springs F/R: Gas/Gas
Brake system: PA
Brakes F/R: Disc/Drum
Steering: Rack & pinion PA
Wheelbase: 267.2cm 105.2in
Track F: 148.6cm 58.5in
Track R: 147.3cm 58.0in
Length: 450.9cm 177.5in
Width: 172.0cm 67.7in
Height: 140.7cm 55.4in
Ground clearance: 19.1cm 7.5in
Kerb weight: 1231.2kg 2712.0lb
Fuel: 72.8L 16.0gal 19.2galUS

415 Austin

Allegro 1750 HL
1977 UK
105.0mph 168.9kmh
0-50mph 80.5kmh: 7.8secs
0-60mph 96.5kmh: 11.4secs
0-1/4 mile: 18.4secs
0-1km: 34.0secs
90.0bhp 67.1kW 91.2PS
@ 5500rpm
103.0lbft 139.6Nm @ 3100rpm
100.7bhp/ton 99.0bhp/tonne
51.5bhp/L 38.4kW/L 52.2PS/L
56.4ft/sec 17.2m/sec
20.0mph 32.2kmh/1000rpm
26.7mpg 22.2mpgUS 10.6L/100km
Petrol 4-stroke piston
1748cc 106.6cu in
In-line 4 2 Carburettor
Compression ratio: 9.5:1
Bore: 76.2mm 3.0in
Stroke: 93.8mm 3.7in
Valve type/No: Overhead 8
Transmission: Manual
No. of forward speeds: 5
Wheels driven: Front
Springs F/R: Gas/Gas
Brake system: PA
Brakes F/R: Disc/Drum
Steering: Rack & pinion
Wheelbase: 245.1cm 96.5in
Track F: 136.1cm 53.6in
Track R: 136.4cm 53.7in
Length: 385.3cm 151.7in
Width: 161.3cm 63.5in
Height: 138.9cm 54.7in
Ground clearance: 17.8cm 7.0in
Kerb weight: 908.9kg 2002.0lb
Fuel: 47.8L 10.5gal 12.6galUS

416 Austin

Maxi 1750
1977 UK
93.0mph 149.6kmh
0-50mph 80.5kmh: 10.5secs
0-60mph 96.5kmh: 15.8secs
0-1/4 mile: 20.1secs
0-1km: 37.6secs
72.0bhp 53.7kW 73.0PS
@ 4900rpm
97.0lbft 131.4Nm @ 2600rpm
74.7bhp/ton 73.4bhp/tonne
41.2bhp/L 30.7kW/L 41.8PS/L
51.3ft/sec 15.6m/sec
19.4mph 31.2kmh/1000rpm
28.8mpg 24.0mpgUS 9.8L/100km
Petrol 4-stroke piston
1748cc 106.6cu in
In-line 4 1 Carburettor
Compression ratio: 8.7:1
Bore: 76.2mm 3.0in
Stroke: 95.7mm 3.8in
Valve type/No: Overhead 8
Transmission: Manual
No. of forward speeds: 5
Wheels driven: Front
Springs F/R: Gas/Gas
Brake system: PA
Brakes F/R: Disc/Drum
Steering: Rack & pinion
Wheelbase: 266.2cm 104.8in
Track F: 136.7cm 53.8in
Track R: 135.1cm 53.2in
Length: 403.9cm 159.0in
Width: 162.6cm 64.0in
Height: 138.4cm 54.5in
Ground clearance: 15.2cm 6.0in
Kerb weight: 980.6kg 2160.0lb
Fuel: 47.8L 10.5gal 12.6galUS

417 Austin

Princess II 2000 HL
1978 UK
100.0mph 160.9kmh
0-50mph 80.5kmh: 10.1secs
0-60mph 96.5kmh: 14.6secs
0-1/4 mile: 19.4secs
0-1km: 36.0secs
93.0bhp 69.3kW 94.3PS
@ 4900rpm
112.0lbft 151.8Nm @ 3400rpm

82.0bhp/ton 80.6bhp/tonne
46.7bhp/L 34.8kW/L 47.3PS/L
47.6ft/sec 14.5m/sec
18.8mph 30.2kmh/1000rpm
24.1mpg 20.1mpgUS 11.7L/100km
Petrol 4-stroke piston
1993cc 121.6cu in
In-line 4 1 Carburettor
Compression ratio: 9.0:1
Bore: 84.4mm 3.3in
Stroke: 89.0mm 3.5in
Valve type/No: Overhead 8
Transmission: Manual
No. of forward speeds: 4
Wheels driven: Front
Springs F/R: Gas/Gas
Brake system: PA
Brakes F/R: Disc/Drum
Steering: Rack & pinion
Wheelbase: 267.2cm 105.2in
Track F: 148.6cm 58.5in
Track R: 147.3cm 58.0in
Length: 450.9cm 177.5in
Width: 172.0cm 67.7in
Height: 140.7cm 55.4in
Ground clearance: 19.1cm 7.5in
Kerb weight: 1153.2kg 2540.0lb
Fuel: 72.8L 16.0gal 19.2galUS

418 Austin

Metro Automatic
1981 UK
92.0mph 148.0kmh
0-50mph 80.5kmh: 13.8secs
0-60mph 96.5kmh: 19.4secs
0-1/4 mile: 22.1secs
0-1km: 40.5secs
60.0bhp 44.7kW 60.8PS
@ 5250rpm
69.0lbft 93.5Nm @ 3200rpm
75.1bhp/ton 73.8bhp/tonne
47.1bhp/L 35.1kW/L 47.7PS/L
46.7ft/sec 14.2m/sec
18.7mph 30.1kmh/1000rpm
27.7mpg 23.1mpgUS 10.2L/100km
Petrol 4-stroke piston
1275cc 77.8cu in
In-line 4 1 Carburettor
Compression ratio: 9.4:1
Bore: 70.6mm 2.8in
Stroke: 81.3mm 3.2in
Valve type/No: Overhead 8
Transmission: Automatic
No. of forward speeds: 4
Wheels driven: Front
Springs F/R: Gas/Gas
Brake system: PA
Brakes F/R: Disc/Drum
Steering: Rack & pinion
Wheelbase: 225.0cm 88.6in
Track F: 127.3cm 50.1in
Track R: 127.5cm 50.2in
Length: 340.6cm 134.1in
Width: 154.7cm 60.9in
Height: 135.9cm 53.5in
Ground clearance: 16.5cm 6.5in
Kerb weight: 812.7kg 1790.0lb
Fuel: 31.8L 7.0gal 8.4galUS

419 Austin

Mini Metro
1981 UK
87.0mph 140.0kmh
0-50mph 80.5kmh: 13.1secs
0-60mph 96.5kmh: 18.9secs
0-1/4 mile: 21.6secs
0-1km: 41.2secs
41.0bhp 30.6kW 41.6PS
@ 5400rpm
51.0lbft 69.1Nm @ 2700rpm
54.8bhp/ton 53.9bhp/tonne
41.1bhp/L 30.6kW/L 41.6PS/L
45.0ft/sec 13.7m/sec
16.3mph 26.2kmh/1000rpm
35.2mpg 29.3mpgUS 8.0L/100km
Petrol 4-stroke piston
998cc 60.9cu in
In-line 4 1 Carburettor
Compression ratio: 8.3:1
Bore: 64.6mm 2.5in
Stroke: 76.2mm 3.0in
Valve type/No: Overhead 8
Transmission: Manual
No. of forward speeds: 4
Wheels driven: Front
Springs F/R: Gas/Gas
Brake system: PA
Brakes F/R: Disc/Drum
Steering: Rack & pinion
Wheelbase: 225.0cm 88.6in
Track F: 127.3cm 50.1in
Track R: 127.5cm 50.2in
Length: 416.8cm 164.1in
Width: 154.7cm 60.9in
Height: 135.9cm 53.5in
Ground clearance: 16.5cm 6.5in
Kerb weight: 760.4kg 1675.0lb
Fuel: 31.8L 7.0gal 8.4galUS

420 Austin

Ambassador 2.0 HL
1982 UK
102.0mph 164.1kmh
0-50mph 80.5kmh: 9.5secs
0-60mph 96.5kmh: 14.3secs
0-1/4 mile: 19.6secs
0-1km: 36.7secs
92.0bhp 68.6kW 93.3PS
@ 4900rpm
114.0lbft 154.5Nm @ 2750rpm
74.0bhp/ton 72.8bhp/tonne
46.1bhp/L 34.4kW/L 46.8PS/L
47.6ft/sec 14.5m/sec
20.3mph 32.7kmh/1000rpm
26.5mpg 22.1mpgUS 10.7L/100km
Petrol 4-stroke piston
1994cc 121.7cu in
In-line 4 1 Carburettor
Compression ratio: 9.0:1
Bore: 84.4mm 3.3in
Stroke: 89.0mm 3.5in
Valve type/No: Overhead 8
Transmission: Manual
No. of forward speeds: 4
Wheels driven: Front
Springs F/R: Gas/Gas
Brake system: PA
Brakes F/R: Disc/Drum
Steering: Rack & pinion PA
Wheelbase: 267.2cm 105.2in
Track F: 147.8cm 58.2in
Track R: 145.8cm 57.4in
Length: 455.4cm 179.3in
Width: 176.3cm 69.4in
Height: 140.2cm 55.2in
Ground clearance: 17.0cm 6.7in
Kerb weight: 1263.9kg 2784.0lb
Fuel: 72.8L 16.0gal 19.2galUS

421 Austin

Maestro 1.6 HLS
1983 UK
105.0mph 168.9kmh
0-50mph 80.5kmh: 8.1secs
0-60mph 96.5kmh: 12.0secs
0-1/4 mile: 18.4secs
0-1km: 34.7secs
81.0bhp 60.4kW 82.1PS
@ 5000rpm
91.0lbft 123.3Nm @ 3500rpm
86.7bhp/ton 85.2bhp/tonne
50.7bhp/L 37.8kW/L 51.4PS/L
47.9ft/sec 14.6m/sec
24.5mph 39.4kmh/1000rpm
32.8mpg 27.3mpgUS 8.6L/100km
Petrol 4-stroke piston
1598cc 97.5cu in
In-line 4 1 Carburettor
Compression ratio: 9.7:1
Bore: 76.2mm 3.0in
Stroke: 87.6mm 3.4in
Valve type/No: Overhead 8
Transmission: Manual
No. of forward speeds: 5
Wheels driven: Front
Springs F/R: Coil/Coil
Brake system: PA
Brakes F/R: Disc/Drum
Steering: Rack & pinion
Wheelbase: 250.7cm 98.7in
Track F: 146.6cm 57.7in
Track R: 144.0cm 56.7in
Length: 405.1cm 159.5in
Width: 168.7cm 66.4in
Height: 143.0cm 56.3in
Ground clearance: 14.7cm 5.8in
Kerb weight: 950.2kg 2093.0lb
Fuel: 53.2L 11.7gal 14.1galUS

422 Austin

Maestro 1600
1983 UK
112.0mph 180.2kmh
0-50mph 80.5kmh: 6.7secs
0-60mph 96.5kmh: 9.6secs
0-1/4 mile: 17.1secs
0-1km: 32.0secs
103.0bhp 76.8kW 104.4PS
@ 6000rpm
100.0lbft 135.5Nm @ 4000rpm
105.3bhp/ton 103.6bhp/tonne
64.5bhp/L 48.1kW/L 65.3PS/L
57.5ft/sec 17.5m/sec
19.9mph 32.0kmh/1000rpm
26.8mpg 22.3mpgUS 10.5L/100km
Petrol 4-stroke piston
1598cc 97.5cu in
In-line 4 2 Carburettor
Compression ratio: 9.7:1
Bore: 76.2mm 3.0in
Stroke: 87.6mm 3.4in
Valve type/No: Overhead 8
Transmission: Manual
No. of forward speeds: 5
Wheels driven: Front
Springs F/R: Coil/Coil
Brake system: PA
Brakes F/R: Disc/Drum
Steering: Rack & pinion
Wheelbase: 250.7cm 98.7in
Track F: 149.9cm 59.0in
Track R: 147.3cm 58.0in
Length: 405.1cm 159.5in
Width: 168.7cm 66.4in
Height: 143.0cm 56.3in
Ground clearance: 14.7cm 5.8in
Kerb weight: 994.3kg 2190.0lb
Fuel: 53.2L 11.7gal 14.1galUS

423 Austin

Montego 1.6L
1984 UK
103.0mph 165.7kmh
0-50mph 80.5kmh: 8.2secs
0-60mph 96.5kmh: 11.9secs
0-1/4 mile: 18.4secs
86.0bhp 64.1kW 87.2PS
@ 5600rpm
97.0lbft 131.4Nm @ 3500rpm
86.6bhp/ton 85.1bhp/tonne
53.8bhp/L 40.1kW/L 54.6PS/L
53.4ft/sec 16.3m/sec
22.2mph 35.7kmh/1000rpm
31.9mpg 26.6mpgUS 8.9L/100km
Petrol 4-stroke piston
1598cc 97.5cu in
In-line 4 1 Carburettor
Compression ratio: 9.7:1
Bore: 76.2mm 3.0in
Stroke: 87.2mm 3.4in
Valve type/No: Overhead 8
Transmission: Manual with overdrive
No. of forward speeds: 6
Wheels driven: Front
Springs F/R: Coil/Coil
Brake system: PA
Brakes F/R: Disc/Drum
Steering: Rack & pinion
Wheelbase: 256.5cm 101.0in
Track F: 148.6cm 58.5in
Track R: 145.8cm 57.4in
Length: 455.9cm 179.5in
Width: 170.9cm 67.3in
Height: 142.0cm 55.9in
Ground clearance: 15.7cm 6.2in
Kerb weight: 1010.1kg 2225.0lb
Fuel: 51.0L 11.2gal 13.5galUS

424 Austin

Montego 2.0 HL
1985 UK
111.0mph 178.6kmh
0-50mph 80.5kmh: 7.5secs
0-60mph 96.5kmh: 10.1secs
0-1/4 mile: 17.6secs
0-1km: 32.6secs
102.0bhp 76.1kW 103.4PS
@ 5500rpm
121.0lbft 164.0Nm @ 3000rpm
97.9bhp/ton 96.3bhp/tonne
51.1bhp/L 38.1kW/L 51.9PS/L
53.5ft/sec 16.3m/sec
26.5mph 42.6kmh/1000rpm
29.4mpg 24.5mpgUS 9.6L/100km
Petrol 4-stroke piston
1994cc 121.7cu in
In-line 4 1 Carburettor
Compression ratio: 9.0:1
Bore: 84.5mm 3.3in
Stroke: 89.0mm 3.5in
Valve type/No: Overhead 8
Transmission: Manual
No. of forward speeds: 5
Wheels driven: Front
Springs F/R: Coil/Coil
Brake system: PA
Brakes F/R: Disc/Drum
Steering: Rack & pinion PA
Wheelbase: 256.5cm 101.0in
Track F: 144.0cm 56.7in
Track R: 145.8cm 57.4in
Length: 446.8cm 175.9in
Width: 170.9cm 67.3in
Height: 142.0cm 55.9in
Ground clearance: 15.7cm 6.2in
Kerb weight: 1059.2kg 2333.0lb
Fuel: 50.0L 11.0gal 13.2galUS

425 Austin

Montego 2.0 Vanden Plas EFI
1986 UK
112.0mph 180.2kmh
0-50mph 80.5kmh: 7.7secs
0-60mph 96.5kmh: 10.9secs
0-1/4 mile: 17.6secs
0-1km: 32.7secs
115.0bhp 85.8kW 116.6PS
@ 5500rpm
134.0lbft 181.6Nm @ 2800rpm
108.8bhp/ton 107.0bhp/tonne
57.7bhp/L 43.0kW/L 58.5PS/L
53.5ft/sec 16.3m/sec
26.8mph 43.1kmh/1000rpm
27.9mpg 23.2mpgUS 10.1L/100km
Petrol 4-stroke piston
1994cc 121.7cu in
In-line 4 fuel injection
Compression ratio: 9.0:1
Bore: 84.5mm 3.3in
Stroke: 89.0mm 3.5in
Valve type/No: Overhead 8
Transmission: Manual
No. of forward speeds: 5
Wheels driven: Front
Springs F/R: Coil/Coil
Brake system: PA
Brakes F/R: Disc/Drum
Steering: Rack & pinion PA
Wheelbase: 256.5cm 101.0in
Track F: 144.0cm 56.7in
Track R: 145.8cm 57.4in
Length: 446.8cm 175.9in
Width: 170.9cm 67.3in
Height: 142.0cm 55.9in
Ground clearance: 15.7cm 6.2in
Kerb weight: 1074.6kg 2367.0lb
Fuel: 50.0L 11.0gal 13.2galUS

426 Austin

Metro 1.3L 3-door
1987 UK
95.0mph 152.9kmh
0-50mph 80.5kmh: 8.5secs
0-60mph 96.5kmh: 13.0secs
0-1/4 mile: 19.4secs
0-1km: 36.5secs
62.0bhp 46.2kW 62.9PS
@ 5300rpm
72.0lbft 97.6Nm @ 3200rpm
78.8bhp/ton 77.5bhp/tonne
48.6bhp/L 36.3kW/L 49.3PS/L
47.1ft/sec 14.4m/sec
18.5mph 29.8kmh/1000rpm
36.9mpg 30.7mpgUS 7.7L/100km
Petrol 4-stroke piston
1275cc 78.0cu in
In-line 4 1 Carburettor
Compression ratio: 9.7:1
Bore: 70.6mm 2.8in
Stroke: 81.3mm 3.2in
Valve type/No: Overhead 8
Transmission: Manual
No. of forward speeds: 4
Wheels driven: Front
Springs F/R: Gas/Gas
Brake system: PA
Brakes F/R: Disc/Drum
Steering: Rack & pinion
Wheelbase: 225.0cm 88.6in
Track F: 127.3cm 50.1in
Track R: 127.5cm 50.2in
Length: 340.4cm 134.0in
Width: 154.7cm 60.9in
Height: 135.9cm 53.5in
Ground clearance: 16.5cm 6.5in
Kerb weight: 800.0kg 1762.1lb
Fuel: 35.5L 7.8gal 9.4galUS

427 Austin
Metro GTa
1989 UK
104.0mph 167.3kmh
0-50mph 80.5kmh: 8.2secs
0-60mph 96.5kmh: 11.8secs
0-1/4 mile: 18.6secs
0-1km: 34.7secs
73.0bhp 54.4kW 74.0PS
@ 6000rpm
73.1lbft 99.0Nm @ 4000rpm
89.4bhp/ton 87.9bhp/tonne
57.2bhp/L 42.7kW/L 58.0PS/L
53.3ft/sec 16.3m/sec
17.6mph 28.3kmh/1000rpm
30.7mpg 25.6mpgUS 9.2L/100km
Petrol 4-stroke piston
1275cc 78.0cu in
In-line 4 1 Carburettor
Compression ratio: 10.5:1
Bore: 70.6mm 2.8in
Stroke: 81.3mm 3.2in
Valve type/No: Overhead 8
Transmission: Manual
No. of forward speeds: 4
Wheels driven: Front
Springs F/R: Gas/Gas
Brake system: PA
Brakes F/R: Disc/Drum
Steering: Rack & pinion
Wheelbase: 225.0cm 88.6in
Track F: 127.3cm 50.1in
Track R: 127.5cm 50.2in
Length: 340.6cm 134.1in
Width: 156.0cm 61.4in
Height: 138.0cm 54.3in
Ground clearance: 16.5cm 6.5in
Kerb weight: 830.0kg 1828.2lb
Fuel: 35.5L 7.8gal 9.4galUS

428 Austin-Healey
100
1953 UK
119.0mph 191.5kmh
0-50mph 80.5kmh: 7.6secs
0-60mph 96.5kmh: 10.3secs
0-1/4 mile: 17.5secs
90.0bhp 67.1kW 91.2PS
@ 4000rpm
144.0lbft 195.1Nm @ 2500rpm
96.0bhp/ton 94.4bhp/tonne
33.8bhp/L 25.2kW/L 34.3PS/L
48.6ft/sec 14.8m/sec
23.8mph 38.3kmh/1000rpm
24.5mpg 20.4mpgUS 11.5L/100km
Petrol 4-stroke piston
2660cc 162.3cu in
In-line 4
Compression ratio: 7.5:1
Bore: 87.3mm 3.4in
Stroke: 111.1mm 4.4in
Valve type/No: Overhead 8
Transmission: Manual with overdrive
No. of forward speeds: 5
Wheels driven: Rear
Springs F/R: Coil/Leaf
Brakes F/R: Drum/Drum
Wheelbase: 228.6cm 90.0in
Track F: 123.7cm 48.7in
Track R: 128.8cm 50.7in
Length: 384.8cm 151.5in
Width: 153.7cm 60.5in
Height: 124.5cm 49.0in
Ground clearance: 15.2cm 6.0in
Kerb weight: 953.4kg 2100.0lb
Fuel: 54.6L 12.0gal 14.4galUS

429 Austin-Healey
100
1954 UK
102.3mph 164.6kmh
0-50mph 80.5kmh: 8.3secs
0-60mph 96.5kmh: 11.7secs
0-1/4 mile: 18.1secs
90.0bhp 67.1kW 91.2PS
@ 4000rpm
144.0lbft 195.1Nm @ 2500rpm
93.8bhp/ton 92.2bhp/tonne
33.8bhp/L 25.2kW/L 34.3PS/L
48.7ft/sec 14.8m/sec
23.9mph 38.5kmh/1000rpm
Petrol 4-stroke piston
2660cc 162.3cu in
In-line 6
Compression ratio: 7.5:1
Bore: 87.4mm 3.4in
Stroke: 111.3mm 4.4in
Valve type/No: Overhead 12
Transmission: Manual
No. of forward speeds: 3
Wheels driven: Rear
Wheelbase: 228.6cm 90.0in
Track F: 124.0cm 48.8in
Track R: 125.7cm 49.5in
Kerb weight: 976.1kg 2150.0lb

430 Austin-Healey
100S
1955 UK
118.6mph 190.8kmh
0-50mph 80.5kmh: 5.6secs
0-60mph 96.5kmh: 7.8secs
0-1/4 mile: 16.1secs
132.0bhp 98.4kW 133.8PS
@ 4700rpm
168.0lbft 227.6Nm @ 2500rpm
139.8bhp/ton 137.5bhp/tonne
49.7bhp/L 37.0kW/L 50.3PS/L
57.2ft/sec 17.4m/sec
26.6mph 42.8kmh/1000rpm
Petrol 4-stroke piston
2658cc 162.2cu in
In-line 4
Compression ratio: 8.3:1
Bore: 87.4mm 3.4in
Stroke: 111.3mm 4.4in
Valve type/No: Overhead 8
Transmission: Manual
No. of forward speeds: 4
Wheels driven: Rear
Wheelbase: 228.6cm 90.0in
Track F: 126.0cm 49.6in
Track R: 129.0cm 50.8in
Kerb weight: 960.2kg 2115.0lb

431 Austin-Healey
100M
1956 UK
109.0mph 175.4kmh
0-50mph 80.5kmh: 7.2secs
0-60mph 96.5kmh: 9.6secs
0-1/4 mile: 17.4secs
110.0bhp 82.0kW 111.5PS
@ 4500rpm
160.0lbft 216.8Nm @ 2500rpm
103.3bhp/ton 101.6bhp/tonne
41.3bhp/L 30.8kW/L 41.9PS/L
54.7ft/sec 16.7m/sec
23.4mph 37.7kmh/1000rpm
Petrol 4-stroke piston
2660cc 162.3cu in
In-line 4
Compression ratio: 8.1:1
Bore: 87.4mm 3.4in
Stroke: 111.3mm 4.4in
Valve type/No: Overhead 8
Transmission: Manual with overdrive
Wheels driven: Rear
Wheelbase: 228.6cm 90.0in
Track F: 124.5cm 49.0in
Track R: 129.0cm 50.8in
Kerb weight: 1082.8kg 2385.0lb

432 Austin-Healey
100/6
1957 UK
105.0mph 168.9kmh
0-50mph 80.5kmh: 8.5secs
0-60mph 96.5kmh: 12.2secs
0-1/4 mile: 18.2secs
102.0bhp 76.1kW 103.4PS
@ 4600rpm
142.0lbft 192.4Nm @ 2400rpm
92.1bhp/ton 90.6bhp/tonne
38.6bhp/L 28.8kW/L 39.2PS/L
44.7ft/sec 13.6m/sec
Petrol 4-stroke piston
2639cc 161.0cu in
In-line 6
Compression ratio: 8.3:1
Bore: 79.4mm 3.1in
Stroke: 88.9mm 3.5in
Valve type/No: Overhead 12
Transmission: Manual with overdrive
Wheels driven: Rear
Wheelbase: 233.7cm 92.0in
Track F: 124.0cm 48.8in
Track R: 127.0cm 50.0in
Kerb weight: 1125.9kg 2480.0lb

433 Austin-Healey
100/6
1958 UK
111.0mph 178.6kmh
0-50mph 80.5kmh: 8.2secs
0-60mph 96.5kmh: 11.2secs
0-1/4 mile: 18.1secs
117.0bhp 87.2kW 118.6PS
@ 4750rpm
149.0lbft 201.9Nm @ 3000rpm
107.6bhp/ton 105.8bhp/tonne
44.3bhp/L 33.1kW/L 44.9PS/L
46.2ft/sec 14.1m/sec
23.2mph 37.3kmh/1000rpm
21.2mpg 17.7mpgUS 13.3L/100km
Petrol 4-stroke piston
2639cc 161.0cu in
In-line 6
Compression ratio: 8.2:1
Bore: 79.4mm 3.1in
Stroke: 89.0mm 3.5in
Valve type/No: Overhead 12
Transmission: Manual with overdrive
No. of forward speeds: 6
Wheels driven: Rear
Springs F/R: Coil/Leaf
Brakes F/R: Drum/Drum
Wheelbase: 233.7cm 92.0in
Track F: 123.7cm 48.7in
Track R: 127.0cm 50.0in
Length: 400.1cm 157.5in
Width: 153.7cm 60.5in
Height: 124.5cm 49.0in
Ground clearance: 14.0cm 5.5in
Kerb weight: 1105.9kg 2436.0lb
Fuel: 54.6L 12.0gal 14.4galUS

434 Austin-Healey
Mille Miglia
1958 UK
109.0mph 175.4kmh
0-50mph 80.5kmh: 7.3secs
0-60mph 96.5kmh: 10.4secs
0-1/4 mile: 17.4secs
117.0bhp 87.2kW 118.6PS
@ 4750rpm
149.0lbft 201.9Nm @ 3000rpm
100.8bhp/ton 99.1bhp/tonne
44.3bhp/L 33.1kW/L 44.9PS/L
39.6ft/sec 12.1m/sec
Petrol 4-stroke piston
2639cc 161.0cu in
In-line 6
Compression ratio: 8.5:1
Bore: 79.4mm 3.1in
Stroke: 76.2mm 3.0in
Valve type/No: Overhead 12
Transmission: Manual with overdrive
Wheels driven: Rear
Wheelbase: 233.7cm 92.0in
Track F: 124.0cm 48.8in
Track R: 127.0cm 50.0in
Kerb weight: 1180.4kg 2600.0lb

435 Austin-Healey
Sprite
1958 UK
81.0mph 130.3kmh
0-50mph 80.5kmh: 13.7secs
0-60mph 96.5kmh: 20.9secs
0-1/4 mile: 21.7secs
50.0bhp 37.3kW 50.7PS
@ 5500rpm
52.0lbft 70.5Nm @ 3000rpm
76.6bhp/ton 75.3bhp/tonne
52.7bhp/L 39.3kW/L 53.5PS/L
45.8ft/sec 14.0m/sec
15.4mph 24.8kmh/1000rpm
34.0mpg 28.3mpgUS 8.3L/100km
Petrol 4-stroke piston
948cc 57.8cu in
In-line 4
Compression ratio: 8.3:1
Bore: 62.9mm 2.5in
Stroke: 76.2mm 3.0in
Valve type/No: Overhead 8
Transmission: Manual
No. of forward speeds: 4
Wheels driven: Rear
Springs F/R: Coil/Leaf
Brakes F/R: Drum/Drum
Wheelbase: 203.2cm 80.0in
Track F: 116.1cm 45.7in
Track R: 113.5cm 44.7in
Length: 348.5cm 137.2in
Width: 134.6cm 53.0in
Height: 126.2cm 49.7in
Ground clearance: 12.7cm 5.0in
Kerb weight: 664.2kg 1463.0lb
Fuel: 27.3L 6.0gal 7.2galUS

436 Austin-Healey
3000
1959 UK
116.0mph 186.6kmh
0-50mph 80.5kmh: 8.0secs
0-60mph 96.5kmh: 11.4secs
0-1/4 mile: 17.9secs
124.0bhp 92.5kW 125.7PS
@ 4600rpm
175.0lbft 237.1Nm @ 3000rpm
110.5bhp/ton 108.7bhp/tonne
42.6bhp/L 31.7kW/L 43.2PS/L
44.7ft/sec 13.6m/sec
23.1mph 37.2kmh/1000rpm
20.0mpg 16.7mpgUS 14.1L/100km
Petrol 4-stroke piston
2912cc 177.7cu in
In-line 6
Compression ratio: 9.0:1
Bore: 83.3mm 3.3in
Stroke: 88.9mm 3.5in
Valve type/No: Overhead 12
Transmission: Manual with overdrive
No. of forward speeds: 6
Wheels driven: Rear
Springs F/R: Coil/Leaf
Brakes F/R: Disc/Drum
Wheelbase: 233.7cm 92.0in
Track F: 123.7cm 48.7in
Track R: 127.0cm 50.0in
Length: 400.1cm 157.5in
Width: 153.7cm 60.5in
Height: 127.0cm 50.0in
Ground clearance: 11.4cm 4.5in
Kerb weight: 1140.9kg 2513.0lb
Fuel: 54.6L 12.0gal 14.4galUS

437 Austin-Healey
Sprite Hardtop
1959 UK
86.0mph 138.4kmh
0-50mph 80.5kmh: 14.9secs
0-60mph 96.5kmh: 23.7secs
0-1/4 mile: 22.3secs
42.5bhp 31.7kW 43.1PS
@ 5500rpm
52.0lbft 70.5Nm @ 3200rpm
63.8bhp/ton 62.8bhp/tonne
44.8bhp/L 33.4kW/L 45.4PS/L
45.8ft/sec 14.0m/sec
15.4mph 24.8kmh/1000rpm
40.3mpg 33.6mpgUS 7.0L/100km
Petrol 4-stroke piston
948cc 57.8cu in
In-line 4 2 Carburettor
Compression ratio: 8.3:1
Bore: 62.9mm 2.5in
Stroke: 76.2mm 3.0in
Valve type/No: Overhead 8
Transmission: Manual
No. of forward speeds: 4
Wheels driven: Rear
Springs F/R: Coil/Leaf
Brakes F/R: Drum/Drum
Wheelbase: 203.2cm 80.0in
Track F: 116.1cm 45.7in
Track R: 113.5cm 44.7in
Length: 348.5cm 137.2in
Width: 134.6cm 53.0in
Height: 126.2cm 49.7in
Ground clearance: 12.7cm 5.0in
Kerb weight: 676.9kg 1491.0lb
Fuel: 27.3L 6.0gal 7.2galUS

438 Austin-Healey
Sebring Sprite
1960 UK
87.4mph 140.6kmh
0-50mph 80.5kmh: 10.5secs
0-60mph 96.5kmh: 14.2secs
0-1/4 mile: 20.0secs
55.0bhp 41.0kW 55.8PS
@ 5800rpm
59.0lbft 79.9Nm @ 3600rpm
83.5bhp/ton 82.1bhp/tonne
58.0bhp/L 43.3kW/L 58.8PS/L
48.3ft/sec 14.7m/sec
14.6mph 23.5kmh/1000rpm
Petrol 4-stroke piston
948cc 57.8cu in
In-line 4 1 Carburettor
Compression ratio: 9.3:1

Bore: 63.0mm 2.5in
Stroke: 76.2mm 3.0in
Valve type/No: Overhead 8
Transmission: Manual
No. of forward speeds: 4
Wheels driven: Rear
Wheelbase: 203.2cm 80.0in
Track F: 117.9cm 46.4in
Track R: 116.3cm 45.8in
Length: 348.0cm 137.0in
Width: 137.2cm 54.0in
Height: 121.9cm 48.0in
Kerb weight: 669.6kg 1475.0lb

439 Austin-Healey

Sprite Supercharged
1960 UK
90.0mph 144.8kmh
0-50mph 80.5kmh: 10.4secs
0-60mph 96.5kmh: 15.3secs
0-1/4 mile: 19.7secs
68.0bhp 50.7kW 68.9PS
@ 5700rpm
65.0lbft 88.1Nm @ 3000rpm
102.2bhp/ton 100.5bhp/tonne
71.7bhp/L 53.5kW/L 72.7PS/L
47.5ft/sec 14.5m/sec
15.4mph 24.8kmh/1000rpm
28.3mpg 23.6mpgUS 10.0L/100km
Petrol 4-stroke piston
948cc 57.8cu in supercharged
In-line 4 2 Carburettor
Compression ratio: 8.3:1
Bore: 62.9mm 2.5in
Stroke: 76.2mm 3.0in
Valve type/No: Overhead 8
Transmission: Manual
No. of forward speeds: 4
Wheels driven: Rear
Springs F/R: Coil/Leaf
Brakes F/R: Drum/Drum
Wheelbase: 203.2cm 80.0in
Track F: 116.1cm 45.7in
Track R: 113.5cm 44.7in
Length: 348.5cm 137.2in
Width: 134.6cm 53.0in
Height: 126.2cm 49.7in
Ground clearance: 12.7cm 5.0in
Kerb weight: 676.9kg 1491.0lb
Fuel: 27.3L 6.0gal 7.2galUS

440 Austin-Healey

3000
1961 UK
115.0mph 185.0kmh
0-50mph 80.5kmh: 9.3secs
0-60mph 96.5kmh: 11.5secs
0-1/4 mile: 18.8secs
130.0bhp 96.9kW 131.8PS
@ 4750rpm
167.0lbft 226.3Nm @ 3000rpm
114.0bhp/ton 112.1bhp/tonne
44.6bhp/L 33.3kW/L 45.3PS/L
46.2ft/sec 14.1m/sec
20.9mph 33.6kmh/1000rpm
17.7mpg 14.7mpgUS 16.0L/100km
Petrol 4-stroke piston
2912cc 177.7cu in
In-line 6
Compression ratio: 9.0:1
Bore: 83.3mm 3.3in
Stroke: 89.0mm 3.5in
Valve type/No: Overhead 12
Transmission: Manual with overdrive
No. of forward speeds: 6
Wheels driven: Rear
Springs F/R: Coil/Leaf
Brakes F/R: Disc/Drum
Wheelbase: 233.7cm 92.0in
Track F: 123.7cm 48.7in
Track R: 127.0cm 50.0in
Length: 400.1cm 157.5in
Width: 153.7cm 60.5in
Height: 137.2cm 54.0in
Ground clearance: 11.4cm 4.5in
Kerb weight: 1160.0kg 2555.0lb
Fuel: 54.6L 12.0gal 14.4galUS

441 Austin-Healey

Sprite Mk II
1961 UK
85.5mph 137.6kmh
0-50mph 80.5kmh: 13.8secs
0-60mph 96.5kmh: 19.8secs
0-1/4 mile: 21.8secs
46.5bhp 34.7kW 47.1PS
@ 5500rpm
53.0lbft 71.8Nm @ 2750rpm
67.6bhp/ton 66.5bhp/tonne
49.0bhp/L 36.6kW/L 49.7PS/L
45.8ft/sec 14.0m/sec
15.3mph 24.6kmh/1000rpm
33.2mpg 27.6mpgUS 8.5L/100km
Petrol 4-stroke piston
948cc 57.8cu in
In-line 4 2 Carburettor
Compression ratio: 9.0:1
Bore: 62.9mm 2.5in
Stroke: 76.2mm 3.0in
Valve type/No: Overhead 8
Transmission: Manual
No. of forward speeds: 4
Wheels driven: Rear
Springs F/R: Coil/Leaf
Brakes F/R: Drum/Drum
Wheelbase: 203.2cm 80.0in
Track F: 116.1cm 45.7in
Track R: 113.5cm 44.7in
Length: 345.4cm 136.0in
Width: 134.6cm 53.0in
Height: 126.2cm 49.7in
Ground clearance: 17.8cm 7.0in
Kerb weight: 699.2kg 1540.0lb
Fuel: 27.3L 6.0gal 7.2galUS

442 Austin-Healey

3000
1962 UK
115.0mph 185.0kmh
0-50mph 80.5kmh: 8.2secs
0-60mph 96.5kmh: 11.2secs
0-1/4 mile: 17.6secs
136.0bhp 101.4kW 137.9PS
@ 4750rpm
167.0lbft 226.3Nm @ 3000rpm
125.4bhp/ton 123.3bhp/tonne
46.7bhp/L 34.8kW/L 47.3PS/L
46.2ft/sec 14.1m/sec
23.7mph 38.1kmh/1000rpm
Petrol 4-stroke piston
2912cc 177.7cu in
In-line 6
Compression ratio: 9.0:1
Bore: 83.3mm 3.3in
Stroke: 88.9mm 3.5in
Valve type/No: Overhead 12
Transmission: Manual with overdrive
Wheels driven: Rear
Wheelbase: 233.7cm 92.0in
Track F: 123.7cm 48.7in
Track R: 127.0cm 50.0in
Length: 400.1cm 157.5in
Width: 153.7cm 60.5in
Height: 127.0cm 50.0in
Ground clearance: 11.4cm 4.5in
Kerb weight: 1103.2kg 2430.0lb

443 Austin-Healey

3000 Mk II
1962 UK
120.0mph 193.1kmh
0-50mph 80.5kmh: 7.8secs
0-60mph 96.5kmh: 10.4secs
0-1/4 mile: 17.8secs
130.0bhp 96.9kW 131.8PS
@ 4750rpm
167.0lbft 226.3Nm @ 3000rpm
113.7bhp/ton 111.8bhp/tonne
44.6bhp/L 33.3kW/L 45.3PS/L
46.2ft/sec 14.1m/sec
25.4mph 40.9kmh/1000rpm
17.1mpg 14.2mpgUS 16.5L/100km
Petrol 4-stroke piston
2912cc 177.7cu in
In-line 6 2 Carburettor
Compression ratio: 9.0:1
Bore: 83.3mm 3.3in
Stroke: 88.9mm 3.5in
Valve type/No: Overhead 12
Transmission: Manual with overdrive
No. of forward speeds: 6
Wheels driven: Rear
Springs F/R: Coil/Leaf
Brake system: PA
Brakes F/R: Disc/Drum
Steering: Cam & peg
Wheelbase: 232.9cm 91.7in
Track F: 123.7cm 48.7in
Track R: 127.0cm 50.0in
Length: 400.1cm 157.5in
Width: 152.4cm 60.0in
Height: 123.7cm 48.7in
Ground clearance: 11.4cm 4.5in
Kerb weight: 1163.1kg 2562.0lb
Fuel: 54.6L 12.0gal 14.4galUS

444 Austin-Healey

Sprite 1100
1963 UK
85.0mph 136.8kmh
0-50mph 80.5kmh: 12.5secs
0-60mph 96.5kmh: 18.3secs
0-1/4 mile: 20.9secs
55.0bhp 41.0kW 55.8PS
@ 5500rpm
61.0lbft 82.7Nm @ 2500rpm
79.0bhp/ton 77.7bhp/tonne
50.1bhp/L 37.3kW/L 50.8PS/L
50.4ft/sec 15.4m/sec
15.4mph 24.8kmh/1000rpm
Petrol 4-stroke piston
1098cc 67.0cu in
In-line 4 1 Carburettor
Compression ratio: 8.9:1
Bore: 64.5mm 2.5in
Stroke: 83.8mm 3.3in
Valve type/No: Overhead 8
Transmission: Manual
No. of forward speeds: 4
Wheels driven: Rear
Wheelbase: 204.5cm 80.5in
Track F: 119.9cm 47.2in
Track R: 114.3cm 45.0in
Length: 350.5cm 138.0in
Width: 137.2cm 54.0in
Height: 121.4cm 47.8in
Ground clearance: 15.7cm 6.2in
Kerb weight: 708.2kg 1560.0lb

445 Austin-Healey

3000 Mk III
1964 UK
122.0mph 196.3kmh
0-50mph 80.5kmh: 7.0secs
0-60mph 96.5kmh: 9.8secs
0-1/4 mile: 17.2secs
148.0bhp 110.4kW 150.0PS
@ 5250rpm
162.0lbft 219.5Nm @ 3500rpm
127.3bhp/ton 125.2bhp/tonne
50.8bhp/L 37.9kW/L 51.5PS/L
51.0ft/sec 15.6m/sec
23.0mph 37.0kmh/1000rpm
20.3mpg 16.9mpgUS 13.9L/100km
Petrol 4-stroke piston
2912cc 177.7cu in
In-line 6 2 Carburettor
Compression ratio: 9.0:1
Bore: 83.3mm 3.3in
Stroke: 88.9mm 3.5in
Valve type/No: Overhead 12
Transmission: Manual with overdrive
No. of forward speeds: 6
Wheels driven: Rear
Springs F/R: Coil/Leaf
Brake system: PA
Brakes F/R: Disc/Drum
Steering: Cam & peg
Wheelbase: 232.9cm 91.7in
Track F: 123.7cm 48.7in
Track R: 127.0cm 50.0in
Length: 400.1cm 157.5in
Width: 152.4cm 60.0in
Height: 123.7cm 48.7in
Ground clearance: 11.4cm 4.5in
Kerb weight: 1182.2kg 2604.0lb
Fuel: 54.6L 12.0gal 14.4galUS

446 Austin-Healey

3000 Mk III
1965 UK
116.0mph 186.6kmh
0-50mph 80.5kmh: 7.0secs
0-60mph 96.5kmh: 9.8secs
0-1/4 mile: 17.4secs
148.0bhp 110.4kW 150.0PS
@ 5250rpm
165.0lbft 223.6Nm @ 3500rpm
125.1bhp/ton 123.0bhp/tonne
50.8bhp/L 37.9kW/L 51.5PS/L
51.0ft/sec 15.6m/sec
23.3mph 37.5kmh/1000rpm
Petrol 4-stroke piston
2912cc 177.7cu in
In-line 6 2 Carburettor
Compression ratio: 9.0:1
Bore: 83.3mm 3.3in
Stroke: 88.9mm 3.5in
Valve type/No: Overhead 12
Transmission: Manual with overdrive
Wheels driven: Rear
Springs F/R: Coil/Leaf
Brakes F/R: Disc/Drum
Steering: Cam & lever
Wheelbase: 233.7cm 92.0in
Track F: 123.7cm 48.7in
Track R: 127.0cm 50.0in
Length: 398.8cm 157.0in
Width: 152.4cm 60.0in
Height: 127.0cm 50.0in
Ground clearance: 11.4cm 4.5in
Kerb weight: 1203.1kg 2650.0lb
Fuel: 54.5L 12.0gal 14.4galUS

447 Austin-Healey

Sprite
1968 UK
93.0mph 149.6kmh
0-60mph 96.5kmh: 14.7secs
0-1/4 mile: 19.9secs
65.0bhp 48.5kW 65.9PS
@ 6000rpm
72.0lbft 97.6Nm @ 3000rpm
93.3bhp/ton 91.8bhp/tonne
51.0bhp/L 38.0kW/L 51.7PS/L
53.3ft/sec 16.3m/sec
15.4mph 24.8kmh/1000rpm
Petrol 4-stroke piston
1275cc 77.8cu in
In-line 4
Bore: 70.6mm 2.8in
Stroke: 81.3mm 3.2in
Valve type/No: Overhead 8
Transmission: Manual
No. of forward speeds: 4
Wheels driven: Rear
Brakes F/R: Disc/Drum
Wheelbase: 203.2cm 80.0in
Track F: 117.6cm 46.3in
Track R: 113.8cm 44.8in
Length: 349.0cm 137.4in
Width: 143.8cm 56.6in
Height: 123.4cm 48.6in
Kerb weight: 708.2kg 1560.0lb

448 Austro Daimler

32/100 Saloon
1931 Austria
81.8mph 131.6kmh
13.0mpg 10.8mpgUS 21.7L/100km
Petrol 4-stroke piston
4624cc 282.1cu in
In-line 8
Bore: 80.0mm 3.1in
Stroke: 115.0mm 4.5in
Transmission: Manual
No. of forward speeds: 4
Wheels driven: Rear
Brakes F/R: Drum/Drum
Wheelbase: 372.1cm 146.5in
Track F: 144.8cm 57.0in
Track R: 144.8cm 57.0in
Length: 495.3cm 195.0in
Width: 180.3cm 71.0in
Height: 162.6cm 64.0in
Kerb weight: 2110.2kg 4648.0lb
Fuel: 100.1L 22.0gal 26.4galUS

449 Auto Union

1000
1958 Germany
80.8mph 130.0kmh
0-50mph 80.5kmh: 14.4secs
0-60mph 96.5kmh: 21.7secs
0-1/4 mile: 22.7secs
50.0bhp 37.3kW 50.7PS
@ 4500rpm
61.5lbft 83.3Nm @ 2250rpm
55.4bhp/ton 54.5bhp/tonne
51.0bhp/L 38.0kW/L 51.7PS/L
37.4ft/sec 11.4m/sec
17.1mph 27.5kmh/1000rpm
Petrol 2-stroke piston
980cc 59.8cu in
In-line 3
Compression ratio: 7.3:1
Bore: 73.9mm 2.9in
Stroke: 75.9mm 3.0in
Transmission: Manual
No. of forward speeds: 4
Wheels driven: Front
Wheelbase: 235.0cm 92.5in
Track F: 129.0cm 50.8in
Track R: 134.9cm 53.1in
Length: 421.6cm 166.0in

Width: 169.7cm 66.8in
Height: 146.6cm 57.7in
Kerb weight: 917.1kg 2020.0lb

450 Auto Union

1000
1959 Germany
80.3mph 129.2kmh
0-50mph 80.5kmh: 15.3secs
0-60mph 96.5kmh: 23.0secs
0-1/4 mile: 22.5secs
44.6bhp 33.3kW 45.2PS
@ 4500rpm
62.0lbft 84.0Nm @ 2250rpm
50.6bhp/ton 49.8bhp/tonne
45.5bhp/L 33.9kW/L 46.1PS/L
37.4ft/sec 11.4m/sec
18.6mph 29.9kmh/1000rpm
26.4mpg 22.0mpgUS 10.7L/100km
Petrol 2-stroke piston
980cc 59.8cu in
In-line 3
Compression ratio: 7.2:1
Bore: 74.0mm 2.9in
Stroke: 76.0mm 3.0in
Valve type/No: Ports
Transmission: Manual
No. of forward speeds: 4
Wheels driven: Front
Springs F/R: Leaf/Leaf
Brakes F/R: Drum/Drum
Wheelbase: 235.0cm 92.5in
Track F: 128.8cm 50.7in
Track R: 134.9cm 53.1in
Length: 422.4cm 166.3in
Width: 169.4cm 66.7in
Height: 146.6cm 57.7in
Ground clearance: 20.3cm 8.0in
Kerb weight: 896.2kg 1974.0lb
Fuel: 44.6L 9.8gal 11.8galUS

451 Auto Union

Universal
1961 Germany
74.0mph 119.1kmh
0-50mph 80.5kmh: 20.4secs
0-60mph 96.5kmh: 35.7secs
0-1/4 mile: 24.0secs
44.0bhp 32.8kW 44.6PS
@ 4500rpm
61.0lbft 82.7Nm @ 2250rpm
45.6bhp/ton 44.8bhp/tonne
44.8bhp/L 33.4kW/L 45.5PS/L
37.4ft/sec 11.4m/sec
16.8mph 27.0kmh/1000rpm
23.1mpg 19.2mpgUS 12.2L/100km
Petrol 2-stroke piston
981cc 59.8cu in
In-line 3
Compression ratio: 7.2:1
Bore: 74.0mm 2.9in
Stroke: 76.0mm 3.0in
Valve type/No: Ports
Transmission: Manual
No. of forward speeds: 4
Wheels driven: Front
Springs F/R: Leaf/Leaf
Brakes F/R: Drum/Drum
Wheelbase: 245.1cm 96.5in
Track F: 127.8cm 50.3in
Track R: 134.6cm 53.0in
Length: 414.0cm 163.0in
Width: 164.6cm 64.8in
Height: 149.4cm 58.8in
Ground clearance: 17.0cm 6.7in
Kerb weight: 982.0kg 2163.0lb
Fuel: 45.5L 10.0gal 12.0galUS

452 Auto Union

Audi
1966 Germany
97.0mph 156.1kmh
0-50mph 80.5kmh: 11.3secs
0-60mph 96.5kmh: 16.5secs
0-1/4 mile: 20.4secs
0-1km: 38.7secs
72.0bhp 53.7kW 73.0PS
@ 5000rpm
94.0lbft 127.4Nm @ 2400rpm
71.0bhp/ton 69.8bhp/tonne
42.5bhp/L 31.7kW/L 43.1PS/L
46.1ft/sec 14.1m/sec
16.7mph 26.9kmh/1000rpm
24.5mpg 20.4mpgUS 11.5L/100km
Petrol 4-stroke piston
1695cc 103.4cu in
In-line 4 1 Carburettor
Compression ratio: 11.2:1
Bore: 80.0mm 3.1in
Stroke: 84.4mm 3.3in
Valve type/No: Overhead 8
Transmission: Manual
No. of forward speeds: 4
Wheels driven: Front
Springs F/R: Torsion bar/Torsion bar
Brakes F/R: Disc/Drum
Steering: Rack & pinion
Wheelbase: 248.9cm 98.0in
Track F: 133.1cm 52.4in
Track R: 132.6cm 52.2in
Length: 440.7cm 173.5in
Width: 162.6cm 64.0in
Height: 146.1cm 57.5in
Ground clearance: 18.8cm 7.4in
Kerb weight: 1031.5kg 2272.0lb
Fuel: 53.2L 11.7gal 14.1galUS

453 Auto Union

Audi Super 90
1967 Germany
102.0mph 164.1kmh
0-50mph 80.5kmh: 8.8secs
0-60mph 96.5kmh: 12.8secs
0-1/4 mile: 18.7secs
0-1km: 35.0secs
90.0bhp 67.1kW 91.2PS
@ 5200rpm
108.0lbft 146.3Nm @ 3000rpm
92.3bhp/ton 90.8bhp/tonne
51.1bhp/L 38.1kW/L 51.8PS/L
48.0ft/sec 14.6m/sec
18.6mph 29.9kmh/1000rpm
21.3mpg 17.7mpgUS 13.3L/100km
Petrol 4-stroke piston
1760cc 107.4cu in
In-line 4 1 Carburettor
Compression ratio: 10.6:1
Bore: 81.5mm 3.2in
Stroke: 84.4mm 3.3in
Valve type/No: Overhead 8
Transmission: Manual
No. of forward speeds: 4
Wheels driven: Front
Springs F/R: Torsion bar/Torsion bar
Brakes F/R: Disc/Drum
Steering: Rack & pinion
Wheelbase: 248.9cm 98.0in
Track F: 133.1cm 52.4in
Track R: 132.6cm 52.2in
Length: 439.4cm 173.0in
Width: 162.6cm 64.0in
Height: 146.1cm 57.5in
Ground clearance: 18.8cm 7.4in
Kerb weight: 991.5kg 2184.0lb
Fuel: 53.5L 11.7gal 14.1galUS

454 Auto Union

100 LS
1969 Germany
108.0mph 173.8kmh
0-50mph 80.5kmh: 8.4secs
0-60mph 96.5kmh: 11.9secs
0-1/4 mile: 18.7secs
0-1km: 35.7secs
100.0bhp 74.6kW 101.4PS
@ 5500rpm
111.0lbft 150.4Nm @ 3200rpm
97.0bhp/ton 95.3bhp/tonne
56.8bhp/L 42.4kW/L 57.6PS/L
50.7ft/sec 15.5m/sec
18.5mph 29.8kmh/1000rpm
23.7mpg 19.7mpgUS 11.9L/100km
Petrol 4-stroke piston
1760cc 107.4cu in
In-line 4 1 Carburettor
Compression ratio: 10.2:1
Bore: 81.5mm 3.2in
Stroke: 84.4mm 3.3in
Valve type/No: Overhead 8
Transmission: Manual
No. of forward speeds: 4
Wheels driven: Front
Springs F/R: Coil/Torsion bar
Brake system: PA
Brakes F/R: Disc/Drum
Steering: Rack & pinion
Wheelbase: 267.5cm 105.3in
Track F: 142.0cm 55.9in
Track R: 142.5cm 56.1in
Length: 462.3cm 182.0in
Width: 172.7cm 68.0in
Height: 141.7cm 55.8in
Ground clearance: 19.6cm 7.7in
Kerb weight: 1048.7kg 2310.0lb
Fuel: 58.2L 12.8gal 15.4galUS

455 Autokraft

AC Cobra Mk IV
1985 UK
0-60mph 96.5kmh: 5.2secs
0-1/4 mile: 13.7secs
300.0bhp 223.7kW 304.2PS
@ 6000rpm
285.0lbft 386.2Nm @ 3800rpm
274.3bhp/ton 269.7bhp/tonne
52.1bhp/L 38.8kW/L 52.8PS/L
Petrol 4-stroke piston
5763cc 351.6cu in
Vee 8 1 Carburettor
Valve type/No: Overhead 16
Transmission: Manual
No. of forward speeds: 5
Wheels driven: Rear
Springs F/R: Coil/Coil
Brake system: PA
Brakes F/R: Disc/Disc
Steering: Rack & pinion
Wheelbase: 228.6cm 90.0in
Track F: 142.2cm 56.0in
Track R: 152.4cm 60.0in
Length: 411.5cm 162.0in
Width: 172.7cm 68.0in
Height: 124.5cm 49.0in
Kerb weight: 1112.3kg 2450.0lb

456 Autokraft

AC Cobra Mk IV
1987 UK
129.0mph 207.6kmh
0-60mph 96.5kmh: 5.0secs
0-1/4 mile: 13.5secs
300.0bhp 223.7kW 304.2PS
@ 6000rpm
285.0lbft 386.2Nm @ 3800rpm
274.3bhp/ton 269.7bhp/tonne
52.1bhp/L 38.8kW/L 52.8PS/L
20.9mph 33.6kmh/1000rpm
Petrol 4-stroke piston
5763cc 351.6cu in
Vee 8 1 Carburettor
Compression ratio: 10.6:1
Valve type/No: Overhead 16
Transmission: Manual
No. of forward speeds: 5
Wheels driven: Rear
Springs F/R: Coil/Coil
Brake system: PA
Brakes F/R: Disc/Disc
Steering: Rack & pinion
Wheelbase: 228.6cm 90.0in
Track F: 142.2cm 56.0in
Track R: 152.4cm 60.0in
Length: 411.5cm 162.0in
Width: 172.7cm 68.0in
Height: 124.5cm 49.0in
Kerb weight: 1112.3kg 2450.0lb

457 Avanti

R2
1963 USA
135.0mph 217.2kmh
0-60mph 96.5kmh: 7.9secs
0-1/4 mile: 16.1secs
280.0bhp 208.8kW 283.9PS
180.7bhp/ton 177.7bhp/tonne
59.1bhp/L 44.1kW/L 59.9PS/L
Petrol 4-stroke piston
4737cc 289.0cu in
Vee 8 1 Carburettor
Compression ratio: 9.1:1
Bore: 90.4mm 3.6in
Stroke: 92.2mm 3.6in
Valve type/No: Overhead 16
Transmission: Manual
No. of forward speeds: 4
Wheels driven: Rear
Springs F/R: Coil/Leaf
Brake system: PA
Brakes F/R: Disc/Drum
Steering: Cam & roller PA
Wheelbase: 276.9cm 109.0in
Track F: 146.1cm 57.5in
Track R: 143.5cm 56.5in
Length: 489.0cm 192.5in
Width: 178.8cm 70.4in
Height: 137.2cm 54.0in
Kerb weight: 1575.4kg 3470.0lb
Fuel: 79.5L 17.5gal 21.0galUS

458 Avanti

II
1966 USA
125.0mph 201.1kmh
0-50mph 80.5kmh: 6.7secs
0-60mph 96.5kmh: 8.8secs
0-1/4 mile: 17.5secs
300.0bhp 223.7kW 304.2PS
@ 5000rpm
360.0lbft 487.8Nm @ 3200rpm
193.1bhp/ton 189.9bhp/tonne
55.9bhp/L 41.7kW/L 56.7PS/L
45.3ft/sec 13.8m/sec
21.5mph 34.6kmh/1000rpm
Petrol 4-stroke piston
5367cc 327.5cu in
Vee 8 1 Carburettor
Compression ratio: 10.5:1
Bore: 108.0mm 4.2in
Stroke: 82.7mm 3.3in
Valve type/No: Overhead 16
Transmission: Automatic
No. of forward speeds: 3
Wheels driven: Rear
Springs F/R: Coil/Coil
Brakes F/R: Disc/Drum
Steering: Cam & lever
Wheelbase: 276.9cm 109.0in
Track F: 145.8cm 57.4in
Track R: 143.8cm 56.6in
Length: 489.0cm 192.5in
Width: 178.8cm 70.4in
Height: 137.2cm 54.0in
Ground clearance: 15.0cm 5.9in
Kerb weight: 1579.9kg 3480.0lb
Fuel: 79.5L 17.5gal 21.0galUS

459 Avanti

II
1969 USA
124.0mph 199.5kmh
0-50mph 80.5kmh: 5.9secs
0-60mph 96.5kmh: 7.5secs
0-1/4 mile: 15.5secs
300.0bhp 223.7kW 304.2PS
@ 4800rpm
380.0lbft 514.9Nm @ 3200rpm
200.6bhp/ton 197.2bhp/tonne
52.3bhp/L 39.0kW/L 53.0PS/L
46.4ft/sec 14.1m/sec
21.5mph 34.6kmh/1000rpm
Petrol 4-stroke piston
5735cc 349.9cu in
Vee 8 1 Carburettor
Compression ratio: 10.3:1
Bore: 101.6mm 4.0in
Stroke: 88.4mm 3.5in
Valve type/No: Overhead 16
Transmission: Automatic
No. of forward speeds: 3
Wheels driven: Rear
Springs F/R: Coil/Leaf
Brake system: PA
Brakes F/R: Disc/Drum
Steering: Cam & lever PA
Wheelbase: 276.9cm 109.0in
Track F: 145.8cm 57.4in
Track R: 143.8cm 56.6in
Length: 489.0cm 192.5in
Width: 178.8cm 70.4in
Height: 137.2cm 54.0in
Kerb weight: 1520.9kg 3350.0lb
Fuel: 79.5L 17.5gal 21.0galUS

460 Avanti

II
1984 USA
130.0mph 209.2kmh
0-50mph 80.5kmh: 6.1secs
0-60mph 96.5kmh: 8.4secs
0-1/4 mile: 16.3secs
180.0bhp 134.2kW 182.5PS
@ 4000rpm
240.0lbft 325.2Nm @ 1600rpm
109.4bhp/ton 107.6bhp/tonne
36.0bhp/L 26.8kW/L 36.5PS/L
38.7ft/sec 11.8m/sec
38.7mph 62.3kmh/1000rpm
16.8mpg 14.0mpgUS 16.8L/100km
Petrol 4-stroke piston
5004cc 305.3cu in
Vee 8 1 Carburettor
Compression ratio: 9.0:1
Bore: 94.9mm 3.7in
Stroke: 88.4mm 3.5in
Valve type/No: Overhead 16
Transmission: Automatic

No. of forward speeds: 4
Wheels driven: Rear
Springs F/R: Coil/Leaf
Brake system: PA
Brakes F/R: Disc/Drum
Steering: Recirculating ball PA
Wheelbase: 276.9cm 109.0in
Track F: 145.8cm 57.4in
Track R: 143.8cm 56.6in
Length: 490.5cm 193.1in
Width: 178.8cm 70.4in
Height: 138.2cm 54.4in
Ground clearance: 10.2cm 4.0in
Kerb weight: 1673.0kg 3685.0lb
Fuel: 71.9L 15.8gal 19.0galUS

461 Bentley
4.5-litre
1929 UK
92.0mph 148.0kmh
100.0bhp 74.6kW 101.4PS
@ 3500rpm
65.4bhp/ton 64.3bhp/tonne
22.7bhp/L 17.0kW/L 23.0PS/L
53.6ft/sec 16.3m/sec
15.0mpg 12.5mpgUS 18.8L/100km
Petrol 4-stroke piston
4398cc 268.3cu in
In-line 4 2 Carburettor
Compression ratio: 5.1:1
Bore: 100.0mm 3.9in
Stroke: 140.0mm 5.5in
Valve type/No: Overhead 8
Transmission: Manual
No. of forward speeds: 4
Wheels driven: Rear
Brakes F/R: Drum/Drum
Wheelbase: 330.2cm 130.0in
Track F: 142.2cm 56.0in
Track R: 142.2cm 56.0in
Length: 438.2cm 172.5in
Width: 174.0cm 68.5in
Height: 157.5cm 62.0in
Kerb weight: 1555.4kg 3426.0lb
Fuel: 72.8L 16.0gal 19.2galUS

462 Bentley
4.5-litre Supercharged
1930 UK
97.8mph 157.4kmh
175.0bhp 130.5kW 177.4PS
@ 3500rpm
94.6bhp/ton 93.0bhp/tonne
39.8bhp/L 29.7kW/L 40.3PS/L
53.6ft/sec 16.3m/sec
11.0mpg 9.2mpgUS 25.7L/100km
Petrol 4-stroke piston
4398cc 268.3cu in supercharged
In-line 4 2 Carburettor
Compression ratio: 5.0:1
Bore: 100.0mm 3.9in
Stroke: 140.0mm 5.5in
Valve type/No: Overhead 8
Transmission: Manual
No. of forward speeds: 4
Wheels driven: Rear
Brakes F/R: Drum/Drum
Wheelbase: 330.2cm 130.0in
Track F: 142.2cm 56.0in
Track R: 142.2cm 56.0in
Length: 468.6cm 184.5in
Width: 174.0cm 68.5in
Height: 142.2cm 56.0in
Kerb weight: 1881.4kg 4144.0lb
Fuel: 72.8L 16.0gal 19.2galUS

463 Bentley
8-litre Saloon
1930 UK
101.1mph 162.7kmh
220.0bhp 164.0kW 223.0PS
@ 3500rpm
91.4bhp/ton 89.9bhp/tonne
27.6bhp/L 20.5kW/L 27.9PS/L
53.6ft/sec 16.3m/sec
10.0mpg 8.3mpgUS 28.2L/100km
Petrol 4-stroke piston
7982cc 487.0cu in
In-line 6 2 Carburettor
Compression ratio: 5.1:1
Bore: 110.0mm 4.3in
Stroke: 140.0mm 5.5in
Valve type/No: Overhead 12
Transmission: Manual
No. of forward speeds: 4
Wheels driven: Rear
Brakes F/R: Drum/Drum
Wheelbase: 365.8cm 144.0in
Track F: 142.0cm 55.9in
Track R: 142.0cm 55.9in
Length: 509.3cm 200.5in
Width: 176.3cm 69.4in
Height: 181.6cm 71.5in
Kerb weight: 2447.1kg 5390.0lb
Fuel: 113.7L 25.0gal 30.0galUS

464 Bentley
Speed Six Weymann
1930 UK
85.7mph 137.9kmh
180.0bhp 134.2kW 182.5PS
@ 3500rpm
80.0bhp/ton 78.7bhp/tonne
27.3bhp/L 20.3kW/L 27.7PS/L
53.6ft/sec 16.3m/sec
12.0mpg 10.0mpgUS 23.5L/100km
Petrol 4-stroke piston
6597cc 402.5cu in
In-line 6 2 Carburettor
Compression ratio: 5.3:1
Bore: 100.0mm 3.9in
Stroke: 140.0mm 5.5in
Valve type/No: Overhead 12
Transmission: Manual
No. of forward speeds: 4
Wheels driven: Rear
Brakes F/R: Drum/Drum
Wheelbase: 336.6cm 132.5in
Track F: 142.2cm 56.0in
Track R: 142.2cm 56.0in
Length: 480.1cm 189.0in
Width: 174.0cm 68.5in
Height: 182.9cm 72.0in
Kerb weight: 2288.2kg 5040.0lb
Fuel: 113.7L 25.0gal 30.0galUS

465 Bentley
Sedan
1934 UK
91.0mph 146.4kmh
0-50mph 80.5kmh: 13.2secs
0-60mph 96.5kmh: 18.8secs
0-1/4 mile: 20.5secs
104.0bhp 77.5kW 105.4PS
@ 3800rpm
167.0lbft 226.3Nm @ 2400rpm
63.8bhp/ton 62.8bhp/tonne
28.3bhp/L 21.1kW/L 28.7PS/L
47.5ft/sec 14.5m/sec
Petrol 4-stroke piston
3669cc 223.9cu in
In-line 6
Compression ratio: 6.0:1
Bore: 82.6mm 3.2in
Stroke: 114.3mm 4.5in
Valve type/No: Overhead 12
Transmission: Manual
No. of forward speeds: 4
Wheels driven: Rear
Wheelbase: 320.0cm 126.0in
Track F: 142.2cm 56.0in
Track R: 142.2cm 56.0in
Kerb weight: 1657.1kg 3650.0lb

466 Bentley
4.25-litre
1936 UK
94.7mph 152.4kmh
0-50mph 80.5kmh: 10.3secs
0-60mph 96.5kmh: 15.5secs
17.0mpg 14.2mpgUS 16.6L/100km
Petrol 4-stroke piston
4255cc 259.6cu in
In-line 6 2 Carburettor
Bore: 88.0mm 3.5in
Stroke: 114.0mm 4.5in
Valve type/No: Overhead 12
Transmission: Manual
No. of forward speeds: 4
Wheels driven: Rear
Brakes F/R: Drum/Drum
Kerb weight: 1700.7kg 3746.0lb
Fuel: 81.9L 18.0gal 21.6galUS

467 Bentley
4.5-litre
1937 UK
91.8mph 147.7kmh
0-50mph 80.5kmh: 12.7secs
0-60mph 96.5kmh: 17.1secs
16.0mpg 13.3mpgUS 17.7L/100km
Petrol 4-stroke piston
4257cc 259.7cu in
In-line 6
Bore: 89.0mm 3.5in
Stroke: 114.0mm 4.5in
Valve type/No: Overhead 12
Transmission: Manual
No. of forward speeds: 4
Wheels driven: Rear
Brakes F/R: Drum/Drum
Kerb weight: 1750.6kg 3856.0lb
Fuel: 81.9L 18.0gal 21.6galUS

468 Bentley
4.25-litre
1938 UK
96.0mph 154.5kmh
0-50mph 80.5kmh: 10.0secs
0-60mph 96.5kmh: 14.2secs
0-1/4 mile: 19.0secs
125.0bhp 93.2kW 126.7PS
@ 3800rpm
205.0lbft 277.8Nm @ 2200rpm
78.9bhp/ton 77.6bhp/tonne
29.4bhp/L 21.9kW/L 29.8PS/L
47.5ft/sec 14.5m/sec
21.1mph 33.9kmh/1000rpm
Petrol 4-stroke piston
4255cc 259.6cu in
In-line 6
Compression ratio: 6.4:1
Bore: 88.9mm 3.5in
Stroke: 114.3mm 4.5in
Valve type/No: Overhead 12
Transmission: Manual
No. of forward speeds: 4
Wheels driven: Rear
Wheelbase: 320.0cm 126.0in
Track F: 116.8cm 46.0in
Track R: 116.8cm 46.0in
Length: 480.1cm 189.0in
Width: 172.7cm 68.0in
Height: 157.5cm 62.0in
Kerb weight: 1611.7kg 3550.0lb

469 Bentley
4.5-litre
1939 UK
92.7mph 149.2kmh
0-50mph 80.5kmh: 11.5secs
0-60mph 96.5kmh: 16.1secs
16.0mpg 13.3mpgUS 17.7L/100km
Petrol 4-stroke piston
4257cc 259.7cu in
In-line 6 2 Carburettor
Bore: 89.0mm 3.5in
Stroke: 114.0mm 4.5in
Valve type/No: Overhead 12
Transmission: Manual
No. of forward speeds: 4
Wheels driven: Rear
Brakes F/R: Drum/Drum
Kerb weight: 1790.1kg 3943.0lb
Fuel: 81.9L 18.0gal 21.6galUS

470 Bentley
4.5-litre Mk VI Saloon
1947 UK
94.0mph 151.2kmh
0-50mph 80.5kmh: 17.5secs
0-60mph 96.5kmh: 25.8secs
16.0mpg 13.3mpgUS 17.7L/100km
Petrol 4-stroke piston
4257cc 259.7cu in
In-line 6
Compression ratio: 6.4:1
Bore: 89.0mm 3.5in
Stroke: 114.0mm 4.5in
Valve type/No: IOE 12
Transmission: Manual
No. of forward speeds: 4
Wheels driven: Rear
Brakes F/R: Drum/Drum
Wheelbase: 304.8cm 120.0in
Track F: 142.7cm 56.2in
Track R: 147.3cm 58.0in
Length: 486.4cm 191.5in
Width: 175.3cm 69.0in
Height: 163.8cm 64.5in
Ground clearance: 18.3cm 7.2in
Kerb weight: 1817.8kg 4004.0lb
Fuel: 81.9L 18.0gal 21.6galUS

471 Bentley
Continental
1952 UK
116.9mph 188.1kmh
0-50mph 80.5kmh: 10.5secs
0-60mph 96.5kmh: 13.5secs
0-1/4 mile: 19.5secs
27.0mph 43.4kmh/1000rpm
19.4mpg 16.2mpgUS 14.6L/100km
Petrol 4-stroke piston
4566cc 278.6cu in
In-line 6
Compression ratio: 7.0:1
Bore: 92.0mm 3.6in
Stroke: 114.3mm 4.5in
Valve type/No: IOE 12
Transmission: Manual
No. of forward speeds: 4
Wheels driven: Rear
Springs F/R: Coil/Leaf
Brake system: PA
Brakes F/R: Drum/Drum
Wheelbase: 304.8cm 120.0in
Track F: 144.0cm 56.7in
Track R: 148.6cm 58.5in
Length: 524.5cm 206.5in
Width: 181.6cm 71.5in
Height: 160.0cm 63.0in
Ground clearance: 17.8cm 7.0in
Kerb weight: 1697.5kg 3739.0lb
Fuel: 81.9L 18.0gal 21.6galUS

472 Bentley
Mk VI
1952 UK
100.0mph 160.9kmh
0-50mph 80.5kmh: 10.2secs
0-60mph 96.5kmh: 15.2secs
22.1mph 35.6kmh/1000rpm
15.0mpg 12.5mpgUS 18.8L/100km
Petrol 4-stroke piston
4566cc 278.6cu in
In-line 6
Compression ratio: 6.4:1
Bore: 92.0mm 3.6in
Stroke: 114.0mm 4.5in
Valve type/No: IOE 12
Transmission: Manual
No. of forward speeds: 4
Wheels driven: Rear
Springs F/R: Coil/Leaf
Brake system: PA
Brakes F/R: Drum/Drum
Wheelbase: 304.8cm 120.0in
Track F: 143.5cm 56.5in
Track R: 148.6cm 58.5in
Length: 487.7cm 192.0in
Width: 177.8cm 70.0in
Height: 167.6cm 66.0in
Ground clearance: 18.3cm 7.2in
Kerb weight: 1851.4kg 4078.0lb
Fuel: 81.9L 18.0gal 21.6galUS

473 Bentley
Sports Saloon
1952 UK
106.5mph 171.4kmh
0-50mph 80.5kmh: 10.0secs
0-60mph 96.5kmh: 13.8secs
0-1/4 mile: 19.1secs
22.0mph 35.4kmh/1000rpm
12.3mpg 10.2mpgUS 23.0L/100km
Petrol 4-stroke piston
4566cc 278.6cu in
In-line 6
Compression ratio: 6.7:1
Bore: 92.0mm 3.6in
Stroke: 114.0mm 4.5in
Valve type/No: IOE 12
Transmission: Manual
No. of forward speeds: 4
Wheels driven: Rear
Springs F/R: Coil/Leaf
Brake system: PA
Brakes F/R: Drum/Drum
Wheelbase: 304.8cm 120.0in
Track F: 144.0cm 56.7in
Track R: 148.8cm 58.6in
Length: 508.0cm 200.0in
Width: 177.8cm 70.0in
Height: 167.6cm 66.0in
Kerb weight: 1916.3kg 4221.0lb
Fuel: 81.9L 18.0gal 21.6galUS

474 Bentley
Sports
1954 UK
106.5mph 171.4kmh
0-50mph 80.5kmh: 10.0secs
0-60mph 96.5kmh: 13.8secs
0-1/4 mile: 19.1secs
22.0mph 35.4kmh/1000rpm
16.0mpg 13.3mpgUS 17.7L/100km
Petrol 4-stroke piston
4566cc 278.6cu in
In-line 6
Compression ratio: 6.7:1
Bore: 92.0mm 3.6in
Stroke: 114.0mm 4.5in
Valve type/No: IOE 12
Transmission: Manual
No. of forward speeds: 4
Wheels driven: Rear
Springs F/R: Coil/Leaf
Brake system: PA
Brakes F/R: Drum/Drum
Wheelbase: 304.8cm 120.0in
Track F: 144.0cm 56.7in
Track R: 148.8cm 58.6in
Length: 508.0cm 200.0in
Width: 177.8cm 70.0in
Height: 167.6cm 66.0in
Kerb weight: 1916.3kg 4221.0lb
Fuel: 81.9L 18.0gal 21.6galUS

475 Bentley
Continental Park Ward DH Coupe
1956 UK
120.5mph 193.9kmh
0-50mph 80.5kmh: 9.3secs
0-60mph 96.5kmh: 12.9secs
0-1/4 mile: 18.8secs
28.4mph 45.7kmh/1000rpm
15.2mpg 12.7mpgUS 18.6L/100km
Petrol 4-stroke piston
4887cc 298.2cu in
In-line 6
Compression ratio: 8.0:1
Bore: 92.2mm 3.6in
Stroke: 114.3mm 4.5in
Valve type/No: IOE 12
Transmission: Manual
No. of forward speeds: 4
Wheels driven: Rear
Springs F/R: Coil/Leaf
Brake system: PA
Brakes F/R: Drum/Drum
Wheelbase: 312.4cm 123.0in
Track F: 147.3cm 58.0in
Track R: 152.4cm 60.0in
Length: 534.7cm 210.5in
Width: 182.9cm 72.0in
Height: 158.8cm 62.5in
Ground clearance: 17.8cm 7.0in
Kerb weight: 1805.1kg 3976.0lb
Fuel: 81.9L 18.0gal 21.6galUS

476 Bentley
Series S
1956 UK
101.0mph 162.5kmh
0-50mph 80.5kmh: 10.3secs
0-60mph 96.5kmh: 14.2secs
0-1/4 mile: 19.7secs
25.0mph 40.2kmh/1000rpm
14.0mpg 11.7mpgUS 20.2L/100km
Petrol 4-stroke piston
4887cc 298.2cu in
In-line 6
Compression ratio: 6.6:1
Bore: 95.2mm 3.8in
Stroke: 114.3mm 4.5in
Valve type/No: IOE 12
Transmission: Manual
No. of forward speeds: 4
Wheels driven: Rear
Springs F/R: Coil/Leaf
Brake system: PA
Brakes F/R: Drum/Drum
Wheelbase: 312.4cm 123.0in
Track F: 147.3cm 58.0in
Track R: 152.4cm 60.0in
Length: 537.7cm 211.7in
Width: 189.7cm 74.7in
Height: 162.6cm 64.0in
Ground clearance: 17.8cm 7.0in
Kerb weight: 1925.9kg 4242.0lb
Fuel: 81.9L 18.0gal 21.6galUS

477 Bentley
S2 Continental
1960 UK
114.5mph 184.2kmh
0-50mph 80.5kmh: 8.9secs
0-60mph 96.5kmh: 12.1secs
0-1/4 mile: 18.6secs
27.0mph 43.4kmh/1000rpm
13.0mpg 10.8mpgUS 21.7L/100km
Petrol 4-stroke piston
6230cc 380.1cu in
Vee 8 2 Carburettor
Compression ratio: 8.0:1
Bore: 104.1mm 4.1in
Stroke: 91.4mm 3.6in
Valve type/No: Overhead 16
Transmission: Manual
No. of forward speeds: 4
Wheels driven: Rear
Springs F/R: Coil/Leaf
Brake system: PA
Brakes F/R: Drum/Drum
Wheelbase: 312.4cm 123.0in
Track F: 148.6cm 58.5in
Track R: 152.4cm 60.0in
Length: 534.7cm 210.5in
Width: 185.4cm 73.0in
Height: 154.9cm 61.0in
Ground clearance: 17.8cm 7.0in
Kerb weight: 2024.8kg 4460.0lb
Fuel: 81.9L 18.0gal 21.6galUS

478 Bentley
T2
1979 UK
120.0mph 193.1kmh
0-50mph 80.5kmh: 6.6secs
0-60mph 96.5kmh: 9.4secs
0-1/4 mile: 17.7secs
0-1km: 32.4secs
26.2mph 42.2kmh/1000rpm
13.6mpg 11.3mpgUS 20.8L/100km
Petrol 4-stroke piston
6748cc 411.7cu in
Vee 8 2 Carburettor
Compression ratio: 8.0:1
Bore: 104.1mm 4.1in
Stroke: 99.1mm 3.9in
Valve type/No: Overhead 16
Transmission: Automatic
No. of forward speeds: 3
Wheels driven: Rear
Springs F/R: Coil/Coil
Brake system: PA
Brakes F/R: Disc/Disc
Steering: Rack & pinion PA
Wheelbase: 304.8cm 120.0in
Track F: 152.4cm 60.0in
Track R: 151.1cm 59.5in
Length: 519.4cm 204.5in
Width: 182.9cm 72.0in
Height: 151.6cm 59.7in
Ground clearance: 16.5cm 6.5in
Kerb weight: 2183.3kg 4809.0lb
Fuel: 106.9L 23.5gal 28.2galUS

479 Bentley
Mulsanne Turbo
1982 UK
135.0mph 217.2kmh
0-50mph 80.5kmh: 5.1secs
0-60mph 96.5kmh: 7.0secs
0-1/4 mile: 15.1secs
0-1km: 27.8secs
298.0bhp 222.2kW 302.1PS
@ 3800rpm
135.5bhp/ton 133.2bhp/tonne
44.1bhp/L 32.9kW/L 44.8PS/L
41.2ft/sec 12.5m/sec
29.9mph 48.1kmh/1000rpm
12.1mpg 10.1mpgUS 23.3L/100km
Petrol 4-stroke piston
6750cc 411.8cu in turbocharged
Vee 8 1 Carburettor
Compression ratio: 8.0:1
Bore: 104.1mm 4.1in
Stroke: 99.1mm 3.9in
Valve type/No: Overhead 16
Transmission: Automatic
No. of forward speeds: 3
Wheels driven: Rear
Springs F/R: Coil/Coil
Brake system: PA
Brakes F/R: Disc/Disc
Steering: Rack & pinion PA
Wheelbase: 306.1cm 120.5in
Track F: 153.7cm 60.5in
Track R: 153.7cm 60.5in
Length: 526.8cm 207.4in
Width: 188.7cm 74.3in
Height: 148.6cm 58.5in
Ground clearance: 16.5cm 6.5in
Kerb weight: 2236.4kg 4926.0lb
Fuel: 106.9L 23.5gal 28.2galUS

480 Bentley
Mulsanne Turbo
1985 UK
134.0mph 215.6kmh
0-50mph 80.5kmh: 5.2secs
0-60mph 96.5kmh: 6.9secs
0-1/4 mile: 15.0secs
0-1km: 27.8secs
298.0bhp 222.2kW 302.1PS
@ 3800rpm
136.3bhp/ton 134.1bhp/tonne
44.1bhp/L 32.9kW/L 44.8PS/L
41.2ft/sec 12.5m/sec
28.7mph 46.2kmh/1000rpm
13.4mpg 11.2mpgUS 21.1L/100km
Petrol 4-stroke piston
6750cc 411.8cu in turbocharged
Vee 8 1 Carburettor
Compression ratio: 8.0:1
Bore: 104.1mm 4.1in
Stroke: 99.1mm 3.9in
Valve type/No: Overhead 16
Transmission: Automatic
No. of forward speeds: 3
Wheels driven: Rear
Springs F/R: Coil/Coil
Brake system: PA
Brakes F/R: Disc/Disc
Steering: Rack & pinion PA
Wheelbase: 306.1cm 120.5in
Track F: 153.7cm 60.5in
Track R: 153.7cm 60.5in
Length: 526.8cm 207.4in
Width: 188.7cm 74.3in
Height: 148.6cm 58.5in
Ground clearance: 16.5cm 6.5in
Kerb weight: 2222.8kg 4896.0lb
Fuel: 108.1L 23.7gal 28.5galUS

481 Bentley
Turbo R
1987 UK
146.0mph 234.9kmh
0-50mph 80.5kmh: 5.2secs
0-60mph 96.5kmh: 7.0secs
0-1/4 mile: 15.4secs
0-1km: 28.3secs
328.0bhp 244.6kW 332.5PS
148.1bhp/ton 145.6bhp/tonne
48.6bhp/L 36.2kW/L 49.3PS/L
35.6mph 57.3kmh/1000rpm
14.2mpg 11.8mpgUS 19.9L/100km
Petrol 4-stroke piston
6750cc 412.0cu in turbocharged
Vee 8 fuel injection
Compression ratio: 8.0:1
Bore: 104.1mm 4.1in
Stroke: 99.1mm 3.9in
Valve type/No: Overhead 16
Transmission: Automatic
No. of forward speeds: 3
Wheels driven: Rear
Springs F/R: Coil/Coil
Brake system: PA ABS
Brakes F/R: Disc/Disc
Steering: Rack & pinion PA
Wheelbase: 306.1cm 120.5in
Track F: 153.8cm 60.6in
Track R: 153.8cm 60.6in
Length: 526.8cm 207.4in
Width: 188.7cm 74.3in
Height: 148.6cm 58.5in
Ground clearance: 16.5cm 6.5in
Kerb weight: 2252.0kg 4960.3lb
Fuel: 108.3L 23.8gal 28.6galUS

482 Bentley
Turbo R
1990 UK
145.0mph 233.3kmh
0-60mph 96.5kmh: 6.7secs
Petrol 4-stroke piston
6750cc 411.8cu in turbocharged
Vee 8 fuel injection
Compression ratio: 8.0:1
Bore: 104.1mm 4.1in
Stroke: 99.1mm 3.9in
Valve type/No: Overhead 16
Transmission: Automatic
No. of forward speeds: 3
Wheels driven: Rear
Springs F/R: Coil/Coil
Brake system: ABS
Brakes F/R: Disc/Disc
Steering: Rack & pinion PA
Wheelbase: 306.1cm 120.5in
Track F: 154.9cm 61.0in
Track R: 154.9cm 61.0in
Length: 526.8cm 207.4in
Width: 200.7cm 79.0in
Height: 148.6cm 58.5in
Kerb weight: 2392.6kg 5270.0lb
Fuel: 107.9L 23.7gal 28.5galUS

483 Bentley
Turbo R
1991 UK
128.0mph 206.0kmh
0-60mph 96.5kmh: 7.1secs
0-1/4 mile: 15.5secs
315.0bhp 234.9kW 319.4PS
@ 4300rpm
485.0lbft 657.2Nm @ 2250rpm
135.3bhp/ton 133.0bhp/tonne
46.7bhp/L 34.8kW/L 47.3PS/L
46.6ft/sec 14.2m/sec
13.8mpg 11.5mpgUS 20.5L/100km
Petrol 4-stroke piston
6750cc 411.8cu in turbocharged
Vee 8 fuel injection
Compression ratio: 8.0:1
Bore: 104.0mm 4.1in
Stroke: 99.1mm 3.9in
Valve type/No: Overhead 16
Transmission: Automatic
No. of forward speeds: 3
Wheels driven: Rear
Springs F/R: Coil/Coil
Brake system: PA ABS
Brakes F/R: Disc/Disc
Steering: Rack & pinion PA
Wheelbase: 306.1cm 120.5in
Track F: 154.9cm 61.0in
Track R: 154.9cm 61.0in
Length: 526.8cm 207.4in
Width: 189.0cm 74.4in
Height: 148.6cm 58.5in
Kerb weight: 2367.6kg 5215.0lb
Fuel: 107.9L 23.7gal 28.5galUS

484 Berkeley
Sports
1957 UK
65.0mph 104.6kmh
0-50mph 80.5kmh: 22.2secs
0-60mph 96.5kmh: 38.3secs
0-1/4 mile: 25.6secs
18.2bhp 13.6kW 18.4PS
@ 5250rpm
21.6lbft 29.3Nm @ 3000rpm
58.2bhp/ton 57.3bhp/tonne
55.5bhp/L 41.4kW/L 56.3PS/L
35.6ft/sec 10.8m/sec
11.7mph 18.8kmh/1000rpm
44.7mpg 37.2mpgUS 6.3L/100km
Petrol 2-stroke piston
328cc 20.0cu in
In-line 2
Compression ratio: 8.2:1
Bore: 58.0mm 2.3in
Stroke: 62.0mm 2.4in
Valve type/No: Ports
Transmission: Manual
No. of forward speeds: 3
Wheels driven: Front
Springs F/R: Coil/Coil
Brakes F/R: Drum/Drum
Wheelbase: 152.4cm 60.0in
Track F: 107.2cm 42.2in
Track R: 106.7cm 42.0in
Length: 312.4cm 123.0in
Width: 127.0cm 50.0in
Height: 108.0cm 42.5in
Ground clearance: 17.8cm 7.0in
Kerb weight: 317.8kg 700.0lb
Fuel: 15.9L 3.5gal 4.2galUS

485 Berkeley
Sports
1958 UK
58.0mph 93.3kmh
0-50mph 80.5kmh: 28.0secs
0-1/4 mile: 25.8secs
18.2bhp 13.6kW 18.4PS

@ 5250rpm
21.6lbft 29.3Nm @ 3000rpm
57.4bhp/ton 56.5bhp/tonne
55.5bhp/L 41.4kW/L 56.3PS/L
35.6ft/sec 10.8m/sec
Petrol 2-stroke piston
328cc 20.0cu in
In-line 2
Compression ratio: 8.2:1
Bore: 57.9mm 2.3in
Stroke: 62.0mm 2.4in
Transmission: Manual
No. of forward speeds: 3
Wheels driven: Front
Wheelbase: 177.8cm 70.0in
Track F: 107.2cm 42.2in
Track R: 106.7cm 42.0in
Kerb weight: 322.3kg 710.0lb

486 Berkeley

Sports 4
1958 UK
83.0mph 133.5kmh
0-50mph 80.5kmh: 14.4secs
0-60mph 96.5kmh: 21.8secs
0-1/4 mile: 22.4secs
30.0bhp 22.4kW 30.4PS
@ 5000rpm
35.4lbft 48.0Nm @ 3500rpm
79.3bhp/ton 78.0bhp/tonne
61.0bhp/L 45.5kW/L 61.8PS/L
33.9ft/sec 10.3m/sec
13.2mph 21.2kmh/1000rpm
33.1mpg 27.6mpgUS 8.5L/100km
Petrol 2-stroke piston
492cc 30.0cu in
In-line 3
Compression ratio: 7.5:1
Bore: 58.0mm 2.3in
Stroke: 62.0mm 2.4in
Valve type/No: Ports
Transmission: Manual
No. of forward speeds: 4
Wheels driven: Front
Springs F/R: Coil/Coil
Brakes F/R: Drum/Drum
Wheelbase: 174.0cm 68.5in
Track F: 107.2cm 42.2in
Track R: 106.7cm 42.0in
Length: 312.4cm 123.0in
Width: 127.0cm 50.0in
Height: 108.0cm 42.5in
Ground clearance: 17.8cm 7.0in
Kerb weight: 384.5kg 847.0lb
Fuel: 22.7L 5.0gal 6.0galUS

487 Berkeley

B95
1960 UK
82.5mph 132.7kmh
0-50mph 80.5kmh: 12.4secs
0-60mph 96.5kmh: 17.2secs
0-1/4 mile: 20.5secs
40.0bhp 29.8kW 40.5PS
@ 5500rpm
42.5lbft 57.6Nm @ 4000rpm
97.9bhp/ton 96.3bhp/tonne
57.8bhp/L 43.1kW/L 58.6PS/L
54.1ft/sec 16.5m/sec
14.9mph 24.0kmh/1000rpm
Petrol 4-stroke piston
692cc 42.2cu in
In-line 2 1 Carburettor
Compression ratio: 7.3:1
Bore: 70.1mm 2.8in
Stroke: 89.9mm 3.5in
Valve type/No: Overhead 4
Transmission: Manual
No. of forward speeds: 4
Wheels driven: Front
Wheelbase: 177.8cm 70.0in
Track F: 107.4cm 42.3in
Track R: 107.4cm 42.3in
Length: 312.4cm 123.0in
Width: 127.0cm 50.0in
Height: 116.8cm 46.0in
Kerb weight: 415.4kg 915.0lb

488 Bertone

Zabrus
1990 Italy
138.0mph 222.0kmh
200.0bhp 149.1kW 202.8PS
@ 5250rpm
200.0lbft 271.0Nm @ 5250rpm
93.4bhp/L 69.7kW/L 94.7PS/L
46.8ft/sec 14.3m/sec
Petrol 4-stroke piston
2141cc 130.6cu in turbocharged
In-line 4
Compression ratio: 7.0:1
Bore: 91.4mm 3.6in
Stroke: 81.6mm 3.2in
Valve type/No: Overhead 8
Transmission: Manual
No. of forward speeds: 5
Wheels driven: 4-wheel drive
Springs F/R: Gas/Gas
Brakes F/R: Disc/Disc
Steering: Rack & pinion
Wheelbase: 265.2cm 104.4in
Track F: 155.4cm 61.2in
Track R: 155.4cm 61.2in
Length: 430.3cm 169.4in
Width: 188.0cm 74.0in
Height: 137.2cm 54.0in
Fuel: 83.3L 18.3gal 22.0galUS

489 Bertone

Emotion Lotus
1991 Italy
170.0mph 273.5kmh
0-60mph 96.5kmh: 5.0secs
264.0bhp 196.9kW 267.7PS
@ 6500rpm
261.0lbft 353.7Nm @ 3900rpm
121.4bhp/L 90.6kW/L 123.1PS/L
54.2ft/sec 16.5m/sec
Petrol 4-stroke piston
2174cc 132.6cu in turbocharged
In-line 4 fuel injection
Compression ratio: 8.0:1
Bore: 95.3mm 3.8in
Stroke: 76.2mm 3.0in
Valve type/No: Overhead 16
Transmission: Manual
No. of forward speeds: 5
Wheels driven: Rear
Springs F/R: Coil/Coil
Brake system: PA ABS
Brakes F/R: Disc/Disc
Steering: Rack & pinion
Wheelbase: 245.1cm 96.5in
Track F: 157.0cm 61.8in
Track R: 159.0cm 62.6in
Length: 406.4cm 160.0in
Width: 190.0cm 74.8in
Height: 109.7cm 43.2in
Fuel: 70.0L 15.4gal 18.5galUS

490 Bianchi

Straight Eight Saloon
1931 Italy
71.4mph 114.9kmh
18.0mpg 15.0mpgUS 15.7L/100km
Petrol 4-stroke piston
2906cc 177.3cu in
In-line 8
Bore: 68.0mm 2.7in
Stroke: 100.0mm 3.9in
Transmission: Manual
No. of forward speeds: 4
Wheels driven: Rear
Brakes F/R: Drum/Drum
Wheelbase: 330.2cm 130.0in
Track F: 143.5cm 56.5in
Track R: 143.5cm 56.5in
Length: 457.2cm 180.0in
Width: 170.2cm 67.0in
Height: 167.6cm 66.0in
Kerb weight: 1627.1kg 3584.0lb
Fuel: 77.3L 17.0gal 20.4galUS

491 Bianchi

12hp Pillarless Saloon
1937 Italy
59.2mph 95.3kmh
0-50mph 80.5kmh: 46.3secs
25.0mpg 20.8mpgUS 11.3L/100km
Petrol 4-stroke piston
1462cc 89.2cu in
In-line 4
Bore: 68.0mm 2.7in
Stroke: 100.0mm 3.9in
Valve type/No: Overhead 8
Transmission: Manual
No. of forward speeds: 4
Wheels driven: Rear
Brakes F/R: Drum/Drum
Kerb weight: 1270.3kg 2798.0lb
Fuel: 40.9L 9.0gal 10.8galUS

492 Bitter

SC
1984 Germany
0-60mph 96.5kmh: 9.2secs
170.0bhp 126.8kW 172.4PS
@ 5800rpm
173.0lbft 234.4Nm @ 4500rpm
114.0bhp/ton 112.1bhp/tonne
57.3bhp/L 42.7kW/L 58.1PS/L
24.6mpg 20.5mpgUS 11.5L/100km
Petrol 4-stroke piston
2968cc 181.1cu in
In-line 6 fuel injection
Valve type/No: Overhead 12
Transmission: Manual
No. of forward speeds: 5
Wheels driven: Rear
Springs F/R: Coil/Coil
Brakes F/R: Disc/Disc
Steering: Recirculating ball PA
Wheelbase: 266.7cm 105.0in
Length: 484.9cm 190.9in
Width: 182.1cm 71.7in
Height: 134.9cm 53.1in
Kerb weight: 1516.4kg 3340.0lb
Fuel: 73.0L 16.1gal 19.3galUS

493 Bitter

SC
1986 Germany
130.0mph 209.2kmh
0-50mph 80.5kmh: 6.1secs
0-60mph 96.5kmh: 8.3secs
0-1/4 mile: 16.4secs
200.0bhp 149.1kW 202.8PS
@ 5100rpm
236.0lbft 319.8Nm @ 3400rpm
128.4bhp/ton 126.2bhp/tonne
52.0bhp/L 38.8kW/L 52.7PS/L
50.4ft/sec 15.4m/sec
25.2mph 40.5kmh/1000rpm
16.8mpg 14.0mpgUS 16.8L/100km
Petrol 4-stroke piston
3848cc 234.8cu in
In-line 6 fuel injection
Compression ratio: 9.5:1
Bore: 95.0mm 3.7in
Stroke: 90.5mm 3.6in
Valve type/No: Overhead 12
Transmission: Manual
No. of forward speeds: 5
Wheels driven: Rear
Springs F/R: Coil/Coil
Brake system: PA
Brakes F/R: Disc/Disc
Steering: Recirculating ball PA
Wheelbase: 268.2cm 105.6in
Track F: 144.3cm 56.8in
Track R: 147.3cm 58.0in
Length: 491.0cm 193.3in
Width: 182.1cm 71.7in
Height: 134.9cm 53.1in
Ground clearance: 10.9cm 4.3in
Kerb weight: 1584.5kg 3490.0lb
Fuel: 73.0L 16.1gal 19.3galUS

494 Bitter

Type 3 Cabrio
1990 Germany
141.0mph 226.9kmh
0-60mph 96.5kmh: 7.6secs
240.0bhp 179.0kW 243.3PS
@ 5800rpm
235.0lbft 318.4Nm @ 4200rpm
180.1bhp/ton 177.1bhp/tonne
80.8bhp/L 60.3kW/L 82.0PS/L
44.3ft/sec 13.5m/sec
Petrol 4-stroke piston
2969cc 181.1cu in
In-line 6 fuel injection
Compression ratio: 10.0:1
Bore: 95.0mm 3.7in
Stroke: 69.8mm 2.7in
Valve type/No: Overhead 24
Transmission: Manual
No. of forward speeds: 5
Wheels driven: Rear
Springs F/R: Coil/Coil
Brake system: PA ABS
Brakes F/R: Disc/Disc
Steering: Rack & pinion PA
Wheelbase: 236.2cm 93.0in
Track F: 148.3cm 58.4in
Track R: 150.6cm 59.3in
Length: 452.1cm 178.0in
Width: 176.8cm 69.6in
Height: 141.7cm 55.8in
Kerb weight: 1355.2kg 2985.0lb
Fuel: 74.9L 16.5gal 19.8galUS

495 Bizzarrini

5300 Spyder
1965 Italy
165.0mph 265.5kmh
0-60mph 96.5kmh: 6.4secs
0-1/4 mile: 14.6secs
350.0bhp 261.0kW 354.8PS
@ 5400rpm
375.0lbft 508.1Nm @ 3500rpm
284.6bhp/ton 279.8bhp/tonne
65.4bhp/L 48.7kW/L 66.3PS/L
48.7ft/sec 14.9m/sec
Petrol 4-stroke piston
5354cc 326.7cu in
Vee 8 1 Carburettor
Compression ratio: 10.2:1
Bore: 102.0mm 4.0in
Stroke: 82.6mm 3.2in
Valve type/No: Overhead 16
Transmission: Manual
No. of forward speeds: 4
Wheels driven: Rear
Springs F/R: Coil/Coil
Brake system: PA
Brakes F/R: Disc/Disc
Steering: Recirculating ball
Wheelbase: 245.1cm 96.5in
Track F: 141.0cm 55.5in
Track R: 144.0cm 56.7in
Length: 439.4cm 173.0in
Width: 173.0cm 68.1in
Height: 111.0cm 43.7in
Kerb weight: 1250.8kg 2755.0lb
Fuel: 132.5L 29.1gal 35.0galUS

496 Bizzarrini

GT America
1966 Italy
145.0mph 233.3kmh
0-50mph 80.5kmh: 4.6secs
0-60mph 96.5kmh: 6.4secs
0-1/4 mile: 14.6secs
400.0bhp 298.3kW 405.5PS
@ 6000rpm
375.0lbft 508.1Nm @ 3600rpm
351.4bhp/ton 345.5bhp/tonne
74.7bhp/L 55.7kW/L 75.7PS/L
54.2ft/sec 16.5m/sec
24.5mph 39.4kmh/1000rpm
Petrol 4-stroke piston
5354cc 326.7cu in
Vee 8 4 Carburettor
Compression ratio: 11.0:1
Bore: 102.0mm 4.0in
Stroke: 82.6mm 3.2in
Valve type/No: Overhead 16
Transmission: Manual
No. of forward speeds: 4
Wheels driven: Rear
Springs F/R: Coil/Coil
Brakes F/R: Disc/Disc
Steering: Recirculating ball
Wheelbase: 244.9cm 96.4in
Track F: 139.7cm 55.0in
Track R: 142.2cm 56.0in
Length: 440.9cm 173.6in
Width: 172.7cm 68.0in
Height: 111.0cm 43.7in
Ground clearance: 12.7cm 5.0in
Kerb weight: 1157.7kg 2550.0lb
Fuel: 132.5L 29.1gal 35.0galUS

497 Bizzarrini

P538
1966 Italy
180.0mph 289.6kmh
350.0bhp 261.0kW 354.8PS
@ 7000rpm
412.6bhp/ton 405.7bhp/tonne
89.1bhp/L 66.4kW/L 90.3PS/L
47.4ft/sec 14.5m/sec
Petrol 4-stroke piston
3929cc 239.7cu in
Vee 12 6 Carburettor
Bore: 82.0mm 3.2in
Stroke: 62.0mm 2.4in
Valve type/No: Overhead 24
Transmission: Manual
No. of forward speeds: 5
Wheels driven: Rear
Springs F/R: Coil/Coil
Brakes F/R: Disc/Disc
Steering: Rack & pinion

Wheelbase: 251.5cm 99.0in
Track F: 165.1cm 65.0in
Track R: 172.7cm 68.0in
Length: 421.6cm 166.0in
Width: 193.0cm 76.0in
Height: 82.6cm 32.5in
Kerb weight: 862.6kg 1900.0lb
Fuel: 227.1L 49.9gal 60.0galUS

498 BMW

501
1956 Germany
101.0mph 162.5kmh
0-50mph 80.5kmh: 12.0secs
0-60mph 96.5kmh: 16.8secs
0-1/4 mile: 22.2secs
100.0bhp 74.6kW 101.4PS
@ 4800rpm
130.0lbft 176.2Nm @ 2500rpm
74.1bhp/ton 72.8bhp/tonne
38.8bhp/L 28.9kW/L 39.3PS/L
39.3ft/sec 12.0m/sec
18.0mph 29.0kmh/1000rpm
19.3mpg 16.1mpgUS 14.6L/100km
Petrol 4-stroke piston
2580cc 157.4cu in
Vee 8
Compression ratio: 7.0:1
Bore: 74.0mm 2.9in
Stroke: 75.0mm 2.9in
Valve type/No: Overhead 16
Transmission: Manual
No. of forward speeds: 4
Wheels driven: Rear
Springs F/R: Torsion bar/Torsion bar
Brakes F/R: Drum/Drum
Wheelbase: 288.3cm 113.5in
Track F: 137.2cm 54.0in
Track R: 144.8cm 57.0in
Length: 480.1cm 189.0in
Width: 180.3cm 71.0in
Height: 154.9cm 61.0in
Ground clearance: 17.8cm 7.0in
Kerb weight: 1372.9kg 3024.0lb
Fuel: 56.9L 12.5gal 15.0galUS

499 BMW

Isetta Motocoupe
1956 Germany
54.0mph 86.9kmh
0-1/4 mile: 29.8secs
12.0bhp 8.9kW 12.2PS
@ 5800rpm
25.0lbft 33.9Nm @ 5800rpm
34.3bhp/ton 33.7bhp/tonne
49.0bhp/L 36.5kW/L 49.7PS/L
43.2ft/sec 13.1m/sec
21.0mph 33.8kmh/1000rpm
61.0mpg 50.8mpgUS 4.6L/100km
Petrol 4-stroke piston
245cc 14.9cu in
Compression ratio: 6.8:1
Bore: 68.0mm 2.7in
Stroke: 68.0mm 2.7in
Valve type/No: Overhead
Transmission: Manual
No. of forward speeds: 3
Wheels driven: Rear
Springs F/R: Coil/Leaf
Brakes F/R: Drum/Drum
Wheelbase: 147.3cm 58.0in
Track F: 119.4cm 47.0in
Track R: 52.1cm 20.5in
Length: 228.6cm 90.0in
Width: 137.2cm 54.0in
Height: 133.4cm 52.5in
Ground clearance: 15.2cm 6.0in
Kerb weight: 355.9kg 784.0lb
Fuel: 10.0L 2.2gal 2.6galUS

500 BMW

507
1957 Germany
124.0mph 199.5kmh
0-50mph 80.5kmh: 6.3secs
0-60mph 96.5kmh: 8.8secs
0-1/4 mile: 16.5secs
155.0bhp 115.6kW 157.1PS
@ 5000rpm
174.0lbft 235.8Nm @ 4000rpm
120.6bhp/ton 118.5bhp/tonne
48.9bhp/L 36.5kW/L 49.6PS/L
41.0ft/sec 12.5m/sec
Petrol 4-stroke piston
3168cc 193.3cu in
Vee 8
Compression ratio: 7.8:1
Bore: 82.0mm 3.2in
Stroke: 74.9mm 2.9in
Valve type/No: Overhead 16
Transmission: Manual
No. of forward speeds: 4
Wheels driven: Rear
Wheelbase: 247.9cm 97.6in
Track F: 144.0cm 56.7in
Track R: 142.0cm 55.9in
Kerb weight: 1307.5kg 2880.0lb

501 BMW

600
1958 Germany
62.8mph 101.0kmh
0-50mph 80.5kmh: 22.4secs
0-1/4 mile: 24.5secs
19.5bhp 14.5kW 19.8PS
@ 4000rpm
28.9lbft 39.2Nm @ 2500rpm
35.4bhp/ton 34.9bhp/tonne
33.3bhp/L 24.8kW/L 33.8PS/L
29.8ft/sec 9.1m/sec
12.4mph 20.0kmh/1000rpm
45.6mpg 38.0mpgUS 6.2L/100km
Petrol 4-stroke piston
585cc 35.7cu in
Flat 2 1 Carburettor
Compression ratio: 6.8:1
Bore: 74.0mm 2.9in
Stroke: 68.0mm 2.7in
Valve type/No: Overhead 4
Transmission: Manual
No. of forward speeds: 4
Wheels driven: Rear
Springs F/R: Coil/Coil
Brakes F/R: Drum/Drum
Wheelbase: 170.2cm 67.0in
Track F: 121.9cm 48.0in
Track R: 115.8cm 45.6in
Length: 289.6cm 114.0in
Width: 139.7cm 55.0in
Height: 137.2cm 54.0in
Ground clearance: 16.5cm 6.5in
Kerb weight: 559.3kg 1232.0lb
Fuel: 22.7L 5.0gal 6.0galUS

502 BMW

Isetta 300
1958 Germany
49.7mph 80.0kmh
0-50mph 80.5kmh: 52.0secs
0-1/4 mile: 27.7secs
13.0bhp 9.7kW 13.2PS
@ 5800rpm
14.0lbft 19.0Nm @ 4200rpm
33.9bhp/ton 33.3bhp/tonne
43.8bhp/L 32.6kW/L 44.4PS/L
46.2ft/sec 14.1m/sec
Petrol 2-stroke piston
297cc 18.1cu in
Compression ratio: 7.0:1
Bore: 71.9mm 2.8in
Stroke: 72.9mm 2.9in
Valve type/No: Overhead
Transmission: Manual
No. of forward speeds: 4
Wheels driven: Rear
Wheelbase: 154.9cm 61.0in
Track F: 119.9cm 47.2in
Track R: 51.8cm 20.4in
Kerb weight: 390.4kg 860.0lb

503 BMW

700
1960 Germany
75.0mph 120.7kmh
0-50mph 80.5kmh: 17.3secs
0-60mph 96.5kmh: 29.0secs
0-1/4 mile: 23.2secs
35.0bhp 26.1kW 35.5PS
@ 5200rpm
37.2lbft 50.4Nm @ 3200rpm
54.4bhp/ton 53.5bhp/tonne
50.3bhp/L 37.5kW/L 51.0PS/L
41.5ft/sec 12.6m/sec
13.8mph 22.2kmh/1000rpm
Petrol 4-stroke piston
696cc 42.5cu in
Flat 2 1 Carburettor
Compression ratio: 7.5:1
Bore: 78.0mm 3.1in
Stroke: 72.9mm 2.9in
Valve type/No: Overhead 4
Transmission: Manual
No. of forward speeds: 4
Wheels driven: Rear
Wheelbase: 212.1cm 83.5in
Track F: 127.0cm 50.0in
Track R: 119.9cm 47.2in
Length: 355.6cm 140.0in
Width: 148.1cm 58.3in
Height: 132.1cm 52.0in
Kerb weight: 653.8kg 1440.0lb

504 BMW

700 Coupe
1962 Germany
82.0mph 131.9kmh
0-50mph 80.5kmh: 15.7secs
0-60mph 96.5kmh: 23.4secs
0-1/4 mile: 22.8secs
40.0bhp 29.8kW 40.5PS
@ 5800rpm
38.0lbft 51.5Nm @ 4000rpm
62.7bhp/ton 61.7bhp/tonne
57.4bhp/L 42.8kW/L 58.2PS/L
46.2ft/sec 14.1m/sec
12.9mph 20.8kmh/1000rpm
35.5mpg 29.6mpgUS 8.0L/100km
Petrol 4-stroke piston
697cc 42.5cu in
Flat 2 2 Carburettor
Compression ratio: 9.0:1
Bore: 78.0mm 3.1in
Stroke: 73.0mm 2.9in
Valve type/No: Overhead 4
Transmission: Manual
No. of forward speeds: 4
Wheels driven: Rear
Springs F/R: Coil/Coil
Brakes F/R: Drum/Drum
Steering: Rack & pinion
Wheelbase: 207.0cm 81.5in
Track F: 127.0cm 50.0in
Track R: 119.9cm 47.2in
Length: 350.5cm 138.0in
Width: 147.8cm 58.2in
Height: 127.0cm 50.0in
Ground clearance: 18.3cm 7.2in
Kerb weight: 648.3kg 1428.0lb
Fuel: 32.3L 7.1gal 8.5galUS

505 BMW

1500
1963 Germany
95.0mph 152.9kmh
0-50mph 80.5kmh: 10.9secs
0-60mph 96.5kmh: 15.0secs
0-1/4 mile: 19.6secs
90.0bhp 67.1kW 91.2PS
@ 5900rpm
87.0lbft 117.9Nm @ 3000rpm
84.3bhp/ton 82.9bhp/tonne
60.0bhp/L 44.8kW/L 60.9PS/L
45.7ft/sec 13.9m/sec
16.0mph 25.7kmh/1000rpm
Petrol 4-stroke piston
1499cc 91.5cu in
In-line 4 1 Carburettor
Compression ratio: 8.8:1
Bore: 82.0mm 3.2in
Stroke: 70.9mm 2.8in
Valve type/No: Overhead 8
Transmission: Manual
No. of forward speeds: 4
Wheels driven: Rear
Wheelbase: 254.8cm 100.3in
Track F: 132.1cm 52.0in
Track R: 137.4cm 54.1in
Length: 452.1cm 178.0in
Width: 171.2cm 67.4in
Height: 142.2cm 56.0in
Ground clearance: 17.5cm 6.9in
Kerb weight: 1085.1kg 2390.0lb

506 BMW

1800 Saloon
1963 Germany
100.6mph 161.9kmh
0-50mph 80.5kmh: 8.9secs
0-60mph 96.5kmh: 13.7secs
0-1/4 mile: 19.0secs
90.0bhp 67.1kW 91.2PS
@ 5250rpm
106.0lbft 143.6Nm @ 3200rpm
85.2bhp/ton 83.8bhp/tonne
50.8bhp/L 37.8kW/L 51.5PS/L
45.9ft/sec 14.0m/sec
16.8mph 27.0kmh/1000rpm
27.2mpg 22.6mpgUS 10.4L/100km
Petrol 4-stroke piston
1773cc 108.2cu in
In-line 4 1 Carburettor
Compression ratio: 8.6:1
Bore: 84.0mm 3.3in
Stroke: 80.0mm 3.1in
Valve type/No: Overhead 8
Transmission: Manual
No. of forward speeds: 4
Wheels driven: Rear
Springs F/R: Coil/Coil
Brake system: PA
Brakes F/R: Disc/Drum
Steering: Worm & roller
Wheelbase: 255.3cm 100.5in
Track F: 132.1cm 52.0in
Track R: 137.2cm 54.0in
Length: 454.7cm 179.0in
Width: 165.1cm 65.0in
Height: 144.0cm 56.7in
Ground clearance: 16.5cm 6.5in
Kerb weight: 1074.2kg 2366.0lb
Fuel: 50.0L 11.0gal 13.2galUS

507 BMW

700 LS
1964 Germany
78.0mph 125.5kmh
0-50mph 80.5kmh: 18.6secs
0-60mph 96.5kmh: 28.0secs
0-1/4 mile: 23.6secs
32.0bhp 23.9kW 32.4PS
@ 5000rpm
37.0lbft 50.1Nm @ 3400rpm
48.5bhp/ton 47.7bhp/tonne
45.9bhp/L 34.2kW/L 46.5PS/L
39.9ft/sec 12.2m/sec
13.8mph 22.2kmh/1000rpm
32.3mpg 26.9mpgUS 8.7L/100km
Petrol 4-stroke piston
697cc 42.5cu in
Flat 2 1 Carburettor
Compression ratio: 7.5:1
Bore: 78.0mm 3.1in
Stroke: 73.0mm 2.9in
Valve type/No: Overhead 4
Transmission: Manual
No. of forward speeds: 4
Wheels driven: Rear
Springs F/R: Coil/Coil
Brakes F/R: Drum/Drum
Steering: Rack & pinion
Wheelbase: 227.8cm 89.7in
Track F: 127.0cm 50.0in
Track R: 114.3cm 45.0in
Length: 386.1cm 152.0in
Width: 148.6cm 58.5in
Height: 135.9cm 53.5in
Ground clearance: 18.3cm 7.2in
Kerb weight: 670.6kg 1477.0lb
Fuel: 27.8L 6.1gal 7.3galUS

508 BMW

1800 Ti
1965 Germany
108.0mph 173.8kmh
0-50mph 80.5kmh: 7.5secs
0-60mph 96.5kmh: 10.9secs
0-1/4 mile: 17.7secs
110.0bhp 82.0kW 111.5PS
@ 5800rpm
109.0lbft 147.7Nm @ 4000rpm
101.9bhp/ton 100.2bhp/tonne
62.0bhp/L 46.3kW/L 62.9PS/L
50.7ft/sec 15.5m/sec
17.1mph 27.5kmh/1000rpm
17.1mpg 14.2mpgUS 16.5L/100km
Petrol 4-stroke piston
1773cc 108.2cu in
In-line 4 2 Carburettor
Compression ratio: 9.5:1
Bore: 84.0mm 3.3in
Stroke: 80.0mm 3.1in
Valve type/No: Overhead 8
Transmission: Manual
No. of forward speeds: 4
Wheels driven: Rear
Springs F/R: Coil/Coil
Brake system: PA
Brakes F/R: Disc/Drum
Steering: Worm & roller
Wheelbase: 255.3cm 100.5in
Track F: 132.1cm 52.0in
Track R: 137.2cm 54.0in
Length: 454.7cm 179.0in
Width: 165.1cm 65.0in
Height: 144.0cm 56.7in

Ground clearance: 16.5cm 6.5in
Kerb weight: 1097.3kg 2417.0lb
Fuel: 52.3L 11.5gal 13.8galUS

509 BMW

2000
1966 Germany
105.0mph 168.9kmh
0-50mph 80.5kmh: 8.1secs
0-60mph 96.5kmh: 11.7secs
0-1/4 mile: 17.7secs
0-1km: 34.0secs
100.0bhp 74.6kW 101.4PS
@ 5500rpm
116.0lbft 157.2Nm @ 3000rpm
91.6bhp/ton 90.0bhp/tonne
50.2bhp/L 37.5kW/L 50.9PS/L
48.1ft/sec 14.7m/sec
16.9mph 27.2kmh/1000rpm
23.3mpg 19.4mpgUS 12.1L/100km
Petrol 4-stroke piston
1990cc 121.4cu in
In-line 4 1 Carburettor
Compression ratio: 8.5:1
Bore: 89.0mm 3.5in
Stroke: 80.0mm 3.1in
Valve type/No: Overhead 8
Transmission: Manual
No. of forward speeds: 4
Wheels driven: Rear
Springs F/R: Coil/Coil
Brake system: PA
Brakes F/R: Disc/Drum
Steering: Worm & roller
Wheelbase: 255.3cm 100.5in
Track F: 132.1cm 52.0in
Track R: 137.2cm 54.0in
Length: 454.7cm 179.0in
Width: 165.1cm 65.0in
Height: 144.0cm 56.7in
Ground clearance: 16.5cm 6.5in
Kerb weight: 1110.5kg 2446.0lb
Fuel: 54.6L 12.0gal 14.4galUS

510 BMW

2000 CS
1966 Germany
115.0mph 185.0kmh
0-50mph 80.5kmh: 8.2secs
0-60mph 96.5kmh: 11.3secs
0-1/4 mile: 18.2secs
135.0bhp 100.7kW 136.9PS
@ 5800rpm
123.0lbft 166.7Nm @ 3600rpm
115.0bhp/ton 113.1bhp/tonne
67.8bhp/L 50.6kW/L 68.8PS/L
50.7ft/sec 15.5m/sec
18.9mph 30.4kmh/1000rpm
Petrol 4-stroke piston
1990cc 121.4cu in
In-line 4 2 Carburettor
Compression ratio: 9.3:1
Bore: 89.0mm 3.5in
Stroke: 80.0mm 3.1in
Valve type/No: Overhead 8
Transmission: Manual
No. of forward speeds: 4
Wheels driven: Rear
Springs F/R: Coil/Coil
Brakes F/R: Disc/Drum
Steering: Worm & roller
Wheelbase: 255.0cm 100.4in
Track F: 133.1cm 52.4in
Track R: 137.9cm 54.3in
Length: 452.9cm 178.3in
Width: 167.4cm 65.9in
Height: 135.9cm 53.5in
Ground clearance: 14.0cm 5.5in
Kerb weight: 1194.0kg 2630.0lb
Fuel: 54.9L 12.1gal 14.5galUS

511 BMW

2000 Ti
1966 Germany
109.0mph 175.4kmh
0-50mph 80.5kmh: 7.2secs
0-60mph 96.5kmh: 10.0secs
0-1/4 mile: 17.3secs
135.0bhp 100.7kW 136.9PS
@ 5800rpm
123.0lbft 166.7Nm @ 3600rpm
121.6bhp/ton 119.6bhp/tonne
67.6bhp/L 50.4kW/L 68.5PS/L
50.7ft/sec 15.5m/sec
17.6mph 28.3kmh/1000rpm
Petrol 4-stroke piston
1997cc 121.8cu in
In-line 4 2 Carburettor
Compression ratio: 9.3:1
Bore: 89.0mm 3.5in
Stroke: 80.0mm 3.1in
Valve type/No: Overhead 8
Transmission: Manual
No. of forward speeds: 4
Wheels driven: Rear
Springs F/R: Coil/Coil
Brake system: PA
Brakes F/R: Disc/Drum
Steering: Worm & roller
Wheelbase: 254.0cm 100.0in
Track F: 138.9cm 54.7in
Track R: 137.7cm 54.2in
Length: 449.6cm 177.0in
Width: 170.2cm 67.0in
Height: 134.6cm 53.0in
Ground clearance: 15.0cm 5.9in
Kerb weight: 1128.6kg 2486.0lb
Fuel: 56.8L 12.5gal 15.0galUS

512 BMW

1600 Coupe
1967 Germany
106.0mph 170.6kmh
0-50mph 80.5kmh: 8.8secs
0-60mph 96.5kmh: 12.5secs
0-1/4 mile: 18.5secs
0-1km: 34.3secs
85.0bhp 63.4kW 86.2PS
@ 5700rpm
91.0lbft 123.3Nm @ 3000rpm
92.8bhp/ton 91.3bhp/tonne
54.0bhp/L 40.3kW/L 54.8PS/L
44.3ft/sec 13.5m/sec
16.3mph 26.2kmh/1000rpm
26.3mpg 21.9mpgUS 10.7L/100km
Petrol 4-stroke piston
1573cc 96.0cu in
In-line 4 1 Carburettor
Compression ratio: 8.6:1
Bore: 84.0mm 3.3in
Stroke: 71.0mm 2.8in
Valve type/No: Overhead 8
Transmission: Manual
No. of forward speeds: 4
Wheels driven: Rear
Springs F/R: Coil/Coil
Brake system: PA
Brakes F/R: Disc/Drum
Steering: Worm & roller
Wheelbase: 250.2cm 98.5in
Track F: 132.1cm 52.0in
Track R: 132.1cm 52.0in
Length: 429.3cm 169.0in
Width: 162.6cm 64.0in
Height: 142.2cm 56.0in
Ground clearance: 16.5cm 6.5in
Kerb weight: 931.1kg 2051.0lb
Fuel: 46.4L 10.2gal 12.3galUS

513 BMW

1600-2
1967 Germany
100.0mph 160.9kmh
0-50mph 80.5kmh: 8.4secs
0-60mph 96.5kmh: 11.6secs
0-1/4 mile: 18.2secs
96.0bhp 71.6kW 97.3PS
@ 5800rpm
91.0lbft 123.3Nm @ 3000rpm
104.9bhp/ton 103.1bhp/tonne
61.0bhp/L 45.5kW/L 61.9PS/L
45.1ft/sec 13.7m/sec
16.3mph 26.2kmh/1000rpm
30.0mpg 25.0mpgUS 9.4L/100km
Petrol 4-stroke piston
1573cc 96.0cu in
In-line 4
Compression ratio: 8.6:1
Bore: 84.0mm 3.3in
Stroke: 71.0mm 2.8in
Valve type/No: Overhead 8
Transmission: Manual
No. of forward speeds: 4
Wheels driven: Rear
Brake system: PA
Brakes F/R: Disc/Drum
Steering: Worm & roller
Wheelbase: 249.9cm 98.4in
Track F: 133.1cm 52.4in
Track R: 133.1cm 52.4in
Length: 417.8cm 164.5in
Width: 159.0cm 62.6in
Height: 137.2cm 54.0in
Kerb weight: 930.7kg 2050.0lb
Fuel: 38.2L 8.4gal 10.1galUS

514 BMW

2000 TiLux
1967 Germany
110.0mph 177.0kmh
0-50mph 80.5kmh: 7.9secs
0-60mph 96.5kmh: 10.7secs
0-1/4 mile: 17.3secs
135.0bhp 100.7kW 136.9PS
@ 5800rpm
123.0lbft 166.7Nm @ 3600rpm
118.1bhp/ton 116.2bhp/tonne
67.8bhp/L 50.6kW/L 68.8PS/L
50.7ft/sec 15.5m/sec
18.4mph 29.6kmh/1000rpm
25.2mpg 21.0mpgUS 11.2L/100km
Petrol 4-stroke piston
1990cc 121.4cu in
In-line 4
Compression ratio: 9.3:1
Bore: 89.0mm 3.5in
Stroke: 80.0mm 3.1in
Valve type/No: Overhead 8
Transmission: Manual
No. of forward speeds: 4
Wheels driven: Rear
Brake system: PA
Brakes F/R: Disc/Drum
Steering: Worm & roller
Wheelbase: 255.0cm 100.4in
Track F: 133.1cm 52.4in
Track R: 137.2cm 54.0in
Length: 450.1cm 177.2in
Width: 170.9cm 67.3in
Height: 141.7cm 55.8in
Kerb weight: 1162.2kg 2560.0lb
Fuel: 45.8L 10.1gal 12.1galUS

515 BMW

2000 CS
1968 Germany
113.0mph 181.8kmh
0-50mph 80.5kmh: 7.7secs
0-60mph 96.5kmh: 10.7secs
0-1/4 mile: 17.6secs
135.0bhp 100.7kW 136.9PS
@ 5800rpm
123.0lbft 166.7Nm @ 3600rpm
116.8bhp/ton 114.8bhp/tonne
67.6bhp/L 50.4kW/L 68.5PS/L
50.7ft/sec 15.5m/sec
18.4mph 29.6kmh/1000rpm
Petrol 4-stroke piston
1997cc 121.8cu in
In-line 4 2 Carburettor
Compression ratio: 9.3:1
Bore: 88.9mm 3.5in
Stroke: 80.0mm 3.1in
Valve type/No: Overhead 8
Transmission: Manual
No. of forward speeds: 4
Wheels driven: Rear
Springs F/R: Coil/Coil
Brake system: PA
Brakes F/R: Disc/Drum
Steering: Worm & roller
Wheelbase: 255.0cm 100.4in
Track F: 133.1cm 52.4in
Track R: 137.2cm 54.0in
Length: 452.1cm 178.0in
Width: 167.1cm 65.8in
Height: 135.9cm 53.5in
Ground clearance: 13.5cm 5.3in
Kerb weight: 1175.9kg 2590.0lb
Fuel: 54.9L 12.1gal 14.5galUS

516 BMW

2002
1968 Germany
108.0mph 173.8kmh
0-50mph 80.5kmh: 8.0secs
0-60mph 96.5kmh: 11.3secs
0-1/4 mile: 17.9secs
113.0bhp 84.3kW 114.6PS
@ 5800rpm
116.0lbft 157.2Nm @ 3000rpm
114.5bhp/ton 112.6bhp/tonne
56.8bhp/L 42.3kW/L 57.6PS/L
50.7ft/sec 15.5m/sec
18.1mph 29.1kmh/1000rpm
Petrol 4-stroke piston
1990cc 121.4cu in
In-line 4 1 Carburettor
Compression ratio: 8.5:1
Bore: 89.0mm 3.5in
Stroke: 80.0mm 3.1in
Valve type/No: Overhead 8
Transmission: Manual
No. of forward speeds: 4
Wheels driven: Rear
Springs F/R: Coil/Coil
Brake system: PA
Brakes F/R: Disc/Drum
Steering: Worm & roller
Wheelbase: 249.9cm 98.4in
Track F: 133.1cm 52.4in
Track R: 133.1cm 52.4in
Length: 422.9cm 166.5in
Width: 159.0cm 62.6in
Height: 137.2cm 54.0in
Ground clearance: 16.0cm 6.3in
Kerb weight: 1003.3kg 2210.0lb
Fuel: 45.8L 10.1gal 12.1galUS

517 BMW

2000 Tilux
1969 Germany
111.0mph 178.6kmh
0-50mph 80.5kmh: 7.3secs
0-60mph 96.5kmh: 10.1secs
0-1/4 mile: 17.6secs
0-1km: 32.0secs
120.0bhp 89.5kW 121.7PS
@ 5800rpm
123.0lbft 166.7Nm @ 3500rpm
105.3bhp/ton 103.6bhp/tonne
60.3bhp/L 45.0kW/L 61.1PS/L
50.7ft/sec 15.5m/sec
18.4mph 29.6kmh/1000rpm
21.2mpg 17.7mpgUS 13.3L/100km
Petrol 4-stroke piston
1990cc 121.4cu in
In-line 4 2 Carburettor
Compression ratio: 9.3:1
Bore: 89.0mm 3.5in
Stroke: 80.0mm 3.1in
Valve type/No: Overhead 8
Transmission: Manual
No. of forward speeds: 4
Wheels driven: Rear
Springs F/R: Coil/Coil
Brake system: PA
Brakes F/R: Disc/Drum
Steering: Worm & roller
Wheelbase: 255.3cm 100.5in
Track F: 132.1cm 52.0in
Track R: 137.2cm 54.0in
Length: 454.7cm 179.0in
Width: 165.1cm 65.0in
Height: 144.0cm 56.7in
Ground clearance: 16.5cm 6.5in
Kerb weight: 1158.6kg 2552.0lb
Fuel: 54.6L 12.0gal 14.4galUS

518 BMW

2002
1969 Germany
104.0mph 167.3kmh
0-50mph 80.5kmh: 7.1secs
0-60mph 96.5kmh: 10.0secs
0-1/4 mile: 17.4secs
113.0bhp 84.3kW 114.6PS
@ 5800rpm
116.0lbft 157.2Nm @ 3000rpm
114.0bhp/ton 112.1bhp/tonne
56.8bhp/L 42.3kW/L 57.5PS/L
50.7ft/sec 15.5m/sec
18.3mph 29.4kmh/1000rpm
Petrol 4-stroke piston
1991cc 121.5cu in
In-line 4 1 Carburettor
Compression ratio: 8.5:1
Bore: 88.9mm 3.5in
Stroke: 80.0mm 3.1in
Valve type/No: Overhead 8
Transmission: Manual
No. of forward speeds: 4
Wheels driven: Rear
Springs F/R: Coil/Coil
Brake system: PA
Brakes F/R: Disc/Drum
Steering: Worm & roller
Wheelbase: 249.9cm 98.4in
Track F: 133.1cm 52.4in
Track R: 133.1cm 52.4in
Length: 422.9cm 166.5in
Width: 159.0cm 62.6in
Height: 137.2cm 54.0in
Kerb weight: 1007.9kg 2220.0lb
Fuel: 45.8L 10.1gal 12.1galUS

519 BMW

2500
1969 Germany
121.0mph 194.7kmh
0-50mph 80.5kmh: 7.0secs
0-60mph 96.5kmh: 9.3secs
0-1/4 mile: 17.2secs
0-1km: 31.6secs
150.0bhp 111.9kW 152.1PS
@ 6000rpm
155.4lbft 210.6Nm @ 3700rpm
114.4bhp/ton 112.5bhp/tonne
60.1bhp/L 44.8kW/L 61.0PS/L
47.0ft/sec 14.3m/sec
19.7mph 31.7kmh/1000rpm
21.8mpg 18.2mpgUS 13.0L/100km
Petrol 4-stroke piston
2494cc 152.2cu in
In-line 6 2 Carburettor
Compression ratio: 9.0:1
Bore: 86.0mm 3.4in
Stroke: 71.6mm 2.8in
Valve type/No: Overhead 12
Transmission: Manual
No. of forward speeds: 4
Wheels driven: Rear
Springs F/R: Coil/Coil
Brake system: PA
Brakes F/R: Disc/Disc
Steering: Worm & roller PA
Wheelbase: 269.2cm 106.0in
Track F: 144.5cm 56.9in
Track R: 146.3cm 57.6in
Length: 469.9cm 185.0in
Width: 175.3cm 69.0in
Height: 144.8cm 57.0in
Ground clearance: 14.0cm 5.5in
Kerb weight: 1333.8kg 2938.0lb
Fuel: 75.1L 16.5gal 19.8galUS

520 BMW

2002 Automatic
1970 Germany
102.0mph 164.1kmh
0-50mph 80.5kmh: 9.8secs
0-60mph 96.5kmh: 13.3secs
0-1/4 mile: 17.9secs
113.0bhp 84.3kW 114.6PS
@ 5800rpm
116.0lbft 157.2Nm @ 3000rpm
111.5bhp/ton 109.6bhp/tonne
56.8bhp/L 42.3kW/L 57.6PS/L
50.7ft/sec 15.5m/sec
17.2mph 27.7kmh/1000rpm
23.4mpg 19.5mpgUS 12.1L/100km
Petrol 4-stroke piston
1990cc 121.4cu in
In-line 4
Compression ratio: 8.5:1
Bore: 89.0mm 3.5in
Stroke: 80.0mm 3.1in
Valve type/No: Overhead 8
Transmission: Automatic
No. of forward speeds: 3
Wheels driven: Rear
Brake system: PA
Brakes F/R: Disc/Drum
Steering: Worm & roller
Wheelbase: 249.9cm 98.4in
Track F: 133.1cm 52.4in
Track R: 133.1cm 52.4in
Length: 422.9cm 166.5in
Width: 159.0cm 62.6in
Height: 137.2cm 54.0in
Kerb weight: 1030.6kg 2270.0lb
Fuel: 45.8L 10.1gal 12.1galUS

521 BMW

2800 CS
1970 Germany
126.0mph 202.7kmh
0-50mph 80.5kmh: 7.4secs
0-60mph 96.5kmh: 9.3secs
0-1/4 mile: 17.4secs
192.0bhp 143.2kW 194.7PS
@ 6000rpm
174.0lbft 235.8Nm @ 3700rpm
143.8bhp/ton 141.4bhp/tonne
68.9bhp/L 51.3kW/L 69.8PS/L
52.5ft/sec 16.0m/sec
19.5mph 31.4kmh/1000rpm
22.8mpg 19.0mpgUS 12.4L/100km
Petrol 4-stroke piston
2788cc 170.1cu in
In-line 6 2 Carburettor
Compression ratio: 9.0:1
Bore: 86.0mm 3.4in
Stroke: 80.0mm 3.1in
Valve type/No: Overhead 12
Transmission: Manual
No. of forward speeds: 4
Wheels driven: Rear
Springs F/R: Coil/Coil
Brake system: PA
Brakes F/R: Disc/Drum
Steering: Worm & roller PA
Wheelbase: 262.4cm 103.3in
Track F: 144.5cm 56.9in
Track R: 140.2cm 55.2in
Length: 466.1cm 183.5in
Width: 164.8cm 64.9in
Height: 136.9cm 53.9in
Ground clearance: 15.0cm 5.9in
Kerb weight: 1357.5kg 2990.0lb
Fuel: 70.0L 15.4gal 18.5galUS

522 BMW

2002
1971 Germany
118.0mph 189.9kmh
0-50mph 80.5kmh: 6.1secs
0-60mph 96.5kmh: 8.3secs
0-1/4 mile: 16.4secs
0-1km: 30.3secs
130.0bhp 96.9kW 131.8PS
@ 5800rpm
131.0lbft 177.5Nm @ 4500rpm
125.9bhp/ton 123.8bhp/tonne
65.3bhp/L 48.7kW/L 66.2PS/L
50.7ft/sec 15.5m/sec
19.5mph 31.4kmh/1000rpm
25.4mpg 21.1mpgUS 11.1L/100km
Petrol 4-stroke piston
1990cc 121.4cu in
In-line 4 fuel injection
Compression ratio: 10.0:1
Bore: 89.0mm 3.5in
Stroke: 80.0mm 3.1in
Valve type/No: Overhead 8
Transmission: Manual
No. of forward speeds: 4
Wheels driven: Rear
Springs F/R: Coil/Coil
Brake system: PA
Brakes F/R: Disc/Drum
Steering: Worm & roller
Wheelbase: 250.2cm 98.5in
Track F: 132.1cm 52.0in
Track R: 132.1cm 52.0in
Length: 431.8cm 170.0in
Width: 163.8cm 64.5in
Height: 139.7cm 55.0in
Ground clearance: 16.5cm 6.5in
Kerb weight: 1049.6kg 2312.0lb
Fuel: 46.0L 10.1gal 12.1galUS

523 BMW

2002 Tii
1971 Germany
120.0mph 193.1kmh
0-50mph 80.5kmh: 6.3secs
0-60mph 96.5kmh: 8.2secs
0-1/4 mile: 16.5secs
0-1km: 30.6secs
130.0bhp 96.9kW 131.8PS
@ 5800rpm
131.0lbft 177.5Nm @ 4500rpm
128.7bhp/ton 126.6bhp/tonne
65.3bhp/L 48.7kW/L 66.2PS/L
50.7ft/sec 15.5m/sec
19.6mph 31.5kmh/1000rpm
24.0mpg 20.0mpgUS 11.8L/100km
Petrol 4-stroke piston
1990cc 121.4cu in
In-line 4 fuel injection
Compression ratio: 10.0:1
Bore: 89.0mm 3.5in
Stroke: 80.0mm 3.1in
Valve type/No: Overhead 8
Transmission: Manual
No. of forward speeds: 4
Wheels driven: Rear
Springs F/R: Coil/Coil
Brake system: PA
Brakes F/R: Disc/Drum
Steering: Worm & roller
Wheelbase: 250.2cm 98.5in
Track F: 132.6cm 52.2in
Track R: 132.6cm 52.2in
Length: 422.9cm 166.5in
Width: 156.2cm 61.5in
Height: 139.7cm 55.0in
Ground clearance: 12.7cm 5.0in
Kerb weight: 1027.1kg 2262.4lb
Fuel: 46.0L 10.1gal 12.1galUS

524 BMW

3.0 CS
1971 Germany
132.0mph 212.4kmh
0-50mph 80.5kmh: 6.1secs
0-60mph 96.5kmh: 8.0secs
0-1/4 mile: 16.2secs
0-1km: 29.5secs
180.0bhp 134.2kW 182.5PS
@ 6000rpm
188.0lbft 254.7Nm @ 3700rpm
133.1bhp/ton 130.8bhp/tonne
60.3bhp/L 45.0kW/L 61.1PS/L
52.5ft/sec 16.0m/sec
20.7mph 33.3kmh/1000rpm
20.8mpg 17.3mpgUS 13.6L/100km
Petrol 4-stroke piston
2985cc 182.1cu in
In-line 6 2 Carburettor
Compression ratio: 9.0:1
Bore: 89.0mm 3.5in
Stroke: 80.0mm 3.1in
Valve type/No: Overhead 12
Transmission: Manual
No. of forward speeds: 4
Wheels driven: Rear
Springs F/R: Coil/Coil
Brake system: PA
Brakes F/R: Disc/Disc
Steering: Ball & nut PA
Wheelbase: 262.4cm 103.3in
Track F: 144.5cm 56.9in
Track R: 140.0cm 55.1in
Length: 465.8cm 183.4in
Width: 167.6cm 66.0in
Height: 136.1cm 53.6in
Ground clearance: 15.2cm 6.0in
Kerb weight: 1375.6kg 3030.0lb
Fuel: 70.1L 15.4gal 18.5galUS

525 BMW

3.0S
1971 Germany
128.0mph 206.0kmh
0-50mph 80.5kmh: 6.1secs
0-60mph 96.5kmh: 8.0secs
0-1/4 mile: 15.9secs
0-1km: 29.5secs
180.0bhp 134.2kW 182.5PS
@ 6000rpm
188.0lbft 254.7Nm @ 3700rpm
129.5bhp/ton 127.3bhp/tonne
60.3bhp/L 45.0kW/L 61.1PS/L
52.5ft/sec 16.0m/sec
20.7mph 33.3kmh/1000rpm
21.3mpg 17.7mpgUS 13.3L/100km
Petrol 4-stroke piston
2985cc 182.1cu in
In-line 6 2 Carburettor
Compression ratio: 9.0:1
Bore: 89.0mm 3.5in
Stroke: 80.0mm 3.1in
Valve type/No: Overhead 12
Transmission: Manual
No. of forward speeds: 4
Wheels driven: Rear
Springs F/R: Coil/Coil
Brake system: PA
Brakes F/R: Disc/Disc
Steering: Ball & nut PA
Wheelbase: 269.2cm 106.0in
Track F: 144.5cm 56.9in
Track R: 146.3cm 57.6in
Length: 469.9cm 185.0in
Width: 175.3cm 69.0in
Height: 144.8cm 57.0in
Ground clearance: 14.0cm 5.5in
Kerb weight: 1413.8kg 3114.0lb
Fuel: 75.1L 16.5gal 19.8galUS

526 BMW

Bavaria
1971 Germany
122.0mph 196.3kmh
0-50mph 80.5kmh: 6.7secs
0-60mph 96.5kmh: 9.3secs
0-1/4 mile: 16.8secs
192.0bhp 143.2kW 194.7PS
@ 6000rpm
200.0lbft 271.0Nm @ 3700rpm
135.7bhp/ton 133.4bhp/tonne
68.9bhp/L 51.3kW/L 69.8PS/L
52.5ft/sec 16.0m/sec
19.4mph 31.2kmh/1000rpm
21.6mpg 18.0mpgUS 13.1L/100km
Petrol 4-stroke piston
2788cc 170.1cu in
In-line 6 2 Carburettor
Compression ratio: 9.0:1
Bore: 86.0mm 3.4in
Stroke: 80.0mm 3.1in
Valve type/No: Overhead 12
Transmission: Manual
No. of forward speeds: 4
Wheels driven: Rear
Springs F/R: Coil/Coil
Brake system: PA
Brakes F/R: Disc/Disc
Steering: Worm & roller PA
Wheelbase: 269.2cm 106.0in
Track F: 144.5cm 56.9in
Track R: 146.3cm 57.6in
Length: 469.9cm 185.0in
Width: 175.0cm 68.9in
Height: 142.5cm 56.1in
Ground clearance: 14.0cm 5.5in
Kerb weight: 1439.2kg 3170.0lb
Fuel: 74.9L 16.5gal 19.8galUS

527 BMW

2002 Tii
1972 Germany
115.0mph 185.0kmh
0-50mph 80.5kmh: 7.7secs
0-60mph 96.5kmh: 9.8secs
0-1/4 mile: 17.3secs
140.0bhp 104.4kW 141.9PS
@ 5800rpm
145.0lbft 196.5Nm @ 4500rpm
135.8bhp/ton 133.5bhp/tonne
70.3bhp/L 52.5kW/L 71.3PS/L
50.7ft/sec 15.5m/sec
19.8mph 31.9kmh/1000rpm
27.3mpg 22.7mpgUS 10.4L/100km
Petrol 4-stroke piston
1990cc 121.4cu in
In-line 4 fuel injection
Compression ratio: 9.0:1
Bore: 89.0mm 3.5in
Stroke: 80.0mm 3.1in
Valve type/No: Overhead 8
Transmission: Manual
No. of forward speeds: 4
Wheels driven: Rear
Springs F/R: Coil/Coil
Brake system: PA
Brakes F/R: Disc/Drum
Steering: Worm & roller
Wheelbase: 249.9cm 98.4in
Track F: 136.7cm 53.8in
Track R: 136.7cm 53.8in
Length: 422.9cm 166.5in
Width: 159.0cm 62.6in
Height: 141.0cm 55.5in
Ground clearance: 16.0cm 6.3in
Kerb weight: 1048.7kg 2310.0lb
Fuel: 45.8L 10.1gal 12.1galUS

528 BMW

2002 TransAm
1972 Germany
118.0mph 189.9kmh
0-50mph 80.5kmh: 5.6secs
0-60mph 96.5kmh: 7.2secs
0-1/4 mile: 14.4secs
200.0bhp 149.1kW 202.8PS
@ 7100rpm
150.0lbft 203.3Nm @ 7100rpm
183.6bhp/ton 180.5bhp/tonne
98.4bhp/L 73.4kW/L 99.8PS/L
62.1ft/sec 18.9m/sec
15.8mph 25.4kmh/1000rpm
4.8mpg 4.0mpgUS 58.8L/100km
Petrol 4-stroke piston
2032cc 124.0cu in
In-line 4
Compression ratio: 12.5:1
Bore: 90.0mm 3.5in
Stroke: 80.0mm 3.1in
Valve type/No: Overhead 8
Transmission: Manual
No. of forward speeds: 5
Wheels driven: Rear
Brakes F/R: Disc/Disc
Steering: Worm & nut
Wheelbase: 250.2cm 98.5in
Track F: 141.7cm 55.8in
Track R: 141.7cm 55.8in
Length: 422.9cm 166.5in
Width: 165.4cm 65.1in
Height: 121.9cm 48.0in

Kerb weight: 1107.8kg 2440.0lb
Fuel: 56.8L 12.5gal 15.0galUS

529 BMW

3.0 CS
1973 Germany
125.0mph 201.1kmh
0-50mph 80.5kmh: 7.3secs
0-60mph 96.5kmh: 10.0secs
0-1/4 mile: 17.2secs
170.0bhp 126.8kW 172.4PS
@ 5800rpm
185.0lbft 250.7Nm @ 3500rpm
119.9bhp/ton 117.9bhp/tonne
56.9bhp/L 42.5kW/L 57.7PS/L
50.7ft/sec 15.5m/sec
19.4mph 31.2kmh/1000rpm
20.4mpg 17.0mpgUS 13.8L/100km
Petrol 4-stroke piston
2985cc 182.1cu in
In-line 6 2 Carburettor
Compression ratio: 8.3:1
Bore: 89.0mm 3.5in
Stroke: 80.0mm 3.1in
Valve type/No: Overhead 12
Transmission: Manual
No. of forward speeds: 4
Wheels driven: Rear
Springs F/R: Coil/Coil
Brake system: PA
Brakes F/R: Disc/Disc
Steering: Worm & roller PA
Wheelbase: 262.4cm 103.3in
Track F: 144.5cm 56.9in
Track R: 140.2cm 55.2in
Length: 473.7cm 186.5in
Width: 164.8cm 64.9in
Height: 136.9cm 53.9in
Ground clearance: 15.0cm 5.9in
Kerb weight: 1441.4kg 3175.0lb
Fuel: 70.0L 15.4gal 18.5galUS

530 BMW

3.0 CSL
1973 Germany
134.0mph 215.6kmh
0-50mph 80.5kmh: 5.7secs
0-60mph 96.5kmh: 7.3secs
0-1/4 mile: 15.7secs
0-1km: 28.7secs
200.0bhp 149.1kW 202.8PS
@ 5500rpm
200.0lbft 271.0Nm @ 4300rpm
155.2bhp/ton 152.6bhp/tonne
66.6bhp/L 49.7kW/L 67.5PS/L
48.1ft/sec 14.7m/sec
22.0mph 35.4kmh/1000rpm
16.7mpg 13.9mpgUS 16.9L/100km
Petrol 4-stroke piston
3003cc 183.2cu in
In-line 6 fuel injection
Compression ratio: 9.5:1
Bore: 89.2mm 3.5in
Stroke: 80.0mm 3.1in
Valve type/No: Overhead 12
Transmission: Manual
No. of forward speeds: 4
Wheels driven: Rear
Springs F/R: Coil/Coil
Brake system: PA
Brakes F/R: Disc/Disc
Steering: Ball & nut PA
Wheelbase: 262.4cm 103.3in
Track F: 144.5cm 56.9in
Track R: 140.0cm 55.1in
Length: 465.8cm 183.4in
Width: 167.6cm 66.0in
Height: 136.1cm 53.6in
Ground clearance: 15.2cm 6.0in
Kerb weight: 1310.7kg 2887.0lb
Fuel: 70.1L 15.4gal 18.5galUS

531 BMW

520i
1973 Germany
116.0mph 186.6kmh
0-50mph 80.5kmh: 7.6secs
0-60mph 96.5kmh: 10.5secs
0-1/4 mile: 17.5secs
0-1km: 32.2secs
130.0bhp 96.9kW 131.8PS
@ 5800rpm
131.0lbft 177.5Nm @ 4500rpm
105.4bhp/ton 103.7bhp/tonne
65.3bhp/L 48.7kW/L 66.2PS/L
50.7ft/sec 15.5m/sec
18.5mph 29.8kmh/1000rpm
22.4mpg 18.7mpgUS 12.6L/100km
Petrol 4-stroke piston
1990cc 121.4cu in
In-line 4 fuel injection
Compression ratio: 9.5:1
Bore: 89.0mm 3.5in
Stroke: 80.0mm 3.1in
Valve type/No: Overhead 8
Transmission: Manual
No. of forward speeds: 4
Wheels driven: Rear
Springs F/R: Coil/Coil
Brake system: PA
Brakes F/R: Disc/Disc
Steering: Worm & roller
Wheelbase: 263.7cm 103.8in
Track F: 140.7cm 55.4in
Track R: 144.3cm 56.8in
Length: 461.8cm 181.8in
Width: 168.9cm 66.5in
Height: 142.2cm 56.0in
Ground clearance: 15.2cm 6.0in
Kerb weight: 1254.0kg 2762.1lb
Fuel: 56.9L 12.5gal 15.0galUS

532 BMW

Bavaria
1973 Germany
124.0mph 199.5kmh
0-60mph 96.5kmh: 10.7secs
0-1/4 mile: 17.8secs
170.0bhp 126.8kW 172.4PS
@ 5800rpm
185.0lbft 250.7Nm @ 3500rpm
117.7bhp/ton 115.7bhp/tonne
56.9bhp/L 42.5kW/L 57.7PS/L
50.7ft/sec 15.5m/sec
20.4mpg 17.0mpgUS 13.8L/100km
Petrol 4-stroke piston
2985cc 182.1cu in
In-line 6 2 Carburettor
Compression ratio: 8.3:1
Bore: 89.0mm 3.5in
Stroke: 80.0mm 3.1in
Valve type/No: Overhead 12
Transmission: Manual
No. of forward speeds: 4
Wheels driven: Rear
Brake system: PA
Brakes F/R: Disc/Disc
Steering: PA
Wheelbase: 269.2cm 106.0in
Track F: 144.5cm 56.9in
Track R: 146.3cm 57.6in
Length: 469.9cm 185.0in
Width: 175.0cm 68.9in
Height: 145.0cm 57.1in
Ground clearance: 14.0cm 5.5in
Kerb weight: 1468.7kg 3235.0lb
Fuel: 74.9L 16.5gal 19.8galUS

533 BMW

2002 Tii
1974 Germany
112.0mph 180.2kmh
0-60mph 96.5kmh: 9.5secs
0-1/4 mile: 17.7secs
125.0bhp 93.2kW 126.7PS
@ 5500rpm
127.0lbft 172.1Nm @ 4000rpm
115.7bhp/ton 113.8bhp/tonne
62.8bhp/L 46.8kW/L 63.7PS/L
18.8mph 30.2kmh/1000rpm
28.2mpg 23.5mpgUS 10.0L/100km
Petrol 4-stroke piston
1990cc 121.4cu in
In-line 4
Valve type/No: Overhead 8
Transmission: Manual
No. of forward speeds: 4
Wheels driven: Rear
Springs F/R: Coil/Coil
Brakes F/R: Disc/Drum
Steering: Worm & roller
Wheelbase: 249.9cm 98.4in
Track F: 134.1cm 52.8in
Track R: 134.1cm 52.8in
Length: 447.0cm 176.0in
Width: 159.0cm 62.6in
Height: 141.0cm 55.5in
Kerb weight: 1098.7kg 2420.0lb
Fuel: 49.2L 10.8gal 13.0galUS

534 BMW

2002 Turbo
1974 Germany
130.0mph 209.2kmh
0-50mph 80.5kmh: 5.7secs
0-60mph 96.5kmh: 7.3secs
0-1/4 mile: 16.0secs
0-1km: 28.9secs
170.0bhp 126.8kW 172.4PS
@ 5800rpm
117.0lbft 158.5Nm @ 4000rpm
156.8bhp/ton 154.2bhp/tonne
85.4bhp/L 63.7kW/L 86.6PS/L
50.7ft/sec 15.5m/sec
20.3mph 32.7kmh/1000rpm
21.7mpg 18.1mpgUS 13.0L/100km
Petrol 4-stroke piston
1990cc 121.4cu in turbocharged
In-line 4 fuel injection
Compression ratio: 6.9:1
Bore: 89.0mm 3.5in
Stroke: 80.0mm 3.1in
Valve type/No: Overhead 8
Transmission: Manual
No. of forward speeds: 5
Wheels driven: Rear
Springs F/R: Coil/Coil
Brake system: PA
Brakes F/R: Disc/Drum
Steering: Worm & roller
Wheelbase: 250.2cm 98.5in
Track F: 137.7cm 54.2in
Track R: 135.9cm 53.5in
Length: 422.1cm 166.2in
Width: 161.8cm 63.7in
Height: 139.7cm 55.0in
Ground clearance: 16.5cm 6.5in
Kerb weight: 1102.8kg 2429.0lb
Fuel: 70.1L 15.4gal 18.5galUS

535 BMW

3.3L
1974 Germany
124.0mph 199.5kmh
0-50mph 80.5kmh: 7.3secs
0-60mph 96.5kmh: 9.9secs
0-1/4 mile: 17.3secs
0-1km: 31.7secs
190.0bhp 141.7kW 192.6PS
@ 5500rpm
213.0lbft 288.6Nm @ 3500rpm
119.9bhp/ton 117.9bhp/tonne
57.7bhp/L 43.0kW/L 58.5PS/L
53.2ft/sec 16.2m/sec
20.8mph 33.5kmh/1000rpm
17.7mpg 14.7mpgUS 16.0L/100km
Petrol 4-stroke piston
3295cc 201.0cu in
In-line 6 2 Carburettor
Compression ratio: 9.0:1
Bore: 89.0mm 3.5in
Stroke: 88.4mm 3.5in
Valve type/No: Overhead 12
Transmission: Automatic
No. of forward speeds: 3
Wheels driven: Rear
Springs F/R: Coil/Coil
Brake system: PA
Brakes F/R: Disc/Disc
Steering: Worm & roller PA
Wheelbase: 279.1cm 109.9in
Track F: 144.5cm 56.9in
Track R: 146.3cm 57.6in
Length: 479.8cm 188.9in
Width: 175.3cm 69.0in
Height: 144.8cm 57.0in
Ground clearance: 14.0cm 5.5in
Kerb weight: 1610.8kg 3548.0lb
Fuel: 75.1L 16.5gal 19.8galUS

536 BMW

525
1974 Germany
119.0mph 191.5kmh
0-50mph 80.5kmh: 7.5secs
0-60mph 96.5kmh: 10.6secs
0-1/4 mile: 17.8secs
0-1km: 32.5secs
145.0bhp 108.1kW 147.0PS
@ 6000rpm
153.3lbft 207.7Nm @ 4000rpm
107.9bhp/ton 106.1bhp/tonne
58.1bhp/L 43.4kW/L 58.9PS/L
47.0ft/sec 14.3m/sec
19.8mph 31.9kmh/1000rpm
23.7mpg 19.7mpgUS 11.9L/100km
Petrol 4-stroke piston
2494cc 152.2cu in
In-line 6 2 Carburettor
Compression ratio: 9.0:1
Bore: 86.0mm 3.4in
Stroke: 71.6mm 2.8in
Valve type/No: Overhead 12
Transmission: Manual
No. of forward speeds: 4
Wheels driven: Rear
Springs F/R: Coil/Coil
Brake system: PA
Brakes F/R: Disc/Disc
Steering: Worm & roller
Wheelbase: 263.7cm 103.8in
Track F: 140.7cm 55.4in
Track R: 144.3cm 56.8in
Length: 461.8cm 181.8in
Width: 168.9cm 66.5in
Height: 142.2cm 56.0in
Ground clearance: 15.2cm 6.0in
Kerb weight: 1367.0kg 3011.0lb
Fuel: 70.1L 15.4gal 18.5galUS

537 BMW

1602L
1975 Germany
96.0mph 154.5kmh
0-50mph 80.5kmh: 9.7secs
0-60mph 96.5kmh: 14.1secs
0-1/4 mile: 19.6secs
0-1km: 39.6secs
85.0bhp 63.4kW 86.2PS
@ 5700rpm
95.0lbft 128.7Nm @ 3500rpm
91.1bhp/ton 89.6bhp/tonne
54.0bhp/L 40.3kW/L 54.8PS/L
52.4ft/sec 16.0m/sec
16.4mph 26.4kmh/1000rpm
25.6mpg 21.3mpgUS 11.0L/100km
Petrol 4-stroke piston
1573cc 96.0cu in
In-line 4 1 Carburettor
Compression ratio: 8.6:1
Bore: 71.0mm 2.8in
Stroke: 84.0mm 3.3in
Valve type/No: Overhead 8
Transmission: Manual
No. of forward speeds: 4
Wheels driven: Rear
Springs F/R: Coil/Coil
Brake system: PA
Brakes F/R: Disc/Drum
Steering: Worm & roller
Wheelbase: 250.2cm 98.5in
Track F: 132.1cm 52.0in
Track R: 132.1cm 52.0in
Length: 422.9cm 166.5in
Width: 162.6cm 64.0in
Height: 142.2cm 56.0in
Ground clearance: 16.5cm 6.5in
Kerb weight: 948.9kg 2090.0lb
Fuel: 50.0L 11.0gal 13.2galUS

538 BMW

525
1975 Germany
119.0mph 191.5kmh
0-50mph 80.5kmh: 8.0secs
0-60mph 96.5kmh: 10.5secs
0-1/4 mile: 17.8secs
138.0bhp 102.9kW 139.9PS
@ 6000rpm
153.0lbft 207.3Nm @ 4000rpm
103.7bhp/ton 102.0bhp/tonne
55.3bhp/L 41.3kW/L 56.1PS/L
47.0ft/sec 14.3m/sec
18.9mph 30.4kmh/1000rpm
22.8mpg 19.0mpgUS 12.4L/100km
Petrol 4-stroke piston
2494cc 152.2cu in
In-line 6
Compression ratio: 9.0:1
Bore: 86.0mm 3.4in
Stroke: 71.6mm 2.8in
Valve type/No: Overhead 12
Transmission: Manual
No. of forward speeds: 4
Wheels driven: Rear
Springs F/R: Coil/Coil
Brake system: PA
Brakes F/R: Disc/Disc
Steering: Worm & roller PA
Wheelbase: 264.2cm 104.0in
Track F: 141.0cm 55.5in
Track R: 144.8cm 57.0in
Length: 462.3cm 182.0in
Width: 168.9cm 66.5in

Height: 142.7cm 56.2in
Kerb weight: 1352.9kg 2980.0lb
Fuel: 71.9L 15.8gal 19.0galUS

539 BMW

530i
1975 Germany
120.0mph 193.1kmh
0-50mph 80.5kmh: 7.4secs
0-60mph 96.5kmh: 10.2secs
0-1/4 mile: 17.5secs
176.0bhp 131.2kW 178.4PS
@ 5500rpm
185.0lbft 250.7Nm @ 4500rpm
118.9bhp/ton 116.9bhp/tonne
59.0bhp/L 44.0kW/L 59.8PS/L
48.1ft/sec 14.7m/sec
20.0mph 32.2kmh/1000rpm
22.8mpg 19.0mpgUS 12.4L/100km
Petrol 4-stroke piston
2985cc 182.1cu in
In-line 6 fuel injection
Compression ratio: 8.1:1
Bore: 89.0mm 3.5in
Stroke: 80.0mm 3.1in
Valve type/No: Overhead 12
Transmission: Manual
No. of forward speeds: 4
Wheels driven: Rear
Springs F/R: Coil/Coil
Brake system: PA
Brakes F/R: Disc/Disc
Steering: Recirculating ball PA
Wheelbase: 263.7cm 103.8in
Track F: 142.2cm 56.0in
Track R: 146.1cm 57.5in
Length: 482.3cm 189.9in
Width: 170.7cm 67.2in
Height: 142.2cm 56.0in
Ground clearance: 16.5cm 6.5in
Kerb weight: 1505.0kg 3315.0lb
Fuel: 70.0L 15.4gal 18.5galUS

540 BMW

633 CSi
1976 Germany
132.0mph 212.4kmh
0-50mph 80.5kmh: 6.1secs
0-60mph 96.5kmh: 8.1secs
0-1/4 mile: 14.9secs
0-1km: 30.3secs
200.0bhp 149.1kW 202.8PS
@ 5500rpm
210.0lbft 284.6Nm @ 4250rpm
136.6bhp/ton 134.3bhp/tonne
62.3bhp/L 46.5kW/L 63.2PS/L
51.8ft/sec 15.8m/sec
22.5mph 36.2kmh/1000rpm
20.6mpg 17.2mpgUS 13.7L/100km
Petrol 4-stroke piston
3210cc 195.8cu in
In-line 6 fuel injection
Compression ratio: 9.0:1
Bore: 89.0mm 3.5in
Stroke: 86.0mm 3.4in
Valve type/No: Overhead 12
Transmission: Manual
No. of forward speeds: 4
Wheels driven: Rear
Springs F/R: Coil/Coil
Brake system: PA
Brakes F/R: Disc/Disc
Steering: Worm & roller PA
Wheelbase: 261.6cm 103.0in
Track F: 142.2cm 56.0in
Track R: 148.6cm 58.5in
Length: 475.5cm 187.2in
Width: 175.3cm 69.0in
Height: 138.4cm 54.5in
Ground clearance: 12.7cm 5.0in
Kerb weight: 1489.1kg 3280.0lb
Fuel: 70.1L 15.4gal 18.5galUS

541 BMW

320
1977 Germany
114.0mph 183.4kmh
0-50mph 80.5kmh: 7.3secs
0-60mph 96.5kmh: 9.8secs
0-1/4 mile: 17.4secs
0-1km: 32.4secs
122.4bhp 91.3kW 124.1PS
@ 6000rpm
118.0lbft 159.9Nm @ 4000rpm
114.2bhp/ton 112.3bhp/tonne
61.5bhp/L 45.9kW/L 62.4PS/L
52.5ft/sec 16.0m/sec
18.8mph 30.2kmh/1000rpm
24.6mpg 20.5mpgUS 11.5L/100km
Petrol 4-stroke piston
1990cc 121.4cu in
In-line 6 1 Carburettor
Compression ratio: 9.2:1
Bore: 66.0mm 2.6in
Stroke: 80.0mm 3.1in
Valve type/No: Overhead 12
Transmission: Manual
No. of forward speeds: 4
Wheels driven: Rear
Springs F/R: Coil/Coil
Brake system: PA
Brakes F/R: Disc/Drum
Steering: Rack & pinion
Wheelbase: 254.0cm 100.0in
Track F: 137.2cm 54.0in
Track R: 137.2cm 54.0in
Length: 434.3cm 171.0in
Width: 160.0cm 63.0in
Height: 137.2cm 54.0in
Ground clearance: 17.8cm 7.0in
Kerb weight: 1090.0kg 2400.9lb
Fuel: 58.2L 12.8gal 15.4galUS

542 BMW

320i
1977 Germany
104.0mph 167.3kmh
0-50mph 80.5kmh: 8.7secs
0-60mph 96.5kmh: 12.0secs
0-1/4 mile: 18.7secs
110.0bhp 82.0kW 111.5PS
@ 5800rpm
112.0lbft 151.8Nm @ 3750rpm
94.6bhp/ton 93.0bhp/tonne
55.3bhp/L 41.2kW/L 56.0PS/L
50.7ft/sec 15.5m/sec
18.2mph 29.3kmh/1000rpm
25.8mpg 21.5mpgUS 10.9L/100km
Petrol 4-stroke piston
1990cc 121.4cu in
In-line 4 fuel injection
Compression ratio: 8.1:1
Bore: 89.0mm 3.5in
Stroke: 80.0mm 3.1in
Valve type/No: Overhead 8
Transmission: Manual
No. of forward speeds: 4
Wheels driven: Rear
Springs F/R: Coil/Coil
Brake system: PA
Brakes F/R: Disc/Drum
Steering: Rack & pinion
Wheelbase: 256.3cm 100.9in
Track F: 138.7cm 54.6in
Track R: 140.0cm 55.1in
Length: 450.9cm 177.5in
Width: 161.0cm 63.4in
Height: 137.9cm 54.3in
Ground clearance: 14.5cm 5.7in
Kerb weight: 1182.7kg 2605.0lb
Fuel: 60.2L 13.2gal 15.9galUS

543 BMW

528
1977 Germany
126.0mph 202.7kmh
0-50mph 80.5kmh: 6.4secs
0-60mph 96.5kmh: 9.0secs
0-1/4 mile: 16.7secs
0-1km: 31.0secs
170.0bhp 126.8kW 172.4PS
@ 5800rpm
172.0lbft 233.1Nm @ 4000rpm
122.4bhp/ton 120.4bhp/tonne
61.0bhp/L 45.5kW/L 61.8PS/L
50.7ft/sec 15.5m/sec
19.8mph 31.9kmh/1000rpm
18.1mpg 15.1mpgUS 15.6L/100km
Petrol 4-stroke piston
2788cc 170.1cu in
In-line 6 1 Carburettor
Compression ratio: 9.0:1
Bore: 86.0mm 3.4in
Stroke: 80.0mm 3.1in
Valve type/No: Overhead 12
Transmission: Manual
No. of forward speeds: 4
Wheels driven: Rear
Springs F/R: Coil/Coil
Brake system: PA
Brakes F/R: Disc/Disc
Steering: Worm & roller PA
Wheelbase: 263.7cm 103.8in
Track F: 140.7cm 55.4in
Track R: 144.3cm 56.8in
Length: 462.3cm 182.0in
Width: 168.9cm 66.5in
Height: 142.2cm 56.0in
Ground clearance: 15.2cm 6.0in
Kerb weight: 1411.9kg 3110.0lb
Fuel: 70.1L 15.4gal 18.5galUS

544 BMW

630 CSi
1977 Germany
122.0mph 196.3kmh
0-50mph 80.5kmh: 7.2secs
0-60mph 96.5kmh: 9.7secs
0-1/4 mile: 17.5secs
176.0bhp 131.2kW 178.4PS
@ 5500rpm
185.0lbft 250.7Nm @ 4500rpm
112.3bhp/ton 110.4bhp/tonne
59.0bhp/L 44.0kW/L 59.8PS/L
48.1ft/sec 14.7m/sec
21.4mph 34.4kmh/1000rpm
21.6mpg 18.0mpgUS 13.1L/100km
Petrol 4-stroke piston
2985cc 182.1cu in
In-line 6 fuel injection
Compression ratio: 8.1:1
Bore: 89.0mm 3.5in
Stroke: 80.0mm 3.1in
Valve type/No: Overhead 12
Transmission: Manual
No. of forward speeds: 4
Wheels driven: Rear
Springs F/R: Coil/Coil
Brake system: PA
Brakes F/R: Disc/Disc
Steering: Recirculating ball PA
Wheelbase: 262.6cm 103.4in
Track F: 142.2cm 56.0in
Track R: 149.4cm 58.8in
Length: 489.5cm 192.7in
Width: 172.5cm 67.9in
Height: 136.4cm 53.7in
Ground clearance: 9.4cm 3.7in
Kerb weight: 1593.5kg 3510.0lb
Fuel: 62.4L 13.7gal 16.5galUS

545 BMW

733i
1977 Germany
122.0mph 196.3kmh
0-50mph 80.5kmh: 6.8secs
0-60mph 96.5kmh: 8.9secs
0-1/4 mile: 16.7secs
0-1km: 30.6secs
197.0bhp 146.9kW 199.7PS
@ 5500rpm
206.0lbft 279.1Nm @ 4250rpm
123.1bhp/ton 121.0bhp/tonne
61.4bhp/L 45.8kW/L 62.2PS/L
51.8ft/sec 15.8m/sec
21.3mph 34.3kmh/1000rpm
19.4mpg 16.2mpgUS 14.6L/100km
Petrol 4-stroke piston
3210cc 195.8cu in
In-line 6 fuel injection
Compression ratio: 9.0:1
Bore: 89.0mm 3.5in
Stroke: 86.0mm 3.4in
Valve type/No: Overhead 12
Transmission: Manual
No. of forward speeds: 4
Wheels driven: Rear
Springs F/R: Coil/Coil
Brake system: PA
Brakes F/R: Disc/Disc
Steering: Recirculating ball PA
Wheelbase: 279.4cm 110.0in
Track F: 150.1cm 59.1in
Track R: 151.4cm 59.6in
Length: 485.9cm 191.3in
Width: 180.1cm 70.9in
Height: 143.0cm 56.3in
Ground clearance: 15.2cm 6.0in
Kerb weight: 1627.6kg 3585.0lb
Fuel: 85.1L 18.7gal 22.5galUS

546 BMW

320i Alpina
1978 Germany
119.0mph 191.5kmh
0-50mph 80.5kmh: 6.2secs
0-60mph 96.5kmh: 8.5secs
0-1/4 mile: 16.5secs
160.0bhp 119.3kW 162.2PS
@ 6400rpm
139.7bhp/ton 137.4bhp/tonne
80.4bhp/L 59.9kW/L 81.5PS/L
56.0ft/sec 17.1m/sec
18.5mph 29.8kmh/1000rpm
22.2mpg 18.5mpgUS 12.7L/100km
Petrol 4-stroke piston
1990cc 121.4cu in
In-line 4
Compression ratio: 10.0:1
Bore: 89.0mm 3.5in
Stroke: 80.0mm 3.1in
Valve type/No: Overhead 8
Transmission: Manual
No. of forward speeds: 5
Wheels driven: Rear
Springs F/R: Coil/Coil
Brake system: PA
Brakes F/R: Disc/Drum
Steering: Rack & pinion
Wheelbase: 256.3cm 100.9in
Track F: 138.7cm 54.6in
Track R: 145.0cm 57.1in
Length: 450.9cm 177.5in
Width: 161.0cm 63.4in
Height: 132.8cm 52.3in
Kerb weight: 1164.5kg 2565.0lb
Fuel: 60.2L 13.2gal 15.9galUS

547 BMW

323i
1978 Germany
126.0mph 202.7kmh
0-50mph 80.5kmh: 6.2secs
0-60mph 96.5kmh: 8.3secs
0-1/4 mile: 16.7secs
0-1km: 30.8secs
142.8bhp 106.5kW 144.8PS
@ 6000rpm
140.0lbft 189.7Nm @ 4500rpm
122.0bhp/ton 120.0bhp/tonne
61.7bhp/L 46.0kW/L 62.5PS/L
50.3ft/sec 15.4m/sec
19.8mph 31.9kmh/1000rpm
19.7mpg 16.4mpgUS 14.3L/100km
Petrol 4-stroke piston
2315cc 141.2cu in
In-line 6 fuel injection
Compression ratio: 9.5:1
Bore: 80.0mm 3.1in
Stroke: 76.8mm 3.0in
Valve type/No: Overhead 12
Transmission: Manual
No. of forward speeds: 4
Wheels driven: Rear
Springs F/R: Coil/Coil
Brake system: PA
Brakes F/R: Disc/Disc
Steering: Rack & pinion
Wheelbase: 254.0cm 100.0in
Track F: 137.2cm 54.0in
Track R: 137.2cm 54.0in
Length: 434.3cm 171.0in
Width: 160.0cm 63.0in
Height: 137.2cm 54.0in
Ground clearance: 17.8cm 7.0in
Kerb weight: 1190.0kg 2621.1lb
Fuel: 58.2L 12.8gal 15.4galUS

548 BMW

333i Alpina
1978 Germany
129.0mph 207.6kmh
0-50mph 80.5kmh: 5.2secs
0-60mph 96.5kmh: 7.0secs
0-1/4 mile: 15.7secs
220.0bhp 164.0kW 223.0PS
@ 6000rpm
228.0lbft 308.9Nm @ 4500rpm
176.6bhp/ton 173.7bhp/tonne
68.5bhp/L 51.1kW/L 69.5PS/L
56.5ft/sec 17.2m/sec
24.0mpg 20.0mpgUS 11.8L/100km
Petrol 4-stroke piston
3210cc 195.8cu in
In-line 6 fuel injection
Compression ratio: 9.5:1
Bore: 89.0mm 3.5in
Stroke: 86.0mm 3.4in
Valve type/No: Overhead 12
Transmission: Manual
No. of forward speeds: 5
Wheels driven: Rear
Springs F/R: Coil/Coil
Brake system: PA
Brakes F/R: Disc/Disc
Steering: Rack & pinion

Wheelbase: 256.3cm 100.9in
Track F: 138.7cm 54.6in
Track R: 145.0cm 57.1in
Length: 450.9cm 177.5in
Width: 161.0cm 63.4in
Height: 132.8cm 52.3in
Kerb weight: 1266.7kg 2790.0lb
Fuel: 60.2L 13.2gal 15.9galUS

549 BMW

528i
1978 Germany
131.0mph 210.8kmh
0-50mph 80.5kmh: 6.6secs
0-60mph 96.5kmh: 8.7secs
0-1/4 mile: 16.8secs
0-1km: 30.4secs
177.0bhp 132.0kW 179.4PS
@ 5800rpm
173.0lbft 234.4Nm @ 4300rpm
121.6bhp/ton 119.6bhp/tonne
63.5bhp/L 47.3kW/L 64.4PS/L
50.7ft/sec 15.5m/sec
20.9mph 33.6kmh/1000rpm
19.2mpg 16.0mpgUS 14.7L/100km
Petrol 4-stroke piston
2788cc 170.1cu in
In-line 6 fuel injection
Compression ratio: 9.0:1
Bore: 86.0mm 3.4in
Stroke: 80.0mm 3.1in
Valve type/No: Overhead 12
Transmission: Manual
No. of forward speeds: 4
Wheels driven: Rear
Springs F/R: Coil/Coil
Brake system: PA
Brakes F/R: Disc/Disc
Steering: Worm & roller PA
Wheelbase: 263.7cm 103.8in
Track F: 140.7cm 55.4in
Track R: 144.3cm 56.8in
Length: 462.3cm 182.0in
Width: 168.9cm 66.5in
Height: 142.2cm 56.0in
Ground clearance: 15.2cm 6.0in
Kerb weight: 1480.0kg 3260.0lb
Fuel: 70.1L 15.4gal 18.5galUS

550 BMW

733i
1978 Germany
118.0mph 189.9kmh
0-50mph 80.5kmh: 6.3secs
0-60mph 96.5kmh: 8.6secs
0-1/4 mile: 17.0secs
177.0bhp 132.0kW 179.4PS
@ 5500rpm
196.0lbft 265.6Nm @ 4000rpm
107.9bhp/ton 106.1bhp/tonne
55.1bhp/L 41.1kW/L 55.9PS/L
51.8ft/sec 15.8m/sec
21.9mph 35.2kmh/1000rpm
22.8mpg 19.0mpgUS 12.4L/100km
Petrol 4-stroke piston
3210cc 195.8cu in
In-line 6 fuel injection
Compression ratio: 8.4:1
Bore: 89.0mm 3.5in
Stroke: 86.0mm 3.4in
Valve type/No: Overhead 12
Transmission: Manual
No. of forward speeds: 4
Wheels driven: Rear
Springs F/R: Coil/Coil
Brakes F/R: Disc/Disc
Steering: Recirculating ball PA
Wheelbase: 279.4cm 110.0in
Track F: 150.1cm 59.1in
Track R: 151.6cm 59.7in
Length: 501.4cm 197.4in
Width: 180.1cm 70.9in
Height: 143.0cm 56.3in
Ground clearance: 17.3cm 6.8in
Kerb weight: 1668.4kg 3675.0lb
Fuel: 85.2L 18.7gal 22.5galUS

551 BMW

528i
1979 Germany
125.0mph 201.1kmh
0-50mph 80.5kmh: 6.0secs
0-60mph 96.5kmh: 8.2secs
0-1/4 mile: 16.7secs
169.0bhp 126.0kW 171.3PS
@ 5500rpm
170.0lbft 230.4Nm @ 4500rpm
111.3bhp/ton 109.5bhp/tonne
60.6bhp/L 45.2kW/L 61.5PS/L
48.1ft/sec 14.7m/sec
21.4mph 34.4kmh/1000rpm
26.4mpg 22.0mpgUS 10.7L/100km
Petrol 4-stroke piston
2788cc 170.1cu in
In-line 6 fuel injection
Compression ratio: 8.2:1
Bore: 86.0mm 3.4in
Stroke: 80.0mm 3.1in
Valve type/No: Overhead 12
Transmission: Manual
No. of forward speeds: 4
Wheels driven: Rear
Springs F/R: Coil/Coil
Brake system: PA
Brakes F/R: Disc/Disc
Steering: Recirculating ball PA
Wheelbase: 263.7cm 103.8in
Track F: 142.2cm 56.0in
Track R: 147.1cm 57.9in
Length: 482.6cm 190.0in
Width: 170.7cm 67.2in
Height: 142.0cm 55.9in
Kerb weight: 1543.6kg 3400.0lb
Fuel: 62.1L 13.6gal 16.4galUS

552 BMW

635 CSi
1979 Germany
140.0mph 225.3kmh
0-50mph 80.5kmh: 6.7secs
0-60mph 96.5kmh: 8.5secs
0-1/4 mile: 16.2secs
0-1km: 29.8secs
218.0bhp 162.6kW 221.0PS
@ 5200rpm
224.0lbft 303.5Nm @ 4000rpm
141.7bhp/ton 139.3bhp/tonne
63.1bhp/L 47.1kW/L 64.0PS/L
47.8ft/sec 14.6m/sec
23.5mph 37.8kmh/1000rpm
17.5mpg 14.6mpgUS 16.1L/100km
Petrol 4-stroke piston
3453cc 210.7cu in
In-line 6 fuel injection
Compression ratio: 9.3:1
Bore: 93.4mm 3.7in
Stroke: 84.0mm 3.3in
Valve type/No: Overhead 12
Transmission: Manual
No. of forward speeds: 5
Wheels driven: Rear
Springs F/R: Coil/Coil
Brake system: PA
Brakes F/R: Disc/Disc
Steering: Ball & nut PA
Wheelbase: 261.6cm 103.0in
Track F: 142.2cm 56.0in
Track R: 148.6cm 58.5in
Length: 475.5cm 187.2in
Width: 175.3cm 69.0in
Height: 138.4cm 54.5in
Ground clearance: 12.7cm 5.0in
Kerb weight: 1564.9kg 3447.0lb
Fuel: 70.5L 15.5gal 18.6galUS

553 BMW

732i
1979 Germany
130.0mph 209.2kmh
0-50mph 80.5kmh: 6.0secs
0-60mph 96.5kmh: 8.0secs
0-1/4 mile: 16.4secs
0-1km: 30.0secs
197.0bhp 146.9kW 199.7PS
@ 5500rpm
210.0lbft 284.6Nm @ 4300rpm
127.1bhp/ton 125.0bhp/tonne
61.4bhp/L 45.8kW/L 62.2PS/L
51.8ft/sec 15.8m/sec
21.2mph 34.1kmh/1000rpm
19.8mpg 16.5mpgUS 14.3L/100km
Petrol 4-stroke piston
3210cc 195.8cu in
In-line 6 fuel injection
Compression ratio: 9.3:1
Bore: 89.0mm 3.5in
Stroke: 86.0mm 3.4in
Valve type/No: Overhead 12
Transmission: Manual
No. of forward speeds: 4
Wheels driven: Rear
Springs F/R: Coil/Coil
Brake system: PA
Brakes F/R: Disc/Disc
Steering: Recirculating ball PA
Wheelbase: 279.4cm 110.0in
Track F: 150.1cm 59.1in
Track R: 151.4cm 59.6in
Length: 485.9cm 191.3in
Width: 180.1cm 70.9in
Height: 143.0cm 56.3in
Ground clearance: 15.2cm 6.0in
Kerb weight: 1575.8kg 3471.0lb
Fuel: 85.1L 18.7gal 22.5galUS

554 BMW

320i
1980 Germany
109.0mph 175.4kmh
0-50mph 80.5kmh: 7.7secs
0-60mph 96.5kmh: 11.1secs
0-1/4 mile: 18.0secs
101.0bhp 75.3kW 102.4PS
@ 5800rpm
100.0lbft 135.5Nm @ 4500rpm
92.9bhp/ton 91.4bhp/tonne
57.2bhp/L 42.6kW/L 58.0PS/L
44.9ft/sec 13.7m/sec
21.1mph 33.9kmh/1000rpm
31.2mpg 26.0mpgUS 9.0L/100km
Petrol 4-stroke piston
1766cc 107.7cu in
In-line 4 fuel injection
Compression ratio: 8.8:1
Bore: 80.0mm 3.1in
Stroke: 70.9mm 2.8in
Valve type/No: Overhead 8
Transmission: Manual
No. of forward speeds: 5
Wheels driven: Rear
Springs F/R: Coil/Coil
Brake system: PA
Brakes F/R: Disc/Drum
Steering: Rack & pinion
Wheelbase: 256.3cm 100.9in
Track F: 138.7cm 54.6in
Track R: 139.7cm 55.0in
Length: 450.9cm 177.5in
Width: 161.0cm 63.4in
Height: 137.9cm 54.3in
Kerb weight: 1105.5kg 2435.0lb
Fuel: 57.9L 12.7gal 15.3galUS

555 BMW

633 CSi
1980 Germany
124.0mph 199.5kmh
0-60mph 96.5kmh: 8.4secs
0-1/4 mile: 16.8secs
174.0bhp 129.7kW 176.4PS
@ 5200rpm
188.0lbft 254.7Nm @ 4200rpm
114.6bhp/ton 112.7bhp/tonne
54.2bhp/L 40.4kW/L 55.0PS/L
49.0ft/sec 14.9m/sec
21.4mph 34.4kmh/1000rpm
22.8mpg 19.0mpgUS 12.4L/100km
Petrol 4-stroke piston
3210cc 195.8cu in
In-line 6 fuel injection
Compression ratio: 8.4:1
Bore: 89.0mm 3.5in
Stroke: 86.1mm 3.4in
Valve type/No: Overhead 12
Transmission: Manual
No. of forward speeds: 4
Wheels driven: Rear
Springs F/R: Coil/Coil
Brake system: PA
Brakes F/R: Disc/Disc
Steering: Recirculating ball PA
Wheelbase: 262.6cm 103.4in
Track F: 142.2cm 56.0in
Track R: 149.4cm 58.8in
Length: 489.5cm 192.7in
Width: 172.5cm 67.9in
Height: 136.4cm 53.7in
Ground clearance: 9.4cm 3.7in
Kerb weight: 1543.6kg 3400.0lb
Fuel: 62.4L 13.7gal 16.5galUS

556 BMW

M1
1980 Germany
156.0mph 251.0kmh
0-50mph 80.5kmh: 4.9secs
0-60mph 96.5kmh: 6.2secs
0-1/4 mile: 14.5secs
235.0bhp 175.2kW 238.3PS
@ 6500rpm
243.0lbft 329.3Nm @ 5000rpm
158.3bhp/ton 155.7bhp/tonne
68.1bhp/L 50.7kW/L 69.0PS/L
59.8ft/sec 18.2m/sec
23.1mph 37.2kmh/1000rpm
15.6mpg 13.0mpgUS 18.1L/100km
Petrol 4-stroke piston
3453cc 210.7cu in
In-line 6 fuel injection
Compression ratio: 9.0:1
Bore: 93.4mm 3.7in
Stroke: 84.0mm 3.3in
Valve type/No: Overhead 24
Transmission: Manual
No. of forward speeds: 5
Wheels driven: Rear
Springs F/R: Coil/Coil
Brake system: PA
Brakes F/R: Disc/Disc
Steering: Rack & pinion
Wheelbase: 256.0cm 100.8in
Track F: 154.9cm 61.0in
Track R: 157.5cm 62.0in
Length: 443.7cm 174.7in
Width: 182.4cm 71.8in
Height: 114.0cm 44.9in
Ground clearance: 12.4cm 4.9in
Kerb weight: 1509.5kg 3325.0lb
Fuel: 115.8L 25.5gal 30.6galUS

557 BMW

323i Hardy & Beck
1981 Germany
125.0mph 201.1kmh
0-50mph 80.5kmh: 6.7secs
0-60mph 96.5kmh: 9.3secs
0-1/4 mile: 16.9secs
162.0bhp 120.8kW 164.2PS
@ 5800rpm
140.0lbft 189.7Nm @ 4500rpm
136.3bhp/ton 134.0bhp/tonne
70.0bhp/L 52.2kW/L 70.9PS/L
48.7ft/sec 14.8m/sec
21.4mph 34.4kmh/1000rpm
24.6mpg 20.5mpgUS 11.5L/100km
Petrol 4-stroke piston
2315cc 141.2cu in
In-line 6 fuel injection
Compression ratio: 9.5:1
Bore: 80.0mm 3.1in
Stroke: 76.8mm 3.0in
Valve type/No: Overhead 12
Transmission: Manual
No. of forward speeds: 5
Wheels driven: Rear
Springs F/R: Coil/Coil
Brake system: PA
Brakes F/R: Disc/Disc
Steering: Rack & pinion
Wheelbase: 256.3cm 100.9in
Track F: 138.7cm 54.6in
Track R: 140.5cm 55.3in
Length: 450.9cm 177.5in
Width: 161.0cm 63.4in
Height: 137.9cm 54.3in
Kerb weight: 1208.5kg 2662.0lb
Fuel: 96.5L 21.2gal 25.5galUS

558 BMW

528i
1981 Germany
134.0mph 215.6kmh
0-50mph 80.5kmh: 6.7secs
0-60mph 96.5kmh: 8.7secs
0-1/4 mile: 16.8secs
0-1km: 30.6secs
184.0bhp 137.2kW 186.5PS
@ 5800rpm
177.0lbft 239.8Nm @ 4200rpm
132.9bhp/ton 130.7bhp/tonne
66.0bhp/L 49.2kW/L 66.9PS/L
50.7ft/sec 15.5m/sec
25.6mph 41.2kmh/1000rpm
23.3mpg 19.4mpgUS 12.1L/100km
Petrol 4-stroke piston
2788cc 170.1cu in
In-line 6 fuel injection
Compression ratio: 9.3:1
Bore: 86.0mm 3.4in
Stroke: 80.0mm 3.1in
Valve type/No: Overhead 12
Transmission: Manual
No. of forward speeds: 5
Wheels driven: Rear
Springs F/R: Coil/Coil
Brake system: PA

Brakes F/R: Disc/Disc
Steering: Recirculating ball PA
Wheelbase: 262.4cm 103.3in
Track F: 143.0cm 56.3in
Track R: 146.1cm 57.5in
Length: 462.0cm 181.9in
Width: 169.9cm 66.9in
Height: 141.5cm 55.7in
Ground clearance: 15.2cm 6.0in
Kerb weight: 1407.8kg 3101.0lb
Fuel: 70.1L 15.4gal 18.5galUS

559 BMW
316
1982 Germany
103.0mph 165.7kmh
0-50mph 80.5kmh: 8.2secs
0-60mph 96.5kmh: 12.1secs
0-1/4 mile: 18.4secs
0-1km: 34.5secs
90.0bhp 67.1kW 91.2PS
@ 5500rpm
103.0lbft 139.6Nm @ 4000rpm
82.8bhp/ton 81.4bhp/tonne
51.0bhp/L 38.0kW/L 51.7PS/L
42.8ft/sec 13.0m/sec
21.4mph 34.4kmh/1000rpm
26.7mpg 22.2mpgUS 10.6L/100km
Petrol 4-stroke piston
1766cc 107.7cu in
In-line 4 1 Carburettor
Compression ratio: 9.5:1
Bore: 89.0mm 3.5in
Stroke: 71.0mm 2.8in
Valve type/No: Overhead 8
Transmission: Manual
No. of forward speeds: 5
Wheels driven: Rear
Springs F/R: Coil/Coil
Brake system: PA
Brakes F/R: Disc/Drum
Steering: Rack & pinion
Wheelbase: 256.5cm 101.0in
Track F: 136.4cm 53.7in
Track R: 137.4cm 54.1in
Length: 435.6cm 171.5in
Width: 161.0cm 63.4in
Height: 137.9cm 54.3in
Ground clearance: 17.8cm 7.0in
Kerb weight: 1105.9kg 2436.0lb
Fuel: 58.2L 12.8gal 15.4galUS

560 BMW
528e
1982 Germany
114.0mph 183.4kmh
0-60mph 96.5kmh: 10.3secs
0-1/4 mile: 17.5secs
121.0bhp 90.2kW 122.7PS
@ 4250rpm
170.0lbft 230.4Nm @ 3250rpm
89.9bhp/ton 88.4bhp/tonne
44.9bhp/L 33.5kW/L 45.6PS/L
37.7ft/sec 11.5m/sec
20.3mph 32.7kmh/1000rpm
28.8mpg 24.0mpgUS 9.8L/100km
Petrol 4-stroke piston
2693cc 164.3cu in
In-line 6 fuel injection
Compression ratio: 9.0:1
Bore: 84.1mm 3.3in
Stroke: 81.0mm 3.2in
Valve type/No: Overhead 12
Transmission: Manual
No. of forward speeds: 5
Wheels driven: Rear
Springs F/R: Coil/Coil
Brake system: PA
Brakes F/R: Disc/Disc
Steering: Recirculating ball PA
Wheelbase: 262.4cm 103.3in
Track F: 143.0cm 56.3in
Track R: 147.1cm 57.9in
Length: 480.1cm 189.0in
Width: 169.9cm 66.9in
Height: 141.5cm 55.7in
Ground clearance: 12.7cm 5.0in
Kerb weight: 1368.8kg 3015.0lb
Fuel: 62.8L 13.8gal 16.6galUS

561 BMW
635 CSi
1982 Germany
141.0mph 226.9kmh
0-50mph 80.5kmh: 5.6secs
0-60mph 96.5kmh: 7.3secs
0-1/4 mile: 15.6secs
0-1km: 28.3secs
218.0bhp 162.6kW 221.0PS
@ 5200rpm
224.0lbft 303.5Nm @ 4000rpm
153.8bhp/ton 151.2bhp/tonne
63.6bhp/L 47.4kW/L 64.4PS/L
49.0ft/sec 14.9m/sec
28.8mph 46.3kmh/1000rpm
21.8mpg 18.2mpgUS 13.0L/100km
Petrol 4-stroke piston
3430cc 209.3cu in
In-line 6 fuel injection
Compression ratio: 10.0:1
Bore: 92.0mm 3.6in
Stroke: 86.0mm 3.4in
Valve type/No: Overhead 12
Transmission: Manual
No. of forward speeds: 5
Wheels driven: Rear
Springs F/R: Coil/Coil
Brake system: PA
Brakes F/R: Disc/Disc
Steering: Ball & nut PA
Wheelbase: 262.6cm 103.4in
Track F: 142.2cm 56.0in
Track R: 148.6cm 58.5in
Length: 475.5cm 187.2in
Width: 172.5cm 67.9in
Height: 136.4cm 53.7in
Ground clearance: 9.4cm 3.7in
Kerb weight: 1441.4kg 3175.0lb
Fuel: 70.1L 15.4gal 18.5galUS

562 BMW
745i
1982 Germany
124.0mph 199.5kmh
0-50mph 80.5kmh: 6.6secs
0-60mph 96.5kmh: 8.5secs
0-1/4 mile: 16.6secs
252.0bhp 187.9kW 255.5PS
@ 5200rpm
280.0lbft 379.4Nm @ 2600rpm
159.9bhp/ton 157.2bhp/tonne
78.5bhp/L 58.5kW/L 79.6PS/L
49.0ft/sec 14.9m/sec
22.6mph 36.4kmh/1000rpm
21.6mpg 18.0mpgUS 13.1L/100km
Petrol 4-stroke piston
3210cc 195.8cu in turbocharged
In-line 6 fuel injection
Compression ratio: 7.0:1
Bore: 89.0mm 3.5in
Stroke: 86.0mm 3.4in
Valve type/No: Overhead 12
Transmission: Automatic
No. of forward speeds: 3
Wheels driven: Rear
Springs F/R: Coil/Coil
Brake system: PA ABS
Brakes F/R: Disc/Disc
Steering: Recirculating ball PA
Wheelbase: 279.4cm 110.0in
Track F: 150.9cm 59.4in
Track R: 151.9cm 59.8in
Length: 485.9cm 191.3in
Width: 180.1cm 70.9in
Height: 143.0cm 56.3in
Kerb weight: 1602.6kg 3530.0lb
Fuel: 84.8L 18.6gal 22.4galUS

563 BMW
318i
1983 Germany
111.0mph 178.6kmh
0-60mph 96.5kmh: 11.6secs
0-1/4 mile: 18.3secs
101.0bhp 75.3kW 102.4PS
@ 5800rpm
103.0lbft 139.6Nm @ 4500rpm
92.0bhp/ton 90.4bhp/tonne
57.2bhp/L 42.6kW/L 58.0PS/L
45.1ft/sec 13.7m/sec
22.2mph 35.7kmh/1000rpm
31.2mpg 26.0mpgUS 9.0L/100km
Petrol 4-stroke piston
1766cc 107.7cu in
In-line 4 fuel injection
Compression ratio: 9.3:1
Bore: 89.0mm 3.5in
Stroke: 71.0mm 2.8in
Valve type/No: Overhead 8
Transmission: Manual
No. of forward speeds: 5
Wheels driven: Rear
Springs F/R: Coil/Coil
Brake system: PA
Brakes F/R: Disc/Drum
Steering: Rack & pinion PA
Wheelbase: 257.0cm 101.2in
Track F: 140.7cm 55.4in
Track R: 141.5cm 55.7in
Length: 449.1cm 176.8in
Width: 164.6cm 64.8in
Height: 137.9cm 54.3in
Ground clearance: 12.2cm 4.8in
Kerb weight: 1116.8kg 2460.0lb
Fuel: 54.9L 12.1gal 14.5galUS

564 BMW
320i
1983 Germany
121.0mph 194.7kmh
0-50mph 80.5kmh: 6.2secs
0-60mph 96.5kmh: 8.0secs
0-1/4 mile: 16.4secs
0-1km: 30.4secs
125.0bhp 93.2kW 126.7PS
@ 5800rpm
123.0lbft 166.7Nm @ 4000rpm
115.1bhp/ton 113.2bhp/tonne
62.8bhp/L 46.8kW/L 63.7PS/L
41.9ft/sec 12.8m/sec
24.0mph 38.6kmh/1000rpm
26.0mpg 21.6mpgUS 10.9L/100km
Petrol 4-stroke piston
1990cc 121.4cu in
In-line 6 fuel injection
Compression ratio: 9.8:1
Bore: 80.0mm 3.1in
Stroke: 66.0mm 2.6in
Valve type/No: Overhead 12
Transmission: Manual
No. of forward speeds: 5
Wheels driven: Rear
Springs F/R: Coil/Coil
Brake system: PA
Brakes F/R: Disc/Drum
Steering: Rack & pinion
Wheelbase: 257.0cm 101.2in
Track F: 140.7cm 55.4in
Track R: 141.5cm 55.7in
Length: 432.6cm 170.3in
Width: 164.6cm 64.8in
Height: 137.9cm 54.3in
Ground clearance: 17.8cm 7.0in
Kerb weight: 1104.1kg 2432.0lb
Fuel: 54.6L 12.0gal 14.4galUS

565 BMW
525E
1983 Germany
113.0mph 181.8kmh
0-50mph 80.5kmh: 7.5secs
0-60mph 96.5kmh: 10.2secs
0-1/4 mile: 17.8secs
0-1km: 32.7secs
125.0bhp 93.2kW 126.7PS
@ 4250rpm
177.0lbft 239.8Nm @ 3250rpm
95.9bhp/ton 94.3bhp/tonne
46.4bhp/L 34.6kW/L 47.1PS/L
37.7ft/sec 11.5m/sec
33.6mph 54.1kmh/1000rpm
26.2mpg 21.8mpgUS 10.8L/100km
Petrol 4-stroke piston
2693cc 164.3cu in
In-line 6 fuel injection
Compression ratio: 11.0:1
Bore: 84.0mm 3.3in
Stroke: 81.0mm 3.2in
Valve type/No: Overhead 12
Transmission: Automatic
No. of forward speeds: 4
Wheels driven: Rear
Springs F/R: Coil/Coil
Brake system: PA
Brakes F/R: Disc/Disc
Steering: Ball & nut PA
Wheelbase: 262.4cm 103.3in
Track F: 143.0cm 56.3in
Track R: 146.1cm 57.5in
Length: 462.0cm 181.9in
Width: 169.9cm 66.9in
Height: 141.5cm 55.7in
Ground clearance: 15.2cm 6.0in
Kerb weight: 1325.2kg 2919.0lb
Fuel: 70.1L 15.4gal 18.5galUS

566 BMW
533i
1983 Germany
134.0mph 215.6kmh
0-50mph 80.5kmh: 6.2secs
0-60mph 96.5kmh: 8.3secs
0-1/4 mile: 16.4secs
181.0bhp 135.0kW 183.5PS
@ 6000rpm
195.0lbft 264.2Nm @ 4000rpm
128.3bhp/ton 126.2bhp/tonne
56.4bhp/L 42.0kW/L 57.2PS/L
56.5ft/sec 17.2m/sec
27.3mph 43.9kmh/1000rpm
22.8mpg 19.0mpgUS 12.4L/100km
Petrol 4-stroke piston
3210cc 195.8cu in
In-line 6 fuel injection
Compression ratio: 8.8:1
Bore: 89.0mm 3.5in
Stroke: 86.0mm 3.4in
Valve type/No: Overhead 12
Transmission: Manual
No. of forward speeds: 5
Wheels driven: Rear
Springs F/R: Coil/Coil
Brakes F/R: Disc/Disc
Steering: Recirculating ball PA
Wheelbase: 262.4cm 103.3in
Track F: 143.0cm 56.3in
Track R: 147.1cm 57.9in
Length: 480.1cm 189.0in
Width: 167.6cm 66.0in
Height: 141.5cm 55.7in
Kerb weight: 1434.6kg 3160.0lb
Fuel: 62.8L 13.8gal 16.6galUS

567 BMW
735i
1983 Germany
131.0mph 210.8kmh
0-50mph 80.5kmh: 5.8secs
0-60mph 96.5kmh: 7.8secs
0-1/4 mile: 15.9secs
0-1km: 29.3secs
218.0bhp 162.6kW 221.0PS
@ 5200rpm
228.0lbft 308.9Nm @ 4000rpm
139.3bhp/ton 137.0bhp/tonne
63.6bhp/L 47.4kW/L 64.4PS/L
49.0ft/sec 14.9m/sec
31.1mph 50.0kmh/1000rpm
19.6mpg 16.3mpgUS 14.4L/100km
Petrol 4-stroke piston
3430cc 209.3cu in
In-line 6 fuel injection
Compression ratio: 10.0:1
Bore: 92.0mm 3.6in
Stroke: 86.0mm 3.4in
Valve type/No: Overhead 12
Transmission: Automatic
No. of forward speeds: 4
Wheels driven: Rear
Springs F/R: Coil/Coil
Brake system: PA
Brakes F/R: Disc/Disc
Steering: Recirculating ball PA
Wheelbase: 279.4cm 110.0in
Track F: 150.1cm 59.1in
Track R: 151.4cm 59.6in
Length: 485.9cm 191.3in
Width: 180.1cm 70.9in
Height: 143.0cm 56.3in
Ground clearance: 15.2cm 6.0in
Kerb weight: 1591.7kg 3506.0lb
Fuel: 100.1L 22.0gal 26.4galUS

568 BMW
318i
1984 Germany
111.0mph 178.6kmh
0-50mph 80.5kmh: 7.5secs
0-60mph 96.5kmh: 10.9secs
0-1/4 mile: 17.9secs
0-1km: 33.4secs
105.0bhp 78.3kW 106.5PS
@ 5800rpm
107.0lbft 145.0Nm @ 4500rpm
96.7bhp/ton 95.1bhp/tonne
59.5bhp/L 44.3kW/L 60.3PS/L
45.1ft/sec 13.7m/sec
22.8mph 36.7kmh/1000rpm
28.5mpg 23.7mpgUS 9.9L/100km
Petrol 4-stroke piston
1766cc 107.7cu in
In-line 4 fuel injection
Compression ratio: 9.5:1
Bore: 89.0mm 3.5in
Stroke: 71.0mm 2.8in
Valve type/No: Overhead 8

Transmission: Manual
No. of forward speeds: 5
Wheels driven: Rear
Springs F/R: Coil/Coil
Brake system: PA
Brakes F/R: Disc/Drum
Steering: Rack & pinion
Wheelbase: 257.0cm 101.2in
Track F: 140.7cm 55.4in
Track R: 141.5cm 55.7in
Length: 432.6cm 170.3in
Width: 164.6cm 64.8in
Height: 137.9cm 54.3in
Ground clearance: 17.8cm 7.0in
Kerb weight: 1104.1kg 2432.0lb
Fuel: 55.1L 12.1gal 14.5galUS

569 BMW
325E
1984 Germany
122.0mph 196.3kmh
0-60mph 96.5kmh: 8.9secs
0-1/4 mile: 16.6secs
121.0bhp 90.2kW 122.7PS
@ 4250rpm
170.0lbft 230.4Nm @ 3250rpm
98.9bhp/ton 97.3bhp/tonne
44.9bhp/L 33.5kW/L 45.6PS/L
37.7ft/sec 11.5m/sec
30.3mph 48.8kmh/1000rpm
33.6mpg 28.0mpgUS 8.4L/100km
Petrol 4-stroke piston
2693cc 164.3cu in
In-line 6 fuel injection
Compression ratio: 9.0:1
Bore: 84.0mm 3.3in
Stroke: 81.0mm 3.2in
Valve type/No: Overhead 12
Transmission: Manual
No. of forward speeds: 5
Wheels driven: Rear
Springs F/R: Coil/Coil
Brakes F/R: Disc/Disc
Steering: Rack & pinion PA
Wheelbase: 257.0cm 101.2in
Track F: 140.7cm 55.4in
Track R: 141.5cm 55.7in
Length: 449.1cm 176.8in
Width: 164.6cm 64.8in
Height: 137.9cm 54.3in
Kerb weight: 1244.0kg 2740.0lb
Fuel: 54.9L 12.1gal 14.5galUS

570 BMW
633 CSi
1984 Germany
125.0mph 201.1kmh
0-50mph 80.5kmh: 6.3secs
0-60mph 96.5kmh: 8.4secs
0-1/4 mile: 16.5secs
181.0bhp 135.0kW 183.5PS
@ 6000rpm
195.0lbft 264.2Nm @ 4000rpm
122.7bhp/ton 120.6bhp/tonne
56.4bhp/L 42.0kW/L 57.2PS/L
56.5ft/sec 17.2m/sec
27.0mph 43.4kmh/1000rpm
24.6mpg 20.5mpgUS 11.5L/100km
Petrol 4-stroke piston
3210cc 195.8cu in
In-line 6 fuel injection
Compression ratio: 8.8:1
Bore: 89.0mm 3.5in
Stroke: 86.0mm 3.4in
Valve type/No: Overhead 12
Transmission: Manual
No. of forward speeds: 5
Wheels driven: Rear
Springs F/R: Coil/Coil
Brakes F/R: Disc/Disc
Steering: Recirculating ball PA
Wheelbase: 262.9cm 103.5in
Track F: 143.0cm 56.3in
Track R: 147.1cm 57.9in
Length: 492.3cm 193.8in
Width: 172.5cm 67.9in
Height: 136.4cm 53.7in
Kerb weight: 1500.5kg 3305.0lb
Fuel: 62.8L 13.8gal 16.6galUS

571 BMW
735i Automatic
1984 Germany
132.0mph 212.4kmh
0-50mph 80.5kmh: 6.1secs
0-60mph 96.5kmh: 8.2secs
0-1/4 mile: 16.3secs
0-1km: 29.5secs
218.0bhp 162.6kW 221.0PS
@ 5200rpm
229.0lbft 310.3Nm @ 4000rpm
134.2bhp/ton 131.9bhp/tonne
63.6bhp/L 47.4kW/L 64.4PS/L
49.0ft/sec 14.9m/sec
30.9mph 49.7kmh/1000rpm
18.8mpg 15.7mpgUS 15.0L/100km
Petrol 4-stroke piston
3430cc 209.3cu in
In-line 6 fuel injection
Compression ratio: 10.0:1
Bore: 92.0mm 3.6in
Stroke: 86.0mm 3.4in
Valve type/No: Overhead 12
Transmission: Automatic
No. of forward speeds: 4
Wheels driven: Rear
Springs F/R: Coil/Coil
Brake system: PA
Brakes F/R: Disc/Disc
Steering: Recirculating ball PA
Wheelbase: 279.4cm 110.0in
Track F: 150.1cm 59.1in
Track R: 151.4cm 59.6in
Length: 485.9cm 191.3in
Width: 180.1cm 70.9in
Height: 143.0cm 56.3in
Ground clearance: 15.2cm 6.0in
Kerb weight: 1652.1kg 3639.0lb
Fuel: 100.1L 22.0gal 26.4galUS

572 BMW
M635 CSi
1984 Germany
158.0mph 254.2kmh
0-50mph 80.5kmh: 4.8secs
0-60mph 96.5kmh: 6.1secs
0-1/4 mile: 14.7secs
0-1km: 26.5secs
286.0bhp 213.3kW 290.0PS
@ 6500rpm
251.0lbft 340.1Nm @ 4500rpm
192.8bhp/ton 189.6bhp/tonne
82.8bhp/L 61.8kW/L 84.0PS/L
59.8ft/sec 18.2m/sec
23.8mph 38.3kmh/1000rpm
17.0mpg 14.2mpgUS 16.6L/100km
Petrol 4-stroke piston
3453cc 210.7cu in
In-line 6 fuel injection
Compression ratio: 10.5:1
Bore: 93.4mm 3.7in
Stroke: 84.0mm 3.3in
Valve type/No: Overhead 24
Transmission: Manual
No. of forward speeds: 5
Wheels driven: Rear
Springs F/R: Coil/Coil
Brake system: PA
Brakes F/R: Disc/Disc
Steering: Recirculating ball PA
Wheelbase: 262.6cm 103.4in
Track F: 143.0cm 56.3in
Track R: 146.3cm 57.6in
Length: 475.5cm 187.2in
Width: 172.5cm 67.9in
Height: 135.4cm 53.3in
Ground clearance: 9.4cm 3.7in
Kerb weight: 1508.2kg 3322.0lb
Fuel: 70.1L 15.4gal 18.5galUS

573 BMW
325i
1985 Germany
132.0mph 212.4kmh
0-50mph 80.5kmh: 5.3secs
0-60mph 96.5kmh: 7.4secs
0-1/4 mile: 15.4secs
0-1km: 28.3secs
171.0bhp 127.5kW 173.4PS
@ 5800rpm
164.0lbft 222.2Nm @ 4000rpm
165.4bhp/ton 162.6bhp/tonne
68.6bhp/L 51.1kW/L 69.5PS/L
47.5ft/sec 14.5m/sec
23.3mph 37.5kmh/1000rpm
24.6mpg 20.5mpgUS 11.5L/100km
Petrol 4-stroke piston
2494cc 152.2cu in
In-line 6 fuel injection
Compression ratio: 9.7:1
Bore: 84.0mm 3.3in
Stroke: 75.0mm 2.9in
Valve type/No: Overhead 12
Transmission: Manual
No. of forward speeds: 5
Wheels driven: Rear
Springs F/R: Coil/Coil
Brake system: PA
Brakes F/R: Disc/Disc
Steering: Rack & pinion PA
Wheelbase: 257.0cm 101.2in
Track F: 140.7cm 55.4in
Track R: 141.5cm 55.7in
Length: 432.6cm 170.3in
Width: 164.6cm 64.8in
Height: 137.9cm 54.3in
Ground clearance: 17.8cm 7.0in
Kerb weight: 1051.5kg 2316.0lb
Fuel: 55.1L 12.1gal 14.5galUS

574 BMW
327S Hardy & Beck
1985 Germany
135.0mph 217.2kmh
0-50mph 80.5kmh: 4.9secs
0-60mph 96.5kmh: 6.9secs
0-1/4 mile: 15.3secs
180.0bhp 134.2kW 182.5PS
@ 6000rpm
175.0lbft 237.1Nm @ 4000rpm
151.6bhp/ton 149.0bhp/tonne
66.8bhp/L 49.8kW/L 67.8PS/L
53.2ft/sec 16.2m/sec
24.0mph 38.6kmh/1000rpm
20.4mpg 17.0mpgUS 13.8L/100km
Petrol 4-stroke piston
2693cc 164.3cu in
In-line 6 fuel injection
Compression ratio: 10.5:1
Bore: 84.0mm 3.3in
Stroke: 81.0mm 3.2in
Valve type/No: Overhead 12
Transmission: Manual
No. of forward speeds: 5
Wheels driven: Rear
Springs F/R: Coil/Coil
Brake system: PA
Brakes F/R: Disc/Disc
Steering: Rack & pinion PA
Wheelbase: 257.0cm 101.2in
Track F: 140.7cm 55.4in
Track R: 141.5cm 55.7in
Length: 432.6cm 170.3in
Width: 164.6cm 64.8in
Height: 137.9cm 54.3in
Kerb weight: 1207.6kg 2660.0lb
Fuel: 45.8L 10.1gal 12.1galUS

575 BMW
732i
1985 Germany
125.0mph 201.1kmh
0-50mph 80.5kmh: 6.8secs
0-60mph 96.5kmh: 9.1secs
0-1/4 mile: 16.9secs
0-1km: 32.0secs
197.0bhp 146.9kW 199.7PS
@ 5500rpm
210.0lbft 284.6Nm @ 4300rpm
131.6bhp/ton 129.4bhp/tonne
61.4bhp/L 45.8kW/L 62.2PS/L
51.8ft/sec 15.8m/sec
29.2mph 47.0kmh/1000rpm
20.3mpg 16.9mpgUS 13.9L/100km
Petrol 4-stroke piston
3210cc 195.8cu in
In-line 6 fuel injection
Compression ratio: 10.0:1
Bore: 89.0mm 3.5in
Stroke: 86.0mm 3.4in
Valve type/No: Overhead 12
Transmission: Automatic
No. of forward speeds: 4
Wheels driven: Rear
Springs F/R: Coil/Coil
Brake system: PA
Brakes F/R: Disc/Disc
Steering: Recirculating ball PA
Wheelbase: 279.4cm 110.0in
Track F: 150.1cm 59.1in
Track R: 151.4cm 59.6in
Length: 485.9cm 191.3in
Width: 180.1cm 70.9in
Height: 143.0cm 56.3in
Ground clearance: 15.2cm 6.0in
Kerb weight: 1521.8kg 3352.0lb
Fuel: 100.1L 22.0gal 26.4galUS

576 BMW
M535i
1985 Germany
146.0mph 234.9kmh
0-50mph 80.5kmh: 5.7secs
0-60mph 96.5kmh: 7.4secs
0-1/4 mile: 15.6secs
0-1km: 28.7secs
218.0bhp 162.6kW 221.0PS
@ 5500rpm
229.0lbft 310.3Nm @ 4000rpm
156.7bhp/ton 154.1bhp/tonne
63.6bhp/L 47.4kW/L 64.4PS/L
51.8ft/sec 15.8m/sec
29.0mph 46.7kmh/1000rpm
17.7mpg 14.7mpgUS 16.0L/100km
Petrol 4-stroke piston
3430cc 209.3cu in
In-line 6 fuel injection
Compression ratio: 10.0:1
Bore: 92.0mm 3.6in
Stroke: 86.0mm 3.4in
Valve type/No: Overhead 12
Transmission: Manual
No. of forward speeds: 5
Wheels driven: Rear
Springs F/R: Coil/Coil
Brake system: PA
Brakes F/R: Disc/Disc
Steering: Recirculating ball PA
Wheelbase: 262.4cm 103.3in
Track F: 143.0cm 56.3in
Track R: 146.1cm 57.5in
Length: 462.0cm 181.9in
Width: 169.9cm 66.9in
Height: 141.5cm 55.7in
Ground clearance: 15.2cm 6.0in
Kerb weight: 1414.7kg 3116.0lb
Fuel: 70.1L 15.4gal 18.5galUS

577 BMW
M635 CSi Hardy & Beck
1985 Germany
145.0mph 233.3kmh
0-50mph 80.5kmh: 4.9secs
0-60mph 96.5kmh: 6.4secs
0-1/4 mile: 15.0secs
281.0bhp 209.5kW 284.9PS
@ 6500rpm
251.0lbft 340.1Nm @ 4500rpm
187.9bhp/ton 184.8bhp/tonne
81.4bhp/L 60.7kW/L 82.5PS/L
59.8ft/sec 18.2m/sec
24.0mph 38.6kmh/1000rpm
19.8mpg 16.5mpgUS 14.3L/100km
Petrol 4-stroke piston
3453cc 210.7cu in
In-line 6 fuel injection
Compression ratio: 10.5:1
Bore: 93.4mm 3.7in
Stroke: 84.0mm 3.3in
Valve type/No: Overhead 24
Transmission: Manual
No. of forward speeds: 5
Wheels driven: Rear
Springs F/R: Coil/Coil
Brake system: ABS
Brakes F/R: Disc/Disc
Steering: Recirculating ball PA
Wheelbase: 262.4cm 103.3in
Track F: 142.0cm 55.9in
Track R: 148.1cm 58.3in
Length: 475.5cm 187.2in
Width: 172.5cm 67.9in
Height: 135.4cm 53.3in
Kerb weight: 1520.9kg 3350.0lb
Fuel: 70.0L 15.4gal 18.5galUS

578 BMW
325 ES
1986 Germany
124.0mph 199.5kmh
0-50mph 80.5kmh: 6.0secs
0-60mph 96.5kmh: 9.0secs
0-1/4 mile: 16.7secs
121.0bhp 90.2kW 122.7PS
@ 4250rpm
170.0lbft 230.4Nm @ 3250rpm
97.3bhp/ton 95.7bhp/tonne
44.9bhp/L 33.5kW/L 45.6PS/L
37.7ft/sec 11.5m/sec
33.6mpg 28.0mpgUS 8.4L/100km
Petrol 4-stroke piston
2693cc 164.3cu in
In-line 6 fuel injection
Compression ratio: 9.0:1
Bore: 84.0mm 3.3in

Stroke: 81.0mm 3.2in
Valve type/No: Overhead 12
Transmission: Manual
No. of forward speeds: 5
Wheels driven: Rear
Springs F/R: Coil/Coil
Brake system: PA ABS
Brakes F/R: Disc/Disc
Steering: Rack & pinion PA
Wheelbase: 257.0cm 101.2in
Track F: 140.7cm 55.4in
Track R: 141.5cm 55.7in
Length: 446.0cm 175.6in
Width: 164.6cm 64.8in
Height: 137.9cm 54.3in
Kerb weight: 1264.4kg 2785.0lb
Fuel: 54.9L 12.1gal 14.5galUS

579 BMW

325i Convertible
1986 Germany
135.0mph 217.2kmh
0-50mph 80.5kmh: 5.8secs
0-60mph 96.5kmh: 8.1secs
0-1/4 mile: 16.1secs
0-1km: 29.4secs
171.0bhp 127.5kW 173.4PS
@ 5800rpm
167.0lbft 226.3Nm @ 4000rpm
148.8bhp/ton 146.3bhp/tonne
68.6bhp/L 51.1kW/L 69.5PS/L
47.5ft/sec 14.5m/sec
23.0mph 37.0kmh/1000rpm
26.5mpg 22.1mpgUS 10.7L/100km
Petrol 4-stroke piston
2494cc 152.0cu in
In-line 6 fuel injection
Compression ratio: 9.7:1
Bore: 84.0mm 3.3in
Stroke: 75.0mm 2.9in
Valve type/No: Side 12
Transmission: Manual
No. of forward speeds: 5
Wheels driven: Rear
Springs F/R: Coil/Coil
Brake system: PA
Brakes F/R: Disc/Disc
Steering: Rack & pinion PA
Wheelbase: 257.0cm 101.2in
Track F: 140.7cm 55.4in
Track R: 141.5cm 55.7in
Length: 432.5cm 170.3in
Width: 164.5cm 64.8in
Height: 138.0cm 54.3in
Ground clearance: 17.8cm 7.0in
Kerb weight: 1169.0kg 2574.9lb
Fuel: 55.1L 12.1gal 14.5galUS

580 BMW

520i
1986 Germany
121.0mph 194.7kmh
0-50mph 80.5kmh: 7.2secs
0-60mph 96.5kmh: 10.5secs
0-1/4 mile: 17.6secs
0-1km: 32.7secs
129.0bhp 96.2kW 130.8PS
@ 5800rpm
128.0lbft 173.4Nm @ 4500rpm
99.8bhp/ton 98.1bhp/tonne
64.8bhp/L 48.3kW/L 65.7PS/L
41.9ft/sec 12.8m/sec
21.5mph 34.6kmh/1000rpm
23.8mpg 19.8mpgUS 11.9L/100km
Petrol 4-stroke piston
1990cc 121.0cu in
In-line 6 fuel injection
Compression ratio: 9.8:1
Bore: 80.0mm 3.1in
Stroke: 66.0mm 2.6in
Valve type/No: Overhead 12
Transmission: Manual
No. of forward speeds: 5
Wheels driven: Rear
Springs F/R: Coil/Coil
Brake system: PA
Brakes F/R: Disc/Drum
Steering: Recirculating ball PA
Wheelbase: 262.5cm 103.3in
Track F: 143.0cm 56.3in
Track R: 146.0cm 57.5in
Length: 462.0cm 181.9in
Width: 170.0cm 66.9in
Height: 141.5cm 55.7in
Ground clearance: 15.2cm 6.0in
Kerb weight: 1315.0kg 2896.5lb
Fuel: 70.1L 15.4gal 18.5galUS

581 BMW

524 TD
1986 Germany
102.0mph 164.1kmh
0-60mph 96.5kmh: 11.0secs
0-1/4 mile: 18.1secs
114.0bhp 85.0kW 115.6PS
@ 4800rpm
155.0lbft 210.0Nm @ 2400rpm
78.7bhp/ton 77.4bhp/tonne
46.7bhp/L 34.8kW/L 47.3PS/L
42.5ft/sec 13.0m/sec
30.6mpg 25.5mpgUS 9.2L/100km
Diesel 4-stroke piston
2443cc 149.0cu in turbocharged
In-line 6 fuel injection
Compression ratio: 22.0:1
Bore: 80.0mm 3.1in
Stroke: 81.0mm 3.2in
Valve type/No: Overhead 12
Transmission: Automatic
No. of forward speeds: 4
Wheels driven: Rear
Springs F/R: Coil/Coil
Brake system: PA
Brakes F/R: Disc/Disc
Steering: Recirculating ball PA
Wheelbase: 262.4cm 103.3in
Track F: 143.0cm 56.3in
Track R: 146.1cm 57.5in
Length: 480.1cm 189.0in
Width: 169.9cm 66.9in
Height: 141.5cm 55.7in
Kerb weight: 1473.2kg 3245.0lb
Fuel: 62.8L 13.8gal 16.6galUS

582 BMW

535i
1986 Germany
131.0mph 210.8kmh
0-60mph 96.5kmh: 7.9secs
0-1/4 mile: 16.1secs
182.0bhp 135.7kW 184.5PS
@ 5400rpm
214.0lbft 290.0Nm @ 4000rpm
126.0bhp/ton 123.9bhp/tonne
53.1bhp/L 39.6kW/L 53.8PS/L
50.8ft/sec 15.5m/sec
20.4mpg 17.0mpgUS 13.8L/100km
Petrol 4-stroke piston
3430cc 209.3cu in
In-line 6 fuel injection
Compression ratio: 8.0:1
Bore: 92.0mm 3.6in
Stroke: 86.0mm 3.4in
Valve type/No: Overhead 12
Transmission: Manual
No. of forward speeds: 5
Wheels driven: Rear
Springs F/R: Coil/Coil
Brake system: ABS
Brakes F/R: Disc/Disc
Steering: Recirculating ball PA
Wheelbase: 262.4cm 103.3in
Track F: 143.0cm 56.3in
Track R: 146.1cm 57.5in
Length: 480.1cm 189.0in
Width: 169.9cm 66.9in
Height: 141.5cm 55.7in
Kerb weight: 1468.7kg 3235.0lb
Fuel: 62.8L 13.8gal 16.6galUS

583 BMW

635 CSi
1986 Germany
131.0mph 210.8kmh
0-60mph 96.5kmh: 8.5secs
0-1/4 mile: 16.3secs
182.0bhp 135.7kW 184.5PS
@ 5400rpm
214.0lbft 290.0Nm @ 4000rpm
119.4bhp/ton 117.4bhp/tonne
53.1bhp/L 39.6kW/L 53.8PS/L
50.8ft/sec 15.5m/sec
21.0mpg 17.5mpgUS 13.4L/100km
Petrol 4-stroke piston
3430cc 209.3cu in
In-line 6 fuel injection
Bore: 92.0mm 3.6in
Stroke: 86.0mm 3.4in
Valve type/No: Overhead 12
Transmission: Manual
No. of forward speeds: 5
Wheels driven: Rear
Springs F/R: Coil/Coil
Brake system: ABS
Brakes F/R: Disc/Disc
Steering: Recirculating ball PA
Wheelbase: 262.9cm 103.5in
Track F: 143.0cm 56.3in
Track R: 147.1cm 57.9in
Length: 492.3cm 193.8in
Width: 172.5cm 67.9in
Height: 136.4cm 53.7in
Kerb weight: 1550.4kg 3415.0lb
Fuel: 62.8L 13.8gal 16.6galUS

584 BMW

735i
1986 Germany
119.0mph 191.5kmh
0-50mph 80.5kmh: 6.7secs
0-60mph 96.5kmh: 9.1secs
0-1/4 mile: 16.7secs
182.0bhp 135.7kW 184.5PS
@ 5400rpm
214.0lbft 290.0Nm @ 4000rpm
115.0bhp/ton 113.1bhp/tonne
53.1bhp/L 39.6kW/L 53.8PS/L
50.8ft/sec 15.5m/sec
20.4mpg 17.0mpgUS 13.8L/100km
Petrol 4-stroke piston
3430cc 209.3cu in
In-line 6 fuel injection
Compression ratio: 8.0:1
Bore: 92.0mm 3.6in
Stroke: 86.0mm 3.4in
Valve type/No: Overhead 12
Transmission: Manual
No. of forward speeds: 5
Wheels driven: Rear
Springs F/R: Coil/Coil
Brake system: ABS
Brakes F/R: Disc/Disc
Steering: Recirculating ball PA
Wheelbase: 279.4cm 110.0in
Track F: 150.1cm 59.1in
Track R: 151.6cm 59.7in
Length: 501.4cm 197.4in
Width: 180.1cm 70.9in
Height: 143.0cm 56.3in
Kerb weight: 1609.4kg 3545.0lb
Fuel: 85.2L 18.7gal 22.5galUS

585 BMW

735i Automatic
1986 Germany
147.0mph 236.5kmh
0-50mph 80.5kmh: 6.7secs
0-60mph 96.5kmh: 9.0secs
0-1/4 mile: 16.7secs
0-1km: 30.1secs
217.0bhp 161.8kW 220.0PS
@ 5700rpm
232.0lbft 314.4Nm @ 4000rpm
125.3bhp/ton 123.2bhp/tonne
63.3bhp/L 47.2kW/L 64.1PS/L
53.7ft/sec 16.3m/sec
28.3mph 45.5kmh/1000rpm
17.5mpg 14.6mpgUS 16.1L/100km
Petrol 4-stroke piston
3430cc 209.0cu in
In-line 6 fuel injection
Compression ratio: 9.2:1
Bore: 92.0mm 3.6in
Stroke: 86.0mm 3.4in
Valve type/No: Overhead 12
Transmission: Automatic
No. of forward speeds: 4
Wheels driven: Rear
Springs F/R: Coil/Coil
Brake system: PA ABS
Brakes F/R: Disc/Disc
Steering: Recirculating ball PA
Wheelbase: 283.2cm 111.5in
Track F: 152.7cm 60.1in
Track R: 155.0cm 61.0in
Length: 491.0cm 193.3in
Width: 184.5cm 72.6in
Height: 141.1cm 55.6in
Ground clearance: 20.3cm 8.0in
Kerb weight: 1761.0kg 3878.8lb
Fuel: 90.1L 19.8gal 23.8galUS

586 BMW

318i 2-door
1987 Germany
116.0mph 186.6kmh
0-50mph 80.5kmh: 6.6secs
0-60mph 96.5kmh: 9.3secs
0-1/4 mile: 16.9secs
0-1km: 31.8secs
115.0bhp 85.8kW 116.6PS
@ 5500rpm
122.0lbft 165.3Nm @ 4250rpm
107.8bhp/ton 106.0bhp/tonne
64.1bhp/L 47.8kW/L 65.0PS/L
48.7ft/sec 14.8m/sec
20.8mph 33.5kmh/1000rpm
27.4mpg 22.8mpgUS 10.3L/100km
Petrol 4-stroke piston
1795cc 110.0cu in
In-line 4 fuel injection
Compression ratio: 8.8:1
Bore: 84.0mm 3.3in
Stroke: 81.0mm 3.2in
Valve type/No: Overhead 8
Transmission: Manual
No. of forward speeds: 5
Wheels driven: Rear
Springs F/R: Coil/Coil
Brake system: PA
Brakes F/R: Disc/Drum
Steering: Rack & pinion PA
Wheelbase: 257.0cm 101.2in
Track F: 140.7cm 55.4in
Track R: 141.5cm 55.7in
Length: 432.5cm 170.3in
Width: 164.5cm 64.8in
Height: 138.0cm 54.3in
Ground clearance: 15.5cm 6.1in
Kerb weight: 1085.0kg 2389.9lb
Fuel: 55.1L 12.1gal 14.5galUS

587 BMW

325i Cabriolet
1987 Germany
130.0mph 209.2kmh
0-60mph 96.5kmh: 7.5secs
168.0bhp 125.3kW 170.3PS
@ 5800rpm
164.0lbft 222.2Nm @ 4300rpm
124.8bhp/ton 122.7bhp/tonne
67.4bhp/L 50.2kW/L 68.3PS/L
47.5ft/sec 14.5m/sec
Petrol 4-stroke piston
2494cc 152.2cu in
In-line 6 fuel injection
Compression ratio: 8.8:1
Bore: 84.0mm 3.3in
Stroke: 75.0mm 2.9in
Valve type/No: Overhead 12
Transmission: Manual
No. of forward speeds: 5
Wheels driven: Rear
Springs F/R: Coil/Coil
Brake system: PA ABS
Brakes F/R: Disc/Disc
Steering: Rack & pinion PA
Wheelbase: 257.0cm 101.2in
Track F: 140.7cm 55.4in
Track R: 141.5cm 55.7in
Length: 446.0cm 175.6in
Width: 164.6cm 64.8in
Height: 136.9cm 53.9in
Kerb weight: 1368.8kg 3015.0lb
Fuel: 54.9L 12.1gal 14.5galUS

588 BMW

730i SE
1987 Germany
132.0mph 212.4kmh
0-50mph 80.5kmh: 7.9secs
0-60mph 96.5kmh: 10.5secs
0-1/4 mile: 17.7secs
0-1km: 32.0secs
197.0bhp 146.9kW 199.7PS
@ 5800rpm
199.0lbft 269.6Nm @ 4000rpm
117.8bhp/ton 115.9bhp/tonne
66.0bhp/L 49.2kW/L 66.9PS/L
50.7ft/sec 15.5m/sec
27.6mph 44.4kmh/1000rpm
20.0mpg 16.7mpgUS 14.1L/100km
Petrol 4-stroke piston
2986cc 182.0cu in
In-line 6 fuel injection
Compression ratio: 9.2:1
Bore: 89.0mm 3.5in
Stroke: 80.0mm 3.1in
Valve type/No: Overhead 12
Transmission: Automatic
No. of forward speeds: 4
Wheels driven: Rear
Springs F/R: Coil/Coil
Brake system: PA ABS
Brakes F/R: Disc/Disc
Steering: Recirculating ball PA
Wheelbase: 283.2cm 111.5in
Track F: 152.7cm 60.1in

Track R: 155.0cm 61.0in
Length: 491.0cm 193.3in
Width: 184.5cm 72.6in
Height: 141.1cm 55.6in
Ground clearance: 20.3cm 8.0in
Kerb weight: 1700.0kg 3744.5lb
Fuel: 90.1L 19.8gal 23.8galUS

589 BMW
750i L
1987 Germany
158.0mph 254.2kmh
0-50mph 80.5kmh: 5.8secs
0-60mph 96.5kmh: 7.7secs
0-1/4 mile: 15.9secs
0-1km: 28.1secs
300.0bhp 223.7kW 304.2PS
@ 5200rpm
332.0lbft 449.9Nm @ 4100rpm
159.3bhp/ton 156.7bhp/tonne
60.1bhp/L 44.8kW/L 61.0PS/L
42.6ft/sec 13.0m/sec
32.1mph 51.6kmh/1000rpm
18.5mpg 15.4mpgUS 15.3L/100km
Petrol 4-stroke piston
4988cc 304.0cu in
Vee 12 fuel injection
Compression ratio: 8.8:1
Bore: 84.0mm 3.3in
Stroke: 75.0mm 2.9in
Valve type/No: Overhead 48
Transmission: Automatic
No. of forward speeds: 4
Wheels driven: Rear
Springs F/R: Coil/Coil
Brake system: PA
Brakes F/R: Disc/Disc
Steering: Recirculating ball PA
Wheelbase: 294.7cm 116.0in
Track F: 152.8cm 60.2in
Track R: 155.6cm 61.3in
Length: 502.4cm 197.8in
Width: 184.5cm 72.6in
Height: 140.0cm 55.1in
Ground clearance: 20.3cm 8.0in
Kerb weight: 1915.0kg 4218.1lb
Fuel: 102.4L 22.5gal 27.0galUS

590 BMW
M3
1987 Germany
140.0mph 225.3kmh
0-50mph 80.5kmh: 5.5secs
0-60mph 96.5kmh: 7.1secs
0-1/4 mile: 15.7secs
0-1km: 28.3secs
200.0bhp 149.1kW 202.8PS
@ 6750rpm
177.0lbft 239.8Nm @ 4750rpm
162.4bhp/ton 159.7bhp/tonne
86.9bhp/L 64.8kW/L 88.1PS/L
62.1ft/sec 18.9m/sec
21.2mph 34.1kmh/1000rpm
20.3mpg 16.9mpgUS 13.9L/100km
Petrol 4-stroke piston
2302cc 140.0cu in
In-line 4 fuel injection
Compression ratio: 10.5:1
Bore: 93.4mm 3.7in
Stroke: 84.0mm 3.3in
Valve type/No: Overhead 16
Transmission: Manual
No. of forward speeds: 5
Wheels driven: Rear
Springs F/R: Coil/Coil
Brake system: PA
Brakes F/R: Disc/Disc
Steering: Rack & pinion PA
Wheelbase: 256.2cm 100.9in
Track F: 141.2cm 55.6in
Track R: 143.3cm 56.4in
Length: 434.5cm 171.1in
Width: 168.0cm 66.1in
Height: 136.5cm 53.7in
Ground clearance: 15.3cm 6.0in
Kerb weight: 1252.0kg 2757.7lb
Fuel: 70.1L 15.4gal 18.5galUS

591 BMW
325i S
1988 Germany
133.0mph 214.0kmh
0-50mph 80.5kmh: 5.6secs
0-60mph 96.5kmh: 7.5secs
0-1/4 mile: 15.7secs
168.0bhp 125.3kW 170.3PS
@ 5800rpm
164.0lbft 222.2Nm @ 4300rpm
133.2bhp/ton 131.0bhp/tonne
67.4bhp/L 50.2kW/L 68.3PS/L
47.5ft/sec 14.5m/sec
24.6mpg 20.5mpgUS 11.5L/100km
Petrol 4-stroke piston
2494cc 152.2cu in
In-line 6 fuel injection
Compression ratio: 8.8:1
Bore: 84.0mm 3.3in
Stroke: 75.0mm 2.9in
Valve type/No: Overhead 12
Transmission: Manual
No. of forward speeds: 5
Wheels driven: Rear
Springs F/R: Coil/Coil
Brake system: PA ABS
Brakes F/R: Disc/Disc
Steering: Rack & pinion PA
Wheelbase: 257.0cm 101.2in
Track F: 140.7cm 55.4in
Track R: 141.5cm 55.7in
Length: 445.0cm 175.2in
Width: 164.6cm 64.8in
Height: 137.9cm 54.3in
Kerb weight: 1282.5kg 2825.0lb
Fuel: 62.1L 13.6gal 16.4galUS

592 BMW
325i X
1988 Germany
127.0mph 204.3kmh
0-50mph 80.5kmh: 5.7secs
0-60mph 96.5kmh: 7.9secs
0-1/4 mile: 15.9secs
168.0bhp 125.3kW 170.3PS
@ 5800rpm
164.0lbft 222.2Nm @ 4300rpm
126.3bhp/ton 124.2bhp/tonne
67.4bhp/L 50.2kW/L 68.3PS/L
47.5ft/sec 14.5m/sec
24.0mpg 20.0mpgUS 11.8L/100km
Petrol 4-stroke piston
2494cc 152.2cu in
In-line 6 fuel injection
Compression ratio: 8.8:1
Bore: 84.0mm 3.3in
Stroke: 75.0mm 2.9in
Valve type/No: Overhead 12
Transmission: Manual
No. of forward speeds: 5
Wheels driven: 4-wheel drive
Springs F/R: Coil/Coil
Brake system: PA ABS
Brakes F/R: Disc/Disc
Steering: Rack & pinion PA
Wheelbase: 257.0cm 101.2in
Track F: 142.0cm 55.9in
Track R: 141.5cm 55.7in
Length: 445.0cm 175.2in
Width: 166.1cm 65.4in
Height: 140.0cm 55.1in
Kerb weight: 1352.9kg 2980.0lb
Fuel: 62.1L 13.6gal 16.4galUS

593 BMW
535i SE
1988 Germany
145.0mph 233.3kmh
0-50mph 80.5kmh: 5.6secs
0-60mph 96.5kmh: 7.4secs
0-1/4 mile: 15.9secs
0-1km: 28.9secs
211.0bhp 157.3kW 213.9PS
@ 5700rpm
225.1lbft 305.0Nm @ 4000rpm
135.2bhp/ton 133.0bhp/tonne
61.5bhp/L 45.9kW/L 62.4PS/L
53.7ft/sec 16.3m/sec
25.1mph 40.4kmh/1000rpm
22.3mpg 18.6mpgUS 12.7L/100km
Petrol 4-stroke piston
3430cc 209.0cu in
In-line 6 fuel injection
Compression ratio: 9.0:1
Bore: 92.0mm 3.6in
Stroke: 86.0mm 3.4in
Valve type/No: Overhead 12
Transmission: Manual
No. of forward speeds: 5
Wheels driven: Rear
Springs F/R: Coil/Coil
Brake system: PA ABS
Brakes F/R: Disc/Disc
Steering: Recirculating ball PA
Wheelbase: 276.1cm 108.7in
Track F: 146.6cm 57.7in
Track R: 148.7cm 58.5in
Length: 472.0cm 185.8in
Width: 175.1cm 68.9in
Height: 141.2cm 55.6in
Ground clearance: 17.9cm 7.0in
Kerb weight: 1587.0kg 3495.6lb
Fuel: 80.1L 17.6gal 21.1galUS

594 BMW
635 CSi
1988 Germany
135.0mph 217.2kmh
0-50mph 80.5kmh: 6.3secs
0-60mph 96.5kmh: 8.4secs
0-1/4 mile: 16.7secs
0-1km: 29.4secs
220.0bhp 164.0kW 223.0PS
@ 5700rpm
232.5lbft 315.0Nm @ 4000rpm
142.0bhp/ton 139.6bhp/tonne
64.1bhp/L 47.8kW/L 65.0PS/L
53.7ft/sec 16.3m/sec
27.3mph 43.9kmh/1000rpm
17.2mpg 14.3mpgUS 16.4L/100km
Petrol 4-stroke piston
3430cc 209.0cu in
In-line 6 fuel injection
Compression ratio: 9.2:1
Bore: 92.0mm 3.6in
Stroke: 86.0mm 3.4in
Valve type/No: Overhead 12
Transmission: Automatic
No. of forward speeds: 4
Wheels driven: Rear
Springs F/R: Coil/Coil
Brake system: PA ABS
Brakes F/R: Disc/Disc
Steering: Ball & nut PA
Wheelbase: 262.5cm 103.3in
Track F: 143.0cm 56.3in
Track R: 146.0cm 57.5in
Length: 481.5cm 189.6in
Width: 172.5cm 67.9in
Height: 136.5cm 53.7in
Ground clearance: 9.5cm 3.7in
Kerb weight: 1576.0kg 3471.4lb
Fuel: 70.1L 15.4gal 18.5galUS

595 BMW
735i
1988 Germany
137.0mph 220.4kmh
0-50mph 80.5kmh: 7.2secs
0-60mph 96.5kmh: 9.3secs
0-1/4 mile: 17.0secs
208.0bhp 155.1kW 210.9PS
@ 5700rpm
225.0lbft 304.9Nm @ 4000rpm
120.1bhp/ton 118.1bhp/tonne
60.6bhp/L 45.2kW/L 61.5PS/L
53.7ft/sec 16.3m/sec
21.6mpg 18.0mpgUS 13.1L/100km
Petrol 4-stroke piston
3430cc 209.3cu in
In-line 6 fuel injection
Compression ratio: 9.0:1
Bore: 92.0mm 3.6in
Stroke: 86.0mm 3.4in
Valve type/No: Overhead 12
Transmission: Automatic
No. of forward speeds: 4
Wheels driven: Rear
Springs F/R: Coil/Coil
Brake system: ABS
Brakes F/R: Disc/Disc
Steering: Recirculating ball PA
Wheelbase: 283.2cm 111.5in
Track F: 152.9cm 60.2in
Track R: 156.0cm 61.4in
Length: 491.0cm 193.3in
Width: 184.4cm 72.6in
Height: 141.2cm 55.6in
Ground clearance: 17.8cm 7.0in
Kerb weight: 1761.5kg 3880.0lb
Fuel: 81.4L 17.9gal 21.5galUS

596 BMW
750i L
1988 Germany
155.0mph 249.4kmh
0-50mph 80.5kmh: 5.2secs
0-60mph 96.5kmh: 6.9secs
0-1/4 mile: 15.2secs
300.0bhp 223.7kW 304.2PS
@ 5200rpm
332.0lbft 449.9Nm @ 4100rpm
158.7bhp/ton 156.0bhp/tonne
60.1bhp/L 44.8kW/L 61.0PS/L
42.6ft/sec 13.0m/sec
19.2mpg 16.0mpgUS 14.7L/100km
Petrol 4-stroke piston
4988cc 304.3cu in
Vee 12 fuel injection
Compression ratio: 8.8:1
Bore: 84.0mm 3.3in
Stroke: 75.0mm 2.9in
Valve type/No: Overhead 24
Transmission: Automatic
No. of forward speeds: 4
Wheels driven: Rear
Springs F/R: Coil/Coil
Brake system: ABS
Brakes F/R: Disc/Disc
Steering: Recirculating ball PA
Wheelbase: 294.6cm 116.0in
Track F: 152.9cm 60.2in
Track R: 155.7cm 61.3in
Length: 502.4cm 197.8in
Width: 184.4cm 72.6in
Height: 140.0cm 55.1in
Kerb weight: 1922.7kg 4235.0lb
Fuel: 90.8L 20.0gal 24.0galUS

597 BMW
M6
1988 Germany
147.0mph 236.5kmh
0-50mph 80.5kmh: 5.3secs
0-60mph 96.5kmh: 7.2secs
0-1/4 mile: 15.3secs
256.0bhp 190.9kW 259.5PS
@ 6500rpm
243.0lbft 329.3Nm @ 4500rpm
160.8bhp/ton 158.2bhp/tonne
74.1bhp/L 55.3kW/L 75.2PS/L
59.8ft/sec 18.2m/sec
15.0mpg 12.5mpgUS 18.8L/100km
Petrol 4-stroke piston
3453cc 210.7cu in
In-line 6 fuel injection
Compression ratio: 9.8:1
Bore: 93.4mm 3.7in
Stroke: 84.0mm 3.3in
Valve type/No: Overhead 24
Transmission: Manual
No. of forward speeds: 5
Wheels driven: Rear
Springs F/R: Coil/Coil
Brake system: ABS
Brakes F/R: Disc/Disc
Steering: Recirculating ball PA
Wheelbase: 262.4cm 103.3in
Track F: 143.0cm 56.3in
Track R: 146.3cm 57.6in
Length: 492.3cm 193.8in
Width: 172.5cm 67.9in
Height: 135.4cm 53.3in
Kerb weight: 1618.5kg 3565.0lb
Fuel: 62.8L 13.8gal 16.6galUS

598 BMW
316i 4-door
1989 Germany
114.0mph 183.4kmh
0-50mph 80.5kmh: 7.1secs
0-60mph 96.5kmh: 10.1secs
0-1/4 mile: 17.4secs
0-1km: 32.4secs
102.0bhp 76.1kW 103.4PS
@ 5500rpm
105.5lbft 143.0Nm @ 4250rpm
93.5bhp/ton 92.0bhp/tonne
63.9bhp/L 47.7kW/L 64.8PS/L
43.2ft/sec 13.2m/sec
20.8mph 33.5kmh/1000rpm
25.3mpg 21.1mpgUS 11.2L/100km
Petrol 4-stroke piston
1596cc 97.0cu in
In-line 4 fuel injection
Compression ratio: 9.0:1
Bore: 84.0mm 3.3in
Stroke: 72.0mm 2.8in
Valve type/No: Overhead 8
Transmission: Manual
No. of forward speeds: 5
Wheels driven: Rear
Springs F/R: Coil/Coil
Brake system: PA ABS
Brakes F/R: Disc/Drum
Steering: Rack & pinion PA
Wheelbase: 257.0cm 101.2in
Track F: 140.7cm 55.4in

Track R: 141.5cm 55.7in
Length: 432.5cm 170.3in
Width: 164.5cm 64.8in
Height: 138.0cm 54.3in
Ground clearance: 15.3cm 6.0in
Kerb weight: 1109.0kg 2442.7lb
Fuel: 55.1L 12.1gal 14.5galUS

599 BMW
325i S
1989 Germany
0-60mph 96.5kmh: 7.5secs
168.0bhp 125.3kW 170.3PS
@ 5800rpm
164.0lbft 222.2Nm @ 4300rpm
133.2bhp/ton 131.0bhp/tonne
67.4bhp/L 50.2kW/L 68.3PS/L
47.5ft/sec 14.5m/sec
24.6mpg 20.5mpgUS 11.5L/100km
Petrol 4-stroke piston
2494cc 152.2cu in
In-line 6 fuel injection
Compression ratio: 8.8:1
Bore: 84.0mm 3.3in
Stroke: 75.0mm 2.9in
Valve type/No: Overhead 12
Transmission: Manual
No. of forward speeds: 5
Wheels driven: Rear
Springs F/R: Coil/Coil
Brake system: PA ABS
Brakes F/R: Disc/Disc
Steering: Rack & pinion PA
Wheelbase: 257.0cm 101.2in
Track F: 140.7cm 55.4in
Track R: 141.5cm 55.7in
Length: 445.0cm 175.2in
Width: 164.6cm 64.8in
Height: 137.9cm 54.3in
Kerb weight: 1282.5kg 2825.0lb
Fuel: 62.1L 13.6gal 16.4galUS

600 BMW
535i
1989 Germany
143.0mph 230.1kmh
0-50mph 80.5kmh: 5.8secs
0-60mph 96.5kmh: 7.7secs
0-1/4 mile: 15.9secs
208.0bhp 155.1kW 210.9PS
@ 5700rpm
225.0lbft 304.9Nm @ 4000rpm
128.0bhp/ton 125.9bhp/tonne
60.6bhp/L 45.2kW/L 61.5PS/L
53.7ft/sec 16.3m/sec
20.4mpg 17.0mpgUS 13.8L/100km
Petrol 4-stroke piston
3430cc 209.3cu in
In-line 6 fuel injection
Compression ratio: 9.0:1
Bore: 92.0mm 3.6in
Stroke: 86.0mm 3.4in
Valve type/No: Overhead 12
Transmission: Manual
No. of forward speeds: 5
Wheels driven: Rear
Springs F/R: Coil/Coil
Brake system: PA ABS
Brakes F/R: Disc/Disc
Steering: Recirculating ball PA
Wheelbase: 276.1cm 108.7in
Track F: 146.6cm 57.7in
Track R: 148.6cm 58.5in
Length: 471.9cm 185.8in
Width: 175.0cm 68.9in
Height: 141.2cm 55.6in
Ground clearance: 17.0cm 6.7in
Kerb weight: 1652.6kg 3640.0lb
Fuel: 79.9L 17.6gal 21.1galUS

601 BMW
535i Automatic
1989 Germany
143.0mph 230.1kmh
0-60mph 96.5kmh: 8.6secs
0-1/4 mile: 16.5secs
208.0bhp 155.1kW 210.9PS
@ 5700rpm
225.0lbft 304.9Nm @ 4000rpm
126.6bhp/ton 124.5bhp/tonne
60.6bhp/L 45.2kW/L 61.5PS/L
53.7ft/sec 16.3m/sec
22.2mpg 18.5mpgUS 12.7L/100km
Petrol 4-stroke piston
3430cc 209.3cu in
In-line 6 fuel injection
Compression ratio: 9.0:1
Bore: 92.0mm 3.6in
Stroke: 86.0mm 3.4in
Valve type/No: Overhead 12
Transmission: Automatic
No. of forward speeds: 4
Wheels driven: Rear
Springs F/R: Coil/Coil
Brake system: PA ABS
Brakes F/R: Disc/Disc
Steering: Recirculating ball PA
Wheelbase: 276.1cm 108.7in
Track F: 146.6cm 57.7in
Track R: 148.6cm 58.5in
Length: 471.9cm 185.8in
Width: 175.0cm 68.9in
Height: 141.2cm 55.6in
Kerb weight: 1670.7kg 3680.0lb
Fuel: 79.9L 17.6gal 21.1galUS

602 BMW
735i Alpina B11
1989 Germany
154.0mph 247.8kmh
0-60mph 96.5kmh: 7.4secs
0-1/4 mile: 15.5secs
250.0bhp 186.4kW 253.5PS
@ 5700rpm
243.0lbft 329.3Nm @ 4000rpm
146.0bhp/ton 143.6bhp/tonne
72.9bhp/L 54.3kW/L 73.9PS/L
53.7ft/sec 16.3m/sec
Petrol 4-stroke piston
3430cc 209.3cu in
In-line 6 fuel injection
Compression ratio: 10.4:1
Bore: 92.0mm 3.6in
Stroke: 86.0mm 3.4in
Valve type/No: Overhead 12
Transmission: Manual
No. of forward speeds: 5
Wheels driven: Rear
Springs F/R: Coil/Coil
Brake system: ABS
Brakes F/R: Disc/Disc
Steering: Recirculating ball PA
Wheelbase: 279.4cm 110.0in
Track F: 150.1cm 59.1in
Track R: 151.6cm 59.7in
Length: 501.4cm 197.4in
Width: 180.1cm 70.9in
Height: 140.5cm 55.3in
Kerb weight: 1741.1kg 3835.0lb
Fuel: 85.2L 18.7gal 22.5galUS

603 BMW
M3
1989 Germany
143.0mph 230.1kmh
0-60mph 96.5kmh: 7.1secs
0-1/4 mile: 15.4secs
192.0bhp 143.2kW 194.7PS
@ 6750rpm
170.0lbft 230.4Nm @ 4750rpm
150.1bhp/ton 147.6bhp/tonne
83.4bhp/L 62.2kW/L 84.6PS/L
62.1ft/sec 18.9m/sec
Petrol 4-stroke piston
2302cc 140.4cu in
In-line 4 fuel injection
Compression ratio: 10.5:1
Bore: 93.4mm 3.7in
Stroke: 84.0mm 3.3in
Valve type/No: Overhead 16
Transmission: Manual
No. of forward speeds: 5
Wheels driven: Rear
Springs F/R: Coil/Coil
Brake system: PA ABS
Brakes F/R: Disc/Disc
Steering: Recirculating ball PA
Wheelbase: 256.5cm 101.0in
Track F: 141.2cm 55.6in
Track R: 142.5cm 56.1in
Length: 434.6cm 171.1in
Width: 167.9cm 66.1in
Height: 136.9cm 53.9in
Kerb weight: 1300.7kg 2865.0lb
Fuel: 54.9L 12.1gal 14.5galUS

604 BMW
M3 Evolution
1989 Germany
148.0mph 238.1kmh
0-50mph 80.5kmh: 5.1secs
0-60mph 96.5kmh: 6.6secs
0-1/4 mile: 15.2secs
0-1km: 27.6secs
220.0bhp 164.0kW 223.0PS
@ 6750rpm
180.8lbft 245.0Nm @ 4750rpm
175.6bhp/ton 172.7bhp/tonne
95.6bhp/L 71.3kW/L 96.9PS/L
62.1ft/sec 18.9m/sec
22.2mph 35.7kmh/1000rpm
26.0mpg 21.6mpgUS 10.9L/100km
Petrol 4-stroke piston
2302cc 140.0cu in
In-line 4 fuel injection
Compression ratio: 11.0:1
Bore: 93.4mm 3.7in
Stroke: 84.0mm 3.3in
Valve type/No: Overhead 16
Transmission: Manual
No. of forward speeds: 5
Wheels driven: Rear
Springs F/R: Coil/Coil
Brake system: PA
Brakes F/R: Disc/Disc
Steering: Rack & pinion PA
Wheelbase: 257.0cm 101.2in
Track F: 140.7cm 55.4in
Track R: 141.5cm 55.7in
Length: 432.5cm 170.3in
Width: 164.5cm 64.8in
Height: 138.0cm 54.3in
Ground clearance: 15.3cm 6.0in
Kerb weight: 1274.0kg 2806.2lb
Fuel: 70.1L 15.4gal 18.5galUS

605 BMW
M3 Hor Technologie
1989 Germany
0-50mph 80.5kmh: 5.9secs
0-60mph 96.5kmh: 8.3secs
0-1/4 mile: 16.1secs
220.0bhp 164.0kW 223.0PS
@ 7000rpm
171.4bhp/ton 168.5bhp/tonne
95.6bhp/L 71.3kW/L 96.9PS/L
64.4ft/sec 19.6m/sec
Petrol 4-stroke piston
2302cc 140.4cu in
In-line 4 fuel injection
Compression ratio: 10.5:1
Bore: 93.4mm 3.7in
Stroke: 84.0mm 3.3in
Valve type/No: Overhead 16
Transmission: Manual
No. of forward speeds: 5
Wheels driven: Rear
Springs F/R: Coil/Coil
Brake system: PA ABS
Brakes F/R: Disc/Disc
Steering: Rack & pinion PA
Wheelbase: 256.5cm 101.0in
Track F: 141.2cm 55.6in
Track R: 142.5cm 56.1in
Length: 434.6cm 171.1in
Width: 167.9cm 66.1in
Height: 134.4cm 52.9in
Kerb weight: 1305.2kg 2875.0lb

606 BMW
M5
1989 Germany
155.0mph 249.4kmh
0-60mph 96.5kmh: 6.3secs
315.0bhp 234.9kW 319.4PS
@ 6900rpm
266.0lbft 360.4Nm @ 4750rpm
184.7bhp/ton 181.6bhp/tonne
89.1bhp/L 66.4kW/L 90.3PS/L
65.0ft/sec 19.8m/sec
Petrol 4-stroke piston
3535cc 215.7cu in
In-line 6 fuel injection
Compression ratio: 10.0:1
Bore: 93.4mm 3.7in
Stroke: 86.0mm 3.4in
Valve type/No: Overhead 24
Transmission: Manual
No. of forward speeds: 5
Wheels driven: Rear
Springs F/R: Coil/Coil
Brake system: ABS
Brakes F/R: Disc/Disc
Steering: Recirculating ball PA
Wheelbase: 276.1cm 108.7in
Track F: 147.3cm 58.0in
Track R: 149.6cm 58.9in
Length: 471.9cm 185.8in
Width: 175.0cm 68.9in
Height: 139.2cm 54.8in
Kerb weight: 1734.3kg 3820.0lb
Fuel: 90.1L 19.8gal 23.8galUS

607 BMW
M635 CSi
1989 Germany
150.0mph 241.4kmh
0-50mph 80.5kmh: 4.6secs
0-60mph 96.5kmh: 6.0secs
0-1/4 mile: 14.6secs
0-1km: 23.6secs
286.0bhp 213.3kW 290.0PS
@ 6500rpm
250.9lbft 340.0Nm @ 4500rpm
185.3bhp/ton 182.2bhp/tonne
82.8bhp/L 61.8kW/L 84.0PS/L
59.8ft/sec 18.2m/sec
24.0mph 38.6kmh/1000rpm
20.6mpg 17.2mpgUS 13.7L/100km
Petrol 4-stroke piston
3453cc 211.0cu in
In-line 6 fuel injection
Compression ratio: 10.5:1
Bore: 93.4mm 3.7in
Stroke: 84.0mm 3.3in
Valve type/No: Overhead 24
Transmission: Manual
No. of forward speeds: 5
Wheels driven: Rear
Springs F/R: Coil/Coil
Brake system: PA
Brakes F/R: Disc/Disc
Steering: Recirculating ball PA
Wheelbase: 262.5cm 103.3in
Track F: 143.0cm 56.3in
Track R: 146.0cm 57.5in
Length: 481.5cm 189.6in
Width: 172.5cm 67.9in
Height: 133.8cm 52.7in
Ground clearance: 9.5cm 3.7in
Kerb weight: 1570.0kg 3458.1lb
Fuel: 70.1L 15.4gal 18.5galUS

608 BMW
Z1
1989 Germany
139.0mph 223.7kmh
0-50mph 80.5kmh: 5.8secs
0-60mph 96.5kmh: 7.9secs
0-1/4 mile: 15.9secs
0-1km: 29.4secs
170.0bhp 126.8kW 172.4PS
@ 5800rpm
163.8lbft 222.0Nm @ 4300rpm
129.3bhp/ton 127.1bhp/tonne
68.2bhp/L 50.8kW/L 69.1PS/L
47.5ft/sec 14.5m/sec
24.8mph 39.9kmh/1000rpm
24.0mpg 20.0mpgUS 11.8L/100km
Petrol 4-stroke piston
2494cc 152.0cu in
In-line 6 fuel injection
Compression ratio: 8.8:1
Bore: 84.0mm 3.3in
Stroke: 75.0mm 2.9in
Valve type/No: Overhead 12
Transmission: Manual
No. of forward speeds: 5
Wheels driven: Rear
Springs F/R: Coil/Coil
Brake system: PA ABS
Brakes F/R: Disc/Drum
Steering: Rack & pinion PA
Wheelbase: 243.8cm 96.0in
Track F: 142.2cm 56.0in
Track R: 144.7cm 57.0in
Length: 392.4cm 154.5in
Width: 170.1cm 67.0in
Height: 124.4cm 49.0in
Ground clearance: 16.5cm 6.5in
Kerb weight: 1337.0kg 2944.9lb
Fuel: 58.2L 12.8gal 15.4galUS

609 BMW
318i S
1990 Germany
125.0mph 201.1kmh
0-50mph 80.5kmh: 6.5secs
0-60mph 96.5kmh: 9.3secs
0-1/4 mile: 16.8secs
0-1km: 30.8secs
136.0bhp 101.4kW 137.9PS
@ 6000rpm
126.9lbft 172.0Nm @ 4600rpm
119.2bhp/ton 117.2bhp/tonne

75.7bhp/L 56.5kW/L 76.8PS/L
53.2ft/sec 16.2m/sec
20.8mph 33.5kmh/1000rpm
27.5mpg 22.9mpgUS 10.3L/100km
Petrol 4-stroke piston
1796cc 110.0cu in
In-line 4 fuel injection
Compression ratio: 10.0:1
Bore: 84.0mm 3.3in
Stroke: 81.0mm 3.2in
Valve type/No: Overhead 16
Transmission: Manual
No. of forward speeds: 5
Wheels driven: Rear
Springs F/R: Coil/Coil
Brake system: PA ABS
Brakes F/R: Disc/Disc
Steering: Rack & pinion PA
Wheelbase: 257.0cm 101.2in
Track F: 140.7cm 55.4in
Track R: 141.5cm 55.7in
Length: 432.5cm 170.3in
Width: 164.5cm 64.8in
Height: 138.0cm 54.3in
Ground clearance: 15.5cm 6.1in
Kerb weight: 1160.0kg 2555.1lb
Fuel: 55.1L 12.1gal 14.5galUS

610 BMW
325i Convertible
1990 Germany
0-50mph 80.5kmh: 5.6secs
0-60mph 96.5kmh: 7.5secs
0-1/4 mile: 15.7secs
168.0bhp 125.3kW 170.3PS
@ 5800rpm
164.0lbft 222.2Nm @ 4300rpm
121.4bhp/ton 119.4bhp/tonne
67.4bhp/L 50.2kW/L 68.3PS/L
47.5ft/sec 14.5m/sec
26.4mpg 22.0mpgUS 10.7L/100km
Petrol 4-stroke piston
2494cc 152.2cu in
In-line 6 fuel injection
Compression ratio: 8.8:1
Bore: 84.0mm 3.3in
Stroke: 75.0mm 2.9in
Valve type/No: Overhead 12
Transmission: Automatic
No. of forward speeds: 4
Wheels driven: Rear
Springs F/R: Coil/Coil
Brake system: PA ABS
Brakes F/R: Disc/Disc
Steering: Rack & pinion PA
Wheelbase: 257.0cm 101.2in
Track F: 140.7cm 55.4in
Track R: 141.5cm 55.7in
Length: 445.0cm 175.2in
Width: 164.6cm 64.8in
Height: 136.9cm 53.9in
Kerb weight: 1407.4kg 3100.0lb
Fuel: 62.1L 13.6gal 16.4galUS

611 BMW
735i Koenig
1990 Germany
158.0mph 254.2kmh
0-60mph 96.5kmh: 6.0secs
290.0bhp 216.2kW 294.0PS
@ 5200rpm
299.0lbft 405.1Nm
164.5bhp/ton 161.7bhp/tonne
84.5bhp/L 63.0kW/L 85.7PS/L
49.0ft/sec 14.9m/sec
Petrol 4-stroke piston
3430cc 209.3cu in supercharged
In-line 6 fuel injection
Compression ratio: 8.0:1
Bore: 92.0mm 3.6in
Stroke: 86.0mm 3.4in
Valve type/No: Overhead 12
Transmission: Automatic
No. of forward speeds: 4
Wheels driven: Rear
Springs F/R: Coil/Coil
Brake system: ABS
Brakes F/R: Disc/Disc
Steering: Recirculating ball PA
Wheelbase: 279.4cm 110.0in
Track F: 150.1cm 59.1in
Track R: 151.6cm 59.7in
Length: 515.6cm 203.0in
Width: 203.2cm 80.0in
Height: 139.7cm 55.0in
Kerb weight: 1793.3kg 3950.0lb
Fuel: 85.2L 18.7gal 22.5galUS

612 BMW
750i
1990 Germany
153.0mph 246.2kmh
0-50mph 80.5kmh: 5.4secs
0-60mph 96.5kmh: 7.3secs
0-1/4 mile: 15.2secs
0-1km: 27.7secs
300.0bhp 223.7kW 304.2PS
@ 5200rpm
332.1lbft 450.0Nm @ 4100rpm
164.9bhp/ton 162.2bhp/tonne
60.1bhp/L 44.8kW/L 61.0PS/L
42.6ft/sec 13.0m/sec
32.1mph 51.6kmh/1000rpm
16.2mpg 13.5mpgUS 17.4L/100km
Petrol 4-stroke piston
4988cc 304.0cu in
Vee 12 fuel injection
Compression ratio: 8.8:1
Bore: 84.0mm 3.3in
Stroke: 75.0mm 2.9in
Valve type/No: Overhead 48
Transmission: Automatic
No. of forward speeds: 4
Wheels driven: Rear
Springs F/R: Coil/Coil
Brake system: PA ABS
Brakes F/R: Disc/Disc
Steering: Recirculating ball PA
Wheelbase: 283.2cm 111.5in
Track F: 152.7cm 60.1in
Track R: 155.0cm 61.0in
Length: 491.0cm 193.3in
Width: 184.5cm 72.6in
Height: 141.1cm 55.6in
Ground clearance: 20.3cm 8.0in
Kerb weight: 1850.0kg 4074.9lb
Fuel: 101.9L 22.4gal 26.9galUS

613 BMW
750i Alpina B12
1990 Germany
171.0mph 275.1kmh
0-60mph 96.5kmh: 6.9secs
350.0bhp 261.0kW 354.8PS
@ 5300rpm
347.0lbft 470.2Nm @ 4000rpm
191.7bhp/ton 188.5bhp/tonne
70.2bhp/L 52.3kW/L 71.1PS/L
43.4ft/sec 13.2m/sec
Petrol 4-stroke piston
4988cc 304.3cu in
Vee 12 fuel injection
Compression ratio: 9.5:1
Bore: 84.0mm 3.3in
Stroke: 75.0mm 2.9in
Valve type/No: Overhead 24
Transmission: Automatic
No. of forward speeds: 4
Wheels driven: Rear
Springs F/R: Coil/Coil
Brake system: ABS
Brakes F/R: Disc/Disc
Steering: Recirculating ball PA
Wheelbase: 283.2cm 111.5in
Track F: 153.9cm 60.6in
Track R: 153.4cm 60.4in
Length: 491.0cm 193.3in
Width: 184.4cm 72.6in
Height: 138.9cm 54.7in
Kerb weight: 1856.9kg 4090.0lb
Fuel: 101.8L 22.4gal 26.9galUS

614 BMW
318i
1991 Germany
123.0mph 197.9kmh
0-50mph 80.5kmh: 7.4secs
0-60mph 96.5kmh: 10.2secs
0-1/4 mile: 17.5secs
0-1km: 32.0secs
113.0bhp 84.3kW 114.6PS
@ 5900rpm
119.6lbft 162.0Nm @ 3000rpm
91.2bhp/ton 89.7bhp/tonne
62.9bhp/L 46.9kW/L 63.8PS/L
52.3ft/sec 15.9m/sec
20.5mph 33.0kmh/1000rpm
27.6mpg 23.0mpgUS 10.2L/100km
Petrol 4-stroke piston
1796cc 110.0cu in
In-line 4 fuel injection
Compression ratio: 8.8:1
Bore: 84.0mm 3.3in
Stroke: 81.0mm 3.2in
Valve type/No: Overhead 8
Transmission: Manual
No. of forward speeds: 5
Wheels driven: Rear
Springs F/R: Coil/Coil
Brake system: PA ABS
Brakes F/R: Disc/Drum
Steering: Rack & pinion PA
Wheelbase: 269.7cm 106.2in
Track F: 140.7cm 55.4in
Track R: 142.0cm 55.9in
Length: 443.2cm 174.5in
Width: 169.7cm 66.8in
Height: 139.2cm 54.8in
Kerb weight: 1260.0kg 2775.3lb
Fuel: 65.1L 14.3gal 17.2galUS

615 BMW
325i SE
1991 Germany
143.0mph 230.1kmh
0-50mph 80.5kmh: 5.3secs
0-60mph 96.5kmh: 7.3secs
0-1/4 mile: 15.8secs
0-1km: 28.3secs
189.0bhp 140.9kW 191.6PS
@ 5900rpm
180.8lbft 245.0Nm @ 4700rpm
144.5bhp/ton 142.1bhp/tonne
75.8bhp/L 56.5kW/L 76.8PS/L
51.0ft/sec 15.5m/sec
22.5mph 36.2kmh/1000rpm
26.6mpg 22.1mpgUS 10.6L/100km
Petrol 4-stroke piston
2494cc 152.0cu in
In-line 6 fuel injection
Compression ratio: 10.0:1
Bore: 84.0mm 3.3in
Stroke: 79.0mm 3.1in
Valve type/No: Overhead 24
Transmission: Manual
No. of forward speeds: 5
Wheels driven: Rear
Springs F/R: Coil/Coil
Brake system: PA ABS
Brakes F/R: Disc/Disc
Steering: Rack & pinion PA
Wheelbase: 269.7cm 106.2in
Track F: 140.7cm 55.4in
Track R: 142.0cm 55.9in
Length: 443.2cm 174.5in
Width: 169.7cm 66.8in
Height: 139.2cm 54.8in
Kerb weight: 1330.0kg 2929.5lb
Fuel: 65.1L 14.3gal 17.2galUS

616 BMW
520i
1991 Germany
130.0mph 209.2kmh
0-50mph 80.5kmh: 6.7secs
0-60mph 96.5kmh: 9.6secs
0-1/4 mile: 17.1secs
0-1km: 31.4secs
150.0bhp 111.9kW 152.1PS
@ 5900rpm
140.2lbft 190.0Nm @ 4700rpm
102.4bhp/ton 100.7bhp/tonne
75.3bhp/L 56.2kW/L 76.4PS/L
42.6ft/sec 13.0m/sec
24.4mph 39.3kmh/1000rpm
22.0mpg 18.3mpgUS 12.8L/100km
Petrol 4-stroke piston
1991cc 121.0cu in
In-line 6 fuel injection
Compression ratio: 10.5:1
Bore: 80.0mm 3.1in
Stroke: 66.0mm 2.6in
Valve type/No: Overhead 24
Transmission: Manual
No. of forward speeds: 5
Wheels driven: Rear
Springs F/R: Coil/Coil
Brake system: PA
Brakes F/R: Disc/Disc
Steering: Recirculating ball PA
Wheelbase: 276.1cm 108.7in
Track F: 146.6cm 57.7in
Track R: 154.9cm 61.0in
Length: 471.9cm 185.8in
Width: 175.0cm 68.9in
Height: 141.2cm 55.6in
Ground clearance: 17.8cm 7.0in
Kerb weight: 1490.0kg 3281.9lb
Fuel: 80.1L 17.6gal 21.1galUS

617 BMW
525i
1991 Germany
128.0mph 206.0kmh
0-50mph 80.5kmh: 6.2secs
0-60mph 96.5kmh: 8.5secs
0-1/4 mile: 16.3secs
189.0bhp 140.9kW 191.6PS
@ 5900rpm
181.0lbft 245.3Nm @ 4700rpm
121.5bhp/ton 119.4bhp/tonne
75.8bhp/L 56.5kW/L 76.8PS/L
48.3ft/sec 14.7m/sec
24.0mpg 20.0mpgUS 11.8L/100km
Petrol 4-stroke piston
2494cc 152.2cu in
In-line 6 fuel injection
Compression ratio: 10.0:1
Bore: 84.0mm 3.3in
Stroke: 75.0mm 2.9in
Valve type/No: Overhead 24
Transmission: Manual
No. of forward speeds: 5
Wheels driven: Rear
Springs F/R: Coil/Coil
Brake system: PA ABS
Brakes F/R: Disc/Disc
Steering: Recirculating ball PA
Wheelbase: 276.1cm 108.7in
Track F: 147.1cm 57.9in
Track R: 149.6cm 58.9in
Length: 471.9cm 185.8in
Width: 175.0cm 68.9in
Height: 141.2cm 55.6in
Kerb weight: 1582.2kg 3485.0lb
Fuel: 79.9L 17.6gal 21.1galUS

618 BMW
525i SE 24v
1991 Germany
141.0mph 226.9kmh
0-50mph 80.5kmh: 6.3secs
0-60mph 96.5kmh: 8.7secs
0-1/4 mile: 16.5secs
0-1km: 29.9secs
192.0bhp 143.2kW 194.7PS
@ 5900rpm
180.8lbft 245.0Nm @ 4700rpm
127.2bhp/ton 125.1bhp/tonne
77.0bhp/L 57.4kW/L 78.0PS/L
48.3ft/sec 14.7m/sec
22.2mph 35.7kmh/1000rpm
21.7mpg 18.1mpgUS 13.0L/100km
Petrol 4-stroke piston
2494cc 152.0cu in
In-line 6 fuel injection
Compression ratio: 10.0:1
Bore: 84.0mm 3.3in
Stroke: 75.0mm 2.9in
Valve type/No: Overhead 24
Transmission: Manual
No. of forward speeds: 5
Wheels driven: Rear
Springs F/R: Coil/Coil
Brake system: PA ABS
Brakes F/R: Disc/Disc
Steering: Recirculating ball PA
Wheelbase: 276.1cm 108.7in
Track F: 146.6cm 57.7in
Track R: 154.9cm 61.0in
Length: 471.9cm 185.8in
Width: 175.0cm 68.9in
Height: 141.2cm 55.6in
Ground clearance: 17.8cm 7.0in
Kerb weight: 1535.0kg 3381.1lb
Fuel: 80.1L 17.6gal 21.1galUS

619 BMW
535i Alpina B10 Bi-Turbo
1991 Germany
179.0mph 288.0kmh
0-60mph 96.5kmh: 5.1secs
0-1/4 mile: 13.6secs
360.0bhp 268.4kW 365.0PS
@ 6000rpm
382.0lbft 517.6Nm @ 4000rpm
216.2bhp/ton 212.6bhp/tonne
105.0bhp/L 78.3kW/L 106.4PS/L
56.5ft/sec 17.2m/sec
Petrol 4-stroke piston
3430cc 209.3cu in turbocharged
In-line 6 fuel injection
Compression ratio: 7.2:1
Bore: 92.0mm 3.6in
Stroke: 86.0mm 3.4in
Valve type/No: Overhead 12
Transmission: Manual

No. of forward speeds: 5
Wheels driven: Rear
Springs F/R: Coil/Coil
Brake system: PA ABS
Brakes F/R: Disc/Disc
Steering: Recirculating ball PA
Wheelbase: 278.1cm 109.5in
Track F: 149.4cm 58.8in
Track R: 148.8cm 58.6in
Length: 475.5cm 187.2in
Width: 176.3cm 69.4in
Height: 140.2cm 55.2in
Kerb weight: 1693.4kg 3730.0lb
Fuel: 109.8L 24.1gal 29.0galUS

620 BMW

850i
1991 Germany
161.0mph 259.0kmh
0-50mph 80.5kmh: 5.3secs
0-60mph 96.5kmh: 7.2secs
0-1/4 mile: 15.3secs
0-1km: 27.2secs
300.0bhp 223.7kW 304.2PS
@ 5200rpm
332.0lbft 449.9Nm @ 4100rpm
162.3bhp/ton 159.6bhp/tonne
60.1bhp/L 44.8kW/L 61.0PS/L
42.6ft/sec 13.0m/sec
31.8mph 51.2kmh/1000rpm
14.4mpg 12.0mpgUS 19.6L/100km
Petrol 4-stroke piston
4988cc 304.3cu in
Vee 12 fuel injection
Compression ratio: 8.8:1
Bore: 84.0mm 3.3in
Stroke: 75.0mm 2.9in
Valve type/No: Overhead 24
Transmission: Automatic
No. of forward speeds: 4
Wheels driven: Rear
Springs F/R: Coil/Coil
Brake system: PA ABS
Brakes F/R: Disc/Disc
Steering: Recirculating ball PA
Wheelbase: 268.2cm 105.6in
Track F: 154.9cm 61.0in
Track R: 154.9cm 61.0in
Length: 477.5cm 188.0in
Width: 185.4cm 73.0in
Height: 131.3cm 51.7in
Ground clearance: 15.2cm 6.0in
Kerb weight: 1880.0kg 4141.0lb
Fuel: 90.1L 19.8gal 23.8galUS

621 BMW

M3 Sport Evolution
1991 Germany
0-60mph 96.5kmh: 6.5secs
0-1/4 mile: 14.8secs
238.0bhp 177.5kW 241.3PS
@ 7000rpm
177.0lbft 239.8Nm @ 4750rpm
201.2bhp/ton 197.8bhp/tonne
96.5bhp/L 71.9kW/L 97.8PS/L
66.7ft/sec 20.3m/sec
24.6mpg 20.5mpgUS 11.5L/100km
Petrol 4-stroke piston
2467cc 150.5cu in
In-line 4 fuel injection
Compression ratio: 10.2:1
Bore: 95.0mm 3.7in
Stroke: 87.0mm 3.4in
Valve type/No: Overhead 16
Transmission: Manual
No. of forward speeds: 5
Wheels driven: Rear
Springs F/R: Coil/Coil
Brake system: PA ABS
Brakes F/R: Disc/Disc
Steering: Rack & pinion PA
Wheelbase: 256.5cm 101.0in
Track F: 141.7cm 55.8in
Track R: 143.0cm 56.3in
Length: 434.6cm 171.1in
Width: 167.9cm 66.1in
Height: 136.9cm 53.9in
Kerb weight: 1203.1kg 2650.0lb
Fuel: 70.0L 15.4gal 18.5galUS

622 BMW

M5
1991 Germany
155.0mph 249.4kmh
0-60mph 96.5kmh: 6.4secs
0-1/4 mile: 15.0secs
310.0bhp 231.2kW 314.3PS
@ 6900rpm
265.0lbft 359.1Nm @ 4750rpm
175.8bhp/ton 172.9bhp/tonne
87.7bhp/L 65.4kW/L 88.9PS/L
65.0ft/sec 19.8m/sec
18.6mpg 15.5mpgUS 15.2L/100km
Petrol 4-stroke piston
3535cc 215.7cu in
In-line 6 fuel injection
Compression ratio: 10.0:1
Bore: 93.4mm 3.7in
Stroke: 86.0mm 3.4in
Valve type/No: Overhead 24
Transmission: Manual
No. of forward speeds: 5
Wheels driven: Rear
Springs F/R: Coil/Coil
Brake system: PA ABS
Brakes F/R: Disc/Disc
Steering: Recirculating ball PA
Wheelbase: 276.1cm 108.7in
Track F: 147.3cm 58.0in
Track R: 149.6cm 58.9in
Length: 471.9cm 185.8in
Width: 175.0cm 68.9in
Height: 140.7cm 55.4in
Kerb weight: 1793.3kg 3950.0lb
Fuel: 90.1L 19.8gal 23.8galUS

623 BMW

325i
1992 Germany
128.0mph 206.0kmh
0-50mph 80.5kmh: 5.9secs
0-60mph 96.5kmh: 7.9secs
0-1/4 mile: 16.1secs
189.0bhp 140.9kW 191.6PS
@ 5900rpm
181.0lbft 245.3Nm @ 4700rpm
137.4bhp/ton 135.2bhp/tonne
75.8bhp/L 56.5kW/L 76.8PS/L
48.3ft/sec 14.7m/sec
26.4mpg 22.0mpgUS 10.7L/100km
Petrol 4-stroke piston
2494cc 152.2cu in
In-line 6 fuel injection
Compression ratio: 10.0:1
Bore: 84.0mm 3.3in
Stroke: 75.0mm 2.9in
Valve type/No: Overhead 24
Transmission: Manual
No. of forward speeds: 5
Wheels driven: Rear
Springs F/R: Coil/Coil
Brake system: PA ABS
Brakes F/R: Disc/Disc
Steering: Rack & pinion PA
Wheelbase: 270.0cm 106.3in
Track F: 140.7cm 55.4in
Track R: 142.0cm 55.9in
Length: 443.2cm 174.5in
Width: 169.7cm 66.8in
Height: 139.2cm 54.8in
Ground clearance: 16.5cm 6.5in
Kerb weight: 1398.3kg 3080.0lb
Fuel: 65.1L 14.3gal 17.2galUS

624 BMW

520i SE Touring
1992 Germany
132.0mph 212.4kmh
0-50mph 80.5kmh: 6.6secs
0-60mph 96.5kmh: 9.2secs
0-1/4 mile: 17.0secs
0-1km: 31.0secs
192.0bhp 143.2kW 194.7PS
@ 5900rpm
180.0lbft 243.9Nm @ 4700rpm
122.8bhp/ton 120.7bhp/tonne
77.0bhp/L 57.4kW/L 78.0PS/L
48.3ft/sec 14.7m/sec
22.9mph 36.8kmh/1000rpm
20.8mpg 17.3mpgUS 13.6L/100km
Petrol 4-stroke piston
2494cc 152.2cu in
In-line 6 fuel injection
Compression ratio: 10.1:1
Bore: 84.0mm 3.3in
Stroke: 75.0mm 2.9in
Valve type/No: Overhead 24
Transmission: Manual
No. of forward speeds: 5
Wheels driven: Rear
Springs F/R: Coil/Coil
Brake system: PA ABS
Brakes F/R: Disc/Disc
Steering: Ball & nut PA
Wheelbase: 276.1cm 108.7in
Track F: 147.0cm 57.9in
Track R: 149.5cm 58.9in
Length: 472.0cm 185.8in
Width: 175.1cm 68.9in
Height: 141.7cm 55.8in
Ground clearance: 17.8cm 7.0in
Kerb weight: 1590.0kg 3502.2lb
Fuel: 80.1L 17.6gal 21.1galUS

625 BMW

850i Manual
1992 Germany
160.0mph 257.4kmh
0-50mph 80.5kmh: 5.3secs
0-60mph 96.5kmh: 7.1secs
0-1/4 mile: 15.5secs
0-1km: 27.5secs
300.0bhp 223.7kW 304.2PS
@ 5200rpm
332.1lbft 450.0Nm @ 4100rpm
161.8bhp/ton 159.1bhp/tonne
60.1bhp/L 44.8kW/L 61.0PS/L
42.6ft/sec 13.0m/sec
30.4mph 48.9kmh/1000rpm
14.7mpg 12.2mpgUS 19.2L/100km
Petrol 4-stroke piston
4988cc 304.0cu in
Vee 12 fuel injection
Compression ratio: 8.8:1
Bore: 84.0mm 3.3in
Stroke: 75.0mm 2.9in
Valve type/No: Overhead 24
Transmission: Manual
No. of forward speeds: 6
Wheels driven: Rear
Springs F/R: Coil/Coil
Brake system: PA ABS
Brakes F/R: Disc/Disc
Steering: Recirculating ball PA
Wheelbase: 268.4cm 105.7in
Track F: 155.2cm 61.1in
Track R: 156.2cm 61.5in
Length: 478.0cm 188.2in
Width: 185.5cm 73.0in
Height: 134.0cm 52.8in
Kerb weight: 1885.0kg 4152.0lb
Fuel: 90.0L 19.8gal 23.8galUS

626 Bond

Equipe GT
1964 UK
83.0mph 133.5kmh
0-50mph 80.5kmh: 12.3secs
0-60mph 96.5kmh: 17.6secs
0-1/4 mile: 20.8secs
63.0bhp 47.0kW 63.9PS
@ 5750rpm
67.0lbft 90.8Nm @ 3500rpm
82.2bhp/ton 80.9bhp/tonne
54.9bhp/L 41.0kW/L 55.7PS/L
47.8ft/sec 14.6m/sec
15.8mph 25.4kmh/1000rpm
30.3mpg 25.2mpgUS 9.3L/100km
Petrol 4-stroke piston
1147cc 70.0cu in
In-line 4 2 Carburettor
Compression ratio: 9.0:1
Bore: 69.3mm 2.7in
Stroke: 76.0mm 3.0in
Valve type/No: Overhead 8
Transmission: Manual
No. of forward speeds: 4
Wheels driven: Rear
Springs F/R: Coil/Leaf
Brakes F/R: Disc/Drum
Steering: Rack & pinion
Wheelbase: 232.4cm 91.5in
Track F: 121.9cm 48.0in
Track R: 121.9cm 48.0in
Length: 398.8cm 157.0in
Width: 152.4cm 60.0in
Height: 134.6cm 53.0in
Ground clearance: 17.0cm 6.7in
Kerb weight: 779.1kg 1716.0lb
Fuel: 45.5L 10.0gal 12.0galUS

627 Bond

Equipe GT 4S
1965 UK
92.0mph 148.0kmh
0-50mph 80.5kmh: 14.1secs
0-60mph 96.5kmh: 20.0secs
0-1/4 mile: 21.4secs
67.0bhp 50.0kW 67.9PS
@ 6000rpm
67.0lbft 90.8Nm @ 3760rpm
81.8bhp/ton 80.5bhp/tonne
58.4bhp/L 43.6kW/L 59.2PS/L
49.8ft/sec 15.2m/sec
15.7mph 25.3kmh/1000rpm
26.7mpg 22.2mpgUS 10.6L/100km
Petrol 4-stroke piston
1147cc 70.0cu in
In-line 4 2 Carburettor
Compression ratio: 9.0:1
Bore: 69.3mm 2.7in
Stroke: 76.0mm 3.0in
Valve type/No: Overhead 8
Transmission: Manual
No. of forward speeds: 4
Wheels driven: Rear
Springs F/R: Coil/Leaf
Brakes F/R: Disc/Drum
Steering: Rack & pinion
Wheelbase: 232.4cm 91.5in
Track F: 121.9cm 48.0in
Track R: 121.9cm 48.0in
Length: 406.4cm 160.0in
Width: 152.4cm 60.0in
Height: 134.6cm 53.0in
Ground clearance: 17.0cm 6.7in
Kerb weight: 832.6kg 1834.0lb
Fuel: 45.5L 10.0gal 12.0galUS

628 Bond

875
1966 UK
82.0mph 131.9kmh
0-50mph 80.5kmh: 11.9secs
0-60mph 96.5kmh: 17.4secs
0-1/4 mile: 20.8secs
0-1km: 39.2secs
34.0bhp 25.3kW 34.5PS
@ 4700rpm
47.0lbft 63.7Nm @ 2800rpm
57.9bhp/ton 56.9bhp/tonne
38.9bhp/L 29.0kW/L 39.4PS/L
31.1ft/sec 9.5m/sec
16.0mph 25.7kmh/1000rpm
34.5mpg 28.7mpgUS 8.2L/100km
Petrol 4-stroke piston
875cc 53.4cu in
In-line 4 1 Carburettor
Compression ratio: 8.0:1
Bore: 68.0mm 2.7in
Stroke: 60.4mm 2.4in
Valve type/No: Overhead 8
Transmission: Manual
No. of forward speeds: 4
Wheels driven: Rear
Springs F/R: Coil/Coil
Brakes F/R: Drum/Drum
Steering: Worm & nut
Wheelbase: 198.1cm 78.0in
Track R: 121.9cm 48.0in
Length: 327.7cm 129.0in
Width: 139.7cm 55.0in
Height: 134.6cm 53.0in
Ground clearance: 17.8cm 7.0in
Kerb weight: 597.0kg 1315.0lb
Fuel: 27.3L 6.0gal 7.2galUS

629 Bond

Bug
1970 UK
77.0mph 123.9kmh
0-50mph 80.5kmh: 13.6secs
0-60mph 96.5kmh: 23.2secs
0-1/4 mile: 21.8secs
0-1km: 42.6secs
31.0bhp 23.1kW 31.4PS
@ 5000rpm
38.0lbft 51.5Nm @ 3000rpm
80.0bhp/ton 78.7bhp/tonne
44.3bhp/L 33.0kW/L 44.9PS/L
33.3ft/sec 10.2m/sec
15.5mph 24.9kmh/1000rpm
35.0mpg 29.1mpgUS 8.1L/100km
Petrol 4-stroke piston
700cc 42.7cu in
In-line 4 1 Carburettor
Compression ratio: 8.4:1
Bore: 60.4mm 2.4in
Stroke: 61.0mm 2.4in
Valve type/No: Overhead 8
Transmission: Manual
No. of forward speeds: 4
Wheels driven: Rear
Springs F/R: Coil/Coil
Brakes F/R: Drum/Drum
Steering: Worm & peg

Wheelbase: 195.6cm 77.0in
Track R: 121.9cm 48.0in
Length: 279.4cm 110.0in
Width: 139.7cm 55.0in
Height: 127.0cm 50.0in
Ground clearance: 20.3cm 8.0in
Kerb weight: 394.1kg 868.0lb
Fuel: 22.7L 5.0gal 6.0galUS

630 Borgward

Isabella 1500
1955 Germany
80.6mph 129.7kmh
0-50mph 80.5kmh: 14.0secs
0-60mph 96.5kmh: 22.4secs
0-1/4 mile: 22.0secs
60.0bhp 44.7kW 60.8PS
@ 4700rpm
82.0lbft 111.1Nm @ 2400rpm
60.3bhp/ton 59.3bhp/tonne
40.2bhp/L 30.0kW/L 40.8PS/L
43.1ft/sec 13.1m/sec
18.2mph 29.3kmh/1000rpm
Petrol 4-stroke piston
1492cc 91.0cu in
In-line 4
Compression ratio: 6.8:1
Bore: 74.9mm 2.9in
Stroke: 83.8mm 3.3in
Valve type/No: Overhead 8
Transmission: Manual
No. of forward speeds: 4
Wheels driven: Rear
Wheelbase: 260.1cm 102.4in
Track F: 133.6cm 52.6in
Track R: 135.9cm 53.5in
Kerb weight: 1012.4kg 2230.0lb

631 Borgward

Isabella TS
1956 Germany
92.8mph 149.3kmh
0-50mph 80.5kmh: 12.0secs
0-60mph 96.5kmh: 16.0secs
0-1/4 mile: 19.8secs
82.0bhp 61.1kW 83.1PS
@ 5200rpm
84.6lbft 114.6Nm @ 3000rpm
79.2bhp/ton 77.8bhp/tonne
54.9bhp/L 41.0kW/L 55.7PS/L
48.1ft/sec 14.7m/sec
Petrol 4-stroke piston
1493cc 91.1cu in
In-line 4
Compression ratio: 8.2:1
Bore: 74.9mm 2.9in
Stroke: 84.6mm 3.3in
Valve type/No: Overhead 8
Transmission: Manual
No. of forward speeds: 4
Wheels driven: Rear
Wheelbase: 260.1cm 102.4in
Track F: 134.1cm 52.8in
Track R: 135.9cm 53.5in
Kerb weight: 1053.3kg 2320.0lb

632 Borgward

Isabella Coupe
1958 Germany
90.2mph 145.1kmh
0-50mph 80.5kmh: 12.5secs
0-60mph 96.5kmh: 17.5secs
0-1/4 mile: 21.4secs
82.0bhp 61.1kW 83.1PS
@ 5200rpm
84.0lbft 113.8Nm @ 3000rpm
74.1bhp/ton 72.8bhp/tonne
54.9bhp/L 41.0kW/L 55.7PS/L
47.7ft/sec 14.5m/sec
17.5mph 28.2kmh/1000rpm
Petrol 4-stroke piston
1493cc 91.1cu in
In-line 4
Compression ratio: 8.2:1
Bore: 74.9mm 2.9in
Stroke: 83.8mm 3.3in
Valve type/No: Overhead 8
Transmission: Manual
No. of forward speeds: 4
Wheels driven: Rear
Wheelbase: 260.1cm 102.4in
Track F: 134.1cm 52.8in
Track R: 135.9cm 53.5in
Length: 439.4cm 173.0in
Width: 172.0cm 67.7in
Height: 135.1cm 53.2in
Kerb weight: 1125.9kg 2480.0lb

633 Borgward

Isabella TS
1958 Germany
91.0mph 146.4kmh
0-50mph 80.5kmh: 13.8secs
0-60mph 96.5kmh: 19.7secs
0-1/4 mile: 21.7secs
75.0bhp 55.9kW 76.0PS
@ 5200rpm
84.6lbft 114.6Nm @ 2800rpm
70.6bhp/ton 69.4bhp/tonne
50.2bhp/L 37.5kW/L 50.9PS/L
48.1ft/sec 14.6m/sec
17.6mph 28.3kmh/1000rpm
33.0mpg 27.5mpgUS 8.6L/100km
Petrol 4-stroke piston
1493cc 91.1cu in
In-line 4
Compression ratio: 8.2:1
Bore: 75.0mm 2.9in
Stroke: 84.5mm 3.3in
Valve type/No: Overhead 8
Transmission: Manual
No. of forward speeds: 4
Wheels driven: Rear
Springs F/R: Coil/Coil
Brakes F/R: Drum/Drum
Wheelbase: 264.2cm 104.0in
Track F: 135.6cm 53.4in
Track R: 138.2cm 54.4in
Length: 443.5cm 174.6in
Width: 173.2cm 68.2in
Height: 151.4cm 59.6in
Ground clearance: 17.8cm 7.0in
Kerb weight: 1080.5kg 2380.0lb
Fuel: 47.8L 10.5gal 12.6galUS

634 Borgward

2.3 Grosse
1960 Germany
101.0mph 162.5kmh
0-50mph 80.5kmh: 9.7secs
0-60mph 96.5kmh: 14.8secs
0-1/4 mile: 19.8secs
100.0bhp 74.6kW 101.4PS
@ 5100rpm
116.0lbft 157.2Nm @ 2000rpm
78.3bhp/ton 77.0bhp/tonne
44.6bhp/L 33.3kW/L 45.3PS/L
47.2ft/sec 14.4m/sec
18.3mph 29.4kmh/1000rpm
19.6mpg 16.3mpgUS 14.4L/100km
Petrol 4-stroke piston
2240cc 136.7cu in
In-line 6
Compression ratio: 8.7:1
Bore: 75.0mm 2.9in
Stroke: 84.5mm 3.3in
Valve type/No: Overhead 12
Transmission: Manual
No. of forward speeds: 4
Wheels driven: Rear
Springs F/R: Gas/Gas
Brakes F/R: Drum/Drum
Wheelbase: 264.9cm 104.3in
Track F: 135.9cm 53.5in
Track R: 136.7cm 53.8in
Length: 471.2cm 185.5in
Width: 173.5cm 68.3in
Height: 142.2cm 56.0in
Ground clearance: 16.8cm 6.6in
Kerb weight: 1299.3kg 2862.0lb
Fuel: 65.1L 14.3gal 17.2galUS

635 Borgward

Isabella TS
1960 Germany
92.8mph 149.3kmh
0-50mph 80.5kmh: 12.0secs
0-60mph 96.5kmh: 16.0secs
0-1/4 mile: 19.8secs
82.0bhp 61.1kW 83.1PS
@ 5200rpm
84.0lbft 113.8Nm @ 3000rpm
79.2bhp/ton 77.8bhp/tonne
54.9bhp/L 41.0kW/L 55.7PS/L
47.7ft/sec 14.5m/sec
17.5mph 28.2kmh/1000rpm
Petrol 4-stroke piston
1493cc 91.1cu in
In-line 4 1 Carburettor
Compression ratio: 8.2:1
Bore: 74.9mm 2.9in
Stroke: 83.8mm 3.3in
Valve type/No: Overhead 8
Transmission: Manual
No. of forward speeds: 4
Wheels driven: Rear
Wheelbase: 260.1cm 102.4in
Track F: 134.1cm 52.8in
Track R: 135.9cm 53.5in
Length: 439.4cm 173.0in
Width: 172.0cm 67.7in
Height: 135.1cm 53.2in
Kerb weight: 1053.3kg 2320.0lb

636 Borgward

Isabella TS Coupe
1960 Germany
98.0mph 157.7kmh
0-50mph 80.5kmh: 12.2secs
0-60mph 96.5kmh: 17.4secs
0-1/4 mile: 20.5secs
75.0bhp 55.9kW 76.0PS
@ 5200rpm
83.8lbft 113.6Nm @ 2800rpm
68.8bhp/ton 67.7bhp/tonne
50.2bhp/L 37.5kW/L 50.9PS/L
48.0ft/sec 14.6m/sec
17.4mph 28.0kmh/1000rpm
27.8mpg 23.1mpgUS 10.2L/100km
Petrol 4-stroke piston
1493cc 91.1cu in
In-line 4
Compression ratio: 8.2:1
Bore: 75.0mm 2.9in
Stroke: 84.3mm 3.3in
Valve type/No: Overhead 8
Transmission: Manual
No. of forward speeds: 4
Wheels driven: Rear
Springs F/R: Coil/Coil
Brakes F/R: Drum/Drum
Wheelbase: 264.2cm 104.0in
Track F: 135.9cm 53.5in
Track R: 138.4cm 54.5in
Length: 440.7cm 173.5in
Width: 170.2cm 67.0in
Height: 146.6cm 57.7in
Ground clearance: 17.8cm 7.0in
Kerb weight: 1107.8kg 2440.0lb
Fuel: 45.5L 10.0gal 12.0galUS

637 Bricklin

SV-1
1975 USA
111.0mph 178.6kmh
0-50mph 80.5kmh: 7.3secs
0-60mph 96.5kmh: 9.9secs
0-1/4 mile: 17.8secs
220.0bhp 164.0kW 223.0PS
@ 4400rpm
315.0lbft 426.8Nm @ 3100rpm
138.6bhp/ton 136.3bhp/tonne
37.3bhp/L 27.8kW/L 37.8PS/L
42.0ft/sec 12.8m/sec
21.4mph 34.4kmh/1000rpm
19.2mpg 16.0mpgUS 14.7L/100km
Petrol 4-stroke piston
5896cc 359.7cu in
Vee 8 1 Carburettor
Compression ratio: 8.5:1
Bore: 103.6mm 4.1in
Stroke: 87.4mm 3.4in
Valve type/No: Overhead 16
Transmission: Manual
No. of forward speeds: 4
Wheels driven: Rear
Springs F/R: Coil/Leaf
Brake system: PA
Brakes F/R: Disc/Drum
Steering: Recirculating ball PA
Wheelbase: 243.8cm 96.0in
Track F: 147.8cm 58.2in
Track R: 144.5cm 56.9in
Length: 452.1cm 178.0in
Width: 171.7cm 67.6in
Height: 124.5cm 49.0in
Ground clearance: 13.0cm 5.1in
Kerb weight: 1614.0kg 3555.0lb
Fuel: 79.5L 17.5gal 21.0galUS

638 Bristol

400
1948 UK
92.0mph 148.0kmh
0-50mph 80.5kmh: 13.5secs
0-60mph 96.5kmh: 19.1secs
80.0bhp 59.7kW 81.1PS
@ 4200rpm
63.3bhp/ton 62.3bhp/tonne
40.6bhp/L 30.3kW/L 41.1PS/L
44.1ft/sec 13.4m/sec
22.0mpg 18.3mpgUS 12.8L/100km
Petrol 4-stroke piston
1971cc 120.3cu in
In-line 6
Compression ratio: 7.5:1
Bore: 66.0mm 2.6in
Stroke: 96.0mm 3.8in
Valve type/No: Overhead 12
Transmission: Manual
No. of forward speeds: 4
Wheels driven: Rear
Brakes F/R: Drum/Drum
Wheelbase: 289.6cm 114.0in
Track F: 131.3cm 51.7in
Track R: 137.2cm 54.0in
Length: 464.8cm 183.0in
Width: 162.6cm 64.0in
Height: 144.8cm 57.0in
Ground clearance: 17.8cm 7.0in
Kerb weight: 1284.8kg 2830.0lb
Fuel: 54.6L 12.0gal 14.4galUS

639 Bristol

401
1952 UK
93.7mph 150.8kmh
0-50mph 80.5kmh: 11.7secs
0-60mph 96.5kmh: 17.4secs
0-1/4 mile: 20.2secs
85.0bhp 63.4kW 86.2PS
@ 4500rpm
106.8lbft 144.7Nm @ 3500rpm
68.3bhp/ton 67.2bhp/tonne
43.1bhp/L 32.2kW/L 43.7PS/L
47.2ft/sec 14.4m/sec
19.8mph 31.9kmh/1000rpm
22.7mpg 18.9mpgUS 12.4L/100km
Petrol 4-stroke piston
1971cc 120.3cu in
In-line 6
Compression ratio: 7.5:1
Bore: 66.0mm 2.6in
Stroke: 96.0mm 3.8in
Valve type/No: Overhead 12
Transmission: Manual
No. of forward speeds: 4
Wheels driven: Rear
Springs F/R: Leaf/Torsion bar
Brakes F/R: Drum/Drum
Wheelbase: 289.6cm 114.0in
Track F: 131.3cm 51.7in
Track R: 137.2cm 54.0in
Length: 486.4cm 191.5in
Width: 170.2cm 67.0in
Height: 152.4cm 60.0in
Ground clearance: 16.5cm 6.5in
Kerb weight: 1264.8kg 2786.0lb
Fuel: 77.3L 17.0gal 20.4galUS

640 Bristol

407
1961 UK
122.0mph 196.3kmh
0-50mph 80.5kmh: 7.4secs
0-60mph 96.5kmh: 9.9secs
0-1/4 mile: 17.4secs
250.0bhp 186.4kW 253.5PS
@ 4400rpm
340.0lbft 460.7Nm @ 2800rpm
153.8bhp/ton 151.3bhp/tonne
48.7bhp/L 36.3kW/L 49.4PS/L
40.5ft/sec 12.3m/sec
23.8mph 38.3kmh/1000rpm
14.1mpg 11.7mpgUS 20.0L/100km
Petrol 4-stroke piston
5130cc 313.0cu in
Vee 8
Compression ratio: 9.0:1
Bore: 98.5mm 3.9in
Stroke: 84.1mm 3.3in
Valve type/No: Overhead 16
Transmission: Automatic
No. of forward speeds: 3
Wheels driven: Rear
Springs F/R: Coil
Brake system: PA
Brakes F/R: Disc/Disc
Wheelbase: 289.6cm 114.0in
Track F: 134.6cm 53.0in
Track R: 138.4cm 54.5in
Length: 505.5cm 199.0in
Width: 172.7cm 68.0in
Height: 152.4cm 60.0in
Ground clearance: 16.5cm 6.5in

Kerb weight: 1652.6kg 3640.0lb
Fuel: 81.9L 18.0gal 21.6galUS

641 British Adler

13.67 Cabriolet
1935 Germany
61.2mph 98.5kmh
0-50mph 80.5kmh: 33.0secs
24.0mpg 20.0mpgUS 11.8L/100km
Petrol 4-stroke piston
1645cc 100.4cu in
In-line 4
Bore: 74.2mm 2.9in
Stroke: 95.0mm 3.7in
Valve type/No: Side 8
Transmission: Manual
No. of forward speeds: 4
Wheels driven: Rear
Brakes F/R: Drum/Drum
Ground clearance: 22.1cm 8.7in
Kerb weight: 1070.1kg 2357.0lb
Fuel: 27.3L 6.0gal 7.2galUS

642 British Salmson

Closed-coupled Saloon
1934 UK
70.3mph 113.1kmh
0-50mph 80.5kmh: 18.4secs
0-60mph 96.5kmh: 27.2secs
55.0bhp 41.0kW 55.8PS
@ 4500rpm
48.9bhp/ton 48.1bhp/tonne
37.4bhp/L 27.9kW/L 37.9PS/L
48.2ft/sec 14.7m/sec
28.0mpg 23.3mpgUS 10.1L/100km
Petrol 4-stroke piston
1470cc 89.7cu in
In-line 4 1 Carburettor
Compression ratio: 5.5:1
Bore: 69.0mm 2.7in
Stroke: 98.0mm 3.9in
Valve type/No: Overhead 8
Transmission: Manual
No. of forward speeds: 4
Wheels driven: Rear
Brakes F/R: Drum/Drum
Kerb weight: 1144.1kg 2520.0lb
Fuel: 45.5L 10.0gal 12.0galUS

643 British Salmson

12hp Four-seater Tourer
1936 UK
75.6mph 121.6kmh
0-50mph 80.5kmh: 17.0secs
0-60mph 96.5kmh: 31.0secs
30.0mpg 25.0mpgUS 9.4L/100km
Petrol 4-stroke piston
1480cc 90.3cu in
In-line 4
Bore: 69.0mm 2.7in
Stroke: 98.0mm 3.9in
Valve type/No: Overhead 8
Transmission: Manual
No. of forward speeds: 4
Wheels driven: Rear
Brakes F/R: Drum/Drum
Kerb weight: 1099.6kg 2422.0lb
Fuel: 45.5L 10.0gal 12.0galUS

644 British Salmson

20.8hp Sports Two-seater
1936 UK
88.2mph 141.9kmh
0-50mph 80.5kmh: 11.9secs
0-60mph 96.5kmh: 19.4secs
19.0mpg 15.8mpgUS 14.9L/100km
Petrol 4-stroke piston
2596cc 158.4cu in
In-line 6
Bore: 75.0mm 2.9in
Stroke: 98.0mm 3.9in
Valve type/No: Overhead 12
Transmission: Manual
No. of forward speeds: 4
Wheels driven: Rear
Brakes F/R: Drum/Drum
Kerb weight: 1342.5kg 2957.0lb
Fuel: 68.2L 15.0gal 18.0galUS

645 British Salmson

14hp Saloon
1937 UK
73.1mph 117.6kmh
0-50mph 80.5kmh: 23.1secs
0-60mph 96.5kmh: 38.5secs
65.0bhp 48.5kW 65.9PS
@ 4500rpm
49.7bhp/ton 48.8bhp/tonne
40.7bhp/L 30.4kW/L 41.3PS/L
48.2ft/sec 14.7m/sec
26.0mpg 21.6mpgUS 10.9L/100km
Petrol 4-stroke piston
1596cc 97.4cu in
In-line 4
Bore: 72.0mm 2.8in
Stroke: 98.0mm 3.9in
Valve type/No: Overhead 8
Transmission: Manual
No. of forward speeds: 4
Wheels driven: Rear
Brakes F/R: Drum/Drum
Kerb weight: 1331.1kg 2932.0lb
Fuel: 45.5L 10.0gal 12.0galUS

646 BSA

FWD Tourer
1932 UK
58.4mph 94.0kmh
38.0mpg 31.6mpgUS 7.4L/100km
Petrol 4-stroke piston
1074cc 65.5cu in
In-line 4 1 Carburettor
Bore: 60.0mm 2.4in
Stroke: 95.0mm 3.7in
Valve type/No: Side 8
Transmission: Manual
No. of forward speeds: 3
Wheels driven: Front
Brakes F/R: Drum/Drum
Wheelbase: 236.2cm 93.0in
Track F: 121.9cm 48.0in
Track R: 121.9cm 48.0in
Length: 378.5cm 149.0in
Width: 144.8cm 57.0in
Height: 149.9cm 59.0in
Kerb weight: 661.0kg 1456.0lb
Fuel: 29.6L 6.5gal 7.8galUS

647 BSA

Scout
1939 UK
65.0mph 104.6kmh
0-50mph 80.5kmh: 28.5secs
32.0bhp 23.9kW 32.4PS
@ 4250rpm
38.5bhp/ton 37.9bhp/tonne
26.6bhp/L 19.8kW/L 27.0PS/L
44.1ft/sec 13.5m/sec
31.0mpg 25.8mpgUS 9.1L/100km
Petrol 4-stroke piston
1203cc 73.4cu in
In-line 4 1 Carburettor
Compression ratio: 6.5:1
Bore: 63.5mm 2.5in
Stroke: 95.0mm 3.7in
Valve type/No: Side 8
Transmission: Manual
No. of forward speeds: 3
Wheels driven: Front
Brakes F/R: Drum/Drum
Kerb weight: 844.9kg 1861.0lb
Fuel: 50.0L 11.0gal 13.2galUS

648 Bugatti

50S
1926 France
121.0mph 194.7kmh
0-50mph 80.5kmh: 5.8secs
0-60mph 96.5kmh: 8.0secs
0-1/4 mile: 15.6secs
250.0bhp 186.4kW 253.5PS
@ 4500rpm
310.0lbft 420.1Nm @ 2800rpm
169.7bhp/ton 166.9bhp/tonne
51.6bhp/L 38.5kW/L 52.4PS/L
52.6ft/sec 16.0m/sec
26.9mph 43.3kmh/1000rpm
Petrol 4-stroke piston
4840cc 295.3cu in
In-line 8
Compression ratio: 7.5:1
Bore: 86.1mm 3.4in
Stroke: 106.9mm 4.2in
Valve type/No: Overhead 16
Transmission: Manual
No. of forward speeds: 3
Wheels driven: Rear
Wheelbase: 309.9cm 122.0in
Track F: 140.0cm 55.1in
Track R: 140.0cm 55.1in
Length: 416.6cm 164.0in
Width: 172.7cm 68.0in
Height: 157.5cm 62.0in
Kerb weight: 1498.2kg 3300.0lb

649 Bugatti

49
1930 France
81.0mph 130.3kmh
0-50mph 80.5kmh: 14.7secs
0-60mph 96.5kmh: 20.2secs
0-1/4 mile: 21.0secs
85.0bhp 63.4kW 86.2PS
@ 3600rpm
160.0lbft 216.8Nm @ 2000rpm
62.4bhp/ton 61.4bhp/tonne
26.1bhp/L 19.5kW/L 26.5PS/L
39.4ft/sec 12.0m/sec
20.2mph 32.5kmh/1000rpm
Petrol 4-stroke piston
3257cc 198.7cu in
In-line 8
Compression ratio: 5.5:1
Bore: 71.9mm 2.8in
Stroke: 100.1mm 3.9in
Valve type/No: Overhead 16
Transmission: Manual
No. of forward speeds: 4
Wheels driven: Rear
Wheelbase: 312.4cm 123.0in
Track F: 127.0cm 50.0in
Track R: 127.0cm 50.0in
Length: 419.1cm 165.0in
Width: 162.6cm 64.0in
Height: 157.5cm 62.0in
Kerb weight: 1384.7kg 3050.0lb

650 Bugatti

5-litre Saloon
1931 France
88.2mph 141.9kmh
12.0mpg 10.0mpgUS 23.5L/100km
Petrol 4-stroke piston
5350cc 326.4cu in
In-line 8
Bore: 81.0mm 3.2in
Stroke: 130.0mm 5.1in
Transmission: Manual
No. of forward speeds: 3
Wheels driven: Rear
Brakes F/R: Drum/Drum
Wheelbase: 350.5cm 138.0in
Track F: 139.7cm 55.0in
Track R: 139.7cm 55.0in
Length: 457.2cm 180.0in
Width: 174.0cm 68.5in
Height: 167.6cm 66.0in
Kerb weight: 1830.5kg 4032.0lb
Fuel: 104.6L 23.0gal 27.6galUS

651 Bugatti

55
1932 France
110.0mph 177.0kmh
0-60mph 96.5kmh: 17.3secs
135.0bhp 100.7kW 136.9PS
@ 5500rpm
114.3bhp/ton 112.4bhp/tonne
59.7bhp/L 44.5kW/L 60.5PS/L
60.2ft/sec 18.3m/sec
Petrol 4-stroke piston
2262cc 138.0cu in supercharged
In-line 8 1 Carburettor
Bore: 60.0mm 2.4in
Stroke: 100.0mm 3.9in
Valve type/No: Overhead 16
Transmission: Manual
No. of forward speeds: 4
Wheels driven: Rear
Springs F/R: Leaf/Leaf
Brakes F/R: Drum/Drum
Steering: Worm & sector
Wheelbase: 275.1cm 108.3in
Track F: 125.0cm 49.2in
Track R: 125.0cm 49.2in
Kerb weight: 1200.8kg 2645.0lb

652 Bugatti

EB110
1991 Italy
214.0mph 344.3kmh
0-60mph 96.5kmh: 3.9secs
600.0bhp 447.4kW 608.3PS
@ 9000rpm
419.0lbft 567.8Nm @ 4200rpm
454.8bhp/ton 447.2bhp/tonne
171.5bhp/L 127.9kW/L 173.9PS/L
55.7ft/sec 17.0m/sec
Petrol 4-stroke piston
3498cc 213.4cu in turbocharged
Vee 12 fuel injection
Compression ratio: 7.5:1
Bore: 81.0mm 3.2in
Stroke: 56.6mm 2.2in
Valve type/No: Overhead 48
Transmission: Manual
No. of forward speeds: 6
Wheels driven: 4-wheel drive
Brake system: ABS
Brakes F/R: Disc/Disc
Steering: Rack & pinion PA
Wheelbase: 255.0cm 100.4in
Track F: 153.9cm 60.6in
Track R: 153.9cm 60.6in
Length: 407.9cm 160.6in
Width: 198.9cm 78.3in
Height: 105.9cm 41.7in
Kerb weight: 1341.6kg 2955.0lb
Fuel: 120.0L 26.4gal 31.7galUS

653 Buick

Empire Saloon
1928 USA
70.0mph 112.6kmh
17.0mpg 14.2mpgUS 16.6L/100km
Petrol 4-stroke piston
3849cc 234.8cu in
In-line 6
Bore: 84.1mm 3.3in
Stroke: 117.5mm 4.6in
Transmission: Manual
No. of forward speeds: 3
Wheels driven: Rear
Brakes F/R: Drum/Drum
Wheelbase: 294.6cm 116.0in
Track F: 142.2cm 56.0in
Track R: 142.2cm 56.0in
Length: 416.6cm 164.0in
Width: 180.3cm 71.0in
Fuel: 61.4L 13.5gal 16.2galUS

654 Buick

28.4hp Saloon
1930 USA
67.1mph 108.0kmh
15.0mpg 12.5mpgUS 18.8L/100km
Petrol 4-stroke piston
4212cc 257.0cu in
In-line 6
Bore: 87.3mm 3.4in
Stroke: 117.5mm 4.6in
Transmission: Manual
No. of forward speeds: 3
Wheels driven: Rear
Brakes F/R: Drum/Drum
Wheelbase: 299.7cm 118.0in
Track F: 144.0cm 56.7in
Track R: 144.0cm 56.7in
Length: 447.0cm 176.0in
Width: 180.3cm 71.0in
Height: 182.9cm 72.0in
Kerb weight: 1697.0kg 3738.0lb
Fuel: 72.8L 16.0gal 19.2galUS

655 Buick

Light Eight Saloon
1930 USA
67.1mph 108.0kmh
17.0mpg 14.2mpgUS 16.6L/100km
Petrol 4-stroke piston
3616cc 220.6cu in
In-line 8
Bore: 73.0mm 2.9in
Stroke: 107.9mm 4.2in
Transmission: Manual
No. of forward speeds: 3
Wheels driven: Rear
Brakes F/R: Drum/Drum
Wheelbase: 289.6cm 114.0in
Track F: 143.5cm 56.5in
Track R: 143.5cm 56.5in
Length: 421.6cm 166.0in
Width: 177.8cm 70.0in
Height: 182.9cm 72.0in
Kerb weight: 1474.6kg 3248.0lb
Fuel: 61.4L 13.5gal 16.2galUS

656 Buick
Straight Eight Saloon
1933 USA
72.5mph 116.7kmh
0-50mph 80.5kmh: 18.8secs
0-60mph 96.5kmh: 26.8secs
17.0mpg 14.2mpgUS 16.6L/100km
Petrol 4-stroke piston
3777cc 230.4cu in
In-line 8
Bore: 74.6mm 2.9in
Stroke: 107.9mm 4.2in
Transmission: Manual
No. of forward speeds: 3
Wheels driven: Rear
Brakes F/R: Drum/Drum
Kerb weight: 1728.8kg 3808.0lb
Fuel: 59.1L 13.0gal 15.6galUS

657 Buick
Light Eight Viceroy Saloon
1935 USA
73.7mph 118.6kmh
0-50mph 80.5kmh: 16.8secs
0-60mph 96.5kmh: 25.0secs
15.0mpg 12.5mpgUS 18.8L/100km
Petrol 4-stroke piston
3854cc 235.1cu in
In-line 8
Bore: 75.4mm 3.0in
Stroke: 107.9mm 4.2in
Valve type/No: Overhead 16
Transmission: Manual
No. of forward speeds: 3
Wheels driven: Rear
Brakes F/R: Drum/Drum
Kerb weight: 1911.3kg 4210.0lb
Fuel: 59.1L 13.0gal 15.6galUS

658 Buick
Century Saloon
1936 USA
81.8mph 131.6kmh
0-50mph 80.5kmh: 11.6secs
0-60mph 96.5kmh: 16.4secs
12.0mpg 10.0mpgUS 23.5L/100km
Petrol 4-stroke piston
5247cc 320.1cu in
In-line 8
Bore: 87.3mm 3.4in
Stroke: 109.5mm 4.3in
Valve type/No: Overhead 16
Transmission: Manual
No. of forward speeds: 3
Wheels driven: Rear
Brakes F/R: Drum/Drum
Kerb weight: 1884.1kg 4150.0lb
Fuel: 60.5L 13.3gal 16.0galUS

659 Buick
Viceroy Saloon
1938 USA
84.9mph 136.6kmh
0-50mph 80.5kmh: 11.9secs
0-60mph 96.5kmh: 17.3secs
15.0mpg 12.5mpgUS 18.8L/100km
Petrol 4-stroke piston
4070cc 248.3cu in
In-line 8
Bore: 78.6mm 3.1in
Stroke: 104.8mm 4.1in
Valve type/No: Overhead 16
Transmission: Manual
No. of forward speeds: 3
Wheels driven: Rear
Brakes F/R: Drum/Drum
Kerb weight: 1735.2kg 3822.0lb
Fuel: 65.5L 14.4gal 17.3galUS

660 Buick
Roadmaster
1954 USA
100.0mph 160.9kmh
0-50mph 80.5kmh: 9.2secs
0-60mph 96.5kmh: 12.6secs
0-1/4 mile: 18.6secs
200.0bhp 149.1kW 202.8PS
@ 4100rpm
309.0lbft 418.7Nm @ 2400rpm
101.3bhp/ton 99.6bhp/tonne
36.2bhp/L 28.5kW/L 38.8PS/L
36.4ft/sec 11.1m/sec
16.0mpg 13.3mpgUS 17.7L/100km
Petrol 4-stroke piston
5230cc 319.1cu in
Vee 8
Compression ratio: 8.5:1
Bore: 101.6mm 4.0in
Stroke: 81.3mm 3.2in
Valve type/No: Overhead 16
Transmission: Automatic
No. of forward speeds: 2
Wheels driven: Rear
Springs F/R: Coil/Coil
Brakes F/R: Drum/Drum
Wheelbase: 322.6cm 127.0in
Track F: 149.9cm 59.0in
Track R: 158.0cm 62.2in
Length: 550.7cm 216.8in
Width: 202.9cm 79.9in
Height: 163.6cm 64.4in
Ground clearance: 16.5cm 6.5in
Kerb weight: 2008.5kg 4424.0lb
Fuel: 75.1L 16.5gal 19.8galUS

661 Buick
Special
1960 USA
105.0mph 168.9kmh
0-50mph 80.5kmh: 8.5secs
0-60mph 96.5kmh: 11.2secs
0-1/4 mile: 17.7secs
150.0bhp 111.9kW 152.1PS
@ 4400rpm
220.0lbft 298.1Nm @ 2400rpm
122.2bhp/ton 120.1bhp/tonne
42.5bhp/L 31.7kW/L 43.0PS/L
34.2ft/sec 10.4m/sec
21.0mph 33.8kmh/1000rpm
Petrol 4-stroke piston
3533cc 215.6cu in
Vee 8 1 Carburettor
Compression ratio: 8.8:1
Bore: 88.9mm 3.5in
Stroke: 71.1mm 2.8in
Valve type/No: Overhead 16
Transmission: Automatic
No. of forward speeds: 3
Wheels driven: Rear
Wheelbase: 284.5cm 112.0in
Track F: 142.2cm 56.0in
Track R: 142.2cm 56.0in
Length: 478.5cm 188.4in
Width: 181.1cm 71.3in
Height: 133.4cm 52.5in
Kerb weight: 1248.5kg 2750.0lb

662 Buick
Special
1961 USA
101.0mph 162.5kmh
0-50mph 80.5kmh: 9.6secs
0-60mph 96.5kmh: 12.9secs
0-1/4 mile: 19.2secs
155.0bhp 115.6kW 157.1PS
@ 4600rpm
220.0lbft 298.1Nm @ 2400rpm
124.8bhp/ton 122.8bhp/tonne
44.0bhp/L 32.8kW/L 44.6PS/L
35.6ft/sec 10.9m/sec
22.8mph 36.7kmh/1000rpm
17.5mpg 14.6mpgUS 16.1L/100km
Petrol 4-stroke piston
3523cc 214.9cu in
Vee 8
Compression ratio: 8.8:1
Bore: 88.9mm 3.5in
Stroke: 70.9mm 2.8in
Valve type/No: Overhead 16
Transmission: Automatic
No. of forward speeds: 2
Wheels driven: Rear
Springs F/R: Coil/Coil
Brakes F/R: Drum/Drum
Wheelbase: 284.5cm 112.0in
Track F: 142.2cm 56.0in
Track R: 142.2cm 56.0in
Length: 478.5cm 188.4in
Width: 181.1cm 71.3in
Height: 133.4cm 52.5in
Ground clearance: 12.4cm 4.9in
Kerb weight: 1262.6kg 2781.0lb
Fuel: 59.1L 13.0gal 15.6galUS

663 Buick
Invicta
1962 USA
115.0mph 185.0kmh
0-50mph 80.5kmh: 6.2secs
0-60mph 96.5kmh: 8.5secs
0-1/4 mile: 16.7secs
325.0bhp 242.3kW 329.5PS
@ 4400rpm
445.0lbft 603.0Nm @ 2800rpm
164.7bhp/ton 162.0bhp/tonne
49.4bhp/L 36.9kW/L 50.1PS/L
44.5ft/sec 13.6m/sec
25.1mph 40.4kmh/1000rpm
Petrol 4-stroke piston
6574cc 401.1cu in
Vee 8 1 Carburettor
Compression ratio: 10.3:1
Bore: 106.4mm 4.2in
Stroke: 92.5mm 3.6in
Valve type/No: Overhead 16
Transmission: Automatic
No. of forward speeds: 2
Wheels driven: Rear
Brake system: PA
Brakes F/R: Drum/Drum
Steering: PA
Wheelbase: 312.4cm 123.0in
Track F: 157.5cm 62.0in
Track R: 154.9cm 61.0in
Length: 543.8cm 214.1in
Width: 198.1cm 78.0in
Height: 143.0cm 56.3in
Ground clearance: 17.8cm 7.0in
Kerb weight: 2006.7kg 4420.0lb

664 Buick
Skylark
1962 USA
107.0mph 172.2kmh
0-50mph 80.5kmh: 7.5secs
0-60mph 96.5kmh: 10.2secs
0-1/4 mile: 17.9secs
190.0bhp 141.7kW 192.6PS
@ 4800rpm
235.0lbft 318.4Nm @ 3000rpm
142.8bhp/ton 140.4bhp/tonne
53.9bhp/L 40.2kW/L 54.7PS/L
37.3ft/sec 11.4m/sec
21.4mph 34.4kmh/1000rpm
Petrol 4-stroke piston
3524cc 215.0cu in
Vee 8
Compression ratio: 11.0:1
Bore: 88.9mm 3.5in
Stroke: 71.1mm 2.8in
Valve type/No: Overhead 16
Transmission: Manual
No. of forward speeds: 4
Wheels driven: Rear
Wheelbase: 284.5cm 112.0in
Track F: 142.2cm 56.0in
Track R: 142.2cm 56.0in
Length: 478.5cm 188.4in
Width: 181.1cm 71.3in
Height: 132.3cm 52.1in
Ground clearance: 12.2cm 4.8in
Kerb weight: 1352.9kg 2980.0lb

665 Buick
Skylark Automatic
1962 USA
105.0mph 168.9kmh
0-50mph 80.5kmh: 8.3secs
0-60mph 96.5kmh: 10.7secs
0-1/4 mile: 17.8secs
190.0bhp 141.7kW 192.6PS
@ 4800rpm
235.0lbft 318.4Nm @ 3000rpm
150.4bhp/ton 147.9bhp/tonne
53.8bhp/L 40.1kW/L 54.6PS/L
37.3ft/sec 11.4m/sec
21.0mph 33.8kmh/1000rpm
Petrol 4-stroke piston
3531cc 215.4cu in
Vee 8
Compression ratio: 11.0:1
Bore: 88.9mm 3.5in
Stroke: 71.1mm 2.8in
Valve type/No: Overhead 16
Transmission: Automatic
No. of forward speeds: 2
Wheels driven: Rear
Brake system: PA
Steering: PA
Wheelbase: 284.5cm 112.0in
Track F: 142.2cm 56.0in
Track R: 142.2cm 56.0in
Length: 478.5cm 188.4in
Width: 181.1cm 71.3in
Height: 132.3cm 52.1in
Ground clearance: 12.2cm 4.8in
Kerb weight: 1284.8kg 2830.0lb
Fuel: 60.6L 13.3gal 16.0galUS

666 Buick
Special V6
1962 USA
95.0mph 152.9kmh
0-50mph 80.5kmh: 11.0secs
0-60mph 96.5kmh: 14.8secs
0-1/4 mile: 19.7secs
135.0bhp 100.7kW 136.9PS
@ 4600rpm
205.0lbft 277.8Nm @ 2400rpm
108.0bhp/ton 106.2bhp/tonne
41.6bhp/L 31.0kW/L 42.1PS/L
40.9ft/sec 12.5m/sec
22.9mph 36.8kmh/1000rpm
Petrol 4-stroke piston
3248cc 198.2cu in
Vee 6 1 Carburettor
Compression ratio: 8.8:1
Bore: 92.2mm 3.6in
Stroke: 81.3mm 3.2in
Valve type/No: Overhead 12
Transmission: Automatic
No. of forward speeds: 2
Wheels driven: Rear
Brakes F/R: Drum/Drum
Wheelbase: 284.5cm 112.0in
Track F: 142.2cm 56.0in
Track R: 142.2cm 56.0in
Length: 478.5cm 188.4in
Width: 181.1cm 71.3in
Height: 134.1cm 52.8in
Ground clearance: 12.4cm 4.9in
Kerb weight: 1271.2kg 2800.0lb
Fuel: 60.6L 13.3gal 16.0galUS

667 Buick
Wildcat
1962 USA
113.0mph 181.8kmh
0-50mph 80.5kmh: 6.8secs
0-60mph 96.5kmh: 8.9secs
0-1/4 mile: 17.0secs
325.0bhp 242.3kW 329.5PS
@ 4400rpm
445.0lbft 603.0Nm @ 2800rpm
167.0bhp/ton 164.2bhp/tonne
49.5bhp/L 36.9kW/L 50.1PS/L
44.5ft/sec 13.6m/sec
25.6mph 41.2kmh/1000rpm
Petrol 4-stroke piston
6571cc 400.9cu in
Vee 8 1 Carburettor
Compression ratio: 10.3:1
Bore: 106.4mm 4.2in
Stroke: 92.5mm 3.6in
Valve type/No: Overhead 16
Transmission: Automatic
No. of forward speeds: 2
Wheels driven: Rear
Brake system: PA
Steering: PA
Wheelbase: 312.4cm 123.0in
Track F: 157.5cm 62.0in
Track R: 154.9cm 61.0in
Length: 543.8cm 214.1in
Width: 198.1cm 78.0in
Height: 143.0cm 56.3in
Ground clearance: 13.2cm 5.2in
Kerb weight: 1979.4kg 4360.0lb
Fuel: 75.7L 16.6gal 20.0galUS

668 Buick
Riviera
1963 USA
123.0mph 197.9kmh
0-50mph 80.5kmh: 5.8secs
0-60mph 96.5kmh: 7.7secs
0-1/4 mile: 16.2secs
340.0bhp 253.5kW 344.7PS
@ 4400rpm
465.0lbft 630.1Nm @ 2800rpm
181.8bhp/ton 178.7bhp/tonne
48.8bhp/L 36.4kW/L 49.5PS/L
44.5ft/sec 13.6m/sec
24.9mph 40.1kmh/1000rpm
Petrol 4-stroke piston
6965cc 424.9cu in
Vee 8 1 Carburettor
Compression ratio: 10.3:1
Bore: 109.5mm 4.3in
Stroke: 92.5mm 3.6in
Valve type/No: Overhead 16
Transmission: Automatic

No. of forward speeds: 2
Wheels driven: Rear
Brake system: PA
Steering: PA
Wheelbase: 297.2cm 117.0in
Track F: 152.4cm 60.0in
Track R: 149.9cm 59.0in
Length: 528.3cm 208.0in
Width: 194.6cm 76.6in
Height: 134.6cm 53.0in
Ground clearance: 14.0cm 5.5in
Kerb weight: 1902.3kg 4190.0lb
Fuel: 75.7L 16.6gal 20.0galUS

669 Buick
Electra 225
1964 USA
120.0mph 193.1kmh
0-50mph 80.5kmh: 6.6secs
0-60mph 96.5kmh: 9.2secs
0-1/4 mile: 17.0secs
325.0bhp 242.3kW 329.5PS
@ 4400rpm
445.0lbft 603.0Nm @ 2800rpm
170.7bhp/ton 167.8bhp/tonne
49.5bhp/L 36.9kW/L 50.1PS/L
44.5ft/sec 13.6m/sec
25.6mph 41.2kmh/1000rpm
Petrol 4-stroke piston
6571cc 400.9cu in
Vee 8 1 Carburettor
Compression ratio: 10.3:1
Bore: 106.3mm 4.2in
Stroke: 92.5mm 3.6in
Valve type/No: Overhead 16
Transmission: Automatic
No. of forward speeds: 3
Wheels driven: Rear
Wheelbase: 320.0cm 126.0in
Track F: 157.5cm 62.0in
Track R: 154.9cm 61.0in
Length: 565.9cm 222.8in
Width: 198.1cm 78.0in
Height: 144.8cm 57.0in
Ground clearance: 15.5cm 6.1in
Kerb weight: 1936.3kg 4265.0lb
Fuel: 75.7L 16.6gal 20.0galUS

670 Buick
Skylark Sports Wagon
1964 USA
99.0mph 159.3kmh
0-50mph 80.5kmh: 7.6secs
0-60mph 96.5kmh: 10.0secs
0-1/4 mile: 17.1secs
250.0bhp 186.4kW 253.5PS
@ 4800rpm
335.0lbft 453.9Nm @ 3000rpm
141.2bhp/ton 138.9bhp/tonne
50.8bhp/L 37.9kW/L 51.6PS/L
45.3ft/sec 13.8m/sec
24.7mph 39.7kmh/1000rpm
Petrol 4-stroke piston
4916cc 299.9cu in
Vee 8 1 Carburettor
Compression ratio: 11.0:1
Bore: 95.3mm 3.8in
Stroke: 86.4mm 3.4in
Valve type/No: Overhead 16
Transmission: Automatic
No. of forward speeds: 2
Wheels driven: Rear
Brake system: PA
Steering: PA
Wheelbase: 304.8cm 120.0in
Track F: 147.3cm 58.0in
Track R: 147.3cm 58.0in
Length: 528.8cm 208.2in
Width: 186.9cm 73.6in
Height: 148.1cm 58.3in
Ground clearance: 15.2cm 6.0in
Kerb weight: 1800.1kg 3965.0lb
Fuel: 75.7L 16.6gal 20.0galUS

671 Buick
Special
1964 USA
93.0mph 149.6kmh
0-50mph 80.5kmh: 12.0secs
0-60mph 96.5kmh: 16.9secs
0-1/4 mile: 20.5secs
155.0bhp 115.6kW 157.1PS
@ 4400rpm
225.0lbft 304.9Nm @ 2400rpm
110.2bhp/ton 108.4bhp/tonne
42.0bhp/L 31.3kW/L 42.6PS/L
41.6ft/sec 12.7m/sec
22.6mph 36.4kmh/1000rpm
Petrol 4-stroke piston
3687cc 224.9cu in
Vee 6 1 Carburettor
Compression ratio: 9.0:1
Bore: 95.3mm 3.8in
Stroke: 86.4mm 3.4in
Valve type/No: Overhead 12
Transmission: Manual
No. of forward speeds: 3
Wheels driven: Rear
Brake system: PA
Steering: PA
Wheelbase: 292.1cm 115.0in
Track F: 147.3cm 58.0in
Track R: 147.3cm 58.0in
Length: 516.9cm 203.5in
Width: 186.4cm 73.4in
Height: 138.2cm 54.4in
Ground clearance: 14.7cm 5.8in
Kerb weight: 1430.1kg 3150.0lb
Fuel: 75.7L 16.6gal 20.0galUS

672 Buick
Wildcat
1964 USA
115.0mph 185.0kmh
0-50mph 80.5kmh: 5.7secs
0-60mph 96.5kmh: 7.7secs
0-1/4 mile: 16.0secs
360.0bhp 268.4kW 365.0PS
@ 4400rpm
465.0lbft 630.1Nm @ 2800rpm
182.4bhp/ton 179.4bhp/tonne
51.7bhp/L 38.5kW/L 52.4PS/L
44.5ft/sec 13.6m/sec
20.7mph 33.3kmh/1000rpm
Petrol 4-stroke piston
6965cc 424.9cu in
Vee 8 2 Carburettor
Compression ratio: 10.3:1
Bore: 109.5mm 4.3in
Stroke: 92.5mm 3.6in
Valve type/No: Overhead 16
Transmission: Manual
No. of forward speeds: 4
Wheels driven: Rear
Brake system: PA
Steering: PA
Wheelbase: 312.4cm 123.0in
Track F: 157.5cm 62.0in
Track R: 154.9cm 61.0in
Length: 555.8cm 218.8in
Width: 198.1cm 78.0in
Height: 141.2cm 55.6in
Ground clearance: 14.7cm 5.8in
Kerb weight: 2006.7kg 4420.0lb
Fuel: 75.7L 16.6gal 20.0galUS

673 Buick
LeSabre 400
1965 USA
106.0mph 170.6kmh
0-50mph 80.5kmh: 6.6secs
0-60mph 96.5kmh: 9.2secs
0-1/4 mile: 17.1secs
250.0bhp 186.4kW 253.5PS
@ 4800rpm
335.0lbft 453.9Nm @ 3000rpm
134.0bhp/ton 131.7bhp/tonne
50.8bhp/L 37.9kW/L 51.6PS/L
45.3ft/sec 13.8m/sec
26.1mph 42.0kmh/1000rpm
Petrol 4-stroke piston
4916cc 299.9cu in
Vee 8 1 Carburettor
Compression ratio: 11.0:1
Bore: 95.3mm 3.8in
Stroke: 86.4mm 3.4in
Valve type/No: Overhead 16
Transmission: Automatic
No. of forward speeds: 3
Wheels driven: Rear
Brake system: PA
Steering: PA
Wheelbase: 312.4cm 123.0in
Track F: 160.0cm 63.0in
Track R: 160.0cm 63.0in
Length: 550.9cm 216.9in
Width: 203.2cm 80.0in
Height: 140.2cm 55.2in
Ground clearance: 14.2cm 5.6in
Kerb weight: 1897.7kg 4180.0lb
Fuel: 94.6L 20.8gal 25.0galUS

674 Buick
Riviera
1965 USA
122.0mph 196.3kmh
0-50mph 80.5kmh: 5.5secs
0-60mph 96.5kmh: 7.4secs
0-1/4 mile: 15.5secs
360.0bhp 268.4kW 365.0PS
@ 4400rpm
465.0lbft 630.1Nm @ 2800rpm
184.6bhp/ton 181.5bhp/tonne
51.8bhp/L 38.6kW/L 52.5PS/L
44.5ft/sec 13.6m/sec
23.8mph 38.3kmh/1000rpm
10.8mpg 9.0mpgUS 26.2L/100km
Petrol 4-stroke piston
6949cc 424.0cu in
Vee 8 2 Carburettor
Compression ratio: 10.2:1
Bore: 109.5mm 4.3in
Stroke: 92.5mm 3.6in
Valve type/No: Overhead 16
Transmission: Automatic
No. of forward speeds: 3
Wheels driven: Rear
Springs F/R: Coil/Coil
Brake system: PA
Brakes F/R: Drum/Drum
Steering: Recirculating ball PA
Wheelbase: 297.2cm 117.0in
Track F: 152.4cm 60.0in
Track R: 149.9cm 59.0in
Length: 533.4cm 210.0in
Width: 193.0cm 76.0in
Height: 139.7cm 55.0in
Ground clearance: 15.2cm 6.0in
Kerb weight: 1983.5kg 4369.0lb
Fuel: 75.5L 16.6gal 19.9galUS

675 Buick
Skylark
1965 USA
106.0mph 170.6kmh
0-50mph 80.5kmh: 7.7secs
0-60mph 96.5kmh: 9.9secs
0-1/4 mile: 17.4secs
250.0bhp 186.4kW 253.5PS
@ 4800rpm
335.0lbft 453.9Nm @ 3000rpm
158.2bhp/ton 155.5bhp/tonne
50.8bhp/L 37.9kW/L 51.6PS/L
45.3ft/sec 13.8m/sec
25.2mph 40.5kmh/1000rpm
Petrol 4-stroke piston
4916cc 299.9cu in
Vee 8 1 Carburettor
Compression ratio: 11.0:1
Bore: 95.3mm 3.8in
Stroke: 86.4mm 3.4in
Valve type/No: Overhead 16
Transmission: Automatic
No. of forward speeds: 2
Wheels driven: Rear
Brake system: PA
Steering: PA
Wheelbase: 292.1cm 115.0in
Track F: 147.3cm 58.0in
Track R: 147.3cm 58.0in
Length: 516.6cm 203.4in
Width: 187.7cm 73.9in
Height: 137.2cm 54.0in
Ground clearance: 13.7cm 5.4in
Kerb weight: 1607.2kg 3540.0lb
Fuel: 75.7L 16.6gal 20.0galUS

676 Buick
Skylark Gran Sport
1965 USA
121.0mph 194.7kmh
0-50mph 80.5kmh: 5.6secs
0-60mph 96.5kmh: 7.4secs
0-1/4 mile: 15.3secs
325.0bhp 242.3kW 329.5PS
@ 4400rpm
445.0lbft 603.0Nm @ 2800rpm
196.8bhp/ton 193.5bhp/tonne
49.5bhp/L 36.9kW/L 50.1PS/L
44.5ft/sec 13.6m/sec
24.1mph 38.8kmh/1000rpm
Petrol 4-stroke piston
6571cc 400.9cu in
Vee 8 1 Carburettor
Compression ratio: 10.3:1
Bore: 106.4mm 4.2in
Stroke: 92.5mm 3.6in
Valve type/No: Overhead 16
Transmission: Automatic
No. of forward speeds: 2
Wheels driven: Rear
Brake system: PA
Brakes F/R: Drum/Drum
Steering: PA
Wheelbase: 292.1cm 115.0in
Track F: 147.3cm 58.0in
Track R: 147.3cm 58.0in
Length: 516.6cm 203.4in
Width: 187.7cm 73.9in
Height: 137.2cm 54.0in
Ground clearance: 13.7cm 5.4in
Kerb weight: 1679.8kg 3700.0lb
Fuel: 75.7L 16.6gal 20.0galUS

677 Buick
Riviera Gran Sport
1966 USA
120.0mph 193.1kmh
0-50mph 80.5kmh: 5.9secs
0-60mph 96.5kmh: 8.2secs
0-1/4 mile: 16.7secs
360.0bhp 268.4kW 365.0PS
@ 4400rpm
465.0lbft 630.1Nm @ 2800rpm
184.3bhp/ton 181.2bhp/tonne
51.7bhp/L 38.5kW/L 52.4PS/L
44.5ft/sec 13.6m/sec
23.6mph 38.0kmh/1000rpm
Petrol 4-stroke piston
6965cc 424.9cu in
Vee 8 2 Carburettor
Compression ratio: 10.3:1
Bore: 109.6mm 4.3in
Stroke: 92.5mm 3.6in
Valve type/No: Overhead 16
Transmission: Automatic
No. of forward speeds: 3
Wheels driven: Rear
Springs F/R: Coil/Coil
Brake system: PA
Brakes F/R: Drum/Drum
Steering: Recirculating ball PA
Wheelbase: 302.3cm 119.0in
Track F: 161.3cm 63.5in
Track R: 160.0cm 63.0in
Length: 536.4cm 211.2in
Width: 200.2cm 78.8in
Height: 135.6cm 53.4in
Ground clearance: 15.2cm 6.0in
Kerb weight: 1986.2kg 4375.0lb
Fuel: 83.3L 18.3gal 22.0galUS

678 Buick
California GS
1967 USA
105.0mph 168.9kmh
0-50mph 80.5kmh: 7.1secs
0-60mph 96.5kmh: 9.3secs
0-1/4 mile: 16.7secs
260.0bhp 193.9kW 263.6PS
@ 4200rpm
365.0lbft 494.6Nm @ 2800rpm
178.9bhp/ton 175.9bhp/tonne
46.6bhp/L 34.8kW/L 47.3PS/L
44.9ft/sec 13.7m/sec
26.2mph 42.2kmh/1000rpm
Petrol 4-stroke piston
5574cc 340.1cu in
Vee 8 1 Carburettor
Compression ratio: 10.3:1
Bore: 95.3mm 3.8in
Stroke: 97.8mm 3.8in
Valve type/No: Overhead 16
Transmission: Automatic
No. of forward speeds: 2
Wheels driven: Rear
Springs F/R: Coil/Coil
Brakes F/R: Drum/Drum
Steering: Recirculating ball
Wheelbase: 292.1cm 115.0in
Track F: 147.3cm 58.0in
Track R: 149.9cm 59.0in
Length: 520.7cm 205.0in
Width: 191.5cm 75.4in
Height: 137.4cm 54.1in
Ground clearance: 16.0cm 6.3in
Kerb weight: 1477.8kg 3255.0lb
Fuel: 75.7L 16.6gal 20.0galUS

679 Buick
GS400
1967 USA
110.0mph 177.0kmh
0-50mph 80.5kmh: 4.8secs
0-60mph 96.5kmh: 6.0secs

0-1/4 mile: 14.7secs
340.0bhp 253.5kW 344.7PS
@ 5000rpm
440.0lbft 596.2Nm @ 3200rpm
202.3bhp/ton 198.9bhp/tonne
51.9bhp/L 38.7kW/L 52.6PS/L
54.2ft/sec 16.5m/sec
19.5mph 31.4kmh/1000rpm
Petrol 4-stroke piston
6551cc 399.7cu in
Vee 8 1 Carburettor
Compression ratio: 10.3:1
Bore: 102.6mm 4.0in
Stroke: 99.1mm 3.9in
Valve type/No: Overhead 16
Transmission: Automatic
No. of forward speeds: 3
Wheels driven: Rear
Springs F/R: Coil/Coil
Brake system: PA
Brakes F/R: Disc/Drum
Steering: Recirculating ball PA
Wheelbase: 292.1cm 115.0in
Track F: 147.3cm 58.0in
Track R: 149.9cm 59.0in
Length: 520.7cm 205.0in
Width: 191.5cm 75.4in
Height: 134.9cm 53.1in
Ground clearance: 17.5cm 6.9in
Kerb weight: 1709.3kg 3765.0lb
Fuel: 75.7L 16.6gal 20.0galUS

680 Buick

Wildcat
1967 USA
125.0mph 201.1kmh
0-50mph 80.5kmh: 6.0secs
0-60mph 96.5kmh: 8.4secs
0-1/4 mile: 15.8secs
360.0bhp 268.4kW 365.0PS
@ 5000rpm
475.0lbft 643.6Nm @ 3200rpm
179.6bhp/ton 176.6bhp/tonne
51.1bhp/L 38.1kW/L 51.8PS/L
54.2ft/sec 16.5m/sec
26.9mph 43.3kmh/1000rpm
Petrol 4-stroke piston
7041cc 429.6cu in
Vee 8 1 Carburettor
Compression ratio: 10.3:1
Bore: 106.4mm 4.2in
Stroke: 99.1mm 3.9in
Valve type/No: Overhead 16
Transmission: Automatic
No. of forward speeds: 3
Wheels driven: Rear
Springs F/R: Coil/Coil
Brake system: PA
Brakes F/R: Drum/Drum
Steering: Recirculating ball PA
Wheelbase: 320.0cm 126.0in
Track F: 161.0cm 63.4in
Track R: 160.0cm 63.0in
Length: 560.1cm 220.5in
Width: 203.2cm 80.0in
Height: 141.5cm 55.7in
Ground clearance: 18.0cm 7.1in
Kerb weight: 2038.5kg 4490.0lb
Fuel: 94.6L 20.8gal 25.0galUS

681 Buick

GS400
1968 USA
110.0mph 177.0kmh
0-50mph 80.5kmh: 5.0secs
0-60mph 96.5kmh: 6.1secs
0-1/4 mile: 14.4secs
345.0bhp 257.3kW 349.8PS
@ 4800rpm
440.0lbft 596.2Nm @ 3200rpm
211.8bhp/ton 208.3bhp/tonne
52.6bhp/L 39.2kW/L 53.4PS/L
52.0ft/sec 15.9m/sec
19.0mph 30.6kmh/1000rpm
Petrol 4-stroke piston
6554cc 399.9cu in
Vee 8 1 Carburettor
Compression ratio: 11.0:1
Bore: 102.6mm 4.0in
Stroke: 99.1mm 3.9in
Valve type/No: Overhead 16
Transmission: Automatic
No. of forward speeds: 3
Wheels driven: Rear
Springs F/R: Coil/Coil
Brakes F/R: Drum/Drum
Steering: Recirculating ball
Wheelbase: 284.5cm 112.0in
Track F: 150.9cm 59.4in
Track R: 149.9cm 59.0in
Length: 509.8cm 200.7in
Width: 192.0cm 75.6in
Height: 134.6cm 53.0in
Ground clearance: 15.5cm 6.1in
Kerb weight: 1656.2kg 3648.0lb
Fuel: 75.7L 16.6gal 20.0galUS

682 Buick

Riviera
1968 USA
118.0mph 189.9kmh
0-50mph 80.5kmh: 8.5secs
0-60mph 96.5kmh: 10.7secs
0-1/4 mile: 16.5secs
360.0bhp 268.4kW 365.0PS
@ 5000rpm
475.0lbft 643.6Nm @ 3200rpm
177.2bhp/ton 174.3bhp/tonne
51.1bhp/L 38.1kW/L 51.8PS/L
54.2ft/sec 16.5m/sec
26.5mph 42.6kmh/1000rpm
Petrol 4-stroke piston
7041cc 429.6cu in
Vee 8 1 Carburettor
Compression ratio: 10.3:1
Bore: 106.4mm 4.2in
Stroke: 99.1mm 3.9in
Valve type/No: Overhead 16
Transmission: Automatic
No. of forward speeds: 3
Wheels driven: Rear
Springs F/R: Coil/Coil
Brake system: PA
Brakes F/R: Disc/Drum
Steering: Recirculating ball PA
Wheelbase: 302.3cm 119.0in
Track F: 161.0cm 63.4in
Track R: 162.6cm 64.0in
Length: 546.6cm 215.2in
Width: 200.2cm 78.8in
Height: 135.6cm 53.4in
Ground clearance: 14.0cm 5.5in
Kerb weight: 2065.7kg 4550.0lb
Fuel: 79.5L 17.5gal 21.0galUS

683 Buick

Riviera
1969 USA
124.0mph 199.5kmh
0-50mph 80.5kmh: 7.4secs
0-60mph 96.5kmh: 10.0secs
0-1/4 mile: 16.5secs
360.0bhp 268.4kW 365.0PS
@ 5000rpm
475.0lbft 643.6Nm @ 3200rpm
174.9bhp/ton 172.0bhp/tonne
51.1bhp/L 38.1kW/L 51.8PS/L
54.2ft/sec 16.5m/sec
26.2mph 42.2kmh/1000rpm
Petrol 4-stroke piston
7046cc 429.9cu in
Vee 8 1 Carburettor
Compression ratio: 10.3:1
Bore: 106.4mm 4.2in
Stroke: 99.0mm 3.9in
Valve type/No: Overhead 16
Transmission: Automatic
No. of forward speeds: 3
Wheels driven: Rear
Springs F/R: Coil/Coil
Brake system: PA
Brakes F/R: Disc/Drum
Steering: Recirculating ball PA
Wheelbase: 302.3cm 119.0in
Track F: 161.0cm 63.4in
Track R: 160.0cm 63.0in
Length: 546.6cm 215.2in
Width: 201.2cm 79.2in
Height: 135.1cm 53.2in
Kerb weight: 2092.9kg 4610.0lb
Fuel: 79.5L 17.5gal 21.0galUS

684 Buick

Skylark
1969 USA
109.0mph 175.4kmh
0-50mph 80.5kmh: 9.5secs
0-60mph 96.5kmh: 11.6secs
0-1/4 mile: 17.8secs
230.0bhp 171.5kW 233.2PS
@ 4400rpm
350.0lbft 474.3Nm @ 2400rpm
143.9bhp/ton 141.5bhp/tonne
40.1bhp/L 29.9kW/L 40.7PS/L
47.1ft/sec 14.3m/sec
30.2mph 48.6kmh/1000rpm
Petrol 4-stroke piston
5735cc 349.9cu in
Vee 8 1 Carburettor
Compression ratio: 9.0:1
Bore: 96.5mm 3.8in
Stroke: 97.8mm 3.8in
Valve type/No: Overhead 16
Transmission: Automatic
No. of forward speeds: 2
Wheels driven: Rear
Springs F/R: Coil/Coil
Brake system: PA
Brakes F/R: Drum/Drum
Steering: Recirculating ball PA
Wheelbase: 284.5cm 112.0in
Track F: 149.9cm 59.0in
Track R: 149.9cm 59.0in
Length: 509.8cm 200.7in
Width: 192.0cm 75.6in
Height: 135.6cm 53.4in
Kerb weight: 1625.3kg 3580.0lb
Fuel: 75.7L 16.6gal 20.0galUS

685 Buick

Sportswagon
1969 USA
113.0mph 181.8kmh
0-50mph 80.5kmh: 6.5secs
0-60mph 96.5kmh: 9.0secs
0-1/4 mile: 17.1secs
340.0bhp 253.5kW 344.7PS
@ 5000rpm
440.0lbft 596.2Nm @ 3200rpm
164.0bhp/ton 161.2bhp/tonne
51.9bhp/L 38.7kW/L 52.6PS/L
54.2ft/sec 16.5m/sec
24.1mph 38.8kmh/1000rpm
Petrol 4-stroke piston
6555cc 399.9cu in
Vee 8 1 Carburettor
Compression ratio: 10.3:1
Bore: 102.6mm 4.0in
Stroke: 99.1mm 3.9in
Valve type/No: Overhead 16
Transmission: Automatic
No. of forward speeds: 3
Wheels driven: Rear
Springs F/R: Coil/Coil
Brake system: PA
Brakes F/R: Drum/Drum
Steering: Recirculating ball PA
Wheelbase: 307.3cm 121.0in
Track F: 150.9cm 59.4in
Track R: 150.9cm 59.4in
Length: 543.8cm 214.1in
Width: 192.0cm 75.6in
Height: 149.6cm 58.9in
Kerb weight: 2108.8kg 4645.0lb
Fuel: 75.7L 16.6gal 20.0galUS

686 Buick

Wildcat
1969 USA
122.0mph 196.3kmh
0-50mph 80.5kmh: 6.5secs
0-60mph 96.5kmh: 9.9secs
0-1/4 mile: 16.5secs
360.0bhp 268.4kW 365.0PS
@ 5000rpm
475.0lbft 643.6Nm @ 3200rpm
193.4bhp/ton 190.2bhp/tonne
51.1bhp/L 38.1kW/L 51.8PS/L
54.2ft/sec 16.5m/sec
26.4mph 42.5kmh/1000rpm
Petrol 4-stroke piston
7046cc 429.9cu in
Vee 8 1 Carburettor
Compression ratio: 10.3:1
Bore: 106.4mm 4.2in
Stroke: 99.1mm 3.9in
Valve type/No: Overhead 16
Transmission: Automatic
No. of forward speeds: 3
Wheels driven: Rear
Springs F/R: Coil/Coil
Brake system: PA
Brakes F/R: Disc/Drum
Steering: Recirculating ball PA
Wheelbase: 312.4cm 123.0in
Track F: 162.6cm 64.0in
Track R: 160.0cm 63.0in
Length: 553.7cm 218.0in
Width: 203.2cm 80.0in
Height: 139.7cm 55.0in
Kerb weight: 1893.2kg 4170.0lb
Fuel: 94.6L 20.8gal 25.0galUS

687 Buick

GS455 Stage 1
1970 USA
129.5mph 208.4kmh
0-50mph 80.5kmh: 5.0secs
0-60mph 96.5kmh: 6.5secs
0-1/4 mile: 14.6secs
360.0bhp 268.4kW 365.0PS
@ 4600rpm
510.0lbft 691.1Nm @ 2800rpm
204.1bhp/ton 200.7bhp/tonne
48.3bhp/L 36.0kW/L 48.9PS/L
49.8ft/sec 15.2m/sec
19.8mph 31.9kmh/1000rpm
Petrol 4-stroke piston
7456cc 454.9cu in
Vee 8 1 Carburettor
Compression ratio: 10.0:1
Bore: 109.5mm 4.3in
Stroke: 99.1mm 3.9in
Valve type/No: Overhead 16
Transmission: Automatic
No. of forward speeds: 3
Wheels driven: Rear
Springs F/R: Coil/Coil
Brake system: PA
Brakes F/R: Drum/Drum
Steering: Recirculating ball PA
Wheelbase: 284.5cm 112.0in
Track F: 150.9cm 59.4in
Track R: 149.9cm 59.0in
Length: 509.8cm 200.7in
Width: 192.0cm 75.6in
Height: 134.6cm 53.0in
Kerb weight: 1793.3kg 3950.0lb
Fuel: 75.7L 16.6gal 20.0galUS

688 Buick

Skylark
1975 USA
101.0mph 162.5kmh
0-50mph 80.5kmh: 10.4secs
0-60mph 96.5kmh: 14.2secs
0-1/4 mile: 19.7secs
110.0bhp 82.0kW 111.5PS
@ 4000rpm
175.0lbft 237.1Nm @ 2000rpm
79.5bhp/ton 78.2bhp/tonne
29.0bhp/L 21.7kW/L 29.5PS/L
37.8ft/sec 11.5m/sec
25.3mph 40.7kmh/1000rpm
25.2mpg 21.0mpgUS 11.2L/100km
Petrol 4-stroke piston
3786cc 231.0cu in
Vee 6
Compression ratio: 8.0:1
Bore: 96.5mm 3.8in
Stroke: 86.4mm 3.4in
Valve type/No: Overhead 12
Transmission: Automatic
No. of forward speeds: 3
Wheels driven: Rear
Springs F/R: Coil/Coil
Brake system: PA
Brakes F/R: Disc/Drum
Steering: Recirculating ball PA
Wheelbase: 246.4cm 97.0in
Track F: 138.9cm 54.7in
Track R: 136.1cm 53.6in
Length: 455.4cm 179.3in
Width: 166.1cm 65.4in
Height: 127.5cm 50.2in
Kerb weight: 1407.4kg 3100.0lb
Fuel: 70.0L 15.4gal 18.5galUS

689 Buick

Opel by Isuzu
1976 Japan
98.0mph 157.7kmh
0-50mph 80.5kmh: 9.2secs
0-60mph 96.5kmh: 13.2secs
0-1/4 mile: 18.8secs
80.0bhp 59.7kW 81.1PS
@ 4800rpm
95.0lbft 128.7Nm @ 3000rpm
83.3bhp/ton 82.0bhp/tonne
44.0bhp/L 32.8kW/L 44.7PS/L
43.1ft/sec 13.1m/sec
18.6mph 29.9kmh/1000rpm
33.0mpg 27.5mpgUS 8.6L/100km
Petrol 4-stroke piston
1816cc 110.8cu in
In-line 4 1 Carburettor

Compression ratio: 8.5:1
Bore: 84.0mm 3.3in
Stroke: 82.0mm 3.2in
Valve type/No: Overhead 8
Transmission: Manual
No. of forward speeds: 4
Wheels driven: Rear
Springs F/R: Coil/Coil
Brake system: PA
Brakes F/R: Disc/Drum
Steering: Rack & pinion
Wheelbase: 239.5cm 94.3in
Track F: 130.6cm 51.4in
Track R: 130.6cm 51.4in
Length: 426.7cm 168.0in
Width: 157.0cm 61.8in
Height: 129.0cm 50.8in
Ground clearance: 10.9cm 4.3in
Kerb weight: 976.1kg 2150.0lb
Fuel: 51.8L 11.4gal 13.7galUS

690 Buick

Skyhawk
1976 USA
101.0mph 162.5kmh
0-50mph 80.5kmh: 10.4secs
0-60mph 96.5kmh: 14.2secs
0-1/4 mile: 19.7secs
110.0bhp 82.0kW 111.5PS
@ 4000rpm
175.0lbft 237.1Nm @ 2000rpm
79.5bhp/ton 78.2bhp/tonne
29.0bhp/L 21.7kW/L 29.5PS/L
37.8ft/sec 11.5m/sec
25.3mph 40.7kmh/1000rpm
25.2mpg 21.0mpgUS 11.2L/100km
Petrol 4-stroke piston
3786cc 231.0cu in
Vee 6
Compression ratio: 8.0:1
Bore: 96.5mm 3.8in
Stroke: 86.4mm 3.4in
Valve type/No: Overhead 12
Transmission: Automatic
No. of forward speeds: 3
Wheels driven: Rear
Springs F/R: Coil/Coil
Brake system: PA
Brakes F/R: Disc/Drum
Steering: Recirculating ball
Wheelbase: 246.4cm 97.0in
Track F: 138.9cm 54.7in
Track R: 136.1cm 53.6in
Length: 455.4cm 179.3in
Width: 166.1cm 65.4in
Height: 127.5cm 50.2in
Kerb weight: 1407.4kg 3100.0lb
Fuel: 70.0L 15.4gal 18.5galUS

691 Buick

Century
1978 USA
107.1mph 172.3kmh
0-50mph 80.5kmh: 8.5secs
0-60mph 96.5kmh: 11.9secs
0-1/4 mile: 18.2secs
0-1km: 34.2secs
145.0bhp 108.1kW 147.0PS
@ 3800rpm
245.0lbft 332.0Nm @ 2400rpm
98.0bhp/ton 96.3bhp/tonne
29.0bhp/L 21.6kW/L 29.4PS/L
36.7ft/sec 11.2m/sec
31.6mph 50.8kmh/1000rpm
16.9mpg 14.1mpgUS 16.7L/100km
Petrol 4-stroke piston
4995cc 304.8cu in
Vee 8 1 Carburettor
Compression ratio: 8.5:1
Bore: 95.0mm 3.7in
Stroke: 88.4mm 3.5in
Valve type/No: Overhead 16
Transmission: Automatic
No. of forward speeds: 3
Wheels driven: Rear
Springs F/R: Coil/Coil
Brake system: PA
Brakes F/R: Disc/Drum
Steering: Recirculating ball PA
Wheelbase: 274.6cm 108.1in
Track F: 148.6cm 58.5in
Track R: 146.8cm 57.8in
Length: 497.6cm 195.9in
Width: 180.6cm 71.1in
Height: 138.7cm 54.6in
Ground clearance: 15.5cm 6.1in
Kerb weight: 1505.1kg 3315.2lb
Fuel: 66.0L 14.5gal 17.4galUS

692 Buick

Riviera S-type
1979 USA
102.0mph 164.1kmh
0-50mph 80.5kmh: 6.8secs
0-60mph 96.5kmh: 9.5secs
0-1/4 mile: 17.5secs
185.0bhp 137.9kW 187.6PS
@ 4200rpm
280.0lbft 379.4Nm @ 2400rpm
104.9bhp/ton 103.2bhp/tonne
48.8bhp/L 36.4kW/L 49.5PS/L
39.7ft/sec 12.1m/sec
26.4mph 42.5kmh/1000rpm
18.0mpg 15.0mpgUS 15.7L/100km
Petrol 4-stroke piston
3791cc 231.3cu in
Vee 6 1 Carburettor
Compression ratio: 8.0:1
Bore: 96.5mm 3.8in
Stroke: 86.4mm 3.4in
Valve type/No: Overhead 12
Transmission: Automatic
No. of forward speeds: 3
Wheels driven: Front
Springs F/R: Torsion bar/Coil
Brake system: PA
Brakes F/R: Disc/Disc
Steering: Recirculating ball PA
Wheelbase: 289.6cm 114.0in
Track F: 150.6cm 59.3in
Track R: 152.4cm 60.0in
Length: 524.8cm 206.6in
Width: 178.8cm 70.4in
Height: 137.9cm 54.3in
Ground clearance: 16.5cm 6.5in
Kerb weight: 1793.3kg 3950.0lb
Fuel: 75.7L 16.6gal 20.0galUS

693 Buick

Century T-type
1983 USA
97.0mph 156.1kmh
0-60mph 96.5kmh: 14.1secs
0-1/4 mile: 19.5secs
110.0bhp 82.0kW 111.5PS
@ 4800rpm
145.0lbft 196.5Nm @ 2600rpm
81.6bhp/ton 80.2bhp/tonne
37.1bhp/L 27.7kW/L 37.6PS/L
35.5ft/sec 10.8m/sec
24.5mph 39.4kmh/1000rpm
24.6mpg 20.5mpgUS 11.5L/100km
Petrol 4-stroke piston
2966cc 181.0cu in
Vee 6 1 Carburettor
Compression ratio: 8.5:1
Bore: 96.5mm 3.8in
Stroke: 67.6mm 2.7in
Valve type/No: Overhead 12
Transmission: Automatic
No. of forward speeds: 3
Wheels driven: Front
Springs F/R: Coil/Coil
Brakes F/R: Disc/Drum
Wheelbase: 266.4cm 104.9in
Track F: 149.1cm 58.7in
Track R: 144.8cm 57.0in
Length: 480.3cm 189.1in
Width: 169.7cm 66.8in
Height: 138.7cm 54.6in
Kerb weight: 1371.1kg 3020.0lb
Fuel: 61.3L 13.5gal 16.2galUS

694 Buick

Electra T-type
1986 USA
0-60mph 96.5kmh: 12.5secs
0-1/4 mile: 19.0secs
125.0bhp 93.2kW 126.7PS
@ 4400rpm
195.0lbft 264.2Nm @ 2000rpm
85.9bhp/ton 84.5bhp/tonne
33.0bhp/L 24.6kW/L 33.5PS/L
41.6ft/sec 12.7m/sec
22.8mpg 19.0mpgUS 12.4L/100km
Petrol 4-stroke piston
3788cc 231.1cu in
Vee 6 fuel injection
Compression ratio: 8.0:1
Bore: 96.5mm 3.8in
Stroke: 86.4mm 3.4in
Valve type/No: Overhead 12
Transmission: Automatic
No. of forward speeds: 4
Wheels driven: Front
Brakes F/R: Disc/Drum
Steering: Rack & pinion PA
Wheelbase: 281.4cm 110.8in
Length: 500.4cm 197.0in
Width: 183.9cm 72.4in
Height: 137.9cm 54.3in
Kerb weight: 1480.0kg 3260.0lb

695 Buick

Reatta
1988 USA
125.0mph 201.1kmh
0-50mph 80.5kmh: 6.3secs
0-60mph 96.5kmh: 8.9secs
0-1/4 mile: 16.8secs
165.0bhp 123.0kW 167.3PS
@ 4800rpm
210.0lbft 284.6Nm @ 2000rpm
109.3bhp/ton 107.5bhp/tonne
43.5bhp/L 32.5kW/L 44.1PS/L
45.3ft/sec 13.8m/sec
19.8mpg 16.5mpgUS 14.3L/100km
Petrol 4-stroke piston
3791cc 231.3cu in
Vee 6 fuel injection
Compression ratio: 8.5:1
Bore: 96.5mm 3.8in
Stroke: 86.4mm 3.4in
Valve type/No: Overhead 12
Transmission: Automatic
No. of forward speeds: 4
Wheels driven: Front
Springs F/R: Coil/Leaf
Brake system: PA ABS
Brakes F/R: Disc/Disc
Steering: Rack & pinion PA
Wheelbase: 250.2cm 98.5in
Track F: 153.2cm 60.3in
Track R: 153.2cm 60.3in
Length: 464.3cm 182.8in
Width: 185.4cm 73.0in
Height: 130.0cm 51.2in
Kerb weight: 1534.5kg 3380.0lb
Fuel: 68.9L 15.1gal 18.2galUS

696 Buick

Regal Custom
1988 USA
0-60mph 96.5kmh: 11.2secs
0-1/4 mile: 18.2secs
130.0bhp 96.9kW 131.8PS
@ 4500rpm
170.0lbft 230.4Nm @ 3600rpm
90.4bhp/ton 88.9bhp/tonne
45.8bhp/L 34.2kW/L 46.5PS/L
37.4ft/sec 11.4m/sec
24.6mpg 20.5mpgUS 11.5L/100km
Petrol 4-stroke piston
2837cc 173.1cu in
Vee 6 fuel injection
Compression ratio: 8.9:1
Bore: 89.0mm 3.5in
Stroke: 76.0mm 3.0in
Valve type/No: Overhead 12
Transmission: Automatic
No. of forward speeds: 4
Wheels driven: Front
Springs F/R: Coil/Leaf
Brake system: PA
Brakes F/R: Disc/Disc
Steering: Rack & pinion PA
Wheelbase: 273.1cm 107.5in
Track F: 151.1cm 59.5in
Track R: 147.3cm 58.0in
Length: 488.2cm 192.2in
Width: 184.2cm 72.5in
Height: 134.6cm 53.0in
Kerb weight: 1461.9kg 3220.0lb
Fuel: 62.4L 13.7gal 16.5galUS

697 Buick

Reatta Turbo Buick Engineering
1989 USA
0-50mph 80.5kmh: 5.0secs
0-60mph 96.5kmh: 6.8secs
0-1/4 mile: 15.5secs
230.0bhp 171.5kW 233.2PS
@ 5100rpm
260.0lbft 352.3Nm @ 2500rpm
151.5bhp/ton 149.0bhp/tonne
60.7bhp/L 45.2kW/L 61.5PS/L
48.2ft/sec 14.7m/sec
Petrol 4-stroke piston
3791cc 231.3cu in turbocharged
Vee 6 fuel injection
Compression ratio: 8.0:1
Bore: 96.5mm 3.8in
Stroke: 86.4mm 3.4in
Valve type/No: Overhead 12
Transmission: Automatic
No. of forward speeds: 4
Wheels driven: Front
Springs F/R: Coil/Leaf
Brake system: PA ABS
Brakes F/R: Disc/Disc
Steering: Rack & pinion PA
Wheelbase: 250.2cm 98.5in
Track F: 153.2cm 60.3in
Track R: 153.2cm 60.3in
Length: 464.3cm 182.8in
Width: 185.4cm 73.0in
Height: 130.0cm 51.2in
Kerb weight: 1543.6kg 3400.0lb

698 Buick

Reatta Convertible
1991 USA
125.0mph 201.1kmh
0-50mph 80.5kmh: 6.3secs
0-60mph 96.5kmh: 8.9secs
0-1/4 mile: 16.8secs
170.0bhp 126.8kW 172.4PS
@ 4800rpm
220.0lbft 298.1Nm @ 3200rpm
105.9bhp/ton 104.2bhp/tonne
44.8bhp/L 33.4kW/L 45.5PS/L
45.3ft/sec 13.8m/sec
19.8mpg 16.5mpgUS 14.3L/100km
Petrol 4-stroke piston
3791cc 231.3cu in
Vee 6 fuel injection
Compression ratio: 8.5:1
Bore: 96.5mm 3.8in
Stroke: 86.4mm 3.4in
Valve type/No: Overhead 12
Transmission: Automatic
No. of forward speeds: 4
Wheels driven: Front
Springs F/R: Coil/Leaf
Brake system: PA ABS
Brakes F/R: Disc/Disc
Steering: Rack & pinion PA
Wheelbase: 250.2cm 98.5in
Track F: 153.2cm 60.3in
Track R: 153.2cm 60.3in
Length: 466.6cm 183.7in
Width: 185.4cm 73.0in
Height: 132.8cm 52.3in
Kerb weight: 1632.1kg 3595.0lb
Fuel: 68.9L 15.1gal 18.2galUS

699 Cadillac

V16 "Madame X"
1930 USA
87.0mph 140.0kmh
0-50mph 80.5kmh: 14.9secs
0-60mph 96.5kmh: 20.0secs
0-1/4 mile: 21.8secs
165.0bhp 123.0kW 167.3PS
@ 3400rpm
320.0lbft 433.6Nm @ 1500rpm
59.6bhp/ton 58.6bhp/tonne
22.3bhp/L 16.6kW/L 22.6PS/L
37.8ft/sec 11.5m/sec
22.8mph 36.7kmh/1000rpm
Petrol 4-stroke piston
7410cc 452.1cu in
Vee 16 1 Carburettor
Compression ratio: 5.5:1
Bore: 76.2mm 3.0in
Stroke: 101.6mm 4.0in
Valve type/No: Overhead 32
Transmission: Manual
No. of forward speeds: 3
Wheels driven: Rear
Wheelbase: 375.9cm 148.0in
Track F: 149.9cm 59.0in
Track R: 151.1cm 59.5in
Length: 589.3cm 232.0in
Width: 188.0cm 74.0in
Height: 188.0cm 74.0in
Ground clearance: 23.4cm 9.2in
Kerb weight: 2814.8kg 6200.0lb

700 Cadillac

V16 Fleetwood Roadster
1931 USA
88.8mph 142.9kmh
0-50mph 80.5kmh: 13.6secs
0-60mph 96.5kmh: 18.8secs

0-1/4 mile: 21.0secs
175.0bhp 130.5kW 177.4PS
@ 3400rpm
360.0lbft 487.8Nm @ 1800rpm
73.6bhp/ton 72.4bhp/tonne
23.6bhp/L 17.6kW/L 23.9PS/L
37.8ft/sec 11.5m/sec
Petrol 4-stroke piston
7410cc 452.1cu in
Vee 16
Compression ratio: 5.5:1
Bore: 76.2mm 3.0in
Stroke: 101.6mm 4.0in
Valve type/No: Overhead 32
Transmission: Manual
No. of forward speeds: 3
Wheels driven: Rear
Wheelbase: 375.9cm 148.0in
Track F: 145.5cm 57.3in
Track R: 151.1cm 59.5in
Kerb weight: 2417.5kg 5325.0lb

701 Cadillac

Eldorado Convertible
1959 USA
115.0mph 185.0kmh
0-60mph 96.5kmh: 10.6secs
0-1/4 mile: 18.2secs
345.0bhp 257.3kW 349.8PS
@ 4800rpm
435.0lbft 589.4Nm @ 3400rpm
152.7bhp/ton 150.2bhp/tonne
54.1bhp/L 40.3kW/L 54.8PS/L
51.6ft/sec 15.7m/sec
Petrol 4-stroke piston
6382cc 389.4cu in
Vee 8 3 Carburettor
Compression ratio: 10.5:1
Bore: 101.6mm 4.0in
Stroke: 98.4mm 3.9in
Valve type/No: Overhead 16
Transmission: Automatic
No. of forward speeds: 3
Wheels driven: Rear
Springs F/R: Gas/Gas
Brake system: PA
Brakes F/R: Drum/Drum
Steering: Recirculating ball PA
Wheelbase: 330.2cm 130.0in
Length: 571.5cm 225.0in
Width: 204.0cm 80.3in
Height: 138.2cm 54.4in
Kerb weight: 2297.2kg 5060.0lb
Fuel: 79.5L 17.5gal 21.0galUS

702 Cadillac

Coupe de Ville
1961 USA
115.0mph 185.0kmh
0-50mph 80.5kmh: 6.8secs
0-60mph 96.5kmh: 9.5secs
0-1/4 mile: 17.1secs
325.0bhp 242.3kW 329.5PS
@ 4800rpm
430.0lbft 582.7Nm @ 3100rpm
152.3bhp/ton 149.8bhp/tonne
50.8bhp/L 37.9kW/L 51.5PS/L
51.6ft/sec 15.7m/sec
26.7mph 43.0kmh/1000rpm
Petrol 4-stroke piston
6394cc 390.1cu in
Vee 8 1 Carburettor
Compression ratio: 10.5:1
Bore: 101.6mm 4.0in
Stroke: 98.3mm 3.9in
Valve type/No: Overhead 16
Transmission: Automatic
No. of forward speeds: 4
Wheels driven: Rear
Brake system: PA
Brakes F/R: Drum/Drum
Steering: PA
Wheelbase: 328.9cm 129.5in
Track F: 154.9cm 61.0in
Track R: 154.9cm 61.0in
Length: 563.9cm 222.0in
Width: 202.7cm 79.8in
Height: 142.0cm 55.9in
Ground clearance: 13.5cm 5.3in
Kerb weight: 2170.1kg 4780.0lb

703 Cadillac

Fleetwood
1961 USA
120.0mph 193.1kmh
0-50mph 80.5kmh: 8.3secs
0-60mph 96.5kmh: 11.2secs
0-1/4 mile: 18.1secs
325.0bhp 242.3kW 329.5PS
@ 4800rpm
430.0lbft 582.7Nm @ 3100rpm
128.4bhp/ton 126.2bhp/tonne
50.9bhp/L 38.0kW/L 51.6PS/L
51.6ft/sec 15.7m/sec
25.2mph 40.5kmh/1000rpm
10.9mpg 9.1mpgUS 25.9L/100km
Petrol 4-stroke piston
6384cc 389.5cu in
Vee 8
Compression ratio: 10.5:1
Bore: 101.6mm 4.0in
Stroke: 98.4mm 3.9in
Valve type/No: Overhead 16
Transmission: Manual
No. of forward speeds: 4
Wheels driven: Rear
Brake system: PA
Brakes F/R: Drum/Drum
Wheelbase: 380.5cm 149.8in
Track F: 154.9cm 61.0in
Track R: 154.9cm 61.0in
Length: 621.8cm 244.8in
Width: 203.2cm 80.0in
Height: 149.9cm 59.0in
Ground clearance: 17.5cm 6.9in
Kerb weight: 2574.2kg 5670.0lb
Fuel: 79.6L 17.5gal 21.0galUS

704 Cadillac

Park Avenue
1963 USA
114.0mph 183.4kmh
0-50mph 80.5kmh: 7.4secs
0-60mph 96.5kmh: 10.0secs
0-1/4 mile: 17.7secs
325.0bhp 242.3kW 329.5PS
@ 4800rpm
430.0lbft 582.7Nm @ 3100rpm
149.9bhp/ton 147.4bhp/tonne
50.8bhp/L 37.9kW/L 51.6PS/L
51.6ft/sec 15.7m/sec
26.2mph 42.2kmh/1000rpm
Petrol 4-stroke piston
6391cc 389.9cu in
Vee 8 1 Carburettor
Compression ratio: 10.5:1
Bore: 101.6mm 4.0in
Stroke: 98.4mm 3.9in
Valve type/No: Overhead 16
Transmission: Automatic
No. of forward speeds: 4
Wheels driven: Rear
Brake system: PA
Steering: PA
Wheelbase: 328.9cm 129.5in
Track F: 154.9cm 61.0in
Track R: 154.9cm 61.0in
Length: 546.1cm 215.0in
Width: 202.9cm 79.9in
Height: 141.7cm 55.8in
Ground clearance: 13.5cm 5.3in
Kerb weight: 2204.2kg 4855.0lb
Fuel: 79.5L 17.5gal 21.0galUS

705 Cadillac

Coupe de Ville
1964 USA
123.0mph 197.9kmh
0-50mph 80.5kmh: 7.0secs
0-60mph 96.5kmh: 9.7secs
0-1/4 mile: 17.0secs
340.0bhp 253.5kW 344.7PS
@ 4600rpm
480.0lbft 650.4Nm @ 3000rpm
152.1bhp/ton 149.6bhp/tonne
48.4bhp/L 36.1kW/L 49.0PS/L
51.1ft/sec 15.6m/sec
25.5mph 41.0kmh/1000rpm
10.9mpg 9.1mpgUS 25.9L/100km
Petrol 4-stroke piston
7030cc 428.9cu in
Vee 8 1 Carburettor
Compression ratio: 10.5:1
Bore: 104.9mm 4.1in
Stroke: 101.6mm 4.0in
Valve type/No: Overhead 16
Transmission: Automatic
No. of forward speeds: 3
Wheels driven: Rear
Springs F/R: Coil/Coil
Brake system: PA
Brakes F/R: Drum/Drum
Steering: Recirculating ball PA
Wheelbase: 327.7cm 129.0in
Track F: 154.9cm 61.0in
Track R: 154.9cm 61.0in
Length: 567.7cm 223.5in
Width: 202.4cm 79.7in
Height: 168.9cm 66.5in
Ground clearance: 13.5cm 5.3in
Kerb weight: 2272.7kg 5006.0lb
Fuel: 97.8L 21.5gal 25.8galUS

706 Cadillac

Sedan de Ville
1964 USA
121.0mph 194.7kmh
0-50mph 80.5kmh: 6.5secs
0-60mph 96.5kmh: 8.5secs
0-1/4 mile: 16.4secs
340.0bhp 253.5kW 344.7PS
@ 4600rpm
480.0lbft 650.4Nm @ 3000rpm
155.4bhp/ton 152.8bhp/tonne
48.4bhp/L 36.1kW/L 49.0PS/L
51.1ft/sec 15.6m/sec
26.0mph 41.8kmh/1000rpm
Petrol 4-stroke piston
7030cc 428.9cu in
Vee 8 1 Carburettor
Compression ratio: 10.5:1
Bore: 104.9mm 4.1in
Stroke: 101.6mm 4.0in
Valve type/No: Overhead 16
Transmission: Automatic
No. of forward speeds: 3
Wheels driven: Rear
Brake system: PA
Steering: PA
Wheelbase: 328.9cm 129.5in
Track F: 154.9cm 61.0in
Track R: 154.9cm 61.0in
Length: 567.7cm 223.5in
Width: 202.4cm 79.7in
Height: 139.2cm 54.8in
Ground clearance: 13.5cm 5.3in
Kerb weight: 2224.6kg 4900.0lb
Fuel: 98.4L 21.6gal 26.0galUS

707 Cadillac

Calais
1966 USA
115.0mph 185.0kmh
0-50mph 80.5kmh: 7.3secs
0-60mph 96.5kmh: 9.4secs
0-1/4 mile: 17.0secs
340.0bhp 253.5kW 344.7PS
@ 4600rpm
480.0lbft 650.4Nm @ 3000rpm
160.0bhp/ton 157.3bhp/tonne
48.4bhp/L 36.1kW/L 49.0PS/L
51.1ft/sec 15.6m/sec
26.0mph 41.8kmh/1000rpm
Petrol 4-stroke piston
7030cc 428.9cu in
Vee 8 1 Carburettor
Compression ratio: 10.5:1
Bore: 104.9mm 4.1in
Stroke: 101.6mm 4.0in
Valve type/No: Overhead 16
Transmission: Automatic
No. of forward speeds: 3
Wheels driven: Rear
Springs F/R: Coil/Coil
Brake system: PA
Brakes F/R: Drum/Drum
Steering: Recirculating ball PA
Wheelbase: 328.9cm 129.5in
Track F: 158.8cm 62.5in
Track R: 158.8cm 62.5in
Length: 569.0cm 224.0in
Width: 203.2cm 80.0in
Height: 138.7cm 54.6in
Ground clearance: 15.2cm 6.0in
Kerb weight: 2161.0kg 4760.0lb
Fuel: 98.4L 21.6gal 26.0galUS

708 Cadillac

Eldorado
1967 USA
120.0mph 193.1kmh
0-50mph 80.5kmh: 6.7secs
0-60mph 96.5kmh: 9.2secs
0-1/4 mile: 17.2secs
340.0bhp 253.5kW 344.7PS
@ 4600rpm
480.0lbft 650.4Nm @ 3000rpm
159.0bhp/ton 156.3bhp/tonne
48.4bhp/L 36.1kW/L 49.1PS/L
51.1ft/sec 15.6m/sec
25.9mph 41.7kmh/1000rpm
Petrol 4-stroke piston
7021cc 428.4cu in
Vee 8 1 Carburettor
Compression ratio: 10.5:1
Bore: 104.9mm 4.1in
Stroke: 101.6mm 4.0in
Valve type/No: Overhead 16
Transmission: Automatic
No. of forward speeds: 3
Wheels driven: Front
Springs F/R: Torsion bar/Leaf
Brake system: PA
Brakes F/R: Disc/Drum
Steering: Recirculating ball PA
Wheelbase: 304.8cm 120.0in
Track F: 161.3cm 63.5in
Track R: 160.0cm 63.0in
Length: 561.3cm 221.0in
Width: 202.9cm 79.9in
Height: 136.7cm 53.8in
Ground clearance: 18.5cm 7.3in
Kerb weight: 2174.7kg 4790.0lb
Fuel: 90.8L 20.0gal 24.0galUS

709 Cadillac

Coupe de Ville
1968 USA
120.0mph 193.1kmh
0-50mph 80.5kmh: 7.1secs
0-60mph 96.5kmh: 9.9secs
0-1/4 mile: 16.9secs
0-1km: 31.2secs
375.0bhp 279.6kW 380.2PS
@ 4400rpm
525.0lbft 711.4Nm @ 3000rpm
169.6bhp/ton 166.8bhp/tonne
48.5bhp/L 36.2kW/L 49.2PS/L
49.6ft/sec 15.1m/sec
28.5mph 45.9kmh/1000rpm
10.4mpg 8.7mpgUS 27.2L/100km
Petrol 4-stroke piston
7729cc 471.6cu in
Vee 8 1 Carburettor
Compression ratio: 10.5:1
Bore: 109.2mm 4.3in
Stroke: 103.1mm 4.1in
Valve type/No: Overhead 16
Transmission: Automatic
No. of forward speeds: 3
Wheels driven: Rear
Springs F/R: Coil/Coil
Brake system: PA
Brakes F/R: Disc/Drum
Steering: Recirculating ball PA
Wheelbase: 328.9cm 129.5in
Track F: 158.8cm 62.5in
Track R: 158.8cm 62.5in
Length: 570.7cm 224.7in
Width: 203.2cm 80.0in
Height: 137.2cm 54.0in
Ground clearance: 17.8cm 7.0in
Kerb weight: 2248.2kg 4952.0lb
Fuel: 98.7L 21.7gal 26.1galUS

710 Cadillac

Seville
1976 USA
109.0mph 175.4kmh
0-50mph 80.5kmh: 9.7secs
0-60mph 96.5kmh: 13.3secs
0-1/4 mile: 19.0secs
180.0bhp 134.2kW 182.5PS
@ 4400rpm
275.0lbft 372.6Nm @ 2000rpm
92.8bhp/ton 91.2bhp/tonne
31.4bhp/L 23.4kW/L 31.8PS/L
41.4ft/sec 12.6m/sec
29.0mph 46.7kmh/1000rpm
19.8mpg 16.5mpgUS 14.3L/100km
Petrol 4-stroke piston
5736cc 350.0cu in
Vee 8 fuel injection
Compression ratio: 8.0:1
Bore: 103.0mm 4.1in
Stroke: 86.0mm 3.4in
Valve type/No: Overhead 16
Transmission: Automatic
No. of forward speeds: 3
Wheels driven: Rear
Springs F/R: Coil/Leaf
Brake system: PA
Brakes F/R: Disc/Drum
Steering: Recirculating ball PA
Wheelbase: 290.3cm 114.3in
Track F: 155.7cm 61.3in

Track R: 149.9cm 59.0in
Length: 518.2cm 204.0in
Width: 182.4cm 71.8in
Height: 138.9cm 54.7in
Ground clearance: 13.7cm 5.4in
Kerb weight: 1972.6kg 4345.0lb
Fuel: 79.5L 17.5gal 21.0galUS

711 Cadillac

Seville Diesel
1978 USA
95.0mph 152.9kmh
0-50mph 80.5kmh: 11.0secs
0-60mph 96.5kmh: 15.7secs
0-1/4 mile: 20.8secs
120.0bhp 89.5kW 121.7PS
@ 3600rpm
220.0lbft 298.1Nm @ 1600rpm
60.7bhp/ton 59.7bhp/tonne
20.9bhp/L 15.6kW/L 21.2PS/L
33.9ft/sec 10.3m/sec
31.0mph 49.9kmh/1000rpm
26.4mpg 22.0mpgUS 10.7L/100km
Diesel 4-stroke piston
5732cc 349.7cu in
Vee 8 fuel injection
Compression ratio: 22.5:1
Bore: 103.0mm 4.1in
Stroke: 86.0mm 3.4in
Valve type/No: Overhead 16
Transmission: Automatic
No. of forward speeds: 3
Wheels driven: Rear
Springs F/R: Coil/Leaf
Brakes F/R: Disc/Disc
Steering: Recirculating ball PA
Wheelbase: 290.3cm 114.3in
Track F: 155.7cm 61.3in
Track R: 149.9cm 59.0in
Length: 518.2cm 204.0in
Width: 182.4cm 71.8in
Height: 138.9cm 54.7in
Kerb weight: 2011.2kg 4430.0lb
Fuel: 79.5L 17.5gal 21.0galUS

712 Cadillac

Seville Diesel
1981 USA
95.0mph 152.9kmh
0-50mph 80.5kmh: 14.4secs
0-60mph 96.5kmh: 21.0secs
0-1/4 mile: 22.4secs
105.0bhp 78.3kW 106.5PS
@ 3200rpm
205.0lbft 277.8Nm @ 1600rpm
55.3bhp/ton 54.3bhp/tonne
18.3bhp/L 13.7kW/L 18.6PS/L
30.1ft/sec 9.2m/sec
31.7mph 51.0kmh/1000rpm
21.0mpg 17.5mpgUS 13.4L/100km
Diesel 4-stroke piston
5732cc 349.7cu in
Vee 8 fuel injection
Compression ratio: 22.5:1
Bore: 103.0mm 4.1in
Stroke: 86.0mm 3.4in
Valve type/No: Overhead 16
Transmission: Automatic
No. of forward speeds: 3
Wheels driven: Front
Springs F/R: Torsion bar/Coil
Brakes F/R: Disc/Disc
Steering: Recirculating ball PA
Wheelbase: 289.6cm 114.0in
Track F: 150.6cm 59.3in
Track R: 153.9cm 60.6in
Length: 522.0cm 205.5in
Width: 181.4cm 71.4in
Height: 137.9cm 54.3in
Ground clearance: 14.0cm 5.5in
Kerb weight: 1931.8kg 4255.0lb
Fuel: 87.1L 19.1gal 23.0galUS

713 Cadillac

Cimarron
1982 USA
94.0mph 151.2kmh
0-50mph 80.5kmh: 10.7secs
0-60mph 96.5kmh: 15.9secs
0-1/4 mile: 20.3secs
85.0bhp 63.4kW 86.2PS
@ 5100rpm
100.0lbft 135.5Nm @ 2800rpm
71.2bhp/ton 70.0bhp/tonne
46.3bhp/L 34.5kW/L 46.9PS/L
41.2ft/sec 12.6m/sec
23.1mph 37.2kmh/1000rpm
26.4mpg 22.0mpgUS 10.7L/100km
Petrol 4-stroke piston
1836cc 112.0cu in
In-line 4 1 Carburettor
Compression ratio: 9.0:1
Bore: 89.0mm 3.5in
Stroke: 74.0mm 2.9in
Valve type/No: Overhead 8
Transmission: Manual
No. of forward speeds: 4
Wheels driven: Front
Springs F/R: Coil/Coil
Brake system: PA
Brakes F/R: Disc/Drum
Steering: Rack & pinion PA
Wheelbase: 257.0cm 101.2in
Track F: 140.7cm 55.4in
Track R: 140.2cm 55.2in
Length: 439.4cm 173.0in
Width: 165.1cm 65.0in
Height: 132.1cm 52.0in
Kerb weight: 1214.4kg 2675.0lb
Fuel: 53.0L 11.6gal 14.0galUS

714 Cadillac

Cimarron
1985 USA
0-60mph 96.5kmh: 10.5secs
0-1/4 mile: 17.9secs
129.0bhp 96.2kW 130.8PS
@ 4800rpm
159.0lbft 215.4Nm @ 3600rpm
102.1bhp/ton 100.4bhp/tonne
45.4bhp/L 33.9kW/L 46.1PS/L
40.0ft/sec 12.2m/sec
27.0mpg 22.5mpgUS 10.5L/100km
Petrol 4-stroke piston
2838cc 173.1cu in
Vee 6 fuel injection
Compression ratio: 8.4:1
Bore: 88.9mm 3.5in
Stroke: 76.2mm 3.0in
Valve type/No: Overhead 12
Transmission: Automatic
No. of forward speeds: 3
Wheels driven: Front
Brakes F/R: Disc/Drum
Steering: Rack & pinion PA
Wheelbase: 257.0cm 101.2in
Length: 439.4cm 173.0in
Width: 165.6cm 65.2in
Height: 132.1cm 52.0in
Kerb weight: 1284.8kg 2830.0lb

715 Cadillac

Allante
1988 USA
119.0mph 191.5kmh
0-60mph 96.5kmh: 9.3secs
0-1/4 mile: 17.1secs
170.0bhp 126.8kW 172.4PS
@ 4300rpm
230.0lbft 311.7Nm @ 3200rpm
109.0bhp/ton 107.1bhp/tonne
41.6bhp/L 31.0kW/L 42.2PS/L
39.5ft/sec 12.0m/sec
26.9mpg 22.4mpgUS 10.5L/100km
Petrol 4-stroke piston
4087cc 249.4cu in
Vee 8 fuel injection
Compression ratio: 8.5:1
Bore: 88.0mm 3.5in
Stroke: 84.0mm 3.3in
Valve type/No: Overhead 16
Transmission: Automatic
No. of forward speeds: 4
Wheels driven: Front
Springs F/R: Coil/Leaf
Brake system: ABS
Brakes F/R: Disc/Disc
Steering: Rack & pinion PA
Wheelbase: 252.5cm 99.4in
Track F: 153.7cm 60.5in
Track R: 153.7cm 60.5in
Length: 453.6cm 178.6in
Width: 186.4cm 73.4in
Height: 132.1cm 52.0in
Kerb weight: 1586.7kg 3495.0lb
Fuel: 83.3L 18.3gal 22.0galUS

716 Cadillac

Allante
1990 USA
130.0mph 209.2kmh
0-50mph 80.5kmh: 6.2secs
0-60mph 96.5kmh: 8.3secs
0-1/4 mile: 16.4secs
200.0bhp 149.1kW 202.8PS
@ 4400rpm
270.0lbft 365.9Nm @ 3200rpm
129.3bhp/ton 127.1bhp/tonne
44.8bhp/L 33.4kW/L 45.4PS/L
40.5ft/sec 12.3m/sec
Petrol 4-stroke piston
4467cc 272.5cu in
Vee 8 fuel injection
Compression ratio: 9.0:1
Bore: 92.0mm 3.6in
Stroke: 84.0mm 3.3in
Valve type/No: Overhead 16
Transmission: Automatic
No. of forward speeds: 4
Wheels driven: Front
Springs F/R: Coil/Leaf
Brake system: PA ABS
Brakes F/R: Disc/Disc
Steering: Rack & pinion PA
Wheelbase: 252.5cm 99.4in
Track F: 153.4cm 60.4in
Track R: 153.4cm 60.4in
Length: 453.9cm 178.7in
Width: 186.7cm 73.5in
Height: 132.6cm 52.2in
Kerb weight: 1573.1kg 3465.0lb
Fuel: 83.3L 18.3gal 22.0galUS

717 Cadillac

Aurora
1990 USA
0-60mph 96.5kmh: 10.0secs
0-1/4 mile: 17.2secs
200.0bhp 149.1kW 202.8PS
@ 4400rpm
270.0lbft 365.9Nm @ 3200rpm
128.0bhp/ton 125.9bhp/tonne
44.8bhp/L 33.4kW/L 45.4PS/L
40.5ft/sec 12.3m/sec
Petrol 4-stroke piston
4467cc 272.5cu in
Vee 8 fuel injection
Compression ratio: 9.0:1
Bore: 92.0mm 3.6in
Stroke: 84.0mm 3.3in
Valve type/No: Overhead 16
Transmission: Automatic
No. of forward speeds: 4
Wheels driven: 4-wheel drive
Springs F/R: Coil/Leaf
Brake system: PA ABS
Brakes F/R: Disc/Disc
Steering: Recirculating ball PA
Wheelbase: 285.0cm 112.2in
Track F: 149.9cm 59.0in
Track R: 153.9cm 60.6in
Length: 484.9cm 190.9in
Width: 188.0cm 74.0in
Height: 140.5cm 55.3in
Kerb weight: 1589.0kg 3500.0lb
Fuel: 71.2L 15.6gal 18.8galUS

718 Cadillac

Eldorado Touring Coupe
1990 USA
125.0mph 201.1kmh
0-50mph 80.5kmh: 6.3secs
0-60mph 96.5kmh: 8.5secs
0-1/4 mile: 16.6secs
180.0bhp 134.2kW 182.5PS
@ 4300rpm
240.0lbft 325.2Nm @ 2600rpm
114.7bhp/ton 112.8bhp/tonne
40.3bhp/L 30.0kW/L 40.9PS/L
39.5ft/sec 12.0m/sec
29.1mpg 24.2mpgUS 9.7L/100km
Petrol 4-stroke piston
4467cc 272.5cu in
Vee 8 fuel injection
Compression ratio: 9.5:1
Bore: 91.9mm 3.6in
Stroke: 84.1mm 3.3in
Valve type/No: Overhead 16
Transmission: Automatic
No. of forward speeds: 4
Wheels driven: Front
Springs F/R: Coil/Leaf
Brake system: PA ABS
Brakes F/R: Disc/Disc
Steering: Rack & pinion PA
Wheelbase: 274.3cm 108.0in
Track F: 152.1cm 59.9in
Track R: 152.1cm 59.9in
Length: 486.2cm 191.4in
Width: 183.9cm 72.4in
Height: 136.4cm 53.7in
Kerb weight: 1595.8kg 3515.0lb
Fuel: 71.2L 15.6gal 18.8galUS

719 Cadillac

Allante
1991 USA
130.0mph 209.2kmh
0-50mph 80.5kmh: 6.2secs
0-60mph 96.5kmh: 8.3secs
0-1/4 mile: 16.4secs
200.0bhp 149.1kW 202.8PS
@ 4400rpm
270.0lbft 365.9Nm @ 3200rpm
126.7bhp/ton 124.6bhp/tonne
44.8bhp/L 33.4kW/L 45.4PS/L
40.5ft/sec 12.3m/sec
19.9mpg 16.6mpgUS 14.2L/100km
Petrol 4-stroke piston
4467cc 272.5cu in
Vee 8 fuel injection
Compression ratio: 9.0:1
Bore: 92.0mm 3.6in
Stroke: 84.0mm 3.3in
Valve type/No: Overhead 16
Transmission: Automatic
No. of forward speeds: 4
Wheels driven: Front
Springs F/R: Coil/Leaf
Brake system: PA ABS
Brakes F/R: Disc/Disc
Steering: Rack & pinion PA
Wheelbase: 252.5cm 99.4in
Track F: 153.4cm 60.4in
Track R: 153.4cm 60.4in
Length: 453.9cm 178.7in
Width: 186.7cm 73.5in
Height: 130.0cm 51.2in
Kerb weight: 1604.9kg 3535.0lb
Fuel: 83.3L 18.3gal 22.0galUS

720 Cadillac

Seville Touring Sedan
1991 USA
125.0mph 201.1kmh
0-60mph 96.5kmh: 8.6secs
0-1/4 mile: 16.6secs
200.0bhp 149.1kW 202.8PS
@ 4100rpm
275.0lbft 372.6Nm @ 3000rpm
125.5bhp/ton 123.4bhp/tonne
40.9bhp/L 30.5kW/L 41.4PS/L
41.2ft/sec 12.6m/sec
22.2mpg 18.5mpgUS 12.7L/100km
Petrol 4-stroke piston
4894cc 298.6cu in
Vee 8 fuel injection
Compression ratio: 9.5:1
Bore: 92.0mm 3.6in
Stroke: 92.0mm 3.6in
Valve type/No: Overhead 16
Transmission: Automatic
No. of forward speeds: 4
Wheels driven: Front
Springs F/R: Coil/Leaf
Brake system: PA ABS
Brakes F/R: Disc/Disc
Steering: Rack & pinion PA
Wheelbase: 274.3cm 108.0in
Track F: 152.1cm 59.9in
Track R: 152.1cm 59.9in
Length: 484.6cm 190.8in
Width: 182.9cm 72.0in
Height: 135.1cm 53.2in
Kerb weight: 1620.8kg 3570.0lb
Fuel: 71.2L 15.6gal 18.8galUS

721 Carbodies

Fairway 2.7 Silver
1989 UK
81.0mph 130.3kmh
0-50mph 80.5kmh: 14.6secs
0-60mph 96.5kmh: 23.6secs
0-1/4 mile: 22.0secs
0-1km: 43.1secs
78.0bhp 58.2kW 79.1PS
@ 4300rpm
127.7lbft 173.0Nm @ 2200rpm
51.4bhp/ton 50.6bhp/tonne
29.3bhp/L 21.8kW/L 29.7PS/L
43.2ft/sec 13.2m/sec
29.5mph 47.5kmh/1000rpm
23.0mpg 19.2mpgUS 12.3L/100km
Diesel 4-stroke piston
2663cc 162.0cu in

In-line 4 fuel injection
Compression ratio: 22.8:1
Bore: 96.0mm 3.8in
Stroke: 92.0mm 3.6in
Valve type/No: Overhead 8
Transmission: Manual
No. of forward speeds: 4
Wheels driven: Rear
Springs F/R: Coil/Leaf
Brake system: PA
Brakes F/R: Drum/Drum
Steering: Worm & roller PA
Wheelbase: 281.0cm 110.6in
Track F: 142.0cm 55.9in
Track R: 142.0cm 55.9in
Length: 458.0cm 180.3in
Width: 175.0cm 68.9in
Height: 177.0cm 69.7in
Ground clearance: 20.4cm 8.0in
Kerb weight: 1542.0kg 3396.5lb
Fuel: 52.3L 11.5gal 13.8galUS

722 Caterham

Super 7
1975 UK
114.0mph 183.4kmh
0-50mph 80.5kmh: 4.5secs
0-60mph 96.5kmh: 6.2secs
0-1/4 mile: 14.9secs
0-1km: 28.2secs
126.0bhp 94.0kW 127.7PS
@ 6500rpm
113.0lbft 153.1Nm @ 5500rpm
242.9bhp/ton 238.8bhp/tonne
79.3bhp/L 59.2kW/L 80.4PS/L
51.8ft/sec 15.8m/sec
17.4mph 28.0kmh/1000rpm
28.3mpg 23.6mpgUS 10.0L/100km
Petrol 4-stroke piston
1588cc 96.9cu in
In-line 4 2 Carburettor
Compression ratio: 10.3:1
Bore: 82.6mm 3.2in
Stroke: 72.8mm 2.9in
Valve type/No: Overhead 8
Transmission: Manual
No. of forward speeds: 4
Wheels driven: Rear
Springs F/R: Coil/Coil
Brakes F/R: Disc/Drum
Steering: Rack & pinion
Wheelbase: 226.1cm 89.0in
Track F: 124.5cm 49.0in
Track R: 134.6cm 53.0in
Length: 337.8cm 133.0in
Width: 154.9cm 61.0in
Height: 94.0cm 37.0in
Kerb weight: 527.5kg 1162.0lb
Fuel: 36.4L 8.0gal 9.6galUS

723 Caterham

1700 Super Sprint
1985 UK
116.0mph 186.6kmh
0-50mph 80.5kmh: 4.2secs
0-60mph 96.5kmh: 5.6secs
0-1/4 mile: 14.6secs
0-1km: 27.7secs
135.0bhp 100.7kW 136.9PS
@ 6000rpm
122.0lbft 165.3Nm @ 4500rpm
252.8bhp/ton 248.6bhp/tonne
79.8bhp/L 59.5kW/L 80.9PS/L
51.0ft/sec 15.5m/sec
18.5mph 29.8kmh/1000rpm
23.5mpg 19.6mpgUS 12.0L/100km
Petrol 4-stroke piston
1691cc 103.2cu in
In-line 4 2 Carburettor
Compression ratio: 10.5:1
Bore: 83.3mm 3.3in
Stroke: 77.6mm 3.1in
Valve type/No: Overhead 8
Transmission: Manual
No. of forward speeds: 4
Wheels driven: Rear
Springs F/R: Coil/Coil
Brakes F/R: Disc/Drum
Steering: Rack & pinion
Wheelbase: 223.5cm 88.0in
Track F: 124.5cm 49.0in
Track R: 132.1cm 52.0in
Length: 339.1cm 133.5in
Width: 157.5cm 62.0in
Height: 108.0cm 42.5in
Ground clearance: 12.7cm 5.0in
Kerb weight: 543.0kg 1196.0lb
Fuel: 36.4L 8.0gal 9.6galUS

724 Caterham

7
1985 UK
100.0mph 160.9kmh
0-60mph 96.5kmh: 7.6secs
0-1/4 mile: 15.7secs
84.0bhp 62.6kW 85.2PS
@ 5000rpm
92.0lbft 124.7Nm @ 3500rpm
167.2bhp/ton 164.5bhp/tonne
52.5bhp/L 39.2kW/L 53.3PS/L
Petrol 4-stroke piston
1599cc 97.6cu in
In-line 4 1 Carburettor
Valve type/No: Overhead 8
Transmission: Manual
No. of forward speeds: 4
Wheels driven: Rear
Springs F/R: Coil/Coil
Brakes F/R: Disc/Drum
Steering: Rack & pinion
Wheelbase: 224.8cm 88.5in
Length: 337.8cm 133.0in
Width: 145.3cm 57.2in
Height: 109.2cm 43.0in
Kerb weight: 510.7kg 1125.0lb
Fuel: 36.3L 8.0gal 9.6galUS

725 Caterham

7 HPC
1990 UK
126.0mph 202.7kmh
0-50mph 80.5kmh: 4.1secs
0-60mph 96.5kmh: 5.2secs
0-1/4 mile: 13.6secs
0-1km: 25.7secs
175.0bhp 130.5kW 177.4PS
@ 6000rpm
155.0lbft 210.0Nm @ 4800rpm
283.4bhp/ton 278.7bhp/tonne
87.6bhp/L 65.3kW/L 88.8PS/L
56.5ft/sec 17.2m/sec
20.2mph 32.5kmh/1000rpm
17.3mpg 14.4mpgUS 16.3L/100km
Petrol 4-stroke piston
1998cc 121.9cu in
In-line 4 2 Carburettor
Compression ratio: 10.5:1
Bore: 86.0mm 3.4in
Stroke: 86.0mm 3.4in
Valve type/No: Overhead 16
Transmission: Manual
No. of forward speeds: 5
Wheels driven: Rear
Springs F/R: Coil/Coil
Brakes F/R: Disc/Disc
Steering: Rack & pinion
Wheelbase: 223.5cm 88.0in
Track F: 124.5cm 49.0in
Track R: 132.1cm 52.0in
Length: 339.1cm 133.5in
Width: 157.5cm 62.0in
Height: 108.0cm 42.5in
Ground clearance: 12.7cm 5.0in
Kerb weight: 627.9kg 1383.0lb
Fuel: 45.5L 10.0gal 12.0galUS

726 Caterham

Super 7
1991 UK
112.0mph 180.2kmh
0-60mph 96.5kmh: 5.6secs
135.0bhp 100.7kW 136.9PS
@ 6000rpm
122.0lbft 165.3Nm @ 4500rpm
236.2bhp/ton 232.3bhp/tonne
79.9bhp/L 59.6kW/L 81.0PS/L
51.0ft/sec 15.5m/sec
Petrol 4-stroke piston
1690cc 103.1cu in
In-line 4 2 Carburettor
Compression ratio: 9.7:1
Bore: 88.3mm 3.5in
Stroke: 77.6mm 3.1in
Valve type/No: Overhead 8
Transmission: Manual
No. of forward speeds: 5
Wheels driven: Rear
Springs F/R: Coil/Coil
Brakes F/R: Disc/Disc
Steering: Rack & pinion
Wheelbase: 224.8cm 88.5in
Track F: 127.0cm 50.0in
Track R: 132.1cm 52.0in
Length: 337.8cm 133.0in
Width: 158.0cm 62.2in
Height: 109.2cm 43.0in
Kerb weight: 581.1kg 1280.0lb
Fuel: 30.3L 6.7gal 8.0galUS

727 Checker

Marathon
1968 USA
103.0mph 165.7kmh
0-50mph 80.5kmh: 10.0secs
0-60mph 96.5kmh: 13.9secs
0-1/4 mile: 19.7secs
200.0bhp 149.1kW 202.8PS
@ 4600rpm
300.0lbft 406.5Nm @ 2400rpm
116.7bhp/ton 114.7bhp/tonne
39.7bhp/L 29.6kW/L 40.3PS/L
41.5ft/sec 12.6m/sec
24.0mph 38.6kmh/1000rpm
Petrol 4-stroke piston
5032cc 307.0cu in
Vee 8
Compression ratio: 9.0:1
Bore: 98.3mm 3.9in
Stroke: 82.5mm 3.2in
Valve type/No: Overhead 16
Transmission: Automatic
No. of forward speeds: 3
Wheels driven: Rear
Brakes F/R: Drum/Drum
Steering: Recirculating ball PA
Wheelbase: 304.8cm 120.0in
Track F: 157.5cm 62.0in
Track R: 158.8cm 62.5in
Length: 506.2cm 199.3in
Width: 193.0cm 76.0in
Height: 159.5cm 62.8in
Kerb weight: 1743.4kg 3840.0lb

728 Checker

Marathon
1969 USA
109.0mph 175.4kmh
0-50mph 80.5kmh: 7.5secs
0-60mph 96.5kmh: 10.3secs
0-1/4 mile: 17.8secs
275.0bhp 205.1kW 278.8PS
@ 4800rpm
355.0lbft 481.0Nm @ 3200rpm
160.6bhp/ton 157.9bhp/tonne
51.3bhp/L 38.3kW/L 52.0PS/L
43.3ft/sec 13.2m/sec
23.6mph 38.0kmh/1000rpm
Petrol 4-stroke piston
5359cc 327.0cu in
Vee 8 1 Carburettor
Compression ratio: 10.0:1
Bore: 101.6mm 4.0in
Stroke: 82.6mm 3.2in
Valve type/No: Overhead 16
Transmission: Automatic
No. of forward speeds: 3
Wheels driven: Rear
Springs F/R: Coil/Leaf
Brake system: PA
Brakes F/R: Drum/Drum
Steering: Recirculating ball PA
Wheelbase: 304.8cm 120.0in
Track F: 152.4cm 60.0in
Track R: 160.0cm 63.0in
Length: 505.5cm 199.0in
Width: 193.0cm 76.0in
Height: 160.0cm 63.0in
Kerb weight: 1741.1kg 3835.0lb
Fuel: 87.1L 19.1gal 23.0galUS

729 Chevrolet

26.3hp Saloon de Luxe
1935 USA
79.6mph 128.1kmh
0-50mph 80.5kmh: 15.0secs
0-60mph 96.5kmh: 20.4secs
18.0mpg 15.0mpgUS 15.7L/100km
Petrol 4-stroke piston
3358cc 204.9cu in
In-line 6
Bore: 84.1mm 3.3in
Stroke: 101.6mm 4.0in
Valve type/No: Overhead 12
Transmission: Manual
No. of forward speeds: 3
Wheels driven: Rear
Brakes F/R: Drum/Drum
Kerb weight: 1556.8kg 3429.0lb
Fuel: 54.6L 12.0gal 14.4galUS

730 Chevrolet

Master de Luxe Sports Sedan
1937 USA
78.9mph 127.0kmh
0-50mph 80.5kmh: 15.2secs
0-60mph 96.5kmh: 22.6secs
18.0mpg 15.0mpgUS 15.7L/100km
Petrol 4-stroke piston
3725cc 227.3cu in
In-line 6
Bore: 88.8mm 3.5in
Stroke: 95.3mm 3.8in
Valve type/No: Overhead 12
Transmission: Manual
No. of forward speeds: 3
Wheels driven: Rear
Brakes F/R: Drum/Drum
Wheelbase: 285.0cm 112.2in
Track F: 144.0cm 56.7in
Track R: 144.0cm 56.7in
Length: 464.8cm 183.0in
Width: 177.8cm 70.0in
Height: 174.0cm 68.5in
Ground clearance: 20.8cm 8.2in
Kerb weight: 1457.3kg 3210.0lb
Fuel: 54.6L 12.0gal 14.4galUS

731 Chevrolet

Master de Luxe Saloon
1938 USA
84.1mph 135.3kmh
0-50mph 80.5kmh: 13.6secs
0-60mph 96.5kmh: 20.4secs
17.0mpg 14.2mpgUS 16.6L/100km
Petrol 4-stroke piston
3548cc 216.5cu in
In-line 6
Bore: 88.9mm 3.5in
Stroke: 95.2mm 3.8in
Valve type/No: Overhead 12
Transmission: Manual
No. of forward speeds: 3
Wheels driven: Rear
Brakes F/R: Drum/Drum
Kerb weight: 1415.6kg 3118.0lb
Fuel: 52.8L 11.6gal 13.9galUS

732 Chevrolet

Corvette
1953 USA
107.1mph 172.3kmh
0-60mph 96.5kmh: 11.0secs
0-1/4 mile: 18.0secs
150.0bhp 111.9kW 152.1PS
@ 4200rpm
223.0lbft 302.2Nm @ 2400rpm
117.9bhp/ton 115.9bhp/tonne
38.8bhp/L 29.0kW/L 39.4PS/L
46.0ft/sec 14.0m/sec
Petrol 4-stroke piston
3861cc 235.6cu in
In-line 6 3 Carburettor
Compression ratio: 8.0:1
Bore: 90.4mm 3.6in
Stroke: 100.1mm 3.9in
Valve type/No: Overhead 12
Transmission: Automatic
No. of forward speeds: 2
Wheels driven: Rear
Springs F/R: Coil/Leaf
Brakes F/R: Drum/Drum
Steering: Recirculating ball
Wheelbase: 259.1cm 102.0in
Track F: 144.8cm 57.0in
Track R: 149.9cm 59.0in
Length: 424.2cm 167.0in
Width: 183.4cm 72.2in
Height: 132.3cm 52.1in
Kerb weight: 1293.9kg 2850.0lb
Fuel: 68.1L 15.0gal 18.0galUS

733 Chevrolet

Corvette
1954 USA
106.4mph 171.2kmh
0-50mph 80.5kmh: 7.7secs
0-60mph 96.5kmh: 11.0secs
0-1/4 mile: 18.0secs
150.0bhp 111.9kW 152.1PS
@ 4200rpm
223.0lbft 302.2Nm @ 2400rpm
116.3bhp/ton 114.3bhp/tonne
38.8bhp/L 29.0kW/L 39.4PS/L
46.0ft/sec 14.0m/sec
22.5mph 36.2kmh/1000rpm

Petrol 4-stroke piston
3861cc 235.6cu in
In-line 6
Compression ratio: 8.0:1
Bore: 90.4mm 3.6in
Stroke: 100.1mm 3.9in
Valve type/No: Overhead 12
Transmission: Automatic
No. of forward speeds: 2
Wheels driven: Rear
Wheelbase: 259.1cm 102.0in
Track F: 144.8cm 57.0in
Track R: 149.9cm 59.0in
Kerb weight: 1312.1kg 2890.0lb

734 Chevrolet

210 Coupe Club V8
1955 USA
104.7mph 168.5kmh
0-50mph 80.5kmh: 7.2secs
0-60mph 96.5kmh: 9.7secs
0-1/4 mile: 17.4secs
180.0bhp 134.2kW 182.5PS
@ 4600rpm
260.0lbft 352.3Nm @ 2800rpm
118.9bhp/ton 116.9bhp/tonne
41.4bhp/L 30.9kW/L 42.0PS/L
38.3ft/sec 11.7m/sec
27.8mph 44.7kmh/1000rpm
Petrol 4-stroke piston
4344cc 265.0cu in
Vee 8
Compression ratio: 8.0:1
Bore: 95.3mm 3.8in
Stroke: 76.2mm 3.0in
Valve type/No: Overhead 16
Transmission: Manual
No. of forward speeds: 3
Wheels driven: Rear
Wheelbase: 292.1cm 115.0in
Track F: 147.3cm 58.0in
Track R: 149.4cm 58.8in
Kerb weight: 1539.1kg 3390.0lb

735 Chevrolet

Corvette V8
1955 USA
116.9mph 188.1kmh
0-50mph 80.5kmh: 6.4secs
0-60mph 96.5kmh: 8.7secs
0-1/4 mile: 16.5secs
195.0bhp 145.4kW 197.7PS
@ 4600rpm
260.0lbft 352.3Nm @ 2800rpm
151.7bhp/ton 149.1bhp/tonne
44.9bhp/L 33.5kW/L 45.5PS/L
38.3ft/sec 11.7m/sec
22.5mph 36.2kmh/1000rpm
Petrol 4-stroke piston
4344cc 265.0cu in
Vee 8
Compression ratio: 8.0:1
Bore: 95.3mm 3.8in
Stroke: 76.2mm 3.0in
Valve type/No: Overhead 16
Transmission: Automatic
No. of forward speeds: 2
Wheels driven: Rear
Wheelbase: 259.1cm 102.0in
Track F: 144.8cm 57.0in
Track R: 149.9cm 59.0in
Kerb weight: 1307.5kg 2880.0lb

736 Chevrolet

210
1956 USA
111.0mph 178.6kmh
0-50mph 80.5kmh: 6.8secs
0-60mph 96.5kmh: 9.0secs
0-1/4 mile: 16.6secs
205.0bhp 152.9kW 207.8PS
@ 4600rpm
268.0lbft 363.1Nm @ 3000rpm
135.9bhp/ton 133.6bhp/tonne
47.2bhp/L 35.2kW/L 47.9PS/L
38.3ft/sec 11.7m/sec
21.6mph 34.8kmh/1000rpm
Petrol 4-stroke piston
4343cc 265.0cu in
Vee 8
Compression ratio: 9.3:1
Bore: 95.3mm 3.8in
Stroke: 76.2mm 3.0in
Valve type/No: Overhead 16
Transmission: Manual
No. of forward speeds: 3
Wheels driven: Rear
Wheelbase: 292.1cm 115.0in
Track F: 147.3cm 58.0in
Track R: 149.4cm 58.8in
Kerb weight: 1534.5kg 3380.0lb

737 Chevrolet

Corvette
1956 USA
129.1mph 207.7kmh
0-50mph 80.5kmh: 5.3secs
0-60mph 96.5kmh: 7.3secs
0-1/4 mile: 15.8secs
225.0bhp 167.8kW 228.1PS
@ 5200rpm
270.0lbft 365.9Nm @ 3600rpm
169.1bhp/ton 166.3bhp/tonne
51.8bhp/L 38.6kW/L 52.5PS/L
43.3ft/sec 13.2m/sec
22.5mph 36.2kmh/1000rpm
Petrol 4-stroke piston
4344cc 265.0cu in
Vee 8
Compression ratio: 9.3:1
Bore: 95.3mm 3.8in
Stroke: 76.2mm 3.0in
Valve type/No: Overhead 16
Transmission: Manual
No. of forward speeds: 3
Wheels driven: Rear
Wheelbase: 259.1cm 102.0in
Track F: 144.0cm 56.7in
Track R: 149.4cm 58.8in
Kerb weight: 1352.9kg 2980.0lb

738 Chevrolet

Corvette Sebring
1956 USA
148.0mph 238.1kmh
0-60mph 96.5kmh: 6.3secs
0-1/4 mile: 14.9secs
225.0bhp 167.8kW 228.1PS
@ 5200rpm
270.0lbft 365.9Nm @ 3600rpm
186.7bhp/ton 183.5bhp/tonne
51.8bhp/L 38.6kW/L 52.5PS/L
43.3ft/sec 13.2m/sec
Petrol 4-stroke piston
4343cc 265.0cu in
Vee 8 2 Carburettor
Compression ratio: 9.3:1
Bore: 95.3mm 3.8in
Stroke: 76.2mm 3.0in
Valve type/No: Overhead 16
Transmission: Manual
No. of forward speeds: 3
Wheels driven: Rear
Springs F/R: Coil/Leaf
Brakes F/R: Drum/Drum
Steering: Recirculating ball
Wheelbase: 259.1cm 102.0in
Track F: 144.8cm 57.0in
Track R: 149.9cm 59.0in
Length: 426.7cm 168.0in
Width: 179.1cm 70.5in
Height: 109.2cm 43.0in
Kerb weight: 1225.8kg 2700.0lb
Fuel: 141.9L 31.2gal 37.5galUS

739 Chevrolet

Corvette
1957 USA
132.0mph 212.4kmh
0-50mph 80.5kmh: 4.7secs
0-60mph 96.5kmh: 5.7secs
0-1/4 mile: 14.3secs
283.0bhp 211.0kW 286.9PS
@ 6200rpm
290.0lbft 393.0Nm @ 4400rpm
220.1bhp/ton 216.4bhp/tonne
61.0bhp/L 45.5kW/L 61.8PS/L
51.7ft/sec 15.7m/sec
Petrol 4-stroke piston
4639cc 283.0cu in
Vee 8 fuel injection
Compression ratio: 10.5:1
Bore: 98.4mm 3.9in
Stroke: 76.2mm 3.0in
Valve type/No: Overhead 16
Transmission: Manual
No. of forward speeds: 4
Wheels driven: Rear
Springs F/R: Coil/Coil
Brakes F/R: Drum/Drum
Steering: Recirculating ball
Wheelbase: 259.1cm 102.0in
Track F: 144.8cm 57.0in
Track R: 149.9cm 59.0in
Length: 426.7cm 168.0in
Width: 179.1cm 70.5in
Height: 129.8cm 51.1in
Kerb weight: 1307.5kg 2880.0lb

740 Chevrolet

Corvette Injection
1957 USA
132.0mph 212.4kmh
0-50mph 80.5kmh: 4.7secs
0-60mph 96.5kmh: 5.7secs
0-1/4 mile: 14.3secs
283.0bhp 211.0kW 286.9PS
@ 6200rpm
290.0lbft 393.0Nm @ 4400rpm
220.1bhp/ton 216.4bhp/tonne
61.0bhp/L 45.5kW/L 61.8PS/L
51.7ft/sec 15.7m/sec
Petrol 4-stroke piston
4639cc 283.0cu in
Vee 8 fuel injection
Compression ratio: 10.5:1
Bore: 98.4mm 3.9in
Stroke: 76.2mm 3.0in
Valve type/No: Overhead 16
Transmission: Manual
No. of forward speeds: 4
Wheels driven: Rear
Wheelbase: 259.1cm 102.0in
Track F: 144.8cm 57.0in
Track R: 149.9cm 59.0in
Kerb weight: 1307.5kg 2880.0lb

741 Chevrolet

Corvette RPO 684/579E
1957 USA
132.0mph 212.4kmh
0-60mph 96.5kmh: 5.7secs
0-1/4 mile: 14.3secs
283.0bhp 211.0kW 286.9PS
@ 6200rpm
290.0lbft 393.0Nm
220.1bhp/ton 216.4bhp/tonne
61.0bhp/L 45.5kW/L 61.9PS/L
51.7ft/sec 15.7m/sec
Petrol 4-stroke piston
4638cc 283.0cu in
Vee 8 fuel injection
Compression ratio: 10.5:1
Bore: 98.3mm 3.9in
Stroke: 76.2mm 3.0in
Valve type/No: Overhead 16
Transmission: Manual
No. of forward speeds: 4
Wheels driven: Rear
Springs F/R: Coil/Leaf
Brakes F/R: Drum/Drum
Steering: Recirculating ball
Wheelbase: 259.1cm 102.0in
Track F: 144.8cm 57.0in
Track R: 149.9cm 59.0in
Length: 426.7cm 168.0in
Width: 179.1cm 70.5in
Height: 129.5cm 51.0in
Kerb weight: 1307.5kg 2880.0lb
Fuel: 62.1L 13.6gal 16.4galUS

742 Chevrolet

Corvair
1959 USA
88.0mph 141.6kmh
0-50mph 80.5kmh: 14.4secs
0-60mph 96.5kmh: 19.5secs
0-1/4 mile: 21.7secs
80.0bhp 59.7kW 81.1PS
@ 4400rpm
125.0lbft 169.4Nm @ 2400rpm
73.1bhp/ton 71.9bhp/tonne
35.0bhp/L 26.1kW/L 35.4PS/L
31.8ft/sec 9.7m/sec
19.9mph 32.0kmh/1000rpm
Petrol 4-stroke piston
2288cc 139.6cu in
Flat 6
Compression ratio: 8.0:1
Bore: 85.9mm 3.4in
Stroke: 66.0mm 2.6in
Valve type/No: Overhead 12
Transmission: Manual
No. of forward speeds: 3
Wheels driven: Rear
Wheelbase: 274.3cm 108.0in
Track F: 137.2cm 54.0in
Track R: 137.2cm 54.0in
Length: 457.2cm 180.0in
Width: 169.9cm 66.9in
Height: 131.6cm 51.8in
Kerb weight: 1112.3kg 2450.0lb

743 Chevrolet

Corvette
1959 USA
128.0mph 206.0kmh
0-50mph 80.5kmh: 5.1secs
0-60mph 96.5kmh: 6.6secs
0-1/4 mile: 14.5secs
290.0bhp 216.2kW 294.0PS
@ 6200rpm
290.0lbft 393.0Nm @ 4400rpm
215.1bhp/ton 211.5bhp/tonne
62.5bhp/L 46.6kW/L 63.4PS/L
51.7ft/sec 15.7m/sec
19.6mph 31.5kmh/1000rpm
Petrol 4-stroke piston
4639cc 283.0cu in
Vee 8 fuel injection
Compression ratio: 10.5:1
Bore: 98.4mm 3.9in
Stroke: 76.2mm 3.0in
Valve type/No: Overhead 16
Transmission: Manual
No. of forward speeds: 4
Wheels driven: Rear
Wheelbase: 259.1cm 102.0in
Track F: 144.8cm 57.0in
Track R: 149.9cm 59.0in
Length: 452.1cm 178.0in
Width: 184.9cm 72.8in
Height: 129.5cm 51.0in
Kerb weight: 1371.1kg 3020.0lb

744 Chevrolet

Corvair 4-speed
1960 USA
87.5mph 140.8kmh
0-50mph 80.5kmh: 11.2secs
0-60mph 96.5kmh: 16.4secs
0-1/4 mile: 20.6secs
80.0bhp 59.7kW 81.1PS
@ 4400rpm
125.0lbft 169.4Nm @ 2400rpm
73.7bhp/ton 72.5bhp/tonne
35.0bhp/L 26.1kW/L 35.4PS/L
31.8ft/sec 9.7m/sec
19.9mph 32.0kmh/1000rpm
Petrol 4-stroke piston
2288cc 139.6cu in
Flat 6 1 Carburettor
Compression ratio: 8.0:1
Bore: 85.9mm 3.4in
Stroke: 66.0mm 2.6in
Valve type/No: Overhead 12
Transmission: Manual
No. of forward speeds: 4
Wheels driven: Rear
Wheelbase: 274.3cm 108.0in
Track F: 137.2cm 54.0in
Track R: 137.2cm 54.0in
Length: 457.2cm 180.0in
Width: 170.2cm 67.0in
Height: 130.8cm 51.5in
Ground clearance: 15.2cm 6.0in
Kerb weight: 1103.2kg 2430.0lb

745 Chevrolet

Corvair Automatic
1960 USA
85.5mph 137.6kmh
0-50mph 80.5kmh: 12.5secs
0-60mph 96.5kmh: 17.5secs
0-1/4 mile: 21.5secs
80.0bhp 59.7kW 81.1PS
@ 4400rpm
125.0lbft 169.4Nm @ 2400rpm
72.3bhp/ton 71.0bhp/tonne
35.0bhp/L 26.1kW/L 35.4PS/L
31.8ft/sec 9.7m/sec
19.9mph 32.0kmh/1000rpm
Petrol 4-stroke piston
2288cc 139.6cu in
Flat 6 1 Carburettor
Compression ratio: 8.0:1
Bore: 85.9mm 3.4in
Stroke: 66.0mm 2.6in
Valve type/No: Overhead 12
Transmission: Automatic
No. of forward speeds: 2
Wheels driven: Rear
Wheelbase: 274.3cm 108.0in
Track F: 137.2cm 54.0in

Track R: 137.2cm 54.0in
Length: 457.2cm 180.0in
Width: 169.9cm 66.9in
Height: 131.6cm 51.8in
Kerb weight: 1125.9kg 2480.0lb

746 Chevrolet

Corvair 700
1961 USA
84.6mph 136.1kmh
0-50mph 80.5kmh: 13.6secs
0-60mph 96.5kmh: 20.6secs
0-1/4 mile: 22.0secs
80.0bhp 59.7kW 81.1PS
@ 4400rpm
125.0lbft 169.4Nm @ 2400rpm
72.7bhp/ton 71.5bhp/tonne
35.0bhp/L 26.1kW/L 35.5PS/L
31.8ft/sec 9.7m/sec
19.8mph 31.9kmh/1000rpm
18.8mpg 15.7mpgUS 15.0L/100km
Petrol 4-stroke piston
2287cc 139.5cu in
Flat 6
Compression ratio: 8.0:1
Bore: 85.7mm 3.4in
Stroke: 66.0mm 2.6in
Valve type/No: Overhead 12
Transmission: Automatic
No. of forward speeds: 2
Wheels driven: Rear
Springs F/R: Coil/Coil
Brake system: PA
Brakes F/R: Drum/Drum
Wheelbase: 274.3cm 108.0in
Track F: 137.2cm 54.0in
Track R: 137.2cm 54.0in
Length: 457.2cm 180.0in
Width: 169.9cm 66.9in
Height: 130.3cm 51.3in
Ground clearance: 15.2cm 6.0in
Kerb weight: 1118.7kg 2464.0lb
Fuel: 40.9L 9.0gal 10.8galUS

747 Chevrolet

Corvair Greenbrier
1961 USA
70.0mph 112.6kmh
0-50mph 80.5kmh: 19.6secs
0-60mph 96.5kmh: 32.2secs
0-1/4 mile: 25.0secs
80.0bhp 59.7kW 81.1PS
@ 4400rpm
128.0lbft 173.4Nm @ 2300rpm
58.9bhp/ton 58.0bhp/tonne
33.7bhp/L 25.1kW/L 34.1PS/L
31.8ft/sec 9.7m/sec
19.4mph 31.2kmh/1000rpm
Petrol 4-stroke piston
2377cc 145.0cu in
Flat 6 1 Carburettor
Compression ratio: 8.0:1
Bore: 87.3mm 3.4in
Stroke: 66.0mm 2.6in
Valve type/No: Overhead 12
Transmission: Automatic
No. of forward speeds: 2
Wheels driven: Rear
Brakes F/R: Drum/Drum
Wheelbase: 241.3cm 95.0in
Track F: 147.3cm 58.0in
Track R: 147.3cm 58.0in
Length: 456.4cm 179.7in
Width: 177.8cm 70.0in
Height: 174.0cm 68.5in
Ground clearance: 16.8cm 6.6in
Kerb weight: 1380.2kg 3040.0lb

748 Chevrolet

Corvair Monza
1961 USA
85.0mph 136.8kmh
0-50mph 80.5kmh: 13.0secs
0-60mph 96.5kmh: 19.7secs
0-1/4 mile: 22.0secs
80.0bhp 59.7kW 81.1PS
@ 4400rpm
128.0lbft 173.4Nm @ 2300rpm
69.6bhp/ton 68.4bhp/tonne
33.7bhp/L 25.1kW/L 34.1PS/L
31.8ft/sec 9.7m/sec
21.6mph 34.8kmh/1000rpm
Petrol 4-stroke piston
2377cc 145.0cu in
Flat 6 1 Carburettor
Compression ratio: 8.0:1
Bore: 87.3mm 3.4in
Stroke: 66.0mm 2.6in
Valve type/No: Overhead 12
Transmission: Automatic
No. of forward speeds: 3
Wheels driven: Rear
Brakes F/R: Drum/Drum
Wheelbase: 274.3cm 108.0in
Track F: 137.2cm 54.0in
Track R: 137.2cm 54.0in
Length: 457.2cm 180.0in
Width: 170.2cm 67.0in
Height: 130.8cm 51.5in
Ground clearance: 15.2cm 6.0in
Kerb weight: 1169.0kg 2575.0lb

749 Chevrolet

Corvair Monza 4-speed
1961 USA
92.0mph 148.0kmh
0-50mph 80.5kmh: 10.4secs
0-60mph 96.5kmh: 15.5secs
0-1/4 mile: 20.3secs
98.0bhp 73.1kW 99.4PS
@ 4600rpm
132.0lbft 178.9Nm @ 2900rpm
86.6bhp/ton 85.1bhp/tonne
41.2bhp/L 30.7kW/L 41.8PS/L
33.2ft/sec 10.1m/sec
21.6mph 34.8kmh/1000rpm
Petrol 4-stroke piston
2377cc 145.0cu in
Flat 6 1 Carburettor
Compression ratio: 8.0:1
Bore: 87.4mm 3.4in
Stroke: 66.0mm 2.6in
Valve type/No: Overhead 12
Transmission: Manual
No. of forward speeds: 4
Wheels driven: Rear
Brakes F/R: Drum/Drum
Wheelbase: 274.3cm 108.0in
Track F: 137.2cm 54.0in
Track R: 137.2cm 54.0in
Length: 457.2cm 180.0in
Width: 170.2cm 67.0in
Height: 130.8cm 51.5in
Ground clearance: 15.2cm 6.0in
Kerb weight: 1150.9kg 2535.0lb

750 Chevrolet

Corvette
1961 USA
128.0mph 206.0kmh
0-50mph 80.5kmh: 5.1secs
0-60mph 96.5kmh: 6.6secs
0-1/4 mile: 14.2secs
315.0bhp 234.9kW 319.4PS
@ 6200rpm
295.0lbft 399.7Nm @ 4700rpm
229.1bhp/ton 225.3bhp/tonne
67.9bhp/L 50.6kW/L 68.8PS/L
51.7ft/sec 15.7m/sec
19.6mph 31.5kmh/1000rpm
Petrol 4-stroke piston
4639cc 283.0cu in
Vee 8
Compression ratio: 11.0:1
Bore: 98.6mm 3.9in
Stroke: 76.2mm 3.0in
Valve type/No: Overhead 16
Transmission: Manual
No. of forward speeds: 4
Wheels driven: Rear
Wheelbase: 259.1cm 102.0in
Track F: 144.8cm 57.0in
Track R: 149.9cm 59.0in
Length: 452.1cm 178.0in
Width: 178.8cm 70.4in
Height: 132.3cm 52.1in
Ground clearance: 17.0cm 6.7in
Kerb weight: 1398.3kg 3080.0lb

751 Chevrolet

Corvette 230
1961 USA
109.0mph 175.4kmh
0-50mph 80.5kmh: 6.6secs
0-60mph 96.5kmh: 7.7secs
0-1/4 mile: 16.5secs
230.0bhp 171.5kW 233.2PS
@ 4800rpm
300.0lbft 406.5Nm @ 3000rpm
170.0bhp/ton 167.2bhp/tonne
49.6bhp/L 37.0kW/L 50.3PS/L
40.0ft/sec 12.2m/sec
22.8mph 36.7kmh/1000rpm
Petrol 4-stroke piston
4639cc 283.0cu in
Vee 8 1 Carburettor
Compression ratio: 9.5:1
Bore: 98.6mm 3.9in
Stroke: 76.2mm 3.0in
Valve type/No: Overhead 16
Transmission: Automatic
No. of forward speeds: 2
Wheels driven: Rear
Brake system: PA
Brakes F/R: Drum/Drum
Wheelbase: 259.1cm 102.0in
Track F: 144.8cm 57.0in
Track R: 149.9cm 59.0in
Length: 452.1cm 178.0in
Width: 178.8cm 70.4in
Height: 131.1cm 51.6in
Ground clearance: 17.0cm 6.7in
Kerb weight: 1375.6kg 3030.0lb

752 Chevrolet

Corvette 270
1961 USA
131.0mph 210.8kmh
0-50mph 80.5kmh: 4.5secs
0-60mph 96.5kmh: 5.9secs
0-1/4 mile: 14.6secs
270.0bhp 201.3kW 273.7PS
@ 6000rpm
285.0lbft 386.2Nm @ 4200rpm
205.0bhp/ton 201.6bhp/tonne
58.2bhp/L 43.4kW/L 59.0PS/L
50.0ft/sec 15.2m/sec
21.9mph 35.2kmh/1000rpm
Petrol 4-stroke piston
4639cc 283.0cu in
Vee 8 2 Carburettor
Compression ratio: 9.5:1
Bore: 98.6mm 3.9in
Stroke: 76.2mm 3.0in
Valve type/No: Overhead 16
Transmission: Manual
No. of forward speeds: 4
Wheels driven: Rear
Brake system: PA
Brakes F/R: Drum/Drum
Steering: PA
Wheelbase: 259.1cm 102.0in
Track F: 144.8cm 57.0in
Track R: 149.9cm 59.0in
Length: 452.1cm 178.0in
Width: 178.8cm 70.4in
Height: 131.1cm 51.6in
Ground clearance: 17.0cm 6.7in
Kerb weight: 1339.3kg 2950.0lb

753 Chevrolet

Corvette 315
1961 USA
128.0mph 206.0kmh
0-50mph 80.5kmh: 4.5secs
0-60mph 96.5kmh: 5.5secs
0-1/4 mile: 14.2secs
315.0bhp 234.9kW 319.4PS
@ 6200rpm
295.0lbft 399.7Nm @ 4700rpm
232.1bhp/ton 228.2bhp/tonne
67.9bhp/L 50.6kW/L 68.8PS/L
51.7ft/sec 15.7m/sec
19.5mph 31.4kmh/1000rpm
Petrol 4-stroke piston
4639cc 283.0cu in
Vee 8 fuel injection
Compression ratio: 11.0:1
Bore: 98.6mm 3.9in
Stroke: 76.2mm 3.0in
Valve type/No: Overhead 16
Transmission: Manual
No. of forward speeds: 4
Wheels driven: Rear
Brake system: PA
Brakes F/R: Drum/Drum
Wheelbase: 259.1cm 102.0in
Track F: 144.8cm 57.0in
Track R: 149.9cm 59.0in
Length: 452.1cm 178.0in
Width: 178.8cm 70.4in
Height: 131.1cm 51.6in
Ground clearance: 17.0cm 6.7in
Kerb weight: 1380.2kg 3040.0lb

754 Chevrolet

Impala
1961 USA
115.0mph 185.0kmh
0-50mph 80.5kmh: 7.8secs
0-60mph 96.5kmh: 10.6secs
0-1/4 mile: 17.2secs
250.0bhp 186.4kW 253.5PS
@ 4400rpm
355.0lbft 481.0Nm @ 2800rpm
140.7bhp/ton 138.4bhp/tonne
43.8bhp/L 32.7kW/L 44.4PS/L
39.7ft/sec 12.1m/sec
24.7mph 39.7kmh/1000rpm
Petrol 4-stroke piston
5705cc 348.1cu in
Vee 8 1 Carburettor
Compression ratio: 9.5:1
Bore: 104.8mm 4.1in
Stroke: 82.6mm 3.2in
Valve type/No: Overhead 16
Transmission: Manual
No. of forward speeds: 3
Wheels driven: Rear
Brake system: PA
Steering: PA
Wheelbase: 302.3cm 119.0in
Track F: 153.2cm 60.3in
Track R: 150.6cm 59.3in
Length: 531.6cm 209.3in
Width: 199.1cm 78.4in
Height: 141.0cm 55.5in
Ground clearance: 15.2cm 6.0in
Kerb weight: 1806.9kg 3980.0lb

755 Chevrolet

Bel Air 409 SS/S
1962 USA
116.0mph 186.6kmh
0-50mph 80.5kmh: 3.0secs
0-60mph 96.5kmh: 4.0secs
0-1/4 mile: 12.2secs
409.0bhp 305.0kW 414.7PS
@ 6000rpm
420.0lbft 569.1Nm @ 4000rpm
261.8bhp/ton 257.4bhp/tonne
61.0bhp/L 45.5kW/L 61.9PS/L
58.3ft/sec 17.8m/sec
17.8mph 28.6kmh/1000rpm
Petrol 4-stroke piston
6702cc 408.9cu in
Vee 8 2 Carburettor
Compression ratio: 11.0:1
Bore: 109.5mm 4.3in
Stroke: 88.9mm 3.5in
Valve type/No: Overhead 16
Transmission: Manual
No. of forward speeds: 4
Wheels driven: Rear
Wheelbase: 302.3cm 119.0in
Track F: 153.2cm 60.3in
Track R: 150.6cm 59.3in
Length: 532.4cm 209.6in
Width: 200.7cm 79.0in
Height: 139.7cm 55.0in
Ground clearance: 16.5cm 6.5in
Kerb weight: 1589.0kg 3500.0lb
Fuel: 75.7L 16.6gal 20.0galUS

756 Chevrolet

Chevy II
1962 USA
92.0mph 148.0kmh
0-50mph 80.5kmh: 9.7secs
0-60mph 96.5kmh: 14.0secs
0-1/4 mile: 19.2secs
120.0bhp 89.5kW 121.7PS
@ 4400rpm
177.0lbft 239.8Nm @ 2400rpm
100.7bhp/ton 99.0bhp/tonne
37.7bhp/L 28.1kW/L 38.2PS/L
39.6ft/sec 12.1m/sec
21.8mph 35.1kmh/1000rpm
Petrol 4-stroke piston
3186cc 194.4cu in
In-line 6 1 Carburettor
Compression ratio: 8.5:1
Bore: 90.4mm 3.6in
Stroke: 82.3mm 3.2in
Valve type/No: Overhead 12
Transmission: Automatic
No. of forward speeds: 2
Wheels driven: Rear
Brakes F/R: Drum/Drum
Wheelbase: 279.4cm 110.0in
Track F: 144.3cm 56.8in
Track R: 143.0cm 56.3in
Length: 464.8cm 183.0in
Width: 179.8cm 70.8in
Height: 139.7cm 55.0in
Ground clearance: 15.2cm 6.0in

Kerb weight: 1212.2kg 2670.0lb

757 Chevrolet
Chevy II Corvette
1962 USA
131.0mph 210.8kmh
0-50mph 80.5kmh: 6.0secs
0-60mph 96.5kmh: 7.3secs
0-1/4 mile: 14.8secs
360.0bhp 268.4kW 365.0PS
@ 6000rpm
352.0lbft 477.0Nm @ 4000rpm
269.7bhp/ton 265.2bhp/tonne
67.2bhp/L 50.1kW/L 68.1PS/L
54.2ft/sec 16.5m/sec
21.9mph 35.2kmh/1000rpm
Petrol 4-stroke piston
5359cc 327.0cu in
Vee 8 fuel injection
Compression ratio: 11.3:1
Bore: 101.6mm 4.0in
Stroke: 82.6mm 3.2in
Valve type/No: Overhead 16
Transmission: Manual
No. of forward speeds: 4
Wheels driven: Rear
Wheelbase: 279.4cm 110.0in
Track F: 144.3cm 56.8in
Track R: 143.0cm 56.3in
Length: 464.8cm 183.0in
Width: 179.8cm 70.8in
Height: 137.2cm 54.0in
Ground clearance: 16.3cm 6.4in
Kerb weight: 1357.5kg 2990.0lb
Fuel: 60.6L 13.3gal 16.0galUS

758 Chevrolet
Chevy II Four Automatic
1962 USA
82.0mph 131.9kmh
0-50mph 80.5kmh: 13.8secs
0-60mph 96.5kmh: 20.0secs
0-1/4 mile: 21.7secs
90.0bhp 67.1kW 91.2PS
@ 4000rpm
152.0lbft 206.0Nm @ 2400rpm
75.8bhp/ton 74.5bhp/tonne
35.9bhp/L 26.8kW/L 36.4PS/L
36.1ft/sec 11.0m/sec
20.0mph 32.2kmh/1000rpm
Petrol 4-stroke piston
2507cc 153.0cu in
In-line 4
Compression ratio: 8.5:1
Bore: 98.6mm 3.9in
Stroke: 82.6mm 3.2in
Valve type/No: Overhead 8
Transmission: Automatic
No. of forward speeds: 2
Wheels driven: Rear
Wheelbase: 279.4cm 110.0in
Track F: 144.3cm 56.8in
Track R: 143.0cm 56.3in
Length: 464.8cm 183.0in
Width: 179.8cm 70.8in
Height: 139.7cm 55.0in
Ground clearance: 15.2cm 6.0in
Kerb weight: 1207.6kg 2660.0lb
Fuel: 60.6L 13.3gal 16.0galUS

759 Chevrolet
Chevy II Four Manual
1962 USA
84.0mph 135.2kmh
0-50mph 80.5kmh: 11.6secs
0-60mph 96.5kmh: 17.0secs
0-1/4 mile: 20.2secs
90.0bhp 67.1kW 91.2PS
@ 4000rpm
152.0lbft 206.0Nm @ 2400rpm
76.4bhp/ton 75.1bhp/tonne
35.9bhp/L 26.8kW/L 36.4PS/L
36.1ft/sec 11.0m/sec
21.8mph 35.1kmh/1000rpm
Petrol 4-stroke piston
2507cc 153.0cu in
In-line 4
Compression ratio: 8.5:1
Bore: 98.6mm 3.9in
Stroke: 82.6mm 3.2in
Valve type/No: Overhead 8
Transmission: Manual
No. of forward speeds: 3
Wheels driven: Rear
Wheelbase: 279.4cm 110.0in
Track F: 144.3cm 56.8in
Track R: 143.0cm 56.3in
Length: 464.8cm 183.0in
Width: 179.8cm 70.8in
Height: 139.7cm 55.0in
Ground clearance: 15.2cm 6.0in
Kerb weight: 1198.6kg 2640.0lb
Fuel: 60.6L 13.3gal 16.0galUS

760 Chevrolet
Chevy II Six Automatic
1962 USA
92.0mph 148.0kmh
0-50mph 80.5kmh: 10.6secs
0-60mph 96.5kmh: 14.5secs
0-1/4 mile: 19.5secs
120.0bhp 89.5kW 121.7PS
@ 4400rpm
177.0lbft 239.8Nm @ 2400rpm
94.3bhp/ton 92.7bhp/tonne
37.7bhp/L 28.1kW/L 38.3PS/L
39.7ft/sec 12.1m/sec
22.9mph 36.8kmh/1000rpm
Petrol 4-stroke piston
3179cc 194.0cu in
In-line 6
Compression ratio: 8.5:1
Bore: 90.4mm 3.6in
Stroke: 82.6mm 3.2in
Valve type/No: Overhead 12
Transmission: Automatic
No. of forward speeds: 2
Wheels driven: Rear
Wheelbase: 279.4cm 110.0in
Track F: 144.3cm 56.8in
Track R: 143.0cm 56.3in
Length: 464.8cm 183.0in
Width: 179.8cm 70.8in
Height: 137.2cm 54.0in
Ground clearance: 16.3cm 6.4in
Kerb weight: 1293.9kg 2850.0lb
Fuel: 60.6L 13.3gal 16.0galUS

761 Chevrolet
Chevy II Six Manual
1962 USA
92.0mph 148.0kmh
0-50mph 80.5kmh: 9.8secs
0-60mph 96.5kmh: 13.0secs
0-1/4 mile: 19.0secs
120.0bhp 89.5kW 121.7PS
@ 4400rpm
177.0lbft 239.8Nm @ 2400rpm
95.0bhp/ton 93.4bhp/tonne
37.7bhp/L 28.1kW/L 38.3PS/L
39.7ft/sec 12.1m/sec
22.9mph 36.8kmh/1000rpm
Petrol 4-stroke piston
3179cc 194.0cu in
In-line 6
Compression ratio: 8.5:1
Bore: 90.4mm 3.6in
Stroke: 82.6mm 3.2in
Valve type/No: Overhead 12
Transmission: Manual
No. of forward speeds: 3
Wheels driven: Rear
Wheelbase: 279.4cm 110.0in
Track F: 144.3cm 56.8in
Track R: 143.0cm 56.3in
Length: 464.8cm 183.0in
Width: 179.8cm 70.8in
Height: 137.2cm 54.0in
Ground clearance: 16.3cm 6.4in
Kerb weight: 1284.8kg 2830.0lb
Fuel: 60.6L 13.3gal 16.0galUS

762 Chevrolet
Corvair Monza
1962 USA
90.0mph 144.8kmh
0-50mph 80.5kmh: 14.7secs
0-60mph 96.5kmh: 21.6secs
0-1/4 mile: 22.8secs
84.0bhp 62.6kW 85.2PS
@ 4400rpm
130.0lbft 176.2Nm @ 2300rpm
73.5bhp/ton 72.3bhp/tonne
35.3bhp/L 26.4kW/L 35.8PS/L
31.8ft/sec 9.7m/sec
19.8mph 31.9kmh/1000rpm
Petrol 4-stroke piston
2376cc 145.0cu in
Flat 6 1 Carburettor
Compression ratio: 9.0:1
Bore: 87.4mm 3.4in
Stroke: 66.0mm 2.6in
Valve type/No: Overhead 12
Transmission: Automatic
No. of forward speeds: 2
Wheels driven: Rear
Wheelbase: 274.3cm 108.0in
Track F: 138.4cm 54.5in
Track R: 138.4cm 54.5in
Length: 457.2cm 180.0in
Width: 170.2cm 67.0in
Height: 130.8cm 51.5in
Ground clearance: 15.2cm 6.0in
Kerb weight: 1162.2kg 2560.0lb
Fuel: 53.0L 11.6gal 14.0galUS

763 Chevrolet
Corvair Monza Coupe
1962 USA
90.0mph 144.8kmh
0-50mph 80.5kmh: 14.7secs
0-60mph 96.5kmh: 21.6secs
0-1/4 mile: 22.8secs
84.0bhp 62.6kW 85.2PS
@ 4400rpm
130.0lbft 176.2Nm @ 2300rpm
73.5bhp/ton 72.3bhp/tonne
35.3bhp/L 26.3kW/L 35.8PS/L
31.8ft/sec 9.7m/sec
19.8mph 31.9kmh/1000rpm
Petrol 4-stroke piston
2377cc 145.0cu in
Flat 6 1 Carburettor
Compression ratio: 9.0:1
Bore: 87.4mm 3.4in
Stroke: 66.0mm 2.6in
Valve type/No: Overhead 12
Transmission: Automatic
No. of forward speeds: 2
Wheels driven: Rear
Brakes F/R: Drum/Drum
Wheelbase: 274.3cm 108.0in
Track F: 138.4cm 54.5in
Track R: 138.4cm 54.5in
Length: 457.2cm 180.0in
Width: 170.2cm 67.0in
Height: 130.8cm 51.5in
Ground clearance: 15.2cm 6.0in
Kerb weight: 1162.2kg 2560.0lb
Fuel: 53.0L 11.6gal 14.0galUS

764 Chevrolet
Corvair Navarro
1962 USA
98.0mph 157.7kmh
0-50mph 80.5kmh: 6.9secs
0-60mph 96.5kmh: 9.3secs
0-1/4 mile: 17.5secs
135.0bhp 100.7kW 136.9PS
@ 4800rpm
119.8bhp/ton 117.8bhp/tonne
49.9bhp/L 37.2kW/L 50.6PS/L
38.0ft/sec 11.6m/sec
18.1mph 29.1kmh/1000rpm
Petrol 4-stroke piston
2704cc 165.0cu in turbocharged
Flat 6
Compression ratio: 8.0:1
Bore: 88.9mm 3.5in
Stroke: 72.4mm 2.8in
Valve type/No: Overhead 12
Transmission: Automatic
No. of forward speeds: 2
Wheels driven: Rear
Wheelbase: 274.3cm 108.0in
Track F: 138.4cm 54.5in
Track R: 138.4cm 54.5in
Length: 457.2cm 180.0in
Width: 170.2cm 67.0in
Height: 130.8cm 51.5in
Ground clearance: 15.2cm 6.0in
Kerb weight: 1146.3kg 2525.0lb
Fuel: 53.0L 11.6gal 14.0galUS

765 Chevrolet
Corvair Spyder
1962 USA
105.0mph 168.9kmh
0-50mph 80.5kmh: 8.3secs
0-60mph 96.5kmh: 10.8secs
0-1/4 mile: 18.5secs
150.0bhp 111.9kW 152.1PS
@ 4400rpm
210.0lbft 284.6Nm @ 3300rpm
132.8bhp/ton 130.6bhp/tonne
63.1bhp/L 47.1kW/L 64.0PS/L
31.8ft/sec 9.7m/sec
19.8mph 31.9kmh/1000rpm
Petrol 4-stroke piston
2376cc 145.0cu in turbocharged
Flat 6 1 Carburettor
Compression ratio: 8.0:1
Bore: 87.4mm 3.4in
Stroke: 66.0mm 2.6in
Valve type/No: Overhead 12
Transmission: Manual
No. of forward speeds: 4
Wheels driven: Rear
Wheelbase: 274.3cm 108.0in
Track F: 138.4cm 54.5in
Track R: 138.4cm 54.5in
Length: 457.2cm 180.0in
Width: 170.2cm 67.0in
Height: 130.8cm 51.5in
Ground clearance: 15.2cm 6.0in
Kerb weight: 1148.6kg 2530.0lb
Fuel: 53.0L 11.6gal 14.0galUS

766 Chevrolet
Corvette
1962 USA
125.0mph 201.1kmh
0-50mph 80.5kmh: 4.5secs
0-60mph 96.5kmh: 5.9secs
0-1/4 mile: 14.0secs
360.0bhp 268.4kW 365.0PS
@ 6000rpm
352.0lbft 477.0Nm @ 4000rpm
261.8bhp/ton 257.4bhp/tonne
67.2bhp/L 50.1kW/L 68.1PS/L
54.2ft/sec 16.5m/sec
19.2mph 30.9kmh/1000rpm
Petrol 4-stroke piston
5359cc 327.0cu in
Vee 8 fuel injection
Compression ratio: 11.3:1
Bore: 101.6mm 4.0in
Stroke: 82.6mm 3.2in
Valve type/No: Overhead 16
Transmission: Manual
No. of forward speeds: 4
Wheels driven: Rear
Wheelbase: 259.1cm 102.0in
Track F: 144.8cm 57.0in
Track R: 149.9cm 59.0in
Length: 448.8cm 176.7in
Width: 178.8cm 70.4in
Height: 132.3cm 52.1in
Ground clearance: 17.0cm 6.7in
Kerb weight: 1398.3kg 3080.0lb
Fuel: 62.1L 13.6gal 16.4galUS

767 Chevrolet
Corvette Sebring
1962 USA
0-60mph 96.5kmh: 5.3secs
0-1/4 mile: 14.2secs
310.0bhp 231.2kW 314.3PS
@ 6200rpm
303.0lbft 410.6Nm @ 5000rpm
217.0bhp/ton 213.4bhp/tonne
57.8bhp/L 43.1kW/L 58.6PS/L
Petrol 4-stroke piston
5360cc 327.0cu in
Vee 8 fuel injection
Valve type/No: Overhead 16
Transmission: Manual
No. of forward speeds: 4
Wheels driven: Rear
Springs F/R: Coil/Leaf
Brakes F/R: Drum/Drum
Steering: Recirculating ball
Wheelbase: 259.1cm 102.0in
Track F: 144.8cm 57.0in
Track R: 149.9cm 59.0in
Length: 448.8cm 176.7in
Width: 178.8cm 70.4in
Height: 134.1cm 52.8in
Kerb weight: 1452.8kg 3200.0lb

768 Chevrolet
Impala SS 409
1962 USA
125.0mph 201.1kmh
0-50mph 80.5kmh: 5.6secs
0-60mph 96.5kmh: 7.3secs
0-1/4 mile: 14.9secs
380.0bhp 283.4kW 385.3PS
@ 5800rpm
420.0lbft 569.1Nm @ 3200rpm
228.2bhp/ton 224.4bhp/tonne
56.7bhp/L 42.3kW/L 57.5PS/L
56.4ft/sec 17.2m/sec
21.0mph 33.8kmh/1000rpm

Petrol 4-stroke piston
6702cc 408.9cu in
Vee 8
Compression ratio: 11.0:1
Bore: 109.5mm 4.3in
Stroke: 88.9mm 3.5in
Valve type/No: Overhead 16
Transmission: Manual
No. of forward speeds: 4
Wheels driven: Rear
Steering: PA
Wheelbase: 302.3cm 119.0in
Track F: 153.2cm 60.3in
Track R: 150.6cm 59.3in
Length: 532.4cm 209.6in
Width: 200.7cm 79.0in
Height: 139.7cm 55.0in
Ground clearance: 16.5cm 6.5in
Kerb weight: 1693.4kg 3730.0lb
Fuel: 75.7L 16.6gal 20.0galUS

769 Chevrolet

Impala Station Wagon
1962 USA
111.0mph 178.6kmh
0-50mph 80.5kmh: 7.6secs
0-60mph 96.5kmh: 9.5secs
0-1/4 mile: 17.5secs
250.0bhp 186.4kW 253.5PS
@ 4400rpm
350.0lbft 474.3Nm @ 2800rpm
136.7bhp/ton 134.5bhp/tonne
46.6bhp/L 34.8kW/L 47.3PS/L
39.7ft/sec 12.1m/sec
25.2mph 40.5kmh/1000rpm
Petrol 4-stroke piston
5359cc 327.0cu in
Vee 8 1 Carburettor
Compression ratio: 10.5:1
Bore: 101.6mm 4.0in
Stroke: 82.6mm 3.2in
Valve type/No: Overhead 16
Transmission: Automatic
No. of forward speeds: 2
Wheels driven: Rear
Brake system: PA
Steering: PA
Wheelbase: 302.3cm 119.0in
Track F: 153.2cm 60.3in
Track R: 150.6cm 59.3in
Length: 532.4cm 209.6in
Width: 200.7cm 79.0in
Height: 142.2cm 56.0in
Ground clearance: 16.5cm 6.5in
Kerb weight: 1859.1kg 4095.0lb
Fuel: 71.9L 15.8gal 19.0galUS

770 Chevrolet

Bel Air
1963 USA
85.0mph 136.8kmh
0-50mph 80.5kmh: 11.3secs
0-60mph 96.5kmh: 17.0secs
0-1/4 mile: 21.0secs
140.0bhp 104.4kW 141.9PS
@ 4400rpm
220.0lbft 298.1Nm @ 1600rpm
88.2bhp/ton 86.8bhp/tonne
37.1bhp/L 27.7kW/L 37.7PS/L
39.7ft/sec 12.1m/sec
24.8mph 39.9kmh/1000rpm
Petrol 4-stroke piston
3769cc 230.0cu in
In-line 6 1 Carburettor
Compression ratio: 8.5:1
Bore: 98.6mm 3.9in
Stroke: 82.6mm 3.2in
Valve type/No: Overhead 12
Transmission: Automatic
No. of forward speeds: 2
Wheels driven: Rear
Brake system: PA
Steering: PA
Wheelbase: 302.3cm 119.0in
Track F: 153.2cm 60.3in
Track R: 150.6cm 59.3in
Length: 534.4cm 210.4in
Width: 201.7cm 79.4in
Height: 141.0cm 55.5in
Ground clearance: 15.2cm 6.0in
Kerb weight: 1613.5kg 3554.0lb
Fuel: 75.7L 16.6gal 20.0galUS

771 Chevrolet

Biscayne V8
1963 USA
105.0mph 168.9kmh
0-50mph 80.5kmh: 7.8secs
0-60mph 96.5kmh: 10.7secs
0-1/4 mile: 17.9secs
195.0bhp 145.4kW 197.7PS
@ 4800rpm
245.0lbft 332.0Nm @ 2400rpm
126.2bhp/ton 124.1bhp/tonne
42.0bhp/L 31.3kW/L 42.6PS/L
40.0ft/sec 12.2m/sec
24.0mph 38.6kmh/1000rpm
Petrol 4-stroke piston
4638cc 283.0cu in
Vee 8 1 Carburettor
Compression ratio: 9.3:1
Bore: 98.6mm 3.9in
Stroke: 76.2mm 3.0in
Valve type/No: Overhead 16
Transmission: Manual
No. of forward speeds: 3
Wheels driven: Rear
Wheelbase: 302.3cm 119.0in
Track F: 153.2cm 60.3in
Track R: 150.6cm 59.3in
Length: 534.4cm 210.4in
Width: 201.7cm 79.4in
Height: 141.0cm 55.5in
Ground clearance: 15.2cm 6.0in
Kerb weight: 1570.8kg 3460.0lb
Fuel: 75.7L 16.6gal 20.0galUS

772 Chevrolet

C-10 Fleetside Pickup
1963 USA
85.0mph 136.8kmh
0-50mph 80.5kmh: 9.4secs
0-60mph 96.5kmh: 14.2secs
0-1/4 mile: 20.0secs
140.0bhp 104.4kW 141.9PS
@ 4400rpm
220.0lbft 298.1Nm @ 1600rpm
92.8bhp/ton 91.2bhp/tonne
37.1bhp/L 27.7kW/L 37.7PS/L
39.7ft/sec 12.1m/sec
28.3mph 45.5kmh/1000rpm
Petrol 4-stroke piston
3769cc 230.0cu in
In-line 6 1 Carburettor
Compression ratio: 8.5:1
Bore: 98.6mm 3.9in
Stroke: 82.6mm 3.2in
Valve type/No: Overhead 12
Transmission: Manual
No. of forward speeds: 3
Wheels driven: Rear
Brakes F/R: Drum/Drum
Wheelbase: 322.6cm 127.0in
Track F: 160.3cm 63.1in
Track R: 154.9cm 61.0in
Length: 523.2cm 206.0in
Width: 200.7cm 79.0in
Height: 180.3cm 71.0in
Ground clearance: 19.3cm 7.6in
Kerb weight: 1534.5kg 3380.0lb
Fuel: 71.9L 15.8gal 19.0galUS

773 Chevrolet

Corvair Monza Convertible
1963 USA
90.0mph 144.8kmh
0-50mph 80.5kmh: 10.5secs
0-60mph 96.5kmh: 15.3secs
0-1/4 mile: 21.1secs
122.0bhp 91.0kW 123.7PS
@ 4400rpm
134.0lbft 181.6Nm @ 2900rpm
103.7bhp/ton 102.0bhp/tonne
51.3bhp/L 38.3kW/L 52.0PS/L
31.8ft/sec 9.7m/sec
22.9mph 36.8kmh/1000rpm
Petrol 4-stroke piston
2377cc 145.0cu in
Flat 6 1 Carburettor
Compression ratio: 9.0:1
Bore: 87.3mm 3.4in
Stroke: 66.0mm 2.6in
Valve type/No: Overhead 12
Transmission: Manual
No. of forward speeds: 4
Wheels driven: Rear
Wheelbase: 274.3cm 108.0in
Track F: 137.2cm 54.0in
Track R: 137.2cm 54.0in
Length: 457.2cm 180.0in
Width: 170.2cm 67.0in
Height: 130.8cm 51.5in
Ground clearance: 15.2cm 6.0in
Kerb weight: 1196.3kg 2635.0lb

774 Chevrolet

Corvair Monza EMPI
1963 USA
93.0mph 149.6kmh
0-50mph 80.5kmh: 11.0secs
0-60mph 96.5kmh: 15.0secs
0-1/4 mile: 19.9secs
102.0bhp 76.1kW 103.4PS
@ 4400rpm
134.0lbft 181.6Nm @ 2800rpm
90.3bhp/ton 88.8bhp/tonne
42.9bhp/L 32.0kW/L 43.5PS/L
31.8ft/sec 9.7m/sec
21.6mph 34.8kmh/1000rpm
Petrol 4-stroke piston
2376cc 145.0cu in
Flat 6 1 Carburettor
Compression ratio: 9.0:1
Bore: 87.4mm 3.4in
Stroke: 66.0mm 2.6in
Valve type/No: Overhead 12
Transmission: Manual
No. of forward speeds: 4
Wheels driven: Rear
Wheelbase: 274.3cm 108.0in
Track F: 138.4cm 54.5in
Track R: 138.4cm 54.5in
Length: 457.2cm 180.0in
Width: 170.2cm 67.0in
Height: 130.8cm 51.5in
Ground clearance: 15.2cm 6.0in
Kerb weight: 1148.6kg 2530.0lb
Fuel: 53.0L 11.6gal 14.0galUS

775 Chevrolet

Corvette
1963 USA
142.0mph 228.5kmh
0-50mph 80.5kmh: 4.5secs
0-60mph 96.5kmh: 5.9secs
0-1/4 mile: 14.9secs
360.0bhp 268.4kW 365.0PS
@ 6000rpm
352.0lbft 477.0Nm @ 4000rpm
266.1bhp/ton 261.7bhp/tonne
67.4bhp/L 50.3kW/L 68.3PS/L
54.2ft/sec 16.5m/sec
21.8mph 35.1kmh/1000rpm
Petrol 4-stroke piston
5340cc 325.8cu in
Vee 8
Compression ratio: 11.3:1
Bore: 101.6mm 4.0in
Stroke: 82.6mm 3.2in
Valve type/No: Overhead 16
Transmission: Manual
No. of forward speeds: 4
Wheels driven: Rear
Wheelbase: 248.9cm 98.0in
Track F: 143.0cm 56.3in
Track R: 144.8cm 57.0in
Length: 445.3cm 175.3in
Width: 176.8cm 69.6in
Height: 126.5cm 49.8in
Ground clearance: 12.7cm 5.0in
Kerb weight: 1375.6kg 3030.0lb

776 Chevrolet

Corvette Grand Sport Roadster
1963 USA
150.0mph 241.4kmh
0-60mph 96.5kmh: 5.0secs
0-1/4 mile: 12.8secs
550.0bhp 410.1kW 557.6PS
@ 6000rpm
560.0bhp/ton 550.7bhp/tonne
78.6bhp/L 58.6kW/L 79.7PS/L
62.5ft/sec 19.0m/sec
Petrol 4-stroke piston
6997cc 426.9cu in
Vee 8 1 Carburettor
Compression ratio: 11.0:1
Bore: 108.0mm 4.2in
Stroke: 95.2mm 3.8in
Valve type/No: Overhead 16
Transmission: Manual
No. of forward speeds: 4
Wheels driven: Rear
Springs F/R: Coil/Leaf
Brakes F/R: Disc/Disc
Steering: Recirculating ball
Wheelbase: 248.9cm 98.0in
Track F: 144.3cm 56.8in
Track R: 146.3cm 57.6in
Length: 445.0cm 175.2in
Width: 175.8cm 69.2in
Kerb weight: 998.8kg 2200.0lb
Fuel: 56.8L 12.5gal 15.0galUS

777 Chevrolet

Corvette Sting Ray
1963 USA
142.0mph 228.5kmh
0-50mph 80.5kmh: 4.5secs
0-60mph 96.5kmh: 5.9secs
0-1/4 mile: 14.9secs
360.0bhp 268.4kW 365.0PS
@ 6000rpm
352.0lbft 477.0Nm @ 4000rpm
266.1bhp/ton 261.7bhp/tonne
67.4bhp/L 50.3kW/L 68.3PS/L
54.2ft/sec 16.5m/sec
21.8mph 35.1kmh/1000rpm
Petrol 4-stroke piston
5340cc 325.8cu in
Vee 8
Compression ratio: 11.3:1
Bore: 101.6mm 4.0in
Stroke: 82.6mm 3.2in
Valve type/No: Overhead 16
Transmission: Manual
No. of forward speeds: 4
Wheels driven: Rear
Wheelbase: 248.9cm 98.0in
Track F: 143.0cm 56.3in
Track R: 144.8cm 57.0in
Length: 445.3cm 175.3in
Width: 176.8cm 69.6in
Height: 126.5cm 49.8in
Ground clearance: 12.7cm 5.0in
Kerb weight: 1375.6kg 3030.0lb

778 Chevrolet

Corvette Sting Ray Automatic
1963 USA
130.0mph 209.2kmh
0-50mph 80.5kmh: 5.6secs
0-60mph 96.5kmh: 7.2secs
0-1/4 mile: 15.5secs
300.0bhp 223.7kW 304.2PS
@ 5000rpm
360.0lbft 487.8Nm @ 3200rpm
220.5bhp/ton 216.8bhp/tonne
56.0bhp/L 41.8kW/L 56.8PS/L
45.1ft/sec 13.8m/sec
23.5mph 37.8kmh/1000rpm
Petrol 4-stroke piston
5354cc 326.7cu in
Vee 8 1 Carburettor
Compression ratio: 10.5:1
Bore: 101.6mm 4.0in
Stroke: 82.6mm 3.2in
Valve type/No: Overhead 16
Transmission: Automatic
No. of forward speeds: 2
Wheels driven: Rear
Brake system: PA
Steering: PA
Wheelbase: 248.9cm 98.0in
Track F: 143.0cm 56.3in
Track R: 144.8cm 57.0in
Length: 445.3cm 175.3in
Width: 176.8cm 69.6in
Height: 126.5cm 49.8in
Ground clearance: 12.7cm 5.0in
Kerb weight: 1383.8kg 3048.0lb
Fuel: 75.7L 16.6gal 20.0galUS

779 Chevrolet

Impala Super Sport 409
1963 USA
124.0mph 199.5kmh
0-50mph 80.5kmh: 5.0secs
0-60mph 96.5kmh: 6.6secs
0-1/4 mile: 15.2secs
340.0bhp 253.5kW 344.7PS
@ 5000rpm
420.0lbft 569.1Nm @ 3200rpm
196.4bhp/ton 193.2bhp/tonne
50.7bhp/L 37.8kW/L 51.4PS/L
48.6ft/sec 14.8m/sec
23.0mph 37.0kmh/1000rpm
Petrol 4-stroke piston
6702cc 408.9cu in
Vee 8 2 Carburettor
Compression ratio: 10.0:1
Bore: 109.5mm 4.3in
Stroke: 88.9mm 3.5in
Valve type/No: Overhead 16
Transmission: Automatic
No. of forward speeds: 2
Wheels driven: Rear
Brake system: PA

Steering: PA
Wheelbase: 302.3cm 119.0in
Track F: 153.2cm 60.3in
Track R: 150.6cm 59.3in
Length: 534.4cm 210.4in
Width: 200.7cm 79.0in
Height: 141.0cm 55.5in
Ground clearance: 15.2cm 6.0in
Kerb weight: 1760.2kg 3877.0lb
Fuel: 75.7L 16.6gal 20.0galUS

780 Chevrolet

Chevelle 300
1964 USA
90.0mph 144.8kmh
0-50mph 80.5kmh: 10.6secs
0-60mph 96.5kmh: 14.3secs
0-1/4 mile: 19.5secs
120.0bhp 89.5kW 121.7PS
@ 4400rpm
177.0lbft 239.8Nm @ 2400rpm
86.7bhp/ton 85.3bhp/tonne
37.7bhp/L 28.1kW/L 38.3PS/L
39.7ft/sec 12.1m/sec
22.9mph 36.8kmh/1000rpm
Petrol 4-stroke piston
3179cc 194.0cu in
In-line 6 1 Carburettor
Compression ratio: 8.5:1
Bore: 90.5mm 3.6in
Stroke: 82.6mm 3.2in
Valve type/No: Overhead 12
Transmission: Manual
No. of forward speeds: 3
Wheels driven: Rear
Wheelbase: 292.1cm 115.0in
Track F: 147.3cm 58.0in
Track R: 147.3cm 58.0in
Length: 492.5cm 193.9in
Width: 189.5cm 74.6in
Height: 138.4cm 54.5in
Ground clearance: 15.2cm 6.0in
Kerb weight: 1407.4kg 3100.0lb
Fuel: 75.7L 16.6gal 20.0galUS

781 Chevrolet

Chevelle Malibu
1964 USA
92.0mph 148.0kmh
0-50mph 80.5kmh: 9.6secs
0-60mph 96.5kmh: 13.4secs
0-1/4 mile: 19.6secs
155.0bhp 115.6kW 157.1PS
@ 4400rpm
215.0lbft 291.3Nm @ 2000rpm
106.3bhp/ton 104.6bhp/tonne
41.1bhp/L 30.7kW/L 41.7PS/L
39.7ft/sec 12.1m/sec
22.9mph 36.8kmh/1000rpm
Petrol 4-stroke piston
3769cc 230.0cu in
In-line 6 1 Carburettor
Compression ratio: 8.5:1
Bore: 98.4mm 3.9in
Stroke: 82.6mm 3.2in
Valve type/No: Overhead 12
Transmission: Automatic
No. of forward speeds: 2
Wheels driven: Rear
Wheelbase: 292.1cm 115.0in
Track F: 147.3cm 58.0in
Track R: 147.3cm 58.0in
Length: 492.5cm 193.9in
Width: 189.5cm 74.6in
Height: 138.4cm 54.5in
Ground clearance: 15.2cm 6.0in
Kerb weight: 1482.3kg 3265.0lb
Fuel: 75.7L 16.6gal 20.0galUS

782 Chevrolet

Chevelle Super Sport
1964 USA
110.0mph 177.0kmh
0-50mph 80.5kmh: 6.6secs
0-60mph 96.5kmh: 8.7secs
0-1/4 mile: 16.2secs
220.0bhp 164.0kW 223.0PS
@ 4800rpm
295.0lbft 399.7Nm @ 3200rpm
145.4bhp/ton 142.9bhp/tonne
47.4bhp/L 35.4kW/L 48.1PS/L
40.0ft/sec 12.2m/sec
25.7mph 41.4kmh/1000rpm
Petrol 4-stroke piston
4638cc 283.0cu in
Vee 8 1 Carburettor
Compression ratio: 9.3:1
Bore: 98.4mm 3.9in
Stroke: 76.2mm 3.0in
Valve type/No: Overhead 16
Transmission: Manual
No. of forward speeds: 4
Wheels driven: Rear
Wheelbase: 292.1cm 115.0in
Track F: 147.3cm 58.0in
Track R: 147.3cm 58.0in
Length: 492.5cm 193.9in
Width: 189.5cm 74.6in
Height: 137.2cm 54.0in
Ground clearance: 15.2cm 6.0in
Kerb weight: 1539.1kg 3390.0lb
Fuel: 75.7L 16.6gal 20.0galUS

783 Chevrolet

Chevy II V8 Station Wagon
1964 USA
104.0mph 167.3kmh
0-50mph 80.5kmh: 10.6secs
0-60mph 96.5kmh: 14.2secs
0-1/4 mile: 19.4secs
195.0bhp 145.4kW 197.7PS
@ 4800rpm
285.0lbft 386.2Nm @ 2400rpm
142.5bhp/ton 140.1bhp/tonne
42.0bhp/L 31.3kW/L 42.6PS/L
40.0ft/sec 12.2m/sec
22.6mph 36.4kmh/1000rpm
Petrol 4-stroke piston
4638cc 283.0cu in
Vee 8 1 Carburettor
Compression ratio: 9.3:1
Bore: 98.4mm 3.9in
Stroke: 76.2mm 3.0in
Valve type/No: Overhead 16
Transmission: Automatic
No. of forward speeds: 2
Wheels driven: Rear
Wheelbase: 279.4cm 110.0in
Track F: 144.3cm 56.8in
Track R: 143.0cm 56.3in
Length: 476.5cm 187.6in
Width: 179.8cm 70.8in
Height: 139.7cm 55.0in
Ground clearance: 13.2cm 5.2in
Kerb weight: 1391.5kg 3065.0lb
Fuel: 60.6L 13.3gal 16.0galUS

784 Chevrolet

Corvair Monza
1964 USA
98.0mph 157.7kmh
0-50mph 80.5kmh: 9.8secs
0-60mph 96.5kmh: 14.0secs
0-1/4 mile: 19.5secs
110.0bhp 82.0kW 111.5PS
@ 4400rpm
160.0lbft 216.8Nm @ 2600rpm
93.3bhp/ton 91.8bhp/tonne
40.9bhp/L 30.5kW/L 41.5PS/L
35.9ft/sec 11.0m/sec
21.4mph 34.4kmh/1000rpm
Petrol 4-stroke piston
2687cc 163.9cu in
Flat 6 2 Carburettor
Compression ratio: 9.3:1
Bore: 87.4mm 3.4in
Stroke: 74.7mm 2.9in
Valve type/No: Overhead 12
Transmission: Manual
No. of forward speeds: 4
Wheels driven: Rear
Wheelbase: 274.3cm 108.0in
Track F: 138.2cm 54.4in
Track R: 140.0cm 55.1in
Length: 457.2cm 180.0in
Width: 170.2cm 67.0in
Height: 129.8cm 51.1in
Ground clearance: 14.5cm 5.7in
Kerb weight: 1198.6kg 2640.0lb
Fuel: 53.0L 11.6gal 14.0galUS

785 Chevrolet

Corvair Sprint
1964 USA
120.0mph 193.1kmh
0-50mph 80.5kmh: 8.3secs
0-60mph 96.5kmh: 11.9secs
0-1/4 mile: 18.4secs
155.0bhp 115.6kW 157.1PS
@ 5000rpm
202.0lbft 273.7Nm @ 3600rpm
136.7bhp/ton 134.4bhp/tonne
57.6bhp/L 43.0kW/L 58.4PS/L
40.8ft/sec 12.4m/sec
20.4mph 32.8kmh/1000rpm
Petrol 4-stroke piston
2689cc 164.1cu in
Flat 6 4 Carburettor
Compression ratio: 9.3:1
Bore: 87.4mm 3.4in
Stroke: 74.7mm 2.9in
Valve type/No: Overhead 12
Transmission: Manual
No. of forward speeds: 4
Wheels driven: Rear
Springs F/R: Coil/Coil
Brakes F/R: Drum/Drum
Steering: Recirculating ball
Wheelbase: 274.3cm 108.0in
Track F: 138.2cm 54.4in
Track R: 140.0cm 55.1in
Length: 457.2cm 180.0in
Width: 170.2cm 67.0in
Height: 129.3cm 50.9in
Ground clearance: 13.7cm 5.4in
Kerb weight: 1153.2kg 2540.0lb
Fuel: 53.0L 11.6gal 14.0galUS

786 Chevrolet

Corvette Sting Ray
1964 USA
148.0mph 238.1kmh
0-50mph 80.5kmh: 5.1secs
0-60mph 96.5kmh: 6.5secs
0-1/4 mile: 14.6secs
360.0bhp 268.4kW 365.0PS
@ 6000rpm
352.0lbft 477.0Nm @ 4000rpm
248.3bhp/ton 244.1bhp/tonne
67.1bhp/L 50.1kW/L 68.1PS/L
54.8ft/sec 16.7m/sec
22.3mph 35.9kmh/1000rpm
14.6mpg 12.2mpgUS 19.3L/100km
Petrol 4-stroke piston
5363cc 327.2cu in
Vee 8 fuel injection
Compression ratio: 11.2:1
Bore: 101.6mm 4.0in
Stroke: 83.5mm 3.3in
Valve type/No: Overhead 16
Transmission: Manual
No. of forward speeds: 4
Wheels driven: Rear
Springs F/R: Coil/Leaf
Brake system: PA
Brakes F/R: Drum/Drum
Steering: Recirculating ball
Wheelbase: 248.9cm 98.0in
Track F: 142.7cm 56.2in
Track R: 144.8cm 57.0in
Length: 445.0cm 175.2in
Width: 176.5cm 69.5in
Height: 124.5cm 49.0in
Ground clearance: 15.2cm 6.0in
Kerb weight: 1474.6kg 3248.0lb
Fuel: 76.0L 16.7gal 20.1galUS

787 Chevrolet

Corvette Sting Ray Automatic
1964 USA
130.0mph 209.2kmh
0-50mph 80.5kmh: 6.1secs
0-60mph 96.5kmh: 8.0secs
0-1/4 mile: 15.2secs
300.0bhp 223.7kW 304.2PS
@ 5000rpm
360.0lbft 487.8Nm @ 3200rpm
220.3bhp/ton 216.6bhp/tonne
56.0bhp/L 41.8kW/L 56.8PS/L
45.0ft/sec 13.7m/sec
23.5mph 37.8kmh/1000rpm
Petrol 4-stroke piston
5356cc 326.8cu in
Vee 8 1 Carburettor
Compression ratio: 10.5:1
Bore: 101.6mm 4.0in
Stroke: 82.3mm 3.2in
Valve type/No: Overhead 16
Transmission: Automatic
No. of forward speeds: 2
Wheels driven: Rear
Springs F/R: Coil/Leaf
Brakes F/R: Drum/Drum
Steering: Recirculating ball
Wheelbase: 248.9cm 98.0in
Track F: 143.0cm 56.3in
Track R: 144.8cm 57.0in
Length: 445.3cm 175.3in
Width: 176.8cm 69.6in
Height: 126.5cm 49.8in
Ground clearance: 12.7cm 5.0in
Kerb weight: 1384.7kg 3050.0lb
Fuel: 75.7L 16.6gal 20.0galUS

788 Chevrolet

Corvette Sting Ray Injection
1964 USA
138.0mph 222.0kmh
0-50mph 80.5kmh: 5.2secs
0-60mph 96.5kmh: 6.3secs
0-1/4 mile: 14.4secs
375.0bhp 279.6kW 380.2PS
@ 6200rpm
360.0lbft 487.8Nm @ 4000rpm
275.4bhp/ton 270.8bhp/tonne
70.0bhp/L 52.2kW/L 71.0PS/L
55.8ft/sec 17.0m/sec
21.3mph 34.3kmh/1000rpm
Petrol 4-stroke piston
5356cc 326.8cu in
Vee 8 fuel injection
Compression ratio: 11.0:1
Bore: 101.6mm 4.0in
Stroke: 82.3mm 3.2in
Valve type/No: Overhead 16
Transmission: Manual
No. of forward speeds: 4
Wheels driven: Rear
Springs F/R: Coil/Leaf
Brakes F/R: Disc/Disc
Steering: Recirculating ball
Wheelbase: 248.9cm 98.0in
Track F: 144.3cm 56.8in
Track R: 146.3cm 57.6in
Length: 444.8cm 175.1in
Width: 176.8cm 69.6in
Height: 126.5cm 49.8in
Ground clearance: 12.7cm 5.0in
Kerb weight: 1384.7kg 3050.0lb
Fuel: 75.7L 16.6gal 20.0galUS

789 Chevrolet

El Camino
1964 USA
110.0mph 177.0kmh
0-50mph 80.5kmh: 7.2secs
0-60mph 96.5kmh: 9.1secs
0-1/4 mile: 16.5secs
220.0bhp 164.0kW 223.0PS
@ 4800rpm
295.0lbft 399.7Nm @ 3200rpm
155.0bhp/ton 152.4bhp/tonne
47.4bhp/L 35.4kW/L 48.1PS/L
40.0ft/sec 12.2m/sec
24.3mph 39.1kmh/1000rpm
Petrol 4-stroke piston
4638cc 283.0cu in
Vee 8 1 Carburettor
Compression ratio: 9.3:1
Bore: 98.4mm 3.9in
Stroke: 76.2mm 3.0in
Valve type/No: Overhead 16
Transmission: Automatic
No. of forward speeds: 2
Wheels driven: Rear
Wheelbase: 292.1cm 115.0in
Track F: 147.3cm 58.0in
Track R: 147.3cm 58.0in
Length: 505.2cm 198.9in
Width: 189.5cm 74.6in
Height: 137.2cm 54.0in
Ground clearance: 16.5cm 6.5in
Kerb weight: 1443.7kg 3180.0lb
Fuel: 75.7L 16.6gal 20.0galUS

790 Chevrolet

Caprice Custom 396
1965 USA
114.0mph 183.4kmh
0-50mph 80.5kmh: 6.5secs
0-60mph 96.5kmh: 8.4secs
0-1/4 mile: 16.5secs
325.0bhp 242.3kW 329.5PS
@ 4800rpm
410.0lbft 555.6Nm @ 3200rpm
166.2bhp/ton 163.4bhp/tonne
50.1bhp/L 37.3kW/L 50.8PS/L
50.1ft/sec 15.3m/sec
28.5mph 45.9kmh/1000rpm
Petrol 4-stroke piston
6489cc 395.9cu in
Vee 8 1 Carburettor
Compression ratio: 10.3:1
Bore: 103.9mm 4.1in
Stroke: 95.5mm 3.8in

Valve type/No: Overhead 16
Transmission: Automatic
No. of forward speeds: 3
Wheels driven: Rear
Brake system: PA
Brakes F/R: Drum/Drum
Steering: PA
Wheelbase: 302.3cm 119.0in
Track F: 158.8cm 62.5in
Track R: 158.5cm 62.4in
Length: 541.3cm 213.1in
Width: 202.2cm 79.6in
Height: 138.4cm 54.5in
Ground clearance: 13.7cm 5.4in
Kerb weight: 1988.5kg 4380.0lb
Fuel: 75.7L 16.6gal 20.0galUS

791 Chevrolet

Chevelle Malibu
1965 USA
91.5mph 147.2kmh
0-50mph 80.5kmh: 10.6secs
0-60mph 96.5kmh: 15.1secs
0-1/4 mile: 20.3secs
140.0bhp 104.4kW 141.9PS
@ 4400rpm
220.0lbft 298.1Nm @ 1600rpm
102.1bhp/ton 100.4bhp/tonne
37.1bhp/L 27.7kW/L 37.7PS/L
39.7ft/sec 12.1m/sec
20.8mph 33.5kmh/1000rpm
16.4mpg 13.7mpgUS 17.2L/100km
Petrol 4-stroke piston
3769cc 230.0cu in
In-line 6 1 Carburettor
Compression ratio: 8.5:1
Bore: 98.4mm 3.9in
Stroke: 82.5mm 3.2in
Valve type/No: Overhead 12
Transmission: Automatic
No. of forward speeds: 2
Wheels driven: Rear
Springs F/R: Coil/Coil
Brakes F/R: Drum/Drum
Steering: Recirculating ball
Wheelbase: 292.1cm 115.0in
Track F: 147.3cm 58.0in
Track R: 147.3cm 58.0in
Length: 499.1cm 196.5in
Width: 188.0cm 74.0in
Height: 143.5cm 56.5in
Kerb weight: 1394.2kg 3071.0lb
Fuel: 76.0L 16.7gal 20.1galUS

792 Chevrolet

Chevelle Malibu 396
1965 USA
130.0mph 209.2kmh
0-50mph 80.5kmh: 4.8secs
0-60mph 96.5kmh: 6.5secs
0-1/4 mile: 14.9secs
375.0bhp 279.6kW 380.2PS
@ 5600rpm
420.0lbft 569.1Nm @ 3600rpm
230.1bhp/ton 226.3bhp/tonne
57.8bhp/L 43.1kW/L 58.6PS/L
58.5ft/sec 17.8m/sec
23.1mph 37.2kmh/1000rpm
Petrol 4-stroke piston
6489cc 395.9cu in
Vee 8 1 Carburettor
Compression ratio: 11.0:1
Bore: 103.9mm 4.1in
Stroke: 95.5mm 3.8in
Valve type/No: Overhead 16
Transmission: Manual
No. of forward speeds: 4
Wheels driven: Rear
Brake system: PA
Brakes F/R: Drum/Drum
Steering: PA
Wheelbase: 292.1cm 115.0in
Track F: 147.3cm 58.0in
Track R: 147.3cm 58.0in
Length: 499.4cm 196.6in
Width: 189.5cm 74.6in
Height: 134.1cm 52.8in
Ground clearance: 11.9cm 4.7in
Kerb weight: 1657.1kg 3650.0lb
Fuel: 75.7L 16.6gal 20.0galUS

793 Chevrolet

Corvair Corsa IECO
1965 USA
106.0mph 170.6kmh
0-50mph 80.5kmh: 8.4secs
0-60mph 96.5kmh: 11.4secs
0-1/4 mile: 18.1secs
156.0bhp 116.3kW 158.2PS
@ 4400rpm
170.0lbft 230.4Nm @ 2800rpm
137.6bhp/ton 135.3bhp/tonne
58.1bhp/L 43.3kW/L 58.9PS/L
35.9ft/sec 11.0m/sec
19.6mph 31.5kmh/1000rpm
Petrol 4-stroke piston
2687cc 163.9cu in
Flat 6 1 Carburettor
Compression ratio: 9.3:1
Bore: 87.4mm 3.4in
Stroke: 74.7mm 2.9in
Valve type/No: Overhead 12
Transmission: Manual
No. of forward speeds: 4
Wheels driven: Rear
Wheelbase: 274.3cm 108.0in
Track F: 139.7cm 55.0in
Track R: 145.3cm 57.2in
Length: 465.6cm 183.3in
Width: 177.0cm 69.7in
Height: 130.0cm 51.2in
Ground clearance: 15.0cm 5.9in
Kerb weight: 1153.2kg 2540.0lb
Fuel: 53.0L 11.6gal 14.0galUS

794 Chevrolet

Corvair Monza
1965 USA
90.0mph 144.8kmh
0-50mph 80.5kmh: 12.5secs
0-60mph 96.5kmh: 17.5secs
0-1/4 mile: 20.9secs
110.0bhp 82.0kW 111.5PS
@ 4400rpm
160.0lbft 216.8Nm @ 2800rpm
94.8bhp/ton 93.2bhp/tonne
40.9bhp/L 30.5kW/L 41.5PS/L
35.9ft/sec 11.0m/sec
20.3mph 32.7kmh/1000rpm
Petrol 4-stroke piston
2687cc 163.9cu in
Flat 6 2 Carburettor
Compression ratio: 9.3:1
Bore: 87.4mm 3.4in
Stroke: 74.7mm 2.9in
Valve type/No: Overhead 12
Transmission: Automatic
No. of forward speeds: 2
Wheels driven: Rear
Wheelbase: 274.3cm 108.0in
Track F: 139.7cm 55.0in
Track R: 145.3cm 57.2in
Length: 465.6cm 183.3in
Width: 177.0cm 69.7in
Height: 130.0cm 51.2in
Ground clearance: 13.7cm 5.4in
Kerb weight: 1180.4kg 2600.0lb
Fuel: 53.0L 11.6gal 14.0galUS

795 Chevrolet

Corvette
1965 USA
136.0mph 218.8kmh
0-50mph 80.5kmh: 4.8secs
0-60mph 96.5kmh: 5.7secs
0-1/4 mile: 14.1secs
425.0bhp 316.9kW 430.9PS
@ 6400rpm
415.0lbft 562.3Nm @ 3400rpm
292.0bhp/ton 287.1bhp/tonne
65.5bhp/L 48.8kW/L 66.4PS/L
66.8ft/sec 20.4m/sec
21.2mph 34.1kmh/1000rpm
Petrol 4-stroke piston
6489cc 395.9cu in
Vee 8 1 Carburettor
Compression ratio: 11.0:1
Bore: 103.9mm 4.1in
Stroke: 95.5mm 3.8in
Valve type/No: Overhead 16
Transmission: Manual
No. of forward speeds: 4
Wheels driven: Rear
Springs F/R: Coil/Leaf
Brake system: PA
Brakes F/R: Disc/Disc
Steering: Recirculating ball PA
Wheelbase: 248.9cm 98.0in
Track F: 144.3cm 56.8in
Track R: 146.3cm 57.6in
Length: 444.8cm 175.1in
Width: 176.8cm 69.6in
Height: 126.5cm 49.8in
Ground clearance: 12.7cm 5.0in
Kerb weight: 1480.0kg 3260.0lb
Fuel: 70.0L 15.4gal 18.5galUS

796 Chevrolet

Corvette 396
1965 USA
136.0mph 218.8kmh
0-50mph 80.5kmh: 4.8secs
0-60mph 96.5kmh: 5.7secs
0-1/4 mile: 14.1secs
425.0bhp 316.9kW 430.9PS
@ 6400rpm
415.0lbft 562.3Nm @ 4000rpm
292.0bhp/ton 287.1bhp/tonne
65.5bhp/L 48.8kW/L 66.4PS/L
66.8ft/sec 20.4m/sec
21.2mph 34.1kmh/1000rpm
Petrol 4-stroke piston
6489cc 395.9cu in
Vee 8 1 Carburettor
Compression ratio: 11.0:1
Bore: 103.9mm 4.1in
Stroke: 95.5mm 3.8in
Valve type/No: Overhead 16
Transmission: Manual
No. of forward speeds: 4
Wheels driven: Rear
Springs F/R: Coil/Leaf
Brake system: PA
Brakes F/R: Disc/Disc
Steering: Recirculating ball PA
Wheelbase: 248.9cm 98.0in
Track F: 144.3cm 56.8in
Track R: 146.3cm 57.6in
Length: 444.8cm 175.1in
Width: 176.8cm 69.6in
Height: 126.5cm 49.8in
Ground clearance: 12.7cm 5.0in
Kerb weight: 1480.0kg 3260.0lb
Fuel: 70.0L 15.4gal 18.5galUS

797 Chevrolet

Corvette Injection
1965 USA
127.0mph 204.3kmh
0-50mph 80.5kmh: 5.1secs
0-60mph 96.5kmh: 6.3secs
0-1/4 mile: 14.6secs
375.0bhp 279.6kW 380.2PS
@ 6200rpm
360.0lbft 487.8Nm @ 4000rpm
260.1bhp/ton 255.7bhp/tonne
70.0bhp/L 52.2kW/L 71.0PS/L
56.0ft/sec 17.1m/sec
19.0mph 30.6kmh/1000rpm
16.2mpg 13.5mpgUS 17.4L/100km
Petrol 4-stroke piston
5356cc 326.8cu in
Vee 8 fuel injection
Compression ratio: 11.0:1
Bore: 102.0mm 4.0in
Stroke: 82.6mm 3.2in
Valve type/No: Overhead 16
Transmission: Manual
No. of forward speeds: 4
Wheels driven: Rear
Springs F/R: Coil/Leaf
Brakes F/R: Disc/Disc
Steering: Recirculating ball
Wheelbase: 248.9cm 98.0in
Track F: 144.3cm 56.8in
Track R: 146.3cm 57.6in
Length: 444.8cm 175.1in
Width: 176.8cm 69.6in
Height: 126.5cm 49.8in
Ground clearance: 12.7cm 5.0in
Kerb weight: 1466.4kg 3230.0lb
Fuel: 70.0L 15.4gal 18.5galUS

798 Chevrolet

Corvette Sting Ray 396
1965 USA
138.0mph 222.0kmh
0-50mph 80.5kmh: 4.8secs
0-60mph 96.5kmh: 6.0secs
0-1/4 mile: 14.1secs
425.0bhp 316.9kW 430.9PS
@ 6400rpm
415.0lbft 562.3Nm @ 4000rpm
292.0bhp/ton 287.1bhp/tonne
65.5bhp/L 48.8kW/L 66.4PS/L
66.8ft/sec 20.4m/sec
21.2mph 34.1kmh/1000rpm
Petrol 4-stroke piston
6489cc 395.9cu in
Vee 8 1 Carburettor
Compression ratio: 11.0:1
Bore: 103.9mm 4.1in
Stroke: 95.5mm 3.8in
Valve type/No: Overhead 16
Transmission: Manual
No. of forward speeds: 4
Wheels driven: Rear
Brake system: PA
Wheelbase: 248.9cm 98.0in
Track F: 144.3cm 56.8in
Track R: 146.3cm 57.6in
Length: 444.8cm 175.1in
Width: 176.8cm 69.6in
Height: 126.5cm 49.8in
Ground clearance: 12.7cm 5.0in
Kerb weight: 1480.0kg 3260.0lb
Fuel: 70.0L 15.4gal 18.5galUS

799 Chevrolet

Impala SS
1965 USA
107.0mph 172.2kmh
0-50mph 80.5kmh: 7.7secs
0-60mph 96.5kmh: 9.8secs
0-1/4 mile: 17.8secs
250.0bhp 186.4kW 253.5PS
@ 4400rpm
350.0lbft 474.3Nm @ 2800rpm
143.6bhp/ton 141.2bhp/tonne
46.6bhp/L 34.8kW/L 47.3PS/L
39.7ft/sec 12.1m/sec
25.4mph 40.9kmh/1000rpm
Petrol 4-stroke piston
5359cc 327.0cu in
Vee 8 1 Carburettor
Compression ratio: 10.5:1
Bore: 101.6mm 4.0in
Stroke: 82.6mm 3.2in
Valve type/No: Overhead 16
Transmission: Automatic
No. of forward speeds: 2
Wheels driven: Rear
Brake system: PA
Steering: PA
Wheelbase: 302.3cm 119.0in
Track F: 158.8cm 62.5in
Track R: 158.5cm 62.4in
Length: 541.0cm 213.0in
Width: 202.2cm 79.6in
Height: 137.4cm 54.1in
Ground clearance: 13.7cm 5.4in
Kerb weight: 1770.6kg 3900.0lb
Fuel: 75.7L 16.6gal 20.0galUS

800 Chevrolet

Bel Air Six
1966 USA
95.0mph 152.9kmh
0-50mph 80.5kmh: 11.4secs
0-60mph 96.5kmh: 15.5secs
0-1/4 mile: 20.5secs
150.0bhp 111.9kW 152.1PS
@ 4200rpm
235.0lbft 318.4Nm @ 1600rpm
94.4bhp/ton 92.8bhp/tonne
36.6bhp/L 27.3kW/L 37.1PS/L
41.2ft/sec 12.6m/sec
25.0mph 40.2kmh/1000rpm
Petrol 4-stroke piston
4097cc 250.0cu in
In-line 6 1 Carburettor
Compression ratio: 8.5:1
Bore: 98.4mm 3.9in
Stroke: 89.7mm 3.5in
Valve type/No: Overhead 12
Transmission: Automatic
No. of forward speeds: 2
Wheels driven: Rear
Springs F/R: Coil/Coil
Brakes F/R: Drum/Drum
Steering: Recirculating ball PA
Wheelbase: 302.3cm 119.0in
Track F: 158.8cm 62.5in
Track R: 158.5cm 62.4in
Length: 541.5cm 213.2in
Width: 203.2cm 80.0in
Height: 140.7cm 55.4in
Ground clearance: 14.5cm 5.7in
Kerb weight: 1616.2kg 3560.0lb
Fuel: 75.7L 16.6gal 20.0galUS

801 Chevrolet

Chevy II Nova SS
1966 USA
123.0mph 197.9kmh

0-50mph 80.5kmh: 5.5secs
0-60mph 96.5kmh: 7.2secs
0-1/4 mile: 15.1secs
350.0bhp 261.0kW 354.8PS
@ 5800rpm
360.0lbft 487.8Nm @ 3600rpm
249.7bhp/ton 245.5bhp/tonne
65.3bhp/L 48.7kW/L 66.2PS/L
52.4ft/sec 16.0m/sec
21.2mph 34.1kmh/1000rpm
Petrol 4-stroke piston
5359cc 327.0cu in
Vee 8 1 Carburettor
Compression ratio: 11.0:1
Bore: 101.6mm 4.0in
Stroke: 82.6mm 3.2in
Valve type/No: Overhead 16
Transmission: Manual
No. of forward speeds: 4
Wheels driven: Rear
Springs F/R: Coil/Leaf
Brake system: PA
Brakes F/R: Drum/Drum
Steering: Recirculating ball PA
Wheelbase: 279.4cm 110.0in
Track F: 144.3cm 56.8in
Track R: 143.0cm 56.3in
Length: 464.8cm 183.0in
Width: 181.1cm 71.3in
Height: 136.7cm 53.8in
Ground clearance: 16.3cm 6.4in
Kerb weight: 1425.6kg 3140.0lb
Fuel: 60.6L 13.3gal 16.0galUS

802 Chevrolet

Corvette
1966 USA
115.0mph 185.0kmh
0-50mph 80.5kmh: 6.4secs
0-60mph 96.5kmh: 8.3secs
0-1/4 mile: 15.7secs
300.0bhp 223.7kW 304.2PS
@ 5000rpm
360.0lbft 487.8Nm @ 3400rpm
209.3bhp/ton 205.8bhp/tonne
56.0bhp/L 41.7kW/L 56.8PS/L
45.1ft/sec 13.8m/sec
22.9mph 36.8kmh/1000rpm
Petrol 4-stroke piston
5359cc 327.0cu in
Vee 8 1 Carburettor
Compression ratio: 10.3:1
Bore: 101.6mm 4.0in
Stroke: 82.6mm 3.2in
Valve type/No: Overhead 16
Transmission: Automatic
No. of forward speeds: 2
Wheels driven: Rear
Springs F/R: Coil/Leaf
Brake system: PA
Brakes F/R: Disc/Disc
Steering: Recirculating ball PA
Wheelbase: 248.9cm 98.0in
Track F: 144.3cm 56.8in
Track R: 146.3cm 57.6in
Length: 444.8cm 175.1in
Width: 175.8cm 69.2in
Height: 126.0cm 49.6in
Ground clearance: 12.7cm 5.0in
Kerb weight: 1457.3kg 3210.0lb
Fuel: 75.7L 16.6gal 20.0galUS

803 Chevrolet

Corvette Convertible
1966 USA
130.0mph 209.2kmh
0-50mph 80.5kmh: 4.6secs
0-60mph 96.5kmh: 5.7secs
0-1/4 mile: 14.0secs
425.0bhp 316.9kW 430.9PS
@ 5600rpm
460.0lbft 623.3Nm @ 4000rpm
291.1bhp/ton 286.3bhp/tonne
60.7bhp/L 45.3kW/L 61.6PS/L
58.5ft/sec 17.8m/sec
22.9mph 36.8kmh/1000rpm
Petrol 4-stroke piston
6997cc 426.9cu in
Vee 8 1 Carburettor
Compression ratio: 11.0:1
Bore: 108.0mm 4.2in
Stroke: 95.5mm 3.8in
Valve type/No: Overhead 16
Transmission: Manual
No. of forward speeds: 4
Wheels driven: Rear
Springs F/R: Coil/Leaf
Brake system: PA
Brakes F/R: Disc/Disc
Steering: Recirculating ball PA
Wheelbase: 248.9cm 98.0in
Track F: 144.3cm 56.8in
Track R: 146.3cm 57.6in
Length: 444.8cm 175.1in
Width: 176.8cm 69.6in
Height: 126.5cm 49.8in
Ground clearance: 12.7cm 5.0in
Kerb weight: 1484.6kg 3270.0lb
Fuel: 75.7L 16.6gal 20.0galUS

804 Chevrolet

Camaro
1967 USA
120.0mph 193.1kmh
0-50mph 80.5kmh: 7.0secs
0-60mph 96.5kmh: 9.1secs
0-1/4 mile: 16.9secs
275.0bhp 205.1kW 278.8PS
@ 4800rpm
355.0lbft 481.0Nm @ 3200rpm
190.1bhp/ton 186.9bhp/tonne
51.2bhp/L 38.2kW/L 51.9PS/L
43.5ft/sec 13.2m/sec
24.2mph 38.9kmh/1000rpm
15.6mpg 13.0mpgUS 18.1L/100km
Petrol 4-stroke piston
5367cc 327.5cu in
Vee 8 1 Carburettor
Compression ratio: 10.5:1
Bore: 108.0mm 4.2in
Stroke: 82.7mm 3.3in
Valve type/No: Overhead 16
Transmission: Manual
No. of forward speeds: 4
Wheels driven: Rear
Springs F/R: Coil/Leaf
Brake system: PA
Brakes F/R: Disc/Drum
Steering: Recirculating ball PA
Wheelbase: 274.6cm 108.1in
Track F: 149.9cm 59.0in
Track R: 149.6cm 58.9in
Length: 464.8cm 183.0in
Width: 181.1cm 71.3in
Height: 129.5cm 51.0in
Kerb weight: 1471.0kg 3240.0lb
Fuel: 70.0L 15.4gal 18.5galUS

805 Chevrolet

Camaro 427 Dana
1967 USA
130.0mph 209.2kmh
0-50mph 80.5kmh: 4.9secs
0-60mph 96.5kmh: 6.3secs
0-1/4 mile: 14.2secs
425.0bhp 316.9kW 430.9PS
@ 5600rpm
460.0lbft 623.3Nm @ 4000rpm
282.7bhp/ton 277.9bhp/tonne
60.8bhp/L 45.3kW/L 61.6PS/L
58.5ft/sec 17.8m/sec
21.4mph 34.4kmh/1000rpm
Petrol 4-stroke piston
6989cc 426.4cu in
Vee 8 1 Carburettor
Compression ratio: 11.0:1
Bore: 108.0mm 4.2in
Stroke: 95.5mm 3.8in
Valve type/No: Overhead 16
Transmission: Manual
No. of forward speeds: 4
Wheels driven: Rear
Springs F/R: Coil/Leaf
Brake system: PA
Brakes F/R: Disc/Drum
Steering: Recirculating ball
Wheelbase: 274.6cm 108.1in
Track F: 149.9cm 59.0in
Track R: 149.6cm 58.9in
Length: 468.9cm 184.6in
Width: 184.2cm 72.5in
Height: 129.5cm 51.0in
Ground clearance: 16.0cm 6.3in
Kerb weight: 1529.1kg 3368.0lb
Fuel: 70.0L 15.4gal 18.5galUS

806 Chevrolet

Camaro Six
1967 USA
104.0mph 167.3kmh
0-50mph 80.5kmh: 8.7secs
0-60mph 96.5kmh: 11.4secs
0-1/4 mile: 18.5secs
155.0bhp 115.6kW 157.1PS
@ 4200rpm
235.0lbft 318.4Nm @ 1600rpm
115.8bhp/ton 113.9bhp/tonne
37.8bhp/L 28.2kW/L 38.3PS/L
41.2ft/sec 12.6m/sec
24.7mph 39.7kmh/1000rpm
Petrol 4-stroke piston
4100cc 250.1cu in
In-line 6 1 Carburettor
Compression ratio: 8.5:1
Bore: 98.4mm 3.9in
Stroke: 89.7mm 3.5in
Valve type/No: Overhead 12
Transmission: Manual
No. of forward speeds: 3
Wheels driven: Rear
Springs F/R: Coil/Leaf
Brake system: PA
Brakes F/R: Drum/Drum
Steering: Recirculating ball PA
Wheelbase: 274.6cm 108.1in
Track F: 149.9cm 59.0in
Track R: 149.6cm 58.9in
Length: 468.9cm 184.6in
Width: 184.2cm 72.5in
Height: 129.5cm 51.0in
Ground clearance: 16.0cm 6.3in
Kerb weight: 1361.1kg 2998.0lb
Fuel: 70.0L 15.4gal 18.5galUS

807 Chevrolet

Camaro SS350
1967 USA
120.0mph 193.1kmh
0-50mph 80.5kmh: 5.8secs
0-60mph 96.5kmh: 7.8secs
0-1/4 mile: 15.8secs
295.0bhp 220.0kW 299.1PS
@ 4800rpm
380.0lbft 514.9Nm @ 3200rpm
205.9bhp/ton 202.4bhp/tonne
51.5bhp/L 38.4kW/L 52.2PS/L
46.4ft/sec 14.1m/sec
23.2mph 37.3kmh/1000rpm
Petrol 4-stroke piston
5730cc 349.6cu in
Vee 8 1 Carburettor
Compression ratio: 10.5:1
Bore: 101.6mm 4.0in
Stroke: 88.4mm 3.5in
Valve type/No: Overhead 16
Transmission: Manual
No. of forward speeds: 4
Wheels driven: Rear
Springs F/R: Coil/Leaf
Brake system: PA
Brakes F/R: Drum/Drum
Steering: Recirculating ball PA
Wheelbase: 274.6cm 108.1in
Track F: 149.9cm 59.0in
Track R: 149.6cm 58.9in
Length: 468.9cm 184.6in
Width: 184.2cm 72.5in
Height: 129.5cm 51.0in
Ground clearance: 16.0cm 6.3in
Kerb weight: 1457.3kg 3210.0lb
Fuel: 70.0L 15.4gal 18.5galUS

808 Chevrolet

Corvette
1967 USA
121.0mph 194.7kmh
0-50mph 80.5kmh: 5.9secs
0-60mph 96.5kmh: 7.8secs
0-1/4 mile: 16.0secs
300.0bhp 223.7kW 304.2PS
@ 5000rpm
360.0lbft 487.8Nm @ 3400rpm
212.7bhp/ton 209.1bhp/tonne
56.0bhp/L 41.8kW/L 56.8PS/L
45.1ft/sec 13.8m/sec
23.1mph 37.2kmh/1000rpm
Petrol 4-stroke piston
5356cc 326.8cu in
Vee 8 1 Carburettor
Compression ratio: 10.3:1
Bore: 102.0mm 4.0in
Stroke: 82.6mm 3.2in
Valve type/No: Overhead 16
Transmission: Manual
No. of forward speeds: 4
Wheels driven: Rear
Springs F/R: Coil/Leaf
Brake system: PA
Brakes F/R: Disc/Disc
Steering: Recirculating ball PA
Wheelbase: 248.9cm 98.0in
Track F: 146.3cm 57.6in
Track R: 148.1cm 58.3in
Length: 444.8cm 175.1in
Width: 176.8cm 69.6in
Height: 126.5cm 49.8in
Ground clearance: 12.7cm 5.0in
Kerb weight: 1434.6kg 3160.0lb
Fuel: 70.0L 15.4gal 18.5galUS

809 Chevrolet

Impala SS427
1967 USA
125.0mph 201.1kmh
0-50mph 80.5kmh: 6.5secs
0-60mph 96.5kmh: 8.4secs
0-1/4 mile: 15.8secs
385.0bhp 287.1kW 390.3PS
@ 5200rpm
460.0lbft 623.3Nm @ 3400rpm
224.9bhp/ton 221.1bhp/tonne
55.0bhp/L 41.0kW/L 55.8PS/L
54.3ft/sec 16.5m/sec
24.0mph 38.6kmh/1000rpm
Petrol 4-stroke piston
6997cc 426.9cu in
Vee 8 1 Carburettor
Compression ratio: 10.3:1
Bore: 108.0mm 4.2in
Stroke: 95.5mm 3.8in
Valve type/No: Overhead 16
Transmission: Automatic
No. of forward speeds: 3
Wheels driven: Rear
Springs F/R: Coil/Coil
Brake system: PA
Brakes F/R: Drum/Drum
Steering: Recirculating ball PA
Wheelbase: 302.3cm 119.0in
Track F: 158.8cm 62.5in
Track R: 158.5cm 62.4in
Length: 541.5cm 213.2in
Width: 202.9cm 79.9in
Height: 138.2cm 54.4in
Ground clearance: 16.3cm 6.4in
Kerb weight: 1741.1kg 3835.0lb
Fuel: 90.8L 20.0gal 24.0galUS

810 Chevrolet

Camaro SS396
1968 USA
121.0mph 194.7kmh
0-50mph 80.5kmh: 6.0secs
0-60mph 96.5kmh: 7.6secs
0-1/4 mile: 15.5secs
325.0bhp 242.3kW 329.5PS
@ 4800rpm
410.0lbft 555.6Nm @ 3200rpm
188.8bhp/ton 185.7bhp/tonne
50.1bhp/L 37.3kW/L 50.8PS/L
50.1ft/sec 15.3m/sec
24.0mph 38.6kmh/1000rpm
Petrol 4-stroke piston
6489cc 395.9cu in
Vee 8 1 Carburettor
Compression ratio: 10.3:1
Bore: 104.0mm 4.1in
Stroke: 95.5mm 3.8in
Valve type/No: Overhead 16
Transmission: Automatic
No. of forward speeds: 3
Wheels driven: Rear
Springs F/R: Coil/Leaf
Brake system: PA
Brakes F/R: Disc/Drum
Steering: Recirculating ball PA
Wheelbase: 274.3cm 108.0in
Track F: 149.9cm 59.0in
Track R: 149.6cm 58.9in
Length: 469.1cm 184.7in
Width: 184.4cm 72.6in
Height: 130.8cm 51.5in
Kerb weight: 1750.2kg 3855.0lb
Fuel: 70.0L 15.4gal 18.5galUS

811 Chevrolet

Camaro Z/28
1968 USA
133.0mph 214.0kmh
0-50mph 80.5kmh: 5.7secs
0-60mph 96.5kmh: 7.4secs
0-1/4 mile: 14.9secs
290.0bhp 216.2kW 294.0PS
@ 5800rpm
290.0lbft 393.0Nm @ 4200rpm
193.6bhp/ton 190.4bhp/tonne

58.6bhp/L 43.7kW/L 59.4PS/L
48.3ft/sec 14.7m/sec
18.4mph 29.6kmh/1000rpm
Petrol 4-stroke piston
4949cc 301.9cu in
Vee 8 1 Carburettor
Compression ratio: 11.0:1
Bore: 101.6mm 4.0in
Stroke: 76.2mm 3.0in
Valve type/No: Overhead 16
Transmission: Manual
No. of forward speeds: 4
Wheels driven: Rear
Springs F/R: Coil/Leaf
Brake system: PA
Brakes F/R: Disc/Drum
Steering: Recirculating ball PA
Wheelbase: 274.3cm 108.0in
Track F: 151.4cm 59.6in
Track R: 151.1cm 59.5in
Length: 468.9cm 184.6in
Width: 183.6cm 72.3in
Height: 129.3cm 50.9in
Kerb weight: 1523.2kg 3355.0lb
Fuel: 70.0L 15.4gal 18.5galUS

812 Chevrolet

Chevelle Malibu
1968 USA
112.0mph 180.2kmh
0-50mph 80.5kmh: 7.0secs
0-60mph 96.5kmh: 9.1secs
0-1/4 mile: 16.8secs
275.0bhp 205.1kW 278.8PS
@ 4800rpm
355.0lbft 481.0Nm @ 3200rpm
152.8bhp/ton 150.3bhp/tonne
51.3bhp/L 38.3kW/L 52.0PS/L
43.3ft/sec 13.2m/sec
22.6mph 36.4kmh/1000rpm
Petrol 4-stroke piston
5359cc 327.0cu in
Vee 8 1 Carburettor
Compression ratio: 10.0:1
Bore: 101.6mm 4.0in
Stroke: 82.5mm 3.2in
Valve type/No: Overhead 16
Transmission: Automatic
No. of forward speeds: 2
Wheels driven: Rear
Springs F/R: Coil/Coil
Brake system: PA
Brakes F/R: Disc/Drum
Steering: Recirculating ball PA
Wheelbase: 284.5cm 112.0in
Track F: 149.9cm 59.0in
Track R: 149.9cm 59.0in
Length: 500.6cm 197.1in
Width: 192.3cm 75.7in
Height: 133.9cm 52.7in
Ground clearance: 12.2cm 4.8in
Kerb weight: 1829.6kg 4030.0lb
Fuel: 75.7L 16.6gal 20.0galUS

813 Chevrolet

Chevelle SS396
1968 USA
120.0mph 193.1kmh
0-50mph 80.5kmh: 5.1secs
0-60mph 96.5kmh: 6.6secs
0-1/4 mile: 14.8secs
375.0bhp 279.6kW 380.2PS
@ 5600rpm
415.0lbft 562.3Nm @ 3600rpm
201.9bhp/ton 198.6bhp/tonne
57.8bhp/L 43.1kW/L 58.6PS/L
58.5ft/sec 17.8m/sec
21.4mph 34.4kmh/1000rpm
Petrol 4-stroke piston
6489cc 395.9cu in
Vee 8 1 Carburettor
Compression ratio: 11.0:1
Bore: 104.0mm 4.1in
Stroke: 95.5mm 3.8in
Valve type/No: Overhead 16
Transmission: Manual
No. of forward speeds: 4
Wheels driven: Rear
Springs F/R: Coil/Coil
Brake system: PA
Brakes F/R: Disc/Drum
Steering: Recirculating ball PA
Wheelbase: 284.5cm 112.0in
Track F: 149.9cm 59.0in
Track R: 149.9cm 59.0in
Length: 500.6cm 197.1in
Width: 192.3cm 75.7in
Height: 133.9cm 52.7in
Ground clearance: 12.2cm 4.8in
Kerb weight: 1888.6kg 4160.0lb
Fuel: 75.7L 16.6gal 20.0galUS

814 Chevrolet

Chevy II
1968 USA
116.0mph 186.6kmh
0-50mph 80.5kmh: 6.8secs
0-60mph 96.5kmh: 8.7secs
0-1/4 mile: 16.5secs
325.0bhp 242.3kW 329.5PS
@ 5600rpm
355.0lbft 481.0Nm @ 3600rpm
214.1bhp/ton 210.5bhp/tonne
60.6bhp/L 45.2kW/L 61.5PS/L
50.6ft/sec 15.4m/sec
20.7mph 33.3kmh/1000rpm
Petrol 4-stroke piston
5359cc 327.0cu in
Vee 8 1 Carburettor
Compression ratio: 11.0:1
Bore: 101.6mm 4.0in
Stroke: 82.6mm 3.2in
Valve type/No: Overhead 16
Transmission: Manual
No. of forward speeds: 4
Wheels driven: Rear
Springs F/R: Coil/Leaf
Brake system: PA
Brakes F/R: Disc/Drum
Steering: Recirculating ball PA
Wheelbase: 281.9cm 111.0in
Track F: 149.9cm 59.0in
Track R: 149.6cm 58.9in
Length: 476.8cm 187.7in
Width: 179.1cm 70.5in
Height: 137.4cm 54.1in
Kerb weight: 1543.6kg 3400.0lb
Fuel: 68.1L 15.0gal 18.0galUS

815 Chevrolet

Corvair Monza
1968 USA
98.0mph 157.7kmh
0-50mph 80.5kmh: 11.2secs
0-60mph 96.5kmh: 15.6secs
0-1/4 mile: 19.8secs
140.0bhp 104.4kW 141.9PS
@ 5200rpm
160.0lbft 216.8Nm @ 3600rpm
119.9bhp/ton 117.9bhp/tonne
52.2bhp/L 38.9kW/L 52.9PS/L
42.5ft/sec 12.9m/sec
20.1mph 32.3kmh/1000rpm
Petrol 4-stroke piston
2683cc 163.7cu in
Flat 6 4 Carburettor
Compression ratio: 9.3:1
Bore: 87.3mm 3.4in
Stroke: 74.7mm 2.9in
Valve type/No: Overhead 12
Transmission: Manual
No. of forward speeds: 4
Wheels driven: Rear
Springs F/R: Coil/Coil
Brakes F/R: Drum/Drum
Steering: Recirculating ball
Wheelbase: 274.3cm 108.0in
Track F: 139.7cm 55.0in
Track R: 143.8cm 56.6in
Length: 465.6cm 183.3in
Width: 177.0cm 69.7in
Height: 130.3cm 51.3in
Ground clearance: 16.3cm 6.4in
Kerb weight: 1187.2kg 2615.0lb
Fuel: 53.0L 11.6gal 14.0galUS

816 Chevrolet

Corvair Sport Coupe
1968 USA
106.0mph 170.6kmh
0-50mph 80.5kmh: 8.3secs
0-60mph 96.5kmh: 11.4secs
0-1/4 mile: 17.9secs
140.0bhp 104.4kW 141.9PS
@ 5200rpm
160.0lbft 216.8Nm @ 3600rpm
119.9bhp/ton 117.9bhp/tonne
52.2bhp/L 38.9kW/L 52.9PS/L
42.5ft/sec 12.9m/sec
20.1mph 32.3kmh/1000rpm
Petrol 4-stroke piston
2683cc 163.7cu in
Flat 6 4 Carburettor
Compression ratio: 9.3:1
Bore: 87.3mm 3.4in
Stroke: 74.7mm 2.9in
Valve type/No: Overhead 12
Transmission: Manual
No. of forward speeds: 4
Wheels driven: Rear
Springs F/R: Coil/Coil
Brake system: PA
Brakes F/R: Drum/Drum
Steering: Recirculating ball
Wheelbase: 274.3cm 108.0in
Track F: 139.7cm 55.0in
Track R: 143.8cm 56.6in
Length: 465.6cm 183.3in
Width: 177.0cm 69.7in
Height: 130.3cm 51.3in
Kerb weight: 1187.2kg 2615.0lb
Fuel: 53.0L 11.6gal 14.0galUS

817 Chevrolet

Corvette
1968 USA
128.0mph 206.0kmh
0-50mph 80.5kmh: 6.1secs
0-60mph 96.5kmh: 7.7secs
0-1/4 mile: 15.6secs
350.0bhp 261.0kW 354.8PS
@ 5800rpm
360.0lbft 487.8Nm @ 3600rpm
240.5bhp/ton 236.5bhp/tonne
65.3bhp/L 48.7kW/L 66.2PS/L
52.4ft/sec 16.0m/sec
21.6mph 34.8kmh/1000rpm
Petrol 4-stroke piston
5356cc 326.8cu in
Vee 8 1 Carburettor
Compression ratio: 11.0:1
Bore: 101.6mm 4.0in
Stroke: 82.6mm 3.2in
Valve type/No: Overhead 16
Transmission: Manual
No. of forward speeds: 4
Wheels driven: Rear
Springs F/R: Coil/Leaf
Brake system: PA
Brakes F/R: Disc/Disc
Steering: Recirculating ball PA
Wheelbase: 248.9cm 98.0in
Track F: 148.1cm 58.3in
Track R: 149.9cm 59.0in
Length: 462.5cm 182.1in
Width: 175.8cm 69.2in
Height: 121.4cm 47.8in
Ground clearance: 12.4cm 4.9in
Kerb weight: 1480.0kg 3260.0lb
Fuel: 75.7L 16.6gal 20.0galUS

818 Chevrolet

Corvette Convertible
1968 USA
142.0mph 228.5kmh
0-50mph 80.5kmh: 5.3secs
0-60mph 96.5kmh: 6.5secs
0-1/4 mile: 13.4secs
435.0bhp 324.4kW 441.0PS
@ 5800rpm
460.0lbft 623.3Nm @ 4000rpm
296.6bhp/ton 291.7bhp/tonne
62.2bhp/L 46.4kW/L 63.0PS/L
60.6ft/sec 18.5m/sec
21.8mph 35.1kmh/1000rpm
Petrol 4-stroke piston
6997cc 426.9cu in
Vee 8 3 Carburettor
Compression ratio: 11.0:1
Bore: 108.0mm 4.2in
Stroke: 95.5mm 3.8in
Valve type/No: Overhead 16
Transmission: Manual
No. of forward speeds: 4
Wheels driven: Rear
Springs F/R: Coil/Leaf
Brake system: PA
Brakes F/R: Disc/Disc
Steering: Recirculating ball PA
Wheelbase: 248.9cm 98.0in
Track F: 148.1cm 58.3in
Track R: 149.9cm 59.0in
Length: 462.5cm 182.1in
Width: 175.8cm 69.2in
Height: 123.4cm 48.6in
Kerb weight: 1491.4kg 3285.0lb
Fuel: 75.7L 16.6gal 20.0galUS

819 Chevrolet

Corvette Coupe
1968 USA
128.0mph 206.0kmh
0-50mph 80.5kmh: 6.5secs
0-60mph 96.5kmh: 8.6secs
0-1/4 mile: 15.8secs
300.0bhp 223.7kW 304.2PS
@ 5000rpm
360.0lbft 487.8Nm @ 3400rpm
199.1bhp/ton 195.8bhp/tonne
56.0bhp/L 41.7kW/L 56.8PS/L
45.1ft/sec 13.8m/sec
25.1mph 40.4kmh/1000rpm
Petrol 4-stroke piston
5359cc 327.0cu in
Vee 8 1 Carburettor
Compression ratio: 10.0:1
Bore: 101.6mm 4.0in
Stroke: 82.6mm 3.2in
Valve type/No: Overhead 16
Transmission: Automatic
No. of forward speeds: 3
Wheels driven: Rear
Springs F/R: Coil/Leaf
Brake system: PA
Brakes F/R: Disc/Disc
Steering: Recirculating ball PA
Wheelbase: 248.9cm 98.0in
Track F: 148.1cm 58.3in
Track R: 149.9cm 59.0in
Length: 462.5cm 182.1in
Width: 175.8cm 69.2in
Height: 121.4cm 47.8in
Kerb weight: 1532.2kg 3375.0lb
Fuel: 75.7L 16.6gal 20.0galUS

820 Chevrolet

Corvette L88
1968 USA
151.0mph 243.0kmh
0-50mph 80.5kmh: 5.6secs
0-60mph 96.5kmh: 6.8secs
0-1/4 mile: 14.1secs
430.0bhp 320.6kW 436.0PS
@ 5800rpm
460.0lbft 623.3Nm @ 4000rpm
282.5bhp/ton 277.7bhp/tonne
61.4bhp/L 45.8kW/L 62.3PS/L
60.4ft/sec 18.4m/sec
13.6mpg 11.3mpgUS 20.8L/100km
Petrol 4-stroke piston
6997cc 426.9cu in
Vee 8 1 Carburettor
Compression ratio: 12.5:1
Bore: 108.0mm 4.2in
Stroke: 95.2mm 3.8in
Valve type/No: Overhead 16
Transmission: Automatic
No. of forward speeds: 3
Wheels driven: Rear
Springs F/R: Coil/Leaf
Brake system: PA
Brakes F/R: Disc/Disc
Steering: Recirculating ball PA
Wheelbase: 248.9cm 98.0in
Track F: 148.1cm 58.3in
Track R: 149.9cm 59.0in
Length: 462.5cm 182.1in
Width: 175.8cm 69.2in
Height: 123.4cm 48.6in
Kerb weight: 1548.1kg 3410.0lb
Fuel: 75.7L 16.6gal 20.0galUS

821 Chevrolet

El Camino
1968 USA
132.0mph 212.4kmh
0-50mph 80.5kmh: 5.5secs
0-60mph 96.5kmh: 6.8secs
0-1/4 mile: 14.8secs
350.0bhp 261.0kW 354.8PS
@ 5200rpm
415.0lbft 562.3Nm @ 3400rpm
208.5bhp/ton 205.0bhp/tonne
53.9bhp/L 40.2kW/L 54.7PS/L
54.3ft/sec 16.5m/sec
22.8mph 36.7kmh/1000rpm
Petrol 4-stroke piston
6489cc 395.9cu in
Vee 8 1 Carburettor
Compression ratio: 10.2:1
Bore: 104.0mm 4.1in
Stroke: 95.5mm 3.8in
Valve type/No: Overhead 16
Transmission: Automatic
No. of forward speeds: 3

Wheels driven: Rear
Springs F/R: Coil/Coil
Brake system: PA
Brakes F/R: Disc/Drum
Steering: Recirculating ball PA
Wheelbase: 294.6cm 116.0in
Track F: 149.9cm 59.0in
Track R: 149.9cm 59.0in
Length: 525.8cm 207.0in
Width: 192.3cm 75.7in
Height: 137.2cm 54.0in
Kerb weight: 1707.0kg 3760.0lb
Fuel: 75.7L 16.6gal 20.0galUS

822 Chevrolet

Impala
1968 USA
96.0mph 154.5kmh
0-50mph 80.5kmh: 10.5secs
0-60mph 96.5kmh: 13.8secs
0-1/4 mile: 18.6secs
200.0bhp 149.1kW 202.8PS
@ 4600rpm
300.0lbft 406.5Nm @ 2400rpm
116.7bhp/ton 114.7bhp/tonne
39.7bhp/L 29.6kW/L 40.3PS/L
41.5ft/sec 12.7m/sec
25.8mph 41.5kmh/1000rpm
Petrol 4-stroke piston
5031cc 307.0cu in
Vee 8 1 Carburettor
Compression ratio: 9.0:1
Bore: 98.6mm 3.9in
Stroke: 82.6mm 3.2in
Valve type/No: Overhead 16
Transmission: Automatic
No. of forward speeds: 2
Wheels driven: Rear
Springs F/R: Coil/Coil
Brakes F/R: Drum/Drum
Steering: Recirculating ball PA
Wheelbase: 302.3cm 119.0in
Track F: 158.8cm 62.5in
Track R: 158.5cm 62.4in
Length: 545.3cm 214.7in
Width: 202.2cm 79.6in
Height: 137.9cm 54.3in
Kerb weight: 1743.4kg 3840.0lb
Fuel: 90.8L 20.0gal 24.0galUS

823 Chevrolet

Malibu 327
1968 USA
115.0mph 185.0kmh
0-50mph 80.5kmh: 7.1secs
0-60mph 96.5kmh: 9.3secs
0-1/4 mile: 17.1secs
275.0bhp 205.1kW 278.8PS
@ 4800rpm
355.0lbft 481.0Nm @ 3200rpm
171.6bhp/ton 168.7bhp/tonne
51.3bhp/L 38.3kW/L 52.1PS/L
43.3ft/sec 13.2m/sec
20.6mph 33.1kmh/1000rpm
Petrol 4-stroke piston
5356cc 326.8cu in
Vee 8 1 Carburettor
Compression ratio: 10.0:1
Bore: 101.6mm 4.0in
Stroke: 82.6mm 3.2in
Valve type/No: Overhead 16
Transmission: Automatic
No. of forward speeds: 2
Wheels driven: Rear
Springs F/R: Coil/Coil
Brake system: PA
Brakes F/R: Disc/Drum
Steering: Recirculating ball PA
Wheelbase: 284.5cm 112.0in
Track F: 149.9cm 59.0in
Track R: 149.9cm 59.0in
Length: 499.9cm 196.8in
Width: 193.0cm 76.0in
Height: 134.1cm 52.8in
Ground clearance: 15.0cm 5.9in
Kerb weight: 1629.9kg 3590.0lb
Fuel: 75.7L 16.6gal 20.0galUS

824 Chevrolet

Camaro SS 396
1969 USA
126.0mph 202.7kmh
0-50mph 80.5kmh: 5.1secs
0-60mph 96.5kmh: 6.8secs
0-1/4 mile: 14.8secs
375.0bhp 279.6kW 380.2PS
@ 5600rpm
415.0lbft 562.3Nm @ 3600rpm
240.7bhp/ton 236.7bhp/tonne
57.8bhp/L 43.1kW/L 58.6PS/L
58.5ft/sec 17.8m/sec
19.9mph 32.0kmh/1000rpm
Petrol 4-stroke piston
6489cc 395.9cu in
Vee 8 1 Carburettor
Compression ratio: 11.0:1
Bore: 104.0mm 4.1in
Stroke: 95.5mm 3.8in
Valve type/No: Overhead 16
Transmission: Manual
No. of forward speeds: 4
Wheels driven: Rear
Springs F/R: Coil/Leaf
Brake system: PA
Brakes F/R: Disc/Drum
Steering: Recirculating ball PA
Wheelbase: 274.3cm 108.0in
Track F: 152.4cm 60.0in
Track R: 152.4cm 60.0in
Length: 472.4cm 186.0in
Width: 188.0cm 74.0in
Height: 132.1cm 52.0in
Kerb weight: 1584.5kg 3490.0lb
Fuel: 70.0L 15.4gal 18.5galUS

825 Chevrolet

Camaro Z/28
1969 USA
120.0mph 193.1kmh
0-50mph 80.5kmh: 6.0secs
0-60mph 96.5kmh: 7.4secs
0-1/4 mile: 15.1secs
290.0bhp 216.2kW 294.0PS
@ 5800rpm
290.0lbft 393.0Nm @ 4200rpm
188.0bhp/ton 184.9bhp/tonne
58.7bhp/L 43.8kW/L 59.5PS/L
48.3ft/sec 14.7m/sec
12.0mpg 10.0mpgUS 23.5L/100km
Petrol 4-stroke piston
4942cc 301.5cu in
Vee 8 1 Carburettor
Compression ratio: 11.0:1
Bore: 101.6mm 4.0in
Stroke: 76.2mm 3.0in
Valve type/No: Overhead 16
Transmission: Manual
No. of forward speeds: 4
Wheels driven: Rear
Springs F/R: Coil/Leaf
Brake system: PA
Brakes F/R: Disc/Disc
Steering: Recirculating ball PA
Wheelbase: 274.3cm 108.0in
Track F: 144.5cm 56.9in
Track R: 151.1cm 59.5in
Length: 472.4cm 186.0in
Width: 188.0cm 74.0in
Height: 131.1cm 51.6in
Kerb weight: 1568.6kg 3455.0lb
Fuel: 70.0L 15.4gal 18.5galUS

826 Chevrolet

Camaro Z/28 Yenko/SC
1969 USA
0-1/4 mile: 11.9secs
450.0bhp 335.6kW 456.2PS
@ 5000rpm
460.0lbft 623.3Nm @ 4000rpm
296.5bhp/ton 291.5bhp/tonne
64.3bhp/L 47.9kW/L 65.2PS/L
52.2ft/sec 15.9m/sec
Petrol 4-stroke piston
6998cc 427.0cu in
Vee 8 1 Carburettor
Compression ratio: 11.0:1
Bore: 107.9mm 4.2in
Stroke: 95.5mm 3.8in
Valve type/No: Overhead 16
Transmission: Manual
No. of forward speeds: 4
Wheels driven: Rear
Springs F/R: Coil/Leaf
Brake system: PA
Brakes F/R: Disc/Drum
Steering: Recirculating ball
Wheelbase: 274.3cm 108.0in
Track F: 151.4cm 59.6in
Track R: 151.1cm 59.5in
Length: 472.4cm 186.0in
Width: 188.0cm 74.0in
Height: 129.8cm 51.1in
Kerb weight: 1543.6kg 3400.0lb
Fuel: 70.0L 15.4gal 18.5galUS

827 Chevrolet

Caprice
1969 USA
126.0mph 202.7kmh
0-50mph 80.5kmh: 5.9secs
0-60mph 96.5kmh: 7.7secs
0-1/4 mile: 15.5secs
390.0bhp 290.8kW 395.4PS
@ 5400rpm
460.0lbft 623.3Nm @ 3600rpm
193.5bhp/ton 190.3bhp/tonne
55.7bhp/L 41.6kW/L 56.5PS/L
56.4ft/sec 17.2m/sec
25.2mph 40.5kmh/1000rpm
Petrol 4-stroke piston
6997cc 426.9cu in
Vee 8 1 Carburettor
Compression ratio: 10.3:1
Bore: 108.0mm 4.2in
Stroke: 95.5mm 3.8in
Valve type/No: Overhead 16
Transmission: Automatic
No. of forward speeds: 3
Wheels driven: Rear
Springs F/R: Coil/Coil
Brake system: PA
Brakes F/R: Disc/Drum
Steering: Recirculating ball PA
Wheelbase: 302.3cm 119.0in
Track F: 157.5cm 62.0in
Track R: 157.5cm 62.0in
Length: 548.6cm 216.0in
Width: 203.2cm 80.0in
Height: 137.2cm 54.0in
Kerb weight: 2049.8kg 4515.0lb
Fuel: 90.8L 20.0gal 24.0galUS

828 Chevrolet

Chevelle Malibu
1969 USA
115.0mph 185.0kmh
0-50mph 80.5kmh: 6.0secs
0-60mph 96.5kmh: 7.8secs
0-1/4 mile: 16.1secs
300.0bhp 223.7kW 304.2PS
@ 4800rpm
380.0lbft 514.9Nm @ 3200rpm
179.9bhp/ton 176.9bhp/tonne
52.3bhp/L 39.0kW/L 53.0PS/L
46.4ft/sec 14.1m/sec
22.1mph 35.6kmh/1000rpm
Petrol 4-stroke piston
5735cc 349.9cu in
Vee 8 1 Carburettor
Compression ratio: 10.3:1
Bore: 101.6mm 4.0in
Stroke: 88.4mm 3.5in
Valve type/No: Overhead 16
Transmission: Automatic
No. of forward speeds: 3
Wheels driven: Rear
Springs F/R: Coil/Coil
Brake system: PA
Brakes F/R: Disc/Drum
Steering: Recirculating ball PA
Wheelbase: 294.6cm 116.0in
Track F: 149.9cm 59.0in
Track R: 149.9cm 59.0in
Length: 510.3cm 200.9in
Width: 193.0cm 76.0in
Height: 135.9cm 53.5in
Kerb weight: 1695.7kg 3735.0lb
Fuel: 75.7L 16.6gal 20.0galUS

829 Chevrolet

Corvette 435hp
1969 USA
122.0mph 196.3kmh
0-50mph 80.5kmh: 4.5secs
0-60mph 96.5kmh: 6.1secs
0-1/4 mile: 14.3secs
435.0bhp 324.4kW 441.0PS
@ 5800rpm
460.0lbft 623.3Nm @ 4000rpm
273.5bhp/ton 269.0bhp/tonne
62.2bhp/L 46.4kW/L 63.0PS/L
60.4ft/sec 18.4m/sec
19.0mph 30.6kmh/1000rpm
12.0mpg 10.0mpgUS 23.5L/100km
Petrol 4-stroke piston
6997cc 426.9cu in
Vee 8
Compression ratio: 11.0:1
Bore: 108.0mm 4.2in
Stroke: 95.2mm 3.8in
Valve type/No: Overhead 16
Transmission: Manual
No. of forward speeds: 4
Wheels driven: Rear
Brakes F/R: Disc/Disc
Steering: Recirculating ball PA
Wheelbase: 248.9cm 98.0in
Track F: 149.1cm 58.7in
Track R: 150.9cm 59.4in
Length: 463.6cm 182.5in
Width: 175.3cm 69.0in
Height: 121.7cm 47.9in
Kerb weight: 1617.1kg 3562.0lb
Fuel: 75.7L 16.6gal 20.0galUS

830 Chevrolet

Corvette L36
1969 USA
134.0mph 215.6kmh
0-50mph 80.5kmh: 5.9secs
0-60mph 96.5kmh: 7.6secs
0-1/4 mile: 15.0secs
390.0bhp 290.8kW 395.4PS
@ 5400rpm
460.0lbft 623.3Nm @ 3600rpm
244.7bhp/ton 240.6bhp/tonne
55.7bhp/L 41.6kW/L 56.5PS/L
56.4ft/sec 17.2m/sec
24.5mph 39.4kmh/1000rpm
15.9mpg 13.2mpgUS 17.8L/100km
Petrol 4-stroke piston
6997cc 426.9cu in
Vee 8 1 Carburettor
Compression ratio: 10.3:1
Bore: 108.0mm 4.2in
Stroke: 95.5mm 3.8in
Valve type/No: Overhead 16
Transmission: Manual
No. of forward speeds: 4
Wheels driven: Rear
Springs F/R: Coil/Leaf
Brake system: PA
Brakes F/R: Disc/Disc
Steering: Recirculating ball
Wheelbase: 248.9cm 98.0in
Track F: 149.1cm 58.7in
Track R: 150.9cm 59.4in
Length: 462.5cm 182.1in
Width: 175.3cm 69.0in
Height: 121.9cm 48.0in
Kerb weight: 1620.8kg 3570.0lb
Fuel: 75.7L 16.6gal 20.0galUS

831 Chevrolet

Corvette L46
1969 USA
119.0mph 191.5kmh
0-50mph 80.5kmh: 5.0secs
0-60mph 96.5kmh: 6.4secs
0-1/4 mile: 14.6secs
350.0bhp 261.0kW 354.8PS
@ 5600rpm
380.0lbft 514.9Nm @ 3800rpm
237.9bhp/ton 234.0bhp/tonne
61.0bhp/L 45.5kW/L 61.9PS/L
54.1ft/sec 16.5m/sec
18.4mph 29.6kmh/1000rpm
16.9mpg 14.1mpgUS 16.7L/100km
Petrol 4-stroke piston
5735cc 349.9cu in
Vee 8 1 Carburettor
Compression ratio: 11.1:1
Bore: 101.6mm 4.0in
Stroke: 88.4mm 3.5in
Valve type/No: Overhead 16
Transmission: Manual
No. of forward speeds: 4
Wheels driven: Rear
Springs F/R: Coil/Leaf
Brake system: PA
Brakes F/R: Disc/Disc
Steering: Recirculating ball
Wheelbase: 248.9cm 98.0in
Track F: 149.1cm 58.7in
Track R: 150.9cm 59.4in
Length: 462.5cm 182.1in
Width: 175.3cm 69.0in
Height: 121.9cm 48.0in
Kerb weight: 1495.9kg 3295.0lb
Fuel: 75.7L 16.6gal 20.0galUS

832 Chevrolet

Corvette L68
1969 USA
137.0mph 220.4kmh
0-50mph 80.5kmh: 5.8secs
0-60mph 96.5kmh: 7.3secs
0-1/4 mile: 14.7secs
400.0bhp 298.3kW 405.5PS

@ 5400rpm
460.0lbft 623.3Nm @ 3600rpm
254.2bhp/ton 249.9bhp/tonne
57.2bhp/L 42.6kW/L 58.0PS/L
56.4ft/sec 17.2m/sec
24.5mph 39.4kmh/1000rpm
15.7mpg 13.1mpgUS 18.0L/100km
Petrol 4-stroke piston
6997cc 426.9cu in
Vee 8 3 Carburettor
Compression ratio: 10.3:1
Bore: 108.0mm 4.2in
Stroke: 95.5mm 3.8in
Valve type/No: Overhead 16
Transmission: Automatic
No. of forward speeds: 3
Wheels driven: Rear
Springs F/R: Coil/Leaf
Brake system: PA
Brakes F/R: Disc/Disc
Steering: Recirculating ball
Wheelbase: 248.9cm 98.0in
Track F: 149.1cm 58.7in
Track R: 150.9cm 59.4in
Length: 462.5cm 182.1in
Width: 175.3cm 69.0in
Height: 121.9cm 48.0in
Kerb weight: 1600.3kg 3525.0lb
Fuel: 75.7L 16.6gal 20.0galUS

833 Chevrolet

Corvette L71
1969 USA
119.0mph 191.5kmh
0-50mph 80.5kmh: 5.4secs
0-60mph 96.5kmh: 7.0secs
0-1/4 mile: 13.9secs
435.0bhp 324.4kW 441.0PS
@ 5800rpm
460.0lbft 623.3Nm @ 4000rpm
273.7bhp/ton 269.1bhp/tonne
62.2bhp/L 46.4kW/L 63.0PS/L
60.6ft/sec 18.5m/sec
18.2mph 29.3kmh/1000rpm
12.5mpg 10.4mpgUS 22.6L/100km
Petrol 4-stroke piston
6997cc 426.9cu in
Vee 8 3 Carburettor
Compression ratio: 11.1:1
Bore: 108.0mm 4.2in
Stroke: 95.5mm 3.8in
Valve type/No: Overhead 16
Transmission: Manual
No. of forward speeds: 4
Wheels driven: Rear
Springs F/R: Coil/Leaf
Brake system: PA
Brakes F/R: Disc/Disc
Steering: Recirculating ball
Wheelbase: 248.9cm 98.0in
Track F: 149.1cm 58.7in
Track R: 150.9cm 59.4in
Length: 462.5cm 182.1in
Width: 175.3cm 69.0in
Height: 121.9cm 48.0in
Kerb weight: 1616.2kg 3560.0lb
Fuel: 75.7L 16.6gal 20.0galUS

834 Chevrolet

Corvette L71/89
1969 USA
141.0mph 226.9kmh
0-50mph 80.5kmh: 5.1secs
0-60mph 96.5kmh: 6.6secs
0-1/4 mile: 14.6secs
435.0bhp 324.4kW 441.0PS
@ 5800rpm
460.0lbft 623.3Nm @ 4000rpm
278.0bhp/ton 273.4bhp/tonne
62.2bhp/L 46.4kW/L 63.0PS/L
60.6ft/sec 18.5m/sec
22.3mph 35.9kmh/1000rpm
15.5mpg 12.9mpgUS 18.2L/100km
Petrol 4-stroke piston
6997cc 426.9cu in
Vee 8 3 Carburettor
Compression ratio: 11.1:1
Bore: 108.0mm 4.2in
Stroke: 95.5mm 3.8in
Valve type/No: Overhead 16
Transmission: Automatic
No. of forward speeds: 3
Wheels driven: Rear
Springs F/R: Coil/Leaf
Brake system: PA
Brakes F/R: Disc/Disc
Steering: Recirculating ball
Wheelbase: 248.9cm 98.0in
Track F: 149.1cm 58.7in
Track R: 150.9cm 59.4in
Length: 462.5cm 182.1in
Width: 175.3cm 69.0in
Height: 121.9cm 48.0in
Kerb weight: 1591.3kg 3505.0lb
Fuel: 75.7L 16.6gal 20.0galUS

835 Chevrolet

Corvette L88
1969 USA
151.0mph 243.0kmh
0-50mph 80.5kmh: 5.6secs
0-60mph 96.5kmh: 6.8secs
0-1/4 mile: 14.1secs
430.0bhp 320.6kW 436.0PS
@ 5200rpm
450.0lbft 609.8Nm @ 4400rpm
282.5bhp/ton 277.7bhp/tonne
61.4bhp/L 45.8kW/L 62.3PS/L
54.3ft/sec 16.5m/sec
22.3mph 35.9kmh/1000rpm
13.6mpg 11.3mpgUS 20.8L/100km
Petrol 4-stroke piston
6997cc 426.9cu in
Vee 8 1 Carburettor
Compression ratio: 12.0:1
Bore: 108.0mm 4.2in
Stroke: 95.5mm 3.8in
Valve type/No: Overhead 16
Transmission: Automatic
No. of forward speeds: 3
Wheels driven: Rear
Springs F/R: Coil/Leaf
Brake system: PA
Brakes F/R: Disc/Disc
Steering: Recirculating ball
Wheelbase: 248.9cm 98.0in
Track F: 149.1cm 58.7in
Track R: 150.9cm 59.4in
Length: 462.5cm 182.1in
Width: 175.3cm 69.0in
Height: 121.9cm 48.0in
Kerb weight: 1548.1kg 3410.0lb
Fuel: 75.7L 16.6gal 20.0galUS

836 Chevrolet

Corvette LT-1
1969 USA
135.0mph 217.2kmh
0-50mph 80.5kmh: 5.6secs
0-60mph 96.5kmh: 7.2secs
0-1/4 mile: 14.4secs
370.0bhp 275.9kW 375.1PS
@ 5800rpm
370.0lbft 501.4Nm @ 4000rpm
255.8bhp/ton 251.5bhp/tonne
64.5bhp/L 48.1kW/L 65.4PS/L
56.1ft/sec 17.1m/sec
20.8mph 33.5kmh/1000rpm
15.4mpg 12.8mpgUS 18.4L/100km
Petrol 4-stroke piston
5735cc 349.9cu in
Vee 8 1 Carburettor
Compression ratio: 11.1:1
Bore: 101.6mm 4.0in
Stroke: 88.4mm 3.5in
Valve type/No: Overhead 16
Transmission: Manual
No. of forward speeds: 4
Wheels driven: Rear
Springs F/R: Coil/Leaf
Brake system: PA
Brakes F/R: Disc/Disc
Steering: Recirculating ball
Wheelbase: 248.9cm 98.0in
Track F: 149.1cm 58.7in
Track R: 150.9cm 59.4in
Length: 462.5cm 182.1in
Width: 175.3cm 69.0in
Height: 121.9cm 48.0in
Kerb weight: 1471.0kg 3240.0lb
Fuel: 75.7L 16.6gal 20.0galUS

837 Chevrolet

Corvette Stingray
1969 USA
132.0mph 212.4kmh
0-60mph 96.5kmh: 8.4secs
0-1/4 mile: 16.0secs
300.0bhp 223.7kW 304.2PS
@ 4800rpm
360.0lbft 487.8Nm @ 3200rpm
191.7bhp/ton 188.5bhp/tonne
52.3bhp/L 39.0kW/L 53.0PS/L
46.4ft/sec 14.1m/sec
17.2mpg 14.3mpgUS 16.4L/100km
Petrol 4-stroke piston
5737cc 350.0cu in
Vee 8
Bore: 101.6mm 4.0in
Stroke: 88.4mm 3.5in
Valve type/No: Overhead 16
Transmission: Automatic
No. of forward speeds: 3
Wheels driven: Rear
Brake system: PA
Brakes F/R: Disc/Disc
Steering: PA
Wheelbase: 248.9cm 98.0in
Track F: 149.1cm 58.7in
Track R: 150.9cm 59.4in
Length: 463.6cm 182.5in
Width: 175.3cm 69.0in
Height: 121.4cm 47.8in
Kerb weight: 1591.3kg 3505.0lb

838 Chevrolet

Corvette ZQ3
1969 USA
126.0mph 202.7kmh
0-50mph 80.5kmh: 7.4secs
0-60mph 96.5kmh: 8.4secs
0-1/4 mile: 16.1secs
300.0bhp 223.7kW 304.2PS
@ 4800rpm
380.0lbft 514.9Nm @ 3200rpm
197.4bhp/ton 194.1bhp/tonne
52.3bhp/L 39.0kW/L 53.0PS/L
46.4ft/sec 14.1m/sec
24.6mph 39.6kmh/1000rpm
18.6mpg 15.5mpgUS 15.2L/100km
Petrol 4-stroke piston
5735cc 349.9cu in
Vee 8 1 Carburettor
Compression ratio: 10.3:1
Bore: 101.6mm 4.0in
Stroke: 88.4mm 3.5in
Valve type/No: Overhead 16
Transmission: Automatic
No. of forward speeds: 3
Wheels driven: Rear
Springs F/R: Coil/Leaf
Brake system: PA
Brakes F/R: Disc/Disc
Steering: Recirculating ball
Wheelbase: 248.9cm 98.0in
Track F: 149.1cm 58.7in
Track R: 150.9cm 59.4in
Length: 462.5cm 182.1in
Width: 175.3cm 69.0in
Height: 121.9cm 48.0in
Kerb weight: 1545.9kg 3405.0lb
Fuel: 75.7L 16.6gal 20.0galUS

839 Chevrolet

Kingswood Estate Wagon
1969 USA
124.0mph 199.5kmh
0-50mph 80.5kmh: 6.9secs
0-60mph 96.5kmh: 9.0secs
0-1/4 mile: 16.3secs
390.0bhp 290.8kW 395.4PS
@ 5400rpm
460.0lbft 623.3Nm @ 3600rpm
173.3bhp/ton 170.4bhp/tonne
55.7bhp/L 41.6kW/L 56.5PS/L
56.4ft/sec 17.2m/sec
29.5mph 47.5kmh/1000rpm
Petrol 4-stroke piston
6997cc 426.9cu in
Vee 8 1 Carburettor
Compression ratio: 10.3:1
Bore: 108.0mm 4.2in
Stroke: 95.5mm 3.8in
Valve type/No: Overhead 16
Transmission: Automatic
No. of forward speeds: 3
Wheels driven: Rear
Springs F/R: Coil/Coil
Brake system: PA
Brakes F/R: Disc/Drum
Steering: Recirculating ball PA
Wheelbase: 302.3cm 119.0in
Track F: 161.3cm 63.5in
Track R: 161.0cm 63.4in
Length: 550.4cm 216.7in
Width: 202.7cm 79.8in
Height: 144.5cm 56.9in
Kerb weight: 2288.2kg 5040.0lb
Fuel: 90.8L 20.0gal 24.0galUS

840 Chevrolet

Camaro
1970 USA
115.0mph 185.0kmh
0-50mph 80.5kmh: 6.7secs
0-60mph 96.5kmh: 8.8secs
0-1/4 mile: 16.6secs
300.0bhp 223.7kW 304.2PS
@ 4800rpm
380.0lbft 514.9Nm @ 3200rpm
183.1bhp/ton 180.0bhp/tonne
52.3bhp/L 39.0kW/L 53.0PS/L
46.4ft/sec 14.1m/sec
23.4mph 37.7kmh/1000rpm
17.3mpg 14.4mpgUS 16.3L/100km
Petrol 4-stroke piston
5735cc 349.9cu in
Vee 8 1 Carburettor
Compression ratio: 10.3:1
Bore: 101.6mm 4.0in
Stroke: 88.4mm 3.5in
Valve type/No: Overhead 16
Transmission: Automatic
No. of forward speeds: 3
Wheels driven: Rear
Springs F/R: Coil/Leaf
Brake system: PA
Brakes F/R: Disc/Drum
Steering: Recirculating ball PA
Wheelbase: 274.3cm 108.0in
Track F: 155.7cm 61.3in
Track R: 152.4cm 60.0in
Length: 477.5cm 188.0in
Width: 189.0cm 74.4in
Height: 128.3cm 50.5in
Ground clearance: 11.4cm 4.5in
Kerb weight: 1666.2kg 3670.0lb
Fuel: 68.1L 15.0gal 18.0galUS

841 Chevrolet

Camaro Z/28
1970 USA
119.0mph 191.5kmh
0-50mph 80.5kmh: 5.2secs
0-60mph 96.5kmh: 6.5secs
0-1/4 mile: 14.5secs
360.0bhp 268.4kW 365.0PS
@ 6000rpm
380.0lbft 514.9Nm @ 4000rpm
225.2bhp/ton 221.5bhp/tonne
62.8bhp/L 46.8kW/L 63.6PS/L
58.0ft/sec 17.7m/sec
18.3mph 29.4kmh/1000rpm
14.2mpg 11.8mpgUS 19.9L/100km
Petrol 4-stroke piston
5735cc 349.9cu in
Vee 8 1 Carburettor
Compression ratio: 11.0:1
Bore: 101.6mm 4.0in
Stroke: 88.4mm 3.5in
Valve type/No: Overhead 16
Transmission: Automatic
No. of forward speeds: 3
Wheels driven: Rear
Springs F/R: Coil/Leaf
Brake system: PA
Brakes F/R: Disc/Drum
Steering: Recirculating ball PA
Wheelbase: 274.3cm 108.0in
Track F: 155.7cm 61.3in
Track R: 152.4cm 60.0in
Length: 477.5cm 188.0in
Width: 189.0cm 74.4in
Height: 128.3cm 50.5in
Kerb weight: 1625.3kg 3580.0lb
Fuel: 68.1L 15.0gal 18.0galUS

842 Chevrolet

Camaro Z/28 RS
1970 USA
118.0mph 189.9kmh
0-60mph 96.5kmh: 5.8secs
0-1/4 mile: 14.2secs
360.0bhp 268.4kW 365.0PS
@ 6000rpm
380.0lbft 514.9Nm @ 4000rpm
253.2bhp/ton 249.0bhp/tonne
62.8bhp/L 46.8kW/L 63.6PS/L
58.0ft/sec 17.7m/sec
Petrol 4-stroke piston
5734cc 349.8cu in
Vee 8 1 Carburettor
Compression ratio: 11.0:1
Bore: 101.6mm 4.0in
Stroke: 88.4mm 3.5in
Valve type/No: Overhead 16
Transmission: Manual

No. of forward speeds: 4
Wheels driven: Rear
Springs F/R: Coil/Leaf
Brake system: PA
Brakes F/R: Disc/Drum
Steering: Recirculating ball
Wheelbase: 274.3cm 108.0in
Track F: 155.7cm 61.3in
Track R: 152.4cm 60.0in
Length: 477.5cm 188.0in
Width: 189.0cm 74.4in
Height: 128.3cm 50.5in
Kerb weight: 1446.0kg 3185.0lb
Fuel: 64.0L 14.1gal 16.9galUS

843 Chevrolet

Chevelle SS396
1970 USA
124.0mph 199.5kmh
0-50mph 80.5kmh: 6.3secs
0-60mph 96.5kmh: 8.1secs
0-1/4 mile: 15.5secs
350.0bhp 261.0kW 354.8PS
@ 5200rpm
415.0lbft 562.3Nm @ 3400rpm
196.5bhp/ton 193.2bhp/tonne
53.1bhp/L 39.6kW/L 53.9PS/L
54.3ft/sec 16.5m/sec
22.2mph 35.7kmh/1000rpm
16.3mpg 13.6mpgUS 17.3L/100km
Petrol 4-stroke piston
6588cc 401.9cu in
Vee 8 1 Carburettor
Compression ratio: 10.3:1
Bore: 104.8mm 4.1in
Stroke: 95.5mm 3.8in
Valve type/No: Overhead 16
Transmission: Automatic
No. of forward speeds: 3
Wheels driven: Rear
Springs F/R: Coil/Coil
Brake system: PA
Brakes F/R: Disc/Drum
Steering: Recirculating ball PA
Wheelbase: 284.5cm 112.0in
Track F: 149.9cm 59.0in
Track R: 149.9cm 59.0in
Length: 500.9cm 197.2in
Width: 193.0cm 76.0in
Height: 134.1cm 52.8in
Kerb weight: 1811.5kg 3990.0lb
Fuel: 75.7L 16.6gal 20.0galUS

844 Chevrolet

Corvette 454
1970 USA
144.0mph 231.7kmh
0-50mph 80.5kmh: 5.3secs
0-60mph 96.5kmh: 7.0secs
0-1/4 mile: 15.0secs
390.0bhp 290.8kW 395.4PS
@ 4800rpm
500.0lbft 677.5Nm @ 3400rpm
233.6bhp/ton 229.7bhp/tonne
52.4bhp/L 39.1kW/L 53.1PS/L
53.3ft/sec 16.2m/sec
25.3mph 40.7kmh/1000rpm
10.8mpg 9.0mpgUS 26.1L/100km
Petrol 4-stroke piston
7440cc 453.9cu in
Vee 8 1 Carburettor
Compression ratio: 10.3:1
Bore: 108.0mm 4.2in
Stroke: 101.5mm 4.0in
Valve type/No: Overhead 16
Transmission: Automatic
No. of forward speeds: 3
Wheels driven: Rear
Springs F/R: Coil/Leaf
Brake system: PA
Brakes F/R: Disc/Disc
Steering: Recirculating ball PA
Wheelbase: 248.9cm 98.0in
Track F: 149.1cm 58.7in
Track R: 150.9cm 59.4in
Length: 463.6cm 182.5in
Width: 175.3cm 69.0in
Height: 120.4cm 47.4in
Ground clearance: 11.4cm 4.5in
Kerb weight: 1698.0kg 3740.0lb
Fuel: 68.1L 15.0gal 18.0galUS

845 Chevrolet

Corvette LT-1
1970 USA
122.0mph 196.3kmh
0-50mph 80.5kmh: 4.4secs
0-60mph 96.5kmh: 5.7secs
0-1/4 mile: 14.2secs
370.0bhp 275.9kW 375.1PS
@ 6000rpm
380.0lbft 514.9Nm @ 4000rpm
248.5bhp/ton 244.4bhp/tonne
64.5bhp/L 48.1kW/L 65.4PS/L
58.0ft/sec 17.7m/sec
18.8mph 30.2kmh/1000rpm
13.2mpg 11.0mpgUS 21.4L/100km
Petrol 4-stroke piston
5735cc 349.9cu in
Vee 8 1 Carburettor
Compression ratio: 11.0:1
Bore: 101.6mm 4.0in
Stroke: 88.4mm 3.5in
Valve type/No: Overhead 16
Transmission: Manual
No. of forward speeds: 4
Wheels driven: Rear
Springs F/R: Coil/Leaf
Brake system: PA
Brakes F/R: Disc/Disc
Steering: Recirculating ball
Wheelbase: 248.9cm 98.0in
Track F: 149.1cm 58.7in
Track R: 150.9cm 59.4in
Length: 463.6cm 182.5in
Width: 175.3cm 69.0in
Height: 120.4cm 47.4in
Kerb weight: 1514.1kg 3335.0lb
Fuel: 75.7L 16.6gal 20.0galUS

846 Chevrolet

Impala
1970 USA
118.0mph 189.9kmh
0-50mph 80.5kmh: 6.6secs
0-60mph 96.5kmh: 9.0secs
0-1/4 mile: 16.8secs
0-1km: 31.2secs
345.0bhp 257.3kW 349.8PS
@ 4400rpm
500.0lbft 677.5Nm @ 3000rpm
175.6bhp/ton 172.7bhp/tonne
46.4bhp/L 34.6kW/L 47.0PS/L
48.6ft/sec 14.8m/sec
31.5mph 50.7kmh/1000rpm
10.3mpg 8.6mpgUS 27.4L/100km
Petrol 4-stroke piston
7440cc 453.9cu in
Vee 8 1 Carburettor
Compression ratio: 10.2:1
Bore: 107.9mm 4.2in
Stroke: 101.0mm 4.0in
Valve type/No: Overhead 16
Transmission: Automatic
No. of forward speeds: 3
Wheels driven: Rear
Springs F/R: Coil/Coil
Brake system: PA
Brakes F/R: Disc/Drum
Steering: Recirculating ball PA
Wheelbase: 302.3cm 119.0in
Track F: 158.8cm 62.5in
Track R: 157.7cm 62.1in
Length: 548.4cm 215.9in
Width: 202.7cm 79.8in
Height: 138.4cm 54.5in
Ground clearance: 15.2cm 6.0in
Kerb weight: 1997.6kg 4400.0lb
Fuel: 95.5L 21.0gal 25.2galUS

847 Chevrolet

Monte Carlo
1970 USA
132.0mph 212.4kmh
0-50mph 80.5kmh: 5.8secs
0-60mph 96.5kmh: 7.7secs
0-1/4 mile: 16.2secs
360.0bhp 268.4kW 365.0PS
@ 4400rpm
500.0lbft 677.5Nm @ 3200rpm
194.8bhp/ton 191.5bhp/tonne
48.4bhp/L 36.1kW/L 49.1PS/L
48.9ft/sec 14.9m/sec
28.6mph 46.0kmh/1000rpm
15.4mpg 12.8mpgUS 18.4L/100km
Petrol 4-stroke piston
7440cc 453.9cu in
Vee 8 1 Carburettor
Compression ratio: 10.3:1
Bore: 108.0mm 4.2in
Stroke: 101.6mm 4.0in
Valve type/No: Overhead 16
Transmission: Automatic
No. of forward speeds: 3
Wheels driven: Rear
Springs F/R: Coil/Coil
Brake system: PA
Brakes F/R: Disc/Drum
Steering: Recirculating ball PA
Wheelbase: 294.6cm 116.0in
Track F: 149.9cm 59.0in
Track R: 149.9cm 59.0in
Length: 522.7cm 205.8in
Width: 192.0cm 75.6in
Height: 134.4cm 52.9in
Kerb weight: 1879.6kg 4140.0lb
Fuel: 75.7L 16.6gal 20.0galUS

848 Chevrolet

Nova SS350
1970 USA
117.0mph 188.3kmh
0-50mph 80.5kmh: 6.9secs
0-60mph 96.5kmh: 9.3secs
0-1/4 mile: 16.5secs
300.0bhp 223.7kW 304.2PS
@ 4800rpm
380.0lbft 514.9Nm @ 3200rpm
191.2bhp/ton 188.0bhp/tonne
52.3bhp/L 39.0kW/L 53.0PS/L
46.4ft/sec 14.1m/sec
23.8mph 38.3kmh/1000rpm
15.9mpg 13.2mpgUS 17.8L/100km
Petrol 4-stroke piston
5735cc 349.9cu in
Vee 8 1 Carburettor
Compression ratio: 10.3:1
Bore: 101.6mm 4.0in
Stroke: 88.4mm 3.5in
Valve type/No: Overhead 16
Transmission: Automatic
No. of forward speeds: 3
Wheels driven: Rear
Springs F/R: Coil/Leaf
Brake system: PA
Brakes F/R: Disc/Drum
Steering: Recirculating ball PA
Wheelbase: 281.9cm 111.0in
Track F: 149.9cm 59.0in
Track R: 149.6cm 58.9in
Length: 481.1cm 189.4in
Width: 183.9cm 72.4in
Height: 133.4cm 52.5in
Kerb weight: 1595.8kg 3515.0lb
Fuel: 68.1L 15.0gal 18.0galUS

849 Chevrolet

Beauville
1971 USA
0-60mph 96.5kmh: 12.7secs
250.0bhp 186.4kW 253.5PS
@ 4600rpm
350.0lbft 474.3Nm @ 3000rpm
124.3bhp/ton 122.2bhp/tonne
43.6bhp/L 32.5kW/L 44.2PS/L
44.7ft/sec 13.6m/sec
Petrol 4-stroke piston
5735cc 349.9cu in
Vee 8
Compression ratio: 8.5:1
Bore: 101.6mm 4.0in
Stroke: 88.9mm 3.5in
Valve type/No: Overhead 16
Transmission: Automatic
No. of forward speeds: 3
Wheels driven: Rear
Wheelbase: 317.5cm 125.0in
Track F: 164.3cm 64.7in
Track R: 175.8cm 69.2in
Length: 510.3cm 200.9in
Width: 202.9cm 79.9in
Height: 204.2cm 80.4in
Ground clearance: 18.5cm 7.3in
Kerb weight: 2045.3kg 4505.0lb

850 Chevrolet

Blazer
1971 USA
98.0mph 157.7kmh
0-60mph 96.5kmh: 14.9secs
200.0bhp 149.1kW 202.8PS
@ 4600rpm
300.0lbft 406.5Nm @ 2400rpm
91.4bhp/ton 89.9bhp/tonne
39.7bhp/L 29.6kW/L 40.3PS/L
44.7ft/sec 13.6m/sec
Petrol 4-stroke piston
5031cc 307.0cu in
Vee 8
Compression ratio: 8.5:1
Bore: 98.4mm 3.9in
Stroke: 88.9mm 3.5in
Valve type/No: Overhead 16
Transmission: Manual
No. of forward speeds: 3
Wheels driven: 4-wheel drive
Brake system: PA
Brakes F/R: Disc/Drum
Steering: Recirculating ball PA
Wheelbase: 264.2cm 104.0in
Track F: 162.6cm 64.0in
Track R: 158.8cm 62.5in
Length: 450.9cm 177.5in
Width: 200.7cm 79.0in
Height: 174.8cm 68.8in
Ground clearance: 22.9cm 9.0in
Kerb weight: 2224.6kg 4900.0lb
Fuel: 79.5L 17.5gal 21.0galUS

851 Chevrolet

Pickup Cheyenne Fleetside
1971 USA
90.0mph 144.8kmh
0-60mph 96.5kmh: 14.9secs
250.0bhp 186.4kW 253.5PS
@ 4600rpm
350.0lbft 474.3Nm @ 3000rpm
119.1bhp/ton 117.2bhp/tonne
43.6bhp/L 32.5kW/L 44.2PS/L
44.7ft/sec 13.6m/sec
Petrol 4-stroke piston
5735cc 349.9cu in
Vee 8
Compression ratio: 8.5:1
Bore: 101.6mm 4.0in
Stroke: 88.9mm 3.5in
Valve type/No: Overhead 16
Transmission: Automatic
No. of forward speeds: 3
Wheels driven: 4-wheel drive
Brake system: PA
Brakes F/R: Disc/Drum
Steering: Recirculating ball PA
Wheelbase: 322.6cm 127.0in
Track F: 162.6cm 64.0in
Track R: 158.8cm 62.5in
Length: 528.3cm 208.0in
Width: 200.7cm 79.0in
Height: 184.2cm 72.5in
Ground clearance: 22.9cm 9.0in
Kerb weight: 2133.8kg 4700.0lb
Fuel: 75.7L 16.6gal 20.0galUS

852 Chevrolet

Vega
1971 USA
88.0mph 141.6kmh
0-50mph 80.5kmh: 12.0secs
0-60mph 96.5kmh: 16.5secs
0-1/4 mile: 20.3secs
90.0bhp 67.1kW 91.2PS
@ 4800rpm
136.0lbft 184.3Nm @ 2400rpm
87.3bhp/ton 85.8bhp/tonne
39.3bhp/L 29.3kW/L 39.9PS/L
48.4ft/sec 14.7m/sec
26.8mph 43.1kmh/1000rpm
24.6mpg 20.5mpgUS 11.5L/100km
Petrol 4-stroke piston
2287cc 139.5cu in
In-line 4 1 Carburettor
Compression ratio: 8.0:1
Bore: 89.0mm 3.5in
Stroke: 92.2mm 3.6in
Valve type/No: Overhead 8
Transmission: Manual
No. of forward speeds: 3
Wheels driven: Rear
Springs F/R: Coil/Coil
Brakes F/R: Disc/Drum
Steering: Recirculating ball
Wheelbase: 246.4cm 97.0in
Track F: 138.7cm 54.6in
Track R: 137.4cm 54.1in
Length: 431.0cm 169.7in
Width: 166.1cm 65.4in
Height: 130.0cm 51.2in
Ground clearance: 11.4cm 4.5in
Kerb weight: 1048.7kg 2310.0lb
Fuel: 40.9L 9.0gal 10.8galUS

853 Chevrolet

Vega 2300
1971 USA
98.0mph 157.7kmh

0-50mph 80.5kmh: 11.0secs
0-60mph 96.5kmh: 16.4secs
0-1/4 mile: 20.5secs
0-1km: 38.3secs
80.0bhp 59.7kW 81.1PS
@ 4400rpm
121.0lbft 164.0Nm @ 2400rpm
79.8bhp/ton 78.5bhp/tonne
35.0bhp/L 26.1kW/L 35.5PS/L
44.4ft/sec 13.5m/sec
23.0mph 37.0kmh/1000rpm
22.3mpg 18.6mpgUS 12.7L/100km
Petrol 4-stroke piston
2286cc 139.5cu in
In-line 4 1 Carburettor
Compression ratio: 8.0:1
Bore: 88.9mm 3.5in
Stroke: 92.1mm 3.6in
Valve type/No: Overhead 8
Transmission: Manual
No. of forward speeds: 4
Wheels driven: Rear
Springs F/R: Coil/Coil
Brakes F/R: Disc/Drum
Steering: Recirculating ball
Wheelbase: 246.4cm 97.0in
Track F: 139.7cm 55.0in
Track R: 136.1cm 53.6in
Length: 429.3cm 169.0in
Width: 166.4cm 65.5in
Height: 129.5cm 51.0in
Ground clearance: 15.2cm 6.0in
Kerb weight: 1019.7kg 2246.0lb
Fuel: 41.9L 9.2gal 11.1galUS

854 Chevrolet

Vega L11
1971 USA
102.0mph 164.1kmh
0-50mph 80.5kmh: 10.2secs
0-60mph 96.5kmh: 14.2secs
0-1/4 mile: 19.3secs
110.0bhp 82.0kW 111.5PS
@ 5200rpm
138.0lbft 187.0Nm @ 3200rpm
106.7bhp/ton 104.9bhp/tonne
48.1bhp/L 35.9kW/L 48.8PS/L
52.4ft/sec 16.0m/sec
18.8mph 30.2kmh/1000rpm
22.3mpg 18.6mpgUS 12.6L/100km
Petrol 4-stroke piston
2287cc 139.5cu in
In-line 4 1 Carburettor
Bore: 89.0mm 3.5in
Stroke: 92.2mm 3.6in
Valve type/No: Overhead 8
Transmission: Manual
No. of forward speeds: 4
Wheels driven: Rear
Springs F/R: Coil/Coil
Brakes F/R: Disc/Drum
Steering: Recirculating ball
Wheelbase: 246.4cm 97.0in
Track F: 138.7cm 54.6in
Track R: 137.4cm 54.1in
Length: 431.0cm 169.7in
Width: 166.1cm 65.4in
Height: 130.0cm 51.2in
Ground clearance: 11.4cm 4.5in
Kerb weight: 1048.7kg 2310.0lb
Fuel: 40.9L 9.0gal 10.8galUS

855 Chevrolet

Camaro Budget
1972 USA
110.0mph 177.0kmh
0-60mph 96.5kmh: 9.8secs
0-1/4 mile: 17.2secs
165.0bhp 123.0kW 167.3PS
@ 4000rpm
280.0lbft 379.4Nm @ 2400rpm
28.8bhp/L 21.4kW/L 29.2PS/L
38.7ft/sec 11.8m/sec
24.6mph 39.6kmh/1000rpm
18.1mpg 15.1mpgUS 15.6L/100km
Petrol 4-stroke piston
5735cc 349.9cu in
Vee 8 1 Carburettor
Compression ratio: 8.5:1
Bore: 101.6mm 4.0in
Stroke: 88.4mm 3.5in
Valve type/No: Overhead 16
Transmission: Manual
No. of forward speeds: 4
Wheels driven: Rear
Springs F/R: Coil/Leaf
Brake system: PA
Brakes F/R: Disc/Drum
Steering: Recirculating ball PA
Wheelbase: 274.3cm 108.0in
Track F: 155.7cm 61.3in
Track R: 152.4cm 60.0in
Length: 477.5cm 188.0in
Width: 189.0cm 74.4in
Height: 128.3cm 50.5in
Ground clearance: 11.4cm 4.5in
Fuel: 68.1L 15.0gal 18.0galUS

856 Chevrolet

Camaro Luxury
1972 USA
107.0mph 172.2kmh
0-60mph 96.5kmh: 10.5secs
0-1/4 mile: 17.6secs
165.0bhp 123.0kW 167.3PS
@ 4000rpm
280.0lbft 379.4Nm @ 2400rpm
28.8bhp/L 21.4kW/L 29.2PS/L
38.7ft/sec 11.8m/sec
27.1mph 43.6kmh/1000rpm
16.3mpg 13.6mpgUS 17.3L/100km
Petrol 4-stroke piston
5735cc 349.9cu in
Vee 8 1 Carburettor
Compression ratio: 8.5:1
Bore: 101.6mm 4.0in
Stroke: 88.4mm 3.5in
Valve type/No: Overhead 16
Transmission: Automatic
No. of forward speeds: 3
Wheels driven: Rear
Springs F/R: Coil/Leaf
Brake system: PA
Brakes F/R: Disc/Drum
Steering: Recirculating ball PA
Wheelbase: 274.3cm 108.0in
Track F: 155.7cm 61.3in
Track R: 152.4cm 60.0in
Length: 477.5cm 188.0in
Width: 189.0cm 74.4in
Height: 128.3cm 50.5in
Ground clearance: 11.4cm 4.5in
Fuel: 68.1L 15.0gal 18.0galUS

857 Chevrolet

Camaro Z/28
1972 USA
124.0mph 199.5kmh
0-60mph 96.5kmh: 7.5secs
0-1/4 mile: 15.5secs
255.0bhp 190.1kW 258.5PS
@ 5600rpm
280.0lbft 379.4Nm @ 4000rpm
44.5bhp/L 33.2kW/L 45.1PS/L
54.1ft/sec 16.5m/sec
19.2mph 30.9kmh/1000rpm
14.8mpg 12.3mpgUS 19.1L/100km
Petrol 4-stroke piston
5735cc 349.9cu in
Vee 8 1 Carburettor
Compression ratio: 9.0:1
Bore: 101.6mm 4.0in
Stroke: 88.4mm 3.5in
Valve type/No: Overhead 16
Transmission: Automatic
No. of forward speeds: 3
Wheels driven: Rear
Springs F/R: Coil/Leaf
Brake system: PA
Brakes F/R: Disc/Drum
Steering: Recirculating ball PA
Wheelbase: 274.3cm 108.0in
Track F: 155.7cm 61.3in
Track R: 152.4cm 60.0in
Length: 477.5cm 188.0in
Width: 189.0cm 74.4in
Height: 128.3cm 50.5in
Ground clearance: 11.4cm 4.5in
Fuel: 68.1L 15.0gal 18.0galUS

858 Chevrolet

Corvette LT-1
1973 USA
124.0mph 199.5kmh
0-50mph 80.5kmh: 5.6secs
0-60mph 96.5kmh: 7.2secs
0-1/4 mile: 15.5secs
250.0bhp 186.4kW 253.5PS
@ 5200rpm
285.0lbft 386.2Nm @ 4000rpm
159.1bhp/ton 156.4bhp/tonne
43.6bhp/L 32.5kW/L 44.2PS/L
50.3ft/sec 15.3m/sec
22.0mph 35.4kmh/1000rpm
17.4mpg 14.5mpgUS 16.2L/100km
Petrol 4-stroke piston
5737cc 350.0cu in
Vee 8 1 Carburettor
Compression ratio: 9.0:1
Bore: 101.6mm 4.0in
Stroke: 88.4mm 3.5in
Valve type/No: Overhead 16
Transmission: Manual
No. of forward speeds: 4
Wheels driven: Rear
Springs F/R: Coil/Leaf
Brake system: PA
Brakes F/R: Disc/Disc
Steering: Recirculating ball PA
Wheelbase: 248.9cm 98.0in
Track F: 149.1cm 58.7in
Track R: 151.1cm 59.5in
Length: 469.1cm 184.7in
Width: 175.3cm 69.0in
Height: 121.2cm 47.7in
Ground clearance: 10.9cm 4.3in
Kerb weight: 1598.1kg 3520.0lb
Fuel: 68.1L 15.0gal 18.0galUS

859 Chevrolet

Monte Carlo
1973 USA
117.0mph 188.3kmh
0-50mph 80.5kmh: 6.5secs
0-60mph 96.5kmh: 8.6secs
0-1/4 mile: 16.6secs
245.0bhp 182.7kW 248.4PS
@ 4000rpm
375.0lbft 508.1Nm @ 2800rpm
124.7bhp/ton 122.6bhp/tonne
32.9bhp/L 24.5kW/L 33.4PS/L
44.4ft/sec 13.5m/sec
27.3mph 43.9kmh/1000rpm
16.8mpg 14.0mpgUS 16.8L/100km
Petrol 4-stroke piston
7441cc 454.0cu in
Vee 8
Compression ratio: 8.3:1
Bore: 108.0mm 4.2in
Stroke: 101.6mm 4.0in
Valve type/No: Overhead 16
Transmission: Automatic
No. of forward speeds: 3
Wheels driven: Rear
Springs F/R: Coil/Coil
Brake system: PA
Brakes F/R: Disc/Drum
Steering: Recirculating ball PA
Wheelbase: 294.6cm 116.0in
Track F: 157.2cm 61.9in
Track R: 155.2cm 61.1in
Length: 534.4cm 210.4in
Width: 197.1cm 77.6in
Height: 133.9cm 52.7in
Kerb weight: 1997.6kg 4400.0lb

860 Chevrolet

Vega
1973 USA
100.0mph 160.9kmh
0-50mph 80.5kmh: 9.5secs
0-60mph 96.5kmh: 13.5secs
0-1/4 mile: 19.1secs
85.0bhp 63.4kW 86.2PS
@ 4800rpm
115.0lbft 155.8Nm @ 2400rpm
76.5bhp/ton 75.2bhp/tonne
37.2bhp/L 27.7kW/L 37.7PS/L
48.3ft/sec 14.7m/sec
23.2mph 37.3kmh/1000rpm
31.2mpg 26.0mpgUS 9.0L/100km
Petrol 4-stroke piston
2287cc 139.5cu in
In-line 4
Compression ratio: 8.0:1
Bore: 89.0mm 3.5in
Stroke: 92.0mm 3.6in
Valve type/No: Overhead 8
Transmission: Manual
No. of forward speeds: 4
Wheels driven: Rear
Springs F/R: Coil/Coil
Brakes F/R: Disc/Drum
Steering: Recirculating ball
Wheelbase: 246.4cm 97.0in
Track F: 140.2cm 55.2in
Track R: 137.4cm 54.1in
Length: 437.4cm 172.2in
Width: 166.1cm 65.4in
Height: 127.0cm 50.0in
Kerb weight: 1130.5kg 2490.0lb
Fuel: 41.6L 9.1gal 11.0galUS

861 Chevrolet

Vega Station Wagon
1973 USA
0-60mph 96.5kmh: 14.6secs
0-1/4 mile: 19.8secs
85.0bhp 63.4kW 86.2PS
@ 4800rpm
115.0lbft 155.8Nm @ 2400rpm
72.8bhp/ton 71.6bhp/tonne
37.2bhp/L 27.7kW/L 37.7PS/L
27.0mpg 22.5mpgUS 10.5L/100km
Petrol 4-stroke piston
2287cc 139.5cu in
In-line 4
Valve type/No: Overhead 8
Transmission: Automatic
No. of forward speeds: 3
Wheels driven: Rear
Brakes F/R: Disc/Drum
Wheelbase: 246.4cm 97.0in
Length: 437.4cm 172.2in
Width: 166.1cm 65.4in
Height: 132.1cm 52.0in
Kerb weight: 1187.2kg 2615.0lb

862 Chevrolet

Corvette
1974 USA
124.0mph 199.5kmh
0-60mph 96.5kmh: 7.4secs
0-1/4 mile: 15.8secs
250.0bhp 186.4kW 253.5PS
@ 5200rpm
285.0lbft 386.2Nm @ 4000rpm
160.5bhp/ton 157.8bhp/tonne
43.6bhp/L 32.5kW/L 44.2PS/L
50.3ft/sec 15.3m/sec
16.2mpg 13.5mpgUS 17.4L/100km
Petrol 4-stroke piston
5737cc 350.0cu in
Vee 8 1 Carburettor
Compression ratio: 9.0:1
Bore: 101.6mm 4.0in
Stroke: 88.4mm 3.5in
Valve type/No: Overhead 16
Transmission: Manual
No. of forward speeds: 4
Wheels driven: Rear
Brake system: PA
Brakes F/R: Disc/Disc
Wheelbase: 248.9cm 98.0in
Track F: 149.1cm 58.7in
Track R: 151.1cm 59.5in
Length: 471.2cm 185.5in
Width: 175.3cm 69.0in
Height: 121.4cm 47.8in
Ground clearance: 10.7cm 4.2in
Kerb weight: 1584.5kg 3490.0lb
Fuel: 68.1L 15.0gal 18.0galUS

863 Chevrolet

Vega
1974 USA
100.0mph 160.9kmh
0-60mph 96.5kmh: 12.4secs
0-1/4 mile: 18.8secs
85.0bhp 63.4kW 86.2PS
@ 4400rpm
122.0lbft 165.3Nm @ 2400rpm
74.4bhp/ton 73.1bhp/tonne
37.2bhp/L 27.7kW/L 37.7PS/L
19.4mph 31.2kmh/1000rpm
25.2mpg 21.0mpgUS 11.2L/100km
Petrol 4-stroke piston
2287cc 139.5cu in
In-line 4
Valve type/No: Overhead 8
Transmission: Manual
No. of forward speeds: 4
Wheels driven: Rear
Springs F/R: Coil/Leaf
Brakes F/R: Disc/Drum
Steering: Recirculating ball
Wheelbase: 246.4cm 97.0in
Track F: 140.2cm 55.2in
Track R: 137.4cm 54.1in
Length: 445.5cm 175.4in
Width: 166.1cm 65.4in
Height: 131.8cm 51.9in
Kerb weight: 1162.2kg 2560.0lb
Fuel: 60.6L 13.3gal 16.0galUS

864 Chevrolet

Monza 2+2 V8
1975 USA

103.0mph 165.7kmh
0-50mph 80.5kmh: 9.7secs
0-60mph 96.5kmh: 13.4secs
0-1/4 mile: 19.5secs
110.0bhp 82.0kW 111.5PS
@ 3600rpm
150.0lbft 203.3Nm @ 2200rpm
77.0bhp/ton 75.7bhp/tonne
25.6bhp/L 19.1kW/L 25.9PS/L
31.0ft/sec 9.4m/sec
23.5mph 37.8kmh/1000rpm
20.4mpg 17.0mpgUS 13.8L/100km
Petrol 4-stroke piston
4302cc 262.5cu in
Vee 8 1 Carburettor
Compression ratio: 8.5:1
Bore: 93.2mm 3.7in
Stroke: 78.7mm 3.1in
Valve type/No: Overhead 16
Transmission: Automatic
No. of forward speeds: 3
Wheels driven: Rear
Springs F/R: Coil/Coil
Brakes F/R: Disc/Drum
Steering: Recirculating ball PA
Wheelbase: 246.4cm 97.0in
Track F: 138.9cm 54.7in
Track R: 136.1cm 53.6in
Length: 455.4cm 179.3in
Width: 166.1cm 65.4in
Height: 127.5cm 50.2in
Ground clearance: 12.4cm 4.9in
Kerb weight: 1452.8kg 3200.0lb
Fuel: 70.0L 15.4gal 18.5galUS

865 Chevrolet

Nova LN
1975 USA
109.0mph 175.4kmh
0-50mph 80.5kmh: 7.7secs
0-60mph 96.5kmh: 10.3secs
0-1/4 mile: 18.0secs
155.0bhp 115.6kW 157.1PS
@ 3800rpm
250.0lbft 338.8Nm @ 2400rpm
88.7bhp/ton 87.2bhp/tonne
27.0bhp/L 20.1kW/L 27.4PS/L
36.7ft/sec 11.2m/sec
23.6mph 38.0kmh/1000rpm
16.2mpg 13.5mpgUS 17.4L/100km
Petrol 4-stroke piston
5737cc 350.0cu in
Vee 8 1 Carburettor
Compression ratio: 8.5:1
Bore: 101.6mm 4.0in
Stroke: 88.4mm 3.5in
Valve type/No: Overhead 16
Transmission: Automatic
No. of forward speeds: 3
Wheels driven: Rear
Springs F/R: Coil/Leaf
Brake system: PA
Brakes F/R: Disc/Drum
Steering: Recirculating ball PA
Wheelbase: 281.9cm 111.0in
Track F: 155.7cm 61.3in
Track R: 149.9cm 59.0in
Length: 502.2cm 197.7in
Width: 183.4cm 72.2in
Height: 137.9cm 54.3in
Ground clearance: 12.2cm 4.8in
Kerb weight: 1777.4kg 3915.0lb
Fuel: 79.5L 17.5gal 21.0galUS

866 Chevrolet

Vega GT
1975 USA
90.0mph 144.8kmh
0-50mph 80.5kmh: 11.3secs
0-60mph 96.5kmh: 15.8secs
0-1/4 mile: 20.8secs
87.0bhp 64.9kW 88.2PS
@ 4400rpm
122.0lbft 165.3Nm @ 2800rpm
71.5bhp/ton 70.3bhp/tonne
38.0bhp/L 28.4kW/L 38.6PS/L
Petrol 4-stroke piston
2287cc 139.5cu in
In-line 4
Transmission: Manual
No. of forward speeds: 4
Wheels driven: Rear
Springs F/R: Coil/Coil
Brakes F/R: Disc/Drum
Wheelbase: 246.4cm 97.0in
Track F: 139.2cm 54.8in
Track R: 136.1cm 53.6in
Length: 445.5cm 175.4in
Width: 166.1cm 65.4in
Height: 131.6cm 51.8in
Kerb weight: 1237.1kg 2725.0lb

867 Chevrolet

Camaro
1976 USA
107.0mph 172.2kmh
0-50mph 80.5kmh: 8.0secs
0-60mph 96.5kmh: 10.1secs
0-1/4 mile: 17.9secs
165.0bhp 123.0kW 167.3PS
@ 3800rpm
260.0lbft 352.3Nm @ 2400rpm
91.9bhp/ton 90.4bhp/tonne
28.8bhp/L 21.4kW/L 29.2PS/L
36.7ft/sec 11.2m/sec
18.0mpg 15.0mpgUS 15.7L/100km
Petrol 4-stroke piston
5736cc 350.0cu in
Vee 8 1 Carburettor
Compression ratio: 8.5:1
Bore: 101.6mm 4.0in
Stroke: 88.4mm 3.5in
Valve type/No: Overhead 16
Transmission: Automatic
No. of forward speeds: 3
Wheels driven: Rear
Springs F/R: Coil/Leaf
Brake system: PA
Brakes F/R: Disc/Drum
Steering: Recirculating ball PA
Wheelbase: 274.3cm 108.0in
Track F: 156.5cm 61.6in
Track R: 153.2cm 60.3in
Length: 496.3cm 195.4in
Width: 189.0cm 74.4in
Height: 125.0cm 49.2in
Ground clearance: 12.7cm 5.0in
Kerb weight: 1825.1kg 4020.0lb
Fuel: 79.5L 17.5gal 21.0galUS

868 Chevrolet

Chevette Rally 1.6
1976 USA
91.0mph 146.4kmh
0-50mph 80.5kmh: 11.7secs
0-60mph 96.5kmh: 16.9secs
0-1/4 mile: 20.2secs
60.0bhp 44.7kW 60.8PS
@ 4800rpm
82.0lbft 111.1Nm @ 3400rpm
63.7bhp/ton 62.6bhp/tonne
37.5bhp/L 28.0kW/L 38.1PS/L
39.7ft/sec 12.1m/sec
16.0mph 25.7kmh/1000rpm
33.0mpg 27.5mpgUS 8.6L/100km
Petrol 4-stroke piston
1598cc 97.5cu in
In-line 4 1 Carburettor
Compression ratio: 8.5:1
Bore: 82.0mm 3.2in
Stroke: 75.7mm 3.0in
Valve type/No: Overhead 8
Transmission: Manual
No. of forward speeds: 4
Wheels driven: Rear
Springs F/R: Coil/Coil
Brakes F/R: Disc/Drum
Steering: Rack & pinion
Wheelbase: 239.5cm 94.3in
Track F: 130.0cm 51.2in
Track R: 130.0cm 51.2in
Length: 403.1cm 158.7in
Width: 157.0cm 61.8in
Height: 132.8cm 52.3in
Ground clearance: 13.5cm 5.3in
Kerb weight: 957.9kg 2110.0lb
Fuel: 49.2L 10.8gal 13.0galUS

869 Chevrolet

Corvette
1976 USA
0-60mph 96.5kmh: 8.1secs
0-1/4 mile: 16.5secs
210.0bhp 156.6kW 212.9PS
@ 5200rpm
255.0lbft 345.5Nm @ 3600rpm
130.3bhp/ton 128.1bhp/tonne
36.6bhp/L 27.3kW/L 37.1PS/L
50.3ft/sec 15.3m/sec
22.1mph 35.6kmh/1000rpm
16.8mpg 14.0mpgUS 16.8L/100km
Petrol 4-stroke piston
5737cc 350.0cu in
Vee 8 1 Carburettor
Compression ratio: 9.0:1
Bore: 101.6mm 4.0in
Stroke: 88.4mm 3.5in
Valve type/No: Overhead 16
Transmission: Manual
No. of forward speeds: 4
Wheels driven: Rear
Springs F/R: Coil/Leaf
Brake system: PA
Brakes F/R: Disc/Disc
Track F: 149.1cm 58.7in
Track R: 151.1cm 59.5in
Length: 470.4cm 185.2in
Width: 175.3cm 69.0in
Height: 121.9cm 48.0in
Ground clearance: 11.2cm 4.4in
Kerb weight: 1638.9kg 3610.0lb
Fuel: 64.3L 14.1gal 17.0galUS

870 Chevrolet

Corvette Greenwood
1976 USA
221.0mph 355.6kmh
0-50mph 80.5kmh: 5.5secs
0-60mph 96.5kmh: 6.2secs
0-1/4 mile: 13.9secs
700.0bhp 522.0kW 709.7PS
@ 6800rpm
620.0lbft 840.1Nm @ 4000rpm
543.5bhp/ton 534.4bhp/tonne
91.5bhp/L 68.2kW/L 92.7PS/L
75.6ft/sec 23.0m/sec
29.6mph 47.6kmh/1000rpm
4.8mpg 4.0mpgUS 58.8L/100km
Petrol 4-stroke piston
7654cc 467.0cu in
Vee 8 fuel injection
Compression ratio: 11.8:1
Bore: 109.5mm 4.3in
Stroke: 101.6mm 4.0in
Valve type/No: Overhead 16
Transmission: Manual
No. of forward speeds: 4
Wheels driven: Rear
Springs F/R: Coil/Coil
Brakes F/R: Disc/Disc
Steering: Recirculating ball
Wheelbase: 248.9cm 98.0in
Track F: 151.1cm 59.5in
Track R: 163.1cm 64.2in
Length: 475.0cm 187.0in
Width: 208.3cm 82.0in
Height: 119.4cm 47.0in
Ground clearance: 7.6cm 3.0in
Kerb weight: 1309.8kg 2885.0lb
Fuel: 121.1L 26.6gal 32.0galUS

871 Chevrolet

Cosworth Vega
1976 USA
112.0mph 180.2kmh
0-50mph 80.5kmh: 8.8secs
0-60mph 96.5kmh: 12.3secs
0-1/4 mile: 18.5secs
110.0bhp 82.0kW 111.5PS
@ 5600rpm
107.0lbft 145.0Nm @ 4800rpm
92.3bhp/ton 90.7bhp/tonne
55.1bhp/L 41.1kW/L 55.8PS/L
49.2ft/sec 15.0m/sec
21.0mph 33.8kmh/1000rpm
24.6mpg 20.5mpgUS 11.5L/100km
Petrol 4-stroke piston
1998cc 121.9cu in
In-line 4
Compression ratio: 8.0:1
Bore: 88.9mm 3.5in
Stroke: 80.3mm 3.2in
Valve type/No: Overhead 16
Transmission: Manual
No. of forward speeds: 5
Wheels driven: Rear
Springs F/R: Coil/Coil
Brakes F/R: Disc/Drum
Steering: Recirculating ball
Wheelbase: 246.4cm 97.0in
Track F: 139.2cm 54.8in
Track R: 136.1cm 53.6in
Length: 445.5cm 175.4in
Width: 166.1cm 65.4in
Height: 127.0cm 50.0in
Kerb weight: 1212.2kg 2670.0lb
Fuel: 60.6L 13.3gal 16.0galUS

872 Chevrolet

Monza
1976 USA
0-60mph 96.5kmh: 10.4secs
0-1/4 mile: 17.3secs
140.0bhp 104.4kW 141.9PS
@ 3800rpm
245.0lbft 332.0Nm @ 2000rpm
96.8bhp/ton 95.2bhp/tonne
28.0bhp/L 20.9kW/L 28.4PS/L
36.7ft/sec 11.2m/sec
23.1mph 37.2kmh/1000rpm
18.0mpg 15.0mpgUS 15.7L/100km
Petrol 4-stroke piston
4996cc 304.8cu in
Vee 8 1 Carburettor
Compression ratio: 8.5:1
Bore: 94.9mm 3.7in
Stroke: 88.4mm 3.5in
Valve type/No: Overhead 16
Transmission: Manual
No. of forward speeds: 4
Wheels driven: Rear
Springs F/R: Coil/Coil
Brake system: PA
Brakes F/R: Disc/Drum
Steering: Recirculating ball
Wheelbase: 246.4cm 97.0in
Track F: 148.3cm 58.4in
Track R: 136.1cm 53.6in
Length: 455.4cm 179.3in
Width: 166.1cm 65.4in
Height: 127.5cm 50.2in
Ground clearance: 12.4cm 4.9in
Kerb weight: 1471.0kg 3240.0lb
Fuel: 70.0L 15.4gal 18.5galUS

873 Chevrolet

Monza 2+2 V8
1976 USA
103.0mph 165.7kmh
0-50mph 80.5kmh: 9.7secs
0-60mph 96.5kmh: 13.4secs
0-1/4 mile: 19.5secs
110.0bhp 82.0kW 111.5PS
@ 3600rpm
150.0lbft 203.3Nm @ 2200rpm
77.0bhp/ton 75.7bhp/tonne
25.6bhp/L 19.1kW/L 25.9PS/L
31.0ft/sec 9.4m/sec
23.5mph 37.8kmh/1000rpm
20.4mpg 17.0mpgUS 13.8L/100km
Petrol 4-stroke piston
4302cc 262.5cu in
Vee 8 1 Carburettor
Compression ratio: 8.5:1
Bore: 93.2mm 3.7in
Stroke: 78.7mm 3.1in
Valve type/No: Overhead 16
Transmission: Automatic
No. of forward speeds: 3
Wheels driven: Rear
Springs F/R: Coil/Coil
Brakes F/R: Disc/Drum
Steering: Recirculating ball PA
Wheelbase: 246.4cm 97.0in
Track F: 138.9cm 54.7in
Track R: 136.1cm 53.6in
Length: 455.4cm 179.3in
Width: 166.1cm 65.4in
Height: 127.5cm 50.2in
Ground clearance: 12.4cm 4.9in
Kerb weight: 1452.8kg 3200.0lb
Fuel: 70.0L 15.4gal 18.5galUS

874 Chevrolet

Monza Mike Keyser
1976 USA
154.0mph 247.8kmh
0-50mph 80.5kmh: 3.8secs
0-60mph 96.5kmh: 4.7secs
0-1/4 mile: 12.1secs
536.0bhp 399.7kW 543.4PS
@ 7200rpm
440.0lbft 596.2Nm @ 6500rpm
448.0bhp/ton 440.5bhp/tonne
93.5bhp/L 69.7kW/L 94.8PS/L
69.6ft/sec 21.2m/sec
22.4mph 36.0kmh/1000rpm
6.0mpg 5.0mpgUS 47.0L/100km
Petrol 4-stroke piston
5735cc 349.9cu in
Vee 8 4 Carburettor
Compression ratio: 11.5:1
Bore: 101.6mm 4.0in
Stroke: 88.4mm 3.5in
Valve type/No: Overhead 16

Transmission: Manual
No. of forward speeds: 4
Wheels driven: Rear
Springs F/R: Coil/Coil
Brakes F/R: Disc/Disc
Steering: Rack & pinion
Wheelbase: 246.4cm 97.0in
Track F: 144.8cm 57.0in
Track R: 142.2cm 56.0in
Length: 455.4cm 179.3in
Width: 200.7cm 79.0in
Height: 121.7cm 47.9in
Ground clearance: 8.9cm 3.5in
Kerb weight: 1216.7kg 2680.0lb
Fuel: 120.0L 26.4gal 31.7galUS

875 Chevrolet

Corvette Sting Ray
1977 USA
132.0mph 212.4kmh
0-50mph 80.5kmh: 5.3secs
0-60mph 96.5kmh: 6.8secs
0-1/4 mile: 15.5secs
210.0bhp 156.6kW 212.9PS
@ 5200rpm
255.0lbft 345.5Nm @ 3600rpm
132.9bhp/ton 130.7bhp/tonne
36.6bhp/L 27.3kW/L 37.1PS/L
50.3ft/sec 15.3m/sec
21.6mph 34.8kmh/1000rpm
18.0mpg 15.0mpgUS 15.7L/100km
Petrol 4-stroke piston
5735cc 349.9cu in
Vee 8
Compression ratio: 9.0:1
Bore: 101.6mm 4.0in
Stroke: 88.4mm 3.5in
Valve type/No: Overhead 16
Transmission: Manual
No. of forward speeds: 4
Wheels driven: Rear
Springs F/R: Coil/Leaf
Brake system: PA
Brakes F/R: Disc/Disc
Steering: Recirculating ball PA
Wheelbase: 248.9cm 98.0in
Track F: 149.1cm 58.7in
Track R: 151.1cm 59.5in
Length: 470.4cm 185.2in
Width: 175.3cm 69.0in
Height: 121.9cm 48.0in
Kerb weight: 1607.2kg 3540.0lb
Fuel: 64.3L 14.1gal 17.0galUS

876 Chevrolet

Blazer
1978 USA
97.0mph 156.1kmh
0-50mph 80.5kmh: 10.3secs
0-60mph 96.5kmh: 14.5secs
0-1/4 mile: 20.0secs
0-1km: 37.0secs
165.0bhp 123.0kW 167.3PS
@ 3800rpm
255.0lbft 345.5Nm @ 2800rpm
158.0bhp/ton 155.4bhp/tonne
28.7bhp/L 21.4kW/L 29.1PS/L
36.7ft/sec 11.2m/sec
24.0mph 38.6kmh/1000rpm
10.6mpg 8.8mpgUS 26.6L/100km
Petrol 4-stroke piston
5740cc 350.2cu in
Vee 8 1 Carburettor
Compression ratio: 8.5:1
Bore: 101.6mm 4.0in
Stroke: 88.4mm 3.5in
Valve type/No: Overhead 16
Transmission: Automatic
No. of forward speeds: 3
Wheels driven: 4-wheel drive
Springs F/R: Leaf/Leaf
Brake system: PA
Brakes F/R: Disc/Drum
Steering: Recirculating ball PA
Wheelbase: 270.5cm 106.5in
Track F: 169.4cm 66.7in
Track R: 161.8cm 63.7in
Length: 468.4cm 184.4in
Width: 202.2cm 79.6in
Height: 182.9cm 72.0in
Ground clearance: 17.8cm 7.0in
Kerb weight: 1061.9kg 2339.0lb
Fuel: 118.3L 26.0gal 31.3galUS

877 Chevrolet

Camaro IROC
1978 USA
152.0mph 244.6kmh
0-50mph 80.5kmh: 3.9secs
0-60mph 96.5kmh: 5.2secs
0-1/4 mile: 13.3secs
450.0bhp 335.6kW 456.2PS
@ 6500rpm
396.0lbft 536.6Nm @ 5000rpm
307.3bhp/ton 302.2bhp/tonne
78.4bhp/L 58.5kW/L 79.5PS/L
63.2ft/sec 19.3m/sec
21.7mph 34.9kmh/1000rpm
5.4mpg 4.5mpgUS 52.3L/100km
Petrol 4-stroke piston
5737cc 350.0cu in
Vee 8 1 Carburettor
Compression ratio: 12.0:1
Bore: 101.6mm 4.0in
Stroke: 88.9mm 3.5in
Valve type/No: Overhead 16
Transmission: Manual
No. of forward speeds: 4
Wheels driven: Rear
Springs F/R: Coil/Coil
Brakes F/R: Disc/Disc
Steering: Recirculating ball
Wheelbase: 274.3cm 108.0in
Track F: 165.1cm 65.0in
Track R: 165.1cm 65.0in
Length: 501.9cm 197.6in
Width: 203.2cm 80.0in
Height: 127.0cm 50.0in
Ground clearance: 15.2cm 6.0in
Kerb weight: 1489.1kg 3280.0lb
Fuel: 124.9L 27.5gal 33.0galUS

878 Chevrolet

Camaro Z/28
1978 USA
0-60mph 96.5kmh: 7.3secs
0-1/4 mile: 15.8secs
185.0bhp 137.9kW 187.6PS
@ 4000rpm
280.0lbft 379.4Nm @ 2400rpm
115.4bhp/ton 113.5bhp/tonne
32.3bhp/L 24.0kW/L 32.7PS/L
38.7ft/sec 11.8m/sec
22.0mph 35.4kmh/1000rpm
17.4mpg 14.5mpgUS 16.2L/100km
Petrol 4-stroke piston
5735cc 349.9cu in
Vee 8 1 Carburettor
Compression ratio: 8.2:1
Bore: 102.0mm 4.0in
Stroke: 88.4mm 3.5in
Valve type/No: Overhead 16
Transmission: Manual
No. of forward speeds: 4
Wheels driven: Rear
Springs F/R: Coil/Leaf
Brake system: PA
Brakes F/R: Disc/Drum
Track F: 156.5cm 61.6in
Track R: 153.2cm 60.3in
Width: 189.2cm 74.5in
Height: 125.0cm 49.2in
Ground clearance: 12.4cm 4.9in
Kerb weight: 1629.9kg 3590.0lb
Fuel: 79.5L 17.5gal 21.0galUS

879 Chevrolet

Malibu
1978 USA
88.0mph 141.6kmh
0-50mph 80.5kmh: 8.0secs
0-60mph 96.5kmh: 11.4secs
0-1/4 mile: 18.5secs
135.0bhp 100.7kW 136.9PS
@ 3800rpm
240.0lbft 325.2Nm @ 2400rpm
87.0bhp/ton 85.6bhp/tonne
27.0bhp/L 20.1kW/L 27.4PS/L
36.7ft/sec 11.2m/sec
26.7mph 43.0kmh/1000rpm
18.0mpg 15.0mpgUS 15.7L/100km
Petrol 4-stroke piston
4996cc 304.8cu in
Vee 8 1 Carburettor
Compression ratio: 8.4:1
Bore: 94.9mm 3.7in
Stroke: 88.4mm 3.5in
Valve type/No: Overhead 16
Transmission: Automatic
No. of forward speeds: 3
Wheels driven: Rear
Springs F/R: Coil/Coil
Brake system: PA
Brakes F/R: Disc/Drum
Steering: Recirculating ball PA
Wheelbase: 274.6cm 108.1in
Track F: 148.6cm 58.5in
Track R: 146.8cm 57.8in
Length: 489.5cm 192.7in
Width: 181.6cm 71.5in
Height: 135.4cm 53.3in
Ground clearance: 13.7cm 5.4in
Kerb weight: 1577.6kg 3475.0lb
Fuel: 66.2L 14.6gal 17.5galUS

880 Chevrolet

Citation X11
1979 USA
108.0mph 173.8kmh
0-60mph 96.5kmh: 9.6secs
0-1/4 mile: 17.8secs
115.0bhp 85.8kW 116.6PS
@ 4800rpm
145.0lbft 196.5Nm @ 2400rpm
94.0bhp/ton 92.4bhp/tonne
40.5bhp/L 30.2kW/L 41.1PS/L
39.9ft/sec 12.2m/sec
26.7mph 43.0kmh/1000rpm
28.8mpg 24.0mpgUS 9.8L/100km
Petrol 4-stroke piston
2837cc 173.1cu in
Vee 6 1 Carburettor
Compression ratio: 8.5:1
Bore: 89.0mm 3.5in
Stroke: 76.0mm 3.0in
Valve type/No: Overhead 12
Transmission: Manual
No. of forward speeds: 4
Wheels driven: Front
Springs F/R: Coil/Coil
Brake system: PA
Brakes F/R: Disc/Drum
Steering: Rack & pinion PA
Wheelbase: 266.4cm 104.9in
Track F: 149.1cm 58.7in
Track R: 144.8cm 57.0in
Length: 448.8cm 176.7in
Width: 173.5cm 68.3in
Height: 134.9cm 53.1in
Ground clearance: 13.7cm 5.4in
Kerb weight: 1244.0kg 2740.0lb
Fuel: 53.0L 11.6gal 14.0galUS

881 Chevrolet

Corvette
1979 USA
132.0mph 212.4kmh
0-50mph 80.5kmh: 4.8secs
0-60mph 96.5kmh: 6.5secs
0-1/4 mile: 15.2secs
220.0bhp 164.0kW 223.0PS
@ 5200rpm
260.0lbft 352.3Nm @ 3600rpm
141.2bhp/ton 138.8bhp/tonne
38.4bhp/L 28.6kW/L 38.9PS/L
50.3ft/sec 15.3m/sec
21.8mph 35.1kmh/1000rpm
18.0mpg 15.0mpgUS 15.7L/100km
Petrol 4-stroke piston
5735cc 349.9cu in
Vee 8
Compression ratio: 8.9:1
Bore: 101.6mm 4.0in
Stroke: 88.4mm 3.5in
Valve type/No: Overhead 16
Transmission: Manual
No. of forward speeds: 4
Wheels driven: Rear
Springs F/R: Coil/Leaf
Brake system: PA
Brakes F/R: Disc/Disc
Steering: Recirculating ball PA
Wheelbase: 248.9cm 98.0in
Track F: 149.1cm 58.7in
Track R: 151.1cm 59.5in
Length: 470.4cm 185.2in
Width: 175.3cm 69.0in
Height: 121.9cm 48.0in
Kerb weight: 1584.5kg 3490.0lb
Fuel: 90.8L 20.0gal 24.0galUS

882 Chevrolet

Corvette Automatic
1979 USA
0-60mph 96.5kmh: 6.6secs
0-1/4 mile: 15.6secs
220.0bhp 164.0kW 223.0PS
@ 5200rpm
260.0lbft 352.3Nm @ 3600rpm
134.8bhp/ton 132.5bhp/tonne
38.4bhp/L 28.6kW/L 38.9PS/L
50.3ft/sec 15.3m/sec
14.4mpg 12.0mpgUS 19.6L/100km
Petrol 4-stroke piston
5735cc 349.9cu in
Vee 8 1 Carburettor
Compression ratio: 8.9:1
Bore: 101.6mm 4.0in
Stroke: 88.4mm 3.5in
Valve type/No: Overhead 16
Transmission: Automatic
No. of forward speeds: 3
Wheels driven: Rear
Brake system: PA
Brakes F/R: Disc/Disc
Wheelbase: 248.9cm 98.0in
Track F: 149.1cm 58.7in
Track R: 151.1cm 59.5in
Length: 470.4cm 185.2in
Width: 175.3cm 69.0in
Height: 121.9cm 48.0in
Kerb weight: 1659.4kg 3655.0lb
Fuel: 90.8L 20.0gal 24.0galUS

883 Chevrolet

Citation
1980 USA
0-60mph 96.5kmh: 10.3secs
0-1/4 mile: 17.6secs
115.0bhp 85.8kW 116.6PS
@ 4800rpm
145.0lbft 196.5Nm @ 2400rpm
94.0bhp/ton 92.4bhp/tonne
40.5bhp/L 30.2kW/L 41.1PS/L
39.9ft/sec 12.2m/sec
25.2mpg 21.0mpgUS 11.2L/100km
Petrol 4-stroke piston
2837cc 173.1cu in
Vee 6 1 Carburettor
Compression ratio: 8.5:1
Bore: 89.0mm 3.5in
Stroke: 76.0mm 3.0in
Valve type/No: Overhead 12
Transmission: Manual
No. of forward speeds: 4
Wheels driven: Front
Brakes F/R: Disc/Drum
Wheelbase: 266.4cm 104.9in
Track F: 149.1cm 58.7in
Track R: 144.8cm 57.0in
Length: 448.8cm 176.7in
Width: 173.5cm 68.3in
Height: 126.5cm 49.8in
Kerb weight: 1244.0kg 2740.0lb
Fuel: 70.0L 15.4gal 18.5galUS

884 Chevrolet

Corvette
1980 USA
130.0mph 209.2kmh
0-60mph 96.5kmh: 7.7secs
0-1/4 mile: 16.0secs
190.0bhp 141.7kW 192.6PS
@ 4400rpm
280.0lbft 379.4Nm @ 2400rpm
127.2bhp/ton 125.1bhp/tonne
33.1bhp/L 24.7kW/L 33.6PS/L
42.5ft/sec 13.0m/sec
25.0mph 40.2kmh/1000rpm
17.4mpg 14.5mpgUS 16.2L/100km
Petrol 4-stroke piston
5735cc 349.9cu in
Vee 8 1 Carburettor
Compression ratio: 8.2:1
Bore: 101.6mm 4.0in
Stroke: 88.4mm 3.5in
Valve type/No: Overhead 16
Transmission: Manual
No. of forward speeds: 4
Wheels driven: Rear
Springs F/R: Coil/Leaf
Brake system: PA
Brakes F/R: Disc/Disc
Steering: Recirculating ball PA
Wheelbase: 248.9cm 98.0in
Track F: 149.1cm 58.7in
Track R: 151.1cm 59.5in
Length: 470.7cm 185.3in
Width: 175.3cm 69.0in
Height: 121.9cm 48.0in
Ground clearance: 10.4cm 4.1in
Kerb weight: 1518.6kg 3345.0lb
Fuel: 90.8L 20.0gal 24.0galUS

885 Chevrolet
Camaro Z/28
1982 USA
115.0mph 185.0kmh
0-60mph 96.5kmh: 9.7secs
0-1/4 mile: 17.5secs
145.0bhp 108.1kW 147.0PS
@ 4000rpm
240.0lbft 325.2Nm @ 2400rpm
95.5bhp/ton 93.9bhp/tonne
29.0bhp/L 21.6kW/L 29.4PS/L
38.7ft/sec 11.8m/sec
23.1mph 37.2kmh/1000rpm
19.2mpg 16.0mpgUS 14.7L/100km
Petrol 4-stroke piston
4998cc 304.9cu in
Vee 8 1 Carburettor
Compression ratio: 8.6:1
Bore: 94.9mm 3.7in
Stroke: 88.4mm 3.5in
Valve type/No: Overhead 16
Transmission: Manual
No. of forward speeds: 4
Wheels driven: Rear
Springs F/R: Coil/Coil
Brake system: PA
Brakes F/R: Disc/Drum
Steering: Recirculating ball PA
Wheelbase: 256.5cm 101.0in
Track F: 154.2cm 60.7in
Track R: 156.5cm 61.6in
Length: 477.0cm 187.8in
Width: 183.1cm 72.1in
Height: 126.5cm 49.8in
Ground clearance: 12.2cm 4.8in
Kerb weight: 1543.6kg 3400.0lb
Fuel: 59.8L 13.1gal 15.8galUS

886 Chevrolet
Corvette
1982 USA
124.0mph 199.5kmh
0-60mph 96.5kmh: 9.2secs
0-1/4 mile: 17.0secs
190.0bhp 141.7kW 192.6PS
@ 4200rpm
280.0lbft 379.4Nm @ 2800rpm
125.4bhp/ton 123.3bhp/tonne
33.1bhp/L 24.7kW/L 33.6PS/L
40.6ft/sec 12.4m/sec
30.0mph 48.3kmh/1000rpm
19.2mpg 16.0mpgUS 14.7L/100km
Petrol 4-stroke piston
5735cc 349.9cu in
Vee 8 1 Carburettor
Compression ratio: 8.2:1
Bore: 101.6mm 4.0in
Stroke: 88.4mm 3.5in
Valve type/No: Overhead 16
Transmission: Manual
No. of forward speeds: 4
Wheels driven: Rear
Springs F/R: Coil/Leaf
Brake system: PA
Brakes F/R: Disc/Disc
Steering: Recirculating ball PA
Wheelbase: 248.9cm 98.0in
Track F: 149.1cm 58.7in
Track R: 151.1cm 59.5in
Length: 470.7cm 185.3in
Width: 175.3cm 69.0in
Height: 121.9cm 48.0in
Ground clearance: 10.4cm 4.1in
Kerb weight: 1541.3kg 3395.0lb
Fuel: 90.8L 20.0gal 24.0galUS

887 Chevrolet
Camaro
1983 USA
125.0mph 201.1kmh
0-60mph 96.5kmh: 9.5secs
0-1/4 mile: 17.5secs
145.0bhp 108.1kW 147.0PS
@ 4000rpm
240.0lbft 325.2Nm @ 2400rpm
95.5bhp/ton 93.9bhp/tonne
29.0bhp/L 21.6kW/L 29.4PS/L
38.7ft/sec 11.8m/sec
21.0mpg 17.5mpgUS 13.4L/100km
Petrol 4-stroke piston
4998cc 304.9cu in
Vee 8 1 Carburettor
Compression ratio: 8.6:1
Bore: 94.9mm 3.7in
Stroke: 88.4mm 3.5in
Valve type/No: Overhead 16
Transmission: Manual
No. of forward speeds: 5
Wheels driven: Rear
Springs F/R: Coil/Coil
Brakes F/R: Disc/Disc
Wheelbase: 256.5cm 101.0in
Track F: 154.2cm 60.7in
Track R: 156.5cm 61.6in
Length: 477.0cm 187.8in
Width: 183.1cm 72.1in
Height: 126.5cm 49.8in
Kerb weight: 1543.6kg 3400.0lb
Fuel: 59.8L 13.1gal 15.8galUS

888 Chevrolet
Camaro Z/28
1983 USA
125.0mph 201.1kmh
0-60mph 96.5kmh: 9.5secs
0-1/4 mile: 17.5secs
145.0bhp 108.1kW 147.0PS
@ 4000rpm
240.0lbft 325.2Nm @ 2400rpm
95.5bhp/ton 93.9bhp/tonne
29.0bhp/L 21.6kW/L 29.4PS/L
38.7ft/sec 11.8m/sec
23.1mph 37.2kmh/1000rpm
19.2mpg 16.0mpgUS 14.7L/100km
Petrol 4-stroke piston
4998cc 304.9cu in
Vee 8 1 Carburettor
Compression ratio: 8.6:1
Bore: 94.9mm 3.7in
Stroke: 88.4mm 3.5in
Valve type/No: Overhead 16
Transmission: Manual
No. of forward speeds: 5
Wheels driven: Rear
Springs F/R: Coil/Coil
Brake system: PA
Brakes F/R: Disc/Drum
Steering: Recirculating ball PA
Wheelbase: 256.5cm 101.0in
Track F: 154.2cm 60.7in
Track R: 156.5cm 61.6in
Length: 477.0cm 187.8in
Width: 183.1cm 72.1in
Height: 126.0cm 49.6in
Ground clearance: 12.2cm 4.8in
Kerb weight: 1543.6kg 3400.0lb
Fuel: 59.8L 13.1gal 15.8galUS

889 Chevrolet
Cavalier CS
1983 USA
100.0mph 160.9kmh
0-60mph 96.5kmh: 13.1secs
0-1/4 mile: 19.1secs
88.0bhp 65.6kW 89.2PS
@ 4800rpm
110.0lbft 149.1Nm @ 2400rpm
75.5bhp/ton 74.3bhp/tonne
44.3bhp/L 33.0kW/L 44.9PS/L
42.0ft/sec 12.8m/sec
32.8mph 52.8kmh/1000rpm
28.8mpg 24.0mpgUS 9.8L/100km
Petrol 4-stroke piston
1987cc 121.2cu in
In-line 4 fuel injection
Compression ratio: 9.3:1
Bore: 89.0mm 3.5in
Stroke: 80.0mm 3.1in
Valve type/No: Overhead 8
Transmission: Manual
No. of forward speeds: 5
Wheels driven: Front
Springs F/R: Coil/Coil
Brake system: PA
Brakes F/R: Disc/Drum
Steering: Rack & pinion PA
Wheelbase: 257.0cm 101.2in
Track F: 140.7cm 55.4in
Track R: 140.2cm 55.2in
Length: 437.9cm 172.4in
Width: 168.4cm 66.3in
Height: 138.2cm 54.4in
Ground clearance: 17.3cm 6.8in
Kerb weight: 1184.9kg 2610.0lb
Fuel: 51.5L 11.3gal 13.6galUS

890 Chevrolet
Citation X11 HO
1983 USA
115.0mph 185.0kmh
0-50mph 80.5kmh: 7.1secs
0-60mph 96.5kmh: 9.9secs
0-1/4 mile: 17.3secs
135.0bhp 100.7kW 136.9PS
@ 5400rpm
145.0lbft 196.5Nm @ 2400rpm
109.0bhp/ton 107.2bhp/tonne
47.6bhp/L 35.5kW/L 48.2PS/L
45.0ft/sec 13.7m/sec
22.6mph 36.4kmh/1000rpm
23.4mpg 19.5mpgUS 12.1L/100km
Petrol 4-stroke piston
2837cc 173.1cu in
Vee 6 1 Carburettor
Compression ratio: 8.9:1
Bore: 89.0mm 3.5in
Stroke: 76.2mm 3.0in
Valve type/No: Overhead 12
Transmission: Manual
No. of forward speeds: 4
Wheels driven: Front
Springs F/R: Coil/Coil
Brake system: PA
Brakes F/R: Disc/Drum
Steering: Rack & pinion PA
Wheelbase: 266.4cm 104.9in
Track F: 149.1cm 58.7in
Track R: 144.8cm 57.0in
Length: 448.8cm 176.7in
Width: 173.5cm 68.3in
Height: 134.9cm 53.1in
Kerb weight: 1259.8kg 2775.0lb
Fuel: 53.0L 11.6gal 14.0galUS

891 Chevrolet
Corvette
1983 USA
137.0mph 220.4kmh
0-60mph 96.5kmh: 7.1secs
0-1/4 mile: 15.5secs
205.0bhp 152.9kW 207.8PS
@ 4300rpm
290.0lbft 393.0Nm @ 2800rpm
143.5bhp/ton 141.1bhp/tonne
35.8bhp/L 26.7kW/L 36.2PS/L
41.6ft/sec 12.7m/sec
32.4mph 52.1kmh/1000rpm
21.6mpg 18.0mpgUS 13.1L/100km
Petrol 4-stroke piston
5733cc 349.8cu in
Vee 8 fuel injection
Compression ratio: 9.0:1
Bore: 101.6mm 4.0in
Stroke: 88.4mm 3.5in
Valve type/No: Overhead 16
Transmission: Automatic
No. of forward speeds: 4
Wheels driven: Rear
Springs F/R: Leaf/Leaf
Brake system: PA
Brakes F/R: Disc/Disc
Steering: Rack & pinion PA
Wheelbase: 244.3cm 96.2in
Track F: 151.4cm 59.6in
Track R: 153.4cm 60.4in
Length: 448.3cm 176.5in
Width: 180.3cm 71.0in
Height: 118.6cm 46.7in
Ground clearance: 12.7cm 5.0in
Kerb weight: 1452.8kg 3200.0lb
Fuel: 75.7L 16.6gal 20.0galUS

892 Chevrolet
Camaro
1984 USA
0-60mph 96.5kmh: 9.5secs
150.0bhp 111.9kW 152.1PS
@ 4000rpm
240.0lbft 325.2Nm @ 2400rpm
108.0bhp/ton 106.2bhp/tonne
30.0bhp/L 22.4kW/L 30.4PS/L
19.2mpg 16.0mpgUS 14.7L/100km
Petrol 4-stroke piston
5002cc 305.2cu in
Vee 8 1 Carburettor
Valve type/No: Overhead 16
Transmission: Manual
No. of forward speeds: 5
Wheels driven: Rear
Springs F/R: Coil/Coil
Brakes F/R: Disc
Steering: Rack & pinion PA
Wheelbase: 256.5cm 101.0in
Length: 477.0cm 187.8in
Width: 184.9cm 72.8in
Height: 127.0cm 50.0in
Kerb weight: 1411.9kg 3110.0lb
Fuel: 60.9L 13.4gal 16.1galUS

893 Chevrolet
Camaro Z/28
1984 USA
110.0mph 177.0kmh
0-50mph 80.5kmh: 5.8secs
0-60mph 96.5kmh: 7.9secs
0-1/4 mile: 16.1secs
190.0bhp 141.7kW 192.6PS
@ 4800rpm
240.0lbft 325.2Nm @ 3200rpm
132.0bhp/ton 129.8bhp/tonne
38.0bhp/L 28.3kW/L 38.5PS/L
46.4ft/sec 14.1m/sec
Petrol 4-stroke piston
4998cc 304.9cu in
Vee 8
Compression ratio: 9.5:1
Bore: 94.9mm 3.7in
Stroke: 88.4mm 3.5in
Valve type/No: Overhead 16
Transmission: Manual
No. of forward speeds: 5
Wheels driven: Rear
Springs F/R: Coil/Coil
Brakes F/R: Disc/Drum
Steering: Rack & pinion PA
Wheelbase: 256.5cm 101.0in
Track F: 154.2cm 60.7in
Track R: 156.5cm 61.6in
Length: 477.0cm 187.8in
Width: 184.9cm 72.8in
Height: 127.0cm 50.0in
Kerb weight: 1464.1kg 3225.0lb

894 Chevrolet
Corvette
1984 USA
145.0mph 233.3kmh
0-50mph 80.5kmh: 4.8secs
0-60mph 96.5kmh: 6.6secs
0-1/4 mile: 15.0secs
0-1km: 27.7secs
201.0bhp 149.9kW 203.8PS
@ 4200rpm
289.0lbft 391.6Nm @ 2700rpm
144.0bhp/ton 141.6bhp/tonne
35.1bhp/L 26.1kW/L 35.5PS/L
40.6ft/sec 12.4m/sec
34.8mph 56.0kmh/1000rpm
16.7mpg 13.9mpgUS 16.9L/100km
Petrol 4-stroke piston
5733cc 349.8cu in
Vee 8 1 Carburettor
Compression ratio: 9.0:1
Bore: 101.6mm 4.0in
Stroke: 88.4mm 3.5in
Valve type/No: Overhead 16
Transmission: Automatic
No. of forward speeds: 4
Wheels driven: Rear
Springs F/R: Leaf/Leaf
Brake system: PA
Brakes F/R: Disc/Disc
Steering: Rack & pinion PA
Wheelbase: 244.3cm 96.2in
Track F: 151.4cm 59.6in
Track R: 153.4cm 60.4in
Length: 448.3cm 176.5in
Width: 180.3cm 71.0in
Height: 118.6cm 46.7in
Ground clearance: 12.7cm 5.0in
Kerb weight: 1419.7kg 3127.0lb
Fuel: 76.0L 16.7gal 20.1galUS

895 Chevrolet
Sprint
1984 Japan
87.0mph 140.0kmh
0-50mph 80.5kmh: 10.0secs
0-60mph 96.5kmh: 14.5secs
0-1/4 mile: 20.3secs
48.0bhp 35.8kW 48.7PS
@ 5100rpm
57.0lbft 77.2Nm @ 3200rpm
67.8bhp/ton 66.7bhp/tonne
48.3bhp/L 36.0kW/L 49.0PS/L
42.9ft/sec 13.1m/sec
19.1mph 30.7kmh/1000rpm
52.8mpg 44.0mpgUS 5.3L/100km
Petrol 4-stroke piston
993cc 60.6cu in
In-line 3 1 Carburettor
Compression ratio: 9.5:1
Bore: 74.0mm 2.9in
Stroke: 77.0mm 3.0in
Valve type/No: Overhead 6
Transmission: Manual

No. of forward speeds: 5
Wheels driven: Front
Springs F/R: Coil/Leaf
Brake system: PA
Brakes F/R: Disc/Drum
Steering: Rack & pinion
Wheelbase: 224.5cm 88.4in
Track F: 133.1cm 52.4in
Track R: 130.0cm 51.2in
Length: 358.4cm 141.1in
Width: 153.2cm 60.3in
Height: 134.9cm 53.1in
Ground clearance: 15.7cm 6.2in
Kerb weight: 719.6kg 1585.0lb
Fuel: 31.4L 6.9gal 8.3galUS

896 Chevrolet

Camaro IROC-Z
1985 USA
135.0mph 217.2kmh
0-60mph 96.5kmh: 8.1secs
0-1/4 mile: 16.5secs
190.0bhp 141.7kW 192.6PS
@ 4800rpm
240.0lbft 325.2Nm @ 3200rpm
123.4bhp/ton 121.3bhp/tonne
38.0bhp/L 28.3kW/L 38.5PS/L
46.4ft/sec 14.1m/sec
31.5mph 50.7kmh/1000rpm
19.2mpg 16.0mpgUS 14.7L/100km
Petrol 4-stroke piston
5001cc 305.1cu in
Vee 8 1 Carburettor
Compression ratio: 9.5:1
Bore: 94.8mm 3.7in
Stroke: 88.4mm 3.5in
Valve type/No: Overhead 16
Transmission: Manual
No. of forward speeds: 5
Wheels driven: Rear
Springs F/R: Coil/Coil
Brakes F/R: Disc/Disc
Steering: Rack & pinion PA
Wheelbase: 256.5cm 101.0in
Track F: 154.2cm 60.7in
Track R: 153.9cm 60.6in
Length: 487.7cm 192.0in
Width: 184.9cm 72.8in
Height: 127.8cm 50.3in
Kerb weight: 1566.3kg 3450.0lb
Fuel: 60.9L 13.4gal 16.1galUS

897 Chevrolet

Corvette
1985 USA
152.0mph 244.6kmh
0-50mph 80.5kmh: 4.6secs
0-60mph 96.5kmh: 6.0secs
0-1/4 mile: 14.8secs
0-1km: 26.9secs
235.0bhp 175.2kW 238.3PS
@ 4100rpm
330.0lbft 447.2Nm @ 2700rpm
165.9bhp/ton 163.1bhp/tonne
41.0bhp/L 30.6kW/L 41.6PS/L
39.6ft/sec 12.1m/sec
35.3mph 56.8kmh/1000rpm
17.6mpg 14.7mpgUS 16.1L/100km
Petrol 4-stroke piston
5733cc 349.8cu in
Vee 8 fuel injection
Compression ratio: 9.0:1
Bore: 101.6mm 4.0in
Stroke: 88.4mm 3.5in
Valve type/No: Overhead 16
Transmission: Manual with overdrive
No. of forward speeds: 7
Wheels driven: Rear
Springs F/R: Leaf/Leaf
Brake system: PA
Brakes F/R: Disc/Disc
Steering: Rack & pinion PA
Wheelbase: 244.3cm 96.2in
Track F: 151.4cm 59.6in
Track R: 153.4cm 60.4in
Length: 448.3cm 176.5in
Width: 180.3cm 71.0in
Height: 118.6cm 46.7in
Ground clearance: 12.7cm 5.0in
Kerb weight: 1440.5kg 3173.0lb
Fuel: 76.0L 16.7gal 20.1galUS

898 Chevrolet

Cavalier Z24
1986 USA
113.0mph 181.8kmh
0-60mph 96.5kmh: 8.5secs
0-1/4 mile: 16.7secs
120.0bhp 89.5kW 121.7PS
@ 4800rpm
155.0lbft 210.0Nm @ 3600rpm
101.4bhp/ton 99.7bhp/tonne
42.3bhp/L 31.5kW/L 42.9PS/L
39.9ft/sec 12.2m/sec
26.4mpg 22.0mpgUS 10.7L/100km
Petrol 4-stroke piston
2837cc 173.1cu in
Vee 6 fuel injection
Compression ratio: 8.9:1
Bore: 89.0mm 3.5in
Stroke: 76.0mm 3.0in
Valve type/No: Overhead 12
Transmission: Manual
No. of forward speeds: 4
Wheels driven: Front
Springs F/R: Coil/Coil
Brake system: PA
Brakes F/R: Disc/Drum
Steering: Rack & pinion PA
Wheelbase: 257.0cm 101.2in
Track F: 140.7cm 55.4in
Track R: 140.2cm 55.2in
Length: 437.9cm 172.4in
Width: 167.6cm 66.0in
Height: 131.8cm 51.9in
Kerb weight: 1203.1kg 2650.0lb
Fuel: 51.5L 11.3gal 13.6galUS

899 Chevrolet

Celebrity CL Eurosport
1986 USA
110.0mph 177.0kmh
0-60mph 96.5kmh: 10.7secs
0-1/4 mile: 17.9secs
125.0bhp 93.2kW 126.7PS
@ 4800rpm
160.0lbft 216.8Nm @ 3600rpm
92.3bhp/ton 90.7bhp/tonne
44.1bhp/L 32.9kW/L 44.7PS/L
39.9ft/sec 12.2m/sec
23.2mpg 19.3mpgUS 12.2L/100km
Petrol 4-stroke piston
2837cc 173.1cu in
Vee 6 fuel injection
Compression ratio: 8.5:1
Bore: 89.0mm 3.5in
Stroke: 76.0mm 3.0in
Valve type/No: Overhead 12
Transmission: Automatic
No. of forward speeds: 4
Wheels driven: Front
Springs F/R: Coil/Coil
Brake system: PA
Brakes F/R: Disc/Drum
Steering: Rack & pinion PA
Wheelbase: 266.4cm 104.9in
Track F: 149.1cm 58.7in
Track R: 144.8cm 57.0in
Length: 478.3cm 188.3in
Width: 176.0cm 69.3in
Height: 137.4cm 54.1in
Kerb weight: 1377.9kg 3035.0lb
Fuel: 59.4L 13.1gal 15.7galUS

900 Chevrolet

Corvette
1986 USA
154.0mph 247.8kmh
0-60mph 96.5kmh: 5.8secs
0-1/4 mile: 14.4secs
230.0bhp 171.5kW 233.2PS
@ 4000rpm
330.0lbft 447.2Nm @ 3200rpm
157.1bhp/ton 154.4bhp/tonne
40.1bhp/L 29.9kW/L 40.7PS/L
38.7ft/sec 11.8m/sec
36.4mph 58.6kmh/1000rpm
19.2mpg 16.0mpgUS 14.7L/100km
Petrol 4-stroke piston
5733cc 349.8cu in
Vee 8 fuel injection
Compression ratio: 9.5:1
Bore: 101.6mm 4.0in
Stroke: 88.4mm 3.5in
Valve type/No: Overhead 16
Transmission: Manual with overdrive
Wheels driven: Rear
Springs F/R: Leaf/Leaf
Brake system: ABS
Brakes F/R: Disc/Disc
Steering: Rack & pinion PA
Wheelbase: 244.3cm 96.2in
Track F: 151.4cm 59.6in
Track R: 153.4cm 60.4in
Length: 448.3cm 176.5in
Width: 180.3cm 71.0in
Height: 118.6cm 46.7in
Kerb weight: 1489.1kg 3280.0lb

901 Chevrolet

Corvette Callaway
1986 USA
178.0mph 286.4kmh
0-50mph 80.5kmh: 3.8secs
0-60mph 96.5kmh: 5.0secs
0-1/4 mile: 13.7secs
345.0bhp 257.3kW 349.8PS
@ 4000rpm
465.0lbft 630.1Nm @ 2800rpm
225.3bhp/ton 221.5bhp/tonne
60.2bhp/L 44.9kW/L 61.0PS/L
38.7ft/sec 11.8m/sec
Petrol 4-stroke piston
5733cc 349.8cu in turbocharged
Vee 8 fuel injection
Compression ratio: 7.5:1
Bore: 101.6mm 4.0in
Stroke: 88.4mm 3.5in
Valve type/No: Overhead 16
Transmission: Manual with overdrive
Wheels driven: Rear
Springs F/R: Leaf/Leaf
Brake system: PA ABS
Brakes F/R: Disc/Disc
Steering: Rack & pinion PA
Wheelbase: 244.3cm 96.2in
Track F: 151.4cm 59.6in
Track R: 153.4cm 60.4in
Length: 448.3cm 176.5in
Width: 180.3cm 71.0in
Height: 118.6cm 46.7in
Kerb weight: 1557.2kg 3430.0lb
Fuel: 75.7L 16.6gal 20.0galUS

902 Chevrolet

Corvette Z51
1986 USA
154.0mph 247.8kmh
0-50mph 80.5kmh: 4.4secs
0-60mph 96.5kmh: 5.8secs
0-1/4 mile: 14.4secs
230.0bhp 171.5kW 233.2PS
@ 4000rpm
330.0lbft 447.2Nm @ 3200rpm
157.1bhp/ton 154.4bhp/tonne
40.1bhp/L 29.9kW/L 40.7PS/L
38.7ft/sec 11.8m/sec
22.8mpg 19.0mpgUS 12.4L/100km
Petrol 4-stroke piston
5733cc 349.8cu in
Vee 8 fuel injection
Compression ratio: 9.5:1
Bore: 101.6mm 4.0in
Stroke: 88.4mm 3.5in
Valve type/No: Overhead 16
Transmission: Manual with overdrive
Wheels driven: Rear
Springs F/R: Leaf/Leaf
Brake system: PA ABS
Brakes F/R: Disc/Disc
Steering: Rack & pinion PA
Wheelbase: 244.3cm 96.2in
Track F: 151.4cm 59.6in
Track R: 153.4cm 60.4in
Length: 448.3cm 176.5in
Width: 180.3cm 71.0in
Height: 118.6cm 46.7in
Kerb weight: 1489.1kg 3280.0lb
Fuel: 75.7L 16.6gal 20.0galUS

903 Chevrolet

Nova CL
1986 USA
95.0mph 152.9kmh
0-50mph 80.5kmh: 9.3secs
0-60mph 96.5kmh: 13.0secs
0-1/4 mile: 18.8secs
70.0bhp 52.2kW 71.0PS
@ 4800rpm
85.0lbft 115.2Nm @ 2800rpm
69.7bhp/ton 68.5bhp/tonne
44.1bhp/L 32.9kW/L 44.7PS/L
40.4ft/sec 12.3m/sec
36.0mpg 30.0mpgUS 7.8L/100km
Petrol 4-stroke piston
1587cc 96.8cu in
In-line 4 1 Carburettor
Compression ratio: 9.0:1
Bore: 81.0mm 3.2in
Stroke: 77.0mm 3.0in
Valve type/No: Overhead 8
Transmission: Manual
No. of forward speeds: 5
Wheels driven: Front
Springs F/R: Coil/Coil
Brake system: PA
Brakes F/R: Disc/Drum
Steering: Rack & pinion PA
Wheelbase: 243.1cm 95.7in
Track F: 142.5cm 56.1in
Track R: 140.5cm 55.3in
Length: 422.4cm 166.3in
Width: 163.6cm 64.4in
Height: 134.1cm 52.8in
Kerb weight: 1021.5kg 2250.0lb
Fuel: 50.0L 11.0gal 13.2galUS

904 Chevrolet

Sprint
1986 Japan
0-60mph 96.5kmh: 13.4secs
0-1/4 mile: 19.1secs
48.0bhp 35.8kW 48.7PS
@ 5100rpm
57.0lbft 77.2Nm @ 3200rpm
67.8bhp/ton 66.7bhp/tonne
48.3bhp/L 36.0kW/L 49.0PS/L
42.9ft/sec 13.1m/sec
19.7mph 31.7kmh/1000rpm
48.6mpg 40.5mpgUS 5.8L/100km
Petrol 4-stroke piston
993cc 60.6cu in
In-line 3 1 Carburettor
Compression ratio: 9.5:1
Bore: 74.0mm 2.9in
Stroke: 77.0mm 3.0in
Valve type/No: Overhead 6
Transmission: Manual
No. of forward speeds: 5
Wheels driven: Front
Springs F/R: Coil/Leaf
Brakes F/R: Disc/Drum
Steering: Rack & pinion
Wheelbase: 224.5cm 88.4in
Track F: 133.1cm 52.4in
Track R: 130.0cm 51.2in
Length: 358.4cm 141.1in
Width: 153.2cm 60.3in
Height: 134.9cm 53.1in
Kerb weight: 719.6kg 1585.0lb
Fuel: 31.4L 6.9gal 8.3galUS

905 Chevrolet

Beretta GT
1987 USA
115.0mph 185.0kmh
0-50mph 80.5kmh: 5.9secs
0-60mph 96.5kmh: 8.3secs
0-1/4 mile: 16.3secs
125.0bhp 93.2kW 126.7PS
@ 4500rpm
160.0lbft 216.8Nm @ 3600rpm
98.1bhp/ton 96.4bhp/tonne
44.1bhp/L 32.9kW/L 44.7PS/L
37.4ft/sec 11.4m/sec
24.0mpg 20.0mpgUS 11.8L/100km
Petrol 4-stroke piston
2837cc 173.1cu in
Vee 6 fuel injection
Compression ratio: 8.9:1
Bore: 89.0mm 3.5in
Stroke: 76.0mm 3.0in
Valve type/No: Overhead 12
Transmission: Manual
No. of forward speeds: 5
Wheels driven: Front
Springs F/R: Coil/Coil
Brake system: PA
Brakes F/R: Disc/Drum
Steering: Rack & pinion PA
Wheelbase: 262.6cm 103.4in
Track F: 141.2cm 55.6in
Track R: 143.5cm 56.5in
Length: 475.5cm 187.2in
Width: 173.2cm 68.2in
Height: 133.6cm 52.6in
Ground clearance: 16.5cm 6.5in
Kerb weight: 1296.2kg 2855.0lb
Fuel: 51.5L 11.3gal 13.6galUS

906 Chevrolet

Camaro IROC-Z
1987 USA
150.0mph 241.4kmh
0-60mph 96.5kmh: 6.6secs

0-1/4 mile: 14.9secs
215.0bhp 160.3kW 218.0PS
@ 4400rpm
295.0lbft 399.7Nm @ 3200rpm
140.4bhp/ton 138.1bhp/tonne
43.0bhp/L 32.1kW/L 43.6PS/L
40.1ft/sec 12.2m/sec
20.1mpg 16.7mpgUS 14.1L/100km
Petrol 4-stroke piston
4999cc 305.0cu in
Vee 8 fuel injection
Compression ratio: 9.3:1
Bore: 94.9mm 3.7in
Stroke: 83.4mm 3.3in
Valve type/No: Overhead 16
Transmission: Manual
No. of forward speeds: 5
Wheels driven: Rear
Springs F/R: Coil/Coil
Brakes F/R: Disc/Disc
Steering: Recirculating ball PA
Wheelbase: 256.5cm 101.0in
Track F: 154.2cm 60.7in
Track R: 153.9cm 60.6in
Length: 487.7cm 192.0in
Width: 184.9cm 72.8in
Height: 127.8cm 50.3in
Kerb weight: 1557.2kg 3430.0lb
Fuel: 58.7L 12.9gal 15.5galUS

907 Chevrolet

Camaro IROC-Z L98
1987 USA
149.0mph 239.7kmh
0-60mph 96.5kmh: 6.8secs
0-1/4 mile: 15.3secs
220.0bhp 164.0kW 223.0PS
@ 4200rpm
320.0lbft 433.6Nm @ 3200rpm
141.2bhp/ton 138.8bhp/tonne
38.4bhp/L 28.6kW/L 38.9PS/L
39.7ft/sec 12.1m/sec
33.1mph 53.3kmh/1000rpm
Petrol 4-stroke piston
5733cc 349.8cu in
Vee 8 fuel injection
Compression ratio: 9.0:1
Bore: 101.6mm 4.0in
Stroke: 86.4mm 3.4in
Valve type/No: Overhead 16
Transmission: Automatic
No. of forward speeds: 4
Wheels driven: Rear
Springs F/R: Coil/Coil
Brakes F/R: Disc/Disc
Steering: Recirculating ball PA
Wheelbase: 256.5cm 101.0in
Track F: 154.2cm 60.7in
Track R: 153.9cm 60.6in
Length: 487.7cm 192.0in
Width: 184.9cm 72.8in
Height: 127.8cm 50.3in
Kerb weight: 1584.5kg 3490.0lb
Fuel: 58.7L 12.9gal 15.5galUS

908 Chevrolet

Corvette
1987 USA
154.0mph 247.8kmh
0-50mph 80.5kmh: 4.3secs
0-60mph 96.5kmh: 5.9secs
0-1/4 mile: 14.5secs
240.0bhp 179.0kW 243.3PS
@ 4000rpm
345.0lbft 467.5Nm @ 3200rpm
163.9bhp/ton 161.2bhp/tonne
41.9bhp/L 31.2kW/L 42.4PS/L
38.7ft/sec 11.8m/sec
21.0mpg 17.5mpgUS 13.4L/100km
Petrol 4-stroke piston
5733cc 349.8cu in
Vee 8 fuel injection
Compression ratio: 9.5:1
Bore: 101.6mm 4.0in
Stroke: 88.4mm 3.5in
Valve type/No: Overhead 16
Transmission: Manual with overdrive
Wheels driven: Rear
Springs F/R: Leaf/Leaf
Brake system: PA ABS
Brakes F/R: Disc/Disc
Steering: Rack & pinion PA
Wheelbase: 244.3cm 96.2in
Track F: 151.4cm 59.6in
Track R: 153.4cm 60.4in
Length: 448.3cm 176.5in
Width: 180.3cm 71.0in
Height: 118.6cm 46.7in
Ground clearance: 11.9cm 4.7in
Kerb weight: 1489.1kg 3280.0lb
Fuel: 75.7L 16.6gal 20.0galUS

909 Chevrolet

Corvette ASC Geneve
1987 USA
154.0mph 247.8kmh
0-60mph 96.5kmh: 5.8secs
0-1/4 mile: 14.4secs
230.0bhp 171.5kW 233.2PS
@ 4000rpm
330.0lbft 447.2Nm @ 3200rpm
153.8bhp/ton 151.2bhp/tonne
40.1bhp/L 29.9kW/L 40.7PS/L
38.7ft/sec 11.8m/sec
Petrol 4-stroke piston
5733cc 349.8cu in
Vee 8 fuel injection
Compression ratio: 9.5:1
Bore: 101.6mm 4.0in
Stroke: 88.4mm 3.5in
Valve type/No: Overhead 16
Transmission: Manual with overdrive
Wheels driven: Rear
Springs F/R: Leaf/Leaf
Brake system: PA ABS
Brakes F/R: Disc/Disc
Steering: Rack & pinion PA
Wheelbase: 244.3cm 96.2in
Track F: 169.7cm 66.8in
Track R: 184.2cm 72.5in
Length: 467.4cm 184.0in
Width: 193.0cm 76.0in
Height: 121.9cm 48.0in
Kerb weight: 1520.9kg 3350.0lb
Fuel: 75.7L 16.6gal 20.0galUS

910 Chevrolet

Corvette Convertible
1987 USA
150.0mph 241.4kmh
0-50mph 80.5kmh: 4.7secs
0-60mph 96.5kmh: 6.3secs
0-1/4 mile: 14.8secs
240.0bhp 179.0kW 243.3PS
@ 4000rpm
345.0lbft 467.5Nm @ 3200rpm
161.9bhp/ton 159.2bhp/tonne
41.9bhp/L 31.2kW/L 42.4PS/L
38.7ft/sec 11.8m/sec
20.4mpg 17.0mpgUS 13.8L/100km
Petrol 4-stroke piston
5733cc 349.8cu in
Vee 8 fuel injection
Compression ratio: 9.5:1
Bore: 101.6mm 4.0in
Stroke: 88.4mm 3.5in
Valve type/No: Overhead 16
Transmission: Manual with overdrive
Wheels driven: Rear
Springs F/R: Leaf/Leaf
Brake system: PA ABS
Brakes F/R: Disc/Disc
Steering: Rack & pinion PA
Wheelbase: 244.3cm 96.2in
Track F: 151.4cm 59.6in
Track R: 153.4cm 60.4in
Length: 448.3cm 176.5in
Width: 180.3cm 71.0in
Height: 117.9cm 46.4in
Ground clearance: 12.7cm 5.0in
Kerb weight: 1507.3kg 3320.0lb
Fuel: 75.7L 16.6gal 20.0galUS

911 Chevrolet

Camaro
1988 USA
0-50mph 80.5kmh: 6.7secs
0-60mph 96.5kmh: 9.3secs
0-1/4 mile: 17.0secs
135.0bhp 100.7kW 136.9PS
@ 4900rpm
160.0lbft 216.8Nm @ 3900rpm
95.7bhp/ton 94.1bhp/tonne
47.6bhp/L 35.5kW/L 48.3PS/L
40.7ft/sec 12.4m/sec
25.2mpg 21.0mpgUS 11.2L/100km
Petrol 4-stroke piston
2835cc 173.0cu in
Vee 6 fuel injection
Compression ratio: 8.9:1
Bore: 89.0mm 3.5in
Stroke: 76.0mm 3.0in
Valve type/No: Overhead 12
Transmission: Manual
No. of forward speeds: 5
Wheels driven: Rear
Springs F/R: Coil/Coil
Brake system: PA
Brakes F/R: Disc/Drum
Steering: Recirculating ball PA
Wheelbase: 256.5cm 101.0in
Track F: 152.4cm 60.0in
Track R: 154.7cm 60.9in
Length: 487.7cm 192.0in
Width: 184.9cm 72.8in
Height: 127.8cm 50.3in
Kerb weight: 1434.6kg 3160.0lb
Fuel: 58.7L 12.9gal 15.5galUS

912 Chevrolet

Camaro IROC-Z 5.0
1988 USA
0-50mph 80.5kmh: 5.0secs
0-60mph 96.5kmh: 6.9secs
0-1/4 mile: 15.4secs
220.0bhp 164.0kW 223.0PS
@ 4400rpm
290.0lbft 393.0Nm @ 3200rpm
148.4bhp/ton 146.0bhp/tonne
44.0bhp/L 32.8kW/L 44.6PS/L
42.5ft/sec 13.0m/sec
18.6mpg 15.5mpgUS 15.2L/100km
Petrol 4-stroke piston
5001cc 305.1cu in
Vee 8 fuel injection
Compression ratio: 9.3:1
Bore: 94.9mm 3.7in
Stroke: 88.4mm 3.5in
Valve type/No: Overhead 16
Transmission: Manual
No. of forward speeds: 5
Wheels driven: Rear
Springs F/R: Coil/Coil
Brake system: PA
Brakes F/R: Disc/Disc
Steering: Recirculating ball PA
Wheelbase: 256.5cm 101.0in
Track F: 152.4cm 60.0in
Track R: 154.7cm 60.9in
Length: 487.7cm 192.0in
Width: 184.9cm 72.8in
Height: 127.8cm 50.3in
Kerb weight: 1507.3kg 3320.0lb
Fuel: 58.7L 12.9gal 15.5galUS

913 Chevrolet

Camaro IROC-Z 5.7
1988 USA
0-50mph 80.5kmh: 4.8secs
0-60mph 96.5kmh: 6.6secs
0-1/4 mile: 15.2secs
230.0bhp 171.5kW 233.2PS
@ 4400rpm
330.0lbft 447.2Nm @ 3200rpm
148.0bhp/ton 145.6bhp/tonne
40.1bhp/L 29.9kW/L 40.7PS/L
42.5ft/sec 13.0m/sec
19.2mpg 16.0mpgUS 14.7L/100km
Petrol 4-stroke piston
5733cc 349.8cu in
Vee 8 fuel injection
Compression ratio: 9.3:1
Bore: 101.6mm 4.0in
Stroke: 88.4mm 3.5in
Valve type/No: Overhead 16
Transmission: Automatic
No. of forward speeds: 4
Wheels driven: Rear
Springs F/R: Coil/Coil
Brake system: PA
Brakes F/R: Disc/Disc
Steering: Recirculating ball PA
Wheelbase: 256.5cm 101.0in
Track F: 152.4cm 60.0in
Track R: 154.7cm 60.9in
Length: 487.7cm 192.0in
Width: 184.9cm 72.8in
Height: 127.8cm 50.3in
Kerb weight: 1579.9kg 3480.0lb
Fuel: 58.7L 12.9gal 15.5galUS

914 Chevrolet

Camaro IROC-Z 8.3-litre
1988 USA
0-1/4 mile: 13.1secs
496.0bhp 369.9kW 502.9PS
@ 5200rpm
550.0lbft 745.3Nm @ 3800rpm
59.8bhp/L 44.6kW/L 60.6PS/L
57.8ft/sec 17.6m/sec
Petrol 4-stroke piston
8292cc 505.9cu in
Vee 8 1 Carburettor
Compression ratio: 9.7:1
Bore: 114.3mm 4.5in
Stroke: 101.6mm 4.0in
Valve type/No: Overhead 16
Transmission: Manual
No. of forward speeds: 6
Wheels driven: Rear

915 Chevrolet

Cavalier Z24 Convertible
1988 USA
120.0mph 193.1kmh
0-50mph 80.5kmh: 5.8secs
0-60mph 96.5kmh: 8.2secs
0-1/4 mile: 16.2secs
125.0bhp 93.2kW 126.7PS
@ 4500rpm
160.0lbft 216.8Nm @ 3600rpm
104.7bhp/ton 102.9bhp/tonne
44.1bhp/L 32.9kW/L 44.7PS/L
37.4ft/sec 11.4m/sec
30.0mpg 25.0mpgUS 9.4L/100km
Petrol 4-stroke piston
2837cc 173.1cu in
Vee 6 fuel injection
Compression ratio: 8.9:1
Bore: 89.0mm 3.5in
Stroke: 76.0mm 3.0in
Valve type/No: Overhead 12
Transmission: Manual
No. of forward speeds: 5
Wheels driven: Front
Springs F/R: Coil/Coil
Brake system: PA
Brakes F/R: Disc/Drum
Steering: Rack & pinion PA
Wheelbase: 257.0cm 101.2in
Track F: 140.7cm 55.4in
Track R: 140.2cm 55.2in
Length: 437.9cm 172.4in
Width: 167.6cm 66.0in
Height: 131.8cm 51.9in
Kerb weight: 1214.4kg 2675.0lb
Fuel: 51.5L 11.3gal 13.6galUS

916 Chevrolet

Corvette
1988 USA
155.0mph 249.4kmh
0-50mph 80.5kmh: 4.3secs
0-60mph 96.5kmh: 6.0secs
0-1/4 mile: 14.6secs
245.0bhp 182.7kW 248.4PS
@ 4300rpm
340.0lbft 460.7Nm @ 3200rpm
164.8bhp/ton 162.1bhp/tonne
42.7bhp/L 31.8kW/L 43.2PS/L
41.6ft/sec 12.7m/sec
21.0mpg 17.5mpgUS 13.4L/100km
Petrol 4-stroke piston
5743cc 350.4cu in
Vee 8 fuel injection
Compression ratio: 9.5:1
Bore: 101.6mm 4.0in
Stroke: 88.4mm 3.5in
Valve type/No: Overhead 16
Transmission: Manual with overdrive
Wheels driven: Rear
Springs F/R: Leaf/Leaf
Brake system: PA ABS
Brakes F/R: Disc/Disc
Steering: Rack & pinion PA
Wheelbase: 244.3cm 96.2in
Track F: 151.4cm 59.6in
Track R: 153.4cm 60.4in
Length: 448.3cm 176.5in
Width: 180.3cm 71.0in
Height: 118.6cm 46.7in
Kerb weight: 1511.8kg 3330.0lb
Fuel: 75.7L 16.6gal 20.0galUS

917 Chevrolet

Corvette Bakeracing SCCA Escort
1988 USA
169.0mph 271.9kmh
0-50mph 80.5kmh: 3.3secs
0-60mph 96.5kmh: 4.5secs
0-1/4 mile: 13.2secs
325.0bhp 242.3kW 329.5PS
@ 4400rpm
410.0lbft 555.6Nm @ 3250rpm
227.5bhp/ton 223.7bhp/tonne

56.6bhp/L 42.2kW/L 57.4PS/L
42.5ft/sec 13.0m/sec
12.0mpg 10.0mpgUS 23.5L/100km
Petrol 4-stroke piston
5743cc 350.4cu in
Vee 8 fuel injection
Compression ratio: 10.0:1
Bore: 101.6mm 4.0in
Stroke: 88.4mm 3.5in
Valve type/No: Overhead 16
Transmission: Manual with overdrive
Wheels driven: Rear
Springs F/R: Leaf/Leaf
Brake system: PA ABS
Brakes F/R: Disc/Disc
Steering: Rack & pinion PA
Wheelbase: 244.3cm 96.2in
Track F: 151.4cm 59.6in
Track R: 153.4cm 60.4in
Length: 448.3cm 176.5in
Width: 180.3cm 71.0in
Height: 116.1cm 45.7in
Kerb weight: 1452.8kg 3200.0lb
Fuel: 75.7L 16.6gal 20.0galUS

918 Chevrolet
Corvette Callaway
1988 USA
191.0mph 307.3kmh
0-60mph 96.5kmh: 4.6secs
0-1/4 mile: 13.0secs
382.0bhp 284.9kW 387.3PS
@ 4250rpm
545.0lbft 738.5Nm @ 2750rpm
248.0bhp/ton 243.9bhp/tonne
66.5bhp/L 49.6kW/L 67.4PS/L
41.1ft/sec 12.5m/sec
Petrol 4-stroke piston
5743cc 350.4cu in turbocharged
Vee 8 fuel injection
Compression ratio: 7.5:1
Bore: 101.6mm 4.0in
Stroke: 88.4mm 3.5in
Valve type/No: Overhead 16
Transmission: Manual with overdrive
Wheels driven: Rear
Springs F/R: Leaf/Leaf
Brake system: PA ABS
Brakes F/R: Disc/Disc
Steering: Rack & pinion PA
Wheelbase: 244.3cm 96.2in
Track F: 151.4cm 59.6in
Track R: 153.4cm 60.4in
Length: 448.3cm 176.5in
Width: 180.3cm 71.0in
Height: 118.6cm 46.7in
Kerb weight: 1566.3kg 3450.0lb
Fuel: 75.7L 16.6gal 20.0galUS

919 Chevrolet
Corvette Convertible
1988 USA
158.0mph 254.2kmh
0-60mph 96.5kmh: 6.0secs
0-1/4 mile: 14.6secs
245.0bhp 182.7kW 248.4PS
@ 4300rpm
340.0lbft 460.7Nm @ 3200rpm
164.3bhp/ton 161.6bhp/tonne
42.7bhp/L 31.9kW/L 43.3PS/L
41.6ft/sec 12.7m/sec
23.2mpg 19.3mpgUS 12.2L/100km
Petrol 4-stroke piston
5733cc 349.8cu in
Vee 8 fuel injection
Compression ratio: 9.5:1
Bore: 101.6mm 4.0in
Stroke: 88.4mm 3.5in
Valve type/No: Overhead 16
Transmission: Manual with overdrive
Wheels driven: Rear
Springs F/R: Leaf/Leaf
Brake system: PA ABS
Brakes F/R: Disc/Disc
Steering: Rack & pinion PA
Wheelbase: 244.3cm 96.2in
Track F: 151.4cm 59.6in
Track R: 153.4cm 60.4in
Length: 448.3cm 176.5in
Width: 180.3cm 71.0in
Height: 117.9cm 46.4in
Kerb weight: 1516.4kg 3340.0lb
Fuel: 75.7L 16.6gal 20.0galUS

920 Chevrolet
Corvette Guldstrand Grand Sport 80
1988 USA
172.0mph 276.7kmh
0-60mph 96.5kmh: 5.2secs
0-1/4 mile: 13.6secs
374.0bhp 278.9kW 379.2PS
@ 5600rpm
442.0lbft 598.9Nm @ 3600rpm
254.2bhp/ton 250.0bhp/tonne
61.3bhp/L 45.7kW/L 62.2PS/L
54.1ft/sec 16.5m/sec
Petrol 4-stroke piston
6096cc 371.9cu in
Vee 8 fuel injection
Compression ratio: 10.0:1
Bore: 104.7mm 4.1in
Stroke: 88.4mm 3.5in
Valve type/No: Overhead 16
Transmission: Manual with overdrive
Wheels driven: Rear
Springs F/R: Leaf/Leaf
Brake system: PA ABS
Brakes F/R: Disc/Disc
Steering: Rack & pinion PA
Wheelbase: 244.3cm 96.2in
Track F: 151.4cm 59.6in
Track R: 153.4cm 60.4in
Length: 448.3cm 176.5in
Width: 180.3cm 71.0in
Height: 117.9cm 46.4in
Kerb weight: 1495.9kg 3295.0lb
Fuel: 75.7L 16.6gal 20.0galUS

921 Chevrolet
Corvette Morrison/Baker Nelson Ledges
1988 USA
127.0mph 204.3kmh
0-50mph 80.5kmh: 3.6secs
0-60mph 96.5kmh: 4.9secs
0-1/4 mile: 13.7secs
360.0bhp 268.4kW 365.0PS
@ 5000rpm
437.0lbft 592.1Nm @ 3500rpm
252.0bhp/ton 247.8bhp/tonne
60.9bhp/L 45.4kW/L 61.8PS/L
48.3ft/sec 14.7m/sec
12.0mpg 10.0mpgUS 23.5L/100km
Petrol 4-stroke piston
5907cc 360.4cu in
Vee 8 fuel injection
Compression ratio: 10.5:1
Bore: 103.1mm 4.1in
Stroke: 88.4mm 3.5in
Valve type/No: Overhead 16
Transmission: Manual
No. of forward speeds: 5
Wheels driven: Rear
Springs F/R: Leaf/Leaf
Brake system: PA ABS
Brakes F/R: Disc/Disc
Steering: Rack & pinion PA
Wheelbase: 244.3cm 96.2in
Track F: 151.4cm 59.6in
Track R: 153.4cm 60.4in
Length: 452.1cm 178.0in
Width: 180.3cm 71.0in
Height: 116.1cm 45.7in
Kerb weight: 1452.8kg 3200.0lb
Fuel: 75.7L 16.6gal 20.0galUS

922 Chevrolet
Corvette Z51
1988 USA
158.0mph 254.2kmh
0-50mph 80.5kmh: 4.3secs
0-60mph 96.5kmh: 6.0secs
0-1/4 mile: 14.6secs
245.0bhp 182.7kW 248.4PS
@ 4300rpm
340.0lbft 460.7Nm @ 3200rpm
164.8bhp/ton 162.1bhp/tonne
42.7bhp/L 31.8kW/L 43.2PS/L
41.6ft/sec 12.7m/sec
21.0mpg 17.5mpgUS 13.4L/100km
Petrol 4-stroke piston
5743cc 350.4cu in
Vee 8 fuel injection
Compression ratio: 9.5:1
Bore: 101.6mm 4.0in
Stroke: 88.4mm 3.5in
Valve type/No: Overhead 16
Transmission: Manual with overdrive
Wheels driven: Rear
Springs F/R: Leaf/Leaf
Brake system: PA ABS
Brakes F/R: Disc/Disc
Steering: Rack & pinion PA
Wheelbase: 244.3cm 96.2in
Track F: 151.4cm 59.6in
Track R: 153.4cm 60.4in
Length: 448.3cm 176.5in
Width: 180.3cm 71.0in
Height: 118.6cm 46.7in
Kerb weight: 1511.8kg 3330.0lb
Fuel: 75.7L 16.6gal 20.0galUS

923 Chevrolet
Nova Twin Cam
1988 Japan
110.0mph 177.0kmh
0-50mph 80.5kmh: 6.3secs
0-60mph 96.5kmh: 8.9secs
0-1/4 mile: 16.7secs
110.0bhp 82.0kW 111.5PS
@ 6600rpm
98.0lbft 132.8Nm @ 4800rpm
103.1bhp/ton 101.4bhp/tonne
69.3bhp/L 51.7kW/L 70.3PS/L
55.5ft/sec 16.9m/sec
31.8mpg 26.5mpgUS 8.9L/100km
Petrol 4-stroke piston
1587cc 96.8cu in
In-line 4 fuel injection
Compression ratio: 9.4:1
Bore: 81.0mm 3.2in
Stroke: 77.0mm 3.0in
Valve type/No: Overhead 16
Transmission: Manual
No. of forward speeds: 5
Wheels driven: Front
Springs F/R: Coil/Coil
Brake system: PA
Brakes F/R: Disc/Disc
Steering: Rack & pinion PA
Wheelbase: 243.1cm 95.7in
Track F: 142.5cm 56.1in
Track R: 140.5cm 55.3in
Length: 422.4cm 166.3in
Width: 163.6cm 64.4in
Height: 134.1cm 52.8in
Kerb weight: 1085.1kg 2390.0lb
Fuel: 50.0L 11.0gal 13.2galUS

924 Chevrolet
Sprint
1988 Japan
0-60mph 96.5kmh: 14.6secs
0-1/4 mile: 19.2secs
48.0bhp 35.8kW 48.7PS
@ 5100rpm
57.0lbft 77.2Nm @ 3200rpm
62.1bhp/ton 61.1bhp/tonne
48.3bhp/L 36.0kW/L 49.0PS/L
42.9ft/sec 13.1m/sec
45.0mpg 37.5mpgUS 6.3L/100km
Petrol 4-stroke piston
993cc 60.6cu in
In-line 3 1 Carburettor
Compression ratio: 9.5:1
Bore: 74.0mm 2.9in
Stroke: 77.0mm 3.0in
Valve type/No: Overhead 6
Transmission: Manual
No. of forward speeds: 5
Wheels driven: Front
Springs F/R: Coil/Coil
Brake system: PA
Brakes F/R: Disc/Drum
Steering: Rack & pinion
Wheelbase: 234.4cm 92.3in
Track F: 133.6cm 52.6in
Track R: 130.0cm 51.2in
Length: 376.9cm 148.4in
Width: 152.9cm 60.2in
Height: 134.9cm 53.1in
Kerb weight: 785.4kg 1730.0lb
Fuel: 32.9L 7.2gal 8.7galUS

925 Chevrolet
Baretta GTU
1989 USA
110.0mph 177.0kmh
0-50mph 80.5kmh: 6.3secs
0-60mph 96.5kmh: 9.0secs
0-1/4 mile: 16.7secs
130.0bhp 96.9kW 131.8PS
@ 4700rpm
160.0lbft 216.8Nm @ 3600rpm
103.3bhp/ton 101.5bhp/tonne
45.8bhp/L 34.2kW/L 46.5PS/L
39.0ft/sec 11.9m/sec
26.4mpg 22.0mpgUS 10.7L/100km
Petrol 4-stroke piston
2837cc 173.1cu in
Vee 6 fuel injection
Compression ratio: 8.9:1
Bore: 89.0mm 3.5in
Stroke: 76.0mm 3.0in
Valve type/No: Overhead 12
Transmission: Manual
No. of forward speeds: 5
Wheels driven: Front
Springs F/R: Coil/Coil
Brake system: PA
Brakes F/R: Disc/Drum
Steering: Rack & pinion PA
Wheelbase: 262.6cm 103.4in
Track F: 141.2cm 55.6in
Track R: 143.5cm 56.5in
Length: 475.5cm 187.2in
Width: 172.7cm 68.0in
Height: 133.6cm 52.6in
Kerb weight: 1280.3kg 2820.0lb
Fuel: 51.5L 11.3gal 13.6galUS

926 Chevrolet
Camaro Gottlieb 1969
1989 USA
203.0mph 326.6kmh
0-50mph 80.5kmh: 3.6secs
0-60mph 96.5kmh: 4.8secs
0-1/4 mile: 12.2secs
798.0bhp 595.1kW 809.1PS
@ 7000rpm
638.0lbft 864.5Nm @ 6500rpm
595.8bhp/ton 585.9bhp/tonne
90.0bhp/L 67.1kW/L 91.3PS/L
82.6ft/sec 25.2m/sec
Petrol 4-stroke piston
8865cc 540.9cu in
Vee 8 1 Carburettor
Compression ratio: 12.8:1
Bore: 114.3mm 4.5in
Stroke: 108.0mm 4.2in
Valve type/No: Overhead 16
Transmission: Manual
No. of forward speeds: 4
Wheels driven: Rear
Springs F/R: Coil/Coil
Brakes F/R: Disc/Disc
Steering: Rack & pinion
Wheelbase: 274.3cm 108.0in
Track F: 144.8cm 57.0in
Track R: 144.8cm 57.0in
Length: 469.1cm 184.7in
Width: 184.2cm 72.5in
Height: 129.5cm 51.0in
Kerb weight: 1362.0kg 3000.0lb

927 Chevrolet
Camaro IROC-Z
1989 USA
145.0mph 233.3kmh
0-50mph 80.5kmh: 4.7secs
0-60mph 96.5kmh: 6.6secs
0-1/4 mile: 14.9secs
230.0bhp 171.5kW 233.2PS
@ 4600rpm
300.0lbft 406.5Nm @ 3200rpm
155.2bhp/ton 152.6bhp/tonne
46.0bhp/L 34.3kW/L 46.6PS/L
44.5ft/sec 13.5m/sec
19.2mpg 16.0mpgUS 14.7L/100km
Petrol 4-stroke piston
5001cc 305.1cu in
Vee 8 fuel injection
Compression ratio: 9.3:1
Bore: 94.9mm 3.7in
Stroke: 88.4mm 3.5in
Valve type/No: Overhead 16
Transmission: Manual
No. of forward speeds: 5
Wheels driven: Rear
Springs F/R: Coil/Coil
Brake system: PA
Brakes F/R: Disc/Disc
Steering: Recirculating ball PA
Wheelbase: 256.5cm 101.0in
Track F: 152.4cm 60.0in
Track R: 154.7cm 60.9in
Length: 487.7cm 192.0in
Width: 184.9cm 72.8in
Height: 127.8cm 50.3in
Kerb weight: 1507.3kg 3320.0lb
Fuel: 58.7L 12.9gal 15.5galUS

928 Chevrolet
Camaro IROC-Z Automatic
1989 USA

145.0mph 233.3kmh
0-50mph 80.5kmh: 4.8secs
0-60mph 96.5kmh: 6.6secs
0-1/4 mile: 15.2secs
240.0bhp 179.0kW 243.3PS
@ 4400rpm
345.0lbft 467.5Nm @ 3200rpm
154.5bhp/ton 151.9bhp/tonne
41.9bhp/L 31.2kW/L 42.4PS/L
42.5ft/sec 13.0m/sec
19.2mpg 16.0mpgUS 14.7L/100km
Petrol 4-stroke piston
5733cc 349.8cu in
Vee 8 fuel injection
Compression ratio: 9.3:1
Bore: 101.6mm 4.0in
Stroke: 88.4mm 3.5in
Valve type/No: Overhead 16
Transmission: Automatic
No. of forward speeds: 4
Wheels driven: Rear
Springs F/R: Coil/Coil
Brake system: PA
Brakes F/R: Disc/Disc
Steering: Recirculating ball PA
Wheelbase: 256.5cm 101.0in
Track F: 152.4cm 60.0in
Track R: 154.7cm 60.9in
Length: 487.7cm 192.0in
Width: 184.9cm 72.8in
Height: 127.8cm 50.3in
Kerb weight: 1579.9kg 3480.0lb
Fuel: 58.7L 12.9gal 15.5galUS

929 Chevrolet

Camaro IROC-Z Chevrolet Engineering
1989 USA
193.0mph 310.5kmh
0-50mph 80.5kmh: 3.7secs
0-60mph 96.5kmh: 4.5secs
0-1/4 mile: 12.8secs
530.0bhp 395.2kW 537.3PS
@ 5000rpm
672.0lbft 910.6Nm @ 4500rpm
320.9bhp/ton 315.5bhp/tonne
63.9bhp/L 47.7kW/L 64.8PS/L
55.6ft/sec 16.9m/sec
Petrol 4-stroke piston
8292cc 505.9cu in
Vee 8 fuel injection
Compression ratio: 9.7:1
Bore: 114.3mm 4.5in
Stroke: 101.6mm 4.0in
Valve type/No: Overhead 16
Transmission: Manual
No. of forward speeds: 6
Wheels driven: Rear
Springs F/R: Coil/Coil
Brake system: PA
Brakes F/R: Disc/Disc
Steering: Recirculating ball PA
Wheelbase: 256.5cm 101.0in
Track F: 152.4cm 60.0in
Track R: 154.7cm 60.9in
Length: 487.7cm 192.0in
Width: 184.9cm 72.8in
Height: 127.8cm 50.3in
Kerb weight: 1679.8kg 3700.0lb

930 Chevrolet

Corvette
1989 USA
149.0mph 239.7kmh
0-50mph 80.5kmh: 4.8secs
0-60mph 96.5kmh: 6.2secs
0-1/4 mile: 14.8secs
245.0bhp 182.7kW 248.4PS
@ 4300rpm
340.0lbft 460.7Nm @ 3200rpm
164.8bhp/ton 162.1bhp/tonne
42.7bhp/L 31.9kW/L 43.3PS/L
41.6ft/sec 12.7m/sec
21.5mpg 17.9mpgUS 13.1L/100km
Petrol 4-stroke piston
5733cc 349.8cu in
Vee 8 fuel injection
Compression ratio: 9.5:1
Bore: 101.6mm 4.0in
Stroke: 88.4mm 3.5in
Valve type/No: Overhead 16
Transmission: Manual
No. of forward speeds: 6
Wheels driven: Rear
Springs F/R: Leaf/Leaf
Brake system: PA ABS
Brakes F/R: Disc/Disc
Steering: Rack & pinion PA
Wheelbase: 244.3cm 96.2in
Track F: 151.4cm 59.6in
Track R: 153.4cm 60.4in
Length: 448.3cm 176.5in
Width: 180.3cm 71.0in
Height: 118.6cm 46.7in
Kerb weight: 1511.8kg 3330.0lb
Fuel: 75.7L 16.6gal 20.0galUS

931 Chevrolet

Corvette Callaway
1989 USA
191.0mph 307.3kmh
0-50mph 80.5kmh: 3.9secs
0-60mph 96.5kmh: 4.9secs
0-1/4 mile: 13.4secs
382.0bhp 284.9kW 387.3PS
@ 4250rpm
562.0lbft 761.5Nm @ 2500rpm
244.5bhp/ton 240.4bhp/tonne
66.6bhp/L 49.7kW/L 67.6PS/L
41.1ft/sec 12.5m/sec
Petrol 4-stroke piston
5733cc 349.8cu in turbocharged
Vee 8 fuel injection
Compression ratio: 7.5:1
Bore: 101.6mm 4.0in
Stroke: 88.4mm 3.5in
Valve type/No: Overhead 16
Transmission: Manual
No. of forward speeds: 6
Wheels driven: Rear
Springs F/R: Leaf/Leaf
Brake system: PA ABS
Brakes F/R: Disc/Disc
Steering: Rack & pinion PA
Wheelbase: 244.3cm 96.2in
Track F: 151.4cm 59.6in
Track R: 153.4cm 60.4in
Length: 448.3cm 176.5in
Width: 180.3cm 71.0in
Height: 118.6cm 46.7in
Kerb weight: 1589.0kg 3500.0lb
Fuel: 75.7L 16.6gal 20.0galUS

932 Chevrolet

Corvette Guldstrand Grand Sport 80
1989 USA
171.0mph 275.1kmh
0-50mph 80.5kmh: 4.0secs
0-60mph 96.5kmh: 5.1secs
0-1/4 mile: 13.5secs
355.0bhp 264.7kW 359.9PS
@ 5200rpm
425.0lbft 575.9Nm @ 4000rpm
238.8bhp/ton 234.8bhp/tonne
58.2bhp/L 43.4kW/L 59.0PS/L
50.3ft/sec 15.3m/sec
Petrol 4-stroke piston
6097cc 372.0cu in
Vee 8 fuel injection
Compression ratio: 9.5:1
Bore: 104.8mm 4.1in
Stroke: 88.4mm 3.5in
Valve type/No: Overhead 16
Transmission: Manual with overdrive
Wheels driven: Rear
Springs F/R: Leaf/Leaf
Brake system: PA ABS
Brakes F/R: Disc/Disc
Steering: Rack & pinion PA
Wheelbase: 244.3cm 96.2in
Track F: 151.4cm 59.6in
Track R: 153.4cm 60.4in
Length: 448.3cm 176.5in
Width: 180.3cm 71.0in
Height: 118.6cm 46.7in
Kerb weight: 1511.8kg 3330.0lb
Fuel: 75.7L 16.6gal 20.0galUS

933 Chevrolet

Corvette L98
1989 USA
155.0mph 249.4kmh
0-60mph 96.5kmh: 6.6secs
0-1/4 mile: 14.8secs
245.0bhp 182.7kW 248.4PS
@ 4300rpm
340.0lbft 460.7Nm @ 3200rpm
164.3bhp/ton 161.6bhp/tonne
42.7bhp/L 31.9kW/L 43.3PS/L
41.6ft/sec 12.7m/sec
23.4mpg 19.5mpgUS 12.1L/100km
Petrol 4-stroke piston
5733cc 349.8cu in
Vee 8 fuel injection
Compression ratio: 9.5:1
Bore: 101.6mm 4.0in
Stroke: 88.4mm 3.5in
Valve type/No: Overhead 16
Transmission: Manual
No. of forward speeds: 6
Wheels driven: Rear
Springs F/R: Leaf/Leaf
Brake system: PA ABS
Brakes F/R: Disc/Disc
Steering: Rack & pinion PA
Wheelbase: 244.3cm 96.2in
Track F: 151.4cm 59.6in
Track R: 153.4cm 60.4in
Length: 446.0cm 175.6in
Width: 180.3cm 71.0in
Height: 117.9cm 46.4in
Kerb weight: 1516.4kg 3340.0lb
Fuel: 75.7L 16.6gal 20.0galUS

934 Chevrolet

Corvette ZR-1
1989 USA
170.0mph 273.5kmh
0-50mph 80.5kmh: 3.6secs
0-60mph 96.5kmh: 4.9secs
0-1/4 mile: 13.4secs
380.0bhp 283.4kW 385.3PS
@ 6200rpm
370.0lbft 501.4Nm @ 4500rpm
241.1bhp/ton 237.1bhp/tonne
66.3bhp/L 49.5kW/L 67.3PS/L
63.0ft/sec 19.2m/sec
Petrol 4-stroke piston
5727cc 349.4cu in
Vee 8 fuel injection
Compression ratio: 11.3:1
Bore: 99.0mm 3.9in
Stroke: 93.0mm 3.7in
Valve type/No: Overhead 32
Transmission: Manual
No. of forward speeds: 6
Wheels driven: Rear
Springs F/R: Leaf/Leaf
Brake system: PA ABS
Brakes F/R: Disc/Disc
Steering: Rack & pinion PA
Wheelbase: 244.3cm 96.2in
Track F: 151.4cm 59.6in
Track R: 153.4cm 60.4in
Length: 448.3cm 176.5in
Width: 180.3cm 71.0in
Height: 118.6cm 46.7in
Kerb weight: 1602.6kg 3530.0lb
Fuel: 75.7L 16.6gal 20.0galUS

935 Chevrolet

Beretta GT
1990 USA
125.0mph 201.1kmh
0-60mph 96.5kmh: 8.6secs
0-1/4 mile: 16.4secs
135.0bhp 100.7kW 136.9PS
@ 4200rpm
180.0lbft 243.9Nm @ 3600rpm
105.7bhp/ton 104.0bhp/tonne
43.1bhp/L 32.1kW/L 43.7PS/L
38.6ft/sec 11.8m/sec
24.0mpg 20.0mpgUS 11.8L/100km
Petrol 4-stroke piston
3135cc 191.3cu in
Vee 6 fuel injection
Compression ratio: 8.8:1
Bore: 89.0mm 3.5in
Stroke: 84.0mm 3.3in
Valve type/No: Overhead 12
Transmission: Manual
No. of forward speeds: 5
Wheels driven: Front
Springs F/R: Coil/Coil
Brake system: PA
Brakes F/R: Disc/Drum
Steering: Rack & pinion PA
Wheelbase: 262.6cm 103.4in
Track F: 141.2cm 55.6in
Track R: 140.0cm 55.1in
Length: 465.8cm 183.4in
Width: 173.2cm 68.2in
Height: 142.7cm 56.2in
Kerb weight: 1298.4kg 2860.0lb
Fuel: 59.0L 13.0gal 15.6galUS

936 Chevrolet

Beretta GTZ
1990 USA
125.0mph 201.1kmh
0-50mph 80.5kmh: 6.3secs
0-60mph 96.5kmh: 8.0secs
0-1/4 mile: 16.4secs
180.0bhp 134.2kW 182.5PS
@ 6200rpm
160.0lbft 216.8Nm @ 5200rpm
140.5bhp/ton 138.1bhp/tonne
79.2bhp/L 59.1kW/L 80.3PS/L
57.7ft/sec 17.6m/sec
25.3mpg 21.1mpgUS 11.1L/100km
Petrol 4-stroke piston
2272cc 138.6cu in
In-line 4 fuel injection
Compression ratio: 10.0:1
Bore: 92.2mm 3.6in
Stroke: 85.1mm 3.3in
Valve type/No: Overhead 16
Transmission: Manual
No. of forward speeds: 5
Wheels driven: Front
Springs F/R: Coil/Coil
Brake system: PA
Brakes F/R: Disc/Drum
Steering: Rack & pinion PA
Wheelbase: 262.6cm 103.4in
Track F: 141.2cm 55.6in
Track R: 143.5cm 56.5in
Length: 475.5cm 187.2in
Width: 172.7cm 68.0in
Height: 133.6cm 52.6in
Kerb weight: 1303.0kg 2870.0lb
Fuel: 51.5L 11.3gal 13.6galUS

937 Chevrolet

Camaro IROC-Z Convertible
1990 USA
120.0mph 193.1kmh
0-50mph 80.5kmh: 6.2secs
0-60mph 96.5kmh: 8.6secs
0-1/4 mile: 16.6secs
195.0bhp 145.4kW 197.7PS
@ 4000rpm
295.0lbft 399.7Nm @ 2800rpm
124.1bhp/ton 122.0bhp/tonne
39.0bhp/L 29.1kW/L 39.5PS/L
38.7ft/sec 11.8m/sec
22.3mpg 18.6mpgUS 12.6L/100km
Petrol 4-stroke piston
5002cc 305.2cu in
Vee 8 fuel injection
Compression ratio: 9.3:1
Bore: 94.9mm 3.7in
Stroke: 88.4mm 3.5in
Valve type/No: Overhead 16
Transmission: Automatic
No. of forward speeds: 4
Wheels driven: Rear
Springs F/R: Coil/Coil
Brake system: PA
Brakes F/R: Disc/Disc
Steering: Recirculating ball PA
Wheelbase: 256.5cm 101.0in
Track F: 152.4cm 60.0in
Track R: 154.7cm 60.9in
Length: 487.7cm 192.0in
Width: 184.9cm 72.8in
Height: 127.8cm 50.3in
Kerb weight: 1598.1kg 3520.0lb
Fuel: 58.7L 12.9gal 15.5galUS

938 Chevrolet

Camaro Z/28
1990 USA
145.0mph 233.3kmh
0-50mph 80.5kmh: 4.8secs
0-60mph 96.5kmh: 6.6secs
0-1/4 mile: 15.2secs
240.0bhp 179.0kW 243.3PS
@ 4400rpm
345.0lbft 467.5Nm @ 3200rpm
153.6bhp/ton 151.0bhp/tonne
41.9bhp/L 31.2kW/L 42.4PS/L
42.5ft/sec 13.0m/sec
19.2mpg 16.0mpgUS 14.7L/100km
Petrol 4-stroke piston
5733cc 349.8cu in
Vee 8 fuel injection
Compression ratio: 9.3:1
Bore: 101.6mm 4.0in
Stroke: 88.4mm 3.5in
Valve type/No: Overhead 16
Transmission: Automatic
No. of forward speeds: 4
Wheels driven: Rear
Springs F/R: Coil/Coil
Brake system: PA
Brakes F/R: Disc/Disc

Steering: Recirculating ball PA
Wheelbase: 256.5cm 101.0in
Track F: 152.4cm 60.0in
Track R: 154.7cm 60.9in
Length: 487.7cm 192.0in
Width: 184.9cm 72.8in
Height: 127.8cm 50.3in
Kerb weight: 1589.0kg 3500.0lb
Fuel: 58.7L 12.9gal 15.5galUS

939 Chevrolet

Cavalier Z24
1990 USA
125.0mph 201.1kmh
0-50mph 80.5kmh: 5.8secs
0-60mph 96.5kmh: 8.1secs
0-1/4 mile: 16.1secs
140.0bhp 104.4kW 141.9PS
@ 4500rpm
185.0lbft 250.7Nm @ 3600rpm
128.8bhp/ton 126.6bhp/tonne
44.7bhp/L 33.3kW/L 45.3PS/L
41.4ft/sec 12.6m/sec
23.1mpg 19.2mpgUS 12.3L/100km
Petrol 4-stroke piston
3135cc 191.3cu in
Vee 6 fuel injection
Compression ratio: 9.0:1
Bore: 89.0mm 3.5in
Stroke: 84.0mm 3.3in
Valve type/No: Overhead 12
Transmission: Manual
No. of forward speeds: 5
Wheels driven: Front
Springs F/R: Coil/Coil
Brake system: PA
Brakes F/R: Disc/Drum
Steering: Rack & pinion PA
Wheelbase: 257.0cm 101.2in
Track F: 141.7cm 55.8in
Track R: 140.2cm 55.2in
Length: 453.6cm 178.6in
Width: 167.6cm 66.0in
Height: 132.1cm 52.0in
Kerb weight: 1105.5kg 2435.0lb
Fuel: 51.5L 11.3gal 13.6galUS

940 Chevrolet

Corvette Callaway
1990 USA
170.0mph 273.5kmh
0-50mph 80.5kmh: 3.9secs
0-60mph 96.5kmh: 5.1secs
0-1/4 mile: 13.4secs
390.0bhp 290.8kW 395.4PS
@ 4250rpm
562.0lbft 761.5Nm @ 2500rpm
256.9bhp/ton 252.7bhp/tonne
68.0bhp/L 50.7kW/L 68.9PS/L
41.1ft/sec 12.5m/sec
21.6mpg 18.0mpgUS 13.1L/100km
Petrol 4-stroke piston
5735cc 349.9cu in turbocharged
Vee 8 fuel injection
Compression ratio: 7.5:1
Bore: 101.6mm 4.0in
Stroke: 88.4mm 3.5in
Valve type/No: Overhead 16
Transmission: Manual
No. of forward speeds: 6
Wheels driven: Rear
Springs F/R: Leaf/Leaf
Brake system: PA
Brakes F/R: Disc/Disc
Steering: Rack & pinion PA
Wheelbase: 244.3cm 96.2in
Track F: 151.4cm 59.6in
Track R: 153.4cm 60.4in
Length: 448.3cm 176.5in
Width: 180.3cm 71.0in
Height: 118.6cm 46.7in
Kerb weight: 1543.6kg 3400.0lb
Fuel: 75.7L 16.6gal 20.0galUS

941 Chevrolet

Corvette Callaway Sledgehammer
1990 USA
255.0mph 410.3kmh
0-60mph 96.5kmh: 3.9secs
0-1/4 mile: 10.6secs
880.0bhp 656.2kW 892.2PS
@ 6250rpm
772.0lbft 1046.1Nm @ 5250rpm
537.1bhp/ton 528.1bhp/tonne
153.5bhp/L 114.5kW/L 155.6PS/L
60.4ft/sec 18.4m/sec
Petrol 4-stroke piston
5733cc 349.8cu in turbocharged
Vee 8 fuel injection
Compression ratio: 7.5:1
Bore: 101.6mm 4.0in
Stroke: 88.4mm 3.5in
Valve type/No: Overhead 16
Transmission: Manual
No. of forward speeds: 6
Wheels driven: Rear
Springs F/R: Leaf/Leaf
Brake system: PA ABS
Brakes F/R: Disc/Disc
Steering: Rack & pinion PA
Wheelbase: 244.3cm 96.2in
Track F: 151.4cm 59.6in
Track R: 153.4cm 60.4in
Length: 448.3cm 176.5in
Width: 180.3cm 71.0in
Height: 118.6cm 46.7in
Kerb weight: 1666.2kg 3670.0lb
Fuel: 75.7L 16.6gal 20.0galUS

942 Chevrolet

Corvette Convertible
1990 USA
0-60mph 96.5kmh: 6.3secs
0-1/4 mile: 14.8secs
245.0bhp 182.7kW 248.4PS
@ 4000rpm
345.0lbft 467.5Nm @ 3200rpm
163.3bhp/ton 160.6bhp/tonne
42.8bhp/L 31.9kW/L 43.4PS/L
Petrol 4-stroke piston
5727cc 349.4cu in
Vee 8
Valve type/No: Overhead 16
Transmission: Manual
No. of forward speeds: 6
Wheels driven: Rear
Brake system: ABS
Kerb weight: 1525.4kg 3360.0lb

943 Chevrolet

Corvette Coupe
1990 USA
0-60mph 96.5kmh: 6.2secs
0-1/4 mile: 14.7secs
250.0bhp 186.4kW 253.5PS
@ 4400rpm
350.0lbft 474.3Nm @ 3200rpm
168.7bhp/ton 165.9bhp/tonne
43.6bhp/L 32.5kW/L 44.3PS/L
Petrol 4-stroke piston
5727cc 349.4cu in
Vee 8
Valve type/No: Overhead 16
Transmission: Automatic
No. of forward speeds: 4
Wheels driven: Rear
Brake system: ABS
Kerb weight: 1507.3kg 3320.0lb

944 Chevrolet

Corvette L98
1990 USA
149.0mph 239.7kmh
0-50mph 80.5kmh: 4.8secs
0-60mph 96.5kmh: 6.3secs
0-1/4 mile: 14.8secs
245.0bhp 182.7kW 248.4PS
@ 4300rpm
340.0lbft 460.7Nm @ 3200rpm
164.8bhp/ton 162.1bhp/tonne
42.7bhp/L 31.9kW/L 43.3PS/L
41.6ft/sec 12.7m/sec
20.9mpg 17.4mpgUS 13.5L/100km
Petrol 4-stroke piston
5735cc 349.9cu in
Vee 8 fuel injection
Compression ratio: 9.5:1
Bore: 101.6mm 4.0in
Stroke: 88.4mm 3.5in
Valve type/No: Overhead 16
Transmission: Manual
No. of forward speeds: 6
Wheels driven: Rear
Springs F/R: Leaf/Leaf
Brake system: PA ABS
Brakes F/R: Disc/Disc
Steering: Rack & pinion PA
Wheelbase: 244.3cm 96.2in
Track F: 151.4cm 59.6in
Track R: 153.4cm 60.4in
Length: 448.3cm 176.5in
Width: 180.3cm 71.0in
Height: 118.6cm 46.7in
Kerb weight: 1511.8kg 3330.0lb
Fuel: 75.7L 16.6gal 20.0galUS

945 Chevrolet

Lumina APV
1990 USA
105.0mph 168.9kmh
0-50mph 80.5kmh: 8.7secs
0-60mph 96.5kmh: 12.6secs
0-1/4 mile: 18.8secs
120.0bhp 89.5kW 121.7PS
@ 4200rpm
175.0lbft 237.1Nm @ 2200rpm
76.8bhp/ton 75.5bhp/tonne
38.3bhp/L 28.5kW/L 38.8PS/L
38.6ft/sec 11.8m/sec
27.0mpg 22.5mpgUS 10.5L/100km
Petrol 4-stroke piston
3135cc 191.3cu in
Vee 6 fuel injection
Compression ratio: 8.5:1
Bore: 89.0mm 3.5in
Stroke: 84.0mm 3.3in
Valve type/No: Overhead 12
Transmission: Automatic
No. of forward speeds: 3
Wheels driven: Front
Springs F/R: Coil/Coil
Brake system: PA
Steering: Rack & pinion PA
Wheelbase: 278.9cm 109.8in
Track F: 149.1cm 58.7in
Track R: 154.7cm 60.9in
Length: 492.5cm 193.9in
Width: 188.5cm 74.2in
Height: 166.4cm 65.5in
Ground clearance: 18.3cm 7.2in
Kerb weight: 1589.0kg 3500.0lb
Fuel: 75.7L 16.6gal 20.0galUS

946 Chevrolet

Baretta GTZ
1991 USA
125.0mph 201.1kmh
0-50mph 80.5kmh: 6.3secs
0-60mph 96.5kmh: 8.0secs
0-1/4 mile: 16.4secs
180.0bhp 134.2kW 182.5PS
@ 6200rpm
160.0lbft 216.8Nm @ 5200rpm
140.5bhp/ton 138.1bhp/tonne
79.6bhp/L 59.4kW/L 80.7PS/L
57.7ft/sec 17.6m/sec
30.0mpg 25.0mpgUS 9.4L/100km
Petrol 4-stroke piston
2260cc 137.9cu in
In-line 4 fuel injection
Compression ratio: 10.0:1
Bore: 92.0mm 3.6in
Stroke: 85.0mm 3.3in
Valve type/No: Overhead 16
Transmission: Manual
No. of forward speeds: 5
Wheels driven: Front
Springs F/R: Coil/Coil
Brake system: PA
Brakes F/R: Disc/Drum
Steering: Rack & pinion PA
Wheelbase: 262.6cm 103.4in
Track F: 141.2cm 55.6in
Track R: 143.8cm 56.6in
Length: 465.8cm 183.4in
Width: 173.2cm 68.2in
Height: 134.4cm 52.9in
Kerb weight: 1303.0kg 2870.0lb
Fuel: 59.0L 13.0gal 15.6galUS

947 Chevrolet

Camaro Z/28 Convertible
1991 USA
120.0mph 193.1kmh
0-50mph 80.5kmh: 6.2secs
0-60mph 96.5kmh: 8.6secs
0-1/4 mile: 16.6secs
195.0bhp 145.4kW 197.7PS
@ 4000rpm
295.0lbft 399.7Nm @ 2800rpm
128.5bhp/ton 126.3bhp/tonne
39.0bhp/L 29.1kW/L 39.5PS/L
38.7ft/sec 11.8m/sec
22.3mpg 18.6mpgUS 12.6L/100km
Petrol 4-stroke piston
5002cc 305.2cu in
Vee 8 fuel injection
Compression ratio: 9.3:1
Bore: 94.9mm 3.7in
Stroke: 88.4mm 3.5in
Valve type/No: Overhead 16
Transmission: Automatic
No. of forward speeds: 4
Wheels driven: Rear
Springs F/R: Coil/Coil
Brake system: PA
Brakes F/R: Disc/Disc
Steering: Recirculating ball PA
Wheelbase: 256.5cm 101.0in
Track F: 152.4cm 60.0in
Track R: 154.7cm 60.9in
Length: 487.7cm 192.0in
Width: 184.9cm 72.8in
Height: 127.8cm 50.3in
Kerb weight: 1543.6kg 3400.0lb
Fuel: 58.7L 12.9gal 15.5galUS

948 Chevrolet

Corvette Callaway
1991 USA
184.0mph 296.1kmh
0-60mph 96.5kmh: 4.9secs
0-1/4 mile: 13.3secs
403.0bhp 300.5kW 408.6PS
@ 4500rpm
575.0lbft 779.1Nm @ 3000rpm
262.4bhp/ton 258.0bhp/tonne
70.3bhp/L 52.4kW/L 71.2PS/L
43.5ft/sec 13.3m/sec
Petrol 4-stroke piston
5735cc 349.9cu in turbocharged
Vee 8 fuel injection
Compression ratio: 7.5:1
Bore: 101.6mm 4.0in
Stroke: 88.4mm 3.5in
Valve type/No: Overhead 16
Transmission: Manual
No. of forward speeds: 6
Wheels driven: Rear
Springs F/R: Leaf/Leaf
Brake system: PA ABS
Brakes F/R: Disc/Disc
Steering: Rack & pinion PA
Wheelbase: 244.3cm 96.2in
Track F: 151.4cm 59.6in
Track R: 153.4cm 60.4in
Length: 448.3cm 176.5in
Width: 180.3cm 71.0in
Height: 118.6cm 46.7in
Kerb weight: 1561.8kg 3440.0lb

949 Chevrolet

Corvette Callaway Speedster
1991 USA
201.0mph 323.4kmh
0-60mph 96.5kmh: 4.4secs
403.0bhp 300.5kW 408.6PS
@ 4500rpm
575.0lbft 779.1Nm @ 3000rpm
282.1bhp/ton 277.4bhp/tonne
70.3bhp/L 52.4kW/L 71.2PS/L
43.5ft/sec 13.3m/sec
Petrol 4-stroke piston
5735cc 349.9cu in turbocharged
Vee 8 fuel injection
Compression ratio: 7.5:1
Bore: 101.6mm 4.0in
Stroke: 88.4mm 3.5in
Valve type/No: Overhead 16
Transmission: Manual
No. of forward speeds: 6
Wheels driven: Rear
Springs F/R: Leaf/Leaf
Brake system: PA ABS
Brakes F/R: Disc/Disc
Steering: Rack & pinion PA
Wheelbase: 234.2cm 92.2in
Track F: 151.4cm 59.6in
Track R: 153.4cm 60.4in
Length: 448.3cm 176.5in
Width: 180.3cm 71.0in
Kerb weight: 1452.8kg 3200.0lb
Fuel: 75.7L 16.6gal 20.0galUS

950 Chevrolet

Corvette Callaway Twin Turbo
1991 USA
0-50mph 80.5kmh: 4.0secs
0-60mph 96.5kmh: 4.9secs
0-1/4 mile: 13.3secs
403.0bhp 300.5kW 408.6PS
@ 4500rpm
575.0lbft 779.1Nm @ 3000rpm
262.4bhp/ton 258.0bhp/tonne

70.3bhp/L 52.4kW/L 71.2PS/L
43.5ft/sec 13.3m/sec
19.2mpg 16.0mpgUS 14.7L/100km
Petrol 4-stroke piston
5735cc 349.9cu in turbocharged
Vee 8 fuel injection
Compression ratio: 7.5:1
Bore: 101.6mm 4.0in
Stroke: 88.4mm 3.5in
Valve type/No: Overhead 16
Transmission: Manual
No. of forward speeds: 6
Wheels driven: Rear
Springs F/R: Leaf/Leaf
Brake system: PA ABS
Brakes F/R: Disc/Disc
Steering: Rack & pinion PA
Wheelbase: 244.3cm 96.2in
Track F: 151.4cm 59.6in
Track R: 153.4cm 60.4in
Length: 448.3cm 176.5in
Width: 180.3cm 71.0in
Height: 118.6cm 46.7in
Kerb weight: 1561.8kg 3440.0lb

951 Chevrolet

Corvette Lingenfelter
1991 USA
204.0mph 328.2kmh
0-60mph 96.5kmh: 3.4secs
0-1/4 mile: 11.8secs
530.0bhp 395.2kW 537.3PS
@ 5500rpm
570.0lbft 772.4Nm @ 4300rpm
341.6bhp/ton 335.9bhp/tonne
79.7bhp/L 59.4kW/L 80.8PS/L
57.3ft/sec 17.5m/sec
Petrol 4-stroke piston
6653cc 405.9cu in
Vee 8 fuel injection
Compression ratio: 10.5:1
Bore: 105.5mm 4.1in
Stroke: 95.3mm 3.8in
Valve type/No: Overhead 16
Transmission: Automatic
No. of forward speeds: 4
Wheels driven: Rear
Springs F/R: Coil/Leaf
Brake system: PA ABS
Brakes F/R: Disc/Disc
Steering: Rack & pinion PA
Wheelbase: 244.3cm 96.2in
Track F: 151.4cm 59.6in
Track R: 153.4cm 60.4in
Length: 453.6cm 178.6in
Width: 181.4cm 71.4in
Height: 118.6cm 46.7in
Kerb weight: 1577.6kg 3475.0lb

952 Chevrolet

Corvette Rick Mears
1991 USA
147.0mph 236.5kmh
0-60mph 96.5kmh: 6.3secs
0-1/4 mile: 14.8secs
245.0bhp 182.7kW 248.4PS
@ 4000rpm
340.0lbft 460.7Nm @ 3200rpm
164.8bhp/ton 162.1bhp/tonne
42.7bhp/L 31.9kW/L 43.3PS/L
38.7ft/sec 11.8m/sec
Petrol 4-stroke piston
5735cc 349.9cu in
Vee 8 fuel injection
Compression ratio: 10.0:1
Bore: 101.6mm 4.0in
Stroke: 88.4mm 3.5in
Valve type/No: Overhead 16
Transmission: Manual
No. of forward speeds: 6
Wheels driven: Rear
Springs F/R: Leaf/Leaf
Brake system: PA ABS
Brakes F/R: Disc/Disc
Steering: Rack & pinion PA
Wheelbase: 244.3cm 96.2in
Track F: 151.4cm 59.6in
Track R: 153.4cm 60.4in
Length: 461.0cm 181.5in
Width: 182.9cm 72.0in
Height: 118.6cm 46.7in
Kerb weight: 1511.8kg 3330.0lb

953 Chevrolet

Corvette ZR-1
1991 USA
154.0mph 247.8kmh
0-50mph 80.5kmh: 3.6secs
0-60mph 96.5kmh: 4.9secs
0-1/4 mile: 13.4secs
375.0bhp 279.6kW 380.2PS
@ 5800rpm
370.0lbft 501.4Nm @ 4800rpm
242.4bhp/ton 238.4bhp/tonne
65.5bhp/L 48.8kW/L 66.4PS/L
59.0ft/sec 18.0m/sec
21.7mpg 18.1mpgUS 13.0L/100km
Petrol 4-stroke piston
5727cc 349.4cu in
Vee 8 fuel injection
Compression ratio: 11.0:1
Bore: 99.0mm 3.9in
Stroke: 93.0mm 3.7in
Valve type/No: Overhead 32
Transmission: Manual
No. of forward speeds: 6
Wheels driven: Rear
Springs F/R: Leaf/Leaf
Brake system: PA ABS
Brakes F/R: Disc/Disc
Steering: Rack & pinion PA
Wheelbase: 244.3cm 96.2in
Track F: 151.4cm 59.6in
Track R: 157.2cm 61.9in
Length: 450.6cm 177.4in
Width: 188.0cm 74.0in
Height: 118.6cm 46.7in
Kerb weight: 1573.1kg 3465.0lb
Fuel: 75.7L 16.6gal 20.0galUS

954 Chevrolet

Corvette ZR-1 Geiger
1991 USA
186.0mph 299.3kmh
0-60mph 96.5kmh: 4.9secs
410.0bhp 305.7kW 415.7PS
@ 5800rpm
370.0lbft 501.4Nm @ 4800rpm
71.6bhp/L 53.4kW/L 72.6PS/L
59.0ft/sec 18.0m/sec
Petrol 4-stroke piston
5727cc 349.4cu in
Vee 8 fuel injection
Compression ratio: 11.0:1
Bore: 99.0mm 3.9in
Stroke: 93.0mm 3.7in
Valve type/No: Overhead 32
Transmission: Manual
No. of forward speeds: 6
Wheels driven: Rear
Springs F/R: Leaf/Leaf
Brake system: PA ABS
Brakes F/R: Disc/Disc
Steering: Rack & pinion PA
Wheelbase: 244.3cm 96.2in
Track F: 151.4cm 59.6in
Length: 473.7cm 186.5in
Width: 180.6cm 71.1in
Height: 118.6cm 46.7in
Fuel: 75.7L 16.6gal 20.0galUS

955 Chevrolet

Corvette ZR-1 SS
1991 USA
0-60mph 96.5kmh: 4.2secs
0-1/4 mile: 12.5secs
425.0bhp 316.9kW 430.9PS
@ 6400rpm
400.0lbft 542.0Nm @ 4000rpm
304.1bhp/ton 299.1bhp/tonne
74.2bhp/L 55.3kW/L 75.2PS/L
65.1ft/sec 19.8m/sec
Petrol 4-stroke piston
5727cc 349.4cu in
Vee 8 fuel injection
Compression ratio: 11.0:1
Bore: 99.0mm 3.9in
Stroke: 93.0mm 3.7in
Valve type/No: Overhead 32
Transmission: Manual
No. of forward speeds: 6
Wheels driven: Rear
Springs F/R: Leaf/Leaf
Brake system: PA ABS
Brakes F/R: Disc/Disc
Steering: Rack & pinion PA
Wheelbase: 244.3cm 96.2in
Track F: 151.4cm 59.6in
Track R: 157.2cm 61.9in
Length: 453.4cm 178.5in
Width: 188.0cm 74.0in
Kerb weight: 1421.0kg 3130.0lb

956 Chevrolet

Corvette ZR-2
1991 USA
185.0mph 297.7kmh
0-60mph 96.5kmh: 4.9secs
0-1/4 mile: 13.3secs
385.0bhp 287.1kW 390.3PS
@ 5200rpm
445.0lbft 603.0Nm @ 3400rpm
244.3bhp/ton 240.2bhp/tonne
51.7bhp/L 38.6kW/L 52.5PS/L
57.8ft/sec 17.6m/sec
Petrol 4-stroke piston
7439cc 453.9cu in
Vee 8 fuel injection
Compression ratio: 9.0:1
Bore: 107.9mm 4.2in
Stroke: 101.6mm 4.0in
Valve type/No: Overhead 16
Transmission: Manual
No. of forward speeds: 6
Wheels driven: Rear
Springs F/R: Leaf/Leaf
Brake system: PA ABS
Brakes F/R: Disc/Disc
Steering: Rack & pinion PA
Wheelbase: 244.3cm 96.2in
Track F: 151.4cm 59.6in
Track R: 157.2cm 61.9in
Length: 453.4cm 178.5in
Width: 188.0cm 74.0in
Height: 115.3cm 45.4in
Kerb weight: 1602.6kg 3530.0lb
Fuel: 75.7L 16.6gal 20.0galUS

957 Chevrolet

Lumina Z34
1991 USA
113.0mph 181.8kmh
0-60mph 96.5kmh: 8.0secs
0-1/4 mile: 15.8secs
210.0bhp 156.6kW 212.9PS
@ 5200rpm
215.0lbft 291.3Nm @ 4000rpm
137.5bhp/ton 135.2bhp/tonne
62.6bhp/L 46.7kW/L 63.5PS/L
47.8ft/sec 14.6m/sec
25.8mpg 21.5mpgUS 10.9L/100km
Petrol 4-stroke piston
3352cc 204.5cu in
Vee 6 fuel injection
Compression ratio: 9.3:1
Bore: 92.0mm 3.6in
Stroke: 84.0mm 3.3in
Valve type/No: Overhead 24
Transmission: Manual
No. of forward speeds: 5
Wheels driven: Front
Springs F/R: Coil/Leaf
Brake system: PA
Brakes F/R: Disc/Disc
Steering: Rack & pinion PA
Wheelbase: 273.1cm 107.5in
Track F: 151.1cm 59.5in
Track R: 147.3cm 58.0in
Length: 506.2cm 199.3in
Width: 182.1cm 71.7in
Height: 135.4cm 53.3in
Kerb weight: 1552.7kg 3420.0lb
Fuel: 62.4L 13.7gal 16.5galUS

958 Chevrolet

Camaro Z28
1992 USA
140.0mph 225.3kmh
0-50mph 80.5kmh: 4.9secs
0-60mph 96.5kmh: 6.7secs
0-1/4 mile: 15.2secs
230.0bhp 171.5kW 233.2PS
@ 4400rpm
300.0lbft 406.5Nm @ 3200rpm
155.2bhp/ton 152.6bhp/tonne
46.0bhp/L 34.3kW/L 46.6PS/L
42.5ft/sec 13.0m/sec
21.6mpg 18.0mpgUS 13.1L/100km
Petrol 4-stroke piston
5002cc 305.2cu in
Vee 8 fuel injection
Compression ratio: 9.3:1
Bore: 94.9mm 3.7in
Stroke: 88.4mm 3.5in
Valve type/No: Overhead 16
Transmission: Manual
No. of forward speeds: 5
Wheels driven: Rear
Springs F/R: Coil/Coil
Brake system: PA
Brakes F/R: Disc/Drum
Steering: Recirculating ball PA
Wheelbase: 256.5cm 101.0in
Track F: 152.4cm 60.0in
Track R: 154.7cm 60.9in
Length: 489.2cm 192.6in
Width: 183.9cm 72.4in
Height: 128.0cm 50.4in
Kerb weight: 1507.3kg 3320.0lb
Fuel: 58.7L 12.9gal 15.5galUS

959 Chevrolet

Corvette LT1
1992 USA
163.0mph 262.3kmh
0-60mph 96.5kmh: 5.7secs
0-1/4 mile: 14.1secs
300.0bhp 223.7kW 304.2PS
@ 5000rpm
330.0lbft 447.2Nm @ 4000rpm
201.8bhp/ton 198.4bhp/tonne
52.3bhp/L 39.0kW/L 53.0PS/L
48.3ft/sec 14.7m/sec
20.4mpg 17.0mpgUS 13.8L/100km
Petrol 4-stroke piston
5733cc 349.8cu in
Vee 8 fuel injection
Compression ratio: 10.5:1
Bore: 101.6mm 4.0in
Stroke: 88.4mm 3.5in
Valve type/No: Overhead 16
Transmission: Manual
No. of forward speeds: 6
Wheels driven: Rear
Springs F/R: Leaf/Leaf
Brake system: PA ABS
Brakes F/R: Disc/Disc
Steering: Rack & pinion PA
Wheelbase: 244.3cm 96.2in
Track F: 146.6cm 57.7in
Track R: 149.9cm 59.0in
Length: 453.6cm 178.6in
Width: 180.3cm 71.0in
Height: 118.6cm 46.7in
Kerb weight: 1511.8kg 3330.0lb
Fuel: 75.7L 16.6gal 20.0galUS

960 Chrysler

65 Saloon
1929 USA
64.0mph 103.0kmh
20.0mpg 16.7mpgUS 14.1L/100km
Petrol 4-stroke piston
3176cc 193.8cu in
In-line 6
Bore: 79.4mm 3.1in
Stroke: 103.0mm 4.1in
Transmission: Manual
No. of forward speeds: 3
Wheels driven: Rear
Brakes F/R: Drum/Drum
Wheelbase: 255.8cm 100.7in
Track F: 142.2cm 56.0in
Track R: 142.2cm 56.0in
Length: 439.9cm 173.2in
Width: 149.9cm 59.0in
Height: 180.3cm 71.0in
Kerb weight: 1366.1kg 3009.0lb
Fuel: 36.4L 8.0gal 9.6galUS

961 Chrysler

75 Saloon
1929 USA
70.0mph 112.6kmh
18.0mpg 15.0mpgUS 15.7L/100km
Petrol 4-stroke piston
4074cc 248.6cu in
In-line 6
Bore: 82.5mm 3.2in
Stroke: 120.0mm 4.7in
Transmission: Manual
No. of forward speeds: 3
Wheels driven: Rear
Brakes F/R: Drum/Drum
Wheelbase: 307.3cm 121.0in
Track F: 142.2cm 56.0in
Track R: 142.2cm 56.0in
Length: 471.2cm 185.5in
Width: 169.4cm 66.7in
Height: 188.0cm 74.0in
Fuel: 54.6L 12.0gal 14.4galUS

962 Chrysler

77 Saloon

1930 USA
75.0mph 120.7kmh
16.0mpg 13.3mpgUS 17.7L/100km
Petrol 4-stroke piston
4396cc 268.2cu in
In-line 6
Bore: 85.7mm 3.4in
Stroke: 127.0mm 5.0in
Transmission: Manual
No. of forward speeds: 4
Wheels driven: Rear
Brakes F/R: Drum/Drum
Wheelbase: 315.0cm 124.0in
Track F: 149.1cm 58.7in
Track R: 149.1cm 58.7in
Length: 481.3cm 189.5in
Width: 175.3cm 69.0in
Height: 185.4cm 73.0in
Kerb weight: 1797.8kg 3960.0lb
Fuel: 68.2L 15.0gal 18.0galUS

963 Chrysler
Eight Saloon
1930 USA
73.1mph 117.6kmh
14.0mpg 11.7mpgUS 20.2L/100km
Petrol 4-stroke piston
3939cc 240.3cu in
In-line 8
Bore: 76.2mm 3.0in
Stroke: 108.0mm 4.2in
Transmission: Manual
No. of forward speeds: 4
Wheels driven: Rear
Brakes F/R: Drum/Drum
Wheelbase: 315.0cm 124.0in
Track F: 142.2cm 56.0in
Track R: 142.2cm 56.0in
Length: 440.4cm 173.4in
Width: 175.3cm 69.0in
Height: 180.3cm 71.0in
Kerb weight: 1620.8kg 3570.0lb
Fuel: 59.1L 13.0gal 15.6galUS

964 Chrysler
Custom Imperial Le Baron
1931 USA
96.0mph 154.5kmh
0-50mph 80.5kmh: 14.5secs
0-60mph 96.5kmh: 20.0secs
0-1/4 mile: 21.5secs
125.0bhp 93.2kW 126.7PS
@ 3200rpm
290.0lbft 393.0Nm @ 1400rpm
58.9bhp/ton 58.0bhp/tonne
19.8bhp/L 14.8kW/L 20.1PS/L
44.4ft/sec 13.5m/sec
24.5mph 39.4kmh/1000rpm
Petrol 4-stroke piston
6308cc 384.9cu in
In-line 8 1 Carburettor
Compression ratio: 5.2:1
Bore: 88.9mm 3.5in
Stroke: 127.0mm 5.0in
Valve type/No: Side 16
Transmission: Manual
No. of forward speeds: 4
Wheels driven: Rear
Brakes F/R: Drum/Drum
Wheelbase: 370.8cm 146.0in
Track F: 147.3cm 58.0in
Track R: 147.3cm 58.0in
Length: 551.2cm 217.0in
Width: 185.4cm 73.0in
Height: 167.6cm 66.0in
Kerb weight: 2156.5kg 4750.0lb

965 Chrysler
Heston Airflow Saloon
1935 USA
88.6mph 142.6kmh
0-50mph 80.5kmh: 12.4secs
0-60mph 96.5kmh: 19.0secs
16.0mpg 13.3mpgUS 17.7L/100km
Petrol 4-stroke piston
4893cc 298.5cu in
In-line 8
Bore: 82.5mm 3.2in
Stroke: 114.3mm 4.5in
Transmission: Manual
No. of forward speeds: 3
Wheels driven: Rear
Brakes F/R: Drum/Drum
Kerb weight: 1890.5kg 4164.0lb
Fuel: 75.1L 16.5gal 19.8galUS

966 Chrysler
23.4hp Wimbledon Saloon
1936 USA
77.5mph 124.7kmh
0-50mph 80.5kmh: 15.2secs
0-60mph 96.5kmh: 22.6secs
20.0mpg 16.7mpgUS 14.1L/100km
Petrol 4-stroke piston
3302cc 201.5cu in
In-line 6
Bore: 79.4mm 3.1in
Stroke: 111.1mm 4.4in
Valve type/No: Side 12
Transmission: Manual
No. of forward speeds: 3
Wheels driven: Rear
Brakes F/R: Drum/Drum
Kerb weight: 1481.4kg 3263.0lb
Fuel: 54.6L 12.0gal 14.4galUS

967 Chrysler
Richmond Touring Saloon
1937 USA
78.9mph 127.0kmh
0-50mph 80.5kmh: 15.7secs
0-60mph 96.5kmh: 23.9secs
18.0mpg 15.0mpgUS 15.7L/100km
Petrol 4-stroke piston
3298cc 201.2cu in
In-line 6
Bore: 79.4mm 3.1in
Stroke: 111.1mm 4.4in
Valve type/No: Side 12
Transmission: Manual
No. of forward speeds: 3
Wheels driven: Rear
Brakes F/R: Drum/Drum
Kerb weight: 1569.5kg 3457.0lb
Fuel: 61.4L 13.5gal 16.2galUS

968 Chrysler
Super Power Saloon
1937 USA
94.7mph 152.4kmh
0-50mph 80.5kmh: 11.7secs
0-60mph 96.5kmh: 16.9secs
12.0mpg 10.0mpgUS 23.5L/100km
Petrol 4-stroke piston
5299cc 323.3cu in
In-line 8
Bore: 82.6mm 3.2in
Stroke: 123.8mm 4.9in
Valve type/No: Side 16
Transmission: Manual
No. of forward speeds: 3
Wheels driven: Rear
Brakes F/R: Drum/Drum
Kerb weight: 1800.6kg 3966.0lb
Fuel: 58.2L 12.8gal 15.4galUS

969 Chrysler
Royal Saloon
1938 USA
83.3mph 134.0kmh
0-50mph 80.5kmh: 13.7secs
0-60mph 96.5kmh: 20.2secs
17.0mpg 14.2mpgUS 16.6L/100km
Petrol 4-stroke piston
3970cc 242.2cu in
In-line 6
Bore: 85.7mm 3.4in
Stroke: 114.3mm 4.5in
Valve type/No: Side 12
Transmission: Manual
No. of forward speeds: 3
Wheels driven: Rear
Brakes F/R: Drum/Drum
Kerb weight: 1567.7kg 3453.0lb
Fuel: 59.1L 13.0gal 15.6galUS

970 Chrysler
Saratoga Club Coupe
1951 USA
104.0mph 167.3kmh
0-60mph 96.5kmh: 10.0secs
0-1/4 mile: 18.7secs
180.0bhp 134.2kW 182.5PS
@ 4000rpm
312.0lbft 422.8Nm @ 2000rpm
102.1bhp/ton 100.4bhp/tonne
33.2bhp/L 24.7kW/L 33.6PS/L
40.3ft/sec 12.3m/sec
15.0mpg 12.5mpgUS 18.8L/100km
Petrol 4-stroke piston
5425cc 331.0cu in
Vee 8
Compression ratio: 7.5:1
Bore: 96.8mm 3.8in
Stroke: 92.1mm 3.6in
Valve type/No: Overhead 16
Transmission: Manual
No. of forward speeds: 4
Wheels driven: Rear
Wheelbase: 318.8cm 125.5in
Track F: 143.0cm 56.3in
Track R: 151.4cm 59.6in
Length: 527.8cm 207.8in
Width: 191.8cm 75.5in
Height: 165.1cm 65.0in
Ground clearance: 21.6cm 8.5in
Kerb weight: 1792.4kg 3948.0lb

971 Chrysler
New Yorker Saloon
1953 USA
107.0mph 172.2kmh
0-50mph 80.5kmh: 10.0secs
0-60mph 96.5kmh: 13.6secs
0-1/4 mile: 19.3secs
180.0bhp 134.2kW 182.5PS
@ 4000rpm
312.0lbft 422.8Nm @ 2000rpm
93.4bhp/ton 91.9bhp/tonne
33.1bhp/L 24.7kW/L 33.6PS/L
40.3ft/sec 12.3m/sec
25.1mph 40.4kmh/1000rpm
16.2mpg 13.5mpgUS 17.4L/100km
Petrol 4-stroke piston
5430cc 331.3cu in
Vee 8
Compression ratio: 7.5:1
Bore: 96.8mm 3.8in
Stroke: 92.1mm 3.6in
Valve type/No: Overhead 16
Transmission: Manual
No. of forward speeds: 4
Wheels driven: Rear
Springs F/R: Coil/Leaf
Brake system: PA
Brakes F/R: Drum/Drum
Wheelbase: 318.8cm 125.5in
Track F: 143.0cm 56.3in
Track R: 151.4cm 59.6in
Length: 535.9cm 211.0in
Width: 194.8cm 76.7in
Height: 159.3cm 62.7in
Ground clearance: 21.6cm 8.5in
Kerb weight: 1959.0kg 4315.0lb
Fuel: 76.0L 16.7gal 20.1galUS

972 Chrysler
Windsor de Luxe
1955 USA
104.5mph 168.1kmh
0-50mph 80.5kmh: 9.7secs
0-60mph 96.5kmh: 13.1secs
0-1/4 mile: 19.0secs
188.0bhp 140.2kW 190.6PS
@ 4400rpm
275.0lbft 372.6Nm @ 2400rpm
97.9bhp/ton 96.3bhp/tonne
38.1bhp/L 28.4kW/L 38.6PS/L
44.4ft/sec 13.5m/sec
22.8mph 36.7kmh/1000rpm
14.1mpg 11.7mpgUS 20.0L/100km
Petrol 4-stroke piston
4933cc 301.0cu in
Vee 8
Compression ratio: 8.0:1
Bore: 92.2mm 3.6in
Stroke: 92.2mm 3.6in
Valve type/No: Overhead 16
Transmission: Automatic
No. of forward speeds: 2
Wheels driven: Rear
Springs F/R: Coil/Leaf
Brake system: PA
Brakes F/R: Drum/Drum
Wheelbase: 320.0cm 126.0in
Track F: 152.9cm 60.2in
Track R: 151.4cm 59.6in
Length: 555.2cm 218.6in
Width: 200.9cm 79.1in
Height: 153.9cm 60.6in
Ground clearance: 15.7cm 6.2in
Kerb weight: 1952.2kg 4300.0lb
Fuel: 73.7L 16.2gal 19.5galUS

973 Chrysler
300-D
1958 USA
135.0mph 217.2kmh
0-50mph 80.5kmh: 6.7secs
0-60mph 96.5kmh: 8.4secs
0-1/4 mile: 16.0secs
380.0bhp 283.4kW 385.3PS
@ 5200rpm
435.0lbft 589.4Nm @ 3600rpm
173.0bhp/ton 170.1bhp/tonne
59.1bhp/L 44.1kW/L 59.9PS/L
56.3ft/sec 17.2m/sec
Petrol 4-stroke piston
6426cc 392.1cu in
Vee 8
Compression ratio: 10.0:1
Bore: 101.6mm 4.0in
Stroke: 99.1mm 3.9in
Valve type/No: Overhead 16
Transmission: Automatic
No. of forward speeds: 3
Wheels driven: Rear
Wheelbase: 320.0cm 126.0in
Track F: 155.4cm 61.2in
Track R: 152.4cm 60.0in
Kerb weight: 2233.7kg 4920.0lb

974 Chrysler
Valiant
1960 Australia
96.0mph 154.5kmh
0-50mph 80.5kmh: 13.1secs
0-60mph 96.5kmh: 17.7secs
0-1/4 mile: 21.1secs
101.0bhp 75.3kW 102.4PS
@ 4400rpm
155.0lbft 210.0Nm @ 2400rpm
80.2bhp/ton 78.9bhp/tonne
36.2bhp/L 27.0kW/L 36.8PS/L
38.3ft/sec 11.7m/sec
21.7mph 34.9kmh/1000rpm
19.1mpg 15.9mpgUS 14.8L/100km
Petrol 4-stroke piston
2786cc 170.0cu in
In-line 6
Compression ratio: 8.5:1
Bore: 83.3mm 3.3in
Stroke: 79.6mm 3.1in
Valve type/No: Overhead 12
Transmission: Automatic
No. of forward speeds: 3
Wheels driven: Rear
Springs F/R: Torsion bar/Leaf
Brake system: PA
Brakes F/R: Drum/Drum
Wheelbase: 270.5cm 106.5in
Track F: 142.2cm 56.0in
Track R: 141.0cm 55.5in
Length: 467.4cm 184.0in
Width: 178.8cm 70.4in
Height: 137.2cm 54.0in
Ground clearance: 15.7cm 6.2in
Kerb weight: 1280.7kg 2821.0lb
Fuel: 59.1L 13.0gal 15.6galUS

975 Chrysler
300-G
1961 USA
131.0mph 210.8kmh
0-50mph 80.5kmh: 6.1secs
0-60mph 96.5kmh: 8.4secs
0-1/4 mile: 16.2secs
375.0bhp 279.6kW 380.2PS
@ 5000rpm
495.0lbft 670.7Nm @ 2800rpm
186.0bhp/ton 182.9bhp/tonne
55.4bhp/L 41.3kW/L 56.2PS/L
52.1ft/sec 15.9m/sec
26.2mph 42.2kmh/1000rpm
Petrol 4-stroke piston
6770cc 413.1cu in
Vee 8 1 Carburettor
Compression ratio: 10.1:1
Bore: 106.2mm 4.2in
Stroke: 95.3mm 3.8in
Valve type/No: Overhead 16
Transmission: Automatic
No. of forward speeds: 3
Wheels driven: Rear
Brake system: PA
Brakes F/R: Drum/Drum
Steering: PA
Wheelbase: 320.0cm 126.0in
Track F: 155.4cm 61.2in
Track R: 155.4cm 61.2in
Length: 558.8cm 220.0in

Width: 201.7cm 79.4in
Height: 142.2cm 56.0in
Ground clearance: 16.0cm 6.3in
Kerb weight: 2049.8kg 4515.0lb

976 Chrysler
Enforcer
1961 USA
130.0mph 209.2kmh
0-50mph 80.5kmh: 6.0secs
0-60mph 96.5kmh: 8.3secs
0-1/4 mile: 16.9secs
325.0bhp 242.3kW 329.5PS
@ 4600rpm
425.0lbft 575.9Nm @ 2800rpm
177.6bhp/ton 174.6bhp/tonne
51.8bhp/L 38.6kW/L 52.5PS/L
43.2ft/sec 13.2m/sec
25.4mph 40.9kmh/1000rpm
Petrol 4-stroke piston
6279cc 383.1cu in
Vee 8 1 Carburettor
Compression ratio: 10.0:1
Bore: 108.0mm 4.2in
Stroke: 85.9mm 3.4in
Valve type/No: Overhead 16
Transmission: Automatic
No. of forward speeds: 3
Wheels driven: Rear
Brakes F/R: Drum/Drum
Wheelbase: 309.9cm 122.0in
Track F: 154.9cm 61.0in
Track R: 151.6cm 59.7in
Length: 548.6cm 216.0in
Width: 201.7cm 79.4in
Height: 139.7cm 55.0in
Ground clearance: 13.2cm 5.2in
Kerb weight: 1861.4kg 4100.0lb

977 Chrysler
Imperial
1961 USA
120.0mph 193.1kmh
0-50mph 80.5kmh: 7.5secs
0-60mph 96.5kmh: 10.0secs
0-1/4 mile: 17.0secs
350.0bhp 261.0kW 354.8PS
@ 4600rpm
470.0lbft 636.9Nm @ 2800rpm
153.4bhp/ton 150.9bhp/tonne
51.7bhp/L 38.5kW/L 52.4PS/L
47.9ft/sec 14.6m/sec
26.5mph 42.6kmh/1000rpm
Petrol 4-stroke piston
6771cc 413.1cu in
Vee 8
Compression ratio: 10.1:1
Bore: 106.4mm 4.2in
Stroke: 95.3mm 3.8in
Valve type/No: Overhead 16
Transmission: Automatic
No. of forward speeds: 3
Wheels driven: Rear
Brake system: PA
Brakes F/R: Drum/Drum
Steering: PA
Wheelbase: 327.7cm 129.0in
Track F: 157.0cm 61.8in
Track R: 158.0cm 62.2in
Length: 577.3cm 227.3in
Width: 207.5cm 81.7in
Height: 144.0cm 56.7in
Ground clearance: 14.2cm 5.6in
Kerb weight: 2319.9kg 5110.0lb

978 Chrysler
Newport
1961 USA
117.0mph 188.3kmh
0-50mph 80.5kmh: 8.0secs
0-60mph 96.5kmh: 10.9secs
0-1/4 mile: 18.1secs
265.0bhp 197.6kW 268.7PS
@ 4400rpm
380.0lbft 514.9Nm @ 2400rpm
140.5bhp/ton 138.1bhp/tonne
44.7bhp/L 33.3kW/L 45.3PS/L
41.3ft/sec 12.6m/sec
26.6mph 42.8kmh/1000rpm
Petrol 4-stroke piston
5934cc 362.0cu in
Vee 8 1 Carburettor
Compression ratio: 9.0:1
Bore: 104.6mm 4.1in
Stroke: 85.9mm 3.4in
Valve type/No: Overhead 16
Transmission: Automatic
No. of forward speeds: 3
Wheels driven: Rear
Brake system: PA
Brakes F/R: Drum/Drum
Steering: PA
Wheelbase: 309.9cm 122.0in
Track F: 154.9cm 61.0in
Track R: 151.6cm 59.7in
Length: 547.6cm 215.6in
Width: 201.7cm 79.4in
Height: 139.7cm 55.0in
Ground clearance: 13.2cm 5.2in
Kerb weight: 1918.1kg 4225.0lb

979 Chrysler
300
1962 USA
120.0mph 193.1kmh
0-50mph 80.5kmh: 6.5secs
0-60mph 96.5kmh: 8.7secs
0-1/4 mile: 16.7secs
340.0bhp 253.5kW 344.7PS
@ 4600rpm
470.0lbft 636.9Nm @ 2800rpm
179.6bhp/ton 176.6bhp/tonne
50.2bhp/L 37.5kW/L 50.9PS/L
47.9ft/sec 14.6m/sec
24.4mph 39.3kmh/1000rpm
Petrol 4-stroke piston
6768cc 412.9cu in
Vee 8 1 Carburettor
Compression ratio: 10.0:1
Bore: 106.4mm 4.2in
Stroke: 95.3mm 3.8in
Valve type/No: Overhead 16
Transmission: Automatic
No. of forward speeds: 3
Wheels driven: Rear
Brake system: PA
Steering: PA
Wheelbase: 309.9cm 122.0in
Track F: 154.7cm 60.9in
Track R: 151.6cm 59.7in
Length: 545.8cm 214.9in
Width: 201.7cm 79.4in
Height: 140.2cm 55.2in
Ground clearance: 13.7cm 5.4in
Kerb weight: 1925.0kg 4240.0lb
Fuel: 87.1L 19.1gal 23.0galUS

980 Chrysler
300-H
1962 USA
133.0mph 214.0kmh
0-50mph 80.5kmh: 6.0secs
0-60mph 96.5kmh: 7.7secs
0-1/4 mile: 16.0secs
380.0bhp 283.4kW 385.3PS
@ 5200rpm
450.0lbft 609.8Nm @ 3600rpm
201.7bhp/ton 198.3bhp/tonne
56.1bhp/L 41.9kW/L 56.9PS/L
54.2ft/sec 16.5m/sec
25.5mph 41.0kmh/1000rpm
Petrol 4-stroke piston
6768cc 412.9cu in
Vee 8
Compression ratio: 10.1:1
Bore: 106.4mm 4.2in
Stroke: 95.3mm 3.8in
Valve type/No: Overhead 16
Transmission: Automatic
No. of forward speeds: 3
Wheels driven: Rear
Brake system: PA
Steering: PA
Wheelbase: 309.9cm 122.0in
Track F: 155.2cm 61.1in
Track R: 152.4cm 60.0in
Length: 546.9cm 215.3in
Width: 201.7cm 79.4in
Height: 141.5cm 55.7in
Ground clearance: 13.5cm 5.3in
Kerb weight: 1915.9kg 4220.0lb
Fuel: 87.1L 19.1gal 23.0galUS

981 Chrysler
300-J
1963 USA
130.0mph 209.2kmh
0-50mph 80.5kmh: 6.4secs
0-60mph 96.5kmh: 7.9secs
0-1/4 mile: 16.5secs
390.0bhp 290.8kW 395.4PS
@ 4800rpm
485.0lbft 657.2Nm @ 3600rpm
197.6bhp/ton 194.3bhp/tonne
57.6bhp/L 43.0kW/L 58.4PS/L
50.0ft/sec 15.2m/sec
25.0mph 40.2kmh/1000rpm
Petrol 4-stroke piston
6768cc 412.9cu in
Vee 8 2 Carburettor
Compression ratio: 9.6:1
Bore: 106.4mm 4.2in
Stroke: 95.3mm 3.8in
Valve type/No: Overhead 16
Transmission: Automatic
No. of forward speeds: 3
Wheels driven: Rear
Brake system: PA
Brakes F/R: Drum/Drum
Steering: PA
Wheelbase: 309.9cm 122.0in
Track F: 154.9cm 61.0in
Track R: 151.6cm 59.7in
Length: 547.4cm 215.5in
Width: 200.7cm 79.0in
Height: 141.2cm 55.6in
Ground clearance: 15.5cm 6.1in
Kerb weight: 2006.7kg 4420.0lb
Fuel: 87.1L 19.1gal 23.0galUS

982 Chrysler
Imperial Le Baron
1964 USA
121.0mph 194.7kmh
0-50mph 80.5kmh: 8.8secs
0-60mph 96.5kmh: 10.4secs
0-1/4 mile: 18.2secs
340.0bhp 253.5kW 344.7PS
@ 4600rpm
470.0lbft 636.9Nm @ 2800rpm
142.6bhp/ton 140.2bhp/tonne
50.2bhp/L 37.5kW/L 50.9PS/L
47.9ft/sec 14.6m/sec
28.4mph 45.7kmh/1000rpm
Petrol 4-stroke piston
6768cc 412.9cu in
Vee 8 1 Carburettor
Compression ratio: 10.1:1
Bore: 106.4mm 4.2in
Stroke: 95.3mm 3.8in
Valve type/No: Overhead 16
Transmission: Automatic
No. of forward speeds: 3
Wheels driven: Rear
Brake system: PA
Brakes F/R: Drum/Drum
Steering: PA
Wheelbase: 327.7cm 129.0in
Track F: 157.0cm 61.8in
Track R: 156.7cm 61.7in
Length: 578.6cm 227.8in
Width: 203.2cm 80.0in
Height: 144.3cm 56.8in
Ground clearance: 14.2cm 5.6in
Kerb weight: 2424.4kg 5340.0lb
Fuel: 87.1L 19.1gal 23.0galUS

983 Chrysler
Newport
1965 USA
110.0mph 177.0kmh
0-50mph 80.5kmh: 7.3secs
0-60mph 96.5kmh: 9.6secs
0-1/4 mile: 17.1secs
315.0bhp 234.9kW 319.4PS
@ 4400rpm
420.0lbft 569.1Nm @ 2800rpm
163.7bhp/ton 161.0bhp/tonne
50.2bhp/L 37.4kW/L 50.9PS/L
41.3ft/sec 12.6m/sec
24.9mph 40.1kmh/1000rpm
Petrol 4-stroke piston
6276cc 382.9cu in
Vee 8 1 Carburettor
Compression ratio: 10.0:1
Bore: 108.0mm 4.2in
Stroke: 85.9mm 3.4in
Valve type/No: Overhead 16
Transmission: Automatic
No. of forward speeds: 3
Wheels driven: Rear
Brake system: PA
Steering: PA
Wheelbase: 315.0cm 124.0in
Track F: 157.5cm 62.0in
Track R: 154.2cm 60.7in
Length: 554.2cm 218.2in
Width: 201.9cm 79.5in
Height: 139.4cm 54.9in
Ground clearance: 13.7cm 5.4in
Kerb weight: 1956.7kg 4310.0lb
Fuel: 94.6L 20.8gal 25.0galUS

984 Chrysler
300
1966 USA
120.0mph 193.1kmh
0-50mph 80.5kmh: 5.8secs
0-60mph 96.5kmh: 7.7secs
0-1/4 mile: 16.1secs
365.0bhp 272.2kW 370.1PS
@ 4600rpm
480.0lbft 650.4Nm @ 3200rpm
173.2bhp/ton 170.3bhp/tonne
50.6bhp/L 37.7kW/L 51.3PS/L
47.9ft/sec 14.6m/sec
25.2mph 40.5kmh/1000rpm
Petrol 4-stroke piston
7210cc 439.9cu in
Vee 8 1 Carburettor
Compression ratio: 10.1:1
Bore: 109.7mm 4.3in
Stroke: 95.3mm 3.8in
Valve type/No: Overhead 16
Transmission: Automatic
No. of forward speeds: 3
Wheels driven: Rear
Springs F/R: Torsion bar/Leaf
Brake system: PA
Brakes F/R: Disc/Drum
Steering: Rack & sector PA
Wheelbase: 315.0cm 124.0in
Track F: 157.5cm 62.0in
Track R: 154.2cm 60.7in
Length: 563.6cm 221.9in
Width: 201.9cm 79.5in
Height: 138.7cm 54.6in
Ground clearance: 18.3cm 7.2in
Kerb weight: 2142.9kg 4720.0lb
Fuel: 94.6L 20.8gal 25.0galUS

985 Chrysler
Turbine
1966 USA
0-60mph 96.5kmh: 10.0secs
130.0bhp 96.9kW 131.8PS
@ 3600rpm
425.0lbft 575.9Nm
74.7bhp/ton 73.4bhp/tonne
Gas turbine
Transmission: Automatic
No. of forward speeds: 3
Wheels driven: Rear
Springs F/R: Coil/Leaf
Brake system: PA
Brakes F/R: Drum/Drum
Steering: Recirculating ball PA
Wheelbase: 279.4cm 110.0in
Track F: 149.9cm 59.0in
Track R: 144.0cm 56.7in
Length: 512.1cm 201.6in
Width: 185.2cm 72.9in
Height: 135.9cm 53.5in
Kerb weight: 1770.6kg 3900.0lb
Fuel: 79.5L 17.5gal 21.0galUS

986 Chrysler
Valiant Premium Auto
1966 Australia
109.0mph 175.4kmh
0-50mph 80.5kmh: 8.3secs
0-60mph 96.5kmh: 11.3secs
0-1/4 mile: 18.0secs
0-1km: 33.5secs
180.0bhp 134.2kW 182.5PS
@ 4200rpm
260.0lbft 352.3Nm @ 1600rpm
128.6bhp/ton 126.4bhp/tonne
40.2bhp/L 30.0kW/L 40.8PS/L
38.6ft/sec 11.8m/sec
22.0mph 35.4kmh/1000rpm
18.1mpg 15.1mpgUS 15.6L/100km
Petrol 4-stroke piston
4473cc 272.9cu in
Vee 8 1 Carburettor
Compression ratio: 8.8:1
Bore: 92.2mm 3.6in
Stroke: 84.2mm 3.3in
Valve type/No: Overhead 16
Transmission: Automatic
No. of forward speeds: 3
Wheels driven: Rear
Springs F/R: Torsion bar/Leaf
Brake system: PA
Brakes F/R: Disc/Drum

Steering: Recirculating ball
Wheelbase: 269.2cm 106.0in
Track F: 142.2cm 56.0in
Track R: 141.5cm 55.7in
Length: 478.0cm 188.2in
Width: 177.8cm 70.0in
Height: 139.7cm 55.0in
Ground clearance: 17.8cm 7.0in
Kerb weight: 1423.7kg 3136.0lb
Fuel: 65.1L 14.3gal 17.2galUS

987 Chrysler

Imperial Crown
1967 USA
117.0mph 188.3kmh
0-50mph 80.5kmh: 7.3secs
0-60mph 96.5kmh: 9.6secs
0-1/4 mile: 17.4secs
350.0bhp 261.0kW 354.8PS
@ 4400rpm
480.0lbft 650.4Nm @ 2800rpm
149.9bhp/ton 147.4bhp/tonne
48.6bhp/L 36.2kW/L 49.3PS/L
45.8ft/sec 14.0m/sec
27.5mph 44.2kmh/1000rpm
Petrol 4-stroke piston
7202cc 439.4cu in
Vee 8 1 Carburettor
Compression ratio: 10.1:1
Bore: 109.7mm 4.3in
Stroke: 95.3mm 3.8in
Valve type/No: Overhead 16
Transmission: Automatic
No. of forward speeds: 3
Wheels driven: Rear
Springs F/R: Torsion bar/Leaf
Brake system: PA
Brakes F/R: Disc/Drum
Steering: Recirculating ball PA
Wheelbase: 322.6cm 127.0in
Track F: 158.5cm 62.4in
Track R: 155.2cm 61.1in
Length: 570.7cm 224.7in
Width: 202.2cm 79.6in
Height: 142.7cm 56.2in
Ground clearance: 14.0cm 5.5in
Kerb weight: 2374.4kg 5230.0lb
Fuel: 94.6L 20.8gal 25.0galUS

988 Chrysler

300
1969 USA
119.0mph 191.5kmh
0-50mph 80.5kmh: 6.5secs
0-60mph 96.5kmh: 8.5secs
0-1/4 mile: 16.1secs
350.0bhp 261.0kW 354.8PS
@ 4400rpm
480.0lbft 650.4Nm @ 2800rpm
176.2bhp/ton 173.2bhp/tonne
48.5bhp/L 36.2kW/L 49.2PS/L
45.8ft/sec 14.0m/sec
25.4mph 40.9kmh/1000rpm
Petrol 4-stroke piston
7210cc 439.9cu in
Vee 8 1 Carburettor
Compression ratio: 10.1:1
Bore: 109.7mm 4.3in
Stroke: 95.3mm 3.8in
Valve type/No: Overhead 16
Transmission: Automatic
No. of forward speeds: 3
Wheels driven: Rear
Springs F/R: Torsion bar/Leaf
Brake system: PA
Brakes F/R: Drum/Drum
Steering: Recirculating ball PA
Wheelbase: 315.0cm 124.0in
Track F: 157.5cm 62.0in
Track R: 152.4cm 60.0in
Length: 571.5cm 225.0in
Width: 200.7cm 79.0in
Height: 139.7cm 55.0in
Kerb weight: 2020.3kg 4450.0lb
Fuel: 90.8L 20.0gal 24.0galUS

989 Chrysler

300-H
1970 USA
127.0mph 204.3kmh
0-50mph 80.5kmh: 5.5secs
0-60mph 96.5kmh: 7.1secs
0-1/4 mile: 15.3secs
375.0bhp 279.6kW 380.2PS
@ 4600rpm
480.0lbft 650.4Nm @ 3200rpm
189.2bhp/ton 186.0bhp/tonne
52.0bhp/L 38.8kW/L 52.7PS/L
47.9ft/sec 14.6m/sec
24.4mph 39.3kmh/1000rpm
15.5mpg 12.9mpgUS 18.2L/100km
Petrol 4-stroke piston
7210cc 439.9cu in
Vee 8 1 Carburettor
Compression ratio: 9.7:1
Bore: 109.7mm 4.3in
Stroke: 95.3mm 3.8in
Valve type/No: Overhead 16
Transmission: Automatic
No. of forward speeds: 3
Wheels driven: Rear
Springs F/R: Torsion bar/Leaf
Brake system: PA
Brakes F/R: Disc/Drum
Steering: Recirculating ball PA
Wheelbase: 315.0cm 124.0in
Track F: 157.7cm 62.1in
Track R: 157.5cm 62.0in
Length: 571.8cm 225.1in
Width: 200.7cm 79.0in
Height: 138.9cm 54.7in
Kerb weight: 2015.8kg 4440.0lb
Fuel: 90.8L 20.0gal 24.0galUS

990 Chrysler

Charger
1970 Australia
116.0mph 186.6kmh
0-50mph 80.5kmh: 7.0secs
0-60mph 96.5kmh: 9.3secs
0-1/4 mile: 16.7secs
0-1km: 30.8secs
230.0bhp 171.5kW 233.2PS
@ 4400rpm
340.0lbft 460.7Nm @ 1600rpm
157.3bhp/ton 154.6bhp/tonne
44.1bhp/L 32.9kW/L 44.8PS/L
40.5ft/sec 12.3m/sec
25.4mph 40.9kmh/1000rpm
14.0mpg 11.7mpgUS 20.2L/100km
Petrol 4-stroke piston
5210cc 317.9cu in
Vee 8 1 Carburettor
Compression ratio: 9.2:1
Bore: 99.3mm 3.9in
Stroke: 84.1mm 3.3in
Valve type/No: Overhead 16
Transmission: Automatic
No. of forward speeds: 3
Wheels driven: Rear
Springs F/R: Torsion bar/Leaf
Brake system: PA
Brakes F/R: Disc/Drum
Steering: Recirculating ball PA
Wheelbase: 264.2cm 104.0in
Track F: 143.5cm 56.5in
Track R: 143.5cm 56.5in
Length: 463.6cm 182.5in
Width: 177.8cm 70.0in
Height: 134.6cm 53.0in
Ground clearance: 19.1cm 7.5in
Kerb weight: 1487.3kg 3276.0lb
Fuel: 79.6L 17.5gal 21.0galUS

991 Chrysler

180
1971 UK
101.0mph 162.5kmh
0-50mph 80.5kmh: 9.1secs
0-60mph 96.5kmh: 13.6secs
0-1/4 mile: 19.0secs
0-1km: 35.5secs
97.0bhp 72.3kW 98.3PS
@ 5600rpm
106.0lbft 143.6Nm @ 3000rpm
93.1bhp/ton 91.5bhp/tonne
51.5bhp/L 38.4kW/L 52.3PS/L
45.9ft/sec 14.0m/sec
18.1mph 29.1kmh/1000rpm
23.5mpg 19.6mpgUS 12.0L/100km
Petrol 4-stroke piston
1882cc 114.8cu in
In-line 4 1 Carburettor
Compression ratio: 9.2:1
Bore: 87.7mm 3.4in
Stroke: 75.0mm 2.9in
Valve type/No: Overhead 8
Transmission: Manual
No. of forward speeds: 4
Wheels driven: Rear
Springs F/R: Coil/Coil
Brake system: PA
Brakes F/R: Disc/Disc
Steering: Rack & pinion
Wheelbase: 266.7cm 105.0in
Track F: 142.2cm 56.0in
Track R: 142.2cm 56.0in
Length: 445.8cm 175.5in
Width: 170.2cm 67.0in
Height: 147.3cm 58.0in
Ground clearance: 14.0cm 5.5in
Kerb weight: 1059.6kg 2334.0lb
Fuel: 65.1L 14.3gal 17.2galUS

992 Chrysler

2-litre
1973 UK
105.0mph 168.9kmh
0-50mph 80.5kmh: 9.4secs
0-60mph 96.5kmh: 12.8secs
0-1/4 mile: 19.2secs
0-1km: 34.9secs
110.0bhp 82.0kW 111.5PS
@ 5600rpm
118.0lbft 159.9Nm @ 3600rpm
100.6bhp/ton 98.9bhp/tonne
55.5bhp/L 41.4kW/L 56.3PS/L
45.9ft/sec 14.0m/sec
18.5mph 29.8kmh/1000rpm
23.1mpg 19.2mpgUS 12.2L/100km
Petrol 4-stroke piston
1981cc 120.9cu in
In-line 4 1 Carburettor
Compression ratio: 9.4:1
Bore: 91.7mm 3.6in
Stroke: 75.0mm 2.9in
Valve type/No: Overhead 8
Transmission: Automatic
No. of forward speeds: 3
Wheels driven: Rear
Springs F/R: Coil/Coil
Brake system: PA
Brakes F/R: Disc/Disc
Steering: Rack & pinion
Wheelbase: 266.7cm 105.0in
Track F: 142.2cm 56.0in
Track R: 142.2cm 56.0in
Length: 445.8cm 175.5in
Width: 170.2cm 67.0in
Height: 147.3cm 58.0in
Ground clearance: 14.0cm 5.5in
Kerb weight: 1112.3kg 2450.0lb
Fuel: 65.1L 14.3gal 17.2galUS

993 Chrysler

Alpine S
1976 UK
105.0mph 168.9kmh
0-50mph 80.5kmh: 9.0secs
0-60mph 96.5kmh: 13.3secs
0-1/4 mile: 19.3secs
0-1km: 36.0secs
85.0bhp 63.4kW 86.2PS
@ 5600rpm
93.0lbft 126.0Nm @ 3000rpm
81.4bhp/ton 80.0bhp/tonne
58.9bhp/L 43.9kW/L 59.8PS/L
47.8ft/sec 14.6m/sec
16.9mph 27.2kmh/1000rpm
29.3mpg 24.4mpgUS 9.6L/100km
Petrol 4-stroke piston
1442cc 88.0cu in
In-line 4 1 Carburettor
Compression ratio: 9.5:1
Bore: 76.7mm 3.0in
Stroke: 78.0mm 3.1in
Valve type/No: Overhead 8
Transmission: Manual
No. of forward speeds: 4
Wheels driven: Front
Springs F/R: Torsion bar/Coil
Brake system: PA
Brakes F/R: Disc/Drum
Steering: Rack & pinion
Wheelbase: 260.4cm 102.5in
Track F: 141.5cm 55.7in
Track R: 138.9cm 54.7in
Length: 424.4cm 167.1in
Width: 167.9cm 66.1in
Height: 140.0cm 55.1in
Ground clearance: 20.3cm 8.0in
Kerb weight: 1062.4kg 2340.0lb
Fuel: 60.1L 13.2gal 15.9galUS

994 Chrysler

Avenger Super 1300
1976 UK
91.0mph 146.4kmh
0-50mph 80.5kmh: 12.5secs
0-60mph 96.5kmh: 17.5secs
0-1/4 mile: 20.6secs
0-1km: 39.0secs
59.0bhp 44.0kW 59.8PS
@ 5000rpm
69.0lbft 93.5Nm @ 2600rpm
69.7bhp/ton 68.6bhp/tonne
45.6bhp/L 34.0kW/L 46.2PS/L
36.5ft/sec 11.1m/sec
16.8mph 27.0kmh/1000rpm
32.6mpg 27.1mpgUS 8.7L/100km
Petrol 4-stroke piston
1295cc 79.0cu in
In-line 4 1 Carburettor
Compression ratio: 8.8:1
Bore: 76.6mm 3.0in
Stroke: 66.7mm 2.6in
Valve type/No: Overhead 8
Transmission: Manual
No. of forward speeds: 4
Wheels driven: Rear
Springs F/R: Coil/Coil
Brake system: PA
Brakes F/R: Disc/Drum
Steering: Rack & pinion
Wheelbase: 248.9cm 98.0in
Track F: 129.5cm 51.0in
Track R: 130.8cm 51.5in
Length: 408.9cm 161.0in
Width: 159.0cm 62.6in
Height: 139.7cm 55.0in
Ground clearance: 14.0cm 5.5in
Kerb weight: 860.3kg 1895.0lb
Fuel: 44.6L 9.8gal 11.8galUS

995 Chrysler

Alpine GL
1977 UK
93.0mph 149.6kmh
0-50mph 80.5kmh: 11.3secs
0-60mph 96.5kmh: 16.9secs
0-1/4 mile: 20.5secs
0-1km: 38.9secs
68.0bhp 50.7kW 68.9PS
@ 5600rpm
79.0lbft 107.0Nm @ 2800rpm
65.7bhp/ton 64.6bhp/tonne
52.5bhp/L 39.2kW/L 53.3PS/L
42.9ft/sec 13.1m/sec
17.6mph 28.3kmh/1000rpm
29.2mpg 24.3mpgUS 9.7L/100km
Petrol 4-stroke piston
1294cc 78.9cu in
In-line 4 1 Carburettor
Compression ratio: 9.5:1
Bore: 76.7mm 3.0in
Stroke: 70.0mm 2.8in
Valve type/No: Overhead 8
Transmission: Manual
No. of forward speeds: 4
Wheels driven: Front
Springs F/R: Torsion bar/Coil
Brake system: PA
Brakes F/R: Disc/Drum
Steering: Rack & pinion
Wheelbase: 260.4cm 102.5in
Track F: 141.5cm 55.7in
Track R: 138.9cm 54.7in
Length: 424.4cm 167.1in
Width: 167.9cm 66.1in
Height: 140.0cm 55.1in
Ground clearance: 20.3cm 8.0in
Kerb weight: 1052.4kg 2318.0lb
Fuel: 60.1L 13.2gal 15.9galUS

996 Chrysler

Avenger 1600 Estate
1977 UK
94.0mph 151.2kmh
0-50mph 80.5kmh: 9.5secs
0-60mph 96.5kmh: 14.1secs
0-1/4 mile: 19.5secs
0-1km: 37.0secs
69.0bhp 51.4kW 70.0PS
@ 4800rpm
91.0lbft 123.3Nm @ 2900rpm
73.4bhp/ton 72.1bhp/tonne
43.2bhp/L 32.2kW/L 43.8PS/L
35.1ft/sec 10.7m/sec
17.6mph 28.3kmh/1000rpm
28.2mpg 23.5mpgUS 10.0L/100km
Petrol 4-stroke piston
1598cc 97.5cu in
In-line 4 1 Carburettor
Compression ratio: 8.8:1
Bore: 87.4mm 3.4in
Stroke: 66.7mm 2.6in

Valve type/No: Overhead 8
Transmission: Manual
No. of forward speeds: 4
Wheels driven: Rear
Springs F/R: Coil/Coil
Brake system: PA
Brakes F/R: Disc/Drum
Steering: Rack & pinion
Wheelbase: 248.9cm 98.0in
Track F: 129.5cm 51.0in
Track R: 130.8cm 51.5in
Length: 414.0cm 163.0in
Width: 158.8cm 62.5in
Height: 139.7cm 55.0in
Ground clearance: 14.0cm 5.5in
Kerb weight: 956.6kg 2107.0lb
Fuel: 44.6L 9.8gal 11.8galUS

997 Chrysler

Sunbeam 1.0LS
1977 UK
80.0mph 128.7kmh
0-50mph 80.5kmh: 15.5secs
0-60mph 96.5kmh: 24.3secs
0-1/4 mile: 22.7secs
0-1km: 43.5secs
42.0bhp 31.3kW 42.6PS
@ 5000rpm
51.0lbft 69.1Nm @ 2600rpm
53.5bhp/ton 52.6bhp/tonne
45.3bhp/L 33.7kW/L 45.9PS/L
32.9ft/sec 10.0m/sec
14.5mph 23.3kmh/1000rpm
31.5mpg 26.2mpgUS 9.0L/100km
Petrol 4-stroke piston
928cc 56.6cu in
In-line 4 1 Carburettor
Compression ratio: 9.0:1
Bore: 70.0mm 2.8in
Stroke: 60.3mm 2.4in
Valve type/No: Overhead 8
Transmission: Manual
No. of forward speeds: 4
Wheels driven: Rear
Springs F/R: Coil/Coil
Brake system: PA
Brakes F/R: Disc/Disc
Steering: Rack & pinion
Wheelbase: 241.3cm 95.0in
Track F: 131.6cm 51.8in
Track R: 130.3cm 51.3in
Length: 382.8cm 150.7in
Width: 160.3cm 63.1in
Height: 139.4cm 54.9in
Ground clearance: 16.5cm 6.5in
Kerb weight: 797.7kg 1757.0lb
Fuel: 40.9L 9.0gal 10.8galUS

998 Chrysler

Sunbeam 1.6S
1977 UK
101.0mph 162.5kmh
0-50mph 80.5kmh: 8.8secs
0-60mph 96.5kmh: 12.9secs
0-1/4 mile: 19.2secs
0-1km: 36.5secs
69.0bhp 51.4kW 70.0PS
@ 4800rpm
91.0lbft 123.3Nm @ 2900rpm
79.1bhp/ton 77.8bhp/tonne
43.2bhp/L 32.2kW/L 43.8PS/L
35.1ft/sec 10.7m/sec
18.4mph 29.6kmh/1000rpm
30.6mpg 25.5mpgUS 9.2L/100km
Petrol 4-stroke piston
1598cc 97.5cu in
In-line 4 1 Carburettor
Compression ratio: 8.8:1
Bore: 87.3mm 3.4in
Stroke: 66.7mm 2.6in
Valve type/No: Overhead 8
Transmission: Manual
No. of forward speeds: 4
Wheels driven: Rear
Springs F/R: Coil/Coil
Brake system: PA
Brakes F/R: Disc/Drum
Steering: Rack & pinion
Wheelbase: 241.3cm 95.0in
Track F: 131.6cm 51.8in
Track R: 130.3cm 51.3in
Length: 382.8cm 150.7in
Width: 160.3cm 63.1in
Height: 139.4cm 54.9in
Ground clearance: 16.5cm 6.5in
Kerb weight: 886.7kg 1953.0lb
Fuel: 40.9L 9.0gal 10.8galUS

999 Chrysler

1300 GL
1978 UK
96.0mph 154.5kmh
0-50mph 80.5kmh: 10.5secs
0-60mph 96.5kmh: 14.8secs
0-1/4 mile: 21.0secs
0-1km: 37.7secs
59.0bhp 44.0kW 59.8PS
@ 5000rpm
69.0lbft 93.5Nm @ 2600rpm
66.0bhp/ton 64.9bhp/tonne
45.6bhp/L 34.0kW/L 46.2PS/L
36.4ft/sec 11.1m/sec
17.6mph 28.3kmh/1000rpm
29.4mpg 24.5mpgUS 9.6L/100km
Petrol 4-stroke piston
1295cc 79.0cu in
In-line 4 1 Carburettor
Compression ratio: 8.8:1
Bore: 78.6mm 3.1in
Stroke: 66.6mm 2.6in
Valve type/No: Overhead 8
Transmission: Manual
No. of forward speeds: 4
Wheels driven: Rear
Springs F/R: Coil/Coil
Brake system: PA
Brakes F/R: Disc/Drum
Steering: Rack & pinion
Wheelbase: 241.3cm 95.0in
Track F: 131.6cm 51.8in
Track R: 130.3cm 51.3in
Length: 382.8cm 150.7in
Width: 160.3cm 63.1in
Height: 139.4cm 54.9in
Ground clearance: 16.5cm 6.5in
Kerb weight: 908.9kg 2002.0lb
Fuel: 40.9L 9.0gal 10.8galUS

1000 Chrysler

Alpine GLS
1978 UK
102.0mph 164.1kmh
0-50mph 80.5kmh: 8.6secs
0-60mph 96.5kmh: 12.6secs
0-1/4 mile: 18.9secs
0-1km: 35.6secs
85.0bhp 63.4kW 86.2PS
@ 5600rpm
94.0lbft 127.4Nm @ 3000rpm
80.7bhp/ton 79.4bhp/tonne
58.9bhp/L 43.9kW/L 59.8PS/L
47.8ft/sec 14.6m/sec
16.9mph 27.2kmh/1000rpm
27.7mpg 23.1mpgUS 10.2L/100km
Petrol 4-stroke piston
1442cc 88.0cu in
In-line 4 1 Carburettor
Compression ratio: 9.5:1
Bore: 76.7mm 3.0in
Stroke: 78.0mm 3.1in
Valve type/No: Overhead 8
Transmission: Manual
No. of forward speeds: 4
Wheels driven: Front
Springs F/R: Torsion bar/Coil
Brake system: PA
Brakes F/R: Disc/Drum
Steering: Rack & pinion
Wheelbase: 260.4cm 102.5in
Track F: 141.5cm 55.7in
Track R: 138.9cm 54.7in
Length: 424.4cm 167.1in
Width: 167.9cm 66.1in
Height: 140.0cm 55.1in
Ground clearance: 20.3cm 8.0in
Kerb weight: 1071.0kg 2359.0lb
Fuel: 60.1L 13.2gal 15.9galUS

1001 Chrysler

Horizon GL
1978 UK
100.0mph 160.9kmh
0-50mph 80.5kmh: 10.0secs
0-60mph 96.5kmh: 15.3secs
0-1/4 mile: 20.3secs
0-1km: 38.3secs
59.0bhp 44.0kW 59.8PS
@ 5600rpm
67.0lbft 90.8Nm @ 3000rpm
63.5bhp/ton 62.4bhp/tonne
52.8bhp/L 39.4kW/L 53.5PS/L
39.8ft/sec 12.1m/sec
16.1mph 25.9kmh/1000rpm
30.9mpg 25.7mpgUS 9.1L/100km
Petrol 4-stroke piston
1118cc 68.2cu in
In-line 4 1 Carburettor
Compression ratio: 9.6:1
Bore: 74.0mm 2.9in
Stroke: 65.0mm 2.6in
Valve type/No: Overhead 8
Transmission: Manual
No. of forward speeds: 4
Wheels driven: Front
Springs F/R: Torsion bar/Coil
Brake system: PA
Brakes F/R: Disc/Drum
Steering: Rack & pinion
Wheelbase: 252.0cm 99.2in
Track F: 141.7cm 55.8in
Track R: 136.9cm 53.9in
Length: 396.0cm 155.9in
Width: 167.9cm 66.1in
Height: 141.0cm 55.5in
Ground clearance: 12.7cm 5.0in
Kerb weight: 944.8kg 2081.0lb
Fuel: 46.9L 10.3gal 12.4galUS

1002 Chrysler

Sunbeam 1600 Ti
1979 UK
112.0mph 180.2kmh
0-50mph 80.5kmh: 7.1secs
0-60mph 96.5kmh: 10.7secs
0-1/4 mile: 18.5secs
0-1km: 33.6secs
100.0bhp 74.6kW 101.4PS
@ 6000rpm
96.0lbft 130.1Nm @ 4600rpm
110.0bhp/ton 108.1bhp/tonne
62.6bhp/L 46.7kW/L 63.4PS/L
43.8ft/sec 13.3m/sec
17.7mph 28.5kmh/1000rpm
22.3mpg 18.6mpgUS 12.7L/100km
Petrol 4-stroke piston
1598cc 97.5cu in
In-line 4 2 Carburettor
Compression ratio: 9.4:1
Bore: 87.3mm 3.4in
Stroke: 66.7mm 2.6in
Valve type/No: Overhead 8
Transmission: Manual
No. of forward speeds: 4
Wheels driven: Rear
Springs F/R: Coil/Coil
Brake system: PA
Brakes F/R: Disc/Drum
Steering: Rack & pinion
Wheelbase: 241.3cm 95.0in
Track F: 131.6cm 51.8in
Track R: 130.3cm 51.3in
Length: 382.8cm 150.7in
Width: 160.3cm 63.1in
Height: 139.4cm 54.9in
Ground clearance: 16.5cm 6.5in
Kerb weight: 924.8kg 2037.0lb
Fuel: 40.9L 9.0gal 10.8galUS

1003 Chrysler

Laser XE
1984 USA
113.0mph 181.8kmh
0-50mph 80.5kmh: 6.0secs
0-60mph 96.5kmh: 8.6secs
0-1/4 mile: 16.2secs
142.0bhp 105.9kW 144.0PS
@ 5600rpm
160.0lbft 216.8Nm @ 3600rpm
113.6bhp/ton 111.7bhp/tonne
64.2bhp/L 47.8kW/L 65.1PS/L
56.3ft/sec 17.2m/sec
25.0mph 40.2kmh/1000rpm
27.6mpg 23.0mpgUS 10.2L/100km
Petrol 4-stroke piston
2213cc 135.0cu in turbocharged
In-line 4 fuel injection
Compression ratio: 8.1:1
Bore: 87.5mm 3.4in
Stroke: 92.0mm 3.6in
Valve type/No: Overhead 8
Transmission: Manual
No. of forward speeds: 5
Wheels driven: Rear
Springs F/R: Coil/Coil
Brake system: PA
Brakes F/R: Disc/Drum
Steering: Rack & pinion PA
Wheelbase: 246.6cm 97.1in
Track F: 146.3cm 57.6in
Track R: 145.3cm 57.2in
Length: 444.5cm 175.0in
Width: 176.0cm 69.3in
Height: 127.8cm 50.3in
Ground clearance: 11.7cm 4.6in
Kerb weight: 1271.2kg 2800.0lb
Fuel: 53.0L 11.6gal 14.0galUS

1004 Chrysler

Le Baron GTS
1985 USA
120.0mph 193.1kmh
0-50mph 80.5kmh: 6.0secs
0-60mph 96.5kmh: 8.2secs
0-1/4 mile: 16.4secs
146.0bhp 108.9kW 148.0PS
@ 5200rpm
168.0lbft 227.6Nm @ 3600rpm
117.6bhp/ton 115.7bhp/tonne
66.0bhp/L 49.2kW/L 66.9PS/L
52.3ft/sec 15.9m/sec
26.3mph 42.3kmh/1000rpm
30.6mpg 25.5mpgUS 9.2L/100km
Petrol 4-stroke piston
2213cc 135.0cu in turbocharged
In-line 4 fuel injection
Compression ratio: 8.2:1
Bore: 87.5mm 3.4in
Stroke: 92.0mm 3.6in
Valve type/No: Overhead 8
Transmission: Manual
No. of forward speeds: 5
Wheels driven: Front
Springs F/R: Coil/Coil
Brake system: PA
Brakes F/R: Disc/Drum
Steering: Rack & pinion PA
Wheelbase: 261.9cm 103.1in
Track F: 146.3cm 57.6in
Track R: 145.3cm 57.2in
Length: 458.2cm 180.4in
Width: 174.0cm 68.5in
Height: 134.6cm 53.0in
Ground clearance: 13.2cm 5.2in
Kerb weight: 1262.1kg 2780.0lb
Fuel: 53.0L 11.6gal 14.0galUS

1005 Chrysler

Laser XT
1986 USA
118.0mph 189.9kmh
0-60mph 96.5kmh: 8.1secs
0-1/4 mile: 16.2secs
146.0bhp 108.9kW 148.0PS
@ 5200rpm
170.0lbft 230.4Nm @ 3600rpm
115.1bhp/ton 113.2bhp/tonne
66.0bhp/L 49.2kW/L 66.9PS/L
52.3ft/sec 15.9m/sec
25.2mpg 21.0mpgUS 11.2L/100km
Petrol 4-stroke piston
2213cc 135.0cu in turbocharged
In-line 4 fuel injection
Compression ratio: 8.1:1
Bore: 87.5mm 3.4in
Stroke: 92.0mm 3.6in
Valve type/No: Overhead 8
Transmission: Manual
No. of forward speeds: 5
Wheels driven: Front
Springs F/R: Coil/Coil
Brake system: PA
Brakes F/R: Disc/Drum
Steering: Rack & pinion PA
Wheelbase: 246.6cm 97.1in
Track F: 146.3cm 57.6in
Track R: 146.3cm 57.6in
Length: 444.5cm 175.0in
Width: 176.0cm 69.3in
Height: 128.0cm 50.4in
Kerb weight: 1289.4kg 2840.0lb
Fuel: 53.0L 11.6gal 14.0galUS

1006 Chrysler

Le Baron Coupe
1987 USA
120.0mph 193.1kmh
0-50mph 80.5kmh: 6.4secs
0-60mph 96.5kmh: 8.8secs
0-1/4 mile: 16.8secs
146.0bhp 108.9kW 148.0PS
@ 5200rpm
170.0lbft 230.4Nm @ 3600rpm
113.4bhp/ton 111.5bhp/tonne
66.0bhp/L 49.2kW/L 66.9PS/L
52.3ft/sec 15.9m/sec
24.6mpg 20.5mpgUS 11.5L/100km
Petrol 4-stroke piston
2213cc 135.0cu in turbocharged

In-line 4 fuel injection
Compression ratio: 8.1:1
Bore: 87.5mm 3.4in
Stroke: 92.0mm 3.6in
Valve type/No: Overhead 8
Transmission: Manual
No. of forward speeds: 5
Wheels driven: Front
Springs F/R: Coil/Coil
Brake system: PA
Brakes F/R: Disc/Drum
Steering: Rack & pinion PA
Wheelbase: 254.8cm 100.3in
Track F: 146.1cm 57.5in
Track R: 146.3cm 57.6in
Length: 469.6cm 184.9in
Width: 173.7cm 68.4in
Height: 129.3cm 50.9in
Ground clearance: 11.7cm 4.6in
Kerb weight: 1309.8kg 2885.0lb
Fuel: 53.0L 11.6gal 14.0galUS

1007 Chrysler

Conquest TSi
1988 Japan
127.0mph 204.3kmh
0-50mph 80.5kmh: 5.1secs
0-60mph 96.5kmh: 7.3secs
0-1/4 mile: 15.4secs
188.0bhp 140.2kW 190.6PS
@ 5000rpm
234.0lbft 317.1Nm @ 2500rpm
135.8bhp/ton 133.6bhp/tonne
73.6bhp/L 54.9kW/L 74.6PS/L
53.6ft/sec 16.3m/sec
24.0mpg 20.0mpgUS 11.8L/100km
Petrol 4-stroke piston
2555cc 155.9cu in turbocharged
In-line 4 fuel injection
Compression ratio: 7.0:1
Bore: 91.1mm 3.6in
Stroke: 98.0mm 3.9in
Valve type/No: Overhead 8
Transmission: Manual
No. of forward speeds: 5
Wheels driven: Rear
Springs F/R: Coil/Coil
Brake system: PA ABS
Brakes F/R: Disc/Disc
Steering: Recirculating ball PA
Wheelbase: 243.6cm 95.9in
Track F: 146.6cm 57.7in
Track R: 145.5cm 57.3in
Length: 439.9cm 173.2in
Width: 173.5cm 68.3in
Height: 127.5cm 50.2in
Kerb weight: 1407.4kg 3100.0lb
Fuel: 74.9L 16.5gal 19.8galUS

1008 Chrysler

TC by Maserati
1989 Italy
135.0mph 217.2kmh
0-60mph 96.5kmh: 6.9secs
0-1/4 mile: 15.4secs
200.0bhp 149.1kW 202.8PS
@ 5500rpm
220.0lbft 298.1Nm @ 3400rpm
139.3bhp/ton 137.0bhp/tonne
90.4bhp/L 67.4kW/L 91.6PS/L
55.3ft/sec 16.9m/sec
24.0mpg 20.0mpgUS 11.8L/100km
Petrol 4-stroke piston
2213cc 135.0cu in turbocharged
In-line 4 fuel injection
Compression ratio: 7.3:1
Bore: 87.5mm 3.4in
Stroke: 92.0mm 3.6in
Valve type/No: Overhead 16
Transmission: Manual
No. of forward speeds: 5
Wheels driven: Front
Springs F/R: Coil/Coil
Brake system: PA ABS
Brakes F/R: Disc/Disc
Steering: Rack & pinion PA
Wheelbase: 237.0cm 93.3in
Track F: 146.3cm 57.6in
Track R: 146.3cm 57.6in
Length: 446.5cm 175.8in
Width: 174.0cm 68.5in
Height: 131.8cm 51.9in
Kerb weight: 1459.6kg 3215.0lb
Fuel: 53.0L 11.6gal 14.0galUS

1009 Cisitalia

Aerodinamica Mille Miglia
1947 Italy
125.0mph 201.1kmh
75.0bhp 55.9kW 76.0PS
@ 5500rpm
115.1bhp/ton 113.1bhp/tonne
68.9bhp/L 51.4kW/L 69.8PS/L
45.1ft/sec 13.7m/sec
Petrol 4-stroke piston
1089cc 66.4cu in
In-line 4 1 Carburettor
Compression ratio: 7.5:1
Bore: 68.0mm 2.7in
Stroke: 75.0mm 2.9in
Valve type/No: Overhead 8
Transmission: Manual
No. of forward speeds: 4
Wheels driven: Rear
Springs F/R: Leaf/Leaf
Brakes F/R: Drum/Drum
Steering: Worm & sector
Wheelbase: 239.8cm 94.4in
Track F: 125.7cm 49.5in
Track R: 124.7cm 49.1in
Length: 415.3cm 163.5in
Width: 145.0cm 57.1in
Height: 135.9cm 53.5in
Kerb weight: 662.8kg 1460.0lb
Fuel: 90.8L 20.0gal 24.0galUS

1010 Citroen

Six Saloon
1930 France
60.8mph 97.8kmh
20.0mpg 16.7mpgUS 14.1L/100km
Petrol 4-stroke piston
2442cc 149.0cu in
In-line 6
Bore: 72.0mm 2.8in
Stroke: 100.0mm 3.9in
Transmission: Manual
No. of forward speeds: 3
Wheels driven: Rear
Brakes F/R: Drum/Drum
Wheelbase: 294.6cm 116.0in
Track F: 142.2cm 56.0in
Track R: 142.2cm 56.0in
Length: 453.4cm 178.5in
Width: 170.2cm 67.0in
Height: 170.2cm 67.0in
Kerb weight: 1398.3kg 3080.0lb
Fuel: 63.7L 14.0gal 16.8galUS

1011 Citroen

Super Model Twelve
1936 France
63.3mph 101.8kmh
0-50mph 80.5kmh: 23.8secs
26.0mpg 21.6mpgUS 10.9L/100km
Petrol 4-stroke piston
1628cc 99.3cu in
In-line 4
Bore: 72.0mm 2.8in
Stroke: 100.0mm 3.9in
Valve type/No: Overhead 8
Transmission: Manual
No. of forward speeds: 3
Wheels driven: Front
Brakes F/R: Drum/Drum
Kerb weight: 1075.1kg 2368.0lb
Fuel: 38.7L 8.5gal 10.2galUS

1012 Citroen

Super Modern Fifteen Saloon
1936 France
72.5mph 116.7kmh
0-50mph 80.5kmh: 23.2secs
0-60mph 96.5kmh: 37.7secs
21.0mpg 17.5mpgUS 13.5L/100km
Petrol 4-stroke piston
1911cc 116.6cu in
In-line 4
Bore: 78.0mm 3.1in
Stroke: 100.0mm 3.9in
Valve type/No: Overhead 8
Transmission: Manual
No. of forward speeds: 3
Wheels driven: Rear
Brakes F/R: Drum/Drum
Kerb weight: 1200.4kg 2644.0lb
Fuel: 45.5L 10.0gal 12.0galUS

1013 Citroen

Sports Twelve Saloon
1937 France
68.7mph 110.5kmh
0-50mph 80.5kmh: 20.9secs
0-60mph 96.5kmh: 36.1secs
23.0mpg 19.2mpgUS 12.3L/100km
Petrol 4-stroke piston
1911cc 116.6cu in
In-line 4
Bore: 78.0mm 3.1in
Stroke: 100.0mm 3.9in
Valve type/No: Overhead 8
Transmission: Manual
No. of forward speeds: 3
Wheels driven: Front
Brakes F/R: Drum/Drum
Kerb weight: 1090.0kg 2401.0lb
Fuel: 40.9L 9.0gal 10.8galUS

1014 Citroen

Light Fifteen Roadster
1940 France
75.0mph 120.7kmh
0-50mph 80.5kmh: 19.6secs
0-60mph 96.5kmh: 34.9secs
25.0mpg 20.8mpgUS 11.3L/100km
Petrol 4-stroke piston
1911cc 116.6cu in
In-line 4
Bore: 78.0mm 3.1in
Stroke: 100.0mm 3.9in
Valve type/No: Overhead 8
Transmission: Manual
No. of forward speeds: 3
Wheels driven: Front
Springs F/R: Torsion bar/Torsion bar
Brakes F/R: Drum/Drum
Wheelbase: 290.8cm 114.5in
Track F: 133.9cm 52.7in
Track R: 133.9cm 52.7in
Length: 426.7cm 168.0in
Width: 166.9cm 65.7in
Ground clearance: 17.8cm 7.0in
Kerb weight: 1107.3kg 2439.0lb
Fuel: 40.9L 9.0gal 10.8galUS

1015 Citroen

Light Fifteen
1948 France
76.0mph 122.3kmh
0-50mph 80.5kmh: 15.6secs
0-60mph 96.5kmh: 20.6secs
55.9bhp 41.7kW 56.7PS
@ 4250rpm
51.0bhp/ton 50.1bhp/tonne
29.2bhp/L 21.8kW/L 29.7PS/L
46.5ft/sec 14.2m/sec
23.0mpg 19.2mpgUS 12.3L/100km
Petrol 4-stroke piston
1911cc 116.6cu in
In-line 4
Compression ratio: 6.2:1
Bore: 78.0mm 3.1in
Stroke: 100.0mm 3.9in
Valve type/No: Overhead 8
Transmission: Manual
No. of forward speeds: 3
Wheels driven: Front
Brakes F/R: Drum/Drum
Wheelbase: 290.8cm 114.5in
Track F: 133.9cm 52.7in
Track R: 133.9cm 52.7in
Length: 431.8cm 170.0in
Width: 165.1cm 65.0in
Height: 152.4cm 60.0in
Ground clearance: 17.8cm 7.0in
Kerb weight: 1115.5kg 2457.0lb
Fuel: 45.5L 10.0gal 12.0galUS

1016 Citroen

Six Saloon
1949 France
83.0mph 133.5kmh
0-50mph 80.5kmh: 14.4secs
0-60mph 96.5kmh: 21.9secs
76.0bhp 56.7kW 77.0PS
@ 3700rpm
137.8lbft 186.7Nm @ 2000rpm
55.2bhp/ton 54.3bhp/tonne
26.5bhp/L 19.8kW/L 26.9PS/L
40.5ft/sec 12.3m/sec
20.0mph 32.2kmh/1000rpm
16.0mpg 13.3mpgUS 17.7L/100km
Petrol 4-stroke piston
2867cc 174.9cu in
In-line 6
Compression ratio: 6.4:1
Bore: 78.0mm 3.1in
Stroke: 100.0mm 3.9in
Valve type/No: Overhead 12
Transmission: Manual
No. of forward speeds: 3
Wheels driven: Front
Brakes F/R: Drum/Drum
Wheelbase: 308.6cm 121.5in
Track F: 148.6cm 58.5in
Track R: 146.1cm 57.5in
Length: 485.1cm 191.0in
Width: 177.8cm 70.0in
Height: 154.9cm 61.0in
Ground clearance: 17.8cm 7.0in
Kerb weight: 1399.2kg 3082.0lb
Fuel: 68.2L 15.0gal 18.0galUS

1017 Citroen

Light Fifteen
1952 France
76.0mph 122.3kmh
0-50mph 80.5kmh: 14.1secs
0-60mph 96.5kmh: 22.1secs
0-1/4 mile: 22.1secs
55.7bhp 41.5kW 56.5PS
@ 4250rpm
90.4lbft 122.5Nm @ 2200rpm
50.6bhp/ton 49.8bhp/tonne
29.1bhp/L 21.7kW/L 29.5PS/L
46.5ft/sec 14.2m/sec
17.4mph 28.0kmh/1000rpm
24.4mpg 20.3mpgUS 11.6L/100km
Petrol 4-stroke piston
1911cc 116.6cu in
In-line 4
Compression ratio: 6.5:1
Bore: 78.0mm 3.1in
Stroke: 100.0mm 3.9in
Valve type/No: Overhead 8
Transmission: Manual
No. of forward speeds: 3
Wheels driven: Front
Springs F/R: Torsion bar/Torsion bar
Brakes F/R: Drum/Drum
Wheelbase: 290.8cm 114.5in
Track F: 133.9cm 52.7in
Track R: 132.6cm 52.2in
Length: 426.7cm 168.0in
Width: 165.6cm 65.2in
Height: 151.1cm 59.5in
Ground clearance: 17.8cm 7.0in
Kerb weight: 1118.7kg 2464.0lb
Fuel: 50.0L 11.0gal 13.2galUS

1018 Citroen

11CV
1953 France
75.0mph 120.7kmh
0-50mph 80.5kmh: 14.7secs
0-60mph 96.5kmh: 21.5secs
0-1/4 mile: 22.4secs
56.0bhp 41.8kW 56.8PS
@ 4250rpm
90.0lbft 122.0Nm @ 2200rpm
53.4bhp/ton 52.5bhp/tonne
29.3bhp/L 21.8kW/L 29.7PS/L
46.5ft/sec 14.2m/sec
17.4mph 28.0kmh/1000rpm
Petrol 4-stroke piston
1911cc 116.6cu in
In-line 4
Compression ratio: 6.5:1
Bore: 78.0mm 3.1in
Stroke: 100.0mm 3.9in
Valve type/No: Overhead 8
Transmission: Manual
No. of forward speeds: 3
Wheels driven: Front
Springs F/R: Torsion bar/Torsion bar
Steering: Rack & pinion
Track F: 134.1cm 52.8in
Track R: 132.8cm 52.3in
Length: 426.7cm 168.0in
Ground clearance: 17.8cm 7.0in
Kerb weight: 1066.9kg 2350.0lb
Fuel: 49.2L 10.8gal 13.0galUS

1019 Citroen

2CV Cabriolet
1953 France
41.0mph 66.0kmh
0-1/4 mile: 37.6secs
9.0bhp 6.7kW 9.1PS

@ 3500rpm
16.6lbft 22.5Nm @ 1800rpm
18.3bhp/ton 18.0bhp/tonne
24.0bhp/L 17.9kW/L 24.3PS/L
23.7ft/sec 7.2m/sec
12.1mph 19.5kmh/1000rpm
63.2mpg 52.6mpgUS 4.5L/100km
Petrol 4-stroke piston
375cc 22.9cu in
Flat 2
Compression ratio: 6.2:1
Bore: 62.0mm 2.4in
Stroke: 62.0mm 2.4in
Valve type/No: Overhead 4
Transmission: Manual
No. of forward speeds: 4
Wheels driven: Front
Springs F/R: Coil/Coil
Brakes F/R: Drum/Drum
Wheelbase: 237.0cm 93.3in
Track F: 126.0cm 49.6in
Track R: 126.0cm 49.6in
Length: 377.7cm 148.7in
Width: 147.6cm 58.1in
Height: 160.0cm 63.0in
Ground clearance: 19.1cm 7.5in
Kerb weight: 499.4kg 1100.0lb
Fuel: 20.0L 4.4gal 5.3galUS

1020 Citroen

Big Fifteen
1953 France
72.0mph 115.8kmh
0-50mph 80.5kmh: 17.9secs
0-60mph 96.5kmh: 29.1secs
0-1/4 mile: 23.3secs
55.7bhp 41.5kW 56.5PS
@ 4250rpm
90.4lbft 122.5Nm @ 2200rpm
47.4bhp/ton 46.6bhp/tonne
29.1bhp/L 21.7kW/L 29.5PS/L
46.5ft/sec 14.2m/sec
17.4mph 28.0kmh/1000rpm
23.6mpg 19.7mpgUS 12.0L/100km
Petrol 4-stroke piston
1911cc 116.6cu in
In-line 4
Compression ratio: 6.5:1
Bore: 78.0mm 3.1in
Stroke: 100.0mm 3.9in
Valve type/No: Overhead 8
Transmission: Manual
No. of forward speeds: 3
Wheels driven: Front
Springs F/R: Torsion bar/Torsion bar
Brakes F/R: Drum/Drum
Wheelbase: 308.6cm 121.5in
Track F: 148.6cm 58.5in
Track R: 148.6cm 58.5in
Length: 473.7cm 186.5in
Width: 177.8cm 70.0in
Height: 154.9cm 61.0in
Ground clearance: 17.8cm 7.0in
Kerb weight: 1194.9kg 2632.0lb
Fuel: 50.0L 11.0gal 13.2galUS

1021 Citroen

Six
1954 France
84.0mph 135.2kmh
0-50mph 80.5kmh: 12.5secs
0-60mph 96.5kmh: 19.3secs
0-1/4 mile: 21.4secs
76.0bhp 56.7kW 77.0PS
@ 3800rpm
138.0lbft 187.0Nm @ 2000rpm
56.2bhp/ton 55.3bhp/tonne
26.5bhp/L 19.8kW/L 26.9PS/L
41.6ft/sec 12.7m/sec
19.9mph 32.0kmh/1000rpm
18.5mpg 15.4mpgUS 15.3L/100km
Petrol 4-stroke piston
2867cc 174.9cu in
In-line 6
Compression ratio: 6.5:1
Bore: 78.0mm 3.1in
Stroke: 100.0mm 3.9in
Valve type/No: Overhead 12
Transmission: Manual
No. of forward speeds: 3
Wheels driven: Front
Springs F/R: Torsion bar/Torsion bar
Brakes F/R: Drum/Drum
Wheelbase: 308.6cm 121.5in
Track F: 148.6cm 58.5in
Track R: 148.6cm 58.5in
Length: 485.1cm 191.0in
Width: 179.1cm 70.5in
Height: 156.2cm 61.5in
Ground clearance: 17.8cm 7.0in
Kerb weight: 1374.3kg 3027.0lb
Fuel: 68.2L 15.0gal 18.0galUS

1022 Citroen

2CV
1955 France
49.2mph 79.2kmh
0-1/4 mile: 29.4secs
12.0bhp 8.9kW 12.2PS
@ 3500rpm
24.0bhp/ton 23.6bhp/tonne
28.2bhp/L 21.1kW/L 28.6PS/L
23.7ft/sec 7.2m/sec
Petrol 4-stroke piston
425cc 25.9cu in
Flat 2
Bore: 66.0mm 2.6in
Stroke: 62.0mm 2.4in
Valve type/No: Overhead 4
Transmission: Manual
No. of forward speeds: 4
Wheels driven: Front
Wheelbase: 237.0cm 93.3in
Track F: 126.0cm 49.6in
Track R: 126.0cm 49.6in
Kerb weight: 508.5kg 1120.0lb

1023 Citroen

DS19
1956 France
88.4mph 142.2kmh
0-50mph 80.5kmh: 13.5secs
0-60mph 96.5kmh: 18.6secs
0-1/4 mile: 22.2secs
75.0bhp 55.9kW 76.0PS
@ 4500rpm
101.0lbft 136.9Nm @ 3000rpm
61.8bhp/ton 60.7bhp/tonne
39.2bhp/L 29.3kW/L 39.8PS/L
49.2ft/sec 15.0m/sec
Petrol 4-stroke piston
1911cc 116.6cu in
In-line 4
Compression ratio: 7.5:1
Bore: 78.0mm 3.1in
Stroke: 100.1mm 3.9in
Valve type/No: Overhead 8
Transmission: Manual
No. of forward speeds: 4
Wheels driven: Front
Wheelbase: 312.4cm 123.0in
Track F: 150.1cm 59.1in
Track R: 130.0cm 51.2in
Kerb weight: 1234.9kg 2720.0lb

1024 Citroen

DS19
1957 France
87.5mph 140.8kmh
0-50mph 80.5kmh: 15.3secs
0-60mph 96.5kmh: 22.1secs
0-1/4 mile: 22.9secs
75.0bhp 55.9kW 76.0PS
@ 4500rpm
101.0lbft 136.9Nm @ 3000rpm
61.6bhp/ton 60.6bhp/tonne
39.2bhp/L 29.3kW/L 39.8PS/L
49.2ft/sec 15.0m/sec
23.0mph 37.0kmh/1000rpm
24.2mpg 20.2mpgUS 11.7L/100km
Petrol 4-stroke piston
1911cc 116.6cu in
In-line 4
Compression ratio: 7.5:1
Bore: 78.0mm 3.1in
Stroke: 100.1mm 3.9in
Valve type/No: Overhead 8
Transmission: Manual
No. of forward speeds: 4
Wheels driven: Front
Springs F/R: Gas/Gas
Brake system: PA
Brakes F/R: Disc/Drum
Steering: PA
Wheelbase: 312.4cm 123.0in
Track F: 150.1cm 59.1in
Track R: 130.0cm 51.2in
Length: 480.1cm 189.0in
Width: 178.3cm 70.2in
Height: 152.1cm 59.9in
Ground clearance: 15.7cm 6.2in
Kerb weight: 1238.1kg 2727.0lb
Fuel: 63.7L 14.0gal 16.8galUS

1025 Citroen

ID19
1958 France
88.0mph 141.6kmh
0-50mph 80.5kmh: 14.0secs
0-60mph 96.5kmh: 21.1secs
0-1/4 mile: 22.3secs
66.0bhp 49.2kW 66.9PS
@ 4500rpm
97.6lbft 132.2Nm @ 2500rpm
54.3bhp/ton 53.4bhp/tonne
34.5bhp/L 25.8kW/L 35.0PS/L
49.2ft/sec 15.0m/sec
23.0mph 37.0kmh/1000rpm
26.3mpg 21.9mpgUS 10.7L/100km
Petrol 4-stroke piston
1911cc 116.6cu in
In-line 4
Compression ratio: 7.5:1
Bore: 78.0mm 3.1in
Stroke: 100.0mm 3.9in
Valve type/No: Overhead 8
Transmission: Manual
No. of forward speeds: 4
Wheels driven: Front
Springs F/R: Gas/Gas
Brake system: PA
Brakes F/R: Disc/Drum
Steering: Rack & pinion PA
Wheelbase: 312.4cm 123.0in
Track F: 149.9cm 59.0in
Track R: 130.0cm 51.2in
Length: 480.1cm 189.0in
Width: 179.1cm 70.5in
Height: 151.9cm 59.8in
Ground clearance: 15.7cm 6.2in
Kerb weight: 1234.9kg 2720.0lb
Fuel: 63.7L 14.0gal 16.8galUS

1026 Citroen

ID Safari
1960 France
87.0mph 140.0kmh
0-50mph 80.5kmh: 15.5secs
0-60mph 96.5kmh: 25.2secs
0-1/4 mile: 22.8secs
66.0bhp 49.2kW 66.9PS
@ 4500rpm
101.3lbft 137.3Nm @ 3000rpm
49.9bhp/ton 49.1bhp/tonne
34.5bhp/L 25.8kW/L 35.0PS/L
49.2ft/sec 15.0m/sec
22.6mph 36.4kmh/1000rpm
21.6mpg 18.0mpgUS 13.1L/100km
Petrol 4-stroke piston
1911cc 116.6cu in
In-line 4
Compression ratio: 7.5:1
Bore: 78.0mm 3.1in
Stroke: 100.0mm 3.9in
Valve type/No: Overhead 8
Transmission: Manual
No. of forward speeds: 4
Wheels driven: Front
Springs F/R: Gas/Gas
Brake system: PA
Brakes F/R: Disc/Drum
Steering: Rack & pinion PA
Wheelbase: 312.4cm 123.0in
Track F: 149.9cm 59.0in
Track R: 130.0cm 51.2in
Length: 497.8cm 196.0in
Width: 179.1cm 70.5in
Height: 152.4cm 60.0in
Ground clearance: 15.7cm 6.2in
Kerb weight: 1344.3kg 2961.0lb
Fuel: 63.7L 14.0gal 16.8galUS

1027 Citroen

ID19
1960 France
87.4mph 140.6kmh
0-50mph 80.5kmh: 13.0secs
0-60mph 96.5kmh: 19.1secs
0-1/4 mile: 22.2secs
66.0bhp 49.2kW 66.9PS
@ 4000rpm
98.0lbft 132.8Nm @ 2500rpm
56.0bhp/ton 55.1bhp/tonne
34.5bhp/L 25.8kW/L 35.0PS/L
43.8ft/sec 13.3m/sec
23.1mph 37.2kmh/1000rpm
Petrol 4-stroke piston
1911cc 116.6cu in
In-line 4 1 Carburettor
Compression ratio: 7.5:1
Bore: 78.0mm 3.1in
Stroke: 100.1mm 3.9in
Valve type/No: Overhead 8
Transmission: Manual
No. of forward speeds: 4
Wheels driven: Front
Wheelbase: 312.4cm 123.0in
Track F: 150.1cm 59.1in
Track R: 130.0cm 51.2in
Length: 480.1cm 189.0in
Width: 179.1cm 70.5in
Height: 147.1cm 57.9in
Kerb weight: 1198.6kg 2640.0lb

1028 Citroen

Bijou
1961 France
50.5mph 81.3kmh
0-1/4 mile: 31.6secs
12.0bhp 8.9kW 12.2PS
@ 4000rpm
17.4lbft 23.6Nm @ 2500rpm
20.2bhp/ton 19.9bhp/tonne
28.2bhp/L 21.1kW/L 28.6PS/L
27.1ft/sec 8.3m/sec
12.1mph 19.5kmh/1000rpm
49.2mpg 41.0mpgUS 5.7L/100km
Petrol 4-stroke piston
425cc 25.9cu in
Flat 2 1 Carburettor
Compression ratio: 7.0:1
Bore: 66.0mm 2.6in
Stroke: 62.0mm 2.4in
Valve type/No: Overhead 4
Transmission: Manual
No. of forward speeds: 4
Wheels driven: Front
Springs F/R: Coil/Coil
Brakes F/R: Drum/Drum
Wheelbase: 237.5cm 93.5in
Track F: 126.0cm 49.6in
Track R: 126.0cm 49.6in
Length: 393.7cm 155.0in
Width: 154.9cm 61.0in
Height: 147.3cm 58.0in
Ground clearance: 19.1cm 7.5in
Kerb weight: 603.8kg 1330.0lb
Fuel: 19.6L 4.3gal 5.2galUS

1029 Citroen

DS
1961 France
95.0mph 152.9kmh
0-50mph 80.5kmh: 13.2secs
0-60mph 96.5kmh: 18.4secs
0-1/4 mile: 21.7secs
83.0bhp 61.9kW 84.1PS
@ 4500rpm
104.8lbft 142.0Nm @ 3500rpm
66.9bhp/ton 65.8bhp/tonne
43.4bhp/L 32.4kW/L 44.0PS/L
49.2ft/sec 15.0m/sec
22.6mph 36.4kmh/1000rpm
29.2mpg 24.3mpgUS 9.7L/100km
Petrol 4-stroke piston
1911cc 116.6cu in
In-line 4
Compression ratio: 8.5:1
Bore: 78.0mm 3.1in
Stroke: 100.0mm 3.9in
Valve type/No: Overhead 8
Transmission: Manual
No. of forward speeds: 4
Wheels driven: Front
Springs F/R: Gas/Gas
Brake system: PA
Brakes F/R: Disc/Drum
Steering: Rack & pinion PA
Wheelbase: 312.4cm 123.0in
Track F: 149.9cm 59.0in
Track R: 130.0cm 51.2in
Length: 480.1cm 189.0in
Width: 179.1cm 70.5in
Height: 151.9cm 59.8in
Ground clearance: 15.7cm 6.2in
Kerb weight: 1262.1kg 2780.0lb
Fuel: 65.1L 14.3gal 17.2galUS

1030 Citroen

Ami 6
1962 France
69.5mph 111.8kmh
0-50mph 80.5kmh: 24.7secs
0-60mph 96.5kmh: 44.0secs
0-1/4 mile: 25.2secs
22.0bhp 16.4kW 22.3PS
@ 4500rpm

29.6lbft 40.1Nm @ 2800rpm
34.5bhp/ton 33.9bhp/tonne
36.5bhp/L 27.3kW/L 37.1PS/L
34.5ft/sec 10.5m/sec
14.4mph 23.2kmh/1000rpm
44.5mpg 37.1mpgUS 6.3L/100km
Petrol 4-stroke piston
602cc 36.7cu in
Flat 2 1 Carburettor
Compression ratio: 7.2:1
Bore: 74.0mm 2.9in
Stroke: 70.0mm 2.8in
Valve type/No: Overhead 4
Transmission: Manual
No. of forward speeds: 4
Wheels driven: Front
Springs F/R: Coil/Coil
Brakes F/R: Drum/Drum
Steering: Rack & pinion
Wheelbase: 239.3cm 94.2in
Track F: 126.0cm 49.6in
Track R: 121.9cm 48.0in
Length: 386.6cm 152.2in
Width: 152.1cm 59.9in
Height: 148.6cm 58.5in
Ground clearance: 19.1cm 7.5in
Kerb weight: 648.3kg 1428.0lb
Fuel: 25.0L 5.5gal 6.6galUS

1031 Citroen
DS
1963 France
98.0mph 157.7kmh
0-50mph 80.5kmh: 14.5secs
0-60mph 96.5kmh: 21.2secs
0-1/4 mile: 22.3secs
83.0bhp 61.9kW 84.1PS
@ 4500rpm
105.0lbft 142.3Nm @ 3500rpm
65.7bhp/ton 64.6bhp/tonne
43.4bhp/L 32.4kW/L 44.0PS/L
49.2ft/sec 15.0m/sec
23.1mph 37.2kmh/1000rpm
24.1mpg 20.1mpgUS 11.7L/100km
Petrol 4-stroke piston
1911cc 116.6cu in
In-line 4 1 Carburettor
Compression ratio: 8.5:1
Bore: 78.0mm 3.1in
Stroke: 100.0mm 3.9in
Valve type/No: Overhead 8
Transmission: Manual
No. of forward speeds: 4
Wheels driven: Front
Springs F/R: Gas/Gas
Brake system: PA
Brakes F/R: Disc/Drum
Steering: Rack & pinion PA
Wheelbase: 312.4cm 123.0in
Track F: 149.9cm 59.0in
Track R: 130.0cm 51.2in
Length: 480.1cm 189.0in
Width: 179.1cm 70.5in
Height: 151.1cm 59.5in
Ground clearance: 15.7cm 6.2in
Kerb weight: 1284.8kg 2830.0lb
Fuel: 63.7L 14.0gal 16.8galUS

1032 Citroen
DS21 Pallas M
1965 France
108.0mph 173.8kmh
0-50mph 80.5kmh: 10.1secs
0-60mph 96.5kmh: 14.4secs
0-1/4 mile: 19.5secs
0-1km: 36.2secs
100.0bhp 74.6kW 101.4PS
@ 5500rpm
121.0lbft 164.0Nm @ 3000rpm
77.8bhp/ton 76.5bhp/tonne
46.0bhp/L 34.3kW/L 46.6PS/L
51.5ft/sec 15.7m/sec
20.7mph 33.3kmh/1000rpm
22.0mpg 18.3mpgUS 12.8L/100km
Petrol 4-stroke piston
2175cc 132.7cu in
In-line 4 1 Carburettor
Compression ratio: 8.7:1
Bore: 90.0mm 3.5in
Stroke: 85.5mm 3.4in
Valve type/No: Overhead 8
Transmission: Manual
No. of forward speeds: 4
Wheels driven: Front
Springs F/R: Gas/Gas
Brake system: PA
Brakes F/R: Disc/Drum
Steering: Rack & pinion PA
Wheelbase: 312.4cm 123.0in
Track F: 149.9cm 59.0in
Track R: 130.0cm 51.2in
Length: 480.1cm 189.0in
Width: 179.1cm 70.5in
Height: 151.1cm 59.5in
Ground clearance: 15.7cm 6.2in
Kerb weight: 1306.6kg 2878.0lb
Fuel: 65.1L 14.3gal 17.2galUS

1033 Citroen
DSM
1965 France
105.0mph 168.9kmh
0-50mph 80.5kmh: 10.3secs
0-60mph 96.5kmh: 15.0secs
0-1/4 mile: 19.9secs
83.0bhp 61.9kW 84.1PS
@ 4500rpm
105.0lbft 142.3Nm @ 3500rpm
66.9bhp/ton 65.8bhp/tonne
43.4bhp/L 32.4kW/L 44.0PS/L
49.2ft/sec 15.0m/sec
22.9mph 36.8kmh/1000rpm
Petrol 4-stroke piston
1911cc 116.6cu in
In-line 4 1 Carburettor
Compression ratio: 8.5:1
Bore: 78.0mm 3.1in
Stroke: 100.1mm 3.9in
Valve type/No: Overhead 8
Transmission: Manual
No. of forward speeds: 4
Wheels driven: Front
Steering: PA
Wheelbase: 312.4cm 123.0in
Track F: 149.9cm 59.0in
Track R: 130.3cm 51.3in
Length: 485.1cm 191.0in
Width: 179.1cm 70.5in
Height: 147.3cm 58.0in
Ground clearance: 16.5cm 6.5in
Kerb weight: 1262.1kg 2780.0lb
Fuel: 64.3L 14.1gal 17.0galUS

1034 Citroen
DS21
1966 France
106.0mph 170.6kmh
0-50mph 80.5kmh: 11.0secs
0-60mph 96.5kmh: 14.8secs
0-1/4 mile: 20.5secs
109.0bhp 81.3kW 110.5PS
@ 5500rpm
128.0lbft 173.4Nm @ 3000rpm
83.3bhp/ton 81.9bhp/tonne
50.1bhp/L 37.4kW/L 50.8PS/L
51.5ft/sec 15.7m/sec
20.7mph 33.3kmh/1000rpm
Petrol 4-stroke piston
2175cc 132.7cu in
In-line 4 1 Carburettor
Compression ratio: 8.8:1
Bore: 90.0mm 3.5in
Stroke: 85.5mm 3.4in
Valve type/No: Overhead 8
No. of forward speeds: 4
Wheels driven: Front
Springs F/R: Gas/Gas
Brakes F/R: Disc/Drum
Steering: Rack & pinion
Wheelbase: 312.4cm 123.0in
Track F: 150.1cm 59.1in
Track R: 130.3cm 51.3in
Length: 491.5cm 193.5in
Width: 179.1cm 70.5in
Height: 142.0cm 55.9in
Ground clearance: 15.0cm 5.9in
Kerb weight: 1330.2kg 2930.0lb
Fuel: 64.3L 14.1gal 17.0galUS

1035 Citroen
Ami 6 Break
1967 France
68.0mph 109.4kmh
0-50mph 80.5kmh: 24.1secs
0-60mph 96.5kmh: 54.7secs
0-1/4 mile: 25.4secs
0-1km: 48.8secs
26.0bhp 19.4kW 26.4PS
@ 4750rpm
30.0lbft 40.7Nm @ 3000rpm
37.6bhp/ton 36.9bhp/tonne
43.2bhp/L 32.2kW/L 43.8PS/L
36.4ft/sec 11.1m/sec
13.4mph 21.6kmh/1000rpm
35.0mpg 29.1mpgUS 8.1L/100km
Petrol 4-stroke piston
602cc 36.7cu in
Flat 2 1 Carburettor
Compression ratio: 7.7:1
Bore: 74.0mm 2.9in
Stroke: 70.0mm 2.8in
Valve type/No: Overhead 4
Transmission: Manual
No. of forward speeds: 4
Wheels driven: Front
Springs F/R: Coil/Coil
Brakes F/R: Drum/Drum
Steering: Rack & pinion
Wheelbase: 239.3cm 94.2in
Track F: 126.0cm 49.6in
Track R: 121.9cm 48.0in
Length: 388.6cm 153.0in
Width: 154.9cm 61.0in
Height: 147.3cm 58.0in
Ground clearance: 19.1cm 7.5in
Kerb weight: 703.7kg 1550.0lb
Fuel: 25.0L 5.5gal 6.6galUS

1036 Citroen
DS21 Safari
1968 France
100.0mph 160.9kmh
0-1/4 mile: 20.5secs
109.0bhp 81.3kW 110.5PS
50.1bhp/L 37.4kW/L 50.8PS/L
24.0mpg 20.0mpgUS 11.8L/100km
Petrol 4-stroke piston
2175cc 132.7cu in
In-line 4
Valve type/No: Overhead 8
Wheels driven: Front
Wheelbase: 312.4cm 123.0in
Length: 499.1cm 196.5in

1037 Citroen
Ami 8 Club
1970 France
73.0mph 117.5kmh
0-50mph 80.5kmh: 19.4secs
0-60mph 96.5kmh: 31.7secs
0-1/4 mile: 24.5secs
0-1km: 46.3secs
32.0bhp 23.9kW 32.4PS
@ 5750rpm
31.0lbft 42.0Nm @ 4000rpm
43.8bhp/ton 43.1bhp/tonne
53.2bhp/L 39.6kW/L 53.9PS/L
44.1ft/sec 13.4m/sec
13.3mph 21.4kmh/1000rpm
32.2mpg 26.8mpgUS 8.8L/100km
Petrol 4-stroke piston
602cc 36.7cu in
Flat 2 1 Carburettor
Compression ratio: 9.0:1
Bore: 74.0mm 2.9in
Stroke: 70.0mm 2.8in
Valve type/No: Overhead 4
Transmission: Manual
No. of forward speeds: 4
Wheels driven: Front
Springs F/R: Coil/Coil
Brakes F/R: Disc/Drum
Steering: Rack & pinion
Wheelbase: 240.0cm 94.5in
Track F: 126.0cm 49.6in
Track R: 121.9cm 48.0in
Length: 398.8cm 157.0in
Width: 152.4cm 60.0in
Height: 152.4cm 60.0in
Ground clearance: 15.2cm 6.0in
Kerb weight: 742.7kg 1636.0lb
Fuel: 30.9L 6.8gal 8.2galUS

1038 Citroen
DS21 EFI 139 Pallas
1970 France
114.0mph 183.4kmh
0-50mph 80.5kmh: 8.5secs
0-60mph 96.5kmh: 11.8secs
0-1/4 mile: 18.5secs
0-1km: 34.3secs
125.0bhp 93.2kW 126.7PS
@ 5250rpm
135.0lbft 182.9Nm @ 3500rpm
94.6bhp/ton 93.0bhp/tonne
57.5bhp/L 42.9kW/L 58.3PS/L
49.1ft/sec 15.0m/sec
20.5mph 33.0kmh/1000rpm
20.9mpg 17.4mpgUS 13.5L/100km
Petrol 4-stroke piston
2175cc 132.7cu in
In-line 4 fuel injection
Compression ratio: 8.5:1
Bore: 90.0mm 3.5in
Stroke: 85.5mm 3.4in
Valve type/No: Overhead 8
Transmission: Manual
No. of forward speeds: 4
Wheels driven: Front
Springs F/R: Gas/Gas
Brake system: PA
Brakes F/R: Disc/Drum
Steering: Rack & pinion PA
Wheelbase: 312.4cm 123.0in
Track F: 149.9cm 59.0in
Track R: 129.5cm 51.0in
Length: 482.6cm 190.0in
Width: 179.1cm 70.5in
Height: 147.3cm 58.0in
Ground clearance: 15.2cm 6.0in
Kerb weight: 1343.8kg 2960.0lb
Fuel: 65.1L 14.3gal 17.2galUS

1039 Citroen
GS
1971 France
92.0mph 148.0kmh
0-50mph 80.5kmh: 12.5secs
0-60mph 96.5kmh: 18.0secs
0-1/4 mile: 21.5secs
0-1km: 39.9secs
55.5bhp 41.4kW 56.3PS
@ 6500rpm
52.0lbft 70.5Nm @ 3500rpm
66.6bhp/ton 65.5bhp/tonne
54.7bhp/L 40.8kW/L 55.4PS/L
41.9ft/sec 12.8m/sec
14.3mph 23.0kmh/1000rpm
23.3mpg 19.4mpgUS 12.1L/100km
Petrol 4-stroke piston
1015cc 61.9cu in
Flat 4 1 Carburettor
Compression ratio: 9.0:1
Bore: 74.0mm 2.9in
Stroke: 59.0mm 2.3in
Valve type/No: Overhead 8
Transmission: Manual
No. of forward speeds: 4
Wheels driven: Front
Springs F/R: Gas/Gas
Brake system: PA
Brakes F/R: Disc/Disc
Steering: Rack & pinion
Wheelbase: 255.0cm 100.4in
Track F: 135.1cm 53.2in
Track R: 132.6cm 52.2in
Length: 381.5cm 150.2in
Width: 160.8cm 63.3in
Height: 137.2cm 54.0in
Ground clearance: 20.3cm 8.0in
Kerb weight: 847.6kg 1867.0lb
Fuel: 43.2L 9.5gal 11.4galUS

1040 Citroen
Safari 21
1971 France
109.0mph 175.4kmh
0-50mph 80.5kmh: 9.6secs
0-60mph 96.5kmh: 13.9secs
0-1/4 mile: 19.5secs
0-1km: 35.9secs
106.0bhp 79.0kW 107.5PS
@ 5500rpm
123.0lbft 166.7Nm @ 3500rpm
75.6bhp/ton 74.4bhp/tonne
48.7bhp/L 36.3kW/L 49.4PS/L
51.5ft/sec 15.7m/sec
20.6mph 33.1kmh/1000rpm
23.1mpg 19.2mpgUS 12.2L/100km
Petrol 4-stroke piston
2175cc 132.7cu in
In-line 4 1 Carburettor
Compression ratio: 8.7:1
Bore: 90.0mm 3.5in
Stroke: 85.5mm 3.4in
Valve type/No: Overhead 8
Transmission: Manual
No. of forward speeds: 4
Wheels driven: Front
Springs F/R: Gas/Gas
Brake system: PA
Brakes F/R: Disc/Drum
Steering: Rack & pinion PA
Wheelbase: 312.4cm 123.0in
Track F: 149.9cm 59.0in
Track R: 130.0cm 51.2in

Length: 497.8cm 196.0in
Width: 180.3cm 71.0in
Height: 160.0cm 63.0in
Ground clearance: 15.2cm 6.0in
Kerb weight: 1425.6kg 3140.0lb
Fuel: 63.7L 14.0gal 16.8galUS

1041 Citroen

Safari SM
1971 France
135.0mph 217.2kmh
0-50mph 80.5kmh: 7.0secs
0-60mph 96.5kmh: 9.0secs
0-1/4 mile: 16.9secs
0-1km: 30.2secs
170.0bhp 126.8kW 172.4PS
@ 5500rpm
170.0lbft 230.4Nm @ 4000rpm
115.5bhp/ton 113.5bhp/tonne
63.7bhp/L 47.5kW/L 64.5PS/L
45.1ft/sec 13.7m/sec
22.6mph 36.4kmh/1000rpm
16.0mpg 13.3mpgUS 17.7L/100km
Petrol 4-stroke piston
2670cc 162.9cu in
Vee 6 3 Carburettor
Compression ratio: 9.0:1
Bore: 87.0mm 3.4in
Stroke: 75.0mm 2.9in
Valve type/No: Overhead 12
Transmission: Manual
No. of forward speeds: 5
Wheels driven: Front
Springs F/R: Gas/Gas
Brake system: PA
Brakes F/R: Disc/Disc
Steering: Rack & pinion PA
Wheelbase: 295.1cm 116.2in
Track F: 152.4cm 60.0in
Track R: 133.6cm 52.6in
Length: 487.7cm 192.0in
Width: 183.4cm 72.2in
Height: 133.4cm 52.5in
Ground clearance: 15.2cm 6.0in
Kerb weight: 1497.3kg 3298.0lb
Fuel: 89.6L 19.7gal 23.7galUS

1042 Citroen

GS
1972 France
90.0mph 144.8kmh
0-50mph 80.5kmh: 13.1secs
0-60mph 96.5kmh: 18.2secs
0-1/4 mile: 21.4secs
56.0bhp 41.8kW 56.8PS
@ 6500rpm
52.0lbft 70.5Nm @ 3500rpm
66.0bhp/ton 64.9bhp/tonne
55.2bhp/L 41.1kW/L 55.9PS/L
41.9ft/sec 12.8m/sec
14.3mph 23.0kmh/1000rpm
25.2mpg 21.0mpgUS 11.2L/100km
Petrol 4-stroke piston
1015cc 61.9cu in
Flat 4 1 Carburettor
Compression ratio: 9.0:1
Bore: 74.0mm 2.9in
Stroke: 59.0mm 2.3in
Valve type/No: Overhead 8
Transmission: Manual
No. of forward speeds: 4
Wheels driven: Front
Springs F/R: Gas/Gas
Brakes F/R: Disc/Disc
Steering: Rack & pinion PA
Wheelbase: 255.0cm 100.4in
Track F: 137.7cm 54.2in
Track R: 132.8cm 52.3in
Length: 412.0cm 162.2in
Width: 160.8cm 63.3in
Height: 134.9cm 53.1in
Ground clearance: 15.5cm 6.1in
Kerb weight: 862.6kg 1900.0lb
Fuel: 43.1L 9.5gal 11.4galUS

1043 Citroen

SM
1972 France
135.0mph 217.2kmh
0-50mph 80.5kmh: 6.8secs
0-60mph 96.5kmh: 9.3secs
0-1/4 mile: 17.4secs
180.0bhp 134.2kW 182.5PS
@ 6250rpm
172.0lbft 233.1Nm @ 4000rpm
123.3bhp/ton 121.2bhp/tonne
67.4bhp/L 50.3kW/L 68.3PS/L
51.2ft/sec 15.6m/sec
21.8mph 35.1kmh/1000rpm
19.1mpg 15.9mpgUS 14.8L/100km
Petrol 4-stroke piston
2670cc 162.9cu in
Vee 6 3 Carburettor
Compression ratio: 9.0:1
Bore: 87.0mm 3.4in
Stroke: 75.0mm 2.9in
Valve type/No: Overhead 12
Transmission: Manual
No. of forward speeds: 5
Wheels driven: Front
Springs F/R: Gas/Gas
Brakes F/R: Disc/Disc
Steering: Rack & pinion PA
Wheelbase: 294.9cm 116.1in
Track F: 152.7cm 60.1in
Track R: 132.6cm 52.2in
Length: 489.2cm 192.6in
Width: 183.6cm 72.3in
Height: 132.3cm 52.1in
Ground clearance: 15.5cm 6.1in
Kerb weight: 1484.6kg 3270.0lb
Fuel: 74.6L 16.4gal 19.7galUS

1044 Citroen

GS 1220
1973 France
96.0mph 154.5kmh
0-50mph 80.5kmh: 10.5secs
0-60mph 96.5kmh: 14.9secs
0-1/4 mile: 20.1secs
0-1km: 37.5secs
60.0bhp 44.7kW 60.8PS
@ 6500rpm
64.0lbft 86.7Nm @ 3250rpm
71.3bhp/ton 70.1bhp/tonne
49.2bhp/L 36.7kW/L 49.9PS/L
46.6ft/sec 14.2m/sec
15.2mph 24.5kmh/1000rpm
24.8mpg 20.7mpgUS 11.4L/100km
Petrol 4-stroke piston
1220cc 74.4cu in
Flat 4 1 Carburettor
Compression ratio: 9.0:1
Bore: 77.0mm 3.0in
Stroke: 65.5mm 2.6in
Valve type/No: Overhead 8
Transmission: Manual
No. of forward speeds: 4
Wheels driven: Front
Springs F/R: Gas/Gas
Brake system: PA
Brakes F/R: Disc/Disc
Steering: Rack & pinion
Wheelbase: 255.0cm 100.4in
Track F: 135.1cm 53.2in
Track R: 132.6cm 52.2in
Length: 381.5cm 150.2in
Width: 160.8cm 63.3in
Height: 137.2cm 54.0in
Ground clearance: 20.3cm 8.0in
Kerb weight: 856.2kg 1886.0lb
Fuel: 43.2L 9.5gal 11.4galUS

1045 Citroen

Safari SM
1973 France
140.0mph 225.3kmh
0-50mph 80.5kmh: 7.2secs
0-60mph 96.5kmh: 9.3secs
0-1/4 mile: 17.1secs
0-1km: 31.0secs
178.0bhp 132.7kW 180.5PS
@ 5500rpm
164.0lbft 222.2Nm @ 4000rpm
117.4bhp/ton 115.5bhp/tonne
66.7bhp/L 49.7kW/L 67.6PS/L
45.1ft/sec 13.7m/sec
23.2mph 37.3kmh/1000rpm
17.9mpg 14.9mpgUS 15.8L/100km
Petrol 4-stroke piston
2670cc 162.9cu in
Vee 6 fuel injection
Compression ratio: 9.0:1
Bore: 87.0mm 3.4in
Stroke: 75.0mm 2.9in
Valve type/No: Overhead 12
Transmission: Manual
No. of forward speeds: 5
Wheels driven: Front
Springs F/R: Gas/Gas
Brake system: PA
Brakes F/R: Disc/Disc
Steering: Rack & pinion PA
Wheelbase: 295.1cm 116.2in
Track F: 152.4cm 60.0in
Track R: 133.6cm 52.6in
Length: 487.7cm 192.0in
Width: 183.4cm 72.2in
Height: 133.4cm 52.5in
Ground clearance: 15.2cm 6.0in
Kerb weight: 1541.3kg 3395.0lb
Fuel: 89.6L 19.7gal 23.7galUS

1046 Citroen

2CV6
1975 France
71.0mph 114.2kmh
0-50mph 80.5kmh: 18.1secs
0-60mph 96.5kmh: 32.7secs
0-1/4 mile: 23.6secs
0-1km: 46.0secs
28.5bhp 21.2kW 28.9PS
@ 5750rpm
30.5lbft 41.3Nm @ 3500rpm
48.1bhp/ton 47.3bhp/tonne
47.3bhp/L 35.3kW/L 48.0PS/L
44.1ft/sec 13.4m/sec
12.4mph 20.0kmh/1000rpm
45.9mpg 38.2mpgUS 6.2L/100km
Petrol 4-stroke piston
602cc 36.7cu in
Flat 2 1 Carburettor
Compression ratio: 8.5:1
Bore: 74.0mm 2.9in
Stroke: 70.0mm 2.8in
Valve type/No: Overhead 4
Transmission: Manual
No. of forward speeds: 4
Wheels driven: Front
Springs F/R: Coil/Coil
Brakes F/R: Drum/Drum
Steering: Rack & pinion
Wheelbase: 240.0cm 94.5in
Track F: 126.0cm 49.6in
Track R: 126.0cm 49.6in
Length: 381.0cm 150.0in
Width: 147.3cm 58.0in
Height: 160.0cm 63.0in
Ground clearance: 20.3cm 8.0in
Kerb weight: 602.5kg 1327.0lb
Fuel: 20.0L 4.4gal 5.3galUS

1047 Citroen

CX 2000
1975 France
112.0mph 180.2kmh
0-50mph 80.5kmh: 8.7secs
0-60mph 96.5kmh: 12.2secs
0-1/4 mile: 18.8secs
0-1km: 34.7secs
102.0bhp 76.1kW 103.4PS
@ 5500rpm
112.0lbft 151.8Nm @ 3000rpm
80.9bhp/ton 79.6bhp/tonne
51.4bhp/L 38.3kW/L 52.1PS/L
51.5ft/sec 15.7m/sec
19.3mph 31.1kmh/1000rpm
23.2mpg 19.3mpgUS 12.2L/100km
Petrol 4-stroke piston
1985cc 121.1cu in
In-line 4 1 Carburettor
Compression ratio: 9.0:1
Bore: 86.0mm 3.4in
Stroke: 85.5mm 3.4in
Valve type/No: Overhead 8
Transmission: Manual
No. of forward speeds: 4
Wheels driven: Front
Springs F/R: Gas/Gas
Brake system: PA
Brakes F/R: Disc/Disc
Steering: Rack & pinion PA
Wheelbase: 284.5cm 112.0in
Track F: 147.3cm 58.0in
Track R: 135.9cm 53.5in
Length: 461.0cm 181.5in
Width: 172.7cm 68.0in
Height: 135.9cm 53.5in
Ground clearance: 15.5cm 6.1in
Kerb weight: 1281.6kg 2823.0lb
Fuel: 68.2L 15.0gal 18.0galUS

1048 Citroen

GS Pallas
1975 France
100.0mph 160.9kmh
0-50mph 80.5kmh: 11.1secs
0-60mph 96.5kmh: 15.9secs
0-1/4 mile: 20.6secs
0-1km: 38.2secs
60.0bhp 44.7kW 60.8PS
@ 5750rpm
67.0lbft 90.8Nm @ 3250rpm
70.0bhp/ton 68.8bhp/tonne
49.2bhp/L 36.7kW/L 49.9PS/L
41.2ft/sec 12.5m/sec
15.2mph 24.5kmh/1000rpm
28.6mpg 23.8mpgUS 9.9L/100km
Petrol 4-stroke piston
1220cc 74.4cu in
Flat 4 1 Carburettor
Compression ratio: 8.2:1
Bore: 77.0mm 3.0in
Stroke: 65.5mm 2.6in
Valve type/No: Overhead 8
Transmission: Manual
No. of forward speeds: 4
Wheels driven: Front
Springs F/R: Gas/Gas
Brake system: PA
Brakes F/R: Disc/Disc
Steering: Rack & pinion
Wheelbase: 255.0cm 100.4in
Track F: 135.1cm 53.2in
Track R: 132.6cm 52.2in
Length: 381.5cm 150.2in
Width: 160.8cm 63.3in
Height: 137.2cm 54.0in
Ground clearance: 20.3cm 8.0in
Kerb weight: 872.1kg 1921.0lb
Fuel: 43.2L 9.5gal 11.4galUS

1049 Citroen

CX 2200 Pallas
1976 France
115.0mph 185.0kmh
0-50mph 80.5kmh: 8.1secs
0-60mph 96.5kmh: 11.6secs
0-1/4 mile: 18.2secs
0-1km: 33.5secs
110.0bhp 82.0kW 111.5PS
@ 5500rpm
123.0lbft 166.7Nm @ 3500rpm
84.4bhp/ton 83.0bhp/tonne
50.6bhp/L 37.7kW/L 51.3PS/L
51.3ft/sec 15.6m/sec
20.0mph 32.2kmh/1000rpm
23.5mpg 19.6mpgUS 12.0L/100km
Petrol 4-stroke piston
2175cc 132.7cu in
In-line 4 1 Carburettor
Compression ratio: 9.0:1
Bore: 90.0mm 3.5in
Stroke: 85.3mm 3.4in
Valve type/No: Overhead 8
Transmission: Manual
No. of forward speeds: 4
Wheels driven: Front
Springs F/R: Gas/Gas
Brake system: PA
Brakes F/R: Disc/Disc
Steering: Rack & pinion PA
Wheelbase: 284.5cm 112.0in
Track F: 147.3cm 58.0in
Track R: 135.9cm 53.5in
Length: 461.0cm 181.5in
Width: 172.7cm 68.0in
Height: 135.9cm 53.5in
Ground clearance: 15.5cm 6.1in
Kerb weight: 1324.8kg 2918.0lb
Fuel: 68.2L 15.0gal 18.0galUS

1050 Citroen

GS X2
1976 France
100.0mph 160.9kmh
0-50mph 80.5kmh: 10.6secs
0-60mph 96.5kmh: 15.4secs
0-1/4 mile: 20.0secs
0-1km: 37.7secs
65.0bhp 48.5kW 65.9PS
@ 5750rpm
67.0lbft 90.8Nm @ 3250rpm
70.3bhp/ton 69.1bhp/tonne
53.2bhp/L 39.7kW/L 53.9PS/L
41.2ft/sec 12.6m/sec
15.2mph 24.5kmh/1000rpm
29.0mpg 24.1mpgUS 9.7L/100km
Petrol 4-stroke piston
1222cc 74.6cu in
Flat 4 1 Carburettor
Compression ratio: 8.7:1
Bore: 77.0mm 3.0in
Stroke: 65.6mm 2.6in
Valve type/No: Overhead 8
Transmission: Manual

No. of forward speeds: 4
Wheels driven: Front
Springs F/R: Gas/Gas
Brake system: PA
Brakes F/R: Disc/Disc
Steering: Rack & pinion
Wheelbase: 255.0cm 100.4in
Track F: 135.1cm 53.2in
Track R: 132.6cm 52.2in
Length: 381.5cm 150.2in
Width: 160.8cm 63.3in
Height: 137.2cm 54.0in
Ground clearance: 20.3cm 8.0in
Kerb weight: 940.7kg 2072.0lb
Fuel: 43.2L 9.5gal 11.4galUS

1051 Citroen

CX 2200 Diesel
1977 France
90.0mph 144.8kmh
0-50mph 80.5kmh: 14.6secs
0-60mph 96.5kmh: 20.8secs
0-1/4 mile: 21.9secs
0-1km: 40.7secs
66.0bhp 49.2kW 66.9PS
@ 4500rpm
92.6lbft 125.5Nm @ 2750rpm
47.1bhp/ton 46.3bhp/tonne
30.3bhp/L 22.6kW/L 30.8PS/L
42.1ft/sec 12.8m/sec
19.3mph 31.1kmh/1000rpm
31.8mpg 26.5mpgUS 8.9L/100km
Diesel 4-stroke piston
2175cc 132.7cu in
In-line 4 fuel injection
Compression ratio: 22.2:1
Bore: 90.0mm 3.5in
Stroke: 85.5mm 3.4in
Valve type/No: Overhead 8
Transmission: Manual
No. of forward speeds: 4
Wheels driven: Front
Springs F/R: Gas/Gas
Brake system: PA
Brakes F/R: Disc/Disc
Steering: Rack & pinion PA
Wheelbase: 284.5cm 112.0in
Track F: 147.3cm 58.0in
Track R: 135.9cm 53.5in
Length: 461.0cm 181.5in
Width: 172.7cm 68.0in
Height: 135.9cm 53.5in
Ground clearance: 15.5cm 6.1in
Kerb weight: 1425.6kg 3140.0lb
Fuel: 68.2L 15.0gal 18.0galUS

1052 Citroen

CX 2400
1977 France
116.0mph 186.6kmh
0-50mph 80.5kmh: 8.1secs
0-60mph 96.5kmh: 11.8secs
0-1/4 mile: 18.1secs
0-1km: 33.5secs
115.0bhp 85.8kW 116.6PS
@ 5500rpm
131.0lbft 177.5Nm @ 3000rpm
86.1bhp/ton 84.7bhp/tonne
49.0bhp/L 36.5kW/L 49.7PS/L
51.5ft/sec 15.7m/sec
21.1mph 33.9kmh/1000rpm
23.5mpg 19.6mpgUS 12.0L/100km
Petrol 4-stroke piston
2347cc 143.2cu in
In-line 4 1 Carburettor
Compression ratio: 8.7:1
Bore: 93.5mm 3.7in
Stroke: 85.5mm 3.4in
Valve type/No: Overhead 8
Transmission: Manual
No. of forward speeds: 4
Wheels driven: Front
Springs F/R: Gas/Gas
Brake system: PA
Brakes F/R: Disc/Disc
Steering: Rack & pinion PA
Wheelbase: 284.5cm 112.0in
Track F: 147.3cm 58.0in
Track R: 135.9cm 53.5in
Length: 461.0cm 181.5in
Width: 172.7cm 68.0in
Height: 135.9cm 53.5in
Ground clearance: 15.5cm 6.1in
Kerb weight: 1357.5kg 2990.0lb
Fuel: 68.2L 15.0gal 18.0galUS

1053 Citroen

CX 2400 GTi
1977 France
118.0mph 189.9kmh
0-50mph 80.5kmh: 7.4secs
0-60mph 96.5kmh: 10.1secs
0-1/4 mile: 17.4secs
0-1km: 32.3secs
128.0bhp 95.4kW 129.8PS
@ 4800rpm
148.0lbft 200.5Nm @ 3600rpm
95.6bhp/ton 94.0bhp/tonne
54.5bhp/L 40.7kW/L 55.3PS/L
44.9ft/sec 13.7m/sec
21.1mph 33.9kmh/1000rpm
21.6mpg 18.0mpgUS 13.1L/100km
Petrol 4-stroke piston
2347cc 143.2cu in
In-line 4 fuel injection
Compression ratio: 9.1:1
Bore: 93.5mm 3.7in
Stroke: 85.5mm 3.4in
Valve type/No: Overhead 8
Transmission: Manual
No. of forward speeds: 5
Wheels driven: Front
Springs F/R: Gas/Gas
Brake system: PA
Brakes F/R: Disc/Disc
Steering: Rack & pinion PA
Wheelbase: 284.5cm 112.0in
Track F: 147.3cm 58.0in
Track R: 135.9cm 53.5in
Length: 464.8cm 183.0in
Width: 172.7cm 68.0in
Height: 135.9cm 53.5in
Ground clearance: 15.5cm 6.1in
Kerb weight: 1362.0kg 3000.0lb
Fuel: 68.2L 15.0gal 18.0galUS

1054 Citroen

CX Pallas C-Matic Injection
1978 France
113.0mph 181.8kmh
0-50mph 80.5kmh: 8.8secs
0-60mph 96.5kmh: 12.2secs
0-1/4 mile: 18.7secs
0-1km: 33.9secs
128.0bhp 95.4kW 129.8PS
@ 4800rpm
145.0lbft 196.5Nm @ 3600rpm
93.6bhp/ton 92.0bhp/tonne
54.5bhp/L 40.7kW/L 55.3PS/L
44.9ft/sec 13.7m/sec
19.2mph 30.9kmh/1000rpm
20.9mpg 17.4mpgUS 13.5L/100km
Petrol 4-stroke piston
2347cc 143.2cu in
In-line 4 fuel injection
Compression ratio: 8.7:1
Bore: 93.5mm 3.7in
Stroke: 85.5mm 3.4in
Valve type/No: Overhead 8
Transmission: Automatic
No. of forward speeds: 3
Wheels driven: Front
Springs F/R: Gas/Gas
Brake system: PA
Brakes F/R: Disc/Disc
Steering: Rack & pinion PA
Wheelbase: 284.5cm 112.0in
Track F: 147.3cm 58.0in
Track R: 135.9cm 53.5in
Length: 462.8cm 182.2in
Width: 172.7cm 68.0in
Height: 130.8cm 51.5in
Ground clearance: 15.5cm 6.1in
Kerb weight: 1390.6kg 3063.0lb
Fuel: 68.2L 15.0gal 18.0galUS

1055 Citroen

Athena
1979 France
110.0mph 177.0kmh
0-50mph 80.5kmh: 8.7secs
0-60mph 96.5kmh: 12.5secs
0-1/4 mile: 18.2secs
0-1km: 33.9secs
106.0bhp 79.0kW 107.5PS
@ 5500rpm
122.0lbft 165.3Nm @ 3250rpm
87.5bhp/ton 86.1bhp/tonne
53.1bhp/L 39.6kW/L 53.9PS/L
49.3ft/sec 15.0m/sec
22.0mph 35.4kmh/1000rpm
26.2mpg 21.8mpgUS 10.8L/100km
Petrol 4-stroke piston
1995cc 121.7cu in
In-line 4 1 Carburettor
Compression ratio: 9.2:1
Bore: 88.0mm 3.5in
Stroke: 82.0mm 3.2in
Valve type/No: Overhead 8
Transmission: Manual
No. of forward speeds: 5
Wheels driven: Front
Springs F/R: Gas/Gas
Brake system: PA
Brakes F/R: Disc/Disc
Steering: Rack & pinion PA
Wheelbase: 284.5cm 112.0in
Track F: 147.3cm 58.0in
Track R: 135.9cm 53.5in
Length: 462.8cm 182.2in
Width: 172.7cm 68.0in
Height: 130.8cm 51.5in
Ground clearance: 15.5cm 6.1in
Kerb weight: 1231.7kg 2713.0lb
Fuel: 68.2L 15.0gal 18.0galUS

1056 Citroen

CX 2500 Diesel Super
1979 France
99.0mph 159.3kmh
0-50mph 80.5kmh: 12.0secs
0-60mph 96.5kmh: 17.0secs
0-1/4 mile: 20.7secs
0-1km: 37.6secs
75.0bhp 55.9kW 76.0PS
@ 4250rpm
111.0lbft 150.4Nm @ 2000rpm
56.8bhp/ton 55.8bhp/tonne
30.0bhp/L 22.4kW/L 30.4PS/L
42.7ft/sec 13.0m/sec
22.7mph 36.5kmh/1000rpm
31.5mpg 26.2mpgUS 9.0L/100km
Diesel 4-stroke piston
2500cc 152.5cu in
In-line 4 fuel injection
Compression ratio: 22.2:1
Bore: 93.0mm 3.7in
Stroke: 92.0mm 3.6in
Valve type/No: Overhead 8
Transmission: Manual
No. of forward speeds: 5
Wheels driven: Front
Springs F/R: Gas/Gas
Brake system: PA
Brakes F/R: Disc/Disc
Steering: Rack & pinion PA
Wheelbase: 284.5cm 112.0in
Track F: 147.3cm 58.0in
Track R: 135.9cm 53.5in
Length: 462.8cm 182.2in
Width: 172.7cm 68.0in
Height: 135.9cm 53.5in
Ground clearance: 15.5cm 6.1in
Kerb weight: 1343.8kg 2960.0lb
Fuel: 68.2L 15.0gal 18.0galUS

1057 Citroen

Visa Club
1979 France
72.0mph 115.8kmh
0-50mph 80.5kmh: 17.1secs
0-60mph 96.5kmh: 27.9secs
0-1/4 mile: 23.2secs
0-1km: 43.7secs
36.0bhp 26.8kW 36.5PS
@ 5500rpm
38.0lbft 51.5Nm @ 3500rpm
48.6bhp/ton 47.8bhp/tonne
55.2bhp/L 41.2kW/L 56.0PS/L
42.2ft/sec 12.8m/sec
13.1mph 21.1kmh/1000rpm
36.1mpg 30.1mpgUS 7.8L/100km
Petrol 4-stroke piston
652cc 39.8cu in
Flat 2 1 Carburettor
Compression ratio: 9.0:1
Bore: 77.0mm 3.0in
Stroke: 70.0mm 2.8in
Valve type/No: Overhead 4
Transmission: Manual
No. of forward speeds: 4
Wheels driven: Front
Springs F/R: Coil/Coil
Brakes F/R: Disc/Drum
Steering: Rack & pinion
Wheelbase: 243.1cm 95.7in
Track F: 129.3cm 50.9in
Track R: 124.2cm 48.9in
Length: 369.1cm 145.3in
Width: 151.1cm 59.5in
Height: 140.7cm 55.4in
Ground clearance: 12.7cm 5.0in
Kerb weight: 753.2kg 1659.0lb
Fuel: 40.0L 8.8gal 10.6galUS

1058 Citroen

CX Pallas
1981 France
116.0mph 186.6kmh
0-50mph 80.5kmh: 8.1secs
0-60mph 96.5kmh: 11.6secs
0-1/4 mile: 18.2secs
0-1km: 32.4secs
128.0bhp 95.4kW 129.8PS
@ 4800rpm
145.0lbft 196.5Nm @ 3600rpm
89.9bhp/ton 88.4bhp/tonne
54.5bhp/L 40.7kW/L 55.3PS/L
44.9ft/sec 13.7m/sec
21.0mph 33.8kmh/1000rpm
21.9mpg 18.2mpgUS 12.9L/100km
Petrol 4-stroke piston
2347cc 143.2cu in
In-line 4 fuel injection
Compression ratio: 9.0:1
Bore: 93.5mm 3.7in
Stroke: 85.5mm 3.4in
Valve type/No: Overhead 8
Transmission: Automatic
No. of forward speeds: 3
Wheels driven: Front
Springs F/R: Gas/Gas
Brake system: PA
Brakes F/R: Disc/Disc
Steering: Rack & pinion PA
Wheelbase: 284.5cm 112.0in
Track F: 147.3cm 58.0in
Track R: 135.9cm 53.5in
Length: 463.6cm 182.5in
Width: 172.7cm 68.0in
Height: 135.9cm 53.5in
Ground clearance: 15.2cm 6.0in
Kerb weight: 1448.3kg 3190.0lb
Fuel: 68.2L 15.0gal 18.0galUS

1059 Citroen

BX14 RE
1983 France
99.0mph 159.3kmh
0-50mph 80.5kmh: 10.3secs
0-60mph 96.5kmh: 15.3secs
0-1/4 mile: 20.3secs
0-1km: 32.3secs
72.0bhp 53.7kW 73.0PS
@ 5750rpm
79.4lbft 107.6Nm @ 3000rpm
85.1bhp/ton 83.6bhp/tonne
52.9bhp/L 39.5kW/L 53.7PS/L
48.4ft/sec 14.8m/sec
19.2mph 30.9kmh/1000rpm
30.5mpg 25.4mpgUS 9.3L/100km
Petrol 4-stroke piston
1360cc 83.0cu in
In-line 4 1 Carburettor
Compression ratio: 9.3:1
Bore: 75.0mm 2.9in
Stroke: 77.0mm 3.0in
Valve type/No: Overhead 8
Transmission: Manual
No. of forward speeds: 5
Wheels driven: Front
Springs F/R: Gas/Gas
Brake system: PA
Brakes F/R: Disc/Disc
Steering: Rack & pinion PA
Wheelbase: 265.4cm 104.5in
Track F: 141.0cm 55.5in
Track R: 135.4cm 53.3in
Length: 422.9cm 166.5in
Width: 165.9cm 65.3in
Height: 135.9cm 53.5in
Ground clearance: 16.3cm 6.4in
Kerb weight: 860.8kg 1896.0lb
Fuel: 44.1L 9.7gal 11.7galUS

1060 Citroen

BX16 TRS
1983 France
112.0mph 180.2kmh
0-50mph 80.5kmh: 7.6secs
0-60mph 96.5kmh: 10.7secs
0-1/4 mile: 17.9secs
0-1km: 33.4secs
92.5bhp 69.0kW 93.8PS
@ 6000rpm
97.0lbft 131.4Nm @ 3500rpm

98.0bhp/ton 96.4bhp/tonne
58.5bhp/L 43.7kW/L 59.3PS/L
47.8ft/sec 14.6m/sec
21.2mph 34.1kmh/1000rpm
30.3mpg 25.2mpgUS 9.3L/100km
Petrol 4-stroke piston
1580cc 96.4cu in
In-line 4 1 Carburettor
Compression ratio: 9.5:1
Bore: 83.0mm 3.3in
Stroke: 73.0mm 2.9in
Valve type/No: Overhead 8
Transmission: Manual
No. of forward speeds: 5
Wheels driven: Front
Springs F/R: Gas/Gas
Brake system: PA
Brakes F/R: Disc/Disc
Steering: Rack & pinion PA
Wheelbase: 265.4cm 104.5in
Track F: 141.0cm 55.5in
Track R: 135.4cm 53.3in
Length: 422.9cm 166.5in
Width: 165.9cm 65.3in
Height: 135.9cm 53.5in
Ground clearance: 16.3cm 6.4in
Kerb weight: 959.8kg 2114.0lb
Fuel: 51.9L 11.4gal 13.7galUS

1061 Citroen

BX19 RD Diesel
1984 France
100.0mph 160.9kmh
0-50mph 80.5kmh: 11.2secs
0-60mph 96.5kmh: 15.6secs
0-1/4 mile: 20.2secs
0-1km: 37.5secs
65.0bhp 48.5kW 65.9PS
@ 4600rpm
88.0lbft 119.2Nm @ 2000rpm
64.4bhp/ton 63.3bhp/tonne
34.1bhp/L 25.4kW/L 34.6PS/L
44.2ft/sec 13.5m/sec
22.5mph 36.2kmh/1000rpm
42.1mpg 35.1mpgUS 6.7L/100km
Diesel 4-stroke piston
1905cc 116.2cu in
In-line 4 fuel injection
Compression ratio: 23.5:1
Bore: 83.0mm 3.3in
Stroke: 88.0mm 3.5in
Valve type/No: Overhead 8
Transmission: Manual
No. of forward speeds: 5
Wheels driven: Front
Springs F/R: Gas/Gas
Brake system: PA
Brakes F/R: Disc/Disc
Steering: Rack & pinion PA
Wheelbase: 265.4cm 104.5in
Track F: 141.0cm 55.5in
Track R: 135.4cm 53.3in
Length: 422.9cm 166.5in
Width: 165.9cm 65.3in
Height: 135.9cm 53.5in
Ground clearance: 16.3cm 6.4in
Kerb weight: 1026.5kg 2261.0lb
Fuel: 51.9L 11.4gal 13.7galUS

1062 Citroen

CX GTi Turbo
1984 France
128.0mph 206.0kmh
0-50mph 80.5kmh: 5.9secs
0-60mph 96.5kmh: 8.6secs
0-1/4 mile: 16.7secs
0-1km: 30.2secs
168.0bhp 125.3kW 170.3PS
@ 5000rpm
217.0lbft 294.0Nm @ 3250rpm
121.1bhp/ton 119.1bhp/tonne
67.9bhp/L 50.7kW/L 68.9PS/L
50.3ft/sec 15.3m/sec
25.2mph 40.5kmh/1000rpm
20.1mpg 16.7mpgUS 14.1L/100km
Petrol 4-stroke piston
2473cc 150.9cu in turbocharged
In-line 4 fuel injection
Compression ratio: 7.7:1
Bore: 93.0mm 3.7in
Stroke: 92.0mm 3.6in
Valve type/No: Overhead 8
Transmission: Manual
No. of forward speeds: 5
Wheels driven: Front
Springs F/R: Gas/Gas
Brake system: PA
Brakes F/R: Disc/Disc
Steering: Rack & pinion PA
Wheelbase: 285.0cm 112.2in
Track F: 147.3cm 58.0in
Track R: 135.9cm 53.5in
Length: 466.1cm 183.5in
Width: 177.0cm 69.7in
Height: 135.9cm 53.5in
Ground clearance: 15.2cm 6.0in
Kerb weight: 1410.6kg 3107.0lb
Fuel: 68.2L 15.0gal 18.0galUS

1063 Citroen

LNA 11RE
1984 France
85.0mph 136.8kmh
0-50mph 80.5kmh: 10.7secs
0-60mph 96.5kmh: 16.0secs
0-1/4 mile: 20.3secs
0-1km: 38.2secs
50.0bhp 37.3kW 50.7PS
@ 5500rpm
62.0lbft 84.0Nm @ 2500rpm
68.4bhp/ton 67.2bhp/tonne
44.5bhp/L 33.2kW/L 45.1PS/L
41.6ft/sec 12.6m/sec
20.7mph 33.3kmh/1000rpm
35.2mpg 29.3mpgUS 8.0L/100km
Petrol 4-stroke piston
1124cc 68.6cu in
In-line 4 1 Carburettor
Compression ratio: 9.7:1
Bore: 72.0mm 2.8in
Stroke: 69.0mm 2.7in
Valve type/No: Overhead 8
Transmission: Manual
No. of forward speeds: 4
Wheels driven: Front
Springs F/R: Coil/Coil
Brake system: PA
Brakes F/R: Disc/Drum
Steering: Rack & pinion
Wheelbase: 223.0cm 87.8in
Track F: 129.0cm 50.8in
Track R: 127.0cm 50.0in
Length: 342.9cm 135.0in
Width: 153.9cm 60.6in
Height: 137.9cm 54.3in
Ground clearance: 13.0cm 5.1in
Kerb weight: 743.6kg 1638.0lb
Fuel: 40.0L 8.8gal 10.6galUS

1064 Citroen

Visa Convertible
1984 France
85.0mph 136.8kmh
0-50mph 80.5kmh: 12.4secs
0-60mph 96.5kmh: 20.1secs
0-1/4 mile: 20.6secs
0-1km: 39.7secs
50.0bhp 37.3kW 50.7PS
@ 5500rpm
62.0lbft 84.0Nm @ 2500rpm
64.1bhp/ton 63.0bhp/tonne
44.5bhp/L 33.2kW/L 45.1PS/L
41.6ft/sec 12.6m/sec
19.0mph 30.6kmh/1000rpm
30.6mpg 25.5mpgUS 9.2L/100km
Petrol 4-stroke piston
1124cc 68.6cu in
In-line 4 1 Carburettor
Compression ratio: 9.7:1
Bore: 72.0mm 2.8in
Stroke: 69.0mm 2.7in
Valve type/No: Overhead 8
Transmission: Manual
No. of forward speeds: 4
Wheels driven: Front
Springs F/R: Coil/Coil
Brake system: PA
Brakes F/R: Disc/Drum
Steering: Rack & pinion
Wheelbase: 242.1cm 95.3in
Track F: 129.3cm 50.9in
Track R: 124.2cm 48.9in
Length: 369.1cm 145.3in
Width: 153.4cm 60.4in
Height: 141.0cm 55.5in
Ground clearance: 12.7cm 5.0in
Kerb weight: 793.6kg 1748.0lb
Fuel: 40.0L 8.8gal 10.6galUS

1065 Citroen

2CV6 Charleston
1985 France
71.0mph 114.2kmh
0-50mph 80.5kmh: 16.9secs
0-60mph 96.5kmh: 27.3secs
0-1/4 mile: 23.0secs
29.0bhp 21.6kW 29.4PS
@ 5750rpm
29.0lbft 39.3Nm @ 3500rpm
51.3bhp/ton 50.5bhp/tonne
48.2bhp/L 35.9kW/L 48.8PS/L
44.1ft/sec 13.4m/sec
12.6mph 20.3kmh/1000rpm
51.0mpg 42.5mpgUS 5.5L/100km
Petrol 4-stroke piston
602cc 36.7cu in
Flat 2 1 Carburettor
Compression ratio: 8.5:1
Bore: 74.0mm 2.9in
Stroke: 70.0mm 2.8in
Valve type/No: Overhead 4
Transmission: Manual
No. of forward speeds: 4
Wheels driven: Front
Springs F/R: Coil/Coil
Brakes F/R: Disc/Drum
Steering: Rack & pinion
Wheelbase: 240.0cm 94.5in
Track F: 126.0cm 49.6in
Track R: 126.0cm 49.6in
Length: 383.0cm 150.8in
Width: 148.1cm 58.3in
Height: 160.0cm 63.0in
Ground clearance: 19.1cm 7.5in
Kerb weight: 574.3kg 1265.0lb
Fuel: 25.0L 5.5gal 6.6galUS

1066 Citroen

BX16 TRS Automatic
1985 France
109.0mph 175.4kmh
0-50mph 80.5kmh: 9.8secs
0-60mph 96.5kmh: 13.5secs
0-1/4 mile: 19.6secs
0-1km: 36.0secs
93.0bhp 69.3kW 94.3PS
@ 6000rpm
101.0lbft 136.9Nm @ 3500rpm
92.7bhp/ton 91.1bhp/tonne
58.9bhp/L 43.9kW/L 59.7PS/L
47.8ft/sec 14.6m/sec
21.3mph 34.3kmh/1000rpm
26.5mpg 22.1mpgUS 10.7L/100km
Petrol 4-stroke piston
1580cc 96.4cu in
In-line 4 1 Carburettor
Compression ratio: 9.5:1
Bore: 83.0mm 3.3in
Stroke: 73.0mm 2.9in
Valve type/No: Overhead 8
Transmission: Automatic
No. of forward speeds: 4
Wheels driven: Front
Springs F/R: Gas/Gas
Brake system: PA
Brakes F/R: Disc/Disc
Steering: Rack & pinion PA
Wheelbase: 265.4cm 104.5in
Track F: 141.0cm 55.5in
Track R: 135.4cm 53.3in
Length: 422.9cm 166.5in
Width: 165.9cm 65.3in
Height: 135.9cm 53.5in
Ground clearance: 16.3cm 6.4in
Kerb weight: 1020.6kg 2248.0lb
Fuel: 51.9L 11.4gal 13.7galUS

1067 Citroen

CX22 TRS
1985 France
113.0mph 181.8kmh
0-50mph 80.5kmh: 7.6secs
0-60mph 96.5kmh: 10.8secs
0-1/4 mile: 17.6secs
0-1km: 32.9secs
115.0bhp 85.8kW 116.6PS
@ 5600rpm
131.0lbft 177.5Nm @ 3250rpm
90.8bhp/ton 89.3bhp/tonne
53.1bhp/L 39.6kW/L 53.9PS/L
54.4ft/sec 16.6m/sec
22.5mph 36.2kmh/1000rpm
26.2mpg 21.8mpgUS 10.8L/100km
Petrol 4-stroke piston
2165cc 132.1cu in
In-line 4 1 Carburettor
Compression ratio: 9.8:1
Bore: 88.0mm 3.5in
Stroke: 89.0mm 3.5in
Valve type/No: Overhead 8
Transmission: Manual
No. of forward speeds: 5
Wheels driven: Front
Springs F/R: Gas/Gas
Brake system: PA
Brakes F/R: Disc/Disc
Steering: Rack & pinion PA
Wheelbase: 285.0cm 112.2in
Track F: 147.3cm 58.0in
Track R: 135.9cm 53.5in
Length: 466.1cm 183.5in
Width: 177.0cm 69.7in
Height: 135.9cm 53.5in
Ground clearance: 15.2cm 6.0in
Kerb weight: 1287.5kg 2836.0lb
Fuel: 68.2L 15.0gal 18.0galUS

1068 Citroen

Visa 14TRS
1985 France
98.0mph 157.7kmh
0-50mph 80.5kmh: 9.8secs
0-60mph 96.5kmh: 14.9secs
0-1/4 mile: 19.5secs
0-1km: 37.2secs
60.0bhp 44.7kW 60.8PS
@ 5000rpm
77.2lbft 104.6Nm @ 2500rpm
77.6bhp/ton 76.3bhp/tonne
44.1bhp/L 32.9kW/L 44.7PS/L
42.1ft/sec 12.8m/sec
21.7mph 34.9kmh/1000rpm
31.3mpg 26.1mpgUS 9.0L/100km
Petrol 4-stroke piston
1360cc 83.0cu in
In-line 4 1 Carburettor
Compression ratio: 9.3:1
Bore: 75.0mm 2.9in
Stroke: 77.0mm 3.0in
Valve type/No: Overhead 8
Transmission: Manual
No. of forward speeds: 5
Wheels driven: Front
Springs F/R: Coil/Coil
Brake system: PA
Brakes F/R: Disc/Drum
Steering: Rack & pinion
Wheelbase: 242.1cm 95.3in
Track F: 129.3cm 50.9in
Track R: 124.2cm 48.9in
Length: 369.1cm 145.3in
Width: 153.4cm 60.4in
Height: 141.0cm 55.5in
Ground clearance: 12.7cm 5.0in
Kerb weight: 785.9kg 1731.0lb
Fuel: 40.0L 8.8gal 10.6galUS

1069 Citroen

Visa 17RD
1985 France
93.0mph 149.6kmh
0-50mph 80.5kmh: 12.7secs
0-60mph 96.5kmh: 19.1secs
0-1/4 mile: 21.1secs
0-1km: 39.4secs
60.0bhp 44.7kW 60.8PS
@ 4600rpm
82.0lbft 111.1Nm @ 2000rpm
67.7bhp/ton 66.6bhp/tonne
33.9bhp/L 25.3kW/L 34.4PS/L
44.2ft/sec 13.5m/sec
22.4mph 36.0kmh/1000rpm
43.9mpg 36.6mpgUS 6.4L/100km
Diesel 4-stroke piston
1769cc 107.9cu in
In-line 4 fuel injection
Compression ratio: 23.0:1
Bore: 80.0mm 3.1in
Stroke: 88.0mm 3.5in
Valve type/No: Overhead 8
Transmission: Manual
No. of forward speeds: 4
Wheels driven: Front
Springs F/R: Coil/Coil
Brake system: PA
Brakes F/R: Disc/Drum
Steering: Rack & pinion
Wheelbase: 242.1cm 95.3in
Track F: 129.3cm 50.9in
Track R: 124.2cm 48.9in
Length: 369.1cm 145.3in
Width: 153.4cm 60.4in
Height: 141.0cm 55.5in
Ground clearance: 12.7cm 5.0in
Kerb weight: 900.7kg 1984.0lb
Fuel: 43.2L 9.5gal 11.4galUS

1070 Citroen
Visa GTi
1985 France
112.0mph 180.2kmh
0-50mph 80.5kmh: 7.0secs
0-60mph 96.5kmh: 9.7secs
0-1/4 mile: 17.4secs
0-1km: 32.6secs
105.0bhp 78.3kW 106.5PS
@ 6250rpm
99.0lbft 134.1Nm @ 4000rpm
116.8bhp/ton 114.9bhp/tonne
66.5bhp/L 49.6kW/L 67.4PS/L
49.8ft/sec 15.2m/sec
18.3mph 29.4kmh/1000rpm
28.8mpg 24.0mpgUS 9.8L/100km
Petrol 4-stroke piston
1580cc 96.4cu in
In-line 4 fuel injection
Compression ratio: 9.8:1
Bore: 83.0mm 3.3in
Stroke: 73.0mm 2.9in
Valve type/No: Overhead 8
Transmission: Manual
No. of forward speeds: 5
Wheels driven: Front
Springs F/R: Coil/Coil
Brake system: PA
Brakes F/R: Disc/Drum
Steering: Rack & pinion
Wheelbase: 242.1cm 95.3in
Track F: 129.3cm 50.9in
Track R: 124.2cm 48.9in
Length: 369.1cm 145.3in
Width: 153.4cm 60.4in
Height: 141.0cm 55.5in
Ground clearance: 12.7cm 5.0in
Kerb weight: 913.9kg 2013.0lb
Fuel: 43.2L 9.5gal 11.4galUS

1071 Citroen
BX19 RD Estate
1986 France
94.0mph 151.2kmh
0-50mph 80.5kmh: 12.2secs
0-60mph 96.5kmh: 17.9secs
0-1/4 mile: 20.8secs
0-1km: 38.7secs
65.0bhp 48.5kW 65.9PS
@ 4600rpm
88.0lbft 119.2Nm @ 2000rpm
62.1bhp/ton 61.0bhp/tonne
34.1bhp/L 25.4kW/L 34.6PS/L
44.2ft/sec 13.5m/sec
21.8mph 35.1kmh/1000rpm
38.4mpg 32.0mpgUS 7.4L/100km
Diesel 4-stroke piston
1905cc 116.2cu in
In-line 4 fuel injection
Compression ratio: 23.5:1
Bore: 83.0mm 3.3in
Stroke: 88.0mm 3.5in
Valve type/No: Overhead 8
Transmission: Manual
No. of forward speeds: 5
Wheels driven: Front
Springs F/R: Gas/Gas
Brake system: PA
Brakes F/R: Disc/Disc
Steering: Rack & pinion PA
Wheelbase: 265.4cm 104.5in
Track F: 141.0cm 55.5in
Track R: 135.4cm 53.3in
Length: 439.9cm 173.2in
Width: 165.6cm 65.2in
Height: 142.7cm 56.2in
Ground clearance: 16.3cm 6.4in
Kerb weight: 1064.6kg 2345.0lb
Fuel: 51.9L 11.4gal 13.7galUS

1072 Citroen
CX25 Ri Familiale Auto
1986 France
116.0mph 186.6kmh
0-50mph 80.5kmh: 8.7secs
0-60mph 96.5kmh: 11.9secs
0-1/4 mile: 18.7secs
0-1km: 34.9secs
138.0bhp 102.9kW 139.9PS
@ 5000rpm
155.0lbft 210.0Nm @ 4000rpm
97.5bhp/ton 95.8bhp/tonne
55.8bhp/L 41.6kW/L 56.6PS/L
50.3ft/sec 15.3m/sec
21.7mph 34.9kmh/1000rpm
20.4mpg 17.0mpgUS 13.8L/100km
Petrol 4-stroke piston
2473cc 151.0cu in
In-line 4 fuel injection
Compression ratio: 8.7:1
Bore: 93.0mm 3.7in
Stroke: 92.0mm 3.6in
Valve type/No: Overhead 8
Transmission: Automatic
No. of forward speeds: 3
Wheels driven: Front
Springs F/R: Gas/Gas
Brake system: PA
Brakes F/R: Disc/Disc
Steering: Rack & pinion PA
Wheelbase: 307.3cm 121.0in
Track F: 147.3cm 58.0in
Track R: 135.9cm 53.5in
Length: 495.2cm 195.0in
Width: 177.0cm 69.7in
Height: 146.5cm 57.7in
Ground clearance: 15.5cm 6.1in
Kerb weight: 1440.0kg 3171.8lb
Fuel: 68.2L 15.0gal 18.0galUS

1073 Citroen
Visa GTi
1986 France
115.0mph 185.0kmh
0-50mph 80.5kmh: 6.5secs
0-60mph 96.5kmh: 9.1secs
0-1/4 mile: 17.1secs
0-1km: 31.7secs
115.0bhp 85.8kW 116.6PS
@ 6250rpm
97.0lbft 131.4Nm @ 4000rpm
133.3bhp/ton 131.1bhp/tonne
72.8bhp/L 54.3kW/L 73.8PS/L
49.8ft/sec 15.2m/sec
18.3mph 29.4kmh/1000rpm
26.2mpg 21.8mpgUS 10.8L/100km
Petrol 4-stroke piston
1580cc 96.0cu in
In-line 4 fuel injection
Compression ratio: 9.8:1
Bore: 83.0mm 3.3in
Stroke: 73.0mm 2.9in
Valve type/No: Overhead 8
Transmission: Manual
No. of forward speeds: 5
Wheels driven: Front
Springs F/R: Coil/Coil
Brake system: PA
Brakes F/R: Disc/Drum
Steering: Rack & pinion
Wheelbase: 242.1cm 95.3in
Track F: 129.2cm 50.9in
Track R: 124.1cm 48.9in
Length: 369.0cm 145.3in
Width: 153.4cm 60.4in
Height: 141.0cm 55.5in
Ground clearance: 13.1cm 5.2in
Kerb weight: 877.0kg 1931.7lb
Fuel: 43.2L 9.5gal 11.4galUS

1074 Citroen
AX GT
1987 France
108.0mph 173.8kmh
0-50mph 80.5kmh: 6.3secs
0-60mph 96.5kmh: 9.0secs
0-1/4 mile: 16.8secs
0-1km: 31.6secs
85.0bhp 63.4kW 86.2PS
@ 6400rpm
85.3lbft 115.6Nm @ 4000rpm
121.3bhp/ton 119.3bhp/tonne
62.5bhp/L 46.6kW/L 63.4PS/L
53.9ft/sec 16.4m/sec
18.2mph 29.3kmh/1000rpm
30.4mpg 25.3mpgUS 9.3L/100km
Petrol 4-stroke piston
1360cc 83.0cu in
In-line 4 1 Carburettor
Compression ratio: 9.3:1
Bore: 75.0mm 2.9in
Stroke: 77.0mm 3.0in
Valve type/No: Overhead 8
Transmission: Manual
No. of forward speeds: 5
Wheels driven: Front
Springs F/R: Coil/Torsion bar
Brake system: PA
Brakes F/R: Disc/Drum
Steering: Rack & pinion
Wheelbase: 228.5cm 90.0in
Track F: 138.0cm 54.3in
Track R: 130.0cm 51.2in
Length: 349.5cm 137.6in
Width: 155.5cm 61.2in
Height: 135.5cm 53.3in
Ground clearance: 11.0cm 4.3in
Kerb weight: 712.3kg 1569.0lb
Fuel: 43.2L 9.5gal 11.4galUS

1075 Citroen
AX11 TRE
1987 France
101.0mph 162.5kmh
0-50mph 80.5kmh: 8.3secs
0-60mph 96.5kmh: 12.6secs
0-1/4 mile: 17.9secs
0-1km: 34.6secs
54.0bhp 40.3kW 54.7PS
@ 5800rpm
65.7lbft 89.0Nm @ 3200rpm
86.9bhp/ton 85.4bhp/tonne
48.0bhp/L 35.8kW/L 48.7PS/L
43.8ft/sec 13.3m/sec
20.2mph 32.5kmh/1000rpm
38.9mpg 32.4mpgUS 7.3L/100km
Petrol 4-stroke piston
1124cc 69.0cu in
In-line 4 1 Carburettor
Compression ratio: 9.4:1
Bore: 72.0mm 2.8in
Stroke: 69.0mm 2.7in
Valve type/No: Overhead 8
Transmission: Manual
No. of forward speeds: 5
Wheels driven: Front
Springs F/R: Coil/Torsion bar
Brake system: PA
Brakes F/R: Disc/Drum
Steering: Rack & pinion
Wheelbase: 228.5cm 90.0in
Track F: 138.0cm 54.3in
Track R: 130.0cm 51.2in
Length: 349.5cm 137.6in
Width: 155.5cm 61.2in
Height: 135.5cm 53.3in
Ground clearance: 11.0cm 4.3in
Kerb weight: 632.0kg 1392.1lb
Fuel: 35.9L 7.9gal 9.5galUS

1076 Citroen
AX14 TRS
1987 France
101.0mph 162.5kmh
0-50mph 80.5kmh: 7.7secs
0-60mph 96.5kmh: 11.0secs
0-1/4 mile: 18.1secs
0-1km: 34.1secs
65.0bhp 48.5kW 65.9PS
@ 5400rpm
83.2lbft 112.7Nm @ 3000rpm
96.9bhp/ton 95.3bhp/tonne
47.8bhp/L 35.6kW/L 48.5PS/L
45.4ft/sec 13.9m/sec
21.6mph 34.8kmh/1000rpm
34.7mpg 28.9mpgUS 8.1L/100km
Petrol 4-stroke piston
1360cc 83.0cu in
In-line 4 1 Carburettor
Compression ratio: 9.3:1
Bore: 75.0mm 2.9in
Stroke: 77.0mm 3.0in
Valve type/No: Overhead 8
Transmission: Manual
No. of forward speeds: 5
Wheels driven: Front
Springs F/R: Coil/Torsion bar
Brake system: PA
Brakes F/R: Disc/Drum
Steering: Rack & pinion
Wheelbase: 228.5cm 90.0in
Track F: 138.0cm 54.3in
Track R: 130.0cm 51.2in
Length: 349.5cm 137.6in
Width: 145.5cm 57.3in
Height: 135.5cm 53.3in
Ground clearance: 11.0cm 4.3in
Kerb weight: 682.0kg 1502.2lb
Fuel: 43.2L 9.5gal 11.4galUS

1077 Citroen
BX GTi 16v
1987 France
133.0mph 214.0kmh
0-50mph 80.5kmh: 5.9secs
0-60mph 96.5kmh: 7.9secs
0-1/4 mile: 16.2secs
0-1km: 29.1secs
155.0bhp 115.6kW 157.1PS
@ 6500rpm
133.0lbft 180.2Nm @ 5000rpm
145.5bhp/ton 143.1bhp/tonne
81.4bhp/L 60.7kW/L 82.5PS/L
62.5ft/sec 19.1m/sec
19.9mph 32.0kmh/1000rpm
29.8mpg 24.8mpgUS 9.5L/100km
Petrol 4-stroke piston
1905cc 116.0cu in
In-line 4 fuel injection
Compression ratio: 10.4:1
Bore: 83.0mm 3.3in
Stroke: 88.0mm 3.5in
Valve type/No: Overhead 16
Transmission: Manual
No. of forward speeds: 5
Wheels driven: Front
Springs F/R: Gas/Gas
Brake system: PA ABS
Brakes F/R: Disc/Disc
Steering: Rack & pinion PA
Wheelbase: 265.5cm 104.5in
Track F: 141.0cm 55.5in
Track R: 135.4cm 53.3in
Length: 422.9cm 166.5in
Width: 165.7cm 65.2in
Height: 136.5cm 53.7in
Ground clearance: 16.2cm 6.4in
Kerb weight: 1083.0kg 2385.5lb
Fuel: 66.0L 14.5gal 17.4galUS

1078 Citroen
CX25 DTR Turbo 2
1987 France
113.0mph 181.8kmh
0-50mph 80.5kmh: 7.3secs
0-60mph 96.5kmh: 10.1secs
0-1/4 mile: 17.8secs
0-1km: 32.8secs
120.0bhp 89.5kW 121.7PS
@ 3900rpm
188.0lbft 254.7Nm @ 2000rpm
90.3bhp/ton 88.8bhp/tonne
48.5bhp/L 36.2kW/L 49.2PS/L
39.2ft/sec 12.0m/sec
28.9mph 46.5kmh/1000rpm
30.1mpg 25.1mpgUS 9.4L/100km
Diesel 4-stroke piston
2473cc 151.0cu in turbocharged
In-line 4 fuel injection
Compression ratio: 21.0:1
Bore: 93.0mm 3.7in
Stroke: 92.0mm 3.6in
Valve type/No: Overhead 8
Transmission: Manual
No. of forward speeds: 5
Wheels driven: Front
Springs F/R: Gas/Gas
Brake system: PA ABS
Brakes F/R: Disc/Disc
Steering: Rack & pinion PA
Wheelbase: 284.5cm 112.0in
Track F: 152.2cm 59.9in
Track R: 136.8cm 53.9in
Length: 465.0cm 183.1in
Width: 177.0cm 69.7in
Height: 136.0cm 53.5in
Ground clearance: 15.3cm 6.0in
Kerb weight: 1351.0kg 2975.8lb
Fuel: 68.2L 15.0gal 18.0galUS

1079 Citroen
AX11 TRE 5DR
1988 France
98.0mph 157.7kmh
0-50mph 80.5kmh: 8.8secs
0-60mph 96.5kmh: 12.6secs
0-1/4 mile: 19.1secs
0-1km: 35.4secs
55.0bhp 41.0kW 55.8PS
@ 5800rpm
65.7lbft 89.0Nm @ 3200rpm
76.6bhp/ton 75.3bhp/tonne
48.9bhp/L 36.5kW/L 49.6PS/L
43.8ft/sec 13.3m/sec
20.1mph 32.3kmh/1000rpm
32.7mpg 27.2mpgUS 8.6L/100km
Petrol 4-stroke piston
1124cc 69.0cu in
In-line 4 1 Carburettor
Compression ratio: 9.4:1
Bore: 72.0mm 2.8in
Stroke: 69.0mm 2.7in
Valve type/No: Overhead 8
Transmission: Manual
No. of forward speeds: 5
Wheels driven: Front
Springs F/R: Coil/Torsion bar

Brake system: PA
Brakes F/R: Disc/Drum
Steering: Rack & pinion
Wheelbase: 228.5cm 90.0in
Track F: 138.0cm 54.3in
Track R: 130.0cm 51.2in
Length: 349.5cm 137.6in
Width: 155.5cm 61.2in
Height: 135.5cm 53.3in
Ground clearance: 11.0cm 4.3in
Kerb weight: 730.0kg 1607.9lb
Fuel: 35.9L 7.9gal 9.5galUS

1080 Citroen

BX DTR Turbo
1988 France
106.0mph 170.6kmh
0-50mph 80.5kmh: 8.7secs
0-60mph 96.5kmh: 11.9secs
0-1/4 mile: 18.3secs
0-1km: 34.0secs
90.0bhp 67.1kW 91.2PS
@ 4300rpm
134.3lbft 182.0Nm @ 2100rpm
85.9bhp/ton 84.5bhp/tonne
50.9bhp/L 37.9kW/L 51.6PS/L
41.3ft/sec 12.6m/sec
25.6mph 41.2kmh/1000rpm
36.2mpg 30.1mpgUS 7.8L/100km
Diesel 4-stroke piston
1769cc 108.0cu in turbocharged
In-line 4 fuel injection
Compression ratio: 22.1:1
Bore: 80.0mm 3.1in
Stroke: 88.0mm 3.5in
Valve type/No: Overhead 8
Transmission: Manual
No. of forward speeds: 5
Wheels driven: Front
Springs F/R: Gas/Gas
Brake system: PA ABS
Brakes F/R: Disc/Disc
Steering: Rack & pinion PA
Wheelbase: 265.5cm 104.5in
Track F: 141.0cm 55.5in
Track R: 135.4cm 53.3in
Length: 422.9cm 166.5in
Width: 165.7cm 65.2in
Height: 136.5cm 53.7in
Ground clearance: 16.2cm 6.4in
Kerb weight: 1065.0kg 2345.8lb
Fuel: 66.0L 14.5gal 17.4galUS

1081 Citroen

AX14 DTR
1989 France
92.0mph 148.0kmh
0-50mph 80.5kmh: 11.4secs
0-60mph 96.5kmh: 16.2secs
0-1/4 mile: 20.3secs
0-1km: 37.5secs
53.7bhp 40.0kW 54.4PS
@ 5000rpm
62.4lbft 84.6Nm @ 2500rpm
73.8bhp/ton 72.6bhp/tonne
39.5bhp/L 29.4kW/L 40.0PS/L
42.1ft/sec 12.8m/sec
20.3mph 32.7kmh/1000rpm
54.7mpg 45.5mpgUS 5.2L/100km
Diesel 4-stroke piston
1360cc 83.0cu in
In-line 4 fuel injection
Compression ratio: 22.0:1
Bore: 75.0mm 2.9in
Stroke: 77.0mm 3.0in
Valve type/No: Overhead 8
Transmission: Manual
No. of forward speeds: 5
Wheels driven: Front
Springs F/R: Coil/Torsion bar
Brakes F/R: Disc/Drum
Steering: Rack & pinion
Wheelbase: 228.5cm 90.0in
Track F: 138.0cm 54.3in
Track R: 130.0cm 51.2in
Length: 349.5cm 137.6in
Width: 155.5cm 61.2in
Height: 135.5cm 53.3in
Ground clearance: 11.0cm 4.3in
Kerb weight: 740.0kg 1630.0lb
Fuel: 43.2L 9.5gal 11.4galUS

1082 Citroen

BX14 TGE
1989 France
102.0mph 164.1kmh
0-50mph 80.5kmh: 9.8secs
0-60mph 96.5kmh: 14.3secs
0-1/4 mile: 19.3secs
0-1km: 36.3secs
73.0bhp 54.4kW 74.0PS
@ 5600rpm
81.9lbft 111.0Nm @ 3000rpm
78.1bhp/ton 76.8bhp/tonne
53.7bhp/L 40.0kW/L 54.4PS/L
47.1ft/sec 14.4m/sec
19.3mph 31.1kmh/1000rpm
34.0mpg 28.3mpgUS 8.3L/100km
Petrol 4-stroke piston
1360cc 83.0cu in
In-line 4 1 Carburettor
Compression ratio: 9.3:1
Bore: 75.0mm 2.9in
Stroke: 77.0mm 3.0in
Valve type/No: Overhead 8
Transmission: Manual
No. of forward speeds: 5
Wheels driven: Front
Springs F/R: Gas/Gas
Brake system: PA
Brakes F/R: Disc/Disc
Steering: Rack & pinion
Wheelbase: 265.5cm 104.5in
Track F: 141.0cm 55.5in
Track R: 135.4cm 53.3in
Length: 422.9cm 166.5in
Width: 165.7cm 65.2in
Height: 136.5cm 53.7in
Ground clearance: 16.2cm 6.4in
Kerb weight: 950.0kg 2092.5lb
Fuel: 44.1L 9.7gal 11.7galUS

1083 Citroen

AX GT5
1990 France
109.0mph 175.4kmh
0-50mph 80.5kmh: 7.4secs
0-60mph 96.5kmh: 10.1secs
0-1/4 mile: 17.6secs
0-1km: 31.9secs
85.0bhp 63.4kW 86.2PS
@ 6400rpm
85.6lbft 116.0Nm @ 4000rpm
106.2bhp/ton 104.4bhp/tonne
62.5bhp/L 46.6kW/L 63.4PS/L
53.9ft/sec 16.4m/sec
18.3mph 29.4kmh/1000rpm
35.9mpg 29.9mpgUS 7.9L/100km
Petrol 4-stroke piston
1360cc 83.0cu in
In-line 4 1 Carburettor
Compression ratio: 9.3:1
Bore: 75.0mm 2.9in
Stroke: 77.0mm 3.0in
Valve type/No: Overhead 8
Transmission: Manual
No. of forward speeds: 5
Wheels driven: Front
Springs F/R: Coil/Torsion bar
Brake system: PA
Brakes F/R: Disc/Drum
Steering: Rack & pinion
Wheelbase: 228.5cm 90.0in
Track F: 138.0cm 54.3in
Track R: 130.0cm 51.2in
Length: 349.5cm 137.6in
Width: 155.5cm 61.2in
Height: 135.5cm 53.3in
Ground clearance: 11.0cm 4.3in
Kerb weight: 814.0kg 1792.9lb
Fuel: 43.2L 9.5gal 11.4galUS

1084 Citroen

BX GTi 4x4
1990 France
116.0mph 186.6kmh
0-50mph 80.5kmh: 7.4secs
0-60mph 96.5kmh: 10.6secs
0-1/4 mile: 17.8secs
0-1km: 32.7secs
125.0bhp 93.2kW 126.7PS
@ 5500rpm
124.7lbft 169.0Nm @ 4500rpm
110.5bhp/ton 108.7bhp/tonne
65.6bhp/L 48.9kW/L 66.5PS/L
52.9ft/sec 16.1m/sec
20.7mph 33.3kmh/1000rpm
26.3mpg 21.9mpgUS 10.7L/100km
Petrol 4-stroke piston
1905cc 116.0cu in
In-line 4 fuel injection
Compression ratio: 9.3:1
Bore: 83.0mm 3.3in
Stroke: 88.0mm 3.5in
Valve type/No: Overhead 8
Transmission: Manual
No. of forward speeds: 5
Wheels driven: 4-wheel drive
Springs F/R: Gas/Gas
Brake system: PA ABS
Brakes F/R: Disc/Disc
Steering: Rack & pinion PA
Wheelbase: 265.4cm 104.5in
Track F: 141.0cm 55.5in
Track R: 135.4cm 53.3in
Length: 422.9cm 166.5in
Width: 168.9cm 66.5in
Height: 136.4cm 53.7in
Ground clearance: 16.3cm 6.4in
Kerb weight: 1150.0kg 2533.0lb
Fuel: 66.0L 14.5gal 17.4galUS

1085 Citroen

CX25 GTi Turbo 2 CX Auto
1990 France
0-60mph 96.5kmh: 8.6secs
0-1/4 mile: 16.5secs
150.0bhp 111.9kW 152.1PS
@ 5000rpm
156.0lbft 211.4Nm @ 4000rpm
105.7bhp/ton 103.9bhp/tonne
60.0bhp/L 44.7kW/L 60.8PS/L
50.3ft/sec 15.3m/sec
Petrol 4-stroke piston
2500cc 152.5cu in turbocharged
In-line 4 fuel injection
Compression ratio: 8.8:1
Bore: 93.0mm 3.7in
Stroke: 92.0mm 3.6in
Valve type/No: Overhead 8
Transmission: Automatic
No. of forward speeds: 5
Wheels driven: Front
Springs F/R: Gas/Gas
Brake system: ABS
Brakes F/R: Disc/Disc
Steering: Rack & pinion PA
Wheelbase: 284.5cm 112.0in
Track F: 152.4cm 60.0in
Track R: 137.2cm 54.0in
Length: 464.8cm 183.0in
Width: 177.0cm 69.7in
Height: 134.6cm 53.0in
Kerb weight: 1443.7kg 3180.0lb
Fuel: 68.1L 15.0gal 18.0galUS

1086 Citroen

XM 2.0SEi
1990 France
122.0mph 196.3kmh
0-50mph 80.5kmh: 8.0secs
0-60mph 96.5kmh: 11.2secs
0-1/4 mile: 19.0secs
0-1km: 33.0secs
130.0bhp 96.9kW 131.8PS
@ 5600rpm
129.2lbft 175.0Nm @ 4800rpm
92.4bhp/ton 90.9bhp/tonne
65.1bhp/L 48.5kW/L 66.0PS/L
52.7ft/sec 16.0m/sec
20.9mph 33.6kmh/1000rpm
25.8mpg 21.5mpgUS 10.9L/100km
Petrol 4-stroke piston
1998cc 122.0cu in
In-line 4 fuel injection
Compression ratio: 8.8:1
Bore: 86.0mm 3.4in
Stroke: 86.0mm 3.4in
Valve type/No: Overhead 8
Transmission: Manual
No. of forward speeds: 5
Wheels driven: Front
Springs F/R: Gas/Gas
Brake system: PA ABS
Brakes F/R: Disc/Disc
Steering: Rack & pinion PA
Wheelbase: 285.0cm 112.2in
Track F: 153.0cm 60.2in
Track R: 145.7cm 57.4in
Length: 470.8cm 185.4in
Width: 179.4cm 70.6in
Height: 138.2cm 54.4in
Ground clearance: 17.9cm 7.0in
Kerb weight: 1430.0kg 3149.8lb
Fuel: 80.1L 17.6gal 21.1galUS

1087 Citroen

AX11 TZX
1991 France
95.0mph 152.9kmh
0-50mph 80.5kmh: 9.4secs
0-60mph 96.5kmh: 13.5secs
0-1/4 mile: 19.5secs
0-1km: 36.2secs
55.0bhp 41.0kW 55.8PS
@ 5800rpm
66.0lbft 89.4Nm @ 3200rpm
75.6bhp/ton 74.3bhp/tonne
48.9bhp/L 36.5kW/L 49.6PS/L
43.8ft/sec 13.3m/sec
20.3mph 32.7kmh/1000rpm
38.8mpg 32.3mpgUS 7.3L/100km
Petrol 4-stroke piston
1124cc 69.0cu in
In-line 4 1 Carburettor
Compression ratio: 9.4:1
Bore: 72.0mm 2.8in
Stroke: 69.0mm 2.7in
Valve type/No: Overhead 8
Transmission: Manual
No. of forward speeds: 5
Wheels driven: Front
Springs F/R: Coil/Coil
Brake system: PA
Brakes F/R: Disc/Drum
Steering: Rack & pinion
Track F: 137.9cm 54.3in
Track R: 130.0cm 51.2in
Length: 350.5cm 138.0in
Width: 177.8cm 70.0in
Height: 134.6cm 53.0in
Ground clearance: 10.9cm 4.3in
Kerb weight: 740.0kg 1630.0lb
Fuel: 36.4L 8.0gal 9.6galUS

1088 Citroen

XM 3.0 SEi Auto
1991 France
135.0mph 217.2kmh
0-50mph 80.5kmh: 7.2secs
0-60mph 96.5kmh: 9.5secs
0-1/4 mile: 17.3secs
0-1km: 30.9secs
170.0bhp 126.8kW 172.4PS
@ 5600rpm
173.4lbft 235.0Nm @ 4600rpm
115.0bhp/ton 113.1bhp/tonne
57.1bhp/L 42.6kW/L 57.9PS/L
44.6ft/sec 13.6m/sec
25.1mph 40.4kmh/1000rpm
18.8mpg 15.7mpgUS 15.0L/100km
Petrol 4-stroke piston
2975cc 182.0cu in
Vee 6 fuel injection
Compression ratio: 9.5:1
Bore: 93.0mm 3.7in
Stroke: 73.0mm 2.9in
Valve type/No: Overhead 12
Transmission: Automatic
No. of forward speeds: 4
Wheels driven: Front
Springs F/R: Gas/Gas
Brake system: PA ABS
Brakes F/R: Disc/Disc
Steering: Rack & pinion PA
Wheelbase: 285.0cm 112.2in
Track F: 153.0cm 60.2in
Track R: 145.7cm 57.4in
Length: 470.8cm 185.4in
Width: 179.4cm 70.6in
Height: 138.2cm 54.4in
Ground clearance: 17.9cm 7.0in
Kerb weight: 1503.0kg 3310.6lb
Fuel: 80.1L 17.6gal 21.1galUS

1089 Citroen

XM V6.24
1991 France
145.0mph 233.3kmh
0-50mph 80.5kmh: 5.8secs
0-60mph 96.5kmh: 7.5secs
0-1/4 mile: 15.5secs
0-1km: 28.7secs
200.0bhp 149.1kW 202.8PS
@ 6000rpm
191.9lbft 260.0Nm @ 3600rpm
133.4bhp/ton 131.1bhp/tonne
67.2bhp/L 50.1kW/L 68.2PS/L
47.8ft/sec 14.6m/sec
22.9mph 36.8kmh/1000rpm
20.8mpg 17.3mpgUS 13.6L/100km
Petrol 4-stroke piston
2975cc 182.0cu in
Vee 6 fuel injection
Compression ratio: 9.5:1
Bore: 93.0mm 3.7in

Stroke: 73.0mm 2.9in
Valve type/No: Overhead 24
Transmission: Manual
No. of forward speeds: 5
Wheels driven: Front
Springs F/R: Gas/Gas
Brake system: PA ABS
Brakes F/R: Disc/Disc
Steering: Rack & pinion PA
Wheelbase: 285.0cm 112.2in
Track F: 152.9cm 60.2in
Track R: 145.5cm 57.3in
Length: 470.7cm 185.3in
Width: 179.3cm 70.6in
Height: 138.2cm 54.4in
Ground clearance: 17.8cm 7.0in
Kerb weight: 1525.0kg 3359.0lb
Fuel: 80.1L 17.6gal 21.1galUS

1090 Citroen

ZX 1.4 Avantage
1991 France
107.0mph 172.2kmh
0-50mph 80.5kmh: 8.3secs
0-60mph 96.5kmh: 11.9secs
0-1/4 mile: 18.7secs
0-1km: 29.6secs
75.0bhp 55.9kW 76.0PS
@ 5800rpm
84.9lbft 115.0Nm @ 3800rpm
75.5bhp/ton 74.3bhp/tonne
55.1bhp/L 41.1kW/L 55.9PS/L
48.8ft/sec 14.9m/sec
20.6mph 33.1kmh/1000rpm
26.5mpg 22.1mpgUS 10.7L/100km
Petrol 4-stroke piston
1360cc 83.0cu in
In-line 4 1 Carburettor
Compression ratio: 9.3:1
Bore: 75.0mm 2.9in
Stroke: 77.0mm 3.0in
Valve type/No: Overhead 8
Transmission: Manual
No. of forward speeds: 5
Wheels driven: Front
Springs F/R: Coil/Torsion bar
Brake system: PA
Brakes F/R: Disc/Drum
Steering: Rack & pinion
Wheelbase: 254.0cm 100.0in
Length: 407.0cm 160.2in
Width: 169.0cm 66.5in
Height: 140.0cm 55.1in
Kerb weight: 1010.0kg 2224.7lb
Fuel: 56.0L 12.3gal 14.8galUS

1091 Citroen

ZX Volcane
1991 France
125.0mph 201.1kmh
0-50mph 80.5kmh: 6.9secs
0-60mph 96.5kmh: 9.1secs
0-1/4 mile: 17.1secs
0-1km: 31.1secs
130.0bhp 96.9kW 131.8PS
@ 6000rpm
118.1lbft 160.0Nm @ 3250rpm
120.2bhp/ton 118.2bhp/tonne
68.2bhp/L 50.9kW/L 69.2PS/L
57.7ft/sec 17.6m/sec
19.9mph 32.0kmh/1000rpm
25.3mpg 21.1mpgUS 11.2L/100km
Petrol 4-stroke piston
1905cc 116.0cu in
In-line 4 fuel injection
Compression ratio: 9.2:1
Bore: 83.0mm 3.3in
Stroke: 88.0mm 3.5in
Valve type/No: Overhead 8
Transmission: Manual
No. of forward speeds: 5
Wheels driven: Front
Springs F/R: Coil/Torsion bar
Brake system: PA
Brakes F/R: Disc/Disc
Steering: Rack & pinion PA
Wheelbase: 254.0cm 100.0in
Length: 407.9cm 160.6in
Width: 170.9cm 67.3in
Height: 138.9cm 54.7in
Ground clearance: 19.1cm 7.5in
Kerb weight: 1100.0kg 2422.9lb
Fuel: 56.0L 12.3gal 14.8galUS

1092 Citroen

AX GTi
1992 France
115.0mph 185.0kmh
0-50mph 80.5kmh: 6.6secs
0-60mph 96.5kmh: 9.3secs
0-1/4 mile: 17.1secs
0-1km: 31.5secs
100.0bhp 74.6kW 101.4PS
@ 6800rpm
90.0lbft 122.0Nm @ 4200rpm
124.0bhp/ton 121.9bhp/tonne
73.5bhp/L 54.8kW/L 74.5PS/L
57.2ft/sec 17.4m/sec
18.5mph 29.8kmh/1000rpm
26.0mpg 21.6mpgUS 10.9L/100km
Petrol 4-stroke piston
1360cc 83.0cu in
In-line 4 fuel injection
Compression ratio: 9.9:1
Bore: 75.0mm 2.9in
Stroke: 77.0mm 3.0in
Valve type/No: Overhead 8
Transmission: Manual
No. of forward speeds: 5
Wheels driven: Front
Springs F/R: Coil/Torsion bar
Brake system: PA ABS
Brakes F/R: Disc/Drum
Steering: Rack & pinion
Wheelbase: 228.5cm 90.0in
Track F: 138.0cm 54.3in
Track R: 130.0cm 51.2in
Length: 350.0cm 137.8in
Width: 156.0cm 61.4in
Height: 135.5cm 53.3in
Ground clearance: 11.0cm 4.3in
Kerb weight: 820.0kg 1806.2lb
Fuel: 43.1L 9.5gal 11.4galUS

1093 Citroen

XM Turbo SD Estate
1992 France
112.0mph 180.2kmh
0-50mph 80.5kmh: 9.6secs
0-60mph 96.5kmh: 13.1secs
0-1/4 mile: 19.5secs
0-1km: 33.9secs
110.0bhp 82.0kW 111.5PS
@ 4300rpm
183.0lbft 248.0Nm @ 2000rpm
65.1bhp/ton 64.1bhp/tonne
52.7bhp/L 39.3kW/L 53.4PS/L
43.2ft/sec 13.2m/sec
32.0mpg 26.6mpgUS 8.8L/100km
Diesel 4-stroke piston
2088cc 127.4cu in turbocharged
In-line 4 fuel injection
Compression ratio: 21.5:1
Bore: 85.0mm 3.3in
Stroke: 92.0mm 3.6in
Valve type/No: Overhead 12
Transmission: Manual
No. of forward speeds: 5
Wheels driven: Front
Springs F/R: Gas/Gas
Brake system: PA
Brakes F/R: Disc/Disc
Steering: Rack & pinion PA
Kerb weight: 1716.9kg 3781.8lb
Fuel: 80.1L 17.6gal 21.1galUS

1094 Cizeta

Moroder V16T
1990 Italy
204.0mph 328.2kmh
0-60mph 96.5kmh: 4.5secs
560.0bhp 417.6kW 567.8PS
@ 8000rpm
398.0lbft 539.3Nm @ 6000rpm
334.5bhp/ton 328.9bhp/tonne
93.4bhp/L 69.7kW/L 94.7PS/L
56.4ft/sec 17.2m/sec
Petrol 4-stroke piston
5995cc 365.8cu in
Vee 16 fuel injection
Compression ratio: 9.3:1
Bore: 86.0mm 3.4in
Stroke: 64.5mm 2.5in
Valve type/No: Overhead 64
Transmission: Manual
No. of forward speeds: 5
Wheels driven: Rear
Springs F/R: Coil/Coil
Brake system: PA
Brakes F/R: Disc/Disc
Steering: Rack & pinion PA
Wheelbase: 269.0cm 105.9in
Track F: 161.0cm 63.4in
Track R: 166.6cm 65.6in
Length: 449.3cm 176.9in
Width: 206.0cm 81.1in
Height: 111.5cm 43.9in
Kerb weight: 1702.5kg 3750.0lb
Fuel: 120.4L 26.5gal 31.8galUS

1095 Clan

Crusader
1971 UK
102.0mph 164.1kmh
0-50mph 80.5kmh: 9.1secs
0-60mph 96.5kmh: 12.5secs
0-1/4 mile: 18.8secs
0-1km: 35.3secs
51.0bhp 38.0kW 51.7PS
@ 6100rpm
52.0lbft 70.5Nm @ 4300rpm
89.4bhp/ton 87.9bhp/tonne
58.3bhp/L 43.5kW/L 59.1PS/L
40.3ft/sec 12.3m/sec
15.1mph 24.3kmh/1000rpm
34.3mpg 28.6mpgUS 8.2L/100km
Petrol 4-stroke piston
875cc 53.4cu in
In-line 4 2 Carburettor
Compression ratio: 10.0:1
Bore: 68.0mm 2.7in
Stroke: 60.4mm 2.4in
Valve type/No: Overhead 8
Transmission: Manual
No. of forward speeds: 4
Wheels driven: Rear
Springs F/R: Coil/Coil
Brake system: PA
Brakes F/R: Drum/Drum
Steering: Rack & pinion
Wheelbase: 208.3cm 82.0in
Track F: 127.0cm 50.0in
Track R: 129.5cm 51.0in
Length: 381.0cm 150.0in
Width: 148.6cm 58.5in
Height: 106.7cm 42.0in
Ground clearance: 14.0cm 5.5in
Kerb weight: 580.2kg 1278.0lb
Fuel: 27.3L 6.0gal 7.2galUS

1096 Consulier

GTP LX
1990 USA
140.0mph 225.3kmh
0-50mph 80.5kmh: 4.2secs
0-60mph 96.5kmh: 5.7secs
0-1/4 mile: 14.2secs
174.0bhp 129.7kW 176.4PS
@ 5200rpm
200.0lbft 271.0Nm @ 2400rpm
166.6bhp/ton 163.8bhp/tonne
78.6bhp/L 58.6kW/L 79.7PS/L
52.3ft/sec 15.9m/sec
21.9mpg 18.2mpgUS 12.9L/100km
Petrol 4-stroke piston
2213cc 135.0cu in turbocharged
In-line 4 fuel injection
Compression ratio: 8.0:1
Bore: 87.5mm 3.4in
Stroke: 92.0mm 3.6in
Valve type/No: Overhead 8
Transmission: Manual
No. of forward speeds: 5
Wheels driven: Rear
Springs F/R: Coil/Coil
Brake system: PA
Brakes F/R: Disc/Disc
Steering: Rack & pinion
Wheelbase: 254.0cm 100.0in
Track F: 153.7cm 60.5in
Track R: 153.7cm 60.5in
Length: 436.9cm 172.0in
Width: 182.9cm 72.0in
Height: 114.3cm 45.0in
Kerb weight: 1062.4kg 2340.0lb
Fuel: 64.3L 14.1gal 17.0galUS

1097 Cord

L-29
1930 USA
77.0mph 123.9kmh
0-50mph 80.5kmh: 16.0secs
0-60mph 96.5kmh: 23.9secs
0-1/4 mile: 23.5secs
125.0bhp 93.2kW 126.7PS
@ 3600rpm
220.0lbft 298.1Nm @ 1800rpm
62.9bhp/ton 61.9bhp/tonne
25.5bhp/L 19.0kW/L 25.9PS/L
45.0ft/sec 13.7m/sec
Petrol 4-stroke piston
4895cc 298.7cu in
In-line 8
Compression ratio: 5.3:1
Bore: 82.6mm 3.2in
Stroke: 114.3mm 4.5in
Valve type/No: Side 16
Transmission: Manual
No. of forward speeds: 3
Wheels driven: Front
Wheelbase: 349.5cm 137.6in
Track F: 147.3cm 58.0in
Track R: 152.4cm 60.0in
Kerb weight: 2020.3kg 4450.0lb

1098 Cord

Front Wheel Drive Phaeton
1931 USA
76.9mph 123.7kmh
12.0mpg 10.0mpgUS 23.5L/100km
Petrol 4-stroke piston
4934cc 301.0cu in
In-line 8
Bore: 83.0mm 3.3in
Stroke: 114.0mm 4.5in
Transmission: Manual
No. of forward speeds: 3
Wheels driven: Front
Brakes F/R: Drum/Drum
Wheelbase: 349.3cm 137.5in
Track F: 152.4cm 60.0in
Track R: 152.4cm 60.0in
Length: 522.0cm 205.5in
Width: 181.6cm 71.5in
Height: 168.9cm 66.5in
Kerb weight: 2023.0kg 4456.0lb
Fuel: 91.0L 20.0gal 24.0galUS

1099 Cord

Front Wheel Drive Saloon
1936 USA
92.4mph 148.7kmh
0-50mph 80.5kmh: 13.7secs
0-60mph 96.5kmh: 20.1secs
16.0mpg 13.3mpgUS 17.7L/100km
Petrol 4-stroke piston
4730cc 288.6cu in
In-line 8
Bore: 88.9mm 3.5in
Stroke: 95.2mm 3.8in
Valve type/No: Side 16
Transmission: Manual
No. of forward speeds: 4
Wheels driven: Front
Brakes F/R: Drum/Drum
Wheelbase: 317.5cm 125.0in
Track F: 142.2cm 56.0in
Track R: 154.9cm 61.0in
Length: 496.6cm 195.5in
Width: 180.3cm 71.0in
Height: 152.4cm 60.0in
Ground clearance: 22.9cm 9.0in
Kerb weight: 1786.0kg 3934.0lb
Fuel: 77.3L 17.0gal 20.4galUS

1100 Cord

812
1937 USA
102.3mph 164.6kmh
0-50mph 80.5kmh: 10.5secs
0-60mph 96.5kmh: 13.5secs
0-1/4 mile: 18.2secs
170.0bhp 126.8kW 172.4PS
@ 3500rpm
260.0lbft 352.3Nm @ 2200rpm
95.2bhp/ton 93.6bhp/tonne
35.9bhp/L 26.8kW/L 36.4PS/L
36.5ft/sec 11.1m/sec
Petrol 4-stroke piston
4732cc 288.7cu in
Vee 8
Compression ratio: 6.5:1
Bore: 88.9mm 3.5in
Stroke: 95.3mm 3.8in
Valve type/No: Side 16
Transmission: Manual
No. of forward speeds: 4
Wheels driven: Front
Wheelbase: 317.5cm 125.0in
Track F: 142.2cm 56.0in
Track R: 154.9cm 61.0in
Kerb weight: 1816.0kg 4000.0lb

1101 Cord
812-S
1937 USA
112.0mph 180.2kmh
0-50mph 80.5kmh: 10.2secs
0-60mph 96.5kmh: 13.7secs
0-1/4 mile: 18.3secs
190.0bhp 141.7kW 192.6PS
@ 4200rpm
272.0lbft 368.6Nm @ 3000rpm
103.4bhp/ton 101.7bhp/tonne
40.1bhp/L 29.9kW/L 40.7PS/L
43.8ft/sec 13.3m/sec
27.2mph 43.8kmh/1000rpm
Petrol 4-stroke piston
4732cc 288.7cu in supercharged
Vee 8 1 Carburettor
Compression ratio: 6.3:1
Bore: 88.9mm 3.5in
Stroke: 95.3mm 3.8in
Valve type/No: Side 16
Transmission: Manual
No. of forward speeds: 4
Wheels driven: Front
Brakes F/R: Drum/Drum
Wheelbase: 317.5cm 125.0in
Track F: 142.2cm 56.0in
Track R: 154.9cm 61.0in
Length: 496.6cm 195.5in
Width: 180.3cm 71.0in
Height: 147.3cm 58.0in
Ground clearance: 22.9cm 9.0in
Kerb weight: 1868.2kg 4115.0lb

1102 Cord
Supercharged Saloon
1937 USA
102.2mph 164.4kmh
0-50mph 80.5kmh: 10.5secs
0-60mph 96.5kmh: 13.2secs
14.0mpg 11.7mpgUS 20.2L/100km
Petrol 4-stroke piston
4730cc 288.6cu in supercharged
In-line 8
Bore: 88.9mm 3.5in
Stroke: 95.2mm 3.8in
Valve type/No: Side 16
Transmission: Manual
No. of forward speeds: 4
Wheels driven: Front
Brakes F/R: Drum/Drum
Kerb weight: 1823.3kg 4016.0lb
Fuel: 79.6L 17.5gal 21.0galUS

1103 Crossley
2-litre Saloon
1929 UK
77.0mph 123.9kmh
61.0bhp 45.5kW 61.8PS
@ 4000rpm
46.0bhp/ton 45.3bhp/tonne
30.6bhp/L 22.8kW/L 31.1PS/L
43.8ft/sec 13.3m/sec
21.0mpg 17.5mpgUS 13.5L/100km
Petrol 4-stroke piston
1991cc 121.5cu in
In-line 6
Compression ratio: 6.5:1
Bore: 65.0mm 2.6in
Stroke: 100.0mm 3.9in
Valve type/No: Overhead 12
Transmission: Manual
No. of forward speeds: 4
Wheels driven: Rear
Brakes F/R: Drum/Drum
Wheelbase: 312.4cm 123.0in
Track F: 142.2cm 56.0in
Track R: 142.2cm 56.0in
Length: 420.9cm 165.7in
Width: 170.2cm 67.0in
Height: 170.2cm 67.0in
Kerb weight: 1347.5kg 2968.0lb
Fuel: 59.1L 13.0gal 15.6galUS

1104 Crossley
10hp Torquay
1934 UK
60.0mph 96.5kmh
0-50mph 80.5kmh: 28.6secs
28.0mpg 23.3mpgUS 10.1L/100km
Petrol 4-stroke piston
1122cc 68.5cu in
In-line 4
Bore: 63.0mm 2.5in
Stroke: 90.0mm 3.5in
Valve type/No: IOE 8
Transmission: Manual
No. of forward speeds: 4
Wheels driven: Rear
Brakes F/R: Drum/Drum
Kerb weight: 1048.7kg 2310.0lb
Fuel: 31.8L 7.0gal 8.4galUS

1105 Crossley
10hp Regis Sports Saloon
1935 UK
65.6mph 105.6kmh
0-50mph 80.5kmh: 32.0secs
28.0mpg 23.3mpgUS 10.1L/100km
Petrol 4-stroke piston
1122cc 68.5cu in
In-line 4
Bore: 63.0mm 2.5in
Stroke: 90.0mm 3.5in
Valve type/No: IOE 8
Transmission: Pre-selector
No. of forward speeds: 4
Wheels driven: Rear
Brakes F/R: Drum/Drum
Kerb weight: 1155.4kg 2545.0lb
Fuel: 31.8L 7.0gal 8.4galUS

1106 Dacia
Duster GLX
1985 Romania
74.0mph 119.1kmh
0-50mph 80.5kmh: 13.8secs
0-60mph 96.5kmh: 22.7secs
0-1/4 mile: 22.6secs
65.0bhp 48.5kW 65.9PS
@ 5250rpm
72.0lbft 97.6Nm @ 3200rpm
54.2bhp/ton 53.3bhp/tonne
46.5bhp/L 34.7kW/L 47.2PS/L
44.2ft/sec 13.5m/sec
15.2mph 24.5kmh/1000rpm
31.1mpg 25.9mpgUS 9.1L/100km
Petrol 4-stroke piston
1397cc 85.2cu in
In-line 4 1 Carburettor
Compression ratio: 9.5:1
Bore: 76.0mm 3.0in
Stroke: 77.0mm 3.0in
Valve type/No: Overhead 8
Transmission: Manual
No. of forward speeds: 4
Wheels driven: 4-wheel engageable
Springs F/R: Coil/Leaf
Brake system: PA
Brakes F/R: Disc/Drum
Steering: Worm & roller
Wheelbase: 240.0cm 94.5in
Track F: 130.3cm 51.3in
Track R: 130.3cm 51.3in
Length: 377.7cm 148.7in
Width: 160.0cm 63.0in
Height: 174.0cm 68.5in
Ground clearance: 22.6cm 8.9in
Kerb weight: 1219.0kg 2685.0lb
Fuel: 45.5L 10.0gal 12.0galUS

1107 DAF
55
1958 Nederlands
82.0mph 131.9kmh
0-50mph 80.5kmh: 15.0secs
0-60mph 96.5kmh: 22.5secs
0-1/4 mile: 22.8secs
0-1km: 43.0secs
46.0bhp 34.3kW 46.6PS
@ 4600rpm
62.0lbft 84.0Nm @ 2800rpm
59.4bhp/ton 58.4bhp/tonne
41.5bhp/L 31.0kW/L 42.1PS/L
36.2ft/sec 11.0m/sec
28.5mpg 23.7mpgUS 9.9L/100km
Petrol 4-stroke piston
1108cc 67.6cu in
In-line 4 1 Carburettor
Compression ratio: 8.5:1
Bore: 70.0mm 2.8in
Stroke: 72.0mm 2.8in
Valve type/No: Overhead 8
Transmission: Continuously variable
Wheels driven: Rear
Springs F/R: Torsion bar/Coil
Brakes F/R: Disc/Drum
Steering: Rack & pinion
Wheelbase: 225.0cm 88.6in
Track F: 128.0cm 50.4in
Track R: 125.0cm 49.2in
Length: 383.5cm 151.0in
Width: 152.4cm 60.0in
Height: 144.8cm 57.0in
Kerb weight: 787.2kg 1734.0lb
Fuel: 38.2L 8.4gal 10.1galUS

1108 DAF
600 de Luxe
1960 Nederlands
57.0mph 91.7kmh
0-50mph 80.5kmh: 20.8secs
0-60mph 96.5kmh: 41.5secs
0-1/4 mile: 28.5secs
22.0bhp 16.4kW 22.3PS
@ 4000rpm
32.6lbft 44.2Nm @ 2700rpm
33.1bhp/ton 32.5bhp/tonne
37.3bhp/L 27.8kW/L 37.8PS/L
28.4ft/sec 8.7m/sec
14.2mph 22.8kmh/1000rpm
Petrol 4-stroke piston
590cc 36.0cu in
Flat 2 1 Carburettor
Compression ratio: 7.1:1
Bore: 75.9mm 3.0in
Stroke: 65.0mm 2.6in
Valve type/No: Overhead 4
Transmission: Continuously variable
Wheels driven: Rear
Springs F/R: Leaf/Coil
Brakes F/R: Drum/Drum
Steering: Rack & pinion
Wheelbase: 205.0cm 80.7in
Track F: 118.1cm 46.5in
Track R: 118.1cm 46.5in
Length: 360.7cm 142.0in
Width: 145.0cm 57.1in
Height: 138.4cm 54.5in
Ground clearance: 17.0cm 6.7in
Kerb weight: 676.5kg 1490.0lb
Fuel: 28.2L 6.2gal 7.4galUS

1109 DAF
Daffodil
1962 Nederlands
63.5mph 102.2kmh
0-50mph 80.5kmh: 21.8secs
0-60mph 96.5kmh: 52.0secs
0-1/4 mile: 25.4secs
30.0bhp 22.4kW 30.4PS
@ 4000rpm
42.0lbft 56.9Nm @ 2800rpm
46.4bhp/ton 45.6bhp/tonne
40.2bhp/L 30.0kW/L 40.8PS/L
28.4ft/sec 8.7m/sec
15.9mph 25.6kmh/1000rpm
33.6mpg 28.0mpgUS 8.4L/100km
Petrol 4-stroke piston
746cc 45.5cu in
Flat 2 1 Carburettor
Compression ratio: 7.1:1
Bore: 85.5mm 3.4in
Stroke: 65.0mm 2.6in
Valve type/No: Overhead 4
Transmission: Continuously variable
Wheels driven: Rear
Springs F/R: Leaf/Coil
Brakes F/R: Drum/Drum
Steering: Rack & pinion
Wheelbase: 205.7cm 81.0in
Track F: 118.1cm 46.5in
Track R: 116.8cm 46.0in
Length: 388.6cm 153.0in
Width: 144.8cm 57.0in
Height: 138.9cm 54.7in
Ground clearance: 17.0cm 6.7in
Kerb weight: 657.8kg 1449.0lb
Fuel: 29.1L 6.4gal 7.7galUS

1110 DAF
Daffodil de Luxe Extra
1962 Nederlands
63.5mph 102.2kmh
0-50mph 80.5kmh: 25.2secs
0-1/4 mile: 25.7secs
26.0bhp 19.4kW 26.4PS
@ 4000rpm
42.0lbft 56.9Nm @ 2800rpm
38.0bhp/ton 37.4bhp/tonne
34.8bhp/L 26.0kW/L 35.3PS/L
28.4ft/sec 8.7m/sec
15.9mph 25.6kmh/1000rpm
34.5mpg 28.7mpgUS 8.2L/100km
Petrol 4-stroke piston
746cc 45.5cu in
Flat 2 1 Carburettor
Compression ratio: 7.5:1
Bore: 88.5mm 3.5in
Stroke: 65.0mm 2.6in
Valve type/No: Overhead 4
Transmission: Continuously variable
Wheels driven: Rear
Springs F/R: Leaf/Coil
Brakes F/R: Drum/Drum
Steering: Rack & pinion
Wheelbase: 205.7cm 81.0in
Track F: 118.1cm 46.5in
Track R: 118.1cm 46.5in
Length: 362.0cm 142.5in
Width: 144.8cm 57.0in
Height: 143.5cm 56.5in
Ground clearance: 15.2cm 6.0in
Kerb weight: 696.0kg 1533.0lb
Fuel: 32.8L 7.2gal 8.6galUS

1111 DAF
44
1967 Nederlands
75.0mph 120.7kmh
0-50mph 80.5kmh: 19.3secs
0-60mph 96.5kmh: 31.2secs
0-1/4 mile: 24.1secs
0-1km: 45.4secs
34.0bhp 25.3kW 34.5PS
@ 4500rpm
51.4lbft 69.6Nm @ 2400rpm
46.4bhp/ton 45.6bhp/tonne
40.3bhp/L 30.0kW/L 40.8PS/L
36.1ft/sec 11.0m/sec
16.3mph 26.2kmh/1000rpm
34.3mpg 28.6mpgUS 8.2L/100km
Petrol 4-stroke piston
844cc 51.5cu in
Flat 2 1 Carburettor
Compression ratio: 7.5:1
Bore: 85.5mm 3.4in
Stroke: 73.5mm 2.9in
Valve type/No: Overhead 4
Transmission: Continuously variable
Wheels driven: Rear
Springs F/R: Leaf/Coil
Brakes F/R: Drum/Drum
Steering: Rack & pinion
Wheelbase: 225.0cm 88.6in
Track F: 128.0cm 50.4in
Track R: 125.0cm 49.2in
Length: 383.5cm 151.0in
Width: 152.4cm 60.0in
Height: 144.8cm 57.0in
Ground clearance: 15.2cm 6.0in
Kerb weight: 745.5kg 1642.0lb
Fuel: 39.8L 8.8gal 10.5galUS

1112 DAF
55 Estate
1971 Nederlands
82.0mph 131.9kmh
0-50mph 80.5kmh: 15.0secs
0-60mph 96.5kmh: 23.1secs
0-1/4 mile: 23.1secs
0-1km: 43.4secs
43.0bhp 32.1kW 43.6PS
@ 4600rpm
62.0lbft 84.0Nm @ 3000rpm
53.5bhp/ton 52.6bhp/tonne
38.8bhp/L 28.9kW/L 39.3PS/L
36.2ft/sec 11.0m/sec
17.4mph 28.0kmh/1000rpm
25.7mpg 21.4mpgUS 11.0L/100km
Petrol 4-stroke piston
1108cc 67.6cu in
In-line 4 1 Carburettor
Compression ratio: 8.5:1
Bore: 70.0mm 2.8in
Stroke: 72.0mm 2.8in
Valve type/No: Overhead 8
Transmission: Continuously variable
Wheels driven: Rear
Springs F/R: Torsion bar/Coil
Brakes F/R: Disc/Drum
Steering: Rack & pinion
Wheelbase: 225.0cm 88.6in
Track F: 128.0cm 50.4in
Track R: 125.0cm 49.2in
Length: 383.5cm 151.0in
Width: 152.4cm 60.0in
Height: 144.8cm 57.0in
Ground clearance: 17.0cm 6.7in
Kerb weight: 816.7kg 1799.0lb
Fuel: 38.2L 8.4gal 10.1galUS

1113 DAF

66SL
1973 Nederlands
83.0mph 133.5kmh
0-50mph 80.5kmh: 14.9secs
0-60mph 96.5kmh: 24.0secs
0-1/4 mile: 22.8secs
0-1km: 43.1secs
47.0bhp 35.0kW 47.6PS
@ 5000rpm
55.0lbft 74.5Nm @ 2700rpm
58.2bhp/ton 57.2bhp/tonne
42.4bhp/L 31.6kW/L 43.0PS/L
39.3ft/sec 12.0m/sec
18.1mph 29.1kmh/1000rpm
26.4mpg 22.0mpgUS 10.7L/100km
Petrol 4-stroke piston
1108cc 67.6cu in
In-line 4 1 Carburettor
Compression ratio: 8.5:1
Bore: 70.0mm 2.8in
Stroke: 72.0mm 2.8in
Valve type/No: Overhead 8
Transmission: Continuously variable
Wheels driven: Rear
Springs F/R: Torsion bar/Leaf
Brakes F/R: Disc/Drum
Steering: Rack & pinion
Wheelbase: 225.0cm 88.6in
Track F: 131.1cm 51.6in
Track R: 124.0cm 48.8in
Length: 387.9cm 152.7in
Width: 153.9cm 60.6in
Height: 144.8cm 57.0in
Kerb weight: 821.3kg 1809.0lb
Fuel: 42.1L 9.2gal 11.1galUS

1114 DAF

66SL 1300
1974 Nederlands
89.0mph 143.2kmh
0-50mph 80.5kmh: 12.2secs
0-60mph 96.5kmh: 19.4secs
0-1/4 mile: 21.3secs
0-1km: 40.6secs
57.0bhp 42.5kW 57.8PS
@ 5200rpm
69.4lbft 94.0Nm @ 2800rpm
68.1bhp/ton 67.0bhp/tonne
44.2bhp/L 33.0kW/L 44.8PS/L
43.8ft/sec 13.3m/sec
18.2mph 29.3kmh/1000rpm
27.1mpg 22.6mpgUS 10.4L/100km
Petrol 4-stroke piston
1289cc 78.6cu in
In-line 4 1 Carburettor
Compression ratio: 8.5:1
Bore: 73.0mm 2.9in
Stroke: 77.0mm 3.0in
Valve type/No: Overhead 8
Transmission: Continuously variable
Wheels driven: Rear
Springs F/R: Torsion bar/Leaf
Brakes F/R: Disc/Drum
Steering: Rack & pinion
Wheelbase: 225.0cm 88.6in
Track F: 131.1cm 51.6in
Track R: 124.0cm 48.8in
Length: 387.9cm 152.7in
Width: 153.9cm 60.6in
Height: 144.8cm 57.0in
Kerb weight: 851.2kg 1875.0lb
Fuel: 42.1L 9.2gal 11.1galUS

1115 Daihatsu

Compagno Berlina
1965 Japan
70.0mph 112.6kmh
0-50mph 80.5kmh: 21.2secs
0-1/4 mile: 24.5secs
41.0bhp 30.6kW 41.6PS
@ 5000rpm
47.0lbft 63.7Nm @ 3600rpm
53.5bhp/ton 52.7bhp/tonne
51.4bhp/L 38.4kW/L 52.2PS/L
36.1ft/sec 11.0m/sec
13.7mph 22.0kmh/1000rpm
34.8mpg 29.0mpgUS 8.1L/100km
Petrol 4-stroke piston
797cc 48.6cu in
In-line 4 1 Carburettor
Compression ratio: 8.0:1
Bore: 62.0mm 2.4in
Stroke: 66.0mm 2.6in
Valve type/No: Overhead 8
Transmission: Manual
No. of forward speeds: 4
Wheels driven: Rear
Springs F/R: Torsion bar/Leaf
Brake system: PA
Brakes F/R: Drum/Drum
Steering: Recirculating ball
Wheelbase: 222.3cm 87.5in
Track F: 118.1cm 46.5in
Track R: 115.6cm 45.5in
Length: 380.2cm 149.7in
Width: 144.8cm 57.0in
Height: 138.4cm 54.5in
Ground clearance: 15.7cm 6.2in
Kerb weight: 778.6kg 1715.0lb
Fuel: 23.7L 5.2gal 6.3galUS

1116 Daihatsu

Charade XTE
1979 Japan
85.0mph 136.8kmh
0-50mph 80.5kmh: 11.2secs
0-60mph 96.5kmh: 16.1secs
0-1/4 mile: 20.6secs
0-1km: 39.2secs
50.0bhp 37.3kW 50.7PS
@ 5500rpm
53.5lbft 72.5Nm @ 3000rpm
73.8bhp/ton 72.6bhp/tonne
50.3bhp/L 37.5kW/L 51.0PS/L
43.8ft/sec 13.4m/sec
18.5mph 29.8kmh/1000rpm
36.5mpg 30.4mpgUS 7.7L/100km
Petrol 4-stroke piston
993cc 60.6cu in
In-line 3 1 Carburettor
Compression ratio: 9.0:1
Bore: 76.0mm 3.0in
Stroke: 73.0mm 2.9in
Valve type/No: Overhead 6
Transmission: Manual
No. of forward speeds: 5
Wheels driven: Rear
Springs F/R: Coil/Coil
Brake system: PA
Brakes F/R: Disc/Drum
Steering: Rack & pinion
Wheelbase: 230.1cm 90.6in
Track F: 130.0cm 51.2in
Track R: 128.0cm 50.4in
Length: 348.5cm 137.2in
Width: 150.9cm 59.4in
Height: 134.6cm 53.0in
Ground clearance: 16.5cm 6.5in
Kerb weight: 688.7kg 1517.0lb
Fuel: 34.1L 7.5gal 9.0galUS

1117 Daihatsu

Domino
1981 Japan
76.0mph 122.3kmh
0-50mph 80.5kmh: 14.9secs
0-60mph 96.5kmh: 26.6secs
0-1/4 mile: 22.8secs
0-1km: 44.4secs
27.0bhp 20.1kW 27.4PS
@ 6000rpm
28.0lbft 37.9Nm @ 3500rpm
48.0bhp/ton 47.2bhp/tonne
49.4bhp/L 36.8kW/L 50.0PS/L
44.7ft/sec 13.6m/sec
11.0mph 17.7kmh/1000rpm
39.1mpg 32.6mpgUS 7.2L/100km
Petrol 4-stroke piston
547cc 33.4cu in
In-line 2 1 Carburettor
Compression ratio: 9.2:1
Bore: 71.6mm 2.8in
Stroke: 68.0mm 2.7in
Valve type/No: Overhead 4
Transmission: Manual
No. of forward speeds: 4
Wheels driven: Front
Springs F/R: Coil/Coil
Brakes F/R: Drum/Drum
Steering: Rack & pinion
Wheelbase: 214.9cm 84.6in
Track F: 120.4cm 47.4in
Track R: 120.9cm 47.6in
Length: 319.5cm 125.8in
Width: 139.4cm 54.9in
Height: 136.4cm 53.7in
Ground clearance: 16.5cm 6.5in
Kerb weight: 572.0kg 1260.0lb
Fuel: 25.9L 5.7gal 6.8galUS

1118 Daihatsu

Charmant 1600LE
1982 Japan
96.0mph 154.5kmh
0-50mph 80.5kmh: 9.0secs
0-60mph 96.5kmh: 13.2secs
0-1/4 mile: 19.2secs
0-1km: 36.0secs
74.0bhp 55.2kW 75.0PS
@ 5400rpm
87.0lbft 117.9Nm @ 3600rpm
79.3bhp/ton 78.0bhp/tonne
46.6bhp/L 34.7kW/L 47.2PS/L
41.4ft/sec 12.6m/sec
19.3mph 31.1kmh/1000rpm
29.3mpg 24.4mpgUS 9.6L/100km
Petrol 4-stroke piston
1588cc 96.9cu in
In-line 4 1 Carburettor
Compression ratio: 9.0:1
Bore: 85.0mm 3.3in
Stroke: 70.0mm 2.8in
Valve type/No: Overhead 8
Transmission: Manual
No. of forward speeds: 5
Wheels driven: Rear
Springs F/R: Coil/Coil
Brake system: PA
Brakes F/R: Disc/Drum
Steering: Recirculating ball
Wheelbase: 240.0cm 94.5in
Track F: 132.1cm 52.0in
Track R: 133.6cm 52.6in
Length: 415.0cm 163.4in
Width: 162.6cm 64.0in
Height: 137.9cm 54.3in
Ground clearance: 15.5cm 6.1in
Kerb weight: 948.9kg 2090.0lb
Fuel: 50.0L 11.0gal 13.2galUS

1119 Daihatsu

Charade CX
1983 Japan
88.0mph 141.6kmh
0-50mph 80.5kmh: 10.9secs
0-60mph 96.5kmh: 15.6secs
0-1/4 mile: 19.7secs
0-1km: 38.1secs
51.0bhp 38.0kW 51.7PS
@ 5600rpm
55.6lbft 75.3Nm @ 3200rpm
69.7bhp/ton 68.5bhp/tonne
51.4bhp/L 38.3kW/L 52.1PS/L
44.6ft/sec 13.6m/sec
20.2mph 32.5kmh/1000rpm
40.2mpg 33.5mpgUS 7.0L/100km
Petrol 4-stroke piston
993cc 60.6cu in
In-line 3 1 Carburettor
Compression ratio: 9.5:1
Bore: 76.0mm 3.0in
Stroke: 73.0mm 2.9in
Valve type/No: Overhead 6
Transmission: Manual
No. of forward speeds: 5
Wheels driven: Front
Springs F/R: Coil/Coil
Brake system: PA
Brakes F/R: Disc/Drum
Steering: Rack & pinion
Wheelbase: 231.9cm 91.3in
Track F: 131.1cm 51.6in
Track R: 134.1cm 52.8in
Length: 355.1cm 139.8in
Width: 154.9cm 61.0in
Height: 143.0cm 56.3in
Ground clearance: 18.0cm 7.1in
Kerb weight: 744.6kg 1640.0lb
Fuel: 35.0L 7.7gal 9.2galUS

1120 Daihatsu

Charade Diesel
1983 Japan
82.0mph 131.9kmh
0-50mph 80.5kmh: 13.2secs
0-60mph 96.5kmh: 20.8secs
0-1/4 mile: 21.9secs
0-1km: 41.3secs
37.0bhp 27.6kW 37.5PS
@ 4600rpm
45.0lbft 61.0Nm @ 3500rpm
48.1bhp/ton 47.3bhp/tonne
37.3bhp/L 27.8kW/L 37.8PS/L
36.7ft/sec 11.2m/sec
18.5mph 29.8kmh/1000rpm
48.5mpg 40.4mpgUS 5.8L/100km
Diesel 4-stroke piston
993cc 60.6cu in
In-line 3 fuel injection
Compression ratio: 25.0:1
Bore: 76.0mm 3.0in
Stroke: 73.0mm 2.9in
Valve type/No: Overhead 6
Transmission: Manual
No. of forward speeds: 5
Wheels driven: Front
Springs F/R: Coil/Coil
Brake system: PA
Brakes F/R: Disc/Drum
Steering: Rack & pinion
Wheelbase: 231.9cm 91.3in
Track F: 131.1cm 51.6in
Track R: 134.1cm 52.8in
Length: 355.1cm 139.8in
Width: 154.9cm 61.0in
Height: 143.0cm 56.3in
Ground clearance: 18.0cm 7.1in
Kerb weight: 781.8kg 1722.0lb
Fuel: 35.0L 7.7gal 9.2galUS

1121 Daihatsu

Charmant 1300LC
1985 Japan
95.0mph 152.9kmh
0-50mph 80.5kmh: 9.8secs
0-60mph 96.5kmh: 14.2secs
0-1/4 mile: 19.5secs
0-1km: 37.6secs
64.0bhp 47.7kW 64.9PS
@ 5400rpm
72.0lbft 97.6Nm @ 3600rpm
74.5bhp/ton 73.3bhp/tonne
49.6bhp/L 37.0kW/L 50.3PS/L
43.0ft/sec 13.1m/sec
19.8mph 31.9kmh/1000rpm
30.9mpg 25.7mpgUS 9.1L/100km
Petrol 4-stroke piston
1290cc 78.7cu in
In-line 4 1 Carburettor
Compression ratio: 9.5:1
Bore: 75.0mm 2.9in
Stroke: 73.0mm 2.9in
Valve type/No: Overhead 8
Transmission: Manual
No. of forward speeds: 5
Wheels driven: Rear
Springs F/R: Coil/Coil
Brake system: PA
Brakes F/R: Disc/Drum
Steering: Rack & pinion
Wheelbase: 240.0cm 94.5in
Track F: 133.1cm 52.4in
Track R: 133.6cm 52.6in
Length: 415.0cm 163.4in
Width: 162.6cm 64.0in
Height: 137.9cm 54.3in
Ground clearance: 15.5cm 6.1in
Kerb weight: 873.0kg 1923.0lb
Fuel: 49.6L 10.9gal 13.1galUS

1122 Daihatsu

Domino
1986 Japan
88.0mph 141.6kmh
0-50mph 80.5kmh: 10.1secs
0-60mph 96.5kmh: 14.7secs
0-1/4 mile: 19.7secs
0-1km: 37.8secs
44.0bhp 32.8kW 44.6PS
@ 5500rpm
50.0lbft 67.8Nm @ 3200rpm
72.6bhp/ton 71.4bhp/tonne
52.0bhp/L 38.8kW/L 52.7PS/L
48.7ft/sec 14.8m/sec
17.8mph 28.6kmh/1000rpm
37.2mpg 31.0mpgUS 7.6L/100km
Petrol 4-stroke piston
846cc 52.0cu in
In-line 3 1 Carburettor
Compression ratio: 9.5:1
Bore: 66.6mm 2.6in
Stroke: 81.0mm 3.2in
Valve type/No: Overhead 6
Transmission: Manual
No. of forward speeds: 5
Wheels driven: Front
Springs F/R: Coil/Coil
Brake system: PA
Brakes F/R: Disc/Drum
Steering: Rack & pinion
Wheelbase: 225.0cm 88.6in
Track F: 121.5cm 47.8in
Track R: 120.5cm 47.4in
Length: 319.5cm 125.8in
Width: 139.5cm 54.9in
Height: 140.0cm 55.1in

Ground clearance: 12.0cm 4.7in
Kerb weight: 616.0kg 1356.8lb
Fuel: 28.2L 6.2gal 7.4galUS

1123 Daihatsu

Charade CX Diesel Turbo
1987 Japan
81.0mph 130.3kmh
0-50mph 80.5kmh: 13.9secs
0-60mph 96.5kmh: 20.9secs
0-1/4 mile: 22.0secs
0-1km: 41.3secs
47.0bhp 35.0kW 47.6PS
@ 4800rpm
63.0lbft 85.4Nm @ 2300rpm
58.1bhp/ton 57.2bhp/tonne
47.3bhp/L 35.3kW/L 48.0PS/L
38.3ft/sec 11.7m/sec
18.5mph 29.8kmh/1000rpm
45.5mpg 37.9mpgUS 6.2L/100km
Diesel 4-stroke piston
993cc 61.0cu in turbocharged
In-line 3 fuel injection
Compression ratio: 21.5:1
Bore: 76.0mm 3.0in
Stroke: 73.0mm 2.9in
Valve type/No: Overhead 6
Transmission: Manual
No. of forward speeds: 5
Wheels driven: Front
Springs F/R: Coil/Coil
Brake system: PA
Brakes F/R: Disc/Drum
Steering: Rack & pinion
Wheelbase: 234.0cm 92.1in
Track F: 138.5cm 54.5in
Track R: 136.5cm 53.7in
Length: 361.0cm 142.1in
Width: 160.0cm 63.0in
Height: 138.5cm 54.5in
Ground clearance: 16.0cm 6.3in
Kerb weight: 822.0kg 1810.6lb
Fuel: 36.9L 8.1gal 9.7galUS

1124 Daihatsu

Charade GT ti
1987 Japan
116.0mph 186.6kmh
0-50mph 80.5kmh: 5.8secs
0-60mph 96.5kmh: 7.9secs
0-1/4 mile: 16.4secs
0-1km: 30.4secs
99.0bhp 73.8kW 100.4PS
@ 6500rpm
95.8lbft 129.8Nm @ 3500rpm
123.1bhp/ton 121.0bhp/tonne
99.7bhp/L 74.3kW/L 101.1PS/L
51.8ft/sec 15.8m/sec
18.4mph 29.6kmh/1000rpm
28.8mpg 24.0mpgUS 9.8L/100km
Petrol 4-stroke piston
993cc 61.0cu in turbocharged
In-line 3 fuel injection
Compression ratio: 7.8:1
Bore: 76.0mm 3.0in
Stroke: 73.0mm 2.9in
Valve type/No: Overhead 12
Transmission: Manual
No. of forward speeds: 5
Wheels driven: Front
Springs F/R: Coil/Coil
Brake system: PA
Brakes F/R: Disc/Disc
Steering: Rack & pinion
Wheelbase: 234.0cm 92.1in
Track F: 138.5cm 54.5in
Track R: 137.5cm 54.1in
Length: 361.0cm 142.1in
Width: 161.5cm 63.6in
Height: 138.5cm 54.5in
Ground clearance: 16.0cm 6.3in
Kerb weight: 818.0kg 1801.8lb
Fuel: 40.0L 8.8gal 10.6galUS

1125 Daihatsu

Fourtrak Estate DT EL
1987 Japan
85.0mph 136.8kmh
0-50mph 80.5kmh: 12.0secs
0-60mph 96.5kmh: 17.9secs
0-1/4 mile: 20.7secs
0-1km: 38.7secs
87.0bhp 64.9kW 88.2PS
@ 3500rpm
155.0lbft 210.0Nm @ 2200rpm
53.3bhp/ton 52.4bhp/tonne
31.5bhp/L 23.5kW/L 31.9PS/L
39.8ft/sec 12.1m/sec
21.5mph 34.6kmh/1000rpm
23.0mpg 19.2mpgUS 12.3L/100km
Diesel 4-stroke piston
2765cc 169.0cu in turbocharged
In-line 4 fuel injection
Compression ratio: 21.5:1
Bore: 92.0mm 3.6in
Stroke: 104.0mm 4.1in
Valve type/No: Overhead 8
Transmission: Manual
No. of forward speeds: 5
Wheels driven: 4-wheel engageable
Springs F/R: Leaf/Leaf
Brake system: PA
Brakes F/R: Disc/Drum
Steering: Ball & nut PA
Wheelbase: 210.0cm 82.7in
Track F: 132.0cm 52.0in
Track R: 130.0cm 51.2in
Length: 412.5cm 162.4in
Width: 158.0cm 62.2in
Height: 191.5cm 75.4in
Ground clearance: 21.0cm 8.3in
Kerb weight: 1660.0kg 3656.4lb
Fuel: 60.1L 13.2gal 15.9galUS

1126 Daihatsu

Charade CLX
1988 Japan
0-60mph 96.5kmh: 15.2secs
0-1/4 mile: 19.5secs
53.0bhp 39.5kW 53.7PS
@ 5200rpm
58.0lbft 78.6Nm @ 3600rpm
62.3bhp/ton 61.3bhp/tonne
53.4bhp/L 39.8kW/L 54.1PS/L
41.5ft/sec 12.6m/sec
43.8mpg 36.5mpgUS 6.4L/100km
Petrol 4-stroke piston
993cc 60.6cu in
In-line 3 fuel injection
Compression ratio: 9.5:1
Bore: 76.0mm 3.0in
Stroke: 73.0mm 2.9in
Valve type/No: Overhead 6
Transmission: Manual
No. of forward speeds: 5
Wheels driven: Front
Springs F/R: Coil/Coil
Brake system: PA
Brakes F/R: Disc/Drum
Steering: Rack & pinion
Wheelbase: 233.9cm 92.1in
Track F: 138.4cm 54.5in
Track R: 136.4cm 53.7in
Length: 368.0cm 144.9in
Width: 161.5cm 63.6in
Height: 138.4cm 54.5in
Kerb weight: 864.9kg 1905.0lb
Fuel: 40.1L 8.8gal 10.6galUS

1127 Daihatsu

Charade Turbo
1988 Japan
96.0mph 154.5kmh
0-50mph 80.5kmh: 8.1secs
0-60mph 96.5kmh: 11.3secs
0-1/4 mile: 18.2secs
0-1km: 34.3secs
67.0bhp 50.0kW 67.9PS
@ 5500rpm
78.2lbft 106.0Nm @ 3500rpm
85.7bhp/ton 84.3bhp/tonne
67.5bhp/L 50.3kW/L 68.4PS/L
43.8ft/sec 13.4m/sec
19.8mph 31.9kmh/1000rpm
29.2mpg 24.3mpgUS 9.7L/100km
Petrol 4-stroke piston
993cc 61.0cu in turbocharged
In-line 3 1 Carburettor
Compression ratio: 8.0:1
Bore: 76.0mm 3.0in
Stroke: 73.0mm 2.9in
Valve type/No: Overhead 6
Transmission: Manual
No. of forward speeds: 5
Wheels driven: Front
Springs F/R: Coil/Coil
Brake system: PA
Brakes F/R: Disc/Drum
Steering: Rack & pinion
Wheelbase: 234.0cm 92.1in
Track F: 138.5cm 54.5in
Track R: 136.5cm 53.7in
Length: 361.0cm 142.1in
Width: 160.0cm 63.0in
Height: 138.5cm 54.5in
Ground clearance: 16.0cm 6.3in
Kerb weight: 795.0kg 1751.1lb
Fuel: 40.0L 8.8gal 10.6galUS

1128 Daihatsu

Charade 1.3 CX
1989 Japan
102.0mph 164.1kmh
0-50mph 80.5kmh: 8.0secs
0-60mph 96.5kmh: 11.2secs
0-1/4 mile: 18.3secs
0-1km: 34.4secs
75.0bhp 55.9kW 76.0PS
@ 6500rpm
75.3lbft 102.0Nm @ 3900rpm
90.8bhp/ton 89.3bhp/tonne
57.9bhp/L 43.2kW/L 58.7PS/L
50.6ft/sec 15.4m/sec
18.4mph 29.6kmh/1000rpm
25.8mpg 21.5mpgUS 10.9L/100km
Petrol 4-stroke piston
1295cc 79.0cu in
In-line 4 1 Carburettor
Compression ratio: 9.5:1
Bore: 76.0mm 3.0in
Stroke: 71.0mm 2.8in
Valve type/No: Overhead 16
Transmission: Manual
No. of forward speeds: 5
Wheels driven: Front
Springs F/R: Coil/Coil
Brake system: PA
Brakes F/R: Disc/Drum
Steering: Rack & pinion
Wheelbase: 234.0cm 92.1in
Track F: 138.5cm 54.5in
Track R: 136.5cm 53.7in
Length: 361.0cm 142.1in
Width: 160.0cm 63.0in
Height: 138.5cm 54.5in
Ground clearance: 16.0cm 6.3in
Kerb weight: 840.0kg 1850.2lb
Fuel: 44.6L 9.8gal 11.8galUS

1129 Daihatsu

Charade CLS
1989 Japan
95.0mph 152.9kmh
0-60mph 96.5kmh: 11.5secs
0-1/4 mile: 18.2secs
80.0bhp 59.7kW 81.1PS
@ 6000rpm
74.0lbft 100.3Nm @ 4400rpm
88.9bhp/ton 87.4bhp/tonne
61.7bhp/L 46.0kW/L 62.6PS/L
46.8ft/sec 14.3m/sec
35.4mpg 29.5mpgUS 8.0L/100km
Petrol 4-stroke piston
1296cc 79.1cu in
In-line 4 fuel injection
Compression ratio: 9.5:1
Bore: 76.0mm 3.0in
Stroke: 71.4mm 2.8in
Valve type/No: Overhead 16
Transmission: Manual
No. of forward speeds: 5
Wheels driven: Front
Springs F/R: Coil/Coil
Brake system: PA
Brakes F/R: Disc/Drum
Steering: Rack & pinion PA
Wheelbase: 233.9cm 92.1in
Track F: 138.4cm 54.5in
Track R: 136.4cm 53.7in
Length: 368.0cm 144.9in
Width: 161.5cm 63.6in
Height: 138.4cm 54.5in
Kerb weight: 914.8kg 2015.0lb
Fuel: 40.1L 8.8gal 10.6galUS

1130 Daihatsu

Sportrak EL
1989 Japan
91.0mph 146.4kmh
0-50mph 80.5kmh: 11.1secs
0-60mph 96.5kmh: 16.1secs
0-1/4 mile: 20.3secs
0-1km: 40.1secs
85.0bhp 63.4kW 86.2PS
@ 6000rpm
93.0lbft 126.0Nm @ 3500rpm
68.3bhp/ton 67.1bhp/tonne
53.5bhp/L 39.9kW/L 54.2PS/L
57.5ft/sec 17.5m/sec
16.9mph 27.2kmh/1000rpm
21.4mpg 17.8mpgUS 13.2L/100km
Petrol 4-stroke piston
1589cc 97.0cu in
In-line 4 1 Carburettor
Compression ratio: 9.5:1
Bore: 76.0mm 3.0in
Stroke: 87.6mm 3.4in
Valve type/No: Overhead 16
Transmission: Manual
No. of forward speeds: 5
Wheels driven: 4-wheel engageable
Springs F/R: Torsion bar/Leaf
Brake system: PA
Brakes F/R: Disc/Drum
Steering: Recirculating ball PA
Wheelbase: 217.5cm 85.6in
Track F: 132.0cm 52.0in
Track R: 132.0cm 52.0in
Length: 368.5cm 145.1in
Width: 158.0cm 62.2in
Height: 172.0cm 67.7in
Ground clearance: 21.0cm 8.3in
Kerb weight: 1266.0kg 2788.5lb
Fuel: 60.1L 13.2gal 15.9galUS

1131 Daihatsu

Applause 16 Xi
1990 Japan
111.0mph 178.6kmh
0-50mph 80.5kmh: 7.2secs
0-60mph 96.5kmh: 10.1secs
0-1/4 mile: 17.6secs
0-1km: 32.6secs
105.0bhp 78.3kW 106.5PS
@ 6000rpm
98.9lbft 134.0Nm @ 4800rpm
107.3bhp/ton 105.5bhp/tonne
66.1bhp/L 49.3kW/L 67.0PS/L
57.7ft/sec 17.6m/sec
20.4mph 32.8kmh/1000rpm
29.0mpg 24.1mpgUS 9.7L/100km
Petrol 4-stroke piston
1589cc 97.0cu in
In-line 4 fuel injection
Compression ratio: 9.5:1
Bore: 76.0mm 3.0in
Stroke: 88.0mm 3.5in
Valve type/No: Overhead 16
Transmission: Manual
No. of forward speeds: 5
Wheels driven: Front
Springs F/R: Coil/Coil
Brake system: PA
Brakes F/R: Disc/Disc
Steering: Rack & pinion PA
Wheelbase: 247.0cm 97.2in
Track F: 142.5cm 56.1in
Track R: 141.5cm 55.7in
Length: 426.0cm 167.7in
Width: 166.0cm 65.4in
Height: 137.5cm 54.1in
Ground clearance: 14.9cm 5.9in
Kerb weight: 995.0kg 2191.6lb
Fuel: 60.1L 13.2gal 15.9galUS

1132 Daimler

30hp Double-six Saloon
1929 UK
75.0mph 120.7kmh
16.0mpg 13.3mpgUS 17.7L/100km
Petrol 4-stroke piston
3744cc 228.4cu in
Vee 12
Bore: 65.0mm 2.6in
Stroke: 94.0mm 3.7in
Transmission: Manual
No. of forward speeds: 4
Wheels driven: Rear
Brakes F/R: Drum/Drum
Wheelbase: 358.1cm 141.0in
Track F: 132.1cm 52.0in
Track R: 132.1cm 52.0in
Length: 482.6cm 190.0in
Width: 165.1cm 65.0in
Height: 182.9cm 72.0in
Fuel: 72.8L 16.0gal 19.2galUS

1133 Daimler

15hp Saloon
1933 UK
66.6mph 107.2kmh
25.0mpg 20.8mpgUS 11.3L/100km
Petrol 4-stroke piston
1805cc 110.1cu in
In-line 6 1 Carburettor

Bore: 63.5mm 2.5in
Stroke: 95.0mm 3.7in
12
Transmission: Manual
No. of forward speeds: 4
Wheels driven: Rear
Brakes F/R: Drum/Drum
Wheelbase: 278.1cm 109.5in
Track F: 128.5cm 50.6in
Track R: 128.5cm 50.6in
Length: 393.7cm 155.0in
Width: 151.1cm 59.5in
Height: 160.0cm 63.0in
Kerb weight: 1207.6kg 2660.0lb
Fuel: 54.6L 12.0gal 14.4galUS

1134 Daimler

15hp Saloon
1936 UK
70.3mph 113.1kmh
0-50mph 80.5kmh: 20.6secs
0-60mph 96.5kmh: 39.8secs
24.0mpg 20.0mpgUS 11.8L/100km
Petrol 4-stroke piston
2003cc 122.2cu in
In-line 6
Bore: 63.5mm 2.5in
Stroke: 105.0mm 4.1in
Valve type/No: Overhead 12
Transmission: Manual
No. of forward speeds: 4
Wheels driven: Rear
Brakes F/R: Drum/Drum
Kerb weight: 1398.3kg 3080.0lb
Fuel: 54.6L 12.0gal 14.4galUS

1135 Daimler

25.7hp Light Straight Eight Coupe
1936 UK
90.0mph 144.8kmh
0-50mph 80.5kmh: 12.4secs
0-60mph 96.5kmh: 18.8secs
15.0mpg 12.5mpgUS 18.8L/100km
Petrol 4-stroke piston
3421cc 208.7cu in
In-line 8
Bore: 72.0mm 2.8in
Stroke: 105.0mm 4.1in
Valve type/No: Overhead 16
Transmission: Manual
No. of forward speeds: 4
Wheels driven: Rear
Brakes F/R: Drum/Drum
Kerb weight: 1791.5kg 3946.0lb
Fuel: 91.0L 20.0gal 24.0galUS

1136 Daimler

18hp 2.5-litre
1938 UK
73.7mph 118.6kmh
0-50mph 80.5kmh: 19.1secs
0-60mph 96.5kmh: 31.0secs
70.0bhp 52.2kW 71.0PS
@ 4200rpm
45.3bhp/ton 44.6bhp/tonne
27.8bhp/L 20.7kW/L 28.1PS/L
50.7ft/sec 15.5m/sec
18.0mpg 15.0mpgUS 15.7L/100km
Petrol 4-stroke piston
2522cc 153.9cu in
In-line 6 1 Carburettor
Compression ratio: 7.0:1
Bore: 69.6mm 2.7in
Stroke: 110.5mm 4.3in
Valve type/No: Overhead 12
Transmission: Manual
No. of forward speeds: 4
Wheels driven: Rear
Brakes F/R: Drum/Drum
Kerb weight: 1569.9kg 3458.0lb
Fuel: 45.5L 10.0gal 12.0galUS

1137 Daimler

24hp Limousine
1938 UK
75.0mph 120.7kmh
0-50mph 80.5kmh: 24.2secs
0-60mph 96.5kmh: 35.9secs
14.0mpg 11.7mpgUS 20.2L/100km
Petrol 4-stroke piston
3317cc 202.4cu in
In-line 6
Bore: 80.0mm 3.1in
Stroke: 110.0mm 4.3in
Valve type/No: Overhead 12
Transmission: Pre-selector
No. of forward speeds: 4
Wheels driven: Rear
Brakes F/R: Drum/Drum
Kerb weight: 2017.6kg 4444.0lb
Fuel: 91.0L 20.0gal 24.0galUS

1138 Daimler

Twenty-Seven Limousine
1946 UK
81.0mph 130.3kmh
0-50mph 80.5kmh: 19.5secs
0-60mph 96.5kmh: 28.7secs
110.0bhp 82.0kW 111.5PS
@ 3600rpm
42.3bhp/ton 41.6bhp/tonne
26.9bhp/L 20.0kW/L 27.2PS/L
47.2ft/sec 14.4m/sec
12.0mpg 10.0mpgUS 23.5L/100km
Petrol 4-stroke piston
4095cc 249.8cu in
In-line 6
Compression ratio: 6.3:1
Bore: 85.0mm 3.3in
Stroke: 120.0mm 4.7in
Valve type/No: Overhead 12
Transmission: Manual
No. of forward speeds: 4
Wheels driven: Rear
Brakes F/R: Drum/Drum
Wheelbase: 350.5cm 138.0in
Track F: 152.4cm 60.0in
Track R: 160.0cm 63.0in
Length: 542.3cm 213.5in
Width: 188.0cm 74.0in
Height: 182.9cm 72.0in
Kerb weight: 2644.1kg 5824.0lb
Fuel: 91.0L 20.0gal 24.0galUS

1139 Daimler

Straight Eight
1948 UK
85.0mph 136.8kmh
0-50mph 80.5kmh: 18.6secs
0-60mph 96.5kmh: 26.0secs
150.0bhp 111.9kW 152.1PS
@ 3600rpm
56.9bhp/ton 55.9bhp/tonne
27.5bhp/L 20.5kW/L 27.8PS/L
47.2ft/sec 14.4m/sec
12.0mpg 10.0mpgUS 23.5L/100km
Petrol 4-stroke piston
5460cc 333.1cu in
In-line 8
Compression ratio: 6.3:1
Bore: 85.1mm 3.3in
Stroke: 120.0mm 4.7in
Valve type/No: Overhead 16
Transmission: Manual
No. of forward speeds: 4
Wheels driven: Rear
Brakes F/R: Drum/Drum
Wheelbase: 373.4cm 147.0in
Track F: 152.4cm 60.0in
Track R: 160.0cm 63.0in
Length: 563.9cm 222.0in
Width: 188.0cm 74.0in
Height: 182.9cm 72.0in
Ground clearance: 17.8cm 7.0in
Kerb weight: 2682.2kg 5908.0lb
Fuel: 91.0L 20.0gal 24.0galUS

1140 Daimler

Conquest
1953 UK
81.0mph 130.3kmh
0-50mph 80.5kmh: 13.0secs
0-60mph 96.5kmh: 20.4secs
0-1/4 mile: 22.3secs
75.0bhp 55.9kW 76.0PS
@ 4000rpm
124.0lbft 168.0Nm @ 2000rpm
54.2bhp/ton 53.3bhp/tonne
30.8bhp/L 23.0kW/L 31.3PS/L
38.9ft/sec 11.8m/sec
17.4mph 28.0kmh/1000rpm
19.7mpg 16.4mpgUS 14.3L/100km
Petrol 4-stroke piston
2433cc 148.4cu in
In-line 6
Compression ratio: 6.6:1
Bore: 76.2mm 3.0in
Stroke: 88.9mm 3.5in
Valve type/No: Overhead 12
Transmission: Manual
No. of forward speeds: 4
Wheels driven: Rear
Springs F/R: Torsion bar/Leaf
Brakes F/R: Drum/Drum
Wheelbase: 264.2cm 104.0in
Track F: 132.1cm 52.0in
Track R: 132.1cm 52.0in
Length: 450.1cm 177.2in
Width: 167.6cm 66.0in
Height: 165.1cm 65.0in
Ground clearance: 17.8cm 7.0in
Kerb weight: 1407.4kg 3100.0lb
Fuel: 68.2L 15.0gal 18.0galUS

1141 Daimler

One-O-Four Ladies' Model
1955 UK
102.5mph 164.9kmh
0-50mph 80.5kmh: 12.2secs
0-60mph 96.5kmh: 16.7secs
0-1/4 mile: 21.0secs
137.0bhp 102.2kW 138.9PS
@ 4400rpm
191.0lbft 258.8Nm @ 2000rpm
74.0bhp/ton 72.8bhp/tonne
39.5bhp/L 29.5kW/L 40.0PS/L
51.9ft/sec 15.8m/sec
22.7mph 36.5kmh/1000rpm
18.0mpg 15.0mpgUS 15.7L/100km
Petrol 4-stroke piston
3468cc 211.6cu in
In-line 6
Compression ratio: 7.6:1
Bore: 82.5mm 3.2in
Stroke: 107.9mm 4.2in
Valve type/No: Overhead 12
Transmission: Manual
No. of forward speeds: 4
Wheels driven: Rear
Springs F/R: Coil/Leaf
Brake system: PA
Brakes F/R: Drum/Drum
Wheelbase: 289.6cm 114.0in
Track F: 142.2cm 56.0in
Track R: 144.8cm 57.0in
Length: 497.8cm 196.0in
Width: 179.1cm 70.5in
Height: 158.8cm 62.5in
Ground clearance: 17.8cm 7.0in
Kerb weight: 1881.4kg 4144.0lb
Fuel: 81.9L 18.0gal 21.6galUS

1142 Daimler

Regency Mk II
1955 UK
85.0mph 136.8kmh
0-50mph 80.5kmh: 12.9secs
0-60mph 96.5kmh: 19.1secs
0-1/4 mile: 21.1secs
107.0bhp 79.8kW 108.5PS
@ 4000rpm
180.0lbft 243.9Nm @ 1600rpm
57.8bhp/ton 56.9bhp/tonne
30.8bhp/L 23.0kW/L 31.3PS/L
47.2ft/sec 14.4m/sec
19.2mph 30.9kmh/1000rpm
17.0mpg 14.2mpgUS 16.6L/100km
Petrol 4-stroke piston
3468cc 211.6cu in
In-line 6
Compression ratio: 6.5:1
Bore: 82.5mm 3.2in
Stroke: 107.9mm 4.2in
Valve type/No: Overhead 12
Transmission: Manual
No. of forward speeds: 4
Wheels driven: Rear
Springs F/R: Coil/Leaf
Brakes F/R: Drum/Drum
Wheelbase: 289.6cm 114.0in
Track F: 142.2cm 56.0in
Track R: 144.8cm 57.0in
Length: 497.8cm 196.0in
Width: 179.1cm 70.5in
Height: 159.3cm 62.7in
Ground clearance: 15.2cm 6.0in
Kerb weight: 1881.4kg 4144.0lb
Fuel: 81.9L 18.0gal 21.6galUS

1143 Daimler

One-O-Four
1957 UK
98.0mph 157.7kmh
0-50mph 80.5kmh: 12.3secs
0-60mph 96.5kmh: 17.3secs
0-1/4 mile: 23.0secs
137.0bhp 102.2kW 138.9PS
@ 4400rpm
191.0lbft 258.8Nm @ 2000rpm
74.9bhp/ton 73.7bhp/tonne
39.5bhp/L 29.5kW/L 40.0PS/L
51.9ft/sec 15.8m/sec
21.2mph 34.1kmh/1000rpm
19.0mpg 15.8mpgUS 14.9L/100km
Petrol 4-stroke piston
3468cc 211.6cu in
In-line 6
Compression ratio: 7.6:1
Bore: 82.5mm 3.2in
Stroke: 107.9mm 4.2in
Valve type/No: Overhead 12
Transmission: Manual
No. of forward speeds: 4
Wheels driven: Rear
Springs F/R: Coil/Leaf
Brake system: PA
Brakes F/R: Drum/Drum
Wheelbase: 289.6cm 114.0in
Track F: 142.2cm 56.0in
Track R: 144.8cm 57.0in
Length: 497.8cm 196.0in
Width: 179.1cm 70.5in
Height: 158.8cm 62.5in
Ground clearance: 17.8cm 7.0in
Kerb weight: 1859.1kg 4095.0lb
Fuel: 81.9L 18.0gal 21.6galUS

1144 Daimler

Majestic
1958 UK
103.5mph 166.5kmh
0-50mph 80.5kmh: 11.2secs
0-60mph 96.5kmh: 15.3secs
0-1/4 mile: 20.2secs
147.0bhp 109.6kW 149.0PS
@ 4400rpm
209.0lbft 283.2Nm @ 2800rpm
83.4bhp/ton 82.0bhp/tonne
38.7bhp/L 28.9kW/L 39.3PS/L
51.9ft/sec 15.8m/sec
21.1mph 33.9kmh/1000rpm
17.6mpg 14.7mpgUS 16.1L/100km
Petrol 4-stroke piston
3794cc 231.5cu in
In-line 6
Compression ratio: 7.5:1
Bore: 86.4mm 3.4in
Stroke: 107.9mm 4.2in
Valve type/No: Overhead 12
Transmission: Automatic
No. of forward speeds: 3
Wheels driven: Rear
Springs F/R: /Leaf
Brake system: PA
Brakes F/R: Disc/Disc
Wheelbase: 289.6cm 114.0in
Track F: 142.2cm 56.0in
Track R: 144.8cm 57.0in
Length: 497.8cm 196.0in
Width: 185.9cm 73.2in
Height: 159.3cm 62.7in
Ground clearance: 17.8cm 7.0in
Kerb weight: 1792.4kg 3948.0lb
Fuel: 81.9L 18.0gal 21.6galUS

1145 Daimler

DK 400B
1959 UK
93.8mph 150.9kmh
0-50mph 80.5kmh: 11.4secs
0-60mph 96.5kmh: 16.3secs
0-1/4 mile: 20.9secs
167.0bhp 124.5kW 169.3PS
@ 3800rpm
260.0lbft 352.3Nm @ 2800rpm
75.4bhp/ton 74.1bhp/tonne
36.2bhp/L 27.0kW/L 36.7PS/L
44.9ft/sec 13.7m/sec
20.8mph 33.5kmh/1000rpm
12.3mpg 10.2mpgUS 23.0L/100km
Petrol 4-stroke piston
4617cc 281.7cu in
In-line 6
Compression ratio: 7.0:1
Bore: 95.2mm 3.8in
Stroke: 107.9mm 4.2in
Valve type/No: Overhead 12
Transmission: Manual
No. of forward speeds: 4
Wheels driven: Rear
Springs F/R: Coil/Leaf
Brake system: PA
Brakes F/R: Drum/Drum

Wheelbase: 330.2cm 130.0in
Track F: 152.4cm 60.0in
Track R: 160.0cm 63.0in
Length: 551.2cm 217.0in
Width: 195.6cm 77.0in
Height: 178.6cm 70.3in
Ground clearance: 17.8cm 7.0in
Kerb weight: 2253.7kg 4964.0lb
Fuel: 91.0L 20.0gal 24.0galUS

1146 Daimler

V8 SP250
1959 UK
122.0mph 196.3kmh
0-50mph 80.5kmh: 7.7secs
0-60mph 96.5kmh: 10.2secs
0-1/4 mile: 17.8secs
140.0bhp 104.4kW 141.9PS
@ 5800rpm
155.0lbft 210.0Nm @ 3600rpm
141.1bhp/ton 138.8bhp/tonne
54.9bhp/L 41.0kW/L 55.7PS/L
44.3ft/sec 13.5m/sec
20.6mph 33.1kmh/1000rpm
29.1mpg 24.2mpgUS 9.7L/100km
Petrol 4-stroke piston
2548cc 155.5cu in
Vee 8
Compression ratio: 8.2:1
Bore: 76.2mm 3.0in
Stroke: 69.8mm 2.7in
Valve type/No: Overhead 16
Transmission: Manual
No. of forward speeds: 4
Wheels driven: Rear
Springs F/R: Coil/Leaf
Brakes F/R: Disc/Disc
Wheelbase: 233.7cm 92.0in
Track F: 127.0cm 50.0in
Track R: 121.9cm 48.0in
Length: 407.7cm 160.5in
Width: 166.4cm 65.5in
Height: 127.5cm 50.2in
Ground clearance: 15.2cm 6.0in
Kerb weight: 1008.8kg 2222.0lb
Fuel: 54.6L 12.0gal 14.4galUS

1147 Daimler

SP250
1960 UK
127.0mph 204.3kmh
0-50mph 80.5kmh: 7.1secs
0-60mph 96.5kmh: 9.1secs
0-1/4 mile: 16.9secs
140.0bhp 104.4kW 141.9PS
@ 5800rpm
155.0lbft 210.0Nm @ 3600rpm
138.8bhp/ton 136.4bhp/tonne
54.9bhp/L 41.0kW/L 55.7PS/L
44.3ft/sec 13.5m/sec
21.2mph 34.1kmh/1000rpm
Petrol 4-stroke piston
2549cc 155.5cu in
Vee 8 1 Carburettor
Compression ratio: 8.2:1
Bore: 76.2mm 3.0in
Stroke: 69.9mm 2.7in
Valve type/No: Overhead 16
Transmission: Manual
No. of forward speeds: 4
Wheels driven: Rear
Wheelbase: 233.7cm 92.0in
Track F: 127.0cm 50.0in
Track R: 121.9cm 48.0in
Length: 408.9cm 161.0in
Width: 153.7cm 60.5in
Height: 127.8cm 50.3in
Kerb weight: 1026.0kg 2260.0lb

1148 Daimler

Majestic Major
1961 UK
120.0mph 193.1kmh
0-50mph 80.5kmh: 7.5secs
0-60mph 96.5kmh: 10.3secs
0-1/4 mile: 17.1secs
220.0bhp 164.0kW 223.0PS
@ 5500rpm
283.0lbft 383.5Nm @ 3200rpm
116.6bhp/ton 114.6bhp/tonne
48.2bhp/L 36.0kW/L 48.9PS/L
48.1ft/sec 14.7m/sec
22.3mph 35.9kmh/1000rpm
14.8mpg 12.3mpgUS 19.1L/100km
Petrol 4-stroke piston
4561cc 278.3cu in
Vee 8
Compression ratio: 8.0:1
Bore: 95.3mm 3.8in
Stroke: 80.0mm 3.1in
Valve type/No: Overhead 16
Transmission: Automatic
No. of forward speeds: 3
Wheels driven: Rear
Springs F/R: Coil/Leaf
Brake system: PA
Brakes F/R: Disc/Disc
Wheelbase: 289.6cm 114.0in
Track F: 144.8cm 57.0in
Track R: 144.8cm 57.0in
Length: 513.1cm 202.0in
Width: 185.9cm 73.2in
Height: 159.3cm 62.7in
Ground clearance: 17.8cm 7.0in
Kerb weight: 1919.5kg 4228.0lb
Fuel: 72.8L 16.0gal 19.2galUS

1149 Daimler

2.5-litre V8 Saloon
1963 UK
112.5mph 181.0kmh
0-50mph 80.5kmh: 10.2secs
0-60mph 96.5kmh: 13.8secs
0-1/4 mile: 19.5secs
140.0bhp 104.4kW 141.9PS
@ 5800rpm
155.0lbft 210.0Nm @ 3600rpm
96.5bhp/ton 94.9bhp/tonne
54.9bhp/L 41.0kW/L 55.7PS/L
44.3ft/sec 13.5m/sec
16.6mph 26.7kmh/1000rpm
17.3mpg 14.4mpgUS 16.3L/100km
Petrol 4-stroke piston
2548cc 155.5cu in
Vee 8 2 Carburettor
Compression ratio: 8.2:1
Bore: 76.2mm 3.0in
Stroke: 69.8mm 2.7in
Valve type/No: Overhead 16
Transmission: Automatic
No. of forward speeds: 3
Wheels driven: Rear
Springs F/R: Coil/Leaf
Brake system: PA
Brakes F/R: Disc/Disc
Steering: Recirculating ball PA
Wheelbase: 271.8cm 107.0in
Track F: 139.7cm 55.0in
Track R: 134.6cm 53.0in
Length: 459.0cm 180.7in
Width: 168.9cm 66.5in
Height: 146.1cm 57.5in
Ground clearance: 17.8cm 7.0in
Kerb weight: 1474.6kg 3248.0lb
Fuel: 54.6L 12.0gal 14.4galUS

1150 Daimler

Limousine
1963 UK
114.0mph 183.4kmh
0-50mph 80.5kmh: 8.2secs
0-60mph 96.5kmh: 11.3secs
0-1/4 mile: 18.0secs
220.0bhp 164.0kW 223.0PS
@ 5500rpm
283.0lbft 383.5Nm @ 3200rpm
105.2bhp/ton 103.5bhp/tonne
48.2bhp/L 36.0kW/L 48.9PS/L
48.1ft/sec 14.7m/sec
22.3mph 35.9kmh/1000rpm
14.7mpg 12.2mpgUS 19.2L/100km
Petrol 4-stroke piston
4561cc 278.3cu in
Vee 8 2 Carburettor
Compression ratio: 8.0:1
Bore: 95.3mm 3.8in
Stroke: 80.0mm 3.1in
Valve type/No: Overhead 16
Transmission: Automatic
No. of forward speeds: 3
Wheels driven: Rear
Springs F/R: Coil/Leaf
Brake system: PA
Brakes F/R: Disc/Disc
Wheelbase: 348.0cm 137.0in
Track F: 144.8cm 57.0in
Track R: 144.8cm 57.0in
Length: 574.0cm 226.0in
Width: 186.7cm 73.5in
Height: 161.3cm 63.5in
Ground clearance: 17.8cm 7.0in
Kerb weight: 2126.1kg 4683.0lb
Fuel: 81.9L 18.0gal 21.6galUS

1151 Daimler

Conquest Century Saloon
1964 UK
88.0mph 141.6kmh
0-50mph 80.5kmh: 11.4secs
0-60mph 96.5kmh: 16.3secs
0-1/4 mile: 20.7secs
100.0bhp 74.6kW 101.4PS
@ 4400rpm
130.0lbft 176.2Nm @ 2500rpm
71.9bhp/ton 70.7bhp/tonne
41.1bhp/L 30.6kW/L 41.7PS/L
42.8ft/sec 13.0m/sec
17.4mph 28.0kmh/1000rpm
18.8mpg 15.7mpgUS 15.0L/100km
Petrol 4-stroke piston
2433cc 148.4cu in
In-line 6
Compression ratio: 7.7:1
Bore: 76.2mm 3.0in
Stroke: 88.9mm 3.5in
Valve type/No: Overhead 12
Transmission: Manual
No. of forward speeds: 4
Wheels driven: Rear
Springs F/R: Torsion bar/Leaf
Brakes F/R: Drum/Drum
Wheelbase: 264.2cm 104.0in
Track F: 132.1cm 52.0in
Track R: 132.1cm 52.0in
Length: 453.9cm 178.7in
Width: 167.6cm 66.0in
Height: 165.1cm 65.0in
Kerb weight: 1415.1kg 3117.0lb
Fuel: 68.2L 15.0gal 18.0galUS

1152 Daimler

2.5-litre V8
1966 UK
115.0mph 185.0kmh
0-50mph 80.5kmh: 11.3secs
0-60mph 96.5kmh: 14.7secs
0-1/4 mile: 19.9secs
0-1km: 36.3secs
140.0bhp 104.4kW 141.9PS
@ 5800rpm
155.0lbft 210.0Nm @ 3600rpm
95.9bhp/ton 94.3bhp/tonne
54.9bhp/L 41.0kW/L 55.7PS/L
44.5ft/sec 13.5m/sec
17.7mph 28.5kmh/1000rpm
19.3mpg 16.1mpgUS 14.6L/100km
Petrol 4-stroke piston
2548cc 155.5cu in
Vee 8 2 Carburettor
Compression ratio: 8.2:1
Bore: 76.0mm 3.0in
Stroke: 70.0mm 2.8in
Valve type/No: Overhead 16
Transmission: Automatic
No. of forward speeds: 3
Wheels driven: Rear
Springs F/R: Coil/Leaf
Brake system: PA
Brakes F/R: Disc/Disc
Steering: Recirculating ball PA
Wheelbase: 271.8cm 107.0in
Track F: 139.7cm 55.0in
Track R: 134.6cm 53.0in
Length: 459.0cm 180.7in
Width: 168.9cm 66.5in
Height: 146.1cm 57.5in
Ground clearance: 17.8cm 7.0in
Kerb weight: 1484.1kg 3269.0lb
Fuel: 54.6L 12.0gal 14.4galUS

1153 Daimler

Sovereign
1972 UK
120.0mph 193.1kmh
0-50mph 80.5kmh: 7.8secs
0-60mph 96.5kmh: 10.4secs
0-1/4 mile: 17.6secs
0-1km: 31.8secs
171.0bhp 127.5kW 173.4PS
@ 4500rpm
234.0lbft 317.1Nm @ 3200rpm
100.8bhp/ton 99.1bhp/tonne
40.4bhp/L 30.1kW/L 40.9PS/L
52.1ft/sec 15.9m/sec
22.9mph 36.8kmh/1000rpm
16.4mpg 13.7mpgUS 17.2L/100km
Petrol 4-stroke piston
4235cc 258.4cu in
In-line 6 2 Carburettor
Compression ratio: 9.0:1
Bore: 92.0mm 3.6in
Stroke: 106.0mm 4.2in
Valve type/No: Overhead 12
Transmission: Automatic
No. of forward speeds: 3
Wheels driven: Rear
Springs F/R: Coil/Coil
Brake system: PA
Brakes F/R: Disc/Disc
Steering: Rack & pinion PA
Wheelbase: 276.4cm 108.8in
Track F: 147.3cm 58.0in
Track R: 148.8cm 58.6in
Length: 481.3cm 189.5in
Width: 176.8cm 69.6in
Height: 134.1cm 52.8in
Ground clearance: 17.8cm 7.0in
Kerb weight: 1725.2kg 3800.0lb
Fuel: 109.2L 24.0gal 28.8galUS

1154 Daimler

Sovereign LWB Automatic
1974 UK
120.0mph 193.1kmh
0-50mph 80.5kmh: 7.6secs
0-60mph 96.5kmh: 10.3secs
0-1/4 mile: 17.8secs
0-1km: 32.3secs
180.0bhp 134.2kW 182.5PS
@ 4500rpm
232.0lbft 314.4Nm @ 3000rpm
107.3bhp/ton 105.6bhp/tonne
42.5bhp/L 31.7kW/L 43.1PS/L
52.1ft/sec 15.9m/sec
22.9mph 36.8kmh/1000rpm
14.3mpg 11.9mpgUS 19.8L/100km
Petrol 4-stroke piston
4235cc 258.4cu in
In-line 6 2 Carburettor
Compression ratio: 7.8:1
Bore: 92.0mm 3.6in
Stroke: 106.0mm 4.2in
Valve type/No: Overhead 12
Transmission: Automatic
No. of forward speeds: 3
Wheels driven: Rear
Springs F/R: Coil/Coil
Brake system: PA
Brakes F/R: Disc/Disc
Steering: Rack & pinion PA
Wheelbase: 286.5cm 112.8in
Track F: 147.3cm 58.0in
Track R: 149.4cm 58.8in
Length: 494.5cm 194.7in
Width: 177.0cm 69.7in
Height: 137.4cm 54.1in
Ground clearance: 17.8cm 7.0in
Kerb weight: 1705.2kg 3756.0lb
Fuel: 100.1L 22.0gal 26.4galUS

1155 Daimler

Double-Six HE
1981 UK
151.0mph 243.0kmh
0-50mph 80.5kmh: 6.4secs
0-60mph 96.5kmh: 8.1secs
0-1/4 mile: 16.2secs
0-1km: 28.9secs
299.0bhp 223.0kW 303.1PS
@ 5500rpm
318.0lbft 430.9Nm @ 3000rpm
158.7bhp/ton 156.1bhp/tonne
55.9bhp/L 41.7kW/L 56.7PS/L
42.2ft/sec 12.8m/sec
26.8mph 43.1kmh/1000rpm
16.4mpg 13.7mpgUS 17.2L/100km
Petrol 4-stroke piston
5345cc 326.1cu in
Vee 12 fuel injection
Compression ratio: 12.5:1
Bore: 90.0mm 3.5in
Stroke: 70.0mm 2.8in
Valve type/No: Overhead 24
Transmission: Automatic
No. of forward speeds: 3
Wheels driven: Rear
Springs F/R: Coil/Coil
Brake system: PA
Brakes F/R: Disc/Disc
Steering: Rack & pinion PA
Wheelbase: 286.5cm 112.8in
Track F: 148.1cm 58.3in
Track R: 149.6cm 58.9in
Length: 496.1cm 195.3in
Width: 177.0cm 69.7in
Height: 137.4cm 54.1in
Ground clearance: 17.8cm 7.0in
Kerb weight: 1915.4kg 4219.0lb

Fuel: 91.0L 20.0gal 24.0galUS

1156 Darracq

Straight Eight Saloon
1932 France
80.1mph 128.9kmh
15.0mpg 12.5mpgUS 18.8L/100km
Petrol 4-stroke piston
3392cc 207.0cu in
In-line 8
Bore: 75.0mm 2.9in
Stroke: 96.0mm 3.8in
Transmission: Manual
No. of forward speeds: 4
Wheels driven: Rear
Brakes F/R: Drum/Drum
Wheelbase: 322.6cm 127.0in
Track F: 147.3cm 58.0in
Track R: 147.3cm 58.0in
Length: 449.6cm 177.0in
Width: 171.5cm 67.5in
Height: 165.1cm 65.0in
Kerb weight: 1576.3kg 3472.0lb
Fuel: 109.2L 24.0gal 28.8galUS

1157 Datsun

1000
1958 Japan
65.6mph 105.6kmh
0-50mph 80.5kmh: 24.5secs
0-60mph 96.5kmh: 46.0secs
0-1/4 mile: 25.0secs
37.0bhp 27.6kW 37.5PS
@ 4400rpm
49.0lbft 66.4Nm @ 2400rpm
39.7bhp/ton 39.0bhp/tonne
37.4bhp/L 27.9kW/L 38.0PS/L
28.4ft/sec 8.6m/sec
14.8mph 23.8kmh/1000rpm
Petrol 4-stroke piston
988cc 60.3cu in
In-line 4
Compression ratio: 7.4:1
Bore: 73.2mm 2.9in
Stroke: 58.9mm 2.3in
Valve type/No: Overhead 8
Transmission: Manual
No. of forward speeds: 4
Wheels driven: Rear
Wheelbase: 222.0cm 87.4in
Track F: 117.1cm 46.1in
Track R: 118.1cm 46.5in
Length: 388.6cm 153.0in
Width: 146.6cm 57.7in
Height: 153.4cm 60.4in
Kerb weight: 948.9kg 2090.0lb

1158 Datsun

Bluebird Station Wagon
1961 Japan
75.0mph 120.7kmh
0-50mph 80.5kmh: 14.9secs
0-60mph 96.5kmh: 27.6secs
0-1/4 mile: 24.0secs
48.0bhp 35.8kW 48.7PS
@ 4800rpm
60.7lbft 82.2Nm @ 2400rpm
50.4bhp/ton 49.5bhp/tonne
40.4bhp/L 30.1kW/L 40.9PS/L
37.2ft/sec 11.3m/sec
14.7mph 23.7kmh/1000rpm
Petrol 4-stroke piston
1189cc 72.5cu in
In-line 4 1 Carburettor
Compression ratio: 7.5:1
Bore: 72.9mm 2.9in
Stroke: 70.9mm 2.8in
Valve type/No: Overhead 8
Transmission: Manual
No. of forward speeds: 3
Wheels driven: Rear
Wheelbase: 228.1cm 89.8in
Track F: 120.9cm 47.6in
Track R: 119.4cm 47.0in
Length: 390.9cm 153.9in
Width: 149.6cm 58.9in
Height: 146.1cm 57.5in
Ground clearance: 18.3cm 7.2in
Kerb weight: 969.3kg 2135.0lb

1159 Datsun

SPL-310
1964 Japan
87.5mph 140.8kmh
0-50mph 80.5kmh: 10.7secs
0-60mph 96.5kmh: 15.5secs
0-1/4 mile: 20.2secs
85.0bhp 63.4kW 86.2PS
@ 5600rpm
92.0lbft 124.7Nm @ 4400rpm
93.8bhp/ton 92.2bhp/tonne
57.1bhp/L 42.6kW/L 57.9PS/L
45.3ft/sec 13.8m/sec
17.5mph 28.2kmh/1000rpm
Petrol 4-stroke piston
1488cc 90.8cu in
In-line 4 2 Carburettor
Compression ratio: 9.0:1
Bore: 80.0mm 3.1in
Stroke: 73.9mm 2.9in
Valve type/No: Overhead 8
Transmission: Manual
No. of forward speeds: 4
Wheels driven: Rear
Springs F/R: Coil/Leaf
Brakes F/R: Drum/Drum
Steering: Cam & lever
Wheelbase: 228.1cm 89.8in
Track F: 121.4cm 47.8in
Track R: 119.6cm 47.1in
Length: 395.2cm 155.6in
Width: 149.6cm 58.9in
Height: 127.5cm 50.2in
Ground clearance: 16.0cm 6.3in
Kerb weight: 921.6kg 2030.0lb
Fuel: 43.1L 9.5gal 11.4galUS

1160 Datsun

1600 Sedan
1967 Japan
85.0mph 136.8kmh
0-50mph 80.5kmh: 13.2secs
0-60mph 96.5kmh: 19.4secs
0-1/4 mile: 21.5secs
96.0bhp 71.6kW 97.3PS
@ 6000rpm
103.0lbft 139.6Nm @ 4000rpm
100.5bhp/ton 98.8bhp/tonne
60.3bhp/L 44.9kW/L 61.1PS/L
43.8ft/sec 13.4m/sec
16.7mph 26.9kmh/1000rpm
Petrol 4-stroke piston
1593cc 97.2cu in
In-line 4 2 Carburettor
Compression ratio: 9.0:1
Bore: 87.1mm 3.4in
Stroke: 66.8mm 2.6in
Valve type/No: Overhead 8
Transmission: Automatic
No. of forward speeds: 3
Wheels driven: Rear
Springs F/R: Coil/Leaf
Brakes F/R: Disc/Drum
Steering: Recirculating ball
Wheelbase: 238.0cm 93.7in
Track F: 120.7cm 47.5in
Track R: 119.9cm 47.2in
Length: 400.1cm 157.5in
Width: 149.1cm 58.7in
Height: 143.0cm 56.3in
Ground clearance: 16.8cm 6.6in
Kerb weight: 971.6kg 2140.0lb
Fuel: 41.6L 9.1gal 11.0galUS

1161 Datsun

1600 Sports
1967 Japan
101.0mph 162.5kmh
0-50mph 80.5kmh: 9.6secs
0-60mph 96.5kmh: 13.3secs
0-1/4 mile: 19.9secs
96.0bhp 71.6kW 97.3PS
@ 6000rpm
103.0lbft 139.6Nm @ 4000rpm
103.1bhp/ton 101.4bhp/tonne
60.2bhp/L 44.9kW/L 61.0PS/L
43.8ft/sec 13.4m/sec
18.4mph 29.6kmh/1000rpm
Petrol 4-stroke piston
1595cc 97.3cu in
In-line 4 2 Carburettor
Compression ratio: 9.0:1
Bore: 87.2mm 3.4in
Stroke: 66.8mm 2.6in
Valve type/No: Overhead 8
Transmission: Manual
No. of forward speeds: 4
Wheels driven: Rear
Springs F/R: Coil/Leaf
Brakes F/R: Disc/Drum
Steering: Cam & lever
Wheelbase: 228.1cm 89.8in
Track F: 127.0cm 50.0in
Track R: 119.6cm 47.1in
Length: 395.2cm 155.6in
Width: 149.6cm 58.9in
Height: 130.6cm 51.4in
Ground clearance: 18.3cm 7.2in
Kerb weight: 946.6kg 2085.0lb
Fuel: 43.1L 9.5gal 11.4galUS

1162 Datsun

2000 Sports
1967 Japan
114.0mph 183.4kmh
0-50mph 80.5kmh: 7.8secs
0-60mph 96.5kmh: 10.2secs
0-1/4 mile: 17.3secs
135.0bhp 100.7kW 136.9PS
@ 6000rpm
145.0lbft 196.5Nm @ 4000rpm
143.3bhp/ton 140.9bhp/tonne
68.1bhp/L 50.8kW/L 69.1PS/L
54.5ft/sec 16.6m/sec
22.0mph 35.4kmh/1000rpm
Petrol 4-stroke piston
1982cc 120.9cu in
In-line 4
Compression ratio: 9.5:1
Bore: 87.2mm 3.4in
Stroke: 83.0mm 3.3in
Valve type/No: Overhead 8
Transmission: Manual
No. of forward speeds: 5
Wheels driven: Rear
Brakes F/R: Disc/Drum
Steering: Cam & lever
Wheelbase: 228.1cm 89.8in
Track F: 127.5cm 50.2in
Track R: 119.9cm 47.2in
Length: 395.5cm 155.7in
Width: 149.6cm 58.9in
Height: 131.1cm 51.6in
Kerb weight: 957.9kg 2110.0lb
Fuel: 43.1L 9.5gal 11.4galUS

1163 Datsun

1600
1968 Japan
95.0mph 152.9kmh
0-50mph 80.5kmh: 10.6secs
0-60mph 96.5kmh: 15.4secs
0-1/4 mile: 20.1secs
0-1km: 37.7secs
96.0bhp 71.6kW 97.3PS
@ 5600rpm
99.6lbft 135.0Nm @ 3600rpm
98.5bhp/ton 96.8bhp/tonne
60.2bhp/L 44.9kW/L 61.0PS/L
45.0ft/sec 13.7m/sec
18.6mph 29.9kmh/1000rpm
28.9mpg 24.1mpgUS 9.8L/100km
Petrol 4-stroke piston
1595cc 97.3cu in
In-line 4 1 Carburettor
Compression ratio: 8.5:1
Bore: 83.0mm 3.3in
Stroke: 73.3mm 2.9in
Valve type/No: Overhead 8
Transmission: Manual
No. of forward speeds: 4
Wheels driven: Rear
Springs F/R: Coil/Leaf
Brakes F/R: Disc/Drum
Steering: Recirculating ball
Wheelbase: 242.1cm 95.3in
Track F: 127.5cm 50.2in
Track R: 126.0cm 49.6in
Length: 419.6cm 165.2in
Width: 156.0cm 61.4in
Height: 137.9cm 54.3in
Ground clearance: 16.0cm 6.3in
Kerb weight: 991.5kg 2184.0lb
Fuel: 45.0L 9.9gal 11.9galUS

1164 Datsun

2000 Sports
1968 USA
114.0mph 183.4kmh
0-50mph 80.5kmh: 7.7secs
0-60mph 96.5kmh: 10.3secs
0-1/4 mile: 17.6secs
135.0bhp 100.7kW 136.9PS
@ 6000rpm
132.0lbft 178.9Nm @ 4400rpm
138.7bhp/ton 136.4bhp/tonne
68.1bhp/L 50.8kW/L 69.1PS/L
54.5ft/sec 16.6m/sec
22.0mph 35.4kmh/1000rpm
Petrol 4-stroke piston
1981cc 120.9cu in
In-line 4 2 Carburettor
Compression ratio: 9.5:1
Bore: 87.1mm 3.4in
Stroke: 83.0mm 3.3in
Valve type/No: Overhead 8
Transmission: Manual
No. of forward speeds: 5
Wheels driven: Rear
Springs F/R: Coil/Leaf
Brakes F/R: Disc/Drum
Steering: Cam & lever
Wheelbase: 228.1cm 89.8in
Track F: 127.5cm 50.2in
Track R: 119.9cm 47.2in
Length: 395.5cm 155.7in
Width: 149.6cm 58.9in
Height: 132.6cm 52.2in
Kerb weight: 989.7kg 2180.0lb
Fuel: 43.1L 9.5gal 11.4galUS

1165 Datsun

510
1968 USA
98.0mph 157.7kmh
0-50mph 80.5kmh: 9.5secs
0-60mph 96.5kmh: 14.0secs
0-1/4 mile: 19.7secs
96.0bhp 71.6kW 97.3PS
@ 5800rpm
100.0lbft 135.5Nm @ 3600rpm
91.0bhp/ton 89.5bhp/tonne
60.2bhp/L 44.9kW/L 61.1PS/L
46.7ft/sec 14.2m/sec
18.4mph 29.6kmh/1000rpm
Petrol 4-stroke piston
1594cc 97.2cu in
In-line 4 1 Carburettor
Compression ratio: 8.5:1
Bore: 83.1mm 3.3in
Stroke: 73.7mm 2.9in
Valve type/No: Overhead 8
Transmission: Manual
No. of forward speeds: 4
Wheels driven: Rear
Springs F/R: Coil/Coil
Brakes F/R: Disc/Drum
Steering: Recirculating ball
Wheelbase: 242.1cm 95.3in
Track F: 128.0cm 50.4in
Track R: 128.0cm 50.4in
Length: 412.0cm 162.2in
Width: 156.0cm 61.4in
Height: 140.0cm 55.1in
Kerb weight: 1072.8kg 2363.0lb
Fuel: 45.8L 10.1gal 12.1galUS

1166 Datsun

510 Sedan
1968 Japan
98.0mph 157.7kmh
0-50mph 80.5kmh: 9.2secs
0-60mph 96.5kmh: 13.5secs
0-1/4 mile: 19.7secs
96.0bhp 71.6kW 97.3PS
@ 5600rpm
100.0lbft 135.5Nm @ 3600rpm
101.0bhp/ton 99.3bhp/tonne
60.2bhp/L 44.9kW/L 61.0PS/L
45.0ft/sec 13.7m/sec
18.4mph 29.6kmh/1000rpm
Petrol 4-stroke piston
1595cc 97.3cu in
In-line 4 1 Carburettor
Compression ratio: 8.5:1
Bore: 83.0mm 3.3in
Stroke: 73.3mm 2.9in
Valve type/No: Overhead 8
Transmission: Manual
No. of forward speeds: 4
Wheels driven: Rear
Springs F/R: Coil/Coil
Brakes F/R: Disc/Drum
Steering: Recirculating ball
Wheelbase: 242.1cm 95.3in
Track F: 128.0cm 50.4in
Track R: 128.0cm 50.4in
Length: 412.0cm 162.2in
Width: 156.0cm 61.4in
Height: 140.0cm 55.1in
Ground clearance: 19.1cm 7.5in
Kerb weight: 967.0kg 2130.0lb
Fuel: 45.8L 10.1gal 12.1galUS

1167 Datsun
510 Station Wagon
1968 USA
89.5mph 144.0kmh
0-50mph 80.5kmh: 12.5secs
0-60mph 96.5kmh: 18.7secs
0-1/4 mile: 21.7secs
96.0bhp 71.6kW 97.3PS
@ 5600rpm
100.0lbft 135.5Nm @ 3600rpm
87.4bhp/ton 85.9bhp/tonne
60.2bhp/L 44.9kW/L 61.1PS/L
45.1ft/sec 13.8m/sec
17.2mph 27.7kmh/1000rpm
Petrol 4-stroke piston
1594cc 97.2cu in
In-line 4 1 Carburettor
Compression ratio: 8.5:1
Bore: 83.1mm 3.3in
Stroke: 73.7mm 2.9in
Valve type/No: Overhead 8
Transmission: Automatic
No. of forward speeds: 3
Wheels driven: Rear
Springs F/R: Coil/Leaf
Brakes F/R: Disc/Drum
Steering: Recirculating ball
Wheelbase: 242.1cm 95.3in
Track F: 127.5cm 50.2in
Track R: 126.0cm 49.6in
Length: 414.5cm 163.2in
Width: 156.0cm 61.4in
Height: 143.5cm 56.5in
Kerb weight: 1117.3kg 2461.0lb
Fuel: 45.8L 10.1gal 12.1galUS

1168 Datsun
1000 de Luxe
1969 Japan
78.0mph 125.5kmh
0-50mph 80.5kmh: 14.1secs
0-60mph 96.5kmh: 21.7secs
0-1/4 mile: 21.7secs
0-1km: 41.2secs
62.0bhp 46.2kW 62.9PS
@ 6000rpm
61.5lbft 83.3Nm @ 4000rpm
88.6bhp/ton 87.1bhp/tonne
62.7bhp/L 46.8kW/L 63.6PS/L
38.7ft/sec 11.8m/sec
14.3mph 23.0kmh/1000rpm
29.3mpg 24.4mpgUS 9.6L/100km
Petrol 4-stroke piston
988cc 60.3cu in
In-line 4 1 Carburettor
Compression ratio: 8.5:1
Bore: 73.0mm 2.9in
Stroke: 59.0mm 2.3in
Valve type/No: Overhead 8
Transmission: Manual
No. of forward speeds: 4
Wheels driven: Rear
Springs F/R: Leaf/Leaf
Brakes F/R: Drum/Drum
Steering: Recirculating ball
Wheelbase: 228.1cm 89.8in
Track F: 119.1cm 46.9in
Track R: 118.4cm 46.6in
Length: 380.0cm 149.6in
Width: 144.5cm 56.9in
Height: 134.6cm 53.0in
Ground clearance: 16.5cm 6.5in
Kerb weight: 711.4kg 1567.0lb
Fuel: 35.0L 7.7gal 9.2galUS

1169 Datsun
1200
1970 Japan
95.0mph 152.9kmh
0-50mph 80.5kmh: 10.8secs
0-60mph 96.5kmh: 15.3secs
0-1/4 mile: 19.9secs
0-1km: 37.8secs
68.0bhp 50.7kW 68.9PS
@ 6000rpm
70.0lbft 94.9Nm @ 3600rpm
95.0bhp/ton 93.4bhp/tonne
58.1bhp/L 43.3kW/L 58.9PS/L
46.0ft/sec 14.0m/sec
16.1mph 25.9kmh/1000rpm
31.2mpg 26.0mpgUS 9.1L/100km
Petrol 4-stroke piston
1171cc 71.4cu in
In-line 4 1 Carburettor
Compression ratio: 9.0:1
Bore: 73.0mm 2.9in
Stroke: 70.0mm 2.8in
Valve type/No: Overhead 8
Transmission: Manual
No. of forward speeds: 4
Wheels driven: Rear
Springs F/R: Coil/Leaf
Brakes F/R: Disc/Drum
Steering: Recirculating ball
Wheelbase: 230.1cm 90.6in
Track F: 121.9cm 48.0in
Track R: 124.5cm 49.0in
Length: 386.1cm 152.0in
Width: 149.9cm 59.0in
Height: 137.2cm 54.0in
Ground clearance: 15.2cm 6.0in
Kerb weight: 727.8kg 1603.0lb
Fuel: 39.8L 8.8gal 10.5galUS

1170 Datsun
1600 Pickup
1970 Japan
90.0mph 144.8kmh
0-50mph 80.5kmh: 10.3secs
0-60mph 96.5kmh: 15.6secs
0-1/4 mile: 20.0secs
96.0bhp 71.6kW 97.3PS
@ 5000rpm
99.8lbft 135.2Nm @ 3600rpm
95.6bhp/ton 94.0bhp/tonne
60.2bhp/L 44.9kW/L 61.0PS/L
40.1ft/sec 12.2m/sec
17.1mph 27.5kmh/1000rpm
27.6mpg 23.0mpgUS 10.2L/100km
Petrol 4-stroke piston
1595cc 97.3cu in
In-line 4
Compression ratio: 8.5:1
Bore: 83.0mm 3.3in
Stroke: 73.3mm 2.9in
Valve type/No: Overhead 8
Transmission: Manual
No. of forward speeds: 4
Wheels driven: Rear
Brakes F/R: Drum/Drum
Steering: Recirculating ball
Wheelbase: 253.0cm 99.6in
Track F: 125.0cm 49.2in
Track R: 126.7cm 49.9in
Length: 432.6cm 170.3in
Width: 157.5cm 62.0in
Height: 154.4cm 60.8in
Kerb weight: 1021.5kg 2250.0lb
Fuel: 40.9L 9.0gal 10.8galUS

1171 Datsun
240Z
1970 Japan
122.0mph 196.3kmh
0-50mph 80.5kmh: 6.6secs
0-60mph 96.5kmh: 8.7secs
0-1/4 mile: 17.1secs
150.0bhp 111.9kW 152.1PS
@ 6000rpm
148.0lbft 200.5Nm @ 4400rpm
142.7bhp/ton 140.3bhp/tonne
62.7bhp/L 46.7kW/L 63.5PS/L
48.2ft/sec 14.7m/sec
21.0mph 33.8kmh/1000rpm
25.2mpg 21.0mpgUS 11.2L/100km
Petrol 4-stroke piston
2393cc 146.0cu in
In-line 6 2 Carburettor
Compression ratio: 9.0:1
Bore: 83.0mm 3.3in
Stroke: 73.3mm 2.9in
Valve type/No: Overhead 12
Transmission: Manual
No. of forward speeds: 4
Wheels driven: Rear
Springs F/R: Coil/Coil
Brake system: PA
Brakes F/R: Disc/Drum
Steering: Rack & pinion
Wheelbase: 230.4cm 90.7in
Track F: 135.4cm 53.3in
Track R: 134.6cm 53.0in
Length: 413.5cm 162.8in
Width: 162.8cm 64.1in
Height: 128.5cm 50.6in
Ground clearance: 14.5cm 5.7in
Kerb weight: 1069.2kg 2355.0lb
Fuel: 60.2L 13.2gal 15.9galUS

1172 Datsun
100A
1971 Japan
87.0mph 140.0kmh
0-50mph 80.5kmh: 11.2secs
0-60mph 96.5kmh: 16.8secs
0-1/4 mile: 20.5secs
0-1km: 38.8secs
59.0bhp 44.0kW 59.8PS
@ 6000rpm
60.0lbft 81.3Nm @ 4000rpm
91.5bhp/ton 89.9bhp/tonne
59.7bhp/L 44.5kW/L 60.5PS/L
38.7ft/sec 11.8m/sec
14.6mph 23.5kmh/1000rpm
34.8mpg 29.0mpgUS 8.1L/100km
Petrol 4-stroke piston
988cc 60.3cu in
In-line 4 1 Carburettor
Compression ratio: 9.0:1
Bore: 73.0mm 2.9in
Stroke: 59.0mm 2.3in
Valve type/No: Overhead 8
Transmission: Manual
No. of forward speeds: 4
Wheels driven: Front
Springs F/R: Coil/Coil
Brakes F/R: Drum/Drum
Steering: Rack & pinion
Wheelbase: 233.4cm 91.9in
Track F: 127.0cm 50.0in
Track R: 123.4cm 48.6in
Length: 360.7cm 142.0in
Width: 147.1cm 57.9in
Height: 132.8cm 52.3in
Ground clearance: 20.1cm 7.9in
Kerb weight: 656.0kg 1445.0lb
Fuel: 35.9L 7.9gal 9.5galUS

1173 Datsun
1200 Coupe
1971 Japan
93.0mph 149.6kmh
0-50mph 80.5kmh: 10.4secs
0-60mph 96.5kmh: 15.1secs
0-1/4 mile: 19.6secs
69.0bhp 51.4kW 70.0PS
@ 6000rpm
70.0lbft 94.9Nm @ 3600rpm
94.0bhp/ton 92.4bhp/tonne
58.9bhp/L 43.9kW/L 59.7PS/L
46.0ft/sec 14.0m/sec
16.4mph 26.4kmh/1000rpm
33.6mpg 28.0mpgUS 8.4L/100km
Petrol 4-stroke piston
1171cc 71.4cu in
In-line 4 1 Carburettor
Compression ratio: 9.0:1
Bore: 73.0mm 2.9in
Stroke: 70.0mm 2.8in
Valve type/No: Overhead 8
Transmission: Manual
No. of forward speeds: 4
Wheels driven: Rear
Springs F/R: Coil/Leaf
Brakes F/R: Disc/Drum
Steering: Recirculating ball
Wheelbase: 230.1cm 90.6in
Track F: 124.0cm 48.8in
Track R: 124.5cm 49.0in
Length: 386.1cm 152.0in
Width: 151.4cm 59.6in
Height: 134.9cm 53.1in
Ground clearance: 17.0cm 6.7in
Kerb weight: 746.8kg 1645.0lb
Fuel: 37.8L 8.3gal 10.0galUS

1174 Datsun
1200 Estate
1971 Japan
89.0mph 143.2kmh
0-50mph 80.5kmh: 11.1secs
0-60mph 96.5kmh: 16.4secs
0-1/4 mile: 20.1secs
0-1km: 38.4secs
68.0bhp 50.7kW 68.9PS
@ 6000rpm
70.0lbft 94.9Nm @ 3600rpm
92.1bhp/ton 90.6bhp/tonne
58.1bhp/L 43.3kW/L 58.9PS/L
46.0ft/sec 14.0m/sec
16.1mph 25.9kmh/1000rpm
27.3mpg 22.7mpgUS 10.3L/100km
Petrol 4-stroke piston
1171cc 71.4cu in
In-line 4 1 Carburettor
Compression ratio: 9.0:1
Bore: 73.0mm 2.9in
Stroke: 70.0mm 2.8in
Valve type/No: Overhead 8
Transmission: Manual
No. of forward speeds: 4
Wheels driven: Rear
Springs F/R: Coil/Leaf
Brakes F/R: Disc/Drum
Steering: Recirculating ball
Wheelbase: 230.1cm 90.6in
Track F: 121.9cm 48.0in
Track R: 124.5cm 49.0in
Length: 386.1cm 152.0in
Width: 149.9cm 59.0in
Height: 141.0cm 55.5in
Ground clearance: 15.2cm 6.0in
Kerb weight: 750.5kg 1653.0lb
Fuel: 38.2L 8.4gal 10.1galUS

1175 Datsun
240Z
1971 Japan
126.0mph 202.7kmh
0-50mph 80.5kmh: 6.0secs
0-60mph 96.5kmh: 8.0secs
0-1/4 mile: 15.8secs
0-1km: 27.7secs
151.0bhp 112.6kW 153.1PS
@ 5600rpm
146.0lbft 197.8Nm @ 4400rpm
148.1bhp/ton 145.6bhp/tonne
63.1bhp/L 47.0kW/L 64.0PS/L
45.1ft/sec 13.8m/sec
21.6mph 34.8kmh/1000rpm
21.4mpg 17.8mpgUS 13.2L/100km
Petrol 4-stroke piston
2393cc 146.0cu in
In-line 6 2 Carburettor
Compression ratio: 9.0:1
Bore: 83.0mm 3.3in
Stroke: 73.7mm 2.9in
Valve type/No: Overhead 12
Transmission: Manual
No. of forward speeds: 5
Wheels driven: Rear
Springs F/R: Coil/Coil
Brake system: PA
Brakes F/R: Disc/Drum
Steering: Rack & pinion
Wheelbase: 229.9cm 90.5in
Track F: 135.9cm 53.5in
Track R: 134.6cm 53.0in
Length: 416.6cm 164.0in
Width: 162.6cm 64.0in
Height: 128.3cm 50.5in
Ground clearance: 20.3cm 8.0in
Kerb weight: 1036.9kg 2284.0lb
Fuel: 60.1L 13.2gal 15.9galUS

1176 Datsun
240Z Automatic
1971 Japan
120.0mph 193.1kmh
0-50mph 80.5kmh: 7.9secs
0-60mph 96.5kmh: 10.4secs
0-1/4 mile: 17.6secs
150.0bhp 111.9kW 152.1PS
@ 6000rpm
148.0lbft 200.5Nm @ 4400rpm
139.7bhp/ton 137.4bhp/tonne
62.7bhp/L 46.7kW/L 63.5PS/L
48.2ft/sec 14.7m/sec
18.8mph 30.2kmh/1000rpm
22.8mpg 19.0mpgUS 12.4L/100km
Petrol 4-stroke piston
2393cc 146.0cu in
In-line 6
Compression ratio: 9.0:1
Bore: 83.0mm 3.3in
Stroke: 73.3mm 2.9in
Valve type/No: Overhead 12
Transmission: Automatic
No. of forward speeds: 3
Wheels driven: Rear
Brake system: PA
Brakes F/R: Disc/Drum
Steering: Rack & pinion
Wheelbase: 230.4cm 90.7in
Track F: 135.4cm 53.3in
Track R: 134.6cm 53.0in
Length: 413.5cm 162.8in
Width: 162.8cm 64.1in
Height: 128.5cm 50.6in
Kerb weight: 1091.9kg 2405.0lb
Fuel: 60.2L 13.2gal 15.9galUS

1177 Datsun
510
1971 Japan
98.0mph 157.7kmh

0-60mph 96.5kmh: 13.9secs
0-1/4 mile: 19.6secs
96.0bhp 71.6kW 97.3PS
@ 5600rpm
100.0lbft 135.5Nm @ 3600rpm
100.5bhp/ton 98.8bhp/tonne
60.2bhp/L 44.9kW/L 61.0PS/L
45.0ft/sec 13.7m/sec
30.4mpg 25.3mpgUS 9.3L/100km
Petrol 4-stroke piston
1595cc 97.3cu in
In-line 4
Bore: 83.0mm 3.3in
Stroke: 73.3mm 2.9in
Valve type/No: Overhead 8
Transmission: Manual
No. of forward speeds: 4
Wheels driven: Rear
Springs F/R: Coil/Coil
Brakes F/R: Disc/Drum
Wheelbase: 242.1cm 95.3in
Track F: 128.0cm 50.4in
Track R: 128.0cm 50.4in
Length: 412.0cm 162.2in
Width: 156.0cm 61.4in
Height: 140.0cm 55.1in
Kerb weight: 971.6kg 2140.0lb
Fuel: 45.8L 10.1gal 12.1galUS

1178 Datsun

180B
1972 Japan
107.0mph 172.2kmh
0-50mph 80.5kmh: 8.8secs
0-60mph 96.5kmh: 12.5secs
0-1/4 mile: 18.5secs
0-1km: 34.1secs
105.0bhp 78.3kW 106.5PS
@ 6000rpm
108.0lbft 146.3Nm @ 3600rpm
104.6bhp/ton 102.9bhp/tonne
59.3bhp/L 44.2kW/L 60.1PS/L
51.2ft/sec 15.6m/sec
18.2mph 29.3kmh/1000rpm
24.9mpg 20.7mpgUS 11.3L/100km
Petrol 4-stroke piston
1770cc 108.0cu in
In-line 4 1 Carburettor
Compression ratio: 8.5:1
Bore: 85.0mm 3.3in
Stroke: 78.0mm 3.1in
Valve type/No: Overhead 8
Transmission: Manual
No. of forward speeds: 4
Wheels driven: Rear
Springs F/R: Coil/Coil
Brake system: PA
Brakes F/R: Disc/Drum
Steering: Recirculating ball
Wheelbase: 249.9cm 98.4in
Track F: 131.1cm 51.6in
Track R: 132.1cm 52.0in
Length: 421.4cm 165.9in
Width: 160.0cm 63.0in
Height: 140.5cm 55.3in
Ground clearance: 18.5cm 7.3in
Kerb weight: 1020.6kg 2248.0lb
Fuel: 54.6L 12.0gal 14.4galUS

1179 Datsun

240C
1972 Japan
104.0mph 167.3kmh
0-50mph 80.5kmh: 8.7secs
0-60mph 96.5kmh: 12.3secs
0-1/4 mile: 18.4secs
0-1km: 34.0secs
130.0bhp 96.9kW 131.8PS
@ 5600rpm
141.0lbft 191.1Nm @ 3600rpm
116.3bhp/ton 114.4bhp/tonne
54.3bhp/L 40.5kW/L 55.1PS/L
45.1ft/sec 13.8m/sec
17.4mph 28.0kmh/1000rpm
21.6mpg 18.0mpgUS 13.1L/100km
Petrol 4-stroke piston
2393cc 146.0cu in
In-line 6 1 Carburettor
Compression ratio: 8.5:1
Bore: 83.0mm 3.3in
Stroke: 73.7mm 2.9in
Valve type/No: Overhead 12
Transmission: Manual
No. of forward speeds: 4
Wheels driven: Rear
Springs F/R: Coil/Leaf
Brake system: PA
Brakes F/R: Disc/Drum
Steering: Recirculating ball
Wheelbase: 279.4cm 110.0in
Track F: 139.2cm 54.8in
Track R: 138.4cm 54.5in
Length: 469.9cm 185.0in
Width: 165.1cm 65.0in
Height: 148.6cm 58.5in
Ground clearance: 17.8cm 7.0in
Kerb weight: 1136.4kg 2503.0lb
Fuel: 65.5L 14.4gal 17.3galUS

1180 Datsun

510 TransAm
1972 Japan
127.0mph 204.3kmh
0-50mph 80.5kmh: 5.6secs
0-60mph 96.5kmh: 7.0secs
0-1/4 mile: 15.2secs
175.0bhp 130.5kW 177.4PS
@ 7800rpm
197.8bhp/ton 194.5bhp/tonne
107.9bhp/L 80.5kW/L 109.4PS/L
67.6ft/sec 20.6m/sec
14.1mph 22.7kmh/1000rpm
8.4mpg 7.0mpgUS 33.6L/100km
Petrol 4-stroke piston
1622cc 99.0cu in
In-line 4
Compression ratio: 11.5:1
Bore: 87.0mm 3.4in
Stroke: 79.3mm 3.1in
Valve type/No: Overhead 8
Transmission: Manual
No. of forward speeds: 5
Wheels driven: Rear
Brakes F/R: Disc/Drum
Steering: Recirculating ball
Wheelbase: 242.1cm 95.3in
Track F: 135.9cm 53.5in
Track R: 135.9cm 53.5in
Length: 412.0cm 162.2in
Width: 168.9cm 66.5in
Height: 121.9cm 48.0in
Kerb weight: 899.8kg 1982.0lb
Fuel: 56.8L 12.5gal 15.0galUS

1181 Datsun

200L
1973 Japan
104.0mph 167.3kmh
0-50mph 80.5kmh: 8.8secs
0-60mph 96.5kmh: 12.6secs
0-1/4 mile: 18.6secs
0-1km: 34.8secs
114.0bhp 85.0kW 115.6PS
@ 5600rpm
124.0lbft 168.0Nm @ 3200rpm
112.9bhp/ton 111.0bhp/tonne
57.3bhp/L 42.7kW/L 58.1PS/L
49.0ft/sec 14.9m/sec
18.0mph 29.0kmh/1000rpm
24.6mpg 20.5mpgUS 11.5L/100km
Petrol 4-stroke piston
1990cc 121.4cu in
In-line 4 1 Carburettor
Compression ratio: 8.3:1
Bore: 89.0mm 3.5in
Stroke: 80.0mm 3.1in
Valve type/No: Overhead 8
Transmission: Manual
No. of forward speeds: 4
Wheels driven: Rear
Springs F/R: /Leaf
Brake system: PA
Brakes F/R: Disc/Drum
Steering: Recirculating ball
Wheelbase: 266.7cm 105.0in
Track F: 134.6cm 53.0in
Track R: 133.9cm 52.7in
Length: 450.1cm 177.2in
Width: 166.9cm 65.7in
Height: 142.2cm 56.0in
Ground clearance: 17.8cm 7.0in
Kerb weight: 1026.9kg 2262.0lb
Fuel: 60.5L 13.3gal 16.0galUS

1182 Datsun

240Z
1973 Japan
115.0mph 185.0kmh
0-50mph 80.5kmh: 7.9secs
0-60mph 96.5kmh: 10.1secs
0-1/4 mile: 17.7secs
129.0bhp 96.2kW 130.8PS
@ 6000rpm
127.0lbft 172.1Nm @ 4400rpm
117.9bhp/ton 116.0bhp/tonne
53.9bhp/L 40.2kW/L 54.7PS/L
48.2ft/sec 14.7m/sec
21.0mph 33.8kmh/1000rpm
22.8mpg 19.0mpgUS 12.4L/100km
Petrol 4-stroke piston
2393cc 146.0cu in
In-line 6 2 Carburettor
Compression ratio: 8.8:1
Bore: 83.0mm 3.3in
Stroke: 73.3mm 2.9in
Valve type/No: Overhead 12
Transmission: Manual
No. of forward speeds: 4
Wheels driven: Rear
Springs F/R: Coil/Coil
Brake system: PA
Brakes F/R: Disc/Drum
Steering: Rack & pinion
Wheelbase: 230.4cm 90.7in
Track F: 134.6cm 53.0in
Track R: 134.6cm 53.0in
Length: 413.5cm 162.8in
Width: 162.8cm 64.1in
Height: 128.5cm 50.6in
Ground clearance: 14.5cm 5.7in
Kerb weight: 1112.3kg 2450.0lb
Fuel: 57.1L 12.6gal 15.1galUS

1183 Datsun

610 1800
1973 Japan
100.0mph 160.9kmh
0-50mph 80.5kmh: 9.8secs
0-60mph 96.5kmh: 14.0secs
0-1/4 mile: 19.4secs
94.0bhp 70.1kW 95.3PS
@ 5600rpm
99.0lbft 134.1Nm @ 3200rpm
91.9bhp/ton 90.4bhp/tonne
53.1bhp/L 39.6kW/L 53.8PS/L
47.8ft/sec 14.6m/sec
17.7mph 28.5kmh/1000rpm
29.4mpg 24.5mpgUS 9.6L/100km
Petrol 4-stroke piston
1770cc 108.0cu in
In-line 4 1 Carburettor
Compression ratio: 8.5:1
Bore: 85.0mm 3.3in
Stroke: 78.0mm 3.1in
Valve type/No: Overhead 8
Transmission: Manual
No. of forward speeds: 4
Wheels driven: Rear
Springs F/R: Coil/Coil
Brake system: PA
Brakes F/R: Disc/Drum
Steering: Recirculating ball
Wheelbase: 249.9cm 98.4in
Track F: 131.1cm 51.6in
Track R: 132.1cm 52.0in
Length: 436.9cm 172.0in
Width: 160.0cm 63.0in
Height: 140.5cm 55.3in
Ground clearance: 18.5cm 7.3in
Kerb weight: 1039.7kg 2290.0lb
Fuel: 54.9L 12.1gal 14.5galUS

1184 Datsun

610 Station Wagon
1973 Japan
0-60mph 96.5kmh: 18.5secs
0-1/4 mile: 22.0secs
94.0bhp 70.1kW 95.3PS
@ 5600rpm
99.0lbft 134.1Nm @ 3200rpm
80.7bhp/ton 79.3bhp/tonne
53.1bhp/L 39.6kW/L 53.8PS/L
26.4mpg 22.0mpgUS 10.7L/100km
Petrol 4-stroke piston
1770cc 108.0cu in
In-line 4
Valve type/No: Overhead 8
Transmission: Automatic
No. of forward speeds: 3
Wheels driven: Rear
Brake system: PA
Brakes F/R: Disc/Drum
Wheelbase: 249.9cm 98.4in
Length: 443.2cm 174.5in
Width: 160.0cm 63.0in
Height: 141.5cm 55.7in
Kerb weight: 1184.9kg 2610.0lb

1185 Datsun

120Y
1974 Japan
96.0mph 154.5kmh
0-50mph 80.5kmh: 10.8secs
0-60mph 96.5kmh: 16.0secs
0-1/4 mile: 21.0secs
0-1km: 38.7secs
52.5bhp 39.1kW 53.2PS
@ 6000rpm
74.0lbft 100.3Nm @ 4000rpm
66.9bhp/ton 65.8bhp/tonne
44.8bhp/L 33.4kW/L 45.5PS/L
46.0ft/sec 14.0m/sec
16.0mph 25.7kmh/1000rpm
31.9mpg 26.6mpgUS 8.9L/100km
Petrol 4-stroke piston
1171cc 71.4cu in
In-line 4 1 Carburettor
Compression ratio: 9.0:1
Bore: 73.0mm 2.9in
Stroke: 70.0mm 2.8in
Valve type/No: Overhead 8
Transmission: Manual
No. of forward speeds: 4
Wheels driven: Rear
Springs F/R: Coil/Leaf
Brakes F/R: Disc/Drum
Steering: Recirculating ball
Wheelbase: 233.7cm 92.0in
Track F: 124.5cm 49.0in
Track R: 124.5cm 49.0in
Length: 395.0cm 155.5in
Width: 154.9cm 61.0in
Height: 137.2cm 54.0in
Ground clearance: 20.3cm 8.0in
Kerb weight: 797.7kg 1757.0lb
Fuel: 47.3L 10.4gal 12.5galUS

1186 Datsun

260Z
1974 Japan
113.0mph 181.8kmh
0-50mph 80.5kmh: 7.6secs
0-60mph 96.5kmh: 10.0secs
0-1/4 mile: 17.9secs
139.0bhp 103.6kW 140.9PS
@ 5200rpm
137.0lbft 185.6Nm @ 4400rpm
116.8bhp/ton 114.9bhp/tonne
54.2bhp/L 40.4kW/L 54.9PS/L
44.9ft/sec 13.7m/sec
21.4mph 34.4kmh/1000rpm
24.0mpg 20.0mpgUS 11.8L/100km
Petrol 4-stroke piston
2565cc 156.5cu in
In-line 6 2 Carburettor
Compression ratio: 8.8:1
Bore: 83.0mm 3.3in
Stroke: 79.0mm 3.1in
Valve type/No: Overhead 12
Transmission: Manual
No. of forward speeds: 4
Wheels driven: Rear
Springs F/R: Coil/Coil
Brake system: PA
Brakes F/R: Disc/Drum
Steering: Rack & pinion
Wheelbase: 230.4cm 90.7in
Track F: 135.4cm 53.3in
Track R: 134.6cm 53.0in
Length: 429.5cm 169.1in
Width: 162.8cm 64.1in
Height: 128.5cm 50.6in
Ground clearance: 14.5cm 5.7in
Kerb weight: 1209.9kg 2665.0lb
Fuel: 59.8L 13.1gal 15.8galUS

1187 Datsun

260Z 2+2
1974 Japan
121.0mph 194.7kmh
0-50mph 80.5kmh: 7.3secs
0-60mph 96.5kmh: 9.9secs
0-1/4 mile: 17.3secs
0-1km: 32.0secs
150.0bhp 111.9kW 152.1PS
@ 5400rpm
158.0lbft 214.1Nm @ 4400rpm
127.7bhp/ton 125.5bhp/tonne
58.5bhp/L 43.6kW/L 59.3PS/L
46.6ft/sec 14.2m/sec
22.6mph 36.4kmh/1000rpm
23.9mpg 19.9mpgUS 11.8L/100km
Petrol 4-stroke piston
2565cc 156.5cu in
In-line 6 2 Carburettor

Compression ratio: 8.3:1
Bore: 83.0mm 3.3in
Stroke: 79.0mm 3.1in
Valve type/No: Overhead 12
Transmission: Manual
No. of forward speeds: 5
Wheels driven: Rear
Springs F/R: Coil/Coil
Brake system: PA
Brakes F/R: Disc/Drum
Steering: Rack & pinion
Wheelbase: 260.6cm 102.6in
Track F: 135.4cm 53.3in
Track R: 134.6cm 53.0in
Length: 442.0cm 174.0in
Width: 152.4cm 60.0in
Height: 128.5cm 50.6in
Ground clearance: 14.0cm 5.5in
Kerb weight: 1194.9kg 2632.0lb
Fuel: 60.1L 13.2gal 15.9galUS

1188 Datsun

710
1974 Japan
96.0mph 154.5kmh
0-50mph 80.5kmh: 10.4secs
0-60mph 96.5kmh: 14.6secs
0-1/4 mile: 20.0secs
93.0bhp 69.3kW 94.3PS
@ 6000rpm
99.0lbft 134.1Nm @ 3200rpm
87.9bhp/ton 86.4bhp/tonne
52.5bhp/L 39.2kW/L 53.3PS/L
51.2ft/sec 15.6m/sec
16.7mph 26.9kmh/1000rpm
26.4mpg 22.0mpgUS 10.7L/100km
Petrol 4-stroke piston
1770cc 108.0cu in
In-line 4 1 Carburettor
Compression ratio: 8.5:1
Bore: 85.0mm 3.3in
Stroke: 78.0mm 3.1in
Valve type/No: Overhead 8
Transmission: Manual
No. of forward speeds: 4
Wheels driven: Rear
Springs F/R: Coil/Leaf
Brake system: PA
Brakes F/R: Disc/Drum
Steering: Recirculating ball
Wheelbase: 245.1cm 96.5in
Track F: 131.1cm 51.6in
Track R: 133.1cm 52.4in
Length: 433.1cm 170.5in
Width: 158.0cm 62.2in
Height: 140.5cm 55.3in
Ground clearance: 17.0cm 6.7in
Kerb weight: 1076.0kg 2370.0lb
Fuel: 50.0L 11.0gal 13.2galUS

1189 Datsun

B210
1974 Japan
91.0mph 146.4kmh
0-50mph 80.5kmh: 11.4secs
0-60mph 96.5kmh: 16.7secs
0-1/4 mile: 20.9secs
67.0bhp 50.0kW 67.9PS
@ 6000rpm
71.0lbft 96.2Nm @ 3600rpm
81.3bhp/ton 80.0bhp/tonne
52.0bhp/L 38.8kW/L 52.7PS/L
50.5ft/sec 15.4m/sec
16.0mph 25.7kmh/1000rpm
33.0mpg 27.5mpgUS 8.6L/100km
Petrol 4-stroke piston
1288cc 78.6cu in
In-line 4 1 Carburettor
Compression ratio: 8.5:1
Bore: 73.0mm 2.9in
Stroke: 77.0mm 3.0in
Valve type/No: Overhead 8
Transmission: Manual
No. of forward speeds: 4
Wheels driven: Rear
Springs F/R: Coil/Leaf
Brake system: PA
Brakes F/R: Disc/Drum
Steering: Recirculating ball
Wheelbase: 233.9cm 92.1in
Track F: 127.5cm 50.2in
Track R: 126.5cm 49.8in
Length: 406.4cm 160.0in
Width: 154.4cm 60.8in
Height: 134.6cm 53.0in
Ground clearance: 17.0cm 6.7in
Kerb weight: 837.6kg 1845.0lb
Fuel: 43.1L 9.5gal 11.4galUS

1190 Datsun

240Z Sharp
1975 Japan
147.0mph 236.5kmh
0-50mph 80.5kmh: 6.0secs
0-60mph 96.5kmh: 7.0secs
0-1/4 mile: 15.8secs
258.0bhp 192.4kW 261.6PS
@ 8250rpm
184.0lbft 249.3Nm @ 6500rpm
262.7bhp/ton 258.3bhp/tonne
105.3bhp/L 78.5kW/L 106.8PS/L
66.5ft/sec 20.3m/sec
17.6mph 28.3kmh/1000rpm
7.2mpg 6.0mpgUS 39.2L/100km
Petrol 4-stroke piston
2450cc 149.5cu in
In-line 6 3 Carburettor
Compression ratio: 11.8:1
Bore: 84.0mm 3.3in
Stroke: 73.7mm 2.9in
Valve type/No: Overhead 12
Transmission: Manual
No. of forward speeds: 5
Wheels driven: Rear
Springs F/R: Coil/Coil
Brakes F/R: Disc/Disc
Steering: Rack & pinion
Wheelbase: 230.4cm 90.7in
Track F: 147.3cm 58.0in
Track R: 161.3cm 63.5in
Length: 434.3cm 171.0in
Width: 208.3cm 82.0in
Height: 124.5cm 49.0in
Ground clearance: 9.1cm 3.6in
Kerb weight: 998.8kg 2200.0lb
Fuel: 83.3L 18.3gal 22.0galUS

1191 Datsun

260C Estate
1975 Japan
100.0mph 160.9kmh
0-50mph 80.5kmh: 10.0secs
0-60mph 96.5kmh: 14.4secs
0-1/4 mile: 19.9secs
0-1km: 37.0secs
138.0bhp 102.9kW 139.9PS
@ 5200rpm
154.0lbft 208.7Nm @ 4000rpm
96.8bhp/ton 95.2bhp/tonne
53.8bhp/L 40.1kW/L 54.5PS/L
44.9ft/sec 13.7m/sec
17.4mph 28.0kmh/1000rpm
20.2mpg 16.8mpgUS 14.0L/100km
Petrol 4-stroke piston
2565cc 156.5cu in
In-line 6 1 Carburettor
Compression ratio: 8.6:1
Bore: 83.0mm 3.3in
Stroke: 79.0mm 3.1in
Valve type/No: Overhead 12
Transmission: Manual
No. of forward speeds: 4
Wheels driven: Rear
Springs F/R: Coil/Leaf
Brake system: PA
Brakes F/R: Disc/Drum
Steering: Recirculating ball
Wheelbase: 269.0cm 105.9in
Track F: 137.4cm 54.1in
Track R: 137.4cm 54.1in
Length: 468.9cm 184.6in
Width: 168.9cm 66.5in
Height: 148.1cm 58.3in
Ground clearance: 18.5cm 7.3in
Kerb weight: 1449.2kg 3192.0lb
Fuel: 56.9L 12.5gal 15.0galUS

1192 Datsun

280Z
1975 Japan
119.0mph 191.5kmh
0-50mph 80.5kmh: 6.9secs
0-60mph 96.5kmh: 9.4secs
0-1/4 mile: 17.3secs
149.0bhp 111.1kW 151.1PS
@ 5600rpm
163.0lbft 220.9Nm @ 4400rpm
116.1bhp/ton 114.1bhp/tonne
54.1bhp/L 40.3kW/L 54.8PS/L
48.4ft/sec 14.7m/sec
20.3mph 32.7kmh/1000rpm
23.4mpg 19.5mpgUS 12.1L/100km
Petrol 4-stroke piston
2754cc 168.0cu in
In-line 6
Compression ratio: 8.3:1
Bore: 86.1mm 3.4in
Stroke: 79.0mm 3.1in
Valve type/No: Overhead 12
Transmission: Manual
No. of forward speeds: 4
Wheels driven: Rear
Springs F/R: Coil/Coil
Brake system: PA
Brakes F/R: Disc/Drum
Steering: Rack & pinion
Wheelbase: 230.4cm 90.7in
Track F: 135.4cm 53.3in
Track R: 134.6cm 53.0in
Length: 439.9cm 173.2in
Width: 163.1cm 64.2in
Height: 129.5cm 51.0in
Kerb weight: 1305.2kg 2875.0lb
Fuel: 65.1L 14.3gal 17.2galUS

1193 Datsun

710
1975 Japan
95.0mph 152.9kmh
0-50mph 80.5kmh: 10.7secs
0-60mph 96.5kmh: 14.9secs
0-1/4 mile: 20.0secs
97.0bhp 72.3kW 98.3PS
@ 5600rpm
102.0lbft 138.2Nm @ 3200rpm
90.7bhp/ton 89.2bhp/tonne
49.7bhp/L 37.0kW/L 50.4PS/L
Petrol 4-stroke piston
1952cc 119.1cu in
In-line 4
Transmission: Manual
No. of forward speeds: 4
Wheels driven: Rear
Springs F/R: Coil/Leaf
Brakes F/R: Disc/Drum
Wheelbase: 245.1cm 96.5in
Track F: 131.1cm 51.6in
Track R: 133.1cm 52.4in
Length: 436.1cm 171.7in
Width: 158.0cm 62.2in
Height: 141.0cm 55.5in
Kerb weight: 1087.3kg 2395.0lb

1194 Datsun

B210
1975 Japan
0-60mph 96.5kmh: 17.3secs
0-1/4 mile: 20.8secs
70.0bhp 52.2kW 71.0PS
@ 6000rpm
75.0lbft 101.6Nm @ 3200rpm
74.8bhp/ton 73.6bhp/tonne
50.1bhp/L 37.4kW/L 50.8PS/L
50.5ft/sec 15.4m/sec
32.4mpg 27.0mpgUS 8.7L/100km
Petrol 4-stroke piston
1397cc 85.2cu in
In-line 4 1 Carburettor
Compression ratio: 8.5:1
Bore: 76.0mm 3.0in
Stroke: 77.0mm 3.0in
Valve type/No: Overhead 8
Transmission: Manual
No. of forward speeds: 4
Wheels driven: Rear
Brake system: PA
Wheelbase: 233.9cm 92.1in
Track F: 127.5cm 50.2in
Track R: 124.5cm 49.0in
Length: 414.0cm 163.0in
Width: 154.4cm 60.8in
Height: 135.9cm 53.5in
Ground clearance: 17.0cm 6.7in
Kerb weight: 951.1kg 2095.0lb
Fuel: 43.9L 9.6gal 11.6galUS

1195 Datsun

140J Violet
1976 Japan
100.0mph 160.9kmh
0-50mph 80.5kmh: 10.6secs
0-60mph 96.5kmh: 15.8secs
0-1/4 mile: 20.2secs
0-1km: 37.3secs
65.0bhp 48.5kW 65.9PS
@ 5800rpm
85.0lbft 115.2Nm @ 3600rpm
71.4bhp/ton 70.2bhp/tonne
45.5bhp/L 33.9kW/L 46.1PS/L
41.9ft/sec 12.8m/sec
16.3mph 26.2kmh/1000rpm
31.5mpg 26.2mpgUS 9.0L/100km
Petrol 4-stroke piston
1428cc 87.1cu in
In-line 4 1 Carburettor
Compression ratio: 9.0:1
Bore: 83.0mm 3.3in
Stroke: 66.0mm 2.6in
Valve type/No: Overhead 8
Transmission: Manual
No. of forward speeds: 4
Wheels driven: Rear
Springs F/R: Coil/Leaf
Brake system: PA
Brakes F/R: Disc/Drum
Steering: Recirculating ball
Wheelbase: 245.1cm 96.5in
Track F: 129.5cm 51.0in
Track R: 130.8cm 51.5in
Length: 411.5cm 162.0in
Width: 157.5cm 62.0in
Height: 137.2cm 54.0in
Ground clearance: 16.5cm 6.5in
Kerb weight: 926.2kg 2040.0lb
Fuel: 50.0L 11.0gal 13.2galUS

1196 Datsun

200L-6
1976 Japan
103.0mph 165.7kmh
0-50mph 80.5kmh: 10.7secs
0-60mph 96.5kmh: 14.8secs
0-1/4 mile: 20.3secs
0-1km: 37.1secs
115.0bhp 85.8kW 116.6PS
@ 5600rpm
120.0lbft 162.6Nm @ 3500rpm
110.0bhp/ton 108.2bhp/tonne
57.6bhp/L 42.9kW/L 58.4PS/L
42.6ft/sec 13.0m/sec
17.0mph 27.4kmh/1000rpm
22.2mpg 18.5mpgUS 12.7L/100km
Petrol 4-stroke piston
1998cc 121.9cu in
In-line 6 1 Carburettor
Compression ratio: 8.6:1
Bore: 78.0mm 3.1in
Stroke: 69.7mm 2.7in
Valve type/No: Overhead 12
Transmission: Automatic
No. of forward speeds: 3
Wheels driven: Rear
Springs F/R: Coil/Leaf
Brake system: PA
Brakes F/R: Disc/Drum
Steering: Recirculating ball
Wheelbase: 266.7cm 105.0in
Track F: 134.6cm 53.0in
Track R: 133.9cm 52.7in
Length: 450.1cm 177.2in
Width: 166.9cm 65.7in
Height: 142.2cm 56.0in
Ground clearance: 17.8cm 7.0in
Kerb weight: 1063.3kg 2342.0lb
Fuel: 60.1L 13.2gal 15.9galUS

1197 Datsun

B210
1976 Japan
0-60mph 96.5kmh: 15.3secs
0-1/4 mile: 20.3secs
70.0bhp 52.2kW 71.0PS
@ 6000rpm
75.0lbft 101.6Nm @ 3600rpm
76.9bhp/ton 75.6bhp/tonne
50.1bhp/L 37.4kW/L 50.8PS/L
50.5ft/sec 15.4m/sec
16.6mph 26.7kmh/1000rpm
36.6mpg 30.5mpgUS 7.7L/100km
Petrol 4-stroke piston
1397cc 85.2cu in
In-line 4 1 Carburettor
Compression ratio: 8.5:1
Bore: 75.9mm 3.0in
Stroke: 77.0mm 3.0in
Valve type/No: Overhead 8
Transmission: Manual
No. of forward speeds: 4
Wheels driven: Rear
Springs F/R: Coil/Leaf
Brake system: PA
Brakes F/R: Disc/Drum
Track F: 127.5cm 50.2in
Track R: 124.5cm 49.0in
Length: 412.0cm 162.2in
Width: 154.4cm 60.8in

Height: 134.4cm 52.9in
Ground clearance: 17.0cm 6.7in
Kerb weight: 926.2kg 2040.0lb
Fuel: 43.9L 9.6gal 11.6galUS

1198 Datsun

B210 Electramotive
1976 Japan
124.0mph 199.5kmh
0-50mph 80.5kmh: 5.0secs
0-60mph 96.5kmh: 6.7secs
0-1/4 mile: 14.8secs
148.0bhp 110.4kW 150.0PS
@ 9000rpm
105.0lbft 142.3Nm @ 7000rpm
204.0bhp/ton 200.6bhp/tonne
114.2bhp/L 85.1kW/L 115.8PS/L
75.7ft/sec 23.1m/sec
13.5mph 21.7kmh/1000rpm
10.8mpg 9.0mpgUS 26.1L/100km
Petrol 4-stroke piston
1296cc 79.1cu in
In-line 4 2 Carburettor
Compression ratio: 13.0:1
Bore: 73.2mm 2.9in
Stroke: 77.0mm 3.0in
Valve type/No: Overhead 8
Transmission: Manual
No. of forward speeds: 5
Wheels driven: Rear
Springs F/R: Coil/Leaf
Brakes F/R: Disc/Drum
Steering: Recirculating ball
Wheelbase: 233.9cm 92.1in
Track F: 134.1cm 52.8in
Track R: 131.6cm 51.8in
Length: 392.7cm 154.6in
Width: 162.6cm 64.0in
Height: 123.2cm 48.5in
Ground clearance: 6.6cm 2.6in
Kerb weight: 737.7kg 1625.0lb
Fuel: 30.3L 6.7gal 8.0galUS

1199 Datsun

F10
1976 Japan
94.0mph 151.2kmh
0-50mph 80.5kmh: 11.1secs
0-60mph 96.5kmh: 15.5secs
0-1/4 mile: 20.1secs
70.0bhp 52.2kW 71.0PS
@ 6000rpm
75.0lbft 101.6Nm @ 3600rpm
82.1bhp/ton 80.7bhp/tonne
50.1bhp/L 37.4kW/L 50.8PS/L
50.5ft/sec 15.4m/sec
18.3mph 29.4kmh/1000rpm
39.0mpg 32.5mpgUS 7.2L/100km
Petrol 4-stroke piston
1397cc 85.2cu in
In-line 4 1 Carburettor
Compression ratio: 8.5:1
Bore: 75.9mm 3.0in
Stroke: 77.0mm 3.0in
Valve type/No: Overhead 8
Transmission: Manual
No. of forward speeds: 5
Wheels driven: Front
Springs F/R: Coil/Coil
Brake system: PA
Brakes F/R: Disc/Drum
Steering: Rack & pinion
Wheelbase: 239.5cm 94.3in
Track F: 128.0cm 50.4in
Track R: 124.5cm 49.0in
Length: 398.5cm 156.9in
Width: 151.9cm 59.8in
Height: 131.6cm 51.8in
Ground clearance: 18.5cm 7.3in
Kerb weight: 867.1kg 1910.0lb
Fuel: 40.1L 8.8gal 10.6galUS

1200 Datsun

180B Bluebird
1977 Japan
103.0mph 165.7kmh
0-50mph 80.5kmh: 9.2secs
0-60mph 96.5kmh: 13.6secs
0-1/4 mile: 19.1secs
0-1km: 35.5secs
88.0bhp 65.6kW 89.2PS
@ 5600rpm
98.3lbft 133.2Nm @ 3600rpm
82.5bhp/ton 81.1bhp/tonne
49.7bhp/L 37.1kW/L 50.4PS/L
47.8ft/sec 14.6m/sec
18.0mph 29.0kmh/1000rpm
27.7mpg 23.1mpgUS 10.2L/100km
Petrol 4-stroke piston
1770cc 108.0cu in
In-line 4 1 Carburettor
Compression ratio: 8.5:1
Bore: 85.0mm 3.3in
Stroke: 78.0mm 3.1in
Valve type/No: Overhead 8
Transmission: Manual
No. of forward speeds: 4
Wheels driven: Rear
Springs F/R: Coil/Coil
Brake system: PA
Brakes F/R: Disc/Drum
Steering: Recirculating ball
Wheelbase: 249.9cm 98.4in
Track F: 134.9cm 53.1in
Track R: 134.6cm 53.0in
Length: 426.0cm 167.7in
Width: 163.1cm 64.2in
Height: 138.9cm 54.7in
Ground clearance: 17.5cm 6.9in
Kerb weight: 1085.1kg 2390.0lb
Fuel: 60.1L 13.2gal 15.9galUS

1201 Datsun

200SX
1977 Japan
98.0mph 157.7kmh
0-50mph 80.5kmh: 9.3secs
0-60mph 96.5kmh: 13.3secs
0-1/4 mile: 19.5secs
97.0bhp 72.3kW 98.3PS
@ 5600rpm
102.0lbft 138.2Nm @ 3200rpm
91.9bhp/ton 90.3bhp/tonne
49.7bhp/L 37.0kW/L 50.4PS/L
52.7ft/sec 16.1m/sec
19.7mph 31.7kmh/1000rpm
28.2mpg 23.5mpgUS 10.0L/100km
Petrol 4-stroke piston
1952cc 119.1cu in
In-line 4
Compression ratio: 8.5:1
Bore: 85.1mm 3.3in
Stroke: 86.1mm 3.4in
Valve type/No: Overhead 8
Transmission: Manual
No. of forward speeds: 5
Wheels driven: Rear
Springs F/R: Coil/Leaf
Brake system: PA
Brakes F/R: Disc/Drum
Steering: Recirculating ball
Wheelbase: 233.7cm 92.0in
Track F: 128.0cm 50.4in
Track R: 126.5cm 49.8in
Length: 431.8cm 170.0in
Width: 160.0cm 63.0in
Height: 130.0cm 51.2in
Kerb weight: 1073.7kg 2365.0lb
Fuel: 59.8L 13.1gal 15.8galUS

1202 Datsun

260Z
1977 Japan
115.0mph 185.0kmh
0-50mph 80.5kmh: 7.4secs
0-60mph 96.5kmh: 10.1secs
0-1/4 mile: 17.9secs
0-1km: 32.7secs
150.0bhp 111.9kW 152.1PS
@ 5400rpm
162.0lbft 219.5Nm @ 3200rpm
131.5bhp/ton 129.3bhp/tonne
58.5bhp/L 43.6kW/L 59.3PS/L
46.6ft/sec 14.2m/sec
23.6mph 38.0kmh/1000rpm
22.4mpg 18.7mpgUS 12.6L/100km
Petrol 4-stroke piston
2565cc 156.5cu in
In-line 6 2 Carburettor
Compression ratio: 9.2:1
Bore: 83.0mm 3.3in
Stroke: 79.0mm 3.1in
Valve type/No: Overhead 12
Transmission: Manual
No. of forward speeds: 5
Wheels driven: Rear
Springs F/R: Coil/Coil
Brake system: PA
Brakes F/R: Disc/Drum
Steering: Rack & pinion
Wheelbase: 230.4cm 90.7in
Track F: 135.9cm 53.5in
Track R: 134.6cm 53.0in
Length: 414.0cm 163.0in
Width: 163.1cm 64.2in
Height: 128.0cm 50.4in
Ground clearance: 20.3cm 8.0in
Kerb weight: 1160.0kg 2555.0lb
Fuel: 65.1L 14.3gal 17.2galUS

1203 Datsun

810 Sedan
1977 Japan
111.0mph 178.6kmh
0-50mph 80.5kmh: 8.8secs
0-60mph 96.5kmh: 12.2secs
0-1/4 mile: 18.7secs
127.0bhp 94.7kW 128.8PS
@ 5600rpm
138.0lbft 187.0Nm @ 4400rpm
104.6bhp/ton 102.8bhp/tonne
53.1bhp/L 39.6kW/L 53.8PS/L
45.1ft/sec 13.8m/sec
21.7mph 34.9kmh/1000rpm
27.6mpg 23.0mpgUS 10.2L/100km
Petrol 4-stroke piston
2393cc 146.0cu in
In-line 6 fuel injection
Compression ratio: 8.6:1
Bore: 83.0mm 3.3in
Stroke: 73.7mm 2.9in
Valve type/No: Overhead 12
Transmission: Manual
No. of forward speeds: 4
Wheels driven: Rear
Springs F/R: Coil/Coil
Brake system: PA
Brakes F/R: Disc/Drum
Steering: Recirculating ball PA
Wheelbase: 264.9cm 104.3in
Track F: 134.9cm 53.1in
Track R: 133.9cm 52.7in
Length: 466.1cm 183.5in
Width: 163.1cm 64.2in
Height: 138.4cm 54.5in
Ground clearance: 16.0cm 6.3in
Kerb weight: 1234.9kg 2720.0lb
Fuel: 64.7L 14.2gal 17.1galUS

1204 Datsun

Cherry F11
1977 Japan
85.0mph 136.8kmh
0-50mph 80.5kmh: 13.8secs
0-60mph 96.5kmh: 20.3secs
0-1/4 mile: 21.7secs
0-1km: 40.3secs
45.0bhp 33.6kW 45.6PS
@ 5600rpm
55.7lbft 75.5Nm @ 4000rpm
61.5bhp/ton 60.5bhp/tonne
45.5bhp/L 34.0kW/L 46.2PS/L
36.1ft/sec 11.0m/sec
15.3mph 24.6kmh/1000rpm
37.2mpg 31.0mpgUS 7.6L/100km
Petrol 4-stroke piston
988cc 60.3cu in
In-line 4 1 Carburettor
Compression ratio: 9.0:1
Bore: 73.0mm 2.9in
Stroke: 59.0mm 2.3in
Valve type/No: Overhead 8
Transmission: Manual
No. of forward speeds: 4
Wheels driven: Front
Springs F/R: Coil/Coil
Brake system: PA
Brakes F/R: Disc/Drum
Steering: Rack & pinion
Wheelbase: 239.5cm 94.3in
Track F: 127.5cm 50.2in
Track R: 124.0cm 48.8in
Length: 382.5cm 150.6in
Width: 150.1cm 59.1in
Height: 134.1cm 52.8in
Ground clearance: 17.8cm 7.0in
Kerb weight: 743.6kg 1638.0lb
Fuel: 40.0L 8.8gal 10.6galUS

1205 Datsun

280Z Scarab
1978 Japan
130.0mph 209.2kmh
0-50mph 80.5kmh: 4.8secs
0-60mph 96.5kmh: 6.2secs
0-1/4 mile: 14.8secs
350.0bhp 261.0kW 354.8PS
@ 5800rpm
360.0lbft 487.8Nm @ 3600rpm
266.2bhp/ton 261.8bhp/tonne
65.3bhp/L 48.7kW/L 66.2PS/L
52.7ft/sec 16.0m/sec
20.7mph 33.3kmh/1000rpm
13.2mpg 11.0mpgUS 21.4L/100km
Petrol 4-stroke piston
5359cc 327.0cu in
Vee 8
Compression ratio: 10.5:1
Bore: 102.0mm 4.0in
Stroke: 83.0mm 3.3in
Valve type/No: Overhead 16
Transmission: Manual
No. of forward speeds: 4
Wheels driven: Rear
Springs F/R: Coil/Coil
Brake system: PA
Brakes F/R: Disc/Drum
Steering: Rack & pinion
Wheelbase: 230.4cm 90.7in
Track F: 143.5cm 56.5in
Track R: 143.5cm 56.5in
Length: 439.9cm 173.2in
Width: 170.2cm 67.0in
Height: 130.6cm 51.4in
Kerb weight: 1337.0kg 2945.0lb
Fuel: 60.2L 13.2gal 15.9galUS

1206 Datsun

510
1978 Japan
98.0mph 157.7kmh
0-50mph 80.5kmh: 8.9secs
0-60mph 96.5kmh: 12.7secs
0-1/4 mile: 19.3secs
97.0bhp 72.3kW 98.3PS
@ 5600rpm
102.0lbft 138.2Nm @ 3200rpm
91.3bhp/ton 89.8bhp/tonne
49.7bhp/L 37.0kW/L 50.4PS/L
52.7ft/sec 16.1m/sec
23.0mph 37.0kmh/1000rpm
30.0mpg 25.0mpgUS 9.4L/100km
Petrol 4-stroke piston
1952cc 119.1cu in
In-line 4 1 Carburettor
Compression ratio: 8.5:1
Bore: 85.1mm 3.3in
Stroke: 86.1mm 3.4in
Valve type/No: Overhead 8
Transmission: Manual
No. of forward speeds: 5
Wheels driven: Rear
Springs F/R: Coil/Coil
Brake system: PA
Brakes F/R: Disc/Drum
Steering: Recirculating ball
Wheelbase: 240.0cm 94.5in
Track F: 133.4cm 52.5in
Track R: 133.1cm 52.4in
Length: 431.5cm 169.9in
Width: 160.0cm 63.0in
Height: 134.9cm 53.1in
Ground clearance: 16.5cm 6.5in
Kerb weight: 1080.5kg 2380.0lb
Fuel: 49.2L 10.8gal 13.0galUS

1207 Datsun

Laurel Six
1978 Japan
95.0mph 152.9kmh
0-50mph 80.5kmh: 9.9secs
0-60mph 96.5kmh: 14.7secs
0-1/4 mile: 20.2secs
0-1km: 37.8secs
108.0bhp 80.5kW 109.5PS
@ 5600rpm
113.0lbft 153.1Nm @ 3600rpm
93.6bhp/ton 92.1bhp/tonne
54.0bhp/L 40.3kW/L 54.8PS/L
42.6ft/sec 13.0m/sec
18.0mph 29.0kmh/1000rpm
21.1mpg 17.6mpgUS 13.4L/100km
Petrol 4-stroke piston
1998cc 121.9cu in
In-line 6 1 Carburettor
Compression ratio: 8.6:1
Bore: 78.0mm 3.1in
Stroke: 69.7mm 2.7in
Valve type/No: Overhead 12
Transmission: Manual
No. of forward speeds: 4
Wheels driven: Rear
Springs F/R: Coil/Coil
Brake system: PA
Brakes F/R: Disc/Drum
Steering: Recirculating ball

Wheelbase: 267.0cm 105.1in
Track F: 137.9cm 54.3in
Track R: 137.2cm 54.0in
Length: 452.4cm 178.1in
Width: 168.4cm 66.3in
Height: 140.5cm 55.3in
Ground clearance: 20.3cm 8.0in
Kerb weight: 1173.1kg 2584.0lb
Fuel: 60.1L 13.2gal 15.9galUS

1208 Datsun

2.4 Laurel Six
1979 Japan
101.0mph 162.5kmh
0-50mph 80.5kmh: 8.0secs
0-60mph 96.5kmh: 11.8secs
0-1/4 mile: 18.2secs
0-1km: 34.1secs
113.0bhp 84.3kW 114.6PS
@ 5200rpm
129.0lbft 174.8Nm @ 3200rpm
92.5bhp/ton 90.9bhp/tonne
47.2bhp/L 35.2kW/L 47.9PS/L
41.9ft/sec 12.8m/sec
22.2mph 35.7kmh/1000rpm
23.3mpg 19.4mpgUS 12.1L/100km
Petrol 4-stroke piston
2393cc 146.0cu in
In-line 6 1 Carburettor
Compression ratio: 8.6:1
Bore: 83.0mm 3.3in
Stroke: 73.7mm 2.9in
Valve type/No: Overhead 12
Transmission: Manual
No. of forward speeds: 5
Wheels driven: Rear
Springs F/R: Coil/Coil
Brake system: PA
Brakes F/R: Disc/Drum
Steering: Recirculating ball PA
Wheelbase: 267.0cm 105.1in
Track F: 137.9cm 54.3in
Track R: 139.4cm 54.9in
Length: 462.5cm 182.1in
Width: 168.9cm 66.5in
Height: 140.0cm 55.1in
Ground clearance: 20.3cm 8.0in
Kerb weight: 1242.6kg 2737.0lb
Fuel: 60.1L 13.2gal 15.9galUS

1209 Datsun

210
1979 Japan
93.0mph 149.6kmh
0-50mph 80.5kmh: 9.7secs
0-60mph 96.5kmh: 14.0secs
0-1/4 mile: 19.7secs
65.0bhp 48.5kW 65.9PS
@ 5600rpm
75.0lbft 101.6Nm @ 3600rpm
71.5bhp/ton 70.3bhp/tonne
46.5bhp/L 34.7kW/L 47.2PS/L
47.1ft/sec 14.4m/sec
18.1mph 29.1kmh/1000rpm
37.8mpg 31.5mpgUS 7.5L/100km
Petrol 4-stroke piston
1397cc 85.2cu in
In-line 4 1 Carburettor
Compression ratio: 8.5:1
Bore: 76.0mm 3.0in
Stroke: 77.0mm 3.0in
Valve type/No: Overhead 8
Transmission: Manual
No. of forward speeds: 4
Wheels driven: Rear
Springs F/R: Coil/Coil
Brake system: PA
Brakes F/R: Disc/Drum
Steering: Recirculating ball
Wheelbase: 233.9cm 92.1in
Track F: 133.1cm 52.4in
Track R: 133.1cm 52.4in
Length: 419.1cm 165.0in
Width: 158.0cm 62.2in
Height: 133.6cm 52.6in
Ground clearance: 19.3cm 7.6in
Kerb weight: 923.9kg 2035.0lb
Fuel: 50.0L 11.0gal 13.2galUS

1210 Datsun

240K
1979 Japan
112.0mph 180.2kmh
0-50mph 80.5kmh: 7.8secs
0-60mph 96.5kmh: 11.0secs
0-1/4 mile: 17.8secs
0-1km: 33.0secs
127.0bhp 94.7kW 128.8PS
@ 5600rpm
132.1lbft 179.0Nm @ 3600rpm
102.8bhp/ton 101.1bhp/tonne
53.1bhp/L 39.6kW/L 53.8PS/L
45.1ft/sec 13.8m/sec
21.2mph 34.1kmh/1000rpm
21.3mpg 17.7mpgUS 13.3L/100km
Petrol 4-stroke piston
2393cc 146.0cu in
In-line 6 fuel injection
Compression ratio: 8.9:1
Bore: 83.0mm 3.3in
Stroke: 73.7mm 2.9in
Valve type/No: Overhead 12
Transmission: Manual
No. of forward speeds: 5
Wheels driven: Rear
Springs F/R: Coil/Coil
Brake system: PA
Brakes F/R: Disc/Disc
Steering: Recirculating ball PA
Wheelbase: 261.6cm 103.0in
Track F: 136.9cm 53.9in
Track R: 135.4cm 53.3in
Length: 460.0cm 181.1in
Width: 162.6cm 64.0in
Height: 136.9cm 53.9in
Ground clearance: 15.5cm 6.1in
Kerb weight: 1256.7kg 2768.0lb
Fuel: 60.1L 13.2gal 15.9galUS

1211 Datsun

280ZX
1979 Japan
121.0mph 194.7kmh
0-50mph 80.5kmh: 6.8secs
0-60mph 96.5kmh: 9.2secs
0-1/4 mile: 17.2secs
135.0bhp 100.7kW 136.9PS
@ 5200rpm
144.0lbft 195.1Nm @ 4400rpm
107.0bhp/ton 105.3bhp/tonne
49.0bhp/L 36.6kW/L 49.7PS/L
44.9ft/sec 13.7m/sec
24.9mph 40.1kmh/1000rpm
26.4mpg 22.0mpgUS 10.7L/100km
Petrol 4-stroke piston
2753cc 168.0cu in
In-line 6 fuel injection
Compression ratio: 8.3:1
Bore: 86.0mm 3.4in
Stroke: 79.0mm 3.1in
Valve type/No: Overhead 12
Transmission: Manual
No. of forward speeds: 5
Wheels driven: Rear
Springs F/R: Coil/Coil
Brake system: PA
Brakes F/R: Disc/Disc
Steering: Rack & pinion
Wheelbase: 231.9cm 91.3in
Track F: 138.4cm 54.5in
Track R: 137.9cm 54.3in
Length: 442.0cm 174.0in
Width: 168.9cm 66.5in
Height: 129.5cm 51.0in
Ground clearance: 15.0cm 5.9in
Kerb weight: 1282.5kg 2825.0lb
Fuel: 79.9L 17.6gal 21.1galUS

1212 Datsun

280ZX 2+2 Automatic
1979 Japan
114.0mph 183.4kmh
0-50mph 80.5kmh: 8.2secs
0-60mph 96.5kmh: 11.3secs
0-1/4 mile: 18.3secs
0-1km: 33.7secs
140.0bhp 104.4kW 141.9PS
@ 5200rpm
149.0lbft 201.9Nm @ 4000rpm
108.8bhp/ton 107.0bhp/tonne
50.8bhp/L 37.9kW/L 51.6PS/L
44.9ft/sec 13.7m/sec
20.1mph 32.3kmh/1000rpm
18.4mpg 15.3mpgUS 15.4L/100km
Petrol 4-stroke piston
2753cc 168.0cu in
In-line 6 fuel injection
Compression ratio: 8.3:1
Bore: 86.0mm 3.4in
Stroke: 79.0mm 3.1in
Valve type/No: Overhead 12
Transmission: Automatic
No. of forward speeds: 3
Wheels driven: Rear
Springs F/R: Coil/Coil
Brake system: PA
Brakes F/R: Disc/Disc
Steering: Recirculating ball PA
Wheelbase: 252.0cm 99.2in
Track F: 139.4cm 54.9in
Track R: 138.9cm 54.7in
Length: 453.9cm 178.7in
Width: 168.9cm 66.5in
Height: 130.0cm 51.2in
Ground clearance: 14.5cm 5.7in
Kerb weight: 1308.0kg 2881.0lb
Fuel: 80.1L 17.6gal 21.1galUS

1213 Datsun

280ZX Automatic
1979 Japan
0-60mph 96.5kmh: 10.2secs
0-1/4 mile: 18.1secs
132.0bhp 98.4kW 133.8PS
@ 5200rpm
144.0lbft 195.1Nm @ 4000rpm
102.0bhp/ton 100.3bhp/tonne
47.9bhp/L 35.7kW/L 48.6PS/L
44.9ft/sec 13.7m/sec
18.6mpg 15.5mpgUS 15.2L/100km
Petrol 4-stroke piston
2753cc 168.0cu in
In-line 6 fuel injection
Compression ratio: 8.3:1
Bore: 86.0mm 3.4in
Stroke: 79.0mm 3.1in
Valve type/No: Overhead 12
Transmission: Automatic
No. of forward speeds: 3
Wheels driven: Rear
Brake system: PA
Brakes F/R: Disc/Disc
Wheelbase: 231.9cm 91.3in
Track F: 138.4cm 54.5in
Track R: 137.9cm 54.3in
Length: 442.0cm 174.0in
Width: 168.9cm 66.5in
Height: 129.5cm 51.0in
Kerb weight: 1316.6kg 2900.0lb
Fuel: 79.9L 17.6gal 21.1galUS

1214 Datsun

310 Coupe
1979 Japan
97.0mph 156.1kmh
0-60mph 96.5kmh: 12.8secs
0-1/4 mile: 19.5secs
65.0bhp 48.5kW 65.9PS
@ 5600rpm
75.0lbft 101.6Nm @ 3600rpm
71.0bhp/ton 69.8bhp/tonne
46.5bhp/L 34.7kW/L 47.2PS/L
47.1ft/sec 14.4m/sec
19.1mph 30.7kmh/1000rpm
37.2mpg 31.0mpgUS 7.6L/100km
Petrol 4-stroke piston
1397cc 85.2cu in
In-line 4 1 Carburettor
Compression ratio: 8.9:1
Bore: 76.0mm 3.0in
Stroke: 77.0mm 3.0in
Valve type/No: Overhead 8
Transmission: Manual
No. of forward speeds: 5
Wheels driven: Front
Springs F/R: Coil/Coil
Brake system: PA
Brakes F/R: Disc/Drum
Steering: Rack & pinion
Wheelbase: 239.5cm 94.3in
Track F: 137.4cm 54.1in
Track R: 134.6cm 53.0in
Length: 412.0cm 162.2in
Width: 162.1cm 63.8in
Height: 132.1cm 52.0in
Ground clearance: 18.0cm 7.1in
Kerb weight: 930.7kg 2050.0lb
Fuel: 50.0L 11.0gal 13.2galUS

1215 Datsun

810 Coupe
1979 Japan
108.0mph 173.8kmh
0-50mph 80.5kmh: 8.7secs
0-60mph 96.5kmh: 11.9secs
0-1/4 mile: 18.7secs
118.0bhp 88.0kW 119.6PS
@ 5200rpm
125.0lbft 169.4Nm @ 4400rpm
91.3bhp/ton 89.8bhp/tonne
49.3bhp/L 36.8kW/L 50.0PS/L
41.9ft/sec 12.8m/sec
23.3mph 37.5kmh/1000rpm
27.6mpg 23.0mpgUS 10.2L/100km
Petrol 4-stroke piston
2393cc 146.0cu in
In-line 6
Compression ratio: 8.6:1
Bore: 83.0mm 3.3in
Stroke: 73.7mm 2.9in
Valve type/No: Overhead 12
Transmission: Manual
No. of forward speeds: 5
Wheels driven: Rear
Springs F/R: Coil/Coil
Brake system: PA
Brakes F/R: Disc/Drum
Steering: Recirculating ball PA
Wheelbase: 264.9cm 104.3in
Track F: 134.6cm 53.0in
Track R: 134.6cm 53.0in
Length: 467.1cm 183.9in
Width: 164.6cm 64.8in
Height: 138.4cm 54.5in
Kerb weight: 1314.3kg 2895.0lb
Fuel: 59.0L 13.0gal 15.6galUS

1216 Datsun

New Sunny
1979 Japan
86.0mph 138.4kmh
0-50mph 80.5kmh: 12.6secs
0-60mph 96.5kmh: 19.1secs
0-1/4 mile: 21.5secs
0-1km: 40.7secs
52.0bhp 38.8kW 52.7PS
@ 5600rpm
58.5lbft 79.3Nm @ 4000rpm
62.0bhp/ton 60.9bhp/tonne
44.4bhp/L 33.1kW/L 45.0PS/L
42.9ft/sec 13.1m/sec
16.9mph 27.2kmh/1000rpm
31.6mpg 26.3mpgUS 8.9L/100km
Petrol 4-stroke piston
1171cc 71.4cu in
In-line 4 1 Carburettor
Compression ratio: 9.0:1
Bore: 73.2mm 2.9in
Stroke: 70.0mm 2.8in
Valve type/No: Overhead 8
Transmission: Manual
No. of forward speeds: 4
Wheels driven: Rear
Springs F/R: Coil/Coil
Brake system: PA
Brakes F/R: Disc/Drum
Steering: Recirculating ball
Wheelbase: 233.9cm 92.1in
Track F: 132.8cm 52.3in
Track R: 129.8cm 51.1in
Length: 400.1cm 157.5in
Width: 159.0cm 62.6in
Height: 135.9cm 53.5in
Ground clearance: 16.5cm 6.5in
Kerb weight: 853.5kg 1880.0lb
Fuel: 50.0L 11.0gal 13.2galUS

1217 Datsun

200SX
1980 Japan
110.0mph 177.0kmh
0-60mph 96.5kmh: 11.6secs
0-1/4 mile: 18.8secs
100.0bhp 74.6kW 101.4PS
@ 5200rpm
112.0lbft 151.8Nm @ 3200rpm
83.3bhp/ton 81.9bhp/tonne
51.2bhp/L 38.2kW/L 51.9PS/L
49.0ft/sec 14.9m/sec
23.3mph 37.5kmh/1000rpm
30.0mpg 25.0mpgUS 9.4L/100km
Petrol 4-stroke piston
1952cc 119.1cu in
In-line 4 fuel injection
Compression ratio: 8.5:1
Bore: 85.1mm 3.3in
Stroke: 86.1mm 3.4in
Valve type/No: Overhead 8
Transmission: Manual
No. of forward speeds: 5
Wheels driven: Rear
Springs F/R: Coil/Coil
Brake system: PA
Brakes F/R: Disc/Disc
Steering: Recirculating ball
Wheelbase: 240.0cm 94.5in

Track F: 134.6cm 53.0in
Track R: 134.6cm 53.0in
Length: 448.1cm 176.4in
Width: 167.9cm 66.1in
Height: 131.1cm 51.6in
Ground clearance: 17.0cm 6.7in
Kerb weight: 1221.3kg 2690.0lb
Fuel: 60.2L 13.2gal 15.9galUS

1218 Datsun

280ZX
1980 Japan
0-60mph 96.5kmh: 9.2secs
0-1/4 mile: 17.2secs
135.0bhp 100.7kW 136.9PS
@ 5200rpm
144.0lbft 195.1Nm @ 4400rpm
107.0bhp/ton 105.3bhp/tonne
49.0bhp/L 36.6kW/L 49.7PS/L
44.9ft/sec 13.7m/sec
24.9mph 40.1kmh/1000rpm
26.4mpg 22.0mpgUS 10.7L/100km
Petrol 4-stroke piston
2753cc 168.0cu in
In-line 6 fuel injection
Bore: 86.0mm 3.4in
Stroke: 79.0mm 3.1in
Valve type/No: Overhead 12
Transmission: Manual
No. of forward speeds: 5
Wheels driven: Rear
Springs F/R: Coil/Coil
Brake system: PA
Brakes F/R: Disc/Disc
Track F: 138.4cm 54.5in
Track R: 137.9cm 54.3in
Width: 168.9cm 66.5in
Height: 129.5cm 51.0in
Kerb weight: 1282.5kg 2825.0lb
Fuel: 79.9L 17.6gal 21.1galUS

1219 Datsun

280ZX Automatic
1980 Japan
111.0mph 178.6kmh
0-60mph 96.5kmh: 10.2secs
0-1/4 mile: 18.1secs
132.0bhp 98.4kW 133.8PS
@ 5200rpm
144.0lbft 195.1Nm @ 4000rpm
102.0bhp/ton 100.3bhp/tonne
47.9bhp/L 35.7kW/L 48.6PS/L
44.9ft/sec 13.7m/sec
20.0mph 32.2kmh/1000rpm
25.2mpg 21.0mpgUS 11.2L/100km
Petrol 4-stroke piston
2753cc 168.0cu in
In-line 6 fuel injection
Compression ratio: 8.6:1
Bore: 86.0mm 3.4in
Stroke: 79.0mm 3.1in
Valve type/No: Overhead 12
Transmission: Automatic
No. of forward speeds: 3
Wheels driven: Rear
Springs F/R: Coil/Coil
Brake system: PA
Brakes F/R: Disc/Disc
Steering: Rack & pinion PA
Wheelbase: 231.9cm 91.3in
Track F: 138.4cm 54.5in
Track R: 137.9cm 54.3in
Length: 442.0cm 174.0in
Width: 168.9cm 66.5in
Height: 129.5cm 51.0in
Ground clearance: 15.0cm 5.9in
Kerb weight: 1316.6kg 2900.0lb
Fuel: 79.9L 17.6gal 21.1galUS

1220 Datsun

280ZX Electramotive
1980 Japan
122.0mph 196.3kmh
0-50mph 80.5kmh: 4.2secs
0-60mph 96.5kmh: 5.7secs
0-1/4 mile: 14.1secs
270.0bhp 201.3kW 273.7PS
@ 7500rpm
202.0lbft 273.7Nm @ 6000rpm
248.9bhp/ton 244.7bhp/tonne
108.6bhp/L 81.0kW/L 110.1PS/L
60.4ft/sec 18.4m/sec
14.3mph 23.0kmh/1000rpm
8.4mpg 7.0mpgUS 33.6L/100km
Petrol 4-stroke piston
2486cc 151.7cu in
In-line 6 3 Carburettor
Compression ratio: 12.5:1
Bore: 84.6mm 3.3in
Stroke: 73.7mm 2.9in
Valve type/No: Overhead 12
Transmission: Manual
No. of forward speeds: 5
Wheels driven: Rear
Springs F/R: Coil/Coil
Brakes F/R: Disc/Disc
Steering: Recirculating ball
Wheelbase: 231.9cm 91.3in
Track F: 147.8cm 58.2in
Track R: 147.8cm 58.2in
Length: 442.0cm 174.0in
Width: 182.9cm 72.0in
Height: 123.7cm 48.7in
Ground clearance: 9.1cm 3.6in
Kerb weight: 1103.2kg 2430.0lb
Fuel: 109.8L 24.1gal 29.0galUS

1221 Datsun

280ZX Sharp
1980 Japan
124.0mph 199.5kmh
0-50mph 80.5kmh: 4.2secs
0-60mph 96.5kmh: 5.6secs
0-1/4 mile: 13.7secs
300.0bhp 223.7kW 304.2PS
@ 7500rpm
245.0lbft 332.0Nm @ 6000rpm
301.3bhp/ton 296.3bhp/tonne
106.5bhp/L 79.4kW/L 107.9PS/L
64.8ft/sec 19.7m/sec
15.9mph 25.6kmh/1000rpm
7.8mpg 6.5mpgUS 36.2L/100km
Petrol 4-stroke piston
2818cc 171.9cu in
In-line 6 3 Carburettor
Compression ratio: 12.7:1
Bore: 87.0mm 3.4in
Stroke: 79.0mm 3.1in
Valve type/No: Overhead 12
Transmission: Manual
No. of forward speeds: 5
Wheels driven: Rear
Springs F/R: Coil/Coil
Brakes F/R: Disc/Disc
Steering: Recirculating ball
Wheelbase: 231.9cm 91.3in
Track F: 149.4cm 58.8in
Track R: 148.8cm 58.6in
Length: 442.0cm 174.0in
Width: 177.8cm 70.0in
Height: 122.9cm 48.4in
Ground clearance: 8.4cm 3.3in
Kerb weight: 1012.4kg 2230.0lb
Fuel: 56.8L 12.5gal 15.0galUS

1222 Datsun

510
1980 Japan
102.0mph 164.1kmh
0-50mph 80.5kmh: 9.2secs
0-60mph 96.5kmh: 12.6secs
0-1/4 mile: 19.7secs
92.0bhp 68.6kW 93.3PS
@ 5200rpm
112.0lbft 151.8Nm @ 2800rpm
84.5bhp/ton 83.0bhp/tonne
47.1bhp/L 35.1kW/L 47.8PS/L
49.0ft/sec 14.9m/sec
25.2mph 40.5kmh/1000rpm
33.6mpg 28.0mpgUS 8.4L/100km
Petrol 4-stroke piston
1952cc 119.1cu in
In-line 4 1 Carburettor
Compression ratio: 8.5:1
Bore: 85.1mm 3.3in
Stroke: 86.1mm 3.4in
Valve type/No: Overhead 8
Transmission: Manual
No. of forward speeds: 5
Wheels driven: Rear
Springs F/R: Coil/Coil
Brake system: PA
Brakes F/R: Disc/Drum
Steering: Recirculating ball
Wheelbase: 240.0cm 94.5in
Track F: 133.6cm 52.6in
Track R: 133.1cm 52.4in
Length: 431.5cm 169.9in
Width: 160.0cm 63.0in
Height: 136.9cm 53.9in
Kerb weight: 1107.8kg 2440.0lb
Fuel: 50.0L 11.0gal 13.2galUS

1223 Datsun

280ZX Turbo
1981 Japan
129.0mph 207.6kmh
0-50mph 80.5kmh: 5.5secs
0-60mph 96.5kmh: 7.4secs
0-1/4 mile: 15.6secs
180.0bhp 134.2kW 182.5PS
@ 5600rpm
203.0lbft 275.1Nm @ 2800rpm
134.6bhp/ton 132.4bhp/tonne
65.4bhp/L 48.8kW/L 66.3PS/L
48.4ft/sec 14.7m/sec
20.1mph 32.3kmh/1000rpm
24.0mpg 20.0mpgUS 11.8L/100km
Petrol 4-stroke piston
2753cc 168.0cu in turbocharged
In-line 4 fuel injection
Compression ratio: 7.4:1
Bore: 86.0mm 3.4in
Stroke: 79.0mm 3.1in
Valve type/No: Overhead 8
Transmission: Automatic
No. of forward speeds: 3
Wheels driven: Rear
Springs F/R: Coil/Coil
Brake system: PA
Brakes F/R: Disc/Disc
Steering: Rack & pinion PA
Wheelbase: 231.9cm 91.3in
Track F: 139.4cm 54.9in
Track R: 138.9cm 54.7in
Length: 442.0cm 174.0in
Width: 168.9cm 66.5in
Height: 129.5cm 51.0in
Kerb weight: 1359.7kg 2995.0lb
Fuel: 79.9L 17.6gal 21.1galUS

1224 Datsun

810 Maxima
1981 Japan
113.0mph 181.8kmh
0-50mph 80.5kmh: 9.2secs
0-60mph 96.5kmh: 12.3secs
0-1/4 mile: 19.0secs
120.0bhp 89.5kW 121.7PS
@ 5200rpm
134.0lbft 181.6Nm @ 2800rpm
91.9bhp/ton 90.4bhp/tonne
50.1bhp/L 37.4kW/L 50.8PS/L
41.9ft/sec 12.8m/sec
19.7mph 31.7kmh/1000rpm
22.8mpg 19.0mpgUS 12.4L/100km
Petrol 4-stroke piston
2393cc 146.0cu in
In-line 6 fuel injection
Compression ratio: 8.9:1
Bore: 83.0mm 3.3in
Stroke: 73.7mm 2.9in
Valve type/No: Overhead 12
Transmission: Automatic
No. of forward speeds: 3
Wheels driven: Rear
Springs F/R: Coil/Coil
Brake system: PA
Brakes F/R: Disc/Disc
Steering: Rack & pinion PA
Wheelbase: 262.6cm 103.4in
Track F: 137.9cm 54.3in
Track R: 135.9cm 53.5in
Length: 465.6cm 183.3in
Width: 165.6cm 65.2in
Height: 138.4cm 54.5in
Ground clearance: 17.0cm 6.7in
Kerb weight: 1327.9kg 2925.0lb
Fuel: 62.1L 13.6gal 16.4galUS

1225 Datsun

280ZX
1982 Japan
123.0mph 197.9kmh
0-50mph 80.5kmh: 6.4secs
0-60mph 96.5kmh: 9.1secs
0-1/4 mile: 16.8secs
145.0bhp 108.1kW 147.0PS
@ 5500rpm
166.0lbft 224.9Nm @ 3000rpm
110.7bhp/ton 108.8bhp/tonne
52.7bhp/L 39.3kW/L 53.4PS/L
47.5ft/sec 14.5m/sec
24.5mph 39.4kmh/1000rpm
28.8mpg 24.0mpgUS 9.8L/100km
Petrol 4-stroke piston
2753cc 168.0cu in
In-line 6 fuel injection
Compression ratio: 8.8:1
Bore: 86.0mm 3.4in
Stroke: 79.0mm 3.1in
Valve type/No: Overhead 12
Transmission: Manual
No. of forward speeds: 5
Wheels driven: Rear
Springs F/R: Coil/Coil
Brake system: PA
Brakes F/R: Disc/Disc
Steering: Rack & pinion PA
Wheelbase: 231.9cm 91.3in
Track F: 137.9cm 54.3in
Track R: 138.9cm 54.7in
Length: 442.0cm 174.0in
Width: 168.9cm 66.5in
Height: 129.5cm 51.0in
Ground clearance: 15.0cm 5.9in
Kerb weight: 1332.5kg 2935.0lb
Fuel: 79.9L 17.6gal 21.1galUS

1226 Datsun

Stanza 1.6 GL
1982 Japan
97.0mph 156.1kmh
0-50mph 80.5kmh: 8.7secs
0-60mph 96.5kmh: 12.0secs
0-1/4 mile: 18.4secs
0-1km: 34.8secs
81.0bhp 60.4kW 82.1PS
@ 5200rpm
96.0lbft 130.1Nm @ 3200rpm
85.8bhp/ton 84.4bhp/tonne
50.7bhp/L 37.8kW/L 51.4PS/L
47.5ft/sec 14.5m/sec
25.2mph 40.5kmh/1000rpm
31.8mpg 26.5mpgUS 8.9L/100km
Petrol 4-stroke piston
1598cc 97.5cu in
In-line 4 1 Carburettor
Compression ratio: 9.0:1
Bore: 78.0mm 3.1in
Stroke: 83.6mm 3.3in
Valve type/No: Overhead 8
Transmission: Manual
No. of forward speeds: 5
Wheels driven: Front
Springs F/R: Coil/Coil
Brake system: PA
Brakes F/R: Disc/Drum
Steering: Rack & pinion
Wheelbase: 246.9cm 97.2in
Track F: 143.0cm 56.3in
Track R: 141.0cm 55.5in
Length: 428.0cm 168.5in
Width: 166.6cm 65.6in
Height: 138.9cm 54.7in
Ground clearance: 16.5cm 6.5in
Kerb weight: 959.8kg 2114.0lb
Fuel: 54.1L 11.9gal 14.3galUS

1227 Datsun

Sunny 1.5 DX
1982 Japan
98.0mph 157.7kmh
0-50mph 80.5kmh: 7.8secs
0-60mph 96.5kmh: 11.0secs
0-1/4 mile: 18.2secs
0-1km: 34.4secs
75.0bhp 55.9kW 76.0PS
@ 5600rpm
90.6lbft 122.8Nm @ 2800rpm
91.9bhp/ton 90.4bhp/tonne
50.4bhp/L 37.6kW/L 51.1PS/L
50.2ft/sec 15.3m/sec
25.3mph 40.7kmh/1000rpm
36.7mpg 30.6mpgUS 7.7L/100km
Petrol 4-stroke piston
1488cc 90.8cu in
In-line 4 1 Carburettor
Compression ratio: 9.8:1
Bore: 76.0mm 3.0in
Stroke: 82.0mm 3.2in
Valve type/No: Overhead 8
Transmission: Manual
No. of forward speeds: 5
Wheels driven: Front
Springs F/R: Coil/Coil
Brake system: PA
Brakes F/R: Disc/Drum
Steering: Rack & pinion
Wheelbase: 240.0cm 94.5in
Track F: 139.4cm 54.9in
Track R: 139.4cm 54.9in
Length: 404.9cm 159.4in
Width: 162.1cm 63.8in
Height: 138.4cm 54.5in
Ground clearance: 15.2cm 6.0in
Kerb weight: 829.9kg 1828.0lb

Fuel: 50.0L 11.0gal 13.2galUS

1228 Datsun
200SX
1983 Japan
108.0mph 173.8kmh
0-50mph 80.5kmh: 8.3secs
0-60mph 96.5kmh: 11.5secs
0-1/4 mile: 18.3secs
102.0bhp 76.1kW 103.4PS
@ 5600rpm
129.0lbft 174.8Nm @ 2800rpm
85.2bhp/ton 83.8bhp/tonne
46.6bhp/L 34.8kW/L 47.3PS/L
56.3ft/sec 17.2m/sec
24.0mph 38.6kmh/1000rpm
29.4mpg 24.5mpgUS 9.6L/100km
Petrol 4-stroke piston
2187cc 133.4cu in
In-line 4 fuel injection
Compression ratio: 8.5:1
Bore: 87.0mm 3.4in
Stroke: 92.0mm 3.6in
Valve type/No: Overhead 8
Transmission: Manual
No. of forward speeds: 5
Wheels driven: Rear
Springs F/R: Coil/Coil
Brake system: PA
Brakes F/R: Disc/Disc
Steering: Recirculating ball PA
Wheelbase: 240.0cm 94.5in
Track F: 134.6cm 53.0in
Track R: 134.6cm 53.0in
Length: 448.1cm 176.4in
Width: 167.9cm 66.1in
Height: 131.1cm 51.6in
Kerb weight: 1216.7kg 2680.0lb
Fuel: 60.2L 13.2gal 15.9galUS

1229 Datsun
280ZX
1983 Japan
124.0mph 199.5kmh
0-50mph 80.5kmh: 7.0secs
0-60mph 96.5kmh: 9.7secs
0-1/4 mile: 17.2secs
145.0bhp 108.1kW 147.0PS
@ 5200rpm
156.0lbft 211.4Nm @ 4000rpm
111.2bhp/ton 109.4bhp/tonne
52.7bhp/L 39.3kW/L 53.4PS/L
44.9ft/sec 13.7m/sec
24.8mph 39.9kmh/1000rpm
26.4mpg 22.0mpgUS 10.7L/100km
Petrol 4-stroke piston
2753cc 168.0cu in
In-line 6 fuel injection
Compression ratio: 8.3:1
Bore: 86.0mm 3.4in
Stroke: 79.0mm 3.1in
Valve type/No: Overhead 12
Transmission: Manual
No. of forward speeds: 5
Wheels driven: Rear
Springs F/R: Coil/Coil
Brake system: PA
Brakes F/R: Disc/Disc
Steering: Rack & pinion PA
Wheelbase: 231.9cm 91.3in
Track F: 139.4cm 54.9in
Track R: 138.9cm 54.7in
Length: 442.0cm 174.0in
Width: 168.9cm 66.5in
Height: 129.5cm 51.0in
Kerb weight: 1325.7kg 2920.0lb
Fuel: 79.9L 17.6gal 21.1galUS

1230 Datsun
280ZX Electramotive
1983 Japan
145.0mph 233.3kmh
0-60mph 96.5kmh: 3.8secs
0-1/4 mile: 11.5secs
580.0bhp 432.5kW 588.0PS
@ 7500rpm
520.0lbft 704.6Nm @ 5500rpm
499.7bhp/ton 491.4bhp/tonne
210.7bhp/L 157.1kW/L 213.6PS/L
64.8ft/sec 19.7m/sec
18.1mph 29.1kmh/1000rpm
4.8mpg 4.0mpgUS 58.8L/100km
Petrol 4-stroke piston
2753cc 168.0cu in turbocharged
In-line 6 fuel injection
Bore: 86.0mm 3.4in
Stroke: 79.0mm 3.1in
Valve type/No: Overhead 12
Transmission: Manual
No. of forward speeds: 5
Wheels driven: Rear
Springs F/R: Coil/Coil
Brakes F/R: Disc/Disc
Steering: Rack & pinion
Wheelbase: 231.9cm 91.3in
Track F: 148.6cm 58.5in
Track R: 147.3cm 58.0in
Length: 442.0cm 174.0in
Width: 185.4cm 73.0in
Height: 122.2cm 48.1in
Ground clearance: 7.6cm 3.0in
Kerb weight: 1180.4kg 2600.0lb
Fuel: 120.0L 26.4gal 31.7galUS

1231 Datsun
280ZX Turbo
1983 Japan
129.0mph 207.6kmh
0-50mph 80.5kmh: 5.8secs
0-60mph 96.5kmh: 7.9secs
0-1/4 mile: 16.1secs
180.0bhp 134.2kW 182.5PS
@ 5600rpm
203.0lbft 275.1Nm @ 2800rpm
134.8bhp/ton 132.6bhp/tonne
65.4bhp/L 48.8kW/L 66.3PS/L
48.4ft/sec 14.7m/sec
27.0mph 43.4kmh/1000rpm
24.6mpg 20.5mpgUS 11.5L/100km
Petrol 4-stroke piston
2753cc 168.0cu in turbocharged
In-line 6 fuel injection
Compression ratio: 7.4:1
Bore: 86.0mm 3.4in
Stroke: 79.0mm 3.1in
Valve type/No: Overhead 12
Transmission: Manual
No. of forward speeds: 5
Wheels driven: Rear
Springs F/R: Coil/Coil
Brake system: PA
Brakes F/R: Disc/Disc
Steering: Rack & pinion PA
Wheelbase: 231.9cm 91.3in
Track F: 138.4cm 54.5in
Track R: 137.9cm 54.3in
Length: 442.0cm 174.0in
Width: 168.9cm 66.5in
Height: 129.5cm 51.0in
Kerb weight: 1357.5kg 2990.0lb
Fuel: 79.9L 17.6gal 21.1galUS

1232 Datsun
Micra GL
1983 Japan
88.0mph 141.6kmh
0-50mph 80.5kmh: 10.0secs
0-60mph 96.5kmh: 15.0secs
0-1/4 mile: 19.6secs
0-1km: 37.3secs
55.0bhp 41.0kW 55.8PS
@ 6000rpm
56.0lbft 75.9Nm @ 3600rpm
84.1bhp/ton 82.7bhp/tonne
55.1bhp/L 41.1kW/L 55.9PS/L
44.7ft/sec 13.6m/sec
22.5mph 36.2kmh/1000rpm
43.7mpg 36.4mpgUS 6.5L/100km
Petrol 4-stroke piston
998cc 60.9cu in
In-line 4 1 Carburettor
Compression ratio: 10.3:1
Bore: 68.0mm 2.7in
Stroke: 68.0mm 2.7in
Valve type/No: Overhead 8
Transmission: Manual
No. of forward speeds: 5
Wheels driven: Front
Springs F/R: Coil/Coil
Brake system: PA
Brakes F/R: Disc/Drum
Steering: Rack & pinion
Wheelbase: 230.1cm 90.6in
Track F: 134.6cm 53.0in
Track R: 133.1cm 52.4in
Length: 364.5cm 143.5in
Width: 156.0cm 61.4in
Height: 139.4cm 54.9in
Ground clearance: 15.2cm 6.0in
Kerb weight: 665.1kg 1465.0lb
Fuel: 40.0L 8.8gal 10.6galUS

1233 De Lorean
DMC 2.8-litre Coupe
1982 UK
109.0mph 175.4kmh
0-60mph 96.5kmh: 10.5secs
0-1/4 mile: 17.9secs
130.0bhp 96.9kW 131.8PS
@ 5500rpm
162.0lbft 219.5Nm @ 2750rpm
102.5bhp/ton 100.8bhp/tonne
45.6bhp/L 34.0kW/L 46.3PS/L
43.8ft/sec 13.4m/sec
25.0mph 40.2kmh/1000rpm
23.4mpg 19.5mpgUS 12.1L/100km
Petrol 4-stroke piston
2849cc 173.8cu in
Vee 6 fuel injection
Compression ratio: 8.8:1
Bore: 91.0mm 3.6in
Stroke: 73.0mm 2.9in
Valve type/No: Overhead 12
Transmission: Manual
No. of forward speeds: 5
Wheels driven: Rear
Springs F/R: Coil/Coil
Brake system: PA
Brakes F/R: Disc/Disc
Steering: Rack & pinion
Wheelbase: 240.8cm 94.8in
Track F: 159.0cm 62.6in
Track R: 158.8cm 62.5in
Length: 426.7cm 168.0in
Width: 198.9cm 78.3in
Height: 114.0cm 44.9in
Ground clearance: 14.2cm 5.6in
Kerb weight: 1289.4kg 2840.0lb
Fuel: 51.1L 11.2gal 13.5galUS

1234 De Soto
Straight Eight Saloon
1931 USA
68.1mph 109.6kmh
16.0mpg 13.3mpgUS 17.7L/100km
Petrol 4-stroke piston
3308cc 201.8cu in
In-line 8
Bore: 73.0mm 2.9in
Stroke: 101.0mm 4.0in
Transmission: Manual
No. of forward speeds: 3
Wheels driven: Rear
Brakes F/R: Drum/Drum
Wheelbase: 292.1cm 115.0in
Track F: 147.3cm 58.0in
Track R: 147.3cm 58.0in
Length: 452.1cm 178.0in
Width: 175.3cm 69.0in
Height: 190.5cm 75.0in
Kerb weight: 1407.4kg 3100.0lb
Fuel: 54.6L 12.0gal 14.4galUS

1235 De Tomaso
Mangusta
1969 Italy
118.0mph 189.9kmh
0-50mph 80.5kmh: 5.4secs
0-60mph 96.5kmh: 7.0secs
0-1/4 mile: 15.1secs
230.0bhp 171.5kW 233.2PS
@ 4800rpm
310.0lbft 420.1Nm @ 2800rpm
168.9bhp/ton 166.1bhp/tonne
46.5bhp/L 34.7kW/L 47.1PS/L
40.0ft/sec 12.2m/sec
22.4mph 36.0kmh/1000rpm
19.8mpg 16.5mpgUS 14.3L/100km
Petrol 4-stroke piston
4949cc 301.9cu in
Vee 8 1 Carburettor
Compression ratio: 10.0:1
Bore: 101.6mm 4.0in
Stroke: 76.2mm 3.0in
Valve type/No: Overhead 16
Transmission: Manual
No. of forward speeds: 5
Wheels driven: Rear
Springs F/R: Coil/Coil
Brakes F/R: Disc/Disc
Steering: Rack & pinion
Wheelbase: 249.9cm 98.4in
Track F: 140.2cm 55.2in
Track R: 145.8cm 57.4in
Length: 426.5cm 167.9in
Width: 184.4cm 72.6in
Height: 106.9cm 42.1in
Ground clearance: 16.0cm 6.3in
Kerb weight: 1384.7kg 3050.0lb
Fuel: 90.1L 19.8gal 23.8galUS

1236 De Tomaso
Pantera
1971 Italy
129.0mph 207.6kmh
0-50mph 80.5kmh: 5.4secs
0-60mph 96.5kmh: 6.8secs
0-1/4 mile: 14.5secs
310.0bhp 231.2kW 314.3PS
@ 5400rpm
380.0lbft 514.9Nm @ 3400rpm
220.1bhp/ton 216.4bhp/tonne
53.8bhp/L 40.1kW/L 54.5PS/L
52.5ft/sec 16.0m/sec
19.8mph 31.9kmh/1000rpm
16.6mpg 13.8mpgUS 17.0L/100km
Petrol 4-stroke piston
5763cc 351.6cu in
Vee 8 1 Carburettor
Compression ratio: 10.7:1
Bore: 102.0mm 4.0in
Stroke: 89.0mm 3.5in
Valve type/No: Overhead 16
Transmission: Manual
No. of forward speeds: 5
Wheels driven: Rear
Springs F/R: Coil/Coil
Brake system: PA
Brakes F/R: Disc/Disc
Steering: Rack & pinion
Wheelbase: 249.9cm 98.4in
Track F: 144.8cm 57.0in
Track R: 146.1cm 57.5in
Length: 425.2cm 167.4in
Width: 181.1cm 71.3in
Height: 112.0cm 44.1in
Ground clearance: 12.7cm 5.0in
Kerb weight: 1432.4kg 3155.0lb
Fuel: 79.5L 17.5gal 21.0galUS

1237 De Tomaso
Pantera
1972 Italy
159.0mph 255.8kmh
0-50mph 80.5kmh: 4.7secs
0-60mph 96.5kmh: 6.2secs
0-1/4 mile: 14.4secs
0-1km: 26.0secs
330.0bhp 246.1kW 334.6PS
@ 5400rpm
325.0lbft 440.4Nm @ 3600rpm
237.5bhp/ton 233.6bhp/tonne
57.3bhp/L 42.7kW/L 58.1PS/L
52.5ft/sec 16.0m/sec
26.3mph 42.3kmh/1000rpm
13.0mpg 10.8mpgUS 21.7L/100km
Petrol 4-stroke piston
5763cc 351.6cu in
Vee 8 1 Carburettor
Compression ratio: 11.0:1
Bore: 101.6mm 4.0in
Stroke: 88.9mm 3.5in
Valve type/No: Overhead 16
Transmission: Manual
No. of forward speeds: 5
Wheels driven: Rear
Springs F/R: Coil/Coil
Brake system: PA
Brakes F/R: Disc/Disc
Steering: Rack & pinion
Wheelbase: 251.5cm 99.0in
Track F: 146.1cm 57.5in
Track R: 144.8cm 57.0in
Length: 425.5cm 167.5in
Width: 182.9cm 72.0in
Height: 109.2cm 43.0in
Ground clearance: 14.5cm 5.7in
Kerb weight: 1412.8kg 3112.0lb
Fuel: 80.1L 17.6gal 21.1galUS

1238 De Tomaso
Pantera
1973 Italy
143.0mph 230.1kmh
0-60mph 96.5kmh: 7.6secs
0-1/4 mile: 15.6secs
264.0bhp 196.9kW 267.7PS
@ 5400rpm
314.0lbft 425.5Nm @ 3600rpm
184.5bhp/ton 181.4bhp/tonne
45.8bhp/L 34.2kW/L 46.4PS/L
52.5ft/sec 16.0m/sec
27.3mph 43.9kmh/1000rpm
12.6mpg 10.5mpgUS 22.4L/100km
Petrol 4-stroke piston

5763cc 351.6cu in
Vee 8 1 Carburettor
Compression ratio: 8.0:1
Bore: 102.0mm 4.0in
Stroke: 89.0mm 3.5in
Valve type/No: Overhead 16
Transmission: Manual
No. of forward speeds: 5
Wheels driven: Rear
Springs F/R: Coil/Coil
Brake system: PA
Brakes F/R: Disc/Disc
Steering: Rack & pinion
Wheelbase: 249.9cm 98.4in
Track F: 144.8cm 57.0in
Track R: 146.1cm 57.5in
Length: 447.0cm 176.0in
Width: 181.1cm 71.3in
Height: 112.0cm 44.1in
Ground clearance: 12.7cm 5.0in
Kerb weight: 1455.1kg 3205.0lb
Fuel: 79.5L 17.5gal 21.0galUS

1239 De Tomaso

Pantera GTS
1974 Italy
159.0mph 255.8kmh
0-50mph 80.5kmh: 5.0secs
0-60mph 96.5kmh: 6.5secs
0-1/4 mile: 14.3secs
335.0bhp 249.8kW 339.6PS
@ 6000rpm
345.0lbft 467.5Nm @ 4000rpm
248.5bhp/ton 244.3bhp/tonne
58.1bhp/L 43.3kW/L 58.9PS/L
58.3ft/sec 17.8m/sec
27.4mph 44.1kmh/1000rpm
14.4mpg 12.0mpgUS 19.6L/100km
Petrol 4-stroke piston
5763cc 351.6cu in
Vee 8 1 Carburettor
Compression ratio: 11.0:1
Bore: 102.0mm 4.0in
Stroke: 89.0mm 3.5in
Valve type/No: Overhead 16
Transmission: Manual
No. of forward speeds: 5
Wheels driven: Rear
Springs F/R: Coil/Coil
Brake system: PA
Brakes F/R: Disc/Disc
Steering: Rack & pinion
Wheelbase: 249.9cm 98.4in
Track F: 145.0cm 57.1in
Track R: 146.8cm 57.8in
Length: 427.0cm 168.1in
Width: 190.0cm 74.8in
Height: 110.0cm 43.3in
Ground clearance: 13.0cm 5.1in
Kerb weight: 1371.1kg 3020.0lb
Fuel: 79.5L 17.5gal 21.0galUS

1240 De Tomaso

Pantera L
1974 Italy
143.0mph 230.1kmh
0-50mph 80.5kmh: 5.6secs
0-60mph 96.5kmh: 7.6secs
0-1/4 mile: 15.6secs
264.0bhp 196.9kW 267.7PS
@ 5400rpm
314.0lbft 425.5Nm @ 3600rpm
184.5bhp/ton 181.4bhp/tonne
45.8bhp/L 34.2kW/L 46.4PS/L
52.5ft/sec 16.0m/sec
27.3mph 43.9kmh/1000rpm
12.6mpg 10.5mpgUS 22.4L/100km
Petrol 4-stroke piston
5763cc 351.6cu in
Vee 8 1 Carburettor
Compression ratio: 8.0:1
Bore: 102.0mm 4.0in
Stroke: 89.0mm 3.5in
Valve type/No: Overhead 16
Transmission: Manual
No. of forward speeds: 5
Wheels driven: Rear
Springs F/R: Coil/Coil
Brake system: PA
Brakes F/R: Disc/Disc
Steering: Rack & pinion
Wheelbase: 249.9cm 98.4in
Track F: 144.8cm 57.0in
Track R: 146.1cm 57.5in
Length: 447.0cm 176.0in
Width: 181.1cm 71.3in
Height: 112.0cm 44.1in
Ground clearance: 12.7cm 5.0in
Kerb weight: 1455.1kg 3205.0lb
Fuel: 79.5L 17.5gal 21.0galUS

1241 De Tomaso

Pantera GT5
1984 Italy
137.0mph 220.4kmh
0-50mph 80.5kmh: 4.3secs
0-60mph 96.5kmh: 5.5secs
0-1/4 mile: 14.0secs
350.0bhp 261.0kW 354.8PS
@ 6000rpm
333.0lbft 451.2Nm @ 3800rpm
241.2bhp/ton 237.2bhp/tonne
60.7bhp/L 45.3kW/L 61.6PS/L
58.3ft/sec 17.8m/sec
22.4mph 36.0kmh/1000rpm
12.0mpg 10.0mpgUS 23.5L/100km
Petrol 4-stroke piston
5763cc 351.6cu in
Vee 8 1 Carburettor
Compression ratio: 8.5:1
Bore: 101.6mm 4.0in
Stroke: 89.0mm 3.5in
Valve type/No: Overhead 16
Transmission: Manual
No. of forward speeds: 5
Wheels driven: Rear
Springs F/R: Coil/Coil
Brake system: PA
Brakes F/R: Disc/Disc
Steering: Rack & pinion
Wheelbase: 251.0cm 98.8in
Track F: 150.9cm 59.4in
Track R: 158.0cm 62.2in
Length: 427.0cm 168.1in
Width: 197.1cm 77.6in
Height: 105.7cm 41.6in
Ground clearance: 8.6cm 3.4in
Kerb weight: 1475.5kg 3250.0lb
Fuel: 79.9L 17.6gal 21.1galUS

1242 De Tomaso

Pantera GT5-S
1986 Italy
165.0mph 265.5kmh
0-50mph 80.5kmh: 4.1secs
0-60mph 96.5kmh: 5.4secs
0-1/4 mile: 13.6secs
0-1km: 25.2secs
300.0bhp 223.7kW 304.2PS
@ 6500rpm
209.0bhp/ton 205.5bhp/tonne
52.1bhp/L 38.8kW/L 52.8PS/L
63.2ft/sec 19.3m/sec
27.0mph 43.4kmh/1000rpm
16.0mpg 13.3mpgUS 17.7L/100km
Petrol 4-stroke piston
5763cc 352.0cu in
Vee 8 1 Carburettor
Compression ratio: 10.5:1
Bore: 101.6mm 4.0in
Stroke: 88.9mm 3.5in
Valve type/No: Overhead 16
Transmission: Manual
No. of forward speeds: 5
Wheels driven: Rear
Springs F/R: Coil/Coil
Brake system: PA
Brakes F/R: Disc/Disc
Steering: Rack & pinion
Wheelbase: 251.4cm 99.0in
Track F: 151.1cm 59.5in
Track R: 157.7cm 62.1in
Length: 426.9cm 168.1in
Width: 196.8cm 77.5in
Height: 109.9cm 43.3in
Ground clearance: 14.5cm 5.7in
Kerb weight: 1460.0kg 3215.9lb
Fuel: 79.6L 17.5gal 21.0galUS

1243 De Tomaso

Pantera Group 3
1989 Italy
168.0mph 270.3kmh
0-50mph 80.5kmh: 3.4secs
0-60mph 96.5kmh: 4.3secs
0-1/4 mile: 12.7secs
465.0bhp 346.7kW 471.4PS
@ 5800rpm
440.0lbft 596.2Nm @ 3800rpm
315.2bhp/ton 309.9bhp/tonne
73.9bhp/L 55.1kW/L 74.9PS/L
60.4ft/sec 18.4m/sec
Petrol 4-stroke piston
6291cc 383.8cu in
Vee 8 4 Carburettor
Compression ratio: 10.1:1
Bore: 102.5mm 4.0in
Stroke: 95.3mm 3.8in
Valve type/No: Overhead 16
Transmission: Manual
No. of forward speeds: 5
Wheels driven: Rear
Springs F/R: Coil/Coil
Brakes F/R: Disc/Disc
Steering: Rack & pinion
Wheelbase: 249.9cm 98.4in
Track F: 157.5cm 62.0in
Track R: 162.6cm 64.0in
Length: 457.2cm 180.0in
Width: 198.1cm 78.0in
Height: 109.2cm 43.0in
Kerb weight: 1500.5kg 3305.0lb

1244 De Tomaso

Pantera GT5 S
1990 Italy
167.0mph 268.7kmh
305.0bhp 227.4kW 309.2PS
@ 5800rpm
333.0lbft 451.2Nm @ 3700rpm
208.9bhp/ton 205.4bhp/tonne
61.7bhp/L 46.0kW/L 62.6PS/L
48.3ft/sec 14.7m/sec
Petrol 4-stroke piston
4942cc 301.5cu in
Vee 8 fuel injection
Compression ratio: 11.0:1
Bore: 101.6mm 4.0in
Stroke: 76.2mm 3.0in
Valve type/No: Overhead 16
Transmission: Manual
No. of forward speeds: 5
Wheels driven: Rear
Springs F/R: Coil/Coil
Brake system: PA
Brakes F/R: Disc/Disc
Steering: Rack & pinion
Wheelbase: 251.5cm 99.0in
Track F: 156.0cm 61.4in
Track R: 156.2cm 61.5in
Length: 427.0cm 168.1in
Width: 197.1cm 77.6in
Height: 110.0cm 43.3in
Kerb weight: 1484.6kg 3270.0lb
Fuel: 79.5L 17.5gal 21.0galUS

1245 Delage

21hp Weymann Saloon
1928 France
70.0mph 112.6kmh
18.0mpg 15.0mpgUS 15.7L/100km
Petrol 4-stroke piston
3180cc 194.0cu in
In-line 6
Bore: 75.0mm 2.9in
Stroke: 120.0mm 4.7in
Transmission: Manual
No. of forward speeds: 4
Wheels driven: Rear
Brakes F/R: Drum/Drum
Wheelbase: 351.8cm 138.5in
Track F: 142.2cm 56.0in
Track R: 142.2cm 56.0in
Length: 471.2cm 185.5in
Width: 167.6cm 66.0in
Fuel: 70.5L 15.5gal 18.6galUS

1246 Delage

18.2hp Saloon
1930 France
64.7mph 104.1kmh
22.0mpg 18.3mpgUS 12.8L/100km
Petrol 4-stroke piston
2516cc 153.5cu in
In-line 6
Bore: 70.0mm 2.8in
Stroke: 109.0mm 4.3in
Transmission: Manual
No. of forward speeds: 4
Wheels driven: Rear
Brakes F/R: Drum/Drum
Wheelbase: 311.2cm 122.5in
Track F: 137.2cm 54.0in
Track R: 137.2cm 54.0in
Length: 411.5cm 162.0in
Width: 157.5cm 62.0in
Height: 167.6cm 66.0in
Kerb weight: 1684.8kg 3711.0lb
Fuel: 95.5L 21.0gal 25.2galUS

1247 Delage

Straight Eight Sports Saloon
1930 France
86.5mph 139.2kmh
14.0mpg 11.7mpgUS 20.2L/100km
Petrol 4-stroke piston
4050cc 247.1cu in
In-line 8
Bore: 77.0mm 3.0in
Stroke: 109.0mm 4.3in
Transmission: Manual
No. of forward speeds: 4
Wheels driven: Rear
Brakes F/R: Drum/Drum
Wheelbase: 330.2cm 130.0in
Track F: 142.2cm 56.0in
Track R: 142.2cm 56.0in
Length: 444.5cm 175.0in
Width: 170.2cm 67.0in
Height: 167.6cm 66.0in
Kerb weight: 1779.7kg 3920.0lb
Fuel: 72.8L 16.0gal 19.2galUS

1248 Delage

Super Sports Straight Eight
1931 France
98.9mph 159.1kmh
14.0mpg 11.7mpgUS 20.2L/100km
Petrol 4-stroke piston
4050cc 247.1cu in
In-line 8
Bore: 77.0mm 3.0in
Stroke: 109.0mm 4.3in
Transmission: Manual
No. of forward speeds: 4
Wheels driven: Rear
Brakes F/R: Drum/Drum
Wheelbase: 309.9cm 122.0in
Track F: 142.2cm 56.0in
Track R: 142.2cm 56.0in
Length: 487.7cm 192.0in
Width: 167.6cm 66.0in
Kerb weight: 1767.0kg 3892.0lb
Fuel: 81.9L 18.0gal 21.6galUS

1249 Delage

D6-11 Sports Saloon
1933 France
73.7mph 118.6kmh
0-60mph 96.5kmh: 31.6secs
20.0mpg 16.7mpgUS 14.1L/100km
Petrol 4-stroke piston
2149cc 131.1cu in
In-line 6
Bore: 75.0mm 2.9in
Stroke: 75.5mm 3.0in
Transmission: Manual
No. of forward speeds: 4
Wheels driven: Rear
Brakes F/R: Drum/Drum
Kerb weight: 1500.0kg 3304.0lb
Fuel: 81.9L 18.0gal 21.6galUS

1250 Delage

D6-70 Sports Coupe
1937 France
83.3mph 134.0kmh
0-50mph 80.5kmh: 14.9secs
0-60mph 96.5kmh: 23.3secs
16.0mpg 13.3mpgUS 17.7L/100km
Petrol 4-stroke piston
2729cc 166.5cu in
In-line 6
Bore: 80.0mm 3.1in
Stroke: 90.5mm 3.6in
Valve type/No: Overhead 12
Transmission: Manual
No. of forward speeds: 4
Wheels driven: Rear
Brakes F/R: Drum/Drum
Kerb weight: 1524.1kg 3357.0lb
Fuel: 81.9L 18.0gal 21.6galUS

1251 Delage

D8-120 Super Sports
1938 France
96.5mph 155.3kmh
0-50mph 80.5kmh: 12.8secs
0-60mph 96.5kmh: 17.6secs
0-1/4 mile: 20.6secs
142.0bhp 105.9kW 144.0PS
@ 4000rpm
250.0lbft 338.8Nm @ 2200rpm
74.5bhp/ton 73.2bhp/tonne

29.9bhp/L 22.3kW/L 30.3PS/L
46.8ft/sec 14.2m/sec
Petrol 4-stroke piston
4744cc 289.4cu in
In-line 8
Compression ratio: 7.3:1
Bore: 84.1mm 3.3in
Stroke: 106.9mm 4.2in
Valve type/No: Overhead 16
Transmission: Manual
No. of forward speeds: 4
Wheels driven: Rear
Wheelbase: 335.0cm 131.9in
Track F: 149.9cm 59.0in
Track R: 149.9cm 59.0in
Kerb weight: 1938.6kg 4270.0lb

1252 Delahaye
23.8hp Drop-head Coupe
1936 France
98.9mph 159.1kmh
0-50mph 80.5kmh: 9.9secs
0-60mph 96.5kmh: 13.7secs
18.0mpg 15.0mpgUS 15.7L/100km
Petrol 4-stroke piston
3227cc 196.9cu in
In-line 6
Bore: 80.0mm 3.1in
Stroke: 107.0mm 4.2in
Valve type/No: Overhead 12
Transmission: Manual
No. of forward speeds: 4
Wheels driven: Rear
Brakes F/R: Drum/Drum
Kerb weight: 1367.0kg 3011.0lb
Fuel: 77.3L 17.0gal 20.4galUS

1253 Delaunay-Belleville
21hp Saloon
1929 France
66.0mph 106.2kmh
18.0mpg 15.0mpgUS 15.7L/100km
Petrol 4-stroke piston
3180cc 194.0cu in
In-line 6
Bore: 75.0mm 2.9in
Stroke: 120.0mm 4.7in
Valve type/No: Overhead 12
Transmission: Manual
No. of forward speeds: 4
Wheels driven: Rear
Brakes F/R: Drum/Drum
Wheelbase: 363.2cm 143.0in
Track F: 139.7cm 55.0in
Track R: 139.7cm 55.0in
Length: 487.7cm 192.0in
Width: 167.6cm 66.0in
Fuel: 72.8L 16.0gal 19.2galUS

1254 Dellow
Mk V
1956 UK
74.0mph 119.1kmh
0-50mph 80.5kmh: 12.5secs
0-60mph 96.5kmh: 20.4secs
0-1/4 mile: 21.2secs
42.0bhp 31.3kW 42.6PS
@ 4500rpm
54.0lbft 73.2Nm @ 2150rpm
71.3bhp/ton 70.1bhp/tonne
35.8bhp/L 26.7kW/L 36.3PS/L
45.4ft/sec 13.8m/sec
16.7mph 26.9kmh/1000rpm
Petrol 4-stroke piston
1172cc 71.5cu in
In-line 4
Compression ratio: 7.0:1
Bore: 63.5mm 2.5in
Stroke: 92.2mm 3.6in
Valve type/No: Side 8
Transmission: Manual
No. of forward speeds: 3
Wheels driven: Rear
Wheelbase: 213.4cm 84.0in
Track F: 114.3cm 45.0in
Track R: 114.3cm 45.0in
Kerb weight: 599.3kg 1320.0lb

1255 Denzel
1300
1957 Austria
99.0mph 159.3kmh
0-50mph 80.5kmh: 9.6secs
0-60mph 96.5kmh: 13.7secs
0-1/4 mile: 18.0secs
65.0bhp 48.5kW 65.9PS
@ 5400rpm
71.0lbft 96.2Nm @ 4400rpm
102.9bhp/ton 101.2bhp/tonne
50.7bhp/L 37.8kW/L 51.4PS/L
39.6ft/sec 12.1m/sec
Petrol 4-stroke piston
1281cc 78.2cu in
Flat 4
Compression ratio: 8.5:1
Bore: 78.0mm 3.1in
Stroke: 67.1mm 2.6in
Valve type/No: Overhead 8
Transmission: Manual
No. of forward speeds: 4
Wheels driven: Rear
Wheelbase: 210.1cm 82.7in
Track F: 131.1cm 51.6in
Track R: 131.1cm 51.6in
Kerb weight: 642.4kg 1415.0lb

1256 Deutsch-Bonnet
Coupe
1957 France
88.0mph 141.6kmh
0-50mph 80.5kmh: 13.9secs
0-60mph 96.5kmh: 21.3secs
0-1/4 mile: 21.5secs
51.0bhp 38.0kW 51.7PS
@ 5700rpm
47.0lbft 63.7Nm @ 3500rpm
77.7bhp/ton 76.4bhp/tonne
59.9bhp/L 44.7kW/L 60.8PS/L
46.7ft/sec 14.2m/sec
Petrol 4-stroke piston
851cc 51.9cu in
Flat 2
Compression ratio: 7.5:1
Bore: 85.1mm 3.3in
Stroke: 74.9mm 2.9in
Valve type/No: Overhead 4
Transmission: Manual
No. of forward speeds: 4
Wheels driven: Rear
Wheelbase: 213.1cm 83.9in
Track F: 121.9cm 48.0in
Track R: 121.9cm 48.0in
Kerb weight: 667.4kg 1470.0lb

1257 Devin
Super Sports
1959 USA
131.0mph 210.8kmh
0-50mph 80.5kmh: 4.7secs
0-60mph 96.5kmh: 5.7secs
0-1/4 mile: 14.0secs
220.0bhp 164.0kW 223.0PS
@ 4800rpm
300.0lbft 406.5Nm @ 3000rpm
227.1bhp/ton 223.3bhp/tonne
47.4bhp/L 35.4kW/L 48.1PS/L
40.0ft/sec 12.2m/sec
21.0mph 33.8kmh/1000rpm
Petrol 4-stroke piston
4639cc 283.0cu in
Vee 8
Compression ratio: 9.5:1
Bore: 98.6mm 3.9in
Stroke: 76.2mm 3.0in
Valve type/No: Overhead 16
Transmission: Manual
No. of forward speeds: 4
Wheels driven: Rear
Wheelbase: 233.7cm 92.0in
Track F: 132.1cm 52.0in
Track R: 139.7cm 55.0in
Length: 416.6cm 164.0in
Width: 160.0cm 63.0in
Height: 111.8cm 44.0in
Kerb weight: 985.2kg 2170.0lb

1258 Devin
VW
1960 USA
72.2mph 116.2kmh
0-50mph 80.5kmh: 15.4secs
0-60mph 96.5kmh: 22.8secs
0-1/4 mile: 22.1secs
36.0bhp 26.8kW 36.5PS
@ 3700rpm
56.0lbft 75.9Nm @ 2000rpm
63.7bhp/ton 62.7bhp/tonne
30.2bhp/L 22.5kW/L 30.6PS/L
25.9ft/sec 7.9m/sec
20.2mph 32.5kmh/1000rpm
Petrol 4-stroke piston
1192cc 72.7cu in
Flat 4 1 Carburettor
Compression ratio: 6.6:1
Bore: 77.0mm 3.0in
Stroke: 64.0mm 2.5in
Valve type/No: Overhead 8
Transmission: Manual
No. of forward speeds: 4
Wheels driven: Rear
Wheelbase: 208.3cm 82.0in
Track F: 130.6cm 51.4in
Track R: 125.0cm 49.2in
Length: 388.6cm 153.0in
Width: 152.4cm 60.0in
Height: 116.8cm 46.0in
Kerb weight: 574.3kg 1265.0lb

1259 DKW
7.1hp Cabriolet
1934 Germany
53.5mph 86.1kmh
0-50mph 80.5kmh: 44.8secs
35.0mpg 29.1mpgUS 8.1L/100km
Petrol 4-stroke piston
684cc 41.7cu in
Flat 2
Bore: 76.0mm 3.0in
Stroke: 76.0mm 3.0in
Valve type/No: Ports
Transmission: Manual
No. of forward speeds: 3
Wheels driven: Front
Brakes F/R: Drum/Drum
Kerb weight: 686.4kg 1512.0lb
Fuel: 27.3L 6.0gal 7.2galUS

1260 DKW
7.1hp Cabriolet
1937 Germany
56.6mph 91.1kmh
0-50mph 80.5kmh: 40.2secs
40.0mpg 33.3mpgUS 7.1L/100km
Petrol 2-stroke piston
684cc 41.7cu in
Flat 2
Bore: 76.0mm 3.0in
Stroke: 76.0mm 3.0in
Valve type/No: Ports
Transmission: Manual
No. of forward speeds: 3
Wheels driven: Front
Brakes F/R: Drum/Drum
Kerb weight: 763.6kg 1682.0lb
Fuel: 31.8L 7.0gal 8.4galUS

1261 DKW
Sonderklasse
1954 Germany
74.5mph 119.9kmh
0-50mph 80.5kmh: 17.5secs
0-60mph 96.5kmh: 26.7secs
0-1/4 mile: 23.5secs
34.0bhp 25.3kW 34.5PS
@ 4000rpm
50.6lbft 68.6Nm @ 2000rpm
38.3bhp/ton 37.7bhp/tonne
37.9bhp/L 28.3kW/L 38.5PS/L
33.2ft/sec 10.1m/sec
17.2mph 27.7kmh/1000rpm
31.5mpg 26.2mpgUS 9.0L/100km
Petrol 2-stroke piston
896cc 54.7cu in
In-line 3
Compression ratio: 6.5:1
Bore: 71.0mm 2.8in
Stroke: 76.0mm 3.0in
Valve type/No: Ports
Transmission: Manual
No. of forward speeds: 4
Wheels driven: Front
Springs F/R: Leaf/Leaf
Brakes F/R: Drum/Drum
Wheelbase: 235.0cm 92.5in
Track F: 119.4cm 47.0in
Track R: 124.5cm 49.0in
Length: 421.6cm 166.0in
Width: 160.0cm 63.0in
Height: 144.8cm 57.0in
Ground clearance: 19.6cm 7.7in
Kerb weight: 902.5kg 1988.0lb
Fuel: 31.8L 7.0gal 8.4galUS

1262 DKW
3-6
1955 Germany
73.8mph 118.7kmh
0-50mph 80.5kmh: 18.2secs
0-60mph 96.5kmh: 28.4secs
0-1/4 mile: 23.9secs
34.0bhp 25.3kW 34.5PS
@ 4000rpm
39.6bhp/ton 38.9bhp/tonne
37.9bhp/L 28.3kW/L 38.5PS/L
33.2ft/sec 10.1m/sec
Petrol 2-stroke piston
896cc 54.7cu in
In-line 3
Bore: 71.1mm 2.8in
Stroke: 75.9mm 3.0in
Transmission: Manual
No. of forward speeds: 4
Wheels driven: Front
Wheelbase: 235.0cm 92.5in
Track F: 119.1cm 46.9in
Track R: 125.0cm 49.2in
Kerb weight: 873.9kg 1925.0lb

1263 DKW
3-6
1956 Germany
77.7mph 125.0kmh
0-50mph 80.5kmh: 16.5secs
0-60mph 96.5kmh: 25.5secs
0-1/4 mile: 23.4secs
42.0bhp 31.3kW 42.6PS
@ 4200rpm
54.2lbft 73.4Nm @ 2800rpm
48.4bhp/ton 47.6bhp/tonne
46.9bhp/L 35.0kW/L 47.5PS/L
34.9ft/sec 10.6m/sec
16.9mph 27.2kmh/1000rpm
Petrol 2-stroke piston
896cc 54.7cu in
In-line 3
Compression ratio: 6.5:1
Bore: 71.1mm 2.8in
Stroke: 75.9mm 3.0in
Transmission: Manual
No. of forward speeds: 4
Wheels driven: Front
Wheelbase: 235.0cm 92.5in
Track F: 129.0cm 50.8in
Track R: 134.9cm 53.1in
Kerb weight: 883.0kg 1945.0lb

1264 DKW
Karavan
1956 Germany
61.9mph 99.6kmh
0-50mph 80.5kmh: 26.1secs
0-60mph 96.5kmh: 60.0secs
0-1/4 mile: 35.8secs
42.0bhp 31.3kW 42.6PS
@ 4200rpm
54.2lbft 73.4Nm @ 2800rpm
32.4bhp/ton 31.9bhp/tonne
46.9bhp/L 35.0kW/L 47.5PS/L
34.9ft/sec 10.6m/sec
Petrol 2-stroke piston
896cc 54.7cu in
In-line 3
Compression ratio: 6.7:1
Bore: 71.1mm 2.8in
Stroke: 75.9mm 3.0in
Transmission: Manual
No. of forward speeds: 4
Wheels driven: Front
Wheelbase: 275.1cm 108.3in
Track F: 136.9cm 53.9in
Track R: 140.0cm 55.1in
Length: 417.1cm 164.2in
Height: 190.0cm 74.8in
Kerb weight: 1316.6kg 2900.0lb

1265 DKW
3-6 Sonderklasse Coupe
1958 Germany
82.0mph 131.9kmh
0-50mph 80.5kmh: 14.3secs
0-60mph 96.5kmh: 22.5secs
0-1/4 mile: 23.1secs
40.0bhp 29.8kW 40.5PS
@ 4250rpm
50.6lbft 68.6Nm @ 2000rpm
45.2bhp/ton 44.5bhp/tonne
44.6bhp/L 33.3kW/L 45.3PS/L
35.3ft/sec 10.8m/sec

17.2mph 27.7kmh/1000rpm
33.2mpg 27.6mpgUS 8.5L/100km
Petrol 2-stroke piston
896cc 54.7cu in
In-line 3
Compression ratio: 7.0:1
Bore: 71.0mm 2.8in
Stroke: 76.0mm 3.0in
Valve type/No: Ports
Transmission: Manual
No. of forward speeds: 4
Wheels driven: Front
Springs F/R: Leaf/Leaf
Brakes F/R: Drum/Drum
Wheelbase: 233.7cm 92.0in
Track F: 127.0cm 50.0in
Track R: 134.6cm 53.0in
Length: 421.6cm 166.0in
Width: 167.6cm 66.0in
Height: 146.1cm 57.5in
Ground clearance: 19.6cm 7.7in
Kerb weight: 899.4kg 1981.0lb
Fuel: 44.6L 9.8gal 11.8galUS

1266 DKW

750
1960 Germany
70.5mph 113.4kmh
0-50mph 80.5kmh: 17.8secs
0-60mph 96.5kmh: 28.4secs
0-1/4 mile: 22.9secs
34.0bhp 25.3kW 34.5PS
@ 4300rpm
47.0lbft 63.7Nm @ 2500rpm
50.1bhp/ton 49.3bhp/tonne
45.9bhp/L 34.2kW/L 46.5PS/L
31.9ft/sec 9.7m/sec
17.4mph 28.0kmh/1000rpm
Petrol 2-stroke piston
741cc 45.2cu in
In-line 3 1 Carburettor
Compression ratio: 8.0:1
Bore: 67.8mm 2.7in
Stroke: 67.8mm 2.7in
Transmission: Manual
No. of forward speeds: 4
Wheels driven: Front
Wheelbase: 217.4cm 85.6in
Track F: 118.1cm 46.5in
Track R: 119.9cm 47.2in
Length: 393.7cm 155.0in
Width: 158.0cm 62.2in
Height: 140.0cm 55.1in
Kerb weight: 690.1kg 1520.0lb

1267 DKW

Junior
1961 Germany
73.0mph 117.5kmh
0-50mph 80.5kmh: 20.2secs
0-60mph 96.5kmh: 37.6secs
0-1/4 mile: 24.0secs
34.0bhp 25.3kW 34.5PS
@ 4300rpm
47.0lbft 63.7Nm @ 2500rpm
49.4bhp/ton 48.6bhp/tonne
45.9bhp/L 34.2kW/L 46.5PS/L
32.0ft/sec 9.7m/sec
17.2mph 27.7kmh/1000rpm
30.1mpg 25.1mpgUS 9.4L/100km
Petrol 2-stroke piston
741cc 45.2cu in
In-line 3
Compression ratio: 8.0:1
Bore: 68.0mm 2.7in
Stroke: 68.0mm 2.7in
Valve type/No: Ports
Transmission: Manual
No. of forward speeds: 4
Wheels driven: Front
Springs F/R: Torsion bar/Torsion bar
Brakes F/R: Drum/Drum
Wheelbase: 215.9cm 85.0in
Track F: 116.8cm 46.0in
Track R: 119.4cm 47.0in
Length: 393.7cm 155.0in
Width: 157.5cm 62.0in
Height: 139.7cm 55.0in
Ground clearance: 15.2cm 6.0in
Kerb weight: 699.2kg 1540.0lb
Fuel: 36.4L 8.0gal 9.6galUS

1268 DKW

Junior de Luxe
1962 Germany
71.0mph 114.2kmh
0-50mph 80.5kmh: 14.3secs
0-60mph 96.5kmh: 24.2secs
0-1/4 mile: 22.4secs
34.0bhp 25.3kW 34.5PS
@ 4000rpm
55.7lbft 75.5Nm @ 2500rpm
48.4bhp/ton 47.5bhp/tonne
42.8bhp/L 31.9kW/L 43.4PS/L
29.8ft/sec 9.1m/sec
17.4mph 28.0kmh/1000rpm
Petrol 2-stroke piston
795cc 48.5cu in
In-line 3
Compression ratio: 7.3:1
Bore: 70.6mm 2.8in
Stroke: 68.1mm 2.7in
Transmission: Manual
No. of forward speeds: 4
Wheels driven: Front
Wheelbase: 217.4cm 85.6in
Track F: 119.9cm 47.2in
Track R: 120.7cm 47.5in
Length: 396.2cm 156.0in
Width: 157.5cm 62.0in
Height: 144.0cm 56.7in
Ground clearance: 16.0cm 6.3in
Kerb weight: 715.0kg 1575.0lb

1269 Dodge

New Six Saloon
1929 USA
64.0mph 103.0kmh
18.0mpg 15.0mpgUS 15.7L/100km
Petrol 4-stroke piston
3410cc 208.0cu in
In-line 6
Bore: 85.7mm 3.4in
Stroke: 98.4mm 3.9in
Transmission: Manual
No. of forward speeds: 3
Wheels driven: Rear
Brakes F/R: Drum/Drum
Wheelbase: 284.5cm 112.0in
Track F: 142.2cm 56.0in
Track R: 142.2cm 56.0in
Length: 429.3cm 169.0in
Width: 167.6cm 66.0in
Height: 170.2cm 67.0in
Kerb weight: 1350.6kg 2975.0lb
Fuel: 45.5L 10.0gal 12.0galUS

1270 Dodge

Eight Saloon
1930 USA
69.2mph 111.3kmh
17.0mpg 14.2mpgUS 16.6L/100km
Petrol 4-stroke piston
3618cc 220.7cu in
In-line 8
Bore: 73.0mm 2.9in
Stroke: 108.0mm 4.2in
Transmission: Manual
No. of forward speeds: 3
Wheels driven: Rear
Brakes F/R: Drum/Drum
Wheelbase: 289.6cm 114.0in
Track F: 144.8cm 57.0in
Track R: 144.8cm 57.0in
Length: 426.7cm 168.0in
Width: 175.3cm 69.0in
Height: 182.9cm 72.0in
Kerb weight: 1449.2kg 3192.0lb
Fuel: 56.9L 12.5gal 15.0galUS

1271 Dodge

Victory Six Touring Saloon
1937 USA
76.9mph 123.7kmh
0-50mph 80.5kmh: 16.7secs
0-60mph 96.5kmh: 26.2secs
18.0mpg 15.0mpgUS 15.7L/100km
Petrol 4-stroke piston
3568cc 217.7cu in
In-line 6
Bore: 82.5mm 3.2in
Stroke: 111.1mm 4.4in
Valve type/No: Side 12
Transmission: Manual
No. of forward speeds: 3
Wheels driven: Rear
Brakes F/R: Drum/Drum
Kerb weight: 1503.6kg 3312.0lb
Fuel: 57.8L 12.7gal 15.3galUS

1272 Dodge

De Luxe Saloon
1938 USA
76.2mph 122.6kmh
0-50mph 80.5kmh: 14.8secs
0-60mph 96.5kmh: 24.8secs
18.0mpg 15.0mpgUS 15.7L/100km
Petrol 4-stroke piston
3570cc 217.8cu in
In-line 6
Bore: 82.5mm 3.2in
Stroke: 111.1mm 4.4in
Valve type/No: Side 12
Transmission: Manual
No. of forward speeds: 3
Wheels driven: Rear
Brakes F/R: Drum/Drum
Kerb weight: 1494.6kg 3292.0lb
Fuel: 59.1L 13.0gal 15.6galUS

1273 Dodge

Custom Royal
1958 USA
108.0mph 173.8kmh
0-50mph 80.5kmh: 8.2secs
0-60mph 96.5kmh: 11.5secs
0-1/4 mile: 16.6secs
245.0bhp 182.7kW 248.4PS
@ 4400rpm
320.0lbft 433.6Nm @ 2400rpm
140.0bhp/ton 137.7bhp/tonne
46.0bhp/L 34.3kW/L 46.7PS/L
46.4ft/sec 14.1m/sec
26.6mph 42.8kmh/1000rpm
14.5mpg 12.1mpgUS 19.5L/100km
Petrol 4-stroke piston
5323cc 324.8cu in
Vee 8 1 Carburettor
Compression ratio: 8.5:1
Bore: 93.7mm 3.7in
Stroke: 96.5mm 3.8in
Valve type/No: Overhead 16
Transmission: Automatic
No. of forward speeds: 3
Wheels driven: Rear
Springs F/R: Torsion bar/Leaf
Brakes F/R: Drum/Drum
Wheelbase: 309.9cm 122.0in
Track F: 154.9cm 61.0in
Track R: 151.6cm 59.7in
Length: 539.0cm 212.2in
Width: 198.1cm 78.0in
Height: 144.0cm 56.7in
Ground clearance: 14.0cm 5.5in
Kerb weight: 1779.7kg 3920.0lb
Fuel: 77.3L 17.0gal 20.4galUS

1274 Dodge

Custom Royal
1959 USA
110.0mph 177.0kmh
0-50mph 80.5kmh: 7.9secs
0-60mph 96.5kmh: 10.5secs
0-1/4 mile: 17.4secs
295.0bhp 220.0kW 299.1PS
@ 4600rpm
390.0lbft 528.5Nm @ 2400rpm
165.2bhp/ton 162.5bhp/tonne
49.9bhp/L 37.2kW/L 50.6PS/L
43.2ft/sec 13.2m/sec
26.6mph 42.8kmh/1000rpm
15.9mpg 13.2mpgUS 17.8L/100km
Petrol 4-stroke piston
5916cc 360.9cu in
Vee 8
Compression ratio: 10.0:1
Bore: 104.6mm 4.1in
Stroke: 85.9mm 3.4in
Valve type/No: Overhead 16
Transmission: Automatic
No. of forward speeds: 3
Wheels driven: Rear
Springs F/R: Torsion bar/Leaf
Brake system: PA
Brakes F/R: Drum/Drum
Wheelbase: 309.9cm 122.0in
Track F: 152.4cm 60.0in
Track R: 151.9cm 59.8in
Length: 552.2cm 217.4in
Width: 182.9cm 72.0in
Height: 144.3cm 56.8in
Ground clearance: 14.0cm 5.5in
Kerb weight: 1815.5kg 3999.0lb
Fuel: 77.3L 17.0gal 20.4galUS

1275 Dodge

Dart
1961 USA
115.0mph 185.0kmh
0-50mph 80.5kmh: 7.5secs
0-60mph 96.5kmh: 10.4secs
0-1/4 mile: 17.7secs
230.0bhp 171.5kW 233.2PS
@ 4400rpm
340.0lbft 460.7Nm @ 2400rpm
132.8bhp/ton 130.6bhp/tonne
44.1bhp/L 32.9kW/L 44.7PS/L
40.5ft/sec 12.3m/sec
26.0mph 41.8kmh/1000rpm
Petrol 4-stroke piston
5213cc 318.1cu in
Vee 8 1 Carburettor
Compression ratio: 9.0:1
Bore: 99.3mm 3.9in
Stroke: 84.1mm 3.3in
Valve type/No: Overhead 16
Transmission: Automatic
No. of forward speeds: 3
Wheels driven: Rear
Brakes F/R: Drum/Drum
Wheelbase: 299.7cm 118.0in
Track F: 156.2cm 61.5in
Track R: 152.9cm 60.2in
Length: 531.9cm 209.4in
Width: 199.9cm 78.7in
Height: 139.2cm 54.8in
Ground clearance: 12.7cm 5.0in
Kerb weight: 1761.5kg 3880.0lb

1276 Dodge

Dart Phoenix
1961 USA
109.0mph 175.4kmh
0-50mph 80.5kmh: 8.5secs
0-60mph 96.5kmh: 11.8secs
0-1/4 mile: 18.2secs
230.0bhp 171.5kW 233.2PS
@ 4400rpm
340.0lbft 460.7Nm @ 2400rpm
145.7bhp/ton 143.3bhp/tonne
44.1bhp/L 32.9kW/L 44.7PS/L
40.5ft/sec 12.3m/sec
26.4mph 42.5kmh/1000rpm
17.3mpg 14.4mpgUS 16.3L/100km
Petrol 4-stroke piston
5212cc 318.0cu in
Vee 8
Compression ratio: 9.0:1
Bore: 99.3mm 3.9in
Stroke: 84.0mm 3.3in
Valve type/No: Overhead 16
Transmission: Automatic
No. of forward speeds: 3
Wheels driven: Rear
Springs F/R: Torsion bar/Leaf
Brake system: PA
Brakes F/R: Drum/Drum
Wheelbase: 299.7cm 118.0in
Track F: 156.2cm 61.5in
Track R: 152.9cm 60.2in
Length: 529.6cm 208.5in
Width: 199.9cm 78.7in
Height: 139.7cm 55.0in
Ground clearance: 13.0cm 5.1in
Kerb weight: 1604.9kg 3535.0lb
Fuel: 77.3L 17.0gal 20.4galUS

1277 Dodge

Lancer
1961 USA
100.0mph 160.9kmh
0-50mph 80.5kmh: 9.5secs
0-60mph 96.5kmh: 13.7secs
0-1/4 mile: 18.8secs
145.0bhp 108.1kW 147.0PS
@ 4000rpm
215.0lbft 291.3Nm @ 2800rpm
117.3bhp/ton 115.3bhp/tonne
39.3bhp/L 29.3kW/L 39.9PS/L
45.9ft/sec 14.0m/sec
22.6mph 36.4kmh/1000rpm
Petrol 4-stroke piston
3688cc 225.0cu in
In-line 6 1 Carburettor
Compression ratio: 8.2:1
Bore: 86.4mm 3.4in
Stroke: 104.8mm 4.1in
Valve type/No: Overhead 12
Transmission: Automatic
No. of forward speeds: 3
Wheels driven: Rear
Wheelbase: 270.5cm 106.5in

Track F: 142.2cm 56.0in
Track R: 141.0cm 55.5in
Length: 479.6cm 188.8in
Width: 183.6cm 72.3in
Height: 135.4cm 53.3in
Ground clearance: 13.7cm 5.4in
Kerb weight: 1257.6kg 2770.0lb

1278 Dodge

Lancer 225 Hyper-Pack
1961 USA
109.0mph 175.4kmh
0-50mph 80.5kmh: 6.1secs
0-60mph 96.5kmh: 8.6secs
0-1/4 mile: 16.4secs
196.0bhp 146.2kW 198.7PS
@ 5200rpm
212.0lbft 287.3Nm @ 4200rpm
164.4bhp/ton 161.7bhp/tonne
53.1bhp/L 39.6kW/L 53.9PS/L
59.7ft/sec 18.2m/sec
18.1mph 29.1kmh/1000rpm
Petrol 4-stroke piston
3688cc 225.0cu in
In-line 6 1 Carburettor
Compression ratio: 8.2:1
Bore: 86.4mm 3.4in
Stroke: 104.8mm 4.1in
Valve type/No: Overhead 12
Transmission: Manual
No. of forward speeds: 3
Wheels driven: Rear
Brakes F/R: Drum/Drum
Wheelbase: 270.5cm 106.5in
Track F: 142.2cm 56.0in
Track R: 141.0cm 55.5in
Length: 480.1cm 189.0in
Width: 183.6cm 72.3in
Height: 135.4cm 53.3in
Ground clearance: 13.7cm 5.4in
Kerb weight: 1212.2kg 2670.0lb

1279 Dodge

Custom 880
1962 USA
119.0mph 191.5kmh
0-50mph 80.5kmh: 7.7secs
0-60mph 96.5kmh: 10.8secs
0-1/4 mile: 16.8secs
265.0bhp 197.6kW 268.7PS
@ 4400rpm
380.0lbft 514.9Nm @ 2400rpm
148.6bhp/ton 146.1bhp/tonne
44.8bhp/L 33.4kW/L 45.4PS/L
41.3ft/sec 12.6m/sec
27.0mph 43.4kmh/1000rpm
Petrol 4-stroke piston
5916cc 360.9cu in
Vee 8 1 Carburettor
Compression ratio: 9.0:1
Bore: 104.6mm 4.1in
Stroke: 85.9mm 3.4in
Valve type/No: Overhead 16
Transmission: Automatic
No. of forward speeds: 3
Wheels driven: Rear
Brake system: PA
Steering: PA
Wheelbase: 309.9cm 122.0in
Track F: 154.7cm 60.9in
Track R: 151.6cm 59.7in
Length: 542.3cm 213.5in
Width: 199.9cm 78.7in
Height: 140.2cm 55.2in
Ground clearance: 13.7cm 5.4in
Kerb weight: 1813.7kg 3995.0lb
Fuel: 87.1L 19.1gal 23.0galUS

1280 Dodge

Dart 413
1962 USA
107.0mph 172.2kmh
0-50mph 80.5kmh: 6.1secs
0-60mph 96.5kmh: 7.4secs
0-1/4 mile: 15.1secs
385.0bhp 287.1kW 390.3PS
@ 5200rpm
455.0lbft 616.5Nm @ 3600rpm
243.6bhp/ton 239.5bhp/tonne
56.9bhp/L 42.4kW/L 57.7PS/L
54.2ft/sec 16.5m/sec
19.1mph 30.7kmh/1000rpm
Petrol 4-stroke piston
6768cc 412.9cu in
Vee 8
Compression ratio: 11.0:1
Bore: 106.4mm 4.2in
Stroke: 95.3mm 3.8in
Valve type/No: Overhead 16
Transmission: Manual
No. of forward speeds: 3
Wheels driven: Rear
Steering: PA
Wheelbase: 294.6cm 116.0in
Track F: 150.9cm 59.4in
Track R: 146.1cm 57.5in
Length: 513.1cm 202.0in
Width: 194.3cm 76.5in
Height: 137.2cm 54.0in
Ground clearance: 15.2cm 6.0in
Kerb weight: 1607.2kg 3540.0lb
Fuel: 75.7L 16.6gal 20.0galUS

1281 Dodge

Dreamer
1962 USA
80.0mph 128.7kmh
0-50mph 80.5kmh: 12.8secs
0-60mph 96.5kmh: 19.3secs
0-1/4 mile: 21.3secs
200.0bhp 149.1kW 202.8PS
@ 3900rpm
286.0lbft 387.5Nm @ 2400rpm
83.9bhp/ton 82.5bhp/tonne
38.4bhp/L 28.6kW/L 38.9PS/L
35.9ft/sec 10.9m/sec
21.8mph 35.1kmh/1000rpm
Petrol 4-stroke piston
5213cc 318.1cu in
Vee 8 1 Carburettor
Compression ratio: 8.3:1
Bore: 99.3mm 3.9in
Stroke: 84.1mm 3.3in
Valve type/No: Overhead 16
Transmission: Automatic
No. of forward speeds: 3
Wheels driven: Rear
Brakes F/R: Drum/Drum
Wheelbase: 309.9cm 122.0in
Track F: 164.3cm 64.7in
Track R: 160.5cm 63.2in
Length: 607.1cm 239.0in
Width: 183.6cm 72.3in
Height: 139.2cm 54.8in
Ground clearance: 19.6cm 7.7in
Kerb weight: 2424.4kg 5340.0lb

1282 Dodge

Lancer Gran Turismo
1962 USA
100.0mph 160.9kmh
0-50mph 80.5kmh: 9.4secs
0-60mph 96.5kmh: 13.2secs
0-1/4 mile: 19.0secs
145.0bhp 108.1kW 147.0PS
@ 4000rpm
215.0lbft 291.3Nm @ 2800rpm
117.3bhp/ton 115.3bhp/tonne
43.4bhp/L 32.4kW/L 44.0PS/L
45.9ft/sec 14.0m/sec
24.2mph 38.9kmh/1000rpm
Petrol 4-stroke piston
3340cc 203.8cu in
In-line 6
Compression ratio: 8.2:1
Bore: 86.4mm 3.4in
Stroke: 104.8mm 4.1in
Valve type/No: Overhead 12
Transmission: Automatic
No. of forward speeds: 3
Wheels driven: Rear
Wheelbase: 270.5cm 106.5in
Track F: 142.0cm 55.9in
Track R: 141.2cm 55.6in
Length: 467.9cm 184.2in
Width: 178.8cm 70.4in
Height: 135.6cm 53.4in
Ground clearance: 14.0cm 5.5in
Kerb weight: 1257.6kg 2770.0lb

1283 Dodge

D-100 Sweptline Pickup
1963 USA
91.0mph 146.4kmh
0-50mph 80.5kmh: 7.4secs
0-60mph 96.5kmh: 10.3secs
0-1/4 mile: 18.1secs
202.0bhp 150.6kW 204.8PS
@ 3900rpm
286.0lbft 387.5Nm @ 2400rpm
118.4bhp/ton 116.5bhp/tonne
38.7bhp/L 28.9kW/L 39.3PS/L
35.9ft/sec 10.9m/sec
21.1mph 33.9kmh/1000rpm
Petrol 4-stroke piston
5213cc 318.1cu in
Vee 8 1 Carburettor
Compression ratio: 8.3:1
Bore: 99.3mm 3.9in
Stroke: 84.1mm 3.3in
Valve type/No: Overhead 16
Transmission: Automatic
No. of forward speeds: 3
Wheels driven: Rear
Steering: PA
Wheelbase: 309.9cm 122.0in
Track F: 164.3cm 64.7in
Track R: 160.5cm 63.2in
Length: 543.6cm 214.0in
Width: 203.2cm 80.0in
Height: 176.5cm 69.5in
Ground clearance: 19.6cm 7.7in
Kerb weight: 1734.3kg 3820.0lb
Fuel: 68.1L 15.0gal 18.0galUS

1284 Dodge

Dart 270
1963 USA
95.0mph 152.9kmh
0-50mph 80.5kmh: 8.5secs
0-60mph 96.5kmh: 13.3secs
0-1/4 mile: 19.3secs
145.0bhp 108.1kW 147.0PS
@ 4000rpm
215.0lbft 291.3Nm @ 2400rpm
112.4bhp/ton 110.5bhp/tonne
39.3bhp/L 29.3kW/L 39.9PS/L
45.8ft/sec 13.9m/sec
22.0mph 35.4kmh/1000rpm
Petrol 4-stroke piston
3687cc 224.9cu in
In-line 6 1 Carburettor
Compression ratio: 8.2:1
Bore: 86.4mm 3.4in
Stroke: 104.6mm 4.1in
Valve type/No: Overhead 12
Transmission: Manual
No. of forward speeds: 3
Wheels driven: Rear
Brakes F/R: Drum/Drum
Wheelbase: 281.9cm 111.0in
Track F: 142.0cm 55.9in
Track R: 141.2cm 55.6in
Length: 497.6cm 195.9in
Width: 177.3cm 69.8in
Height: 137.2cm 54.0in
Ground clearance: 14.5cm 5.7in
Kerb weight: 1312.1kg 2890.0lb
Fuel: 68.1L 15.0gal 18.0galUS

1285 Dodge

Dart GT 225 Smogburner
1963 USA
100.0mph 160.9kmh
0-50mph 80.5kmh: 10.0secs
0-60mph 96.5kmh: 14.4secs
0-1/4 mile: 20.0secs
145.0bhp 108.1kW 147.0PS
@ 4000rpm
215.0lbft 291.3Nm @ 2400rpm
115.6bhp/ton 113.7bhp/tonne
39.3bhp/L 29.3kW/L 39.9PS/L
45.9ft/sec 14.0m/sec
24.1mph 38.8kmh/1000rpm
Petrol 4-stroke piston
3687cc 224.9cu in
In-line 6 1 Carburettor
Compression ratio: 8.2:1
Bore: 86.4mm 3.4in
Stroke: 104.9mm 4.1in
Valve type/No: Overhead 12
Transmission: Automatic
No. of forward speeds: 3
Wheels driven: Rear
Brakes F/R: Drum/Drum
Wheelbase: 281.9cm 111.0in
Track F: 142.0cm 55.9in
Track R: 141.2cm 55.6in
Length: 497.6cm 195.9in
Width: 177.3cm 69.8in
Height: 137.2cm 54.0in
Ground clearance: 14.5cm 5.7in
Kerb weight: 1275.7kg 2810.0lb
Fuel: 68.1L 15.0gal 18.0galUS

1286 Dodge

Polara
1963 USA
115.0mph 185.0kmh
0-50mph 80.5kmh: 7.2secs
0-60mph 96.5kmh: 9.6secs
0-1/4 mile: 17.2secs
305.0bhp 227.4kW 309.2PS
@ 4600rpm
410.0lbft 555.6Nm @ 2400rpm
181.2bhp/ton 178.2bhp/tonne
48.6bhp/L 36.2kW/L 49.3PS/L
43.2ft/sec 13.2m/sec
24.0mph 38.6kmh/1000rpm
Petrol 4-stroke piston
6276cc 382.9cu in
Vee 8 1 Carburettor
Compression ratio: 10.0:1
Bore: 108.0mm 4.2in
Stroke: 85.9mm 3.4in
Valve type/No: Overhead 16
Transmission: Automatic
No. of forward speeds: 3
Wheels driven: Rear
Brake system: PA
Steering: PA
Wheelbase: 302.3cm 119.0in
Track F: 150.9cm 59.4in
Track R: 146.1cm 57.5in
Length: 528.8cm 208.2in
Width: 194.3cm 76.5in
Height: 136.9cm 53.9in
Kerb weight: 1711.6kg 3770.0lb
Fuel: 75.7L 16.6gal 20.0galUS

1287 Dodge

Ramcharger 426 Super/Stock
1963 USA
115.0mph 185.0kmh
0-50mph 80.5kmh: 3.3secs
0-60mph 96.5kmh: 4.2secs
0-1/4 mile: 12.5secs
425.0bhp 316.9kW 430.9PS
@ 5600rpm
480.0lbft 650.4Nm @ 4400rpm
295.8bhp/ton 290.9bhp/tonne
60.9bhp/L 45.4kW/L 61.7PS/L
58.3ft/sec 17.8m/sec
17.7mph 28.5kmh/1000rpm
Petrol 4-stroke piston
6981cc 425.9cu in
Vee 8 2 Carburettor
Compression ratio: 13.5:1
Bore: 108.0mm 4.2in
Stroke: 95.3mm 3.8in
Valve type/No: Overhead 16
Transmission: Automatic
No. of forward speeds: 3
Wheels driven: Rear
Brakes F/R: Drum/Drum
Wheelbase: 302.3cm 119.0in
Track F: 151.1cm 59.5in
Track R: 146.1cm 57.5in
Length: 528.6cm 208.1in
Width: 194.3cm 76.5in
Height: 137.4cm 54.1in
Ground clearance: 13.5cm 5.3in
Kerb weight: 1461.0kg 3218.0lb
Fuel: 75.7L 16.6gal 20.0galUS

1288 Dodge

Dart GT
1964 USA
102.0mph 164.1kmh
0-50mph 80.5kmh: 8.2secs
0-60mph 96.5kmh: 12.1secs
0-1/4 mile: 17.5secs
180.0bhp 134.2kW 182.5PS
@ 4200rpm
260.0lbft 352.3Nm @ 1600rpm
128.0bhp/ton 125.9bhp/tonne
40.2bhp/L 29.9kW/L 40.7PS/L
38.6ft/sec 11.8m/sec
24.1mph 38.8kmh/1000rpm
Petrol 4-stroke piston
4482cc 273.5cu in
Vee 8 1 Carburettor
Compression ratio: 8.8:1
Bore: 92.2mm 3.6in
Stroke: 84.1mm 3.3in
Valve type/No: Overhead 16
Transmission: Manual
No. of forward speeds: 4
Wheels driven: Rear
Steering: PA
Wheelbase: 281.9cm 111.0in
Track F: 142.0cm 55.9in
Track R: 141.2cm 55.6in
Length: 498.6cm 196.3in
Width: 177.3cm 69.8in

Height: 137.2cm 54.0in
Ground clearance: 14.7cm 5.8in
Kerb weight: 1430.1kg 3150.0lb
Fuel: 68.1L 15.0gal 18.0galUS

1289 Dodge

Polara
1964 USA
118.0mph 189.9kmh
0-50mph 80.5kmh: 6.3secs
0-60mph 96.5kmh: 8.4secs
0-1/4 mile: 16.2secs
330.0bhp 246.1kW 334.6PS
@ 4600rpm
425.0lbft 575.9Nm @ 2800rpm
198.7bhp/ton 195.4bhp/tonne
52.6bhp/L 39.2kW/L 53.3PS/L
43.2ft/sec 13.2m/sec
23.6mph 38.0kmh/1000rpm
Petrol 4-stroke piston
6276cc 382.9cu in
Vee 8 1 Carburettor
Compression ratio: 10.0:1
Bore: 108.0mm 4.2in
Stroke: 85.9mm 3.4in
Valve type/No: Overhead 16
Transmission: Automatic
No. of forward speeds: 3
Wheels driven: Rear
Brake system: PA
Steering: PA
Wheelbase: 302.3cm 119.0in
Track F: 151.1cm 59.5in
Track R: 151.4cm 59.6in
Length: 532.9cm 209.8in
Width: 190.2cm 74.9in
Height: 140.0cm 55.1in
Ground clearance: 13.5cm 5.3in
Kerb weight: 1688.9kg 3720.0lb
Fuel: 71.9L 15.8gal 19.0galUS

1290 Dodge

Polara 500
1964 USA
125.0mph 201.1kmh
0-50mph 80.5kmh: 5.5secs
0-60mph 96.5kmh: 7.2secs
0-1/4 mile: 15.2secs
365.0bhp 272.2kW 370.1PS
@ 4800rpm
470.0lbft 636.9Nm @ 3200rpm
202.4bhp/ton 199.0bhp/tonne
52.3bhp/L 39.0kW/L 53.0PS/L
50.0ft/sec 15.2m/sec
23.6mph 38.0kmh/1000rpm
Petrol 4-stroke piston
6981cc 425.9cu in
Vee 8 1 Carburettor
Compression ratio: 10.3:1
Bore: 108.0mm 4.2in
Stroke: 95.3mm 3.8in
Valve type/No: Overhead 16
Transmission: Manual
No. of forward speeds: 4
Wheels driven: Rear
Brake system: PA
Steering: PA
Wheelbase: 302.3cm 119.0in
Track F: 151.1cm 59.5in
Track R: 151.1cm 59.5in
Length: 532.9cm 209.8in
Width: 190.2cm 74.9in
Height: 138.2cm 54.4in
Ground clearance: 13.5cm 5.3in
Kerb weight: 1834.2kg 4040.0lb
Fuel: 71.9L 15.8gal 19.0galUS

1291 Dodge

Safari Super Sport
1964 USA
50.2mph 80.8kmh
0-50mph 80.5kmh: 40.2secs
0-1/4 mile: 29.3secs
125.0bhp 93.2kW 126.7PS
@ 3600rpm
216.0lbft 292.7Nm @ 1200rpm
56.4bhp/ton 55.4bhp/tonne
30.4bhp/L 22.7kW/L 30.8PS/L
45.0ft/sec 13.7m/sec
17.9mph 28.8kmh/1000rpm
Petrol 4-stroke piston
4113cc 250.9cu in
In-line 6 1 Carburettor
Compression ratio: 7.1:1
Bore: 87.4mm 3.4in
Stroke: 114.3mm 4.5in
Valve type/No: Side 12
Transmission: Manual
No. of forward speeds: 4
Wheels driven: 4-wheel engageable
Wheelbase: 320.0cm 126.0in
Track F: 164.6cm 64.8in
Track R: 164.6cm 64.8in
Length: 502.7cm 197.9in
Width: 197.6cm 77.8in
Height: 204.5cm 80.5in
Ground clearance: 39.4cm 15.5in
Kerb weight: 2254.1kg 4965.0lb
Fuel: 75.7L 16.6gal 20.0galUS

1292 Dodge

A-100 Super/Surfer
1965 USA
90.0mph 144.8kmh
0-50mph 80.5kmh: 9.5secs
0-60mph 96.5kmh: 13.1secs
0-1/4 mile: 19.7secs
174.0bhp 129.7kW 176.4PS
@ 3900rpm
246.0lbft 333.3Nm @ 2000rpm
104.2bhp/ton 102.5bhp/tonne
38.8bhp/L 28.9kW/L 39.4PS/L
35.9ft/sec 10.9m/sec
22.1mph 35.6kmh/1000rpm
Petrol 4-stroke piston
4482cc 273.5cu in
Vee 8 1 Carburettor
Compression ratio: 8.8:1
Bore: 92.2mm 3.6in
Stroke: 84.1mm 3.3in
Valve type/No: Overhead 16
Transmission: Automatic
No. of forward speeds: 3
Wheels driven: Rear
Wheelbase: 228.6cm 90.0in
Track F: 152.9cm 60.2in
Track R: 152.7cm 60.1in
Length: 434.3cm 171.0in
Width: 193.3cm 76.1in
Height: 198.6cm 78.2in
Ground clearance: 16.5cm 6.5in
Kerb weight: 1698.0kg 3740.0lb
Fuel: 79.5L 17.5gal 21.0galUS

1293 Dodge

Coronet
1965 USA
99.0mph 159.3kmh
0-50mph 80.5kmh: 8.4secs
0-60mph 96.5kmh: 11.8secs
0-1/4 mile: 18.3secs
180.0bhp 134.2kW 182.5PS
@ 4200rpm
260.0lbft 352.3Nm @ 1600rpm
120.7bhp/ton 118.7bhp/tonne
40.2bhp/L 30.0kW/L 40.8PS/L
38.6ft/sec 11.8m/sec
24.7mph 39.7kmh/1000rpm
Petrol 4-stroke piston
4474cc 273.0cu in
Vee 8 1 Carburettor
Compression ratio: 8.8:1
Bore: 92.2mm 3.6in
Stroke: 84.1mm 3.3in
Valve type/No: Overhead 16
Transmission: Automatic
No. of forward speeds: 3
Wheels driven: Rear
Steering: PA
Wheelbase: 297.2cm 117.0in
Track F: 151.1cm 59.5in
Track R: 148.6cm 58.5in
Length: 518.7cm 204.2in
Width: 190.5cm 75.0in
Height: 139.4cm 54.9in
Ground clearance: 13.0cm 5.1in
Kerb weight: 1516.4kg 3340.0lb
Fuel: 71.9L 15.8gal 19.0galUS

1294 Dodge

Coronet 426-S
1965 USA
120.0mph 193.1kmh
0-50mph 80.5kmh: 6.1secs
0-60mph 96.5kmh: 7.8secs
0-1/4 mile: 15.4secs
365.0bhp 272.2kW 370.1PS
@ 4800rpm
470.0lbft 636.9Nm @ 3200rpm
210.5bhp/ton 207.0bhp/tonne
52.3bhp/L 39.0kW/L 53.0PS/L
50.0ft/sec 15.2m/sec
23.6mph 38.0kmh/1000rpm
Petrol 4-stroke piston
6981cc 425.9cu in
Vee 8 1 Carburettor
Compression ratio: 10.3:1
Bore: 108.0mm 4.2in
Stroke: 95.3mm 3.8in
Valve type/No: Overhead 16
Transmission: Manual
No. of forward speeds: 4
Wheels driven: Rear
Wheelbase: 297.2cm 117.0in
Track F: 151.1cm 59.5in
Track R: 148.6cm 58.5in
Length: 518.7cm 204.2in
Width: 190.5cm 75.0in
Height: 137.7cm 54.2in
Ground clearance: 13.0cm 5.1in
Kerb weight: 1763.3kg 3884.0lb
Fuel: 71.9L 15.8gal 19.0galUS

1295 Dodge

Coronet 440
1965 USA
105.0mph 168.9kmh
0-50mph 80.5kmh: 6.9secs
0-60mph 96.5kmh: 9.3secs
0-1/4 mile: 17.0secs
265.0bhp 197.6kW 268.7PS
@ 4400rpm
380.0lbft 514.9Nm @ 2400rpm
163.5bhp/ton 160.8bhp/tonne
44.8bhp/L 33.4kW/L 45.4PS/L
41.3ft/sec 12.6m/sec
23.9mph 38.5kmh/1000rpm
Petrol 4-stroke piston
5916cc 360.9cu in
Vee 8 1 Carburettor
Compression ratio: 9.0:1
Bore: 104.6mm 4.1in
Stroke: 85.9mm 3.4in
Valve type/No: Overhead 16
Transmission: Automatic
No. of forward speeds: 3
Wheels driven: Rear
Brake system: PA
Steering: PA
Wheelbase: 297.2cm 117.0in
Track F: 151.1cm 59.5in
Track R: 148.6cm 58.5in
Length: 518.7cm 204.2in
Width: 190.5cm 75.0in
Height: 139.4cm 54.9in
Ground clearance: 13.0cm 5.1in
Kerb weight: 1648.0kg 3630.0lb
Fuel: 71.9L 15.8gal 19.0galUS

1296 Dodge

Coronet 500
1965 USA
115.0mph 185.0kmh
0-50mph 80.5kmh: 6.2secs
0-60mph 96.5kmh: 8.0secs
0-1/4 mile: 15.8secs
330.0bhp 246.1kW 334.6PS
@ 4600rpm
425.0lbft 575.9Nm @ 2800rpm
197.6bhp/ton 194.3bhp/tonne
52.6bhp/L 39.2kW/L 53.3PS/L
43.2ft/sec 13.2m/sec
23.9mph 38.5kmh/1000rpm
Petrol 4-stroke piston
6276cc 382.9cu in
Vee 8 1 Carburettor
Compression ratio: 10.0:1
Bore: 108.0mm 4.2in
Stroke: 85.9mm 3.4in
Valve type/No: Overhead 16
Transmission: Automatic
No. of forward speeds: 3
Wheels driven: Rear
Brake system: PA
Steering: PA
Wheelbase: 297.2cm 117.0in
Track F: 151.1cm 59.5in
Track R: 148.6cm 58.5in
Length: 518.7cm 204.2in
Width: 190.5cm 75.0in
Height: 137.7cm 54.2in
Ground clearance: 13.0cm 5.1in
Kerb weight: 1698.0kg 3740.0lb
Fuel: 71.9L 15.8gal 19.0galUS

1297 Dodge

Dart GT
1965 USA
115.0mph 185.0kmh
0-50mph 80.5kmh: 7.4secs
0-60mph 96.5kmh: 9.3secs
0-1/4 mile: 16.4secs
235.0bhp 175.2kW 238.3PS
@ 5200rpm
280.0lbft 379.4Nm @ 4000rpm
164.0bhp/ton 161.2bhp/tonne
52.4bhp/L 39.1kW/L 53.2PS/L
47.8ft/sec 14.6m/sec
21.7mph 34.9kmh/1000rpm
Petrol 4-stroke piston
4482cc 273.5cu in
Vee 8 1 Carburettor
Compression ratio: 10.5:1
Bore: 92.2mm 3.6in
Stroke: 84.1mm 3.3in
Valve type/No: Overhead 16
Transmission: Manual
No. of forward speeds: 4
Wheels driven: Rear
Brakes F/R: Disc/Drum
Steering: PA
Wheelbase: 281.9cm 111.0in
Track F: 142.0cm 55.9in
Track R: 141.2cm 55.6in
Length: 498.9cm 196.4in
Width: 177.3cm 69.8in
Height: 136.7cm 53.8in
Ground clearance: 14.0cm 5.5in
Kerb weight: 1457.3kg 3210.0lb
Fuel: 68.1L 15.0gal 18.0galUS

1298 Dodge

Charger
1966 USA
120.0mph 193.1kmh
0-50mph 80.5kmh: 5.6secs
0-60mph 96.5kmh: 7.2secs
0-1/4 mile: 15.6secs
325.0bhp 242.3kW 329.5PS
@ 4800rpm
425.0lbft 575.9Nm @ 2800rpm
182.5bhp/ton 179.4bhp/tonne
51.8bhp/L 38.6kW/L 52.5PS/L
45.1ft/sec 13.7m/sec
23.3mph 37.5kmh/1000rpm
Petrol 4-stroke piston
6276cc 382.9cu in
Vee 8 1 Carburettor
Compression ratio: 10.0:1
Bore: 108.0mm 4.2in
Stroke: 85.9mm 3.4in
Valve type/No: Overhead 16
Transmission: Automatic
No. of forward speeds: 3
Wheels driven: Rear
Springs F/R: Torsion bar/Leaf
Brake system: PA
Brakes F/R: Drum/Drum
Steering: Rack & sector PA
Wheelbase: 297.2cm 117.0in
Track F: 151.1cm 59.5in
Track R: 148.6cm 58.5in
Length: 517.1cm 203.6in
Width: 191.3cm 75.3in
Height: 134.6cm 53.0in
Ground clearance: 19.8cm 7.8in
Kerb weight: 1811.5kg 3990.0lb
Fuel: 71.9L 15.8gal 19.0galUS

1299 Dodge

Charger
1967 USA
134.0mph 215.6kmh
0-50mph 80.5kmh: 5.1secs
0-60mph 96.5kmh: 6.4secs
0-1/4 mile: 14.2secs
425.0bhp 316.9kW 430.9PS
@ 5000rpm
490.0lbft 664.0Nm @ 4000rpm
228.8bhp/ton 225.0bhp/tonne
61.0bhp/L 45.5kW/L 61.8PS/L
52.1ft/sec 15.9m/sec
22.4mph 36.0kmh/1000rpm
Petrol 4-stroke piston
6971cc 425.3cu in
Vee 8 2 Carburettor
Compression ratio: 10.3:1
Bore: 108.0mm 4.2in
Stroke: 95.3mm 3.8in
Valve type/No: Overhead 16
Transmission: Automatic
No. of forward speeds: 3
Wheels driven: Rear
Springs F/R: Torsion bar/Leaf
Brake system: PA

Brakes F/R: Disc/Drum
Steering: Recirculating ball PA
Wheelbase: 297.2cm 117.0in
Track F: 151.1cm 59.5in
Track R: 148.6cm 58.5in
Length: 517.1cm 203.6in
Width: 191.3cm 75.3in
Height: 136.7cm 53.8in
Ground clearance: 15.5cm 6.1in
Kerb weight: 1888.6kg 4160.0lb
Fuel: 71.9L 15.8gal 19.0galUS

1300 Dodge

Coronet R/T
1967 USA
113.0mph 181.8kmh
0-50mph 80.5kmh: 6.5secs
0-60mph 96.5kmh: 8.6secs
0-1/4 mile: 16.6secs
375.0bhp 279.6kW 380.2PS
@ 4600rpm
480.0lbft 650.4Nm @ 3200rpm
219.3bhp/ton 215.7bhp/tonne
52.0bhp/L 38.8kW/L 52.8PS/L
47.9ft/sec 14.6m/sec
23.1mph 37.2kmh/1000rpm
Petrol 4-stroke piston
7206cc 439.7cu in
Vee 8 1 Carburettor
Compression ratio: 10.0:1
Bore: 110.0mm 4.3in
Stroke: 95.2mm 3.8in
Valve type/No: Overhead 16
Transmission: Automatic
No. of forward speeds: 3
Wheels driven: Rear
Springs F/R: Torsion bar/Leaf
Brake system: PA
Brakes F/R: Disc/Drum
Steering: Recirculating ball PA
Wheelbase: 297.2cm 117.0in
Track F: 151.1cm 59.5in
Track R: 148.6cm 58.5in
Length: 515.6cm 203.0in
Width: 191.3cm 75.3in
Height: 136.9cm 53.9in
Ground clearance: 14.0cm 5.5in
Kerb weight: 1738.8kg 3830.0lb
Fuel: 71.9L 15.8gal 19.0galUS

1301 Dodge

Dart 270
1967 USA
96.0mph 154.5kmh
0-50mph 80.5kmh: 11.0secs
0-60mph 96.5kmh: 15.1secs
0-1/4 mile: 19.3secs
145.0bhp 108.1kW 147.0PS
@ 4000rpm
214.0lbft 290.0Nm @ 2400rpm
97.5bhp/ton 95.9bhp/tonne
39.4bhp/L 29.4kW/L 39.9PS/L
45.9ft/sec 14.0m/sec
23.1mph 37.2kmh/1000rpm
Petrol 4-stroke piston
3680cc 224.5cu in
In-line 6 1 Carburettor
Compression ratio: 8.4:1
Bore: 86.4mm 3.4in
Stroke: 104.8mm 4.1in
Valve type/No: Overhead 12
Transmission: Automatic
No. of forward speeds: 3
Wheels driven: Rear
Springs F/R: Torsion bar/Leaf
Brakes F/R: Drum/Drum
Steering: Recirculating ball PA
Wheelbase: 281.9cm 111.0in
Track F: 145.8cm 57.4in
Track R: 141.2cm 55.6in
Length: 496.3cm 195.4in
Width: 177.0cm 69.7in
Height: 136.1cm 53.6in
Ground clearance: 18.0cm 7.1in
Kerb weight: 1511.8kg 3330.0lb
Fuel: 68.1L 15.0gal 18.0galUS

1302 Dodge

Monaco Wagon
1967 USA
108.0mph 173.8kmh
0-50mph 80.5kmh: 8.5secs
0-60mph 96.5kmh: 11.5secs
0-1/4 mile: 18.0secs
325.0bhp 242.3kW 329.5PS
@ 4800rpm
425.0lbft 575.9Nm @ 2800rpm
156.9bhp/ton 154.3bhp/tonne
51.7bhp/L 38.5kW/L 52.4PS/L
45.1ft/sec 13.7m/sec
24.0mph 38.6kmh/1000rpm
Petrol 4-stroke piston
6287cc 383.6cu in
Vee 8 1 Carburettor
Compression ratio: 10.0:1
Bore: 108.0mm 4.2in
Stroke: 85.9mm 3.4in
Valve type/No: Overhead 16
Transmission: Automatic
No. of forward speeds: 3
Wheels driven: Rear
Springs F/R: Torsion bar/Leaf
Brake system: PA
Brakes F/R: Drum/Drum
Steering: Rack & sector PA
Wheelbase: 309.9cm 122.0in
Track F: 157.5cm 62.0in
Track R: 154.2cm 60.7in
Length: 562.1cm 221.3in
Width: 202.7cm 79.8in
Height: 143.3cm 56.4in
Ground clearance: 13.5cm 5.3in
Kerb weight: 2106.6kg 4640.0lb
Fuel: 83.3L 18.3gal 22.0galUS

1303 Dodge

Charger R/T
1968 USA
132.0mph 212.4kmh
0-50mph 80.5kmh: 5.9secs
0-60mph 96.5kmh: 7.6secs
0-1/4 mile: 15.4secs
425.0bhp 316.9kW 430.9PS
@ 5000rpm
490.0lbft 664.0Nm @ 4000rpm
241.6bhp/ton 237.6bhp/tonne
60.9bhp/L 45.4kW/L 61.8PS/L
52.1ft/sec 15.9m/sec
24.3mph 39.1kmh/1000rpm
Petrol 4-stroke piston
6974cc 425.5cu in
Vee 8 2 Carburettor
Compression ratio: 10.3:1
Bore: 108.0mm 4.2in
Stroke: 95.3mm 3.8in
Valve type/No: Overhead 16
Transmission: Automatic
No. of forward speeds: 3
Wheels driven: Rear
Springs F/R: Torsion bar/Leaf
Brake system: PA
Brakes F/R: Disc/Drum
Steering: Recirculating ball PA
Wheelbase: 297.2cm 117.0in
Track F: 151.1cm 59.5in
Track R: 150.4cm 59.2in
Length: 528.3cm 208.0in
Width: 194.6cm 76.6in
Height: 135.1cm 53.2in
Ground clearance: 16.8cm 6.6in
Kerb weight: 1788.8kg 3940.0lb
Fuel: 71.9L 15.8gal 19.0galUS

1304 Dodge

Coronet R/T
1968 USA
123.0mph 197.9kmh
0-50mph 80.5kmh: 5.0secs
0-60mph 96.5kmh: 6.6secs
0-1/4 mile: 14.7secs
375.0bhp 279.6kW 380.2PS
@ 4600rpm
480.0lbft 650.4Nm @ 3200rpm
218.5bhp/ton 214.8bhp/tonne
52.0bhp/L 38.8kW/L 52.7PS/L
47.9ft/sec 14.6m/sec
23.5mph 37.8kmh/1000rpm
Petrol 4-stroke piston
7210cc 439.9cu in
Vee 8 1 Carburettor
Compression ratio: 10.0:1
Bore: 109.7mm 4.3in
Stroke: 95.3mm 3.8in
Valve type/No: Overhead 16
Transmission: Automatic
No. of forward speeds: 3
Wheels driven: Rear
Springs F/R: Torsion bar/Leaf
Brake system: PA
Brakes F/R: Disc/Drum
Steering: Recirculating ball PA
Wheelbase: 297.2cm 117.0in
Track F: 151.1cm 59.5in
Track R: 150.4cm 59.2in
Length: 524.8cm 206.6in
Width: 194.8cm 76.7in
Height: 133.4cm 52.5in
Ground clearance: 16.0cm 6.3in
Kerb weight: 1745.6kg 3845.0lb
Fuel: 71.9L 15.8gal 19.0galUS

1305 Dodge

Dart GTS
1968 USA
122.0mph 196.3kmh
0-50mph 80.5kmh: 5.0secs
0-60mph 96.5kmh: 6.3secs
0-1/4 mile: 14.7secs
275.0bhp 205.1kW 278.8PS
@ 5000rpm
340.0lbft 460.7Nm @ 3200rpm
186.4bhp/ton 183.3bhp/tonne
49.3bhp/L 36.8kW/L 50.0PS/L
46.0ft/sec 14.0m/sec
23.2mph 37.3kmh/1000rpm
Petrol 4-stroke piston
5572cc 340.0cu in
Vee 8 1 Carburettor
Compression ratio: 10.5:1
Bore: 102.6mm 4.0in
Stroke: 84.1mm 3.3in
Valve type/No: Overhead 16
Transmission: Automatic
No. of forward speeds: 3
Wheels driven: Rear
Springs F/R: Torsion bar/Leaf
Brake system: PA
Brakes F/R: Disc/Drum
Steering: Recirculating ball PA
Wheelbase: 281.9cm 111.0in
Track F: 145.8cm 57.4in
Track R: 141.2cm 55.6in
Length: 496.3cm 195.4in
Width: 177.0cm 69.7in
Height: 134.4cm 52.9in
Ground clearance: 15.5cm 6.1in
Kerb weight: 1500.5kg 3305.0lb
Fuel: 68.1L 15.0gal 18.0galUS

1306 Dodge

Dart GTS 340
1968 USA
122.0mph 196.3kmh
0-50mph 80.5kmh: 5.0secs
0-60mph 96.5kmh: 6.3secs
0-1/4 mile: 14.7secs
275.0bhp 205.1kW 278.8PS
@ 5000rpm
186.4bhp/ton 183.3bhp/tonne
49.3bhp/L 36.8kW/L 50.0PS/L
46.0ft/sec 14.0m/sec
23.2mph 37.3kmh/1000rpm
Petrol 4-stroke piston
5572cc 340.0cu in
Vee 8
Compression ratio: 10.5:1
Bore: 102.6mm 4.0in
Stroke: 84.1mm 3.3in
Valve type/No: Overhead 16
Transmission: Automatic
No. of forward speeds: 3
Wheels driven: Rear
Springs F/R: Torsion bar/Leaf
Brake system: PA
Brakes F/R: Disc/Drum
Steering: Recirculating ball PA
Wheelbase: 281.9cm 111.0in
Length: 496.3cm 195.4in
Width: 177.0cm 69.7in
Height: 134.4cm 52.9in
Kerb weight: 1500.5kg 3305.0lb

1307 Dodge

Coronet 500 Station Wagon
1969 USA
126.0mph 202.7kmh
0-50mph 80.5kmh: 4.8secs
0-60mph 96.5kmh: 6.5secs
0-1/4 mile: 16.0secs
330.0bhp 246.1kW 334.6PS
@ 5000rpm
425.0lbft 575.9Nm @ 3200rpm
175.6bhp/ton 172.6bhp/tonne
52.6bhp/L 39.2kW/L 53.3PS/L
46.9ft/sec 14.3m/sec
25.3mph 40.7kmh/1000rpm
Petrol 4-stroke piston
6276cc 382.9cu in
Vee 8 1 Carburettor
Compression ratio: 10.0:1
Bore: 108.0mm 4.2in
Stroke: 85.9mm 3.4in
Valve type/No: Overhead 16
Transmission: Automatic
No. of forward speeds: 3
Wheels driven: Rear
Springs F/R: Coil/Leaf
Brake system: PA
Brakes F/R: Drum/Drum
Steering: Recirculating ball PA
Wheelbase: 297.2cm 117.0in
Track F: 151.1cm 59.5in
Track R: 148.6cm 58.5in
Length: 524.8cm 206.6in
Width: 194.6cm 76.6in
Height: 144.8cm 57.0in
Kerb weight: 1911.3kg 4210.0lb
Fuel: 71.9L 15.8gal 19.0galUS

1308 Dodge

Hemi Charger 500 Automatic
1969 USA
136.0mph 218.8kmh
0-50mph 80.5kmh: 4.4secs
0-60mph 96.5kmh: 5.7secs
0-1/4 mile: 13.9secs
425.0bhp 316.9kW 430.9PS
@ 5000rpm
490.0lbft 664.0Nm @ 4000rpm
241.0bhp/ton 237.0bhp/tonne
60.9bhp/L 45.4kW/L 61.7PS/L
52.1ft/sec 15.9m/sec
23.9mph 38.5kmh/1000rpm
Petrol 4-stroke piston
6981cc 425.9cu in
Vee 8 2 Carburettor
Compression ratio: 10.3:1
Bore: 108.0mm 4.2in
Stroke: 95.3mm 3.8in
Valve type/No: Overhead 16
Transmission: Automatic
No. of forward speeds: 3
Wheels driven: Rear
Springs F/R: Torsion bar/Leaf
Brake system: PA
Brakes F/R: Disc/Drum
Steering: Recirculating ball PA
Wheelbase: 297.2cm 117.0in
Track F: 152.4cm 60.0in
Track R: 149.9cm 59.0in
Length: 528.3cm 208.0in
Width: 195.6cm 77.0in
Height: 134.6cm 53.0in
Kerb weight: 1793.3kg 3950.0lb
Fuel: 71.9L 15.8gal 19.0galUS

1309 Dodge

Hemi Charger 500 Manual
1969 USA
134.0mph 215.6kmh
0-50mph 80.5kmh: 4.4secs
0-60mph 96.5kmh: 5.7secs
0-1/4 mile: 13.7secs
425.0bhp 316.9kW 430.9PS
@ 5000rpm
490.0lbft 664.0Nm @ 4000rpm
236.5bhp/ton 232.6bhp/tonne
60.9bhp/L 45.4kW/L 61.7PS/L
52.1ft/sec 15.9m/sec
21.8mph 35.1kmh/1000rpm
Petrol 4-stroke piston
6981cc 425.9cu in
Vee 8 2 Carburettor
Compression ratio: 10.3:1
Bore: 108.0mm 4.2in
Stroke: 95.3mm 3.8in
Valve type/No: Overhead 16
Transmission: Manual
No. of forward speeds: 4
Wheels driven: Rear
Springs F/R: Torsion bar/Leaf
Brake system: PA
Brakes F/R: Disc/Drum
Steering: Recirculating ball PA
Wheelbase: 297.2cm 117.0in
Track F: 152.4cm 60.0in
Track R: 149.9cm 59.0in
Length: 528.3cm 208.0in
Width: 195.6cm 77.0in
Height: 134.6cm 53.0in
Kerb weight: 1827.3kg 4025.0lb
Fuel: 71.9L 15.8gal 19.0galUS

1310 Dodge

Monaco

1969 USA
127.0mph 204.3kmh
0-50mph 80.5kmh: 5.9secs
0-60mph 96.5kmh: 7.6secs
0-1/4 mile: 15.5secs
375.0bhp 279.6kW 380.2PS
@ 4600rpm
480.0lbft 650.4Nm @ 3200rpm
189.2bhp/ton 186.0bhp/tonne
52.0bhp/L 38.8kW/L 52.7PS/L
47.9ft/sec 14.6m/sec
24.9mph 40.1kmh/1000rpm
Petrol 4-stroke piston
7210cc 439.9cu in
Vee 8 1 Carburettor
Compression ratio: 10.1:1
Bore: 109.7mm 4.3in
Stroke: 95.3mm 3.8in
Valve type/No: Overhead 16
Transmission: Automatic
No. of forward speeds: 3
Wheels driven: Rear
Springs F/R: Torsion bar/Leaf
Brake system: PA
Brakes F/R: Disc/Drum
Steering: Recirculating ball PA
Wheelbase: 309.9cm 122.0in
Track F: 157.5cm 62.0in
Track R: 154.9cm 61.0in
Length: 561.3cm 221.0in
Width: 200.7cm 79.0in
Height: 139.7cm 55.0in
Kerb weight: 2015.8kg 4440.0lb
Fuel: 90.8L 20.0gal 24.0galUS

1311 Dodge

Super Bee
1969 USA
110.2mph 177.3kmh
0-50mph 80.5kmh: 5.3secs
0-60mph 96.5kmh: 6.6secs
0-1/4 mile: 14.7secs
335.0bhp 249.8kW 339.6PS
@ 5200rpm
425.0lbft 575.9Nm @ 3400rpm
211.1bhp/ton 207.6bhp/tonne
53.4bhp/L 39.8kW/L 54.1PS/L
48.8ft/sec 14.9m/sec
19.0mph 30.6kmh/1000rpm
Petrol 4-stroke piston
6276cc 382.9cu in
Vee 8 1 Carburettor
Compression ratio: 10.0:1
Bore: 108.0mm 4.2in
Stroke: 85.9mm 3.4in
Valve type/No: Overhead 16
Transmission: Automatic
No. of forward speeds: 3
Wheels driven: Rear
Springs F/R: Torsion bar/Leaf
Brake system: PA
Brakes F/R: Disc/Drum
Steering: Recirculating ball PA
Wheelbase: 297.2cm 117.0in
Track F: 151.1cm 59.5in
Track R: 150.4cm 59.2in
Length: 524.8cm 206.6in
Width: 194.8cm 76.7in
Height: 134.9cm 53.1in
Kerb weight: 1614.0kg 3555.0lb
Fuel: 71.9L 15.8gal 19.0galUS

1312 Dodge

Super Bee Six-Pack
1969 USA
117.0mph 188.3kmh
0-50mph 80.5kmh: 4.2secs
0-60mph 96.5kmh: 6.3secs
0-1/4 mile: 13.8secs
390.0bhp 290.8kW 395.4PS
@ 4700rpm
390.0lbft 528.5Nm @ 3600rpm
227.2bhp/ton 223.4bhp/tonne
54.1bhp/L 40.3kW/L 54.8PS/L
49.0ft/sec 14.9m/sec
19.4mph 31.2kmh/1000rpm
Petrol 4-stroke piston
7210cc 439.9cu in
Vee 8 3 Carburettor
Compression ratio: 10.1:1
Bore: 109.7mm 4.3in
Stroke: 95.3mm 3.8in
Valve type/No: Overhead 16
Transmission: Automatic
No. of forward speeds: 3
Wheels driven: Rear
Springs F/R: Torsion bar/Leaf
Brake system: PA
Brakes F/R: Drum/Drum
Steering: Recirculating ball PA
Wheelbase: 297.2cm 117.0in
Track F: 149.9cm 59.0in
Track R: 149.9cm 59.0in
Length: 525.8cm 207.0in
Width: 195.6cm 77.0in
Height: 134.6cm 53.0in
Kerb weight: 1745.6kg 3845.0lb
Fuel: 71.9L 15.8gal 19.0galUS

1313 Dodge

Swinger
1969 USA
121.0mph 194.7kmh
0-50mph 80.5kmh: 5.4secs
0-60mph 96.5kmh: 6.9secs
0-1/4 mile: 14.3secs
275.0bhp 205.1kW 278.8PS
@ 5000rpm
340.0lbft 460.7Nm @ 3200rpm
186.1bhp/ton 183.0bhp/tonne
49.3bhp/L 36.8kW/L 50.0PS/L
46.0ft/sec 14.0m/sec
22.3mph 35.9kmh/1000rpm
Petrol 4-stroke piston
5572cc 340.0cu in
Vee 8 1 Carburettor
Compression ratio: 10.5:1
Bore: 102.6mm 4.0in
Stroke: 84.1mm 3.3in
Valve type/No: Overhead 16
Transmission: Automatic
No. of forward speeds: 3
Wheels driven: Rear
Springs F/R: Torsion bar/Leaf
Brake system: PA
Brakes F/R: Disc/Drum
Steering: Recirculating ball PA
Wheelbase: 281.9cm 111.0in
Track F: 145.8cm 57.4in
Track R: 141.2cm 55.6in
Length: 496.3cm 195.4in
Width: 176.8cm 69.6in
Height: 138.2cm 54.4in
Kerb weight: 1502.7kg 3310.0lb
Fuel: 68.1L 15.0gal 18.0galUS

1314 Dodge

Challenger R/T
1970 USA
128.0mph 206.0kmh
0-50mph 80.5kmh: 5.8secs
0-60mph 96.5kmh: 7.1secs
0-1/4 mile: 14.6secs
390.0bhp 290.8kW 395.4PS
@ 5200rpm
490.0lbft 664.0Nm @ 3200rpm
224.0bhp/ton 220.3bhp/tonne
54.1bhp/L 40.3kW/L 54.8PS/L
54.2ft/sec 16.5m/sec
21.0mph 33.8kmh/1000rpm
12.9mpg 10.7mpgUS 22.0L/100km
Petrol 4-stroke piston
7210cc 439.9cu in
Vee 8 3 Carburettor
Compression ratio: 10.5:1
Bore: 109.8mm 4.3in
Stroke: 95.3mm 3.8in
Valve type/No: Overhead 16
Transmission: Manual
No. of forward speeds: 4
Wheels driven: Rear
Springs F/R: Torsion bar/Leaf
Brake system: PA
Brakes F/R: Disc/Drum
Steering: Recirculating ball PA
Wheelbase: 279.4cm 110.0in
Track F: 151.6cm 59.7in
Track R: 154.2cm 60.7in
Length: 485.9cm 191.3in
Width: 193.3cm 76.1in
Height: 128.5cm 50.6in
Kerb weight: 1770.6kg 3900.0lb
Fuel: 68.1L 15.0gal 18.0galUS

1315 Dodge

Charger R/T
1970 USA
115.0mph 185.0kmh
0-50mph 80.5kmh: 5.8secs
0-60mph 96.5kmh: 7.2secs
0-1/4 mile: 14.7secs
375.0bhp 279.6kW 380.2PS
@ 4600rpm
480.0lbft 650.4Nm @ 3200rpm
201.4bhp/ton 198.1bhp/tonne
52.0bhp/L 38.8kW/L 52.7PS/L
47.9ft/sec 14.6m/sec
20.9mph 33.6kmh/1000rpm
13.9mpg 11.6mpgUS 20.3L/100km
Petrol 4-stroke piston
7210cc 439.9cu in
Vee 8 1 Carburettor
Compression ratio: 9.7:1
Bore: 109.8mm 4.3in
Stroke: 95.3mm 3.8in
Valve type/No: Overhead 16
Transmission: Automatic
No. of forward speeds: 3
Wheels driven: Rear
Springs F/R: Torsion bar/Leaf
Brake system: PA
Brakes F/R: Disc/Drum
Steering: Recirculating ball PA
Wheelbase: 297.2cm 117.0in
Track F: 151.6cm 59.7in
Track R: 150.4cm 59.2in
Length: 528.3cm 208.0in
Width: 194.6cm 76.6in
Height: 134.6cm 53.0in
Kerb weight: 1893.2kg 4170.0lb
Fuel: 71.9L 15.8gal 19.0galUS

1316 Dodge

Colt
1971 Japan
96.0mph 154.5kmh
0-50mph 80.5kmh: 9.2secs
0-60mph 96.5kmh: 13.4secs
0-1/4 mile: 19.3secs
100.0bhp 74.6kW 101.4PS
@ 5600rpm
105.0lbft 142.3Nm @ 3600rpm
106.4bhp/ton 104.6bhp/tonne
62.6bhp/L 46.7kW/L 63.5PS/L
52.7ft/sec 16.0m/sec
18.5mph 29.8kmh/1000rpm
32.2mpg 26.8mpgUS 8.8L/100km
Petrol 4-stroke piston
1597cc 97.4cu in
In-line 4 1 Carburettor
Compression ratio: 8.5:1
Bore: 76.9mm 3.0in
Stroke: 86.0mm 3.4in
Valve type/No: Overhead 8
Transmission: Manual
No. of forward speeds: 4
Wheels driven: Rear
Springs F/R: Coil/Leaf
Brakes F/R: Disc/Drum
Steering: Recirculating ball
Wheelbase: 242.1cm 95.3in
Track F: 128.5cm 50.6in
Track R: 128.5cm 50.6in
Length: 407.9cm 160.6in
Width: 156.0cm 61.4in
Height: 136.1cm 53.6in
Ground clearance: 17.5cm 6.9in
Kerb weight: 955.7kg 2105.0lb
Fuel: 54.9L 12.1gal 14.5galUS

1317 Dodge

Pickup Power Wagon
1971 USA
82.0mph 131.9kmh
0-60mph 96.5kmh: 23.0secs
140.0bhp 104.4kW 141.9PS
@ 3900rpm
215.0lbft 291.3Nm @ 1600rpm
76.7bhp/ton 75.4bhp/tonne
38.0bhp/L 28.3kW/L 38.5PS/L
44.7ft/sec 13.6m/sec
16.8mpg 14.0mpgUS 16.8L/100km
Petrol 4-stroke piston
3687cc 224.9cu in
In-line 6
Compression ratio: 8.4:1
Bore: 86.3mm 3.4in
Stroke: 104.9mm 4.1in
Valve type/No: Overhead 12
Transmission: Manual
No. of forward speeds: 3
Wheels driven: 4-wheel drive
Brake system: PA
Brakes F/R: Drum/Drum
Steering: Recirculating ball PA
Wheelbase: 289.6cm 114.0in
Track F: 158.8cm 62.5in
Track R: 158.8cm 62.5in
Length: 467.9cm 184.2in
Width: 202.7cm 79.8in
Height: 180.8cm 71.2in
Ground clearance: 20.3cm 8.0in
Kerb weight: 1856.9kg 4090.0lb
Fuel: 87.1L 19.1gal 23.0galUS

1318 Dodge

Super/Surver Van
1971 USA
174.0bhp 129.7kW 176.4PS
@ 3900rpm
246.0lbft 333.3Nm @ 2000rpm
104.2bhp/ton 102.5bhp/tonne
38.8bhp/L 28.9kW/L 39.4PS/L
35.9ft/sec 10.9m/sec
Petrol 4-stroke piston
4482cc 273.5cu in
Vee 8
Compression ratio: 8.8:1
Bore: 92.2mm 3.6in
Stroke: 84.1mm 3.3in
Valve type/No: Overhead 16
Transmission: Automatic
No. of forward speeds: 3
Wheels driven: Rear
Wheelbase: 228.6cm 90.0in
Track F: 152.9cm 60.2in
Track R: 152.7cm 60.1in
Length: 434.3cm 171.0in
Width: 193.3cm 76.1in
Height: 198.6cm 78.2in
Ground clearance: 16.5cm 6.5in
Kerb weight: 1698.0kg 3740.0lb

1319 Dodge

Colt Station Wagon
1973 Japan
0-60mph 96.5kmh: 14.4secs
0-1/4 mile: 19.4secs
83.0bhp 61.9kW 84.1PS
@ 5600rpm
89.0lbft 120.6Nm @ 3600rpm
81.7bhp/ton 80.4bhp/tonne
52.0bhp/L 38.7kW/L 52.7PS/L
30.6mpg 25.5mpgUS 9.2L/100km
Petrol 4-stroke piston
1597cc 97.4cu in
In-line 4
Valve type/No: Overhead 8
Transmission: Manual
No. of forward speeds: 4
Wheels driven: Rear
Brakes F/R: Disc/Drum
Wheelbase: 242.1cm 95.3in
Length: 409.4cm 161.2in
Width: 156.0cm 61.4in
Height: 141.0cm 55.5in
Kerb weight: 1032.8kg 2275.0lb

1320 Dodge

Colt GT 2-litre
1974 Japan
102.0mph 164.1kmh
0-50mph 80.5kmh: 10.2secs
0-60mph 96.5kmh: 14.1secs
0-1/4 mile: 19.9secs
94.0bhp 70.1kW 95.3PS
@ 5500rpm
108.0lbft 146.3Nm @ 3600rpm
89.6bhp/ton 88.1bhp/tonne
47.1bhp/L 35.1kW/L 47.8PS/L
54.1ft/sec 16.5m/sec
18.9mph 30.4kmh/1000rpm
24.0mpg 20.0mpgUS 11.8L/100km
Petrol 4-stroke piston
1995cc 121.7cu in
In-line 4 1 Carburettor
Compression ratio: 8.5:1
Bore: 84.0mm 3.3in
Stroke: 90.0mm 3.5in
Valve type/No: Overhead 8
Transmission: Automatic
No. of forward speeds: 3
Wheels driven: Rear
Springs F/R: Coil/Leaf
Brake system: PA
Brakes F/R: Disc/Drum
Steering: Recirculating ball
Wheelbase: 242.1cm 95.3in
Track F: 131.6cm 51.8in
Track R: 130.0cm 51.2in
Length: 437.4cm 172.2in
Width: 161.5cm 63.6in
Height: 134.9cm 53.1in
Ground clearance: 18.0cm 7.1in
Kerb weight: 1066.9kg 2350.0lb
Fuel: 51.1L 11.2gal 13.5galUS

1321 Dodge
Colt GT
1975 Japan
97.0mph 156.1kmh
0-50mph 80.5kmh: 11.5secs
0-60mph 96.5kmh: 16.7secs
0-1/4 mile: 20.3secs
89.0bhp 66.4kW 90.2PS
@ 5200rpm
105.0lbft 142.3Nm @ 3000rpm
84.5bhp/ton 83.1bhp/tonne
44.6bhp/L 33.3kW/L 45.2PS/L
51.1ft/sec 15.6m/sec
22.4mph 36.0kmh/1000rpm
21.6mpg 18.0mpgUS 13.1L/100km
Petrol 4-stroke piston
1995cc 121.7cu in
In-line 4
Compression ratio: 8.5:1
Bore: 84.0mm 3.3in
Stroke: 90.0mm 3.5in
Valve type/No: Overhead 8
Transmission: Manual
No. of forward speeds: 5
Wheels driven: Rear
Springs F/R: Coil/Leaf
Brake system: PA
Brakes F/R: Disc/Drum
Steering: Recirculating ball
Wheelbase: 242.1cm 95.3in
Track F: 131.6cm 51.8in
Track R: 130.3cm 51.3in
Length: 434.6cm 171.1in
Width: 161.5cm 63.6in
Height: 135.9cm 53.5in
Kerb weight: 1071.4kg 2360.0lb
Fuel: 51.1L 11.2gal 13.5galUS

1322 Dodge
Colt Lancer
1977 Japan
96.0mph 154.5kmh
0-50mph 80.5kmh: 8.7secs
0-60mph 96.5kmh: 12.8secs
0-1/4 mile: 19.0secs
83.0bhp 61.9kW 84.1PS
@ 5500rpm
89.0lbft 120.6Nm @ 3500rpm
89.4bhp/ton 87.9bhp/tonne
52.0bhp/L 38.7kW/L 52.7PS/L
51.8ft/sec 15.8m/sec
18.2mph 29.3kmh/1000rpm
37.8mpg 31.5mpgUS 7.5L/100km
Petrol 4-stroke piston
1597cc 97.4cu in
In-line 4 1 Carburettor
Compression ratio: 8.5:1
Bore: 77.0mm 3.0in
Stroke: 86.1mm 3.4in
Valve type/No: Overhead 8
Transmission: Manual
No. of forward speeds: 5
Wheels driven: Rear
Springs F/R: Coil/Leaf
Brake system: PA
Brakes F/R: Disc/Drum
Steering: Recirculating ball
Wheelbase: 233.9cm 92.1in
Track F: 130.0cm 51.2in
Track R: 127.0cm 50.0in
Length: 413.0cm 162.6in
Width: 153.4cm 60.4in
Height: 135.9cm 53.5in
Ground clearance: 16.5cm 6.5in
Kerb weight: 944.3kg 2080.0lb
Fuel: 50.0L 11.0gal 13.2galUS

1323 Dodge
Colt Hatchback
1979 Japan
95.0mph 152.9kmh
0-60mph 96.5kmh: 10.4secs
0-1/4 mile: 18.0secs
80.0bhp 59.7kW 81.1PS
@ 5200rpm
87.0lbft 117.9Nm @ 3000rpm
91.9bhp/ton 90.4bhp/tonne
50.1bhp/L 37.4kW/L 50.8PS/L
49.0ft/sec 14.9m/sec
17.6mph 28.3kmh/1000rpm
38.4mpg 32.0mpgUS 7.4L/100km
Petrol 4-stroke piston
1597cc 97.4cu in
In-line 4 1 Carburettor
Compression ratio: 8.5:1
Bore: 76.9mm 3.0in
Stroke: 86.0mm 3.4in
Valve type/No: Overhead 8
Transmission: Manual
No. of forward speeds: 4
Wheels driven: Front
Springs F/R: Coil/Coil
Brake system: PA
Brakes F/R: Disc/Drum
Steering: Rack & pinion
Wheelbase: 230.1cm 90.6in
Track F: 136.9cm 53.9in
Track R: 134.1cm 52.8in
Length: 398.5cm 156.9in
Width: 158.5cm 62.4in
Height: 128.5cm 50.6in
Ground clearance: 10.9cm 4.3in
Kerb weight: 885.3kg 1950.0lb
Fuel: 37.8L 8.3gal 10.0galUS

1324 Dodge
Aires Wagon
1981 USA
100.0mph 160.9kmh
0-60mph 96.5kmh: 13.1secs
0-1/4 mile: 19.2secs
84.0bhp 62.6kW 85.2PS
@ 4800rpm
111.0lbft 150.4Nm @ 2800rpm
72.1bhp/ton 70.9bhp/tonne
38.0bhp/L 28.3kW/L 38.5PS/L
48.3ft/sec 14.7m/sec
25.0mph 40.2kmh/1000rpm
32.4mpg 27.0mpgUS 8.7L/100km
Petrol 4-stroke piston
2213cc 135.0cu in
In-line 4 1 Carburettor
Compression ratio: 8.5:1
Bore: 87.5mm 3.4in
Stroke: 92.0mm 3.6in
Valve type/No: Overhead 8
Transmission: Manual
No. of forward speeds: 4
Wheels driven: Front
Springs F/R: Coil/Coil
Brake system: PA
Brakes F/R: Disc/Drum
Steering: Rack & pinion
Wheelbase: 253.0cm 99.6in
Track F: 146.3cm 57.6in
Track R: 144.8cm 57.0in
Length: 447.5cm 176.2in
Width: 174.2cm 68.6in
Height: 134.1cm 52.8in
Ground clearance: 11.4cm 4.5in
Kerb weight: 1184.9kg 2610.0lb
Fuel: 49.2L 10.8gal 13.0galUS

1325 Dodge
Challenger
1982 Japan
109.0mph 175.4kmh
0-60mph 96.5kmh: 12.1secs
0-1/4 mile: 18.4secs
100.0bhp 74.6kW 101.4PS
@ 5000rpm
137.0lbft 185.6Nm @ 2500rpm
80.6bhp/ton 79.2bhp/tonne
39.1bhp/L 29.2kW/L 39.7PS/L
53.6ft/sec 16.3m/sec
25.8mpg 21.5mpgUS 10.9L/100km
Petrol 4-stroke piston
2555cc 155.9cu in
In-line 4 1 Carburettor
Compression ratio: 8.2:1
Bore: 91.1mm 3.6in
Stroke: 98.0mm 3.9in
Valve type/No: Overhead 8
Transmission: Manual
No. of forward speeds: 5
Wheels driven: Rear
Springs F/R: Coil/Coil
Brakes F/R: Disc/Disc
Wheelbase: 253.0cm 99.6in
Track F: 137.4cm 54.1in
Track R: 135.4cm 53.3in
Length: 457.2cm 180.0in
Width: 167.4cm 65.9in
Height: 134.1cm 52.8in
Kerb weight: 1262.1kg 2780.0lb
Fuel: 59.8L 13.1gal 15.8galUS

1326 Dodge
Charger 2.2
1982 USA
105.0mph 168.9kmh
0-50mph 80.5kmh: 7.5secs
0-60mph 96.5kmh: 10.1secs
0-1/4 mile: 17.8secs
84.0bhp 62.6kW 85.2PS
@ 4800rpm
111.0lbft 150.4Nm @ 2400rpm
79.4bhp/ton 78.1bhp/tonne
38.0bhp/L 28.3kW/L 38.5PS/L
48.3ft/sec 14.7m/sec
21.0mph 33.8kmh/1000rpm
25.2mpg 21.0mpgUS 11.2L/100km
Petrol 4-stroke piston
2213cc 135.0cu in
In-line 4 1 Carburettor
Compression ratio: 8.5:1
Bore: 87.5mm 3.4in
Stroke: 92.0mm 3.6in
Valve type/No: Overhead 8
Transmission: Manual
No. of forward speeds: 4
Wheels driven: Front
Springs F/R: Coil/Coil
Brake system: PA
Brakes F/R: Disc/Drum
Steering: Rack & pinion PA
Wheelbase: 245.4cm 96.6in
Track F: 142.5cm 56.1in
Track R: 141.2cm 55.6in
Length: 442.0cm 174.0in
Width: 169.4cm 66.7in
Height: 129.0cm 50.8in
Kerb weight: 1076.0kg 2370.0lb
Fuel: 49.2L 10.8gal 13.0galUS

1327 Dodge
600ES
1983 USA
100.0mph 160.9kmh
0-60mph 96.5kmh: 11.8secs
0-1/4 mile: 18.5secs
94.0bhp 70.1kW 95.3PS
@ 5200rpm
117.0lbft 158.5Nm @ 3200rpm
76.0bhp/ton 74.7bhp/tonne
42.5bhp/L 31.7kW/L 43.1PS/L
52.3ft/sec 15.9m/sec
26.1mph 42.0kmh/1000rpm
18.6mpg 15.5mpgUS 15.2L/100km
Petrol 4-stroke piston
2213cc 135.0cu in
In-line 4 1 Carburettor
Compression ratio: 9.0:1
Bore: 87.5mm 3.4in
Stroke: 92.0mm 3.6in
Valve type/No: Overhead 8
Transmission: Manual
No. of forward speeds: 5
Wheels driven: Front
Springs F/R: Coil/Coil
Brakes F/R: Disc/Drum
Wheelbase: 261.6cm 103.0in
Track F: 146.3cm 57.6in
Track R: 144.8cm 57.0in
Length: 475.5cm 187.2in
Width: 173.5cm 68.3in
Height: 134.4cm 52.9in
Kerb weight: 1257.6kg 2770.0lb
Fuel: 49.2L 10.8gal 13.0galUS

1328 Dodge
Shelby Charger
1983 USA
111.0mph 178.6kmh
0-50mph 80.5kmh: 7.3secs
0-60mph 96.5kmh: 10.0secs
0-1/4 mile: 17.5secs
107.0bhp 79.8kW 108.5PS
@ 5600rpm
127.0lbft 172.1Nm @ 3600rpm
98.4bhp/ton 96.8bhp/tonne
48.3bhp/L 36.1kW/L 49.0PS/L
56.3ft/sec 17.2m/sec
24.0mph 38.6kmh/1000rpm
26.4mpg 22.0mpgUS 10.7L/100km
Petrol 4-stroke piston
2213cc 135.0cu in
In-line 4 1 Carburettor
Compression ratio: 9.6:1
Bore: 87.5mm 3.4in
Stroke: 92.0mm 3.6in
Valve type/No: Overhead 8
Transmission: Manual
No. of forward speeds: 5
Wheels driven: Front
Springs F/R: Coil/Coil
Brake system: PA
Brakes F/R: Disc/Drum
Steering: Rack & pinion PA
Wheelbase: 245.4cm 96.6in
Track F: 142.5cm 56.1in
Track R: 141.2cm 55.6in
Length: 441.2cm 173.7in
Width: 169.4cm 66.7in
Height: 126.7cm 49.9in
Kerb weight: 1105.5kg 2435.0lb
Fuel: 49.2L 10.8gal 13.0galUS

1329 Dodge
Colt Vista
1984 Japan
97.0mph 156.1kmh
0-50mph 80.5kmh: 8.8secs
0-60mph 96.5kmh: 13.2secs
0-1/4 mile: 19.0secs
88.0bhp 65.6kW 89.2PS
@ 5000rpm
108.0lbft 146.3Nm @ 3500rpm
74.1bhp/ton 72.9bhp/tonne
44.1bhp/L 32.9kW/L 44.7PS/L
48.1ft/sec 14.7m/sec
22.6mph 36.4kmh/1000rpm
31.2mpg 26.0mpgUS 9.0L/100km
Petrol 4-stroke piston
1997cc 121.8cu in
In-line 4 1 Carburettor
Compression ratio: 8.5:1
Bore: 85.0mm 3.3in
Stroke: 88.0mm 3.5in
Valve type/No: Overhead 8
Transmission: Manual
No. of forward speeds: 4
Wheels driven: Front
Springs F/R: Coil/Coil
Brake system: PA
Brakes F/R: Disc/Drum
Steering: Rack & pinion PA
Wheelbase: 262.4cm 103.3in
Track F: 141.0cm 55.5in
Track R: 137.4cm 54.1in
Length: 443.5cm 174.6in
Width: 164.1cm 64.6in
Height: 151.9cm 59.8in
Ground clearance: 14.0cm 5.5in
Kerb weight: 1207.6kg 2660.0lb
Fuel: 50.0L 11.0gal 13.2galUS

1330 Dodge
Conquest
1984 Japan
0-60mph 96.5kmh: 9.2secs
145.0bhp 108.1kW 147.0PS
@ 5000rpm
185.0lbft 250.7Nm @ 2500rpm
116.0bhp/ton 114.1bhp/tonne
56.7bhp/L 42.3kW/L 57.5PS/L
26.4mpg 22.0mpgUS 10.7L/100km
Petrol 4-stroke piston
2555cc 155.9cu in turbocharged
In-line 4 fuel injection
Valve type/No: Overhead 8
Transmission: Manual
No. of forward speeds: 5
Wheels driven: Rear
Springs F/R: Coil/Coil
Brakes F/R: Disc/Disc
Steering: Recirculating ball PA
Wheelbase: 243.6cm 95.9in
Length: 439.9cm 173.2in
Width: 168.4cm 66.3in
Height: 127.5cm 50.2in
Kerb weight: 1271.2kg 2800.0lb
Fuel: 74.9L 16.5gal 19.8galUS

1331 Dodge
Daytona Turbo Z
1984 USA
101.0mph 162.5kmh
0-50mph 80.5kmh: 6.0secs
0-60mph 96.5kmh: 8.6secs
0-1/4 mile: 16.2secs
142.0bhp 105.9kW 144.0PS
@ 5600rpm
160.0lbft 216.8Nm @ 3600rpm
113.6bhp/ton 111.7bhp/tonne
64.2bhp/L 47.8kW/L 65.1PS/L
56.3ft/sec 17.2m/sec
Petrol 4-stroke piston
2213cc 135.0cu in turbocharged
In-line 4
Compression ratio: 8.1:1
Bore: 87.5mm 3.4in
Stroke: 92.0mm 3.6in
Valve type/No: Overhead 8
Transmission: Manual
No. of forward speeds: 5
Wheels driven: Front

Springs F/R: Coil/Coil
Brakes F/R: Disc/Drum
Steering: Rack & pinion PA
Wheelbase: 232.9cm 91.7in
Track F: 146.3cm 57.6in
Track R: 145.3cm 57.2in
Length: 444.5cm 175.0in
Width: 176.0cm 69.3in
Height: 127.8cm 50.3in
Kerb weight: 1271.2kg 2800.0lb

1332 Dodge
Omni GLH
1985 USA
110.0mph 177.0kmh
0-50mph 80.5kmh: 6.8secs
0-60mph 96.5kmh: 9.4secs
0-1/4 mile: 17.2secs
110.0bhp 82.0kW 111.5PS
@ 5600rpm
129.0lbft 174.8Nm @ 3600rpm
105.7bhp/ton 104.0bhp/tonne
49.7bhp/L 37.1kW/L 50.4PS/L
56.3ft/sec 17.2m/sec
24.0mph 38.6kmh/1000rpm
30.6mpg 25.5mpgUS 9.2L/100km
Petrol 4-stroke piston
2213cc 135.0cu in
In-line 4 1 Carburettor
Compression ratio: 9.6:1
Bore: 87.5mm 3.4in
Stroke: 92.0mm 3.6in
Valve type/No: Overhead 8
Transmission: Manual
No. of forward speeds: 5
Wheels driven: Front
Springs F/R: Coil/Coil
Brakes F/R: Disc/Drum
Steering: Rack & pinion PA
Wheelbase: 251.7cm 99.1in
Track F: 142.5cm 56.1in
Track R: 141.5cm 55.7in
Length: 411.7cm 162.1in
Width: 168.1cm 66.2in
Height: 134.6cm 53.0in
Kerb weight: 1057.8kg 2330.0lb
Fuel: 49.2L 10.8gal 13.0galUS

1333 Dodge
Colt Turbo
1986 Japan
0-60mph 96.5kmh: 9.2secs
0-1/4 mile: 16.8secs
102.0bhp 76.1kW 103.4PS
@ 5500rpm
122.0lbft 165.3Nm @ 3000rpm
63.9bhp/L 47.6kW/L 64.7PS/L
32.4mpg 27.0mpgUS 8.7L/100km
Petrol 4-stroke piston
1597cc 97.4cu in turbocharged
In-line 5
Valve type/No: Overhead 10
Transmission: Manual
No. of forward speeds: 5
Wheels driven: Front
Brakes F/R: Disc/Drum
Steering: Rack & pinion PA
Wheelbase: 238.0cm 93.7in
Length: 424.9cm 167.3in
Width: 162.1cm 63.8in
Height: 129.0cm 50.8in

1334 Dodge
Omni GLH
1986 USA
0-60mph 96.5kmh: 8.1secs
0-1/4 mile: 16.2secs
146.0bhp 108.9kW 148.0PS
@ 5200rpm
168.0lbft 227.6Nm @ 3200rpm
66.0bhp/L 49.2kW/L 66.9PS/L
25.2mpg 21.0mpgUS 11.2L/100km
Petrol 4-stroke piston
2213cc 135.0cu in turbocharged
In-line 4
Valve type/No: Overhead 8
Transmission: Manual
No. of forward speeds: 5
Wheels driven: Front
Brakes F/R: Disc/Drum
Steering: Rack & pinion PA
Wheelbase: 251.7cm 99.1in
Length: 414.5cm 163.2in
Width: 168.1cm 66.2in
Height: 134.6cm 53.0in

1335 Dodge
Shelby GLH-S
1986 USA
120.0mph 193.1kmh
0-50mph 80.5kmh: 4.9secs
0-60mph 96.5kmh: 6.7secs
0-1/4 mile: 15.3secs
175.0bhp 130.5kW 177.4PS
@ 5300rpm
175.0lbft 237.1Nm @ 2200rpm
154.3bhp/ton 151.8bhp/tonne
79.1bhp/L 59.0kW/L 80.2PS/L
53.3ft/sec 16.2m/sec
24.0mpg 20.0mpgUS 11.8L/100km
Petrol 4-stroke piston
2213cc 135.0cu in turbocharged
In-line 4 fuel injection
Compression ratio: 8.5:1
Bore: 87.5mm 3.4in
Stroke: 92.0mm 3.6in
Valve type/No: Overhead 8
Transmission: Manual
No. of forward speeds: 5
Wheels driven: Front
Springs F/R: Coil/Coil
Brake system: PA
Brakes F/R: Disc/Drum
Steering: Rack & pinion PA
Wheelbase: 251.7cm 99.1in
Track F: 142.5cm 56.1in
Track R: 142.5cm 56.1in
Length: 414.5cm 163.2in
Width: 162.1cm 63.8in
Height: 134.6cm 53.0in
Kerb weight: 1153.2kg 2540.0lb
Fuel: 49.2L 10.8gal 13.0galUS

1336 Dodge
Daytona Shelby Z
1988 USA
120.0mph 193.1kmh
0-50mph 80.5kmh: 5.2secs
0-60mph 96.5kmh: 7.2secs
0-1/4 mile: 15.5secs
174.0bhp 129.7kW 176.4PS
@ 5200rpm
200.0lbft 271.0Nm @ 2400rpm
137.2bhp/ton 134.9bhp/tonne
78.6bhp/L 58.6kW/L 79.7PS/L
52.3ft/sec 15.9m/sec
27.6mpg 23.0mpgUS 10.2L/100km
Petrol 4-stroke piston
2213cc 135.0cu in turbocharged
In-line 4 fuel injection
Compression ratio: 8.0:1
Bore: 87.5mm 3.4in
Stroke: 92.0mm 3.6in
Valve type/No: Overhead 8
Transmission: Manual
No. of forward speeds: 5
Wheels driven: Rear
Springs F/R: Coil/Coil
Brake system: PA
Brakes F/R: Disc/Drum
Steering: Rack & pinion PA
Wheelbase: 246.6cm 97.1in
Track F: 146.3cm 57.6in
Track R: 146.3cm 57.6in
Length: 446.8cm 175.9in
Width: 177.3cm 69.8in
Height: 129.0cm 50.8in
Kerb weight: 1289.4kg 2840.0lb
Fuel: 53.0L 11.6gal 14.0galUS

1337 Dodge
Lancer Shelby
1988 USA
118.0mph 189.9kmh
0-50mph 80.5kmh: 5.5secs
0-60mph 96.5kmh: 7.6secs
0-1/4 mile: 15.8secs
174.0bhp 129.7kW 176.4PS
@ 5200rpm
200.0lbft 271.0Nm @ 2400rpm
140.2bhp/ton 137.9bhp/tonne
78.6bhp/L 58.6kW/L 79.7PS/L
52.3ft/sec 15.9m/sec
25.8mpg 21.5mpgUS 10.9L/100km
Petrol 4-stroke piston
2213cc 135.0cu in turbocharged
In-line 4 fuel injection
Compression ratio: 8.0:1
Bore: 87.5mm 3.4in
Stroke: 92.0mm 3.6in
Valve type/No: Overhead 8
Transmission: Manual
No. of forward speeds: 5
Wheels driven: Front
Springs F/R: Coil/Coil
Brake system: PA
Brakes F/R: Disc/Drum
Steering: Rack & pinion PA
Wheelbase: 261.9cm 103.1in
Track F: 146.3cm 57.6in
Track R: 145.3cm 57.2in
Length: 458.0cm 180.3in
Width: 173.5cm 68.3in
Height: 134.6cm 53.0in
Kerb weight: 1262.1kg 2780.0lb
Fuel: 53.0L 11.6gal 14.0galUS

1338 Dodge
Shelby CSX
1988 USA
135.0mph 217.2kmh
0-50mph 80.5kmh: 5.0secs
0-60mph 96.5kmh: 6.9secs
0-1/4 mile: 14.9secs
175.0bhp 130.5kW 177.4PS
@ 5300rpm
200.0lbft 271.0Nm @ 2200rpm
155.6bhp/ton 153.0bhp/tonne
79.1bhp/L 59.0kW/L 80.2PS/L
53.3ft/sec 16.2m/sec
25.8mpg 21.5mpgUS 10.9L/100km
Petrol 4-stroke piston
2213cc 135.0cu in turbocharged
In-line 4 fuel injection
Compression ratio: 8.0:1
Bore: 87.5mm 3.4in
Stroke: 92.0mm 3.6in
Valve type/No: Overhead 8
Transmission: Manual
No. of forward speeds: 5
Wheels driven: Front
Springs F/R: Coil/Coil
Brake system: PA
Brakes F/R: Disc/Disc
Steering: Rack & pinion PA
Wheelbase: 246.4cm 97.0in
Track F: 148.8cm 58.6in
Track R: 147.8cm 58.2in
Length: 436.1cm 171.7in
Width: 170.9cm 67.3in
Height: 132.1cm 52.0in
Kerb weight: 1144.1kg 2520.0lb
Fuel: 53.0L 11.6gal 14.0galUS

1339 Dodge
Daytona Shelby
1989 USA
125.0mph 201.1kmh
0-50mph 80.5kmh: 5.6secs
0-60mph 96.5kmh: 7.5secs
0-1/4 mile: 15.9secs
174.0bhp 129.7kW 176.4PS
@ 5200rpm
200.0lbft 271.0Nm @ 2400rpm
128.8bhp/ton 126.7bhp/tonne
78.6bhp/L 58.6kW/L 79.7PS/L
52.3ft/sec 15.9m/sec
20.3mpg 16.9mpgUS 13.9L/100km
Petrol 4-stroke piston
2213cc 135.0cu in turbocharged
In-line 4 fuel injection
Compression ratio: 8.1:1
Bore: 87.5mm 3.4in
Stroke: 92.0mm 3.6in
Valve type/No: Overhead 8
Transmission: Manual
No. of forward speeds: 5
Wheels driven: Front
Springs F/R: Coil/Coil
Brake system: PA
Brakes F/R: Disc/Disc
Steering: Rack & pinion PA
Wheelbase: 246.4cm 97.0in
Track F: 146.3cm 57.6in
Track R: 146.3cm 57.6in
Length: 455.4cm 179.3in
Width: 176.0cm 69.3in
Height: 130.3cm 51.3in
Kerb weight: 1373.3kg 3025.0lb
Fuel: 53.0L 11.6gal 14.0galUS

1340 Dodge
Shadow ES Turbo
1989 USA
115.0mph 185.0kmh
0-50mph 80.5kmh: 5.5secs
0-60mph 96.5kmh: 7.7secs
0-1/4 mile: 16.0secs
150.0bhp 111.9kW 152.1PS
@ 4800rpm
180.0lbft 243.9Nm @ 2000rpm
121.7bhp/ton 119.7bhp/tonne
60.0bhp/L 44.7kW/L 60.8PS/L
54.5ft/sec 16.6m/sec
22.8mpg 19.0mpgUS 12.4L/100km
Petrol 4-stroke piston
2501cc 152.6cu in turbocharged
In-line 4 fuel injection
Compression ratio: 7.8:1
Bore: 87.5mm 3.4in
Stroke: 104.0mm 4.1in
Valve type/No: Overhead 8
Transmission: Manual
No. of forward speeds: 5
Wheels driven: Front
Springs F/R: Coil/Coil
Brake system: PA
Brakes F/R: Disc/Drum
Steering: Rack & pinion PA
Wheelbase: 246.4cm 97.0in
Track F: 146.3cm 57.6in
Track R: 145.3cm 57.2in
Length: 434.6cm 171.1in
Width: 170.9cm 67.3in
Height: 133.9cm 52.7in
Kerb weight: 1253.0kg 2760.0lb
Fuel: 53.0L 11.6gal 14.0galUS

1341 Dodge
Shelby CSX
1989 USA
140.0mph 225.3kmh
0-60mph 96.5kmh: 7.6secs
0-1/4 mile: 15.7secs
175.0bhp 130.5kW 177.4PS
@ 5200rpm
210.0lbft 284.6Nm @ 2400rpm
140.7bhp/ton 138.4bhp/tonne
79.1bhp/L 59.0kW/L 80.2PS/L
52.3ft/sec 15.9m/sec
24.6mpg 20.5mpgUS 11.5L/100km
Petrol 4-stroke piston
2213cc 135.0cu in turbocharged
In-line 4 fuel injection
Compression ratio: 8.1:1
Bore: 87.5mm 3.4in
Stroke: 92.0mm 3.6in
Valve type/No: Overhead 8
Transmission: Manual
No. of forward speeds: 5
Wheels driven: Front
Springs F/R: Coil/Coil
Brake system: PA
Brakes F/R: Disc/Disc
Steering: Rack & pinion PA
Wheelbase: 246.4cm 97.0in
Track F: 147.6cm 58.1in
Track R: 146.6cm 57.7in
Length: 436.1cm 171.7in
Width: 170.9cm 67.3in
Height: 133.9cm 52.7in
Kerb weight: 1264.4kg 2785.0lb
Fuel: 53.0L 11.6gal 14.0galUS

1342 Dodge
Shelby CSX VNT
1989 USA
120.0mph 193.1kmh
0-50mph 80.5kmh: 5.2secs
0-60mph 96.5kmh: 7.2secs
0-1/4 mile: 15.6secs
175.0bhp 130.5kW 177.4PS
@ 5300rpm
200.0lbft 271.0Nm @ 3700rpm
141.3bhp/ton 138.9bhp/tonne
79.1bhp/L 59.0kW/L 80.2PS/L
53.3ft/sec 16.2m/sec
24.1mpg 20.1mpgUS 11.7L/100km
Petrol 4-stroke piston
2213cc 135.0cu in turbocharged
In-line 4 fuel injection
Compression ratio: 8.1:1
Bore: 87.5mm 3.4in
Stroke: 92.0mm 3.6in
Valve type/No: Overhead 8
Transmission: Manual
No. of forward speeds: 5
Wheels driven: Front
Springs F/R: Coil/Coil
Brake system: PA
Brakes F/R: Disc/Disc
Steering: Rack & pinion PA
Wheelbase: 246.4cm 97.0in
Track F: 147.6cm 58.1in
Track R: 146.6cm 57.7in
Length: 434.6cm 171.1in

Width: 170.9cm 67.3in
Height: 133.9cm 52.7in
Kerb weight: 1259.8kg 2775.0lb
Fuel: 53.0L 11.6gal 14.0galUS

1343 Dodge

Daytona ES
1990 USA
125.0mph 201.1kmh
0-60mph 96.5kmh: 8.4secs
0-1/4 mile: 16.2secs
141.0bhp 105.1kW 143.0PS
@ 5000rpm
171.0lbft 231.7Nm @ 2800rpm
104.2bhp/ton 102.5bhp/tonne
47.4bhp/L 35.4kW/L 48.1PS/L
41.5ft/sec 12.7m/sec
24.6mpg 20.5mpgUS 11.5L/100km
Petrol 4-stroke piston
2972cc 181.3cu in
Vee 6 fuel injection
Compression ratio: 8.9:1
Bore: 91.1mm 3.6in
Stroke: 76.0mm 3.0in
Valve type/No: Overhead 12
Transmission: Manual
No. of forward speeds: 5
Wheels driven: Front
Springs F/R: Coil/Coil
Brake system: PA
Brakes F/R: Disc/Disc
Steering: Rack & pinion PA
Wheelbase: 246.4cm 97.0in
Track F: 146.1cm 57.5in
Track R: 146.3cm 57.6in
Length: 455.2cm 179.2in
Width: 176.0cm 69.3in
Height: 127.3cm 50.1in
Kerb weight: 1375.6kg 3030.0lb
Fuel: 53.0L 11.6gal 14.0galUS

1344 Dodge

Daytona Shelby
1990 USA
135.0mph 217.2kmh
0-60mph 96.5kmh: 7.6secs
0-1/4 mile: 16.0secs
174.0bhp 129.7kW 176.4PS
@ 5200rpm
210.0lbft 284.6Nm @ 2400rpm
128.2bhp/ton 126.1bhp/tonne
78.6bhp/L 58.6kW/L 79.7PS/L
52.3ft/sec 15.9m/sec
27.6mpg 23.0mpgUS 10.2L/100km
Petrol 4-stroke piston
2213cc 135.0cu in turbocharged
In-line 4 fuel injection
Compression ratio: 8.0:1
Bore: 87.5mm 3.4in
Stroke: 92.0mm 3.6in
Valve type/No: Overhead 8
Transmission: Manual
No. of forward speeds: 5
Wheels driven: Front
Springs F/R: Coil/Coil
Brake system: PA
Brakes F/R: Disc/Disc
Steering: Rack & pinion PA
Wheelbase: 246.4cm 97.0in
Track F: 146.1cm 57.5in
Track R: 146.3cm 57.6in
Length: 455.2cm 179.2in
Width: 176.0cm 69.3in
Height: 127.3cm 50.1in
Kerb weight: 1380.2kg 3040.0lb
Fuel: 53.0L 11.6gal 14.0galUS

1345 Dodge

Shadow ES VNT
1990 USA
130.0mph 209.2kmh
0-50mph 80.5kmh: 5.4secs
0-60mph 96.5kmh: 7.3secs
0-1/4 mile: 15.7secs
174.0bhp 129.7kW 176.4PS
@ 5200rpm
210.0lbft 284.6Nm @ 2400rpm
152.8bhp/ton 150.3bhp/tonne
78.6bhp/L 58.6kW/L 79.7PS/L
52.3ft/sec 15.9m/sec
26.3mpg 21.9mpgUS 10.7L/100km
Petrol 4-stroke piston
2213cc 135.0cu in turbocharged
In-line 4 fuel injection
Compression ratio: 8.0:1
Bore: 87.5mm 3.4in
Stroke: 92.0mm 3.6in
Valve type/No: Overhead 8
Transmission: Manual
No. of forward speeds: 5
Wheels driven: Front
Springs F/R: Coil/Coil
Brake system: PA
Brakes F/R: Disc/Disc
Steering: Rack & pinion PA
Wheelbase: 246.4cm 97.0in
Track F: 146.3cm 57.6in
Track R: 145.3cm 57.2in
Length: 436.1cm 171.7in
Width: 170.9cm 67.3in
Height: 128.0cm 50.4in
Kerb weight: 1157.7kg 2550.0lb
Fuel: 53.0L 11.6gal 14.0galUS

1346 Dodge

Spirit R/T
1991 USA
140.0mph 225.3kmh
0-60mph 96.5kmh: 6.5secs
0-1/4 mile: 15.0secs
224.0bhp 167.0kW 227.1PS
@ 6000rpm
217.0lbft 294.0Nm @ 2800rpm
160.6bhp/ton 157.9bhp/tonne
101.6bhp/L 75.8kW/L 103.0PS/L
60.3ft/sec 18.4m/sec
25.8mpg 21.5mpgUS 10.9L/100km
Petrol 4-stroke piston
2205cc 134.5cu in turbocharged
In-line 4 fuel injection
Compression ratio: 8.5:1
Bore: 87.4mm 3.4in
Stroke: 92.0mm 3.6in
Valve type/No: Overhead 16
Transmission: Manual
No. of forward speeds: 5
Wheels driven: Front
Springs F/R: Coil/Coil
Brake system: PA
Brakes F/R: Disc/Disc
Steering: Rack & pinion PA
Wheelbase: 262.4cm 103.3in
Track F: 146.3cm 57.6in
Track R: 145.3cm 57.2in
Length: 460.2cm 181.2in
Width: 173.0cm 68.1in
Height: 135.9cm 53.5in
Kerb weight: 1418.7kg 3125.0lb
Fuel: 60.6L 13.3gal 16.0galUS

1347 Dodge

Stealth R/T Turbo
1991 Japan
159.0mph 255.8kmh
0-50mph 80.5kmh: 4.8secs
0-60mph 96.5kmh: 6.3secs
0-1/4 mile: 14.7secs
300.0bhp 223.7kW 304.2PS
@ 6000rpm
307.0lbft 416.0Nm @ 2500rpm
177.1bhp/ton 174.1bhp/tonne
100.9bhp/L 75.3kW/L 102.3PS/L
49.8ft/sec 15.2m/sec
21.6mpg 18.0mpgUS 13.1L/100km
Petrol 4-stroke piston
2972cc 181.3cu in turbocharged
Vee 6 fuel injection
Compression ratio: 8.0:1
Bore: 91.1mm 3.6in
Stroke: 76.0mm 3.0in
Valve type/No: Overhead 24
Transmission: Manual
No. of forward speeds: 5
Wheels driven: 4-wheel drive
Springs F/R: Coil/Coil
Brake system: PA ABS
Brakes F/R: Disc/Disc
Steering: Rack & pinion PA
Wheelbase: 246.9cm 97.2in
Track F: 156.0cm 61.4in
Track R: 158.0cm 62.2in
Length: 458.5cm 180.5in
Width: 183.9cm 72.4in
Height: 124.7cm 49.1in
Kerb weight: 1722.9kg 3795.0lb
Fuel: 74.9L 16.5gal 19.8galUS

1348 Dodge

Viper
1992 USA
190.0mph 305.7kmh
0-60mph 96.5kmh: 4.1secs
0-1/4 mile: 12.5secs
400.0bhp 298.3kW 405.5PS
@ 5500rpm
450.0lbft 609.8Nm @ 2200rpm
299.7bhp/ton 294.7bhp/tonne
50.1bhp/L 37.3kW/L 50.8PS/L
59.3ft/sec 18.1m/sec
Petrol 4-stroke piston
7989cc 487.4cu in
Vee 10 fuel injection
Bore: 101.6mm 4.0in
Stroke: 98.6mm 3.9in
Valve type/No: Overhead 20
Transmission: Manual
No. of forward speeds: 6
Wheels driven: Rear
Springs F/R: Coil/Coil
Brakes F/R: Disc/Disc
Steering: Rack & pinion
Wheelbase: 244.3cm 96.2in
Track F: 151.4cm 59.6in
Track R: 154.4cm 60.8in
Length: 436.9cm 172.0in
Width: 192.0cm 75.6in
Height: 117.3cm 46.2in
Kerb weight: 1357.5kg 2990.0lb

1349 Dove

GTR4
1963 UK
110.0mph 177.0kmh
0-50mph 80.5kmh: 8.8secs
0-60mph 96.5kmh: 12.0secs
0-1/4 mile: 18.4secs
100.0bhp 74.6kW 101.4PS
@ 4600rpm
127.0lbft 172.1Nm @ 3350rpm
84.2bhp/ton 82.8bhp/tonne
46.8bhp/L 34.9kW/L 47.4PS/L
46.3ft/sec 14.1m/sec
25.0mph 40.2kmh/1000rpm
24.1mpg 20.1mpgUS 11.7L/100km
Petrol 4-stroke piston
2138cc 130.4cu in
In-line 4 2 Carburettor
Compression ratio: 9.0:1
Bore: 86.0mm 3.4in
Stroke: 92.0mm 3.6in
Valve type/No: Overhead 8
Transmission: Manual with overdrive
No. of forward speeds: 6
Wheels driven: Rear
Springs F/R: Coil/Leaf
Brakes F/R: Disc/Drum
Steering: Rack & pinion
Wheelbase: 213.4cm 84.0in
Track F: 127.0cm 50.0in
Track R: 124.5cm 49.0in
Length: 396.2cm 156.0in
Width: 146.1cm 57.5in
Height: 132.1cm 52.0in
Ground clearance: 15.2cm 6.0in
Kerb weight: 1207.6kg 2660.0lb
Fuel: 68.2L 15.0gal 18.0galUS

1350 Du Pont

Speedster
1929 USA
97.0mph 156.1kmh
0-50mph 80.5kmh: 12.1secs
0-60mph 96.5kmh: 16.2secs
0-1/4 mile: 19.8secs
140.0bhp 104.4kW 141.9PS
@ 3600rpm
260.0lbft 352.3Nm @ 2000rpm
82.5bhp/ton 81.1bhp/tonne
26.4bhp/L 19.7kW/L 26.8PS/L
45.0ft/sec 13.7m/sec
24.6mph 39.6kmh/1000rpm
Petrol 4-stroke piston
5295cc 323.1cu in
In-line 8 1 Carburettor
Compression ratio: 6.0:1
Bore: 85.9mm 3.4in
Stroke: 114.4mm 4.5in
Valve type/No: Side 16
Transmission: Manual
No. of forward speeds: 4
Wheels driven: Rear
Wheelbase: 309.9cm 122.0in
Track F: 147.3cm 58.0in
Track R: 147.3cm 58.0in
Length: 495.3cm 195.0in
Width: 182.9cm 72.0in
Height: 160.0cm 63.0in
Kerb weight: 1725.2kg 3800.0lb

1351 Du Pont

Town Car
1930 USA
76.0mph 122.3kmh
0-50mph 80.5kmh: 15.6secs
0-60mph 96.5kmh: 22.5secs
0-1/4 mile: 22.5secs
114.0bhp 85.0kW 115.6PS
@ 3200rpm
245.0lbft 332.0Nm @ 1800rpm
52.1bhp/ton 51.2bhp/tonne
21.5bhp/L 16.0kW/L 21.8PS/L
40.0ft/sec 12.2m/sec
22.3mph 35.9kmh/1000rpm
Petrol 4-stroke piston
5295cc 323.1cu in
In-line 8
Compression ratio: 5.3:1
Bore: 85.9mm 3.4in
Stroke: 114.3mm 4.5in
Valve type/No: Side 16
Transmission: Manual
No. of forward speeds: 4
Wheels driven: Rear
Wheelbase: 358.1cm 141.0in
Track F: 147.3cm 58.0in
Track R: 147.3cm 58.0in
Length: 546.1cm 215.0in
Width: 182.9cm 72.0in
Height: 172.7cm 68.0in
Kerb weight: 2224.6kg 4900.0lb

1352 Duesenberg

J Coupe
1930 USA
115.0mph 185.0kmh
0-50mph 80.5kmh: 6.3secs
0-60mph 96.5kmh: 8.6secs
0-1/4 mile: 16.3secs
265.0bhp 197.6kW 268.7PS
@ 4200rpm
374.0lbft 506.8Nm @ 2000rpm
118.7bhp/ton 116.7bhp/tonne
38.5bhp/L 28.7kW/L 39.0PS/L
55.4ft/sec 16.9m/sec
Petrol 4-stroke piston
6885cc 420.1cu in
In-line 8
Compression ratio: 5.7:1
Bore: 95.3mm 3.8in
Stroke: 120.7mm 4.7in
Valve type/No: Overhead 16
Transmission: Manual
No. of forward speeds: 3
Wheels driven: Rear
Wheelbase: 362.0cm 142.5in
Track F: 152.4cm 60.0in
Track R: 152.4cm 60.0in
Kerb weight: 2270.0kg 5000.0lb

1353 Duesenberg

SJ Town Car
1938 USA
106.0mph 170.6kmh
0-50mph 80.5kmh: 7.9secs
0-60mph 96.5kmh: 9.8secs
0-1/4 mile: 16.8secs
320.0bhp 238.6kW 324.4PS
@ 4200rpm
425.0lbft 575.9Nm @ 2400rpm
112.0bhp/ton 110.1bhp/tonne
46.5bhp/L 34.7kW/L 47.1PS/L
55.4ft/sec 16.9m/sec
23.1mph 37.2kmh/1000rpm
Petrol 4-stroke piston
6885cc 420.1cu in supercharged
In-line 8
Compression ratio: 5.7:1
Bore: 95.3mm 3.8in
Stroke: 120.7mm 4.7in
Valve type/No: Overhead 16
Transmission: Manual
No. of forward speeds: 3
Wheels driven: Rear
Wheelbase: 389.9cm 153.5in
Track F: 152.4cm 60.0in
Track R: 152.4cm 60.0in
Length: 624.8cm 246.0in
Width: 188.0cm 74.0in
Height: 177.8cm 70.0in
Kerb weight: 2905.6kg 6400.0lb

1354 Eagle

Premier ES
1988 USA

125.0mph 201.1kmh
0-60mph 96.5kmh: 10.5secs
0-1/4 mile: 17.7secs
150.0bhp 111.9kW 152.1PS
@ 5000rpm
171.0lbft 231.7Nm @ 3750rpm
110.5bhp/ton 108.7bhp/tonne
50.4bhp/L 37.6kW/L 51.1PS/L
39.9ft/sec 12.2m/sec
22.8mpg 19.0mpgUS 12.4L/100km
Petrol 4-stroke piston
2975cc 181.5cu in
Vee 6 fuel injection
Compression ratio: 9.3:1
Bore: 93.0mm 3.7in
Stroke: 73.0mm 2.9in
Valve type/No: Overhead 12
Transmission: Automatic
No. of forward speeds: 4
Wheels driven: Front
Springs F/R: Coil/Torsion bar
Brake system: PA
Brakes F/R: Disc/Drum
Steering: Rack & pinion PA
Wheelbase: 268.0cm 105.5in
Track F: 147.8cm 58.2in
Track R: 145.0cm 57.1in
Length: 489.5cm 192.7in
Width: 177.3cm 69.8in
Height: 142.0cm 55.9in
Kerb weight: 1380.2kg 3040.0lb
Fuel: 64.3L 14.1gal 17.0galUS

1355 Eagle

Talon
1990 USA
143.0mph 230.1kmh
0-50mph 80.5kmh: 4.9secs
0-60mph 96.5kmh: 6.8secs
0-1/4 mile: 15.3secs
195.0bhp 145.4kW 197.7PS
@ 6000rpm
203.0lbft 275.1Nm @ 3000rpm
138.9bhp/ton 136.6bhp/tonne
97.6bhp/L 72.8kW/L 99.0PS/L
57.7ft/sec 17.6m/sec
19.8mpg 16.5mpgUS 14.3L/100km
Petrol 4-stroke piston
1997cc 121.8cu in turbocharged
In-line 4 fuel injection
Compression ratio: 7.8:1
Bore: 85.0mm 3.3in
Stroke: 88.0mm 3.5in
Valve type/No: Overhead 16
Transmission: Manual
No. of forward speeds: 5
Wheels driven: 4-wheel drive
Springs F/R: Coil/Coil
Brake system: PA
Brakes F/R: Disc/Disc
Steering: Rack & pinion PA
Wheelbase: 246.9cm 97.2in
Track F: 146.6cm 57.7in
Track R: 145.0cm 57.1in
Length: 433.1cm 170.5in
Width: 169.4cm 66.7in
Height: 130.6cm 51.4in
Kerb weight: 1427.8kg 3145.0lb
Fuel: 60.2L 13.2gal 15.9galUS

1356 Eagle

GTP
1991 USA
200.0mph 321.8kmh
0-60mph 96.5kmh: 5.0secs
0-1/4 mile: 13.8secs
345.0bhp 257.3kW 349.8PS
@ 5600rpm
340.0lbft 460.7Nm @ 3200rpm
396.3bhp/ton 389.7bhp/tonne
60.2bhp/L 44.9kW/L 61.0PS/L
54.1ft/sec 16.5m/sec
Petrol 4-stroke piston
5733cc 349.8cu in
Vee 8 1 Carburettor
Compression ratio: 9.0:1
Bore: 101.6mm 4.0in
Stroke: 88.4mm 3.5in
Valve type/No: Overhead 16
Transmission: Manual
No. of forward speeds: 4
Wheels driven: Rear
Springs F/R: Coil/Coil
Brakes F/R: Disc/Disc
Steering: Rack & pinion
Wheelbase: 270.5cm 106.5in
Track F: 160.0cm 63.0in
Track R: 154.9cm 61.0in
Length: 477.5cm 188.0in
Width: 200.7cm 79.0in
Height: 104.1cm 41.0in
Kerb weight: 885.3kg 1950.0lb
Fuel: 60.6L 13.3gal 16.0galUS

1357 Eagle

Talon TSi 4WD
1991 USA
143.0mph 230.1kmh
0-50mph 80.5kmh: 4.9secs
0-60mph 96.5kmh: 6.8secs
0-1/4 mile: 15.3secs
195.0bhp 145.4kW 197.7PS
@ 6000rpm
203.0lbft 275.1Nm @ 3000rpm
140.9bhp/ton 138.5bhp/tonne
97.6bhp/L 72.8kW/L 99.0PS/L
57.7ft/sec 17.6m/sec
19.8mpg 16.5mpgUS 14.3L/100km
Petrol 4-stroke piston
1997cc 121.8cu in turbocharged
In-line 4 fuel injection
Compression ratio: 7.8:1
Bore: 85.0mm 3.3in
Stroke: 88.0mm 3.5in
Valve type/No: Overhead 16
Transmission: Manual
No. of forward speeds: 5
Wheels driven: 4-wheel drive
Springs F/R: Coil/Coil
Brake system: PA ABS
Brakes F/R: Disc/Disc
Steering: Rack & pinion PA
Wheelbase: 246.9cm 97.2in
Track F: 146.6cm 57.7in
Track R: 145.5cm 57.3in
Length: 437.9cm 172.4in
Width: 169.9cm 66.9in
Height: 132.1cm 52.0in
Kerb weight: 1407.4kg 3100.0lb
Fuel: 60.2L 13.2gal 15.9galUS

1358 Elva

Courier
1958 UK
98.5mph 158.5kmh
0-50mph 80.5kmh: 8.3secs
0-60mph 96.5kmh: 12.7secs
0-1/4 mile: 18.2secs
72.0bhp 53.7kW 73.0PS
@ 5000rpm
77.4lbft 104.9Nm @ 3500rpm
103.8bhp/ton 102.0bhp/tonne
48.3bhp/L 36.1kW/L 49.0PS/L
48.6ft/sec 14.8m/sec
19.6mph 31.5kmh/1000rpm
29.8mpg 24.8mpgUS 9.5L/100km
Petrol 4-stroke piston
1489cc 90.8cu in
In-line 4
Compression ratio: 8.3:1
Bore: 73.0mm 2.9in
Stroke: 89.0mm 3.5in
Valve type/No: Overhead 8
Transmission: Manual
No. of forward speeds: 4
Wheels driven: Rear
Springs F/R: Coil/Coil
Brakes F/R: Drum/Drum
Wheelbase: 231.1cm 91.0in
Track F: 127.5cm 50.2in
Track R: 127.0cm 50.0in
Length: 384.8cm 151.5in
Width: 151.1cm 59.5in
Height: 125.7cm 49.5in
Ground clearance: 8.9cm 3.5in
Kerb weight: 705.5kg 1554.0lb
Fuel: 40.9L 9.0gal 10.8galUS

1359 Enfield

8000 Electric
1976 UK
37.0mph 59.5kmh
8.0bhp 6.0kW 8.2PS
8.4bhp/ton 8.2bhp/tonne
DC electric
No. of forward speeds: 1
Wheels driven: Rear
Springs F/R: Coil/Coil
Brakes F/R: Drum/Drum
Wheelbase: 172.7cm 68.0in
Track F: 121.9cm 48.0in
Track R: 121.9cm 48.0in
Length: 284.5cm 112.0in
Width: 142.2cm 56.0in
Height: 142.2cm 56.0in
Ground clearance: 12.7cm 5.0in
Kerb weight: 976.3kg 2150.4lb

1360 Essex

Terraplane Tourer
1932 USA
73.7mph 118.6kmh
24.0mpg 20.0mpgUS 11.8L/100km
Petrol 4-stroke piston
2560cc 156.2cu in
In-line 6
Bore: 67.4mm 2.7in
Stroke: 121.0mm 4.8in
Transmission: Manual
No. of forward speeds: 3
Wheels driven: Rear
Brakes F/R: Drum/Drum
Wheelbase: 269.2cm 106.0in
Track F: 130.8cm 51.5in
Track R: 138.4cm 54.5in
Length: 421.6cm 166.0in
Width: 167.6cm 66.0in
Height: 106.7cm 42.0in
Kerb weight: 1017.0kg 2240.0lb
Fuel: 43.2L 9.5gal 11.4galUS

1361 Essex

Terraplane Straight Eight
1933 USA
82.5mph 132.7kmh
0-50mph 80.5kmh: 11.0secs
0-60mph 96.5kmh: 16.0secs
17.0mpg 14.2mpgUS 16.6L/100km
Petrol 4-stroke piston
4010cc 244.7cu in
In-line 8
Bore: 75.0mm 2.9in
Stroke: 114.0mm 4.5in
Transmission: Manual
No. of forward speeds: 3
Wheels driven: Rear
Brakes F/R: Drum/Drum
Kerb weight: 1228.1kg 2705.0lb
Fuel: 59.1L 13.0gal 15.6galUS

1362 Evans

Series I
1990 USA
0-60mph 96.5kmh: 4.6secs
0-1/4 mile: 12.9secs
300.0bhp 223.7kW 304.2PS
@ 4000rpm
360.0lbft 487.8Nm @ 3200rpm
293.4bhp/ton 288.6bhp/tonne
52.3bhp/L 39.0kW/L 53.0PS/L
38.7ft/sec 11.8m/sec
Petrol 4-stroke piston
5735cc 349.9cu in
Vee 8 fuel injection
Compression ratio: 9.5:1
Bore: 101.6mm 4.0in
Stroke: 88.4mm 3.5in
Valve type/No: Overhead 16
Transmission: Manual
No. of forward speeds: 5
Wheels driven: Rear
Springs F/R: Coil/Coil
Brakes F/R: Disc/Disc
Steering: Rack & pinion
Wheelbase: 266.7cm 105.0in
Track F: 193.0cm 76.0in
Track R: 193.0cm 76.0in
Length: 424.2cm 167.0in
Width: 200.7cm 79.0in
Height: 104.1cm 41.0in
Kerb weight: 1039.7kg 2290.0lb

1363 Excalibur

SS
1964 USA
125.0mph 201.1kmh
0-50mph 80.5kmh: 5.6secs
0-60mph 96.5kmh: 7.0secs
0-1/4 mile: 15.0secs
289.0bhp 215.5kW 293.0PS
@ 4800rpm
257.9bhp/ton 253.6bhp/tonne
61.0bhp/L 45.5kW/L 61.8PS/L
48.4ft/sec 14.7m/sec
22.7mph 36.5kmh/1000rpm
Petrol 4-stroke piston
4738cc 289.1cu in supercharged
Vee 8 1 Carburettor
Compression ratio: 9.0:1
Bore: 90.4mm 3.6in
Stroke: 92.2mm 3.6in
Valve type/No: Overhead 16
Transmission: Manual
No. of forward speeds: 4
Wheels driven: Rear
Springs F/R: Coil/Leaf
Brakes F/R: Disc/Drum
Steering: Cam & lever
Wheelbase: 276.9cm 109.0in
Track F: 145.8cm 57.4in
Track R: 143.8cm 56.6in
Length: 425.5cm 167.5in
Width: 170.2cm 67.0in
Height: 124.5cm 49.0in
Ground clearance: 11.4cm 4.5in
Kerb weight: 1139.5kg 2510.0lb
Fuel: 56.8L 12.5gal 15.0galUS

1364 Facel Vega

Coupe
1956 France
121.1mph 194.8kmh
0-50mph 80.5kmh: 7.2secs
0-60mph 96.5kmh: 9.3secs
0-1/4 mile: 17.0secs
255.0bhp 190.1kW 258.5PS
@ 4400rpm
350.0lbft 474.3Nm @ 3200rpm
140.7bhp/ton 138.3bhp/tonne
47.1bhp/L 35.1kW/L 47.8PS/L
46.4ft/sec 14.1m/sec
Petrol 4-stroke piston
5410cc 330.1cu in
Vee 8
Compression ratio: 8.5:1
Bore: 94.5mm 3.7in
Stroke: 96.5mm 3.8in
Valve type/No: Overhead 16
Transmission: Automatic
No. of forward speeds: 2
Wheels driven: Rear
Wheelbase: 262.9cm 103.5in
Track F: 136.9cm 53.9in
Track R: 137.9cm 54.3in
Kerb weight: 1843.2kg 4060.0lb

1365 Facel Vega

FVS
1958 France
135.5mph 218.0kmh
0-50mph 80.5kmh: 7.0secs
0-60mph 96.5kmh: 9.6secs
0-1/4 mile: 16.1secs
325.0bhp 242.3kW 329.5PS
@ 4600rpm
430.0lbft 582.7Nm @ 2800rpm
177.3bhp/ton 174.3bhp/tonne
56.0bhp/L 41.8kW/L 56.8PS/L
46.3ft/sec 14.1m/sec
27.3mph 43.9kmh/1000rpm
14.4mpg 12.0mpgUS 19.6L/100km
Petrol 4-stroke piston
5801cc 353.9cu in
Vee 8
Compression ratio: 9.2:1
Bore: 100.0mm 3.9in
Stroke: 92.0mm 3.6in
Valve type/No: Overhead 16
Transmission: Manual
No. of forward speeds: 4
Wheels driven: Rear
Springs F/R: Coil/Leaf
Brake system: PA
Brakes F/R: Drum/Drum
Wheelbase: 265.9cm 104.7in
Track F: 142.2cm 56.0in
Track R: 144.8cm 57.0in
Length: 459.7cm 181.0in
Width: 179.6cm 70.7in
Height: 135.9cm 53.5in
Ground clearance: 17.8cm 7.0in
Kerb weight: 1864.6kg 4107.0lb
Fuel: 100.1L 22.0gal 26.4galUS

1366 Facel Vega

HK-500
1960 France
130.0mph 209.2kmh
0-50mph 80.5kmh: 7.1secs
0-60mph 96.5kmh: 9.7secs
0-1/4 mile: 17.0secs
330.0bhp 246.1kW 334.6PS
@ 4600rpm

460.0lbft 623.3Nm @ 2800rpm
177.3bhp/ton 174.3bhp/tonne
52.6bhp/L 39.2kW/L 53.3PS/L
43.2ft/sec 13.2m/sec
23.8mph 38.3kmh/1000rpm
Petrol 4-stroke piston
6279cc 383.1cu in
Vee 8 1 Carburettor
Compression ratio: 10.0:1
Bore: 107.8mm 4.2in
Stroke: 85.9mm 3.4in
Valve type/No: Overhead 16
Transmission: Automatic
No. of forward speeds: 3
Wheels driven: Rear
Wheelbase: 265.9cm 104.7in
Track F: 141.0cm 55.5in
Track R: 146.1cm 57.5in
Length: 459.7cm 181.0in
Width: 179.8cm 70.8in
Height: 136.7cm 53.8in
Kerb weight: 1893.2kg 4170.0lb

1367 Facel Vega

Facellia 1600
1961 France
114.0mph 183.4kmh
0-50mph 80.5kmh: 10.2secs
0-60mph 96.5kmh: 13.7secs
0-1/4 mile: 18.9secs
115.0bhp 85.8kW 116.6PS
@ 6400rpm
105.5lbft 143.0Nm @ 4100rpm
104.5bhp/ton 102.8bhp/tonne
69.9bhp/L 52.1kW/L 70.8PS/L
54.6ft/sec 16.6m/sec
18.1mph 29.1kmh/1000rpm
Petrol 4-stroke piston
1646cc 100.4cu in
In-line 4 1 Carburettor
Compression ratio: 9.4:1
Bore: 82.0mm 3.2in
Stroke: 78.0mm 3.1in
Valve type/No: Overhead 8
Transmission: Manual
No. of forward speeds: 4
Wheels driven: Rear
Wheelbase: 244.9cm 96.4in
Track F: 130.0cm 51.2in
Track R: 128.0cm 50.4in
Length: 416.6cm 164.0in
Width: 156.0cm 61.4in
Height: 130.0cm 51.2in
Ground clearance: 17.8cm 7.0in
Kerb weight: 1119.1kg 2465.0lb

1368 Facel Vega

Facel II
1962 France
133.0mph 214.0kmh
0-50mph 80.5kmh: 5.9secs
0-60mph 96.5kmh: 7.8secs
0-1/4 mile: 15.8secs
355.0bhp 264.7kW 359.9PS
@ 4800rpm
195.9bhp/ton 192.6bhp/tonne
56.5bhp/L 42.1kW/L 57.3PS/L
50.3ft/sec 15.3m/sec
26.8mph 43.1kmh/1000rpm
13.1mpg 10.9mpgUS 21.6L/100km
Petrol 4-stroke piston
6286cc 383.5cu in
Vee 8 1 Carburettor
Compression ratio: 10.0:1
Bore: 107.9mm 4.2in
Stroke: 95.8mm 3.8in
Valve type/No: Overhead 16
Transmission: Automatic
No. of forward speeds: 3
Wheels driven: Rear
Springs F/R: Coil/Leaf
Brake system: PA
Brakes F/R: Disc/Disc
Wheelbase: 266.7cm 105.0in
Track F: 141.0cm 55.5in
Track R: 146.1cm 57.5in
Length: 459.7cm 181.0in
Width: 180.3cm 71.0in
Height: 135.9cm 53.5in
Ground clearance: 14.0cm 5.5in
Kerb weight: 1843.2kg 4060.0lb
Fuel: 100.1L 22.0gal 26.4galUS

1369 Fairthorpe

Zeta
1961 UK
119.0mph 191.5kmh
0-50mph 80.5kmh: 5.8secs
0-60mph 96.5kmh: 7.9secs
0-1/4 mile: 15.8secs
143.0bhp 106.6kW 145.0PS
@ 5800rpm
162.0lbft 219.5Nm @ 3500rpm
174.7bhp/ton 171.7bhp/tonne
56.0bhp/L 41.8kW/L 56.8PS/L
50.4ft/sec 15.4m/sec
20.2mph 32.5kmh/1000rpm
18.1mpg 15.1mpgUS 15.6L/100km
Petrol 4-stroke piston
2553cc 155.8cu in
In-line 6 6 Carburettor
Compression ratio: 9.0:1
Bore: 82.5mm 3.2in
Stroke: 79.5mm 3.1in
Valve type/No: Overhead 12
Transmission: Manual
No. of forward speeds: 4
Wheels driven: Rear
Springs F/R: Coil/Coil
Brakes F/R: Disc/Drum
Wheelbase: 222.3cm 87.5in
Track F: 132.1cm 52.0in
Track R: 115.6cm 45.5in
Length: 355.6cm 140.0in
Width: 147.3cm 58.0in
Height: 116.8cm 46.0in
Ground clearance: 17.8cm 7.0in
Kerb weight: 832.6kg 1834.0lb
Fuel: 45.5L 10.0gal 12.0galUS

1370 Ferguson

R5
1966 UK
104.0mph 167.3kmh
0-50mph 80.5kmh: 10.8secs
0-60mph 96.5kmh: 14.7secs
0-1/4 mile: 20.0secs
0-1km: 37.0secs
111.0bhp 82.8kW 112.5PS
@ 5350rpm
128.0lbft 173.4Nm @ 3500rpm
77.4bhp/ton 76.1bhp/tonne
50.2bhp/L 37.4kW/L 50.9PS/L
45.6ft/sec 13.9m/sec
18.0mph 29.0kmh/1000rpm
18.6mpg 15.5mpgUS 15.2L/100km
Petrol 4-stroke piston
2212cc 135.0cu in
Flat 4 2 Carburettor
Compression ratio: 8.6:1
Bore: 95.0mm 3.7in
Stroke: 78.0mm 3.1in
Valve type/No: Overhead 8
Transmission: Manual
No. of forward speeds: 3
Wheels driven: 4-wheel drive
Springs F/R: Coil/Coil
Brake system: PA
Brakes F/R: Disc/Disc
Steering: Rack & pinion
Wheelbase: 269.2cm 106.0in
Track F: 144.8cm 57.0in
Track R: 142.2cm 56.0in
Length: 457.2cm 180.0in
Width: 172.7cm 68.0in
Height: 147.3cm 58.0in
Ground clearance: 19.1cm 7.5in
Kerb weight: 1458.2kg 3212.0lb
Fuel: 59.1L 13.0gal 15.6galUS

1371 Ferrari

166 Mille Miglia Barchetta
1948 Italy
125.0mph 201.1kmh
0-50mph 80.5kmh: 7.3secs
0-60mph 96.5kmh: 10.0secs
0-1/4 mile: 16.3secs
130.0bhp 96.9kW 131.8PS
@ 7000rpm
117.0lbft 158.5Nm @ 5000rpm
189.1bhp/ton 185.9bhp/tonne
65.2bhp/L 48.6kW/L 66.1PS/L
44.9ft/sec 13.7m/sec
19.2mph 30.9kmh/1000rpm
Petrol 4-stroke piston
1995cc 121.7cu in
Vee 12
Compression ratio: 8.5:1
Bore: 59.9mm 2.4in
Stroke: 58.7mm 2.3in
Valve type/No: Overhead 24
Transmission: Manual with overdrive
Wheels driven: Rear
Wheelbase: 220.0cm 86.6in
Track F: 126.5cm 49.8in
Track R: 119.9cm 47.2in
Length: 360.7cm 142.0in
Width: 152.4cm 60.0in
Height: 106.7cm 42.0in
Kerb weight: 699.2kg 1540.0lb

1372 Ferrari

212 Touring
1952 Italy
123.0mph 197.9kmh
0-50mph 80.5kmh: 5.2secs
0-60mph 96.5kmh: 7.1secs
0-1/4 mile: 15.3secs
170.0bhp 126.8kW 172.4PS
@ 7200rpm
192.8bhp/ton 189.6bhp/tonne
66.3bhp/L 49.5kW/L 67.3PS/L
46.2ft/sec 14.1m/sec
18.5mph 29.8kmh/1000rpm
24.0mpg 20.0mpgUS 11.8L/100km
Petrol 4-stroke piston
2562cc 156.3cu in
Vee 12 3 Carburettor
Compression ratio: 7.5:1
Bore: 68.0mm 2.7in
Stroke: 58.8mm 2.3in
Valve type/No: Overhead 24
Transmission: Manual
No. of forward speeds: 5
Wheels driven: Rear
Wheelbase: 224.8cm 88.5in
Track F: 126.7cm 49.9in
Track R: 125.0cm 49.2in
Length: 378.5cm 149.0in
Height: 96.5cm 38.0in
Ground clearance: 17.0cm 6.7in
Kerb weight: 896.6kg 1975.0lb
Fuel: 189.2L 41.6gal 50.0galUS

1373 Ferrari

375 Indianapolis
1952 Italy
180.0mph 289.6kmh
0-60mph 96.5kmh: 5.8secs
390.0bhp 290.8kW 395.4PS
@ 7500rpm
507.9bhp/ton 499.4bhp/tonne
86.8bhp/L 64.7kW/L 88.0PS/L
61.0ft/sec 18.6m/sec
Petrol 4-stroke piston
4494cc 274.2cu in
Vee 12 3 Carburettor
Compression ratio: 12.0:1
Bore: 80.0mm 3.1in
Stroke: 74.5mm 2.9in
Valve type/No: Overhead 24
Transmission: Manual
No. of forward speeds: 4
Wheels driven: Rear
Springs F/R: Leaf/Leaf
Brakes F/R: Drum/Drum
Steering: Worm & sector
Wheelbase: 241.8cm 95.2in
Track F: 127.8cm 50.3in
Track R: 125.0cm 49.2in
Length: 383.0cm 150.8in
Width: 158.8cm 62.5in
Height: 111.0cm 43.7in
Kerb weight: 780.9kg 1720.0lb
Fuel: 198.3L 43.6gal 52.4galUS

1374 Ferrari

212 Coupe
1953 Italy
128.0mph 206.0kmh
0-50mph 80.5kmh: 6.8secs
0-60mph 96.5kmh: 8.2secs
0-1/4 mile: 15.5secs
170.0bhp 126.8kW 172.4PS
@ 6500rpm
152.0lbft 206.0Nm @ 5250rpm
182.2bhp/ton 179.2bhp/tonne
66.3bhp/L 49.5kW/L 67.3PS/L
41.7ft/sec 12.7m/sec
17.8mph 28.6kmh/1000rpm
Petrol 4-stroke piston
2562cc 156.3cu in
Vee 12
Compression ratio: 8.4:1
Bore: 68.1mm 2.7in
Stroke: 58.7mm 2.3in
Valve type/No: Overhead 24
Transmission: Manual
No. of forward speeds: 5
Wheels driven: Rear
Wheelbase: 225.0cm 88.6in
Track F: 127.8cm 50.3in
Track R: 125.0cm 49.2in
Length: 375.9cm 148.0in
Width: 156.0cm 61.4in
Height: 129.5cm 51.0in
Kerb weight: 948.9kg 2090.0lb

1375 Ferrari

4.1 Coupe
1953 Italy
150.0mph 241.4kmh
0-50mph 80.5kmh: 4.7secs
0-60mph 96.5kmh: 6.1secs
0-1/4 mile: 15.5secs
260.0bhp 193.9kW 263.6PS
@ 6500rpm
284.1bhp/ton 279.4bhp/tonne
63.4bhp/L 47.3kW/L 64.3PS/L
48.4ft/sec 14.8m/sec
22.6mph 36.4kmh/1000rpm
Petrol 4-stroke piston
4102cc 250.3cu in
Vee 12
Compression ratio: 8.0:1
Bore: 80.0mm 3.1in
Stroke: 68.1mm 2.7in
Valve type/No: Overhead 24
Transmission: Manual
No. of forward speeds: 5
Wheels driven: Rear
Wheelbase: 243.8cm 96.0in
Track F: 127.0cm 50.0in
Track R: 125.2cm 49.3in
Kerb weight: 930.7kg 2050.0lb

1376 Ferrari

250 Mille Miglia
1954 Italy
135.0mph 217.2kmh
0-50mph 80.5kmh: 4.0secs
0-60mph 96.5kmh: 5.1secs
0-1/4 mile: 14.4secs
240.0bhp 179.0kW 243.3PS
@ 7200rpm
178.0lbft 241.2Nm @ 5250rpm
262.2bhp/ton 257.9bhp/tonne
81.3bhp/L 60.6kW/L 82.4PS/L
46.2ft/sec 14.1m/sec
19.1mph 30.7kmh/1000rpm
Petrol 4-stroke piston
2953cc 180.2cu in
Vee 12
Compression ratio: 9.0:1
Bore: 72.3mm 2.8in
Stroke: 58.7mm 2.3in
Valve type/No: Overhead 24
Transmission: Manual
No. of forward speeds: 4
Wheels driven: Rear
Wheelbase: 242.6cm 95.5in
Track F: 130.0cm 51.2in
Track R: 132.1cm 52.0in
Kerb weight: 930.7kg 2050.0lb

1377 Ferrari

412 MI
1956 Italy
174.0mph 280.0kmh
0-60mph 96.5kmh: 5.2secs
415.0bhp 309.5kW 420.8PS
@ 7600rpm
510.8bhp/ton 502.2bhp/tonne
103.2bhp/L 76.9kW/L 104.6PS/L
59.7ft/sec 18.2m/sec
Petrol 4-stroke piston
4023cc 245.4cu in
Vee 12 6 Carburettor
Compression ratio: 9.9:1
Bore: 77.0mm 3.0in
Stroke: 72.0mm 2.8in
Valve type/No: Overhead 24
Transmission: Manual
No. of forward speeds: 4
Wheels driven: Rear
Springs F/R: Coil
Brakes F/R: Drum/Drum
Steering: Worm & sector
Wheelbase: 235.0cm 92.5in
Track F: 129.5cm 51.0in
Track R: 131.1cm 51.6in
Length: 420.4cm 165.5in
Width: 165.1cm 65.0in
Height: 104.1cm 41.0in
Kerb weight: 826.3kg 1820.0lb

Fuel: 162.8L 35.8gal 43.0galUS

1378 Ferrari

250 Testa Rossa
1957 Italy
168.0mph 270.3kmh
0-60mph 96.5kmh: 4.5secs
0-1/4 mile: 13.0secs
300.0bhp 223.7kW 304.2PS
@ 7200rpm
220.0lbft 298.1Nm @ 6200rpm
324.6bhp/ton 319.2bhp/tonne
101.6bhp/L 75.8kW/L 103.0PS/L
46.2ft/sec 14.1m/sec
Petrol 4-stroke piston
2953cc 180.2cu in
Vee 12 6 Carburettor
Bore: 73.0mm 2.9in
Stroke: 58.8mm 2.3in
Valve type/No: Overhead 24
Transmission: Manual
No. of forward speeds: 4
Wheels driven: Rear
Springs F/R: Coil/Coil
Brakes F/R: Drum/Drum
Steering: Worm & peg
Wheelbase: 235.0cm 92.5in
Track F: 129.8cm 51.1in
Track R: 129.8cm 51.1in
Length: 412.8cm 162.5in
Width: 165.1cm 65.0in
Height: 100.3cm 39.5in
Kerb weight: 939.8kg 2070.0lb

1379 Ferrari

TRC 2500 Testa Rossa
1957 Italy
130.0mph 209.2kmh
0-50mph 80.5kmh: 4.7secs
0-60mph 96.5kmh: 5.8secs
0-1/4 mile: 13.3secs
220.0bhp 164.0kW 223.0PS
@ 6500rpm
189.0lbft 256.1Nm @ 5500rpm
304.2bhp/ton 299.1bhp/tonne
88.1bhp/L 65.7kW/L 89.3PS/L
61.4ft/sec 18.7m/sec
Petrol 4-stroke piston
2498cc 152.4cu in
In-line 4
Compression ratio: 9.0:1
Bore: 94.0mm 3.7in
Stroke: 86.4mm 3.4in
Valve type/No: Overhead 16
Transmission: Manual
No. of forward speeds: 4
Wheels driven: Rear
Wheelbase: 225.0cm 88.6in
Track F: 130.3cm 51.3in
Track R: 125.0cm 49.2in
Kerb weight: 735.5kg 1620.0lb

1380 Ferrari

250 GT Cabriolet
1958 Italy
126.0mph 202.7kmh
0-60mph 96.5kmh: 7.1secs
0-1/4 mile: 15.5secs
240.0bhp 179.0kW 243.3PS
@ 7000rpm
181.0lbft 245.3Nm @ 5500rpm
199.1bhp/ton 195.8bhp/tonne
81.3bhp/L 60.6kW/L 82.4PS/L
44.9ft/sec 13.7m/sec
Petrol 4-stroke piston
2953cc 180.2cu in
Vee 12 3 Carburettor
Compression ratio: 9.2:1
Bore: 72.9mm 2.9in
Stroke: 58.7mm 2.3in
Valve type/No: Overhead 24
Transmission: Manual
No. of forward speeds: 4
Wheels driven: Rear
Springs F/R: Coil/Leaf
Brakes F/R: Drum/Drum
Steering: Worm & sector
Wheelbase: 260.1cm 102.4in
Track F: 135.4cm 53.3in
Track R: 134.9cm 53.1in
Length: 439.4cm 173.0in
Width: 165.1cm 65.0in
Height: 139.7cm 55.0in
Kerb weight: 1225.8kg 2700.0lb
Fuel: 99.9L 22.0gal 26.4galUS

1381 Ferrari

250 GT Coupe
1958 Italy
126.0mph 202.7kmh
0-60mph 96.5kmh: 7.1secs
0-1/4 mile: 15.5secs
260.0bhp 193.9kW 263.6PS
@ 7000rpm
195.0lbft 264.2Nm @ 5000rpm
200.8bhp/ton 197.5bhp/tonne
88.0bhp/L 65.7kW/L 89.3PS/L
44.9ft/sec 13.7m/sec
Petrol 4-stroke piston
2953cc 180.2cu in
Vee 12 3 Carburettor
Compression ratio: 9.2:1
Bore: 72.9mm 2.9in
Stroke: 58.7mm 2.3in
Valve type/No: Overhead 24
Transmission: Manual
No. of forward speeds: 4
Wheels driven: Rear
Springs F/R: Coil/Leaf
Brakes F/R: Drum/Drum
Steering: Worm & sector
Wheelbase: 260.1cm 102.4in
Track F: 135.4cm 53.3in
Track R: 134.9cm 53.1in
Length: 439.4cm 173.0in
Width: 165.1cm 65.0in
Height: 139.7cm 55.0in
Kerb weight: 1316.6kg 2900.0lb
Fuel: 99.9L 22.0gal 26.4galUS

1382 Ferrari

250 Testa Rossa
1958 Italy
140.0mph 225.3kmh
0-60mph 96.5kmh: 6.0secs
300.0bhp 223.7kW 304.2PS
@ 7200rpm
381.8bhp/ton 375.4bhp/tonne
101.6bhp/L 75.8kW/L 103.0PS/L
44.0ft/sec 13.4m/sec
Petrol 4-stroke piston
2953cc 180.2cu in
Vee 12 6 Carburettor
Compression ratio: 9.8:1
Bore: 73.0mm 2.9in
Stroke: 55.8mm 2.2in
Valve type/No: Overhead 24
Transmission: Manual
No. of forward speeds: 4
Wheels driven: Rear
Springs F/R: Coil/Leaf
Brakes F/R: Drum/Drum
Steering: Worm & sector
Wheelbase: 235.0cm 92.5in
Track F: 130.8cm 51.5in
Track R: 130.0cm 51.2in
Length: 412.8cm 162.5in
Width: 165.1cm 65.0in
Height: 100.3cm 39.5in
Kerb weight: 799.0kg 1760.0lb
Fuel: 128.7L 28.3gal 34.0galUS

1383 Ferrari

250 GT Berlinetta SWB
1960 Italy
0-60mph 96.5kmh: 6.3secs
0-1/4 mile: 14.3secs
241.0bhp 179.7kW 244.3PS
@ 7000rpm
183.0lbft 248.0Nm @ 5500rpm
226.8bhp/ton 223.0bhp/tonne
81.6bhp/L 60.9kW/L 82.7PS/L
Petrol 4-stroke piston
2953cc 180.2cu in
Vee 12 6 Carburettor
Valve type/No: Overhead 24
Transmission: Manual
No. of forward speeds: 4
Wheels driven: Rear
Springs F/R: Coil/Leaf
Brakes F/R: Disc/Disc
Steering: Worm & sector
Wheelbase: 240.0cm 94.5in
Track F: 135.4cm 53.3in
Track R: 134.9cm 53.1in
Length: 415.3cm 163.5in
Width: 165.1cm 65.0in
Height: 128.3cm 50.5in
Kerb weight: 1080.5kg 2380.0lb

1384 Ferrari

250 GT Coupe
1960 Italy
126.0mph 202.7kmh
0-50mph 80.5kmh: 5.4secs
0-60mph 96.5kmh: 7.1secs
0-1/4 mile: 15.5secs
240.0bhp 179.0kW 243.3PS
@ 7000rpm
181.0lbft 245.3Nm @ 5500rpm
199.1bhp/ton 195.8bhp/tonne
81.3bhp/L 60.6kW/L 82.4PS/L
44.9ft/sec 13.7m/sec
17.8mph 28.6kmh/1000rpm
Petrol 4-stroke piston
2953cc 180.2cu in
Vee 12 1 Carburettor
Compression ratio: 8.5:1
Bore: 73.0mm 2.9in
Stroke: 58.8mm 2.3in
Valve type/No: Overhead 24
Transmission: Manual with overdrive
Wheels driven: Rear
Wheelbase: 260.1cm 102.4in
Track F: 135.4cm 53.3in
Track R: 134.9cm 53.1in
Length: 439.4cm 173.0in
Width: 165.1cm 65.0in
Height: 139.7cm 55.0in
Kerb weight: 1225.8kg 2700.0lb

1385 Ferrari

250 GT 2+2
1962 Italy
150.0mph 241.4kmh
0-50mph 80.5kmh: 6.3secs
0-60mph 96.5kmh: 8.0secs
0-1/4 mile: 16.3secs
240.0bhp 179.0kW 243.3PS
@ 7000rpm
181.0lbft 245.3Nm @ 5000rpm
173.4bhp/ton 170.5bhp/tonne
81.3bhp/L 60.6kW/L 82.4PS/L
44.9ft/sec 13.7m/sec
28.0mph 45.1kmh/1000rpm
Petrol 4-stroke piston
2953cc 180.2cu in
Vee 12
Compression ratio: 8.8:1
Bore: 72.9mm 2.9in
Stroke: 58.6mm 2.3in
Valve type/No: Overhead 24
Transmission: Manual with overdrive
Wheels driven: Rear
Wheelbase: 260.1cm 102.4in
Track F: 137.7cm 54.2in
Track R: 138.7cm 54.6in
Length: 469.9cm 185.0in
Width: 170.9cm 67.3in
Height: 134.1cm 52.8in
Ground clearance: 14.5cm 5.7in
Kerb weight: 1407.4kg 3100.0lb

1386 Ferrari

250 GTO
1962 Italy
175.0mph 281.6kmh
0-60mph 96.5kmh: 5.9secs
390.0bhp 290.8kW 395.4PS
@ 7500rpm
367.8bhp/ton 361.7bhp/tonne
98.3bhp/L 73.3kW/L 99.7PS/L
58.3ft/sec 17.7m/sec
Petrol 4-stroke piston
3967cc 242.0cu in
Vee 12 3 Carburettor
Compression ratio: 9.7:1
Bore: 77.0mm 3.0in
Stroke: 71.0mm 2.8in
Valve type/No: Overhead 24
Transmission: Manual
No. of forward speeds: 4
Wheels driven: Rear
Springs F/R: Coil/Leaf
Brakes F/R: Disc/Disc
Steering: Recirculating ball
Wheelbase: 240.0cm 94.5in
Track F: 135.1cm 53.2in
Track R: 134.6cm 53.0in
Length: 439.9cm 173.2in
Width: 167.4cm 65.9in
Height: 124.5cm 49.0in
Kerb weight: 1078.2kg 2375.0lb
Fuel: 143.8L 31.6gal 38.0galUS

1387 Ferrari

4.9
1962 Italy
165.0mph 265.5kmh
0-50mph 80.5kmh: 5.3secs
0-60mph 96.5kmh: 6.6secs
0-1/4 mile: 14.6secs
360.0bhp 268.4kW 365.0PS
@ 7000rpm
311.0lbft 421.4Nm @ 5000rpm
227.1bhp/ton 223.4bhp/tonne
72.5bhp/L 54.1kW/L 73.6PS/L
52.1ft/sec 15.9m/sec
24.2mph 38.9kmh/1000rpm
Petrol 4-stroke piston
4962cc 302.7cu in
Vee 12
Compression ratio: 8.5:1
Bore: 87.9mm 3.5in
Stroke: 68.1mm 2.7in
Valve type/No: Overhead 24
Transmission: Manual
No. of forward speeds: 4
Wheels driven: Rear
Wheelbase: 259.8cm 102.3in
Track F: 148.3cm 58.4in
Track R: 147.8cm 58.2in
Length: 477.0cm 187.8in
Width: 188.0cm 74.0in
Height: 135.9cm 53.5in
Ground clearance: 12.7cm 5.0in
Kerb weight: 1611.7kg 3550.0lb

1388 Ferrari

250 GT Berlinetta Lusso
1963 Italy
150.0mph 241.4kmh
0-50mph 80.5kmh: 6.2secs
0-60mph 96.5kmh: 8.0secs
0-1/4 mile: 16.1secs
290.0bhp 216.2kW 294.0PS
@ 7500rpm
215.0lbft 291.3Nm @ 5500rpm
216.9bhp/ton 213.3bhp/tonne
98.2bhp/L 73.2kW/L 99.6PS/L
48.1ft/sec 14.7m/sec
18.8mph 30.2kmh/1000rpm
17.4mpg 14.5mpgUS 16.2L/100km
Petrol 4-stroke piston
2953cc 180.2cu in
Vee 12 3 Carburettor
Compression ratio: 9.3:1
Bore: 73.0mm 2.9in
Stroke: 58.8mm 2.3in
Valve type/No: Overhead 24
Transmission: Manual
No. of forward speeds: 4
Wheels driven: Rear
Springs F/R: Coil/Leaf
Brake system: PA
Brakes F/R: Disc/Disc
Steering: Worm & roller
Wheelbase: 239.8cm 94.4in
Track F: 139.7cm 55.0in
Track R: 139.2cm 54.8in
Length: 440.7cm 173.5in
Width: 165.1cm 65.0in
Height: 129.0cm 50.8in
Ground clearance: 11.9cm 4.7in
Kerb weight: 1359.7kg 2995.0lb
Fuel: 113.5L 25.0gal 30.0galUS

1389 Ferrari

400 Super America
1963 Italy
180.0mph 289.6kmh
0-50mph 80.5kmh: 6.0secs
0-60mph 96.5kmh: 7.8secs
0-1/4 mile: 15.8secs
420.0bhp 313.2kW 425.8PS
@ 7500rpm
295.0lbft 399.7Nm @ 5500rpm
281.7bhp/ton 277.0bhp/tonne
91.5bhp/L 68.2kW/L 92.8PS/L
58.3ft/sec 17.8m/sec
24.5mph 39.4kmh/1000rpm
Petrol 4-stroke piston
4590cc 280.0cu in
Vee 12
Compression ratio: 9.6:1
Bore: 82.8mm 3.3in
Stroke: 71.1mm 2.8in
Valve type/No: Overhead 24
Transmission: Manual with overdrive
Wheels driven: Rear
Wheelbase: 241.8cm 95.2in
Track F: 135.9cm 53.5in

Track R: 134.6cm 53.0in
Length: 467.4cm 184.0in
Width: 177.8cm 70.0in
Height: 130.0cm 51.2in
Ground clearance: 14.0cm 5.5in
Kerb weight: 1516.4kg 3340.0lb

1390 Ferrari
365 GTC
1965 Italy
151.0mph 243.0kmh
0-50mph 80.5kmh: 4.9secs
0-60mph 96.5kmh: 6.3secs
0-1/4 mile: 14.5secs
0-1km: 26.0secs
320.0bhp 238.6kW 324.4PS
@ 6600rpm
268.0lbft 363.1Nm @ 5000rpm
224.1bhp/ton 220.4bhp/tonne
72.9bhp/L 54.4kW/L 73.9PS/L
51.3ft/sec 15.6m/sec
22.8mph 36.7kmh/1000rpm
11.9mpg 9.9mpgUS 23.7L/100km
Petrol 4-stroke piston
4390cc 267.8cu in
Vee 12 3 Carburettor
Compression ratio: 8.8:1
Bore: 81.0mm 3.2in
Stroke: 71.0mm 2.8in
Valve type/No: Overhead 24
Transmission: Manual
No. of forward speeds: 5
Wheels driven: Rear
Springs F/R: Coil/Coil
Brake system: PA
Brakes F/R: Disc/Disc
Steering: Worm & roller
Wheelbase: 240.0cm 94.5in
Track F: 140.2cm 55.2in
Track R: 141.7cm 55.8in
Length: 449.6cm 177.0in
Width: 167.6cm 66.0in
Height: 128.3cm 50.5in
Kerb weight: 1451.9kg 3198.0lb
Fuel: 90.1L 19.8gal 23.8galUS

1391 Ferrari
275 GTS
1966 Italy
145.0mph 233.3kmh
0-50mph 80.5kmh: 5.7secs
0-60mph 96.5kmh: 7.2secs
0-1/4 mile: 15.7secs
260.0bhp 193.9kW 263.6PS
@ 7000rpm
202.0lbft 273.7Nm @ 5000rpm
196.8bhp/ton 193.5bhp/tonne
79.1bhp/L 59.0kW/L 80.2PS/L
44.9ft/sec 13.7m/sec
20.6mph 33.1kmh/1000rpm
Petrol 4-stroke piston
3286cc 200.5cu in
Vee 12 3 Carburettor
Compression ratio: 9.2:1
Bore: 77.0mm 3.0in
Stroke: 58.8mm 2.3in
Valve type/No: Overhead 24
Transmission: Manual
No. of forward speeds: 5
Wheels driven: Rear
Springs F/R: Coil/Coil
Brakes F/R: Disc/Disc
Steering: Worm & roller
Wheelbase: 240.0cm 94.5in
Track F: 137.7cm 54.2in
Track R: 139.2cm 54.8in
Length: 435.1cm 171.3in
Width: 167.4cm 65.9in
Height: 131.1cm 51.6in
Ground clearance: 14.0cm 5.5in
Kerb weight: 1343.8kg 2960.0lb
Fuel: 85.9L 18.9gal 22.7galUS

1392 Ferrari
275 GTS/4 NART
1967 Italy
155.0mph 249.4kmh
0-60mph 96.5kmh: 6.7secs
0-1/4 mile: 14.7secs
330.0bhp 246.1kW 334.6PS
@ 8000rpm
240.0lbft 325.2Nm @ 6000rpm
301.1bhp/ton 296.1bhp/tonne
100.4bhp/L 74.9kW/L 101.8PS/L
51.3ft/sec 15.7m/sec
19.6mph 31.5kmh/1000rpm
Petrol 4-stroke piston
3286cc 200.5cu in
Vee 12 6 Carburettor
Compression ratio: 9.2:1
Bore: 77.0mm 3.0in
Stroke: 58.8mm 2.3in
Valve type/No: Overhead 24
Transmission: Manual
No. of forward speeds: 5
Wheels driven: Rear
Springs F/R: Coil/Coil
Brakes F/R: Disc/Disc
Steering: Worm & roller
Wheelbase: 240.0cm 94.5in
Track F: 140.2cm 55.2in
Track R: 141.7cm 55.8in
Length: 440.9cm 173.6in
Width: 172.5cm 67.9in
Height: 124.5cm 49.0in
Ground clearance: 11.9cm 4.7in
Kerb weight: 1114.6kg 2455.0lb
Fuel: 93.9L 20.6gal 24.8galUS

1393 Ferrari
330 GTS
1968 Italy
146.0mph 234.9kmh
0-50mph 80.5kmh: 5.5secs
0-60mph 96.5kmh: 6.9secs
0-1/4 mile: 14.9secs
345.0bhp 257.3kW 349.8PS
@ 7000rpm
277.0lbft 375.3Nm @ 5000rpm
248.9bhp/ton 244.7bhp/tonne
87.0bhp/L 64.8kW/L 88.2PS/L
54.4ft/sec 16.6m/sec
22.1mph 35.6kmh/1000rpm
Petrol 4-stroke piston
3967cc 242.0cu in
Vee 12 3 Carburettor
Compression ratio: 8.8:1
Bore: 77.0mm 3.0in
Stroke: 71.0mm 2.8in
Valve type/No: Overhead 24
Transmission: Manual
No. of forward speeds: 5
Wheels driven: Rear
Springs F/R: Coil/Coil
Brake system: PA
Brakes F/R: Disc/Disc
Steering: Worm & roller
Wheelbase: 240.0cm 94.5in
Track F: 140.2cm 55.2in
Track R: 141.7cm 55.8in
Length: 443.0cm 174.4in
Width: 167.4cm 65.9in
Height: 125.0cm 49.2in
Ground clearance: 12.4cm 4.9in
Kerb weight: 1409.7kg 3105.0lb
Fuel: 90.1L 19.8gal 23.8galUS

1394 Ferrari
365 GTS 2+2
1969 Italy
152.0mph 244.6kmh
0-50mph 80.5kmh: 5.7secs
0-60mph 96.5kmh: 7.1secs
0-1/4 mile: 14.7secs
368.0bhp 274.4kW 373.1PS
@ 6600rpm
308.0lbft 417.3Nm @ 5000rpm
205.0bhp/ton 201.6bhp/tonne
83.8bhp/L 62.5kW/L 85.0PS/L
51.3ft/sec 15.6m/sec
21.1mph 33.9kmh/1000rpm
12.0mpg 10.0mpgUS 23.5L/100km
Petrol 4-stroke piston
4390cc 267.8cu in
Vee 12 3 Carburettor
Compression ratio: 8.8:1
Bore: 81.0mm 3.2in
Stroke: 71.0mm 2.8in
Valve type/No: Overhead 24
Transmission: Manual
No. of forward speeds: 5
Wheels driven: Rear
Springs F/R: Coil/Coil
Brake system: PA
Brakes F/R: Disc/Disc
Steering: Recirculating ball
Wheelbase: 264.9cm 104.3in
Track F: 143.8cm 56.6in
Track R: 146.8cm 57.8in
Length: 498.1cm 196.1in
Width: 179.1cm 70.5in
Height: 134.6cm 53.0in
Ground clearance: 13.0cm 5.1in
Kerb weight: 1825.1kg 4020.0lb
Fuel: 99.9L 22.0gal 26.4galUS

1395 Ferrari
Daytona Sportwagen
1969 Italy
173.0mph 278.4kmh
0-60mph 96.5kmh: 5.9secs
0-1/4 mile: 13.8secs
352.0bhp 262.5kW 356.9PS
@ 7500rpm
315.0lbft 426.8Nm @ 5500rpm
213.1bhp/ton 209.5bhp/tonne
80.2bhp/L 59.8kW/L 81.3PS/L
58.3ft/sec 17.7m/sec
Petrol 4-stroke piston
4390cc 267.8cu in
Vee 12 6 Carburettor
Compression ratio: 8.8:1
Bore: 81.0mm 3.2in
Stroke: 71.0mm 2.8in
Valve type/No: Overhead 24
Transmission: Manual
No. of forward speeds: 5
Wheels driven: Rear
Springs F/R: Coil/Coil
Brake system: PA
Brakes F/R: Disc/Disc
Steering: Recirculating ball
Wheelbase: 240.0cm 94.5in
Track F: 144.0cm 56.7in
Track R: 142.5cm 56.1in
Length: 475.0cm 187.0in
Width: 176.0cm 69.3in
Height: 124.5cm 49.0in
Kerb weight: 1679.8kg 3700.0lb
Fuel: 99.9L 22.0gal 26.4galUS

1396 Ferrari
365 GTB/4 Daytona
1970 Italy
173.0mph 278.4kmh
0-50mph 80.5kmh: 4.3secs
0-60mph 96.5kmh: 5.9secs
0-1/4 mile: 13.8secs
405.0bhp 302.0kW 410.6PS
@ 7500rpm
365.0lbft 494.6Nm @ 5500rpm
252.0bhp/ton 247.8bhp/tonne
92.3bhp/L 68.8kW/L 93.5PS/L
58.3ft/sec 17.7m/sec
24.8mph 39.9kmh/1000rpm
14.4mpg 12.0mpgUS 19.6L/100km
Petrol 4-stroke piston
4390cc 267.8cu in
Vee 12 6 Carburettor
Compression ratio: 9.3:1
Bore: 81.0mm 3.2in
Stroke: 71.0mm 2.8in
Valve type/No: Overhead 24
Transmission: Manual
No. of forward speeds: 5
Wheels driven: Rear
Springs F/R: Coil/Coil
Brake system: PA
Brakes F/R: Disc/Disc
Steering: Recirculating ball
Wheelbase: 240.0cm 94.5in
Track F: 144.0cm 56.7in
Track R: 142.5cm 56.1in
Length: 442.5cm 174.2in
Width: 176.0cm 69.3in
Height: 124.5cm 49.0in
Ground clearance: 13.0cm 5.1in
Kerb weight: 1634.4kg 3600.0lb
Fuel: 99.9L 22.0gal 26.4galUS

1397 Ferrari
Daytona
1971 Italy
175.0mph 281.6kmh
0-50mph 80.5kmh: 4.3secs
0-60mph 96.5kmh: 5.4secs
0-1/4 mile: 13.7secs
0-1km: 24.3secs
352.0bhp 262.5kW 356.9PS
@ 7500rpm
318.0lbft 430.9Nm @ 5500rpm
223.4bhp/ton 219.6bhp/tonne
80.2bhp/L 59.8kW/L 81.3PS/L
58.3ft/sec 17.7m/sec
24.6mph 39.6kmh/1000rpm
12.4mpg 10.3mpgUS 22.8L/100km
Petrol 4-stroke piston
4390cc 267.8cu in
Vee 12 6 Carburettor
Compression ratio: 9.3:1
Bore: 81.0mm 3.2in
Stroke: 71.0mm 2.8in
Valve type/No: Overhead 24
Transmission: Manual
No. of forward speeds: 5
Wheels driven: Rear
Springs F/R: Coil/Coil
Brake system: PA
Brakes F/R: Disc/Disc
Steering: Worm & nut
Wheelbase: 240.0cm 94.5in
Track F: 143.5cm 56.5in
Track R: 142.2cm 56.0in
Length: 442.0cm 174.0in
Width: 175.8cm 69.2in
Height: 124.5cm 49.0in
Ground clearance: 11.4cm 4.5in
Kerb weight: 1602.6kg 3530.0lb
Fuel: 127.4L 28.0gal 33.6galUS

1398 Ferrari
Daytona Cannonball
1971 Italy
173.0mph 278.4kmh
0-60mph 96.5kmh: 5.6secs
0-1/4 mile: 13.8secs
352.0bhp 262.5kW 356.9PS
@ 7500rpm
320.0lbft 433.6Nm @ 5500rpm
219.0bhp/ton 215.4bhp/tonne
80.2bhp/L 59.8kW/L 81.3PS/L
58.3ft/sec 17.7m/sec
Petrol 4-stroke piston
4390cc 267.8cu in
Vee 12 6 Carburettor
Compression ratio: 8.8:1
Bore: 81.0mm 3.2in
Stroke: 71.0mm 2.8in
Valve type/No: Overhead 48
Transmission: Manual
No. of forward speeds: 5
Wheels driven: Rear
Springs F/R: Coil/Coil
Brake system: PA
Brakes F/R: Disc/Disc
Steering: Worm & peg
Wheelbase: 239.8cm 94.4in
Track F: 143.8cm 56.6in
Track R: 142.5cm 56.1in
Length: 442.5cm 174.2in
Width: 176.0cm 69.3in
Height: 124.5cm 49.0in
Kerb weight: 1634.4kg 3600.0lb
Fuel: 99.9L 22.0gal 26.4galUS

1399 Ferrari
246 GT Dino
1972 Italy
141.0mph 226.9kmh
0-50mph 80.5kmh: 6.2secs
0-60mph 96.5kmh: 7.9secs
0-1/4 mile: 15.9secs
175.0bhp 130.5kW 177.4PS
@ 7000rpm
160.0lbft 216.8Nm @ 5500rpm
141.5bhp/ton 139.2bhp/tonne
72.4bhp/L 54.0kW/L 73.4PS/L
45.9ft/sec 14.0m/sec
18.2mph 29.3kmh/1000rpm
15.3mpg 12.7mpgUS 18.5L/100km
Petrol 4-stroke piston
2418cc 147.5cu in
Vee 6 3 Carburettor
Compression ratio: 9.0:1
Bore: 92.5mm 3.6in
Stroke: 60.0mm 2.4in
Valve type/No: Overhead 12
Transmission: Manual
No. of forward speeds: 5
Wheels driven: Rear
Springs F/R: Coil/Coil
Brake system: PA
Brakes F/R: Disc/Disc
Steering: Rack & pinion
Wheelbase: 233.9cm 92.1in
Track F: 142.7cm 56.2in
Track R: 143.0cm 56.3in
Length: 420.1cm 165.4in
Width: 170.2cm 67.0in
Height: 113.3cm 44.6in
Ground clearance: 11.9cm 4.7in
Kerb weight: 1257.6kg 2770.0lb
Fuel: 70.4L 15.5gal 18.6galUS

1400 Ferrari
365 GTC4
1972 Italy
152.0mph 244.6kmh
0-50mph 80.5kmh: 5.2secs
0-60mph 96.5kmh: 7.3secs
0-1/4 mile: 15.7secs
320.0bhp 238.6kW 324.4PS
@ 6200rpm
318.0lbft 430.9Nm @ 4000rpm
187.4bhp/ton 184.3bhp/tonne
72.9bhp/L 54.4kW/L 73.9PS/L
48.2ft/sec 14.7m/sec
24.5mph 39.4kmh/1000rpm
15.1mpg 12.6mpgUS 18.7L/100km
Petrol 4-stroke piston
4390cc 267.8cu in
Vee 12 6 Carburettor
Compression ratio: 8.8:1
Bore: 81.0mm 3.2in
Stroke: 71.0mm 2.8in
Valve type/No: Overhead 24
Transmission: Manual
No. of forward speeds: 5
Wheels driven: Rear
Springs F/R: Coil/Coil
Brake system: PA
Brakes F/R: Disc/Disc
Steering: Recirculating ball PA
Wheelbase: 249.4cm 98.2in
Track F: 147.8cm 58.2in
Track R: 147.8cm 58.2in
Length: 454.7cm 179.0in
Width: 177.8cm 70.0in
Height: 126.7cm 49.9in
Ground clearance: 11.9cm 4.7in
Kerb weight: 1736.5kg 3825.0lb
Fuel: 104.5L 23.0gal 27.6galUS

1401 Ferrari
246 GTS Dino
1974 Italy
141.0mph 226.9kmh
0-60mph 96.5kmh: 8.0secs
0-1/4 mile: 16.2secs
195.0bhp 145.4kW 197.7PS
@ 7600rpm
166.0lbft 224.9Nm @ 5500rpm
150.1bhp/ton 147.6bhp/tonne
80.6bhp/L 60.1kW/L 81.8PS/L
49.8ft/sec 15.2m/sec
18.6mpg 15.5mpgUS 15.2L/100km
Petrol 4-stroke piston
2418cc 147.5cu in
Vee 6 3 Carburettor
Compression ratio: 9.0:1
Bore: 92.5mm 3.6in
Stroke: 60.0mm 2.4in
Valve type/No: Overhead 12
Transmission: Manual
No. of forward speeds: 5
Wheels driven: Rear
Brake system: PA
Brakes F/R: Disc/Disc
Wheelbase: 233.9cm 92.1in
Track F: 145.3cm 57.2in
Track R: 145.5cm 57.3in
Length: 420.1cm 165.4in
Width: 174.0cm 68.5in
Height: 113.3cm 44.6in
Ground clearance: 11.9cm 4.7in
Kerb weight: 1321.1kg 2910.0lb
Fuel: 70.4L 15.5gal 18.6galUS

1402 Ferrari
308 GT4 Dino
1974 Italy
152.0mph 244.6kmh
0-50mph 80.5kmh: 5.1secs
0-60mph 96.5kmh: 6.4secs
0-1/4 mile: 14.6secs
242.0bhp 180.5kW 245.4PS
@ 7700rpm
185.0bhp/ton 181.9bhp/tonne
82.7bhp/L 61.7kW/L 83.9PS/L
59.9ft/sec 18.2m/sec
22.2mph 35.7kmh/1000rpm
15.0mpg 12.5mpgUS 18.8L/100km
Petrol 4-stroke piston
2926cc 178.5cu in
Vee 8
Compression ratio: 8.8:1
Bore: 81.0mm 3.2in
Stroke: 71.0mm 2.8in
Valve type/No: Overhead 16
Transmission: Manual
No. of forward speeds: 5
Wheels driven: Rear
Springs F/R: Coil/Coil
Brake system: PA
Brakes F/R: Disc/Disc
Steering: Rack & pinion
Wheelbase: 255.0cm 100.4in
Track F: 147.1cm 57.9in
Track R: 146.1cm 57.5in
Length: 431.8cm 170.0in
Width: 180.3cm 71.0in
Height: 118.1cm 46.5in
Kerb weight: 1330.2kg 2930.0lb
Fuel: 83.3L 18.3gal 22.0galUS

1403 Ferrari
365 GTB/4 Competitione
1974 Italy
186.0mph 299.3kmh
0-50mph 80.5kmh: 4.5secs
0-60mph 96.5kmh: 5.8secs
0-1/4 mile: 14.5secs
402.0bhp 299.8kW 407.6PS
@ 8300rpm
282.3bhp/ton 277.6bhp/tonne
91.6bhp/L 68.3kW/L 92.8PS/L
64.6ft/sec 19.6m/sec
25.3mph 40.7kmh/1000rpm
6.6mpg 5.5mpgUS 42.8L/100km
Petrol 4-stroke piston
4390cc 267.8cu in
Vee 12 6 Carburettor
Compression ratio: 10.1:1
Bore: 81.0mm 3.2in
Stroke: 71.0mm 2.8in
Valve type/No: Overhead 24
Transmission: Manual
No. of forward speeds: 5
Wheels driven: Rear
Springs F/R: Coil/Coil
Brake system: PA
Brakes F/R: Disc/Disc
Steering: Recirculating ball
Wheelbase: 240.0cm 94.5in
Track F: 149.1cm 58.7in
Track R: 147.6cm 58.1in
Length: 429.5cm 169.1in
Width: 176.0cm 69.3in
Height: 124.5cm 49.0in
Ground clearance: 13.0cm 5.1in
Kerb weight: 1448.3kg 3190.0lb
Fuel: 98.4L 21.6gal 26.0galUS

1404 Ferrari
365 GTB/4 Daytona
1974 Italy
0-60mph 96.5kmh: 7.2secs
0-1/4 mile: 15.7secs
352.0bhp 262.5kW 356.9PS
@ 7500rpm
319.0lbft 432.2Nm @ 5500rpm
218.1bhp/ton 214.5bhp/tonne
80.2bhp/L 59.8kW/L 81.3PS/L
58.3ft/sec 17.7m/sec
24.0mph 38.6kmh/1000rpm
12.6mpg 10.5mpgUS 22.4L/100km
Petrol 4-stroke piston
4390cc 267.8cu in
Vee 12
Compression ratio: 9.3:1
Bore: 81.0mm 3.2in
Stroke: 71.0mm 2.8in
Valve type/No: Overhead 24
Transmission: Manual
No. of forward speeds: 5
Wheels driven: Rear
Brakes F/R: Disc/Disc
Steering: Recirculating ball
Track F: 144.0cm 56.7in
Track R: 142.5cm 56.1in
Length: 442.5cm 174.2in
Kerb weight: 1641.2kg 3615.0lb
Fuel: 99.9L 22.0gal 26.4galUS

1405 Ferrari
308 Dino GT4
1975 Italy
138.0mph 222.0kmh
0-60mph 96.5kmh: 8.0secs
0-1/4 mile: 16.1secs
240.0bhp 179.0kW 243.3PS
@ 6600rpm
195.0lbft 264.2Nm @ 5000rpm
166.2bhp/ton 163.4bhp/tonne
82.0bhp/L 61.2kW/L 83.2PS/L
51.3ft/sec 15.6m/sec
16.2mpg 13.5mpgUS 17.4L/100km
Petrol 4-stroke piston
2926cc 178.5cu in
Vee 8 4 Carburettor
Compression ratio: 8.8:1
Bore: 81.0mm 3.2in
Stroke: 71.0mm 2.8in
Valve type/No: Overhead 16
Transmission: Manual
No. of forward speeds: 5
Wheels driven: Rear
Brake system: PA
Wheelbase: 255.0cm 100.4in
Track F: 146.1cm 57.5in
Track R: 146.1cm 57.5in
Length: 430.0cm 169.3in
Width: 180.3cm 71.0in
Height: 118.1cm 46.5in
Kerb weight: 1468.7kg 3235.0lb
Fuel: 83.3L 18.3gal 22.0galUS

1406 Ferrari
365 GT4 2+2
1975 Italy
150.0mph 241.4kmh
0-50mph 80.5kmh: 5.6secs
0-60mph 96.5kmh: 7.1secs
0-1/4 mile: 15.2secs
0-1km: 27.5secs
320.0bhp 238.6kW 324.4PS
@ 6200rpm
318.0lbft 430.9Nm @ 4000rpm
180.9bhp/ton 177.9bhp/tonne
72.9bhp/L 54.4kW/L 73.9PS/L
48.2ft/sec 14.7m/sec
22.8mph 36.7kmh/1000rpm
11.0mpg 9.2mpgUS 25.7L/100km
Petrol 4-stroke piston
4390cc 267.8cu in
Vee 12 6 Carburettor
Compression ratio: 8.8:1
Bore: 81.0mm 3.2in
Stroke: 71.0mm 2.8in
Valve type/No: Overhead 24
Transmission: Manual
No. of forward speeds: 5
Wheels driven: Rear
Springs F/R: Coil/Coil
Brake system: PA
Brakes F/R: Disc/Disc
Steering: Rack & pinion PA
Wheelbase: 269.2cm 106.0in
Track F: 147.1cm 57.9in
Track R: 149.9cm 59.0in
Length: 480.1cm 189.0in
Width: 180.3cm 71.0in
Height: 132.1cm 52.0in
Ground clearance: 10.2cm 4.0in
Kerb weight: 1799.2kg 3963.0lb
Fuel: 118.3L 26.0gal 31.3galUS

1407 Ferrari
512 BB
1975 Italy
175.0mph 281.6kmh
0-50mph 80.5kmh: 5.8secs
0-60mph 96.5kmh: 7.2secs
0-1/4 mile: 15.5secs
344.0bhp 256.5kW 348.8PS
@ 7200rpm
302.0lbft 409.2Nm @ 3900rpm
225.3bhp/ton 221.5bhp/tonne
78.4bhp/L 58.4kW/L 79.4PS/L
56.0ft/sec 17.0m/sec
25.2mph 40.5kmh/1000rpm
14.4mpg 12.0mpgUS 19.6L/100km
Petrol 4-stroke piston
4390cc 267.8cu in
Flat 12 4 Carburettor
Compression ratio: 8.8:1
Bore: 81.0mm 3.2in
Stroke: 71.0mm 2.8in
Valve type/No: Overhead 24
Transmission: Manual
No. of forward speeds: 5
Wheels driven: Rear
Springs F/R: Coil/Coil
Brake system: PA
Brakes F/R: Disc/Disc
Steering: Rack & pinion
Wheelbase: 249.9cm 98.4in
Track F: 150.1cm 59.1in
Track R: 151.1cm 59.5in
Length: 436.1cm 171.7in
Width: 180.1cm 70.9in
Height: 112.0cm 44.1in
Ground clearance: 12.4cm 4.9in
Kerb weight: 1552.7kg 3420.0lb
Fuel: 120.0L 26.4gal 31.7galUS

1408 Ferrari
308 GT4 Dino
1976 Italy
138.0mph 222.0kmh
0-60mph 96.5kmh: 8.0secs
0-1/4 mile: 16.1secs
240.0bhp 179.0kW 243.3PS
@ 6600rpm
195.0lbft 264.2Nm @ 5000rpm
166.2bhp/ton 163.4bhp/tonne
82.0bhp/L 61.2kW/L 83.2PS/L
51.3ft/sec 15.6m/sec
16.2mpg 13.5mpgUS 17.4L/100km
Petrol 4-stroke piston
2926cc 178.5cu in
Vee 8 4 Carburettor
Compression ratio: 8.8:1
Bore: 81.0mm 3.2in
Stroke: 71.0mm 2.8in
Valve type/No: Overhead 16
Transmission: Manual
No. of forward speeds: 5
Wheels driven: Rear
Springs F/R: Coil/Coil
Brake system: PA
Brakes F/R: Disc/Disc
Steering: Rack & pinion
Wheelbase: 255.0cm 100.4in
Track F: 146.1cm 57.5in
Track R: 146.1cm 57.5in
Length: 430.0cm 169.3in
Width: 180.3cm 71.0in
Height: 118.1cm 46.5in
Ground clearance: 15.2cm 6.0in
Kerb weight: 1468.7kg 3235.0lb
Fuel: 83.3L 18.3gal 22.0galUS

1409 Ferrari
308 GTB
1976 Italy
154.0mph 247.8kmh
0-50mph 80.5kmh: 5.1secs
0-60mph 96.5kmh: 6.5secs
0-1/4 mile: 14.8secs
0-1km: 26.9secs
255.0bhp 190.1kW 258.5PS
@ 7700rpm
210.0lbft 284.6Nm @ 5000rpm
199.0bhp/ton 195.7bhp/tonne
87.1bhp/L 65.0kW/L 88.3PS/L
59.9ft/sec 18.2m/sec
21.8mph 35.1kmh/1000rpm
19.2mpg 16.0mpgUS 14.7L/100km
Petrol 4-stroke piston
2927cc 178.6cu in
Vee 8 4 Carburettor
Compression ratio: 8.8:1
Bore: 81.0mm 3.2in
Stroke: 71.0mm 2.8in
Valve type/No: Overhead 16
Transmission: Manual
No. of forward speeds: 5
Wheels driven: Rear
Springs F/R: Coil/Coil
Brake system: PA
Brakes F/R: Disc/Disc
Steering: Rack & pinion
Wheelbase: 239.0cm 94.1in
Track F: 146.8cm 57.8in
Track R: 145.8cm 57.4in
Length: 422.9cm 166.5in
Width: 172.0cm 67.7in
Height: 111.8cm 44.0in
Ground clearance: 12.7cm 5.0in
Kerb weight: 1303.0kg 2870.0lb
Fuel: 74.2L 16.3gal 19.6galUS

1410 Ferrari
Dino 308 GT4 2+2
1976 Italy
154.0mph 247.8kmh
0-50mph 80.5kmh: 5.4secs
0-60mph 96.5kmh: 6.9secs
0-1/4 mile: 14.9secs
0-1km: 27.6secs
250.0bhp 186.4kW 253.5PS
@ 7700rpm
210.0lbft 284.6Nm @ 5000rpm
191.6bhp/ton 188.4bhp/tonne
85.4bhp/L 63.7kW/L 86.6PS/L
59.9ft/sec 18.2m/sec
21.1mph 33.9kmh/1000rpm
19.8mpg 16.5mpgUS 14.3L/100km
Petrol 4-stroke piston

2927cc 178.6cu in
Vee 8 4 Carburettor
Compression ratio: 8.8:1
Bore: 81.0mm 3.2in
Stroke: 71.0mm 2.8in
Valve type/No: Overhead 16
Transmission: Manual
No. of forward speeds: 5
Wheels driven: Rear
Springs F/R: Coil/Coil
Brake system: PA
Brakes F/R: Disc/Disc
Steering: Rack & pinion
Wheelbase: 255.0cm 100.4in
Track F: 146.1cm 57.5in
Track R: 146.1cm 57.5in
Length: 430.0cm 169.3in
Width: 180.3cm 71.0in
Height: 118.1cm 46.5in
Ground clearance: 12.7cm 5.0in
Kerb weight: 1327.0kg 2923.0lb
Fuel: 78.3L 17.2gal 20.7galUS

1411 Ferrari

308 GTB
1977 Italy
132.0mph 212.4kmh
0-50mph 80.5kmh: 7.4secs
0-60mph 96.5kmh: 9.4secs
0-1/4 mile: 16.7secs
240.0bhp 179.0kW 243.3PS
@ 6600rpm
195.0lbft 264.2Nm @ 5000rpm
174.3bhp/ton 171.4bhp/tonne
82.0bhp/L 61.2kW/L 83.2PS/L
51.3ft/sec 15.6m/sec
20.7mph 33.3kmh/1000rpm
15.6mpg 13.0mpgUS 18.1L/100km
Petrol 4-stroke piston
2926cc 178.5cu in
Vee 8 4 Carburettor
Compression ratio: 8.8:1
Bore: 81.0mm 3.2in
Stroke: 71.0mm 2.8in
Valve type/No: Overhead 16
Transmission: Manual
No. of forward speeds: 5
Wheels driven: Rear
Springs F/R: Coil/Coil
Brake system: PA
Brakes F/R: Disc/Disc
Steering: Rack & pinion
Wheelbase: 233.9cm 92.1in
Track F: 146.1cm 57.5in
Track R: 146.1cm 57.5in
Length: 422.9cm 166.5in
Width: 172.0cm 67.7in
Height: 112.0cm 44.1in
Ground clearance: 7.6cm 3.0in
Kerb weight: 1400.6kg 3085.0lb
Fuel: 79.9L 17.6gal 21.1galUS

1412 Ferrari

308 GTS
1978 Italy
145.0mph 233.3kmh
0-50mph 80.5kmh: 5.3secs
0-60mph 96.5kmh: 7.3secs
0-1/4 mile: 15.8secs
205.0bhp 152.9kW 207.8PS
@ 6600rpm
181.0lbft 245.3Nm @ 5000rpm
138.9bhp/ton 136.6bhp/tonne
70.0bhp/L 52.2kW/L 71.0PS/L
51.3ft/sec 15.6m/sec
20.7mph 33.3kmh/1000rpm
18.0mpg 15.0mpgUS 15.7L/100km
Petrol 4-stroke piston
2927cc 178.6cu in
Vee 8
Compression ratio: 8.8:1
Bore: 81.0mm 3.2in
Stroke: 71.0mm 2.8in
Valve type/No: Overhead 16
Transmission: Manual
No. of forward speeds: 5
Wheels driven: Rear
Springs F/R: Coil/Coil
Brake system: PA
Brakes F/R: Disc/Disc
Steering: Rack & pinion
Wheelbase: 233.9cm 92.1in
Track F: 146.1cm 57.5in
Track R: 146.1cm 57.5in
Length: 437.9cm 172.4in
Width: 172.0cm 67.7in
Height: 112.0cm 44.1in
Kerb weight: 1500.5kg 3305.0lb
Fuel: 79.9L 17.6gal 21.1galUS

1413 Ferrari

512 BB
1978 Italy
163.0mph 262.3kmh
0-50mph 80.5kmh: 4.7secs
0-60mph 96.5kmh: 6.2secs
0-1/4 mile: 13.6secs
0-1km: 25.0secs
360.0bhp 268.4kW 365.0PS
@ 6200rpm
332.0lbft 449.9Nm @ 4600rpm
235.4bhp/ton 231.5bhp/tonne
72.8bhp/L 54.3kW/L 73.8PS/L
52.9ft/sec 16.1m/sec
27.2mph 43.8kmh/1000rpm
15.7mpg 13.1mpgUS 18.0L/100km
Petrol 4-stroke piston
4942cc 301.5cu in
Vee 12 4 Carburettor
Compression ratio: 9.2:1
Bore: 82.0mm 3.2in
Stroke: 78.0mm 3.1in
Valve type/No: Overhead 24
Transmission: Manual
No. of forward speeds: 5
Wheels driven: Rear
Springs F/R: Coil/Coil
Brake system: PA
Brakes F/R: Disc/Disc
Steering: Rack & pinion
Wheelbase: 250.2cm 98.5in
Track F: 149.9cm 59.0in
Track R: 156.2cm 61.5in
Length: 439.9cm 173.2in
Width: 182.9cm 72.0in
Height: 111.8cm 44.0in
Ground clearance: 14.0cm 5.5in
Kerb weight: 1554.9kg 3425.0lb
Fuel: 110.1L 24.2gal 29.1galUS

1414 Ferrari

308 GT4 Dino
1980 Italy
138.0mph 222.0kmh
0-50mph 80.5kmh: 5.7secs
0-60mph 96.5kmh: 7.8secs
0-1/4 mile: 16.0secs
205.0bhp 152.9kW 207.8PS
@ 6600rpm
181.0lbft 245.3Nm @ 5000rpm
134.9bhp/ton 132.6bhp/tonne
70.1bhp/L 52.2kW/L 71.0PS/L
51.3ft/sec 15.6m/sec
20.7mph 33.3kmh/1000rpm
16.8mpg 14.0mpgUS 16.8L/100km
Petrol 4-stroke piston
2926cc 178.5cu in
Vee 8 4 Carburettor
Compression ratio: 8.8:1
Bore: 81.0mm 3.2in
Stroke: 71.0mm 2.8in
Valve type/No: Overhead 16
Transmission: Manual
No. of forward speeds: 5
Wheels driven: Rear
Springs F/R: Coil/Coil
Brake system: PA
Brakes F/R: Disc/Disc
Steering: Rack & pinion
Wheelbase: 255.0cm 100.4in
Track F: 147.1cm 57.9in
Track R: 147.1cm 57.9in
Length: 448.8cm 176.7in
Width: 170.9cm 67.3in
Height: 120.9cm 47.6in
Kerb weight: 1545.9kg 3405.0lb
Fuel: 74.9L 16.5gal 19.8galUS

1415 Ferrari

308 GTSi
1981 Italy
147.0mph 236.5kmh
0-50mph 80.5kmh: 6.1secs
0-60mph 96.5kmh: 7.9secs
0-1/4 mile: 16.1secs
205.0bhp 152.9kW 207.8PS
@ 6600rpm
181.0lbft 245.3Nm @ 5000rpm
141.3bhp/ton 138.9bhp/tonne
70.1bhp/L 52.2kW/L 71.0PS/L
51.3ft/sec 15.6m/sec
18.8mph 30.2kmh/1000rpm
13.8mpg 11.5mpgUS 20.5L/100km
Petrol 4-stroke piston
2926cc 178.5cu in
Vee 8 fuel injection
Compression ratio: 8.8:1
Bore: 81.0mm 3.2in
Stroke: 71.0mm 2.8in
Valve type/No: Overhead 16
Transmission: Manual
No. of forward speeds: 5
Wheels driven: Rear
Springs F/R: Coil/Coil
Brake system: PA
Brakes F/R: Disc/Disc
Steering: Rack & pinion
Wheelbase: 233.9cm 92.1in
Track F: 146.8cm 57.8in
Track R: 146.8cm 57.8in
Length: 442.5cm 174.2in
Width: 172.0cm 67.7in
Height: 112.0cm 44.1in
Kerb weight: 1475.5kg 3250.0lb
Fuel: 70.0L 15.4gal 18.5galUS

1416 Ferrari

288 GTO
1982 Italy
180.0mph 289.6kmh
0-60mph 96.5kmh: 5.0secs
0-1/4 mile: 14.1secs
394.0bhp 293.8kW 399.5PS
@ 7000rpm
366.0lbft 495.9Nm @ 3800rpm
306.4bhp/ton 301.3bhp/tonne
138.0bhp/L 102.9kW/L 139.9PS/L
54.4ft/sec 16.6m/sec
Petrol 4-stroke piston
2855cc 174.2cu in turbocharged
Vee 8 fuel injection
Compression ratio: 7.6:1
Bore: 80.0mm 3.1in
Stroke: 71.0mm 2.8in
Valve type/No: Overhead 32
Transmission: Manual
No. of forward speeds: 5
Wheels driven: Rear
Springs F/R: Coil/Coil
Brakes F/R: Disc/Disc
Steering: Rack & pinion
Wheelbase: 245.1cm 96.5in
Track F: 156.0cm 61.4in
Track R: 156.2cm 61.5in
Length: 429.0cm 168.9in
Width: 191.0cm 75.2in
Height: 112.0cm 44.1in
Kerb weight: 1307.5kg 2880.0lb
Fuel: 120.0L 26.4gal 31.7galUS

1417 Ferrari

512 BB
1982 Italy
168.0mph 270.3kmh
0-60mph 96.5kmh: 5.1secs
0-1/4 mile: 13.5secs
360.0bhp 268.4kW 365.0PS
@ 6200rpm
333.0lbft 451.2Nm @ 4600rpm
232.4bhp/ton 228.5bhp/tonne
72.8bhp/L 54.3kW/L 73.8PS/L
52.9ft/sec 16.1m/sec
Petrol 4-stroke piston
4942cc 301.5cu in
Flat 12 4 Carburettor
Compression ratio: 9.2:1
Bore: 82.0mm 3.2in
Stroke: 78.0mm 3.1in
Valve type/No: Overhead 48
Transmission: Manual
No. of forward speeds: 5
Wheels driven: Rear
Springs F/R: Coil/Coil
Brakes F/R: Disc/Disc
Wheelbase: 249.9cm 98.4in
Track F: 149.9cm 59.0in
Track R: 156.2cm 61.5in
Length: 464.3cm 182.8in
Width: 182.9cm 72.0in
Height: 111.8cm 44.0in
Kerb weight: 1575.4kg 3470.0lb
Fuel: 120.0L 26.4gal 31.7galUS

1418 Ferrari

Mondial 8
1982 Italy
135.0mph 217.2kmh
0-50mph 80.5kmh: 7.1secs
0-60mph 96.5kmh: 9.4secs
0-1/4 mile: 17.1secs
205.0bhp 152.9kW 207.8PS
@ 6600rpm
181.0lbft 245.3Nm @ 4600rpm
126.1bhp/ton 124.0bhp/tonne
70.1bhp/L 52.2kW/L 71.0PS/L
51.3ft/sec 15.6m/sec
20.7mph 33.3kmh/1000rpm
15.6mpg 13.0mpgUS 18.1L/100km
Petrol 4-stroke piston
2926cc 178.5cu in
Vee 8 fuel injection
Compression ratio: 8.8:1
Bore: 81.0mm 3.2in
Stroke: 71.0mm 2.8in
Valve type/No: Overhead 16
Transmission: Manual
No. of forward speeds: 5
Wheels driven: Rear
Springs F/R: Coil/Coil
Brake system: PA
Brakes F/R: Disc/Disc
Steering: Rack & pinion
Wheelbase: 264.9cm 104.3in
Track F: 149.4cm 58.8in
Track R: 151.6cm 59.7in
Length: 458.0cm 180.3in
Width: 179.1cm 70.5in
Height: 125.0cm 49.2in
Ground clearance: 12.4cm 4.9in
Kerb weight: 1652.6kg 3640.0lb
Fuel: 84.0L 18.5gal 22.2galUS

1419 Ferrari

308 GTBi Quattrovalvole
1983 Italy
142.0mph 228.5kmh
0-60mph 96.5kmh: 6.8secs
0-1/4 mile: 15.2secs
230.0bhp 171.5kW 233.2PS
@ 6800rpm
188.0lbft 254.7Nm @ 5500rpm
158.5bhp/ton 155.9bhp/tonne
78.6bhp/L 58.6kW/L 79.7PS/L
52.9ft/sec 16.1m/sec
19.2mpg 16.0mpgUS 14.7L/100km
Petrol 4-stroke piston
2926cc 178.5cu in
Vee 8 fuel injection
Compression ratio: 8.8:1
Bore: 81.0mm 3.2in
Stroke: 71.0mm 2.8in
Valve type/No: Overhead 32
Transmission: Manual
No. of forward speeds: 5
Wheels driven: Rear
Springs F/R: Coil/Coil
Brakes F/R: Disc/Disc
Wheelbase: 233.9cm 92.1in
Track F: 146.8cm 57.8in
Track R: 146.8cm 57.8in
Length: 442.5cm 174.2in
Width: 172.0cm 67.7in
Height: 112.0cm 44.1in
Kerb weight: 1475.5kg 3250.0lb
Fuel: 70.0L 15.4gal 18.5galUS

1420 Ferrari

308 GTSi Targa
1983 Italy
140.0mph 225.3kmh
0-50mph 80.5kmh: 6.1secs
0-60mph 96.5kmh: 7.9secs
0-1/4 mile: 16.1secs
205.0bhp 152.9kW 207.8PS
@ 6600rpm
181.0lbft 245.3Nm @ 5000rpm
141.3bhp/ton 138.9bhp/tonne
70.1bhp/L 52.2kW/L 71.0PS/L
51.3ft/sec 15.6m/sec
18.8mph 30.2kmh/1000rpm
13.8mpg 11.5mpgUS 20.5L/100km
Petrol 4-stroke piston
2926cc 178.5cu in
Vee 8 fuel injection
Compression ratio: 8.8:1
Bore: 81.0mm 3.2in
Stroke: 71.0mm 2.8in
Valve type/No: Overhead 16
Transmission: Manual
No. of forward speeds: 5
Wheels driven: Rear
Springs F/R: Coil/Coil
Brake system: PA
Brakes F/R: Disc/Disc
Steering: Rack & pinion
Wheelbase: 233.9cm 92.1in

Track F: 146.8cm 57.8in
Track R: 146.8cm 57.8in
Length: 442.5cm 174.2in
Width: 172.0cm 67.7in
Height: 112.0cm 44.1in
Kerb weight: 1475.5kg 3250.0lb
Fuel: 70.0L 15.4gal 18.5galUS

1421 Ferrari

288 GTO
1984 Italy
189.0mph 304.1kmh
0-50mph 80.5kmh: 4.1secs
0-60mph 96.5kmh: 5.0secs
0-1/4 mile: 14.1secs
400.0bhp 298.3kW 405.5PS
@ 7000rpm
366.0lbft 495.9Nm @ 3800rpm
350.7bhp/ton 344.8bhp/tonne
140.1bhp/L 104.5kW/L 142.0PS/L
54.4ft/sec 16.6m/sec
32.7mph 52.6kmh/1000rpm
16.2mpg 13.5mpgUS 17.4L/100km
Petrol 4-stroke piston
2855cc 174.2cu in turbocharged
Vee 8 fuel injection
Compression ratio: 7.6:1
Bore: 80.0mm 3.1in
Stroke: 71.0mm 2.8in
Valve type/No: Overhead 32
Transmission: Manual
No. of forward speeds: 5
Wheels driven: Rear
Springs F/R: Coil/Coil
Brake system: PA
Brakes F/R: Disc/Disc
Steering: Rack & pinion
Wheelbase: 245.1cm 96.5in
Track F: 156.0cm 61.4in
Track R: 156.2cm 61.5in
Length: 429.0cm 168.9in
Width: 191.0cm 75.2in
Height: 112.0cm 44.1in
Ground clearance: 12.7cm 5.0in
Kerb weight: 1160.0kg 2555.0lb
Fuel: 120.0L 26.4gal 31.7galUS

1422 Ferrari

512 BBi
1984 Italy
0-60mph 96.5kmh: 6.0secs
340.0bhp 253.5kW 344.7PS
@ 6000rpm
333.0lbft 451.2Nm @ 4200rpm
225.0bhp/ton 221.2bhp/tonne
68.8bhp/L 51.3kW/L 69.7PS/L
12.0mpg 10.0mpgUS 23.5L/100km
Petrol 4-stroke piston
4943cc 301.6cu in
Flat 12 fuel injection
Valve type/No: Overhead 48
Transmission: Manual
No. of forward speeds: 5
Wheels driven: Rear
Springs F/R: Coil/Coil
Brakes F/R: Disc/Disc
Steering: Rack & pinion
Wheelbase: 249.9cm 98.4in
Length: 439.9cm 173.2in
Width: 182.9cm 72.0in
Height: 112.0cm 44.1in
Kerb weight: 1536.8kg 3385.0lb
Fuel: 120.0L 26.4gal 31.7galUS

1423 Ferrari

GTO
1984 Italy
180.0mph 289.6kmh
0-60mph 96.5kmh: 5.0secs
0-1/4 mile: 14.1secs
400.0bhp 298.3kW 405.5PS
@ 7000rpm
366.0lbft 495.9Nm @ 3800rpm
350.7bhp/ton 344.8bhp/tonne
140.1bhp/L 104.5kW/L 142.0PS/L
54.4ft/sec 16.6m/sec
32.7mph 52.6kmh/1000rpm
15.6mpg 13.0mpgUS 18.1L/100km
Petrol 4-stroke piston
2855cc 174.2cu in turbocharged
Vee 8 fuel injection
Compression ratio: 7.6:1
Bore: 80.0mm 3.1in
Stroke: 71.0mm 2.8in
Valve type/No: Overhead 32
Transmission: Manual
No. of forward speeds: 5
Wheels driven: Rear
Springs F/R: Coil/Coil
Brake system: PA
Brakes F/R: Disc/Disc
Steering: Rack & pinion
Wheelbase: 245.1cm 96.5in
Track F: 156.0cm 61.4in
Track R: 156.2cm 61.5in
Length: 429.0cm 168.9in
Width: 191.0cm 75.2in
Height: 112.0cm 44.1in
Ground clearance: 12.7cm 5.0in
Kerb weight: 1160.0kg 2555.0lb
Fuel: 120.0L 26.4gal 31.7galUS

1424 Ferrari

Mondial Cabriolet Quattrovalvole
1984 Italy
138.0mph 222.0kmh
0-50mph 80.5kmh: 5.5secs
0-60mph 96.5kmh: 7.6secs
0-1/4 mile: 16.0secs
230.0bhp 171.5kW 233.2PS
@ 6800rpm
188.0lbft 254.7Nm @ 5500rpm
145.3bhp/ton 142.9bhp/tonne
78.6bhp/L 58.6kW/L 79.7PS/L
52.9ft/sec 16.1m/sec
20.3mph 32.7kmh/1000rpm
16.2mpg 13.5mpgUS 17.4L/100km
Petrol 4-stroke piston
2927cc 178.6cu in
Vee 8 fuel injection
Compression ratio: 8.6:1
Bore: 81.0mm 3.2in
Stroke: 71.0mm 2.8in
Valve type/No: Overhead 32
Transmission: Manual
No. of forward speeds: 5
Wheels driven: Rear
Springs F/R: Coil/Coil
Brake system: PA
Brakes F/R: Disc/Disc
Steering: Rack & pinion
Wheelbase: 264.9cm 104.3in
Track F: 151.4cm 59.6in
Track R: 153.4cm 60.4in
Length: 464.1cm 182.7in
Width: 179.1cm 70.5in
Height: 126.0cm 49.6in
Ground clearance: 11.7cm 4.6in
Kerb weight: 1609.4kg 3545.0lb
Fuel: 70.0L 15.4gal 18.5galUS

1425 Ferrari

365 GTB Goldsmith
1985 Italy
177.0mph 284.8kmh
0-60mph 96.5kmh: 5.1secs
0-1/4 mile: 13.7secs
400.0bhp 298.3kW 405.5PS
@ 7500rpm
440.0lbft 596.2Nm @ 5500rpm
285.3bhp/ton 280.6bhp/tonne
91.1bhp/L 68.0kW/L 92.4PS/L
58.3ft/sec 17.7m/sec
15.6mpg 13.0mpgUS 18.1L/100km
Petrol 4-stroke piston
4389cc 267.8cu in
Vee 12 6 Carburettor
Compression ratio: 9.8:1
Bore: 81.0mm 3.2in
Stroke: 71.0mm 2.8in
Valve type/No: Overhead 24
Transmission: Manual
No. of forward speeds: 5
Wheels driven: Rear
Springs F/R: Coil/Coil
Brake system: PA
Brakes F/R: Disc/Disc
Steering: Rack & pinion
Wheelbase: 233.9cm 92.1in
Track F: 146.8cm 57.8in
Track R: 146.8cm 57.8in
Length: 442.5cm 174.2in
Width: 172.0cm 67.7in
Height: 108.0cm 42.5in
Kerb weight: 1425.6kg 3140.0lb
Fuel: 70.0L 15.4gal 18.5galUS

1426 Ferrari

Testa Rossa
1985 Italy
178.0mph 286.4kmh
0-50mph 80.5kmh: 4.2secs
0-60mph 96.5kmh: 5.3secs
0-1/4 mile: 13.6secs
380.0bhp 283.4kW 385.3PS
@ 5750rpm
354.0lbft 479.7Nm @ 4500rpm
232.6bhp/ton 228.7bhp/tonne
76.9bhp/L 57.3kW/L 78.0PS/L
49.0ft/sec 14.9m/sec
26.1mph 42.0kmh/1000rpm
14.4mpg 12.0mpgUS 19.6L/100km
Petrol 4-stroke piston
4942cc 301.5cu in
Flat 12 fuel injection
Compression ratio: 8.7:1
Bore: 82.0mm 3.2in
Stroke: 78.0mm 3.1in
Valve type/No: Overhead 48
Transmission: Manual
No. of forward speeds: 5
Wheels driven: Rear
Springs F/R: Coil/Coil
Brake system: PA
Brakes F/R: Disc/Disc
Steering: Rack & pinion
Wheelbase: 255.0cm 100.4in
Track F: 151.9cm 59.8in
Track R: 166.1cm 65.4in
Length: 448.6cm 176.6in
Width: 197.6cm 77.8in
Height: 113.0cm 44.5in
Ground clearance: 13.0cm 5.1in
Kerb weight: 1661.6kg 3660.0lb
Fuel: 104.8L 23.0gal 27.7galUS

1427 Ferrari

3.2 Mondial
1986 Italy
145.0mph 233.3kmh
0-60mph 96.5kmh: 7.1secs
0-1/4 mile: 15.3secs
260.0bhp 193.9kW 263.6PS
@ 7000rpm
213.0lbft 288.6Nm @ 5500rpm
164.3bhp/ton 161.5bhp/tonne
81.6bhp/L 60.9kW/L 82.8PS/L
56.4ft/sec 17.2m/sec
19.4mph 31.2kmh/1000rpm
Petrol 4-stroke piston
3185cc 194.3cu in
Vee 8 fuel injection
Compression ratio: 9.2:1
Bore: 83.0mm 3.3in
Stroke: 73.6mm 2.9in
Valve type/No: Overhead 32
Transmission: Manual
No. of forward speeds: 5
Wheels driven: Rear
Springs F/R: Coil/Coil
Brakes F/R: Disc/Disc
Steering: Rack & pinion
Wheelbase: 264.9cm 104.3in
Track F: 151.4cm 59.6in
Track R: 153.4cm 60.4in
Length: 464.1cm 182.7in
Width: 179.1cm 70.5in
Height: 126.0cm 49.6in
Kerb weight: 1609.4kg 3545.0lb

1428 Ferrari

328 GTB
1986 Italy
155.0mph 249.4kmh
0-60mph 96.5kmh: 6.6secs
0-1/4 mile: 14.6secs
260.0bhp 193.9kW 263.6PS
@ 7000rpm
213.0lbft 288.6Nm @ 5500rpm
185.5bhp/ton 182.4bhp/tonne
81.6bhp/L 60.9kW/L 82.8PS/L
Petrol 4-stroke piston
3185cc 194.3cu in
Vee 8 fuel injection
Valve type/No: Overhead 32
Transmission: Manual
No. of forward speeds: 5
Wheels driven: Rear
Springs F/R: Coil/Coil
Brakes F/R: Disc/Disc
Steering: Rack & pinion
Wheelbase: 235.0cm 92.5in
Length: 429.5cm 169.1in
Width: 172.0cm 67.7in
Height: 112.0cm 44.1in
Kerb weight: 1425.6kg 3140.0lb
Fuel: 51.5L 11.3gal 13.6galUS

1429 Ferrari

Mondial 3.2
1986 Italy
149.0mph 239.7kmh
0-60mph 96.5kmh: 7.4secs
0-1/4 mile: 15.0secs
260.0bhp 193.9kW 263.6PS
@ 7000rpm
213.0lbft 288.6Nm @ 5500rpm
171.3bhp/ton 168.4bhp/tonne
81.6bhp/L 60.9kW/L 82.8PS/L
Petrol 4-stroke piston
3185cc 194.3cu in
Vee 8 fuel injection
Valve type/No: Overhead 32
Transmission: Manual
No. of forward speeds: 5
Wheels driven: Rear
Springs F/R: Coil/Coil
Brakes F/R: Disc/Disc
Steering: Rack & pinion
Wheelbase: 264.9cm 104.3in
Length: 453.4cm 178.5in
Width: 179.1cm 70.5in
Height: 125.0cm 49.2in
Kerb weight: 1543.6kg 3400.0lb
Fuel: 60.2L 13.2gal 15.9galUS

1430 Ferrari

Mondial 3.2QV
1986 Italy
144.0mph 231.7kmh
0-50mph 80.5kmh: 5.3secs
0-60mph 96.5kmh: 6.8secs
0-1/4 mile: 14.9secs
0-1km: 27.4secs
270.0bhp 201.3kW 273.7PS
@ 7000rpm
224.0lbft 303.5Nm @ 5500rpm
185.9bhp/ton 182.8bhp/tonne
84.7bhp/L 63.2kW/L 85.9PS/L
56.4ft/sec 17.2m/sec
20.9mph 33.6kmh/1000rpm
16.8mpg 14.0mpgUS 16.8L/100km
Petrol 4-stroke piston
3186cc 194.0cu in
Vee 8 1 Carburettor
Compression ratio: 9.8:1
Bore: 83.0mm 3.3in
Stroke: 73.6mm 2.9in
Valve type/No: Overhead 32
Transmission: Manual
No. of forward speeds: 5
Wheels driven: Rear
Springs F/R: Coil/Coil
Brake system: PA
Brakes F/R: Disc/Disc
Steering: Rack & pinion
Wheelbase: 264.9cm 104.3in
Track F: 151.8cm 59.8in
Track R: 150.8cm 59.4in
Length: 453.3cm 178.5in
Width: 179.5cm 70.7in
Height: 123.4cm 48.6in
Ground clearance: 15.3cm 6.0in
Kerb weight: 1477.0kg 3253.3lb
Fuel: 80.1L 17.6gal 21.1galUS

1431 Ferrari

328 GTS
1987 Italy
149.0mph 239.7kmh
0-60mph 96.5kmh: 5.9secs
0-1/4 mile: 14.4secs
260.0bhp 193.9kW 263.6PS
@ 7000rpm
213.0lbft 288.6Nm @ 5500rpm
183.7bhp/ton 180.7bhp/tonne
81.6bhp/L 60.9kW/L 82.8PS/L
56.4ft/sec 17.2m/sec
19.9mph 32.0kmh/1000rpm
19.8mpg 16.5mpgUS 14.3L/100km
Petrol 4-stroke piston
3185cc 194.3cu in
Vee 8 fuel injection
Compression ratio: 9.2:1
Bore: 83.0mm 3.3in
Stroke: 73.6mm 2.9in
Valve type/No: Overhead 32
Transmission: Manual
No. of forward speeds: 5
Wheels driven: Rear
Springs F/R: Coil/Coil
Brake system: PA
Brakes F/R: Disc/Disc
Steering: Rack & pinion
Wheelbase: 235.0cm 92.5in

Track F: 147.3cm 58.0in
Track R: 146.8cm 57.8in
Length: 428.5cm 168.7in
Width: 173.0cm 68.1in
Height: 112.8cm 44.4in
Ground clearance: 10.2cm 4.0in
Kerb weight: 1439.2kg 3170.0lb
Fuel: 70.0L 15.4gal 18.5galUS

1432 Ferrari

412
1987 Italy
147.0mph 236.5kmh
0-60mph 96.5kmh: 6.7secs
0-1/4 mile: 14.9secs
340.0bhp 253.5kW 344.7PS
@ 6000rpm
333.0lbft 451.2Nm @ 4200rpm
191.4bhp/ton 188.2bhp/tonne
68.8bhp/L 51.3kW/L 69.7PS/L
51.2ft/sec 15.6m/sec
23.5mph 37.8kmh/1000rpm
10.8mpg 9.0mpgUS 26.1L/100km
Petrol 4-stroke piston
4942cc 301.5cu in
Vee 12 fuel injection
Compression ratio: 9.6:1
Bore: 82.0mm 3.2in
Stroke: 78.0mm 3.1in
Valve type/No: Overhead 24
Transmission: Manual
No. of forward speeds: 5
Wheels driven: Rear
Springs F/R: Coil/Coil
Brake system: PA ABS
Brakes F/R: Disc/Disc
Steering: Rack & pinion PA
Wheelbase: 270.0cm 106.3in
Track F: 148.1cm 58.3in
Track R: 149.9cm 59.0in
Length: 481.1cm 189.4in
Width: 179.8cm 70.8in
Height: 131.3cm 51.7in
Kerb weight: 1806.9kg 3980.0lb
Fuel: 109.8L 24.1gal 29.0galUS

1433 Ferrari

Mondial Cabriolet 3.2
1987 Italy
145.0mph 233.3kmh
0-60mph 96.5kmh: 7.0secs
0-1/4 mile: 15.2secs
260.0bhp 193.9kW 263.6PS
@ 7000rpm
213.0lbft 288.6Nm @ 5500rpm
164.3bhp/ton 161.5bhp/tonne
81.6bhp/L 60.9kW/L 82.8PS/L
56.4ft/sec 17.2m/sec
19.4mph 31.2kmh/1000rpm
19.2mpg 16.0mpgUS 14.7L/100km
Petrol 4-stroke piston
3185cc 194.3cu in
Vee 8 fuel injection
Compression ratio: 9.2:1
Bore: 83.0mm 3.3in
Stroke: 73.6mm 2.9in
Valve type/No: Overhead 32
Transmission: Manual
No. of forward speeds: 5
Wheels driven: Rear
Springs F/R: Coil/Coil
Brake system: PA
Brakes F/R: Disc/Disc
Steering: Rack & pinion
Wheelbase: 264.9cm 104.3in
Track F: 151.4cm 59.6in
Track R: 153.4cm 60.4in
Length: 464.1cm 182.7in
Width: 179.1cm 70.5in
Height: 126.0cm 49.6in
Ground clearance: 11.7cm 4.6in
Kerb weight: 1609.4kg 3545.0lb
Fuel: 70.0L 15.4gal 18.5galUS

1434 Ferrari

308 Norwood Bonneville GTO
1988 Italy
198.0mph 318.6kmh
0-60mph 96.5kmh: 3.7secs
0-1/4 mile: 12.3secs
671.0bhp 500.4kW 680.3PS
@ 7850rpm
502.0lbft 680.2Nm @ 5250rpm
589.4bhp/ton 579.6bhp/tonne
111.8bhp/L 83.4kW/L 113.4PS/L
77.6ft/sec 23.6m/sec
Petrol 4-stroke piston
6000cc 366.1cu in
Vee 8 fuel injection
Compression ratio: 13.2:1
Bore: 104.9mm 4.1in
Stroke: 90.4mm 3.6in
Valve type/No: Overhead 16
Transmission: Manual
No. of forward speeds: 5
Wheels driven: Rear
Springs F/R: Coil/Coil
Brake system: PA
Brakes F/R: Disc/Disc
Steering: Rack & pinion
Wheelbase: 245.1cm 96.5in
Track F: 149.4cm 58.8in
Track R: 158.8cm 62.5in
Length: 429.0cm 168.9in
Width: 191.0cm 75.2in
Height: 112.0cm 44.1in
Kerb weight: 1157.7kg 2550.0lb
Fuel: 56.8L 12.5gal 15.0galUS

1435 Ferrari

F40
1988 Italy
201.0mph 323.4kmh
478.0bhp 356.4kW 484.6PS
@ 7000rpm
425.0lbft 575.9Nm @ 4000rpm
441.5bhp/ton 434.2bhp/tonne
162.8bhp/L 121.4kW/L 165.1PS/L
53.3ft/sec 16.2m/sec
Petrol 4-stroke piston
2936cc 179.1cu in turbocharged
Vee 8 fuel injection
Compression ratio: 7.8:1
Bore: 82.0mm 3.2in
Stroke: 69.5mm 2.7in
Valve type/No: Overhead 32
Transmission: Manual
No. of forward speeds: 5
Wheels driven: Rear
Springs F/R: Coil/Coil
Brake system: PA
Brakes F/R: Disc/Disc
Steering: Rack & pinion
Wheelbase: 245.1cm 96.5in
Track F: 159.5cm 62.8in
Track R: 161.0cm 63.4in
Length: 443.0cm 174.4in
Width: 198.1cm 78.0in
Height: 113.0cm 44.5in
Kerb weight: 1100.9kg 2425.0lb
Fuel: 119.6L 26.3gal 31.6galUS

1436 Ferrari

Mondial Cabriolet
1988 Italy
145.0mph 233.3kmh
0-50mph 80.5kmh: 5.4secs
0-60mph 96.5kmh: 7.0secs
0-1/4 mile: 15.2secs
260.0bhp 193.9kW 263.6PS
@ 7000rpm
213.0lbft 288.6Nm @ 5500rpm
164.3bhp/ton 161.5bhp/tonne
81.6bhp/L 60.9kW/L 82.8PS/L
56.4ft/sec 17.2m/sec
19.2mpg 16.0mpgUS 14.7L/100km
Petrol 4-stroke piston
3185cc 194.3cu in
Vee 8 fuel injection
Compression ratio: 9.2:1
Bore: 83.0mm 3.3in
Stroke: 73.6mm 2.9in
Valve type/No: Overhead 32
Transmission: Manual
No. of forward speeds: 5
Wheels driven: Rear
Springs F/R: Coil/Coil
Brake system: PA
Brakes F/R: Disc/Disc
Steering: Rack & pinion
Wheelbase: 264.9cm 104.3in
Track F: 151.4cm 59.6in
Track R: 153.4cm 60.4in
Length: 464.1cm 182.7in
Width: 179.1cm 70.5in
Height: 126.0cm 49.6in
Kerb weight: 1609.4kg 3545.0lb
Fuel: 70.0L 15.4gal 18.5galUS

1437 Ferrari

Testa Rossa
1988 Italy
181.0mph 291.2kmh
0-50mph 80.5kmh: 3.9secs
0-60mph 96.5kmh: 5.3secs
0-1/4 mile: 13.3secs
380.0bhp 283.4kW 385.3PS
@ 5750rpm
354.0lbft 479.7Nm @ 4500rpm
232.6bhp/ton 228.7bhp/tonne
76.9bhp/L 57.3kW/L 78.0PS/L
49.0ft/sec 14.9m/sec
14.4mpg 12.0mpgUS 19.6L/100km
Petrol 4-stroke piston
4942cc 301.5cu in
Flat 12 fuel injection
Compression ratio: 8.7:1
Bore: 82.0mm 3.2in
Stroke: 78.0mm 3.1in
Valve type/No: Overhead 48
Transmission: Manual
No. of forward speeds: 5
Wheels driven: Rear
Springs F/R: Coil/Coil
Brake system: PA
Brakes F/R: Disc/Disc
Steering: Rack & pinion
Wheelbase: 255.0cm 100.4in
Track F: 151.9cm 59.8in
Track R: 166.1cm 65.4in
Length: 448.6cm 176.6in
Width: 197.1cm 77.6in
Height: 113.0cm 44.5in
Kerb weight: 1661.6kg 3660.0lb
Fuel: 104.8L 23.0gal 27.7galUS

1438 Ferrari

Testa Rossa Straman Spyder
1988 Italy
181.0mph 291.2kmh
0-60mph 96.5kmh: 5.3secs
0-1/4 mile: 13.3secs
380.0bhp 283.4kW 385.3PS
@ 5750rpm
354.0lbft 479.7Nm @ 4500rpm
221.7bhp/ton 218.0bhp/tonne
76.9bhp/L 57.3kW/L 78.0PS/L
49.0ft/sec 14.9m/sec
Petrol 4-stroke piston
4942cc 301.5cu in
Flat 12 fuel injection
Compression ratio: 8.7:1
Bore: 82.0mm 3.2in
Stroke: 78.0mm 3.1in
Valve type/No: Overhead 48
Transmission: Manual
No. of forward speeds: 5
Wheels driven: Rear
Springs F/R: Coil/Coil
Brake system: PA
Brakes F/R: Disc/Disc
Steering: Rack & pinion
Wheelbase: 255.0cm 100.4in
Track F: 151.9cm 59.8in
Track R: 166.1cm 65.4in
Length: 448.6cm 176.6in
Width: 197.1cm 77.6in
Height: 114.3cm 45.0in
Kerb weight: 1743.4kg 3840.0lb
Fuel: 104.8L 23.0gal 27.7galUS

1439 Ferrari

308 Norwood
1989 Italy
182.0mph 292.8kmh
0-50mph 80.5kmh: 3.8secs
0-60mph 96.5kmh: 4.7secs
0-1/4 mile: 12.7secs
450.0bhp 335.6kW 456.2PS
@ 6700rpm
311.1bhp/ton 305.9bhp/tonne
153.8bhp/L 114.7kW/L 155.9PS/L
52.1ft/sec 15.9m/sec
Petrol 4-stroke piston
2926cc 178.5cu in turbocharged
Vee 8 fuel injection
Compression ratio: 8.0:1
Bore: 81.0mm 3.2in
Stroke: 71.0mm 2.8in
Valve type/No: Overhead 16
Transmission: Manual
No. of forward speeds: 5
Wheels driven: Rear
Springs F/R: Coil/Coil
Brake system: PA
Brakes F/R: Disc/Disc
Steering: Rack & pinion
Wheelbase: 233.9cm 92.1in
Track F: 146.8cm 57.8in
Track R: 146.8cm 57.8in
Length: 442.5cm 174.2in
Width: 172.0cm 67.7in
Height: 112.0cm 44.1in
Kerb weight: 1471.0kg 3240.0lb

1440 Ferrari

Mondial 3.2 Cabriolet
1989 Italy
145.0mph 233.3kmh
0-50mph 80.5kmh: 5.4secs
0-60mph 96.5kmh: 7.0secs
0-1/4 mile: 15.2secs
260.0bhp 193.9kW 263.6PS
@ 7000rpm
213.0lbft 288.6Nm @ 5500rpm
164.3bhp/ton 161.5bhp/tonne
81.6bhp/L 60.9kW/L 82.8PS/L
56.4ft/sec 17.2m/sec
19.2mpg 16.0mpgUS 14.7L/100km
Petrol 4-stroke piston
3185cc 194.3cu in
Vee 8 fuel injection
Compression ratio: 9.2:1
Bore: 83.0mm 3.3in
Stroke: 73.6mm 2.9in
Valve type/No: Overhead 32
Transmission: Manual
No. of forward speeds: 5
Wheels driven: Rear
Springs F/R: Coil/Coil
Brake system: PA
Brakes F/R: Disc/Disc
Steering: Rack & pinion
Wheelbase: 264.9cm 104.3in
Track F: 151.4cm 59.6in
Track R: 153.4cm 60.4in
Length: 464.1cm 182.7in
Width: 179.1cm 70.5in
Height: 126.0cm 49.6in
Kerb weight: 1609.4kg 3545.0lb
Fuel: 70.0L 15.4gal 18.5galUS

1441 Ferrari

Mondial t
1989 Italy
0-50mph 80.5kmh: 4.6secs
0-60mph 96.5kmh: 5.9secs
0-1/4 mile: 14.2secs
296.0bhp 220.7kW 300.1PS
@ 7200rpm
238.0lbft 322.5Nm @ 4200rpm
86.9bhp/L 64.8kW/L 88.1PS/L
59.0ft/sec 18.0m/sec
Petrol 4-stroke piston
3405cc 207.7cu in
Vee 8 fuel injection
Compression ratio: 10.4:1
Bore: 85.0mm 3.3in
Stroke: 75.0mm 2.9in
Valve type/No: Overhead 32
Transmission: Manual
No. of forward speeds: 5
Wheels driven: Rear
Springs F/R: Coil/Coil
Brake system: PA ABS
Brakes F/R: Disc/Disc
Steering: Rack & pinion PA
Wheelbase: 264.9cm 104.3in
Track F: 152.1cm 59.9in
Track R: 156.0cm 61.4in
Length: 453.4cm 178.5in
Width: 180.8cm 71.2in
Height: 123.4cm 48.6in
Fuel: 85.9L 18.9gal 22.7galUS

1442 Ferrari

Testa Rossa
1989 Italy
174.0mph 280.0kmh
0-50mph 80.5kmh: 4.1secs
0-60mph 96.5kmh: 5.2secs
0-1/4 mile: 13.5secs
0-1km: 23.8secs
390.0bhp 290.8kW 395.4PS
@ 6300rpm
363.1lbft 492.0Nm @ 4500rpm
237.6bhp/ton 233.7bhp/tonne
78.9bhp/L 58.8kW/L 80.0PS/L
53.7ft/sec 16.4m/sec
26.5mph 42.6kmh/1000rpm
16.6mpg 13.8mpgUS 17.0L/100km
Petrol 4-stroke piston
4942cc 302.0cu in
Flat 12 fuel injection
Compression ratio: 9.3:1

Bore: 82.0mm 3.2in
Stroke: 78.0mm 3.1in
Valve type/No: Overhead 48
Transmission: Manual
No. of forward speeds: 5
Wheels driven: Rear
Springs F/R: Coil/Coil
Brake system: PA
Brakes F/R: Disc/Disc
Steering: Rack & pinion
Wheelbase: 255.0cm 100.4in
Track F: 151.8cm 59.8in
Track R: 166.1cm 65.4in
Length: 448.5cm 176.6in
Width: 196.6cm 77.4in
Height: 113.0cm 44.5in
Ground clearance: 12.6cm 5.0in
Kerb weight: 1669.0kg 3676.2lb
Fuel: 113.7L 25.0gal 30.0galUS

1443 Ferrari

Testa Rossa Gemballa
1989 Italy
185.0mph 297.7kmh
0-60mph 96.5kmh: 5.3secs
0-1/4 mile: 13.3secs
380.0bhp 283.4kW 385.3PS
@ 5750rpm
354.0lbft 479.7Nm @ 4500rpm
231.3bhp/ton 227.4bhp/tonne
76.9bhp/L 57.3kW/L 78.0PS/L
49.0ft/sec 14.9m/sec
Petrol 4-stroke piston
4942cc 301.5cu in
Vee 12 fuel injection
Compression ratio: 8.7:1
Bore: 82.0mm 3.2in
Stroke: 78.0mm 3.1in
Valve type/No: Overhead 48
Transmission: Manual
No. of forward speeds: 5
Wheels driven: Rear
Springs F/R: Coil/Coil
Brake system: PA
Brakes F/R: Disc/Disc
Steering: Rack & pinion PA
Wheelbase: 255.0cm 100.4in
Track F: 151.9cm 59.8in
Track R: 168.7cm 66.4in
Length: 460.0cm 181.1in
Width: 210.1cm 82.7in
Height: 113.0cm 44.5in
Kerb weight: 1670.7kg 3680.0lb
Fuel: 104.8L 23.0gal 27.7galUS

1444 Ferrari

Testa Rossa Norwood
1989 Italy
210.0mph 337.9kmh
0-50mph 80.5kmh: 4.0secs
0-60mph 96.5kmh: 4.7secs
0-1/4 mile: 12.1secs
943.0bhp 703.2kW 956.1PS
@ 10000rpm
570.9bhp/ton 561.4bhp/tonne
190.8bhp/L 142.3kW/L 193.5PS/L
85.3ft/sec 26.0m/sec
Petrol 4-stroke piston
4942cc 301.5cu in turbocharged
Flat 12 fuel injection
Compression ratio: 8.2:1
Bore: 82.0mm 3.2in
Stroke: 78.0mm 3.1in
Valve type/No: Overhead 48
Transmission: Manual
No. of forward speeds: 5
Wheels driven: Rear
Springs F/R: Coil/Coil
Brake system: PA
Brakes F/R: Disc/Disc
Steering: Rack & pinion
Wheelbase: 255.0cm 100.4in
Track F: 151.9cm 59.8in
Track R: 166.1cm 65.4in
Length: 448.6cm 176.6in
Width: 197.1cm 77.6in
Height: 113.0cm 44.5in
Kerb weight: 1679.8kg 3700.0lb

1445 Ferrari

348tb
1990 Italy
164.0mph 263.9kmh
0-50mph 80.5kmh: 4.4secs
0-60mph 96.5kmh: 5.6secs
0-1/4 mile: 13.8secs
0-1km: 25.3secs
300.0bhp 223.7kW 304.2PS
@ 7200rpm
238.4lbft 323.0Nm @ 4200rpm
208.2bhp/ton 204.8bhp/tonne
88.1bhp/L 65.7kW/L 89.3PS/L
59.0ft/sec 18.0m/sec
23.3mph 37.5kmh/1000rpm
18.4mpg 15.3mpgUS 15.4L/100km
Petrol 4-stroke piston
3405cc 208.0cu in
Vee 8 fuel injection
Compression ratio: 10.4:1
Bore: 85.0mm 3.3in
Stroke: 75.0mm 2.9in
Valve type/No: Overhead 32
Transmission: Manual
No. of forward speeds: 5
Wheels driven: Rear
Springs F/R: Coil/Coil
Brake system: PA ABS
Brakes F/R: Disc/Disc
Steering: Rack & pinion
Wheelbase: 245.0cm 96.5in
Track F: 150.2cm 59.1in
Track R: 157.8cm 62.1in
Length: 423.0cm 166.5in
Width: 189.4cm 74.6in
Height: 117.0cm 46.1in
Kerb weight: 1465.0kg 3226.9lb
Fuel: 95.0L 20.9gal 25.1galUS

1446 Ferrari

F40
1990 Italy
200.0mph 321.8kmh
0-60mph 96.5kmh: 4.5secs
0-1/4 mile: 11.6secs
478.0bhp 356.4kW 484.6PS
@ 7000rpm
425.0lbft 575.9Nm @ 4000rpm
441.5bhp/ton 434.2bhp/tonne
162.8bhp/L 121.4kW/L 165.1PS/L
53.3ft/sec 16.2m/sec
Petrol 4-stroke piston
2936cc 179.1cu in turbocharged
Vee 8 fuel injection
Compression ratio: 7.8:1
Bore: 82.0mm 3.2in
Stroke: 69.5mm 2.7in
Valve type/No: Overhead 32
Transmission: Manual
No. of forward speeds: 5
Wheels driven: Rear
Springs F/R: Coil/Coil
Brakes F/R: Disc/Disc
Steering: Rack & pinion
Wheelbase: 245.1cm 96.5in
Track F: 159.5cm 62.8in
Track R: 161.0cm 63.4in
Length: 443.0cm 174.4in
Width: 198.1cm 78.0in
Height: 113.0cm 44.5in
Kerb weight: 1100.9kg 2425.0lb
Fuel: 117.3L 25.8gal 31.0galUS

1447 Ferrari

Mondial
1990 Italy
154.0mph 247.8kmh
0-50mph 80.5kmh: 5.1secs
0-60mph 96.5kmh: 6.6secs
0-1/4 mile: 15.0secs
300.0bhp 223.7kW 304.2PS
@ 7000rpm
229.0lbft 310.3Nm @ 4000rpm
194.2bhp/ton 191.0bhp/tonne
88.1bhp/L 65.7kW/L 89.3PS/L
57.4ft/sec 17.5m/sec
Petrol 4-stroke piston
3405cc 207.7cu in
Vee 8 fuel injection
Compression ratio: 10.4:1
Bore: 85.0mm 3.3in
Stroke: 75.0mm 2.9in
Valve type/No: Overhead 32
Transmission: Manual
No. of forward speeds: 5
Wheels driven: Rear
Springs F/R: Coil/Coil
Brake system: ABS
Brakes F/R: Disc/Disc
Steering: Rack & pinion PA
Wheelbase: 264.9cm 104.3in
Track F: 152.1cm 59.9in
Track R: 156.0cm 61.4in
Length: 453.4cm 178.5in
Width: 181.1cm 71.3in
Height: 123.4cm 48.6in
Kerb weight: 1570.8kg 3460.0lb
Fuel: 85.2L 18.7gal 22.5galUS

1448 Ferrari

Pininfarina Mythos
1990 Italy
180.0mph 289.6kmh
0-60mph 96.5kmh: 6.2secs
380.0bhp 283.4kW 385.3PS
@ 5750rpm
354.0lbft 479.7Nm @ 4500rpm
309.0bhp/ton 303.8bhp/tonne
76.9bhp/L 57.3kW/L 78.0PS/L
49.0ft/sec 14.9m/sec
Petrol 4-stroke piston
4942cc 301.5cu in
Flat 12 fuel injection
Compression ratio: 8.7:1
Bore: 82.0mm 3.2in
Stroke: 78.0mm 3.1in
Valve type/No: Overhead 48
Transmission: Manual
No. of forward speeds: 5
Wheels driven: Rear
Springs F/R: Coil/Coil
Brake system: PA
Brakes F/R: Disc/Disc
Steering: Rack & pinion
Wheelbase: 255.0cm 100.4in
Track F: 151.9cm 59.8in
Track R: 172.7cm 68.0in
Length: 430.5cm 169.5in
Width: 209.8cm 82.6in
Height: 106.4cm 41.9in
Kerb weight: 1250.8kg 2755.0lb
Fuel: 115.1L 25.3gal 30.4galUS

1449 Ferrari

348tb
1991 Italy
171.0mph 275.1kmh
0-50mph 80.5kmh: 4.7secs
0-60mph 96.5kmh: 6.0secs
0-1/4 mile: 14.3secs
300.0bhp 223.7kW 304.2PS
@ 7000rpm
229.0lbft 310.3Nm @ 4000rpm
205.5bhp/ton 202.1bhp/tonne
88.1bhp/L 65.7kW/L 89.3PS/L
57.4ft/sec 17.5m/sec
19.2mpg 16.0mpgUS 14.7L/100km
Petrol 4-stroke piston
3405cc 207.7cu in
Vee 8 fuel injection
Compression ratio: 10.4:1
Bore: 85.0mm 3.3in
Stroke: 75.0mm 2.9in
Valve type/No: Overhead 32
Transmission: Manual
No. of forward speeds: 5
Wheels driven: Rear
Springs F/R: Coil/Coil
Brake system: PA ABS
Brakes F/R: Disc/Disc
Steering: Rack & pinion
Wheelbase: 245.1cm 96.5in
Track F: 150.4cm 59.2in
Track R: 158.0cm 62.2in
Length: 423.4cm 166.7in
Width: 189.5cm 74.6in
Height: 117.1cm 46.1in
Ground clearance: 14.0cm 5.5in
Kerb weight: 1484.6kg 3270.0lb
Fuel: 87.8L 19.3gal 23.2galUS

1450 Ferrari

F40
1991 Italy
196.0mph 315.4kmh
0-50mph 80.5kmh: 2.8secs
0-60mph 96.5kmh: 3.8secs
0-1/4 mile: 11.8secs
478.0bhp 356.4kW 484.6PS
@ 7000rpm
425.0lbft 575.9Nm @ 4500rpm
359.3bhp/ton 353.3bhp/tonne
162.8bhp/L 121.4kW/L 165.1PS/L
53.3ft/sec 16.2m/sec
15.6mpg 13.0mpgUS 18.1L/100km
Petrol 4-stroke piston
2936cc 179.1cu in turbocharged
Vee 8 fuel injection
Compression ratio: 7.7:1
Bore: 82.0mm 3.2in
Stroke: 69.5mm 2.7in
Valve type/No: Overhead 32
Transmission: Manual
No. of forward speeds: 5
Wheels driven: Rear
Springs F/R: Coil/Coil
Brake system: PA
Brakes F/R: Disc/Disc
Steering: Rack & pinion
Wheelbase: 245.1cm 96.5in
Track F: 159.5cm 62.8in
Track R: 161.0cm 63.4in
Length: 443.0cm 174.4in
Width: 198.1cm 78.0in
Height: 113.0cm 44.5in
Ground clearance: 10.9cm 4.3in
Kerb weight: 1352.9kg 2980.0lb
Fuel: 120.0L 26.4gal 31.7galUS

1451 Ferrari

GTO Norwood
1991 Italy
199.0mph 320.2kmh
0-1/4 mile: 11.8secs
1600.0bhp 1193.1kW 1622.2PS
@ 7200rpm
900.0lbft 1219.5Nm @ 5600rpm
1257.5bhp/ton 1236.6bhp/tonne
190.7bhp/L 142.2kW/L 193.3PS/L
89.8ft/sec 27.4m/sec
Petrol 4-stroke piston
8390cc 511.9cu in turbocharged
Vee 8 fuel injection
Compression ratio: 7.0:1
Bore: 100.0mm 3.9in
Stroke: 114.0mm 4.5in
Valve type/No: Overhead 32
Transmission: Manual
No. of forward speeds: 4
Wheels driven: Rear
Springs F/R: Coil/Coil
Brakes F/R: Disc/Disc
Steering: Rack & pinion
Wheelbase: 245.1cm 96.5in
Track F: 156.0cm 61.4in
Track R: 156.2cm 61.5in
Length: 429.0cm 168.9in
Width: 191.0cm 75.2in
Height: 106.7cm 42.0in
Kerb weight: 1293.9kg 2850.0lb

1452 Ferrari

Mondial t
1991 Italy
154.0mph 247.8kmh
0-50mph 80.5kmh: 5.1secs
0-60mph 96.5kmh: 6.6secs
0-1/4 mile: 15.0secs
300.0bhp 223.7kW 304.2PS
@ 7200rpm
237.0lbft 321.1Nm @ 4200rpm
207.7bhp/ton 204.3bhp/tonne
88.1bhp/L 65.7kW/L 89.3PS/L
59.0ft/sec 18.0m/sec
Petrol 4-stroke piston
3405cc 207.7cu in
Vee 8 fuel injection
Compression ratio: 10.4:1
Bore: 85.0mm 3.3in
Stroke: 75.0mm 2.9in
Valve type/No: Overhead 32
Transmission: Manual
No. of forward speeds: 5
Wheels driven: Rear
Springs F/R: Coil/Coil
Brake system: ABS
Brakes F/R: Disc/Disc
Steering: Rack & pinion
Wheelbase: 264.9cm 104.3in
Track F: 152.1cm 59.9in
Track R: 156.0cm 61.4in
Length: 453.4cm 178.5in
Width: 180.8cm 71.2in
Height: 123.4cm 48.6in
Kerb weight: 1468.7kg 3235.0lb
Fuel: 85.2L 18.7gal 22.5galUS

1453 Ferrari

Mondial t Cabriolet
1991 Italy
154.0mph 247.8kmh
0-60mph 96.5kmh: 6.6secs
0-1/4 mile: 15.0secs
300.0bhp 223.7kW 304.2PS
@ 7000rpm
229.0lbft 310.3Nm @ 4000rpm

184.6bhp/ton 181.5bhp/tonne
88.1bhp/L 65.7kW/L 89.3PS/L
57.4ft/sec 17.5m/sec
18.0mpg 15.0mpgUS 15.7L/100km
Petrol 4-stroke piston
3405cc 207.7cu in
Vee 8 fuel injection
Compression ratio: 10.4:1
Bore: 85.0mm 3.3in
Stroke: 75.0mm 2.9in
Valve type/No: Overhead 32
Transmission: Manual
No. of forward speeds: 5
Wheels driven: Rear
Springs F/R: Coil/Coil
Brake system: PA ABS
Brakes F/R: Disc/Disc
Steering: Rack & pinion PA
Wheelbase: 264.9cm 104.3in
Track F: 152.1cm 59.9in
Track R: 156.0cm 61.4in
Length: 453.4cm 178.5in
Width: 181.1cm 71.3in
Height: 123.4cm 48.6in
Kerb weight: 1652.6kg 3640.0lb
Fuel: 85.2L 18.7gal 22.5galUS

1454 Fiat
17/50 Saloon
1928 Italy
55.0mph 88.5kmh
17.0mpg 14.2mpgUS 16.6L/100km
Petrol 4-stroke piston
2244cc 136.9cu in
In-line 6
Bore: 68.0mm 2.7in
Stroke: 103.0mm 4.1in
Transmission: Manual
No. of forward speeds: 4
Wheels driven: Rear
Brakes F/R: Drum/Drum
Wheelbase: 289.6cm 114.0in
Track F: 142.2cm 56.0in
Track R: 142.2cm 56.0in
Length: 408.9cm 161.0in
Width: 172.7cm 68.0in
Height: 180.3cm 71.0in
Kerb weight: 1220.3kg 2688.0lb
Fuel: 52.3L 11.5gal 13.8galUS

1455 Fiat
Balilla Pillarless Saloon
1934 Italy
57.5mph 92.5kmh
0-50mph 80.5kmh: 34.0secs
35.0mpg 29.1mpgUS 8.1L/100km
Petrol 4-stroke piston
995cc 60.7cu in
In-line 4
Bore: 65.0mm 2.6in
Stroke: 75.0mm 2.9in
Transmission: Manual
No. of forward speeds: 4
Wheels driven: Rear
Brakes F/R: Drum/Drum
Kerb weight: 788.1kg 1736.0lb
Fuel: 31.8L 7.0gal 8.4galUS

1456 Fiat
1500 Saloon
1935 Italy
71.4mph 114.9kmh
0-50mph 80.5kmh: 27.0secs
25.0mpg 20.8mpgUS 11.3L/100km
Petrol 4-stroke piston
1493cc 91.1cu in
In-line 6
Bore: 65.0mm 2.6in
Stroke: 75.0mm 2.9in
Valve type/No: Overhead 12
Transmission: Manual
No. of forward speeds: 4
Wheels driven: Rear
Brakes F/R: Drum/Drum
Ground clearance: 20.3cm 8.0in
Kerb weight: 1042.8kg 2297.0lb
Fuel: 45.5L 10.0gal 12.0galUS

1457 Fiat
Balilla Sports Two-seater
1935 Italy
73.7mph 118.6kmh
0-50mph 80.5kmh: 18.6secs
0-60mph 96.5kmh: 30.4secs
30.0mpg 25.0mpgUS 9.4L/100km
Petrol 4-stroke piston
995cc 60.7cu in
In-line 4
Bore: 65.0mm 2.6in
Stroke: 75.0mm 2.9in
Valve type/No: Overhead 8
Transmission: Manual
No. of forward speeds: 4
Wheels driven: Rear
Brakes F/R: Drum/Drum
Kerb weight: 657.4kg 1448.0lb
Fuel: 45.5L 10.0gal 12.0galUS

1458 Fiat
500 Convertible Saloon
1936 Italy
52.6mph 84.6kmh
0-50mph 80.5kmh: 63.6secs
42.0mpg 35.0mpgUS 6.7L/100km
Petrol 4-stroke piston
570cc 34.8cu in
In-line 4
Bore: 52.0mm 2.0in
Stroke: 67.0mm 2.6in
Valve type/No: Side 8
Transmission: Manual
No. of forward speeds: 4
Wheels driven: Rear
Brakes F/R: Drum/Drum
Kerb weight: 538.0kg 1185.0lb
Fuel: 21.6L 4.7gal 5.7galUS

1459 Fiat
1500 Pillarless Saloon
1937 Italy
75.0mph 120.7kmh
0-50mph 80.5kmh: 20.3secs
0-60mph 96.5kmh: 36.6secs
23.0mpg 19.2mpgUS 12.3L/100km
Petrol 4-stroke piston
1493cc 91.1cu in
In-line 6
Bore: 65.0mm 2.6in
Stroke: 75.0mm 2.9in
Valve type/No: Overhead 12
Transmission: Manual
No. of forward speeds: 4
Wheels driven: Rear
Brakes F/R: Drum/Drum
Ground clearance: 20.3cm 8.0in
Kerb weight: 1108.2kg 2441.0lb
Fuel: 45.5L 10.0gal 12.0galUS

1460 Fiat
Balilla Pillarless Saloon
1937 Italy
72.0mph 115.8kmh
0-50mph 80.5kmh: 23.0secs
0-60mph 96.5kmh: 39.5secs
30.0mpg 25.0mpgUS 9.4L/100km
Petrol 4-stroke piston
1089cc 66.4cu in
In-line 4
Bore: 68.0mm 2.7in
Stroke: 75.0mm 2.9in
Valve type/No: Overhead 8
Transmission: Manual
No. of forward speeds: 4
Wheels driven: Rear
Brakes F/R: Drum/Drum
Kerb weight: 885.7kg 1951.0lb
Fuel: 38.7L 8.5gal 10.2galUS

1461 Fiat
1400 Saloon
1950 Italy
76.9mph 123.7kmh
0-50mph 80.5kmh: 18.5secs
0-60mph 96.5kmh: 27.5secs
44.0bhp 32.8kW 44.6PS
@ 4400rpm
64.2lbft 87.0Nm @ 2700rpm
38.6bhp/ton 38.0bhp/tonne
31.5bhp/L 23.5kW/L 32.0PS/L
31.8ft/sec 9.7m/sec
15.9mph 25.6kmh/1000rpm
26.0mpg 21.6mpgUS 10.9L/100km
Petrol 4-stroke piston
1395cc 85.1cu in
In-line 4 1 Carburettor
Compression ratio: 6.7:1
Bore: 82.0mm 3.2in
Stroke: 66.0mm 2.6in
Valve type/No: Overhead 8
Transmission: Manual
No. of forward speeds: 4
Wheels driven: Rear
Brakes F/R: Drum/Drum
Wheelbase: 264.9cm 104.3in
Track F: 130.8cm 51.5in
Track R: 132.1cm 52.0in
Length: 423.9cm 166.9in
Width: 153.7cm 60.5in
Height: 150.1cm 59.1in
Ground clearance: 17.0cm 6.7in
Kerb weight: 1158.6kg 2552.0lb
Fuel: 47.8L 10.5gal 12.6galUS

1462 Fiat
500C Convertible (Topolino)
1951 Italy
60.3mph 97.0kmh
0-50mph 80.5kmh: 37.8secs
16.5bhp 12.3kW 16.7PS
@ 4400rpm
21.7lbft 29.4Nm @ 2900rpm
27.5bhp/ton 27.0bhp/tonne
29.0bhp/L 21.6kW/L 29.4PS/L
32.3ft/sec 9.8m/sec
13.5mph 21.7kmh/1000rpm
44.0mpg 36.6mpgUS 6.4L/100km
Petrol 4-stroke piston
569cc 34.7cu in
In-line 4 1 Carburettor
Compression ratio: 6.4:1
Bore: 52.0mm 2.0in
Stroke: 67.0mm 2.6in
Valve type/No: Overhead 8
Transmission: Manual
No. of forward speeds: 4
Wheels driven: Rear
Brakes F/R: Drum/Drum
Wheelbase: 199.9cm 78.7in
Track F: 111.5cm 43.9in
Track R: 108.2cm 42.6in
Length: 324.4cm 127.7in
Width: 128.3cm 50.5in
Height: 137.7cm 54.2in
Ground clearance: 14.2cm 5.6in
Kerb weight: 610.2kg 1344.0lb
Fuel: 23.0L 5.0gal 6.1galUS

1463 Fiat
1400
1952 Italy
76.3mph 122.8kmh
0-1/4 mile: 25.2secs
44.0bhp 32.8kW 44.6PS
@ 4400rpm
31.6bhp/L 23.5kW/L 32.0PS/L
31.8ft/sec 9.7m/sec
30.0mpg 25.0mpgUS 9.4L/100km
Petrol 4-stroke piston
1393cc 85.0cu in
In-line 4
Compression ratio: 6.5:1
Bore: 81.3mm 3.2in
Stroke: 66.0mm 2.6in
Valve type/No: Overhead 8
Transmission: Manual
No. of forward speeds: 4
Wheels driven: Rear
Wheelbase: 264.9cm 104.3in
Track F: 130.8cm 51.5in
Track R: 132.1cm 52.0in
Length: 424.2cm 167.0in
Height: 151.9cm 59.8in
Ground clearance: 16.5cm 6.5in

1464 Fiat
500C Convertible
1952 Italy
60.3mph 97.0kmh
0-50mph 80.5kmh: 37.8secs
16.5bhp 12.3kW 16.7PS
@ 4400rpm
21.7lbft 29.4Nm @ 2900rpm
27.5bhp/ton 27.0bhp/tonne
29.0bhp/L 21.6kW/L 29.4PS/L
32.3ft/sec 9.8m/sec
13.5mph 21.7kmh/1000rpm
41.0mpg 34.1mpgUS 6.9L/100km
Petrol 4-stroke piston
569cc 34.7cu in
In-line 4 1 Carburettor
Compression ratio: 6.4:1
Bore: 52.0mm 2.0in
Stroke: 67.0mm 2.6in
Valve type/No: Overhead 8
Transmission: Manual
No. of forward speeds: 4
Wheels driven: Rear
Brakes F/R: Drum/Drum
Wheelbase: 199.9cm 78.7in
Track F: 111.5cm 43.9in
Track R: 108.2cm 42.6in
Length: 324.4cm 127.7in
Width: 128.5cm 50.6in
Height: 137.7cm 54.2in
Ground clearance: 14.2cm 5.6in
Kerb weight: 610.2kg 1344.0lb
Fuel: 23.0L 5.0gal 6.1galUS

1465 Fiat
1100
1953 Italy
76.0mph 122.3kmh
0-50mph 80.5kmh: 19.8secs
0-60mph 96.5kmh: 32.7secs
0-1/4 mile: 24.5secs
36.0bhp 26.8kW 36.5PS
@ 4400rpm
50.5lbft 68.4Nm @ 2500rpm
44.7bhp/ton 43.9bhp/tonne
33.1bhp/L 24.7kW/L 33.5PS/L
36.1ft/sec 11.0m/sec
15.8mph 25.4kmh/1000rpm
36.2mpg 30.1mpgUS 7.8L/100km
Petrol 4-stroke piston
1089cc 66.4cu in
In-line 4
Compression ratio: 6.7:1
Bore: 68.0mm 2.7in
Stroke: 75.0mm 2.9in
Valve type/No: Overhead 8
Transmission: Manual
No. of forward speeds: 4
Wheels driven: Rear
Springs F/R: Coil/Leaf
Brakes F/R: Drum/Drum
Wheelbase: 233.7cm 92.0in
Track F: 121.9cm 48.0in
Track R: 121.2cm 47.7in
Length: 377.4cm 148.6in
Width: 143.0cm 56.3in
Height: 151.1cm 59.5in
Ground clearance: 15.7cm 6.2in
Kerb weight: 819.0kg 1804.0lb
Fuel: 31.8L 7.0gal 8.4galUS

1466 Fiat
1900
1953 Italy
86.0mph 138.4kmh
0-50mph 80.5kmh: 14.8secs
0-60mph 96.5kmh: 22.2secs
0-1/4 mile: 23.0secs
59.0bhp 44.0kW 59.8PS
@ 3700rpm
96.0lbft 130.1Nm @ 2600rpm
51.1bhp/ton 50.3bhp/tonne
31.0bhp/L 23.1kW/L 31.5PS/L
36.4ft/sec 11.1m/sec
22.1mph 35.6kmh/1000rpm
25.0mpg 20.8mpgUS 11.3L/100km
Petrol 4-stroke piston
1901cc 116.0cu in
In-line 4
Compression ratio: 6.7:1
Bore: 82.0mm 3.2in
Stroke: 90.0mm 3.5in
Valve type/No: Overhead 8
Transmission: Manual
No. of forward speeds: 5
Wheels driven: Rear
Springs F/R: Coil/Coil
Brakes F/R: Drum/Drum
Wheelbase: 265.2cm 104.4in
Track F: 132.6cm 52.2in
Track R: 132.1cm 52.0in
Length: 430.3cm 169.4in
Width: 166.9cm 65.7in
Height: 152.4cm 60.0in
Ground clearance: 18.3cm 7.2in
Kerb weight: 1173.6kg 2585.0lb
Fuel: 47.8L 10.5gal 12.6galUS

1467 Fiat
1100 TV Saloon
1954 Italy
84.0mph 135.2kmh
0-50mph 80.5kmh: 14.1secs
0-60mph 96.5kmh: 21.5secs
0-1/4 mile: 22.2secs
50.0bhp 37.3kW 50.7PS

@ 5200rpm
56.0lbft 75.9Nm @ 3200rpm
60.0bhp/ton 59.0bhp/tonne
45.9bhp/L 34.2kW/L 46.5PS/L
42.6ft/sec 13.0m/sec
15.8mph 25.4kmh/1000rpm
33.5mpg 27.9mpgUS 8.4L/100km
Petrol 4-stroke piston
1089cc 66.4cu in
In-line 4 1 Carburettor
Compression ratio: 7.6:1
Bore: 68.0mm 2.7in
Stroke: 75.0mm 2.9in
Valve type/No: Overhead 8
Transmission: Manual
No. of forward speeds: 4
Wheels driven: Rear
Springs F/R: Coil/Leaf
Brakes F/R: Drum/Drum
Wheelbase: 234.2cm 92.2in
Track F: 122.9cm 48.4in
Track R: 120.9cm 47.6in
Length: 377.4cm 148.6in
Width: 146.1cm 57.5in
Height: 148.6cm 58.5in
Ground clearance: 15.5cm 6.1in
Kerb weight: 846.7kg 1865.0lb
Fuel: 39.8L 8.8gal 10.5galUS

1468 Fiat

8V
1954 Italy
120.0mph 193.1kmh
0-50mph 80.5kmh: 9.3secs
0-60mph 96.5kmh: 12.6secs
0-1/4 mile: 21.5secs
115.0bhp 85.8kW 116.6PS
@ 6000rpm
106.7lbft 144.6Nm @ 4600rpm
110.1bhp/ton 108.2bhp/tonne
57.6bhp/L 43.0kW/L 58.4PS/L
40.2ft/sec 12.3m/sec
16.8mph 27.0kmh/1000rpm
15.5mpg 12.9mpgUS 18.2L/100km
Petrol 4-stroke piston
1996cc 121.8cu in
Vee 8
Compression ratio: 8.5:1
Bore: 72.0mm 2.8in
Stroke: 61.3mm 2.4in
Valve type/No: Overhead 16
Transmission: Manual
No. of forward speeds: 4
Wheels driven: Rear
Springs F/R: Coil/Coil
Brakes F/R: Drum/Drum
Wheelbase: 240.0cm 94.5in
Track F: 128.8cm 50.7in
Track R: 128.8cm 50.7in
Length: 402.8cm 158.6in
Width: 156.7cm 61.7in
Height: 130.6cm 51.4in
Ground clearance: 15.0cm 5.9in
Kerb weight: 1062.4kg 2340.0lb
Fuel: 79.6L 17.5gal 21.0galUS

1469 Fiat

600
1955 Italy
59.5mph 95.7kmh
0-50mph 80.5kmh: 35.5secs
0-1/4 mile: 27.3secs
21.5bhp 16.0kW 21.8PS
@ 4600rpm
28.9lbft 39.2Nm @ 2800rpm
37.4bhp/ton 36.8bhp/tonne
34.0bhp/L 25.3kW/L 34.4PS/L
28.1ft/sec 8.6m/sec
13.7mph 22.0kmh/1000rpm
49.0mpg 40.8mpgUS 5.8L/100km
Petrol 4-stroke piston
633cc 38.6cu in
In-line 4 1 Carburettor
Compression ratio: 7.0:1
Bore: 60.0mm 2.4in
Stroke: 56.0mm 2.2in
Valve type/No: Overhead 8
Transmission: Manual
No. of forward speeds: 4
Wheels driven: Rear
Springs F/R: Leaf/Coil
Brakes F/R: Drum/Drum
Wheelbase: 199.9cm 78.7in
Track F: 114.3cm 45.0in
Track R: 116.1cm 45.7in
Length: 321.3cm 126.5in
Width: 137.2cm 54.0in
Height: 141.0cm 55.5in
Ground clearance: 16.0cm 6.3in
Kerb weight: 584.7kg 1288.0lb
Fuel: 27.3L 6.0gal 7.2galUS

1470 Fiat

1100
1957 Italy
73.7mph 118.6kmh
0-50mph 80.5kmh: 19.6secs
0-60mph 96.5kmh: 29.5secs
0-1/4 mile: 23.1secs
40.0bhp 29.8kW 40.5PS
@ 4400rpm
51.4lbft 69.6Nm @ 2700rpm
46.7bhp/ton 45.9bhp/tonne
36.7bhp/L 27.4kW/L 37.2PS/L
36.1ft/sec 11.0m/sec
Petrol 4-stroke piston
1089cc 66.4cu in
In-line 4
Compression ratio: 7.0:1
Bore: 68.1mm 2.7in
Stroke: 74.9mm 2.9in
Valve type/No: Overhead 8
Transmission: Manual
No. of forward speeds: 4
Wheels driven: Rear
Wheelbase: 233.9cm 92.1in
Track F: 122.7cm 48.3in
Track R: 121.2cm 47.7in
Kerb weight: 871.7kg 1920.0lb

1471 Fiat

1100 Saloon
1957 Italy
77.0mph 123.9kmh
0-50mph 80.5kmh: 18.6secs
0-60mph 96.5kmh: 29.8secs
0-1/4 mile: 23.8secs
40.0bhp 29.8kW 40.5PS
@ 4400rpm
51.3lbft 69.5Nm @ 2700rpm
47.9bhp/ton 47.1bhp/tonne
36.7bhp/L 27.4kW/L 37.2PS/L
36.1ft/sec 11.0m/sec
15.8mph 25.4kmh/1000rpm
34.2mpg 28.5mpgUS 8.3L/100km
Petrol 4-stroke piston
1089cc 66.4cu in
In-line 4 1 Carburettor
Compression ratio: 7.1:1
Bore: 68.0mm 2.7in
Stroke: 75.0mm 2.9in
Valve type/No: Overhead 8
Transmission: Manual
No. of forward speeds: 4
Wheels driven: Rear
Springs F/R: Coil/Leaf
Brakes F/R: Drum/Drum
Wheelbase: 234.2cm 92.2in
Track F: 122.9cm 48.4in
Track R: 120.9cm 47.6in
Length: 377.4cm 148.6in
Width: 146.1cm 57.5in
Height: 148.6cm 58.5in
Ground clearance: 15.5cm 6.1in
Kerb weight: 848.5kg 1869.0lb
Fuel: 37.5L 8.2gal 9.9galUS

1472 Fiat

600
1957 Italy
60.3mph 97.0kmh
0-50mph 80.5kmh: 28.5secs
0-60mph 96.5kmh: 54.0secs
0-1/4 mile: 26.1secs
21.5bhp 16.0kW 21.8PS
@ 4600rpm
28.9lbft 39.2Nm @ 2800rpm
36.2bhp/ton 35.6bhp/tonne
34.0bhp/L 25.3kW/L 34.4PS/L
28.1ft/sec 8.6m/sec
Petrol 4-stroke piston
633cc 38.6cu in
In-line 4
Compression ratio: 7.0:1
Bore: 59.9mm 2.4in
Stroke: 55.9mm 2.2in
Valve type/No: Overhead 8
Transmission: Manual
No. of forward speeds: 4
Wheels driven: Rear
Wheelbase: 199.9cm 78.7in
Track F: 114.3cm 45.0in
Track R: 115.3cm 45.4in
Kerb weight: 603.8kg 1330.0lb

1473 Fiat

600 Multipla
1957 Italy
55.0mph 88.5kmh
0-50mph 80.5kmh: 50.7secs
0-1/4 mile: 29.7secs
21.5bhp 16.0kW 21.8PS
@ 4600rpm
28.9lbft 39.2Nm @ 2800rpm
29.7bhp/ton 29.2bhp/tonne
34.0bhp/L 25.3kW/L 34.4PS/L
28.1ft/sec 8.6m/sec
13.7mph 22.0kmh/1000rpm
39.4mpg 32.8mpgUS 7.2L/100km
Petrol 4-stroke piston
633cc 38.6cu in
In-line 4 1 Carburettor
Compression ratio: 7.0:1
Bore: 60.0mm 2.4in
Stroke: 56.0mm 2.2in
Valve type/No: Overhead 8
Transmission: Manual
No. of forward speeds: 4
Wheels driven: Rear
Springs F/R: Coil/Coil
Brakes F/R: Drum/Drum
Wheelbase: 199.9cm 78.7in
Track F: 114.8cm 45.2in
Track R: 111.8cm 44.0in
Length: 353.1cm 139.0in
Width: 145.3cm 57.2in
Height: 158.0cm 62.2in
Ground clearance: 14.0cm 5.5in
Kerb weight: 737.3kg 1624.0lb
Fuel: 27.3L 6.0gal 7.2galUS

1474 Fiat

Multipla
1957 Italy
58.8mph 94.6kmh
0-50mph 80.5kmh: 32.3secs
0-1/4 mile: 27.3secs
21.5bhp 16.0kW 21.8PS
@ 4600rpm
28.9lbft 39.2Nm @ 2800rpm
30.9bhp/ton 30.4bhp/tonne
34.0bhp/L 25.3kW/L 34.4PS/L
28.1ft/sec 8.6m/sec
Petrol 4-stroke piston
633cc 38.6cu in
In-line 4
Compression ratio: 7.0:1
Bore: 59.9mm 2.4in
Stroke: 55.9mm 2.2in
Valve type/No: Overhead 8
Transmission: Manual
No. of forward speeds: 4
Wheels driven: Rear
Wheelbase: 199.9cm 78.7in
Track F: 122.4cm 48.2in
Track R: 115.3cm 45.4in
Kerb weight: 708.2kg 1560.0lb

1475 Fiat

1200 Gran Luce
1958 Italy
89.0mph 143.2kmh
0-50mph 80.5kmh: 14.2secs
0-60mph 96.5kmh: 19.9secs
0-1/4 mile: 21.6secs
55.0bhp 41.0kW 55.8PS
@ 5300rpm
60.0lbft 81.3Nm @ 3000rpm
60.9bhp/ton 59.9bhp/tonne
45.0bhp/L 33.6kW/L 45.7PS/L
43.4ft/sec 13.2m/sec
15.8mph 25.4kmh/1000rpm
34.5mpg 28.7mpgUS 8.2L/100km
Petrol 4-stroke piston
1221cc 74.5cu in
In-line 4 1 Carburettor
Compression ratio: 8.1:1
Bore: 72.0mm 2.8in
Stroke: 75.0mm 2.9in
Valve type/No: Overhead 8
Transmission: Manual
No. of forward speeds: 4
Wheels driven: Rear
Springs F/R: Coil/Leaf
Brakes F/R: Drum/Drum
Wheelbase: 233.9cm 92.1in
Track F: 123.2cm 48.5in
Track R: 121.4cm 47.8in
Length: 391.9cm 154.3in
Width: 145.8cm 57.4in
Height: 146.8cm 57.8in
Ground clearance: 13.0cm 5.1in
Kerb weight: 918.4kg 2023.0lb
Fuel: 38.2L 8.4gal 10.1galUS

1476 Fiat

1200 TV Spyder
1958 Italy
89.2mph 143.5kmh
0-50mph 80.5kmh: 12.8secs
0-60mph 96.5kmh: 18.8secs
0-1/4 mile: 21.0secs
60.0bhp 44.7kW 60.8PS
@ 5300rpm
60.0lbft 81.3Nm @ 3000rpm
66.9bhp/ton 65.7bhp/tonne
49.1bhp/L 36.6kW/L 49.8PS/L
43.4ft/sec 13.2m/sec
16.2mph 26.1kmh/1000rpm
Petrol 4-stroke piston
1221cc 74.5cu in
In-line 4
Compression ratio: 8.0:1
Bore: 71.9mm 2.8in
Stroke: 74.9mm 2.9in
Valve type/No: Overhead 8
Transmission: Manual
No. of forward speeds: 4
Wheels driven: Rear
Wheelbase: 233.9cm 92.1in
Track F: 122.7cm 48.3in
Track R: 121.2cm 47.7in
Length: 391.2cm 154.0in
Width: 145.8cm 57.4in
Height: 128.0cm 50.4in
Kerb weight: 912.5kg 2010.0lb

1477 Fiat

500
1958 Italy
54.0mph 86.9kmh
0-1/4 mile: 31.9secs
13.0bhp 9.7kW 13.2PS
@ 4000rpm
20.2lbft 27.4Nm @ 2500rpm
28.1bhp/ton 27.6bhp/tonne
27.1bhp/L 20.2kW/L 27.5PS/L
30.7ft/sec 9.3m/sec
12.5mph 20.1kmh/1000rpm
55.5mpg 46.2mpgUS 5.1L/100km
Petrol 4-stroke piston
479cc 29.2cu in
In-line 2 1 Carburettor
Compression ratio: 6.5:1
Bore: 66.0mm 2.6in
Stroke: 70.0mm 2.8in
Valve type/No: Overhead 4
Transmission: Manual
No. of forward speeds: 4
Wheels driven: Rear
Springs F/R: Leaf/Coil
Brakes F/R: Drum/Drum
Wheelbase: 184.2cm 72.5in
Track F: 112.0cm 44.1in
Track R: 113.3cm 44.6in
Length: 294.6cm 116.0in
Width: 132.1cm 52.0in
Height: 132.3cm 52.1in
Ground clearance: 13.0cm 5.1in
Kerb weight: 470.3kg 1036.0lb
Fuel: 20.5L 4.5gal 5.4galUS

1478 Fiat

750 Abarth
1958 Italy
76.0mph 122.3kmh
0-50mph 80.5kmh: 13.4secs
0-60mph 96.5kmh: 19.6secs
0-1/4 mile: 21.6secs
41.5bhp 30.9kW 42.1PS
@ 5500rpm
39.8lbft 53.9Nm @ 4000rpm
68.9bhp/ton 67.7bhp/tonne
55.6bhp/L 41.4kW/L 56.3PS/L
38.5ft/sec 11.7m/sec
14.8mph 23.8kmh/1000rpm
Petrol 4-stroke piston
747cc 45.6cu in
In-line 4
Compression ratio: 9.0:1
Bore: 61.0mm 2.4in
Stroke: 64.0mm 2.5in
Valve type/No: Overhead 8
Transmission: Manual
No. of forward speeds: 4

Wheels driven: Rear
Wheelbase: 199.9cm 78.7in
Track F: 115.1cm 45.3in
Track R: 115.3cm 45.4in
Length: 331.5cm 130.5in
Width: 137.9cm 54.3in
Height: 140.5cm 55.3in
Kerb weight: 612.9kg 1350.0lb

1479 Fiat

Abarth 750GT Zagato
1958 Italy
87.1mph 140.1kmh
0-50mph 80.5kmh: 12.8secs
0-60mph 96.5kmh: 17.3secs
0-1/4 mile: 20.9secs
43.0bhp 32.1kW 43.6PS
@ 5800rpm
40.0lbft 54.2Nm @ 4000rpm
77.1bhp/ton 75.8bhp/tonne
57.6bhp/L 42.9kW/L 58.4PS/L
40.6ft/sec 12.4m/sec
15.8mph 25.4kmh/1000rpm
Petrol 4-stroke piston
747cc 45.6cu in
In-line 4
Compression ratio: 9.8:1
Bore: 61.0mm 2.4in
Stroke: 64.0mm 2.5in
Valve type/No: Overhead 8
Transmission: Manual
No. of forward speeds: 4
Wheels driven: Rear
Wheelbase: 199.9cm 78.7in
Track F: 115.1cm 45.3in
Track R: 115.3cm 45.4in
Length: 325.1cm 128.0in
Width: 137.9cm 54.3in
Height: 119.9cm 47.2in
Kerb weight: 567.5kg 1250.0lb

1480 Fiat

Abarth Zagato
1958 Italy
87.1mph 140.1kmh
0-50mph 80.5kmh: 12.8secs
0-60mph 96.5kmh: 17.3secs
0-1/4 mile: 20.9secs
43.0bhp 32.1kW 43.6PS
@ 5800rpm
40.0lbft 54.2Nm @ 4000rpm
77.1bhp/ton 75.8bhp/tonne
57.6bhp/L 42.9kW/L 58.4PS/L
40.6ft/sec 12.4m/sec
15.8mph 25.4kmh/1000rpm
Petrol 4-stroke piston
747cc 45.6cu in
In-line 4
Compression ratio: 9.8:1
Bore: 61.0mm 2.4in
Stroke: 64.0mm 2.5in
Valve type/No: Overhead 8
Transmission: Manual
No. of forward speeds: 4
Wheels driven: Rear
Wheelbase: 199.9cm 78.7in
Track F: 115.1cm 45.3in
Track R: 115.3cm 45.4in
Length: 325.1cm 128.0in
Width: 137.9cm 54.3in
Height: 119.9cm 47.2in
Kerb weight: 567.5kg 1250.0lb

1481 Fiat

1200 Gran Luce
1959 Italy
84.1mph 135.3kmh
0-50mph 80.5kmh: 14.0secs
0-60mph 96.5kmh: 20.0secs
0-1/4 mile: 21.2secs
60.0bhp 44.7kW 60.8PS
@ 5300rpm
60.0lbft 81.3Nm @ 3000rpm
65.6bhp/ton 64.5bhp/tonne
49.1bhp/L 36.6kW/L 49.8PS/L
43.4ft/sec 13.2m/sec
16.2mph 26.1kmh/1000rpm
Petrol 4-stroke piston
1221cc 74.5cu in
In-line 4
Compression ratio: 8.5:1
Bore: 71.9mm 2.8in
Stroke: 74.9mm 2.9in
Valve type/No: Overhead 8
Transmission: Manual
No. of forward speeds: 4
Wheels driven: Rear
Wheelbase: 233.9cm 92.1in
Track F: 122.7cm 48.3in
Track R: 121.2cm 47.7in
Length: 391.2cm 154.0in
Width: 145.8cm 57.4in
Height: 146.8cm 57.8in
Kerb weight: 930.7kg 2050.0lb

1482 Fiat

500
1959 Italy
61.0mph 98.1kmh
0-1/4 mile: 29.0secs
16.5bhp 12.3kW 16.7PS
@ 4000rpm
20.3lbft 27.5Nm @ 2500rpm
33.2bhp/ton 32.6bhp/tonne
34.4bhp/L 25.7kW/L 34.9PS/L
30.7ft/sec 9.3m/sec
12.8mph 20.6kmh/1000rpm
53.2mpg 44.3mpgUS 5.3L/100km
Petrol 4-stroke piston
479cc 29.2cu in
In-line 2 1 Carburettor
Compression ratio: 7.0:1
Bore: 66.0mm 2.6in
Stroke: 70.0mm 2.8in
Valve type/No: Overhead 4
Transmission: Manual
No. of forward speeds: 4
Wheels driven: Rear
Springs F/R: Leaf/Coil
Brakes F/R: Drum/Drum
Wheelbase: 184.2cm 72.5in
Track F: 112.0cm 44.1in
Track R: 113.3cm 44.6in
Length: 294.6cm 116.0in
Width: 132.1cm 52.0in
Height: 132.3cm 52.1in
Ground clearance: 13.0cm 5.1in
Kerb weight: 505.3kg 1113.0lb
Fuel: 20.5L 4.5gal 5.4galUS

1483 Fiat

500 Nuova
1959 Italy
66.6mph 107.2kmh
0-50mph 80.5kmh: 17.8secs
0-60mph 96.5kmh: 37.2secs
0-1/4 mile: 25.0secs
21.5bhp 16.0kW 21.8PS
@ 4500rpm
22.0lbft 29.8Nm @ 3000rpm
45.4bhp/ton 44.7bhp/tonne
44.9bhp/L 33.5kW/L 45.5PS/L
34.5ft/sec 10.5m/sec
14.0mph 22.5kmh/1000rpm
Petrol 4-stroke piston
479cc 29.2cu in
In-line 2
Compression ratio: 8.5:1
Bore: 66.0mm 2.6in
Stroke: 70.1mm 2.8in
Valve type/No: Overhead 4
Transmission: Manual
No. of forward speeds: 4
Wheels driven: Rear
Wheelbase: 183.9cm 72.4in
Track F: 112.0cm 44.1in
Track R: 113.5cm 44.7in
Length: 297.2cm 117.0in
Width: 132.8cm 52.3in
Height: 132.8cm 52.3in
Kerb weight: 481.2kg 1060.0lb

1484 Fiat

1500
1960 Italy
104.0mph 167.3kmh
0-50mph 80.5kmh: 10.7secs
0-60mph 96.5kmh: 15.2secs
0-1/4 mile: 20.3secs
80.0bhp 59.7kW 81.1PS
@ 4000rpm
77.4lbft 104.9Nm @ 4000rpm
83.1bhp/ton 81.7bhp/tonne
53.7bhp/L 40.0kW/L 54.4PS/L
34.1ft/sec 10.4m/sec
16.7mph 26.9kmh/1000rpm
24.1mpg 20.1mpgUS 11.7L/100km
Petrol 4-stroke piston
1491cc 91.0cu in
In-line 4
Compression ratio: 8.7:1
Bore: 78.0mm 3.1in
Stroke: 78.0mm 3.1in
Valve type/No: Overhead 8
Transmission: Manual
No. of forward speeds: 4
Wheels driven: Rear
Springs F/R: Coil/Leaf
Brakes F/R: Drum/Drum
Wheelbase: 233.9cm 92.1in
Track F: 124.0cm 48.8in
Track R: 119.9cm 47.2in
Length: 401.8cm 158.2in
Width: 152.1cm 59.9in
Height: 130.0cm 51.2in
Ground clearance: 12.2cm 4.8in
Kerb weight: 978.8kg 2156.0lb
Fuel: 40.0L 8.8gal 10.6galUS

1485 Fiat

2100
1960 Italy
93.0mph 149.6kmh
0-50mph 80.5kmh: 10.2secs
0-60mph 96.5kmh: 14.5secs
0-1/4 mile: 19.7secs
95.0bhp 70.8kW 96.3PS
@ 5000rpm
123.0lbft 166.7Nm @ 3000rpm
76.0bhp/ton 74.7bhp/tonne
46.2bhp/L 34.5kW/L 46.9PS/L
40.1ft/sec 12.2m/sec
16.5mph 26.5kmh/1000rpm
Petrol 4-stroke piston
2054cc 125.3cu in
In-line 6 1 Carburettor
Compression ratio: 8.8:1
Bore: 77.0mm 3.0in
Stroke: 73.4mm 2.9in
Valve type/No: Overhead 12
Transmission: Manual
No. of forward speeds: 4
Wheels driven: Rear
Wheelbase: 264.9cm 104.3in
Track F: 134.1cm 52.8in
Track R: 130.8cm 51.5in
Length: 447.0cm 176.0in
Width: 162.1cm 63.8in
Height: 147.1cm 57.9in
Kerb weight: 1271.2kg 2800.0lb

1486 Fiat

600
1960 Italy
66.0mph 106.2kmh
0-50mph 80.5kmh: 31.6secs
0-1/4 mile: 27.0secs
28.5bhp 21.2kW 28.9PS
@ 4600rpm
28.9lbft 39.2Nm @ 3000rpm
48.4bhp/ton 47.6bhp/tonne
45.0bhp/L 33.6kW/L 45.7PS/L
28.1ft/sec 8.6m/sec
12.8mph 20.6kmh/1000rpm
38.8mpg 32.3mpgUS 7.3L/100km
Petrol 4-stroke piston
633cc 38.6cu in
In-line 4 1 Carburettor
Compression ratio: 7.5:1
Bore: 60.0mm 2.4in
Stroke: 56.0mm 2.2in
Valve type/No: Overhead 8
Transmission: Manual
No. of forward speeds: 4
Wheels driven: Rear
Springs F/R: Leaf/Coil
Brakes F/R: Drum/Drum
Wheelbase: 199.9cm 78.7in
Track F: 114.8cm 45.2in
Track R: 115.3cm 45.4in
Length: 328.4cm 129.3in
Width: 137.9cm 54.3in
Height: 140.5cm 55.3in
Ground clearance: 15.7cm 6.2in
Kerb weight: 599.3kg 1320.0lb
Fuel: 27.3L 6.0gal 7.2galUS

1487 Fiat

Abarth 850
1960 Italy
100.0mph 160.9kmh
0-50mph 80.5kmh: 12.2secs
0-60mph 96.5kmh: 17.6secs
0-1/4 mile: 20.6secs
52.0bhp 38.8kW 52.7PS
@ 6000rpm
51.3lbft 69.5Nm @ 4500rpm
86.6bhp/ton 85.2bhp/tonne
62.4bhp/L 46.5kW/L 63.3PS/L
45.3ft/sec 13.8m/sec
16.3mph 26.2kmh/1000rpm
Petrol 4-stroke piston
833cc 50.8cu in
In-line 4 1 Carburettor
Compression ratio: 9.0:1
Bore: 62.0mm 2.4in
Stroke: 69.1mm 2.7in
Valve type/No: Overhead 8
Transmission: Manual
No. of forward speeds: 4
Wheels driven: Rear
Wheelbase: 199.9cm 78.7in
Track F: 115.1cm 45.3in
Track R: 115.3cm 45.4in
Length: 335.3cm 132.0in
Width: 142.0cm 55.9in
Height: 118.9cm 46.8in
Kerb weight: 610.6kg 1345.0lb

1488 Fiat

Abarth Twin Cam
1960 Italy
102.0mph 164.1kmh
0-50mph 80.5kmh: 8.0secs
0-60mph 96.5kmh: 11.2secs
0-1/4 mile: 18.0secs
61.0bhp 45.5kW 61.8PS
@ 7000rpm
50.5lbft 68.4Nm @ 5000rpm
102.0bhp/ton 100.3bhp/tonne
81.7bhp/L 60.9kW/L 82.8PS/L
49.0ft/sec 14.9m/sec
12.7mph 20.4kmh/1000rpm
Petrol 4-stroke piston
747cc 45.6cu in
In-line 4
Compression ratio: 9.7:1
Bore: 61.0mm 2.4in
Stroke: 64.0mm 2.5in
Valve type/No: Overhead 8
Transmission: Manual
No. of forward speeds: 4
Wheels driven: Rear
Wheelbase: 199.9cm 78.7in
Track F: 115.1cm 45.3in
Track R: 115.3cm 45.4in
Length: 345.4cm 136.0in
Width: 134.9cm 53.1in
Height: 115.8cm 45.6in
Kerb weight: 608.4kg 1340.0lb

1489 Fiat

1200 Spider
1961 Italy
90.0mph 144.8kmh
0-50mph 80.5kmh: 13.2secs
0-60mph 96.5kmh: 19.1secs
0-1/4 mile: 21.0secs
63.0bhp 47.0kW 63.9PS
@ 5300rpm
60.0lbft 81.3Nm @ 3000rpm
71.6bhp/ton 70.4bhp/tonne
51.6bhp/L 38.5kW/L 52.3PS/L
43.4ft/sec 13.2m/sec
16.2mph 26.1kmh/1000rpm
Petrol 4-stroke piston
1221cc 74.5cu in
In-line 4 1 Carburettor
Compression ratio: 8.3:1
Bore: 71.9mm 2.8in
Stroke: 74.9mm 2.9in
Valve type/No: Overhead 8
Transmission: Manual
No. of forward speeds: 4
Wheels driven: Rear
Wheelbase: 233.9cm 92.1in
Track F: 122.7cm 48.3in
Track R: 121.2cm 47.7in
Length: 403.1cm 158.7in
Width: 151.9cm 59.8in
Height: 130.0cm 51.2in
Ground clearance: 12.7cm 5.0in
Kerb weight: 894.4kg 1970.0lb

1490 Fiat

1300
1961 Italy
90.5mph 145.6kmh
0-50mph 80.5kmh: 13.1secs
0-60mph 96.5kmh: 19.2secs
0-1/4 mile: 21.4secs
65.0bhp 48.5kW 65.9PS
@ 5200rpm
68.7lbft 93.1Nm @ 3400rpm

69.3bhp/ton 68.2bhp/tonne
50.2bhp/L 37.4kW/L 50.9PS/L
45.2ft/sec 13.8m/sec
16.1mph 25.9kmh/1000rpm
24.7mpg 20.6mpgUS 11.4L/100km
Petrol 4-stroke piston
1295cc 79.0cu in
In-line 4
Compression ratio: 8.8:1
Bore: 72.0mm 2.8in
Stroke: 79.5mm 3.1in
Valve type/No: Overhead 8
Transmission: Manual
No. of forward speeds: 4
Wheels driven: Rear
Springs F/R: Coil/Leaf
Brakes F/R: Disc/Drum
Wheelbase: 241.8cm 95.2in
Track F: 129.5cm 51.0in
Track R: 127.3cm 50.1in
Length: 402.8cm 158.6in
Width: 154.9cm 61.0in
Height: 142.2cm 56.0in
Ground clearance: 16.5cm 6.5in
Kerb weight: 953.4kg 2100.0lb
Fuel: 45.0L 9.9gal 11.9galUS

1491 Fiat

1500
1961 Italy
92.4mph 148.7kmh
0-50mph 80.5kmh: 10.4secs
0-60mph 96.5kmh: 15.3secs
0-1/4 mile: 19.7secs
72.0bhp 53.7kW 73.0PS
@ 5200rpm
75.0lbft 101.6Nm @ 3400rpm
76.8bhp/ton 75.5bhp/tonne
48.6bhp/L 36.2kW/L 49.3PS/L
45.2ft/sec 13.8m/sec
16.1mph 25.9kmh/1000rpm
25.5mpg 21.2mpgUS 11.1L/100km
Petrol 4-stroke piston
1481cc 90.4cu in
In-line 4
Compression ratio: 8.8:1
Bore: 77.0mm 3.0in
Stroke: 79.5mm 3.1in
Valve type/No: Overhead 8
Transmission: Manual
No. of forward speeds: 4
Wheels driven: Rear
Springs F/R: Coil/Leaf
Brakes F/R: Disc/Drum
Wheelbase: 241.8cm 95.2in
Track F: 129.5cm 51.0in
Track R: 127.3cm 50.1in
Length: 402.8cm 158.6in
Width: 154.9cm 61.0in
Height: 142.2cm 56.0in
Ground clearance: 16.5cm 6.5in
Kerb weight: 953.4kg 2100.0lb
Fuel: 45.0L 9.9gal 11.9galUS

1492 Fiat

500 Giardiniera
1961 Italy
60.0mph 96.5kmh
0-50mph 80.5kmh: 38.1secs
0-1/4 mile: 27.7secs
17.5bhp 13.0kW 17.7PS
@ 4600rpm
21.7lbft 29.4Nm @ 3200rpm
31.5bhp/ton 30.9bhp/tonne
35.1bhp/L 26.1kW/L 35.5PS/L
35.3ft/sec 10.7m/sec
12.7mph 20.4kmh/1000rpm
46.8mpg 39.0mpgUS 6.0L/100km
Petrol 4-stroke piston
499cc 30.4cu in
In-line 2
Compression ratio: 7.0:1
Bore: 67.4mm 2.6in
Stroke: 70.0mm 2.8in
Valve type/No: Overhead 4
Transmission: Manual
No. of forward speeds: 4
Wheels driven: Rear
Springs F/R: Leaf/Coil
Brakes F/R: Drum/Drum
Wheelbase: 194.1cm 76.4in
Track F: 112.0cm 44.1in
Track R: 113.0cm 44.5in
Length: 318.0cm 125.2in
Width: 132.3cm 52.1in
Height: 135.1cm 53.2in
Ground clearance: 13.2cm 5.2in
Kerb weight: 565.7kg 1246.0lb
Fuel: 20.9L 4.6gal 5.5galUS

1493 Fiat

600D
1961 Italy
68.0mph 109.4kmh
0-50mph 80.5kmh: 23.8secs
0-1/4 mile: 24.9secs
29.0bhp 21.6kW 29.4PS
@ 4800rpm
40.0lbft 54.2Nm @ 2800rpm
48.1bhp/ton 47.3bhp/tonne
37.8bhp/L 28.2kW/L 38.3PS/L
33.3ft/sec 10.2m/sec
14.1mph 22.7kmh/1000rpm
38.0mpg 31.6mpgUS 7.4L/100km
Petrol 4-stroke piston
767cc 46.8cu in
In-line 4 1 Carburettor
Compression ratio: 7.5:1
Bore: 62.0mm 2.4in
Stroke: 63.5mm 2.5in
Valve type/No: Overhead 8
Transmission: Manual
No. of forward speeds: 4
Wheels driven: Rear
Springs F/R: Leaf/Coil
Brakes F/R: Drum/Drum
Wheelbase: 199.9cm 78.7in
Track F: 114.8cm 45.2in
Track R: 115.3cm 45.4in
Length: 327.7cm 129.0in
Width: 137.9cm 54.3in
Height: 140.5cm 55.3in
Ground clearance: 15.7cm 6.2in
Kerb weight: 613.3kg 1351.0lb
Fuel: 27.3L 6.0gal 7.2galUS

1494 Fiat

2300
1962 Italy
101.0mph 162.5kmh
0-50mph 80.5kmh: 8.4secs
0-60mph 96.5kmh: 12.3secs
0-1/4 mile: 18.5secs
105.0bhp 78.3kW 106.5PS
@ 5300rpm
123.0lbft 166.7Nm @ 2800rpm
84.4bhp/ton 83.0bhp/tonne
46.1bhp/L 34.4kW/L 46.7PS/L
46.1ft/sec 14.0m/sec
17.0mph 27.4kmh/1000rpm
21.3mpg 17.7mpgUS 13.3L/100km
Petrol 4-stroke piston
2279cc 139.0cu in
In-line 6 1 Carburettor
Compression ratio: 8.8:1
Bore: 78.0mm 3.1in
Stroke: 79.5mm 3.1in
Valve type/No: Overhead 12
Transmission: Manual
No. of forward speeds: 4
Wheels driven: Rear
Springs F/R: Torsion bar/Leaf
Brake system: PA
Brakes F/R: Disc/Disc
Steering: Worm & roller
Wheelbase: 265.2cm 104.4in
Track F: 134.6cm 53.0in
Track R: 130.8cm 51.5in
Length: 448.6cm 176.6in
Width: 161.8cm 63.7in
Height: 146.8cm 57.8in
Ground clearance: 13.5cm 5.3in
Kerb weight: 1264.8kg 2786.0lb
Fuel: 60.1L 13.2gal 15.9galUS

1495 Fiat

1100
1963 Italy
83.0mph 133.5kmh
0-50mph 80.5kmh: 16.0secs
0-60mph 96.5kmh: 25.4secs
0-1/4 mile: 22.4secs
55.0bhp 41.0kW 55.8PS
@ 5200rpm
53.0lbft 71.8Nm @ 3500rpm
59.8bhp/ton 58.8bhp/tonne
50.5bhp/L 37.7kW/L 51.2PS/L
42.6ft/sec 13.0m/sec
16.1mph 25.9kmh/1000rpm
Petrol 4-stroke piston
1089cc 66.4cu in
In-line 4 1 Carburettor
Compression ratio: 7.9:1
Bore: 68.1mm 2.7in
Stroke: 74.9mm 2.9in
Valve type/No: Overhead 8
Transmission: Manual
No. of forward speeds: 4
Wheels driven: Rear
Wheelbase: 233.9cm 92.1in
Track F: 123.2cm 48.5in
Track R: 121.7cm 47.9in
Length: 391.2cm 154.0in
Width: 145.8cm 57.4in
Height: 146.8cm 57.8in
Ground clearance: 13.0cm 5.1in
Kerb weight: 935.2kg 2060.0lb

1496 Fiat

1100D
1963 Italy
81.0mph 130.3kmh
0-50mph 80.5kmh: 14.0secs
0-60mph 96.5kmh: 22.5secs
0-1/4 mile: 21.5secs
50.0bhp 37.3kW 50.7PS
@ 5000rpm
56.4lbft 76.4Nm @ 2500rpm
58.6bhp/ton 57.6bhp/tonne
40.9bhp/L 30.5kW/L 41.5PS/L
41.0ft/sec 12.5m/sec
16.2mph 26.1kmh/1000rpm
28.2mpg 23.5mpgUS 10.0L/100km
Petrol 4-stroke piston
1221cc 74.5cu in
In-line 4 1 Carburettor
Compression ratio: 8.1:1
Bore: 72.0mm 2.8in
Stroke: 75.0mm 2.9in
Valve type/No: Overhead 8
Transmission: Manual
No. of forward speeds: 4
Wheels driven: Rear
Springs F/R: Coil/Leaf
Brakes F/R: Drum/Drum
Steering: Worm & roller
Wheelbase: 235.0cm 92.5in
Track F: 123.2cm 48.5in
Track R: 121.4cm 47.8in
Length: 391.9cm 154.3in
Width: 145.8cm 57.4in
Height: 146.8cm 57.8in
Ground clearance: 13.0cm 5.1in
Kerb weight: 867.6kg 1911.0lb
Fuel: 38.2L 8.4gal 10.1galUS

1497 Fiat

1500L
1964 Italy
90.0mph 144.8kmh
0-50mph 80.5kmh: 13.4secs
0-60mph 96.5kmh: 19.0secs
0-1/4 mile: 21.1secs
72.0bhp 53.7kW 73.0PS
@ 5200rpm
75.0lbft 101.6Nm @ 3400rpm
61.4bhp/ton 60.4bhp/tonne
48.6bhp/L 36.2kW/L 49.3PS/L
45.2ft/sec 13.8m/sec
17.1mph 27.5kmh/1000rpm
23.7mpg 19.7mpgUS 11.9L/100km
Petrol 4-stroke piston
1481cc 90.4cu in
In-line 4
Compression ratio: 8.8:1
Bore: 77.0mm 3.0in
Stroke: 79.5mm 3.1in
Valve type/No: Overhead 8
Transmission: Manual
No. of forward speeds: 4
Wheels driven: Rear
Springs F/R: Torsion bar/Leaf
Brake system: PA
Brakes F/R: Disc/Disc
Steering: Worm & roller
Wheelbase: 265.2cm 104.4in
Track F: 134.6cm 53.0in
Track R: 130.8cm 51.5in
Length: 448.8cm 176.7in
Width: 161.8cm 63.7in
Height: 146.6cm 57.7in
Ground clearance: 13.2cm 5.2in
Kerb weight: 1191.7kg 2625.0lb
Fuel: 60.1L 13.2gal 15.9galUS

1498 Fiat

500D
1964 Italy
61.0mph 98.1kmh
0-50mph 80.5kmh: 31.0secs
0-1/4 mile: 26.6secs
17.5bhp 13.0kW 17.7PS
@ 4400rpm
22.4lbft 30.4Nm @ 3500rpm
35.4bhp/ton 34.8bhp/tonne
35.1bhp/L 26.1kW/L 35.5PS/L
33.7ft/sec 10.3m/sec
12.7mph 20.4kmh/1000rpm
46.0mpg 38.3mpgUS 6.1L/100km
Petrol 4-stroke piston
499cc 30.4cu in
In-line 2 1 Carburettor
Compression ratio: 7.1:1
Bore: 67.4mm 2.6in
Stroke: 70.0mm 2.8in
Valve type/No: Overhead 4
Transmission: Manual
No. of forward speeds: 4
Wheels driven: Rear
Springs F/R: Leaf/Coil
Brakes F/R: Drum/Drum
Steering: Worm & sector
Wheelbase: 184.2cm 72.5in
Track F: 112.0cm 44.1in
Track R: 113.3cm 44.6in
Length: 296.4cm 116.7in
Width: 132.1cm 52.0in
Height: 133.4cm 52.5in
Ground clearance: 16.5cm 6.5in
Kerb weight: 502.1kg 1106.0lb
Fuel: 20.9L 4.6gal 5.5galUS

1499 Fiat

850 Super
1964 Italy
78.0mph 125.5kmh
0-50mph 80.5kmh: 17.0secs
0-60mph 96.5kmh: 26.8secs
0-1/4 mile: 22.9secs
37.0bhp 27.6kW 37.5PS
@ 5100rpm
40.5lbft 54.9Nm @ 3400rpm
54.7bhp/ton 53.8bhp/tonne
43.9bhp/L 32.7kW/L 44.5PS/L
35.4ft/sec 10.8m/sec
13.8mph 22.2kmh/1000rpm
35.5mpg 29.6mpgUS 8.0L/100km
Petrol 4-stroke piston
843cc 51.4cu in
In-line 4 1 Carburettor
Compression ratio: 8.8:1
Bore: 65.0mm 2.6in
Stroke: 63.5mm 2.5in
Valve type/No: Overhead 8
Transmission: Manual
No. of forward speeds: 4
Wheels driven: Rear
Springs F/R: Leaf/Coil
Brakes F/R: Drum/Drum
Steering: Worm & roller
Wheelbase: 203.2cm 80.0in
Track F: 114.6cm 45.1in
Track R: 121.2cm 47.7in
Length: 356.9cm 140.5in
Width: 142.2cm 56.0in
Height: 135.9cm 53.5in
Kerb weight: 688.3kg 1516.0lb
Fuel: 30.0L 6.6gal 7.9galUS

1500 Fiat

1500
1965 Italy
94.0mph 151.2kmh
0-50mph 80.5kmh: 11.6secs
0-60mph 96.5kmh: 16.2secs
0-1/4 mile: 19.9secs
75.0bhp 55.9kW 76.0PS
@ 5400rpm
79.0lbft 107.0Nm @ 3200rpm
78.9bhp/ton 77.6bhp/tonne
50.6bhp/L 37.8kW/L 51.3PS/L
46.6ft/sec 14.2m/sec
16.4mph 26.4kmh/1000rpm
26.8mpg 22.3mpgUS 10.5L/100km
Petrol 4-stroke piston
1481cc 90.4cu in
In-line 4 1 Carburettor
Compression ratio: 8.8:1
Bore: 77.0mm 3.0in
Stroke: 79.0mm 3.1in
Valve type/No: Overhead 8
Transmission: Manual
No. of forward speeds: 4
Wheels driven: Rear
Springs F/R: Coil/Leaf
Brake system: PA

Brakes F/R: Disc/Drum
Steering: Worm & roller
Wheelbase: 242.6cm 95.5in
Track F: 129.5cm 51.0in
Track R: 127.0cm 50.0in
Length: 407.4cm 160.4in
Width: 154.4cm 60.8in
Height: 144.0cm 56.7in
Ground clearance: 12.7cm 5.0in
Kerb weight: 966.1kg 2128.0lb
Fuel: 45.5L 10.0gal 12.0galUS

1501 Fiat

1500 Spider
1965 Italy
94.0mph 151.2kmh
0-50mph 80.5kmh: 10.8secs
0-60mph 96.5kmh: 17.0secs
0-1/4 mile: 20.2secs
80.0bhp 59.7kW 81.1PS
@ 5200rpm
87.0lbft 117.9Nm @ 3200rpm
84.5bhp/ton 83.1bhp/tonne
54.0bhp/L 40.3kW/L 54.8PS/L
45.2ft/sec 13.8m/sec
17.4mph 28.0kmh/1000rpm
Petrol 4-stroke piston
1481cc 90.4cu in
In-line 4 1 Carburettor
Compression ratio: 8.8:1
Bore: 77.0mm 3.0in
Stroke: 79.5mm 3.1in
Valve type/No: Overhead 8
Transmission: Manual
No. of forward speeds: 4
Wheels driven: Rear
Springs F/R: Coil/Leaf
Brakes F/R: Disc/Drum
Steering: Worm & roller
Wheelbase: 233.9cm 92.1in
Track F: 122.9cm 48.4in
Track R: 122.9cm 48.4in
Length: 408.4cm 160.8in
Width: 151.9cm 59.8in
Height: 129.0cm 50.8in
Ground clearance: 11.9cm 4.7in
Kerb weight: 962.5kg 2120.0lb
Fuel: 37.8L 8.3gal 10.0galUS

1502 Fiat

Abarth OT 1600
1965 Italy
136.0mph 218.8kmh
0-50mph 80.5kmh: 5.1secs
0-60mph 96.5kmh: 7.3secs
0-1/4 mile: 14.5secs
154.0bhp 114.8kW 156.1PS
@ 7600rpm
123.0lbft 166.7Nm @ 5200rpm
193.1bhp/ton 189.9bhp/tonne
96.7bhp/L 72.1kW/L 98.1PS/L
57.0ft/sec 17.4m/sec
18.4mph 29.6kmh/1000rpm
Petrol 4-stroke piston
1592cc 97.1cu in
In-line 4 2 Carburettor
Compression ratio: 9.5:1
Bore: 86.1mm 3.4in
Stroke: 68.6mm 2.7in
Valve type/No: Overhead 8
Transmission: Manual
No. of forward speeds: 4
Wheels driven: Rear
Springs F/R: Leaf/Coil
Brakes F/R: Disc/Disc
Steering: Worm & sector
Wheelbase: 202.7cm 79.8in
Track F: 116.1cm 45.7in
Track R: 132.1cm 52.0in
Length: 357.4cm 140.7in
Width: 142.5cm 56.1in
Height: 137.4cm 54.1in
Ground clearance: 19.6cm 7.7in
Kerb weight: 810.8kg 1786.0lb
Fuel: 32.2L 7.1gal 8.5galUS

1503 Fiat

1100R
1966 Italy
81.0mph 130.3kmh
0-50mph 80.5kmh: 14.6secs
0-60mph 96.5kmh: 21.6secs
0-1/4 mile: 22.4secs
53.0bhp 39.5kW 53.7PS
@ 5200rpm
57.0lbft 77.2Nm @ 3200rpm
62.8bhp/ton 61.8bhp/tonne
48.7bhp/L 36.3kW/L 49.3PS/L
42.6ft/sec 13.0m/sec
15.4mph 24.8kmh/1000rpm
Petrol 4-stroke piston
1089cc 66.4cu in
In-line 4 1 Carburettor
Compression ratio: 8.1:1
Bore: 68.1mm 2.7in
Stroke: 74.9mm 2.9in
Valve type/No: Overhead 8
Transmission: Manual
No. of forward speeds: 4
Wheels driven: Rear
Brakes F/R: Disc/Drum
Steering: Worm & sector
Wheelbase: 234.2cm 92.2in
Track F: 123.2cm 48.5in
Track R: 121.4cm 47.8in
Length: 396.5cm 156.1in
Width: 146.6cm 57.7in
Height: 138.4cm 54.5in
Kerb weight: 858.1kg 1890.0lb
Fuel: 37.8L 8.3gal 10.0galUS

1504 Fiat

500F
1966 Italy
61.0mph 98.1kmh
0-50mph 80.5kmh: 35.8secs
0-1/4 mile: 26.7secs
0-1km: 53.0secs
18.0bhp 13.4kW 18.2PS
@ 4600rpm
22.4lbft 30.4Nm @ 3000rpm
35.7bhp/ton 35.1bhp/tonne
36.1bhp/L 26.9kW/L 36.6PS/L
35.3ft/sec 10.7m/sec
12.7mph 20.4kmh/1000rpm
42.8mpg 35.6mpgUS 6.6L/100km
Petrol 4-stroke piston
499cc 30.4cu in
In-line 2 1 Carburettor
Compression ratio: 7.1:1
Bore: 67.4mm 2.6in
Stroke: 70.0mm 2.8in
Valve type/No: Overhead 4
Transmission: Manual
No. of forward speeds: 4
Wheels driven: Rear
Springs F/R: Leaf/Coil
Brakes F/R: Drum/Drum
Steering: Worm & sector
Wheelbase: 184.2cm 72.5in
Track F: 111.8cm 44.0in
Track R: 113.0cm 44.5in
Length: 297.2cm 117.0in
Width: 132.1cm 52.0in
Height: 133.4cm 52.5in
Ground clearance: 13.2cm 5.2in
Kerb weight: 513.0kg 1130.0lb
Fuel: 20.9L 4.6gal 5.5galUS

1505 Fiat

850 Coupe
1966 Italy
90.0mph 144.8kmh
0-50mph 80.5kmh: 12.4secs
0-60mph 96.5kmh: 18.2secs
0-1/4 mile: 21.0secs
0-1km: 41.0secs
47.0bhp 35.0kW 47.6PS
@ 6200rpm
44.0lbft 59.6Nm @ 3600rpm
65.5bhp/ton 64.4bhp/tonne
55.7bhp/L 41.6kW/L 56.5PS/L
43.1ft/sec 13.1m/sec
14.0mph 22.5kmh/1000rpm
32.5mpg 27.1mpgUS 8.7L/100km
Petrol 4-stroke piston
843cc 51.4cu in
In-line 4 1 Carburettor
Compression ratio: 9.3:1
Bore: 65.0mm 2.6in
Stroke: 63.5mm 2.5in
Valve type/No: Overhead 8
Transmission: Manual
No. of forward speeds: 4
Wheels driven: Rear
Springs F/R: Leaf/Coil
Brakes F/R: Disc/Drum
Steering: Worm & roller
Wheelbase: 202.7cm 79.8in
Track F: 115.8cm 45.6in
Track R: 121.2cm 47.7in
Length: 364.5cm 143.5in
Width: 150.1cm 59.1in
Height: 130.8cm 51.5in
Ground clearance: 15.2cm 6.0in
Kerb weight: 729.6kg 1607.0lb
Fuel: 30.0L 6.6gal 7.9galUS

1506 Fiat

Abarth 595
1966 Italy
76.0mph 122.3kmh
0-50mph 80.5kmh: 15.3secs
0-60mph 96.5kmh: 27.2secs
0-1/4 mile: 22.7secs
27.0bhp 20.1kW 27.4PS
@ 5000rpm
33.0lbft 44.7Nm @ 3500rpm
53.5bhp/ton 52.6bhp/tonne
45.4bhp/L 33.9kW/L 46.1PS/L
38.3ft/sec 11.7m/sec
12.7mph 20.4kmh/1000rpm
33.6mpg 28.0mpgUS 8.4L/100km
Petrol 4-stroke piston
594cc 36.2cu in
In-line 2 1 Carburettor
Compression ratio: 9.2:1
Bore: 73.5mm 2.9in
Stroke: 70.0mm 2.8in
Valve type/No: Overhead 4
Transmission: Manual
No. of forward speeds: 4
Wheels driven: Rear
Springs F/R: Leaf/Coil
Brakes F/R: Drum/Drum
Steering: Worm & sector
Wheelbase: 184.2cm 72.5in
Track F: 111.8cm 44.0in
Track R: 113.0cm 44.5in
Length: 297.2cm 117.0in
Width: 132.1cm 52.0in
Height: 133.4cm 52.5in
Ground clearance: 13.2cm 5.2in
Kerb weight: 513.0kg 1130.0lb
Fuel: 20.9L 4.6gal 5.5galUS

1507 Fiat

124
1967 Italy
85.0mph 136.8kmh
0-50mph 80.5kmh: 11.1secs
0-60mph 96.5kmh: 15.9secs
0-1/4 mile: 20.1secs
0-1km: 38.7secs
60.0bhp 44.7kW 60.8PS
@ 5600rpm
64.0lbft 86.7Nm @ 3400rpm
73.2bhp/ton 72.0bhp/tonne
50.1bhp/L 37.4kW/L 50.8PS/L
43.7ft/sec 13.3m/sec
15.1mph 24.3kmh/1000rpm
26.8mpg 22.3mpgUS 10.5L/100km
Petrol 4-stroke piston
1197cc 73.0cu in
In-line 4 1 Carburettor
Compression ratio: 8.8:1
Bore: 73.0mm 2.9in
Stroke: 71.5mm 2.8in
Valve type/No: Overhead 8
Transmission: Manual
No. of forward speeds: 4
Wheels driven: Rear
Springs F/R: Coil/Coil
Brakes F/R: Disc/Disc
Steering: Worm & roller
Wheelbase: 242.1cm 95.3in
Track F: 132.6cm 52.2in
Track R: 130.0cm 51.2in
Length: 401.3cm 158.0in
Width: 157.5cm 62.0in
Height: 144.8cm 57.0in
Ground clearance: 15.2cm 6.0in
Kerb weight: 833.5kg 1836.0lb
Fuel: 38.7L 8.5gal 10.2galUS

1508 Fiat

125
1967 Italy
100.0mph 160.9kmh
0-50mph 80.5kmh: 9.4secs
0-60mph 96.5kmh: 13.4secs
0-1/4 mile: 19.0secs
0-1km: 35.3secs
90.0bhp 67.1kW 91.2PS
@ 5600rpm
94.0lbft 127.4Nm @ 3400rpm
92.0bhp/ton 90.5bhp/tonne
56.0bhp/L 41.7kW/L 56.7PS/L
49.0ft/sec 14.9m/sec
16.6mph 26.7kmh/1000rpm
24.5mpg 20.4mpgUS 11.5L/100km
Petrol 4-stroke piston
1608cc 98.1cu in
In-line 4 1 Carburettor
Compression ratio: 8.8:1
Bore: 80.0mm 3.1in
Stroke: 80.0mm 3.1in
Valve type/No: Overhead 8
Transmission: Manual
No. of forward speeds: 4
Wheels driven: Rear
Springs F/R: Coil/Leaf
Brake system: PA
Brakes F/R: Disc/Disc
Steering: Worm & roller
Wheelbase: 250.4cm 98.6in
Track F: 131.3cm 51.7in
Track R: 129.0cm 50.8in
Length: 422.1cm 166.2in
Width: 161.0cm 63.4in
Height: 139.4cm 54.9in
Ground clearance: 17.5cm 6.9in
Kerb weight: 994.7kg 2191.0lb
Fuel: 45.0L 9.9gal 11.9galUS

1509 Fiat

124 Sport Coupe
1968 Italy
105.0mph 168.9kmh
0-50mph 80.5kmh: 9.0secs
0-60mph 96.5kmh: 12.6secs
0-1/4 mile: 18.8secs
0-1km: 34.9secs
90.0bhp 67.1kW 91.2PS
@ 6500rpm
80.0lbft 108.4Nm @ 4000rpm
97.2bhp/ton 95.6bhp/tonne
62.6bhp/L 46.7kW/L 63.5PS/L
50.7ft/sec 15.5m/sec
16.1mph 25.9kmh/1000rpm
22.2mpg 18.5mpgUS 12.7L/100km
Petrol 4-stroke piston
1438cc 87.7cu in
In-line 4 1 Carburettor
Compression ratio: 8.9:1
Bore: 80.0mm 3.1in
Stroke: 71.5mm 2.8in
Valve type/No: Overhead 8
Transmission: Manual
No. of forward speeds: 5
Wheels driven: Rear
Springs F/R: Coil/Coil
Brake system: PA
Brakes F/R: Disc/Disc
Steering: Worm & roller
Wheelbase: 241.3cm 95.0in
Track F: 134.6cm 53.0in
Track R: 131.3cm 51.7in
Length: 411.5cm 162.0in
Width: 167.1cm 65.8in
Height: 132.8cm 52.3in
Ground clearance: 17.8cm 7.0in
Kerb weight: 941.6kg 2074.0lb
Fuel: 44.6L 9.8gal 11.8galUS

1510 Fiat

124 Sport Spider
1968 Italy
106.0mph 170.6kmh
0-50mph 80.5kmh: 8.3secs
0-60mph 96.5kmh: 11.9secs
0-1/4 mile: 18.3secs
96.0bhp 71.6kW 97.3PS
@ 6500rpm
82.5lbft 111.8Nm @ 4000rpm
102.9bhp/ton 101.2bhp/tonne
66.8bhp/L 49.8kW/L 67.7PS/L
50.7ft/sec 15.5m/sec
17.5mph 28.2kmh/1000rpm
Petrol 4-stroke piston
1438cc 87.7cu in
In-line 4 1 Carburettor
Compression ratio: 8.9:1
Bore: 80.0mm 3.1in
Stroke: 71.5mm 2.8in
Valve type/No: Overhead 8
Transmission: Manual
No. of forward speeds: 5
Wheels driven: Rear
Springs F/R: Coil/Coil
Brakes F/R: Disc/Disc
Steering: Worm & roller
Wheelbase: 228.1cm 89.8in
Track F: 134.6cm 53.0in
Track R: 131.6cm 51.8in
Length: 397.0cm 156.3in
Width: 161.3cm 63.5in

Height: 125.0cm 49.2in
Ground clearance: 11.9cm 4.7in
Kerb weight: 948.9kg 2090.0lb
Fuel: 44.7L 9.8gal 11.8galUS

1511 Fiat

124 Station Wagon
1968 Italy
85.0mph 136.8kmh
0-1/4 mile: 20.5secs
65.0bhp 48.5kW 65.9PS
54.3bhp/L 40.5kW/L 55.0PS/L
31.2mpg 26.0mpgUS 9.0L/100km
Petrol 4-stroke piston
1197cc 73.0cu in
In-line 4
Valve type/No: Overhead 8
Wheels driven: Rear
Wheelbase: 242.1cm 95.3in
Length: 403.1cm 158.7in

1512 Fiat

850 Idromatic
1968 Italy
77.0mph 123.9kmh
0-50mph 80.5kmh: 17.3secs
0-60mph 96.5kmh: 25.5secs
0-1/4 mile: 23.3secs
42.0bhp 31.3kW 42.6PS
@ 5300rpm
44.0lbft 59.6Nm @ 3600rpm
61.5bhp/ton 60.5bhp/tonne
51.4bhp/L 38.3kW/L 52.1PS/L
36.8ft/sec 11.2m/sec
13.0mph 20.9kmh/1000rpm
33.6mpg 28.0mpgUS 8.4L/100km
Petrol 4-stroke piston
817cc 49.8cu in
In-line 4
Compression ratio: 8.8:1
Bore: 63.9mm 2.5in
Stroke: 63.5mm 2.5in
Valve type/No: Overhead 8
No. of forward speeds: 4
Wheels driven: Rear
Brakes F/R: Drum/Drum
Steering: Worm & sector
Wheelbase: 202.7cm 79.8in
Track F: 114.6cm 45.1in
Track R: 112.0cm 44.1in
Length: 357.4cm 140.7in
Width: 142.5cm 56.1in
Height: 138.4cm 54.5in
Kerb weight: 694.6kg 1530.0lb
Fuel: 29.9L 6.6gal 7.9galUS

1513 Fiat

850 Special
1968 Italy
84.0mph 135.2kmh
0-50mph 80.5kmh: 12.9secs
0-60mph 96.5kmh: 19.0secs
0-1/4 mile: 21.3secs
0-1km: 40.8secs
47.0bhp 35.0kW 47.6PS
@ 6200rpm
44.0lbft 59.6Nm @ 3600rpm
68.1bhp/ton 67.0bhp/tonne
55.7bhp/L 41.6kW/L 56.5PS/L
43.1ft/sec 13.1m/sec
13.7mph 22.0kmh/1000rpm
29.0mpg 24.1mpgUS 9.7L/100km
Petrol 4-stroke piston
843cc 51.4cu in
In-line 4 1 Carburettor
Compression ratio: 9.3:1
Bore: 65.0mm 2.6in
Stroke: 63.5mm 2.5in
Valve type/No: Overhead 8
Transmission: Manual
No. of forward speeds: 4
Wheels driven: Rear
Springs F/R: Leaf/Coil
Brakes F/R: Disc/Drum
Steering: Worm & sector
Wheelbase: 203.2cm 80.0in
Track F: 114.6cm 45.1in
Track R: 121.2cm 47.7in
Length: 356.9cm 140.5in
Width: 142.2cm 56.0in
Height: 135.9cm 53.5in
Kerb weight: 701.9kg 1546.0lb
Fuel: 30.0L 6.6gal 7.9galUS

1514 Fiat

850 Spider
1968 Italy
84.0mph 135.2kmh
0-50mph 80.5kmh: 13.2secs
0-60mph 96.5kmh: 20.0secs
0-1/4 mile: 21.7secs
52.0bhp 38.8kW 52.7PS
@ 6200rpm
45.6lbft 61.8Nm @ 4000rpm
71.0bhp/ton 69.8bhp/tonne
63.6bhp/L 47.5kW/L 64.5PS/L
43.1ft/sec 13.1m/sec
13.6mph 21.9kmh/1000rpm
Petrol 4-stroke piston
817cc 49.8cu in
In-line 4 1 Carburettor
Compression ratio: 9.3:1
Bore: 63.9mm 2.5in
Stroke: 63.5mm 2.5in
Valve type/No: Overhead 8
Transmission: Manual
No. of forward speeds: 4
Wheels driven: Rear
Springs F/R: Leaf/Coil
Brakes F/R: Disc/Drum
Steering: Worm & sector
Wheelbase: 202.7cm 79.8in
Track F: 119.6cm 47.1in
Track R: 125.0cm 49.2in
Length: 378.2cm 148.9in
Width: 149.9cm 59.0in
Height: 121.9cm 48.0in
Ground clearance: 13.5cm 5.3in
Kerb weight: 744.6kg 1640.0lb
Fuel: 29.9L 6.6gal 7.9galUS

1515 Fiat

124 Coupe
1969 Italy
104.0mph 167.3kmh
0-50mph 80.5kmh: 10.0secs
0-60mph 96.5kmh: 14.2secs
0-1/4 mile: 18.6secs
96.0bhp 71.6kW 97.3PS
@ 6500rpm
83.0lbft 112.5Nm @ 5000rpm
101.0bhp/ton 99.3bhp/tonne
66.7bhp/L 49.7kW/L 67.6PS/L
50.7ft/sec 15.5m/sec
17.8mph 28.6kmh/1000rpm
Petrol 4-stroke piston
1439cc 87.8cu in
In-line 4 1 Carburettor
Compression ratio: 8.9:1
Bore: 80.0mm 3.1in
Stroke: 71.4mm 2.8in
Valve type/No: Overhead 8
Transmission: Manual
No. of forward speeds: 5
Wheels driven: Rear
Springs F/R: Coil/Coil
Brake system: PA
Brakes F/R: Disc/Disc
Steering: Worm & roller
Wheelbase: 242.1cm 95.3in
Track F: 134.6cm 53.0in
Track R: 131.6cm 51.8in
Length: 411.5cm 162.0in
Width: 167.1cm 65.8in
Height: 134.1cm 52.8in
Kerb weight: 967.0kg 2130.0lb
Fuel: 44.7L 9.8gal 11.8galUS

1516 Fiat

124 Estate Car
1969 Italy
86.0mph 138.4kmh
0-50mph 80.5kmh: 12.2secs
0-60mph 96.5kmh: 17.8secs
0-1/4 mile: 20.4secs
0-1km: 39.0secs
60.0bhp 44.7kW 60.8PS
@ 5600rpm
64.0lbft 86.7Nm @ 3400rpm
65.8bhp/ton 64.7bhp/tonne
50.1bhp/L 37.4kW/L 50.8PS/L
43.7ft/sec 13.3m/sec
14.8mph 23.8kmh/1000rpm
26.2mpg 21.8mpgUS 10.8L/100km
Petrol 4-stroke piston
1197cc 73.0cu in
In-line 4 1 Carburettor
Compression ratio: 8.8:1
Bore: 73.0mm 2.9in
Stroke: 71.5mm 2.8in
Valve type/No: Overhead 8
Transmission: Manual
No. of forward speeds: 4
Wheels driven: Rear
Springs F/R: Coil/Coil
Brakes F/R: Disc/Disc
Steering: Worm & roller
Wheelbase: 241.3cm 95.0in
Track F: 129.5cm 51.0in
Track R: 129.5cm 51.0in
Length: 464.8cm 183.0in
Width: 162.6cm 64.0in
Height: 142.0cm 55.9in
Ground clearance: 11.9cm 4.7in
Kerb weight: 926.6kg 2041.0lb
Fuel: 46.4L 10.2gal 12.3galUS

1517 Fiat

125 Special
1969 Italy
106.0mph 170.6kmh
0-50mph 80.5kmh: 7.7secs
0-60mph 96.5kmh: 11.9secs
0-1/4 mile: 18.1secs
0-1km: 34.2secs
100.0bhp 74.6kW 101.4PS
@ 6000rpm
96.0lbft 130.1Nm @ 4000rpm
101.0bhp/ton 99.3bhp/tonne
62.2bhp/L 46.4kW/L 63.0PS/L
52.5ft/sec 16.0m/sec
19.0mph 30.6kmh/1000rpm
23.1mpg 19.2mpgUS 12.2L/100km
Petrol 4-stroke piston
1608cc 98.1cu in
In-line 4 1 Carburettor
Compression ratio: 8.8:1
Bore: 80.0mm 3.1in
Stroke: 80.0mm 3.1in
Valve type/No: Overhead 8
Transmission: Manual
No. of forward speeds: 5
Wheels driven: Rear
Springs F/R: Coil/Leaf
Brake system: PA
Brakes F/R: Disc/Disc
Steering: Worm & roller
Wheelbase: 250.4cm 98.6in
Track F: 131.3cm 51.7in
Track R: 129.0cm 50.8in
Length: 422.1cm 166.2in
Width: 161.0cm 63.4in
Height: 144.0cm 56.7in
Ground clearance: 11.9cm 4.7in
Kerb weight: 1007.0kg 2218.0lb
Fuel: 50.0L 11.0gal 13.2galUS

1518 Fiat

850 Coupe
1969 Italy
95.0mph 152.9kmh
0-50mph 80.5kmh: 10.8secs
0-60mph 96.5kmh: 15.6secs
0-1/4 mile: 20.4secs
0-1km: 38.3secs
52.0bhp 38.8kW 52.7PS
@ 6500rpm
47.7lbft 64.6Nm @ 4000rpm
72.4bhp/ton 71.2bhp/tonne
57.6bhp/L 42.9kW/L 58.4PS/L
48.4ft/sec 14.7m/sec
13.8mph 22.2kmh/1000rpm
34.1mpg 28.4mpgUS 8.3L/100km
Petrol 4-stroke piston
903cc 55.1cu in
In-line 4 1 Carburettor
Compression ratio: 9.5:1
Bore: 65.0mm 2.6in
Stroke: 68.0mm 2.7in
Valve type/No: Overhead 8
Transmission: Manual
No. of forward speeds: 4
Wheels driven: Rear
Springs F/R: Leaf/Coil
Brakes F/R: Disc/Drum
Steering: Worm & sector
Wheelbase: 202.7cm 79.8in
Track F: 114.6cm 45.1in
Track R: 121.2cm 47.7in
Length: 363.2cm 143.0in
Width: 149.9cm 59.0in
Height: 130.0cm 51.2in
Ground clearance: 13.5cm 5.3in
Kerb weight: 730.0kg 1608.0lb
Fuel: 30.0L 6.6gal 7.9galUS

1519 Fiat

Abarth 1300
1969 Italy
106.0mph 170.6kmh
0-50mph 80.5kmh: 8.5secs
0-60mph 96.5kmh: 12.5secs
0-1/4 mile: 18.5secs
86.0bhp 64.1kW 87.2PS
@ 6000rpm
79.0lbft 107.0Nm @ 3500rpm
109.8bhp/ton 107.9bhp/tonne
67.2bhp/L 50.1kW/L 68.1PS/L
46.8ft/sec 14.3m/sec
16.1mph 25.9kmh/1000rpm
28.2mpg 23.5mpgUS 10.0L/100km
Petrol 4-stroke piston
1280cc 78.1cu in
In-line 4
Compression ratio: 10.5:1
Bore: 75.5mm 3.0in
Stroke: 71.5mm 2.8in
Valve type/No: Overhead 8
Transmission: Manual
No. of forward speeds: 4
Wheels driven: Rear
Brakes F/R: Disc/Drum
Steering: Worm & sector
Wheelbase: 202.7cm 79.8in
Track F: 130.6cm 51.4in
Track R: 132.1cm 52.0in
Length: 360.7cm 142.0in
Width: 149.9cm 59.0in
Height: 130.0cm 51.2in
Kerb weight: 796.8kg 1755.0lb
Fuel: 29.9L 6.6gal 7.9galUS

1520 Fiat

124 Coupe 1600
1970 Italy
112.0mph 180.2kmh
0-50mph 80.5kmh: 7.4secs
0-60mph 96.5kmh: 10.7secs
0-1/4 mile: 17.8secs
0-1km: 33.0secs
110.0bhp 82.0kW 111.5PS
@ 6400rpm
101.0lbft 136.9Nm @ 3800rpm
111.3bhp/ton 109.4bhp/tonne
68.4bhp/L 51.0kW/L 69.4PS/L
56.0ft/sec 17.1m/sec
17.5mph 28.2kmh/1000rpm
23.6mpg 19.7mpgUS 12.0L/100km
Petrol 4-stroke piston
1608cc 98.1cu in
In-line 4 2 Carburettor
Compression ratio: 9.9:1
Bore: 80.0mm 3.1in
Stroke: 80.0mm 3.1in
Valve type/No: Overhead 8
Transmission: Manual
No. of forward speeds: 5
Wheels driven: Rear
Springs F/R: Coil/Coil
Brake system: PA
Brakes F/R: Disc/Disc
Steering: Worm & roller
Wheelbase: 241.3cm 95.0in
Track F: 134.6cm 53.0in
Track R: 131.3cm 51.7in
Length: 411.5cm 162.0in
Width: 167.1cm 65.8in
Height: 132.8cm 52.3in
Ground clearance: 17.8cm 7.0in
Kerb weight: 1005.2kg 2214.0lb
Fuel: 45.0L 9.9gal 11.9galUS

1521 Fiat

124 Special
1970 Italy
90.0mph 144.8kmh
0-50mph 80.5kmh: 10.2secs
0-60mph 96.5kmh: 14.3secs
0-1/4 mile: 19.2secs
76.0bhp 56.7kW 77.0PS
@ 5400rpm
81.0lbft 109.8Nm @ 3300rpm
81.6bhp/ton 80.3bhp/tonne
52.8bhp/L 39.4kW/L 53.6PS/L
42.1ft/sec 12.9m/sec
15.3mph 24.6kmh/1000rpm
26.9mpg 22.4mpgUS 10.5L/100km
Petrol 4-stroke piston
1438cc 87.7cu in
In-line 4
Compression ratio: 9.0:1
Bore: 80.0mm 3.1in
Stroke: 71.5mm 2.8in

Transmission: Manual
No. of forward speeds: 4
Wheels driven: Rear
Brakes F/R: Disc/Disc
Steering: Worm & roller
Wheelbase: 242.1cm 95.3in
Track F: 133.1cm 52.4in
Track R: 130.0cm 51.2in
Length: 403.4cm 158.8in
Width: 162.6cm 64.0in
Height: 136.7cm 53.8in
Ground clearance: 6.9cm 2.7in
Kerb weight: 946.6kg 2085.0lb
Fuel: 39.0L 8.6gal 10.3galUS

1522 Fiat

124 Spider
1970 Italy
106.0mph 170.6kmh
0-60mph 96.5kmh: 11.9secs
0-1/4 mile: 18.3secs
96.0bhp 71.6kW 97.3PS
@ 6500rpm
82.5lbft 111.8Nm @ 4000rpm
102.9bhp/ton 101.2bhp/tonne
66.8bhp/L 49.8kW/L 67.7PS/L
50.7ft/sec 15.5m/sec
29.2mpg 24.3mpgUS 9.7L/100km
Petrol 4-stroke piston
1438cc 87.7cu in
In-line 4
Bore: 80.0mm 3.1in
Stroke: 71.5mm 2.8in
Valve type/No: Overhead 8
Transmission: Manual
No. of forward speeds: 5
Wheels driven: Rear
Brakes F/R: Disc/Disc
Wheelbase: 228.1cm 89.8in
Track F: 134.6cm 53.0in
Track R: 131.6cm 51.8in
Length: 397.0cm 156.3in
Width: 161.3cm 63.5in
Height: 125.0cm 49.2in
Kerb weight: 948.9kg 2090.0lb
Fuel: 44.7L 9.8gal 11.8galUS

1523 Fiat

128 4-door
1970 Italy
87.0mph 140.0kmh
0-50mph 80.5kmh: 10.5secs
0-60mph 96.5kmh: 16.3secs
0-1/4 mile: 19.8secs
0-1km: 38.0secs
55.0bhp 41.0kW 55.8PS
@ 6000rpm
57.0lbft 77.2Nm @ 3000rpm
68.4bhp/ton 67.2bhp/tonne
49.3bhp/L 36.7kW/L 50.0PS/L
36.5ft/sec 11.1m/sec
15.2mph 24.5kmh/1000rpm
29.2mpg 24.3mpgUS 9.7L/100km
Petrol 4-stroke piston
1116cc 68.1cu in
In-line 4 1 Carburettor
Compression ratio: 8.8:1
Bore: 80.0mm 3.1in
Stroke: 55.5mm 2.2in
Valve type/No: Overhead 8
Transmission: Manual
No. of forward speeds: 4
Wheels driven: Front
Springs F/R: Coil/Leaf
Brake system: PA
Brakes F/R: Disc/Drum
Steering: Rack & pinion
Wheelbase: 246.4cm 97.0in
Track F: 130.8cm 51.5in
Track R: 128.3cm 50.5in
Length: 383.5cm 151.0in
Width: 153.7cm 60.5in
Height: 143.5cm 56.5in
Ground clearance: 14.5cm 5.7in
Kerb weight: 818.1kg 1802.0lb
Fuel: 37.8L 8.3gal 10.0galUS

1524 Fiat

850 Racer
1970 Italy
84.0mph 135.2kmh
0-50mph 80.5kmh: 12.0secs
0-60mph 96.5kmh: 17.9secs
0-1/4 mile: 21.0secs
58.0bhp 43.2kW 58.8PS
@ 6400rpm
47.7lbft 64.6Nm @ 4000rpm
76.9bhp/ton 75.6bhp/tonne
64.2bhp/L 47.9kW/L 65.1PS/L
47.6ft/sec 14.5m/sec
13.6mph 21.9kmh/1000rpm
37.2mpg 31.0mpgUS 7.6L/100km
Petrol 4-stroke piston
903cc 55.1cu in
In-line 4 1 Carburettor
Compression ratio: 9.5:1
Bore: 65.0mm 2.6in
Stroke: 68.0mm 2.7in
Valve type/No: Overhead 8
Transmission: Manual
No. of forward speeds: 4
Wheels driven: Rear
Springs F/R: Leaf/Coil
Brakes F/R: Disc/Drum
Steering: Worm & sector
Wheelbase: 202.7cm 79.8in
Track F: 119.6cm 47.1in
Track R: 125.0cm 49.2in
Length: 378.2cm 148.9in
Width: 149.9cm 59.0in
Height: 121.9cm 48.0in
Ground clearance: 13.5cm 5.3in
Kerb weight: 767.3kg 1690.0lb
Fuel: 29.9L 6.6gal 7.9galUS

1525 Fiat

124 Special T
1971 Italy
102.0mph 164.1kmh
0-50mph 80.5kmh: 8.3secs
0-60mph 96.5kmh: 12.0secs
0-1/4 mile: 18.4secs
0-1km: 34.0secs
80.0bhp 59.7kW 81.1PS
@ 5800rpm
81.0lbft 109.8Nm @ 4000rpm
88.7bhp/ton 87.2bhp/tonne
55.6bhp/L 41.5kW/L 56.4PS/L
45.1ft/sec 13.7m/sec
15.7mph 25.3kmh/1000rpm
24.2mpg 20.2mpgUS 11.7L/100km
Petrol 4-stroke piston
1438cc 87.7cu in
In-line 4 1 Carburettor
Compression ratio: 8.9:1
Bore: 80.0mm 3.1in
Stroke: 71.0mm 2.8in
Valve type/No: Overhead 8
Transmission: Manual
No. of forward speeds: 4
Wheels driven: Rear
Springs F/R: Coil/Coil
Brake system: PA
Brakes F/R: Disc/Disc
Steering: Worm & roller
Wheelbase: 241.3cm 95.0in
Track F: 132.6cm 52.2in
Track R: 130.0cm 51.2in
Length: 401.3cm 158.0in
Width: 157.5cm 62.0in
Height: 144.8cm 57.0in
Ground clearance: 15.2cm 6.0in
Kerb weight: 917.1kg 2020.0lb
Fuel: 39.1L 8.6gal 10.3galUS

1526 Fiat

124 Spider 1600
1971 Italy
112.0mph 180.2kmh
0-50mph 80.5kmh: 9.0secs
0-60mph 96.5kmh: 12.2secs
0-1/4 mile: 18.6secs
104.0bhp 77.5kW 105.4PS
@ 6000rpm
94.0lbft 127.4Nm @ 4200rpm
106.4bhp/ton 104.6bhp/tonne
64.7bhp/L 48.2kW/L 65.6PS/L
52.5ft/sec 16.0m/sec
17.7mph 28.5kmh/1000rpm
27.9mpg 23.2mpgUS 10.1L/100km
Petrol 4-stroke piston
1608cc 98.1cu in
In-line 4 1 Carburettor
Compression ratio: 8.5:1
Bore: 80.0mm 3.1in
Stroke: 80.0mm 3.1in
Valve type/No: Overhead 8
Transmission: Manual
No. of forward speeds: 5
Wheels driven: Rear
Springs F/R: Coil/Coil
Brake system: PA
Brakes F/R: Disc/Disc
Steering: Worm & roller
Wheelbase: 228.1cm 89.8in
Track F: 134.4cm 52.9in
Track R: 131.6cm 51.8in
Length: 397.0cm 156.3in
Width: 161.3cm 63.5in
Height: 125.0cm 49.2in
Ground clearance: 12.4cm 4.9in
Kerb weight: 994.3kg 2190.0lb
Fuel: 45.0L 9.9gal 11.9galUS

1527 Fiat

124 Sport Coupe
1971 Italy
112.0mph 180.2kmh
0-60mph 96.5kmh: 12.4secs
0-1/4 mile: 18.6secs
104.0bhp 77.5kW 105.4PS
@ 6000rpm
94.0lbft 127.4Nm @ 4200rpm
104.9bhp/ton 103.2bhp/tonne
64.7bhp/L 48.2kW/L 65.6PS/L
52.5ft/sec 16.0m/sec
26.5mpg 22.1mpgUS 10.6L/100km
Petrol 4-stroke piston
1608cc 98.1cu in
In-line 4
Bore: 80.0mm 3.1in
Stroke: 80.0mm 3.1in
Valve type/No: Overhead 8
Transmission: Manual
No. of forward speeds: 5
Wheels driven: Rear
Springs F/R: Coil/Coil
Brakes F/R: Disc/Disc
Wheelbase: 242.1cm 95.3in
Track F: 134.6cm 53.0in
Track R: 131.6cm 51.8in
Length: 412.2cm 162.3in
Width: 167.1cm 65.8in
Height: 134.1cm 52.8in
Kerb weight: 1007.9kg 2220.0lb
Fuel: 44.7L 9.8gal 11.8galUS

1528 Fiat

127
1971 Italy
85.0mph 136.8kmh
0-50mph 80.5kmh: 12.2secs
0-60mph 96.5kmh: 17.4secs
0-1/4 mile: 19.7secs
0-1km: 39.5secs
47.0bhp 35.0kW 47.6PS
@ 6200rpm
46.0lbft 62.3Nm @ 3500rpm
67.9bhp/ton 66.8bhp/tonne
52.0bhp/L 38.8kW/L 52.8PS/L
46.2ft/sec 14.0m/sec
14.0mph 22.5kmh/1000rpm
32.0mpg 26.6mpgUS 8.8L/100km
Petrol 4-stroke piston
903cc 55.1cu in
In-line 4 1 Carburettor
Compression ratio: 9.0:1
Bore: 65.0mm 2.6in
Stroke: 68.0mm 2.7in
Valve type/No: Overhead 8
Transmission: Manual
No. of forward speeds: 4
Wheels driven: Front
Springs F/R: Coil/Leaf
Brakes F/R: Disc/Drum
Steering: Rack & pinion
Wheelbase: 222.3cm 87.5in
Track F: 129.5cm 51.0in
Track R: 127.0cm 50.0in
Length: 360.7cm 142.0in
Width: 152.4cm 60.0in
Height: 138.4cm 54.5in
Ground clearance: 19.1cm 7.5in
Kerb weight: 703.7kg 1550.0lb
Fuel: 30.0L 6.6gal 7.9galUS

1529 Fiat

128
1971 Italy
85.0mph 136.8kmh
0-50mph 80.5kmh: 11.8secs
0-60mph 96.5kmh: 17.0secs
0-1/4 mile: 20.5secs
55.0bhp 41.0kW 55.8PS
@ 6000rpm
57.0lbft 77.2Nm @ 3600rpm
68.4bhp/ton 67.3bhp/tonne
49.3bhp/L 36.7kW/L 50.0PS/L
36.5ft/sec 11.1m/sec
15.1mph 24.3kmh/1000rpm
41.6mpg 34.6mpgUS 6.8L/100km
Petrol 4-stroke piston
1116cc 68.1cu in
In-line 4 1 Carburettor
Compression ratio: 8.8:1
Bore: 80.0mm 3.1in
Stroke: 55.5mm 2.2in
Valve type/No: Overhead 8
Transmission: Manual
No. of forward speeds: 4
Wheels driven: Front
Springs F/R: Coil/Leaf
Brakes F/R: Disc/Drum
Steering: Rack & pinion
Wheelbase: 244.9cm 96.4in
Track F: 130.8cm 51.5in
Track R: 130.6cm 51.4in
Length: 385.6cm 151.8in
Width: 159.0cm 62.6in
Height: 142.0cm 55.9in
Ground clearance: 14.5cm 5.7in
Kerb weight: 817.2kg 1800.0lb
Fuel: 37.8L 8.3gal 10.0galUS

1530 Fiat

124
1972 Italy
96.0mph 154.5kmh
0-50mph 80.5kmh: 10.6secs
0-60mph 96.5kmh: 14.6secs
0-1/4 mile: 20.2secs
0-1km: 37.5secs
60.0bhp 44.7kW 60.8PS
@ 5600rpm
64.0lbft 86.7Nm @ 3400rpm
68.5bhp/ton 67.4bhp/tonne
50.1bhp/L 37.4kW/L 50.8PS/L
43.7ft/sec 13.3m/sec
15.0mph 24.1kmh/1000rpm
26.5mpg 22.1mpgUS 10.7L/100km
Petrol 4-stroke piston
1197cc 73.0cu in
In-line 4 1 Carburettor
Compression ratio: 8.8:1
Bore: 73.0mm 2.9in
Stroke: 71.5mm 2.8in
Valve type/No: Overhead 8
Transmission: Manual
No. of forward speeds: 4
Wheels driven: Rear
Springs F/R: Coil/Coil
Brake system: PA
Brakes F/R: Disc/Disc
Steering: Worm & roller
Wheelbase: 241.3cm 95.0in
Track F: 132.6cm 52.2in
Track R: 130.0cm 51.2in
Length: 401.3cm 158.0in
Width: 157.5cm 62.0in
Height: 144.8cm 57.0in
Ground clearance: 15.2cm 6.0in
Kerb weight: 890.3kg 1961.0lb
Fuel: 38.7L 8.5gal 10.2galUS

1531 Fiat

128 Coupe 1300
1972 Italy
101.0mph 162.5kmh
0-50mph 80.5kmh: 8.9secs
0-60mph 96.5kmh: 13.1secs
0-1/4 mile: 18.8secs
0-1km: 35.2secs
75.0bhp 55.9kW 76.0PS
@ 6600rpm
68.0lbft 92.1Nm @ 3600rpm
93.5bhp/ton 91.9bhp/tonne
58.1bhp/L 43.4kW/L 58.9PS/L
40.1ft/sec 12.2m/sec
15.0mph 24.1kmh/1000rpm
28.5mpg 23.7mpgUS 9.9L/100km
Petrol 4-stroke piston
1290cc 78.7cu in
In-line 4 1 Carburettor
Compression ratio: 8.9:1
Bore: 86.0mm 3.4in
Stroke: 55.5mm 2.2in
Valve type/No: Overhead 8
Transmission: Manual
No. of forward speeds: 4
Wheels driven: Front
Springs F/R: Coil/Leaf
Brake system: PA
Brakes F/R: Disc/Drum
Steering: Rack & pinion
Wheelbase: 222.3cm 87.5in
Track F: 133.1cm 52.4in

Track R: 133.4cm 52.5in
Length: 381.0cm 150.0in
Width: 156.2cm 61.5in
Height: 130.8cm 51.5in
Ground clearance: 19.1cm 7.5in
Kerb weight: 815.8kg 1797.0lb
Fuel: 50.0L 11.0gal 13.2galUS

1532 Fiat
128 SL 1300 Coupe
1972 Italy
87.5mph 140.8kmh
0-50mph 80.5kmh: 10.5secs
0-60mph 96.5kmh: 15.2secs
0-1/4 mile: 20.5secs
51.0bhp 38.0kW 51.7PS
@ 5600rpm
62.0lbft 84.0Nm @ 3000rpm
61.9bhp/ton 60.9bhp/tonne
39.5bhp/L 29.5kW/L 40.1PS/L
34.1ft/sec 10.4m/sec
14.9mph 24.0kmh/1000rpm
34.8mpg 29.0mpgUS 8.1L/100km
Petrol 4-stroke piston
1290cc 78.7cu in
In-line 4 1 Carburettor
Compression ratio: 8.5:1
Bore: 86.0mm 3.4in
Stroke: 55.5mm 2.2in
Valve type/No: Overhead 8
Transmission: Manual
No. of forward speeds: 4
Wheels driven: Front
Springs F/R: Coil/Leaf
Brake system: PA
Brakes F/R: Disc/Drum
Steering: Rack & pinion
Wheelbase: 222.3cm 87.5in
Track F: 132.6cm 52.2in
Track R: 133.4cm 52.5in
Length: 381.0cm 150.0in
Width: 156.0cm 61.4in
Height: 131.1cm 51.6in
Ground clearance: 13.0cm 5.1in
Kerb weight: 837.6kg 1845.0lb
Fuel: 36.3L 8.0gal 9.6galUS

1533 Fiat
130 Automatic
1972 Italy
114.0mph 183.4kmh
0-50mph 80.5kmh: 8.6secs
0-60mph 96.5kmh: 11.4secs
0-1/4 mile: 18.4secs
0-1km: 33.6secs
165.0bhp 123.0kW 167.3PS
@ 5600rpm
184.0lbft 249.3Nm @ 3400rpm
103.4bhp/ton 101.7bhp/tonne
51.0bhp/L 38.0kW/L 51.7PS/L
40.4ft/sec 12.3m/sec
19.6mph 31.5kmh/1000rpm
15.7mpg 13.1mpgUS 18.0L/100km
Petrol 4-stroke piston
3235cc 197.4cu in
Vee 6 1 Carburettor
Compression ratio: 9.0:1
Bore: 102.0mm 4.0in
Stroke: 66.0mm 2.6in
Valve type/No: Overhead 12
Transmission: Automatic
No. of forward speeds: 3
Wheels driven: Rear
Springs F/R: Torsion bar/Coil
Brake system: PA
Brakes F/R: Disc/Disc
Steering: Worm & roller PA
Wheelbase: 271.8cm 107.0in
Track F: 146.6cm 57.7in
Track R: 146.6cm 57.7in
Length: 475.0cm 187.0in
Width: 180.3cm 71.0in
Height: 147.3cm 58.0in
Ground clearance: 20.3cm 8.0in
Kerb weight: 1622.6kg 3574.0lb
Fuel: 79.6L 17.5gal 21.0galUS

1534 Fiat
124 Spider
1973 Italy
101.0mph 162.5kmh
0-50mph 80.5kmh: 9.4secs
0-60mph 96.5kmh: 12.5secs
0-1/4 mile: 19.3secs
94.0bhp 70.1kW 95.3PS
@ 5600rpm
94.0lbft 127.4Nm @ 4000rpm
96.6bhp/ton 95.0bhp/tonne
58.5bhp/L 43.6kW/L 59.3PS/L
Petrol 4-stroke piston
1608cc 98.1cu in
In-line 4
Transmission: Manual
No. of forward speeds: 5
Wheels driven: Rear
Springs F/R: Coil/Coil
Brakes F/R: Disc/Disc
Wheelbase: 228.1cm 89.8in
Track F: 134.6cm 53.0in
Track R: 131.6cm 51.8in
Length: 397.0cm 156.3in
Width: 161.3cm 63.5in
Height: 125.0cm 49.2in
Kerb weight: 989.7kg 2180.0lb

1535 Fiat
124 Spider 1600
1973 Italy
106.0mph 170.6kmh
0-50mph 80.5kmh: 9.0secs
0-60mph 96.5kmh: 12.2secs
0-1/4 mile: 18.6secs
90.0bhp 67.1kW 91.2PS
@ 6600rpm
87.0lbft 117.9Nm @ 3600rpm
92.0bhp/ton 90.5bhp/tonne
56.5bhp/L 42.1kW/L 57.3PS/L
57.0ft/sec 17.4m/sec
17.7mph 28.5kmh/1000rpm
27.9mpg 23.2mpgUS 10.1L/100km
Petrol 4-stroke piston
1592cc 97.1cu in
In-line 4 1 Carburettor
Compression ratio: 8.5:1
Bore: 80.0mm 3.1in
Stroke: 79.0mm 3.1in
Valve type/No: Overhead 8
Transmission: Manual
No. of forward speeds: 5
Wheels driven: Rear
Springs F/R: Coil/Coil
Brake system: PA
Brakes F/R: Disc/Disc
Steering: Worm & roller
Wheelbase: 228.1cm 89.8in
Track F: 134.4cm 52.9in
Track R: 131.6cm 51.8in
Length: 397.0cm 156.3in
Width: 161.3cm 63.5in
Height: 125.0cm 49.2in
Ground clearance: 12.4cm 4.9in
Kerb weight: 994.3kg 2190.0lb
Fuel: 45.0L 9.9gal 11.9galUS

1536 Fiat
124 Sport Coupe 1800
1973 Italy
108.0mph 173.8kmh
0-50mph 80.5kmh: 8.0secs
0-60mph 96.5kmh: 10.5secs
0-1/4 mile: 17.4secs
0-1km: 32.1secs
118.0bhp 88.0kW 119.6PS
@ 6000rpm
111.0lbft 150.4Nm @ 4000rpm
119.9bhp/ton 117.9bhp/tonne
67.2bhp/L 50.1kW/L 68.1PS/L
52.0ft/sec 15.8m/sec
17.5mph 28.2kmh/1000rpm
24.6mpg 20.5mpgUS 11.5L/100km
Petrol 4-stroke piston
1756cc 107.1cu in
In-line 4 1 Carburettor
Compression ratio: 9.8:1
Bore: 84.0mm 3.3in
Stroke: 79.2mm 3.1in
Valve type/No: Overhead 8
Transmission: Manual
No. of forward speeds: 5
Wheels driven: Rear
Springs F/R: Coil/Coil
Brake system: PA
Brakes F/R: Disc/Disc
Steering: Worm & roller
Wheelbase: 242.1cm 95.3in
Track F: 134.6cm 53.0in
Track R: 131.3cm 51.7in
Length: 416.6cm 164.0in
Width: 166.9cm 65.7in
Height: 133.9cm 52.7in
Ground clearance: 15.2cm 6.0in
Kerb weight: 1001.1kg 2205.0lb
Fuel: 44.6L 9.8gal 11.8galUS

1537 Fiat
124 Station Wagon
1973 Italy
0-60mph 96.5kmh: 13.8secs
0-1/4 mile: 19.2secs
70.0bhp 52.2kW 71.0PS
@ 5400rpm
81.0lbft 109.8Nm @ 3300rpm
70.5bhp/ton 69.3bhp/tonne
48.7bhp/L 36.3kW/L 49.3PS/L
30.0mpg 25.0mpgUS 9.4L/100km
Petrol 4-stroke piston
1438cc 87.7cu in
In-line 4
Valve type/No: Overhead 8
Transmission: Manual
No. of forward speeds: 4
Wheels driven: Rear
Brake system: PA
Brakes F/R: Disc/Disc
Wheelbase: 242.6cm 95.5in
Length: 412.0cm 162.2in
Width: 162.6cm 64.0in
Height: 144.0cm 56.7in
Kerb weight: 1010.1kg 2225.0lb

1538 Fiat
124S Automatic
1973 Italy
94.0mph 151.2kmh
0-50mph 80.5kmh: 10.3secs
0-60mph 96.5kmh: 14.8secs
0-1/4 mile: 20.2secs
0-1km: 37.8secs
75.0bhp 55.9kW 76.0PS
@ 5400rpm
81.7lbft 110.7Nm @ 3500rpm
82.2bhp/ton 80.8bhp/tonne
50.6bhp/L 37.7kW/L 51.3PS/L
42.1ft/sec 12.9m/sec
15.8mph 25.4kmh/1000rpm
26.6mpg 22.1mpgUS 10.6L/100km
Petrol 4-stroke piston
1483cc 90.5cu in
In-line 4 1 Carburettor
Compression ratio: 9.0:1
Bore: 80.0mm 3.1in
Stroke: 71.5mm 2.8in
Valve type/No: Overhead 8
Transmission: Automatic
No. of forward speeds: 3
Wheels driven: Rear
Springs F/R: Coil/Coil
Brake system: PA
Brakes F/R: Disc/Disc
Steering: Worm & roller
Wheelbase: 242.1cm 95.3in
Track F: 132.6cm 52.2in
Track R: 130.0cm 51.2in
Length: 401.3cm 158.0in
Width: 157.5cm 62.0in
Height: 144.8cm 57.0in
Ground clearance: 15.2cm 6.0in
Kerb weight: 928.0kg 2044.0lb
Fuel: 37.8L 8.3gal 10.0galUS

1539 Fiat
126
1973 Italy
65.0mph 104.6kmh
0-50mph 80.5kmh: 24.5secs
0-60mph 96.5kmh: 62.2secs
0-1/4 mile: 25.6secs
0-1km: 50.1secs
23.0bhp 17.1kW 23.3PS
@ 4800rpm
29.0lbft 39.3Nm @ 3400rpm
40.5bhp/ton 39.9bhp/tonne
38.7bhp/L 28.9kW/L 39.3PS/L
36.8ft/sec 11.2m/sec
13.7mph 22.0kmh/1000rpm
36.8mpg 30.6mpgUS 7.7L/100km
Petrol 4-stroke piston
594cc 36.2cu in
In-line 2 1 Carburettor
Compression ratio: 7.5:1
Bore: 73.5mm 2.9in
Stroke: 70.0mm 2.8in
Valve type/No: Overhead 4
Transmission: Manual
No. of forward speeds: 4
Wheels driven: Rear
Springs F/R: Leaf/Coil
Brakes F/R: Drum/Drum
Steering: Worm & sector
Wheelbase: 184.7cm 72.7in
Track F: 114.3cm 45.0in
Track R: 120.1cm 47.3in
Length: 305.1cm 120.1in
Width: 137.7cm 54.2in
Height: 133.4cm 52.5in
Ground clearance: 14.0cm 5.5in
Kerb weight: 577.0kg 1271.0lb
Fuel: 20.9L 4.6gal 5.5galUS

1540 Fiat
128 Station Wagon
1973 Italy
0-60mph 96.5kmh: 17.1secs
0-1/4 mile: 20.4secs
55.0bhp 41.0kW 55.8PS
@ 6000rpm
57.0lbft 77.2Nm @ 3000rpm
64.8bhp/ton 63.8bhp/tonne
49.3bhp/L 36.7kW/L 50.0PS/L
36.6mpg 30.5mpgUS 7.7L/100km
Petrol 4-stroke piston
1116cc 68.1cu in
In-line 4
Valve type/No: Overhead 8
Transmission: Manual
No. of forward speeds: 4
Wheels driven: Front
Brakes F/R: Disc/Drum
Wheelbase: 244.9cm 96.4in
Length: 391.7cm 154.2in
Width: 159.0cm 62.6in
Height: 142.2cm 56.0in
Kerb weight: 862.6kg 1900.0lb

1541 Fiat
132 1800 Special
1973 Italy
106.0mph 170.6kmh
0-50mph 80.5kmh: 7.3secs
0-60mph 96.5kmh: 10.6secs
0-1/4 mile: 17.8secs
0-1km: 33.5secs
105.0bhp 78.3kW 106.5PS
@ 6000rpm
104.0lbft 140.9Nm @ 4200rpm
98.1bhp/ton 96.5bhp/tonne
59.8bhp/L 44.6kW/L 60.6PS/L
52.0ft/sec 15.8m/sec
19.0mph 30.6kmh/1000rpm
23.2mpg 19.3mpgUS 12.2L/100km
Petrol 4-stroke piston
1756cc 107.1cu in
In-line 4 1 Carburettor
Compression ratio: 8.9:1
Bore: 84.0mm 3.3in
Stroke: 79.2mm 3.1in
Valve type/No: Overhead 8
Transmission: Manual
No. of forward speeds: 5
Wheels driven: Rear
Springs F/R: Coil/Coil
Brake system: PA
Brakes F/R: Disc/Disc
Steering: Worm & roller
Wheelbase: 254.0cm 100.0in
Track F: 132.1cm 52.0in
Track R: 132.1cm 52.0in
Length: 436.9cm 172.0in
Width: 162.6cm 64.0in
Height: 142.2cm 56.0in
Ground clearance: 20.3cm 8.0in
Kerb weight: 1088.2kg 2397.0lb
Fuel: 56.0L 12.3gal 14.8galUS

1542 Fiat
132 GLS
1974 Italy
107.0mph 172.2kmh
0-50mph 80.5kmh: 7.1secs
0-60mph 96.5kmh: 10.4secs
0-1/4 mile: 17.9secs
0-1km: 33.5secs
107.0bhp 79.8kW 108.5PS
@ 6000rpm
104.0lbft 140.9Nm @ 4000rpm
99.5bhp/ton 97.8bhp/tonne
60.9bhp/L 45.4kW/L 61.8PS/L
52.0ft/sec 15.8m/sec
18.0mph 29.0kmh/1000rpm
23.8mpg 19.8mpgUS 11.9L/100km
Petrol 4-stroke piston
1756cc 107.1cu in
In-line 4 1 Carburettor
Compression ratio: 8.9:1
Bore: 84.0mm 3.3in
Stroke: 79.2mm 3.1in
Valve type/No: Overhead 8

Transmission: Manual
No. of forward speeds: 5
Wheels driven: Rear
Springs F/R: Coil/Coil
Brake system: PA
Brakes F/R: Disc/Disc
Steering: Worm & roller
Wheelbase: 254.0cm 100.0in
Track F: 132.1cm 52.0in
Track R: 132.1cm 52.0in
Length: 436.9cm 172.0in
Width: 162.6cm 64.0in
Height: 142.2cm 56.0in
Ground clearance: 20.3cm 8.0in
Kerb weight: 1093.7kg 2409.0lb
Fuel: 55.1L 12.1gal 14.5galUS

1543 Fiat

X1/9
1974 Italy
93.0mph 149.6kmh
0-50mph 80.5kmh: 11.3secs
0-60mph 96.5kmh: 15.3secs
0-1/4 mile: 20.1secs
66.5bhp 49.6kW 67.4PS
@ 6200rpm
68.0lbft 92.1Nm @ 3600rpm
74.7bhp/ton 73.4bhp/tonne
51.5bhp/L 38.4kW/L 52.3PS/L
37.7ft/sec 11.5m/sec
16.2mph 26.1kmh/1000rpm
36.0mpg 30.0mpgUS 7.8L/100km
Petrol 4-stroke piston
1290cc 78.7cu in
In-line 4 1 Carburettor
Compression ratio: 8.5:1
Bore: 86.0mm 3.4in
Stroke: 55.5mm 2.2in
Valve type/No: Overhead 8
Transmission: Manual
No. of forward speeds: 4
Wheels driven: Rear
Springs F/R: Coil/Coil
Brakes F/R: Disc/Disc
Steering: Rack & pinion
Wheelbase: 220.2cm 86.7in
Track F: 133.4cm 52.5in
Track R: 134.4cm 52.9in
Length: 389.9cm 153.5in
Width: 157.0cm 61.8in
Height: 117.1cm 46.1in
Ground clearance: 12.7cm 5.0in
Kerb weight: 905.7kg 1995.0lb
Fuel: 46.2L 10.1gal 12.2galUS

1544 Fiat

124 Special TC
1975 Italy
92.0mph 148.0kmh
0-50mph 80.5kmh: 11.2secs
0-60mph 96.5kmh: 15.2secs
0-1/4 mile: 20.2secs
78.0bhp 58.2kW 79.1PS
@ 6000rpm
85.0lbft 115.2Nm @ 3600rpm
77.3bhp/ton 76.0bhp/tonne
49.0bhp/L 36.5kW/L 49.7PS/L
52.0ft/sec 15.8m/sec
16.1mph 25.9kmh/1000rpm
26.4mpg 22.0mpgUS 10.7L/100km
Petrol 4-stroke piston
1592cc 97.1cu in
In-line 4
Compression ratio: 8.0:1
Bore: 80.0mm 3.1in
Stroke: 79.2mm 3.1in
Valve type/No: Overhead 8
Transmission: Manual
No. of forward speeds: 4
Wheels driven: Rear
Springs F/R: Coil/Coil
Brake system: PA
Brakes F/R: Disc/Disc
Steering: Worm & roller
Wheelbase: 242.1cm 95.3in
Track F: 133.1cm 52.4in
Track R: 130.0cm 51.2in
Length: 420.6cm 165.6in
Width: 164.8cm 64.9in
Height: 142.0cm 55.9in
Kerb weight: 1026.0kg 2260.0lb
Fuel: 36.3L 8.0gal 9.6galUS

1545 Fiat

124 Sport Coupe 1800
1975 Italy
107.0mph 172.2kmh
0-50mph 80.5kmh: 9.2secs
0-60mph 96.5kmh: 13.2secs
0-1/4 mile: 18.6secs
92.5bhp 69.0kW 93.8PS
@ 6200rpm
92.0lbft 124.7Nm @ 3000rpm
87.8bhp/ton 86.3bhp/tonne
52.7bhp/L 39.3kW/L 53.4PS/L
53.7ft/sec 16.4m/sec
17.9mph 28.8kmh/1000rpm
29.4mpg 24.5mpgUS 9.6L/100km
Petrol 4-stroke piston
1756cc 107.1cu in
In-line 4 1 Carburettor
Compression ratio: 8.0:1
Bore: 84.0mm 3.3in
Stroke: 79.2mm 3.1in
Valve type/No: Overhead 8
Transmission: Manual
No. of forward speeds: 5
Wheels driven: Rear
Springs F/R: Coil/Coil
Brake system: PA
Brakes F/R: Disc/Disc
Steering: Worm & roller
Wheelbase: 242.1cm 95.3in
Track F: 134.6cm 53.0in
Track R: 131.6cm 51.8in
Length: 434.3cm 171.0in
Width: 167.1cm 65.8in
Height: 134.1cm 52.8in
Ground clearance: 12.4cm 4.9in
Kerb weight: 1071.4kg 2360.0lb
Fuel: 43.1L 9.5gal 11.4galUS

1546 Fiat

128
1975 Italy
0-60mph 96.5kmh: 14.7secs
0-1/4 mile: 19.8secs
66.0bhp 49.2kW 66.9PS
@ 6200rpm
68.0lbft 92.1Nm @ 3600rpm
75.2bhp/ton 74.0bhp/tonne
51.2bhp/L 38.2kW/L 51.9PS/L
37.7ft/sec 11.5m/sec
29.4mpg 24.5mpgUS 9.6L/100km
Petrol 4-stroke piston
1290cc 78.7cu in
In-line 4 1 Carburettor
Compression ratio: 8.5:1
Bore: 86.0mm 3.4in
Stroke: 55.5mm 2.2in
Valve type/No: Overhead 8
Transmission: Manual
No. of forward speeds: 4
Wheels driven: Front
Brake system: PA
Wheelbase: 244.9cm 96.4in
Track F: 130.8cm 51.5in
Track R: 130.6cm 51.4in
Length: 399.3cm 157.2in
Width: 159.0cm 62.6in
Height: 142.0cm 55.9in
Ground clearance: 14.5cm 5.7in
Kerb weight: 892.1kg 1965.0lb
Fuel: 37.8L 8.3gal 10.0galUS

1547 Fiat

128 Special
1975 Italy
92.0mph 148.0kmh
0-50mph 80.5kmh: 9.6secs
0-60mph 96.5kmh: 13.9secs
0-1/4 mile: 19.1secs
0-1km: 36.8secs
60.5bhp 45.1kW 61.3PS
@ 6000rpm
66.5lbft 90.1Nm @ 3000rpm
75.4bhp/ton 74.1bhp/tonne
46.9bhp/L 35.0kW/L 47.5PS/L
36.5ft/sec 11.1m/sec
15.2mph 24.5kmh/1000rpm
32.6mpg 27.1mpgUS 8.7L/100km
Petrol 4-stroke piston
1290cc 78.7cu in
In-line 4 1 Carburettor
Compression ratio: 8.9:1
Bore: 86.0mm 3.4in
Stroke: 55.5mm 2.2in
Valve type/No: Overhead 8
Transmission: Manual
No. of forward speeds: 4
Wheels driven: Front
Springs F/R: Coil/Leaf
Brake system: PA
Brakes F/R: Disc/Drum
Steering: Rack & pinion
Wheelbase: 246.4cm 97.0in
Track F: 130.8cm 51.5in
Track R: 128.3cm 50.5in
Length: 383.5cm 151.0in
Width: 153.7cm 60.5in
Height: 143.5cm 56.5in
Ground clearance: 14.5cm 5.7in
Kerb weight: 816.3kg 1798.0lb
Fuel: 37.8L 8.3gal 10.0galUS

1548 Fiat

131 1300S
1975 Italy
94.0mph 151.2kmh
0-50mph 80.5kmh: 11.1secs
0-60mph 96.5kmh: 16.1secs
0-1/4 mile: 20.4secs
0-1km: 38.8secs
65.0bhp 48.5kW 65.9PS
@ 5400rpm
75.0lbft 101.6Nm @ 3000rpm
69.5bhp/ton 68.3bhp/tonne
50.1bhp/L 37.4kW/L 50.8PS/L
42.1ft/sec 12.9m/sec
15.7mph 25.3kmh/1000rpm
25.5mpg 21.2mpgUS 11.1L/100km
Petrol 4-stroke piston
1297cc 79.1cu in
In-line 4 1 Carburettor
Compression ratio: 9.2:1
Bore: 76.0mm 3.0in
Stroke: 71.5mm 2.8in
Valve type/No: Overhead 8
Transmission: Manual
No. of forward speeds: 4
Wheels driven: Rear
Springs F/R: Coil/Coil
Brake system: PA
Brakes F/R: Disc/Drum
Steering: Rack & pinion
Wheelbase: 248.9cm 98.0in
Track F: 137.2cm 54.0in
Track R: 137.2cm 54.0in
Length: 426.7cm 168.0in
Width: 165.1cm 65.0in
Height: 139.7cm 55.0in
Ground clearance: 17.8cm 7.0in
Kerb weight: 951.1kg 2095.0lb
Fuel: 50.0L 11.0gal 13.2galUS

1549 Fiat

133
1975 Italy
78.0mph 125.5kmh
0-50mph 80.5kmh: 16.5secs
0-60mph 96.5kmh: 28.9secs
0-1/4 mile: 22.9secs
0-1km: 44.4secs
37.0bhp 27.6kW 37.5PS
@ 5000rpm
40.5lbft 54.9Nm @ 3400rpm
53.8bhp/ton 52.9bhp/tonne
43.9bhp/L 32.7kW/L 44.5PS/L
34.7ft/sec 10.6m/sec
13.8mph 22.2kmh/1000rpm
36.0mpg 30.0mpgUS 7.8L/100km
Petrol 4-stroke piston
843cc 51.4cu in
In-line 4 1 Carburettor
Compression ratio: 9.0:1
Bore: 65.0mm 2.6in
Stroke: 63.5mm 2.5in
Valve type/No: Overhead 8
Transmission: Manual
No. of forward speeds: 4
Wheels driven: Rear
Springs F/R: Leaf/Coil
Brakes F/R: Drum/Drum
Steering: Worm & sector
Wheelbase: 203.2cm 80.0in
Track F: 114.3cm 45.0in
Track R: 120.7cm 47.5in
Length: 353.1cm 139.0in
Width: 142.2cm 56.0in
Height: 132.1cm 52.0in
Kerb weight: 699.2kg 1540.0lb
Fuel: 30.0L 6.6gal 7.9galUS

1550 Fiat

124 Spider
1976 Italy
100.0mph 160.9kmh
0-60mph 96.5kmh: 14.8secs
0-1/4 mile: 20.0secs
86.0bhp 64.1kW 87.2PS
@ 6200rpm
90.0lbft 122.0Nm @ 2800rpm
85.4bhp/ton 84.0bhp/tonne
49.0bhp/L 36.5kW/L 49.6PS/L
53.7ft/sec 16.4m/sec
26.4mpg 22.0mpgUS 10.7L/100km
Petrol 4-stroke piston
1756cc 107.1cu in
In-line 4 1 Carburettor
Compression ratio: 8.0:1
Bore: 84.0mm 3.3in
Stroke: 79.2mm 3.1in
Valve type/No: Overhead 8
Transmission: Manual
No. of forward speeds: 5
Wheels driven: Rear
Wheelbase: 227.8cm 89.7in
Track F: 135.1cm 53.2in
Track R: 132.1cm 52.0in
Length: 414.3cm 163.1in
Width: 161.3cm 63.5in
Height: 125.0cm 49.2in
Kerb weight: 1023.8kg 2255.0lb
Fuel: 43.1L 9.5gal 11.4galUS

1551 Fiat

124 Sport Spider
1976 Italy
95.0mph 152.9kmh
0-50mph 80.5kmh: 10.7secs
0-60mph 96.5kmh: 24.8secs
0-1/4 mile: 20.0secs
86.0bhp 64.1kW 87.2PS
@ 6200rpm
90.0lbft 122.0Nm @ 2800rpm
78.9bhp/ton 77.6bhp/tonne
49.0bhp/L 36.5kW/L 49.6PS/L
53.7ft/sec 16.4m/sec
27.6mpg 23.0mpgUS 10.2L/100km
Petrol 4-stroke piston
1756cc 107.1cu in
In-line 4 1 Carburettor
Compression ratio: 8.0:1
Bore: 84.0mm 3.3in
Stroke: 79.2mm 3.1in
Valve type/No: Overhead 8
Transmission: Manual
No. of forward speeds: 5
Wheels driven: Rear
Springs F/R: Coil/Coil
Brake system: PA
Brakes F/R: Disc/Disc
Steering: Worm & roller
Wheelbase: 227.8cm 89.7in
Track F: 135.1cm 53.2in
Track R: 132.1cm 52.0in
Length: 414.3cm 163.1in
Width: 161.3cm 63.5in
Height: 125.0cm 49.2in
Ground clearance: 11.9cm 4.7in
Kerb weight: 1107.8kg 2440.0lb
Fuel: 43.1L 9.5gal 11.4galUS

1552 Fiat

128 3P
1976 Italy
102.0mph 164.1kmh
0-50mph 80.5kmh: 8.1secs
0-60mph 96.5kmh: 11.7secs
0-1/4 mile: 18.4secs
0-1km: 34.6secs
73.0bhp 54.4kW 74.0PS
@ 6000rpm
74.0lbft 100.3Nm @ 3900rpm
87.0bhp/ton 85.6bhp/tonne
56.6bhp/L 42.2kW/L 57.4PS/L
36.5ft/sec 11.1m/sec
14.9mph 24.0kmh/1000rpm
32.7mpg 27.2mpgUS 8.6L/100km
Petrol 4-stroke piston
1290cc 78.7cu in
In-line 4 1 Carburettor
Compression ratio: 9.2:1
Bore: 86.0mm 3.4in
Stroke: 55.5mm 2.2in
Valve type/No: Overhead 8
Transmission: Manual
No. of forward speeds: 4
Wheels driven: Front
Springs F/R: Coil/Leaf
Brake system: PA
Brakes F/R: Disc/Drum
Steering: Rack & pinion
Wheelbase: 222.3cm 87.5in
Track F: 133.1cm 52.4in
Track R: 133.4cm 52.5in

Length: 382.3cm 150.5in
Width: 156.2cm 61.5in
Height: 127.0cm 50.0in
Ground clearance: 15.2cm 6.0in
Kerb weight: 853.1kg 1879.0lb
Fuel: 50.0L 11.0gal 13.2galUS

1553 Fiat

128 Estate
1976 Italy
89.0mph 143.2kmh
0-50mph 80.5kmh: 9.6secs
0-60mph 96.5kmh: 15.3secs
0-1/4 mile: 19.6secs
0-1km: 37.7secs
60.0bhp 44.7kW 60.8PS
@ 6000rpm
71.0lbft 96.2Nm @ 3200rpm
73.7bhp/ton 72.5bhp/tonne
46.5bhp/L 34.7kW/L 47.2PS/L
36.7ft/sec 11.2m/sec
15.1mph 24.3kmh/1000rpm
32.5mpg 27.1mpgUS 8.7L/100km
Petrol 4-stroke piston
1290cc 78.7cu in
In-line 4 1 Carburettor
Compression ratio: 9.2:1
Bore: 86.0mm 3.4in
Stroke: 56.0mm 2.2in
Valve type/No: Overhead 8
Transmission: Manual
No. of forward speeds: 4
Wheels driven: Front
Springs F/R: Coil/Leaf
Brake system: PA
Brakes F/R: Disc/Drum
Steering: Rack & pinion
Wheelbase: 244.9cm 96.4in
Track F: 130.8cm 51.5in
Track R: 131.1cm 51.6in
Length: 384.0cm 151.2in
Width: 159.0cm 62.6in
Height: 142.0cm 55.9in
Ground clearance: 15.2cm 6.0in
Kerb weight: 827.6kg 1823.0lb
Fuel: 40.0L 8.8gal 10.6galUS

1554 Fiat

131
1976 Italy
99.0mph 159.3kmh
0-50mph 80.5kmh: 9.6secs
0-60mph 96.5kmh: 13.7secs
0-1/4 mile: 19.3secs
83.0bhp 61.9kW 84.1PS
@ 5800rpm
89.0lbft 120.6Nm @ 2800rpm
78.1bhp/ton 76.8bhp/tonne
47.3bhp/L 35.2kW/L 47.9PS/L
50.3ft/sec 15.3m/sec
18.2mph 29.3kmh/1000rpm
25.8mpg 21.5mpgUS 10.9L/100km
Petrol 4-stroke piston
1756cc 107.1cu in
In-line 4 1 Carburettor
Compression ratio: 8.0:1
Bore: 84.0mm 3.3in
Stroke: 79.2mm 3.1in
Valve type/No: Overhead 8
Transmission: Manual
No. of forward speeds: 5
Wheels driven: Rear
Springs F/R: Coil/Coil
Brake system: PA
Brakes F/R: Disc/Drum
Steering: Rack & pinion
Wheelbase: 248.9cm 98.0in
Track F: 137.4cm 54.1in
Track R: 131.8cm 51.9in
Length: 436.1cm 171.7in
Width: 164.1cm 64.6in
Height: 136.4cm 53.7in
Ground clearance: 12.2cm 4.8in
Kerb weight: 1080.5kg 2380.0lb
Fuel: 46.2L 10.1gal 12.2galUS

1555 Fiat

127 1050 CL
1977 Italy
88.0mph 141.6kmh
0-50mph 80.5kmh: 11.6secs
0-60mph 96.5kmh: 17.6secs
0-1/4 mile: 20.8secs
0-1km: 39.5secs
50.0bhp 37.3kW 50.7PS
@ 5600rpm
57.0lbft 77.2Nm @ 3000rpm
66.4bhp/ton 65.3bhp/tonne
47.7bhp/L 35.5kW/L 48.3PS/L
35.5ft/sec 10.8m/sec
15.8mph 25.4kmh/1000rpm
30.7mpg 25.6mpgUS 9.2L/100km
Petrol 4-stroke piston
1049cc 64.0cu in
In-line 4 1 Carburettor
Compression ratio: 9.3:1
Bore: 76.0mm 3.0in
Stroke: 57.8mm 2.3in
Valve type/No: Overhead 8
Transmission: Manual
No. of forward speeds: 4
Wheels driven: Front
Springs F/R: Coil/Leaf
Brakes F/R: Disc/Drum
Steering: Rack & pinion
Wheelbase: 222.3cm 87.5in
Track F: 129.5cm 51.0in
Track R: 127.0cm 50.0in
Length: 360.7cm 142.0in
Width: 152.4cm 60.0in
Height: 138.4cm 54.5in
Ground clearance: 19.1cm 7.5in
Kerb weight: 765.9kg 1687.0lb
Fuel: 30.0L 6.6gal 7.9galUS

1556 Fiat

131
1977 Italy
98.0mph 157.7kmh
0-60mph 96.5kmh: 13.4secs
0-1/4 mile: 19.5secs
86.0bhp 64.1kW 87.2PS
@ 6200rpm
90.0lbft 122.0Nm @ 2800rpm
80.9bhp/ton 79.6bhp/tonne
49.0bhp/L 36.5kW/L 49.6PS/L
53.7ft/sec 16.4m/sec
Petrol 4-stroke piston
1756cc 107.1cu in
In-line 4 1 Carburettor
Compression ratio: 8.2:1
Bore: 84.0mm 3.3in
Stroke: 79.2mm 3.1in
Valve type/No: Overhead 8
Transmission: Manual
No. of forward speeds: 5
Wheels driven: Rear
Brakes F/R: Disc/Drum
Wheelbase: 248.9cm 98.0in
Track F: 137.4cm 54.1in
Track R: 131.8cm 51.9in
Length: 436.1cm 171.7in
Width: 164.1cm 64.6in
Height: 136.4cm 53.7in
Kerb weight: 1080.5kg 2380.0lb
Fuel: 46.2L 10.1gal 12.2galUS

1557 Fiat

X1/9
1977 Italy
100.0mph 160.9kmh
0-50mph 80.5kmh: 8.7secs
0-60mph 96.5kmh: 12.7secs
0-1/4 mile: 18.8secs
0-1km: 35.7secs
73.0bhp 54.4kW 74.0PS
@ 6000rpm
72.0lbft 97.6Nm @ 3400rpm
81.3bhp/ton 80.0bhp/tonne
56.6bhp/L 42.2kW/L 57.4PS/L
36.5ft/sec 11.1m/sec
16.6mph 26.7kmh/1000rpm
30.7mpg 25.6mpgUS 9.2L/100km
Petrol 4-stroke piston
1290cc 78.7cu in
In-line 4 1 Carburettor
Compression ratio: 8.9:1
Bore: 86.0mm 3.4in
Stroke: 55.5mm 2.2in
Valve type/No: Overhead 8
Transmission: Manual
No. of forward speeds: 4
Wheels driven: Rear
Springs F/R: Coil/Coil
Brakes F/R: Disc/Disc
Steering: Rack & pinion
Wheelbase: 220.2cm 86.7in
Track F: 133.4cm 52.5in
Track R: 133.4cm 52.5in
Length: 382.8cm 150.7in
Width: 156.7cm 61.7in
Height: 116.8cm 46.0in
Ground clearance: 12.7cm 5.0in
Kerb weight: 913.0kg 2011.0lb
Fuel: 47.8L 10.5gal 12.6galUS

1558 Fiat

127 Sport
1978 Italy
98.0mph 157.7kmh
0-50mph 80.5kmh: 9.5secs
0-60mph 96.5kmh: 13.8secs
0-1/4 mile: 19.2secs
0-1km: 36.5secs
70.0bhp 52.2kW 71.0PS
@ 6500rpm
61.5lbft 83.3Nm @ 4500rpm
92.3bhp/ton 90.7bhp/tonne
66.7bhp/L 49.8kW/L 67.6PS/L
41.2ft/sec 12.5m/sec
14.5mph 23.3kmh/1000rpm
34.1mpg 28.4mpgUS 8.3L/100km
Petrol 4-stroke piston
1049cc 64.0cu in
In-line 4 1 Carburettor
Compression ratio: 9.8:1
Bore: 76.0mm 3.0in
Stroke: 57.8mm 2.3in
Valve type/No: Overhead 8
Transmission: Manual
No. of forward speeds: 4
Wheels driven: Front
Springs F/R: Coil/Leaf
Brake system: PA
Brakes F/R: Disc/Drum
Steering: Rack & pinion
Wheelbase: 222.3cm 87.5in
Track F: 129.5cm 51.0in
Track R: 127.0cm 50.0in
Length: 360.7cm 142.0in
Width: 152.4cm 60.0in
Height: 138.4cm 54.5in
Ground clearance: 19.1cm 7.5in
Kerb weight: 771.3kg 1699.0lb
Fuel: 30.5L 6.7gal 8.0galUS

1559 Fiat

131 Supermirafiori
1978 Italy
105.0mph 168.9kmh
0-50mph 80.5kmh: 8.3secs
0-60mph 96.5kmh: 11.9secs
0-1/4 mile: 18.8secs
0-1km: 34.4secs
96.0bhp 71.6kW 97.3PS
@ 6000rpm
94.0lbft 127.4Nm @ 3800rpm
92.3bhp/ton 90.7bhp/tonne
60.6bhp/L 45.2kW/L 61.4PS/L
46.7ft/sec 14.2m/sec
19.9mph 32.0kmh/1000rpm
23.2mpg 19.3mpgUS 12.2L/100km
Petrol 4-stroke piston
1585cc 96.7cu in
In-line 4 1 Carburettor
Compression ratio: 9.0:1
Bore: 84.0mm 3.3in
Stroke: 71.0mm 2.8in
Valve type/No: Overhead 8
Transmission: Manual
No. of forward speeds: 5
Wheels driven: Rear
Springs F/R: Coil/Coil
Brake system: PA
Brakes F/R: Disc/Drum
Steering: Rack & pinion
Wheelbase: 248.9cm 98.0in
Track F: 137.2cm 54.0in
Track R: 132.1cm 52.0in
Length: 426.7cm 168.0in
Width: 165.1cm 65.0in
Height: 139.7cm 55.0in
Ground clearance: 17.8cm 7.0in
Kerb weight: 1057.8kg 2330.0lb
Fuel: 50.0L 11.0gal 13.2galUS

1560 Fiat

132 2000 GLS
1978 Italy
108.0mph 173.8kmh
0-50mph 80.5kmh: 7.1secs
0-60mph 96.5kmh: 10.0secs
0-1/4 mile: 18.1secs
0-1km: 33.6secs
112.0bhp 83.5kW 113.5PS
@ 5600rpm
116.0lbft 157.2Nm @ 3000rpm
97.9bhp/ton 96.3bhp/tonne
56.1bhp/L 41.9kW/L 56.9PS/L
55.1ft/sec 16.8m/sec
22.7mph 36.5kmh/1000rpm
22.5mpg 18.7mpgUS 12.6L/100km
Petrol 4-stroke piston
1995cc 121.7cu in
In-line 4 1 Carburettor
Compression ratio: 8.9:1
Bore: 84.0mm 3.3in
Stroke: 90.0mm 3.5in
Valve type/No: Overhead 8
Transmission: Manual
No. of forward speeds: 5
Wheels driven: Rear
Springs F/R: Coil/Coil
Brake system: PA
Brakes F/R: Disc/Drum
Steering: Recirculating ball PA
Wheelbase: 254.0cm 100.0in
Track F: 132.1cm 52.0in
Track R: 132.1cm 52.0in
Length: 436.9cm 172.0in
Width: 162.6cm 64.0in
Height: 142.2cm 56.0in
Ground clearance: 20.3cm 8.0in
Kerb weight: 1163.1kg 2562.0lb
Fuel: 56.0L 12.3gal 14.8galUS

1561 Fiat

Super Brava
1978 Italy
102.0mph 164.1kmh
0-50mph 80.5kmh: 8.3secs
0-60mph 96.5kmh: 12.1secs
0-1/4 mile: 18.8secs
83.0bhp 61.9kW 84.1PS
@ 5800rpm
89.0lbft 120.6Nm @ 2800rpm
74.2bhp/ton 73.0bhp/tonne
47.3bhp/L 35.2kW/L 47.9PS/L
50.3ft/sec 15.3m/sec
19.4mph 31.2kmh/1000rpm
28.2mpg 23.5mpgUS 10.0L/100km
Petrol 4-stroke piston
1756cc 107.1cu in
In-line 4
Compression ratio: 8.0:1
Bore: 84.0mm 3.3in
Stroke: 79.2mm 3.1in
Valve type/No: Overhead 8
Transmission: Manual
No. of forward speeds: 5
Wheels driven: Rear
Springs F/R: Coil/Coil
Brake system: PA
Brakes F/R: Disc/Drum
Steering: Rack & pinion
Wheelbase: 248.9cm 98.0in
Track F: 137.7cm 54.2in
Track R: 131.8cm 51.9in
Length: 437.9cm 172.4in
Width: 164.1cm 64.6in
Height: 138.2cm 54.4in
Kerb weight: 1137.3kg 2505.0lb
Fuel: 46.2L 10.1gal 12.2galUS

1562 Fiat

124 Spider
1979 Italy
102.0mph 164.1kmh
0-50mph 80.5kmh: 7.3secs
0-60mph 96.5kmh: 10.6secs
0-1/4 mile: 18.1secs
80.0bhp 59.7kW 81.1PS
@ 5000rpm
104.0lbft 140.9Nm @ 3000rpm
75.8bhp/ton 74.5bhp/tonne
40.1bhp/L 29.9kW/L 40.7PS/L
49.2ft/sec 15.0m/sec
19.4mph 31.2kmh/1000rpm
25.2mpg 21.0mpgUS 11.2L/100km
Petrol 4-stroke piston
1995cc 121.7cu in
In-line 4 1 Carburettor
Compression ratio: 8.1:1
Bore: 84.0mm 3.3in
Stroke: 90.0mm 3.5in
Valve type/No: Overhead 8
Transmission: Manual
No. of forward speeds: 5
Wheels driven: Rear
Springs F/R: Coil/Coil
Brake system: PA
Brakes F/R: Disc/Disc
Steering: Worm & roller
Wheelbase: 227.8cm 89.7in
Track F: 135.1cm 53.2in
Track R: 132.1cm 52.0in

Length: 414.0cm 163.0in
Width: 161.3cm 63.5in
Height: 122.4cm 48.2in
Kerb weight: 1073.7kg 2365.0lb
Fuel: 43.1L 9.5gal 11.4galUS

1563 Fiat

124 Sports Spider
1979 Italy
108.0mph 173.8kmh
0-50mph 80.5kmh: 8.1secs
0-60mph 96.5kmh: 11.5secs
0-1/4 mile: 18.6secs
83.0bhp 61.9kW 84.1PS
@ 5800rpm
89.0lbft 120.6Nm @ 2800rpm
78.9bhp/ton 77.6bhp/tonne
47.3bhp/L 35.2kW/L 47.9PS/L
50.3ft/sec 15.3m/sec
18.6mph 29.9kmh/1000rpm
28.2mpg 23.5mpgUS 10.0L/100km
Petrol 4-stroke piston
1756cc 107.1cu in
In-line 4
Compression ratio: 8.0:1
Bore: 84.0mm 3.3in
Stroke: 79.2mm 3.1in
Valve type/No: Overhead 8
Transmission: Manual
No. of forward speeds: 5
Wheels driven: Rear
Springs F/R: Coil/Coil
Brake system: PA
Brakes F/R: Disc/Disc
Steering: Worm & roller
Wheelbase: 227.8cm 89.7in
Track F: 135.1cm 53.2in
Track R: 132.1cm 52.0in
Length: 414.0cm 163.0in
Width: 161.3cm 63.5in
Height: 125.0cm 49.2in
Kerb weight: 1069.2kg 2355.0lb
Fuel: 43.1L 9.5gal 11.4galUS

1564 Fiat

126 de Ville
1979 Italy
68.0mph 109.4kmh
0-50mph 80.5kmh: 20.5secs
0-60mph 96.5kmh: 42.1secs
0-1/4 mile: 24.8secs
0-1km: 49.5secs
24.0bhp 17.9kW 24.3PS
@ 4500rpm
30.5lbft 41.3Nm @ 3000rpm
40.0bhp/ton 39.3bhp/tonne
36.8bhp/L 27.4kW/L 37.3PS/L
34.5ft/sec 10.5m/sec
14.0mph 22.5kmh/1000rpm
37.1mpg 30.9mpgUS 7.6L/100km
Petrol 4-stroke piston
652cc 39.8cu in
In-line 2 1 Carburettor
Compression ratio: 7.5:1
Bore: 77.0mm 3.0in
Stroke: 70.0mm 2.8in
Valve type/No: Overhead 4
Transmission: Manual
No. of forward speeds: 4
Wheels driven: Rear
Springs F/R: Leaf/Coil
Brakes F/R: Drum/Drum
Steering: Rack & pinion
Wheelbase: 183.6cm 72.3in
Track F: 114.3cm 45.0in
Track R: 120.1cm 47.3in
Length: 312.9cm 123.2in
Width: 138.4cm 54.5in
Height: 135.9cm 53.5in
Ground clearance: 14.0cm 5.5in
Kerb weight: 610.2kg 1344.0lb
Fuel: 20.9L 4.6gal 5.5galUS

1565 Fiat

Mirafiori Sport
1979 Italy
112.0mph 180.2kmh
0-50mph 80.5kmh: 7.3secs
0-60mph 96.5kmh: 10.7secs
0-1/4 mile: 17.5secs
0-1km: 33.0secs
115.0bhp 85.8kW 116.6PS
@ 5800rpm
123.0lbft 166.7Nm @ 3600rpm
102.2bhp/ton 100.5bhp/tonne
57.6bhp/L 43.0kW/L 58.4PS/L
57.0ft/sec 17.4m/sec
19.9mph 32.0kmh/1000rpm
22.5mpg 18.7mpgUS 12.6L/100km
Petrol 4-stroke piston
1995cc 121.7cu in
In-line 4 1 Carburettor
Compression ratio: 8.9:1
Bore: 84.0mm 3.3in
Stroke: 90.0mm 3.5in
Valve type/No: Overhead 8
Transmission: Manual
No. of forward speeds: 5
Wheels driven: Rear
Springs F/R: Coil/Coil
Brake system: PA
Brakes F/R: Disc/Drum
Steering: Rack & pinion
Wheelbase: 248.9cm 98.0in
Track F: 137.2cm 54.0in
Track R: 132.1cm 52.0in
Length: 426.7cm 168.0in
Width: 165.1cm 65.0in
Height: 139.7cm 55.0in
Ground clearance: 17.8cm 7.0in
Kerb weight: 1144.1kg 2520.0lb
Fuel: 49.6L 10.9gal 13.1galUS

1566 Fiat

Strada
1979 Italy
107.0mph 172.2kmh
0-60mph 96.5kmh: 12.3secs
0-1/4 mile: 19.0secs
69.0bhp 51.4kW 70.0PS
@ 5100rpm
77.0lbft 104.3Nm @ 2500rpm
67.6bhp/ton 66.5bhp/tonne
46.1bhp/L 34.3kW/L 46.7PS/L
35.7ft/sec 10.9m/sec
21.3mph 34.3kmh/1000rpm
36.0mpg 30.0mpgUS 7.8L/100km
Petrol 4-stroke piston
1498cc 91.4cu in
In-line 4 1 Carburettor
Compression ratio: 8.5:1
Bore: 86.4mm 3.4in
Stroke: 63.9mm 2.5in
Valve type/No: Overhead 8
Transmission: Manual
No. of forward speeds: 5
Wheels driven: Front
Springs F/R: Coil/Leaf
Brake system: PA
Brakes F/R: Disc/Drum
Steering: Rack & pinion
Wheelbase: 244.9cm 96.4in
Track F: 140.0cm 55.1in
Track R: 141.0cm 55.5in
Length: 408.9cm 161.0in
Width: 164.8cm 64.9in
Height: 134.6cm 53.0in
Ground clearance: 16.5cm 6.5in
Kerb weight: 1037.4kg 2285.0lb
Fuel: 45.8L 10.1gal 12.1galUS

1567 Fiat

Strada 65CL
1979 Italy
88.0mph 141.6kmh
0-50mph 80.5kmh: 10.3secs
0-60mph 96.5kmh: 15.6secs
0-1/4 mile: 19.8secs
0-1km: 37.5secs
65.0bhp 48.5kW 65.9PS
@ 5800rpm
72.0lbft 97.6Nm @ 3500rpm
72.8bhp/ton 71.6bhp/tonne
50.0bhp/L 37.3kW/L 50.6PS/L
35.3ft/sec 10.7m/sec
19.8mph 31.9kmh/1000rpm
27.6mpg 23.0mpgUS 10.2L/100km
Petrol 4-stroke piston
1301cc 79.4cu in
In-line 4 1 Carburettor
Compression ratio: 9.1:1
Bore: 86.4mm 3.4in
Stroke: 55.5mm 2.2in
Valve type/No: Overhead 8
Transmission: Manual
No. of forward speeds: 5
Wheels driven: Front
Springs F/R: Coil/Coil
Brake system: PA
Brakes F/R: Disc/Drum
Steering: Rack & pinion
Wheelbase: 244.9cm 96.4in
Track F: 140.0cm 55.1in
Track R: 141.0cm 55.5in
Length: 393.7cm 155.0in
Width: 165.1cm 65.0in
Height: 134.6cm 53.0in
Ground clearance: 15.2cm 6.0in
Kerb weight: 908.0kg 2000.0lb
Fuel: 51.0L 11.2gal 13.5galUS

1568 Fiat

Strada 75CL
1979 Italy
99.0mph 159.3kmh
0-50mph 80.5kmh: 8.6secs
0-60mph 96.5kmh: 13.3secs
0-1/4 mile: 18.9secs
0-1km: 36.7secs
75.0bhp 55.9kW 76.0PS
@ 5800rpm
87.0lbft 117.9Nm @ 3000rpm
83.0bhp/ton 81.6bhp/tonne
50.0bhp/L 37.3kW/L 50.7PS/L
40.6ft/sec 12.3m/sec
20.9mph 33.6kmh/1000rpm
28.6mpg 23.8mpgUS 9.9L/100km
Petrol 4-stroke piston
1499cc 91.5cu in
In-line 4 1 Carburettor
Compression ratio: 9.0:1
Bore: 86.4mm 3.4in
Stroke: 63.9mm 2.5in
Valve type/No: Overhead 8
Transmission: Manual
No. of forward speeds: 5
Wheels driven: Front
Springs F/R: Coil/Leaf
Brake system: PA
Brakes F/R: Disc/Drum
Steering: Rack & pinion
Wheelbase: 244.9cm 96.4in
Track F: 140.0cm 55.1in
Track R: 141.0cm 55.5in
Length: 393.7cm 155.0in
Width: 165.1cm 65.0in
Height: 140.0cm 55.1in
Ground clearance: 15.2cm 6.0in
Kerb weight: 919.3kg 2025.0lb
Fuel: 51.0L 11.2gal 13.5galUS

1569 Fiat

X1/9 1300
1979 Italy
90.0mph 144.8kmh
0-50mph 80.5kmh: 9.4secs
0-60mph 96.5kmh: 13.3secs
0-1/4 mile: 19.8secs
61.0bhp 45.5kW 61.8PS
@ 5800rpm
67.0lbft 90.8Nm @ 4000rpm
66.2bhp/ton 65.1bhp/tonne
47.3bhp/L 35.3kW/L 47.9PS/L
35.3ft/sec 10.7m/sec
16.2mph 26.1kmh/1000rpm
36.6mpg 30.5mpgUS 7.7L/100km
Petrol 4-stroke piston
1290cc 78.7cu in
In-line 4 1 Carburettor
Compression ratio: 8.5:1
Bore: 86.0mm 3.4in
Stroke: 55.5mm 2.2in
Valve type/No: Overhead 8
Transmission: Manual
No. of forward speeds: 4
Wheels driven: Rear
Springs F/R: Coil/Coil
Brakes F/R: Disc/Disc
Steering: Rack & pinion
Wheelbase: 220.2cm 86.7in
Track F: 133.4cm 52.5in
Track R: 134.4cm 52.9in
Length: 402.6cm 158.5in
Width: 157.0cm 61.8in
Height: 117.1cm 46.1in
Ground clearance: 12.7cm 5.0in
Kerb weight: 937.5kg 2065.0lb
Fuel: 46.2L 10.1gal 12.2galUS

1570 Fiat

X1/9 1500
1979 Italy
112.0mph 180.2kmh
0-50mph 80.5kmh: 8.0secs
0-60mph 96.5kmh: 11.0secs
0-1/4 mile: 17.8secs
0-1km: 33.0secs
85.0bhp 63.4kW 86.2PS
@ 6000rpm
86.8lbft 117.6Nm @ 3200rpm
94.7bhp/ton 93.1bhp/tonne
56.7bhp/L 42.3kW/L 57.5PS/L
42.0ft/sec 12.8m/sec
18.2mph 29.3kmh/1000rpm
26.1mpg 21.7mpgUS 10.8L/100km
Petrol 4-stroke piston
1498cc 91.4cu in
In-line 4 1 Carburettor
Compression ratio: 9.2:1
Bore: 86.4mm 3.4in
Stroke: 63.9mm 2.5in
Valve type/No: Overhead 8
Transmission: Manual
No. of forward speeds: 5
Wheels driven: Rear
Springs F/R: Coil/Coil
Brakes F/R: Disc/Disc
Steering: Rack & pinion
Wheelbase: 220.2cm 86.7in
Track F: 135.6cm 53.4in
Track R: 135.1cm 53.2in
Length: 397.0cm 156.3in
Width: 157.0cm 61.8in
Height: 118.1cm 46.5in
Ground clearance: 12.7cm 5.0in
Kerb weight: 912.5kg 2010.0lb
Fuel: 49.1L 10.8gal 13.0galUS

1571 Fiat

Brava Abarth Rally
1980 Italy
113.0mph 181.8kmh
0-50mph 80.5kmh: 5.2secs
0-60mph 96.5kmh: 6.9secs
0-1/4 mile: 15.2secs
230.0bhp 171.5kW 233.2PS
@ 7500rpm
166.0lbft 224.9Nm @ 5750rpm
245.3bhp/ton 241.2bhp/tonne
115.3bhp/L 86.0kW/L 116.9PS/L
73.7ft/sec 22.5m/sec
15.0mph 24.1kmh/1000rpm
14.4mpg 12.0mpgUS 19.6L/100km
Petrol 4-stroke piston
1995cc 121.7cu in
In-line 4 fuel injection
Compression ratio: 11.0:1
Bore: 84.0mm 3.3in
Stroke: 90.0mm 3.5in
Valve type/No: Overhead 16
Transmission: Manual
No. of forward speeds: 5
Wheels driven: Rear
Springs F/R: Coil/Coil
Brakes F/R: Disc/Disc
Steering: Rack & pinion
Wheelbase: 248.9cm 98.0in
Track F: 146.1cm 57.5in
Track R: 139.7cm 55.0in
Length: 418.1cm 164.6in
Width: 172.0cm 67.7in
Height: 137.2cm 54.0in
Ground clearance: 21.6cm 8.5in
Kerb weight: 953.4kg 2100.0lb
Fuel: 58.7L 12.9gal 15.5galUS

1572 Fiat

127 1050 Super
1981 Italy
88.0mph 141.6kmh
0-50mph 80.5kmh: 11.4secs
0-60mph 96.5kmh: 16.1secs
0-1/4 mile: 20.2secs
0-1km: 37.8secs
50.0bhp 37.3kW 50.7PS
@ 5600rpm
57.0lbft 77.2Nm @ 3000rpm
67.6bhp/ton 66.5bhp/tonne
47.7bhp/L 35.5kW/L 48.3PS/L
35.5ft/sec 10.8m/sec
18.3mph 29.4kmh/1000rpm
38.7mpg 32.2mpgUS 7.3L/100km
Petrol 4-stroke piston
1049cc 64.0cu in
In-line 4 1 Carburettor
Compression ratio: 9.3:1
Bore: 76.0mm 3.0in
Stroke: 57.8mm 2.3in
Valve type/No: Overhead 8
Transmission: Manual
No. of forward speeds: 5
Wheels driven: Front
Springs F/R: Coil/Leaf
Brakes F/R: Disc/Drum
Steering: Rack & pinion
Wheelbase: 222.5cm 87.6in

Track F: 129.8cm 51.1in
Track R: 130.3cm 51.3in
Length: 371.1cm 146.1in
Width: 155.2cm 61.1in
Height: 136.9cm 53.9in
Ground clearance: 19.1cm 7.5in
Kerb weight: 751.8kg 1656.0lb
Fuel: 30.0L 6.6gal 7.9galUS

1573 Fiat

Brava
1981 Italy
108.0mph 173.8kmh
0-50mph 80.5kmh: 8.8secs
0-60mph 96.5kmh: 12.9secs
0-1/4 mile: 18.9secs
102.0bhp 76.1kW 103.4PS
@ 5500rpm
110.0lbft 149.1Nm @ 3000rpm
86.5bhp/ton 85.1bhp/tonne
51.1bhp/L 38.1kW/L 51.8PS/L
54.1ft/sec 16.5m/sec
21.1mph 33.9kmh/1000rpm
27.6mpg 23.0mpgUS 10.2L/100km
Petrol 4-stroke piston
1995cc 121.7cu in
In-line 4 fuel injection
Compression ratio: 8.1:1
Bore: 84.0mm 3.3in
Stroke: 90.0mm 3.5in
Valve type/No: Overhead 8
Transmission: Manual
No. of forward speeds: 5
Wheels driven: Rear
Springs F/R: Coil/Coil
Brake system: PA
Brakes F/R: Disc/Drum
Steering: Rack & pinion PA
Wheelbase: 248.9cm 98.0in
Track F: 137.7cm 54.2in
Track R: 131.8cm 51.9in
Length: 437.9cm 172.4in
Width: 165.1cm 65.0in
Height: 138.2cm 54.4in
Kerb weight: 1198.6kg 2640.0lb
Fuel: 46.2L 10.1gal 12.2galUS

1574 Fiat

Panda
1981 Italy
89.0mph 143.2kmh
0-50mph 80.5kmh: 10.1secs
0-60mph 96.5kmh: 16.2secs
0-1/4 mile: 20.6secs
0-1km: 39.3secs
45.0bhp 33.6kW 45.6PS
@ 5600rpm
47.0lbft 63.7Nm @ 3000rpm
65.2bhp/ton 64.1bhp/tonne
49.8bhp/L 37.2kW/L 50.5PS/L
42.3ft/sec 12.9m/sec
15.8mph 25.4kmh/1000rpm
38.7mpg 32.2mpgUS 7.3L/100km
Petrol 4-stroke piston
903cc 55.1cu in
In-line 4 1 Carburettor
Compression ratio: 9.0:1
Bore: 65.0mm 2.6in
Stroke: 69.0mm 2.7in
Valve type/No: Overhead 8
Transmission: Manual
No. of forward speeds: 4
Wheels driven: Front
Springs F/R: Coil/Leaf
Brakes F/R: Disc/Drum
Steering: Rack & pinion
Wheelbase: 215.9cm 85.0in
Track F: 125.0cm 49.2in
Track R: 125.0cm 49.2in
Length: 337.8cm 133.0in
Width: 146.1cm 57.5in
Height: 144.0cm 56.7in
Ground clearance: 16.5cm 6.5in
Kerb weight: 701.9kg 1546.0lb
Fuel: 35.3L 7.7gal 9.3galUS

1575 Fiat

Mirafiori 1400CL
1982 Italy
92.0mph 148.0kmh
0-50mph 80.5kmh: 9.5secs
0-60mph 96.5kmh: 14.5secs
0-1/4 mile: 20.5secs
0-1km: 37.8secs
70.0bhp 52.2kW 71.0PS
@ 5000rpm
79.6lbft 107.9Nm @ 3000rpm
72.8bhp/ton 71.6bhp/tonne
51.2bhp/L 38.2kW/L 51.9PS/L
39.0ft/sec 11.9m/sec
19.8mph 31.9kmh/1000rpm
26.8mpg 22.3mpgUS 10.5L/100km
Petrol 4-stroke piston
1367cc 83.4cu in
In-line 4 1 Carburettor
Compression ratio: 9.0:1
Bore: 78.0mm 3.1in
Stroke: 71.5mm 2.8in
Valve type/No: Overhead 8
Transmission: Manual
No. of forward speeds: 5
Wheels driven: Rear
Springs F/R: Coil/Coil
Brake system: PA
Brakes F/R: Disc/Drum
Steering: Rack & pinion
Wheelbase: 248.9cm 98.0in
Track F: 138.7cm 54.6in
Track R: 132.6cm 52.2in
Length: 426.2cm 167.8in
Width: 164.3cm 64.7in
Height: 141.2cm 55.6in
Ground clearance: 17.8cm 7.0in
Kerb weight: 977.9kg 2154.0lb
Fuel: 53.2L 11.7gal 14.1galUS

1576 Fiat

Spider 2000
1982 Italy
115.0mph 185.0kmh
0-50mph 80.5kmh: 7.2secs
0-60mph 96.5kmh: 9.9secs
0-1/4 mile: 17.3secs
102.0bhp 76.1kW 103.4PS
@ 5500rpm
110.0lbft 149.1Nm @ 3000rpm
95.8bhp/ton 94.2bhp/tonne
51.1bhp/L 38.1kW/L 51.8PS/L
54.1ft/sec 16.5m/sec
19.4mph 31.2kmh/1000rpm
31.2mpg 26.0mpgUS 9.0L/100km
Petrol 4-stroke piston
1995cc 121.7cu in
In-line 4 fuel injection
Compression ratio: 8.1:1
Bore: 84.0mm 3.3in
Stroke: 90.0mm 3.5in
Valve type/No: Overhead 8
Transmission: Manual
No. of forward speeds: 5
Wheels driven: Rear
Springs F/R: Coil/Coil
Brake system: PA
Brakes F/R: Disc/Disc
Steering: Worm & roller
Wheelbase: 227.8cm 89.7in
Track F: 135.1cm 53.2in
Track R: 132.1cm 52.0in
Length: 414.0cm 163.0in
Width: 161.3cm 63.5in
Height: 122.4cm 48.2in
Kerb weight: 1082.8kg 2385.0lb
Fuel: 43.1L 9.5gal 11.4galUS

1577 Fiat

Spider Turbo
1982 Italy
104.0mph 167.3kmh
0-50mph 80.5kmh: 7.3secs
0-60mph 96.5kmh: 9.4secs
0-1/4 mile: 17.1secs
120.0bhp 89.5kW 121.7PS
@ 6000rpm
130.0lbft 176.2Nm @ 3600rpm
112.7bhp/ton 110.8bhp/tonne
60.1bhp/L 44.8kW/L 61.0PS/L
59.0ft/sec 18.0m/sec
17.1mph 27.5kmh/1000rpm
26.4mpg 22.0mpgUS 10.7L/100km
Petrol 4-stroke piston
1995cc 121.7cu in turbocharged
In-line 4 fuel injection
Compression ratio: 8.1:1
Bore: 84.0mm 3.3in
Stroke: 90.0mm 3.5in
Valve type/No: Overhead 8
Transmission: Manual
No. of forward speeds: 5
Wheels driven: Rear
Springs F/R: Coil/Coil
Brake system: PA
Brakes F/R: Disc/Disc
Steering: Worm & roller
Wheelbase: 227.8cm 89.7in
Track F: 135.1cm 53.2in
Track R: 132.1cm 52.0in
Length: 414.0cm 163.0in
Width: 161.3cm 63.5in
Height: 122.4cm 48.2in
Kerb weight: 1082.8kg 2385.0lb
Fuel: 43.1L 9.5gal 11.4galUS

1578 Fiat

Strada Super 85
1982 Italy
99.0mph 159.3kmh
0-50mph 80.5kmh: 9.0secs
0-60mph 96.5kmh: 12.4secs
0-1/4 mile: 18.5secs
0-1km: 34.5secs
85.0bhp 63.4kW 86.2PS
@ 5800rpm
87.0lbft 117.9Nm @ 3800rpm
91.4bhp/ton 89.9bhp/tonne
56.7bhp/L 42.3kW/L 57.5PS/L
40.6ft/sec 12.3m/sec
19.8mph 31.9kmh/1000rpm
31.3mpg 26.1mpgUS 9.0L/100km
Petrol 4-stroke piston
1498cc 91.4cu in
In-line 4 1 Carburettor
Compression ratio: 9.0:1
Bore: 86.4mm 3.4in
Stroke: 63.9mm 2.5in
Valve type/No: Overhead 8
Transmission: Manual
No. of forward speeds: 5
Wheels driven: Front
Springs F/R: Coil/Leaf
Brake system: PA
Brakes F/R: Disc/Drum
Steering: Rack & pinion
Wheelbase: 244.9cm 96.4in
Track F: 140.0cm 55.1in
Track R: 141.0cm 55.5in
Length: 393.7cm 155.0in
Width: 165.1cm 65.0in
Height: 140.0cm 55.1in
Ground clearance: 15.2cm 6.0in
Kerb weight: 945.7kg 2083.0lb
Fuel: 50.0L 11.0gal 13.2galUS

1579 Fiat

X1/9
1982 Italy
108.0mph 173.8kmh
0-50mph 80.5kmh: 8.9secs
0-60mph 96.5kmh: 12.4secs
0-1/4 mile: 18.6secs
75.0bhp 55.9kW 76.0PS
@ 5500rpm
80.0lbft 108.4Nm @ 3000rpm
77.8bhp/ton 76.5bhp/tonne
50.1bhp/L 37.3kW/L 50.8PS/L
38.5ft/sec 11.7m/sec
17.6mph 28.3kmh/1000rpm
32.4mpg 27.0mpgUS 8.7L/100km
Petrol 4-stroke piston
1498cc 91.4cu in
In-line 4 fuel injection
Compression ratio: 8.5:1
Bore: 86.4mm 3.4in
Stroke: 63.9mm 2.5in
Valve type/No: Overhead 8
Transmission: Manual
No. of forward speeds: 5
Wheels driven: Rear
Springs F/R: Coil/Coil
Brakes F/R: Disc/Disc
Steering: Rack & pinion
Wheelbase: 220.2cm 86.7in
Track F: 135.4cm 53.3in
Track R: 136.1cm 53.6in
Length: 396.7cm 156.2in
Width: 157.0cm 61.8in
Height: 118.1cm 46.5in
Kerb weight: 980.6kg 2160.0lb
Fuel: 46.2L 10.1gal 12.2galUS

1580 Fiat

Spider 2000
1983 Italy
109.0mph 175.4kmh
0-50mph 80.5kmh: 8.1secs
0-60mph 96.5kmh: 10.9secs
0-1/4 mile: 17.9secs
102.0bhp 76.1kW 103.4PS
@ 5500rpm
110.0lbft 149.1Nm @ 3000rpm
96.0bhp/ton 94.4bhp/tonne
51.1bhp/L 38.1kW/L 51.8PS/L
54.1ft/sec 16.5m/sec
17.9mph 28.8kmh/1000rpm
30.0mpg 25.0mpgUS 9.4L/100km
Petrol 4-stroke piston
1995cc 121.7cu in
In-line 4 fuel injection
Compression ratio: 8.1:1
Bore: 84.0mm 3.3in
Stroke: 90.0mm 3.5in
Valve type/No: Overhead 8
Transmission: Manual
No. of forward speeds: 5
Wheels driven: Rear
Springs F/R: Coil/Coil
Brake system: PA
Brakes F/R: Disc/Disc
Steering: Worm & roller
Wheelbase: 227.8cm 89.7in
Track F: 135.1cm 53.2in
Track R: 132.1cm 52.0in
Length: 414.0cm 163.0in
Width: 161.3cm 63.5in
Height: 122.4cm 48.2in
Kerb weight: 1080.5kg 2380.0lb
Fuel: 43.1L 9.5gal 11.4galUS

1581 Fiat

Strada 60 Comfort ES
1983 Italy
96.0mph 154.5kmh
0-50mph 80.5kmh: 10.4secs
0-60mph 96.5kmh: 14.7secs
0-1/4 mile: 19.7secs
0-1km: 37.5secs
55.0bhp 41.0kW 55.8PS
@ 5600rpm
65.0lbft 88.1Nm @ 2900rpm
68.2bhp/ton 67.0bhp/tonne
49.3bhp/L 36.7kW/L 50.0PS/L
34.1ft/sec 10.4m/sec
19.7mph 31.7kmh/1000rpm
38.9mpg 32.4mpgUS 7.3L/100km
Petrol 4-stroke piston
1116cc 68.1cu in
In-line 4 1 Carburettor
Compression ratio: 9.6:1
Bore: 80.0mm 3.1in
Stroke: 55.5mm 2.2in
Valve type/No: Overhead 8
Transmission: Manual
No. of forward speeds: 5
Wheels driven: Front
Springs F/R: Coil/Leaf
Brake system: PA
Brakes F/R: Disc/Drum
Steering: Rack & pinion
Wheelbase: 244.3cm 96.2in
Track F: 141.0cm 55.5in
Track R: 141.5cm 55.7in
Length: 401.3cm 158.0in
Width: 165.1cm 65.0in
Height: 140.5cm 55.3in
Ground clearance: 15.2cm 6.0in
Kerb weight: 820.4kg 1807.0lb
Fuel: 55.1L 12.1gal 14.5galUS

1582 Fiat

Uno 55 S
1983 Italy
95.0mph 152.9kmh
0-50mph 80.5kmh: 9.1secs
0-60mph 96.5kmh: 14.1secs
0-1/4 mile: 19.4secs
0-1km: 36.5secs
55.0bhp 41.0kW 55.8PS
@ 5600rpm
64.0lbft 86.7Nm @ 2900rpm
72.1bhp/ton 70.9bhp/tonne
49.3bhp/L 36.7kW/L 50.0PS/L
34.1ft/sec 10.4m/sec
21.7mph 34.9kmh/1000rpm
35.8mpg 29.8mpgUS 7.9L/100km
Petrol 4-stroke piston
1116cc 68.1cu in
In-line 4 1 Carburettor
Compression ratio: 9.2:1
Bore: 80.0mm 3.1in
Stroke: 55.5mm 2.2in
Valve type/No: Overhead 8
Transmission: Manual
No. of forward speeds: 5
Wheels driven: Front
Springs F/R: Coil/Coil
Brake system: PA
Brakes F/R: Disc/Drum

Steering: Rack & pinion
Wheelbase: 236.2cm 93.0in
Track F: 134.1cm 52.8in
Track R: 130.0cm 51.2in
Length: 364.5cm 143.5in
Width: 155.4cm 61.2in
Height: 143.3cm 56.4in
Ground clearance: 15.0cm 5.9in
Kerb weight: 775.4kg 1708.0lb
Fuel: 41.9L 9.2gal 11.1galUS

1583 Fiat

Uno 70 SX
1983 Italy
103.0mph 165.7kmh
0-50mph 80.5kmh: 8.0secs
0-60mph 96.5kmh: 12.1secs
0-1/4 mile: 18.6secs
0-1km: 34.6secs
70.0bhp 52.2kW 71.0PS
@ 5700rpm
74.0lbft 100.3Nm @ 2900rpm
90.6bhp/ton 89.1bhp/tonne
53.8bhp/L 40.1kW/L 54.5PS/L
34.7ft/sec 10.5m/sec
21.7mph 34.9kmh/1000rpm
35.4mpg 29.5mpgUS 8.0L/100km
Petrol 4-stroke piston
1301cc 79.4cu in
In-line 4 1 Carburettor
Compression ratio: 9.0:1
Bore: 86.4mm 3.4in
Stroke: 55.5mm 2.2in
Valve type/No: Overhead 8
Transmission: Manual
No. of forward speeds: 5
Wheels driven: Front
Springs F/R: Coil/Coil
Brake system: PA
Brakes F/R: Disc/Drum
Steering: Rack & pinion
Wheelbase: 236.2cm 93.0in
Track F: 134.1cm 52.8in
Track R: 130.0cm 51.2in
Length: 364.5cm 143.5in
Width: 154.9cm 61.0in
Height: 143.3cm 56.4in
Ground clearance: 15.0cm 5.9in
Kerb weight: 785.4kg 1730.0lb
Fuel: 41.9L 9.2gal 11.1galUS

1584 Fiat

Regata 100 S
1984 Italy
110.0mph 177.0kmh
0-50mph 80.5kmh: 7.3secs
0-60mph 96.5kmh: 9.9secs
0-1/4 mile: 17.7secs
0-1km: 32.6secs
100.0bhp 74.6kW 101.4PS
@ 5900rpm
98.0lbft 132.8Nm @ 3800rpm
98.8bhp/ton 97.1bhp/tonne
63.1bhp/L 47.0kW/L 64.0PS/L
46.0ft/sec 14.1m/sec
21.0mph 33.8kmh/1000rpm
29.1mpg 24.2mpgUS 9.7L/100km
Petrol 4-stroke piston
1585cc 96.7cu in
In-line 4 1 Carburettor
Compression ratio: 9.3:1
Bore: 84.0mm 3.3in
Stroke: 71.5mm 2.8in
Valve type/No: Overhead 8
Transmission: Manual
No. of forward speeds: 5
Wheels driven: Front
Springs F/R: Coil/Leaf
Brake system: PA
Brakes F/R: Disc/Drum
Steering: Rack & pinion
Wheelbase: 244.9cm 96.4in
Track F: 141.5cm 55.7in
Track R: 141.2cm 55.6in
Length: 426.0cm 167.7in
Width: 165.1cm 65.0in
Height: 142.0cm 55.9in
Ground clearance: 15.2cm 6.0in
Kerb weight: 1029.7kg 2268.0lb
Fuel: 54.6L 12.0gal 14.4galUS

1585 Fiat

Regata 70 ES
1984 Italy
100.0mph 160.9kmh
0-50mph 80.5kmh: 9.2secs
0-60mph 96.5kmh: 13.2secs
0-1/4 mile: 18.7secs
0-1km: 35.5secs
64.0bhp 47.7kW 64.9PS
@ 5800rpm
74.0lbft 100.3Nm @ 2900rpm
71.6bhp/ton 70.4bhp/tonne
49.3bhp/L 36.7kW/L 49.9PS/L
35.1ft/sec 10.7m/sec
20.1mph 32.3kmh/1000rpm
35.5mpg 29.6mpgUS 8.0L/100km
Petrol 4-stroke piston
1299cc 79.3cu in
In-line 4 1 Carburettor
Compression ratio: 9.5:1
Bore: 86.4mm 3.4in
Stroke: 55.4mm 2.2in
Valve type/No: Overhead 8
Transmission: Manual
No. of forward speeds: 5
Wheels driven: Front
Springs F/R: Coil/Leaf
Brake system: PA
Brakes F/R: Disc/Drum
Steering: Rack & pinion
Wheelbase: 244.9cm 96.4in
Track F: 141.5cm 55.7in
Track R: 141.2cm 55.6in
Length: 426.0cm 167.7in
Width: 165.1cm 65.0in
Height: 142.0cm 55.9in
Ground clearance: 15.2cm 6.0in
Kerb weight: 908.9kg 2002.0lb
Fuel: 54.6L 12.0gal 14.4galUS

1586 Fiat

Strada Abarth 130TC
1984 Italy
123.0mph 197.9kmh
0-50mph 80.5kmh: 6.0secs
0-60mph 96.5kmh: 8.2secs
0-1/4 mile: 16.2secs
0-1km: 29.8secs
130.0bhp 96.9kW 131.8PS
@ 5900rpm
130.0lbft 176.2Nm @ 3600rpm
134.3bhp/ton 132.1bhp/tonne
65.2bhp/L 48.6kW/L 66.1PS/L
58.0ft/sec 17.7m/sec
19.8mph 31.9kmh/1000rpm
26.3mpg 21.9mpgUS 10.7L/100km
Petrol 4-stroke piston
1995cc 121.7cu in
In-line 4 2 Carburettor
Compression ratio: 9.4:1
Bore: 84.0mm 3.3in
Stroke: 90.0mm 3.5in
Valve type/No: Overhead 8
Transmission: Manual
No. of forward speeds: 5
Wheels driven: Front
Springs F/R: Coil/Leaf
Brake system: PA
Brakes F/R: Disc/Drum
Steering: Rack & pinion
Wheelbase: 244.1cm 96.1in
Track F: 142.0cm 55.9in
Track R: 142.0cm 55.9in
Length: 401.3cm 158.0in
Width: 166.4cm 65.5in
Height: 138.9cm 54.7in
Ground clearance: 15.2cm 6.0in
Kerb weight: 984.3kg 2168.0lb
Fuel: 55.1L 12.1gal 14.5galUS

1587 Fiat

X1/9
1984 Italy
108.0mph 173.8kmh
0-50mph 80.5kmh: 8.8secs
0-60mph 96.5kmh: 12.3secs
0-1/4 mile: 18.5secs
75.0bhp 55.9kW 76.0PS
@ 5500rpm
80.0lbft 108.4Nm @ 3000rpm
75.3bhp/ton 74.1bhp/tonne
50.1bhp/L 37.3kW/L 50.8PS/L
38.5ft/sec 11.7m/sec
17.6mph 28.3kmh/1000rpm
32.4mpg 27.0mpgUS 8.7L/100km
Petrol 4-stroke piston
1498cc 91.4cu in
In-line 4 fuel injection
Compression ratio: 8.5:1
Bore: 86.4mm 3.4in
Stroke: 63.9mm 2.5in
Valve type/No: Overhead 8
Transmission: Manual
No. of forward speeds: 5
Wheels driven: Rear
Springs F/R: Coil/Coil
Brake system: PA
Brakes F/R: Disc/Disc
Steering: Rack & pinion
Wheelbase: 220.2cm 86.7in
Track F: 135.4cm 53.3in
Track R: 136.1cm 53.6in
Length: 397.0cm 156.3in
Width: 157.0cm 61.8in
Height: 118.9cm 46.8in
Kerb weight: 1012.4kg 2230.0lb
Fuel: 46.2L 10.1gal 12.2galUS

1588 Fiat

Uno 70 SX
1985 Italy
105.0mph 168.9kmh
0-50mph 80.5kmh: 7.7secs
0-60mph 96.5kmh: 11.3secs
0-1/4 mile: 18.5secs
0-1km: 34.3secs
68.0bhp 50.7kW 68.9PS
@ 5700rpm
74.0lbft 100.3Nm @ 2900rpm
85.7bhp/ton 84.3bhp/tonne
52.3bhp/L 39.0kW/L 53.1PS/L
34.7ft/sec 10.5m/sec
21.0mph 33.8kmh/1000rpm
35.7mpg 29.7mpgUS 7.9L/100km
Petrol 4-stroke piston
1299cc 79.3cu in
In-line 4 1 Carburettor
Compression ratio: 9.0:1
Bore: 86.4mm 3.4in
Stroke: 55.5mm 2.2in
Valve type/No: Overhead 8
Transmission: Manual
No. of forward speeds: 5
Wheels driven: Front
Springs F/R: Coil/Coil
Brake system: PA
Brakes F/R: Disc/Drum
Steering: Rack & pinion
Wheelbase: 236.2cm 93.0in
Track F: 134.1cm 52.8in
Track R: 130.0cm 51.2in
Length: 364.5cm 143.5in
Width: 154.9cm 61.0in
Height: 143.3cm 56.4in
Ground clearance: 15.0cm 5.9in
Kerb weight: 806.8kg 1777.0lb
Fuel: 41.9L 9.2gal 11.1galUS

1589 Fiat

Uno Turbo ie
1985 Italy
122.0mph 196.3kmh
0-50mph 80.5kmh: 6.4secs
0-60mph 96.5kmh: 9.1secs
0-1/4 mile: 16.7secs
0-1km: 31.0secs
105.0bhp 78.3kW 106.5PS
@ 5750rpm
108.0lbft 146.3Nm @ 3200rpm
184.6bhp/ton 181.5bhp/tonne
80.8bhp/L 60.3kW/L 82.0PS/L
40.1ft/sec 12.2m/sec
20.0mph 32.2kmh/1000rpm
26.1mpg 21.7mpgUS 10.8L/100km
Petrol 4-stroke piston
1299cc 79.3cu in turbocharged
In-line 4 fuel injection
Compression ratio: 7.6:1
Bore: 80.5mm 3.2in
Stroke: 63.8mm 2.5in
Valve type/No: Overhead 8
Transmission: Manual
No. of forward speeds: 5
Wheels driven: Front
Springs F/R: Coil/Coil
Brake system: PA
Brakes F/R: Disc/Disc
Steering: Rack & pinion
Wheelbase: 236.2cm 93.0in
Track F: 134.1cm 52.8in
Track R: 130.0cm 51.2in
Length: 364.5cm 143.5in
Width: 154.9cm 61.0in
Height: 143.3cm 56.4in
Ground clearance: 15.0cm 5.9in
Kerb weight: 578.4kg 1274.0lb
Fuel: 50.0L 11.0gal 13.2galUS

1590 Fiat

X1/9
1985 Italy
105.0mph 168.9kmh
0-60mph 96.5kmh: 12.3secs
0-1/4 mile: 18.5secs
75.0bhp 55.9kW 76.0PS
@ 5500rpm
80.0lbft 108.4Nm @ 3000rpm
75.3bhp/ton 74.1bhp/tonne
50.1bhp/L 37.3kW/L 50.8PS/L
38.5ft/sec 11.7m/sec
17.6mph 28.3kmh/1000rpm
30.4mpg 25.3mpgUS 9.3L/100km
Petrol 4-stroke piston
1498cc 91.4cu in
In-line 4 fuel injection
Bore: 86.4mm 3.4in
Stroke: 63.9mm 2.5in
Valve type/No: Overhead 8
Transmission: Manual
No. of forward speeds: 5
Wheels driven: Rear
Springs F/R: Coil/Coil
Brakes F/R: Disc/Disc
Steering: Rack & pinion
Wheelbase: 220.2cm 86.7in
Track F: 135.4cm 53.3in
Track R: 136.1cm 53.6in
Length: 397.0cm 156.3in
Width: 157.0cm 61.8in
Height: 118.9cm 46.8in
Kerb weight: 1012.4kg 2230.0lb

1591 Fiat

X1/9VS
1985 Italy
117.0mph 188.3kmh
0-50mph 80.5kmh: 7.8secs
0-60mph 96.5kmh: 10.8secs
0-1/4 mile: 17.0secs
0-1km: 31.9secs
85.0bhp 63.4kW 86.2PS
@ 6000rpm
87.0lbft 117.9Nm @ 3200rpm
94.7bhp/ton 93.1bhp/tonne
56.7bhp/L 42.3kW/L 57.5PS/L
42.0ft/sec 12.8m/sec
18.2mph 29.3kmh/1000rpm
26.8mpg 22.3mpgUS 10.5L/100km
Petrol 4-stroke piston
1498cc 91.4cu in
In-line 4 1 Carburettor
Compression ratio: 9.2:1
Bore: 86.4mm 3.4in
Stroke: 63.9mm 2.5in
Valve type/No: Overhead 8
Transmission: Manual
No. of forward speeds: 5
Wheels driven: Rear
Springs F/R: Coil/Coil
Brake system: PA
Brakes F/R: Disc/Disc
Steering: Rack & pinion
Wheelbase: 220.2cm 86.7in
Track F: 135.6cm 53.4in
Track R: 135.1cm 53.2in
Length: 397.0cm 156.3in
Width: 157.0cm 61.8in
Height: 118.1cm 46.5in
Ground clearance: 12.7cm 5.0in
Kerb weight: 912.5kg 2010.0lb
Fuel: 48.9L 10.7gal 12.9galUS

1592 Fiat

Panda 1000 S
1986 Italy
89.0mph 143.2kmh
0-50mph 80.5kmh: 11.1secs
0-60mph 96.5kmh: 16.0secs
0-1/4 mile: 20.2secs
0-1km: 38.2secs
45.0bhp 33.6kW 45.6PS
@ 5000rpm
59.0lbft 79.9Nm @ 2750rpm
60.7bhp/ton 59.7bhp/tonne
45.0bhp/L 33.6kW/L 45.7PS/L
35.6ft/sec 10.8m/sec
18.8mph 30.2kmh/1000rpm
34.0mpg 28.3mpgUS 8.3L/100km
Petrol 4-stroke piston
999cc 61.0cu in
In-line 4 1 Carburettor
Compression ratio: 9.8:1
Bore: 70.0mm 2.8in
Stroke: 64.9mm 2.6in
Valve type/No: Overhead 8

Transmission: Manual
No. of forward speeds: 5
Wheels driven: Front
Springs F/R: Coil/Coil
Brakes F/R: Disc/Drum
Steering: Rack & pinion
Wheelbase: 215.9cm 85.0in
Track F: 125.1cm 49.3in
Track R: 125.1cm 49.3in
Length: 337.8cm 133.0in
Width: 146.1cm 57.5in
Height: 144.2cm 56.8in
Ground clearance: 16.5cm 6.5in
Kerb weight: 754.0kg 1660.8lb
Fuel: 40.0L 8.8gal 10.6galUS

1593 Fiat

Panda 750 L
1986 Italy
80.0mph 128.7kmh
0-50mph 80.5kmh: 13.2secs
0-60mph 96.5kmh: 20.6secs
0-1/4 mile: 22.1secs
0-1km: 42.4secs
34.0bhp 25.3kW 34.5PS
@ 2250rpm
42.0lbft 56.9Nm @ 3000rpm
45.9bhp/ton 45.1bhp/tonne
44.2bhp/L 33.0kW/L 44.8PS/L
14.2ft/sec 4.3m/sec
18.8mph 30.2kmh/1000rpm
35.5mpg 29.6mpgUS 8.0L/100km
Petrol 4-stroke piston
769cc 47.0cu in
In-line 4 1 Carburettor
Compression ratio: 9.4:1
Bore: 65.0mm 2.6in
Stroke: 58.0mm 2.3in
Valve type/No: Overhead 8
Transmission: Manual
No. of forward speeds: 4
Wheels driven: Front
Springs F/R: Coil/Coil
Brakes F/R: Disc/Drum
Steering: Rack & pinion
Wheelbase: 215.9cm 85.0in
Track F: 125.1cm 49.3in
Track R: 125.1cm 49.3in
Length: 337.8cm 133.0in
Width: 146.1cm 57.5in
Height: 144.2cm 56.8in
Ground clearance: 16.5cm 6.5in
Kerb weight: 754.0kg 1660.8lb
Fuel: 40.0L 8.8gal 10.6galUS

1594 Fiat

Regata DS
1986 Italy
96.0mph 154.5kmh
0-50mph 80.5kmh: 10.6secs
0-60mph 96.5kmh: 15.6secs
0-1/4 mile: 19.9secs
0-1km: 37.7secs
65.0bhp 48.5kW 65.9PS
@ 4600rpm
88.0lbft 119.2Nm @ 2000rpm
63.9bhp/ton 62.8bhp/tonne
33.7bhp/L 25.1kW/L 34.2PS/L
45.2ft/sec 13.8m/sec
21.6mph 34.8kmh/1000rpm
41.8mpg 34.8mpgUS 6.8L/100km
Diesel 4-stroke piston
1929cc 118.0cu in
In-line 4 fuel injection
Compression ratio: 21.0:1
Bore: 82.6mm 3.2in
Stroke: 90.0mm 3.5in
Valve type/No: Overhead 8
Transmission: Manual
No. of forward speeds: 5
Wheels driven: Front
Springs F/R: Coil/Leaf
Brake system: PA
Brakes F/R: Disc/Drum
Steering: Rack & pinion PA
Wheelbase: 244.8cm 96.4in
Track F: 141.4cm 55.7in
Track R: 141.2cm 55.6in
Length: 426.0cm 167.7in
Width: 165.0cm 65.0in
Height: 142.0cm 55.9in
Ground clearance: 15.2cm 6.0in
Kerb weight: 1035.0kg 2279.7lb
Fuel: 55.1L 12.1gal 14.5galUS

1595 Fiat

Croma ie Super
1987 Italy
121.0mph 194.7kmh
0-50mph 80.5kmh: 7.2secs
0-60mph 96.5kmh: 9.9secs
0-1/4 mile: 17.3secs
0-1km: 31.7secs
120.0bhp 89.5kW 121.7PS
@ 5250rpm
123.0lbft 166.7Nm @ 3300rpm
101.8bhp/ton 100.1bhp/tonne
60.1bhp/L 44.8kW/L 61.0PS/L
51.6ft/sec 15.7m/sec
24.9mph 40.1kmh/1000rpm
29.0mpg 24.1mpgUS 9.7L/100km
Petrol 4-stroke piston
1995cc 122.0cu in
In-line 4 fuel injection
Compression ratio: 9.8:1
Bore: 84.0mm 3.3in
Stroke: 90.0mm 3.5in
Valve type/No: Overhead 8
Transmission: Manual
No. of forward speeds: 5
Wheels driven: Front
Springs F/R: Coil/Coil
Brake system: PA
Brakes F/R: Disc/Drum
Steering: Rack & pinion PA
Wheelbase: 266.0cm 104.7in
Track F: 148.2cm 58.3in
Track R: 147.2cm 58.0in
Length: 449.5cm 177.0in
Width: 176.0cm 69.3in
Height: 143.3cm 56.4in
Ground clearance: 17.9cm 7.0in
Kerb weight: 1199.0kg 2641.0lb
Fuel: 70.1L 15.4gal 18.5galUS

1596 Fiat

Regata 100S ie
1987 Italy
107.0mph 172.2kmh
0-50mph 80.5kmh: 8.4secs
0-60mph 96.5kmh: 12.0secs
0-1/4 mile: 18.6secs
0-1km: 34.7secs
100.0bhp 74.6kW 101.4PS
@ 6000rpm
94.0lbft 127.4Nm @ 4000rpm
98.7bhp/ton 97.1bhp/tonne
63.1bhp/L 47.0kW/L 64.0PS/L
46.8ft/sec 14.3m/sec
21.9mph 35.2kmh/1000rpm
25.9mpg 21.6mpgUS 10.9L/100km
Petrol 4-stroke piston
1585cc 97.0cu in
In-line 4 fuel injection
Compression ratio: 9.7:1
Bore: 84.0mm 3.3in
Stroke: 71.5mm 2.8in
Valve type/No: Overhead 8
Transmission: Manual
No. of forward speeds: 5
Wheels driven: Front
Springs F/R: Coil/Leaf
Brake system: PA
Brakes F/R: Disc/Drum
Steering: Rack & pinion PA
Wheelbase: 245.5cm 96.7in
Track F: 140.0cm 55.1in
Track R: 139.5cm 54.9in
Length: 426.0cm 167.7in
Width: 165.0cm 65.0in
Height: 141.2cm 55.6in
Ground clearance: 15.2cm 6.0in
Kerb weight: 1030.0kg 2268.7lb
Fuel: 55.1L 12.1gal 14.5galUS

1597 Fiat

Uno Selecta
1987 Italy
91.0mph 146.4kmh
0-50mph 80.5kmh: 11.7secs
0-60mph 96.5kmh: 16.6secs
0-1/4 mile: 21.1secs
0-1km: 41.0secs
59.0bhp 44.0kW 59.8PS
@ 5700rpm
64.0lbft 86.7Nm @ 3000rpm
77.9bhp/ton 76.6bhp/tonne
52.9bhp/L 39.4kW/L 53.6PS/L
34.7ft/sec 10.5m/sec
25.7mph 41.4kmh/1000rpm
34.9mpg 29.1mpgUS 8.1L/100km
Petrol 4-stroke piston
1116cc 68.0cu in
In-line 4 1 Carburettor
Compression ratio: 9.2:1
Bore: 80.0mm 3.1in
Stroke: 55.5mm 2.2in
Valve type/No: Overhead 8
Transmission: Continuously variable
Wheels driven: Front
Springs F/R: Coil/Torsion bar
Brake system: PA
Brakes F/R: Disc/Drum
Steering: Rack & pinion
Wheelbase: 236.2cm 93.0in
Track F: 133.9cm 52.7in
Track R: 130.9cm 51.5in
Length: 364.4cm 143.5in
Width: 155.5cm 61.2in
Height: 142.0cm 55.9in
Ground clearance: 15.0cm 5.9in
Kerb weight: 770.0kg 1696.0lb
Fuel: 42.0L 9.2gal 11.1galUS

1598 Fiat

Tipo 1.4
1988 Italy
101.0mph 162.5kmh
0-50mph 80.5kmh: 9.2secs
0-60mph 96.5kmh: 13.1secs
0-1/4 mile: 19.1secs
0-1km: 35.5secs
72.0bhp 53.7kW 73.0PS
@ 6000rpm
78.2lbft 106.0Nm @ 2900rpm
73.4bhp/ton 72.1bhp/tonne
52.5bhp/L 39.1kW/L 53.2PS/L
44.5ft/sec 13.5m/sec
20.6mph 33.1kmh/1000rpm
32.2mpg 26.8mpgUS 8.8L/100km
Petrol 4-stroke piston
1372cc 84.0cu in
In-line 4 1 Carburettor
Compression ratio: 9.2:1
Bore: 80.5mm 3.2in
Stroke: 67.7mm 2.7in
Valve type/No: Overhead 8
Transmission: Manual
No. of forward speeds: 5
Wheels driven: Front
Springs F/R: Coil/Coil
Brake system: PA
Brakes F/R: Disc/Drum
Steering: Rack & pinion
Wheelbase: 254.0cm 100.0in
Track F: 142.9cm 56.3in
Track R: 141.5cm 55.7in
Length: 395.8cm 155.8in
Width: 170.0cm 66.9in
Height: 144.5cm 56.9in
Ground clearance: 15.2cm 6.0in
Kerb weight: 998.0kg 2198.2lb
Fuel: 60.0L 13.2gal 15.8galUS

1599 Fiat

X1/9
1988 Italy
107.0mph 172.2kmh
0-50mph 80.5kmh: 8.6secs
0-60mph 96.5kmh: 12.0secs
0-1/4 mile: 18.4secs
75.0bhp 55.9kW 76.0PS
@ 5500rpm
79.0lbft 107.0Nm @ 3000rpm
76.0bhp/ton 74.7bhp/tonne
50.1bhp/L 37.3kW/L 50.8PS/L
38.5ft/sec 11.7m/sec
28.2mpg 23.5mpgUS 10.0L/100km
Petrol 4-stroke piston
1498cc 91.4cu in
In-line 4 fuel injection
Compression ratio: 8.5:1
Bore: 86.4mm 3.4in
Stroke: 63.9mm 2.5in
Valve type/No: Overhead 8
Transmission: Manual
No. of forward speeds: 5
Wheels driven: Rear
Springs F/R: Coil/Coil
Brake system: PA
Brakes F/R: Disc/Disc
Steering: Rack & pinion
Wheelbase: 220.2cm 86.7in
Track F: 135.4cm 53.3in
Track R: 136.1cm 53.6in
Length: 397.0cm 156.3in
Width: 157.0cm 61.8in
Height: 118.9cm 46.8in
Kerb weight: 1003.3kg 2210.0lb
Fuel: 46.2L 10.1gal 12.2galUS

1600 Fiat

Tipo 1.6 DGT SX
1989 Italy
107.0mph 172.2kmh
0-50mph 80.5kmh: 8.1secs
0-60mph 96.5kmh: 11.3secs
0-1/4 mile: 18.4secs
0-1km: 33.9secs
83.0bhp 61.9kW 84.1PS
@ 6000rpm
95.9lbft 130.0Nm @ 2900rpm
80.4bhp/ton 79.0bhp/tonne
52.5bhp/L 39.2kW/L 53.3PS/L
44.2ft/sec 13.5m/sec
21.8mph 35.1kmh/1000rpm
30.4mpg 25.3mpgUS 9.3L/100km
Petrol 4-stroke piston
1580cc 96.0cu in
In-line 4 1 Carburettor
Compression ratio: 9.2:1
Bore: 86.4mm 3.4in
Stroke: 67.4mm 2.6in
Valve type/No: Overhead 8
Transmission: Manual
No. of forward speeds: 5
Wheels driven: Front
Springs F/R: Coil/Coil
Brake system: PA
Brakes F/R: Disc/Drum
Steering: Rack & pinion
Wheelbase: 254.0cm 100.0in
Track F: 142.9cm 56.3in
Track R: 141.5cm 55.7in
Length: 395.8cm 155.8in
Width: 170.0cm 66.9in
Height: 144.5cm 56.9in
Ground clearance: 15.2cm 6.0in
Kerb weight: 1050.0kg 2312.8lb
Fuel: 55.1L 12.1gal 14.5galUS

1601 Fiat

X1/9
1989 Italy
107.0mph 172.2kmh
0-50mph 80.5kmh: 8.7secs
0-60mph 96.5kmh: 12.3secs
0-1/4 mile: 18.6secs
75.0bhp 55.9kW 76.0PS
@ 5500rpm
79.0lbft 107.0Nm @ 3000rpm
76.0bhp/ton 74.7bhp/tonne
50.1bhp/L 37.3kW/L 50.8PS/L
38.5ft/sec 11.7m/sec
28.2mpg 23.5mpgUS 10.0L/100km
Petrol 4-stroke piston
1498cc 91.4cu in
In-line 4 fuel injection
Compression ratio: 8.5:1
Bore: 86.4mm 3.4in
Stroke: 63.9mm 2.5in
Valve type/No: Overhead 8
Transmission: Manual
No. of forward speeds: 5
Wheels driven: Rear
Springs F/R: Coil/Coil
Brake system: PA
Brakes F/R: Disc/Disc
Steering: Rack & pinion
Wheelbase: 220.2cm 86.7in
Track F: 135.4cm 53.3in
Track R: 136.1cm 53.6in
Length: 397.0cm 156.3in
Width: 157.0cm 61.8in
Height: 118.9cm 46.8in
Kerb weight: 1003.3kg 2210.0lb
Fuel: 46.2L 10.1gal 12.2galUS

1602 Fiat

Croma CHT
1990 Italy
116.0mph 186.6kmh
0-50mph 80.5kmh: 8.2secs
0-60mph 96.5kmh: 11.6secs
0-1/4 mile: 18.2secs
0-1km: 33.4secs
98.0bhp 73.1kW 99.4PS
@ 5250rpm
123.2lbft 167.0Nm @ 2750rpm
84.7bhp/ton 83.3bhp/tonne
49.1bhp/L 36.6kW/L 49.8PS/L
51.6ft/sec 15.7m/sec
24.5mph 39.4kmh/1000rpm
28.3mpg 23.6mpgUS 10.0L/100km
Petrol 4-stroke piston

1995cc 122.0cu in
In-line 4 1 Carburettor
Compression ratio: 9.5:1
Bore: 84.0mm 3.3in
Stroke: 90.0mm 3.5in
Valve type/No: Overhead 8
Transmission: Manual
No. of forward speeds: 5
Wheels driven: Front
Springs F/R: Coil/Coil
Brake system: PA
Brakes F/R: Disc/Disc
Steering: Rack & pinion PA
Wheelbase: 266.0cm 104.7in
Track F: 149.0cm 58.7in
Track R: 148.2cm 58.3in
Length: 449.5cm 177.0in
Width: 176.0cm 69.3in
Height: 143.3cm 56.4in
Ground clearance: 17.9cm 7.0in
Kerb weight: 1177.0kg 2592.5lb
Fuel: 70.1L 15.4gal 18.5galUS

1603 Fiat
Tempra 1.6 SX
1990 Italy
113.0mph 181.8kmh
0-50mph 80.5kmh: 8.6secs
0-60mph 96.5kmh: 12.2secs
0-1/4 mile: 18.7secs
0-1km: 34.6secs
86.0bhp 64.1kW 87.2PS
@ 6000rpm
95.9lbft 130.0Nm @ 2900rpm
75.4bhp/ton 74.1bhp/tonne
54.4bhp/L 40.6kW/L 55.1PS/L
44.0ft/sec 13.4m/sec
18.8mph 30.2kmh/1000rpm
28.1mpg 23.4mpgUS 10.1L/100km
Petrol 4-stroke piston
1581cc 96.0cu in
In-line 4 1 Carburettor
Compression ratio: 9.2:1
Bore: 86.0mm 3.4in
Stroke: 67.0mm 2.6in
Valve type/No: Overhead 8
Transmission: Manual
No. of forward speeds: 5
Wheels driven: Front
Springs F/R: Coil/Coil
Brake system: PA
Brakes F/R: Disc/Drum
Steering: Rack & pinion PA
Wheelbase: 254.0cm 100.0in
Track F: 142.5cm 56.1in
Track R: 141.5cm 55.7in
Length: 435.4cm 171.4in
Width: 169.5cm 66.7in
Height: 144.5cm 56.9in
Kerb weight: 1160.0kg 2555.1lb
Fuel: 65.1L 14.3gal 17.2galUS

1604 Fiat
Uno 60S
1990 Italy
97.0mph 156.1kmh
0-50mph 80.5kmh: 9.3secs
0-60mph 96.5kmh: 14.2secs
0-1/4 mile: 19.6secs
0-1km: 36.5secs
57.0bhp 42.5kW 57.8PS
@ 5500rpm
64.2lbft 87.0Nm @ 2900rpm
72.3bhp/ton 71.1bhp/tonne
51.4bhp/L 38.4kW/L 52.2PS/L
43.2ft/sec 13.2m/sec
21.7mph 34.9kmh/1000rpm
39.0mpg 32.5mpgUS 7.2L/100km
Petrol 4-stroke piston
1108cc 68.0cu in
In-line 4 1 Carburettor
Compression ratio: 9.6:1
Bore: 70.0mm 2.8in
Stroke: 72.0mm 2.8in
Valve type/No: Overhead 8
Transmission: Manual
No. of forward speeds: 5
Wheels driven: Front
Springs F/R: Coil/Torsion bar
Brake system: PA
Brakes F/R: Disc/Drum
Steering: Rack & pinion
Wheelbase: 236.2cm 93.0in
Track F: 134.4cm 52.9in
Track R: 130.0cm 51.2in
Length: 368.8cm 145.2in
Width: 155.7cm 61.3in
Height: 141.5cm 55.7in
Ground clearance: 15.0cm 5.9in
Kerb weight: 802.0kg 1766.5lb
Fuel: 41.9L 9.2gal 11.1galUS

1605 Fiat
Uno Turbo ie
1990 Italy
128.0mph 206.0kmh
0-50mph 80.5kmh: 6.0secs
0-60mph 96.5kmh: 8.3secs
0-1/4 mile: 16.4secs
0-1km: 30.1secs
118.0bhp 88.0kW 119.6PS
@ 6000rpm
118.8lbft 161.0Nm @ 3500rpm
127.1bhp/ton 125.0bhp/tonne
86.0bhp/L 64.1kW/L 87.2PS/L
44.2ft/sec 13.5m/sec
20.9mph 33.6kmh/1000rpm
25.9mpg 21.6mpgUS 10.9L/100km
Petrol 4-stroke piston
1372cc 84.0cu in turbocharged
In-line 4 fuel injection
Compression ratio: 7.7:1
Bore: 80.5mm 3.2in
Stroke: 67.4mm 2.6in
Valve type/No: Overhead 8
Transmission: Manual
No. of forward speeds: 5
Wheels driven: Front
Springs F/R: Coil/Coil
Brake system: PA
Brakes F/R: Disc/Drum
Steering: Rack & pinion
Wheelbase: 236.2cm 93.0in
Track F: 135.1cm 53.2in
Track R: 130.6cm 51.4in
Length: 368.9cm 145.2in
Width: 156.2cm 61.5in
Height: 140.5cm 55.3in
Ground clearance: 17.9cm 7.0in
Kerb weight: 944.0kg 2079.3lb
Fuel: 50.0L 11.0gal 13.2galUS

1606 Fiat
Tipo 1.8ie DGT SX
1992 Italy
120.0mph 193.0kmh
0-50mph 80.5kmh: 7.6secs
0-60mph 96.5kmh: 10.5secs
0-1/4 mile: 17.9secs
0-1km: 32.7secs
110.0bhp 82.0kW 111.5PS
@ 6000rpm
104.8lbft 142.0Nm @ 2500rpm
94.0bhp/ton 92.4bhp/tonne
62.6bhp/L 46.7kW/L 63.5PS/L
52.0ft/sec 15.8m/sec
19.5mph 31.4kmh/1000rpm
28.6mpg 23.8mpgUS 9.9L/100km
Petrol 4-stroke piston
1756cc 107.0cu in
In-line 4 fuel injection
Compression ratio: 9.5:1
Bore: 84.0mm 3.3in
Stroke: 79.2mm 3.1in
Valve type/No: Overhead 8
Transmission: Manual
No. of forward speeds: 5
Wheels driven: Front
Springs F/R: Coil/Coil
Brake system: PA ABS
Brakes F/R: Disc/Drum
Steering: Rack & pinion PA
Wheelbase: 254.0cm 100.0in
Track F: 142.9cm 56.3in
Track R: 141.5cm 55.7in
Length: 395.8cm 155.8in
Width: 170.0cm 66.9in
Height: 144.5cm 56.9in
Ground clearance: 15.2cm 6.0in
Kerb weight: 1190.0kg 2621.1lb
Fuel: 54.9L 12.1gal 14.5galUS

1607 Fiberfab
Jamaican Buick V8
1969 USA
100.0mph 160.9kmh
0-50mph 80.5kmh: 7.0secs
0-60mph 96.5kmh: 9.2secs
0-1/4 mile: 16.7secs
150.0bhp 111.9kW 152.1PS
@ 4400rpm
220.0lbft 298.1Nm @ 2400rpm
166.2bhp/ton 163.4bhp/tonne
42.5bhp/L 31.7kW/L 43.0PS/L
34.2ft/sec 10.4m/sec
20.7mph 33.3kmh/1000rpm
18.0mpg 15.0mpgUS 15.7L/100km
Petrol 4-stroke piston
3533cc 215.6cu in
Vee 8 1 Carburettor
Compression ratio: 8.8:1
Bore: 89.0mm 3.5in
Stroke: 71.2mm 2.8in
Valve type/No: Overhead 16
Transmission: Automatic
No. of forward speeds: 2
Wheels driven: Rear
Springs F/R: Coil/Leaf
Brakes F/R: Drum/Drum
Steering: Rack & pinion
Wheelbase: 238.8cm 94.0in
Track F: 132.6cm 52.2in
Track R: 130.3cm 51.3in
Length: 415.3cm 163.5in
Width: 161.3cm 63.5in
Height: 111.8cm 44.0in
Ground clearance: 9.9cm 3.9in
Kerb weight: 918.0kg 2022.0lb
Fuel: 45.4L 10.0gal 12.0galUS

1608 Ford
Model T
1915 USA
44.0mph 70.8kmh
0-1/4 mile: 32.0secs
20.0bhp 14.9kW 20.3PS
@ 1600rpm
82.0lbft 111.1Nm @ 900rpm
27.1bhp/ton 26.7bhp/tonne
6.9bhp/L 5.1kW/L 7.0PS/L
17.8ft/sec 5.4m/sec
24.5mph 39.4kmh/1000rpm
Petrol 4-stroke piston
2897cc 176.7cu in
In-line 4 1 Carburettor
Compression ratio: 4.0:1
Bore: 95.3mm 3.8in
Stroke: 101.6mm 4.0in
Valve type/No: Side 8
Transmission: Manual
No. of forward speeds: 2
Wheels driven: Rear
Brakes F/R: Drum/Drum
Wheelbase: 251.5cm 99.0in
Track F: 142.2cm 56.0in
Track R: 142.2cm 56.0in
Length: 342.9cm 135.0in
Width: 167.6cm 66.0in
Height: 180.3cm 71.0in
Ground clearance: 24.1cm 9.5in
Kerb weight: 749.1kg 1650.0lb

1609 Ford
24 Saloon
1930 UK
64.2mph 103.3kmh
40.0bhp 29.8kW 40.5PS
@ 2200rpm
37.3bhp/ton 36.7bhp/tonne
12.2bhp/L 9.1kW/L 12.3PS/L
26.0ft/sec 7.9m/sec
22.0mpg 18.3mpgUS 12.8L/100km
Petrol 4-stroke piston
3283cc 200.3cu in
In-line 4 1 Carburettor
Bore: 98.4mm 3.9in
Stroke: 108.0mm 4.2in
Valve type/No: Side 8
Transmission: Manual
No. of forward speeds: 3
Wheels driven: Rear
Brakes F/R: Drum/Drum
Wheelbase: 262.9cm 103.5in
Track F: 142.2cm 56.0in
Track R: 142.2cm 56.0in
Length: 384.8cm 151.5in
Width: 170.2cm 67.0in
Height: 183.4cm 72.2in
Kerb weight: 1089.6kg 2400.0lb
Fuel: 40.9L 9.0gal 10.8galUS

1610 Ford
V8
1932 UK
78.2mph 125.8kmh
65.0bhp 48.5kW 65.9PS
@ 3400rpm
56.5bhp/ton 55.5bhp/tonne
17.9bhp/L 13.4kW/L 18.2PS/L
35.3ft/sec 10.8m/sec
16.0mpg 13.3mpgUS 17.7L/100km
Petrol 4-stroke piston
3622cc 221.0cu in
Vee 8
Compression ratio: 6.3:1
Bore: 77.8mm 3.1in
Stroke: 95.0mm 3.7in
Valve type/No: Side 16
Transmission: Manual
No. of forward speeds: 3
Wheels driven: Rear
Brakes F/R: Drum/Drum
Wheelbase: 269.2cm 106.0in
Track F: 145.3cm 57.2in
Track R: 144.3cm 56.8in
Length: 420.4cm 165.5in
Width: 170.2cm 67.0in
Height: 177.8cm 70.0in
Kerb weight: 1170.9kg 2579.0lb
Fuel: 50.0L 11.0gal 13.2galUS

1611 Ford
8 Tudor Saloon
1933 UK
58.8mph 94.6kmh
22.0bhp 16.4kW 22.3PS
@ 4000rpm
33.2bhp/ton 32.6bhp/tonne
23.6bhp/L 17.6kW/L 23.9PS/L
40.4ft/sec 12.3m/sec
35.0mpg 29.1mpgUS 8.1L/100km
Petrol 4-stroke piston
933cc 56.9cu in
In-line 4
Bore: 56.6mm 2.2in
Stroke: 92.5mm 3.6in
Valve type/No: Side 8
Transmission: Manual
No. of forward speeds: 3
Wheels driven: Rear
Brakes F/R: Drum/Drum
Kerb weight: 673.7kg 1484.0lb
Fuel: 29.6L 6.5gal 7.8galUS

1612 Ford
10 de Luxe Saloon
1934 UK
66.1mph 106.4kmh
0-50mph 80.5kmh: 18.2secs
0-60mph 96.5kmh: 33.4secs
35.0mpg 29.1mpgUS 8.1L/100km
Petrol 4-stroke piston
1172cc 71.5cu in
In-line 4
Bore: 63.5mm 2.5in
Stroke: 92.6mm 3.6in
Transmission: Manual
No. of forward speeds: 3
Wheels driven: Rear
Brakes F/R: Drum/Drum
Kerb weight: 788.1kg 1736.0lb
Fuel: 29.6L 6.5gal 7.8galUS

1613 Ford
Model A
1934 USA
62.0mph 99.8kmh
0-50mph 80.5kmh: 18.3secs
0-60mph 96.5kmh: 29.0secs
0-1/4 mile: 23.0secs
40.0bhp 29.8kW 40.5PS
@ 2200rpm
114.0lbft 154.5Nm @ 1200rpm
37.6bhp/ton 37.0bhp/tonne
12.2bhp/L 9.1kW/L 12.3PS/L
26.0ft/sec 7.9m/sec
Petrol 4-stroke piston
3287cc 200.5cu in
In-line 4
Compression ratio: 4.4:1
Bore: 98.4mm 3.9in
Stroke: 108.0mm 4.2in
Valve type/No: Side 8
Transmission: Manual
No. of forward speeds: 3
Wheels driven: Rear
Wheelbase: 262.9cm 103.5in
Track F: 142.2cm 56.0in
Track R: 142.2cm 56.0in
Kerb weight: 1080.5kg 2380.0lb

1614 Ford
V8 Touring Saloon

1936 UK
87.3mph 140.5kmh
0-50mph 80.5kmh: 11.3secs
0-60mph 96.5kmh: 17.5secs
17.0mpg 14.2mpgUS 16.6L/100km
Petrol 4-stroke piston
3622cc 221.0cu in
Vee 8
Bore: 77.8mm 3.1in
Stroke: 95.2mm 3.8in
Valve type/No: Side 16
Transmission: Manual
No. of forward speeds: 3
Wheels driven: Rear
Brakes F/R: Drum/Drum
Wheelbase: 284.5cm 112.0in
Track F: 140.2cm 55.2in
Track R: 147.3cm 58.0in
Length: 470.4cm 185.2in
Width: 176.5cm 69.5in
Height: 172.7cm 68.0in
Ground clearance: 21.6cm 8.5in
Kerb weight: 1424.2kg 3137.0lb
Fuel: 52.3L 11.5gal 13.8galUS

1615 Ford
10
1937 UK
65.6mph 105.6kmh
0-50mph 80.5kmh: 24.7secs
0-60mph 96.5kmh: 47.9secs
30.0bhp 22.4kW 30.4PS
@ 4000rpm
36.9bhp/ton 36.2bhp/tonne
25.6bhp/L 19.1kW/L 26.0PS/L
40.4ft/sec 12.3m/sec
33.0mpg 27.5mpgUS 8.6L/100km
Petrol 4-stroke piston
1172cc 71.5cu in
In-line 4 1 Carburettor
Compression ratio: 6.1:1
Bore: 63.5mm 2.5in
Stroke: 92.5mm 3.6in
Valve type/No: Side 8
Transmission: Manual
No. of forward speeds: 3
Wheels driven: Rear
Brakes F/R: Drum/Drum
Kerb weight: 827.6kg 1823.0lb
Fuel: 31.8L 7.0gal 8.4galUS

1616 Ford
Prefect
1938 UK
65.2mph 104.9kmh
0-50mph 80.5kmh: 25.0secs
30.0bhp 22.4kW 30.4PS
@ 4000rpm
36.4bhp/ton 35.8bhp/tonne
25.6bhp/L 19.1kW/L 26.0PS/L
40.4ft/sec 12.3m/sec
35.0mpg 29.1mpgUS 8.1L/100km
Petrol 4-stroke piston
1172cc 71.5cu in
In-line 4
Compression ratio: 6.1:1
Bore: 63.5mm 2.5in
Stroke: 92.5mm 3.6in
Valve type/No: Side 8
Transmission: Manual
No. of forward speeds: 3
Wheels driven: Rear
Brakes F/R: Drum/Drum
Kerb weight: 837.2kg 1844.0lb
Fuel: 31.8L 7.0gal 8.4galUS

1617 Ford
V8 30
1938 UK
87.3mph 140.5kmh
0-50mph 80.5kmh: 11.8secs
0-60mph 96.5kmh: 17.4secs
65.0bhp 48.5kW 65.9PS
@ 3400rpm
47.5bhp/ton 46.7bhp/tonne
17.9bhp/L 13.4kW/L 18.2PS/L
35.4ft/sec 10.8m/sec
17.0mpg 14.2mpgUS 16.6L/100km
Petrol 4-stroke piston
3622cc 221.0cu in
Vee 8
Compression ratio: 6.3:1
Bore: 77.8mm 3.1in
Stroke: 95.2mm 3.8in
Valve type/No: Side 16
Transmission: Manual
No. of forward speeds: 3
Wheels driven: Rear
Brakes F/R: Drum/Drum
Kerb weight: 1391.1kg 3064.0lb
Fuel: 54.6L 12.0gal 14.4galUS

1618 Ford
8
1939 UK
60.4mph 97.2kmh
0-50mph 80.5kmh: 35.3secs
23.4bhp 17.4kW 23.7PS
@ 4000rpm
30.9bhp/ton 30.4bhp/tonne
25.1bhp/L 18.7kW/L 25.4PS/L
40.4ft/sec 12.3m/sec
36.0mpg 30.0mpgUS 7.8L/100km
Petrol 4-stroke piston
933cc 56.9cu in
In-line 4
Compression ratio: 6.3:1
Bore: 56.6mm 2.2in
Stroke: 92.5mm 3.6in
Valve type/No: Side 8
Transmission: Manual
No. of forward speeds: 3
Wheels driven: Rear
Brakes F/R: Drum/Drum
Kerb weight: 769.5kg 1695.0lb
Fuel: 31.8L 7.0gal 8.4galUS

1619 Ford
Tudor Sedan
1947 USA
81.3mph 130.8kmh
0-50mph 80.5kmh: 13.5secs
0-60mph 96.5kmh: 21.0secs
100.0bhp 74.6kW 101.4PS
@ 3800rpm
70.2bhp/ton 69.0bhp/tonne
25.5bhp/L 19.0kW/L 25.8PS/L
39.6ft/sec 12.1m/sec
Petrol 4-stroke piston
3923cc 239.3cu in
Vee 8 1 Carburettor
Compression ratio: 6.8:1
Bore: 81.0mm 3.2in
Stroke: 95.3mm 3.8in
Valve type/No: Side 16
Transmission: Manual
No. of forward speeds: 3
Wheels driven: Rear
Springs F/R: Leaf/Leaf
Brakes F/R: Drum/Drum
Wheelbase: 289.6cm 114.0in
Track F: 147.3cm 58.0in
Track R: 152.4cm 60.0in
Length: 503.4cm 198.2in
Width: 185.7cm 73.1in
Ground clearance: 18.0cm 7.1in
Kerb weight: 1448.3kg 3190.0lb
Fuel: 64.3L 14.1gal 17.0galUS

1620 Ford
Prefect
1948 UK
61.0mph 98.1kmh
0-50mph 80.5kmh: 27.4secs
30.1bhp 22.4kW 30.5PS
@ 4000rpm
38.2bhp/ton 37.6bhp/tonne
25.7bhp/L 19.2kW/L 26.0PS/L
40.4ft/sec 12.3m/sec
32.0mpg 26.6mpgUS 8.8L/100km
Petrol 4-stroke piston
1172cc 71.5cu in
In-line 4
Compression ratio: 6.1:1
Bore: 63.5mm 2.5in
Stroke: 92.5mm 3.6in
Valve type/No: Side 8
Transmission: Manual
No. of forward speeds: 3
Wheels driven: Rear
Brakes F/R: Drum/Drum
Wheelbase: 238.8cm 94.0in
Track F: 114.3cm 45.0in
Track R: 114.3cm 45.0in
Length: 395.0cm 155.5in
Width: 144.8cm 57.0in
Height: 161.3cm 63.5in
Ground clearance: 22.1cm 8.7in
Kerb weight: 800.9kg 1764.0lb
Fuel: 31.8L 7.0gal 8.4galUS

1621 Ford
V8 Pilot
1948 UK
82.5mph 132.7kmh
0-50mph 80.5kmh: 13.1secs
0-60mph 96.5kmh: 20.5secs
85.0bhp 63.4kW 86.2PS
@ 3500rpm
55.6bhp/ton 54.7bhp/tonne
23.5bhp/L 17.5kW/L 23.8PS/L
36.5ft/sec 11.1m/sec
17.0mpg 14.2mpgUS 16.6L/100km
Petrol 4-stroke piston
3622cc 221.0cu in
Vee 8
Compression ratio: 6.1:1
Bore: 77.8mm 3.1in
Stroke: 95.3mm 3.8in
Valve type/No: Side 16
Transmission: Manual
No. of forward speeds: 3
Wheels driven: Rear
Brakes F/R: Drum/Drum
Wheelbase: 274.8cm 108.2in
Track F: 142.2cm 56.0in
Track R: 147.3cm 58.0in
Length: 443.7cm 174.7in
Width: 176.5cm 69.5in
Height: 167.6cm 66.0in
Ground clearance: 20.3cm 8.0in
Kerb weight: 1554.0kg 3423.0lb
Fuel: 56.9L 12.5gal 15.0galUS

1622 Ford
Anglia 10 Saloon
1949 UK
63.0mph 101.4kmh
0-50mph 80.5kmh: 28.3secs
30.1bhp 22.4kW 30.5PS
@ 4000rpm
39.5bhp/ton 38.8bhp/tonne
25.7bhp/L 19.2kW/L 26.0PS/L
40.4ft/sec 12.3m/sec
30.0mpg 25.0mpgUS 9.4L/100km
Petrol 4-stroke piston
1172cc 71.5cu in
In-line 4
Compression ratio: 6.1:1
Bore: 63.5mm 2.5in
Stroke: 92.5mm 3.6in
Valve type/No: Side 8
Transmission: Manual
No. of forward speeds: 3
Wheels driven: Rear
Brakes F/R: Drum/Drum
Wheelbase: 228.6cm 90.0in
Track F: 114.3cm 45.0in
Track R: 114.3cm 45.0in
Length: 389.9cm 153.5in
Width: 144.8cm 57.0in
Height: 160.0cm 63.0in
Ground clearance: 22.6cm 8.9in
Kerb weight: 775.4kg 1708.0lb
Fuel: 31.8L 7.0gal 8.4galUS

1623 Ford
Anglia 8 Saloon
1949 UK
59.0mph 94.9kmh
0-50mph 80.5kmh: 48.1secs
23.4bhp 17.4kW 23.7PS
@ 4000rpm
36.4lbft 49.3Nm @ 2300rpm
31.1bhp/ton 30.5bhp/tonne
25.1bhp/L 18.7kW/L 25.4PS/L
40.4ft/sec 12.3m/sec
13.7mph 22.0kmh/1000rpm
36.0mpg 30.0mpgUS 7.8L/100km
Petrol 4-stroke piston
933cc 56.9cu in
In-line 4
Compression ratio: 6.3:1
Bore: 56.6mm 2.2in
Stroke: 92.5mm 3.6in
Valve type/No: Side 8
Transmission: Manual
No. of forward speeds: 3
Wheels driven: Rear
Brakes F/R: Drum/Drum
Wheelbase: 228.6cm 90.0in
Track F: 114.3cm 45.0in
Track R: 114.3cm 45.0in
Length: 386.6cm 152.2in
Width: 142.0cm 55.9in
Height: 163.1cm 64.2in
Ground clearance: 22.4cm 8.8in
Kerb weight: 765.9kg 1687.0lb
Fuel: 31.8L 7.0gal 8.4galUS

1624 Ford
Consul
1951 UK
0-50mph 80.5kmh: 19.5secs
0-60mph 96.5kmh: 31.6secs
0-1/4 mile: 23.9secs
47.0bhp 35.0kW 47.6PS
@ 4400rpm
44.2bhp/ton 43.5bhp/tonne
31.2bhp/L 23.2kW/L 31.6PS/L
36.7ft/sec 11.2m/sec
Petrol 4-stroke piston
1508cc 92.0cu in
In-line 4
Bore: 79.4mm 3.1in
Stroke: 76.2mm 3.0in
Transmission: Manual
No. of forward speeds: 3
Wheels driven: Rear
Wheelbase: 254.0cm 100.0in
Track F: 127.0cm 50.0in
Track R: 124.5cm 49.0in
Length: 412.8cm 162.5in
Width: 162.6cm 64.0in
Height: 152.4cm 60.0in
Ground clearance: 16.8cm 6.6in
Kerb weight: 1080.5kg 2380.0lb

1625 Ford
Comete
1952 France
84.0mph 135.2kmh
0-50mph 80.5kmh: 16.6secs
0-60mph 96.5kmh: 24.5secs
0-1/4 mile: 23.1secs
63.0bhp 47.0kW 63.9PS
@ 4500rpm
94.0lbft 127.4Nm @ 2300rpm
47.9bhp/ton 47.1bhp/tonne
29.2bhp/L 21.8kW/L 29.6PS/L
38.7ft/sec 11.8m/sec
17.2mph 27.7kmh/1000rpm
20.0mpg 16.7mpgUS 14.1L/100km
Petrol 4-stroke piston
2158cc 131.7cu in
Vee 8
Compression ratio: 7.2:1
Bore: 66.0mm 2.6in
Stroke: 78.8mm 3.1in
Valve type/No: Side 16
Transmission: Manual
No. of forward speeds: 4
Wheels driven: Rear
Springs F/R: Coil/Leaf
Brakes F/R: Drum/Drum
Wheelbase: 269.2cm 106.0in
Track F: 135.1cm 53.2in
Track R: 138.2cm 54.4in
Length: 462.3cm 182.0in
Width: 173.2cm 68.2in
Height: 142.2cm 56.0in
Ground clearance: 19.1cm 7.5in
Kerb weight: 1338.4kg 2948.0lb
Fuel: 59.1L 13.0gal 15.6galUS

1626 Ford
Customline 6
1952 USA
83.2mph 133.9kmh
0-1/4 mile: 21.8secs
101.0bhp 75.3kW 102.4PS
@ 3500rpm
28.7bhp/L 21.4kW/L 29.1PS/L
35.0ft/sec 10.7m/sec
30.0mpg 25.0mpgUS 9.4L/100km
Petrol 4-stroke piston
3523cc 214.9cu in
In-line 6
Compression ratio: 7.0:1
Bore: 91.2mm 3.6in
Stroke: 91.4mm 3.6in
Valve type/No: Overhead 12
Transmission: Manual
No. of forward speeds: 3
Wheels driven: Rear
Wheelbase: 292.1cm 115.0in
Track F: 147.3cm 58.0in
Track R: 142.2cm 56.0in
Length: 502.4cm 197.8in
Width: 187.7cm 73.9in
Height: 158.2cm 62.3in
Ground clearance: 17.8cm 7.0in

1627 Ford
Customline 8
1952 USA
83.3mph 134.0kmh
0-1/4 mile: 22.2secs
110.0bhp 82.0kW 111.5PS
@ 3800rpm
28.1bhp/L 20.9kW/L 28.5PS/L
39.6ft/sec 12.1m/sec
Petrol 4-stroke piston
3917cc 239.0cu in
Vee 8
Compression ratio: 7.2:1
Bore: 80.9mm 3.2in
Stroke: 95.3mm 3.8in
Valve type/No: Side 16
Transmission: Automatic
Wheels driven: Rear
Wheelbase: 292.1cm 115.0in
Track F: 147.3cm 58.0in
Track R: 142.2cm 56.0in
Length: 502.4cm 197.8in
Width: 187.7cm 73.9in
Height: 158.2cm 62.3in
Ground clearance: 17.8cm 7.0in

1628 Ford
Zephyr Sedan
1953 UK
79.5mph 127.9kmh
0-50mph 80.5kmh: 14.3secs
0-60mph 96.5kmh: 20.1secs
0-1/4 mile: 21.1secs
68.0bhp 50.7kW 68.9PS
@ 4000rpm
112.0lbft 151.8Nm @ 2000rpm
58.6bhp/ton 57.6bhp/tonne
30.1bhp/L 22.4kW/L 30.5PS/L
33.3ft/sec 10.2m/sec
16.3mph 26.2kmh/1000rpm
Petrol 4-stroke piston
2262cc 138.0cu in
In-line 6
Compression ratio: 6.8:1
Bore: 79.2mm 3.1in
Stroke: 76.2mm 3.0in
Valve type/No: Overhead 12
Transmission: Manual
No. of forward speeds: 3
Wheels driven: Rear
Wheelbase: 264.2cm 104.0in
Track F: 127.0cm 50.0in
Track R: 124.5cm 49.0in
Kerb weight: 1180.4kg 2600.0lb

1629 Ford
Zephyr Sedan Modified
1953 UK
91.4mph 147.1kmh
0-50mph 80.5kmh: 9.0secs
0-60mph 96.5kmh: 13.1secs
0-1/4 mile: 18.9secs
85.0bhp 63.4kW 86.2PS
@ 4000rpm
112.0lbft 151.8Nm @ 2000rpm
73.2bhp/ton 72.0bhp/tonne
37.6bhp/L 28.0kW/L 38.1PS/L
33.3ft/sec 10.2m/sec
16.3mph 26.2kmh/1000rpm
Petrol 4-stroke piston
2262cc 138.0cu in
In-line 6 2 Carburettor
Compression ratio: 7.8:1
Bore: 79.2mm 3.1in
Stroke: 76.2mm 3.0in
Valve type/No: Overhead 12
Transmission: Manual
No. of forward speeds: 3
Wheels driven: Rear
Wheelbase: 264.2cm 104.0in
Track F: 127.0cm 50.0in
Track R: 124.5cm 49.0in
Kerb weight: 1180.4kg 2600.0lb

1630 Ford
Anglia Saloon
1954 UK
70.0mph 112.6kmh
0-50mph 80.5kmh: 19.7secs
0-60mph 96.5kmh: 33.2secs
0-1/4 mile: 24.3secs
36.0bhp 26.8kW 36.5PS
@ 4500rpm
52.0lbft 70.5Nm @ 2500rpm
47.4bhp/ton 46.6bhp/tonne
30.7bhp/L 22.9kW/L 31.1PS/L
45.5ft/sec 13.9m/sec
14.9mph 24.0kmh/1000rpm
29.7mpg 24.7mpgUS 9.5L/100km
Petrol 4-stroke piston
1172cc 71.5cu in
In-line 4
Compression ratio: 7.0:1
Bore: 63.5mm 2.5in
Stroke: 92.5mm 3.6in
Valve type/No: Side 8
Transmission: Manual
No. of forward speeds: 3
Wheels driven: Rear
Springs F/R: Coil/Leaf
Brakes F/R: Drum/Drum
Wheelbase: 221.0cm 87.0in
Track F: 121.9cm 48.0in
Track R: 120.7cm 47.5in
Length: 384.0cm 151.2in
Width: 153.7cm 60.5in
Height: 149.1cm 58.7in
Ground clearance: 17.8cm 7.0in
Kerb weight: 772.2kg 1701.0lb
Fuel: 31.8L 7.0gal 8.4galUS

1631 Ford
Popular
1954 UK
61.0mph 98.1kmh
0-50mph 80.5kmh: 29.2secs
0-1/4 mile: 26.3secs
30.1bhp 22.4kW 30.5PS
@ 4000rpm
46.4lbft 62.9Nm @ 2400rpm
41.7bhp/ton 41.0bhp/tonne
25.7bhp/L 19.2kW/L 26.0PS/L
40.4ft/sec 12.3m/sec
13.9mph 22.4kmh/1000rpm
35.0mpg 29.1mpgUS 8.1L/100km
Petrol 4-stroke piston
1172cc 72.0cu in
In-line 4
Compression ratio: 6.1:1
Bore: 63.5mm 2.5in
Stroke: 92.5mm 3.6in
Valve type/No: Side 8
Transmission: Manual
No. of forward speeds: 3
Wheels driven: Rear
Springs F/R: Leaf/Leaf
Brakes F/R: Drum/Drum
Wheelbase: 228.6cm 90.0in
Track F: 114.3cm 45.0in
Track R: 114.3cm 45.0in
Length: 384.8cm 151.5in
Width: 143.5cm 56.5in
Height: 163.1cm 64.2in
Ground clearance: 22.1cm 8.7in
Kerb weight: 734.1kg 1617.0lb
Fuel: 31.8L 7.0gal 8.4galUS

1632 Ford
Anglia
1955 UK
71.1mph 114.4kmh
0-50mph 80.5kmh: 18.7secs
0-60mph 96.5kmh: 29.8secs
0-1/4 mile: 24.0secs
36.0bhp 26.8kW 36.5PS
@ 4500rpm
54.0lbft 73.2Nm @ 2150rpm
46.7bhp/ton 46.0bhp/tonne
30.7bhp/L 22.9kW/L 31.1PS/L
45.5ft/sec 13.9m/sec
15.0mph 24.1kmh/1000rpm
Petrol 4-stroke piston
1172cc 71.5cu in
In-line 4
Compression ratio: 7.0:1
Bore: 63.5mm 2.5in
Stroke: 92.5mm 3.6in
Valve type/No: Side 8
Transmission: Manual
No. of forward speeds: 3
Wheels driven: Rear
Wheelbase: 221.0cm 87.0in
Track F: 121.9cm 48.0in
Track R: 120.7cm 47.5in
Kerb weight: 783.1kg 1725.0lb

1633 Ford
Prefect
1955 UK
73.0mph 117.5kmh
0-50mph 80.5kmh: 18.4secs
0-60mph 96.5kmh: 31.0secs
0-1/4 mile: 23.8secs
39.0bhp 29.1kW 39.5PS
@ 5000rpm
52.8lbft 71.5Nm @ 2700rpm
48.7bhp/ton 47.9bhp/tonne
39.1bhp/L 29.2kW/L 39.7PS/L
26.5ft/sec 8.1m/sec
14.8mph 23.8kmh/1000rpm
34.1mpg 28.4mpgUS 8.3L/100km
Petrol 4-stroke piston
997cc 61.0cu in
In-line 4 1 Carburettor
Compression ratio: 8.9:1
Bore: 81.0mm 3.2in
Stroke: 48.4mm 1.9in
Valve type/No: Overhead 8
Transmission: Manual
No. of forward speeds: 4
Wheels driven: Rear
Springs F/R: Coil/Leaf
Brakes F/R: Drum/Drum
Wheelbase: 221.0cm 87.0in
Track F: 121.9cm 48.0in
Track R: 120.7cm 47.5in
Length: 380.2cm 149.7in
Width: 154.2cm 60.7in
Height: 151.1cm 59.5in
Ground clearance: 16.3cm 6.4in
Kerb weight: 813.6kg 1792.0lb
Fuel: 31.8L 7.0gal 8.4galUS

1634 Ford
Prefect 1172cc
1955 UK
70.0mph 112.6kmh
0-50mph 80.5kmh: 21.8secs
0-60mph 96.5kmh: 38.9secs
0-1/4 mile: 24.3secs
36.0bhp 26.8kW 36.5PS
@ 4500rpm
52.0lbft 70.5Nm @ 2500rpm
46.4bhp/ton 45.7bhp/tonne
30.7bhp/L 22.9kW/L 31.1PS/L
45.5ft/sec 13.9m/sec
14.9mph 24.0kmh/1000rpm
33.8mpg 28.1mpgUS 8.4L/100km
Petrol 4-stroke piston
1172cc 71.5cu in
In-line 4 1 Carburettor
Compression ratio: 7.0:1
Bore: 63.5mm 2.5in
Stroke: 92.5mm 3.6in
Valve type/No: Side 8
Transmission: Manual
No. of forward speeds: 3
Wheels driven: Rear
Springs F/R: Coil/Leaf
Brakes F/R: Drum/Drum
Wheelbase: 221.0cm 87.0in
Track F: 121.9cm 48.0in
Track R: 120.7cm 47.5in
Length: 384.0cm 151.2in
Width: 153.9cm 60.6in
Height: 149.1cm 58.7in
Ground clearance: 17.8cm 7.0in
Kerb weight: 788.1kg 1736.0lb
Fuel: 31.8L 7.0gal 8.4galUS

1635 Ford
Thunderbird
1955 USA
110.1mph 177.2kmh
0-50mph 80.5kmh: 7.6secs
0-60mph 96.5kmh: 9.5secs
0-1/4 mile: 17.1secs
198.0bhp 147.6kW 200.7PS
@ 4400rpm
286.0lbft 387.5Nm @ 2500rpm
136.9bhp/ton 134.6bhp/tonne
41.3bhp/L 30.8kW/L 41.9PS/L
40.3ft/sec 12.3m/sec
24.2mph 38.9kmh/1000rpm
Petrol 4-stroke piston
4788cc 292.1cu in
Vee 8
Compression ratio: 8.5:1
Bore: 95.3mm 3.8in
Stroke: 83.8mm 3.3in
Valve type/No: Overhead 16
Transmission: Automatic
No. of forward speeds: 3
Wheels driven: Rear
Wheelbase: 259.1cm 102.0in
Track F: 142.2cm 56.0in
Track R: 142.2cm 56.0in
Kerb weight: 1471.0kg 3240.0lb

1636 Ford
Zodiac
1955 UK
84.0mph 135.2kmh
0-50mph 80.5kmh: 13.5secs
0-60mph 96.5kmh: 20.4secs
0-1/4 mile: 21.5secs
71.0bhp 52.9kW 72.0PS
@ 4200rpm
112.0lbft 151.8Nm @ 2000rpm
59.8bhp/ton 58.8bhp/tonne
31.4bhp/L 23.4kW/L 31.8PS/L
35.0ft/sec 10.7m/sec
16.1mph 25.9kmh/1000rpm
23.7mpg 19.7mpgUS 11.9L/100km
Petrol 4-stroke piston
2262cc 138.0cu in
In-line 6
Compression ratio: 7.5:1
Bore: 79.4mm 3.1in
Stroke: 76.2mm 3.0in
Valve type/No: Overhead 12
Transmission: Manual
No. of forward speeds: 3
Wheels driven: Rear
Springs F/R: Coil/Leaf
Brakes F/R: Drum/Drum
Wheelbase: 264.2cm 104.0in
Track F: 127.0cm 50.0in
Track R: 124.5cm 49.0in
Length: 436.4cm 171.8in
Width: 162.3cm 63.9in
Height: 154.2cm 60.7in
Ground clearance: 18.0cm 7.1in
Kerb weight: 1207.6kg 2660.0lb
Fuel: 40.9L 9.0gal 10.8galUS

1637 Ford
Anglia
1956 UK
69.5mph 111.8kmh
0-50mph 80.5kmh: 17.8secs
0-60mph 96.5kmh: 30.0secs
0-1/4 mile: 24.0secs
36.0bhp 26.8kW 36.5PS
@ 4500rpm
54.0lbft 73.2Nm @ 2150rpm
46.9bhp/ton 46.1bhp/tonne
30.7bhp/L 22.9kW/L 31.1PS/L
45.5ft/sec 13.9m/sec
20.2mph 32.5kmh/1000rpm
Petrol 4-stroke piston
1172cc 71.5cu in
In-line 4
Compression ratio: 7.0:1
Bore: 63.5mm 2.5in
Stroke: 92.5mm 3.6in
Valve type/No: Side 8
Transmission: Manual
No. of forward speeds: 3
Wheels driven: Rear
Wheelbase: 221.0cm 87.0in
Track F: 121.9cm 48.0in
Track R: 120.7cm 47.5in
Kerb weight: 780.9kg 1720.0lb

1638 Ford
Consul Mk II
1956 UK
79.0mph 127.1kmh
0-50mph 80.5kmh: 15.8secs
0-60mph 96.5kmh: 25.0secs
0-1/4 mile: 23.1secs
59.0bhp 44.0kW 59.8PS
@ 4200rpm
92.0lbft 124.7Nm @ 2300rpm
53.6bhp/ton 52.7bhp/tonne
34.6bhp/L 25.8kW/L 35.1PS/L
36.5ft/sec 11.1m/sec
16.6mph 26.7kmh/1000rpm
29.0mpg 24.1mpgUS 9.7L/100km
Petrol 4-stroke piston
1703cc 103.9cu in
In-line 4
Compression ratio: 7.8:1
Bore: 82.5mm 3.2in
Stroke: 79.5mm 3.1in
Valve type/No: Overhead 8
Transmission: Manual
No. of forward speeds: 3
Wheels driven: Rear
Springs F/R: Coil/Leaf
Brakes F/R: Drum/Drum
Wheelbase: 265.4cm 104.5in
Track F: 134.6cm 53.0in
Track R: 132.1cm 52.0in
Length: 436.9cm 172.0in

Width: 170.2cm 67.0in
Height: 156.2cm 61.5in
Ground clearance: 16.5cm 6.5in
Kerb weight: 1118.7kg 2464.0lb
Fuel: 50.0L 11.0gal 13.2galUS

1639 Ford

Interceptor Coupe
1956 USA
111.0mph 178.6kmh
0-50mph 80.5kmh: 6.9secs
0-60mph 96.5kmh: 8.8secs
0-1/4 mile: 16.4secs
292.0bhp 217.7kW 296.0PS
@ 4600rpm
289.0lbft 391.6Nm @ 2600rpm
191.0bhp/ton 187.8bhp/tonne
61.0bhp/L 45.5kW/L 61.9PS/L
41.9ft/sec 12.8m/sec
18.7mph 30.1kmh/1000rpm
18.3mpg 15.2mpgUS 15.5L/100km
Petrol 4-stroke piston
4785cc 291.9cu in
Vee 8
Compression ratio: 9.0:1
Bore: 95.3mm 3.8in
Stroke: 83.2mm 3.3in
Valve type/No: Overhead 16
Transmission: Manual
No. of forward speeds: 3
Wheels driven: Rear
Wheelbase: 293.4cm 115.5in
Track F: 147.3cm 58.0in
Track R: 142.2cm 56.0in
Kerb weight: 1554.9kg 3425.0lb

1640 Ford

Taunus 15M
1956 Germany
78.5mph 126.3kmh
0-50mph 80.5kmh: 14.5secs
0-60mph 96.5kmh: 22.8secs
0-1/4 mile: 21.4secs
60.0bhp 44.7kW 60.8PS
@ 4500rpm
81.7lbft 110.7Nm @ 2000rpm
68.7bhp/ton 67.6bhp/tonne
40.0bhp/L 29.9kW/L 40.6PS/L
34.9ft/sec 10.6m/sec
16.1mph 25.9kmh/1000rpm
31.5mpg 26.2mpgUS 9.0L/100km
Petrol 4-stroke piston
1498cc 91.4cu in
In-line 4
Compression ratio: 7.0:1
Bore: 82.0mm 3.2in
Stroke: 70.9mm 2.8in
Valve type/No: Overhead 8
Transmission: Manual
No. of forward speeds: 3
Wheels driven: Rear
Springs F/R: Coil/Leaf
Brakes F/R: Drum/Drum
Wheelbase: 248.9cm 98.0in
Track F: 121.9cm 48.0in
Track R: 121.9cm 48.0in
Length: 406.4cm 160.0in
Width: 157.5cm 62.0in
Height: 154.9cm 61.0in
Ground clearance: 15.7cm 6.2in
Kerb weight: 888.0kg 1956.0lb
Fuel: 40.9L 9.0gal 10.8galUS

1641 Ford

Thunderbird
1956 USA
116.0mph 186.6kmh
0-50mph 80.5kmh: 7.4secs
0-60mph 96.5kmh: 10.2secs
0-1/4 mile: 17.5secs
225.0bhp 167.8kW 228.1PS
@ 4600rpm
324.0lbft 439.0Nm @ 2600rpm
145.2bhp/ton 142.7bhp/tonne
44.0bhp/L 32.8kW/L 44.6PS/L
44.0ft/sec 13.4m/sec
25.0mph 40.2kmh/1000rpm
16.5mpg 13.7mpgUS 17.1L/100km
Petrol 4-stroke piston
5115cc 312.1cu in
Vee 8 1 Carburettor
Compression ratio: 9.0:1
Bore: 96.5mm 3.8in
Stroke: 87.4mm 3.4in
Valve type/No: Overhead 16
Transmission: Automatic
No. of forward speeds: 3
Wheels driven: Rear
Springs F/R: Coil/Leaf
Brakes F/R: Drum/Drum
Wheelbase: 259.1cm 102.0in
Track F: 142.2cm 56.0in
Track R: 142.2cm 56.0in
Length: 470.4cm 185.2in
Width: 178.3cm 70.2in
Height: 132.6cm 52.2in
Ground clearance: 15.0cm 5.9in
Kerb weight: 1576.3kg 3472.0lb
Fuel: 61.9L 13.6gal 16.3galUS

1642 Ford

Zephyr
1956 UK
86.0mph 138.4kmh
0-50mph 80.5kmh: 12.3secs
0-60mph 96.5kmh: 17.9secs
0-1/4 mile: 20.5secs
86.0bhp 64.1kW 87.2PS
@ 4200rpm
136.0lbft 184.3Nm @ 2000rpm
71.1bhp/ton 69.9bhp/tonne
33.7bhp/L 25.1kW/L 34.1PS/L
36.5ft/sec 11.1m/sec
25.3mph 40.7kmh/1000rpm
24.1mpg 20.1mpgUS 11.7L/100km
Petrol 4-stroke piston
2553cc 155.8cu in
In-line 6 1 Carburettor
Compression ratio: 7.8:1
Bore: 82.5mm 3.2in
Stroke: 79.5mm 3.1in
Valve type/No: Overhead 12
Transmission: Manual with overdrive
No. of forward speeds: 6
Wheels driven: Rear
Springs F/R: Coil/Leaf
Brakes F/R: Drum/Drum
Wheelbase: 271.8cm 107.0in
Track F: 134.6cm 53.0in
Track R: 132.1cm 52.0in
Length: 453.1cm 178.4in
Width: 174.8cm 68.8in
Height: 157.0cm 61.8in
Ground clearance: 17.3cm 6.8in
Kerb weight: 1229.9kg 2709.0lb
Fuel: 50.0L 11.0gal 13.2galUS

1643 Ford

Zodiac Automatic
1957 UK
84.6mph 136.1kmh
0-50mph 80.5kmh: 14.3secs
0-60mph 96.5kmh: 20.9secs
0-1/4 mile: 22.5secs
85.0bhp 63.4kW 86.2PS
@ 4400rpm
133.0lbft 180.2Nm @ 2000rpm
65.9bhp/ton 64.8bhp/tonne
33.3bhp/L 24.8kW/L 33.8PS/L
38.3ft/sec 11.7m/sec
19.1mph 30.7kmh/1000rpm
23.1mpg 19.2mpgUS 12.2L/100km
Petrol 4-stroke piston
2553cc 155.8cu in
In-line 6 1 Carburettor
Compression ratio: 7.8:1
Bore: 82.5mm 3.2in
Stroke: 79.5mm 3.1in
Valve type/No: Overhead 12
Transmission: Automatic
No. of forward speeds: 3
Wheels driven: Rear
Springs F/R: Coil/Leaf
Brakes F/R: Drum/Drum
Wheelbase: 271.8cm 107.0in
Track F: 134.6cm 53.0in
Track R: 132.1cm 52.0in
Length: 458.5cm 180.5in
Width: 174.5cm 68.7in
Height: 157.5cm 62.0in
Ground clearance: 17.0cm 6.7in
Kerb weight: 1312.5kg 2891.0lb
Fuel: 47.8L 10.5gal 12.6galUS

1644 Ford

Anglia de Luxe
1958 UK
72.0mph 115.8kmh
0-50mph 80.5kmh: 22.0secs
0-60mph 96.5kmh: 32.4secs
0-1/4 mile: 25.6secs
36.0bhp 26.8kW 36.5PS
@ 4500rpm
53.0lbft 71.8Nm @ 2500rpm
45.7bhp/ton 44.9bhp/tonne
30.7bhp/L 22.9kW/L 31.1PS/L
45.5ft/sec 13.9m/sec
14.8mph 23.8kmh/1000rpm
30.1mpg 25.1mpgUS 9.4L/100km
Petrol 4-stroke piston
1172cc 71.5cu in
In-line 4 1 Carburettor
Compression ratio: 7.0:1
Bore: 63.5mm 2.5in
Stroke: 92.5mm 3.6in
Valve type/No: Side 8
Transmission: Automatic
No. of forward speeds: 3
Wheels driven: Rear
Springs F/R: Coil/Leaf
Brakes F/R: Drum/Drum
Wheelbase: 221.0cm 87.0in
Track F: 121.9cm 48.0in
Track R: 120.7cm 47.5in
Length: 384.0cm 151.2in
Width: 153.7cm 60.5in
Height: 149.1cm 58.7in
Ground clearance: 17.8cm 7.0in
Kerb weight: 800.9kg 1764.0lb
Fuel: 31.8L 7.0gal 8.4galUS

1645 Ford

Consul
1958 UK
80.6mph 129.7kmh
0-50mph 80.5kmh: 15.6secs
0-60mph 96.5kmh: 25.4secs
0-1/4 mile: 22.7secs
59.0bhp 44.0kW 59.8PS
@ 4400rpm
91.0lbft 123.3Nm @ 2300rpm
53.4bhp/ton 52.5bhp/tonne
34.6bhp/L 25.8kW/L 35.1PS/L
38.3ft/sec 11.7m/sec
16.9mph 27.2kmh/1000rpm
31.4mpg 26.1mpgUS 9.0L/100km
Petrol 4-stroke piston
1703cc 103.9cu in
In-line 4 1 Carburettor
Compression ratio: 7.8:1
Bore: 82.5mm 3.2in
Stroke: 79.5mm 3.1in
Valve type/No: Overhead 8
Transmission: Manual
No. of forward speeds: 3
Wheels driven: Rear
Springs F/R: Coil/Leaf
Brakes F/R: Drum/Drum
Wheelbase: 265.4cm 104.5in
Track F: 134.6cm 53.0in
Track R: 132.1cm 52.0in
Length: 436.9cm 172.0in
Width: 174.5cm 68.7in
Height: 156.2cm 61.5in
Ground clearance: 16.5cm 6.5in
Kerb weight: 1122.7kg 2473.0lb
Fuel: 47.8L 10.5gal 12.6galUS

1646 Ford

Fairlane 500
1958 USA
92.0mph 148.0kmh
0-50mph 80.5kmh: 10.6secs
0-60mph 96.5kmh: 15.1secs
0-1/4 mile: 20.0secs
176.0bhp 131.2kW 178.4PS
@ 4400rpm
264.0lbft 357.7Nm @ 2400rpm
105.7bhp/ton 103.9bhp/tonne
39.5bhp/L 29.4kW/L 40.0PS/L
40.3ft/sec 12.3m/sec
23.8mph 38.3kmh/1000rpm
16.1mpg 13.4mpgUS 17.5L/100km
Petrol 4-stroke piston
4458cc 272.0cu in
Vee 8 1 Carburettor
Compression ratio: 7.1:1
Bore: 92.1mm 3.6in
Stroke: 83.8mm 3.3in
Valve type/No: Overhead 16
Transmission: Automatic
No. of forward speeds: 3
Wheels driven: Rear
Springs F/R: Coil/Leaf
Brakes F/R: Drum/Drum
Wheelbase: 299.7cm 118.0in
Track F: 149.9cm 59.0in
Track R: 143.5cm 56.5in
Length: 527.1cm 207.5in
Width: 195.6cm 77.0in
Height: 143.5cm 56.5in
Ground clearance: 18.0cm 7.1in
Kerb weight: 1693.9kg 3731.0lb
Fuel: 72.8L 16.0gal 19.2galUS

1647 Ford

Taunus 17M
1958 Germany
79.0mph 127.1kmh
0-50mph 80.5kmh: 12.8secs
0-60mph 96.5kmh: 18.5secs
0-1/4 mile: 21.0secs
67.0bhp 50.0kW 67.9PS
@ 4400rpm
97.0lbft 131.4Nm @ 2200rpm
68.1bhp/ton 66.9bhp/tonne
39.5bhp/L 29.4kW/L 40.0PS/L
36.9ft/sec 11.2m/sec
17.9mph 28.8kmh/1000rpm
Petrol 4-stroke piston
1698cc 103.6cu in
In-line 4
Compression ratio: 7.1:1
Bore: 84.1mm 3.3in
Stroke: 76.7mm 3.0in
Valve type/No: Overhead 8
Transmission: Manual
No. of forward speeds: 3
Wheels driven: Rear
Wheelbase: 260.1cm 102.4in
Track F: 127.0cm 50.0in
Track R: 127.0cm 50.0in
Length: 436.9cm 172.0in
Width: 166.9cm 65.7in
Height: 150.1cm 59.1in
Kerb weight: 1001.1kg 2205.0lb

1648 Ford

Zephyr Estate
1958 UK
84.0mph 135.2kmh
0-50mph 80.5kmh: 12.6secs
0-60mph 96.5kmh: 18.7secs
0-1/4 mile: 20.9secs
90.0bhp 67.1kW 91.2PS
@ 4400rpm
137.0lbft 185.6Nm @ 2000rpm
71.0bhp/ton 69.8bhp/tonne
35.2bhp/L 26.3kW/L 35.7PS/L
38.3ft/sec 11.7m/sec
27.3mph 43.9kmh/1000rpm
25.0mpg 20.8mpgUS 11.3L/100km
Petrol 4-stroke piston
2553cc 155.8cu in
In-line 6 1 Carburettor
Compression ratio: 7.8:1
Bore: 82.5mm 3.2in
Stroke: 79.5mm 3.1in
Valve type/No: Overhead 12
Transmission: Manual with overdrive
No. of forward speeds: 6
Wheels driven: Rear
Springs F/R: Coil/Leaf
Brakes F/R: Drum/Drum
Wheelbase: 271.8cm 107.0in
Track F: 134.6cm 53.0in
Track R: 132.1cm 52.0in
Length: 453.4cm 178.5in
Width: 174.8cm 68.8in
Height: 157.5cm 62.0in
Ground clearance: 17.3cm 6.8in
Kerb weight: 1288.4kg 2838.0lb
Fuel: 47.8L 10.5gal 12.6galUS

1649 Ford

Anglia
1959 UK
79.0mph 127.1kmh
0-50mph 80.5kmh: 17.8secs
0-60mph 96.5kmh: 29.4secs
0-1/4 mile: 23.0secs
39.0bhp 29.1kW 39.5PS
@ 5000rpm
52.5lbft 71.1Nm @ 2700rpm
52.0bhp/ton 51.1bhp/tonne
39.2bhp/L 29.2kW/L 39.7PS/L
26.5ft/sec 8.1m/sec
16.0mph 25.7kmh/1000rpm
36.1mpg 30.1mpgUS 7.8L/100km
Petrol 4-stroke piston
996cc 60.8cu in
In-line 4 1 Carburettor
Compression ratio: 8.9:1
Bore: 80.9mm 3.2in
Stroke: 48.4mm 1.9in

Valve type/No: Overhead 8
Transmission: Manual
No. of forward speeds: 4
Wheels driven: Rear
Springs F/R: Coil/Leaf
Brakes F/R: Drum/Drum
Wheelbase: 229.9cm 90.5in
Track F: 116.8cm 46.0in
Track R: 116.3cm 45.8in
Length: 389.9cm 153.5in
Width: 145.5cm 57.3in
Height: 143.8cm 56.6in
Ground clearance: 16.3cm 6.4in
Kerb weight: 762.7kg 1680.0lb
Fuel: 31.8L 7.0gal 8.4galUS

1650 Ford

Falcon
1959 USA
87.0mph 140.0kmh
0-50mph 80.5kmh: 12.8secs
0-60mph 96.5kmh: 17.7secs
0-1/4 mile: 20.8secs
85.0bhp 63.4kW 86.2PS
@ 4000rpm
138.0lbft 187.0Nm @ 2000rpm
80.2bhp/ton 78.8bhp/tonne
35.9bhp/L 26.8kW/L 36.4PS/L
27.8ft/sec 8.5m/sec
21.6mph 34.8kmh/1000rpm
Petrol 4-stroke piston
2366cc 144.4cu in
In-line 6
Compression ratio: 8.7:1
Bore: 88.9mm 3.5in
Stroke: 63.5mm 2.5in
Valve type/No: Overhead 12
Transmission: Manual
No. of forward speeds: 3
Wheels driven: Rear
Wheelbase: 278.1cm 109.5in
Track F: 139.7cm 55.0in
Track R: 138.4cm 54.5in
Length: 460.0cm 181.1in
Width: 177.8cm 70.0in
Height: 138.4cm 54.5in
Kerb weight: 1078.2kg 2375.0lb

1651 Ford

Popular II
1959 UK
69.0mph 111.0kmh
0-50mph 80.5kmh: 20.8secs
0-60mph 96.5kmh: 36.4secs
0-1/4 mile: 24.4secs
36.0bhp 26.8kW 36.5PS
@ 4500rpm
53.0lbft 71.8Nm @ 2500rpm
48.0bhp/ton 47.2bhp/tonne
30.7bhp/L 22.9kW/L 31.1PS/L
45.5ft/sec 13.9m/sec
14.9mph 24.0kmh/1000rpm
29.6mpg 24.6mpgUS 9.5L/100km
Petrol 4-stroke piston
1172cc 71.5cu in
In-line 4 1 Carburettor
Compression ratio: 7.0:1
Bore: 63.5mm 2.5in
Stroke: 92.5mm 3.6in
Valve type/No: Side 8
Transmission: Manual
No. of forward speeds: 3
Wheels driven: Rear
Springs F/R: Coil/Leaf
Brakes F/R: Drum/Drum
Wheelbase: 221.0cm 87.0in
Track F: 121.9cm 48.0in
Track R: 120.7cm 47.5in
Length: 380.2cm 149.7in
Width: 153.7cm 60.5in
Height: 149.1cm 58.7in
Ground clearance: 17.8cm 7.0in
Kerb weight: 762.7kg 1680.0lb
Fuel: 31.8L 7.0gal 8.4galUS

1652 Ford

Taunus 17M Estate
1959 Germany
82.5mph 132.7kmh
0-50mph 80.5kmh: 14.6secs
0-60mph 96.5kmh: 23.5secs
0-1/4 mile: 22.5secs
67.0bhp 50.0kW 67.9PS
@ 4400rpm
97.0lbft 131.4Nm @ 2200rpm
62.8bhp/ton 61.8bhp/tonne
39.5bhp/L 29.4kW/L 40.0PS/L
36.9ft/sec 11.2m/sec
17.3mph 27.8kmh/1000rpm
27.0mpg 22.5mpgUS 10.5L/100km
Petrol 4-stroke piston
1698cc 103.6cu in
In-line 4 1 Carburettor
Compression ratio: 7.2:1
Bore: 84.0mm 3.3in
Stroke: 76.6mm 3.0in
Valve type/No: Overhead 8
Transmission: Manual
No. of forward speeds: 3
Wheels driven: Rear
Springs F/R: Coil/Leaf
Brakes F/R: Drum/Drum
Wheelbase: 260.4cm 102.5in
Track F: 127.0cm 50.0in
Track R: 127.0cm 50.0in
Length: 442.0cm 174.0in
Width: 141.5cm 55.7in
Height: 151.1cm 59.5in
Ground clearance: 12.7cm 5.0in
Kerb weight: 1084.6kg 2389.0lb
Fuel: 45.0L 9.9gal 11.9galUS

1653 Ford

Thunderbird
1959 USA
120.0mph 193.1kmh
0-50mph 80.5kmh: 6.6secs
0-60mph 96.5kmh: 8.2secs
0-1/4 mile: 16.2secs
350.0bhp 261.0kW 354.8PS
@ 4800rpm
490.0lbft 664.0Nm @ 3100rpm
179.0bhp/ton 176.0bhp/tonne
49.6bhp/L 37.0kW/L 50.3PS/L
49.3ft/sec 15.0m/sec
25.1mph 40.4kmh/1000rpm
Petrol 4-stroke piston
7049cc 430.1cu in
Vee 8
Compression ratio: 10.0:1
Bore: 109.2mm 4.3in
Stroke: 94.0mm 3.7in
Valve type/No: Overhead 16
Transmission: Automatic
No. of forward speeds: 3
Wheels driven: Rear
Wheelbase: 287.0cm 113.0in
Track F: 152.4cm 60.0in
Track R: 144.8cm 57.0in
Length: 521.7cm 205.4in
Width: 195.6cm 77.0in
Height: 133.4cm 52.5in
Kerb weight: 1988.5kg 4380.0lb

1654 Ford

Anglia
1960 UK
74.0mph 119.1kmh
0-50mph 80.5kmh: 18.5secs
0-60mph 96.5kmh: 29.1secs
0-1/4 mile: 24.0secs
41.0bhp 30.6kW 41.6PS
@ 5000rpm
52.5lbft 71.1Nm @ 2700rpm
54.8bhp/ton 53.9bhp/tonne
41.2bhp/L 30.7kW/L 41.7PS/L
26.5ft/sec 8.1m/sec
16.1mph 25.9kmh/1000rpm
Petrol 4-stroke piston
996cc 60.8cu in
In-line 4 1 Carburettor
Compression ratio: 8.9:1
Bore: 81.0mm 3.2in
Stroke: 48.5mm 1.9in
Valve type/No: Overhead 8
Transmission: Manual
No. of forward speeds: 4
Wheels driven: Rear
Wheelbase: 229.9cm 90.5in
Track F: 116.8cm 46.0in
Track R: 116.8cm 46.0in
Length: 389.9cm 153.5in
Width: 143.5cm 56.5in
Height: 142.2cm 56.0in
Kerb weight: 760.9kg 1676.0lb

1655 Ford

Consul Mk II
1960 UK
78.6mph 126.5kmh
0-50mph 80.5kmh: 14.1secs
0-60mph 96.5kmh: 22.5secs
0-1/4 mile: 22.8secs
59.0bhp 44.0kW 59.8PS
@ 4200rpm
92.0lbft 124.7Nm @ 2300rpm
52.0bhp/ton 51.2bhp/tonne
34.6bhp/L 25.8kW/L 35.1PS/L
36.5ft/sec 11.1m/sec
16.7mph 26.9kmh/1000rpm
Petrol 4-stroke piston
1703cc 103.9cu in
In-line 4 1 Carburettor
Compression ratio: 7.8:1
Bore: 82.6mm 3.2in
Stroke: 79.4mm 3.1in
Valve type/No: Overhead 8
Transmission: Manual
No. of forward speeds: 3
Wheels driven: Rear
Wheelbase: 265.4cm 104.5in
Track F: 134.6cm 53.0in
Track R: 132.1cm 52.0in
Length: 401.3cm 158.0in
Width: 174.2cm 68.6in
Height: 150.9cm 59.4in
Kerb weight: 1153.2kg 2540.0lb

1656 Ford

Falcon
1960 USA
91.0mph 146.4kmh
0-50mph 80.5kmh: 12.4secs
0-60mph 96.5kmh: 18.6secs
0-1/4 mile: 21.3secs
90.0bhp 67.1kW 91.2PS
@ 4200rpm
138.0lbft 187.0Nm @ 2000rpm
82.5bhp/ton 81.1bhp/tonne
38.0bhp/L 28.4kW/L 38.6PS/L
29.2ft/sec 8.9m/sec
21.5mph 34.6kmh/1000rpm
23.3mpg 19.4mpgUS 12.1L/100km
Petrol 4-stroke piston
2365cc 144.3cu in
In-line 6 1 Carburettor
Compression ratio: 8.7:1
Bore: 88.9mm 3.5in
Stroke: 63.5mm 2.5in
Valve type/No: Overhead 12
Transmission: Manual
No. of forward speeds: 3
Wheels driven: Rear
Springs F/R: Coil/Leaf
Brake system: PA
Brakes F/R: Drum/Drum
Wheelbase: 278.1cm 109.5in
Track F: 139.7cm 55.0in
Track R: 137.2cm 54.0in
Length: 459.7cm 181.0in
Width: 177.8cm 70.0in
Height: 143.5cm 56.5in
Ground clearance: 17.5cm 6.9in
Kerb weight: 1109.1kg 2443.0lb
Fuel: 54.6L 12.0gal 14.4galUS

1657 Ford

Falcon Automatic
1960 USA
86.0mph 138.4kmh
0-50mph 80.5kmh: 14.3secs
0-60mph 96.5kmh: 22.9secs
0-1/4 mile: 22.2secs
90.0bhp 67.1kW 91.2PS
@ 4200rpm
138.0lbft 187.0Nm @ 2000rpm
82.5bhp/ton 81.1bhp/tonne
38.0bhp/L 28.4kW/L 38.6PS/L
29.2ft/sec 8.9m/sec
21.5mph 34.6kmh/1000rpm
22.1mpg 18.4mpgUS 12.8L/100km
Petrol 4-stroke piston
2365cc 144.3cu in
In-line 6 1 Carburettor
Compression ratio: 8.7:1
Bore: 88.9mm 3.5in
Stroke: 63.5mm 2.5in
Valve type/No: Overhead 12
Transmission: Automatic
No. of forward speeds: 2
Wheels driven: Rear
Springs F/R: Coil/Leaf
Brake system: PA
Brakes F/R: Drum/Drum
Wheelbase: 278.1cm 109.5in
Track F: 139.7cm 55.0in
Track R: 137.2cm 54.0in
Length: 459.7cm 181.0in
Width: 177.8cm 70.0in
Height: 143.5cm 56.5in
Ground clearance: 17.5cm 6.9in
Kerb weight: 1109.1kg 2443.0lb
Fuel: 54.6L 12.0gal 14.4galUS

1658 Ford

Galaxie
1960 USA
108.0mph 173.8kmh
0-50mph 80.5kmh: 10.2secs
0-60mph 96.5kmh: 13.6secs
0-1/4 mile: 18.6secs
225.0bhp 167.8kW 228.1PS
@ 4400rpm
324.0lbft 439.0Nm @ 2200rpm
124.1bhp/ton 122.1bhp/tonne
41.3bhp/L 30.8kW/L 41.9PS/L
42.0ft/sec 12.8m/sec
25.0mph 40.2kmh/1000rpm
16.5mpg 13.7mpgUS 17.1L/100km
Petrol 4-stroke piston
5441cc 332.0cu in
Vee 8 1 Carburettor
Compression ratio: 8.9:1
Bore: 101.6mm 4.0in
Stroke: 87.3mm 3.4in
Valve type/No: Overhead 16
Transmission: Automatic
No. of forward speeds: 3
Wheels driven: Rear
Springs F/R: Coil/Leaf
Brake system: PA
Brakes F/R: Drum/Drum
Wheelbase: 302.3cm 119.0in
Track F: 154.9cm 61.0in
Track R: 152.4cm 60.0in
Length: 542.8cm 213.7in
Width: 207.0cm 81.5in
Height: 139.7cm 55.0in
Ground clearance: 17.8cm 7.0in
Kerb weight: 1843.2kg 4060.0lb
Fuel: 75.1L 16.5gal 19.8galUS

1659 Ford

Taunus 17M
1960 Germany
79.0mph 127.1kmh
0-50mph 80.5kmh: 12.8secs
0-60mph 96.5kmh: 18.5secs
0-1/4 mile: 21.0secs
67.0bhp 50.0kW 67.9PS
@ 4400rpm
97.0lbft 131.4Nm @ 2200rpm
68.1bhp/ton 66.9bhp/tonne
39.5bhp/L 29.4kW/L 40.0PS/L
36.9ft/sec 11.2m/sec
17.9mph 28.8kmh/1000rpm
Petrol 4-stroke piston
1698cc 103.6cu in
In-line 4 1 Carburettor
Compression ratio: 7.1:1
Bore: 84.1mm 3.3in
Stroke: 76.7mm 3.0in
Valve type/No: Overhead 8
Transmission: Manual
No. of forward speeds: 3
Wheels driven: Rear
Wheelbase: 260.1cm 102.4in
Track F: 127.0cm 50.0in
Track R: 127.0cm 50.0in
Length: 436.9cm 172.0in
Width: 166.9cm 65.7in
Height: 150.1cm 59.1in
Kerb weight: 1001.1kg 2205.0lb

1660 Ford

Zephyr
1960 UK
91.0mph 146.4kmh
0-50mph 80.5kmh: 11.2secs
0-60mph 96.5kmh: 16.5secs
0-1/4 mile: 20.9secs
85.0bhp 63.4kW 86.2PS
@ 4400rpm
133.0lbft 180.2Nm @ 2000rpm
70.4bhp/ton 69.2bhp/tonne
33.3bhp/L 24.8kW/L 33.8PS/L
38.3ft/sec 11.7m/sec
26.4mph 42.5kmh/1000rpm
23.7mpg 19.7mpgUS 11.9L/100km
Petrol 4-stroke piston
2553cc 155.8cu in
In-line 6 1 Carburettor
Compression ratio: 7.8:1
Bore: 82.5mm 3.2in
Stroke: 79.5mm 3.1in

Valve type/No: Overhead 12
Transmission: Manual with overdrive
No. of forward speeds: 6
Wheels driven: Rear
Springs F/R: Coil/Leaf
Brake system: PA
Brakes F/R: Disc/Drum
Wheelbase: 271.8cm 107.0in
Track F: 134.6cm 53.0in
Track R: 132.1cm 52.0in
Length: 454.7cm 179.0in
Width: 174.8cm 68.8in
Height: 153.9cm 60.6in
Ground clearance: 17.3cm 6.8in
Kerb weight: 1228.1kg 2705.0lb
Fuel: 47.8L 10.5gal 12.6galUS

1661 Ford

Consul Capri
1961 UK
82.5mph 132.7kmh
0-50mph 80.5kmh: 14.0secs
0-60mph 96.5kmh: 21.3secs
0-1/4 mile: 21.7secs
54.0bhp 40.3kW 54.7PS
@ 4900rpm
74.0lbft 100.3Nm @ 2500rpm
58.9bhp/ton 57.9bhp/tonne
40.3bhp/L 30.0kW/L 40.9PS/L
34.8ft/sec 10.6m/sec
16.5mph 26.5kmh/1000rpm
27.9mpg 23.2mpgUS 10.1L/100km
Petrol 4-stroke piston
1340cc 81.8cu in
In-line 4 1 Carburettor
Compression ratio: 8.5:1
Bore: 81.0mm 3.2in
Stroke: 65.1mm 2.6in
Valve type/No: Overhead 8
Transmission: Manual
No. of forward speeds: 4
Wheels driven: Rear
Springs F/R: Coil/Leaf
Brakes F/R: Disc/Drum
Steering: Recirculating ball
Wheelbase: 251.5cm 99.0in
Track F: 125.7cm 49.5in
Track R: 125.7cm 49.5in
Length: 433.8cm 170.8in
Width: 165.6cm 65.2in
Height: 137.2cm 54.0in
Ground clearance: 15.2cm 6.0in
Kerb weight: 933.0kg 2055.0lb
Fuel: 40.9L 9.0gal 10.8galUS

1662 Ford

Econoline
1961 USA
75.0mph 120.7kmh
0-50mph 80.5kmh: 16.2secs
0-60mph 96.5kmh: 25.8secs
0-1/4 mile: 23.3secs
85.0bhp 63.4kW 86.2PS
@ 4200rpm
134.0lbft 181.6Nm @ 2000rpm
66.3bhp/ton 65.2bhp/tonne
35.9bhp/L 26.8kW/L 36.4PS/L
29.2ft/sec 8.9m/sec
18.2mph 29.3kmh/1000rpm
Petrol 4-stroke piston
2366cc 144.4cu in
In-line 6 1 Carburettor
Compression ratio: 8.7:1
Bore: 88.9mm 3.5in
Stroke: 63.5mm 2.5in
Valve type/No: Overhead 12
Transmission: Manual
No. of forward speeds: 3
Wheels driven: Rear
Brakes F/R: Drum/Drum
Wheelbase: 228.6cm 90.0in
Track F: 152.4cm 60.0in
Track R: 152.4cm 60.0in
Length: 427.7cm 168.4in
Width: 188.0cm 74.0in
Height: 199.4cm 78.5in
Ground clearance: 18.8cm 7.4in
Kerb weight: 1303.0kg 2870.0lb

1663 Ford

Galaxie
1961 USA
122.0mph 196.3kmh
0-50mph 80.5kmh: 7.2secs
0-60mph 96.5kmh: 9.5secs
0-1/4 mile: 17.0secs
300.0bhp 223.7kW 304.2PS
@ 4600rpm
427.0lbft 578.6Nm @ 2800rpm
169.7bhp/ton 166.9bhp/tonne
47.0bhp/L 35.0kW/L 47.6PS/L
48.3ft/sec 14.7m/sec
26.1mph 42.0kmh/1000rpm
Petrol 4-stroke piston
6386cc 389.6cu in
Vee 8 1 Carburettor
Compression ratio: 9.6:1
Bore: 102.9mm 4.0in
Stroke: 96.0mm 3.8in
Valve type/No: Overhead 16
Transmission: Automatic
No. of forward speeds: 3
Wheels driven: Rear
Wheelbase: 302.3cm 119.0in
Track F: 154.9cm 61.0in
Track R: 152.4cm 60.0in
Length: 533.4cm 210.0in
Width: 202.9cm 79.9in
Height: 139.7cm 55.0in
Ground clearance: 14.0cm 5.5in
Kerb weight: 1797.8kg 3960.0lb

1664 Ford

Taunus 17M
1961 Germany
87.0mph 140.0kmh
0-50mph 80.5kmh: 13.4secs
0-60mph 96.5kmh: 19.7secs
0-1/4 mile: 21.5secs
60.0bhp 44.7kW 60.8PS
@ 4500rpm
95.5lbft 129.4Nm @ 2200rpm
64.5bhp/ton 63.5bhp/tonne
35.3bhp/L 26.3kW/L 35.8PS/L
37.7ft/sec 11.5m/sec
20.0mph 32.2kmh/1000rpm
30.5mpg 25.4mpgUS 9.3L/100km
Petrol 4-stroke piston
1698cc 103.6cu in
In-line 4 1 Carburettor
Compression ratio: 7.1:1
Bore: 84.0mm 3.3in
Stroke: 76.7mm 3.0in
Valve type/No: Overhead 8
Transmission: Manual
No. of forward speeds: 4
Wheels driven: Rear
Springs F/R: Coil/Leaf
Brakes F/R: Drum/Drum
Wheelbase: 262.9cm 103.5in
Track F: 129.5cm 51.0in
Track R: 128.8cm 50.7in
Length: 445.0cm 175.2in
Width: 167.1cm 65.8in
Height: 144.8cm 57.0in
Ground clearance: 17.8cm 7.0in
Kerb weight: 945.2kg 2082.0lb
Fuel: 45.5L 10.0gal 12.0galUS

1665 Ford

Thunderbird
1961 USA
120.0mph 193.1kmh
0-50mph 80.5kmh: 7.0secs
0-60mph 96.5kmh: 9.3secs
0-1/4 mile: 16.8secs
300.0bhp 223.7kW 304.2PS
@ 4600rpm
427.0lbft 578.6Nm @ 2800rpm
159.9bhp/ton 157.2bhp/tonne
46.9bhp/L 35.0kW/L 47.6PS/L
48.3ft/sec 14.7m/sec
26.1mph 42.0kmh/1000rpm
13.7mpg 11.4mpgUS 20.6L/100km
Petrol 4-stroke piston
6392cc 390.0cu in
Vee 8 1 Carburettor
Compression ratio: 9.6:1
Bore: 109.2mm 4.3in
Stroke: 96.0mm 3.8in
Valve type/No: Overhead 16
Transmission: Automatic
No. of forward speeds: 3
Wheels driven: Rear
Springs F/R: Coil/Leaf
Brake system: PA
Brakes F/R: Drum/Drum
Steering: Recirculating ball
Wheelbase: 287.0cm 113.0in
Track F: 154.9cm 61.0in
Track R: 152.4cm 60.0in
Length: 520.7cm 205.0in
Width: 193.0cm 76.0in
Height: 133.4cm 52.5in
Ground clearance: 13.2cm 5.2in
Kerb weight: 1908.2kg 4203.0lb
Fuel: 72.8L 16.0gal 19.2galUS

1666 Ford

Anglia de Luxe Estate
1962 UK
73.0mph 117.5kmh
0-50mph 80.5kmh: 20.1secs
0-60mph 96.5kmh: 36.4secs
0-1/4 mile: 23.9secs
39.0bhp 29.1kW 39.5PS
@ 5000rpm
55.5lbft 75.2Nm @ 2700rpm
48.7bhp/ton 47.9bhp/tonne
39.2bhp/L 29.2kW/L 39.7PS/L
26.5ft/sec 8.1m/sec
15.3mph 24.6kmh/1000rpm
30.8mpg 25.6mpgUS 9.2L/100km
Petrol 4-stroke piston
996cc 60.8cu in
In-line 4 1 Carburettor
Compression ratio: 8.9:1
Bore: 81.0mm 3.2in
Stroke: 48.4mm 1.9in
Valve type/No: Overhead 8
Transmission: Manual
No. of forward speeds: 4
Wheels driven: Rear
Springs F/R: Coil/Leaf
Brakes F/R: Drum/Drum
Steering: Recirculating ball
Wheelbase: 229.9cm 90.5in
Track F: 116.8cm 46.0in
Track R: 116.3cm 45.8in
Length: 391.7cm 154.2in
Width: 145.5cm 57.3in
Height: 146.1cm 57.5in
Ground clearance: 16.3cm 6.4in
Kerb weight: 813.6kg 1792.0lb
Fuel: 31.8L 7.0gal 8.4galUS

1667 Ford

Anglia Super
1962 UK
84.0mph 135.2kmh
0-50mph 80.5kmh: 13.7secs
0-60mph 96.5kmh: 20.8secs
0-1/4 mile: 21.8secs
48.5bhp 36.2kW 49.2PS
@ 4800rpm
63.0lbft 85.4Nm @ 2700rpm
64.2bhp/ton 63.1bhp/tonne
40.5bhp/L 30.2kW/L 41.0PS/L
30.5ft/sec 9.3m/sec
16.0mph 25.7kmh/1000rpm
31.4mpg 26.1mpgUS 9.0L/100km
Petrol 4-stroke piston
1198cc 73.1cu in
In-line 4 1 Carburettor
Compression ratio: 8.7:1
Bore: 81.0mm 3.2in
Stroke: 58.2mm 2.3in
Valve type/No: Overhead 8
Transmission: Manual
No. of forward speeds: 4
Wheels driven: Rear
Springs F/R: Coil/Leaf
Brakes F/R: Drum/Drum
Steering: Recirculating ball
Wheelbase: 229.9cm 90.5in
Track F: 116.8cm 46.0in
Track R: 116.3cm 45.8in
Length: 389.9cm 153.5in
Width: 145.5cm 57.3in
Height: 146.1cm 57.5in
Ground clearance: 16.3cm 6.4in
Kerb weight: 768.2kg 1692.0lb
Fuel: 31.8L 7.0gal 8.4galUS

1668 Ford

Consul Capri
1962 UK
82.0mph 131.9kmh
0-50mph 80.5kmh: 13.7secs
0-60mph 96.5kmh: 20.8secs
0-1/4 mile: 21.5secs
57.0bhp 42.5kW 57.8PS
@ 5000rpm
74.0lbft 100.3Nm @ 2500rpm
62.0bhp/ton 60.9bhp/tonne
42.5bhp/L 31.7kW/L 43.1PS/L
35.6ft/sec 10.8m/sec
16.2mph 26.1kmh/1000rpm
Petrol 4-stroke piston
1340cc 81.8cu in
In-line 4
Compression ratio: 8.5:1
Bore: 81.0mm 3.2in
Stroke: 65.0mm 2.6in
Valve type/No: Overhead 8
Transmission: Manual
No. of forward speeds: 4
Wheels driven: Rear
Wheelbase: 251.5cm 99.0in
Track F: 125.7cm 49.5in
Track R: 125.7cm 49.5in
Length: 433.8cm 170.8in
Width: 165.6cm 65.2in
Height: 137.2cm 54.0in
Ground clearance: 15.2cm 6.0in
Kerb weight: 935.2kg 2060.0lb

1669 Ford

Consul Cortina
1962 UK
77.0mph 123.9kmh
0-50mph 80.5kmh: 14.8secs
0-60mph 96.5kmh: 22.5secs
0-1/4 mile: 22.4secs
48.5bhp 36.2kW 49.2PS
@ 4800rpm
63.0lbft 85.4Nm @ 2700rpm
60.6bhp/ton 59.6bhp/tonne
40.5bhp/L 30.2kW/L 41.0PS/L
30.5ft/sec 9.3m/sec
16.1mph 25.9kmh/1000rpm
30.2mpg 25.1mpgUS 9.4L/100km
Petrol 4-stroke piston
1198cc 73.1cu in
In-line 4 1 Carburettor
Compression ratio: 8.7:1
Bore: 81.0mm 3.2in
Stroke: 58.2mm 2.3in
Valve type/No: Overhead 8
Transmission: Manual
No. of forward speeds: 4
Wheels driven: Rear
Springs F/R: Coil/Leaf
Brakes F/R: Drum/Drum
Steering: Recirculating ball
Wheelbase: 248.9cm 98.0in
Track F: 125.7cm 49.5in
Track R: 125.7cm 49.5in
Length: 433.1cm 170.5in
Width: 160.0cm 63.0in
Height: 144.8cm 57.0in
Ground clearance: 16.5cm 6.5in
Kerb weight: 813.6kg 1792.0lb
Fuel: 36.4L 8.0gal 9.6galUS

1670 Ford

Country Sedan
1962 USA
90.0mph 144.8kmh
0-50mph 80.5kmh: 10.8secs
0-60mph 96.5kmh: 14.3secs
0-1/4 mile: 19.6secs
170.0bhp 126.8kW 172.4PS
@ 4200rpm
279.0lbft 378.0Nm @ 2200rpm
90.3bhp/ton 88.8bhp/tonne
35.5bhp/L 26.5kW/L 36.0PS/L
38.5ft/sec 11.7m/sec
25.8mph 41.5kmh/1000rpm
Petrol 4-stroke piston
4785cc 291.9cu in
Vee 8 1 Carburettor
Compression ratio: 8.8:1
Bore: 95.3mm 3.8in
Stroke: 83.8mm 3.3in
Valve type/No: Overhead 16
Transmission: Automatic
No. of forward speeds: 2
Wheels driven: Rear
Brake system: PA
Steering: PA
Wheelbase: 302.3cm 119.0in
Track F: 154.9cm 61.0in
Track R: 152.4cm 60.0in
Length: 531.6cm 209.3in
Width: 201.2cm 79.2in
Height: 144.3cm 56.8in
Ground clearance: 14.2cm 5.6in
Kerb weight: 1913.6kg 4215.0lb
Fuel: 75.7L 16.6gal 20.0galUS

1671 Ford

Fairlane 500
1962 USA
94.0mph 151.2kmh
0-50mph 80.5kmh: 9.8secs
0-60mph 96.5kmh: 14.8secs

0-1/4 mile: 19.9secs
145.0bhp 108.1kW 147.0PS
@ 4400rpm
216.0lbft 292.7Nm @ 2200rpm
103.6bhp/ton 101.8bhp/tonne
40.0bhp/L 29.8kW/L 40.6PS/L
35.1ft/sec 10.7m/sec
22.2mph 35.7kmh/1000rpm
15.7mpg 13.1mpgUS 18.0L/100km
Petrol 4-stroke piston
3622cc 221.0cu in
Vee 8 1 Carburettor
Compression ratio: 8.7:1
Bore: 88.9mm 3.5in
Stroke: 72.8mm 2.9in
Valve type/No: Overhead 16
Transmission: Automatic
No. of forward speeds: 2
Wheels driven: Rear
Springs F/R: Coil/Leaf
Brake system: PA
Brakes F/R: Drum/Drum
Steering: Recirculating ball
Wheelbase: 293.4cm 115.5in
Track F: 144.8cm 57.0in
Track R: 142.2cm 56.0in
Length: 500.4cm 197.0in
Width: 181.1cm 71.3in
Height: 146.1cm 57.5in
Ground clearance: 22.9cm 9.0in
Kerb weight: 1423.7kg 3136.0lb
Fuel: 60.1L 13.2gal 15.9galUS

1672 Ford

Fairlane 500 Sports Coupe
1962 USA
103.0mph 165.7kmh
0-50mph 80.5kmh: 8.9secs
0-60mph 96.5kmh: 12.1secs
0-1/4 mile: 18.9secs
164.0bhp 122.3kW 166.3PS
@ 4400rpm
258.0lbft 349.6Nm @ 2200rpm
116.6bhp/ton 114.7bhp/tonne
38.5bhp/L 28.7kW/L 39.0PS/L
35.1ft/sec 10.7m/sec
22.1mph 35.6kmh/1000rpm
Petrol 4-stroke piston
4261cc 260.0cu in
Vee 8 1 Carburettor
Compression ratio: 8.7:1
Bore: 96.5mm 3.8in
Stroke: 72.9mm 2.9in
Valve type/No: Overhead 16
Transmission: Automatic
No. of forward speeds: 2
Wheels driven: Rear
Brake system: PA
Steering: PA
Wheelbase: 293.4cm 115.5in
Track F: 144.8cm 57.0in
Track R: 142.2cm 56.0in
Length: 501.9cm 197.6in
Width: 190.5cm 75.0in
Height: 141.0cm 55.5in
Ground clearance: 14.5cm 5.7in
Kerb weight: 1430.1kg 3150.0lb
Fuel: 60.6L 13.3gal 16.0galUS

1673 Ford

Fairlane V8
1962 USA
94.0mph 151.2kmh
0-50mph 80.5kmh: 11.1secs
0-60mph 96.5kmh: 15.5secs
0-1/4 mile: 20.3secs
143.0bhp 106.6kW 145.0PS
@ 4600rpm
217.0lbft 294.0Nm @ 2200rpm
112.0bhp/ton 110.1bhp/tonne
39.5bhp/L 29.4kW/L 40.0PS/L
36.7ft/sec 11.2m/sec
23.5mph 37.8kmh/1000rpm
Petrol 4-stroke piston
3621cc 220.9cu in
Vee 8 1 Carburettor
Compression ratio: 8.5:1
Bore: 88.9mm 3.5in
Stroke: 72.9mm 2.9in
Valve type/No: Overhead 16
Transmission: Automatic
No. of forward speeds: 2
Wheels driven: Rear
Brake system: PA
Brakes F/R: Drum/Drum
Wheelbase: 293.4cm 115.5in
Track F: 144.8cm 57.0in
Track R: 142.2cm 56.0in
Length: 500.4cm 197.0in
Width: 181.1cm 71.3in
Height: 141.0cm 55.5in
Ground clearance: 14.5cm 5.7in
Kerb weight: 1298.4kg 2860.0lb

1674 Ford

Falcon 144 Automatic
1962 USA
76.4mph 122.9kmh
0-60mph 96.5kmh: 24.5secs
0-1/4 mile: 22.7secs
85.0bhp 63.4kW 86.2PS
75.4bhp/ton 74.1bhp/tonne
36.0bhp/L 26.9kW/L 36.5PS/L
22.0mph 35.4kmh/1000rpm
Petrol 4-stroke piston
2360cc 144.0cu in
In-line 6
Valve type/No: Overhead 12
Transmission: Automatic
No. of forward speeds: 2
Wheels driven: Rear
Wheelbase: 278.1cm 109.5in
Track F: 139.7cm 55.0in
Track R: 138.4cm 54.5in
Length: 460.0cm 181.1in
Width: 179.3cm 70.6in
Height: 138.4cm 54.5in
Ground clearance: 15.0cm 5.9in
Kerb weight: 1146.3kg 2525.0lb

1675 Ford

Falcon 144 Manual
1962 USA
82.0mph 131.9kmh
0-50mph 80.5kmh: 12.5secs
0-60mph 96.5kmh: 19.0secs
0-1/4 mile: 21.0secs
85.0bhp 63.4kW 86.2PS
75.4bhp/ton 74.1bhp/tonne
36.0bhp/L 26.9kW/L 36.5PS/L
22.0mph 35.4kmh/1000rpm
Petrol 4-stroke piston
2360cc 144.0cu in
In-line 6
Valve type/No: Overhead 12
Transmission: Manual
No. of forward speeds: 3
Wheels driven: Rear
Wheelbase: 278.1cm 109.5in
Track F: 139.7cm 55.0in
Track R: 138.4cm 54.5in
Length: 460.0cm 181.1in
Width: 179.3cm 70.6in
Height: 138.4cm 54.5in
Ground clearance: 15.0cm 5.9in
Kerb weight: 1146.3kg 2525.0lb

1676 Ford

Falcon 170 Automatic
1962 USA
84.0mph 135.2kmh
0-50mph 80.5kmh: 12.8secs
0-60mph 96.5kmh: 17.7secs
0-1/4 mile: 20.6secs
101.0bhp 75.3kW 102.4PS
@ 4400rpm
156.0lbft 211.4Nm @ 2400rpm
89.6bhp/ton 88.1bhp/tonne
36.2bhp/L 27.0kW/L 36.7PS/L
35.9ft/sec 11.0m/sec
22.0mph 35.4kmh/1000rpm
Petrol 4-stroke piston
2788cc 170.1cu in
In-line 6
Compression ratio: 8.7:1
Bore: 86.4mm 3.4in
Stroke: 74.7mm 2.9in
Valve type/No: Overhead 12
Transmission: Automatic
No. of forward speeds: 2
Wheels driven: Rear
Wheelbase: 278.1cm 109.5in
Track F: 139.7cm 55.0in
Track R: 138.4cm 54.5in
Length: 460.0cm 181.1in
Width: 179.3cm 70.6in
Height: 138.4cm 54.5in
Ground clearance: 15.0cm 5.9in
Kerb weight: 1146.3kg 2525.0lb

1677 Ford

Falcon 170 Manual
1962 USA
90.0mph 144.8kmh
0-60mph 96.5kmh: 17.5secs
0-1/4 mile: 20.4secs
101.0bhp 75.3kW 102.4PS
@ 4400rpm
156.0lbft 211.4Nm @ 2400rpm
89.6bhp/ton 88.1bhp/tonne
36.2bhp/L 27.0kW/L 36.8PS/L
35.9ft/sec 11.0m/sec
22.0mph 35.4kmh/1000rpm
Petrol 4-stroke piston
2786cc 170.0cu in
In-line 6
Compression ratio: 8.7:1
Bore: 86.4mm 3.4in
Stroke: 74.7mm 2.9in
Valve type/No: Overhead 12
Transmission: Manual
No. of forward speeds: 3
Wheels driven: Rear
Wheelbase: 278.1cm 109.5in
Track F: 139.7cm 55.0in
Track R: 138.4cm 54.5in
Length: 460.0cm 181.1in
Width: 179.3cm 70.6in
Height: 138.4cm 54.5in
Ground clearance: 15.0cm 5.9in
Kerb weight: 1146.3kg 2525.0lb

1678 Ford

Galaxie
1962 USA
115.0mph 185.0kmh
0-50mph 80.5kmh: 7.9secs
0-60mph 96.5kmh: 10.5secs
0-1/4 mile: 17.8secs
300.0bhp 223.7kW 304.2PS
@ 4600rpm
427.0lbft 578.6Nm @ 2800rpm
169.1bhp/ton 166.2bhp/tonne
47.0bhp/L 35.0kW/L 47.6PS/L
48.3ft/sec 14.7m/sec
25.4mph 40.9kmh/1000rpm
Petrol 4-stroke piston
6386cc 389.6cu in
Vee 8
Compression ratio: 9.6:1
Bore: 102.9mm 4.0in
Stroke: 96.0mm 3.8in
Valve type/No: Overhead 16
Transmission: Automatic
No. of forward speeds: 3
Wheels driven: Rear
Brake system: PA
Steering: PA
Wheelbase: 302.3cm 119.0in
Track F: 154.9cm 61.0in
Track R: 152.4cm 60.0in
Length: 518.7cm 204.2in
Width: 201.2cm 79.2in
Height: 139.2cm 54.8in
Ground clearance: 14.0cm 5.5in
Kerb weight: 1804.6kg 3975.0lb

1679 Ford

Galaxie 406
1962 USA
130.0mph 209.2kmh
0-50mph 80.5kmh: 5.4secs
0-60mph 96.5kmh: 7.0secs
0-1/4 mile: 15.3secs
405.0bhp 302.0kW 410.6PS
@ 5800rpm
448.0lbft 607.0Nm @ 3500rpm
233.8bhp/ton 229.9bhp/tonne
60.9bhp/L 45.4kW/L 61.7PS/L
60.9ft/sec 18.6m/sec
22.8mph 36.7kmh/1000rpm
Petrol 4-stroke piston
6653cc 405.9cu in
Vee 8
Compression ratio: 10.9:1
Bore: 104.9mm 4.1in
Stroke: 96.0mm 3.8in
Valve type/No: Overhead 16
Transmission: Manual
No. of forward speeds: 4
Wheels driven: Rear
Wheelbase: 302.3cm 119.0in
Track F: 154.9cm 61.0in
Track R: 152.4cm 60.0in
Length: 530.9cm 209.0in
Width: 202.9cm 79.9in
Height: 139.2cm 54.8in
Ground clearance: 14.0cm 5.5in
Kerb weight: 1761.5kg 3880.0lb
Fuel: 75.7L 16.6gal 20.0galUS

1680 Ford

Thunderbird Sports Roadster
1962 USA
119.0mph 191.5kmh
0-50mph 80.5kmh: 8.3secs
0-60mph 96.5kmh: 12.4secs
0-1/4 mile: 18.7secs
300.0bhp 223.7kW 304.2PS
@ 4600rpm
427.0lbft 578.6Nm @ 2800rpm
143.3bhp/ton 140.9bhp/tonne
46.9bhp/L 35.0kW/L 47.6PS/L
48.3ft/sec 14.7m/sec
25.8mph 41.5kmh/1000rpm
Petrol 4-stroke piston
6391cc 389.9cu in
Vee 8 1 Carburettor
Compression ratio: 9.6:1
Bore: 102.9mm 4.0in
Stroke: 96.0mm 3.8in
Valve type/No: Overhead 16
Transmission: Automatic
No. of forward speeds: 3
Wheels driven: Rear
Brake system: PA
Steering: PA
Wheelbase: 287.0cm 113.0in
Track F: 154.9cm 61.0in
Track R: 152.4cm 60.0in
Length: 520.7cm 205.0in
Width: 192.8cm 75.9in
Height: 135.4cm 53.3in
Ground clearance: 13.2cm 5.2in
Kerb weight: 2129.3kg 4690.0lb
Fuel: 75.7L 16.6gal 20.0galUS

1681 Ford

Zephyr 4
1962 UK
84.5mph 136.0kmh
0-50mph 80.5kmh: 13.4secs
0-60mph 96.5kmh: 19.6secs
0-1/4 mile: 21.4secs
68.0bhp 50.7kW 68.9PS
@ 4800rpm
93.5lbft 126.7Nm @ 3000rpm
59.8bhp/ton 58.8bhp/tonne
39.9bhp/L 29.8kW/L 40.5PS/L
41.7ft/sec 12.7m/sec
18.4mph 29.6kmh/1000rpm
23.8mpg 19.8mpgUS 11.9L/100km
Petrol 4-stroke piston
1703cc 103.9cu in
In-line 4 1 Carburettor
Compression ratio: 8.3:1
Bore: 82.5mm 3.2in
Stroke: 79.5mm 3.1in
Valve type/No: Overhead 8
Transmission: Manual
No. of forward speeds: 4
Wheels driven: Rear
Springs F/R: Coil/Leaf
Brake system: PA
Brakes F/R: Disc/Drum
Steering: Recirculating ball
Wheelbase: 271.8cm 107.0in
Track F: 134.6cm 53.0in
Track R: 132.1cm 52.0in
Length: 457.2cm 180.0in
Width: 175.3cm 69.0in
Height: 146.1cm 57.5in
Ground clearance: 17.3cm 6.8in
Kerb weight: 1156.3kg 2547.0lb
Fuel: 54.6L 12.0gal 14.4galUS

1682 Ford

Zephyr 4 Automatic
1962 UK
77.0mph 123.9kmh
0-50mph 80.5kmh: 15.3secs
0-60mph 96.5kmh: 23.3secs
0-1/4 mile: 22.9secs
68.0bhp 50.7kW 68.9PS
@ 4800rpm
93.5lbft 126.7Nm @ 3000rpm
59.8bhp/ton 58.8bhp/tonne
39.9bhp/L 29.8kW/L 40.5PS/L
41.7ft/sec 12.7m/sec
20.3mph 32.7kmh/1000rpm
23.1mpg 19.2mpgUS 12.2L/100km
Petrol 4-stroke piston
1703cc 103.9cu in

In-line 4 1 Carburettor
Compression ratio: 8.3:1
Bore: 82.5mm 3.2in
Stroke: 79.5mm 3.1in
Valve type/No: Overhead 8
Transmission: Automatic
No. of forward speeds: 3
Wheels driven: Rear
Springs F/R: Coil/Leaf
Brake system: PA
Brakes F/R: Disc/Drum
Steering: Recirculating ball
Wheelbase: 271.8cm 107.0in
Track F: 134.6cm 53.0in
Track R: 132.1cm 52.0in
Length: 457.2cm 180.0in
Width: 175.3cm 69.0in
Height: 146.1cm 57.5in
Ground clearance: 17.3cm 6.8in
Kerb weight: 1156.3kg 2547.0lb
Fuel: 54.6L 12.0gal 14.4galUS

1683 Ford

Zodiac Mk III
1962 UK
103.5mph 166.5kmh
0-50mph 80.5kmh: 10.0secs
0-60mph 96.5kmh: 13.5secs
0-1/4 mile: 19.2secs
109.0bhp 81.3kW 110.5PS
@ 4800rpm
137.0lbft 185.6Nm @ 2400rpm
86.8bhp/ton 85.3bhp/tonne
42.7bhp/L 31.8kW/L 43.3PS/L
41.7ft/sec 12.7m/sec
20.3mph 32.7kmh/1000rpm
19.1mpg 15.9mpgUS 14.8L/100km
Petrol 4-stroke piston
2553cc 155.8cu in
In-line 6 1 Carburettor
Compression ratio: 8.5:1
Bore: 82.6mm 3.2in
Stroke: 79.5mm 3.1in
Valve type/No: Overhead 12
Transmission: Manual
No. of forward speeds: 4
Wheels driven: Rear
Springs F/R: Coil/Leaf
Brake system: PA
Brakes F/R: Disc/Drum
Steering: Recirculating ball
Wheelbase: 271.8cm 107.0in
Track F: 134.6cm 53.0in
Track R: 132.1cm 52.0in
Length: 460.2cm 181.2in
Width: 175.3cm 69.0in
Height: 146.1cm 57.5in
Ground clearance: 17.3cm 6.8in
Kerb weight: 1277.6kg 2814.0lb
Fuel: 54.6L 12.0gal 14.4galUS

1684 Ford

Capri GT
1963 UK
97.0mph 156.1kmh
0-50mph 80.5kmh: 9.1secs
0-60mph 96.5kmh: 13.7secs
0-1/4 mile: 19.1secs
78.0bhp 58.2kW 79.1PS
@ 6200rpm
91.0lbft 123.3Nm @ 3600rpm
80.8bhp/ton 79.4bhp/tonne
52.1bhp/L 38.8kW/L 52.8PS/L
49.4ft/sec 15.1m/sec
16.5mph 26.5kmh/1000rpm
26.7mpg 22.2mpgUS 10.6L/100km
Petrol 4-stroke piston
1498cc 91.4cu in
In-line 4 1 Carburettor
Compression ratio: 9.0:1
Bore: 81.0mm 3.2in
Stroke: 73.0mm 2.9in
Valve type/No: Overhead 8
Transmission: Manual
No. of forward speeds: 4
Wheels driven: Rear
Springs F/R: Coil/Leaf
Brake system: PA
Brakes F/R: Disc/Drum
Steering: Recirculating ball
Wheelbase: 251.5cm 99.0in
Track F: 125.7cm 49.5in
Track R: 125.7cm 49.5in
Length: 432.3cm 170.2in
Width: 165.6cm 65.2in
Height: 138.4cm 54.5in
Ground clearance: 16.5cm 6.5in
Kerb weight: 982.0kg 2163.0lb
Fuel: 40.9L 9.0gal 10.8galUS

1685 Ford

Consul Corsair GT
1963 UK
96.0mph 154.5kmh
0-50mph 80.5kmh: 10.0secs
0-60mph 96.5kmh: 14.3secs
0-1/4 mile: 19.5secs
78.0bhp 58.2kW 79.1PS
@ 5200rpm
91.0lbft 123.3Nm @ 3600rpm
85.9bhp/ton 84.5bhp/tonne
52.1bhp/L 38.8kW/L 52.8PS/L
41.3ft/sec 12.6m/sec
17.4mph 28.0kmh/1000rpm
25.9mpg 21.6mpgUS 10.9L/100km
Petrol 4-stroke piston
1498cc 91.4cu in
In-line 4 1 Carburettor
Compression ratio: 9.0:1
Bore: 81.0mm 3.2in
Stroke: 72.7mm 2.9in
Valve type/No: Overhead 8
Transmission: Manual
No. of forward speeds: 4
Wheels driven: Rear
Springs F/R: Coil/Leaf
Brake system: PA
Brakes F/R: Disc/Drum
Steering: Recirculating ball
Wheelbase: 256.5cm 101.0in
Track F: 127.0cm 50.0in
Track R: 125.7cm 49.5in
Length: 448.3cm 176.5in
Width: 161.3cm 63.5in
Height: 145.3cm 57.2in
Ground clearance: 17.0cm 6.7in
Kerb weight: 923.0kg 2033.0lb
Fuel: 36.4L 8.0gal 9.6galUS

1686 Ford

Consul Cortina
1963 UK
75.0mph 120.7kmh
0-50mph 80.5kmh: 15.3secs
0-60mph 96.5kmh: 24.4secs
0-1/4 mile: 22.5secs
53.0bhp 39.5kW 53.7PS
@ 4800rpm
66.0lbft 89.4Nm @ 2700rpm
66.9bhp/ton 65.8bhp/tonne
44.2bhp/L 33.0kW/L 44.9PS/L
30.5ft/sec 9.3m/sec
15.7mph 25.3kmh/1000rpm
Petrol 4-stroke piston
1198cc 73.1cu in
In-line 4 1 Carburettor
Compression ratio: 8.7:1
Bore: 81.0mm 3.2in
Stroke: 58.2mm 2.3in
Valve type/No: Overhead 8
Transmission: Manual
No. of forward speeds: 4
Wheels driven: Rear
Wheelbase: 249.4cm 98.2in
Track F: 125.7cm 49.5in
Track R: 125.7cm 49.5in
Length: 427.5cm 168.3in
Width: 158.8cm 62.5in
Height: 143.8cm 56.6in
Ground clearance: 14.0cm 5.5in
Kerb weight: 805.8kg 1775.0lb

1687 Ford

Consul Cortina 1500
1963 UK
81.0mph 130.3kmh
0-50mph 80.5kmh: 12.5secs
0-60mph 96.5kmh: 19.0secs
0-1/4 mile: 21.0secs
64.0bhp 47.7kW 64.9PS
@ 4600rpm
85.0lbft 115.2Nm @ 2300rpm
77.9bhp/ton 76.6bhp/tonne
42.7bhp/L 31.9kW/L 43.3PS/L
36.5ft/sec 11.1m/sec
17.4mph 28.0kmh/1000rpm
Petrol 4-stroke piston
1498cc 91.4cu in
In-line 4 1 Carburettor
Compression ratio: 8.3:1
Bore: 81.0mm 3.2in
Stroke: 72.6mm 2.9in
Valve type/No: Overhead 8
Transmission: Manual
No. of forward speeds: 4
Wheels driven: Rear
Wheelbase: 249.4cm 98.2in
Track F: 125.7cm 49.5in
Track R: 125.7cm 49.5in
Length: 427.5cm 168.3in
Width: 158.8cm 62.5in
Height: 143.8cm 56.6in
Ground clearance: 14.0cm 5.5in
Kerb weight: 835.4kg 1840.0lb
Fuel: 37.8L 8.3gal 10.0galUS

1688 Ford

Cortina Estate de Luxe
1963 UK
78.5mph 126.3kmh
0-50mph 80.5kmh: 16.1secs
0-60mph 96.5kmh: 25.5secs
0-1/4 mile: 23.3secs
48.5bhp 36.2kW 49.2PS
@ 4800rpm
63.0lbft 85.4Nm @ 2700rpm
54.6bhp/ton 53.7bhp/tonne
40.5bhp/L 30.2kW/L 41.0PS/L
30.5ft/sec 9.3m/sec
16.1mph 25.9kmh/1000rpm
29.5mpg 24.6mpgUS 9.6L/100km
Petrol 4-stroke piston
1198cc 73.1cu in
In-line 4 1 Carburettor
Compression ratio: 8.7:1
Bore: 81.0mm 3.2in
Stroke: 58.2mm 2.3in
Valve type/No: Overhead 8
Transmission: Manual
No. of forward speeds: 4
Wheels driven: Rear
Springs F/R: Coil/Leaf
Brakes F/R: Drum/Drum
Steering: Recirculating ball
Wheelbase: 248.9cm 98.0in
Track F: 125.7cm 49.5in
Track R: 125.7cm 49.5in
Length: 433.1cm 170.5in
Width: 160.0cm 63.0in
Height: 144.8cm 57.0in
Ground clearance: 16.5cm 6.5in
Kerb weight: 902.5kg 1988.0lb
Fuel: 36.4L 8.0gal 9.6galUS

1689 Ford

Cortina Lotus
1963 UK
107.5mph 173.0kmh
0-50mph 80.5kmh: 7.3secs
0-60mph 96.5kmh: 9.9secs
0-1/4 mile: 17.4secs
105.0bhp 78.3kW 106.5PS
@ 5500rpm
108.0lbft 146.3Nm @ 4000rpm
129.2bhp/ton 127.1bhp/tonne
67.4bhp/L 50.3kW/L 68.3PS/L
43.7ft/sec 13.3m/sec
17.4mph 28.0kmh/1000rpm
20.8mpg 17.3mpgUS 13.6L/100km
Petrol 4-stroke piston
1558cc 95.1cu in
In-line 4 2 Carburettor
Compression ratio: 9.5:1
Bore: 82.5mm 3.2in
Stroke: 72.7mm 2.9in
Valve type/No: Overhead 8
Transmission: Manual
No. of forward speeds: 4
Wheels driven: Rear
Springs F/R: Coil/Coil
Brake system: PA
Brakes F/R: Disc/Drum
Steering: Recirculating ball
Wheelbase: 250.2cm 98.5in
Track F: 130.8cm 51.5in
Track R: 128.3cm 50.5in
Length: 421.6cm 166.0in
Width: 158.8cm 62.5in
Height: 139.7cm 55.0in
Ground clearance: 13.5cm 5.3in
Kerb weight: 826.3kg 1820.0lb
Fuel: 36.4L 8.0gal 9.6galUS

1690 Ford

Cortina Super
1963 UK
82.0mph 131.9kmh
0-50mph 80.5kmh: 12.8secs
0-60mph 96.5kmh: 19.0secs
0-1/4 mile: 20.8secs
59.5bhp 44.4kW 60.3PS
@ 4600rpm
81.5lbft 110.4Nm @ 2300rpm
72.4bhp/ton 71.1bhp/tonne
39.7bhp/L 29.6kW/L 40.3PS/L
36.7ft/sec 11.2m/sec
17.4mph 28.0kmh/1000rpm
27.2mpg 22.6mpgUS 10.4L/100km
Petrol 4-stroke piston
1498cc 91.4cu in
In-line 4 1 Carburettor
Compression ratio: 8.3:1
Bore: 81.0mm 3.2in
Stroke: 72.8mm 2.9in
Valve type/No: Overhead 8
Transmission: Manual
No. of forward speeds: 4
Wheels driven: Rear
Springs F/R: Coil/Leaf
Brakes F/R: Drum/Drum
Steering: Recirculating ball
Wheelbase: 248.9cm 98.0in
Track F: 125.7cm 49.5in
Track R: 125.7cm 49.5in
Length: 433.1cm 170.5in
Width: 160.0cm 63.0in
Height: 144.8cm 57.0in
Ground clearance: 16.5cm 6.5in
Kerb weight: 836.3kg 1842.0lb
Fuel: 36.4L 8.0gal 9.6galUS

1691 Ford

Econoline
1963 USA
85.0bhp 63.4kW 86.2PS
@ 4200rpm
134.0lbft 181.6Nm @ 2000rpm
66.3bhp/ton 65.2bhp/tonne
35.9bhp/L 26.8kW/L 36.4PS/L
29.2ft/sec 8.9m/sec
Petrol 4-stroke piston
2365cc 144.3cu in
In-line 6
Compression ratio: 8.7:1
Bore: 88.9mm 3.5in
Stroke: 63.5mm 2.5in
Valve type/No: Overhead 12
Transmission: Manual
No. of forward speeds: 3
Wheels driven: Rear
Wheelbase: 228.6cm 90.0in
Track F: 152.4cm 60.0in
Track R: 152.4cm 60.0in
Length: 427.7cm 168.4in
Width: 188.0cm 74.0in
Height: 199.4cm 78.5in
Ground clearance: 18.8cm 7.4in
Kerb weight: 1303.0kg 2870.0lb

1692 Ford

F-100 Styleside Pickup
1963 USA
85.0mph 136.8kmh
0-50mph 80.5kmh: 10.3secs
0-60mph 96.5kmh: 15.0secs
0-1/4 mile: 20.1secs
160.0bhp 119.3kW 162.2PS
@ 4000rpm
270.0lbft 365.9Nm @ 2000rpm
101.7bhp/ton 100.0bhp/tonne
33.4bhp/L 24.9kW/L 33.9PS/L
36.7ft/sec 11.2m/sec
21.9mph 35.2kmh/1000rpm
Petrol 4-stroke piston
4785cc 291.9cu in
Vee 8 1 Carburettor
Compression ratio: 8.0:1
Bore: 95.3mm 3.8in
Stroke: 83.8mm 3.3in
Valve type/No: Overhead 16
Transmission: Manual
No. of forward speeds: 4
Wheels driven: Rear
Wheelbase: 309.9cm 122.0in
Track F: 152.4cm 60.0in
Track R: 152.4cm 60.0in
Length: 511.8cm 201.5in
Width: 202.7cm 79.8in
Height: 193.8cm 76.3in
Ground clearance: 19.8cm 7.8in
Kerb weight: 1600.3kg 3525.0lb

1693 Ford

Fairlane Squire Wagon
1963 USA

90.0mph 144.8kmh
0-50mph 80.5kmh: 11.5secs
0-60mph 96.5kmh: 16.4secs
0-1/4 mile: 20.7secs
164.0bhp 122.3kW 166.3PS
@ 4400rpm
258.0lbft 349.6Nm @ 2200rpm
106.5bhp/ton 104.7bhp/tonne
38.5bhp/L 28.7kW/L 39.0PS/L
35.1ft/sec 10.7m/sec
23.1mph 37.2kmh/1000rpm
Petrol 4-stroke piston
4261cc 260.0cu in
Vee 8 1 Carburettor
Compression ratio: 8.7:1
Bore: 96.5mm 3.8in
Stroke: 72.9mm 2.9in
Valve type/No: Overhead 16
Transmission: Automatic
No. of forward speeds: 2
Wheels driven: Rear
Brake system: PA
Brakes F/R: Drum/Drum
Steering: PA
Wheelbase: 293.4cm 115.5in
Track F: 144.8cm 57.0in
Track R: 142.2cm 56.0in
Length: 512.6cm 201.8in
Width: 181.1cm 71.3in
Height: 143.8cm 56.6in
Ground clearance: 14.5cm 5.7in
Kerb weight: 1566.3kg 3450.0lb
Fuel: 60.6L 13.3gal 16.0galUS

1694 Ford

Falcon Futura
1963 USA
82.0mph 131.9kmh
0-50mph 80.5kmh: 15.6secs
0-60mph 96.5kmh: 21.6secs
0-1/4 mile: 22.2secs
101.0bhp 75.3kW 102.4PS
@ 4400rpm
156.0lbft 211.4Nm @ 2400rpm
80.1bhp/ton 78.7bhp/tonne
36.2bhp/L 27.0kW/L 36.8PS/L
35.9ft/sec 11.0m/sec
22.0mph 35.4kmh/1000rpm
Petrol 4-stroke piston
2786cc 170.0cu in
In-line 6 1 Carburettor
Compression ratio: 8.7:1
Bore: 88.9mm 3.5in
Stroke: 74.7mm 2.9in
Valve type/No: Overhead 12
Transmission: Automatic
No. of forward speeds: 2
Wheels driven: Rear
Wheelbase: 278.1cm 109.5in
Track F: 139.7cm 55.0in
Track R: 138.4cm 54.5in
Length: 460.0cm 181.1in
Width: 179.3cm 70.6in
Height: 136.9cm 53.9in
Ground clearance: 15.0cm 5.9in
Kerb weight: 1282.5kg 2825.0lb
Fuel: 53.0L 11.6gal 14.0galUS

1695 Ford

Falcon Futura V8
1963 USA
123.0mph 197.9kmh
0-50mph 80.5kmh: 7.2secs
0-60mph 96.5kmh: 9.3secs
0-1/4 mile: 16.6secs
260.0bhp 193.9kW 263.6PS
@ 5800rpm
269.0lbft 364.5Nm @ 4500rpm
213.5bhp/ton 209.9bhp/tonne
61.0bhp/L 45.5kW/L 61.9PS/L
46.2ft/sec 14.1m/sec
20.5mph 33.0kmh/1000rpm
Petrol 4-stroke piston
4261cc 260.0cu in
Vee 8 1 Carburettor
Compression ratio: 9.2:1
Bore: 96.5mm 3.8in
Stroke: 72.9mm 2.9in
Valve type/No: Overhead 16
Transmission: Manual
No. of forward speeds: 4
Wheels driven: Rear
Brakes F/R: Drum/Drum
Wheelbase: 278.1cm 109.5in
Track F: 139.7cm 55.0in
Track R: 137.2cm 54.0in
Length: 460.0cm 181.1in
Width: 179.3cm 70.6in
Height: 138.4cm 54.5in
Ground clearance: 15.0cm 5.9in
Kerb weight: 1238.5kg 2728.0lb
Fuel: 53.0L 11.6gal 14.0galUS

1696 Ford

Falcon Sprint Convertible
1963 USA
107.0mph 172.2kmh
0-50mph 80.5kmh: 7.9secs
0-60mph 96.5kmh: 11.2secs
0-1/4 mile: 17.8secs
164.0bhp 122.3kW 166.3PS
@ 4400rpm
258.0lbft 349.6Nm @ 2200rpm
120.1bhp/ton 118.1bhp/tonne
38.5bhp/L 28.7kW/L 39.0PS/L
35.1ft/sec 10.7m/sec
22.8mph 36.7kmh/1000rpm
16.1mpg 13.4mpgUS 17.5L/100km
Petrol 4-stroke piston
4261cc 260.0cu in
Vee 8 1 Carburettor
Compression ratio: 8.8:1
Bore: 96.0mm 3.8in
Stroke: 73.0mm 2.9in
Valve type/No: Overhead 16
Transmission: Manual
No. of forward speeds: 4
Wheels driven: Rear
Springs F/R: Coil/Leaf
Brake system: PA
Brakes F/R: Drum/Drum
Steering: Recirculating ball
Wheelbase: 278.1cm 109.5in
Track F: 139.7cm 55.0in
Track R: 142.2cm 56.0in
Length: 462.3cm 182.0in
Width: 181.6cm 71.5in
Height: 142.2cm 56.0in
Ground clearance: 15.2cm 6.0in
Kerb weight: 1388.8kg 3059.0lb
Fuel: 52.3L 11.5gal 13.8galUS

1697 Ford

Falcon V8
1963 USA
123.0mph 197.9kmh
0-50mph 80.5kmh: 6.3secs
0-60mph 96.5kmh: 8.5secs
0-1/4 mile: 16.0secs
260.0bhp 193.9kW 263.6PS
@ 5800rpm
269.0lbft 364.5Nm @ 4500rpm
219.8bhp/ton 216.1bhp/tonne
61.0bhp/L 45.5kW/L 61.9PS/L
45.9ft/sec 14.0m/sec
20.5mph 33.0kmh/1000rpm
Petrol 4-stroke piston
4261cc 260.0cu in
Vee 8 1 Carburettor
Compression ratio: 9.2:1
Bore: 96.5mm 3.8in
Stroke: 72.3mm 2.8in
Valve type/No: Overhead 16
Transmission: Manual
No. of forward speeds: 4
Wheels driven: Rear
Wheelbase: 278.1cm 109.5in
Track F: 139.7cm 55.0in
Track R: 137.2cm 54.0in
Length: 460.0cm 181.1in
Width: 179.3cm 70.6in
Height: 135.9cm 53.5in
Ground clearance: 20.1cm 7.9in
Kerb weight: 1203.1kg 2650.0lb

1698 Ford

Fastback NASCAR
1963 USA
155.0mph 249.4kmh
0-50mph 80.5kmh: 4.7secs
0-60mph 96.5kmh: 6.3secs
0-1/4 mile: 14.2secs
410.0bhp 305.7kW 415.7PS
@ 5600rpm
476.0lbft 645.0Nm @ 3400rpm
247.2bhp/ton 243.1bhp/tonne
58.6bhp/L 43.7kW/L 59.4PS/L
58.8ft/sec 17.9m/sec
23.9mph 38.5kmh/1000rpm
Petrol 4-stroke piston
6997cc 426.9cu in
Vee 8 1 Carburettor
Compression ratio: 11.5:1
Bore: 107.6mm 4.2in
Stroke: 96.1mm 3.8in
Valve type/No: Overhead 16
Transmission: Manual
No. of forward speeds: 4
Wheels driven: Rear
Wheelbase: 302.3cm 119.0in
Track F: 154.9cm 61.0in
Track R: 152.4cm 60.0in
Length: 533.1cm 209.9in
Width: 202.9cm 79.9in
Height: 138.4cm 54.5in
Ground clearance: 13.2cm 5.2in
Kerb weight: 1686.6kg 3715.0lb
Fuel: 82.9L 18.2gal 21.9galUS

1699 Ford

Galaxie 500 XL
1963 USA
105.0mph 168.9kmh
0-50mph 80.5kmh: 9.1secs
0-60mph 96.5kmh: 12.3secs
0-1/4 mile: 19.0secs
195.0bhp 145.4kW 197.7PS
@ 4400rpm
282.0lbft 382.1Nm @ 2400rpm
116.0bhp/ton 114.1bhp/tonne
41.2bhp/L 30.7kW/L 41.7PS/L
35.1ft/sec 10.7m/sec
23.8mph 38.3kmh/1000rpm
Petrol 4-stroke piston
4736cc 289.0cu in
Vee 8 1 Carburettor
Compression ratio: 8.7:1
Bore: 101.6mm 4.0in
Stroke: 72.9mm 2.9in
Valve type/No: Overhead 16
Transmission: Automatic
No. of forward speeds: 3
Wheels driven: Rear
Steering: PA
Wheelbase: 302.3cm 119.0in
Track F: 154.9cm 61.0in
Track R: 152.4cm 60.0in
Length: 533.1cm 209.9in
Width: 202.9cm 79.9in
Height: 138.4cm 54.5in
Ground clearance: 13.2cm 5.2in
Kerb weight: 1709.3kg 3765.0lb
Fuel: 75.7L 16.6gal 20.0galUS

1700 Ford

Zephyr 6 Estate
1963 UK
91.0mph 146.4kmh
0-50mph 80.5kmh: 11.2secs
0-60mph 96.5kmh: 16.1secs
0-1/4 mile: 20.0secs
98.0bhp 73.1kW 99.4PS
@ 4750rpm
134.0lbft 181.6Nm @ 2000rpm
75.9bhp/ton 74.6bhp/tonne
38.4bhp/L 28.6kW/L 38.9PS/L
41.3ft/sec 12.6m/sec
26.2mph 42.2kmh/1000rpm
18.9mpg 15.7mpgUS 14.9L/100km
Petrol 4-stroke piston
2553cc 155.8cu in
In-line 6 1 Carburettor
Compression ratio: 8.3:1
Bore: 82.5mm 3.2in
Stroke: 79.5mm 3.1in
Valve type/No: Overhead 12
Transmission: Manual with overdrive
No. of forward speeds: 7
Wheels driven: Rear
Springs F/R: Coil/Leaf
Brake system: PA
Brakes F/R: Disc/Drum
Steering: Recirculating ball
Wheelbase: 271.8cm 107.0in
Track F: 134.6cm 53.0in
Track R: 132.1cm 52.0in
Length: 457.2cm 180.0in
Width: 175.3cm 69.0in
Height: 148.6cm 58.5in
Ground clearance: 17.3cm 6.8in
Kerb weight: 13[illegible]3.4kg 2893.0lb
Fuel: 56.9L 12.5gal 15.0galUS

1701 Ford

Consul Corsair
1964 UK
87.1mph 140.1kmh
0-50mph 80.5kmh: 12.2secs
0-60mph 96.5kmh: 17.8secs
0-1/4 mile: 20.6secs
58.5bhp 43.6kW 59.3PS
@ 4600rpm
81.5lbft 110.4Nm @ 2300rpm
66.7bhp/ton 65.6bhp/tonne
39.0bhp/L 29.1kW/L 39.5PS/L
36.7ft/sec 11.2m/sec
17.4mph 28.0kmh/1000rpm
28.6mpg 23.8mpgUS 9.9L/100km
Petrol 4-stroke piston
1500cc 91.5cu in
In-line 4 1 Carburettor
Compression ratio: 8.3:1
Bore: 81.0mm 3.2in
Stroke: 72.8mm 2.9in
Valve type/No: Overhead 8
Transmission: Manual
No. of forward speeds: 4
Wheels driven: Rear
Springs F/R: Coil/Leaf
Brakes F/R: Disc/Drum
Steering: Recirculating ball
Wheelbase: 256.5cm 101.0in
Track F: 127.0cm 50.0in
Track R: 125.7cm 49.5in
Length: 448.3cm 176.5in
Width: 161.3cm 63.5in
Height: 145.3cm 57.2in
Ground clearance: 17.0cm 6.7in
Kerb weight: 891.7kg 1964.0lb
Fuel: 36.4L 8.0gal 9.6galUS

1702 Ford

Cortina Super
1964 UK
82.5mph 132.7kmh
0-50mph 80.5kmh: 13.6secs
0-60mph 96.5kmh: 21.8secs
0-1/4 mile: 21.1secs
59.5bhp 44.4kW 60.3PS
@ 4600rpm
81.5lbft 110.4Nm @ 2300rpm
71.0bhp/ton 69.9bhp/tonne
39.7bhp/L 29.6kW/L 40.2PS/L
36.7ft/sec 11.2m/sec
17.4mph 28.0kmh/1000rpm
24.8mpg 20.7mpgUS 11.4L/100km
Petrol 4-stroke piston
1500cc 91.5cu in
In-line 4 1 Carburettor
Compression ratio: 8.3:1
Bore: 81.0mm 3.2in
Stroke: 72.8mm 2.9in
Valve type/No: Overhead 8
Transmission: Automatic
No. of forward speeds: 3
Wheels driven: Rear
Springs F/R: Coil/Leaf
Brakes F/R: Drum/Drum
Steering: Recirculating ball
Wheelbase: 248.9cm 98.0in
Track F: 125.7cm 49.5in
Track R: 125.7cm 49.5in
Length: 433.1cm 170.5in
Width: 160.0cm 63.0in
Height: 144.8cm 57.0in
Ground clearance: 16.5cm 6.5in
Kerb weight: 851.7kg 1876.0lb
Fuel: 36.4L 8.0gal 9.6galUS

1703 Ford

Custom 500
1964 USA
105.0mph 168.9kmh
0-50mph 80.5kmh: 10.7secs
0-60mph 96.5kmh: 15.2secs
0-1/4 mile: 20.1secs
195.0bhp 145.4kW 197.7PS
@ 4400rpm
282.0lbft 382.1Nm @ 2400rpm
114.8bhp/ton 112.9bhp/tonne
41.2bhp/L 30.7kW/L 41.7PS/L
35.1ft/sec 10.7m/sec
23.8mph 38.3kmh/1000rpm
Petrol 4-stroke piston
4736cc 289.0cu in
Vee 8 1 Carburettor
Compression ratio: 9.0:1
Bore: 101.6mm 4.0in
Stroke: 72.9mm 2.9in
Valve type/No: Overhead 16
Transmission: Automatic
No. of forward speeds: 3
Wheels driven: Rear
Steering: PA
Wheelbase: 302.3cm 119.0in
Track F: 154.9cm 61.0in

Track R: 152.4cm 60.0in
Length: 532.9cm 209.8in
Width: 203.2cm 80.0in
Height: 143.5cm 56.5in
Ground clearance: 13.5cm 5.3in
Kerb weight: 1727.5kg 3805.0lb
Fuel: 75.7L 16.6gal 20.0galUS

1704 Ford
Falcon Sprint
1964 USA
105.0mph 168.9kmh
0-50mph 80.5kmh: 8.8secs
0-60mph 96.5kmh: 12.1secs
0-1/4 mile: 18.0secs
164.0bhp 122.3kW 166.3PS
@ 4400rpm
258.0lbft 349.6Nm @ 2200rpm
117.7bhp/ton 115.8bhp/tonne
38.5bhp/L 28.7kW/L 39.0PS/L
35.1ft/sec 10.7m/sec
22.2mph 35.7kmh/1000rpm
Petrol 4-stroke piston
4261cc 260.0cu in
Vee 8 1 Carburettor
Compression ratio: 8.7:1
Bore: 96.5mm 3.8in
Stroke: 72.9mm 2.9in
Valve type/No: Overhead 16
Transmission: Manual
No. of forward speeds: 4
Wheels driven: Rear
Steering: PA
Wheelbase: 278.1cm 109.5in
Track F: 141.2cm 55.6in
Track R: 142.2cm 56.0in
Length: 461.3cm 181.6in
Width: 181.9cm 71.6in
Height: 138.4cm 54.5in
Ground clearance: 14.0cm 5.5in
Kerb weight: 1416.5kg 3120.0lb
Fuel: 53.0L 11.6gal 14.0galUS

1705 Ford
Galaxie 500
1964 USA
120.0mph 193.1kmh
0-50mph 80.5kmh: 7.7secs
0-60mph 96.5kmh: 9.5secs
0-1/4 mile: 16.6secs
304.0bhp 226.7kW 308.2PS
@ 4600rpm
427.0lbft 578.6Nm @ 2800rpm
156.6bhp/ton 154.0bhp/tonne
47.6bhp/L 35.5kW/L 48.2PS/L
48.3ft/sec 14.7m/sec
28.6mph 46.0kmh/1000rpm
11.7mpg 9.7mpgUS 24.1L/100km
Petrol 4-stroke piston
6390cc 389.9cu in
Vee 8 1 Carburettor
Compression ratio: 9.6:1
Bore: 102.9mm 4.0in
Stroke: 96.0mm 3.8in
Valve type/No: Overhead 16
Transmission: Automatic
No. of forward speeds: 3
Wheels driven: Rear
Springs F/R: Coil/Leaf
Brake system: PA
Brakes F/R: Drum/Drum
Steering: Recirculating ball PA
Wheelbase: 302.3cm 119.0in
Track F: 154.9cm 61.0in
Track R: 152.4cm 60.0in
Length: 530.9cm 209.0in
Width: 203.2cm 80.0in
Height: 142.2cm 56.0in
Ground clearance: 15.2cm 6.0in
Kerb weight: 1973.5kg 4347.0lb
Fuel: 63.7L 14.0gal 16.8galUS

1706 Ford
Mustang
1964 USA
110.0mph 177.0kmh
0-50mph 80.5kmh: 6.3secs
0-60mph 96.5kmh: 9.0secs
0-1/4 mile: 16.5secs
210.0bhp 156.6kW 212.9PS
@ 4400rpm
300.0lbft 406.5Nm @ 2400rpm
160.5bhp/ton 157.9bhp/tonne
44.3bhp/L 33.1kW/L 45.0PS/L
35.1ft/sec 10.7m/sec
24.7mph 39.7kmh/1000rpm
Petrol 4-stroke piston
4736cc 289.0cu in
Vee 8 1 Carburettor
Compression ratio: 9.0:1
Bore: 101.6mm 4.0in
Stroke: 72.9mm 2.9in
Valve type/No: Overhead 16
Transmission: Manual
No. of forward speeds: 4
Wheels driven: Rear
Springs F/R: Coil/Leaf
Brakes F/R: Drum/Drum
Steering: Recirculating ball
Wheelbase: 274.3cm 108.0in
Track F: 142.2cm 56.0in
Track R: 142.2cm 56.0in
Length: 461.3cm 181.6in
Width: 172.7cm 68.0in
Height: 129.8cm 51.1in
Ground clearance: 14.0cm 5.5in
Kerb weight: 1330.2kg 2930.0lb
Fuel: 60.6L 13.3gal 16.0galUS

1707 Ford
Mustang 271hp
1964 USA
120.0mph 193.1kmh
0-50mph 80.5kmh: 6.3secs
0-60mph 96.5kmh: 8.3secs
0-1/4 mile: 15.9secs
271.0bhp 202.1kW 274.8PS
@ 3000rpm
57.2bhp/L 42.7kW/L 58.0PS/L
23.9ft/sec 7.3m/sec
Petrol 4-stroke piston
4736cc 289.0cu in
Vee 8 1 Carburettor
Compression ratio: 9.0:1
Bore: 101.6mm 4.0in
Stroke: 72.9mm 2.9in
Valve type/No: Overhead 16
Transmission: Manual
No. of forward speeds: 4
Wheels driven: Rear
Springs F/R: Coil/Leaf
Brakes F/R: Drum/Drum
Steering: Recirculating ball
Wheelbase: 274.3cm 108.0in
Track F: 142.2cm 56.0in
Track R: 142.2cm 56.0in
Length: 461.3cm 181.6in
Width: 172.7cm 68.0in
Height: 129.8cm 51.1in
Ground clearance: 14.0cm 5.5in
Fuel: 60.6L 13.3gal 16.0galUS

1708 Ford
Mustang Convertible
1964 USA
116.5mph 187.4kmh
0-50mph 80.5kmh: 6.2secs
0-60mph 96.5kmh: 8.2secs
0-1/4 mile: 16.0secs
271.0bhp 202.1kW 274.8PS
@ 6000rpm
312.0lbft 422.8Nm @ 3400rpm
195.6bhp/ton 192.4bhp/tonne
57.3bhp/L 42.7kW/L 58.1PS/L
47.8ft/sec 14.6m/sec
18.3mph 29.4kmh/1000rpm
12.8mpg 10.7mpgUS 22.1L/100km
Petrol 4-stroke piston
4727cc 288.4cu in
Vee 8 1 Carburettor
Compression ratio: 10.5:1
Bore: 101.6mm 4.0in
Stroke: 73.0mm 2.9in
Valve type/No: Overhead 16
Transmission: Manual
No. of forward speeds: 4
Wheels driven: Rear
Springs F/R: Coil/Leaf
Brakes F/R: Drum/Drum
Steering: Recirculating ball
Wheelbase: 274.3cm 108.0in
Track F: 142.2cm 56.0in
Track R: 142.2cm 56.0in
Length: 462.3cm 182.0in
Width: 175.3cm 69.0in
Height: 132.1cm 52.0in
Ground clearance: 15.2cm 6.0in
Kerb weight: 1408.8kg 3103.0lb
Fuel: 58.2L 12.8gal 15.4galUS

1709 Ford
Zephyr 6
1964 UK
95.0mph 152.9kmh
0-50mph 80.5kmh: 11.7secs
0-60mph 96.5kmh: 16.5secs
0-1/4 mile: 20.5secs
98.0bhp 73.1kW 99.4PS
@ 4750rpm
134.0lbft 181.6Nm @ 2000rpm
79.6bhp/ton 78.3bhp/tonne
38.4bhp/L 28.6kW/L 38.9PS/L
41.3ft/sec 12.6m/sec
20.3mph 32.7kmh/1000rpm
19.1mpg 15.9mpgUS 14.8L/100km
Petrol 4-stroke piston
2553cc 155.8cu in
In-line 6 1 Carburettor
Compression ratio: 8.3:1
Bore: 82.6mm 3.2in
Stroke: 79.5mm 3.1in
Valve type/No: Overhead 12
Transmission: Automatic
No. of forward speeds: 3
Wheels driven: Rear
Springs F/R: Coil/Leaf
Brake system: PA
Brakes F/R: Disc/Drum
Steering: Recirculating ball
Wheelbase: 271.8cm 107.0in
Track F: 134.6cm 53.0in
Track R: 135.9cm 53.5in
Length: 463.6cm 182.5in
Width: 175.3cm 69.0in
Height: 146.1cm 57.5in
Ground clearance: 17.3cm 6.8in
Kerb weight: 1252.1kg 2758.0lb
Fuel: 54.6L 12.0gal 14.4galUS

1710 Ford
Anglia Estate
1965 UK
79.0mph 127.1kmh
0-50mph 80.5kmh: 15.4secs
0-60mph 96.5kmh: 24.2secs
0-1/4 mile: 22.4secs
50.0bhp 37.3kW 50.7PS
@ 4900rpm
65.0lbft 88.1Nm @ 2700rpm
62.0bhp/ton 61.0bhp/tonne
41.7bhp/L 31.1kW/L 42.3PS/L
31.2ft/sec 9.5m/sec
15.3mph 24.6kmh/1000rpm
32.9mpg 27.4mpgUS 8.6L/100km
Petrol 4-stroke piston
1198cc 73.1cu in
In-line 4 1 Carburettor
Compression ratio: 9.0:1
Bore: 81.0mm 3.2in
Stroke: 58.2mm 2.3in
Valve type/No: Overhead 8
Transmission: Manual
No. of forward speeds: 4
Wheels driven: Rear
Springs F/R: Coil/Leaf
Brakes F/R: Drum/Drum
Steering: Recirculating ball
Wheelbase: 229.9cm 90.5in
Track F: 116.8cm 46.0in
Track R: 116.3cm 45.8in
Length: 392.4cm 154.5in
Width: 145.5cm 57.3in
Height: 146.1cm 57.5in
Ground clearance: 16.3cm 6.4in
Kerb weight: 819.9kg 1806.0lb
Fuel: 31.8L 7.0gal 8.4galUS

1711 Ford
Corsair GT
1965 UK
89.0mph 143.2kmh
0-50mph 80.5kmh: 10.4secs
0-60mph 96.5kmh: 14.7secs
0-1/4 mile: 19.6secs
88.0bhp 65.6kW 89.2PS
@ 4750rpm
116.0lbft 157.2Nm @ 2750rpm
91.0bhp/ton 89.5bhp/tonne
44.1bhp/L 32.9kW/L 44.7PS/L
37.6ft/sec 11.5m/sec
17.9mph 28.8kmh/1000rpm
22.8mpg 19.0mpgUS 12.4L/100km
Petrol 4-stroke piston
1996cc 121.8cu in
Vee 4 1 Carburettor
Compression ratio: 8.9:1
Bore: 93.7mm 3.7in
Stroke: 72.4mm 2.8in
Valve type/No: Overhead 8
Transmission: Manual
No. of forward speeds: 4
Wheels driven: Rear
Springs F/R: Coil/Leaf
Brake system: PA
Brakes F/R: Disc/Drum
Steering: Recirculating ball
Wheelbase: 256.5cm 101.0in
Track F: 127.0cm 50.0in
Track R: 125.7cm 49.5in
Length: 448.3cm 176.5in
Width: 161.3cm 63.5in
Height: 145.3cm 57.2in
Ground clearance: 17.0cm 6.7in
Kerb weight: 983.4kg 2166.0lb
Fuel: 45.5L 10.0gal 12.0galUS

1712 Ford
Cortina GT
1965 UK
94.0mph 151.2kmh
0-50mph 80.5kmh: 9.5secs
0-60mph 96.5kmh: 13.9secs
0-1/4 mile: 18.7secs
78.0bhp 58.2kW 79.1PS
@ 5200rpm
91.0lbft 123.3Nm @ 3600rpm
89.1bhp/ton 87.7bhp/tonne
52.0bhp/L 38.8kW/L 52.8PS/L
41.5ft/sec 12.6m/sec
17.4mph 28.0kmh/1000rpm
26.2mpg 21.8mpgUS 10.8L/100km
Petrol 4-stroke piston
1499cc 91.5cu in
In-line 4 1 Carburettor
Compression ratio: 9.0:1
Bore: 81.0mm 3.2in
Stroke: 72.8mm 2.9in
Valve type/No: Overhead 8
Transmission: Manual
No. of forward speeds: 4
Wheels driven: Rear
Springs F/R: Coil/Leaf
Brakes F/R: Disc/Drum
Steering: Recirculating ball
Wheelbase: 248.9cm 98.0in
Track F: 125.7cm 49.5in
Track R: 125.7cm 49.5in
Length: 433.1cm 170.5in
Width: 160.0cm 63.0in
Height: 144.8cm 57.0in
Ground clearance: 16.5cm 6.5in
Kerb weight: 889.8kg 1960.0lb
Fuel: 36.4L 8.0gal 9.6galUS

1713 Ford
Fairlane 500
1965 USA
96.0mph 154.5kmh
0-50mph 80.5kmh: 8.6secs
0-60mph 96.5kmh: 11.9secs
0-1/4 mile: 17.8secs
200.0bhp 149.1kW 202.8PS
@ 4400rpm
282.0lbft 382.1Nm @ 2400rpm
136.2bhp/ton 133.9bhp/tonne
42.2bhp/L 31.5kW/L 42.8PS/L
35.1ft/sec 10.7m/sec
25.2mph 40.5kmh/1000rpm
Petrol 4-stroke piston
4736cc 289.0cu in
Vee 8 1 Carburettor
Compression ratio: 9.3:1
Bore: 101.6mm 4.0in
Stroke: 72.9mm 2.9in
Valve type/No: Overhead 16
Transmission: Automatic
No. of forward speeds: 3
Wheels driven: Rear
Brake system: PA
Brakes F/R: Drum/Drum
Steering: PA
Wheelbase: 294.6cm 116.0in
Track F: 144.8cm 57.0in
Track R: 142.2cm 56.0in
Length: 505.0cm 198.8in
Width: 187.5cm 73.8in
Height: 139.4cm 54.9in
Ground clearance: 13.7cm 5.4in
Kerb weight: 1493.7kg 3290.0lb
Fuel: 60.6L 13.3gal 16.0galUS

1714 Ford
Galaxie 500 XL 427
1965 USA
136.0mph 218.8kmh
0-50mph 80.5kmh: 3.3secs

0-60mph 96.5kmh: 4.8secs
0-1/4 mile: 14.9secs
425.0bhp 316.9kW 430.9PS
@ 6000rpm
480.0lbft 650.4Nm @ 3700rpm
232.4bhp/ton 228.5bhp/tonne
60.7bhp/L 45.3kW/L 61.6PS/L
63.0ft/sec 19.2m/sec
22.7mph 36.5kmh/1000rpm
Petrol 4-stroke piston
6997cc 426.9cu in
Vee 8 2 Carburettor
Compression ratio: 11.1:1
Bore: 107.4mm 4.2in
Stroke: 96.0mm 3.8in
Valve type/No: Overhead 16
Transmission: Manual
No. of forward speeds: 4
Wheels driven: Rear
Wheelbase: 302.3cm 119.0in
Track F: 157.5cm 62.0in
Track R: 157.5cm 62.0in
Length: 533.4cm 210.0in
Width: 196.3cm 77.3in
Height: 138.9cm 54.7in
Ground clearance: 15.0cm 5.9in
Kerb weight: 1859.6kg 4096.0lb
Fuel: 75.7L 16.6gal 20.0galUS

1715 Ford

Galaxie LTD
1965 USA
116.0mph 186.6kmh
0-50mph 80.5kmh: 6.8secs
0-60mph 96.5kmh: 9.4secs
0-1/4 mile: 17.2secs
300.0bhp 223.7kW 304.2PS
@ 4600rpm
427.0lbft 578.6Nm @ 2800rpm
161.5bhp/ton 158.8bhp/tonne
46.9bhp/L 35.0kW/L 47.6PS/L
48.3ft/sec 14.7m/sec
25.2mph 40.5kmh/1000rpm
Petrol 4-stroke piston
6391cc 389.9cu in
Vee 8 1 Carburettor
Compression ratio: 9.7:1
Bore: 102.9mm 4.0in
Stroke: 96.0mm 3.8in
Valve type/No: Overhead 16
Transmission: Automatic
No. of forward speeds: 3
Wheels driven: Rear
Brake system: PA
Brakes F/R: Drum/Drum
Steering: PA
Wheelbase: 302.3cm 119.0in
Track F: 157.5cm 62.0in
Track R: 157.5cm 62.0in
Length: 533.4cm 210.0in
Width: 196.3cm 77.3in
Height: 138.9cm 54.7in
Ground clearance: 14.0cm 5.5in
Kerb weight: 1888.6kg 4160.0lb
Fuel: 75.7L 16.6gal 20.0galUS

1716 Ford

Mustang
1965 USA
90.0mph 144.8kmh
0-50mph 80.5kmh: 10.8secs
0-60mph 96.5kmh: 15.1secs
0-1/4 mile: 19.5secs
120.0bhp 89.5kW 121.7PS
@ 4400rpm
190.0lbft 257.5Nm @ 2400rpm
100.7bhp/ton 99.0bhp/tonne
36.6bhp/L 27.3kW/L 37.1PS/L
38.3ft/sec 11.7m/sec
23.6mph 38.0kmh/1000rpm
Petrol 4-stroke piston
3277cc 199.9cu in
In-line 6 1 Carburettor
Compression ratio: 9.2:1
Bore: 93.6mm 3.7in
Stroke: 79.5mm 3.1in
Valve type/No: Overhead 12
Transmission: Automatic
No. of forward speeds: 3
Wheels driven: Rear
Brakes F/R: Drum/Drum
Steering: PA
Wheelbase: 274.3cm 108.0in
Track F: 140.7cm 55.4in
Track R: 142.2cm 56.0in
Length: 461.3cm 181.6in
Width: 173.2cm 68.2in
Height: 129.8cm 51.1in
Ground clearance: 14.0cm 5.5in
Kerb weight: 1212.2kg 2670.0lb
Fuel: 60.6L 13.3gal 16.0galUS

1717 Ford

Mustang 6
1965 USA
90.0mph 144.8kmh
0-50mph 80.5kmh: 9.2secs
0-60mph 96.5kmh: 12.5secs
0-1/4 mile: 20.0secs
101.0bhp 75.3kW 102.4PS
@ 4400rpm
156.0lbft 211.4Nm @ 2400rpm
81.1bhp/ton 79.7bhp/tonne
36.2bhp/L 27.0kW/L 36.8PS/L
35.9ft/sec 11.0m/sec
20.0mph 32.2kmh/1000rpm
Petrol 4-stroke piston
2786cc 170.0cu in
In-line 6 1 Carburettor
Compression ratio: 8.7:1
Bore: 88.9mm 3.5in
Stroke: 74.7mm 2.9in
Valve type/No: Overhead 12
Transmission: Automatic
No. of forward speeds: 3
Wheels driven: Rear
Brakes F/R: Drum/Drum
Wheelbase: 274.3cm 108.0in
Track F: 140.7cm 55.4in
Track R: 142.2cm 56.0in
Length: 461.3cm 181.6in
Width: 172.7cm 68.0in
Height: 129.5cm 51.0in
Ground clearance: 14.0cm 5.5in
Kerb weight: 1266.7kg 2790.0lb
Fuel: 60.6L 13.3gal 16.0galUS

1718 Ford

Mustang Convertible
1965 USA
101.0mph 162.5kmh
0-50mph 80.5kmh: 8.8secs
0-60mph 96.5kmh: 11.2secs
0-1/4 mile: 18.8secs
164.0bhp 122.3kW 166.3PS
@ 4400rpm
258.0lbft 349.6Nm @ 5200rpm
124.5bhp/ton 122.4bhp/tonne
38.5bhp/L 28.7kW/L 39.0PS/L
35.1ft/sec 10.7m/sec
24.0mph 38.6kmh/1000rpm
Petrol 4-stroke piston
4260cc 259.9cu in
Vee 8 1 Carburettor
Compression ratio: 8.7:1
Bore: 96.5mm 3.8in
Stroke: 72.9mm 2.9in
Valve type/No: Overhead 16
Transmission: Automatic
No. of forward speeds: 3
Wheels driven: Rear
Wheelbase: 274.3cm 108.0in
Track F: 142.2cm 56.0in
Track R: 142.2cm 56.0in
Length: 461.3cm 181.6in
Width: 172.7cm 68.0in
Height: 129.5cm 51.0in
Ground clearance: 14.0cm 5.5in
Kerb weight: 1339.3kg 2950.0lb
Fuel: 60.6L 13.3gal 16.0galUS

1719 Ford

Mustang Convertible V8
1965 USA
111.0mph 178.6kmh
0-50mph 80.5kmh: 6.9secs
0-60mph 96.5kmh: 8.9secs
0-1/4 mile: 17.0secs
210.0bhp 156.6kW 212.9PS
@ 4400rpm
300.0lbft 406.5Nm @ 2400rpm
154.2bhp/ton 151.7bhp/tonne
44.3bhp/L 33.1kW/L 45.0PS/L
35.1ft/sec 10.7m/sec
24.1mph 38.8kmh/1000rpm
Petrol 4-stroke piston
4736cc 289.0cu in
Vee 8 1 Carburettor
Compression ratio: 9.0:1
Bore: 101.6mm 4.0in
Stroke: 72.9mm 2.9in
Valve type/No: Overhead 16
Transmission: Manual
No. of forward speeds: 4
Wheels driven: Rear
Brakes F/R: Drum/Drum
Wheelbase: 274.3cm 108.0in
Track F: 142.2cm 56.0in
Track R: 142.2cm 56.0in
Length: 461.3cm 181.6in
Width: 172.7cm 68.0in
Height: 129.5cm 51.0in
Ground clearance: 14.0cm 5.5in
Kerb weight: 1384.7kg 3050.0lb
Fuel: 60.6L 13.3gal 16.0galUS

1720 Ford

Mustang Coupe
1965 USA
109.0mph 175.4kmh
0-50mph 80.5kmh: 6.9secs
0-60mph 96.5kmh: 9.0secs
0-1/4 mile: 17.0secs
200.0bhp 149.1kW 202.8PS
@ 4400rpm
282.0lbft 382.1Nm @ 2400rpm
152.9bhp/ton 150.3bhp/tonne
42.2bhp/L 31.5kW/L 42.8PS/L
35.1ft/sec 10.7m/sec
24.7mph 39.7kmh/1000rpm
Petrol 4-stroke piston
4737cc 289.0cu in
Vee 8 1 Carburettor
Compression ratio: 9.3:1
Bore: 101.6mm 4.0in
Stroke: 72.9mm 2.9in
Valve type/No: Overhead 16
Transmission: Manual
No. of forward speeds: 4
Wheels driven: Rear
Wheelbase: 274.3cm 108.0in
Track F: 142.2cm 56.0in
Track R: 142.2cm 56.0in
Length: 461.3cm 181.6in
Width: 172.7cm 68.0in
Height: 129.8cm 51.1in
Ground clearance: 14.0cm 5.5in
Kerb weight: 1330.2kg 2930.0lb
Fuel: 60.6L 13.3gal 16.0galUS

1721 Ford

Mustang Coupe Automatic
1965 USA
110.0mph 177.0kmh
0-50mph 80.5kmh: 6.1secs
0-60mph 96.5kmh: 8.5secs
0-1/4 mile: 16.8secs
225.0bhp 167.8kW 228.1PS
@ 4800rpm
305.0lbft 413.3Nm @ 3200rpm
174.4bhp/ton 171.5bhp/tonne
47.5bhp/L 35.4kW/L 48.2PS/L
38.3ft/sec 11.7m/sec
24.4mph 39.3kmh/1000rpm
Petrol 4-stroke piston
4737cc 289.0cu in
Vee 8 1 Carburettor
Compression ratio: 10.0:1
Bore: 101.6mm 4.0in
Stroke: 72.9mm 2.9in
Valve type/No: Overhead 16
Transmission: Automatic
No. of forward speeds: 3
Wheels driven: Rear
Brakes F/R: Disc/Drum
Wheelbase: 274.3cm 108.0in
Track F: 142.2cm 56.0in
Track R: 142.2cm 56.0in
Length: 461.3cm 181.6in
Width: 172.7cm 68.0in
Height: 129.5cm 51.0in
Ground clearance: 14.0cm 5.5in
Kerb weight: 1312.1kg 2890.0lb
Fuel: 60.6L 13.3gal 16.0galUS

1722 Ford

Mustang Fastback
1965 USA
120.0mph 193.1kmh
0-50mph 80.5kmh: 6.3secs
0-60mph 96.5kmh: 8.3secs
0-1/4 mile: 15.9secs
271.0bhp 202.1kW 274.8PS
@ 6000rpm
312.0lbft 422.8Nm @ 3400rpm
199.0bhp/ton 195.7bhp/tonne
57.2bhp/L 42.7kW/L 58.0PS/L
47.8ft/sec 14.6m/sec
18.5mph 29.8kmh/1000rpm
Petrol 4-stroke piston
4737cc 289.0cu in
Vee 8 1 Carburettor
Compression ratio: 10.5:1
Bore: 101.6mm 4.0in
Stroke: 72.9mm 2.9in
Valve type/No: Overhead 16
Transmission: Manual
No. of forward speeds: 4
Wheels driven: Rear
Wheelbase: 274.3cm 108.0in
Track F: 142.2cm 56.0in
Track R: 142.2cm 56.0in
Length: 461.3cm 181.6in
Width: 172.7cm 68.0in
Height: 129.8cm 51.1in
Ground clearance: 14.0cm 5.5in
Kerb weight: 1384.7kg 3050.0lb
Fuel: 60.6L 13.3gal 16.0galUS

1723 Ford

Mustang High Performance
1965 USA
120.0mph 193.1kmh
0-50mph 80.5kmh: 6.3secs
0-60mph 96.5kmh: 8.3secs
0-1/4 mile: 15.9secs
271.0bhp 202.1kW 274.8PS
@ 6000rpm
312.0lbft 422.8Nm @ 3400rpm
199.0bhp/ton 195.7bhp/tonne
57.2bhp/L 42.7kW/L 58.0PS/L
47.8ft/sec 14.6m/sec
18.5mph 29.8kmh/1000rpm
Petrol 4-stroke piston
4736cc 289.0cu in
Vee 8 1 Carburettor
Compression ratio: 10.5:1
Bore: 101.6mm 4.0in
Stroke: 72.9mm 2.9in
Valve type/No: Overhead 16
Transmission: Manual
No. of forward speeds: 4
Wheels driven: Rear
Wheelbase: 274.3cm 108.0in
Track F: 142.2cm 56.0in
Track R: 142.2cm 56.0in
Length: 461.3cm 181.6in
Width: 172.7cm 68.0in
Height: 129.8cm 51.1in
Ground clearance: 14.0cm 5.5in
Kerb weight: 1384.7kg 3050.0lb
Fuel: 60.6L 13.3gal 16.0galUS

1724 Ford

Mustang V8 4.2-litre
1965 USA
101.0mph 162.5kmh
0-50mph 80.5kmh: 8.8secs
0-60mph 96.5kmh: 11.2secs
0-1/4 mile: 18.8secs
164.0bhp 122.3kW 166.3PS
@ 4400rpm
258.0lbft 349.6Nm @ 2200rpm
124.5bhp/ton 122.4bhp/tonne
38.5bhp/L 28.7kW/L 39.0PS/L
35.1ft/sec 10.7m/sec
24.0mph 38.6kmh/1000rpm
Petrol 4-stroke piston
4261cc 260.0cu in
Vee 8 1 Carburettor
Compression ratio: 8.7:1
Bore: 96.5mm 3.8in
Stroke: 72.9mm 2.9in
Valve type/No: Overhead 16
Transmission: Automatic
No. of forward speeds: 3
Wheels driven: Rear
Brakes F/R: Drum/Drum
Wheelbase: 274.3cm 108.0in
Track F: 142.2cm 56.0in
Track R: 142.2cm 56.0in
Length: 461.3cm 181.6in
Width: 172.7cm 68.0in
Height: 129.8cm 51.1in
Ground clearance: 14.0cm 5.5in
Kerb weight: 1339.3kg 2950.0lb
Fuel: 60.6L 13.3gal 16.0galUS

1725 Ford

Mustang V8 4.7-litre
1965 USA
110.0mph 177.0kmh
0-50mph 80.5kmh: 6.1secs
0-60mph 96.5kmh: 8.5secs
0-1/4 mile: 16.8secs

225.0bhp 167.8kW 228.1PS
@ 4800rpm
305.0lbft 413.3Nm @ 3200rpm
174.4bhp/ton 171.5bhp/tonne
47.5bhp/L 35.4kW/L 48.2PS/L
38.3ft/sec 11.7m/sec
24.4mph 39.3kmh/1000rpm
Petrol 4-stroke piston
4736cc 289.0cu in
Vee 8 1 Carburettor
Compression ratio: 10.0:1
Bore: 101.6mm 4.0in
Stroke: 72.9mm 2.9in
Valve type/No: Overhead 16
Transmission: Automatic
No. of forward speeds: 3
Wheels driven: Rear
Brake system: PA
Brakes F/R: Disc/Drum
Steering: PA
Wheelbase: 274.3cm 108.0in
Track F: 142.2cm 56.0in
Track R: 142.2cm 56.0in
Length: 461.3cm 181.6in
Width: 172.7cm 68.0in
Height: 129.8cm 51.1in
Ground clearance: 14.0cm 5.5in
Kerb weight: 1312.1kg 2890.0lb
Fuel: 60.6L 13.3gal 16.0galUS

1726 Ford

Taunus 20M
1965 Germany
100.0mph 160.9kmh
0-50mph 80.5kmh: 10.1secs
0-60mph 96.5kmh: 14.8secs
0-1/4 mile: 19.6secs
85.0bhp 63.4kW 86.2PS
@ 5000rpm
113.0lbft 153.1Nm @ 3500rpm
83.5bhp/ton 82.1bhp/tonne
42.5bhp/L 31.7kW/L 43.1PS/L
32.8ft/sec 10.0m/sec
19.2mph 30.9kmh/1000rpm
20.2mpg 16.8mpgUS 14.0L/100km
Petrol 4-stroke piston
1998cc 121.9cu in
Vee 6 1 Carburettor
Compression ratio: 8.0:1
Bore: 84.0mm 3.3in
Stroke: 60.0mm 2.4in
Valve type/No: Overhead 12
Transmission: Manual
No. of forward speeds: 3
Wheels driven: Rear
Springs F/R: Coil/Leaf
Brakes F/R: Disc/Drum
Steering: Recirculating ball
Wheelbase: 270.5cm 106.5in
Track F: 143.0cm 56.3in
Track R: 140.0cm 55.1in
Length: 463.6cm 182.5in
Width: 166.4cm 65.5in
Height: 147.8cm 58.2in
Kerb weight: 1035.1kg 2280.0lb
Fuel: 45.0L 9.9gal 11.9galUS

1727 Ford

Thunderbird
1965 USA
115.0mph 185.0kmh
0-50mph 80.5kmh: 7.8secs
0-60mph 96.5kmh: 10.3secs
0-1/4 mile: 17.5secs
300.0bhp 223.7kW 304.2PS
@ 4600rpm
427.0lbft 578.6Nm @ 2800rpm
145.6bhp/ton 143.2bhp/tonne
46.9bhp/L 35.0kW/L 47.6PS/L
48.3ft/sec 14.7m/sec
25.4mph 40.9kmh/1000rpm
Petrol 4-stroke piston
6391cc 389.9cu in
Vee 8 1 Carburettor
Compression ratio: 10.8:1
Bore: 102.9mm 4.0in
Stroke: 96.0mm 3.8in
Valve type/No: Overhead 16
Transmission: Automatic
No. of forward speeds: 3
Wheels driven: Rear
Brake system: PA
Steering: PA
Wheelbase: 287.5cm 113.2in
Track F: 154.9cm 61.0in
Track R: 152.4cm 60.0in
Length: 521.7cm 205.4in
Width: 195.8cm 77.1in
Height: 133.4cm 52.5in
Ground clearance: 14.0cm 5.5in
Kerb weight: 2095.2kg 4615.0lb
Fuel: 83.3L 18.3gal 22.0galUS

1728 Ford

Zodiac Executive
1965 UK
97.0mph 156.1kmh
0-50mph 80.5kmh: 10.7secs
0-60mph 96.5kmh: 15.2secs
0-1/4 mile: 20.1secs
109.0bhp 81.3kW 110.5PS
@ 4800rpm
137.0lbft 185.6Nm @ 2400rpm
86.2bhp/ton 84.7bhp/tonne
42.7bhp/L 31.8kW/L 43.2PS/L
41.7ft/sec 12.7m/sec
20.3mph 32.7kmh/1000rpm
17.7mpg 14.7mpgUS 16.0L/100km
Petrol 4-stroke piston
2555cc 155.9cu in
In-line 6 1 Carburettor
Compression ratio: 8.3:1
Bore: 82.6mm 3.2in
Stroke: 79.5mm 3.1in
Valve type/No: Overhead 12
Transmission: Automatic
No. of forward speeds: 3
Wheels driven: Rear
Springs F/R: Coil/Leaf
Brake system: PA
Brakes F/R: Disc/Drum
Steering: Recirculating ball
Wheelbase: 271.8cm 107.0in
Track F: 134.6cm 53.0in
Track R: 135.9cm 53.5in
Length: 463.6cm 182.5in
Width: 175.3cm 69.0in
Height: 146.1cm 57.5in
Ground clearance: 17.3cm 6.8in
Kerb weight: 1286.2kg 2833.0lb
Fuel: 54.6L 12.0gal 14.4galUS

1729 Ford

Bronco
1966 USA
74.0mph 119.1kmh
0-50mph 80.5kmh: 14.9secs
0-60mph 96.5kmh: 22.6secs
0-1/4 mile: 21.9secs
105.0bhp 78.3kW 106.5PS
@ 4400rpm
158.0lbft 214.1Nm @ 2400rpm
71.8bhp/ton 70.6bhp/tonne
37.7bhp/L 28.1kW/L 38.2PS/L
35.9ft/sec 11.0m/sec
17.5mph 28.2kmh/1000rpm
Petrol 4-stroke piston
2786cc 170.0cu in
In-line 6 1 Carburettor
Compression ratio: 9.1:1
Bore: 88.9mm 3.5in
Stroke: 74.7mm 2.9in
Valve type/No: Overhead 12
Transmission: Manual
No. of forward speeds: 3
Wheels driven: 4-wheel drive
Springs F/R: Coil/Leaf
Brakes F/R: Drum/Drum
Steering: Worm & roller
Wheelbase: 233.7cm 92.0in
Track F: 144.8cm 57.0in
Track R: 144.8cm 57.0in
Length: 386.3cm 152.1in
Width: 174.8cm 68.8in
Height: 181.4cm 71.4in
Ground clearance: 16.8cm 6.6in
Kerb weight: 1487.8kg 3277.0lb
Fuel: 54.9L 12.1gal 14.5galUS

1730 Ford

Corsair GT Estate
1966 UK
94.0mph 151.2kmh
0-50mph 80.5kmh: 10.5secs
0-60mph 96.5kmh: 15.0secs
0-1/4 mile: 19.7secs
88.0bhp 65.6kW 89.2PS
@ 4750rpm
116.5lbft 157.9Nm @ 2750rpm
83.8bhp/ton 82.4bhp/tonne
44.1bhp/L 32.9kW/L 44.7PS/L
37.6ft/sec 11.5m/sec
17.9mph 28.8kmh/1000rpm
24.8mpg 20.7mpgUS 11.4L/100km
Petrol 4-stroke piston
1996cc 121.8cu in
Vee 4 1 Carburettor
Compression ratio: 8.9:1
Bore: 93.7mm 3.7in
Stroke: 72.4mm 2.8in
Valve type/No: Overhead 8
Transmission: Manual
No. of forward speeds: 4
Wheels driven: Rear
Springs F/R: Coil/Leaf
Brake system: PA
Brakes F/R: Disc/Drum
Steering: Recirculating ball
Wheelbase: 256.5cm 101.0in
Track F: 127.0cm 50.0in
Track R: 125.7cm 49.5in
Length: 448.3cm 176.5in
Width: 161.3cm 63.5in
Height: 147.3cm 58.0in
Ground clearance: 17.0cm 6.7in
Kerb weight: 1067.8kg 2352.0lb
Fuel: 45.5L 10.0gal 12.0galUS

1731 Ford

Cortina 1300 de Luxe
1966 UK
83.0mph 133.5kmh
0-50mph 80.5kmh: 14.5secs
0-60mph 96.5kmh: 21.4secs
0-1/4 mile: 22.2secs
0-1km: 42.0secs
53.5bhp 39.9kW 54.2PS
@ 5000rpm
71.0lbft 96.2Nm @ 2500rpm
63.1bhp/ton 62.0bhp/tonne
41.2bhp/L 30.8kW/L 41.8PS/L
34.4ft/sec 10.5m/sec
15.8mph 25.4kmh/1000rpm
26.8mpg 22.3mpgUS 10.5L/100km
Petrol 4-stroke piston
1297cc 79.1cu in
In-line 4 1 Carburettor
Compression ratio: 9.0:1
Bore: 81.0mm 3.2in
Stroke: 63.0mm 2.5in
Valve type/No: Overhead 8
Transmission: Manual
No. of forward speeds: 4
Wheels driven: Rear
Springs F/R: Coil/Leaf
Brakes F/R: Disc/Drum
Steering: Recirculating ball
Wheelbase: 248.9cm 98.0in
Track F: 133.4cm 52.5in
Track R: 129.5cm 51.0in
Length: 426.7cm 168.0in
Width: 165.1cm 65.0in
Height: 143.5cm 56.5in
Ground clearance: 16.5cm 6.5in
Kerb weight: 862.6kg 1900.0lb
Fuel: 45.5L 10.0gal 12.0galUS

1732 Ford

Cortina Lotus
1966 UK
100.0mph 160.9kmh
0-50mph 80.5kmh: 7.2secs
0-60mph 96.5kmh: 9.7secs
0-1/4 mile: 17.6secs
115.0bhp 85.8kW 116.6PS
@ 5700rpm
108.0lbft 146.3Nm @ 4000rpm
125.0bhp/ton 123.0bhp/tonne
73.8bhp/L 55.0kW/L 74.8PS/L
45.3ft/sec 13.8m/sec
17.5mph 28.2kmh/1000rpm
Petrol 4-stroke piston
1558cc 95.1cu in
In-line 4 2 Carburettor
Compression ratio: 9.5:1
Bore: 82.6mm 3.2in
Stroke: 72.6mm 2.9in
Valve type/No: Overhead 8
Transmission: Manual
No. of forward speeds: 4
Wheels driven: Rear
Springs F/R: Coil/Leaf
Brake system: PA
Brakes F/R: Disc/Drum
Steering: Recirculating ball
Wheelbase: 248.9cm 98.0in
Track F: 130.8cm 51.5in
Track R: 128.3cm 50.5in
Length: 427.5cm 168.3in
Width: 158.8cm 62.5in
Height: 135.6cm 53.4in
Ground clearance: 13.5cm 5.3in
Kerb weight: 935.2kg 2060.0lb
Fuel: 36.3L 8.0gal 9.6galUS

1733 Ford

Cortina Super Estate
1966 UK
83.0mph 133.5kmh
0-50mph 80.5kmh: 13.9secs
0-60mph 96.5kmh: 20.5secs
0-1/4 mile: 21.5secs
0-1km: 40.8secs
61.5bhp 45.9kW 62.3PS
@ 4700rpm
81.5lbft 110.4Nm @ 2300rpm
68.1bhp/ton 67.0bhp/tonne
41.0bhp/L 30.6kW/L 41.6PS/L
37.5ft/sec 11.4m/sec
17.3mph 27.8kmh/1000rpm
24.7mpg 20.6mpgUS 11.4L/100km
Petrol 4-stroke piston
1500cc 91.5cu in
In-line 4 1 Carburettor
Compression ratio: 9.0:1
Bore: 81.0mm 3.2in
Stroke: 72.8mm 2.9in
Valve type/No: Overhead 8
Transmission: Manual
No. of forward speeds: 4
Wheels driven: Rear
Springs F/R: Coil/Leaf
Brakes F/R: Disc/Drum
Steering: Recirculating ball
Wheelbase: 248.9cm 98.0in
Track F: 125.7cm 49.5in
Track R: 125.7cm 49.5in
Length: 431.8cm 170.0in
Width: 160.0cm 63.0in
Height: 144.8cm 57.0in
Ground clearance: 16.5cm 6.5in
Kerb weight: 918.0kg 2022.0lb
Fuel: 36.4L 8.0gal 9.6galUS

1734 Ford

Custom 500
1966 USA
95.0mph 152.9kmh
0-50mph 80.5kmh: 11.2secs
0-60mph 96.5kmh: 16.3secs
0-1/4 mile: 20.7secs
150.0bhp 111.9kW 152.1PS
@ 4000rpm
234.0lbft 317.1Nm @ 2200rpm
92.3bhp/ton 90.8bhp/tonne
38.1bhp/L 28.4kW/L 38.7PS/L
35.3ft/sec 10.8m/sec
25.4mph 40.9kmh/1000rpm
Petrol 4-stroke piston
3933cc 240.0cu in
In-line 6 1 Carburettor
Compression ratio: 9.2:1
Bore: 101.6mm 4.0in
Stroke: 80.8mm 3.2in
Valve type/No: Overhead 12
Transmission: Automatic
No. of forward speeds: 3
Wheels driven: Rear
Springs F/R: Coil/Coil
Brakes F/R: Drum/Drum
Steering: Recirculating ball PA
Wheelbase: 302.3cm 119.0in
Track F: 157.5cm 62.0in
Track R: 157.5cm 62.0in
Length: 533.4cm 210.0in
Width: 200.7cm 79.0in
Height: 141.2cm 55.6in
Ground clearance: 15.2cm 6.0in
Kerb weight: 1652.6kg 3640.0lb
Fuel: 94.6L 20.8gal 25.0galUS

1735 Ford

Fairlane GTA
1966 USA
115.0mph 185.0kmh
0-50mph 80.5kmh: 6.5secs
0-60mph 96.5kmh: 8.6secs
0-1/4 mile: 15.4secs
335.0bhp 249.8kW 339.6PS
@ 4800rpm
427.0lbft 578.6Nm @ 3200rpm
214.4bhp/ton 210.8bhp/tonne
52.4bhp/L 39.1kW/L 53.1PS/L
50.4ft/sec 15.4m/sec
23.0mph 37.0kmh/1000rpm
Petrol 4-stroke piston

6391cc 389.9cu in
Vee 8 1 Carburettor
Compression ratio: 10.5:1
Bore: 102.9mm 4.0in
Stroke: 96.0mm 3.8in
Valve type/No: Overhead 16
Transmission: Automatic
No. of forward speeds: 3
Wheels driven: Rear
Springs F/R: Coil/Leaf
Brake system: PA
Brakes F/R: Drum/Drum
Steering: Recirculating ball PA
Wheelbase: 294.6cm 116.0in
Track F: 147.3cm 58.0in
Track R: 147.3cm 58.0in
Length: 500.4cm 197.0in
Width: 188.2cm 74.1in
Height: 139.7cm 55.0in
Ground clearance: 16.5cm 6.5in
Kerb weight: 1589.0kg 3500.0lb
Fuel: 75.7L 16.6gal 20.0galUS

1736 Ford
Falcon Ranchero Custom
1966 USA
95.0mph 152.9kmh
0-50mph 80.5kmh: 7.7secs
0-60mph 96.5kmh: 10.3secs
0-1/4 mile: 17.7secs
225.0bhp 167.8kW 228.1PS
@ 4800rpm
305.0lbft 413.3Nm @ 3200rpm
171.1bhp/ton 168.3bhp/tonne
47.5bhp/L 35.4kW/L 48.2PS/L
38.3ft/sec 11.7m/sec
24.8mph 39.9kmh/1000rpm
Petrol 4-stroke piston
4736cc 289.0cu in
Vee 8 1 Carburettor
Compression ratio: 10.0:1
Bore: 101.6mm 4.0in
Stroke: 72.9mm 2.9in
Valve type/No: Overhead 16
Transmission: Automatic
No. of forward speeds: 3
Wheels driven: Rear
Springs F/R: Coil/Leaf
Brake system: PA
Brakes F/R: Drum/Drum
Steering: Recirculating ball PA
Wheelbase: 287.0cm 113.0in
Track F: 147.3cm 58.0in
Track R: 147.3cm 58.0in
Length: 501.7cm 197.5in
Width: 189.7cm 74.7in
Height: 142.7cm 56.2in
Ground clearance: 15.0cm 5.9in
Kerb weight: 1337.0kg 2945.0lb
Fuel: 75.7L 16.6gal 20.0galUS

1737 Ford
Galaxie 7-litre
1966 USA
116.0mph 186.6kmh
0-50mph 80.5kmh: 6.2secs
0-60mph 96.5kmh: 8.0secs
0-1/4 mile: 16.4secs
345.0bhp 257.3kW 349.8PS
@ 4600rpm
462.0lbft 626.0Nm @ 2800rpm
187.7bhp/ton 184.5bhp/tonne
49.2bhp/L 36.7kW/L 49.9PS/L
50.9ft/sec 15.5m/sec
24.1mph 38.8kmh/1000rpm
Petrol 4-stroke piston
7014cc 427.9cu in
Vee 8 1 Carburettor
Compression ratio: 10.5:1
Bore: 104.9mm 4.1in
Stroke: 101.1mm 4.0in
Valve type/No: Overhead 16
Transmission: Automatic
No. of forward speeds: 3
Wheels driven: Rear
Springs F/R: Coil/Coil
Brake system: PA
Brakes F/R: Disc/Drum
Steering: Recirculating ball PA
Wheelbase: 302.3cm 119.0in
Track F: 157.5cm 62.0in
Track R: 157.5cm 62.0in
Length: 533.4cm 210.0in
Width: 200.7cm 79.0in
Height: 138.9cm 54.7in
Kerb weight: 1869.6kg 4118.0lb
Fuel: 94.6L 20.8gal 25.0galUS

1738 Ford
GT40 Super Street
1966 UK
164.0mph 263.9kmh
0-50mph 80.5kmh: 4.3secs
0-60mph 96.5kmh: 5.3secs
0-1/4 mile: 14.2secs
335.0bhp 249.8kW 339.6PS
@ 6250rpm
329.0lbft 445.8Nm @ 3200rpm
366.0bhp/ton 359.9bhp/tonne
70.7bhp/L 52.7kW/L 71.7PS/L
49.8ft/sec 15.2m/sec
23.4mph 37.7kmh/1000rpm
Petrol 4-stroke piston
4736cc 289.0cu in
Vee 8 4 Carburettor
Compression ratio: 9.1:1
Bore: 101.7mm 4.0in
Stroke: 72.9mm 2.9in
Valve type/No: Overhead 16
Transmission: Manual
No. of forward speeds: 5
Wheels driven: Rear
Springs F/R: Coil/Coil
Brakes F/R: Disc/Disc
Steering: Rack & pinion
Wheelbase: 241.3cm 95.0in
Track F: 137.2cm 54.0in
Track R: 137.2cm 54.0in
Length: 418.1cm 164.6in
Width: 177.8cm 70.0in
Height: 102.9cm 40.5in
Ground clearance: 12.2cm 4.8in
Kerb weight: 930.7kg 2050.0lb
Fuel: 140.0L 30.8gal 37.0galUS

1739 Ford
Thunderbird Town Landau
1966 USA
117.0mph 188.3kmh
0-50mph 80.5kmh: 6.8secs
0-60mph 96.5kmh: 9.4secs
0-1/4 mile: 16.9secs
345.0bhp 257.3kW 349.8PS
@ 4600rpm
462.0lbft 626.0Nm @ 2800rpm
159.7bhp/ton 157.0bhp/tonne
49.2bhp/L 36.7kW/L 49.9PS/L
50.9ft/sec 15.5m/sec
26.5mph 42.6kmh/1000rpm
Petrol 4-stroke piston
7014cc 427.9cu in
Vee 8 1 Carburettor
Compression ratio: 10.0:1
Bore: 104.9mm 4.1in
Stroke: 101.2mm 4.0in
Valve type/No: Overhead 16
Transmission: Automatic
No. of forward speeds: 3
Wheels driven: Rear
Springs F/R: Coil/Leaf
Brake system: PA
Brakes F/R: Disc/Drum
Steering: Recirculating ball PA
Wheelbase: 287.0cm 113.0in
Track F: 154.9cm 61.0in
Track R: 152.4cm 60.0in
Length: 521.7cm 205.4in
Width: 196.3cm 77.3in
Height: 133.6cm 52.6in
Ground clearance: 18.8cm 7.4in
Kerb weight: 2197.4kg 4840.0lb
Fuel: 83.3L 18.3gal 22.0galUS

1740 Ford
Zephyr 6 Mk IV
1966 UK
102.0mph 164.1kmh
0-50mph 80.5kmh: 10.6secs
0-60mph 96.5kmh: 14.6secs
0-1/4 mile: 19.6secs
0-1km: 36.3secs
112.0bhp 83.5kW 113.5PS
@ 4750rpm
137.5lbft 186.3Nm @ 3000rpm
86.6bhp/ton 85.2bhp/tonne
44.9bhp/L 33.5kW/L 45.5PS/L
31.3ft/sec 9.5m/sec
19.4mph 31.2kmh/1000rpm
19.4mpg 16.2mpgUS 14.6L/100km
Petrol 4-stroke piston
2495cc 152.2cu in
Vee 6 1 Carburettor
Compression ratio: 9.0:1
Bore: 93.7mm 3.7in
Stroke: 60.3mm 2.4in
Valve type/No: Overhead 12
Transmission: Manual
No. of forward speeds: 4
Wheels driven: Rear
Springs F/R: Coil/Coil
Brake system: PA
Brakes F/R: Disc/Disc
Steering: Recirculating ball
Wheelbase: 292.1cm 115.0in
Track F: 144.8cm 57.0in
Track R: 147.3cm 58.0in
Length: 469.9cm 185.0in
Width: 181.1cm 71.3in
Height: 148.6cm 58.5in
Ground clearance: 15.2cm 6.0in
Kerb weight: 1314.8kg 2896.0lb
Fuel: 68.2L 15.0gal 18.0galUS

1741 Ford
Corsair 2000E
1967 UK
98.0mph 157.7kmh
0-50mph 80.5kmh: 9.3secs
0-60mph 96.5kmh: 13.5secs
0-1/4 mile: 18.8secs
0-1km: 35.6secs
97.0bhp 72.3kW 98.3PS
@ 5000rpm
113.5lbft 153.8Nm @ 3000rpm
96.4bhp/ton 94.8bhp/tonne
48.6bhp/L 36.2kW/L 49.3PS/L
39.6ft/sec 12.1m/sec
17.8mph 28.6kmh/1000rpm
20.5mpg 17.1mpgUS 13.8L/100km
Petrol 4-stroke piston
1996cc 121.8cu in
Vee 4 1 Carburettor
Compression ratio: 8.9:1
Bore: 93.7mm 3.7in
Stroke: 72.4mm 2.8in
Valve type/No: Overhead 8
Transmission: Manual
No. of forward speeds: 4
Wheels driven: Rear
Springs F/R: Coil/Leaf
Brake system: PA
Brakes F/R: Disc/Drum
Steering: Recirculating ball
Wheelbase: 256.5cm 101.0in
Track F: 127.0cm 50.0in
Track R: 125.7cm 49.5in
Length: 448.3cm 176.5in
Width: 161.3cm 63.5in
Height: 145.5cm 57.3in
Ground clearance: 17.0cm 6.7in
Kerb weight: 1023.3kg 2254.0lb
Fuel: 45.5L 10.0gal 12.0galUS

1742 Ford
Cortina 1600E
1967 UK
100.0mph 160.9kmh
0-50mph 80.5kmh: 9.1secs
0-60mph 96.5kmh: 13.1secs
0-1/4 mile: 18.8secs
0-1km: 35.5secs
88.0bhp 65.6kW 89.2PS
@ 5400rpm
96.0lbft 130.1Nm @ 3600rpm
91.5bhp/ton 90.0bhp/tonne
55.0bhp/L 41.0kW/L 55.8PS/L
45.9ft/sec 14.0m/sec
17.1mph 27.5kmh/1000rpm
25.1mpg 20.9mpgUS 11.3L/100km
Petrol 4-stroke piston
1599cc 97.6cu in
In-line 4 1 Carburettor
Compression ratio: 9.0:1
Bore: 81.0mm 3.2in
Stroke: 77.6mm 3.1in
Valve type/No: Overhead 8
Transmission: Manual
No. of forward speeds: 4
Wheels driven: Rear
Springs F/R: Coil/Leaf
Brakes F/R: Disc/Drum
Steering: Recirculating ball
Wheelbase: 248.9cm 98.0in
Track F: 133.4cm 52.5in
Track R: 129.5cm 51.0in
Length: 431.8cm 170.0in
Width: 165.1cm 65.0in
Height: 142.2cm 56.0in
Ground clearance: 16.5cm 6.5in
Kerb weight: 978.0kg 2154.2lb
Fuel: 45.5L 10.0gal 12.0galUS

1743 Ford
Cortina GT
1967 UK
91.0mph 146.4kmh
0-50mph 80.5kmh: 11.2secs
0-60mph 96.5kmh: 14.5secs
0-1/4 mile: 19.1secs
78.0bhp 58.2kW 79.1PS
@ 5200rpm
97.0lbft 131.4Nm @ 3600rpm
85.6bhp/ton 84.2bhp/tonne
52.0bhp/L 38.8kW/L 52.7PS/L
41.5ft/sec 12.6m/sec
16.6mph 26.7kmh/1000rpm
Petrol 4-stroke piston
1500cc 91.5cu in
In-line 4 1 Carburettor
Compression ratio: 9.0:1
Bore: 81.0mm 3.2in
Stroke: 72.8mm 2.9in
Valve type/No: Overhead 8
Transmission: Manual
No. of forward speeds: 4
Wheels driven: Rear
Springs F/R: Coil/Leaf
Brakes F/R: Disc/Drum
Steering: Recirculating ball
Wheelbase: 248.9cm 98.0in
Track F: 133.4cm 52.5in
Track R: 129.5cm 51.0in
Length: 426.7cm 168.0in
Width: 164.8cm 64.9in
Height: 144.5cm 56.9in
Kerb weight: 926.2kg 2040.0lb
Fuel: 45.0L 9.9gal 11.9galUS

1744 Ford
Cortina Lotus
1967 UK
105.0mph 168.9kmh
0-50mph 80.5kmh: 7.9secs
0-60mph 96.5kmh: 11.0secs
0-1/4 mile: 18.2secs
0-1km: 32.2secs
109.5bhp 81.6kW 111.0PS
@ 6000rpm
106.5lbft 144.3Nm @ 4500rpm
113.9bhp/ton 112.0bhp/tonne
70.2bhp/L 52.3kW/L 71.2PS/L
47.8ft/sec 14.6m/sec
17.8mph 28.6kmh/1000rpm
22.2mpg 18.5mpgUS 12.7L/100km
Petrol 4-stroke piston
1560cc 95.2cu in
In-line 4 2 Carburettor
Compression ratio: 9.5:1
Bore: 82.6mm 3.2in
Stroke: 72.8mm 2.9in
Valve type/No: Overhead 8
Transmission: Manual
No. of forward speeds: 4
Wheels driven: Rear
Springs F/R: Coil/Leaf
Brake system: PA
Brakes F/R: Disc/Drum
Steering: Recirculating ball
Wheelbase: 248.9cm 98.0in
Track F: 135.9cm 53.5in
Track R: 132.1cm 52.0in
Length: 426.7cm 168.0in
Width: 165.1cm 65.0in
Height: 137.2cm 54.0in
Ground clearance: 12.7cm 5.0in
Kerb weight: 978.0kg 2154.2lb
Fuel: 45.5L 10.0gal 12.0galUS

1745 Ford
Cortina Super Estate
1967 UK
82.0mph 131.9kmh
0-50mph 80.5kmh: 16.7secs
0-60mph 96.5kmh: 24.6secs
0-1/4 mile: 23.1secs
0-1km: 43.4secs
61.5bhp 45.9kW 62.3PS
@ 4700rpm
83.5lbft 113.1Nm @ 2500rpm
63.9bhp/ton 62.9bhp/tonne
41.0bhp/L 30.6kW/L 41.6PS/L
37.5ft/sec 11.4m/sec
17.4mph 28.0kmh/1000rpm
22.4mpg 18.7mpgUS 12.6L/100km
Petrol 4-stroke piston
1500cc 91.5cu in
In-line 4 1 Carburettor
Compression ratio: 9.0:1
Bore: 81.0mm 3.2in

Stroke: 72.8mm 2.9in
Valve type/No: Overhead 8
Transmission: Automatic
No. of forward speeds: 3
Wheels driven: Rear
Springs F/R: Coil/Leaf
Brakes F/R: Disc/Drum
Steering: Recirculating ball
Wheelbase: 248.9cm 98.0in
Track F: 133.4cm 52.5in
Track R: 129.5cm 51.0in
Length: 431.8cm 170.0in
Width: 165.1cm 65.0in
Height: 144.8cm 57.0in
Ground clearance: 16.5cm 6.5in
Kerb weight: 978.0kg 2154.2lb
Fuel: 36.4L 8.0gal 9.6galUS

1746 Ford

Fairlane Ranchero
1967 USA
108.0mph 173.8kmh
0-50mph 80.5kmh: 7.0secs
0-60mph 96.5kmh: 9.8secs
0-1/4 mile: 16.4secs
315.0bhp 234.9kW 319.4PS
@ 4600rpm
427.0lbft 578.6Nm @ 2800rpm
198.8bhp/ton 195.4bhp/tonne
49.3bhp/L 36.8kW/L 50.0PS/L
48.3ft/sec 14.7m/sec
26.0mph 41.8kmh/1000rpm
Petrol 4-stroke piston
6385cc 389.6cu in
Vee 8 1 Carburettor
Compression ratio: 10.5:1
Bore: 102.9mm 4.0in
Stroke: 96.0mm 3.8in
Valve type/No: Overhead 16
Transmission: Automatic
No. of forward speeds: 3
Wheels driven: Rear
Springs F/R: Coil/Leaf
Brake system: PA
Brakes F/R: Disc/Drum
Steering: Recirculating ball PA
Wheelbase: 287.0cm 113.0in
Track F: 148.3cm 58.4in
Track R: 147.6cm 58.1in
Length: 507.7cm 199.9in
Width: 188.0cm 74.0in
Height: 142.7cm 56.2in
Ground clearance: 15.7cm 6.2in
Kerb weight: 1611.7kg 3550.0lb
Fuel: 75.7L 16.6gal 20.0galUS

1747 Ford

Mustang
1967 USA
110.0mph 177.0kmh
0-50mph 80.5kmh: 7.4secs
0-60mph 96.5kmh: 9.7secs
0-1/4 mile: 17.4secs
225.0bhp 167.8kW 228.1PS
@ 4400rpm
282.0lbft 382.1Nm @ 2400rpm
169.1bhp/ton 166.3bhp/tonne
47.5bhp/L 35.4kW/L 48.2PS/L
38.1ft/sec 11.6m/sec
25.1mph 40.4kmh/1000rpm
16.8mpg 14.0mpgUS 16.8L/100km
Petrol 4-stroke piston
4736cc 289.0cu in
Vee 8
Compression ratio: 9.8:1
Bore: 93.3mm 3.7in
Stroke: 79.3mm 3.1in
Valve type/No: Overhead 16
Transmission: Manual
No. of forward speeds: 4
Wheels driven: Rear
Brakes F/R: Disc/Drum
Steering: Recirculating ball
Wheelbase: 274.3cm 108.0in
Track F: 147.6cm 58.1in
Track R: 147.6cm 58.1in
Length: 466.3cm 183.6in
Width: 180.1cm 70.9in
Height: 131.1cm 51.6in
Kerb weight: 1352.9kg 2980.0lb
Fuel: 64.3L 14.1gal 17.0galUS

1748 Ford

Mustang 390 Fastback
1967 USA
113.0mph 181.8kmh
0-50mph 80.5kmh: 5.8secs
0-60mph 96.5kmh: 7.8secs
0-1/4 mile: 15.5secs
335.0bhp 249.8kW 339.6PS
@ 4800rpm
427.0lbft 578.6Nm @ 3200rpm
220.7bhp/ton 217.0bhp/tonne
52.5bhp/L 39.1kW/L 53.2PS/L
50.4ft/sec 15.4m/sec
22.5mph 36.2kmh/1000rpm
Petrol 4-stroke piston
6381cc 389.3cu in
Vee 8 1 Carburettor
Compression ratio: 10.5:1
Bore: 102.9mm 4.0in
Stroke: 96.0mm 3.8in
Valve type/No: Overhead 16
Transmission: Automatic
No. of forward speeds: 3
Wheels driven: Rear
Springs F/R: Coil/Leaf
Brake system: PA
Brakes F/R: Disc/Drum
Steering: Recirculating ball PA
Wheelbase: 274.3cm 108.0in
Track F: 147.6cm 58.1in
Track R: 147.6cm 58.1in
Length: 466.3cm 183.6in
Width: 180.1cm 70.9in
Height: 131.6cm 51.8in
Ground clearance: 16.5cm 6.5in
Kerb weight: 1543.6kg 3400.0lb
Fuel: 64.3L 14.1gal 17.0galUS

1749 Ford

Thunderbird
1967 USA
120.0mph 193.1kmh
0-50mph 80.5kmh: 7.5secs
0-60mph 96.5kmh: 9.8secs
0-1/4 mile: 16.4secs
345.0bhp 257.3kW 349.8PS
@ 4600rpm
462.0lbft 626.0Nm @ 2800rpm
168.4bhp/ton 165.6bhp/tonne
49.4bhp/L 36.8kW/L 50.1PS/L
50.9ft/sec 15.5m/sec
25.6mph 41.2kmh/1000rpm
Petrol 4-stroke piston
6986cc 426.2cu in
Vee 8 1 Carburettor
Compression ratio: 10.5:1
Bore: 104.9mm 4.1in
Stroke: 101.2mm 4.0in
Valve type/No: Overhead 16
Transmission: Automatic
No. of forward speeds: 3
Wheels driven: Rear
Springs F/R: Coil/Coil
Brake system: PA
Brakes F/R: Disc/Drum
Steering: Recirculating ball PA
Wheelbase: 297.2cm 117.0in
Track F: 157.5cm 62.0in
Track R: 157.5cm 62.0in
Length: 531.9cm 209.4in
Width: 196.1cm 77.2in
Height: 136.7cm 53.8in
Ground clearance: 16.5cm 6.5in
Kerb weight: 2083.9kg 4590.0lb
Fuel: 91.2L 20.0gal 24.1galUS

1750 Ford

Zodiac Executive
1967 UK
102.0mph 164.1kmh
0-50mph 80.5kmh: 9.2secs
0-60mph 96.5kmh: 13.1secs
0-1/4 mile: 18.6secs
0-1km: 35.3secs
136.0bhp 101.4kW 137.9PS
@ 4740rpm
181.5lbft 245.9Nm @ 3000rpm
99.7bhp/ton 98.1bhp/tonne
45.4bhp/L 33.9kW/L 46.1PS/L
37.5ft/sec 11.4m/sec
19.7mph 31.7kmh/1000rpm
17.2mpg 14.3mpgUS 16.4L/100km
Petrol 4-stroke piston
2994cc 182.7cu in
Vee 6 1 Carburettor
Compression ratio: 8.9:1
Bore: 93.7mm 3.7in
Stroke: 72.4mm 2.8in
Valve type/No: Overhead 12
Transmission: Automatic
No. of forward speeds: 3
Wheels driven: Rear
Springs F/R: Coil/Coil
Brake system: PA
Brakes F/R: Disc/Disc
Steering: Recirculating ball PA
Wheelbase: 292.1cm 115.0in
Track F: 144.8cm 57.0in
Track R: 147.3cm 58.0in
Length: 469.9cm 185.0in
Width: 181.1cm 71.3in
Height: 148.6cm 58.5in
Ground clearance: 15.2cm 6.0in
Kerb weight: 1386.5kg 3054.0lb
Fuel: 68.2L 15.0gal 18.0galUS

1751 Ford

Cortina 1300 de Luxe
1968 UK
86.0mph 138.4kmh
0-50mph 80.5kmh: 12.4secs
0-60mph 96.5kmh: 18.2secs
0-1/4 mile: 20.7secs
0-1km: 40.1secs
57.5bhp 42.9kW 58.3PS
@ 5000rpm
74.5lbft 100.9Nm @ 2500rpm
59.8bhp/ton 58.8bhp/tonne
44.3bhp/L 33.1kW/L 44.9PS/L
34.4ft/sec 10.5m/sec
15.8mph 25.4kmh/1000rpm
24.9mpg 20.7mpgUS 11.3L/100km
Petrol 4-stroke piston
1297cc 79.1cu in
In-line 4 1 Carburettor
Compression ratio: 9.0:1
Bore: 80.9mm 3.2in
Stroke: 63.0mm 2.5in
Valve type/No: Overhead 8
Transmission: Manual
No. of forward speeds: 4
Wheels driven: Rear
Springs F/R: Coil/Leaf
Brakes F/R: Disc/Drum
Steering: Recirculating ball
Wheelbase: 248.9cm 98.0in
Track F: 133.4cm 52.5in
Track R: 132.8cm 52.3in
Length: 426.7cm 168.0in
Width: 165.1cm 65.0in
Height: 143.5cm 56.5in
Ground clearance: 16.5cm 6.5in
Kerb weight: 978.0kg 2154.2lb
Fuel: 45.5L 10.0gal 12.0galUS

1752 Ford

Cortina GT
1968 UK
102.0mph 164.1kmh
0-50mph 80.5kmh: 11.3secs
0-60mph 96.5kmh: 14.9secs
0-1/4 mile: 18.8secs
89.0bhp 66.4kW 90.2PS
@ 5500rpm
103.0lbft 139.6Nm @ 4000rpm
98.2bhp/ton 96.6bhp/tonne
55.7bhp/L 41.5kW/L 56.4PS/L
46.7ft/sec 14.2m/sec
16.8mph 27.0kmh/1000rpm
Petrol 4-stroke piston
1599cc 97.6cu in
In-line 4 1 Carburettor
Compression ratio: 9.6:1
Bore: 81.0mm 3.2in
Stroke: 77.6mm 3.1in
Valve type/No: Overhead 8
Transmission: Manual
No. of forward speeds: 4
Wheels driven: Rear
Springs F/R: Coil/Leaf
Brakes F/R: Disc/Drum
Steering: Recirculating ball
Wheelbase: 248.9cm 98.0in
Track F: 133.4cm 52.5in
Track R: 129.5cm 51.0in
Length: 426.7cm 168.0in
Width: 164.8cm 64.9in
Height: 139.7cm 55.0in
Kerb weight: 921.6kg 2030.0lb
Fuel: 45.4L 10.0gal 12.0galUS

1753 Ford

Cortina GT Estate
1968 UK
97.0mph 156.1kmh
0-50mph 80.5kmh: 9.6secs
0-60mph 96.5kmh: 14.2secs
0-1/4 mile: 19.3secs
0-1km: 35.9secs
88.0bhp 65.6kW 89.2PS
@ 5400rpm
96.0lbft 130.1Nm @ 3600rpm
91.5bhp/ton 90.0bhp/tonne
55.1bhp/L 41.1kW/L 55.8PS/L
45.9ft/sec 14.0m/sec
17.1mph 27.5kmh/1000rpm
23.6mpg 19.7mpgUS 12.0L/100km
Petrol 4-stroke piston
1598cc 97.5cu in
In-line 4 1 Carburettor
Compression ratio: 9.0:1
Bore: 80.9mm 3.2in
Stroke: 77.6mm 3.1in
Valve type/No: Overhead 8
Transmission: Manual
No. of forward speeds: 4
Wheels driven: Rear
Springs F/R: Coil/Leaf
Brakes F/R: Disc/Drum
Steering: Recirculating ball
Wheelbase: 248.9cm 98.0in
Track F: 133.4cm 52.5in
Track R: 129.5cm 51.0in
Length: 431.8cm 170.0in
Width: 165.1cm 65.0in
Height: 144.8cm 57.0in
Ground clearance: 16.5cm 6.5in
Kerb weight: 978.0kg 2154.2lb
Fuel: 36.4L 8.0gal 9.6galUS

1754 Ford

Cortina Race-proved Savage
1968 UK
108.0mph 173.8kmh
0-50mph 80.5kmh: 6.6secs
0-60mph 96.5kmh: 9.2secs
0-1/4 mile: 16.8secs
0-1km: 31.5secs
136.0bhp 101.4kW 137.9PS
@ 4750rpm
182.0lbft 246.6Nm @ 3000rpm
129.3bhp/ton 127.1bhp/tonne
45.4bhp/L 33.9kW/L 46.1PS/L
37.6ft/sec 11.5m/sec
19.5mph 31.4kmh/1000rpm
20.7mpg 17.2mpgUS 13.6L/100km
Petrol 4-stroke piston
2994cc 182.7cu in
Vee 6 1 Carburettor
Compression ratio: 8.9:1
Bore: 93.7mm 3.7in
Stroke: 72.4mm 2.8in
Valve type/No: Overhead 12
Transmission: Manual
No. of forward speeds: 4
Wheels driven: Rear
Springs F/R: Coil/Leaf
Brake system: PA
Brakes F/R: Disc/Drum
Steering: Recirculating ball
Wheelbase: 248.9cm 98.0in
Track F: 133.4cm 52.5in
Track R: 132.8cm 52.3in
Length: 426.7cm 168.0in
Width: 165.1cm 65.0in
Height: 143.5cm 56.5in
Ground clearance: 16.5cm 6.5in
Kerb weight: 1069.6kg 2356.0lb
Fuel: 45.5L 10.0gal 12.0galUS

1755 Ford

Cortina Station Wagon
1968 UK
85.0mph 136.8kmh
0-1/4 mile: 20.0secs
76.0bhp 56.7kW 77.0PS
47.5bhp/L 35.4kW/L 48.2PS/L
26.4mpg 22.0mpgUS 10.7L/100km
Petrol 4-stroke piston
1599cc 97.6cu in
In-line 4
Valve type/No: Overhead 8
Wheels driven: Rear
Wheelbase: 248.9cm 98.0in
Length: 426.7cm 168.0in

1756 Ford

Escort
1968 UK
80.0mph 128.7kmh
0-50mph 80.5kmh: 14.5secs
0-60mph 96.5kmh: 22.3secs
0-1/4 mile: 22.1secs

0-1km: 42.4secs
49.5bhp 36.9kW 50.2PS
@ 5500rpm
58.5lbft 79.3Nm @ 3000rpm
65.1bhp/ton 64.0bhp/tonne
45.1bhp/L 33.6kW/L 45.7PS/L
32.1ft/sec 9.8m/sec
15.1mph 24.3kmh/1000rpm
27.6mpg 23.0mpgUS 10.2L/100km
Petrol 4-stroke piston
1098cc 67.0cu in
In-line 4 1 Carburettor
Compression ratio: 9.0:1
Bore: 81.0mm 3.2in
Stroke: 53.3mm 2.1in
Valve type/No: Overhead 8
Transmission: Manual
No. of forward speeds: 4
Wheels driven: Rear
Springs F/R: Coil/Leaf
Brake system: PA
Brakes F/R: Disc/Drum
Steering: Rack & pinion
Wheelbase: 240.0cm 94.5in
Track F: 124.5cm 49.0in
Track R: 127.0cm 50.0in
Length: 406.4cm 160.0in
Width: 157.0cm 61.8in
Height: 139.7cm 55.0in
Ground clearance: 16.0cm 6.3in
Kerb weight: 773.6kg 1704.0lb
Fuel: 40.9L 9.0gal 10.8galUS

1757 Ford
Escort 1300
1968 UK
85.0mph 136.8kmh
0-50mph 80.5kmh: 13.2secs
0-60mph 96.5kmh: 19.4secs
0-1/4 mile: 22.0secs
0-1km: 41.6secs
58.0bhp 43.2kW 58.8PS
@ 5000rpm
71.5lbft 96.9Nm @ 2500rpm
72.8bhp/ton 71.6bhp/tonne
44.7bhp/L 33.3kW/L 45.3PS/L
34.4ft/sec 10.5m/sec
15.1mph 24.3kmh/1000rpm
25.0mpg 20.8mpgUS 11.3L/100km
Petrol 4-stroke piston
1297cc 79.1cu in
In-line 4 1 Carburettor
Compression ratio: 9.0:1
Bore: 81.0mm 3.2in
Stroke: 63.0mm 2.5in
Valve type/No: Overhead 8
Transmission: Automatic
No. of forward speeds: 3
Wheels driven: Rear
Springs F/R: Coil/Leaf
Brake system: PA
Brakes F/R: Disc/Drum
Steering: Rack & pinion
Wheelbase: 240.0cm 94.5in
Track F: 131.3cm 51.7in
Track R: 132.1cm 52.0in
Length: 406.4cm 160.0in
Width: 157.0cm 61.8in
Height: 137.2cm 54.0in
Ground clearance: 15.2cm 6.0in
Kerb weight: 810.4kg 1785.0lb
Fuel: 40.9L 9.0gal 10.8galUS

1758 Ford
Escort Twin Cam
1968 UK
113.0mph 181.8kmh
0-50mph 80.5kmh: 7.2secs
0-60mph 96.5kmh: 9.9secs
0-1/4 mile: 17.2secs
0-1km: 31.9secs
109.5bhp 81.6kW 111.0PS
@ 6000rpm
106.5lbft 144.3Nm @ 4500rpm
131.0bhp/ton 128.8bhp/tonne
70.3bhp/L 52.4kW/L 71.3PS/L
47.8ft/sec 14.6m/sec
17.8mph 28.6kmh/1000rpm
21.5mpg 17.9mpgUS 13.1L/100km
Petrol 4-stroke piston
1558cc 95.1cu in
In-line 4 2 Carburettor
Compression ratio: 9.5:1
Bore: 82.5mm 3.2in
Stroke: 72.8mm 2.9in
Valve type/No: Overhead 8
Transmission: Manual
No. of forward speeds: 4
Wheels driven: Rear
Springs F/R: Coil/Leaf
Brake system: PA
Brakes F/R: Disc/Drum
Steering: Rack & pinion
Wheelbase: 240.0cm 94.5in
Track F: 131.3cm 51.7in
Track R: 132.1cm 52.0in
Length: 406.4cm 160.0in
Width: 157.0cm 61.8in
Height: 137.2cm 54.0in
Ground clearance: 15.2cm 6.0in
Kerb weight: 849.9kg 1872.0lb
Fuel: 40.9L 9.0gal 10.8galUS

1759 Ford
Galaxie
1968 USA
95.0mph 152.9kmh
0-50mph 80.5kmh: 8.6secs
0-60mph 96.5kmh: 12.0secs
0-1/4 mile: 18.9secs
210.0bhp 156.6kW 212.9PS
@ 4600rpm
300.0lbft 406.5Nm @ 2600rpm
125.4bhp/ton 123.3bhp/tonne
42.4bhp/L 31.6kW/L 43.0PS/L
38.3ft/sec 11.7m/sec
26.0mph 41.8kmh/1000rpm
Petrol 4-stroke piston
4949cc 301.9cu in
Vee 8 1 Carburettor
Compression ratio: 9.0:1
Bore: 101.6mm 4.0in
Stroke: 76.2mm 3.0in
Valve type/No: Overhead 16
Transmission: Automatic
No. of forward speeds: 3
Wheels driven: Rear
Springs F/R: Coil/Coil
Brakes F/R: Drum/Drum
Steering: Recirculating ball PA
Wheelbase: 302.3cm 119.0in
Track F: 157.5cm 62.0in
Track R: 157.5cm 62.0in
Length: 541.8cm 213.3in
Width: 198.1cm 78.0in
Height: 138.2cm 54.4in
Kerb weight: 1702.5kg 3750.0lb
Fuel: 94.6L 20.8gal 25.0galUS

1760 Ford
GT40
1968 UK
205.0mph 329.8kmh
0-60mph 96.5kmh: 5.0secs
0-1/4 mile: 12.5secs
380.0bhp 283.4kW 385.3PS
@ 6500rpm
330.0lbft 447.2Nm @ 5500rpm
342.5bhp/ton 336.8bhp/tonne
80.2bhp/L 59.8kW/L 81.3PS/L
51.8ft/sec 15.8m/sec
Petrol 4-stroke piston
4736cc 289.0cu in
Vee 8 4 Carburettor
Compression ratio: 10.5:1
Bore: 101.6mm 4.0in
Stroke: 72.9mm 2.9in
Valve type/No: Overhead 16
Transmission: Manual
No. of forward speeds: 5
Wheels driven: Rear
Springs F/R: Coil/Coil
Brakes F/R: Disc/Disc
Steering: Rack & pinion
Wheelbase: 241.3cm 95.0in
Track F: 139.7cm 55.0in
Track R: 139.7cm 55.0in
Length: 417.8cm 164.5in
Width: 177.8cm 70.0in
Height: 101.6cm 40.0in
Kerb weight: 1128.2kg 2485.0lb
Fuel: 140.0L 30.8gal 37.0galUS

1761 Ford
Mustang 428 Cobra Jet
1968 USA
0-60mph 96.5kmh: 5.9secs
0-1/4 mile: 13.6secs
335.0bhp 249.8kW 339.6PS
@ 5400rpm
440.0lbft 596.2Nm @ 3400rpm
224.7bhp/ton 220.9bhp/tonne
47.7bhp/L 35.6kW/L 48.4PS/L
59.7ft/sec 18.2m/sec
Petrol 4-stroke piston
7019cc 428.2cu in
Vee 8 1 Carburettor
Compression ratio: 10.6:1
Bore: 104.9mm 4.1in
Stroke: 101.1mm 4.0in
Valve type/No: Overhead 16
Transmission: Automatic
No. of forward speeds: 3
Wheels driven: Rear
Springs F/R: Coil/Leaf
Brake system: PA
Brakes F/R: Disc/Drum
Steering: Recirculating ball PA
Wheelbase: 274.3cm 108.0in
Track F: 147.3cm 58.0in
Track R: 147.3cm 58.0in
Length: 466.3cm 183.6in
Width: 180.1cm 70.9in
Height: 131.1cm 51.6in
Kerb weight: 1516.4kg 3340.0lb
Fuel: 64.3L 14.1gal 17.0galUS

1762 Ford
Mustang Fastback
1968 USA
113.0mph 181.8kmh
0-50mph 80.5kmh: 6.6secs
0-60mph 96.5kmh: 8.7secs
0-1/4 mile: 16.7secs
230.0bhp 171.5kW 233.2PS
@ 4800rpm
310.0lbft 420.1Nm @ 2800rpm
161.0bhp/ton 158.3bhp/tonne
46.5bhp/L 34.7kW/L 47.1PS/L
40.0ft/sec 12.2m/sec
23.6mph 38.0kmh/1000rpm
Petrol 4-stroke piston
4949cc 301.9cu in
Vee 8 1 Carburettor
Compression ratio: 10.0:1
Bore: 101.6mm 4.0in
Stroke: 76.2mm 3.0in
Valve type/No: Overhead 16
Transmission: Automatic
No. of forward speeds: 3
Wheels driven: Rear
Springs F/R: Coil/Leaf
Brake system: PA
Brakes F/R: Disc/Drum
Steering: Recirculating ball
Wheelbase: 274.3cm 108.0in
Track F: 148.6cm 58.5in
Track R: 148.6cm 58.5in
Length: 466.3cm 183.6in
Width: 180.1cm 70.9in
Height: 130.6cm 51.4in
Kerb weight: 1452.8kg 3200.0lb
Fuel: 60.6L 13.3gal 16.0galUS

1763 Ford
Torino
1968 USA
111.0mph 178.6kmh
0-50mph 80.5kmh: 6.0secs
0-60mph 96.5kmh: 7.7secs
0-1/4 mile: 15.8secs
315.0bhp 234.9kW 319.4PS
@ 4600rpm
427.0lbft 578.6Nm @ 2800rpm
187.7bhp/ton 184.5bhp/tonne
49.3bhp/L 36.8kW/L 50.0PS/L
48.3ft/sec 14.7m/sec
22.3mph 35.9kmh/1000rpm
Petrol 4-stroke piston
6384cc 389.5cu in
Vee 8 1 Carburettor
Compression ratio: 10.5:1
Bore: 102.9mm 4.0in
Stroke: 96.0mm 3.8in
Valve type/No: Overhead 16
Transmission: Automatic
No. of forward speeds: 3
Wheels driven: Rear
Springs F/R: Coil/Leaf
Brakes F/R: Drum/Drum
Steering: Recirculating ball
Wheelbase: 294.6cm 116.0in
Track F: 149.4cm 58.8in
Track R: 148.6cm 58.5in
Length: 510.5cm 201.0in
Width: 189.5cm 74.6in
Height: 135.6cm 53.4in
Ground clearance: 15.2cm 6.0in
Kerb weight: 1707.0kg 3760.0lb
Fuel: 75.7L 16.6gal 20.0galUS

1764 Ford
XL Fastback 428
1968 USA
123.0mph 197.9kmh
0-50mph 80.5kmh: 6.2secs
0-60mph 96.5kmh: 8.2secs
0-1/4 mile: 16.7secs
340.0bhp 253.5kW 344.7PS
@ 4600rpm
462.0lbft 626.0Nm @ 2800rpm
179.8bhp/ton 176.8bhp/tonne
48.6bhp/L 36.3kW/L 49.3PS/L
50.9ft/sec 15.5m/sec
28.4mph 45.7kmh/1000rpm
Petrol 4-stroke piston
6990cc 426.5cu in
Vee 8 1 Carburettor
Compression ratio: 10.5:1
Bore: 104.9mm 4.1in
Stroke: 101.1mm 4.0in
Valve type/No: Overhead 16
Transmission: Automatic
No. of forward speeds: 3
Wheels driven: Rear
Springs F/R: Coil/Coil
Brake system: PA
Brakes F/R: Disc/Drum
Steering: Recirculating ball PA
Wheelbase: 302.3cm 119.0in
Track F: 157.5cm 62.0in
Track R: 157.5cm 62.0in
Length: 541.8cm 213.3in
Width: 198.1cm 78.0in
Height: 138.2cm 54.4in
Ground clearance: 16.8cm 6.6in
Kerb weight: 1923.1kg 4236.0lb
Fuel: 94.6L 20.8gal 25.0galUS

1765 Ford
Zephyr de Luxe
1968 UK
99.0mph 159.3kmh
0-50mph 80.5kmh: 12.1secs
0-60mph 96.5kmh: 17.7secs
0-1/4 mile: 20.3secs
0-1km: 39.6secs
88.0bhp 65.6kW 89.2PS
@ 4750rpm
116.0lbft 157.2Nm @ 2750rpm
69.3bhp/ton 68.1bhp/tonne
44.1bhp/L 32.9kW/L 44.7PS/L
31.3ft/sec 9.5m/sec
19.7mph 31.7kmh/1000rpm
21.1mpg 17.6mpgUS 13.4L/100km
Petrol 4-stroke piston
1996cc 121.8cu in
Vee 4 1 Carburettor
Compression ratio: 8.9:1
Bore: 93.7mm 3.7in
Stroke: 60.3mm 2.4in
Valve type/No: Overhead 8
Transmission: Manual
No. of forward speeds: 4
Wheels driven: Rear
Springs F/R: Coil/Coil
Brake system: PA
Brakes F/R: Disc/Disc
Steering: Recirculating ball
Wheelbase: 292.1cm 115.0in
Track F: 144.8cm 57.0in
Track R: 147.3cm 58.0in
Length: 469.9cm 185.0in
Width: 181.1cm 71.3in
Height: 147.6cm 58.1in
Ground clearance: 15.2cm 6.0in
Kerb weight: 1291.2kg 2844.0lb
Fuel: 68.2L 15.0gal 18.0galUS

1766 Ford
Capri 1600 GT
1969 UK
98.0mph 157.7kmh
0-50mph 80.5kmh: 9.4secs
0-60mph 96.5kmh: 13.4secs
0-1/4 mile: 18.8secs
0-1km: 35.5secs
88.0bhp 65.6kW 89.2PS
@ 5400rpm
96.0lbft 130.1Nm @ 3600rpm
96.0bhp/ton 94.4bhp/tonne
55.0bhp/L 41.0kW/L 55.8PS/L
45.4ft/sec 13.9m/sec
17.9mph 28.8kmh/1000rpm
24.8mpg 20.7mpgUS 11.4L/100km
Petrol 4-stroke piston
1599cc 97.6cu in
In-line 4 1 Carburettor

Compression ratio: 9.0:1
Bore: 81.0mm 3.2in
Stroke: 77.0mm 3.0in
Valve type/No: Overhead 8
Transmission: Manual
No. of forward speeds: 4
Wheels driven: Rear
Springs F/R: Coil/Leaf
Brake system: PA
Brakes F/R: Disc/Drum
Steering: Rack & pinion
Wheelbase: 256.0cm 100.8in
Track F: 134.6cm 53.0in
Track R: 132.1cm 52.0in
Length: 428.0cm 168.5in
Width: 164.6cm 64.8in
Height: 128.8cm 50.7in
Ground clearance: 11.4cm 4.5in
Kerb weight: 932.1kg 2053.0lb
Fuel: 47.8L 10.5gal 12.6galUS

1767 Ford

Capri 2000 GT
1969 UK
107.0mph 172.2kmh
0-50mph 80.5kmh: 7.5secs
0-60mph 96.5kmh: 10.6secs
0-1/4 mile: 18.2secs
0-1km: 33.6secs
92.5bhp 69.0kW 93.8PS
@ 5500rpm
104.0lbft 140.9Nm @ 3600rpm
93.7bhp/ton 92.1bhp/tonne
46.3bhp/L 34.6kW/L 47.0PS/L
43.5ft/sec 13.3m/sec
19.0mph 30.6kmh/1000rpm
22.0mpg 18.3mpgUS 12.8L/100km
Petrol 4-stroke piston
1996cc 121.8cu in
Vee 4 1 Carburettor
Compression ratio: 8.9:1
Bore: 93.7mm 3.7in
Stroke: 72.4mm 2.8in
Valve type/No: Overhead 8
Transmission: Manual
No. of forward speeds: 4
Wheels driven: Rear
Springs F/R: Coil/Leaf
Brake system: PA
Brakes F/R: Disc/Drum
Steering: Rack & pinion
Wheelbase: 256.0cm 100.8in
Track F: 134.6cm 53.0in
Track R: 132.1cm 52.0in
Length: 428.0cm 168.5in
Width: 164.6cm 64.8in
Height: 128.8cm 50.7in
Ground clearance: 11.4cm 4.5in
Kerb weight: 1004.2kg 2212.0lb
Fuel: 47.8L 10.5gal 12.6galUS

1768 Ford

Capri 3000 GT XLR
1969 UK
115.0mph 185.0kmh
0-50mph 80.5kmh: 7.6secs
0-60mph 96.5kmh: 10.3secs
0-1/4 mile: 17.6secs
0-1km: 32.3secs
136.0bhp 101.4kW 137.9PS
@ 4750rpm
181.0lbft 245.3Nm @ 3000rpm
132.0bhp/ton 129.8bhp/tonne
45.4bhp/L 33.9kW/L 46.1PS/L
37.6ft/sec 11.5m/sec
20.7mph 33.3kmh/1000rpm
19.3mpg 16.1mpgUS 14.6L/100km
Petrol 4-stroke piston
2994cc 182.7cu in
Vee 6 1 Carburettor
Compression ratio: 8.9:1
Bore: 93.7mm 3.7in
Stroke: 72.4mm 2.8in
Valve type/No: Overhead 12
Transmission: Manual
No. of forward speeds: 4
Wheels driven: Rear
Springs F/R: Coil/Leaf
Brake system: PA
Brakes F/R: Disc/Drum
Steering: Rack & pinion
Wheelbase: 256.0cm 100.8in
Track F: 134.6cm 53.0in
Track R: 132.1cm 52.0in
Length: 428.0cm 168.5in
Width: 164.6cm 64.8in
Height: 128.8cm 50.7in
Ground clearance: 11.4cm 4.5in
Kerb weight: 1047.4kg 2307.0lb
Fuel: 63.7L 14.0gal 16.8galUS

1769 Ford

Cortina 1100
1969 UK
72.0mph 115.8kmh
0-50mph 80.5kmh: 17.7secs
0-60mph 96.5kmh: 27.1secs
0-1/4 mile: 23.7secs
0-1km: 45.1secs
49.5bhp 36.9kW 50.2PS
@ 5500rpm
59.0lbft 79.9Nm @ 3000rpm
57.7bhp/ton 56.8bhp/tonne
45.1bhp/L 33.6kW/L 45.7PS/L
32.1ft/sec 9.8m/sec
15.2mph 24.5kmh/1000rpm
22.3mpg 18.6mpgUS 12.7L/100km
Petrol 4-stroke piston
1098cc 67.0cu in
In-line 4 1 Carburettor
Compression ratio: 9.0:1
Bore: 81.0mm 3.2in
Stroke: 53.3mm 2.1in
Valve type/No: Overhead 8
Transmission: Manual
No. of forward speeds: 4
Wheels driven: Rear
Springs F/R: Coil/Leaf
Brakes F/R: Disc/Drum
Steering: Recirculating ball
Wheelbase: 248.9cm 98.0in
Track F: 133.4cm 52.5in
Track R: 129.5cm 51.0in
Length: 431.8cm 170.0in
Width: 165.1cm 65.0in
Height: 144.8cm 57.0in
Ground clearance: 16.5cm 6.5in
Kerb weight: 871.7kg 1920.0lb
Fuel: 45.5L 10.0gal 12.0galUS

1770 Ford

Cortina 1600 GT
1969 UK
96.0mph 154.5kmh
0-50mph 80.5kmh: 10.0secs
0-60mph 96.5kmh: 14.2secs
0-1/4 mile: 19.8secs
89.5bhp 66.7kW 90.7PS
@ 5400rpm
98.0lbft 132.8Nm @ 3600rpm
98.0bhp/ton 96.4bhp/tonne
56.0bhp/L 41.7kW/L 56.7PS/L
45.9ft/sec 14.0m/sec
17.5mph 28.2kmh/1000rpm
26.4mpg 22.0mpgUS 10.7L/100km
Petrol 4-stroke piston
1599cc 97.6cu in
In-line 4 1 Carburettor
Compression ratio: 9.0:1
Bore: 81.0mm 3.2in
Stroke: 77.6mm 3.1in
Valve type/No: Overhead 8
Transmission: Manual
No. of forward speeds: 4
Wheels driven: Rear
Springs F/R: Coil/Leaf
Brake system: PA
Brakes F/R: Disc/Drum
Steering: Recirculating ball
Wheelbase: 248.9cm 98.0in
Track F: 133.4cm 52.5in
Track R: 131.6cm 51.8in
Length: 426.7cm 168.0in
Width: 164.8cm 64.9in
Height: 138.9cm 54.7in
Ground clearance: 13.2cm 5.2in
Kerb weight: 928.4kg 2045.0lb
Fuel: 45.4L 10.0gal 12.0galUS

1771 Ford

Fairlane 351
1969 USA
119.0mph 191.5kmh
0-50mph 80.5kmh: 7.6secs
0-60mph 96.5kmh: 10.1secs
0-1/4 mile: 17.4secs
250.0bhp 186.4kW 253.5PS
@ 4600rpm
355.0lbft 481.0Nm @ 2600rpm
161.8bhp/ton 159.1bhp/tonne
43.5bhp/L 32.4kW/L 44.1PS/L
44.7ft/sec 13.6m/sec
25.8mph 41.5kmh/1000rpm
Petrol 4-stroke piston
5752cc 350.9cu in
Vee 8 1 Carburettor
Compression ratio: 9.5:1
Bore: 101.6mm 4.0in
Stroke: 88.9mm 3.5in
Valve type/No: Overhead 16
Transmission: Automatic
No. of forward speeds: 3
Wheels driven: Rear
Springs F/R: Coil/Leaf
Brake system: PA
Brakes F/R: Disc/Drum
Steering: Recirculating ball PA
Wheelbase: 294.6cm 116.0in
Track F: 149.4cm 58.8in
Track R: 148.6cm 58.5in
Length: 515.6cm 203.0in
Width: 189.5cm 74.6in
Height: 133.1cm 52.4in
Kerb weight: 1570.8kg 3460.0lb
Fuel: 75.7L 16.6gal 20.0galUS

1772 Ford

Fairlane Cobra
1969 USA
125.5mph 201.9kmh
0-50mph 80.5kmh: 5.9secs
0-60mph 96.5kmh: 7.3secs
0-1/4 mile: 14.9secs
335.0bhp 249.8kW 339.6PS
@ 5200rpm
440.0lbft 596.2Nm @ 3400rpm
195.2bhp/ton 191.9bhp/tonne
47.8bhp/L 35.6kW/L 48.4PS/L
57.5ft/sec 17.5m/sec
20.9mph 33.6kmh/1000rpm
12.2mpg 10.2mpgUS 23.1L/100km
Petrol 4-stroke piston
7014cc 427.9cu in
Vee 8 1 Carburettor
Compression ratio: 10.6:1
Bore: 105.0mm 4.1in
Stroke: 101.2mm 4.0in
Valve type/No: Overhead 16
Transmission: Manual
No. of forward speeds: 4
Wheels driven: Rear
Springs F/R: Coil/Leaf
Brake system: PA
Brakes F/R: Disc/Drum
Steering: Recirculating ball PA
Wheelbase: 294.6cm 116.0in
Track F: 149.4cm 58.8in
Track R: 148.6cm 58.5in
Length: 510.8cm 201.1in
Width: 190.0cm 74.8in
Height: 132.6cm 52.2in
Kerb weight: 1745.6kg 3845.0lb
Fuel: 75.7L 16.6gal 20.0galUS

1773 Ford

LTD
1969 USA
123.0mph 197.9kmh
0-50mph 80.5kmh: 7.2secs
0-60mph 96.5kmh: 9.1secs
0-1/4 mile: 16.7secs
360.0bhp 268.4kW 365.0PS
@ 4600rpm
480.0lbft 650.4Nm @ 2800rpm
176.6bhp/ton 173.7bhp/tonne
51.2bhp/L 38.2kW/L 51.9PS/L
45.9ft/sec 14.0m/sec
26.8mph 43.1kmh/1000rpm
Petrol 4-stroke piston
7030cc 428.9cu in
Vee 8 1 Carburettor
Compression ratio: 10.5:1
Bore: 110.7mm 4.4in
Stroke: 91.2mm 3.6in
Valve type/No: Overhead 16
Transmission: Automatic
No. of forward speeds: 3
Wheels driven: Rear
Springs F/R: Coil/Coil
Brake system: PA
Brakes F/R: Disc/Drum
Steering: Recirculating ball PA
Wheelbase: 307.3cm 121.0in
Track F: 160.0cm 63.0in
Track R: 162.6cm 64.0in
Length: 543.6cm 214.0in
Width: 203.2cm 80.0in
Height: 137.2cm 54.0in
Kerb weight: 2072.5kg 4565.0lb
Fuel: 94.6L 20.8gal 25.0galUS

1774 Ford

Maverick
1969 USA
95.0mph 152.9kmh
0-50mph 80.5kmh: 10.6secs
0-60mph 96.5kmh: 14.5secs
0-1/4 mile: 19.5secs
120.0bhp 89.5kW 121.7PS
@ 4000rpm
190.0lbft 257.5Nm @ 2200rpm
105.0bhp/ton 103.2bhp/tonne
36.6bhp/L 27.3kW/L 37.1PS/L
34.8ft/sec 10.6m/sec
26.1mph 42.0kmh/1000rpm
24.6mpg 20.5mpgUS 11.5L/100km
Petrol 4-stroke piston
3277cc 199.9cu in
In-line 6 1 Carburettor
Compression ratio: 8.7:1
Bore: 93.4mm 3.7in
Stroke: 79.5mm 3.1in
Valve type/No: Overhead 12
Transmission: Automatic
No. of forward speeds: 3
Wheels driven: Rear
Springs F/R: Coil/Leaf
Brake system: PA
Brakes F/R: Drum/Drum
Steering: Recirculating ball
Wheelbase: 261.6cm 103.0in
Track F: 141.0cm 55.5in
Track R: 141.0cm 55.5in
Length: 455.7cm 179.4in
Width: 179.3cm 70.6in
Height: 132.8cm 52.3in
Ground clearance: 13.2cm 5.2in
Kerb weight: 1162.2kg 2560.0lb
Fuel: 60.6L 13.3gal 16.0galUS

1775 Ford

Mustang 428 Mach I
1969 USA
121.0mph 194.7kmh
0-50mph 80.5kmh: 4.4secs
0-60mph 96.5kmh: 5.5secs
0-1/4 mile: 13.9secs
335.0bhp 249.8kW 339.6PS
@ 5200rpm
440.0lbft 596.2Nm @ 3400rpm
219.4bhp/ton 215.8bhp/tonne
47.8bhp/L 35.6kW/L 48.4PS/L
57.5ft/sec 17.5m/sec
19.4mph 31.2kmh/1000rpm
Petrol 4-stroke piston
7014cc 427.9cu in
Vee 8 1 Carburettor
Compression ratio: 10.2:1
Bore: 104.9mm 4.1in
Stroke: 101.1mm 4.0in
Valve type/No: Overhead 16
Transmission: Automatic
No. of forward speeds: 3
Wheels driven: Rear
Springs F/R: Coil/Leaf
Brake system: PA
Brakes F/R: Disc/Drum
Steering: Recirculating ball PA
Wheelbase: 274.3cm 108.0in
Track F: 149.9cm 59.0in
Track R: 149.9cm 59.0in
Length: 475.0cm 187.0in
Width: 182.4cm 71.8in
Height: 127.8cm 50.3in
Kerb weight: 1552.7kg 3420.0lb
Fuel: 75.7L 16.6gal 20.0galUS

1776 Ford

Mustang Boss 302
1969 USA
118.0mph 189.9kmh
0-50mph 80.5kmh: 5.0secs
0-60mph 96.5kmh: 6.9secs
0-1/4 mile: 14.9secs
290.0bhp 216.2kW 294.0PS
@ 5800rpm
290.0lbft 393.0Nm @ 4300rpm
199.3bhp/ton 195.9bhp/tonne
58.6bhp/L 43.7kW/L 59.4PS/L
48.3ft/sec 14.7m/sec
19.8mph 31.9kmh/1000rpm
Petrol 4-stroke piston
4949cc 301.9cu in
Vee 8 1 Carburettor
Compression ratio: 10.5:1
Bore: 101.6mm 4.0in
Stroke: 76.2mm 3.0in
Valve type/No: Overhead 16

Transmission: Manual
No. of forward speeds: 4
Wheels driven: Rear
Springs F/R: Coil/Leaf
Brake system: PA
Brakes F/R: Disc/Drum
Steering: Recirculating ball
Wheelbase: 274.3cm 108.0in
Track F: 148.6cm 58.5in
Track R: 148.6cm 58.5in
Length: 476.0cm 187.4in
Width: 182.4cm 71.8in
Height: 127.8cm 50.3in
Kerb weight: 1480.0kg 3260.0lb
Fuel: 75.7L 16.6gal 20.0galUS

1777 Ford

Mustang Boss 429
1969 USA
118.0mph 189.9kmh
0-50mph 80.5kmh: 5.8secs
0-60mph 96.5kmh: 7.1secs
0-1/4 mile: 14.1secs
375.0bhp 279.6kW 380.2PS
@ 5200rpm
410.0lbft 555.6Nm @ 3400rpm
236.0bhp/ton 232.0bhp/tonne
53.3bhp/L 39.8kW/L 54.1PS/L
51.9ft/sec 15.8m/sec
19.1mph 30.7kmh/1000rpm
Petrol 4-stroke piston
7030cc 428.9cu in
Vee 8 1 Carburettor
Compression ratio: 10.5:1
Bore: 110.7mm 4.4in
Stroke: 91.2mm 3.6in
Valve type/No: Overhead 16
Transmission: Manual
No. of forward speeds: 4
Wheels driven: Rear
Springs F/R: Coil/Leaf
Brake system: PA
Brakes F/R: Disc/Drum
Steering: Recirculating ball PA
Wheelbase: 274.3cm 108.0in
Track F: 150.6cm 59.3in
Track R: 148.6cm 58.5in
Length: 475.0cm 187.0in
Width: 182.9cm 72.0in
Height: 129.5cm 51.0in
Kerb weight: 1616.2kg 3560.0lb
Fuel: 68.1L 15.0gal 18.0galUS

1778 Ford

Mustang Grande
1969 USA
119.2mph 191.8kmh
0-50mph 80.5kmh: 6.3secs
0-60mph 96.5kmh: 8.0secs
0-1/4 mile: 15.6secs
290.0bhp 216.2kW 294.0PS
@ 4800rpm
385.0lbft 521.7Nm @ 3200rpm
207.9bhp/ton 204.4bhp/tonne
50.4bhp/L 37.6kW/L 51.1PS/L
46.7ft/sec 14.2m/sec
27.1mph 43.6kmh/1000rpm
Petrol 4-stroke piston
5752cc 350.9cu in
Vee 8 1 Carburettor
Compression ratio: 10.7:1
Bore: 101.6mm 4.0in
Stroke: 88.9mm 3.5in
Valve type/No: Overhead 16
Transmission: Automatic
No. of forward speeds: 3
Wheels driven: Rear
Springs F/R: Coil/Leaf
Brake system: PA
Brakes F/R: Disc/Drum
Steering: Recirculating ball PA
Wheelbase: 274.3cm 108.0in
Track F: 148.6cm 58.5in
Track R: 148.6cm 58.5in
Length: 476.0cm 187.4in
Width: 181.1cm 71.3in
Height: 130.3cm 51.3in
Kerb weight: 1418.7kg 3125.0lb
Fuel: 75.7L 16.6gal 20.0galUS

1779 Ford

Thunderbird
1969 USA
126.0mph 202.7kmh
0-50mph 80.5kmh: 7.7secs
0-60mph 96.5kmh: 9.8secs
0-1/4 mile: 16.8secs
360.0bhp 268.4kW 365.0PS
@ 4600rpm
480.0lbft 650.4Nm @ 2800rpm
177.5bhp/ton 174.5bhp/tonne
51.2bhp/L 38.2kW/L 51.9PS/L
45.9ft/sec 14.0m/sec
29.2mph 47.0kmh/1000rpm
Petrol 4-stroke piston
7030cc 428.9cu in
Vee 8 1 Carburettor
Compression ratio: 10.0:1
Bore: 110.7mm 4.4in
Stroke: 91.2mm 3.6in
Valve type/No: Overhead 16
Transmission: Automatic
No. of forward speeds: 3
Wheels driven: Rear
Springs F/R: Coil/Coil
Brake system: PA
Brakes F/R: Disc/Drum
Steering: Recirculating ball PA
Wheelbase: 291.3cm 114.7in
Track F: 157.5cm 62.0in
Track R: 157.5cm 62.0in
Length: 525.5cm 206.9in
Width: 196.3cm 77.3in
Height: 132.8cm 52.3in
Kerb weight: 2062.5kg 4543.0lb
Fuel: 91.2L 20.0gal 24.1galUS

1780 Ford

Capri 1300 GT
1970 UK
94.0mph 151.2kmh
0-50mph 80.5kmh: 10.4secs
0-60mph 96.5kmh: 14.8secs
0-1/4 mile: 19.5secs
0-1km: 36.6secs
64.0bhp 47.7kW 64.9PS
@ 5800rpm
65.0lbft 88.1Nm @ 4000rpm
71.0bhp/ton 69.8bhp/tonne
49.3bhp/L 36.8kW/L 50.0PS/L
40.0ft/sec 12.2m/sec
16.4mph 26.4kmh/1000rpm
24.3mpg 20.2mpgUS 11.6L/100km
Petrol 4-stroke piston
1297cc 79.1cu in
In-line 4 1 Carburettor
Compression ratio: 9.2:1
Bore: 81.0mm 3.2in
Stroke: 63.0mm 2.5in
Valve type/No: Overhead 8
Transmission: Manual
No. of forward speeds: 4
Wheels driven: Rear
Springs F/R: Coil/Leaf
Brake system: PA
Brakes F/R: Disc/Drum
Steering: Rack & pinion
Wheelbase: 256.0cm 100.8in
Track F: 134.6cm 53.0in
Track R: 132.1cm 52.0in
Length: 428.0cm 168.5in
Width: 164.6cm 64.8in
Height: 128.8cm 50.7in
Ground clearance: 11.4cm 4.5in
Kerb weight: 917.1kg 2020.0lb
Fuel: 47.8L 10.5gal 12.6galUS

1781 Ford

Capri 1600
1970 UK
90.0mph 144.8kmh
0-50mph 80.5kmh: 11.4secs
0-60mph 96.5kmh: 17.3secs
0-1/4 mile: 20.4secs
71.0bhp 52.9kW 72.0PS
@ 5000rpm
91.0lbft 123.3Nm @ 2800rpm
74.5bhp/ton 73.2bhp/tonne
44.4bhp/L 33.1kW/L 45.0PS/L
42.5ft/sec 12.9m/sec
16.5mph 26.5kmh/1000rpm
29.3mpg 24.4mpgUS 9.6L/100km
Petrol 4-stroke piston
1599cc 97.6cu in
In-line 4 1 Carburettor
Compression ratio: 8.0:1
Bore: 81.0mm 3.2in
Stroke: 77.6mm 3.1in
Valve type/No: Overhead 8
Transmission: Manual
No. of forward speeds: 4
Wheels driven: Rear
Springs F/R: Coil/Leaf
Brake system: PA
Brakes F/R: Disc/Drum
Steering: Rack & pinion
Wheelbase: 256.0cm 100.8in
Track F: 134.6cm 53.0in
Track R: 132.1cm 52.0in
Length: 426.2cm 167.8in
Width: 164.6cm 64.8in
Height: 132.1cm 52.0in
Ground clearance: 15.2cm 6.0in
Kerb weight: 969.3kg 2135.0lb
Fuel: 45.4L 10.0gal 12.0galUS

1782 Ford

Capri Plus 50
1970 Germany
108.0mph 173.8kmh
0-50mph 80.5kmh: 6.7secs
0-60mph 96.5kmh: 9.2secs
0-1/4 mile: 17.0secs
125.0bhp 93.2kW 126.7PS
@ 6000rpm
121.0lbft 164.0Nm @ 5100rpm
78.2bhp/L 58.3kW/L 79.3PS/L
51.0ft/sec 15.5m/sec
18.0mpg 15.0mpgUS 15.7L/100km
Petrol 4-stroke piston
1599cc 97.6cu in
In-line 4 2 Carburettor
Compression ratio: 11.0:1
Bore: 81.0mm 3.2in
Stroke: 77.6mm 3.1in
Valve type/No: Overhead 8
Wheels driven: Rear

1783 Ford

Cortina 2000 GXL
1970 UK
105.0mph 168.9kmh
0-50mph 80.5kmh: 7.8secs
0-60mph 96.5kmh: 10.7secs
0-1/4 mile: 18.1secs
0-1km: 33.9secs
98.0bhp 73.1kW 99.4PS
@ 5500rpm
111.0lbft 150.4Nm @ 3500rpm
93.6bhp/ton 92.0bhp/tonne
49.2bhp/L 36.7kW/L 49.8PS/L
46.3ft/sec 14.1m/sec
19.9mph 32.0kmh/1000rpm
25.1mpg 20.9mpgUS 11.3L/100km
Petrol 4-stroke piston
1993cc 121.6cu in
In-line 4 1 Carburettor
Compression ratio: 9.2:1
Bore: 90.8mm 3.6in
Stroke: 77.0mm 3.0in
Valve type/No: Overhead 8
Transmission: Manual
No. of forward speeds: 4
Wheels driven: Rear
Springs F/R: Coil/Leaf
Brake system: PA
Brakes F/R: Disc/Drum
Steering: Rack & pinion
Wheelbase: 268.0cm 105.5in
Track F: 142.2cm 56.0in
Track R: 142.2cm 56.0in
Length: 426.0cm 167.7in
Width: 170.2cm 67.0in
Height: 132.1cm 52.0in
Ground clearance: 17.8cm 7.0in
Kerb weight: 1065.1kg 2346.0lb
Fuel: 54.6L 12.0gal 14.4galUS

1784 Ford

Escort 1300 Super Estate
1970 UK
83.0mph 133.5kmh
0-50mph 80.5kmh: 13.7secs
0-60mph 96.5kmh: 20.1secs
0-1/4 mile: 21.6secs
0-1km: 41.4secs
58.0bhp 43.2kW 58.8PS
@ 5000rpm
71.5lbft 96.9Nm @ 2500rpm
69.0bhp/ton 67.9bhp/tonne
44.7bhp/L 33.3kW/L 45.3PS/L
34.4ft/sec 10.5m/sec
15.5mph 24.9kmh/1000rpm
28.3mpg 23.6mpgUS 10.0L/100km
Petrol 4-stroke piston
1297cc 79.1cu in
In-line 4 1 Carburettor
Compression ratio: 9.0:1
Bore: 81.0mm 3.2in
Stroke: 63.0mm 2.5in
Valve type/No: Overhead 8
Transmission: Manual
No. of forward speeds: 4
Wheels driven: Rear
Springs F/R: Coil/Leaf
Brake system: PA
Brakes F/R: Disc/Drum
Steering: Rack & pinion
Wheelbase: 240.0cm 94.5in
Track F: 131.3cm 51.7in
Track R: 132.1cm 52.0in
Length: 414.0cm 163.0in
Width: 157.0cm 61.8in
Height: 137.2cm 54.0in
Ground clearance: 15.2cm 6.0in
Kerb weight: 854.4kg 1882.0lb
Fuel: 40.9L 9.0gal 10.8galUS

1785 Ford

Escort 1600 RS
1970 UK
113.0mph 181.8kmh
0-50mph 80.5kmh: 6.8secs
0-60mph 96.5kmh: 8.9secs
0-1/4 mile: 16.7secs
0-1km: 31.2secs
120.0bhp 89.5kW 121.7PS
@ 6500rpm
112.0lbft 151.8Nm @ 4000rpm
140.0bhp/ton 137.7bhp/tonne
74.9bhp/L 55.9kW/L 76.0PS/L
55.2ft/sec 16.8m/sec
17.7mph 28.5kmh/1000rpm
21.5mpg 17.9mpgUS 13.1L/100km
Petrol 4-stroke piston
1601cc 97.7cu in
In-line 4 2 Carburettor
Compression ratio: 10.0:1
Bore: 81.0mm 3.2in
Stroke: 77.6mm 3.1in
Valve type/No: Overhead 8
Transmission: Manual
No. of forward speeds: 4
Wheels driven: Rear
Springs F/R: Coil/Leaf
Brake system: PA
Brakes F/R: Disc/Drum
Steering: Rack & pinion
Wheelbase: 240.0cm 94.5in
Track F: 131.3cm 51.7in
Track R: 132.1cm 52.0in
Length: 406.4cm 160.0in
Width: 157.0cm 61.8in
Height: 137.2cm 54.0in
Ground clearance: 15.2cm 6.0in
Kerb weight: 871.7kg 1920.0lb
Fuel: 40.9L 9.0gal 10.8galUS

1786 Ford

Maverick
1970 Germany
99.0mph 159.3kmh
0-50mph 80.5kmh: 10.1secs
0-60mph 96.5kmh: 14.3secs
0-1/4 mile: 19.8secs
0-1km: 37.1secs
122.0bhp 91.0kW 123.7PS
@ 4000rpm
190.0lbft 257.5Nm @ 2200rpm
107.1bhp/ton 105.3bhp/tonne
37.3bhp/L 27.8kW/L 37.8PS/L
34.8ft/sec 10.6m/sec
26.6mph 42.8kmh/1000rpm
18.8mpg 15.7mpgUS 15.0L/100km
Petrol 4-stroke piston
3273cc 199.7cu in
In-line 6 1 Carburettor
Compression ratio: 8.3:1
Bore: 93.5mm 3.7in
Stroke: 79.5mm 3.1in
Valve type/No: Overhead 12
Transmission: Automatic
No. of forward speeds: 3
Wheels driven: Rear
Springs F/R: Coil/Leaf
Brake system: PA
Brakes F/R: Drum/Drum
Steering: Recirculating ball
Wheelbase: 261.6cm 103.0in
Track F: 141.0cm 55.5in
Track R: 141.0cm 55.5in
Length: 455.9cm 179.5in
Width: 179.1cm 70.5in
Height: 133.4cm 52.5in
Ground clearance: 14.0cm 5.5in
Kerb weight: 1158.6kg 2552.0lb
Fuel: 60.5L 13.3gal 16.0galUS

1787 Ford

Mustang Boss 302
1970 USA
0-50mph 80.5kmh: 4.6secs
0-60mph 96.5kmh: 5.8secs
0-1/4 mile: 14.4secs
290.0bhp 216.2kW 294.0PS
@ 5800rpm
290.0lbft 393.0Nm @ 4300rpm
191.3bhp/ton 188.1bhp/tonne
58.6bhp/L 43.7kW/L 59.4PS/L
48.3ft/sec 14.7m/sec
12.0mpg 10.0mpgUS 23.5L/100km
Petrol 4-stroke piston
4950cc 302.0cu in
Vee 8 1 Carburettor
Compression ratio: 10.5:1
Bore: 101.6mm 4.0in
Stroke: 76.2mm 3.0in
Valve type/No: Overhead 16
Transmission: Manual
No. of forward speeds: 4
Wheels driven: Rear
Springs F/R: Coil/Leaf
Brakes F/R: Disc/Drum
Steering: Recirculating ball
Wheelbase: 274.3cm 108.0in
Track F: 148.6cm 58.5in
Track R: 148.6cm 58.5in
Length: 476.0cm 187.4in
Width: 182.4cm 71.8in
Height: 127.8cm 50.3in
Kerb weight: 1541.3kg 3395.0lb
Fuel: 75.7L 16.6gal 20.0galUS

1788 Ford

Torino GT
1970 USA
115.0mph 185.0kmh
0-50mph 80.5kmh: 6.0secs
0-60mph 96.5kmh: 8.1secs
0-1/4 mile: 15.6secs
300.0bhp 223.7kW 304.2PS
@ 5400rpm
380.0lbft 514.9Nm @ 3400rpm
175.5bhp/ton 172.5bhp/tonne
52.2bhp/L 38.9kW/L 52.9PS/L
52.5ft/sec 16.0m/sec
22.9mph 36.8kmh/1000rpm
15.4mpg 12.8mpgUS 18.4L/100km
Petrol 4-stroke piston
5752cc 350.9cu in
Vee 8 1 Carburettor
Compression ratio: 11.0:1
Bore: 102.1mm 4.0in
Stroke: 88.9mm 3.5in
Valve type/No: Overhead 16
Transmission: Manual
No. of forward speeds: 4
Wheels driven: Rear
Springs F/R: Coil/Leaf
Brake system: PA
Brakes F/R: Disc/Drum
Steering: Recirculating ball PA
Wheelbase: 297.2cm 117.0in
Track F: 153.7cm 60.5in
Track R: 152.4cm 60.0in
Length: 523.7cm 206.2in
Width: 195.1cm 76.8in
Height: 129.5cm 51.0in
Kerb weight: 1738.8kg 3830.0lb
Fuel: 75.7L 16.6gal 20.0galUS

1789 Ford

1600 GT
1971 UK
100.0mph 160.9kmh
0-50mph 80.5kmh: 9.3secs
0-60mph 96.5kmh: 13.3secs
0-1/4 mile: 19.0secs
0-1km: 35.2secs
86.0bhp 64.1kW 87.2PS
@ 5500rpm
92.0lbft 124.7Nm @ 4000rpm
88.4bhp/ton 87.0bhp/tonne
54.0bhp/L 40.3kW/L 54.7PS/L
39.7ft/sec 12.1m/sec
17.9mph 28.8kmh/1000rpm
25.3mpg 21.1mpgUS 11.2L/100km
Petrol 4-stroke piston
1593cc 97.2cu in
In-line 4 1 Carburettor
Compression ratio: 9.2:1
Bore: 87.7mm 3.4in
Stroke: 66.0mm 2.6in
Valve type/No: Overhead 8
Transmission: Manual
No. of forward speeds: 4
Wheels driven: Rear
Springs F/R: Coil/Leaf
Brake system: PA
Brakes F/R: Disc/Drum
Steering: Rack & pinion
Wheelbase: 257.8cm 101.5in
Track F: 142.2cm 56.0in
Track R: 142.2cm 56.0in
Length: 426.0cm 167.7in
Width: 170.2cm 67.0in
Height: 132.1cm 52.0in
Ground clearance: 17.8cm 7.0in
Kerb weight: 988.8kg 2178.0lb
Fuel: 54.6L 12.0gal 14.4galUS

1790 Ford

Bronco
1971 USA
90.0mph 144.8kmh
0-60mph 96.5kmh: 14.5secs
205.0bhp 152.9kW 207.8PS
@ 4600rpm
300.0lbft 406.5Nm @ 2600rpm
133.9bhp/ton 131.6bhp/tonne
41.4bhp/L 30.9kW/L 42.0PS/L
38.3ft/sec 11.7m/sec
Petrol 4-stroke piston
4949cc 301.9cu in
Vee 8
Compression ratio: 8.6:1
Bore: 101.6mm 4.0in
Stroke: 76.2mm 3.0in
Valve type/No: Overhead 16
Transmission: Manual
No. of forward speeds: 3
Wheels driven: 4-wheel drive
Brakes F/R: Drum/Drum
Steering: Worm & roller
Wheelbase: 233.7cm 92.0in
Track F: 145.8cm 57.4in
Track R: 145.8cm 57.4in
Length: 386.3cm 152.1in
Width: 174.8cm 68.8in
Height: 179.6cm 70.7in
Ground clearance: 21.6cm 8.5in
Kerb weight: 1557.2kg 3430.0lb
Fuel: 47.3L 10.4gal 12.5galUS

1791 Ford

Capri 2000
1971 Germany
108.0mph 173.8kmh
0-50mph 80.5kmh: 8.1secs
0-60mph 96.5kmh: 11.5secs
0-1/4 mile: 18.5secs
100.0bhp 74.6kW 101.4PS
@ 5600rpm
120.0lbft 162.6Nm @ 3600rpm
101.4bhp/ton 99.7bhp/tonne
50.2bhp/L 37.4kW/L 50.9PS/L
47.1ft/sec 14.4m/sec
19.0mph 30.6kmh/1000rpm
30.6mpg 25.5mpgUS 9.2L/100km
Petrol 4-stroke piston
1993cc 121.6cu in
In-line 4 1 Carburettor
Compression ratio: 8.6:1
Bore: 91.0mm 3.6in
Stroke: 77.0mm 3.0in
Valve type/No: Overhead 8
Transmission: Manual
No. of forward speeds: 4
Wheels driven: Rear
Springs F/R: Coil/Leaf
Brake system: PA
Brakes F/R: Disc/Drum
Steering: Rack & pinion
Wheelbase: 256.0cm 100.8in
Track F: 134.6cm 53.0in
Track R: 132.1cm 52.0in
Length: 426.2cm 167.8in
Width: 164.6cm 64.8in
Height: 132.1cm 52.0in
Kerb weight: 1003.3kg 2210.0lb
Fuel: 45.4L 10.0gal 12.0galUS

1792 Ford

Econoline Chateau Wagon
1971 USA
0-60mph 96.5kmh: 15.3secs
205.0bhp 152.9kW 207.8PS
@ 4600rpm
300.0lbft 406.5Nm @ 2600rpm
102.5bhp/ton 100.8bhp/tonne
41.4bhp/L 30.9kW/L 42.0PS/L
38.3ft/sec 11.7m/sec
Petrol 4-stroke piston
4949cc 301.9cu in
Vee 8
Compression ratio: 9.0:1
Bore: 101.6mm 4.0in
Stroke: 76.2mm 3.0in
Valve type/No: Overhead 16
Transmission: Automatic
No. of forward speeds: 3
Wheels driven: Rear
Wheelbase: 313.7cm 123.5in
Track F: 172.7cm 68.0in
Track R: 170.2cm 67.0in
Length: 475.2cm 187.1in
Width: 201.9cm 79.5in
Height: 197.6cm 77.8in
Ground clearance: 16.5cm 6.5in
Kerb weight: 2033.9kg 4480.0lb

1793 Ford

Escort 1300 GT
1971 UK
98.0mph 157.7kmh
0-50mph 80.5kmh: 8.5secs
0-60mph 96.5kmh: 12.4secs
0-1/4 mile: 19.0secs
0-1km: 36.0secs
72.0bhp 53.7kW 73.0PS
@ 6000rpm
68.0lbft 92.1Nm @ 4000rpm
94.5bhp/ton 93.0bhp/tonne
55.5bhp/L 41.4kW/L 56.3PS/L
41.3ft/sec 12.6m/sec
15.0mph 24.1kmh/1000rpm
25.4mpg 21.1mpgUS 11.1L/100km
Petrol 4-stroke piston
1297cc 79.1cu in
In-line 4 1 Carburettor
Compression ratio: 9.0:1
Bore: 81.0mm 3.2in
Stroke: 63.0mm 2.5in
Valve type/No: Overhead 8
Transmission: Manual
No. of forward speeds: 4
Wheels driven: Rear
Springs F/R: Coil/Leaf
Brake system: PA
Brakes F/R: Disc/Drum
Steering: Rack & pinion
Wheelbase: 240.0cm 94.5in
Track F: 124.5cm 49.0in
Track R: 127.0cm 50.0in
Length: 406.4cm 160.0in
Width: 157.0cm 61.8in
Height: 137.2cm 54.0in
Ground clearance: 15.2cm 6.0in
Kerb weight: 774.5kg 1706.0lb
Fuel: 40.9L 9.0gal 10.8galUS

1794 Ford

Escort 1300 XL
1971 UK
87.0mph 140.0kmh
0-50mph 80.5kmh: 11.8secs
0-60mph 96.5kmh: 17.6secs
0-1/4 mile: 20.8secs
0-1km: 39.5secs
57.0bhp 42.5kW 57.8PS
@ 5500rpm
67.0lbft 90.8Nm @ 3000rpm
71.0bhp/ton 69.8bhp/tonne
43.9bhp/L 32.8kW/L 44.6PS/L
37.9ft/sec 11.5m/sec
16.0mph 25.7kmh/1000rpm
26.7mpg 22.2mpgUS 10.6L/100km
Petrol 4-stroke piston
1297cc 79.1cu in
In-line 4 1 Carburettor
Compression ratio: 9.0:1
Bore: 81.0mm 3.2in
Stroke: 63.0mm 2.5in
Valve type/No: Overhead 8
Transmission: Manual
No. of forward speeds: 4
Wheels driven: Rear
Springs F/R: Coil/Leaf
Brake system: PA
Brakes F/R: Disc/Drum
Steering: Rack & pinion
Wheelbase: 240.0cm 94.5in
Track F: 124.5cm 49.0in
Track R: 127.0cm 50.0in
Length: 406.4cm 160.0in
Width: 157.0cm 61.8in
Height: 137.2cm 54.0in
Ground clearance: 15.2cm 6.0in
Kerb weight: 816.3kg 1798.0lb
Fuel: 40.9L 9.0gal 10.8galUS

1795 Ford

Escort Sport
1971 UK
96.0mph 154.5kmh
0-50mph 80.5kmh: 9.2secs
0-60mph 96.5kmh: 13.8secs
0-1/4 mile: 18.9secs
0-1km: 35.8secs
72.0bhp 53.7kW 73.0PS
@ 6000rpm
68.0lbft 92.1Nm @ 4000rpm
91.4bhp/ton 89.9bhp/tonne
55.5bhp/L 41.4kW/L 56.3PS/L
41.3ft/sec 12.6m/sec
16.3mph 26.2kmh/1000rpm
25.0mpg 20.8mpgUS 11.3L/100km
Petrol 4-stroke piston
1297cc 79.1cu in
In-line 4 1 Carburettor
Compression ratio: 9.0:1
Bore: 81.0mm 3.2in
Stroke: 63.0mm 2.5in
Valve type/No: Overhead 8
Transmission: Manual
No. of forward speeds: 4
Wheels driven: Rear
Springs F/R: Coil/Leaf
Brake system: PA
Brakes F/R: Disc/Drum
Steering: Rack & pinion
Wheelbase: 240.0cm 94.5in
Track F: 124.5cm 49.0in
Track R: 127.0cm 50.0in
Length: 397.5cm 156.5in
Width: 157.0cm 61.8in
Height: 137.2cm 54.0in
Ground clearance: 15.2cm 6.0in
Kerb weight: 800.9kg 1764.0lb
Fuel: 40.9L 9.0gal 10.8galUS

1796 Ford

Mustang TransAm
1971 USA
151.0mph 243.0kmh
0-60mph 96.5kmh: 5.5secs
0-1/4 mile: 12.0secs
460.0bhp 343.0kW 466.4PS
@ 7500rpm
360.0lbft 487.8Nm @ 6000rpm
318.0bhp/ton 312.7bhp/tonne
93.1bhp/L 69.4kW/L 94.4PS/L
62.5ft/sec 19.0m/sec
20.0mph 32.2kmh/1000rpm
4.8mpg 4.0mpgUS 58.8L/100km
Petrol 4-stroke piston
4942cc 301.5cu in
Vee 8 1 Carburettor
Compression ratio: 10.5:1
Bore: 101.6mm 4.0in
Stroke: 76.2mm 3.0in
Valve type/No: Overhead 16
Transmission: Manual
No. of forward speeds: 4
Wheels driven: Rear
Springs F/R: Coil/Leaf
Brakes F/R: Disc/Disc
Steering: Recirculating ball
Wheelbase: 274.3cm 108.0in
Track F: 148.6cm 58.5in
Track R: 148.6cm 58.5in
Length: 476.0cm 187.4in
Width: 182.1cm 71.7in
Height: 120.7cm 47.5in
Ground clearance: 6.4cm 2.5in
Kerb weight: 1471.0kg 3240.0lb
Fuel: 83.3L 18.3gal 22.0galUS

1797 Ford

Pickup 4WD
1971 USA
77.0mph 123.9kmh
140.0bhp 104.4kW 141.9PS
@ 4000rpm
230.0lbft 311.7Nm @ 2200rpm
35.6bhp/L 26.5kW/L 36.1PS/L
35.3ft/sec 10.8m/sec
Petrol 4-stroke piston
3933cc 240.0cu in
In-line 6
Compression ratio: 8.9:1
Bore: 101.6mm 4.0in
Stroke: 80.8mm 3.2in
Valve type/No: Overhead 12

Transmission: Manual
No. of forward speeds: 4
Wheels driven: 4-wheel drive
Brake system: PA
Brakes F/R: Drum/Drum
Steering: Recirculating ball PA
Wheelbase: 292.1cm 115.0in
Track F: 163.6cm 64.4in
Track R: 153.4cm 60.4in
Length: 476.5cm 187.6in
Width: 201.7cm 79.4in
Height: 188.7cm 74.3in
Ground clearance: 19.8cm 7.8in
Fuel: 70.0L 15.4gal 18.5galUS

1798 Ford

Pinto
1971 USA
78.0mph 125.5kmh
0-50mph 80.5kmh: 13.2secs
0-60mph 96.5kmh: 20.0secs
0-1/4 mile: 21.3secs
75.0bhp 55.9kW 76.0PS
@ 5000rpm
96.0lbft 130.1Nm @ 3000rpm
82.3bhp/ton 81.0bhp/tonne
46.9bhp/L 35.0kW/L 47.5PS/L
42.5ft/sec 12.9m/sec
18.6mph 29.9kmh/1000rpm
26.4mpg 22.0mpgUS 10.7L/100km
Petrol 4-stroke piston
1599cc 97.6cu in
In-line 4 1 Carburettor
Compression ratio: 8.4:1
Bore: 81.0mm 3.2in
Stroke: 77.6mm 3.1in
Valve type/No: Overhead 8
Transmission: Manual
No. of forward speeds: 4
Wheels driven: Rear
Springs F/R: Coil/Leaf
Brakes F/R: Drum/Drum
Steering: Rack & pinion
Wheelbase: 238.8cm 94.0in
Track F: 139.7cm 55.0in
Track R: 139.7cm 55.0in
Length: 414.0cm 163.0in
Width: 176.3cm 69.4in
Height: 127.3cm 50.1in
Ground clearance: 13.0cm 5.1in
Kerb weight: 926.2kg 2040.0lb
Fuel: 41.6L 9.1gal 11.0galUS

1799 Ford

Pinto 1600
1971 USA
82.0mph 131.9kmh
0-60mph 96.5kmh: 18.0secs
0-1/4 mile: 21.1secs
75.0bhp 55.9kW 76.0PS
@ 5000rpm
96.0lbft 130.1Nm @ 3000rpm
82.3bhp/ton 81.0bhp/tonne
46.9bhp/L 35.0kW/L 47.5PS/L
42.5ft/sec 12.9m/sec
27.1mpg 22.6mpgUS 10.4L/100km
Petrol 4-stroke piston
1599cc 97.6cu in
In-line 4
Bore: 81.0mm 3.2in
Stroke: 77.6mm 3.1in
Valve type/No: Overhead 8
Transmission: Manual
No. of forward speeds: 4
Wheels driven: Rear
Springs F/R: Coil/Leaf
Brakes F/R: Drum/Drum
Wheelbase: 238.8cm 94.0in
Track F: 139.7cm 55.0in
Track R: 139.7cm 55.0in
Length: 414.0cm 163.0in
Width: 176.3cm 69.4in
Height: 127.3cm 50.1in
Kerb weight: 926.2kg 2040.0lb
Fuel: 41.6L 9.1gal 11.0galUS

1800 Ford

Pinto 2-litre
1971 USA
102.0mph 164.1kmh
0-50mph 80.5kmh: 8.1secs
0-60mph 96.5kmh: 11.4secs
0-1/4 mile: 18.2secs
100.0bhp 74.6kW 101.4PS
@ 5600rpm
120.0lbft 162.6Nm @ 3600rpm
104.4bhp/ton 102.7bhp/tonne
50.2bhp/L 37.4kW/L 50.9PS/L
47.1ft/sec 14.4m/sec
19.0mph 30.6kmh/1000rpm
27.0mpg 22.5mpgUS 10.5L/100km
Petrol 4-stroke piston
1993cc 121.6cu in
In-line 4
Compression ratio: 8.6:1
Bore: 91.0mm 3.6in
Stroke: 77.0mm 3.0in
Valve type/No: Overhead 8
Transmission: Manual
No. of forward speeds: 4
Wheels driven: Rear
Brakes F/R: Disc/Drum
Steering: Rack & pinion
Wheelbase: 238.8cm 94.0in
Track F: 139.7cm 55.0in
Track R: 139.7cm 55.0in
Length: 414.0cm 163.0in
Width: 176.3cm 69.4in
Height: 127.3cm 50.1in
Kerb weight: 973.8kg 2145.0lb
Fuel: 41.6L 9.1gal 11.0galUS

1801 Ford

1600 XL Auto
1972 UK
87.0mph 140.0kmh
0-50mph 80.5kmh: 13.9secs
0-60mph 96.5kmh: 20.4secs
0-1/4 mile: 21.9secs
68.0bhp 50.7kW 68.9PS
@ 5200rpm
85.0lbft 115.2Nm @ 2600rpm
62.1bhp/ton 61.1bhp/tonne
42.5bhp/L 31.7kW/L 43.1PS/L
44.2ft/sec 13.4m/sec
16.3mph 26.2kmh/1000rpm
22.7mpg 18.9mpgUS 12.4L/100km
Petrol 4-stroke piston
1599cc 97.6cu in
In-line 4 1 Carburettor
Compression ratio: 9.0:1
Bore: 81.0mm 3.2in
Stroke: 77.6mm 3.1in
Valve type/No: Overhead 8
Transmission: Automatic
No. of forward speeds: 3
Wheels driven: Rear
Springs F/R: Coil/Coil
Brake system: PA
Brakes F/R: Disc/Drum
Steering: Rack & pinion
Wheelbase: 257.8cm 101.5in
Track F: 142.2cm 56.0in
Track R: 142.2cm 56.0in
Length: 434.3cm 171.0in
Width: 170.2cm 67.0in
Height: 132.1cm 52.0in
Ground clearance: 17.8cm 7.0in
Kerb weight: 1113.2kg 2452.0lb
Fuel: 54.1L 11.9gal 14.3galUS

1802 Ford

Capri 1600 XL
1972 UK
100.0mph 160.9kmh
0-50mph 80.5kmh: 9.0secs
0-60mph 96.5kmh: 12.9secs
0-1/4 mile: 18.9secs
0-1km: 35.5secs
72.0bhp 53.7kW 73.0PS
@ 5500rpm
87.0lbft 117.9Nm @ 2700rpm
76.0bhp/ton 74.8bhp/tonne
45.2bhp/L 33.7kW/L 45.8PS/L
39.7ft/sec 12.1m/sec
16.8mph 27.0kmh/1000rpm
27.4mpg 22.8mpgUS 10.3L/100km
Petrol 4-stroke piston
1593cc 97.2cu in
In-line 4 1 Carburettor
Compression ratio: 9.2:1
Bore: 87.6mm 3.4in
Stroke: 66.0mm 2.6in
Valve type/No: Overhead 8
Transmission: Manual
No. of forward speeds: 4
Wheels driven: Rear
Springs F/R: Coil/Leaf
Brake system: PA
Brakes F/R: Disc/Drum
Steering: Rack & pinion
Wheelbase: 256.0cm 100.8in
Track F: 134.6cm 53.0in
Track R: 132.1cm 52.0in
Length: 428.0cm 168.5in
Width: 164.6cm 64.8in
Height: 128.8cm 50.7in
Ground clearance: 11.4cm 4.5in
Kerb weight: 962.9kg 2121.0lb
Fuel: 47.8L 10.5gal 12.6galUS

1803 Ford

Capri 2600 V6
1972 Germany
110.0mph 177.0kmh
0-50mph 80.5kmh: 7.7secs
0-60mph 96.5kmh: 10.4secs
0-1/4 mile: 17.7secs
107.0bhp 79.8kW 108.5PS
@ 5000rpm
130.0lbft 176.2Nm @ 3400rpm
102.9bhp/ton 101.1bhp/tonne
42.0bhp/L 31.3kW/L 42.5PS/L
36.5ft/sec 11.1m/sec
20.3mph 32.7kmh/1000rpm
28.8mpg 24.0mpgUS 9.8L/100km
Petrol 4-stroke piston
2550cc 155.6cu in
Vee 6 1 Carburettor
Compression ratio: 8.2:1
Bore: 90.0mm 3.5in
Stroke: 66.8mm 2.6in
Valve type/No: Overhead 12
Transmission: Manual
No. of forward speeds: 4
Wheels driven: Rear
Springs F/R: Coil/Leaf
Brake system: PA
Brakes F/R: Disc/Drum
Steering: Rack & pinion
Wheelbase: 256.0cm 100.8in
Track F: 134.6cm 53.0in
Track R: 132.1cm 52.0in
Length: 426.2cm 167.8in
Width: 164.6cm 64.8in
Height: 132.1cm 52.0in
Ground clearance: 15.2cm 6.0in
Kerb weight: 1057.8kg 2330.0lb
Fuel: 45.4L 10.0gal 12.0galUS

1804 Ford

Capri 3000E
1972 UK
122.0mph 196.3kmh
0-50mph 80.5kmh: 6.5secs
0-60mph 96.5kmh: 8.4secs
0-1/4 mile: 16.2secs
0-1km: 30.3secs
138.0bhp 102.9kW 139.9PS
@ 5000rpm
174.0lbft 235.8Nm @ 3000rpm
127.2bhp/ton 125.1bhp/tonne
46.1bhp/L 34.4kW/L 46.7PS/L
39.6ft/sec 12.1m/sec
21.6mph 34.8kmh/1000rpm
21.5mpg 17.9mpgUS 13.1L/100km
Petrol 4-stroke piston
2994cc 182.7cu in
Vee 6 1 Carburettor
Compression ratio: 8.9:1
Bore: 93.7mm 3.7in
Stroke: 72.4mm 2.8in
Valve type/No: Overhead 12
Transmission: Manual
No. of forward speeds: 4
Wheels driven: Rear
Springs F/R: Coil/Leaf
Brake system: PA
Brakes F/R: Disc/Drum
Steering: Rack & pinion
Wheelbase: 256.0cm 100.8in
Track F: 134.6cm 53.0in
Track R: 132.1cm 52.0in
Length: 428.0cm 168.5in
Width: 164.6cm 64.8in
Height: 128.8cm 50.7in
Ground clearance: 11.4cm 4.5in
Kerb weight: 1103.2kg 2430.0lb
Fuel: 57.8L 12.7gal 15.3galUS

1805 Ford

Capri RS2600
1972 Germany
126.0mph 202.7kmh
0-50mph 80.5kmh: 5.6secs
0-60mph 96.5kmh: 7.3secs
0-1/4 mile: 15.0secs
150.0bhp 111.9kW 152.1PS
@ 5800rpm
165.0lbft 223.6Nm @ 3500rpm
145.1bhp/ton 142.7bhp/tonne
56.9bhp/L 42.4kW/L 57.7PS/L
43.8ft/sec 13.3m/sec
20.0mph 32.2kmh/1000rpm
23.4mpg 19.5mpgUS 12.1L/100km
Petrol 4-stroke piston
2637cc 160.9cu in
Vee 6 fuel injection
Compression ratio: 10.0:1
Bore: 90.0mm 3.5in
Stroke: 69.0mm 2.7in
Valve type/No: Overhead 12
Transmission: Manual
No. of forward speeds: 4
Wheels driven: Rear
Springs F/R: Coil/Leaf
Brake system: PA
Brakes F/R: Disc/Drum
Steering: Rack & pinion
Wheelbase: 256.0cm 100.8in
Track F: 137.7cm 54.2in
Track R: 135.1cm 53.2in
Length: 419.1cm 165.0in
Width: 164.6cm 64.8in
Height: 126.2cm 49.7in
Ground clearance: 10.2cm 4.0in
Kerb weight: 1051.0kg 2315.0lb
Fuel: 57.9L 12.7gal 15.3galUS

1806 Ford

Consul 2000L
1972 UK
98.0mph 157.7kmh
0-50mph 80.5kmh: 9.4secs
0-60mph 96.5kmh: 14.1secs
0-1/4 mile: 19.2secs
0-1km: 34.0secs
82.0bhp 61.1kW 83.1PS
@ 5000rpm
106.0lbft 143.6Nm @ 3000rpm
78.1bhp/ton 76.8bhp/tonne
41.1bhp/L 30.6kW/L 41.6PS/L
39.6ft/sec 12.1m/sec
17.8mph 28.6kmh/1000rpm
23.3mpg 19.4mpgUS 12.1L/100km
Petrol 4-stroke piston
1996cc 121.8cu in
Vee 4 1 Carburettor
Compression ratio: 8.9:1
Bore: 93.7mm 3.7in
Stroke: 72.4mm 2.8in
Valve type/No: Overhead 8
Transmission: Manual
No. of forward speeds: 4
Wheels driven: Rear
Springs F/R: Coil/Coil
Brake system: PA
Brakes F/R: Disc/Drum
Steering: Rack & pinion
Wheelbase: 276.9cm 109.0in
Track F: 151.1cm 59.5in
Track R: 153.7cm 60.5in
Length: 466.1cm 183.5in
Width: 179.1cm 70.5in
Height: 141.2cm 55.6in
Ground clearance: 20.3cm 8.0in
Kerb weight: 1067.8kg 2352.0lb
Fuel: 65.1L 14.3gal 17.2galUS

1807 Ford

Cortina 1300L
1972 UK
87.0mph 140.0kmh
0-50mph 80.5kmh: 13.3secs
0-60mph 96.5kmh: 19.8secs
0-1/4 mile: 21.4secs
0-1km: 40.3secs
57.0bhp 42.5kW 57.8PS
@ 5500rpm
74.0lbft 100.3Nm @ 3000rpm
56.1bhp/ton 55.1bhp/tonne
43.9bhp/L 32.7kW/L 44.5PS/L
37.9ft/sec 11.5m/sec
16.7mph 26.9kmh/1000rpm
24.8mpg 20.7mpgUS 11.4L/100km
Petrol 4-stroke piston
1298cc 79.2cu in
In-line 4 1 Carburettor
Compression ratio: 9.0:1
Bore: 81.0mm 3.2in
Stroke: 63.0mm 2.5in
Valve type/No: Overhead 8
Transmission: Manual
No. of forward speeds: 4
Wheels driven: Rear
Springs F/R: Coil/Coil

Brake system: PA
Brakes F/R: Disc/Drum
Steering: Rack & pinion
Wheelbase: 257.8cm 101.5in
Track F: 142.2cm 56.0in
Track R: 142.2cm 56.0in
Length: 426.0cm 167.7in
Width: 170.2cm 67.0in
Height: 132.1cm 52.0in
Ground clearance: 17.8cm 7.0in
Kerb weight: 1033.8kg 2277.0lb
Fuel: 54.1L 11.9gal 14.3galUS

1808 Ford
Granada GXL
1972 UK
113.0mph 181.8kmh
0-50mph 80.5kmh: 6.9secs
0-60mph 96.5kmh: 9.1secs
0-1/4 mile: 16.8secs
0-1km: 31.4secs
138.0bhp 102.9kW 139.9PS
@ 5000rpm
174.0lbft 235.8Nm @ 3000rpm
100.6bhp/ton 98.9bhp/tonne
46.1bhp/L 34.4kW/L 46.7PS/L
39.6ft/sec 12.1m/sec
21.2mph 34.1kmh/1000rpm
19.1mpg 15.9mpgUS 14.8L/100km
Petrol 4-stroke piston
2994cc 182.7cu in
Vee 6 1 Carburettor
Compression ratio: 8.9:1
Bore: 93.7mm 3.7in
Stroke: 72.4mm 2.8in
Valve type/No: Overhead 12
Transmission: Manual
No. of forward speeds: 4
Wheels driven: Rear
Springs F/R: Coil/Coil
Brake system: PA
Brakes F/R: Disc/Drum
Steering: Rack & pinion PA
Wheelbase: 276.9cm 109.0in
Track F: 151.1cm 59.5in
Track R: 153.7cm 60.5in
Length: 466.1cm 183.5in
Width: 179.1cm 70.5in
Height: 141.2cm 55.6in
Ground clearance: 20.3cm 8.0in
Kerb weight: 1395.1kg 3073.0lb
Fuel: 65.1L 14.3gal 17.2galUS

1809 Ford
LTD
1972 USA
110.0mph 177.0kmh
0-50mph 80.5kmh: 8.7secs
0-60mph 96.5kmh: 11.8secs
0-1/4 mile: 18.4secs
172.0bhp 128.3kW 174.4PS
@ 4000rpm
298.0lbft 403.8Nm @ 2200rpm
86.6bhp/ton 85.1bhp/tonne
26.2bhp/L 19.5kW/L 26.6PS/L
44.4ft/sec 13.5m/sec
29.2mph 47.0kmh/1000rpm
13.0mpg 10.8mpgUS 21.8L/100km
Petrol 4-stroke piston
6560cc 400.2cu in
Vee 8 1 Carburettor
Compression ratio: 8.4:1
Bore: 101.6mm 4.0in
Stroke: 101.6mm 4.0in
Valve type/No: Overhead 16
Transmission: Automatic
No. of forward speeds: 3
Wheels driven: Rear
Springs F/R: Coil/Coil
Brake system: PA
Brakes F/R: Disc/Drum
Steering: Recirculating ball PA
Wheelbase: 307.3cm 121.0in
Track F: 160.8cm 63.3in
Track R: 163.3cm 64.3in
Length: 554.7cm 218.4in
Width: 201.2cm 79.2in
Height: 134.6cm 53.0in
Ground clearance: 11.4cm 4.5in
Kerb weight: 2020.3kg 4450.0lb
Fuel: 83.3L 18.3gal 22.0galUS

1810 Ford
Mustang Grande
1972 USA
110.0mph 177.0kmh
0-50mph 80.5kmh: 7.7secs
0-60mph 96.5kmh: 10.4secs
0-1/4 mile: 17.7secs
0-1km: 32.6secs
143.0bhp 106.6kW 145.0PS
@ 4000rpm
243.0lbft 329.3Nm @ 2000rpm
98.3bhp/ton 96.6bhp/tonne
28.9bhp/L 21.6kW/L 29.3PS/L
33.3ft/sec 10.2m/sec
26.4mph 42.5kmh/1000rpm
15.1mpg 12.6mpgUS 18.7L/100km
Petrol 4-stroke piston
4945cc 301.7cu in
Vee 8 1 Carburettor
Compression ratio: 8.5:1
Bore: 101.6mm 4.0in
Stroke: 76.2mm 3.0in
Valve type/No: Overhead 16
Transmission: Automatic
No. of forward speeds: 3
Wheels driven: Rear
Springs F/R: Coil/Leaf
Brake system: PA
Brakes F/R: Disc/Drum
Steering: Recirculating ball PA
Wheelbase: 276.9cm 109.0in
Track F: 156.2cm 61.5in
Track R: 154.9cm 61.0in
Length: 481.3cm 189.5in
Width: 190.0cm 74.8in
Height: 134.1cm 52.8in
Ground clearance: 15.2cm 6.0in
Kerb weight: 1480.0kg 3260.0lb
Fuel: 74.2L 16.3gal 19.6galUS

1811 Ford
Capri 3000 GXL
1973 UK
122.0mph 196.3kmh
0-50mph 80.5kmh: 6.0secs
0-60mph 96.5kmh: 8.3secs
0-1/4 mile: 16.6secs
0-1km: 30.6secs
148.0bhp 110.4kW 150.0PS
@ 5300rpm
173.0lbft 234.4Nm @ 3000rpm
131.6bhp/ton 129.4bhp/tonne
49.4bhp/L 36.9kW/L 50.1PS/L
42.0ft/sec 12.8m/sec
21.7mph 34.9kmh/1000rpm
20.7mpg 17.2mpgUS 13.6L/100km
Petrol 4-stroke piston
2994cc 182.7cu in
Vee 6 1 Carburettor
Compression ratio: 8.9:1
Bore: 93.7mm 3.7in
Stroke: 72.4mm 2.8in
Valve type/No: Overhead 12
Transmission: Manual
No. of forward speeds: 4
Wheels driven: Rear
Springs F/R: Coil/Leaf
Brake system: PA
Brakes F/R: Disc/Drum
Steering: Rack & pinion
Wheelbase: 256.0cm 100.8in
Track F: 134.6cm 53.0in
Track R: 132.1cm 52.0in
Length: 428.0cm 168.5in
Width: 164.6cm 64.8in
Height: 128.8cm 50.7in
Ground clearance: 11.4cm 4.5in
Kerb weight: 1143.6kg 2519.0lb
Fuel: 61.4L 13.5gal 16.2galUS

1812 Ford
Consul 3000 GT
1973 UK
114.0mph 183.4kmh
0-50mph 80.5kmh: 6.9secs
0-60mph 96.5kmh: 9.0secs
0-1/4 mile: 16.7secs
0-1km: 31.5secs
138.0bhp 102.9kW 139.9PS
@ 5000rpm
174.0lbft 235.8Nm @ 3000rpm
103.9bhp/ton 102.2bhp/tonne
46.1bhp/L 34.4kW/L 46.7PS/L
39.6ft/sec 12.1m/sec
21.2mph 34.1kmh/1000rpm
20.0mpg 16.7mpgUS 14.1L/100km
Petrol 4-stroke piston
2994cc 182.7cu in
Vee 6 1 Carburettor
Compression ratio: 9.0:1
Bore: 93.7mm 3.7in
Stroke: 72.4mm 2.8in
Valve type/No: Overhead 12
Transmission: Manual
No. of forward speeds: 4
Wheels driven: Rear
Springs F/R: Coil/Coil
Brake system: PA
Brakes F/R: Disc/Drum
Steering: Rack & pinion
Wheelbase: 276.9cm 109.0in
Track F: 151.1cm 59.5in
Track R: 153.7cm 60.5in
Length: 466.1cm 183.5in
Width: 179.1cm 70.5in
Height: 141.2cm 55.6in
Ground clearance: 20.3cm 8.0in
Kerb weight: 1350.6kg 2975.0lb
Fuel: 65.1L 14.3gal 17.2galUS

1813 Ford
Cortina 1600 XL
1973 UK
93.0mph 149.6kmh
0-50mph 80.5kmh: 10.0secs
0-60mph 96.5kmh: 14.7secs
0-1/4 mile: 19.7secs
0-1km: 37.4secs
68.0bhp 50.7kW 68.9PS
@ 5200rpm
85.0lbft 115.2Nm @ 2600rpm
68.3bhp/ton 67.2bhp/tonne
42.5bhp/L 31.7kW/L 43.1PS/L
44.2ft/sec 13.4m/sec
17.3mph 27.8kmh/1000rpm
24.6mpg 20.5mpgUS 11.5L/100km
Petrol 4-stroke piston
1599cc 97.6cu in
In-line 4 1 Carburettor
Compression ratio: 9.0:1
Bore: 81.0mm 3.2in
Stroke: 77.6mm 3.1in
Valve type/No: Overhead 8
Transmission: Manual
No. of forward speeds: 4
Wheels driven: Rear
Springs F/R: Coil/Coil
Brake system: PA
Brakes F/R: Disc/Drum
Steering: Rack & pinion
Wheelbase: 257.8cm 101.5in
Track F: 142.2cm 56.0in
Track R: 142.2cm 56.0in
Length: 426.0cm 167.7in
Width: 170.2cm 67.0in
Height: 132.1cm 52.0in
Ground clearance: 17.8cm 7.0in
Kerb weight: 1012.4kg 2230.0lb
Fuel: 54.1L 11.9gal 14.3galUS

1814 Ford
Cortina 1600 XL Estate
1973 UK
96.0mph 154.5kmh
0-50mph 80.5kmh: 10.2secs
0-60mph 96.5kmh: 15.1secs
0-1/4 mile: 19.9secs
0-1km: 37.4secs
72.0bhp 53.7kW 73.0PS
@ 5500rpm
87.0lbft 117.9Nm @ 3000rpm
72.0bhp/ton 70.8bhp/tonne
45.2bhp/L 33.7kW/L 45.8PS/L
39.7ft/sec 12.1m/sec
17.1mph 27.5kmh/1000rpm
23.7mpg 19.7mpgUS 11.9L/100km
Petrol 4-stroke piston
1593cc 97.2cu in
In-line 4 1 Carburettor
Compression ratio: 9.2:1
Bore: 87.7mm 3.4in
Stroke: 66.0mm 2.6in
Valve type/No: Overhead 8
Transmission: Manual
No. of forward speeds: 4
Wheels driven: Rear
Springs F/R: Coil/Coil
Brake system: PA
Brakes F/R: Disc/Drum
Steering: Rack & pinion
Wheelbase: 257.8cm 101.5in
Track F: 142.2cm 56.0in
Track R: 142.2cm 56.0in
Length: 426.0cm 167.7in
Width: 170.2cm 67.0in
Height: 132.1cm 52.0in
Ground clearance: 17.8cm 7.0in
Kerb weight: 1017.0kg 2240.0lb
Fuel: 54.1L 11.9gal 14.3galUS

1815 Ford
Cortina 2000 Estate
1973 UK
101.0mph 162.5kmh
0-50mph 80.5kmh: 9.3secs
0-60mph 96.5kmh: 12.9secs
0-1/4 mile: 19.3secs
0-1km: 35.3secs
98.0bhp 73.1kW 99.4PS
@ 5500rpm
111.4lbft 150.9Nm @ 3500rpm
87.1bhp/ton 85.7bhp/tonne
49.2bhp/L 36.7kW/L 49.8PS/L
46.3ft/sec 14.1m/sec
16.8mph 27.0kmh/1000rpm
23.3mpg 19.4mpgUS 12.1L/100km
Petrol 4-stroke piston
1993cc 121.6cu in
In-line 4 1 Carburettor
Compression ratio: 9.2:1
Bore: 90.8mm 3.6in
Stroke: 76.9mm 3.0in
Valve type/No: Overhead 8
Transmission: Automatic
No. of forward speeds: 3
Wheels driven: Rear
Springs F/R: Coil/Coil
Brake system: PA
Brakes F/R: Disc/Drum
Steering: Rack & pinion
Wheelbase: 257.8cm 101.5in
Track F: 142.2cm 56.0in
Track R: 142.2cm 56.0in
Length: 437.9cm 172.4in
Width: 170.2cm 67.0in
Height: 132.1cm 52.0in
Ground clearance: 17.8cm 7.0in
Kerb weight: 1144.1kg 2520.0lb
Fuel: 54.6L 12.0gal 14.4galUS

1816 Ford
Cortina 2000E
1973 UK
105.0mph 168.9kmh
0-50mph 80.5kmh: 7.6secs
0-60mph 96.5kmh: 10.6secs
0-1/4 mile: 17.7secs
0-1km: 33.8secs
98.0bhp 73.1kW 99.4PS
@ 5700rpm
111.0lbft 150.4Nm @ 3500rpm
93.6bhp/ton 92.0bhp/tonne
49.2bhp/L 36.7kW/L 49.8PS/L
48.0ft/sec 14.6m/sec
18.2mph 29.3kmh/1000rpm
24.1mpg 20.1mpgUS 11.7L/100km
Petrol 4-stroke piston
1993cc 121.6cu in
In-line 4 1 Carburettor
Compression ratio: 9.2:1
Bore: 90.8mm 3.6in
Stroke: 76.9mm 3.0in
Valve type/No: Overhead 8
Transmission: Manual
No. of forward speeds: 4
Wheels driven: Rear
Springs F/R: Coil/Coil
Brake system: PA
Brakes F/R: Disc/Drum
Steering: Rack & pinion
Wheelbase: 257.8cm 101.5in
Track F: 142.2cm 56.0in
Track R: 142.2cm 56.0in
Length: 426.0cm 167.7in
Width: 170.2cm 67.0in
Height: 132.1cm 52.0in
Ground clearance: 17.8cm 7.0in
Kerb weight: 1065.1kg 2346.0lb
Fuel: 54.1L 11.9gal 14.3galUS

1817 Ford
Escort RS2000
1973 UK
111.0mph 178.6kmh
0-50mph 80.5kmh: 6.9secs
0-60mph 96.5kmh: 9.0secs
0-1/4 mile: 17.1secs
0-1km: 32.3secs
100.0bhp 74.6kW 101.4PS
@ 5750rpm
108.0lbft 146.3Nm @ 3500rpm
113.2bhp/ton 111.4bhp/tonne
50.2bhp/L 37.4kW/L 50.9PS/L
48.4ft/sec 14.7m/sec
18.7mph 30.1kmh/1000rpm
26.6mpg 22.1mpgUS 10.6L/100km
Petrol 4-stroke piston

1993cc 121.6cu in
In-line 4 1 Carburettor
Compression ratio: 9.2:1
Bore: 90.8mm 3.6in
Stroke: 76.9mm 3.0in
Valve type/No: Overhead 8
Transmission: Manual
No. of forward speeds: 4
Wheels driven: Rear
Springs F/R: Coil/Leaf
Brake system: PA
Brakes F/R: Disc/Drum
Steering: Rack & pinion
Wheelbase: 240.0cm 94.5in
Track F: 124.5cm 49.0in
Track R: 127.0cm 50.0in
Length: 406.4cm 160.0in
Width: 157.0cm 61.8in
Height: 137.2cm 54.0in
Ground clearance: 15.2cm 6.0in
Kerb weight: 898.0kg 1978.0lb
Fuel: 40.9L 9.0gal 10.8galUS

1818 Ford
Granada Estate Auto
1973 UK
109.0mph 175.4kmh
0-50mph 80.5kmh: 8.6secs
0-60mph 96.5kmh: 11.5secs
0-1/4 mile: 18.4secs
0-1km: 34.0secs
138.0bhp 102.9kW 139.9PS
@ 5000rpm
174.0lbft 235.8Nm @ 3000rpm
96.2bhp/ton 94.6bhp/tonne
46.1bhp/L 34.4kW/L 46.7PS/L
39.6ft/sec 12.1m/sec
21.2mph 34.1kmh/1000rpm
17.4mpg 14.5mpgUS 16.2L/100km
Petrol 4-stroke piston
2994cc 182.7cu in
Vee 6 1 Carburettor
Compression ratio: 9.0:1
Bore: 93.7mm 3.7in
Stroke: 72.4mm 2.8in
Valve type/No: Overhead 12
Transmission: Automatic
No. of forward speeds: 3
Wheels driven: Rear
Springs F/R: Coil/Coil
Brake system: PA
Brakes F/R: Disc/Drum
Steering: Rack & pinion PA
Wheelbase: 276.9cm 109.0in
Track F: 151.1cm 59.5in
Track R: 153.7cm 60.5in
Length: 467.4cm 184.0in
Width: 179.1cm 70.5in
Height: 141.2cm 55.6in
Ground clearance: 12.7cm 5.0in
Kerb weight: 1458.2kg 3212.0lb
Fuel: 65.1L 14.3gal 17.2galUS

1819 Ford
Pinto Pangra
1973 USA
123.0mph 197.9kmh
0-50mph 80.5kmh: 6.2secs
0-60mph 96.5kmh: 7.7secs
0-1/4 mile: 15.7secs
175.0bhp 130.5kW 177.4PS
@ 5500rpm
220.0lbft 298.1Nm @ 3600rpm
169.3bhp/ton 166.5bhp/tonne
87.8bhp/L 65.5kW/L 89.0PS/L
46.3ft/sec 14.1m/sec
18.8mph 30.2kmh/1000rpm
22.2mpg 18.5mpgUS 12.7L/100km
Petrol 4-stroke piston
1993cc 121.6cu in turbocharged
In-line 4 1 Carburettor
Compression ratio: 7.0:1
Bore: 91.0mm 3.6in
Stroke: 77.0mm 3.0in
Valve type/No: Overhead 8
Transmission: Manual
No. of forward speeds: 4
Wheels driven: Rear
Springs F/R: Coil/Leaf
Brakes F/R: Disc/Drum
Steering: Rack & pinion
Wheelbase: 239.3cm 94.2in
Track F: 144.8cm 57.0in
Track R: 144.8cm 57.0in
Length: 422.7cm 166.4in
Width: 176.3cm 69.4in
Height: 127.3cm 50.1in
Ground clearance: 6.4cm 2.5in
Kerb weight: 1051.0kg 2315.0lb
Fuel: 41.6L 9.1gal 11.0galUS

1820 Ford
Pinto Station Wagon
1973 USA
0-60mph 96.5kmh: 15.4secs
0-1/4 mile: 20.0secs
85.0bhp 63.4kW 86.2PS
@ 5600rpm
98.0lbft 132.8Nm @ 3800rpm
76.5bhp/ton 75.2bhp/tonne
42.6bhp/L 31.8kW/L 43.2PS/L
25.8mpg 21.5mpgUS 10.9L/100km
Petrol 4-stroke piston
1993cc 121.6cu in
In-line 4
Valve type/No: Overhead 8
Transmission: Manual
No. of forward speeds: 4
Wheels driven: Rear
Brakes F/R: Disc/Drum
Wheelbase: 239.3cm 94.2in
Length: 441.7cm 173.9in
Width: 177.0cm 69.7in
Height: 130.3cm 51.3in
Kerb weight: 1130.5kg 2490.0lb

1821 Ford
Capri 2800 V6
1974 Germany
111.0mph 178.6kmh
0-50mph 80.5kmh: 7.9secs
0-60mph 96.5kmh: 10.8secs
0-1/4 mile: 18.0secs
119.0bhp 88.7kW 120.6PS
@ 5200rpm
147.0lbft 199.2Nm @ 2800rpm
103.5bhp/ton 101.8bhp/tonne
42.6bhp/L 31.8kW/L 43.2PS/L
39.0ft/sec 11.9m/sec
20.3mph 32.7kmh/1000rpm
24.0mpg 20.0mpgUS 11.8L/100km
Petrol 4-stroke piston
2792cc 170.3cu in
Vee 6
Compression ratio: 8.2:1
Bore: 93.0mm 3.7in
Stroke: 68.5mm 2.7in
Valve type/No: Overhead 12
Transmission: Manual
No. of forward speeds: 4
Wheels driven: Rear
Springs F/R: Coil/Leaf
Brake system: PA
Brakes F/R: Disc/Drum
Steering: Rack & pinion
Wheelbase: 256.0cm 100.8in
Track F: 135.4cm 53.3in
Track R: 132.8cm 52.3in
Length: 449.6cm 177.0in
Width: 164.6cm 64.8in
Height: 128.3cm 50.5in
Kerb weight: 1169.0kg 2575.0lb
Fuel: 48.1L 10.6gal 12.7galUS

1822 Ford
Capri II 1600 GT
1974 UK
106.0mph 170.6kmh
0-50mph 80.5kmh: 8.1secs
0-60mph 96.5kmh: 11.4secs
0-1/4 mile: 18.2secs
0-1km: 34.2secs
88.0bhp 65.6kW 89.2PS
@ 5700rpm
92.0lbft 124.7Nm @ 4000rpm
88.8bhp/ton 87.3bhp/tonne
55.2bhp/L 41.2kW/L 56.0PS/L
41.2ft/sec 12.5m/sec
18.0mph 29.0kmh/1000rpm
27.4mpg 22.8mpgUS 10.3L/100km
Petrol 4-stroke piston
1593cc 97.2cu in
In-line 4 1 Carburettor
Compression ratio: 9.2:1
Bore: 87.7mm 3.4in
Stroke: 66.0mm 2.6in
Valve type/No: Overhead 8
Transmission: Manual
No. of forward speeds: 4
Wheels driven: Rear
Springs F/R: Coil/Leaf
Brake system: PA
Brakes F/R: Disc/Drum
Steering: Rack & pinion
Wheelbase: 256.5cm 101.0in
Track F: 134.6cm 53.0in
Track R: 138.4cm 54.5in
Length: 434.3cm 171.0in
Width: 170.2cm 67.0in
Height: 129.5cm 51.0in
Ground clearance: 15.2cm 6.0in
Kerb weight: 1007.9kg 2220.0lb
Fuel: 57.8L 12.7gal 15.3galUS

1823 Ford
Escort 1100L
1974 UK
84.0mph 135.2kmh
0-50mph 80.5kmh: 13.2secs
0-60mph 96.5kmh: 19.8secs
0-1/4 mile: 21.6secs
0-1km: 40.9secs
48.0bhp 35.8kW 48.7PS
@ 5500rpm
55.0lbft 74.5Nm @ 3000rpm
63.1bhp/ton 62.0bhp/tonne
43.7bhp/L 32.6kW/L 44.3PS/L
31.9ft/sec 9.7m/sec
16.2mph 26.1kmh/1000rpm
29.4mpg 24.5mpgUS 9.6L/100km
Petrol 4-stroke piston
1098cc 67.0cu in
In-line 4 1 Carburettor
Compression ratio: 9.0:1
Bore: 81.0mm 3.2in
Stroke: 53.0mm 2.1in
Valve type/No: Overhead 8
Transmission: Manual
No. of forward speeds: 4
Wheels driven: Rear
Springs F/R: Coil/Leaf
Brake system: PA
Brakes F/R: Disc/Drum
Steering: Rack & pinion
Wheelbase: 240.0cm 94.5in
Track F: 124.5cm 49.0in
Track R: 127.0cm 50.0in
Length: 406.4cm 160.0in
Width: 157.0cm 61.8in
Height: 137.2cm 54.0in
Ground clearance: 15.2cm 6.0in
Kerb weight: 773.6kg 1704.0lb
Fuel: 40.9L 9.0gal 10.8galUS

1824 Ford
Granada Ghia Coupe
1974 UK
111.0mph 178.6kmh
0-50mph 80.5kmh: 7.2secs
0-60mph 96.5kmh: 10.3secs
0-1/4 mile: 17.8secs
0-1km: 32.9secs
138.0bhp 102.9kW 139.9PS
@ 5000rpm
174.0lbft 235.8Nm @ 3000rpm
101.3bhp/ton 99.6bhp/tonne
46.1bhp/L 34.4kW/L 46.7PS/L
39.6ft/sec 12.1m/sec
21.3mph 34.3kmh/1000rpm
18.7mpg 15.6mpgUS 15.1L/100km
Petrol 4-stroke piston
2994cc 182.7cu in
Vee 6 1 Carburettor
Compression ratio: 8.9:1
Bore: 93.7mm 3.7in
Stroke: 72.4mm 2.8in
Valve type/No: Overhead 12
Transmission: Automatic
No. of forward speeds: 3
Wheels driven: Rear
Springs F/R: Coil/Coil
Brake system: PA
Brakes F/R: Disc/Drum
Steering: Rack & pinion PA
Wheelbase: 276.9cm 109.0in
Track F: 149.9cm 59.0in
Track R: 153.7cm 60.5in
Length: 466.1cm 183.5in
Width: 179.1cm 70.5in
Height: 138.7cm 54.6in
Ground clearance: 20.3cm 8.0in
Kerb weight: 1385.1kg 3051.0lb
Fuel: 65.1L 14.3gal 17.2galUS

1825 Ford
Granada GXL
1974 UK
110.0mph 177.0kmh
0-50mph 80.5kmh: 9.0secs
0-60mph 96.5kmh: 11.7secs
138.0bhp 102.9kW 139.9PS
@ 5000rpm
174.0lbft 235.8Nm @ 3000rpm
99.7bhp/ton 98.0bhp/tonne
46.1bhp/L 34.4kW/L 46.7PS/L
39.6ft/sec 12.1m/sec
20.7mph 33.3kmh/1000rpm
19.2mpg 16.0mpgUS 14.7L/100km
Petrol 4-stroke piston
2994cc 182.7cu in
Vee 6
Compression ratio: 8.9:1
Bore: 93.7mm 3.7in
Stroke: 72.4mm 2.8in
Valve type/No: Overhead 12
Transmission: Automatic
No. of forward speeds: 3
Wheels driven: Rear
Springs F/R: Coil/Coil
Brakes F/R: Disc/Drum
Steering: Rack & pinion PA
Wheelbase: 276.9cm 109.0in
Track F: 151.1cm 59.5in
Track R: 153.7cm 60.5in
Length: 457.2cm 180.0in
Width: 179.1cm 70.5in
Height: 136.9cm 53.9in
Kerb weight: 1407.4kg 3100.0lb
Fuel: 65.1L 14.3gal 17.2galUS

1826 Ford
Mustang II Ghia
1974 USA
102.0mph 164.1kmh
0-50mph 80.5kmh: 9.1secs
0-60mph 96.5kmh: 13.0secs
0-1/4 mile: 19.0secs
0-1km: 35.7secs
105.0bhp 78.3kW 106.5PS
@ 4600rpm
140.0lbft 189.7Nm @ 3200rpm
71.9bhp/ton 70.7bhp/tonne
37.5bhp/L 28.0kW/L 38.0PS/L
34.5ft/sec 10.5m/sec
18.7mph 30.1kmh/1000rpm
20.7mpg 17.2mpgUS 13.6L/100km
Petrol 4-stroke piston
2798cc 170.7cu in
In-line 6 1 Carburettor
Compression ratio: 8.2:1
Bore: 93.0mm 3.7in
Stroke: 68.6mm 2.7in
Valve type/No: Overhead 12
Transmission: Automatic
No. of forward speeds: 3
Wheels driven: Rear
Springs F/R: Coil/Leaf
Brake system: PA
Brakes F/R: Disc/Drum
Steering: Rack & pinion PA
Wheelbase: 248.9cm 98.0in
Track F: 137.2cm 54.0in
Track R: 139.7cm 55.0in
Length: 449.6cm 177.0in
Width: 177.8cm 70.0in
Height: 132.1cm 52.0in
Ground clearance: 19.1cm 7.5in
Kerb weight: 1485.9kg 3273.0lb
Fuel: 48.7L 10.7gal 12.9galUS

1827 Ford
Mustang II Mach I
1974 USA
99.0mph 159.3kmh
0-50mph 80.5kmh: 10.0secs
0-60mph 96.5kmh: 13.8secs
0-1/4 mile: 19.4secs
119.0bhp 88.7kW 120.6PS
@ 5200rpm
147.0lbft 199.2Nm @ 2800rpm
85.4bhp/ton 84.0bhp/tonne
42.6bhp/L 31.8kW/L 43.2PS/L
39.0ft/sec 11.9m/sec
19.5mph 31.4kmh/1000rpm
19.8mpg 16.5mpgUS 14.3L/100km
Petrol 4-stroke piston
2792cc 170.3cu in
Vee 6 1 Carburettor
Compression ratio: 8.2:1
Bore: 93.0mm 3.7in
Stroke: 68.5mm 2.7in
Valve type/No: Overhead 12
Transmission: Manual
No. of forward speeds: 4
Wheels driven: Rear
Springs F/R: Coil/Leaf

Brake system: PA
Brakes F/R: Disc/Drum
Steering: Rack & pinion PA
Wheelbase: 244.3cm 96.2in
Track F: 141.2cm 55.6in
Track R: 141.7cm 55.8in
Length: 444.5cm 175.0in
Width: 178.3cm 70.2in
Height: 126.0cm 49.6in
Ground clearance: 11.4cm 4.5in
Kerb weight: 1416.5kg 3120.0lb
Fuel: 49.2L 10.8gal 13.0galUS

1828 Ford

Capri 2000S GT
1975 UK
110.0mph 177.0kmh
0-50mph 80.5kmh: 7.5secs
0-60mph 96.5kmh: 10.4secs
0-1/4 mile: 17.9secs
0-1km: 33.8secs
99.0bhp 73.8kW 100.4PS
@ 5200rpm
111.0lbft 150.4Nm @ 3500rpm
97.6bhp/ton 95.9bhp/tonne
49.7bhp/L 37.0kW/L 50.4PS/L
43.8ft/sec 13.3m/sec
19.6mph 31.5kmh/1000rpm
24.0mpg 20.0mpgUS 11.8L/100km
Petrol 4-stroke piston
1993cc 121.6cu in
In-line 4 1 Carburettor
Compression ratio: 9.2:1
Bore: 90.8mm 3.6in
Stroke: 76.9mm 3.0in
Valve type/No: Overhead 8
Transmission: Manual
No. of forward speeds: 4
Wheels driven: Rear
Springs F/R: Coil/Leaf
Brake system: PA
Brakes F/R: Disc/Drum
Steering: Rack & pinion
Wheelbase: 256.5cm 101.0in
Track F: 134.6cm 53.0in
Track R: 138.4cm 54.5in
Length: 434.3cm 171.0in
Width: 170.2cm 67.0in
Height: 129.5cm 51.0in
Ground clearance: 15.2cm 6.0in
Kerb weight: 1031.9kg 2273.0lb
Fuel: 57.8L 12.7gal 15.3galUS

1829 Ford

Consul 2000L
1975 UK
100.0mph 160.9kmh
0-50mph 80.5kmh: 8.5secs
0-60mph 96.5kmh: 12.0secs
0-1/4 mile: 18.6secs
0-1km: 32.5secs
99.0bhp 73.8kW 100.4PS
@ 5500rpm
111.0lbft 150.4Nm @ 3500rpm
92.7bhp/ton 91.2bhp/tonne
49.7bhp/L 37.0kW/L 50.4PS/L
46.3ft/sec 14.1m/sec
18.8mph 30.2kmh/1000rpm
23.2mpg 19.3mpgUS 12.2L/100km
Petrol 4-stroke piston
1993cc 121.6cu in
In-line 4 1 Carburettor
Compression ratio: 9.0:1
Bore: 90.8mm 3.6in
Stroke: 76.9mm 3.0in
Valve type/No: Overhead 8
Transmission: Manual
No. of forward speeds: 4
Wheels driven: Rear
Springs F/R: Coil/Coil
Brake system: PA
Brakes F/R: Disc/Drum
Steering: Rack & pinion
Wheelbase: 276.9cm 109.0in
Track F: 151.1cm 59.5in
Track R: 153.7cm 60.5in
Length: 466.1cm 183.5in
Width: 179.1cm 70.5in
Height: 141.2cm 55.6in
Ground clearance: 20.3cm 8.0in
Kerb weight: 1086.0kg 2392.0lb
Fuel: 65.1L 14.3gal 17.2galUS

1830 Ford

Cortina 1300L
1975 UK
92.0mph 148.0kmh
0-50mph 80.5kmh: 10.8secs
0-60mph 96.5kmh: 16.4secs
0-1/4 mile: 20.3secs
0-1km: 38.7secs
57.0bhp 42.5kW 57.8PS
@ 5500rpm
67.0lbft 90.8Nm @ 3000rpm
57.5bhp/ton 56.5bhp/tonne
43.9bhp/L 32.8kW/L 44.6PS/L
37.9ft/sec 11.5m/sec
15.1mph 24.3kmh/1000rpm
27.0mpg 22.5mpgUS 10.5L/100km
Petrol 4-stroke piston
1297cc 79.1cu in
In-line 4 1 Carburettor
Compression ratio: 9.0:1
Bore: 81.0mm 3.2in
Stroke: 63.0mm 2.5in
Valve type/No: Overhead 8
Transmission: Manual
No. of forward speeds: 4
Wheels driven: Rear
Springs F/R: Coil/Coil
Brake system: PA
Brakes F/R: Disc/Drum
Steering: Rack & pinion
Wheelbase: 257.8cm 101.5in
Track F: 142.2cm 56.0in
Track R: 142.2cm 56.0in
Length: 426.0cm 167.7in
Width: 170.2cm 67.0in
Height: 139.7cm 55.0in
Ground clearance: 17.8cm 7.0in
Kerb weight: 1007.9kg 2220.0lb
Fuel: 54.1L 11.9gal 14.3galUS

1831 Ford

Cortina 2000E Estate
1975 UK
103.0mph 165.7kmh
0-50mph 80.5kmh: 8.5secs
0-60mph 96.5kmh: 12.6secs
0-1/4 mile: 17.8secs
0-1km: 37.8secs
98.0bhp 73.1kW 99.4PS
@ 5500rpm
111.0lbft 150.4Nm @ 3500rpm
87.1bhp/ton 85.7bhp/tonne
49.2bhp/L 36.7kW/L 49.8PS/L
48.1ft/sec 14.7m/sec
17.9mph 28.8kmh/1000rpm
25.3mpg 21.1mpgUS 11.2L/100km
Petrol 4-stroke piston
1993cc 121.6cu in
In-line 4 1 Carburettor
Compression ratio: 9.2:1
Bore: 90.8mm 3.6in
Stroke: 79.9mm 3.1in
Valve type/No: Overhead 8
Transmission: Manual
No. of forward speeds: 4
Wheels driven: Rear
Springs F/R: Coil/Coil
Brake system: PA
Brakes F/R: Disc/Drum
Steering: Rack & pinion
Wheelbase: 257.8cm 101.5in
Track F: 142.2cm 56.0in
Track R: 142.2cm 56.0in
Length: 437.1cm 172.1in
Width: 170.2cm 67.0in
Height: 132.1cm 52.0in
Ground clearance: 17.8cm 7.0in
Kerb weight: 1144.1kg 2520.0lb
Fuel: 54.1L 11.9gal 14.3galUS

1832 Ford

Escort 1.3 Ghia
1975 UK
96.0mph 154.5kmh
0-50mph 80.5kmh: 9.0secs
0-60mph 96.5kmh: 13.5secs
0-1/4 mile: 19.9secs
0-1km: 36.3secs
70.0bhp 52.2kW 71.0PS
@ 5500rpm
68.0lbft 92.1Nm @ 4000rpm
79.8bhp/ton 78.4bhp/tonne
54.0bhp/L 40.2kW/L 54.7PS/L
37.9ft/sec 11.5m/sec
15.9mph 25.6kmh/1000rpm
29.3mpg 24.4mpgUS 9.6L/100km
Petrol 4-stroke piston
1297cc 79.1cu in
In-line 4 1 Carburettor
Compression ratio: 9.2:1
Bore: 81.0mm 3.2in
Stroke: 63.0mm 2.5in
Valve type/No: Overhead 8
Transmission: Manual
No. of forward speeds: 4
Wheels driven: Rear
Springs F/R: Coil/Leaf
Brake system: PA
Brakes F/R: Disc/Drum
Steering: Rack & pinion
Wheelbase: 240.0cm 94.5in
Track F: 127.0cm 50.0in
Track R: 129.5cm 51.0in
Length: 397.5cm 156.5in
Width: 153.7cm 60.5in
Height: 141.0cm 55.5in
Ground clearance: 14.0cm 5.5in
Kerb weight: 892.6kg 1966.0lb
Fuel: 40.9L 9.0gal 10.8galUS

1833 Ford

Escort RS1800
1975 UK
114.0mph 183.4kmh
0-50mph 80.5kmh: 6.6secs
0-60mph 96.5kmh: 9.0secs
0-1/4 mile: 16.9secs
0-1km: 31.4secs
115.0bhp 85.8kW 116.6PS
@ 6000rpm
120.0lbft 162.6Nm @ 4000rpm
127.8bhp/ton 125.6bhp/tonne
62.3bhp/L 46.5kW/L 63.2PS/L
51.0ft/sec 15.5m/sec
18.5mph 29.8kmh/1000rpm
26.5mpg 22.1mpgUS 10.7L/100km
Petrol 4-stroke piston
1845cc 112.6cu in
In-line 4 1 Carburettor
Compression ratio: 9.0:1
Bore: 86.7mm 3.4in
Stroke: 77.6mm 3.1in
Valve type/No: Overhead 8
Transmission: Manual
No. of forward speeds: 4
Wheels driven: Rear
Springs F/R: Coil/Leaf
Brake system: PA
Brakes F/R: Disc/Drum
Steering: Rack & pinion
Wheelbase: 240.0cm 94.5in
Track F: 127.0cm 50.0in
Track R: 129.5cm 51.0in
Length: 397.5cm 156.5in
Width: 153.7cm 60.5in
Height: 141.0cm 55.5in
Ground clearance: 14.0cm 5.5in
Kerb weight: 915.3kg 2016.0lb
Fuel: 40.9L 9.0gal 10.8galUS

1834 Ford

Granada 2000 GL
1975 UK
96.0mph 154.5kmh
0-50mph 80.5kmh: 10.6secs
0-60mph 96.5kmh: 14.7secs
0-1/4 mile: 20.5secs
0-1km: 37.5secs
98.0bhp 73.1kW 99.4PS
@ 5200rpm
111.0lbft 150.4Nm @ 3500rpm
78.6bhp/ton 77.3bhp/tonne
49.2bhp/L 36.7kW/L 49.8PS/L
43.8ft/sec 13.3m/sec
18.4mph 29.6kmh/1000rpm
20.1mpg 16.7mpgUS 14.1L/100km
Petrol 4-stroke piston
1993cc 121.6cu in
In-line 4 1 Carburettor
Compression ratio: 9.2:1
Bore: 90.8mm 3.6in
Stroke: 76.9mm 3.0in
Valve type/No: Overhead 8
Transmission: Automatic
No. of forward speeds: 3
Wheels driven: Rear
Springs F/R: Coil/Coil
Brake system: PA
Brakes F/R: Disc/Drum
Steering: Rack & pinion PA
Wheelbase: 276.9cm 109.0in
Track F: 151.1cm 59.5in
Track R: 153.7cm 60.5in
Length: 467.4cm 184.0in
Width: 179.1cm 70.5in
Height: 138.7cm 54.6in
Ground clearance: 12.7cm 5.0in
Kerb weight: 1268.0kg 2793.0lb
Fuel: 65.1L 14.3gal 17.2galUS

1835 Ford

Granada 5-litre
1975 USA
101.0mph 162.5kmh
0-50mph 80.5kmh: 8.8secs
0-60mph 96.5kmh: 12.0secs
0-1/4 mile: 18.7secs
129.0bhp 96.2kW 130.8PS
@ 3800rpm
220.0lbft 298.1Nm @ 1800rpm
79.3bhp/ton 77.9bhp/tonne
26.1bhp/L 19.4kW/L 26.4PS/L
31.7ft/sec 9.6m/sec
24.0mph 38.6kmh/1000rpm
15.0mpg 12.5mpgUS 18.8L/100km
Petrol 4-stroke piston
4950cc 302.0cu in
Vee 8 1 Carburettor
Compression ratio: 8.0:1
Bore: 101.6mm 4.0in
Stroke: 76.2mm 3.0in
Valve type/No: Overhead 16
Transmission: Automatic
No. of forward speeds: 3
Wheels driven: Rear
Springs F/R: Coil/Leaf
Brake system: PA
Brakes F/R: /Drum
Steering: Recirculating ball PA
Wheelbase: 279.1cm 109.9in
Track F: 148.6cm 58.5in
Track R: 146.6cm 57.7in
Length: 502.2cm 197.7in
Width: 180.8cm 71.2in
Height: 135.4cm 53.3in
Ground clearance: 12.7cm 5.0in
Kerb weight: 1654.8kg 3645.0lb
Fuel: 73.8L 16.2gal 19.5galUS

1836 Ford

Pinto 2300
1975 USA
93.0mph 149.6kmh
0-50mph 80.5kmh: 10.4secs
0-60mph 96.5kmh: 15.2secs
0-1/4 mile: 19.8secs
102.0bhp 76.1kW 103.4PS
@ 5200rpm
122.0lbft 165.3Nm @ 3200rpm
91.6bhp/ton 90.0bhp/tonne
44.4bhp/L 33.1kW/L 45.0PS/L
Petrol 4-stroke piston
2298cc 140.2cu in
In-line 4
Transmission: Manual
No. of forward speeds: 4
Wheels driven: Rear
Springs F/R: Coil/Leaf
Brakes F/R: Disc/Drum
Wheelbase: 240.0cm 94.5in
Track F: 139.7cm 55.0in
Track R: 141.7cm 55.8in
Length: 429.3cm 169.0in
Width: 176.3cm 69.4in
Height: 128.3cm 50.5in
Kerb weight: 1132.7kg 2495.0lb

1837 Ford

Capri 1300
1976 UK
88.0mph 141.6kmh
0-50mph 80.5kmh: 12.4secs
0-60mph 96.5kmh: 18.8secs
0-1/4 mile: 21.0secs
0-1km: 39.8secs
49.5bhp 36.9kW 50.2PS
@ 5000rpm
64.0lbft 86.7Nm @ 3000rpm
50.9bhp/ton 50.1bhp/tonne
38.2bhp/L 28.5kW/L 38.7PS/L
34.4ft/sec 10.5m/sec
16.3mph 26.2kmh/1000rpm
28.7mpg 23.9mpgUS 9.8L/100km
Petrol 4-stroke piston
1297cc 79.1cu in
In-line 4 1 Carburettor
Compression ratio: 9.2:1
Bore: 81.0mm 3.2in
Stroke: 63.0mm 2.5in
Valve type/No: Overhead 8
Transmission: Manual
No. of forward speeds: 4
Wheels driven: Rear

Springs F/R: Coil/Leaf
Brake system: PA
Brakes F/R: Disc/Drum
Steering: Rack & pinion
Wheelbase: 256.5cm 101.0in
Track F: 134.6cm 53.0in
Track R: 138.4cm 54.5in
Length: 434.3cm 171.0in
Width: 170.2cm 67.0in
Height: 129.5cm 51.0in
Ground clearance: 15.2cm 6.0in
Kerb weight: 988.8kg 2178.0lb
Fuel: 59.1L 13.0gal 15.6galUS

1838 Ford

Capri 3000S
1976 UK
118.0mph 189.9kmh
0-50mph 80.5kmh: 6.4secs
0-60mph 96.5kmh: 8.6secs
0-1/4 mile: 16.6secs
0-1km: 30.6secs
138.0bhp 102.9kW 139.9PS
@ 5000rpm
174.0lbft 235.8Nm @ 3000rpm
116.8bhp/ton 114.9bhp/tonne
46.1bhp/L 34.4kW/L 46.7PS/L
39.6ft/sec 12.1m/sec
21.8mph 35.1kmh/1000rpm
19.5mpg 16.2mpgUS 14.5L/100km
Petrol 4-stroke piston
2994cc 182.7cu in
Vee 6 1 Carburettor
Compression ratio: 9.0:1
Bore: 93.7mm 3.7in
Stroke: 72.4mm 2.8in
Valve type/No: Overhead 12
Transmission: Manual
No. of forward speeds: 4
Wheels driven: Rear
Springs F/R: Coil/Leaf
Brake system: PA
Brakes F/R: Disc/Drum
Steering: Rack & pinion PA
Wheelbase: 256.5cm 101.0in
Track F: 134.6cm 53.0in
Track R: 138.4cm 54.5in
Length: 435.6cm 171.5in
Width: 170.2cm 67.0in
Height: 129.5cm 51.0in
Ground clearance: 15.2cm 6.0in
Kerb weight: 1201.3kg 2646.0lb
Fuel: 59.1L 13.0gal 15.6galUS

1839 Ford

Capri II 2.8 V6
1976 Germany
108.0mph 173.8kmh
0-50mph 80.5kmh: 7.7secs
0-60mph 96.5kmh: 10.6secs
0-1/4 mile: 18.0secs
109.0bhp 81.3kW 110.5PS
@ 4800rpm
146.0lbft 197.8Nm @ 3000rpm
90.9bhp/ton 89.4bhp/tonne
39.0bhp/L 29.1kW/L 39.6PS/L
36.0ft/sec 11.0m/sec
21.0mph 33.8kmh/1000rpm
23.4mpg 19.5mpgUS 12.1L/100km
Petrol 4-stroke piston
2792cc 170.3cu in
Vee 6 1 Carburettor
Compression ratio: 8.2:1
Bore: 93.0mm 3.7in
Stroke: 68.5mm 2.7in
Valve type/No: Overhead 12
Transmission: Manual
No. of forward speeds: 4
Wheels driven: Rear
Springs F/R: Coil/Leaf
Brake system: PA
Brakes F/R: Disc/Drum
Steering: Rack & pinion PA
Wheelbase: 256.0cm 100.8in
Track F: 135.4cm 53.3in
Track R: 138.4cm 54.5in
Length: 444.0cm 174.8in
Width: 169.9cm 66.9in
Height: 129.5cm 51.0in
Ground clearance: 12.4cm 4.9in
Kerb weight: 1219.0kg 2685.0lb
Fuel: 48.1L 10.6gal 12.7galUS

1840 Ford

Capri V6 Black Gold
1976 Germany
130.0mph 209.2kmh
0-50mph 80.5kmh: 5.9secs
0-60mph 96.5kmh: 7.7secs
170.0bhp 126.8kW 172.4PS
@ 6000rpm
170.0lbft 230.4Nm @ 4000rpm
157.4bhp/ton 154.7bhp/tonne
60.9bhp/L 45.4kW/L 61.7PS/L
45.0ft/sec 13.7m/sec
21.0mph 33.8kmh/1000rpm
20.4mpg 17.0mpgUS 13.8L/100km
Petrol 4-stroke piston
2792cc 170.3cu in
Vee 6
Compression ratio: 10.5:1
Bore: 93.0mm 3.7in
Stroke: 68.5mm 2.7in
Valve type/No: Overhead 12
Transmission: Manual
No. of forward speeds: 4
Wheels driven: Rear
Springs F/R: Coil/Leaf
Brake system: PA
Brakes F/R: Disc/Drum
Steering: Rack & pinion
Wheelbase: 256.0cm 100.8in
Track F: 135.4cm 53.3in
Track R: 138.4cm 54.5in
Length: 435.6cm 171.5in
Width: 169.9cm 66.9in
Height: 127.0cm 50.0in
Kerb weight: 1098.7kg 2420.0lb
Fuel: 48.1L 10.6gal 12.7galUS

1841 Ford

Cobra II Kemp
1976 USA
153.0mph 246.2kmh
0-50mph 80.5kmh: 3.4secs
0-60mph 96.5kmh: 4.1secs
0-1/4 mile: 12.1secs
570.0bhp 425.0kW 577.9PS
@ 7000rpm
530.0lbft 718.2Nm @ 4600rpm
476.4bhp/ton 468.5bhp/tonne
99.1bhp/L 73.9kW/L 100.4PS/L
68.1ft/sec 20.7m/sec
21.0mph 33.8kmh/1000rpm
6.0mpg 5.0mpgUS 47.0L/100km
Petrol 4-stroke piston
5753cc 351.0cu in
Vee 8 fuel injection
Compression ratio: 12.5:1
Bore: 101.6mm 4.0in
Stroke: 88.9mm 3.5in
Valve type/No: Overhead 16
Transmission: Manual
No. of forward speeds: 4
Wheels driven: Rear
Springs F/R: Coil/Coil
Brakes F/R: Disc/Disc
Steering: Rack & pinion
Wheelbase: 245.9cm 96.8in
Track F: 147.3cm 58.0in
Track R: 147.3cm 58.0in
Length: 434.3cm 171.0in
Width: 189.2cm 74.5in
Height: 109.2cm 43.0in
Ground clearance: 7.4cm 2.9in
Kerb weight: 1216.7kg 2680.0lb
Fuel: 120.0L 26.4gal 31.7galUS

1842 Ford

Cortina 2.0 Ghia
1976 UK
103.0mph 165.7kmh
0-50mph 80.5kmh: 7.6secs
0-60mph 96.5kmh: 11.0secs
0-1/4 mile: 17.9secs
0-1km: 34.0secs
98.0bhp 73.1kW 99.4PS
@ 5200rpm
111.0lbft 150.4Nm @ 3500rpm
92.0bhp/ton 90.4bhp/tonne
49.2bhp/L 36.7kW/L 49.8PS/L
43.8ft/sec 13.3m/sec
17.8mph 28.6kmh/1000rpm
24.1mpg 20.1mpgUS 11.7L/100km
Petrol 4-stroke piston
1993cc 121.6cu in
In-line 4 1 Carburettor
Compression ratio: 9.2:1
Bore: 90.8mm 3.6in
Stroke: 77.0mm 3.0in
Valve type/No: Overhead 8
Transmission: Manual
No. of forward speeds: 4
Wheels driven: Rear
Springs F/R: Coil/Coil
Brake system: PA
Brakes F/R: Disc/Drum
Steering: Rack & pinion
Wheelbase: 257.8cm 101.5in
Track F: 144.5cm 56.9in
Track R: 142.2cm 56.0in
Length: 432.6cm 170.3in
Width: 169.9cm 66.9in
Height: 132.1cm 52.0in
Ground clearance: 17.8cm 7.0in
Kerb weight: 1083.7kg 2387.0lb
Fuel: 54.1L 11.9gal 14.3galUS

1843 Ford

Escort 1300 GL
1976 UK
92.0mph 148.0kmh
0-50mph 80.5kmh: 10.6secs
0-60mph 96.5kmh: 16.4secs
0-1/4 mile: 20.7secs
0-1km: 39.5secs
57.0bhp 42.5kW 57.8PS
@ 5500rpm
67.0lbft 90.8Nm @ 3000rpm
66.0bhp/ton 64.9bhp/tonne
43.9bhp/L 32.8kW/L 44.6PS/L
37.9ft/sec 11.5m/sec
17.1mph 27.5kmh/1000rpm
27.6mpg 23.0mpgUS 10.2L/100km
Petrol 4-stroke piston
1297cc 79.1cu in
In-line 4 1 Carburettor
Compression ratio: 9.2:1
Bore: 81.0mm 3.2in
Stroke: 63.0mm 2.5in
Valve type/No: Overhead 8
Transmission: Manual
No. of forward speeds: 4
Wheels driven: Rear
Springs F/R: Coil/Leaf
Brake system: PA
Brakes F/R: Disc/Drum
Steering: Rack & pinion
Wheelbase: 240.0cm 94.5in
Track F: 127.0cm 50.0in
Track R: 129.5cm 51.0in
Length: 397.5cm 156.5in
Width: 153.7cm 60.5in
Height: 141.0cm 55.5in
Ground clearance: 14.0cm 5.5in
Kerb weight: 878.0kg 1934.0lb
Fuel: 40.9L 9.0gal 10.8galUS

1844 Ford

Escort RS2000
1976 UK
112.0mph 180.2kmh
0-50mph 80.5kmh: 6.4secs
0-60mph 96.5kmh: 8.6secs
0-1/4 mile: 16.7secs
0-1km: 31.7secs
110.0bhp 82.0kW 111.5PS
@ 5500rpm
119.0lbft 161.2Nm @ 4000rpm
118.7bhp/ton 116.8bhp/tonne
55.2bhp/L 41.2kW/L 56.0PS/L
46.3ft/sec 14.1m/sec
18.6mph 29.9kmh/1000rpm
24.7mpg 20.6mpgUS 11.4L/100km
Petrol 4-stroke piston
1993cc 121.6cu in
In-line 4 1 Carburettor
Compression ratio: 9.2:1
Bore: 90.8mm 3.6in
Stroke: 76.9mm 3.0in
Valve type/No: Overhead 8
Transmission: Manual
No. of forward speeds: 4
Wheels driven: Rear
Springs F/R: Coil/Leaf
Brake system: PA
Brakes F/R: Disc/Drum
Steering: Rack & pinion
Wheelbase: 240.0cm 94.5in
Track F: 127.0cm 50.0in
Track R: 129.5cm 51.0in
Length: 414.3cm 163.1in
Width: 153.7cm 60.5in
Height: 141.0cm 55.5in
Ground clearance: 14.0cm 5.5in
Kerb weight: 942.0kg 2075.0lb
Fuel: 40.9L 9.0gal 10.8galUS

1845 Ford

Fiesta
1976 UK
91.0mph 146.4kmh
0-50mph 80.5kmh: 13.5secs
0-60mph 96.5kmh: 19.6secs
0-1/4 mile: 20.8secs
0-1km: 39.7secs
45.0bhp 33.6kW 45.6PS
@ 6000rpm
47.7lbft 64.6Nm @ 3000rpm
61.6bhp/ton 60.6bhp/tonne
47.0bhp/L 35.1kW/L 47.7PS/L
36.5ft/sec 11.1m/sec
14.9mph 24.0kmh/1000rpm
31.8mpg 26.5mpgUS 8.9L/100km
Petrol 4-stroke piston
957cc 58.4cu in
In-line 4 1 Carburettor
Compression ratio: 9.0:1
Bore: 74.0mm 2.9in
Stroke: 55.7mm 2.2in
Valve type/No: Overhead 8
Transmission: Manual
No. of forward speeds: 4
Wheels driven: Front
Springs F/R: Coil/Coil
Brake system: PA
Brakes F/R: Disc/Drum
Steering: Rack & pinion
Wheelbase: 228.6cm 90.0in
Track F: 133.4cm 52.5in
Track R: 132.6cm 52.2in
Length: 356.9cm 140.5in
Width: 156.2cm 61.5in
Height: 134.6cm 53.0in
Ground clearance: 15.2cm 6.0in
Kerb weight: 742.3kg 1635.0lb
Fuel: 34.1L 7.5gal 9.0galUS

1846 Ford

Granada 3000 S
1976 UK
116.0mph 186.6kmh
0-50mph 80.5kmh: 6.8secs
0-60mph 96.5kmh: 9.2secs
0-1/4 mile: 17.3secs
0-1km: 32.2secs
138.0bhp 102.9kW 139.9PS
@ 5000rpm
174.0lbft 235.8Nm @ 3000rpm
102.3bhp/ton 100.5bhp/tonne
46.1bhp/L 34.4kW/L 46.7PS/L
39.6ft/sec 12.1m/sec
21.2mph 34.1kmh/1000rpm
21.3mpg 17.7mpgUS 13.3L/100km
Petrol 4-stroke piston
2994cc 182.7cu in
Vee 6 1 Carburettor
Compression ratio: 9.0:1
Bore: 93.7mm 3.7in
Stroke: 72.4mm 2.8in
Valve type/No: Overhead 12
Transmission: Manual
No. of forward speeds: 4
Wheels driven: Rear
Springs F/R: Coil/Coil
Brake system: PA
Brakes F/R: Disc/Drum
Steering: Rack & pinion PA
Wheelbase: 276.9cm 109.0in
Track F: 151.1cm 59.5in
Track R: 153.7cm 60.5in
Length: 466.1cm 183.5in
Width: 179.1cm 70.5in
Height: 141.2cm 55.6in
Ground clearance: 12.7cm 5.0in
Kerb weight: 1372.4kg 3023.0lb
Fuel: 65.1L 14.3gal 17.2galUS

1847 Ford

Mustang II
1976 USA
0-60mph 96.5kmh: 10.4secs
0-1/4 mile: 17.7secs
134.0bhp 99.9kW 135.9PS
@ 3600rpm
247.0lbft 334.7Nm @ 1800rpm
95.0bhp/ton 93.4bhp/tonne
27.1bhp/L 20.2kW/L 27.4PS/L
30.0ft/sec 9.1m/sec
23.1mph 37.2kmh/1000rpm
16.8mpg 14.0mpgUS 16.8L/100km
Petrol 4-stroke piston
4950cc 302.0cu in
Vee 8 1 Carburettor
Compression ratio: 8.0:1

Bore: 101.6mm 4.0in
Stroke: 76.2mm 3.0in
Valve type/No: Overhead 16
Transmission: Manual
No. of forward speeds: 4
Wheels driven: Rear
Springs F/R: Coil/Leaf
Brake system: PA
Brakes F/R: Disc/Drum
Steering: Rack & pinion PA
Wheelbase: 244.3cm 96.2in
Track F: 141.2cm 55.6in
Track R: 141.7cm 55.8in
Length: 444.5cm 175.0in
Width: 178.3cm 70.2in
Height: 126.2cm 49.7in
Ground clearance: 12.7cm 5.0in
Kerb weight: 1434.6kg 3160.0lb
Fuel: 49.2L 10.8gal 13.0galUS

1848 Ford

Mustang II V8
1976 USA
106.0mph 170.6kmh
0-50mph 80.5kmh: 7.5secs
0-60mph 96.5kmh: 10.5secs
0-1/4 mile: 17.9secs
133.0bhp 99.2kW 134.8PS
@ 3600rpm
223.0lbft 302.2Nm @ 2000rpm
91.2bhp/ton 89.7bhp/tonne
26.9bhp/L 20.0kW/L 27.2PS/L
30.0ft/sec 9.1m/sec
22.2mph 35.7kmh/1000rpm
15.6mpg 13.0mpgUS 18.1L/100km
Petrol 4-stroke piston
4952cc 302.1cu in
Vee 8 1 Carburettor
Compression ratio: 8.0:1
Bore: 101.7mm 4.0in
Stroke: 76.2mm 3.0in
Valve type/No: Overhead 16
Transmission: Automatic
No. of forward speeds: 3
Wheels driven: Rear
Springs F/R: Coil/Leaf
Brake system: PA
Brakes F/R: Disc/Drum
Steering: Rack & pinion PA
Wheelbase: 244.3cm 96.2in
Track F: 140.0cm 55.1in
Track R: 140.5cm 55.3in
Length: 444.5cm 175.0in
Width: 178.3cm 70.2in
Height: 126.2cm 49.7in
Ground clearance: 12.7cm 5.0in
Kerb weight: 1482.3kg 3265.0lb
Fuel: 62.4L 13.7gal 16.5galUS

1849 Ford

Cortina 2.3 Ghia
1977 UK
104.0mph 167.3kmh
0-50mph 80.5kmh: 8.6secs
0-60mph 96.5kmh: 12.2secs
0-1/4 mile: 18.8secs
0-1km: 35.4secs
108.0bhp 80.5kW 109.5PS
@ 5000rpm
130.0lbft 176.2Nm @ 3000rpm
96.5bhp/ton 94.9bhp/tonne
47.1bhp/L 35.1kW/L 47.7PS/L
32.9ft/sec 10.0m/sec
19.6mph 31.5kmh/1000rpm
22.8mpg 19.0mpgUS 12.4L/100km
Petrol 4-stroke piston
2293cc 139.9cu in
Vee 6 1 Carburettor
Compression ratio: 8.7:1
Bore: 90.0mm 3.5in
Stroke: 60.1mm 2.4in
Valve type/No: Overhead 12
Transmission: Automatic
No. of forward speeds: 3
Wheels driven: Rear
Springs F/R: Coil/Coil
Brake system: PA
Brakes F/R: Disc/Drum
Steering: Rack & pinion
Wheelbase: 257.8cm 101.5in
Track F: 144.5cm 56.9in
Track R: 142.2cm 56.0in
Length: 432.6cm 170.3in
Width: 169.9cm 66.9in
Height: 132.1cm 52.0in
Ground clearance: 17.8cm 7.0in
Kerb weight: 1138.2kg 2507.0lb
Fuel: 54.6L 12.0gal 14.4galUS

1850 Ford

Escort 1300 GL
1977 UK
93.0mph 149.6kmh
0-50mph 80.5kmh: 10.4secs
0-60mph 96.5kmh: 16.0secs
0-1/4 mile: 20.4secs
0-1km: 38.7secs
57.0bhp 42.5kW 57.8PS
@ 5500rpm
67.0lbft 90.8Nm @ 3000rpm
66.9bhp/ton 65.8bhp/tonne
43.9bhp/L 32.8kW/L 44.6PS/L
37.9ft/sec 11.5m/sec
17.1mph 27.5kmh/1000rpm
32.5mpg 27.1mpgUS 8.7L/100km
Petrol 4-stroke piston
1297cc 79.1cu in
In-line 4 1 Carburettor
Compression ratio: 9.2:1
Bore: 81.0mm 3.2in
Stroke: 63.0mm 2.5in
Valve type/No: Overhead 8
Transmission: Manual
No. of forward speeds: 4
Wheels driven: Rear
Springs F/R: Coil/Leaf
Brake system: PA
Brakes F/R: Disc/Drum
Steering: Rack & pinion
Wheelbase: 240.0cm 94.5in
Track F: 130.0cm 51.2in
Track R: 132.6cm 52.2in
Length: 397.5cm 156.5in
Width: 153.7cm 60.5in
Height: 141.0cm 55.5in
Ground clearance: 14.0cm 5.5in
Kerb weight: 866.2kg 1908.0lb
Fuel: 40.9L 9.0gal 10.8galUS

1851 Ford

Escort 1600 Sport
1977 UK
104.0mph 167.3kmh
0-50mph 80.5kmh: 8.6secs
0-60mph 96.5kmh: 12.3secs
0-1/4 mile: 18.6secs
0-1km: 35.0secs
84.0bhp 62.6kW 85.2PS
@ 5500rpm
92.0lbft 124.7Nm @ 3500rpm
98.3bhp/ton 96.7bhp/tonne
52.6bhp/L 39.2kW/L 53.3PS/L
46.9ft/sec 14.3m/sec
18.4mph 29.6kmh/1000rpm
34.3mpg 28.6mpgUS 8.2L/100km
Petrol 4-stroke piston
1598cc 97.5cu in
In-line 4 1 Carburettor
Compression ratio: 9.0:1
Bore: 81.0mm 3.2in
Stroke: 78.0mm 3.1in
Valve type/No: Overhead 8
Transmission: Manual
No. of forward speeds: 4
Wheels driven: Rear
Springs F/R: Coil/Leaf
Brake system: PA
Brakes F/R: Disc/Drum
Steering: Rack & pinion
Wheelbase: 240.0cm 94.5in
Track F: 127.0cm 50.0in
Track R: 129.5cm 51.0in
Length: 397.5cm 156.5in
Width: 153.7cm 60.5in
Height: 141.0cm 55.5in
Ground clearance: 14.0cm 5.5in
Kerb weight: 869.0kg 1914.0lb
Fuel: 40.9L 9.0gal 10.8galUS

1852 Ford

Fiesta 1000
1977 UK
81.0mph 130.3kmh
0-50mph 80.5kmh: 12.1secs
0-60mph 96.5kmh: 19.0secs
0-1/4 mile: 21.0secs
0-1km: 40.5secs
40.0bhp 29.8kW 40.5PS
@ 5500rpm
47.0lbft 63.7Nm @ 2700rpm
55.4bhp/ton 54.5bhp/tonne
41.8bhp/L 31.2kW/L 42.4PS/L
33.5ft/sec 10.2m/sec
15.1mph 24.3kmh/1000rpm
35.2mpg 29.3mpgUS 8.0L/100km
Petrol 4-stroke piston
957cc 58.4cu in
In-line 4 1 Carburettor
Compression ratio: 8.3:1
Bore: 74.0mm 2.9in
Stroke: 55.7mm 2.2in
Valve type/No: Overhead 8
Transmission: Manual
No. of forward speeds: 4
Wheels driven: Front
Springs F/R: Coil/Coil
Brake system: PA
Brakes F/R: Disc/Drum
Steering: Rack & pinion
Wheelbase: 228.6cm 90.0in
Track F: 133.4cm 52.5in
Track R: 132.6cm 52.2in
Length: 356.9cm 140.5in
Width: 156.2cm 61.5in
Height: 134.6cm 53.0in
Ground clearance: 15.2cm 6.0in
Kerb weight: 734.0kg 1616.7lb
Fuel: 34.1L 7.5gal 9.0galUS

1853 Ford

Fiesta 1100 Ghia
1977 UK
88.0mph 141.6kmh
0-50mph 80.5kmh: 10.5secs
0-60mph 96.5kmh: 15.7secs
0-1/4 mile: 20.0secs
0-1km: 38.4secs
53.0bhp 39.5kW 53.7PS
@ 6000rpm
59.0lbft 79.9Nm @ 3000rpm
70.2bhp/ton 69.0bhp/tonne
47.4bhp/L 35.4kW/L 48.1PS/L
42.7ft/sec 13.0m/sec
15.5mph 24.9kmh/1000rpm
33.5mpg 27.9mpgUS 8.4L/100km
Petrol 4-stroke piston
1117cc 68.1cu in
In-line 4 1 Carburettor
Compression ratio: 9.0:1
Bore: 74.0mm 2.9in
Stroke: 65.0mm 2.6in
Valve type/No: Overhead 8
Transmission: Manual
No. of forward speeds: 4
Wheels driven: Front
Springs F/R: Coil/Coil
Brake system: PA
Brakes F/R: Disc/Drum
Steering: Rack & pinion
Wheelbase: 228.6cm 90.0in
Track F: 133.4cm 52.5in
Track R: 132.6cm 52.2in
Length: 356.9cm 140.5in
Width: 156.2cm 61.5in
Height: 134.6cm 53.0in
Ground clearance: 15.2cm 6.0in
Kerb weight: 768.0kg 1691.6lb
Fuel: 34.1L 7.5gal 9.0galUS

1854 Ford

Fiesta 1300 S
1977 UK
100.0mph 160.9kmh
0-50mph 80.5kmh: 9.3secs
0-60mph 96.5kmh: 13.7secs
0-1/4 mile: 19.3secs
0-1km: 36.0secs
66.0bhp 49.2kW 66.9PS
@ 5600rpm
68.0lbft 92.1Nm @ 3250rpm
83.8bhp/ton 82.4bhp/tonne
50.8bhp/L 37.9kW/L 51.6PS/L
38.6ft/sec 11.8m/sec
16.8mph 27.0kmh/1000rpm
31.6mpg 26.3mpgUS 8.9L/100km
Petrol 4-stroke piston
1298cc 79.2cu in
In-line 4 1 Carburettor
Compression ratio: 9.2:1
Bore: 81.0mm 3.2in
Stroke: 63.0mm 2.5in
Valve type/No: Overhead 8
Transmission: Manual
No. of forward speeds: 4
Wheels driven: Front
Springs F/R: Coil/Coil
Brake system: PA
Brakes F/R: Disc/Drum
Steering: Rack & pinion
Wheelbase: 228.6cm 90.0in
Track F: 133.4cm 52.5in
Track R: 132.6cm 52.2in
Length: 363.7cm 143.2in
Width: 156.2cm 61.5in
Height: 134.6cm 53.0in
Ground clearance: 15.2cm 6.0in
Kerb weight: 800.9kg 1764.0lb
Fuel: 34.1L 7.5gal 9.0galUS

1855 Ford

Fiesta Ghia
1977 Germany
101.0mph 162.5kmh
0-50mph 80.5kmh: 7.7secs
0-60mph 96.5kmh: 11.5secs
0-1/4 mile: 18.2secs
66.0bhp 49.2kW 66.9PS
@ 5000rpm
82.0lbft 111.1Nm @ 3200rpm
80.6bhp/ton 79.2bhp/tonne
41.3bhp/L 30.8kW/L 41.8PS/L
42.6ft/sec 13.0m/sec
20.5mph 33.0kmh/1000rpm
42.0mpg 35.0mpgUS 6.7L/100km
Petrol 4-stroke piston
1599cc 97.6cu in
In-line 4 1 Carburettor
Compression ratio: 8.5:1
Bore: 81.0mm 3.2in
Stroke: 78.0mm 3.1in
Valve type/No: Overhead 8
Transmission: Manual
No. of forward speeds: 4
Wheels driven: Front
Springs F/R: Coil/Coil
Brake system: PA
Brakes F/R: Disc/Drum
Steering: Rack & pinion
Wheelbase: 228.6cm 90.0in
Track F: 133.4cm 52.5in
Track R: 132.1cm 52.0in
Length: 373.6cm 147.1in
Width: 156.7cm 61.7in
Height: 132.8cm 52.3in
Ground clearance: 17.8cm 7.0in
Kerb weight: 833.1kg 1835.0lb
Fuel: 37.8L 8.3gal 10.0galUS

1856 Ford

Granada 2.3 GL Auto
1977 UK
100.0mph 160.9kmh
0-50mph 80.5kmh: 10.1secs
0-60mph 96.5kmh: 14.5secs
0-1/4 mile: 19.6secs
0-1km: 36.9secs
108.0bhp 80.5kW 109.5PS
@ 5000rpm
130.0lbft 176.2Nm @ 3000rpm
82.5bhp/ton 81.1bhp/tonne
47.1bhp/L 35.1kW/L 47.7PS/L
32.9ft/sec 10.0m/sec
19.6mph 31.5kmh/1000rpm
20.6mpg 17.2mpgUS 13.7L/100km
Petrol 4-stroke piston
2293cc 139.9cu in
Vee 6 1 Carburettor
Compression ratio: 8.7:1
Bore: 90.0mm 3.5in
Stroke: 60.1mm 2.4in
Valve type/No: Overhead 12
Transmission: Automatic
No. of forward speeds: 3
Wheels driven: Rear
Springs F/R: Coil/Coil
Brake system: PA
Brakes F/R: Disc/Drum
Steering: Rack & pinion PA
Wheelbase: 276.9cm 109.0in
Track F: 151.1cm 59.5in
Track R: 153.7cm 60.5in
Length: 463.3cm 182.4in
Width: 179.1cm 70.5in
Height: 138.4cm 54.5in
Ground clearance: 17.8cm 7.0in
Kerb weight: 1331.1kg 2932.0lb
Fuel: 65.1L 14.3gal 17.2galUS

1857 Ford

Capri 1600S
1978 UK
101.0mph 162.5kmh
0-50mph 80.5kmh: 9.0secs
0-60mph 96.5kmh: 12.7secs
0-1/4 mile: 19.0secs
0-1km: 35.4secs
88.0bhp 65.6kW 89.2PS
@ 5700rpm
92.0lbft 124.7Nm @ 4000rpm

86.0bhp/ton 84.5bhp/tonne
55.2bhp/L 41.2kW/L 56.0PS/L
41.2ft/sec 12.5m/sec
18.0mph 29.0kmh/1000rpm
27.6mpg 23.0mpgUS 10.2L/100km
Petrol 4-stroke piston
1593cc 97.2cu in
In-line 4 1 Carburettor
Compression ratio: 9.2:1
Bore: 87.7mm 3.4in
Stroke: 66.0mm 2.6in
Valve type/No: Overhead 8
Transmission: Manual
No. of forward speeds: 4
Wheels driven: Rear
Springs F/R: Coil/Leaf
Brake system: PA
Brakes F/R: Disc/Drum
Steering: Rack & pinion
Wheelbase: 256.5cm 101.0in
Track F: 134.6cm 53.0in
Track R: 138.4cm 54.5in
Length: 435.1cm 171.3in
Width: 170.2cm 67.0in
Height: 129.5cm 51.0in
Ground clearance: 15.2cm 6.0in
Kerb weight: 1041.0kg 2293.0lb
Fuel: 59.1L 13.0gal 15.6galUS

1858 Ford

Granada 2.0L
1978 UK
103.0mph 165.7kmh
0-50mph 80.5kmh: 8.4secs
0-60mph 96.5kmh: 11.9secs
0-1/4 mile: 18.5secs
0-1km: 33.7secs
99.0bhp 73.8kW 100.4PS
@ 5200rpm
111.0lbft 150.4Nm @ 4000rpm
81.1bhp/ton 79.7bhp/tonne
49.7bhp/L 37.0kW/L 50.4PS/L
43.8ft/sec 13.3m/sec
18.5mph 29.8kmh/1000rpm
21.2mpg 17.7mpgUS 13.3L/100km
Petrol 4-stroke piston
1993cc 121.6cu in
In-line 4 1 Carburettor
Compression ratio: 9.2:1
Bore: 90.3mm 3.6in
Stroke: 76.9mm 3.0in
Valve type/No: Overhead 8
Transmission: Manual
No. of forward speeds: 4
Wheels driven: Rear
Springs F/R: Coil/Coil
Brake system: PA
Brakes F/R: Disc/Drum
Steering: Rack & pinion PA
Wheelbase: 276.9cm 109.0in
Track F: 151.1cm 59.5in
Track R: 153.7cm 60.5in
Length: 463.3cm 182.4in
Width: 179.1cm 70.5in
Height: 138.4cm 54.5in
Ground clearance: 17.8cm 7.0in
Kerb weight: 1241.7kg 2735.0lb
Fuel: 66.4L 14.6gal 17.5galUS

1859 Ford

Granada 2.1D
1978 UK
88.0mph 141.6kmh
0-50mph 80.5kmh: 18.1secs
0-60mph 96.5kmh: 27.2secs
0-1/4 mile: 23.4secs
0-1km: 46.0secs
63.0bhp 47.0kW 63.9PS
@ 4500rpm
90.0lbft 122.0Nm @ 2000rpm
48.1bhp/ton 47.3bhp/tonne
29.8bhp/L 22.2kW/L 30.2PS/L
40.9ft/sec 12.4m/sec
18.5mph 29.8kmh/1000rpm
30.1mpg 25.1mpgUS 9.4L/100km
Diesel 4-stroke piston
2112cc 128.9cu in
In-line 4 fuel injection
Compression ratio: 22.8:1
Bore: 90.0mm 3.5in
Stroke: 83.0mm 3.3in
Valve type/No: Overhead 8
Transmission: Manual
No. of forward speeds: 4
Wheels driven: Rear
Springs F/R: Coil/Coil
Brake system: PA
Brakes F/R: Disc/Drum
Steering: Rack & pinion PA
Wheelbase: 276.9cm 109.0in
Track F: 150.9cm 59.4in
Track R: 153.7cm 60.5in
Length: 458.2cm 180.4in
Width: 179.1cm 70.5in
Height: 138.4cm 54.5in
Ground clearance: 17.8cm 7.0in
Kerb weight: 1332.5kg 2935.0lb
Fuel: 66.4L 14.6gal 17.5galUS

1860 Ford

Granada 2.8i S
1978 UK
117.0mph 188.3kmh
0-50mph 80.5kmh: 6.5secs
0-60mph 96.5kmh: 8.9secs
0-1/4 mile: 16.7secs
0-1km: 31.2secs
160.0bhp 119.3kW 162.2PS
@ 5700rpm
162.0lbft 219.5Nm @ 4300rpm
120.6bhp/ton 118.6bhp/tonne
57.3bhp/L 42.7kW/L 58.1PS/L
42.7ft/sec 13.0m/sec
20.7mph 33.3kmh/1000rpm
20.8mpg 17.3mpgUS 13.6L/100km
Petrol 4-stroke piston
2792cc 170.3cu in
Vee 6 fuel injection
Compression ratio: 9.2:1
Bore: 93.0mm 3.7in
Stroke: 68.5mm 2.7in
Valve type/No: Overhead 12
Transmission: Manual
No. of forward speeds: 4
Wheels driven: Rear
Springs F/R: Coil/Coil
Brake system: PA
Brakes F/R: Disc/Drum
Steering: Rack & pinion PA
Wheelbase: 276.9cm 109.0in
Track F: 151.1cm 59.5in
Track R: 153.7cm 60.5in
Length: 463.3cm 182.4in
Width: 179.1cm 70.5in
Height: 138.4cm 54.5in
Ground clearance: 17.8cm 7.0in
Kerb weight: 1348.8kg 2971.0lb
Fuel: 65.1L 14.3gal 17.2galUS

1861 Ford

Capri 2000S
1979 UK
107.0mph 172.2kmh
0-50mph 80.5kmh: 7.8secs
0-60mph 96.5kmh: 10.8secs
0-1/4 mile: 17.7secs
0-1km: 33.3secs
98.0bhp 73.1kW 99.4PS
@ 5200rpm
111.0lbft 150.4Nm @ 3500rpm
96.6bhp/ton 95.0bhp/tonne
49.2bhp/L 36.7kW/L 49.8PS/L
43.8ft/sec 13.3m/sec
19.5mph 31.4kmh/1000rpm
25.6mpg 21.3mpgUS 11.0L/100km
Petrol 4-stroke piston
1993cc 121.6cu in
In-line 4 1 Carburettor
Compression ratio: 9.2:1
Bore: 90.3mm 3.6in
Stroke: 77.0mm 3.0in
Valve type/No: Overhead 8
Transmission: Manual
No. of forward speeds: 4
Wheels driven: Rear
Springs F/R: Coil/Leaf
Brake system: PA
Brakes F/R: Disc/Drum
Steering: Rack & pinion
Wheelbase: 256.5cm 101.0in
Track F: 134.6cm 53.0in
Track R: 138.4cm 54.5in
Length: 435.1cm 171.3in
Width: 170.2cm 67.0in
Height: 129.5cm 51.0in
Ground clearance: 15.2cm 6.0in
Kerb weight: 1031.9kg 2273.0lb
Fuel: 59.1L 13.0gal 15.6galUS

1862 Ford

Cortina 1600L
1979 UK
94.0mph 151.2kmh
0-50mph 80.5kmh: 8.8secs
0-60mph 96.5kmh: 13.6secs
0-1/4 mile: 18.9secs
0-1km: 34.4secs
75.5bhp 56.3kW 76.5PS
@ 5500rpm
87.5lbft 118.6Nm @ 2800rpm
79.0bhp/ton 77.7bhp/tonne
47.4bhp/L 35.3kW/L 48.0PS/L
39.7ft/sec 12.1m/sec
17.7mph 28.5kmh/1000rpm
29.3mpg 24.4mpgUS 9.6L/100km
Petrol 4-stroke piston
1593cc 97.2cu in
In-line 4 1 Carburettor
Compression ratio: 9.2:1
Bore: 87.7mm 3.4in
Stroke: 66.0mm 2.6in
Valve type/No: Overhead 8
Transmission: Manual
No. of forward speeds: 4
Wheels driven: Rear
Springs F/R: Coil/Coil
Brake system: PA
Brakes F/R: Disc/Drum
Steering: Rack & pinion
Wheelbase: 257.8cm 101.5in
Track F: 144.5cm 56.9in
Track R: 142.7cm 56.2in
Length: 434.1cm 170.9in
Width: 169.4cm 66.7in
Height: 136.4cm 53.7in
Ground clearance: 17.8cm 7.0in
Kerb weight: 971.6kg 2140.0lb
Fuel: 54.6L 12.0gal 14.4galUS

1863 Ford

Cortina 2.3 Ghia S
1979 UK
109.0mph 175.4kmh
0-50mph 80.5kmh: 7.4secs
0-60mph 96.5kmh: 10.5secs
0-1/4 mile: 18.0secs
0-1km: 33.5secs
116.0bhp 86.5kW 117.6PS
@ 5000rpm
132.0lbft 178.9Nm @ 3000rpm
105.1bhp/ton 103.4bhp/tonne
50.6bhp/L 37.7kW/L 51.3PS/L
32.9ft/sec 10.0m/sec
19.5mph 31.4kmh/1000rpm
22.6mpg 18.8mpgUS 12.5L/100km
Petrol 4-stroke piston
2293cc 139.9cu in
Vee 6 1 Carburettor
Compression ratio: 9.2:1
Bore: 90.3mm 3.6in
Stroke: 60.1mm 2.4in
Valve type/No: Overhead 12
Transmission: Manual
No. of forward speeds: 4
Wheels driven: Rear
Springs F/R: Coil/Coil
Brake system: PA
Brakes F/R: Disc/Drum
Steering: Rack & pinion PA
Wheelbase: 257.8cm 101.5in
Track F: 144.5cm 56.9in
Track R: 142.2cm 56.0in
Length: 432.6cm 170.3in
Width: 169.9cm 66.9in
Height: 132.1cm 52.0in
Ground clearance: 17.8cm 7.0in
Kerb weight: 1122.3kg 2472.0lb
Fuel: 54.6L 12.0gal 14.4galUS

1864 Ford

Fiesta Healey
1979 Germany
108.0mph 173.8kmh
0-50mph 80.5kmh: 7.0secs
0-60mph 96.5kmh: 9.6secs
0-1/4 mile: 17.4secs
105.0bhp 78.3kW 106.5PS
@ 6200rpm
125.1bhp/ton 123.0bhp/tonne
65.7bhp/L 49.0kW/L 66.6PS/L
52.9ft/sec 16.1m/sec
18.2mph 29.3kmh/1000rpm
32.4mpg 27.0mpgUS 8.7L/100km
Petrol 4-stroke piston
1599cc 97.6cu in
In-line 4 1 Carburettor
Compression ratio: 10.1:1
Bore: 81.0mm 3.2in
Stroke: 78.0mm 3.1in
Valve type/No: Overhead 8
Transmission: Manual
No. of forward speeds: 4
Wheels driven: Front
Springs F/R: Coil/Coil
Brakes F/R: Disc/Drum
Steering: Rack & pinion
Wheelbase: 228.6cm 90.0in
Track F: 137.9cm 54.3in
Track R: 135.6cm 53.4in
Length: 373.6cm 147.1in
Width: 161.0cm 63.4in
Height: 132.6cm 52.2in
Kerb weight: 853.5kg 1880.0lb
Fuel: 37.8L 8.3gal 10.0galUS

1865 Ford

Granada 2.8i GLS Estate
1979 UK
111.0mph 178.6kmh
0-50mph 80.5kmh: 7.4secs
0-60mph 96.5kmh: 10.0secs
0-1/4 mile: 17.4secs
0-1km: 32.1secs
160.0bhp 119.3kW 162.2PS
@ 5700rpm
162.0lbft 219.5Nm @ 4300rpm
112.3bhp/ton 110.4bhp/tonne
57.3bhp/L 42.7kW/L 58.1PS/L
42.7ft/sec 13.0m/sec
20.7mph 33.3kmh/1000rpm
20.5mpg 17.1mpgUS 13.8L/100km
Petrol 4-stroke piston
2792cc 170.3cu in
Vee 6 fuel injection
Compression ratio: 9.2:1
Bore: 93.0mm 3.7in
Stroke: 68.5mm 2.7in
Valve type/No: Overhead 12
Transmission: Manual
No. of forward speeds: 4
Wheels driven: Rear
Springs F/R: Coil/Coil
Brake system: PA
Brakes F/R: Disc/Drum
Steering: Rack & pinion PA
Wheelbase: 276.9cm 109.0in
Track F: 150.9cm 59.4in
Track R: 153.7cm 60.5in
Length: 476.0cm 187.4in
Width: 179.3cm 70.6in
Height: 137.9cm 54.3in
Ground clearance: 17.8cm 7.0in
Kerb weight: 1449.2kg 3192.0lb
Fuel: 66.4L 14.6gal 17.5galUS

1866 Ford

Mustang Ghia Turbo
1979 USA
102.0mph 164.1kmh
0-50mph 80.5kmh: 8.9secs
0-60mph 96.5kmh: 12.0secs
0-1/4 mile: 18.3secs
0-1km: 34.0secs
120.0bhp 89.5kW 121.7PS
@ 5400rpm
135.0lbft 182.9Nm @ 3200rpm
96.8bhp/ton 95.2bhp/tonne
52.1bhp/L 38.9kW/L 52.9PS/L
46.9ft/sec 14.3m/sec
21.1mph 33.9kmh/1000rpm
18.9mpg 15.7mpgUS 14.9L/100km
Petrol 4-stroke piston
2301cc 140.4cu in turbocharged
In-line 4 1 Carburettor
Compression ratio: 9.0:1
Bore: 96.0mm 3.8in
Stroke: 79.4mm 3.1in
Valve type/No: Overhead 8
Transmission: Manual
No. of forward speeds: 4
Wheels driven: Rear
Springs F/R: Coil/Coil
Brake system: PA
Brakes F/R: Disc/Drum
Steering: Rack & pinion PA
Wheelbase: 255.0cm 100.4in
Track F: 143.8cm 56.6in
Track R: 144.8cm 57.0in
Length: 454.9cm 179.1in
Width: 171.2cm 67.4in
Height: 130.8cm 51.5in
Ground clearance: 12.7cm 5.0in
Kerb weight: 1260.3kg 2776.0lb
Fuel: 47.3L 10.4gal 12.5galUS

1867 Ford
Mustang Turbo
1979 USA
121.0mph 194.7kmh
0-60mph 96.5kmh: 10.4secs
0-1/4 mile: 17.8secs
130.0bhp 96.9kW 131.8PS
@ 5400rpm
145.0lbft 196.5Nm @ 3000rpm
103.4bhp/ton 101.7bhp/tonne
56.6bhp/L 42.2kW/L 57.3PS/L
46.9ft/sec 14.3m/sec
21.5mph 34.6kmh/1000rpm
23.4mpg 19.5mpgUS 12.1L/100km
Petrol 4-stroke piston
2298cc 140.2cu in turbocharged
In-line 4 1 Carburettor
Compression ratio: 9.0:1
Bore: 96.0mm 3.8in
Stroke: 79.4mm 3.1in
Valve type/No: Overhead 8
Transmission: Manual
No. of forward speeds: 4
Wheels driven: Rear
Springs F/R: Coil/Coil
Brake system: PA
Brakes F/R: Disc/Drum
Steering: Rack & pinion PA
Wheelbase: 255.0cm 100.4in
Track F: 143.8cm 56.6in
Track R: 144.8cm 57.0in
Length: 454.9cm 179.1in
Width: 171.2cm 67.4in
Height: 131.1cm 51.6in
Kerb weight: 1278.0kg 2815.0lb
Fuel: 47.3L 10.4gal 12.5galUS

1868 Ford
Fairmont
1980 USA
0-60mph 96.5kmh: 13.8secs
0-1/4 mile: 19.4secs
94.0bhp 70.1kW 95.3PS
@ 4000rpm
157.0lbft 212.7Nm @ 2000rpm
72.6bhp/ton 71.4bhp/tonne
28.7bhp/L 21.4kW/L 29.1PS/L
34.8ft/sec 10.6m/sec
21.6mpg 18.0mpgUS 13.1L/100km
Petrol 4-stroke piston
3272cc 199.6cu in
In-line 6 1 Carburettor
Compression ratio: 8.6:1
Bore: 93.5mm 3.7in
Stroke: 79.4mm 3.1in
Valve type/No: Overhead 12
Transmission: Automatic
No. of forward speeds: 3
Wheels driven: Rear
Brakes F/R: Disc/Drum
Wheelbase: 268.0cm 105.5in
Track F: 143.8cm 56.6in
Track R: 144.8cm 57.0in
Length: 496.6cm 195.5in
Width: 180.3cm 71.0in
Height: 136.1cm 53.6in
Kerb weight: 1316.6kg 2900.0lb
Fuel: 53.0L 11.6gal 14.0galUS

1869 Ford
Fiesta
1980 Germany
0-60mph 96.5kmh: 10.5secs
0-1/4 mile: 17.9secs
66.0bhp 49.2kW 66.9PS
@ 5000rpm
82.0lbft 111.1Nm @ 3200rpm
81.2bhp/ton 79.9bhp/tonne
41.3bhp/L 30.8kW/L 41.8PS/L
42.5ft/sec 12.9m/sec
33.0mpg 27.5mpgUS 8.6L/100km
Petrol 4-stroke piston
1599cc 97.6cu in
In-line 4 1 Carburettor
Compression ratio: 8.6:1
Bore: 81.0mm 3.2in
Stroke: 77.6mm 3.1in
Valve type/No: Overhead 8
Transmission: Manual
No. of forward speeds: 4
Wheels driven: Front
Brakes F/R: Disc/Drum
Wheelbase: 228.6cm 90.0in
Track F: 133.4cm 52.5in
Track R: 132.1cm 52.0in
Length: 373.6cm 147.1in
Width: 154.9cm 61.0in
Height: 132.8cm 52.3in
Kerb weight: 826.3kg 1820.0lb
Fuel: 37.8L 8.3gal 10.0galUS

1870 Ford
Mustang Turbo
1980 USA
121.0mph 194.7kmh
0-60mph 96.5kmh: 10.4secs
0-1/4 mile: 17.8secs
21.5mph 34.6kmh/1000rpm
23.4mpg 19.5mpgUS 12.1L/100km
Petrol 4-stroke piston
2298cc 140.2cu in turbocharged
In-line 4 1 Carburettor
Compression ratio: 9.0:1
Bore: 96.0mm 3.8in
Stroke: 79.4mm 3.1in
Valve type/No: Overhead 8
Transmission: Manual
No. of forward speeds: 4
Wheels driven: Rear
Springs F/R: Coil/Coil
Brake system: PA
Brakes F/R: Disc/Drum
Steering: Rack & pinion PA
Wheelbase: 255.0cm 100.4in
Track F: 143.8cm 56.6in
Track R: 144.8cm 57.0in
Length: 454.9cm 179.1in
Width: 171.2cm 67.4in
Height: 131.1cm 51.6in
Ground clearance: 14.5cm 5.7in
Kerb weight: 1278.0kg 2815.0lb
Fuel: 47.3L 10.4gal 12.5galUS

1871 Ford
Capri 2.8 Injection
1981 UK
129.0mph 207.6kmh
0-50mph 80.5kmh: 6.0secs
0-60mph 96.5kmh: 7.9secs
0-1/4 mile: 16.2secs
0-1km: 30.0secs
160.0bhp 119.3kW 162.2PS
@ 5700rpm
162.0lbft 219.5Nm @ 4200rpm
136.8bhp/ton 134.5bhp/tonne
57.3bhp/L 42.7kW/L 58.1PS/L
42.7ft/sec 13.0m/sec
21.1mph 33.9kmh/1000rpm
21.3mpg 17.7mpgUS 13.3L/100km
Petrol 4-stroke piston
2792cc 170.3cu in
Vee 6 fuel injection
Compression ratio: 9.2:1
Bore: 93.0mm 3.7in
Stroke: 68.5mm 2.7in
Valve type/No: Overhead 12
Transmission: Manual
No. of forward speeds: 4
Wheels driven: Rear
Springs F/R: Coil/Leaf
Brake system: PA
Brakes F/R: Disc/Drum
Steering: Rack & pinion PA
Wheelbase: 256.5cm 101.0in
Track F: 134.6cm 53.0in
Track R: 138.4cm 54.5in
Length: 435.1cm 171.3in
Width: 170.2cm 67.0in
Height: 129.5cm 51.0in
Ground clearance: 15.2cm 6.0in
Kerb weight: 1189.5kg 2620.0lb
Fuel: 59.1L 13.0gal 15.6galUS

1872 Ford
Cortina 2.0 GL
1981 UK
103.0mph 165.7kmh
0-50mph 80.5kmh: 7.7secs
0-60mph 96.5kmh: 10.3secs
0-1/4 mile: 17.7secs
0-1km: 33.1secs
101.0bhp 75.3kW 102.4PS
@ 5200rpm
112.0lbft 151.8Nm @ 4000rpm
102.0bhp/ton 100.3bhp/tonne
50.7bhp/L 37.8kW/L 51.4PS/L
43.8ft/sec 13.3m/sec
17.9mph 28.8kmh/1000rpm
29.2mpg 24.3mpgUS 9.7L/100km
Petrol 4-stroke piston
1993cc 121.6cu in
In-line 4 1 Carburettor
Compression ratio: 9.2:1
Bore: 90.8mm 3.6in
Stroke: 76.9mm 3.0in
Valve type/No: Overhead 8
Transmission: Manual
No. of forward speeds: 4
Wheels driven: Rear
Springs F/R: Coil/Coil
Brake system: PA
Brakes F/R: Disc/Drum
Steering: Rack & pinion
Wheelbase: 257.8cm 101.5in
Track F: 144.0cm 56.7in
Track R: 142.0cm 55.9in
Length: 437.9cm 172.4in
Width: 169.9cm 66.9in
Height: 136.1cm 53.6in
Ground clearance: 15.2cm 6.0in
Kerb weight: 1007.4kg 2219.0lb
Fuel: 54.6L 12.0gal 14.4galUS

1873 Ford
Escort
1981 USA
0-60mph 96.5kmh: 13.9secs
0-1/4 mile: 19.2secs
65.0bhp 48.5kW 65.9PS
@ 5200rpm
85.0lbft 115.2Nm @ 3200rpm
69.3bhp/ton 68.2bhp/tonne
40.7bhp/L 30.3kW/L 41.2PS/L
45.2ft/sec 13.8m/sec
30.0mpg 25.0mpgUS 9.4L/100km
Petrol 4-stroke piston
1598cc 97.5cu in
In-line 4 1 Carburettor
Compression ratio: 8.8:1
Bore: 80.0mm 3.1in
Stroke: 79.5mm 3.1in
Valve type/No: Overhead 8
Transmission: Manual
No. of forward speeds: 4
Wheels driven: Front
Brakes F/R: Disc/Drum
Wheelbase: 239.3cm 94.2in
Track F: 138.9cm 54.7in
Track R: 142.2cm 56.0in
Length: 416.3cm 163.9in
Width: 167.4cm 65.9in
Height: 135.4cm 53.3in
Kerb weight: 953.4kg 2100.0lb
Fuel: 37.8L 8.3gal 10.0galUS

1874 Ford
Escort 1.6L Estate
1981 UK
104.0mph 167.3kmh
0-50mph 80.5kmh: 8.4secs
0-60mph 96.5kmh: 11.9secs
0-1/4 mile: 18.7secs
0-1km: 34.6secs
79.0bhp 58.9kW 80.1PS
@ 5800rpm
92.0lbft 124.7Nm @ 3000rpm
95.5bhp/ton 94.0bhp/tonne
49.5bhp/L 36.9kW/L 50.2PS/L
50.4ft/sec 15.4m/sec
19.2mph 30.9kmh/1000rpm
32.1mpg 26.7mpgUS 8.8L/100km
Petrol 4-stroke piston
1597cc 97.4cu in
In-line 4 1 Carburettor
Compression ratio: 9.5:1
Bore: 80.0mm 3.1in
Stroke: 79.5mm 3.1in
Valve type/No: Overhead 8
Transmission: Manual
No. of forward speeds: 4
Wheels driven: Front
Springs F/R: Coil/Coil
Brake system: PA
Brakes F/R: Disc/Drum
Steering: Rack & pinion
Wheelbase: 239.8cm 94.4in
Track F: 138.4cm 54.5in
Track R: 143.0cm 56.3in
Length: 403.4cm 158.8in
Width: 164.1cm 64.6in
Height: 137.9cm 54.3in
Ground clearance: 17.8cm 7.0in
Kerb weight: 840.8kg 1852.0lb
Fuel: 40.0L 8.8gal 10.6galUS

1875 Ford
Fiesta Popular
1981 UK
81.0mph 130.3kmh
0-50mph 80.5kmh: 12.3secs
0-60mph 96.5kmh: 19.6secs
0-1/4 mile: 20.8secs
0-1km: 40.7secs
40.0bhp 29.8kW 40.5PS
@ 5000rpm
47.0lbft 63.7Nm @ 2700rpm
56.6bhp/ton 55.7bhp/tonne
41.8bhp/L 31.2kW/L 42.4PS/L
30.4ft/sec 9.3m/sec
15.1mph 24.3kmh/1000rpm
31.4mpg 26.1mpgUS 9.0L/100km
Petrol 4-stroke piston
957cc 58.4cu in
In-line 4 1 Carburettor
Compression ratio: 8.3:1
Bore: 74.0mm 2.9in
Stroke: 55.7mm 2.2in
Valve type/No: Overhead 8
Transmission: Manual
No. of forward speeds: 4
Wheels driven: Front
Springs F/R: Coil/Coil
Brake system: PA
Brakes F/R: Disc/Drum
Steering: Rack & pinion
Wheelbase: 228.6cm 90.0in
Track F: 133.4cm 52.5in
Track R: 132.6cm 52.2in
Length: 356.9cm 140.5in
Width: 156.2cm 61.5in
Height: 134.6cm 53.0in
Ground clearance: 15.2cm 6.0in
Kerb weight: 718.2kg 1582.0lb
Fuel: 34.1L 7.5gal 9.0galUS

1876 Ford
Fiesta XR2
1981 UK
106.0mph 170.6kmh
0-50mph 80.5kmh: 6.9secs
0-60mph 96.5kmh: 9.4secs
0-1/4 mile: 17.4secs
0-1km: 33.0secs
84.0bhp 62.6kW 85.2PS
@ 5500rpm
91.0lbft 123.3Nm @ 2800rpm
101.8bhp/ton 100.1bhp/tonne
52.6bhp/L 39.2kW/L 53.3PS/L
46.7ft/sec 14.2m/sec
18.4mph 29.6kmh/1000rpm
28.8mpg 24.0mpgUS 9.8L/100km
Petrol 4-stroke piston
1598cc 97.5cu in
In-line 4 1 Carburettor
Compression ratio: 9.0:1
Bore: 81.0mm 3.2in
Stroke: 77.6mm 3.1in
Valve type/No: Overhead 8
Transmission: Manual
No. of forward speeds: 4
Wheels driven: Front
Springs F/R: Coil/Coil
Brake system: PA
Brakes F/R: Disc/Drum
Steering: Rack & pinion
Wheelbase: 229.6cm 90.4in
Track F: 134.9cm 53.1in
Track R: 133.6cm 52.6in
Length: 371.9cm 146.4in
Width: 158.0cm 62.2in
Height: 137.2cm 54.0in
Ground clearance: 15.2cm 6.0in
Kerb weight: 839.0kg 1848.0lb
Fuel: 34.1L 7.5gal 9.0galUS

1877 Ford
Granada 2.8i
1981 UK
119.0mph 191.5kmh
0-50mph 80.5kmh: 7.0secs
0-60mph 96.5kmh: 9.2secs
0-1/4 mile: 17.3secs
0-1km: 31.3secs
160.0bhp 119.3kW 162.2PS
@ 5700rpm
162.0lbft 219.5Nm @ 4200rpm
116.3bhp/ton 114.3bhp/tonne
57.3bhp/L 42.7kW/L 58.1PS/L
42.7ft/sec 13.0m/sec
20.6mph 33.1kmh/1000rpm
23.8mpg 19.8mpgUS 11.9L/100km
Petrol 4-stroke piston
2792cc 170.3cu in
Vee 6 fuel injection
Compression ratio: 9.2:1
Bore: 93.0mm 3.7in

Stroke: 68.5mm 2.7in
Valve type/No: Overhead 12
Transmission: Manual
No. of forward speeds: 4
Wheels driven: Rear
Springs F/R: Coil/Coil
Brake system: PA
Brakes F/R: Disc/Drum
Steering: Rack & pinion PA
Wheelbase: 276.9cm 109.0in
Track F: 151.6cm 59.7in
Track R: 153.7cm 60.5in
Length: 474.0cm 186.6in
Width: 179.3cm 70.6in
Height: 137.9cm 54.3in
Ground clearance: 17.8cm 7.0in
Kerb weight: 1399.2kg 3082.0lb
Fuel: 65.1L 14.3gal 17.2galUS

1878 Ford

Escort 1600 GL
1982 UK
103.0mph 165.7kmh
0-50mph 80.5kmh: 8.0secs
0-60mph 96.5kmh: 11.1secs
0-1/4 mile: 18.6secs
0-1km: 34.6secs
79.0bhp 58.9kW 80.1PS
@ 5800rpm
92.0lbft 124.7Nm @ 3000rpm
87.1bhp/ton 85.6bhp/tonne
49.5bhp/L 36.9kW/L 50.2PS/L
50.4ft/sec 15.4m/sec
24.2mph 38.9kmh/1000rpm
32.1mpg 26.7mpgUS 8.8L/100km
Petrol 4-stroke piston
1597cc 97.4cu in
In-line 4 1 Carburettor
Compression ratio: 9.5:1
Bore: 79.9mm 3.1in
Stroke: 79.5mm 3.1in
Valve type/No: Overhead 8
Transmission: Manual
No. of forward speeds: 5
Wheels driven: Front
Springs F/R: Coil/Coil
Brake system: PA
Brakes F/R: Disc/Drum
Steering: Rack & pinion
Wheelbase: 239.8cm 94.4in
Track F: 138.4cm 54.5in
Track R: 143.0cm 56.3in
Length: 397.0cm 156.3in
Width: 158.8cm 62.5in
Height: 133.6cm 52.6in
Ground clearance: 17.8cm 7.0in
Kerb weight: 922.5kg 2032.0lb
Fuel: 40.0L 8.8gal 10.6galUS

1879 Ford

Granada 2.3L Estate
1982 UK
101.0mph 162.5kmh
0-50mph 80.5kmh: 9.4secs
0-60mph 96.5kmh: 12.6secs
0-1/4 mile: 19.0secs
0-1km: 35.8secs
108.0bhp 80.5kW 109.5PS
@ 5000rpm
130.0lbft 176.2Nm @ 3000rpm
79.6bhp/ton 78.3bhp/tonne
47.1bhp/L 35.1kW/L 47.7PS/L
32.8ft/sec 10.0m/sec
20.3mph 32.7kmh/1000rpm
19.7mpg 16.4mpgUS 14.3L/100km
Petrol 4-stroke piston
2294cc 140.0cu in
Vee 6 1 Carburettor
Compression ratio: 8.7:1
Bore: 90.0mm 3.5in
Stroke: 60.0mm 2.4in
Valve type/No: Overhead 12
Transmission: Manual
No. of forward speeds: 4
Wheels driven: Rear
Springs F/R: Coil/Coil
Brake system: PA
Brakes F/R: Disc/Drum
Steering: Rack & pinion PA
Wheelbase: 276.9cm 109.0in
Track F: 151.1cm 59.5in
Track R: 153.7cm 60.5in
Length: 475.2cm 187.1in
Width: 179.1cm 70.5in
Height: 138.2cm 54.4in
Ground clearance: 17.8cm 7.0in
Kerb weight: 1379.2kg 3038.0lb
Fuel: 61.9L 13.6gal 16.3galUS

1880 Ford

Mustang 4.2
1982 USA
114.0mph 183.4kmh
0-50mph 80.5kmh: 9.0secs
0-60mph 96.5kmh: 12.4secs
0-1/4 mile: 18.8secs
115.0bhp 85.8kW 116.6PS
@ 3400rpm
195.0lbft 264.2Nm @ 2200rpm
85.3bhp/ton 83.9bhp/tonne
27.5bhp/L 20.5kW/L 27.8PS/L
28.3ft/sec 8.6m/sec
30.0mph 48.3kmh/1000rpm
20.4mpg 17.0mpgUS 13.8L/100km
Petrol 4-stroke piston
4186cc 255.4cu in
Vee 8 1 Carburettor
Compression ratio: 8.2:1
Bore: 93.5mm 3.7in
Stroke: 76.2mm 3.0in
Valve type/No: Overhead 16
Transmission: Automatic
No. of forward speeds: 3
Wheels driven: Rear
Springs F/R: Coil/Coil
Brake system: PA
Brakes F/R: Disc/Drum
Steering: Rack & pinion PA
Wheelbase: 255.0cm 100.4in
Track F: 143.8cm 56.6in
Track R: 144.8cm 57.0in
Length: 454.9cm 179.1in
Width: 175.5cm 69.1in
Height: 131.1cm 51.6in
Ground clearance: 14.5cm 5.7in
Kerb weight: 1371.1kg 3020.0lb
Fuel: 47.3L 10.4gal 12.5galUS

1881 Ford

Mustang GT 5.0
1982 USA
118.0mph 189.9kmh
0-60mph 96.5kmh: 8.0secs
0-1/4 mile: 16.3secs
157.0bhp 117.1kW 159.2PS
@ 4200rpm
240.0lbft 325.2Nm @ 2400rpm
112.4bhp/ton 110.5bhp/tonne
31.8bhp/L 23.7kW/L 32.2PS/L
35.0ft/sec 10.7m/sec
31.6mph 50.8kmh/1000rpm
18.6mpg 15.5mpgUS 15.2L/100km
Petrol 4-stroke piston
4942cc 301.5cu in
Vee 8 1 Carburettor
Compression ratio: 8.3:1
Bore: 101.6mm 4.0in
Stroke: 76.2mm 3.0in
Valve type/No: Overhead 16
Transmission: Manual
No. of forward speeds: 4
Wheels driven: Rear
Springs F/R: Coil/Coil
Brake system: PA
Brakes F/R: Disc/Drum
Steering: Rack & pinion PA
Wheelbase: 255.0cm 100.4in
Track F: 143.8cm 56.6in
Track R: 144.8cm 57.0in
Length: 454.9cm 179.1in
Width: 175.5cm 69.1in
Height: 130.6cm 51.4in
Ground clearance: 11.9cm 4.7in
Kerb weight: 1421.0kg 3130.0lb
Fuel: 58.3L 12.8gal 15.4galUS

1882 Ford

Sierra 1.6L
1982 UK
104.0mph 167.3kmh
0-50mph 80.5kmh: 9.3secs
0-60mph 96.5kmh: 13.0secs
0-1/4 mile: 19.1secs
0-1km: 35.8secs
75.0bhp 55.9kW 76.0PS
@ 5300rpm
88.0lbft 119.2Nm @ 2900rpm
71.2bhp/ton 70.0bhp/tonne
47.0bhp/L 35.1kW/L 47.7PS/L
38.3ft/sec 11.7m/sec
23.7mph 38.1kmh/1000rpm
33.0mpg 27.5mpgUS 8.6L/100km
Petrol 4-stroke piston
1594cc 97.2cu in
In-line 4 1 Carburettor
Compression ratio: 9.2:1
Bore: 86.7mm 3.4in
Stroke: 66.0mm 2.6in
Valve type/No: Overhead 8
Transmission: Manual
No. of forward speeds: 5
Wheels driven: Rear
Springs F/R: Coil/Coil
Brake system: PA
Brakes F/R: Disc/Drum
Steering: Rack & pinion
Wheelbase: 260.9cm 102.7in
Track F: 145.3cm 57.2in
Track R: 146.8cm 57.8in
Length: 439.4cm 173.0in
Width: 172.0cm 67.7in
Height: 136.1cm 53.6in
Ground clearance: 17.8cm 7.0in
Kerb weight: 1071.4kg 2360.0lb
Fuel: 60.1L 13.2gal 15.9galUS

1883 Ford

Sierra 2.3 Ghia Automatic
1982 UK
115.0mph 185.0kmh
0-50mph 80.5kmh: 8.7secs
0-60mph 96.5kmh: 11.9secs
0-1/4 mile: 18.7secs
0-1km: 34.5secs
114.0bhp 85.0kW 115.6PS
@ 5300rpm
130.0lbft 176.2Nm @ 3000rpm
97.2bhp/ton 95.6bhp/tonne
49.7bhp/L 37.1kW/L 50.4PS/L
34.9ft/sec 10.6m/sec
21.7mph 34.9kmh/1000rpm
20.9mpg 17.4mpgUS 13.5L/100km
Petrol 4-stroke piston
2294cc 140.0cu in
Vee 6 1 Carburettor
Compression ratio: 9.0:1
Bore: 90.0mm 3.5in
Stroke: 60.1mm 2.4in
Valve type/No: Overhead 12
Transmission: Automatic
No. of forward speeds: 3
Wheels driven: Rear
Springs F/R: Coil/Coil
Brake system: PA
Brakes F/R: Disc/Drum
Steering: Rack & pinion
Wheelbase: 260.9cm 102.7in
Track F: 145.3cm 57.2in
Track R: 146.8cm 57.8in
Length: 439.4cm 173.0in
Width: 172.0cm 67.7in
Height: 136.1cm 53.6in
Ground clearance: 17.8cm 7.0in
Kerb weight: 1192.7kg 2627.0lb
Fuel: 60.1L 13.2gal 15.9galUS

1884 Ford

Escort 1.6 GL Automatic
1983 UK
104.0mph 167.3kmh
0-50mph 80.5kmh: 8.8secs
0-60mph 96.5kmh: 12.2secs
0-1/4 mile: 18.8secs
0-1km: 35.4secs
79.0bhp 58.9kW 80.1PS
@ 5800rpm
92.0lbft 124.7Nm @ 3000rpm
87.1bhp/ton 85.6bhp/tonne
49.5bhp/L 36.9kW/L 50.2PS/L
50.4ft/sec 15.4m/sec
19.8mph 31.9kmh/1000rpm
25.6mpg 21.3mpgUS 11.0L/100km
Petrol 4-stroke piston
1597cc 97.4cu in
In-line 4 1 Carburettor
Compression ratio: 9.5:1
Bore: 80.0mm 3.1in
Stroke: 79.5mm 3.1in
Valve type/No: Overhead 8
Transmission: Automatic
No. of forward speeds: 3
Wheels driven: Front
Springs F/R: Coil/Coil
Brake system: PA
Brakes F/R: Disc/Drum
Steering: Rack & pinion
Wheelbase: 239.8cm 94.4in
Track F: 138.4cm 54.5in
Track R: 143.0cm 56.3in
Length: 397.0cm 156.3in
Width: 158.8cm 62.5in
Height: 133.6cm 52.6in
Ground clearance: 17.8cm 7.0in
Kerb weight: 922.5kg 2032.0lb
Fuel: 40.0L 8.8gal 10.6galUS

1885 Ford

Escort XR3i
1983 UK
118.0mph 189.9kmh
0-50mph 80.5kmh: 6.1secs
0-60mph 96.5kmh: 8.6secs
0-1/4 mile: 16.7secs
0-1km: 30.9secs
105.0bhp 78.3kW 106.5PS
@ 6000rpm
101.0lbft 136.9Nm @ 4800rpm
116.0bhp/ton 114.1bhp/tonne
65.8bhp/L 49.1kW/L 66.7PS/L
52.2ft/sec 15.9m/sec
20.2mph 32.5kmh/1000rpm
30.5mpg 25.4mpgUS 9.3L/100km
Petrol 4-stroke piston
1596cc 97.4cu in
In-line 4 fuel injection
Compression ratio: 9.5:1
Bore: 80.0mm 3.1in
Stroke: 79.5mm 3.1in
Valve type/No: Overhead 8
Transmission: Manual
No. of forward speeds: 5
Wheels driven: Front
Springs F/R: Coil/Coil
Brake system: PA
Brakes F/R: Disc/Drum
Steering: Rack & pinion
Wheelbase: 239.8cm 94.4in
Track F: 138.4cm 54.5in
Track R: 143.0cm 56.3in
Length: 405.9cm 159.8in
Width: 158.8cm 62.5in
Height: 133.6cm 52.6in
Ground clearance: 17.8cm 7.0in
Kerb weight: 920.3kg 2027.0lb
Fuel: 48.2L 10.6gal 12.7galUS

1886 Ford

Fiesta 1.1 Ghia
1983 UK
90.0mph 144.8kmh
0-50mph 80.5kmh: 11.6secs
0-60mph 96.5kmh: 16.8secs
0-1/4 mile: 20.6secs
0-1km: 39.2secs
50.0bhp 37.3kW 50.7PS
@ 5000rpm
61.0lbft 82.7Nm @ 2700rpm
63.5bhp/ton 62.4bhp/tonne
44.8bhp/L 33.4kW/L 45.4PS/L
35.6ft/sec 10.8m/sec
21.7mph 34.9kmh/1000rpm
37.2mpg 31.0mpgUS 7.6L/100km
Petrol 4-stroke piston
1117cc 68.1cu in
In-line 4 1 Carburettor
Compression ratio: 9.5:1
Bore: 73.9mm 2.9in
Stroke: 64.9mm 2.6in
Valve type/No: Overhead 8
Transmission: Manual
No. of forward speeds: 5
Wheels driven: Front
Springs F/R: Coil/Coil
Brake system: PA
Brakes F/R: Disc/Drum
Steering: Rack & pinion
Wheelbase: 228.9cm 90.1in
Track F: 136.9cm 53.9in
Track R: 132.1cm 52.0in
Length: 371.6cm 146.3in
Width: 154.9cm 61.0in
Height: 133.6cm 52.6in
Ground clearance: 15.2cm 6.0in
Kerb weight: 800.9kg 1764.0lb
Fuel: 34.1L 7.5gal 9.0galUS

1887 Ford

Granada 2.5 Diesel Estate
1983 UK
89.0mph 143.2kmh
0-50mph 80.5kmh: 12.2secs
0-60mph 96.5kmh: 17.5secs
0-1/4 mile: 20.7secs
0-1km: 39.5secs
69.0bhp 51.4kW 70.0PS
@ 4200rpm
109.0lbft 147.7Nm @ 2000rpm
49.3bhp/ton 48.5bhp/tonne
27.6bhp/L 20.6kW/L 28.0PS/L

43.2ft/sec 13.2m/sec
23.1mph 37.2kmh/1000rpm
27.5mpg 22.9mpgUS 10.3L/100km
Diesel 4-stroke piston
2498cc 152.4cu in
In-line 4 fuel injection
Compression ratio: 22.0:1
Bore: 90.0mm 3.5in
Stroke: 94.0mm 3.7in
Valve type/No: Overhead 8
Transmission: Manual
No. of forward speeds: 5
Wheels driven: Rear
Springs F/R: Coil/Coil
Brake system: PA
Brakes F/R: Disc/Drum
Steering: Rack & pinion PA
Wheelbase: 276.9cm 109.0in
Track F: 151.1cm 59.5in
Track R: 153.7cm 60.5in
Length: 475.2cm 187.1in
Width: 179.1cm 70.5in
Height: 138.2cm 54.4in
Ground clearance: 17.8cm 7.0in
Kerb weight: 1423.7kg 3136.0lb
Fuel: 61.9L 13.6gal 16.3galUS

1888 Ford

Mustang GT 5.0
1983 USA
125.0mph 201.1kmh
0-50mph 80.5kmh: 5.7secs
0-60mph 96.5kmh: 7.8secs
0-1/4 mile: 16.1secs
177.0bhp 132.0kW 179.4PS
@ 4200rpm
247.0lbft 334.7Nm @ 2600rpm
126.7bhp/ton 124.6bhp/tonne
35.8bhp/L 26.7kW/L 36.3PS/L
35.0ft/sec 10.7m/sec
30.0mph 48.3kmh/1000rpm
18.6mpg 15.5mpgUS 15.2L/100km
Petrol 4-stroke piston
4942cc 301.5cu in
Vee 8 1 Carburettor
Compression ratio: 8.3:1
Bore: 101.6mm 4.0in
Stroke: 76.2mm 3.0in
Valve type/No: Overhead 16
Transmission: Manual
No. of forward speeds: 5
Wheels driven: Rear
Springs F/R: Coil/Coil
Brake system: PA
Brakes F/R: Disc/Drum
Steering: Rack & pinion PA
Wheelbase: 255.0cm 100.4in
Track F: 143.8cm 56.6in
Track R: 144.8cm 57.0in
Length: 454.9cm 179.1in
Width: 175.5cm 69.1in
Height: 131.8cm 51.9in
Kerb weight: 1421.0kg 3130.0lb
Fuel: 58.3L 12.8gal 15.4galUS

1889 Ford

Orion 1.6 GL
1983 UK
113.0mph 181.8kmh
0-50mph 80.5kmh: 7.8secs
0-60mph 96.5kmh: 10.4secs
0-1/4 mile: 17.8secs
0-1km: 33.1secs
79.0bhp 58.9kW 80.1PS
@ 5800rpm
93.0lbft 126.0Nm @ 3000rpm
88.4bhp/ton 87.0bhp/tonne
49.5bhp/L 36.9kW/L 50.2PS/L
50.4ft/sec 15.4m/sec
24.2mph 38.9kmh/1000rpm
33.2mpg 27.6mpgUS 8.5L/100km
Petrol 4-stroke piston
1597cc 97.4cu in
In-line 4 1 Carburettor
Compression ratio: 9.5:1
Bore: 80.0mm 3.1in
Stroke: 79.5mm 3.1in
Valve type/No: Overhead 8
Transmission: Manual
No. of forward speeds: 5
Wheels driven: Front
Springs F/R: Coil/Coil
Brake system: PA
Brakes F/R: Disc/Drum
Steering: Rack & pinion
Wheelbase: 240.0cm 94.5in
Track F: 140.0cm 55.1in
Track R: 142.2cm 56.0in
Length: 419.1cm 165.0in
Width: 158.8cm 62.5in
Height: 133.4cm 52.5in
Ground clearance: 17.8cm 7.0in
Kerb weight: 908.4kg 2001.0lb
Fuel: 47.8L 10.5gal 12.6galUS

1890 Ford

Sierra XR4i
1983 UK
129.0mph 207.6kmh
0-50mph 80.5kmh: 5.8secs
0-60mph 96.5kmh: 7.7secs
0-1/4 mile: 15.9secs
0-1km: 29.3secs
150.0bhp 111.9kW 152.1PS
@ 5700rpm
161.0lbft 218.2Nm @ 3800rpm
126.5bhp/ton 124.4bhp/tonne
53.7bhp/L 40.1kW/L 54.5PS/L
42.7ft/sec 13.0m/sec
22.5mph 36.2kmh/1000rpm
21.4mpg 17.8mpgUS 13.2L/100km
Petrol 4-stroke piston
2792cc 170.3cu in
Vee 6 fuel injection
Compression ratio: 9.2:1
Bore: 93.0mm 3.7in
Stroke: 68.5mm 2.7in
Valve type/No: Overhead 12
Transmission: Manual
No. of forward speeds: 5
Wheels driven: Rear
Springs F/R: Coil/Coil
Brake system: PA
Brakes F/R: Disc/Drum
Steering: Rack & pinion
Wheelbase: 260.6cm 102.6in
Track F: 145.0cm 57.1in
Track R: 146.6cm 57.7in
Length: 445.8cm 175.5in
Width: 172.7cm 68.0in
Height: 139.2cm 54.8in
Ground clearance: 17.8cm 7.0in
Kerb weight: 1205.8kg 2656.0lb
Fuel: 60.1L 13.2gal 15.9galUS

1891 Ford

Thunderbird Turbo Coupe
1983 USA
119.0mph 191.5kmh
0-60mph 96.5kmh: 9.7secs
0-1/4 mile: 17.1secs
142.0bhp 105.9kW 144.0PS
@ 5000rpm
172.0lbft 233.1Nm @ 3800rpm
100.3bhp/ton 98.7bhp/tonne
61.7bhp/L 46.0kW/L 62.6PS/L
43.5ft/sec 13.2m/sec
23.3mph 37.5kmh/1000rpm
Petrol 4-stroke piston
2300cc 140.3cu in turbocharged
In-line 4 fuel injection
Compression ratio: 8.0:1
Bore: 96.0mm 3.8in
Stroke: 79.4mm 3.1in
Valve type/No: Overhead 8
Transmission: Manual
No. of forward speeds: 5
Wheels driven: Rear
Springs F/R: Coil/Coil
Brake system: PA
Brakes F/R: Disc/Drum
Steering: Rack & pinion PA
Wheelbase: 263.7cm 103.8in
Track F: 147.6cm 58.1in
Track R: 148.6cm 58.5in
Length: 501.9cm 197.6in
Width: 180.6cm 71.1in
Height: 135.1cm 53.2in
Ground clearance: 12.2cm 4.8in
Kerb weight: 1439.2kg 3170.0lb
Fuel: 68.1L 15.0gal 18.0galUS

1892 Ford

Fiesta 1.3L CVH
1984 UK
104.0mph 167.3kmh
0-50mph 80.5kmh: 8.1secs
0-60mph 96.5kmh: 12.1secs
0-1/4 mile: 18.3secs
0-1km: 34.5secs
69.0bhp 51.4kW 70.0PS
@ 6000rpm
74.0lbft 100.3Nm @ 4000rpm
89.9bhp/ton 88.4bhp/tonne
53.2bhp/L 39.7kW/L 53.9PS/L
42.3ft/sec 12.9m/sec
22.6mph 36.4kmh/1000rpm
28.1mpg 23.4mpgUS 10.1L/100km
Petrol 4-stroke piston
1297cc 79.1cu in
In-line 4 1 Carburettor
Compression ratio: 9.5:1
Bore: 79.9mm 3.1in
Stroke: 64.5mm 2.5in
Valve type/No: Overhead 8
Transmission: Manual
No. of forward speeds: 5
Wheels driven: Front
Springs F/R: Coil/Coil
Brake system: PA
Brakes F/R: Disc/Drum
Steering: Rack & pinion
Wheelbase: 228.9cm 90.1in
Track F: 136.7cm 53.8in
Track R: 132.1cm 52.0in
Length: 364.7cm 143.6in
Width: 154.9cm 61.0in
Height: 132.6cm 52.2in
Ground clearance: 15.2cm 6.0in
Kerb weight: 780.9kg 1720.0lb
Fuel: 34.1L 7.5gal 9.0galUS

1893 Ford

Fiesta 1.6L Diesel
1984 UK
92.0mph 148.0kmh
0-50mph 80.5kmh: 10.6secs
0-60mph 96.5kmh: 15.8secs
0-1/4 mile: 19.9secs
0-1km: 37.9secs
54.0bhp 40.3kW 54.7PS
@ 4800rpm
70.0lbft 94.9Nm @ 3000rpm
63.1bhp/ton 62.0bhp/tonne
33.6bhp/L 25.0kW/L 34.0PS/L
42.0ft/sec 12.8m/sec
24.9mph 40.1kmh/1000rpm
46.8mpg 39.0mpgUS 6.0L/100km
Diesel 4-stroke piston
1608cc 98.1cu in
In-line 4 fuel injection
Compression ratio: 22.5:1
Bore: 80.0mm 3.1in
Stroke: 80.0mm 3.1in
Valve type/No: Overhead 8
Transmission: Manual
No. of forward speeds: 5
Wheels driven: Front
Springs F/R: Coil/Coil
Brake system: PA
Brakes F/R: Disc/Drum
Steering: Rack & pinion
Wheelbase: 228.9cm 90.1in
Track F: 136.7cm 53.8in
Track R: 132.1cm 52.0in
Length: 364.7cm 143.6in
Width: 154.9cm 61.0in
Height: 132.6cm 52.2in
Ground clearance: 15.2cm 6.0in
Kerb weight: 870.8kg 1918.0lb
Fuel: 34.1L 7.5gal 9.0galUS

1894 Ford

Fiesta XR2
1984 UK
112.0mph 180.2kmh
0-50mph 80.5kmh: 7.0secs
0-60mph 96.5kmh: 10.2secs
0-1/4 mile: 17.5secs
0-1km: 32.4secs
96.0bhp 71.6kW 97.3PS
@ 6000rpm
98.0lbft 132.8Nm @ 4000rpm
116.2bhp/ton 114.2bhp/tonne
60.1bhp/L 44.8kW/L 60.9PS/L
52.2ft/sec 15.9m/sec
23.0mph 37.0kmh/1000rpm
29.9mpg 24.9mpgUS 9.4L/100km
Petrol 4-stroke piston
1597cc 97.4cu in
In-line 4 1 Carburettor
Compression ratio: 9.5:1
Bore: 79.9mm 3.1in
Stroke: 79.5mm 3.1in
Valve type/No: Overhead 8
Transmission: Manual
No. of forward speeds: 5
Wheels driven: Front
Springs F/R: Coil/Coil
Brake system: PA
Brakes F/R: Disc/Drum
Steering: Rack & pinion
Wheelbase: 228.9cm 90.1in
Track F: 138.4cm 54.5in
Track R: 133.9cm 52.7in
Length: 371.1cm 146.1in
Width: 162.1cm 63.8in
Height: 133.4cm 52.5in
Ground clearance: 15.2cm 6.0in
Kerb weight: 840.3kg 1851.0lb
Fuel: 40.0L 8.8gal 10.6galUS

1895 Ford

Mustang GT
1984 USA
111.0mph 178.6kmh
0-50mph 80.5kmh: 5.7secs
0-60mph 96.5kmh: 7.5secs
0-1/4 mile: 16.6secs
210.0bhp 156.6kW 212.9PS
@ 4400rpm
268.0lbft 363.1Nm @ 3200rpm
149.3bhp/ton 146.8bhp/tonne
42.5bhp/L 31.7kW/L 43.1PS/L
36.7ft/sec 11.2m/sec
Petrol 4-stroke piston
4942cc 301.5cu in
Vee 8
Compression ratio: 8.4:1
Bore: 101.6mm 4.0in
Stroke: 76.2mm 3.0in
Valve type/No: Overhead 16
Transmission: Manual
No. of forward speeds: 5
Wheels driven: Rear
Springs F/R: Coil/Coil
Brakes F/R: Disc/Drum
Steering: Rack & pinion PA
Wheelbase: 255.0cm 100.4in
Track F: 143.8cm 56.6in
Track R: 144.8cm 57.0in
Length: 454.9cm 179.1in
Width: 175.5cm 69.1in
Height: 130.6cm 51.4in
Kerb weight: 1430.1kg 3150.0lb

1896 Ford

Mustang GT 5.0
1984 USA
0-60mph 96.5kmh: 7.0secs
205.0bhp 152.9kW 207.8PS
@ 4600rpm
265.0lbft 359.1Nm @ 3200rpm
146.7bhp/ton 144.3bhp/tonne
41.5bhp/L 30.9kW/L 42.1PS/L
19.2mpg 16.0mpgUS 14.7L/100km
Petrol 4-stroke piston
4942cc 301.5cu in
Vee 8 1 Carburettor
Valve type/No: Overhead 16
Transmission: Manual
No. of forward speeds: 5
Wheels driven: Rear
Springs F/R: Coil/Coil
Brakes F/R: Disc/Drum
Steering: Rack & pinion PA
Wheelbase: 255.0cm 100.4in
Length: 454.9cm 179.1in
Width: 175.5cm 69.1in
Height: 131.8cm 51.9in
Kerb weight: 1421.0kg 3130.0lb
Fuel: 58.3L 12.8gal 15.4galUS

1897 Ford

Mustang SVO
1984 USA
134.0mph 215.6kmh
0-60mph 96.5kmh: 7.7secs
0-1/4 mile: 15.8secs
175.0bhp 130.5kW 177.4PS
@ 4500rpm
210.0lbft 284.6Nm @ 3000rpm
126.9bhp/ton 124.7bhp/tonne
76.1bhp/L 56.7kW/L 77.1PS/L
39.1ft/sec 11.9m/sec
23.3mph 37.5kmh/1000rpm
25.2mpg 21.0mpgUS 11.2L/100km
Petrol 4-stroke piston
2300cc 140.3cu in turbocharged
In-line 4 fuel injection
Compression ratio: 8.0:1
Bore: 96.0mm 3.8in
Stroke: 79.4mm 3.1in
Valve type/No: Overhead 8
Transmission: Manual
No. of forward speeds: 5

Wheels driven: Rear
Springs F/R: Coil/Coil
Brake system: PA
Brakes F/R: Disc/Disc
Steering: Rack & pinion PA
Wheelbase: 255.3cm 100.5in
Track F: 146.8cm 57.8in
Track R: 148.1cm 58.3in
Length: 459.7cm 181.0in
Width: 175.5cm 69.1in
Height: 131.8cm 51.9in
Ground clearance: 12.4cm 4.9in
Kerb weight: 1402.9kg 3090.0lb
Fuel: 58.3L 12.8gal 15.4galUS

1898 Ford

Sierra XR4i
1984 Germany
125.0mph 201.1kmh
0-60mph 96.5kmh: 8.3secs
0-1/4 mile: 16.4secs
150.0bhp 111.9kW 152.1PS
@ 5700rpm
159.0lbft 215.4Nm @ 3800rpm
130.0bhp/ton 127.8bhp/tonne
53.7bhp/L 40.1kW/L 54.5PS/L
42.7ft/sec 13.0m/sec
22.2mph 35.7kmh/1000rpm
20.4mpg 17.0mpgUS 13.8L/100km
Petrol 4-stroke piston
2792cc 170.3cu in
Vee 6 fuel injection
Compression ratio: 9.2:1
Bore: 93.0mm 3.7in
Stroke: 68.5mm 2.7in
Valve type/No: Overhead 12
Transmission: Manual
No. of forward speeds: 5
Wheels driven: Rear
Springs F/R: Coil/Coil
Brake system: PA
Brakes F/R: Disc/Drum
Steering: Rack & pinion PA
Wheelbase: 260.9cm 102.7in
Track F: 145.3cm 57.2in
Track R: 146.8cm 57.8in
Length: 446.0cm 175.6in
Width: 172.0cm 67.7in
Height: 139.2cm 54.8in
Ground clearance: 14.7cm 5.8in
Kerb weight: 1173.6kg 2585.0lb
Fuel: 60.2L 13.2gal 15.9galUS

1899 Ford

Tempo GLX
1984 USA
100.0mph 160.9kmh
0-60mph 96.5kmh: 13.6secs
0-1/4 mile: 18.9secs
84.0bhp 62.6kW 85.2PS
@ 4400rpm
118.0lbft 159.9Nm @ 2600rpm
74.1bhp/ton 72.8bhp/tonne
36.4bhp/L 27.1kW/L 36.9PS/L
40.5ft/sec 12.3m/sec
26.5mph 42.6kmh/1000rpm
28.8mpg 24.0mpgUS 9.8L/100km
Petrol 4-stroke piston
2307cc 140.8cu in
In-line 4 1 Carburettor
Compression ratio: 9.0:1
Bore: 93.5mm 3.7in
Stroke: 84.0mm 3.3in
Valve type/No: Overhead 8
Transmission: Manual
No. of forward speeds: 5
Wheels driven: Front
Springs F/R: Coil/Coil
Brake system: PA
Brakes F/R: Disc/Drum
Steering: Rack & pinion PA
Wheelbase: 253.7cm 99.9in
Track F: 138.9cm 54.7in
Track R: 146.3cm 57.6in
Length: 447.5cm 176.2in
Width: 173.5cm 68.3in
Height: 133.9cm 52.7in
Ground clearance: 12.7cm 5.0in
Kerb weight: 1153.2kg 2540.0lb
Fuel: 53.0L 11.6gal 14.0galUS

1900 Ford

Escort GL
1985 USA
0-60mph 96.5kmh: 11.7secs
0-1/4 mile: 18.1secs
86.0bhp 64.1kW 87.2PS
@ 4800rpm
100.0lbft 135.5Nm @ 3000rpm
80.9bhp/ton 79.6bhp/tonne
46.3bhp/L 34.5kW/L 46.9PS/L
46.1ft/sec 14.1m/sec
34.2mpg 28.5mpgUS 8.3L/100km
Petrol 4-stroke piston
1859cc 113.4cu in
In-line 4 1 Carburettor
Compression ratio: 9.0:1
Bore: 82.0mm 3.2in
Stroke: 88.0mm 3.5in
Valve type/No: Overhead 8
Transmission: Manual
No. of forward speeds: 5
Wheels driven: Front
Brakes F/R: Disc/Drum
Steering: Rack & pinion PA
Wheelbase: 239.3cm 94.2in
Length: 423.9cm 166.9in
Width: 167.4cm 65.9in
Height: 135.4cm 53.3in
Kerb weight: 1080.5kg 2380.0lb

1901 Ford

Escort RS Turbo
1985 UK
128.0mph 206.0kmh
0-50mph 80.5kmh: 5.7secs
0-60mph 96.5kmh: 8.1secs
0-1/4 mile: 16.2secs
0-1km: 29.6secs
132.0bhp 98.4kW 133.8PS
@ 6000rpm
133.0lbft 180.2Nm @ 3000rpm
137.5bhp/ton 135.2bhp/tonne
82.6bhp/L 61.6kW/L 83.8PS/L
52.2ft/sec 15.9m/sec
20.3mph 32.7kmh/1000rpm
26.8mpg 22.3mpgUS 10.5L/100km
Petrol 4-stroke piston
1597cc 97.4cu in turbocharged
In-line 4 fuel injection
Compression ratio: 8.3:1
Bore: 80.0mm 3.1in
Stroke: 79.5mm 3.1in
Valve type/No: Overhead 8
Transmission: Manual
No. of forward speeds: 5
Wheels driven: Front
Springs F/R: Coil/Coil
Brake system: PA
Brakes F/R: Disc/Drum
Steering: Rack & pinion
Wheelbase: 239.8cm 94.4in
Track F: 138.4cm 54.5in
Track R: 143.0cm 56.3in
Length: 405.9cm 159.8in
Width: 158.8cm 62.5in
Height: 133.6cm 52.6in
Ground clearance: 17.8cm 7.0in
Kerb weight: 976.1kg 2150.0lb
Fuel: 48.2L 10.6gal 12.7galUS

1902 Ford

Fiesta XR2
1985 UK
116.0mph 186.6kmh
0-50mph 80.5kmh: 6.8secs
0-60mph 96.5kmh: 9.3secs
0-1/4 mile: 17.1secs
0-1km: 31.8secs
96.0bhp 71.6kW 97.3PS
@ 6000rpm
98.0lbft 132.8Nm @ 4000rpm
116.2bhp/ton 114.2bhp/tonne
60.1bhp/L 44.8kW/L 60.9PS/L
52.2ft/sec 15.9m/sec
23.0mph 37.0kmh/1000rpm
31.0mpg 25.8mpgUS 9.1L/100km
Petrol 4-stroke piston
1597cc 97.4cu in
In-line 4 1 Carburettor
Compression ratio: 9.5:1
Bore: 79.9mm 3.1in
Stroke: 79.5mm 3.1in
Valve type/No: Overhead 8
Transmission: Manual
No. of forward speeds: 5
Wheels driven: Front
Springs F/R: Coil/Coil
Brake system: PA
Brakes F/R: Disc/Drum
Steering: Rack & pinion
Wheelbase: 228.9cm 90.1in
Track F: 136.9cm 53.9in
Track R: 132.1cm 52.0in
Length: 371.1cm 146.1in
Width: 162.1cm 63.8in
Height: 133.6cm 52.6in
Ground clearance: 15.2cm 6.0in
Kerb weight: 840.3kg 1851.0lb
Fuel: 40.0L 8.8gal 10.6galUS

1903 Ford

Granada Scorpio
1985 UK
127.0mph 204.3kmh
0-50mph 80.5kmh: 7.1secs
0-60mph 96.5kmh: 9.5secs
0-1/4 mile: 16.9secs
0-1km: 29.5secs
150.0bhp 111.9kW 152.1PS
@ 5800rpm
161.0lbft 218.2Nm @ 3000rpm
112.9bhp/ton 111.0bhp/tonne
53.7bhp/L 40.1kW/L 54.5PS/L
43.5ft/sec 13.2m/sec
25.4mph 40.9kmh/1000rpm
21.9mpg 18.2mpgUS 12.9L/100km
Petrol 4-stroke piston
2792cc 170.3cu in
Vee 6 fuel injection
Compression ratio: 9.2:1
Bore: 93.0mm 3.7in
Stroke: 68.5mm 2.7in
Valve type/No: Overhead 12
Transmission: Manual
No. of forward speeds: 5
Wheels driven: Rear
Springs F/R: Coil/Coil
Brake system: PA ABS
Brakes F/R: Disc/Disc
Steering: Rack & pinion PA
Wheelbase: 276.1cm 108.7in
Track F: 147.6cm 58.1in
Track R: 149.1cm 58.7in
Length: 466.9cm 183.8in
Width: 176.5cm 69.5in
Height: 145.0cm 57.1in
Ground clearance: 17.8cm 7.0in
Kerb weight: 1351.1kg 2976.0lb
Fuel: 70.1L 15.4gal 18.5galUS

1904 Ford

Granada Scorpio 4x4
1985 UK
125.0mph 201.1kmh
0-50mph 80.5kmh: 7.0secs
0-60mph 96.5kmh: 9.4secs
0-1/4 mile: 16.9secs
0-1km: 31.1secs
150.0bhp 111.9kW 152.1PS
@ 5800rpm
161.0lbft 218.2Nm @ 3000rpm
105.4bhp/ton 103.7bhp/tonne
53.7bhp/L 40.1kW/L 54.5PS/L
43.5ft/sec 13.2m/sec
24.1mph 38.8kmh/1000rpm
19.2mpg 16.0mpgUS 14.7L/100km
Petrol 4-stroke piston
2792cc 170.3cu in
Vee 6 fuel injection
Compression ratio: 9.2:1
Bore: 93.0mm 3.7in
Stroke: 68.5mm 2.7in
Valve type/No: Overhead 12
Transmission: Manual
No. of forward speeds: 5
Wheels driven: 4-wheel drive
Springs F/R: Coil/Coil
Brake system: PA
Brakes F/R: Disc/Disc
Steering: Rack & pinion PA
Wheelbase: 276.1cm 108.7in
Track F: 147.6cm 58.1in
Track R: 149.1cm 58.7in
Length: 466.9cm 183.8in
Width: 176.5cm 69.5in
Height: 145.0cm 57.1in
Ground clearance: 17.8cm 7.0in
Kerb weight: 1446.9kg 3187.0lb
Fuel: 70.1L 15.4gal 18.5galUS

1905 Ford

Mustang GT
1985 USA
135.0mph 217.2kmh
0-60mph 96.5kmh: 7.2secs
0-1/4 mile: 15.9secs
210.0bhp 156.6kW 212.9PS
@ 4600rpm
265.0lbft 359.1Nm @ 3400rpm
147.5bhp/ton 145.0bhp/tonne
42.5bhp/L 31.7kW/L 43.1PS/L
38.3ft/sec 11.7m/sec
34.7mph 55.8kmh/1000rpm
18.6mpg 15.5mpgUS 15.2L/100km
Petrol 4-stroke piston
4942cc 301.5cu in
Vee 8 1 Carburettor
Compression ratio: 8.3:1
Bore: 101.6mm 4.0in
Stroke: 76.2mm 3.0in
Valve type/No: Overhead 16
Transmission: Manual
No. of forward speeds: 5
Wheels driven: Rear
Springs F/R: Coil/Coil
Brakes F/R: Disc/Drum
Steering: Rack & pinion PA
Wheelbase: 255.3cm 100.5in
Track F: 143.8cm 56.6in
Track R: 144.8cm 57.0in
Length: 455.4cm 179.3in
Width: 175.5cm 69.1in
Height: 132.3cm 52.1in
Kerb weight: 1448.3kg 3190.0lb
Fuel: 58.3L 12.8gal 15.4galUS

1906 Ford

Sierra 1.8 Ghia
1985 UK
103.0mph 165.7kmh
0-50mph 80.5kmh: 8.2secs
0-60mph 96.5kmh: 12.2secs
0-1/4 mile: 18.0secs
0-1km: 34.1secs
90.0bhp 67.1kW 91.2PS
@ 5300rpm
100.0lbft 135.5Nm @ 3300rpm
79.4bhp/ton 78.0bhp/tonne
50.1bhp/L 37.4kW/L 50.8PS/L
44.6ft/sec 13.6m/sec
24.4mph 39.3kmh/1000rpm
26.8mpg 22.3mpgUS 10.5L/100km
Petrol 4-stroke piston
1796cc 109.6cu in
In-line 4 1 Carburettor
Compression ratio: 9.5:1
Bore: 86.2mm 3.4in
Stroke: 77.0mm 3.0in
Valve type/No: Overhead 8
Transmission: Manual
No. of forward speeds: 5
Wheels driven: Rear
Springs F/R: Coil/Coil
Brake system: PA
Brakes F/R: Disc/Drum
Steering: Rack & pinion
Wheelbase: 260.6cm 102.6in
Track F: 145.0cm 57.1in
Track R: 146.6cm 57.7in
Length: 445.8cm 175.5in
Width: 172.7cm 68.0in
Height: 139.2cm 54.8in
Ground clearance: 17.8cm 7.0in
Kerb weight: 1153.2kg 2540.0lb
Fuel: 59.1L 13.0gal 15.6galUS

1907 Ford

Sierra 2.0i S
1985 UK
118.0mph 189.9kmh
0-50mph 80.5kmh: 6.4secs
0-60mph 96.5kmh: 9.2secs
0-1/4 mile: 16.9secs
0-1km: 31.5secs
115.0bhp 85.8kW 116.6PS
@ 5500rpm
118.0lbft 159.9Nm @ 4000rpm
120.3bhp/ton 118.3bhp/tonne
57.7bhp/L 43.0kW/L 58.5PS/L
46.3ft/sec 14.1m/sec
20.7mph 33.3kmh/1000rpm
23.4mpg 19.5mpgUS 12.1L/100km
Petrol 4-stroke piston
1993cc 121.6cu in
In-line 4 fuel injection
Compression ratio: 9.2:1
Bore: 90.8mm 3.6in
Stroke: 77.0mm 3.0in
Valve type/No: Overhead 8
Transmission: Manual
No. of forward speeds: 5
Wheels driven: Rear
Springs F/R: Coil/Coil
Brake system: PA
Brakes F/R: Disc/Drum
Steering: Rack & pinion

Wheelbase: 260.6cm 102.6in
Track F: 145.0cm 57.1in
Track R: 146.6cm 57.7in
Length: 445.8cm 175.5in
Width: 172.7cm 68.0in
Height: 139.2cm 54.8in
Ground clearance: 17.8cm 7.0in
Kerb weight: 972.0kg 2141.0lb
Fuel: 60.1L 13.2gal 15.9galUS

1908 Ford
Aerostar XLT
1986 USA
90.0mph 144.8kmh
0-60mph 96.5kmh: 14.4secs
0-1/4 mile: 19.5secs
115.0bhp 85.8kW 116.6PS
@ 4600rpm
150.0lbft 203.3Nm @ 2600rpm
97.6bhp/ton 95.9bhp/tonne
41.0bhp/L 30.6kW/L 41.6PS/L
34.5ft/sec 10.5m/sec
22.2mpg 18.5mpgUS 12.7L/100km
Petrol 4-stroke piston
2802cc 171.0cu in
Vee 6 1 Carburettor
Compression ratio: 8.7:1
Bore: 93.0mm 3.7in
Stroke: 68.6mm 2.7in
Valve type/No: Overhead 12
Transmission: Manual
No. of forward speeds: 5
Wheels driven: Rear
Springs F/R: Coil/Coil
Brake system: PA
Brakes F/R: Disc/Drum
Steering: Rack & pinion PA
Wheelbase: 302.0cm 118.9in
Track F: 156.2cm 61.5in
Track R: 152.4cm 60.0in
Length: 444.2cm 174.9in
Width: 182.1cm 71.7in
Height: 184.4cm 72.6in
Ground clearance: 16.0cm 6.3in
Kerb weight: 1198.6kg 2640.0lb
Fuel: 64.3L 14.1gal 17.0galUS

1909 Ford
Escort 1.4 GL
1986 UK
104.0mph 167.3kmh
0-50mph 80.5kmh: 8.4secs
0-60mph 96.5kmh: 12.4secs
0-1/4 mile: 18.5secs
0-1km: 35.1secs
75.0bhp 55.9kW 76.0PS
@ 5600rpm
80.0lbft 108.4Nm @ 4000rpm
87.5bhp/ton 86.0bhp/tonne
53.9bhp/L 40.2kW/L 54.6PS/L
45.6ft/sec 13.9m/sec
22.5mph 36.2kmh/1000rpm
34.6mpg 28.8mpgUS 8.2L/100km
Petrol 4-stroke piston
1392cc 85.0cu in
In-line 4 1 Carburettor
Compression ratio: 9.5:1
Bore: 77.2mm 3.0in
Stroke: 74.3mm 2.9in
Valve type/No: Overhead 8
Transmission: Manual
No. of forward speeds: 5
Wheels driven: Front
Springs F/R: Coil/Coil
Brake system: PA ABS
Brakes F/R: Disc/Drum
Steering: Rack & pinion
Wheelbase: 239.8cm 94.4in
Track F: 138.4cm 54.5in
Track R: 143.0cm 56.3in
Length: 402.0cm 158.3in
Width: 158.8cm 62.5in
Height: 136.9cm 53.9in
Ground clearance: 17.9cm 7.0in
Kerb weight: 872.0kg 1920.7lb
Fuel: 48.2L 10.6gal 12.7galUS

1910 Ford
Escort L
1986 USA
0-60mph 96.5kmh: 11.4secs
0-1/4 mile: 18.2secs
86.0bhp 64.1kW 87.2PS
@ 4800rpm
100.0lbft 135.5Nm @ 3000rpm
83.6bhp/ton 82.2bhp/tonne
46.3bhp/L 34.5kW/L 46.9PS/L
46.1ft/sec 14.1m/sec
25.0mph 40.2kmh/1000rpm
35.1mpg 29.2mpgUS 8.1L/100km
Petrol 4-stroke piston
1859cc 113.4cu in
In-line 4 1 Carburettor
Compression ratio: 9.0:1
Bore: 82.0mm 3.2in
Stroke: 88.0mm 3.5in
Valve type/No: Overhead 8
Transmission: Manual
No. of forward speeds: 5
Wheels driven: Front
Springs F/R: Coil/Coil
Brake system: PA
Brakes F/R: Disc/Drum
Steering: Rack & pinion
Wheelbase: 239.3cm 94.2in
Track F: 138.9cm 54.7in
Track R: 142.2cm 56.0in
Length: 416.3cm 163.9in
Width: 167.4cm 65.9in
Height: 135.4cm 53.3in
Kerb weight: 1046.5kg 2305.0lb
Fuel: 49.2L 10.8gal 13.0galUS

1911 Ford
Escort RS Turbo
1986 UK
125.0mph 201.1kmh
0-50mph 80.5kmh: 6.1secs
0-60mph 96.5kmh: 9.2secs
0-1/4 mile: 16.8secs
0-1km: 30.2secs
132.0bhp 98.4kW 133.8PS
@ 5750rpm
132.7lbft 179.8Nm @ 2750rpm
132.0bhp/ton 129.8bhp/tonne
82.6bhp/L 61.6kW/L 83.8PS/L
50.0ft/sec 15.2m/sec
22.5mph 36.2kmh/1000rpm
27.4mpg 22.8mpgUS 10.3L/100km
Petrol 4-stroke piston
1597cc 97.0cu in turbocharged
In-line 4 fuel injection
Compression ratio: 8.2:1
Bore: 79.6mm 3.1in
Stroke: 79.5mm 3.1in
Valve type/No: Overhead 8
Transmission: Manual
No. of forward speeds: 5
Wheels driven: Front
Springs F/R: Coil/Coil
Brake system: PA ABS
Brakes F/R: Disc/Drum
Steering: Rack & pinion PA
Wheelbase: 239.8cm 94.4in
Track F: 138.4cm 54.5in
Track R: 143.0cm 56.3in
Length: 404.6cm 159.3in
Width: 183.3cm 72.2in
Height: 134.8cm 53.1in
Ground clearance: 17.9cm 7.0in
Kerb weight: 1017.0kg 2240.1lb
Fuel: 48.2L 10.6gal 12.7galUS

1912 Ford
Escort XR3i
1986 UK
118.0mph 189.9kmh
0-50mph 80.5kmh: 7.0secs
0-60mph 96.5kmh: 9.6secs
0-1/4 mile: 17.0secs
0-1km: 31.3secs
105.0bhp 78.3kW 106.5PS
@ 6000rpm
104.0lbft 140.9Nm @ 4800rpm
110.6bhp/ton 108.8bhp/tonne
65.7bhp/L 49.0kW/L 66.7PS/L
52.2ft/sec 15.9m/sec
20.2mph 32.5kmh/1000rpm
30.8mpg 25.6mpgUS 9.2L/100km
Petrol 4-stroke piston
1597cc 97.0cu in
In-line 4 fuel injection
Compression ratio: 9.5:1
Bore: 79.9mm 3.1in
Stroke: 79.5mm 3.1in
Valve type/No: Overhead 8
Transmission: Manual
No. of forward speeds: 5
Wheels driven: Front
Springs F/R: Coil/Coil
Brake system: PA
Brakes F/R: Disc/Drum
Steering: Rack & pinion
Wheelbase: 179.0cm 70.5in
Track F: 138.4cm 54.5in
Track R: 143.0cm 56.3in
Length: 404.6cm 159.3in
Width: 158.8cm 62.5in
Height: 134.8cm 53.1in
Ground clearance: 17.9cm 7.0in
Kerb weight: 965.0kg 2125.5lb
Fuel: 48.2L 10.6gal 12.7galUS

1913 Ford
Mustang GT 5.0
1986 USA
135.0mph 217.2kmh
0-60mph 96.5kmh: 6.9secs
0-1/4 mile: 15.0secs
200.0bhp 149.1kW 202.8PS
@ 4000rpm
285.0lbft 386.2Nm @ 3500rpm
142.7bhp/ton 140.3bhp/tonne
40.5bhp/L 30.2kW/L 41.0PS/L
Petrol 4-stroke piston
4942cc 301.5cu in
Vee 8 fuel injection
Valve type/No: Overhead 16
Transmission: Manual
No. of forward speeds: 5
Wheels driven: Rear
Springs F/R: Coil/Coil
Brakes F/R: Disc/Drum
Steering: Rack & pinion PA
Wheelbase: 255.3cm 100.5in
Length: 456.9cm 179.9in
Width: 175.5cm 69.1in
Height: 132.3cm 52.1in
Kerb weight: 1425.6kg 3140.0lb
Fuel: 58.3L 12.8gal 15.4galUS

1914 Ford
Mustang Saleen
1986 USA
0-60mph 96.5kmh: 7.0secs
0-1/4 mile: 15.8secs
210.0bhp 156.6kW 212.9PS
@ 4600rpm
265.0lbft 359.1Nm @ 3400rpm
42.5bhp/L 31.7kW/L 43.1PS/L
18.6mpg 15.5mpgUS 15.2L/100km
Petrol 4-stroke piston
4942cc 301.5cu in
Vee 8
Valve type/No: Overhead 16
Transmission: Manual
No. of forward speeds: 5
Wheels driven: Rear
Brakes F/R: Disc/Drum
Steering: Rack & pinion PA
Wheelbase: 255.3cm 100.5in
Length: 455.4cm 179.3in
Width: 175.5cm 69.1in
Height: 132.3cm 52.1in

1915 Ford
Mustang SVO
1986 USA
134.0mph 215.6kmh
0-60mph 96.5kmh: 7.1secs
0-1/4 mile: 15.2secs
200.0bhp 149.1kW 202.8PS
@ 5000rpm
240.0lbft 325.2Nm @ 3200rpm
142.7bhp/ton 140.3bhp/tonne
87.0bhp/L 64.8kW/L 88.2PS/L
Petrol 4-stroke piston
2300cc 140.3cu in turbocharged
In-line 4 fuel injection
Valve type/No: Overhead 8
Transmission: Manual
No. of forward speeds: 5
Wheels driven: Rear
Springs F/R: Coil/Coil
Brakes F/R: Disc/Disc
Steering: Rack & pinion PA
Wheelbase: 255.3cm 100.5in
Length: 459.2cm 180.8in
Width: 175.5cm 69.1in
Height: 132.3cm 52.1in
Kerb weight: 1425.6kg 3140.0lb
Fuel: 58.3L 12.8gal 15.4galUS

1916 Ford
Orion 1.4 GL
1986 UK
106.0mph 170.6kmh
0-50mph 80.5kmh: 8.8secs
0-60mph 96.5kmh: 12.8secs
0-1/4 mile: 19.1secs
0-1km: 42.9secs
75.0bhp 55.9kW 76.0PS
@ 5600rpm
80.0lbft 108.4Nm @ 4000rpm
80.4bhp/ton 79.0bhp/tonne
53.9bhp/L 40.2kW/L 54.6PS/L
45.6ft/sec 13.9m/sec
22.4mph 36.0kmh/1000rpm
31.0mpg 25.8mpgUS 9.1L/100km
Petrol 4-stroke piston
1392cc 85.0cu in
In-line 4 1 Carburettor
Compression ratio: 9.5:1
Bore: 77.2mm 3.0in
Stroke: 74.3mm 2.9in
Valve type/No: Overhead 8
Transmission: Manual
No. of forward speeds: 5
Wheels driven: Front
Springs F/R: Coil/Coil
Brake system: PA
Brakes F/R: Disc/Drum
Steering: Rack & pinion
Wheelbase: 240.0cm 94.5in
Track F: 140.0cm 55.1in
Track R: 140.0cm 55.1in
Length: 421.3cm 165.9in
Width: 183.3cm 72.2in
Height: 138.9cm 54.7in
Ground clearance: 17.9cm 7.0in
Kerb weight: 949.0kg 2090.3lb
Fuel: 46.9L 10.3gal 12.4galUS

1917 Ford
RS200
1986 UK
140.0mph 225.3kmh
0-50mph 80.5kmh: 4.8secs
0-60mph 96.5kmh: 6.1secs
0-1/4 mile: 15.0secs
0-1km: 27.4secs
230.0bhp 171.5kW 233.2PS
@ 6000rpm
280.0lbft 379.4Nm @ 4500rpm
181.9bhp/ton 178.8bhp/tonne
127.8bhp/L 95.3kW/L 129.5PS/L
51.0ft/sec 15.5m/sec
20.1mph 32.3kmh/1000rpm
18.3mpg 15.2mpgUS 15.4L/100km
Petrol 4-stroke piston
1800cc 110.0cu in turbocharged
In-line 4 fuel injection
Compression ratio: 8.2:1
Bore: 86.0mm 3.4in
Stroke: 77.6mm 3.1in
Valve type/No: Overhead 16
Transmission: Manual
No. of forward speeds: 5
Wheels driven: 4-wheel drive
Springs F/R: Coil/Coil
Brakes F/R: Disc/Disc
Steering: Rack & pinion PA
Wheelbase: 253.0cm 99.6in
Track F: 147.3cm 58.0in
Track R: 149.9cm 59.0in
Length: 399.8cm 157.4in
Width: 175.3cm 69.0in
Height: 132.1cm 52.0in
Ground clearance: 17.8cm 7.0in
Kerb weight: 1286.0kg 2832.6lb
Fuel: 90.1L 19.8gal 23.8galUS

1918 Ford
Sierra Ghia 4x4 Estate
1986 UK
124.0mph 199.5kmh
0-50mph 80.5kmh: 7.0secs
0-60mph 96.5kmh: 9.5secs
0-1/4 mile: 17.6secs
0-1km: 32.1secs
150.0bhp 111.9kW 152.1PS
@ 5700rpm
216.0lbft 292.7Nm @ 3800rpm
114.7bhp/ton 112.8bhp/tonne
53.7bhp/L 40.1kW/L 54.5PS/L
42.7ft/sec 13.0m/sec
22.9mph 36.8kmh/1000rpm
21.0mpg 17.5mpgUS 13.5L/100km
Petrol 4-stroke piston
2792cc 170.0cu in
Vee 6 fuel injection
Compression ratio: 9.2:1
Bore: 93.0mm 3.7in
Stroke: 68.5mm 2.7in

Valve type/No: Overhead 12
Transmission: Manual
No. of forward speeds: 5
Wheels driven: 4-wheel drive
Springs F/R: Coil/Coil
Brake system: PA ABS
Brakes F/R: Disc/Disc
Steering: Rack & pinion PA
Wheelbase: 260.8cm 102.7in
Track F: 146.8cm 57.8in
Track R: 146.6cm 57.7in
Length: 452.1cm 178.0in
Width: 192.0cm 75.6in
Height: 150.6cm 59.3in
Ground clearance: 17.9cm 7.0in
Kerb weight: 1330.0kg 2929.5lb
Fuel: 60.1L 13.2gal 15.9galUS

1919 Ford

Festiva L
1987 Japan
95.0mph 152.9kmh
0-50mph 80.5kmh: 7.2secs
0-60mph 96.5kmh: 10.2secs
0-1/4 mile: 17.8secs
58.0bhp 43.2kW 58.8PS
@ 5000rpm
73.0lbft 98.9Nm @ 3500rpm
75.5bhp/ton 74.3bhp/tonne
43.8bhp/L 32.7kW/L 44.4PS/L
45.7ft/sec 13.9m/sec
44.4mpg 37.0mpgUS 6.4L/100km
Petrol 4-stroke piston
1324cc 80.8cu in
In-line 4 1 Carburettor
Compression ratio: 9.0:1
Bore: 71.0mm 2.8in
Stroke: 83.6mm 3.3in
Valve type/No: Overhead 8
Transmission: Manual
No. of forward speeds: 4
Wheels driven: Front
Springs F/R: Coil/Coil
Brake system: PA
Brakes F/R: Disc/Drum
Steering: Rack & pinion
Wheelbase: 229.1cm 90.2in
Track F: 140.0cm 55.1in
Track R: 138.4cm 54.5in
Length: 356.9cm 140.5in
Width: 160.5cm 63.2in
Height: 140.5cm 55.3in
Kerb weight: 780.9kg 1720.0lb
Fuel: 37.8L 8.3gal 10.0galUS

1920 Ford

Fiesta 1.1 Ghia Auto
1987 UK
88.0mph 141.6kmh
0-50mph 80.5kmh: 10.9secs
0-60mph 96.5kmh: 15.8secs
0-1/4 mile: 20.4secs
0-1km: 38.8secs
50.0bhp 37.3kW 50.7PS
@ 5000rpm
61.0lbft 82.7Nm @ 2700rpm
62.4bhp/ton 61.3bhp/tonne
44.8bhp/L 33.4kW/L 45.4PS/L
35.6ft/sec 10.8m/sec
25.7mph 41.4kmh/1000rpm
35.0mpg 29.1mpgUS 8.1L/100km
Petrol 4-stroke piston
1117cc 68.0cu in
In-line 4 1 Carburettor
Compression ratio: 9.5:1
Bore: 74.0mm 2.9in
Stroke: 64.9mm 2.6in
Valve type/No: Overhead 8
Transmission: Automatic
Wheels driven: Front
Springs F/R: Coil/Coil
Brake system: PA
Brakes F/R: Disc/Drum
Steering: Rack & pinion
Wheelbase: 228.8cm 90.1in
Track F: 136.7cm 53.8in
Track R: 132.1cm 52.0in
Length: 364.8cm 143.6in
Width: 172.4cm 67.9in
Height: 133.5cm 52.6in
Ground clearance: 15.2cm 6.0in
Kerb weight: 815.0kg 1795.1lb
Fuel: 40.0L 8.8gal 10.6galUS

1921 Ford

Granada 2.4i Ghia
1987 UK
122.0mph 196.3kmh
0-50mph 80.5kmh: 7.2secs
0-60mph 96.5kmh: 9.5secs
0-1/4 mile: 17.4secs
0-1km: 32.0secs
130.0bhp 96.9kW 131.8PS
@ 5800rpm
142.0lbft 192.4Nm @ 3000rpm
98.7bhp/ton 97.0bhp/tonne
54.3bhp/L 40.5kW/L 55.1PS/L
45.6ft/sec 13.9m/sec
23.6mph 38.0kmh/1000rpm
21.5mpg 17.9mpgUS 13.1L/100km
Petrol 4-stroke piston
2393cc 146.0cu in
Vee 6 fuel injection
Compression ratio: 9.5:1
Bore: 84.0mm 3.3in
Stroke: 72.0mm 2.8in
Valve type/No: Overhead 12
Transmission: Manual
No. of forward speeds: 5
Wheels driven: Rear
Springs F/R: Coil/Coil
Brake system: PA
Brakes F/R: Disc/Disc
Steering: Rack & pinion PA
Wheelbase: 276.1cm 108.7in
Track F: 147.7cm 58.1in
Track R: 149.2cm 58.7in
Length: 466.9cm 183.8in
Width: 176.6cm 69.5in
Height: 145.0cm 57.1in
Ground clearance: 17.9cm 7.0in
Kerb weight: 1340.0kg 2951.5lb
Fuel: 70.1L 15.4gal 18.5galUS

1922 Ford

Granada Scorpio 2.9 EX
1987 UK
126.0mph 202.7kmh
0-50mph 80.5kmh: 6.2secs
0-60mph 96.5kmh: 9.8secs
0-1/4 mile: 17.6secs
0-1km: 31.5secs
150.0bhp 111.9kW 152.1PS
@ 5700rpm
172.0lbft 233.1Nm @ 3000rpm
106.3bhp/ton 104.5bhp/tonne
51.1bhp/L 38.1kW/L 51.8PS/L
44.8ft/sec 13.7m/sec
26.2mph 42.2kmh/1000rpm
24.0mpg 20.0mpgUS 11.8L/100km
Petrol 4-stroke piston
2933cc 179.0cu in
Vee 6 fuel injection
Compression ratio: 9.5:1
Bore: 93.0mm 3.7in
Stroke: 72.0mm 2.8in
Valve type/No: Overhead 12
Transmission: Automatic
No. of forward speeds: 4
Wheels driven: Rear
Springs F/R: Coil/Coil
Brake system: PA
Brakes F/R: Disc/Disc
Steering: Rack & pinion PA
Wheelbase: 276.1cm 108.7in
Track F: 147.7cm 58.1in
Track R: 149.2cm 58.7in
Length: 466.9cm 183.8in
Width: 176.6cm 69.5in
Height: 145.0cm 57.1in
Ground clearance: 17.9cm 7.0in
Kerb weight: 1435.0kg 3160.8lb
Fuel: 70.1L 15.4gal 18.5galUS

1923 Ford

Mustang GT
1987 USA
148.0mph 238.1kmh
0-60mph 96.5kmh: 6.7secs
0-1/4 mile: 15.3secs
225.0bhp 167.8kW 228.1PS
@ 4400rpm
300.0lbft 406.5Nm @ 3000rpm
154.1bhp/ton 151.6bhp/tonne
45.5bhp/L 33.9kW/L 46.2PS/L
36.7ft/sec 11.2m/sec
37.0mph 59.5kmh/1000rpm
Petrol 4-stroke piston
4942cc 301.5cu in
Vee 8 fuel injection
Compression ratio: 9.0:1
Bore: 101.6mm 4.0in
Stroke: 76.2mm 3.0in
Valve type/No: Overhead 16
Transmission: Manual
No. of forward speeds: 5
Wheels driven: Rear
Springs F/R: Coil/Coil
Brakes F/R: Disc/Drum
Steering: Rack & pinion PA
Wheelbase: 255.3cm 100.5in
Track F: 143.8cm 56.6in
Track R: 144.8cm 57.0in
Length: 455.4cm 179.3in
Width: 175.5cm 69.1in
Height: 132.3cm 52.1in
Kerb weight: 1484.6kg 3270.0lb
Fuel: 58.3L 12.8gal 15.4galUS

1924 Ford

Mustang LX 5.0
1987 USA
0-50mph 80.5kmh: 4.3secs
0-60mph 96.5kmh: 6.0secs
0-1/4 mile: 14.5secs
225.0bhp 167.8kW 228.1PS
@ 4000rpm
300.0lbft 406.5Nm @ 3200rpm
156.3bhp/ton 153.7bhp/tonne
45.4bhp/L 33.9kW/L 46.1PS/L
33.3ft/sec 10.2m/sec
19.7mpg 16.4mpgUS 14.3L/100km
Petrol 4-stroke piston
4950cc 302.0cu in
Vee 8 fuel injection
Compression ratio: 9.2:1
Bore: 101.6mm 4.0in
Stroke: 76.2mm 3.0in
Valve type/No: Overhead 16
Transmission: Manual
No. of forward speeds: 5
Wheels driven: Rear
Springs F/R: Coil/Coil
Brakes F/R: Disc/Drum
Steering: Rack & pinion PA
Wheelbase: 255.3cm 100.5in
Track F: 143.8cm 56.6in
Track R: 144.8cm 57.0in
Length: 456.2cm 179.6in
Width: 175.5cm 69.1in
Height: 132.3cm 52.1in
Kerb weight: 1464.1kg 3225.0lb
Fuel: 58.3L 12.8gal 15.4galUS

1925 Ford

Sierra Sapphire 2.0 Ghia
1987 UK
117.0mph 188.3kmh
0-50mph 80.5kmh: 6.7secs
0-60mph 96.5kmh: 9.6secs
0-1/4 mile: 17.3secs
0-1km: 31.8secs
115.0bhp 85.8kW 116.6PS
@ 5500rpm
118.0lbft 159.9Nm @ 4000rpm
102.6bhp/ton 100.9bhp/tonne
57.7bhp/L 43.0kW/L 58.5PS/L
46.3ft/sec 14.1m/sec
21.9mph 35.2kmh/1000rpm
26.8mpg 22.3mpgUS 10.5L/100km
Petrol 4-stroke piston
1993cc 122.0cu in
In-line 4 fuel injection
Compression ratio: 9.2:1
Bore: 90.8mm 3.6in
Stroke: 77.0mm 3.0in
Valve type/No: Overhead 8
Transmission: Manual
No. of forward speeds: 5
Wheels driven: Rear
Springs F/R: Coil/Coil
Brake system: PA
Brakes F/R: Disc/Drum
Steering: Rack & pinion
Wheelbase: 260.8cm 102.7in
Track F: 145.0cm 57.1in
Track R: 146.6cm 57.7in
Length: 446.7cm 175.9in
Width: 192.0cm 75.6in
Height: 135.8cm 53.5in
Ground clearance: 17.9cm 7.0in
Kerb weight: 1140.0kg 2511.0lb
Fuel: 60.1L 13.2gal 15.9galUS

1926 Ford

Thunderbird Bondurant 5.0
1987 USA
139.0mph 223.7kmh
0-50mph 80.5kmh: 5.3secs
0-60mph 96.5kmh: 6.8secs
0-1/4 mile: 15.2secs
225.0bhp 167.8kW 228.1PS
@ 4000rpm
300.0lbft 406.5Nm @ 3200rpm
140.0bhp/ton 137.7bhp/tonne
45.4bhp/L 33.9kW/L 46.1PS/L
33.3ft/sec 10.2m/sec
Petrol 4-stroke piston
4950cc 302.0cu in
Vee 8 fuel injection
Compression ratio: 9.2:1
Bore: 101.6mm 4.0in
Stroke: 76.2mm 3.0in
Valve type/No: Overhead 16
Transmission: Manual
No. of forward speeds: 5
Wheels driven: Rear
Springs F/R: Coil/Coil
Brake system: ABS
Brakes F/R: Disc/Disc
Steering: Rack & pinion PA
Wheelbase: 264.7cm 104.2in
Track F: 147.6cm 58.1in
Track R: 148.6cm 58.5in
Length: 513.3cm 202.1in
Width: 180.6cm 71.1in
Height: 135.6cm 53.4in
Kerb weight: 1634.4kg 3600.0lb
Fuel: 68.9L 15.1gal 18.2galUS

1927 Ford

Thunderbird Turbo Coupe
1987 USA
131.0mph 210.8kmh
0-50mph 80.5kmh: 5.9secs
0-60mph 96.5kmh: 8.5secs
0-1/4 mile: 16.3secs
190.0bhp 141.7kW 192.6PS
@ 4600rpm
240.0lbft 325.2Nm @ 3400rpm
122.1bhp/ton 120.1bhp/tonne
82.8bhp/L 61.7kW/L 83.9PS/L
39.9ft/sec 12.1m/sec
20.4mpg 17.0mpgUS 13.8L/100km
Petrol 4-stroke piston
2295cc 140.0cu in turbocharged
In-line 4 fuel injection
Compression ratio: 8.0:1
Bore: 96.0mm 3.8in
Stroke: 79.2mm 3.1in
Valve type/No: Overhead 8
Transmission: Manual
No. of forward speeds: 5
Wheels driven: Rear
Springs F/R: Coil/Coil
Brake system: ABS
Brakes F/R: Disc/Disc
Steering: Rack & pinion PA
Wheelbase: 264.7cm 104.2in
Track F: 147.6cm 58.1in
Track R: 148.6cm 58.5in
Length: 513.3cm 202.1in
Width: 180.6cm 71.1in
Height: 135.6cm 53.4in
Kerb weight: 1582.2kg 3485.0lb
Fuel: 68.9L 15.1gal 18.2galUS

1928 Ford

Mustang Cartech Turbo
1988 USA
177.0mph 284.8kmh
0-60mph 96.5kmh: 4.9secs
0-1/4 mile: 13.3secs
392.0bhp 292.3kW 397.4PS
@ 5000rpm
550.0lbft 745.3Nm @ 4200rpm
310.3bhp/ton 305.1bhp/tonne
79.3bhp/L 59.1kW/L 80.4PS/L
41.7ft/sec 12.7m/sec
Petrol 4-stroke piston
4942cc 301.5cu in turbocharged
Vee 8 fuel injection
Compression ratio: 9.2:1
Bore: 101.6mm 4.0in
Stroke: 76.2mm 3.0in
Valve type/No: Overhead 16
Transmission: Manual
No. of forward speeds: 5
Wheels driven: Rear
Springs F/R: Coil/Coil
Brake system: PA
Brakes F/R: Disc/Drum
Steering: Rack & pinion PA
Wheelbase: 255.3cm 100.5in
Track F: 145.3cm 57.2in
Track R: 147.3cm 58.0in

Length: 456.2cm 179.6in
Width: 175.5cm 69.1in
Height: 128.5cm 50.6in
Kerb weight: 1284.8kg 2830.0lb
Fuel: 96.1L 21.1gal 25.4galUS

1929 Ford

Mustang Convertible Saleen
1988 USA
149.0mph 239.7kmh
0-60mph 96.5kmh: 6.0secs
0-1/4 mile: 14.5secs
225.0bhp 167.8kW 228.1PS
@ 4000rpm
300.0lbft 406.5Nm @ 3200rpm
168.8bhp/ton 166.0bhp/tonne
45.4bhp/L 33.9kW/L 46.1PS/L
33.3ft/sec 10.2m/sec
Petrol 4-stroke piston
4950cc 302.0cu in
Vee 8 fuel injection
Compression ratio: 9.2:1
Bore: 101.6mm 4.0in
Stroke: 76.2mm 3.0in
Valve type/No: Overhead 16
Transmission: Manual
No. of forward speeds: 5
Wheels driven: Rear
Springs F/R: Coil/Coil
Brake system: PA
Brakes F/R: Disc/Disc
Steering: Rack & pinion PA
Wheelbase: 255.3cm 100.5in
Track F: 147.1cm 57.9in
Track R: 149.1cm 58.7in
Length: 456.2cm 179.6in
Width: 175.5cm 69.1in
Height: 127.0cm 50.0in
Kerb weight: 1355.2kg 2985.0lb
Fuel: 58.3L 12.8gal 15.4galUS

1930 Ford

Mustang GT
1988 USA
148.0mph 238.1kmh
0-50mph 80.5kmh: 4.3secs
0-60mph 96.5kmh: 6.0secs
0-1/4 mile: 14.6secs
225.0bhp 167.8kW 228.1PS
@ 4000rpm
300.0lbft 406.5Nm @ 3200rpm
154.1bhp/ton 151.6bhp/tonne
45.4bhp/L 33.9kW/L 46.1PS/L
33.3ft/sec 10.2m/sec
19.2mpg 16.0mpgUS 14.7L/100km
Petrol 4-stroke piston
4950cc 302.0cu in
Vee 8 fuel injection
Compression ratio: 9.2:1
Bore: 101.6mm 4.0in
Stroke: 76.2mm 3.0in
Valve type/No: Overhead 16
Transmission: Manual
No. of forward speeds: 5
Wheels driven: Rear
Springs F/R: Coil/Coil
Brake system: PA
Brakes F/R: Disc/Drum
Steering: Rack & pinion PA
Wheelbase: 255.3cm 100.5in
Track F: 143.8cm 56.6in
Track R: 144.8cm 57.0in
Length: 455.4cm 179.3in
Width: 175.5cm 69.1in
Height: 132.3cm 52.1in
Kerb weight: 1484.6kg 3270.0lb
Fuel: 58.3L 12.8gal 15.4galUS

1931 Ford

Mustang JBA/Saleen
1988 USA
0-1/4 mile: 13.9secs
280.0bhp 208.8kW 283.9PS
@ 4500rpm
330.0lbft 447.2Nm @ 3500rpm
56.7bhp/L 42.2kW/L 57.4PS/L
37.5ft/sec 11.4m/sec
Petrol 4-stroke piston
4942cc 301.5cu in
Vee 8 fuel injection
Compression ratio: 9.2:1
Bore: 101.6mm 4.0in
Stroke: 76.2mm 3.0in
Valve type/No: Overhead 16
Transmission: Manual
No. of forward speeds: 5
Wheels driven: Rear

1932 Ford

Mustang Kaufmann
1988 USA
0-1/4 mile: 13.5secs
350.0bhp 261.0kW 354.8PS
@ 5400rpm
410.0lbft 555.6Nm @ 4100rpm
60.9bhp/L 45.4kW/L 61.7PS/L
52.5ft/sec 16.0m/sec
Petrol 4-stroke piston
5751cc 350.9cu in
Vee 8 1 Carburettor
Compression ratio: 8.8:1
Bore: 101.6mm 4.0in
Stroke: 88.9mm 3.5in
Valve type/No: Overhead 16
Transmission: Manual
No. of forward speeds: 5
Wheels driven: Rear

1933 Ford

Probe GT
1988 USA
131.0mph 210.8kmh
0-60mph 96.5kmh: 7.3secs
0-1/4 mile: 15.6secs
145.0bhp 108.1kW 147.0PS
@ 4300rpm
190.0lbft 257.5Nm @ 3500rpm
110.7bhp/ton 108.8bhp/tonne
66.4bhp/L 49.5kW/L 67.3PS/L
44.2ft/sec 13.5m/sec
24.0mpg 20.0mpgUS 11.8L/100km
Petrol 4-stroke piston
2184cc 133.2cu in turbocharged
In-line 4 fuel injection
Compression ratio: 7.8:1
Bore: 86.0mm 3.4in
Stroke: 94.0mm 3.7in
Valve type/No: Overhead 12
Transmission: Manual
No. of forward speeds: 5
Wheels driven: Front
Springs F/R: Coil/Coil
Brake system: PA ABS
Brakes F/R: Disc/Disc
Steering: Rack & pinion PA
Wheelbase: 251.5cm 99.0in
Track F: 145.5cm 57.3in
Track R: 146.6cm 57.7in
Length: 449.6cm 177.0in
Width: 174.0cm 68.5in
Height: 131.6cm 51.8in
Kerb weight: 1332.5kg 2935.0lb
Fuel: 57.1L 12.6gal 15.1galUS

1934 Ford

Sierra RS Cosworth
1988 UK
143.0mph 230.1kmh
0-50mph 80.5kmh: 4.4secs
0-60mph 96.5kmh: 5.8secs
0-1/4 mile: 14.4secs
0-1km: 26.8secs
204.0bhp 152.1kW 206.8PS
@ 6000rpm
205.0lbft 277.8Nm @ 4500rpm
171.8bhp/ton 168.9bhp/tonne
102.4bhp/L 76.3kW/L 103.8PS/L
50.5ft/sec 15.4m/sec
22.9mph 36.8kmh/1000rpm
20.3mpg 16.9mpgUS 13.9L/100km
Petrol 4-stroke piston
1993cc 121.6cu in turbocharged
In-line 4 fuel injection
Compression ratio: 8.0:1
Bore: 90.8mm 3.6in
Stroke: 76.9mm 3.0in
Valve type/No: Overhead 16
Transmission: Manual
No. of forward speeds: 5
Wheels driven: Rear
Springs F/R: Coil/Coil
Brake system: PA ABS
Brakes F/R: Disc/Disc
Steering: Rack & pinion PA
Wheelbase: 260.9cm 102.7in
Track F: 144.3cm 56.8in
Track R: 146.1cm 57.5in
Length: 449.3cm 176.9in
Width: 169.7cm 66.8in
Height: 137.7cm 54.2in
Ground clearance: 17.8cm 7.0in
Kerb weight: 1207.6kg 2660.0lb
Fuel: 60.1L 13.2gal 15.9galUS

1935 Ford

Taurus 3.8
1988 USA
115.0mph 185.0kmh
0-50mph 80.5kmh: 6.8secs
0-60mph 96.5kmh: 9.3secs
0-1/4 mile: 17.2secs
140.0bhp 104.4kW 141.9PS
@ 3800rpm
215.0lbft 291.3Nm @ 2200rpm
95.6bhp/ton 94.0bhp/tonne
36.9bhp/L 27.5kW/L 37.4PS/L
35.8ft/sec 10.9m/sec
21.0mpg 17.5mpgUS 13.4L/100km
Petrol 4-stroke piston
3797cc 231.7cu in
Vee 6 fuel injection
Compression ratio: 9.0:1
Bore: 96.8mm 3.8in
Stroke: 86.0mm 3.4in
Valve type/No: Overhead 12
Transmission: Automatic
No. of forward speeds: 4
Wheels driven: Front
Springs F/R: Coil/Coil
Brake system: PA
Brakes F/R: Disc/Drum
Steering: Rack & pinion PA
Wheelbase: 269.2cm 106.0in
Track F: 156.5cm 61.6in
Track R: 153.7cm 60.5in
Length: 478.5cm 188.4in
Width: 179.8cm 70.8in
Height: 137.9cm 54.3in
Kerb weight: 1489.1kg 3280.0lb
Fuel: 60.6L 13.3gal 16.0galUS

1936 Ford

Escort 1.3L 3-door
1989 UK
97.0mph 156.1kmh
0-50mph 80.5kmh: 9.8secs
0-60mph 96.5kmh: 14.1secs
0-1/4 mile: 19.8secs
0-1km: 35.1secs
63.0bhp 47.0kW 63.9PS
@ 5000rpm
74.5lbft 101.0Nm @ 3000rpm
76.9bhp/ton 75.6bhp/tonne
48.6bhp/L 36.2kW/L 49.2PS/L
41.2ft/sec 12.6m/sec
22.1mph 35.6kmh/1000rpm
36.1mpg 30.1mpgUS 7.8L/100km
Petrol 4-stroke piston
1297cc 79.0cu in
In-line 4 1 Carburettor
Compression ratio: 9.5:1
Bore: 74.0mm 2.9in
Stroke: 75.5mm 3.0in
Valve type/No: Overhead 8
Transmission: Manual
No. of forward speeds: 5
Wheels driven: Front
Springs F/R: Coil/Coil
Brake system: PA
Brakes F/R: Disc/Drum
Steering: Rack & pinion
Wheelbase: 239.8cm 94.4in
Track F: 138.4cm 54.5in
Track R: 143.0cm 56.3in
Length: 402.0cm 158.3in
Width: 158.8cm 62.5in
Height: 136.9cm 53.9in
Ground clearance: 17.9cm 7.0in
Kerb weight: 833.0kg 1834.8lb
Fuel: 48.2L 10.6gal 12.7galUS

1937 Ford

Fiesta 1.1LX 5-door
1989 UK
93.0mph 149.6kmh
0-50mph 80.5kmh: 10.5secs
0-60mph 96.5kmh: 15.3secs
0-1/4 mile: 20.0secs
0-1km: 37.7secs
55.0bhp 41.0kW 55.8PS
@ 5200rpm
63.5lbft 86.0Nm @ 2700rpm
63.9bhp/ton 62.9bhp/tonne
49.2bhp/L 36.7kW/L 49.9PS/L
42.9ft/sec 13.1m/sec
20.3mph 32.7kmh/1000rpm
33.2mpg 27.6mpgUS 8.5L/100km
Petrol 4-stroke piston
1118cc 68.0cu in
In-line 4 1 Carburettor
Compression ratio: 9.5:1
Bore: 68.7mm 2.7in
Stroke: 75.5mm 3.0in
Valve type/No: Overhead 8
Transmission: Manual
No. of forward speeds: 5
Wheels driven: Front
Springs F/R: Coil/Coil
Brake system: PA
Brakes F/R: Disc/Disc
Steering: Rack & pinion
Wheelbase: 244.6cm 96.3in
Length: 374.3cm 147.4in
Width: 185.4cm 73.0in
Height: 132.0cm 52.0in
Ground clearance: 18.5cm 7.3in
Kerb weight: 875.0kg 1927.3lb
Fuel: 41.9L 9.2gal 11.1galUS

1938 Ford

Fiesta 1.4 Ghia
1989 UK
100.0mph 160.9kmh
0-50mph 80.5kmh: 9.4secs
0-60mph 96.5kmh: 13.4secs
0-1/4 mile: 19.1secs
0-1km: 35.9secs
75.0bhp 55.9kW 76.0PS
@ 5600rpm
80.4lbft 109.0Nm @ 4000rpm
85.7bhp/ton 84.3bhp/tonne
53.9bhp/L 40.2kW/L 54.6PS/L
45.3ft/sec 13.8m/sec
20.6mph 33.1kmh/1000rpm
28.1mpg 23.4mpgUS 10.1L/100km
Petrol 4-stroke piston
1392cc 85.0cu in
In-line 4 1 Carburettor
Compression ratio: 9.5:1
Bore: 77.0mm 3.0in
Stroke: 74.0mm 2.9in
Valve type/No: Overhead 8
Transmission: Manual
No. of forward speeds: 5
Wheels driven: Front
Springs F/R: Coil/Coil
Brake system: PA
Brakes F/R: Disc/Drum
Steering: Rack & pinion
Wheelbase: 244.6cm 96.3in
Length: 374.3cm 147.4in
Width: 185.4cm 73.0in
Height: 132.0cm 52.0in
Ground clearance: 18.5cm 7.3in
Kerb weight: 890.0kg 1960.3lb
Fuel: 41.9L 9.2gal 11.1galUS

1939 Ford

Fiesta 1.6S
1989 UK
110.0mph 177.0kmh
0-50mph 80.5kmh: 7.3secs
0-60mph 96.5kmh: 10.2secs
0-1/4 mile: 18.0secs
0-1km: 33.0secs
90.0bhp 67.1kW 91.2PS
@ 5800rpm
98.2lbft 133.0Nm @ 4000rpm
103.6bhp/ton 101.9bhp/tonne
56.4bhp/L 42.0kW/L 57.2PS/L
50.4ft/sec 15.4m/sec
21.4mph 34.4kmh/1000rpm
29.0mpg 24.1mpgUS 9.7L/100km
Petrol 4-stroke piston
1596cc 97.0cu in
In-line 4 1 Carburettor
Compression ratio: 9.5:1
Bore: 80.0mm 3.1in
Stroke: 79.5mm 3.1in
Valve type/No: Overhead 8
Transmission: Manual
No. of forward speeds: 5
Wheels driven: Front
Springs F/R: Coil/Coil
Brake system: PA ABS
Brakes F/R: Disc/Drum
Steering: Rack & pinion
Wheelbase: 244.6cm 96.3in
Length: 374.3cm 147.4in
Width: 185.4cm 73.0in
Height: 132.0cm 52.0in
Ground clearance: 18.5cm 7.3in
Kerb weight: 883.0kg 1944.9lb
Fuel: 42.1L 9.2gal 11.1galUS

1940 Ford

Mustang 5.0 Cartech Turbo

1989 USA
185.0mph 297.7kmh
0-50mph 80.5kmh: 4.4secs
0-60mph 96.5kmh: 5.4secs
0-1/4 mile: 13.4secs
470.0bhp 350.5kW 476.5PS
@ 5500rpm
445.0lbft 603.0Nm @ 5200rpm
319.0bhp/ton 313.7bhp/tonne
95.1bhp/L 70.9kW/L 96.4PS/L
45.8ft/sec 14.0m/sec
Petrol 4-stroke piston
4942cc 301.5cu in turbocharged
Vee 8 fuel injection
Compression ratio: 9.2:1
Bore: 101.6mm 4.0in
Stroke: 76.2mm 3.0in
Valve type/No: Overhead 16
Transmission: Manual
No. of forward speeds: 5
Wheels driven: Rear
Springs F/R: Coil/Coil
Brake system: PA
Brakes F/R: Disc/Drum
Steering: Rack & pinion PA
Wheelbase: 255.3cm 100.5in
Track F: 144.0cm 56.7in
Track R: 144.8cm 57.0in
Length: 456.2cm 179.6in
Width: 175.5cm 69.1in
Height: 132.3cm 52.1in
Kerb weight: 1498.2kg 3300.0lb

1941 Ford
Mustang Saleen SSC
1989 USA
0-50mph 80.5kmh: 4.6secs
0-60mph 96.5kmh: 6.3secs
0-1/4 mile: 14.5secs
292.0bhp 217.7kW 296.0PS
@ 5200rpm
327.0lbft 443.1Nm @ 3500rpm
191.2bhp/ton 188.1bhp/tonne
59.1bhp/L 44.1kW/L 59.9PS/L
43.3ft/sec 13.2m/sec
Petrol 4-stroke piston
4942cc 301.5cu in
Vee 8 fuel injection
Compression ratio: 10.2:1
Bore: 101.6mm 4.0in
Stroke: 76.2mm 3.0in
Valve type/No: Overhead 16
Transmission: Manual
No. of forward speeds: 5
Wheels driven: Rear
Springs F/R: Coil/Coil
Brake system: PA
Brakes F/R: Disc/Disc
Steering: Rack & pinion PA
Wheelbase: 255.3cm 100.5in
Track F: 145.5cm 57.3in
Track R: 146.8cm 57.8in
Length: 456.2cm 179.6in
Width: 175.5cm 69.1in
Height: 129.5cm 51.0in
Kerb weight: 1552.7kg 3420.0lb

1942 Ford
Mustang SVO J Bittle American
1989 USA
173.0mph 278.4kmh
0-50mph 80.5kmh: 4.2secs
0-60mph 96.5kmh: 5.2secs
0-1/4 mile: 13.4secs
510.0bhp 380.3kW 517.1PS
@ 7900rpm
368.0lbft 498.6Nm @ 6400rpm
355.9bhp/ton 349.9bhp/tonne
101.2bhp/L 75.5kW/L 102.6PS/L
65.8ft/sec 20.1m/sec
Petrol 4-stroke piston
5040cc 307.5cu in
Vee 8 1 Carburettor
Compression ratio: 13.0:1
Bore: 102.6mm 4.0in
Stroke: 76.2mm 3.0in
Valve type/No: Overhead 16
Transmission: Manual
No. of forward speeds: 4
Wheels driven: Rear
Springs F/R: Coil/Coil
Brakes F/R: Disc/Disc
Steering: Rack & pinion
Wheelbase: 255.3cm 100.5in
Track F: 160.0cm 63.0in
Track R: 160.0cm 63.0in
Length: 456.2cm 179.6in
Width: 196.9cm 77.5in
Height: 129.5cm 51.0in
Kerb weight: 1457.3kg 3210.0lb

1943 Ford
Probe GT Suspension Techniques/ HKS
1989 USA
0-50mph 80.5kmh: 4.9secs
0-60mph 96.5kmh: 6.7secs
0-1/4 mile: 15.0secs
220.0bhp 164.0kW 223.0PS
@ 4000rpm
240.0lbft 325.2Nm @ 3500rpm
167.0bhp/ton 164.3bhp/tonne
100.7bhp/L 75.1kW/L 102.1PS/L
41.1ft/sec 12.5m/sec
Petrol 4-stroke piston
2184cc 133.2cu in turbocharged
In-line 4 fuel injection
Compression ratio: 7.8:1
Bore: 86.0mm 3.4in
Stroke: 94.0mm 3.7in
Valve type/No: Overhead 12
Transmission: Manual
No. of forward speeds: 5
Wheels driven: Front
Springs F/R: Coil/Coil
Brake system: PA ABS
Brakes F/R: Disc/Disc
Steering: Rack & pinion PA
Wheelbase: 251.5cm 99.0in
Track F: 145.5cm 57.3in
Track R: 146.6cm 57.7in
Length: 449.6cm 177.0in
Width: 174.0cm 68.5in
Height: 131.6cm 51.8in
Kerb weight: 1339.3kg 2950.0lb

1944 Ford
Sierra Sapphire 2000E
1989 UK
120.0mph 193.1kmh
0-50mph 80.5kmh: 7.1secs
0-60mph 96.5kmh: 10.0secs
0-1/4 mile: 17.3secs
0-1km: 32.2secs
125.0bhp 93.2kW 126.7PS
@ 5600rpm
128.4lbft 174.0Nm @ 2500rpm
104.0bhp/ton 102.3bhp/tonne
62.6bhp/L 46.6kW/L 63.4PS/L
52.7ft/sec 16.0m/sec
21.7mph 34.9kmh/1000rpm
28.8mpg 24.0mpgUS 9.8L/100km
Petrol 4-stroke piston
1998cc 122.0cu in
In-line 4 fuel injection
Compression ratio: 10.3:1
Bore: 86.0mm 3.4in
Stroke: 86.0mm 3.4in
Valve type/No: Overhead 8
Transmission: Manual
No. of forward speeds: 5
Wheels driven: Rear
Springs F/R: Coil/Coil
Brake system: PA ABS
Brakes F/R: Disc/Drum
Steering: Rack & pinion PA
Wheelbase: 260.8cm 102.7in
Track F: 145.0cm 57.1in
Track R: 146.6cm 57.7in
Length: 446.7cm 175.9in
Width: 192.0cm 75.6in
Height: 135.8cm 53.5in
Ground clearance: 17.9cm 7.0in
Kerb weight: 1222.0kg 2691.6lb
Fuel: 60.1L 13.2gal 15.9galUS

1945 Ford
Sierra XR 4x4
1989 UK
130.0mph 209.2kmh
0-50mph 80.5kmh: 6.2secs
0-60mph 96.5kmh: 8.6secs
0-1/4 mile: 16.6secs
0-1km: 30.4secs
150.0bhp 111.9kW 152.1PS
@ 5700rpm
172.7lbft 234.0Nm @ 3000rpm
126.1bhp/ton 124.0bhp/tonne
51.1bhp/L 38.1kW/L 51.8PS/L
44.8ft/sec 13.7m/sec
22.4mph 36.0kmh/1000rpm
17.0mpg 14.2mpgUS 16.6L/100km
Petrol 4-stroke piston
2933cc 179.0cu in
Vee 6 fuel injection
Compression ratio: 9.5:1
Bore: 93.0mm 3.7in
Stroke: 72.0mm 2.8in
Valve type/No: Overhead 12
Transmission: Manual
No. of forward speeds: 5
Wheels driven: 4-wheel drive
Springs F/R: Coil/Coil
Brake system: PA
Brakes F/R: Disc/Disc
Steering: Rack & pinion PA
Wheelbase: 260.6cm 102.6in
Track F: 146.8cm 57.8in
Track R: 146.6cm 57.7in
Length: 445.8cm 175.5in
Width: 172.8cm 68.0in
Height: 137.8cm 54.3in
Ground clearance: 17.9cm 7.0in
Kerb weight: 1210.0kg 2665.2lb
Fuel: 60.1L 13.2gal 15.9galUS

1946 Ford
Taurus SHO
1989 USA
140.0mph 225.3kmh
0-50mph 80.5kmh: 5.0secs
0-60mph 96.5kmh: 6.6secs
0-1/4 mile: 15.2secs
220.0bhp 164.0kW 223.0PS
@ 6000rpm
200.0lbft 271.0Nm @ 4800rpm
148.9bhp/ton 146.4bhp/tonne
73.7bhp/L 54.9kW/L 74.7PS/L
52.5ft/sec 16.0m/sec
26.4mpg 22.0mpgUS 10.7L/100km
Petrol 4-stroke piston
2986cc 182.2cu in
Vee 6 fuel injection
Compression ratio: 9.8:1
Bore: 89.0mm 3.5in
Stroke: 80.0mm 3.1in
Valve type/No: Overhead 24
Transmission: Manual
No. of forward speeds: 5
Wheels driven: Front
Springs F/R: Coil/Coil
Brake system: PA
Brakes F/R: Disc/Disc
Steering: Rack & pinion PA
Wheelbase: 269.2cm 106.0in
Track F: 156.5cm 61.6in
Track R: 153.7cm 60.5in
Length: 478.5cm 188.4in
Width: 179.8cm 70.8in
Height: 137.9cm 54.3in
Ground clearance: 14.0cm 5.5in
Kerb weight: 1502.7kg 3310.0lb
Fuel: 70.4L 15.5gal 18.6galUS

1947 Ford
Thunderbird Super Coupe
1989 USA
140.0mph 225.3kmh
0-50mph 80.5kmh: 5.5secs
0-60mph 96.5kmh: 7.4secs
0-1/4 mile: 15.9secs
210.0bhp 156.6kW 212.9PS
@ 4000rpm
315.0lbft 426.8Nm @ 2600rpm
124.8bhp/ton 122.7bhp/tonne
55.3bhp/L 41.2kW/L 56.1PS/L
37.7ft/sec 11.5m/sec
20.4mpg 17.0mpgUS 13.8L/100km
Petrol 4-stroke piston
3797cc 231.7cu in supercharged
Vee 6 fuel injection
Compression ratio: 8.2:1
Bore: 96.8mm 3.8in
Stroke: 86.0mm 3.4in
Valve type/No: Overhead 12
Transmission: Manual
No. of forward speeds: 5
Wheels driven: Rear
Springs F/R: Coil/Coil
Brake system: PA ABS
Brakes F/R: Disc/Disc
Steering: Rack & pinion PA
Wheelbase: 287.0cm 113.0in
Track F: 156.0cm 61.4in
Track R: 152.9cm 60.2in
Length: 504.7cm 198.7in
Width: 184.7cm 72.7in
Height: 133.9cm 52.7in
Ground clearance: 13.7cm 5.4in
Kerb weight: 1711.6kg 3770.0lb
Fuel: 71.9L 15.8gal 19.0galUS

1948 Ford
Thunderbird Super Coupe Ford Engineering
1989 USA
160.0mph 257.4kmh
0-50mph 80.5kmh: 4.0secs
0-60mph 96.5kmh: 5.2secs
0-1/4 mile: 14.1secs
330.0bhp 246.1kW 334.6PS
@ 5500rpm
403.0lbft 546.1Nm @ 4000rpm
201.6bhp/ton 198.2bhp/tonne
86.9bhp/L 64.8kW/L 88.1PS/L
51.8ft/sec 15.8m/sec
Petrol 4-stroke piston
3797cc 231.7cu in supercharged
Vee 6 fuel injection
Compression ratio: 8.0:1
Bore: 96.8mm 3.8in
Stroke: 86.0mm 3.4in
Valve type/No: Overhead 12
Transmission: Manual
No. of forward speeds: 5
Wheels driven: Rear
Springs F/R: Coil/Coil
Brake system: PA ABS
Brakes F/R: Disc/Disc
Steering: Rack & pinion PA
Wheelbase: 287.0cm 113.0in
Track F: 156.0cm 61.4in
Track R: 152.9cm 60.2in
Length: 504.7cm 198.7in
Width: 184.7cm 72.7in
Height: 132.1cm 52.0in
Kerb weight: 1664.8kg 3667.0lb

1949 Ford
Fiesta RS Turbo
1990 UK
132.0mph 212.4kmh
0-50mph 80.5kmh: 5.9secs
0-60mph 96.5kmh: 7.9secs
0-1/4 mile: 16.1secs
0-1km: 28.9secs
133.0bhp 99.2kW 134.8PS
@ 5500rpm
135.1lbft 183.0Nm @ 2400rpm
148.6bhp/ton 146.1bhp/tonne
83.3bhp/L 62.1kW/L 84.5PS/L
47.8ft/sec 14.6m/sec
20.8mph 33.5kmh/1000rpm
23.6mpg 19.7mpgUS 12.0L/100km
Petrol 4-stroke piston
1596cc 97.0cu in turbocharged
In-line 4 fuel injection
Compression ratio: 8.2:1
Bore: 80.0mm 3.1in
Stroke: 79.5mm 3.1in
Valve type/No: Overhead 8
Transmission: Manual
No. of forward speeds: 5
Wheels driven: Front
Springs F/R: Coil/Coil
Brake system: PA ABS
Brakes F/R: Disc/Drum
Steering: Rack & pinion
Wheelbase: 244.6cm 96.3in
Track F: 143.0cm 56.3in
Track R: 137.7cm 54.2in
Length: 380.0cm 149.6in
Width: 163.1cm 64.2in
Height: 132.1cm 52.0in
Ground clearance: 18.5cm 7.3in
Kerb weight: 910.0kg 2004.4lb
Fuel: 42.1L 9.2gal 11.1galUS

1950 Ford
Fiesta XR2i
1990 UK
120.0mph 193.1kmh
0-50mph 80.5kmh: 6.3secs
0-60mph 96.5kmh: 8.9secs
0-1/4 mile: 16.7secs
0-1km: 30.8secs
110.0bhp 82.0kW 111.5PS
@ 6000rpm
101.8lbft 138.0Nm @ 2800rpm
121.9bhp/ton 119.8bhp/tonne
68.9bhp/L 51.4kW/L 69.9PS/L
52.2ft/sec 15.9m/sec
20.3mph 32.7kmh/1000rpm
28.4mpg 23.6mpgUS 9.9L/100km
Petrol 4-stroke piston
1596cc 97.0cu in
In-line 4 fuel injection
Compression ratio: 9.7:1
Bore: 80.0mm 3.1in

Stroke: 79.5mm 3.1in
Valve type/No: Overhead 8
Transmission: Manual
No. of forward speeds: 5
Wheels driven: Front
Springs F/R: Coil/Coil
Brake system: PA ABS
Brakes F/R: Disc/Disc
Steering: Rack & pinion
Wheelbase: 244.6cm 96.3in
Length: 374.4cm 147.4in
Width: 185.4cm 73.0in
Height: 132.1cm 52.0in
Ground clearance: 18.5cm 7.3in
Kerb weight: 918.0kg 2022.0lb
Fuel: 41.9L 9.2gal 11.1galUS

1951 Ford
Granada 2.5 GL Diesel
1990 UK
107.0mph 172.2kmh
0-50mph 80.5kmh: 9.4secs
0-60mph 96.5kmh: 13.4secs
0-1/4 mile: 19.2secs
0-1km: 35.5secs
92.0bhp 68.6kW 93.3PS
@ 4150rpm
150.6lbft 204.0Nm @ 2250rpm
67.3bhp/ton 66.2bhp/tonne
36.8bhp/L 27.5kW/L 37.3PS/L
40.8ft/sec 12.4m/sec
24.3mph 39.1kmh/1000rpm
30.6mpg 25.5mpgUS 9.2L/100km
Diesel 4-stroke piston
2498cc 152.0cu in turbocharged
In-line 4 fuel injection
Compression ratio: 21.1:1
Bore: 94.0mm 3.7in
Stroke: 90.0mm 3.5in
Valve type/No: Overhead 8
Transmission: Manual
No. of forward speeds: 5
Wheels driven: Rear
Springs F/R: Coil/Coil
Brake system: PA ABS
Brakes F/R: Disc/Disc
Steering: Rack & pinion PA
Wheelbase: 276.1cm 1u8.7in
Track F: 147.7cm 58.1in
Track R: 149.2cm 58.7in
Length: 466.9cm 183.8in
Width: 176.6cm 69.5in
Height: 145.0cm 57.1in
Ground clearance: 17.9cm 7.0in
Kerb weight: 1390.0kg 3061.7lb
Fuel: 70.1L 15.4gal 18.5galUS

1952 Ford
Granada Ghia X 2.9 EFi Saloon
1990 UK
125.0mph 201.1kmh
0-50mph 80.5kmh: 7.0secs
0-60mph 96.5kmh: 9.5secs
0-1/4 mile: 17.3secs
0-1km: 31.8secs
150.0bhp 111.9kW 152.1PS
@ 5700rpm
172.0lbft 233.0Nm @ 5900rpm
113.8bhp/ton 111.9bhp/tonne
51.1bhp/L 38.1kW/L 51.8PS/L
44.8ft/sec 13.7m/sec
26.4mph 42.5kmh/1000rpm
18.9mpg 15.7mpgUS 14.9L/100km
Petrol 4-stroke piston
2933cc 179.0cu in
Vee 6 fuel injection
Compression ratio: 9.5:1
Bore: 93.0mm 3.7in
Stroke: 72.0mm 2.8in
Valve type/No: Overhead 12
Transmission: Automatic
No. of forward speeds: 4
Wheels driven: Rear
Springs F/R: Coil/Coil
Brake system: PA ABS
Brakes F/R: Disc/Disc
Steering: Rack & pinion PA
Wheelbase: 226.1cm 89.0in
Track F: 147.7cm 58.1in
Track R: 149.2cm 58.7in
Length: 466.9cm 183.8in
Width: 176.6cm 69.5in
Height: 145.0cm 57.1in
Ground clearance: 17.9cm 7.0in
Kerb weight: 1340.0kg 2951.5lb
Fuel: 70.1L 15.4gal 18.5galUS

1953 Ford
Granada Scorpio 2.0i Auto
1990 UK
114.0mph 183.4kmh
0-50mph 80.5kmh: 8.5secs
0-60mph 96.5kmh: 11.6secs
0-1/4 mile: 18.6secs
0-1km: 33.9secs
125.0bhp 93.2kW 126.7PS
@ 5600rpm
128.4lbft 174.0Nm @ 2500rpm
92.4bhp/ton 90.9bhp/tonne
62.6bhp/L 46.6kW/L 63.4PS/L
52.7ft/sec 16.0m/sec
24.4mph 39.3kmh/1000rpm
25.2mpg 21.0mpgUS 11.2L/100km
Petrol 4-stroke piston
1998cc 122.0cu in
In-line 4 fuel injection
Compression ratio: 10.3:1
Bore: 86.0mm 3.4in
Stroke: 86.0mm 3.4in
Valve type/No: Overhead 8
Transmission: Automatic
No. of forward speeds: 4
Wheels driven: Rear
Springs F/R: Coil/Coil
Brake system: PA ABS
Brakes F/R: Disc/Disc
Steering: Rack & pinion PA
Wheelbase: 276.1cm 108.7in
Track F: 147.6cm 58.1in
Track R: 149.1cm 58.7in
Length: 466.3cm 183.6in
Width: 196.3cm 77.3in
Height: 139.2cm 54.8in
Ground clearance: 17.8cm 7.0in
Kerb weight: 1375.0kg 3028.6lb
Fuel: 70.1L 15.4gal 18.5galUS

1954 Ford
Mustang GT Convertible
1990 USA
135.0mph 217.2kmh
0-50mph 80.5kmh: 6.0secs
0-60mph 96.5kmh: 8.0secs
0-1/4 mile: 16.1secs
225.0bhp 167.8kW 228.1PS
@ 4000rpm
300.0lbft 406.5Nm @ 3200rpm
144.4bhp/ton 142.0bhp/tonne
45.5bhp/L 33.9kW/L 46.2PS/L
33.3ft/sec 10.2m/sec
17.2mpg 14.3mpgUS 16.4L/100km
Petrol 4-stroke piston
4942cc 301.5cu in
Vee 8 fuel injection
Compression ratio: 9.2:1
Bore: 101.1mm 4.0in
Stroke: 76.2mm 3.0in
Valve type/No: Overhead 16
Transmission: Automatic
No. of forward speeds: 4
Wheels driven: Rear
Springs F/R: Coil/Coil
Brake system: PA
Brakes F/R: Disc/Drum
Steering: Rack & pinion PA
Wheelbase: 255.3cm 100.5in
Track F: 143.8cm 56.6in
Track R: 144.8cm 57.0in
Length: 456.2cm 179.6in
Width: 175.5cm 69.1in
Height: 132.3cm 52.1in
Kerb weight: 1584.5kg 3490.0lb
Fuel: 58.3L 12.8gal 15.4galUS

1955 Ford
Mustang LX 5.0L
1990 USA
148.0mph 238.1kmh
0-50mph 80.5kmh: 4.9secs
0-60mph 96.5kmh: 6.6secs
0-1/4 mile: 15.3secs
225.0bhp 167.8kW 228.1PS
@ 4000rpm
300.0lbft 406.5Nm @ 3200rpm
153.7bhp/ton 151.1bhp/tonne
45.5bhp/L 33.9kW/L 46.2PS/L
33.3ft/sec 10.2m/sec
20.4mpg 17.0mpgUS 13.8L/100km
Petrol 4-stroke piston
4942cc 301.5cu in
Vee 8 fuel injection
Compression ratio: 9.2:1
Bore: 101.1mm 4.0in
Stroke: 76.2mm 3.0in
Valve type/No: Overhead 16
Transmission: Manual
No. of forward speeds: 5
Wheels driven: Rear
Springs F/R: Coil/Coil
Brake system: PA
Brakes F/R: Disc/Drum
Steering: Rack & pinion PA
Wheelbase: 255.3cm 100.5in
Track F: 143.8cm 56.6in
Track R: 144.8cm 57.0in
Length: 456.2cm 179.6in
Width: 175.5cm 69.1in
Height: 132.3cm 52.1in
Kerb weight: 1489.1kg 3280.0lb
Fuel: 58.3L 12.8gal 15.4galUS

1956 Ford
Probe GT
1990 USA
131.0mph 210.8kmh
0-60mph 96.5kmh: 7.6secs
0-1/4 mile: 16.0secs
145.0bhp 108.1kW 147.0PS
@ 4300rpm
190.0lbft 257.5Nm @ 3500rpm
110.7bhp/ton 108.8bhp/tonne
66.4bhp/L 49.5kW/L 67.3PS/L
44.2ft/sec 13.5m/sec
28.1mpg 23.4mpgUS 10.1L/100km
Petrol 4-stroke piston
2184cc 133.2cu in turbocharged
In-line 4 fuel injection
Compression ratio: 7.8:1
Bore: 86.0mm 3.4in
Stroke: 94.0mm 3.7in
Valve type/No: Overhead 12
Transmission: Manual
No. of forward speeds: 5
Wheels driven: Front
Springs F/R: Coil/Coil
Brake system: PA ABS
Brakes F/R: Disc/Disc
Steering: Rack & pinion PA
Wheelbase: 251.5cm 99.0in
Track F: 145.5cm 57.3in
Track R: 146.6cm 57.7in
Length: 449.6cm 177.0in
Width: 174.0cm 68.5in
Height: 131.6cm 51.8in
Kerb weight: 1332.5kg 2935.0lb
Fuel: 57.1L 12.6gal 15.1galUS

1957 Ford
Probe LX
1990 USA
130.0mph 209.2kmh
0-60mph 96.5kmh: 8.2secs
0-1/4 mile: 16.2secs
140.0bhp 104.4kW 141.9PS
@ 4800rpm
160.0lbft 216.8Nm @ 3000rpm
108.1bhp/ton 106.3bhp/tonne
48.5bhp/L 36.2kW/L 49.2PS/L
42.0ft/sec 12.8m/sec
25.2mpg 21.0mpgUS 11.2L/100km
Petrol 4-stroke piston
2886cc 176.1cu in
Vee 6 fuel injection
Compression ratio: 9.3:1
Bore: 89.0mm 3.5in
Stroke: 80.0mm 3.1in
Valve type/No: Overhead 12
Transmission: Manual
No. of forward speeds: 5
Wheels driven: Front
Springs F/R: Coil/Coil
Brake system: PA ABS
Brakes F/R: Disc/Disc
Steering: Rack & pinion PA
Wheelbase: 251.5cm 99.0in
Track F: 145.5cm 57.3in
Track R: 146.6cm 57.7in
Length: 449.6cm 177.0in
Width: 172.5cm 67.9in
Height: 131.8cm 51.9in
Kerb weight: 1316.6kg 2900.0lb
Fuel: 57.1L 12.6gal 15.1galUS

1958 Ford
Sierra Sapphire Cosworth 4x4
1990 UK
146.0mph 234.9kmh
0-50mph 80.5kmh: 4.8secs
0-60mph 96.5kmh: 6.6secs
0-1/4 mile: 14.3secs
0-1km: 26.8secs
220.0bhp 164.0kW 223.0PS
@ 6250rpm
214.0lbft 290.0Nm @ 3500rpm
171.4bhp/ton 168.6bhp/tonne
110.4bhp/L 82.3kW/L 111.9PS/L
52.6ft/sec 16.0m/sec
22.2mph 35.7kmh/1000rpm
21.6mpg 18.0mpgUS 13.1L/100km
Petrol 4-stroke piston
1993cc 122.0cu in turbocharged
In-line 4 fuel injection
Compression ratio: 8.0:1
Bore: 91.0mm 3.6in
Stroke: 77.0mm 3.0in
Valve type/No: Overhead 16
Transmission: Manual
No. of forward speeds: 5
Wheels driven: 4-wheel drive
Springs F/R: Coil/Coil
Brake system: PA ABS
Brakes F/R: Disc/Disc
Steering: Rack & pinion PA
Wheelbase: 260.9cm 102.7in
Track F: 144.3cm 56.8in
Track R: 146.1cm 57.5in
Length: 423.9cm 166.9in
Width: 169.7cm 66.8in
Height: 137.7cm 54.2in
Ground clearance: 17.8cm 7.0in
Kerb weight: 1305.0kg 2874.4lb
Fuel: 59.1L 13.0gal 15.6galUS

1959 Ford
Crown Victoria LX
1991 USA
125.0mph 201.1kmh
0-50mph 80.5kmh: 7.2secs
0-60mph 96.5kmh: 9.9secs
0-1/4 mile: 17.4secs
210.0bhp 156.6kW 212.9PS
@ 4600rpm
270.0lbft 365.9Nm @ 3400rpm
117.2bhp/ton 115.2bhp/tonne
45.6bhp/L 34.0kW/L 46.3PS/L
45.2ft/sec 13.8m/sec
27.0mpg 22.5mpgUS 10.5L/100km
Petrol 4-stroke piston
4601cc 280.7cu in
Vee 8 fuel injection
Compression ratio: 9.0:1
Bore: 90.2mm 3.5in
Stroke: 90.0mm 3.5in
Valve type/No: Overhead 16
Transmission: Automatic
No. of forward speeds: 4
Wheels driven: Rear
Springs F/R: Coil/Coil
Brake system: PA ABS
Brakes F/R: Disc/Disc
Steering: Recirculating ball PA
Wheelbase: 290.6cm 114.4in
Track F: 159.5cm 62.8in
Track R: 160.8cm 63.3in
Length: 539.5cm 212.4in
Width: 197.6cm 77.8in
Height: 144.0cm 56.7in
Ground clearance: 15.5cm 6.1in
Kerb weight: 1822.8kg 4015.0lb
Fuel: 75.7L 16.6gal 20.0galUS

1960 Ford
Escort 1.4LX
1991 UK
108.0mph 173.8kmh
0-50mph 80.5kmh: 9.2secs
0-60mph 96.5kmh: 12.8secs
0-1/4 mile: 18.8secs
0-1km: 34.2secs
73.0bhp 54.4kW 74.0PS
@ 5500rpm
79.7lbft 108.0Nm @ 4000rpm
73.5bhp/ton 72.3bhp/tonne
52.4bhp/L 39.1kW/L 53.2PS/L
44.8ft/sec 13.6m/sec
22.8mph 36.7kmh/1000rpm
29.0mpg 24.1mpgUS 9.7L/100km
Petrol 4-stroke piston
1392cc 85.0cu in
In-line 4 1 Carburettor
Compression ratio: 8.5:1
Bore: 77.2mm 3.0in
Stroke: 74.3mm 2.9in
Valve type/No: Overhead 8
Transmission: Manual
No. of forward speeds: 5
Wheels driven: Front

Springs F/R: Coil/Torsion bar
Brake system: PA ABS
Brakes F/R: Disc/Drum
Steering: Rack & pinion
Wheelbase: 252.5cm 99.4in
Track F: 143.8cm 56.6in
Track R: 146.1cm 57.5in
Length: 403.6cm 158.9in
Width: 168.4cm 66.3in
Height: 135.1cm 53.2in
Kerb weight: 1010.0kg 2224.7lb
Fuel: 55.1L 12.1gal 14.5galUS

1961 Ford

Escort 1.6 Ghia Estate
1991 UK
108.0mph 173.8kmh
0-50mph 80.5kmh: 8.7secs
0-60mph 96.5kmh: 12.3secs
0-1/4 mile: 18.9secs
0-1km: 34.7secs
90.0bhp 67.1kW 91.2PS
@ 5800rpm
95.9lbft 130.0Nm @ 4000rpm
82.1bhp/ton 80.7bhp/tonne
56.4bhp/L 42.0kW/L 57.1PS/L
50.7ft/sec 15.5m/sec
22.7mph 36.5kmh/1000rpm
27.8mpg 23.1mpgUS 10.2L/100km
Petrol 4-stroke piston
1597cc 97.0cu in
In-line 4 1 Carburettor
Compression ratio: 9.5:1
Bore: 80.0mm 3.1in
Stroke: 80.0mm 3.1in
Valve type/No: Overhead 8
Transmission: Manual
No. of forward speeds: 5
Wheels driven: Front
Springs F/R: Coil/Coil
Brake system: PA ABS
Brakes F/R: Disc/Drum
Steering: Rack & pinion PA
Wheelbase: 252.5cm 99.4in
Track F: 143.8cm 56.6in
Track R: 146.1cm 57.5in
Length: 428.8cm 168.8in
Width: 168.4cm 66.3in
Height: 135.1cm 53.2in
Kerb weight: 1115.0kg 2455.9lb
Fuel: 55.1L 12.1gal 14.5galUS

1962 Ford

Escort Cabriolet
1991 UK
116.0mph 186.6kmh
0-50mph 80.5kmh: 7.3secs
0-60mph 96.5kmh: 10.2secs
0-1/4 mile: 17.7secs
0-1km: 32.6secs
108.0bhp 80.5kW 109.5PS
@ 6000rpm
104.1lbft 141.0Nm @ 4500rpm
98.3bhp/ton 96.7bhp/tonne
67.7bhp/L 50.5kW/L 68.6PS/L
52.2ft/sec 15.9m/sec
22.7mph 36.5kmh/1000rpm
28.6mpg 23.8mpgUS 9.9L/100km
Petrol 4-stroke piston
1596cc 97.0cu in
In-line 4 fuel injection
Compression ratio: 9.7:1
Bore: 80.0mm 3.1in
Stroke: 79.5mm 3.1in
Valve type/No: Overhead 8
Transmission: Manual
No. of forward speeds: 5
Wheels driven: Front
Springs F/R: Coil/Coil
Brake system: PA
Brakes F/R: Disc/Drum
Steering: Rack & pinion PA
Wheelbase: 251.5cm 99.0in
Track F: 144.8cm 57.0in
Track R: 144.8cm 57.0in
Length: 403.9cm 159.0in
Width: 170.2cm 67.0in
Height: 139.7cm 55.0in
Kerb weight: 1117.0kg 2460.3lb
Fuel: 66.0L 14.5gal 17.4galUS

1963 Ford

Escort GT
1991 USA
120.0mph 193.1kmh
0-50mph 80.5kmh: 6.6secs
0-60mph 96.5kmh: 8.9secs
0-1/4 mile: 16.8secs
127.0bhp 94.7kW 128.8PS
@ 6500rpm
114.0lbft 154.5Nm @ 4500rpm
113.6bhp/ton 111.7bhp/tonne
69.0bhp/L 51.5kW/L 70.0PS/L
60.5ft/sec 18.4m/sec
33.6mpg 28.0mpgUS 8.4L/100km
Petrol 4-stroke piston
1840cc 112.3cu in
In-line 4 fuel injection
Compression ratio: 9.0:1
Bore: 83.0mm 3.3in
Stroke: 85.0mm 3.3in
Valve type/No: Overhead 16
Transmission: Manual
No. of forward speeds: 5
Wheels driven: Front
Springs F/R: Coil/Coil
Brake system: PA
Brakes F/R: Disc/Disc
Steering: Rack & pinion PA
Wheelbase: 249.9cm 98.4in
Track F: 143.5cm 56.5in
Track R: 143.5cm 56.5in
Length: 434.1cm 170.9in
Width: 169.4cm 66.7in
Height: 133.4cm 52.5in
Ground clearance: 13.0cm 5.1in
Kerb weight: 1137.3kg 2505.0lb
Fuel: 45.0L 9.9gal 11.9galUS

1964 Ford

Escort Millen
1991 USA
0-60mph 96.5kmh: 6.2secs
0-1/4 mile: 14.8secs
220.0bhp 164.0kW 223.0PS
@ 6000rpm
245.0lbft 332.0Nm @ 3500rpm
189.9bhp/ton 186.7bhp/tonne
119.6bhp/L 89.2kW/L 121.2PS/L
55.8ft/sec 17.0m/sec
Petrol 4-stroke piston
1840cc 112.3cu in turbocharged
In-line 4 fuel injection
Compression ratio: 7.9:1
Bore: 83.0mm 3.3in
Stroke: 85.0mm 3.3in
Valve type/No: Overhead 16
Transmission: Manual
No. of forward speeds: 5
Wheels driven: Front
Brake system: PA
Brakes F/R: Disc/Disc
Steering: Rack & pinion
Wheelbase: 249.9cm 98.4in
Track F: 143.5cm 56.5in
Track R: 143.5cm 56.5in
Length: 434.1cm 170.9in
Width: 167.4cm 65.9in
Height: 133.4cm 52.5in
Kerb weight: 1178.1kg 2595.0lb
Fuel: 45.0L 9.9gal 11.9galUS

1965 Ford

Festiva Shogun
1991 USA
0-60mph 96.5kmh: 5.3secs
0-1/4 mile: 14.0secs
220.0bhp 164.0kW 223.0PS
@ 6000rpm
200.0lbft 271.0Nm @ 4800rpm
191.7bhp/ton 188.5bhp/tonne
73.7bhp/L 54.9kW/L 74.7PS/L
52.5ft/sec 16.0m/sec
Petrol 4-stroke piston
2986cc 182.2cu in
Vee 6 fuel injection
Compression ratio: 9.8:1
Bore: 89.0mm 3.5in
Stroke: 80.0mm 3.1in
Valve type/No: Overhead 24
Transmission: Manual
No. of forward speeds: 5
Wheels driven: Rear
Brake system: PA
Brakes F/R: Disc/Disc
Steering: Rack & pinion
Wheelbase: 231.1cm 91.0in
Track F: 142.2cm 56.0in
Track R: 157.5cm 62.0in
Length: 365.8cm 144.0in
Width: 186.7cm 73.5in
Height: 135.1cm 53.2in
Kerb weight: 1166.8kg 2570.0lb
Fuel: 56.8L 12.5gal 15.0galUS

1966 Ford

Mustang Holdener
1991 USA
174.0mph 280.0kmh
0-60mph 96.5kmh: 4.9secs
0-1/4 mile: 13.3secs
450.0bhp 335.6kW 456.2PS
@ 5600rpm
420.0lbft 569.1Nm @ 4300rpm
362.6bhp/ton 356.5bhp/tonne
91.1bhp/L 67.9kW/L 92.3PS/L
46.7ft/sec 14.2m/sec
Petrol 4-stroke piston
4942cc 301.5cu in supercharged
Vee 8
Compression ratio: 8.0:1
Bore: 101.0mm 4.0in
Stroke: 76.2mm 3.0in
Valve type/No: Overhead 16
Transmission: Manual
No. of forward speeds: 5
Wheels driven: Rear
Springs F/R: Coil/Coil
Brake system: PA
Brakes F/R: Disc/Drum
Steering: Rack & pinion PA
Wheelbase: 255.3cm 100.5in
Track F: 143.8cm 56.6in
Track R: 144.8cm 57.0in
Length: 456.2cm 179.6in
Width: 175.5cm 69.1in
Height: 132.3cm 52.1in
Kerb weight: 1262.1kg 2780.0lb

1967 Ford

Mustang NOS/Saleen
1991 USA
186.0mph 299.3kmh
0-60mph 96.5kmh: 5.7secs
0-1/4 mile: 14.1secs
310.0bhp 231.2kW 314.3PS
@ 6000rpm
323.0lbft 437.7Nm @ 4500rpm
231.8bhp/ton 228.0bhp/tonne
62.7bhp/L 46.8kW/L 63.6PS/L
50.0ft/sec 15.2m/sec
Petrol 4-stroke piston
4942cc 301.5cu in
Vee 8 fuel injection
Compression ratio: 9.2:1
Bore: 101.6mm 4.0in
Stroke: 76.2mm 3.0in
Valve type/No: Overhead 16
Transmission: Manual
No. of forward speeds: 5
Wheels driven: Rear
Springs F/R: Coil/Coil
Brake system: PA
Brakes F/R: Disc/Disc
Steering: Rack & pinion PA
Wheelbase: 255.3cm 100.5in
Track F: 147.1cm 57.9in
Track R: 149.1cm 58.7in
Length: 456.2cm 179.6in
Width: 175.5cm 69.1in
Height: 127.0cm 50.0in
Kerb weight: 1359.7kg 2995.0lb

1968 Ford

Orion 1.6i Ghia
1991 UK
121.0mph 194.7kmh
0-50mph 80.5kmh: 7.2secs
0-60mph 96.5kmh: 10.0secs
0-1/4 mile: 17.6secs
0-1km: 32.2secs
108.0bhp 80.5kW 109.5PS
@ 6000rpm
101.8lbft 138.0Nm @ 4500rpm
102.6bhp/ton 100.9bhp/tonne
67.7bhp/L 50.5kW/L 68.6PS/L
52.2ft/sec 15.9m/sec
22.8mph 36.7kmh/1000rpm
29.2mpg 24.3mpgUS 9.7L/100km
Petrol 4-stroke piston
1596cc 97.0cu in
In-line 4 fuel injection
Compression ratio: 9.7:1
Bore: 80.0mm 3.1in
Stroke: 79.5mm 3.1in
Valve type/No: Overhead 8
Transmission: Manual
No. of forward speeds: 5
Wheels driven: Front
Springs F/R: Coil/Coil
Brake system: PA ABS
Brakes F/R: Disc/Drum
Steering: Rack & pinion PA
Wheelbase: 252.5cm 99.4in
Track F: 144.0cm 56.7in
Track R: 143.9cm 56.7in
Length: 422.9cm 166.5in
Width: 187.5cm 73.8in
Height: 134.5cm 53.0in
Kerb weight: 1070.0kg 2356.8lb
Fuel: 55.1L 12.1gal 14.5galUS

1969 Ford

Probe GT
1991 USA
120.0mph 193.1kmh
0-60mph 96.5kmh: 7.4secs
0-1/4 mile: 15.4secs
145.0bhp 108.1kW 147.0PS
@ 4300rpm
190.0lbft 257.5Nm @ 3500rpm
112.0bhp/ton 110.1bhp/tonne
66.4bhp/L 49.5kW/L 67.3PS/L
44.2ft/sec 13.5m/sec
24.6mpg 20.5mpgUS 11.5L/100km
Petrol 4-stroke piston
2184cc 133.2cu in turbocharged
In-line 4 fuel injection
Compression ratio: 7.8:1
Bore: 86.0mm 3.4in
Stroke: 94.0mm 3.7in
Valve type/No: Overhead 12
Transmission: Automatic
No. of forward speeds: 4
Wheels driven: Front
Springs F/R: Coil/Coil
Brake system: PA ABS
Brakes F/R: Disc/Disc
Steering: Rack & pinion PA
Wheelbase: 251.5cm 99.0in
Track F: 145.5cm 57.3in
Track R: 146.6cm 57.7in
Length: 449.6cm 177.0in
Width: 174.0cm 68.5in
Height: 131.6cm 51.8in
Kerb weight: 1316.6kg 2900.0lb
Fuel: 57.1L 12.6gal 15.1galUS

1970 Ford

Scorpio 24v
1991 UK
140.0mph 225.3kmh
0-50mph 80.5kmh: 6.5secs
0-60mph 96.5kmh: 8.5secs
0-1/4 mile: 16.6secs
0-1km: 30.1secs
195.0bhp 145.4kW 197.7PS
@ 5750rpm
203.0lbft 275.0Nm @ 4500rpm
133.1bhp/ton 130.9bhp/tonne
66.4bhp/L 49.5kW/L 67.4PS/L
45.2ft/sec 13.8m/sec
25.5mph 41.0kmh/1000rpm
21.0mpg 17.5mpgUS 13.5L/100km
Petrol 4-stroke piston
2935cc 179.0cu in
Vee 6 fuel injection
Compression ratio: 9.7:1
Bore: 93.0mm 3.7in
Stroke: 72.0mm 2.8in
Valve type/No: Overhead 24
Transmission: Automatic
No. of forward speeds: 4
Wheels driven: Rear
Springs F/R: Coil/Coil
Brake system: PA ABS
Brakes F/R: Disc/Disc
Steering: Rack & pinion PA
Wheelbase: 276.1cm 108.7in
Track F: 147.7cm 58.1in
Track R: 150.0cm 59.1in
Length: 474.4cm 186.8in
Width: 176.6cm 69.5in
Height: 145.0cm 57.1in
Ground clearance: 17.9cm 7.0in
Kerb weight: 1490.0kg 3281.9lb
Fuel: 70.0L 15.4gal 18.5galUS

1971 Ford

Taurus SHO
1991 USA
140.0mph 225.3kmh
0-60mph 96.5kmh: 7.6secs
0-1/4 mile: 15.9secs
220.0bhp 164.0kW 223.0PS
@ 6200rpm
200.0lbft 271.0Nm @ 4800rpm
144.5bhp/ton 142.1bhp/tonne

73.7bhp/L 54.9kW/L 74.7PS/L
54.2ft/sec 16.5m/sec
26.4mpg 22.0mpgUS 10.7L/100km
Petrol 4-stroke piston
2986cc 182.2cu in
Vee 6 fuel injection
Compression ratio: 9.8:1
Bore: 89.0mm 3.5in
Stroke: 80.0mm 3.1in
Valve type/No: Overhead 24
Transmission: Manual
No. of forward speeds: 5
Wheels driven: Front
Springs F/R: Coil/Coil
Brake system: PA ABS
Brakes F/R: Disc/Disc
Steering: Rack & pinion PA
Wheelbase: 269.2cm 106.0in
Track F: 156.5cm 61.6in
Track R: 153.7cm 60.5in
Length: 478.5cm 188.4in
Width: 179.8cm 70.8in
Height: 137.9cm 54.3in
Kerb weight: 1548.1kg 3410.0lb
Fuel: 60.6L 13.3gal 16.0galUS

1972 Ford
Thunderbird LX
1991 USA
145.0mph 233.3kmh
0-60mph 96.5kmh: 9.0secs
0-1/4 mile: 16.7secs
200.0bhp 149.1kW 202.8PS
@ 4000rpm
275.0lbft 372.6Nm @ 3000rpm
116.1bhp/ton 114.1bhp/tonne
40.5bhp/L 30.2kW/L 41.0PS/L
33.3ft/sec 10.2m/sec
20.4mpg 17.0mpgUS 13.8L/100km
Petrol 4-stroke piston
4942cc 301.5cu in
Vee 8 fuel injection
Compression ratio: 9.0:1
Bore: 101.6mm 4.0in
Stroke: 76.2mm 3.0in
Valve type/No: Overhead 16
Transmission: Automatic
No. of forward speeds: 4
Wheels driven: Rear
Springs F/R: Coil/Coil
Brake system: PA ABS
Brakes F/R: Disc/Disc
Steering: Rack & pinion PA
Wheelbase: 287.0cm 113.0in
Track F: 156.5cm 61.6in
Track R: 152.9cm 60.2in
Length: 504.7cm 198.7in
Width: 184.7cm 72.7in
Height: 133.9cm 52.7in
Kerb weight: 1752.4kg 3860.0lb
Fuel: 71.9L 15.8gal 19.0galUS

1973 Ford
Escort RS2000
1992 UK
131.1mph 211.0kmh
0-50mph 80.5kmh: 6.0secs
0-60mph 96.5kmh: 8.3secs
0-1/4 mile: 16.4secs
0-1km: 29.7secs
150.0bhp 111.9kW 152.1PS
@ 6000rpm
140.2lbft 190.0Nm @ 4500rpm
135.6bhp/ton 133.3bhp/tonne
75.1bhp/L 56.0kW/L 76.1PS/L
56.5ft/sec 17.2m/sec
20.2mph 32.5kmh/1000rpm
26.4mpg 22.0mpgUS 10.7L/100km
Petrol 4-stroke piston
1998cc 122.0cu in
In-line 4 fuel injection
Compression ratio: 10.3:1
Bore: 86.0mm 3.4in
Stroke: 86.0mm 3.4in
Valve type/No: Overhead 16
Transmission: Manual
No. of forward speeds: 5
Wheels driven: Front
Springs F/R: Coil/Coil
Brake system: PA ABS
Brakes F/R: Disc/Disc
Steering: Rack & pinion PA
Wheelbase: 251.5cm 99.0in
Track F: 144.8cm 57.0in
Track R: 144.8cm 57.0in
Length: 403.9cm 159.0in
Width: 170.2cm 67.0in
Height: 139.7cm 55.0in
Kerb weight: 1125.0kg 2478.0lb
Fuel: 54.6L 12.0gal 14.4galUS

1974 Ford
Escort XR3i
1992 UK
125.0mph 201.1kmh
0-50mph 80.5kmh: 6.3secs
0-60mph 96.5kmh: 8.6secs
0-1/4 mile: 16.7secs
0-1km: 30.5secs
130.0bhp 96.9kW 131.8PS
@ 6250rpm
119.0lbft 161.2Nm @ 4500rpm
72.4bhp/L 54.0kW/L 73.4PS/L
60.1ft/sec 18.3m/sec
20.2mph 32.5kmh/1000rpm
28.6mpg 23.8mpgUS 9.9L/100km
Petrol 4-stroke piston
1796cc 109.6cu in
In-line 4 fuel injection
Compression ratio: 10.0:1
Bore: 80.6mm 3.2in
Stroke: 88.0mm 3.5in
Valve type/No: Overhead 16
Transmission: Manual
No. of forward speeds: 5
Wheels driven: Front
Springs F/R: Coil/Coil
Brake system: PA
Brakes F/R: Disc/Disc
Steering: Rack & pinion PA
Wheelbase: 252.5cm 99.4in
Track F: 144.3cm 56.8in
Track R: 143.9cm 56.7in
Length: 404.0cm 159.1in
Width: 169.2cm 66.6in
Height: 139.7cm 55.0in
Fuel: 68.2L 15.0gal 18.0galUS

1975 Ford
Mustang LX
1992 USA
140.0mph 225.3kmh
0-50mph 80.5kmh: 5.4secs
0-60mph 96.5kmh: 7.1secs
0-1/4 mile: 15.5secs
225.0bhp 167.8kW 228.1PS
@ 4200rpm
300.0lbft 406.5Nm @ 3200rpm
156.8bhp/ton 154.1bhp/tonne
45.5bhp/L 33.9kW/L 46.2PS/L
35.0ft/sec 10.7m/sec
22.8mpg 19.0mpgUS 12.4L/100km
Petrol 4-stroke piston
4942cc 301.5cu in
Vee 8 fuel injection
Compression ratio: 9.0:1
Bore: 101.6mm 4.0in
Stroke: 76.2mm 3.0in
Valve type/No: Overhead 16
Transmission: Manual
No. of forward speeds: 5
Wheels driven: Rear
Springs F/R: Coil/Coil
Brake system: PA
Brakes F/R: Disc/Drum
Steering: Rack & pinion PA
Wheelbase: 255.3cm 100.5in
Track F: 143.8cm 56.6in
Track R: 144.8cm 57.0in
Length: 456.2cm 179.6in
Width: 173.5cm 68.3in
Height: 132.3cm 52.1in
Kerb weight: 1459.6kg 3215.0lb
Fuel: 58.3L 12.8gal 15.4galUS

1976 Ford
Taurus LX
1992 USA
126.0mph 202.7kmh
0-60mph 96.5kmh: 10.4secs
0-1/4 mile: 17.7secs
140.0bhp 104.4kW 141.9PS
@ 3800rpm
215.0lbft 291.3Nm @ 2200rpm
94.7bhp/ton 93.2bhp/tonne
36.9bhp/L 27.5kW/L 37.4PS/L
35.8ft/sec 10.9m/sec
21.0mpg 17.5mpgUS 13.4L/100km
Petrol 4-stroke piston
3791cc 231.3cu in
Vee 6 fuel injection
Compression ratio: 9.0:1
Bore: 96.8mm 3.8in
Stroke: 86.0mm 3.4in
Valve type/No: Overhead 12
Transmission: Automatic
No. of forward speeds: 4
Wheels driven: Front
Springs F/R: Coil/Coil
Brake system: PA ABS
Brakes F/R: Disc/Disc
Steering: Rack & pinion PA
Wheelbase: 269.2cm 106.0in
Track F: 156.5cm 61.6in
Track R: 153.7cm 60.5in
Length: 487.7cm 192.0in
Width: 180.8cm 71.2in
Height: 137.4cm 54.1in
Kerb weight: 1502.7kg 3310.0lb
Fuel: 60.6L 13.3gal 16.0galUS

1977 Franklin
29.4hp Saloon
1929 USA
64.0mph 103.0kmh
16.0mpg 13.3mpgUS 17.7L/100km
Petrol 4-stroke piston
4497cc 274.4cu in
In-line 6
Bore: 88.9mm 3.5in
Stroke: 120.7mm 4.7in
Transmission: Manual
No. of forward speeds: 3
Wheels driven: Rear
Brakes F/R: Drum/Drum
Wheelbase: 317.5cm 125.0in
Track F: 147.3cm 58.0in
Track R: 147.3cm 58.0in
Length: 490.2cm 193.0in
Width: 195.6cm 77.0in
Height: 190.5cm 75.0in
Kerb weight: 1784.2kg 3930.0lb
Fuel: 81.9L 18.0gal 21.6galUS

1978 Frazer
Saloon
1949 USA
83.0mph 133.5kmh
0-50mph 80.5kmh: 14.2secs
0-60mph 96.5kmh: 21.8secs
112.0bhp 83.5kW 113.5PS
@ 3600rpm
69.1bhp/ton 67.9bhp/tonne
30.2bhp/L 22.5kW/L 30.6PS/L
43.7ft/sec 13.3m/sec
17.0mpg 14.2mpgUS 16.6L/100km
Petrol 4-stroke piston
3706cc 226.1cu in
In-line 6
Compression ratio: 7.3:1
Bore: 84.1mm 3.3in
Stroke: 111.1mm 4.4in
Valve type/No: Side 12
Transmission: Manual with overdrive
No. of forward speeds: 6
Wheels driven: Rear
Springs F/R: Coil
Brakes F/R: Drum/Drum
Wheelbase: 313.7cm 123.5in
Track F: 147.3cm 58.0in
Track R: 152.4cm 60.0in
Length: 527.1cm 207.5in
Width: 185.2cm 72.9in
Height: 166.9cm 65.7in
Ground clearance: 18.3cm 7.2in
Kerb weight: 1649.4kg 3633.0lb
Fuel: 76.4L 16.8gal 20.2galUS

1979 Frazer-Nash
Super Sports
1930 UK
77.2mph 124.2kmh
47.0bhp 35.0kW 47.6PS
@ 4000rpm
60.6bhp/ton 59.6bhp/tonne
31.4bhp/L 23.4kW/L 31.8PS/L
43.8ft/sec 13.3m/sec
30.0mpg 25.0mpgUS 9.4L/100km
Petrol 4-stroke piston
1496cc 91.3cu in
In-line 4 1 Carburettor
Bore: 69.0mm 2.7in
Stroke: 100.0mm 3.9in
Valve type/No: Overhead 8
Transmission: Manual
No. of forward speeds: 4
Wheels driven: Rear
Brakes F/R: Drum/Drum
Wheelbase: 269.2cm 106.0in
Track F: 121.9cm 48.0in
Track R: 121.9cm 48.0in
Kerb weight: 788.1kg 1736.0lb
Fuel: 45.5L 10.0gal 12.0galUS

1980 Frazer-Nash
Boulogne II
1931 UK
87.3mph 140.5kmh
28.0mpg 23.3mpgUS 10.1L/100km
Petrol 4-stroke piston
1496cc 91.3cu in
In-line 4
Bore: 69.0mm 2.7in
Stroke: 100.0mm 3.9in
Valve type/No: Overhead 8
Transmission: Manual
No. of forward speeds: 4
Wheels driven: Rear
Brakes F/R: Drum/Drum
Wheelbase: 251.5cm 99.0in
Track F: 116.8cm 46.0in
Track R: 116.8cm 46.0in
Length: 381.0cm 150.0in
Width: 127.0cm 50.0in
Height: 101.6cm 40.0in
Kerb weight: 737.3kg 1624.0lb
Fuel: 54.6L 12.0gal 14.4galUS

1981 Frazer-Nash
1.5-litre
1933 UK
87.3mph 140.5kmh
0-50mph 80.5kmh: 12.6secs
0-60mph 96.5kmh: 16.0secs
24.0mpg 20.0mpgUS 11.8L/100km
Petrol 4-stroke piston
1498cc 91.4cu in
In-line 6 3 Carburettor
Bore: 57.0mm 2.2in
Stroke: 97.9mm 3.8in
Valve type/No: Overhead 12
Transmission: Manual
No. of forward speeds: 4
Wheels driven: Rear
Brakes F/R: Drum/Drum
Kerb weight: 940.7kg 2072.0lb
Fuel: 59.1L 13.0gal 15.6galUS

1982 Frazer-Nash
TT Replica
1933 UK
86.5mph 139.2kmh
0-50mph 80.5kmh: 11.2secs
0-60mph 96.5kmh: 18.0secs
32.0mpg 26.6mpgUS 8.8L/100km
Petrol 4-stroke piston
1496cc 91.3cu in
In-line 4
Bore: 69.0mm 2.7in
Stroke: 100.0mm 3.9in
Transmission: Manual
No. of forward speeds: 4
Wheels driven: Rear
Brakes F/R: Drum/Drum
Kerb weight: 839.0kg 1848.0lb
Fuel: 54.6L 12.0gal 14.4galUS

1983 Frazer-Nash
14hp Sports Tourer
1934 UK
84.5mph 136.0kmh
0-50mph 80.5kmh: 10.6secs
0-60mph 96.5kmh: 14.0secs
26.0mpg 21.6mpgUS 10.9L/100km
Petrol 4-stroke piston
1657cc 101.1cu in
In-line 6
Bore: 60.0mm 2.4in
Stroke: 97.9mm 3.8in
Transmission: Manual
No. of forward speeds: 4
Wheels driven: Rear
Brakes F/R: Drum/Drum
Kerb weight: 889.8kg 1960.0lb
Fuel: 54.6L 12.0gal 14.4galUS

1984 Frazer-Nash
1.5-litre
1937 UK
87.3mph 140.5kmh
0-50mph 80.5kmh: 9.8secs

0-60mph 96.5kmh: 13.8secs
25.0mpg 20.8mpgUS 11.3L/100km
Petrol 4-stroke piston
1496cc 91.3cu in
In-line 6 3 Carburettor
Bore: 57.0mm 2.2in
Stroke: 97.9mm 3.8in
Valve type/No: Overhead 12
Transmission: Manual
No. of forward speeds: 4
Wheels driven: Rear
Brakes F/R: Drum/Drum
Kerb weight: 996.1kg 2194.0lb
Fuel: 54.6L 12.0gal 14.4galUS

1985 Frazer-Nash
Targa Florio Turismo
1953 UK
116.0mph 186.6kmh
0-50mph 80.5kmh: 8.0secs
0-60mph 96.5kmh: 10.4secs
0-1/4 mile: 17.8secs
100.0bhp 74.6kW 101.4PS
@ 5250rpm
118.0lbft 159.9Nm @ 3750rpm
115.5bhp/ton 113.6bhp/tonne
50.7bhp/L 37.8kW/L 51.4PS/L
55.1ft/sec 16.8m/sec
20.6mph 33.1kmh/1000rpm
21.2mpg 17.7mpgUS 13.3L/100km
Petrol 4-stroke piston
1971cc 120.3cu in
In-line 6
Compression ratio: 7.5:1
Bore: 66.0mm 2.6in
Stroke: 96.0mm 3.8in
Valve type/No: Overhead 12
Transmission: Manual
No. of forward speeds: 4
Wheels driven: Rear
Springs F/R: Leaf/Torsion bar
Brakes F/R: Drum/Drum
Wheelbase: 243.8cm 96.0in
Track F: 121.9cm 48.0in
Track R: 127.0cm 50.0in
Length: 381.0cm 150.0in
Width: 147.3cm 58.0in
Height: 129.5cm 51.0in
Ground clearance: 15.7cm 6.2in
Kerb weight: 880.3kg 1939.0lb
Fuel: 54.6L 12.0gal 14.4galUS

1986 Frazer-Nash
Targa Florio Fast Roadster
1955 UK
114.0mph 183.4kmh
0-50mph 80.5kmh: 7.3secs
0-60mph 96.5kmh: 9.6secs
0-1/4 mile: 17.4secs
105.0bhp 78.3kW 106.5PS
@ 5000rpm
123.0lbft 166.7Nm @ 3750rpm
126.3bhp/ton 124.2bhp/tonne
53.3bhp/L 39.7kW/L 54.0PS/L
52.5ft/sec 16.0m/sec
21.5mph 34.6kmh/1000rpm
20.5mpg 17.1mpgUS 13.8L/100km
Petrol 4-stroke piston
1971cc 120.3cu in
In-line 6
Compression ratio: 8.5:1
Bore: 66.0mm 2.6in
Stroke: 96.0mm 3.8in
Valve type/No: Overhead 12
Transmission: Manual
No. of forward speeds: 4
Wheels driven: Rear
Springs F/R: Leaf/Torsion bar
Brakes F/R: Drum/Drum
Wheelbase: 243.8cm 96.0in
Track F: 121.9cm 48.0in
Track R: 121.9cm 48.0in
Length: 381.0cm 150.0in
Width: 144.8cm 57.0in
Height: 129.5cm 51.0in
Ground clearance: 16.5cm 6.5in
Kerb weight: 845.3kg 1862.0lb
Fuel: 77.3L 17.0gal 20.4galUS

1987 Frazer-Nash BMW
12.5hp Saloon
1935 Germany
75.0mph 120.7kmh
0-50mph 80.5kmh: 16.6secs
0-60mph 96.5kmh: 26.2secs
27.0mpg 22.5mpgUS 10.5L/100km
Petrol 4-stroke piston
1490cc 90.9cu in
In-line 6
Bore: 58.0mm 2.3in
Stroke: 94.0mm 3.7in
Valve type/No: Overhead 12
Transmission: Manual
No. of forward speeds: 4
Wheels driven: Rear
Brakes F/R: Drum/Drum
Kerb weight: 890.7kg 1962.0lb
Fuel: 38.7L 8.5gal 10.2galUS

1988 Frazer-Nash BMW
Type 55 Cabriolet
1935 Germany
80.3mph 129.2kmh
0-50mph 80.5kmh: 12.6secs
0-60mph 96.5kmh: 17.6secs
24.0mpg 20.0mpgUS 11.8L/100km
Petrol 4-stroke piston
1911cc 116.6cu in
In-line 6
Bore: 65.0mm 2.6in
Stroke: 96.0mm 3.8in
Valve type/No: Overhead 12
Transmission: Manual
No. of forward speeds: 4
Wheels driven: Rear
Brakes F/R: Drum/Drum
Kerb weight: 902.5kg 1988.0lb
Fuel: 45.5L 10.0gal 12.0galUS

1989 Frazer-Nash BMW
Grand Prix Two-seater
1937 Germany
103.4mph 166.4kmh
0-50mph 80.5kmh: 6.9secs
0-60mph 96.5kmh: 9.5secs
18.0mpg 15.0mpgUS 15.7L/100km
Petrol 4-stroke piston
1971cc 120.3cu in
In-line 6
Bore: 66.0mm 2.6in
Stroke: 96.0mm 3.8in
Valve type/No: Overhead 12
Transmission: Manual
No. of forward speeds: 4
Wheels driven: Rear
Brakes F/R: Drum/Drum
Kerb weight: 743.6kg 1638.0lb
Fuel: 45.5L 10.0gal 12.0galUS

1990 Frazer-Nash BMW
Type 326 Saloon
1938 Germany
76.2mph 122.6kmh
0-50mph 80.5kmh: 17.0secs
0-60mph 96.5kmh: 29.5secs
25.0mpg 20.8mpgUS 11.3L/100km
Petrol 4-stroke piston
1971cc 120.3cu in
In-line 6
Bore: 66.0mm 2.6in
Stroke: 96.0mm 3.8in
Valve type/No: Overhead 12
Transmission: Manual
No. of forward speeds: 4
Wheels driven: Rear
Brakes F/R: Drum/Drum
Kerb weight: 1115.0kg 2456.0lb
Fuel: 61.4L 13.5gal 16.2galUS

1991 Frazer-Nash BMW
Type 327 Cabriolet
1939 Germany
96.7mph 155.6kmh
0-50mph 80.5kmh: 11.2secs
0-60mph 96.5kmh: 15.2secs
85.0bhp 63.4kW 86.2PS
@ 4500rpm
76.9bhp/ton 75.6bhp/tonne
43.1bhp/L 32.2kW/L 43.7PS/L
47.2ft/sec 14.4m/sec
22.0mpg 18.3mpgUS 12.8L/100km
Petrol 4-stroke piston
1971cc 120.3cu in
In-line 6 3 Carburettor
Compression ratio: 7.5:1
Bore: 66.0mm 2.6in
Stroke: 96.0mm 3.8in
Valve type/No: Overhead 12
Transmission: Manual
No. of forward speeds: 4
Wheels driven: Rear
Brakes F/R: Drum/Drum
Kerb weight: 1124.6kg 2477.0lb
Fuel: 54.6L 12.0gal 14.4galUS

1992 Frazer-Nash BMW
2000TI
1967 Germany
110.0mph 177.0kmh
0-50mph 80.5kmh: 7.7secs
0-60mph 96.5kmh: 10.8secs
0-1/4 mile: 17.7secs
0-1km: 32.9secs
135.0bhp 100.7kW 136.9PS
@ 5800rpm
123.0lbft 166.7Nm @ 3600rpm
122.2bhp/ton 120.2bhp/tonne
67.8bhp/L 50.6kW/L 68.8PS/L
50.7ft/sec 15.5m/sec
18.4mph 29.6kmh/1000rpm
21.1mpg 17.6mpgUS 13.4L/100km
Petrol 4-stroke piston
1990cc 121.4cu in
In-line 4 2 Carburettor
Compression ratio: 9.3:1
Bore: 89.0mm 3.5in
Stroke: 80.0mm 3.1in
Valve type/No: Overhead 8
Transmission: Manual
No. of forward speeds: 4
Wheels driven: Rear
Springs F/R: Coil/Coil
Brake system: PA
Brakes F/R: Disc/Drum
Steering: Worm & roller
Wheelbase: 255.3cm 100.5in
Track F: 132.1cm 52.0in
Track R: 137.2cm 54.0in
Length: 454.7cm 179.0in
Width: 165.1cm 65.0in
Height: 144.0cm 56.7in
Ground clearance: 16.5cm 6.5in
Kerb weight: 1123.2kg 2474.0lb
Fuel: 54.6L 12.0gal 14.4galUS

1993 Frisky
Coupe
1958 UK
56.0mph 90.1kmh
0-50mph 80.5kmh: 33.1secs
0-1/4 mile: 27.2secs
16.0bhp 11.9kW 16.2PS
@ 5500rpm
18.0lbft 24.4Nm @ 4000rpm
47.4bhp/ton 46.6bhp/tonne
49.4bhp/L 36.8kW/L 50.1PS/L
38.2ft/sec 11.6m/sec
56.5mpg 47.0mpgUS 5.0L/100km
Petrol 2-stroke piston
324cc 19.8cu in
In-line 2
Compression ratio: 7.2:1
Bore: 57.0mm 2.2in
Stroke: 63.5mm 2.5in
Valve type/No: Ports
Transmission: Manual
No. of forward speeds: 4
Wheels driven: Rear
Springs F/R: Rubber/Coil
Brakes F/R: Drum/Drum
Wheelbase: 152.4cm 60.0in
Track F: 122.4cm 48.2in
Track R: 81.3cm 32.0in
Length: 285.8cm 112.5in
Width: 141.0cm 55.5in
Height: 124.5cm 49.0in
Ground clearance: 16.5cm 6.5in
Kerb weight: 343.2kg 756.0lb
Fuel: 15.9L 3.5gal 4.2galUS

1994 Geo
Storm GSi
1991 Japan
120.0mph 193.1kmh
0-60mph 96.5kmh: 9.3secs
0-1/4 mile: 16.9secs
130.0bhp 96.9kW 131.8PS
@ 7000rpm
102.0lbft 138.2Nm @ 5800rpm
118.9bhp/ton 116.9bhp/tonne
81.9bhp/L 61.0kW/L 83.0PS/L
60.5ft/sec 18.4m/sec
32.4mpg 27.0mpgUS 8.7L/100km
Petrol 4-stroke piston
1588cc 96.9cu in
In-line 4 fuel injection
Compression ratio: 9.8:1
Bore: 80.0mm 3.1in
Stroke: 79.0mm 3.1in
Valve type/No: Overhead 16
Transmission: Manual
No. of forward speeds: 5
Wheels driven: Front
Springs F/R: Coil/Coil
Brake system: PA
Brakes F/R: Disc/Disc
Steering: Rack & pinion PA
Wheelbase: 245.1cm 96.5in
Track F: 143.0cm 56.3in
Track R: 140.2cm 55.2in
Length: 415.0cm 163.4in
Width: 169.4cm 66.7in
Height: 129.8cm 51.1in
Kerb weight: 1112.3kg 2450.0lb
Fuel: 46.9L 10.3gal 12.4galUS

1995 Gilbern
GT
1961 UK
91.0mph 146.4kmh
0-50mph 80.5kmh: 12.6secs
0-60mph 96.5kmh: 17.4secs
0-1/4 mile: 20.9secs
68.0bhp 50.7kW 68.9PS
@ 5700rpm
64.8lbft 87.8Nm @ 3000rpm
96.3bhp/ton 94.7bhp/tonne
71.7bhp/L 53.5kW/L 72.7PS/L
47.5ft/sec 14.5m/sec
15.4mph 24.8kmh/1000rpm
28.3mpg 23.6mpgUS 10.0L/100km
Petrol 4-stroke piston
948cc 57.8cu in
In-line 4 1 Carburettor
Compression ratio: 8.3:1
Bore: 62.9mm 2.5in
Stroke: 76.2mm 3.0in
Valve type/No: Overhead 8
Transmission: Manual
No. of forward speeds: 4
Wheels driven: Rear
Springs F/R: Coil/Coil
Brakes F/R: Disc/Drum
Wheelbase: 236.2cm 93.0in
Track F: 127.0cm 50.0in
Track R: 125.7cm 49.5in
Length: 381.0cm 150.0in
Width: 152.4cm 60.0in
Height: 133.4cm 52.5in
Ground clearance: 16.5cm 6.5in
Kerb weight: 718.2kg 1582.0lb
Fuel: 40.9L 9.0gal 10.8galUS

1996 Gilbern
Invader
1969 UK
116.0mph 186.6kmh
0-50mph 80.5kmh: 7.4secs
0-60mph 96.5kmh: 10.7secs
0-1/4 mile: 17.8secs
0-1km: 32.6secs
140.0bhp 104.4kW 141.9PS
@ 4750rpm
181.5lbft 245.9Nm @ 3000rpm
127.7bhp/ton 125.6bhp/tonne
46.8bhp/L 34.9kW/L 47.4PS/L
37.6ft/sec 11.5m/sec
21.1mph 33.9kmh/1000rpm
19.6mpg 16.3mpgUS 14.4L/100km
Petrol 4-stroke piston
2994cc 182.7cu in
Vee 6 1 Carburettor
Compression ratio: 8.9:1
Bore: 93.7mm 3.7in
Stroke: 72.4mm 2.8in
Valve type/No: Overhead 12
Transmission: Manual with overdrive
No. of forward speeds: 6
Wheels driven: Rear
Springs F/R: Coil/Coil
Brake system: PA
Brakes F/R: Disc/Drum

Steering: Rack & pinion
Wheelbase: 235.5cm 92.7in
Track F: 137.2cm 54.0in
Track R: 133.4cm 52.5in
Length: 403.9cm 159.0in
Width: 165.1cm 65.0in
Height: 129.5cm 51.0in
Ground clearance: 15.2cm 6.0in
Kerb weight: 1115.0kg 2456.0lb
Fuel: 63.7L 14.0gal 16.8galUS

1997 Ginetta

G21S
1976 UK
119.0mph 191.5kmh
0-50mph 80.5kmh: 6.5secs
0-60mph 96.5kmh: 9.2secs
0-1/4 mile: 17.0secs
0-1km: 32.0secs
98.0bhp 73.1kW 99.4PS
@ 5000rpm
106.0lbft 143.6Nm @ 4000rpm
122.2bhp/ton 120.1bhp/tonne
56.8bhp/L 42.4kW/L 57.6PS/L
45.1ft/sec 13.7m/sec
22.5mph 36.2kmh/1000rpm
25.5mpg 21.2mpgUS 11.1L/100km
Petrol 4-stroke piston
1725cc 105.2cu in
In-line 4 2 Carburettor
Compression ratio: 9.6:1
Bore: 81.5mm 3.2in
Stroke: 82.5mm 3.2in
Valve type/No: Overhead 8
Transmission: Manual with overdrive
No. of forward speeds: 6
Wheels driven: Rear
Springs F/R: Coil/Coil
Brakes F/R: Disc/Drum
Steering: Rack & pinion
Wheelbase: 231.1cm 91.0in
Track F: 128.8cm 50.7in
Track R: 129.5cm 51.0in
Length: 397.5cm 156.5in
Width: 160.0cm 63.0in
Height: 116.8cm 46.0in
Ground clearance: 12.7cm 5.0in
Kerb weight: 815.8kg 1797.0lb
Fuel: 45.5L 10.0gal 12.0galUS

1998 Ginetta

G32
1990 UK
116.0mph 186.6kmh
0-50mph 80.5kmh: 6.4secs
0-60mph 96.5kmh: 9.0secs
0-1/4 mile: 16.8secs
0-1km: 31.4secs
110.0bhp 82.0kW 111.5PS
@ 6000rpm
104.1lbft 141.0Nm @ 2800rpm
127.1bhp/ton 125.0bhp/tonne
68.8bhp/L 51.3kW/L 69.8PS/L
52.2ft/sec 15.9m/sec
22.6mph 36.4kmh/1000rpm
23.3mpg 19.4mpgUS 12.1L/100km
Petrol 4-stroke piston
1598cc 97.0cu in
In-line 4 fuel injection
Compression ratio: 9.5:1
Bore: 80.0mm 3.1in
Stroke: 79.5mm 3.1in
Valve type/No: Overhead 8
Transmission: Manual
No. of forward speeds: 5
Wheels driven: Rear
Springs F/R: Coil/Coil
Brake system: PA
Brakes F/R: Disc/Disc
Steering: Rack & pinion PA
Wheelbase: 221.0cm 87.0in
Track F: 139.7cm 55.0in
Track R: 139.7cm 55.0in
Length: 375.9cm 148.0in
Width: 165.1cm 65.0in
Height: 116.8cm 46.0in
Kerb weight: 880.0kg 1938.3lb
Fuel: 44.1L 9.7gal 11.7galUS

1999 Glas

1300GT
1965 Germany
98.0mph 157.7kmh
0-50mph 80.5kmh: 8.4secs
0-60mph 96.5kmh: 12.5secs
0-1/4 mile: 18.9secs
88.0bhp 65.6kW 89.2PS
@ 5500rpm
94.0lbft 127.4Nm @ 3500rpm
102.9bhp/ton 101.2bhp/tonne
68.8bhp/L 51.3kW/L 69.7PS/L
43.8ft/sec 13.4m/sec
17.1mph 27.5kmh/1000rpm
Petrol 4-stroke piston
1280cc 78.1cu in
In-line 4 2 Carburettor
Compression ratio: 9.3:1
Bore: 74.9mm 2.9in
Stroke: 72.9mm 2.9in
Valve type/No: Overhead 8
Transmission: Manual
No. of forward speeds: 4
Wheels driven: Rear
Springs F/R: Coil/Leaf
Brakes F/R: Disc/Drum
Steering: Worm & roller
Wheelbase: 231.9cm 91.3in
Track F: 125.7cm 49.5in
Track R: 120.1cm 47.3in
Length: 404.9cm 159.4in
Width: 154.9cm 61.0in
Height: 128.0cm 50.4in
Ground clearance: 15.2cm 6.0in
Kerb weight: 869.4kg 1915.0lb
Fuel: 55.6L 12.2gal 14.7galUS

2000 Glas

1700GT
1966 Germany
112.0mph 180.2kmh
0-50mph 80.5kmh: 8.3secs
0-60mph 96.5kmh: 11.2secs
0-1/4 mile: 18.2secs
112.0bhp 83.5kW 113.5PS
@ 5500rpm
108.0lbft 146.3Nm @ 3000rpm
124.8bhp/ton 122.7bhp/tonne
66.6bhp/L 49.7kW/L 67.5PS/L
20.0mph 32.2kmh/1000rpm
Petrol 4-stroke piston
1682cc 102.6cu in
In-line 4 2 carburettor
Compression ratio: 9.7:1
Bore: 78.0mm 3.1in
Valve type/No: Overhead 8
Transmission: Manual
No. of forward speeds: 4
Wheels driven: Rear
Springs F/R: Coil/Leaf
Brakes F/R: Disc/Drum
Steering: Worm & roller
Wheelbase: 233.7cm 92.0in
Track F: 126.0cm 49.6in
Track R: 119.9cm 47.2in
Length: 410.5cm 161.6in
Width: 155.4cm 61.2in
Height: 128.0cm 50.4in
Ground clearance: 15.0cm 5.9in
Kerb weight: 912.5kg 2010.0lb
Fuel: 55.6L 12.2gal 14.7galUS

2001 Glas

L1700
1974 Germany
91.0mph 146.4kmh
0-50mph 80.5kmh: 11.8secs
0-60mph 96.5kmh: 17.1secs
0-1/4 mile: 20.5secs
80.0bhp 59.7kW 81.1PS
@ 4800rpm
99.8lbft 135.2Nm @ 2500rpm
79.7bhp/ton 78.3bhp/tonne
47.6bhp/L 35.5kW/L 48.2PS/L
46.1ft/sec 14.1m/sec
18.0mph 29.0kmh/1000rpm
28.9mpg 24.1mpgUS 9.8L/100km
Petrol 4-stroke piston
1682cc 102.6cu in
In-line 4 1 Carburettor
Compression ratio: 8.5:1
Bore: 78.0mm 3.1in
Stroke: 88.0mm 3.5in
Valve type/No: Overhead 8
Transmission: Manual
No. of forward speeds: 4
Wheels driven: Rear
Springs F/R: Coil/Leaf
Brakes F/R: Disc/Drum
Steering: Worm & roller
Wheelbase: 250.2cm 98.5in
Track F: 131.8cm 51.9in
Track R: 131.8cm 51.9in
Length: 454.7cm 179.0in
Width: 156.2cm 61.5in
Height: 138.4cm 54.5in
Ground clearance: 15.2cm 6.0in
Kerb weight: 1021.0kg 2249.0lb
Fuel: 57.8L 12.7gal 15.3galUS

2002 GM

Impact
1990 USA
75.0mph 120.7kmh
0-60mph 96.5kmh: 8.0secs
0-1/4 mile: 16.7secs
57.0bhp 42.5kW 57.8PS
@ 6600rpm
47.0lbft 63.7Nm @ 6000rpm
58.0bhp/ton 57.1bhp/tonne
AC electric
No. of forward speeds: 1
Wheels driven: Front
Springs F/R: Coil/Coil
Brakes F/R: Disc/Drum
Steering: Rack & pinion
Wheelbase: 241.3cm 95.0in
Track F: 147.1cm 57.9in
Track R: 122.9cm 48.4in
Length: 464.8cm 183.0in
Width: 173.2cm 68.2in
Height: 120.7cm 47.5in
Kerb weight: 998.8kg 2200.0lb

2003 GMC

Safari Cargo Mover
1985 USA
95.0mph 152.9kmh
0-50mph 80.5kmh: 8.3secs
0-60mph 96.5kmh: 11.9secs
0-1/4 mile: 18.4secs
145.0bhp 108.1kW 147.0PS
@ 4000rpm
225.0lbft 304.9Nm @ 2400rpm
86.1bhp/ton 84.7bhp/tonne
33.7bhp/L 25.1kW/L 34.2PS/L
38.7ft/sec 11.8m/sec
33.5mph 53.9kmh/1000rpm
16.8mpg 14.0mpgUS 16.8L/100km
Petrol 4-stroke piston
4300cc 262.4cu in
Vee 6 1 Carburettor
Compression ratio: 9.3:1
Bore: 101.6mm 4.0in
Stroke: 88.4mm 3.5in
Valve type/No: Overhead 12
Transmission: Automatic
No. of forward speeds: 4
Wheels driven: Rear
Springs F/R: Coil/Leaf
Brake system: PA
Brakes F/R: Disc/Drum
Steering: Recirculating ball PA
Wheelbase: 281.9cm 111.0in
Track F: 165.4cm 65.1in
Track R: 165.4cm 65.1in
Length: 449.1cm 176.8in
Width: 195.6cm 77.0in
Height: 182.1cm 71.7in
Ground clearance: 18.5cm 7.3in
Kerb weight: 1711.6kg 3770.0lb
Fuel: 102.2L 22.5gal 27.0galUS

2004 Goggomobil

TS400
1959 Germany
61.0mph 98.1kmh
0-50mph 80.5kmh: 28.5secs
0-1/4 mile: 26.0secs
20.0bhp 14.9kW 20.3PS
@ 5000rpm
23.9lbft 32.4Nm @ 3900rpm
44.8bhp/ton 44.0bhp/tonne
51.0bhp/L 38.0kW/L 51.7PS/L
30.6ft/sec 9.3m/sec
10.9mph 17.5kmh/1000rpm
47.8mpg 39.8mpgUS 5.9L/100km
Petrol 2-stroke piston
392cc 23.9cu in
In-line 2 1 Carburettor
Compression ratio: 6.0:1
Bore: 67.0mm 2.6in
Stroke: 56.0mm 2.2in
Valve type/No: Ports
Transmission: Manual
No. of forward speeds: 4
Wheels driven: Rear
Springs F/R: Coil/Coil
Brakes F/R: Drum/Drum
Wheelbase: 179.6cm 70.7in
Track F: 109.2cm 43.0in
Track R: 109.2cm 43.0in
Length: 303.5cm 119.5in
Width: 136.4cm 53.7in
Height: 121.9cm 48.0in
Ground clearance: 19.6cm 7.7in
Kerb weight: 454.4kg 1001.0lb
Fuel: 25.0L 5.5gal 6.6galUS

2005 Goliath

1100 Sedan
1957 Germany
75.6mph 121.6kmh
0-50mph 80.5kmh: 16.0secs
0-60mph 96.5kmh: 24.6secs
0-1/4 mile: 22.9secs
40.0bhp 29.8kW 40.5PS
@ 4250rpm
59.3lbft 80.4Nm @ 2750rpm
44.6bhp/ton 43.8bhp/tonne
36.6bhp/L 27.3kW/L 37.1PS/L
29.7ft/sec 9.1m/sec
Petrol 4-stroke piston
1094cc 66.7cu in
Flat 4
Compression ratio: 7.3:1
Bore: 73.9mm 2.9in
Stroke: 64.0mm 2.5in
Valve type/No: Overhead 8
Transmission: Manual
No. of forward speeds: 4
Wheels driven: Front
Wheelbase: 227.1cm 89.4in
Track F: 129.0cm 50.8in
Track R: 125.0cm 49.2in
Kerb weight: 912.5kg 2010.0lb

2006 Goliath

900
1957 Germany
72.0mph 115.8kmh
0-50mph 80.5kmh: 19.4secs
0-60mph 96.5kmh: 32.0secs
0-1/4 mile: 23.7secs
40.0bhp 29.8kW 40.5PS
@ 4000rpm
54.0lbft 73.2Nm @ 2750rpm
43.5bhp/ton 42.8bhp/tonne
45.1bhp/L 33.7kW/L 45.8PS/L
35.0ft/sec 10.7m/sec
Petrol 2-stroke piston
886cc 54.1cu in
In-line 2 fuel injection
Compression ratio: 7.4:1
Bore: 84.1mm 3.3in
Stroke: 80.0mm 3.1in
Transmission: Manual
No. of forward speeds: 4
Wheels driven: Front
Wheelbase: 229.9cm 90.5in
Track F: 125.0cm 49.2in
Track R: 125.0cm 49.2in
Kerb weight: 935.2kg 2060.0lb

2007 Goliath

Tiger
1959 Germany
84.0mph 135.2kmh
0-50mph 80.5kmh: 13.7secs
0-60mph 96.5kmh: 18.5secs
0-1/4 mile: 21.8secs
61.0bhp 45.5kW 61.8PS
@ 5000rpm
60.0lbft 81.3Nm @ 4000rpm
67.6bhp/ton 66.5bhp/tonne
55.8bhp/L 41.6kW/L 56.6PS/L
35.0ft/sec 10.7m/sec
17.0mph 27.4kmh/1000rpm
Petrol 4-stroke piston
1093cc 66.7cu in
Flat 4
Compression ratio: 7.9:1
Bore: 73.9mm 2.9in
Stroke: 64.0mm 2.5in
Valve type/No: Overhead 8
Transmission: Manual
No. of forward speeds: 4
Wheels driven: Front
Wheelbase: 227.1cm 89.4in
Track F: 129.0cm 50.8in
Track R: 125.0cm 49.2in
Length: 421.6cm 166.0in
Width: 163.1cm 64.2in
Height: 136.9cm 53.9in
Kerb weight: 917.1kg 2020.0lb

2008 Gordon
GT
1960 UK
142.0mph 228.5kmh
0-50mph 80.5kmh: 6.3secs
0-60mph 96.5kmh: 7.7secs
0-1/4 mile: 15.6secs
290.0bhp 216.2kW 294.0PS
@ 6250rpm
300.0lbft 406.5Nm @ 3000rpm
206.2bhp/ton 202.8bhp/tonne
62.5bhp/L 46.6kW/L 63.4PS/L
52.1ft/sec 15.9m/sec
22.3mph 35.9kmh/1000rpm
14.2mpg 11.8mpgUS 19.9L/100km
Petrol 4-stroke piston
4639cc 283.0cu in
Vee 8
Compression ratio: 9.5:1
Bore: 98.4mm 3.9in
Stroke: 76.2mm 3.0in
Valve type/No: Overhead 16
Transmission: Manual
No. of forward speeds: 4
Wheels driven: Rear
Springs F/R: Coil/Coil
Brakes F/R: Disc/Disc
Wheelbase: 259.1cm 102.0in
Track F: 139.7cm 55.0in
Track R: 139.7cm 55.0in
Length: 472.4cm 186.0in
Width: 172.7cm 68.0in
Height: 134.6cm 53.0in
Ground clearance: 20.3cm 8.0in
Kerb weight: 1430.1kg 3150.0lb
Fuel: 81.9L 18.0gal 21.6galUS

2009 Gordon Keeble
GK1
1965 UK
137.0mph 220.4kmh
0-50mph 80.5kmh: 5.5secs
0-60mph 96.5kmh: 7.5secs
0-1/4 mile: 15.6secs
300.0bhp 223.7kW 304.2PS
@ 5000rpm
360.0lbft 487.8Nm @ 3000rpm
212.4bhp/ton 208.8bhp/tonne
56.0bhp/L 41.8kW/L 56.8PS/L
45.1ft/sec 13.7m/sec
25.8mph 41.5kmh/1000rpm
14.5mpg 12.1mpgUS 19.5L/100km
Petrol 4-stroke piston
5355cc 326.7cu in
Vee 8 1 Carburettor
Compression ratio: 10.5:1
Bore: 101.6mm 4.0in
Stroke: 82.5mm 3.2in
Valve type/No: Overhead 16
Transmission: Manual
No. of forward speeds: 4
Wheels driven: Rear
Springs F/R: Coil/Coil
Brake system: PA
Brakes F/R: Disc/Disc
Steering: Worm & wheel
Wheelbase: 259.1cm 102.0in
Track F: 139.7cm 55.0in
Track R: 139.7cm 55.0in
Length: 481.3cm 189.5in
Width: 172.7cm 68.0in
Height: 137.2cm 54.0in
Ground clearance: 12.7cm 5.0in
Kerb weight: 1436.5kg 3164.0lb
Fuel: 100.1L 22.0gal 26.4galUS

2010 Graham
Blue Streak Saloon
1932 USA
80.3mph 129.2kmh
15.0mpg 12.5mpgUS 18.8L/100km
Petrol 4-stroke piston
3960cc 241.6cu in
In-line 8
Bore: 79.3mm 3.1in
Stroke: 101.6mm 4.0in
Transmission: Manual
No. of forward speeds: 3
Wheels driven: Rear
Brakes F/R: Drum/Drum
Wheelbase: 312.4cm 123.0in
Track F: 154.9cm 61.0in
Track R: 154.9cm 61.0in
Length: 495.3cm 195.0in
Width: 185.4cm 73.0in
Height: 177.8cm 70.0in
Kerb weight: 1703.4kg 3752.0lb
Fuel: 68.2L 15.0gal 18.0galUS

2011 Graham
21.6hp Saloon
1935 USA
75.6mph 121.6kmh
0-50mph 80.5kmh: 17.0secs
0-60mph 96.5kmh: 24.0secs
22.0mpg 18.3mpgUS 12.8L/100km
Petrol 4-stroke piston
2780cc 169.6cu in
In-line 8
Bore: 76.2mm 3.0in
Stroke: 101.6mm 4.0in
Valve type/No: Side 16
Transmission: Manual
No. of forward speeds: 3
Wheels driven: Rear
Brakes F/R: Drum/Drum
Kerb weight: 1259.8kg 2775.0lb
Fuel: 45.5L 10.0gal 12.0galUS

2012 Graham
33.8hp Supercharged Saloon
1935 USA
91.8mph 147.7kmh
0-50mph 80.5kmh: 10.6secs
0-60mph 96.5kmh: 15.8secs
15.0mpg 12.5mpgUS 18.8L/100km
Petrol 4-stroke piston
4350cc 265.4cu in supercharged
In-line 8
Bore: 82.5mm 3.2in
Stroke: 101.6mm 4.0in
Valve type/No: Side 16
Transmission: Manual
No. of forward speeds: 3
Wheels driven: Rear
Brakes F/R: Drum/Drum
Ground clearance: 21.6cm 8.5in
Kerb weight: 1722.5kg 3794.0lb
Fuel: 68.2L 15.0gal 18.0galUS

2013 Graham
26hp Supercharged Saloon
1936 USA
89.1mph 143.4kmh
0-50mph 80.5kmh: 9.9secs
0-60mph 96.5kmh: 14.5secs
20.0mpg 16.7mpgUS 14.1L/100km
Petrol 4-stroke piston
3569cc 217.7cu in supercharged
In-line 6
Bore: 82.5mm 3.2in
Stroke: 111.1mm 4.4in
Valve type/No: Side 12
Transmission: Manual
No. of forward speeds: 3
Wheels driven: Rear
Brakes F/R: Drum/Drum
Wheelbase: 304.8cm 120.0in
Track F: 144.0cm 56.7in
Track R: 155.4cm 61.2in
Length: 500.4cm 197.0in
Width: 190.5cm 75.0in
Height: 167.6cm 66.0in
Ground clearance: 20.3cm 8.0in
Kerb weight: 1503.2kg 3311.0lb
Fuel: 54.6L 12.0gal 14.4galUS

2014 Graham
26hp Supercharged Saloon
1938 USA
91.8mph 147.7kmh
0-50mph 80.5kmh: 10.6secs
0-60mph 96.5kmh: 16.4secs
16.0mpg 13.3mpgUS 17.7L/100km
Petrol 4-stroke piston
3556cc 217.0cu in supercharged
In-line 6
Bore: 82.5mm 3.2in
Stroke: 111.1mm 4.4in
Valve type/No: Side 12
Transmission: Manual
No. of forward speeds: 3
Wheels driven: Rear
Brakes F/R: Drum/Drum
Wheelbase: 304.8cm 120.0in
Track F: 144.0cm 56.7in
Track R: 155.4cm 61.2in
Length: 500.4cm 197.0in
Width: 190.5cm 75.0in
Height: 167.6cm 66.0in
Ground clearance: 20.3cm 8.0in
Kerb weight: 1624.4kg 3578.0lb
Fuel: 54.6L 12.0gal 14.4galUS

2015 Graham-Paige
21.6hp Saloon
1929 USA
62.0mph 99.8kmh
20.0mpg 16.7mpgUS 14.1L/100km
Petrol 4-stroke piston
3128cc 190.8cu in
In-line 6
Bore: 76.2mm 3.0in
Stroke: 114.3mm 4.5in
Transmission: Manual
No. of forward speeds: 4
Wheels driven: Rear
Brakes F/R: Drum/Drum
Wheelbase: 284.5cm 112.0in
Track F: 146.1cm 57.5in
Track R: 146.1cm 57.5in
Length: 430.5cm 169.5in
Width: 174.0cm 68.5in
Height: 182.9cm 72.0in
Kerb weight: 915.3kg 2016.0lb
Fuel: 50.0L 11.0gal 13.2galUS

2016 Graham-Paige
Straight Eight
1929 USA
76.0mph 122.3kmh
12.0mpg 10.0mpgUS 23.5L/100km
Petrol 4-stroke piston
5274cc 321.8cu in
In-line 8
Bore: 85.7mm 3.4in
Stroke: 114.3mm 4.5in
Transmission: Manual
No. of forward speeds: 4
Wheels driven: Rear
Brakes F/R: Drum/Drum
Wheelbase: 342.9cm 135.0in
Track F: 142.2cm 56.0in
Track R: 142.2cm 56.0in
Length: 500.4cm 197.0in
Width: 177.8cm 70.0in
Height: 185.4cm 73.0in
Fuel: 84.2L 18.5gal 22.2galUS

2017 HE
16/60 Sports Four-seater
1929 UK
78.0mph 125.5kmh
22.0mpg 18.3mpgUS 12.8L/100km
Petrol 4-stroke piston
2290cc 139.7cu in
In-line 6
Bore: 65.0mm 2.6in
Stroke: 115.0mm 4.5in
Transmission: Manual
No. of forward speeds: 4
Wheels driven: Rear
Brakes F/R: Drum/Drum
Kerb weight: 1372.9kg 3024.0lb
Fuel: 81.9L 18.0gal 21.6galUS

2018 HE
Supercharged Six Coupe
1930 UK
66.4mph 106.8kmh
18.0mpg 15.0mpgUS 15.7L/100km
Petrol 4-stroke piston
1419cc 86.6cu in supercharged
In-line 6
Bore: 56.0mm 2.2in
Stroke: 96.0mm 3.8in
Valve type/No: Side 12
Transmission: Manual
No. of forward speeds: 4
Wheels driven: Rear
Brakes F/R: Drum/Drum
Wheelbase: 294.6cm 116.0in
Track F: 132.1cm 52.0in
Track R: 132.1cm 52.0in
Length: 419.1cm 165.0in
Width: 165.1cm 65.0in
Height: 162.6cm 64.0in
Kerb weight: 1322.0kg 2912.0lb
Fuel: 56.9L 12.5gal 15.0galUS

2019 Healey
2.4-litre Roadster
1948 UK
102.0mph 164.1kmh
0-50mph 80.5kmh: 10.2secs
0-60mph 96.5kmh: 14.7secs
104.0bhp 77.5kW 105.4PS
@ 4500rpm
89.9bhp/ton 88.4bhp/tonne
42.6bhp/L 31.7kW/L 43.2PS/L
59.0ft/sec 18.0m/sec
22.0mpg 18.3mpgUS 12.8L/100km
Petrol 4-stroke piston
2443cc 149.0cu in
In-line 4
Compression ratio: 6.9:1
Bore: 80.5mm 3.2in
Stroke: 120.0mm 4.7in
Valve type/No: Overhead 8
Transmission: Manual
No. of forward speeds: 4
Wheels driven: Rear
Brakes F/R: Drum/Drum
Wheelbase: 259.1cm 102.0in
Track F: 137.2cm 54.0in
Track R: 134.6cm 53.0in
Length: 426.7cm 168.0in
Width: 166.4cm 65.5in
Height: 139.7cm 55.0in
Ground clearance: 17.8cm 7.0in
Kerb weight: 1175.9kg 2590.0lb
Fuel: 61.4L 13.5gal 16.2galUS

2020 Healey
Tickford Saloon
1952 UK
104.6mph 168.3kmh
0-50mph 80.5kmh: 10.5secs
0-60mph 96.5kmh: 14.6secs
0-1/4 mile: 19.3secs
106.0bhp 79.0kW 107.5PS
@ 4800rpm
136.0lbft 184.3Nm @ 3000rpm
80.2bhp/ton 78.8bhp/tonne
43.4bhp/L 32.3kW/L 44.0PS/L
62.9ft/sec 19.2m/sec
20.6mph 33.1kmh/1000rpm
22.0mpg 18.3mpgUS 12.8L/100km
Petrol 4-stroke piston
2443cc 149.0cu in
In-line 4
Compression ratio: 6.8:1
Bore: 80.5mm 3.2in
Stroke: 120.0mm 4.7in
Valve type/No: Overhead 8
Transmission: Manual
No. of forward speeds: 4
Wheels driven: Rear
Springs F/R: Coil/Coil
Brakes F/R: Drum/Drum
Wheelbase: 259.1cm 102.0in
Track F: 137.2cm 54.0in
Track R: 139.7cm 55.0in
Length: 449.6cm 177.0in
Width: 170.2cm 67.0in
Height: 139.7cm 55.0in
Ground clearance: 17.8cm 7.0in
Kerb weight: 1344.3kg 2961.0lb
Fuel: 72.8L 16.0gal 19.2galUS

2021 Healey
Sports Convertible
1953 UK
100.0mph 160.9kmh
0-50mph 80.5kmh: 9.7secs
0-60mph 96.5kmh: 13.5secs
0-1/4 mile: 19.9secs
106.0bhp 79.0kW 107.5PS
@ 4200rpm
140.0lbft 189.7Nm @ 2000rpm
85.3bhp/ton 83.9bhp/tonne
35.4bhp/L 26.4kW/L 35.9PS/L
41.3ft/sec 12.6m/sec
20.6mph 33.1kmh/1000rpm
23.8mpg 19.8mpgUS 11.9L/100km
Petrol 4-stroke piston
2993cc 183.0cu in
In-line 6 2 Carburettor
Compression ratio: 7.0:1
Bore: 84.0mm 3.3in
Stroke: 90.0mm 3.5in
Valve type/No: Overhead 12
Transmission: Manual
No. of forward speeds: 4
Wheels driven: Rear
Springs F/R: Coil/Coil
Brakes F/R: Drum/Drum
Steering: Worm & roller
Wheelbase: 259.1cm 102.0in
Track F: 134.6cm 53.0in

Track R: 139.7cm 55.0in
Length: 442.0cm 174.0in
Width: 165.1cm 65.0in
Height: 142.2cm 56.0in
Ground clearance: 17.8cm 7.0in
Kerb weight: 1263.5kg 2783.0lb
Fuel: 72.8L 16.0gal 19.2galUS

2022 Hillman
Safety Saloon
1928 UK
56.0mph 90.1kmh
25.0mpg 20.8mpgUS 11.3L/100km
Petrol 4-stroke piston
1954cc 119.2cu in
In-line 4
Bore: 72.0mm 2.8in
Stroke: 120.0mm 4.7in
Valve type/No: Side 8
Transmission: Manual
No. of forward speeds: 4
Wheels driven: Rear
Brakes F/R: Drum/Drum
Wheelbase: 289.6cm 114.0in
Track F: 142.2cm 56.0in
Track R: 142.2cm 56.0in
Length: 411.5cm 162.0in
Width: 173.2cm 68.2in
Kerb weight: 1093.2kg 2408.0lb
Fuel: 54.6L 12.0gal 14.4galUS

2023 Hillman
Segrave Saloon
1929 UK
57.0mph 91.7kmh
16.0mpg 13.3mpgUS 17.7L/100km
Petrol 4-stroke piston
2620cc 159.8cu in
In-line 8
Bore: 63.0mm 2.5in
Stroke: 105.0mm 4.1in
Valve type/No: Overhead 16
Transmission: Manual
No. of forward speeds: 4
Wheels driven: Rear
Brakes F/R: Drum/Drum
Wheelbase: 306.1cm 120.5in
Track F: 142.2cm 56.0in
Track R: 142.2cm 56.0in
Length: 432.3cm 170.2in
Width: 173.2cm 68.2in
Height: 172.7cm 68.0in
Kerb weight: 1576.3kg 3472.0lb
Fuel: 63.7L 14.0gal 16.8galUS

2024 Hillman
Straight Eight Saloon
1929 UK
65.0mph 104.6kmh
19.0mpg 15.8mpgUS 14.9L/100km
Petrol 4-stroke piston
2620cc 159.8cu in
In-line 8
Bore: 63.0mm 2.5in
Stroke: 105.0mm 4.1in
Transmission: Manual
No. of forward speeds: 4
Wheels driven: Rear
Brakes F/R: Drum/Drum
Wheelbase: 304.8cm 120.0in
Track F: 142.2cm 56.0in
Track R: 142.2cm 56.0in
Length: 430.5cm 169.5in
Width: 173.2cm 68.2in
Height: 174.0cm 68.5in
Kerb weight: 1563.6kg 3444.0lb
Fuel: 54.6L 12.0gal 14.4galUS

2025 Hillman
Minx Sports Tourer
1932 UK
60.8mph 97.8kmh
32.0mpg 26.6mpgUS 8.8L/100km
Petrol 4-stroke piston
1185cc 72.3cu in
In-line 4
Bore: 63.0mm 2.5in
Stroke: 95.0mm 3.7in
Valve type/No: Side 8
Transmission: Manual
No. of forward speeds: 3
Wheels driven: Rear
Brakes F/R: Drum/Drum
Wheelbase: 233.7cm 92.0in
Track F: 121.9cm 48.0in
Track R: 121.9cm 48.0in
Length: 340.4cm 134.0in
Width: 147.3cm 58.0in
Height: 167.6cm 66.0in
Kerb weight: 845.3kg 1862.0lb
Fuel: 35.3L 7.7gal 9.3galUS

2026 Hillman
Wizard 65 Saloon de Luxe
1932 UK
66.1mph 106.4kmh
18.0mpg 15.0mpgUS 15.7L/100km
Petrol 4-stroke piston
2110cc 128.7cu in
In-line 6
Bore: 65.0mm 2.6in
Stroke: 106.0mm 4.2in
Valve type/No: Side 12
Transmission: Manual
No. of forward speeds: 4
Wheels driven: Rear
Brakes F/R: Drum/Drum
Wheelbase: 281.9cm 111.0in
Track F: 142.2cm 56.0in
Track R: 142.2cm 56.0in
Length: 410.2cm 161.5in
Width: 172.7cm 68.0in
Height: 179.1cm 70.5in
Kerb weight: 1449.2kg 3192.0lb
Fuel: 66.0L 14.5gal 17.4galUS

<H>2027 Hillman
20/70 Limousine
1934 UK
68.4mph 110.1kmh
0-50mph 80.5kmh: 18.2secs
0-60mph 96.5kmh: 28.6secs
18.0mpg 15.0mpgUS 15.7L/100km
Petrol 4-stroke piston
2810cc 171.4cu in
In-line 6
Bore: 75.0mm 2.9in
Stroke: 106.0mm 4.2in
Transmission: Manual
No. of forward speeds: 4
Wheels driven: Rear
Brakes F/R: Drum/Drum
Kerb weight: 1627.1kg 3584.0lb
Fuel: 63.7L 14.0gal 16.8galUS

2028 Hillman
Aero Minx Coupe
1934 UK
72.5mph 116.7kmh
0-50mph 80.5kmh: 22.2secs
27.0mpg 22.5mpgUS 10.5L/100km
Petrol 4-stroke piston
1185cc 72.3cu in
In-line 4
Bore: 63.0mm 2.5in
Stroke: 95.0mm 3.7in
Valve type/No: Side 8
Transmission: Manual
No. of forward speeds: 4
Wheels driven: Rear
Brakes F/R: Drum/Drum
Kerb weight: 889.8kg 1960.0lb
Fuel: 36.4L 8.0gal 9.6galUS

2029 Hillman
20/27 Sports Saloon
1935 UK
72.0mph 115.8kmh
0-50mph 80.5kmh: 15.2secs
0-60mph 96.5kmh: 24.0secs
18.0mpg 15.0mpgUS 15.7L/100km
Petrol 4-stroke piston
2810cc 171.4cu in
In-line 6
Bore: 75.0mm 2.9in
Stroke: 106.0mm 4.2in
Valve type/No: Side 12
Transmission: Manual
No. of forward speeds: 4
Wheels driven: Rear
Brakes F/R: Drum/Drum
Kerb weight: 1510.5kg 3327.0lb
Fuel: 63.7L 14.0gal 16.8galUS

2030 Hillman
Aero Minx Cresta Saloon
1935 UK
71.4mph 114.9kmh
0-50mph 80.5kmh: 23.0secs
0-60mph 96.5kmh: 37.8secs
26.0mpg 21.6mpgUS 10.9L/100km
Petrol 4-stroke piston
1185cc 72.3cu in
In-line 4
Bore: 63.0mm 2.5in
Stroke: 95.0mm 3.7in
Valve type/No: Side 8
Transmission: Manual
No. of forward speeds: 4
Wheels driven: Rear
Brakes F/R: Drum/Drum
Kerb weight: 898.0kg 1978.0lb
Fuel: 36.4L 8.0gal 9.6galUS

2031 Hillman
Hawk Sports Saloon
1936 UK
75.0mph 120.7kmh
0-50mph 80.5kmh: 17.7secs
0-60mph 96.5kmh: 27.9secs
18.0mpg 15.0mpgUS 15.7L/100km
Petrol 4-stroke piston
3181cc 194.1cu in
In-line 6
Bore: 75.0mm 2.9in
Stroke: 120.0mm 4.7in
Valve type/No: Side 12
Transmission: Manual
No. of forward speeds: 4
Wheels driven: Rear
Brakes F/R: Drum/Drum
Kerb weight: 1659.4kg 3655.0lb
Fuel: 63.7L 14.0gal 16.8galUS

2032 Hillman
80 Limousine
1937 UK
73.7mph 118.6kmh
0-50mph 80.5kmh: 17.3secs
0-60mph 96.5kmh: 26.4secs
18.0mpg 15.0mpgUS 15.7L/100km
Petrol 4-stroke piston
3181cc 194.1cu in
In-line 6
Bore: 75.0mm 2.9in
Stroke: 120.0mm 4.7in
Valve type/No: Side 12
Transmission: Manual
No. of forward speeds: 4
Wheels driven: Rear
Brakes F/R: Drum/Drum
Kerb weight: 1801.5kg 3968.0lb
Fuel: 63.7L 14.0gal 16.8galUS

2033 Hillman
Minx Saloon de Luxe
1937 UK
62.5mph 100.6kmh
0-50mph 80.5kmh: 29.4secs
32.0mpg 26.6mpgUS 8.8L/100km
Petrol 4-stroke piston
1185cc 72.3cu in
In-line 4
Bore: 63.0mm 2.5in
Stroke: 95.0mm 3.7in
Valve type/No: Overhead 8
Transmission: Manual
No. of forward speeds: 4
Wheels driven: Rear
Brakes F/R: Drum/Drum
Kerb weight: 958.8kg 2112.0lb
Fuel: 35.3L 7.7gal 9.3galUS

2034 Hillman
Minx Saloon
1947 UK
63.0mph 101.4kmh
0-50mph 80.5kmh: 29.3secs
35.0bhp 26.1kW 35.5PS
@ 4100rpm
37.6bhp/ton 37.0bhp/tonne
29.6bhp/L 22.0kW/L 30.0PS/L
42.6ft/sec 13.0m/sec
35.0mpg 29.1mpgUS 8.1L/100km
Petrol 4-stroke piston
1184cc 72.2cu in
In-line 4
Compression ratio: 6.3:1
Bore: 63.0mm 2.5in
Stroke: 95.0mm 3.7in
Valve type/No: Side 8
Transmission: Manual
No. of forward speeds: 4
Wheels driven: Rear
Brakes F/R: Drum/Drum
Wheelbase: 233.7cm 92.0in
Track F: 120.9cm 47.6in
Track R: 123.2cm 48.5in
Length: 396.2cm 156.0in
Width: 153.7cm 60.5in
Height: 158.8cm 62.5in
Ground clearance: 15.7cm 6.2in
Kerb weight: 947.0kg 2086.0lb
Fuel: 32.8L 7.2gal 8.6galUS

2035 Hillman
Minx Saloon
1949 UK
67.0mph 107.8kmh
0-50mph 80.5kmh: 23.9secs
0-60mph 96.5kmh: 40.2secs
37.5bhp 28.0kW 38.0PS
@ 4200rpm
58.3lbft 79.0Nm @ 2200rpm
39.6bhp/ton 38.9bhp/tonne
29.6bhp/L 22.1kW/L 30.1PS/L
43.6ft/sec 13.3m/sec
14.2mph 22.8kmh/1000rpm
30.0mpg 25.0mpgUS 9.4L/100km
Petrol 4-stroke piston
1265cc 77.2cu in
In-line 4
Compression ratio: 6.6:1
Bore: 65.0mm 2.6in
Stroke: 95.0mm 3.7in
Valve type/No: Side 8
Transmission: Manual
No. of forward speeds: 4
Wheels driven: Rear
Brakes F/R: Drum/Drum
Wheelbase: 236.2cm 93.0in
Track F: 122.9cm 48.4in
Track R: 123.2cm 48.5in
Length: 399.3cm 157.2in
Width: 157.5cm 62.0in
Height: 152.4cm 60.0in
Ground clearance: 17.8cm 7.0in
Kerb weight: 962.9kg 2121.0lb
Fuel: 33.0L 7.2gal 8.7galUS

2036 Hillman
Minx Estate
1951 UK
69.0mph 111.0kmh
37.5bhp 28.0kW 38.0PS
@ 4200rpm
58.3lbft 79.0Nm @ 2200rpm
37.4bhp/ton 36.8bhp/tonne
29.6bhp/L 22.1kW/L 30.1PS/L
43.6ft/sec 13.3m/sec
14.3mph 23.0kmh/1000rpm
31.0mpg 25.8mpgUS 9.1L/100km
Petrol 4-stroke piston
1265cc 77.2cu in
In-line 4 1 Carburettor
Compression ratio: 6.6:1
Bore: 65.0mm 2.6in
Stroke: 95.0mm 3.7in
Valve type/No: Side 8
Transmission: Manual
No. of forward speeds: 4
Wheels driven: Rear
Brakes F/R: Drum/Drum
Wheelbase: 236.2cm 93.0in
Track F: 123.4cm 48.6in
Track R: 128.3cm 50.5in
Length: 416.6cm 164.0in
Width: 157.5cm 62.0in
Height: 166.9cm 65.7in
Ground clearance: 17.8cm 7.0in
Kerb weight: 1018.8kg 2244.0lb
Fuel: 32.8L 7.2gal 8.6galUS

2037 Hillman
Minx Sedan
1951 UK
0-60mph 96.5kmh: 40.0secs
0-1/4 mile: 25.0secs
38.0bhp 28.3kW 38.5PS
@ 4200rpm
49.0lbft 66.4Nm @ 2400rpm
41.1bhp/ton 40.4bhp/tonne
30.0bhp/L 22.4kW/L 30.5PS/L
43.6ft/sec 13.3m/sec
25.2mpg 21.0mpgUS 11.2L/100km
Petrol 4-stroke piston
1265cc 77.2cu in

In-line 4
Compression ratio: 6.6:1
Bore: 65.1mm 2.6in
Stroke: 95.0mm 3.7in
Transmission: Manual
No. of forward speeds: 4
Wheels driven: Rear
Wheelbase: 236.2cm 93.0in
Track F: 123.2cm 48.5in
Track R: 123.2cm 48.5in
Length: 406.4cm 160.0in
Width: 157.5cm 62.0in
Height: 167.1cm 65.8in
Ground clearance: 17.8cm 7.0in
Kerb weight: 940.7kg 2072.0lb

2038 Hillman

Minx Convertible
1952 UK
70.0mph 112.6kmh
0-50mph 80.5kmh: 20.3secs
0-60mph 96.5kmh: 32.3secs
37.5bhp 28.0kW 38.0PS
@ 4200rpm
58.3lbft 79.0Nm @ 2200rpm
39.2bhp/ton 38.5bhp/tonne
29.6bhp/L 22.1kW/L 30.1PS/L
43.6ft/sec 13.3m/sec
14.3mph 23.0kmh/1000rpm
26.0mpg 21.6mpgUS 10.9L/100km
Petrol 4-stroke piston
1265cc 77.2cu in
In-line 4
Compression ratio: 6.6:1
Bore: 65.0mm 2.6in
Stroke: 95.0mm 3.7in
Valve type/No: Side 8
Transmission: Manual
No. of forward speeds: 4
Wheels driven: Rear
Brakes F/R: Drum/Drum
Wheelbase: 236.2cm 93.0in
Track F: 122.9cm 48.4in
Track R: 123.2cm 48.5in
Length: 400.1cm 157.5in
Width: 157.5cm 62.0in
Height: 148.6cm 58.5in
Ground clearance: 17.8cm 7.0in
Kerb weight: 973.4kg 2144.0lb
Fuel: 32.8L 7.2gal 8.6galUS

2039 Hillman

Minx Califonian Coupe
1953 UK
70.5mph 113.4kmh
0-50mph 80.5kmh: 21.0secs
0-60mph 96.5kmh: 34.7secs
0-1/4 mile: 24.8secs
37.5bhp 28.0kW 38.0PS
@ 4200rpm
58.3lbft 79.0Nm @ 2200rpm
37.8bhp/ton 37.2bhp/tonne
29.6bhp/L 22.1kW/L 30.1PS/L
43.6ft/sec 13.3m/sec
14.2mph 22.8kmh/1000rpm
29.0mpg 24.1mpgUS 9.7L/100km
Petrol 4-stroke piston
1265cc 77.0cu in
In-line 4
Compression ratio: 6.6:1
Bore: 65.0mm 2.6in
Stroke: 95.0mm 3.7in
Valve type/No: Side 8
Transmission: Manual
No. of forward speeds: 4
Wheels driven: Rear
Springs F/R: Coil/Leaf
Brakes F/R: Drum/Drum
Wheelbase: 236.2cm 93.0in
Track F: 123.4cm 48.6in
Track R: 123.2cm 48.5in
Length: 400.1cm 157.5in
Width: 161.3cm 63.5in
Height: 148.6cm 58.5in
Ground clearance: 17.8cm 7.0in
Kerb weight: 1007.4kg 2219.0lb
Fuel: 33.0L 7.2gal 8.7galUS

2040 Hillman

Minx Supercharged
1954 UK
80.0mph 128.7kmh
0-50mph 80.5kmh: 13.1secs
0-60mph 96.5kmh: 20.2secs
0-1/4 mile: 20.9secs
37.5bhp 28.0kW 38.0PS
@ 4200rpm
35.9bhp/ton 35.3bhp/tonne
29.6bhp/L 22.1kW/L 30.1PS/L
43.6ft/sec 13.3m/sec
Petrol 4-stroke piston
1265cc 77.2cu in supercharged
In-line 4
Bore: 65.0mm 2.6in
Stroke: 95.0mm 3.7in
Valve type/No: Overhead 8
Transmission: Manual
No. of forward speeds: 4
Wheels driven: Rear
Wheelbase: 236.2cm 93.0in
Track F: 123.4cm 48.6in
Track R: 123.4cm 48.6in
Kerb weight: 1062.4kg 2340.0lb

2041 Hillman

Husky
1955 UK
68.0mph 109.4kmh
0-50mph 80.5kmh: 27.5secs
0-1/4 mile: 26.3secs
35.0bhp 26.1kW 35.5PS
@ 4100rpm
55.5lbft 75.2Nm @ 2200rpm
38.4bhp/ton 37.7bhp/tonne
27.7bhp/L 20.6kW/L 28.1PS/L
42.6ft/sec 13.0m/sec
15.0mph 24.1kmh/1000rpm
34.7mpg 28.9mpgUS 8.1L/100km
Petrol 4-stroke piston
1265cc 77.0cu in
In-line 4 1 Carburettor
Compression ratio: 6.6:1
Bore: 65.0mm 2.6in
Stroke: 95.0mm 3.7in
Valve type/No: Side 8
Transmission: Manual
No. of forward speeds: 4
Wheels driven: Rear
Springs F/R: Coil/Leaf
Brakes F/R: Drum/Drum
Wheelbase: 213.4cm 84.0in
Track F: 123.7cm 48.7in
Track R: 123.2cm 48.5in
Length: 369.6cm 145.5in
Width: 157.5cm 62.0in
Height: 154.9cm 61.0in
Ground clearance: 16.5cm 6.5in
Kerb weight: 928.0kg 2044.0lb
Fuel: 28.4L 6.3gal 7.5galUS

2042 Hillman

Minx de Luxe
1955 UK
74.5mph 119.9kmh
0-50mph 80.5kmh: 18.5secs
0-60mph 96.5kmh: 29.7secs
0-1/4 mile: 23.9secs
43.0bhp 32.1kW 43.6PS
@ 4400rpm
66.3lbft 89.8Nm @ 2200rpm
44.0bhp/ton 43.2bhp/tonne
30.9bhp/L 23.1kW/L 31.4PS/L
36.7ft/sec 11.2m/sec
15.3mph 24.6kmh/1000rpm
34.7mpg 28.9mpgUS 8.1L/100km
Petrol 4-stroke piston
1390cc 84.8cu in
In-line 4 1 Carburettor
Compression ratio: 9.0:1
Bore: 76.2mm 3.0in
Stroke: 76.2mm 3.0in
Valve type/No: Overhead 8
Transmission: Manual
No. of forward speeds: 4
Wheels driven: Rear
Springs F/R: Coil/Leaf
Brakes F/R: Drum/Drum
Wheelbase: 236.2cm 93.0in
Track F: 123.4cm 48.6in
Track R: 123.2cm 48.5in
Length: 405.1cm 159.5in
Width: 161.3cm 63.5in
Height: 154.9cm 61.0in
Ground clearance: 17.8cm 7.0in
Kerb weight: 994.7kg 2191.0lb
Fuel: 32.8L 7.2gal 8.6galUS

2043 Hillman

Minx de Luxe
1956 UK
82.7mph 133.1kmh
0-50mph 80.5kmh: 17.6secs
0-60mph 96.5kmh: 27.7secs
0-1/4 mile: 23.5secs
47.5bhp 35.4kW 48.2PS
@ 4600rpm
69.7lbft 94.4Nm @ 2400rpm
48.7bhp/ton 47.9bhp/tonne
34.2bhp/L 25.5kW/L 34.6PS/L
38.3ft/sec 11.7m/sec
15.3mph 24.6kmh/1000rpm
34.3mpg 28.6mpgUS 8.2L/100km
Petrol 4-stroke piston
1390cc 84.8cu in
In-line 4 1 Carburettor
Compression ratio: 8.0:1
Bore: 76.2mm 3.0in
Stroke: 76.2mm 3.0in
Valve type/No: Overhead 8
Transmission: Manual
No. of forward speeds: 4
Wheels driven: Rear
Springs F/R: Coil/Leaf
Brakes F/R: Drum/Drum
Wheelbase: 243.8cm 96.0in
Track F: 124.5cm 49.0in
Track R: 123.2cm 48.5in
Length: 407.7cm 160.5in
Width: 154.2cm 60.7in
Height: 151.1cm 59.5in
Ground clearance: 17.8cm 7.0in
Kerb weight: 991.5kg 2184.0lb
Fuel: 32.8L 7.2gal 8.6galUS

2044 Hillman

Minx Convertible
1957 UK
92.0mph 148.0kmh
0-50mph 80.5kmh: 13.5secs
0-60mph 96.5kmh: 18.9secs
0-1/4 mile: 21.6secs
68.0bhp 50.7kW 68.9PS
@ 5000rpm
68.4bhp/ton 67.3bhp/tonne
48.9bhp/L 36.5kW/L 49.6PS/L
41.7ft/sec 12.7m/sec
20.3mph 32.7kmh/1000rpm
26.8mpg 22.3mpgUS 10.5L/100km
Petrol 4-stroke piston
1390cc 84.8cu in
In-line 4
Compression ratio: 8.6:1
Bore: 76.2mm 3.0in
Stroke: 76.2mm 3.0in
Valve type/No: Overhead 8
Transmission: Manual with overdrive
No. of forward speeds: 6
Wheels driven: Rear
Springs F/R: Coil/Leaf
Brakes F/R: Drum/Drum
Wheelbase: 243.8cm 96.0in
Track F: 124.5cm 49.0in
Track R: 123.2cm 48.5in
Length: 407.7cm 160.5in
Width: 154.2cm 60.7in
Height: 147.3cm 58.0in
Ground clearance: 17.8cm 7.0in
Kerb weight: 1010.6kg 2226.0lb
Fuel: 31.8L 7.0gal 8.4galUS

2045 Hillman

Hunter Husky
1958 UK
74.0mph 119.1kmh
0-50mph 80.5kmh: 21.8secs
0-60mph 96.5kmh: 31.4secs
0-1/4 mile: 24.3secs
40.0bhp 29.8kW 40.5PS
@ 4000rpm
66.4lbft 90.0Nm @ 1600rpm
41.8bhp/ton 41.1bhp/tonne
28.8bhp/L 21.5kW/L 29.2PS/L
33.3ft/sec 10.2m/sec
15.1mph 24.3kmh/1000rpm
33.6mpg 28.0mpgUS 8.4L/100km
Petrol 4-stroke piston
1390cc 84.8cu in
In-line 4 1 Carburettor
Compression ratio: 7.0:1
Bore: 76.2mm 3.0in
Stroke: 76.2mm 3.0in
Valve type/No: Overhead 8
Transmission: Manual
No. of forward speeds: 4
Wheels driven: Rear
Springs F/R: Coil/Leaf
Brakes F/R: Drum/Drum
Wheelbase: 218.4cm 86.0in
Track F: 124.5cm 49.0in
Track R: 123.2cm 48.5in
Length: 379.7cm 149.5in
Width: 153.7cm 60.5in
Height: 157.5cm 62.0in
Ground clearance: 16.5cm 6.5in
Kerb weight: 972.5kg 2142.0lb
Fuel: 28.2L 6.2gal 7.4galUS

2046 Hillman

Husky
1958 UK
73.8mph 118.7kmh
0-50mph 80.5kmh: 15.2secs
0-60mph 96.5kmh: 23.7secs
0-1/4 mile: 22.2secs
46.0bhp 34.3kW 46.6PS
@ 4400rpm
71.0lbft 96.2Nm @ 2000rpm
47.0bhp/ton 46.3bhp/tonne
33.1bhp/L 24.7kW/L 33.5PS/L
36.7ft/sec 11.2m/sec
15.4mph 24.8kmh/1000rpm
Petrol 4-stroke piston
1390cc 84.8cu in
In-line 4
Compression ratio: 8.0:1
Bore: 76.2mm 3.0in
Stroke: 76.2mm 3.0in
Valve type/No: Overhead 8
Transmission: Manual
No. of forward speeds: 4
Wheels driven: Rear
Wheelbase: 218.4cm 86.0in
Track F: 123.2cm 48.5in
Track R: 123.2cm 48.5in
Length: 386.1cm 152.0in
Width: 153.7cm 60.5in
Height: 154.4cm 60.8in
Kerb weight: 994.3kg 2190.0lb

2047 Hillman

Minx Estate
1958 UK
79.5mph 127.9kmh
0-50mph 80.5kmh: 18.4secs
0-60mph 96.5kmh: 28.4secs
0-1/4 mile: 24.1secs
47.5bhp 35.4kW 48.2PS
@ 4600rpm
69.7lbft 94.4Nm @ 2400rpm
45.5bhp/ton 44.7bhp/tonne
34.2bhp/L 25.5kW/L 34.6PS/L
38.3ft/sec 11.7m/sec
14.2mph 22.8kmh/1000rpm
29.0mpg 24.1mpgUS 9.7L/100km
Petrol 4-stroke piston
1390cc 84.8cu in
In-line 4 1 Carburettor
Compression ratio: 8.0:1
Bore: 76.2mm 3.0in
Stroke: 76.2mm 3.0in
Valve type/No: Overhead 8
Transmission: Manual
No. of forward speeds: 4
Wheels driven: Rear
Springs F/R: Coil/Leaf
Brakes F/R: Drum/Drum
Wheelbase: 243.8cm 96.0in
Track F: 124.5cm 49.0in
Track R: 123.2cm 48.5in
Length: 407.7cm 160.5in
Width: 154.2cm 60.7in
Height: 149.9cm 59.0in
Ground clearance: 17.8cm 7.0in
Kerb weight: 1061.4kg 2338.0lb
Fuel: 33.0L 7.2gal 8.7galUS

2048 Hillman

Minx Series II
1958 UK
76.0mph 122.3kmh
0-50mph 80.5kmh: 18.8secs
0-60mph 96.5kmh: 29.2secs
0-1/4 mile: 24.5secs
47.5bhp 35.4kW 48.2PS
@ 4400rpm
72.0lbft 97.6Nm @ 2200rpm
48.1bhp/ton 47.3bhp/tonne
34.2bhp/L 25.5kW/L 34.6PS/L
36.7ft/sec 11.2m/sec
15.3mph 24.6kmh/1000rpm
32.5mpg 27.1mpgUS 8.7L/100km
Petrol 4-stroke piston
1390cc 84.8cu in
In-line 4 1 Carburettor
Compression ratio: 8.0:1
Bore: 76.2mm 3.0in

Stroke: 76.2mm 3.0in
Valve type/No: Overhead 8
Transmission: Manual
No. of forward speeds: 4
Wheels driven: Rear
Springs F/R: Coil/Leaf
Brakes F/R: Drum/Drum
Wheelbase: 243.8cm 96.0in
Track F: 124.5cm 49.0in
Track R: 123.2cm 48.5in
Length: 411.5cm 162.0in
Width: 154.2cm 60.7in
Height: 151.1cm 59.5in
Ground clearance: 17.8cm 7.0in
Kerb weight: 1004.2kg 2212.0lb
Fuel: 33.0L 7.2gal 8.7galUS

2049 Hillman
Minx Series III Convertible
1958 UK
82.0mph 131.9kmh
0-50mph 80.5kmh: 17.2secs
0-60mph 96.5kmh: 26.6secs
0-1/4 mile: 23.2secs
49.2bhp 36.7kW 49.9PS
@ 4400rpm
78.3lbft 106.1Nm @ 2100rpm
48.1bhp/ton 47.3bhp/tonne
32.9bhp/L 24.6kW/L 33.4PS/L
36.7ft/sec 11.2m/sec
16.1mph 25.9kmh/1000rpm
28.6mpg 23.8mpgUS 9.9L/100km
Petrol 4-stroke piston
1494cc 91.1cu in
In-line 4
Compression ratio: 8.5:1
Bore: 79.0mm 3.1in
Stroke: 76.2mm 3.0in
Valve type/No: Overhead 8
Transmission: Manual
No. of forward speeds: 4
Wheels driven: Rear
Springs F/R: Coil/Leaf
Brakes F/R: Drum/Drum
Wheelbase: 243.8cm 96.0in
Track F: 124.5cm 49.0in
Track R: 123.2cm 48.5in
Length: 411.5cm 162.0in
Width: 154.2cm 60.7in
Height: 147.3cm 58.0in
Ground clearance: 14.5cm 5.7in
Kerb weight: 1039.2kg 2289.0lb
Fuel: 32.8L 7.2gal 8.6galUS

2050 Hillman
Minx Series IIIA Easidrive
1959 UK
79.0mph 127.1kmh
0-50mph 80.5kmh: 17.3secs
0-60mph 96.5kmh: 26.7secs
0-1/4 mile: 23.8secs
53.0bhp 39.5kW 53.7PS
@ 4600rpm
83.0lbft 112.5Nm @ 2000rpm
49.4bhp/ton 48.6bhp/tonne
35.5bhp/L 26.4kW/L 36.0PS/L
38.3ft/sec 11.7m/sec
16.1mph 25.9kmh/1000rpm
28.1mpg 23.4mpgUS 10.1L/100km
Petrol 4-stroke piston
1494cc 91.1cu in
In-line 4
Compression ratio: 8.5:1
Bore: 79.0mm 3.1in
Stroke: 76.2mm 3.0in
Valve type/No: Overhead 8
Transmission: Automatic
No. of forward speeds: 4
Wheels driven: Rear
Springs F/R: Coil/Leaf
Brakes F/R: Drum/Drum
Wheelbase: 243.8cm 96.0in
Track F: 124.5cm 49.0in
Track R: 123.2cm 48.5in
Length: 411.5cm 162.0in
Width: 154.2cm 60.7in
Height: 151.1cm 59.5in
Ground clearance: 17.8cm 7.0in
Kerb weight: 1090.0kg 2401.0lb
Fuel: 32.8L 7.2gal 8.6galUS

2051 Hillman
Easidrive
1960 UK
78.5mph 126.3kmh
0-50mph 80.5kmh: 17.0secs
0-60mph 96.5kmh: 25.0secs
0-1/4 mile: 23.5secs
57.0bhp 42.5kW 57.8PS
@ 4600rpm
83.0lbft 112.5Nm @ 2000rpm
52.5bhp/ton 51.7bhp/tonne
38.1bhp/L 28.4kW/L 38.7PS/L
38.3ft/sec 11.7m/sec
16.3mph 26.2kmh/1000rpm
Petrol 4-stroke piston
1494cc 91.1cu in
In-line 4 1 Carburettor
Compression ratio: 8.5:1
Bore: 74.4mm 2.9in
Stroke: 76.2mm 3.0in
Valve type/No: Overhead 8
Transmission: Automatic
No. of forward speeds: 3
Wheels driven: Rear
Wheelbase: 243.8cm 96.0in
Track F: 124.5cm 49.0in
Track R: 123.2cm 48.5in
Length: 411.5cm 162.0in
Width: 154.4cm 60.8in
Height: 151.1cm 59.5in
Kerb weight: 1103.2kg 2430.0lb

2052 Hillman
Hunter Husky Series II
1960 UK
75.0mph 120.7kmh
0-50mph 80.5kmh: 18.2secs
0-60mph 96.5kmh: 30.0secs
0-1/4 mile: 23.2secs
51.0bhp 38.0kW 51.7PS
@ 4400rpm
72.0lbft 97.6Nm @ 2200rpm
53.3bhp/ton 52.4bhp/tonne
36.7bhp/L 27.4kW/L 37.2PS/L
36.7ft/sec 11.2m/sec
15.9mph 25.6kmh/1000rpm
24.8mpg 20.7mpgUS 11.4L/100km
Petrol 4-stroke piston
1390cc 84.8cu in
In-line 4 1 Carburettor
Compression ratio: 8.0:1
Bore: 76.2mm 3.0in
Stroke: 76.2mm 3.0in
Valve type/No: Overhead 8
Transmission: Manual
No. of forward speeds: 4
Wheels driven: Rear
Springs F/R: Coil/Leaf
Brakes F/R: Drum/Drum
Wheelbase: 218.4cm 86.0in
Track F: 124.5cm 49.0in
Track R: 123.2cm 48.5in
Length: 379.7cm 149.5in
Width: 153.7cm 60.5in
Height: 151.1cm 59.5in
Ground clearance: 16.5cm 6.5in
Kerb weight: 972.5kg 2142.0lb
Fuel: 28.2L 6.2gal 7.4galUS

2053 Hillman
Super Minx
1962 UK
86.0mph 138.4kmh
0-50mph 80.5kmh: 14.9secs
0-60mph 96.5kmh: 22.2secs
0-1/4 mile: 21.9secs
62.0bhp 46.2kW 62.9PS
@ 4800rpm
84.4lbft 114.4Nm @ 2800rpm
58.3bhp/ton 57.4bhp/tonne
38.9bhp/L 29.0kW/L 39.5PS/L
40.0ft/sec 12.2m/sec
16.2mph 26.1kmh/1000rpm
23.9mpg 19.9mpgUS 11.8L/100km
Petrol 4-stroke piston
1592cc 97.1cu in
In-line 4 1 Carburettor
Compression ratio: 8.3:1
Bore: 81.5mm 3.2in
Stroke: 76.2mm 3.0in
Valve type/No: Overhead 8
Transmission: Manual
No. of forward speeds: 4
Wheels driven: Rear
Springs F/R: Coil/Leaf
Brakes F/R: Drum/Drum
Steering: Recirculating ball
Wheelbase: 256.5cm 101.0in
Track F: 130.8cm 51.5in
Track R: 123.2cm 48.5in
Length: 419.1cm 165.0in
Width: 158.0cm 62.2in
Height: 147.8cm 58.2in
Ground clearance: 16.5cm 6.5in
Kerb weight: 1080.5kg 2380.0lb
Fuel: 50.0L 11.0gal 13.2galUS

2054 Hillman
Super Minx Mk II
1962 UK
85.0mph 136.8kmh
0-50mph 80.5kmh: 14.9secs
0-60mph 96.5kmh: 22.5secs
0-1/4 mile: 22.7secs
62.0bhp 46.2kW 62.9PS
@ 4400rpm
86.3lbft 116.9Nm @ 2500rpm
58.8bhp/ton 57.9bhp/tonne
38.9bhp/L 29.0kW/L 39.5PS/L
36.7ft/sec 11.2m/sec
17.6mph 28.3kmh/1000rpm
24.0mpg 20.0mpgUS 11.8L/100km
Petrol 4-stroke piston
1592cc 97.1cu in
In-line 4 1 Carburettor
Compression ratio: 8.3:1
Bore: 81.5mm 3.2in
Stroke: 76.2mm 3.0in
Valve type/No: Overhead 8
Transmission: Manual
No. of forward speeds: 4
Wheels driven: Rear
Springs F/R: Coil/Leaf
Brakes F/R: Disc/Drum
Steering: Recirculating ball
Wheelbase: 256.5cm 101.0in
Track F: 130.8cm 51.5in
Track R: 123.2cm 48.5in
Length: 419.1cm 165.0in
Width: 158.0cm 62.2in
Height: 147.8cm 58.2in
Ground clearance: 16.5cm 6.5in
Kerb weight: 1071.4kg 2360.0lb
Fuel: 47.8L 10.5gal 12.6galUS

2055 Hillman
Hunter Husky III
1963 UK
76.0mph 122.3kmh
0-50mph 80.5kmh: 20.1secs
0-60mph 96.5kmh: 35.9secs
0-1/4 mile: 24.5secs
40.5bhp 30.2kW 41.1PS
@ 4200rpm
71.6lbft 97.0Nm @ 1800rpm
43.3bhp/ton 42.6bhp/tonne
29.1bhp/L 21.7kW/L 29.5PS/L
35.0ft/sec 10.7m/sec
17.2mph 27.7kmh/1000rpm
26.9mpg 22.4mpgUS 10.5L/100km
Petrol 4-stroke piston
1390cc 84.8cu in
In-line 4 1 Carburettor
Compression ratio: 8.0:1
Bore: 76.2mm 3.0in
Stroke: 76.2mm 3.0in
Valve type/No: Overhead 8
Transmission: Manual
No. of forward speeds: 4
Wheels driven: Rear
Springs F/R: Coil/Leaf
Brakes F/R: Drum/Drum
Steering: Recirculating ball
Wheelbase: 218.4cm 86.0in
Track F: 124.5cm 49.0in
Track R: 123.2cm 48.5in
Length: 383.5cm 151.0in
Width: 153.7cm 60.5in
Height: 152.4cm 60.0in
Ground clearance: 16.5cm 6.5in
Kerb weight: 950.2kg 2093.0lb
Fuel: 28.2L 6.2gal 7.4galUS

2056 Hillman
Imp de Luxe
1963 UK
83.0mph 133.5kmh
0-50mph 80.5kmh: 14.7secs
0-60mph 96.5kmh: 23.7secs
0-1/4 mile: 21.8secs
39.0bhp 29.1kW 39.5PS
@ 5000rpm
52.0lbft 70.5Nm @ 2800rpm
55.7bhp/ton 54.8bhp/tonne
44.6bhp/L 33.2kW/L 45.2PS/L
33.1ft/sec 10.1m/sec
15.2mph 24.5kmh/1000rpm
38.1mpg 31.7mpgUS 7.4L/100km
Petrol 4-stroke piston
875cc 53.4cu in
In-line 4 1 Carburettor
Compression ratio: 10.0:1
Bore: 68.0mm 2.7in
Stroke: 60.4mm 2.4in
Valve type/No: Overhead 8
Transmission: Manual
No. of forward speeds: 4
Wheels driven: Rear
Springs F/R: Coil/Coil
Brakes F/R: Drum/Drum
Steering: Rack & pinion
Wheelbase: 208.3cm 82.0in
Track F: 124.7cm 49.1in
Track R: 121.7cm 47.9in
Length: 358.1cm 141.0in
Width: 152.9cm 60.2in
Height: 138.4cm 54.5in
Ground clearance: 15.7cm 6.2in
Kerb weight: 711.9kg 1568.0lb
Fuel: 27.3L 6.0gal 7.2galUS

2057 Hillman
Minx Series V Automatic
1964 UK
79.0mph 127.1kmh
0-50mph 80.5kmh: 18.0secs
0-60mph 96.5kmh: 28.8secs
0-1/4 mile: 24.8secs
58.0bhp 43.2kW 58.8PS
@ 4400rpm
86.3lbft 116.9Nm @ 2500rpm
58.3bhp/ton 57.4bhp/tonne
36.4bhp/L 27.2kW/L 36.9PS/L
36.7ft/sec 11.2m/sec
17.6mph 28.3kmh/1000rpm
24.7mpg 20.6mpgUS 11.4L/100km
Petrol 4-stroke piston
1592cc 97.1cu in
In-line 4 1 Carburettor
Compression ratio: 8.3:1
Bore: 81.5mm 3.2in
Stroke: 76.2mm 3.0in
Valve type/No: Overhead 8
Transmission: Automatic
No. of forward speeds: 3
Wheels driven: Rear
Springs F/R: Coil/Leaf
Brakes F/R: Disc/Drum
Steering: Recirculating ball
Wheelbase: 243.8cm 96.0in
Track F: 131.3cm 51.7in
Track R: 123.2cm 48.5in
Length: 417.8cm 164.5in
Width: 154.2cm 60.7in
Height: 147.3cm 58.0in
Ground clearance: 15.2cm 6.0in
Kerb weight: 1011.1kg 2227.0lb
Fuel: 45.5L 10.0gal 12.0galUS

2058 Hillman
Super Minx Convertible
1964 UK
80.0mph 128.7kmh
0-50mph 80.5kmh: 15.8secs
0-60mph 96.5kmh: 22.6secs
0-1/4 mile: 22.5secs
58.0bhp 43.2kW 58.8PS
@ 4400rpm
86.3lbft 116.9Nm @ 2500rpm
52.1bhp/ton 51.3bhp/tonne
36.4bhp/L 27.2kW/L 36.9PS/L
36.7ft/sec 11.2m/sec
16.2mph 26.1kmh/1000rpm
20.0mpg 16.7mpgUS 14.1L/100km
Petrol 4-stroke piston
1592cc 97.1cu in
In-line 4 1 Carburettor
Compression ratio: 8.3:1
Bore: 81.5mm 3.2in
Stroke: 76.2mm 3.0in
Valve type/No: Overhead 8
Transmission: Manual
No. of forward speeds: 4
Wheels driven: Rear
Springs F/R: Coil/Leaf
Brakes F/R: Disc/Drum
Steering: Recirculating ball
Wheelbase: 256.5cm 101.0in
Track F: 130.8cm 51.5in
Track R: 123.2cm 48.5in
Length: 419.1cm 165.0in
Width: 158.0cm 62.2in
Height: 147.8cm 58.2in
Ground clearance: 16.5cm 6.5in
Kerb weight: 1131.4kg 2492.0lb
Fuel: 47.8L 10.5gal 12.6galUS

2059 Hillman
Super Minx III
1964 UK
83.6mph 134.5kmh
0-50mph 80.5kmh: 14.6secs
0-60mph 96.5kmh: 22.9secs
0-1/4 mile: 21.9secs
58.0bhp 43.2kW 58.8PS
@ 4400rpm
86.3lbft 116.9Nm @ 2500rpm
54.9bhp/ton 54.0bhp/tonne
36.4bhp/L 27.2kW/L 36.9PS/L
36.7ft/sec 11.2m/sec
16.2mph 26.1kmh/1000rpm
24.6mpg 20.5mpgUS 11.5L/100km
Petrol 4-stroke piston
1592cc 97.1cu in
In-line 4 1 Carburettor
Compression ratio: 8.3:1
Bore: 81.5mm 3.2in
Stroke: 76.2mm 3.0in
Valve type/No: Overhead 8
Transmission: Manual
No. of forward speeds: 4
Wheels driven: Rear
Springs F/R: Coil/Leaf
Brakes F/R: Disc/Drum
Steering: Recirculating ball
Wheelbase: 256.5cm 101.0in
Track F: 130.8cm 51.5in
Track R: 123.2cm 48.5in
Length: 419.1cm 165.0in
Width: 158.0cm 62.2in
Height: 147.8cm 58.2in
Ground clearance: 16.5cm 6.5in
Kerb weight: 1073.7kg 2365.0lb
Fuel: 47.8L 10.5gal 12.6galUS

2060 Hillman
Minx Series VI de Luxe
1965 UK
84.0mph 135.2kmh
0-50mph 80.5kmh: 14.0secs
0-60mph 96.5kmh: 20.5secs
0-1/4 mile: 21.8secs
58.5bhp 43.6kW 59.3PS
@ 4200rpm
92.2lbft 124.9Nm @ 2200rpm
57.9bhp/ton 56.9bhp/tonne
33.9bhp/L 25.3kW/L 34.4PS/L
37.9ft/sec 11.6m/sec
17.4mph 28.0kmh/1000rpm
24.4mpg 20.3mpgUS 11.6L/100km
Petrol 4-stroke piston
1725cc 105.2cu in
In-line 4 1 Carburettor
Compression ratio: 8.4:1
Bore: 81.5mm 3.2in
Stroke: 82.5mm 3.2in
Valve type/No: Overhead 8
Transmission: Manual
No. of forward speeds: 4
Wheels driven: Rear
Springs F/R: Coil/Leaf
Brakes F/R: Disc/Drum
Steering: Recirculating ball
Wheelbase: 243.8cm 96.0in
Track F: 131.3cm 51.7in
Track R: 123.2cm 48.5in
Length: 417.8cm 164.5in
Width: 154.2cm 60.7in
Height: 147.3cm 58.0in
Ground clearance: 15.2cm 6.0in
Kerb weight: 1027.4kg 2263.0lb
Fuel: 45.5L 10.0gal 12.0galUS

2061 Hillman
Super Imp
1965 UK
81.0mph 130.3kmh
0-50mph 80.5kmh: 16.0secs
0-60mph 96.5kmh: 25.4secs
0-1/4 mile: 22.8secs
39.0bhp 29.1kW 39.5PS
@ 5000rpm
52.0lbft 70.5Nm @ 2800rpm
54.2bhp/ton 53.3bhp/tonne
44.6bhp/L 33.2kW/L 45.2PS/L
33.1ft/sec 10.1m/sec
15.2mph 24.5kmh/1000rpm
35.5mpg 29.6mpgUS 8.0L/100km
Petrol 4-stroke piston
875cc 53.4cu in
In-line 4 1 Carburettor
Compression ratio: 10.0:1
Bore: 68.0mm 2.7in
Stroke: 60.4mm 2.4in
Valve type/No: Overhead 8
Transmission: Manual
No. of forward speeds: 4
Wheels driven: Rear
Springs F/R: Coil/Coil
Brakes F/R: Drum/Drum
Steering: Rack & pinion
Wheelbase: 208.3cm 82.0in
Track F: 124.7cm 49.1in
Track R: 121.7cm 47.9in
Length: 358.1cm 141.0in
Width: 152.9cm 60.2in
Height: 138.4cm 54.5in
Ground clearance: 15.7cm 6.2in
Kerb weight: 732.3kg 1613.0lb
Fuel: 27.3L 6.0gal 7.2galUS

2062 Hillman
Super Minx Estate
1966 UK
86.0mph 138.4kmh
0-50mph 80.5kmh: 12.7secs
0-60mph 96.5kmh: 19.2secs
0-1/4 mile: 21.4secs
0-1km: 40.5secs
65.0bhp 48.5kW 65.9PS
@ 4800rpm
91.0lbft 123.3Nm @ 2400rpm
58.1bhp/ton 57.1bhp/tonne
37.7bhp/L 28.1kW/L 38.2PS/L
43.3ft/sec 13.2m/sec
20.7mph 33.3kmh/1000rpm
20.0mpg 16.7mpgUS 14.1L/100km
Petrol 4-stroke piston
1725cc 105.2cu in
In-line 4 1 Carburettor
Compression ratio: 8.4:1
Bore: 81.5mm 3.2in
Stroke: 82.5mm 3.2in
Valve type/No: Overhead 8
Transmission: Manual with overdrive
No. of forward speeds: 6
Wheels driven: Rear
Springs F/R: Coil/Leaf
Brakes F/R: Disc/Drum
Steering: Recirculating ball
Wheelbase: 256.5cm 101.0in
Track F: 129.8cm 51.1in
Track R: 123.2cm 48.5in
Length: 424.2cm 167.0in
Width: 160.0cm 63.0in
Height: 148.6cm 58.5in
Ground clearance: 16.5cm 6.5in
Kerb weight: 1137.7kg 2506.0lb
Fuel: 47.8L 10.5gal 12.6galUS

2063 Hillman
Estate
1967 UK
89.0mph 143.2kmh
0-50mph 80.5kmh: 13.6secs
0-60mph 96.5kmh: 19.9secs
0-1/4 mile: 21.5secs
0-1km: 41.2secs
60.0bhp 44.7kW 60.8PS
@ 4800rpm
80.5lbft 109.1Nm @ 2600rpm
61.4bhp/ton 60.3bhp/tonne
40.1bhp/L 29.9kW/L 40.7PS/L
37.6ft/sec 11.5m/sec
16.0mph 25.7kmh/1000rpm
28.7mpg 23.9mpgUS 9.8L/100km
Petrol 4-stroke piston
1496cc 91.3cu in
In-line 4 1 Carburettor
Compression ratio: 8.4:1
Bore: 81.5mm 3.2in
Stroke: 71.6mm 2.8in
Valve type/No: Overhead 8
Transmission: Manual
No. of forward speeds: 4
Wheels driven: Rear
Springs F/R: Coil/Leaf
Brakes F/R: Disc/Drum
Steering: Recirculating ball
Wheelbase: 250.2cm 98.5in
Track F: 132.1cm 52.0in
Track R: 132.1cm 52.0in
Length: 435.6cm 171.5in
Width: 161.3cm 63.5in
Height: 144.8cm 57.0in
Ground clearance: 17.0cm 6.7in
Kerb weight: 994.3kg 2190.0lb
Fuel: 45.5L 10.0gal 12.0galUS

2064 Hillman
Hunter Husky
1967 UK
79.0mph 127.1kmh
0-50mph 80.5kmh: 15.9secs
0-60mph 96.5kmh: 24.2secs
0-1/4 mile: 22.8secs
0-1km: 43.3secs
39.0bhp 29.1kW 39.5PS
@ 5000rpm
52.0lbft 70.5Nm @ 2800rpm
53.1bhp/ton 52.2bhp/tonne
44.6bhp/L 33.2kW/L 45.2PS/L
33.1ft/sec 10.1m/sec
15.1mph 24.3kmh/1000rpm
33.8mpg 28.1mpgUS 8.4L/100km
Petrol 4-stroke piston
875cc 53.4cu in
In-line 4 1 Carburettor
Compression ratio: 10.0:1
Bore: 68.0mm 2.7in
Stroke: 60.4mm 2.4in
Valve type/No: Overhead 8
Transmission: Manual
No. of forward speeds: 4
Wheels driven: Rear
Springs F/R: Coil/Coil
Brakes F/R: Drum/Drum
Steering: Rack & pinion
Wheelbase: 208.3cm 82.0in
Track F: 124.7cm 49.1in
Track R: 121.7cm 47.9in
Length: 358.1cm 141.0in
Width: 152.9cm 60.2in
Height: 147.3cm 58.0in
Ground clearance: 15.7cm 6.2in
Kerb weight: 746.4kg 1644.0lb
Fuel: 27.3L 6.0gal 7.2galUS

2065 Hillman
Imp Californian
1967 UK
81.0mph 130.3kmh
0-50mph 80.5kmh: 14.4secs
0-60mph 96.5kmh: 22.1secs
0-1/4 mile: 21.9secs
0-1km: 41.8secs
39.0bhp 29.1kW 39.5PS
@ 5000rpm
52.0lbft 70.5Nm @ 2800rpm
56.0bhp/ton 55.1bhp/tonne
44.6bhp/L 33.2kW/L 45.2PS/L
33.1ft/sec 10.1m/sec
15.2mph 24.5kmh/1000rpm
34.6mpg 28.8mpgUS 8.2L/100km
Petrol 4-stroke piston
875cc 53.4cu in
In-line 4 1 Carburettor
Compression ratio: 10.0:1
Bore: 68.0mm 2.7in
Stroke: 60.4mm 2.4in
Valve type/No: Overhead 8
Transmission: Manual
No. of forward speeds: 4
Wheels driven: Rear
Springs F/R: Coil/Coil
Brakes F/R: Drum/Drum
Steering: Rack & pinion
Wheelbase: 208.3cm 82.0in
Track F: 124.7cm 49.1in
Track R: 121.7cm 47.9in
Length: 342.9cm 135.0in
Width: 152.9cm 60.2in
Height: 129.5cm 51.0in
Ground clearance: 15.7cm 6.2in
Kerb weight: 708.2kg 1560.0lb
Fuel: 27.3L 6.0gal 7.2galUS

2066 Hillman
Minx
1967 UK
86.0mph 138.4kmh
0-50mph 80.5kmh: 12.0secs
0-60mph 96.5kmh: 17.8secs
0-1/4 mile: 20.9secs
0-1km: 40.2secs
60.0bhp 44.7kW 60.8PS
@ 4800rpm
80.5lbft 109.1Nm @ 2600rpm
63.6bhp/ton 62.6bhp/tonne
40.1bhp/L 29.9kW/L 40.7PS/L
37.6ft/sec 11.5m/sec
17.4mph 28.0kmh/1000rpm
27.1mpg 22.6mpgUS 10.4L/100km
Petrol 4-stroke piston
1496cc 91.3cu in
In-line 4 1 Carburettor
Compression ratio: 8.4:1
Bore: 81.5mm 3.2in
Stroke: 71.6mm 2.8in
Valve type/No: Overhead 8
Transmission: Manual
No. of forward speeds: 4
Wheels driven: Rear
Springs F/R: Coil/Leaf
Brakes F/R: Disc/Drum
Steering: Recirculating ball
Wheelbase: 250.2cm 98.5in
Track F: 132.1cm 52.0in
Track R: 132.1cm 52.0in
Length: 435.6cm 171.5in
Width: 161.3cm 63.5in
Height: 142.2cm 56.0in
Ground clearance: 17.0cm 6.7in
Kerb weight: 958.8kg 2112.0lb
Fuel: 45.5L 10.0gal 12.0galUS

2067 Hillman
GT
1969 UK
96.0mph 154.5kmh
0-50mph 80.5kmh: 9.5secs
0-60mph 96.5kmh: 13.9secs
0-1/4 mile: 19.4secs
0-1km: 36.2secs
88.0bhp 65.6kW 89.2PS
@ 5200rpm
100.0lbft 135.5Nm @ 4000rpm
93.5bhp/ton 91.9bhp/tonne
51.0bhp/L 38.0kW/L 51.7PS/L
46.9ft/sec 14.3m/sec
17.3mph 27.8kmh/1000rpm
22.6mpg 18.8mpgUS 12.5L/100km
Petrol 4-stroke piston
1725cc 105.2cu in
In-line 4 2 Carburettor
Compression ratio: 9.2:1
Bore: 81.5mm 3.2in
Stroke: 82.5mm 3.2in
Valve type/No: Overhead 8
Transmission: Manual with overdrive
No. of forward speeds: 6
Wheels driven: Rear
Springs F/R: Coil/Leaf
Brake system: PA
Brakes F/R: Disc/Drum
Steering: Recirculating ball
Wheelbase: 250.2cm 98.5in
Track F: 132.1cm 52.0in
Track R: 132.1cm 52.0in
Length: 435.6cm 171.5in
Width: 161.3cm 63.5in
Height: 142.2cm 56.0in
Ground clearance: 17.0cm 6.7in
Kerb weight: 957.5kg 2109.0lb
Fuel: 45.5L 10.0gal 12.0galUS

2068 Hillman
Hunter Mk II
1969 UK
91.0mph 146.4kmh
0-50mph 80.5kmh: 9.6secs
0-60mph 96.5kmh: 13.6secs
0-1/4 mile: 19.5secs
0-1km: 37.1secs
74.0bhp 55.2kW 75.0PS
@ 5000rpm
96.0lbft 130.1Nm @ 3000rpm
80.8bhp/ton 79.5bhp/tonne
42.9bhp/L 32.0kW/L 43.5PS/L
45.1ft/sec 13.8m/sec
17.4mph 28.0kmh/1000rpm
25.2mpg 21.0mpgUS 11.2L/100km
Petrol 4-stroke piston
1725cc 105.2cu in
In-line 4 1 Carburettor
Compression ratio: 9.2:1
Bore: 81.5mm 3.2in
Stroke: 82.5mm 3.2in
Valve type/No: Overhead 8
Transmission: Manual
No. of forward speeds: 4
Wheels driven: Rear
Springs F/R: Coil/Leaf
Brake system: PA
Brakes F/R: Disc/Drum
Steering: Recirculating ball
Wheelbase: 250.2cm 98.5in
Track F: 132.1cm 52.0in
Track R: 132.1cm 52.0in
Length: 435.6cm 171.5in
Width: 161.3cm 63.5in
Height: 142.2cm 56.0in
Ground clearance: 17.0cm 6.7in

Kerb weight: 931.1kg 2051.0lb
Fuel: 45.5L 10.0gal 12.0galUS

2069 Hillman

Avenger GL
1970 UK
97.0mph 156.1kmh
0-50mph 80.5kmh: 10.7secs
0-60mph 96.5kmh: 15.6secs
0-1/4 mile: 20.1secs
0-1km: 38.3secs
63.0bhp 47.0kW 63.9PS
@ 5000rpm
80.0lbft 108.4Nm @ 3000rpm
74.2bhp/ton 72.9bhp/tonne
42.1bhp/L 31.4kW/L 42.6PS/L
35.1ft/sec 10.7m/sec
16.1mph 25.9kmh/1000rpm
27.8mpg 23.1mpgUS 10.2L/100km
Petrol 4-stroke piston
1498cc 91.4cu in
In-line 4 1 Carburettor
Compression ratio: 9.2:1
Bore: 86.1mm 3.4in
Stroke: 64.3mm 2.5in
Valve type/No: Overhead 8
Transmission: Manual
No. of forward speeds: 4
Wheels driven: Rear
Springs F/R: Coil/Coil
Brakes F/R: Disc/Drum
Steering: Rack & pinion
Wheelbase: 248.9cm 98.0in
Track F: 129.5cm 51.0in
Track R: 130.8cm 51.5in
Length: 408.9cm 161.0in
Width: 158.8cm 62.5in
Height: 135.9cm 53.5in
Ground clearance: 14.0cm 5.5in
Kerb weight: 864.0kg 1903.0lb
Fuel: 40.9L 9.0gal 10.8galUS

2070 Hillman

Avenger GT
1970 UK
98.0mph 157.7kmh
0-50mph 80.5kmh: 8.7secs
0-60mph 96.5kmh: 12.5secs
0-1/4 mile: 18.5secs
0-1km: 35.1secs
75.0bhp 55.9kW 76.0PS
@ 5400rpm
81.0lbft 109.8Nm @ 3750rpm
86.5bhp/ton 85.1bhp/tonne
50.1bhp/L 37.3kW/L 50.8PS/L
37.9ft/sec 11.6m/sec
16.9mph 27.2kmh/1000rpm
26.9mpg 22.4mpgUS 10.5L/100km
Petrol 4-stroke piston
1498cc 91.4cu in
In-line 4 2 Carburettor
Compression ratio: 9.2:1
Bore: 86.1mm 3.4in
Stroke: 64.3mm 2.5in
Valve type/No: Overhead 8
Transmission: Manual
No. of forward speeds: 4
Wheels driven: Rear
Springs F/R: Coil/Coil
Brakes F/R: Disc/Drum
Steering: Rack & pinion
Wheelbase: 248.9cm 98.0in
Track F: 129.5cm 51.0in
Track R: 130.8cm 51.5in
Length: 408.9cm 161.0in
Width: 158.8cm 62.5in
Height: 135.9cm 53.5in
Ground clearance: 14.0cm 5.5in
Kerb weight: 881.2kg 1941.0lb
Fuel: 45.5L 10.0gal 12.0galUS

2071 Hillman

Avenger Super
1970 UK
84.0mph 135.2kmh
0-50mph 80.5kmh: 13.0secs
0-60mph 96.5kmh: 19.8secs
0-1/4 mile: 21.4secs
0-1km: 40.8secs
53.0bhp 39.5kW 53.7PS
@ 5000rpm
66.0lbft 89.4Nm @ 3000rpm
62.6bhp/ton 61.6bhp/tonne
42.5bhp/L 31.7kW/L 43.1PS/L
35.1ft/sec 10.7m/sec
14.3mph 23.0kmh/1000rpm
22.9mpg 19.1mpgUS 12.3L/100km
Petrol 4-stroke piston
1248cc 76.1cu in
In-line 4 1 Carburettor
Compression ratio: 9.2:1
Bore: 78.6mm 3.1in
Stroke: 64.3mm 2.5in
Valve type/No: Overhead 8
Transmission: Manual
No. of forward speeds: 4
Wheels driven: Rear
Springs F/R: Coil/Coil
Brakes F/R: Disc/Drum
Steering: Rack & pinion
Wheelbase: 248.9cm 98.0in
Track F: 129.5cm 51.0in
Track R: 130.8cm 51.5in
Length: 408.9cm 161.0in
Width: 158.8cm 62.5in
Height: 135.9cm 53.5in
Ground clearance: 14.0cm 5.5in
Kerb weight: 860.8kg 1896.0lb
Fuel: 40.9L 9.0gal 10.8galUS

2072 Hillman

Hunter Super
1971 UK
89.0mph 143.2kmh
0-50mph 80.5kmh: 11.0secs
0-60mph 96.5kmh: 16.2secs
0-1/4 mile: 20.2secs
0-1km: 38.2secs
61.0bhp 45.5kW 61.8PS
@ 4700rpm
85.0lbft 115.2Nm @ 2600rpm
66.6bhp/ton 65.4bhp/tonne
35.4bhp/L 26.4kW/L 35.9PS/L
42.4ft/sec 12.9m/sec
17.4mph 28.0kmh/1000rpm
23.4mpg 19.5mpgUS 12.1L/100km
Petrol 4-stroke piston
1725cc 105.2cu in
In-line 4 1 Carburettor
Compression ratio: 9.2:1
Bore: 81.5mm 3.2in
Stroke: 82.5mm 3.2in
Valve type/No: Overhead 8
Transmission: Manual
No. of forward speeds: 4
Wheels driven: Rear
Springs F/R: Coil/Leaf
Brake system: PA
Brakes F/R: Disc/Drum
Steering: Recirculating ball
Wheelbase: 250.2cm 98.5in
Track F: 132.1cm 52.0in
Track R: 132.1cm 52.0in
Length: 435.6cm 171.5in
Width: 161.3cm 63.5in
Height: 142.2cm 56.0in
Ground clearance: 17.0cm 6.7in
Kerb weight: 932.1kg 2053.0lb
Fuel: 45.5L 10.0gal 12.0galUS

2073 Hillman

Imp de Luxe
1971 UK
81.0mph 130.3kmh
0-50mph 80.5kmh: 14.0secs
0-60mph 96.5kmh: 21.1secs
0-1/4 mile: 21.0secs
0-1km: 40.4secs
37.0bhp 27.6kW 37.5PS
@ 4800rpm
49.0lbft 66.4Nm @ 2600rpm
55.4bhp/ton 54.5bhp/tonne
42.3bhp/L 31.5kW/L 42.9PS/L
31.7ft/sec 9.7m/sec
15.1mph 24.3kmh/1000rpm
32.4mpg 27.0mpgUS 8.7L/100km
Petrol 4-stroke piston
875cc 53.4cu in
In-line 4 1 Carburettor
Compression ratio: 10.0:1
Bore: 68.0mm 2.7in
Stroke: 60.4mm 2.4in
Valve type/No: Overhead 8
Transmission: Manual
No. of forward speeds: 4
Wheels driven: Rear
Springs F/R: Coil/Coil
Brakes F/R: Drum/Drum
Steering: Rack & pinion
Wheelbase: 208.3cm 82.0in
Track F: 128.3cm 50.5in
Track R: 123.2cm 48.5in
Length: 353.1cm 139.0in
Width: 152.9cm 60.2in
Height: 138.4cm 54.5in
Ground clearance: 15.2cm 6.0in
Kerb weight: 678.7kg 1495.0lb
Fuel: 27.3L 6.0gal 7.2galUS

2074 Hillman

Avenger Estate
1972 UK
87.0mph 140.0kmh
0-50mph 80.5kmh: 11.5secs
0-60mph 96.5kmh: 16.6secs
0-1/4 mile: 20.2secs
0-1km: 38.5secs
63.0bhp 47.0kW 63.9PS
@ 5000rpm
83.0lbft 112.5Nm @ 3000rpm
70.8bhp/ton 69.6bhp/tonne
42.1bhp/L 31.4kW/L 42.6PS/L
35.1ft/sec 10.7m/sec
16.1mph 25.9kmh/1000rpm
25.1mpg 20.9mpgUS 11.3L/100km
Petrol 4-stroke piston
1498cc 91.4cu in
In-line 4 1 Carburettor
Compression ratio: 9.2:1
Bore: 86.1mm 3.4in
Stroke: 64.3mm 2.5in
Valve type/No: Overhead 8
Transmission: Manual
No. of forward speeds: 4
Wheels driven: Rear
Springs F/R: Coil/Coil
Brake system: PA
Brakes F/R: Disc/Drum
Steering: Rack & pinion
Wheelbase: 248.9cm 98.0in
Track F: 129.5cm 51.0in
Track R: 130.8cm 51.5in
Length: 414.0cm 163.0in
Width: 158.8cm 62.5in
Height: 133.4cm 52.5in
Ground clearance: 14.0cm 5.5in
Kerb weight: 904.8kg 1993.0lb
Fuel: 40.9L 9.0gal 10.8galUS

2075 Hillman

Hunter GLS
1972 UK
110.0mph 177.0kmh
0-50mph 80.5kmh: 7.1secs
0-60mph 96.5kmh: 10.5secs
0-1/4 mile: 17.4secs
0-1km: 32.9secs
93.0bhp 69.3kW 94.3PS
@ 5200rpm
106.0lbft 143.6Nm @ 4000rpm
98.5bhp/ton 96.9bhp/tonne
53.9bhp/L 40.2kW/L 54.7PS/L
46.9ft/sec 14.3m/sec
21.6mph 34.8kmh/1000rpm
21.5mpg 17.9mpgUS 13.1L/100km
Petrol 4-stroke piston
1725cc 105.2cu in
In-line 4 2 Carburettor
Compression ratio: 9.6:1
Bore: 81.5mm 3.2in
Stroke: 82.5mm 3.2in
Valve type/No: Overhead 8
Transmission: Manual
No. of forward speeds: 4
Wheels driven: Rear
Springs F/R: Coil/Leaf
Brake system: PA
Brakes F/R: Disc/Drum
Steering: Recirculating ball
Wheelbase: 250.2cm 98.5in
Track F: 132.1cm 52.0in
Track R: 132.1cm 52.0in
Length: 426.7cm 168.0in
Width: 161.3cm 63.5in
Height: 142.2cm 56.0in
Ground clearance: 17.0cm 6.7in
Kerb weight: 959.8kg 2114.0lb
Fuel: 45.5L 10.0gal 12.0galUS

2076 Hillman

Avenger DL
1973 UK
88.0mph 141.6kmh
0-50mph 80.5kmh: 12.0secs
0-60mph 96.5kmh: 17.0secs
0-1/4 mile: 20.4secs
0-1km: 38.7secs
63.0bhp 47.0kW 63.9PS
@ 5000rpm
80.0lbft 108.4Nm @ 3000rpm
77.1bhp/ton 75.8bhp/tonne
42.1bhp/L 31.4kW/L 42.6PS/L
35.1ft/sec 10.7m/sec
16.0mph 25.7kmh/1000rpm
29.8mpg 24.8mpgUS 9.5L/100km
Petrol 4-stroke piston
1498cc 91.4cu in
In-line 4 1 Carburettor
Compression ratio: 9.2:1
Bore: 86.1mm 3.4in
Stroke: 64.3mm 2.5in
Valve type/No: Overhead 8
Transmission: Manual
No. of forward speeds: 4
Wheels driven: Rear
Springs F/R: Coil/Coil
Brakes F/R: Disc/Drum
Steering: Rack & pinion
Wheelbase: 248.9cm 98.0in
Track F: 129.5cm 51.0in
Track R: 130.8cm 51.5in
Length: 410.2cm 161.5in
Width: 158.8cm 62.5in
Height: 134.6cm 53.0in
Ground clearance: 14.0cm 5.5in
Kerb weight: 831.3kg 1831.0lb
Fuel: 45.5L 10.0gal 12.0galUS

2077 Hillman

Avenger GLS
1973 UK
98.0mph 157.7kmh
0-50mph 80.5kmh: 9.0secs
0-60mph 96.5kmh: 13.5secs
0-1/4 mile: 19.3secs
0-1km: 36.1secs
78.0bhp 58.2kW 79.1PS
@ 5600rpm
81.0lbft 109.8Nm @ 3750rpm
90.1bhp/ton 88.6bhp/tonne
52.1bhp/L 38.8kW/L 52.8PS/L
39.4ft/sec 12.0m/sec
16.9mph 27.2kmh/1000rpm
24.4mpg 20.3mpgUS 11.6L/100km
Petrol 4-stroke piston
1498cc 91.4cu in
In-line 4 2 Carburettor
Compression ratio: 9.2:1
Bore: 86.1mm 3.4in
Stroke: 64.3mm 2.5in
Valve type/No: Overhead 8
Transmission: Manual
No. of forward speeds: 4
Wheels driven: Rear
Springs F/R: Coil/Coil
Brake system: PA
Brakes F/R: Disc/Drum
Steering: Rack & pinion
Wheelbase: 248.9cm 98.0in
Track F: 129.5cm 51.0in
Track R: 130.8cm 51.5in
Length: 408.9cm 161.0in
Width: 158.8cm 62.5in
Height: 139.7cm 55.0in
Ground clearance: 14.0cm 5.5in
Kerb weight: 880.8kg 1940.0lb
Fuel: 45.5L 10.0gal 12.0galUS

2078 Hillman

Avenger 1300 GL
1974 UK
87.0mph 140.0kmh
0-50mph 80.5kmh: 11.8secs
0-60mph 96.5kmh: 17.5secs
0-1/4 mile: 20.9secs
0-1km: 39.7secs
57.0bhp 42.5kW 57.8PS
@ 5000rpm
69.0lbft 93.5Nm @ 2800rpm
67.8bhp/ton 66.7bhp/tonne
44.0bhp/L 32.8kW/L 44.6PS/L
36.5ft/sec 11.1m/sec
15.0mph 24.1kmh/1000rpm
27.9mpg 23.2mpgUS 10.1L/100km
Petrol 4-stroke piston
1295cc 79.0cu in
In-line 4 1 Carburettor
Compression ratio: 8.6:1
Bore: 78.6mm 3.1in
Stroke: 66.7mm 2.6in
Valve type/No: Overhead 8
Transmission: Manual
No. of forward speeds: 4
Wheels driven: Rear
Springs F/R: Coil/Coil
Brake system: PA

Brakes F/R: Disc/Drum
Steering: Rack & pinion
Wheelbase: 248.9cm 98.0in
Track F: 129.5cm 51.0in
Track R: 130.8cm 51.5in
Length: 408.9cm 161.0in
Width: 158.8cm 62.5in
Height: 135.9cm 53.5in
Ground clearance: 14.0cm 5.5in
Kerb weight: 854.4kg 1882.0lb
Fuel: 45.5L 10.0gal 12.0galUS

2079 Hillman

Avenger 1600 GLS
1974 UK
94.0mph 151.2kmh
0-50mph 80.5kmh: 10.4secs
0-60mph 96.5kmh: 14.5secs
0-1/4 mile: 19.8secs
0-1km: 36.8secs
81.0bhp 60.4kW 82.1PS
@ 5500rpm
86.0lbft 116.5Nm @ 3400rpm
91.0bhp/ton 89.5bhp/tonne
50.6bhp/L 37.7kW/L 51.3PS/L
40.2ft/sec 12.2m/sec
16.8mph 27.0kmh/1000rpm
22.1mpg 18.4mpgUS 12.8L/100km
Petrol 4-stroke piston
1600cc 97.6cu in
In-line 4 2 Carburettor
Compression ratio: 8.6:1
Bore: 87.3mm 3.4in
Stroke: 66.7mm 2.6in
Valve type/No: Overhead 8
Transmission: Automatic
No. of forward speeds: 4
Wheels driven: Rear
Springs F/R: Coil/Coil
Brake system: PA
Brakes F/R: Disc/Drum
Steering: Rack & pinion
Wheelbase: 248.9cm 98.0in
Track F: 129.5cm 51.0in
Track R: 130.8cm 51.5in
Length: 408.9cm 161.0in
Width: 158.8cm 62.5in
Height: 139.7cm 55.0in
Ground clearance: 14.0cm 5.5in
Kerb weight: 905.3kg 1994.0lb
Fuel: 45.5L 10.0gal 12.0galUS

2080 Hillman

Avenger GLS
1975 UK
102.0mph 164.1kmh
0-50mph 80.5kmh: 8.5secs
0-60mph 96.5kmh: 12.2secs
0-1/4 mile: 19.0secs
0-1km: 35.5secs
81.0bhp 60.4kW 82.1PS
@ 5000rpm
86.0lbft 116.5Nm @ 3400rpm
92.0bhp/ton 90.5bhp/tonne
50.6bhp/L 37.7kW/L 51.3PS/L
36.4ft/sec 11.1m/sec
16.8mph 27.0kmh/1000rpm
28.3mpg 23.6mpgUS 10.0L/100km
Petrol 4-stroke piston
1600cc 97.6cu in
In-line 4 2 Carburettor
Compression ratio: 8.6:1
Bore: 87.3mm 3.4in
Stroke: 66.6mm 2.6in
Valve type/No: Overhead 8
Transmission: Manual
No. of forward speeds: 4
Wheels driven: Rear
Springs F/R: Coil/Coil
Brake system: PA
Brakes F/R: Disc/Drum
Steering: Rack & pinion
Wheelbase: 248.9cm 98.0in
Track F: 129.5cm 51.0in
Track R: 130.8cm 51.5in
Length: 410.2cm 161.5in
Width: 158.8cm 62.5in
Height: 135.9cm 53.5in
Ground clearance: 14.0cm 5.5in
Kerb weight: 894.8kg 1971.0lb
Fuel: 45.5L 10.0gal 12.0galUS

2081 Hillman

Hunter Super
1975 UK
94.0mph 151.2kmh
0-50mph 80.5kmh: 10.0secs
0-60mph 96.5kmh: 14.3secs
0-1/4 mile: 19.7secs
0-1km: 36.9secs
72.0bhp 53.7kW 73.0PS
@ 5000rpm
90.0lbft 122.0Nm @ 3000rpm
80.6bhp/ton 79.3bhp/tonne
41.7bhp/L 31.1kW/L 42.3PS/L
45.1ft/sec 13.8m/sec
17.7mph 28.5kmh/1000rpm
24.3mpg 20.2mpgUS 11.6L/100km
Petrol 4-stroke piston
1725cc 105.2cu in
In-line 4 1 Carburettor
Compression ratio: 9.2:1
Bore: 81.5mm 3.2in
Stroke: 82.5mm 3.2in
Valve type/No: Overhead 8
Transmission: Manual
No. of forward speeds: 4
Wheels driven: Rear
Springs F/R: Coil/Leaf
Brake system: PA
Brakes F/R: Disc/Drum
Steering: Recirculating ball
Wheelbase: 250.2cm 98.5in
Track F: 132.1cm 52.0in
Track R: 132.1cm 52.0in
Length: 426.7cm 168.0in
Width: 161.3cm 63.5in
Height: 142.2cm 56.0in
Ground clearance: 17.0cm 6.7in
Kerb weight: 908.0kg 2000.0lb
Fuel: 45.5L 10.0gal 12.0galUS

2082 Hillman

Avenger 1600 Super
1976 UK
97.0mph 156.1kmh
0-50mph 80.5kmh: 9.2secs
0-60mph 96.5kmh: 13.2secs
0-1/4 mile: 19.4secs
0-1km: 36.0secs
69.0bhp 51.4kW 70.0PS
@ 5000rpm
87.0lbft 117.9Nm @ 2900rpm
80.6bhp/ton 79.2bhp/tonne
43.1bhp/L 32.2kW/L 43.7PS/L
36.5ft/sec 11.1m/sec
17.7mph 28.5kmh/1000rpm
28.3mpg 23.6mpgUS 10.0L/100km
Petrol 4-stroke piston
1600cc 97.6cu in
In-line 4 1 Carburettor
Compression ratio: 8.6:1
Bore: 87.3mm 3.4in
Stroke: 66.7mm 2.6in
Valve type/No: Overhead 8
Transmission: Manual
No. of forward speeds: 4
Wheels driven: Rear
Springs F/R: Coil/Coil
Brake system: PA
Brakes F/R: Disc/Drum
Steering: Rack & pinion
Wheelbase: 248.9cm 98.0in
Track F: 129.5cm 51.0in
Track R: 130.8cm 51.5in
Length: 408.9cm 161.0in
Width: 158.8cm 62.5in
Height: 139.7cm 55.0in
Ground clearance: 14.0cm 5.5in
Kerb weight: 870.8kg 1918.0lb
Fuel: 45.5L 10.0gal 12.0galUS

2083 Hispano-Suiza

30/120 Saloon
1934 Spain
82.9mph 133.4kmh
0-50mph 80.5kmh: 12.2secs
0-60mph 96.5kmh: 19.6secs
120.0bhp 89.5kW 121.7PS
68.6bhp/ton 67.4bhp/tonne
24.5bhp/L 18.3kW/L 24.8PS/L
14.0mpg 11.7mpgUS 20.2L/100km
Petrol 4-stroke piston
4900cc 299.0cu in
In-line 6
Bore: 100.0mm 3.9in
Stroke: 110.0mm 4.3in
Transmission: Manual
No. of forward speeds: 3
Wheels driven: Rear
Brakes F/R: Drum/Drum
Kerb weight: 1779.7kg 3920.0lb
Fuel: 100.1L 22.0gal 26.4galUS

2084 Hispano-Suiza

54/220
1934 Spain
100.0mph 160.9kmh
0-50mph 80.5kmh: 9.4secs
0-60mph 96.5kmh: 12.0secs
220.0bhp 164.0kW 223.0PS
112.8bhp/ton 110.9bhp/tonne
23.3bhp/L 17.4kW/L 23.7PS/L
10.0mpg 8.3mpgUS 28.2L/100km
Petrol 4-stroke piston
9420cc 574.7cu in
Vee 12
Bore: 100.0mm 3.9in
Stroke: 100.0mm 3.9in
Valve type/No: Overhead 24
Transmission: Manual
No. of forward speeds: 3
Wheels driven: Rear
Brakes F/R: Drum/Drum
Kerb weight: 1983.1kg 4368.0lb
Fuel: 127.4L 28.0gal 33.6galUS

2085 Holden

Saloon
1952 Australia
80.0mph 128.7kmh
0-50mph 80.5kmh: 13.8secs
0-60mph 96.5kmh: 20.7secs
60.0bhp 44.7kW 60.8PS
@ 3800rpm
100.0lbft 135.5Nm @ 2000rpm
59.8bhp/ton 58.8bhp/tonne
27.6bhp/L 20.6kW/L 28.0PS/L
33.0ft/sec 10.1m/sec
19.5mph 31.4kmh/1000rpm
28.0mpg 23.3mpgUS 10.1L/100km
Petrol 4-stroke piston
2171cc 132.5cu in
In-line 4
Compression ratio: 6.5:1
Bore: 76.2mm 3.0in
Stroke: 79.4mm 3.1in
Valve type/No: Overhead 8
Transmission: Manual
No. of forward speeds: 3
Wheels driven: Rear
Brakes F/R: Drum/Drum
Wheelbase: 261.6cm 103.0in
Track F: 134.6cm 53.0in
Track R: 137.2cm 54.0in
Length: 436.9cm 172.0in
Width: 169.7cm 66.8in
Height: 156.7cm 61.7in
Ground clearance: 21.6cm 8.5in
Kerb weight: 1020.1kg 2247.0lb
Fuel: 43.2L 9.5gal 11.4galUS

2086 Holden

Brougham
1969 Australia
106.0mph 170.6kmh
0-50mph 80.5kmh: 8.9secs
0-60mph 96.5kmh: 11.9secs
0-1/4 mile: 18.9secs
0-1km: 34.4secs
210.0bhp 156.6kW 212.9PS
@ 4600rpm
300.0lbft 406.5Nm @ 2400rpm
151.9bhp/ton 149.4bhp/tonne
41.8bhp/L 31.2kW/L 42.4PS/L
41.5ft/sec 12.7m/sec
25.4mph 40.9kmh/1000rpm
15.0mpg 12.5mpgUS 18.8L/100km
Petrol 4-stroke piston
5025cc 306.6cu in
Vee 8 1 Carburettor
Compression ratio: 8.7:1
Bore: 98.4mm 3.9in
Stroke: 82.5mm 3.2in
Valve type/No: Overhead 16
Transmission: Automatic
No. of forward speeds: 2
Wheels driven: Rear
Springs F/R: Coil/Leaf
Brake system: PA
Brakes F/R: Disc/Drum
Steering: Recirculating ball PA
Wheelbase: 283.2cm 111.5in
Track F: 145.3cm 57.2in
Track R: 145.3cm 57.2in
Length: 487.7cm 192.0in
Width: 181.4cm 71.4in
Height: 142.2cm 56.0in
Ground clearance: 16.5cm 6.5in
Kerb weight: 1406.0kg 3097.0lb
Fuel: 75.1L 16.5gal 19.8galUS

2087 Honda

S600
1965 Japan
90.0mph 144.8kmh
0-50mph 80.5kmh: 11.5secs
0-60mph 96.5kmh: 17.8secs
0-1/4 mile: 20.7secs
57.0bhp 42.5kW 57.8PS
@ 8500rpm
37.5lbft 50.8Nm @ 5500rpm
77.8bhp/ton 76.6bhp/tonne
94.1bhp/L 70.1kW/L 95.4PS/L
60.4ft/sec 18.4m/sec
9.9mph 15.9kmh/1000rpm
Petrol 4-stroke piston
606cc 37.0cu in
In-line 4 4 Carburettor
Compression ratio: 9.5:1
Bore: 54.6mm 2.1in
Stroke: 65.0mm 2.6in
Valve type/No: Overhead 8
Transmission: Manual
No. of forward speeds: 4
Wheels driven: Rear
Springs F/R: Torsion bar/Coil
Brakes F/R: Drum/Drum
Steering: Rack & pinion
Wheelbase: 200.7cm 79.0in
Track F: 115.1cm 45.3in
Track R: 112.8cm 44.4in
Length: 330.2cm 130.0in
Width: 143.0cm 56.3in
Height: 120.1cm 47.3in
Ground clearance: 16.0cm 6.3in
Kerb weight: 744.6kg 1640.0lb
Fuel: 25.0L 5.5gal 6.6galUS

2088 Honda

S800
1967 Japan
96.0mph 154.5kmh
0-50mph 80.5kmh: 9.5secs
0-60mph 96.5kmh: 13.4secs
0-1/4 mile: 18.8secs
0-1km: 35.8secs
70.0bhp 52.2kW 71.0PS
@ 8000rpm
48.5lbft 65.7Nm @ 6000rpm
92.6bhp/ton 91.0bhp/tonne
88.5bhp/L 66.0kW/L 89.7PS/L
61.3ft/sec 18.7m/sec
11.8mph 19.0kmh/1000rpm
24.6mpg 20.5mpgUS 11.5L/100km
Petrol 4-stroke piston
791cc 48.3cu in
In-line 4 2 Carburettor
Compression ratio: 9.2:1
Bore: 60.0mm 2.4in
Stroke: 70.0mm 2.8in
Valve type/No: Overhead 8
Transmission: Manual
No. of forward speeds: 4
Wheels driven: Rear
Springs F/R: Torsion bar/Coil
Brakes F/R: Disc/Drum
Steering: Rack & pinion
Wheelbase: 199.9cm 78.7in
Track F: 115.1cm 45.3in
Track R: 115.1cm 45.3in
Length: 333.5cm 131.3in
Width: 140.0cm 55.1in
Height: 121.4cm 47.8in
Ground clearance: 15.2cm 6.0in
Kerb weight: 769.1kg 1694.0lb
Fuel: 35.0L 7.7gal 9.2galUS

2089 Honda

N360
1968 Japan
74.0mph 119.1kmh
0-50mph 80.5kmh: 16.5secs
0-60mph 96.5kmh: 29.3secs
0-1/4 mile: 22.9secs
0-1km: 44.7secs
27.0bhp 20.1kW 27.4PS
@ 8000rpm
24.0lbft 32.5Nm @ 5500rpm
54.0bhp/ton 53.1bhp/tonne
76.3bhp/L 56.9kW/L 77.3PS/L
50.7ft/sec 15.4m/sec
8.8mph 14.2kmh/1000rpm
39.4mpg 32.8mpgUS 7.2L/100km
Petrol 4-stroke piston
354cc 21.6cu in
In-line 2 1 Carburettor
Compression ratio: 8.6:1
Bore: 62.5mm 2.5in

Stroke: 57.8mm 2.3in
Valve type/No: Overhead 4
Transmission: Manual
No. of forward speeds: 4
Wheels driven: Front
Springs F/R: Coil/Leaf
Brakes F/R: Drum/Drum
Steering: Rack & pinion
Wheelbase: 198.6cm 78.2in
Track F: 115.1cm 45.3in
Track R: 111.0cm 43.7in
Length: 299.7cm 118.0in
Width: 129.5cm 51.0in
Height: 134.6cm 53.0in
Ground clearance: 15.2cm 6.0in
Kerb weight: 508.0kg 1119.0lb
Fuel: 25.9L 5.7gal 6.8galUS

2090 Honda

600
1970 Japan
73.0mph 117.5kmh
0-50mph 80.5kmh: 15.3secs
0-60mph 96.5kmh: 23.4secs
0-1/4 mile: 22.0secs
36.0bhp 26.8kW 36.5PS
@ 6000rpm
32.0lbft 43.4Nm @ 4000rpm
59.5bhp/ton 58.5bhp/tonne
60.2bhp/L 44.9kW/L 61.0PS/L
45.7ft/sec 13.9m/sec
12.7mph 20.4kmh/1000rpm
38.0mpg 31.6mpgUS 7.4L/100km
Petrol 4-stroke piston
598cc 36.5cu in
In-line 2 1 Carburettor
Compression ratio: 8.6:1
Bore: 74.0mm 2.9in
Stroke: 69.6mm 2.7in
Valve type/No: Overhead 4
Transmission: Manual
No. of forward speeds: 4
Wheels driven: Front
Springs F/R: Coil/Leaf
Brake system: PA
Brakes F/R: Disc/Drum
Steering: Rack & pinion
Wheelbase: 199.9cm 78.7in
Track F: 117.1cm 46.1in
Track R: 112.5cm 44.3in
Length: 317.5cm 125.0in
Width: 133.4cm 52.5in
Height: 133.1cm 52.4in
Ground clearance: 13.5cm 5.3in
Kerb weight: 615.2kg 1355.0lb
Fuel: 26.1L 5.7gal 6.9galUS

2091 Honda

600 Coupe
1972 Japan
78.0mph 125.5kmh
0-50mph 80.5kmh: 15.3secs
0-60mph 96.5kmh: 23.6secs
0-1/4 mile: 23.9secs
32.0bhp 23.9kW 32.4PS
@ 6000rpm
32.0lbft 43.4Nm @ 4000rpm
52.1bhp/ton 51.3bhp/tonne
53.5bhp/L 39.9kW/L 54.2PS/L
45.7ft/sec 13.9m/sec
12.0mph 19.3kmh/1000rpm
51.6mpg 43.0mpgUS 5.5L/100km
Petrol 4-stroke piston
598cc 36.5cu in
In-line 2 1 Carburettor
Compression ratio: 8.5:1
Bore: 74.0mm 2.9in
Stroke: 69.6mm 2.7in
Valve type/No: Overhead 4
Transmission: Manual
No. of forward speeds: 4
Wheels driven: Front
Springs F/R: Coil/Leaf
Brake system: PA
Brakes F/R: Disc/Drum
Steering: Rack & pinion
Wheelbase: 199.9cm 78.7in
Track F: 116.6cm 45.9in
Track R: 112.5cm 44.3in
Length: 311.9cm 122.8in
Width: 129.5cm 51.0in
Height: 128.0cm 50.4in
Ground clearance: 15.5cm 6.1in
Kerb weight: 624.2kg 1375.0lb
Fuel: 26.1L 5.7gal 6.9galUS

2092 Honda

Civic
1973 Japan
91.0mph 146.4kmh
0-50mph 80.5kmh: 10.0secs
0-60mph 96.5kmh: 14.1secs
0-1/4 mile: 19.2secs
50.0bhp 37.3kW 50.7PS
@ 5500rpm
59.0lbft 79.9Nm @ 3000rpm
69.6bhp/ton 68.4bhp/tonne
42.7bhp/L 31.9kW/L 43.3PS/L
45.7ft/sec 13.9m/sec
15.8mph 25.4kmh/1000rpm
36.0mpg 30.0mpgUS 7.8L/100km
Petrol 4-stroke piston
1170cc 71.4cu in
In-line 4 1 Carburettor
Compression ratio: 8.3:1
Bore: 70.0mm 2.8in
Stroke: 76.0mm 3.0in
Valve type/No: Overhead 8
Transmission: Manual
No. of forward speeds: 4
Wheels driven: Front
Springs F/R: Coil/Coil
Brake system: PA
Brakes F/R: Disc/Drum
Steering: Rack & pinion
Wheelbase: 220.0cm 86.6in
Track F: 130.0cm 51.2in
Track R: 128.0cm 50.4in
Length: 355.1cm 139.8in
Width: 150.1cm 59.1in
Height: 134.6cm 53.0in
Ground clearance: 18.0cm 7.1in
Kerb weight: 730.9kg 1610.0lb
Fuel: 37.8L 8.3gal 10.0galUS

2093 Honda

Civic Hondamatic
1973 Japan
86.0mph 138.4kmh
0-50mph 80.5kmh: 12.9secs
0-60mph 96.5kmh: 18.3secs
0-1/4 mile: 21.5secs
0-1km: 40.3secs
60.0bhp 44.7kW 60.8PS
@ 5500rpm
58.0lbft 78.6Nm @ 3500rpm
90.2bhp/ton 88.7bhp/tonne
51.3bhp/L 38.2kW/L 52.0PS/L
45.7ft/sec 13.9m/sec
15.7mph 25.3kmh/1000rpm
32.8mpg 27.3mpgUS 8.6L/100km
Petrol 4-stroke piston
1170cc 71.4cu in
In-line 4 1 Carburettor
Compression ratio: 8.0:1
Bore: 70.0mm 2.8in
Stroke: 76.0mm 3.0in
Valve type/No: Overhead 8
Transmission: Automatic
No. of forward speeds: 2
Wheels driven: Front
Springs F/R: Coil/Coil
Brake system: PA
Brakes F/R: Disc/Drum
Steering: Rack & pinion
Wheelbase: 220.2cm 86.7in
Track F: 130.0cm 51.2in
Track R: 127.0cm 50.0in
Length: 355.6cm 140.0in
Width: 149.9cm 59.0in
Height: 133.9cm 52.7in
Ground clearance: 15.2cm 6.0in
Kerb weight: 676.5kg 1490.0lb
Fuel: 38.2L 8.4gal 10.1galUS

2094 Honda

Civic CVCC
1975 Japan
91.0mph 146.4kmh
0-50mph 80.5kmh: 10.5secs
0-60mph 96.5kmh: 15.0secs
0-1/4 mile: 20.1secs
53.0bhp 39.5kW 53.7PS
@ 5000rpm
68.0lbft 92.1Nm @ 3000rpm
65.0bhp/ton 64.0bhp/tonne
35.6bhp/L 26.6kW/L 36.1PS/L
47.4ft/sec 14.4m/sec
21.4mph 34.4kmh/1000rpm
43.8mpg 36.5mpgUS 6.4L/100km
Petrol 4-stroke piston
1487cc 90.7cu in
In-line 4 1 Carburettor
Compression ratio: 8.1:1
Bore: 74.0mm 2.9in
Stroke: 86.5mm 3.4in
Valve type/No: Overhead 12
Transmission: Manual
No. of forward speeds: 5
Wheels driven: Front
Springs F/R: Coil/Coil
Brake system: PA
Brakes F/R: Disc/Drum
Steering: Rack & pinion
Wheelbase: 220.0cm 86.6in
Track F: 130.0cm 51.2in
Track R: 128.0cm 50.4in
Length: 381.0cm 150.0in
Width: 150.6cm 59.3in
Height: 132.6cm 52.2in
Ground clearance: 17.0cm 6.7in
Kerb weight: 828.5kg 1825.0lb
Fuel: 41.6L 9.1gal 11.0galUS

2095 Honda

Accord
1976 Japan
90.0mph 144.8kmh
0-50mph 80.5kmh: 10.7secs
0-60mph 96.5kmh: 15.4secs
0-1/4 mile: 19.5secs
68.0bhp 50.7kW 68.9PS
@ 5000rpm
85.0lbft 115.2Nm @ 3000rpm
74.5bhp/ton 73.2bhp/tonne
42.6bhp/L 31.7kW/L 43.2PS/L
50.8ft/sec 15.5m/sec
21.5mph 34.6kmh/1000rpm
38.4mpg 32.0mpgUS 7.4L/100km
Petrol 4-stroke piston
1597cc 97.4cu in
In-line 4 1 Carburettor
Compression ratio: 8.0:1
Bore: 73.9mm 2.9in
Stroke: 93.0mm 3.7in
Valve type/No: Overhead 12
Transmission: Manual
No. of forward speeds: 5
Wheels driven: Front
Springs F/R: Coil/Coil
Brake system: PA
Brakes F/R: Disc/Drum
Steering: Rack & pinion
Wheelbase: 238.0cm 93.7in
Track F: 140.0cm 55.1in
Track R: 138.9cm 54.7in
Length: 413.5cm 162.8in
Width: 162.1cm 63.8in
Height: 133.1cm 52.4in
Ground clearance: 16.5cm 6.5in
Kerb weight: 928.4kg 2045.0lb
Fuel: 50.0L 11.0gal 13.2galUS

2096 Honda

Accord
1977 Japan
95.0mph 152.9kmh
0-50mph 80.5kmh: 11.0secs
0-60mph 96.5kmh: 17.0secs
0-1/4 mile: 20.0secs
0-1km: 37.9secs
80.0bhp 59.7kW 81.1PS
@ 5300rpm
92.0lbft 124.7Nm @ 3700rpm
92.2bhp/ton 90.6bhp/tonne
50.0bhp/L 37.3kW/L 50.7PS/L
53.9ft/sec 16.4m/sec
17.6mph 28.3kmh/1000rpm
25.5mpg 21.2mpgUS 11.1L/100km
Petrol 4-stroke piston
1600cc 97.6cu in
In-line 4 1 Carburettor
Compression ratio: 8.4:1
Bore: 74.0mm 2.9in
Stroke: 93.0mm 3.7in
Valve type/No: Overhead 8
Transmission: Automatic
No. of forward speeds: 2
Wheels driven: Front
Springs F/R: Coil/Coil
Brake system: PA
Brakes F/R: Disc/Drum
Steering: Rack & pinion
Wheelbase: 238.0cm 93.7in
Track F: 140.0cm 55.1in
Track R: 138.9cm 54.7in
Length: 413.5cm 162.8in
Width: 162.1cm 63.8in
Height: 133.1cm 52.4in
Ground clearance: 16.5cm 6.5in
Kerb weight: 882.6kg 1944.0lb
Fuel: 50.0L 11.0gal 13.2galUS

2097 Honda

Civic 1500
1977 Japan
97.0mph 156.1kmh
0-50mph 80.5kmh: 9.4secs
0-60mph 96.5kmh: 13.7secs
0-1/4 mile: 19.0secs
0-1km: 35.9secs
70.0bhp 52.2kW 71.0PS
@ 5500rpm
76.0lbft 103.0Nm @ 4000rpm
91.6bhp/ton 90.1bhp/tonne
47.0bhp/L 35.1kW/L 47.7PS/L
52.1ft/sec 15.9m/sec
17.2mph 27.7kmh/1000rpm
30.3mpg 25.2mpgUS 9.3L/100km
Petrol 4-stroke piston
1488cc 90.8cu in
In-line 4 1 Carburettor
Compression ratio: 8.6:1
Bore: 74.0mm 2.9in
Stroke: 86.5mm 3.4in
Valve type/No: Overhead 8
Transmission: Manual
No. of forward speeds: 4
Wheels driven: Front
Springs F/R: Coil/Coil
Brake system: PA
Brakes F/R: Disc/Drum
Steering: Rack & pinion
Wheelbase: 220.2cm 86.7in
Track F: 130.0cm 51.2in
Track R: 128.3cm 50.5in
Length: 355.6cm 140.0in
Width: 149.9cm 59.0in
Height: 133.9cm 52.7in
Ground clearance: 15.2cm 6.0in
Kerb weight: 776.8kg 1711.0lb
Fuel: 41.4L 9.1gal 10.9galUS

2098 Honda

Accord
1978 Japan
90.0mph 144.8kmh
0-60mph 96.5kmh: 13.8secs
0-1/4 mile: 19.7secs
68.0bhp 50.7kW 68.9PS
@ 5000rpm
85.0lbft 115.2Nm @ 3500rpm
72.9bhp/ton 71.7bhp/tonne
42.6bhp/L 31.7kW/L 43.2PS/L
50.8ft/sec 15.5m/sec
33.0mpg 27.5mpgUS 8.6L/100km
Petrol 4-stroke piston
1597cc 97.4cu in
In-line 4 1 Carburettor
Compression ratio: 8.0:1
Bore: 74.0mm 2.9in
Stroke: 93.0mm 3.7in
Valve type/No: Overhead 12
Transmission: Manual
No. of forward speeds: 5
Wheels driven: Front
Brakes F/R: Disc/Drum
Wheelbase: 238.0cm 93.7in
Track F: 140.0cm 55.1in
Track R: 138.9cm 54.7in
Length: 413.5cm 162.8in
Width: 162.1cm 63.8in
Height: 133.1cm 52.4in
Kerb weight: 948.9kg 2090.0lb
Fuel: 49.2L 10.8gal 13.0galUS

2099 Honda

Civic
1978 Japan
95.0mph 152.9kmh
0-50mph 80.5kmh: 9.8secs
0-60mph 96.5kmh: 14.5secs
0-1/4 mile: 19.4secs
0-1km: 37.4secs
60.0bhp 44.7kW 60.8PS
@ 5500rpm
62.0lbft 84.0Nm @ 3000rpm
83.3bhp/ton 81.9bhp/tonne
48.5bhp/L 36.1kW/L 49.1PS/L
45.7ft/sec 13.9m/sec
16.0mph 25.7kmh/1000rpm
29.3mpg 24.4mpgUS 9.6L/100km
Petrol 4-stroke piston
1238cc 75.5cu in
In-line 4 1 Carburettor
Compression ratio: 8.1:1

Bore: 72.0mm 2.8in
Stroke: 76.0mm 3.0in
Valve type/No: Overhead 8
Transmission: Manual
No. of forward speeds: 4
Wheels driven: Front
Springs F/R: Coil/Coil
Brake system: PA
Brakes F/R: Disc/Drum
Steering: Rack & pinion
Wheelbase: 220.2cm 86.7in
Track F: 130.0cm 51.2in
Track R: 128.3cm 50.5in
Length: 355.6cm 140.0in
Width: 149.9cm 59.0in
Height: 133.9cm 52.7in
Ground clearance: 15.2cm 6.0in
Kerb weight: 732.3kg 1613.0lb
Fuel: 36.4L 8.0gal 9.6galUS

2100 Honda
Accord 4-door
1979 Japan
106.0mph 170.6kmh
0-50mph 80.5kmh: 8.3secs
0-60mph 96.5kmh: 12.0secs
0-1/4 mile: 18.8secs
72.0bhp 53.7kW 73.0PS
@ 4500rpm
94.0lbft 127.4Nm @ 3000rpm
72.8bhp/ton 71.6bhp/tonne
41.1bhp/L 30.7kW/L 41.7PS/L
46.2ft/sec 14.1m/sec
22.2mph 35.7kmh/1000rpm
36.0mpg 30.0mpgUS 7.8L/100km
Petrol 4-stroke piston
1751cc 106.8cu in
In-line 4 1 Carburettor
Compression ratio: 8.0:1
Bore: 77.0mm 3.0in
Stroke: 94.0mm 3.7in
Valve type/No: Overhead 12
Transmission: Manual
No. of forward speeds: 5
Wheels driven: Front
Springs F/R: Coil/Coil
Brake system: PA
Brakes F/R: Disc/Drum
Steering: Rack & pinion PA
Wheelbase: 238.0cm 93.7in
Track F: 141.0cm 55.5in
Track R: 140.0cm 55.1in
Length: 440.4cm 173.4in
Width: 162.1cm 63.8in
Height: 135.4cm 53.3in
Kerb weight: 1005.6kg 2215.0lb
Fuel: 50.0L 11.0gal 13.2galUS

2101 Honda
Prelude
1979 Japan
101.0mph 162.5kmh
0-50mph 80.5kmh: 8.3secs
0-60mph 96.5kmh: 11.3secs
0-1/4 mile: 18.6secs
0-1km: 35.0secs
80.0bhp 59.7kW 81.1PS
@ 5300rpm
126.5lbft 171.4Nm @ 3500rpm
88.3bhp/ton 86.8bhp/tonne
49.9bhp/L 37.2kW/L 50.6PS/L
49.9ft/sec 15.2m/sec
20.6mph 33.1kmh/1000rpm
30.4mpg 25.3mpgUS 9.3L/100km
Petrol 4-stroke piston
1602cc 97.7cu in
In-line 4 1 Carburettor
Compression ratio: 8.4:1
Bore: 77.0mm 3.0in
Stroke: 86.0mm 3.4in
Valve type/No: Overhead 8
Transmission: Manual
No. of forward speeds: 5
Wheels driven: Front
Springs F/R: Coil/Coil
Brake system: PA
Brakes F/R: Disc/Drum
Steering: Rack & pinion
Wheelbase: 231.9cm 91.3in
Track F: 140.0cm 55.1in
Track R: 141.0cm 55.5in
Length: 408.9cm 161.0in
Width: 163.6cm 64.4in
Height: 129.5cm 51.0in
Ground clearance: 17.0cm 6.7in
Kerb weight: 921.6kg 2030.0lb
Fuel: 51.0L 11.2gal 13.5galUS

2102 Honda
Civic
1980 Japan
0-60mph 96.5kmh: 10.8secs
0-1/4 mile: 18.3secs
63.0bhp 47.0kW 63.9PS
@ 5000rpm
77.0lbft 104.3Nm @ 3000rpm
78.4bhp/ton 77.1bhp/tonne
42.3bhp/L 31.6kW/L 42.9PS/L
47.4ft/sec 14.4m/sec
33.6mpg 28.0mpgUS 8.4L/100km
Petrol 4-stroke piston
1488cc 90.8cu in
In-line 4 1 Carburettor
Compression ratio: 7.9:1
Bore: 74.0mm 2.9in
Stroke: 86.5mm 3.4in
Valve type/No: Overhead 12
Transmission: Manual
No. of forward speeds: 5
Wheels driven: Front
Brakes F/R: Disc/Drum
Wheelbase: 220.0cm 86.6in
Track F: 130.0cm 51.2in
Track R: 128.0cm 50.4in
Length: 377.4cm 148.6in
Width: 150.6cm 59.3in
Height: 133.1cm 52.4in
Kerb weight: 817.2kg 1800.0lb
Fuel: 40.1L 8.8gal 10.6galUS

2103 Honda
Civic GL 1500
1980 Japan
99.0mph 159.3kmh
0-60mph 96.5kmh: 12.0secs
0-1/4 mile: 18.4secs
67.0bhp 50.0kW 67.9PS
@ 5000rpm
79.0lbft 107.0Nm @ 3000rpm
79.4bhp/ton 78.1bhp/tonne
45.0bhp/L 33.6kW/L 45.6PS/L
47.4ft/sec 14.4m/sec
23.1mph 37.2kmh/1000rpm
33.0mpg 27.5mpgUS 8.6L/100km
Petrol 4-stroke piston
1488cc 90.8cu in
In-line 4 1 Carburettor
Compression ratio: 8.9:1
Bore: 74.0mm 2.9in
Stroke: 86.5mm 3.4in
Valve type/No: Overhead 12
Transmission: Manual
No. of forward speeds: 5
Wheels driven: Front
Springs F/R: Coil/Coil
Brake system: PA
Brakes F/R: Disc/Drum
Steering: Rack & pinion
Wheelbase: 225.0cm 88.6in
Track F: 135.9cm 53.5in
Track R: 136.9cm 53.9in
Length: 375.9cm 148.0in
Width: 158.0cm 62.2in
Height: 134.6cm 53.0in
Ground clearance: 16.5cm 6.5in
Kerb weight: 858.1kg 1890.0lb
Fuel: 40.9L 9.0gal 10.8galUS

2104 Honda
Prelude
1980 Japan
101.0mph 162.5kmh
0-60mph 96.5kmh: 11.5secs
0-1/4 mile: 18.7secs
72.0bhp 53.7kW 73.0PS
@ 4500rpm
93.0lbft 126.0Nm @ 3000rpm
75.0bhp/ton 73.8bhp/tonne
41.1bhp/L 30.7kW/L 41.7PS/L
46.2ft/sec 14.1m/sec
21.8mph 35.1kmh/1000rpm
28.2mpg 23.5mpgUS 10.0L/100km
Petrol 4-stroke piston
1751cc 106.8cu in
In-line 4 1 Carburettor
Compression ratio: 8.0:1
Bore: 77.0mm 3.0in
Stroke: 94.0mm 3.7in
Valve type/No: Overhead 12
Transmission: Manual
No. of forward speeds: 5
Wheels driven: Front
Springs F/R: Coil/Coil
Brake system: PA
Brakes F/R: Disc/Drum
Steering: Rack & pinion
Wheelbase: 231.9cm 91.3in
Track F: 140.0cm 55.1in
Track R: 141.0cm 55.5in
Length: 410.0cm 161.4in
Width: 163.6cm 64.4in
Height: 129.5cm 51.0in
Ground clearance: 16.8cm 6.6in
Kerb weight: 976.1kg 2150.0lb
Fuel: 50.0L 11.0gal 13.2galUS

2105 Honda
Accord
1981 Japan
0-60mph 96.5kmh: 13.4secs
0-1/4 mile: 19.2secs
68.0bhp 50.7kW 68.9PS
@ 4500rpm
94.0lbft 127.4Nm @ 2500rpm
65.1bhp/ton 64.0bhp/tonne
38.8bhp/L 29.0kW/L 39.4PS/L
46.2ft/sec 14.1m/sec
29.4mpg 24.5mpgUS 9.6L/100km
Petrol 4-stroke piston
1751cc 106.8cu in
In-line 4 1 Carburettor
Compression ratio: 8.0:1
Bore: 77.0mm 3.0in
Stroke: 94.0mm 3.7in
Valve type/No: Overhead 12
Transmission: Manual
No. of forward speeds: 5
Wheels driven: Front
Brakes F/R: Disc/Drum
Wheelbase: 238.0cm 93.7in
Track F: 141.0cm 55.5in
Track R: 140.0cm 55.1in
Length: 436.6cm 171.9in
Width: 162.1cm 63.8in
Height: 135.4cm 53.3in
Kerb weight: 1062.4kg 2340.0lb
Fuel: 50.0L 11.0gal 13.2galUS

2106 Honda
Civic 4-door Sedan
1981 Japan
90.0mph 144.8kmh
0-50mph 80.5kmh: 10.2secs
0-60mph 96.5kmh: 15.1secs
0-1/4 mile: 19.9secs
67.0bhp 50.0kW 67.9PS
@ 5000rpm
79.0lbft 107.0Nm @ 3000rpm
72.8bhp/ton 71.6bhp/tonne
45.0bhp/L 33.6kW/L 45.6PS/L
47.4ft/sec 14.4m/sec
16.7mph 26.9kmh/1000rpm
31.8mpg 26.5mpgUS 8.9L/100km
Petrol 4-stroke piston
1488cc 90.8cu in
In-line 4 1 Carburettor
Compression ratio: 8.8:1
Bore: 74.0mm 2.9in
Stroke: 86.5mm 3.4in
Valve type/No: Overhead 12
Transmission: Automatic
No. of forward speeds: 3
Wheels driven: Front
Springs F/R: Coil/Coil
Brake system: PA
Brakes F/R: Disc/Drum
Steering: Rack & pinion
Wheelbase: 231.9cm 91.3in
Track F: 135.9cm 53.5in
Track R: 137.9cm 54.3in
Length: 408.9cm 161.0in
Width: 158.0cm 62.2in
Height: 137.7cm 54.2in
Ground clearance: 16.5cm 6.5in
Kerb weight: 935.2kg 2060.0lb
Fuel: 46.2L 10.1gal 12.2galUS

2107 Honda
Prelude
1981 Japan
103.0mph 165.7kmh
0-60mph 96.5kmh: 11.5secs
0-1/4 mile: 18.3secs
73.0bhp 54.4kW 74.0PS
@ 4500rpm
93.0lbft 126.0Nm @ 3500rpm
76.1bhp/ton 74.8bhp/tonne
41.7bhp/L 31.1kW/L 42.3PS/L
46.2ft/sec 14.1m/sec
19.4mph 31.2kmh/1000rpm
34.8mpg 29.0mpgUS 8.1L/100km
Petrol 4-stroke piston
1751cc 106.8cu in
In-line 4 1 Carburettor
Compression ratio: 8.8:1
Bore: 77.0mm 3.0in
Stroke: 94.0mm 3.7in
Valve type/No: Overhead 12
Transmission: Manual
No. of forward speeds: 5
Wheels driven: Front
Springs F/R: Coil/Coil
Brake system: PA
Brakes F/R: Disc/Drum
Steering: Rack & pinion
Wheelbase: 231.9cm 91.3in
Track F: 140.0cm 55.1in
Track R: 141.0cm 55.5in
Length: 410.0cm 161.4in
Width: 163.6cm 64.4in
Height: 129.5cm 51.0in
Ground clearance: 16.8cm 6.6in
Kerb weight: 976.1kg 2150.0lb
Fuel: 50.0L 11.0gal 13.2galUS

2108 Honda
Quintet
1981 Japan
96.0mph 154.5kmh
0-50mph 80.5kmh: 8.7secs
0-60mph 96.5kmh: 12.2secs
0-1/4 mile: 18.7secs
0-1km: 35.4secs
79.0bhp 58.9kW 80.1PS
@ 5300rpm
93.0lbft 126.0Nm @ 3500rpm
86.0bhp/ton 84.5bhp/tonne
49.3bhp/L 36.8kW/L 50.0PS/L
49.9ft/sec 15.2m/sec
20.6mph 33.1kmh/1000rpm
25.8mpg 21.5mpgUS 10.9L/100km
Petrol 4-stroke piston
1602cc 97.7cu in
In-line 4 1 Carburettor
Compression ratio: 8.4:1
Bore: 77.0mm 3.0in
Stroke: 86.0mm 3.4in
Valve type/No: Overhead 8
Transmission: Manual
No. of forward speeds: 5
Wheels driven: Front
Springs F/R: Coil/Coil
Brake system: PA
Brakes F/R: Disc/Drum
Steering: Rack & pinion
Wheelbase: 236.2cm 93.0in
Track F: 135.9cm 53.5in
Track R: 137.9cm 54.3in
Length: 411.0cm 161.8in
Width: 160.8cm 63.3in
Height: 135.4cm 53.3in
Ground clearance: 16.0cm 6.3in
Kerb weight: 934.3kg 2058.0lb
Fuel: 50.0L 11.0gal 13.2galUS

2109 Honda
Accord
1982 Japan
98.0mph 157.7kmh
0-60mph 96.5kmh: 13.0secs
0-1/4 mile: 18.8secs
75.0bhp 55.9kW 76.0PS
@ 4500rpm
96.0lbft 130.1Nm @ 3500rpm
73.2bhp/ton 72.0bhp/tonne
42.8bhp/L 31.9kW/L 43.4PS/L
46.2ft/sec 14.1m/sec
22.2mph 35.7kmh/1000rpm
31.8mpg 26.5mpgUS 8.9L/100km
Petrol 4-stroke piston
1751cc 106.8cu in
In-line 4 1 Carburettor
Compression ratio: 8.8:1
Bore: 77.0mm 3.0in
Stroke: 94.0mm 3.7in
Valve type/No: Overhead 12
Transmission: Manual
No. of forward speeds: 5
Wheels driven: Front
Springs F/R: Coil/Coil
Brake system: PA
Brakes F/R: Disc/Drum
Steering: Rack & pinion PA
Wheelbase: 245.1cm 96.5in
Track F: 143.0cm 56.3in
Track R: 142.0cm 55.9in
Length: 440.9cm 173.6in
Width: 165.1cm 65.0in

Height: 137.4cm 54.1in
Ground clearance: 16.5cm 6.5in
Kerb weight: 1041.9kg 2295.0lb
Fuel: 59.8L 13.1gal 15.8galUS

2110 Honda
Accord LX
1982 Japan
98.0mph 157.7kmh
0-60mph 96.5kmh: 13.0secs
0-1/4 mile: 18.0secs
75.0bhp 55.9kW 76.0PS
@ 4500rpm
96.0lbft 130.1Nm @ 3000rpm
74.8bhp/ton 73.6bhp/tonne
42.8bhp/L 31.9kW/L 43.4PS/L
46.2ft/sec 14.1m/sec
28.2mpg 23.5mpgUS 10.0L/100km
Petrol 4-stroke piston
1751cc 106.8cu in
In-line 4 1 Carburettor
Compression ratio: 8.8:1
Bore: 77.0mm 3.0in
Stroke: 94.0mm 3.7in
Valve type/No: Overhead 12
Transmission: Manual
No. of forward speeds: 5
Wheels driven: Front
Springs F/R: Coil/Coil
Brakes F/R: Disc/Drum
Wheelbase: 245.1cm 96.5in
Track F: 143.0cm 56.3in
Track R: 142.0cm 55.9in
Length: 421.1cm 165.8in
Width: 165.1cm 65.0in
Height: 135.4cm 53.3in
Kerb weight: 1019.2kg 2245.0lb
Fuel: 59.8L 13.1gal 15.8galUS

2111 Honda
CRX 1.5
1983 Japan
104.0mph 167.3kmh
0-60mph 96.5kmh: 10.1secs
0-1/4 mile: 17.6secs
76.0bhp 56.7kW 77.0PS
@ 6000rpm
84.0lbft 113.8Nm @ 3500rpm
93.8bhp/ton 92.2bhp/tonne
51.1bhp/L 38.1kW/L 51.8PS/L
56.8ft/sec 17.3m/sec
20.8mph 33.5kmh/1000rpm
42.0mpg 35.0mpgUS 6.7L/100km
Petrol 4-stroke piston
1488cc 90.8cu in
In-line 4 1 Carburettor
Compression ratio: 9.2:1
Bore: 74.0mm 2.9in
Stroke: 86.5mm 3.4in
Valve type/No: Overhead 12
Transmission: Manual
No. of forward speeds: 5
Wheels driven: Front
Springs F/R: Torsion bar/Coil
Brake system: PA
Brakes F/R: Disc/Drum
Steering: Rack & pinion
Wheelbase: 220.0cm 86.6in
Track F: 140.0cm 55.1in
Track R: 141.5cm 55.7in
Length: 367.5cm 144.7in
Width: 162.6cm 64.0in
Height: 129.0cm 50.8in
Ground clearance: 16.5cm 6.5in
Kerb weight: 824.0kg 1815.0lb
Fuel: 37.8L 8.3gal 10.0galUS

2112 Honda
Prelude EX ALB
1983 Japan
107.0mph 172.2kmh
0-50mph 80.5kmh: 7.9secs
0-60mph 96.5kmh: 10.9secs
0-1/4 mile: 18.0secs
0-1km: 33.0secs
101.0bhp 75.3kW 102.4PS
@ 5500rpm
113.0lbft 153.1Nm @ 3500rpm
97.4bhp/ton 95.8bhp/tonne
55.2bhp/L 41.2kW/L 56.0PS/L
54.7ft/sec 16.7m/sec
22.4mph 36.0kmh/1000rpm
24.9mpg 20.7mpgUS 11.3L/100km
Petrol 4-stroke piston
1829cc 111.6cu in
In-line 4 2 Carburettor
Compression ratio: 9.5:1
Bore: 80.0mm 3.1in
Stroke: 91.0mm 3.6in
Valve type/No: Overhead 8
Transmission: Automatic
No. of forward speeds: 4
Wheels driven: Front
Springs F/R: Coil/Coil
Brake system: PA
Brakes F/R: Disc/Disc
Steering: Rack & pinion PA
Wheelbase: 245.1cm 96.5in
Track F: 147.1cm 57.9in
Track R: 147.1cm 57.9in
Length: 429.3cm 169.0in
Width: 168.9cm 66.5in
Height: 129.5cm 51.0in
Ground clearance: 15.2cm 6.0in
Kerb weight: 1054.6kg 2323.0lb
Fuel: 60.1L 13.2gal 15.9galUS

2113 Honda
Civic CRX
1984 Japan
115.0mph 185.0kmh
0-50mph 80.5kmh: 6.1secs
0-60mph 96.5kmh: 8.5secs
0-1/4 mile: 16.8secs
0-1km: 31.8secs
100.0bhp 74.6kW 101.4PS
@ 5750rpm
96.0lbft 130.1Nm @ 4500rpm
119.8bhp/ton 117.8bhp/tonne
67.2bhp/L 50.1kW/L 68.1PS/L
54.5ft/sec 16.6m/sec
21.4mph 34.4kmh/1000rpm
32.3mpg 26.9mpgUS 8.7L/100km
Petrol 4-stroke piston
1488cc 90.8cu in
In-line 4 fuel injection
Compression ratio: 8.7:1
Bore: 74.0mm 2.9in
Stroke: 86.5mm 3.4in
Valve type/No: Overhead 12
Transmission: Manual
No. of forward speeds: 5
Wheels driven: Front
Springs F/R: Torsion bar/Coil
Brake system: PA
Brakes F/R: Disc/Drum
Steering: Rack & pinion
Wheelbase: 220.0cm 86.6in
Track F: 140.0cm 55.1in
Track R: 141.5cm 55.7in
Length: 367.5cm 144.7in
Width: 162.6cm 64.0in
Height: 129.0cm 50.8in
Ground clearance: 16.5cm 6.5in
Kerb weight: 848.5kg 1869.0lb
Fuel: 40.9L 9.0gal 10.8galUS

2114 Honda
Civic DL
1984 Japan
98.0mph 157.7kmh
0-50mph 80.5kmh: 7.6secs
0-60mph 96.5kmh: 10.7secs
0-1/4 mile: 18.0secs
0-1km: 34.1secs
71.0bhp 52.9kW 72.0PS
@ 6000rpm
77.0lbft 104.3Nm @ 3500rpm
88.1bhp/ton 86.6bhp/tonne
52.9bhp/L 39.4kW/L 53.6PS/L
51.2ft/sec 15.6m/sec
24.6mph 39.6kmh/1000rpm
32.1mpg 26.7mpgUS 8.8L/100km
Petrol 4-stroke piston
1342cc 81.9cu in
In-line 4 1 Carburettor
Compression ratio: 8.7:1
Bore: 74.0mm 2.9in
Stroke: 78.0mm 3.1in
Valve type/No: Overhead 12
Transmission: Manual
No. of forward speeds: 5
Wheels driven: Front
Springs F/R: Torsion bar/Coil
Brake system: PA
Brakes F/R: Disc/Drum
Steering: Rack & pinion
Wheelbase: 238.0cm 93.7in
Track F: 139.7cm 55.0in
Track R: 141.5cm 55.7in
Length: 381.0cm 150.0in
Width: 163.6cm 64.4in
Height: 134.1cm 52.8in
Ground clearance: 16.5cm 6.5in
Kerb weight: 819.9kg 1806.0lb
Fuel: 45.0L 9.9gal 11.9galUS

2115 Honda
Jazz
1984 Japan
89.0mph 143.2kmh
0-50mph 80.5kmh: 8.7secs
0-60mph 96.5kmh: 13.4secs
0-1/4 mile: 18.8secs
0-1km: 35.9secs
56.0bhp 41.8kW 56.8PS
@ 5000rpm
69.0lbft 93.5Nm @ 3500rpm
80.6bhp/ton 79.3bhp/tonne
45.5bhp/L 33.9kW/L 46.1PS/L
49.2ft/sec 15.0m/sec
22.0mph 35.4kmh/1000rpm
35.3mpg 29.4mpgUS 8.0L/100km
Petrol 4-stroke piston
1231cc 75.1cu in
In-line 4 1 Carburettor
Compression ratio: 10.2:1
Bore: 66.0mm 2.6in
Stroke: 90.0mm 3.5in
Valve type/No: Overhead 8
Transmission: Manual
No. of forward speeds: 5
Wheels driven: Front
Springs F/R: Coil/Coil
Brake system: PA
Brakes F/R: Disc/Drum
Steering: Rack & pinion
Wheelbase: 222.0cm 87.4in
Track F: 136.9cm 53.9in
Track R: 136.9cm 53.9in
Length: 338.1cm 133.1in
Width: 157.0cm 61.8in
Height: 147.1cm 57.9in
Ground clearance: 16.0cm 6.3in
Kerb weight: 706.4kg 1556.0lb
Fuel: 40.9L 9.0gal 10.8galUS

2116 Honda
Prelude
1984 Japan
108.0mph 173.8kmh
0-60mph 96.5kmh: 9.7secs
0-1/4 mile: 17.2secs
100.0bhp 74.6kW 101.4PS
@ 5500rpm
109.0lbft 147.7Nm @ 4000rpm
102.7bhp/ton 101.0bhp/tonne
54.7bhp/L 40.8kW/L 55.4PS/L
54.7ft/sec 16.7m/sec
21.6mph 34.8kmh/1000rpm
30.6mpg 25.5mpgUS 9.2L/100km
Petrol 4-stroke piston
1829cc 111.6cu in
In-line 4 2 Carburettor
Compression ratio: 9.4:1
Bore: 80.0mm 3.1in
Stroke: 91.0mm 3.6in
Valve type/No: Overhead 8
Transmission: Manual
No. of forward speeds: 5
Wheels driven: Front
Springs F/R: Coil/Coil
Brakes F/R: Disc/Drum
Steering: Rack & pinion
Wheelbase: 245.1cm 96.5in
Track F: 147.1cm 57.9in
Track R: 147.1cm 57.9in
Length: 429.0cm 168.9in
Width: 168.9cm 66.5in
Height: 129.5cm 51.0in
Kerb weight: 989.7kg 2180.0lb
Fuel: 59.8L 13.1gal 15.8galUS

2117 Honda
Accord 2.0 EXi
1985 Japan
117.0mph 188.3kmh
0-50mph 80.5kmh: 7.0secs
0-60mph 96.5kmh: 9.9secs
0-1/4 mile: 17.2secs
0-1km: 32.1secs
122.0bhp 91.0kW 123.7PS
@ 5000rpm
122.0lbft 165.3Nm @ 5000rpm
108.1bhp/ton 106.3bhp/tonne
62.4bhp/L 46.5kW/L 63.3PS/L
49.7ft/sec 15.2m/sec
21.5mph 34.6kmh/1000rpm
24.3mpg 20.2mpgUS 11.6L/100km
Petrol 4-stroke piston
1955cc 119.3cu in
In-line 4 fuel injection
Compression ratio: 9.4:1
Bore: 82.7mm 3.3in
Stroke: 91.0mm 3.6in
Valve type/No: Overhead 12
Transmission: Manual
No. of forward speeds: 5
Wheels driven: Front
Springs F/R: Coil/Coil
Brake system: PA
Brakes F/R: Disc/Disc
Steering: Rack & pinion PA
Wheelbase: 259.8cm 102.3in
Track F: 147.3cm 58.0in
Track R: 147.3cm 58.0in
Length: 453.4cm 178.5in
Width: 169.4cm 66.7in
Height: 135.4cm 53.3in
Ground clearance: 17.8cm 7.0in
Kerb weight: 1147.3kg 2527.0lb
Fuel: 60.1L 13.2gal 15.9galUS

2118 Honda
Accord EX Automatic
1985 Japan
104.0mph 167.3kmh
0-50mph 80.5kmh: 8.9secs
0-60mph 96.5kmh: 12.0secs
0-1/4 mile: 19.0secs
0-1km: 35.1secs
100.0bhp 74.6kW 101.4PS
@ 5800rpm
108.0lbft 146.3Nm @ 3500rpm
95.2bhp/ton 93.6bhp/tonne
54.6bhp/L 40.7kW/L 55.4PS/L
57.7ft/sec 17.6m/sec
23.9mph 38.5kmh/1000rpm
23.4mpg 19.5mpgUS 12.1L/100km
Petrol 4-stroke piston
1830cc 111.6cu in
In-line 4 1 Carburettor
Compression ratio: 9.1:1
Bore: 80.0mm 3.1in
Stroke: 91.0mm 3.6in
Valve type/No: Overhead 12
Transmission: Automatic
No. of forward speeds: 4
Wheels driven: Front
Springs F/R: Coil/Coil
Brake system: PA
Brakes F/R: Disc/Disc
Steering: Rack & pinion PA
Wheelbase: 245.1cm 96.5in
Track F: 143.0cm 56.3in
Track R: 142.2cm 56.0in
Length: 445.5cm 175.4in
Width: 166.6cm 65.6in
Height: 135.4cm 53.3in
Ground clearance: 16.5cm 6.5in
Kerb weight: 1067.8kg 2352.0lb
Fuel: 60.1L 13.2gal 15.9galUS

2119 Honda
Accord SEi
1985 Japan
108.0mph 173.8kmh
0-60mph 96.5kmh: 9.8secs
0-1/4 mile: 17.3secs
101.0bhp 75.3kW 102.4PS
@ 5800rpm
108.0lbft 146.3Nm @ 2500rpm
92.7bhp/ton 91.2bhp/tonne
55.2bhp/L 41.2kW/L 56.0PS/L
57.0ft/sec 17.4m/sec
29.4mpg 24.5mpgUS 9.6L/100km
Petrol 4-stroke piston
1829cc 111.6cu in
In-line 4 fuel injection
Bore: 80.0mm 3.1in
Stroke: 90.0mm 3.5in
Valve type/No: Overhead 8
Transmission: Manual
No. of forward speeds: 5
Wheels driven: Front
Springs F/R: Coil/Coil
Brake system: PA
Brakes F/R: Disc/Drum
Steering: Rack & pinion PA
Wheelbase: 245.1cm 96.5in
Track F: 143.0cm 56.3in
Track R: 142.0cm 55.9in
Length: 445.5cm 175.4in
Width: 165.1cm 65.0in
Height: 137.4cm 54.1in
Kerb weight: 1107.8kg 2440.0lb
Fuel: 60.2L 13.2gal 15.9galUS

2120 Honda
Civic GT
1985 Japan
112.0mph 180.2kmh
0-50mph 80.5kmh: 7.0secs
0-60mph 96.5kmh: 9.9secs
0-1/4 mile: 17.5secs
0-1km: 32.3secs
100.0bhp 74.6kW 101.4PS
@ 5750rpm
96.0lbft 130.1Nm @ 4500rpm
119.5bhp/ton 117.5bhp/tonne
67.2bhp/L 50.1kW/L 68.1PS/L
54.5ft/sec 16.6m/sec
21.4mph 34.4kmh/1000rpm
30.5mpg 25.4mpgUS 9.3L/100km
Petrol 4-stroke piston
1488cc 90.8cu in
In-line 4 fuel injection
Compression ratio: 8.7:1
Bore: 74.0mm 2.9in
Stroke: 86.5mm 3.4in
Valve type/No: Overhead 12
Transmission: Manual
No. of forward speeds: 5
Wheels driven: Front
Springs F/R: Torsion bar/Coil
Brake system: PA
Brakes F/R: Disc/Disc
Steering: Rack & pinion
Wheelbase: 238.0cm 93.7in
Track F: 139.7cm 55.0in
Track R: 141.5cm 55.7in
Length: 381.0cm 150.0in
Width: 163.6cm 64.4in
Height: 134.4cm 52.9in
Ground clearance: 16.5cm 6.5in
Kerb weight: 850.8kg 1874.0lb
Fuel: 45.0L 9.9gal 11.9galUS

2121 Honda
Civic S
1985 Japan
100.0mph 160.9kmh
0-50mph 80.5kmh: 7.1secs
0-60mph 96.5kmh: 11.1secs
0-1/4 mile: 18.2secs
76.0bhp 56.7kW 77.0PS
@ 6000rpm
84.0lbft 113.8Nm @ 3500rpm
87.5bhp/ton 86.1bhp/tonne
51.1bhp/L 38.1kW/L 51.8PS/L
56.8ft/sec 17.3m/sec
20.8mph 33.5kmh/1000rpm
33.6mpg 28.0mpgUS 8.4L/100km
Petrol 4-stroke piston
1488cc 90.8cu in
In-line 4 1 Carburettor
Compression ratio: 9.2:1
Bore: 74.0mm 2.9in
Stroke: 86.5mm 3.4in
Valve type/No: Overhead 12
Transmission: Manual
No. of forward speeds: 5
Wheels driven: Front
Springs F/R: Torsion bar/Coil
Brakes F/R: Disc/Drum
Steering: Rack & pinion
Wheelbase: 238.0cm 93.7in
Track F: 140.0cm 55.1in
Track R: 141.5cm 55.7in
Length: 381.0cm 150.0in
Width: 162.3cm 63.9in
Height: 133.6cm 52.6in
Kerb weight: 883.0kg 1945.0lb
Fuel: 45.0L 9.9gal 11.9galUS

2122 Honda
Civic Shuttle
1985 Japan
107.0mph 172.2kmh
0-50mph 80.5kmh: 8.3secs
0-60mph 96.5kmh: 11.2secs
0-1/4 mile: 18.1secs
0-1km: 34.0secs
85.0bhp 63.4kW 86.2PS
@ 6000rpm
93.0lbft 126.0Nm @ 3500rpm
96.3bhp/ton 94.6bhp/tonne
57.1bhp/L 42.6kW/L 57.9PS/L
56.8ft/sec 17.3m/sec
21.5mph 34.6kmh/1000rpm
31.8mpg 26.5mpgUS 8.9L/100km
Petrol 4-stroke piston
1488cc 90.8cu in
In-line 4 1 Carburettor
Compression ratio: 8.7:1
Bore: 74.0mm 2.9in
Stroke: 86.5mm 3.4in
Valve type/No: Overhead 12
Transmission: Manual
No. of forward speeds: 5
Wheels driven: Front
Springs F/R: Coil/Torsion bar
Brake system: PA
Brakes F/R: Disc/Drum
Steering: Rack & pinion
Wheelbase: 245.1cm 96.5in
Track F: 140.0cm 55.1in
Track R: 141.5cm 55.7in
Length: 399.0cm 157.1in
Width: 165.1cm 65.0in
Height: 141.5cm 55.7in
Ground clearance: 16.5cm 6.5in
Kerb weight: 898.0kg 1978.0lb
Fuel: 46.0L 10.1gal 12.1galUS

2123 Honda
Civic Wagon
1985 Japan
98.0mph 157.7kmh
0-50mph 80.5kmh: 8.3secs
0-60mph 96.5kmh: 11.9secs
0-1/4 mile: 18.5secs
76.0bhp 56.7kW 77.0PS
@ 6000rpm
84.0lbft 113.8Nm @ 3500rpm
80.1bhp/ton 78.8bhp/tonne
51.1bhp/L 38.1kW/L 51.8PS/L
56.8ft/sec 17.3m/sec
20.8mph 33.5kmh/1000rpm
33.6mpg 28.0mpgUS 8.4L/100km
Petrol 4-stroke piston
1488cc 90.8cu in
In-line 4 1 Carburettor
Compression ratio: 9.2:1
Bore: 74.0mm 2.9in
Stroke: 86.5mm 3.4in
Valve type/No: Overhead 12
Transmission: Manual
No. of forward speeds: 5
Wheels driven: Front
Springs F/R: Torsion bar/Coil
Brake system: PA
Brakes F/R: Disc/Drum
Steering: Rack & pinion
Wheelbase: 245.1cm 96.5in
Track F: 140.0cm 55.1in
Track R: 141.5cm 55.7in
Length: 399.0cm 157.1in
Width: 162.3cm 63.9in
Height: 148.1cm 58.3in
Ground clearance: 14.7cm 5.8in
Kerb weight: 964.7kg 2125.0lb
Fuel: 45.8L 10.1gal 12.1galUS

2124 Honda
CRX Si
1985 Japan
115.0mph 185.0kmh
0-60mph 96.5kmh: 8.7secs
0-1/4 mile: 16.7secs
91.0bhp 67.9kW 92.3PS
@ 5500rpm
93.0lbft 126.0Nm @ 4500rpm
107.8bhp/ton 106.0bhp/tonne
61.2bhp/L 45.6kW/L 62.0PS/L
52.1ft/sec 15.9m/sec
20.8mph 33.5kmh/1000rpm
42.0mpg 35.0mpgUS 6.7L/100km
Petrol 4-stroke piston
1488cc 90.8cu in
In-line 4 fuel injection
Bore: 74.0mm 2.9in
Stroke: 86.5mm 3.4in
Valve type/No: Overhead 8
Transmission: Manual
No. of forward speeds: 5
Wheels driven: Front
Springs F/R: Torsion bar/Coil
Brake system: PA
Brakes F/R: Disc/Drum
Steering: Rack & pinion
Wheelbase: 220.0cm 86.6in
Track F: 140.0cm 55.1in
Track R: 141.5cm 55.7in
Length: 367.5cm 144.7in
Width: 162.3cm 63.9in
Height: 129.0cm 50.8in
Kerb weight: 858.1kg 1890.0lb

2125 Honda
Prelude
1985 Japan
112.0mph 180.2kmh
0-50mph 80.5kmh: 4.7secs
0-60mph 96.5kmh: 9.4secs
0-1/4 mile: 17.1secs
100.0bhp 74.6kW 101.4PS
@ 5500rpm
108.0lbft 146.3Nm @ 4000rpm
102.7bhp/ton 101.0bhp/tonne
54.7bhp/L 40.8kW/L 55.4PS/L
54.7ft/sec 16.7m/sec
21.6mph 34.8kmh/1000rpm
33.6mpg 28.0mpgUS 8.4L/100km
Petrol 4-stroke piston
1829cc 111.6cu in
In-line 4 1 Carburettor
Compression ratio: 9.4:1
Bore: 80.0mm 3.1in
Stroke: 91.0mm 3.6in
Valve type/No: Overhead 8
Transmission: Manual
No. of forward speeds: 5
Wheels driven: Front
Springs F/R: Coil/Coil
Brake system: PA
Brakes F/R: Disc/Disc
Steering: Rack & pinion PA
Wheelbase: 245.1cm 96.5in
Track F: 147.1cm 57.9in
Track R: 147.1cm 57.9in
Length: 429.0cm 168.9in
Width: 168.9cm 66.5in
Height: 129.5cm 51.0in
Kerb weight: 989.7kg 2180.0lb
Fuel: 59.8L 13.1gal 15.8galUS

2126 Honda
Accord LXi
1986 Japan
108.0mph 173.8kmh
0-60mph 96.5kmh: 9.8secs
0-1/4 mile: 17.3secs
110.0bhp 82.0kW 111.5PS
@ 5500rpm
114.0lbft 154.5Nm @ 4500rpm
87.7bhp/ton 86.2bhp/tonne
56.3bhp/L 42.0kW/L 57.0PS/L
54.7ft/sec 16.7m/sec
28.8mpg 24.0mpgUS 9.8L/100km
Petrol 4-stroke piston
1955cc 119.3cu in
In-line 4 fuel injection
Compression ratio: 8.8:1
Bore: 82.7mm 3.3in
Stroke: 91.0mm 3.6in
Valve type/No: Overhead 8
Transmission: Manual
No. of forward speeds: 5
Wheels driven: Front
Springs F/R: Coil/Coil
Brakes F/R: Disc/Drum
Steering: Rack & pinion PA
Wheelbase: 260.1cm 102.4in
Track F: 148.1cm 58.3in
Track R: 147.6cm 58.1in
Length: 453.4cm 178.5in
Width: 169.4cm 66.7in
Height: 135.4cm 53.3in
Ground clearance: 16.0cm 6.3in
Kerb weight: 1275.7kg 2810.0lb
Fuel: 60.2L 13.2gal 15.9galUS

2127 Honda
Civic Hatchback
1986 Japan
0-60mph 96.5kmh: 13.6secs
0-1/4 mile: 19.3secs
60.0bhp 44.7kW 60.8PS
@ 5500rpm
73.0lbft 98.9Nm @ 3500rpm
68.8bhp/ton 67.6bhp/tonne
44.7bhp/L 33.3kW/L 45.3PS/L
46.9ft/sec 14.3m/sec
22.2mph 35.7kmh/1000rpm
39.2mpg 32.6mpgUS 7.2L/100km
Petrol 4-stroke piston
1342cc 81.9cu in
In-line 4 1 Carburettor
Compression ratio: 10.0:1
Bore: 74.0mm 2.9in
Stroke: 78.0mm 3.1in
Valve type/No: Overhead 12
Transmission: Manual
No. of forward speeds: 4
Wheels driven: Front
Springs F/R: Torsion bar/Coil
Brake system: PA
Brakes F/R: Disc/Drum
Steering: Rack & pinion
Wheelbase: 238.0cm 93.7in
Track F: 140.0cm 55.1in
Track R: 141.5cm 55.7in
Length: 381.0cm 150.0in
Width: 162.3cm 63.9in
Height: 133.6cm 52.6in
Kerb weight: 887.6kg 1955.0lb
Fuel: 45.0L 9.9gal 11.9galUS

2128 Honda
CRX Coupe 1.6i 16
1986 Japan
125.0mph 201.1kmh
0-50mph 80.5kmh: 5.9secs
0-60mph 96.5kmh: 8.0secs
0-1/4 mile: 16.2secs
0-1km: 29.7secs
125.0bhp 93.2kW 126.7PS
@ 6500rpm
103.0lbft 139.6Nm @ 5500rpm
141.2bhp/ton 138.9bhp/tonne
78.6bhp/L 58.6kW/L 79.7PS/L
63.9ft/sec 19.5m/sec
19.4mph 31.2kmh/1000rpm
30.0mpg 25.0mpgUS 9.4L/100km
Petrol 4-stroke piston
1590cc 97.0cu in
In-line 4 fuel injection
Compression ratio: 9.3:1
Bore: 75.0mm 2.9in
Stroke: 90.0mm 3.5in
Valve type/No: Overhead 16
Transmission: Manual
No. of forward speeds: 5
Wheels driven: Front
Springs F/R: Torsion bar/Coil
Brake system: PA
Brakes F/R: Disc/Drum
Steering: Rack & pinion
Wheelbase: 220.0cm 86.6in
Track F: 140.0cm 55.1in
Track R: 141.5cm 55.7in
Length: 375.5cm 147.8in
Width: 163.0cm 64.2in
Height: 129.0cm 50.8in
Ground clearance: 15.3cm 6.0in
Kerb weight: 900.0kg 1982.4lb
Fuel: 40.9L 9.0gal 10.8galUS

2129 Honda
CRX Si
1986 Japan
116.0mph 186.6kmh
0-50mph 80.5kmh: 6.3secs
0-60mph 96.5kmh: 8.9secs
0-1/4 mile: 16.7secs
91.0bhp 67.9kW 92.3PS
@ 5500rpm
93.0lbft 126.0Nm @ 4500rpm
104.3bhp/ton 102.5bhp/tonne
61.2bhp/L 45.6kW/L 62.0PS/L
52.1ft/sec 15.9m/sec
37.8mpg 31.5mpgUS 7.5L/100km
Petrol 4-stroke piston
1488cc 90.8cu in
In-line 4 fuel injection
Compression ratio: 8.7:1
Bore: 73.9mm 2.9in
Stroke: 86.5mm 3.4in
Valve type/No: Overhead 8
Transmission: Manual
No. of forward speeds: 5
Wheels driven: Front
Springs F/R: Torsion bar/Coil
Brake system: PA
Brakes F/R: Disc/Drum
Steering: Rack & pinion
Wheelbase: 220.0cm 86.6in
Track F: 140.0cm 55.1in
Track R: 141.5cm 55.7in
Length: 375.4cm 147.8in
Width: 162.3cm 63.9in
Height: 129.0cm 50.8in
Kerb weight: 887.6kg 1955.0lb
Fuel: 40.9L 9.0gal 10.8galUS

2130 Honda
CRX Si Jackson Turbo
1986 Japan
0-60mph 96.5kmh: 5.7secs
0-1/4 mile: 14.4secs
201.0bhp 149.9kW 203.8PS
@ 6000rpm
221.8bhp/ton 218.1bhp/tonne

126.4bhp/L 94.3kW/L 128.2PS/L
32.4mpg 27.0mpgUS 8.7L/100km
Petrol 4-stroke piston
1590cc 97.0cu in turbocharged
In-line 4
Valve type/No: Overhead 16
Transmission: Manual
No. of forward speeds: 5
Wheels driven: Front
Brakes F/R: Disc/Drum
Steering: Rack & pinion
Length: 375.4cm 147.8in
Kerb weight: 921.6kg 2030.0lb

2131 Honda

Integra 1.5
1986 Japan
102.0mph 164.1kmh
0-50mph 80.5kmh: 8.2secs
0-60mph 96.5kmh: 11.8secs
0-1/4 mile: 18.2secs
0-1km: 34.5secs
85.0bhp 63.4kW 86.2PS
@ 6000rpm
87.0lbft 117.9Nm @ 3750rpm
85.6bhp/ton 84.2bhp/tonne
57.1bhp/L 42.6kW/L 57.9PS/L
56.8ft/sec 17.3m/sec
21.2mph 34.1kmh/1000rpm
29.1mpg 24.2mpgUS 9.7L/100km
Petrol 4-stroke piston
1488cc 91.0cu in
In-line 4 1 Carburettor
Compression ratio: 8.7:1
Bore: 74.0mm 2.9in
Stroke: 86.5mm 3.4in
Valve type/No: Overhead 12
Transmission: Manual
No. of forward speeds: 5
Wheels driven: Front
Springs F/R: Torsion bar/Coil
Brake system: PA
Brakes F/R: Disc/Drum
Steering: Rack & pinion
Wheelbase: 252.0cm 99.2in
Track F: 142.0cm 55.9in
Track R: 141.5cm 55.7in
Length: 435.0cm 171.3in
Width: 166.5cm 65.6in
Height: 134.5cm 53.0in
Ground clearance: 15.3cm 6.0in
Kerb weight: 1010.0kg 2224.7lb
Fuel: 50.0L 11.0gal 13.2galUS

2132 Honda

Integra EX 16
1986 Japan
119.0mph 191.5kmh
0-50mph 80.5kmh: 6.4secs
0-60mph 96.5kmh: 8.6secs
0-1/4 mile: 17.0secs
0-1km: 30.8secs
125.0bhp 93.2kW 126.7PS
@ 6500rpm
103.0lbft 139.6Nm @ 5500rpm
124.6bhp/ton 122.5bhp/tonne
78.6bhp/L 58.6kW/L 79.7PS/L
63.9ft/sec 19.5m/sec
18.4mph 29.6kmh/1000rpm
27.5mpg 22.9mpgUS 10.3L/100km
Petrol 4-stroke piston
1590cc 97.0cu in
In-line 4 fuel injection
Compression ratio: 9.3:1
Bore: 75.0mm 2.9in
Stroke: 90.0mm 3.5in
Valve type/No: Overhead 16
Transmission: Manual
No. of forward speeds: 5
Wheels driven: Front
Springs F/R: Torsion bar/Coil
Brake system: PA
Brakes F/R: Disc/Disc
Steering: Rack & pinion PA
Wheelbase: 252.0cm 99.2in
Track F: 142.0cm 55.9in
Track R: 141.5cm 55.7in
Length: 435.0cm 171.3in
Width: 166.5cm 65.6in
Height: 134.5cm 53.0in
Ground clearance: 15.3cm 6.0in
Kerb weight: 1020.0kg 2246.7lb
Fuel: 50.0L 11.0gal 13.2galUS

2133 Honda

Legend
1986 Japan
127.0mph 204.3kmh
0-50mph 80.5kmh: 6.0secs
0-60mph 96.5kmh: 8.0secs
0-1/4 mile: 16.5secs
0-1km: 30.0secs
173.0bhp 129.0kW 175.4PS
@ 6000rpm
160.0lbft 216.8Nm @ 5000rpm
127.5bhp/ton 125.4bhp/tonne
69.4bhp/L 51.7kW/L 70.4PS/L
49.2ft/sec 15.0m/sec
24.2mph 38.9kmh/1000rpm
21.5mpg 17.9mpgUS 13.1L/100km
Petrol 4-stroke piston
2493cc 152.0cu in
Vee 6 fuel injection
Compression ratio: 9.6:1
Bore: 84.0mm 3.3in
Stroke: 75.0mm 2.9in
Valve type/No: Overhead 24
Transmission: Manual
No. of forward speeds: 5
Wheels driven: Front
Springs F/R: Coil/Coil
Brake system: PA
Brakes F/R: Disc/Disc
Steering: Rack & pinion PA
Wheelbase: 276.0cm 108.7in
Track F: 149.0cm 58.7in
Track R: 145.0cm 57.1in
Length: 481.0cm 189.4in
Width: 173.5cm 68.3in
Height: 139.0cm 54.7in
Ground clearance: 15.0cm 5.9in
Kerb weight: 1380.0kg 3039.6lb
Fuel: 68.2L 15.0gal 18.0galUS

2134 Honda

Prelude 2.0 Si
1986 Japan
0-60mph 96.5kmh: 9.1secs
0-1/4 mile: 16.8secs
110.0bhp 82.0kW 111.5PS
@ 5500rpm
114.0lbft 154.5Nm @ 4500rpm
102.2bhp/ton 100.5bhp/tonne
56.3bhp/L 42.0kW/L 57.0PS/L
54.7ft/sec 16.7m/sec
31.2mpg 26.0mpgUS 9.0L/100km
Petrol 4-stroke piston
1955cc 119.3cu in
In-line 4 fuel injection
Compression ratio: 8.8:1
Bore: 82.7mm 3.3in
Stroke: 91.0mm 3.6in
Valve type/No: Overhead 8
Transmission: Manual
No. of forward speeds: 5
Wheels driven: Front
Brakes F/R: Disc/Disc
Steering: Rack & pinion PA
Wheelbase: 245.1cm 96.5in
Length: 436.9cm 172.0in
Width: 169.9cm 66.9in
Height: 129.5cm 51.0in
Kerb weight: 1094.1kg 2410.0lb

2135 Honda

Ballade EX
1987 Japan
99.0mph 159.3kmh
0-50mph 80.5kmh: 7.9secs
0-60mph 96.5kmh: 11.1secs
0-1/4 mile: 18.5secs
0-1km: 34.8secs
85.0bhp 63.4kW 86.2PS
@ 6000rpm
93.0lbft 126.0Nm @ 3500rpm
93.4bhp/ton 91.9bhp/tonne
57.1bhp/L 42.6kW/L 57.9PS/L
56.8ft/sec 17.3m/sec
22.0mph 35.4kmh/1000rpm
33.3mpg 27.7mpgUS 8.5L/100km
Petrol 4-stroke piston
1488cc 91.0cu in
In-line 4 1 Carburettor
Compression ratio: 8.7:1
Bore: 74.0mm 2.9in
Stroke: 86.5mm 3.4in
Valve type/No: Overhead 12
Transmission: Manual
No. of forward speeds: 5
Wheels driven: Front
Springs F/R: Torsion bar/Coil
Brake system: PA
Brakes F/R: Disc/Drum
Steering: Rack & pinion PA
Wheelbase: 245.0cm 96.5in
Track F: 141.5cm 55.7in
Track R: 140.0cm 55.1in
Length: 414.5cm 163.2in
Width: 163.5cm 64.4in
Height: 139.5cm 54.9in
Ground clearance: 17.9cm 7.0in
Kerb weight: 925.0kg 2037.4lb
Fuel: 45.5L 10.0gal 12.0galUS

2136 Honda

Civic 1.4 GL 3-door
1987 Japan
108.0mph 173.8kmh
0-50mph 80.5kmh: 7.0secs
0-60mph 96.5kmh: 9.7secs
0-1/4 mile: 17.4secs
0-1km: 32.2secs
90.0bhp 67.1kW 91.2PS
@ 6300rpm
82.5lbft 111.8Nm @ 4500rpm
101.5bhp/ton 99.8bhp/tonne
64.5bhp/L 48.1kW/L 65.4PS/L
54.4ft/sec 16.6m/sec
20.1mph 32.3kmh/1000rpm
34.7mpg 28.9mpgUS 8.1L/100km
Petrol 4-stroke piston
1396cc 85.0cu in
In-line 4 2 Carburettor
Compression ratio: 9.3:1
Bore: 75.0mm 2.9in
Stroke: 79.0mm 3.1in
Valve type/No: Overhead 16
Transmission: Manual
No. of forward speeds: 5
Wheels driven: Front
Springs F/R: Coil/Coil
Brake system: PA
Brakes F/R: Disc/Drum
Steering: Rack & pinion PA
Wheelbase: 250.0cm 98.4in
Track F: 145.0cm 57.1in
Track R: 145.5cm 57.3in
Length: 396.5cm 156.1in
Width: 168.0cm 66.1in
Height: 133.0cm 52.4in
Ground clearance: 15.3cm 6.0in
Kerb weight: 902.0kg 1986.8lb
Fuel: 43.2L 9.5gal 11.4galUS

2137 Honda

Legend Coupe
1987 Japan
133.0mph 214.0kmh
0-50mph 80.5kmh: 6.0secs
0-60mph 96.5kmh: 8.0secs
0-1/4 mile: 16.4secs
0-1km: 29.8secs
177.0bhp 132.0kW 179.4PS
@ 6000rpm
165.0lbft 223.6Nm @ 4500rpm
126.8bhp/ton 124.6bhp/tonne
66.2bhp/L 49.3kW/L 67.1PS/L
49.2ft/sec 15.0m/sec
22.6mph 36.4kmh/1000rpm
20.3mpg 16.9mpgUS 13.9L/100km
Petrol 4-stroke piston
2675cc 163.0cu in
Vee 6 fuel injection
Compression ratio: 9.0:1
Bore: 87.0mm 3.4in
Stroke: 75.0mm 2.9in
Valve type/No: Overhead 24
Transmission: Manual
No. of forward speeds: 5
Wheels driven: Front
Springs F/R: Coil/Coil
Brake system: PA ABS
Brakes F/R: Disc/Disc
Steering: Rack & pinion PA
Wheelbase: 270.5cm 106.5in
Track F: 150.0cm 59.1in
Track R: 150.0cm 59.1in
Length: 477.5cm 188.0in
Width: 174.5cm 68.7in
Height: 137.0cm 53.9in
Ground clearance: 17.9cm 7.0in
Kerb weight: 1420.0kg 3127.7lb
Fuel: 68.2L 15.0gal 18.0galUS

2138 Honda

Prelude 2.0 Si
1987 Japan
127.0mph 204.3kmh
0-50mph 80.5kmh: 6.7secs
0-60mph 96.5kmh: 9.3secs
0-1/4 mile: 16.8secs
135.0bhp 100.7kW 136.9PS
@ 6200rpm
127.0lbft 172.1Nm @ 4500rpm
111.8bhp/ton 109.9bhp/tonne
68.9bhp/L 51.4kW/L 69.9PS/L
64.4ft/sec 19.6m/sec
26.4mpg 22.0mpgUS 10.7L/100km
Petrol 4-stroke piston
1958cc 119.5cu in
In-line 4 fuel injection
Compression ratio: 9.0:1
Bore: 81.0mm 3.2in
Stroke: 95.0mm 3.7in
Valve type/No: Overhead 16
Transmission: Manual
No. of forward speeds: 5
Wheels driven: Front
Springs F/R: Coil/Coil
Brake system: PA
Brakes F/R: Disc/Disc
Steering: Rack & pinion PA
Wheelbase: 256.5cm 101.0in
Track F: 148.1cm 58.3in
Track R: 147.1cm 57.9in
Length: 446.0cm 175.6in
Width: 170.9cm 67.3in
Height: 129.5cm 51.0in
Ground clearance: 14.5cm 5.7in
Kerb weight: 1228.1kg 2705.0lb
Fuel: 60.2L 13.2gal 15.9galUS

2139 Honda

Prelude 2.0i 16
1987 Japan
128.0mph 206.0kmh
0-50mph 80.5kmh: 6.2secs
0-60mph 96.5kmh: 8.5secs
0-1/4 mile: 16.4secs
0-1km: 30.0secs
150.0bhp 111.9kW 152.1PS
@ 6000rpm
133.0lbft 180.2Nm @ 5500rpm
133.6bhp/ton 131.3bhp/tonne
76.6bhp/L 57.1kW/L 77.7PS/L
62.3ft/sec 19.0m/sec
20.7mph 33.3kmh/1000rpm
21.0mpg 17.5mpgUS 13.5L/100km
Petrol 4-stroke piston
1958cc 119.0cu in
In-line 4 fuel injection
Compression ratio: 10.5:1
Bore: 81.0mm 3.2in
Stroke: 95.0mm 3.7in
Valve type/No: Overhead 16
Transmission: Manual
No. of forward speeds: 5
Wheels driven: Front
Springs F/R: Coil/Coil
Brake system: PA
Brakes F/R: Disc/Disc
Steering: Rack & pinion PA
Wheelbase: 256.5cm 101.0in
Track F: 148.0cm 58.3in
Track R: 147.0cm 57.9in
Length: 446.0cm 175.6in
Width: 169.5cm 66.7in
Height: 129.5cm 51.0in
Ground clearance: 14.5cm 5.7in
Kerb weight: 1142.0kg 2515.4lb
Fuel: 59.6L 13.1gal 15.7galUS

2140 Honda

Civic CRX
1988 Japan
125.0mph 201.1kmh
0-50mph 80.5kmh: 6.0secs
0-60mph 96.5kmh: 8.0secs
0-1/4 mile: 16.2secs
0-1km: 29.9secs
130.0bhp 96.9kW 131.8PS
@ 6800rpm
105.0lbft 142.3Nm @ 5700rpm
146.5bhp/ton 144.1bhp/tonne
81.8bhp/L 61.0kW/L 82.9PS/L
66.9ft/sec 20.4m/sec
19.2mph 30.9kmh/1000rpm
29.6mpg 24.6mpgUS 9.5L/100km
Petrol 4-stroke piston
1590cc 97.0cu in
In-line 4 fuel injection
Compression ratio: 9.5:1
Bore: 75.0mm 2.9in
Stroke: 90.0mm 3.5in
Valve type/No: Overhead 16
Transmission: Manual

No. of forward speeds: 5
Wheels driven: Front
Springs F/R: Coil/Coil
Brake system: PA
Brakes F/R: Disc/Disc
Steering: Rack & pinion
Wheelbase: 229.9cm 90.5in
Track F: 144.8cm 57.0in
Track R: 145.3cm 57.2in
Length: 377.4cm 148.6in
Width: 167.4cm 65.9in
Height: 127.0cm 50.0in
Ground clearance: 15.7cm 6.2in
Kerb weight: 902.1kg 1987.0lb
Fuel: 45.0L 9.9gal 11.9galUS

2141 Honda
CRX Si
1988 Japan
125.0mph 201.1kmh
0-50mph 80.5kmh: 5.9secs
0-60mph 96.5kmh: 8.2secs
0-1/4 mile: 16.4secs
105.0bhp 78.3kW 106.5PS
@ 6000rpm
98.0lbft 132.8Nm @ 5000rpm
111.2bhp/ton 109.3bhp/tonne
66.0bhp/L 49.2kW/L 67.0PS/L
59.0ft/sec 18.0m/sec
37.2mpg 31.0mpgUS 7.6L/100km
Petrol 4-stroke piston
1590cc 97.0cu in
In-line 4 fuel injection
Compression ratio: 9.1:1
Bore: 75.0mm 2.9in
Stroke: 90.0mm 3.5in
Valve type/No: Overhead 16
Transmission: Manual
No. of forward speeds: 5
Wheels driven: Front
Springs F/R: Coil/Coil
Brake system: PA
Brakes F/R: Disc/Drum
Steering: Rack & pinion PA
Wheelbase: 230.1cm 90.6in
Track F: 145.0cm 57.1in
Track R: 145.0cm 57.1in
Length: 375.4cm 147.8in
Width: 166.9cm 65.7in
Height: 127.0cm 50.0in
Ground clearance: 16.5cm 6.5in
Kerb weight: 960.2kg 2115.0lb
Fuel: 45.0L 9.9gal 11.9galUS

2142 Honda
CRX Si Jackson
1988 Japan
125.0mph 201.1kmh
0-60mph 96.5kmh: 8.0secs
0-1/4 mile: 16.2secs
131.0bhp 97.7kW 132.8PS
@ 6500rpm
134.9bhp/ton 132.7bhp/tonne
82.4bhp/L 61.4kW/L 83.5PS/L
63.9ft/sec 19.5m/sec
34.8mpg 29.0mpgUS 8.1L/100km
Petrol 4-stroke piston
1590cc 97.0cu in
In-line 4 fuel injection
Compression ratio: 9.1:1
Bore: 75.0mm 2.9in
Stroke: 90.0mm 3.5in
Valve type/No: Overhead 16
Transmission: Manual
No. of forward speeds: 5
Wheels driven: Front
Springs F/R: Coil/Coil
Brake system: PA
Brakes F/R: Disc/Drum
Steering: Rack & pinion
Wheelbase: 230.1cm 90.6in
Track F: 145.0cm 57.1in
Track R: 145.0cm 57.1in
Length: 375.4cm 147.8in
Width: 166.9cm 65.7in
Height: 127.0cm 50.0in
Kerb weight: 987.4kg 2175.0lb
Fuel: 45.0L 9.9gal 11.9galUS

2143 Honda
Legend Saloon Automatic
1988 Japan
128.0mph 206.0kmh
0-50mph 80.5kmh: 6.5secs
0-60mph 96.5kmh: 8.6secs
0-1/4 mile: 17.1secs
0-1km: 30.9secs
177.0bhp 132.0kW 179.4PS
@ 6000rpm
165.3lbft 224.0Nm @ 4500rpm
127.2bhp/ton 125.1bhp/tonne
66.2bhp/L 49.3kW/L 67.1PS/L
49.2ft/sec 15.0m/sec
21.1mph 33.9kmh/1000rpm
18.4mpg 15.3mpgUS 15.4L/100km
Petrol 4-stroke piston
2675cc 163.0cu in
Vee 6 fuel injection
Compression ratio: 9.0:1
Bore: 87.0mm 3.4in
Stroke: 75.0mm 2.9in
Valve type/No: Overhead 24
Transmission: Automatic
No. of forward speeds: 4
Wheels driven: Front
Springs F/R: Coil/Coil
Brake system: PA ABS
Brakes F/R: Disc/Disc
Steering: Rack & pinion PA
Wheelbase: 276.0cm 108.7in
Track F: 149.0cm 58.7in
Track R: 145.0cm 57.1in
Length: 481.0cm 189.4in
Width: 173.5cm 68.3in
Height: 139.0cm 54.7in
Ground clearance: 15.0cm 5.9in
Kerb weight: 1415.0kg 3116.7lb
Fuel: 68.2L 15.0gal 18.0galUS

2144 Honda
Shuttle 1.6i RT4 4WD
1988 Japan
107.0mph 172.2kmh
0-50mph 80.5kmh: 6.8secs
0-60mph 96.5kmh: 10.0secs
0-1/4 mile: 17.1secs
0-1km: 32.3secs
116.0bhp 86.5kW 117.6PS
@ 6300rpm
104.1lbft 141.0Nm @ 5300rpm
107.7bhp/ton 105.9bhp/tonne
73.0bhp/L 54.4kW/L 74.0PS/L
61.9ft/sec 18.9m/sec
19.2mph 30.9kmh/1000rpm
22.9mpg 19.1mpgUS 12.3L/100km
Petrol 4-stroke piston
1590cc 97.0cu in
In-line 4 fuel injection
Compression ratio: 9.1:1
Bore: 75.0mm 2.9in
Stroke: 90.0mm 3.5in
Valve type/No: Overhead 16
Transmission: Manual
No. of forward speeds: 5
Wheels driven: 4-wheel drive
Springs F/R: Coil/Coil
Brake system: PA
Brakes F/R: Disc/Drum
Steering: Rack & pinion PA
Wheelbase: 250.0cm 98.4in
Track F: 144.0cm 56.7in
Track R: 145.0cm 57.1in
Length: 410.5cm 161.6in
Width: 169.0cm 66.5in
Height: 151.5cm 59.6in
Ground clearance: 19.0cm 7.5in
Kerb weight: 1095.0kg 2411.9lb
Fuel: 45.0L 9.9gal 11.9galUS

2145 Honda
Civic Si
1989 Japan
115.0mph 185.0kmh
0-50mph 80.5kmh: 6.6secs
0-60mph 96.5kmh: 9.4secs
0-1/4 mile: 17.0secs
108.0bhp 80.5kW 109.5PS
@ 6000rpm
100.0lbft 135.5Nm @ 5000rpm
107.0bhp/ton 105.3bhp/tonne
67.9bhp/L 50.6kW/L 68.9PS/L
59.0ft/sec 18.0m/sec
34.2mpg 28.5mpgUS 8.3L/100km
Petrol 4-stroke piston
1590cc 97.0cu in
In-line 4 fuel injection
Compression ratio: 9.1:1
Bore: 75.0mm 2.9in
Stroke: 90.0mm 3.5in
Valve type/No: Overhead 16
Transmission: Manual
No. of forward speeds: 5
Wheels driven: Front
Springs F/R: Coil/Coil
Brake system: PA
Brakes F/R: Disc/Drum
Steering: Rack & pinion
Wheelbase: 249.9cm 98.4in
Track F: 145.0cm 57.1in
Track R: 145.5cm 57.3in
Length: 396.5cm 156.1in
Width: 166.6cm 65.6in
Height: 133.4cm 52.5in
Kerb weight: 1026.0kg 2260.0lb
Fuel: 45.0L 9.9gal 11.9galUS

2146 Honda
Civic Si HKS
1989 Japan
0-50mph 80.5kmh: 5.8secs
0-60mph 96.5kmh: 8.0secs
0-1/4 mile: 16.2secs
135.0bhp 100.7kW 136.9PS
@ 6000rpm
108.0lbft 146.3Nm @ 4000rpm
139.3bhp/ton 137.0bhp/tonne
90.7bhp/L 67.6kW/L 92.0PS/L
56.8ft/sec 17.3m/sec
Petrol 4-stroke piston
1488cc 90.8cu in turbocharged
In-line 4 fuel injection
Compression ratio: 8.7:1
Bore: 73.9mm 2.9in
Stroke: 86.5mm 3.4in
Valve type/No: Overhead 12
Transmission: Manual
No. of forward speeds: 5
Wheels driven: Front
Springs F/R: Torsion bar/Coil
Brake system: PA
Brakes F/R: Disc/Drum
Steering: Rack & pinion
Wheelbase: 238.0cm 93.7in
Track F: 140.0cm 55.1in
Track R: 141.5cm 55.7in
Length: 381.0cm 150.0in
Width: 162.3cm 63.9in
Height: 133.6cm 52.6in
Kerb weight: 985.2kg 2170.0lb

2147 Honda
CRX Si HKS
1989 Japan
0-50mph 80.5kmh: 5.3secs
0-60mph 96.5kmh: 7.4secs
0-1/4 mile: 15.4secs
182.0bhp 135.7kW 184.5PS
@ 5500rpm
158.0lbft 214.1Nm @ 4000rpm
192.3bhp/ton 189.1bhp/tonne
122.3bhp/L 91.2kW/L 124.0PS/L
52.1ft/sec 15.9m/sec
Petrol 4-stroke piston
1488cc 90.8cu in turbocharged
In-line 4 fuel injection
Compression ratio: 8.0:1
Bore: 73.9mm 2.9in
Stroke: 86.5mm 3.4in
Valve type/No: Overhead 12
Transmission: Manual
No. of forward speeds: 5
Wheels driven: Front
Springs F/R: Torsion bar/Coil
Brake system: PA
Brakes F/R: Disc/Drum
Steering: Rack & pinion
Wheelbase: 220.0cm 86.6in
Track F: 140.0cm 55.1in
Track R: 141.5cm 55.7in
Length: 375.4cm 147.8in
Width: 162.3cm 63.9in
Height: 129.0cm 50.8in
Kerb weight: 962.5kg 2120.0lb

2148 Honda
Prelude Si 4WS
1989 Japan
127.0mph 204.3kmh
0-50mph 80.5kmh: 6.8secs
0-60mph 96.5kmh: 9.4secs
0-1/4 mile: 17.0secs
135.0bhp 100.7kW 136.9PS
@ 6200rpm
127.0lbft 172.1Nm @ 4500rpm
111.8bhp/ton 109.9bhp/tonne
68.9bhp/L 51.4kW/L 69.9PS/L
64.4ft/sec 19.6m/sec
24.6mpg 20.5mpgUS 11.5L/100km
Petrol 4-stroke piston
1958cc 119.5cu in
In-line 4 fuel injection
Compression ratio: 9.0:1
Bore: 81.0mm 3.2in
Stroke: 95.0mm 3.7in
Valve type/No: Overhead 16
Transmission: Manual
No. of forward speeds: 5
Wheels driven: Front
Springs F/R: Coil/Coil
Brake system: PA
Brakes F/R: Disc/Disc
Steering: Rack & pinion PA
Wheelbase: 256.5cm 101.0in
Track F: 148.1cm 58.3in
Track R: 147.1cm 57.9in
Length: 446.0cm 175.6in
Width: 169.4cm 66.7in
Height: 129.5cm 51.0in
Kerb weight: 1228.1kg 2705.0lb
Fuel: 60.2L 13.2gal 15.9galUS

2149 Honda
Shuttle 1.4 GL Automatic
1989 Japan
100.0mph 160.9kmh
0-50mph 80.5kmh: 8.8secs
0-60mph 96.5kmh: 12.2secs
0-1/4 mile: 19.1secs
0-1km: 35.4secs
90.0bhp 67.1kW 91.2PS
@ 6300rpm
82.7lbft 112.0Nm @ 4500rpm
93.3bhp/ton 91.7bhp/tonne
64.5bhp/L 48.1kW/L 65.4PS/L
54.4ft/sec 16.6m/sec
20.9mph 33.6kmh/1000rpm
23.3mpg 19.4mpgUS 12.1L/100km
Petrol 4-stroke piston
1396cc 85.0cu in
In-line 4 1 Carburettor
Compression ratio: 9.3:1
Bore: 75.0mm 2.9in
Stroke: 79.0mm 3.1in
Valve type/No: Overhead 16
Transmission: Automatic
No. of forward speeds: 4
Wheels driven: Front
Springs F/R: Coil/Coil
Brake system: PA
Brakes F/R: Disc/Drum
Steering: Rack & pinion PA
Wheelbase: 250.0cm 98.4in
Track F: 144.0cm 56.7in
Track R: 145.0cm 57.1in
Length: 410.5cm 161.6in
Width: 169.0cm 66.5in
Height: 151.5cm 59.6in
Ground clearance: 19.0cm 7.5in
Kerb weight: 981.0kg 2160.8lb
Fuel: 45.0L 9.9gal 11.9galUS

2150 Honda
Accord 2.0 EXi
1990 Japan
125.0mph 201.1kmh
0-50mph 80.5kmh: 7.1secs
0-60mph 96.5kmh: 9.9secs
0-1/4 mile: 17.5secs
0-1km: 31.9secs
133.0bhp 99.2kW 134.8PS
@ 5300rpm
132.1lbft 179.0Nm @ 5000rpm
106.5bhp/ton 104.7bhp/tonne
66.6bhp/L 49.7kW/L 67.5PS/L
50.9ft/sec 15.5m/sec
22.7mph 36.5kmh/1000rpm
26.1mpg 21.7mpgUS 10.8L/100km
Petrol 4-stroke piston
1997cc 122.0cu in
In-line 4 fuel injection
Compression ratio: 9.5:1
Bore: 85.0mm 3.3in
Stroke: 88.0mm 3.5in
Valve type/No: Overhead 16
Transmission: Manual
No. of forward speeds: 5
Wheels driven: Front
Springs F/R: Coil/Coil
Brake system: PA ABS
Brakes F/R: Disc/Drum
Steering: Rack & pinion PA
Wheelbase: 272.0cm 107.1in
Track F: 147.5cm 58.1in
Track R: 148.0cm 58.3in
Length: 468.5cm 184.4in
Width: 169.5cm 66.7in

Height: 139.0cm 54.7in
Kerb weight: 1270.0kg 2797.4lb
Fuel: 65.1L 14.3gal 17.2galUS

2151 Honda
Concerto 1.6i 16
1990 Japan
121.0mph 194.7kmh
0-50mph 80.5kmh: 6.8secs
0-60mph 96.5kmh: 9.3secs
0-1/4 mile: 17.2secs
0-1km: 31.6secs
130.0bhp 96.9kW 131.8PS
@ 6800rpm
105.5lbft 143.0Nm @ 5700rpm
116.0bhp/ton 114.0bhp/tonne
81.8bhp/L 61.0kW/L 82.9PS/L
66.9ft/sec 20.4m/sec
18.1mph 29.1kmh/1000rpm
25.7mpg 21.4mpgUS 11.0L/100km
Petrol 4-stroke piston
1590cc 97.0cu in
In-line 4 fuel injection
Compression ratio: 9.5:1
Bore: 75.0mm 2.9in
Stroke: 90.0mm 3.5in
Valve type/No: Overhead 16
Transmission: Manual
No. of forward speeds: 5
Wheels driven: Front
Springs F/R: Coil/Coil
Brake system: PA ABS
Brakes F/R: Disc/Disc
Steering: Rack & pinion PA
Wheelbase: 255.0cm 100.4in
Track F: 147.5cm 58.1in
Track R: 147.0cm 57.9in
Length: 426.5cm 167.9in
Width: 194.0cm 76.4in
Height: 140.0cm 55.1in
Ground clearance: 15.0cm 5.9in
Kerb weight: 1140.0kg 2511.0lb
Fuel: 55.1L 12.1gal 14.5galUS

2152 Honda
CRX 1.6i VT
1990 Japan
132.0mph 212.4kmh
0-50mph 80.5kmh: 6.2secs
0-60mph 96.5kmh: 8.0secs
0-1/4 mile: 16.4secs
0-1km: 29.6secs
150.0bhp 111.9kW 152.1PS
@ 7600rpm
106.3lbft 144.0Nm @ 7100rpm
148.8bhp/ton 146.3bhp/tonne
94.0bhp/L 70.1kW/L 95.3PS/L
64.0ft/sec 19.5m/sec
18.7mph 30.1kmh/1000rpm
28.1mpg 23.4mpgUS 10.1L/100km
Petrol 4-stroke piston
1595cc 97.0cu in
In-line 4 fuel injection
Compression ratio: 10.2:1
Bore: 81.0mm 3.2in
Stroke: 77.0mm 3.0in
Valve type/No: Overhead 16
Transmission: Manual
No. of forward speeds: 5
Wheels driven: Front
Springs F/R: Coil/Coil
Brake system: PA ABS
Brakes F/R: Disc/Disc
Steering: Rack & pinion
Wheelbase: 229.9cm 90.5in
Track F: 145.3cm 57.2in
Track R: 145.3cm 57.2in
Length: 377.4cm 148.6in
Width: 167.4cm 65.9in
Height: 127.0cm 50.0in
Kerb weight: 1025.0kg 2257.7lb
Fuel: 45.0L 9.9gal 11.9galUS

2153 Honda
Civic 1.5 VEi
1991 Japan
112.0mph 180.2kmh
0-50mph 80.5kmh: 7.6secs
0-60mph 96.5kmh: 11.2secs
0-1/4 mile: 17.8secs
0-1km: 33.3secs
90.0bhp 67.1kW 91.2PS
@ 5500rpm
95.0lbft 128.7Nm @ 4500rpm
94.8bhp/ton 93.2bhp/tonne
60.3bhp/L 44.9kW/L 61.1PS/L
50.9ft/sec 15.5m/sec
23.6mph 38.0kmh/1000rpm
31.9mpg 26.6mpgUS 8.9L/100km
Petrol 4-stroke piston
1493cc 91.1cu in
In-line 4 fuel injection
Compression ratio: 9.3:1
Bore: 75.0mm 2.9in
Stroke: 84.5mm 3.3in
Valve type/No: Overhead 16
Transmission: Manual
No. of forward speeds: 5
Wheels driven: Front
Springs F/R: Coil/Coil
Brake system: PA
Brakes F/R: Disc/Drum
Steering: Rack & pinion PA
Wheelbase: 257.0cm 101.2in
Track F: 147.3cm 58.0in
Track R: 146.6cm 57.7in
Length: 407.9cm 160.6in
Width: 169.4cm 66.7in
Height: 134.6cm 53.0in
Kerb weight: 965.2kg 2126.0lb
Fuel: 45.0L 9.9gal 11.9galUS

2154 Honda
Civic 1.6i VT
1991 Japan
128.0mph 206.0kmh
0-50mph 80.5kmh: 5.9secs
0-60mph 96.5kmh: 7.6secs
0-1/4 mile: 16.1secs
0-1km: 29.3secs
150.0bhp 111.9kW 152.1PS
@ 7600rpm
106.3lbft 144.0Nm @ 7100rpm
146.7bhp/ton 144.2bhp/tonne
94.0bhp/L 70.1kW/L 95.3PS/L
64.4ft/sec 19.6m/sec
18.7mph 30.1kmh/1000rpm
30.0mpg 25.0mpgUS 9.4L/100km
Petrol 4-stroke piston
1595cc 97.0cu in
In-line 4 fuel injection
Compression ratio: 10.2:1
Bore: 81.0mm 3.2in
Stroke: 77.4mm 3.0in
Valve type/No: Overhead 16
Transmission: Manual
No. of forward speeds: 5
Wheels driven: Front
Springs F/R: Coil/Coil
Brake system: PA
Brakes F/R: Disc/Disc
Steering: Rack & pinion
Wheelbase: 249.9cm 98.4in
Track F: 145.0cm 57.1in
Track R: 145.5cm 57.3in
Length: 396.5cm 156.1in
Width: 167.9cm 66.1in
Height: 133.1cm 52.4in
Ground clearance: 16.0cm 6.3in
Kerb weight: 1040.0kg 2290.7lb
Fuel: 45.0L 9.9gal 11.9galUS

2155 Honda
Legend
1991 Japan
142.0mph 228.5kmh
0-50mph 80.5kmh: 6.3secs
0-60mph 96.5kmh: 8.2secs
0-1/4 mile: 16.5secs
0-1km: 29.6secs
205.0bhp 152.9kW 207.8PS
@ 5500rpm
216.2lbft 293.0Nm @ 4400rpm
129.5bhp/ton 127.3bhp/tonne
63.9bhp/L 47.7kW/L 64.8PS/L
50.6ft/sec 15.4m/sec
25.6mph 41.2kmh/1000rpm
19.1mpg 15.9mpgUS 14.8L/100km
Petrol 4-stroke piston
3206cc 196.0cu in
Vee 6 fuel injection
Compression ratio: 9.6:1
Bore: 90.0mm 3.5in
Stroke: 84.0mm 3.3in
Valve type/No: Overhead 24
Transmission: Automatic
No. of forward speeds: 4
Wheels driven: Front
Springs F/R: Coil/Coil
Brake system: PA ABS
Brakes F/R: Disc/Disc
Steering: Rack & pinion PA
Wheelbase: 290.8cm 114.5in
Track F: 154.9cm 61.0in
Track R: 153.9cm 60.6in
Length: 494.8cm 194.8in
Width: 180.8cm 71.2in
Height: 141.0cm 55.5in
Ground clearance: 15.0cm 5.9in
Kerb weight: 1610.0kg 3546.3lb
Fuel: 68.0L 14.9gal 18.0galUS

2156 Honda
NSX
1991 Japan
162.0mph 260.7kmh
0-50mph 80.5kmh: 4.4secs
0-60mph 96.5kmh: 5.8secs
0-1/4 mile: 14.2secs
0-1km: 25.5secs
270.0bhp 201.3kW 273.7PS
@ 7100rpm
210.3lbft 285.0Nm @ 3500rpm
204.9bhp/ton 201.5bhp/tonne
90.7bhp/L 67.6kW/L 91.9PS/L
60.5ft/sec 18.5m/sec
23.0mph 37.0kmh/1000rpm
19.6mpg 16.3mpgUS 14.4L/100km
Petrol 4-stroke piston
2977cc 182.0cu in
Vee 6 fuel injection
Compression ratio: 10.2:1
Bore: 90.0mm 3.5in
Stroke: 78.0mm 3.1in
Valve type/No: Overhead 24
Transmission: Manual
No. of forward speeds: 5
Wheels driven: Rear
Springs F/R: Coil/Coil
Brake system: PA ABS
Brakes F/R: Disc/Disc
Steering: Rack & pinion
Wheelbase: 253.0cm 99.6in
Track F: 150.9cm 59.4in
Track R: 152.9cm 60.2in
Length: 440.4cm 173.4in
Width: 181.1cm 71.3in
Height: 117.1cm 46.1in
Ground clearance: 13.5cm 5.3in
Kerb weight: 1340.0kg 2951.5lb
Fuel: 70.1L 15.4gal 18.5galUS

2157 Honda
Prelude Si
1991 Japan
130.0mph 209.2kmh
0-50mph 80.5kmh: 6.3secs
0-60mph 96.5kmh: 8.8secs
0-1/4 mile: 16.4secs
140.0bhp 104.4kW 141.9PS
@ 5800rpm
135.0lbft 182.9Nm @ 5000rpm
115.9bhp/ton 114.0bhp/tonne
68.1bhp/L 50.8kW/L 69.0PS/L
60.3ft/sec 18.4m/sec
28.8mpg 24.0mpgUS 9.8L/100km
Petrol 4-stroke piston
2056cc 125.4cu in
In-line 4 fuel injection
Compression ratio: 9.4:1
Bore: 83.0mm 3.3in
Stroke: 95.0mm 3.7in
Valve type/No: Overhead 16
Transmission: Manual
No. of forward speeds: 5
Wheels driven: Front
Springs F/R: Coil/Coil
Brake system: PA ABS
Brakes F/R: Disc/Disc
Steering: Rack & pinion PA
Wheelbase: 256.5cm 101.0in
Track F: 148.1cm 58.3in
Track R: 147.1cm 57.9in
Length: 451.1cm 177.6in
Width: 170.9cm 67.3in
Height: 129.5cm 51.0in
Kerb weight: 1228.1kg 2705.0lb
Fuel: 60.2L 13.2gal 15.9galUS

2158 Honda
Legend Coupe
1992 Japan
143.0mph 230.1kmh
0-50mph 80.5kmh: 6.2secs
0-60mph 96.5kmh: 8.1secs
0-1/4 mile: 16.3secs
0-1km: 29.3secs
205.0bhp 152.9kW 207.8PS
@ 5500rpm
216.0lbft 292.7Nm @ 4400rpm
133.6bhp/ton 131.4bhp/tonne
63.9bhp/L 47.7kW/L 64.8PS/L
50.6ft/sec 15.4m/sec
25.6mph 41.2kmh/1000rpm
21.5mpg 17.9mpgUS 13.1L/100km
Petrol 4-stroke piston
3206cc 195.6cu in
Vee 6 fuel injection
Compression ratio: 9.6:1
Bore: 90.0mm 3.5in
Stroke: 84.0mm 3.3in
Valve type/No: Overhead 24
Transmission: Automatic
No. of forward speeds: 4
Wheels driven: Front
Springs F/R: Coil/Coil
Brake system: PA
Brakes F/R: Disc/Disc
Steering: Rack & pinion PA
Wheelbase: 283.0cm 111.4in
Track F: 154.9cm 61.0in
Track R: 153.9cm 60.6in
Length: 488.4cm 192.3in
Width: 180.8cm 71.2in
Height: 136.9cm 53.9in
Ground clearance: 15.0cm 5.9in
Kerb weight: 1559.9kg 3436.0lb
Fuel: 68.2L 15.0gal 18.0galUS

2159 Honda
NSX Auto
1992 Japan
158.0mph 254.2kmh
0-50mph 80.5kmh: 5.1secs
0-60mph 96.5kmh: 6.8secs
0-1/4 mile: 14.9secs
0-1km: 29.6secs
255.0bhp 190.1kW 258.5PS
@ 6800rpm
209.6lbft 284.0Nm @ 5400rpm
189.3bhp/ton 186.1bhp/tonne
85.7bhp/L 63.9kW/L 86.8PS/L
58.0ft/sec 17.7m/sec
22.8mph 36.7kmh/1000rpm
18.3mpg 15.2mpgUS 15.4L/100km
Petrol 4-stroke piston
2977cc 182.0cu in
Vee 6 fuel injection
Compression ratio: 10.2:1
Bore: 90.0mm 3.5in
Stroke: 78.0mm 3.1in
Valve type/No: Overhead 24
Transmission: Automatic
No. of forward speeds: 4
Wheels driven: Rear
Springs F/R: Coil/Coil
Brake system: PA ABS
Brakes F/R: Disc/Disc
Steering: Rack & pinion PA
Wheelbase: 253.0cm 99.6in
Track F: 151.0cm 59.4in
Track R: 153.0cm 60.2in
Length: 440.5cm 173.4in
Width: 181.0cm 71.3in
Height: 117.0cm 46.1in
Ground clearance: 13.4cm 5.3in
Kerb weight: 1370.0kg 3017.6lb
Fuel: 70.0L 15.4gal 18.5galUS

2160 Honda
Prelude Si 4WS
1992 Japan
126.0mph 202.7kmh
0-50mph 80.5kmh: 5.8secs
0-60mph 96.5kmh: 7.9secs
0-1/4 mile: 16.0secs
160.0bhp 119.3kW 162.2PS
@ 5800rpm
156.0lbft 211.4Nm @ 4500rpm
123.6bhp/ton 121.5bhp/tonne
70.8bhp/L 52.8kW/L 71.8PS/L
60.3ft/sec 18.4m/sec
28.8mpg 24.0mpgUS 9.8L/100km
Petrol 4-stroke piston
2259cc 137.8cu in
In-line 4 fuel injection
Compression ratio: 9.8:1
Bore: 87.0mm 3.4in
Stroke: 95.0mm 3.7in
Valve type/No: Overhead 16
Transmission: Manual
No. of forward speeds: 5
Wheels driven: Front
Springs F/R: Coil/Coil
Brake system: PA ABS
Brakes F/R: Disc/Disc

Steering: Rack & pinion PA
Wheelbase: 255.0cm 100.4in
Track F: 152.4cm 60.0in
Track R: 151.4cm 59.6in
Length: 444.0cm 174.8in
Width: 176.5cm 69.5in
Height: 129.0cm 50.8in
Ground clearance: 15.0cm 5.9in
Kerb weight: 1316.6kg 2900.0lb
Fuel: 60.2L 13.2gal 15.9galUS

2161 Hotchkiss
3.5-litre Coupe
1933 France
80.3mph 129.2kmh
0-50mph 80.5kmh: 17.2secs
0-60mph 96.5kmh: 25.0secs
17.0mpg 14.2mpgUS 16.6L/100km
Petrol 4-stroke piston
3485cc 212.6cu in
In-line 6
Bore: 86.0mm 3.4in
Stroke: 100.0mm 3.9in
Transmission: Manual
No. of forward speeds: 4
Wheels driven: Rear
Brakes F/R: Drum/Drum
Kerb weight: 1563.6kg 3444.0lb
Fuel: 81.9L 18.0gal 21.6galUS

2162 Hotchkiss
Paris-Nice Speed Model
1934 France
93.2mph 150.0kmh
0-50mph 80.5kmh: 11.2secs
0-60mph 96.5kmh: 14.0secs
17.0mpg 14.2mpgUS 16.6L/100km
Petrol 4-stroke piston
3485cc 212.6cu in
In-line 6
Bore: 86.0mm 3.4in
Stroke: 100.0mm 3.9in
Transmission: Manual
No. of forward speeds: 4
Wheels driven: Rear
Brakes F/R: Drum/Drum
Kerb weight: 1372.9kg 3024.0lb
Fuel: 81.9L 18.0gal 21.6galUS

2163 Hotchkiss
Paris-Nice Saloon
1935 France
95.7mph 154.0kmh
0-50mph 80.5kmh: 10.8secs
0-60mph 96.5kmh: 13.8secs
14.0mpg 11.7mpgUS 20.2L/100km
Petrol 4-stroke piston
3485cc 212.6cu in
In-line 6
Bore: 86.0mm 3.4in
Stroke: 100.0mm 3.9in
Valve type/No: Overhead 12
Transmission: Manual
No. of forward speeds: 4
Wheels driven: Rear
Brakes F/R: Drum/Drum
Kerb weight: 1534.5kg 3380.0lb
Fuel: 81.9L 18.0gal 21.6galUS

2164 Hotchkiss
28hp Cabourg Saloon
1937 France
88.2mph 141.9kmh
0-50mph 80.5kmh: 13.0secs
0-60mph 96.5kmh: 18.1secs
17.0mpg 14.2mpgUS 16.6L/100km
Petrol 4-stroke piston
3485cc 212.6cu in
In-line 6
Bore: 86.0mm 3.4in
Stroke: 100.0mm 3.9in
Valve type/No: Overhead 12
Transmission: Manual
No. of forward speeds: 4
Wheels driven: Rear
Brakes F/R: Drum/Drum
Kerb weight: 1580.4kg 3481.0lb
Fuel: 81.9L 18.0gal 21.6galUS

2165 Hotchkiss
3.5-litre Saloon
1938 France
94.7mph 152.4kmh
0-50mph 80.5kmh: 9.7secs
0-60mph 96.5kmh: 13.7secs
17.0mpg 14.2mpgUS 16.6L/100km
Petrol 4-stroke piston
3485cc 212.6cu in
In-line 6
Bore: 86.0mm 3.4in
Stroke: 100.0mm 3.9in
Valve type/No: Overhead 12
Transmission: Manual
No. of forward speeds: 4
Wheels driven: Rear
Brakes F/R: Drum/Drum
Kerb weight: 1396.0kg 3075.0lb
Fuel: 81.9L 18.0gal 21.6galUS

2166 HRG
12hp Sports Two-seater
1937 UK
85.7mph 137.9kmh
0-50mph 80.5kmh: 9.8secs
0-60mph 96.5kmh: 14.3secs
28.0mpg 23.3mpgUS 10.1L/100km
Petrol 4-stroke piston
1496cc 91.3cu in
In-line 4
Bore: 69.0mm 2.7in
Stroke: 100.0mm 3.9in
Valve type/No: Overhead 8
Transmission: Manual
No. of forward speeds: 4
Wheels driven: Rear
Brakes F/R: Drum/Drum
Kerb weight: 738.2kg 1626.0lb
Fuel: 68.2L 15.0gal 18.0galUS

2167 HRG
1.5-litre
1938 UK
86.5mph 139.2kmh
0-50mph 80.5kmh: 11.3secs
0-60mph 96.5kmh: 16.2secs
58.0bhp 43.2kW 58.8PS
@ 4200rpm
78.2bhp/ton 76.9bhp/tonne
38.8bhp/L 28.9kW/L 39.3PS/L
46.0ft/sec 14.0m/sec
28.0mpg 23.3mpgUS 10.1L/100km
Petrol 4-stroke piston
1496cc 91.3cu in
In-line 4 2 Carburettor
Compression ratio: 7.5:1
Bore: 69.0mm 2.7in
Stroke: 100.0mm 3.9in
Valve type/No: Overhead 8
Transmission: Manual
No. of forward speeds: 4
Wheels driven: Rear
Brakes F/R: Drum/Drum
Kerb weight: 754.1kg 1661.0lb
Fuel: 63.7L 14.0gal 16.8galUS

2168 HRG
1.5-litre
1948 UK
83.0mph 133.5kmh
0-50mph 80.5kmh: 12.0secs
0-60mph 96.5kmh: 18.1secs
61.0bhp 45.5kW 61.8PS
@ 4800rpm
78.1bhp/ton 76.8bhp/tonne
40.8bhp/L 30.4kW/L 41.3PS/L
54.1ft/sec 16.5m/sec
26.0mpg 21.6mpgUS 10.9L/100km
Petrol 4-stroke piston
1496cc 91.3cu in
In-line 4
Compression ratio: 7.2:1
Bore: 68.0mm 2.7in
Stroke: 103.0mm 4.1in
Valve type/No: Overhead 8
Transmission: Manual
No. of forward speeds: 4
Wheels driven: Rear
Brakes F/R: Drum/Drum
Wheelbase: 261.6cm 103.0in
Track F: 121.9cm 48.0in
Track R: 114.3cm 45.0in
Length: 365.8cm 144.0in
Width: 139.7cm 55.0in
Height: 127.0cm 50.0in
Ground clearance: 17.8cm 7.0in
Kerb weight: 794.5kg 1750.0lb
Fuel: 40.9L 9.0gal 10.8galUS

2169 Hudson
Straight Eight Roadster
1930 USA
69.2mph 111.3kmh
18.0mpg 15.0mpgUS 15.7L/100km
Petrol 4-stroke piston
3504cc 213.8cu in
In-line 8
Bore: 69.8mm 2.7in
Stroke: 114.3mm 4.5in
Transmission: Manual
No. of forward speeds: 3
Wheels driven: Rear
Brakes F/R: Drum/Drum
Wheelbase: 302.3cm 119.0in
Track F: 147.3cm 58.0in
Track R: 147.3cm 58.0in
Length: 472.4cm 186.0in
Width: 175.3cm 69.0in
Height: 174.0cm 68.5in
Kerb weight: 1347.5kg 2968.0lb
Fuel: 61.4L 13.5gal 16.2galUS

2170 Hudson
Terraplane
1934 USA
84.9mph 136.6kmh
0-50mph 80.5kmh: 10.8secs
0-60mph 96.5kmh: 17.0secs
16.0mpg 13.3mpgUS 17.7L/100km
Petrol 4-stroke piston
4168cc 254.3cu in
In-line 8
Bore: 76.0mm 3.0in
Stroke: 114.0mm 4.5in
Transmission: Manual
No. of forward speeds: 3
Wheels driven: Rear
Brakes F/R: Drum/Drum
Kerb weight: 1318.9kg 2905.0lb
Fuel: 59.1L 13.0gal 15.6galUS

2171 Hudson
Eight Saloon
1935 USA
87.3mph 140.5kmh
0-50mph 80.5kmh: 11.2secs
0-60mph 96.5kmh: 17.6secs
18.0mpg 15.0mpgUS 15.7L/100km
Petrol 4-stroke piston
4168cc 254.3cu in
In-line 8
Bore: 76.0mm 3.0in
Stroke: 114.0mm 4.5in
Valve type/No: Side 16
Transmission: Manual
No. of forward speeds: 3
Wheels driven: Rear
Brakes F/R: Drum/Drum
Kerb weight: 1485.0kg 3271.0lb
Fuel: 59.1L 13.0gal 15.6galUS

2172 Hudson
Terraplane Big Six Saloon
1935 USA
80.3mph 129.2kmh
0-50mph 80.5kmh: 15.4secs
0-60mph 96.5kmh: 23.0secs
20.0mpg 16.7mpgUS 14.1L/100km
Petrol 4-stroke piston
3455cc 210.8cu in
In-line 6
Bore: 76.2mm 3.0in
Stroke: 127.0mm 5.0in
Valve type/No: Side 12
Transmission: Manual
No. of forward speeds: 3
Wheels driven: Rear
Brakes F/R: Drum/Drum
Ground clearance: 20.8cm 8.2in
Kerb weight: 1398.3kg 3080.0lb
Fuel: 56.9L 12.5gal 15.0galUS

2173 Hudson
22hp Six Saloon
1936 USA
82.5mph 132.7kmh
0-50mph 80.5kmh: 14.7secs
0-60mph 96.5kmh: 23.0secs
18.0mpg 15.0mpgUS 15.7L/100km
Petrol 4-stroke piston
3455cc 210.8cu in
In-line 6
Bore: 76.2mm 3.0in
Stroke: 127.0mm 5.0in
Valve type/No: Side 12
Transmission: Manual
No. of forward speeds: 3
Wheels driven: Rear
Brakes F/R: Drum/Drum
Kerb weight: 1472.3kg 3243.0lb
Fuel: 61.4L 13.5gal 16.2galUS

2174 Hudson
Terraplane Saloon
1937 USA
75.6mph 121.6kmh
0-50mph 80.5kmh: 17.2secs
0-60mph 96.5kmh: 28.5secs
19.0mpg 15.8mpgUS 14.9L/100km
Petrol 4-stroke piston
2723cc 166.1cu in
In-line 6
Bore: 67.4mm 2.7in
Stroke: 127.0mm 5.0in
Valve type/No: Side 12
Transmission: Manual
No. of forward speeds: 3
Wheels driven: Rear
Brakes F/R: Drum/Drum
Kerb weight: 1433.3kg 3157.0lb
Fuel: 61.4L 13.5gal 16.2galUS

2175 Hudson
22hp Six Special Saloon
1938 USA
81.8mph 131.6kmh
0-50mph 80.5kmh: 13.0secs
0-60mph 96.5kmh: 20.5secs
17.0mpg 14.2mpgUS 16.6L/100km
Petrol 4-stroke piston
3455cc 210.8cu in
In-line 6
Bore: 76.2mm 3.0in
Stroke: 127.0mm 5.0in
Valve type/No: Side 12
Transmission: Manual
No. of forward speeds: 3
Wheels driven: Rear
Brakes F/R: Drum/Drum
Kerb weight: 1528.6kg 3367.0lb
Fuel: 61.4L 13.5gal 16.2galUS

2176 Hudson
Commodore
1949 USA
91.0mph 146.4kmh
0-50mph 80.5kmh: 11.5secs
0-60mph 96.5kmh: 18.4secs
128.0bhp 95.4kW 129.8PS
@ 4200rpm
198.0lbft 268.3Nm @ 1600rpm
74.5bhp/ton 73.2bhp/tonne
30.7bhp/L 22.9kW/L 31.1PS/L
52.5ft/sec 16.0m/sec
18.0mph 29.0kmh/1000rpm
15.0mpg 12.5mpgUS 18.8L/100km
Petrol 4-stroke piston
4168cc 254.0cu in
In-line 8 1 Carburettor
Compression ratio: 6.5:1
Bore: 76.2mm 3.0in
Stroke: 114.3mm 4.5in
Valve type/No: Side 16
Transmission: Manual with overdrive
No. of forward speeds: 6
Wheels driven: Rear
Springs F/R: Coil/Leaf
Brakes F/R: Drum/Drum
Steering: Worm & roller
Wheelbase: 315.0cm 124.0in
Track F: 151.1cm 59.5in
Track R: 142.2cm 56.0in
Length: 527.1cm 207.5in
Width: 190.5cm 75.0in
Height: 152.4cm 60.0in
Ground clearance: 20.3cm 8.0in
Kerb weight: 1747.9kg 3850.0lb
Fuel: 75.1L 16.5gal 19.8galUS

2177 Hudson
Hornet
1952 USA
92.9mph 149.5kmh
0-1/4 mile: 20.7secs
145.0bhp 108.1kW 147.0PS
@ 3800rpm

257.0lbft 348.2Nm @ 1800rpm
28.7bhp/L 21.4kW/L 29.1PS/L
47.5ft/sec 14.5m/sec
Petrol 4-stroke piston
5050cc 308.1cu in
In-line 6
Compression ratio: 7.2:1
Bore: 96.8mm 3.8in
Stroke: 114.3mm 4.5in
Valve type/No: Side 12
Transmission: Automatic
No. of forward speeds: 4
Wheels driven: Rear
Wheelbase: 314.7cm 123.9in
Track F: 148.6cm 58.5in
Track R: 141.0cm 55.5in
Length: 511.8cm 201.5in
Width: 195.8cm 77.1in
Height: 153.4cm 60.4in
Ground clearance: 20.6cm 8.1in

2178 Hudson Super Jet

1953 USA
88.5mph 142.4kmh
0-50mph 80.5kmh: 9.7secs
0-60mph 96.5kmh: 15.1secs
0-1/4 mile: 20.1secs
104.0bhp 77.5kW 105.4PS
@ 4000rpm
158.0lbft 214.1Nm @ 1600rpm
78.2bhp/ton 76.9bhp/tonne
31.4bhp/L 23.4kW/L 31.8PS/L
52.8ft/sec 16.1m/sec
26.3mph 42.3kmh/1000rpm
Petrol 4-stroke piston
3311cc 202.0cu in
In-line 6
Compression ratio: 7.5:1
Bore: 76.2mm 3.0in
Stroke: 120.7mm 4.7in
Valve type/No: Side 12
Transmission: Manual
No. of forward speeds: 3
Wheels driven: Rear
Wheelbase: 266.7cm 105.0in
Track F: 143.5cm 56.5in
Track R: 137.2cm 54.0in
Kerb weight: 1352.9kg 2980.0lb

2179 Hudson

Rambler
1956 USA
84.0mph 135.2kmh
0-50mph 80.5kmh: 13.3secs
0-60mph 96.5kmh: 18.9secs
0-1/4 mile: 21.0secs
90.0bhp 67.1kW 91.2PS
@ 3800rpm
150.0lbft 203.3Nm @ 1600rpm
74.5bhp/ton 73.3bhp/tonne
28.1bhp/L 20.9kW/L 28.5PS/L
44.9ft/sec 13.7m/sec
35.0mph 56.3kmh/1000rpm
23.0mpg 19.2mpgUS 12.3L/100km
Petrol 4-stroke piston
3205cc 195.5cu in
In-line 6
Compression ratio: 7.3:1
Bore: 79.4mm 3.1in
Stroke: 107.9mm 4.2in
Valve type/No: Side 12
Transmission: Manual
No. of forward speeds: 3
Wheels driven: Rear
Springs F/R: Coil/Leaf
Brakes F/R: Drum/Drum
Wheelbase: 274.3cm 108.0in
Track F: 138.9cm 54.7in
Track R: 134.6cm 53.0in
Length: 473.7cm 186.5in
Width: 186.7cm 73.5in
Height: 150.9cm 59.4in
Ground clearance: 20.6cm 8.1in
Kerb weight: 1228.5kg 2706.0lb
Fuel: 75.1L 16.5gal 19.8galUS

2180 Humber

Snipe
1929 UK
75.0mph 120.7kmh
17.0mpg 14.2mpgUS 16.6L/100km
Petrol 4-stroke piston
3948cc 240.9cu in
In-line 6 1 Carburettor
Compression ratio: 5.8:1
Bore: 80.0mm 3.1in
Stroke: 116.0mm 4.6in
Valve type/No: IOE 12
Transmission: Manual
No. of forward speeds: 4
Wheels driven: Rear
Brakes F/R: Drum/Drum
Wheelbase: 304.8cm 120.0in
Track F: 142.2cm 56.0in
Track R: 142.2cm 56.0in
Length: 433.6cm 170.7in
Width: 172.7cm 68.0in
Height: 177.8cm 70.0in
Kerb weight: 1563.6kg 3444.0lb
Fuel: 54.6L 12.0gal 14.4galUS

2181 Humber

16/60 Saloon
1932 UK
64.7mph 104.1kmh
22.0mpg 18.3mpgUS 12.8L/100km
Petrol 4-stroke piston
2276cc 138.9cu in
In-line 6 1 Carburettor
Bore: 67.5mm 2.7in
Stroke: 106.0mm 4.2in
Valve type/No: IOE 12
Transmission: Manual
No. of forward speeds: 4
Wheels driven: Rear
Brakes F/R: Drum/Drum
Wheelbase: 311.2cm 122.5in
Track F: 142.2cm 56.0in
Track R: 142.2cm 56.0in
Length: 439.4cm 173.0in
Width: 172.7cm 68.0in
Height: 182.9cm 72.0in
Kerb weight: 1678.0kg 3696.0lb
Fuel: 63.7L 14.0gal 16.8galUS

2182 Humber

Pullman Limousine
1932 UK
67.1mph 108.0kmh
17.0mpg 14.2mpgUS 16.6L/100km
Petrol 4-stroke piston
3499cc 213.5cu in
In-line 6 1 Carburettor
Compression ratio: 5.8:1
Bore: 80.0mm 3.1in
Stroke: 116.0mm 4.6in
Valve type/No: IOE 12
Transmission: Manual
No. of forward speeds: 4
Wheels driven: Rear
Brakes F/R: Drum/Drum
Wheelbase: 335.3cm 132.0in
Track F: 142.2cm 56.0in
Track R: 142.2cm 56.0in
Length: 490.2cm 193.0in
Width: 185.4cm 73.0in
Height: 193.0cm 76.0in
Kerb weight: 1817.8kg 4004.0lb
Fuel: 72.8L 16.0gal 19.2galUS

2183 Humber

12 Vogue
1934 UK
66.1mph 106.4kmh
0-50mph 80.5kmh: 26.8secs
42.0bhp 31.3kW 42.6PS
@ 3800rpm
36.1bhp/ton 35.5bhp/tonne
25.2bhp/L 18.8kW/L 25.5PS/L
45.7ft/sec 13.9m/sec
28.0mpg 23.3mpgUS 10.1L/100km
Petrol 4-stroke piston
1669cc 101.8cu in
In-line 4 1 Carburettor
Compression ratio: 5.6:1
Bore: 69.5mm 2.7in
Stroke: 110.0mm 4.3in
Valve type/No: Side 8
Transmission: Manual
No. of forward speeds: 4
Wheels driven: Rear
Brakes F/R: Drum/Drum
Kerb weight: 1182.2kg 2604.0lb
Fuel: 45.5L 10.0gal 12.0galUS

2184 Humber

12 Six-light Saloon
1935 UK
68.7mph 110.5kmh
0-50mph 80.5kmh: 24.0secs
0-60mph 96.5kmh: 38.8secs
25.0mpg 20.8mpgUS 11.3L/100km
Petrol 4-stroke piston
1669cc 101.8cu in
In-line 4
Bore: 69.5mm 2.7in
Stroke: 110.0mm 4.3in
Valve type/No: Side 8
Transmission: Manual
No. of forward speeds: 4
Wheels driven: Rear
Brakes F/R: Drum/Drum
Kerb weight: 1289.8kg 2841.0lb
Fuel: 45.5L 10.0gal 12.0galUS

2185 Humber

Snipe Sports Saloon
1935 UK
80.3mph 129.2kmh
0-50mph 80.5kmh: 17.6secs
0-60mph 96.5kmh: 25.8secs
16.0mpg 13.3mpgUS 17.7L/100km
Petrol 4-stroke piston
3498cc 213.4cu in
In-line 6
Bore: 80.0mm 3.1in
Stroke: 116.0mm 4.6in
Valve type/No: Side 12
Transmission: Manual
No. of forward speeds: 4
Wheels driven: Rear
Brakes F/R: Drum/Drum
Kerb weight: 1908.6kg 4204.0lb
Fuel: 63.7L 14.0gal 16.8galUS

2186 Humber

Pullman Limousine
1936 UK
78.2mph 125.8kmh
0-50mph 80.5kmh: 17.7secs
0-60mph 96.5kmh: 27.2secs
15.0mpg 12.5mpgUS 18.8L/100km
Petrol 4-stroke piston
4086cc 249.3cu in
In-line 6
Bore: 85.0mm 3.3in
Stroke: 120.0mm 4.7in
Valve type/No: Side 12
Transmission: Manual
No. of forward speeds: 4
Wheels driven: Rear
Brakes F/R: Drum/Drum
Kerb weight: 2081.6kg 4585.0lb
Fuel: 72.8L 16.0gal 19.2galUS

2187 Humber

Snipe Sports Saloon
1936 UK
86.5mph 139.2kmh
0-50mph 80.5kmh: 16.6secs
0-60mph 96.5kmh: 24.8secs
15.0mpg 12.5mpgUS 18.8L/100km
Petrol 4-stroke piston
4086cc 249.3cu in
In-line 6
Bore: 85.0mm 3.3in
Stroke: 120.0mm 4.7in
Valve type/No: Side 12
Transmission: Manual
No. of forward speeds: 4
Wheels driven: Rear
Brakes F/R: Drum/Drum
Kerb weight: 2008.5kg 4424.0lb
Fuel: 72.8L 16.0gal 19.2galUS

2188 Humber

Snipe Drop-head Foursome
1937 UK
81.8mph 131.6kmh
0-50mph 80.5kmh: 15.1secs
0-60mph 96.5kmh: 23.7secs
100.0bhp 74.6kW 101.4PS
@ 3400rpm
52.3bhp/ton 51.5bhp/tonne
24.5bhp/L 18.2kW/L 24.8PS/L
44.6ft/sec 13.6m/sec
15.0mpg 12.5mpgUS 18.8L/100km
Petrol 4-stroke piston
4086cc 249.3cu in
In-line 6
Bore: 85.0mm 3.3in
Stroke: 120.0mm 4.7in
Valve type/No: Side 12
Transmission: Manual
No. of forward speeds: 4
Wheels driven: Rear
Brakes F/R: Drum/Drum
Kerb weight: 1943.1kg 4280.0lb
Fuel: 72.8L 16.0gal 19.2galUS

2189 Humber

16.9hp Saloon
1938 UK
70.8mph 113.9kmh
0-50mph 80.5kmh: 19.8secs
0-60mph 96.5kmh: 31.2secs
20.0mpg 16.7mpgUS 14.1L/100km
Petrol 4-stroke piston
2576cc 157.2cu in
In-line 6
Bore: 67.5mm 2.7in
Stroke: 120.0mm 4.7in
Valve type/No: Side 12
Transmission: Manual
No. of forward speeds: 4
Wheels driven: Rear
Brakes F/R: Drum/Drum
Kerb weight: 1559.9kg 3436.0lb
Fuel: 59.1L 13.0gal 15.6galUS

2190 Humber

Snipe Sports Saloon
1938 UK
78.9mph 127.0kmh
0-50mph 80.5kmh: 16.4secs
0-60mph 96.5kmh: 24.4secs
75.0bhp 55.9kW 76.0PS
@ 3300rpm
47.9bhp/ton 47.1bhp/tonne
23.6bhp/L 17.6kW/L 23.9PS/L
43.3ft/sec 13.2m/sec
18.0mpg 15.0mpgUS 15.7L/100km
Petrol 4-stroke piston
3181cc 194.1cu in
In-line 6
Bore: 75.0mm 2.9in
Stroke: 120.0mm 4.7in
Valve type/No: Side 12
Transmission: Manual
No. of forward speeds: 4
Wheels driven: Rear
Brakes F/R: Drum/Drum
Kerb weight: 1593.1kg 3509.0lb
Fuel: 59.1L 13.0gal 15.6galUS

2191 Humber

Hawk Saloon
1947 UK
64.0mph 103.0kmh
0-50mph 80.5kmh: 24.9secs
56.0bhp 41.8kW 56.8PS
@ 3800rpm
42.3bhp/ton 41.6bhp/tonne
28.8bhp/L 21.5kW/L 29.2PS/L
45.7ft/sec 13.9m/sec
21.0mpg 17.5mpgUS 13.5L/100km
Petrol 4-stroke piston
1944cc 118.6cu in
In-line 4
Compression ratio: 6.4:1
Bore: 75.0mm 2.9in
Stroke: 110.0mm 4.3in
Valve type/No: Side 8
Transmission: Manual
No. of forward speeds: 4
Wheels driven: Rear
Brakes F/R: Drum/Drum
Wheelbase: 289.6cm 114.0in
Track F: 141.7cm 55.8in
Track R: 142.2cm 56.0in
Length: 457.2cm 180.0in
Width: 175.3cm 69.0in
Height: 165.1cm 65.0in
Ground clearance: 19.1cm 7.5in
Kerb weight: 1347.5kg 2968.0lb
Fuel: 63.7L 14.0gal 16.8galUS

2192 Humber

Hawk
1949 UK
72.0mph 115.8kmh
0-50mph 80.5kmh: 21.2secs
0-60mph 96.5kmh: 34.4secs
56.0bhp 41.8kW 56.8PS
@ 3800rpm
96.7lbft 131.0Nm @ 2000rpm

44.4bhp/ton 43.6bhp/tonne
28.8bhp/L 21.5kW/L 29.2PS/L
45.7ft/sec 13.9m/sec
16.3mph 26.2kmh/1000rpm
24.0mpg 20.0mpgUS 11.8L/100km
Petrol 4-stroke piston
1944cc 118.6cu in
In-line 4 1 Carburettor
Compression ratio: 6.4:1
Bore: 75.0mm 2.9in
Stroke: 110.0mm 4.3in
Valve type/No: Side 8
Transmission: Manual
No. of forward speeds: 4
Wheels driven: Rear
Springs F/R: Coil/Leaf
Brakes F/R: Drum/Drum
Wheelbase: 268.0cm 105.5in
Track F: 142.2cm 56.0in
Track R: 144.8cm 57.0in
Length: 442.0cm 174.0in
Width: 177.8cm 70.0in
Height: 163.1cm 64.2in
Ground clearance: 17.0cm 6.7in
Kerb weight: 1283.9kg 2828.0lb
Fuel: 45.5L 10.0gal 12.0galUS

2193 Humber

Imperial
1949 UK
79.0mph 127.1kmh
0-50mph 80.5kmh: 18.1secs
0-60mph 96.5kmh: 26.5secs
100.0bhp 74.6kW 101.4PS
@ 3400rpm
197.5lbft 267.6Nm @ 1200rpm
48.6bhp/ton 47.8bhp/tonne
24.5bhp/L 18.2kW/L 24.8PS/L
44.6ft/sec 13.6m/sec
20.9mph 33.6kmh/1000rpm
13.0mpg 10.8mpgUS 21.7L/100km
Petrol 4-stroke piston
4086cc 249.3cu in
In-line 6
Compression ratio: 6.2:1
Bore: 85.0mm 3.3in
Stroke: 120.0mm 4.7in
Valve type/No: Side 12
Transmission: Manual
No. of forward speeds: 4
Wheels driven: Rear
Brakes F/R: Drum/Drum
Wheelbase: 332.7cm 131.0in
Track F: 147.1cm 57.9in
Track R: 158.8cm 62.5in
Length: 534.7cm 210.5in
Width: 189.2cm 74.5in
Height: 175.3cm 69.0in
Ground clearance: 19.1cm 7.5in
Kerb weight: 2091.1kg 4606.0lb
Fuel: 68.2L 15.0gal 18.0galUS

2194 Humber

Imperial Saloon
1949 UK
79.0mph 127.1kmh
0-50mph 80.5kmh: 18.1secs
0-60mph 96.5kmh: 26.5secs
100.0bhp 74.6kW 101.4PS
@ 3400rpm
197.5lbft 267.6Nm @ 1200rpm
48.6bhp/ton 47.8bhp/tonne
24.5bhp/L 18.2kW/L 24.8PS/L
44.6ft/sec 13.6m/sec
20.9mph 33.6kmh/1000rpm
14.0mpg 11.7mpgUS 20.2L/100km
Petrol 4-stroke piston
4086cc 249.3cu in
In-line 6
Compression ratio: 6.2:1
Bore: 85.0mm 3.3in
Stroke: 120.0mm 4.7in
Valve type/No: Side 12
Transmission: Manual
No. of forward speeds: 4
Wheels driven: Rear
Brakes F/R: Drum/Drum
Wheelbase: 332.7cm 131.0in
Track F: 147.1cm 57.9in
Track R: 158.0cm 62.2in
Length: 534.7cm 210.5in
Width: 199.4cm 78.5in
Height: 175.3cm 69.0in
Ground clearance: 19.1cm 7.5in
Kerb weight: 2091.1kg 4606.0lb
Fuel: 68.2L 15.0gal 18.0galUS

2195 Humber

Super Snipe
1949 UK
80.5mph 129.5kmh
0-50mph 80.5kmh: 14.5secs
0-60mph 96.5kmh: 22.7secs
100.0bhp 74.6kW 101.4PS
@ 3400rpm
59.0bhp/ton 58.1bhp/tonne
24.5bhp/L 18.2kW/L 24.8PS/L
44.6ft/sec 13.6m/sec
14.0mpg 11.7mpgUS 20.2L/100km
Petrol 4-stroke piston
4086cc 249.3cu in
In-line 6
Compression ratio: 6.2:1
Bore: 85.0mm 3.3in
Stroke: 120.0mm 4.7in
Valve type/No: Side 12
Transmission: Manual
No. of forward speeds: 4
Wheels driven: Rear
Brakes F/R: Drum/Drum
Wheelbase: 298.5cm 117.5in
Track F: 147.1cm 57.9in
Track R: 154.9cm 61.0in
Length: 476.3cm 187.5in
Width: 189.2cm 74.5in
Height: 166.9cm 65.7in
Ground clearance: 17.8cm 7.0in
Kerb weight: 1722.5kg 3794.0lb
Fuel: 68.2L 15.0gal 18.0galUS

2196 Humber

Hawk
1951 UK
72.2mph 116.2kmh
0-50mph 80.5kmh: 18.2secs
0-60mph 96.5kmh: 27.9secs
0-1/4 mile: 26.0secs
58.0bhp 43.2kW 58.8PS
@ 3400rpm
47.1bhp/ton 46.3bhp/tonne
25.6bhp/L 19.1kW/L 25.9PS/L
40.9ft/sec 12.5m/sec
Petrol 4-stroke piston
2267cc 138.3cu in
In-line 4 1 Carburettor
Bore: 81.0mm 3.2in
Stroke: 110.0mm 4.3in
Valve type/No: Side 8
Transmission: Manual
No. of forward speeds: 4
Wheels driven: Rear
Wheelbase: 268.0cm 105.5in
Track F: 142.2cm 56.0in
Track R: 144.8cm 57.0in
Length: 442.0cm 174.0in
Width: 179.8cm 70.8in
Height: 163.8cm 64.5in
Ground clearance: 18.3cm 7.2in
Kerb weight: 1252.1kg 2758.0lb

2197 Humber

Pullman Limousine
1952 UK
82.0mph 131.9kmh
0-50mph 80.5kmh: 17.0secs
0-60mph 96.5kmh: 26.2secs
0-1/4 mile: 23.2secs
100.0bhp 74.6kW 101.4PS
@ 3400rpm
197.5lbft 267.6Nm @ 1200rpm
46.5bhp/ton 45.7bhp/tonne
24.5bhp/L 18.2kW/L 24.8PS/L
44.6ft/sec 13.6m/sec
20.9mph 33.6kmh/1000rpm
16.9mpg 14.1mpgUS 16.7L/100km
Petrol 4-stroke piston
4086cc 249.3cu in
In-line 6
Compression ratio: 6.2:1
Bore: 85.0mm 3.3in
Stroke: 120.0mm 4.7in
Valve type/No: Side 12
Transmission: Manual
No. of forward speeds: 4
Wheels driven: Rear
Springs F/R: Leaf/Leaf
Brakes F/R: Drum/Drum
Wheelbase: 332.7cm 131.0in
Track F: 147.3cm 58.0in
Track R: 158.8cm 62.5in
Length: 538.2cm 211.9in
Width: 189.2cm 74.5in
Height: 175.3cm 69.0in
Ground clearance: 19.1cm 7.5in
Kerb weight: 2186.5kg 4816.0lb
Fuel: 68.2L 15.0gal 18.0galUS

2198 Humber

Super Snipe
1952 UK
84.0mph 135.2kmh
0-50mph 80.5kmh: 14.5secs
0-60mph 96.5kmh: 21.2secs
100.0bhp 74.6kW 101.4PS
@ 3400rpm
197.5lbft 267.6Nm @ 1200rpm
56.2bhp/ton 55.2bhp/tonne
24.5bhp/L 18.2kW/L 24.8PS/L
44.6ft/sec 13.6m/sec
20.0mph 32.2kmh/1000rpm
16.0mpg 13.3mpgUS 17.7L/100km
Petrol 4-stroke piston
4086cc 249.3cu in
In-line 6
Compression ratio: 6.2:1
Bore: 85.0mm 3.3in
Stroke: 120.0mm 4.7in
Valve type/No: Side 12
Transmission: Manual
No. of forward speeds: 4
Wheels driven: Rear
Wheelbase: 298.5cm 117.5in
Track F: 147.1cm 57.9in
Track R: 154.9cm 61.0in
Length: 484.4cm 190.7in
Width: 189.7cm 74.7in
Height: 166.9cm 65.7in
Ground clearance: 17.8cm 7.0in
Kerb weight: 1810.1kg 3987.0lb
Fuel: 68.2L 15.0gal 18.0galUS

2199 Humber

Super Snipe
1953 UK
87.8mph 141.3kmh
0-50mph 80.5kmh: 11.5secs
0-60mph 96.5kmh: 17.5secs
0-1/4 mile: 20.8secs
113.0bhp 84.3kW 114.6PS
@ 3400rpm
207.0lbft 280.5Nm @ 1400rpm
62.9bhp/ton 61.8bhp/tonne
27.3bhp/L 20.4kW/L 27.7PS/L
41.3ft/sec 12.6m/sec
21.5mph 34.6kmh/1000rpm
Petrol 4-stroke piston
4139cc 252.5cu in
In-line 6
Compression ratio: 6.5:1
Bore: 89.0mm 3.5in
Stroke: 111.0mm 4.4in
Valve type/No: Overhead 12
Transmission: Manual
No. of forward speeds: 4
Wheels driven: Rear
Wheelbase: 294.1cm 115.8in
Track F: 147.1cm 57.9in
Track R: 142.7cm 56.2in
Kerb weight: 1827.3kg 4025.0lb

2200 Humber

Super Snipe Mk IV
1953 UK
91.0mph 146.4kmh
0-50mph 80.5kmh: 11.5secs
0-60mph 96.5kmh: 16.0secs
0-1/4 mile: 20.5secs
116.0bhp 86.5kW 117.6PS
@ 3600rpm
211.0lbft 285.9Nm @ 1400rpm
65.3bhp/ton 64.3bhp/tonne
28.0bhp/L 20.9kW/L 28.4PS/L
43.7ft/sec 13.3m/sec
22.5mph 36.2kmh/1000rpm
16.0mpg 13.3mpgUS 17.7L/100km
Petrol 4-stroke piston
4138cc 252.5cu in
In-line 6
Compression ratio: 7.1:1
Bore: 88.9mm 3.5in
Stroke: 111.1mm 4.4in
Valve type/No: Overhead 12
Transmission: Manual
No. of forward speeds: 4
Wheels driven: Rear
Springs F/R: Coil/Leaf
Brakes F/R: Drum/Drum
Wheelbase: 293.9cm 115.7in
Track F: 147.1cm 57.9in
Track R: 142.7cm 56.2in
Length: 500.4cm 197.0in
Width: 186.7cm 73.5in
Height: 167.6cm 66.0in
Ground clearance: 18.8cm 7.4in
Kerb weight: 1805.1kg 3976.0lb
Fuel: 68.2L 15.0gal 18.0galUS

2201 Humber

Hawk Mk VI
1954 UK
84.0mph 135.2kmh
0-50mph 80.5kmh: 15.9secs
0-60mph 96.5kmh: 23.8secs
0-1/4 mile: 22.5secs
70.0bhp 52.2kW 71.0PS
@ 4000rpm
119.3lbft 161.7Nm @ 2200rpm
49.7bhp/ton 48.8bhp/tonne
30.9bhp/L 23.0kW/L 31.3PS/L
48.1ft/sec 14.7m/sec
21.8mph 35.1kmh/1000rpm
26.6mpg 22.1mpgUS 10.6L/100km
Petrol 4-stroke piston
2267cc 138.3cu in
In-line 4
Compression ratio: 7.0:1
Bore: 81.0mm 3.2in
Stroke: 110.0mm 4.3in
Valve type/No: Overhead 8
Transmission: Manual with overdrive
No. of forward speeds: 5
Wheels driven: Rear
Springs F/R: Coil/Leaf
Brakes F/R: Drum/Drum
Wheelbase: 268.0cm 105.5in
Track F: 142.2cm 56.0in
Track R: 144.8cm 57.0in
Length: 458.5cm 180.5in
Width: 182.9cm 72.0in
Height: 165.1cm 65.0in
Ground clearance: 18.0cm 7.1in
Kerb weight: 1433.3kg 3157.0lb
Fuel: 45.5L 10.0gal 12.0galUS

2202 Humber

Hawk Estate
1956 UK
81.7mph 131.5kmh
0-50mph 80.5kmh: 17.4secs
0-60mph 96.5kmh: 26.7secs
0-1/4 mile: 23.3secs
75.0bhp 55.9kW 76.0PS
@ 4000rpm
119.3lbft 161.7Nm @ 2200rpm
47.4bhp/ton 46.6bhp/tonne
33.1bhp/L 24.7kW/L 33.5PS/L
48.1ft/sec 14.7m/sec
22.0mph 35.4kmh/1000rpm
25.7mpg 21.4mpgUS 11.0L/100km
Petrol 4-stroke piston
2267cc 138.3cu in
In-line 4
Compression ratio: 7.0:1
Bore: 81.0mm 3.2in
Stroke: 110.0mm 4.3in
Valve type/No: Overhead 8
Transmission: Manual with overdrive
No. of forward speeds: 5
Wheels driven: Rear
Springs F/R: Coil/Leaf
Brakes F/R: Drum/Drum
Wheelbase: 268.0cm 105.5in
Track F: 142.2cm 56.0in
Track R: 144.8cm 57.0in
Length: 463.6cm 182.5in
Width: 157.5cm 62.0in
Height: 165.6cm 65.2in
Ground clearance: 19.1cm 7.5in
Kerb weight: 1608.1kg 3542.0lb
Fuel: 45.5L 10.0gal 12.0galUS

2203 Humber

Hawk
1957 UK
84.0mph 135.2kmh
0-50mph 80.5kmh: 16.2secs
0-60mph 96.5kmh: 23.4secs
0-1/4 mile: 23.3secs
78.0bhp 58.2kW 79.1PS
@ 4400rpm
120.0lbft 162.6Nm @ 2300rpm
54.5bhp/ton 53.6bhp/tonne
34.4bhp/L 25.7kW/L 34.9PS/L
52.9ft/sec 16.1m/sec
18.3mph 29.4kmh/1000rpm
21.0mpg 17.5mpgUS 13.5L/100km

Petrol 4-stroke piston
2267cc 138.3cu in
In-line 4
Compression ratio: 7.5:1
Bore: 81.0mm 3.2in
Stroke: 110.0mm 4.3in
Valve type/No: Overhead 8
Transmission: Automatic
No. of forward speeds: 3
Wheels driven: Rear
Springs F/R: Coil/Leaf
Brakes F/R: Drum/Drum
Wheelbase: 279.4cm 110.0in
Track F: 142.2cm 56.0in
Track R: 141.0cm 55.5in
Length: 468.6cm 184.5in
Width: 176.5cm 69.5in
Height: 154.9cm 61.0in
Ground clearance: 15.2cm 6.0in
Kerb weight: 1455.5kg 3206.0lb
Fuel: 52.3L 11.5gal 13.8galUS

2204 Humber

Hawk Estate
1958 UK
81.0mph 130.3kmh
0-50mph 80.5kmh: 16.3secs
0-60mph 96.5kmh: 25.7secs
0-1/4 mile: 23.1secs
78.0bhp 58.2kW 79.1PS
@ 4400rpm
120.0lbft 162.6Nm @ 2300rpm
52.8bhp/ton 51.9bhp/tonne
34.4bhp/L 25.7kW/L 34.9PS/L
52.9ft/sec 16.1m/sec
21.8mph 35.1kmh/1000rpm
20.1mpg 16.7mpgUS 14.1L/100km
Petrol 4-stroke piston
2267cc 138.3cu in
In-line 4
Compression ratio: 7.5:1
Bore: 81.0mm 3.2in
Stroke: 110.0mm 4.3in
Valve type/No: Overhead 8
Transmission: Manual with overdrive
No. of forward speeds: 5
Wheels driven: Rear
Springs F/R: Coil/Leaf
Brakes F/R: Drum/Drum
Wheelbase: 279.4cm 110.0in
Track F: 142.2cm 56.0in
Track R: 141.0cm 55.5in
Length: 468.6cm 184.5in
Width: 176.5cm 69.5in
Height: 157.5cm 62.0in
Ground clearance: 17.8cm 7.0in
Kerb weight: 1503.2kg 3311.0lb
Fuel: 56.9L 12.5gal 15.0galUS

2205 Humber

Super Snipe
1958 UK
94.5mph 152.1kmh
0-50mph 80.5kmh: 13.1secs
0-60mph 96.5kmh: 19.0secs
0-1/4 mile: 21.0secs
105.0bhp 78.3kW 106.5PS
@ 5000rpm
138.3lbft 187.4Nm @ 1600rpm
68.4bhp/ton 67.3bhp/tonne
39.6bhp/L 29.5kW/L 40.2PS/L
45.1ft/sec 13.8m/sec
22.4mph 36.0kmh/1000rpm
18.2mpg 15.2mpgUS 15.5L/100km
Petrol 4-stroke piston
2651cc 161.7cu in
In-line 6
Compression ratio: 7.5:1
Bore: 82.5mm 3.2in
Stroke: 82.5mm 3.2in
Valve type/No: Overhead 12
Transmission: Manual with overdrive
No. of forward speeds: 5
Wheels driven: Rear
Springs F/R: Coil/Leaf
Brake system: PA
Brakes F/R: Drum/Drum
Steering: Recirculating ball
Wheelbase: 279.4cm 110.0in
Track F: 143.5cm 56.5in
Track R: 141.0cm 55.5in
Length: 469.1cm 184.7in
Width: 177.0cm 69.7in
Height: 154.9cm 61.0in
Ground clearance: 17.8cm 7.0in
Kerb weight: 1560.8kg 3438.0lb
Fuel: 56.9L 12.5gal 15.0galUS

2206 Humber

Super Snipe
1959 UK
90.0mph 144.8kmh
0-50mph 80.5kmh: 13.2secs
0-60mph 96.5kmh: 18.0secs
0-1/4 mile: 21.5secs
112.0bhp 83.5kW 113.5PS
@ 5000rpm
138.0lbft 187.0Nm @ 2100rpm
71.5bhp/ton 70.3bhp/tonne
42.2bhp/L 31.5kW/L 42.8PS/L
45.1ft/sec 13.8m/sec
17.6mph 28.3kmh/1000rpm
Petrol 4-stroke piston
2651cc 161.7cu in
In-line 6
Compression ratio: 7.5:1
Bore: 82.6mm 3.2in
Stroke: 82.6mm 3.2in
Valve type/No: Overhead 12
Transmission: Automatic
No. of forward speeds: 3
Wheels driven: Rear
Wheelbase: 279.4cm 110.0in
Track F: 143.5cm 56.5in
Track R: 141.0cm 55.5in
Length: 469.9cm 185.0in
Width: 177.3cm 69.8in
Height: 154.9cm 61.0in
Kerb weight: 1593.5kg 3510.0lb

2207 Humber

Super Snipe Estate
1960 UK
96.0mph 154.5kmh
0-50mph 80.5kmh: 13.7secs
0-60mph 96.5kmh: 18.7secs
0-1/4 mile: 21.9secs
129.0bhp 96.2kW 130.8PS
@ 4800rpm
161.6lbft 219.0Nm @ 1800rpm
77.9bhp/ton 76.6bhp/tonne
43.5bhp/L 32.4kW/L 44.1PS/L
43.3ft/sec 13.2m/sec
18.6mph 29.9kmh/1000rpm
16.9mpg 14.1mpgUS 16.7L/100km
Petrol 4-stroke piston
2965cc 180.9cu in
In-line 6
Compression ratio: 8.0:1
Bore: 87.3mm 3.4in
Stroke: 82.5mm 3.2in
Valve type/No: Overhead 12
Transmission: Automatic
No. of forward speeds: 3
Wheels driven: Rear
Springs F/R: Coil/Leaf
Brake system: PA
Brakes F/R: Disc/Drum
Steering: Recirculating ball
Wheelbase: 279.4cm 110.0in
Track F: 144.5cm 56.9in
Track R: 141.2cm 55.6in
Length: 469.1cm 184.7in
Width: 176.5cm 69.5in
Height: 157.5cm 62.0in
Ground clearance: 17.8cm 7.0in
Kerb weight: 1684.3kg 3710.0lb
Fuel: 56.9L 12.5gal 15.0galUS

2208 Humber

3-litre
1961 UK
100.0mph 160.9kmh
0-50mph 80.5kmh: 14.4secs
0-60mph 96.5kmh: 20.5secs
0-1/4 mile: 22.2secs
129.0bhp 96.2kW 130.8PS
@ 4800rpm
162.0lbft 219.5Nm @ 1800rpm
80.0bhp/ton 78.7bhp/tonne
43.5bhp/L 32.4kW/L 44.1PS/L
43.3ft/sec 13.2m/sec
18.5mph 29.8kmh/1000rpm
Petrol 4-stroke piston
2965cc 180.9cu in
In-line 6 1 Carburettor
Compression ratio: 8.0:1
Bore: 87.4mm 3.4in
Stroke: 82.6mm 3.2in
Valve type/No: Overhead 12
Transmission: Automatic
No. of forward speeds: 3
Wheels driven: Rear
Wheelbase: 279.4cm 110.0in
Track F: 143.5cm 56.5in
Track R: 141.0cm 55.5in
Length: 477.5cm 188.0in
Width: 179.1cm 70.5in
Height: 154.9cm 61.0in
Ground clearance: 17.8cm 7.0in
Kerb weight: 1638.9kg 3610.0lb

2209 Humber

Super Snipe Series III
1961 UK
101.5mph 163.3kmh
0-50mph 80.5kmh: 10.1secs
0-60mph 96.5kmh: 14.3secs
0-1/4 mile: 19.5secs
129.0bhp 96.2kW 130.8PS
@ 4800rpm
161.6lbft 219.0Nm @ 1800rpm
86.0bhp/ton 84.6bhp/tonne
43.5bhp/L 32.4kW/L 44.1PS/L
43.3ft/sec 13.2m/sec
22.4mph 36.0kmh/1000rpm
17.7mpg 14.7mpgUS 16.0L/100km
Petrol 4-stroke piston
2965cc 180.9cu in
In-line 6
Compression ratio: 8.0:1
Bore: 87.3mm 3.4in
Stroke: 82.5mm 3.2in
Valve type/No: Overhead 12
Transmission: Manual with overdrive
No. of forward speeds: 5
Wheels driven: Rear
Springs F/R: Coil/Leaf
Brake system: PA
Brakes F/R: Disc/Drum
Steering: Recirculating ball
Wheelbase: 279.4cm 110.0in
Track F: 144.5cm 56.9in
Track R: 141.0cm 55.5in
Length: 477.5cm 188.0in
Width: 176.5cm 69.5in
Height: 154.9cm 61.0in
Ground clearance: 17.8cm 7.0in
Kerb weight: 1525.4kg 3360.0lb
Fuel: 56.9L 12.5gal 15.0galUS

2210 Humber

Hawk III
1963 UK
86.0mph 138.4kmh
0-50mph 80.5kmh: 14.4secs
0-60mph 96.5kmh: 21.3secs
0-1/4 mile: 21.9secs
73.0bhp 54.4kW 74.0PS
@ 4400rpm
120.3lbft 163.0Nm @ 2300rpm
51.7bhp/ton 50.8bhp/tonne
32.2bhp/L 24.0kW/L 32.6PS/L
52.9ft/sec 16.1m/sec
23.3mph 37.5kmh/1000rpm
19.1mpg 15.9mpgUS 14.8L/100km
Petrol 4-stroke piston
2267cc 138.3cu in
In-line 4 1 Carburettor
Compression ratio: 7.5:1
Bore: 81.0mm 3.2in
Stroke: 110.0mm 4.3in
Valve type/No: Overhead 8
Transmission: Manual with overdrive
No. of forward speeds: 6
Wheels driven: Rear
Springs F/R: Coil/Leaf
Brake system: PA
Brakes F/R: Disc/Drum
Steering: Recirculating ball
Wheelbase: 279.4cm 110.0in
Track F: 142.2cm 56.0in
Track R: 141.0cm 55.5in
Length: 464.8cm 183.0in
Width: 172.7cm 68.0in
Height: 157.5cm 62.0in
Ground clearance: 15.2cm 6.0in
Kerb weight: 1436.5kg 3164.0lb
Fuel: 72.8L 16.0gal 19.2galUS

2211 Humber

Sceptre
1963 UK
90.0mph 144.8kmh
0-50mph 80.5kmh: 11.6secs
0-60mph 96.5kmh: 17.1secs
0-1/4 mile: 20.3secs
80.0bhp 59.7kW 81.1PS
@ 5200rpm
91.0lbft 123.3Nm @ 3500rpm
73.3bhp/ton 72.0bhp/tonne
50.2bhp/L 37.5kW/L 50.9PS/L
43.3ft/sec 13.2m/sec
20.2mph 32.5kmh/1000rpm
22.8mpg 19.0mpgUS 12.4L/100km
Petrol 4-stroke piston
1592cc 97.1cu in
In-line 4 2 Carburettor
Compression ratio: 9.0:1
Bore: 81.5mm 3.2in
Stroke: 76.2mm 3.0in
Valve type/No: Overhead 8
Transmission: Manual with overdrive
No. of forward speeds: 6
Wheels driven: Rear
Springs F/R: Coil/Leaf
Brake system: PA
Brakes F/R: Disc/Drum
Steering: Recirculating ball
Wheelbase: 256.5cm 101.0in
Track F: 130.8cm 51.5in
Track R: 123.2cm 48.5in
Length: 420.4cm 165.5in
Width: 158.0cm 62.2in
Height: 144.8cm 57.0in
Ground clearance: 16.5cm 6.5in
Kerb weight: 1110.5kg 2446.0lb
Fuel: 47.8L 10.5gal 12.6galUS

2212 Humber

Imperial
1965 UK
102.0mph 164.1kmh
0-50mph 80.5kmh: 11.6secs
0-60mph 96.5kmh: 16.2secs
0-1/4 mile: 20.7secs
128.5bhp 95.8kW 130.3PS
@ 5000rpm
167.0lbft 226.3Nm @ 2600rpm
78.8bhp/ton 77.5bhp/tonne
43.3bhp/L 32.3kW/L 43.9PS/L
45.1ft/sec 13.8m/sec
18.8mph 30.2kmh/1000rpm
17.5mpg 14.6mpgUS 16.1L/100km
Petrol 4-stroke piston
2965cc 180.9cu in
In-line 6 2 Carburettor
Compression ratio: 8.0:1
Bore: 87.3mm 3.4in
Stroke: 82.5mm 3.2in
Valve type/No: Overhead 12
Transmission: Automatic
No. of forward speeds: 3
Wheels driven: Rear
Springs F/R: Coil/Leaf
Brake system: PA
Brakes F/R: Disc/Drum
Steering: Recirculating ball PA
Wheelbase: 279.4cm 110.0in
Track F: 144.8cm 57.0in
Track R: 141.0cm 55.5in
Length: 477.5cm 188.0in
Width: 176.5cm 69.5in
Height: 154.9cm 61.0in
Ground clearance: 17.8cm 7.0in
Kerb weight: 1657.5kg 3651.0lb
Fuel: 72.8L 16.0gal 19.2galUS

2213 Humber

Sceptre II Automatic
1966 UK
91.0mph 146.4kmh
0-50mph 80.5kmh: 11.8secs
0-60mph 96.5kmh: 16.9secs
0-1/4 mile: 21.3secs
0-1km: 39.3secs
85.0bhp 63.4kW 86.2PS
@ 5500rpm
99.0lbft 134.1Nm @ 3500rpm
79.8bhp/ton 78.4bhp/tonne
49.3bhp/L 36.7kW/L 50.0PS/L
49.6ft/sec 15.1m/sec
17.8mph 28.6kmh/1000rpm
20.9mpg 17.4mpgUS 13.5L/100km
Petrol 4-stroke piston
1725cc 105.2cu in
In-line 4 1 Carburettor
Compression ratio: 9.2:1
Bore: 81.5mm 3.2in
Stroke: 82.5mm 3.2in
Valve type/No: Overhead 8
Transmission: Automatic
No. of forward speeds: 3
Wheels driven: Rear
Springs F/R: Coil/Leaf
Brake system: PA
Brakes F/R: Disc/Drum
Steering: Recirculating ball

Wheelbase: 256.5cm 101.0in
Track F: 130.8cm 51.5in
Track R: 123.2cm 48.5in
Length: 420.4cm 165.5in
Width: 158.0cm 62.2in
Height: 144.8cm 57.0in
Ground clearance: 16.5cm 6.5in
Kerb weight: 1083.7kg 2387.0lb
Fuel: 47.8L 10.5gal 12.6galUS

2214 Humber

Sceptre
1967 UK
102.0mph 164.1kmh
0-50mph 80.5kmh: 9.4secs
0-60mph 96.5kmh: 13.1secs
0-1/4 mile: 19.3secs
0-1km: 36.2secs
88.0bhp 65.6kW 89.2PS
@ 5200rpm
100.0lbft 135.5Nm @ 4000rpm
91.6bhp/ton 90.0bhp/tonne
51.0bhp/L 38.0kW/L 51.7PS/L
46.9ft/sec 14.3m/sec
17.8mph 28.6kmh/1000rpm
25.0mpg 20.8mpgUS 11.3L/100km
Petrol 4-stroke piston
1725cc 105.2cu in
In-line 4 2 Carburettor
Compression ratio: 9.2:1
Bore: 81.5mm 3.2in
Stroke: 82.5mm 3.2in
Valve type/No: Overhead 8
Transmission: Manual with overdrive
No. of forward speeds: 6
Wheels driven: Rear
Springs F/R: Coil/Leaf
Brake system: PA
Brakes F/R: Disc/Drum
Steering: Recirculating ball
Wheelbase: 250.2cm 98.5in
Track F: 132.1cm 52.0in
Track R: 132.1cm 52.0in
Length: 435.6cm 171.5in
Width: 161.3cm 63.5in
Height: 142.2cm 56.0in
Ground clearance: 15.2cm 6.0in
Kerb weight: 977.5kg 2153.0lb
Fuel: 45.5L 10.0gal 12.0galUS

2215 Humber

Sceptre Estate
1974 UK
97.0mph 156.1kmh
0-50mph 80.5kmh: 9.2secs
0-60mph 96.5kmh: 13.5secs
0-1/4 mile: 19.2secs
0-1km: 36.4secs
82.0bhp 61.1kW 83.1PS
@ 5200rpm
93.0lbft 126.0Nm @ 3300rpm
80.7bhp/ton 79.3bhp/tonne
47.5bhp/L 35.4kW/L 48.2PS/L
46.9ft/sec 14.3m/sec
21.6mph 34.8kmh/1000rpm
24.5mpg 20.4mpgUS 11.5L/100km
Petrol 4-stroke piston
1725cc 105.2cu in
In-line 4 2 Carburettor
Compression ratio: 9.2:1
Bore: 81.5mm 3.2in
Stroke: 82.5mm 3.2in
Valve type/No: Overhead 8
Transmission: Manual with overdrive
No. of forward speeds: 6
Wheels driven: Rear
Springs F/R: Coil/Leaf
Brake system: PA
Brakes F/R: Disc/Drum
Steering: Recirculating ball
Wheelbase: 250.2cm 98.5in
Track F: 132.1cm 52.0in
Track R: 132.1cm 52.0in
Length: 435.6cm 171.5in
Width: 161.3cm 63.5in
Height: 144.8cm 57.0in
Ground clearance: 17.0cm 6.7in
Kerb weight: 1033.8kg 2277.0lb
Fuel: 45.5L 10.0gal 12.0galUS

2216 Hupmobile

Straight Eight Limousine
1930 USA
70.8mph 113.9kmh
15.0mpg 12.5mpgUS 18.8L/100km
Petrol 4-stroke piston
4401cc 268.5cu in
In-line 8
Bore: 76.2mm 3.0in
Stroke: 120.7mm 4.7in
Transmission: Manual
No. of forward speeds: 3
Wheels driven: Rear
Brakes F/R: Drum/Drum
Wheelbase: 330.2cm 130.0in
Track F: 147.3cm 58.0in
Track R: 147.3cm 58.0in
Length: 502.9cm 198.0in
Width: 175.3cm 69.0in
Height: 182.9cm 72.0in
Kerb weight: 1932.2kg 4256.0lb
Fuel: 54.6L 12.0gal 14.4galUS

2217 Hupmobile

29.4hp Saloon
1935 USA
78.2mph 125.8kmh
0-50mph 80.5kmh: 11.6secs
0-60mph 96.5kmh: 16.6secs
16.0mpg 13.3mpgUS 17.7L/100km
Petrol 4-stroke piston
4032cc 246.0cu in
In-line 6
Bore: 89.0mm 3.5in
Stroke: 108.0mm 4.2in
Valve type/No: Side 12
Transmission: Manual
No. of forward speeds: 3
Wheels driven: Rear
Brakes F/R: Drum/Drum
Ground clearance: 20.3cm 8.0in
Kerb weight: 1407.4kg 3100.0lb
Fuel: 54.6L 12.0gal 14.4galUS

2218 Hupmobile

32.5hp Saloon
1935 USA
78.2mph 125.8kmh
0-50mph 80.5kmh: 15.6secs
0-60mph 96.5kmh: 20.0secs
14.0mpg 11.7mpgUS 20.2L/100km
Petrol 4-stroke piston
4976cc 303.6cu in
In-line 8
Bore: 81.0mm 3.2in
Stroke: 120.7mm 4.7in
Valve type/No: Side 16
Transmission: Manual
No. of forward speeds: 3
Wheels driven: Rear
Brakes F/R: Drum/Drum
Ground clearance: 20.3cm 8.0in
Kerb weight: 1890.9kg 4165.0lb
Fuel: 72.8L 16.0gal 19.2galUS

2219 Hyundai

Pony 1400 TLS
1982 Korea
91.0mph 146.4kmh
0-50mph 80.5kmh: 10.6secs
0-60mph 96.5kmh: 14.8secs
0-1/4 mile: 19.6secs
0-1km: 37.2secs
67.0bhp 50.0kW 67.9PS
@ 6300rpm
40.4lbft 54.7Nm @ 4000rpm
70.4bhp/ton 69.2bhp/tonne
46.6bhp/L 34.7kW/L 47.2PS/L
59.3ft/sec 18.1m/sec
17.0mph 27.4kmh/1000rpm
29.5mpg 24.6mpgUS 9.6L/100km
Petrol 4-stroke piston
1439cc 87.8cu in
In-line 4 1 Carburettor
Compression ratio: 9.0:1
Bore: 73.0mm 2.9in
Stroke: 86.0mm 3.4in
Valve type/No: Overhead 8
Transmission: Manual
No. of forward speeds: 4
Wheels driven: Rear
Springs F/R: Coil/Leaf
Brake system: PA
Brakes F/R: Disc/Drum
Steering: Recirculating ball
Wheelbase: 233.9cm 92.1in
Track F: 127.8cm 50.3in
Track R: 124.7cm 49.1in
Length: 397.0cm 156.3in
Width: 155.7cm 61.3in
Height: 135.9cm 53.5in
Ground clearance: 16.5cm 6.5in
Kerb weight: 968.4kg 2133.0lb
Fuel: 45.0L 9.9gal 11.9galUS

2220 Hyundai

Stellar 1600 GSL
1984 Korea
100.0mph 160.9kmh
0-50mph 80.5kmh: 10.0secs
0-60mph 96.5kmh: 14.7secs
0-1/4 mile: 19.6secs
0-1km: 36.8secs
73.0bhp 54.4kW 74.0PS
@ 5200rpm
101.0lbft 136.9Nm @ 4000rpm
71.9bhp/ton 70.7bhp/tonne
45.7bhp/L 34.1kW/L 46.3PS/L
49.0ft/sec 14.9m/sec
20.1mph 32.3kmh/1000rpm
30.2mpg 25.1mpgUS 9.4L/100km
Petrol 4-stroke piston
1597cc 97.4cu in
In-line 4 1 Carburettor
Compression ratio: 8.5:1
Bore: 76.9mm 3.0in
Stroke: 86.0mm 3.4in
Valve type/No: Overhead 8
Transmission: Manual
No. of forward speeds: 5
Wheels driven: Rear
Springs F/R: Coil/Coil
Brake system: PA
Brakes F/R: Disc/Drum
Steering: Rack & pinion
Wheelbase: 257.8cm 101.5in
Track F: 144.5cm 56.9in
Track R: 142.5cm 56.1in
Length: 441.7cm 173.9in
Width: 171.7cm 67.6in
Height: 137.2cm 54.0in
Ground clearance: 17.8cm 7.0in
Kerb weight: 1032.4kg 2274.0lb
Fuel: 54.1L 11.9gal 14.3galUS

2221 Hyundai

Pony 1.5 GLS
1985 Korea
98.0mph 157.7kmh
0-50mph 80.5kmh: 9.8secs
0-60mph 96.5kmh: 14.4secs
0-1/4 mile: 19.3secs
0-1km: 36.0secs
71.0bhp 52.9kW 72.0PS
@ 5500rpm
82.0lbft 111.1Nm @ 3500rpm
77.3bhp/ton 76.0bhp/tonne
48.4bhp/L 36.1kW/L 49.0PS/L
49.3ft/sec 15.0m/sec
24.3mph 39.1kmh/1000rpm
29.8mpg 24.8mpgUS 9.5L/100km
Petrol 4-stroke piston
1468cc 89.6cu in
In-line 4 1 Carburettor
Compression ratio: 9.5:1
Bore: 75.5mm 3.0in
Stroke: 82.0mm 3.2in
Valve type/No: Overhead 8
Transmission: Manual
No. of forward speeds: 5
Wheels driven: Front
Springs F/R: Coil/Coil
Brake system: PA
Brakes F/R: Disc/Drum
Steering: Rack & pinion
Wheelbase: 238.0cm 93.7in
Track F: 137.4cm 54.1in
Track R: 133.9cm 52.7in
Length: 398.5cm 156.9in
Width: 159.5cm 62.8in
Height: 137.9cm 54.3in
Ground clearance: 20.3cm 8.0in
Kerb weight: 934.3kg 2058.0lb
Fuel: 40.0L 8.8gal 10.6galUS

2222 Hyundai

Excel GL
1986 Korea
0-60mph 96.5kmh: 14.0secs
0-1/4 mile: 19.4secs
68.0bhp 50.7kW 68.9PS
@ 5500rpm
82.0lbft 111.1Nm @ 3500rpm
70.4bhp/ton 69.2bhp/tonne
46.3bhp/L 34.5kW/L 47.0PS/L
49.3ft/sec 15.0m/sec
21.8mph 35.1kmh/1000rpm
35.9mpg 29.9mpgUS 7.9L/100km
Petrol 4-stroke piston
1468cc 89.6cu in
In-line 4 1 Carburettor
Compression ratio: 9.5:1
Bore: 75.5mm 3.0in
Stroke: 82.0mm 3.2in
Valve type/No: Overhead 8
Transmission: Manual
No. of forward speeds: 5
Wheels driven: Front
Springs F/R: Coil/Coil
Brake system: PA
Brakes F/R: Disc/Drum
Steering: Rack & pinion
Wheelbase: 238.0cm 93.7in
Track F: 137.4cm 54.1in
Track R: 134.1cm 52.8in
Length: 408.7cm 160.9in
Width: 160.3cm 63.1in
Height: 137.4cm 54.1in
Kerb weight: 982.9kg 2165.0lb
Fuel: 40.1L 8.8gal 10.6galUS

2223 Hyundai

Excel GLS
1986 Korea
92.0mph 148.0kmh
0-60mph 96.5kmh: 12.9secs
0-1/4 mile: 19.0secs
68.0bhp 50.7kW 68.9PS
@ 5500rpm
82.0lbft 111.1Nm @ 3500rpm
68.3bhp/ton 67.2bhp/tonne
46.3bhp/L 34.5kW/L 47.0PS/L
49.3ft/sec 15.0m/sec
37.8mpg 31.5mpgUS 7.5L/100km
Petrol 4-stroke piston
1468cc 89.6cu in
In-line 4 1 Carburettor
Compression ratio: 9.5:1
Bore: 75.5mm 3.0in
Stroke: 82.0mm 3.2in
Valve type/No: Overhead 8
Transmission: Manual
No. of forward speeds: 5
Wheels driven: Front
Springs F/R: Coil/Coil
Brake system: PA
Brakes F/R: Disc/Drum
Steering: Rack & pinion
Wheelbase: 238.0cm 93.7in
Track F: 137.4cm 54.1in
Track R: 134.1cm 52.8in
Length: 408.7cm 160.9in
Width: 160.3cm 63.1in
Height: 137.4cm 54.1in
Kerb weight: 1012.4kg 2230.0lb
Fuel: 40.1L 8.8gal 10.6galUS

2224 Hyundai

Sonata 2.0i GLS
1989 Korea
108.0mph 173.8kmh
0-50mph 80.5kmh: 8.5secs
0-60mph 96.5kmh: 11.7secs
0-1/4 mile: 18.9secs
0-1km: 34.5secs
100.0bhp 74.6kW 101.4PS
@ 5000rpm
121.0lbft 164.0Nm @ 3500rpm
83.2bhp/ton 81.8bhp/tonne
50.1bhp/L 37.3kW/L 50.8PS/L
48.1ft/sec 14.7m/sec
22.3mph 35.9kmh/1000rpm
23.0mpg 19.2mpgUS 12.3L/100km
Petrol 4-stroke piston
1997cc 122.0cu in
In-line 4 fuel injection
Compression ratio: 8.6:1
Bore: 85.0mm 3.3in
Stroke: 88.0mm 3.5in
Valve type/No: Overhead 8
Transmission: Manual
No. of forward speeds: 5
Wheels driven: Front
Springs F/R: Coil/Coil
Brake system: PA
Brakes F/R: Disc/Drum
Steering: Rack & pinion PA
Wheelbase: 265.0cm 104.3in
Track F: 145.5cm 57.3in
Track R: 144.0cm 56.7in
Length: 468.0cm 184.3in
Width: 175.1cm 68.9in
Height: 141.1cm 55.6in
Ground clearance: 16.0cm 6.3in
Kerb weight: 1222.0kg 2691.6lb
Fuel: 60.1L 13.2gal 15.9galUS

2225 Hyundai
Sonata 2.4i GLS
1990 Korea
115.0mph 185.0kmh
0-50mph 80.5kmh: 9.1secs
0-60mph 96.5kmh: 12.3secs
0-1/4 mile: 19.0secs
0-1km: 34.5secs
115.0bhp 85.8kW 116.6PS
@ 4500rpm
141.7lbft 192.0Nm @ 3500rpm
90.0bhp/ton 88.5bhp/tonne
48.9bhp/L 36.5kW/L 49.6PS/L
49.2ft/sec 15.0m/sec
26.1mph 42.0kmh/1000rpm
22.7mpg 18.9mpgUS 12.4L/100km
Petrol 4-stroke piston
2351cc 143.0cu in
In-line 4 fuel injection
Compression ratio: 8.6:1
Bore: 86.5mm 3.4in
Stroke: 100.0mm 3.9in
Valve type/No: Overhead 8
Transmission: Automatic
No. of forward speeds: 4
Wheels driven: Front
Springs F/R: Coil/Coil
Brake system: PA
Brakes F/R: Disc/Drum
Steering: Rack & pinion PA
Wheelbase: 265.0cm 104.3in
Track F: 145.5cm 57.3in
Track R: 144.0cm 56.7in
Length: 468.0cm 184.3in
Width: 175.1cm 68.9in
Height: 141.1cm 55.6in
Ground clearance: 16.0cm 6.3in
Kerb weight: 1300.0kg 2863.4lb
Fuel: 60.1L 13.2gal 15.9galUS

2226 Hyundai
Lantra 1.6 Cdi
1991 Korea
114.0mph 183.4kmh
0-50mph 80.5kmh: 7.4secs
0-60mph 96.5kmh: 10.9secs
0-1/4 mile: 18.1secs
0-1km: 33.4secs
112.0bhp 83.5kW 113.5PS
@ 6200rpm
103.3lbft 140.0Nm @ 4500rpm
102.6bhp/ton 100.9bhp/tonne
70.2bhp/L 52.3kW/L 71.1PS/L
50.8ft/sec 15.5m/sec
18.9mph 30.4kmh/1000rpm
27.1mpg 22.6mpgUS 10.4L/100km
Petrol 4-stroke piston
1596cc 97.0cu in
In-line 4 fuel injection
Compression ratio: 9.2:1
Bore: 82.0mm 3.2in
Stroke: 75.0mm 2.9in
Valve type/No: Overhead 16
Transmission: Manual
No. of forward speeds: 5
Wheels driven: Front
Springs F/R: Coil/Coil
Brake system: PA
Brakes F/R: Disc/Drum
Steering: Rack & pinion PA
Wheelbase: 250.2cm 98.5in
Track F: 143.0cm 56.3in
Track R: 143.0cm 56.3in
Length: 435.9cm 171.6in
Width: 166.9cm 65.7in
Height: 138.4cm 54.5in
Ground clearance: 16.0cm 6.3in
Kerb weight: 1110.0kg 2444.9lb
Fuel: 52.0L 11.4gal 13.7galUS

2227 Hyundai
S Coupe GSi
1991 Korea
105.0mph 168.9kmh
0-50mph 80.5kmh: 8.9secs
0-60mph 96.5kmh: 12.5secs
0-1/4 mile: 18.5secs
0-1km: 34.7secs
82.0bhp 61.1kW 83.1PS
@ 5500rpm
87.8lbft 119.0Nm @ 4000rpm
85.1bhp/ton 83.7bhp/tonne
55.9bhp/L 41.7kW/L 56.6PS/L
49.3ft/sec 15.0m/sec
19.4mph 31.2kmh/1000rpm
30.8mpg 25.6mpgUS 9.2L/100km
Petrol 4-stroke piston
1468cc 90.0cu in
In-line 4 fuel injection
Compression ratio: 9.4:1
Bore: 75.5mm 3.0in
Stroke: 82.0mm 3.2in
Valve type/No: Overhead 8
Transmission: Manual
No. of forward speeds: 5
Wheels driven: Front
Springs F/R: Coil/Coil
Brake system: PA
Brakes F/R: Disc/Drum
Steering: Rack & pinion PA
Wheelbase: 238.3cm 93.8in
Track F: 139.0cm 54.7in
Track R: 134.0cm 52.8in
Length: 421.3cm 165.9in
Width: 162.6cm 64.0in
Height: 132.8cm 52.3in
Ground clearance: 16.6cm 6.5in
Kerb weight: 980.0kg 2158.6lb
Fuel: 45.0L 9.9gal 11.9galUS

2228 Hyundai
X2 1.5 GSi
1991 Korea
100.0mph 160.9kmh
0-50mph 80.5kmh: 9.4secs
0-60mph 96.5kmh: 13.7secs
0-1/4 mile: 19.1secs
0-1km: 36.4secs
83.0bhp 61.9kW 84.1PS
@ 5500rpm
88.6lbft 120.0Nm @ 4000rpm
83.2bhp/ton 81.8bhp/tonne
56.5bhp/L 42.2kW/L 57.3PS/L
49.3ft/sec 15.0m/sec
21.0mph 33.8kmh/1000rpm
28.0mpg 23.3mpgUS 10.1L/100km
Petrol 4-stroke piston
1468cc 90.0cu in
In-line 4 fuel injection
Compression ratio: 9.4:1
Bore: 76.0mm 3.0in
Stroke: 82.0mm 3.2in
Valve type/No: Overhead 8
Transmission: Manual
No. of forward speeds: 5
Wheels driven: Front
Springs F/R: Coil/Coil
Brake system: PA
Brakes F/R: Disc/Drum
Steering: Rack & pinion PA
Wheelbase: 238.3cm 93.8in
Track F: 138.9cm 54.7in
Track R: 133.9cm 52.7in
Length: 410.0cm 161.4in
Width: 160.5cm 63.2in
Height: 137.7cm 54.2in
Kerb weight: 1015.0kg 2235.7lb
Fuel: 45.0L 9.9gal 11.9galUS

2229 IAD
Venus
1990 UK
165.0mph 265.5kmh
0-60mph 96.5kmh: 5.0secs
172.0bhp 128.3kW 174.4PS
@ 6000rpm
163.0lbft 220.9Nm @ 5000rpm
79.1bhp/L 59.0kW/L 80.2PS/L
50.0ft/sec 15.2m/sec
Petrol 4-stroke piston
2174cc 132.6cu in
In-line 4 2 Carburettor
Compression ratio: 10.9:1
Bore: 95.3mm 3.8in
Stroke: 76.2mm 3.0in
Valve type/No: Overhead 16
Transmission: Manual
No. of forward speeds: 5
Wheels driven: Rear
Springs F/R: Coil/Coil
Brakes F/R: Disc/Disc
Steering: Rack & pinion PA
Wheelbase: 269.5cm 106.1in
Track F: 167.9cm 66.1in
Track R: 167.9cm 66.1in
Length: 398.8cm 157.0in
Width: 195.1cm 76.8in
Height: 111.0cm 43.7in

2230 Infiniti
M30
1990 Japan
128.0mph 206.0kmh
0-50mph 80.5kmh: 7.5secs
0-60mph 96.5kmh: 10.4secs
0-1/4 mile: 17.5secs
162.0bhp 120.8kW 164.2PS
@ 5200rpm
180.0lbft 243.9Nm @ 3600rpm
108.8bhp/ton 107.0bhp/tonne
54.5bhp/L 40.7kW/L 55.3PS/L
47.2ft/sec 14.4m/sec
24.0mpg 20.0mpgUS 11.8L/100km
Petrol 4-stroke piston
2971cc 181.3cu in
Vee 6 fuel injection
Compression ratio: 9.0:1
Bore: 87.1mm 3.4in
Stroke: 83.1mm 3.3in
Valve type/No: Overhead 12
Transmission: Automatic
No. of forward speeds: 4
Wheels driven: Rear
Springs F/R: Coil/Coil
Brake system: PA ABS
Brakes F/R: Disc/Disc
Steering: Rack & pinion PA
Wheelbase: 261.6cm 103.0in
Track F: 143.5cm 56.5in
Track R: 143.5cm 56.5in
Length: 479.6cm 188.8in
Width: 168.9cm 66.5in
Height: 137.9cm 54.3in
Kerb weight: 1514.1kg 3335.0lb
Fuel: 65.1L 14.3gal 17.2galUS

2231 Infiniti
Q45
1990 Japan
150.0mph 241.4kmh
0-60mph 96.5kmh: 6.9secs
0-1/4 mile: 15.4secs
278.0bhp 207.3kW 281.9PS
@ 6000rpm
292.0lbft 395.7Nm @ 4000rpm
155.1bhp/ton 152.5bhp/tonne
61.9bhp/L 46.1kW/L 62.7PS/L
54.3ft/sec 16.5m/sec
20.7mpg 17.2mpgUS 13.7L/100km
Petrol 4-stroke piston
4494cc 274.2cu in
Vee 8 fuel injection
Compression ratio: 10.2:1
Bore: 93.0mm 3.7in
Stroke: 82.7mm 3.3in
Valve type/No: Overhead 32
Transmission: Automatic
No. of forward speeds: 4
Wheels driven: Rear
Springs F/R: Coil/Coil
Brake system: PA ABS
Brakes F/R: Disc/Disc
Steering: Rack & pinion PA
Wheelbase: 287.5cm 113.2in
Track F: 157.0cm 61.8in
Track R: 157.0cm 61.8in
Length: 507.5cm 199.8in
Width: 182.6cm 71.9in
Height: 143.0cm 56.3in
Kerb weight: 1822.8kg 4015.0lb
Fuel: 85.2L 18.7gal 22.5galUS

2232 Infiniti
G20
1991 Japan
130.0mph 209.2kmh
0-50mph 80.5kmh: 7.4secs
0-60mph 96.5kmh: 10.0secs
0-1/4 mile: 17.6secs
140.0bhp 104.4kW 141.9PS
@ 6400rpm
132.0lbft 178.9Nm @ 4800rpm
104.5bhp/ton 102.8bhp/tonne
70.1bhp/L 52.2kW/L 71.0PS/L
60.3ft/sec 18.3m/sec
28.8mpg 24.0mpgUS 9.8L/100km
Petrol 4-stroke piston
1998cc 121.9cu in
In-line 4 fuel injection
Compression ratio: 9.5:1
Bore: 86.0mm 3.4in
Stroke: 86.0mm 3.4in
Valve type/No: Overhead 16
Transmission: Manual
No. of forward speeds: 5
Wheels driven: Front
Springs F/R: Coil/Coil
Brake system: PA ABS
Brakes F/R: Disc/Disc
Steering: Rack & pinion PA
Wheelbase: 255.0cm 100.4in
Track F: 147.1cm 57.9in
Track R: 146.1cm 57.5in
Length: 444.0cm 174.8in
Width: 169.4cm 66.7in
Height: 138.9cm 54.7in
Ground clearance: 15.7cm 6.2in
Kerb weight: 1362.0kg 3000.0lb
Fuel: 60.2L 13.2gal 15.9galUS

2233 Innocenti
S
1964 Italy
85.0mph 136.8kmh
0-50mph 80.5kmh: 12.6secs
0-60mph 96.5kmh: 18.4secs
0-1/4 mile: 21.0secs
58.0bhp 43.2kW 58.8PS
@ 5700rpm
60.0lbft 81.3Nm @ 3000rpm
83.3bhp/ton 81.9bhp/tonne
52.8bhp/L 39.4kW/L 53.5PS/L
52.2ft/sec 15.9m/sec
15.2mph 24.5kmh/1000rpm
Petrol 4-stroke piston
1098cc 67.0cu in
In-line 4 2 Carburettor
Compression ratio: 9.0:1
Bore: 64.5mm 2.5in
Stroke: 83.8mm 3.3in
Valve type/No: Overhead 8
Transmission: Manual
No. of forward speeds: 4
Wheels driven: Rear
Springs F/R: Coil/Leaf
Brakes F/R: Disc/Drum
Steering: Rack & pinion
Wheelbase: 203.2cm 80.0in
Track F: 118.9cm 46.8in
Track R: 116.3cm 45.8in
Length: 345.4cm 136.0in
Width: 147.3cm 58.0in
Height: 119.4cm 47.0in
Ground clearance: 14.0cm 5.5in
Kerb weight: 708.2kg 1560.0lb
Fuel: 28.4L 6.2gal 7.5galUS

2234 International
Scout
1961 USA
80.0mph 128.7kmh
0-50mph 80.5kmh: 14.0secs
0-60mph 96.5kmh: 20.1secs
0-1/4 mile: 21.7secs
87.0bhp 64.9kW 88.2PS
@ 4000rpm
135.0lbft 182.9Nm @ 2400rpm
69.6bhp/ton 68.4bhp/tonne
34.9bhp/L 26.0kW/L 35.4PS/L
35.8ft/sec 10.9m/sec
18.6mph 29.9kmh/1000rpm
Petrol 4-stroke piston
2492cc 152.0cu in
In-line 4 1 Carburettor
Compression ratio: 8.2:1
Bore: 98.6mm 3.9in
Stroke: 81.8mm 3.2in
Valve type/No: Overhead 8
Transmission: Manual
No. of forward speeds: 3
Wheels driven: 4-wheel drive
Brakes F/R: Drum/Drum
Wheelbase: 254.0cm 100.0in
Track F: 140.0cm 55.1in
Track R: 140.0cm 55.1in
Length: 391.2cm 154.0in
Width: 174.2cm 68.6in
Height: 170.2cm 67.0in
Ground clearance: 22.9cm 9.0in
Kerb weight: 1271.2kg 2800.0lb

2235 International
Travelall
1962 USA
85.0mph 136.8kmh
0-50mph 80.5kmh: 13.0secs
0-60mph 96.5kmh: 18.2secs
0-1/4 mile: 20.9secs
155.0bhp 115.6kW 157.1PS
@ 4400rpm
227.0lbft 307.6Nm @ 2800rpm
84.1bhp/ton 82.7bhp/tonne
35.6bhp/L 26.5kW/L 36.1PS/L
39.4ft/sec 12.0m/sec
21.6mph 34.8kmh/1000rpm
Petrol 4-stroke piston

4356cc 265.8cu in
Vee 8 1 Carburettor
Compression ratio: 8.4:1
Bore: 91.9mm 3.6in
Stroke: 81.8mm 3.2in
Valve type/No: Overhead 16
Transmission: Manual
No. of forward speeds: 4
Wheels driven: Rear
Brake system: PA
Wheelbase: 302.3cm 119.0in
Track F: 158.0cm 62.2in
Track R: 158.8cm 62.5in
Length: 513.1cm 202.0in
Width: 191.8cm 75.5in
Height: 176.0cm 69.3in
Ground clearance: 19.8cm 7.8in
Kerb weight: 1875.0kg 4130.0lb
Fuel: 71.9L 15.8gal 19.0galUS

2236 International
900 Pickup
1963 USA
81.0mph 130.3kmh
0-50mph 80.5kmh: 18.5secs
0-60mph 96.5kmh: 27.5secs
0-1/4 mile: 24.5secs
93.0bhp 69.3kW 94.3PS
@ 4400rpm
142.0lbft 192.4Nm @ 2400rpm
66.8bhp/ton 65.7bhp/tonne
37.3bhp/L 27.8kW/L 37.8PS/L
39.4ft/sec 12.0m/sec
19.7mph 31.7kmh/1000rpm
Petrol 4-stroke piston
2491cc 152.0cu in
In-line 4 1 Carburettor
Compression ratio: 8.0:1
Bore: 98.4mm 3.9in
Stroke: 81.8mm 3.2in
Valve type/No: Overhead 8
Transmission: Manual
No. of forward speeds: 3
Wheels driven: Rear
Wheelbase: 271.8cm 107.0in
Track F: 153.7cm 60.5in
Track R: 153.7cm 60.5in
Length: 453.9cm 178.7in
Width: 198.1cm 78.0in
Height: 175.3cm 69.0in
Ground clearance: 19.1cm 7.5in
Kerb weight: 1416.5kg 3120.0lb
Fuel: 56.8L 12.5gal 15.0galUS

2237 International
Pickup 4WD 1210 Camper Special
1971 USA
90.0mph 144.8kmh
0-60mph 96.5kmh: 18.0secs
253.0bhp 188.7kW 256.5PS
@ 4200rpm
381.0lbft 516.3Nm @ 2800rpm
108.8bhp/ton 107.0bhp/tonne
39.4bhp/L 29.4kW/L 39.9PS/L
42.7ft/sec 13.0m/sec
9.4mpg 7.8mpgUS 30.2L/100km
Petrol 4-stroke piston
6424cc 391.9cu in
Vee 8
Compression ratio: 8.0:1
Bore: 104.9mm 4.1in
Stroke: 93.0mm 3.7in
Valve type/No: Overhead 16
Transmission: Manual
No. of forward speeds: 4
Wheels driven: 4-wheel drive
Brake system: PA
Brakes F/R: Drum/Drum
Steering: Recirculating ball PA
Wheelbase: 332.7cm 131.0in
Track F: 160.0cm 63.0in
Track R: 160.0cm 63.0in
Length: 512.3cm 201.7in
Width: 200.2cm 78.8in
Height: 182.4cm 71.8in
Ground clearance: 22.9cm 9.0in
Kerb weight: 2365.3kg 5210.0lb
Fuel: 60.6L 13.3gal 16.0galUS

2238 International
Scout
1971 USA
92.0mph 148.0kmh
0-60mph 96.5kmh: 12.5secs
193.0bhp 143.9kW 195.7PS
@ 4400rpm
276.0lbft 374.0Nm @ 2800rpm
116.8bhp/ton 114.9bhp/tonne
38.7bhp/L 28.9kW/L 39.3PS/L
39.4ft/sec 12.0m/sec
Petrol 4-stroke piston
4982cc 304.0cu in
Vee 8
Compression ratio: 8.2:1
Bore: 98.6mm 3.9in
Stroke: 81.9mm 3.2in
Valve type/No: Overhead 16
Transmission: Automatic
No. of forward speeds: 3
Wheels driven: 4-wheel drive
Brakes F/R: Drum/Drum
Steering: Worm & roller
Wheelbase: 254.0cm 100.0in
Track F: 141.5cm 55.7in
Track R: 141.5cm 55.7in
Length: 391.2cm 154.0in
Width: 174.2cm 68.6in
Height: 168.4cm 66.3in
Ground clearance: 21.1cm 8.3in
Kerb weight: 1679.8kg 3700.0lb
Fuel: 37.8L 8.3gal 10.0galUS

2239 International
Travelall 1210
1971 USA
90.0mph 144.8kmh
0-60mph 96.5kmh: 16.3secs
253.0bhp 188.7kW 256.5PS
@ 4200rpm
381.0lbft 516.3Nm @ 2800rpm
99.4bhp/ton 97.8bhp/tonne
39.4bhp/L 29.4kW/L 39.9PS/L
42.7ft/sec 13.0m/sec
9.0mpg 7.5mpgUS 31.4L/100km
Petrol 4-stroke piston
6424cc 391.9cu in
Vee 8
Compression ratio: 8.0:1
Bore: 104.9mm 4.1in
Stroke: 93.0mm 3.7in
Valve type/No: Overhead 16
Transmission: Automatic
No. of forward speeds: 3
Wheels driven: 4-wheel drive
Brake system: PA
Brakes F/R: Drum/Drum
Steering: Recirculating ball PA
Wheelbase: 302.3cm 119.0in
Track F: 160.0cm 63.0in
Track R: 160.0cm 63.0in
Length: 523.2cm 206.0in
Width: 200.2cm 78.8in
Height: 175.3cm 69.0in
Ground clearance: 21.6cm 8.5in
Kerb weight: 2587.8kg 5700.0lb
Fuel: 60.6L 13.3gal 16.0galUS

2240 International
Scout
1972 USA
95.0mph 152.9kmh
0-60mph 96.5kmh: 14.2secs
144.0bhp 107.4kW 146.0PS
@ 3600rpm
263.0lbft 356.4Nm @ 2000rpm
74.1bhp/ton 72.8bhp/tonne
25.5bhp/L 19.0kW/L 25.8PS/L
36.6ft/sec 11.2m/sec
Petrol 4-stroke piston
5654cc 345.0cu in
Vee 8
Compression ratio: 8.1:1
Bore: 98.6mm 3.9in
Stroke: 93.0mm 3.7in
Valve type/No: Overhead 16
Transmission: Automatic
No. of forward speeds: 3
Wheels driven: 4-wheel drive
Brake system: PA
Brakes F/R: Drum/Drum
Steering: Worm & roller PA
Wheelbase: 254.0cm 100.0in
Track F: 145.0cm 57.1in
Track R: 145.0cm 57.1in
Length: 420.9cm 165.7in
Width: 177.8cm 70.0in
Height: 168.7cm 66.4in
Ground clearance: 21.6cm 8.5in
Kerb weight: 1977.2kg 4355.0lb
Fuel: 71.9L 15.8gal 19.0galUS

2241 Invicta
4.5-litre
1928 UK
68.0mph 109.4kmh
110.0bhp 82.0kW 111.5PS
@ 3200rpm
75.9bhp/ton 74.6bhp/tonne
24.6bhp/L 18.4kW/L 25.0PS/L
42.2ft/sec 12.9m/sec
Petrol 4-stroke piston
4467cc 272.5cu in
In-line 6
Bore: 88.5mm 3.5in
Stroke: 120.6mm 4.7in
Valve type/No: Overhead 12
Transmission: Manual
No. of forward speeds: 4
Wheels driven: Rear
Brakes F/R: Drum/Drum
Wheelbase: 304.8cm 120.0in
Track F: 132.1cm 52.0in
Track R: 132.1cm 52.0in
Length: 436.9cm 172.0in
Width: 172.7cm 68.0in
Height: 160.0cm 63.0in
Kerb weight: 1474.6kg 3248.0lb
Fuel: 63.7L 14.0gal 16.8galUS

2242 Invicta
4.5-litre
1931 UK
92.0mph 148.0kmh
0-50mph 80.5kmh: 9.5secs
0-60mph 96.5kmh: 14.8secs
0-1/4 mile: 19.5secs
110.0bhp 82.0kW 111.5PS
@ 3200rpm
200.0lbft 271.0Nm @ 1800rpm
75.8bhp/ton 74.5bhp/tonne
24.6bhp/L 18.4kW/L 25.0PS/L
42.2ft/sec 12.9m/sec
25.2mph 40.5kmh/1000rpm
Petrol 4-stroke piston
4467cc 272.5cu in
In-line 6
Compression ratio: 6.0:1
Bore: 88.4mm 3.5in
Stroke: 120.7mm 4.7in
Valve type/No: Overhead 12
Transmission: Manual
No. of forward speeds: 4
Wheels driven: Rear
Wheelbase: 299.7cm 118.0in
Track F: 142.2cm 56.0in
Track R: 142.2cm 56.0in
Length: 426.7cm 168.0in
Width: 172.7cm 68.0in
Height: 134.6cm 53.0in
Kerb weight: 1475.5kg 3250.0lb

2243 Irmsher
GT
1989 Germany
150.0mph 241.4kmh
0-60mph 96.5kmh: 7.9secs
200.0bhp 149.1kW 202.8PS
@ 5200rpm
210.0lbft 284.6Nm @ 4200rpm
153.1bhp/ton 150.6bhp/tonne
55.7bhp/L 41.5kW/L 56.5PS/L
48.4ft/sec 14.7m/sec
Petrol 4-stroke piston
3590cc 219.0cu in
In-line 6 fuel injection
Compression ratio: 9.4:1
Bore: 95.0mm 3.7in
Stroke: 85.0mm 3.3in
Valve type/No: Overhead 12
Transmission: Manual
No. of forward speeds: 5
Wheels driven: Rear
Springs F/R: Coil/Coil
Brake system: PA ABS
Brakes F/R: Disc/Disc
Steering: Rack & pinion PA
Wheelbase: 273.1cm 107.5in
Track F: 145.0cm 57.1in
Track R: 146.8cm 57.8in
Length: 459.0cm 180.7in
Width: 177.8cm 70.0in
Height: 133.9cm 52.7in
Kerb weight: 1328.4kg 2926.0lb
Fuel: 74.9L 16.5gal 19.8galUS

2244 Isdera
Imperator
1988 Germany
176.0mph 283.2kmh
0-60mph 96.5kmh: 5.0secs
0-1/4 mile: 13.3secs
390.0bhp 290.8kW 395.4PS
@ 5500rpm
387.0lbft 524.4Nm @ 4100rpm
317.1bhp/ton 311.8bhp/tonne
70.3bhp/L 52.4kW/L 71.3PS/L
57.0ft/sec 17.4m/sec
Petrol 4-stroke piston
5547cc 338.4cu in
Vee 8 fuel injection
Compression ratio: 9.8:1
Bore: 96.5mm 3.8in
Stroke: 94.8mm 3.7in
Valve type/No: Overhead 32
Transmission: Manual
No. of forward speeds: 5
Wheels driven: Rear
Springs F/R: Coil/Coil
Brake system: PA
Brakes F/R: Disc/Disc
Steering: Rack & pinion PA
Wheelbase: 240.0cm 94.5in
Track F: 147.1cm 57.9in
Track R: 139.7cm 55.0in
Length: 421.6cm 166.0in
Width: 182.9cm 72.0in
Height: 113.3cm 44.6in
Kerb weight: 1250.8kg 2755.0lb
Fuel: 113.5L 25.0gal 30.0galUS

2245 Iso
Grifo A3L Berlinetta
1963 Italy
153.0mph 246.2kmh
0-60mph 96.5kmh: 6.2secs
350.0bhp 261.0kW 354.8PS
@ 5800rpm
360.0lbft 487.8Nm @ 3600rpm
324.0bhp/ton 318.6bhp/tonne
65.3bhp/L 48.7kW/L 66.2PS/L
52.4ft/sec 16.0m/sec
Petrol 4-stroke piston
5359cc 327.0cu in
Vee 8 1 Carburettor
Compression ratio: 11.0:1
Bore: 101.6mm 4.0in
Stroke: 82.6mm 3.2in
Valve type/No: Overhead 16
Transmission: Manual
No. of forward speeds: 5
Wheels driven: Rear
Springs F/R: Coil/Coil
Brakes F/R: Disc/Disc
Steering: Recirculating ball
Wheelbase: 249.9cm 98.4in
Track F: 141.0cm 55.5in
Track R: 141.0cm 55.5in
Length: 443.0cm 174.4in
Width: 177.0cm 69.7in
Height: 119.9cm 47.2in
Kerb weight: 1098.7kg 2420.0lb
Fuel: 94.6L 20.8gal 25.0galUS

2246 Iso
GT
1964 Italy
135.0mph 217.2kmh
0-50mph 80.5kmh: 6.5secs
0-60mph 96.5kmh: 8.2secs
0-1/4 mile: 15.9secs
300.0bhp 223.7kW 304.2PS
@ 5000rpm
360.0lbft 487.8Nm @ 3200rpm
197.4bhp/ton 194.1bhp/tonne
56.0bhp/L 41.8kW/L 56.8PS/L
45.1ft/sec 13.8m/sec
24.5mph 39.4kmh/1000rpm
Petrol 4-stroke piston
5356cc 326.8cu in
Vee 8 1 Carburettor
Compression ratio: 10.5:1
Bore: 101.6mm 4.0in
Stroke: 82.6mm 3.2in
Valve type/No: Overhead 16
Transmission: Manual
No. of forward speeds: 4
Wheels driven: Rear
Springs F/R: Coil/Coil
Brakes F/R: Disc/Disc
Steering: Worm & sector
Wheelbase: 269.2cm 106.0in
Track F: 141.2cm 55.6in
Track R: 141.2cm 55.6in

Length: 476.0cm 187.4in
Width: 175.0cm 68.9in
Height: 134.1cm 52.8in
Ground clearance: 11.9cm 4.7in
Kerb weight: 1545.9kg 3405.0lb
Fuel: 94.6L 20.8gal 25.0galUS

2247 Iso

Rivolta IR-340
1964 Italy
142.0mph 228.5kmh
0-50mph 80.5kmh: 6.3secs
0-60mph 96.5kmh: 8.0secs
0-1/4 mile: 15.9secs
340.0bhp 253.5kW 344.7PS
@ 6000rpm
344.0lbft 466.1Nm @ 4000rpm
222.5bhp/ton 218.8bhp/tonne
63.4bhp/L 47.3kW/L 64.3PS/L
54.2ft/sec 16.5m/sec
22.8mph 36.7kmh/1000rpm
12.1mpg 10.1mpgUS 23.3L/100km
Petrol 4-stroke piston
5359cc 327.0cu in
Vee 8 1 Carburettor
Compression ratio: 11.2:1
Bore: 101.6mm 4.0in
Stroke: 82.6mm 3.2in
Valve type/No: Overhead 16
Transmission: Manual
No. of forward speeds: 4
Wheels driven: Rear
Springs F/R: Coil/Coil
Brake system: PA
Brakes F/R: Disc/Disc
Steering: Recirculating ball
Wheelbase: 269.7cm 106.2in
Track F: 141.0cm 55.5in
Track R: 141.0cm 55.5in
Length: 480.1cm 189.0in
Width: 175.3cm 69.0in
Height: 134.6cm 53.0in
Ground clearance: 11.9cm 4.7in
Kerb weight: 1554.0kg 3423.0lb
Fuel: 95.5L 21.0gal 25.2galUS

2248 Iso

Grifo GL 365
1966 Italy
163.0mph 262.3kmh
0-50mph 80.5kmh: 5.7secs
0-60mph 96.5kmh: 7.4secs
0-1/4 mile: 14.9secs
0-1km: 27.1secs
365.0bhp 272.2kW 370.1PS
@ 6200rpm
360.0lbft 487.8Nm @ 4000rpm
257.3bhp/ton 253.1bhp/tonne
68.1bhp/L 50.8kW/L 69.0PS/L
56.0ft/sec 17.1m/sec
25.2mph 40.5kmh/1000rpm
15.7mpg 13.1mpgUS 18.0L/100km
Petrol 4-stroke piston
5359cc 327.0cu in
Vee 8 1 Carburettor
Compression ratio: 11.0:1
Bore: 101.6mm 4.0in
Stroke: 82.6mm 3.2in
Valve type/No: Overhead 16
Transmission: Manual
No. of forward speeds: 4
Wheels driven: Rear
Springs F/R: Coil/Coil
Brake system: PA
Brakes F/R: Disc/Disc
Steering: Recirculating ball
Wheelbase: 250.2cm 98.5in
Track F: 141.0cm 55.5in
Track R: 141.0cm 55.5in
Length: 443.7cm 174.7in
Width: 176.5cm 69.5in
Height: 119.4cm 47.0in
Ground clearance: 11.9cm 4.7in
Kerb weight: 1442.4kg 3177.0lb
Fuel: 100.1L 22.0gal 26.4galUS

2249 Iso

Rivolta S4
1969 Italy
123.0mph 197.9kmh
0-50mph 80.5kmh: 5.6secs
0-60mph 96.5kmh: 7.8secs
0-1/4 mile: 16.3secs
300.0bhp 223.7kW 304.2PS
@ 5000rpm
361.0lbft 489.2Nm @ 3200rpm
181.6bhp/ton 178.6bhp/tonne
56.0bhp/L 41.8kW/L 56.8PS/L
45.1ft/sec 13.8m/sec
26.1mph 42.0kmh/1000rpm
18.1mpg 15.1mpgUS 15.6L/100km
Petrol 4-stroke piston
5356cc 326.8cu in
Vee 8 1 Carburettor
Compression ratio: 10.5:1
Bore: 101.6mm 4.0in
Stroke: 82.6mm 3.2in
Valve type/No: Overhead 16
Transmission: Manual
No. of forward speeds: 4
Wheels driven: Rear
Springs F/R: Coil/Coil
Brake system: PA
Brakes F/R: Disc/Disc
Steering: Recirculating ball
Wheelbase: 285.0cm 112.2in
Track F: 141.0cm 55.5in
Track R: 141.0cm 55.5in
Length: 497.1cm 195.7in
Width: 178.1cm 70.1in
Height: 132.1cm 52.0in
Ground clearance: 11.9cm 4.7in
Kerb weight: 1679.8kg 3700.0lb
Fuel: 99.9L 22.0gal 26.4galUS

2250 Iso

Grifo GL
1971 Italy
157.0mph 252.6kmh
0-60mph 96.5kmh: 7.2secs
0-1/4 mile: 15.7secs
350.0bhp 261.0kW 354.8PS
@ 5800rpm
360.0lbft 487.8Nm @ 3600rpm
223.0bhp/ton 219.3bhp/tonne
65.4bhp/L 48.7kW/L 66.3PS/L
52.4ft/sec 16.0m/sec
Petrol 4-stroke piston
5354cc 326.7cu in
Vee 8 1 Carburettor
Compression ratio: 11.0:1
Bore: 101.6mm 4.0in
Stroke: 82.6mm 3.2in
Valve type/No: Overhead 16
Transmission: Manual
No. of forward speeds: 5
Wheels driven: Rear
Springs F/R: Coil/Coil
Brakes F/R: Disc/Disc
Steering: Recirculating ball
Wheelbase: 248.9cm 98.0in
Track F: 141.0cm 55.5in
Track R: 141.0cm 55.5in
Length: 444.0cm 174.8in
Width: 176.5cm 69.5in
Height: 119.4cm 47.0in
Kerb weight: 1595.8kg 3515.0lb
Fuel: 87.1L 19.1gal 23.0galUS

2251 Iso

Rivolta Fidia
1974 Italy
0-50mph 80.5kmh: 6.1secs
0-60mph 96.5kmh: 8.1secs
0-1/4 mile: 16.2secs
0-1km: 29.3secs
325.0bhp 242.3kW 329.5PS
@ 5800rpm
360.0lbft 487.8Nm @ 3800rpm
184.6bhp/ton 181.5bhp/tonne
56.3bhp/L 42.0kW/L 57.1PS/L
56.4ft/sec 17.2m/sec
22.9mph 36.8kmh/1000rpm
11.7mpg 9.7mpgUS 24.1L/100km
Petrol 4-stroke piston
5768cc 351.9cu in
Vee 8 1 Carburettor
Compression ratio: 8.6:1
Bore: 101.6mm 4.0in
Stroke: 88.9mm 3.5in
Valve type/No: Overhead 16
Transmission: Automatic
No. of forward speeds: 3
Wheels driven: Rear
Springs F/R: Coil/Coil
Brake system: PA
Brakes F/R: Disc/Disc
Steering: Recirculating ball PA
Wheelbase: 284.5cm 112.0in
Track F: 143.5cm 56.5in
Track R: 143.8cm 56.6in
Length: 500.4cm 197.0in
Width: 177.8cm 70.0in
Height: 137.2cm 54.0in
Ground clearance: 12.7cm 5.0in
Kerb weight: 1790.1kg 3943.0lb
Fuel: 100.1L 22.0gal 26.4galUS

2252 Isuzu

I-Mark LS
1983 Japan
84.0mph 135.2kmh
0-50mph 80.5kmh: 13.5secs
0-60mph 96.5kmh: 19.9secs
0-1/4 mile: 21.7secs
51.0bhp 38.0kW 51.7PS
@ 5000rpm
72.0lbft 97.6Nm @ 3000rpm
48.2bhp/ton 47.4bhp/tonne
28.0bhp/L 20.9kW/L 28.4PS/L
44.9ft/sec 13.7m/sec
22.7mph 36.5kmh/1000rpm
45.6mpg 38.0mpgUS 6.2L/100km
Diesel 4-stroke piston
1819cc 111.0cu in
In-line 4 fuel injection
Compression ratio: 22.0:1
Bore: 84.0mm 3.3in
Stroke: 82.0mm 3.2in
Valve type/No: Overhead 8
Transmission: Manual
No. of forward speeds: 5
Wheels driven: Rear
Springs F/R: Coil/Coil
Brake system: PA
Brakes F/R: Disc/Drum
Steering: Rack & pinion PA
Wheelbase: 239.5cm 94.3in
Track F: 130.6cm 51.4in
Track R: 130.6cm 51.4in
Length: 433.6cm 170.7in
Width: 157.0cm 61.8in
Height: 135.9cm 53.5in
Kerb weight: 1076.0kg 2370.0lb
Fuel: 51.8L 11.4gal 13.7galUS

2253 Isuzu

Impulse
1984 Japan
100.0mph 160.9kmh
0-60mph 96.5kmh: 12.9secs
0-1/4 mile: 19.0secs
90.0bhp 67.1kW 91.2PS
@ 5000rpm
108.0lbft 146.3Nm @ 3000rpm
73.8bhp/ton 72.6bhp/tonne
46.2bhp/L 34.4kW/L 46.8PS/L
44.9ft/sec 13.7m/sec
20.7mph 33.3kmh/1000rpm
34.8mpg 29.0mpgUS 8.1L/100km
Petrol 4-stroke piston
1949cc 118.9cu in
In-line 4 fuel injection
Compression ratio: 9.2:1
Bore: 87.0mm 3.4in
Stroke: 82.0mm 3.2in
Valve type/No: Overhead 8
Transmission: Manual
No. of forward speeds: 5
Wheels driven: Rear
Springs F/R: Coil/Coil
Brake system: PA
Brakes F/R: Disc/Disc
Steering: Rack & pinion PA
Wheelbase: 243.8cm 96.0in
Track F: 135.6cm 53.4in
Track R: 136.9cm 53.9in
Length: 438.4cm 172.6in
Width: 165.6cm 65.2in
Height: 130.6cm 51.4in
Ground clearance: 14.0cm 5.5in
Kerb weight: 1239.4kg 2730.0lb
Fuel: 57.1L 12.6gal 15.1galUS

2254 Isuzu

I-Mark
1986 Japan
0-60mph 96.5kmh: 12.0secs
0-1/4 mile: 19.0secs
70.0bhp 52.2kW 71.0PS
@ 5400rpm
87.0lbft 117.9Nm @ 3400rpm
78.4bhp/ton 77.1bhp/tonne
47.6bhp/L 35.5kW/L 48.2PS/L
46.6ft/sec 14.2m/sec
42.6mpg 35.5mpgUS 6.6L/100km
Petrol 4-stroke piston
1471cc 89.7cu in
In-line 4 1 Carburettor
Compression ratio: 9.6:1
Bore: 77.0mm 3.0in
Stroke: 79.0mm 3.1in
Valve type/No: Overhead 8
Transmission: Manual
No. of forward speeds: 5
Wheels driven: Front
Brakes F/R: Disc/Drum
Steering: Rack & pinion PA
Wheelbase: 240.0cm 94.5in
Length: 396.0cm 155.9in
Width: 161.3cm 63.5in
Height: 137.4cm 54.1in
Kerb weight: 908.0kg 2000.0lb

2255 Isuzu

Impulse Sports Coupe
1986 Japan
100.0mph 160.9kmh
0-60mph 96.5kmh: 12.9secs
0-1/4 mile: 19.0secs
90.0bhp 67.1kW 91.2PS
@ 5000rpm
108.0lbft 146.3Nm @ 3000rpm
73.8bhp/ton 72.6bhp/tonne
46.2bhp/L 34.4kW/L 46.8PS/L
44.9ft/sec 13.7m/sec
34.8mpg 29.0mpgUS 8.1L/100km
Petrol 4-stroke piston
1949cc 118.9cu in
In-line 4 fuel injection
Compression ratio: 9.2:1
Bore: 87.0mm 3.4in
Stroke: 82.0mm 3.2in
Valve type/No: Overhead 8
Transmission: Manual
No. of forward speeds: 5
Wheels driven: Rear
Springs F/R: Coil/Coil
Brake system: PA
Brakes F/R: Disc/Disc
Steering: Rack & pinion PA
Wheelbase: 243.8cm 96.0in
Track F: 135.4cm 53.3in
Track R: 137.9cm 54.3in
Length: 438.4cm 172.6in
Width: 165.6cm 65.2in
Height: 130.6cm 51.4in
Kerb weight: 1239.4kg 2730.0lb
Fuel: 57.1L 12.6gal 15.1galUS

2256 Isuzu

Impulse Turbo
1986 Japan
130.0mph 209.2kmh
0-60mph 96.5kmh: 8.5secs
0-1/4 mile: 16.4secs
140.0bhp 104.4kW 141.9PS
@ 5400rpm
166.0lbft 224.9Nm @ 3000rpm
108.9bhp/ton 107.1bhp/tonne
70.2bhp/L 52.4kW/L 71.2PS/L
48.4ft/sec 14.8m/sec
31.2mpg 26.0mpgUS 9.0L/100km
Petrol 4-stroke piston
1994cc 121.7cu in turbocharged
In-line 4 fuel injection
Compression ratio: 7.9:1
Bore: 88.0mm 3.5in
Stroke: 82.0mm 3.2in
Valve type/No: Overhead 8
Transmission: Manual
No. of forward speeds: 5
Wheels driven: Rear
Springs F/R: Coil/Coil
Brake system: PA
Brakes F/R: Disc/Disc
Steering: Rack & pinion PA
Wheelbase: 243.8cm 96.0in
Track F: 135.4cm 53.3in
Track R: 137.9cm 54.3in
Length: 438.4cm 172.6in
Width: 165.6cm 65.2in
Height: 130.6cm 51.4in
Kerb weight: 1307.5kg 2880.0lb
Fuel: 57.1L 12.6gal 15.1galUS

2257 Isuzu

Trooper 3-door TD
1987 Japan
80.0mph 128.7kmh
0-50mph 80.5kmh: 16.6secs
0-60mph 96.5kmh: 26.1secs
0-1/4 mile: 22.4secs
0-1km: 43.2secs
74.0bhp 55.2kW 75.0PS
@ 4000rpm

114.2lbft 154.7Nm @ 2500rpm
45.5bhp/ton 44.7bhp/tonne
33.1bhp/L 24.7kW/L 33.5PS/L
40.2ft/sec 12.3m/sec
20.6mph 33.1kmh/1000rpm
22.3mpg 18.6mpgUS 12.7L/100km
Diesel 4-stroke piston
2238cc 137.0cu in turbocharged
In-line 4 fuel injection
Compression ratio: 21.0:1
Bore: 88.0mm 3.5in
Stroke: 92.0mm 3.6in
Valve type/No: Overhead 8
Transmission: Manual
No. of forward speeds: 5
Wheels driven: 4-wheel engageable
Springs F/R: Torsion bar/Leaf
Brake system: PA
Brakes F/R: Disc/Drum
Steering: Recirculating ball PA
Wheelbase: 230.1cm 90.6in
Track F: 139.4cm 54.9in
Track R: 140.0cm 55.1in
Length: 426.7cm 168.0in
Width: 167.6cm 66.0in
Height: 152.4cm 60.0in
Ground clearance: 22.6cm 8.9in
Kerb weight: 1655.0kg 3645.4lb
Fuel: 83.3L 18.3gal 22.0galUS

2258 Isuzu
I-Mark RS Turbo
1988 Japan
0-60mph 96.5kmh: 8.9secs
0-1/4 mile: 16.8secs
110.0bhp 82.0kW 111.5PS
@ 5400rpm
120.0lbft 162.6Nm @ 3500rpm
110.2bhp/ton 108.4bhp/tonne
74.8bhp/L 55.8kW/L 75.8PS/L
46.6ft/sec 14.2m/sec
27.6mpg 23.0mpgUS 10.2L/100km
Petrol 4-stroke piston
1471cc 89.7cu in turbocharged
In-line 4 fuel injection
Compression ratio: 8.0:1
Bore: 77.0mm 3.0in
Stroke: 79.0mm 3.1in
Valve type/No: Overhead 8
Transmission: Manual
No. of forward speeds: 5
Wheels driven: Front
Springs F/R: Coil/Coil
Brake system: PA
Brakes F/R: Disc/Drum
Steering: Rack & pinion PA
Wheelbase: 240.0cm 94.5in
Track F: 140.7cm 55.4in
Track R: 138.7cm 54.6in
Length: 399.8cm 157.4in
Width: 161.3cm 63.5in
Height: 137.4cm 54.1in
Kerb weight: 1014.7kg 2235.0lb
Fuel: 42.0L 9.2gal 11.1galUS

2259 Isuzu
Impulse Turbo
1988 Japan
125.0mph 201.1kmh
0-50mph 80.5kmh: 6.3secs
0-60mph 96.5kmh: 8.8secs
0-1/4 mile: 16.6secs
140.0bhp 104.4kW 141.9PS
@ 5400rpm
166.0lbft 224.9Nm @ 3000rpm
105.6bhp/ton 103.8bhp/tonne
70.2bhp/L 52.4kW/L 71.2PS/L
48.4ft/sec 14.8m/sec
30.6mpg 25.5mpgUS 9.2L/100km
Petrol 4-stroke piston
1994cc 121.7cu in turbocharged
In-line 4 fuel injection
Compression ratio: 7.9:1
Bore: 88.0mm 3.5in
Stroke: 82.0mm 3.2in
Valve type/No: Overhead 8
Transmission: Manual
No. of forward speeds: 5
Wheels driven: Rear
Springs F/R: Coil/Coil
Brake system: PA
Brakes F/R: Disc/Disc
Steering: Rack & pinion PA
Wheelbase: 244.1cm 96.1in
Track F: 135.4cm 53.3in
Track R: 137.9cm 54.3in
Length: 438.4cm 172.6in
Width: 166.9cm 65.7in
Height: 130.6cm 51.4in
Kerb weight: 1348.4kg 2970.0lb
Fuel: 57.1L 12.6gal 15.1galUS

2260 Isuzu
Impulse XS
1990 Japan
120.0mph 193.1kmh
0-60mph 96.5kmh: 9.3secs
0-1/4 mile: 16.9secs
130.0bhp 96.9kW 131.8PS
@ 6800rpm
102.0lbft 138.2Nm @ 4600rpm
118.9bhp/ton 116.9bhp/tonne
81.9bhp/L 61.0kW/L 83.0PS/L
58.7ft/sec 17.9m/sec
28.8mpg 24.0mpgUS 9.8L/100km
Petrol 4-stroke piston
1588cc 96.9cu in
In-line 4 fuel injection
Compression ratio: 9.8:1
Bore: 80.0mm 3.1in
Stroke: 79.0mm 3.1in
Valve type/No: Overhead 16
Transmission: Manual
No. of forward speeds: 5
Wheels driven: Front
Springs F/R: Coil/Coil
Brake system: PA
Brakes F/R: Disc/Disc
Steering: Rack & pinion PA
Wheelbase: 245.1cm 96.5in
Track F: 143.0cm 56.3in
Track R: 140.7cm 55.4in
Length: 421.6cm 166.0in
Width: 169.4cm 66.7in
Height: 129.8cm 51.1in
Kerb weight: 1112.3kg 2450.0lb
Fuel: 46.9L 10.3gal 12.4galUS

2261 Isuzu
Impulse RS
1991 Japan
120.0mph 193.1kmh
0-60mph 96.5kmh: 8.6secs
0-1/4 mile: 16.6secs
160.0bhp 119.3kW 162.2PS
@ 6600rpm
150.0lbft 203.3Nm @ 4800rpm
131.3bhp/ton 129.1bhp/tonne
100.8bhp/L 75.1kW/L 102.1PS/L
57.0ft/sec 17.4m/sec
29.9mpg 24.9mpgUS 9.4L/100km
Petrol 4-stroke piston
1588cc 96.9cu in turbocharged
In-line 4 fuel injection
Compression ratio: 8.5:1
Bore: 80.0mm 3.1in
Stroke: 79.0mm 3.1in
Valve type/No: Overhead 16
Transmission: Manual
No. of forward speeds: 5
Wheels driven: 4-wheel drive
Springs F/R: Coil/Coil
Brake system: PA ABS
Brakes F/R: Disc/Disc
Steering: Rack & pinion PA
Wheelbase: 245.1cm 96.5in
Track F: 143.0cm 56.3in
Track R: 140.5cm 55.3in
Length: 421.9cm 166.1in
Width: 169.4cm 66.7in
Height: 131.6cm 51.8in
Kerb weight: 1239.4kg 2730.0lb
Fuel: 46.9L 10.3gal 12.4galUS

2262 Ital Design
Aztec
1990 Italy
150.0mph 241.4kmh
250.0bhp 186.4kW 253.5PS
@ 6200rpm
230.0lbft 311.7Nm
112.3bhp/L 83.7kW/L 113.9PS/L
58.6ft/sec 17.9m/sec
Petrol 4-stroke piston
2226cc 135.8cu in turbocharged
In-line 5 fuel injection
Bore: 81.0mm 3.2in
Stroke: 86.4mm 3.4in
Valve type/No: Overhead 20
Transmission: Manual
No. of forward speeds: 5
Wheels driven: 4-wheel drive
Springs F/R: Coil/Coil
Brakes F/R: Disc/Disc
Wheelbase: 260.1cm 102.4in
Track F: 166.9cm 65.7in
Track R: 165.9cm 65.3in
Length: 441.5cm 173.8in
Width: 197.1cm 77.6in
Height: 157.5cm 62.0in
Fuel: 95.0L 20.9gal 25.1galUS

2263 Jaguar
SS1 Sports Tourer
1931 UK
84.5mph 136.0kmh
0-50mph 80.5kmh: 16.8secs
0-60mph 96.5kmh: 23.0secs
0-1/4 mile: 22.4secs
70.0bhp 52.2kW 71.0PS
@ 4500rpm
125.0lbft 169.4Nm @ 2500rpm
52.8bhp/ton 51.9bhp/tonne
26.3bhp/L 19.6kW/L 26.6PS/L
52.1ft/sec 15.9m/sec
Petrol 4-stroke piston
2664cc 162.5cu in
In-line 6
Compression ratio: 7.0:1
Bore: 72.9mm 2.9in
Stroke: 105.9mm 4.2in
Valve type/No: Side 12
Transmission: Manual
No. of forward speeds: 4
Wheels driven: Rear
Wheelbase: 302.3cm 119.0in
Track F: 135.9cm 53.5in
Track R: 135.9cm 53.5in
Kerb weight: 1347.5kg 2968.0lb

2264 Jaguar
SS 2.5-litre
1936 UK
88.2mph 141.9kmh
0-50mph 80.5kmh: 12.0secs
0-60mph 96.5kmh: 17.4secs
21.0mpg 17.5mpgUS 13.5L/100km
Petrol 4-stroke piston
2664cc 162.5cu in
In-line 6
Bore: 73.0mm 2.9in
Stroke: 106.0mm 4.2in
Valve type/No: Overhead 12
Transmission: Manual
No. of forward speeds: 4
Wheels driven: Rear
Brakes F/R: Drum/Drum
Kerb weight: 1532.7kg 3376.0lb
Fuel: 63.7L 14.0gal 16.8galUS

2265 Jaguar
SS 100 2.5-litre
1937 UK
94.7mph 152.4kmh
0-50mph 80.5kmh: 13.5secs
0-60mph 96.5kmh: 18.3secs
18.0mpg 15.0mpgUS 15.7L/100km
Petrol 4-stroke piston
2664cc 162.5cu in
In-line 6
Bore: 73.0mm 2.9in
Stroke: 106.0mm 4.2in
Valve type/No: Overhead 12
Transmission: Manual
No. of forward speeds: 4
Wheels driven: Rear
Brakes F/R: Drum/Drum
Kerb weight: 1204.5kg 2653.0lb
Fuel: 68.2L 15.0gal 18.0galUS

2266 Jaguar
SS 1.5-litre
1938 UK
74.3mph 119.5kmh
0-50mph 80.5kmh: 17.0secs
0-60mph 96.5kmh: 25.1secs
65.0bhp 48.5kW 65.9PS
@ 4500rpm
48.8bhp/ton 47.9bhp/tonne
36.6bhp/L 27.3kW/L 37.1PS/L
52.1ft/sec 15.9m/sec
25.0mpg 20.8mpgUS 11.3L/100km
Petrol 4-stroke piston
1776cc 108.4cu in
In-line 4 1 Carburettor
Bore: 73.0mm 2.9in
Stroke: 106.0mm 4.2in
Valve type/No: Side 8
Transmission: Manual
No. of forward speeds: 4
Wheels driven: Rear
Brakes F/R: Drum/Drum
Kerb weight: 1355.6kg 2986.0lb
Fuel: 63.7L 14.0gal 16.8galUS

2267 Jaguar
SS 100 3.5-litre
1938 UK
101.1mph 162.7kmh
0-50mph 80.5kmh: 7.4secs
0-60mph 96.5kmh: 10.4secs
125.0bhp 93.2kW 126.7PS
@ 4250rpm
104.2bhp/ton 102.5bhp/tonne
35.9bhp/L 26.7kW/L 36.3PS/L
51.1ft/sec 15.6m/sec
16.0mpg 13.3mpgUS 17.7L/100km
Petrol 4-stroke piston
3486cc 212.7cu in
In-line 6 2 Carburettor
Compression ratio: 7.2:1
Bore: 82.0mm 3.2in
Stroke: 110.0mm 4.3in
Valve type/No: Overhead 12
Transmission: Manual
No. of forward speeds: 4
Wheels driven: Rear
Brakes F/R: Drum/Drum
Kerb weight: 1219.9kg 2687.0lb
Fuel: 68.2L 15.0gal 18.0galUS

2268 Jaguar
SS 2.5-litre
1940 UK
90.0mph 144.8kmh
0-50mph 80.5kmh: 13.4secs
0-60mph 96.5kmh: 19.5secs
104.0bhp 77.5kW 105.4PS
@ 4500rpm
61.7bhp/ton 60.6bhp/tonne
39.0bhp/L 29.1kW/L 39.6PS/L
52.1ft/sec 15.9m/sec
20.0mpg 16.7mpgUS 14.1L/100km
Petrol 4-stroke piston
2664cc 162.5cu in
In-line 6 2 Carburettor
Bore: 73.0mm 2.9in
Stroke: 106.0mm 4.2in
Valve type/No: Overhead 12
Transmission: Manual
No. of forward speeds: 4
Wheels driven: Rear
Brakes F/R: Drum/Drum
Kerb weight: 1714.8kg 3777.0lb
Fuel: 63.7L 14.0gal 16.8galUS

2269 Jaguar
SS1 2.5-litre
1940 UK
83.3mph 134.0kmh
0-50mph 80.5kmh: 15.8secs
0-60mph 96.5kmh: 24.0secs
19.0mpg 15.8mpgUS 14.9L/100km
Petrol 4-stroke piston
2664cc 162.5cu in
In-line 6 2 Carburettor
Bore: 73.0mm 2.9in
Stroke: 106.0mm 4.2in
Valve type/No: Side 12
Transmission: Manual
No. of forward speeds: 4
Wheels driven: Rear
Brakes F/R: Drum/Drum
Kerb weight: 1381.5kg 3043.0lb
Fuel: 54.6L 12.0gal 14.4galUS

2270 Jaguar
3.5-litre
1948 UK
91.0mph 146.4kmh
0-50mph 80.5kmh: 11.9secs
0-60mph 96.5kmh: 16.8secs
125.0bhp 93.2kW 126.7PS
@ 4250rpm
76.9bhp/ton 75.6bhp/tonne
35.9bhp/L 26.7kW/L 36.4PS/L
51.1ft/sec 15.6m/sec
16.0mpg 13.3mpgUS 17.7L/100km
Petrol 4-stroke piston
3485cc 212.6cu in
In-line 6

Compression ratio: 7.2:1
Bore: 82.0mm 3.2in
Stroke: 110.0mm 4.3in
Valve type/No: Overhead 12
Transmission: Manual
No. of forward speeds: 4
Wheels driven: Rear
Brakes F/R: Drum/Drum
Wheelbase: 304.8cm 120.0in
Track F: 137.2cm 54.0in
Track R: 142.2cm 56.0in
Length: 472.4cm 186.0in
Width: 167.6cm 66.0in
Height: 154.9cm 61.0in
Ground clearance: 17.8cm 7.0in
Kerb weight: 1652.6kg 3640.0lb
Fuel: 63.7L 14.0gal 16.8galUS

2271 Jaguar

Mk IV
1948 UK
91.0mph 146.4kmh
0-50mph 80.5kmh: 11.9secs
0-60mph 96.5kmh: 16.8secs
0-1/4 mile: 20.5secs
125.0bhp 93.2kW 126.7PS
@ 4250rpm
184.0lbft 249.3Nm @ 2000rpm
76.9bhp/ton 75.6bhp/tonne
35.9bhp/L 26.7kW/L 36.4PS/L
51.1ft/sec 15.6m/sec
Petrol 4-stroke piston
3485cc 212.6cu in
In-line 6
Compression ratio: 7.2:1
Bore: 82.0mm 3.2in
Stroke: 110.0mm 4.3in
Valve type/No: Overhead 12
Transmission: Manual
No. of forward speeds: 4
Wheels driven: Rear
Wheelbase: 304.8cm 120.0in
Track F: 137.2cm 54.0in
Track R: 142.2cm 56.0in
Kerb weight: 1652.6kg 3640.0lb

2272 Jaguar

3.5-litre Mk V
1949 UK
91.0mph 146.4kmh
0-50mph 80.5kmh: 13.5secs
0-60mph 96.5kmh: 18.9secs
120.0bhp 89.5kW 121.7PS
@ 4500rpm
180.0lbft 243.9Nm @ 2300rpm
72.3bhp/ton 71.1bhp/tonne
34.4bhp/L 25.7kW/L 34.9PS/L
54.1ft/sec 16.5m/sec
19.0mph 30.6kmh/1000rpm
15.0mpg 12.5mpgUS 18.8L/100km
Petrol 4-stroke piston
3485cc 212.6cu in
In-line 6 2 Carburettor
Compression ratio: 6.7:1
Bore: 82.0mm 3.2in
Stroke: 110.0mm 4.3in
Valve type/No: Overhead 12
Transmission: Manual
No. of forward speeds: 4
Wheels driven: Rear
Springs F/R: Torsion bar/Leaf
Brakes F/R: Drum/Drum
Wheelbase: 304.8cm 120.0in
Track F: 142.2cm 56.0in
Track R: 146.1cm 57.5in
Length: 475.0cm 187.0in
Width: 174.0cm 68.5in
Height: 158.8cm 62.5in
Ground clearance: 17.8cm 7.0in
Kerb weight: 1687.5kg 3717.0lb
Fuel: 63.7L 14.0gal 16.8galUS

2273 Jaguar

XK120
1950 UK
126.0mph 202.7kmh
0-50mph 80.5kmh: 8.3secs
0-60mph 96.5kmh: 12.0secs
160.0bhp 119.3kW 162.2PS
@ 5100rpm
195.0lbft 264.2Nm @ 2500rpm
122.8bhp/ton 120.7bhp/tonne
46.5bhp/L 34.7kW/L 47.1PS/L
59.1ft/sec 18.0m/sec
22.0mph 35.4kmh/1000rpm
16.0mpg 13.3mpgUS 17.7L/100km
Petrol 4-stroke piston
3442cc 210.0cu in
In-line 6 2 Carburettor
Compression ratio: 8.0:1
Bore: 83.0mm 3.3in
Stroke: 106.0mm 4.2in
Valve type/No: Overhead 12
Transmission: Manual
No. of forward speeds: 4
Wheels driven: Rear
Springs F/R: Torsion bar/Leaf
Brakes F/R: Drum/Drum
Wheelbase: 259.1cm 102.0in
Track F: 129.5cm 51.0in
Track R: 127.0cm 50.0in
Length: 439.4cm 173.0in
Width: 156.2cm 61.5in
Height: 133.4cm 52.5in
Ground clearance: 18.3cm 7.2in
Kerb weight: 1325.2kg 2919.0lb
Fuel: 68.2L 15.0gal 18.0galUS

2274 Jaguar

C Type
1951 UK
151.0mph 243.0kmh
0-60mph 96.5kmh: 6.6secs
200.0bhp 149.1kW 202.8PS
@ 5800rpm
220.0lbft 298.1Nm @ 3900rpm
200.0bhp/ton 196.7bhp/tonne
58.1bhp/L 43.3kW/L 58.9PS/L
67.2ft/sec 20.5m/sec
Petrol 4-stroke piston
3442cc 210.0cu in
In-line 6 2 Carburettor
Compression ratio: 8.0:1
Bore: 83.0mm 3.3in
Stroke: 106.0mm 4.2in
Valve type/No: Overhead 12
Transmission: Manual
No. of forward speeds: 4
Wheels driven: Rear
Springs F/R: Torsion bar/Torsion bar
Brakes F/R: Drum/Drum
Steering: Rack & pinion
Wheelbase: 243.8cm 96.0in
Track F: 129.5cm 51.0in
Track R: 129.5cm 51.0in
Length: 398.8cm 157.0in
Width: 163.8cm 64.5in
Height: 108.0cm 42.5in
Kerb weight: 1017.0kg 2240.0lb
Fuel: 189.2L 41.6gal 50.0galUS

2275 Jaguar

XK120
1951 UK
122.0mph 196.3kmh
0-50mph 80.5kmh: 8.3secs
0-60mph 96.5kmh: 11.7secs
0-1/4 mile: 18.3secs
160.0bhp 119.3kW 162.2PS
@ 5400rpm
195.0lbft 264.2Nm @ 2500rpm
118.9bhp/ton 116.9bhp/tonne
46.5bhp/L 34.7kW/L 47.1PS/L
62.5ft/sec 19.1m/sec
22.1mph 35.6kmh/1000rpm
22.8mpg 19.0mpgUS 12.4L/100km
Petrol 4-stroke piston
3442cc 210.0cu in
In-line 6 2 Carburettor
Compression ratio: 8.0:1
Bore: 83.0mm 3.3in
Stroke: 106.0mm 4.2in
Valve type/No: Overhead 12
Transmission: Manual
No. of forward speeds: 4
Wheels driven: Rear
Springs F/R: Torsion bar/Leaf
Brakes F/R: Drum/Drum
Steering: Recirculating ball
Wheelbase: 259.1cm 102.0in
Track F: 129.5cm 51.0in
Track R: 127.0cm 50.0in
Length: 439.4cm 173.0in
Width: 156.2cm 61.5in
Height: 133.4cm 52.5in
Ground clearance: 18.0cm 7.1in
Kerb weight: 1368.8kg 3015.0lb
Fuel: 68.1L 15.0gal 18.0galUS

2276 Jaguar

XK140
1951 UK
125.0mph 201.1kmh
0-50mph 80.5kmh: 6.5secs
0-60mph 96.5kmh: 8.4secs
0-1/4 mile: 16.6secs
210.0bhp 156.6kW 212.9PS
@ 5750rpm
213.0lbft 288.6Nm @ 4000rpm
150.0bhp/ton 147.5bhp/tonne
61.0bhp/L 45.5kW/L 61.9PS/L
66.6ft/sec 20.3m/sec
23.1mph 37.2kmh/1000rpm
Petrol 4-stroke piston
3442cc 210.0cu in
In-line 6
Compression ratio: 8.0:1
Bore: 83.1mm 3.3in
Stroke: 105.9mm 4.2in
Valve type/No: Overhead 12
Transmission: Manual
No. of forward speeds: 4
Wheels driven: Rear
Wheelbase: 259.1cm 102.0in
Track F: 129.5cm 51.0in
Track R: 128.3cm 50.5in
Length: 449.6cm 177.0in
Width: 156.2cm 61.5in
Height: 133.4cm 52.5in
Ground clearance: 18.0cm 7.1in
Kerb weight: 1423.3kg 3135.0lb

2277 Jaguar

Mk VII
1952 UK
103.0mph 165.7kmh
0-50mph 80.5kmh: 9.3secs
0-60mph 96.5kmh: 13.4secs
0-1/4 mile: 19.3secs
160.0bhp 119.3kW 162.2PS
@ 5200rpm
195.0lbft 264.2Nm @ 2500rpm
92.0bhp/ton 90.5bhp/tonne
46.5bhp/L 34.7kW/L 47.1PS/L
60.2ft/sec 18.4m/sec
19.3mph 31.1kmh/1000rpm
19.0mpg 15.8mpgUS 14.9L/100km
Petrol 4-stroke piston
3442cc 210.0cu in
In-line 6
Compression ratio: 8.0:1
Bore: 83.0mm 3.3in
Stroke: 106.0mm 4.2in
Valve type/No: Overhead 12
Transmission: Manual
No. of forward speeds: 4
Wheels driven: Rear
Springs F/R: Torsion bar/Leaf
Brake system: PA
Brakes F/R: Drum/Drum
Wheelbase: 304.8cm 120.0in
Track F: 142.2cm 56.0in
Track R: 146.1cm 57.5in
Length: 499.1cm 196.5in
Width: 185.4cm 73.0in
Height: 160.0cm 63.0in
Ground clearance: 19.1cm 7.5in
Kerb weight: 1768.8kg 3896.0lb
Fuel: 77.3L 17.0gal 20.4galUS

2278 Jaguar

Mk VII
1953 UK
104.0mph 167.3kmh
0-50mph 80.5kmh: 9.9secs
0-60mph 96.5kmh: 13.6secs
0-1/4 mile: 19.3secs
160.0bhp 119.3kW 162.2PS
@ 5200rpm
195.0lbft 264.2Nm @ 2500rpm
92.7bhp/ton 91.2bhp/tonne
46.5bhp/L 34.7kW/L 47.1PS/L
60.2ft/sec 18.4m/sec
23.4mph 37.7kmh/1000rpm
20.0mpg 16.7mpgUS 14.1L/100km
Petrol 4-stroke piston
3442cc 210.0cu in
In-line 6
Compression ratio: 8.0:1
Bore: 83.0mm 3.3in
Stroke: 106.0mm 4.2in
Valve type/No: Overhead 12
Transmission: Manual with overdrive
No. of forward speeds: 5
Wheels driven: Rear
Springs F/R: Torsion bar/Leaf
Brakes F/R: Drum/Drum
Wheelbase: 304.8cm 120.0in
Track F: 143.5cm 56.5in
Track R: 147.3cm 58.0in
Length: 499.1cm 196.5in
Width: 185.4cm 73.0in
Height: 160.0cm 63.0in
Ground clearance: 19.1cm 7.5in
Kerb weight: 1754.3kg 3864.0lb
Fuel: 77.3L 17.0gal 20.4galUS

2279 Jaguar

XK120 Coupe
1953 UK
121.0mph 194.7kmh
0-50mph 80.5kmh: 7.5secs
0-60mph 96.5kmh: 9.9secs
0-1/4 mile: 17.3secs
180.0bhp 134.2kW 182.5PS
@ 5300rpm
203.0lbft 275.1Nm @ 4000rpm
132.8bhp/ton 130.5bhp/tonne
52.3bhp/L 39.0kW/L 53.0PS/L
61.4ft/sec 18.7m/sec
21.3mph 34.3kmh/1000rpm
16.2mpg 13.5mpgUS 17.4L/100km
Petrol 4-stroke piston
3442cc 210.0cu in
In-line 6
Compression ratio: 8.0:1
Bore: 83.0mm 3.3in
Stroke: 106.0mm 4.2in
Valve type/No: Overhead 12
Transmission: Manual
No. of forward speeds: 4
Wheels driven: Rear
Springs F/R: Torsion bar/Leaf
Brakes F/R: Drum/Drum
Wheelbase: 259.1cm 102.0in
Track F: 129.5cm 51.0in
Track R: 127.0cm 50.0in
Length: 439.4cm 173.0in
Width: 157.5cm 62.0in
Height: 135.9cm 53.5in
Ground clearance: 18.3cm 7.2in
Kerb weight: 1378.8kg 3037.0lb
Fuel: 63.7L 14.0gal 16.8galUS

2280 Jaguar

XK120C
1953 UK
141.0mph 226.9kmh
0-50mph 80.5kmh: 5.0secs
0-60mph 96.5kmh: 6.6secs
0-1/4 mile: 15.3secs
210.0bhp 156.6kW 212.9PS
@ 6000rpm
220.0lbft 298.1Nm @ 4000rpm
210.0bhp/ton 206.5bhp/tonne
61.0bhp/L 45.5kW/L 61.9PS/L
69.5ft/sec 21.2m/sec
21.4mph 34.4kmh/1000rpm
Petrol 4-stroke piston
3442cc 210.0cu in
In-line 6
Compression ratio: 8.0:1
Bore: 83.1mm 3.3in
Stroke: 105.9mm 4.2in
Valve type/No: Overhead 12
Transmission: Manual
No. of forward speeds: 4
Wheels driven: Rear
Wheelbase: 243.8cm 96.0in
Track F: 129.5cm 51.0in
Track R: 127.0cm 50.0in
Kerb weight: 1017.0kg 2240.0lb

2281 Jaguar

XK120M
1953 UK
120.8mph 194.4kmh
0-50mph 80.5kmh: 6.7secs
0-60mph 96.5kmh: 8.5secs
0-1/4 mile: 16.7secs
180.0bhp 134.2kW 182.5PS
@ 5300rpm
203.0lbft 275.1Nm @ 4000rpm
130.1bhp/ton 127.9bhp/tonne
52.3bhp/L 39.0kW/L 53.0PS/L
61.4ft/sec 18.7m/sec
21.3mph 34.3kmh/1000rpm
18.3mpg 15.2mpgUS 15.5L/100km
Petrol 4-stroke piston
3442cc 210.0cu in
In-line 6
Compression ratio: 8.0:1
Bore: 83.0mm 3.3in
Stroke: 106.0mm 4.2in
Valve type/No: Overhead 12

Transmission: Manual
No. of forward speeds: 4
Wheels driven: Rear
Wheelbase: 259.1cm 102.0in
Track F: 129.5cm 51.0in
Track R: 127.0cm 50.0in
Kerb weight: 1407.4kg 3100.0lb

2282 Jaguar

Mk VII
1955 UK
106.3mph 171.0kmh
0-50mph 80.5kmh: 8.4secs
0-60mph 96.5kmh: 11.6secs
0-1/4 mile: 18.5secs
190.0bhp 141.7kW 192.6PS
@ 5500rpm
203.0lbft 275.1Nm @ 3000rpm
105.7bhp/ton 104.0bhp/tonne
55.2bhp/L 41.2kW/L 56.0PS/L
63.7ft/sec 19.4m/sec
19.4mph 31.2kmh/1000rpm
Petrol 4-stroke piston
3441cc 209.9cu in
In-line 6
Compression ratio: 8.0:1
Bore: 83.0mm 3.3in
Stroke: 105.9mm 4.2in
Valve type/No: Overhead 12
Transmission: Automatic
No. of forward speeds: 3
Wheels driven: Rear
Wheelbase: 304.8cm 120.0in
Track F: 142.2cm 56.0in
Track R: 146.1cm 57.5in
Kerb weight: 1827.3kg 4025.0lb

2283 Jaguar

XK140MC
1955 UK
120.3mph 193.6kmh
0-50mph 80.5kmh: 6.5secs
0-60mph 96.5kmh: 8.4secs
0-1/4 mile: 16.6secs
210.0bhp 156.6kW 212.9PS
@ 5750rpm
213.0lbft 288.6Nm @ 4000rpm
150.0bhp/ton 147.5bhp/tonne
61.0bhp/L 45.5kW/L 61.9PS/L
66.6ft/sec 20.3m/sec
23.1mph 37.2kmh/1000rpm
Petrol 4-stroke piston
3442cc 210.0cu in
In-line 6
Compression ratio: 8.0:1
Bore: 83.1mm 3.3in
Stroke: 105.9mm 4.2in
Valve type/No: Overhead 12
Transmission: Manual
No. of forward speeds: 4
Wheels driven: Rear
Wheelbase: 259.1cm 102.0in
Track F: 129.5cm 51.0in
Track R: 128.3cm 50.5in
Kerb weight: 1423.3kg 3135.0lb

2284 Jaguar

2.4 Sedan
1956 UK
101.1mph 162.7kmh
0-50mph 80.5kmh: 10.0secs
0-60mph 96.5kmh: 13.1secs
0-1/4 mile: 19.0secs
112.0bhp 83.5kW 113.5PS
@ 5750rpm
140.0lbft 189.7Nm @ 2000rpm
82.4bhp/ton 81.0bhp/tonne
45.1bhp/L 33.6kW/L 45.7PS/L
48.1ft/sec 14.7m/sec
Petrol 4-stroke piston
2483cc 151.5cu in
In-line 6
Compression ratio: 8.0:1
Bore: 83.1mm 3.3in
Stroke: 76.5mm 3.0in
Valve type/No: Overhead 12
Transmission: Manual
No. of forward speeds: 4
Wheels driven: Rear
Wheelbase: 272.8cm 107.4in
Track F: 138.7cm 54.6in
Track R: 127.3cm 50.1in
Kerb weight: 1382.4kg 3045.0lb

2285 Jaguar

D Type
1956 UK
192.0mph 308.9kmh
0-60mph 96.5kmh: 4.7secs
0-1/4 mile: 13.7secs
285.0bhp 212.5kW 288.9PS
@ 5750rpm
242.0lbft 327.9Nm @ 4000rpm
298.3bhp/ton 293.3bhp/tonne
75.4bhp/L 56.2kW/L 76.4PS/L
66.6ft/sec 20.3m/sec
Petrol 4-stroke piston
3781cc 230.7cu in
In-line 6 3 Carburettor
Compression ratio: 9.0:1
Bore: 87.0mm 3.4in
Stroke: 106.0mm 4.2in
Valve type/No: Overhead 12
Transmission: Manual
No. of forward speeds: 4
Wheels driven: Rear
Springs F/R: Torsion bar/Torsion bar
Brakes F/R: Disc/Disc
Steering: Rack & pinion
Wheelbase: 230.1cm 90.6in
Track F: 127.0cm 50.0in
Track R: 127.0cm 50.0in
Length: 410.2cm 161.5in
Width: 166.1cm 65.4in
Height: 114.3cm 45.0in
Kerb weight: 971.6kg 2140.0lb

2286 Jaguar

Mk VII Auto
1956 UK
103.0mph 165.7kmh
0-50mph 80.5kmh: 10.1secs
0-60mph 96.5kmh: 14.3secs
0-1/4 mile: 19.7secs
190.0bhp 141.7kW 192.6PS
@ 5500rpm
203.0lbft 275.1Nm @ 3000rpm
108.0bhp/ton 106.2bhp/tonne
55.2bhp/L 41.2kW/L 56.0PS/L
63.7ft/sec 19.4m/sec
19.3mph 31.1kmh/1000rpm
18.5mpg 15.4mpgUS 15.3L/100km
Petrol 4-stroke piston
3442cc 210.0cu in
In-line 6
Compression ratio: 8.0:1
Bore: 83.0mm 3.3in
Stroke: 106.0mm 4.2in
Valve type/No: Overhead 12
Transmission: Automatic
No. of forward speeds: 3
Wheels driven: Rear
Springs F/R: Torsion bar/Leaf
Brake system: PA
Brakes F/R: Drum/Drum
Wheelbase: 304.8cm 120.0in
Track F: 142.2cm 56.0in
Track R: 147.3cm 58.0in
Length: 499.1cm 196.5in
Width: 185.4cm 73.0in
Height: 160.0cm 63.0in
Ground clearance: 19.1cm 7.5in
Kerb weight: 1789.2kg 3941.0lb
Fuel: 77.3L 17.0gal 20.4galUS

2287 Jaguar

XK 140
1956 UK
129.5mph 208.4kmh
0-50mph 80.5kmh: 7.5secs
0-60mph 96.5kmh: 11.0secs
0-1/4 mile: 17.4secs
210.0bhp 156.6kW 212.9PS
@ 5750rpm
213.0lbft 288.6Nm @ 4000rpm
150.0bhp/ton 147.5bhp/tonne
61.0bhp/L 45.5kW/L 61.9PS/L
66.6ft/sec 20.3m/sec
25.1mph 40.4kmh/1000rpm
21.7mpg 18.1mpgUS 13.0L/100km
Petrol 4-stroke piston
3442cc 210.0cu in
In-line 6
Compression ratio: 8.0:1
Bore: 83.0mm 3.3in
Stroke: 106.0mm 4.2in
Valve type/No: Overhead 12
Transmission: Manual with overdrive
No. of forward speeds: 5
Wheels driven: Rear
Springs F/R: Torsion bar/Leaf
Brakes F/R: Drum/Drum
Wheelbase: 259.1cm 102.0in
Track F: 130.8cm 51.5in
Track R: 130.6cm 51.4in
Length: 447.0cm 176.0in
Width: 163.8cm 64.5in
Height: 139.7cm 55.0in
Ground clearance: 18.3cm 7.2in
Kerb weight: 1423.7kg 3136.0lb
Fuel: 63.7L 14.0gal 16.8galUS

2288 Jaguar

2.4 Saloon
1957 UK
104.0mph 167.3kmh
0-50mph 80.5kmh: 11.5secs
0-60mph 96.5kmh: 15.8secs
0-1/4 mile: 20.5secs
112.0bhp 83.5kW 113.5PS
@ 5750rpm
140.0lbft 189.7Nm @ 2000rpm
82.6bhp/ton 81.2bhp/tonne
45.1bhp/L 33.6kW/L 45.7PS/L
48.1ft/sec 14.7m/sec
23.0mph 37.0kmh/1000rpm
23.1mpg 19.2mpgUS 12.2L/100km
Petrol 4-stroke piston
2483cc 151.5cu in
In-line 6
Compression ratio: 8.0:1
Bore: 83.0mm 3.3in
Stroke: 76.5mm 3.0in
Valve type/No: Overhead 12
Transmission: Manual with overdrive
No. of forward speeds: 5
Wheels driven: Rear
Springs F/R: Coil/Leaf
Brake system: PA
Brakes F/R: Drum/Drum
Wheelbase: 272.8cm 107.4in
Track F: 138.7cm 54.6in
Track R: 127.3cm 50.1in
Length: 459.0cm 180.7in
Width: 169.4cm 66.7in
Height: 146.1cm 57.5in
Ground clearance: 17.8cm 7.0in
Kerb weight: 1379.2kg 3038.0lb
Fuel: 54.6L 12.0gal 14.4galUS

2289 Jaguar

Mk VIII
1957 UK
109.0mph 175.4kmh
0-50mph 80.5kmh: 8.7secs
0-60mph 96.5kmh: 11.6secs
0-1/4 mile: 18.4secs
190.0bhp 141.7kW 192.6PS
@ 5500rpm
203.0lbft 275.1Nm @ 3000rpm
105.3bhp/ton 103.6bhp/tonne
55.2bhp/L 41.2kW/L 56.0PS/L
63.7ft/sec 19.4m/sec
19.3mph 31.1kmh/1000rpm
17.9mpg 14.9mpgUS 15.8L/100km
Petrol 4-stroke piston
3442cc 210.0cu in
In-line 6
Compression ratio: 8.0:1
Bore: 83.0mm 3.3in
Stroke: 106.0mm 4.2in
Valve type/No: Overhead 12
Transmission: Automatic
No. of forward speeds: 3
Wheels driven: Rear
Springs F/R: Torsion bar/Leaf
Brake system: PA
Brakes F/R: Drum/Drum
Wheelbase: 304.8cm 120.0in
Track F: 143.5cm 56.5in
Track R: 147.3cm 58.0in
Length: 499.1cm 196.5in
Width: 185.4cm 73.0in
Height: 160.0cm 63.0in
Ground clearance: 19.1cm 7.5in
Kerb weight: 1834.2kg 4040.0lb
Fuel: 77.3L 17.0gal 20.4galUS

2290 Jaguar

XK150
1957 UK
121.6mph 195.7kmh
0-50mph 80.5kmh: 7.3secs
0-60mph 96.5kmh: 9.5secs
0-1/4 mile: 17.1secs
210.0bhp 156.6kW 212.9PS
@ 5500rpm
216.0lbft 292.7Nm @ 3000rpm
152.2bhp/ton 149.7bhp/tonne
61.0bhp/L 45.5kW/L 61.9PS/L
63.7ft/sec 19.4m/sec
Petrol 4-stroke piston
3442cc 210.0cu in
In-line 6
Compression ratio: 8.0:1
Bore: 83.1mm 3.3in
Stroke: 105.9mm 4.2in
Valve type/No: Overhead 12
Transmission: Manual
No. of forward speeds: 4
Wheels driven: Rear
Wheelbase: 259.1cm 102.0in
Track F: 131.1cm 51.6in
Track R: 131.1cm 51.6in
Kerb weight: 1402.9kg 3090.0lb

2291 Jaguar

XKSS
1957 UK
149.0mph 239.7kmh
0-50mph 80.5kmh: 4.1secs
0-60mph 96.5kmh: 5.2secs
0-1/4 mile: 14.1secs
260.0bhp 193.9kW 263.6PS
@ 6000rpm
260.0lbft 352.3Nm @ 4000rpm
261.2bhp/ton 256.8bhp/tonne
75.5bhp/L 56.3kW/L 76.6PS/L
69.5ft/sec 21.2m/sec
Petrol 4-stroke piston
3442cc 210.0cu in
In-line 6
Compression ratio: 9.0:1
Bore: 83.1mm 3.3in
Stroke: 105.9mm 4.2in
Valve type/No: Overhead 12
Transmission: Manual
No. of forward speeds: 4
Wheels driven: Rear
Wheelbase: 230.1cm 90.6in
Track F: 127.0cm 50.0in
Track R: 121.9cm 48.0in
Kerb weight: 1012.4kg 2230.0lb

2292 Jaguar

3.4
1958 UK
121.0mph 194.7kmh
0-50mph 80.5kmh: 7.0secs
0-60mph 96.5kmh: 9.1secs
0-1/4 mile: 17.2secs
210.0bhp 156.6kW 212.9PS
@ 5500rpm
216.0lbft 292.7Nm @ 3000rpm
147.4bhp/ton 144.9bhp/tonne
62.8bhp/L 46.9kW/L 63.7PS/L
63.7ft/sec 19.4m/sec
26.4mph 42.5kmh/1000rpm
16.0mpg 13.3mpgUS 17.7L/100km
Petrol 4-stroke piston
3342cc 203.9cu in
In-line 6 2 Carburettor
Compression ratio: 8.0:1
Bore: 83.0mm 3.3in
Stroke: 106.0mm 4.2in
Valve type/No: Overhead 12
Transmission: Manual with overdrive
No. of forward speeds: 5
Wheels driven: Rear
Springs F/R: Coil/Leaf
Brake system: PA
Brakes F/R: Disc/Disc
Steering: Recirculating ball
Wheelbase: 272.8cm 107.4in
Track F: 138.7cm 54.6in
Track R: 127.5cm 50.2in
Length: 459.0cm 180.7in
Width: 169.4cm 66.7in
Height: 146.1cm 57.5in
Ground clearance: 17.8cm 7.0in
Kerb weight: 1449.2kg 3192.0lb
Fuel: 54.6L 12.0gal 14.4galUS

2293 Jaguar

XK150
1958 UK
125.5mph 201.9kmh
0-50mph 80.5kmh: 6.5secs
0-60mph 96.5kmh: 8.5secs
0-1/4 mile: 16.9secs
210.0bhp 156.6kW 212.9PS
@ 5500rpm
216.0lbft 292.7Nm @ 3000rpm

145.8bhp/ton 143.4bhp/tonne
61.0bhp/L 45.5kW/L 61.9PS/L
63.7ft/sec 19.4m/sec
25.1mph 40.4kmh/1000rpm
20.5mpg 17.1mpgUS 13.8L/100km
Petrol 4-stroke piston
3442cc 210.0cu in
In-line 6
Compression ratio: 8.0:1
Bore: 83.0mm 3.3in
Stroke: 106.0mm 4.2in
Valve type/No: Overhead 12
Transmission: Manual with overdrive
No. of forward speeds: 5
Wheels driven: Rear
Springs F/R: Torsion bar/Leaf
Brake system: PA
Brakes F/R: Disc/Disc
Wheelbase: 259.1cm 102.0in
Track F: 131.1cm 51.6in
Track R: 131.1cm 51.6in
Length: 449.6cm 177.0in
Width: 163.8cm 64.5in
Height: 139.7cm 55.0in
Ground clearance: 18.3cm 7.2in
Kerb weight: 1464.6kg 3226.0lb
Fuel: 63.7L 14.0gal 16.8galUS

2294 Jaguar

XK150S
1958 UK
136.0mph 218.8kmh
0-50mph 80.5kmh: 5.6secs
0-60mph 96.5kmh: 7.3secs
0-1/4 mile: 15.1secs
250.0bhp 186.4kW 253.5PS
@ 5500rpm
240.0lbft 325.2Nm @ 4500rpm
177.2bhp/ton 174.3bhp/tonne
72.6bhp/L 54.2kW/L 73.6PS/L
63.7ft/sec 19.4m/sec
25.6mph 41.2kmh/1000rpm
Petrol 4-stroke piston
3442cc 210.0cu in
In-line 6
Compression ratio: 9.0:1
Bore: 83.1mm 3.3in
Stroke: 105.9mm 4.2in
Valve type/No: Overhead 12
Transmission: Manual with overdrive
Wheels driven: Rear
Wheelbase: 259.1cm 102.0in
Track F: 131.1cm 51.6in
Track R: 130.6cm 51.4in
Length: 449.6cm 177.0in
Width: 163.8cm 64.5in
Height: 137.2cm 54.0in
Kerb weight: 1434.6kg 3160.0lb

2295 Jaguar

XK150S
1959 UK
136.0mph 218.8kmh
0-50mph 80.5kmh: 6.2secs
0-60mph 96.5kmh: 8.9secs
0-1/4 mile: 16.2secs
250.0bhp 186.4kW 253.5PS
@ 5500rpm
240.0lbft 325.2Nm @ 4500rpm
172.4bhp/ton 169.5bhp/tonne
72.6bhp/L 54.2kW/L 73.6PS/L
63.7ft/sec 19.4m/sec
26.4mph 42.5kmh/1000rpm
17.0mpg 14.2mpgUS 16.6L/100km
Petrol 4-stroke piston
3442cc 210.0cu in
In-line 6
Compression ratio: 9.0:1
Bore: 83.0mm 3.3in
Stroke: 106.0mm 4.2in
Valve type/No: Overhead 12
Transmission: Manual with overdrive
No. of forward speeds: 5
Wheels driven: Rear
Springs F/R: Torsion bar/Leaf
Brake system: PA
Brakes F/R: Disc/Disc
Wheelbase: 259.1cm 102.0in
Track F: 131.3cm 51.7in
Track R: 131.1cm 51.6in
Length: 447.0cm 176.0in
Width: 163.8cm 64.5in
Height: 133.4cm 52.5in
Ground clearance: 18.0cm 7.1in
Kerb weight: 1474.6kg 3248.0lb
Fuel: 63.7L 14.0gal 16.8galUS

2296 Jaguar

3.4
1960 UK
120.0mph 193.1kmh
0-50mph 80.5kmh: 7.9secs
0-60mph 96.5kmh: 10.4secs
0-1/4 mile: 17.6secs
210.0bhp 156.6kW 212.9PS
@ 5500rpm
216.0lbft 292.7Nm @ 3000rpm
143.8bhp/ton 141.4bhp/tonne
61.0bhp/L 45.5kW/L 61.9PS/L
63.7ft/sec 19.4m/sec
26.6mph 42.8kmh/1000rpm
Petrol 4-stroke piston
3442cc 210.0cu in
In-line 6 1 Carburettor
Compression ratio: 8.0:1
Bore: 83.1mm 3.3in
Stroke: 105.9mm 4.2in
Valve type/No: Overhead 12
Transmission: Manual with overdrive
Wheels driven: Rear
Wheelbase: 272.8cm 107.4in
Track F: 139.7cm 55.0in
Track R: 135.6cm 53.4in
Length: 459.7cm 181.0in
Width: 169.4cm 66.7in
Height: 146.1cm 57.5in
Kerb weight: 1484.6kg 3270.0lb

2297 Jaguar

3.8 Sedan
1960 UK
125.0mph 201.1kmh
0-50mph 80.5kmh: 7.0secs
0-60mph 96.5kmh: 9.2secs
0-1/4 mile: 17.0secs
220.0bhp 164.0kW 223.0PS
@ 5500rpm
240.0lbft 325.2Nm @ 3000rpm
144.9bhp/ton 142.5bhp/tonne
58.2bhp/L 43.4kW/L 59.0PS/L
63.7ft/sec 19.4m/sec
26.5mph 42.6kmh/1000rpm
Petrol 4-stroke piston
3781cc 230.7cu in
In-line 6 1 Carburettor
Compression ratio: 8.0:1
Bore: 87.1mm 3.4in
Stroke: 106.0mm 4.2in
Valve type/No: Overhead 12
Transmission: Manual with overdrive
Wheels driven: Front
Wheelbase: 272.8cm 107.4in
Track F: 141.0cm 55.5in
Track R: 137.4cm 54.1in
Length: 459.7cm 181.0in
Width: 169.7cm 66.8in
Height: 145.8cm 57.4in
Kerb weight: 1543.6kg 3400.0lb

2298 Jaguar

E Type Coupe
1961 UK
151.7mph 244.1kmh
0-50mph 80.5kmh: 5.6secs
0-60mph 96.5kmh: 6.9secs
0-1/4 mile: 14.7secs
265.0bhp 197.6kW 268.7PS
@ 5500rpm
260.0lbft 352.3Nm @ 4000rpm
219.7bhp/ton 216.0bhp/tonne
70.1bhp/L 52.3kW/L 71.1PS/L
63.7ft/sec 19.4m/sec
23.0mph 37.0kmh/1000rpm
17.9mpg 14.9mpgUS 15.8L/100km
Petrol 4-stroke piston
3781cc 230.7cu in
In-line 6
Compression ratio: 9.0:1
Bore: 87.0mm 3.4in
Stroke: 106.0mm 4.2in
Valve type/No: Overhead 12
Transmission: Manual
No. of forward speeds: 4
Wheels driven: Rear
Springs F/R: Torsion bar/Coil
Brake system: PA
Brakes F/R: Disc/Disc
Wheelbase: 243.8cm 96.0in
Track F: 127.0cm 50.0in
Track R: 127.0cm 50.0in
Length: 445.3cm 175.3in
Width: 165.6cm 65.2in
Height: 121.9cm 48.0in
Ground clearance: 12.7cm 5.0in
Kerb weight: 1226.7kg 2702.0lb
Fuel: 63.7L 14.0gal 16.8galUS

2299 Jaguar

XKE
1961 UK
150.0mph 241.4kmh
0-50mph 80.5kmh: 5.7secs
0-60mph 96.5kmh: 7.4secs
0-1/4 mile: 15.2secs
265.0bhp 197.6kW 268.7PS
@ 5500rpm
260.0lbft 352.3Nm @ 4000rpm
218.2bhp/ton 214.6bhp/tonne
70.1bhp/L 52.3kW/L 71.1PS/L
63.7ft/sec 19.4m/sec
23.6mph 38.0kmh/1000rpm
Petrol 4-stroke piston
3781cc 230.7cu in
In-line 6 1 Carburettor
Compression ratio: 9.0:1
Bore: 87.1mm 3.4in
Stroke: 105.9mm 4.2in
Valve type/No: Overhead 24
Transmission: Manual
No. of forward speeds: 4
Wheels driven: Rear
Wheelbase: 243.8cm 96.0in
Track F: 127.0cm 50.0in
Track R: 127.0cm 50.0in
Length: 445.3cm 175.3in
Width: 165.6cm 65.2in
Height: 122.2cm 48.1in
Ground clearance: 14.0cm 5.5in
Kerb weight: 1234.9kg 2720.0lb

2300 Jaguar

Mk X
1962 UK
120.0mph 193.1kmh
0-50mph 80.5kmh: 9.1secs
0-60mph 96.5kmh: 12.1secs
0-1/4 mile: 18.5secs
250.0bhp 186.4kW 253.5PS
@ 5500rpm
250.0lbft 338.8Nm @ 4000rpm
134.0bhp/ton 131.8bhp/tonne
66.1bhp/L 49.3kW/L 67.0PS/L
63.7ft/sec 19.4m/sec
21.2mph 34.1kmh/1000rpm
14.1mpg 11.7mpgUS 20.0L/100km
Petrol 4-stroke piston
3781cc 230.7cu in
In-line 6 3 Carburettor
Compression ratio: 8.0:1
Bore: 87.0mm 3.4in
Stroke: 106.0mm 4.2in
Valve type/No: Overhead 12
Transmission: Automatic
No. of forward speeds: 3
Wheels driven: Rear
Springs F/R: Coil/Coil
Brake system: PA
Brakes F/R: Disc/Disc
Steering: Recirculating ball PA
Wheelbase: 304.8cm 120.0in
Track F: 147.3cm 58.0in
Track R: 147.3cm 58.0in
Length: 523.2cm 206.0in
Width: 193.0cm 76.0in
Height: 138.9cm 54.7in
Ground clearance: 13.7cm 5.4in
Kerb weight: 1897.3kg 4179.0lb
Fuel: 91.0L 20.0gal 24.0galUS

2301 Jaguar

3.8 Mk II
1963 UK
126.0mph 202.7kmh
0-50mph 80.5kmh: 6.4secs
0-60mph 96.5kmh: 8.5secs
0-1/4 mile: 16.3secs
220.0bhp 164.0kW 223.0PS
@ 5500rpm
240.0lbft 325.2Nm @ 3000rpm
147.1bhp/ton 144.6bhp/tonne
58.2bhp/L 43.4kW/L 59.0PS/L
63.7ft/sec 19.4m/sec
26.4mph 42.5kmh/1000rpm
15.7mpg 13.1mpgUS 18.0L/100km
Petrol 4-stroke piston
3781cc 230.7cu in
In-line 6
Compression ratio: 8.0:1
Bore: 87.0mm 3.4in
Stroke: 106.0mm 4.2in
Valve type/No: Overhead 12
Transmission: Manual with overdrive
No. of forward speeds: 5
Wheels driven: Rear
Springs F/R: Coil/Leaf
Brake system: PA
Brakes F/R: Disc/Disc
Wheelbase: 272.5cm 107.3in
Track F: 139.7cm 55.0in
Track R: 135.4cm 53.3in
Length: 459.0cm 180.7in
Width: 169.4cm 66.7in
Height: 146.1cm 57.5in
Ground clearance: 17.8cm 7.0in
Kerb weight: 1520.9kg 3350.0lb
Fuel: 54.6L 12.0gal 14.4galUS

2302 Jaguar

3.8 Mk II Automatic
1963 UK
120.6mph 194.0kmh
0-50mph 80.5kmh: 7.2secs
0-60mph 96.5kmh: 9.8secs
0-1/4 mile: 17.2secs
220.0bhp 164.0kW 223.0PS
@ 5500rpm
240.0lbft 325.2Nm @ 3000rpm
143.1bhp/ton 140.7bhp/tonne
58.2bhp/L 43.4kW/L 59.0PS/L
63.7ft/sec 19.4m/sec
21.4mph 34.4kmh/1000rpm
17.3mpg 14.4mpgUS 16.3L/100km
Petrol 4-stroke piston
3781cc 230.7cu in
In-line 6 2 Carburettor
Compression ratio: 8.0:1
Bore: 87.0mm 3.4in
Stroke: 106.0mm 4.2in
Valve type/No: Overhead 12
Transmission: Automatic
No. of forward speeds: 3
Wheels driven: Rear
Springs F/R: Coil/Leaf
Brake system: PA
Brakes F/R: Disc/Disc
Steering: Recirculating ball PA
Wheelbase: 271.8cm 107.0in
Track F: 139.7cm 55.0in
Track R: 134.6cm 53.0in
Length: 459.0cm 180.7in
Width: 168.9cm 66.5in
Height: 146.1cm 57.5in
Ground clearance: 17.8cm 7.0in
Kerb weight: 1563.6kg 3444.0lb
Fuel: 54.6L 12.0gal 14.4galUS

2303 Jaguar

E Type Coupe
1963 UK
155.0mph 249.4kmh
0-50mph 80.5kmh: 5.5secs
0-60mph 96.5kmh: 7.2secs
0-1/4 mile: 15.1secs
265.0bhp 197.6kW 268.7PS
@ 5500rpm
260.0lbft 352.3Nm @ 4000rpm
212.0bhp/ton 208.5bhp/tonne
70.1bhp/L 52.3kW/L 71.1PS/L
63.7ft/sec 19.4m/sec
24.4mph 39.3kmh/1000rpm
18.6mpg 15.5mpgUS 15.2L/100km
Petrol 4-stroke piston
3781cc 230.7cu in
In-line 6 3 Carburettor
Compression ratio: 9.0:1
Bore: 87.0mm 3.4in
Stroke: 106.0mm 4.2in
Valve type/No: Overhead 12
Transmission: Manual
No. of forward speeds: 4
Wheels driven: Rear
Springs F/R: Torsion bar/Coil
Brake system: PA
Brakes F/R: Disc/Disc
Steering: Rack & pinion
Wheelbase: 243.8cm 96.0in
Track F: 127.0cm 50.0in
Track R: 127.0cm 50.0in
Length: 445.3cm 175.3in
Width: 165.6cm 65.2in
Height: 121.9cm 48.0in
Ground clearance: 14.0cm 5.5in
Kerb weight: 1271.2kg 2800.0lb
Fuel: 63.7L 14.0gal 16.8galUS

2304 Jaguar
3.8S Sedan
1964 UK
116.0mph 186.6kmh
0-50mph 80.5kmh: 9.0secs
0-60mph 96.5kmh: 11.5secs
0-1/4 mile: 18.9secs
220.0bhp 164.0kW 223.0PS
@ 5500rpm
240.0lbft 325.2Nm @ 3000rpm
132.1bhp/ton 129.9bhp/tonne
58.2bhp/L 43.4kW/L 59.0PS/L
63.7ft/sec 19.4m/sec
21.4mph 34.4kmh/1000rpm
Petrol 4-stroke piston
3781cc 230.7cu in
In-line 6 2 Carburettor
Compression ratio: 9.0:1
Bore: 87.0mm 3.4in
Stroke: 105.9mm 4.2in
Valve type/No: Overhead 12
Transmission: Automatic
No. of forward speeds: 3
Wheels driven: Rear
Springs F/R: Coil/Coil
Brakes F/R: Disc/Disc
Steering: Recirculating ball
Wheelbase: 272.3cm 107.2in
Track F: 140.5cm 55.3in
Track R: 134.1cm 52.8in
Length: 477.0cm 187.8in
Width: 169.7cm 66.8in
Height: 138.4cm 54.5in
Ground clearance: 17.8cm 7.0in
Kerb weight: 1693.4kg 3730.0lb
Fuel: 62.4L 13.7gal 16.5galUS

2305 Jaguar
4.2 litre Mk X
1964 UK
123.0mph 197.9kmh
0-50mph 80.5kmh: 7.2secs
0-60mph 96.5kmh: 9.9secs
0-1/4 mile: 17.0secs
265.0bhp 197.6kW 268.7PS
@ 5400rpm
283.0lbft 383.5Nm @ 4000rpm
143.0bhp/ton 140.6bhp/tonne
62.6bhp/L 46.7kW/L 63.4PS/L
62.5ft/sec 19.1m/sec
21.4mph 34.4kmh/1000rpm
14.5mpg 12.1mpgUS 19.5L/100km
Petrol 4-stroke piston
4235cc 258.4cu in
In-line 6 3 Carburettor
Compression ratio: 9.0:1
Bore: 92.0mm 3.6in
Stroke: 106.0mm 4.2in
Valve type/No: Overhead 12
Transmission: Automatic
No. of forward speeds: 3
Wheels driven: Rear
Springs F/R: Coil/Coil
Brake system: PA
Brakes F/R: Disc/Disc
Steering: Recirculating ball PA
Wheelbase: 304.8cm 120.0in
Track F: 147.3cm 58.0in
Track R: 147.3cm 58.0in
Length: 523.2cm 206.0in
Width: 193.0cm 76.0in
Height: 138.9cm 54.7in
Ground clearance: 13.7cm 5.4in
Kerb weight: 1884.5kg 4151.0lb
Fuel: 91.0L 20.0gal 24.0galUS

2306 Jaguar
XKE
1964 UK
150.0mph 241.4kmh
0-50mph 80.5kmh: 5.7secs
0-60mph 96.5kmh: 7.4secs
0-1/4 mile: 15.6secs
265.0bhp 197.6kW 268.7PS
@ 5500rpm
260.0lbft 352.3Nm @ 4000rpm
204.7bhp/ton 201.3bhp/tonne
70.1bhp/L 52.3kW/L 71.1PS/L
63.7ft/sec 19.4m/sec
23.6mph 38.0kmh/1000rpm
Petrol 4-stroke piston
3781cc 230.7cu in
In-line 6 3 Carburettor
Compression ratio: 9.0:1
Bore: 87.1mm 3.4in
Stroke: 105.9mm 4.2in
Valve type/No: Overhead 12
Transmission: Manual
No. of forward speeds: 4
Wheels driven: Rear
Springs F/R: Torsion bar/Coil
Brakes F/R: Disc/Disc
Steering: Rack & pinion
Wheelbase: 243.8cm 96.0in
Track F: 127.0cm 50.0in
Track R: 127.0cm 50.0in
Length: 444.5cm 175.0in
Width: 165.6cm 65.2in
Height: 122.2cm 48.1in
Ground clearance: 14.0cm 5.5in
Kerb weight: 1316.6kg 2900.0lb
Fuel: 62.4L 13.7gal 16.5galUS

2307 Jaguar
3.8S
1965 UK
123.0mph 197.9kmh
0-50mph 80.5kmh: 7.5secs
0-60mph 96.5kmh: 10.4secs
0-1/4 mile: 17.5secs
210.0bhp 156.6kW 212.9PS
@ 5500rpm
240.0lbft 325.2Nm @ 3000rpm
129.0bhp/ton 126.8bhp/tonne
55.5bhp/L 41.4kW/L 56.3PS/L
63.7ft/sec 19.4m/sec
25.9mph 41.7kmh/1000rpm
12.8mpg 10.7mpgUS 22.1L/100km
Petrol 4-stroke piston
3781cc 230.7cu in
In-line 6 2 Carburettor
Compression ratio: 8.0:1
Bore: 87.0mm 3.4in
Stroke: 106.0mm 4.2in
Valve type/No: Overhead 12
Transmission: Manual with overdrive
No. of forward speeds: 5
Wheels driven: Rear
Springs F/R: Coil/Coil
Brake system: PA
Brakes F/R: Disc/Disc
Steering: Recirculating ball
Wheelbase: 272.8cm 107.4in
Track F: 140.2cm 55.2in
Track R: 137.7cm 54.2in
Length: 477.0cm 187.8in
Width: 169.4cm 66.7in
Height: 138.4cm 54.5in
Ground clearance: 17.8cm 7.0in
Kerb weight: 1655.7kg 3647.0lb
Fuel: 63.7L 14.0gal 16.8galUS

2308 Jaguar
4.2 litre Mk X Overdrive
1965 UK
124.0mph 199.5kmh
0-50mph 80.5kmh: 7.9secs
0-60mph 96.5kmh: 10.4secs
0-1/4 mile: 17.4secs
265.0bhp 197.6kW 268.7PS
@ 5400rpm
283.0lbft 383.5Nm @ 4000rpm
146.8bhp/ton 144.3bhp/tonne
62.6bhp/L 46.7kW/L 63.4PS/L
62.5ft/sec 19.1m/sec
26.1mph 42.0kmh/1000rpm
16.0mpg 13.3mpgUS 17.7L/100km
Petrol 4-stroke piston
4235cc 258.4cu in
In-line 6 3 Carburettor
Compression ratio: 9.0:1
Bore: 92.1mm 3.6in
Stroke: 106.0mm 4.2in
Valve type/No: Overhead 12
Transmission: Manual with overdrive
No. of forward speeds: 5
Wheels driven: Rear
Springs F/R: Coil/Coil
Brake system: PA
Brakes F/R: Disc/Disc
Steering: Recirculating ball PA
Wheelbase: 304.8cm 120.0in
Track F: 147.3cm 58.0in
Track R: 147.3cm 58.0in
Length: 523.2cm 206.0in
Width: 193.0cm 76.0in
Height: 138.9cm 54.7in
Ground clearance: 13.7cm 5.4in
Kerb weight: 1836.0kg 4044.0lb
Fuel: 91.0L 20.0gal 24.0galUS

2309 Jaguar
E Type 4.2
1965 UK
156.0mph 251.0kmh
0-50mph 80.5kmh: 5.5secs
0-60mph 96.5kmh: 7.6secs
0-1/4 mile: 15.1secs
265.0bhp 197.6kW 268.7PS
@ 5400rpm
283.0lbft 383.5Nm @ 4000rpm
205.3bhp/ton 201.8bhp/tonne
62.6bhp/L 46.7kW/L 63.4PS/L
62.5ft/sec 19.1m/sec
24.4mph 39.3kmh/1000rpm
17.1mpg 14.2mpgUS 16.5L/100km
Petrol 4-stroke piston
4235cc 258.4cu in
In-line 6 3 Carburettor
Compression ratio: 9.0:1
Bore: 92.0mm 3.6in
Stroke: 106.0mm 4.2in
Valve type/No: Overhead 12
Transmission: Manual
No. of forward speeds: 4
Wheels driven: Rear
Springs F/R: Torsion bar/Coil
Brake system: PA
Brakes F/R: Disc/Disc
Steering: Rack & pinion
Wheelbase: 243.8cm 96.0in
Track F: 127.0cm 50.0in
Track R: 127.0cm 50.0in
Length: 445.3cm 175.3in
Width: 165.6cm 65.2in
Height: 121.9cm 48.0in
Ground clearance: 14.0cm 5.5in
Kerb weight: 1313.0kg 2892.0lb
Fuel: 63.7L 14.0gal 16.8galUS

2310 Jaguar
XKE 4.2 2+2
1966 UK
128.0mph 206.0kmh
0-50mph 80.5kmh: 6.4secs
0-60mph 96.5kmh: 8.3secs
0-1/4 mile: 16.7secs
265.0bhp 197.6kW 268.7PS
@ 5400rpm
283.0lbft 383.5Nm @ 4000rpm
192.1bhp/ton 188.9bhp/tonne
62.6bhp/L 46.7kW/L 63.4PS/L
62.5ft/sec 19.1m/sec
23.0mph 37.0kmh/1000rpm
Petrol 4-stroke piston
4235cc 258.4cu in
In-line 6 3 Carburettor
Compression ratio: 9.0:1
Bore: 92.1mm 3.6in
Stroke: 106.0mm 4.2in
Valve type/No: Overhead 24
Transmission: Automatic
No. of forward speeds: 3
Wheels driven: Rear
Springs F/R: Torsion bar/Coil
Brakes F/R: Disc/Disc
Steering: Rack & pinion
Wheelbase: 266.7cm 105.0in
Track F: 127.0cm 50.0in
Track R: 127.0cm 50.0in
Length: 468.1cm 184.3in
Width: 165.9cm 65.3in
Height: 127.3cm 50.1in
Ground clearance: 14.0cm 5.5in
Kerb weight: 1402.9kg 3090.0lb
Fuel: 63.6L 14.0gal 16.8galUS

2311 Jaguar
420
1967 UK
126.0mph 202.7kmh
0-50mph 80.5kmh: 7.0secs
0-60mph 96.5kmh: 9.9secs
0-1/4 mile: 16.7secs
0-1km: 31.0secs
245.0bhp 182.7kW 248.4PS
@ 5500rpm
283.0lbft 383.5Nm @ 3750rpm
149.2bhp/ton 146.7bhp/tonne
57.8bhp/L 43.1kW/L 58.6PS/L
63.7ft/sec 19.4m/sec
25.9mph 41.7kmh/1000rpm
15.7mpg 13.1mpgUS 18.0L/100km
Petrol 4-stroke piston
4235cc 258.4cu in
In-line 6 2 Carburettor
Compression ratio: 8.0:1
Bore: 92.7mm 3.6in
Stroke: 106.0mm 4.2in
Valve type/No: Overhead 12
Transmission: Manual with overdrive
No. of forward speeds: 5
Wheels driven: Rear
Springs F/R: Coil/Coil
Brake system: PA
Brakes F/R: Disc/Disc
Steering: Rack & pinion PA
Wheelbase: 272.8cm 107.4in
Track F: 140.2cm 55.2in
Track R: 137.7cm 54.2in
Length: 477.0cm 187.8in
Width: 169.4cm 66.7in
Height: 138.4cm 54.5in
Ground clearance: 17.8cm 7.0in
Kerb weight: 1669.8kg 3678.0lb
Fuel: 63.7L 14.0gal 16.8galUS

2312 Jaguar
E Type Roadster
1967 UK
141.0mph 226.9kmh
0-50mph 80.5kmh: 5.6secs
0-60mph 96.5kmh: 7.4secs
0-1/4 mile: 15.0secs
265.0bhp 197.6kW 268.7PS
@ 5400rpm
283.0lbft 383.5Nm @ 4000rpm
208.4bhp/ton 204.9bhp/tonne
62.6bhp/L 46.7kW/L 63.4PS/L
62.5ft/sec 19.1m/sec
24.8mph 39.9kmh/1000rpm
21.8mpg 18.2mpgUS 13.0L/100km
Petrol 4-stroke piston
4235cc 258.4cu in
In-line 6 3 Carburettor
Compression ratio: 9.0:1
Bore: 92.0mm 3.6in
Stroke: 106.0mm 4.2in
Valve type/No: Overhead 12
Transmission: Manual
No. of forward speeds: 4
Wheels driven: Rear
Springs F/R: Torsion bar/Coil
Brake system: PA
Brakes F/R: Disc/Disc
Steering: Rack & pinion
Wheelbase: 243.8cm 96.0in
Track F: 127.0cm 50.0in
Track R: 127.0cm 50.0in
Length: 445.3cm 175.3in
Width: 165.6cm 65.2in
Height: 121.9cm 48.0in
Ground clearance: 14.0cm 5.5in
Kerb weight: 1293.0kg 2848.0lb
Fuel: 63.7L 14.0gal 16.8galUS

2313 Jaguar
XJ13
1967 UK
184.0mph 296.1kmh
472.0bhp 352.0kW 478.5PS
@ 7250rpm
381.0lbft 516.3Nm @ 5500rpm
480.6bhp/ton 472.6bhp/tonne
94.6bhp/L 70.5kW/L 95.9PS/L
55.6ft/sec 16.9m/sec
Petrol 4-stroke piston
4991cc 304.5cu in
Vee 12 fuel injection
Compression ratio: 10.4:1
Bore: 87.0mm 3.4in
Stroke: 70.0mm 2.8in
Valve type/No: Overhead 24
Transmission: Manual
No. of forward speeds: 5
Wheels driven: Rear
Springs F/R: Coil/Coil
Brakes F/R: Disc/Disc
Steering: Rack & pinion
Wheelbase: 241.3cm 95.0in
Track F: 142.2cm 56.0in
Track R: 142.2cm 56.0in
Length: 481.3cm 189.5in
Width: 180.3cm 71.0in
Height: 100.3cm 39.5in
Kerb weight: 998.8kg 2200.0lb
Fuel: 151.4L 33.3gal 40.0galUS

2314 Jaguar
240
1968 UK
107.0mph 172.2kmh
0-50mph 80.5kmh: 9.3secs
0-60mph 96.5kmh: 12.5secs
0-1/4 mile: 18.7secs
133.0bhp 99.2kW 134.8PS

@ 5500rpm
146.0lbft 197.8Nm @ 3700rpm
90.4bhp/ton 88.9bhp/tonne
53.6bhp/L 39.9kW/L 54.3PS/L
46.0ft/sec 14.0m/sec
21.8mph 35.1kmh/1000rpm
18.4mpg 15.3mpgUS 15.4L/100km
Petrol 4-stroke piston
2483cc 151.5cu in
In-line 6 2 Carburettor
Compression ratio: 8.0:1
Bore: 83.0mm 3.3in
Stroke: 76.5mm 3.0in
Valve type/No: Overhead 12
Transmission: Manual with overdrive
No. of forward speeds: 5
Wheels driven: Rear
Springs F/R: Coil/Leaf
Brake system: PA
Brakes F/R: Disc/Disc
Steering: Recirculating ball
Wheelbase: 272.8cm 107.4in
Track F: 139.7cm 55.0in
Track R: 135.6cm 53.4in
Length: 454.7cm 179.0in
Width: 169.4cm 66.7in
Height: 144.8cm 57.0in
Ground clearance: 17.8cm 7.0in
Kerb weight: 1496.4kg 3296.0lb
Fuel: 54.6L 12.0gal 14.4galUS

2315 Jaguar

420 Sedan
1968 UK
120.0mph 193.1kmh
0-50mph 80.5kmh: 7.8secs
0-60mph 96.5kmh: 11.0secs
0-1/4 mile: 17.1secs
245.0bhp 182.7kW 248.4PS
@ 5500rpm
282.0lbft 382.1Nm @ 3750rpm
144.8bhp/ton 142.4bhp/tonne
57.8bhp/L 43.1kW/L 58.6PS/L
63.7ft/sec 19.4m/sec
25.3mph 40.7kmh/1000rpm
Petrol 4-stroke piston
4235cc 258.4cu in
In-line 6 2 Carburettor
Compression ratio: 9.0:1
Bore: 92.1mm 3.6in
Stroke: 106.0mm 4.2in
Valve type/No: Overhead 12
Transmission: Manual with overdrive
Wheels driven: Rear
Springs F/R: Coil/Coil
Brakes F/R: Disc/Disc
Steering: Worm & roller PA
Wheelbase: 272.8cm 107.4in
Track F: 140.2cm 55.2in
Track R: 142.7cm 56.2in
Length: 477.0cm 187.8in
Width: 169.7cm 66.8in
Height: 138.4cm 54.5in
Ground clearance: 15.2cm 6.0in
Kerb weight: 1720.7kg 3790.0lb
Fuel: 62.4L 13.7gal 16.5galUS

2316 Jaguar

XJ6 4.2 Automatic
1969 UK
120.0mph 193.1kmh
0-50mph 80.5kmh: 7.6secs
0-60mph 96.5kmh: 10.1secs
0-1/4 mile: 17.5secs
0-1km: 31.9secs
245.0bhp 182.7kW 248.4PS
@ 5500rpm
283.0lbft 383.5Nm @ 3750rpm
151.3bhp/ton 148.8bhp/tonne
57.8bhp/L 43.1kW/L 58.6PS/L
63.7ft/sec 19.4m/sec
22.9mph 36.8kmh/1000rpm
15.2mpg 12.7mpgUS 18.6L/100km
Petrol 4-stroke piston
4235cc 258.4cu in
In-line 6 2 Carburettor
Compression ratio: 9.0:1
Bore: 92.1mm 3.6in
Stroke: 106.0mm 4.2in
Valve type/No: Overhead 12
Transmission: Automatic
No. of forward speeds: 3
Wheels driven: Rear
Springs F/R: Coil/Coil
Brake system: PA
Brakes F/R: Disc/Disc
Steering: Rack & pinion PA
Wheelbase: 276.4cm 108.8in
Track F: 147.3cm 58.0in
Track R: 148.8cm 58.6in
Length: 481.3cm 189.5in
Width: 176.8cm 69.6in
Height: 134.1cm 52.8in
Ground clearance: 17.8cm 7.0in
Kerb weight: 1646.7kg 3627.0lb
Fuel: 104.6L 23.0gal 27.6galUS

2317 Jaguar

XKE Coupe
1969 UK
119.0mph 191.5kmh
0-50mph 80.5kmh: 6.1secs
0-60mph 96.5kmh: 8.0secs
0-1/4 mile: 15.7secs
246.0bhp 183.4kW 249.4PS
@ 5500rpm
263.0lbft 356.4Nm @ 3000rpm
182.6bhp/ton 179.5bhp/tonne
58.1bhp/L 43.3kW/L 58.9PS/L
63.7ft/sec 19.4m/sec
21.2mph 34.1kmh/1000rpm
19.1mpg 15.9mpgUS 14.8L/100km
Petrol 4-stroke piston
4235cc 258.4cu in
In-line 6 2 Carburettor
Compression ratio: 9.0:1
Bore: 92.1mm 3.6in
Stroke: 106.0mm 4.2in
Valve type/No: Overhead 12
Transmission: Manual
No. of forward speeds: 4
Wheels driven: Rear
Springs F/R: Torsion bar/Coil
Brakes F/R: Disc/Disc
Steering: Rack & pinion
Wheelbase: 243.8cm 96.0in
Track F: 127.0cm 50.0in
Track R: 127.0cm 50.0in
Length: 445.3cm 175.3in
Width: 165.6cm 65.2in
Height: 122.2cm 48.1in
Ground clearance: 14.0cm 5.5in
Kerb weight: 1370.2kg 3018.0lb
Fuel: 63.6L 14.0gal 16.8galUS

2318 Jaguar

XJ6
1970 UK
120.0mph 193.1kmh
0-50mph 80.5kmh: 7.6secs
0-60mph 96.5kmh: 10.1secs
0-1/4 mile: 17.3secs
245.0bhp 182.7kW 248.4PS
@ 5500rpm
283.0lbft 383.5Nm @ 3750rpm
147.5bhp/ton 145.1bhp/tonne
57.8bhp/L 43.1kW/L 58.6PS/L
63.7ft/sec 19.4m/sec
16.3mpg 13.6mpgUS 17.3L/100km
Petrol 4-stroke piston
4235cc 258.4cu in
In-line 6 2 Carburettor
Compression ratio: 8.0:1
Bore: 92.1mm 3.6in
Stroke: 106.0mm 4.2in
Valve type/No: Overhead 12
Transmission: Automatic
No. of forward speeds: 3
Wheels driven: Rear
Springs F/R: Coil/Coil
Brake system: PA
Brakes F/R: Disc/Disc
Steering: Rack & pinion PA
Wheelbase: 276.4cm 108.8in
Track F: 147.3cm 58.0in
Track R: 148.8cm 58.6in
Length: 481.3cm 189.5in
Width: 176.8cm 69.6in
Height: 134.1cm 52.8in
Ground clearance: 15.2cm 6.0in
Kerb weight: 1688.9kg 3720.0lb
Fuel: 104.5L 23.0gal 27.6galUS

2319 Jaguar

E Type V12
1971 UK
143.0mph 230.1kmh
0-50mph 80.5kmh: 4.9secs
0-60mph 96.5kmh: 6.8secs
0-1/4 mile: 14.6secs
0-1km: 26.6secs
272.0bhp 202.8kW 275.8PS
@ 5850rpm
304.0lbft 411.9Nm @ 3600rpm
184.1bhp/ton 181.1bhp/tonne
50.9bhp/L 38.0kW/L 51.6PS/L
44.8ft/sec 13.6m/sec
24.7mph 39.7kmh/1000rpm
15.2mpg 12.7mpgUS 18.6L/100km
Petrol 4-stroke piston
5343cc 326.0cu in
Vee 12 4 Carburettor
Compression ratio: 9.0:1
Bore: 90.0mm 3.5in
Stroke: 70.0mm 2.8in
Valve type/No: Overhead 24
Transmission: Manual
No. of forward speeds: 4
Wheels driven: Rear
Springs F/R: Torsion bar/Coil
Brake system: PA
Brakes F/R: Disc/Disc
Steering: Rack & pinion
Wheelbase: 266.7cm 105.0in
Track F: 138.4cm 54.5in
Track R: 134.6cm 53.0in
Length: 468.6cm 184.5in
Width: 167.6cm 66.0in
Height: 129.5cm 51.0in
Ground clearance: 12.7cm 5.0in
Kerb weight: 1502.3kg 3309.0lb
Fuel: 81.9L 18.0gal 21.6galUS

2320 Jaguar

XJ6 4.2
1971 UK
123.0mph 197.9kmh
0-50mph 80.5kmh: 6.5secs
0-60mph 96.5kmh: 8.7secs
0-1/4 mile: 16.5secs
0-1km: 30.4secs
245.0bhp 182.7kW 248.4PS
@ 5500rpm
283.0lbft 383.5Nm @ 3750rpm
150.4bhp/ton 147.9bhp/tonne
57.8bhp/L 43.1kW/L 58.6PS/L
63.7ft/sec 19.4m/sec
27.5mph 44.2kmh/1000rpm
16.0mpg 13.3mpgUS 17.7L/100km
Petrol 4-stroke piston
4235cc 258.4cu in
In-line 6 2 Carburettor
Compression ratio: 9.0:1
Bore: 92.1mm 3.6in
Stroke: 106.0mm 4.2in
Valve type/No: Overhead 12
Transmission: Manual with overdrive
No. of forward speeds: 5
Wheels driven: Rear
Springs F/R: Coil/Coil
Brake system: PA
Brakes F/R: Disc/Disc
Steering: Rack & pinion PA
Wheelbase: 276.4cm 108.8in
Track F: 147.3cm 58.0in
Track R: 148.8cm 58.6in
Length: 481.3cm 189.5in
Width: 176.8cm 69.6in
Height: 134.1cm 52.8in
Ground clearance: 17.8cm 7.0in
Kerb weight: 1656.2kg 3648.0lb
Fuel: 109.2L 24.0gal 28.8galUS

2321 Jaguar

XJ12
1972 UK
142.0mph 228.5kmh
0-50mph 80.5kmh: 6.6secs
0-60mph 96.5kmh: 8.3secs
265.0bhp 197.6kW 268.7PS
@ 6000rpm
301.0lbft 407.9Nm @ 3500rpm
150.3bhp/ton 147.8bhp/tonne
49.6bhp/L 37.0kW/L 50.3PS/L
46.0ft/sec 14.0m/sec
12.4mpg 10.3mpgUS 22.8L/100km
Petrol 4-stroke piston
5343cc 326.0cu in
Vee 12 4 Carburettor
Compression ratio: 9.0:1
Bore: 90.0mm 3.5in
Stroke: 70.0mm 2.8in
Valve type/No: Overhead 24
Transmission: Automatic
No. of forward speeds: 3
Wheels driven: Rear
Springs F/R: Coil/Coil
Brake system: PA
Brakes F/R: Disc/Disc
Steering: Rack & pinion PA
Wheelbase: 276.4cm 108.8in
Track F: 147.3cm 58.0in
Track R: 148.8cm 58.6in
Length: 481.3cm 189.5in
Width: 176.8cm 69.6in
Height: 134.1cm 52.8in
Kerb weight: 1793.3kg 3950.0lb
Fuel: 90.8L 20.0gal 24.0galUS

2322 Jaguar

XJ6
1972 UK
115.0mph 185.0kmh
0-50mph 80.5kmh: 8.0secs
0-60mph 96.5kmh: 10.7secs
0-1/4 mile: 17.1secs
186.0bhp 138.7kW 188.6PS
@ 4500rpm
240.0lbft 325.2Nm @ 3750rpm
107.2bhp/ton 105.4bhp/tonne
43.9bhp/L 32.7kW/L 44.5PS/L
52.1ft/sec 15.9m/sec
20.9mph 33.6kmh/1000rpm
18.3mpg 15.2mpgUS 15.5L/100km
Petrol 4-stroke piston
4235cc 258.4cu in
In-line 6 2 Carburettor
Compression ratio: 8.0:1
Bore: 92.1mm 3.6in
Stroke: 105.9mm 4.2in
Valve type/No: Overhead 12
Transmission: Automatic
No. of forward speeds: 3
Wheels driven: Rear
Springs F/R: Coil/Coil
Brake system: PA
Brakes F/R: Disc/Disc
Steering: Rack & pinion PA
Wheelbase: 276.4cm 108.8in
Track F: 147.3cm 58.0in
Track R: 148.8cm 58.6in
Length: 481.3cm 189.5in
Width: 176.8cm 69.6in
Height: 134.1cm 52.8in
Ground clearance: 15.2cm 6.0in
Kerb weight: 1763.8kg 3885.0lb
Fuel: 104.1L 22.9gal 27.5galUS

2323 Jaguar

XKE V12
1972 UK
135.0mph 217.2kmh
0-50mph 80.5kmh: 6.0secs
0-60mph 96.5kmh: 7.4secs
0-1/4 mile: 15.4secs
250.0bhp 186.4kW 253.5PS
@ 6000rpm
288.0lbft 390.2Nm @ 3500rpm
165.7bhp/ton 162.9bhp/tonne
46.8bhp/L 34.9kW/L 47.4PS/L
46.0ft/sec 14.0m/sec
22.2mph 35.7kmh/1000rpm
17.4mpg 14.5mpgUS 16.2L/100km
Petrol 4-stroke piston
5343cc 326.0cu in
Vee 12 4 Carburettor
Compression ratio: 9.0:1
Bore: 90.0mm 3.5in
Stroke: 70.0mm 2.8in
Valve type/No: Overhead 24
Transmission: Manual
No. of forward speeds: 4
Wheels driven: Rear
Springs F/R: Torsion bar/Coil
Brake system: PA
Brakes F/R: Disc/Disc
Steering: Rack & pinion PA
Wheelbase: 265.9cm 104.7in
Track F: 138.2cm 54.4in
Track R: 135.6cm 53.4in
Length: 468.4cm 184.4in
Width: 167.9cm 66.1in
Height: 122.2cm 48.1in
Ground clearance: 14.0cm 5.5in
Kerb weight: 1534.5kg 3380.0lb
Fuel: 76.8L 16.9gal 20.3galUS

2324 Jaguar

XJ12
1973 UK
148.0mph 238.1kmh
0-50mph 80.5kmh: 5.9secs
0-60mph 96.5kmh: 7.4secs
0-1/4 mile: 15.7secs
0-1km: 28.2secs
253.0bhp 188.7kW 256.5PS

@ 6000rpm
302.0lbft 409.2Nm @ 3500rpm
145.3bhp/ton 142.9bhp/tonne
47.3bhp/L 35.3kW/L 48.0PS/L
46.0ft/sec 14.0m/sec
22.9mph 36.8kmh/1000rpm
11.4mpg 9.5mpgUS 24.8L/100km
Petrol 4-stroke piston
5343cc 326.0cu in
Vee 12 4 Carburettor
Compression ratio: 9.0:1
Bore: 90.0mm 3.5in
Stroke: 70.0mm 2.8in
Valve type/No: Overhead 24
Transmission: Automatic
No. of forward speeds: 3
Wheels driven: Rear
Springs F/R: Coil/Coil
Brake system: PA
Brakes F/R: Disc/Disc
Steering: Rack & pinion PA
Wheelbase: 276.4cm 108.8in
Track F: 147.3cm 58.0in
Track R: 148.8cm 58.6in
Length: 481.3cm 189.5in
Width: 176.8cm 69.6in
Height: 134.1cm 52.8in
Ground clearance: 17.8cm 7.0in
Kerb weight: 1770.6kg 3900.0lb
Fuel: 91.0L 20.0gal 24.0galUS

2325 Jaguar

XKE V12
1974 UK
138.0mph 222.0kmh
0-60mph 96.5kmh: 8.0secs
0-1/4 mile: 16.2secs
241.0bhp 179.7kW 244.3PS
@ 5750rpm
285.0lbft 386.2Nm @ 3500rpm
156.5bhp/ton 153.9bhp/tonne
45.1bhp/L 33.6kW/L 45.7PS/L
44.1ft/sec 13.4m/sec
14.4mpg 12.0mpgUS 19.6L/100km
Petrol 4-stroke piston
5343cc 326.0cu in
Vee 12 4 Carburettor
Compression ratio: 7.8:1
Bore: 90.0mm 3.5in
Stroke: 70.0mm 2.8in
Valve type/No: Overhead 24
Transmission: Manual
No. of forward speeds: 4
Wheels driven: Rear
Brake system: PA
Brakes F/R: Disc/Disc
Steering: PA
Wheelbase: 265.9cm 104.7in
Track F: 138.2cm 54.4in
Track R: 135.6cm 53.4in
Length: 468.4cm 184.4in
Width: 167.9cm 66.1in
Height: 122.2cm 48.1in
Ground clearance: 14.0cm 5.5in
Kerb weight: 1566.3kg 3450.0lb
Fuel: 76.8L 16.9gal 20.3galUS

2326 Jaguar

XJ12L
1975 UK
131.0mph 210.8kmh
0-50mph 80.5kmh: 7.0secs
0-60mph 96.5kmh: 9.1secs
0-1/4 mile: 17.3secs
244.0bhp 181.9kW 247.4PS
@ 5750rpm
331.0lbft 448.5Nm @ 4000rpm
126.4bhp/ton 124.3bhp/tonne
45.7bhp/L 34.0kW/L 46.3PS/L
44.1ft/sec 13.4m/sec
22.4mph 36.0kmh/1000rpm
13.8mpg 11.5mpgUS 20.5L/100km
Petrol 4-stroke piston
5343cc 326.0cu in
Vee 12
Compression ratio: 7.8:1
Bore: 90.0mm 3.5in
Stroke: 70.0mm 2.8in
Valve type/No: Overhead 24
Transmission: Automatic
No. of forward speeds: 3
Wheels driven: Rear
Springs F/R: Coil/Coil
Brake system: PA
Brakes F/R: Disc/Disc
Steering: Rack & pinion PA
Wheelbase: 286.5cm 112.8in
Track F: 147.3cm 58.0in
Track R: 148.8cm 58.6in
Length: 505.0cm 198.8in
Width: 177.0cm 69.7in
Height: 137.4cm 54.1in
Kerb weight: 1963.5kg 4325.0lb
Fuel: 90.8L 20.0gal 24.0galUS

2327 Jaguar

XJ3.4
1975 UK
120.0mph 193.1kmh
0-50mph 80.5kmh: 7.8secs
0-60mph 96.5kmh: 10.9secs
0-1/4 mile: 18.0secs
161.0bhp 120.1kW 163.2PS
@ 5000rpm
189.0lbft 256.1Nm @ 3500rpm
97.3bhp/ton 95.6bhp/tonne
46.8bhp/L 34.9kW/L 47.4PS/L
57.9ft/sec 17.7m/sec
27.6mph 44.4kmh/1000rpm
16.7mpg 13.9mpgUS 16.9L/100km
Petrol 4-stroke piston
3442cc 210.0cu in
In-line 6 2 Carburettor
Compression ratio: 8.8:1
Bore: 83.0mm 3.3in
Stroke: 106.0mm 4.2in
Valve type/No: Overhead 12
Transmission: Manual with overdrive
No. of forward speeds: 5
Wheels driven: Rear
Springs F/R: Coil/Coil
Brake system: PA
Brakes F/R: Disc/Disc
Steering: Rack & pinion PA
Wheelbase: 286.5cm 112.8in
Track F: 147.3cm 58.0in
Track R: 149.4cm 58.8in
Length: 494.5cm 194.7in
Width: 177.0cm 69.7in
Height: 137.4cm 54.1in
Ground clearance: 17.8cm 7.0in
Kerb weight: 1683.4kg 3708.0lb
Fuel: 91.0L 20.0gal 24.0galUS

2328 Jaguar

XJ5.3C
1975 UK
148.0mph 238.1kmh
0-50mph 80.5kmh: 6.5secs
0-60mph 96.5kmh: 8.3secs
0-1/4 mile: 16.0secs
285.0bhp 212.5kW 288.9PS
@ 5750rpm
294.0lbft 398.4Nm @ 3500rpm
155.9bhp/ton 153.3bhp/tonne
53.3bhp/L 39.8kW/L 54.1PS/L
44.1ft/sec 13.4m/sec
24.7mph 39.7kmh/1000rpm
13.8mpg 11.5mpgUS 20.5L/100km
Petrol 4-stroke piston
5343cc 326.0cu in
Vee 12 fuel injection
Compression ratio: 9.0:1
Bore: 90.0mm 3.5in
Stroke: 70.0mm 2.8in
Valve type/No: Overhead 24
Transmission: Automatic
No. of forward speeds: 3
Wheels driven: Rear
Springs F/R: Coil/Coil
Brake system: PA
Brakes F/R: Disc/Disc
Steering: Rack & pinion PA
Wheelbase: 276.4cm 108.8in
Track F: 147.3cm 58.0in
Track R: 148.8cm 58.6in
Length: 484.4cm 190.7in
Width: 177.0cm 69.7in
Height: 134.6cm 53.0in
Ground clearance: 17.8cm 7.0in
Kerb weight: 1859.1kg 4095.0lb
Fuel: 91.0L 20.0gal 24.0galUS

2329 Jaguar

XJ12C
1976 UK
139.0mph 223.7kmh
0-50mph 80.5kmh: 6.8secs
0-60mph 96.5kmh: 8.8secs
0-1/4 mile: 16.5secs
244.0bhp 181.9kW 247.4PS
@ 5250rpm
269.0lbft 364.5Nm @ 4500rpm
130.3bhp/ton 128.1bhp/tonne
45.7bhp/L 34.0kW/L 46.3PS/L
40.2ft/sec 12.2m/sec
22.2mph 35.7kmh/1000rpm
16.2mpg 13.5mpgUS 17.4L/100km
Petrol 4-stroke piston
5343cc 326.0cu in
Vee 12
Compression ratio: 8.0:1
Bore: 90.0mm 3.5in
Stroke: 70.0mm 2.8in
Valve type/No: Overhead 24
Transmission: Automatic
No. of forward speeds: 3
Wheels driven: Rear
Springs F/R: Coil/Coil
Brake system: PA
Brakes F/R: Disc/Disc
Steering: Rack & pinion PA
Wheelbase: 276.4cm 108.8in
Track F: 147.3cm 58.0in
Track R: 148.8cm 58.6in
Length: 495.3cm 195.0in
Width: 177.3cm 69.8in
Height: 137.4cm 54.1in
Kerb weight: 1904.5kg 4195.0lb
Fuel: 90.8L 20.0gal 24.0galUS

2330 Jaguar

XJS
1976 UK
154.0mph 247.8kmh
0-50mph 80.5kmh: 5.2secs
0-60mph 96.5kmh: 6.9secs
0-1/4 mile: 15.2secs
0-1km: 27.3secs
285.0bhp 212.5kW 288.9PS
@ 5500rpm
294.0lbft 398.4Nm @ 3500rpm
163.6bhp/ton 160.9bhp/tonne
53.3bhp/L 39.8kW/L 54.1PS/L
42.2ft/sec 12.8m/sec
24.7mph 39.7kmh/1000rpm
15.4mpg 12.8mpgUS 18.3L/100km
Petrol 4-stroke piston
5343cc 326.0cu in
Vee 12 fuel injection
Compression ratio: 9.0:1
Bore: 90.0mm 3.5in
Stroke: 70.0mm 2.8in
Valve type/No: Overhead 24
Transmission: Manual
No. of forward speeds: 4
Wheels driven: Rear
Springs F/R: Coil/Coil
Brake system: PA
Brakes F/R: Disc/Disc
Steering: Rack & pinion PA
Wheelbase: 259.1cm 102.0in
Track F: 148.8cm 58.6in
Track R: 147.3cm 58.0in
Length: 486.9cm 191.7in
Width: 179.3cm 70.6in
Height: 127.0cm 50.0in
Ground clearance: 14.0cm 5.5in
Kerb weight: 1771.5kg 3902.0lb
Fuel: 91.0L 20.0gal 24.0galUS

2331 Jaguar

XJ4.2
1977 UK
119.0mph 191.5kmh
0-50mph 80.5kmh: 7.9secs
0-60mph 96.5kmh: 10.6secs
0-1/4 mile: 17.9secs
180.0bhp 134.2kW 182.5PS
@ 4500rpm
232.0lbft 314.4Nm @ 3000rpm
104.0bhp/ton 102.2bhp/tonne
42.5bhp/L 31.7kW/L 43.1PS/L
52.1ft/sec 15.9m/sec
22.9mph 36.8kmh/1000rpm
15.0mpg 12.5mpgUS 18.8L/100km
Petrol 4-stroke piston
4235cc 258.4cu in
In-line 6 2 Carburettor
Compression ratio: 8.5:1
Bore: 92.1mm 3.6in
Stroke: 106.0mm 4.2in
Valve type/No: Overhead 12
Transmission: Automatic
No. of forward speeds: 3
Wheels driven: Rear
Springs F/R: Coil/Coil
Brake system: PA
Brakes F/R: Disc/Disc
Steering: Rack & pinion PA
Wheelbase: 286.5cm 112.8in
Track F: 147.3cm 58.0in
Track R: 149.4cm 58.8in
Length: 494.5cm 194.7in
Width: 177.0cm 69.7in
Height: 137.4cm 54.1in
Ground clearance: 17.8cm 7.0in
Kerb weight: 1760.6kg 3878.0lb
Fuel: 91.0L 20.0gal 24.0galUS

2332 Jaguar

XJS Automatic
1977 UK
143.0mph 230.1kmh
0-50mph 80.5kmh: 5.9secs
0-60mph 96.5kmh: 7.5secs
0-1/4 mile: 15.7secs
0-1km: 27.8secs
285.0bhp 212.5kW 288.9PS
@ 5500rpm
294.0lbft 398.4Nm @ 3500rpm
165.1bhp/ton 162.4bhp/tonne
53.3bhp/L 39.8kW/L 54.1PS/L
42.2ft/sec 12.8m/sec
24.7mph 39.7kmh/1000rpm
14.0mpg 11.7mpgUS 20.2L/100km
Petrol 4-stroke piston
5343cc 326.0cu in
Vee 12 fuel injection
Compression ratio: 9.0:1
Bore: 90.0mm 3.5in
Stroke: 70.0mm 2.8in
Valve type/No: Overhead 24
Transmission: Automatic
No. of forward speeds: 3
Wheels driven: Rear
Springs F/R: Coil/Coil
Brake system: PA
Brakes F/R: Disc/Disc
Steering: Rack & pinion PA
Wheelbase: 259.1cm 102.0in
Track F: 148.8cm 58.6in
Track R: 147.3cm 58.0in
Length: 486.9cm 191.7in
Width: 179.3cm 70.6in
Height: 127.0cm 50.0in
Ground clearance: 14.0cm 5.5in
Kerb weight: 1755.2kg 3866.0lb
Fuel: 91.0L 20.0gal 24.0galUS

2333 Jaguar

XJS Tullius
1977 UK
180.0mph 289.6kmh
0-50mph 80.5kmh: 4.3secs
0-60mph 96.5kmh: 5.0secs
0-1/4 mile: 13.6secs
475.0bhp 354.2kW 481.6PS
@ 7600rpm
360.0lbft 487.8Nm @ 5500rpm
339.9bhp/ton 334.3bhp/tonne
88.9bhp/L 66.3kW/L 90.1PS/L
58.3ft/sec 17.7m/sec
22.2mph 35.7kmh/1000rpm
4.8mpg 4.0mpgUS 58.8L/100km
Petrol 4-stroke piston
5343cc 326.0cu in
Vee 12 6 Carburettor
Compression ratio: 11.5:1
Bore: 90.0mm 3.5in
Stroke: 70.0mm 2.8in
Valve type/No: Overhead 24
Transmission: Manual
No. of forward speeds: 4
Wheels driven: Rear
Springs F/R: Coil/Coil
Brakes F/R: Disc/Disc
Steering: Rack & pinion
Wheelbase: 259.1cm 102.0in
Track F: 152.4cm 60.0in
Track R: 153.9cm 60.6in
Length: 486.9cm 191.7in
Width: 190.0cm 74.8in
Height: 120.7cm 47.5in
Ground clearance: 7.6cm 3.0in
Kerb weight: 1421.0kg 3130.0lb
Fuel: 113.5L 25.0gal 30.0galUS

2334 Jaguar

XJ12L
1978 UK
128.0mph 206.0kmh
0-50mph 80.5kmh: 6.8secs
0-60mph 96.5kmh: 8.8secs
0-1/4 mile: 17.0secs
244.0bhp 181.9kW 247.4PS

@ 5250rpm
269.0lbft 364.5Nm @ 4500rpm
128.1bhp/ton 126.0bhp/tonne
45.7bhp/L 34.0kW/L 46.3PS/L
40.2ft/sec 12.2m/sec
22.4mph 36.0kmh/1000rpm
15.6mpg 13.0mpgUS 18.1L/100km
Petrol 4-stroke piston
5343cc 326.0cu in
Vee 12
Compression ratio: 8.0:1
Bore: 90.0mm 3.5in
Stroke: 70.0mm 2.8in
Valve type/No: Overhead 24
Transmission: Automatic
No. of forward speeds: 3
Wheels driven: Rear
Springs F/R: Coil/Coil
Brake system: PA
Brakes F/R: Disc/Disc
Steering: Rack & pinion PA
Wheelbase: 286.5cm 112.8in
Track F: 147.8cm 58.2in
Track R: 149.4cm 58.8in
Length: 509.3cm 200.5in
Width: 177.3cm 69.8in
Height: 137.4cm 54.1in
Kerb weight: 1936.3kg 4265.0lb
Fuel: 96.1L 21.1gal 25.4galUS

2335 Jaguar

XJ5.3 Automatic
1978 UK
148.0mph 238.1kmh
0-50mph 80.5kmh: 6.0secs
0-60mph 96.5kmh: 7.8secs
0-1/4 mile: 15.7secs
0-1km: 28.4secs
285.0bhp 212.5kW 288.9PS
@ 5750rpm
294.0lbft 398.4Nm @ 4000rpm
155.0bhp/ton 152.4bhp/tonne
53.3bhp/L 39.8kW/L 54.1PS/L
44.1ft/sec 13.4m/sec
24.7mph 39.7kmh/1000rpm
13.2mpg 11.0mpgUS 21.4L/100km
Petrol 4-stroke piston
5343cc 326.0cu in
Vee 12 fuel injection
Compression ratio: 9.0:1
Bore: 90.0mm 3.5in
Stroke: 70.0mm 2.8in
Valve type/No: Overhead 24
Transmission: Automatic
No. of forward speeds: 3
Wheels driven: Rear
Springs F/R: Coil/Coil
Brake system: PA
Brakes F/R: Disc/Disc
Steering: Rack & pinion PA
Wheelbase: 286.5cm 112.8in
Track F: 147.3cm 58.0in
Track R: 149.4cm 58.8in
Length: 494.5cm 194.7in
Width: 177.0cm 69.7in
Height: 137.4cm 54.1in
Ground clearance: 17.8cm 7.0in
Kerb weight: 1870.0kg 4119.0lb
Fuel: 100.6L 22.1gal 26.6galUS

2336 Jaguar

XJ6 4.2
1979 UK
130.0mph 209.2kmh
0-50mph 80.5kmh: 7.4secs
0-60mph 96.5kmh: 10.0secs
0-1/4 mile: 17.4secs
0-1km: 31.6secs
205.0bhp 152.9kW 207.8PS
@ 5000rpm
236.0lbft 319.8Nm @ 3700rpm
118.5bhp/ton 116.5bhp/tonne
48.4bhp/L 36.1kW/L 49.1PS/L
57.9ft/sec 17.7m/sec
24.7mph 39.7kmh/1000rpm
16.8mpg 14.0mpgUS 16.8L/100km
Petrol 4-stroke piston
4235cc 258.4cu in
In-line 6 fuel injection
Compression ratio: 8.7:1
Bore: 92.1mm 3.6in
Stroke: 106.0mm 4.2in
Valve type/No: Overhead 12
Transmission: Automatic
No. of forward speeds: 3
Wheels driven: Rear
Springs F/R: Coil/Coil
Brake system: PA
Brakes F/R: Disc/Disc
Steering: Rack & pinion PA
Wheelbase: 286.5cm 112.8in
Track F: 148.1cm 58.3in
Track R: 149.6cm 58.9in
Length: 496.1cm 195.3in
Width: 177.0cm 69.7in
Height: 137.4cm 54.1in
Kerb weight: 1759.2kg 3875.0lb
Fuel: 91.0L 20.0gal 24.0galUS

2337 Jaguar

XJ6L
1979 UK
116.0mph 186.6kmh
0-60mph 96.5kmh: 7.4secs
0-1/4 mile: 17.7secs
176.0bhp 131.2kW 178.4PS
@ 4750rpm
219.0lbft 296.7Nm @ 2500rpm
99.1bhp/ton 97.4bhp/tonne
41.6bhp/L 31.0kW/L 42.1PS/L
55.0ft/sec 16.8m/sec
23.2mph 37.3kmh/1000rpm
21.0mpg 17.5mpgUS 13.4L/100km
Petrol 4-stroke piston
4235cc 258.4cu in
In-line 6
Compression ratio: 7.8:1
Bore: 92.1mm 3.6in
Stroke: 105.9mm 4.2in
Valve type/No: Overhead 12
Transmission: Automatic
No. of forward speeds: 3
Wheels driven: Rear
Springs F/R: Coil/Coil
Brake system: PA
Brakes F/R: Disc/Disc
Steering: Rack & pinion PA
Wheelbase: 286.5cm 112.8in
Track F: 147.8cm 58.2in
Track R: 149.4cm 58.8in
Length: 509.3cm 200.5in
Width: 177.3cm 69.8in
Height: 137.4cm 54.1in
Kerb weight: 1806.9kg 3980.0lb
Fuel: 96.1L 21.1gal 25.4galUS

2338 Jaguar

XJS
1979 UK
137.0mph 220.4kmh
0-50mph 80.5kmh: 6.6secs
0-60mph 96.5kmh: 8.6secs
0-1/4 mile: 16.7secs
244.0bhp 181.9kW 247.4PS
@ 5250rpm
269.0lbft 364.5Nm @ 4500rpm
140.5bhp/ton 138.2bhp/tonne
45.7bhp/L 34.0kW/L 46.3PS/L
40.2ft/sec 12.2m/sec
22.1mph 35.6kmh/1000rpm
13.8mpg 11.5mpgUS 20.5L/100km
Petrol 4-stroke piston
5343cc 326.0cu in
Vee 12 fuel injection
Compression ratio: 7.8:1
Bore: 90.0mm 3.5in
Stroke: 70.0mm 2.8in
Valve type/No: Overhead 24
Transmission: Automatic
No. of forward speeds: 3
Wheels driven: Rear
Springs F/R: Coil/Coil
Brake system: PA
Brakes F/R: Disc/Disc
Steering: Rack & pinion PA
Wheelbase: 259.1cm 102.0in
Track F: 147.3cm 58.0in
Track R: 148.8cm 58.6in
Length: 486.9cm 191.7in
Width: 179.3cm 70.6in
Height: 126.2cm 49.7in
Ground clearance: 12.7cm 5.0in
Kerb weight: 1766.1kg 3890.0lb
Fuel: 87.1L 19.1gal 23.0galUS

2339 Jaguar

XJ6 Series III
1980 UK
117.0mph 188.3kmh
0-50mph 80.5kmh: 7.9secs
0-60mph 96.5kmh: 10.6secs
0-1/4 mile: 18.2secs
176.0bhp 131.2kW 178.4PS
@ 4750rpm
219.0lbft 296.7Nm @ 2500rpm
96.9bhp/ton 95.2bhp/tonne
41.6bhp/L 31.0kW/L 42.1PS/L
55.0ft/sec 16.8m/sec
22.6mph 36.4kmh/1000rpm
16.2mpg 13.5mpgUS 17.4L/100km
Petrol 4-stroke piston
4235cc 258.4cu in
In-line 6 fuel injection
Compression ratio: 7.8:1
Bore: 92.1mm 3.6in
Stroke: 106.0mm 4.2in
Valve type/No: Overhead 12
Transmission: Automatic
No. of forward speeds: 3
Wheels driven: Rear
Springs F/R: Coil/Coil
Brake system: PA
Brakes F/R: Disc/Disc
Steering: Rack & pinion PA
Wheelbase: 286.5cm 112.8in
Track F: 148.1cm 58.3in
Track R: 149.6cm 58.9in
Length: 506.7cm 199.5in
Width: 177.0cm 69.7in
Height: 137.7cm 54.2in
Kerb weight: 1847.8kg 4070.0lb
Fuel: 96.1L 21.1gal 25.4galUS

2340 Jaguar

XJS
1981 UK
139.0mph 223.7kmh
0-50mph 80.5kmh: 6.1secs
0-60mph 96.5kmh: 7.8secs
0-1/4 mile: 15.9secs
262.0bhp 195.4kW 265.6PS
@ 5000rpm
289.0lbft 391.6Nm @ 4000rpm
150.9bhp/ton 148.3bhp/tonne
49.0bhp/L 36.6kW/L 49.7PS/L
38.3ft/sec 11.7m/sec
24.5mph 39.4kmh/1000rpm
18.0mpg 15.0mpgUS 15.7L/100km
Petrol 4-stroke piston
5343cc 326.0cu in
Vee 12 fuel injection
Compression ratio: 9.0:1
Bore: 90.0mm 3.5in
Stroke: 70.0mm 2.8in
Valve type/No: Overhead 24
Transmission: Automatic
No. of forward speeds: 3
Wheels driven: Rear
Springs F/R: Coil
Brake system: PA
Brakes F/R: Disc/Disc
Steering: Rack & pinion PA
Wheelbase: 259.1cm 102.0in
Track F: 148.8cm 58.6in
Track R: 148.8cm 58.6in
Length: 488.2cm 192.2in
Width: 179.3cm 70.6in
Height: 121.4cm 47.8in
Kerb weight: 1766.1kg 3890.0lb
Fuel: 90.8L 20.0gal 24.0galUS

2341 Jaguar

XJS Automatic
1981 UK
154.0mph 247.8kmh
0-50mph 80.5kmh: 5.1secs
0-60mph 96.5kmh: 6.6secs
0-1/4 mile: 14.9secs
0-1km: 27.1secs
296.0bhp 220.7kW 300.1PS
@ 5400rpm
318.0lbft 430.9Nm @ 3900rpm
170.4bhp/ton 167.6bhp/tonne
55.4bhp/L 41.3kW/L 56.2PS/L
41.4ft/sec 12.6m/sec
24.7mph 39.7kmh/1000rpm
14.3mpg 11.9mpgUS 19.8L/100km
Petrol 4-stroke piston
5343cc 326.0cu in
Vee 12 fuel injection
Compression ratio: 10.0:1
Bore: 90.0mm 3.5in
Stroke: 70.0mm 2.8in
Valve type/No: Overhead 24
Transmission: Automatic
No. of forward speeds: 3
Wheels driven: Rear
Springs F/R: Coil/Coil
Brake system: PA
Brakes F/R: Disc/Disc
Steering: Rack & pinion PA
Wheelbase: 259.1cm 102.0in
Track F: 148.8cm 58.6in
Track R: 147.3cm 58.0in
Length: 461.5cm 181.7in
Width: 179.3cm 70.6in
Height: 127.0cm 50.0in
Ground clearance: 14.0cm 5.5in
Kerb weight: 1766.1kg 3890.0lb
Fuel: 91.0L 20.0gal 24.0galUS

2342 Jaguar

XJS HE
1982 UK
157.0mph 252.6kmh
0-50mph 80.5kmh: 5.2secs
0-60mph 96.5kmh: 6.5secs
0-1/4 mile: 14.9secs
0-1km: 26.9secs
299.0bhp 223.0kW 303.1PS
@ 5500rpm
318.0lbft 430.9Nm @ 3000rpm
175.1bhp/ton 172.2bhp/tonne
55.9bhp/L 41.7kW/L 56.7PS/L
42.2ft/sec 12.8m/sec
26.9mph 43.3kmh/1000rpm
16.0mpg 13.3mpgUS 17.7L/100km
Petrol 4-stroke piston
5345cc 326.1cu in
Vee 12 fuel injection
Compression ratio: 12.5:1
Bore: 90.0mm 3.5in
Stroke: 70.0mm 2.8in
Valve type/No: Overhead 24
Transmission: Automatic
No. of forward speeds: 3
Wheels driven: Rear
Springs F/R: Coil/Coil
Brake system: PA
Brakes F/R: Disc/Disc
Steering: Rack & pinion PA
Wheelbase: 259.1cm 102.0in
Track F: 148.8cm 58.6in
Track R: 147.3cm 58.0in
Length: 474.2cm 186.7in
Width: 179.3cm 70.6in
Height: 127.0cm 50.0in
Ground clearance: 14.0cm 5.5in
Kerb weight: 1736.1kg 3824.0lb
Fuel: 91.0L 20.0gal 24.0galUS

2343 Jaguar

XJS
1983 UK
140.0mph 225.3kmh
0-50mph 80.5kmh: 6.3secs
0-60mph 96.5kmh: 8.2secs
0-1/4 mile: 16.3secs
262.0bhp 195.4kW 265.6PS
@ 5000rpm
290.0lbft 393.0Nm @ 3000rpm
150.9bhp/ton 148.3bhp/tonne
49.0bhp/L 36.6kW/L 49.7PS/L
38.3ft/sec 11.7m/sec
26.3mph 42.3kmh/1000rpm
16.2mpg 13.5mpgUS 17.4L/100km
Petrol 4-stroke piston
5343cc 326.0cu in
Vee 12 fuel injection
Compression ratio: 11.5:1
Bore: 90.0mm 3.5in
Stroke: 70.0mm 2.8in
Valve type/No: Overhead 24
Transmission: Automatic
No. of forward speeds: 3
Wheels driven: Rear
Springs F/R: Coil/Coil
Brake system: PA
Brakes F/R: Disc/Disc
Steering: Rack & pinion PA
Wheelbase: 259.1cm 102.0in
Track F: 148.8cm 58.6in
Track R: 150.4cm 59.2in
Length: 485.9cm 191.3in
Width: 179.3cm 70.6in
Height: 126.0cm 49.6in
Kerb weight: 1766.1kg 3890.0lb
Fuel: 90.8L 20.0gal 24.0galUS

2344 Jaguar

XJ6 Vanden Plas
1984 UK
117.0mph 188.3kmh
0-50mph 80.5kmh: 9.1secs
0-60mph 96.5kmh: 12.3secs
0-1/4 mile: 18.9secs

176.0bhp 131.2kW 178.4PS
@ 4750rpm
219.0lbft 296.7Nm @ 2500rpm
92.8bhp/ton 91.2bhp/tonne
41.6bhp/L 31.0kW/L 42.1PS/L
55.0ft/sec 16.8m/sec
27.3mph 43.9kmh/1000rpm
21.0mpg 17.5mpgUS 13.4L/100km
Petrol 4-stroke piston
4235cc 258.4cu in
In-line 6 fuel injection
Compression ratio: 8.1:1
Bore: 92.1mm 3.6in
Stroke: 106.0mm 4.2in
Valve type/No: Overhead 12
Transmission: Automatic
No. of forward speeds: 3
Wheels driven: Rear
Springs F/R: Coil/Coil
Brake system: PA
Brakes F/R: Disc/Disc
Steering: Rack & pinion PA
Wheelbase: 287.0cm 113.0in
Track F: 148.1cm 58.3in
Track R: 149.6cm 58.9in
Length: 507.0cm 199.6in
Width: 176.8cm 69.6in
Height: 134.1cm 52.8in
Kerb weight: 1929.5kg 4250.0lb
Fuel: 89.3L 19.6gal 23.6galUS

2345 Jaguar
XJS 3.6
1984 UK
142.0mph 228.5kmh
0-50mph 80.5kmh: 5.6secs
0-60mph 96.5kmh: 7.4secs
0-1/4 mile: 15.9secs
0-1km: 28.6secs
225.0bhp 167.8kW 228.1PS
@ 5300rpm
240.0lbft 325.2Nm @ 4000rpm
140.9bhp/ton 138.5bhp/tonne
62.7bhp/L 46.7kW/L 63.5PS/L
53.3ft/sec 16.2m/sec
28.8mph 46.3kmh/1000rpm
17.6mpg 14.7mpgUS 16.1L/100km
Petrol 4-stroke piston
3590cc 219.0cu in
In-line 6 fuel injection
Compression ratio: 9.6:1
Bore: 91.0mm 3.6in
Stroke: 92.0mm 3.6in
Valve type/No: Overhead 24
Transmission: Manual
No. of forward speeds: 5
Wheels driven: Rear
Springs F/R: Coil/Coil
Brake system: PA
Brakes F/R: Disc/Disc
Steering: Rack & pinion PA
Wheelbase: 259.1cm 102.0in
Track F: 148.1cm 58.3in
Track R: 149.6cm 58.9in
Length: 474.5cm 186.8in
Width: 179.3cm 70.6in
Height: 127.0cm 50.0in
Ground clearance: 14.0cm 5.5in
Kerb weight: 1624.0kg 3577.0lb
Fuel: 91.0L 20.0gal 24.0galUS

2346 Jaguar
XJS HE
1984 UK
140.0mph 225.3kmh
0-50mph 80.5kmh: 6.3secs
0-60mph 96.5kmh: 8.2secs
0-1/4 mile: 16.3secs
262.0bhp 195.4kW 265.6PS
@ 5000rpm
290.0lbft 393.0Nm @ 3000rpm
150.9bhp/ton 148.3bhp/tonne
49.0bhp/L 36.6kW/L 49.7PS/L
38.3ft/sec 11.7m/sec
26.3mph 42.3kmh/1000rpm
16.2mpg 13.5mpgUS 17.4L/100km
Petrol 4-stroke piston
5343cc 326.0cu in
Vee 12 fuel injection
Compression ratio: 11.5:1
Bore: 90.0mm 3.5in
Stroke: 70.0mm 2.8in
Valve type/No: Overhead 24
Transmission: Automatic
No. of forward speeds: 3
Wheels driven: Rear
Springs F/R: Coil/Coil
Brake system: PA
Brakes F/R: Disc/Disc
Steering: Rack & pinion PA
Wheelbase: 259.1cm 102.0in
Track F: 148.8cm 58.6in
Track R: 150.4cm 59.2in
Length: 485.9cm 191.3in
Width: 179.3cm 70.6in
Height: 126.0cm 49.6in
Kerb weight: 1766.1kg 3890.0lb
Fuel: 90.8L 20.0gal 24.0galUS

2347 Jaguar
XJS HE Cabriolet
1985 UK
146.0mph 234.9kmh
0-50mph 80.5kmh: 6.2secs
0-60mph 96.5kmh: 7.7secs
0-1/4 mile: 15.9secs
0-1km: 28.5secs
295.0bhp 220.0kW 299.1PS
@ 5500rpm
320.0lbft 433.6Nm @ 3250rpm
168.0bhp/ton 165.2bhp/tonne
55.2bhp/L 41.2kW/L 56.0PS/L
42.2ft/sec 12.8m/sec
26.8mph 43.1kmh/1000rpm
14.5mpg 12.1mpgUS 19.5L/100km
Petrol 4-stroke piston
5345cc 326.1cu in
Vee 12 fuel injection
Compression ratio: 12.5:1
Bore: 90.0mm 3.5in
Stroke: 70.0mm 2.8in
Valve type/No: Overhead 24
Transmission: Automatic
No. of forward speeds: 3
Wheels driven: Rear
Springs F/R: Coil/Coil
Brake system: PA
Brakes F/R: Disc/Disc
Steering: Rack & pinion PA
Wheelbase: 259.1cm 102.0in
Track F: 148.1cm 58.3in
Track R: 149.6cm 58.9in
Length: 474.5cm 186.8in
Width: 179.3cm 70.6in
Height: 127.0cm 50.0in
Ground clearance: 14.0cm 5.5in
Kerb weight: 1785.6kg 3933.0lb
Fuel: 91.0L 20.0gal 24.0galUS

2348 Jaguar
XJ6 3.6
1986 UK
140.0mph 225.3kmh
0-50mph 80.5kmh: 7.4secs
0-60mph 96.5kmh: 9.8secs
0-1/4 mile: 15.8secs
0-1km: 28.9secs
221.0bhp 164.8kW 224.1PS
@ 5250rpm
248.0lbft 336.0Nm @ 4000rpm
133.2bhp/ton 131.0bhp/tonne
61.6bhp/L 45.9kW/L 62.4PS/L
52.8ft/sec 16.1m/sec
28.1mph 45.2kmh/1000rpm
20.7mpg 17.2mpgUS 13.6L/100km
Petrol 4-stroke piston
3590cc 219.0cu in
In-line 6 fuel injection
Compression ratio: 9.6:1
Bore: 91.0mm 3.6in
Stroke: 92.0mm 3.6in
Valve type/No: Overhead 24
Transmission: Manual
No. of forward speeds: 5
Wheels driven: Rear
Springs F/R: Coil/Coil
Brake system: PA
Brakes F/R: Disc/Disc
Steering: Rack & pinion PA
Wheelbase: 287.0cm 113.0in
Track F: 150.0cm 59.1in
Track R: 149.8cm 59.0in
Length: 498.8cm 196.4in
Width: 200.5cm 78.9in
Height: 138.0cm 54.3in
Ground clearance: 12.0cm 4.7in
Kerb weight: 1687.0kg 3715.9lb
Fuel: 89.2L 19.6gal 23.6galUS

2349 Jaguar
XJS
1986 UK
132.0mph 212.4kmh
0-60mph 96.5kmh: 8.7secs
0-1/4 mile: 16.5secs
262.0bhp 195.4kW 265.6PS
@ 5000rpm
290.0lbft 393.0Nm @ 3000rpm
148.0bhp/ton 145.5bhp/tonne
49.0bhp/L 36.6kW/L 49.7PS/L
38.3ft/sec 11.7m/sec
15.9mpg 13.2mpgUS 17.8L/100km
Petrol 4-stroke piston
5343cc 326.0cu in
Vee 12 fuel injection
Bore: 90.0mm 3.5in
Stroke: 70.0mm 2.8in
Valve type/No: Overhead 24
Transmission: Automatic
No. of forward speeds: 3
Wheels driven: Rear
Springs F/R: Coil/Coil
Brake system: PA
Brakes F/R: Disc/Disc
Steering: Rack & pinion PA
Wheelbase: 259.1cm 102.0in
Track F: 148.8cm 58.6in
Track R: 150.4cm 59.2in
Length: 486.9cm 191.7in
Width: 179.3cm 70.6in
Height: 120.9cm 47.6in
Kerb weight: 1800.1kg 3965.0lb
Fuel: 90.8L 20.0gal 24.0galUS

2350 Jaguar
XJSC
1986 UK
141.0mph 226.9kmh
0-50mph 80.5kmh: 6.8secs
0-60mph 96.5kmh: 8.8secs
0-1/4 mile: 16.7secs
262.0bhp 195.4kW 265.6PS
@ 5000rpm
290.0lbft 393.0Nm @ 3000rpm
146.3bhp/ton 143.9bhp/tonne
49.0bhp/L 36.6kW/L 49.7PS/L
38.3ft/sec 11.7m/sec
15.6mpg 13.0mpgUS 18.1L/100km
Petrol 4-stroke piston
5343cc 326.0cu in
Vee 12 fuel injection
Compression ratio: 11.5:1
Bore: 90.0mm 3.5in
Stroke: 70.0mm 2.8in
Valve type/No: Overhead 24
Transmission: Automatic
No. of forward speeds: 3
Wheels driven: Rear
Springs F/R: Coil/Coil
Brake system: PA
Brakes F/R: Disc/Disc
Steering: Rack & pinion PA
Wheelbase: 259.1cm 102.0in
Track F: 148.8cm 58.6in
Track R: 150.4cm 59.2in
Length: 486.9cm 191.7in
Width: 179.3cm 70.6in
Height: 121.4cm 47.8in
Kerb weight: 1820.5kg 4010.0lb
Fuel: 90.8L 20.0gal 24.0galUS

2351 Jaguar
XJSC HE
1986 UK
150.0mph 241.4kmh
0-60mph 96.5kmh: 7.2secs
0-1/4 mile: 15.7secs
295.0bhp 220.0kW 299.1PS
@ 5500rpm
320.0lbft 433.6Nm @ 3250rpm
170.7bhp/ton 167.9bhp/tonne
55.2bhp/L 41.2kW/L 56.0PS/L
42.2ft/sec 12.8m/sec
26.3mph 42.3kmh/1000rpm
16.2mpg 13.5mpgUS 17.4L/100km
Petrol 4-stroke piston
5343cc 326.0cu in
Vee 12 fuel injection
Compression ratio: 12.5:1
Bore: 90.0mm 3.5in
Stroke: 70.0mm 2.8in
Valve type/No: Overhead 24
Transmission: Automatic
No. of forward speeds: 3
Wheels driven: Rear
Springs F/R: Coil/Coil
Brakes F/R: Disc/Disc
Steering: Rack & pinion PA
Wheelbase: 259.1cm 102.0in
Track F: 148.8cm 58.6in
Track R: 150.4cm 59.2in
Length: 476.5cm 187.6in
Width: 179.3cm 70.6in
Height: 126.2cm 49.7in
Kerb weight: 1757.0kg 3870.0lb

2352 Jaguar
XJ6
1987 UK
130.0mph 209.2kmh
0-50mph 80.5kmh: 8.3secs
0-60mph 96.5kmh: 11.5secs
0-1/4 mile: 18.3secs
181.0bhp 135.0kW 183.5PS
@ 4750rpm
221.0lbft 299.5Nm @ 3750rpm
103.6bhp/ton 101.8bhp/tonne
50.4bhp/L 37.6kW/L 51.1PS/L
47.8ft/sec 14.6m/sec
21.0mpg 17.5mpgUS 13.4L/100km
Petrol 4-stroke piston
3590cc 219.0cu in
In-line 6 fuel injection
Compression ratio: 8.2:1
Bore: 91.0mm 3.6in
Stroke: 92.0mm 3.6in
Valve type/No: Overhead 24
Transmission: Automatic
No. of forward speeds: 4
Wheels driven: Rear
Springs F/R: Coil/Coil
Brake system: PA ABS
Brakes F/R: Disc/Disc
Steering: Rack & pinion PA
Wheelbase: 287.0cm 113.0in
Track F: 150.1cm 59.1in
Track R: 149.9cm 59.0in
Length: 498.9cm 196.4in
Width: 200.4cm 78.9in
Height: 137.9cm 54.3in
Ground clearance: 11.9cm 4.7in
Kerb weight: 1777.4kg 3915.0lb
Fuel: 87.8L 19.3gal 23.2galUS

2353 Jaguar
XJ6 2.9
1987 UK
118.0mph 189.9kmh
0-50mph 80.5kmh: 7.0secs
0-60mph 96.5kmh: 9.9secs
0-1/4 mile: 17.5secs
0-1km: 32.0secs
165.0bhp 123.0kW 167.3PS
@ 5600rpm
176.0lbft 238.5Nm @ 4000rpm
101.2bhp/ton 99.5bhp/tonne
56.5bhp/L 42.1kW/L 57.3PS/L
45.7ft/sec 14.0m/sec
26.6mph 42.8kmh/1000rpm
19.3mpg 16.1mpgUS 14.6L/100km
Petrol 4-stroke piston
2919cc 178.0cu in
In-line 6 fuel injection
Compression ratio: 12.6:1
Bore: 91.0mm 3.6in
Stroke: 74.8mm 2.9in
Valve type/No: Overhead 12
Transmission: Manual
No. of forward speeds: 5
Wheels driven: Rear
Springs F/R: Coil/Coil
Brake system: PA
Brakes F/R: Disc/Drum
Steering: Rack & pinion PA
Wheelbase: 287.0cm 113.0in
Track F: 150.0cm 59.1in
Track R: 149.8cm 59.0in
Length: 498.8cm 196.4in
Width: 200.5cm 78.9in
Height: 138.0cm 54.3in
Ground clearance: 12.0cm 4.7in
Kerb weight: 1658.0kg 3652.0lb
Fuel: 88.7L 19.5gal 23.4galUS

2354 Jaguar
XJS 3.6 Automatic
1987 UK
134.0mph 215.6kmh
0-50mph 80.5kmh: 5.8secs
0-60mph 96.5kmh: 7.8secs
0-1/4 mile: 16.0secs
0-1km: 29.4secs
221.0bhp 164.8kW 224.1PS
@ 5250rpm
248.0lbft 336.0Nm @ 4000rpm
139.6bhp/ton 137.3bhp/tonne

61.6bhp/L 45.9kW/L 62.4PS/L
52.8ft/sec 16.1m/sec
29.1mph 46.8kmh/1000rpm
18.0mpg 15.0mpgUS 15.7L/100km
Petrol 4-stroke piston
3590cc 219.0cu in
In-line 6 fuel injection
Compression ratio: 9.6:1
Bore: 91.0mm 3.6in
Stroke: 92.0mm 3.6in
Valve type/No: Overhead 24
Transmission: Automatic
No. of forward speeds: 4
Wheels driven: Rear
Springs F/R: Coil/Coil
Brake system: PA
Brakes F/R: Disc/Disc
Steering: Rack & pinion PA
Wheelbase: 259.1cm 102.0in
Track F: 148.1cm 58.3in
Track R: 149.6cm 58.9in
Length: 476.4cm 187.6in
Width: 179.3cm 70.6in
Height: 126.4cm 49.8in
Ground clearance: 14.0cm 5.5in
Kerb weight: 1610.0kg 3546.3lb
Fuel: 91.0L 20.0gal 24.0galUS

2355 Jaguar
XJS
1988 UK
140.0mph 225.3kmh
0-50mph 80.5kmh: 6.7secs
0-60mph 96.5kmh: 8.6secs
0-1/4 mile: 16.5secs
262.0bhp 195.4kW 265.6PS
@ 5000rpm
290.0lbft 393.0Nm @ 5000rpm
145.3bhp/ton 142.8bhp/tonne
49.0bhp/L 36.6kW/L 49.7PS/L
38.3ft/sec 11.7m/sec
16.8mpg 14.0mpgUS 16.8L/100km
Petrol 4-stroke piston
5344cc 326.0cu in
Vee 12 fuel injection
Compression ratio: 11.5:1
Bore: 90.0mm 3.5in
Stroke: 70.0mm 2.8in
Valve type/No: Overhead 24
Transmission: Automatic
No. of forward speeds: 3
Wheels driven: Rear
Springs F/R: Coil/Coil
Brake system: PA
Brakes F/R: Disc/Disc
Steering: Rack & pinion PA
Wheelbase: 259.1cm 102.0in
Track F: 148.8cm 58.6in
Track R: 150.4cm 59.2in
Length: 486.9cm 191.7in
Width: 179.3cm 70.6in
Height: 121.4cm 47.8in
Kerb weight: 1834.2kg 4040.0lb
Fuel: 90.8L 20.0gal 24.0galUS

2356 Jaguar
XJS Koenig
1988 UK
150.0mph 241.4kmh
0-60mph 96.5kmh: 7.5secs
0-1/4 mile: 15.5secs
280.0bhp 208.8kW 283.9PS
@ 5000rpm
300.0lbft 406.5Nm @ 3000rpm
155.6bhp/ton 153.0bhp/tonne
52.4bhp/L 39.1kW/L 53.1PS/L
38.3ft/sec 11.7m/sec
Petrol 4-stroke piston
5343cc 326.0cu in
Vee 12 fuel injection
Compression ratio: 11.5:1
Bore: 90.0mm 3.5in
Stroke: 70.0mm 2.8in
Valve type/No: Overhead 24
Transmission: Automatic
No. of forward speeds: 3
Wheels driven: Rear
Springs F/R: Coil/Coil
Brake system: PA
Brakes F/R: Disc/Disc
Steering: Rack & pinion PA
Wheelbase: 259.1cm 102.0in
Length: 486.9cm 191.7in
Width: 214.6cm 84.5in
Height: 121.4cm 47.8in
Kerb weight: 1829.6kg 4030.0lb
Fuel: 90.8L 20.0gal 24.0galUS

2357 Jaguar
XJS V12 Convertible
1988 UK
146.0mph 234.9kmh
0-50mph 80.5kmh: 6.3secs
0-60mph 96.5kmh: 8.0secs
0-1/4 mile: 16.3secs
0-1km: 29.2secs
291.0bhp 217.0kW 295.0PS
@ 5500rpm
317.3lbft 430.0Nm @ 3000rpm
161.3bhp/ton 158.6bhp/tonne
54.4bhp/L 40.6kW/L 55.2PS/L
42.2ft/sec 12.8m/sec
26.2mph 42.2kmh/1000rpm
13.8mpg 11.5mpgUS 20.5L/100km
Petrol 4-stroke piston
5345cc 326.0cu in
Vee 12 fuel injection
Compression ratio: 12.5:1
Bore: 90.0mm 3.5in
Stroke: 70.0mm 2.8in
Valve type/No: Overhead 24
Transmission: Automatic
No. of forward speeds: 3
Wheels driven: Rear
Springs F/R: Coil/Coil
Brake system: PA ABS
Brakes F/R: Disc/Disc
Steering: Rack & pinion PA
Wheelbase: 259.0cm 102.0in
Track F: 148.1cm 58.3in
Track R: 149.6cm 58.9in
Length: 476.5cm 187.6in
Width: 179.3cm 70.6in
Height: 126.2cm 49.7in
Ground clearance: 14.0cm 5.5in
Kerb weight: 1835.0kg 4041.8lb
Fuel: 81.9L 18.0gal 21.6galUS

2358 Jaguar
4.0 Sovereign
1989 UK
141.0mph 226.9kmh
0-50mph 80.5kmh: 6.3secs
0-60mph 96.5kmh: 8.3secs
0-1/4 mile: 16.0secs
0-1km: 29.2secs
235.0bhp 175.2kW 238.3PS
@ 4750rpm
285.6lbft 387.0Nm @ 3750rpm
136.6bhp/ton 134.3bhp/tonne
59.0bhp/L 44.0kW/L 59.9PS/L
53.0ft/sec 16.1m/sec
29.0mph 46.7kmh/1000rpm
18.5mpg 15.4mpgUS 15.3L/100km
Petrol 4-stroke piston
3980cc 243.0cu in
In-line 6 fuel injection
Compression ratio: 9.5:1
Bore: 91.0mm 3.6in
Stroke: 102.0mm 4.0in
Valve type/No: Overhead 24
Transmission: Automatic
No. of forward speeds: 4
Wheels driven: Rear
Springs F/R: Coil/Coil
Brake system: PA ABS
Brakes F/R: Disc/Disc
Steering: Rack & pinion PA
Wheelbase: 287.0cm 113.0in
Track F: 150.0cm 59.1in
Track R: 149.8cm 59.0in
Length: 498.8cm 196.4in
Width: 201.5cm 79.3in
Height: 138.0cm 54.3in
Ground clearance: 12.0cm 4.7in
Kerb weight: 1750.0kg 3854.6lb
Fuel: 89.2L 19.6gal 23.6galUS

2359 Jaguar
XJ220
1989 UK
200.0mph 321.8kmh
0-60mph 96.5kmh: 3.5secs
530.0bhp 395.2kW 537.3PS
@ 7000rpm
400.0lbft 542.0Nm @ 5000rpm
345.1bhp/ton 339.4bhp/tonne
85.2bhp/L 63.5kW/L 86.4PS/L
59.7ft/sec 18.2m/sec
Petrol 4-stroke piston
6222cc 379.6cu in
Vee 12
Compression ratio: 10.0:1
Bore: 92.0mm 3.6in
Stroke: 78.0mm 3.1in
Valve type/No: Overhead 48
Transmission: Manual
No. of forward speeds: 5
Wheels driven: 4-wheel drive
Springs F/R: Coil/Coil
Brake system: ABS
Brakes F/R: Disc/Disc
Steering: Rack & pinion
Wheelbase: 284.5cm 112.0in
Length: 513.1cm 202.0in
Width: 199.9cm 78.7in
Height: 115.1cm 45.3in
Kerb weight: 1561.8kg 3440.0lb

2360 Jaguar
XJS Convertible
1989 UK
150.0mph 241.4kmh
0-60mph 96.5kmh: 8.7secs
0-1/4 mile: 16.2secs
262.0bhp 195.4kW 265.6PS
@ 5000rpm
290.0lbft 393.0Nm @ 5000rpm
140.1bhp/ton 137.7bhp/tonne
49.0bhp/L 36.6kW/L 49.7PS/L
38.3ft/sec 11.7m/sec
Petrol 4-stroke piston
5344cc 326.0cu in
Vee 12 fuel injection
Compression ratio: 11.5:1
Bore: 90.0mm 3.5in
Stroke: 70.0mm 2.8in
Valve type/No: Overhead 24
Transmission: Automatic
No. of forward speeds: 3
Wheels driven: Rear
Springs F/R: Coil/Coil
Brake system: PA ABS
Brakes F/R: Disc/Disc
Steering: Rack & pinion PA
Wheelbase: 259.1cm 102.0in
Track F: 148.8cm 58.6in
Track R: 150.4cm 59.2in
Length: 486.9cm 191.7in
Width: 179.3cm 70.6in
Height: 121.4cm 47.8in
Kerb weight: 1902.3kg 4190.0lb
Fuel: 90.8L 20.0gal 24.0galUS

2361 Jaguar
XJS V12 Convertible
1989 UK
141.0mph 226.9kmh
0-60mph 96.5kmh: 9.9secs
0-1/4 mile: 17.5secs
262.0bhp 195.4kW 265.6PS
@ 5000rpm
290.0lbft 393.0Nm @ 5000rpm
141.2bhp/ton 138.9bhp/tonne
49.0bhp/L 36.5kW/L 49.7PS/L
38.3ft/sec 11.7m/sec
15.6mpg 13.0mpgUS 18.1L/100km
Petrol 4-stroke piston
5345cc 326.1cu in
Vee 12 fuel injection
Compression ratio: 11.5:1
Bore: 90.0mm 3.5in
Stroke: 70.0mm 2.8in
Valve type/No: Overhead 24
Transmission: Automatic
No. of forward speeds: 3
Wheels driven: Rear
Springs F/R: Coil/Coil
Brake system: PA ABS
Brakes F/R: Disc/Disc
Steering: Rack & pinion PA
Wheelbase: 259.1cm 102.0in
Track F: 148.8cm 58.6in
Track R: 150.4cm 59.2in
Length: 486.9cm 191.7in
Width: 179.3cm 70.6in
Height: 125.5cm 49.4in
Kerb weight: 1886.4kg 4155.0lb
Fuel: 81.8L 18.0gal 21.6galUS

2362 Jaguar
XJ6 Vanden Plas
1990 UK
136.0mph 218.8kmh
0-60mph 96.5kmh: 9.2secs
0-1/4 mile: 16.9secs
223.0bhp 166.3kW 226.1PS
@ 4750rpm
278.0lbft 376.7Nm @ 3650rpm
120.2bhp/ton 118.2bhp/tonne
56.0bhp/L 41.8kW/L 56.8PS/L
53.0ft/sec 16.1m/sec
21.6mpg 18.0mpgUS 13.1L/100km
Petrol 4-stroke piston
3980cc 242.8cu in
In-line 6 fuel injection
Compression ratio: 9.6:1
Bore: 91.0mm 3.6in
Stroke: 102.0mm 4.0in
Valve type/No: Overhead 24
Transmission: Automatic
No. of forward speeds: 4
Wheels driven: Rear
Springs F/R: Coil/Coil
Brake system: PA ABS
Brakes F/R: Disc/Disc
Steering: Rack & pinion PA
Wheelbase: 287.0cm 113.0in
Track F: 150.1cm 59.1in
Track R: 149.9cm 59.0in
Length: 498.9cm 196.4in
Width: 200.4cm 78.9in
Height: 137.9cm 54.3in
Kerb weight: 1886.4kg 4155.0lb
Fuel: 87.8L 19.3gal 23.2galUS

2363 Jaguar
XJR 4.0
1990 UK
143.0mph 230.1kmh
0-50mph 80.5kmh: 6.3secs
0-60mph 96.5kmh: 8.3secs
0-1/4 mile: 16.6secs
0-1km: 29.1secs
251.0bhp 187.2kW 254.5PS
@ 5250rpm
278.2lbft 377.0Nm @ 4000rpm
142.6bhp/ton 140.2bhp/tonne
63.1bhp/L 47.0kW/L 63.9PS/L
58.6ft/sec 17.8m/sec
29.0mph 46.7kmh/1000rpm
17.2mpg 14.3mpgUS 16.4L/100km
Petrol 4-stroke piston
3980cc 243.0cu in
In-line 6 fuel injection
Compression ratio: 9.7:1
Bore: 91.0mm 3.6in
Stroke: 102.0mm 4.0in
Valve type/No: Overhead 24
Transmission: Automatic
No. of forward speeds: 4
Wheels driven: Rear
Springs F/R: Coil/Coil
Brake system: PA ABS
Brakes F/R: Disc/Disc
Steering: Rack & pinion PA
Wheelbase: 287.0cm 113.0in
Track F: 150.1cm 59.1in
Track R: 149.9cm 59.0in
Length: 498.9cm 196.4in
Width: 201.4cm 79.3in
Height: 137.9cm 54.3in
Ground clearance: 11.9cm 4.7in
Kerb weight: 1790.0kg 3942.7lb
Fuel: 89.2L 19.6gal 23.6galUS

2364 Jaguar
XJRS
1990 UK
150.0mph 241.4kmh
0-60mph 96.5kmh: 7.7secs
0-1/4 mile: 17.5secs
286.0bhp 213.3kW 290.0PS
@ 5150rpm
310.0lbft 420.1Nm @ 2800rpm
161.4bhp/ton 158.7bhp/tonne
53.5bhp/L 39.9kW/L 54.3PS/L
39.5ft/sec 12.0m/sec
Petrol 4-stroke piston
5344cc 326.0cu in
Vee 12 fuel injection
Compression ratio: 11.5:1
Bore: 90.0mm 3.5in
Stroke: 70.0mm 2.8in
Valve type/No: Overhead 24
Transmission: Automatic
No. of forward speeds: 3
Wheels driven: Rear
Springs F/R: Coil/Coil
Brake system: PA ABS
Brakes F/R: Disc/Disc
Steering: Rack & pinion PA
Wheelbase: 259.1cm 102.0in
Track F: 150.1cm 59.1in
Track R: 151.6cm 59.7in
Length: 476.5cm 187.6in
Width: 188.2cm 74.1in
Height: 126.2cm 49.7in

Kerb weight: 1802.4kg 3970.0lb
Fuel: 90.8L 20.0gal 24.0galUS

2365 Jaguar
XJS
1990 UK
135.0mph 217.2kmh
0-50mph 80.5kmh: 7.7secs
0-60mph 96.5kmh: 9.9secs
0-1/4 mile: 17.5secs
262.0bhp 195.4kW 265.6PS
@ 5000rpm
290.0lbft 393.0Nm @ 3000rpm
146.2bhp/ton 143.7bhp/tonne
49.0bhp/L 36.6kW/L 49.7PS/L
38.3ft/sec 11.7m/sec
22.5mpg 18.7mpgUS 12.6L/100km
Petrol 4-stroke piston
5344cc 326.0cu in
Vee 12 fuel injection
Compression ratio: 11.5:1
Bore: 90.0mm 3.5in
Stroke: 70.0mm 2.8in
Valve type/No: Overhead 24
Transmission: Automatic
No. of forward speeds: 3
Wheels driven: Rear
Springs F/R: Coil/Coil
Brake system: PA ABS
Brakes F/R: Disc/Disc
Steering: Rack & pinion PA
Wheelbase: 259.1cm 102.0in
Track F: 148.8cm 58.6in
Track R: 150.4cm 59.2in
Length: 486.9cm 191.7in
Width: 179.3cm 70.6in
Height: 121.4cm 47.8in
Kerb weight: 1822.8kg 4015.0lb
Fuel: 90.8L 20.0gal 24.0galUS

2366 Jaguar
XJS Lister Le Mans
1990 UK
200.0mph 321.8kmh
0-60mph 96.5kmh: 4.4secs
0-1/4 mile: 12.6secs
496.0bhp 369.9kW 502.9PS
@ 6200rpm
500.0lbft 677.5Nm @ 3850rpm
279.9bhp/ton 275.2bhp/tonne
70.9bhp/L 52.9kW/L 71.9PS/L
57.0ft/sec 17.4m/sec
Petrol 4-stroke piston
6996cc 426.8cu in
Vee 12 fuel injection
Compression ratio: 11.2:1
Bore: 94.0mm 3.7in
Stroke: 84.0mm 3.3in
Valve type/No: Overhead 24
Transmission: Manual
No. of forward speeds: 5
Wheels driven: Rear
Springs F/R: Coil/Coil
Brake system: PA ABS
Brakes F/R: Disc/Disc
Steering: Rack & pinion PA
Wheelbase: 259.1cm 102.0in
Track F: 186.7cm 73.5in
Track R: 193.0cm 76.0in
Length: 466.6cm 183.7in
Width: 196.9cm 77.5in
Height: 120.7cm 47.5in
Kerb weight: 1802.4kg 3970.0lb
Fuel: 128.3L 28.2gal 33.9galUS

2367 Jaguar
XJS Railton
1990 UK
135.0mph 217.2kmh
0-60mph 96.5kmh: 9.9secs
0-1/4 mile: 17.5secs
286.0bhp 213.3kW 290.0PS
@ 5000rpm
310.0lbft 420.1Nm @ 5000rpm
153.4bhp/ton 150.9bhp/tonne
53.5bhp/L 39.9kW/L 54.3PS/L
38.3ft/sec 11.7m/sec
Petrol 4-stroke piston
5344cc 326.0cu in
Vee 12 fuel injection
Compression ratio: 11.5:1
Bore: 90.0mm 3.5in
Stroke: 70.0mm 2.8in
Valve type/No: Overhead 24
Transmission: Automatic
No. of forward speeds: 3
Wheels driven: Rear
Springs F/R: Coil/Coil
Brake system: PA ABS
Brakes F/R: Disc/Disc
Steering: Rack & pinion PA
Wheelbase: 259.1cm 102.0in
Track F: 148.8cm 58.6in
Track R: 150.4cm 59.2in
Length: 480.1cm 189.0in
Width: 181.9cm 71.6in
Height: 121.4cm 47.8in
Kerb weight: 1895.4kg 4175.0lb
Fuel: 90.8L 20.0gal 24.0galUS

2368 Jaguar
XJ6 3.2
1991 UK
136.0mph 218.8kmh
0-50mph 80.5kmh: 6.1secs
0-60mph 96.5kmh: 8.3secs
0-1/4 mile: 16.1secs
0-1km: 29.7secs
200.0bhp 149.1kW 202.8PS
@ 5250rpm
219.9lbft 298.0Nm @ 4000rpm
121.8bhp/ton 119.8bhp/tonne
61.7bhp/L 46.0kW/L 62.6PS/L
47.7ft/sec 14.5m/sec
26.6mph 42.8kmh/1000rpm
19.9mpg 16.6mpgUS 14.2L/100km
Petrol 4-stroke piston
3239cc 198.0cu in
In-line 6 fuel injection
Compression ratio: 9.7:1
Bore: 91.0mm 3.6in
Stroke: 83.0mm 3.3in
Valve type/No: Overhead 24
Transmission: Manual
No. of forward speeds: 5
Wheels driven: Rear
Springs F/R: Coil/Coil
Brake system: PA ABS
Brakes F/R: Disc/Disc
Steering: Rack & pinion PA
Wheelbase: 287.0cm 113.0in
Track F: 150.0cm 59.1in
Track R: 149.8cm 59.0in
Length: 498.8cm 196.4in
Width: 201.5cm 79.3in
Height: 138.0cm 54.3in
Ground clearance: 12.0cm 4.7in
Kerb weight: 1670.0kg 3678.4lb
Fuel: 86.4L 19.0gal 22.8galUS

2369 Jaguar
XJR15
1991 UK
185.0mph 297.7kmh
450.0bhp 335.6kW 456.2PS
@ 6250rpm
420.0lbft 569.1Nm @ 4500rpm
436.4bhp/ton 429.1bhp/tonne
75.1bhp/L 56.0kW/L 76.1PS/L
53.6ft/sec 16.3m/sec
Petrol 4-stroke piston
5993cc 365.6cu in
Vee 12 fuel injection
Compression ratio: 11.0:1
Bore: 90.0mm 3.5in
Stroke: 78.4mm 3.1in
Valve type/No: Overhead 24
Transmission: Manual
No. of forward speeds: 6
Wheels driven: Rear
Springs F/R: Coil/Coil
Brakes F/R: Disc/Disc
Steering: Rack & pinion
Wheelbase: 271.8cm 107.0in
Length: 479.8cm 188.9in
Width: 190.0cm 74.8in
Height: 110.0cm 43.3in
Kerb weight: 1048.7kg 2310.0lb
Fuel: 120.0L 26.4gal 31.7galUS

2370 Jaguar
XJS
1991 UK
147.0mph 236.5kmh
0-60mph 96.5kmh: 7.8secs
280.0bhp 208.8kW 283.9PS
@ 5550rpm
306.0lbft 414.6Nm @ 2800rpm
155.8bhp/ton 153.2bhp/tonne
52.4bhp/L 39.1kW/L 53.1PS/L
42.5ft/sec 12.9m/sec
Petrol 4-stroke piston
5345cc 326.1cu in
Vee 12 fuel injection
Compression ratio: 11.5:1
Bore: 90.0mm 3.5in
Stroke: 70.0mm 2.8in
Valve type/No: Overhead 24
Transmission: Automatic
No. of forward speeds: 3
Wheels driven: Rear
Springs F/R: Coil/Coil
Brake system: PA ABS
Brakes F/R: Disc/Disc
Steering: Rack & pinion PA
Wheelbase: 259.1cm 102.0in
Track F: 148.8cm 58.6in
Track R: 150.4cm 59.2in
Length: 476.5cm 187.6in
Width: 188.2cm 74.1in
Height: 125.5cm 49.4in
Kerb weight: 1827.3kg 4025.0lb
Fuel: 88.9L 19.5gal 23.5galUS

2371 Jaguar
XJS 4.0 Auto
1991 UK
138.0mph 222.0kmh
0-50mph 80.5kmh: 6.6secs
0-60mph 96.5kmh: 8.7secs
0-1/4 mile: 16.7secs
0-1km: 30.0secs
223.0bhp 166.3kW 226.1PS
@ 4750rpm
278.2lbft 377.0Nm @ 3650rpm
140.7bhp/ton 138.3bhp/tonne
56.0bhp/L 41.8kW/L 56.8PS/L
53.0ft/sec 16.1m/sec
29.1mph 46.8kmh/1000rpm
18.8mpg 15.7mpgUS 15.0L/100km
Petrol 4-stroke piston
3980cc 243.0cu in
In-line 6 fuel injection
Compression ratio: 9.5:1
Bore: 91.0mm 3.6in
Stroke: 102.0mm 4.0in
Valve type/No: Overhead 24
Transmission: Automatic
No. of forward speeds: 4
Wheels driven: Rear
Springs F/R: Coil/Coil
Brake system: PA ABS
Brakes F/R: Disc/Disc
Steering: Rack & pinion PA
Wheelbase: 259.1cm 102.0in
Track F: 148.9cm 58.6in
Track R: 150.4cm 59.2in
Length: 476.4cm 187.6in
Width: 179.3cm 70.6in
Height: 124.7cm 49.1in
Ground clearance: 12.8cm 5.0in
Kerb weight: 1612.0kg 3550.7lb
Fuel: 55.1L 12.1gal 14.5galUS

2372 Jaguar
XJS Convertible
1991 UK
135.0mph 217.2kmh
0-50mph 80.5kmh: 7.7secs
0-60mph 96.5kmh: 9.9secs
0-1/4 mile: 17.5secs
262.0bhp 195.4kW 265.6PS
@ 5000rpm
290.0lbft 393.0Nm @ 3000rpm
136.5bhp/ton 134.2bhp/tonne
49.0bhp/L 36.6kW/L 49.7PS/L
38.3ft/sec 11.7m/sec
22.5mpg 18.7mpgUS 12.6L/100km
Petrol 4-stroke piston
5344cc 326.0cu in
Vee 12 fuel injection
Compression ratio: 11.5:1
Bore: 90.0mm 3.5in
Stroke: 70.0mm 2.8in
Valve type/No: Overhead 24
Transmission: Automatic
No. of forward speeds: 3
Wheels driven: Rear
Springs F/R: Coil/Coil
Brake system: PA ABS
Brakes F/R: Disc/Disc
Steering: Rack & pinion PA
Wheelbase: 259.1cm 102.0in
Track F: 128.5cm 50.6in
Track R: 150.4cm 59.2in
Length: 486.9cm 191.7in
Width: 179.3cm 70.6in
Height: 121.4cm 47.8in
Kerb weight: 1952.2kg 4300.0lb
Fuel: 90.8L 20.0gal 24.0galUS

2373 Jeep
Wagoneer
1964 USA
92.0mph 148.0kmh
0-50mph 80.5kmh: 11.0secs
0-60mph 96.5kmh: 15.5secs
0-1/4 mile: 20.0secs
140.0bhp 104.4kW 141.9PS
@ 4000rpm
210.0lbft 284.6Nm @ 1750rpm
78.9bhp/ton 77.6bhp/tonne
37.8bhp/L 28.2kW/L 38.3PS/L
48.8ft/sec 14.9m/sec
18.8mph 30.2kmh/1000rpm
14.8mpg 12.3mpgUS 19.1L/100km
Petrol 4-stroke piston
3708cc 226.2cu in
In-line 6 1 Carburettor
Compression ratio: 8.5:1
Bore: 84.9mm 3.3in
Stroke: 111.5mm 4.4in
Valve type/No: Overhead 12
Transmission: Manual
No. of forward speeds: 3
Wheels driven: 4-wheel drive
Springs F/R: Torsion bar/Leaf
Brake system: PA
Brakes F/R: Drum/Drum
Steering: Cam & lever PA
Wheelbase: 279.4cm 110.0in
Track F: 144.8cm 57.0in
Track R: 144.8cm 57.0in
Length: 462.3cm 182.0in
Width: 191.8cm 75.5in
Height: 171.5cm 67.5in
Ground clearance: 17.8cm 7.0in
Kerb weight: 1805.1kg 3976.0lb
Fuel: 75.5L 16.6gal 19.9galUS

2374 Jeep
CJ-5
1971 USA
92.0mph 148.0kmh
0-60mph 96.5kmh: 11.2secs
160.0bhp 119.3kW 162.2PS
@ 4200rpm
235.0lbft 318.4Nm @ 2400rpm
140.5bhp/ton 138.2bhp/tonne
43.4bhp/L 32.4kW/L 44.0PS/L
51.0ft/sec 15.5m/sec
19.2mpg 16.0mpgUS 14.7L/100km
Petrol 4-stroke piston
3687cc 224.9cu in
Vee 6
Compression ratio: 9.0:1
Bore: 95.3mm 3.8in
Stroke: 111.1mm 4.4in
Valve type/No: Overhead 12
Transmission: Manual
No. of forward speeds: 3
Wheels driven: 4-wheel drive
Brakes F/R: Drum/Drum
Steering: Cam & lever
Wheelbase: 205.7cm 81.0in
Track F: 122.9cm 48.4in
Track R: 122.9cm 48.4in
Length: 344.4cm 135.6in
Width: 157.0cm 61.8in
Height: 176.5cm 69.5in
Ground clearance: 21.6cm 8.5in
Kerb weight: 1157.7kg 2550.0lb
Fuel: 53.0L 11.6gal 14.0galUS

2375 Jeep
Commando
1971 USA
94.0mph 151.2kmh
0-60mph 96.5kmh: 16.4secs
160.0bhp 119.3kW 162.2PS
@ 4200rpm
235.0lbft 318.4Nm @ 2400rpm
112.7bhp/ton 110.8bhp/tonne
43.4bhp/L 32.4kW/L 44.0PS/L
51.0ft/sec 15.5m/sec
15.6mpg 13.0mpgUS 18.1L/100km
Petrol 4-stroke piston
3687cc 224.9cu in
Vee 6
Compression ratio: 9.0:1
Bore: 95.3mm 3.8in
Stroke: 111.1mm 4.4in
Valve type/No: Overhead 12
Transmission: Automatic
No. of forward speeds: 3
Wheels driven: 4-wheel drive
Brake system: PA
Brakes F/R: Drum/Drum

Steering: Recirculating ball PA
Wheelbase: 256.8cm 101.1in
Track F: 127.0cm 50.0in
Track R: 127.0cm 50.0in
Length: 427.7cm 168.4in
Width: 165.6cm 65.2in
Height: 158.5cm 62.4in
Ground clearance: 19.1cm 7.5in
Kerb weight: 1443.7kg 3180.0lb
Fuel: 56.8L 12.5gal 15.0galUS

2376 Jeep
Gladiator Pickup J-2500 Townside
1971 USA
88.0mph 141.6kmh
0-60mph 96.5kmh: 11.9secs
245.0bhp 182.7kW 248.4PS
@ 4400rpm
365.0lbft 494.6Nm @ 2600rpm
135.8bhp/ton 133.6bhp/tonne
41.5bhp/L 31.0kW/L 42.1PS/L
42.0ft/sec 12.8m/sec
13.2mpg 11.0mpgUS 21.4L/100km
Petrol 4-stroke piston
5899cc 359.9cu in
Vee 8
Compression ratio: 8.4:1
Bore: 103.6mm 4.1in
Stroke: 87.4mm 3.4in
Valve type/No: Overhead 16
Transmission: Manual
No. of forward speeds: 4
Wheels driven: 4-wheel drive
Brakes F/R: Drum/Drum
Steering: Worm & roller PA
Wheelbase: 304.8cm 120.0in
Track F: 161.3cm 63.5in
Track R: 162.1cm 63.8in
Length: 479.0cm 188.6in
Width: 200.4cm 78.9in
Height: 176.5cm 69.5in
Ground clearance: 19.1cm 7.5in
Kerb weight: 1834.2kg 4040.0lb
Fuel: 75.7L 16.6gal 20.0galUS

2377 Jeep
Wagoneer
1971 USA
91.0mph 146.4kmh
0-50mph 80.5kmh: 9.1secs
0-60mph 96.5kmh: 12.9secs
0-1/4 mile: 18.8secs
230.0bhp 171.5kW 233.2PS
@ 4400rpm
350.0lbft 474.3Nm @ 2400rpm
122.8bhp/ton 120.8bhp/tonne
40.1bhp/L 29.9kW/L 40.7PS/L
47.1ft/sec 14.3m/sec
21.8mph 35.1kmh/1000rpm
16.8mpg 14.0mpgUS 16.8L/100km
Petrol 4-stroke piston
5730cc 349.6cu in
Vee 8 1 Carburettor
Compression ratio: 9.0:1
Bore: 96.5mm 3.8in
Stroke: 97.8mm 3.8in
Valve type/No: Overhead 16
Transmission: Automatic
No. of forward speeds: 3
Wheels driven: 4-wheel drive
Springs F/R: Leaf/Leaf
Brake system: PA
Brakes F/R: Drum/Drum
Steering: Recirculating ball PA
Wheelbase: 279.4cm 110.0in
Track F: 144.8cm 57.0in
Track R: 144.8cm 57.0in
Length: 467.4cm 184.0in
Width: 192.0cm 75.6in
Height: 165.9cm 65.3in
Ground clearance: 19.8cm 7.8in
Kerb weight: 1904.5kg 4195.0lb
Fuel: 83.3L 18.3gal 22.0galUS

2378 Jeep
Wagoneer 1414C
1971 USA
97.0mph 156.1kmh
0-60mph 96.5kmh: 14.2secs
245.0bhp 182.7kW 248.4PS
@ 4400rpm
365.0lbft 494.6Nm @ 2600rpm
133.2bhp/ton 131.0bhp/tonne
41.5bhp/L 31.0kW/L 42.1PS/L
42.0ft/sec 12.8m/sec
14.7mpg 12.2mpgUS 19.3L/100km
Petrol 4-stroke piston
5899cc 359.9cu in
Vee 8
Compression ratio: 8.4:1
Bore: 103.6mm 4.1in
Stroke: 87.4mm 3.4in
Valve type/No: Overhead 16
Transmission: Automatic
No. of forward speeds: 3
Wheels driven: 4-wheel drive
Brake system: PA
Brakes F/R: Drum/Drum
Steering: Recirculating ball PA
Wheelbase: 279.4cm 110.0in
Track F: 144.8cm 57.0in
Track R: 144.8cm 57.0in
Length: 466.6cm 183.7in
Width: 192.0cm 75.6in
Height: 165.9cm 65.3in
Ground clearance: 19.1cm 7.5in
Kerb weight: 1870.5kg 4120.0lb
Fuel: 83.3L 18.3gal 22.0galUS

2379 Jeep
CJ-5 V8
1972 USA
82.0mph 131.9kmh
0-60mph 96.5kmh: 13.0secs
150.0bhp 111.9kW 152.1PS
@ 4200rpm
245.0lbft 332.0Nm @ 2500rpm
114.5bhp/ton 112.6bhp/tonne
30.1bhp/L 22.4kW/L 30.5PS/L
40.1ft/sec 12.2m/sec
18.0mpg 15.0mpgUS 15.7L/100km
Petrol 4-stroke piston
4982cc 304.0cu in
Vee 8
Compression ratio: 8.3:1
Bore: 95.3mm 3.8in
Stroke: 87.4mm 3.4in
Valve type/No: Overhead 16
Transmission: Manual
No. of forward speeds: 3
Wheels driven: 4-wheel drive
Brake system: PA
Brakes F/R: Drum/Drum
Steering: Recirculating ball PA
Wheelbase: 213.4cm 84.0in
Track F: 130.8cm 51.5in
Track R: 127.0cm 50.0in
Length: 352.8cm 138.9in
Width: 157.0cm 61.8in
Height: 176.5cm 69.5in
Ground clearance: 21.6cm 8.5in
Kerb weight: 1332.5kg 2935.0lb
Fuel: 62.4L 13.7gal 16.5galUS

2380 Jeep
Commando
1972 USA
88.0mph 141.6kmh
0-60mph 96.5kmh: 13.8secs
150.0bhp 111.9kW 152.1PS
@ 4200rpm
245.0lbft 332.0Nm @ 2500rpm
93.2bhp/ton 91.6bhp/tonne
30.1bhp/L 22.4kW/L 30.5PS/L
40.1ft/sec 12.2m/sec
14.4mpg 12.0mpgUS 19.6L/100km
Petrol 4-stroke piston
4982cc 304.0cu in
Vee 8
Compression ratio: 8.3:1
Bore: 95.3mm 3.8in
Stroke: 87.4mm 3.4in
Valve type/No: Overhead 16
Transmission: Automatic
No. of forward speeds: 3
Wheels driven: 4-wheel drive
Brake system: PA
Brakes F/R: Drum/Drum
Steering: Recirculating ball PA
Wheelbase: 264.2cm 104.0in
Track F: 130.8cm 51.5in
Track R: 127.0cm 50.0in
Length: 443.2cm 174.5in
Width: 165.6cm 65.2in
Height: 158.5cm 62.4in
Ground clearance: 21.6cm 8.5in
Kerb weight: 1636.7kg 3605.0lb
Fuel: 62.4L 13.7gal 16.5galUS

2381 Jeep
CJ6
1974 USA
82.0mph 131.9kmh
0-50mph 80.5kmh: 11.3secs
0-60mph 96.5kmh: 16.5secs
0-1/4 mile: 20.3secs
0-1km: 39.1secs
100.0bhp 74.6kW 101.4PS
@ 3600rpm
185.0lbft 250.7Nm @ 1800rpm
75.6bhp/ton 74.4bhp/tonne
26.3bhp/L 19.6kW/L 26.6PS/L
35.0ft/sec 10.7m/sec
21.4mph 34.4kmh/1000rpm
13.7mpg 11.4mpgUS 20.6L/100km
Petrol 4-stroke piston
3805cc 232.1cu in
In-line 6 1 Carburettor
Compression ratio: 8.0:1
Bore: 95.3mm 3.8in
Stroke: 88.9mm 3.5in
Valve type/No: Overhead 12
Transmission: Manual
No. of forward speeds: 3
Wheels driven: 4-wheel drive
Springs F/R: Leaf/Leaf
Brakes F/R: Drum/Drum
Steering: Worm & roller
Wheelbase: 264.2cm 104.0in
Track F: 130.8cm 51.5in
Track R: 127.0cm 50.0in
Length: 403.6cm 158.9in
Width: 147.1cm 57.9in
Height: 173.5cm 68.3in
Ground clearance: 20.3cm 8.0in
Kerb weight: 1344.3kg 2961.0lb
Fuel: 58.7L 12.9gal 15.5galUS

2382 Jeep
Wagoneer
1974 USA
90.0mph 144.8kmh
0-50mph 80.5kmh: 8.8secs
0-60mph 96.5kmh: 11.9secs
0-1/4 mile: 18.8secs
195.0bhp 145.4kW 197.7PS
@ 4400rpm
295.0lbft 399.7Nm @ 2900rpm
97.6bhp/ton 96.0bhp/tonne
33.0bhp/L 24.6kW/L 33.5PS/L
42.0ft/sec 12.8m/sec
25.8mph 41.5kmh/1000rpm
14.4mpg 12.0mpgUS 19.6L/100km
Petrol 4-stroke piston
5900cc 360.0cu in
Vee 8 1 Carburettor
Compression ratio: 8.3:1
Bore: 103.6mm 4.1in
Stroke: 87.4mm 3.4in
Valve type/No: Overhead 16
Transmission: Automatic
No. of forward speeds: 3
Wheels driven: 4-wheel drive
Springs F/R: Leaf/Leaf
Brake system: PA
Brakes F/R: Disc/Drum
Steering: Recirculating ball PA
Wheelbase: 276.9cm 109.0in
Track F: 149.9cm 59.0in
Track R: 146.1cm 57.5in
Length: 466.6cm 183.7in
Width: 192.0cm 75.6in
Height: 165.9cm 65.3in
Ground clearance: 21.1cm 8.3in
Kerb weight: 2031.6kg 4475.0lb
Fuel: 83.3L 18.3gal 22.0galUS

2383 Jeep
Cherokee Chief
1978 USA
92.0mph 148.0kmh
0-50mph 80.5kmh: 8.4secs
0-60mph 96.5kmh: 12.2secs
0-1/4 mile: 18.7secs
0-1km: 35.8secs
175.0bhp 130.5kW 177.4PS
@ 4000rpm
280.0lbft 379.4Nm @ 2800rpm
86.8bhp/ton 85.4bhp/tonne
29.7bhp/L 22.1kW/L 30.1PS/L
38.2ft/sec 11.6m/sec
21.5mph 34.6kmh/1000rpm
12.5mpg 10.4mpgUS 22.6L/100km
Petrol 4-stroke piston
5896cc 359.7cu in
Vee 8 1 Carburettor
Compression ratio: 8.2:1
Bore: 103.6mm 4.1in
Stroke: 87.4mm 3.4in
Valve type/No: Overhead 16
Transmission: Automatic
No. of forward speeds: 3
Wheels driven: 4-wheel drive
Springs F/R: Leaf/Leaf
Brake system: PA
Brakes F/R: Disc/Drum
Steering: Recirculating ball PA
Wheelbase: 276.1cm 108.7in
Track F: 150.9cm 59.4in
Track R: 146.8cm 57.8in
Length: 466.1cm 183.5in
Width: 200.4cm 78.9in
Height: 171.7cm 67.6in
Ground clearance: 19.6cm 7.7in
Kerb weight: 2049.8kg 4515.0lb
Fuel: 83.3L 18.3gal 22.0galUS

2384 Jensen
3.5-litre Saloon
1936 UK
82.5mph 132.7kmh
0-50mph 80.5kmh: 13.7secs
0-60mph 96.5kmh: 20.0secs
16.0mpg 13.3mpgUS 17.7L/100km
Petrol 4-stroke piston
3622cc 221.0cu in
Vee 8 2 Carburettor
Compression ratio: 6.3:1
Bore: 78.0mm 3.1in
Stroke: 95.2mm 3.8in
Valve type/No: Side 16
Transmission: Manual with overdrive
No. of forward speeds: 6
Wheels driven: Rear
Brakes F/R: Drum/Drum
Kerb weight: 1613.1kg 3553.0lb
Fuel: 81.9L 18.0gal 21.6galUS

2385 Jensen
3.5-litre Tourer
1938 UK
89.1mph 143.4kmh
0-50mph 80.5kmh: 11.4secs
0-60mph 96.5kmh: 19.2secs
17.0mpg 14.2mpgUS 16.6L/100km
Petrol 4-stroke piston
3622cc 221.0cu in
Vee 8 2 Carburettor
Compression ratio: 6.3:1
Bore: 77.8mm 3.1in
Stroke: 95.2mm 3.8in
Valve type/No: Side 16
Transmission: Manual with overdrive
No. of forward speeds: 6
Wheels driven: Rear
Brakes F/R: Drum/Drum
Kerb weight: 1534.5kg 3380.0lb
Fuel: 91.0L 20.0gal 24.0galUS

2386 Jensen
Interceptor Cabriolet
1951 UK
102.0mph 164.1kmh
0-50mph 80.5kmh: 10.6secs
0-60mph 96.5kmh: 13.7secs
130.0bhp 96.9kW 131.8PS
@ 3700rpm
212.0lbft 287.3Nm @ 2200rpm
88.1bhp/ton 86.7bhp/tonne
32.6bhp/L 24.3kW/L 33.0PS/L
44.9ft/sec 13.7m/sec
24.0mph 38.6kmh/1000rpm
20.0mpg 16.7mpgUS 14.1L/100km
Petrol 4-stroke piston
3993cc 243.6cu in
In-line 6
Compression ratio: 6.8:1
Bore: 87.3mm 3.4in
Stroke: 111.1mm 4.4in
Valve type/No: Overhead 12
Transmission: Manual
No. of forward speeds: 4
Wheels driven: Rear
Brakes F/R: Drum/Drum
Wheelbase: 285.0cm 112.2in
Track F: 137.2cm 54.0in
Track R: 145.5cm 57.3in
Length: 477.5cm 188.0in
Width: 167.6cm 66.0in
Height: 147.3cm 58.0in
Ground clearance: 17.8cm 7.0in
Kerb weight: 1500.0kg 3304.0lb
Fuel: 56.9L 12.5gal 15.0galUS

2387 Jensen
541
1956 UK
112.0mph 180.2kmh
0-50mph 80.5kmh: 9.2secs
0-60mph 96.5kmh: 12.1secs
0-1/4 mile: 18.5secs
28.1mph 45.2kmh/1000rpm
20.0mpg 16.7mpgUS 14.1L/100km
Petrol 4-stroke piston
3993cc 243.6cu in
In-line 6
Compression ratio: 7.4:1
Bore: 87.0mm 3.4in
Stroke: 111.0mm 4.4in
Valve type/No: Overhead 12
Transmission: Manual with overdrive
No. of forward speeds: 5
Wheels driven: Rear
Springs F/R: Coil/Leaf
Brake system: PA
Brakes F/R: Drum/Drum
Wheelbase: 266.7cm 105.0in
Track F: 131.6cm 51.8in
Track R: 131.6cm 51.8in
Length: 447.0cm 176.0in
Width: 160.0cm 63.0in
Height: 134.6cm 53.0in
Ground clearance: 17.8cm 7.0in
Kerb weight: 1423.7kg 3136.0lb
Fuel: 68.2L 15.0gal 18.0galUS

2388 Jensen
541R
1958 UK
127.5mph 205.1kmh
0-50mph 80.5kmh: 7.6secs
0-60mph 96.5kmh: 10.6secs
0-1/4 mile: 17.5secs
30.0mph 48.3kmh/1000rpm
18.0mpg 15.0mpgUS 15.7L/100km
Petrol 4-stroke piston
3993cc 243.6cu in
In-line 6
Compression ratio: 7.6:1
Bore: 87.0mm 3.4in
Stroke: 111.0mm 4.4in
Valve type/No: Overhead 12
Transmission: Manual with overdrive
No. of forward speeds: 5
Wheels driven: Rear
Springs F/R: Coil/Leaf
Brakes F/R: Disc/Disc
Wheelbase: 266.7cm 105.0in
Track F: 131.6cm 51.8in
Track R: 130.3cm 51.3in
Length: 447.0cm 176.0in
Width: 160.0cm 63.0in
Height: 134.6cm 53.0in
Ground clearance: 17.8cm 7.0in
Kerb weight: 1480.9kg 3262.0lb
Fuel: 68.2L 15.0gal 18.0galUS

2389 Jensen
541S Automatic
1961 UK
110.0mph 177.0kmh
0-50mph 80.5kmh: 9.2secs
0-60mph 96.5kmh: 12.4secs
0-1/4 mile: 18.8secs
26.0mph 41.8kmh/1000rpm
15.5mpg 12.9mpgUS 18.2L/100km
Petrol 4-stroke piston
3993cc 243.6cu in
In-line 6
Compression ratio: 7.4:1
Bore: 87.0mm 3.4in
Stroke: 111.0mm 4.4in
Valve type/No: Overhead 12
Transmission: Automatic
No. of forward speeds: 4
Wheels driven: Rear
Springs F/R: Coil/Leaf
Brake system: PA
Brakes F/R: Disc/Disc
Wheelbase: 266.7cm 105.0in
Track F: 137.9cm 54.3in
Track R: 140.2cm 55.2in
Length: 452.1cm 178.0in
Width: 170.2cm 67.0in
Height: 137.9cm 54.3in
Ground clearance: 17.8cm 7.0in
Kerb weight: 1550.9kg 3416.0lb
Fuel: 68.2L 15.0gal 18.0galUS

2390 Jensen
CV8
1963 UK
133.0mph 214.0kmh
0-50mph 80.5kmh: 6.3secs
0-60mph 96.5kmh: 8.4secs
0-1/4 mile: 16.0secs
305.0bhp 227.4kW 309.2PS
@ 4800rpm
395.0lbft 535.2Nm @ 3000rpm
194.4bhp/ton 191.2bhp/tonne
51.6bhp/L 38.4kW/L 52.3PS/L
45.2ft/sec 13.8m/sec
26.0mph 41.8kmh/1000rpm
14.4mpg 12.0mpgUS 19.6L/100km
Petrol 4-stroke piston
5916cc 360.9cu in
Vee 8 1 Carburettor
Compression ratio: 9.0:1
Bore: 105.0mm 4.1in
Stroke: 86.0mm 3.4in
Valve type/No: Overhead 16
Transmission: Automatic
No. of forward speeds: 3
Wheels driven: Rear
Springs F/R: Coil/Leaf
Brake system: PA
Brakes F/R: Disc/Disc
Steering: Rack & pinion
Wheelbase: 266.7cm 105.0in
Track F: 142.2cm 56.0in
Track R: 144.8cm 57.0in
Length: 468.6cm 184.5in
Width: 171.5cm 67.5in
Height: 139.7cm 55.0in
Ground clearance: 19.1cm 7.5in
Kerb weight: 1595.4kg 3514.0lb
Fuel: 72.8L 16.0gal 19.2galUS

2391 Jensen
Interceptor
1967 UK
133.0mph 214.0kmh
0-50mph 80.5kmh: 5.9secs
0-60mph 96.5kmh: 7.3secs
0-1/4 mile: 15.7secs
0-1km: 28.4secs
325.0bhp 242.3kW 329.5PS
@ 4600rpm
425.0lbft 575.9Nm @ 2800rpm
196.9bhp/ton 193.6bhp/tonne
51.8bhp/L 38.6kW/L 52.5PS/L
43.3ft/sec 13.2m/sec
25.6mph 41.2kmh/1000rpm
13.6mpg 11.3mpgUS 20.8L/100km
Petrol 4-stroke piston
6276cc 382.9cu in
Vee 8 1 Carburettor
Compression ratio: 10.0:1
Bore: 108.0mm 4.2in
Stroke: 86.0mm 3.4in
Valve type/No: Overhead 16
Transmission: Automatic
No. of forward speeds: 3
Wheels driven: Rear
Springs F/R: Coil/Leaf
Brake system: PA
Brakes F/R: Disc/Disc
Steering: Rack & pinion
Wheelbase: 266.7cm 105.0in
Track F: 142.2cm 56.0in
Track R: 144.8cm 57.0in
Length: 477.5cm 188.0in
Width: 175.3cm 69.0in
Height: 134.6cm 53.0in
Ground clearance: 12.7cm 5.0in
Kerb weight: 1678.4kg 3697.0lb
Fuel: 72.8L 16.0gal 19.2galUS

2392 Jensen
FF
1968 UK
130.0mph 209.2kmh
0-50mph 80.5kmh: 6.2secs
0-60mph 96.5kmh: 8.4secs
0-1/4 mile: 15.9secs
0-1km: 29.3secs
325.0bhp 242.3kW 329.5PS
@ 4600rpm
425.0lbft 575.9Nm @ 2800rpm
182.9bhp/ton 179.8bhp/tonne
51.8bhp/L 38.6kW/L 52.5PS/L
43.3ft/sec 13.2m/sec
25.6mph 41.2kmh/1000rpm
13.6mpg 11.3mpgUS 20.8L/100km
Petrol 4-stroke piston
6276cc 382.9cu in
Vee 8 1 Carburettor
Compression ratio: 10.0:1
Bore: 108.0mm 4.2in
Stroke: 86.0mm 3.4in
Valve type/No: Overhead 16
Transmission: Automatic
No. of forward speeds: 3
Wheels driven: 4-wheel drive
Springs F/R: Coil/Leaf
Brake system: PA
Brakes F/R: Disc/Disc
Steering: Rack & pinion PA
Wheelbase: 276.9cm 109.0in
Track F: 144.5cm 56.9in
Track R: 144.5cm 56.9in
Length: 485.1cm 191.0in
Width: 177.8cm 70.0in
Height: 134.6cm 53.0in
Ground clearance: 12.7cm 5.0in
Kerb weight: 1807.4kg 3981.0lb
Fuel: 72.8L 16.0gal 19.2galUS

2393 Jensen
Interceptor
1969 UK
137.0mph 220.4kmh
0-50mph 80.5kmh: 5.0secs
0-60mph 96.5kmh: 6.4secs
0-1/4 mile: 15.0secs
0-1km: 27.7secs
330.0bhp 246.1kW 334.6PS
@ 4600rpm
425.0lbft 575.9Nm @ 2800rpm
200.0bhp/ton 196.7bhp/tonne
52.6bhp/L 39.2kW/L 53.3PS/L
43.3ft/sec 13.2m/sec
26.4mph 42.5kmh/1000rpm
12.9mpg 10.7mpgUS 21.9L/100km
Petrol 4-stroke piston
6276cc 382.9cu in
Vee 8 1 Carburettor
Compression ratio: 10.0:1
Bore: 108.0mm 4.2in
Stroke: 86.0mm 3.4in
Valve type/No: Overhead 16
Transmission: Automatic
No. of forward speeds: 3
Wheels driven: Rear
Springs F/R: Coil/Leaf
Brake system: PA
Brakes F/R: Disc/Disc
Steering: Rack & pinion PA
Wheelbase: 266.7cm 105.0in
Track F: 142.2cm 56.0in
Track R: 144.5cm 56.9in
Length: 477.5cm 188.0in
Width: 177.8cm 70.0in
Height: 134.6cm 53.0in
Ground clearance: 12.7cm 5.0in
Kerb weight: 1677.5kg 3695.0lb
Fuel: 72.8L 16.0gal 19.2galUS

2394 Jensen
FF II
1970 UK
141.0mph 226.9kmh
0-50mph 80.5kmh: 6.2secs
0-60mph 96.5kmh: 8.1secs
0-1/4 mile: 15.8secs
0-1km: 28.9secs
330.0bhp 246.1kW 334.6PS
@ 5000rpm
425.0lbft 575.9Nm @ 2800rpm
174.7bhp/ton 171.8bhp/tonne
52.6bhp/L 39.2kW/L 53.3PS/L
47.1ft/sec 14.3m/sec
26.4mph 42.5kmh/1000rpm
11.9mpg 9.9mpgUS 23.7L/100km
Petrol 4-stroke piston
6276cc 382.9cu in
Vee 8 1 Carburettor
Compression ratio: 10.0:1
Bore: 108.0mm 4.2in
Stroke: 86.0mm 3.4in
Valve type/No: Overhead 16
Transmission: Automatic
No. of forward speeds: 3
Wheels driven: 4-wheel drive
Springs F/R: Coil/Leaf
Brake system: PA
Brakes F/R: Disc/Disc
Steering: Rack & pinion PA
Wheelbase: 276.9cm 109.0in
Track F: 144.5cm 56.9in
Track R: 144.5cm 56.9in
Length: 485.1cm 191.0in
Width: 177.8cm 70.0in
Height: 134.6cm 53.0in
Ground clearance: 12.7cm 5.0in
Kerb weight: 1920.4kg 4230.0lb
Fuel: 91.0L 20.0gal 24.0galUS

2395 Jensen
Interceptor II
1970 UK
122.0mph 196.3kmh
0-50mph 80.5kmh: 5.3secs
0-60mph 96.5kmh: 7.1secs
0-1/4 mile: 15.7secs
330.0bhp 246.1kW 334.6PS
@ 4600rpm
425.0lbft 575.9Nm @ 2800rpm
200.0bhp/ton 196.7bhp/tonne
52.6bhp/L 39.2kW/L 53.3PS/L
43.3ft/sec 13.2m/sec
14.9mpg 12.4mpgUS 19.0L/100km
Petrol 4-stroke piston
6276cc 382.9cu in
Vee 8 1 Carburettor
Compression ratio: 10.0:1
Bore: 108.0mm 4.2in
Stroke: 86.0mm 3.4in
Valve type/No: Overhead 16
Transmission: Automatic
No. of forward speeds: 3
Wheels driven: Rear
Springs F/R: Coil/Leaf
Brake system: PA
Brakes F/R: Disc/Disc
Steering: Rack & pinion PA
Wheelbase: 261.6cm 103.0in
Track F: 141.7cm 55.8in
Track R: 143.5cm 56.5in
Length: 477.5cm 188.0in
Width: 177.5cm 69.9in
Height: 134.6cm 53.0in
Ground clearance: 12.7cm 5.0in
Kerb weight: 1677.5kg 3695.0lb
Fuel: 75.7L 16.6gal 20.0galUS

2396 Jensen
Interceptor
1971 UK
136.0mph 218.8kmh
0-50mph 80.5kmh: 5.8secs
0-60mph 96.5kmh: 7.4secs
0-1/4 mile: 16.0secs
330.0bhp 246.1kW 334.6PS
@ 5000rpm
425.0lbft 575.9Nm @ 2800rpm
189.3bhp/ton 186.1bhp/tonne
52.6bhp/L 39.2kW/L 53.3PS/L
47.1ft/sec 14.3m/sec
27.2mph 43.8kmh/1000rpm
14.4mpg 12.0mpgUS 19.6L/100km
Petrol 4-stroke piston
6276cc 382.9cu in
Vee 8 1 Carburettor
Compression ratio: 10.0:1
Bore: 108.0mm 4.2in
Stroke: 86.0mm 3.4in
Valve type/No: Overhead 16
Transmission: Automatic
No. of forward speeds: 3
Wheels driven: Rear
Springs F/R: Coil/Leaf
Brake system: PA
Brakes F/R: Disc/Disc
Steering: Rack & pinion PA
Wheelbase: 267.5cm 105.3in
Track F: 143.0cm 56.3in
Track R: 145.5cm 57.3in
Length: 475.0cm 187.0in
Width: 177.8cm 70.0in
Height: 134.6cm 53.0in
Ground clearance: 14.0cm 5.5in
Kerb weight: 1772.9kg 3905.0lb
Fuel: 90.8L 20.0gal 24.0galUS

2397 Jensen
SP
1971 UK
145.0mph 233.3kmh
0-50mph 80.5kmh: 5.4secs
0-60mph 96.5kmh: 6.9secs
0-1/4 mile: 14.8secs
0-1km: 26.7secs
330.0bhp 246.1kW 334.6PS
@ 4700rpm
490.0lbft 664.0Nm @ 3200rpm
187.9bhp/ton 184.8bhp/tonne
45.8bhp/L 34.1kW/L 46.4PS/L
49.1ft/sec 15.0m/sec

26.7mph 43.0kmh/1000rpm
13.0mpg 10.8mpgUS 21.7L/100km
Petrol 4-stroke piston
7212cc 440.0cu in
Vee 8 3 Carburettor
Compression ratio: 10.3:1
Bore: 109.8mm 4.3in
Stroke: 95.5mm 3.8in
Valve type/No: Overhead 16
Transmission: Automatic
No. of forward speeds: 3
Wheels driven: Rear
Springs F/R: Coil/Leaf
Brake system: PA
Brakes F/R: Disc/Disc
Steering: Rack & pinion PA
Wheelbase: 266.7cm 105.0in
Track F: 142.2cm 56.0in
Track R: 144.5cm 56.9in
Length: 477.5cm 188.0in
Width: 177.8cm 70.0in
Height: 134.6cm 53.0in
Ground clearance: 12.7cm 5.0in
Kerb weight: 1786.0kg 3934.0lb
Fuel: 91.0L 20.0gal 24.0galUS

2398 Jensen

Healey
1973 UK
125.0mph 201.1kmh
0-50mph 80.5kmh: 7.1secs
0-60mph 96.5kmh: 9.7secs
0-1/4 mile: 17.3secs
140.0bhp 104.4kW 141.9PS
@ 6500rpm
130.0lbft 176.2Nm @ 5000rpm
145.5bhp/ton 143.1bhp/tonne
71.0bhp/L 52.9kW/L 71.9PS/L
49.3ft/sec 15.0m/sec
18.2mph 29.3kmh/1000rpm
29.4mpg 24.5mpgUS 9.6L/100km
Petrol 4-stroke piston
1973cc 120.4cu in
In-line 4 2 Carburettor
Compression ratio: 8.4:1
Bore: 95.2mm 3.8in
Stroke: 69.3mm 2.7in
Valve type/No: Overhead 8
Transmission: Manual
No. of forward speeds: 4
Wheels driven: Rear
Springs F/R: Coil/Coil
Brake system: PA
Brakes F/R: Disc/Drum
Steering: Rack & pinion
Wheelbase: 233.7cm 92.0in
Track F: 135.4cm 53.3in
Track R: 133.4cm 52.5in
Length: 411.5cm 162.0in
Width: 160.8cm 63.3in
Height: 121.4cm 47.8in
Ground clearance: 12.7cm 5.0in
Kerb weight: 978.4kg 2155.0lb
Fuel: 49.2L 10.8gal 13.0galUS

2399 Jensen

Healey Huffaker
1974 UK
134.0mph 215.6kmh
0-50mph 80.5kmh: 5.3secs
0-60mph 96.5kmh: 7.2secs
0-1/4 mile: 15.1secs
196.0bhp 146.2kW 198.7PS
@ 7000rpm
155.0lbft 210.0Nm @ 5000rpm
219.5bhp/ton 215.9bhp/tonne
99.3bhp/L 74.1kW/L 100.7PS/L
53.1ft/sec 16.2m/sec
17.1mph 27.5kmh/1000rpm
8.4mpg 7.0mpgUS 33.6L/100km
Petrol 4-stroke piston
1973cc 120.4cu in
In-line 4 2 Carburettor
Compression ratio: 11.5:1
Bore: 95.2mm 3.8in
Stroke: 69.3mm 2.7in
Valve type/No: Overhead 8
Transmission: Manual
No. of forward speeds: 4
Wheels driven: Rear
Springs F/R: Coil/Coil
Brakes F/R: Disc/Drum
Steering: Rack & pinion
Wheelbase: 233.7cm 92.0in
Track F: 140.5cm 55.3in
Track R: 138.4cm 54.5in
Length: 411.5cm 162.0in
Width: 160.8cm 63.3in
Height: 112.3cm 44.2in
Ground clearance: 10.2cm 4.0in
Kerb weight: 908.0kg 2000.0lb
Fuel: 45.4L 10.0gal 12.0galUS

2400 Jensen

Interceptor III
1974 UK
133.0mph 214.0kmh
0-50mph 80.5kmh: 7.6secs
0-60mph 96.5kmh: 10.4secs
0-1/4 mile: 17.3secs
220.0bhp 164.0kW 223.0PS
@ 3600rpm
350.0lbft 474.3Nm @ 2400rpm
122.6bhp/ton 120.5bhp/tonne
30.5bhp/L 22.7kW/L 30.9PS/L
37.5ft/sec 11.4m/sec
26.6mph 42.8kmh/1000rpm
13.8mpg 11.5mpgUS 20.5L/100km
Petrol 4-stroke piston
7212cc 440.0cu in
Vee 8 1 Carburettor
Compression ratio: 8.2:1
Bore: 109.7mm 4.3in
Stroke: 95.3mm 3.8in
Valve type/No: Overhead 16
Transmission: Automatic
No. of forward speeds: 3
Wheels driven: Rear
Springs F/R: Coil/Leaf
Brake system: PA
Brakes F/R: Disc/Disc
Steering: Rack & pinion PA
Wheelbase: 266.7cm 105.0in
Track F: 142.5cm 56.1in
Track R: 144.5cm 56.9in
Length: 472.4cm 186.0in
Width: 175.3cm 69.0in
Height: 134.6cm 53.0in
Ground clearance: 12.7cm 5.0in
Kerb weight: 1825.1kg 4020.0lb
Fuel: 90.8L 20.0gal 24.0galUS

2401 Jensen

Interceptor III Convertible
1974 UK
126.0mph 202.7kmh
0-50mph 80.5kmh: 5.5secs
0-60mph 96.5kmh: 7.6secs
0-1/4 mile: 15.8secs
0-1km: 28.8secs
280.0bhp 208.8kW 283.9PS
@ 4800rpm
380.0lbft 514.9Nm @ 3200rpm
156.9bhp/ton 154.3bhp/tonne
38.8bhp/L 28.9kW/L 39.4PS/L
50.0ft/sec 15.2m/sec
24.8mph 39.9kmh/1000rpm
12.5mpg 10.4mpgUS 22.6L/100km
Petrol 4-stroke piston
7212cc 440.0cu in
Vee 8 1 Carburettor
Compression ratio: 8.2:1
Bore: 108.7mm 4.3in
Stroke: 95.2mm 3.8in
Valve type/No: Overhead 16
Transmission: Automatic
No. of forward speeds: 3
Wheels driven: Rear
Springs F/R: Coil/Leaf
Brake system: PA
Brakes F/R: Disc/Disc
Steering: Rack & pinion PA
Wheelbase: 266.7cm 105.0in
Track F: 142.2cm 56.0in
Track R: 144.5cm 56.9in
Length: 477.5cm 188.0in
Width: 177.8cm 70.0in
Height: 134.6cm 53.0in
Ground clearance: 12.7cm 5.0in
Kerb weight: 1814.6kg 3997.0lb
Fuel: 91.0L 20.0gal 24.0galUS

2402 Jensen

GT
1976 UK
120.0mph 193.1kmh
0-50mph 80.5kmh: 6.7secs
0-60mph 96.5kmh: 8.7secs
0-1/4 mile: 16.7secs
0-1km: 30.9secs
144.0bhp 107.4kW 146.0PS
@ 6500rpm
134.0lbft 181.6Nm @ 5000rpm
133.4bhp/ton 131.2bhp/tonne
73.0bhp/L 54.4kW/L 74.0PS/L
49.3ft/sec 15.0m/sec
19.4mph 31.2kmh/1000rpm
19.5mpg 16.2mpgUS 14.5L/100km
Petrol 4-stroke piston
1973cc 120.4cu in
In-line 4 2 Carburettor
Compression ratio: 8.4:1
Bore: 95.2mm 3.8in
Stroke: 69.3mm 2.7in
Valve type/No: Overhead 8
Transmission: Manual
No. of forward speeds: 5
Wheels driven: Rear
Springs F/R: Coil/Coil
Brake system: PA
Brakes F/R: Disc/Disc
Steering: Rack & pinion
Wheelbase: 233.7cm 92.0in
Track F: 135.1cm 53.2in
Track R: 133.4cm 52.5in
Length: 421.6cm 166.0in
Width: 160.5cm 63.2in
Height: 123.2cm 48.5in
Ground clearance: 12.7cm 5.0in
Kerb weight: 1097.3kg 2417.0lb
Fuel: 53.2L 11.7gal 14.1galUS

2403 Jensen

Interceptor III Convertible
1976 UK
120.0mph 193.1kmh
0-50mph 80.5kmh: 6.8secs
0-60mph 96.5kmh: 9.3secs
0-1/4 mile: 17.2secs
215.0bhp 160.3kW 218.0PS
@ 6200rpm
330.0lbft 447.2Nm @ 3200rpm
114.0bhp/ton 112.1bhp/tonne
29.8bhp/L 22.2kW/L 30.2PS/L
64.6ft/sec 19.7m/sec
23.5mph 37.8kmh/1000rpm
15.0mpg 12.5mpgUS 18.8L/100km
Petrol 4-stroke piston
7212cc 440.0cu in
Vee 8
Compression ratio: 8.2:1
Bore: 109.7mm 4.3in
Stroke: 95.3mm 3.8in
Valve type/No: Overhead 16
Transmission: Automatic
No. of forward speeds: 3
Wheels driven: Rear
Springs F/R: Coil/Leaf
Brake system: PA
Brakes F/R: Disc/Disc
Steering: Rack & pinion PA
Wheelbase: 266.7cm 105.0in
Track F: 142.5cm 56.1in
Track R: 144.5cm 56.9in
Length: 472.4cm 186.0in
Width: 175.3cm 69.0in
Height: 134.6cm 53.0in
Ground clearance: 12.7cm 5.0in
Kerb weight: 1918.1kg 4225.0lb
Fuel: 90.8L 20.0gal 24.0galUS

2404 Jensen

GT
1977 UK
113.0mph 181.8kmh
0-50mph 80.5kmh: 8.3secs
0-60mph 96.5kmh: 11.2secs
0-1/4 mile: 18.2secs
140.0bhp 104.4kW 141.9PS
@ 6500rpm
130.0lbft 176.2Nm @ 5000rpm
127.5bhp/ton 125.3bhp/tonne
71.0bhp/L 52.9kW/L 71.9PS/L
49.1ft/sec 15.0m/sec
19.2mph 30.9kmh/1000rpm
25.2mpg 21.0mpgUS 11.2L/100km
Petrol 4-stroke piston
1973cc 120.4cu in
In-line 4 2 Carburettor
Compression ratio: 8.4:1
Bore: 95.2mm 3.8in
Stroke: 69.2mm 2.7in
Valve type/No: Overhead 8
Transmission: Manual
No. of forward speeds: 5
Wheels driven: Rear
Springs F/R: Coil/Coil
Brake system: PA
Brakes F/R: Disc/Drum
Steering: Rack & pinion
Wheelbase: 233.7cm 92.0in
Track F: 135.4cm 53.3in
Track R: 133.4cm 52.5in
Length: 421.4cm 165.9in
Width: 160.8cm 63.3in
Height: 123.2cm 48.5in
Ground clearance: 11.4cm 4.5in
Kerb weight: 1116.8kg 2460.0lb
Fuel: 53.0L 11.6gal 14.0galUS

2405 Jensen-Healey

2-litre
1972 UK
120.0mph 193.1kmh
0-50mph 80.5kmh: 5.9secs
0-60mph 96.5kmh: 7.8secs
0-1/4 mile: 16.2secs
0-1km: 29.8secs
140.0bhp 104.4kW 141.9PS
@ 6500rpm
130.0lbft 176.2Nm @ 5000rpm
147.4bhp/ton 144.9bhp/tonne
71.0bhp/L 52.9kW/L 71.9PS/L
49.3ft/sec 15.0m/sec
18.1mph 29.1kmh/1000rpm
21.0mpg 17.5mpgUS 13.5L/100km
Petrol 4-stroke piston
1973cc 120.4cu in
In-line 4 2 Carburettor
Compression ratio: 8.4:1
Bore: 95.2mm 3.8in
Stroke: 69.3mm 2.7in
Valve type/No: Overhead 8
Transmission: Manual
No. of forward speeds: 4
Wheels driven: Rear
Springs F/R: Coil/Coil
Brake system: PA
Brakes F/R: Disc/Drum
Steering: Rack & pinion
Wheelbase: 233.7cm 92.0in
Track F: 135.1cm 53.2in
Track R: 133.4cm 52.5in
Length: 411.5cm 162.0in
Width: 160.5cm 63.2in
Height: 121.9cm 48.0in
Ground clearance: 12.7cm 5.0in
Kerb weight: 966.1kg 2128.0lb
Fuel: 50.0L 11.0gal 13.2galUS

2406 Jowett

7hp Curlew de Luxe
1935 UK
54.5mph 87.7kmh
37.0mpg 30.8mpgUS 7.6L/100km
Petrol 4-stroke piston
907cc 55.3cu in
Flat 2
Bore: 75.4mm 3.0in
Stroke: 101.6mm 4.0in
Valve type/No: Side 4
Transmission: Manual
No. of forward speeds: 4
Wheels driven: Rear
Brakes F/R: Drum/Drum
Kerb weight: 850.8kg 1874.0lb
Fuel: 27.3L 6.0gal 7.2galUS

2407 Jowett

De Luxe Saloon
1937 UK
61.6mph 99.1kmh
0-50mph 80.5kmh: 24.6secs
32.0bhp 23.9kW 32.4PS
@ 4000rpm
34.6bhp/ton 34.0bhp/tonne
27.4bhp/L 20.5kW/L 27.8PS/L
40.2ft/sec 12.3m/sec
32.0mpg 26.6mpgUS 8.8L/100km
Petrol 4-stroke piston
1166cc 71.1cu in
Flat 4
Bore: 63.5mm 2.5in
Stroke: 92.0mm 3.6in
Valve type/No: Side 8
Transmission: Manual
No. of forward speeds: 4
Wheels driven: Rear
Brakes F/R: Drum/Drum
Kerb weight: 941.1kg 2073.0lb
Fuel: 31.8L 7.0gal 8.4galUS

2408 Jowett

8hp

1939 UK
56.2mph 90.4kmh
0-50mph 80.5kmh: 40.0secs
17.0bhp 12.7kW 17.2PS
@ 3500rpm
20.5bhp/ton 20.1bhp/tonne
17.9bhp/L 13.4kW/L 18.2PS/L
38.9ft/sec 11.8m/sec
41.0mpg 34.1mpgUS 6.9L/100km
Petrol 4-stroke piston
947cc 57.8cu in
Flat 2
Bore: 77.0mm 3.0in
Stroke: 101.5mm 4.0in
Valve type/No: Side 4
Transmission: Manual
No. of forward speeds: 4
Wheels driven: Rear
Brakes F/R: Drum/Drum
Kerb weight: 844.4kg 1860.0lb
Fuel: 31.8L 7.0gal 8.4galUS

2409 Jowett

Javelin
1948 UK
76.0mph 122.3kmh
0-50mph 80.5kmh: 17.0secs
0-60mph 96.5kmh: 25.4secs
50.0bhp 37.3kW 50.7PS
@ 4100rpm
49.7bhp/ton 48.9bhp/tonne
33.6bhp/L 25.1kW/L 34.1PS/L
40.3ft/sec 12.3m/sec
29.0mpg 24.1mpgUS 9.7L/100km
Petrol 4-stroke piston
1486cc 90.7cu in
Flat 4
Compression ratio: 7.0:1
Bore: 72.5mm 2.8in
Stroke: 90.0mm 3.5in
Valve type/No: Overhead 8
Transmission: Manual
No. of forward speeds: 4
Wheels driven: Rear
Brakes F/R: Drum/Drum
Wheelbase: 259.1cm 102.0in
Track F: 129.5cm 51.0in
Track R: 124.5cm 49.0in
Length: 426.7cm 168.0in
Width: 154.9cm 61.0in
Height: 153.7cm 60.5in
Ground clearance: 19.6cm 7.7in
Kerb weight: 1023.3kg 2254.0lb
Fuel: 36.4L 8.0gal 9.6galUS

2410 Jowett

Jupiter
1953 UK
86.2mph 138.7kmh
0-50mph 80.5kmh: 10.4secs
0-60mph 96.5kmh: 15.1secs
0-1/4 mile: 20.4secs
60.0bhp 44.7kW 60.8PS
@ 4500rpm
65.2bhp/ton 64.1bhp/tonne
40.4bhp/L 30.1kW/L 40.9PS/L
44.2ft/sec 13.5m/sec
16.9mph 27.2kmh/1000rpm
30.0mpg 25.0mpgUS 9.4L/100km
Petrol 4-stroke piston
1486cc 90.7cu in
Flat 4
Compression ratio: 8.0:1
Bore: 72.5mm 2.8in
Stroke: 90.0mm 3.5in
Valve type/No: Overhead 8
Transmission: Manual
No. of forward speeds: 4
Wheels driven: Rear
Wheelbase: 236.2cm 93.0in
Track F: 128.3cm 50.5in
Track R: 125.7cm 49.5in
Kerb weight: 936.1kg 2062.0lb

2411 Jowett

Jupiter Mk IA
1953 UK
85.0mph 136.8kmh
0-50mph 80.5kmh: 11.7secs
0-60mph 96.5kmh: 16.8secs
0-1/4 mile: 20.7secs
62.5bhp 46.6kW 63.4PS
@ 4500rpm
84.0lbft 113.8Nm @ 3000rpm
66.0bhp/ton 64.9bhp/tonne
42.1bhp/L 31.4kW/L 42.7PS/L
44.2ft/sec 13.5m/sec
17.0mph 27.4kmh/1000rpm
21.8mpg 18.2mpgUS 13.0L/100km
Petrol 4-stroke piston
1485cc 90.6cu in
Flat 4 2 Carburettor
Compression ratio: 8.0:1
Bore: 72.5mm 2.8in
Stroke: 90.0mm 3.5in
Valve type/No: Overhead 8
Transmission: Manual
No. of forward speeds: 4
Wheels driven: Rear
Springs F/R: Torsion bar/Torsion bar
Brakes F/R: Drum/Drum
Wheelbase: 236.2cm 93.0in
Track F: 132.1cm 52.0in
Track R: 133.4cm 52.5in
Length: 426.7cm 168.0in
Width: 157.5cm 62.0in
Height: 142.2cm 56.0in
Ground clearance: 20.3cm 8.0in
Kerb weight: 962.9kg 2121.0lb
Fuel: 45.5L 10.0gal 12.0galUS

2412 Kaiser

Henry J
1950 USA
0-1/4 mile: 21.5secs
68.0bhp 50.7kW 68.9PS
@ 4000rpm
109.0lbft 147.7Nm @ 1800rpm
65.1bhp/ton 64.0bhp/tonne
30.9bhp/L 23.1kW/L 31.3PS/L
48.6ft/sec 14.8m/sec
Petrol 4-stroke piston
2199cc 134.2cu in
In-line 6 1 Carburettor
Compression ratio: 7.0:1
Bore: 79.4mm 3.1in
Stroke: 111.1mm 4.4in
Valve type/No: Side 12
Transmission: Manual
No. of forward speeds: 3
Wheels driven: Rear
Springs F/R: Coil/Leaf
Brakes F/R: Drum/Drum
Steering: Worm & roller
Wheelbase: 254.0cm 100.0in
Track F: 137.2cm 54.0in
Track R: 137.2cm 54.0in
Length: 443.2cm 174.5in
Width: 177.8cm 70.0in
Height: 151.6cm 59.7in
Ground clearance: 19.8cm 7.8in
Kerb weight: 1062.8kg 2341.0lb
Fuel: 49.2L 10.8gal 13.0galUS

2413 Kaiser

Henry J de Luxe
1950 USA
0-1/4 mile: 21.5secs
80.0bhp 59.7kW 81.1PS
@ 3800rpm
133.0lbft 180.2Nm @ 1600rpm
76.5bhp/ton 75.3bhp/tonne
30.3bhp/L 22.6kW/L 30.7PS/L
36.9ft/sec 11.3m/sec
Petrol 4-stroke piston
2638cc 160.9cu in
In-line 6 1 Carburettor
Compression ratio: 7.0:1
Bore: 79.4mm 3.1in
Stroke: 88.9mm 3.5in
Valve type/No: Side 12
Transmission: Manual
No. of forward speeds: 3
Wheels driven: Rear
Springs F/R: Coil/Leaf
Brakes F/R: Drum/Drum
Steering: Worm & roller
Wheelbase: 254.0cm 100.0in
Track F: 137.2cm 54.0in
Track R: 137.2cm 54.0in
Length: 443.2cm 174.5in
Width: 177.8cm 70.0in
Height: 151.6cm 59.7in
Ground clearance: 19.8cm 7.8in
Kerb weight: 1062.8kg 2341.0lb
Fuel: 49.2L 10.8gal 13.0galUS

2414 Kaiser

Henry J 6
1952 USA
82.0mph 131.9kmh
0-50mph 80.5kmh: 15.8secs
0-60mph 96.5kmh: 24.0secs
80.0bhp 59.7kW 81.1PS
@ 3800rpm
133.0lbft 180.2Nm @ 1600rpm
72.0bhp/ton 70.8bhp/tonne
30.3bhp/L 22.6kW/L 30.7PS/L
36.9ft/sec 11.3m/sec
17.1mph 27.5kmh/1000rpm
18.0mpg 15.0mpgUS 15.7L/100km
Petrol 4-stroke piston
2638cc 160.9cu in
In-line 6
Compression ratio: 7.0:1
Bore: 79.4mm 3.1in
Stroke: 88.9mm 3.5in
Valve type/No: Side 12
Transmission: Manual with overdrive
No. of forward speeds: 6
Wheels driven: Rear
Wheelbase: 254.0cm 100.0in
Track F: 137.2cm 54.0in
Track R: 137.2cm 54.0in
Length: 443.2cm 174.5in
Width: 177.8cm 70.0in
Height: 151.6cm 59.7in
Ground clearance: 16.5cm 6.5in
Kerb weight: 1130.0kg 2489.0lb
Fuel: 45.5L 10.0gal 12.0galUS

2415 Kaiser

Jeepster
1967 USA
87.0mph 140.0kmh
0-50mph 80.5kmh: 9.1secs
0-60mph 96.5kmh: 12.6secs
0-1/4 mile: 19.2secs
160.0bhp 119.3kW 162.2PS
@ 4200rpm
235.0lbft 318.4Nm @ 2400rpm
119.5bhp/ton 117.5bhp/tonne
43.4bhp/L 32.3kW/L 44.0PS/L
39.7ft/sec 12.1m/sec
23.8mph 38.3kmh/1000rpm
Petrol 4-stroke piston
3690cc 225.1cu in
Vee 6 1 Carburettor
Compression ratio: 9.0:1
Bore: 95.3mm 3.8in
Stroke: 86.4mm 3.4in
Valve type/No: Overhead 12
Transmission: Automatic
No. of forward speeds: 3
Wheels driven: 4-wheel drive
Springs F/R: Leaf/Leaf
Brake system: PA
Brakes F/R: Drum/Drum
Steering: Cam & roller
Wheelbase: 256.5cm 101.0in
Track F: 127.0cm 50.0in
Track R: 127.0cm 50.0in
Length: 445.3cm 175.3in
Width: 165.6cm 65.2in
Height: 162.8cm 64.1in
Ground clearance: 19.1cm 7.5in
Kerb weight: 1362.0kg 3000.0lb
Fuel: 56.8L 12.5gal 15.0galUS

2416 Kissel

8-65 Gold Bug
1927 USA
78.0mph 125.5kmh
0-50mph 80.5kmh: 17.8secs
0-60mph 96.5kmh: 23.5secs
0-1/4 mile: 23.0secs
65.0bhp 48.5kW 65.9PS
@ 3200rpm
175.0lbft 237.1Nm @ 1800rpm
42.8bhp/ton 42.1bhp/tonne
16.0bhp/L 12.0kW/L 16.3PS/L
42.2ft/sec 12.9m/sec
20.4mph 32.8kmh/1000rpm
Petrol 4-stroke piston
4049cc 247.0cu in
In-line 8
Compression ratio: 5.5:1
Bore: 73.2mm 2.9in
Stroke: 120.7mm 4.7in
Valve type/No: Side 16
Transmission: Manual
No. of forward speeds: 3
Wheels driven: Rear
Wheelbase: 297.2cm 117.0in
Track F: 142.2cm 56.0in
Track R: 142.2cm 56.0in
Length: 444.5cm 175.0in
Width: 172.7cm 68.0in
Height: 172.7cm 68.0in
Kerb weight: 1543.6kg 3400.0lb

2417 Koenig

Competition
1989 Germany
217.0mph 349.2kmh
0-60mph 96.5kmh: 4.0secs
800.0bhp 596.6kW 811.1PS
@ 6250rpm
664.0lbft 899.7Nm @ 5000rpm
512.0bhp/ton 503.5bhp/tonne
161.9bhp/L 120.7kW/L 164.1PS/L
53.3ft/sec 16.2m/sec
Petrol 4-stroke piston
4942cc 301.5cu in
turbochargedsupercharged
Flat 12 fuel injection
Compression ratio: 7.5:1
Bore: 82.0mm 3.2in
Stroke: 78.0mm 3.1in
Valve type/No: Overhead 48
Transmission: Manual
No. of forward speeds: 5
Wheels driven: Rear
Springs F/R: Coil/Coil
Brake system: PA
Brakes F/R: Disc/Disc
Steering: Rack & pinion
Wheelbase: 255.0cm 100.4in
Track F: 185.9cm 73.2in
Track R: 215.9cm 85.0in
Length: 442.0cm 174.0in
Width: 219.5cm 86.4in
Height: 114.0cm 44.9in
Kerb weight: 1589.0kg 3500.0lb
Fuel: 104.8L 23.0gal 27.7galUS

2418 Koenig

Competition Evolution
1990 Germany
230.0mph 370.1kmh
0-60mph 96.5kmh: 3.5secs
1000.0bhp 745.7kW 1013.9PS
@ 6700rpm
738.0lbft 1000.0Nm @ 4500rpm
640.0bhp/ton 629.3bhp/tonne
202.3bhp/L 150.9kW/L 205.1PS/L
57.5ft/sec 17.5m/sec
Petrol 4-stroke piston
4942cc 301.5cu in turbocharged
Flat 12 fuel injection
Compression ratio: 7.5:1
Bore: 82.0mm 3.2in
Stroke: 78.4mm 3.1in
Valve type/No: Overhead 48
Transmission: Manual
No. of forward speeds: 5
Wheels driven: Rear
Springs F/R: Coil/Coil
Brake system: PA ABS
Brakes F/R: Disc/Disc
Steering: Rack & pinion
Wheelbase: 255.0cm 100.4in
Track F: 185.9cm 73.2in
Track R: 215.9cm 85.0in
Length: 460.5cm 181.3in
Width: 219.5cm 86.4in
Height: 115.8cm 45.6in
Kerb weight: 1589.0kg 3500.0lb
Fuel: 100.3L 22.0gal 26.5galUS

2419 Koenig

C62
1991 Germany
235.0mph 378.1kmh
0-60mph 96.5kmh: 3.5secs
588.0bhp 438.5kW 596.2PS
@ 6300rpm
533.0lbft 722.2Nm @ 4500rpm
543.1bhp/ton 534.1bhp/tonne
174.6bhp/L 130.2kW/L 177.0PS/L
Petrol 4-stroke piston
3368cc 205.5cu in turbocharged
Flat 6 fuel injection
Transmission: Manual
No. of forward speeds: 5
Wheels driven: Rear
Springs F/R: Coil/Coil
Brakes F/R: Disc/Disc
Steering: Rack & pinion
Length: 495.8cm 195.2in
Width: 205.2cm 80.8in
Height: 111.8cm 44.0in
Kerb weight: 1100.9kg 2425.0lb

2420 Kurtis

Hornet Roadster

1953 USA
101.1mph 162.7kmh
0-50mph 80.5kmh: 6.0secs
0-60mph 96.5kmh: 7.7secs
0-1/4 mile: 16.3secs
160.0bhp 119.3kW 162.2PS
@ 4000rpm
257.0lbft 348.2Nm @ 1800rpm
158.2bhp/ton 155.6bhp/tonne
31.7bhp/L 23.6kW/L 32.1PS/L
50.0ft/sec 15.2m/sec
28.5mph 45.9kmh/1000rpm
Petrol 4-stroke piston
5049cc 308.0cu in
In-line 6
Compression ratio: 7.7:1
Bore: 96.8mm 3.8in
Stroke: 114.3mm 4.5in
Valve type/No: Side 12
Transmission: Manual
No. of forward speeds: 3
Wheels driven: Rear
Wheelbase: 254.0cm 100.0in
Track F: 147.3cm 58.0in
Track R: 142.2cm 56.0in
Kerb weight: 1028.3kg 2265.0lb

2421 La Salle

Enclosed Drive Limousine
1930 USA
70.3mph 113.1kmh
11.0mpg 9.2mpgUS 25.7L/100km
Petrol 4-stroke piston
5573cc 340.0cu in
Vee 8
Bore: 84.1mm 3.3in
Stroke: 125.4mm 4.9in
Valve type/No: Side 16
Transmission: Manual
No. of forward speeds: 3
Wheels driven: Rear
Brakes F/R: Drum/Drum
Wheelbase: 340.4cm 134.0in
Track F: 144.8cm 57.0in
Track R: 144.8cm 57.0in
Length: 514.4cm 202.5in
Width: 186.7cm 73.5in
Height: 190.5cm 75.0in
Kerb weight: 2345.4kg 5166.0lb
Fuel: 84.2L 18.5gal 22.2galUS

2422 La Salle

37-50 V8 Saloon
1938 USA
88.2mph 141.9kmh
0-50mph 80.5kmh: 12.5secs
0-60mph 96.5kmh: 18.7secs
14.0mpg 11.7mpgUS 20.2L/100km
Petrol 4-stroke piston
5277cc 322.0cu in
Vee 8
Bore: 85.7mm 3.4in
Stroke: 114.3mm 4.5in
Valve type/No: Side 16
Transmission: Manual
No. of forward speeds: 3
Wheels driven: Rear
Brakes F/R: Drum/Drum
Kerb weight: 1867.3kg 4113.0lb
Fuel: 79.6L 17.5gal 21.0galUS

2423 Lada

1200
1975 USSR
90.0mph 144.8kmh
0-50mph 80.5kmh: 12.8secs
0-60mph 96.5kmh: 18.4secs
0-1/4 mile: 21.2secs
0-1km: 40.7secs
62.0bhp 46.2kW 62.9PS
@ 5600rpm
64.0lbft 86.7Nm @ 3400rpm
68.4bhp/ton 67.3bhp/tonne
51.7bhp/L 38.6kW/L 52.5PS/L
40.4ft/sec 12.3m/sec
15.3mph 24.6kmh/1000rpm
28.3mpg 23.6mpgUS 10.0L/100km
Petrol 4-stroke piston
1198cc 73.1cu in
In-line 4 1 Carburettor
Compression ratio: 8.8:1
Bore: 76.0mm 3.0in
Stroke: 66.0mm 2.6in
Valve type/No: Overhead 8
Transmission: Manual
No. of forward speeds: 4
Wheels driven: Rear
Springs F/R: Coil/Coil
Brakes F/R: Disc/Drum
Steering: Worm & roller
Wheelbase: 242.6cm 95.5in
Track F: 132.6cm 52.2in
Track R: 130.0cm 51.2in
Length: 401.3cm 158.0in
Width: 157.5cm 62.0in
Height: 144.8cm 57.0in
Ground clearance: 17.0cm 6.7in
Kerb weight: 921.6kg 2030.0lb
Fuel: 38.7L 8.5gal 10.2galUS

2424 Lada

1500
1976 USSR
96.0mph 154.5kmh
0-50mph 80.5kmh: 9.6secs
0-60mph 96.5kmh: 13.8secs
0-1/4 mile: 19.4secs
0-1km: 36.5secs
75.0bhp 55.9kW 76.0PS
@ 5600rpm
77.5lbft 105.0Nm @ 3500rpm
74.0bhp/ton 72.7bhp/tonne
51.6bhp/L 38.5kW/L 52.4PS/L
49.0ft/sec 14.9m/sec
16.8mph 27.0kmh/1000rpm
26.8mpg 22.3mpgUS 10.5L/100km
Petrol 4-stroke piston
1452cc 88.6cu in
In-line 4 1 Carburettor
Compression ratio: 8.8:1
Bore: 76.0mm 3.0in
Stroke: 80.0mm 3.1in
Valve type/No: Overhead 8
Transmission: Manual
No. of forward speeds: 4
Wheels driven: Rear
Springs F/R: Coil/Coil
Brake system: PA
Brakes F/R: Disc/Drum
Steering: Worm & roller
Wheelbase: 242.6cm 95.5in
Track F: 132.6cm 52.2in
Track R: 130.0cm 51.2in
Length: 401.3cm 158.0in
Width: 157.5cm 62.0in
Height: 144.8cm 57.0in
Ground clearance: 17.0cm 6.7in
Kerb weight: 1031.0kg 2271.0lb
Fuel: 38.7L 8.5gal 10.2galUS

2425 Lada

1300 ES
1978 USSR
89.0mph 143.2kmh
0-50mph 80.5kmh: 11.3secs
0-60mph 96.5kmh: 16.6secs
0-1/4 mile: 20.7secs
0-1km: 39.8secs
67.0bhp 50.0kW 67.9PS
@ 5600rpm
69.0lbft 93.5Nm @ 3400rpm
69.6bhp/ton 68.4bhp/tonne
51.8bhp/L 38.6kW/L 52.5PS/L
40.4ft/sec 12.3m/sec
15.7mph 25.3kmh/1000rpm
24.1mpg 20.1mpgUS 11.7L/100km
Petrol 4-stroke piston
1294cc 78.9cu in
In-line 4 1 Carburettor
Compression ratio: 8.5:1
Bore: 79.0mm 3.1in
Stroke: 66.0mm 2.6in
Valve type/No: Overhead 8
Transmission: Manual
No. of forward speeds: 4
Wheels driven: Rear
Springs F/R: Coil/Coil
Brakes F/R: Disc/Drum
Steering: Worm & roller
Wheelbase: 242.6cm 95.5in
Track F: 132.6cm 52.2in
Track R: 130.0cm 51.2in
Length: 406.4cm 160.0in
Width: 157.5cm 62.0in
Height: 144.8cm 57.0in
Ground clearance: 17.0cm 6.7in
Kerb weight: 978.8kg 2156.0lb
Fuel: 38.7L 8.5gal 10.2galUS

2426 Lada

Niva 1600
1979 USSR
78.0mph 125.5kmh
0-50mph 80.5kmh: 14.3secs
0-60mph 96.5kmh: 22.4secs
0-1/4 mile: 22.2secs
0-1km: 42.6secs
78.0bhp 58.2kW 79.1PS
@ 5400rpm
88.0lbft 119.2Nm @ 3000rpm
67.1bhp/ton 66.0bhp/tonne
49.7bhp/L 37.0kW/L 50.4PS/L
47.2ft/sec 14.4m/sec
16.1mph 25.9kmh/1000rpm
20.0mpg 16.7mpgUS 14.1L/100km
Petrol 4-stroke piston
1570cc 95.8cu in
In-line 4 1 Carburettor
Compression ratio: 8.5:1
Bore: 79.0mm 3.1in
Stroke: 80.0mm 3.1in
Valve type/No: Overhead 8
Transmission: Manual
No. of forward speeds: 4
Wheels driven: 4-wheel drive
Springs F/R: Coil/Coil
Brake system: PA
Brakes F/R: Disc/Drum
Steering: Worm & roller
Wheelbase: 219.7cm 86.5in
Track F: 142.2cm 56.0in
Track R: 139.7cm 55.0in
Length: 370.8cm 146.0in
Width: 167.6cm 66.0in
Height: 163.8cm 64.5in
Ground clearance: 23.4cm 9.2in
Kerb weight: 1182.2kg 2604.0lb
Fuel: 45.0L 9.9gal 11.9galUS

2427 Lada

Riva 1500 Estate
1986 USSR
89.0mph 143.2kmh
0-50mph 80.5kmh: 11.0secs
0-60mph 96.5kmh: 16.4secs
0-1/4 mile: 20.3secs
0-1km: 38.3secs
71.0bhp 52.9kW 72.0PS
@ 5600rpm
78.0lbft 105.7Nm @ 3400rpm
68.1bhp/ton 67.0bhp/tonne
48.9bhp/L 36.5kW/L 49.6PS/L
49.0ft/sec 14.9m/sec
20.0mph 32.2kmh/1000rpm
30.1mpg 25.1mpgUS 9.4L/100km
Petrol 4-stroke piston
1452cc 89.0cu in
In-line 4 1 Carburettor
Compression ratio: 8.5:1
Bore: 76.0mm 3.0in
Stroke: 80.0mm 3.1in
Valve type/No: Overhead 8
Transmission: Manual
No. of forward speeds: 5
Wheels driven: Rear
Springs F/R: Coil/Coil
Brake system: PA
Brakes F/R: Disc/Drum
Steering: Worm & roller
Wheelbase: 242.4cm 95.4in
Track F: 136.5cm 53.7in
Track R: 132.1cm 52.0in
Length: 411.5cm 162.0in
Width: 162.0cm 63.8in
Height: 145.8cm 57.4in
Ground clearance: 17.9cm 7.0in
Kerb weight: 1060.0kg 2334.8lb
Fuel: 45.5L 10.0gal 12.0galUS

2428 Lada

Niva Cossack Cabrio
1987 USSR
81.0mph 130.3kmh
0-50mph 80.5kmh: 12.5secs
0-60mph 96.5kmh: 18.9secs
0-1/4 mile: 21.1secs
0-1km: 40.6secs
78.0bhp 58.2kW 79.1PS
@ 5400rpm
88.0lbft 119.2Nm @ 3400rpm
73.8bhp/ton 72.6bhp/tonne
49.7bhp/L 37.1kW/L 50.4PS/L
47.2ft/sec 14.4m/sec
19.2mph 30.9kmh/1000rpm
18.8mpg 15.7mpgUS 15.0L/100km
Petrol 4-stroke piston
1569cc 96.0cu in
In-line 4 1 Carburettor
Compression ratio: 8.5:1
Bore: 79.0mm 3.1in
Stroke: 80.0mm 3.1in
Valve type/No: Overhead 8
Transmission: Manual
No. of forward speeds: 5
Wheels driven: 4-wheel drive
Springs F/R: Coil/Coil
Brake system: PA
Brakes F/R: Disc/Drum
Steering: Worm & roller
Wheelbase: 219.7cm 86.5in
Track F: 142.2cm 56.0in
Track R: 139.7cm 55.0in
Length: 370.8cm 146.0in
Width: 167.6cm 66.0in
Height: 163.8cm 64.5in
Ground clearance: 23.5cm 9.3in
Kerb weight: 1075.0kg 2367.8lb
Fuel: 45.5L 10.0gal 12.0galUS

2429 Lada

Samara 1300 SL
1987 USSR
96.0mph 154.5kmh
0-50mph 80.5kmh: 9.5secs
0-60mph 96.5kmh: 14.0secs
0-1/4 mile: 19.6secs
0-1km: 36.5secs
65.0bhp 48.5kW 65.9PS
@ 5600rpm
70.8lbft 95.9Nm @ 3300rpm
71.6bhp/ton 70.4bhp/tonne
50.5bhp/L 37.6kW/L 51.2PS/L
43.6ft/sec 13.2m/sec
20.9mph 33.6kmh/1000rpm
31.1mpg 25.9mpgUS 9.1L/100km
Petrol 4-stroke piston
1288cc 79.0cu in
In-line 4 1 Carburettor
Compression ratio: 9.9:1
Bore: 76.0mm 3.0in
Stroke: 71.0mm 2.8in
Valve type/No: Overhead 8
Transmission: Manual
No. of forward speeds: 5
Wheels driven: Front
Springs F/R: Coil/Coil
Brake system: PA
Brakes F/R: Disc/Drum
Steering: Rack & pinion
Wheelbase: 246.0cm 96.9in
Track F: 139.0cm 54.7in
Track R: 136.0cm 53.5in
Length: 400.6cm 157.7in
Width: 162.0cm 63.8in
Height: 133.5cm 52.6in
Ground clearance: 15.2cm 6.0in
Kerb weight: 923.0kg 2033.0lb
Fuel: 43.2L 9.5gal 11.4galUS

2430 Lada

Samara 1300L 5-door
1989 USSR
94.0mph 151.2kmh
0-50mph 80.5kmh: 9.4secs
0-60mph 96.5kmh: 13.4secs
0-1/4 mile: 19.5secs
0-1km: 36.6secs
65.0bhp 48.5kW 65.9PS
@ 5600rpm
71.6lbft 97.0Nm @ 3500rpm
70.8bhp/ton 69.7bhp/tonne
50.5bhp/L 37.6kW/L 51.2PS/L
43.6ft/sec 13.2m/sec
20.9mph 33.6kmh/1000rpm
30.5mpg 25.4mpgUS 9.3L/100km
Petrol 4-stroke piston
1288cc 79.0cu in
In-line 4 1 Carburettor
Compression ratio: 9.9:1
Bore: 76.0mm 3.0in
Stroke: 71.0mm 2.8in
Valve type/No: Overhead 8
Transmission: Manual
No. of forward speeds: 5
Wheels driven: Front
Springs F/R: Coil/Coil
Brake system: PA
Brakes F/R: Disc/Drum
Steering: Rack & pinion
Wheelbase: 246.0cm 96.9in
Track F: 139.0cm 54.7in
Track R: 136.0cm 53.5in
Length: 400.6cm 157.7in
Width: 162.0cm 63.8in
Height: 133.5cm 52.6in
Ground clearance: 15.2cm 6.0in

Kerb weight: 933.0kg 2055.1lb
Fuel: 43.2L 9.5gal 11.4galUS

2431 Lago

America
1959 France
118.0mph 189.9kmh
0-50mph 80.5kmh: 7.9secs
0-60mph 96.5kmh: 10.6secs
0-1/4 mile: 17.4secs
138.0bhp 102.9kW 139.9PS
@ 5000rpm
156.0lbft 211.4Nm @ 2600rpm
116.6bhp/ton 114.7bhp/tonne
55.7bhp/L 41.6kW/L 56.5PS/L
41.0ft/sec 12.5m/sec
20.9mph 33.6kmh/1000rpm
Petrol 4-stroke piston
2476cc 151.1cu in
Vee 8
Compression ratio: 7.6:1
Bore: 72.4mm 2.8in
Stroke: 74.9mm 2.9in
Valve type/No: Overhead 16
Transmission: Manual
No. of forward speeds: 4
Wheels driven: Rear
Wheelbase: 249.9cm 98.4in
Track F: 130.0cm 51.2in
Track R: 130.0cm 51.2in
Length: 421.6cm 166.0in
Width: 164.1cm 64.6in
Height: 133.1cm 52.4in
Kerb weight: 1203.1kg 2650.0lb

2432 Lagonda

3-litre Tourer
1929 UK
80.0mph 128.7kmh
20.0mpg 16.7mpgUS 14.1L/100km
Petrol 4-stroke piston
2931cc 178.8cu in
In-line 6 1 Carburettor
Bore: 72.0mm 2.8in
Stroke: 120.0mm 4.7in
Valve type/No: Overhead 12
Transmission: Manual
No. of forward speeds: 4
Wheels driven: Rear
Brakes F/R: Drum/Drum
Wheelbase: 327.7cm 129.0in
Track F: 142.2cm 56.0in
Track R: 142.2cm 56.0in
Length: 459.7cm 181.0in
Width: 170.2cm 67.0in
Height: 172.7cm 68.0in
Kerb weight: 1550.9kg 3416.0lb
Fuel: 91.0L 20.0gal 24.0galUS

2433 Lagonda

2-litre Supercharged
1930 UK
88.2mph 141.9kmh
18.0mpg 15.0mpgUS 15.7L/100km
Petrol 4-stroke piston
1954cc 119.2cu in supercharged
In-line 4
Bore: 72.0mm 2.8in
Stroke: 120.0mm 4.7in
Valve type/No: Overhead 8
Transmission: Manual
No. of forward speeds: 4
Wheels driven: Rear
Brakes F/R: Drum/Drum
Wheelbase: 304.8cm 120.0in
Track F: 142.2cm 56.0in
Track R: 142.2cm 56.0in
Length: 434.3cm 171.0in
Width: 170.2cm 67.0in
Height: 167.6cm 66.0in
Kerb weight: 1474.6kg 3248.0lb
Fuel: 91.0L 20.0gal 24.0galUS

2434 Lagonda

3-litre Special Tourer
1931 UK
82.9mph 133.4kmh
20.0mpg 16.7mpgUS 14.1L/100km
Petrol 4-stroke piston
2931cc 178.8cu in
In-line 6
Bore: 72.0mm 2.8in
Stroke: 120.0mm 4.7in
Valve type/No: Side 12
Transmission: Manual
No. of forward speeds: 4
Wheels driven: Rear
Brakes F/R: Drum/Drum
Wheelbase: 327.7cm 129.0in
Track F: 142.2cm 56.0in
Track R: 142.2cm 56.0in
Length: 444.5cm 175.0in
Width: 167.6cm 66.0in
Height: 170.2cm 67.0in
Kerb weight: 1538.1kg 3388.0lb
Fuel: 91.0L 20.0gal 24.0galUS

2435 Lagonda

16/80 Tourer
1933 UK
77.5mph 124.7kmh
0-50mph 80.5kmh: 17.2secs
0-60mph 96.5kmh: 26.2secs
68.0bhp 50.7kW 68.9PS
@ 4500rpm
45.3bhp/ton 44.6bhp/tonne
34.1bhp/L 25.5kW/L 34.6PS/L
49.2ft/sec 15.0m/sec
20.0mpg 16.7mpgUS 14.1L/100km
Petrol 4-stroke piston
1991cc 121.5cu in
In-line 6 2 Carburettor
Compression ratio: 6.5:1
Bore: 65.0mm 2.6in
Stroke: 100.0mm 3.9in
Valve type/No: Overhead 12
Transmission: Manual
No. of forward speeds: 4
Wheels driven: Rear
Brakes F/R: Drum/Drum
Kerb weight: 1525.4kg 3360.0lb
Fuel: 63.7L 14.0gal 16.8galUS

2436 Lagonda

3.5-litre Tourer
1934 UK
83.7mph 134.7kmh
0-50mph 80.5kmh: 17.6secs
0-60mph 96.5kmh: 27.2secs
18.0mpg 15.0mpgUS 15.7L/100km
Petrol 4-stroke piston
3619cc 220.8cu in
In-line 6
Bore: 80.0mm 3.1in
Stroke: 120.0mm 4.7in
Transmission: Manual
No. of forward speeds: 4
Wheels driven: Rear
Brakes F/R: Drum/Drum
Kerb weight: 1627.1kg 3584.0lb
Fuel: 91.0L 20.0gal 24.0galUS

2437 Lagonda

Le Mans
1934 UK
110.0mph 177.0kmh
0-50mph 80.5kmh: 10.7secs
0-60mph 96.5kmh: 15.5secs
0-1/4 mile: 19.5secs
122.0bhp 91.0kW 123.7PS
@ 3600rpm
210.0lbft 284.6Nm @ 1800rpm
73.4bhp/ton 72.1bhp/tonne
27.5bhp/L 20.5kW/L 27.9PS/L
47.2ft/sec 14.4m/sec
28.7mph 46.2kmh/1000rpm
Petrol 4-stroke piston
4429cc 270.2cu in
In-line 6 1 Carburettor
Compression ratio: 7.5:1
Bore: 88.4mm 3.5in
Stroke: 119.9mm 4.7in
Valve type/No: Overhead 12
Transmission: Manual
No. of forward speeds: 4
Wheels driven: Rear
Wheelbase: 312.4cm 123.0in
Track F: 143.3cm 56.4in
Track R: 146.8cm 57.8in
Length: 431.8cm 170.0in
Width: 171.5cm 67.5in
Height: 144.8cm 57.0in
Kerb weight: 1691.1kg 3725.0lb

2438 Lagonda

Rapier Four-seater Tourer
1934 UK
74.0mph 119.1kmh
0-50mph 80.5kmh: 15.6secs
0-60mph 96.5kmh: 27.4secs
26.0mpg 21.6mpgUS 10.9L/100km
Petrol 4-stroke piston
1104cc 67.4cu in
In-line 4
Bore: 62.5mm 2.5in
Stroke: 90.0mm 3.5in
Transmission: Manual
No. of forward speeds: 4
Wheels driven: Rear
Brakes F/R: Drum/Drum
Kerb weight: 864.4kg 1904.0lb
Fuel: 36.4L 8.0gal 9.6galUS

2439 Lagonda

Rapide Tourer
1935 UK
100.5mph 161.7kmh
0-50mph 80.5kmh: 9.4secs
0-60mph 96.5kmh: 14.6secs
150.0bhp 111.9kW 152.1PS
90.4bhp/ton 88.9bhp/tonne
33.6bhp/L 25.0kW/L 34.0PS/L
15.0mpg 12.5mpgUS 18.8L/100km
Petrol 4-stroke piston
4467cc 272.5cu in
In-line 6 2 Carburettor
Compression ratio: 7.5:1
Bore: 88.5mm 3.5in
Stroke: 120.6mm 4.7in
Valve type/No: Overhead 12
Transmission: Manual
No. of forward speeds: 4
Wheels driven: Rear
Brakes F/R: Drum/Drum
Ground clearance: 17.8cm 7.0in
Kerb weight: 1686.6kg 3715.0lb
Fuel: 91.0L 20.0gal 24.0galUS

2440 Lagonda

4.5-litre Tourer
1936 UK
96.7mph 155.6kmh
0-50mph 80.5kmh: 12.4secs
0-60mph 96.5kmh: 17.2secs
16.0mpg 13.3mpgUS 17.7L/100km
Petrol 4-stroke piston
4453cc 271.7cu in
In-line 6
Bore: 88.5mm 3.5in
Stroke: 120.6mm 4.7in
Valve type/No: Overhead 12
Transmission: Manual
No. of forward speeds: 4
Wheels driven: Rear
Brakes F/R: Drum/Drum
Kerb weight: 1827.3kg 4025.0lb
Fuel: 91.0L 20.0gal 24.0galUS

2441 Lagonda

Rapide
1937 UK
104.2mph 167.7kmh
0-50mph 80.5kmh: 10.1secs
0-60mph 96.5kmh: 13.1secs
0-1/4 mile: 19.0secs
150.0bhp 111.9kW 152.1PS
@ 4000rpm
210.0lbft 284.6Nm @ 2000rpm
94.5bhp/ton 92.9bhp/tonne
33.6bhp/L 25.0kW/L 34.0PS/L
52.8ft/sec 16.1m/sec
Petrol 4-stroke piston
4467cc 272.5cu in
In-line 6
Compression ratio: 7.5:1
Bore: 88.9mm 3.5in
Stroke: 120.7mm 4.7in
Valve type/No: Overhead 12
Transmission: Manual
No. of forward speeds: 4
Wheels driven: Rear
Wheelbase: 327.7cm 129.0in
Track F: 146.8cm 57.8in
Track R: 146.8cm 57.8in
Kerb weight: 1614.9kg 3557.0lb

2442 Lagonda

4.5-litre
1938 UK
95.7mph 154.0kmh
0-50mph 80.5kmh: 11.3secs
0-60mph 96.5kmh: 16.4secs
150.0bhp 111.9kW 152.1PS
77.4bhp/ton 76.1bhp/tonne
33.7bhp/L 25.1kW/L 34.1PS/L
12.0mpg 10.0mpgUS 23.5L/100km
Petrol 4-stroke piston
4453cc 271.7cu in
In-line 6 2 Carburettor
Compression ratio: 7.5:1
Bore: 88.5mm 3.5in
Stroke: 120.6mm 4.7in
Valve type/No: Overhead 12
Transmission: Manual
No. of forward speeds: 4
Wheels driven: Rear
Brakes F/R: Drum/Drum
Kerb weight: 1969.9kg 4339.0lb
Fuel: 91.0L 20.0gal 24.0galUS

2443 Lagonda

4.5-litre 12 Cylinder Saloon
1938 UK
103.4mph 166.4kmh
0-50mph 80.5kmh: 9.7secs
0-60mph 96.5kmh: 12.9secs
12.0mpg 10.0mpgUS 23.5L/100km
Petrol 4-stroke piston
4480cc 273.3cu in
Vee 12
Bore: 75.0mm 2.9in
Stroke: 85.0mm 3.3in
Valve type/No: Overhead 24
Transmission: Manual
No. of forward speeds: 4
Wheels driven: Rear
Brakes F/R: Drum/Drum
Kerb weight: 2014.8kg 4438.0lb
Fuel: 91.0L 20.0gal 24.0galUS

2444 Lagonda

Saloon de Ville
1938 UK
100.0mph 160.9kmh
0-50mph 80.5kmh: 11.1secs
0-60mph 96.5kmh: 14.8secs
175.0bhp 130.5kW 177.4PS
@ 5500rpm
84.0bhp/ton 82.6bhp/tonne
39.1bhp/L 29.1kW/L 39.6PS/L
50.9ft/sec 15.5m/sec
12.0mpg 10.0mpgUS 23.5L/100km
Petrol 4-stroke piston
4480cc 273.3cu in
Vee 12 2 Carburettor
Compression ratio: 7.0:1
Bore: 75.0mm 2.9in
Stroke: 84.5mm 3.3in
Valve type/No: Overhead 24
Transmission: Manual
No. of forward speeds: 4
Wheels driven: Rear
Brakes F/R: Drum/Drum
Kerb weight: 2118.8kg 4667.0lb
Fuel: 91.0L 20.0gal 24.0galUS

2445 Lagonda

Rapide
1939 UK
110.1mph 177.2kmh
0-50mph 80.5kmh: 9.5secs
0-60mph 96.5kmh: 12.5secs
0-1/4 mile: 18.7secs
180.0bhp 134.2kW 182.5PS
@ 5500rpm
220.0lbft 298.1Nm @ 2800rpm
94.9bhp/ton 93.3bhp/tonne
40.2bhp/L 30.0kW/L 40.7PS/L
50.9ft/sec 15.5m/sec
Petrol 4-stroke piston
4480cc 273.3cu in
Vee 12
Compression ratio: 7.0:1
Bore: 74.9mm 2.9in
Stroke: 84.6mm 3.3in
Valve type/No: Overhead 24
Transmission: Manual
No. of forward speeds: 4
Wheels driven: Rear
Wheelbase: 315.0cm 124.0in
Track F: 152.4cm 60.0in
Track R: 152.4cm 60.0in
Kerb weight: 1929.5kg 4250.0lb

2446 Lagonda

Drop-head Coupe

1940 UK
94.7mph 152.4kmh
0-50mph 80.5kmh: 10.2secs
0-60mph 96.5kmh: 13.1secs
175.0bhp 130.5kW 177.4PS
@ 5500rpm
89.5bhp/ton 88.0bhp/tonne
39.1bhp/L 29.1kW/L 39.6PS/L
50.9ft/sec 15.5m/sec
13.0mpg 10.8mpgUS 21.7L/100km
Petrol 4-stroke piston
4480cc 273.3cu in
Vee 12
Compression ratio: 7.0:1
Bore: 75.0mm 2.9in
Stroke: 84.5mm 3.3in
Transmission: Manual
No. of forward speeds: 4
Wheels driven: Rear
Springs F/R: Torsion bar/Leaf
Brakes F/R: Drum/Drum
Kerb weight: 1989.0kg 4381.0lb
Fuel: 91.0L 20.0gal 24.0galUS

2447 Lagonda

2.5-litre Saloon
1949 UK
91.0mph 146.4kmh
0-50mph 80.5kmh: 12.3secs
0-60mph 96.5kmh: 18.2secs
105.0bhp 78.3kW 106.5PS
@ 5000rpm
125.0lbft 169.4Nm @ 3000rpm
70.3bhp/ton 69.1bhp/tonne
40.7bhp/L 30.3kW/L 41.3PS/L
49.2ft/sec 15.0m/sec
17.5mph 28.2kmh/1000rpm
18.0mpg 15.0mpgUS 15.7L/100km
Petrol 4-stroke piston
2580cc 157.4cu in
In-line 6
Compression ratio: 6.5:1
Bore: 78.0mm 3.1in
Stroke: 90.0mm 3.5in
Valve type/No: Overhead 12
Transmission: Manual
No. of forward speeds: 4
Wheels driven: Rear
Brakes F/R: Drum/Drum
Wheelbase: 288.3cm 113.5in
Track F: 143.3cm 56.4in
Track R: 144.0cm 56.7in
Length: 477.5cm 188.0in
Width: 172.7cm 68.0in
Height: 157.5cm 62.0in
Ground clearance: 17.8cm 7.0in
Kerb weight: 1519.1kg 3346.0lb
Fuel: 86.4L 19.0gal 22.8galUS

2448 Lagonda

3-litre Saloon
1956 UK
101.0mph 162.5kmh
0-50mph 80.5kmh: 11.4secs
0-60mph 96.5kmh: 15.8secs
0-1/4 mile: 20.5secs
140.0bhp 104.4kW 141.9PS
@ 5000rpm
178.0lbft 241.2Nm @ 3000rpm
83.0bhp/ton 81.6bhp/tonne
47.9bhp/L 35.7kW/L 48.6PS/L
49.2ft/sec 15.0m/sec
17.8mph 28.6kmh/1000rpm
17.5mpg 14.6mpgUS 16.1L/100km
Petrol 4-stroke piston
2922cc 178.3cu in
In-line 6
Compression ratio: 8.2:1
Bore: 83.0mm 3.3in
Stroke: 90.0mm 3.5in
Valve type/No: Overhead 12
Transmission: Manual
No. of forward speeds: 4
Wheels driven: Rear
Springs F/R: Coil/Torsion bar
Brake system: PA
Brakes F/R: Drum/Drum
Wheelbase: 288.3cm 113.5in
Track F: 144.0cm 56.7in
Track R: 144.0cm 56.7in
Length: 497.8cm 196.0in
Width: 176.5cm 69.5in
Height: 157.5cm 62.0in
Ground clearance: 17.8cm 7.0in
Kerb weight: 1716.1kg 3780.0lb
Fuel: 86.4L 19.0gal 22.8galUS

2449 Lamborghini

350GT
1965 Italy
152.0mph 244.6kmh
0-50mph 80.5kmh: 5.1secs
0-60mph 96.5kmh: 6.8secs
0-1/4 mile: 14.9secs
336.0bhp 250.6kW 340.7PS
@ 6500rpm
254.0lbft 344.2Nm @ 5700rpm
348.4bhp/ton 342.6bhp/tonne
97.0bhp/L 72.3kW/L 98.3PS/L
44.1ft/sec 13.4m/sec
21.7mph 34.9kmh/1000rpm
Petrol 4-stroke piston
3464cc 211.3cu in
Vee 12 6 Carburettor
Compression ratio: 9.5:1
Bore: 77.0mm 3.0in
Stroke: 62.0mm 2.4in
Valve type/No: Overhead 24
Transmission: Manual
No. of forward speeds: 5
Wheels driven: Rear
Springs F/R: Coil/Coil
Brakes F/R: Disc/Disc
Steering: Worm & roller
Wheelbase: 245.1cm 96.5in
Track F: 137.9cm 54.3in
Track R: 137.9cm 54.3in
Length: 449.6cm 177.0in
Width: 173.0cm 68.1in
Height: 121.9cm 48.0in
Ground clearance: 13.0cm 5.1in
Kerb weight: 980.6kg 2160.0lb
Fuel: 79.5L 17.5gal 21.0galUS

2450 Lamborghini

400GT
1966 Italy
156.0mph 251.0kmh
0-50mph 80.5kmh: 5.5secs
0-60mph 96.5kmh: 7.5secs
0-1/4 mile: 15.5secs
360.0bhp 268.4kW 365.0PS
@ 6500rpm
290.0lbft 393.0Nm @ 5000rpm
252.0bhp/ton 247.8bhp/tonne
91.6bhp/L 68.3kW/L 92.9PS/L
44.1ft/sec 13.4m/sec
23.8mph 38.3kmh/1000rpm
Petrol 4-stroke piston
3929cc 239.7cu in
Vee 12 6 Carburettor
Compression ratio: 9.5:1
Bore: 82.0mm 3.2in
Stroke: 62.0mm 2.4in
Valve type/No: Overhead 24
Transmission: Manual
No. of forward speeds: 5
Wheels driven: Rear
Springs F/R: Coil/Coil
Brakes F/R: Disc/Disc
Steering: Worm & cam
Wheelbase: 254.8cm 100.3in
Track F: 138.4cm 54.5in
Track R: 138.4cm 54.5in
Length: 468.6cm 184.5in
Width: 172.7cm 68.0in
Height: 128.5cm 50.6in
Ground clearance: 12.7cm 5.0in
Kerb weight: 1452.8kg 3200.0lb
Fuel: 60.6L 13.3gal 16.0galUS

2451 Lamborghini

Miura
1967 Italy
180.0mph 289.6kmh
0-60mph 96.5kmh: 5.5secs
0-1/4 mile: 13.9secs
325.0bhp 242.3kW 329.5PS
@ 7000rpm
286.0lbft 387.5Nm @ 5500rpm
256.3bhp/ton 252.1bhp/tonne
82.7bhp/L 61.7kW/L 83.9PS/L
47.4ft/sec 14.5m/sec
Petrol 4-stroke piston
3929cc 239.7cu in
Vee 12 6 Carburettor
Compression ratio: 10.7:1
Bore: 82.0mm 3.2in
Stroke: 62.0mm 2.4in
Valve type/No: Overhead 24
Transmission: Manual
No. of forward speeds: 5
Wheels driven: Rear
Springs F/R: Coil/Coil
Brakes F/R: Disc/Disc
Steering: Rack & pinion
Wheelbase: 246.6cm 97.1in
Track F: 140.0cm 55.1in
Track R: 151.4cm 59.6in
Length: 434.8cm 171.2in
Width: 176.3cm 69.4in
Height: 109.0cm 42.9in
Kerb weight: 1289.4kg 2840.0lb
Fuel: 79.5L 17.5gal 21.0galUS

2452 Lamborghini

Miura
1968 Italy
163.0mph 262.3kmh
0-60mph 96.5kmh: 6.3secs
0-1/4 mile: 14.5secs
400.0bhp 298.3kW 405.5PS
@ 7000rpm
300.0lbft 406.5Nm @ 5000rpm
314.4bhp/ton 309.1bhp/tonne
101.8bhp/L 75.9kW/L 103.2PS/L
47.4ft/sec 14.5m/sec
24.0mph 38.6kmh/1000rpm
Petrol 4-stroke piston
3929cc 239.7cu in
Vee 12 6 Carburettor
Compression ratio: 9.5:1
Bore: 82.0mm 3.2in
Stroke: 62.0mm 2.4in
Valve type/No: Overhead 24
Transmission: Manual
No. of forward speeds: 5
Wheels driven: Rear
Springs F/R: Coil/Coil
Brakes F/R: Disc/Disc
Steering: Rack & pinion
Wheelbase: 249.9cm 98.4in
Track F: 140.0cm 55.1in
Track R: 140.0cm 55.1in
Length: 435.9cm 171.6in
Width: 176.0cm 69.3in
Height: 105.4cm 41.5in
Ground clearance: 13.0cm 5.1in
Kerb weight: 1293.9kg 2850.0lb
Fuel: 95.0L 20.9gal 25.1galUS

2453 Lamborghini

Espada
1969 Italy
158.0mph 254.2kmh
0-50mph 80.5kmh: 5.2secs
0-60mph 96.5kmh: 6.5secs
0-1/4 mile: 15.0secs
390.0bhp 290.8kW 395.4PS
@ 7000rpm
320.0lbft 433.6Nm @ 5000rpm
237.7bhp/ton 233.7bhp/tonne
99.3bhp/L 74.0kW/L 100.6PS/L
47.4ft/sec 14.5m/sec
20.8mph 33.5kmh/1000rpm
13.0mpg 10.8mpgUS 21.8L/100km
Petrol 4-stroke piston
3929cc 239.7cu in
Vee 12 6 Carburettor
Compression ratio: 9.8:1
Bore: 82.0mm 3.2in
Stroke: 62.0mm 2.4in
Valve type/No: Overhead 24
Transmission: Manual
No. of forward speeds: 5
Wheels driven: Rear
Springs F/R: Coil/Coil
Steering: Worm & cam
Wheelbase: 264.9cm 104.3in
Track F: 149.1cm 58.7in
Track R: 149.1cm 58.7in
Length: 472.9cm 186.2in
Width: 185.9cm 73.2in
Height: 118.4cm 46.6in
Ground clearance: 12.7cm 5.0in
Kerb weight: 1668.4kg 3675.0lb
Fuel: 78.0L 17.1gal 20.6galUS

2454 Lamborghini

Espada
1970 Italy
150.0mph 241.4kmh
0-60mph 96.5kmh: 7.8secs
325.0bhp 242.3kW 329.5PS
@ 6500rpm
275.0lbft 372.6Nm @ 4500rpm
223.3bhp/ton 219.6bhp/tonne
82.7bhp/L 61.7kW/L 83.9PS/L
44.1ft/sec 13.4m/sec
Petrol 4-stroke piston
3929cc 239.7cu in
Vee 12 6 Carburettor
Compression ratio: 9.5:1
Bore: 82.0mm 3.2in
Stroke: 62.0mm 2.4in
Valve type/No: Overhead 24
Transmission: Manual
No. of forward speeds: 5
Wheels driven: Rear
Springs F/R: Coil/Coil
Brake system: PA
Brakes F/R: Disc/Disc
Steering: Worm & sector
Wheelbase: 264.9cm 104.3in
Track F: 149.1cm 58.7in
Track R: 149.1cm 58.7in
Length: 471.9cm 185.8in
Width: 180.8cm 71.2in
Height: 117.9cm 46.4in
Kerb weight: 1480.0kg 3260.0lb
Fuel: 99.9L 22.0gal 26.4galUS

2455 Lamborghini

Miura P400S
1970 Italy
173.0mph 278.4kmh
0-50mph 80.5kmh: 5.1secs
0-60mph 96.5kmh: 6.7secs
0-1/4 mile: 14.5secs
0-1km: 26.1secs
370.0bhp 275.9kW 375.1PS
@ 7700rpm
286.0lbft 387.5Nm @ 5500rpm
289.6bhp/ton 284.8bhp/tonne
94.2bhp/L 70.2kW/L 95.5PS/L
52.2ft/sec 15.9m/sec
22.8mph 36.7kmh/1000rpm
13.4mpg 11.2mpgUS 21.1L/100km
Petrol 4-stroke piston
3929cc 239.7cu in
Vee 12 4 Carburettor
Compression ratio: 10.7:1
Bore: 82.0mm 3.2in
Stroke: 62.0mm 2.4in
Valve type/No: Overhead 24
Transmission: Manual
No. of forward speeds: 5
Wheels driven: Rear
Springs F/R: Coil/Coil
Brake system: PA
Brakes F/R: Disc/Disc
Steering: Rack & pinion
Wheelbase: 250.4cm 98.6in
Track F: 141.7cm 55.8in
Track R: 141.7cm 55.8in
Length: 435.6cm 171.5in
Width: 180.3cm 71.0in
Height: 106.7cm 42.0in
Ground clearance: 12.7cm 5.0in
Kerb weight: 1299.3kg 2862.0lb
Fuel: 77.3L 17.0gal 20.4galUS

2456 Lamborghini

Miura S
1970 Italy
168.0mph 270.3kmh
0-50mph 80.5kmh: 4.1secs
0-60mph 96.5kmh: 5.5secs
0-1/4 mile: 13.9secs
430.0bhp 320.6kW 436.0PS
@ 7350rpm
330.0lbft 447.2Nm @ 5000rpm
331.6bhp/ton 326.0bhp/tonne
109.4bhp/L 81.6kW/L 111.0PS/L
49.8ft/sec 15.2m/sec
24.2mph 38.9kmh/1000rpm
16.7mpg 13.9mpgUS 16.9L/100km
Petrol 4-stroke piston
3929cc 239.7cu in
Vee 12 4 Carburettor
Compression ratio: 10.2:1
Bore: 82.0mm 3.2in
Stroke: 62.0mm 2.4in
Valve type/No: Overhead 24
Transmission: Manual
No. of forward speeds: 5
Wheels driven: Rear
Springs F/R: Coil/Coil
Brake system: PA
Brakes F/R: Disc/Disc
Steering: Rack & pinion
Wheelbase: 249.9cm 98.4in
Track F: 140.0cm 55.1in
Track R: 140.0cm 55.1in
Length: 435.9cm 171.6in
Width: 176.0cm 69.3in
Height: 105.4cm 41.5in

Ground clearance: 13.0cm 5.1in
Kerb weight: 1318.9kg 2905.0lb
Fuel: 95.0L 20.9gal 25.1galUS

2457 Lamborghini

Jarama 400GT
1972 Italy
152.0mph 244.6kmh
0-50mph 80.5kmh: 5.4secs
0-60mph 96.5kmh: 7.2secs
0-1/4 mile: 15.6secs
350.0bhp 261.0kW 354.8PS
@ 7500rpm
289.0lbft 391.6Nm @ 5500rpm
217.8bhp/ton 214.1bhp/tonne
89.1bhp/L 66.4kW/L 90.3PS/L
50.8ft/sec 15.5m/sec
21.0mph 33.8kmh/1000rpm
13.1mpg 10.9mpgUS 21.6L/100km
Petrol 4-stroke piston
3929cc 239.7cu in
Vee 12 6 Carburettor
Compression ratio: 10.7:1
Bore: 82.0mm 3.2in
Stroke: 62.0mm 2.4in
Valve type/No: Overhead 24
Transmission: Manual
No. of forward speeds: 5
Wheels driven: Rear
Springs F/R: Coil/Coil
Brake system: PA
Brakes F/R: Disc/Disc
Steering: Worm & sector
Wheelbase: 237.5cm 93.5in
Track F: 149.1cm 58.7in
Track R: 149.1cm 58.7in
Length: 448.3cm 176.5in
Width: 181.6cm 71.5in
Height: 119.1cm 46.9in
Ground clearance: 11.4cm 4.5in
Kerb weight: 1634.4kg 3600.0lb
Fuel: 99.9L 22.0gal 26.4galUS

2458 Lamborghini

Bravo
1973 Italy
170.0mph 273.5kmh
300.0bhp 223.7kW 304.2PS
@ 7800rpm
237.0lbft 321.1Nm @ 4000rpm
281.2bhp/ton 276.5bhp/tonne
100.1bhp/L 74.7kW/L 101.5PS/L
55.0ft/sec 16.8m/sec
Petrol 4-stroke piston
2996cc 182.8cu in
Vee 8 4 Carburettor
Compression ratio: 10.0:1
Bore: 86.0mm 3.4in
Stroke: 64.5mm 2.5in
Valve type/No: Overhead 16
Transmission: Manual
No. of forward speeds: 5
Wheels driven: Rear
Springs F/R: Coil/Coil
Brakes F/R: Disc/Disc
Steering: Rack & pinion
Wheelbase: 225.3cm 88.7in
Track F: 147.3cm 58.0in
Track R: 153.9cm 60.6in
Length: 373.9cm 147.2in
Width: 188.2cm 74.1in
Height: 104.1cm 41.0in
Kerb weight: 1085.1kg 2390.0lb

2459 Lamborghini

Jarama 400GT
1973 Italy
152.0mph 244.6kmh
0-60mph 96.5kmh: 7.2secs
0-1/4 mile: 15.6secs
350.0bhp 261.0kW 354.8PS
@ 7500rpm
289.0lbft 391.6Nm @ 5500rpm
217.8bhp/ton 214.1bhp/tonne
89.1bhp/L 66.4kW/L 90.3PS/L
50.8ft/sec 15.5m/sec
Petrol 4-stroke piston
3929cc 239.7cu in
Vee 12 6 Carburettor
Compression ratio: 10.7:1
Bore: 82.0mm 3.2in
Stroke: 62.0mm 2.4in
Valve type/No: Overhead 24
Transmission: Manual
No. of forward speeds: 5
Wheels driven: Rear
Springs F/R: Coil/Coil
Brake system: PA
Brakes F/R: Disc/Disc
Steering: Worm & sector PA
Wheelbase: 237.5cm 93.5in
Track F: 149.1cm 58.7in
Track R: 149.1cm 58.7in
Length: 448.3cm 176.5in
Width: 181.6cm 71.5in
Height: 119.1cm 46.9in
Kerb weight: 1634.4kg 3600.0lb
Fuel: 99.9L 22.0gal 26.4galUS

2460 Lamborghini

Urraco S
1974 Italy
144.0mph 231.7kmh
0-50mph 80.5kmh: 6.7secs
0-60mph 96.5kmh: 8.5secs
0-1/4 mile: 16.6secs
0-1km: 30.1secs
220.0bhp 164.0kW 223.0PS
@ 7500rpm
166.0lbft 224.9Nm @ 5750rpm
170.9bhp/ton 168.0bhp/tonne
89.3bhp/L 66.6kW/L 90.6PS/L
43.5ft/sec 13.2m/sec
19.2mph 30.9kmh/1000rpm
18.7mpg 15.6mpgUS 15.1L/100km
Petrol 4-stroke piston
2463cc 150.3cu in
Vee 8 4 Carburettor
Compression ratio: 10.4:1
Bore: 86.0mm 3.4in
Stroke: 53.0mm 2.1in
Valve type/No: Overhead 16
Transmission: Manual
No. of forward speeds: 5
Wheels driven: Rear
Springs F/R: Coil/Coil
Brakes F/R: Disc/Disc
Steering: Rack & pinion
Wheelbase: 245.1cm 96.5in
Track F: 146.1cm 57.5in
Track R: 146.1cm 57.5in
Length: 424.7cm 167.2in
Width: 176.0cm 69.3in
Height: 111.0cm 43.7in
Ground clearance: 19.1cm 7.5in
Kerb weight: 1309.3kg 2884.0lb
Fuel: 80.1L 17.6gal 21.1galUS

2461 Lamborghini

Countach
1976 Italy
192.0mph 308.9kmh
0-50mph 80.5kmh: 5.5secs
0-60mph 96.5kmh: 6.8secs
0-1/4 mile: 14.4secs
375.0bhp 279.6kW 380.2PS
@ 8000rpm
266.0lbft 360.4Nm @ 5000rpm
278.1bhp/ton 273.5bhp/tonne
95.4bhp/L 71.2kW/L 96.8PS/L
54.2ft/sec 16.5m/sec
23.3mph 37.5kmh/1000rpm
14.4mpg 12.0mpgUS 19.6L/100km
Petrol 4-stroke piston
3929cc 239.7cu in
Vee 12 6 Carburettor
Compression ratio: 10.5:1
Bore: 82.0mm 3.2in
Stroke: 62.0mm 2.4in
Valve type/No: Overhead 24
Transmission: Manual
No. of forward speeds: 5
Wheels driven: Rear
Springs F/R: Coil/Coil
Brake system: PA
Brakes F/R: Disc/Disc
Steering: Rack & pinion
Wheelbase: 245.1cm 96.5in
Track F: 150.1cm 59.1in
Track R: 151.9cm 59.8in
Length: 414.0cm 163.0in
Width: 189.0cm 74.4in
Height: 106.9cm 42.1in
Ground clearance: 12.4cm 4.9in
Kerb weight: 1371.1kg 3020.0lb
Fuel: 120.0L 26.4gal 31.7galUS

2462 Lamborghini

Silhouette 3000
1976 Italy
147.0mph 236.5kmh
0-50mph 80.5kmh: 5.1secs
0-60mph 96.5kmh: 6.8secs
0-1/4 mile: 15.2secs
260.0bhp 193.9kW 263.6PS
@ 7500rpm
203.0lbft 275.1Nm @ 3500rpm
211.8bhp/ton 208.2bhp/tonne
86.8bhp/L 64.7kW/L 88.0PS/L
52.9ft/sec 16.1m/sec
20.0mph 32.2kmh/1000rpm
13.8mpg 11.5mpgUS 20.5L/100km
Petrol 4-stroke piston
2996cc 182.8cu in
Vee 8
Compression ratio: 10.0:1
Bore: 86.0mm 3.4in
Stroke: 64.5mm 2.5in
Valve type/No: Overhead 16
Transmission: Manual
No. of forward speeds: 5
Wheels driven: Rear
Springs F/R: Coil/Coil
Brake system: PA
Brakes F/R: Disc/Disc
Steering: Rack & pinion
Wheelbase: 245.1cm 96.5in
Track F: 148.1cm 58.3in
Track R: 153.7cm 60.5in
Length: 439.9cm 173.2in
Width: 165.4cm 65.1in
Height: 111.5cm 43.9in
Kerb weight: 1248.5kg 2750.0lb
Fuel: 77.6L 17.1gal 20.5galUS

2463 Lamborghini

Urraco
1976 Italy
124.0mph 199.5kmh
0-60mph 96.5kmh: 10.1secs
0-1/4 mile: 17.9secs
175.0bhp 130.5kW 177.4PS
@ 7500rpm
139.0lbft 188.3Nm @ 5750rpm
128.1bhp/ton 126.0bhp/tonne
71.0bhp/L 53.0kW/L 72.0PS/L
43.5ft/sec 13.2m/sec
15.6mpg 13.0mpgUS 18.1L/100km
Petrol 4-stroke piston
2463cc 150.3cu in
Vee 8 4 Carburettor
Compression ratio: 10.4:1
Bore: 86.0mm 3.4in
Stroke: 53.0mm 2.1in
Valve type/No: Overhead 16
Transmission: Manual
No. of forward speeds: 5
Wheels driven: Rear
Springs F/R: Coil/Coil
Brakes F/R: Disc/Disc
Steering: Rack & pinion
Wheelbase: 245.1cm 96.5in
Track F: 146.1cm 57.5in
Track R: 146.1cm 57.5in
Length: 424.9cm 167.3in
Width: 176.0cm 69.3in
Height: 110.7cm 43.6in
Ground clearance: 12.4cm 4.9in
Kerb weight: 1389.2kg 3060.0lb
Fuel: 83.3L 18.3gal 22.0galUS

2464 Lamborghini

Countach S
1979 Italy
164.0mph 263.9kmh
0-50mph 80.5kmh: 4.6secs
0-60mph 96.5kmh: 5.9secs
0-1/4 mile: 14.6secs
325.0bhp 242.3kW 329.5PS
@ 7500rpm
260.0lbft 352.3Nm @ 5500rpm
229.6bhp/ton 225.8bhp/tonne
82.7bhp/L 61.7kW/L 83.9PS/L
50.8ft/sec 15.5m/sec
22.5mph 36.2kmh/1000rpm
13.2mpg 11.0mpgUS 21.4L/100km
Petrol 4-stroke piston
3929cc 239.7cu in
Vee 12 6 Carburettor
Compression ratio: 10.5:1
Bore: 82.0mm 3.2in
Stroke: 62.0mm 2.4in
Valve type/No: Overhead 24
Transmission: Manual
No. of forward speeds: 5
Wheels driven: Rear
Springs F/R: Coil/Coil
Brake system: PA
Brakes F/R: Disc/Disc
Steering: Rack & pinion
Wheelbase: 245.1cm 96.5in
Track F: 149.1cm 58.7in
Track R: 163.3cm 64.3in
Length: 414.0cm 163.0in
Width: 199.9cm 78.7in
Height: 106.9cm 42.1in
Ground clearance: 12.4cm 4.9in
Kerb weight: 1439.2kg 3170.0lb
Fuel: 120.0L 26.4gal 31.7galUS

2465 Lamborghini

Countach LP 500S
1982 Italy
165.0mph 265.5kmh
0-50mph 80.5kmh: 4.4secs
0-60mph 96.5kmh: 5.6secs
0-1/4 mile: 14.0secs
0-1km: 24.9secs
375.0bhp 279.6kW 380.2PS
@ 7000rpm
302.0lbft 409.2Nm @ 4500rpm
288.4bhp/ton 283.5bhp/tonne
78.9bhp/L 58.8kW/L 80.0PS/L
52.9ft/sec 16.1m/sec
24.5mph 39.4kmh/1000rpm
14.6mpg 12.2mpgUS 19.3L/100km
Petrol 4-stroke piston
4754cc 290.0cu in
Vee 12 6 Carburettor
Compression ratio: 9.2:1
Bore: 85.5mm 3.4in
Stroke: 69.0mm 2.7in
Valve type/No: Overhead 24
Transmission: Manual
No. of forward speeds: 5
Wheels driven: Rear
Springs F/R: Coil/Coil
Brake system: PA
Brakes F/R: Disc/Disc
Steering: Rack & pinion
Wheelbase: 245.1cm 96.5in
Track F: 149.1cm 58.7in
Track R: 160.5cm 63.2in
Length: 413.8cm 162.9in
Width: 199.9cm 78.7in
Height: 106.9cm 42.1in
Ground clearance: 12.4cm 4.9in
Kerb weight: 1322.5kg 2913.0lb
Fuel: 120.1L 26.4gal 31.7galUS

2466 Lamborghini

Countach S
1982 Italy
150.0mph 241.4kmh
0-60mph 96.5kmh: 5.7secs
0-1/4 mile: 14.1secs
325.0bhp 242.3kW 329.5PS
@ 7500rpm
260.0lbft 352.3Nm @ 5500rpm
229.6bhp/ton 225.8bhp/tonne
82.7bhp/L 61.7kW/L 83.9PS/L
50.8ft/sec 15.5m/sec
Petrol 4-stroke piston
3929cc 239.7cu in
Vee 12 6 Carburettor
Compression ratio: 10.5:1
Bore: 82.0mm 3.2in
Stroke: 62.0mm 2.4in
Valve type/No: Overhead 24
Transmission: Manual
No. of forward speeds: 5
Wheels driven: Rear
Springs F/R: Coil/Coil
Brakes F/R: Disc/Disc
Wheelbase: 245.1cm 96.5in
Track F: 149.1cm 58.7in
Track R: 163.3cm 64.3in
Length: 464.8cm 183.0in
Width: 199.9cm 78.7in
Height: 106.9cm 42.1in
Kerb weight: 1439.2kg 3170.0lb
Fuel: 120.0L 26.4gal 31.7galUS

2467 Lamborghini

Jalpa
1982 Italy
133.0mph 214.0kmh
0-60mph 96.5kmh: 7.3secs
0-1/4 mile: 15.4secs
250.0bhp 186.4kW 253.5PS
@ 7000rpm
235.0lbft 318.4Nm @ 3250rpm
169.4bhp/ton 166.6bhp/tonne
71.7bhp/L 53.5kW/L 72.7PS/L
57.4ft/sec 17.5m/sec

20.4mph 32.8kmh/1000rpm
14.4mpg 12.0mpgUS 19.6L/100km
Petrol 4-stroke piston
3485cc 212.6cu in
Vee 8 4 Carburettor
Compression ratio: 9.0:1
Bore: 86.0mm 3.4in
Stroke: 75.0mm 2.9in
Valve type/No: Overhead 16
Transmission: Manual
No. of forward speeds: 5
Wheels driven: Rear
Springs F/R: Coil/Coil
Brake system: PA
Brakes F/R: Disc/Disc
Steering: Rack & pinion
Wheelbase: 245.1cm 96.5in
Track F: 148.1cm 58.3in
Track R: 153.7cm 60.5in
Length: 421.6cm 166.0in
Width: 165.4cm 65.1in
Height: 111.5cm 43.9in
Ground clearance: 12.7cm 5.0in
Kerb weight: 1500.5kg 3305.0lb
Fuel: 77.6L 17.1gal 20.5galUS

2468 Lamborghini

Countach
1985 Italy
179.0mph 288.0kmh
0-50mph 80.5kmh: 3.5secs
0-60mph 96.5kmh: 4.9secs
0-1/4 mile: 13.0secs
0-1km: 23.3secs
455.0bhp 339.3kW 461.3PS
@ 7000rpm
369.0lbft 500.0Nm @ 5200rpm
319.7bhp/ton 314.4bhp/tonne
88.1bhp/L 65.7kW/L 89.3PS/L
57.4ft/sec 17.5m/sec
24.4mph 39.3kmh/1000rpm
13.7mpg 11.4mpgUS 20.6L/100km
Petrol 4-stroke piston
5167cc 315.2cu in
Vee 12 6 Carburettor
Compression ratio: 9.5:1
Bore: 85.5mm 3.4in
Stroke: 75.0mm 2.9in
Valve type/No: Overhead 48
Transmission: Manual
No. of forward speeds: 5
Wheels driven: Rear
Springs F/R: Coil/Coil
Brake system: PA
Brakes F/R: Disc/Disc
Steering: Rack & pinion
Wheelbase: 245.1cm 96.5in
Track F: 149.1cm 58.7in
Track R: 160.5cm 63.2in
Length: 413.8cm 162.9in
Width: 199.9cm 78.7in
Height: 106.9cm 42.1in
Ground clearance: 12.4cm 4.9in
Kerb weight: 1447.3kg 3188.0lb
Fuel: 120.1L 26.4gal 31.7galUS

2469 Lamborghini

Countach 5000S
1986 Italy
173.0mph 278.4kmh
0-60mph 96.5kmh: 5.2secs
0-1/4 mile: 13.7secs
420.0bhp 313.2kW 425.8PS
@ 7000rpm
341.0lbft 462.1Nm @ 5000rpm
286.4bhp/ton 281.6bhp/tonne
81.3bhp/L 60.6kW/L 82.4PS/L
57.4ft/sec 17.5m/sec
23.4mph 37.7kmh/1000rpm
12.0mpg 10.0mpgUS 23.5L/100km
Petrol 4-stroke piston
5167cc 315.2cu in
Vee 12 fuel injection
Compression ratio: 9.5:1
Bore: 85.5mm 3.4in
Stroke: 75.0mm 2.9in
Valve type/No: Overhead 48
Transmission: Manual
No. of forward speeds: 5
Wheels driven: Rear
Springs F/R: Coil/Coil
Brake system: PA
Brakes F/R: Disc/Disc
Steering: Rack & pinion
Wheelbase: 249.9cm 98.4in
Track F: 153.7cm 60.5in
Track R: 160.5cm 63.2in
Length: 420.1cm 165.4in
Width: 199.9cm 78.7in
Height: 106.9cm 42.1in
Ground clearance: 12.4cm 4.9in
Kerb weight: 1491.4kg 3285.0lb
Fuel: 120.0L 26.4gal 31.7galUS

2470 Lamborghini

Jalpa 3500
1986 Italy
145.0mph 233.3kmh
0-50mph 80.5kmh: 4.9secs
0-60mph 96.5kmh: 6.2secs
0-1/4 mile: 14.7secs
0-1km: 26.8secs
255.0bhp 190.1kW 258.5PS
@ 7000rpm
231.0lbft 313.0Nm @ 3500rpm
184.3bhp/ton 181.2bhp/tonne
73.2bhp/L 54.6kW/L 74.2PS/L
57.4ft/sec 17.5m/sec
20.6mph 33.1kmh/1000rpm
15.9mpg 13.2mpgUS 17.8L/100km
Petrol 4-stroke piston
3485cc 213.0cu in
Vee 8 4 Carburettor
Compression ratio: 9.2:1
Bore: 86.0mm 3.4in
Stroke: 75.0mm 2.9in
Valve type/No: Overhead 16
Transmission: Manual
No. of forward speeds: 5
Wheels driven: Rear
Springs F/R: Coil/Coil
Brake system: PA
Brakes F/R: Disc/Disc
Steering: Rack & pinion
Wheelbase: 245.0cm 96.5in
Track F: 150.0cm 59.1in
Track R: 154.4cm 60.8in
Length: 433.0cm 170.5in
Width: 188.0cm 74.0in
Height: 114.0cm 44.9in
Ground clearance: 10.2cm 4.0in
Kerb weight: 1407.0kg 3099.1lb
Fuel: 80.1L 17.6gal 21.1galUS

2471 Lamborghini

Jalpa
1988 Italy
154.0mph 247.8kmh
0-60mph 96.5kmh: 6.8secs
0-1/4 mile: 15.5secs
247.0bhp 184.2kW 250.4PS
@ 7000rpm
260.0lbft 352.3Nm @ 3400rpm
167.4bhp/ton 164.6bhp/tonne
70.9bhp/L 52.8kW/L 71.9PS/L
57.4ft/sec 17.5m/sec
16.2mpg 13.5mpgUS 17.4L/100km
Petrol 4-stroke piston
3485cc 212.6cu in
Vee 8 4 Carburettor
Compression ratio: 9.0:1
Bore: 86.0mm 3.4in
Stroke: 75.0mm 2.9in
Valve type/No: Overhead 16
Transmission: Manual
No. of forward speeds: 5
Wheels driven: Rear
Springs F/R: Coil/Coil
Brake system: PA
Brakes F/R: Disc/Disc
Steering: Rack & pinion
Wheelbase: 245.1cm 96.5in
Track F: 148.1cm 58.3in
Track R: 153.7cm 60.5in
Length: 421.6cm 166.0in
Width: 165.4cm 65.1in
Height: 111.5cm 43.9in
Ground clearance: 12.7cm 5.0in
Kerb weight: 1500.5kg 3305.0lb
Fuel: 79.9L 17.6gal 21.1galUS

2472 Lamborghini

LM129
1988 Italy
124.0mph 199.5kmh
0-50mph 80.5kmh: 6.1secs
0-60mph 96.5kmh: 7.8secs
0-1/4 mile: 15.8secs
415.0bhp 309.5kW 420.8PS
@ 6900rpm
363.0lbft 491.9Nm @ 4600rpm
139.3bhp/ton 136.9bhp/tonne
80.3bhp/L 59.9kW/L 81.4PS/L
56.5ft/sec 17.2m/sec
9.0mpg 7.5mpgUS 31.4L/100km
Petrol 4-stroke piston
5167cc 315.2cu in
Vee 12 6 Carburettor
Compression ratio: 9.5:1
Bore: 85.5mm 3.4in
Stroke: 75.0mm 2.9in
Valve type/No: Overhead 48
Transmission: Manual
No. of forward speeds: 5
Wheels driven: 4-wheel drive
Springs F/R: Coil/Coil
Brake system: PA
Brakes F/R: Disc/Drum
Steering: Recirculating ball PA
Wheelbase: 300.0cm 118.1in
Track F: 161.5cm 63.6in
Track R: 161.5cm 63.6in
Length: 495.0cm 194.9in
Width: 204.0cm 80.3in
Height: 183.9cm 72.4in
Kerb weight: 3030.4kg 6675.0lb
Fuel: 230.1L 50.6gal 60.8galUS

2473 Lamborghini

Countach 25th Anniversary
1989 Italy
179.0mph 288.0kmh
0-50mph 80.5kmh: 3.8secs
0-60mph 96.5kmh: 4.7secs
0-1/4 mile: 12.9secs
455.0bhp 339.3kW 461.3PS
@ 7000rpm
368.0lbft 498.6Nm @ 5000rpm
310.7bhp/ton 305.5bhp/tonne
88.1bhp/L 65.7kW/L 89.3PS/L
57.4ft/sec 17.5m/sec
12.0mpg 10.0mpgUS 23.5L/100km
Petrol 4-stroke piston
5167cc 315.2cu in
Vee 12 6 Carburettor
Compression ratio: 9.5:1
Bore: 85.5mm 3.4in
Stroke: 75.0mm 2.9in
Valve type/No: Overhead 48
Transmission: Manual
No. of forward speeds: 5
Wheels driven: Rear
Springs F/R: Coil/Coil
Brake system: PA
Brakes F/R: Disc/Disc
Steering: Rack & pinion
Wheelbase: 245.1cm 96.5in
Track F: 153.7cm 60.5in
Track R: 160.5cm 63.2in
Length: 420.1cm 165.4in
Width: 199.9cm 78.7in
Height: 106.9cm 42.1in
Kerb weight: 1489.1kg 3280.0lb
Fuel: 120.0L 26.4gal 31.7galUS

2474 Lamborghini

Diablo
1990 Italy
202.0mph 325.0kmh
485.0bhp 361.7kW 491.7PS
@ 7000rpm
428.0lbft 579.9Nm @ 5200rpm
298.5bhp/ton 293.5bhp/tonne
85.0bhp/L 63.4kW/L 86.2PS/L
61.2ft/sec 18.7m/sec
Petrol 4-stroke piston
5707cc 348.2cu in
Vee 12 fuel injection
Compression ratio: 10.0:1
Bore: 87.0mm 3.4in
Stroke: 80.0mm 3.1in
Valve type/No: Overhead 48
Transmission: Manual
No. of forward speeds: 5
Wheels driven: Rear
Springs F/R: Coil/Coil
Brakes F/R: Disc/Disc
Steering: Rack & pinion
Wheelbase: 264.9cm 104.3in
Track F: 150.9cm 59.4in
Track R: 164.1cm 64.6in
Length: 446.0cm 175.6in
Width: 204.0cm 80.3in
Height: 110.5cm 43.5in
Kerb weight: 1652.6kg 3640.0lb
Fuel: 99.9L 22.0gal 26.4galUS

2475 Lamborghini

Diablo
1991 Italy
202.0mph 325.0kmh
0-50mph 80.5kmh: 3.8secs
0-60mph 96.5kmh: 4.5secs
0-1/4 mile: 13.3secs
492.0bhp 366.9kW 498.8PS
@ 6800rpm
428.0lbft 579.9Nm @ 5200rpm
304.4bhp/ton 299.4bhp/tonne
86.2bhp/L 64.3kW/L 87.4PS/L
59.5ft/sec 18.1m/sec
13.2mpg 11.0mpgUS 21.4L/100km
Petrol 4-stroke piston
5707cc 348.2cu in
Vee 12 fuel injection
Compression ratio: 10.0:1
Bore: 87.0mm 3.4in
Stroke: 80.0mm 3.1in
Valve type/No: Overhead 48
Transmission: Manual
No. of forward speeds: 5
Wheels driven: Rear
Springs F/R: Coil/Coil
Brake system: PA
Brakes F/R: Disc/Disc
Steering: Rack & pinion
Wheelbase: 264.9cm 104.3in
Track F: 150.9cm 59.4in
Track R: 164.1cm 64.6in
Length: 446.0cm 175.6in
Width: 204.0cm 80.3in
Height: 110.5cm 43.5in
Ground clearance: 14.0cm 5.5in
Kerb weight: 1643.5kg 3620.0lb
Fuel: 99.9L 22.0gal 26.4galUS

2476 Lammas-Graham

Drop-head Coupe
1937 UK
94.7mph 152.4kmh
0-50mph 80.5kmh: 11.6secs
0-60mph 96.5kmh: 16.2secs
128.0bhp 95.4kW 129.8PS
@ 4400rpm
79.0bhp/ton 77.7bhp/tonne
35.9bhp/L 26.8kW/L 36.4PS/L
53.4ft/sec 16.3m/sec
18.0mpg 15.0mpgUS 15.7L/100km
Petrol 4-stroke piston
3562cc 217.3cu in supercharged
In-line 6
Bore: 82.5mm 3.2in
Stroke: 111.1mm 4.4in
Valve type/No: Side 12
Transmission: Manual
No. of forward speeds: 3
Wheels driven: Rear
Brakes F/R: Drum/Drum
Kerb weight: 1648.0kg 3630.0lb
Fuel: 54.6L 12.0gal 14.4galUS

2477 Lanchester

15/18 Saloon
1932 UK
71.4mph 114.9kmh
20.0mpg 16.7mpgUS 14.1L/100km
Petrol 4-stroke piston
2504cc 152.8cu in
In-line 6
Bore: 69.5mm 2.7in
Stroke: 110.0mm 4.3in
Valve type/No: Overhead 12
Transmission: Pre-selector
No. of forward speeds: 4
Wheels driven: Rear
Brakes F/R: Drum/Drum
Wheelbase: 292.1cm 115.0in
Track F: 142.2cm 56.0in
Track R: 142.2cm 56.0in
Length: 420.4cm 165.5in
Width: 156.2cm 61.5in
Height: 175.3cm 69.0in
Kerb weight: 1582.6kg 3486.0lb
Fuel: 72.8L 16.0gal 19.2galUS

2478 Lanchester

18 Saloon
1935 UK
71.4mph 114.9kmh
0-50mph 80.5kmh: 19.0secs
0-60mph 96.5kmh: 36.8secs
20.0mpg 16.7mpgUS 14.1L/100km
Petrol 4-stroke piston
2390cc 145.8cu in

In-line 6
Bore: 69.5mm 2.7in
Stroke: 105.0mm 4.1in
Valve type/No: Overhead 12
Transmission: Manual
No. of forward speeds: 4
Wheels driven: Rear
Brakes F/R: Drum/Drum
Kerb weight: 1614.4kg 3556.0lb
Fuel: 81.9L 18.0gal 21.6galUS

2479 Lanchester

18
1937 UK
70.8mph 113.9kmh
0-50mph 80.5kmh: 24.4secs
0-60mph 96.5kmh: 36.8secs
62.0bhp 46.2kW 62.9PS
@ 3600rpm
38.8bhp/ton 38.1bhp/tonne
24.2bhp/L 18.0kW/L 24.5PS/L
41.3ft/sec 12.6m/sec
17.0mpg 14.2mpgUS 16.6L/100km
Petrol 4-stroke piston
2565cc 156.5cu in
In-line 6
Bore: 72.0mm 2.8in
Stroke: 105.0mm 4.1in
Valve type/No: Overhead 12
Transmission: Manual
No. of forward speeds: 4
Wheels driven: Rear
Brakes F/R: Drum/Drum
Kerb weight: 1625.3kg 3580.0lb
Fuel: 91.0L 20.0gal 24.0galUS

2480 Lanchester

SS 2.5-litre
1937 UK
89.1mph 143.4kmh
0-50mph 80.5kmh: 11.3secs
0-60mph 96.5kmh: 16.5secs
104.0bhp 77.5kW 105.4PS
@ 4500rpm
65.8bhp/ton 64.7bhp/tonne
39.0bhp/L 29.1kW/L 39.6PS/L
52.1ft/sec 15.9m/sec
20.0mpg 16.7mpgUS 14.1L/100km
Petrol 4-stroke piston
2664cc 162.5cu in
In-line 6 2 Carburettor
Bore: 73.0mm 2.9in
Stroke: 106.0mm 4.2in
Valve type/No: Overhead 12
Transmission: Manual
No. of forward speeds: 4
Wheels driven: Rear
Brakes F/R: Drum/Drum
Kerb weight: 1606.2kg 3538.0lb
Fuel: 63.7L 14.0gal 16.8galUS

2481 Lanchester

11 Saloon
1938 UK
63.3mph 101.8kmh
0-50mph 80.5kmh: 35.8secs
26.0mpg 21.6mpgUS 10.9L/100km
Petrol 4-stroke piston
1444cc 88.1cu in
In-line 4
Bore: 66.0mm 2.6in
Stroke: 105.4mm 4.1in
Valve type/No: Overhead 8
Transmission: Pre-selector
No. of forward speeds: 4
Wheels driven: Rear
Brakes F/R: Drum/Drum
Kerb weight: 1272.1kg 2802.0lb
Fuel: 45.5L 10.0gal 12.0galUS

2482 Lanchester

Roadrider de Luxe Saloon
1938 UK
73.7mph 118.6kmh
0-50mph 80.5kmh: 20.8secs
0-60mph 96.5kmh: 33.1secs
21.0mpg 17.5mpgUS 13.5L/100km
Petrol 4-stroke piston
1809cc 110.4cu in
In-line 6
Bore: 61.5mm 2.4in
Stroke: 101.6mm 4.0in
Valve type/No: Overhead 12
Transmission: Pre-selector
No. of forward speeds: 4
Wheels driven: Rear
Brakes F/R: Drum/Drum
Kerb weight: 1429.2kg 3148.0lb
Fuel: 54.6L 12.0gal 14.4galUS

2483 Lanchester

Roadrider de Luxe Saloon
1940 UK
68.0mph 109.4kmh
0-50mph 80.5kmh: 25.8secs
0-60mph 96.5kmh: 33.2secs
0-1/4 mile: 25.4secs
52.0bhp 38.8kW 52.7PS
@ 4200rpm
36.8bhp/ton 36.1bhp/tonne
28.7bhp/L 21.4kW/L 29.1PS/L
46.7ft/sec 14.2m/sec
23.0mpg 19.2mpgUS 12.3L/100km
Petrol 4-stroke piston
1809cc 110.4cu in
In-line 6
Bore: 61.5mm 2.4in
Stroke: 101.6mm 4.0in
Valve type/No: Overhead 12
Transmission: Pre-selector
No. of forward speeds: 4
Wheels driven: Rear
Brakes F/R: Drum/Drum
Wheelbase: 279.4cm 110.0in
Track F: 132.1cm 52.0in
Track R: 132.1cm 52.0in
Length: 375.9cm 148.0in
Width: 163.8cm 64.5in
Height: 158.8cm 62.5in
Ground clearance: 15.2cm 6.0in
Kerb weight: 1438.3kg 3168.0lb
Fuel: 54.6L 12.0gal 14.4galUS

2484 Lanchester

10
1949 UK
69.0mph 111.0kmh
0-50mph 80.5kmh: 25.9secs
0-60mph 96.5kmh: 44.7secs
40.0bhp 29.8kW 40.5PS
@ 4200rpm
35.0bhp/ton 34.4bhp/tonne
31.1bhp/L 23.2kW/L 31.5PS/L
46.7ft/sec 14.2m/sec
25.0mpg 20.8mpgUS 11.3L/100km
Petrol 4-stroke piston
1287cc 78.5cu in
In-line 4
Compression ratio: 7.1:1
Bore: 63.5mm 2.5in
Stroke: 101.6mm 4.0in
Valve type/No: Overhead 8
Transmission: Manual
No. of forward speeds: 4
Wheels driven: Rear
Brakes F/R: Drum/Drum
Wheelbase: 251.5cm 99.0in
Track F: 121.9cm 48.0in
Track R: 121.9cm 48.0in
Length: 401.8cm 158.2in
Width: 147.3cm 58.0in
Height: 158.8cm 62.5in
Ground clearance: 15.2cm 6.0in
Kerb weight: 1161.3kg 2558.0lb
Fuel: 36.4L 8.0gal 9.6galUS

2485 Lancia

27.6hp Astura Saloon
1934 Italy
83.1mph 133.7kmh
0-50mph 80.5kmh: 14.0secs
0-60mph 96.5kmh: 19.6secs
17.0mpg 14.2mpgUS 16.6L/100km
Petrol 4-stroke piston
2972cc 181.3cu in
Vee 8
Bore: 74.6mm 2.9in
Stroke: 85.0mm 3.3in
Transmission: Manual
No. of forward speeds: 4
Wheels driven: Rear
Brakes F/R: Drum/Drum
Kerb weight: 1512.7kg 3332.0lb
Fuel: 63.7L 14.0gal 16.8galUS

2486 Lancia

Augusta Saloon
1934 Italy
66.1mph 106.4kmh
0-50mph 80.5kmh: 22.6secs
30.0mpg 25.0mpgUS 9.4L/100km
Petrol 4-stroke piston
1194cc 72.8cu in
Vee 4
Bore: 69.5mm 2.7in
Stroke: 78.0mm 3.1in
Valve type/No: Overhead 8
Transmission: Manual
No. of forward speeds: 4
Wheels driven: Rear
Brakes F/R: Drum/Drum
Kerb weight: 826.3kg 1820.0lb
Fuel: 45.5L 10.0gal 12.0galUS

2487 Lancia

Aprilia Pillarless Saloon
1937 Italy
81.0mph 130.3kmh
0-50mph 80.5kmh: 15.4secs
0-60mph 96.5kmh: 25.2secs
25.0mpg 20.8mpgUS 11.3L/100km
Petrol 4-stroke piston
1352cc 82.5cu in
Vee 4
Bore: 72.0mm 2.8in
Stroke: 83.0mm 3.3in
Valve type/No: Overhead 8
Transmission: Manual
No. of forward speeds: 4
Wheels driven: Rear
Brakes F/R: Drum/Drum
Kerb weight: 891.7kg 1964.0lb
Fuel: 50.0L 11.0gal 13.2galUS

2488 Lancia

Aprilia Saloon
1938 Italy
81.8mph 131.6kmh
0-50mph 80.5kmh: 15.3secs
0-60mph 96.5kmh: 22.8secs
28.0mpg 23.3mpgUS 10.1L/100km
Petrol 4-stroke piston
1352cc 82.5cu in
Vee 4
Bore: 72.0mm 2.8in
Stroke: 83.0mm 3.3in
Valve type/No: Overhead 8
Transmission: Manual
No. of forward speeds: 4
Wheels driven: Rear
Brakes F/R: Drum/Drum
Kerb weight: 914.8kg 2015.0lb
Fuel: 50.0L 11.0gal 13.2galUS

2489 Lancia

Aurelia 2-litre Saloon
1952 Italy
92.0mph 148.0kmh
0-50mph 80.5kmh: 13.2secs
0-60mph 96.5kmh: 18.0secs
0-1/4 mile: 21.4secs
70.0bhp 52.2kW 71.0PS
@ 4500rpm
94.0lbft 127.4Nm @ 2500rpm
61.6bhp/ton 60.5bhp/tonne
35.2bhp/L 26.2kW/L 35.6PS/L
40.1ft/sec 12.2m/sec
18.0mph 29.0kmh/1000rpm
24.5mpg 20.4mpgUS 11.5L/100km
Petrol 4-stroke piston
1991cc 121.5cu in
Vee 6
Compression ratio: 7.8:1
Bore: 72.0mm 2.8in
Stroke: 81.5mm 3.2in
Valve type/No: Overhead 12
Transmission: Manual
No. of forward speeds: 4
Wheels driven: Rear
Springs F/R: Coil/Coil
Brakes F/R: Drum/Drum
Wheelbase: 285.8cm 112.5in
Track F: 127.8cm 50.3in
Track R: 130.0cm 51.2in
Length: 442.0cm 174.0in
Width: 156.2cm 61.5in
Height: 149.9cm 59.0in
Ground clearance: 15.2cm 6.0in
Kerb weight: 1156.3kg 2547.0lb
Fuel: 59.1L 13.0gal 15.6galUS

2490 Lancia

Aurelia Gran Turismo 2500
1955 Italy
112.0mph 180.2kmh
0-50mph 80.5kmh: 8.4secs
0-60mph 96.5kmh: 12.3secs
0-1/4 mile: 19.1secs
118.0bhp 88.0kW 119.6PS
@ 5000rpm
134.0lbft 181.6Nm @ 3500rpm
100.4bhp/ton 98.7bhp/tonne
48.1bhp/L 35.9kW/L 48.8PS/L
46.8ft/sec 14.2m/sec
22.0mph 35.4kmh/1000rpm
19.0mpg 15.8mpgUS 14.9L/100km
Petrol 4-stroke piston
2451cc 149.5cu in
Vee 6
Compression ratio: 8.0:1
Bore: 78.0mm 3.1in
Stroke: 85.5mm 3.4in
Valve type/No: Overhead 12
Transmission: Manual
No. of forward speeds: 4
Wheels driven: Rear
Springs F/R: Coil/Leaf
Brakes F/R: Drum/Drum
Wheelbase: 265.2cm 104.4in
Track F: 127.8cm 50.3in
Track R: 130.0cm 51.2in
Length: 426.7cm 168.0in
Width: 154.9cm 61.0in
Height: 135.9cm 53.5in
Ground clearance: 15.2cm 6.0in
Kerb weight: 1195.4kg 2633.0lb
Fuel: 77.3L 17.0gal 20.4galUS

2491 Lancia

Spyder
1955 Italy
108.0mph 173.8kmh
0-50mph 80.5kmh: 8.7secs
0-60mph 96.5kmh: 12.5secs
0-1/4 mile: 18.5secs
110.0bhp 82.0kW 111.5PS
@ 5100rpm
134.0lbft 181.6Nm @ 3000rpm
98.6bhp/ton 96.9bhp/tonne
44.9bhp/L 33.5kW/L 45.5PS/L
47.7ft/sec 14.5m/sec
21.4mph 34.4kmh/1000rpm
Petrol 4-stroke piston
2451cc 149.5cu in
Vee 6
Compression ratio: 8.0:1
Bore: 78.0mm 3.1in
Stroke: 85.6mm 3.4in
Valve type/No: Overhead 12
Transmission: Manual
No. of forward speeds: 4
Wheels driven: Front
Wheelbase: 244.9cm 96.4in
Track F: 129.0cm 50.8in
Track R: 130.0cm 51.2in
Kerb weight: 1135.0kg 2500.0lb

2492 Lancia

Aurelia GT 2500
1958 Italy
113.0mph 181.8kmh
0-50mph 80.5kmh: 10.0secs
0-60mph 96.5kmh: 14.0secs
0-1/4 mile: 19.6secs
118.0bhp 88.0kW 119.6PS
@ 5000rpm
126.5lbft 171.4Nm @ 3500rpm
92.8bhp/ton 91.2bhp/tonne
48.1bhp/L 35.9kW/L 48.8PS/L
46.8ft/sec 14.2m/sec
20.5mph 33.0kmh/1000rpm
23.6mpg 19.7mpgUS 12.0L/100km
Petrol 4-stroke piston
2451cc 149.5cu in
Vee 6
Compression ratio: 8.4:1
Bore: 78.0mm 3.1in
Stroke: 85.5mm 3.4in
Valve type/No: Overhead 12
Transmission: Manual
No. of forward speeds: 4
Wheels driven: Rear
Springs F/R: Coil/Leaf
Brakes F/R: Drum/Drum
Wheelbase: 265.2cm 104.4in
Track F: 127.8cm 50.3in
Track R: 130.0cm 51.2in
Length: 436.9cm 172.0in

Width: 154.9cm 61.0in
Height: 135.9cm 53.5in
Ground clearance: 15.2cm 6.0in
Kerb weight: 1293.4kg 2849.0lb
Fuel: 75.1L 16.5gal 19.8galUS

2493 Lancia

Flaminia
1958 Italy
103.0mph 165.7kmh
0-50mph 80.5kmh: 11.3secs
0-60mph 96.5kmh: 15.6secs
0-1/4 mile: 20.2secs
112.0bhp 83.5kW 113.5PS
@ 4800rpm
141.0lbft 191.1Nm @ 3000rpm
69.5bhp/ton 68.3bhp/tonne
45.6bhp/L 34.0kW/L 46.2PS/L
42.8ft/sec 13.0m/sec
21.0mph 33.8kmh/1000rpm
20.8mpg 17.3mpgUS 13.6L/100km
Petrol 4-stroke piston
2458cc 150.0cu in
Vee 6
Compression ratio: 7.8:1
Bore: 80.0mm 3.1in
Stroke: 81.5mm 3.2in
Valve type/No: Overhead 12
Transmission: Manual
No. of forward speeds: 4
Wheels driven: Rear
Springs F/R: Coil/Leaf
Brakes F/R: Drum/Drum
Wheelbase: 287.0cm 113.0in
Track F: 137.2cm 54.0in
Track R: 137.2cm 54.0in
Length: 485.1cm 191.0in
Width: 175.3cm 69.0in
Height: 146.1cm 57.5in
Ground clearance: 14.0cm 5.5in
Kerb weight: 1638.9kg 3610.0lb
Fuel: 56.9L 12.5gal 15.0galUS

2494 Lancia

Appia Sedan
1959 Italy
81.8mph 131.6kmh
0-50mph 80.5kmh: 15.0secs
0-60mph 96.5kmh: 23.0secs
0-1/4 mile: 22.5secs
43.5bhp 32.4kW 44.1PS
@ 4800rpm
56.4lbft 76.4Nm @ 3000rpm
50.0bhp/ton 49.1bhp/tonne
39.9bhp/L 29.8kW/L 40.5PS/L
39.5ft/sec 12.0m/sec
17.7mph 28.5kmh/1000rpm
Petrol 4-stroke piston
1090cc 66.5cu in
Vee 4
Compression ratio: 7.2:1
Bore: 68.1mm 2.7in
Stroke: 75.2mm 3.0in
Valve type/No: Overhead 8
Transmission: Manual
No. of forward speeds: 4
Wheels driven: Rear
Wheelbase: 251.0cm 98.8in
Track F: 117.9cm 46.4in
Track R: 118.1cm 46.5in
Length: 401.3cm 158.0in
Width: 149.4cm 58.8in
Height: 140.5cm 55.3in
Kerb weight: 885.3kg 1950.0lb

2495 Lancia

Flaminia
1959 Italy
100.0mph 160.9kmh
0-50mph 80.5kmh: 11.7secs
0-60mph 96.5kmh: 15.5secs
0-1/4 mile: 20.0secs
112.0bhp 83.5kW 113.5PS
@ 4800rpm
142.0lbft 192.4Nm @ 3000rpm
72.5bhp/ton 71.3bhp/tonne
45.6bhp/L 34.0kW/L 46.2PS/L
42.8ft/sec 13.0m/sec
19.5mph 31.4kmh/1000rpm
Petrol 4-stroke piston
2458cc 150.0cu in
Vee 6
Compression ratio: 7.8:1
Bore: 80.0mm 3.1in
Stroke: 81.5mm 3.2in
Valve type/No: Overhead 12
Transmission: Manual
No. of forward speeds: 4
Wheels driven: Front
Wheelbase: 287.0cm 113.0in
Track F: 136.7cm 53.8in
Track R: 136.9cm 53.9in
Length: 485.1cm 191.0in
Width: 175.0cm 68.9in
Height: 146.1cm 57.5in
Kerb weight: 1570.8kg 3460.0lb

2496 Lancia

Flaminia Coupe
1960 Italy
107.0mph 172.2kmh
0-50mph 80.5kmh: 10.1secs
0-60mph 96.5kmh: 13.6secs
0-1/4 mile: 19.1secs
119.0bhp 88.7kW 120.6PS
@ 5100rpm
137.0lbft 185.6Nm @ 3500rpm
81.6bhp/ton 80.3bhp/tonne
48.4bhp/L 36.1kW/L 49.1PS/L
45.5ft/sec 13.9m/sec
18.7mph 30.1kmh/1000rpm
20.1mpg 16.7mpgUS 14.1L/100km
Petrol 4-stroke piston
2458cc 150.0cu in
Vee 6
Compression ratio: 9.0:1
Bore: 80.0mm 3.1in
Stroke: 81.5mm 3.2in
Valve type/No: Overhead 12
Transmission: Manual
No. of forward speeds: 4
Wheels driven: Rear
Springs F/R: Coil/Leaf
Brake system: PA
Brakes F/R: Disc/Disc
Wheelbase: 276.1cm 108.7in
Track F: 137.2cm 54.0in
Track R: 137.2cm 54.0in
Length: 468.6cm 184.5in
Width: 174.0cm 68.5in
Height: 142.0cm 55.9in
Ground clearance: 10.2cm 4.0in
Kerb weight: 1482.8kg 3266.0lb
Fuel: 56.9L 12.5gal 15.0galUS

2497 Lancia

Zagato
1960 Italy
118.0mph 189.9kmh
0-50mph 80.5kmh: 9.5secs
0-60mph 96.5kmh: 13.2secs
0-1/4 mile: 19.0secs
131.0bhp 97.7kW 132.8PS
@ 5100rpm
137.0lbft 185.6Nm @ 3500rpm
104.8bhp/ton 103.0bhp/tonne
53.3bhp/L 39.7kW/L 54.0PS/L
45.5ft/sec 13.9m/sec
20.1mph 32.3kmh/1000rpm
Petrol 4-stroke piston
2458cc 150.0cu in
Vee 6 1 Carburettor
Compression ratio: 9.0:1
Bore: 80.0mm 3.1in
Stroke: 81.5mm 3.2in
Valve type/No: Overhead 12
Transmission: Manual
No. of forward speeds: 4
Wheels driven: Rear
Wheelbase: 252.0cm 99.2in
Track F: 136.7cm 53.8in
Track R: 127.0cm 50.0in
Length: 449.6cm 177.0in
Width: 162.6cm 64.0in
Height: 128.0cm 50.4in
Kerb weight: 1271.2kg 2800.0lb

2498 Lancia

Flavia
1961 Italy
96.0mph 154.5kmh
0-50mph 80.5kmh: 13.7secs
0-60mph 96.5kmh: 18.7secs
0-1/4 mile: 22.0secs
78.0bhp 58.2kW 79.1PS
@ 5200rpm
82.0lbft 111.1Nm @ 3500rpm
66.8bhp/ton 65.7bhp/tonne
52.0bhp/L 38.8kW/L 52.7PS/L
40.4ft/sec 12.3m/sec
18.1mph 29.1kmh/1000rpm
25.4mpg 21.1mpgUS 11.1L/100km
Petrol 4-stroke piston
1500cc 91.5cu in
Flat 4
Compression ratio: 8.3:1
Bore: 82.0mm 3.2in
Stroke: 71.0mm 2.8in
Valve type/No: Overhead 8
Transmission: Manual
No. of forward speeds: 4
Wheels driven: Front
Springs F/R: Leaf/Leaf
Brake system: PA
Brakes F/R: Disc/Disc
Wheelbase: 264.9cm 104.3in
Track F: 130.0cm 51.2in
Track R: 128.0cm 50.4in
Length: 457.7cm 180.2in
Width: 160.5cm 63.2in
Height: 150.1cm 59.1in
Ground clearance: 12.7cm 5.0in
Kerb weight: 1187.2kg 2615.0lb
Fuel: 47.8L 10.5gal 12.6galUS

2499 Lancia

Appia III
1962 Italy
82.0mph 131.9kmh
0-50mph 80.5kmh: 15.2secs
0-60mph 96.5kmh: 23.7secs
0-1/4 mile: 22.5secs
48.0bhp 35.8kW 48.7PS
@ 5200rpm
63.0lbft 85.4Nm @ 3000rpm
52.1bhp/ton 51.2bhp/tonne
44.0bhp/L 32.8kW/L 44.6PS/L
42.6ft/sec 13.0m/sec
15.8mph 25.4kmh/1000rpm
32.6mpg 27.1mpgUS 8.7L/100km
Petrol 4-stroke piston
1090cc 66.5cu in
Vee 4
Compression ratio: 7.8:1
Bore: 68.0mm 2.7in
Stroke: 75.0mm 2.9in
Valve type/No: Overhead 8
Transmission: Manual
No. of forward speeds: 4
Springs F/R: Coil/Leaf
Brakes F/R: Drum/Drum
Wheelbase: 251.0cm 98.8in
Track F: 117.6cm 46.3in
Track R: 118.1cm 46.5in
Length: 401.8cm 158.2in
Width: 147.8cm 58.2in
Height: 144.3cm 56.8in
Ground clearance: 10.7cm 4.2in
Kerb weight: 937.5kg 2065.0lb
Fuel: 38.7L 8.5gal 10.2galUS

2500 Lancia

Flaminia Sedan
1962 Italy
105.0mph 168.9kmh
0-50mph 80.5kmh: 10.2secs
0-60mph 96.5kmh: 14.5secs
0-1/4 mile: 20.1secs
110.0bhp 82.0kW 111.5PS
@ 5200rpm
139.0lbft 188.3Nm @ 3000rpm
70.7bhp/ton 69.5bhp/tonne
44.7bhp/L 33.4kW/L 45.4PS/L
46.4ft/sec 14.1m/sec
20.0mph 32.2kmh/1000rpm
20.2mpg 16.8mpgUS 14.0L/100km
Petrol 4-stroke piston
2458cc 150.0cu in
Vee 6 1 Carburettor
Compression ratio: 8.4:1
Bore: 80.0mm 3.1in
Stroke: 81.5mm 3.2in
Valve type/No: Overhead 12
Transmission: Manual
No. of forward speeds: 4
Wheels driven: Rear
Springs F/R: Coil/Leaf
Brake system: PA
Brakes F/R: Disc/Disc
Steering: Worm & roller
Wheelbase: 287.0cm 113.0in
Track F: 137.2cm 54.0in
Track R: 137.2cm 54.0in
Length: 485.1cm 191.0in
Width: 175.3cm 69.0in
Height: 142.2cm 56.0in
Ground clearance: 14.0cm 5.5in
Kerb weight: 1582.6kg 3486.0lb
Fuel: 57.8L 12.7gal 15.3galUS

2501 Lancia

Flavia Coupe
1964 Italy
107.0mph 172.2kmh
0-50mph 80.5kmh: 9.4secs
0-60mph 96.5kmh: 13.2secs
0-1/4 mile: 19.1secs
92.0bhp 68.6kW 93.3PS
@ 5200rpm
108.0lbft 146.3Nm @ 3000rpm
82.6bhp/ton 81.3bhp/tonne
51.1bhp/L 38.1kW/L 51.8PS/L
42.0ft/sec 12.8m/sec
18.9mph 30.4kmh/1000rpm
22.9mpg 19.1mpgUS 12.3L/100km
Petrol 4-stroke piston
1800cc 109.8cu in
Flat 4 1 Carburettor
Compression ratio: 9.0:1
Bore: 88.0mm 3.5in
Stroke: 74.0mm 2.9in
Valve type/No: Overhead 8
Transmission: Manual
No. of forward speeds: 4
Wheels driven: Front
Springs F/R: Leaf/Leaf
Brake system: PA
Brakes F/R: Disc/Disc
Steering: Worm & roller
Wheelbase: 247.9cm 97.6in
Track F: 130.0cm 51.2in
Track R: 128.0cm 50.4in
Length: 448.3cm 176.5in
Width: 161.3cm 63.5in
Height: 134.6cm 53.0in
Ground clearance: 15.2cm 6.0in
Kerb weight: 1132.3kg 2494.0lb
Fuel: 47.8L 10.5gal 12.6galUS

2502 Lancia

Fulvia
1964 Italy
85.0mph 136.8kmh
0-50mph 80.5kmh: 15.7secs
0-60mph 96.5kmh: 23.5secs
0-1/4 mile: 22.9secs
58.0bhp 43.2kW 58.8PS
@ 5800rpm
62.0lbft 84.0Nm @ 4000rpm
59.9bhp/ton 58.9bhp/tonne
53.2bhp/L 39.6kW/L 53.9PS/L
42.5ft/sec 12.9m/sec
14.7mph 23.7kmh/1000rpm
24.3mpg 20.2mpgUS 11.6L/100km
Petrol 4-stroke piston
1091cc 66.6cu in
Vee 4 1 Carburettor
Compression ratio: 7.8:1
Bore: 72.0mm 2.8in
Stroke: 67.0mm 2.6in
Valve type/No: Overhead 8
Transmission: Manual
No. of forward speeds: 4
Wheels driven: Front
Springs F/R: Leaf/Leaf
Brakes F/R: Disc/Disc
Steering: Worm & roller
Wheelbase: 247.7cm 97.5in
Track F: 130.0cm 51.2in
Track R: 128.3cm 50.5in
Length: 414.0cm 163.0in
Width: 154.9cm 61.0in
Height: 139.7cm 55.0in
Ground clearance: 12.7cm 5.0in
Kerb weight: 985.2kg 2170.0lb
Fuel: 38.7L 8.5gal 10.2galUS

2503 Lancia

Fulvia 2C
1964 Italy
94.0mph 151.2kmh
0-50mph 80.5kmh: 13.0secs
0-60mph 96.5kmh: 18.2secs
0-1/4 mile: 21.1secs
71.0bhp 52.9kW 72.0PS
@ 6000rpm
68.0lbft 92.1Nm @ 4300rpm
73.3bhp/ton 72.1bhp/tonne
65.1bhp/L 48.5kW/L 66.0PS/L
44.0ft/sec 13.4m/sec
15.3mph 24.6kmh/1000rpm
24.3mpg 20.2mpgUS 11.6L/100km
Petrol 4-stroke piston
1091cc 66.6cu in
Vee 4 2 Carburettor
Compression ratio: 9.0:1
Bore: 72.0mm 2.8in

Stroke: 67.0mm 2.6in
Valve type/No: Overhead 8
Transmission: Manual
No. of forward speeds: 4
Wheels driven: Front
Springs F/R: Leaf/Leaf
Brakes F/R: Disc/Disc
Steering: Worm & roller
Wheelbase: 247.7cm 97.5in
Track F: 130.0cm 51.2in
Track R: 128.3cm 50.5in
Length: 414.0cm 163.0in
Width: 154.9cm 61.0in
Height: 139.7cm 55.0in
Ground clearance: 12.7cm 5.0in
Kerb weight: 985.2kg 2170.0lb
Fuel: 38.7L 8.5gal 10.2galUS

2504 Lancia

Flaminia Coupe 3B
1965 Italy
115.0mph 185.0kmh
0-50mph 80.5kmh: 9.3secs
0-60mph 96.5kmh: 12.7secs
0-1/4 mile: 18.7secs
140.0bhp 104.4kW 141.9PS
@ 5400rpm
163.0lbft 220.9Nm @ 3000rpm
94.9bhp/ton 93.3bhp/tonne
50.4bhp/L 37.6kW/L 51.1PS/L
48.1ft/sec 14.7m/sec
20.6mph 33.1kmh/1000rpm
16.2mpg 13.5mpgUS 17.4L/100km
Petrol 4-stroke piston
2775cc 169.3cu in
Vee 6 1 Carburettor
Compression ratio: 9.0:1
Bore: 85.0mm 3.3in
Stroke: 81.5mm 3.2in
Valve type/No: Overhead 12
Transmission: Manual
No. of forward speeds: 4
Wheels driven: Rear
Springs F/R: Coil/Leaf
Brake system: PA
Brakes F/R: Disc/Disc
Steering: Worm & roller
Wheelbase: 274.8cm 108.2in
Track F: 137.2cm 54.0in
Track R: 137.2cm 54.0in
Length: 467.4cm 184.0in
Width: 172.7cm 68.0in
Height: 142.2cm 56.0in
Ground clearance: 16.5cm 6.5in
Kerb weight: 1500.0kg 3304.0lb
Fuel: 57.8L 12.7gal 15.3galUS

2505 Lancia

Flavia Zagato Sport
1965 Italy
115.0mph 185.0kmh
0-50mph 80.5kmh: 8.5secs
0-60mph 96.5kmh: 11.9secs
0-1/4 mile: 18.3secs
100.0bhp 74.6kW 101.4PS
@ 5200rpm
120.0lbft 162.6Nm @ 3000rpm
97.0bhp/ton 95.3bhp/tonne
55.6bhp/L 41.4kW/L 56.3PS/L
42.0ft/sec 12.8m/sec
19.5mph 31.4kmh/1000rpm
20.5mpg 17.1mpgUS 13.8L/100km
Petrol 4-stroke piston
1800cc 109.8cu in
Flat 4 2 Carburettor
Compression ratio: 9.0:1
Bore: 88.0mm 3.5in
Stroke: 74.0mm 2.9in
Valve type/No: Overhead 8
Transmission: Manual
No. of forward speeds: 4
Wheels driven: Front
Springs F/R: Leaf/Leaf
Brake system: PA
Brakes F/R: Disc/Disc
Steering: Worm & roller
Wheelbase: 247.7cm 97.5in
Track F: 130.0cm 51.2in
Track R: 128.0cm 50.4in
Length: 442.0cm 174.0in
Width: 165.1cm 65.0in
Height: 129.5cm 51.0in
Ground clearance: 12.7cm 5.0in
Kerb weight: 1048.7kg 2310.0lb
Fuel: 47.8L 10.5gal 12.6galUS

2506 Lancia

Fulvia Coupe
1966 Italy
104.0mph 167.3kmh
0-50mph 80.5kmh: 10.7secs
0-60mph 96.5kmh: 15.8secs
0-1/4 mile: 20.0secs
0-1km: 37.2secs
80.0bhp 59.7kW 81.1PS
@ 6000rpm
66.6lbft 90.2Nm @ 4000rpm
86.4bhp/ton 85.0bhp/tonne
65.8bhp/L 49.1kW/L 66.7PS/L
44.0ft/sec 13.4m/sec
16.2mph 26.1kmh/1000rpm
28.3mpg 23.6mpgUS 10.0L/100km
Petrol 4-stroke piston
1216cc 74.2cu in
Vee 4 2 Carburettor
Compression ratio: 9.0:1
Bore: 76.0mm 3.0in
Stroke: 67.0mm 2.6in
Valve type/No: Overhead 8
Transmission: Manual
No. of forward speeds: 4
Wheels driven: Front
Springs F/R: Leaf/Leaf
Brake system: PA
Brakes F/R: Disc/Disc
Steering: Worm & roller
Wheelbase: 232.9cm 91.7in
Track F: 131.3cm 51.7in
Track R: 128.3cm 50.5in
Length: 397.5cm 156.5in
Width: 157.5cm 62.0in
Height: 129.5cm 51.0in
Ground clearance: 17.8cm 7.0in
Kerb weight: 941.1kg 2073.0lb
Fuel: 38.7L 8.5gal 10.2galUS

2507 Lancia

Flavia Injection
1967 Italy
105.0mph 168.9kmh
0-50mph 80.5kmh: 10.5secs
0-60mph 96.5kmh: 15.0secs
0-1/4 mile: 19.7secs
0-1km: 36.3secs
102.0bhp 76.1kW 103.4PS
@ 5200rpm
112.7lbft 152.7Nm @ 3500rpm
85.0bhp/ton 83.6bhp/tonne
56.7bhp/L 42.3kW/L 57.4PS/L
42.0ft/sec 12.8m/sec
18.8mph 30.2kmh/1000rpm
25.3mpg 21.1mpgUS 11.2L/100km
Petrol 4-stroke piston
1800cc 109.8cu in
Flat 4 fuel injection
Compression ratio: 9.0:1
Bore: 88.0mm 3.5in
Stroke: 74.0mm 2.9in
Valve type/No: Overhead 8
Transmission: Manual
No. of forward speeds: 4
Wheels driven: Front
Springs F/R: Leaf/Leaf
Brake system: PA
Brakes F/R: Disc/Disc
Steering: Worm & roller
Wheelbase: 264.9cm 104.3in
Track F: 132.1cm 52.0in
Track R: 127.8cm 50.3in
Length: 458.0cm 180.3in
Width: 161.0cm 63.4in
Height: 149.9cm 59.0in
Ground clearance: 22.9cm 9.0in
Kerb weight: 1219.9kg 2687.0lb
Fuel: 54.6L 12.0gal 14.4galUS

2508 Lancia

Fulvia 1.3 Rallye
1967 Italy
104.0mph 167.3kmh
0-50mph 80.5kmh: 9.1secs
0-60mph 96.5kmh: 12.6secs
0-1/4 mile: 18.6secs
87.0bhp 64.9kW 88.2PS
@ 6000rpm
84.0lbft 113.8Nm @ 4500rpm
93.2bhp/ton 91.7bhp/tonne
67.0bhp/L 50.0kW/L 68.0PS/L
45.7ft/sec 13.9m/sec
17.2mph 27.7kmh/1000rpm
Petrol 4-stroke piston
1298cc 79.2cu in
Vee 4 1 Carburettor
Compression ratio: 9.0:1
Bore: 77.0mm 3.0in
Stroke: 69.7mm 2.7in
Valve type/No: Overhead 8
Transmission: Manual
No. of forward speeds: 4
Wheels driven: Front
Springs F/R: Leaf/Leaf
Brakes F/R: Disc/Disc
Steering: Worm & roller
Wheelbase: 232.9cm 91.7in
Track F: 130.0cm 51.2in
Track R: 128.0cm 50.4in
Length: 397.5cm 156.5in
Width: 155.4cm 61.2in
Height: 130.0cm 51.2in
Ground clearance: 11.9cm 4.7in
Kerb weight: 948.9kg 2090.0lb
Fuel: 37.8L 8.3gal 10.0galUS

2509 Lancia

Fulvia 1.3 Zagato
1967 Italy
109.0mph 175.4kmh
0-50mph 80.5kmh: 9.0secs
0-60mph 96.5kmh: 13.0secs
0-1/4 mile: 19.1secs
87.0bhp 64.9kW 88.2PS
@ 6000rpm
84.0lbft 113.8Nm @ 4500rpm
96.7bhp/ton 95.1bhp/tonne
67.0bhp/L 50.0kW/L 68.0PS/L
45.7ft/sec 13.9m/sec
18.2mph 29.3kmh/1000rpm
Petrol 4-stroke piston
1298cc 79.2cu in
Vee 4 1 Carburettor
Compression ratio: 9.0:1
Bore: 77.0mm 3.0in
Stroke: 69.7mm 2.7in
Valve type/No: Overhead 8
Transmission: Manual
No. of forward speeds: 4
Wheels driven: Front
Springs F/R: Leaf/Leaf
Brakes F/R: Disc/Disc
Steering: Worm & roller
Wheelbase: 232.9cm 91.7in
Track F: 130.0cm 51.2in
Track R: 128.0cm 50.4in
Length: 408.9cm 161.0in
Width: 157.0cm 61.8in
Height: 119.9cm 47.2in
Ground clearance: 11.9cm 4.7in
Kerb weight: 914.8kg 2015.0lb
Fuel: 37.8L 8.3gal 10.0galUS

2510 Lancia

Fulvia Coupe
1969 Italy
109.0mph 175.4kmh
0-50mph 80.5kmh: 7.5secs
0-60mph 96.5kmh: 9.9secs
0-1/4 mile: 17.6secs
0-1km: 32.7secs
115.0bhp 85.8kW 116.6PS
@ 6200rpm
112.0lbft 151.8Nm @ 4500rpm
130.3bhp/ton 128.1bhp/tonne
72.6bhp/L 54.1kW/L 73.6PS/L
50.8ft/sec 15.5m/sec
18.6mph 29.9kmh/1000rpm
22.9mpg 19.1mpgUS 12.3L/100km
Petrol 4-stroke piston
1584cc 96.6cu in
Vee 4 2 Carburettor
Compression ratio: 10.5:1
Bore: 82.0mm 3.2in
Stroke: 75.0mm 2.9in
Valve type/No: Overhead 8
Transmission: Manual
No. of forward speeds: 5
Wheels driven: Front
Springs F/R: Leaf/Leaf
Brake system: PA
Brakes F/R: Disc/Disc
Steering: Worm & roller
Wheelbase: 232.9cm 91.7in
Track F: 131.3cm 51.7in
Track R: 128.3cm 50.5in
Length: 397.5cm 156.5in
Width: 162.6cm 64.0in
Height: 129.5cm 51.0in
Ground clearance: 12.7cm 5.0in
Kerb weight: 897.6kg 1977.0lb
Fuel: 38.7L 8.5gal 10.2galUS

2511 Lancia

Fulvia Sedan
1970 Italy
102.0mph 164.1kmh
0-50mph 80.5kmh: 10.8secs
0-60mph 96.5kmh: 15.6secs
0-1/4 mile: 19.7secs
0-1km: 36.9secs
87.0bhp 64.9kW 88.2PS
@ 6000rpm
84.0lbft 113.8Nm @ 4500rpm
82.6bhp/ton 81.2bhp/tonne
67.0bhp/L 50.0kW/L 68.0PS/L
45.7ft/sec 13.9m/sec
16.8mph 27.0kmh/1000rpm
24.1mpg 20.1mpgUS 11.7L/100km
Petrol 4-stroke piston
1298cc 79.2cu in
Vee 4 2 Carburettor
Compression ratio: 9.0:1
Bore: 77.0mm 3.0in
Stroke: 69.7mm 2.7in
Valve type/No: Overhead 8
Transmission: Manual
No. of forward speeds: 4
Wheels driven: Front
Springs F/R: Leaf/Leaf
Brake system: PA
Brakes F/R: Disc/Disc
Steering: Worm & roller
Wheelbase: 250.2cm 98.5in
Track F: 130.0cm 51.2in
Track R: 128.0cm 50.4in
Length: 415.3cm 163.5in
Width: 155.4cm 61.2in
Height: 140.0cm 55.1in
Ground clearance: 19.1cm 7.5in
Kerb weight: 1071.4kg 2360.0lb
Fuel: 42.3L 9.3gal 11.2galUS

2512 Lancia

Fulvia Sedan
1971 Italy
102.0mph 164.1kmh
0-50mph 80.5kmh: 9.7secs
0-60mph 96.5kmh: 13.9secs
0-1/4 mile: 19.1secs
0-1km: 36.0secs
85.0bhp 63.4kW 86.2PS
@ 6000rpm
83.0lbft 112.5Nm @ 4500rpm
80.7bhp/ton 79.3bhp/tonne
65.5bhp/L 48.8kW/L 66.4PS/L
45.7ft/sec 13.9m/sec
16.8mph 27.0kmh/1000rpm
22.4mpg 18.7mpgUS 12.6L/100km
Petrol 4-stroke piston
1298cc 79.2cu in
Vee 4 2 Carburettor
Compression ratio: 9.0:1
Bore: 77.0mm 3.0in
Stroke: 69.7mm 2.7in
Valve type/No: Overhead 8
Transmission: Manual
No. of forward speeds: 5
Wheels driven: Front
Springs F/R: Leaf/Leaf
Brake system: PA
Brakes F/R: Disc/Disc
Steering: Worm & roller
Wheelbase: 250.2cm 98.5in
Track F: 130.0cm 51.2in
Track R: 128.0cm 50.4in
Length: 415.3cm 163.5in
Width: 155.4cm 61.2in
Height: 140.0cm 55.1in
Ground clearance: 19.6cm 7.7in
Kerb weight: 1071.4kg 2360.0lb
Fuel: 42.3L 9.3gal 11.2galUS

2513 Lancia

2000
1972 Italy
116.0mph 186.6kmh
0-50mph 80.5kmh: 7.8secs
0-60mph 96.5kmh: 10.4secs
0-1/4 mile: 17.9secs
0-1km: 33.0secs
125.0bhp 93.2kW 126.7PS
@ 5800rpm
127.0lbft 172.1Nm @ 3700rpm
103.1bhp/ton 101.4bhp/tonne
62.8bhp/L 46.8kW/L 63.6PS/L
50.7ft/sec 15.5m/sec
19.0mph 30.6kmh/1000rpm
20.1mpg 16.7mpgUS 14.1L/100km
Petrol 4-stroke piston

1991cc 121.5cu in
Flat 4 fuel injection
Compression ratio: 9.2:1
Bore: 89.0mm 3.5in
Stroke: 80.0mm 3.1in
Valve type/No: Overhead 8
Transmission: Manual
No. of forward speeds: 5
Wheels driven: Front
Springs F/R: Leaf/Leaf
Brake system: PA
Brakes F/R: Disc/Disc
Steering: Recirculating ball PA
Wheelbase: 267.5cm 105.3in
Track F: 133.1cm 52.4in
Track R: 128.8cm 50.7in
Length: 430.0cm 169.3in
Width: 160.8cm 63.3in
Height: 145.8cm 57.4in
Ground clearance: 15.2cm 6.0in
Kerb weight: 1232.6kg 2715.0lb
Fuel: 55.1L 12.1gal 14.5galUS

2514 Lancia
Beta 1800
1973 Italy
109.0mph 175.4kmh
0-50mph 80.5kmh: 7.8secs
0-60mph 96.5kmh: 10.7secs
0-1/4 mile: 17.9secs
0-1km: 33.1secs
110.0bhp 82.0kW 111.5PS
@ 6000rpm
106.0lbft 143.6Nm @ 3000rpm
101.8bhp/ton 100.1bhp/tonne
62.6bhp/L 46.7kW/L 63.5PS/L
52.0ft/sec 15.8m/sec
18.2mph 29.3kmh/1000rpm
24.3mpg 20.2mpgUS 11.6L/100km
Petrol 4-stroke piston
1756cc 107.1cu in
In-line 4 1 Carburettor
Compression ratio: 8.9:1
Bore: 84.0mm 3.3in
Stroke: 79.2mm 3.1in
Valve type/No: Overhead 8
Transmission: Manual
No. of forward speeds: 5
Wheels driven: Front
Springs F/R: Coil/Coil
Brake system: PA
Brakes F/R: Disc/Disc
Steering: Rack & pinion
Wheelbase: 253.7cm 99.9in
Track F: 140.5cm 55.3in
Track R: 139.2cm 54.8in
Length: 429.0cm 168.9in
Width: 168.9cm 66.5in
Height: 140.0cm 55.1in
Ground clearance: 14.0cm 5.5in
Kerb weight: 1099.1kg 2421.0lb
Fuel: 51.9L 11.4gal 13.7galUS

2515 Lancia
Fulvia Coupe S3
1974 Italy
116.0mph 186.6kmh
0-50mph 80.5kmh: 7.8secs
0-60mph 96.5kmh: 10.4secs
0-1/4 mile: 17.9secs
0-1km: 33.0secs
90.0bhp 67.1kW 91.2PS
@ 6000rpm
84.0lbft 113.8Nm @ 5000rpm
94.2bhp/ton 92.6bhp/tonne
69.3bhp/L 51.7kW/L 70.3PS/L
45.7ft/sec 13.9m/sec
19.0mph 30.6kmh/1000rpm
20.1mpg 16.7mpgUS 14.1L/100km
Petrol 4-stroke piston
1298cc 79.2cu in
Vee 4 2 Carburettor
Compression ratio: 9.5:1
Bore: 77.0mm 3.0in
Stroke: 69.7mm 2.7in
Valve type/No: Overhead 8
Transmission: Manual
No. of forward speeds: 5
Wheels driven: Front
Springs F/R: Leaf/Leaf
Brake system: PA
Brakes F/R: Disc/Disc
Steering: Recirculating ball PA
Wheelbase: 267.5cm 105.3in
Track F: 133.1cm 52.4in
Track R: 128.8cm 50.7in
Length: 430.0cm 169.3in
Width: 160.8cm 63.3in
Height: 145.8cm 57.4in
Ground clearance: 15.2cm 6.0in
Kerb weight: 971.6kg 2140.0lb
Fuel: 55.1L 12.1gal 14.5galUS

2516 Lancia
Beta 1600 Coupe
1975 Italy
113.0mph 181.8kmh
0-50mph 80.5kmh: 7.4secs
0-60mph 96.5kmh: 10.4secs
0-1/4 mile: 17.3secs
0-1km: 32.9secs
108.0bhp 80.5kW 109.5PS
@ 6000rpm
100.0lbft 135.5Nm @ 4500rpm
108.7bhp/ton 106.9bhp/tonne
67.8bhp/L 50.6kW/L 68.8PS/L
52.0ft/sec 15.8m/sec
18.3mph 29.4kmh/1000rpm
24.0mpg 20.0mpgUS 11.8L/100km
Petrol 4-stroke piston
1592cc 97.1cu in
In-line 4 1 Carburettor
Compression ratio: 9.8:1
Bore: 80.0mm 3.1in
Stroke: 79.2mm 3.1in
Valve type/No: Overhead 8
Transmission: Manual
No. of forward speeds: 5
Wheels driven: Front
Springs F/R: Coil/Coil
Brake system: PA
Brakes F/R: Disc/Disc
Steering: Rack & pinion
Wheelbase: 235.0cm 92.5in
Track F: 140.5cm 55.3in
Track R: 139.2cm 54.8in
Length: 399.3cm 157.2in
Width: 164.8cm 64.9in
Height: 128.5cm 50.6in
Ground clearance: 13.5cm 5.3in
Kerb weight: 1010.6kg 2226.0lb
Fuel: 51.0L 11.2gal 13.5galUS

2517 Lancia
Beta Monte Carlo
1975 Italy
120.0mph 193.1kmh
0-50mph 80.5kmh: 7.0secs
0-60mph 96.5kmh: 9.8secs
0-1/4 mile: 16.0secs
0-1km: 30.2secs
120.0bhp 89.5kW 121.7PS
@ 6000rpm
121.0lbft 164.0Nm @ 3500rpm
117.4bhp/ton 115.4bhp/tonne
60.1bhp/L 44.8kW/L 61.0PS/L
59.0ft/sec 18.0m/sec
19.5mph 31.4kmh/1000rpm
25.2mpg 21.0mpgUS 11.2L/100km
Petrol 4-stroke piston
1995cc 121.7cu in
In-line 4 1 Carburettor
Compression ratio: 8.9:1
Bore: 84.0mm 3.3in
Stroke: 90.0mm 3.5in
Valve type/No: Overhead 8
Transmission: Manual
No. of forward speeds: 5
Wheels driven: Rear
Springs F/R: Coil/Coil
Brake system: PA
Brakes F/R: Disc/Disc
Steering: Rack & pinion
Wheelbase: 230.1cm 90.6in
Track F: 141.2cm 55.6in
Track R: 146.3cm 57.6in
Length: 381.3cm 150.1in
Width: 169.7cm 66.8in
Height: 118.4cm 46.6in
Ground clearance: 14.0cm 5.5in
Kerb weight: 1039.7kg 2290.0lb
Fuel: 59.1L 13.0gal 15.6galUS

2518 Lancia
Beta 1300
1976 Italy
102.0mph 164.1kmh
0-50mph 80.5kmh: 9.8secs
0-60mph 96.5kmh: 13.8secs
0-1/4 mile: 19.6secs
0-1km: 36.6secs
82.0bhp 61.1kW 83.1PS
@ 6200rpm
79.5lbft 107.7Nm @ 3300rpm
77.8bhp/ton 76.5bhp/tonne
63.2bhp/L 47.1kW/L 64.1PS/L
48.2ft/sec 14.7m/sec
16.5mph 26.5kmh/1000rpm
29.6mpg 24.6mpgUS 9.5L/100km
Petrol 4-stroke piston
1297cc 79.1cu in
In-line 4 1 Carburettor
Compression ratio: 8.9:1
Bore: 76.0mm 3.0in
Stroke: 71.0mm 2.8in
Valve type/No: Overhead 8
Transmission: Manual
No. of forward speeds: 5
Wheels driven: Front
Springs F/R: Coil/Coil
Brake system: PA
Brakes F/R: Disc/Disc
Steering: Rack & pinion
Wheelbase: 253.7cm 99.9in
Track F: 140.5cm 55.3in
Track R: 139.2cm 54.8in
Length: 429.3cm 169.0in
Width: 168.9cm 66.5in
Height: 139.7cm 55.0in
Ground clearance: 14.0cm 5.5in
Kerb weight: 1071.4kg 2360.0lb
Fuel: 51.9L 11.4gal 13.7galUS

2519 Lancia
Beta 2000
1976 Italy
114.0mph 183.4kmh
0-50mph 80.5kmh: 7.0secs
0-60mph 96.5kmh: 10.1secs
0-1/4 mile: 17.5secs
0-1km: 31.9secs
119.0bhp 88.7kW 120.6PS
@ 5500rpm
127.4lbft 172.6Nm @ 2800rpm
109.2bhp/ton 107.4bhp/tonne
59.6bhp/L 44.5kW/L 60.5PS/L
54.1ft/sec 16.5m/sec
19.1mph 30.7kmh/1000rpm
24.0mpg 20.0mpgUS 11.8L/100km
Petrol 4-stroke piston
1995cc 121.7cu in
In-line 4 1 Carburettor
Compression ratio: 8.9:1
Bore: 84.0mm 3.3in
Stroke: 90.0mm 3.5in
Valve type/No: Overhead 8
Transmission: Manual
No. of forward speeds: 5
Wheels driven: Front
Springs F/R: Coil/Coil
Brake system: PA
Brakes F/R: Disc/Disc
Steering: Rack & pinion
Wheelbase: 253.7cm 99.9in
Track F: 140.5cm 55.3in
Track R: 139.2cm 54.8in
Length: 429.3cm 169.0in
Width: 168.9cm 66.5in
Height: 139.7cm 55.0in
Ground clearance: 14.0cm 5.5in
Kerb weight: 1107.8kg 2440.0lb
Fuel: 51.9L 11.4gal 13.7galUS

2520 Lancia
Beta Coupe
1976 Italy
109.0mph 175.4kmh
0-50mph 80.5kmh: 9.7secs
0-60mph 96.5kmh: 13.2secs
0-1/4 mile: 19.1secs
86.0bhp 64.1kW 87.2PS
@ 6200rpm
90.0lbft 122.0Nm @ 2800rpm
77.5bhp/ton 76.2bhp/tonne
49.0bhp/L 36.5kW/L 49.6PS/L
53.7ft/sec 16.4m/sec
17.9mph 28.8kmh/1000rpm
28.8mpg 24.0mpgUS 9.8L/100km
Petrol 4-stroke piston
1756cc 107.1cu in
In-line 4
Compression ratio: 8.2:1
Bore: 84.0mm 3.3in
Stroke: 79.2mm 3.1in
Valve type/No: Overhead 8
Transmission: Manual
No. of forward speeds: 5
Wheels driven: Front
Springs F/R: Coil/Coil
Brake system: PA
Brakes F/R: Disc/Disc
Steering: Rack & pinion
Wheelbase: 235.0cm 92.5in
Track F: 140.7cm 55.4in
Track R: 139.2cm 54.8in
Length: 423.4cm 166.7in
Width: 165.1cm 65.0in
Height: 128.5cm 50.6in
Kerb weight: 1128.2kg 2485.0lb
Fuel: 47.3L 10.4gal 12.5galUS

2521 Lancia
Beta Sedan
1976 Italy
104.0mph 167.3kmh
0-50mph 80.5kmh: 9.8secs
0-60mph 96.5kmh: 13.6secs
0-1/4 mile: 19.1secs
86.0bhp 64.1kW 87.2PS
@ 6200rpm
90.0lbft 122.0Nm @ 2800rpm
71.2bhp/ton 70.0bhp/tonne
49.0bhp/L 36.5kW/L 49.6PS/L
53.7ft/sec 16.4m/sec
16.9mph 27.2kmh/1000rpm
25.8mpg 21.5mpgUS 10.9L/100km
Petrol 4-stroke piston
1756cc 107.1cu in
In-line 4 1 Carburettor
Compression ratio: 8.2:1
Bore: 84.0mm 3.3in
Stroke: 79.2mm 3.1in
Valve type/No: Overhead 8
Transmission: Manual
No. of forward speeds: 5
Wheels driven: Front
Springs F/R: Coil/Coil
Brake system: PA
Brakes F/R: Disc/Disc
Steering: Rack & pinion
Wheelbase: 254.0cm 100.0in
Track F: 140.7cm 55.4in
Track R: 139.2cm 54.8in
Length: 452.1cm 178.0in
Width: 168.9cm 66.5in
Height: 140.0cm 55.1in
Ground clearance: 14.0cm 5.5in
Kerb weight: 1228.1kg 2705.0lb
Fuel: 47.3L 10.4gal 12.5galUS

2522 Lancia
Beta
1977 Italy
102.0mph 164.1kmh
0-60mph 96.5kmh: 13.8secs
0-1/4 mile: 19.6secs
86.0bhp 64.1kW 87.2PS
@ 6200rpm
90.0lbft 122.0Nm @ 2800rpm
69.5bhp/ton 68.4bhp/tonne
49.0bhp/L 36.5kW/L 49.6PS/L
53.7ft/sec 16.4m/sec
Petrol 4-stroke piston
1756cc 107.1cu in
In-line 4 1 Carburettor
Compression ratio: 8.2:1
Bore: 84.0mm 3.3in
Stroke: 79.2mm 3.1in
Valve type/No: Overhead 8
Transmission: Manual
No. of forward speeds: 5
Wheels driven: Front
Brakes F/R: Disc/Disc
Wheelbase: 254.0cm 100.0in
Track F: 140.7cm 55.4in
Track R: 139.2cm 54.8in
Length: 452.1cm 178.0in
Width: 168.9cm 66.5in
Height: 140.0cm 55.1in
Kerb weight: 1257.6kg 2770.0lb
Fuel: 47.3L 10.4gal 12.5galUS

2523 Lancia
Beta HPE 2000
1977 Italy
116.0mph 186.6kmh
0-50mph 80.5kmh: 7.5secs
0-60mph 96.5kmh: 10.6secs
0-1/4 mile: 17.7secs
0-1km: 32.8secs
119.0bhp 88.7kW 120.6PS
@ 5500rpm
128.0lbft 173.4Nm @ 2800rpm
111.1bhp/ton 109.2bhp/tonne
59.6bhp/L 44.5kW/L 60.5PS/L
54.1ft/sec 16.5m/sec

19.6mph 31.5kmh/1000rpm
20.3mpg 16.9mpgUS 13.9L/100km
Petrol 4-stroke piston
1995cc 121.7cu in
In-line 4 1 Carburettor
Compression ratio: 8.9:1
Bore: 84.0mm 3.3in
Stroke: 90.0mm 3.5in
Valve type/No: Overhead 8
Transmission: Manual
No. of forward speeds: 5
Wheels driven: Front
Springs F/R: Coil/Coil
Brake system: PA
Brakes F/R: Disc/Disc
Steering: Rack & pinion
Wheelbase: 254.0cm 100.0in
Track F: 140.5cm 55.3in
Track R: 139.2cm 54.8in
Length: 428.5cm 168.7in
Width: 165.1cm 65.0in
Height: 127.0cm 50.0in
Ground clearance: 13.5cm 5.3in
Kerb weight: 1089.6kg 2400.0lb
Fuel: 51.9L 11.4gal 13.7galUS

2524 Lancia
Beta Scorpion
1977 Italy
104.0mph 167.3kmh
0-50mph 80.5kmh: 9.5secs
0-60mph 96.5kmh: 13.4secs
0-1/4 mile: 19.1secs
81.0bhp 60.4kW 82.1PS
@ 5900rpm
89.0lbft 120.6Nm @ 3200rpm
76.4bhp/ton 75.1bhp/tonne
46.1bhp/L 34.4kW/L 46.8PS/L
51.1ft/sec 15.6m/sec
18.1mph 29.1kmh/1000rpm
23.4mpg 19.5mpgUS 12.1L/100km
Petrol 4-stroke piston
1756cc 107.1cu in
In-line 4 1 Carburettor
Compression ratio: 8.0:1
Bore: 84.0mm 3.3in
Stroke: 79.2mm 3.1in
Valve type/No: Overhead 8
Transmission: Manual
No. of forward speeds: 5
Wheels driven: Rear
Springs F/R: Coil/Coil
Brake system: PA
Brakes F/R: Disc/Disc
Steering: Rack & pinion
Wheelbase: 230.1cm 90.6in
Track F: 141.2cm 55.6in
Track R: 145.5cm 57.3in
Length: 396.5cm 156.1in
Width: 169.7cm 66.8in
Height: 119.1cm 46.9in
Ground clearance: 12.7cm 5.0in
Kerb weight: 1078.2kg 2375.0lb
Fuel: 56.8L 12.5gal 15.0galUS

2525 Lancia
Gamma
1977 Italy
121.0mph 194.7kmh
0-50mph 80.5kmh: 7.2secs
0-60mph 96.5kmh: 9.7secs
0-1/4 mile: 16.6secs
140.0bhp 104.4kW 141.9PS
@ 5400rpm
153.0lbft 207.3Nm @ 3000rpm
107.8bhp/ton 106.0bhp/tonne
56.4bhp/L 42.0kW/L 57.1PS/L
44.8ft/sec 13.7m/sec
21.4mph 34.4kmh/1000rpm
24.0mpg 20.0mpgUS 11.8L/100km
Petrol 4-stroke piston
2484cc 151.6cu in
Flat 4
Compression ratio: 9.0:1
Bore: 102.0mm 4.0in
Stroke: 76.0mm 3.0in
Valve type/No: Overhead 8
Transmission: Manual
No. of forward speeds: 5
Wheels driven: Front
Springs F/R: Coil/Coil
Brake system: PA
Brakes F/R: Disc/Disc
Steering: Rack & pinion PA
Wheelbase: 267.0cm 105.1in
Track F: 145.0cm 57.1in
Track R: 144.0cm 56.7in
Length: 458.0cm 180.3in
Width: 173.0cm 68.1in
Height: 141.0cm 55.5in
Kerb weight: 1321.1kg 2910.0lb
Fuel: 62.8L 13.8gal 16.6galUS

2526 Lancia
Gamma Berlina
1978 Italy
120.0mph 193.1kmh
0-50mph 80.5kmh: 7.3secs
0-60mph 96.5kmh: 10.1secs
0-1/4 mile: 17.5secs
0-1km: 32.3secs
140.0bhp 104.4kW 141.9PS
@ 5400rpm
153.0lbft 207.3Nm @ 3000rpm
102.7bhp/ton 101.0bhp/tonne
56.4bhp/L 42.0kW/L 57.1PS/L
44.8ft/sec 13.7m/sec
20.9mph 33.6kmh/1000rpm
19.1mpg 15.9mpgUS 14.8L/100km
Petrol 4-stroke piston
2484cc 151.6cu in
Flat 4 1 Carburettor
Compression ratio: 9.0:1
Bore: 102.0mm 4.0in
Stroke: 76.0mm 3.0in
Valve type/No: Overhead 8
Transmission: Manual
No. of forward speeds: 5
Wheels driven: Front
Springs F/R: Coil/Coil
Brake system: PA
Brakes F/R: Disc/Disc
Steering: Rack & pinion PA
Wheelbase: 267.0cm 105.1in
Track F: 145.0cm 57.1in
Track R: 144.0cm 56.7in
Length: 458.0cm 180.3in
Width: 173.0cm 68.1in
Height: 141.0cm 55.5in
Ground clearance: 14.0cm 5.5in
Kerb weight: 1385.6kg 3052.0lb
Fuel: 59.1L 13.0gal 15.6galUS

2527 Lancia
Beta 2000 Automatic
1979 Italy
109.0mph 175.4kmh
0-50mph 80.5kmh: 8.3secs
0-60mph 96.5kmh: 11.4secs
0-1/4 mile: 18.6secs
0-1km: 34.5secs
115.0bhp 85.8kW 116.6PS
@ 5500rpm
129.0lbft 174.8Nm @ 2800rpm
99.1bhp/ton 97.5bhp/tonne
57.6bhp/L 43.0kW/L 58.4PS/L
54.1ft/sec 16.5m/sec
18.7mph 30.1kmh/1000rpm
23.1mpg 19.2mpgUS 12.2L/100km
Petrol 4-stroke piston
1995cc 121.7cu in
In-line 4 1 Carburettor
Compression ratio: 8.9:1
Bore: 84.0mm 3.3in
Stroke: 90.0mm 3.5in
Valve type/No: Overhead 8
Transmission: Automatic
No. of forward speeds: 3
Wheels driven: Front
Springs F/R: Coil/Coil
Brake system: PA
Brakes F/R: Disc/Disc
Steering: Rack & pinion
Wheelbase: 254.0cm 100.0in
Track F: 140.7cm 55.4in
Track R: 139.2cm 54.8in
Length: 429.5cm 169.1in
Width: 170.7cm 67.2in
Height: 140.0cm 55.1in
Ground clearance: 14.0cm 5.5in
Kerb weight: 1179.9kg 2599.0lb
Fuel: 51.9L 11.4gal 13.7galUS

2528 Lancia
Beta HPE 1600
1979 Italy
106.0mph 170.6kmh
0-50mph 80.5kmh: 8.4secs
0-60mph 96.5kmh: 11.3secs
0-1/4 mile: 18.0secs
0-1km: 33.3secs
100.0bhp 74.6kW 101.4PS
@ 5800rpm
99.0lbft 134.1Nm @ 3000rpm
98.7bhp/ton 97.0bhp/tonne
63.1bhp/L 47.0kW/L 64.0PS/L
45.3ft/sec 13.8m/sec
18.3mph 29.4kmh/1000rpm
25.4mpg 21.1mpgUS 11.1L/100km
Petrol 4-stroke piston
1585cc 96.7cu in
In-line 4 1 Carburettor
Compression ratio: 9.4:1
Bore: 84.0mm 3.3in
Stroke: 71.5mm 2.8in
Valve type/No: Overhead 8
Transmission: Manual
No. of forward speeds: 5
Wheels driven: Front
Springs F/R: Coil/Coil
Brake system: PA
Brakes F/R: Disc/Disc
Steering: Rack & pinion
Wheelbase: 254.0cm 100.0in
Track F: 140.5cm 55.3in
Track R: 139.2cm 54.8in
Length: 428.5cm 168.7in
Width: 165.1cm 65.0in
Height: 131.1cm 51.6in
Ground clearance: 13.5cm 5.3in
Kerb weight: 1030.6kg 2270.0lb
Fuel: 49.1L 10.8gal 13.0galUS

2529 Lancia
HPE
1979 Italy
101.0mph 162.5kmh
0-50mph 80.5kmh: 9.4secs
0-60mph 96.5kmh: 13.3secs
0-1/4 mile: 19.6secs
83.0bhp 61.9kW 84.1PS
@ 5800rpm
89.0lbft 120.6Nm @ 2800rpm
68.1bhp/ton 67.0bhp/tonne
47.3bhp/L 35.2kW/L 47.9PS/L
50.3ft/sec 15.3m/sec
17.1mph 27.5kmh/1000rpm
30.0mpg 25.0mpgUS 9.4L/100km
Petrol 4-stroke piston
1756cc 107.1cu in
In-line 4 1 Carburettor
Compression ratio: 8.0:1
Bore: 84.0mm 3.3in
Stroke: 79.2mm 3.1in
Valve type/No: Overhead 8
Transmission: Manual
No. of forward speeds: 5
Wheels driven: Front
Springs F/R: Coil/Coil
Brake system: PA
Brakes F/R: Disc/Disc
Steering: Rack & pinion PA
Wheelbase: 254.0cm 100.0in
Track F: 140.7cm 55.4in
Track R: 139.2cm 54.8in
Length: 453.4cm 178.5in
Width: 165.1cm 65.0in
Height: 128.5cm 50.6in
Ground clearance: 11.9cm 4.7in
Kerb weight: 1239.4kg 2730.0lb
Fuel: 47.3L 10.4gal 12.5galUS

2530 Lancia
Zagato
1980 Italy
111.0mph 178.6kmh
0-50mph 80.5kmh: 9.0secs
0-60mph 96.5kmh: 12.5secs
0-1/4 mile: 19.0secs
83.0bhp 61.9kW 84.1PS
@ 5400rpm
101.0lbft 136.9Nm @ 2900rpm
68.9bhp/ton 67.7bhp/tonne
41.6bhp/L 31.0kW/L 42.2PS/L
53.1ft/sec 16.2m/sec
18.7mph 30.1kmh/1000rpm
24.6mpg 20.5mpgUS 11.5L/100km
Petrol 4-stroke piston
1995cc 121.7cu in
In-line 4 1 Carburettor
Compression ratio: 8.1:1
Bore: 84.0mm 3.3in
Stroke: 90.0mm 3.5in
Valve type/No: Overhead 8
Transmission: Manual
No. of forward speeds: 5
Wheels driven: Front
Springs F/R: Coil/Coil
Brake system: PA
Brakes F/R: Disc/Disc
Steering: Rack & pinion PA
Wheelbase: 235.0cm 92.5in
Track F: 140.7cm 55.4in
Track R: 139.2cm 54.8in
Length: 418.1cm 164.6in
Width: 164.1cm 64.6in
Height: 126.2cm 49.7in
Kerb weight: 1225.8kg 2700.0lb
Fuel: 47.3L 10.4gal 12.5galUS

2531 Lancia
Montecarlo Group 5 Turbo
1981 Italy
140.0mph 225.3kmh
0-50mph 80.5kmh: 3.1secs
0-60mph 96.5kmh: 3.6secs
0-1/4 mile: 11.3secs
400.0bhp 298.3kW 405.5PS
@ 8800rpm
390.0lbft 528.5Nm @ 6000rpm
520.9bhp/ton 512.2bhp/tonne
280.7bhp/L 209.3kW/L 284.6PS/L
65.0ft/sec 19.8m/sec
15.6mph 25.1kmh/1000rpm
5.6mpg 4.7mpgUS 50.0L/100km
Petrol 4-stroke piston
1425cc 86.9cu in turbocharged
In-line 4 fuel injection
Compression ratio: 7.0:1
Bore: 82.0mm 3.2in
Stroke: 67.5mm 2.7in
Valve type/No: Overhead 16
Transmission: Manual
No. of forward speeds: 5
Wheels driven: Rear
Springs F/R: Coil/Coil
Brakes F/R: Disc/Disc
Steering: Rack & pinion
Wheelbase: 230.1cm 90.6in
Track F: 146.3cm 57.6in
Track R: 157.0cm 61.8in
Length: 460.0cm 181.1in
Width: 198.9cm 78.3in
Height: 110.0cm 43.3in
Ground clearance: 6.1cm 2.4in
Kerb weight: 780.9kg 1720.0lb
Fuel: 120.0L 26.4gal 31.7galUS

2532 Lancia
Montecarlo Spyder
1981 Italy
120.0mph 193.1kmh
0-50mph 80.5kmh: 6.0secs
0-60mph 96.5kmh: 8.6secs
0-1/4 mile: 16.4secs
0-1km: 30.7secs
120.0bhp 89.5kW 121.7PS
@ 6000rpm
125.9lbft 170.6Nm @ 3400rpm
122.5bhp/ton 120.4bhp/tonne
60.1bhp/L 44.8kW/L 61.0PS/L
59.0ft/sec 18.0m/sec
19.7mph 31.7kmh/1000rpm
25.0mpg 20.8mpgUS 11.3L/100km
Petrol 4-stroke piston
1995cc 121.7cu in
In-line 4 1 Carburettor
Compression ratio: 9.3:1
Bore: 84.0mm 3.3in
Stroke: 90.0mm 3.5in
Valve type/No: Overhead 8
Transmission: Manual
No. of forward speeds: 5
Wheels driven: Rear
Springs F/R: Coil/Coil
Brakes F/R: Disc/Disc
Steering: Rack & pinion
Wheelbase: 230.1cm 90.6in
Track F: 141.2cm 55.6in
Track R: 146.3cm 57.6in
Length: 381.3cm 150.1in
Width: 169.7cm 66.8in
Height: 118.4cm 46.6in
Ground clearance: 14.0cm 5.5in
Kerb weight: 996.5kg 2195.0lb
Fuel: 59.1L 13.0gal 15.6galUS

2533 Lancia
Trevi 2000
1981 Italy
114.0mph 183.4kmh
0-50mph 80.5kmh: 8.1secs
0-60mph 96.5kmh: 11.1secs
0-1/4 mile: 17.7secs
0-1km: 33.1secs
150.0bhp 111.9kW 152.1PS

@ 5500rpm
129.0lbft 174.8Nm @ 2800rpm
129.0bhp/ton 126.8bhp/tonne
75.2bhp/L 56.1kW/L 76.2PS/L
54.1ft/sec 16.5m/sec
19.3mph 31.1kmh/1000rpm
25.5mpg 21.2mpgUS 11.1L/100km
Petrol 4-stroke piston
1995cc 121.7cu in
In-line 4 1 Carburettor
Compression ratio: 8.9:1
Bore: 84.0mm 3.3in
Stroke: 90.0mm 3.5in
Valve type/No: Overhead 8
Transmission: Manual
No. of forward speeds: 5
Wheels driven: Front
Springs F/R: Coil/Coil
Brake system: PA
Brakes F/R: Disc/Disc
Steering: Rack & pinion PA
Wheelbase: 254.0cm 100.0in
Track F: 140.5cm 55.3in
Track R: 139.2cm 54.8in
Length: 435.6cm 171.5in
Width: 170.4cm 67.1in
Height: 140.0cm 55.1in
Ground clearance: 14.0cm 5.5in
Kerb weight: 1182.7kg 2605.0lb
Fuel: 49.1L 10.8gal 13.0galUS

2534 Lancia

Beta Coupe
1982 Italy
111.0mph 178.6kmh
0-50mph 80.5kmh: 8.4secs
0-60mph 96.5kmh: 11.6secs
0-1/4 mile: 18.3secs
108.0bhp 80.5kW 109.5PS
@ 5500rpm
114.0lbft 154.5Nm @ 2500rpm
90.6bhp/ton 89.1bhp/tonne
54.1bhp/L 40.4kW/L 54.9PS/L
54.1ft/sec 16.5m/sec
17.1mph 27.5kmh/1000rpm
25.2mpg 21.0mpgUS 11.2L/100km
Petrol 4-stroke piston
1995cc 121.7cu in
In-line 4 fuel injection
Compression ratio: 8.3:1
Bore: 84.0mm 3.3in
Stroke: 90.0mm 3.5in
Valve type/No: Overhead 8
Wheels driven: Front
Springs F/R: Coil/Coil
Brake system: PA
Brakes F/R: Disc/Disc
Steering: Rack & pinion PA
Wheelbase: 235.0cm 92.5in
Track F: 140.7cm 55.4in
Track R: 139.2cm 54.8in
Length: 422.9cm 166.5in
Width: 165.1cm 65.0in
Height: 128.5cm 50.6in
Kerb weight: 1212.2kg 2670.0lb
Fuel: 50.0L 11.0gal 13.2galUS

2535 Lancia

Delta Automatic
1982 Italy
97.0mph 156.1kmh
0-50mph 80.5kmh: 10.3secs
0-60mph 96.5kmh: 14.0secs
0-1/4 mile: 20.2secs
0-1km: 37.2secs
85.0bhp 63.4kW 86.2PS
@ 6200rpm
90.0lbft 122.0Nm @ 3500rpm
85.0bhp/ton 83.6bhp/tonne
56.7bhp/L 42.3kW/L 57.5PS/L
43.4ft/sec 13.2m/sec
17.6mph 28.3kmh/1000rpm
26.6mpg 22.1mpgUS 10.6L/100km
Petrol 4-stroke piston
1498cc 91.4cu in
In-line 4 1 Carburettor
Compression ratio: 9.2:1
Bore: 86.4mm 3.4in
Stroke: 63.9mm 2.5in
Valve type/No: Overhead 8
Transmission: Automatic
No. of forward speeds: 3
Wheels driven: Front
Springs F/R: Coil/Coil
Brake system: PA
Brakes F/R: Disc/Drum
Steering: Rack & pinion
Wheelbase: 247.4cm 97.4in
Track F: 140.0cm 55.1in
Track R: 140.0cm 55.1in
Length: 388.6cm 153.0in
Width: 162.1cm 63.8in
Height: 137.9cm 54.3in
Ground clearance: 15.2cm 6.0in
Kerb weight: 1017.0kg 2240.0lb
Fuel: 45.5L 10.0gal 12.0galUS

2536 Lancia

Prisma 1600
1983 Italy
109.0mph 175.4kmh
0-50mph 80.5kmh: 7.6secs
0-60mph 96.5kmh: 10.8secs
0-1/4 mile: 17.8secs
0-1km: 33.1secs
105.0bhp 78.3kW 106.5PS
@ 5800rpm
100.0lbft 135.5Nm @ 3300rpm
106.0bhp/ton 104.3bhp/tonne
66.2bhp/L 49.4kW/L 67.2PS/L
45.3ft/sec 13.8m/sec
18.7mph 30.1kmh/1000rpm
26.5mpg 22.1mpgUS 10.7L/100km
Petrol 4-stroke piston
1585cc 96.7cu in
In-line 4 1 Carburettor
Compression ratio: 9.3:1
Bore: 84.0mm 3.3in
Stroke: 71.5mm 2.8in
Valve type/No: Overhead 8
Transmission: Manual
No. of forward speeds: 5
Wheels driven: Front
Springs F/R: Coil/Coil
Brake system: PA
Brakes F/R: Disc/Disc
Steering: Rack & pinion
Wheelbase: 247.4cm 97.4in
Track F: 140.0cm 55.1in
Track R: 140.0cm 55.1in
Length: 418.1cm 164.6in
Width: 162.1cm 63.8in
Height: 138.4cm 54.5in
Ground clearance: 15.2cm 6.0in
Kerb weight: 1007.0kg 2218.0lb
Fuel: 45.0L 9.9gal 11.9galUS

2537 Lancia

Rally
1984 Italy
128.0mph 206.0kmh
0-50mph 80.5kmh: 5.4secs
0-60mph 96.5kmh: 7.1secs
0-1/4 mile: 15.9secs
205.0bhp 152.9kW 207.8PS
@ 7000rpm
167.0lbft 226.3Nm @ 5000rpm
180.8bhp/ton 177.8bhp/tonne
102.8bhp/L 76.6kW/L 104.2PS/L
68.8ft/sec 21.0m/sec
18.3mph 29.4kmh/1000rpm
24.0mpg 20.0mpgUS 11.8L/100km
Petrol 4-stroke piston
1995cc 121.7cu in supercharged
In-line 4 1 Carburettor
Compression ratio: 7.5:1
Bore: 84.0mm 3.3in
Stroke: 90.0mm 3.5in
Valve type/No: Overhead 16
Transmission: Manual
No. of forward speeds: 5
Wheels driven: Rear
Springs F/R: Coil/Coil
Brake system: PA
Brakes F/R: Disc/Disc
Steering: Rack & pinion
Wheelbase: 244.1cm 96.1in
Track F: 150.9cm 59.4in
Track R: 149.1cm 58.7in
Length: 391.4cm 154.1in
Width: 184.9cm 72.8in
Height: 124.5cm 49.0in
Ground clearance: 13.2cm 5.2in
Kerb weight: 1153.2kg 2540.0lb
Fuel: 70.0L 15.4gal 18.5galUS

2538 Lancia

Coupe 2000ie
1985 Italy
113.0mph 181.8kmh
0-50mph 80.5kmh: 6.7secs
0-60mph 96.5kmh: 9.2secs
0-1/4 mile: 17.1secs
0-1km: 31.5secs
122.0bhp 91.0kW 123.7PS
@ 5500rpm
129.0lbft 174.8Nm @ 2800rpm
168.7bhp/ton 165.9bhp/tonne
61.1bhp/L 45.6kW/L 62.0PS/L
54.1ft/sec 16.5m/sec
19.2mph 30.9kmh/1000rpm
27.7mpg 23.1mpgUS 10.2L/100km
Petrol 4-stroke piston
1995cc 121.7cu in
In-line 4 fuel injection
Compression ratio: 8.9:1
Bore: 84.0mm 3.3in
Stroke: 90.0mm 3.5in
Valve type/No: Overhead 8
Transmission: Manual
No. of forward speeds: 5
Wheels driven: Front
Springs F/R: Coil/Coil
Brake system: PA
Brakes F/R: Disc/Disc
Steering: Rack & pinion PA
Wheelbase: 235.0cm 92.5in
Track F: 140.7cm 55.4in
Track R: 139.2cm 54.8in
Length: 399.5cm 157.3in
Width: 165.1cm 65.0in
Height: 128.5cm 50.6in
Ground clearance: 13.5cm 5.3in
Kerb weight: 735.5kg 1620.0lb
Fuel: 51.9L 11.4gal 13.7galUS

2539 Lancia

Thema 2.0 ie LX Turbo
1985 Italy
140.0mph 225.3kmh
0-50mph 80.5kmh: 5.9secs
0-60mph 96.5kmh: 7.6secs
0-1/4 mile: 16.0secs
0-1km: 29.3secs
165.0bhp 123.0kW 167.3PS
@ 5750rpm
208.0lbft 281.8Nm @ 2750rpm
137.6bhp/ton 135.3bhp/tonne
82.7bhp/L 61.7kW/L 83.8PS/L
56.5ft/sec 17.2m/sec
24.6mph 39.6kmh/1000rpm
21.9mpg 18.2mpgUS 12.9L/100km
Petrol 4-stroke piston
1995cc 121.7cu in turbocharged
In-line 4 fuel injection
Compression ratio: 8.0:1
Bore: 84.0mm 3.3in
Stroke: 90.0mm 3.5in
Valve type/No: Overhead 8
Transmission: Manual
No. of forward speeds: 5
Wheels driven: Front
Springs F/R: Coil/Coil
Brake system: PA
Brakes F/R: Disc/Disc
Steering: Rack & pinion PA
Wheelbase: 265.9cm 104.7in
Track F: 148.8cm 58.6in
Track R: 148.3cm 58.4in
Length: 459.2cm 180.8in
Width: 177.5cm 69.9in
Height: 143.3cm 56.4in
Ground clearance: 17.8cm 7.0in
Kerb weight: 1219.4kg 2686.0lb
Fuel: 68.2L 15.0gal 18.0galUS

2540 Lancia

Y10 Turbo
1985 Italy
111.0mph 178.6kmh
0-50mph 80.5kmh: 8.6secs
0-60mph 96.5kmh: 11.8secs
85.0bhp 63.4kW 86.2PS
@ 5750rpm
90.0lbft 122.0Nm @ 2750rpm
109.5bhp/ton 107.7bhp/tonne
81.0bhp/L 60.4kW/L 82.1PS/L
36.4ft/sec 11.1m/sec
18.6mph 29.9kmh/1000rpm
32.3mpg 26.9mpgUS 8.7L/100km
Petrol 4-stroke piston
1049cc 64.0cu in turbocharged
In-line 4 1 Carburettor
Compression ratio: 7.0:1
Bore: 76.0mm 3.0in
Stroke: 57.8mm 2.3in
Valve type/No: Overhead 8
Transmission: Manual
No. of forward speeds: 5
Wheels driven: Front
Springs F/R: Coil/Coil
Brake system: PA
Brakes F/R: Disc/Drum
Steering: Rack & pinion
Wheelbase: 215.9cm 85.0in
Track F: 128.0cm 50.4in
Track R: 127.8cm 50.3in
Length: 339.1cm 133.5in
Width: 150.6cm 59.3in
Height: 124.5cm 49.0in
Ground clearance: 15.2cm 6.0in
Kerb weight: 789.0kg 1738.0lb
Fuel: 46.9L 10.3gal 12.4galUS

2541 Lancia

Delta HF 4WD
1986 Italy
130.0mph 209.2kmh
0-50mph 80.5kmh: 4.9secs
0-60mph 96.5kmh: 6.6secs
0-1/4 mile: 15.2secs
0-1km: 29.0secs
165.0bhp 123.0kW 167.3PS
@ 5250rpm
188.0lbft 254.7Nm @ 2500rpm
135.3bhp/ton 133.1bhp/tonne
82.7bhp/L 61.7kW/L 83.8PS/L
51.6ft/sec 15.7m/sec
23.9mph 38.5kmh/1000rpm
19.8mpg 16.5mpgUS 14.3L/100km
Petrol 4-stroke piston
1995cc 122.0cu in
In-line 4 fuel injection
Compression ratio: 8.0:1
Bore: 84.0mm 3.3in
Stroke: 90.0mm 3.5in
Valve type/No: Overhead 8
Transmission: Manual
No. of forward speeds: 5
Wheels driven: 4-wheel drive
Springs F/R: Coil/Coil
Brake system: PA
Brakes F/R: Disc/Disc
Steering: Rack & pinion PA
Wheelbase: 247.5cm 97.4in
Track F: 140.2cm 55.2in
Track R: 140.0cm 55.1in
Length: 389.5cm 153.3in
Width: 162.0cm 63.8in
Height: 138.0cm 54.3in
Ground clearance: 15.2cm 6.0in
Kerb weight: 1240.0kg 2731.3lb
Fuel: 56.9L 12.5gal 15.0galUS

2542 Lancia

Delta HF Turbo ie
1986 Italy
122.0mph 196.3kmh
0-50mph 80.5kmh: 6.0secs
0-60mph 96.5kmh: 8.5secs
0-1/4 mile: 16.1secs
0-1km: 30.1secs
140.0bhp 104.4kW 141.9PS
@ 5500rpm
141.0lbft 191.1Nm @ 3500rpm
133.8bhp/ton 131.6bhp/tonne
88.3bhp/L 65.9kW/L 89.5PS/L
42.9ft/sec 13.1m/sec
20.9mph 33.6kmh/1000rpm
24.5mpg 20.4mpgUS 11.5L/100km
Petrol 4-stroke piston
1585cc 97.0cu in turbocharged
In-line 4 fuel injection
Compression ratio: 8.0:1
Bore: 84.0mm 3.3in
Stroke: 71.5mm 2.8in
Valve type/No: Overhead 8
Transmission: Manual
No. of forward speeds: 5
Wheels driven: Front
Springs F/R: Coil/Coil
Brake system: PA
Brakes F/R: Disc/Disc
Steering: Rack & pinion
Wheelbase: 247.5cm 97.4in
Track F: 140.2cm 55.2in
Track R: 140.0cm 55.1in
Length: 389.5cm 153.3in
Width: 162.0cm 63.8in
Height: 138.0cm 54.3in
Ground clearance: 15.2cm 6.0in
Kerb weight: 1064.0kg 2343.6lb
Fuel: 57.3L 12.6gal 15.1galUS

2543 Lancia

Prisma 1600ie LX

1986 Italy
119.0mph 191.5kmh
0-50mph 80.5kmh: 6.9secs
0-60mph 96.5kmh: 9.5secs
0-1/4 mile: 17.3secs
0-1km: 31.7secs
108.0bhp 80.5kW 109.5PS
@ 5900rpm
135.4lbft 183.5Nm @ 3500rpm
103.8bhp/ton 102.1bhp/tonne
68.1bhp/L 50.8kW/L 69.1PS/L
46.0ft/sec 14.1m/sec
18.6mph 29.9kmh/1000rpm
27.1mpg 22.6mpgUS 10.4L/100km
Petrol 4-stroke piston
1585cc 97.0cu in
In-line 4 fuel injection
Compression ratio: 9.7:1
Bore: 84.0mm 3.3in
Stroke: 71.5mm 2.8in
Valve type/No: Overhead 8
Transmission: Manual
No. of forward speeds: 5
Wheels driven: Front
Springs F/R: Coil/Coil
Brake system: PA
Brakes F/R: Disc/Disc
Steering: Rack & pinion
Wheelbase: 247.5cm 97.4in
Track F: 140.0cm 55.1in
Track R: 140.0cm 55.1in
Length: 418.0cm 164.6in
Width: 162.0cm 63.8in
Height: 138.5cm 54.5in
Ground clearance: 15.2cm 6.0in
Kerb weight: 1058.0kg 2330.4lb
Fuel: 56.9L 12.5gal 15.0galUS

2544 Lancia
Thema 2.0ie
1986 Italy
118.0mph 189.9kmh
0-50mph 80.5kmh: 7.1secs
0-60mph 96.5kmh: 10.3secs
0-1/4 mile: 17.3secs
0-1km: 31.9secs
120.0bhp 89.5kW 121.7PS
@ 5250rpm
123.0lbft 166.7Nm @ 3300rpm
103.2bhp/ton 101.5bhp/tonne
60.1bhp/L 44.8kW/L 61.0PS/L
51.6ft/sec 15.7m/sec
21.6mph 34.8kmh/1000rpm
25.9mpg 21.6mpgUS 10.9L/100km
Petrol 4-stroke piston
1995cc 121.7cu in
In-line 4 fuel injection
Compression ratio: 9.8:1
Bore: 84.0mm 3.3in
Stroke: 90.0mm 3.5in
Valve type/No: Overhead 8
Transmission: Manual
No. of forward speeds: 5
Wheels driven: Front
Springs F/R: Coil/Coil
Brake system: PA
Brakes F/R: Disc/Disc
Steering: Rack & pinion PA
Wheelbase: 265.9cm 104.7in
Track F: 148.8cm 58.6in
Track R: 148.3cm 58.4in
Length: 459.2cm 180.8in
Width: 177.5cm 69.9in
Height: 143.3cm 56.4in
Ground clearance: 17.8cm 7.0in
Kerb weight: 1182.2kg 2604.0lb
Fuel: 70.1L 15.4gal 18.5galUS

2545 Lancia
Y10 Fire
1986 Italy
94.0mph 151.2kmh
0-50mph 80.5kmh: 11.7secs
0-60mph 96.5kmh: 16.7secs
0-1/4 mile: 20.6secs
0-1km: 38.6secs
45.0bhp 33.6kW 45.6PS
@ 5000rpm
59.0lbft 79.9Nm @ 2750rpm
58.7bhp/ton 57.7bhp/tonne
45.0bhp/L 33.6kW/L 45.7PS/L
35.6ft/sec 10.8m/sec
21.3mph 34.3kmh/1000rpm
40.6mpg 33.8mpgUS 7.0L/100km
Petrol 4-stroke piston
999cc 60.9cu in
In-line 4 1 Carburettor
Compression ratio: 9.8:1
Bore: 70.0mm 2.8in
Stroke: 64.9mm 2.6in
Valve type/No: Overhead 8
Transmission: Manual
No. of forward speeds: 5
Wheels driven: Front
Springs F/R: Coil/Coil
Brake system: PA
Brakes F/R: Disc/Drum
Steering: Rack & pinion
Wheelbase: 215.9cm 85.0in
Track F: 128.0cm 50.4in
Track R: 127.8cm 50.3in
Length: 339.1cm 133.5in
Width: 150.6cm 59.3in
Height: 124.5cm 49.0in
Ground clearance: 15.2cm 6.0in
Kerb weight: 779.5kg 1717.0lb
Fuel: 46.9L 10.3gal 12.4galUS

2546 Lancia
Thema 8.32
1987 Italy
149.0mph 239.7kmh
0-60mph 96.5kmh: 6.8secs
215.0bhp 160.3kW 218.0PS
@ 6750rpm
209.0lbft 283.2Nm @ 4500rpm
156.4bhp/ton 153.8bhp/tonne
73.4bhp/L 54.8kW/L 74.5PS/L
52.5ft/sec 16.0m/sec
Petrol 4-stroke piston
2927cc 178.6cu in
Vee 8 fuel injection
Compression ratio: 10.5:1
Bore: 81.0mm 3.2in
Stroke: 71.0mm 2.8in
Valve type/No: Overhead 32
Transmission: Manual
No. of forward speeds: 5
Wheels driven: Front
Springs F/R: Coil/Coil
Brake system: PA ABS
Brakes F/R: Disc/Disc
Steering: Rack & pinion PA
Wheelbase: 267.0cm 105.1in
Track F: 149.9cm 59.0in
Track R: 148.8cm 58.6in
Length: 491.0cm 193.3in
Width: 173.7cm 68.4in
Height: 143.8cm 56.6in
Kerb weight: 1398.3kg 3080.0lb
Fuel: 70.4L 15.5gal 18.6galUS

2547 Lancia
Delta HF Integrale
1988 Italy
130.0mph 209.2kmh
0-50mph 80.5kmh: 4.7secs
0-60mph 96.5kmh: 6.4secs
0-1/4 mile: 14.8secs
0-1km: 27.9secs
185.0bhp 137.9kW 187.6PS
@ 5300rpm
223.6lbft 303.0Nm @ 3500rpm
148.5bhp/ton 146.0bhp/tonne
92.7bhp/L 69.1kW/L 94.0PS/L
52.1ft/sec 15.9m/sec
23.4mph 37.7kmh/1000rpm
17.6mpg 14.7mpgUS 16.1L/100km
Petrol 4-stroke piston
1995cc 122.0cu in turbocharged
In-line 4 fuel injection
Compression ratio: 8.0:1
Bore: 87.0mm 3.4in
Stroke: 90.0mm 3.5in
Valve type/No: Side 8
Transmission: Manual
No. of forward speeds: 5
Wheels driven: 4-wheel drive
Springs F/R: Coil/Coil
Brake system: PA
Brakes F/R: Disc/Disc
Steering: Rack & pinion PA
Wheelbase: 248.0cm 97.6in
Track F: 142.6cm 56.1in
Track R: 140.6cm 55.4in
Length: 390.0cm 153.5in
Width: 170.0cm 66.9in
Height: 138.0cm 54.3in
Ground clearance: 15.2cm 6.0in
Kerb weight: 1267.0kg 2790.7lb
Fuel: 56.9L 12.5gal 15.0galUS

2548 Lancia
Thema 8.32
1988 Italy
140.0mph 225.3kmh
0-50mph 80.5kmh: 5.5secs
0-60mph 96.5kmh: 7.2secs
0-1/4 mile: 15.2secs
0-1km: 28.4secs
215.0bhp 160.3kW 218.0PS
@ 6750rpm
209.6lbft 284.0Nm @ 4500rpm
153.6bhp/ton 151.1bhp/tonne
73.4bhp/L 54.8kW/L 74.5PS/L
52.5ft/sec 16.0m/sec
21.8mph 35.1kmh/1000rpm
15.6mpg 13.0mpgUS 18.1L/100km
Petrol 4-stroke piston
2927cc 179.0cu in
Vee 8 fuel injection
Compression ratio: 10.5:1
Bore: 81.0mm 3.2in
Stroke: 71.0mm 2.8in
Valve type/No: Overhead 32
Transmission: Manual
No. of forward speeds: 5
Wheels driven: Front
Springs F/R: Coil/Coil
Brake system: PA ABS
Brakes F/R: Disc/Disc
Steering: Rack & pinion PA
Wheelbase: 266.0cm 104.7in
Track F: 149.4cm 58.8in
Track R: 148.4cm 58.4in
Length: 459.0cm 180.7in
Width: 173.3cm 68.2in
Height: 143.3cm 56.4in
Ground clearance: 17.9cm 7.0in
Kerb weight: 1423.0kg 3134.4lb
Fuel: 70.1L 15.4gal 18.5galUS

2549 Lancia
Delta Integrale 16v
1989 Italy
129.0mph 207.6kmh
0-50mph 80.5kmh: 4.7secs
0-60mph 96.5kmh: 6.3secs
0-1/4 mile: 14.9secs
0-1km: 28.2secs
200.0bhp 149.1kW 202.8PS
@ 5500rpm
219.9lbft 298.0Nm @ 3000rpm
157.4bhp/ton 154.8bhp/tonne
100.2bhp/L 74.8kW/L 101.6PS/L
54.1ft/sec 16.5m/sec
23.1mph 37.2kmh/1000rpm
19.1mpg 15.9mpgUS 14.8L/100km
Petrol 4-stroke piston
1995cc 122.0cu in turbocharged
In-line 4 fuel injection
Compression ratio: 8.0:1
Bore: 84.0mm 3.3in
Stroke: 90.0mm 3.5in
Valve type/No: Overhead 16
Transmission: Manual
No. of forward speeds: 5
Wheels driven: 4-wheel drive
Springs F/R: Coil/Coil
Brake system: PA ABS
Brakes F/R: Disc/Disc
Steering: Rack & pinion PA
Wheelbase: 248.0cm 97.6in
Track F: 144.8cm 57.0in
Track R: 144.0cm 56.7in
Length: 389.5cm 153.3in
Width: 168.6cm 66.4in
Height: 136.5cm 53.7in
Ground clearance: 15.2cm 6.0in
Kerb weight: 1292.0kg 2845.8lb
Fuel: 56.9L 12.5gal 15.0galUS

2550 Lancia
Thema 2.0ie 16v
1989 Italy
126.0mph 202.7kmh
0-50mph 80.5kmh: 6.6secs
0-60mph 96.5kmh: 8.8secs
0-1/4 mile: 16.7secs
0-1km: 30.3secs
150.0bhp 111.9kW 152.1PS
@ 6000rpm
138.7lbft 188.0Nm @ 4000rpm
117.3bhp/ton 115.4bhp/tonne
75.2bhp/L 56.1kW/L 76.2PS/L
59.0ft/sec 18.0m/sec
21.8mph 35.1kmh/1000rpm
24.4mpg 20.3mpgUS 11.6L/100km
Petrol 4-stroke piston
1995cc 122.0cu in
In-line 4 fuel injection
Compression ratio: 9.8:1
Bore: 84.0mm 3.3in
Stroke: 90.0mm 3.5in
Valve type/No: Overhead 16
Transmission: Manual
No. of forward speeds: 5
Wheels driven: Front
Springs F/R: Coil/Coil
Brake system: PA
Brakes F/R: Disc/Disc
Steering: Rack & pinion PA
Wheelbase: 266.0cm 104.7in
Track F: 148.2cm 58.3in
Track R: 147.2cm 58.0in
Length: 459.0cm 180.7in
Width: 175.2cm 69.0in
Height: 143.3cm 56.4in
Ground clearance: 17.9cm 7.0in
Kerb weight: 1300.0kg 2863.4lb
Fuel: 70.1L 15.4gal 18.5galUS

2551 Lancia
Dedra 1.8i
1990 Italy
118.0mph 189.9kmh
0-50mph 80.5kmh: 8.3secs
0-60mph 96.5kmh: 11.5secs
0-1/4 mile: 18.1secs
0-1km: 33.6secs
110.0bhp 82.0kW 111.5PS
@ 6000rpm
104.8lbft 142.0Nm @ 3000rpm
90.2bhp/ton 88.7bhp/tonne
62.6bhp/L 46.7kW/L 63.5PS/L
52.0ft/sec 15.8m/sec
19.4mph 31.2kmh/1000rpm
25.2mpg 21.0mpgUS 11.2L/100km
Petrol 4-stroke piston
1756cc 107.0cu in
In-line 4 fuel injection
Compression ratio: 9.5:1
Bore: 84.0mm 3.3in
Stroke: 79.2mm 3.1in
Valve type/No: Overhead 8
Transmission: Manual
No. of forward speeds: 5
Wheels driven: Front
Springs F/R: Coil/Coil
Brake system: PA ABS
Brakes F/R: Disc/Disc
Steering: Rack & pinion PA
Wheelbase: 254.0cm 100.0in
Track F: 143.5cm 56.5in
Track R: 141.5cm 55.7in
Length: 434.1cm 170.9in
Width: 169.9cm 66.9in
Height: 142.7cm 56.2in
Kerb weight: 1240.0kg 2731.3lb
Fuel: 63.2L 13.9gal 16.7galUS

2552 Lancia
Dedra 2.0ie
1990 Italy
126.0mph 202.7kmh
0-50mph 80.5kmh: 7.1secs
0-60mph 96.5kmh: 10.0secs
0-1/4 mile: 17.6secs
0-1km: 31.5secs
120.0bhp 89.5kW 121.7PS
@ 5750rpm
119.6lbft 162.0Nm @ 3300rpm
96.8bhp/ton 95.2bhp/tonne
60.1bhp/L 44.8kW/L 61.0PS/L
56.5ft/sec 17.2m/sec
21.9mph 35.2kmh/1000rpm
23.7mpg 19.7mpgUS 11.9L/100km
Petrol 4-stroke piston
1995cc 122.0cu in
In-line 4 fuel injection
Compression ratio: 9.5:1
Bore: 84.0mm 3.3in
Stroke: 90.0mm 3.5in
Valve type/No: Overhead 8
Transmission: Manual
No. of forward speeds: 5
Wheels driven: Front
Springs F/R: Coil/Coil
Brake system: PA ABS
Brakes F/R: Disc/Drum
Steering: Rack & pinion PA
Wheelbase: 254.0cm 100.0in
Track F: 143.5cm 56.5in
Track R: 141.5cm 55.7in
Length: 434.1cm 170.9in
Width: 169.9cm 66.9in

Height: 142.7cm 56.2in
Kerb weight: 1260.0kg 2775.3lb
Fuel: 63.2L 13.9gal 16.7galUS

2553 Lancia

Thema 2.0ie 16v SE Turbo
1990 Italy
143.0mph 230.1kmh
0-50mph 80.5kmh: 5.3secs
0-60mph 96.5kmh: 6.8secs
0-1/4 mile: 15.2secs
0-1km: 27.7secs
185.0bhp 137.9kW 187.6PS
@ 5500rpm
236.2lbft 320.0Nm @ 3500rpm
136.8bhp/ton 134.5bhp/tonne
92.7bhp/L 69.1kW/L 94.0PS/L
54.1ft/sec 16.5m/sec
24.7mph 39.7kmh/1000rpm
21.1mpg 17.6mpgUS 13.4L/100km
Petrol 4-stroke piston
1995cc 122.0cu in turbocharged
In-line 4 fuel injection
Compression ratio: 8.0:1
Bore: 84.0mm 3.3in
Stroke: 90.0mm 3.5in
Valve type/No: Overhead 16
Transmission: Manual
No. of forward speeds: 5
Wheels driven: Front
Springs F/R: Coil/Coil
Brake system: PA ABS
Brakes F/R: Disc/Disc
Steering: Rack & pinion PA
Wheelbase: 266.0cm 104.7in
Track F: 148.2cm 58.3in
Track R: 147.2cm 58.0in
Length: 459.0cm 180.7in
Width: 175.2cm 69.0in
Height: 143.3cm 56.4in
Ground clearance: 17.8cm 7.0in
Kerb weight: 1375.0kg 3028.6lb
Fuel: 70.1L 15.4gal 18.5galUS

2554 Lancia

Y10 GTie
1990 Italy
107.0mph 172.2kmh
0-50mph 80.5kmh: 8.0secs
0-60mph 96.5kmh: 11.5secs
0-1/4 mile: 18.1secs
0-1km: 33.8secs
78.0bhp 58.2kW 79.1PS
@ 5750rpm
75.3lbft 102.0Nm @ 3250rpm
91.2bhp/ton 89.7bhp/tonne
59.9bhp/L 44.7kW/L 60.8PS/L
45.2ft/sec 13.8m/sec
19.2mph 30.9kmh/1000rpm
29.8mpg 24.8mpgUS 9.5L/100km
Petrol 4-stroke piston
1301cc 79.0cu in
In-line 4 fuel injection
Compression ratio: 9.5:1
Bore: 76.0mm 3.0in
Stroke: 72.0mm 2.8in
Valve type/No: Overhead 8
Transmission: Manual
No. of forward speeds: 5
Wheels driven: Front
Springs F/R: Coil/Coil
Brake system: PA
Brakes F/R: Disc/Drum
Steering: Rack & pinion
Wheelbase: 215.9cm 85.0in
Track F: 128.2cm 50.5in
Track R: 127.8cm 50.3in
Length: 339.2cm 133.5in
Width: 150.7cm 59.3in
Height: 124.5cm 49.0in
Ground clearance: 14.0cm 5.5in
Kerb weight: 870.0kg 1916.3lb
Fuel: 46.9L 10.3gal 12.4galUS

2555 Lancia

Dedra 2000 Turbo
1991 Italy
133.0mph 214.0kmh
0-50mph 80.5kmh: 5.5secs
0-60mph 96.5kmh: 7.4secs
0-1/4 mile: 15.9secs
0-1km: 28.8secs
165.0bhp 123.0kW 167.3PS
@ 5500rpm
182.3lbft 247.0Nm @ 3000rpm
126.2bhp/ton 124.1bhp/tonne
82.7bhp/L 61.7kW/L 83.8PS/L
54.1ft/sec 16.5m/sec
22.5mph 36.2kmh/1000rpm
22.1mpg 18.4mpgUS 12.8L/100km
Petrol 4-stroke piston
1995cc 122.0cu in turbocharged
In-line 4 fuel injection
Compression ratio: 7.5:1
Bore: 84.0mm 3.3in
Stroke: 90.0mm 3.5in
Valve type/No: Overhead 8
Transmission: Manual
No. of forward speeds: 5
Wheels driven: Front
Springs F/R: Coil/Coil
Brake system: PA ABS
Brakes F/R: Disc/Disc
Steering: Rack & pinion PA
Wheelbase: 254.0cm 100.0in
Track F: 143.6cm 56.5in
Track R: 141.5cm 55.7in
Length: 434.3cm 171.0in
Width: 170.0cm 66.9in
Height: 143.0cm 56.3in
Kerb weight: 1330.0kg 2929.5lb
Fuel: 63.0L 13.8gal 16.6galUS

2556 Land-Rover

Station Wagon
1955 UK
59.5mph 95.7kmh
0-50mph 80.5kmh: 24.9secs
0-1/4 mile: 25.4secs
52.0bhp 38.8kW 52.7PS
@ 4000rpm
101.0lbft 136.9Nm @ 1500rpm
39.2bhp/ton 38.6bhp/tonne
26.0bhp/L 19.4kW/L 26.4PS/L
45.9ft/sec 14.0m/sec
15.0mph 24.1kmh/1000rpm
21.0mpg 17.5mpgUS 13.5L/100km
Petrol 4-stroke piston
1997cc 121.8cu in
In-line 4
Compression ratio: 6.7:1
Bore: 77.8mm 3.1in
Stroke: 105.0mm 4.1in
Valve type/No: IOE 8
Transmission: Manual
No. of forward speeds: 4
Wheels driven: 4-wheel drive
Springs F/R: Leaf/Leaf
Brakes F/R: Drum/Drum
Wheelbase: 218.4cm 86.0in
Track F: 127.0cm 50.0in
Track R: 127.0cm 50.0in
Length: 357.4cm 140.7in
Width: 158.8cm 62.5in
Height: 198.1cm 78.0in
Ground clearance: 20.3cm 8.0in
Kerb weight: 1347.5kg 2968.0lb
Fuel: 45.5L 10.0gal 12.0galUS

2557 Land-Rover

Series III
1971 UK
73.0mph 117.5kmh
0-50mph 80.5kmh: 17.0secs
0-60mph 96.5kmh: 31.7secs
0-1/4 mile: 22.9secs
0-1km: 44.5secs
86.0bhp 64.1kW 87.2PS
@ 4500rpm
132.0lbft 178.9Nm @ 1750rpm
53.6bhp/ton 52.9bhp/tonne
32.8bhp/L 24.4kW/L 33.2PS/L
45.4ft/sec 13.8m/sec
16.2mph 26.1kmh/1000rpm
14.9mpg 12.4mpgUS 19.0L/100km
Petrol 4-stroke piston
2625cc 160.2cu in
In-line 6 1 Carburettor
Compression ratio: 7.8:1
Bore: 77.8mm 3.1in
Stroke: 92.1mm 3.6in
Valve type/No: Overhead 12
Transmission: Manual
No. of forward speeds: 4
Wheels driven: 4-wheel engageable
Springs F/R: Leaf/Leaf
Brake system: PA
Brakes F/R: Drum/Drum
Steering: Recirculating ball
Wheelbase: 276.9cm 109.0in
Track F: 133.4cm 52.5in
Track R: 133.4cm 52.5in
Length: 444.5cm 175.0in
Width: 167.6cm 66.0in
Height: 200.7cm 79.0in
Ground clearance: 25.4cm 10.0in
Kerb weight: 1626.2kg 3582.0lb
Fuel: 50.0L 11.0gal 13.2galUS

2558 Land-Rover

SWB
1973 UK
68.0mph 109.4kmh
0-50mph 80.5kmh: 16.8secs
0-60mph 96.5kmh: 29.1secs
0-1/4 mile: 22.6secs
0-1km: 44.2secs
70.5bhp 52.6kW 71.5PS
@ 4000rpm
119.3lbft 161.7Nm @ 1500rpm
51.1bhp/ton 50.2bhp/tonne
30.8bhp/L 23.0kW/L 31.3PS/L
39.3ft/sec 12.0m/sec
16.3mph 26.2kmh/1000rpm
18.0mpg 15.0mpgUS 15.7L/100km
Petrol 4-stroke piston
2286cc 139.5cu in
In-line 4 1 Carburettor
Compression ratio: 8.0:1
Bore: 90.5mm 3.6in
Stroke: 89.9mm 3.5in
Valve type/No: Overhead 8
Transmission: Manual
No. of forward speeds: 4
Wheels driven: 4-wheel engageable
Springs F/R: Leaf/Leaf
Brakes F/R: Drum/Drum
Steering: Recirculating ball
Wheelbase: 223.5cm 88.0in
Track F: 133.4cm 52.5in
Track R: 133.4cm 52.5in
Length: 354.3cm 139.5in
Width: 167.6cm 66.0in
Height: 200.7cm 79.0in
Ground clearance: 25.4cm 10.0in
Kerb weight: 1402.9kg 3090.0lb
Fuel: 45.5L 10.0gal 12.0galUS

2559 Land-Rover

County
1982 UK
86.0mph 138.4kmh
0-50mph 80.5kmh: 15.2secs
0-60mph 96.5kmh: 26.1secs
91.0bhp 67.9kW 92.3PS
@ 3500rpm
166.0lbft 224.9Nm @ 2000rpm
54.3bhp/ton 53.4bhp/tonne
25.8bhp/L 19.2kW/L 26.1PS/L
27.2ft/sec 8.3m/sec
19.0mph 30.6kmh/1000rpm
13.9mpg 11.6mpgUS 20.3L/100km
Petrol 4-stroke piston
3528cc 215.2cu in
Vee 8 2 Carburettor
Compression ratio: 8.1:1
Bore: 88.9mm 3.5in
Stroke: 71.1mm 2.8in
Valve type/No: Overhead 16
Transmission: Manual
No. of forward speeds: 4
Wheels driven: 4-wheel drive
Springs F/R: Leaf/Leaf
Brake system: PA
Brakes F/R: Drum/Drum
Steering: Recirculating ball
Wheelbase: 276.9cm 109.0in
Track F: 133.4cm 52.5in
Track R: 133.4cm 52.5in
Length: 444.5cm 175.0in
Width: 168.9cm 66.5in
Height: 200.7cm 79.0in
Ground clearance: 20.8cm 8.2in
Kerb weight: 1703.4kg 3752.0lb
Fuel: 68.2L 15.0gal 18.0galUS

2560 Land-Rover

Ninety County Turbo Diesel
1987 UK
76.0mph 122.3kmh
0-50mph 80.5kmh: 14.2secs
0-60mph 96.5kmh: 22.3secs
0-1/4 mile: 22.1secs
0-1km: 42.3secs
85.0bhp 63.4kW 86.2PS
@ 4000rpm
150.0lbft 203.3Nm @ 1800rpm
50.5bhp/ton 49.7bhp/tonne
34.1bhp/L 25.4kW/L 34.5PS/L
42.4ft/sec 12.9m/sec
20.2mph 32.5kmh/1000rpm
18.0mpg 15.0mpgUS 15.7L/100km
Diesel 4-stroke piston
2494cc 152.0cu in turbocharged
In-line 4 fuel injection
Compression ratio: 21.0:1
Bore: 90.5mm 3.6in
Stroke: 97.0mm 3.8in
Valve type/No: Overhead 8
Transmission: Manual
No. of forward speeds: 5
Wheels driven: 4-wheel drive
Springs F/R: Coil/Coil
Brake system: PA
Brakes F/R: Disc/Drum
Steering: Worm & roller PA
Wheelbase: 236.0cm 92.9in
Track F: 148.6cm 58.5in
Track R: 148.6cm 58.5in
Length: 388.3cm 152.9in
Width: 179.0cm 70.5in
Height: 198.9cm 78.3in
Ground clearance: 25.4cm 10.0in
Kerb weight: 1710.0kg 3766.5lb
Fuel: 54.6L 12.0gal 14.4galUS

2561 Land-Rover

One Ten County V8
1987 UK
88.0mph 141.6kmh
0-50mph 80.5kmh: 10.4secs
0-60mph 96.5kmh: 15.1secs
0-1/4 mile: 19.8secs
0-1km: 37.9secs
134.0bhp 99.9kW 135.9PS
@ 5000rpm
187.0lbft 253.4Nm @ 2500rpm
68.1bhp/ton 66.9bhp/tonne
38.0bhp/L 28.3kW/L 38.5PS/L
38.9ft/sec 11.8m/sec
23.0mph 37.0kmh/1000rpm
13.4mpg 11.2mpgUS 21.1L/100km
Petrol 4-stroke piston
3528cc 215.0cu in
Vee 8 2 Carburettor
Compression ratio: 8.0:1
Bore: 88.9mm 3.5in
Stroke: 71.1mm 2.8in
Valve type/No: Overhead 16
Transmission: Manual
No. of forward speeds: 5
Wheels driven: 4-wheel drive
Springs F/R: Coil/Coil
Brake system: PA
Brakes F/R: Disc/Drum
Steering: Worm & roller PA
Wheelbase: 279.4cm 110.0in
Track F: 148.6cm 58.5in
Track R: 148.6cm 58.5in
Length: 459.9cm 181.1in
Width: 179.0cm 70.5in
Height: 203.5cm 80.1in
Ground clearance: 38.1cm 15.0in
Kerb weight: 2002.0kg 4409.7lb
Fuel: 79.6L 17.5gal 21.0galUS

2562 Land-Rover

Ninety County V8
1989 UK
92.0mph 148.0kmh
0-50mph 80.5kmh: 8.9secs
0-60mph 96.5kmh: 13.6secs
0-1/4 mile: 18.8secs
0-1km: 35.5secs
134.0bhp 99.9kW 135.9PS
@ 5000rpm
186.7lbft 253.0Nm @ 2500rpm
81.5bhp/ton 80.1bhp/tonne
38.0bhp/L 28.3kW/L 38.5PS/L
38.9ft/sec 11.8m/sec
21.1mph 33.9kmh/1000rpm
12.1mpg 10.1mpgUS 23.3L/100km
Petrol 4-stroke piston
3528cc 215.0cu in
Vee 8 2 Carburettor
Compression ratio: 8.0:1
Bore: 88.9mm 3.5in
Stroke: 71.1mm 2.8in
Valve type/No: Overhead 16
Transmission: Manual
No. of forward speeds: 5
Wheels driven: 4-wheel engageable
Springs F/R: Coil/Coil
Brake system: PA
Brakes F/R: Disc/Drum
Steering: Worm & roller

Wheelbase: 236.0cm 92.9in
Track F: 148.6cm 58.5in
Track R: 148.6cm 58.5in
Length: 388.3cm 152.9in
Width: 179.0cm 70.5in
Height: 198.9cm 78.3in
Ground clearance: 25.5cm 10.0in
Kerb weight: 1672.0kg 3682.8lb
Fuel: 54.6L 12.0gal 14.4galUS

2563 Land-Rover

Discovery TDi
1990 UK
92.0mph 148.0kmh
0-50mph 80.5kmh: 11.5secs
0-60mph 96.5kmh: 17.1secs
0-1/4 mile: 20.5secs
0-1km: 38.8secs
111.0bhp 82.8kW 112.5PS
@ 4000rpm
195.6lbft 265.0Nm @ 1800rpm
56.1bhp/ton 55.2bhp/tonne
44.5bhp/L 33.2kW/L 45.1PS/L
42.4ft/sec 12.9m/sec
25.1mph 40.4kmh/1000rpm
23.9mpg 19.9mpgUS 11.8L/100km
Diesel 4-stroke piston
2495cc 152.0cu in turbocharged
In-line 4 fuel injection
Compression ratio: 19.5:1
Bore: 90.5mm 3.6in
Stroke: 97.0mm 3.8in
Valve type/No: Overhead 8
Transmission: Manual
No. of forward speeds: 5
Wheels driven: 4-wheel drive
Springs F/R: Coil/Coil
Brake system: PA
Brakes F/R: Disc/Disc
Steering: Recirculating ball PA
Wheelbase: 254.0cm 100.0in
Track F: 148.6cm 58.5in
Track R: 148.6cm 58.5in
Length: 452.1cm 178.0in
Width: 179.3cm 70.6in
Height: 191.9cm 75.6in
Ground clearance: 19.1cm 7.5in
Kerb weight: 2012.0kg 4431.7lb
Fuel: 88.7L 19.5gal 23.4galUS

2564 Land-Rover

Discovery V8
1990 UK
99.0mph 159.3kmh
0-50mph 80.5kmh: 8.7secs
0-60mph 96.5kmh: 12.8secs
0-1/4 mile: 18.8secs
0-1km: 35.7secs
145.0bhp 108.1kW 147.0PS
@ 5000rpm
191.9lbft 260.0Nm @ 2800rpm
78.3bhp/ton 77.0bhp/tonne
41.1bhp/L 30.6kW/L 41.7PS/L
38.9ft/sec 11.8m/sec
25.1mph 40.4kmh/1000rpm
14.0mpg 11.7mpgUS 20.2L/100km
Petrol 4-stroke piston
3528cc 215.0cu in
Vee 8 2 Carburettor
Compression ratio: 8.0:1
Bore: 88.9mm 3.5in
Stroke: 71.1mm 2.8in
Valve type/No: Overhead 16
Transmission: Manual
No. of forward speeds: 5
Wheels driven: 4-wheel drive
Springs F/R: Coil/Coil
Brake system: PA
Brakes F/R: Disc/Disc
Steering: Recirculating ball PA
Wheelbase: 254.0cm 100.0in
Track F: 148.6cm 58.5in
Track R: 148.6cm 58.5in
Length: 452.1cm 178.0in
Width: 179.3cm 70.6in
Height: 191.9cm 75.6in
Ground clearance: 19.1cm 7.5in
Kerb weight: 1882.0kg 4145.4lb
Fuel: 88.7L 19.5gal 23.4galUS

2565 Land Rover

Discovery V8i 5DR
1991 UK
107.0mph 172.2kmh
0-50mph 80.5kmh: 8.2secs
0-60mph 96.5kmh: 11.7secs
0-1/4 mile: 17.7secs
0-1km: 33.6secs
164.0bhp 122.3kW 166.3PS
@ 4750rpm
211.8lbft 287.0Nm @ 2600rpm
88.5bhp/ton 87.0bhp/tonne
46.5bhp/L 34.7kW/L 47.1PS/L
36.9ft/sec 11.2m/sec
25.1mph 40.4kmh/1000rpm
16.5mpg 13.7mpgUS 17.1L/100km
Petrol 4-stroke piston
3528cc 215.0cu in
Vee 8 fuel injection
Compression ratio: 9.4:1
Bore: 89.0mm 3.5in
Stroke: 71.0mm 2.8in
Valve type/No: Overhead 16
Transmission: Manual
No. of forward speeds: 5
Wheels driven: 4-wheel drive
Springs F/R: Coil/Coil
Brake system: PA
Brakes F/R: Disc/Disc
Steering: Recirculating ball PA
Wheelbase: 254.0cm 100.0in
Track F: 148.6cm 58.5in
Track R: 148.6cm 58.5in
Length: 452.1cm 178.0in
Width: 179.3cm 70.6in
Height: 191.9cm 75.6in
Ground clearance: 19.0cm 7.5in
Kerb weight: 1885.0kg 4152.0lb
Fuel: 88.7L 19.5gal 23.4galUS

2566 Lea-Francis

12/40 Saloon
1929 UK
60.0mph 96.5kmh
38.0bhp 28.3kW 38.5PS
@ 4000rpm
36.2bhp/ton 35.6bhp/tonne
25.4bhp/L 18.9kW/L 25.8PS/L
43.8ft/sec 13.3m/sec
24.0mpg 20.0mpgUS 11.8L/100km
Petrol 4-stroke piston
1496cc 91.3cu in
In-line 4 1 Carburettor
Compression ratio: 5.6:1
Bore: 69.0mm 2.7in
Stroke: 100.0mm 3.9in
Valve type/No: Overhead 8
Transmission: Manual
No. of forward speeds: 4
Wheels driven: Rear
Brakes F/R: Drum/Drum
Wheelbase: 281.9cm 111.0in
Track F: 127.0cm 50.0in
Track R: 127.0cm 50.0in
Length: 406.4cm 160.0in
Width: 162.6cm 64.0in
Height: 170.2cm 67.0in
Kerb weight: 1067.8kg 2352.0lb
Fuel: 29.6L 6.5gal 7.8galUS

2567 Lea-Francis

Hyper-sports
1929 UK
85.0mph 136.8kmh
20.0mpg 16.7mpgUS 14.1L/100km
Petrol 4-stroke piston
1496cc 91.3cu in supercharged
In-line 4 1 Carburettor
Bore: 69.0mm 2.7in
Stroke: 100.0mm 3.9in
Valve type/No: Side 8
Transmission: Manual
No. of forward speeds: 4
Wheels driven: Rear
Brakes F/R: Drum/Drum
Wheelbase: 281.9cm 111.0in
Track F: 127.0cm 50.0in
Track R: 127.0cm 50.0in
Length: 406.4cm 160.0in
Width: 162.6cm 64.0in
Kerb weight: 1004.2kg 2212.0lb
Fuel: 45.5L 10.0gal 12.0galUS

2568 Lea-Francis

2-litre Saloon
1933 UK
72.5mph 116.7kmh
0-50mph 80.5kmh: 19.4secs
22.0mpg 18.3mpgUS 12.8L/100km
Petrol 4-stroke piston
1991cc 121.5cu in
In-line 6
Bore: 65.0mm 2.6in
Stroke: 100.0mm 3.9in
Transmission: Manual
No. of forward speeds: 4
Wheels driven: Rear
Brakes F/R: Drum/Drum
Kerb weight: 1233.1kg 2716.0lb
Fuel: 45.5L 10.0gal 12.0galUS

2569 Lea-Francis

Sports
1948 UK
87.0mph 140.0kmh
0-50mph 80.5kmh: 13.3secs
0-60mph 96.5kmh: 19.2secs
77.0bhp 57.4kW 78.1PS
@ 5100rpm
61.7bhp/ton 60.7bhp/tonne
43.6bhp/L 32.5kW/L 44.2PS/L
55.8ft/sec 17.0m/sec
21.0mpg 17.5mpgUS 13.5L/100km
Petrol 4-stroke piston
1767cc 107.8cu in
In-line 4
Compression ratio: 7.2:1
Bore: 75.0mm 2.9in
Stroke: 100.0mm 3.9in
Valve type/No: Overhead 8
Transmission: Manual
No. of forward speeds: 4
Wheels driven: Rear
Brakes F/R: Drum/Drum
Wheelbase: 251.5cm 99.0in
Track F: 130.8cm 51.5in
Track R: 133.1cm 52.4in
Length: 396.2cm 156.0in
Width: 160.0cm 63.0in
Height: 142.2cm 56.0in
Ground clearance: 17.8cm 7.0in
Kerb weight: 1268.0kg 2793.0lb
Fuel: 50.0L 11.0gal 13.2galUS

2570 Lexus

LS400
1990 Japan
148.0mph 238.1kmh
0-50mph 80.5kmh: 6.3secs
0-60mph 96.5kmh: 8.3secs
0-1/4 mile: 16.3secs
0-1km: 29.1secs
241.0bhp 179.7kW 244.3PS
@ 5400rpm
258.3lbft 350.0Nm @ 4400rpm
138.9bhp/ton 136.5bhp/tonne
60.7bhp/L 45.3kW/L 61.6PS/L
48.7ft/sec 14.8m/sec
27.1mph 43.6kmh/1000rpm
19.7mpg 16.4mpgUS 14.3L/100km
Petrol 4-stroke piston
3969cc 242.0cu in
Vee 8 fuel injection
Compression ratio: 10.0:1
Bore: 87.5mm 3.4in
Stroke: 82.5mm 3.2in
Valve type/No: Overhead 32
Transmission: Automatic
No. of forward speeds: 4
Wheels driven: Rear
Springs F/R: Coil/Coil
Brake system: PA ABS
Brakes F/R: Disc/Disc
Steering: Rack & pinion PA
Wheelbase: 281.4cm 110.8in
Track F: 156.5cm 61.6in
Track R: 155.4cm 61.2in
Length: 499.4cm 196.6in
Width: 181.9cm 71.6in
Height: 142.5cm 56.1in
Ground clearance: 15.7cm 6.2in
Kerb weight: 1765.0kg 3887.7lb
Fuel: 85.1L 18.7gal 22.5galUS

2571 Lexus

SC400
1991 Japan
150.0mph 241.4kmh
0-50mph 80.5kmh: 5.3secs
0-60mph 96.5kmh: 6.9secs
0-1/4 mile: 15.2secs
250.0bhp 186.4kW 253.5PS
@ 5600rpm
260.0lbft 352.3Nm @ 4400rpm
153.8bhp/ton 151.3bhp/tonne
63.0bhp/L 47.0kW/L 63.9PS/L
50.6ft/sec 15.4m/sec
24.0mpg 20.0mpgUS 11.8L/100km
Petrol 4-stroke piston
3969cc 242.2cu in
Vee 8 fuel injection
Compression ratio: 10.0:1
Bore: 87.5mm 3.4in
Stroke: 82.5mm 3.2in
Valve type/No: Overhead 32
Transmission: Automatic
No. of forward speeds: 4
Wheels driven: Rear
Springs F/R: Coil/Coil
Brake system: PA ABS
Brakes F/R: Disc/Disc
Steering: Rack & pinion PA
Wheelbase: 269.0cm 105.9in
Track F: 152.1cm 59.9in
Track R: 152.4cm 60.0in
Length: 485.4cm 191.1in
Width: 179.1cm 70.5in
Height: 133.6cm 52.6in
Ground clearance: 14.0cm 5.5in
Kerb weight: 1652.6kg 3640.0lb
Fuel: 78.0L 17.1gal 20.6galUS

2572 Lexus

ES300
1992 Japan
135.0mph 217.2kmh
0-50mph 80.5kmh: 6.8secs
0-60mph 96.5kmh: 9.0secs
0-1/4 mile: 17.0secs
185.0bhp 137.9kW 187.6PS
@ 5200rpm
195.0lbft 264.2Nm @ 4400rpm
121.5bhp/ton 119.5bhp/tonne
62.5bhp/L 46.6kW/L 63.4PS/L
46.7ft/sec 14.2m/sec
25.2mpg 21.0mpgUS 11.2L/100km
Petrol 4-stroke piston
2959cc 180.5cu in
Vee 6 fuel injection
Compression ratio: 9.6:1
Bore: 87.5mm 3.4in
Stroke: 82.0mm 3.2in
Valve type/No: Overhead 24
Transmission: Automatic
No. of forward speeds: 4
Wheels driven: Front
Springs F/R: Coil/Coil
Brake system: PA ABS
Brakes F/R: Disc/Disc
Steering: Rack & pinion PA
Wheelbase: 261.9cm 103.1in
Track F: 154.9cm 61.0in
Track R: 149.9cm 59.0in
Length: 477.0cm 187.8in
Width: 177.8cm 70.0in
Height: 136.9cm 53.9in
Ground clearance: 13.0cm 5.1in
Kerb weight: 1548.1kg 3410.0lb
Fuel: 70.0L 15.4gal 18.5galUS

2573 Lincoln

39.2hp Town Saloon
1930 USA
79.6mph 128.1kmh
12.0mpg 10.0mpgUS 23.5L/100km
Petrol 4-stroke piston
6321cc 385.7cu in
In-line 8
Bore: 89.0mm 3.5in
Stroke: 127.0mm 5.0in
Transmission: Manual
No. of forward speeds: 3
Wheels driven: Rear
Brakes F/R: Drum/Drum
Wheelbase: 345.4cm 136.0in
Track F: 142.2cm 56.0in
Track R: 142.2cm 56.0in
Length: 515.6cm 203.0in
Width: 177.8cm 70.0in
Height: 188.5cm 74.2in
Kerb weight: 2338.1kg 5150.0lb
Fuel: 72.8L 16.0gal 19.2galUS

2574 Lincoln

39.2hp Saloon
1931 USA
84.9mph 136.6kmh
11.0mpg 9.2mpgUS 25.7L/100km
Petrol 4-stroke piston
6304cc 384.6cu in
In-line 8
Bore: 89.0mm 3.5in
Stroke: 127.0mm 5.0in
Transmission: Manual

No. of forward speeds: 3
Wheels driven: Rear
Brakes F/R: Drum/Drum
Wheelbase: 368.3cm 145.0in
Track F: 152.4cm 60.0in
Track R: 152.4cm 60.0in
Length: 538.5cm 212.0in
Width: 182.9cm 72.0in
Height: 177.8cm 70.0in
Kerb weight: 2538.3kg 5591.0lb
Fuel: 104.6L 23.0gal 27.6galUS

2575 Lincoln

Twelve Cylinder Town Sedan
1932 USA
95.7mpn 154.0kmh
10.0mpg 8.3mpgUS 28.2L/100km
Petrol 4-stroke piston
7238cc 441.6cu in
Vee 12
Bore: 82.0mm 3.2in
Stroke: 114.0mm 4.5in
Transmission: Manual
No. of forward speeds: 3
Wheels driven: Rear
Brakes F/R: Drum/Drum
Wheelbase: 368.3cm 145.0in
Track F: 152.4cm 60.0in
Track R: 152.4cm 60.0in
Length: 513.1cm 202.0in
Width: 182.9cm 72.0in
Height: 182.9cm 72.0in
Kerb weight: 2696.3kg 5939.0lb
Fuel: 104.6L 23.0gal 27.6galUS

2576 Lincoln

Zephyr Saloon
1936 USA
90.9mph 146.3kmh
0-50mph 80.5kmh: 10.8secs
0-60mph 96.5kmh: 16.0secs
16.0mpg 13.3mpgUS 17.7L/100km
Petrol 4-stroke piston
4375cc 266.9cu in
Vee 12
Bore: 69.8mm 2.7in
Stroke: 95.2mm 3.8in
Valve type/No: Side 24
Transmission: Manual
No. of forward speeds: 3
Wheels driven: Rear
Brakes F/R: Drum/Drum
Kerb weight: 1671.6kg 3682.0lb
Fuel: 59.1L 13.0gal 15.6galUS

2577 Lincoln

Zephyr Saloon
1938 USA
90.0mph 144.8kmh
0-50mph 80.5kmh: 10.3secs
0-60mph 96.5kmh: 15.5secs
15.0mpg 12.5mpgUS 18.8L/100km
Petrol 4-stroke piston
4378cc 267.1cu in
Vee 12
Bore: 70.0mm 2.8in
Stroke: 95.0mm 3.7in
Valve type/No: Side 24
Transmission: Manual
No. of forward speeds: 3
Wheels driven: Rear
Brakes F/R: Drum/Drum
Kerb weight: 1698.4kg 3741.0lb
Fuel: 72.8L 16.0gal 19.2galUS

2578 Lincoln

Cosmopolitan Sedan
1953 USA
108.1mph 173.9kmh
0-50mph 80.5kmh: 10.7secs
0-60mph 96.5kmh: 14.4secs
0-1/4 mile: 19.8secs
205.0bhp 152.9kW 207.8PS
@ 4200rpm
308.0lbft 417.3Nm @ 2650rpm
103.4bhp/ton 101.7bhp/tonne
39.4bhp/L 29.4kW/L 39.9PS/L
40.8ft/sec 12.4m/sec
25.5mph 41.0kmh/1000rpm
Petrol 4-stroke piston
5203cc 317.4cu in
Vee 8
Compression ratio: 8.0:1
Bore: 96.5mm 3.8in
Stroke: 88.9mm 3.5in
Valve type/No: Overhead 16
Transmission: Automatic
No. of forward speeds: 4
Wheels driven: Rear
Wheelbase: 312.4cm 123.0in
Track F: 148.6cm 58.5in
Track R: 148.6cm 58.5in
Kerb weight: 2015.8kg 4440.0lb

2579 Lincoln

Continental Mk III
1958 USA
116.0mph 186.6kmh
0-50mph 80.5kmh: 6.2secs
0-60mph 96.5kmh: 8.7secs
0-1/4 mile: 16.3secs
375.0bhp 279.6kW 380.2PS
@ 4800rpm
490.0lbft 664.0Nm @ 3100rpm
159.1bhp/ton 156.4bhp/tonne
53.2bhp/L 39.7kW/L 53.9PS/L
49.3ft/sec 15.0m/sec
29.0mph 46.7kmh/1000rpm
Petrol 4-stroke piston
7049cc 430.1cu in
Vee 8
Compression ratio: 10.5:1
Bore: 109.2mm 4.3in
Stroke: 94.0mm 3.7in
Valve type/No: Overhead 16
Transmission: Automatic
No. of forward speeds: 3
Wheels driven: Rear
Wheelbase: 332.7cm 131.0in
Track F: 154.9cm 61.0in
Track R: 154.9cm 61.0in
Length: 581.7cm 229.0in
Width: 203.5cm 80.1in
Height: 144.5cm 56.9in
Kerb weight: 2397.1kg 5280.0lb

2580 Lincoln

Continental
1961 USA
117.0mph 188.3kmh
0-50mph 80.5kmh: 8.0secs
0-60mph 96.5kmh: 11.2secs
0-1/4 mile: 18.2secs
300.0bhp 223.7kW 304.2PS
@ 4100rpm
465.0lbft 630.1Nm @ 2000rpm
128.7bhp/ton 126.6bhp/tonne
42.6bhp/L 31.7kW/L 43.1PS/L
42.1ft/sec 12.8m/sec
28.0mph 45.1kmh/1000rpm
Petrol 4-stroke piston
7049cc 430.1cu in
Vee 8 1 Carburettor
Compression ratio: 10.0:1
Bore: 109.2mm 4.3in
Stroke: 94.0mm 3.7in
Valve type/No: Overhead 16
Transmission: Automatic
No. of forward speeds: 3
Wheels driven: Rear
Brake system: PA
Brakes F/R: Drum/Drum
Steering: PA
Wheelbase: 312.4cm 123.0in
Track F: 157.7cm 62.1in
Track R: 154.9cm 61.0in
Length: 539.5cm 212.4in
Width: 199.6cm 78.6in
Height: 135.9cm 53.5in
Ground clearance: 14.0cm 5.5in
Kerb weight: 2369.9kg 5220.0lb

2581 Lincoln

Continental
1964 USA
121.0mph 194.7kmh
0-50mph 80.5kmh: 9.0secs
0-60mph 96.5kmh: 11.8secs
0-1/4 mile: 18.1secs
320.0bhp 238.6kW 324.4PS
@ 4600rpm
459.0lbft 622.0Nm @ 2600rpm
135.0bhp/ton 132.7bhp/tonne
45.4bhp/L 33.9kW/L 46.0PS/L
47.3ft/sec 14.4m/sec
28.7mph 46.2kmh/1000rpm
Petrol 4-stroke piston
7046cc 429.9cu in
Vee 8 1 Carburettor
Compression ratio: 10.1:1
Bore: 109.2mm 4.3in
Stroke: 94.0mm 3.7in
Valve type/No: Overhead 16
Transmission: Automatic
No. of forward speeds: 3
Wheels driven: Rear
Brake system: PA
Brakes F/R: Drum/Drum
Steering: PA
Wheelbase: 320.0cm 126.0in
Track F: 157.7cm 62.1in
Track R: 154.9cm 61.0in
Length: 549.4cm 216.3in
Width: 199.6cm 78.6in
Height: 137.7cm 54.2in
Ground clearance: 13.2cm 5.2in
Kerb weight: 2410.7kg 5310.0lb
Fuel: 88.9L 19.5gal 23.5galUS

2582 Lincoln

Continental Limousine
1976 USA
104.0mph 167.3kmh
0-50mph 80.5kmh: 8.6secs
0-60mph 96.5kmh: 11.6secs
0-1/4 mile: 18.2secs
208.0bhp 155.1kW 210.9PS
@ 4000rpm
338.0lbft 458.0Nm @ 2800rpm
79.0bhp/ton 77.6bhp/tonne
27.6bhp/L 20.6kW/L 28.0PS/L
42.8ft/sec 13.0m/sec
26.7mph 43.0kmh/1000rpm
12.6mpg 10.5mpgUS 22.4L/100km
Petrol 4-stroke piston
7538cc 459.9cu in
Vee 8 1 Carburettor
Compression ratio: 8.0:1
Bore: 110.8mm 4.4in
Stroke: 97.8mm 3.8in
Valve type/No: Overhead 16
Transmission: Automatic
No. of forward speeds: 3
Wheels driven: Rear
Springs F/R: Coil/Coil
Brake system: PA
Brakes F/R: Disc/Drum
Steering: Recirculating ball PA
Wheelbase: 370.8cm 146.0in
Track F: 163.3cm 64.3in
Track R: 163.3cm 64.3in
Length: 632.2cm 248.9in
Width: 202.2cm 79.6in
Height: 141.0cm 55.5in
Ground clearance: 13.5cm 5.3in
Kerb weight: 2678.6kg 5900.0lb
Fuel: 88.9L 19.5gal 23.5galUS

2583 Lincoln

Continental Mk VII
1984 USA
0-60mph 96.5kmh: 13.0secs
140.0bhp 104.4kW 141.9PS
@ 3400rpm
255.0lbft 345.5Nm @ 1800rpm
86.5bhp/ton 85.1bhp/tonne
28.3bhp/L 21.1kW/L 28.7PS/L
Petrol 4-stroke piston
4942cc 301.5cu in
Vee 8 fuel injection
Valve type/No: Overhead 16
Transmission: Automatic
No. of forward speeds: 4
Wheels driven: Rear
Springs F/R: Gas/Gas
Brakes F/R: Disc/Disc
Steering: Rack & pinion PA
Wheelbase: 275.8cm 108.6in
Length: 515.1cm 202.8in
Width: 178.3cm 70.2in
Height: 137.2cm 54.0in
Kerb weight: 1645.7kg 3625.0lb
Fuel: 84.4L 18.5gal 22.3galUS

2584 Lincoln

Continental Mk VII LSC
1985 USA
120.0mph 193.1kmh
0-50mph 80.5kmh: 6.7secs
0-60mph 96.5kmh: 8.9secs
0-1/4 mile: 16.9secs
180.0bhp 134.2kW 182.5PS
@ 4200rpm
260.0lbft 352.3Nm @ 2600rpm
107.9bhp/ton 106.1bhp/tonne
36.4bhp/L 27.2kW/L 36.9PS/L
35.0ft/sec 10.7m/sec
34.0mph 54.7kmh/1000rpm
19.2mpg 16.0mpgUS 14.7L/100km
Petrol 4-stroke piston
4942cc 301.5cu in
Vee 8 fuel injection
Compression ratio: 8.3:1
Bore: 101.6mm 4.0in
Stroke: 76.2mm 3.0in
Valve type/No: Overhead 16
Transmission: Automatic
No. of forward speeds: 4
Wheels driven: Rear
Springs F/R: Gas/Gas
Brake system: PA ABS
Brakes F/R: Disc/Disc
Steering: Rack & pinion PA
Wheelbase: 275.6cm 108.5in
Track F: 148.3cm 58.4in
Track R: 149.9cm 59.0in
Length: 515.1cm 202.8in
Width: 180.1cm 70.9in
Height: 137.7cm 54.2in
Ground clearance: 14.2cm 5.6in
Kerb weight: 1695.7kg 3735.0lb
Fuel: 83.6L 18.4gal 22.1galUS

2585 Lincoln

Continental Mk VII LSC
1986 USA
0-60mph 96.5kmh: 8.4secs
0-1/4 mile: 16.6secs
200.0bhp 149.1kW 202.8PS
@ 4000rpm
285.0lbft 386.2Nm @ 3000rpm
119.9bhp/ton 117.9bhp/tonne
40.4bhp/L 30.1kW/L 41.0PS/L
19.2mpg 16.0mpgUS 14.7L/100km
Petrol 4-stroke piston
4949cc 301.9cu in
Vee 8
Valve type/No: Overhead 16
Transmission: Automatic
No. of forward speeds: 4
Wheels driven: Rear
Brake system: ABS
Brakes F/R: Disc/Disc
Steering: Rack & pinion PA
Length: 515.1cm 202.8in
Kerb weight: 1695.7kg 3735.0lb

2586 Lincoln

Continental Mk VII
1989 USA
125.0mph 201.1kmh
0-50mph 80.5kmh: 6.0secs
0-60mph 96.5kmh: 8.0secs
0-1/4 mile: 16.3secs
225.0bhp 167.8kW 228.1PS
@ 4200rpm
300.0lbft 406.5Nm @ 3200rpm
133.9bhp/ton 131.6bhp/tonne
45.5bhp/L 33.9kW/L 46.2PS/L
35.0ft/sec 10.7m/sec
19.2mpg 16.0mpgUS 14.7L/100km
Petrol 4-stroke piston
4942cc 301.5cu in
Vee 8 fuel injection
Compression ratio: 9.0:1
Bore: 101.6mm 4.0in
Stroke: 76.2mm 3.0in
Valve type/No: Overhead 16
Transmission: Automatic
No. of forward speeds: 4
Wheels driven: Rear
Springs F/R: Gas/Gas
Brake system: PA ABS
Brakes F/R: Disc/Disc
Steering: Rack & pinion PA
Wheelbase: 275.6cm 108.5in
Track F: 148.3cm 58.4in
Track R: 149.9cm 59.0in
Length: 515.1cm 202.8in
Width: 180.1cm 70.9in
Height: 137.7cm 54.2in
Kerb weight: 1709.3kg 3765.0lb
Fuel: 83.6L 18.4gal 22.1galUS

2587 Lincoln

Continental Mk VII LSC
1990 USA
125.0mph 201.1kmh
0-50mph 80.5kmh: 6.1secs
0-60mph 96.5kmh: 8.3secs
0-1/4 mile: 16.3secs
225.0bhp 167.8kW 228.1PS

@ 4200rpm
300.0lbft 406.5Nm @ 4200rpm
133.9bhp/ton 131.6bhp/tonne
45.5bhp/L 33.9kW/L 46.2PS/L
35.0ft/sec 10.7m/sec
19.2mpg 16.0mpgUS 14.7L/100km
Petrol 4-stroke piston
4942cc 301.5cu in
Vee 8 fuel injection
Compression ratio: 9.0:1
Bore: 101.6mm 4.0in
Stroke: 76.2mm 3.0in
Valve type/No: Overhead 16
Transmission: Automatic
No. of forward speeds: 4
Wheels driven: Rear
Springs F/R: Gas/Gas
Brake system: PA ABS
Brakes F/R: Disc/Disc
Steering: Rack & pinion PA
Wheelbase: 275.6cm 108.5in
Track F: 148.3cm 58.4in
Track R: 149.9cm 59.0in
Length: 515.1cm 202.8in
Width: 180.1cm 70.9in
Height: 137.7cm 54.2in
Kerb weight: 1709.3kg 3765.0lb
Fuel: 83.6L 18.4gal 22.1galUS

2588 Lloyd

LP 600
1958 Germany
63.4mph 102.0kmh
0-50mph 80.5kmh: 26.9secs
0-1/4 mile: 24.1secs
19.0bhp 14.2kW 19.3PS
@ 4500rpm
28.2lbft 38.2Nm @ 2500rpm
35.2bhp/ton 34.6bhp/tonne
31.9bhp/L 23.8kW/L 32.3PS/L
31.5ft/sec 9.6m/sec
12.5mph 20.1kmh/1000rpm
47.3mpg 39.4mpgUS 6.0L/100km
Petrol 4-stroke piston
596cc 36.4cu in
In-line 2 1 Carburettor
Compression ratio: 6.6:1
Bore: 77.0mm 3.0in
Stroke: 64.0mm 2.5in
Valve type/No: Overhead 4
Transmission: Manual
No. of forward speeds: 3
Wheels driven: Front
Springs F/R: Leaf/Leaf
Brakes F/R: Drum/Drum
Wheelbase: 199.4cm 78.5in
Track F: 105.4cm 41.5in
Track R: 110.0cm 43.3in
Length: 335.3cm 132.0in
Width: 141.0cm 55.5in
Height: 139.7cm 55.0in
Ground clearance: 12.7cm 5.0in
Kerb weight: 548.4kg 1208.0lb
Fuel: 25.0L 5.5gal 6.6galUS

2589 Lotus

11 Le Mans
1957 UK
112.5mph 181.0kmh
0-50mph 80.5kmh: 7.9secs
0-60mph 96.5kmh: 10.9secs
0-1/4 mile: 17.9secs
83.0bhp 61.9kW 84.1PS
@ 6800rpm
74.5lbft 100.9Nm @ 4400rpm
182.4bhp/ton 179.4bhp/tonne
75.6bhp/L 56.4kW/L 76.6PS/L
49.5ft/sec 15.1m/sec
18.0mph 29.0kmh/1000rpm
47.8mpg 39.8mpgUS 5.9L/100km
Petrol 4-stroke piston
1098cc 67.0cu in
In-line 4
Compression ratio: 9.8:1
Bore: 72.4mm 2.8in
Stroke: 66.6mm 2.6in
Valve type/No: Overhead 8
Transmission: Manual
No. of forward speeds: 4
Wheels driven: Rear
Springs F/R: Coil/Coil
Brakes F/R: Disc/Disc
Wheelbase: 215.9cm 85.0in
Track F: 118.1cm 46.5in
Track R: 119.4cm 47.0in
Length: 340.4cm 134.0in
Width: 152.4cm 60.0in
Height: 94.0cm 37.0in
Ground clearance: 12.7cm 5.0in
Kerb weight: 462.6kg 1019.0lb
Fuel: 81.9L 18.0gal 21.6galUS

2590 Lotus

Mk XI
1957 UK
0-50mph 80.5kmh: 6.7secs
0-60mph 96.5kmh: 9.0secs
0-1/4 mile: 16.0secs
83.0bhp 61.9kW 84.1PS
@ 6800rpm
74.5lbft 100.9Nm @ 4400rpm
185.9bhp/ton 182.8bhp/tonne
75.6bhp/L 56.4kW/L 76.6PS/L
49.7ft/sec 15.1m/sec
Petrol 4-stroke piston
1098cc 67.0cu in
In-line 4
Compression ratio: 9.8:1
Bore: 72.4mm 2.8in
Stroke: 66.8mm 2.6in
Valve type/No: Overhead 8
Transmission: Manual
No. of forward speeds: 4
Wheels driven: Rear
Wheelbase: 215.9cm 85.0in
Track F: 118.1cm 46.5in
Track R: 119.4cm 47.0in
Kerb weight: 454.0kg 1000.0lb

2591 Lotus

Sports
1957 UK
97.8mph 157.4kmh
0-50mph 80.5kmh: 10.6secs
0-60mph 96.5kmh: 14.2secs
0-1/4 mile: 19.2secs
40.0bhp 29.8kW 40.5PS
@ 4600rpm
52.0lbft 70.5Nm @ 2500rpm
92.4bhp/ton 90.8bhp/tonne
34.1bhp/L 25.4kW/L 34.6PS/L
46.5ft/sec 14.2m/sec
Petrol 4-stroke piston
1172cc 71.5cu in
In-line 4
Compression ratio: 7.0:1
Bore: 63.5mm 2.5in
Stroke: 92.5mm 3.6in
Valve type/No: Side 8
Transmission: Manual
No. of forward speeds: 3
Wheels driven: Rear
Wheelbase: 215.9cm 85.0in
Track F: 118.1cm 46.5in
Track R: 119.4cm 47.0in
Kerb weight: 440.4kg 970.0lb

2592 Lotus

Elite
1960 UK
115.0mph 185.0kmh
0-50mph 80.5kmh: 8.5secs
0-60mph 96.5kmh: 12.2secs
0-1/4 mile: 18.0secs
75.0bhp 55.9kW 76.0PS
@ 6100rpm
70.0lbft 94.9Nm @ 3300rpm
118.3bhp/ton 116.3bhp/tonne
61.5bhp/L 45.8kW/L 62.3PS/L
44.4ft/sec 13.5m/sec
18.0mph 29.0kmh/1000rpm
Petrol 4-stroke piston
1220cc 74.4cu in
In-line 4
Compression ratio: 9.5:1
Bore: 76.2mm 3.0in
Stroke: 66.5mm 2.6in
Valve type/No: Overhead 8
Transmission: Manual
No. of forward speeds: 4
Wheels driven: Rear
Wheelbase: 223.5cm 88.0in
Track F: 119.4cm 47.0in
Track R: 119.4cm 47.0in
Length: 365.8cm 144.0in
Width: 147.3cm 58.0in
Height: 116.8cm 46.0in
Kerb weight: 644.7kg 1420.0lb

2593 Lotus

7
1961 UK
85.0mph 136.8kmh
0-50mph 80.5kmh: 9.2secs
0-60mph 96.5kmh: 14.3secs
0-1/4 mile: 19.2secs
40.0bhp 29.8kW 40.5PS
@ 5000rpm
50.0lbft 67.8Nm @ 2500rpm
93.3bhp/ton 91.8bhp/tonne
42.2bhp/L 31.5kW/L 42.8PS/L
41.7ft/sec 12.7m/sec
14.6mph 23.5kmh/1000rpm
Petrol 4-stroke piston
948cc 57.8cu in
In-line 4
Compression ratio: 8.3:1
Bore: 63.0mm 2.5in
Stroke: 76.2mm 3.0in
Valve type/No: Overhead 8
Transmission: Manual
No. of forward speeds: 4
Wheels driven: Rear
Wheelbase: 223.5cm 88.0in
Track F: 123.2cm 48.5in
Track R: 123.2cm 48.5in
Length: 335.3cm 132.0in
Width: 148.1cm 58.3in
Height: 109.2cm 43.0in
Ground clearance: 15.7cm 6.2in
Kerb weight: 435.8kg 960.0lb

2594 Lotus

Super 7
1961 UK
103.6mph 166.7kmh
0-50mph 80.5kmh: 5.6secs
0-60mph 96.5kmh: 7.6secs
0-1/4 mile: 15.8secs
85.0bhp 63.4kW 86.2PS
@ 6000rpm
197.1bhp/ton 193.8bhp/tonne
63.4bhp/L 47.3kW/L 64.3PS/L
42.7ft/sec 13.0m/sec
16.0mph 25.7kmh/1000rpm
22.9mpg 19.1mpgUS 12.3L/100km
Petrol 4-stroke piston
1340cc 81.8cu in
In-line 4
Compression ratio: 9.5:1
Bore: 81.0mm 3.2in
Stroke: 65.1mm 2.6in
Valve type/No: Overhead 8
Transmission: Manual
No. of forward speeds: 4
Wheels driven: Rear
Springs F/R: Coil/Coil
Brakes F/R: Drum/Drum
Wheelbase: 223.5cm 88.0in
Track F: 119.4cm 47.0in
Track R: 119.4cm 47.0in
Length: 246.4cm 97.0in
Width: 142.2cm 56.0in
Height: 71.1cm 28.0in
Ground clearance: 16.5cm 6.5in
Kerb weight: 438.6kg 966.0lb
Fuel: 22.7L 5.0gal 6.0galUS

2595 Lotus

Super 7
1962 UK
102.0mph 164.1kmh
0-50mph 80.5kmh: 7.4secs
0-60mph 96.5kmh: 9.9secs
0-1/4 mile: 16.9secs
90.0bhp 67.1kW 91.2PS
@ 6000rpm
198.6bhp/ton 195.3bhp/tonne
67.2bhp/L 50.1kW/L 68.1PS/L
42.7ft/sec 13.0m/sec
16.1mph 25.9kmh/1000rpm
Petrol 4-stroke piston
1340cc 81.8cu in
In-line 4
Compression ratio: 9.5:1
Bore: 81.0mm 3.2in
Stroke: 65.0mm 2.6in
Valve type/No: Overhead 8
Transmission: Manual
No. of forward speeds: 4
Wheels driven: Rear
Wheelbase: 223.5cm 88.0in
Track F: 120.7cm 47.5in
Track R: 123.2cm 48.5in
Length: 333.2cm 131.2in
Width: 145.3cm 57.2in
Height: 113.5cm 44.7in
Ground clearance: 12.7cm 5.0in
Kerb weight: 460.8kg 1015.0lb

2596 Lotus

Elan 1600
1963 UK
107.0mph 172.2kmh
0-50mph 80.5kmh: 6.4secs
0-60mph 96.5kmh: 8.5secs
0-1/4 mile: 16.9secs
105.0bhp 78.3kW 106.5PS
@ 5500rpm
108.0lbft 146.3Nm @ 4000rpm
156.8bhp/ton 154.2bhp/tonne
67.4bhp/L 50.3kW/L 68.3PS/L
43.7ft/sec 13.3m/sec
17.0mph 27.4kmh/1000rpm
Petrol 4-stroke piston
1558cc 95.1cu in
In-line 4 1 Carburettor
Compression ratio: 9.5:1
Bore: 82.6mm 3.2in
Stroke: 72.6mm 2.9in
Valve type/No: Overhead 8
Transmission: Manual
No. of forward speeds: 4
Wheels driven: Rear
Wheelbase: 213.4cm 84.0in
Track F: 119.4cm 47.0in
Track R: 125.7cm 49.5in
Length: 368.8cm 145.2in
Width: 142.2cm 56.0in
Height: 114.3cm 45.0in
Ground clearance: 15.2cm 6.0in
Kerb weight: 681.0kg 1500.0lb

2597 Lotus

Elite
1963 UK
115.0mph 185.0kmh
0-50mph 80.5kmh: 9.0secs
0-60mph 96.5kmh: 11.8secs
0-1/4 mile: 18.3secs
80.0bhp 59.7kW 81.1PS
@ 6100rpm
75.0lbft 101.6Nm @ 4750rpm
122.7bhp/ton 120.7bhp/tonne
65.8bhp/L 49.1kW/L 66.7PS/L
44.4ft/sec 13.5m/sec
16.5mph 26.5kmh/1000rpm
Petrol 4-stroke piston
1216cc 74.2cu in
In-line 4 1 Carburettor
Compression ratio: 10.0:1
Bore: 76.2mm 3.0in
Stroke: 66.5mm 2.6in
Valve type/No: Overhead 8
Transmission: Manual
No. of forward speeds: 4
Wheels driven: Rear
Wheelbase: 224.0cm 88.2in
Track F: 119.4cm 47.0in
Track R: 122.4cm 48.2in
Length: 373.4cm 147.0in
Width: 148.6cm 58.5in
Height: 119.4cm 47.0in
Ground clearance: 12.7cm 5.0in
Kerb weight: 662.8kg 1460.0lb

2598 Lotus

Cortina
1964 UK
106.0mph 170.6kmh
0-50mph 80.5kmh: 7.8secs
0-60mph 96.5kmh: 10.5secs
0-1/4 mile: 17.5secs
105.0bhp 78.3kW 106.5PS
@ 5500rpm
108.0lbft 146.3Nm @ 4000rpm
121.9bhp/ton 119.8bhp/tonne
67.4bhp/L 50.3kW/L 68.3PS/L
43.7ft/sec 13.3m/sec
17.3mph 27.8kmh/1000rpm
Petrol 4-stroke piston
1558cc 95.1cu in
In-line 4 2 Carburettor
Compression ratio: 9.5:1
Bore: 82.6mm 3.2in
Stroke: 72.6mm 2.9in
Valve type/No: Overhead 8
Transmission: Manual
No. of forward speeds: 4
Wheels driven: Rear
Springs F/R: Coil/Coil
Brakes F/R: Disc/Drum
Steering: Recirculating ball
Wheelbase: 249.9cm 98.4in
Track F: 131.1cm 51.6in
Track R: 127.5cm 50.2in
Length: 426.7cm 168.0in

Width: 158.8cm 62.5in
Height: 136.9cm 53.9in
Ground clearance: 13.5cm 5.3in
Kerb weight: 876.2kg 1930.0lb
Fuel: 36.3L 8.0gal 9.6galUS

2599 Lotus

Elan 1600
1964 UK
115.0mph 185.0kmh
0-50mph 80.5kmh: 6.6secs
0-60mph 96.5kmh: 8.7secs
0-1/4 mile: 16.4secs
105.0bhp 78.3kW 106.5PS
@ 5500rpm
108.0lbft 146.3Nm @ 4000rpm
155.1bhp/ton 152.6bhp/tonne
67.4bhp/L 50.3kW/L 68.3PS/L
43.7ft/sec 13.3m/sec
17.1mph 27.5kmh/1000rpm
27.9mpg 23.2mpgUS 10.1L/100km
Petrol 4-stroke piston
1558cc 95.1cu in
In-line 4 2 Carburettor
Compression ratio: 9.5:1
Bore: 82.5mm 3.2in
Stroke: 72.7mm 2.9in
Valve type/No: Overhead 8
Transmission: Manual
No. of forward speeds: 4
Wheels driven: Rear
Springs F/R: Coil/Coil
Brakes F/R: Disc/Disc
Steering: Rack & pinion
Wheelbase: 213.4cm 84.0in
Track F: 119.4cm 47.0in
Track R: 119.4cm 47.0in
Length: 368.3cm 145.0in
Width: 144.8cm 57.0in
Height: 115.6cm 45.5in
Ground clearance: 15.2cm 6.0in
Kerb weight: 688.3kg 1516.0lb
Fuel: 45.5L 10.0gal 12.0galUS

2600 Lotus

Elan Coupe SE
1967 UK
123.0mph 197.9kmh
0-50mph 80.5kmh: 6.0secs
0-60mph 96.5kmh: 7.6secs
0-1/4 mile: 15.7secs
0-1km: 29.0secs
115.0bhp 85.8kW 116.6PS
@ 6000rpm
108.0lbft 146.3Nm @ 4000rpm
163.7bhp/ton 160.9bhp/tonne
73.8bhp/L 55.0kW/L 74.8PS/L
47.8ft/sec 14.6m/sec
17.6mph 28.3kmh/1000rpm
26.0mpg 21.6mpgUS 10.9L/100km
Petrol 4-stroke piston
1558cc 95.1cu in
In-line 4 2 Carburettor
Compression ratio: 9.5:1
Bore: 82.6mm 3.2in
Stroke: 72.8mm 2.9in
Valve type/No: Overhead 8
Transmission: Manual
No. of forward speeds: 4
Wheels driven: Rear
Springs F/R: Coil/Coil
Brake system: PA
Brakes F/R: Disc/Disc
Steering: Rack & pinion
Wheelbase: 213.4cm 84.0in
Track F: 119.4cm 47.0in
Track R: 122.9cm 48.4in
Length: 368.8cm 145.2in
Width: 142.2cm 56.0in
Height: 117.3cm 46.2in
Ground clearance: 15.2cm 6.0in
Kerb weight: 714.6kg 1574.0lb
Fuel: 45.5L 10.0gal 12.0galUS

2601 Lotus

Elan SE
1967 UK
119.0mph 191.5kmh
0-50mph 80.5kmh: 6.3secs
0-60mph 96.5kmh: 8.0secs
0-1/4 mile: 16.4secs
115.0bhp 85.8kW 116.6PS
@ 6000rpm
108.0lbft 146.3Nm @ 4000rpm
163.0bhp/ton 160.3bhp/tonne
73.8bhp/L 55.0kW/L 74.8PS/L
47.8ft/sec 14.6m/sec
18.0mph 29.0kmh/1000rpm
Petrol 4-stroke piston
1558cc 95.1cu in
In-line 4 2 Carburettor
Compression ratio: 9.5:1
Bore: 82.6mm 3.2in
Stroke: 72.8mm 2.9in
Valve type/No: Overhead 8
Transmission: Manual
No. of forward speeds: 4
Wheels driven: Rear
Springs F/R: Coil/Coil
Brakes F/R: Disc/Disc
Steering: Rack & pinion
Wheelbase: 213.4cm 84.0in
Track F: 119.6cm 47.1in
Track R: 122.9cm 48.4in
Length: 368.3cm 145.0in
Width: 142.2cm 56.0in
Height: 114.8cm 45.2in
Ground clearance: 15.2cm 6.0in
Kerb weight: 717.3kg 1580.0lb
Fuel: 45.4L 10.0gal 12.0galUS

2602 Lotus

Elan +2
1968 UK
118.0mph 189.9kmh
0-50mph 80.5kmh: 6.8secs
0-60mph 96.5kmh: 8.9secs
0-1/4 mile: 16.6secs
0-1km: 30.6secs
118.0' hp 88.0kW 119.6PS
@ 6000rpm
108.0lbft 146.3Nm @ 4000rpm
136.7bhp/ton 134.4bhp/tonne
75.7bhp/L 56.5kW/L 76.8PS/L
47.8ft/sec 14.6m/sec
18.0mph 29.0kmh/1000rpm
27.1mpg 22.6mpgUS 10.4L/100km
Petrol 4-stroke piston
1558cc 95.1cu in
In-line 4 2 Carburettor
Compression ratio: 9.5:1
Bore: 82.6mm 3.2in
Stroke: 72.8mm 2.9in
Valve type/No: Overhead 8
Transmission: Manual
No. of forward speeds: 4
Wheels driven: Rear
Springs F/R: Coil/Coil
Brake system: PA
Brakes F/R: Disc/Disc
Steering: Rack & pinion
Wheelbase: 243.8cm 96.0in
Track F: 137.2cm 54.0in
Track R: 139.7cm 55.0in
Length: 426.7cm 168.0in
Width: 161.3cm 63.5in
Height: 119.4cm 47.0in
Ground clearance: 15.2cm 6.0in
Kerb weight: 878.0kg 1934.0lb
Fuel: 59.1L 13.0gal 15.6galUS

2603 Lotus

Elan S4 Drophead SE
1969 UK
124.0mph 199.5kmh
0-50mph 80.5kmh: 6.0secs
0-60mph 96.5kmh: 7.8secs
0-1/4 mile: 15.9secs
0-1km: 29.4secs
115.0bhp 85.8kW 116.6PS
@ 6250rpm
108.0lbft 146.3Nm @ 4000rpm
166.7bhp/ton 163.9bhp/tonne
73.8bhp/L 55.0kW/L 74.8PS/L
49.8ft/sec 15.2m/sec
17.4mph 28.0kmh/1000rpm
30.0mpg 25.0mpgUS 9.4L/100km
Petrol 4-stroke piston
1558cc 95.1cu in
In-line 4 2 Carburettor
Compression ratio: 9.5:1
Bore: 82.6mm 3.2in
Stroke: 72.8mm 2.9in
Valve type/No: Overhead 8
Transmission: Manual
No. of forward speeds: 4
Wheels driven: Rear
Springs F/R: Coil/Coil
Brake system: PA
Brakes F/R: Disc/Disc
Steering: Rack & pinion
Wheelbase: 213.4cm 84.0in
Track F: 119.4cm 47.0in
Track R: 122.9cm 48.4in
Length: 368.8cm 145.2in
Width: 142.2cm 56.0in
Height: 116.8cm 46.0in
Ground clearance: 15.2cm 6.0in
Kerb weight: 701.4kg 1545.0lb
Fuel: 42.1L 9.2gal 11.1galUS

2604 Lotus

Elan S4 SE
1969 UK
110.0mph 177.0kmh
0-50mph 80.5kmh: 6.5secs
0-60mph 96.5kmh: 9.4secs
0-1/4 mile: 16.8secs
110.0bhp 82.0kW 111.5PS
@ 6000rpm
104.0lbft 140.9Nm @ 4500rpm
151.2bhp/ton 148.6bhp/tonne
70.6bhp/L 52.6kW/L 71.6PS/L
47.7ft/sec 14.5m/sec
16.9mph 27.2kmh/1000rpm
32.7mpg 27.2mpgUS 8.6L/100km
Petrol 4-stroke piston
1558cc 95.1cu in
In-line 4 2 Carburettor
Compression ratio: 9.5:1
Bore: 82.5mm 3.2in
Stroke: 72.7mm 2.9in
Valve type/No: Overhead 8
Transmission: Manual
No. of forward speeds: 4
Wheels driven: Rear
Springs F/R: Coil/Coil
Brake system: PA
Brakes F/R: Disc/Disc
Steering: Rack & pinion
Wheelbase: 213.4cm 84.0in
Track F: 119.6cm 47.1in
Track R: 122.9cm 48.4in
Length: 368.3cm 145.0in
Width: 142.2cm 56.0in
Height: 114.8cm 45.2in
Ground clearance: 15.2cm 6.0in
Kerb weight: 740.0kg 1630.0lb
Fuel: 45.4L 10.0gal 12.0galUS

2605 Lotus

7 Twin Cam SS
1970 UK
106.0mph 170.6kmh
0-50mph 80.5kmh: 5.1secs
0-60mph 96.5kmh: 7.1secs
0-1/4 mile: 15.5secs
0-1km: 29.8secs
125.0bhp 93.2kW 126.7PS
@ 6200rpm
116.0lbft 157.2Nm @ 4500rpm
222.6bhp/ton 218.9bhp/tonne
80.2bhp/L 59.8kW/L 81.3PS/L
49.4ft/sec 15.0m/sec
18.1mph 29.1kmh/1000rpm
19.2mpg 16.0mpgUS 14.7L/100km
Petrol 4-stroke piston
1558cc 95.1cu in
In-line 4 2 Carburettor
Compression ratio: 9.5:1
Bore: 82.6mm 3.2in
Stroke: 72.8mm 2.9in
Valve type/No: Overhead 8
Transmission: Manual
No. of forward speeds: 4
Wheels driven: Rear
Springs F/R: Coil/Coil
Brakes F/R: Disc/Drum
Steering: Rack & pinion
Wheelbase: 226.1cm 89.0in
Track F: 124.5cm 49.0in
Track R: 132.1cm 52.0in
Length: 337.8cm 133.0in
Width: 154.9cm 61.0in
Height: 94.0cm 37.0in
Ground clearance: 7.6cm 3.0in
Kerb weight: 571.1kg 1258.0lb
Fuel: 36.4L 8.0gal 9.6galUS

2606 Lotus

Europa S2
1970 UK
109.0mph 175.4kmh
0-50mph 80.5kmh: 7.8secs
0-60mph 96.5kmh: 11.2secs
0-1/4 mile: 18.2secs
82.0bhp 61.1kW 83.1PS
@ 6500rpm
80.0lbft 108.4Nm @ 4000rpm
125.8bhp/ton 123.7bhp/tonne
55.8bhp/L 41.6kW/L 56.6PS/L
57.6ft/sec 17.5m/sec
17.6mph 28.3kmh/1000rpm
37.2mpg 31.0mpgUS 7.6L/100km
Petrol 4-stroke piston
1470cc 89.7cu in
In-line 4 1 Carburettor
Compression ratio: 10.3:1
Bore: 76.0mm 3.0in
Stroke: 81.0mm 3.2in
Valve type/No: Overhead 8
Transmission: Manual
No. of forward speeds: 4
Wheels driven: Rear
Springs F/R: Coil/Coil
Brakes F/R: Disc/Drum
Steering: Rack & pinion
Wheelbase: 231.1cm 91.0in
Track F: 134.6cm 53.0in
Track R: 134.6cm 53.0in
Length: 399.3cm 157.2in
Width: 163.8cm 64.5in
Height: 108.0cm 42.5in
Ground clearance: 16.5cm 6.5in
Kerb weight: 662.8kg 1460.0lb
Fuel: 34.1L 7.5gal 9.0galUS

2607 Lotus

Super 7 Twincam
1970 UK
96.0mph 154.5kmh
0-50mph 80.5kmh: 5.6secs
0-60mph 96.5kmh: 7.7secs
0-1/4 mile: 15.7secs
125.0bhp 93.2kW 126.7PS
@ 6200rpm
116.0lbft 157.2Nm @ 4500rpm
231.4bhp/ton 227.5bhp/tonne
80.2bhp/L 59.8kW/L 81.3PS/L
49.4ft/sec 15.0m/sec
17.3mph 27.8kmh/1000rpm
24.0mpg 20.0mpgUS 11.8L/100km
Petrol 4-stroke piston
1558cc 95.1cu in
In-line 4 2 Carburettor
Compression ratio: 9.5:1
Bore: 82.6mm 3.2in
Stroke: 72.8mm 2.9in
Valve type/No: Overhead 8
Transmission: Manual
No. of forward speeds: 4
Wheels driven: Rear
Springs F/R: Coil/Coil
Brakes F/R: Disc/Drum
Steering: Rack & pinion
Wheelbase: 226.1cm 89.0in
Track F: 124.5cm 49.0in
Track R: 132.1cm 52.0in
Length: 337.8cm 133.0in
Width: 154.9cm 61.0in
Height: 94.0cm 37.0in
Ground clearance: 7.6cm 3.0in
Kerb weight: 549.3kg 1210.0lb
Fuel: 36.3L 8.0gal 9.6galUS

2608 Lotus

Elan Sprint
1971 UK
118.0mph 189.9kmh
0-50mph 80.5kmh: 5.2secs
0-60mph 96.5kmh: 7.0secs
0-1/4 mile: 15.0secs
0-1km: 28.1secs
126.0bhp 94.0kW 127.7PS
@ 6500rpm
113.0lbft 153.1Nm @ 5500rpm
178.6bhp/ton 175.6bhp/tonne
80.9bhp/L 60.3kW/L 82.0PS/L
51.8ft/sec 15.8m/sec
17.4mph 28.0kmh/1000rpm
25.5mpg 21.2mpgUS 11.1L/100km
Petrol 4-stroke piston
1558cc 95.1cu in
In-line 4 2 Carburettor
Compression ratio: 10.3:1
Bore: 82.6mm 3.2in
Stroke: 72.8mm 2.9in
Valve type/No: Overhead 8
Transmission: Manual
No. of forward speeds: 4
Wheels driven: Rear
Springs F/R: Coil/Coil
Brake system: PA
Brakes F/R: Disc/Disc
Steering: Rack & pinion
Wheelbase: 213.4cm 84.0in

Track F: 119.4cm 47.0in
Track R: 122.9cm 48.4in
Length: 368.8cm 145.2in
Width: 142.2cm 56.0in
Height: 116.8cm 46.0in
Ground clearance: 15.2cm 6.0in
Kerb weight: 717.3kg 1580.0lb
Fuel: 42.1L 9.2gal 11.1galUS

2609 Lotus
Europa S2
1971 UK
110.0mph 177.0kmh
0-50mph 80.5kmh: 7.4secs
0-60mph 96.5kmh: 10.7secs
0-1/4 mile: 17.3secs
0-1km: 32.6secs
78.0bhp 58.2kW 79.1PS
@ 6000rpm
76.0lbft 103.0Nm @ 4000rpm
119.3bhp/ton 117.3bhp/tonne
53.1bhp/L 39.6kW/L 53.8PS/L
53.2ft/sec 16.2m/sec
18.0mph 29.0kmh/1000rpm
25.1mpg 20.9mpgUS 11.3L/100km
Petrol 4-stroke piston
1470cc 89.7cu in
In-line 4 1 Carburettor
Compression ratio: 10.2:1
Bore: 76.0mm 3.0in
Stroke: 81.0mm 3.2in
Valve type/No: Overhead 8
Transmission: Manual
No. of forward speeds: 4
Wheels driven: Rear
Springs F/R: Coil/Coil
Brakes F/R: Disc/Drum
Steering: Rack & pinion
Wheelbase: 231.1cm 91.0in
Track F: 134.6cm 53.0in
Track R: 134.6cm 53.0in
Length: 398.8cm 157.0in
Width: 163.8cm 64.5in
Height: 109.2cm 43.0in
Ground clearance: 16.5cm 6.5in
Kerb weight: 665.1kg 1465.0lb
Fuel: 31.8L 7.0gal 8.4galUS

2610 Lotus
Plus 2S 130
1971 UK
121.0mph 194.7kmh
0-50mph 80.5kmh: 5.6secs
0-60mph 96.5kmh: 7.4secs
0-1/4 mile: 15.4secs
0-1km: 26.8secs
126.0bhp 94.0kW 127.7PS
@ 6500rpm
113.0lbft 153.1Nm @ 5500rpm
144.4bhp/ton 142.0bhp/tonne
80.9bhp/L 60.3kW/L 82.0PS/L
51.8ft/sec 15.8m/sec
17.8mph 28.6kmh/1000rpm
23.3mpg 19.4mpgUS 12.1L/100km
Petrol 4-stroke piston
1558cc 95.1cu in
In-line 4 2 Carburettor
Compression ratio: 10.3:1
Bore: 86.2mm 3.4in
Stroke: 72.8mm 2.9in
Valve type/No: Overhead 8
Transmission: Manual
No. of forward speeds: 4
Wheels driven: Rear
Springs F/R: Coil/Coil
Brake system: PA
Brakes F/R: Disc/Disc
Steering: Rack & pinion
Wheelbase: 243.8cm 96.0in
Track F: 137.2cm 54.0in
Track R: 139.7cm 55.0in
Length: 426.7cm 168.0in
Width: 161.3cm 63.5in
Height: 119.4cm 47.0in
Ground clearance: 15.2cm 6.0in
Kerb weight: 887.1kg 1954.0lb
Fuel: 59.1L 13.0gal 15.6galUS

2611 Lotus
Elan Plus 2S 130
1972 UK
110.0mph 177.0kmh
0-50mph 80.5kmh: 7.5secs
0-60mph 96.5kmh: 9.8secs
0-1/4 mile: 17.6secs
113.0bhp 84.3kW 114.6PS
@ 6500rpm
108.0lbft 146.3Nm @ 4000rpm
128.2bhp/ton 126.0bhp/tonne
72.5bhp/L 54.1kW/L 73.5PS/L
51.8ft/sec 15.8m/sec
19.8mph 31.9kmh/1000rpm
25.0mpg 20.8mpgUS 11.3L/100km
Petrol 4-stroke piston
1558cc 95.1cu in
In-line 4 2 Carburettor
Compression ratio: 9.5:1
Bore: 82.5mm 3.2in
Stroke: 72.8mm 2.9in
Valve type/No: Overhead 8
Transmission: Manual
No. of forward speeds: 4
Wheels driven: Rear
Springs F/R: Coil/Coil
Brakes F/R: Disc/Disc
Steering: Rack & pinion
Wheelbase: 243.8cm 96.0in
Track F: 137.2cm 54.0in
Track R: 139.7cm 55.0in
Length: 426.7cm 168.0in
Width: 161.3cm 63.5in
Height: 119.4cm 47.0in
Ground clearance: 15.2cm 6.0in
Kerb weight: 896.6kg 1975.0lb
Fuel: 59.0L 13.0gal 15.6galUS

2612 Lotus
Elan Sprint
1972 UK
112.0mph 180.2kmh
0-50mph 80.5kmh: 5.9secs
0-60mph 96.5kmh: 8.4secs
0-1/4 mile: 16.0secs
113.0bhp 84.3kW 114.6PS
@ 6500rpm
108.0lbft 146.3Nm @ 4000rpm
154.3bhp/ton 151.8bhp/tonne
72.5bhp/L 54.1kW/L 73.5PS/L
51.8ft/sec 15.8m/sec
17.4mph 28.0kmh/1000rpm
26.4mpg 22.0mpgUS 10.7L/100km
Petrol 4-stroke piston
1558cc 95.1cu in
In-line 4 2 Carburettor
Compression ratio: 9.5:1
Bore: 82.5mm 3.2in
Stroke: 72.8mm 2.9in
Valve type/No: Overhead 8
Transmission: Manual
No. of forward speeds: 4
Wheels driven: Rear
Springs F/R: Coil/Coil
Brakes F/R: Disc/Disc
Steering: Rack & pinion
Wheelbase: 213.4cm 84.0in
Track F: 119.6cm 47.1in
Track R: 122.9cm 48.4in
Length: 368.3cm 145.0in
Width: 142.2cm 56.0in
Height: 114.8cm 45.2in
Ground clearance: 15.2cm 6.0in
Kerb weight: 744.6kg 1640.0lb
Fuel: 45.4L 10.0gal 12.0galUS

2613 Lotus
Europa
1972 UK
114.0mph 183.4kmh
0-50mph 80.5kmh: 6.0secs
0-60mph 96.5kmh: 8.3secs
0-1/4 mile: 15.5secs
113.0bhp 84.3kW 114.6PS
@ 6500rpm
104.0lbft 140.9Nm @ 5000rpm
162.8bhp/ton 160.1bhp/tonne
72.5bhp/L 54.1kW/L 73.5PS/L
51.8ft/sec 15.8m/sec
27.3mpg 22.7mpgUS 10.4L/100km
Petrol 4-stroke piston
1558cc 95.1cu in
In-line 4 2 Carburettor
Compression ratio: 9.5:1
Bore: 82.5mm 3.2in
Stroke: 72.8mm 2.9in
Valve type/No: Overhead 8
Transmission: Manual
No. of forward speeds: 4
Wheels driven: Rear
Springs F/R: Coil/Coil
Brake system: PA
Brakes F/R: Disc/Drum
Steering: Rack & pinion
Wheelbase: 238.8cm 94.0in
Length: 399.5cm 157.3in
Width: 163.8cm 64.5in
Height: 108.0cm 42.5in
Ground clearance: 10.9cm 4.3in
Kerb weight: 706.0kg 1555.0lb
Fuel: 56.8L 12.5gal 15.0galUS

2614 Lotus
Europa Twin Cam
1972 UK
120.0mph 193.1kmh
0-50mph 80.5kmh: 5.6secs
0-60mph 96.5kmh: 7.0secs
0-1/4 mile: 15.6secs
0-1km: 29.5secs
105.0bhp 78.3kW 106.5PS
@ 6000rpm
103.0lbft 139.6Nm @ 4500rpm
148.1bhp/ton 145.6bhp/tonne
67.4bhp/L 50.3kW/L 68.3PS/L
47.7ft/sec 14.5m/sec
18.2mph 29.3kmh/1000rpm
23.3mpg 19.4mpgUS 12.1L/100km
Petrol 4-stroke piston
1558cc 95.1cu in
In-line 4 2 Carburettor
Compression ratio: 9.5:1
Bore: 82.5mm 3.2in
Stroke: 72.7mm 2.9in
Valve type/No: Overhead 8
Transmission: Manual
No. of forward speeds: 4
Wheels driven: Rear
Springs F/R: Coil/Coil
Brake system: PA
Brakes F/R: Disc/Drum
Steering: Rack & pinion
Wheelbase: 233.7cm 92.0in
Track F: 135.9cm 53.5in
Track R: 134.6cm 53.0in
Length: 400.1cm 157.5in
Width: 163.8cm 64.5in
Height: 128.3cm 50.5in
Ground clearance: 15.2cm 6.0in
Kerb weight: 720.9kg 1588.0lb
Fuel: 56.9L 12.5gal 15.0galUS

2615 Lotus
Plus 2S 130/5
1972 UK
121.0mph 194.7kmh
0-50mph 80.5kmh: 5.7secs
0-60mph 96.5kmh: 7.5secs
0-1/4 mile: 16.0secs
0-1km: 29.3secs
126.0bhp 94.0kW 127.7PS
@ 6500rpm
113.0lbft 153.1Nm @ 5500rpm
144.0bhp/ton 141.6bhp/tonne
80.9bhp/L 60.3kW/L 82.0PS/L
51.8ft/sec 15.8m/sec
22.3mph 35.9kmh/1000rpm
25.6mpg 21.3mpgUS 11.0L/100km
Petrol 4-stroke piston
1558cc 95.1cu in
In-line 4 2 Carburettor
Compression ratio: 10.3:1
Bore: 86.2mm 3.4in
Stroke: 72.8mm 2.9in
Valve type/No: Overhead 8
Transmission: Manual
No. of forward speeds: 5
Wheels driven: Rear
Springs F/R: Coil/Coil
Brake system: PA
Brakes F/R: Disc/Disc
Steering: Rack & pinion
Wheelbase: 243.8cm 96.0in
Track F: 137.2cm 54.0in
Track R: 139.7cm 55.0in
Length: 426.7cm 168.0in
Width: 161.3cm 63.5in
Height: 119.4cm 47.0in
Ground clearance: 15.2cm 6.0in
Kerb weight: 889.8kg 1960.0lb
Fuel: 59.1L 13.0gal 15.6galUS

2616 Lotus
Europa Special 5-speed
1973 UK
117.0mph 188.3kmh
0-50mph 80.5kmh: 7.2secs
0-60mph 96.5kmh: 9.6secs
0-1/4 mile: 17.0secs
113.0bhp 84.3kW 114.6PS
@ 6500rpm
104.0lbft 140.9Nm @ 5000rpm
152.0bhp/ton 149.5bhp/tonne
72.5bhp/L 54.1kW/L 73.5PS/L
51.8ft/sec 15.8m/sec
20.9mph 33.6kmh/1000rpm
33.0mpg 27.5mpgUS 8.6L/100km
Petrol 4-stroke piston
1558cc 95.1cu in
In-line 4 2 Carburettor
Compression ratio: 9.5:1
Bore: 82.5mm 3.2in
Stroke: 72.8mm 2.9in
Valve type/No: Overhead 8
Transmission: Manual
No. of forward speeds: 5
Wheels driven: Rear
Springs F/R: Coil/Coil
Brake system: PA
Brakes F/R: /Drum
Steering: Rack & pinion
Wheelbase: 233.7cm 92.0in
Track F: 138.4cm 54.5in
Track R: 137.2cm 54.0in
Length: 400.1cm 157.5in
Width: 163.8cm 64.5in
Height: 108.0cm 42.5in
Ground clearance: 15.2cm 6.0in
Kerb weight: 755.9kg 1665.0lb
Fuel: 56.8L 12.5gal 15.0galUS

2617 Lotus
Elite
1975 UK
119.0mph 191.5kmh
0-50mph 80.5kmh: 8.1secs
0-60mph 96.5kmh: 11.1secs
0-1/4 mile: 18.4secs
140.0bhp 104.4kW 141.9PS
@ 6600rpm
130.0lbft 176.2Nm @ 5000rpm
121.3bhp/ton 119.3bhp/tonne
71.0bhp/L 52.9kW/L 71.9PS/L
49.9ft/sec 15.2m/sec
23.3mph 37.5kmh/1000rpm
26.4mpg 22.0mpgUS 10.7L/100km
Petrol 4-stroke piston
1973cc 120.4cu in
In-line 4 2 Carburettor
Compression ratio: 8.4:1
Bore: 95.2mm 3.8in
Stroke: 69.2mm 2.7in
Valve type/No: Overhead 16
Transmission: Manual
No. of forward speeds: 5
Wheels driven: Rear
Springs F/R: Coil/Coil
Brake system: PA
Brakes F/R: Disc/Drum
Steering: Rack & pinion
Wheelbase: 248.4cm 97.8in
Track F: 148.6cm 58.5in
Track R: 149.9cm 59.0in
Length: 455.9cm 179.5in
Width: 180.3cm 71.0in
Height: 120.7cm 47.5in
Ground clearance: 12.2cm 4.8in
Kerb weight: 1173.6kg 2585.0lb
Fuel: 66.2L 14.6gal 17.5galUS

2618 Lotus
Elite 503
1975 UK
126.0mph 202.7kmh
0-50mph 80.5kmh: 5.9secs
0-60mph 96.5kmh: 7.8secs
0-1/4 mile: 16.4secs
0-1km: 30.3secs
155.0bhp 115.6kW 157.1PS
@ 6500rpm
135.0lbft 182.9Nm @ 5000rpm
136.0bhp/ton 133.8bhp/tonne
78.6bhp/L 58.6kW/L 79.6PS/L
49.3ft/sec 15.0m/sec
20.8mph 33.5kmh/1000rpm
20.9mpg 17.4mpgUS 13.5L/100km
Petrol 4-stroke piston
1973cc 120.4cu in
In-line 4 2 Carburettor
Compression ratio: 9.5:1
Bore: 95.3mm 3.8in
Stroke: 69.2mm 2.7in
Valve type/No: Overhead 16
Transmission: Manual
No. of forward speeds: 5
Wheels driven: Rear
Springs F/R: Coil/Coil
Brake system: PA
Brakes F/R: Disc/Disc

Steering: Rack & pinion
Wheelbase: 248.4cm 97.8in
Track F: 148.6cm 58.5in
Track R: 149.9cm 59.0in
Length: 445.8cm 175.5in
Width: 181.6cm 71.5in
Height: 120.7cm 47.5in
Ground clearance: 11.7cm 4.6in
Kerb weight: 1158.6kg 2552.0lb
Fuel: 67.1L 14.7gal 17.7galUS

2619 Lotus

Eclat 523
1977 UK
129.0mph 207.6kmh
0-50mph 80.5kmh: 5.9secs
0-60mph 96.5kmh: 7.9secs
0-1/4 mile: 16.2secs
0-1km: 29.8secs
160.0bhp 119.3kW 162.2PS
@ 6200rpm
140.0lbft 189.7Nm @ 4900rpm
146.9bhp/ton 144.5bhp/tonne
81.1bhp/L 60.5kW/L 82.2PS/L
47.0ft/sec 14.3m/sec
22.9mph 36.8kmh/1000rpm
20.7mpg 17.2mpgUS 13.6L/100km
Petrol 4-stroke piston
1973cc 120.4cu in
In-line 4 2 Carburettor
Compression ratio: 9.5:1
Bore: 95.3mm 3.8in
Stroke: 69.2mm 2.7in
Valve type/No: Overhead 8
Transmission: Manual
No. of forward speeds: 5
Wheels driven: Rear
Springs F/R: Coil/Coil
Brake system: PA
Brakes F/R: Disc/Disc
Steering: Rack & pinion PA
Wheelbase: 248.4cm 97.8in
Track F: 148.6cm 58.5in
Track R: 149.9cm 59.0in
Length: 445.8cm 175.5in
Width: 181.6cm 71.5in
Height: 120.7cm 47.5in
Ground clearance: 11.7cm 4.6in
Kerb weight: 1107.3kg 2439.0lb
Fuel: 67.1L 14.7gal 17.7galUS

2620 Lotus

Esprit
1977 UK
124.0mph 199.5kmh
0-50mph 80.5kmh: 6.3secs
0-60mph 96.5kmh: 8.4secs
0-1/4 mile: 16.3secs
0-1km: 30.2secs
160.0bhp 119.3kW 162.2PS
@ 6200rpm
140.0lbft 189.7Nm @ 4900rpm
157.5bhp/ton 154.9bhp/tonne
81.1bhp/L 60.5kW/L 82.2PS/L
46.8ft/sec 14.3m/sec
21.8mph 35.1kmh/1000rpm
23.3mpg 19.4mpgUS 12.1L/100km
Petrol 4-stroke piston
1973cc 120.4cu in
In-line 4 2 Carburettor
Compression ratio: 9.5:1
Bore: 95.3mm 3.8in
Stroke: 69.2mm 2.7in
Valve type/No: Overhead 8
Transmission: Manual
No. of forward speeds: 5
Wheels driven: Rear
Springs F/R: Coil/Coil
Brake system: PA
Brakes F/R: Disc/Disc
Steering: Rack & pinion
Wheelbase: 243.8cm 96.0in
Track F: 151.1cm 59.5in
Track R: 151.1cm 59.5in
Length: 419.1cm 165.0in
Width: 185.4cm 73.0in
Height: 111.0cm 43.7in
Ground clearance: 14.0cm 5.5in
Kerb weight: 1032.8kg 2275.0lb
Fuel: 68.2L 15.0gal 18.0galUS

2621 Lotus

Esprit 16v
1977 UK
120.0mph 193.1kmh
0-50mph 80.5kmh: 6.7secs
0-60mph 96.5kmh: 9.2secs
0-1/4 mile: 17.0secs
140.0bhp 104.4kW 141.9PS
@ 6500rpm
130.0lbft 176.2Nm @ 5000rpm
133.4bhp/ton 131.2bhp/tonne
71.0bhp/L 52.9kW/L 71.9PS/L
49.1ft/sec 15.0m/sec
21.4mph 34.4kmh/1000rpm
33.0mpg 27.5mpgUS 8.6L/100km
Petrol 4-stroke piston
1973cc 120.4cu in
In-line 4 2 Carburettor
Compression ratio: 8.4:1
Bore: 95.2mm 3.8in
Stroke: 69.2mm 2.7in
Valve type/No: Overhead 16
Transmission: Manual
No. of forward speeds: 5
Wheels driven: Rear
Springs F/R: Coil/Coil
Brake system: PA
Brakes F/R: Disc/Disc
Steering: Rack & pinion
Wheelbase: 243.8cm 96.0in
Track F: 151.1cm 59.5in
Track R: 151.1cm 59.5in
Length: 426.0cm 167.7in
Width: 185.9cm 73.2in
Height: 111.3cm 43.8in
Ground clearance: 15.2cm 6.0in
Kerb weight: 1066.9kg 2350.0lb
Fuel: 67.0L 14.7gal 17.7galUS

2622 Lotus

Sprint
1977 UK
120.0mph 193.1kmh
0-50mph 80.5kmh: 7.5secs
0-60mph 96.5kmh: 9.7secs
0-1/4 mile: 17.7secs
140.0bhp 104.4kW 141.9PS
@ 6500rpm
130.0lbft 176.2Nm @ 5000rpm
131.2bhp/ton 129.0bhp/tonne
71.0bhp/L 52.9kW/L 71.9PS/L
44.8ft/sec 13.6m/sec
18.2mph 29.3kmh/1000rpm
27.6mpg 23.0mpgUS 10.2L/100km
Petrol 4-stroke piston
1973cc 120.4cu in
In-line 4
Compression ratio: 8.4:1
Bore: 95.2mm 3.8in
Stroke: 62.9mm 2.5in
Valve type/No: Overhead 8
Transmission: Manual
No. of forward speeds: 4
Wheels driven: Rear
Springs F/R: Coil/Coil
Brake system: PA
Brakes F/R: Disc/Drum
Steering: Rack & pinion
Wheelbase: 248.4cm 97.8in
Track F: 148.6cm 58.5in
Track R: 149.9cm 59.0in
Length: 445.8cm 175.5in
Width: 181.6cm 71.5in
Height: 120.1cm 47.3in
Kerb weight: 1085.1kg 2390.0lb
Fuel: 56.0L 12.3gal 14.8galUS

2623 Lotus

Elite V8
1978 UK
148.0mph 238.1kmh
0-50mph 80.5kmh: 5.3secs
0-60mph 96.5kmh: 7.7secs
0-1/4 mile: 15.7secs
220.0bhp 164.0kW 223.0PS
@ 5700rpm
240.0lbft 325.2Nm @ 3800rpm
190.6bhp/ton 187.5bhp/tonne
61.6bhp/L 46.0kW/L 62.5PS/L
44.3ft/sec 13.5m/sec
23.3mph 37.5kmh/1000rpm
18.0mpg 15.0mpgUS 15.7L/100km
Petrol 4-stroke piston
3569cc 217.7cu in
Vee 8
Compression ratio: 8.5:1
Bore: 89.4mm 3.5in
Stroke: 71.1mm 2.8in
Valve type/No: Overhead 16
Transmission: Manual
No. of forward speeds: 5
Wheels driven: Rear
Springs F/R: Coil/Coil
Brake system: PA
Brakes F/R: Disc/Drum
Steering: Rack & pinion
Wheelbase: 248.4cm 97.8in
Track F: 148.6cm 58.5in
Track R: 149.9cm 59.0in
Length: 455.9cm 179.5in
Width: 180.3cm 71.0in
Height: 120.7cm 47.5in
Kerb weight: 1173.6kg 2585.0lb
Fuel: 66.2L 14.6gal 17.5galUS

2624 Lotus

Elite
1979 UK
125.0mph 201.1kmh
0-50mph 80.5kmh: 7.5secs
0-60mph 96.5kmh: 9.7secs
0-1/4 mile: 17.7secs
140.0bhp 104.4kW 141.9PS
@ 6600rpm
130.0lbft 176.2Nm @ 5000rpm
121.3bhp/ton 119.3bhp/tonne
71.0bhp/L 52.9kW/L 71.9PS/L
49.9ft/sec 15.2m/sec
23.3mph 37.5kmh/1000rpm
27.6mpg 23.0mpgUS 10.2L/100km
Petrol 4-stroke piston
1973cc 120.4cu in
In-line 4 2 Carburettor
Compression ratio: 8.4:1
Bore: 95.2mm 3.8in
Stroke: 69.2mm 2.7in
Valve type/No: Overhead 8
Transmission: Manual
No. of forward speeds: 5
Wheels driven: Rear
Springs F/R: Coil/Coil
Brake system: PA
Brakes F/R: Disc/Drum
Steering: Rack & pinion PA
Wheelbase: 248.4cm 97.8in
Track F: 148.6cm 58.5in
Track R: 149.9cm 59.0in
Length: 455.9cm 179.5in
Width: 180.3cm 71.0in
Height: 120.7cm 47.5in
Ground clearance: 12.2cm 4.8in
Kerb weight: 1173.6kg 2585.0lb
Fuel: 66.2L 14.6gal 17.5galUS

2625 Lotus

Esprit S2
1979 UK
135.0mph 217.2kmh
0-50mph 80.5kmh: 5.9secs
0-60mph 96.5kmh: 8.0secs
0-1/4 mile: 16.0secs
0-1km: 29.4secs
160.0bhp 119.3kW 162.2PS
@ 6500rpm
140.0lbft 189.7Nm @ 5000rpm
153.6bhp/ton 151.0bhp/tonne
81.1bhp/L 60.5kW/L 82.2PS/L
49.1ft/sec 15.0m/sec
21.8mph 35.1kmh/1000rpm
19.4mpg 16.2mpgUS 14.6L/100km
Petrol 4-stroke piston
1973cc 120.4cu in
In-line 4 2 Carburettor
Compression ratio: 9.5:1
Bore: 95.2mm 3.8in
Stroke: 69.2mm 2.7in
Valve type/No: Overhead 8
Transmission: Manual
No. of forward speeds: 5
Wheels driven: Rear
Springs F/R: Coil/Coil
Brake system: PA
Brakes F/R: Disc/Disc
Steering: Rack & pinion
Wheelbase: 243.8cm 96.0in
Track F: 151.1cm 59.5in
Track R: 151.1cm 59.5in
Length: 419.1cm 165.0in
Width: 185.4cm 73.0in
Height: 111.0cm 43.7in
Ground clearance: 14.0cm 5.5in
Kerb weight: 1059.6kg 2334.0lb
Fuel: 67.1L 14.7gal 17.7galUS

2626 Lotus

Eclat
1980 UK
125.0mph 201.1kmh
0-60mph 96.5kmh: 9.7secs
0-1/4 mile: 17.7secs
120.0bhp 89.5kW 121.7PS
@ 6200rpm
118.0lbft 159.9Nm @ 4500rpm
107.1bhp/ton 105.3bhp/tonne
60.8bhp/L 45.3kW/L 61.7PS/L
46.8ft/sec 14.3m/sec
23.3mph 37.5kmh/1000rpm
27.6mpg 23.0mpgUS 10.2L/100km
Petrol 4-stroke piston
1973cc 120.4cu in
In-line 4 2 Carburettor
Compression ratio: 8.4:1
Bore: 95.2mm 3.8in
Stroke: 69.2mm 2.7in
Valve type/No: Overhead 16
Transmission: Manual
No. of forward speeds: 5
Wheels driven: Rear
Springs F/R: Coil/Coil
Brake system: PA
Brakes F/R: Disc/Drum
Steering: Rack & pinion PA
Wheelbase: 248.4cm 97.8in
Track F: 148.6cm 58.5in
Track R: 149.9cm 59.0in
Length: 456.4cm 179.7in
Width: 181.6cm 71.5in
Height: 120.7cm 47.5in
Ground clearance: 12.2cm 4.8in
Kerb weight: 1139.5kg 2510.0lb
Fuel: 67.0L 14.7gal 17.7galUS

2627 Lotus

Esprit Turbo
1981 UK
149.0mph 239.7kmh
0-50mph 80.5kmh: 4.7secs
0-60mph 96.5kmh: 6.1secs
0-1/4 mile: 14.6secs
0-1km: 26.7secs
210.0bhp 156.6kW 212.9PS
@ 6000rpm
200.0lbft 271.0Nm @ 4000rpm
177.3bhp/ton 174.3bhp/tonne
96.6bhp/L 72.0kW/L 97.9PS/L
50.0ft/sec 15.2m/sec
22.7mph 36.5kmh/1000rpm
18.0mpg 15.0mpgUS 15.7L/100km
Petrol 4-stroke piston
2174cc 132.6cu in turbocharged
In-line 4 2 Carburettor
Compression ratio: 7.5:1
Bore: 95.3mm 3.8in
Stroke: 76.2mm 3.0in
Valve type/No: Overhead 16
Transmission: Manual
No. of forward speeds: 5
Wheels driven: Rear
Springs F/R: Coil/Coil
Brake system: PA
Brakes F/R: Disc/Disc
Steering: Rack & pinion
Wheelbase: 243.8cm 96.0in
Track F: 153.7cm 60.5in
Track R: 155.4cm 61.2in
Length: 419.1cm 165.0in
Width: 185.4cm 73.0in
Height: 111.8cm 44.0in
Ground clearance: 12.7cm 5.0in
Kerb weight: 1204.5kg 2653.0lb
Fuel: 86.4L 19.0gal 22.8galUS

2628 Lotus

Eclat Excel
1983 UK
131.0mph 210.8kmh
0-50mph 80.5kmh: 5.5secs
0-60mph 96.5kmh: 7.1secs
0-1/4 mile: 15.4secs
0-1km: 28.5secs
160.0bhp 119.3kW 162.2PS
@ 6500rpm
160.0lbft 216.8Nm @ 5000rpm
144.6bhp/ton 142.2bhp/tonne
73.6bhp/L 54.9kW/L 74.6PS/L
54.2ft/sec 16.5m/sec
21.2mph 34.1kmh/1000rpm
19.5mpg 16.2mpgUS 14.5L/100km
Petrol 4-stroke piston
2174cc 132.6cu in
In-line 4 2 Carburettor
Compression ratio: 9.4:1
Bore: 95.3mm 3.8in
Stroke: 76.2mm 3.0in
Valve type/No: Overhead 16

Transmission: Manual
No. of forward speeds: 5
Wheels driven: Rear
Springs F/R: Coil/Coil
Brake system: PA
Brakes F/R: Disc/Disc
Steering: Rack & pinion
Wheelbase: 248.4cm 97.8in
Track F: 146.1cm 57.5in
Track R: 146.1cm 57.5in
Length: 437.6cm 172.3in
Width: 181.6cm 71.5in
Height: 120.4cm 47.4in
Ground clearance: 12.2cm 4.8in
Kerb weight: 1125.0kg 2478.0lb
Fuel: 66.9L 14.7gal 17.7galUS

2629 Lotus
Esprit Turbo
1983 UK
148.0mph 238.1kmh
0-60mph 96.5kmh: 6.6secs
0-1/4 mile: 15.3secs
205.0bhp 152.9kW 207.8PS
@ 6000rpm
194.0lbft 262.9Nm @ 5000rpm
169.4bhp/ton 166.6bhp/tonne
94.3bhp/L 70.3kW/L 95.6PS/L
50.0ft/sec 15.2m/sec
22.6mph 36.4kmh/1000rpm
21.0mpg 17.5mpgUS 13.4L/100km
Petrol 4-stroke piston
2174cc 132.6cu in turbocharged
In-line 4 2 Carburettor
Compression ratio: 7.5:1
Bore: 95.3mm 3.8in
Stroke: 76.2mm 3.0in
Valve type/No: Overhead 16
Transmission: Manual
No. of forward speeds: 5
Wheels driven: Rear
Springs F/R: Coil/Coil
Brake system: PA
Brakes F/R: Disc/Disc
Steering: Rack & pinion
Wheelbase: 243.8cm 96.0in
Track F: 153.7cm 60.5in
Track R: 155.4cm 61.2in
Length: 429.3cm 169.0in
Width: 185.4cm 73.0in
Height: 113.0cm 44.5in
Ground clearance: 14.7cm 5.8in
Kerb weight: 1230.3kg 2710.0lb
Fuel: 85.9L 18.9gal 22.7galUS

2630 Lotus
Esprit Turbo
1986 UK
152.0mph 244.6kmh
0-50mph 80.5kmh: 4.4secs
0-60mph 96.5kmh: 5.6secs
0-1/4 mile: 14.3secs
215.0bhp 160.3kW 218.0PS
@ 6250rpm
194.0lbft 262.9Nm @ 5000rpm
175.1bhp/ton 172.2bhp/tonne
98.9bhp/L 73.7kW/L 100.3PS/L
52.1ft/sec 15.9m/sec
18.6mpg 15.5mpgUS 15.2L/100km
Petrol 4-stroke piston
2174cc 132.6cu in turbocharged
In-line 4 fuel injection
Compression ratio: 8.5:1
Bore: 95.3mm 3.8in
Stroke: 76.2mm 3.0in
Valve type/No: Overhead 16
Transmission: Manual
No. of forward speeds: 5
Wheels driven: Rear
Springs F/R: Coil/Coil
Brake system: PA
Brakes F/R: Disc/Disc
Steering: Rack & pinion
Wheelbase: 243.8cm 96.0in
Track F: 153.7cm 60.5in
Track R: 155.4cm 61.2in
Length: 429.3cm 169.0in
Width: 185.4cm 73.0in
Height: 113.0cm 44.5in
Ground clearance: 14.7cm 5.8in
Kerb weight: 1248.5kg 2750.0lb
Fuel: 85.9L 18.9gal 22.7galUS

2631 Lotus
Excel SE
1986 UK
134.0mph 215.6kmh
0-50mph 80.5kmh: 5.2secs
0-60mph 96.5kmh: 6.8secs
0-1/4 mile: 15.3secs
0-1km: 28.1secs
180.0bhp 134.2kW 182.5PS
@ 6500rpm
165.0lbft 223.6Nm @ 5000rpm
156.2bhp/ton 153.6bhp/tonne
82.8bhp/L 61.7kW/L 83.9PS/L
54.2ft/sec 16.5m/sec
21.0mph 33.8kmh/1000rpm
19.6mpg 16.3mpgUS 14.4L/100km
Petrol 4-stroke piston
2174cc 132.6cu in
In-line 4 2 Carburettor
Compression ratio: 10.9:1
Bore: 95.3mm 3.8in
Stroke: 76.2mm 3.0in
Valve type/No: Overhead 16
Transmission: Manual
No. of forward speeds: 5
Wheels driven: Rear
Springs F/R: Coil/Coil
Brake system: PA
Brakes F/R: Disc/Disc
Steering: Rack & pinion PA
Wheelbase: 248.2cm 97.7in
Track F: 147.8cm 58.2in
Track R: 147.8cm 58.2in
Length: 439.7cm 173.1in
Width: 181.6cm 71.5in
Height: 120.7cm 47.5in
Ground clearance: 12.2cm 4.8in
Kerb weight: 1171.8kg 2581.0lb
Fuel: 66.9L 14.7gal 17.7galUS

2632 Lotus
Elan Autocrosser
1987 UK
115.0mph 185.0kmh
0-50mph 80.5kmh: 4.2secs
0-60mph 96.5kmh: 5.3secs
0-1/4 mile: 13.9secs
163.0bhp 121.5kW 165.3PS
@ 8000rpm
118.0lbft 159.9Nm @ 7000rpm
259.9bhp/ton 255.5bhp/tonne
102.3bhp/L 76.2kW/L 103.7PS/L
63.8ft/sec 19.4m/sec
7.2mpg 6.0mpgUS 39.2L/100km
Petrol 4-stroke piston
1594cc 97.2cu in
In-line 4 2 Carburettor
Compression ratio: 14.0:1
Bore: 83.5mm 3.3in
Stroke: 72.8mm 2.9in
Valve type/No: Overhead 16
Transmission: Manual
No. of forward speeds: 4
Wheels driven: Rear
Springs F/R: Coil/Coil
Brakes F/R: Disc/Disc
Steering: Rack & pinion
Wheelbase: 213.4cm 84.0in
Track F: 128.3cm 50.5in
Track R: 132.1cm 52.0in
Length: 368.3cm 145.0in
Width: 161.3cm 63.5in
Height: 109.2cm 43.0in
Ground clearance: 6.4cm 2.5in
Kerb weight: 637.9kg 1405.0lb
Fuel: 38.6L 8.5gal 10.2galUS

2633 Lotus
Esprit Turbo HC
1987 UK
146.0mph 234.9kmh
0-50mph 80.5kmh: 4.4secs
0-60mph 96.5kmh: 5.6secs
0-1/4 mile: 14.4secs
0-1km: 26.2secs
215.0bhp 160.3kW 218.0PS
@ 6000rpm
220.0lbft 298.1Nm @ 4250rpm
190.6bhp/ton 187.4bhp/tonne
98.9bhp/L 73.7kW/L 100.3PS/L
50.0ft/sec 15.2m/sec
22.5mph 36.2kmh/1000rpm
20.9mpg 17.4mpgUS 13.5L/100km
Petrol 4-stroke piston
2174cc 133.0cu in turbocharged
In-line 4 1 Carburettor
Compression ratio: 8.0:1
Bore: 95.3mm 3.8in
Stroke: 76.2mm 3.0in
Valve type/No: Overhead 16
Transmission: Manual
No. of forward speeds: 5
Wheels driven: Rear
Springs F/R: Coil/Coil
Brake system: PA
Brakes F/R: Disc/Disc
Steering: Rack & pinion
Wheelbase: 243.8cm 96.0in
Track F: 151.1cm 59.5in
Track R: 151.1cm 59.5in
Length: 422.4cm 166.3in
Width: 185.4cm 73.0in
Height: 101.7cm 40.0in
Kerb weight: 1147.0kg 2526.4lb
Fuel: 86.0L 18.9gal 22.7galUS

2634 Lotus
Excel SA
1987 UK
128.0mph 206.0kmh
0-50mph 80.5kmh: 6.2secs
0-60mph 96.5kmh: 8.2secs
0-1/4 mile: 16.9secs
0-1km: 31.0secs
180.0bhp 134.2kW 182.5PS
@ 6500rpm
165.0lbft 223.6Nm @ 5000rpm
155.5bhp/ton 152.9bhp/tonne
82.8bhp/L 61.7kW/L 83.9PS/L
54.2ft/sec 16.5m/sec
25.0mph 40.2kmh/1000rpm
22.2mpg 18.5mpgUS 12.7L/100km
Petrol 4-stroke piston
2174cc 133.0cu in
In-line 4 2 Carburettor
Compression ratio: 10.9:1
Bore: 95.3mm 3.8in
Stroke: 76.2mm 3.0in
Valve type/No: Overhead 16
Transmission: Automatic
No. of forward speeds: 4
Wheels driven: Rear
Springs F/R: Coil/Coil
Brake system: PA
Brakes F/R: Disc/Disc
Steering: Rack & pinion PA
Wheelbase: 248.3cm 97.8in
Track F: 147.9cm 58.2in
Track R: 147.9cm 58.2in
Length: 439.8cm 173.1in
Width: 181.6cm 71.5in
Height: 120.7cm 47.5in
Ground clearance: 12.2cm 4.8in
Kerb weight: 1177.0kg 2592.5lb
Fuel: 66.9L 14.7gal 17.7galUS

2635 Lotus
Esprit Turbo
1988 UK
153.0mph 246.2kmh
0-50mph 80.5kmh: 4.3secs
0-60mph 96.5kmh: 5.4secs
0-1/4 mile: 13.7secs
0-1km: 25.0secs
215.0bhp 160.3kW 218.0PS
@ 6000rpm
220.0lbft 298.1Nm @ 4250rpm
157.8bhp/ton 155.2bhp/tonne
98.9bhp/L 73.7kW/L 100.3PS/L
50.0ft/sec 15.2m/sec
23.7mph 38.1kmh/1000rpm
20.4mpg 17.0mpgUS 13.8L/100km
Petrol 4-stroke piston
2174cc 132.6cu in turbocharged
In-line 4 2 Carburettor
Compression ratio: 8.0:1
Bore: 95.3mm 3.8in
Stroke: 76.2mm 3.0in
Valve type/No: Overhead 16
Transmission: Manual
No. of forward speeds: 5
Wheels driven: Rear
Springs F/R: Coil/Coil
Brake system: PA
Brakes F/R: Disc/Disc
Steering: Rack & pinion
Wheelbase: 243.8cm 96.0in
Track F: 152.4cm 60.0in
Track R: 155.4cm 61.2in
Length: 433.1cm 170.5in
Width: 185.9cm 73.2in
Height: 115.1cm 45.3in
Ground clearance: 14.7cm 5.8in
Kerb weight: 1385.6kg 3052.0lb
Fuel: 78.7L 17.3gal 20.8galUS

2636 Lotus
Esprit Turbo
1989 UK
156.0mph 251.0kmh
0-60mph 96.5kmh: 5.2secs
0-1/4 mile: 13.6secs
228.0bhp 170.0kW 231.2PS
@ 6500rpm
218.0lbft 295.4Nm @ 4000rpm
179.5bhp/ton 176.5bhp/tonne
104.9bhp/L 78.2kW/L 106.3PS/L
54.2ft/sec 16.5m/sec
20.4mpg 17.0mpgUS 13.8L/100km
Petrol 4-stroke piston
2174cc 132.6cu in turbocharged
In-line 4 fuel injection
Compression ratio: 8.0:1
Bore: 95.3mm 3.8in
Stroke: 76.2mm 3.0in
Valve type/No: Overhead 16
Transmission: Manual
No. of forward speeds: 5
Wheels driven: Rear
Springs F/R: Coil/Coil
Brake system: PA
Brakes F/R: Disc/Disc
Steering: Rack & pinion PA
Wheelbase: 243.8cm 96.0in
Track F: 152.4cm 60.0in
Track R: 155.4cm 61.2in
Length: 433.1cm 170.5in
Width: 185.9cm 73.2in
Height: 115.1cm 45.3in
Kerb weight: 1291.6kg 2845.0lb
Fuel: 70.0L 15.4gal 18.5galUS

2637 Lotus
Esprit Turbo SE
1989 UK
161.0mph 259.0kmh
0-50mph 80.5kmh: 3.8secs
0-60mph 96.5kmh: 4.9secs
0-1/4 mile: 13.5secs
0-1km: 25.3secs
264.0bhp 196.9kW 267.7PS
@ 6500rpm
261.3lbft 354.0Nm @ 3900rpm
201.9bhp/ton 198.5bhp/tonne
121.4bhp/L 90.6kW/L 123.1PS/L
54.2ft/sec 16.5m/sec
23.1mph 37.2kmh/1000rpm
23.5mpg 19.6mpgUS 12.0L/100km
Petrol 4-stroke piston
2174cc 133.0cu in turbocharged
In-line 4 fuel injection
Compression ratio: 8.1:1
Bore: 93.5mm 3.7in
Stroke: 76.2mm 3.0in
Valve type/No: Overhead 16
Transmission: Manual
No. of forward speeds: 5
Wheels driven: Rear
Springs F/R: Coil/Coil
Brake system: PA
Brakes F/R: Disc/Disc
Steering: Rack & pinion
Wheelbase: 243.8cm 96.0in
Track F: 152.4cm 60.0in
Track R: 155.4cm 61.2in
Length: 433.0cm 170.5in
Width: 186.0cm 73.2in
Height: 115.0cm 45.3in
Ground clearance: 14.6cm 5.7in
Kerb weight: 1330.0kg 2929.5lb
Fuel: 70.1L 15.4gal 18.5galUS

2638 Lotus
Elan
1990 UK
137.0mph 220.4kmh
0-60mph 96.5kmh: 6.7secs
0-1/4 mile: 15.4secs
165.0bhp 123.0kW 167.3PS
@ 6600rpm
148.0lbft 200.5Nm @ 4200rpm
164.3bhp/ton 161.5bhp/tonne
103.9bhp/L 77.5kW/L 105.3PS/L
57.0ft/sec 17.4m/sec
Petrol 4-stroke piston
1588cc 96.9cu in turbocharged
In-line 4 fuel injection
Compression ratio: 8.2:1
Bore: 80.0mm 3.1in
Stroke: 79.0mm 3.1in
Valve type/No: Overhead 16
Transmission: Manual
No. of forward speeds: 5

Wheels driven: Front
Springs F/R: Coil/Coil
Brakes F/R: Disc/Disc
Steering: Rack & pinion PA
Wheelbase: 225.0cm 88.6in
Track F: 148.6cm 58.5in
Track R: 148.6cm 58.5in
Length: 380.2cm 149.7in
Width: 173.5cm 68.3in
Height: 122.9cm 48.4in
Kerb weight: 1021.5kg 2250.0lb
Fuel: 38.6L 8.5gal 10.2galUS

2639 Lotus

Elan SE
1990 UK
137.0mph 220.4kmh
0-50mph 80.5kmh: 5.0secs
0-60mph 96.5kmh: 6.5secs
0-1/4 mile: 15.0secs
0-1km: 27.4secs
165.0bhp 123.0kW 167.3PS
@ 6600rpm
147.6lbft 200.0Nm @ 4200rpm
164.0bhp/ton 161.3bhp/tonne
103.9bhp/L 77.5kW/L 105.3PS/L
57.0ft/sec 17.4m/sec
20.8mph 33.5kmh/1000rpm
20.1mpg 16.7mpgUS 14.1L/100km
Petrol 4-stroke piston
1588cc 97.0cu in turbocharged
In-line 4 fuel injection
Compression ratio: 8.2:1
Bore: 80.0mm 3.1in
Stroke: 79.0mm 3.1in
Valve type/No: Overhead 16
Transmission: Manual
No. of forward speeds: 5
Wheels driven: Front
Springs F/R: Coil/Coil
Brake system: PA
Brakes F/R: Disc/Disc
Steering: Rack & pinion PA
Wheelbase: 225.0cm 88.6in
Track F: 148.6cm 58.5in
Track R: 148.6cm 58.5in
Length: 380.2cm 149.7in
Width: 188.7cm 74.3in
Height: 122.9cm 48.4in
Ground clearance: 13.0cm 5.1in
Kerb weight: 1023.0kg 2253.3lb
Fuel: 46.4L 10.2gal 12.3galUS

2640 Lotus

Esprit Turbo SE
1990 UK
165.0mph 265.5kmh
0-50mph 80.5kmh: 4.1secs
0-60mph 96.5kmh: 5.1secs
0-1/4 mile: 13.7secs
264.0bhp 196.9kW 267.7PS
@ 6500rpm
261.0lbft 353.7Nm @ 3900rpm
206.4bhp/ton 203.0bhp/tonne
121.4bhp/L 90.6kW/L 123.1PS/L
54.2ft/sec 16.5m/sec
19.8mpg 16.5mpgUS 14.3L/100km
Petrol 4-stroke piston
2174cc 132.6cu in turbocharged
In-line 4 fuel injection
Compression ratio: 8.0:1
Bore: 95.3mm 3.8in
Stroke: 76.2mm 3.0in
Valve type/No: Overhead 16
Transmission: Manual
No. of forward speeds: 5
Wheels driven: Rear
Springs F/R: Coil/Coil
Brake system: PA
Brakes F/R: Disc/Disc
Steering: Rack & pinion PA
Wheelbase: 243.8cm 96.0in
Track F: 152.4cm 60.0in
Track R: 155.4cm 61.2in
Length: 433.1cm 170.5in
Width: 185.9cm 73.2in
Height: 115.1cm 45.3in
Kerb weight: 1300.7kg 2865.0lb
Fuel: 70.0L 15.4gal 18.5galUS

2641 Lotus

Elan SE
1991 UK
137.0mph 220.4kmh
0-50mph 80.5kmh: 5.1secs
0-60mph 96.5kmh: 6.6secs
0-1/4 mile: 15.2secs
162.0bhp 120.8kW 164.2PS
@ 6600rpm
148.0lbft 200.5Nm @ 4200rpm
148.1bhp/ton 145.6bhp/tonne
102.0bhp/L 76.1kW/L 103.4PS/L
57.0ft/sec 17.4m/sec
31.2mpg 26.0mpgUS 9.0L/100km
Petrol 4-stroke piston
1588cc 96.9cu in turbocharged
In-line 4 fuel injection
Compression ratio: 8.2:1
Bore: 80.0mm 3.1in
Stroke: 79.0mm 3.1in
Valve type/No: Overhead 16
Transmission: Manual
No. of forward speeds: 5
Wheels driven: Front
Springs F/R: Coil/Coil
Brake system: PA ABS
Brakes F/R: Disc/Disc
Steering: Rack & pinion PA
Wheelbase: 225.0cm 88.6in
Track F: 148.6cm 58.5in
Track R: 148.6cm 58.5in
Length: 386.6cm 152.2in
Width: 173.2cm 68.2in
Height: 122.9cm 48.4in
Ground clearance: 12.7cm 5.0in
Kerb weight: 1112.3kg 2450.0lb
Fuel: 38.6L 8.5gal 10.2galUS

2642 Lynx

D Type
1987 UK
150.0mph 241.4kmh
0-60mph 96.5kmh: 5.3secs
0-1/4 mile: 13.9secs
285.0bhp 212.5kW 288.9PS
@ 5300rpm
299.7bhp/ton 294.7bhp/tonne
75.4bhp/L 56.2kW/L 76.4PS/L
61.4ft/sec 18.7m/sec
Petrol 4-stroke piston
3781cc 230.7cu in
In-line 6 3 Carburettor
Compression ratio: 9.0:1
Bore: 87.0mm 3.4in
Stroke: 106.0mm 4.2in
Valve type/No: Overhead 12
Transmission: Manual
No. of forward speeds: 4
Wheels driven: Rear
Springs F/R: Torsion bar/Coil
Brake system: PA
Brakes F/R: Disc/Disc
Steering: Rack & pinion
Wheelbase: 229.9cm 90.5in
Track F: 127.0cm 50.0in
Track R: 127.0cm 50.0in
Length: 391.2cm 154.0in
Width: 168.9cm 66.5in
Height: 80.0cm 31.5in
Kerb weight: 967.0kg 2130.0lb
Fuel: 100.3L 22.0gal 26.5galUS

2643 Lynx

XJS Eventer
1988 UK
151.0mph 243.0kmh
0-60mph 96.5kmh: 7.6secs
0-1/4 mile: 15.6secs
295.0bhp 220.0kW 299.1PS
@ 5500rpm
320.0lbft 433.6Nm @ 3250rpm
166.4bhp/ton 163.7bhp/tonne
55.2bhp/L 41.2kW/L 56.0PS/L
42.2ft/sec 12.8m/sec
Petrol 4-stroke piston
5345cc 326.1cu in
Vee 12 fuel injection
Compression ratio: 11.5:1
Bore: 90.0mm 3.5in
Stroke: 70.0mm 2.8in
Valve type/No: Overhead 24
Transmission: Automatic
No. of forward speeds: 3
Wheels driven: Rear
Springs F/R: Coil/Coil
Brake system: PA
Brakes F/R: Disc/Disc
Steering: Rack & pinion PA
Wheelbase: 259.1cm 102.0in
Track F: 148.8cm 58.6in
Track R: 150.4cm 59.2in
Length: 476.5cm 187.6in
Width: 179.3cm 70.6in
Height: 128.8cm 50.7in
Kerb weight: 1802.4kg 3970.0lb
Fuel: 84.0L 18.5gal 22.2galUS

2644 Marcos

1800
1965 UK
118.0mph 189.9kmh
0-50mph 80.5kmh: 7.0secs
0-60mph 96.5kmh: 9.1secs
0-1/4 mile: 16.5secs
114.0bhp 85.0kW 115.6PS
@ 5800rpm
110.0lbft 149.1Nm @ 4200rpm
151.1bhp/ton 148.6bhp/tonne
64.0bhp/L 47.8kW/L 64.9PS/L
50.7ft/sec 15.5m/sec
21.7mph 34.9kmh/1000rpm
26.0mpg 21.6mpgUS 10.9L/100km
Petrol 4-stroke piston
1780cc 108.6cu in
In-line 4 2 Carburettor
Compression ratio: 10.0:1
Bore: 84.1mm 3.3in
Stroke: 80.0mm 3.1in
Valve type/No: Overhead 8
Transmission: Manual with overdrive
No. of forward speeds: 5
Wheels driven: Rear
Springs F/R: Coil/Coil
Brakes F/R: Disc/Drum
Steering: Rack & pinion
Wheelbase: 226.1cm 89.0in
Track F: 124.5cm 49.0in
Track R: 125.7cm 49.5in
Length: 407.7cm 160.5in
Width: 161.8cm 63.7in
Height: 120.7cm 47.5in
Ground clearance: 10.2cm 4.0in
Kerb weight: 767.3kg 1690.0lb
Fuel: 54.6L 12.0gal 14.4galUS

2645 Marcos

1600GT
1968 UK
112.0mph 180.2kmh
0-50mph 80.5kmh: 8.0secs
0-60mph 96.5kmh: 11.4secs
0-1/4 mile: 17.6secs
0-1km: 33.3secs
88.0bhp 65.6kW 89.2PS
@ 5400rpm
96.0lbft 130.1Nm @ 3600rpm
120.9bhp/ton 118.9bhp/tonne
55.1bhp/L 41.1kW/L 55.8PS/L
45.3ft/sec 13.8m/sec
17.8mph 28.6kmh/1000rpm
21.5mpg 17.9mpgUS 13.1L/100km
Petrol 4-stroke piston
1598cc 97.5cu in
In-line 4 1 Carburettor
Compression ratio: 9.0:1
Bore: 81.0mm 3.2in
Stroke: 76.6mm 3.0in
Valve type/No: Overhead 8
Transmission: Manual
No. of forward speeds: 4
Wheels driven: Rear
Springs F/R: Coil/Coil
Brakes F/R: Disc/Drum
Steering: Rack & pinion
Wheelbase: 226.1cm 89.0in
Track F: 128.3cm 50.5in
Track R: 132.1cm 52.0in
Length: 407.7cm 160.5in
Width: 161.8cm 63.7in
Height: 104.1cm 41.0in
Ground clearance: 11.4cm 4.5in
Kerb weight: 740.0kg 1630.0lb
Fuel: 45.5L 10.0gal 12.0galUS

2646 Marcos

3-litre Volvo
1971 UK
120.0mph 193.1kmh
0-50mph 80.5kmh: 5.8secs
0-60mph 96.5kmh: 7.5secs
0-1/4 mile: 15.9secs
0-1km: 28.9secs
130.0bhp 96.9kW 131.8PS
@ 5000rpm
152.0lbft 206.0Nm @ 2500rpm
143.6bhp/ton 141.2bhp/tonne
43.6bhp/L 32.5kW/L 44.3PS/L
43.8ft/sec 13.3m/sec
21.8mph 35.1kmh/1000rpm
22.3mpg 18.6mpgUS 12.7L/100km
Petrol 4-stroke piston
2978cc 181.7cu in
In-line 6 2 Carburettor
Compression ratio: 9.2:1
Bore: 88.9mm 3.5in
Stroke: 80.0mm 3.1in
Valve type/No: Overhead 12
Transmission: Manual
No. of forward speeds: 4
Wheels driven: Rear
Springs F/R: Coil/Coil
Brakes F/R: Disc/Drum
Steering: Rack & pinion
Wheelbase: 226.1cm 89.0in
Track F: 128.3cm 50.5in
Track R: 132.1cm 52.0in
Length: 407.7cm 160.5in
Width: 161.8cm 63.7in
Height: 104.1cm 41.0in
Ground clearance: 11.4cm 4.5in
Kerb weight: 920.7kg 2028.0lb
Fuel: 54.6L 12.0gal 14.4galUS

2647 Marendaz

15/90 Special Tourer
1935 UK
84.1mph 135.3kmh
0-50mph 80.5kmh: 10.6secs
0-60mph 96.5kmh: 15.8secs
19.0mpg 15.8mpgUS 14.9L/100km
Petrol 4-stroke piston
1991cc 121.5cu in
In-line 6 3 Carburettor
Bore: 65.0mm 2.6in
Stroke: 100.0mm 3.9in
Valve type/No: IOE 12
Transmission: Manual
No. of forward speeds: 4
Wheels driven: Rear
Brakes F/R: Drum/Drum
Ground clearance: 21.6cm 8.5in
Kerb weight: 1121.8kg 2471.0lb
Fuel: 54.6L 12.0gal 14.4galUS

2648 Marmon

Roosevelt Saloon
1929 USA
65.0mph 104.6kmh
18.0mpg 15.0mpgUS 15.7L/100km
Petrol 4-stroke piston
3310cc 201.9cu in
In-line 8
Bore: 69.8mm 2.7in
Stroke: 107.9mm 4.2in
Transmission: Manual
No. of forward speeds: 3
Wheels driven: Rear
Brakes F/R: Drum/Drum
Wheelbase: 286.3cm 112.7in
Track F: 142.2cm 56.0in
Track R: 142.2cm 56.0in
Length: 436.4cm 171.8in
Width: 177.8cm 70.0in
Height: 176.8cm 69.6in
Kerb weight: 1223.5kg 2695.0lb
Fuel: 54.6L 12.0gal 14.4galUS

2649 Marmon

69 Saloon
1930 USA
68.4mph 110.1kmh
16.0mpg 13.3mpgUS 17.7L/100km
Petrol 4-stroke piston
3460cc 211.1cu in
In-line 8
Bore: 71.4mm 2.8in
Stroke: 108.0mm 4.2in
Transmission: Manual
No. of forward speeds: 3
Wheels driven: Rear
Brakes F/R: Drum/Drum
Wheelbase: 297.2cm 117.0in
Track F: 144.0cm 56.7in
Track R: 144.0cm 56.7in
Length: 457.2cm 180.0in
Width: 177.8cm 70.0in
Height: 178.8cm 70.4in
Kerb weight: 1408.8kg 3103.0lb
Fuel: 59.1L 13.0gal 15.6galUS

2650 Marmon

79 Saloon
1930 USA

72.5mph 116.7kmh
12.0mpg 10.0mpgUS 23.5L/100km
Petrol 4-stroke piston
4968cc 303.1cu in
In-line 8
Bore: 81.0mm 3.2in
Stroke: 120.6mm 4.7in
Transmission: Manual
No. of forward speeds: 4
Wheels driven: Rear
Brakes F/R: Drum/Drum
Wheelbase: 317.5cm 125.0in
Track F: 147.3cm 58.0in
Track R: 147.3cm 58.0in
Length: 485.1cm 191.0in
Width: 177.8cm 70.0in
Height: 177.8cm 70.0in
Kerb weight: 1855.9kg 4088.0lb
Fuel: 81.9L 18.0gal 21.6galUS

2651 Marmon

16
1932 USA
105.0mph 168.9kmh
0-50mph 80.5kmh: 9.4secs
0-60mph 96.5kmh: 14.0secs
0-1/4 mile: 18.8secs
200.0bhp 149.1kW 202.8PS
@ 3400rpm
390.0lbft 528.5Nm @ 1800rpm
84.5bhp/ton 83.1bhp/tonne
24.9bhp/L 18.5kW/L 25.2PS/L
37.8ft/sec 11.5m/sec
25.6mph 41.2kmh/1000rpm
Petrol 4-stroke piston
8046cc 490.9cu in
Vee 16
Compression ratio: 6.0:1
Bore: 79.5mm 3.1in
Stroke: 101.6mm 4.0in
Valve type/No: Overhead 32
Transmission: Manual
No. of forward speeds: 3
Wheels driven: Rear
Wheelbase: 368.3cm 145.0in
Track F: 147.3cm 58.0in
Track R: 147.3cm 58.0in
Length: 533.4cm 210.0in
Width: 182.9cm 72.0in
Height: 172.7cm 68.0in
Kerb weight: 2406.2kg 5300.0lb

2652 Maserati

A6G/54 Frua Gran Sport
1954 Italy
125.0mph 201.1kmh
150.0bhp 111.9kW 152.1PS
@ 6000rpm
181.4bhp/ton 178.4bhp/tonne
75.5bhp/L 56.3kW/L 76.6PS/L
47.2ft/sec 14.4m/sec
Petrol 4-stroke piston
1986cc 121.2cu in
In-line 6 3 Carburettor
Compression ratio: 8.0:1
Bore: 76.5mm 3.0in
Stroke: 72.0mm 2.8in
Valve type/No: Overhead 12
Transmission: Manual
No. of forward speeds: 4
Wheels driven: Rear
Brakes F/R: Drum/Drum
Steering: Worm & sector
Wheelbase: 255.3cm 100.5in
Kerb weight: 840.8kg 1852.0lb
Fuel: 62.8L 13.8gal 16.6galUS

2653 Maserati

GT Coupe
1959 Italy
129.0mph 207.6kmh
0-50mph 80.5kmh: 6.2secs
0-60mph 96.5kmh: 7.5secs
0-1/4 mile: 15.5secs
230.0bhp 171.5kW 233.2PS
@ 5500rpm
224.0lbft 303.5Nm @ 4500rpm
162.0bhp/ton 159.3bhp/tonne
66.0bhp/L 49.2kW/L 66.9PS/L
60.2ft/sec 18.3m/sec
23.4mph 37.7kmh/1000rpm
Petrol 4-stroke piston
3485cc 212.6cu in
In-line 6
Compression ratio: 8.2:1
Bore: 86.1mm 3.4in
Stroke: 100.1mm 3.9in
Valve type/No: Overhead 12
Transmission: Manual
No. of forward speeds: 4
Wheels driven: Rear
Wheelbase: 259.6cm 102.2in
Track F: 138.9cm 54.7in
Track R: 135.9cm 53.5in
Length: 469.9cm 185.0in
Width: 161.8cm 63.7in
Height: 130.0cm 51.2in
Kerb weight: 1443.7kg 3180.0lb

2654 Maserati

3500GT
1961 Italy
127.0mph 204.3kmh
0-50mph 80.5kmh: 5.0secs
0-60mph 96.5kmh: 8.1secs
0-1/4 mile: 16.1secs
230.0bhp 171.5kW 233.2PS
@ 5500rpm
224.0lbft 303.5Nm @ 4500rpm
164.1bhp/ton 161.3bhp/tonne
66.0bhp/L 49.2kW/L 66.9PS/L
60.2ft/sec 18.3m/sec
23.2mph 37.3kmh/1000rpm
Petrol 4-stroke piston
3485cc 212.6cu in
In-line 6
Compression ratio: 8.2:1
Bore: 86.1mm 3.4in
Stroke: 100.1mm 3.9in
Valve type/No: Overhead 12
Transmission: Manual
No. of forward speeds: 4
Wheels driven: Rear
Wheelbase: 259.8cm 102.3in
Track F: 138.9cm 54.7in
Track R: 135.9cm 53.5in
Length: 442.0cm 174.0in
Width: 152.4cm 60.0in
Height: 137.2cm 54.0in
Ground clearance: 13.0cm 5.1in
Kerb weight: 1425.6kg 3140.0lb

2655 Maserati

3500 GTI Sebring
1963 Italy
138.0mph 222.0kmh
0-50mph 80.5kmh: 6.4secs
0-60mph 96.5kmh: 8.4secs
0-1/4 mile: 16.0secs
235.0bhp 175.2kW 238.3PS
@ 5500rpm
232.0lbft 314.4Nm @ 4000rpm
158.0bhp/ton 155.3bhp/tonne
67.4bhp/L 50.3kW/L 68.4PS/L
60.2ft/sec 18.3m/sec
24.7mph 39.7kmh/1000rpm
14.8mpg 12.3mpgUS 19.1L/100km
Petrol 4-stroke piston
3485cc 212.6cu in
In-line 6 fuel injection
Compression ratio: 8.5:1
Bore: 86.0mm 3.4in
Stroke: 100.0mm 3.9in
Valve type/No: Overhead 12
Transmission: Manual
No. of forward speeds: 5
Wheels driven: Rear
Springs F/R: Coil/Leaf
Brake system: PA
Brakes F/R: Disc/Disc
Steering: Recirculating ball
Wheelbase: 250.2cm 98.5in
Track F: 138.9cm 54.7in
Track R: 135.4cm 53.3in
Length: 447.0cm 176.0in
Width: 165.9cm 65.3in
Height: 132.1cm 52.0in
Ground clearance: 11.4cm 4.5in
Kerb weight: 1512.7kg 3332.0lb
Fuel: 83.3L 18.3gal 22.0galUS

2656 Maserati

Quattroporte
1968 Italy
130.0mph 209.2kmh
0-50mph 80.5kmh: 6.2secs
0-60mph 96.5kmh: 8.3secs
0-1/4 mile: 16.4secs
290.0bhp 216.2kW 294.0PS
@ 5200rpm
260.0lbft 352.3Nm @ 4000rpm
167.8bhp/ton 165.0bhp/tonne
70.1bhp/L 52.3kW/L 71.1PS/L
48.4ft/sec 14.7m/sec
26.6mph 42.8kmh/1000rpm
Petrol 4-stroke piston
4136cc 252.3cu in
Vee 8 4 Carburettor
Compression ratio: 8.5:1
Bore: 88.0mm 3.5in
Stroke: 85.0mm 3.3in
Valve type/No: Overhead 16
Transmission: Manual
No. of forward speeds: 5
Wheels driven: Rear
Springs F/R: Coil/Leaf
Brake system: PA
Brakes F/R: Disc/Disc
Steering: Recirculating ball
Wheelbase: 275.1cm 108.3in
Track F: 135.9cm 53.5in
Track R: 141.0cm 55.5in
Length: 499.9cm 196.8in
Width: 172.7cm 68.0in
Height: 135.9cm 53.5in
Ground clearance: 14.5cm 5.7in
Kerb weight: 1757.9kg 3872.0lb
Fuel: 94.6L 20.8gal 25.0galUS

2657 Maserati

Indy
1970 Italy
136.0mph 218.8kmh
0-50mph 80.5kmh: 5.8secs
0-60mph 96.5kmh: 7.4secs
0-1/4 mile: 15.5secs
330.0bhp 246.1kW 334.6PS
@ 5000rpm
325.0lbft 440.4Nm @ 4000rpm
213.3bhp/ton 209.8bhp/tonne
69.9bhp/L 52.1kW/L 70.9PS/L
46.5ft/sec 14.2m/sec
25.3mph 40.7kmh/1000rpm
15.6mpg 13.0mpgUS 18.1L/100km
Petrol 4-stroke piston
4719cc 287.9cu in
Vee 8 4 Carburettor
Compression ratio: 8.8:1
Bore: 94.0mm 3.7in
Stroke: 85.0mm 3.3in
Valve type/No: Overhead 16
Transmission: Manual
No. of forward speeds: 5
Wheels driven: Rear
Springs F/R: Coil/Leaf
Brake system: PA
Brakes F/R: Disc/Disc
Steering: Recirculating ball
Wheelbase: 259.8cm 102.3in
Track F: 147.8cm 58.2in
Track R: 135.9cm 53.5in
Length: 474.0cm 186.6in
Width: 175.8cm 69.2in
Height: 121.9cm 48.0in
Ground clearance: 11.9cm 4.7in
Kerb weight: 1573.1kg 3465.0lb
Fuel: 100.3L 22.0gal 26.5galUS

2658 Maserati

Ghibli
1971 Italy
154.0mph 247.8kmh
0-50mph 80.5kmh: 7.5secs
0-60mph 96.5kmh: 9.5secs
0-1/4 mile: 15.1secs
340.0bhp 253.5kW 344.7PS
@ 5500rpm
326.0lbft 441.7Nm @ 4000rpm
203.4bhp/ton 200.0bhp/tonne
72.0bhp/L 53.7kW/L 73.0PS/L
51.2ft/sec 15.6m/sec
23.4mph 37.7kmh/1000rpm
14.2mpg 11.8mpgUS 19.9L/100km
Petrol 4-stroke piston
4719cc 287.9cu in
Vee 8 4 Carburettor
Compression ratio: 8.8:1
Bore: 94.0mm 3.7in
Stroke: 85.0mm 3.3in
Valve type/No: Overhead 16
Transmission: Manual
No. of forward speeds: 5
Wheels driven: Rear
Springs F/R: Coil/Leaf
Brake system: PA
Brakes F/R: Disc/Disc
Steering: Recirculating ball PA
Wheelbase: 255.0cm 100.4in
Track F: 144.0cm 56.7in
Track R: 140.7cm 55.4in
Length: 459.0cm 180.7in
Width: 180.1cm 70.9in
Height: 118.4cm 46.6in
Ground clearance: 11.9cm 4.7in
Kerb weight: 1700.2kg 3745.0lb
Fuel: 100.3L 22.0gal 26.5galUS

2659 Maserati

Indy
1971 Italy
157.0mph 252.6kmh
0-50mph 80.5kmh: 5.6secs
0-60mph 96.5kmh: 7.5secs
0-1/4 mile: 15.6secs
0-1km: 28.7secs
290.0bhp 216.2kW 294.0PS
@ 5500rpm
282.0lbft 382.1Nm @ 3800rpm
178.6bhp/ton 175.6bhp/tonne
61.4bhp/L 45.8kW/L 62.3PS/L
51.2ft/sec 15.6m/sec
26.0mph 41.8kmh/1000rpm
13.9mpg 11.6mpgUS 20.3L/100km
Petrol 4-stroke piston
4719cc 287.9cu in
Vee 8 4 Carburettor
Compression ratio: 8.5:1
Bore: 93.9mm 3.7in
Stroke: 85.0mm 3.3in
Valve type/No: Overhead 16
Transmission: Manual
No. of forward speeds: 5
Wheels driven: Rear
Springs F/R: Coil/Leaf
Brake system: PA
Brakes F/R: Disc/Disc
Steering: Recirculating ball PA
Wheelbase: 268.0cm 105.5in
Track F: 144.8cm 57.0in
Track R: 144.8cm 57.0in
Length: 487.7cm 192.0in
Width: 177.8cm 70.0in
Height: 129.5cm 51.0in
Ground clearance: 15.2cm 6.0in
Kerb weight: 1651.6kg 3638.0lb
Fuel: 100.1L 22.0gal 26.4galUS

2660 Maserati

Bora
1973 Italy
162.0mph 260.7kmh
0-50mph 80.5kmh: 5.0secs
0-60mph 96.5kmh: 6.5secs
0-1/4 mile: 14.6secs
0-1km: 26.4secs
310.0bhp 231.2kW 314.3PS
@ 6000rpm
340.0lbft 460.7Nm @ 4200rpm
198.1bhp/ton 194.8bhp/tonne
65.7bhp/L 49.0kW/L 66.6PS/L
55.8ft/sec 17.0m/sec
28.0mph 45.1kmh/1000rpm
11.9mpg 9.9mpgUS 23.7L/100km
Petrol 4-stroke piston
4719cc 287.9cu in
Vee 8 4 Carburettor
Compression ratio: 8.5:1
Bore: 93.9mm 3.7in
Stroke: 85.0mm 3.3in
Valve type/No: Overhead 16
Transmission: Manual
No. of forward speeds: 5
Wheels driven: Rear
Springs F/R: Coil/Coil
Brake system: PA
Brakes F/R: Disc/Disc
Steering: Rack & pinion
Wheelbase: 259.8cm 102.3in
Track F: 147.3cm 58.0in
Track R: 144.5cm 56.9in
Length: 434.3cm 171.0in
Width: 177.8cm 70.0in
Height: 115.6cm 45.5in
Ground clearance: 12.7cm 5.0in
Kerb weight: 1591.7kg 3506.0lb
Fuel: 90.1L 19.8gal 23.8galUS

2661 Maserati

Merak
1974 Italy
133.0mph 214.0kmh
0-50mph 80.5kmh: 7.0secs
0-60mph 96.5kmh: 9.5secs
0-1/4 mile: 17.2secs
182.0bhp 135.7kW 184.5PS

@ 6000rpm
185.0lbft 250.7Nm @ 3000rpm
126.8bhp/ton 124.7bhp/tonne
61.4bhp/L 45.8kW/L 62.2PS/L
49.2ft/sec 15.0m/sec
23.1mph 37.2kmh/1000rpm
20.4mpg 17.0mpgUS 13.8L/100km
Petrol 4-stroke piston
2965cc 180.9cu in
Vee 6 3 Carburettor
Compression ratio: 8.8:1
Bore: 91.6mm 3.6in
Stroke: 75.0mm 2.9in
Valve type/No: Overhead 12
Transmission: Manual
No. of forward speeds: 5
Wheels driven: Rear
Springs F/R: Coil/Coil
Brakes F/R: Disc/Disc
Steering: Rack & pinion
Wheelbase: 259.8cm 102.3in
Track F: 147.3cm 58.0in
Track R: 144.5cm 56.9in
Length: 451.6cm 177.8in
Width: 176.8cm 69.6in
Height: 113.3cm 44.6in
Ground clearance: 11.7cm 4.6in
Kerb weight: 1459.6kg 3215.0lb
Fuel: 87.1L 19.1gal 23.0galUS

2662 Maserati

Khamsin Automatic
1975 Italy
130.0mph 209.2kmh
0-50mph 80.5kmh: 5.9secs
0-60mph 96.5kmh: 7.5secs
0-1/4 mile: 15.8secs
0-1km: 27.9secs
320.0bhp 238.6kW 324.4PS
@ 5500rpm
354.0lbft 479.7Nm @ 4000rpm
198.1bhp/ton 194.8bhp/tonne
64.9bhp/L 48.4kW/L 65.8PS/L
53.5ft/sec 16.3m/sec
23.6mph 38.0kmh/1000rpm
15.1mpg 12.6mpgUS 18.7L/100km
Petrol 4-stroke piston
4930cc 300.8cu in
Vee 8 4 Carburettor
Compression ratio: 8.5:1
Bore: 93.9mm 3.7in
Stroke: 89.0mm 3.5in
Valve type/No: Overhead 16
Transmission: Automatic
No. of forward speeds: 3
Wheels driven: Rear
Springs F/R: Coil/Coil
Brake system: PA
Brakes F/R: Disc/Disc
Steering: Rack & pinion PA
Wheelbase: 255.0cm 100.4in
Track F: 144.0cm 56.7in
Track R: 147.1cm 57.9in
Length: 439.9cm 173.2in
Width: 180.1cm 70.9in
Height: 124.5cm 49.0in
Ground clearance: 14.0cm 5.5in
Kerb weight: 1643.0kg 3619.0lb
Fuel: 90.1L 19.8gal 23.8galUS

2663 Maserati

Merak
1975 Italy
135.0mph 217.2kmh
0-50mph 80.5kmh: 6.0secs
0-60mph 96.5kmh: 8.2secs
0-1/4 mile: 16.0secs
0-1km: 29.2secs
190.0bhp 141.7kW 192.6PS
@ 6000rpm
188.0lbft 254.7Nm @ 4000rpm
133.2bhp/ton 131.0bhp/tonne
64.1bhp/L 47.8kW/L 64.9PS/L
49.2ft/sec 15.0m/sec
21.6mph 34.8kmh/1000rpm
17.4mpg 14.5mpgUS 16.2L/100km
Petrol 4-stroke piston
2966cc 181.0cu in
Vee 6 2 Carburettor
Compression ratio: 8.7:1
Bore: 91.6mm 3.6in
Stroke: 75.0mm 2.9in
Valve type/No: Overhead 12
Transmission: Manual
No. of forward speeds: 5
Wheels driven: Rear
Springs F/R: Coil/Coil
Brake system: PA
Brakes F/R: Disc/Disc
Steering: Rack & pinion
Wheelbase: 259.6cm 102.2in
Track F: 147.1cm 57.9in
Track R: 145.0cm 57.1in
Length: 432.8cm 170.4in
Width: 173.0cm 68.1in
Height: 115.6cm 45.5in
Ground clearance: 12.7cm 5.0in
Kerb weight: 1450.1kg 3194.0lb
Fuel: 84.6L 18.6gal 22.4galUS

2664 Maserati

Bora
1976 Italy
163.0mph 262.3kmh
0-50mph 80.5kmh: 5.8secs
0-60mph 96.5kmh: 7.2secs
0-1/4 mile: 15.2secs
300.0bhp 223.7kW 304.2PS
@ 6000rpm
325.0lbft 440.4Nm @ 4200rpm
188.2bhp/ton 185.1bhp/tonne
63.6bhp/L 47.4kW/L 64.4PS/L
55.8ft/sec 17.0m/sec
27.3mph 43.9kmh/1000rpm
13.8mpg 11.5mpgUS 20.5L/100km
Petrol 4-stroke piston
4719cc 287.9cu in
Vee 8 1 Carburettor
Compression ratio: 8.5:1
Bore: 93.9mm 3.7in
Stroke: 85.0mm 3.3in
Valve type/No: Overhead 16
Transmission: Manual
No. of forward speeds: 5
Wheels driven: Rear
Springs F/R: Coil/Coil
Brake system: PA
Brakes F/R: Disc/Disc
Steering: Rack & pinion
Wheelbase: 259.6cm 102.2in
Track F: 147.3cm 58.0in
Track R: 144.8cm 57.0in
Length: 432.8cm 170.4in
Width: 173.0cm 68.1in
Height: 113.3cm 44.6in
Ground clearance: 13.0cm 5.1in
Kerb weight: 1620.8kg 3570.0lb
Fuel: 99.9L 22.0gal 26.4galUS

2665 Maserati

Khamsin
1976 Italy
140.0mph 225.3kmh
0-50mph 80.5kmh: 6.0secs
0-60mph 96.5kmh: 8.0secs
0-1/4 mile: 16.2secs
315.0bhp 234.9kW 319.4PS
@ 5000rpm
308.0lbft 417.3Nm @ 3500rpm
188.9bhp/ton 185.8bhp/tonne
63.9bhp/L 47.6kW/L 64.8PS/L
48.6ft/sec 14.8m/sec
23.5mph 37.8kmh/1000rpm
13.8mpg 11.5mpgUS 20.5L/100km
Petrol 4-stroke piston
4930cc 300.8cu in
Vee 8 4 Carburettor
Compression ratio: 8.0:1
Bore: 93.9mm 3.7in
Stroke: 89.0mm 3.5in
Valve type/No: Overhead 16
Transmission: Manual
No. of forward speeds: 5
Wheels driven: Rear
Springs F/R: Coil/Coil
Brakes F/R: Disc/Disc
Steering: Rack & pinion PA
Wheelbase: 254.8cm 100.3in
Track F: 143.8cm 56.6in
Track R: 146.6cm 57.7in
Length: 457.2cm 180.0in
Width: 180.3cm 71.0in
Height: 119.4cm 47.0in
Ground clearance: 12.7cm 5.0in
Kerb weight: 1695.7kg 3735.0lb
Fuel: 85.9L 18.9gal 22.7galUS

2666 Maserati

Khamsin
1978 Italy
160.0mph 257.4kmh
0-50mph 80.5kmh: 4.9secs
0-60mph 96.5kmh: 6.5secs
0-1/4 mile: 14.8secs
0-1km: 26.6secs
320.0bhp 238.6kW 324.4PS
@ 5500rpm
354.0lbft 479.7Nm @ 4000rpm
192.5bhp/ton 189.3bhp/tonne
64.9bhp/L 48.4kW/L 65.8PS/L
53.5ft/sec 16.3m/sec
26.5mph 42.6kmh/1000rpm
14.3mpg 11.9mpgUS 19.8L/100km
Petrol 4-stroke piston
4930cc 300.8cu in
Vee 8 4 Carburettor
Compression ratio: 8.5:1
Bore: 93.9mm 3.7in
Stroke: 89.0mm 3.5in
Valve type/No: Overhead 16
Transmission: Manual
No. of forward speeds: 5
Wheels driven: Rear
Springs F/R: Coil/Coil
Brake system: PA
Brakes F/R: Disc/Disc
Steering: Rack & pinion PA
Wheelbase: 255.0cm 100.4in
Track F: 144.0cm 56.7in
Track R: 147.1cm 57.9in
Length: 439.9cm 173.2in
Width: 180.1cm 70.9in
Height: 124.5cm 49.0in
Ground clearance: 14.0cm 5.5in
Kerb weight: 1690.7kg 3724.0lb
Fuel: 95.5L 21.0gal 25.2galUS

2667 Maserati

Kyalami
1978 Italy
147.0mph 236.5kmh
0-50mph 80.5kmh: 6.0secs
0-60mph 96.5kmh: 7.6secs
0-1/4 mile: 15.8secs
0-1km: 28.9secs
270.0bhp 201.3kW 273.7PS
@ 6000rpm
289.0lbft 391.6Nm @ 3800rpm
157.7bhp/ton 155.0bhp/tonne
65.3bhp/L 48.7kW/L 66.2PS/L
55.8ft/sec 17.0m/sec
24.4mph 39.3kmh/1000rpm
15.3mpg 12.7mpgUS 18.5L/100km
Petrol 4-stroke piston
4136cc 252.3cu in
Vee 8 4 Carburettor
Compression ratio: 8.5:1
Bore: 88.0mm 3.5in
Stroke: 85.0mm 3.3in
Valve type/No: Overhead 16
Transmission: Manual
No. of forward speeds: 5
Wheels driven: Rear
Springs F/R: Coil/Coil
Brake system: PA
Brakes F/R: Disc/Disc
Steering: Rack & pinion PA
Wheelbase: 256.5cm 101.0in
Track F: 152.9cm 60.2in
Track R: 152.9cm 60.2in
Length: 457.7cm 180.2in
Width: 184.7cm 72.7in
Height: 124.5cm 49.0in
Ground clearance: 12.7cm 5.0in
Kerb weight: 1741.5kg 3836.0lb
Fuel: 91.9L 20.2gal 24.3galUS

2668 Maserati

Merak
1978 Italy
141.0mph 226.9kmh
0-50mph 80.5kmh: 6.8secs
0-60mph 96.5kmh: 9.1secs
0-1/4 mile: 17.0secs
182.0bhp 135.7kW 184.5PS
@ 6000rpm
180.0lbft 243.9Nm @ 4000rpm
128.0bhp/ton 125.9bhp/tonne
61.4bhp/L 45.8kW/L 62.2PS/L
49.2ft/sec 15.0m/sec
23.8mph 38.3kmh/1000rpm
16.8mpg 14.0mpgUS 16.8L/100km
Petrol 4-stroke piston
2965cc 180.9cu in
Vee 6
Compression ratio: 8.5:1
Bore: 91.6mm 3.6in
Stroke: 75.0mm 2.9in
Valve type/No: Overhead 12
Transmission: Manual
No. of forward speeds: 5
Wheels driven: Rear
Springs F/R: Coil/Coil
Brake system: PA
Brakes F/R: Disc/Disc
Steering: Rack & pinion
Wheelbase: 259.8cm 102.3in
Track F: 147.3cm 58.0in
Track R: 144.5cm 56.9in
Length: 457.2cm 180.0in
Width: 176.8cm 69.6in
Height: 113.3cm 44.6in
Kerb weight: 1446.0kg 3185.0lb
Fuel: 87.1L 19.1gal 23.0galUS

2669 Maserati

Khamsin
1979 Italy
140.0mph 225.3kmh
0-50mph 80.5kmh: 5.7secs
0-60mph 96.5kmh: 7.3secs
0-1/4 mile: 15.7secs
315.0bhp 234.9kW 319.4PS
@ 5000rpm
308.0lbft 417.3Nm @ 3500rpm
185.7bhp/ton 182.6bhp/tonne
63.9bhp/L 47.6kW/L 64.8PS/L
48.6ft/sec 14.8m/sec
22.8mph 36.7kmh/1000rpm
13.8mpg 11.5mpgUS 20.5L/100km
Petrol 4-stroke piston
4930cc 300.8cu in
Vee 8 4 Carburettor
Compression ratio: 8.5:1
Bore: 93.9mm 3.7in
Stroke: 89.0mm 3.5in
Valve type/No: Overhead 16
Transmission: Manual
No. of forward speeds: 5
Wheels driven: Rear
Springs F/R: Coil/Coil
Brakes F/R: Disc/Disc
Steering: Rack & pinion PA
Wheelbase: 254.8cm 100.3in
Track F: 143.8cm 56.6in
Track R: 146.6cm 57.7in
Length: 457.2cm 180.0in
Width: 180.3cm 71.0in
Height: 119.4cm 47.0in
Ground clearance: 12.7cm 5.0in
Kerb weight: 1725.2kg 3800.0lb
Fuel: 85.9L 18.9gal 22.7galUS

2670 Maserati

Merak SS
1981 Italy
147.0mph 236.5kmh
0-50mph 80.5kmh: 6.2secs
0-60mph 96.5kmh: 7.7secs
0-1/4 mile: 15.8secs
0-1km: 28.7secs
208.0bhp 155.1kW 210.9PS
@ 5800rpm
188.0lbft 254.7Nm @ 4500rpm
152.2bhp/ton 149.6bhp/tonne
70.1bhp/L 52.3kW/L 71.1PS/L
47.5ft/sec 14.5m/sec
22.1mph 35.6kmh/1000rpm
17.9mpg 14.9mpgUS 15.8L/100km
Petrol 4-stroke piston
2965cc 180.9cu in
Vee 6 3 Carburettor
Compression ratio: 8.7:1
Bore: 91.6mm 3.6in
Stroke: 75.0mm 2.9in
Valve type/No: Overhead 12
Transmission: Manual
No. of forward speeds: 5
Wheels driven: Rear
Springs F/R: Coil/Coil
Brake system: PA
Brakes F/R: Disc/Disc
Steering: Rack & pinion
Wheelbase: 259.6cm 102.2in
Length: 432.8cm 170.4in
Width: 173.0cm 68.1in
Height: 115.6cm 45.5in
Ground clearance: 12.7cm 5.0in
Kerb weight: 1390.1kg 3062.0lb
Fuel: 85.1L 18.7gal 22.5galUS

2671 Maserati

Quattroporte
1983 Italy
123.0mph 197.9kmh
0-60mph 96.5kmh: 9.3secs

0-1/4 mile: 17.1secs
288.0bhp 214.8kW 292.0PS
@ 5600rpm
308.0lbft 417.3Nm @ 3000rpm
135.8bhp/ton 133.5bhp/tonne
58.4bhp/L 43.6kW/L 59.2PS/L
54.4ft/sec 16.6m/sec
21.4mph 34.4kmh/1000rpm
10.8mpg 9.0mpgUS 26.1L/100km
Petrol 4-stroke piston
4930cc 300.8cu in
Vee 8 4 Carburettor
Compression ratio: 8.5:1
Bore: 93.9mm 3.7in
Stroke: 89.0mm 3.5in
Valve type/No: Overhead 16
Transmission: Automatic
No. of forward speeds: 3
Wheels driven: Rear
Springs F/R: Coil
Brake system: PA
Brakes F/R: Disc/Disc
Steering: Rack & pinion PA
Wheelbase: 279.9cm 110.2in
Track F: 152.4cm 60.0in
Track R: 152.4cm 60.0in
Length: 497.8cm 196.0in
Width: 189.0cm 74.4in
Height: 134.9cm 53.1in
Ground clearance: 11.4cm 4.5in
Kerb weight: 2156.5kg 4750.0lb
Fuel: 99.9L 22.0gal 26.4galUS

2672 Maserati

Biturbo
1985 Italy
125.0mph 201.1kmh
0-50mph 80.5kmh: 5.5secs
0-60mph 96.5kmh: 7.2secs
0-1/4 mile: 15.7secs
185.0bhp 137.9kW 187.6PS
@ 5500rpm
208.0lbft 281.8Nm @ 3000rpm
174.5bhp/ton 171.6bhp/tonne
74.3bhp/L 55.4kW/L 75.3PS/L
37.9ft/sec 11.5m/sec
21.8mph 35.1kmh/1000rpm
21.6mpg 18.0mpgUS 13.1L/100km
Petrol 4-stroke piston
2491cc 152.0cu in turbocharged
Vee 6 1 Carburettor
Compression ratio: 8.0:1
Bore: 91.6mm 3.6in
Stroke: 63.0mm 2.5in
Valve type/No: Overhead 18
Transmission: Manual
No. of forward speeds: 5
Wheels driven: Rear
Springs F/R: Coil/Coil
Brake system: PA
Brakes F/R: Disc/Disc
Steering: Rack & pinion
Wheelbase: 251.2cm 98.9in
Track F: 142.0cm 55.9in
Track R: 143.0cm 56.3in
Length: 420.4cm 165.5in
Width: 171.5cm 67.5in
Height: 130.6cm 51.4in
Kerb weight: 1078.2kg 2375.0lb
Fuel: 71.9L 15.8gal 19.0galUS

2673 Maserati

Biturbo Automatic
1985 Italy
0-60mph 96.5kmh: 7.3secs
0-1/4 mile: 15.6secs
185.0bhp 137.9kW 187.6PS
@ 5500rpm
208.0lbft 281.8Nm @ 3000rpm
151.8bhp/ton 149.3bhp/tonne
74.3bhp/L 55.4kW/L 75.3PS/L
18.0mpg 15.0mpgUS 15.7L/100km
Petrol 4-stroke piston
2491cc 152.0cu in turbocharged
Vee 6
Valve type/No: Overhead 12
Transmission: Automatic
No. of forward speeds: 3
Wheels driven: Rear
Brakes F/R: Disc/Disc
Steering: Rack & pinion
Length: 420.4cm 165.5in
Kerb weight: 1239.4kg 2730.0lb

2674 Maserati

Biturbo E
1985 Italy
129.0mph 207.6kmh
0-50mph 80.5kmh: 5.0secs
0-60mph 96.5kmh: 6.3secs
0-1/4 mile: 15.0secs
205.0bhp 152.9kW 207.8PS
@ 5250rpm
260.0lbft 352.3Nm @ 3500rpm
165.5bhp/ton 162.7bhp/tonne
82.3bhp/L 61.4kW/L 83.4PS/L
36.2ft/sec 11.0m/sec
23.1mph 37.2kmh/1000rpm
21.6mpg 18.0mpgUS 13.1L/100km
Petrol 4-stroke piston
2491cc 152.0cu in turbocharged
Vee 6 1 Carburettor
Compression ratio: 8.0:1
Bore: 91.6mm 3.6in
Stroke: 63.0mm 2.5in
Valve type/No: Overhead 12
Transmission: Manual
No. of forward speeds: 5
Wheels driven: Rear
Springs F/R: Coil/Coil
Brake system: PA
Brakes F/R: Disc/Disc
Steering: Rack & pinion
Wheelbase: 251.2cm 98.9in
Track F: 142.0cm 55.9in
Track R: 143.0cm 56.3in
Length: 420.4cm 165.5in
Width: 171.5cm 67.5in
Height: 127.0cm 50.0in
Kerb weight: 1259.8kg 2775.0lb
Fuel: 75.7L 16.6gal 20.0galUS

2675 Maserati

Biturbo Spyder
1987 Italy
128.0mph 206.0kmh
0-50mph 80.5kmh: 5.3secs
0-60mph 96.5kmh: 7.2secs
0-1/4 mile: 16.0secs
0-1km: 29.5secs
192.0bhp 143.2kW 194.7PS
@ 5500rpm
220.0lbft 298.1Nm @ 3000rpm
156.8bhp/ton 154.2bhp/tonne
77.1bhp/L 57.5kW/L 78.1PS/L
37.9ft/sec 11.5m/sec
22.9mph 36.8kmh/1000rpm
18.5mpg 15.4mpgUS 15.3L/100km
Petrol 4-stroke piston
2491cc 152.0cu in turbocharged
Vee 6 1 Carburettor
Compression ratio: 7.4:1
Bore: 91.6mm 3.6in
Stroke: 63.0mm 2.5in
Valve type/No: Overhead 18
Transmission: Manual
No. of forward speeds: 5
Wheels driven: Rear
Springs F/R: Coil/Coil
Brake system: PA
Brakes F/R: Disc/Disc
Steering: Rack & pinion PA
Wheelbase: 240.0cm 94.5in
Track F: 142.0cm 55.9in
Track R: 143.1cm 56.3in
Length: 404.3cm 159.2in
Width: 171.4cm 67.5in
Height: 131.0cm 51.6in
Ground clearance: 12.5cm 4.9in
Kerb weight: 1245.0kg 2742.3lb
Fuel: 80.1L 17.6gal 21.1galUS

2676 Maserati

430
1988 Italy
130.0mph 209.2kmh
0-60mph 96.5kmh: 6.5secs
225.0bhp 167.8kW 228.1PS
@ 5500rpm
266.0lbft 360.4Nm @ 3500rpm
192.4bhp/ton 189.2bhp/tonne
80.6bhp/L 60.1kW/L 81.8PS/L
40.3ft/sec 12.3m/sec
Petrol 4-stroke piston
2790cc 170.2cu in turbocharged
Vee 6 fuel injection
Compression ratio: 7.4:1
Bore: 94.0mm 3.7in
Stroke: 67.0mm 2.6in
Valve type/No: Overhead 12
Transmission: Manual
No. of forward speeds: 5
Wheels driven: Rear
Springs F/R: Coil/Coil
Brake system: PA
Brakes F/R: Disc/Disc
Steering: Rack & pinion PA
Wheelbase: 260.1cm 102.4in
Track F: 144.3cm 56.8in
Track R: 145.3cm 57.2in
Length: 439.9cm 173.2in
Width: 173.0cm 68.1in
Height: 130.8cm 51.5in
Kerb weight: 1189.5kg 2620.0lb
Fuel: 81.8L 18.0gal 21.6galUS

2677 Maserati

Biturbo
1988 Italy
129.0mph 207.6kmh
0-50mph 80.5kmh: 5.3secs
0-60mph 96.5kmh: 6.9secs
0-1/4 mile: 15.3secs
187.0bhp 139.4kW 189.6PS
@ 5500rpm
240.0lbft 325.2Nm @ 3000rpm
157.8bhp/ton 155.1bhp/tonne
75.1bhp/L 56.0kW/L 76.1PS/L
37.9ft/sec 11.5m/sec
16.2mpg 13.5mpgUS 17.4L/100km
Petrol 4-stroke piston
2491cc 152.0cu in turbocharged
Vee 6 fuel injection
Compression ratio: 7.3:1
Bore: 91.6mm 3.6in
Stroke: 63.0mm 2.5in
Valve type/No: Overhead 12
Transmission: Manual
No. of forward speeds: 5
Wheels driven: Rear
Springs F/R: Coil/Coil
Brake system: PA
Brakes F/R: Disc/Disc
Steering: Rack & pinion PA
Wheelbase: 251.5cm 99.0in
Track F: 142.0cm 55.9in
Track R: 143.3cm 56.4in
Length: 415.3cm 163.5in
Width: 171.5cm 67.5in
Height: 130.6cm 51.4in
Kerb weight: 1205.4kg 2655.0lb
Fuel: 66.6L 14.6gal 17.6galUS

2678 Maserati

430
1989 Italy
145.0mph 233.3kmh
0-60mph 96.5kmh: 6.3secs
0-1/4 mile: 15.0secs
225.0bhp 167.8kW 228.1PS
@ 5600rpm
246.0lbft 333.3Nm @ 3500rpm
165.0bhp/ton 162.2bhp/tonne
80.6bhp/L 60.1kW/L 81.8PS/L
41.1ft/sec 12.5m/sec
20.4mpg 17.0mpgUS 13.8L/100km
Petrol 4-stroke piston
2790cc 170.2cu in turbocharged
Vee 6 fuel injection
Compression ratio: 7.7:1
Bore: 94.0mm 3.7in
Stroke: 67.0mm 2.6in
Valve type/No: Overhead 18
Transmission: Manual
No. of forward speeds: 5
Wheels driven: Rear
Springs F/R: Coil/Coil
Brake system: PA
Brakes F/R: Disc/Disc
Steering: Rack & pinion PA
Wheelbase: 260.1cm 102.4in
Track F: 144.3cm 56.8in
Track R: 145.3cm 57.2in
Length: 439.9cm 173.2in
Width: 173.0cm 68.1in
Height: 135.9cm 53.5in
Kerb weight: 1387.0kg 3055.0lb
Fuel: 75.7L 16.6gal 20.0galUS

2679 Maserati

Spyder
1989 Italy
130.0mph 209.2kmh
0-50mph 80.5kmh: 5.2secs
0-60mph 96.5kmh: 6.7secs
0-1/4 mile: 15.2secs
225.0bhp 167.8kW 228.1PS
@ 5600rpm
246.0lbft 333.3Nm @ 3500rpm
168.0bhp/ton 165.2bhp/tonne
80.6bhp/L 60.1kW/L 81.8PS/L
41.1ft/sec 12.5m/sec
18.6mpg 15.5mpgUS 15.2L/100km
Petrol 4-stroke piston
2790cc 170.2cu in turbocharged
Vee 6 fuel injection
Compression ratio: 7.4:1
Bore: 94.0mm 3.7in
Stroke: 67.0mm 2.6in
Valve type/No: Overhead 18
Transmission: Manual
No. of forward speeds: 5
Wheels driven: Rear
Springs F/R: Coil/Coil
Brake system: PA
Brakes F/R: Disc/Disc
Steering: Rack & pinion PA
Wheelbase: 240.0cm 94.5in
Track F: 150.1cm 59.1in
Track R: 147.6cm 58.1in
Length: 404.4cm 159.2in
Width: 171.5cm 67.5in
Height: 131.1cm 51.6in
Kerb weight: 1362.0kg 3000.0lb
Fuel: 68.1L 15.0gal 18.0galUS

2680 Maserati

228
1990 Italy
142.0mph 228.5kmh
0-50mph 80.5kmh: 5.2secs
0-60mph 96.5kmh: 6.7secs
0-1/4 mile: 15.2secs
225.0bhp 167.8kW 228.1PS
@ 5600rpm
246.0lbft 333.3Nm @ 3500rpm
166.9bhp/ton 164.1bhp/tonne
80.6bhp/L 60.1kW/L 81.8PS/L
41.1ft/sec 12.5m/sec
18.6mpg 15.5mpgUS 15.2L/100km
Petrol 4-stroke piston
2790cc 170.2cu in turbocharged
Vee 6 fuel injection
Compression ratio: 7.4:1
Bore: 94.0mm 3.7in
Stroke: 67.0mm 2.6in
Valve type/No: Overhead 18
Transmission: Manual
No. of forward speeds: 5
Wheels driven: Rear
Springs F/R: Coil/Coil
Brake system: PA
Brakes F/R: Disc/Disc
Steering: Rack & pinion PA
Wheelbase: 260.1cm 102.4in
Track F: 153.9cm 60.6in
Track R: 154.9cm 61.0in
Length: 446.0cm 175.6in
Width: 186.4cm 73.4in
Height: 133.1cm 52.4in
Kerb weight: 1371.1kg 3020.0lb
Fuel: 65.9L 14.5gal 17.4galUS

2681 Maserati

Shamal
1990 Italy
160.0mph 257.4kmh
325.0bhp 242.3kW 329.5PS
@ 6000rpm
320.0lbft 433.6Nm @ 3000rpm
256.3bhp/ton 252.1bhp/tonne
101.0bhp/L 75.3kW/L 102.4PS/L
52.5ft/sec 16.0m/sec
Petrol 4-stroke piston
3217cc 196.3cu in turbocharged
Vee 8 fuel injection
Compression ratio: 7.5:1
Bore: 80.0mm 3.1in
Stroke: 80.0mm 3.1in
Valve type/No: Overhead 32
Transmission: Manual
No. of forward speeds: 6
Wheels driven: Rear
Springs F/R: Coil/Coil
Brakes F/R: Disc/Disc
Steering: Rack & pinion PA
Wheelbase: 240.0cm 94.5in
Track F: 152.9cm 60.2in
Track R: 152.7cm 60.1in
Length: 410.2cm 161.5in
Width: 194.1cm 76.4in
Height: 127.0cm 50.0in
Kerb weight: 1289.4kg 2840.0lb

2682 Matra
M530A
1969 France
97.0mph 156.1kmh
0-50mph 80.5kmh: 10.5secs
0-60mph 96.5kmh: 15.6secs
0-1/4 mile: 19.9secs
0-1km: 37.2secs
73.0bhp 54.4kW 74.0PS
@ 4800rpm
96.6lbft 130.9Nm @ 2800rpm
84.7bhp/ton 83.3bhp/tonne
43.0bhp/L 32.0kW/L 43.6PS/L
35.1ft/sec 10.7m/sec
19.8mph 31.9kmh/1000rpm
26.9mpg 22.4mpgUS 10.5L/100km
Petrol 4-stroke piston
1699cc 103.7cu in
Vee 4 1 Carburettor
Compression ratio: 9.0:1
Bore: 90.0mm 3.5in
Stroke: 66.8mm 2.6in
Valve type/No: Overhead 8
Transmission: Manual
No. of forward speeds: 4
Wheels driven: Rear
Springs F/R: Coil/Coil
Brakes F/R: Disc/Disc
Steering: Rack & pinion
Wheelbase: 257.8cm 101.5in
Track F: 133.9cm 52.7in
Track R: 134.9cm 53.1in
Length: 419.1cm 165.0in
Width: 156.0cm 61.4in
Height: 124.5cm 49.0in
Ground clearance: 14.0cm 5.5in
Kerb weight: 876.2kg 1930.0lb
Fuel: 45.5L 10.0gal 12.0galUS

2683 Matra
Rancho
1978 France
92.0mph 148.0kmh
0-50mph 80.5kmh: 9.6secs
0-60mph 96.5kmh: 14.9secs
0-1/4 mile: 20.0secs
0-1km: 37.8secs
80.0bhp 59.7kW 81.1PS
@ 5600rpm
88.5lbft 119.9Nm @ 3000rpm
68.4bhp/ton 67.3bhp/tonne
55.5bhp/L 41.4kW/L 56.3PS/L
47.8ft/sec 14.6m/sec
18.3mph 29.4kmh/1000rpm
25.7mpg 21.4mpgUS 11.0L/100km
Petrol 4-stroke piston
1442cc 88.0cu in
In-line 4 1 Carburettor
Compression ratio: 9.5:1
Bore: 76.7mm 3.0in
Stroke: 78.0mm 3.1in
Valve type/No: Overhead 8
Transmission: Manual
No. of forward speeds: 4
Wheels driven: Front
Springs F/R: Torsion bar/Torsion bar
Brake system: PA
Brakes F/R: Disc/Drum
Steering: Rack & pinion
Wheelbase: 252.0cm 99.2in
Track F: 141.0cm 55.5in
Track R: 135.1cm 53.2in
Length: 431.5cm 169.9in
Width: 166.4cm 65.5in
Height: 173.5cm 68.3in
Ground clearance: 21.6cm 8.5in
Kerb weight: 1189.5kg 2620.0lb
Fuel: 60.1L 13.2gal 15.9galUS

2684 Matra-Simca
Bagheera
1975 France
102.0mph 164.1kmh
0-50mph 80.5kmh: 8.5secs
0-60mph 96.5kmh: 12.3secs
0-1/4 mile: 18.7secs
0-1km: 37.5secs
84.0bhp 62.6kW 85.2PS
@ 6000rpm
78.0lbft 105.7Nm @ 4400rpm
87.2bhp/ton 85.8bhp/tonne
64.9bhp/L 48.4kW/L 65.8PS/L
46.0ft/sec 14.0m/sec
17.7mph 28.5kmh/1000rpm
31.0mpg 25.8mpgUS 9.1L/100km
Petrol 4-stroke piston
1294cc 78.9cu in
In-line 4 1 Carburettor
Compression ratio: 9.8:1
Bore: 76.7mm 3.0in
Stroke: 70.0mm 2.8in
Valve type/No: Overhead 8
Transmission: Manual
No. of forward speeds: 4
Wheels driven: Rear
Springs F/R: Torsion bar/Torsion bar
Brake system: PA
Brakes F/R: Disc/Disc
Steering: Rack & pinion
Wheelbase: 231.9cm 91.3in
Track F: 140.2cm 55.2in
Track R: 144.3cm 56.8in
Length: 408.9cm 161.0in
Width: 175.8cm 69.2in
Height: 119.9cm 47.2in
Kerb weight: 979.3kg 2157.0lb
Fuel: 60.1L 13.2gal 15.9galUS

2685 Mazda
110S Coupe
1968 Japan
118.0mph 189.9kmh
0-50mph 80.5kmh: 7.7secs
0-60mph 96.5kmh: 10.2secs
0-1/4 mile: 17.7secs
0-1km: 32.7secs
110.0bhp 82.0kW 111.5PS
@ 7000rpm
96.0lbft 130.1Nm @ 3500rpm
116.7bhp/ton 114.8bhp/tonne
112.0bhp/L 83.5kW/L 113.6PS/L
17.1mph 27.5kmh/1000rpm
17.8mpg 14.8mpgUS 15.9L/100km
Petrol Wankel rotary
982cc 59.9cu in
Rotary 2 1 Carburettor
Compression ratio: 9.4:1
Transmission: Manual
No. of forward speeds: 4
Wheels driven: Rear
Springs F/R: Coil/Leaf
Brake system: PA
Brakes F/R: Disc/Drum
Steering: Rack & pinion
Wheelbase: 218.4cm 86.0in
Track F: 125.0cm 49.2in
Track R: 124.5cm 49.0in
Length: 414.0cm 163.0in
Width: 157.5cm 62.0in
Ground clearance: 12.7cm 5.0in
Kerb weight: 958.4kg 2111.0lb
Fuel: 56.9L 12.5gal 15.0galUS

2686 Mazda
1500 de Luxe
1968 Japan
92.0mph 148.0kmh
0-50mph 80.5kmh: 12.7secs
0-60mph 96.5kmh: 18.0secs
0-1/4 mile: 20.7secs
0-1km: 39.3secs
78.0bhp 58.2kW 79.1PS
@ 5500rpm
85.0lbft 115.2Nm @ 2500rpm
72.9bhp/ton 71.7bhp/tonne
52.3bhp/L 39.0kW/L 53.1PS/L
46.9ft/sec 14.3m/sec
17.1mph 27.5kmh/1000rpm
26.2mpg 21.8mpgUS 10.8L/100km
Petrol 4-stroke piston
1490cc 90.9cu in
In-line 4 1 Carburettor
Compression ratio: 8.2:1
Bore: 78.0mm 3.1in
Stroke: 78.0mm 3.1in
Valve type/No: Overhead 8
Transmission: Manual
No. of forward speeds: 4
Wheels driven: Rear
Springs F/R: Coil/Leaf
Brakes F/R: Drum/Drum
Steering: Recirculating ball
Wheelbase: 252.0cm 99.2in
Track F: 132.8cm 52.3in
Track R: 132.1cm 52.0in
Length: 436.9cm 172.0in
Width: 162.6cm 64.0in
Ground clearance: 17.8cm 7.0in
Kerb weight: 1087.8kg 2396.0lb
Fuel: 50.0L 11.0gal 13.2galUS

2687 Mazda
1200 de Luxe
1970 Japan
87.0mph 140.0kmh
0-50mph 80.5kmh: 11.4secs
0-60mph 96.5kmh: 17.2secs
0-1/4 mile: 20.3secs
0-1km: 38.5secs
73.0bhp 54.4kW 74.0PS
@ 6000rpm
72.0lbft 97.6Nm @ 3000rpm
91.9bhp/ton 90.3bhp/tonne
62.4bhp/L 46.6kW/L 63.3PS/L
49.8ft/sec 15.2m/sec
15.4mph 24.8kmh/1000rpm
29.2mpg 24.3mpgUS 9.7L/100km
Petrol 4-stroke piston
1169cc 71.3cu in
In-line 4 1 Carburettor
Compression ratio: 8.6:1
Bore: 70.0mm 2.8in
Stroke: 76.0mm 3.0in
Valve type/No: Overhead 8
Transmission: Manual
No. of forward speeds: 4
Wheels driven: Rear
Springs F/R: Coil/Leaf
Brakes F/R: Disc/Drum
Steering: Recirculating ball
Wheelbase: 226.6cm 89.2in
Track F: 120.7cm 47.5in
Track R: 119.4cm 47.0in
Length: 379.7cm 149.5in
Width: 149.9cm 59.0in
Height: 141.0cm 55.5in
Ground clearance: 19.1cm 7.5in
Kerb weight: 808.1kg 1780.0lb
Fuel: 40.0L 8.8gal 10.6galUS

2688 Mazda
1800
1971 Japan
85.0mph 136.8kmh
0-50mph 80.5kmh: 12.1secs
0-60mph 96.5kmh: 17.5secs
0-1/4 mile: 20.5secs
98.0bhp 73.1kW 99.4PS
@ 5500rpm
108.0lbft 146.3Nm @ 3000rpm
90.5bhp/ton 89.0bhp/tonne
54.6bhp/L 40.7kW/L 55.3PS/L
56.5ft/sec 17.2m/sec
18.6mph 29.9kmh/1000rpm
24.3mpg 20.2mpgUS 11.6L/100km
Petrol 4-stroke piston
1796cc 109.6cu in
In-line 4 1 Carburettor
Compression ratio: 8.6:1
Bore: 78.0mm 3.1in
Stroke: 94.0mm 3.7in
Valve type/No: Overhead 8
Transmission: Manual
No. of forward speeds: 4
Wheels driven: Rear
Springs F/R: Coil/Leaf
Brake system: PA
Brakes F/R: Disc/Drum
Steering: Recirculating ball
Wheelbase: 249.9cm 98.4in
Track F: 133.1cm 52.4in
Track R: 132.1cm 52.0in
Length: 436.9cm 172.0in
Width: 163.1cm 64.2in
Height: 143.0cm 56.3in
Ground clearance: 18.0cm 7.1in
Kerb weight: 1100.9kg 2425.0lb
Fuel: 50.0L 11.0gal 13.2galUS

2689 Mazda
Rotary
1971 Japan
94.0mph 151.2kmh
0-50mph 80.5kmh: 9.4secs
0-60mph 96.5kmh: 13.5secs
0-1/4 mile: 19.0secs
100.0bhp 74.6kW 101.4PS
@ 7000rpm
92.0lbft 124.7Nm @ 4000rpm
111.4bhp/ton 109.6bhp/tonne
101.8bhp/L 75.9kW/L 103.2PS/L
16.4mph 26.4kmh/1000rpm
18.0mpg 15.0mpgUS 15.7L/100km
Petrol Wankel rotary
982cc 59.9cu in
Rotary 2 1 Carburettor
Compression ratio: 9.4:1
Transmission: Manual
No. of forward speeds: 4
Wheels driven: Rear
Springs F/R: Coil/Leaf
Brakes F/R: Disc/Drum
Steering: Recirculating ball
Wheelbase: 226.1cm 89.0in
Track F: 119.9cm 47.2in
Track R: 119.1cm 46.9in
Length: 383.0cm 150.8in
Width: 148.1cm 58.3in
Height: 134.6cm 53.0in
Ground clearance: 16.0cm 6.3in
Kerb weight: 912.5kg 2010.0lb
Fuel: 50.0L 11.0gal 13.2galUS

2690 Mazda
RX-2
1971 Japan
119.0mph 191.5kmh
0-50mph 80.5kmh: 7.2secs
0-60mph 96.5kmh: 10.0secs
0-1/4 mile: 17.6secs
130.0bhp 96.9kW 131.8PS
@ 7000rpm
116.0lbft 157.2Nm @ 4000rpm
125.8bhp/ton 123.7bhp/tonne
113.4bhp/L 84.6kW/L 115.0PS/L
17.0mph 27.4kmh/1000rpm
23.3mpg 19.4mpgUS 12.1L/100km
Petrol Wankel rotary
1146cc 69.9cu in
Rotary 2 1 Carburettor
Compression ratio: 9.4:1
Transmission: Manual
No. of forward speeds: 4
Wheels driven: Rear
Springs F/R: Coil/Coil
Brakes F/R: Disc/Drum
Steering: Recirculating ball
Wheelbase: 246.9cm 97.2in
Track F: 128.5cm 50.6in
Track R: 127.8cm 50.3in
Length: 414.5cm 163.2in
Width: 158.0cm 62.2in
Height: 139.4cm 54.9in
Ground clearance: 16.0cm 6.3in
Kerb weight: 1051.0kg 2315.0lb
Fuel: 65.5L 14.4gal 17.3galUS

2691 Mazda
RX-2
1972 Japan
116.0mph 186.6kmh
0-50mph 80.5kmh: 7.8secs
0-60mph 96.5kmh: 10.3secs
0-1/4 mile: 17.8secs
0-1km: 32.0secs
120.0bhp 89.5kW 121.7PS
@ 7000rpm
100.0lbft 135.5Nm @ 4000rpm
123.2bhp/ton 121.1bhp/tonne
104.7bhp/L 78.1kW/L 106.2PS/L
17.2mph 27.7kmh/1000rpm
17.8mpg 14.8mpgUS 15.9L/100km
Petrol Wankel rotary
1146cc 69.9cu in
Rotary 2 1 Carburettor
Compression ratio: 9.4:1
Transmission: Manual
No. of forward speeds: 4
Wheels driven: Rear
Springs F/R: Coil/Coil
Brake system: PA
Brakes F/R: Disc/Drum
Steering: Recirculating ball
Wheelbase: 247.7cm 97.5in
Track F: 128.5cm 50.6in
Track R: 128.0cm 50.4in
Length: 414.0cm 163.0in
Width: 157.5cm 62.0in
Height: 142.2cm 56.0in
Ground clearance: 16.0cm 6.3in
Kerb weight: 990.6kg 2182.0lb
Fuel: 66.0L 14.5gal 17.4galUS

2692 Mazda
RX-3
1972 Japan
112.0mph 180.2kmh
0-50mph 80.5kmh: 7.9secs
0-60mph 96.5kmh: 10.9secs
0-1/4 mile: 17.8secs
90.0bhp 67.1kW 91.2PS
@ 6000rpm
96.0lbft 130.1Nm @ 4000rpm
97.9bhp/ton 96.2bhp/tonne
78.5bhp/L 58.6kW/L 79.6PS/L
17.2mph 27.7kmh/1000rpm
21.6mpg 18.0mpgUS 13.1L/100km

Petrol Wankel rotary
1146cc 69.9cu in
Rotary 2 1 Carburettor
Compression ratio: 9.4:1
Transmission: Manual
No. of forward speeds: 4
Wheels driven: Rear
Springs F/R: Coil/Leaf
Brake system: PA
Brakes F/R: Disc/Drum
Steering: Recirculating ball
Wheelbase: 231.1cm 91.0in
Track F: 130.0cm 51.2in
Track R: 128.0cm 50.4in
Length: 406.4cm 160.0in
Width: 160.0cm 63.0in
Height: 137.7cm 54.2in
Ground clearance: 16.5cm 6.5in
Kerb weight: 935.2kg 2060.0lb
Fuel: 59.0L 13.0gal 15.6galUS

2693 Mazda

RX-3 Station Wagon
1973 Japan
0-60mph 96.5kmh: 12.1secs
0-1/4 mile: 18.4secs
90.0bhp 67.1kW 91.2PS
@ 6000rpm
96.0lbft 130.1Nm @ 4000rpm
86.7bhp/ton 85.3bhp/tonne
78.5bhp/L 58.6kW/L 79.6PS/L
21.6mpg 18.0mpgUS 13.1L/100km
Petrol Wankel rotary
1146cc 69.9cu in
Rotary 2
Transmission: Manual
No. of forward speeds: 4
Wheels driven: Rear
Brake system: PA
Brakes F/R: Disc/Drum
Wheelbase: 231.1cm 91.0in
Length: 414.0cm 163.0in
Width: 160.0cm 63.0in
Height: 139.7cm 55.0in
Kerb weight: 1055.5kg 2325.0lb

2694 Mazda

RX-4
1973 Japan
109.0mph 175.4kmh
0-50mph 80.5kmh: 7.6secs
0-60mph 96.5kmh: 10.8secs
0-1/4 mile: 17.8secs
0-1km: 33.1secs
130.0bhp 96.9kW 131.8PS
@ 7000rpm
115.0lbft 155.8Nm @ 4000rpm
123.6bhp/ton 121.5bhp/tonne
113.4bhp/L 84.6kW/L 115.0PS/L
17.4mph 28.0kmh/1000rpm
16.2mpg 13.5mpgUS 17.4L/100km
Petrol Wankel rotary
1146cc 69.9cu in
Rotary 2 1 Carburettor
Compression ratio: 9.4:1
Transmission: Manual
No. of forward speeds: 4
Wheels driven: Rear
Springs F/R: Coil/Leaf
Brake system: PA
Brakes F/R: Disc/Drum
Steering: Recirculating ball
Wheelbase: 251.5cm 99.0in
Track F: 137.2cm 54.0in
Track R: 137.2cm 54.0in
Length: 424.2cm 167.0in
Width: 165.1cm 65.0in
Height: 142.2cm 56.0in
Ground clearance: 17.8cm 7.0in
Kerb weight: 1069.6kg 2356.0lb
Fuel: 65.1L 14.3gal 17.2galUS

2695 Mazda

1300
1974 Japan
94.0mph 151.2kmh
0-50mph 80.5kmh: 9.6secs
0-60mph 96.5kmh: 15.1secs
0-1/4 mile: 19.8secs
0-1km: 37.4secs
69.0bhp 51.4kW 70.0PS
@ 6200rpm
68.0lbft 92.1Nm @ 4000rpm
85.6bhp/ton 84.1bhp/tonne
54.2bhp/L 40.4kW/L 55.0PS/L
51.5ft/sec 15.7m/sec
16.0mph 25.7kmh/1000rpm
25.7mpg 21.4mpgUS 11.0L/100km
Petrol 4-stroke piston
1272cc 77.6cu in
In-line 4 1 Carburettor
Compression ratio: 9.2:1
Bore: 73.0mm 2.9in
Stroke: 76.0mm 3.0in
Valve type/No: Overhead 8
Transmission: Manual
No. of forward speeds: 4
Wheels driven: Rear
Springs F/R: Coil/Leaf
Brakes F/R: Disc/Drum
Steering: Ball & nut
Wheelbase: 226.1cm 89.0in
Track F: 127.0cm 50.0in
Track R: 124.5cm 49.0in
Length: 386.1cm 152.0in
Width: 154.9cm 61.0in
Height: 139.7cm 55.0in
Ground clearance: 15.2cm 6.0in
Kerb weight: 819.9kg 1806.0lb
Fuel: 40.0L 8.8gal 10.6galUS

2696 Mazda

929
1974 Japan
94.0mph 151.2kmh
0-50mph 80.5kmh: 9.6secs
0-60mph 96.5kmh: 14.0secs
0-1/4 mile: 19.6secs
0-1km: 36.9secs
83.0bhp 61.9kW 84.1PS
@ 5000rpm
99.0lbft 134.1Nm @ 3000rpm
71.9bhp/ton 70.7bhp/tonne
46.9bhp/L 35.0kW/L 47.6PS/L
48.1ft/sec 14.7m/sec
17.5mph 28.2kmh/1000rpm
22.5mpg 18.7mpgUS 12.6L/100km
Petrol 4-stroke piston
1769cc 107.9cu in
In-line 4 1 Carburettor
Compression ratio: 8.6:1
Bore: 80.0mm 3.1in
Stroke: 88.0mm 3.5in
Valve type/No: Overhead 8
Transmission: Manual
No. of forward speeds: 4
Wheels driven: Rear
Springs F/R: Coil/Leaf
Brake system: PA
Brakes F/R: Disc/Drum
Steering: Recirculating ball
Wheelbase: 256.5cm 101.0in
Track F: 137.2cm 54.0in
Track R: 137.2cm 54.0in
Length: 440.7cm 173.5in
Width: 165.1cm 65.0in
Height: 142.2cm 56.0in
Ground clearance: 17.8cm 7.0in
Kerb weight: 1174.5kg 2587.0lb
Fuel: 65.1L 14.3gal 17.2galUS

2697 Mazda

Rotary Pickup
1974 Japan
103.0mph 165.7kmh
0-50mph 80.5kmh: 8.0secs
0-60mph 96.5kmh: 11.0secs
0-1/4 mile: 18.3secs
110.0bhp 82.0kW 111.5PS
@ 6000rpm
117.0lbft 158.5Nm @ 3500rpm
86.0bhp/ton 84.6bhp/tonne
84.1bhp/L 62.7kW/L 85.3PS/L
15.9mph 25.6kmh/1000rpm
19.8mpg 16.5mpgUS 14.3L/100km
Petrol Wankel rotary
1308cc 79.8cu in
Rotary 2 1 Carburettor
Compression ratio: 9.2:1
Transmission: Manual
No. of forward speeds: 4
Wheels driven: Rear
Springs F/R: Coil/Leaf
Brake system: PA
Brakes F/R: Disc/Drum
Steering: Recirculating ball
Wheelbase: 264.2cm 104.0in
Track F: 144.8cm 57.0in
Track R: 142.2cm 56.0in
Length: 439.4cm 173.0in
Width: 170.2cm 67.0in
Height: 154.9cm 61.0in
Ground clearance: 20.3cm 8.0in
Kerb weight: 1300.7kg 2865.0lb
Fuel: 77.2L 17.0gal 20.4galUS

2698 Mazda

RX-4 Coupe
1974 Japan
117.0mph 188.3kmh
0-50mph 80.5kmh: 7.1secs
0-60mph 96.5kmh: 9.7secs
0-1/4 mile: 17.4secs
110.0bhp 82.0kW 111.5PS
@ 6000rpm
117.0lbft 158.5Nm @ 3500rpm
94.0bhp/ton 92.5bhp/tonne
84.1bhp/L 62.7kW/L 85.3PS/L
17.2mph 27.7kmh/1000rpm
21.0mpg 17.5mpgUS 13.4L/100km
Petrol Wankel rotary
1308cc 79.8cu in
Rotary 2 1 Carburettor
Compression ratio: 9.2:1
Transmission: Manual
No. of forward speeds: 4
Wheels driven: Rear
Springs F/R: Coil/Leaf
Brake system: PA
Brakes F/R: Disc/Drum
Steering: Recirculating ball
Wheelbase: 251.5cm 99.0in
Track F: 137.2cm 54.0in
Track R: 137.2cm 54.0in
Length: 449.6cm 177.0in
Width: 167.6cm 66.0in
Height: 137.2cm 54.0in
Ground clearance: 17.8cm 7.0in
Kerb weight: 1189.5kg 2620.0lb
Fuel: 64.0L 14.1gal 16.9galUS

2699 Mazda

RX-4 Station Wagon
1974 Japan
0-60mph 96.5kmh: 11.7secs
0-1/4 mile: 18.0secs
110.0bhp 82.0kW 111.5PS
@ 6000rpm
117.0lbft 158.5Nm @ 3500rpm
84.4bhp/ton 83.0bhp/tonne
84.1bhp/L 62.7kW/L 85.3PS/L
20.4mpg 17.0mpgUS 13.8L/100km
Petrol Wankel rotary
1308cc 79.8cu in
Rotary 2
Transmission: Manual
No. of forward speeds: 4
Wheels driven: Rear
Brakes F/R: Disc/Drum
Wheelbase: 251.5cm 99.0in
Length: 467.4cm 184.0in
Width: 165.1cm 65.0in
Height: 142.2cm 56.0in
Kerb weight: 1325.7kg 2920.0lb

2700 Mazda

808
1975 Japan
97.0mph 156.1kmh
0-50mph 80.5kmh: 11.0secs
0-60mph 96.5kmh: 15.6secs
0-1/4 mile: 20.3secs
70.0bhp 52.2kW 71.0PS
@ 5000rpm
82.0lbft 111.1Nm @ 3500rpm
74.3bhp/ton 73.1bhp/tonne
44.0bhp/L 32.8kW/L 44.6PS/L
45.4ft/sec 13.8m/sec
18.1mph 29.1kmh/1000rpm
25.2mpg 21.0mpgUS 11.2L/100km
Petrol 4-stroke piston
1590cc 97.0cu in
In-line 4 1 Carburettor
Compression ratio: 8.6:1
Bore: 78.0mm 3.1in
Stroke: 83.0mm 3.3in
Valve type/No: Overhead 8
Transmission: Manual
No. of forward speeds: 4
Wheels driven: Rear
Springs F/R: Coil/Leaf
Brake system: PA
Brakes F/R: Disc/Drum
Steering: Recirculating ball
Wheelbase: 231.1cm 91.0in
Track F: 129.5cm 51.0in
Track R: 129.5cm 51.0in
Length: 426.7cm 168.0in
Width: 160.0cm 63.0in
Height: 134.6cm 53.0in
Ground clearance: 15.2cm 6.0in
Kerb weight: 957.9kg 2110.0lb
Fuel: 44.3L 9.7gal 11.7galUS

2701 Mazda

Cosmo
1976 Japan
111.0mph 178.6kmh
0-50mph 80.5kmh: 8.4secs
0-60mph 96.5kmh: 11.2secs
0-1/4 mile: 18.1secs
110.0bhp 82.0kW 111.5PS
@ 6000rpm
120.0lbft 162.6Nm @ 4000rpm
88.2bhp/ton 86.7bhp/tonne
84.1bhp/L 62.7kW/L 85.3PS/L
21.5mph 34.6kmh/1000rpm
24.6mpg 20.5mpgUS 11.5L/100km
Petrol Wankel rotary
1308cc 79.8cu in
Rotary 2 1 Carburettor
Compression ratio: 9.2:1
Transmission: Manual
No. of forward speeds: 5
Wheels driven: Rear
Springs F/R: Coil/Coil
Brake system: PA
Brakes F/R: Disc/Disc
Steering: Recirculating ball
Wheelbase: 251.5cm 99.0in
Track F: 137.2cm 54.0in
Track R: 137.2cm 54.0in
Length: 462.3cm 182.0in
Width: 167.6cm 66.0in
Height: 132.1cm 52.0in
Ground clearance: 15.2cm 6.0in
Kerb weight: 1268.9kg 2795.0lb
Fuel: 64.0L 14.1gal 16.9galUS

2702 Mazda

323
1977 Japan
90.0mph 144.8kmh
0-50mph 80.5kmh: 9.9secs
0-60mph 96.5kmh: 14.7secs
0-1/4 mile: 19.6secs
0-1km: 37.4secs
60.0bhp 44.7kW 60.8PS
@ 5500rpm
68.7lbft 93.1Nm @ 3500rpm
72.2bhp/ton 71.0bhp/tonne
47.2bhp/L 35.2kW/L 47.8PS/L
45.7ft/sec 13.9m/sec
16.4mph 26.4kmh/1000rpm
27.9mpg 23.2mpgUS 10.1L/100km
Petrol 4-stroke piston
1272cc 77.6cu in
In-line 4 1 Carburettor
Compression ratio: 9.2:1
Bore: 73.0mm 2.9in
Stroke: 76.0mm 3.0in
Valve type/No: Overhead 8
Transmission: Manual
No. of forward speeds: 4
Wheels driven: Rear
Springs F/R: Coil/Coil
Brake system: PA
Brakes F/R: Disc/Drum
Steering: Recirculating ball
Wheelbase: 231.4cm 91.1in
Track F: 129.5cm 51.0in
Track R: 131.1cm 51.6in
Length: 391.9cm 154.3in
Width: 160.5cm 63.2in
Height: 136.9cm 53.9in
Ground clearance: 16.0cm 6.3in
Kerb weight: 845.3kg 1862.0lb
Fuel: 40.0L 8.8gal 10.6galUS

2703 Mazda

GLC
1977 Japan
91.0mph 146.4kmh
0-50mph 80.5kmh: 11.1secs
0-60mph 96.5kmh: 16.2secs
0-1/4 mile: 20.4secs
49.0bhp 36.5kW 49.7PS
@ 5000rpm
63.0lbft 85.4Nm @ 3000rpm
55.2bhp/ton 54.2bhp/tonne
38.5bhp/L 28.7kW/L 39.1PS/L
41.5ft/sec 12.7m/sec
21.4mph 34.4kmh/1000rpm
41.4mpg 34.5mpgUS 6.8L/100km
Petrol 4-stroke piston

1272cc 77.6cu in
In-line 4 1 Carburettor
Compression ratio: 9.2:1
Bore: 73.0mm 2.9in
Stroke: 76.0mm 3.0in
Valve type/No: Overhead 8
Transmission: Manual
No. of forward speeds: 5
Wheels driven: Rear
Springs F/R: Coil/Coil
Brake system: PA
Brakes F/R: Disc/Drum
Steering: Recirculating ball
Wheelbase: 231.4cm 91.1in
Track F: 129.5cm 51.0in
Track R: 131.1cm 51.6in
Length: 391.9cm 154.3in
Width: 160.5cm 63.2in
Height: 136.9cm 53.9in
Ground clearance: 16.0cm 6.3in
Kerb weight: 903.5kg 1990.0lb
Fuel: 40.1L 8.8gal 10.6galUS

2704 Mazda

RX-4
1977 Japan
112.0mph 180.2kmh
0-60mph 96.5kmh: 12.4secs
0-1/4 mile: 18.8secs
110.0bhp 82.0kW 111.5PS
@ 6000rpm
120.0lbft 162.6Nm @ 4000rpm
90.6bhp/ton 89.1bhp/tonne
84.1bhp/L 62.7kW/L 85.3PS/L
Petrol Wankel rotary
1308cc 79.8cu in
Rotary 2 1 Carburettor
Compression ratio: 9.2:1
Transmission: Manual
No. of forward speeds: 5
Wheels driven: Rear
Brakes F/R: Disc/Drum
Wheelbase: 251.5cm 99.0in
Track F: 137.2cm 54.0in
Track R: 137.2cm 54.0in
Length: 454.7cm 179.0in
Width: 165.1cm 65.0in
Height: 142.2cm 56.0in
Kerb weight: 1234.9kg 2720.0lb
Fuel: 64.0L 14.1gal 16.9galUS

2705 Mazda

RX-7
1978 Japan
122.0mph 196.3kmh
0-50mph 80.5kmh: 6.7secs
0-60mph 96.5kmh: 9.2secs
0-1/4 mile: 17.0secs
100.0bhp 74.6kW 101.4PS
@ 6000rpm
105.0lbft 142.3Nm @ 4000rpm
92.6bhp/ton 91.0bhp/tonne
87.3bhp/L 65.1kW/L 88.5PS/L
20.9mph 33.6kmh/1000rpm
26.4mpg 22.0mpgUS 10.7L/100km
Petrol Wankel rotary
1146cc 69.9cu in
Rotary 2 1 Carburettor
Compression ratio: 9.4:1
Transmission: Manual
No. of forward speeds: 5
Wheels driven: Rear
Springs F/R: Coil/Coil
Brake system: PA
Brakes F/R: Disc/Drum
Steering: Recirculating ball
Wheelbase: 242.1cm 95.3in
Track F: 142.0cm 55.9in
Track R: 140.0cm 55.1in
Length: 428.5cm 168.7in
Width: 167.4cm 65.9in
Height: 126.0cm 49.6in
Ground clearance: 15.5cm 6.1in
Kerb weight: 1098.7kg 2420.0lb
Fuel: 54.9L 12.1gal 14.5galUS

2706 Mazda

1.4 SP
1979 Japan
88.0mph 141.6kmh
0-50mph 80.5kmh: 9.4secs
0-60mph 96.5kmh: 14.4secs
0-1/4 mile: 19.5secs
0-1km: 37.0secs
70.0bhp 52.2kW 71.0PS
@ 5700rpm
80.0lbft 108.4Nm @ 3200rpm
82.7bhp/ton 81.3bhp/tonne
49.5bhp/L 36.9kW/L 50.2PS/L
47.3ft/sec 14.4m/sec
20.2mph 32.5kmh/1000rpm
29.2mpg 24.3mpgUS 9.7L/100km
Petrol 4-stroke piston
1415cc 86.3cu in
In-line 4 1 Carburettor
Compression ratio: 9.0:1
Bore: 77.0mm 3.0in
Stroke: 76.0mm 3.0in
Valve type/No: Overhead 8
Transmission: Manual
No. of forward speeds: 5
Wheels driven: Rear
Springs F/R: Coil/Coil
Brake system: PA
Brakes F/R: Disc/Drum
Steering: Recirculating ball
Wheelbase: 231.4cm 91.1in
Track F: 129.5cm 51.0in
Track R: 131.1cm 51.6in
Length: 391.9cm 154.3in
Width: 160.5cm 63.2in
Height: 136.9cm 53.9in
Ground clearance: 16.0cm 6.3in
Kerb weight: 860.8kg 1896.0lb
Fuel: 45.0L 9.9gal 11.9galUS

2707 Mazda

626 Coupe
1979 Japan
105.0mph 168.9kmh
0-60mph 96.5kmh: 10.7secs
0-1/4 mile: 18.3secs
80.0bhp 59.7kW 81.1PS
@ 4500rpm
105.0lbft 142.3Nm @ 2500rpm
71.7bhp/ton 70.5bhp/tonne
40.6bhp/L 30.3kW/L 41.2PS/L
48.2ft/sec 14.7m/sec
22.1mph 35.6kmh/1000rpm
34.8mpg 29.0mpgUS 8.1L/100km
Petrol 4-stroke piston
1970cc 120.2cu in
In-line 4 1 Carburettor
Compression ratio: 8.6:1
Bore: 80.0mm 3.1in
Stroke: 98.0mm 3.9in
Valve type/No: Overhead 8
Transmission: Manual
No. of forward speeds: 5
Wheels driven: Rear
Springs F/R: Coil/Coil
Brake system: PA
Brakes F/R: Disc/Drum
Steering: Recirculating ball
Wheelbase: 251.0cm 98.8in
Track F: 136.9cm 53.9in
Track R: 137.9cm 54.3in
Length: 441.5cm 173.8in
Width: 166.1cm 65.4in
Height: 135.4cm 53.3in
Ground clearance: 15.5cm 6.1in
Kerb weight: 1135.0kg 2500.0lb
Fuel: 54.9L 12.1gal 14.5galUS

2708 Mazda

GLC Wagon
1979 Japan
96.0mph 154.5kmh
0-50mph 80.5kmh: 9.0secs
0-60mph 96.5kmh: 13.5secs
0-1/4 mile: 19.4secs
65.0bhp 48.5kW 65.9PS
@ 5000rpm
76.0lbft 103.0Nm @ 3000rpm
68.7bhp/ton 67.5bhp/tonne
45.9bhp/L 34.2kW/L 46.6PS/L
41.5ft/sec 12.7m/sec
22.2mph 35.7kmh/1000rpm
39.6mpg 33.0mpgUS 7.1L/100km
Petrol 4-stroke piston
1415cc 86.3cu in
In-line 4
Compression ratio: 9.0:1
Bore: 77.0mm 3.0in
Stroke: 76.0mm 3.0in
Valve type/No: Overhead 8
Transmission: Manual
No. of forward speeds: 5
Wheels driven: Rear
Springs F/R: Coil/Leaf
Brake system: PA
Brakes F/R: Disc/Drum
Steering: Recirculating ball
Wheelbase: 231.4cm 91.1in
Track F: 129.5cm 51.0in
Track R: 131.1cm 51.6in
Length: 414.5cm 163.2in
Width: 160.5cm 63.2in
Height: 142.5cm 56.1in
Kerb weight: 962.5kg 2120.0lb
Fuel: 45.0L 9.9gal 11.9galUS

2709 Mazda

Montrose 1600 GLS
1979 Japan
101.0mph 162.5kmh
0-50mph 80.5kmh: 9.4secs
0-60mph 96.5kmh: 13.6secs
0-1/4 mile: 19.6secs
0-1km: 36.5secs
75.0bhp 55.9kW 76.0PS
@ 5500rpm
88.2lbft 119.5Nm @ 3500rpm
72.8bhp/ton 71.6bhp/tonne
47.3bhp/L 35.3kW/L 47.9PS/L
50.0ft/sec 15.2m/sec
17.2mph 27.7kmh/1000rpm
24.9mpg 20.7mpgUS 11.3L/100km
Petrol 4-stroke piston
1586cc 96.8cu in
In-line 4 1 Carburettor
Compression ratio: 8.6:1
Bore: 78.0mm 3.1in
Stroke: 83.0mm 3.3in
Valve type/No: Overhead 8
Transmission: Manual
No. of forward speeds: 4
Wheels driven: Rear
Springs F/R: Coil/Coil
Brake system: PA
Brakes F/R: Disc/Drum
Steering: Recirculating ball
Wheelbase: 251.0cm 98.8in
Track F: 137.2cm 54.0in
Track R: 137.9cm 54.3in
Length: 430.5cm 169.5in
Width: 166.1cm 65.4in
Height: 134.6cm 53.0in
Ground clearance: 15.5cm 6.1in
Kerb weight: 1047.4kg 2307.0lb
Fuel: 55.1L 12.1gal 14.5galUS

2710 Mazda

RX-7
1979 Japan
115.0mph 185.0kmh
0-50mph 80.5kmh: 6.9secs
0-60mph 96.5kmh: 10.1secs
0-1/4 mile: 17.5secs
0-1km: 32.3secs
105.0bhp 78.3kW 106.5PS
@ 6000rpm
106.0lbft 143.6Nm @ 4000rpm
104.2bhp/ton 102.4bhp/tonne
91.6bhp/L 68.3kW/L 92.9PS/L
21.1mph 33.9kmh/1000rpm
18.2mpg 15.2mpgUS 15.5L/100km
Petrol Wankel rotary
1146cc 69.9cu in
Rotary 2 1 Carburettor
Compression ratio: 9.4:1
Transmission: Manual
No. of forward speeds: 5
Wheels driven: Rear
Springs F/R: Coil/Coil
Brake system: PA
Brakes F/R: Disc/Drum
Steering: Recirculating ball
Wheelbase: 242.1cm 95.3in
Track F: 142.0cm 55.9in
Track R: 140.0cm 55.1in
Length: 428.5cm 168.7in
Width: 167.4cm 65.9in
Height: 126.0cm 49.6in
Ground clearance: 16.0cm 6.3in
Kerb weight: 1025.1kg 2258.0lb
Fuel: 55.1L 12.1gal 14.5galUS

2711 Mazda

RX-7 GS
1979 Japan
0-60mph 96.5kmh: 9.7secs
0-1/4 mile: 17.7secs
100.0bhp 74.6kW 101.4PS
@ 6000rpm
105.0lbft 142.3Nm @ 4000rpm
92.0bhp/ton 90.5bhp/tonne
87.3bhp/L 65.1kW/L 88.5PS/L
19.2mpg 16.0mpgUS 14.7L/100km
Petrol Wankel rotary
1146cc 69.9cu in
Rotary 2 1 Carburettor
Compression ratio: 9.4:1
Transmission: Automatic
No. of forward speeds: 3
Wheels driven: Rear
Brake system: PA
Brakes F/R: Disc/Drum
Wheelbase: 242.1cm 95.3in
Track F: 142.0cm 55.9in
Track R: 140.0cm 55.1in
Length: 428.5cm 168.7in
Width: 167.4cm 65.9in
Height: 126.0cm 49.6in
Kerb weight: 1105.5kg 2435.0lb
Fuel: 54.9L 12.1gal 14.5galUS

2712 Mazda

626
1980 Japan
0-60mph 96.5kmh: 14.4secs
0-1/4 mile: 19.6secs
75.0bhp 55.9kW 76.0PS
@ 4500rpm
105.0lbft 142.3Nm @ 2500rpm
65.1bhp/ton 64.0bhp/tonne
38.1bhp/L 28.4kW/L 38.6PS/L
48.2ft/sec 14.7m/sec
28.2mpg 23.5mpgUS 10.0L/100km
Petrol 4-stroke piston
1970cc 120.2cu in
In-line 4 1 Carburettor
Compression ratio: 8.6:1
Bore: 80.0mm 3.1in
Stroke: 98.0mm 3.9in
Valve type/No: Overhead 8
Transmission: Manual
No. of forward speeds: 5
Wheels driven: Rear
Brakes F/R: Disc/Drum
Wheelbase: 251.0cm 98.8in
Track F: 136.9cm 53.9in
Track R: 137.9cm 54.3in
Length: 428.5cm 168.7in
Width: 165.1cm 65.0in
Height: 126.0cm 49.6in
Kerb weight: 1171.3kg 2580.0lb
Fuel: 54.9L 12.1gal 14.5galUS

2713 Mazda

Montrose GLS Coupe
1980 Japan
108.0mph 173.8kmh
0-50mph 80.5kmh: 9.1secs
0-60mph 96.5kmh: 12.9secs
0-1/4 mile: 19.0secs
0-1km: 35.3secs
90.0bhp 67.1kW 91.2PS
@ 4800rpm
113.0lbft 153.1Nm @ 2500rpm
84.4bhp/ton 83.0bhp/tonne
45.7bhp/L 34.1kW/L 46.3PS/L
51.5ft/sec 15.7m/sec
21.6mph 34.8kmh/1000rpm
27.9mpg 23.2mpgUS 10.1L/100km
Petrol 4-stroke piston
1970cc 120.2cu in
In-line 4 1 Carburettor
Compression ratio: 8.6:1
Bore: 80.0mm 3.1in
Stroke: 98.0mm 3.9in
Valve type/No: Overhead 8
Transmission: Manual
No. of forward speeds: 5
Wheels driven: Rear
Springs F/R: Coil/Coil
Brake system: PA
Brakes F/R: Disc/Drum
Steering: Recirculating ball
Wheelbase: 251.0cm 98.8in
Track F: 137.2cm 54.0in
Track R: 137.9cm 54.3in
Length: 430.5cm 169.5in
Width: 166.1cm 65.4in
Height: 134.6cm 53.0in
Ground clearance: 15.5cm 6.1in
Kerb weight: 1084.6kg 2389.0lb
Fuel: 55.1L 12.1gal 14.5galUS

2714 Mazda

RX-7
1980 Japan
122.0mph 196.3kmh
0-60mph 96.5kmh: 9.2secs
0-1/4 mile: 17.0secs

100.0bhp 74.6kW 101.4PS
@ 6000rpm
105.0lbft 142.3Nm @ 4000rpm
92.6bhp/ton 91.0bhp/tonne
87.3bhp/L 65.1kW/L 88.5PS/L
20.9mph 33.6kmh/1000rpm
26.4mpg 22.0mpgUS 10.7L/100km
Petrol Wankel rotary
1146cc 69.9cu in
Rotary 2 1 Carburettor
Compression ratio: 9.4:1
Transmission: Manual
No. of forward speeds: 5
Wheels driven: Rear
Springs F/R: Coil/Coil
Brake system: PA
Brakes F/R: Disc/Drum
Steering: Recirculating ball
Wheelbase: 242.1cm 95.3in
Track F: 142.0cm 55.9in
Track R: 140.0cm 55.1in
Length: 428.5cm 168.7in
Width: 167.4cm 65.9in
Height: 126.0cm 49.6in
Ground clearance: 15.5cm 6.1in
Kerb weight: 1098.7kg 2420.0lb
Fuel: 54.9L 12.1gal 14.5galUS

2715 Mazda

RX-7 Racer
1980 Japan
133.0mph 214.0kmh
0-50mph 80.5kmh: 4.2secs
0-60mph 96.5kmh: 5.3secs
0-1/4 mile: 14.1secs
270.0bhp 201.3kW 273.7PS
@ 9000rpm
166.0lbft 224.9Nm @ 7500rpm
271.8bhp/ton 267.3bhp/tonne
235.6bhp/L 175.7kW/L 238.9PS/L
14.8mph 23.8kmh/1000rpm
7.8mpg 6.5mpgUS 36.2L/100km
Petrol Wankel rotary
1146cc 69.9cu in
Rotary 2 1 Carburettor
Compression ratio: 9.4:1
Transmission: Manual
No. of forward speeds: 5
Wheels driven: Rear
Springs F/R: Coil/Coil
Brake system: PA
Brakes F/R: Disc/Disc
Steering: Recirculating ball
Wheelbase: 242.1cm 95.3in
Track F: 153.7cm 60.5in
Track R: 157.5cm 62.0in
Length: 428.5cm 168.7in
Width: 191.8cm 75.5in
Height: 116.8cm 46.0in
Ground clearance: 7.6cm 3.0in
Kerb weight: 1010.1kg 2225.0lb
Fuel: 109.8L 24.1gal 29.0galUS

2716 Mazda

323 1300
1981 Japan
94.0mph 151.2kmh
0-50mph 80.5kmh: 8.9secs
0-60mph 96.5kmh: 13.1secs
0-1/4 mile: 18.9secs
0-1km: 35.9secs
68.0bhp 50.7kW 68.9PS
@ 6000rpm
70.0lbft 94.9Nm @ 3500rpm
81.5bhp/ton 80.1bhp/tonne
52.5bhp/L 39.1kW/L 53.2PS/L
45.7ft/sec 13.9m/sec
17.4mph 28.0kmh/1000rpm
31.8mpg 26.5mpgUS 8.9L/100km
Petrol 4-stroke piston
1296cc 79.1cu in
In-line 4 1 Carburettor
Compression ratio: 9.2:1
Bore: 77.0mm 3.0in
Stroke: 69.6mm 2.7in
Valve type/No: Overhead 8
Transmission: Manual
No. of forward speeds: 4
Wheels driven: Front
Springs F/R: Coil/Coil
Brake system: PA
Brakes F/R: Disc/Drum
Steering: Rack & pinion
Wheelbase: 236.5cm 93.1in
Track F: 138.9cm 54.7in
Track R: 139.4cm 54.9in
Length: 395.5cm 155.7in
Width: 163.1cm 64.2in
Height: 137.4cm 54.1in
Ground clearance: 15.5cm 6.1in
Kerb weight: 848.5kg 1869.0lb
Fuel: 40.9L 9.0gal 10.8galUS

2717 Mazda

GLC
1981 Japan
90.0mph 144.8kmh
0-50mph 80.5kmh: 9.7secs
0-60mph 96.5kmh: 14.3secs
0-1/4 mile: 19.4secs
68.0bhp 50.7kW 68.9PS
@ 5000rpm
82.0lbft 111.1Nm @ 3000rpm
72.5bhp/ton 71.3bhp/tonne
45.6bhp/L 34.0kW/L 46.3PS/L
43.8ft/sec 13.3m/sec
22.6mph 36.4kmh/1000rpm
31.8mpg 26.5mpgUS 8.9L/100km
Petrol 4-stroke piston
1490cc 90.9cu in
In-line 4 1 Carburettor
Compression ratio: 9.0:1
Bore: 77.0mm 3.0in
Stroke: 80.0mm 3.1in
Valve type/No: Overhead 8
Transmission: Manual
No. of forward speeds: 5
Wheels driven: Front
Springs F/R: Coil/Coil
Brake system: PA
Brakes F/R: Disc/Drum
Steering: Rack & pinion
Wheelbase: 236.5cm 93.1in
Track F: 138.9cm 54.7in
Track R: 139.4cm 54.9in
Length: 423.4cm 166.7in
Width: 163.1cm 64.2in
Height: 137.4cm 54.1in
Kerb weight: 953.4kg 2100.0lb
Fuel: 42.0L 9.2gal 11.1galUS

2718 Mazda

GLC Sport
1981 Japan
96.0mph 154.5kmh
0-60mph 96.5kmh: 13.9secs
0-1/4 mile: 19.3secs
68.0bhp 50.7kW 68.9PS
@ 5000rpm
82.0lbft 111.1Nm @ 3000rpm
73.1bhp/ton 71.8bhp/tonne
45.6bhp/L 34.0kW/L 46.3PS/L
43.8ft/sec 13.3m/sec
23.1mph 37.2kmh/1000rpm
31.8mpg 26.5mpgUS 8.9L/100km
Petrol 4-stroke piston
1490cc 90.9cu in
In-line 4 1 Carburettor
Compression ratio: 9.0:1
Bore: 77.0mm 3.0in
Stroke: 80.0mm 3.1in
Valve type/No: Overhead 8
Transmission: Manual
No. of forward speeds: 5
Wheels driven: Front
Springs F/R: Coil/Coil
Brake system: PA
Brakes F/R: Disc/Drum
Steering: Rack & pinion
Wheelbase: 236.5cm 93.1in
Track F: 138.9cm 54.7in
Track R: 139.4cm 54.9in
Length: 404.1cm 159.1in
Width: 163.1cm 64.2in
Height: 137.4cm 54.1in
Ground clearance: 15.5cm 6.1in
Kerb weight: 946.6kg 2085.0lb
Fuel: 42.0L 9.2gal 11.1galUS

2719 Mazda

RX-7 GSL
1981 Japan
118.0mph 189.9kmh
0-50mph 80.5kmh: 6.8secs
0-60mph 96.5kmh: 9.7secs
0-1/4 mile: 17.1secs
100.0bhp 74.6kW 101.4PS
@ 6000rpm
105.0lbft 142.3Nm @ 4000rpm
91.2bhp/ton 89.7bhp/tonne
87.3bhp/L 65.1kW/L 88.5PS/L
19.7mph 31.7kmh/1000rpm
25.2mpg 21.0mpgUS 11.2L/100km
Petrol Wankel rotary
1146cc 69.9cu in
Rotary 2 1 Carburettor
Compression ratio: 9.4:1
Transmission: Manual
No. of forward speeds: 5
Wheels driven: Rear
Springs F/R: Coil/Coil
Brake system: PA
Brakes F/R: Disc/Disc
Steering: Recirculating ball
Wheelbase: 242.1cm 95.3in
Track F: 142.0cm 55.9in
Track R: 140.0cm 55.1in
Length: 432.1cm 170.1in
Width: 166.9cm 65.7in
Height: 126.0cm 49.6in
Kerb weight: 1114.6kg 2455.0lb
Fuel: 62.8L 13.8gal 16.6galUS

2720 Mazda

RX-7
1982 Japan
126.0mph 202.7kmh
0-50mph 80.5kmh: 6.0secs
0-60mph 96.5kmh: 8.6secs
0-1/4 mile: 16.3secs
0-1km: 30.2secs
115.0bhp 85.8kW 116.6PS
@ 6000rpm
112.0lbft 151.8Nm @ 4000rpm
109.5bhp/ton 107.7bhp/tonne
100.3bhp/L 74.8kW/L 101.7PS/L
20.9mph 33.6kmh/1000rpm
22.0mpg 18.3mpgUS 12.8L/100km
Petrol Wankel rotary
1146cc 69.9cu in
Rotary 2 1 Carburettor
Compression ratio: 9.4:1
Valve type/No: Ports
Transmission: Manual
No. of forward speeds: 5
Wheels driven: Rear
Springs F/R: Coil/Coil
Brake system: PA
Brakes F/R: Disc/Disc
Steering: Recirculating ball
Wheelbase: 242.1cm 95.3in
Track F: 142.0cm 55.9in
Track R: 140.0cm 55.1in
Length: 432.1cm 170.1in
Width: 167.4cm 65.9in
Height: 126.0cm 49.6in
Ground clearance: 16.0cm 6.3in
Kerb weight: 1067.8kg 2352.0lb
Fuel: 55.1L 12.1gal 14.5galUS

2721 Mazda

626
1983 Japan
105.0mph 168.9kmh
0-60mph 96.5kmh: 12.4secs
0-1/4 mile: 18.6secs
83.0bhp 61.9kW 84.1PS
@ 4800rpm
110.0lbft 149.1Nm @ 2500rpm
73.0bhp/ton 71.8bhp/tonne
41.5bhp/L 31.0kW/L 42.1PS/L
45.2ft/sec 13.8m/sec
21.8mph 35.1kmh/1000rpm
32.4mpg 27.0mpgUS 8.7L/100km
Petrol 4-stroke piston
1998cc 121.9cu in
In-line 4 1 Carburettor
Compression ratio: 8.6:1
Bore: 86.0mm 3.4in
Stroke: 86.0mm 3.4in
Valve type/No: Overhead 8
Transmission: Manual
No. of forward speeds: 5
Wheels driven: Front
Springs F/R: Coil/Coil
Brake system: PA
Brakes F/R: Disc/Drum
Steering: Rack & pinion PA
Wheelbase: 251.0cm 98.8in
Track F: 143.0cm 56.3in
Track R: 142.5cm 56.1in
Length: 441.5cm 173.8in
Width: 168.9cm 66.5in
Height: 136.4cm 53.7in
Ground clearance: 16.5cm 6.5in
Kerb weight: 1155.4kg 2545.0lb
Fuel: 59.8L 13.1gal 15.8galUS

2722 Mazda

626 1600 LX
1983 Japan
102.0mph 164.1kmh
0-50mph 80.5kmh: 8.7secs
0-60mph 96.5kmh: 12.3secs
0-1/4 mile: 18.9secs
0-1km: 35.0secs
81.0bhp 60.4kW 82.1PS
@ 5500rpm
88.0lbft 119.2Nm @ 4000rpm
78.7bhp/ton 77.4bhp/tonne
51.0bhp/L 38.1kW/L 51.7PS/L
46.3ft/sec 14.1m/sec
21.0mph 33.8kmh/1000rpm
30.6mpg 25.5mpgUS 9.2L/100km
Petrol 4-stroke piston
1587cc 96.8cu in
In-line 4 1 Carburettor
Compression ratio: 9.0:1
Bore: 81.0mm 3.2in
Stroke: 77.0mm 3.0in
Valve type/No: Overhead 8
Transmission: Manual
No. of forward speeds: 5
Wheels driven: Front
Springs F/R: Coil/Coil
Brake system: PA
Brakes F/R: Disc/Drum
Steering: Rack & pinion
Wheelbase: 251.0cm 98.8in
Track F: 143.0cm 56.3in
Track R: 142.5cm 56.1in
Length: 443.0cm 174.4in
Width: 168.9cm 66.5in
Height: 139.7cm 55.0in
Ground clearance: 15.2cm 6.0in
Kerb weight: 1046.0kg 2304.0lb
Fuel: 59.1L 13.0gal 15.6galUS

2723 Mazda

RX-7
1983 Japan
118.0mph 189.9kmh
0-50mph 80.5kmh: 6.8secs
0-60mph 96.5kmh: 9.7secs
0-1/4 mile: 17.1secs
100.0bhp 74.6kW 101.4PS
@ 6000rpm
105.0lbft 142.3Nm @ 4000rpm
91.6bhp/ton 90.1bhp/tonne
87.3bhp/L 65.1kW/L 88.5PS/L
19.7mph 31.7kmh/1000rpm
25.2mpg 21.0mpgUS 11.2L/100km
Petrol Wankel rotary
1146cc 69.9cu in
Rotary 2 1 Carburettor
Compression ratio: 9.4:1
Transmission: Manual
No. of forward speeds: 5
Wheels driven: Rear
Springs F/R: Coil/Coil
Brake system: PA
Brakes F/R: Disc/Drum
Steering: Recirculating ball
Wheelbase: 242.1cm 95.3in
Track F: 142.0cm 55.9in
Track R: 140.0cm 55.1in
Length: 432.1cm 170.1in
Width: 166.9cm 65.7in
Height: 126.0cm 49.6in
Kerb weight: 1110.0kg 2445.0lb
Fuel: 62.8L 13.8gal 16.6galUS

2724 Mazda

RX-7
1984 Japan
126.0mph 202.7kmh
0-60mph 96.5kmh: 8.5secs
0-1/4 mile: 16.4secs
135.0bhp 100.7kW 136.9PS
@ 6000rpm
133.0lbft 180.2Nm @ 2750rpm
114.5bhp/ton 112.6bhp/tonne
103.2bhp/L 77.0kW/L 104.6PS/L
22.2mpg 18.5mpgUS 12.7L/100km
Petrol Wankel rotary
1308cc 79.8cu in
Rotary 2 fuel injection
Compression ratio: 9.4:1
Transmission: Manual
No. of forward speeds: 5
Wheels driven: Rear
Springs F/R: Coil/Coil
Brakes F/R: Disc/Disc
Steering: Rack & pinion PA
Wheelbase: 242.1cm 95.3in

Track F: 142.0cm 55.9in
Track R: 140.0cm 55.1in
Length: 432.1cm 170.1in
Width: 166.9cm 65.7in
Height: 126.0cm 49.6in
Kerb weight: 1198.6kg 2640.0lb
Fuel: 62.8L 13.8gal 16.6galUS

2725 Mazda

RX-7 GSL SE
1984 Japan
106.0mph 170.6kmh
0-50mph 80.5kmh: 6.0secs
0-60mph 96.5kmh: 8.5secs
0-1/4 mile: 16.4secs
135.0bhp 100.7kW 136.9PS
@ 6000rpm
133.0lbft 180.2Nm @ 2750rpm
114.5bhp/ton 112.6bhp/tonne
103.2bhp/L 77.0kW/L 104.6PS/L
21.6mpg 18.0mpgUS 13.1L/100km
Petrol Wankel rotary
1308cc 79.8cu in
Rotary 2 fuel injection
Compression ratio: 9.4:1
Transmission: Manual
No. of forward speeds: 5
Wheels driven: Rear
Springs F/R: Coil/Coil
Brakes F/R: Disc/Disc
Steering: Recirculating ball
Wheelbase: 242.1cm 95.3in
Track F: 142.0cm 55.9in
Track R: 140.0cm 55.1in
Length: 432.1cm 170.1in
Width: 166.9cm 65.7in
Height: 126.0cm 49.6in
Kerb weight: 1198.6kg 2640.0lb
Fuel: 62.8L 13.8gal 16.6galUS

2726 Mazda

323 1.5 GLX
1985 Japan
98.0mph 157.7kmh
0-50mph 80.5kmh: 9.1secs
0-60mph 96.5kmh: 13.0secs
0-1/4 mile: 19.2secs
0-1km: 35.8secs
75.0bhp 55.9kW 76.0PS
@ 5500rpm
85.0lbft 115.2Nm @ 3500rpm
81.4bhp/ton 80.1bhp/tonne
50.3bhp/L 37.5kW/L 51.0PS/L
48.1ft/sec 14.7m/sec
22.0mph 35.4kmh/1000rpm
31.4mpg 26.1mpgUS 9.0L/100km
Petrol 4-stroke piston
1490cc 90.9cu in
In-line 4 1 Carburettor
Compression ratio: 9.0:1
Bore: 77.0mm 3.0in
Stroke: 80.0mm 3.1in
Valve type/No: Overhead 8
Transmission: Manual
No. of forward speeds: 5
Wheels driven: Front
Springs F/R: Coil/Coil
Brake system: PA
Brakes F/R: Disc/Drum
Steering: Rack & pinion
Wheelbase: 240.0cm 94.5in
Track F: 138.9cm 54.7in
Track R: 141.5cm 55.7in
Length: 419.4cm 165.1in
Width: 164.3cm 64.7in
Height: 138.9cm 54.7in
Ground clearance: 15.5cm 6.1in
Kerb weight: 936.6kg 2063.0lb
Fuel: 45.0L 9.9gal 11.9galUS

2727 Mazda

323 1.6i
1985 Japan
115.0mph 185.0kmh
0-50mph 80.5kmh: 6.9secs
0-60mph 96.5kmh: 9.8secs
0-1/4 mile: 17.7secs
0-1km: 32.7secs
103.5bhp 77.2kW 104.9PS
@ 6000rpm
101.0lbft 136.9Nm @ 4200rpm
107.0bhp/ton 105.2bhp/tonne
64.8bhp/L 48.3kW/L 65.7PS/L
54.8ft/sec 16.7m/sec
19.6mph 31.5kmh/1000rpm
28.9mpg 24.1mpgUS 9.8L/100km
Petrol 4-stroke piston
1597cc 97.4cu in
In-line 4 fuel injection
Compression ratio: 10.5:1
Bore: 78.0mm 3.1in
Stroke: 83.6mm 3.3in
Valve type/No: Overhead 8
Transmission: Manual
No. of forward speeds: 5
Wheels driven: Front
Springs F/R: Coil/Coil
Brake system: PA
Brakes F/R: Disc/Disc
Steering: Rack & pinion
Wheelbase: 240.0cm 94.5in
Track F: 138.9cm 54.7in
Track R: 141.5cm 55.7in
Length: 399.0cm 157.1in
Width: 164.3cm 64.7in
Height: 138.9cm 54.7in
Ground clearance: 15.5cm 6.1in
Kerb weight: 983.4kg 2166.0lb
Fuel: 45.0L 9.9gal 11.9galUS

2728 Mazda

RX-7 GSL
1985 Japan
120.0mph 193.1kmh
0-60mph 96.5kmh: 9.9secs
0-1/4 mile: 17.4secs
100.0bhp 74.6kW 101.4PS
@ 6000rpm
107.0lbft 145.0Nm @ 4000rpm
89.6bhp/ton 88.1bhp/tonne
87.3bhp/L 65.1kW/L 88.5PS/L
20.0mph 32.2kmh/1000rpm
27.7mpg 23.1mpgUS 10.2L/100km
Petrol Wankel rotary
1146cc 69.9cu in
Rotary 2 1 Carburettor
Transmission: Manual
No. of forward speeds: 5
Wheels driven: Rear
Springs F/R: Coil/Coil
Brakes F/R: Disc/Drum
Steering: Recirculating ball
Wheelbase: 242.1cm 95.3in
Track F: 142.0cm 55.9in
Track R: 140.0cm 55.1in
Length: 432.1cm 170.1in
Width: 166.9cm 65.7in
Height: 126.0cm 49.6in
Kerb weight: 1135.0kg 2500.0lb

2729 Mazda

323 1.5 GLX Estate
1986 Japan
98.0mph 157.7kmh
0-50mph 80.5kmh: 8.5secs
0-60mph 96.5kmh: 12.3secs
0-1/4 mile: 19.4secs
0-1km: 36.3secs
74.0bhp 55.2kW 75.0PS
@ 5500rpm
84.6lbft 114.6Nm @ 3500rpm
77.7bhp/ton 76.4bhp/tonne
49.7bhp/L 37.0kW/L 50.4PS/L
48.1ft/sec 14.7m/sec
21.8mph 35.1kmh/1000rpm
20.4mpg 17.0mpgUS 13.8L/100km
Petrol 4-stroke piston
1490cc 91.0cu in
In-line 4 1 Carburettor
Compression ratio: 9.0:1
Bore: 77.0mm 3.0in
Stroke: 80.0mm 3.1in
Valve type/No: Overhead 8
Transmission: Manual
No. of forward speeds: 5
Wheels driven: Front
Springs F/R: Coil/Coil
Brake system: PA
Brakes F/R: Disc/Drum
Steering: Rack & pinion
Wheelbase: 240.0cm 94.5in
Track F: 139.0cm 54.7in
Track R: 141.5cm 55.7in
Length: 422.5cm 166.3in
Width: 164.5cm 64.8in
Height: 143.0cm 56.3in
Ground clearance: 15.5cm 6.1in
Kerb weight: 969.0kg 2134.4lb
Fuel: 45.0L 9.9gal 11.9galUS

2730 Mazda

323 1.6i
1986 Japan
0-60mph 96.5kmh: 10.0secs
0-1/4 mile: 17.6secs
82.0bhp 61.1kW 83.1PS
@ 5000rpm
92.0lbft 124.7Nm @ 2500rpm
85.6bhp/ton 84.2bhp/tonne
51.3bhp/L 38.3kW/L 52.1PS/L
45.7ft/sec 13.9m/sec
17.1mph 27.5kmh/1000rpm
32.8mpg 27.3mpgUS 8.6L/100km
Petrol 4-stroke piston
1597cc 97.4cu in
In-line 4 fuel injection
Compression ratio: 9.3:1
Bore: 78.0mm 3.1in
Stroke: 83.6mm 3.3in
Valve type/No: Overhead 8
Transmission: Manual
No. of forward speeds: 4
Wheels driven: Front
Springs F/R: Torsion bar/Coil
Brake system: PA
Brakes F/R: Disc/Drum
Steering: Rack & pinion
Wheelbase: 240.0cm 94.5in
Track F: 138.9cm 54.7in
Track R: 141.5cm 55.7in
Length: 411.0cm 161.8in
Width: 164.6cm 64.8in
Height: 138.9cm 54.7in
Kerb weight: 973.8kg 2145.0lb
Fuel: 45.0L 9.9gal 11.9galUS

2731 Mazda

323 LX
1986 Japan
104.0mph 167.3kmh
0-60mph 96.5kmh: 11.1secs
0-1/4 mile: 18.2secs
82.0bhp 61.1kW 83.1PS
@ 5000rpm
92.0lbft 124.7Nm @ 2500rpm
79.7bhp/ton 78.4bhp/tonne
51.3bhp/L 38.3kW/L 52.1PS/L
45.7ft/sec 13.9m/sec
29.4mpg 24.5mpgUS 9.6L/100km
Petrol 4-stroke piston
1597cc 97.4cu in
In-line 4 fuel injection
Compression ratio: 9.3:1
Bore: 78.0mm 3.1in
Stroke: 83.6mm 3.3in
Valve type/No: Overhead 8
Transmission: Automatic
No. of forward speeds: 3
Wheels driven: Front
Springs F/R: Coil/Coil
Brake system: PA
Brakes F/R: Disc/Drum
Steering: Rack & pinion PA
Wheelbase: 240.0cm 94.5in
Track F: 138.9cm 54.7in
Track R: 141.5cm 55.7in
Length: 411.0cm 161.8in
Width: 164.6cm 64.8in
Height: 138.9cm 54.7in
Kerb weight: 1046.5kg 2305.0lb
Fuel: 45.0L 9.9gal 11.9galUS

2732 Mazda

323 Turbo 4x4 Lux
1986 Japan
125.0mph 201.1kmh
0-50mph 80.5kmh: 5.6secs
0-60mph 96.5kmh: 7.9secs
0-1/4 mile: 16.5secs
0-1km: 29.6secs
148.0bhp 110.4kW 150.0PS
@ 6000rpm
143.8lbft 194.9Nm @ 5000rpm
135.7bhp/ton 133.4bhp/tonne
92.7bhp/L 69.1kW/L 94.0PS/L
54.8ft/sec 16.7m/sec
20.2mph 32.5kmh/1000rpm
21.3mpg 17.7mpgUS 13.3L/100km
Petrol 4-stroke piston
1597cc 97.0cu in turbocharged
In-line 4 fuel injection
Compression ratio: 7.9:1
Bore: 78.0mm 3.1in
Stroke: 83.6mm 3.3in
Valve type/No: Overhead 16
Transmission: Manual
No. of forward speeds: 5
Wheels driven: 4-wheel drive
Springs F/R: Coil/Coil
Brake system: PA
Brakes F/R: Disc/Disc
Steering: Rack & pinion PA
Wheelbase: 240.0cm 94.5in
Track F: 140.5cm 55.3in
Track R: 142.5cm 56.1in
Length: 399.0cm 157.1in
Width: 164.5cm 64.8in
Height: 135.5cm 53.3in
Ground clearance: 15.3cm 6.0in
Kerb weight: 1109.0kg 2442.7lb
Fuel: 52.8L 11.6gal 13.9galUS

2733 Mazda

626 2.0i 5-door
1986 Japan
121.0mph 194.7kmh
0-50mph 80.5kmh: 7.5secs
0-60mph 96.5kmh: 9.8secs
0-1/4 mile: 17.8secs
0-1km: 32.4secs
118.0bhp 88.0kW 119.6PS
@ 5400rpm
125.8lbft 170.5Nm @ 4000rpm
101.9bhp/ton 100.2bhp/tonne
59.1bhp/L 44.0kW/L 59.9PS/L
50.8ft/sec 15.5m/sec
21.8mph 35.1kmh/1000rpm
29.5mpg 24.6mpgUS 9.6L/100km
Petrol 4-stroke piston
1998cc 122.0cu in
In-line 4 fuel injection
Compression ratio: 10.0:1
Bore: 86.0mm 3.4in
Stroke: 86.0mm 3.4in
Valve type/No: Overhead 8
Transmission: Manual
No. of forward speeds: 5
Wheels driven: Front
Springs F/R: Coil/Coil
Brake system: PA
Brakes F/R: Disc/Disc
Steering: Rack & pinion PA
Wheelbase: 251.0cm 98.8in
Track F: 143.0cm 56.3in
Track R: 142.5cm 56.1in
Length: 443.0cm 174.4in
Width: 169.0cm 66.5in
Height: 136.4cm 53.7in
Ground clearance: 16.5cm 6.5in
Kerb weight: 1178.0kg 2594.7lb
Fuel: 59.1L 13.0gal 15.6galUS

2734 Mazda

626 GT
1986 Japan
120.0mph 193.1kmh
0-50mph 80.5kmh: 5.6secs
0-60mph 96.5kmh: 7.8secs
0-1/4 mile: 16.0secs
120.0bhp 89.5kW 121.7PS
@ 5000rpm
150.0lbft 203.3Nm @ 3000rpm
100.1bhp/ton 98.4bhp/tonne
60.1bhp/L 44.8kW/L 60.9PS/L
47.1ft/sec 14.3m/sec
28.8mpg 24.0mpgUS 9.8L/100km
Petrol 4-stroke piston
1998cc 121.9cu in turbocharged
In-line 4 fuel injection
Compression ratio: 7.8:1
Bore: 86.0mm 3.4in
Stroke: 86.0mm 3.4in
Valve type/No: Overhead 8
Transmission: Manual
No. of forward speeds: 5
Wheels driven: Front
Springs F/R: Coil/Coil
Brake system: PA
Brakes F/R: Disc/Disc
Steering: Rack & pinion PA
Wheelbase: 251.0cm 98.8in
Track F: 143.0cm 56.3in
Track R: 142.5cm 56.1in
Length: 451.6cm 177.8in
Width: 168.9cm 66.5in
Height: 136.4cm 53.7in
Kerb weight: 1219.0kg 2685.0lb
Fuel: 59.8L 13.1gal 15.8galUS

2735 Mazda

RX-7
1986 Japan
135.0mph 217.2kmh
0-50mph 80.5kmh: 5.7secs
0-60mph 96.5kmh: 8.5secs

0-1/4 mile: 16.2secs
0-1km: 29.8secs
150.0bhp 111.9kW 152.1PS
@ 6500rpm
134.5lbft 182.2Nm @ 3000rpm
124.9bhp/ton 122.8bhp/tonne
114.7bhp/L 85.5kW/L 116.3PS/L
21.4mph 34.4kmh/1000rpm
18.7mpg 15.6mpgUS 15.1L/100km
Petrol Wankel rotary
1308cc 80.0cu in
Rotary 2 fuel injection
Compression ratio: 9.4:1
Valve type/No: Ports
Transmission: Manual
No. of forward speeds: 5
Wheels driven: Rear
Springs F/R: Coil/Coil
Brake system: PA
Brakes F/R: Disc/Disc
Steering: Rack & pinion
Wheelbase: 243.0cm 95.7in
Track F: 145.0cm 57.1in
Track R: 144.0cm 56.7in
Length: 429.0cm 168.9in
Width: 169.0cm 66.5in
Height: 126.5cm 49.8in
Ground clearance: 16.0cm 6.3in
Kerb weight: 1221.0kg 2689.4lb
Fuel: 63.2L 13.9gal 16.7galUS

2736 Mazda
RX-7 GXL
1986 Japan
128.0mph 206.0kmh
0-60mph 96.5kmh: 7.9secs
0-1/4 mile: 16.1secs
146.0bhp 108.9kW 148.0PS
@ 6500rpm
138.0lbft 187.0Nm @ 3500rpm
121.1bhp/ton 119.1bhp/tonne
111.6bhp/L 83.2kW/L 113.2PS/L
22.8mpg 19.0mpgUS 12.4L/100km
Petrol Wankel rotary
1308cc 79.8cu in
Rotary 2 fuel injection
Compression ratio: 9.4:1
Transmission: Manual
No. of forward speeds: 5
Wheels driven: Rear
Springs F/R: Coil/Coil
Brake system: PA
Brakes F/R: Disc/Disc
Steering: Rack & pinion PA
Wheelbase: 243.1cm 95.7in
Track F: 145.0cm 57.1in
Track R: 144.0cm 56.7in
Length: 429.0cm 168.9in
Width: 168.9cm 66.5in
Height: 126.5cm 49.8in
Ground clearance: 14.7cm 5.8in
Kerb weight: 1225.8kg 2700.0lb
Fuel: 62.8L 13.8gal 16.6galUS

2737 Mazda
RX-7 Turbo
1986 Japan
150.0mph 241.4kmh
0-50mph 80.5kmh: 5.1secs
0-60mph 96.5kmh: 6.6secs
0-1/4 mile: 15.2secs
182.0bhp 135.7kW 184.5PS
@ 6500rpm
183.0lbft 248.0Nm @ 3500rpm
144.1bhp/ton 141.6bhp/tonne
139.1bhp/L 103.8kW/L 141.1PS/L
23.1mpg 19.2mpgUS 12.3L/100km
Petrol Wankel rotary
1308cc 79.8cu in turbocharged
Rotary 2 fuel injection
Compression ratio: 8.5:1
Transmission: Manual
No. of forward speeds: 5
Wheels driven: Rear
Springs F/R: Coil/Coil
Brake system: PA
Brakes F/R: Disc/Disc
Steering: Rack & pinion PA
Wheelbase: 243.1cm 95.7in
Track F: 145.0cm 57.1in
Track R: 144.0cm 56.7in
Length: 429.0cm 168.9in
Width: 168.9cm 66.5in
Height: 126.5cm 49.8in
Kerb weight: 1284.8kg 2830.0lb
Fuel: 62.8L 13.8gal 16.6galUS

2738 Mazda
323 1.5 GLX
1987 Japan
101.0mph 162.5kmh
0-50mph 80.5kmh: 7.7secs
0-60mph 96.5kmh: 11.1secs
0-1/4 mile: 18.2secs
0-1km: 34.0secs
72.0bhp 53.7kW 73.0PS
@ 5700rpm
82.0lbft 111.1Nm @ 2200rpm
77.2bhp/ton 75.9bhp/tonne
48.1bhp/L 35.8kW/L 48.7PS/L
48.6ft/sec 14.8m/sec
22.0mph 35.4kmh/1000rpm
30.1mpg 25.1mpgUS 9.4L/100km
Petrol 4-stroke piston
1498cc 91.0cu in
In-line 4 1 Carburettor
Compression ratio: 9.0:1
Bore: 74.0mm 2.9in
Stroke: 78.0mm 3.1in
Valve type/No: Overhead 8
Transmission: Manual
No. of forward speeds: 5
Wheels driven: Front
Springs F/R: Coil/Coil
Brake system: PA
Brakes F/R: Disc/Drum
Steering: Rack & pinion PA
Wheelbase: 240.0cm 94.5in
Track F: 140.5cm 55.3in
Track R: 142.5cm 56.1in
Length: 419.5cm 165.2in
Width: 164.5cm 64.8in
Height: 139.0cm 54.7in
Ground clearance: 15.3cm 6.0in
Kerb weight: 948.0kg 2088.1lb
Fuel: 47.8L 10.5gal 12.6galUS

2739 Mazda
626 2.0 GLS Executive
1987 Japan
113.0mph 181.8kmh
0-50mph 80.5kmh: 7.6secs
0-60mph 96.5kmh: 10.4secs
0-1/4 mile: 17.9secs
0-1km: 32.7secs
108.0bhp 80.5kW 109.5PS
@ 5300rpm
121.0lbft 164.0Nm @ 3300rpm
91.8bhp/ton 90.3bhp/tonne
54.0bhp/L 40.3kW/L 54.8PS/L
49.9ft/sec 15.2m/sec
20.7mph 33.3kmh/1000rpm
24.8mpg 20.7mpgUS 11.4L/100km
Petrol 4-stroke piston
1998cc 122.0cu in
In-line 4 1 Carburettor
Compression ratio: 9.5:1
Bore: 86.0mm 3.4in
Stroke: 86.0mm 3.4in
Valve type/No: Overhead 12
Transmission: Manual
No. of forward speeds: 5
Wheels driven: Front
Springs F/R: Coil/Coil
Brake system: PA
Brakes F/R: Disc/Disc
Steering: Rack & pinion PA
Wheelbase: 257.5cm 101.4in
Track F: 145.5cm 57.3in
Track R: 146.5cm 57.7in
Length: 451.5cm 177.8in
Width: 169.0cm 66.5in
Height: 137.5cm 54.1in
Ground clearance: 16.5cm 6.5in
Kerb weight: 1196.0kg 2634.4lb
Fuel: 60.1L 13.2gal 15.9galUS

2740 Mazda
RX-7 Turbo
1987 Japan
0-60mph 96.5kmh: 6.6secs
0-1/4 mile: 15.2secs
182.0bhp 135.7kW 184.5PS
@ 6500rpm
183.0lbft 248.0Nm @ 3500rpm
144.1bhp/ton 141.6bhp/tonne
139.1bhp/L 103.8kW/L 141.1PS/L
23.1mpg 19.2mpgUS 12.3L/100km
Petrol Wankel rotary
1308cc 79.8cu in turbocharged
Rotary 2
Transmission: Manual
No. of forward speeds: 5
Wheels driven: Rear
Brake system: ABS
Brakes F/R: Disc/Disc
Steering: Rack & pinion PA
Length: 429.0cm 168.9in
Kerb weight: 1284.8kg 2830.0lb

2741 Mazda
121 1.3 LX Sun Top
1988 Japan
92.0mph 148.0kmh
0-50mph 80.5kmh: 7.7secs
0-60mph 96.5kmh: 11.0secs
0-1/4 mile: 18.1secs
0-1km: 34.3secs
65.0bhp 48.5kW 65.9PS
@ 5600rpm
76.0lbft 103.0Nm @ 3600rpm
84.5bhp/ton 83.1bhp/tonne
49.1bhp/L 36.6kW/L 49.8PS/L
51.2ft/sec 15.6m/sec
22.0mph 35.4kmh/1000rpm
30.8mpg 25.6mpgUS 9.2L/100km
Petrol 4-stroke piston
1324cc 81.0cu in
In-line 4 1 Carburettor
Compression ratio: 9.4:1
Bore: 71.0mm 2.8in
Stroke: 83.6mm 3.3in
Valve type/No: Overhead 8
Transmission: Manual
No. of forward speeds: 5
Wheels driven: Front
Springs F/R: Coil/Coil
Brake system: PA
Brakes F/R: Disc/Drum
Steering: Rack & pinion
Wheelbase: 229.5cm 90.4in
Track F: 140.0cm 55.1in
Track R: 138.5cm 54.5in
Length: 347.5cm 136.8in
Width: 160.5cm 63.2in
Height: 150.5cm 59.3in
Ground clearance: 17.9cm 7.0in
Kerb weight: 782.0kg 1722.5lb
Fuel: 38.2L 8.4gal 10.1galUS

2742 Mazda
323 GTX
1988 Japan
119.0mph 191.5kmh
0-60mph 96.5kmh: 8.7secs
0-1/4 mile: 16.7secs
132.0bhp 98.4kW 133.8PS
@ 6000rpm
136.0lbft 184.3Nm @ 3000rpm
111.8bhp/ton 109.9bhp/tonne
82.6bhp/L 61.6kW/L 83.8PS/L
54.8ft/sec 16.7m/sec
25.8mpg 21.5mpgUS 10.9L/100km
Petrol 4-stroke piston
1597cc 97.4cu in turbocharged
In-line 4 fuel injection
Compression ratio: 7.9:1
Bore: 78.0mm 3.1in
Stroke: 83.6mm 3.3in
Valve type/No: Overhead 16
Transmission: Manual
No. of forward speeds: 5
Wheels driven: 4-wheel drive
Springs F/R: Coil/Coil
Brake system: PA
Brakes F/R: Disc/Disc
Steering: Rack & pinion PA
Wheelbase: 240.0cm 94.5in
Track F: 140.0cm 55.1in
Track R: 142.5cm 56.1in
Length: 411.0cm 161.8in
Width: 164.6cm 64.8in
Height: 139.4cm 54.9in
Kerb weight: 1200.8kg 2645.0lb
Fuel: 50.0L 11.0gal 13.2galUS

2743 Mazda
323 Turbo 4x4
1988 Japan
124.0mph 199.5kmh
0-50mph 80.5kmh: 5.8secs
0-60mph 96.5kmh: 7.8secs
0-1/4 mile: 15.9secs
0-1km: 29.8secs
148.0bhp 110.4kW 150.0PS
@ 6000rpm
144.0lbft 195.1Nm @ 5000rpm
128.6bhp/ton 126.5bhp/tonne
92.7bhp/L 69.1kW/L 94.0PS/L
55.2ft/sec 16.8m/sec
20.2mph 32.5kmh/1000rpm
20.7mpg 17.2mpgUS 13.6L/100km
Petrol 4-stroke piston
1597cc 97.0cu in turbocharged
In-line 4 fuel injection
Compression ratio: 7.9:1
Bore: 78.0mm 3.1in
Stroke: 84.0mm 3.3in
Valve type/No: Overhead 16
Transmission: Manual
No. of forward speeds: 5
Wheels driven: 4-wheel drive
Springs F/R: Coil/Coil
Brake system: PA
Brakes F/R: Disc/Disc
Steering: Rack & pinion PA
Wheelbase: 240.0cm 94.5in
Track F: 140.5cm 55.3in
Track R: 142.5cm 56.1in
Length: 399.0cm 157.1in
Width: 164.5cm 64.8in
Height: 133.5cm 52.6in
Ground clearance: 15.3cm 6.0in
Kerb weight: 1170.0kg 2577.0lb
Fuel: 52.8L 11.6gal 13.9galUS

2744 Mazda
626 2.0 GLX Executive Estate
1988 Japan
110.0mph 177.0kmh
0-50mph 80.5kmh: 8.5secs
0-60mph 96.5kmh: 11.7secs
0-1/4 mile: 18.1secs
0-1km: 33.3secs
108.0bhp 80.5kW 109.5PS
@ 5300rpm
121.0lbft 164.0Nm @ 3300rpm
88.0bhp/ton 86.5bhp/tonne
54.0bhp/L 40.3kW/L 54.8PS/L
49.9ft/sec 15.2m/sec
21.6mph 34.8kmh/1000rpm
22.9mpg 19.1mpgUS 12.3L/100km
Petrol 4-stroke piston
1998cc 122.0cu in
In-line 4 1 Carburettor
Compression ratio: 9.5:1
Bore: 86.0mm 3.4in
Stroke: 86.0mm 3.4in
Valve type/No: Overhead 12
Transmission: Manual
No. of forward speeds: 5
Wheels driven: Front
Springs F/R: Coil/Coil
Brake system: PA
Brakes F/R: Disc/Disc
Steering: Rack & pinion PA
Wheelbase: 257.5cm 101.4in
Track F: 145.5cm 57.3in
Track R: 146.5cm 57.7in
Length: 459.0cm 180.7in
Width: 169.0cm 66.5in
Height: 143.0cm 56.3in
Ground clearance: 16.5cm 6.5in
Kerb weight: 1248.0kg 2748.9lb
Fuel: 60.1L 13.2gal 15.9galUS

2745 Mazda
626 2.0i GT 4WS
1988 Japan
124.0mph 199.5kmh
0-50mph 80.5kmh: 6.9secs
0-60mph 96.5kmh: 9.4secs
0-1/4 mile: 17.3secs
0-1km: 31.6secs
146.0bhp 108.9kW 148.0PS
@ 6000rpm
134.3lbft 182.0Nm @ 4000rpm
112.5bhp/ton 110.6bhp/tonne
73.1bhp/L 54.5kW/L 74.1PS/L
56.5ft/sec 17.2m/sec
20.3mph 32.7kmh/1000rpm
24.5mpg 20.4mpgUS 11.5L/100km
Petrol 4-stroke piston
1998cc 122.0cu in
In-line 4 fuel injection
Compression ratio: 10.0:1
Bore: 86.0mm 3.4in
Stroke: 86.0mm 3.4in
Valve type/No: Overhead 16
Transmission: Manual
No. of forward speeds: 5
Wheels driven: Front
Springs F/R: Coil/Coil
Brake system: PA ABS
Brakes F/R: Disc/Disc
Steering: Rack & pinion PA
Wheelbase: 257.5cm 101.4in

Track F: 145.5cm 57.3in
Track R: 146.5cm 57.7in
Length: 451.5cm 177.8in
Width: 169.0cm 66.5in
Height: 137.5cm 54.1in
Ground clearance: 16.5cm 6.5in
Kerb weight: 1320.0kg 2907.5lb
Fuel: 60.1L 13.2gal 15.9galUS

2746 Mazda

929
1988 Japan
121.0mph 194.7kmh
0-60mph 96.5kmh: 10.5secs
0-1/4 mile: 17.5secs
158.0bhp 117.8kW 160.2PS
@ 5500rpm
170.0lbft 230.4Nm @ 4000rpm
102.4bhp/ton 100.7bhp/tonne
53.5bhp/L 39.9kW/L 54.2PS/L
46.6ft/sec 14.2m/sec
22.2mpg 18.5mpgUS 12.7L/100km
Petrol 4-stroke piston
2954cc 180.2cu in
Vee 6 fuel injection
Compression ratio: 8.5:1
Bore: 90.0mm 3.5in
Stroke: 77.4mm 3.0in
Valve type/No: Overhead 18
Transmission: Automatic
No. of forward speeds: 4
Wheels driven: Rear
Springs F/R: Coil/Coil
Brake system: PA ABS
Brakes F/R: Disc/Disc
Steering: Rack & pinion PA
Wheelbase: 271.0cm 106.7in
Track F: 144.5cm 56.9in
Track R: 146.1cm 57.5in
Length: 490.5cm 193.1in
Width: 169.9cm 66.9in
Height: 139.4cm 54.9in
Kerb weight: 1568.6kg 3455.0lb
Fuel: 70.0L 15.4gal 18.5galUS

2747 Mazda

MX-6
1988 Japan
131.0mph 210.8kmh
0-60mph 96.5kmh: 7.5secs
0-1/4 mile: 15.7secs
145.0bhp 108.1kW 147.0PS
@ 4300rpm
190.0lbft 257.5Nm @ 3500rpm
115.6bhp/ton 113.7bhp/tonne
66.4bhp/L 49.5kW/L 67.3PS/L
44.2ft/sec 13.5m/sec
24.0mpg 20.0mpgUS 11.8L/100km
Petrol 4-stroke piston
2184cc 133.2cu in turbocharged
In-line 4 fuel injection
Compression ratio: 7.8:1
Bore: 86.0mm 3.4in
Stroke: 94.0mm 3.7in
Valve type/No: Overhead 12
Transmission: Manual
No. of forward speeds: 5
Wheels driven: Front
Springs F/R: Coil/Coil
Brake system: PA
Brakes F/R: Disc/Disc
Steering: Rack & pinion PA
Wheelbase: 251.5cm 99.0in
Track F: 145.5cm 57.3in
Track R: 146.6cm 57.7in
Length: 449.6cm 177.0in
Width: 168.9cm 66.5in
Height: 135.9cm 53.5in
Ground clearance: 14.0cm 5.5in
Kerb weight: 1275.7kg 2810.0lb
Fuel: 60.2L 13.2gal 15.9galUS

2748 Mazda

MX-6 GT
1988 Japan
131.0mph 210.8kmh
0-50mph 80.5kmh: 5.2secs
0-60mph 96.5kmh: 7.2secs
0-1/4 mile: 15.5secs
145.0bhp 108.1kW 147.0PS
@ 4300rpm
190.0lbft 257.5Nm @ 3500rpm
120.1bhp/ton 118.1bhp/tonne
66.4bhp/L 49.5kW/L 67.3PS/L
44.2ft/sec 13.5m/sec
28.8mpg 24.0mpgUS 9.8L/100km
Petrol 4-stroke piston
2184cc 133.2cu in turbocharged
In-line 4 fuel injection
Compression ratio: 7.8:1
Bore: 86.0mm 3.4in
Stroke: 94.0mm 3.7in
Valve type/No: Overhead 8
Transmission: Manual
No. of forward speeds: 5
Wheels driven: Front
Springs F/R: Coil/Coil
Brake system: PA
Brakes F/R: Disc/Disc
Steering: Rack & pinion PA
Wheelbase: 251.5cm 99.0in
Track F: 145.5cm 57.3in
Track R: 146.6cm 57.7in
Length: 449.6cm 177.0in
Width: 168.9cm 66.5in
Height: 135.9cm 53.5in
Kerb weight: 1228.1kg 2705.0lb
Fuel: 60.2L 13.2gal 15.9galUS

2749 Mazda

RX-7 Convertible
1988 Japan
125.0mph 201.1kmh
0-50mph 80.5kmh: 7.2secs
0-60mph 96.5kmh: 9.7secs
0-1/4 mile: 17.5secs
146.0bhp 108.9kW 148.0PS
@ 6500rpm
138.0lbft 187.0Nm @ 3500rpm
107.9bhp/ton 106.1bhp/tonne
111.6bhp/L 83.2kW/L 113.2PS/L
19.2mpg 16.0mpgUS 14.7L/100km
Petrol Wankel rotary
1308cc 79.8cu in
Rotary 2 fuel injection
Compression ratio: 9.4:1
Transmission: Manual
No. of forward speeds: 5
Wheels driven: Rear
Springs F/R: Coil/Coil
Brake system: PA
Brakes F/R: Disc/Disc
Steering: Rack & pinion PA
Wheelbase: 243.1cm 95.7in
Track F: 145.0cm 57.1in
Track R: 144.0cm 56.7in
Length: 429.0cm 168.9in
Width: 168.9cm 66.5in
Height: 126.5cm 49.8in
Ground clearance: 12.2cm 4.8in
Kerb weight: 1375.6kg 3030.0lb
Fuel: 62.8L 13.8gal 16.6galUS

2750 Mazda

RX-7 GTU
1988 Japan
128.0mph 206.0kmh
0-60mph 96.5kmh: 8.5secs
0-1/4 mile: 16.5secs
146.0bhp 108.9kW 148.0PS
@ 6500rpm
138.0lbft 187.0Nm @ 3500rpm
118.7bhp/ton 116.7bhp/tonne
111.6bhp/L 83.2kW/L 113.2PS/L
25.2mpg 21.0mpgUS 11.2L/100km
Petrol Wankel rotary
1308cc 79.8cu in
Rotary 2 fuel injection
Compression ratio: 9.4:1
Transmission: Manual
No. of forward speeds: 5
Wheels driven: Rear
Springs F/R: Coil/Coil
Brake system: PA
Brakes F/R: Disc/Disc
Steering: Rack & pinion
Wheelbase: 243.1cm 95.7in
Track F: 145.0cm 57.1in
Track R: 144.0cm 56.7in
Length: 429.0cm 168.9in
Width: 168.9cm 66.5in
Height: 126.5cm 49.8in
Kerb weight: 1250.8kg 2755.0lb
Fuel: 62.8L 13.8gal 16.6galUS

2751 Mazda

RX-7 Turbo
1988 Japan
140.0mph 225.3kmh
0-50mph 80.5kmh: 5.1secs
0-60mph 96.5kmh: 6.6secs
0-1/4 mile: 15.1secs
182.0bhp 135.7kW 184.5PS
@ 6500rpm
183.0lbft 248.0Nm @ 3500rpm
143.0bhp/ton 140.7bhp/tonne
139.1bhp/L 103.8kW/L 141.1PS/L
22.8mpg 19.0mpgUS 12.4L/100km
Petrol Wankel rotary
1308cc 79.8cu in turbocharged
Rotary 2 fuel injection
Compression ratio: 8.5:1
Transmission: Manual
No. of forward speeds: 5
Wheels driven: Rear
Springs F/R: Coil/Coil
Brake system: PA ABS
Brakes F/R: Disc/Disc
Steering: Rack & pinion PA
Wheelbase: 243.1cm 95.7in
Track F: 145.0cm 57.1in
Track R: 144.0cm 56.7in
Length: 429.0cm 168.9in
Width: 168.9cm 66.5in
Height: 126.5cm 49.8in
Kerb weight: 1293.9kg 2850.0lb
Fuel: 62.8L 13.8gal 16.6galUS

2752 Mazda

323 1.6i
1989 Japan
116.0mph 186.6kmh
0-50mph 80.5kmh: 6.3secs
0-60mph 96.5kmh: 8.8secs
0-1/4 mile: 16.7secs
0-1km: 33.4secs
105.0bhp 78.3kW 106.5PS
@ 6000rpm
101.8lbft 138.0Nm @ 4200rpm
109.6bhp/ton 107.8bhp/tonne
65.7bhp/L 49.0kW/L 66.7PS/L
54.8ft/sec 16.7m/sec
19.6mph 31.5kmh/1000rpm
27.5mpg 22.9mpgUS 10.3L/100km
Petrol 4-stroke piston
1597cc 97.0cu in
In-line 4 fuel injection
Compression ratio: 10.5:1
Bore: 78.0mm 3.1in
Stroke: 83.6mm 3.3in
Valve type/No: Overhead 8
Transmission: Manual
No. of forward speeds: 5
Wheels driven: Front
Springs F/R: Coil/Coil
Brake system: PA
Brakes F/R: Disc/Disc
Steering: Rack & pinion PA
Wheelbase: 240.0cm 94.5in
Track F: 140.5cm 55.3in
Track R: 142.5cm 56.1in
Length: 399.0cm 157.1in
Width: 164.5cm 64.8in
Height: 135.5cm 53.3in
Ground clearance: 15.3cm 6.0in
Kerb weight: 974.0kg 2145.4lb
Fuel: 48.2L 10.6gal 12.7galUS

2753 Mazda

323 1.8 GT
1989 Japan
128.0mph 206.0kmh
0-50mph 80.5kmh: 6.3secs
0-60mph 96.5kmh: 8.6secs
0-1/4 mile: 16.8secs
0-1km: 30.3secs
140.0bhp 104.4kW 141.9PS
@ 6500rpm
120.3lbft 163.0Nm @ 4700rpm
132.1bhp/ton 129.9bhp/tonne
76.1bhp/L 56.7kW/L 77.1PS/L
60.5ft/sec 18.4m/sec
19.3mph 31.1kmh/1000rpm
28.6mpg 23.8mpgUS 9.9L/100km
Petrol 4-stroke piston
1840cc 112.0cu in
In-line 4 fuel injection
Compression ratio: 9.8:1
Bore: 83.0mm 3.3in
Stroke: 85.0mm 3.3in
Valve type/No: Overhead 16
Transmission: Manual
No. of forward speeds: 5
Wheels driven: Front
Springs F/R: Coil/Coil
Brake system: PA
Brakes F/R: Disc/Disc
Steering: Rack & pinion PA
Wheelbase: 250.0cm 98.4in
Track F: 143.0cm 56.3in
Track R: 143.5cm 56.5in
Length: 426.0cm 167.7in
Width: 167.5cm 65.9in
Height: 133.5cm 52.6in
Ground clearance: 19.0cm 7.5in
Kerb weight: 1078.0kg 2374.4lb
Fuel: 55.0L 12.1gal 14.5galUS

2754 Mazda

MPV
1989 Japan
110.0mph 177.0kmh
0-50mph 80.5kmh: 8.5secs
0-60mph 96.5kmh: 11.7secs
0-1/4 mile: 18.4secs
150.0bhp 111.9kW 152.1PS
@ 5000rpm
165.0lbft 223.6Nm @ 4000rpm
87.6bhp/ton 86.1bhp/tonne
50.8bhp/L 37.9kW/L 51.5PS/L
42.4ft/sec 12.9m/sec
25.2mpg 21.0mpgUS 11.2L/100km
Petrol 4-stroke piston
2954cc 180.2cu in
Vee 6 fuel injection
Compression ratio: 8.5:1
Bore: 90.0mm 3.5in
Stroke: 77.4mm 3.0in
Valve type/No: Overhead 18
Transmission: Automatic
No. of forward speeds: 4
Wheels driven: Rear
Springs F/R: Coil/Coil
Brake system: PA
Brakes F/R: Disc/Drum
Steering: Rack & pinion PA
Wheelbase: 280.4cm 110.4in
Track F: 152.4cm 60.0in
Track R: 153.9cm 60.6in
Length: 446.5cm 175.8in
Width: 182.6cm 71.9in
Height: 173.0cm 68.1in
Ground clearance: 15.7cm 6.2in
Kerb weight: 1741.1kg 3835.0lb
Fuel: 74.2L 16.3gal 19.6galUS

2755 Mazda

MX-5 Miata
1989 Japan
117.0mph 188.3kmh
0-50mph 80.5kmh: 7.0secs
0-60mph 96.5kmh: 9.5secs
0-1/4 mile: 17.0secs
116.0bhp 86.5kW 117.6PS
@ 6500rpm
100.0lbft 135.5Nm @ 5500rpm
117.8bhp/ton 115.9bhp/tonne
72.6bhp/L 54.2kW/L 73.6PS/L
59.4ft/sec 18.1m/sec
30.6mpg 25.5mpgUS 9.2L/100km
Petrol 4-stroke piston
1597cc 97.4cu in
In-line 4 fuel injection
Compression ratio: 9.4:1
Bore: 78.0mm 3.1in
Stroke: 83.6mm 3.3in
Valve type/No: Overhead 16
Transmission: Manual
No. of forward speeds: 5
Wheels driven: Rear
Springs F/R: Coil/Coil
Brake system: PA
Brakes F/R: Disc/Disc
Steering: Rack & pinion PA
Wheelbase: 226.6cm 89.2in
Track F: 141.0cm 55.5in
Track R: 142.7cm 56.2in
Length: 394.7cm 155.4in
Width: 167.4cm 65.9in
Height: 122.4cm 48.2in
Ground clearance: 11.4cm 4.5in
Kerb weight: 1001.1kg 2205.0lb
Fuel: 45.0L 9.9gal 11.9galUS

2756 Mazda

MX-6 GT 4WS
1989 Japan
124.0mph 199.5kmh
0-50mph 80.5kmh: 6.0secs
0-60mph 96.5kmh: 8.2secs
0-1/4 mile: 16.0secs
145.0bhp 108.1kW 147.0PS
@ 4300rpm
190.0lbft 257.5Nm @ 3500rpm
112.4bhp/ton 110.5bhp/tonne

66.4bhp/L 49.5kW/L 67.3PS/L
44.2ft/sec 13.5m/sec
22.8mpg 19.0mpgUS 12.4L/100km
Petrol 4-stroke piston
2184cc 133.2cu in turbocharged
In-line 4 fuel injection
Compression ratio: 7.8:1
Bore: 86.0mm 3.4in
Stroke: 94.0mm 3.7in
Valve type/No: Overhead 12
Transmission: Manual
No. of forward speeds: 5
Wheels driven: Front
Springs F/R: Coil/Coil
Brake system: PA
Brakes F/R: Disc/Disc
Steering: Rack & pinion PA
Wheelbase: 251.5cm 99.0in
Track F: 145.5cm 57.3in
Track R: 146.6cm 57.7in
Length: 449.6cm 177.0in
Width: 168.9cm 66.5in
Height: 135.9cm 53.5in
Kerb weight: 1312.1kg 2890.0lb
Fuel: 60.2L 13.2gal 15.9galUS

2757 Mazda

RX-7 Convertible Racing Beat
1989 Japan
0-50mph 80.5kmh: 4.4secs
0-60mph 96.5kmh: 5.8secs
0-1/4 mile: 14.3secs
241.0bhp 179.7kW 244.3PS
@ 5500rpm
238.0lbft 322.5Nm @ 5500rpm
211.7bhp/ton 208.2bhp/tonne
184.2bhp/L 137.4kW/L 186.8PS/L
Petrol Wankel rotary
1308cc 79.8cu in
Rotary 2 fuel injection
Compression ratio: 8.5:1
Transmission: Automatic
No. of forward speeds: 4
Wheels driven: Rear
Springs F/R: Coil/Coil
Brake system: PA
Brakes F/R: Disc/Disc
Steering: Rack & pinion
Wheelbase: 243.1cm 95.7in
Track F: 145.0cm 57.1in
Track R: 144.0cm 56.7in
Length: 436.4cm 171.8in
Width: 185.7cm 73.1in
Height: 119.9cm 47.2in
Kerb weight: 1157.7kg 2550.0lb

2758 Mazda

RX-7 GTUs
1989 Japan
130.0mph 209.2kmh
0-60mph 96.5kmh: 8.6secs
0-1/4 mile: 16.7secs
160.0bhp 119.3kW 162.2PS
@ 7000rpm
140.0lbft 189.7Nm @ 4000rpm
129.1bhp/ton 127.0bhp/tonne
122.3bhp/L 91.2kW/L 124.0PS/L
22.8mpg 19.0mpgUS 12.4L/100km
Petrol Wankel rotary
1308cc 79.8cu in
Rotary 2 fuel injection
Compression ratio: 9.7:1
Transmission: Manual
No. of forward speeds: 5
Wheels driven: Rear
Springs F/R: Coil/Coil
Brake system: PA
Brakes F/R: Disc/Disc
Steering: Rack & pinion PA
Wheelbase: 243.1cm 95.7in
Track F: 145.0cm 57.1in
Track R: 144.0cm 56.7in
Length: 431.5cm 169.9in
Width: 168.9cm 66.5in
Height: 126.5cm 49.8in
Kerb weight: 1259.8kg 2775.0lb
Fuel: 70.0L 15.4gal 18.5galUS

2759 Mazda

RX-7 Turbo II
1989 Japan
150.0mph 241.4kmh
0-50mph 80.5kmh: 5.0secs
0-60mph 96.5kmh: 6.7secs
0-1/4 mile: 14.9secs
0-1km: 27.0secs
200.0bhp 149.1kW 202.8PS
@ 6500rpm
195.6lbft 265.0Nm @ 3500rpm
152.9bhp/ton 150.4bhp/tonne
152.9bhp/L 114.0kW/L 155.0PS/L
24.3mph 39.1kmh/1000rpm
14.3mpg 11.9mpgUS 19.8L/100km
Petrol Wankel rotary
1308cc 80.0cu in turbocharged
Rotary 2 fuel injection
Compression ratio: 9.0:1
Valve type/No: Ports
Transmission: Manual
No. of forward speeds: 5
Wheels driven: Rear
Springs F/R: Coil/Coil
Brake system: PA ABS
Brakes F/R: Disc/Disc
Steering: Rack & pinion PA
Wheelbase: 243.0cm 95.7in
Track F: 145.0cm 57.1in
Track R: 144.0cm 56.7in
Length: 431.5cm 169.9in
Width: 169.0cm 66.5in
Height: 126.5cm 49.8in
Ground clearance: 16.0cm 6.3in
Kerb weight: 1330.0kg 2929.5lb
Fuel: 71.9L 15.8gal 19.0galUS

2760 Mazda

MX-5 Miata Millen
1990 Japan
126.0mph 202.7kmh
0-60mph 96.5kmh: 6.4secs
0-1/4 mile: 14.7secs
230.0bhp 171.5kW 233.2PS
@ 5500rpm
235.0lbft 318.4Nm @ 5000rpm
230.0bhp/ton 226.2bhp/tonne
144.0bhp/L 107.4kW/L 146.0PS/L
50.3ft/sec 15.3m/sec
18.0mpg 15.0mpgUS 15.7L/100km
Petrol 4-stroke piston
1597cc 97.4cu in turbocharged
In-line 4 fuel injection
Compression ratio: 7.2:1
Bore: 78.0mm 3.1in
Stroke: 83.6mm 3.3in
Valve type/No: Overhead 16
Transmission: Manual
No. of forward speeds: 5
Wheels driven: Rear
Springs F/R: Coil/Coil
Brake system: PA
Brakes F/R: Disc/Disc
Steering: Rack & pinion
Wheelbase: 226.6cm 89.2in
Track F: 143.3cm 56.4in
Track R: 144.5cm 56.9in
Length: 394.7cm 155.4in
Width: 167.4cm 65.9in
Height: 117.6cm 46.3in
Kerb weight: 1017.0kg 2240.0lb
Fuel: 45.0L 9.9gal 11.9galUS

2761 Mazda

MX-6 GT
1990 Japan
124.0mph 199.5kmh
0-50mph 80.5kmh: 6.0secs
0-60mph 96.5kmh: 8.2secs
0-1/4 mile: 16.0secs
145.0bhp 108.1kW 147.0PS
@ 4300rpm
190.0lbft 257.5Nm @ 3500rpm
112.4bhp/ton 110.5bhp/tonne
66.4bhp/L 49.5kW/L 67.3PS/L
44.2ft/sec 13.5m/sec
22.8mpg 19.0mpgUS 12.4L/100km
Petrol 4-stroke piston
2184cc 133.2cu in turbocharged
In-line 4 fuel injection
Compression ratio: 7.8:1
Bore: 86.0mm 3.4in
Stroke: 94.0mm 3.7in
Valve type/No: Overhead 12
Transmission: Manual
No. of forward speeds: 5
Wheels driven: Front
Springs F/R: Coil/Coil
Brake system: PA
Brakes F/R: Disc/Disc
Steering: Rack & pinion PA
Wheelbase: 251.5cm 99.0in
Track F: 145.5cm 57.3in
Track R: 146.6cm 57.7in
Length: 449.6cm 177.0in
Width: 168.9cm 66.5in
Height: 135.9cm 53.5in
Kerb weight: 1312.1kg 2890.0lb
Fuel: 60.2L 13.2gal 15.9galUS

2762 Mazda

Protege
1990 Japan
130.0mph 209.2kmh
0-60mph 96.5kmh: 9.1secs
0-1/4 mile: 16.8secs
125.0bhp 93.2kW 126.7PS
@ 6500rpm
114.0lbft 154.5Nm @ 4500rpm
112.2bhp/ton 110.3bhp/tonne
68.0bhp/L 50.7kW/L 68.9PS/L
60.5ft/sec 18.4m/sec
31.2mpg 26.0mpgUS 9.0L/100km
Petrol 4-stroke piston
1839cc 112.2cu in
In-line 4 fuel injection
Compression ratio: 9.0:1
Bore: 83.0mm 3.3in
Stroke: 85.0mm 3.3in
Valve type/No: Overhead 16
Transmission: Manual
No. of forward speeds: 5
Wheels driven: Front
Springs F/R: Coil/Coil
Brake system: PA
Brakes F/R: Disc/Disc
Steering: Rack & pinion PA
Wheelbase: 249.9cm 98.4in
Track F: 143.0cm 56.3in
Track R: 143.5cm 56.5in
Length: 435.6cm 171.5in
Width: 167.4cm 65.9in
Height: 137.4cm 54.1in
Kerb weight: 1132.7kg 2495.0lb
Fuel: 54.9L 12.1gal 14.5galUS

2763 Mazda

RX-7 Convertible
1990 Japan
0-60mph 96.5kmh: 9.1secs
0-1/4 mile: 17.1secs
160.0bhp 119.3kW 162.2PS
@ 7000rpm
140.0lbft 189.7Nm @ 4000rpm
118.3bhp/ton 116.3bhp/tonne
122.3bhp/L 91.2kW/L 124.0PS/L
22.8mpg 19.0mpgUS 12.4L/100km
Petrol Wankel rotary
1308cc 79.8cu in
Rotary 2
Transmission: Manual
No. of forward speeds: 5
Wheels driven: Rear
Springs F/R: Coil/Coil
Brakes F/R: Disc/Disc
Steering: Rack & pinion PA
Wheelbase: 243.1cm 95.7in
Track F: 145.0cm 57.1in
Track R: 144.0cm 56.7in
Length: 431.5cm 169.9in
Width: 168.9cm 66.5in
Height: 126.5cm 49.8in
Kerb weight: 1375.6kg 3030.0lb

2764 Mazda

RX-7 Turbo
1990 Japan
140.0mph 225.3kmh
0-50mph 80.5kmh: 4.8secs
0-60mph 96.5kmh: 6.4secs
0-1/4 mile: 15.0secs
200.0bhp 149.1kW 202.8PS
@ 6500rpm
196.0lbft 265.6Nm @ 3500rpm
150.1bhp/ton 147.6bhp/tonne
152.9bhp/L 114.0kW/L 155.0PS/L
19.2mpg 16.0mpgUS 14.7L/100km
Petrol Wankel rotary
1308cc 79.8cu in turbocharged
Rotary 2 fuel injection
Compression ratio: 9.0:1
Transmission: Manual
No. of forward speeds: 5
Wheels driven: Rear
Springs F/R: Coil/Coil
Brake system: PA ABS
Brakes F/R: Disc/Disc
Steering: Rack & pinion PA
Wheelbase: 243.1cm 95.7in
Track F: 145.0cm 57.1in
Track R: 144.0cm 56.7in
Length: 431.5cm 169.9in
Width: 168.9cm 66.5in
Height: 126.5cm 49.8in
Kerb weight: 1355.2kg 2985.0lb
Fuel: 70.0L 15.4gal 18.5galUS

2765 Mazda

121 GSX
1991 Japan
91.0mph 146.4kmh
0-50mph 80.5kmh: 10.9secs
0-60mph 96.5kmh: 15.3secs
0-1/4 mile: 20.4secs
0-1km: 38.4secs
72.4bhp 54.0kW 73.4PS
@ 6000rpm
78.2lbft 106.0Nm @ 3700rpm
86.9bhp/ton 85.5bhp/tonne
54.7bhp/L 40.8kW/L 55.4PS/L
54.8ft/sec 16.7m/sec
24.7mph 39.7kmh/1000rpm
30.7mpg 25.6mpgUS 9.2L/100km
Petrol 4-stroke piston
1324cc 81.0cu in
In-line 4 fuel injection
Compression ratio: 9.4:1
Bore: 71.0mm 2.8in
Stroke: 83.6mm 3.3in
Valve type/No: Overhead 16
Transmission: Automatic
No. of forward speeds: 4
Wheels driven: Front
Springs F/R: Coil/Coil
Brake system: PA
Brakes F/R: Disc/Drum
Steering: Rack & pinion
Wheelbase: 239.0cm 94.1in
Track F: 142.0cm 55.9in
Track R: 140.0cm 55.1in
Length: 381.0cm 150.0in
Width: 165.0cm 65.0in
Height: 147.0cm 57.9in
Ground clearance: 14.8cm 5.8in
Kerb weight: 847.0kg 1865.6lb
Fuel: 43.0L 9.4gal 11.4galUS

2766 Mazda

323 1.8 GT
1991 Japan
123.0mph 197.9kmh
0-50mph 80.5kmh: 5.9secs
0-60mph 96.5kmh: 7.8secs
0-1/4 mile: 16.3secs
0-1km: 29.9secs
140.0bhp 104.4kW 141.9PS
@ 6500rpm
120.3lbft 163.0Nm @ 4700rpm
132.1bhp/ton 129.9bhp/tonne
76.1bhp/L 56.7kW/L 77.1PS/L
60.5ft/sec 18.4m/sec
19.3mph 31.1kmh/1000rpm
28.5mpg 23.7mpgUS 9.9L/100km
Petrol 4-stroke piston
1840cc 112.0cu in
In-line 4 fuel injection
Compression ratio: 9.8:1
Bore: 83.0mm 3.3in
Stroke: 85.0mm 3.3in
Valve type/No: Overhead 16
Transmission: Manual
No. of forward speeds: 5
Wheels driven: Front
Springs F/R: Coil/Coil
Brake system: PA
Brakes F/R: Disc/Disc
Steering: Rack & pinion PA
Wheelbase: 245.0cm 96.5in
Track F: 143.0cm 56.3in
Track R: 143.5cm 56.5in
Length: 399.5cm 157.3in
Width: 167.5cm 65.9in
Height: 138.0cm 54.3in
Ground clearance: 19.0cm 7.5in
Kerb weight: 1078.0kg 2374.4lb
Fuel: 55.0L 12.1gal 14.5galUS

2767 Mazda

MX-3 V6
1991 Japan
125.0mph 201.1kmh
0-50mph 80.5kmh: 6.6secs
0-60mph 96.5kmh: 8.9secs
0-1/4 mile: 16.9secs
0-1km: 31.2secs
134.0bhp 99.9kW 135.9PS
@ 6800rpm

118.0lbft 159.9Nm @ 5300rpm
122.7bhp/ton 120.6bhp/tonne
72.6bhp/L 54.2kW/L 73.6PS/L
51.8ft/sec 15.8m/sec
18.8mph 30.2kmh/1000rpm
25.0mpg 20.8mpgUS 11.3L/100km
Petrol 4-stroke piston
1845cc 112.6cu in
Vee 6 fuel injection
Compression ratio: 9.2:1
Bore: 75.0mm 2.9in
Stroke: 69.6mm 2.7in
Valve type/No: Overhead 24
Transmission: Manual
No. of forward speeds: 5
Wheels driven: Front
Springs F/R: Coil/Coil
Brake system: PA ABS
Brakes F/R: Disc/Disc
Steering: Rack & pinion PA
Wheelbase: 245.5cm 96.7in
Track F: 146.0cm 57.5in
Track R: 146.5cm 57.7in
Length: 422.0cm 166.1in
Width: 169.5cm 66.7in
Height: 131.0cm 51.6in
Ground clearance: 13.0cm 5.1in
Kerb weight: 1110.9kg 2447.0lb
Fuel: 50.0L 11.0gal 13.2galUS

2768 Mazda

RX-7 Cartech
1991 Japan
178.0mph 286.4kmh
0-60mph 96.5kmh: 5.5secs
0-1/4 mile: 13.9secs
344.0bhp 256.5kW 348.8PS
@ 6500rpm
285.0lbft 386.2Nm @ 4900rpm
270.4bhp/ton 265.9bhp/tonne
263.0bhp/L 196.1kW/L 266.6PS/L
Petrol Wankel rotary
1308cc 79.8cu in turbocharged
Rotary 2 fuel injection
Compression ratio: 9.0:1
Transmission: Manual
No. of forward speeds: 5
Wheels driven: Rear
Springs F/R: Coil/Coil
Brake system: PA ABS
Brakes F/R: Disc/Disc
Steering: Rack & pinion PA
Wheelbase: 243.1cm 95.7in
Track F: 145.0cm 57.1in
Track R: 144.0cm 56.7in
Length: 431.5cm 169.9in
Width: 168.9cm 66.5in
Height: 123.2cm 48.5in
Kerb weight: 1293.9kg 2850.0lb

2769 Mazda

RX-7 Infini IV
1991 Japan
112.0mph 180.2kmh
0-60mph 96.5kmh: 7.0secs
0-1/4 mile: 14.9secs
215.0bhp 160.3kW 218.0PS
@ 6500rpm
206.0lbft 279.1Nm @ 3500rpm
173.9bhp/ton 171.0bhp/tonne
164.4bhp/L 122.6kW/L 166.6PS/L
17.4mpg 14.5mpgUS 16.2L/100km
Petrol Wankel rotary
1308cc 79.8cu in
Rotary 2 fuel injection
Compression ratio: 9.0:1
Transmission: Manual
No. of forward speeds: 5
Wheels driven: Rear
Springs F/R: Coil/Coil
Brake system: PA
Brakes F/R: Disc/Disc
Steering: Rack & pinion PA
Wheelbase: 243.1cm 95.7in
Track F: 145.0cm 57.1in
Track R: 144.0cm 56.7in
Length: 431.5cm 169.9in
Width: 168.9cm 66.5in
Height: 126.5cm 49.8in
Kerb weight: 1257.6kg 2770.0lb
Fuel: 70.0L 15.4gal 18.5galUS

2770 Mazda

RX-7 Mariah Mode Six
1991 Japan
170.0mph 273.5kmh
0-60mph 96.5kmh: 4.8secs
380.0bhp 283.4kW 385.3PS
@ 6800rpm
330.0lbft 447.2Nm @ 6000rpm
279.1bhp/ton 274.4bhp/tonne
290.5bhp/L 216.6kW/L 294.5PS/L
Petrol Wankel rotary
1308cc 79.8cu in turbocharged
Rotary 2 fuel injection
Compression ratio: 9.0:1
Transmission: Manual
No. of forward speeds: 5
Wheels driven: Rear
Springs F/R: Coil/Coil
Brake system: PA ABS
Brakes F/R: Disc/Disc
Steering: Rack & pinion PA
Wheelbase: 243.1cm 95.7in
Track F: 153.2cm 60.3in
Track R: 153.7cm 60.5in
Length: 431.5cm 169.9in
Width: 168.9cm 66.5in
Height: 123.2cm 48.5in
Kerb weight: 1384.7kg 3050.0lb
Fuel: 70.0L 15.4gal 18.5galUS

2771 Mazda

RX-7 Turbo
1991 Japan
149.0mph 239.7kmh
0-50mph 80.5kmh: 4.8secs
0-60mph 96.5kmh: 6.4secs
0-1/4 mile: 15.0secs
200.0bhp 149.1kW 202.8PS
@ 6500rpm
196.0lbft 265.6Nm @ 3500rpm
149.8bhp/ton 147.3bhp/tonne
152.9bhp/L 114.0kW/L 155.0PS/L
19.2mpg 16.0mpgUS 14.7L/100km
Petrol Wankel rotary
1308cc 79.8cu in turbocharged
Rotary 2 fuel injection
Compression ratio: 9.0:1
Transmission: Manual
No. of forward speeds: 5
Wheels driven: Rear
Springs F/R: Coil/Coil
Brake system: PA ABS
Brakes F/R: Disc/Disc
Steering: Rack & pinion PA
Wheelbase: 243.1cm 95.7in
Track F: 145.0cm 57.1in
Track R: 144.0cm 56.7in
Length: 431.5cm 169.9in
Width: 168.9cm 66.5in
Height: 126.5cm 49.8in
Kerb weight: 1357.5kg 2990.0lb
Fuel: 70.0L 15.4gal 18.5galUS

2772 Mazda

MX-3 1.6 Auto
1992 Japan
102.0mph 164.1kmh
0-50mph 80.5kmh: 9.7secs
0-60mph 96.5kmh: 13.4secs
0-1/4 mile: 19.6secs
0-1km: 36.0secs
88.0bhp 65.6kW 89.2PS
@ 5300rpm
99.0lbft 134.1Nm @ 4000rpm
82.1bhp/ton 80.7bhp/tonne
55.1bhp/L 41.1kW/L 55.8PS/L
48.4ft/sec 14.8m/sec
25.2mph 40.5kmh/1000rpm
27.9mpg 23.2mpgUS 10.1L/100km
Petrol 4-stroke piston
1598cc 97.5cu in
In-line 4 fuel injection
Compression ratio: 9.0:1
Bore: 78.0mm 3.1in
Stroke: 83.6mm 3.3in
Valve type/No: Overhead 16
Transmission: Automatic
No. of forward speeds: 4
Wheels driven: Front
Springs F/R: Coil/Coil
Brake system: PA
Brakes F/R: Disc/Disc
Steering: Rack & pinion PA
Wheelbase: 245.6cm 96.7in
Track F: 146.1cm 57.5in
Track R: 146.6cm 57.7in
Length: 421.9cm 166.1in
Width: 169.4cm 66.7in
Height: 131.1cm 51.6in
Kerb weight: 1090.0kg 2401.0lb
Fuel: 50.0L 11.0gal 13.2galUS

2773 Mazda

MX-3 GS
1992 Japan
120.0mph 193.1kmh
0-50mph 80.5kmh: 6.6secs
0-60mph 96.5kmh: 9.2secs
0-1/4 mile: 16.8secs
130.0bhp 96.9kW 131.8PS
@ 6500rpm
115.0lbft 155.8Nm @ 4500rpm
114.4bhp/ton 112.5bhp/tonne
70.5bhp/L 52.6kW/L 71.5PS/L
49.5ft/sec 15.1m/sec
28.8mpg 24.0mpgUS 9.8L/100km
Petrol 4-stroke piston
1844cc 112.5cu in
Vee 6 fuel injection
Compression ratio: 9.2:1
Bore: 75.0mm 2.9in
Stroke: 69.6mm 2.7in
Valve type/No: Overhead 24
Transmission: Manual
No. of forward speeds: 5
Wheels driven: Front
Springs F/R: Coil/Coil
Brake system: PA
Brakes F/R: Disc/Disc
Steering: Rack & pinion PA
Wheelbase: 244.6cm 96.3in
Track F: 146.1cm 57.5in
Track R: 146.6cm 57.7in
Length: 420.9cm 165.7in
Width: 169.4cm 66.7in
Height: 131.1cm 51.6in
Ground clearance: 13.0cm 5.1in
Kerb weight: 1155.4kg 2545.0lb
Fuel: 50.0L 11.0gal 13.2galUS

2774 Mercedes-Benz

36/220-S
1928 Germany
108.0mph 173.8kmh
0-50mph 80.5kmh: 11.3secs
0-60mph 96.5kmh: 14.0secs
0-1/4 mile: 19.2secs
180.0bhp 134.2kW 182.5PS
@ 3200rpm
390.0lbft 528.5Nm @ 1800rpm
82.3bhp/ton 80.9bhp/tonne
26.5bhp/L 19.8kW/L 26.9PS/L
52.5ft/sec 16.0m/sec
35.1mph 56.5kmh/1000rpm
Petrol 4-stroke piston
6789cc 414.2cu in
In-line 6
Compression ratio: 5.0:1
Bore: 98.0mm 3.9in
Stroke: 150.1mm 5.9in
Valve type/No: Overhead 12
Transmission: Manual
No. of forward speeds: 4
Wheels driven: Rear
Wheelbase: 340.1cm 133.9in
Track F: 142.0cm 55.9in
Track R: 142.0cm 55.9in
Length: 508.0cm 200.0in
Width: 172.7cm 68.0in
Height: 152.4cm 60.0in
Kerb weight: 2224.6kg 4900.0lb

2775 Mercedes-Benz

32/90 Saloon
1929 Germany
75.0mph 120.7kmh
16.0mpg 13.3mpgUS 17.7L/100km
Petrol 4-stroke piston
4624cc 282.1cu in
In-line 8
Bore: 80.0mm 3.1in
Stroke: 115.0mm 4.5in
Transmission: Manual
No. of forward speeds: 4
Wheels driven: Rear
Brakes F/R: Drum/Drum
Wheelbase: 367.0cm 144.5in
Track F: 142.2cm 56.0in
Track R: 142.2cm 56.0in
Length: 487.7cm 192.0in
Width: 175.3cm 69.0in
Height: 186.7cm 73.5in
Kerb weight: 2135.6kg 4704.0lb
Fuel: 109.2L 24.0gal 28.8galUS

2776 Mercedes-Benz

SSKL
1929 Germany
120.0mph 193.1kmh
0-50mph 80.5kmh: 6.7secs
0-60mph 96.5kmh: 9.5secs
0-1/4 mile: 17.0secs
250.0bhp 186.4kW 253.5PS
@ 3200rpm
420.0lbft 569.1Nm @ 1800rpm
160.0bhp/ton 157.3bhp/tonne
35.4bhp/L 26.4kW/L 35.9PS/L
52.5ft/sec 16.0m/sec
36.2mph 58.2kmh/1000rpm
Petrol 4-stroke piston
7069cc 431.3cu in
In-line 6 1 Carburettor
Compression ratio: 5.8:1
Bore: 100.1mm 3.9in
Stroke: 150.1mm 5.9in
Valve type/No: Overhead 12
Transmission: Manual
No. of forward speeds: 4
Wheels driven: Rear
Wheelbase: 294.9cm 116.1in
Track F: 142.0cm 55.9in
Track R: 142.0cm 55.9in
Length: 434.3cm 171.0in
Width: 162.6cm 64.0in
Height: 137.2cm 54.0in
Kerb weight: 1589.0kg 3500.0lb

2777 Mercedes-Benz

32/90 Limousine
1930 Germany
62.5mph 100.6kmh
12.0mpg 10.0mpgUS 23.5L/100km
Petrol 4-stroke piston
4592cc 280.2cu in
In-line 8
Bore: 80.0mm 3.1in
Stroke: 115.0mm 4.5in
Transmission: Manual
No. of forward speeds: 4
Wheels driven: Rear
Brakes F/R: Drum/Drum
Wheelbase: 373.4cm 147.0in
Track F: 144.8cm 57.0in
Track R: 144.8cm 57.0in
Length: 495.3cm 195.0in
Width: 181.6cm 71.5in
Height: 181.6cm 71.5in
Kerb weight: 2135.6kg 4704.0lb
Fuel: 109.2L 24.0gal 28.8galUS

2778 Mercedes-Benz

21/60 Coupe
1931 Germany
62.5mph 100.6kmh
25.0mpg 20.8mpgUS 11.3L/100km
Petrol 4-stroke piston
2650cc 161.7cu in
In-line 6
Bore: 74.0mm 2.9in
Stroke: 100.0mm 3.9in
Transmission: Manual
No. of forward speeds: 3
Wheels driven: Rear
Brakes F/R: Drum/Drum
Wheelbase: 283.2cm 111.5in
Track F: 142.2cm 56.0in
Track R: 142.2cm 56.0in
Length: 426.7cm 168.0in
Width: 167.6cm 66.0in
Height: 177.8cm 70.0in
Kerb weight: 1525.4kg 3360.0lb
Fuel: 54.6L 12.0gal 14.4galUS

2779 Mercedes-Benz

12hp Rear-engined Saloon
1934 Germany
55.5mph 89.3kmh
0-50mph 80.5kmh: 37.2secs
30.0mpg 25.0mpgUS 9.4L/100km
Petrol 4-stroke piston
1308cc 79.8cu in
In-line 4
Bore: 70.0mm 2.8in
Stroke: 85.0mm 3.3in
Transmission: Manual
No. of forward speeds: 4
Wheels driven: Rear
Brakes F/R: Drum/Drum
Kerb weight: 813.6kg 1792.0lb
Fuel: 34.1L 7.5gal 9.0galUS

2780 Mercedes-Benz
Type 290 Cabriolet
1935 Germany
72.5mph 116.7kmh
0-50mph 80.5kmh: 25.6secs
0-60mph 96.5kmh: 44.4secs
15.0mpg 12.5mpgUS 18.8L/100km
Petrol 4-stroke piston
2867cc 174.9cu in
In-line 6
Bore: 78.0mm 3.1in
Stroke: 100.0mm 3.9in
Valve type/No: Side 12
Transmission: Manual
No. of forward speeds: 4
Wheels driven: Rear
Brakes F/R: Drum/Drum
Kerb weight: 1870.5kg 4120.0lb
Fuel: 55.7L 12.2gal 14.7galUS

2781 Mercedes-Benz
20.8hp Diesel Saloon
1936 Germany
56.2mph 90.4kmh
0-50mph 80.5kmh: 51.7secs
28.0mpg 23.3mpgUS 10.1L/100km
Diesel 4-stroke piston
2550cc 155.6cu in
In-line 4
Bore: 90.0mm 3.5in
Stroke: 100.0mm 3.9in
Valve type/No: Overhead 8
Transmission: Manual
No. of forward speeds: 4
Wheels driven: Rear
Brakes F/R: Drum/Drum
Kerb weight: 1667.1kg 3672.0lb
Fuel: 45.5L 10.0gal 12.0galUS

2782 Mercedes-Benz
Type 500 Supercharged
1936 Germany
100.5mph 161.7kmh
0-50mph 80.5kmh: 13.4secs
0-60mph 96.5kmh: 16.5secs
12.0mpg 10.0mpgUS 23.5L/100km
Petrol 4-stroke piston
5018cc 306.2cu in supercharged
In-line 8
Bore: 86.0mm 3.4in
Stroke: 108.0mm 4.2in
Valve type/No: Overhead 16
Transmission: Manual
No. of forward speeds: 4
Wheels driven: Rear
Brakes F/R: Drum/Drum
Kerb weight: 2478.8kg 5460.0lb
Fuel: 109.2L 24.0gal 28.8galUS

2783 Mercedes-Benz
Type 230 Saloon
1937 Germany
70.3mph 113.1kmh
0-50mph 80.5kmh: 22.3secs
0-60mph 96.5kmh: 39.3secs
21.0mpg 17.5mpgUS 13.5L/100km
Petrol 4-stroke piston
2228cc 135.9cu in
In-line 6
Bore: 72.5mm 2.8in
Stroke: 90.0mm 3.5in
Valve type/No: Side 12
Transmission: Manual
No. of forward speeds: 4
Wheels driven: Rear
Brakes F/R: Drum/Drum
Kerb weight: 1500.9kg 3306.0lb
Fuel: 45.5L 10.0gal 12.0galUS

2784 Mercedes-Benz
Type 320 Saloon
1938 Germany
77.5mph 124.7kmh
0-50mph 80.5kmh: 19.5secs
0-60mph 96.5kmh: 32.0secs
16.0mpg 13.3mpgUS 17.7L/100km
Petrol 4-stroke piston
3208cc 195.7cu in
In-line 6
Bore: 82.5mm 3.2in
Stroke: 100.0mm 3.9in
Valve type/No: Side 12
Transmission: Manual
No. of forward speeds: 4
Wheels driven: Rear
Brakes F/R: Drum/Drum
Kerb weight: 2016.7kg 4442.0lb
Fuel: 71.7L 15.7gal 18.9galUS

2785 Mercedes-Benz
Type 540
1938 Germany
104.6mph 168.3kmh
0-50mph 80.5kmh: 11.7secs
0-60mph 96.5kmh: 16.4secs
8.0mpg 6.7mpgUS 35.3L/100km
Petrol 4-stroke piston
5401cc 329.5cu in
In-line 8
Bore: 88.0mm 3.5in
Stroke: 111.0mm 4.4in
Valve type/No: Overhead 16
Transmission: Manual
No. of forward speeds: 4
Wheels driven: Rear
Brakes F/R: Drum/Drum
Kerb weight: 2631.4kg 5796.0lb
Fuel: 120.6L 26.5gal 31.8galUS

2786 Mercedes-Benz
170S
1952 Germany
70.4mph 113.3kmh
0-1/4 mile: 27.5secs
52.0bhp 38.8kW 52.7PS
@ 4500rpm
43.3bhp/ton 42.6bhp/tonne
29.4bhp/L 22.0kW/L 29.8PS/L
49.2ft/sec 15.0m/sec
Petrol 4-stroke piston
1766cc 107.7cu in
In-line 4
Compression ratio: 6.5:1
Bore: 74.6mm 2.9in
Stroke: 100.0mm 3.9in
Valve type/No: Side 8
Transmission: Manual
No. of forward speeds: 4
Wheels driven: Rear
Springs F/R: Coil/Coil
Wheelbase: 284.5cm 112.0in
Track F: 131.3cm 51.7in
Track R: 142.0cm 55.9in
Length: 445.3cm 175.3in
Width: 168.4cm 66.3in
Height: 161.0cm 63.4in
Ground clearance: 18.5cm 7.3in
Kerb weight: 1221.3kg 2690.0lb

2787 Mercedes-Benz
300
1952 Germany
105.0mph 168.9kmh
0-50mph 80.5kmh: 11.7secs
0-60mph 96.5kmh: 16.4secs
0-1/4 mile: 20.0secs
114.0bhp 85.0kW 115.6PS
@ 4600rpm
145.0lbft 196.5Nm @ 2500rpm
65.9bhp/ton 64.8bhp/tonne
38.0bhp/L 28.4kW/L 38.6PS/L
44.2ft/sec 13.5m/sec
18.4mph 29.6kmh/1000rpm
15.3mpg 12.7mpgUS 18.5L/100km
Petrol 4-stroke piston
2996cc 182.8cu in
In-line 6
Compression ratio: 6.4:1
Bore: 85.0mm 3.3in
Stroke: 88.0mm 3.5in
Valve type/No: Overhead 12
Transmission: Manual
No. of forward speeds: 4
Wheels driven: Rear
Springs F/R: Coil/Coil
Brakes F/R: Drum/Drum
Wheelbase: 304.8cm 120.0in
Track F: 144.0cm 56.7in
Track R: 152.4cm 60.0in
Length: 495.3cm 195.0in
Width: 184.2cm 72.5in
Height: 160.0cm 63.0in
Ground clearance: 17.3cm 6.8in
Kerb weight: 1758.8kg 3874.0lb
Fuel: 72.1L 15.8gal 19.0galUS

2788 Mercedes-Benz
300SL Carrera Panamericana
1952 Germany
150.0mph 241.4kmh
0-60mph 96.5kmh: 7.8secs
173.0bhp 129.0kW 175.4PS
@ 5200rpm
188.0lbft 254.7Nm @ 4200rpm
202.5bhp/ton 199.1bhp/tonne
57.7bhp/L 43.1kW/L 58.5PS/L
50.0ft/sec 15.2m/sec
Petrol 4-stroke piston
2996cc 182.8cu in
In-line 6 3 Carburettor
Compression ratio: 8.0:1
Bore: 85.0mm 3.3in
Stroke: 88.0mm 3.5in
Valve type/No: Overhead 12
Transmission: Manual
No. of forward speeds: 4
Wheels driven: Rear
Springs F/R: Coil/Coil
Brakes F/R: Drum/Drum
Steering: Recirculating ball
Wheelbase: 240.0cm 94.5in
Track F: 138.2cm 54.4in
Track R: 144.5cm 56.9in
Length: 421.6cm 166.0in
Width: 177.8cm 70.0in
Height: 126.5cm 49.8in
Kerb weight: 869.0kg 1914.0lb
Fuel: 170.3L 37.4gal 45.0galUS

2789 Mercedes-Benz
300 Sedan
1953 Germany
98.5mph 158.5kmh
0-50mph 80.5kmh: 11.2secs
0-60mph 96.5kmh: 16.1secs
0-1/4 mile: 20.2secs
115.0bhp 85.8kW 116.6PS
@ 4600rpm
144.0lbft 195.1Nm @ 4600rpm
65.2bhp/ton 64.1bhp/tonne
38.4bhp/L 28.6kW/L 38.9PS/L
44.2ft/sec 13.5m/sec
19.8mpg 16.5mpgUS 14.3L/100km
Petrol 4-stroke piston
2996cc 182.8cu in
In-line 6
Compression ratio: 6.4:1
Bore: 85.0mm 3.3in
Stroke: 88.0mm 3.5in
Valve type/No: Overhead 12
Transmission: Manual
No. of forward speeds: 4
Wheels driven: Rear
Wheelbase: 304.8cm 120.0in
Track F: 143.8cm 56.6in
Track R: 152.4cm 60.0in
Length: 487.7cm 192.0in
Width: 160.0cm 63.0in
Height: 185.4cm 73.0in
Ground clearance: 18.5cm 7.3in
Kerb weight: 1793.3kg 3950.0lb

2790 Mercedes-Benz
180 Saloon
1954 Germany
77.0mph 123.9kmh
0-50mph 80.5kmh: 18.6secs
0-60mph 96.5kmh: 29.9secs
0-1/4 mile: 23.9secs
52.0bhp 38.8kW 52.7PS
@ 4000rpm
82.5lbft 111.8Nm @ 1800rpm
45.8bhp/ton 45.1bhp/tonne
29.4bhp/L 21.9kW/L 29.8PS/L
43.8ft/sec 13.3m/sec
19.5mph 31.4kmh/1000rpm
29.4mpg 24.5mpgUS 9.6L/100km
Petrol 4-stroke piston
1767cc 107.8cu in
In-line 4
Compression ratio: 6.7:1
Bore: 75.0mm 2.9in
Stroke: 100.0mm 3.9in
Valve type/No: Side 8
Transmission: Manual
No. of forward speeds: 4
Wheels driven: Rear
Springs F/R: Coil/Coil
Brakes F/R: Drum/Drum
Wheelbase: 266.7cm 105.0in
Track F: 142.2cm 56.0in
Track R: 145.3cm 57.2in
Length: 449.6cm 177.0in
Width: 174.0cm 68.5in
Height: 163.8cm 64.5in
Ground clearance: 20.3cm 8.0in
Kerb weight: 1153.6kg 2541.0lb
Fuel: 57.8L 12.7gal 15.3galUS

2791 Mercedes-Benz
190SL
1955 Germany
99.8mph 160.6kmh
0-50mph 80.5kmh: 9.3secs
0-60mph 96.5kmh: 13.0secs
0-1/4 mile: 19.3secs
120.0bhp 89.5kW 121.7PS
@ 5700rpm
101.0lbft 136.9Nm @ 3800rpm
107.5bhp/ton 105.7bhp/tonne
63.3bhp/L 47.2kW/L 64.1PS/L
52.1ft/sec 15.9m/sec
18.2mph 29.3kmh/1000rpm
Petrol 4-stroke piston
1897cc 115.7cu in
In-line 4
Compression ratio: 8.5:1
Bore: 85.1mm 3.3in
Stroke: 83.6mm 3.3in
Valve type/No: Overhead 8
Transmission: Manual
No. of forward speeds: 4
Wheels driven: Rear
Wheelbase: 240.0cm 94.5in
Track F: 143.0cm 56.3in
Track R: 148.1cm 58.3in
Kerb weight: 1135.0kg 2500.0lb

2792 Mercedes-Benz
300B
1955 Germany
102.0mph 164.1kmh
0-50mph 80.5kmh: 11.6secs
0-60mph 96.5kmh: 15.9secs
0-1/4 mile: 20.4secs
136.0bhp 101.4kW 137.9PS
@ 4500rpm
173.0lbft 234.4Nm @ 2700rpm
75.3bhp/ton 74.0bhp/tonne
45.4bhp/L 33.8kW/L 46.0PS/L
43.2ft/sec 13.2m/sec
17.4mph 28.0kmh/1000rpm
16.8mpg 14.0mpgUS 16.8L/100km
Petrol 4-stroke piston
2996cc 182.8cu in
In-line 6
Compression ratio: 7.5:1
Bore: 85.0mm 3.3in
Stroke: 88.0mm 3.5in
Valve type/No: Overhead 12
Transmission: Manual
No. of forward speeds: 4
Wheels driven: Rear
Springs F/R: Coil/Coil
Brakes F/R: Drum/Drum
Wheelbase: 304.8cm 120.0in
Track F: 147.3cm 58.0in
Track R: 152.4cm 60.0in
Length: 508.0cm 200.0in
Width: 184.2cm 72.5in
Height: 160.0cm 63.0in
Ground clearance: 21.6cm 8.5in
Kerb weight: 1836.9kg 4046.0lb
Fuel: 66.0L 14.5gal 17.4galUS

2793 Mercedes-Benz
300SL
1955 Germany
135.0mph 217.2kmh
0-50mph 80.5kmh: 7.0secs
0-60mph 96.5kmh: 8.8secs
0-1/4 mile: 16.1secs
240.0bhp 179.0kW 243.3PS
@ 6100rpm
217.0lbft 294.0Nm @ 4800rpm
194.9bhp/ton 191.7bhp/tonne
80.1bhp/L 59.7kW/L 81.2PS/L
58.6ft/sec 17.9m/sec
22.2mph 35.7kmh/1000rpm
18.4mpg 15.3mpgUS 15.4L/100km
Petrol 4-stroke piston
2996cc 182.8cu in
In-line 6
Compression ratio: 8.5:1
Bore: 85.0mm 3.3in
Stroke: 88.0mm 3.5in
Valve type/No: Overhead 12
Transmission: Manual
No. of forward speeds: 4

Wheels driven: Rear
Springs F/R: Coil/Coil
Brakes F/R: Drum/Drum
Wheelbase: 238.8cm 94.0in
Track F: 138.4cm 54.5in
Track R: 143.5cm 56.5in
Length: 444.5cm 175.0in
Width: 177.8cm 70.0in
Height: 129.5cm 51.0in
Ground clearance: 13.2cm 5.2in
Kerb weight: 1252.1kg 2758.0lb
Fuel: 127.4L 28.0gal 33.6galUS

2794 Mercedes-Benz

300SL Coupe
1955 Germany
146.0mph 234.9kmh
0-50mph 80.5kmh: 6.3secs
0-60mph 96.5kmh: 8.2secs
0-1/4 mile: 16.0secs
243.0bhp 181.2kW 246.4PS
@ 6100rpm
217.0lbft 294.0Nm @ 4800rpm
183.9bhp/ton 180.8bhp/tonne
81.1bhp/L 60.5kW/L 82.2PS/L
58.6ft/sec 17.9m/sec
21.4mph 34.4kmh/1000rpm
Petrol 4-stroke piston
2996cc 182.8cu in
In-line 6 fuel injection
Compression ratio: 8.3:1
Bore: 85.0mm 3.3in
Stroke: 88.0mm 3.5in
Valve type/No: Overhead 12
Transmission: Manual
No. of forward speeds: 4
Wheels driven: Rear
Springs F/R: Coil/Coil
Brake system: PA
Brakes F/R: Drum/Drum
Steering: Recirculating ball
Wheelbase: 240.0cm 94.5in
Track F: 138.4cm 54.5in
Track R: 143.5cm 56.5in
Length: 446.3cm 175.7in
Width: 179.3cm 70.6in
Height: 130.0cm 51.2in
Ground clearance: 13.0cm 5.1in
Kerb weight: 1343.8kg 2960.0lb
Fuel: 130.6L 28.7gal 34.5galUS

2795 Mercedes-Benz

300SLR
1955 Germany
180.0mph 289.6kmh
302.0bhp 225.2kW 306.2PS
@ 7500rpm
219.0lbft 296.7Nm @ 5950rpm
348.7bhp/ton 342.9bhp/tonne
101.3bhp/L 75.5kW/L 102.7PS/L
64.0ft/sec 19.5m/sec
Petrol 4-stroke piston
2982cc 181.9cu in
In-line 8 fuel injection
Compression ratio: 9.5:1
Bore: 78.0mm 3.1in
Stroke: 78.0mm 3.1in
Valve type/No: Overhead 32
Transmission: Manual
No. of forward speeds: 5
Wheels driven: Rear
Springs F/R: Torsion bar/Torsion bar
Brake system: PA
Brakes F/R: Drum/Drum
Wheelbase: 237.0cm 93.3in
Track F: 133.1cm 52.4in
Track R: 138.2cm 54.4in
Kerb weight: 880.8kg 1940.0lb
Fuel: 264.9L 58.2gal 70.0galUS

2796 Mercedes-Benz

219
1957 Germany
90.8mph 146.1kmh
0-50mph 80.5kmh: 10.6secs
0-60mph 96.5kmh: 15.0secs
0-1/4 mile: 20.3secs
92.0bhp 68.6kW 93.3PS
@ 4800rpm
116.0lbft 157.2Nm @ 2400rpm
74.7bhp/ton 73.4bhp/tonne
41.9bhp/L 31.3kW/L 42.5PS/L
38.3ft/sec 11.7m/sec
Petrol 4-stroke piston
2195cc 133.9cu in
In-line 6
Compression ratio: 7.6:1
Bore: 80.0mm 3.1in
Stroke: 72.9mm 2.9in
Valve type/No: Overhead 12
Transmission: Manual
No. of forward speeds: 4
Wheels driven: Rear
Wheelbase: 275.1cm 108.3in
Track F: 143.0cm 56.3in
Track R: 147.1cm 57.9in
Kerb weight: 1253.0kg 2760.0lb

2797 Mercedes-Benz

180D
1958 Germany
68.1mph 109.6kmh
0-50mph 80.5kmh: 20.2secs
0-60mph 96.5kmh: 32.3secs
0-1/4 mile: 26.0secs
46.0bhp 34.3kW 46.6PS
@ 3500rpm
76.7lbft 103.9Nm @ 2000rpm
38.3bhp/ton 37.7bhp/tonne
26.0bhp/L 19.4kW/L 26.4PS/L
38.3ft/sec 11.7m/sec
Diesel 4-stroke piston
1767cc 107.8cu in
In-line 4
Compression ratio: 19.0:1
Bore: 75.2mm 3.0in
Stroke: 100.1mm 3.9in
Valve type/No: Overhead 8
Transmission: Manual
No. of forward speeds: 4
Wheels driven: Rear
Wheelbase: 264.9cm 104.3in
Track F: 142.0cm 55.9in
Track R: 145.8cm 57.4in
Kerb weight: 1221.3kg 2690.0lb

2798 Mercedes-Benz

190SL
1958 Germany
109.2mph 175.7kmh
0-50mph 80.5kmh: 10.3secs
0-60mph 96.5kmh: 13.3secs
0-1/4 mile: 17.8secs
120.0bhp 89.5kW 121.7PS
@ 5700rpm
107.0lbft 145.0Nm @ 2800rpm
110.8bhp/ton 109.0bhp/tonne
63.3bhp/L 47.2kW/L 64.1PS/L
52.1ft/sec 15.9m/sec
18.4mph 29.6kmh/1000rpm
22.4mpg 18.7mpgUS 12.6L/100km
Petrol 4-stroke piston
1897cc 115.7cu in
In-line 4
Compression ratio: 8.5:1
Bore: 85.0mm 3.3in
Stroke: 83.6mm 3.3in
Valve type/No: Overhead 8
Transmission: Manual
No. of forward speeds: 4
Wheels driven: Rear
Springs F/R: Coil/Coil
Brake system: PA
Brakes F/R: Drum/Drum
Wheelbase: 240.0cm 94.5in
Track F: 142.7cm 56.2in
Track R: 146.8cm 57.8in
Length: 422.1cm 166.2in
Width: 174.0cm 68.5in
Height: 132.1cm 52.0in
Ground clearance: 15.7cm 6.2in
Kerb weight: 1100.9kg 2425.0lb
Fuel: 65.1L 14.3gal 17.2galUS

2799 Mercedes-Benz

220S
1958 Germany
101.0mph 162.5kmh
0-50mph 80.5kmh: 12.4secs
0-60mph 96.5kmh: 15.8secs
0-1/4 mile: 21.0secs
120.0bhp 89.5kW 121.7PS
@ 5200rpm
137.0lbft 185.6Nm @ 3600rpm
92.7bhp/ton 91.2bhp/tonne
54.7bhp/L 40.8kW/L 55.4PS/L
41.5ft/sec 12.6m/sec
17.9mph 28.8kmh/1000rpm
25.1mpg 20.9mpgUS 11.3L/100km
Petrol 4-stroke piston
2195cc 133.9cu in
In-line 6
Compression ratio: 8.7:1
Bore: 80.0mm 3.1in
Stroke: 72.8mm 2.9in
Valve type/No: Overhead 12
Transmission: Manual
No. of forward speeds: 4
Wheels driven: Rear
Springs F/R: Coil/Coil
Brake system: PA
Brakes F/R: Drum/Drum
Wheelbase: 281.9cm 111.0in
Track F: 143.0cm 56.3in
Track R: 146.8cm 57.8in
Length: 469.9cm 185.0in
Width: 174.0cm 68.5in
Height: 156.2cm 61.5in
Ground clearance: 21.6cm 8.5in
Kerb weight: 1315.7kg 2898.0lb
Fuel: 63.7L 14.0gal 16.8galUS

2800 Mercedes-Benz

300SL Roadster
1958 Germany
130.0mph 209.2kmh
0-50mph 80.5kmh: 5.7secs
0-60mph 96.5kmh: 7.0secs
0-1/4 mile: 15.5secs
250.0bhp 186.4kW 253.5PS
@ 6200rpm
228.0lbft 308.9Nm @ 5000rpm
182.1bhp/ton 179.1bhp/tonne
83.4bhp/L 62.2kW/L 84.6PS/L
59.6ft/sec 18.2m/sec
Petrol 4-stroke piston
2996cc 182.8cu in
In-line 6 fuel injection
Compression ratio: 9.5:1
Bore: 85.1mm 3.3in
Stroke: 87.9mm 3.5in
Valve type/No: Overhead 12
Transmission: Manual
No. of forward speeds: 4
Wheels driven: Rear
Wheelbase: 240.0cm 94.5in
Track F: 139.7cm 55.0in
Track R: 144.8cm 57.0in
Kerb weight: 1396.0kg 3075.0lb

2801 Mercedes-Benz

220SE
1959 Germany
107.6mph 173.1kmh
0-50mph 80.5kmh: 8.7secs
0-60mph 96.5kmh: 11.9secs
0-1/4 mile: 17.9secs
134.0bhp 99.9kW 135.9PS
@ 5000rpm
151.8lbft 205.7Nm @ 4100rpm
101.7bhp/ton 100.0bhp/tonne
61.0bhp/L 45.5kW/L 61.9PS/L
39.9ft/sec 12.1m/sec
17.9mph 28.8kmh/1000rpm
22.8mpg 19.0mpgUS 12.4L/100km
Petrol 4-stroke piston
2195cc 133.9cu in
In-line 6
Compression ratio: 8.7:1
Bore: 80.0mm 3.1in
Stroke: 72.8mm 2.9in
Valve type/No: Overhead 12
Transmission: Manual
No. of forward speeds: 4
Wheels driven: Rear
Springs F/R: Coil/Coil
Brake system: PA
Brakes F/R: Drum/Drum
Wheelbase: 274.8cm 108.2in
Track F: 147.1cm 57.9in
Track R: 148.3cm 58.4in
Length: 488.2cm 192.2in
Width: 179.3cm 70.6in
Height: 150.9cm 59.4in
Ground clearance: 19.8cm 7.8in
Kerb weight: 1339.3kg 2950.0lb
Fuel: 65.1L 14.3gal 17.2galUS

2802 Mercedes-Benz

190SL
1960 Germany
106.0mph 170.6kmh
0-50mph 80.5kmh: 10.3secs
0-60mph 96.5kmh: 13.5secs
0-1/4 mile: 18.9secs
120.0bhp 89.5kW 121.7PS
@ 5700rpm
105.0lbft 142.3Nm @ 3200rpm
105.4bhp/ton 103.6bhp/tonne
63.3bhp/L 47.2kW/L 64.1PS/L
52.1ft/sec 15.9m/sec
18.5mph 29.8kmh/1000rpm
Petrol 4-stroke piston
1897cc 115.7cu in
In-line 4 1 Carburettor
Compression ratio: 8.5:1
Bore: 85.1mm 3.3in
Stroke: 83.6mm 3.3in
Valve type/No: Overhead 8
Transmission: Manual
No. of forward speeds: 4
Wheels driven: Rear
Wheelbase: 240.0cm 94.5in
Track F: 142.7cm 56.2in
Track R: 147.3cm 58.0in
Length: 429.3cm 169.0in
Width: 174.0cm 68.5in
Height: 132.1cm 52.0in
Kerb weight: 1157.7kg 2550.0lb

2803 Mercedes-Benz

220
1960 Germany
96.0mph 154.5kmh
0-50mph 80.5kmh: 10.6secs
0-60mph 96.5kmh: 15.0secs
0-1/4 mile: 20.3secs
105.0bhp 78.3kW 106.5PS
@ 5000rpm
133.0lbft 180.2Nm @ 3300rpm
81.4bhp/ton 80.0bhp/tonne
47.8bhp/L 35.7kW/L 48.5PS/L
39.9ft/sec 12.1m/sec
18.7mph 30.1kmh/1000rpm
Petrol 4-stroke piston
2195cc 133.9cu in
In-line 6 1 Carburettor
Compression ratio: 8.7:1
Bore: 80.0mm 3.1in
Stroke: 72.9mm 2.9in
Valve type/No: Overhead 12
Transmission: Manual
No. of forward speeds: 4
Wheels driven: Rear
Wheelbase: 275.1cm 108.3in
Track F: 147.1cm 57.9in
Track R: 148.6cm 58.5in
Length: 488.2cm 192.2in
Width: 179.6cm 70.7in
Height: 150.9cm 59.4in
Kerb weight: 1312.1kg 2890.0lb

2804 Mercedes-Benz

220SE
1960 Germany
105.5mph 169.7kmh
0-50mph 80.5kmh: 8.8secs
0-60mph 96.5kmh: 12.2secs
0-1/4 mile: 18.5secs
134.0bhp 99.9kW 135.9PS
@ 5000rpm
152.0lbft 206.0Nm @ 4100rpm
99.4bhp/ton 97.7bhp/tonne
61.0bhp/L 45.5kW/L 61.9PS/L
39.9ft/sec 12.1m/sec
18.1mph 29.1kmh/1000rpm
Petrol 4-stroke piston
2195cc 133.9cu in
In-line 6 fuel injection
Compression ratio: 8.7:1
Bore: 80.0mm 3.1in
Stroke: 72.9mm 2.9in
Valve type/No: Overhead 12
Transmission: Manual
No. of forward speeds: 4
Wheels driven: Rear
Wheelbase: 275.1cm 108.3in
Track F: 147.1cm 57.9in
Track R: 148.6cm 58.5in
Length: 488.2cm 192.2in
Width: 179.6cm 70.7in
Height: 150.9cm 59.4in
Kerb weight: 1371.1kg 3020.0lb

2805 Mercedes-Benz

190
1961 Germany
88.0mph 141.6kmh
0-50mph 80.5kmh: 11.9secs
0-60mph 96.5kmh: 17.8secs
0-1/4 mile: 20.6secs
80.0bhp 59.7kW 81.1PS
@ 5000rpm
114.0lbft 154.5Nm @ 3000rpm

70.3bhp/ton 69.2bhp/tonne
42.2bhp/L 31.4kW/L 42.8PS/L
45.7ft/sec 13.9m/sec
18.0mph 29.0kmh/1000rpm
21.9mpg 18.2mpgUS 12.9L/100km
Petrol 4-stroke piston
1897cc 115.7cu in
In-line 4
Compression ratio: 8.5:1
Bore: 85.0mm 3.3in
Stroke: 83.6mm 3.3in
Valve type/No: Overhead 8
Transmission: Manual
No. of forward speeds: 4
Wheels driven: Rear
Springs F/R: Coil/Coil
Brakes F/R: Drum/Drum
Wheelbase: 264.9cm 104.3in
Track F: 143.0cm 56.3in
Track R: 147.3cm 58.0in
Length: 450.3cm 177.3in
Width: 174.0cm 68.5in
Height: 156.2cm 61.5in
Ground clearance: 19.1cm 7.5in
Kerb weight: 1156.8kg 2548.0lb
Fuel: 56.0L 12.3gal 14.8galUS

2806 Mercedes-Benz

220SE Coupe
1961 Germany
108.0mph 173.8kmh
0-50mph 80.5kmh: 8.8secs
0-60mph 96.5kmh: 12.4secs
0-1/4 mile: 18.5secs
120.0bhp 89.5kW 121.7PS
@ 5000rpm
151.8lbft 205.7Nm @ 4100rpm
86.6bhp/ton 85.1bhp/tonne
54.7bhp/L 40.8kW/L 55.4PS/L
39.9ft/sec 12.1m/sec
17.6mph 28.3kmh/1000rpm
22.4mpg 18.7mpgUS 12.6L/100km
Petrol 4-stroke piston
2195cc 133.9cu in
In-line 6
Compression ratio: 8.7:1
Bore: 80.0mm 3.1in
Stroke: 72.8mm 2.9in
Valve type/No: Overhead 12
Transmission: Manual
No. of forward speeds: 4
Wheels driven: Rear
Springs F/R: Coil/Coil
Brake system: PA
Brakes F/R: Disc/Drum
Wheelbase: 274.8cm 108.2in
Track F: 148.3cm 58.4in
Track R: 148.6cm 58.5in
Length: 488.2cm 192.2in
Width: 184.7cm 72.7in
Height: 142.2cm 56.0in
Ground clearance: 20.1cm 7.9in
Kerb weight: 1409.2kg 3104.0lb
Fuel: 65.1L 14.3gal 17.2galUS

2807 Mercedes-Benz

300SL Roadster
1961 Germany
130.0mph 209.2kmh
0-50mph 80.5kmh: 6.2secs
0-60mph 96.5kmh: 7.6secs
0-1/4 mile: 16.2secs
250.0bhp 186.4kW 253.5PS
@ 6200rpm
228.0lbft 308.9Nm @ 5000rpm
183.6bhp/ton 180.5bhp/tonne
83.4bhp/L 62.2kW/L 84.6PS/L
59.6ft/sec 18.2m/sec
20.8mph 33.5kmh/1000rpm
Petrol 4-stroke piston
2996cc 182.8cu in
In-line 6
Compression ratio: 9.5:1
Bore: 85.1mm 3.3in
Stroke: 87.9mm 3.5in
Valve type/No: Overhead 12
Transmission: Manual
No. of forward speeds: 4
Wheels driven: Rear
Wheelbase: 240.0cm 94.5in
Track F: 139.7cm 55.0in
Track R: 144.8cm 57.0in
Length: 457.2cm 180.0in
Width: 179.1cm 70.5in
Height: 129.5cm 51.0in
Ground clearance: 12.7cm 5.0in
Kerb weight: 1384.7kg 3050.0lb

2808 Mercedes-Benz

300SE
1962 Germany
109.0mph 175.4kmh
0-50mph 80.5kmh: 8.5secs
0-60mph 96.5kmh: 11.4secs
0-1/4 mile: 18.0secs
185.0bhp 137.9kW 187.6PS
@ 5200rpm
205.0lbft 277.8Nm @ 4000rpm
123.5bhp/ton 121.5bhp/tonne
61.7bhp/L 46.0kW/L 62.6PS/L
50.1ft/sec 15.3m/sec
18.4mph 29.6kmh/1000rpm
Petrol 4-stroke piston
2996cc 182.8cu in
In-line 6 fuel injection
Compression ratio: 9.0:1
Bore: 84.8mm 3.3in
Stroke: 88.1mm 3.5in
Valve type/No: Overhead 12
Transmission: Automatic
No. of forward speeds: 4
Wheels driven: Rear
Brake system: PA
Steering: PA
Wheelbase: 275.1cm 108.3in
Track F: 148.3cm 58.4in
Track R: 149.1cm 58.7in
Length: 487.7cm 192.0in
Width: 179.6cm 70.7in
Height: 146.1cm 57.5in
Ground clearance: 18.3cm 7.2in
Kerb weight: 1523.2kg 3355.0lb
Fuel: 65.1L 14.3gal 17.2galUS

2809 Mercedes-Benz

190C Automatic
1963 Germany
85.0mph 136.8kmh
0-50mph 80.5kmh: 13.5secs
0-60mph 96.5kmh: 19.5secs
0-1/4 mile: 21.5secs
90.0bhp 67.1kW 91.2PS
@ 5200rpm
113.0lbft 153.1Nm @ 2700rpm
72.7bhp/ton 71.5bhp/tonne
47.4bhp/L 35.4kW/L 48.1PS/L
47.5ft/sec 14.5m/sec
16.5mph 26.5kmh/1000rpm
24.6mpg 20.5mpgUS 11.5L/100km
Petrol 4-stroke piston
1897cc 115.7cu in
In-line 4 1 Carburettor
Compression ratio: 8.7:1
Bore: 85.0mm 3.3in
Stroke: 83.6mm 3.3in
Valve type/No: Overhead 8
Transmission: Automatic
No. of forward speeds: 4
Wheels driven: Rear
Springs F/R: Coil/Coil
Brake system: PA
Brakes F/R: Drum/Drum
Steering: Recirculating ball
Wheelbase: 275.1cm 108.3in
Track F: 146.8cm 57.8in
Track R: 148.6cm 58.5in
Length: 469.9cm 185.0in
Width: 179.6cm 70.7in
Height: 150.9cm 59.4in
Ground clearance: 19.1cm 7.5in
Kerb weight: 1258.5kg 2772.0lb
Fuel: 52.3L 11.5gal 13.8galUS

2810 Mercedes-Benz

230SL
1963 Germany
124.0mph 199.5kmh
0-50mph 80.5kmh: 7.0secs
0-60mph 96.5kmh: 9.7secs
0-1/4 mile: 17.3secs
170.0bhp 126.8kW 172.4PS
@ 5600rpm
159.0lbft 215.4Nm @ 4500rpm
126.5bhp/ton 124.4bhp/tonne
73.7bhp/L 55.0kW/L 74.7PS/L
44.6ft/sec 13.6m/sec
19.8mph 31.9kmh/1000rpm
Petrol 4-stroke piston
2306cc 140.7cu in
In-line 6 1 Carburettor
Compression ratio: 9.3:1
Bore: 82.0mm 3.2in
Stroke: 72.9mm 2.9in
Valve type/No: Overhead 12
Transmission: Manual
No. of forward speeds: 4
Wheels driven: Rear
Wheelbase: 240.0cm 94.5in
Track F: 148.6cm 58.5in
Track R: 148.6cm 58.5in
Length: 428.8cm 168.8in
Width: 178.1cm 70.1in
Height: 131.6cm 51.8in
Ground clearance: 17.0cm 6.7in
Kerb weight: 1366.5kg 3010.0lb

2811 Mercedes-Benz

230SL
1964 Germany
121.0mph 194.7kmh
0-50mph 80.5kmh: 7.5secs
0-60mph 96.5kmh: 10.7secs
0-1/4 mile: 17.5secs
150.0bhp 111.9kW 152.1PS
@ 5500rpm
159.0lbft 215.4Nm @ 4500rpm
114.6bhp/ton 112.6bhp/tonne
65.0bhp/L 48.5kW/L 65.9PS/L
43.8ft/sec 13.3m/sec
19.6mph 31.5kmh/1000rpm
22.3mpg 18.6mpgUS 12.7L/100km
Petrol 4-stroke piston
2306cc 140.7cu in
In-line 6 fuel injection
Compression ratio: 9.3:1
Bore: 82.0mm 3.2in
Stroke: 72.8mm 2.9in
Valve type/No: Overhead 12
Transmission: Manual
No. of forward speeds: 4
Wheels driven: Rear
Springs F/R: Coil/Coil
Brake system: PA
Brakes F/R: Disc/Drum
Steering: Recirculating ball PA
Wheelbase: 240.0cm 94.5in
Track F: 148.6cm 58.5in
Track R: 148.6cm 58.5in
Length: 429.3cm 169.0in
Width: 175.8cm 69.2in
Height: 131.3cm 51.7in
Ground clearance: 17.8cm 7.0in
Kerb weight: 1331.6kg 2933.0lb
Fuel: 65.1L 14.3gal 17.2galUS

2812 Mercedes-Benz

300SE LWB
1964 Germany
115.3mph 185.5kmh
0-50mph 80.5kmh: 7.7secs
0-60mph 96.5kmh: 10.4secs
0-1/4 mile: 17.6secs
185.0bhp 137.9kW 187.6PS
@ 5500rpm
205.0lbft 277.8Nm @ 4100rpm
115.4bhp/ton 113.5bhp/tonne
61.7bhp/L 46.0kW/L 62.6PS/L
52.9ft/sec 16.1m/sec
18.8mph 30.2kmh/1000rpm
15.1mpg 12.6mpgUS 18.7L/100km
Petrol 4-stroke piston
2996cc 182.8cu in
In-line 6 fuel injection
Compression ratio: 8.8:1
Bore: 85.0mm 3.3in
Stroke: 88.0mm 3.5in
Valve type/No: Overhead 12
Transmission: Automatic
No. of forward speeds: 4
Wheels driven: Rear
Springs F/R: Gas/Gas
Brake system: PA
Brakes F/R: Disc/Disc
Steering: Recirculating ball PA
Wheelbase: 285.8cm 112.5in
Track F: 148.6cm 58.5in
Track R: 149.1cm 58.7in
Length: 497.8cm 196.0in
Width: 179.6cm 70.7in
Height: 147.3cm 58.0in
Ground clearance: 18.3cm 7.2in
Kerb weight: 1630.3kg 3591.0lb
Fuel: 81.9L 18.0gal 21.6galUS

2813 Mercedes-Benz

190D
1965 Germany
80.0mph 128.7kmh
0-50mph 80.5kmh: 22.3secs
0-60mph 96.5kmh: 38.7secs
0-1/4 mile: 25.1secs
60.0bhp 44.7kW 60.8PS
@ 4200rpm
87.0lbft 117.9Nm @ 2400rpm
46.3bhp/ton 45.6bhp/tonne
30.2bhp/L 22.5kW/L 30.6PS/L
38.4ft/sec 11.7m/sec
16.5mph 26.5kmh/1000rpm
32.2mpg 26.8mpgUS 8.8L/100km
Diesel 4-stroke piston
1988cc 121.3cu in
In-line 4 fuel injection
Compression ratio: 21.0:1
Bore: 87.0mm 3.4in
Stroke: 83.6mm 3.3in
Valve type/No: Overhead 8
Transmission: Manual
No. of forward speeds: 4
Wheels driven: Rear
Springs F/R: Coil/Coil
Brake system: PA
Brakes F/R: Disc/Drum
Steering: Recirculating ball
Wheelbase: 275.1cm 108.3in
Track F: 146.8cm 57.8in
Track R: 148.6cm 58.5in
Length: 469.9cm 185.0in
Width: 179.6cm 70.7in
Height: 150.9cm 59.4in
Ground clearance: 19.1cm 7.5in
Kerb weight: 1316.6kg 2900.0lb
Fuel: 51.9L 11.4gal 13.7galUS

2814 Mercedes-Benz

220SE
1965 Germany
106.0mph 170.6kmh
0-50mph 80.5kmh: 9.2secs
0-60mph 96.5kmh: 12.5secs
0-1/4 mile: 18.5secs
120.0bhp 89.5kW 121.7PS
@ 4800rpm
140.0lbft 189.7Nm @ 3900rpm
86.5bhp/ton 85.0bhp/tonne
54.7bhp/L 40.8kW/L 55.4PS/L
38.3ft/sec 11.6m/sec
18.1mph 29.1kmh/1000rpm
16.8mpg 14.0mpgUS 16.8L/100km
Petrol 4-stroke piston
2195cc 133.9cu in
In-line 6 fuel injection
Compression ratio: 8.7:1
Bore: 80.0mm 3.1in
Stroke: 72.8mm 2.9in
Valve type/No: Overhead 12
Transmission: Automatic
No. of forward speeds: 4
Wheels driven: Rear
Springs F/R: Coil/Coil
Brake system: PA
Brakes F/R: Disc/Drum
Steering: Recirculating ball PA
Wheelbase: 275.1cm 108.3in
Track F: 148.1cm 58.3in
Track R: 148.6cm 58.5in
Length: 487.4cm 191.9in
Width: 179.6cm 70.7in
Height: 147.3cm 58.0in
Ground clearance: 19.6cm 7.7in
Kerb weight: 1411.0kg 3108.0lb
Fuel: 65.1L 14.3gal 17.2galUS

2815 Mercedes-Benz

230SL Automatic
1965 Germany
115.0mph 185.0kmh
0-50mph 80.5kmh: 8.2secs
0-60mph 96.5kmh: 11.0secs
0-1/4 mile: 17.7secs
170.0bhp 126.8kW 172.4PS
@ 5600rpm
159.0lbft 215.4Nm @ 4500rpm
131.1bhp/ton 128.9bhp/tonne
73.7bhp/L 55.0kW/L 74.7PS/L
44.6ft/sec 13.6m/sec
19.8mph 31.9kmh/1000rpm
Petrol 4-stroke piston
2306cc 140.7cu in
In-line 6 fuel injection
Compression ratio: 9.3:1
Bore: 82.0mm 3.2in
Stroke: 72.9mm 2.9in
Valve type/No: Overhead 12
Transmission: Automatic
No. of forward speeds: 4
Wheels driven: Rear
Springs F/R: Coil/Coil

Brakes F/R: Disc/Drum
Steering: PA
Wheelbase: 240.0cm 94.5in
Track F: 148.6cm 58.5in
Track R: 148.6cm 58.5in
Length: 429.3cm 169.0in
Width: 176.0cm 69.3in
Height: 130.6cm 51.4in
Ground clearance: 14.0cm 5.5in
Kerb weight: 1318.9kg 2905.0lb
Fuel: 65.1L 14.3gal 17.2galUS

2816 Mercedes-Benz

600
1965 Germany
115.0mph 185.0kmh
0-50mph 80.5kmh: 7.3secs
0-60mph 96.5kmh: 10.0secs
0-1/4 mile: 17.2secs
300.0bhp 223.7kW 304.2PS
@ 4100rpm
434.0lbft 588.1Nm @ 3000rpm
122.4bhp/ton 120.4bhp/tonne
47.4bhp/L 35.3kW/L 48.1PS/L
42.6ft/sec 13.0m/sec
25.0mph 40.2kmh/1000rpm
Petrol 4-stroke piston
6329cc 386.1cu in
Vee 8 fuel injection
Compression ratio: 9.0:1
Bore: 103.1mm 4.1in
Stroke: 95.0mm 3.7in
Valve type/No: Overhead 16
Transmission: Automatic
No. of forward speeds: 4
Wheels driven: Rear
Springs F/R: Gas/Gas
Brakes F/R: Disc/Disc
Steering: PA
Wheelbase: 320.0cm 126.0in
Track F: 158.8cm 62.5in
Track R: 157.7cm 62.1in
Length: 553.7cm 218.0in
Width: 195.1cm 76.8in
Height: 151.1cm 59.5in
Ground clearance: 18.5cm 7.3in
Kerb weight: 2492.5kg 5490.0lb
Fuel: 112.0L 24.6gal 29.6galUS

2817 Mercedes-Benz

230 Automatic
1966 Germany
96.0mph 154.5kmh
0-50mph 80.5kmh: 10.6secs
0-60mph 96.5kmh: 15.1secs
0-1/4 mile: 19.8secs
0-1km: 37.6secs
105.0bhp 78.3kW 106.5PS
@ 5200rpm
128.0lbft 173.4Nm @ 3600rpm
80.1bhp/ton 78.8bhp/tonne
45.5bhp/L 33.9kW/L 46.2PS/L
41.5ft/sec 12.6m/sec
17.1mph 27.5kmh/1000rpm
17.6mpg 14.7mpgUS 16.1L/100km
Petrol 4-stroke piston
2306cc 140.7cu in
In-line 6 2 Carburettor
Compression ratio: 9.0:1
Bore: 82.0mm 3.2in
Stroke: 72.8mm 2.9in
Valve type/No: Overhead 12
Transmission: Automatic
No. of forward speeds: 4
Wheels driven: Rear
Springs F/R: Coil/Coil
Brake system: PA
Brakes F/R: Disc/Drum
Steering: Recirculating ball
Wheelbase: 275.1cm 108.3in
Track F: 146.8cm 57.8in
Track R: 148.6cm 58.5in
Length: 469.9cm 185.0in
Width: 179.6cm 70.7in
Height: 150.9cm 59.4in
Ground clearance: 19.1cm 7.5in
Kerb weight: 1332.5kg 2935.0lb
Fuel: 65.1L 14.3gal 17.2galUS

2818 Mercedes-Benz

250S
1966 Germany
110.0mph 177.0kmh
0-50mph 80.5kmh: 10.0secs
0-60mph 96.5kmh: 14.0secs
0-1/4 mile: 19.8secs
146.0bhp 108.9kW 148.0PS
@ 5600rpm
157.0lbft 212.7Nm @ 4200rpm
99.1bhp/ton 97.4bhp/tonne
58.5bhp/L 43.6kW/L 59.3PS/L
48.2ft/sec 14.7m/sec
17.6mph 28.3kmh/1000rpm
Petrol 4-stroke piston
2496cc 152.3cu in
In-line 6 2 Carburettor
Compression ratio: 9.0:1
Bore: 82.0mm 3.2in
Stroke: 78.8mm 3.1in
Valve type/No: Overhead 12
Transmission: Automatic
No. of forward speeds: 4
Wheels driven: Rear
Springs F/R: Coil/Coil
Brakes F/R: Disc/Disc
Steering: Recirculating ball PA
Wheelbase: 274.8cm 108.2in
Track F: 148.1cm 58.3in
Track R: 148.3cm 58.4in
Length: 490.0cm 192.9in
Width: 181.1cm 71.3in
Height: 144.0cm 56.7in
Ground clearance: 15.0cm 5.9in
Kerb weight: 1498.2kg 3300.0lb
Fuel: 83.3L 18.3gal 22.0galUS

2819 Mercedes-Benz

300D
1966 Germany
91.0mph 146.4kmh
0-50mph 80.5kmh: 14.0secs
0-60mph 96.5kmh: 20.8secs
0-1/4 mile: 21.7secs
0-1km: 40.8secs
80.0bhp 59.7kW 81.1PS
@ 4000rpm
126.6lbft 171.5Nm @ 2400rpm
54.5bhp/ton 53.6bhp/tonne
26.6bhp/L 19.8kW/L 27.0PS/L
40.4ft/sec 12.3m/sec
20.8mph 33.5kmh/1000rpm
27.2mpg 22.6mpgUS 10.4L/100km
Diesel 4-stroke piston
3005cc 183.3cu in
In-line 6 fuel injection
Compression ratio: 21.0:1
Bore: 91.0mm 3.6in
Stroke: 92.4mm 3.6in
Valve type/No: Overhead 12
Transmission: Automatic
No. of forward speeds: 4
Wheels driven: Rear
Springs F/R: Coil/Coil
Brake system: PA
Brakes F/R: Disc/Disc
Steering: Recirculating ball PA
Wheelbase: 279.4cm 110.0in
Track F: 148.8cm 58.6in
Track R: 144.5cm 56.9in
Length: 472.4cm 186.0in
Width: 178.6cm 70.3in
Height: 143.8cm 56.6in
Ground clearance: 16.5cm 6.5in
Kerb weight: 1493.7kg 3290.0lb
Fuel: 78.3L 17.2gal 20.7galUS

2820 Mercedes-Benz

250SE
1967 Germany
116.0mph 186.6kmh
0-50mph 80.5kmh: 7.9secs
0-60mph 96.5kmh: 10.8secs
0-1/4 mile: 17.9secs
0-1km: 30.7secs
150.0bhp 111.9kW 152.1PS
@ 5500rpm
159.0lbft 215.4Nm @ 4200rpm
100.7bhp/ton 99.0bhp/tonne
60.1bhp/L 44.8kW/L 60.9PS/L
47.4ft/sec 14.4m/sec
17.7mph 28.5kmh/1000rpm
17.4mpg 14.5mpgUS 16.2L/100km
Petrol 4-stroke piston
2496cc 152.3cu in
In-line 6 fuel injection
Compression ratio: 9.3:1
Bore: 82.0mm 3.2in
Stroke: 78.8mm 3.1in
Valve type/No: Overhead 12
Transmission: Automatic
No. of forward speeds: 4
Wheels driven: Rear
Springs F/R: Coil/Coil
Brake system: PA
Brakes F/R: Disc/Disc
Steering: Recirculating ball PA
Wheelbase: 274.8cm 108.2in
Track F: 147.8cm 58.2in
Track R: 147.8cm 58.2in
Length: 490.2cm 193.0in
Width: 180.8cm 71.2in
Height: 144.0cm 56.7in
Ground clearance: 15.2cm 6.0in
Kerb weight: 1515.0kg 3337.0lb
Fuel: 81.9L 18.0gal 21.6galUS

2821 Mercedes-Benz

600
1967 Germany
132.0mph 212.4kmh
0-50mph 80.5kmh: 7.4secs
0-60mph 96.5kmh: 9.7secs
0-1/4 mile: 17.3secs
0-1km: 31.2secs
250.0bhp 186.4kW 253.5PS
@ 4000rpm
369.0lbft 500.0Nm @ 2800rpm
104.1bhp/ton 102.3bhp/tonne
39.5bhp/L 29.5kW/L 40.0PS/L
41.6ft/sec 12.7m/sec
25.1mph 40.4kmh/1000rpm
11.6mpg 9.7mpgUS 24.4L/100km
Petrol 4-stroke piston
6329cc 386.1cu in
Vee 8 fuel injection
Compression ratio: 9.0:1
Bore: 103.0mm 4.1in
Stroke: 95.0mm 3.7in
Valve type/No: Overhead 16
Transmission: Automatic
No. of forward speeds: 4
Wheels driven: Rear
Springs F/R: Gas/Gas
Brake system: PA
Brakes F/R: Disc/Disc
Steering: Recirculating ball PA
Wheelbase: 320.0cm 126.0in
Track F: 158.8cm 62.5in
Track R: 158.8cm 62.5in
Length: 553.7cm 218.0in
Width: 195.1cm 76.8in
Height: 149.6cm 58.9in
Ground clearance: 17.8cm 7.0in
Kerb weight: 2442.5kg 5380.0lb
Fuel: 111.9L 24.6gal 29.6galUS

2822 Mercedes-Benz

220
1968 Germany
95.0mph 152.9kmh
0-50mph 80.5kmh: 11.0secs
0-60mph 96.5kmh: 15.8secs
0-1/4 mile: 20.7secs
116.0bhp 86.5kW 117.6PS
@ 5200rpm
142.0lbft 192.4Nm @ 3000rpm
86.3bhp/ton 84.9bhp/tonne
52.8bhp/L 39.4kW/L 53.5PS/L
52.6ft/sec 16.0m/sec
17.0mph 27.4kmh/1000rpm
Petrol 4-stroke piston
2197cc 134.0cu in
In-line 4 2 Carburettor
Compression ratio: 9.0:1
Bore: 87.0mm 3.4in
Stroke: 92.4mm 3.6in
Valve type/No: Overhead 8
Transmission: Automatic
No. of forward speeds: 4
Wheels driven: Rear
Springs F/R: Coil/Coil
Brake system: PA
Brakes F/R: Disc/Disc
Steering: Recirculating ball
Wheelbase: 275.1cm 108.3in
Track F: 144.3cm 56.8in
Track R: 144.0cm 56.7in
Length: 468.6cm 184.5in
Width: 177.0cm 69.7in
Height: 144.0cm 56.7in
Ground clearance: 10.7cm 4.2in
Kerb weight: 1366.5kg 3010.0lb
Fuel: 65.1L 14.3gal 17.2galUS

2823 Mercedes-Benz

250
1968 Germany
109.0mph 175.4kmh
0-50mph 80.5kmh: 9.9secs
0-60mph 96.5kmh: 13.8secs
0-1/4 mile: 19.8secs
146.0bhp 108.9kW 148.0PS
@ 5600rpm
161.0lbft 218.2Nm @ 3800rpm
103.8bhp/ton 102.1bhp/tonne
58.5bhp/L 43.6kW/L 59.3PS/L
48.2ft/sec 14.7m/sec
17.0mph 27.4kmh/1000rpm
Petrol 4-stroke piston
2496cc 152.3cu in
In-line 6 2 Carburettor
Compression ratio: 9.0:1
Bore: 82.0mm 3.2in
Stroke: 78.8mm 3.1in
Valve type/No: Overhead 12
Transmission: Automatic
No. of forward speeds: 4
Wheels driven: Rear
Springs F/R: Coil/Coil
Brake system: PA
Brakes F/R: Disc/Disc
Steering: Recirculating ball PA
Wheelbase: 275.1cm 108.3in
Track F: 144.3cm 56.8in
Track R: 144.0cm 56.7in
Length: 468.6cm 184.5in
Width: 177.0cm 69.7in
Height: 144.0cm 56.7in
Ground clearance: 10.7cm 4.2in
Kerb weight: 1430.1kg 3150.0lb
Fuel: 65.1L 14.3gal 17.2galUS

2824 Mercedes-Benz

250 Automatic
1968 Germany
110.0mph 177.0kmh
0-50mph 80.5kmh: 9.3secs
0-60mph 96.5kmh: 12.7secs
0-1/4 mile: 19.0secs
0-1km: 34.9secs
130.0bhp 96.9kW 131.8PS
@ 5300rpm
147.0lbft 199.2Nm @ 3600rpm
94.8bhp/ton 93.3bhp/tonne
52.1bhp/L 38.8kW/L 52.8PS/L
45.6ft/sec 13.9m/sec
17.7mph 28.5kmh/1000rpm
17.3mpg 14.4mpgUS 16.3L/100km
Petrol 4-stroke piston
2496cc 152.3cu in
In-line 6 2 Carburettor
Compression ratio: 9.0:1
Bore: 82.0mm 3.2in
Stroke: 78.8mm 3.1in
Valve type/No: Overhead 12
Transmission: Automatic
No. of forward speeds: 4
Wheels driven: Rear
Springs F/R: Coil/Coil
Brake system: PA
Brakes F/R: Disc/Disc
Steering: Recirculating ball PA
Wheelbase: 274.8cm 108.2in
Track F: 148.1cm 58.3in
Track R: 148.6cm 58.5in
Length: 468.6cm 184.5in
Width: 181.1cm 71.3in
Height: 144.0cm 56.7in
Ground clearance: 17.8cm 7.0in
Kerb weight: 1393.8kg 3070.0lb
Fuel: 65.1L 14.3gal 17.2galUS

2825 Mercedes-Benz

280SL
1968 Germany
114.0mph 183.4kmh
0-50mph 80.5kmh: 7.6secs
0-60mph 96.5kmh: 10.3secs
0-1/4 mile: 17.3secs
180.0bhp 134.2kW 182.5PS
@ 5700rpm
193.0lbft 261.5Nm @ 4500rpm
129.2bhp/ton 127.1bhp/tonne
64.8bhp/L 48.3kW/L 65.7PS/L
49.1ft/sec 15.0m/sec
17.6mph 28.3kmh/1000rpm
Petrol 4-stroke piston
2778cc 169.5cu in
In-line 6 fuel injection
Compression ratio: 9.5:1
Bore: 86.5mm 3.4in
Stroke: 78.8mm 3.1in
Valve type/No: Overhead 12
Transmission: Automatic
No. of forward speeds: 4
Wheels driven: Rear

Springs F/R: Coil/Coil
Brakes F/R: Disc/Disc
Steering: Recirculating ball PA
Wheelbase: 240.0cm 94.5in
Track F: 148.1cm 58.3in
Track R: 148.6cm 58.5in
Length: 428.8cm 168.8in
Width: 177.8cm 70.0in
Height: 130.6cm 51.4in
Ground clearance: 12.7cm 5.0in
Kerb weight: 1416.5kg 3120.0lb
Fuel: 82.1L 18.0gal 21.7galUS

2826 Mercedes-Benz

220
1969 Germany
102.0mph 164.1kmh
0-50mph 80.5kmh: 10.1secs
0-60mph 96.5kmh: 13.6secs
0-1/4 mile: 19.0secs
0-1km: 35.5secs
105.0bhp 78.3kW 106.5PS
@ 5000rpm
132.0lbft 178.9Nm @ 2800rpm
78.6bhp/ton 77.2bhp/tonne
47.8bhp/L 35.6kW/L 48.5PS/L
47.8ft/sec 14.6m/sec
17.6mph 28.3kmh/1000rpm
20.2mpg 16.8mpgUS 14.0L/100km
Petrol 4-stroke piston
2197cc 134.0cu in
In-line 4 1 Carburettor
Compression ratio: 9.0:1
Bore: 87.0mm 3.4in
Stroke: 87.4mm 3.4in
Valve type/No: Overhead 8
Transmission: Manual
No. of forward speeds: 4
Wheels driven: Rear
Springs F/R: Coil/Coil
Brake system: PA
Brakes F/R: Disc/Disc
Steering: Recirculating ball
Wheelbase: 274.8cm 108.2in
Track F: 148.1cm 58.3in
Track R: 148.6cm 58.5in
Length: 468.6cm 184.5in
Width: 181.1cm 71.3in
Height: 144.0cm 56.7in
Ground clearance: 17.8cm 7.0in
Kerb weight: 1359.3kg 2994.0lb
Fuel: 65.1L 14.3gal 17.2galUS

2827 Mercedes-Benz

280SL
1969 Germany
114.0mph 183.4kmh
0-60mph 96.5kmh: 9.9secs
0-1/4 mile: 17.1secs
180.0bhp 134.2kW 182.5PS
@ 5700rpm
193.0lbft 261.5Nm @ 4500rpm
129.2bhp/ton 127.1bhp/tonne
64.8bhp/L 48.3kW/L 65.7PS/L
49.1ft/sec 15.0m/sec
18.6mpg 15.5mpgUS 15.2L/100km
Petrol 4-stroke piston
2778cc 169.5cu in
In-line 6
Bore: 86.5mm 3.4in
Stroke: 78.8mm 3.1in
Valve type/No: Overhead 12
Transmission: Automatic
No. of forward speeds: 4
Wheels driven: Rear
Brake system: PA
Brakes F/R: Disc/Disc
Steering: PA
Wheelbase: 240.0cm 94.5in
Track F: 148.1cm 58.3in
Track R: 148.6cm 58.5in
Length: 428.8cm 168.8in
Width: 177.8cm 70.0in
Height: 130.6cm 51.4in
Kerb weight: 1416.5kg 3120.0lb

2828 Mercedes-Benz

300SEL 6.3
1969 Germany
134.0mph 215.6kmh
0-50mph 80.5kmh: 5.3secs
0-60mph 96.5kmh: 7.1secs
0-1/4 mile: 15.5secs
0-1km: 28.3secs
250.0bhp 186.4kW 253.5PS
@ 4000rpm
369.0lbft 500.0Nm @ 2800rpm
146.6bhp/ton 144.1bhp/tonne
39.5bhp/L 29.4kW/L 40.0PS/L
41.6ft/sec 12.7m/sec
24.8mph 39.9kmh/1000rpm
15.1mpg 12.6mpgUS 18.7L/100km
Petrol 4-stroke piston
6332cc 386.3cu in
Vee 8 fuel injection
Compression ratio: 9.0:1
Bore: 103.0mm 4.1in
Stroke: 95.0mm 3.7in
Valve type/No: Overhead 16
Transmission: Automatic
No. of forward speeds: 4
Wheels driven: Rear
Springs F/R: Gas/Gas
Brake system: PA
Brakes F/R: Disc/Disc
Steering: Recirculating ball PA
Wheelbase: 284.5cm 112.0in
Track F: 148.1cm 58.3in
Track R: 148.3cm 58.4in
Length: 500.1cm 196.9in
Width: 181.1cm 71.3in
Height: 146.1cm 57.5in
Ground clearance: 15.2cm 6.0in
Kerb weight: 1734.3kg 3820.0lb
Fuel: 105.1L 23.1gal 27.8galUS

2829 Mercedes-Benz

250 Coupe
1970 Germany
115.0mph 185.0kmh
0-50mph 80.5kmh: 10.2secs
0-60mph 96.5kmh: 13.6secs
0-1/4 mile: 19.0secs
157.0bhp 117.1kW 159.2PS
@ 5400rpm
181.0lbft 245.3Nm @ 3800rpm
99.4bhp/ton 97.7bhp/tonne
56.5bhp/L 42.1kW/L 57.3PS/L
46.5ft/sec 14.2m/sec
17.9mph 28.8kmh/1000rpm
19.2mpg 16.0mpgUS 14.7L/100km
Petrol 4-stroke piston
2778cc 169.5cu in
In-line 6 2 Carburettor
Compression ratio: 9.0:1
Bore: 86.5mm 3.4in
Stroke: 78.8mm 3.1in
Valve type/No: Overhead 12
Transmission: Automatic
No. of forward speeds: 4
Wheels driven: Rear
Springs F/R: Coil/Coil
Brake system: PA
Brakes F/R: Disc/Disc
Steering: Recirculating ball PA
Wheelbase: 275.1cm 108.3in
Track F: 144.3cm 56.8in
Track R: 144.0cm 56.7in
Length: 468.6cm 184.5in
Width: 177.0cm 69.7in
Height: 139.4cm 54.9in
Ground clearance: 10.7cm 4.2in
Kerb weight: 1606.2kg 3538.0lb
Fuel: 65.1L 14.3gal 17.2galUS

2830 Mercedes-Benz

280SE
1970 Germany
116.0mph 186.6kmh
0-50mph 80.5kmh: 8.2secs
0-60mph 96.5kmh: 11.2secs
0-1/4 mile: 17.8secs
0-1km: 32.8secs
160.0bhp 119.3kW 162.2PS
@ 5500rpm
177.0lbft 239.8Nm @ 4250rpm
103.9bhp/ton 102.1bhp/tonne
57.6bhp/L 42.9kW/L 58.4PS/L
47.4ft/sec 14.4m/sec
18.8mph 30.2kmh/1000rpm
17.5mpg 14.6mpgUS 16.1L/100km
Petrol 4-stroke piston
2778cc 169.5cu in
In-line 6 fuel injection
Compression ratio: 9.5:1
Bore: 86.5mm 3.4in
Stroke: 78.8mm 3.1in
Valve type/No: Overhead 12
Transmission: Automatic
No. of forward speeds: 4
Wheels driven: Rear
Springs F/R: Coil/Coil
Brake system: PA
Brakes F/R: Disc/Disc
Steering: Recirculating ball PA
Wheelbase: 274.8cm 108.2in
Track F: 148.1cm 58.3in
Track R: 148.6cm 58.5in
Length: 490.0cm 192.9in
Width: 181.1cm 71.3in
Height: 144.0cm 56.7in
Ground clearance: 15.2cm 6.0in
Kerb weight: 1566.3kg 3450.0lb
Fuel: 81.9L 18.0gal 21.6galUS

2831 Mercedes-Benz

280SE 3.5
1970 Germany
125.0mph 201.1kmh
0-50mph 80.5kmh: 7.0secs
0-60mph 96.5kmh: 9.3secs
0-1/4 mile: 17.2secs
230.0bhp 171.5kW 233.2PS
@ 6050rpm
231.0lbft 313.0Nm @ 4200rpm
139.2bhp/ton 136.9bhp/tonne
65.7bhp/L 49.0kW/L 66.6PS/L
43.5ft/sec 13.3m/sec
19.4mph 31.2kmh/1000rpm
19.0mpg 15.8mpgUS 14.9L/100km
Petrol 4-stroke piston
3499cc 213.5cu in
Vee 8 fuel injection
Compression ratio: 9.5:1
Bore: 92.0mm 3.6in
Stroke: 65.8mm 2.6in
Valve type/No: Overhead 16
Transmission: Automatic
No. of forward speeds: 4
Wheels driven: Rear
Springs F/R: Coil/Coil
Brake system: PA
Brakes F/R: Disc/Disc
Steering: Recirculating ball PA
Wheelbase: 275.1cm 108.3in
Track F: 148.3cm 58.4in
Track R: 148.6cm 58.5in
Length: 490.5cm 193.1in
Width: 184.4cm 72.6in
Height: 140.5cm 55.3in
Ground clearance: 16.8cm 6.6in
Kerb weight: 1679.8kg 3700.0lb
Fuel: 82.1L 18.0gal 21.7galUS

2832 Mercedes-Benz

280SL
1970 Germany
121.0mph 194.7kmh
0-50mph 80.5kmh: 7.1secs
0-60mph 96.5kmh: 9.3secs
0-1/4 mile: 17.0secs
0-1km: 31.3secs
170.0bhp 126.8kW 172.4PS
@ 5750rpm
177.0lbft 239.8Nm @ 4500rpm
122.0bhp/ton 120.0bhp/tonne
61.2bhp/L 45.6kW/L 62.0PS/L
49.5ft/sec 15.1m/sec
18.6mph 29.9kmh/1000rpm
19.0mpg 15.8mpgUS 14.9L/100km
Petrol 4-stroke piston
2778cc 169.5cu in
In-line 6 fuel injection
Compression ratio: 9.5:1
Bore: 86.5mm 3.4in
Stroke: 78.8mm 3.1in
Valve type/No: Overhead 12
Transmission: Automatic
No. of forward speeds: 4
Wheels driven: Rear
Springs F/R: Coil/Coil
Brake system: PA
Brakes F/R: Disc/Disc
Steering: Recirculating ball PA
Wheelbase: 241.3cm 95.0in
Track F: 148.1cm 58.3in
Track R: 148.6cm 58.5in
Length: 431.8cm 170.0in
Width: 180.3cm 71.0in
Height: 134.6cm 53.0in
Ground clearance: 17.8cm 7.0in
Kerb weight: 1416.5kg 3120.0lb
Fuel: 81.9L 18.0gal 21.6galUS

2833 Mercedes-Benz

220D
1971 Germany
84.0mph 135.2kmh
0-50mph 80.5kmh: 18.0secs
0-60mph 96.5kmh: 27.5secs
0-1/4 mile: 23.9secs
65.0bhp 48.5kW 65.9PS
@ 4200rpm
96.0lbft 130.1Nm @ 2400rpm
47.1bhp/ton 46.3bhp/tonne
29.6bhp/L 22.1kW/L 30.0PS/L
42.5ft/sec 12.9m/sec
17.7mph 28.5kmh/1000rpm
30.5mpg 25.4mpgUS 9.3L/100km
Diesel 4-stroke piston
2197cc 134.0cu in
In-line 4 fuel injection
Compression ratio: 21.0:1
Bore: 87.0mm 3.4in
Stroke: 92.4mm 3.6in
Valve type/No: Overhead 8
Transmission: Manual
No. of forward speeds: 4
Wheels driven: Rear
Springs F/R: Coil/Coil
Brake system: PA
Brakes F/R: Disc/Disc
Steering: Recirculating ball
Wheelbase: 275.1cm 108.3in
Track F: 144.3cm 56.8in
Track R: 144.0cm 56.7in
Length: 468.6cm 184.5in
Width: 177.0cm 69.7in
Height: 144.0cm 56.7in
Ground clearance: 17.3cm 6.8in
Kerb weight: 1402.9kg 3090.0lb
Fuel: 65.1L 14.3gal 17.2galUS

2834 Mercedes-Benz

300SL
1971 Germany
126.0mph 202.7kmh
0-50mph 80.5kmh: 7.0secs
0-60mph 96.5kmh: 9.3secs
0-1/4 mile: 17.0secs
0-1km: 31.0secs
200.0bhp 149.1kW 202.8PS
@ 5800rpm
211.0lbft 285.9Nm @ 4000rpm
131.6bhp/ton 129.4bhp/tonne
57.2bhp/L 42.6kW/L 57.9PS/L
41.7ft/sec 12.7m/sec
19.4mph 31.2kmh/1000rpm
14.7mpg 12.2mpgUS 19.2L/100km
Petrol 4-stroke piston
3499cc 213.5cu in
Vee 8 fuel injection
Compression ratio: 9.5:1
Bore: 92.0mm 3.6in
Stroke: 65.8mm 2.6in
Valve type/No: Overhead 16
Transmission: Automatic
No. of forward speeds: 4
Wheels driven: Rear
Springs F/R: Coil/Coil
Brake system: PA
Brakes F/R: Disc/Disc
Steering: Recirculating ball PA
Wheelbase: 246.1cm 96.9in
Track F: 145.3cm 57.2in
Track R: 144.0cm 56.7in
Length: 437.1cm 172.1in
Width: 179.1cm 70.5in
Height: 134.6cm 53.0in
Ground clearance: 17.8cm 7.0in
Kerb weight: 1545.9kg 3405.0lb
Fuel: 90.1L 19.8gal 23.8galUS

2835 Mercedes-Benz

280SE 3.5
1972 Germany
128.0mph 206.0kmh
0-50mph 80.5kmh: 6.3secs
0-60mph 96.5kmh: 8.4secs
0-1/4 mile: 16.4secs
0-1km: 30.0secs
200.0bhp 149.1kW 202.8PS
@ 5800rpm
211.0lbft 285.9Nm @ 4000rpm
128.7bhp/ton 126.5bhp/tonne
57.2bhp/L 42.6kW/L 57.9PS/L
41.7ft/sec 12.7m/sec
21.3mph 34.3kmh/1000rpm
16.0mpg 13.3mpgUS 17.7L/100km
Petrol 4-stroke piston
3499cc 213.5cu in
Vee 8 fuel injection
Compression ratio: 9.5:1
Bore: 92.0mm 3.6in
Stroke: 65.8mm 2.6in
Valve type/No: Overhead 16

Transmission: Automatic
No. of forward speeds: 4
Wheels driven: Rear
Springs F/R: Coil/Coil
Brake system: PA
Brakes F/R: Disc/Disc
Steering: Recirculating ball PA
Wheelbase: 284.5cm 112.0in
Track F: 148.1cm 58.3in
Track R: 148.3cm 58.4in
Length: 500.1cm 196.9in
Width: 181.1cm 71.3in
Height: 141.0cm 55.5in
Ground clearance: 15.2cm 6.0in
Kerb weight: 1580.4kg 3481.0lb
Fuel: 81.9L 18.0gal 21.6galUS

2836 Mercedes-Benz

280SEL
1972 Germany
118.0mph 189.9kmh
0-50mph 80.5kmh: 8.6secs
0-60mph 96.5kmh: 11.2secs
0-1/4 mile: 18.1secs
230.0bhp 171.5kW 233.2PS
@ 5000rpm
279.0lbft 378.0Nm @ 3200rpm
136.5bhp/ton 134.2bhp/tonne
50.9bhp/L 37.9kW/L 51.6PS/L
46.5ft/sec 14.2m/sec
22.6mph 36.4kmh/1000rpm
13.8mpg 11.5mpgUS 20.5L/100km
Petrol 4-stroke piston
4520cc 275.8cu in
Vee 8 fuel injection
Compression ratio: 8.0:1
Bore: 92.0mm 3.6in
Stroke: 85.0mm 3.3in
Valve type/No: Overhead 16
Transmission: Automatic
No. of forward speeds: 3
Wheels driven: Rear
Springs F/R: Coil/Coil
Brake system: PA
Brakes F/R: Disc/Disc
Steering: Recirculating ball PA
Wheelbase: 285.0cm 112.2in
Track F: 148.3cm 58.4in
Track R: 148.6cm 58.5in
Length: 500.1cm 196.9in
Width: 181.1cm 71.3in
Height: 144.0cm 56.7in
Ground clearance: 15.0cm 5.9in
Kerb weight: 1713.8kg 3775.0lb
Fuel: 81.4L 17.9gal 21.5galUS

2837 Mercedes-Benz

350SL
1972 Germany
124.0mph 199.5kmh
0-50mph 80.5kmh: 8.2secs
0-60mph 96.5kmh: 10.5secs
0-1/4 mile: 17.9secs
230.0bhp 171.5kW 233.2PS
@ 5000rpm
279.0lbft 378.0Nm @ 3200rpm
140.4bhp/ton 138.0bhp/tonne
50.9bhp/L 37.9kW/L 51.6PS/L
46.5ft/sec 14.2m/sec
23.1mph 37.2kmh/1000rpm
18.3mpg 15.2mpgUS 15.5L/100km
Petrol 4-stroke piston
4520cc 275.8cu in
Vee 8 fuel injection
Compression ratio: 8.0:1
Bore: 92.0mm 3.6in
Stroke: 85.0mm 3.3in
Valve type/No: Overhead 16
Transmission: Automatic
No. of forward speeds: 3
Wheels driven: Rear
Springs F/R: Coil/Coil
Brake system: PA
Brakes F/R: Disc/Disc
Steering: Recirculating ball PA
Wheelbase: 246.1cm 96.9in
Track F: 145.3cm 57.2in
Track R: 144.0cm 56.7in
Length: 437.1cm 172.1in
Width: 179.1cm 70.5in
Height: 130.0cm 51.2in
Ground clearance: 16.5cm 6.5in
Kerb weight: 1666.2kg 3670.0lb
Fuel: 90.1L 19.8gal 23.8galUS

2838 Mercedes-Benz

230/4
1973 Germany
112.0mph 180.2kmh
0-50mph 80.5kmh: 9.4secs
0-60mph 96.5kmh: 13.4secs
0-1/4 mile: 19.2secs
0-1km: 35.6secs
110.0bhp 82.0kW 111.5PS
@ 4800rpm
137.0lbft 185.6Nm @ 2500rpm
83.3bhp/ton 81.9bhp/tonne
47.7bhp/L 35.6kW/L 48.3PS/L
43.9ft/sec 13.4m/sec
19.5mph 31.4kmh/1000rpm
22.7mpg 18.9mpgUS 12.4L/100km
Petrol 4-stroke piston
2307cc 140.8cu in
In-line 4 1 Carburettor
Compression ratio: 9.0:1
Bore: 93.8mm 3.7in
Stroke: 83.6mm 3.3in
Valve type/No: Overhead 8
Transmission: Manual
No. of forward speeds: 4
Wheels driven: Rear
Springs F/R: Coil/Coil
Brake system: PA
Brakes F/R: Disc/Disc
Steering: Recirculating ball
Wheelbase: 275.1cm 108.3in
Track F: 144.8cm 57.0in
Track R: 148.6cm 58.5in
Length: 468.1cm 184.3in
Width: 177.0cm 69.7in
Height: 144.0cm 56.7in
Ground clearance: 17.8cm 7.0in
Kerb weight: 1342.5kg 2957.0lb
Fuel: 65.1L 14.3gal 17.2galUS

2839 Mercedes-Benz

280
1973 Germany
110.0mph 177.0kmh
0-60mph 96.5kmh: 11.7secs
0-1/4 mile: 18.5secs
130.0bhp 96.9kW 131.8PS
@ 5000rpm
150.0lbft 203.3Nm @ 3500rpm
86.9bhp/ton 85.5bhp/tonne
47.3bhp/L 35.3kW/L 48.0PS/L
43.1ft/sec 13.1m/sec
17.4mpg 14.5mpgUS 16.2L/100km
Petrol 4-stroke piston
2746cc 167.5cu in
In-line 6 1 Carburettor
Compression ratio: 8.0:1
Bore: 86.0mm 3.4in
Stroke: 78.8mm 3.1in
Valve type/No: Overhead 12
Transmission: Automatic
No. of forward speeds: 4
Wheels driven: Rear
Brake system: PA
Brakes F/R: Disc/Disc
Wheelbase: 275.1cm 108.3in
Track F: 144.3cm 56.8in
Track R: 144.0cm 56.7in
Length: 468.6cm 184.5in
Width: 177.0cm 69.7in
Height: 144.0cm 56.7in
Ground clearance: 16.5cm 6.5in
Kerb weight: 1520.9kg 3350.0lb
Fuel: 65.1L 14.3gal 17.2galUS

2840 Mercedes-Benz

280CE Auto
1973 Germany
126.0mph 202.7kmh
0-50mph 80.5kmh: 6.8secs
0-60mph 96.5kmh: 8.9secs
0-1/4 mile: 16.9secs
0-1km: 30.9secs
185.0bhp 137.9kW 187.6PS
@ 6000rpm
166.0lbft 224.9Nm @ 4500rpm
124.7bhp/ton 122.6bhp/tonne
67.4bhp/L 50.2kW/L 68.3PS/L
51.7ft/sec 15.8m/sec
19.7mph 31.7kmh/1000rpm
17.6mpg 14.7mpgUS 16.1L/100km
Petrol 4-stroke piston
2746cc 167.5cu in
In-line 6 fuel injection
Compression ratio: 9.0:1
Bore: 86.0mm 3.4in
Stroke: 78.8mm 3.1in
Valve type/No: Overhead 12
Transmission: Automatic
No. of forward speeds: 4
Wheels driven: Rear
Springs F/R: Coil/Coil
Brake system: PA
Brakes F/R: Disc/Disc
Steering: Recirculating ball PA
Wheelbase: 276.9cm 109.0in
Track F: 144.8cm 57.0in
Track R: 144.8cm 57.0in
Length: 464.8cm 183.0in
Width: 175.3cm 69.0in
Height: 142.2cm 56.0in
Ground clearance: 20.3cm 8.0in
Kerb weight: 1509.1kg 3324.0lb
Fuel: 77.3L 17.0gal 20.4galUS

2841 Mercedes-Benz

280SE
1973 Germany
121.0mph 194.7kmh
0-50mph 80.5kmh: 7.3secs
0-60mph 96.5kmh: 9.7secs
0-1/4 mile: 17.3secs
0-1km: 31.5secs
185.0bhp 137.9kW 187.6PS
@ 6000rpm
165.0lbft 223.6Nm @ 4500rpm
112.7bhp/ton 110.8bhp/tonne
67.4bhp/L 50.2kW/L 68.3PS/L
51.7ft/sec 15.8m/sec
19.9mph 32.0kmh/1000rpm
16.7mpg 13.9mpgUS 16.9L/100km
Petrol 4-stroke piston
2746cc 167.5cu in
In-line 6 fuel injection
Compression ratio: 9.0:1
Bore: 86.0mm 3.4in
Stroke: 78.8mm 3.1in
Valve type/No: Overhead 12
Transmission: Automatic
No. of forward speeds: 4
Wheels driven: Rear
Springs F/R: Coil/Coil
Brake system: PA
Brakes F/R: Disc/Disc
Steering: Recirculating ball PA
Wheelbase: 286.5cm 112.8in
Track F: 152.4cm 60.0in
Track R: 150.6cm 59.3in
Length: 496.1cm 195.3in
Width: 186.2cm 73.3in
Height: 142.2cm 56.0in
Ground clearance: 14.7cm 5.8in
Kerb weight: 1668.9kg 3676.0lb
Fuel: 96.0L 21.1gal 25.4galUS

2842 Mercedes-Benz

450SE
1973 Germany
127.0mph 204.3kmh
0-50mph 80.5kmh: 8.0secs
0-60mph 96.5kmh: 10.6secs
0-1/4 mile: 17.5secs
190.0bhp 141.7kW 192.6PS
@ 4750rpm
240.0lbft 325.2Nm @ 3000rpm
105.6bhp/ton 103.8bhp/tonne
42.0bhp/L 31.3kW/L 42.6PS/L
34.2ft/sec 10.4m/sec
22.4mph 36.0kmh/1000rpm
15.6mpg 13.0mpgUS 18.1L/100km
Petrol 4-stroke piston
4520cc 275.8cu in
Vee 8 fuel injection
Compression ratio: 8.0:1
Bore: 92.0mm 3.6in
Stroke: 65.8mm 2.6in
Valve type/No: Overhead 16
Transmission: Automatic
No. of forward speeds: 3
Wheels driven: Rear
Springs F/R: Coil/Coil
Brake system: PA
Brakes F/R: Disc/Disc
Steering: Recirculating ball PA
Wheelbase: 286.5cm 112.8in
Track F: 152.4cm 60.0in
Track R: 150.6cm 59.3in
Length: 496.1cm 195.3in
Width: 186.9cm 73.6in
Height: 142.5cm 56.1in
Ground clearance: 14.7cm 5.8in
Kerb weight: 1829.6kg 4030.0lb
Fuel: 96.1L 21.1gal 25.4galUS

2843 Mercedes-Benz

450SLC
1973 Germany
124.0mph 199.5kmh
0-50mph 80.5kmh: 8.4secs
0-60mph 96.5kmh: 10.9secs
0-1/4 mile: 18.4secs
195.0bhp 145.4kW 197.7PS
@ 4500rpm
259.0lbft 350.9Nm @ 3000rpm
114.3bhp/ton 112.4bhp/tonne
43.1bhp/L 32.2kW/L 43.7PS/L
41.9ft/sec 12.7m/sec
24.0mph 38.6kmh/1000rpm
18.6mpg 15.5mpgUS 15.2L/100km
Petrol 4-stroke piston
4520cc 275.8cu in
Vee 8 fuel injection
Compression ratio: 8.0:1
Bore: 92.0mm 3.6in
Stroke: 85.0mm 3.3in
Valve type/No: Overhead 16
Transmission: Automatic
No. of forward speeds: 3
Wheels driven: Rear
Springs F/R: Coil/Coil
Brake system: PA
Brakes F/R: Disc/Disc
Steering: Recirculating ball PA
Wheelbase: 281.9cm 111.0in
Track F: 145.3cm 57.2in
Track R: 144.0cm 56.7in
Length: 474.0cm 186.6in
Width: 179.1cm 70.5in
Height: 133.1cm 52.4in
Ground clearance: 13.7cm 5.4in
Kerb weight: 1734.3kg 3820.0lb
Fuel: 90.1L 19.8gal 23.8galUS

2844 Mercedes-Benz

280E
1974 Germany
128.0mph 206.0kmh
0-50mph 80.5kmh: 6.7secs
0-60mph 96.5kmh: 10.1secs
0-1/4 mile: 17.3secs
0-1km: 31.6secs
185.0bhp 137.9kW 187.6PS
@ 6000rpm
175.8lbft 238.2Nm @ 4500rpm
123.0bhp/ton 120.9bhp/tonne
67.4bhp/L 50.2kW/L 68.3PS/L
51.7ft/sec 15.8m/sec
21.5mph 34.6kmh/1000rpm
21.1mpg 17.6mpgUS 13.4L/100km
Petrol 4-stroke piston
2746cc 167.5cu in
In-line 6 fuel injection
Compression ratio: 9.0:1
Bore: 86.0mm 3.4in
Stroke: 78.8mm 3.1in
Valve type/No: Overhead 12
Transmission: Manual
No. of forward speeds: 5
Wheels driven: Rear
Springs F/R: Coil/Coil
Brake system: PA
Brakes F/R: Disc/Disc
Steering: Recirculating ball PA
Wheelbase: 275.1cm 108.3in
Track F: 144.8cm 57.0in
Track R: 144.0cm 56.7in
Length: 468.1cm 184.3in
Width: 177.0cm 69.7in
Height: 144.0cm 56.7in
Ground clearance: 17.8cm 7.0in
Kerb weight: 1530.0kg 3370.0lb
Fuel: 77.3L 17.0gal 20.4galUS

2845 Mercedes-Benz

450SEL
1974 Germany
136.0mph 218.8kmh
0-50mph 80.5kmh: 7.0secs
0-60mph 96.5kmh: 9.1secs
0-1/4 mile: 16.7secs
0-1km: 30.5secs
225.0bhp 167.8kW 228.1PS
@ 5000rpm
278.0lbft 376.7Nm @ 3000rpm
129.1bhp/ton 126.9bhp/tonne
49.8bhp/L 37.1kW/L 50.5PS/L
46.5ft/sec 14.2m/sec
24.0mph 38.6kmh/1000rpm
14.7mpg 12.2mpgUS 19.2L/100km
Petrol 4-stroke piston

4520cc 275.8cu in
Vee 8 fuel injection
Compression ratio: 8.8:1
Bore: 92.0mm 3.6in
Stroke: 85.0mm 3.3in
Valve type/No: Overhead 16
Transmission: Automatic
No. of forward speeds: 3
Wheels driven: Rear
Springs F/R: Coil/Coil
Brake system: PA
Brakes F/R: Disc/Disc
Steering: Recirculating ball PA
Wheelbase: 295.9cm 116.5in
Track F: 150.6cm 59.3in
Track R: 152.4cm 60.0in
Length: 506.0cm 199.2in
Width: 189.5cm 74.6in
Height: 143.0cm 56.3in
Ground clearance: 17.8cm 7.0in
Kerb weight: 1772.4kg 3904.0lb
Fuel: 95.5L 21.0gal 25.2galUS

2846 Mercedes-Benz

450SL
1974 Germany
124.0mph 199.5kmh
0-60mph 96.5kmh: 10.2secs
0-1/4 mile: 17.7secs
190.0bhp 141.7kW 192.6PS
@ 4750rpm
232.0lbft 314.4Nm @ 3000rpm
118.5bhp/ton 116.6bhp/tonne
42.0bhp/L 31.3kW/L 42.6PS/L
44.2ft/sec 13.5m/sec
17.4mpg 14.5mpgUS 16.2L/100km
Petrol 4-stroke piston
4520cc 275.8cu in
Vee 8 fuel injection
Compression ratio: 8.0:1
Bore: 92.0mm 3.6in
Stroke: 85.0mm 3.3in
Valve type/No: Overhead 16
Transmission: Automatic
No. of forward speeds: 3
Wheels driven: Rear
Brake system: PA
Brakes F/R: Disc/Disc
Steering: PA
Wheelbase: 246.1cm 96.9in
Track F: 145.3cm 57.2in
Track R: 144.0cm 56.7in
Length: 463.0cm 182.3in
Width: 179.1cm 70.5in
Height: 130.0cm 51.2in
Ground clearance: 16.5cm 6.5in
Kerb weight: 1629.9kg 3590.0lb
Fuel: 90.1L 19.8gal 23.8galUS

2847 Mercedes-Benz

280S
1975 Germany
103.0mph 165.7kmh
0-50mph 80.5kmh: 11.8secs
0-60mph 96.5kmh: 16.3secs
0-1/4 mile: 21.1secs
120.0bhp 89.5kW 121.7PS
@ 4800rpm
143.0lbft 193.8Nm @ 2800rpm
69.1bhp/ton 67.9bhp/tonne
43.7bhp/L 32.6kW/L 44.3PS/L
41.3ft/sec 12.6m/sec
19.2mph 30.9kmh/1000rpm
18.0mpg 15.0mpgUS 15.7L/100km
Petrol 4-stroke piston
2746cc 167.5cu in
In-line 6
Compression ratio: 8.0:1
Bore: 86.0mm 3.4in
Stroke: 78.8mm 3.1in
Valve type/No: Overhead 12
Transmission: Automatic
No. of forward speeds: 4
Wheels driven: Rear
Springs F/R: Coil/Coil
Brake system: PA
Brakes F/R: Disc/Disc
Steering: Recirculating ball PA
Wheelbase: 286.5cm 112.8in
Track F: 152.4cm 60.0in
Track R: 150.6cm 59.3in
Length: 522.0cm 205.5in
Width: 186.9cm 73.6in
Height: 142.5cm 56.1in
Kerb weight: 1766.1kg 3890.0lb
Fuel: 96.1L 21.1gal 25.4galUS

2848 Mercedes-Benz

300D
1975 Germany
89.0mph 143.2kmh
0-50mph 80.5kmh: 13.7secs
0-60mph 96.5kmh: 20.3secs
0-1/4 mile: 22.0secs
77.0bhp 57.4kW 78.1PS
@ 4000rpm
115.0lbft 155.8Nm @ 2400rpm
49.2bhp/ton 48.4bhp/tonne
25.6bhp/L 19.1kW/L 26.0PS/L
40.4ft/sec 12.3m/sec
19.7mph 31.7kmh/1000rpm
29.4mpg 24.5mpgUS 9.6L/100km
Diesel 4-stroke piston
3006cc 183.4cu in
In-line 5
Compression ratio: 21.0:1
Bore: 90.9mm 3.6in
Stroke: 92.5mm 3.6in
Valve type/No: Overhead 10
Transmission: Automatic
No. of forward speeds: 4
Wheels driven: Rear
Springs F/R: Coil/Coil
Brake system: PA
Brakes F/R: Disc/Disc
Steering: Recirculating ball PA
Wheelbase: 275.1cm 108.3in
Track F: 144.8cm 57.0in
Track R: 144.0cm 56.7in
Length: 496.6cm 195.5in
Width: 177.0cm 69.7in
Height: 144.0cm 56.7in
Kerb weight: 1591.3kg 3505.0lb
Fuel: 65.1L 14.3gal 17.2galUS

2849 Mercedes-Benz

450SLC
1975 Germany
136.0mph 218.8kmh
0-50mph 80.5kmh: 6.9secs
0-60mph 96.5kmh: 9.0secs
0-1/4 mile: 16.9secs
0-1km: 30.2secs
225.0bhp 167.8kW 228.1PS
@ 5000rpm
278.0lbft 376.7Nm @ 3000rpm
136.8bhp/ton 134.5bhp/tonne
49.8bhp/L 37.1kW/L 50.5PS/L
46.5ft/sec 14.2m/sec
24.0mph 38.6kmh/1000rpm
14.1mpg 11.7mpgUS 20.0L/100km
Petrol 4-stroke piston
4520cc 275.8cu in
Vee 8 fuel injection
Compression ratio: 8.8:1
Bore: 92.0mm 3.6in
Stroke: 85.0mm 3.3in
Valve type/No: Overhead 16
Transmission: Automatic
No. of forward speeds: 3
Wheels driven: Rear
Springs F/R: Coil/Coil
Brake system: PA
Brakes F/R: Disc/Disc
Steering: Recirculating ball PA
Wheelbase: 281.9cm 111.0in
Track F: 145.3cm 57.2in
Track R: 144.0cm 56.7in
Length: 474.0cm 186.6in
Width: 179.1cm 70.5in
Height: 133.1cm 52.4in
Ground clearance: 21.6cm 8.5in
Kerb weight: 1673.0kg 3685.0lb
Fuel: 90.1L 19.8gal 23.8galUS

2850 Mercedes-Benz

280E
1976 Germany
118.0mph 189.9kmh
0-50mph 80.5kmh: 8.1secs
0-60mph 96.5kmh: 11.0secs
0-1/4 mile: 18.0secs
0-1km: 33.0secs
177.0bhp 132.0kW 179.4PS
@ 6000rpm
172.0lbft 233.1Nm @ 4500rpm
123.1bhp/ton 121.1bhp/tonne
64.5bhp/L 48.1kW/L 65.3PS/L
51.7ft/sec 15.8m/sec
20.2mph 32.5kmh/1000rpm
16.9mpg 14.1mpgUS 16.7L/100km
Petrol 4-stroke piston
2746cc 167.5cu in
In-line 6 fuel injection
Compression ratio: 8.7:1
Bore: 86.0mm 3.4in
Stroke: 78.8mm 3.1in
Valve type/No: Overhead 12
Transmission: Automatic
No. of forward speeds: 4
Wheels driven: Rear
Springs F/R: Coil/Coil
Brake system: PA
Brakes F/R: Disc/Disc
Steering: Recirculating ball PA
Wheelbase: 279.4cm 110.0in
Track F: 148.8cm 58.6in
Track R: 144.5cm 56.9in
Length: 472.4cm 186.0in
Width: 178.6cm 70.3in
Height: 143.8cm 56.6in
Ground clearance: 16.5cm 6.5in
Kerb weight: 1461.9kg 3220.0lb
Fuel: 80.1L 17.6gal 21.1galUS

2851 Mercedes-Benz

450SL
1976 Germany
117.0mph 188.3kmh
0-50mph 80.5kmh: 8.5secs
0-60mph 96.5kmh: 10.9secs
0-1/4 mile: 18.4secs
180.0bhp 134.2kW 182.5PS
@ 4750rpm
220.0lbft 298.1Nm @ 3000rpm
106.7bhp/ton 104.9bhp/tonne
39.8bhp/L 29.7kW/L 40.4PS/L
44.2ft/sec 13.5m/sec
19.8mpg 16.5mpgUS 14.3L/100km
Petrol 4-stroke piston
4520cc 275.8cu in
Vee 8 fuel injection
Compression ratio: 8.0:1
Bore: 91.9mm 3.6in
Stroke: 85.1mm 3.3in
Valve type/No: Overhead 16
Transmission: Automatic
No. of forward speeds: 3
Wheels driven: Rear
Springs F/R: Coil/Coil
Brake system: PA
Brakes F/R: Disc/Disc
Steering: Recirculating ball PA
Wheelbase: 246.1cm 96.9in
Track F: 145.3cm 57.2in
Track R: 144.0cm 56.7in
Length: 463.0cm 182.3in
Width: 179.1cm 70.5in
Height: 130.0cm 51.2in
Ground clearance: 13.5cm 5.3in
Kerb weight: 1716.1kg 3780.0lb
Fuel: 90.1L 19.8gal 23.8galUS

2852 Mercedes-Benz

230C
1977 Germany
101.0mph 162.5kmh
0-50mph 80.5kmh: 9.9secs
0-60mph 96.5kmh: 14.0secs
0-1/4 mile: 19.2secs
0-1km: 36.3secs
109.0bhp 81.3kW 110.5PS
@ 4800rpm
136.7lbft 185.2Nm @ 3000rpm
79.5bhp/ton 78.2bhp/tonne
47.2bhp/L 35.2kW/L 47.9PS/L
43.9ft/sec 13.4m/sec
19.0mph 30.6kmh/1000rpm
18.7mpg 15.6mpgUS 15.1L/100km
Petrol 4-stroke piston
2307cc 140.8cu in
In-line 4 1 Carburettor
Compression ratio: 9.1:1
Bore: 93.7mm 3.7in
Stroke: 83.6mm 3.3in
Valve type/No: Overhead 8
Transmission: Automatic
No. of forward speeds: 4
Wheels driven: Rear
Springs F/R: Coil/Coil
Brake system: PA
Brakes F/R: Disc/Disc
Steering: Recirculating ball PA
Wheelbase: 276.9cm 109.0in
Track F: 144.8cm 57.0in
Track R: 144.8cm 57.0in
Length: 464.8cm 183.0in
Width: 175.3cm 69.0in
Height: 142.2cm 56.0in
Ground clearance: 20.3cm 8.0in
Kerb weight: 1393.8kg 3070.0lb
Fuel: 65.1L 14.3gal 17.2galUS

2853 Mercedes-Benz

280E
1977 Germany
108.0mph 173.8kmh
0-50mph 80.5kmh: 8.5secs
0-60mph 96.5kmh: 11.4secs
0-1/4 mile: 18.6secs
137.0bhp 102.2kW 138.9PS
@ 5750rpm
142.0lbft 192.4Nm @ 4600rpm
86.1bhp/ton 84.6bhp/tonne
49.9bhp/L 37.2kW/L 50.6PS/L
49.5ft/sec 15.1m/sec
21.4mph 34.4kmh/1000rpm
20.4mpg 17.0mpgUS 13.8L/100km
Petrol 4-stroke piston
2746cc 167.5cu in
In-line 6 fuel injection
Compression ratio: 8.0:1
Bore: 86.0mm 3.4in
Stroke: 78.8mm 3.1in
Valve type/No: Overhead 12
Transmission: Automatic
No. of forward speeds: 4
Wheels driven: Rear
Springs F/R: Coil/Coil
Brake system: PA
Brakes F/R: Disc/Disc
Steering: Recirculating ball PA
Wheelbase: 279.4cm 110.0in
Track F: 148.8cm 58.6in
Track R: 144.5cm 56.9in
Length: 484.9cm 190.9in
Width: 178.6cm 70.3in
Height: 143.8cm 56.6in
Ground clearance: 17.3cm 6.8in
Kerb weight: 1618.5kg 3565.0lb
Fuel: 79.9L 17.6gal 21.1galUS

2854 Mercedes-Benz

600SE
1977 Germany
137.0mph 220.4kmh
0-50mph 80.5kmh: 6.3secs
0-60mph 96.5kmh: 8.2secs
0-1/4 mile: 16.4secs
250.0bhp 186.4kW 253.5PS
@ 4000rpm
360.0lbft 487.8Nm @ 2500rpm
131.1bhp/ton 129.0bhp/tonne
36.6bhp/L 27.3kW/L 37.1PS/L
41.6ft/sec 12.7m/sec
27.5mph 44.2kmh/1000rpm
15.6mpg 13.0mpgUS 18.1L/100km
Petrol 4-stroke piston
6834cc 417.0cu in
Vee 8 fuel injection
Compression ratio: 8.1:1
Bore: 107.0mm 4.2in
Stroke: 95.0mm 3.7in
Valve type/No: Overhead 16
Transmission: Automatic
No. of forward speeds: 3
Wheels driven: Rear
Springs F/R: Gas/Gas
Brake system: PA
Brakes F/R: Disc/Disc
Steering: Recirculating ball PA
Wheelbase: 295.9cm 116.5in
Track F: 152.1cm 59.9in
Track R: 150.6cm 59.3in
Length: 533.4cm 210.0in
Width: 186.9cm 73.6in
Height: 141.0cm 55.5in
Ground clearance: 14.7cm 5.8in
Kerb weight: 1938.6kg 4270.0lb
Fuel: 96.1L 21.1gal 25.4galUS

2855 Mercedes-Benz

200
1978 Germany
97.0mph 156.1kmh
0-50mph 80.5kmh: 10.5secs
0-60mph 96.5kmh: 15.3secs
0-1/4 mile: 20.2secs
0-1km: 37.8secs
94.0bhp 70.1kW 95.3PS
@ 4800rpm
97.0lbft 131.4Nm @ 3000rpm
71.0bhp/ton 69.8bhp/tonne
47.3bhp/L 35.3kW/L 47.9PS/L
43.9ft/sec 13.4m/sec
18.3mph 29.4kmh/1000rpm
22.1mpg 18.4mpgUS 12.8L/100km
Petrol 4-stroke piston
1988cc 121.3cu in
In-line 4 1 Carburettor

Compression ratio: 9.0:1
Bore: 86.0mm 3.4in
Stroke: 83.6mm 3.3in
Valve type/No: Overhead 8
Transmission: Manual
No. of forward speeds: 4
Wheels driven: Rear
Springs F/R: Coil/Coil
Brake system: PA
Brakes F/R: Disc/Disc
Steering: Recirculating ball PA
Wheelbase: 279.4cm 110.0in
Track F: 148.6cm 58.5in
Track R: 144.8cm 57.0in
Length: 472.4cm 186.0in
Width: 178.3cm 70.2in
Height: 143.5cm 56.5in
Ground clearance: 16.5cm 6.5in
Kerb weight: 1347.0kg 2967.0lb
Fuel: 65.1L 14.3gal 17.2galUS

2856 Mercedes-Benz

300CD
1978 Germany
95.0mph 152.9kmh
0-50mph 80.5kmh: 11.8secs
0-60mph 96.5kmh: 17.1secs
0-1/4 mile: 21.2secs
77.0bhp 57.4kW 78.1PS
@ 4000rpm
115.0lbft 155.8Nm @ 2400rpm
49.0bhp/ton 48.2bhp/tonne
25.6bhp/L 19.1kW/L 26.0PS/L
40.4ft/sec 12.3m/sec
19.7mph 31.7kmh/1000rpm
28.8mpg 24.0mpgUS 9.8L/100km
Diesel 4-stroke piston
3005cc 183.3cu in
In-line 5 fuel injection
Compression ratio: 21.0:1
Bore: 91.0mm 3.6in
Stroke: 92.4mm 3.6in
Valve type/No: Overhead 10
Transmission: Automatic
No. of forward speeds: 4
Wheels driven: Rear
Springs F/R: Coil/Coil
Brake system: PA
Brakes F/R: Disc/Disc
Steering: Recirculating ball PA
Wheelbase: 271.0cm 106.7in
Track F: 148.8cm 58.6in
Track R: 144.5cm 56.9in
Length: 476.3cm 187.5in
Width: 178.6cm 70.3in
Height: 139.4cm 54.9in
Kerb weight: 1598.1kg 3520.0lb
Fuel: 79.9L 17.6gal 21.1galUS

2857 Mercedes-Benz

300SD
1978 Germany
110.0mph 177.0kmh
0-50mph 80.5kmh: 8.8secs
0-60mph 96.5kmh: 12.7secs
0-1/4 mile: 19.3secs
110.0bhp 82.0kW 111.5PS
@ 4200rpm
168.0lbft 227.6Nm @ 2400rpm
63.4bhp/ton 62.4bhp/tonne
36.7bhp/L 27.4kW/L 37.2PS/L
42.5ft/sec 12.9m/sec
23.3mph 37.5kmh/1000rpm
30.0mpg 25.0mpgUS 9.4L/100km
Diesel 4-stroke piston
2998cc 182.9cu in turbocharged
In-line 5 fuel injection
Compression ratio: 21.5:1
Bore: 90.9mm 3.6in
Stroke: 92.4mm 3.6in
Valve type/No: Overhead 10
Transmission: Automatic
No. of forward speeds: 4
Wheels driven: Rear
Springs F/R: Coil/Coil
Brake system: PA
Brakes F/R: Disc/Disc
Steering: Recirculating ball PA
Wheelbase: 286.5cm 112.8in
Track F: 152.1cm 59.9in
Track R: 150.6cm 59.3in
Length: 522.0cm 205.5in
Width: 186.9cm 73.6in
Height: 142.5cm 56.1in
Kerb weight: 1763.8kg 3885.0lb
Fuel: 82.1L 18.0gal 21.7galUS

2858 Mercedes-Benz

450SEL
1978 Germany
129.0mph 207.6kmh
0-60mph 96.5kmh: 9.3secs
0-1/4 mile: 17.2secs
180.0bhp 134.2kW 182.5PS
@ 4750rpm
220.0lbft 298.1Nm @ 3000rpm
101.6bhp/ton 99.9bhp/tonne
39.8bhp/L 29.7kW/L 40.4PS/L
44.2ft/sec 13.5m/sec
Petrol 4-stroke piston
4520cc 275.8cu in
Vee 8 fuel injection
Compression ratio: 8.0:1
Bore: 92.0mm 3.6in
Stroke: 85.0mm 3.3in
Valve type/No: Overhead 16
Transmission: Automatic
No. of forward speeds: 3
Wheels driven: Rear
Brakes F/R: Disc/Disc
Wheelbase: 296.4cm 116.7in
Track F: 152.1cm 59.9in
Track R: 150.6cm 59.3in
Length: 531.9cm 209.4in
Width: 186.9cm 73.6in
Height: 143.0cm 56.3in
Kerb weight: 1802.4kg 3970.0lb
Fuel: 95.8L 21.0gal 25.3galUS

2859 Mercedes-Benz

250T
1979 Germany
113.0mph 181.8kmh
0-50mph 80.5kmh: 8.6secs
0-60mph 96.5kmh: 12.4secs
0-1/4 mile: 19.0secs
0-1km: 35.0secs
140.0bhp 104.4kW 141.9PS
@ 5500rpm
142.0lbft 192.4Nm @ 3500rpm
92.4bhp/ton 90.8bhp/tonne
55.4bhp/L 41.3kW/L 56.2PS/L
43.5ft/sec 13.3m/sec
19.5mph 31.4kmh/1000rpm
18.1mpg 15.1mpgUS 15.6L/100km
Petrol 4-stroke piston
2525cc 154.1cu in
In-line 6 1 Carburettor
Compression ratio: 9.0:1
Bore: 86.0mm 3.4in
Stroke: 72.4mm 2.8in
Valve type/No: Overhead 12
Transmission: Automatic
No. of forward speeds: 4
Wheels driven: Rear
Springs F/R: Coil/Coil
Brake system: PA
Brakes F/R: Disc/Disc
Steering: Recirculating ball PA
Wheelbase: 279.4cm 110.0in
Track F: 148.6cm 58.5in
Track R: 144.8cm 57.0in
Length: 472.4cm 186.0in
Width: 178.3cm 70.2in
Height: 142.5cm 56.1in
Ground clearance: 16.5cm 6.5in
Kerb weight: 1541.3kg 3395.0lb
Fuel: 70.1L 15.4gal 18.5galUS

2860 Mercedes-Benz

280CE
1979 Germany
129.0mph 207.6kmh
0-50mph 80.5kmh: 7.5secs
0-60mph 96.5kmh: 10.4secs
0-1/4 mile: 17.5secs
0-1km: 31.9secs
185.0bhp 137.9kW 187.6PS
@ 5800rpm
177.0lbft 239.8Nm @ 4500rpm
122.2bhp/ton 120.2bhp/tonne
67.4bhp/L 50.2kW/L 68.3PS/L
49.9ft/sec 15.2m/sec
20.0mph 32.2kmh/1000rpm
20.8mpg 17.3mpgUS 13.6L/100km
Petrol 4-stroke piston
2746cc 167.5cu in
In-line 6 fuel injection
Compression ratio: 9.0:1
Bore: 86.0mm 3.4in
Stroke: 78.8mm 3.1in
Valve type/No: Overhead 12
Transmission: Automatic
No. of forward speeds: 4
Wheels driven: Rear
Springs F/R: Coil/Coil
Brake system: PA
Brakes F/R: Disc/Disc
Steering: Recirculating ball PA
Wheelbase: 271.0cm 106.7in
Track F: 148.8cm 58.6in
Track R: 144.5cm 56.9in
Length: 464.1cm 182.7in
Width: 178.6cm 70.3in
Height: 139.4cm 54.9in
Ground clearance: 16.5cm 6.5in
Kerb weight: 1539.1kg 3390.0lb
Fuel: 80.1L 17.6gal 21.1galUS

2861 Mercedes-Benz

300TD
1979 Germany
97.0mph 156.1kmh
0-60mph 96.5kmh: 18.1secs
0-1/4 mile: 21.6secs
77.0bhp 57.4kW 78.1PS
@ 4000rpm
115.0lbft 155.8Nm @ 2400rpm
45.1bhp/ton 44.4bhp/tonne
25.7bhp/L 19.1kW/L 26.0PS/L
40.4ft/sec 12.3m/sec
20.5mph 33.0kmh/1000rpm
27.6mpg 23.0mpgUS 10.2L/100km
Diesel 4-stroke piston
2998cc 182.9cu in
In-line 5 fuel injection
Compression ratio: 21.0:1
Bore: 90.9mm 3.6in
Stroke: 92.4mm 3.6in
Valve type/No: Overhead 10
Transmission: Automatic
No. of forward speeds: 4
Wheels driven: Rear
Springs F/R: Coil/Coil
Brake system: PA
Brakes F/R: Disc/Disc
Steering: Recirculating ball PA
Wheelbase: 279.4cm 110.0in
Track F: 148.8cm 58.6in
Track R: 145.3cm 57.2in
Length: 484.9cm 190.9in
Width: 178.6cm 70.3in
Height: 147.1cm 57.9in
Ground clearance: 15.0cm 5.9in
Kerb weight: 1734.3kg 3820.0lb
Fuel: 81.0L 17.8gal 21.4galUS

2862 Mercedes-Benz

450SEL 6.9
1979 Germany
140.0mph 225.3kmh
0-50mph 80.5kmh: 5.6secs
0-60mph 96.5kmh: 7.3secs
0-1/4 mile: 15.4secs
0-1km: 28.2secs
286.0bhp 213.3kW 290.0PS
@ 4250rpm
405.0lbft 548.8Nm @ 3000rpm
157.8bhp/ton 155.2bhp/tonne
41.8bhp/L 31.2kW/L 42.4PS/L
44.1ft/sec 13.5m/sec
24.0mph 38.6kmh/1000rpm
13.6mpg 11.3mpgUS 20.8L/100km
Petrol 4-stroke piston
6834cc 417.0cu in
Vee 8 fuel injection
Compression ratio: 8.8:1
Bore: 107.0mm 4.2in
Stroke: 95.0mm 3.7in
Valve type/No: Overhead 16
Transmission: Automatic
No. of forward speeds: 3
Wheels driven: Rear
Springs F/R: Gas/Gas
Brake system: PA
Brakes F/R: Disc/Disc
Steering: Recirculating ball PA
Wheelbase: 295.9cm 116.5in
Track F: 150.6cm 59.3in
Track R: 152.4cm 60.0in
Length: 506.0cm 199.2in
Width: 189.5cm 74.6in
Height: 143.0cm 56.3in
Ground clearance: 17.8cm 7.0in
Kerb weight: 1843.2kg 4060.0lb
Fuel: 96.0L 21.1gal 25.4galUS

2863 Mercedes-Benz

450SL
1979 Germany
117.0mph 188.3kmh
0-50mph 80.5kmh: 7.5secs
0-60mph 96.5kmh: 10.0secs
0-1/4 mile: 17.8secs
180.0bhp 134.2kW 182.5PS
@ 4750rpm
220.0lbft 298.1Nm @ 3000rpm
106.9bhp/ton 105.2bhp/tonne
39.8bhp/L 29.7kW/L 40.4PS/L
44.2ft/sec 13.5m/sec
23.5mph 37.8kmh/1000rpm
18.0mpg 15.0mpgUS 15.7L/100km
Petrol 4-stroke piston
4520cc 275.8cu in
Vee 8 fuel injection
Compression ratio: 8.0:1
Bore: 92.0mm 3.6in
Stroke: 85.0mm 3.3in
Valve type/No: Overhead 16
Transmission: Automatic
No. of forward speeds: 3
Wheels driven: Rear
Springs F/R: Coil/Coil
Brake system: PA
Brakes F/R: Disc/Disc
Steering: Recirculating ball PA
Wheelbase: 246.1cm 96.9in
Track F: 145.3cm 57.2in
Track R: 144.0cm 56.7in
Length: 463.0cm 182.3in
Width: 179.1cm 70.5in
Height: 129.0cm 50.8in
Ground clearance: 13.5cm 5.3in
Kerb weight: 1711.6kg 3770.0lb
Fuel: 95.8L 21.0gal 25.3galUS

2864 Mercedes-Benz

450SL
1980 Germany
112.0mph 180.2kmh
0-60mph 96.5kmh: 11.7secs
0-1/4 mile: 18.6secs
160.0bhp 119.3kW 162.2PS
@ 4200rpm
230.0lbft 311.7Nm @ 2500rpm
99.1bhp/ton 97.5bhp/tonne
35.4bhp/L 26.4kW/L 35.9PS/L
39.1ft/sec 11.9m/sec
25.0mph 40.2kmh/1000rpm
19.2mpg 16.0mpgUS 14.7L/100km
Petrol 4-stroke piston
4520cc 275.8cu in
Vee 8 fuel injection
Compression ratio: 8.0:1
Bore: 92.0mm 3.6in
Stroke: 85.0mm 3.3in
Valve type/No: Overhead 16
Transmission: Automatic
No. of forward speeds: 3
Wheels driven: Rear
Springs F/R: Coil/Coil
Brake system: PA
Brakes F/R: Disc/Disc
Steering: Recirculating ball PA
Wheelbase: 246.1cm 96.9in
Track F: 145.3cm 57.2in
Track R: 144.0cm 56.7in
Length: 463.0cm 182.3in
Width: 179.1cm 70.5in
Height: 129.0cm 50.8in
Ground clearance: 13.5cm 5.3in
Kerb weight: 1641.2kg 3615.0lb
Fuel: 90.1L 19.8gal 23.8galUS

2865 Mercedes-Benz

230E
1981 Germany
113.0mph 181.8kmh
0-50mph 80.5kmh: 7.1secs
0-60mph 96.5kmh: 10.3secs
0-1/4 mile: 18.0secs
0-1km: 33.2secs
136.0bhp 101.4kW 137.9PS
@ 5100rpm
151.0lbft 204.6Nm @ 3500rpm
100.3bhp/ton 98.6bhp/tonne
59.2bhp/L 44.1kW/L 60.0PS/L
44.8ft/sec 13.6m/sec
19.8mph 31.9kmh/1000rpm
21.9mpg 18.2mpgUS 12.9L/100km
Petrol 4-stroke piston
2299cc 140.3cu in
In-line 4 fuel injection
Compression ratio: 9.0:1
Bore: 95.5mm 3.8in
Stroke: 80.2mm 3.2in
Valve type/No: Overhead 8

Transmission: Manual
No. of forward speeds: 4
Wheels driven: Rear
Springs F/R: Coil/Coil
Brake system: PA
Brakes F/R: Disc/Disc
Steering: Recirculating ball PA
Wheelbase: 279.4cm 110.0in
Track F: 148.6cm 58.5in
Track R: 144.8cm 57.0in
Length: 472.4cm 186.0in
Width: 178.3cm 70.2in
Height: 143.5cm 56.5in
Ground clearance: 16.5cm 6.5in
Kerb weight: 1379.2kg 3038.0lb
Fuel: 71.4L 15.7gal 18.9galUS

2866 Mercedes-Benz

230TE
1981 Germany
108.0mph 173.8kmh
0-50mph 80.5kmh: 9.0secs
0-60mph 96.5kmh: 12.9secs
0-1/4 mile: 18.6secs
0-1km: 34.7secs
136.0bhp 101.4kW 137.9PS
@ 5100rpm
146.0lbft 197.8Nm @ 3500rpm
88.5bhp/ton 87.0bhp/tonne
59.2bhp/L 44.1kW/L 60.0PS/L
44.8ft/sec 13.6m/sec
20.0mph 32.2kmh/1000rpm
22.5mpg 18.7mpgUS 12.6L/100km
Petrol 4-stroke piston
2299cc 140.3cu in
In-line 4 fuel injection
Compression ratio: 9.0:1
Bore: 95.5mm 3.8in
Stroke: 80.2mm 3.2in
Valve type/No: Overhead 8
Transmission: Automatic
No. of forward speeds: 4
Wheels driven: Rear
Springs F/R: Coil/Coil
Brake system: PA
Brakes F/R: Disc/Disc
Steering: Recirculating ball PA
Wheelbase: 279.4cm 110.0in
Track F: 148.6cm 58.5in
Track R: 144.8cm 57.0in
Length: 472.4cm 186.0in
Width: 178.3cm 70.2in
Height: 142.5cm 56.1in
Ground clearance: 16.5cm 6.5in
Kerb weight: 1563.6kg 3444.0lb
Fuel: 70.1L 15.4gal 18.5galUS

2867 Mercedes-Benz

300GD
1981 Germany
83.0mph 133.5kmh
0-50mph 80.5kmh: 15.6secs
0-60mph 96.5kmh: 23.7secs
0-1/4 mile: 22.6secs
0-1km: 43.2secs
80.0bhp 59.7kW 81.1PS
@ 4000rpm
126.5lbft 171.4Nm @ 2400rpm
39.1bhp/ton 38.4bhp/tonne
26.7bhp/L 19.9kW/L 27.0PS/L
40.4ft/sec 12.3m/sec
17.3mph 27.8kmh/1000rpm
19.3mpg 16.1mpgUS 14.6L/100km
Diesel 4-stroke piston
2998cc 182.9cu in
In-line 5 fuel injection
Compression ratio: 21.0:1
Bore: 90.9mm 3.6in
Stroke: 92.4mm 3.6in
Valve type/No: Overhead 10
Transmission: Manual
No. of forward speeds: 4
Wheels driven: 4-wheel engageable
Springs F/R: Coil/Coil
Brake system: PA
Brakes F/R: Disc/Drum
Steering: Recirculating ball PA
Wheelbase: 240.0cm 94.5in
Track F: 142.5cm 56.1in
Track R: 142.5cm 56.1in
Length: 414.5cm 163.2in
Width: 169.9cm 66.9in
Height: 198.4cm 78.1in
Ground clearance: 21.6cm 8.5in
Kerb weight: 2081.6kg 4585.0lb
Fuel: 68.2L 15.0gal 18.0galUS

2868 Mercedes-Benz

300TD
1981 Germany
102.0mph 164.1kmh
0-50mph 80.5kmh: 9.3secs
0-60mph 96.5kmh: 13.2secs
0-1/4 mile: 19.0secs
120.0bhp 89.5kW 121.7PS
@ 4350rpm
170.0lbft 230.4Nm @ 2400rpm
70.6bhp/ton 69.5bhp/tonne
40.0bhp/L 29.8kW/L 40.6PS/L
44.0ft/sec 13.4m/sec
22.6mph 36.4kmh/1000rpm
30.0mpg 25.0mpgUS 9.4L/100km
Diesel 4-stroke piston
2998cc 182.9cu in turbocharged
In-line 5 fuel injection
Compression ratio: 21.5:1
Bore: 90.0mm 3.5in
Stroke: 92.4mm 3.6in
Valve type/No: Overhead 10
Transmission: Automatic
No. of forward speeds: 4
Wheels driven: Rear
Springs F/R: Coil/Coil
Brake system: PA
Brakes F/R: Disc/Disc
Steering: Recirculating ball PA
Wheelbase: 279.4cm 110.0in
Track F: 148.8cm 58.6in
Track R: 145.3cm 57.2in
Length: 482.6cm 190.0in
Width: 178.6cm 70.3in
Height: 147.1cm 57.9in
Kerb weight: 1727.5kg 3805.0lb
Fuel: 70.0L 15.4gal 18.5galUS

2869 Mercedes-Benz

380SEL
1981 Germany
115.0mph 185.0kmh
0-60mph 96.5kmh: 10.1secs
0-1/4 mile: 17.7secs
155.0bhp 115.6kW 157.1PS
@ 4750rpm
196.0lbft 265.6Nm @ 2750rpm
91.0bhp/ton 89.5bhp/tonne
40.4bhp/L 30.1kW/L 40.9PS/L
41.0ft/sec 12.5m/sec
26.1mph 42.0kmh/1000rpm
21.6mpg 18.0mpgUS 13.1L/100km
Petrol 4-stroke piston
3839cc 234.2cu in
Vee 8 fuel injection
Compression ratio: 8.3:1
Bore: 88.0mm 3.5in
Stroke: 78.9mm 3.1in
Valve type/No: Overhead 16
Transmission: Automatic
No. of forward speeds: 4
Wheels driven: Rear
Springs F/R: Coil/Coil
Brake system: PA
Brakes F/R: Disc/Disc
Steering: Recirculating ball PA
Wheelbase: 307.6cm 121.1in
Track F: 154.4cm 60.8in
Track R: 151.6cm 59.7in
Length: 528.6cm 208.1in
Width: 182.1cm 71.7in
Height: 144.0cm 56.7in
Ground clearance: 15.2cm 6.0in
Kerb weight: 1732.0kg 3815.0lb
Fuel: 90.1L 19.8gal 23.8galUS

2870 Mercedes-Benz

380SEC
1982 Germany
132.0mph 212.4kmh
0-50mph 80.5kmh: 7.0secs
0-60mph 96.5kmh: 9.1secs
0-1/4 mile: 16.6secs
0-1km: 30.5secs
204.0bhp 152.1kW 206.8PS
@ 5250rpm
232.0lbft 314.4Nm @ 3250rpm
130.3bhp/ton 128.1bhp/tonne
53.1bhp/L 39.6kW/L 53.9PS/L
45.3ft/sec 13.8m/sec
28.5mph 45.9kmh/1000rpm
20.0mpg 16.7mpgUS 14.1L/100km
Petrol 4-stroke piston
3839cc 234.2cu in
Vee 8 fuel injection
Compression ratio: 9.4:1
Bore: 88.0mm 3.5in
Stroke: 78.9mm 3.1in
Valve type/No: Overhead 16
Transmission: Automatic
No. of forward speeds: 4
Wheels driven: Rear
Springs F/R: Coil/Coil
Brake system: PA
Brakes F/R: Disc/Disc
Steering: Recirculating ball PA
Wheelbase: 282.4cm 111.2in
Track F: 154.4cm 60.8in
Track R: 151.6cm 59.7in
Length: 491.0cm 193.3in
Width: 182.9cm 72.0in
Height: 140.7cm 55.4in
Ground clearance: 15.5cm 6.1in
Kerb weight: 1592.2kg 3507.0lb
Fuel: 90.1L 19.8gal 23.8galUS

2871 Mercedes-Benz

380SL
1982 Germany
110.0mph 177.0kmh
0-60mph 96.5kmh: 11.5secs
0-1/4 mile: 18.6secs
155.0bhp 115.6kW 157.1PS
@ 4750rpm
196.0lbft 265.6Nm @ 2750rpm
99.3bhp/ton 97.7bhp/tonne
40.4bhp/L 30.1kW/L 40.9PS/L
41.0ft/sec 12.5m/sec
26.1mph 42.0kmh/1000rpm
21.0mpg 17.5mpgUS 13.4L/100km
Petrol 4-stroke piston
3839cc 234.2cu in
Vee 8 fuel injection
Compression ratio: 8.3:1
Bore: 88.0mm 3.5in
Stroke: 78.9mm 3.1in
Valve type/No: Overhead 16
Transmission: Automatic
No. of forward speeds: 4
Wheels driven: Rear
Springs F/R: Coil/Coil
Brake system: PA
Brakes F/R: Disc/Disc
Steering: Recirculating ball PA
Wheelbase: 246.1cm 96.9in
Track F: 145.3cm 57.2in
Track R: 144.0cm 56.7in
Length: 463.0cm 182.3in
Width: 179.1cm 70.5in
Height: 129.0cm 50.8in
Kerb weight: 1586.7kg 3495.0lb
Fuel: 85.2L 18.7gal 22.5galUS

2872 Mercedes-Benz

190
1983 Germany
110.0mph 177.0kmh
0-50mph 80.5kmh: 9.3secs
0-60mph 96.5kmh: 13.4secs
0-1/4 mile: 19.5secs
0-1km: 36.4secs
88.0bhp 65.6kW 89.2PS
@ 5000rpm
122.0lbft 165.3Nm @ 2500rpm
79.2bhp/ton 77.9bhp/tonne
44.1bhp/L 32.9kW/L 44.7PS/L
43.9ft/sec 13.4m/sec
21.3mph 34.3kmh/1000rpm
29.2mpg 24.3mpgUS 9.7L/100km
Petrol 4-stroke piston
1997cc 121.8cu in
In-line 4 1 Carburettor
Compression ratio: 9.0:1
Bore: 89.0mm 3.5in
Stroke: 80.2mm 3.2in
Valve type/No: Overhead 8
Transmission: Manual
No. of forward speeds: 4
Wheels driven: Rear
Springs F/R: Coil/Coil
Brake system: PA
Brakes F/R: Disc/Disc
Steering: Recirculating ball
Wheelbase: 266.4cm 104.9in
Track F: 142.7cm 56.2in
Track R: 141.5cm 55.7in
Length: 442.0cm 174.0in
Width: 167.9cm 66.1in
Height: 138.2cm 54.4in
Ground clearance: 15.5cm 6.1in
Kerb weight: 1130.0kg 2489.0lb
Fuel: 55.1L 12.1gal 14.5galUS

2873 Mercedes-Benz

190E
1983 Germany
123.0mph 197.9kmh
0-50mph 80.5kmh: 7.1secs
0-60mph 96.5kmh: 9.7secs
0-1/4 mile: 17.4secs
0-1km: 32.6secs
122.0bhp 91.0kW 123.7PS
@ 5100rpm
131.0lbft 177.5Nm @ 3500rpm
106.2bhp/ton 104.4bhp/tonne
61.1bhp/L 45.6kW/L 61.9PS/L
44.8ft/sec 13.6m/sec
27.3mph 43.9kmh/1000rpm
27.9mpg 23.2mpgUS 10.1L/100km
Petrol 4-stroke piston
1997cc 121.8cu in
In-line 4 fuel injection
Compression ratio: 9.1:1
Bore: 89.0mm 3.5in
Stroke: 80.2mm 3.2in
Valve type/No: Overhead 8
Transmission: Manual
No. of forward speeds: 5
Wheels driven: Rear
Springs F/R: Coil/Coil
Brake system: PA
Brakes F/R: Disc/Disc
Steering: Recirculating ball PA
Wheelbase: 266.4cm 104.9in
Track F: 142.7cm 56.2in
Track R: 141.5cm 55.7in
Length: 442.0cm 174.0in
Width: 167.9cm 66.1in
Height: 138.2cm 54.4in
Ground clearance: 15.5cm 6.1in
Kerb weight: 1168.6kg 2574.0lb
Fuel: 55.1L 12.1gal 14.5galUS

2874 Mercedes-Benz

280SE
1983 Germany
129.0mph 207.6kmh
0-50mph 80.5kmh: 6.5secs
0-60mph 96.5kmh: 8.7secs
0-1/4 mile: 16.9secs
0-1km: 31.1secs
183.0bhp 136.5kW 185.5PS
@ 5800rpm
240.0lbft 325.2Nm @ 4500rpm
115.5bhp/ton 113.5bhp/tonne
66.6bhp/L 49.7kW/L 67.6PS/L
49.9ft/sec 15.2m/sec
25.7mph 41.4kmh/1000rpm
19.0mpg 15.8mpgUS 14.9L/100km
Petrol 4-stroke piston
2746cc 167.5cu in
In-line 6 fuel injection
Compression ratio: 9.0:1
Bore: 86.0mm 3.4in
Stroke: 78.8mm 3.1in
Valve type/No: Overhead 12
Transmission: Manual
No. of forward speeds: 5
Wheels driven: Rear
Springs F/R: Coil/Coil
Brake system: PA
Brakes F/R: Disc/Disc
Steering: Recirculating ball PA
Wheelbase: 293.1cm 115.4in
Track F: 154.4cm 60.8in
Track R: 151.6cm 59.7in
Length: 499.6cm 196.7in
Width: 181.6cm 71.5in
Height: 143.5cm 56.5in
Ground clearance: 15.0cm 5.9in
Kerb weight: 1611.7kg 3550.0lb
Fuel: 90.1L 19.8gal 23.8galUS

2875 Mercedes-Benz

380SL
1983 Germany
110.0mph 177.0kmh
0-60mph 96.5kmh: 10.9secs
0-1/4 mile: 18.4secs
155.0bhp 115.6kW 157.1PS
@ 4750rpm
196.0lbft 265.6Nm @ 2750rpm
99.3bhp/ton 97.7bhp/tonne
40.4bhp/L 30.1kW/L 40.9PS/L
41.0ft/sec 12.5m/sec
26.1mph 42.0kmh/1000rpm
22.8mpg 19.0mpgUS 12.4L/100km
Petrol 4-stroke piston
3839cc 234.2cu in
Vee 8 fuel injection

Compression ratio: 8.3:1
Bore: 88.0mm 3.5in
Stroke: 78.9mm 3.1in
Valve type/No: Overhead 16
Transmission: Automatic
No. of forward speeds: 4
Wheels driven: Rear
Springs F/R: Coil/Coil
Brake system: PA
Brakes F/R: Disc/Disc
Steering: Recirculating ball PA
Wheelbase: 245.9cm 96.8in
Track F: 145.3cm 57.2in
Track R: 144.0cm 56.7in
Length: 463.0cm 182.3in
Width: 179.1cm 70.5in
Height: 129.0cm 50.8in
Kerb weight: 1586.7kg 3495.0lb
Fuel: 85.2L 18.7gal 22.5galUS

2876 Mercedes-Benz

190E
1984 Germany
114.0mph 183.4kmh
0-50mph 80.5kmh: 7.8secs
0-60mph 96.5kmh: 11.2secs
0-1/4 mile: 18.1secs
113.0bhp 84.3kW 114.6PS
@ 5000rpm
133.0lbft 180.2Nm @ 3500rpm
94.3bhp/ton 92.7bhp/tonne
49.1bhp/L 36.6kW/L 49.8PS/L
43.9ft/sec 13.4m/sec
26.7mph 43.0kmh/1000rpm
32.4mpg 27.0mpgUS 8.7L/100km
Petrol 4-stroke piston
2299cc 140.3cu in
In-line 4 fuel injection
Compression ratio: 8.0:1
Bore: 95.5mm 3.8in
Stroke: 80.3mm 3.2in
Valve type/No: Overhead 8
Transmission: Manual
No. of forward speeds: 5
Wheels driven: Rear
Springs F/R: Coil/Coil
Brake system: PA
Brakes F/R: Disc/Disc
Steering: Recirculating ball PA
Wheelbase: 266.4cm 104.9in
Track F: 142.7cm 56.2in
Track R: 141.5cm 55.7in
Length: 444.5cm 175.0in
Width: 167.9cm 66.1in
Height: 138.2cm 54.4in
Ground clearance: 15.5cm 6.1in
Kerb weight: 1219.0kg 2685.0lb
Fuel: 62.4L 13.7gal 16.5galUS

2877 Mercedes-Benz

500SEC
1984 Germany
136.0mph 218.8kmh
0-50mph 80.5kmh: 6.6secs
0-60mph 96.5kmh: 9.0secs
0-1/4 mile: 17.0secs
184.0bhp 137.2kW 186.5PS
@ 4500rpm
247.0lbft 334.7Nm @ 2000rpm
112.8bhp/ton 110.9bhp/tonne
37.0bhp/L 27.6kW/L 37.5PS/L
41.9ft/sec 12.7m/sec
27.9mph 44.9kmh/1000rpm
19.8mpg 16.5mpgUS 14.3L/100km
Petrol 4-stroke piston
4973cc 303.4cu in
Vee 8 fuel injection
Compression ratio: 8.0:1
Bore: 95.6mm 3.8in
Stroke: 85.0mm 3.3in
Valve type/No: Overhead 16
Transmission: Automatic
No. of forward speeds: 4
Wheels driven: Rear
Springs F/R: Coil/Coil
Brake system: PA
Brakes F/R: Disc/Disc
Steering: Recirculating ball PA
Wheelbase: 284.5cm 112.0in
Track F: 154.4cm 60.8in
Track R: 151.6cm 59.7in
Length: 506.0cm 199.2in
Width: 182.9cm 72.0in
Height: 140.7cm 55.4in
Kerb weight: 1659.4kg 3655.0lb
Fuel: 90.1L 19.8gal 23.8galUS

2878 Mercedes-Benz

190E 2.3
1985 Germany
114.0mph 183.4kmh
0-60mph 96.5kmh: 9.9secs
0-1/4 mile: 17.5secs
120.0bhp 89.5kW 121.7PS
@ 5000rpm
136.0lbft 184.3Nm @ 3500rpm
98.5bhp/ton 96.8bhp/tonne
52.2bhp/L 38.9kW/L 52.9PS/L
43.9ft/sec 13.4m/sec
26.4mpg 22.0mpgUS 10.7L/100km
Petrol 4-stroke piston
2299cc 140.3cu in
In-line 4 fuel injection
Bore: 95.5mm 3.8in
Stroke: 80.3mm 3.2in
Valve type/No: Overhead 8
Transmission: Manual
No. of forward speeds: 5
Wheels driven: Rear
Springs F/R: Coil/Coil
Brake system: PA ABS
Brakes F/R: Disc/Disc
Steering: Recirculating ball PA
Wheelbase: 266.4cm 104.9in
Track F: 142.7cm 56.2in
Track R: 141.5cm 55.7in
Length: 444.5cm 175.0in
Width: 167.9cm 66.1in
Height: 138.2cm 54.4in
Kerb weight: 1239.4kg 2730.0lb
Fuel: 62.4L 13.7gal 16.5galUS

2879 Mercedes-Benz

190E 2.3-16
1985 Germany
145.0mph 233.3kmh
0-50mph 80.5kmh: 6.0secs
0-60mph 96.5kmh: 8.0secs
0-1/4 mile: 16.0secs
0-1km: 29.1secs
185.0bhp 137.9kW 187.6PS
@ 6200rpm
173.0lbft 234.4Nm @ 4500rpm
140.3bhp/ton 137.9bhp/tonne
80.5bhp/L 60.0kW/L 81.6PS/L
54.4ft/sec 16.6m/sec
22.5mph 36.2kmh/1000rpm
23.5mpg 19.6mpgUS 12.0L/100km
Petrol 4-stroke piston
2299cc 140.3cu in
In-line 4 fuel injection
Compression ratio: 10.5:1
Bore: 95.5mm 3.8in
Stroke: 80.2mm 3.2in
Valve type/No: Overhead 16
Transmission: Manual
No. of forward speeds: 5
Wheels driven: Rear
Springs F/R: Coil/Coil
Brake system: PA
Brakes F/R: Disc/Disc
Steering: Recirculating ball PA
Wheelbase: 266.4cm 104.9in
Track F: 142.7cm 56.2in
Track R: 142.7cm 56.2in
Length: 443.0cm 174.4in
Width: 170.7cm 67.2in
Height: 136.1cm 53.6in
Ground clearance: 15.5cm 6.1in
Kerb weight: 1341.1kg 2954.0lb
Fuel: 70.1L 15.4gal 18.5galUS

2880 Mercedes-Benz

190E BBS/Callaway Turbo
1985 Germany
0-60mph 96.5kmh: 9.2secs
0-1/4 mile: 16.6secs
190.0bhp 141.7kW 192.6PS
147.3bhp/ton 144.8bhp/tonne
82.6bhp/L 61.6kW/L 83.8PS/L
24.6mpg 20.5mpgUS 11.5L/100km
Petrol 4-stroke piston
2299cc 140.3cu in turbocharged
In-line 4 fuel injection
Compression ratio: 8.0:1
Bore: 95.5mm 3.8in
Stroke: 80.3mm 3.2in
Valve type/No: Overhead 8
Transmission: Manual
No. of forward speeds: 5
Wheels driven: Rear
Brake system: ABS
Brakes F/R: Disc/Disc
Steering: Recirculating ball PA
Wheelbase: 266.4cm 104.9in
Length: 444.5cm 175.0in
Width: 167.9cm 66.1in
Height: 138.2cm 54.4in
Kerb weight: 1312.1kg 2890.0lb

2881 Mercedes-Benz

300E
1985 Germany
143.0mph 230.1kmh
0-50mph 80.5kmh: 6.2secs
0-60mph 96.5kmh: 8.4secs
0-1/4 mile: 17.1secs
0-1km: 30.5secs
190.0bhp 141.7kW 192.6PS
@ 5600rpm
192.0lbft 260.2Nm @ 4250rpm
131.6bhp/ton 129.4bhp/tonne
64.1bhp/L 47.8kW/L 65.0PS/L
49.2ft/sec 15.0m/sec
23.3mph 37.5kmh/1000rpm
22.7mpg 18.9mpgUS 12.4L/100km
Petrol 4-stroke piston
2962cc 180.7cu in
In-line 6 fuel injection
Compression ratio: 10.0:1
Bore: 88.5mm 3.5in
Stroke: 80.2mm 3.2in
Valve type/No: Overhead 12
Transmission: Automatic
No. of forward speeds: 4
Wheels driven: Rear
Springs F/R: Coil/Coil
Brake system: PA
Brakes F/R: Disc/Disc
Steering: Recirculating ball PA
Wheelbase: 279.9cm 110.2in
Track F: 149.6cm 58.9in
Track R: 148.8cm 58.6in
Length: 474.0cm 186.6in
Width: 174.0cm 68.5in
Height: 144.0cm 56.7in
Ground clearance: 17.8cm 7.0in
Kerb weight: 1468.2kg 3234.0lb
Fuel: 70.1L 15.4gal 18.5galUS

2882 Mercedes-Benz

500SEL
1985 Germany
133.0mph 214.0kmh
0-50mph 80.5kmh: 6.0secs
0-60mph 96.5kmh: 8.0secs
0-1/4 mile: 16.3secs
0-1km: 29.9secs
231.0bhp 172.3kW 234.2PS
@ 4750rpm
298.0lbft 403.8Nm @ 3200rpm
133.9bhp/ton 131.7bhp/tonne
46.4bhp/L 34.6kW/L 47.1PS/L
44.2ft/sec 13.5m/sec
32.2mph 51.8kmh/1000rpm
15.7mpg 13.1mpgUS 18.0L/100km
Petrol 4-stroke piston
4973cc 303.4cu in
Vee 8 fuel injection
Compression ratio: 9.2:1
Bore: 96.5mm 3.8in
Stroke: 85.0mm 3.3in
Valve type/No: Overhead 16
Transmission: Automatic
No. of forward speeds: 4
Wheels driven: Rear
Springs F/R: Coil/Coil
Brake system: PA
Brakes F/R: Disc/Disc
Steering: Recirculating ball PA
Wheelbase: 307.1cm 120.9in
Track F: 154.4cm 60.8in
Track R: 151.6cm 59.7in
Length: 513.6cm 202.2in
Width: 182.1cm 71.7in
Height: 144.0cm 56.7in
Ground clearance: 15.5cm 6.1in
Kerb weight: 1754.3kg 3864.0lb
Fuel: 90.1L 19.8gal 23.8galUS

2883 Mercedes-Benz

190E 2.3-16
1986 Germany
139.0mph 223.7kmh
0-50mph 80.5kmh: 5.7secs
0-60mph 96.5kmh: 7.8secs
0-1/4 mile: 16.2secs
167.0bhp 124.5kW 169.3PS
@ 5800rpm
162.0lbft 219.5Nm @ 4750rpm
124.1bhp/ton 122.0bhp/tonne
72.6bhp/L 54.2kW/L 73.6PS/L
50.9ft/sec 15.5m/sec
25.2mpg 21.0mpgUS 11.2L/100km
Petrol 4-stroke piston
2299cc 140.3cu in
In-line 4 fuel injection
Compression ratio: 8.0:1
Bore: 95.5mm 3.8in
Stroke: 80.3mm 3.2in
Valve type/No: Overhead 16
Transmission: Manual
No. of forward speeds: 5
Wheels driven: Rear
Springs F/R: Coil/Coil
Brake system: PA ABS
Brakes F/R: Disc/Disc
Steering: Recirculating ball PA
Wheelbase: 266.4cm 104.9in
Track F: 144.5cm 56.9in
Track R: 143.0cm 56.3in
Length: 443.0cm 174.4in
Width: 170.7cm 67.2in
Height: 136.1cm 53.6in
Ground clearance: 12.7cm 5.0in
Kerb weight: 1368.8kg 3015.0lb
Fuel: 79.5L 17.5gal 21.0galUS

2884 Mercedes-Benz

200
1986 Germany
121.0mph 194.7kmh
0-50mph 80.5kmh: 9.0secs
0-60mph 96.5kmh: 13.0secs
0-1/4 mile: 19.1secs
0-1km: 34.9secs
109.0bhp 81.3kW 110.5PS
@ 5200rpm
125.0lbft 169.4Nm @ 2500rpm
83.9bhp/ton 82.5bhp/tonne
54.6bhp/L 40.7kW/L 55.3PS/L
45.6ft/sec 13.9m/sec
26.4mph 42.5kmh/1000rpm
23.6mpg 19.7mpgUS 12.0L/100km
Petrol 4-stroke piston
1997cc 121.8cu in
In-line 4 1 Carburettor
Compression ratio: 9.0:1
Bore: 89.0mm 3.5in
Stroke: 80.2mm 3.2in
Valve type/No: Overhead 8
Transmission: Manual
No. of forward speeds: 5
Wheels driven: Rear
Springs F/R: Coil/Coil
Brake system: PA
Brakes F/R: Disc/Disc
Steering: Recirculating ball PA
Wheelbase: 279.9cm 110.2in
Track F: 149.6cm 58.9in
Track R: 148.8cm 58.6in
Length: 474.0cm 186.6in
Width: 174.0cm 68.5in
Height: 144.0cm 56.7in
Ground clearance: 15.2cm 6.0in
Kerb weight: 1321.1kg 2910.0lb
Fuel: 70.1L 15.4gal 18.5galUS

2885 Mercedes-Benz

300E
1986 Germany
140.0mph 225.3kmh
0-60mph 96.5kmh: 7.5secs
0-1/4 mile: 16.0secs
177.0bhp 132.0kW 179.4PS
@ 5700rpm
137.0lbft 185.6Nm @ 5750rpm
123.1bhp/ton 121.1bhp/tonne
59.8bhp/L 44.6kW/L 60.6PS/L
50.0ft/sec 15.3m/sec
29.6mph 47.6kmh/1000rpm
26.4mpg 22.0mpgUS 10.7L/100km
Petrol 4-stroke piston
2962cc 180.7cu in
In-line 6 fuel injection
Compression ratio: 9.2:1
Bore: 88.5mm 3.5in
Stroke: 80.3mm 3.2in
Valve type/No: Overhead 12
Transmission: Manual
No. of forward speeds: 5
Wheels driven: Rear
Springs F/R: Coil/Coil
Brake system: PA ABS
Brakes F/R: Disc/Disc
Steering: Recirculating ball PA
Wheelbase: 279.9cm 110.2in

Track F: 149.6cm 58.9in
Track R: 148.8cm 58.6in
Length: 475.5cm 187.2in
Width: 174.0cm 68.5in
Height: 144.5cm 56.9in
Kerb weight: 1461.9kg 3220.0lb
Fuel: 70.0L 15.4gal 18.5galUS

2886 Mercedes-Benz

300TE
1986 Germany
127.0mph 204.3kmh
0-50mph 80.5kmh: 6.3secs
0-60mph 96.5kmh: 8.7secs
0-1/4 mile: 17.1secs
0-1km: 31.0secs
188.0bhp 140.2kW 190.6PS
@ 5700rpm
191.0lbft 258.8Nm @ 4400rpm
123.1bhp/ton 121.1bhp/tonne
63.5bhp/L 47.3kW/L 64.3PS/L
50.0ft/sec 15.2m/sec
23.3mph 37.5kmh/1000rpm
21.5mpg 17.9mpgUS 13.1L/100km
Petrol 4-stroke piston
2962cc 181.0cu in
In-line 6 fuel injection
Compression ratio: 9.2:1
Bore: 88.5mm 3.5in
Stroke: 80.2mm 3.2in
Valve type/No: Overhead 12
Transmission: Automatic
No. of forward speeds: 4
Wheels driven: Rear
Springs F/R: Coil/Coil
Brake system: PA
Brakes F/R: Disc/Disc
Steering: Recirculating ball PA
Wheelbase: 280.0cm 110.2in
Track F: 149.7cm 58.9in
Track R: 148.8cm 58.6in
Length: 476.5cm 187.6in
Width: 174.0cm 68.5in
Height: 149.0cm 58.7in
Ground clearance: 17.9cm 7.0in
Kerb weight: 1553.0kg 3420.7lb
Fuel: 79.1L 17.4gal 20.9galUS

2887 Mercedes-Benz

420SE
1986 Germany
138.0mph 222.0kmh
0-50mph 80.5kmh: 5.8secs
0-60mph 96.5kmh: 7.6secs
0-1/4 mile: 16.1secs
0-1km: 29.0secs
218.0bhp 162.6kW 221.0PS
@ 5200rpm
243.0lbft 329.3Nm @ 3750rpm
135.2bhp/ton 132.9bhp/tonne
51.9bhp/L 38.7kW/L 52.7PS/L
44.9ft/sec 13.7m/sec
29.8mph 47.9kmh/1000rpm
18.4mpg 15.3mpgUS 15.4L/100km
Petrol 4-stroke piston
4196cc 256.0cu in
Vee 8 fuel injection
Compression ratio: 9.0:1
Bore: 92.0mm 3.6in
Stroke: 78.9mm 3.1in
Valve type/No: Overhead 16
Transmission: Automatic
No. of forward speeds: 4
Wheels driven: Rear
Springs F/R: Coil/Coil
Brake system: PA
Brakes F/R: Disc/Disc
Steering: Recirculating ball PA
Wheelbase: 293.5cm 115.6in
Track F: 155.5cm 61.2in
Track R: 152.7cm 60.1in
Length: 502.0cm 197.6in
Width: 182.0cm 71.7in
Height: 143.7cm 56.6in
Ground clearance: 17.9cm 7.0in
Kerb weight: 1640.0kg 3612.3lb
Fuel: 102.8L 22.6gal 27.2galUS

2888 Mercedes-Benz

560SEC
1986 Germany
145.0mph 233.3kmh
0-60mph 96.5kmh: 7.0secs
0-1/4 mile: 15.5secs
238.0bhp 177.5kW 241.3PS
@ 5200rpm
287.0lbft 388.9Nm @ 3500rpm
140.7bhp/ton 138.3bhp/tonne
42.9bhp/L 32.0kW/L 43.5PS/L
53.9ft/sec 16.4m/sec
17.4mpg 14.5mpgUS 16.2L/100km
Petrol 4-stroke piston
5547cc 338.4cu in
Vee 8 fuel injection
Bore: 96.5mm 3.8in
Stroke: 94.8mm 3.7in
Valve type/No: Overhead 16
Transmission: Automatic
No. of forward speeds: 4
Wheels driven: Rear
Springs F/R: Coil/Coil
Brake system: PA ABS
Brakes F/R: Disc/Disc
Steering: Recirculating ball PA
Wheelbase: 284.5cm 112.0in
Track F: 155.4cm 61.2in
Track R: 152.7cm 60.1in
Length: 483.1cm 190.2in
Width: 182.9cm 72.0in
Height: 141.2cm 55.6in
Kerb weight: 1720.7kg 3790.0lb
Fuel: 90.1L 19.8gal 23.8galUS

2889 Mercedes-Benz

560SEL
1986 Germany
151.0mph 243.0kmh
0-50mph 80.5kmh: 5.5secs
0-60mph 96.5kmh: 7.1secs
0-1/4 mile: 15.8secs
0-1km: 28.4secs
295.0bhp 220.0kW 299.1PS
@ 5000rpm
335.0lbft 453.9Nm @ 3750rpm
168.5bhp/ton 165.7bhp/tonne
53.2bhp/L 39.7kW/L 53.9PS/L
51.8ft/sec 15.8m/sec
28.2mph 45.4kmh/1000rpm
18.6mpg 15.5mpgUS 15.2L/100km
Petrol 4-stroke piston
5547cc 338.0cu in
Vee 8 fuel injection
Compression ratio: 10.0:1
Bore: 96.5mm 3.8in
Stroke: 94.8mm 3.7in
Valve type/No: Overhead 16
Transmission: Automatic
No. of forward speeds: 4
Wheels driven: Rear
Springs F/R: Coil/Coil
Brake system: PA
Brakes F/R: Disc/Disc
Steering: Recirculating ball PA
Wheelbase: 307.0cm 120.9in
Track F: 155.5cm 61.2in
Track R: 152.7cm 60.1in
Length: 516.0cm 203.1in
Width: 200.6cm 79.0in
Height: 144.6cm 56.9in
Ground clearance: 15.1cm 5.9in
Kerb weight: 1780.0kg 3920.7lb
Fuel: 90.1L 19.8gal 23.8galUS

2890 Mercedes-Benz

560SL
1986 Germany
130.0mph 209.2kmh
0-60mph 96.5kmh: 7.5secs
0-1/4 mile: 15.8secs
227.0bhp 169.3kW 230.1PS
@ 4750rpm
279.0lbft 378.0Nm @ 3250rpm
138.5bhp/ton 136.2bhp/tonne
40.9bhp/L 30.5kW/L 41.5PS/L
49.2ft/sec 15.0m/sec
18.0mpg 15.0mpgUS 15.7L/100km
Petrol 4-stroke piston
5547cc 338.4cu in
Vee 8 fuel injection
Compression ratio: 9.0:1
Bore: 96.5mm 3.8in
Stroke: 94.8mm 3.7in
Valve type/No: Overhead 16
Transmission: Automatic
No. of forward speeds: 4
Wheels driven: Rear
Springs F/R: Coil/Coil
Brake system: PA ABS
Brakes F/R: Disc/Disc
Steering: Recirculating ball PA
Wheelbase: 245.6cm 96.7in
Track F: 146.3cm 57.6in
Track R: 146.6cm 57.7in
Length: 458.0cm 180.3in
Width: 179.1cm 70.5in
Height: 129.0cm 50.8in
Kerb weight: 1666.2kg 3670.0lb
Fuel: 85.2L 18.7gal 22.5galUS

2891 Mercedes-Benz

190E 2.6
1987 Germany
134.0mph 215.6kmh
0-50mph 80.5kmh: 6.2secs
0-60mph 96.5kmh: 8.3secs
0-1/4 mile: 16.5secs
0-1km: 30.1secs
166.0bhp 123.8kW 168.3PS
@ 5800rpm
168.0lbft 227.6Nm @ 4600rpm
134.5bhp/ton 132.3bhp/tonne
63.9bhp/L 47.6kW/L 64.8PS/L
50.9ft/sec 15.5m/sec
23.2mph 37.3kmh/1000rpm
21.0mpg 17.5mpgUS 13.5L/100km
Petrol 4-stroke piston
2599cc 159.0cu in
In-line 6 fuel injection
Compression ratio: 9.2:1
Bore: 82.9mm 3.3in
Stroke: 80.2mm 3.2in
Valve type/No: Overhead 12
Transmission: Automatic
No. of forward speeds: 4
Wheels driven: Rear
Springs F/R: Coil/Coil
Brake system: PA
Brakes F/R: Disc/Disc
Steering: Recirculating ball PA
Wheelbase: 266.5cm 104.9in
Track F: 142.9cm 56.3in
Track R: 142.9cm 56.3in
Length: 443.0cm 174.4in
Width: 170.6cm 67.2in
Height: 136.1cm 53.6in
Ground clearance: 15.5cm 6.1in
Kerb weight: 1255.0kg 2764.3lb
Fuel: 55.1L 12.1gal 14.5galUS

2892 Mercedes-Benz

300CE
1987 Germany
141.0mph 226.9kmh
0-50mph 80.5kmh: 5.6secs
0-60mph 96.5kmh: 7.5secs
0-1/4 mile: 16.0secs
0-1km: 29.0secs
188.0bhp 140.2kW 190.6PS
@ 5700rpm
191.6lbft 259.6Nm @ 4400rpm
130.1bhp/ton 127.9bhp/tonne
63.5bhp/L 47.3kW/L 64.3PS/L
50.0ft/sec 15.3m/sec
23.3mph 37.5kmh/1000rpm
21.4mpg 17.8mpgUS 13.2L/100km
Petrol 4-stroke piston
2962cc 181.0cu in
In-line 6 fuel injection
Compression ratio: 9.2:1
Bore: 88.5mm 3.5in
Stroke: 80.3mm 3.2in
Valve type/No: Overhead 12
Transmission: Automatic
No. of forward speeds: 4
Wheels driven: Rear
Springs F/R: Coil/Coil
Brake system: PA ABS
Brakes F/R: Disc/Disc
Steering: Recirculating ball PA
Wheelbase: 271.5cm 106.9in
Track F: 149.7cm 58.9in
Track R: 148.8cm 58.6in
Length: 465.5cm 183.3in
Width: 188.4cm 74.2in
Height: 141.0cm 55.5in
Ground clearance: 19.0cm 7.5in
Kerb weight: 1470.0kg 3237.9lb
Fuel: 70.1L 15.4gal 18.5galUS

2893 Mercedes-Benz

300TD
1987 Germany
115.0mph 185.0kmh
0-50mph 80.5kmh: 7.2secs
0-60mph 96.5kmh: 10.3secs
0-1/4 mile: 17.5secs
143.0bhp 106.6kW 145.0PS
@ 4600rpm
195.0lbft 264.2Nm @ 2400rpm
86.2bhp/ton 84.8bhp/tonne
47.7bhp/L 35.6kW/L 48.4PS/L
42.3ft/sec 12.9m/sec
26.4mpg 22.0mpgUS 10.7L/100km
Diesel 4-stroke piston
2996cc 182.8cu in turbocharged
In-line 6 fuel injection
Compression ratio: 22.0:1
Bore: 87.0mm 3.4in
Stroke: 84.0mm 3.3in
Valve type/No: Overhead 12
Transmission: Automatic
No. of forward speeds: 4
Wheels driven: Rear
Springs F/R: Coil/Coil
Brake system: PA ABS
Brakes F/R: /Disc
Steering: Recirculating ball PA
Wheelbase: 279.9cm 110.2in
Track F: 149.6cm 58.9in
Track R: 148.8cm 58.6in
Length: 478.0cm 188.2in
Width: 174.0cm 68.5in
Height: 151.9cm 59.8in
Kerb weight: 1686.6kg 3715.0lb
Fuel: 71.9L 15.8gal 19.0galUS

2894 Mercedes-Benz

420SEL
1987 Germany
131.0mph 210.8kmh
0-50mph 80.5kmh: 6.7secs
0-60mph 96.5kmh: 8.7secs
0-1/4 mile: 16.7secs
201.0bhp 149.9kW 203.8PS
@ 5200rpm
228.0lbft 308.9Nm @ 3600rpm
115.9bhp/ton 114.0bhp/tonne
47.9bhp/L 35.7kW/L 48.6PS/L
44.9ft/sec 13.7m/sec
19.2mpg 16.0mpgUS 14.7L/100km
Petrol 4-stroke piston
4196cc 256.0cu in
Vee 8 fuel injection
Compression ratio: 9.0:1
Bore: 92.0mm 3.6in
Stroke: 78.9mm 3.1in
Valve type/No: Overhead 16
Transmission: Automatic
No. of forward speeds: 4
Wheels driven: Rear
Springs F/R: Coil/Coil
Brake system: PA ABS
Brakes F/R: Disc/Disc
Steering: Recirculating ball PA
Wheelbase: 307.6cm 121.1in
Track F: 155.4cm 61.2in
Track R: 152.7cm 60.1in
Length: 528.6cm 208.1in
Width: 182.1cm 71.7in
Height: 144.0cm 56.7in
Kerb weight: 1763.8kg 3885.0lb
Fuel: 90.1L 19.8gal 23.8galUS

2895 Mercedes-Benz

560SEC Cabriolet Straman
1987 Germany
146.0mph 234.9kmh
0-60mph 96.5kmh: 6.9secs
0-1/4 mile: 15.4secs
238.0bhp 177.5kW 241.3PS
@ 4800rpm
287.0lbft 388.9Nm @ 3500rpm
134.1bhp/ton 131.9bhp/tonne
42.9bhp/L 32.0kW/L 43.5PS/L
49.7ft/sec 15.2m/sec
Petrol 4-stroke piston
5547cc 338.4cu in
Vee 8 fuel injection
Compression ratio: 9.0:1
Bore: 96.5mm 3.8in
Stroke: 94.8mm 3.7in
Valve type/No: Overhead 16
Transmission: Automatic
No. of forward speeds: 4
Wheels driven: Rear
Springs F/R: Coil/Coil
Brake system: PA ABS
Brakes F/R: Disc/Disc
Steering: Recirculating ball PA
Wheelbase: 284.5cm 112.0in
Track F: 155.4cm 61.2in
Track R: 152.7cm 60.1in
Length: 506.0cm 199.2in
Width: 182.9cm 72.0in
Height: 139.7cm 55.0in
Kerb weight: 1804.6kg 3975.0lb
Fuel: 90.1L 19.8gal 23.8galUS

2896 Mercedes-Benz

260E Auto
1988 Germany
134.0mph 215.6kmh
0-50mph 80.5kmh: 6.7secs
0-60mph 96.5kmh: 8.8secs
0-1/4 mile: 16.9secs
0-1km: 30.5secs
166.0bhp 123.8kW 168.3PS
@ 5800rpm
168.3lbft 228.0Nm @ 4600rpm
118.6bhp/ton 116.6bhp/tonne
63.9bhp/L 47.6kW/L 64.8PS/L
50.9ft/sec 15.5m/sec
21.9mph 35.2kmh/1000rpm
23.1mpg 19.2mpgUS 12.2L/100km
Petrol 4-stroke piston
2599cc 159.0cu in
In-line 6 fuel injection
Compression ratio: 9.2:1
Bore: 82.9mm 3.3in
Stroke: 80.2mm 3.2in
Valve type/No: Overhead 12
Transmission: Automatic
No. of forward speeds: 4
Wheels driven: Rear
Springs F/R: Coil/Coil
Brake system: PA ABS
Brakes F/R: Disc/Disc
Steering: Recirculating ball PA
Wheelbase: 280.0cm 110.2in
Track F: 149.7cm 58.9in
Track R: 148.8cm 58.6in
Length: 474.0cm 186.6in
Width: 188.4cm 74.2in
Height: 144.6cm 56.9in
Ground clearance: 17.9cm 7.0in
Kerb weight: 1423.0kg 3134.4lb
Fuel: 70.1L 15.4gal 18.5galUS

2897 Mercedes-Benz

300CE
1988 Germany
137.0mph 220.4kmh
0-60mph 96.5kmh: 8.0secs
177.0bhp 132.0kW 179.4PS
@ 5700rpm
188.0lbft 254.7Nm @ 4400rpm
119.8bhp/ton 117.8bhp/tonne
59.8bhp/L 44.6kW/L 60.6PS/L
50.0ft/sec 15.3m/sec
Petrol 4-stroke piston
2962cc 180.7cu in
In-line 6 fuel injection
Compression ratio: 9.2:1
Bore: 88.5mm 3.5in
Stroke: 80.3mm 3.2in
Valve type/No: Overhead 12
Transmission: Automatic
No. of forward speeds: 4
Wheels driven: Rear
Springs F/R: Coil/Coil
Brake system: PA ABS
Brakes F/R: Disc/Disc
Steering: Recirculating ball PA
Wheelbase: 271.5cm 106.9in
Track F: 149.6cm 58.9in
Track R: 148.8cm 58.6in
Length: 467.1cm 183.9in
Width: 174.0cm 68.5in
Height: 141.0cm 55.5in
Kerb weight: 1502.7kg 3310.0lb
Fuel: 70.0L 15.4gal 18.5galUS

2898 Mercedes-Benz

300E 4Matic
1988 Germany
136.0mph 218.8kmh
0-50mph 80.5kmh: 6.3secs
0-60mph 96.5kmh: 8.3secs
0-1/4 mile: 16.3secs
0-1km: 29.6secs
188.0bhp 140.2kW 190.6PS
@ 5700rpm
191.9lbft 260.0Nm @ 4400rpm
122.7bhp/ton 120.7bhp/tonne
63.5bhp/L 47.3kW/L 64.3PS/L
50.0ft/sec 15.2m/sec
23.5mph 37.8kmh/1000rpm
18.6mpg 15.5mpgUS 15.2L/100km
Petrol 4-stroke piston
2962cc 181.0cu in
In-line 6 fuel injection
Compression ratio: 9.2:1
Bore: 88.5mm 3.5in
Stroke: 80.2mm 3.2in
Valve type/No: Overhead 12
Transmission: Automatic
No. of forward speeds: 4
Wheels driven: Rear
Springs F/R: Coil/Coil
Brake system: PA ABS
Brakes F/R: Disc/Disc
Steering: Recirculating ball PA
Wheelbase: 280.0cm 110.2in
Track F: 149.7cm 58.9in
Track R: 148.8cm 58.6in
Length: 474.0cm 186.6in
Width: 188.4cm 74.2in
Height: 144.6cm 56.9in
Ground clearance: 17.9cm 7.0in
Kerb weight: 1558.0kg 3431.7lb
Fuel: 70.1L 15.4gal 18.5galUS

2899 Mercedes-Benz

300E AMG Hammer
1988 Germany
183.0mph 294.4kmh
0-60mph 96.5kmh: 5.2secs
0-1/4 mile: 13.6secs
375.0bhp 279.6kW 380.2PS
@ 5500rpm
407.0lbft 551.5Nm @ 4000rpm
231.1bhp/ton 227.2bhp/tonne
63.0bhp/L 47.0kW/L 63.9PS/L
57.0ft/sec 17.4m/sec
Petrol 4-stroke piston
5953cc 363.2cu in
Vee 8 fuel injection
Compression ratio: 9.8:1
Bore: 100.0mm 3.9in
Stroke: 94.8mm 3.7in
Valve type/No: Overhead 32
Transmission: Automatic
No. of forward speeds: 4
Wheels driven: Rear
Springs F/R: Coil/Coil
Brake system: PA ABS
Brakes F/R: Disc/Disc
Steering: Recirculating ball PA
Wheelbase: 279.9cm 110.2in
Track F: 149.6cm 58.9in
Track R: 148.8cm 58.6in
Length: 474.0cm 186.6in
Width: 174.0cm 68.5in
Height: 137.4cm 54.1in
Kerb weight: 1650.3kg 3635.0lb
Fuel: 70.0L 15.4gal 18.5galUS

2900 Mercedes-Benz

190
1989 Germany
110.0mph 177.0kmh
0-50mph 80.5kmh: 8.0secs
0-60mph 96.5kmh: 11.2secs
0-1/4 mile: 17.8secs
0-1km: 33.2secs
105.0bhp 78.3kW 106.5PS
@ 5200rpm
125.5lbft 170.0Nm @ 2500rpm
94.5bhp/ton 92.9bhp/tonne
52.6bhp/L 39.2kW/L 53.3PS/L
45.5ft/sec 13.9m/sec
26.1mph 42.0kmh/1000rpm
28.0mpg 23.3mpgUS 10.1L/100km
Petrol 4-stroke piston
1997cc 122.0cu in
In-line 4 1 Carburettor
Compression ratio: 9.1:1
Bore: 89.0mm 3.5in
Stroke: 80.0mm 3.1in
Valve type/No: Overhead 8
Transmission: Manual
No. of forward speeds: 5
Wheels driven: Rear
Springs F/R: Coil/Coil
Brake system: PA ABS
Brakes F/R: Disc/Disc
Steering: Recirculating ball PA
Wheelbase: 266.5cm 104.9in
Track F: 143.7cm 56.6in
Track R: 141.8cm 55.8in
Length: 442.0cm 174.0in
Width: 183.5cm 72.2in
Height: 139.0cm 54.7in
Ground clearance: 15.5cm 6.1in
Kerb weight: 1130.0kg 2489.0lb
Fuel: 55.1L 12.1gal 14.5galUS

2901 Mercedes-Benz

190E 2.5-16
1989 Germany
144.0mph 231.7kmh
0-50mph 80.5kmh: 5.4secs
0-60mph 96.5kmh: 7.2secs
0-1/4 mile: 15.1secs
0-1km: 28.3secs
197.0bhp 146.9kW 199.7PS
@ 6200rpm
176.4lbft 239.0Nm @ 4500rpm
147.3bhp/ton 144.8bhp/tonne
78.9bhp/L 58.8kW/L 80.0PS/L
59.2ft/sec 18.0m/sec
22.5mph 36.2kmh/1000rpm
22.0mpg 18.3mpgUS 12.8L/100km
Petrol 4-stroke piston
2498cc 152.0cu in
In-line 4 fuel injection
Compression ratio: 9.7:1
Bore: 95.5mm 3.8in
Stroke: 87.3mm 3.4in
Valve type/No: Overhead 16
Transmission: Manual
No. of forward speeds: 5
Wheels driven: Rear
Springs F/R: Coil/Coil
Brake system: PA ABS
Brakes F/R: Disc/Disc
Steering: Recirculating ball PA
Wheelbase: 226.5cm 89.2in
Track F: 144.6cm 56.9in
Track R: 142.9cm 56.3in
Length: 443.0cm 174.4in
Width: 160.6cm 63.2in
Height: 136.1cm 53.6in
Ground clearance: 15.5cm 6.1in
Kerb weight: 1360.0kg 2995.6lb
Fuel: 70.1L 15.4gal 18.5galUS

2902 Mercedes-Benz

190E 2.6
1989 Germany
129.0mph 207.6kmh
0-60mph 96.5kmh: 8.7secs
0-1/4 mile: 16.8secs
158.0bhp 117.8kW 160.2PS
@ 5800rpm
162.0lbft 219.5Nm @ 4600rpm
117.4bhp/ton 115.4bhp/tonne
60.8bhp/L 45.3kW/L 61.6PS/L
50.9ft/sec 15.5m/sec
24.6mpg 20.5mpgUS 11.5L/100km
Petrol 4-stroke piston
2599cc 158.6cu in
In-line 6 fuel injection
Compression ratio: 9.2:1
Bore: 82.9mm 3.3in
Stroke: 80.3mm 3.2in
Valve type/No: Overhead 12
Transmission: Automatic
No. of forward speeds: 4
Wheels driven: Rear
Springs F/R: Coil/Coil
Brake system: PA ABS
Brakes F/R: Disc/Disc
Steering: Recirculating ball PA
Wheelbase: 266.4cm 104.9in
Track F: 143.8cm 56.6in
Track R: 141.7cm 55.8in
Length: 444.8cm 175.1in
Width: 168.9cm 66.5in
Height: 138.9cm 54.7in
Kerb weight: 1368.8kg 3015.0lb
Fuel: 54.9L 12.1gal 14.5galUS

2903 Mercedes-Benz

190E AMG Baby Hammer
1989 Germany
140.0mph 225.3kmh
0-60mph 96.5kmh: 7.0secs
0-1/4 mile: 15.5secs
234.0bhp 174.5kW 237.2PS
@ 5750rpm
234.0lbft 317.1Nm @ 4500rpm
184.9bhp/ton 181.8bhp/tonne
73.0bhp/L 54.4kW/L 74.0PS/L
52.9ft/sec 16.1m/sec
Petrol 4-stroke piston
3205cc 195.5cu in
In-line 6 fuel injection
Compression ratio: 10.0:1
Bore: 90.0mm 3.5in
Stroke: 84.0mm 3.3in
Valve type/No: Overhead 12
Transmission: Automatic
No. of forward speeds: 4
Wheels driven: Rear
Springs F/R: Coil/Coil
Brake system: PA ABS
Brakes F/R: Disc/Disc
Steering: Recirculating ball PA
Wheelbase: 266.4cm 104.9in
Track F: 145.5cm 57.3in
Track R: 143.0cm 56.3in
Length: 444.8cm 175.1in
Width: 167.9cm 66.1in
Height: 135.9cm 53.5in
Kerb weight: 1287.1kg 2835.0lb
Fuel: 61.7L 13.6gal 16.3galUS

2904 Mercedes-Benz

200E Automatic
1989 Germany
120.0mph 193.1kmh
0-50mph 80.5kmh: 8.9secs
0-60mph 96.5kmh: 12.3secs
0-1/4 mile: 18.5secs
0-1km: 33.6secs
122.0bhp 91.0kW 123.7PS
@ 5100rpm
131.4lbft 178.0Nm @ 3500rpm
89.3bhp/ton 87.8bhp/tonne
61.1bhp/L 45.6kW/L 61.9PS/L
44.8ft/sec 13.6m/sec
20.7mph 33.3kmh/1000rpm
23.3mpg 19.4mpgUS 12.1L/100km
Petrol 4-stroke piston
1997cc 122.0cu in
In-line 4 fuel injection
Compression ratio: 9.1:1
Bore: 89.0mm 3.5in
Stroke: 80.2mm 3.2in
Valve type/No: Overhead 8
Transmission: Automatic
No. of forward speeds: 4
Wheels driven: Rear
Springs F/R: Coil/Coil
Brake system: PA ABS
Brakes F/R: Disc/Disc
Steering: Recirculating ball PA
Wheelbase: 280.0cm 110.2in
Track F: 149.7cm 58.9in
Track R: 148.8cm 58.6in
Length: 447.0cm 176.0in
Width: 188.4cm 74.2in
Height: 144.6cm 56.9in
Ground clearance: 17.9cm 7.0in
Kerb weight: 1390.0kg 3061.7lb
Fuel: 70.1L 15.4gal 18.5galUS

2905 Mercedes-Benz

300CE Cabriolet Straman
1989 Germany
137.0mph 220.4kmh
0-60mph 96.5kmh: 8.5secs
177.0bhp 132.0kW 179.4PS
@ 5700rpm
188.0lbft 254.7Nm @ 4400rpm
120.1bhp/ton 118.1bhp/tonne
59.8bhp/L 44.6kW/L 60.6PS/L
50.0ft/sec 15.3m/sec
Petrol 4-stroke piston
2962cc 180.7cu in
In-line 6 fuel injection
Compression ratio: 9.2:1
Bore: 88.5mm 3.5in
Stroke: 80.3mm 3.2in
Valve type/No: Overhead 12
Transmission: Automatic
No. of forward speeds: 4
Wheels driven: Rear
Springs F/R: Coil/Coil
Brake system: PA ABS
Brakes F/R: Disc/Disc
Steering: Recirculating ball PA
Wheelbase: 271.5cm 106.9in
Track F: 149.6cm 58.9in
Track R: 148.8cm 58.6in
Length: 467.1cm 183.9in
Width: 174.0cm 68.5in
Height: 141.0cm 55.5in
Kerb weight: 1498.2kg 3300.0lb
Fuel: 79.1L 17.4gal 20.9galUS

2906 Mercedes-Benz

300E
1989 Germany
140.0mph 225.3kmh
0-60mph 96.5kmh: 8.3secs
0-1/4 mile: 16.4secs
177.0bhp 132.0kW 179.4PS
@ 5700rpm
188.0lbft 254.7Nm @ 4400rpm
121.4bhp/ton 119.4bhp/tonne
59.8bhp/L 44.6kW/L 60.6PS/L
50.0ft/sec 15.3m/sec

24.6mpg 20.5mpgUS 11.5L/100km
Petrol 4-stroke piston
2962cc 180.7cu in
In-line 6 fuel injection
Compression ratio: 9.2:1
Bore: 88.5mm 3.5in
Stroke: 80.3mm 3.2in
Valve type/No: Overhead 12
Transmission: Automatic
No. of forward speeds: 4
Wheels driven: Rear
Springs F/R: Coil/Coil
Brake system: PA ABS
Brakes F/R: Disc/Disc
Steering: Recirculating ball PA
Wheelbase: 279.9cm 110.2in
Track F: 149.6cm 58.9in
Track R: 148.8cm 58.6in
Length: 475.5cm 187.2in
Width: 174.0cm 68.5in
Height: 144.5cm 56.9in
Kerb weight: 1482.3kg 3265.0lb
Fuel: 70.0L 15.4gal 18.5galUS

2907 Mercedes-Benz

560SL
1989 Germany
137.0mph 220.4kmh
0-60mph 96.5kmh: 6.8secs
0-1/4 mile: 15.2secs
227.0bhp 169.3kW 230.1PS
@ 4750rpm
279.0lbft 378.0Nm @ 3250rpm
142.4bhp/ton 140.1bhp/tonne
40.9bhp/L 30.5kW/L 41.5PS/L
49.2ft/sec 15.0m/sec
19.8mpg 16.5mpgUS 14.3L/100km
Petrol 4-stroke piston
5547cc 338.4cu in
Vee 8 fuel injection
Compression ratio: 9.0:1
Bore: 96.5mm 3.8in
Stroke: 94.8mm 3.7in
Valve type/No: Overhead 16
Transmission: Automatic
No. of forward speeds: 4
Wheels driven: Rear
Springs F/R: Coil/Coil
Brake system: PA ABS
Brakes F/R: Disc/Disc
Steering: Recirculating ball PA
Wheelbase: 245.6cm 96.7in
Track F: 146.6cm 57.7in
Track R: 146.6cm 57.7in
Length: 458.0cm 180.3in
Width: 179.1cm 70.5in
Height: 129.8cm 51.1in
Kerb weight: 1620.8kg 3570.0lb
Fuel: 85.2L 18.7gal 22.5galUS

2908 Mercedes-Benz

190E 2.5-16 Evolution II
1990 Germany
155.0mph 249.4kmh
0-60mph 96.5kmh: 7.1secs
235.0bhp 175.2kW 238.3PS
@ 7200rpm
181.0lbft 245.3Nm @ 5000rpm
178.1bhp/ton 175.2bhp/tonne
95.4bhp/L 71.1kW/L 96.7PS/L
65.2ft/sec 19.9m/sec
Petrol 4-stroke piston
2463cc 150.3cu in
In-line 4 fuel injection
Compression ratio: 10.5:1
Bore: 97.3mm 3.8in
Stroke: 82.8mm 3.3in
Valve type/No: Overhead 16
Transmission: Manual
No. of forward speeds: 5
Wheels driven: Rear
Springs F/R: Coil/Coil
Brake system: PA ABS
Brakes F/R: Disc/Disc
Steering: Recirculating ball PA
Wheelbase: 266.4cm 104.9in
Track F: 147.6cm 58.1in
Track R: 147.6cm 58.1in
Length: 452.9cm 178.3in
Width: 172.0cm 67.7in
Height: 134.1cm 52.8in
Kerb weight: 1341.6kg 2955.0lb
Fuel: 70.0L 15.4gal 18.5galUS

2909 Mercedes-Benz

300CE
1990 Germany
151.0mph 243.0kmh
0-60mph 96.5kmh: 8.5secs
0-1/4 mile: 16.6secs
217.0bhp 161.8kW 220.0PS
@ 6400rpm
195.0lbft 264.2Nm @ 4600rpm
139.3bhp/ton 137.0bhp/tonne
73.3bhp/L 54.6kW/L 74.3PS/L
56.2ft/sec 17.1m/sec
23.4mpg 19.5mpgUS 12.1L/100km
Petrol 4-stroke piston
2962cc 180.7cu in
In-line 6 fuel injection
Compression ratio: 10.0:1
Bore: 88.5mm 3.5in
Stroke: 80.3mm 3.2in
Valve type/No: Overhead 24
Transmission: Automatic
No. of forward speeds: 4
Wheels driven: Rear
Springs F/R: Coil/Coil
Brake system: PA ABS
Brakes F/R: Disc/Disc
Steering: Recirculating ball PA
Wheelbase: 271.5cm 106.9in
Track F: 150.1cm 59.1in
Track R: 149.1cm 58.7in
Length: 467.1cm 183.9in
Width: 174.0cm 68.5in
Height: 139.4cm 54.9in
Kerb weight: 1584.5kg 3490.0lb

2910 Mercedes-Benz

300CE AMG Hammer
1990 Germany
185.0mph 297.7kmh
0-60mph 96.5kmh: 5.0secs
0-1/4 mile: 13.2secs
375.0bhp 279.6kW 380.2PS
@ 5500rpm
407.0lbft 551.5Nm @ 4000rpm
226.4bhp/ton 222.6bhp/tonne
63.0bhp/L 47.0kW/L 63.9PS/L
57.0ft/sec 17.4m/sec
Petrol 4-stroke piston
5953cc 363.2cu in
Vee 8 fuel injection
Compression ratio: 9.2:1
Bore: 100.1mm 3.9in
Stroke: 94.7mm 3.7in
Valve type/No: Overhead 32
Transmission: Automatic
No. of forward speeds: 4
Wheels driven: Rear
Springs F/R: Coil/Coil
Brake system: PA ABS
Brakes F/R: Disc/Disc
Steering: Recirculating ball PA
Wheelbase: 271.5cm 106.9in
Track F: 151.1cm 59.5in
Track R: 150.1cm 59.1in
Length: 466.1cm 183.5in
Width: 174.0cm 68.5in
Height: 136.9cm 53.9in
Kerb weight: 1684.3kg 3710.0lb
Fuel: 70.0L 15.4gal 18.5galUS

2911 Mercedes-Benz

300D
1990 Germany
115.0mph 185.0kmh
0-50mph 80.5kmh: 10.9secs
0-60mph 96.5kmh: 15.5secs
0-1/4 mile: 20.5secs
0-1km: 36.8secs
109.0bhp 81.3kW 110.5PS
@ 4600rpm
136.5lbft 185.0Nm @ 2800rpm
74.1bhp/ton 72.9bhp/tonne
36.8bhp/L 27.4kW/L 37.3PS/L
42.3ft/sec 12.9m/sec
25.0mph 40.2kmh/1000rpm
28.6mpg 23.8mpgUS 9.9L/100km
Diesel 4-stroke piston
2962cc 181.0cu in
In-line 6 fuel injection
Compression ratio: 22.0:1
Bore: 87.0mm 3.4in
Stroke: 84.0mm 3.3in
Valve type/No: Overhead 12
Transmission: Automatic
No. of forward speeds: 4
Wheels driven: Rear
Springs F/R: Coil/Coil
Brake system: PA ABS
Brakes F/R: Disc/Disc
Steering: Recirculating ball PA
Wheelbase: 280.0cm 110.2in
Track F: 149.7cm 58.9in
Track R: 148.8cm 58.6in
Length: 474.0cm 186.6in
Width: 188.4cm 74.2in
Height: 144.6cm 56.9in
Ground clearance: 17.9cm 7.0in
Kerb weight: 1495.0kg 3292.9lb
Fuel: 70.1L 15.4gal 18.5galUS

2912 Mercedes-Benz

300E-24
1990 Germany
148.0mph 238.1kmh
0-50mph 80.5kmh: 6.0secs
0-60mph 96.5kmh: 7.8secs
0-1/4 mile: 16.0secs
0-1km: 28.8secs
231.0bhp 172.3kW 234.2PS
@ 6300rpm
200.0lbft 271.0Nm @ 4600rpm
152.5bhp/ton 150.0bhp/tonne
78.0bhp/L 58.2kW/L 79.1PS/L
55.3ft/sec 16.8m/sec
21.9mph 35.2kmh/1000rpm
18.5mpg 15.4mpgUS 15.3L/100km
Petrol 4-stroke piston
2962cc 181.0cu in
In-line 6 fuel injection
Compression ratio: 10.1:1
Bore: 88.5mm 3.5in
Stroke: 80.2mm 3.2in
Valve type/No: Overhead 24
Transmission: Manual
No. of forward speeds: 5
Wheels driven: Rear
Springs F/R: Coil/Coil
Brake system: PA ABS
Brakes F/R: Disc/Disc
Steering: Recirculating ball PA
Wheelbase: 280.0cm 110.2in
Track F: 149.7cm 58.9in
Track R: 148.8cm 58.6in
Length: 474.0cm 186.6in
Width: 188.4cm 74.2in
Height: 144.6cm 56.9in
Ground clearance: 17.9cm 7.0in
Kerb weight: 1540.0kg 3392.1lb
Fuel: 70.1L 15.4gal 18.5galUS

2913 Mercedes-Benz

500SL
1990 Germany
160.0mph 257.4kmh
0-50mph 80.5kmh: 4.7secs
0-60mph 96.5kmh: 5.9secs
0-1/4 mile: 14.4secs
0-1km: 25.3secs
326.0bhp 243.1kW 330.5PS
@ 5500rpm
339.5lbft 460.0Nm @ 4000rpm
175.2bhp/ton 172.3bhp/tonne
65.5bhp/L 48.9kW/L 66.5PS/L
51.2ft/sec 15.6m/sec
28.3mph 45.5kmh/1000rpm
16.2mpg 13.5mpgUS 17.4L/100km
Petrol 4-stroke piston
4973cc 303.0cu in
Vee 8 fuel injection
Compression ratio: 10.0:1
Bore: 96.5mm 3.8in
Stroke: 85.0mm 3.3in
Valve type/No: Overhead 32
Transmission: Automatic
No. of forward speeds: 5
Wheels driven: Rear
Springs F/R: Coil/Coil
Brake system: PA ABS
Brakes F/R: Disc/Disc
Steering: Recirculating ball PA
Wheelbase: 251.5cm 99.0in
Track F: 153.5cm 60.4in
Track R: 152.3cm 60.0in
Length: 447.0cm 176.0in
Width: 181.2cm 71.3in
Height: 130.3cm 51.3in
Ground clearance: 15.3cm 6.0in
Kerb weight: 1892.0kg 4167.4lb
Fuel: 90.1L 19.8gal 23.8galUS

2914 Mercedes-Benz

190E 1.8 Auto
1991 Germany
120.0mph 193.1kmh
0-50mph 80.5kmh: 8.8secs
0-60mph 96.5kmh: 12.3secs
0-1/4 mile: 19.1secs
0-1km: 34.4secs
109.0bhp 81.3kW 110.5PS
@ 5500rpm
110.7lbft 150.0Nm @ 3700rpm
90.5bhp/ton 89.0bhp/tonne
60.7bhp/L 45.2kW/L 61.5PS/L
43.2ft/sec 13.2m/sec
20.4mph 32.8kmh/1000rpm
26.1mpg 21.7mpgUS 10.8L/100km
Petrol 4-stroke piston
1797cc 110.0cu in
In-line 4 fuel injection
Compression ratio: 9.1:1
Bore: 89.0mm 3.5in
Stroke: 72.0mm 2.8in
Valve type/No: Overhead 8
Transmission: Automatic
No. of forward speeds: 4
Wheels driven: Rear
Springs F/R: Coil/Coil
Brake system: PA
Brakes F/R: Disc/Disc
Steering: Recirculating ball PA
Wheelbase: 266.4cm 104.9in
Track F: 143.8cm 56.6in
Track R: 141.7cm 55.8in
Length: 442.0cm 174.0in
Width: 183.4cm 72.2in
Height: 138.9cm 54.7in
Ground clearance: 15.5cm 6.1in
Kerb weight: 1225.0kg 2698.2lb
Fuel: 55.1L 12.1gal 14.5galUS

2915 Mercedes-Benz

190E 2.3
1991 Germany
0-60mph 96.5kmh: 11.4secs
0-1/4 mile: 18.4secs
130.0bhp 96.9kW 131.8PS
@ 5100rpm
146.0lbft 197.8Nm @ 3500rpm
97.5bhp/ton 95.9bhp/tonne
56.5bhp/L 42.2kW/L 57.3PS/L
44.8ft/sec 13.6m/sec
30.4mpg 25.3mpgUS 9.3L/100km
Petrol 4-stroke piston
2299cc 140.3cu in
In-line 4
Bore: 95.5mm 3.8in
Stroke: 80.3mm 3.2in
Valve type/No: Overhead 8
Transmission: Manual
No. of forward speeds: 5
Wheels driven: Rear
Springs F/R: Coil/Coil
Brake system: ABS
Brakes F/R: Disc/Disc
Steering: Recirculating ball PA
Wheelbase: 266.4cm 104.9in
Track F: 143.8cm 56.6in
Track R: 141.7cm 55.8in
Length: 444.8cm 175.1in
Width: 167.9cm 66.1in
Height: 143.8cm 56.6in
Kerb weight: 1355.2kg 2985.0lb

2916 Mercedes-Benz

190E 2.5-16 Evolution II
1991 Germany
0-60mph 96.5kmh: 6.9secs
0-1/4 mile: 15.3secs
232.0bhp 173.0kW 235.2PS
@ 7200rpm
181.0lbft 245.3Nm @ 5000rpm
175.9bhp/ton 172.9bhp/tonne
94.2bhp/L 70.2kW/L 95.5PS/L
65.2ft/sec 19.9m/sec
21.6mpg 18.0mpgUS 13.1L/100km
Petrol 4-stroke piston
2463cc 150.3cu in
In-line 4 fuel injection
Compression ratio: 9.7:1
Bore: 97.3mm 3.8in
Stroke: 82.8mm 3.3in
Valve type/No: Overhead 16
Transmission: Manual
No. of forward speeds: 5
Wheels driven: Rear
Springs F/R: Coil/Coil
Brake system: PA ABS
Brakes F/R: Disc/Disc
Steering: Recirculating ball PA
Wheelbase: 266.4cm 104.9in
Track F: 147.6cm 58.1in
Track R: 147.6cm 58.1in

Length: 454.4cm 178.9in
Width: 172.0cm 67.7in
Height: 132.6cm 52.2in
Kerb weight: 1341.6kg 2955.0lb
Fuel: 70.0L 15.4gal 18.5galUS

2917 Mercedes-Benz

300SL-24 5-speed Auto
1991 Germany
135.0mph 217.2kmh
0-50mph 80.5kmh: 6.5secs
0-60mph 96.5kmh: 8.6secs
0-1/4 mile: 16.7secs
0-1km: 29.9secs
231.0bhp 172.3kW 234.2PS
@ 6300rpm
201.5lbft 273.0Nm @ 4600rpm
130.9bhp/ton 128.7bhp/tonne
78.0bhp/L 58.2kW/L 79.1PS/L
55.1ft/sec 16.8m/sec
28.9mph 46.5kmh/1000rpm
19.2mpg 16.0mpgUS 14.7L/100km
Petrol 4-stroke piston
2960cc 181.0cu in
In-line 6 fuel injection
Compression ratio: 10.0:1
Bore: 89.0mm 3.5in
Stroke: 80.0mm 3.1in
Valve type/No: Overhead 24
Transmission: Automatic
No. of forward speeds: 5
Wheels driven: Rear
Springs F/R: Coil/Coil
Brake system: PA ABS
Brakes F/R: Disc/Disc
Steering: Recirculating ball PA
Wheelbase: 251.5cm 99.0in
Track F: 153.4cm 60.4in
Track R: 152.1cm 59.9in
Length: 446.8cm 175.9in
Width: 181.1cm 71.3in
Height: 130.0cm 51.2in
Ground clearance: 15.2cm 6.0in
Kerb weight: 1795.0kg 3953.7lb
Fuel: 80.1L 17.6gal 21.1galUS

2918 Mercedes-Benz

400SE
1991 Germany
146.0mph 234.9kmh
0-50mph 80.5kmh: 6.4secs
0-60mph 96.5kmh: 8.4secs
0-1/4 mile: 16.5secs
0-1km: 29.6secs
286.0bhp 213.3kW 290.0PS
@ 5700rpm
302.0lbft 409.2Nm @ 3900rpm
137.2bhp/ton 134.9bhp/tonne
68.2bhp/L 50.8kW/L 69.1PS/L
49.2ft/sec 15.0m/sec
27.7mph 44.6kmh/1000rpm
14.6mpg 12.2mpgUS 19.3L/100km
Petrol 4-stroke piston
4196cc 256.0cu in
Vee 8 fuel injection
Compression ratio: 10.0:1
Bore: 92.0mm 3.6in
Stroke: 79.0mm 3.1in
Valve type/No: Overhead 32
Transmission: Automatic
No. of forward speeds: 4
Wheels driven: Rear
Springs F/R: Coil/Coil
Brake system: PA
Brakes F/R: Disc/Disc
Steering: Recirculating ball PA
Wheelbase: 303.8cm 119.6in
Track F: 160.0cm 63.0in
Track R: 157.2cm 61.9in
Length: 511.0cm 201.2in
Width: 188.5cm 74.2in
Height: 149.6cm 58.9in
Kerb weight: 2120.2kg 4670.0lb
Fuel: 100.1L 22.0gal 26.4galUS

2919 Mercedes-Benz

500E
1991 Germany
159.0mph 255.8kmh
0-50mph 80.5kmh: 4.9secs
0-60mph 96.5kmh: 6.3secs
0-1/4 mile: 14.7secs
0-1km: 26.3secs
326.0bhp 243.1kW 330.5PS
@ 5700rpm
354.0lbft 479.7Nm @ 3900rpm
191.7bhp/ton 188.5bhp/tonne
65.5bhp/L 48.9kW/L 66.5PS/L
53.0ft/sec 16.1m/sec
26.4mph 42.5kmh/1000rpm
16.5mpg 13.7mpgUS 17.1L/100km
Petrol 4-stroke piston
4973cc 303.4cu in
Vee 8 fuel injection
Compression ratio: 10.0:1
Bore: 97.0mm 3.8in
Stroke: 85.0mm 3.3in
Valve type/No: Overhead 32
Transmission: Automatic
No. of forward speeds: 4
Wheels driven: Rear
Springs F/R: Coil/Coil
Brake system: PA ABS
Brakes F/R: Disc/Disc
Steering: Rack & pinion PA
Wheelbase: 279.9cm 110.2in
Track F: 149.6cm 58.9in
Track R: 148.8cm 58.6in
Length: 474.0cm 186.6in
Width: 188.5cm 74.2in
Height: 144.5cm 56.9in
Ground clearance: 17.8cm 7.0in
Kerb weight: 1729.7kg 3810.0lb
Fuel: 90.1L 19.8gal 23.8galUS

2920 Mercedes-Benz

500SL
1991 Germany
155.0mph 249.4kmh
0-50mph 80.5kmh: 4.9secs
0-60mph 96.5kmh: 6.4secs
0-1/4 mile: 14.9secs
322.0bhp 240.1kW 326.5PS
@ 5500rpm
332.0lbft 449.9Nm @ 4000rpm
179.9bhp/ton 176.9bhp/tonne
64.7bhp/L 48.3kW/L 65.6PS/L
51.2ft/sec 15.6m/sec
19.2mpg 16.0mpgUS 14.7L/100km
Petrol 4-stroke piston
4973cc 303.4cu in
Vee 8 fuel injection
Compression ratio: 10.0:1
Bore: 96.5mm 3.8in
Stroke: 85.0mm 3.3in
Valve type/No: Overhead 32
Transmission: Automatic
No. of forward speeds: 4
Wheels driven: Rear
Springs F/R: Coil/Coil
Brake system: PA ABS
Brakes F/R: Disc/Disc
Steering: Recirculating ball PA
Wheelbase: 251.5cm 99.0in
Track F: 153.4cm 60.4in
Track R: 152.4cm 60.0in
Length: 447.0cm 176.0in
Width: 181.1cm 71.3in
Height: 128.8cm 50.7in
Kerb weight: 1820.5kg 4010.0lb
Fuel: 79.9L 17.6gal 21.1galUS

2921 Mercedes-Benz

G-Wagen 300 GD LWB
1991 Germany
84.0mph 135.2kmh
0-50mph 80.5kmh: 16.1secs
0-60mph 96.5kmh: 25.4secs
0-1/4 mile: 23.4secs
0-1km: 43.6secs
113.0bhp 84.3kW 114.6PS
@ 4600rpm
141.0lbft 191.0Nm @ 2900rpm
50.1bhp/ton 49.3bhp/tonne
37.7bhp/L 28.1kW/L 38.2PS/L
42.3ft/sec 12.9m/sec
20.5mph 33.0kmh/1000rpm
17.1mpg 14.2mpgUS 16.5L/100km
Diesel 4-stroke piston
2996cc 183.0cu in
In-line 6 fuel injection
Compression ratio: 22.0:1
Bore: 87.0mm 3.4in
Stroke: 84.0mm 3.3in
Valve type/No: Overhead 12
Transmission: Manual
No. of forward speeds: 5
Wheels driven: 4-wheel drive
Springs F/R: Coil/Coil
Brake system: PA ABS
Brakes F/R: Disc/Drum
Steering: Recirculating ball PA
Wheelbase: 285.0cm 112.2in
Track F: 142.5cm 56.1in
Track R: 142.5cm 56.1in
Length: 439.4cm 173.0in
Width: 169.9cm 66.9in
Height: 197.6cm 77.8in
Ground clearance: 20.8cm 8.2in
Kerb weight: 2293.0kg 5050.7lb
Fuel: 95.1L 20.9gal 25.1galUS

2922 Mercedes-Benz

500SEL
1992 Germany
155.0mph 249.4kmh
0-50mph 80.5kmh: 5.6secs
0-60mph 96.5kmh: 7.5secs
0-1/4 mile: 15.8secs
322.0bhp 240.1kW 326.5PS
@ 5700rpm
354.0lbft 479.7Nm @ 3900rpm
148.6bhp/ton 146.1bhp/tonne
64.7bhp/L 48.3kW/L 65.6PS/L
13.8mpg 11.5mpgUS 20.5L/100km
Petrol 4-stroke piston
4973cc 303.4cu in
Vee 8 fuel injection
Compression ratio: 10.0:1
Transmission: Automatic
No. of forward speeds: 4
Wheels driven: Rear
Springs F/R: Coil/Coil
Brake system: PA ABS
Brakes F/R: Disc/Disc
Steering: Recirculating ball PA
Wheelbase: 313.9cm 123.6in
Track F: 160.3cm 63.1in
Track R: 157.5cm 62.0in
Length: 521.2cm 205.2in
Width: 188.7cm 74.3in
Height: 149.6cm 58.9in
Ground clearance: 17.8cm 7.0in
Kerb weight: 2204.2kg 4855.0lb
Fuel: 99.9L 22.0gal 26.4galUS

2923 Mercedes-Benz

600SEL
1992 Germany
155.0mph 249.4kmh
0-60mph 96.5kmh: 6.1secs
408.0bhp 304.2kW 413.7PS
@ 5200rpm
428.0lbft 579.9Nm @ 3800rpm
189.2bhp/ton 186.1bhp/tonne
68.1bhp/L 50.8kW/L 69.1PS/L
45.6ft/sec 13.9m/sec
Petrol 4-stroke piston
5987cc 365.3cu in
Vee 12 fuel injection
Compression ratio: 10.0:1
Bore: 89.0mm 3.5in
Stroke: 80.2mm 3.2in
Valve type/No: Overhead 48
Transmission: Automatic
No. of forward speeds: 4
Wheels driven: Rear
Springs F/R: Coil/Coil
Brake system: ABS
Brakes F/R: Disc/Disc
Steering: Recirculating ball PA
Wheelbase: 313.9cm 123.6in
Track F: 160.3cm 63.1in
Track R: 157.5cm 62.0in
Length: 521.2cm 205.2in
Width: 188.7cm 74.3in
Height: 149.1cm 58.7in
Kerb weight: 2192.8kg 4830.0lb
Fuel: 112.4L 24.7gal 29.7galUS

2924 Mercury

Coupe
1949 USA
86.5mph 139.2kmh
0-50mph 80.5kmh: 12.3secs
0-60mph 96.5kmh: 19.2secs
110.0bhp 82.0kW 111.5PS
@ 3600rpm
200.0lbft 271.0Nm @ 2000rpm
69.7bhp/ton 68.5bhp/tonne
26.3bhp/L 19.6kW/L 26.6PS/L
40.0ft/sec 12.2m/sec
21.0mph 33.8kmh/1000rpm
15.0mpg 12.5mpgUS 18.8L/100km
Petrol 4-stroke piston
4185cc 255.3cu in
Vee 8 1 Carburettor
Compression ratio: 6.8:1
Bore: 81.0mm 3.2in
Stroke: 101.6mm 4.0in
Valve type/No: Side 16
Transmission: Manual
No. of forward speeds: 3
Wheels driven: Rear
Brakes F/R: Drum/Drum
Wheelbase: 299.7cm 118.0in
Track F: 148.6cm 58.5in
Track R: 152.4cm 60.0in
Length: 525.8cm 207.0in
Width: 194.3cm 76.5in
Height: 160.0cm 63.0in
Ground clearance: 19.6cm 7.7in
Kerb weight: 1604.9kg 3535.0lb
Fuel: 70.5L 15.5gal 18.6galUS

2925 Mercury

Comet
1960 USA
79.0mph 127.1kmh
0-50mph 80.5kmh: 13.6secs
0-60mph 96.5kmh: 21.0secs
0-1/4 mile: 21.5secs
90.0bhp 67.1kW 91.2PS
@ 4200rpm
138.0lbft 187.0Nm @ 2000rpm
79.8bhp/ton 78.5bhp/tonne
38.0bhp/L 28.4kW/L 38.6PS/L
29.2ft/sec 8.9m/sec
18.7mph 30.1kmh/1000rpm
Petrol 4-stroke piston
2366cc 144.4cu in
In-line 6 1 Carburettor
Compression ratio: 8.7:1
Bore: 88.9mm 3.5in
Stroke: 63.5mm 2.5in
Valve type/No: Overhead 12
Transmission: Automatic
No. of forward speeds: 2
Wheels driven: Rear
Wheelbase: 289.6cm 114.0in
Track F: 139.7cm 55.0in
Track R: 138.4cm 54.5in
Length: 495.0cm 194.9in
Width: 178.8cm 70.4in
Height: 138.4cm 54.5in
Kerb weight: 1146.3kg 2525.0lb

2926 Mercury

Comet
1961 USA
85.0mph 136.8kmh
0-50mph 80.5kmh: 10.7secs
0-60mph 96.5kmh: 15.2secs
0-1/4 mile: 20.2secs
101.0bhp 75.3kW 102.4PS
@ 4400rpm
156.0lbft 211.4Nm @ 2400rpm
92.0bhp/ton 90.4bhp/tonne
36.2bhp/L 27.0kW/L 36.7PS/L
35.9ft/sec 11.0m/sec
20.0mph 32.2kmh/1000rpm
Petrol 4-stroke piston
2788cc 170.1cu in
In-line 6
Compression ratio: 8.7:1
Bore: 88.9mm 3.5in
Stroke: 74.7mm 2.9in
Valve type/No: Overhead 12
Transmission: Automatic
No. of forward speeds: 2
Wheels driven: Rear
Brakes F/R: Drum/Drum
Wheelbase: 289.6cm 114.0in
Track F: 139.7cm 55.0in
Track R: 138.4cm 54.5in
Length: 495.3cm 195.0in
Width: 178.8cm 70.4in
Height: 138.4cm 54.5in
Ground clearance: 15.2cm 6.0in
Kerb weight: 1116.8kg 2460.0lb

2927 Mercury

Comet 170
1961 USA
89.0mph 143.2kmh
0-50mph 80.5kmh: 13.2secs
0-60mph 96.5kmh: 19.2secs
0-1/4 mile: 20.7secs
101.0bhp 75.3kW 102.4PS
@ 4400rpm
156.0lbft 211.4Nm @ 2400rpm
88.7bhp/ton 87.2bhp/tonne
36.3bhp/L 27.1kW/L 36.8PS/L
35.9ft/sec 11.0m/sec
19.1mph 30.7kmh/1000rpm

Petrol 4-stroke piston
2780cc 169.6cu in
In-line 6
Compression ratio: 8.7:1
Bore: 88.9mm 3.5in
Stroke: 74.7mm 2.9in
Valve type/No: Overhead 12
Transmission: Automatic
No. of forward speeds: 2
Wheels driven: Rear
Wheelbase: 289.6cm 114.0in
Track F: 139.7cm 55.0in
Track R: 138.4cm 54.5in
Length: 494.8cm 194.8in
Width: 178.8cm 70.4in
Height: 138.4cm 54.5in
Ground clearance: 19.1cm 7.5in
Kerb weight: 1157.7kg 2550.0lb

2928 Mercury
Meteor 800
1961 USA
100.0mph 160.9kmh
0-50mph 80.5kmh: 12.6secs
0-60mph 96.5kmh: 16.6secs
0-1/4 mile: 20.0secs
175.0bhp 130.5kW 177.4PS
@ 4200rpm
279.0lbft 378.0Nm @ 2200rpm
97.0bhp/ton 95.4bhp/tonne
36.6bhp/L 27.3kW/L 37.1PS/L
38.5ft/sec 11.7m/sec
25.7mph 41.4kmh/1000rpm
Petrol 4-stroke piston
4787cc 292.1cu in
Vee 8 1 Carburettor
Compression ratio: 8.8:1
Bore: 95.3mm 3.8in
Stroke: 83.8mm 3.3in
Valve type/No: Overhead 16
Transmission: Automatic
Wheels driven: Rear
Brake system: PA
Brakes F/R: Drum/Drum
Steering: PA
Wheelbase: 304.8cm 120.0in
Track F: 154.9cm 61.0in
Track R: 152.4cm 60.0in
Length: 545.1cm 214.6in
Width: 202.9cm 79.9in
Height: 140.0cm 55.1in
Ground clearance: 13.7cm 5.4in
Kerb weight: 1834.2kg 4040.0lb

2929 Mercury
Meteor
1962 USA
93.0mph 149.6kmh
0-50mph 80.5kmh: 11.0secs
0-60mph 96.5kmh: 15.0secs
0-1/4 mile: 19.5secs
145.0bhp 108.1kW 147.0PS
@ 4400rpm
216.0lbft 292.7Nm @ 2200rpm
101.2bhp/ton 99.5bhp/tonne
40.0bhp/L 29.8kW/L 40.6PS/L
35.1ft/sec 10.7m/sec
21.2mph 34.1kmh/1000rpm
Petrol 4-stroke piston
3622cc 221.0cu in
Vee 8
Compression ratio: 8.7:1
Bore: 88.9mm 3.5in
Stroke: 72.9mm 2.9in
Valve type/No: Overhead 16
Transmission: Automatic
No. of forward speeds: 2
Wheels driven: Rear
Brake system: PA
Steering: PA
Wheelbase: 295.9cm 116.5in
Track F: 144.8cm 57.0in
Track R: 142.2cm 56.0in
Length: 517.7cm 203.8in
Width: 181.1cm 71.3in
Height: 141.7cm 55.8in
Ground clearance: 15.2cm 6.0in
Kerb weight: 1457.3kg 3210.0lb
Fuel: 60.6L 13.3gal 16.0galUS

2930 Mercury
S-55 406
1962 USA
130.0mph 209.2kmh
0-50mph 80.5kmh: 5.7secs
0-60mph 96.5kmh: 8.0secs
0-1/4 mile: 16.1secs
405.0bhp 302.0kW 410.6PS
@ 5800rpm
448.0lbft 607.0Nm @ 3500rpm
212.0bhp/ton 208.4bhp/tonne
60.9bhp/L 45.4kW/L 61.7PS/L
60.9ft/sec 18.6m/sec
22.4mph 36.0kmh/1000rpm
Petrol 4-stroke piston
6653cc 405.9cu in
Vee 8 3 Carburettor
Compression ratio: 10.9:1
Bore: 104.9mm 4.1in
Stroke: 96.0mm 3.8in
Valve type/No: Overhead 16
Transmission: Manual
No. of forward speeds: 4
Wheels driven: Rear
Wheelbase: 302.3cm 119.0in
Track F: 154.9cm 61.0in
Track R: 152.4cm 60.0in
Length: 530.9cm 209.0in
Width: 202.9cm 79.9in
Height: 144.8cm 57.0in
Ground clearance: 14.0cm 5.5in
Kerb weight: 1943.1kg 4280.0lb
Fuel: 75.7L 16.6gal 20.0galUS

2931 Mercury
Comet S-22 Sportster
1963 USA
103.0mph 165.7kmh
0-50mph 80.5kmh: 10.5secs
0-60mph 96.5kmh: 14.5secs
0-1/4 mile: 19.3secs
164.0bhp 122.3kW 166.3PS
@ 4400rpm
258.0lbft 349.6Nm @ 2200rpm
123.1bhp/ton 121.0bhp/tonne
38.5bhp/L 28.7kW/L 39.0PS/L
35.1ft/sec 10.7m/sec
22.1mph 35.6kmh/1000rpm
Petrol 4-stroke piston
4261cc 260.0cu in
Vee 8 1 Carburettor
Compression ratio: 8.7:1
Bore: 96.5mm 3.8in
Stroke: 72.9mm 2.9in
Valve type/No: Overhead 16
Transmission: Automatic
No. of forward speeds: 2
Wheels driven: Rear
Brake system: PA
Brakes F/R: Drum/Drum
Steering: PA
Wheelbase: 289.6cm 114.0in
Track F: 139.7cm 55.0in
Track R: 138.4cm 54.5in
Length: 494.8cm 194.8in
Width: 178.8cm 70.4in
Height: 138.4cm 54.5in
Ground clearance: 15.0cm 5.9in
Kerb weight: 1355.2kg 2985.0lb
Fuel: 53.0L 11.6gal 14.0galUS

2932 Mercury
Super Marauder S-55
1963 USA
113.0mph 181.8kmh
0-50mph 80.5kmh: 5.4secs
0-60mph 96.5kmh: 7.0secs
0-1/4 mile: 15.1secs
425.0bhp 316.9kW 430.9PS
@ 6000rpm
480.0lbft 650.4Nm @ 3700rpm
229.1bhp/ton 225.3bhp/tonne
60.7bhp/L 45.3kW/L 61.6PS/L
63.0ft/sec 19.2m/sec
18.8mph 30.2kmh/1000rpm
Petrol 4-stroke piston
6997cc 426.9cu in
Vee 8 2 Carburettor
Compression ratio: 11.5:1
Bore: 107.4mm 4.2in
Stroke: 96.0mm 3.8in
Valve type/No: Overhead 16
Transmission: Automatic
No. of forward speeds: 4
Wheels driven: Rear
Wheelbase: 304.8cm 120.0in
Track F: 154.9cm 61.0in
Track R: 152.4cm 60.0in
Length: 546.1cm 215.0in
Width: 203.2cm 80.0in
Height: 141.0cm 55.5in
Ground clearance: 14.0cm 5.5in
Kerb weight: 1886.4kg 4155.0lb
Fuel: 75.7L 16.6gal 20.0galUS

2933 Mercury
Comet A/FX
1964 USA
133.0mph 214.0kmh
0-50mph 80.5kmh: 3.2secs
0-60mph 96.5kmh: 4.2secs
0-1/4 mile: 12.0secs
425.0bhp 316.9kW 430.9PS
@ 6000rpm
480.0lbft 650.4Nm @ 3700rpm
308.6bhp/ton 303.4bhp/tonne
60.7bhp/L 45.3kW/L 61.6PS/L
63.0ft/sec 19.2m/sec
18.9mph 30.4kmh/1000rpm
Petrol 4-stroke piston
6997cc 426.9cu in
Vee 8 2 Carburettor
Compression ratio: 11.5:1
Bore: 107.6mm 4.2in
Stroke: 96.1mm 3.8in
Valve type/No: Overhead 16
Transmission: Manual
No. of forward speeds: 4
Wheels driven: Rear
Brakes F/R: Drum/Drum
Wheelbase: 284.5cm 112.0in
Track F: 141.2cm 55.6in
Track R: 142.2cm 56.0in
Length: 495.6cm 195.1in
Width: 181.4cm 71.4in
Height: 136.1cm 53.6in
Ground clearance: 14.0cm 5.5in
Kerb weight: 1400.6kg 3085.0lb
Fuel: 75.7L 16.6gal 20.0galUS

2934 Mercury
Comet Caliente
1964 USA
109.0mph 175.4kmh
0-50mph 80.5kmh: 9.1secs
0-60mph 96.5kmh: 11.8secs
0-1/4 mile: 16.5secs
210.0bhp 156.6kW 212.9PS
@ 4400rpm
300.0lbft 406.5Nm @ 2800rpm
148.4bhp/ton 145.9bhp/tonne
44.3bhp/L 33.1kW/L 45.0PS/L
35.1ft/sec 10.7m/sec
24.8mph 39.9kmh/1000rpm
Petrol 4-stroke piston
4736cc 289.0cu in
Vee 8 1 Carburettor
Compression ratio: 9.0:1
Bore: 101.6mm 4.0in
Stroke: 72.9mm 2.9in
Valve type/No: Overhead 16
Transmission: Automatic
No. of forward speeds: 3
Wheels driven: Rear
Brake system: PA
Steering: PA
Wheelbase: 289.6cm 114.0in
Track F: 141.2cm 55.6in
Track R: 142.2cm 56.0in
Length: 495.6cm 195.1in
Width: 181.4cm 71.4in
Height: 136.1cm 53.6in
Ground clearance: 14.0cm 5.5in
Kerb weight: 1439.2kg 3170.0lb
Fuel: 75.7L 16.6gal 20.0galUS

2935 Mercury
Comet Cyclone 4-speed
1964 USA
109.0mph 175.4kmh
0-50mph 80.5kmh: 7.7secs
0-60mph 96.5kmh: 10.2secs
0-1/4 mile: 16.4secs
210.0bhp 156.6kW 212.9PS
@ 4400rpm
300.0lbft 406.5Nm @ 2800rpm
44.3bhp/L 33.1kW/L 45.0PS/L
21.7mph 34.9kmh/1000rpm
Petrol 4-stroke piston
4736cc 289.0cu in
Vee 8
Valve type/No: Overhead 16
Transmission: Manual
No. of forward speeds: 4
Wheels driven: Rear
Wheelbase: 289.6cm 114.0in
Track F: 141.2cm 55.6in
Track R: 142.2cm 56.0in
Length: 495.6cm 195.1in
Width: 181.4cm 71.4in
Height: 136.1cm 53.6in
Fuel: 75.7L 16.6gal 20.0galUS

2936 Mercury
Comet Cyclone Automatic
1964 USA
0-50mph 80.5kmh: 9.1secs
0-60mph 96.5kmh: 11.8secs
0-1/4 mile: 16.5secs
210.0bhp 156.6kW 212.9PS
@ 4400rpm
300.0lbft 406.5Nm @ 2800rpm
44.3bhp/L 33.1kW/L 45.0PS/L
21.7mph 34.9kmh/1000rpm
Petrol 4-stroke piston
4736cc 289.0cu in
Vee 8
Valve type/No: Overhead 16
Transmission: Automatic
Wheels driven: Rear
Wheelbase: 289.6cm 114.0in
Track F: 141.2cm 55.6in
Track R: 142.2cm 56.0in
Length: 495.6cm 195.1in
Width: 181.4cm 71.4in
Height: 136.1cm 53.6in
Fuel: 75.7L 16.6gal 20.0galUS

2937 Mercury
Park Lane
1964 USA
116.0mph 186.6kmh
0-50mph 80.5kmh: 7.1secs
0-60mph 96.5kmh: 9.3secs
0-1/4 mile: 16.9secs
300.0bhp 223.7kW 304.2PS
@ 4600rpm
427.0lbft 578.6Nm @ 2800rpm
154.1bhp/ton 151.6bhp/tonne
46.9bhp/L 35.0kW/L 47.6PS/L
48.3ft/sec 14.7m/sec
25.8mph 41.5kmh/1000rpm
Petrol 4-stroke piston
6391cc 389.9cu in
Vee 8 1 Carburettor
Compression ratio: 9.7:1
Bore: 102.9mm 4.0in
Stroke: 96.0mm 3.8in
Valve type/No: Overhead 16
Transmission: Automatic
No. of forward speeds: 3
Wheels driven: Rear
Brake system: PA
Brakes F/R: Drum/Drum
Steering: PA
Wheelbase: 304.8cm 120.0in
Track F: 154.9cm 61.0in
Track R: 152.4cm 60.0in
Length: 547.4cm 215.5in
Width: 203.2cm 80.0in
Height: 144.0cm 56.7in
Ground clearance: 14.0cm 5.5in
Kerb weight: 1979.4kg 4360.0lb
Fuel: 75.7L 16.6gal 20.0galUS

2938 Mercury
Monterey
1965 USA
106.0mph 170.6kmh
0-50mph 80.5kmh: 8.8secs
0-60mph 96.5kmh: 12.2secs
0-1/4 mile: 17.7secs
250.0bhp 186.4kW 253.5PS
@ 4400rpm
378.0lbft 512.2Nm @ 2400rpm
138.6bhp/ton 136.3bhp/tonne
39.1bhp/L 29.2kW/L 39.7PS/L
46.2ft/sec 14.1m/sec
26.5mph 42.6kmh/1000rpm
Petrol 4-stroke piston
6391cc 389.9cu in
Vee 8 1 Carburettor
Compression ratio: 9.4:1
Bore: 103.0mm 4.1in
Stroke: 96.0mm 3.8in
Valve type/No: Overhead 16
Transmission: Automatic
No. of forward speeds: 3
Wheels driven: Rear
Wheelbase: 312.4cm 123.0in
Track F: 157.5cm 62.0in
Track R: 157.5cm 62.0in
Length: 554.7cm 218.4in
Width: 202.2cm 79.6in
Height: 140.2cm 55.2in
Ground clearance: 15.0cm 5.9in
Kerb weight: 1834.2kg 4040.0lb
Fuel: 79.5L 17.5gal 21.0galUS

2939 Mercury

Park Lane
1965 USA
115.0mph 185.0kmh
0-50mph 80.5kmh: 7.2secs
0-60mph 96.5kmh: 9.5secs
0-1/4 mile: 16.9secs
300.0bhp 223.7kW 304.2PS
@ 4600rpm
427.0lbft 578.6Nm @ 2800rpm
160.4bhp/ton 157.7bhp/tonne
46.9bhp/L 35.0kW/L 47.6PS/L
48.3ft/sec 14.7m/sec
26.5mph 42.6kmh/1000rpm
Petrol 4-stroke piston
6391cc 389.9cu in
Vee 8 1 Carburettor
Compression ratio: 10.0:1
Bore: 103.0mm 4.1in
Stroke: 96.0mm 3.8in
Valve type/No: Overhead 16
Transmission: Automatic
No. of forward speeds: 3
Wheels driven: Rear
Wheelbase: 312.4cm 123.0in
Track F: 157.5cm 62.0in
Track R: 157.5cm 62.0in
Length: 554.7cm 218.4in
Width: 201.7cm 79.4in
Height: 140.0cm 55.1in
Ground clearance: 15.0cm 5.9in
Kerb weight: 1902.3kg 4190.0lb
Fuel: 79.5L 17.5gal 21.0galUS

2940 Mercury

Comet Cyclone GT
1966 USA
120.0mph 193.1kmh
0-50mph 80.5kmh: 4.8secs
0-60mph 96.5kmh: 6.6secs
0-1/4 mile: 15.2secs
335.0bhp 249.8kW 339.6PS
@ 4800rpm
427.0lbft 578.6Nm @ 3200rpm
209.6bhp/ton 206.1bhp/tonne
52.4bhp/L 39.1kW/L 53.1PS/L
50.4ft/sec 15.4m/sec
23.7mph 38.1kmh/1000rpm
Petrol 4-stroke piston
6391cc 389.9cu in
Vee 8 1 Carburettor
Compression ratio: 10.5:1
Bore: 103.0mm 4.1in
Stroke: 96.0mm 3.8in
Valve type/No: Overhead 16
Transmission: Automatic
No. of forward speeds: 3
Wheels driven: Rear
Springs F/R: Coil/Leaf
Brake system: PA
Steering: Recirculating ball PA
Wheelbase: 294.6cm 116.0in
Track F: 148.1cm 58.3in
Track R: 148.1cm 58.3in
Length: 515.6cm 203.0in
Width: 187.5cm 73.8in
Height: 137.9cm 54.3in
Ground clearance: 16.5cm 6.5in
Kerb weight: 1625.3kg 3580.0lb
Fuel: 75.7L 16.6gal 20.0galUS

2941 Mercury

Cougar
1967 USA
110.0mph 177.0kmh
0-50mph 80.5kmh: 7.9secs
0-60mph 96.5kmh: 10.7secs
0-1/4 mile: 18.0secs
200.0bhp 149.1kW 202.8PS
@ 4400rpm
282.0lbft 382.1Nm @ 2400rpm
136.6bhp/ton 134.3bhp/tonne
42.2bhp/L 31.5kW/L 42.8PS/L
35.1ft/sec 10.7m/sec
27.5mph 44.2kmh/1000rpm
Petrol 4-stroke piston
4738cc 289.1cu in
Vee 8 1 Carburettor
Compression ratio: 9.3:1
Bore: 101.7mm 4.0in
Stroke: 72.9mm 2.9in
Valve type/No: Overhead 16
Transmission: Manual
No. of forward speeds: 4
Wheels driven: Rear
Springs F/R: Coil/Leaf
Brake system: PA
Brakes F/R: Disc/Drum
Steering: Recirculating ball PA
Wheelbase: 281.9cm 111.0in
Track F: 147.6cm 58.1in
Track R: 147.6cm 58.1in
Length: 483.4cm 190.3in
Width: 180.8cm 71.2in
Height: 131.6cm 51.8in
Ground clearance: 16.0cm 6.3in
Kerb weight: 1489.1kg 3280.0lb
Fuel: 64.3L 14.1gal 17.0galUS

2942 Mercury

Cougar Group 2
1967 USA
125.0mph 201.1kmh
0-50mph 80.5kmh: 5.6secs
0-60mph 96.5kmh: 7.2secs
0-1/4 mile: 15.8secs
341.0bhp 254.3kW 345.7PS
@ 5800rpm
300.0lbft 406.5Nm @ 4000rpm
237.0bhp/ton 233.0bhp/tonne
72.0bhp/L 53.7kW/L 73.0PS/L
46.2ft/sec 14.1m/sec
17.7mph 28.5kmh/1000rpm
Petrol 4-stroke piston
4736cc 289.0cu in
Vee 8 2 Carburettor
Compression ratio: 10.5:1
Bore: 101.6mm 4.0in
Stroke: 72.9mm 2.9in
Valve type/No: Overhead 16
Transmission: Manual
No. of forward speeds: 4
Wheels driven: Rear
Springs F/R: Coil/Leaf
Brakes F/R: Disc/Drum
Steering: Recirculating ball
Wheelbase: 281.9cm 111.0in
Track F: 147.6cm 58.1in
Track R: 147.6cm 58.1in
Length: 483.4cm 190.3in
Width: 180.8cm 71.2in
Height: 131.6cm 51.8in
Ground clearance: 12.7cm 5.0in
Kerb weight: 1463.2kg 3223.0lb
Fuel: 64.3L 14.1gal 17.0galUS

2943 Mercury

Cougar GT
1967 USA
115.0mph 185.0kmh
0-50mph 80.5kmh: 5.8secs
0-60mph 96.5kmh: 7.7secs
0-1/4 mile: 15.9secs
320.0bhp 238.6kW 324.4PS
@ 4800rpm
427.0lbft 578.6Nm @ 3200rpm
203.1bhp/ton 199.7bhp/tonne
50.1bhp/L 37.4kW/L 50.8PS/L
50.4ft/sec 15.4m/sec
24.0mph 38.6kmh/1000rpm
Petrol 4-stroke piston
6385cc 389.6cu in
Vee 8 1 Carburettor
Compression ratio: 10.5:1
Bore: 102.9mm 4.0in
Stroke: 96.0mm 3.8in
Valve type/No: Overhead 16
Transmission: Automatic
No. of forward speeds: 3
Wheels driven: Rear
Springs F/R: Coil/Leaf
Brake system: PA
Brakes F/R: Disc/Drum
Steering: Recirculating ball PA
Wheelbase: 281.9cm 111.0in
Track F: 147.6cm 58.1in
Track R: 147.6cm 58.1in
Length: 483.4cm 190.3in
Width: 180.8cm 71.2in
Height: 131.6cm 51.8in
Ground clearance: 14.7cm 5.8in
Kerb weight: 1602.6kg 3530.0lb
Fuel: 64.3L 14.1gal 17.0galUS

2944 Mercury

Marquis
1967 USA
120.0mph 193.1kmh
0-50mph 80.5kmh: 7.4secs
0-60mph 96.5kmh: 9.4secs
0-1/4 mile: 16.8secs
330.0bhp 246.1kW 334.6PS
@ 4600rpm
444.0lbft 601.6Nm @ 2800rpm
165.2bhp/ton 162.4bhp/tonne
48.9bhp/L 36.5kW/L 49.6PS/L
50.9ft/sec 15.5m/sec
28.3mph 45.5kmh/1000rpm
Petrol 4-stroke piston
6742cc 411.3cu in
Vee 8 1 Carburettor
Compression ratio: 10.5:1
Bore: 103.0mm 4.1in
Stroke: 101.2mm 4.0in
Valve type/No: Overhead 16
Transmission: Automatic
No. of forward speeds: 3
Wheels driven: Rear
Springs F/R: Coil/Coil
Brake system: PA
Brakes F/R: Disc/Drum
Steering: Recirculating ball PA
Wheelbase: 312.4cm 123.0in
Track F: 157.5cm 62.0in
Track R: 157.5cm 62.0in
Length: 555.0cm 218.5in
Width: 198.6cm 78.2in
Height: 142.5cm 56.1in
Ground clearance: 17.0cm 6.7in
Kerb weight: 2031.6kg 4475.0lb
Fuel: 94.6L 20.8gal 25.0galUS

2945 Mercury

Cougar
1968 USA
107.0mph 172.2kmh
0-50mph 80.5kmh: 7.6secs
0-60mph 96.5kmh: 10.0secs
0-1/4 mile: 17.4secs
230.0bhp 171.5kW 233.2PS
@ 4800rpm
310.0lbft 420.1Nm @ 2800rpm
152.2bhp/ton 149.7bhp/tonne
46.5bhp/L 34.7kW/L 47.1PS/L
40.0ft/sec 12.2m/sec
25.4mph 40.9kmh/1000rpm
Petrol 4-stroke piston
4949cc 301.9cu in
Vee 8 1 Carburettor
Compression ratio: 10.0:1
Bore: 101.6mm 4.0in
Stroke: 76.2mm 3.0in
Valve type/No: Overhead 16
Transmission: Automatic
No. of forward speeds: 3
Wheels driven: Rear
Springs F/R: Coil/Leaf
Brake system: PA
Brakes F/R: Disc/Drum
Steering: Recirculating ball
Wheelbase: 281.9cm 111.0in
Track F: 148.6cm 58.5in
Track R: 148.6cm 58.5in
Length: 483.4cm 190.3in
Width: 181.1cm 71.3in
Height: 131.3cm 51.7in
Kerb weight: 1536.8kg 3385.0lb
Fuel: 60.6L 13.3gal 16.0galUS

2946 Mercury

Cougar XR-7
1968 USA
122.0mph 196.3kmh
0-50mph 80.5kmh: 5.4secs
0-60mph 96.5kmh: 7.1secs
0-1/4 mile: 15.1secs
390.0bhp 290.8kW 395.4PS
@ 5600rpm
460.0lbft 623.3Nm @ 3200rpm
238.6bhp/ton 234.6bhp/tonne
55.7bhp/L 41.6kW/L 56.5PS/L
58.8ft/sec 17.9m/sec
21.8mph 35.1kmh/1000rpm
Petrol 4-stroke piston
6997cc 426.9cu in
Vee 8 1 Carburettor
Compression ratio: 10.9:1
Bore: 107.4mm 4.2in
Stroke: 96.0mm 3.8in
Valve type/No: Overhead 16
Transmission: Automatic
No. of forward speeds: 3
Wheels driven: Rear
Springs F/R: Coil/Leaf
Brake system: PA
Brakes F/R: Disc/Drum
Steering: Recirculating ball PA
Wheelbase: 281.9cm 111.0in
Track F: 148.6cm 58.5in
Track R: 148.6cm 58.5in
Length: 483.4cm 190.3in
Width: 181.1cm 71.3in
Height: 131.3cm 51.7in
Kerb weight: 1662.5kg 3662.0lb
Fuel: 60.6L 13.3gal 16.0galUS

2947 Mercury

Cyclone
1968 USA
117.0mph 188.3kmh
0-50mph 80.5kmh: 4.8secs
0-60mph 96.5kmh: 6.2secs
0-1/4 mile: 14.4secs
335.0bhp 249.8kW 339.6PS
@ 5600rpm
445.0lbft 603.0Nm @ 3400rpm
200.6bhp/ton 197.3bhp/tonne
47.8bhp/L 35.6kW/L 48.4PS/L
61.9ft/sec 18.9m/sec
19.5mph 31.4kmh/1000rpm
Petrol 4-stroke piston
7014cc 427.9cu in
Vee 8 1 Carburettor
Compression ratio: 10.7:1
Bore: 104.9mm 4.1in
Stroke: 101.1mm 4.0in
Valve type/No: Overhead 16
Transmission: Automatic
No. of forward speeds: 3
Wheels driven: Rear
Springs F/R: Coil/Leaf
Brake system: PA
Brakes F/R: Disc/Drum
Steering: Recirculating ball PA
Wheelbase: 294.6cm 116.0in
Track F: 149.9cm 59.0in
Track R: 149.9cm 59.0in
Length: 516.9cm 203.5in
Width: 187.5cm 73.8in
Height: 138.4cm 54.5in
Kerb weight: 1698.0kg 3740.0lb
Fuel: 75.7L 16.6gal 20.0galUS

2948 Mercury

Marquis Brougham
1969 USA
114.0mph 183.4kmh
0-50mph 80.5kmh: 6.4secs
0-60mph 96.5kmh: 8.2secs
0-1/4 mile: 16.3secs
360.0bhp 268.4kW 365.0PS
@ 4600rpm
480.0lbft 650.4Nm @ 2800rpm
160.2bhp/ton 157.5bhp/tonne
51.2bhp/L 38.2kW/L 51.9PS/L
45.9ft/sec 14.0m/sec
28.4mph 45.7kmh/1000rpm
Petrol 4-stroke piston
7030cc 428.9cu in
Vee 8 1 Carburettor
Compression ratio: 10.0:1
Bore: 110.7mm 4.4in
Stroke: 91.2mm 3.6in
Valve type/No: Overhead 16
Transmission: Automatic
No. of forward speeds: 3
Wheels driven: Rear
Springs F/R: Coil/Coil
Brake system: PA
Brakes F/R: Disc/Drum
Steering: Recirculating ball PA
Wheelbase: 315.0cm 124.0in
Track F: 160.0cm 63.0in
Track R: 162.6cm 64.0in
Length: 569.0cm 224.0in
Width: 203.2cm 80.0in
Height: 137.2cm 54.0in
Kerb weight: 2285.9kg 5035.0lb
Fuel: 94.6L 20.8gal 25.0galUS

2949 Mercury

Marquis Marauder X-100
1969 USA
126.0mph 202.7kmh
0-50mph 80.5kmh: 5.9secs
0-60mph 96.5kmh: 7.5secs
0-1/4 mile: 15.2secs
360.0bhp 268.4kW 365.0PS
@ 4600rpm
480.0lbft 650.4Nm @ 2800rpm
188.0bhp/ton 184.8bhp/tonne
51.2bhp/L 38.2kW/L 51.9PS/L
45.9ft/sec 14.0m/sec
28.1mph 45.2kmh/1000rpm
Petrol 4-stroke piston
7030cc 428.9cu in

Vee 8 1 Carburettor
Compression ratio: 10.0:1
Bore: 110.7mm 4.4in
Stroke: 91.2mm 3.6in
Valve type/No: Overhead 16
Transmission: Automatic
No. of forward speeds: 3
Wheels driven: Rear
Springs F/R: Coil/Coil
Brake system: PA
Brakes F/R: Disc/Drum
Steering: Recirculating ball PA
Wheelbase: 307.3cm 121.0in
Track F: 160.0cm 63.0in
Track R: 162.6cm 64.0in
Length: 556.3cm 219.0in
Width: 203.2cm 80.0in
Height: 134.6cm 53.0in
Kerb weight: 1947.7kg 4290.0lb
Fuel: 94.6L 20.8gal 25.0galUS

2950 Mercury

Cougar Eliminator
1970 USA
104.0mph 167.3kmh
0-50mph 80.5kmh: 6.0secs
0-60mph 96.5kmh: 7.6secs
0-1/4 mile: 15.8secs
290.0bhp 216.2kW 294.0PS
@ 5800rpm
290.0lbft 393.0Nm @ 4300rpm
179.9bhp/ton 176.9bhp/tonne
58.6bhp/L 43.7kW/L 59.4PS/L
48.3ft/sec 14.7m/sec
17.3mph 27.8kmh/1000rpm
12.7mpg 10.6mpgUS 22.2L/100km
Petrol 4-stroke piston
4949cc 301.9cu in
Vee 8 1 Carburettor
Compression ratio: 10.5:1
Bore: 101.6mm 4.0in
Stroke: 76.2mm 3.0in
Valve type/No: Overhead 16
Transmission: Manual
No. of forward speeds: 4
Wheels driven: Rear
Springs F/R: Coil/Leaf
Brake system: PA
Brakes F/R: Disc/Drum
Steering: Recirculating ball PA
Wheelbase: 282.2cm 111.1in
Track F: 148.6cm 58.5in
Track R: 148.6cm 58.5in
Length: 498.1cm 196.1in
Width: 188.2cm 74.1in
Height: 129.8cm 51.1in
Kerb weight: 1638.9kg 3610.0lb
Fuel: 83.3L 18.3gal 22.0galUS

2951 Mercury

Bobcat 2.3-litre
1975 USA
92.0mph 148.0kmh
0-50mph 80.5kmh: 10.5secs
0-60mph 96.5kmh: 15.4secs
0-1/4 mile: 19.9secs
83.0bhp 61.9kW 84.1PS
@ 4800rpm
109.0lbft 147.7Nm @ 2800rpm
68.3bhp/ton 67.2bhp/tonne
36.1bhp/L 26.9kW/L 36.6PS/L
41.7ft/sec 12.7m/sec
20.5mph 33.0kmh/1000rpm
21.0mpg 17.5mpgUS 13.4L/100km
Petrol 4-stroke piston
2298cc 140.2cu in
In-line 4 1 Carburettor
Compression ratio: 8.4:1
Bore: 96.0mm 3.8in
Stroke: 79.4mm 3.1in
Valve type/No: Overhead 8
Transmission: Manual
No. of forward speeds: 4
Wheels driven: Rear
Springs F/R: Coil/Leaf
Brake system: PA
Brakes F/R: Disc/Drum
Steering: Rack & pinion
Wheelbase: 240.0cm 94.5in
Track F: 139.7cm 55.0in
Track R: 141.7cm 55.8in
Length: 429.3cm 169.0in
Width: 176.3cm 69.4in
Height: 128.3cm 50.5in
Ground clearance: 18.3cm 7.2in
Kerb weight: 1234.9kg 2720.0lb
Fuel: 49.2L 10.8gal 13.0galUS

2952 Mercury

Capri II 2.8 V6
1975 USA
108.0mph 173.8kmh
0-50mph 80.5kmh: 7.7secs
0-60mph 96.5kmh: 10.6secs
0-1/4 mile: 18.0secs
109.0bhp 81.3kW 110.5PS
@ 4800rpm
146.0lbft 197.8Nm @ 3000rpm
90.9bhp/ton 89.4bhp/tonne
39.0bhp/L 29.1kW/L 39.6PS/L
36.0ft/sec 11.0m/sec
21.0mph 33.8kmh/1000rpm
23.4mpg 19.5mpgUS 12.1L/100km
Petrol 4-stroke piston
2792cc 170.3cu in
Vee 6 1 Carburettor
Compression ratio: 8.2:1
Bore: 93.0mm 3.7in
Stroke: 68.5mm 2.7in
Valve type/No: Overhead 12
Transmission: Manual
No. of forward speeds: 4
Wheels driven: Rear
Springs F/R: Coil/Leaf
Brake system: PA
Brakes F/R: Disc/Drum
Steering: Rack & pinion PA
Wheelbase: 256.0cm 100.8in
Track F: 135.4cm 53.3in
Track R: 138.4cm 54.5in
Length: 444.0cm 174.8in
Width: 169.9cm 66.9in
Height: 129.5cm 51.0in
Ground clearance: 12.4cm 4.9in
Kerb weight: 1219.0kg 2685.0lb
Fuel: 48.1L 10.6gal 12.7galUS

2953 Mercury

Monarch
1977 USA
100.0mph 160.9kmh
0-50mph 80.5kmh: 8.1secs
0-60mph 96.5kmh: 11.3secs
0-1/4 mile: 17.9secs
0-1km: 33.5secs
134.0bhp 99.9kW 135.9PS
@ 3600rpm
245.0lbft 332.0Nm @ 1600rpm
85.4bhp/ton 84.0bhp/tonne
27.1bhp/L 20.2kW/L 27.5PS/L
30.0ft/sec 9.1m/sec
29.6mph 47.6kmh/1000rpm
12.5mpg 10.4mpgUS 22.6L/100km
Petrol 4-stroke piston
4942cc 301.5cu in
Vee 8 1 Carburettor
Compression ratio: 8.4:1
Bore: 101.6mm 4.0in
Stroke: 76.2mm 3.0in
Valve type/No: Overhead 16
Transmission: Automatic
No. of forward speeds: 3
Wheels driven: Rear
Springs F/R: Coil/Leaf
Brake system: PA
Brakes F/R: Disc/Drum
Steering: Recirculating ball PA
Wheelbase: 279.4cm 110.0in
Track F: 157.5cm 62.0in
Track R: 157.5cm 62.0in
Length: 508.0cm 200.0in
Width: 188.0cm 74.0in
Height: 134.6cm 53.0in
Ground clearance: 12.7cm 5.0in
Kerb weight: 1595.4kg 3514.0lb
Fuel: 72.8L 16.0gal 19.2galUS

2954 Mercury

Zephyr
1977 USA
96.0mph 154.5kmh
0-50mph 80.5kmh: 11.4secs
0-60mph 96.5kmh: 15.8secs
0-1/4 mile: 20.6secs
92.0bhp 68.6kW 93.3PS
@ 5000rpm
121.0lbft 164.0Nm @ 3000rpm
72.2bhp/ton 71.0bhp/tonne
40.0bhp/L 29.8kW/L 40.6PS/L
43.5ft/sec 13.2m/sec
24.0mph 38.6kmh/1000rpm
26.4mpg 22.0mpgUS 10.7L/100km
Petrol 4-stroke piston
2300cc 140.3cu in
In-line 4
Compression ratio: 9.0:1
Bore: 96.0mm 3.8in
Stroke: 79.4mm 3.1in
Valve type/No: Overhead 8
Transmission: Manual
No. of forward speeds: 4
Wheels driven: Rear
Springs F/R: Coil/Coil
Brake system: PA
Brakes F/R: Disc/Drum
Steering: Rack & pinion
Wheelbase: 268.0cm 105.5in
Track F: 143.8cm 56.6in
Track R: 144.8cm 57.0in
Length: 492.3cm 193.8in
Width: 178.3cm 70.2in
Height: 135.9cm 53.5in
Kerb weight: 1296.2kg 2855.0lb
Fuel: 60.6L 13.3gal 16.0galUS

2955 Mercury

LN7
1981 USA
91.0mph 146.4kmh
0-50mph 80.5kmh: 10.6secs
0-60mph 96.5kmh: 15.0secs
0-1/4 mile: 20.0secs
70.0bhp 52.2kW 71.0PS
@ 5200rpm
88.0lbft 119.2Nm @ 3000rpm
69.1bhp/ton 67.9bhp/tonne
43.8bhp/L 32.7kW/L 44.4PS/L
45.2ft/sec 13.8m/sec
20.0mph 32.2kmh/1000rpm
27.6mpg 23.0mpgUS 10.2L/100km
Petrol 4-stroke piston
1598cc 97.5cu in
In-line 4 1 Carburettor
Compression ratio: 8.8:1
Bore: 80.0mm 3.1in
Stroke: 79.5mm 3.1in
Valve type/No: Overhead 8
Transmission: Manual
No. of forward speeds: 4
Wheels driven: Front
Springs F/R: Coil/Coil
Brake system: PA
Brakes F/R: Disc/Drum
Steering: Rack & pinion PA
Wheelbase: 239.3cm 94.2in
Track F: 138.9cm 54.7in
Track R: 142.2cm 56.0in
Length: 432.6cm 170.3in
Width: 167.4cm 65.9in
Height: 128.3cm 50.5in
Kerb weight: 1030.6kg 2270.0lb
Fuel: 42.8L 9.4gal 11.3galUS

2956 Mercury

Lynx Hatchback RS
1981 USA
98.0mph 157.7kmh
0-60mph 96.5kmh: 13.9secs
0-1/4 mile: 19.2secs
65.0bhp 48.5kW 65.9PS
@ 5200rpm
85.0lbft 115.2Nm @ 3200rpm
68.0bhp/ton 66.9bhp/tonne
40.7bhp/L 30.3kW/L 41.2PS/L
45.2ft/sec 13.8m/sec
22.2mph 35.7kmh/1000rpm
29.4mpg 24.5mpgUS 9.6L/100km
Petrol 4-stroke piston
1598cc 97.5cu in
In-line 4 1 Carburettor
Compression ratio: 8.8:1
Bore: 80.0mm 3.1in
Stroke: 79.5mm 3.1in
Valve type/No: Overhead 8
Transmission: Manual
No. of forward speeds: 4
Wheels driven: Front
Springs F/R: Coil/Coil
Brake system: PA
Brakes F/R: Disc/Drum
Steering: Rack & pinion
Wheelbase: 239.3cm 94.2in
Track F: 138.9cm 54.7in
Track R: 142.2cm 56.0in
Length: 416.3cm 163.9in
Width: 167.4cm 65.9in
Height: 135.4cm 53.3in
Ground clearance: 13.2cm 5.2in
Kerb weight: 971.6kg 2140.0lb
Fuel: 37.8L 8.3gal 10.0galUS

2957 Mercury

Capri
1983 USA
126.0mph 202.7kmh
0-60mph 96.5kmh: 7.8secs
0-1/4 mile: 16.1secs
177.0bhp 132.0kW 179.4PS
@ 4200rpm
247.0lbft 334.7Nm @ 2600rpm
126.7bhp/ton 124.6bhp/tonne
35.8bhp/L 26.7kW/L 36.3PS/L
35.0ft/sec 10.7m/sec
22.2mpg 18.5mpgUS 12.7L/100km
Petrol 4-stroke piston
4942cc 301.5cu in
Vee 8 1 Carburettor
Compression ratio: 8.3:1
Bore: 101.6mm 4.0in
Stroke: 76.2mm 3.0in
Valve type/No: Overhead 16
Transmission: Manual
No. of forward speeds: 5
Wheels driven: Rear
Springs F/R: Coil/Coil
Brakes F/R: Disc/Drum
Wheelbase: 255.0cm 100.4in
Track F: 143.8cm 56.6in
Track R: 144.8cm 57.0in
Length: 454.9cm 179.1in
Width: 175.5cm 69.1in
Height: 131.8cm 51.9in
Kerb weight: 1421.0kg 3130.0lb
Fuel: 58.3L 12.8gal 15.4galUS

2958 Mercury

Sable LS
1986 USA
115.0mph 185.0kmh
0-60mph 96.5kmh: 11.7secs
0-1/4 mile: 18.7secs
140.0bhp 104.4kW 141.9PS
@ 4800rpm
160.0lbft 216.8Nm @ 3000rpm
95.6bhp/ton 94.0bhp/tonne
46.9bhp/L 35.0kW/L 47.5PS/L
42.0ft/sec 12.8m/sec
23.8mpg 19.8mpgUS 11.9L/100km
Petrol 4-stroke piston
2986cc 182.2cu in
Vee 6 fuel injection
Compression ratio: 9.3:1
Bore: 89.0mm 3.5in
Stroke: 80.0mm 3.1in
Valve type/No: Overhead 12
Transmission: Automatic
No. of forward speeds: 4
Wheels driven: Front
Springs F/R: Coil/Coil
Brake system: PA
Brakes F/R: Disc/Drum
Steering: Rack & pinion PA
Wheelbase: 269.2cm 106.0in
Track F: 156.2cm 61.5in
Track R: 153.7cm 60.5in
Length: 484.9cm 190.9in
Width: 180.1cm 70.9in
Height: 138.2cm 54.4in
Kerb weight: 1489.1kg 3280.0lb
Fuel: 60.6L 13.3gal 16.0galUS

2959 Mercury

Tracer
1987 Japan
105.0mph 168.9kmh
0-50mph 80.5kmh: 7.4secs
0-60mph 96.5kmh: 10.3secs
0-1/4 mile: 17.6secs
82.0bhp 61.1kW 83.1PS
@ 5000rpm
92.0lbft 124.7Nm @ 2500rpm
80.0bhp/ton 78.7bhp/tonne
51.3bhp/L 38.3kW/L 52.1PS/L
45.7ft/sec 13.9m/sec
39.6mpg 33.0mpgUS 7.1L/100km
Petrol 4-stroke piston
1597cc 97.4cu in
In-line 4 fuel injection
Compression ratio: 9.3:1
Bore: 78.0mm 3.1in
Stroke: 83.6mm 3.3in
Valve type/No: Overhead 8
Transmission: Manual
No. of forward speeds: 5
Wheels driven: Front
Springs F/R: Coil/Coil
Brake system: PA
Brakes F/R: Disc/Drum

Steering: Rack & pinion PA
Wheelbase: 240.5cm 94.7in
Track F: 139.4cm 54.9in
Track R: 142.2cm 56.0in
Length: 411.5cm 162.0in
Width: 165.6cm 65.2in
Height: 134.6cm 53.0in
Ground clearance: 15.2cm 6.0in
Kerb weight: 1041.9kg 2295.0lb
Fuel: 45.0L 9.9gal 11.9galUS

2960 Mercury

Cougar XR-7
1989 USA
143.0mph 230.1kmh
0-50mph 80.5kmh: 5.5secs
0-60mph 96.5kmh: 7.4secs
0-1/4 mile: 15.9secs
210.0bhp 156.6kW 212.9PS
@ 4000rpm
315.0lbft 426.8Nm @ 2600rpm
126.8bhp/ton 124.7bhp/tonne
55.3bhp/L 41.2kW/L 56.1PS/L
37.7ft/sec 11.5m/sec
20.4mpg 17.0mpgUS 13.8L/100km
Petrol 4-stroke piston
3797cc 231.7cu in supercharged
Vee 6 fuel injection
Compression ratio: 8.2:1
Bore: 96.8mm 3.8in
Stroke: 86.0mm 3.4in
Valve type/No: Overhead 12
Transmission: Manual
No. of forward speeds: 5
Wheels driven: Rear
Springs F/R: Coil/Coil
Brake system: PA ABS
Brakes F/R: Disc/Disc
Steering: Rack & pinion PA
Wheelbase: 287.0cm 113.0in
Track F: 156.0cm 61.4in
Track R: 152.9cm 60.2in
Length: 504.7cm 198.7in
Width: 184.7cm 72.7in
Height: 133.9cm 52.7in
Kerb weight: 1684.3kg 3710.0lb
Fuel: 71.9L 15.8gal 19.0galUS

2961 Mercury

Capri XR-2
1990 Australia
124.0mph 199.5kmh
0-60mph 96.5kmh: 8.3secs
0-1/4 mile: 16.3secs
132.0bhp 98.4kW 133.8PS
@ 6000rpm
136.0lbft 184.3Nm @ 3000rpm
113.3bhp/ton 111.4bhp/tonne
82.6bhp/L 61.6kW/L 83.7PS/L
54.8ft/sec 16.7m/sec
30.0mpg 25.0mpgUS 9.4L/100km
Petrol 4-stroke piston
1598cc 97.5cu in turbocharged
In-line 4 fuel injection
Compression ratio: 7.9:1
Bore: 78.0mm 3.1in
Stroke: 83.6mm 3.3in
Valve type/No: Overhead 16
Transmission: Manual
No. of forward speeds: 5
Wheels driven: Front
Springs F/R: Coil/Coil
Brake system: PA
Brakes F/R: Disc/Disc
Steering: Rack & pinion PA
Wheelbase: 240.5cm 94.7in
Track F: 139.4cm 54.9in
Track R: 142.2cm 56.0in
Length: 421.9cm 166.1in
Width: 164.1cm 64.6in
Height: 127.5cm 50.2in
Kerb weight: 1184.9kg 2610.0lb
Fuel: 42.0L 9.2gal 11.1galUS

2962 Mercury

Tracer LTS
1991 USA
125.0mph 201.1kmh
0-60mph 96.5kmh: 9.1secs
0-1/4 mile: 17.0secs
127.0bhp 94.7kW 128.8PS
@ 6500rpm
114.0lbft 154.5Nm @ 4500rpm
112.9bhp/ton 111.0bhp/tonne
69.0bhp/L 51.5kW/L 70.0PS/L
60.5ft/sec 18.4m/sec
32.4mpg 27.0mpgUS 8.7L/100km
Petrol 4-stroke piston
1840cc 112.3cu in
In-line 4 fuel injection
Compression ratio: 9.0:1
Bore: 83.0mm 3.3in
Stroke: 85.0mm 3.3in
Valve type/No: Overhead 16
Transmission: Manual
No. of forward speeds: 5
Wheels driven: Front
Springs F/R: Coil/Coil
Brake system: PA
Brakes F/R: Disc/Disc
Steering: Rack & pinion PA
Wheelbase: 249.9cm 98.4in
Track F: 143.5cm 56.5in
Track R: 143.5cm 56.5in
Length: 434.1cm 170.9in
Width: 169.4cm 66.7in
Height: 133.9cm 52.7in
Kerb weight: 1144.1kg 2520.0lb
Fuel: 45.0L 9.9gal 11.9galUS

2963 Merkur

XR4Ti
1985 Germany
120.0mph 193.1kmh
0-50mph 80.5kmh: 5.7secs
0-60mph 96.5kmh: 7.9secs
0-1/4 mile: 16.0secs
170.0bhp 126.8kW 172.4PS
@ 5200rpm
195.0lbft 264.2Nm @ 3800rpm
129.1bhp/ton 126.9bhp/tonne
74.1bhp/L 55.3kW/L 75.2PS/L
45.1ft/sec 13.7m/sec
21.4mph 34.4kmh/1000rpm
27.6mpg 23.0mpgUS 10.2L/100km
Petrol 4-stroke piston
2293cc 139.9cu in turbocharged
In-line 4 fuel injection
Compression ratio: 8.0:1
Bore: 96.0mm 3.8in
Stroke: 79.2mm 3.1in
Valve type/No: Overhead 8
Transmission: Manual
No. of forward speeds: 5
Wheels driven: Rear
Springs F/R: Coil/Coil
Brake system: PA
Brakes F/R: Disc/Drum
Steering: Rack & pinion PA
Wheelbase: 260.9cm 102.7in
Track F: 145.3cm 57.2in
Track R: 146.8cm 57.8in
Length: 453.1cm 178.4in
Width: 172.7cm 68.0in
Height: 139.2cm 54.8in
Kerb weight: 1339.3kg 2950.0lb
Fuel: 56.8L 12.5gal 15.0galUS

2964 Merkur

Scorpio
1987 Germany
130.0mph 209.2kmh
0-50mph 80.5kmh: 7.4secs
0-60mph 96.5kmh: 10.1secs
0-1/4 mile: 17.5secs
144.0bhp 107.4kW 146.0PS
@ 5500rpm
162.0lbft 219.5Nm @ 3000rpm
97.9bhp/ton 96.3bhp/tonne
49.1bhp/L 36.6kW/L 49.8PS/L
43.2ft/sec 13.2m/sec
25.2mpg 21.0mpgUS 11.2L/100km
Petrol 4-stroke piston
2933cc 178.9cu in
Vee 6 fuel injection
Compression ratio: 9.0:1
Bore: 93.0mm 3.7in
Stroke: 72.0mm 2.8in
Valve type/No: Overhead 12
Transmission: Automatic
No. of forward speeds: 4
Wheels driven: Rear
Springs F/R: Coil/Coil
Brake system: PA ABS
Brakes F/R: Disc/Disc
Steering: Rack & pinion PA
Wheelbase: 276.1cm 108.7in
Track F: 147.6cm 58.1in
Track R: 147.6cm 58.1in
Length: 473.5cm 186.4in
Width: 176.5cm 69.5in
Height: 138.9cm 54.7in
Ground clearance: 15.2cm 6.0in
Kerb weight: 1495.9kg 3295.0lb
Fuel: 64.0L 14.1gal 16.9galUS

2965 Merkur

XR4Ti
1988 Germany
120.0mph 193.1kmh
0-50mph 80.5kmh: 5.9secs
0-60mph 96.5kmh: 8.1secs
0-1/4 mile: 16.2secs
170.0bhp 126.8kW 172.4PS
@ 5200rpm
195.0lbft 264.2Nm @ 3800rpm
129.1bhp/ton 126.9bhp/tonne
74.1bhp/L 55.3kW/L 75.2PS/L
45.1ft/sec 13.7m/sec
28.8mpg 24.0mpgUS 9.8L/100km
Petrol 4-stroke piston
2293cc 139.9cu in turbocharged
In-line 4 fuel injection
Compression ratio: 8.0:1
Bore: 96.0mm 3.8in
Stroke: 79.2mm 3.1in
Valve type/No: Overhead 8
Transmission: Manual
No. of forward speeds: 5
Wheels driven: Rear
Springs F/R: Coil/Coil
Brake system: PA
Brakes F/R: Disc/Drum
Steering: Rack & pinion PA
Wheelbase: 260.9cm 102.7in
Track F: 145.3cm 57.2in
Track R: 146.8cm 57.8in
Length: 453.1cm 178.4in
Width: 172.7cm 68.0in
Height: 139.2cm 54.8in
Kerb weight: 1339.3kg 2950.0lb
Fuel: 56.8L 12.5gal 15.0galUS

2966 Messerschmitt (FMR)

Tg 500
1958 Germany
68.0mph 109.4kmh
0-50mph 80.5kmh: 16.7secs
0-60mph 96.5kmh: 27.8secs
0-1/4 mile: 22.8secs
24.0bhp 17.9kW 24.3PS
@ 5000rpm
24.6lbft 33.3Nm @ 4000rpm
63.5bhp/ton 62.4bhp/tonne
49.0bhp/L 36.5kW/L 49.6PS/L
38.3ft/sec 11.7m/sec
18.0mph 29.0kmh/1000rpm
43.8mpg 36.5mpgUS 6.4L/100km
Petrol 2-stroke piston
490cc 29.9cu in
In-line 2 1 Carburettor
Compression ratio: 6.5:1
Bore: 67.0mm 2.6in
Stroke: 70.0mm 2.8in
Valve type/No: Ports
Transmission: Manual
No. of forward speeds: 4
Wheels driven: Rear
Springs F/R: Rubber/Coil
Brakes F/R: Drum/Drum
Wheelbase: 189.2cm 74.5in
Track F: 111.8cm 44.0in
Track R: 104.1cm 41.0in
Length: 304.8cm 120.0in
Width: 129.5cm 51.0in
Height: 127.0cm 50.0in
Ground clearance: 15.2cm 6.0in
Kerb weight: 384.5kg 847.0lb
Fuel: 29.6L 6.5gal 7.8galUS

2967 Meyers

Manx
1965 USA
70.0mph 112.6kmh
0-50mph 80.5kmh: 14.4secs
0-60mph 96.5kmh: 22.7secs
0-1/4 mile: 21.0secs
50.0bhp 37.3kW 50.7PS
@ 3900rpm
70.0lbft 94.9Nm @ 2400rpm
82.3bhp/ton 81.0bhp/tonne
33.5bhp/L 25.0kW/L 33.9PS/L
29.5ft/sec 9.0m/sec
21.0mph 33.8kmh/1000rpm
Petrol 4-stroke piston
1493cc 91.1cu in
Flat 4 1 Carburettor
Compression ratio: 7.8:1
Bore: 83.1mm 3.3in
Stroke: 69.1mm 2.7in
Valve type/No: Overhead 8
Transmission: Manual
No. of forward speeds: 4
Wheels driven: Rear
Brakes F/R: Drum/Drum
Wheelbase: 198.1cm 78.0in
Track F: 138.4cm 54.5in
Track R: 133.4cm 52.5in
Length: 313.7cm 123.5in
Width: 158.2cm 62.3in
Height: 129.0cm 50.8in
Ground clearance: 17.8cm 7.0in
Kerb weight: 617.4kg 1360.0lb
Fuel: 53.0L 11.6gal 14.0galUS

2968 MG

Midget
1929 UK
64.0mph 103.0kmh
20.0bhp 14.9kW 20.3PS
@ 4000rpm
40.0bhp/ton 39.3bhp/tonne
23.6bhp/L 17.6kW/L 23.9PS/L
36.3ft/sec 11.1m/sec
38.0mpg 31.6mpgUS 7.4L/100km
Petrol 4-stroke piston
847cc 51.7cu in
In-line 4 1 Carburettor
Bore: 57.0mm 2.2in
Stroke: 83.0mm 3.3in
Valve type/No: Overhead 8
Transmission: Manual
No. of forward speeds: 3
Wheels driven: Rear
Brakes F/R: Drum/Drum
Wheelbase: 198.1cm 78.0in
Track F: 105.4cm 41.5in
Track R: 105.4cm 41.5in
Length: 312.4cm 123.0in
Width: 127.0cm 50.0in
Height: 137.2cm 54.0in
Kerb weight: 508.5kg 1120.0lb
Fuel: 20.5L 4.5gal 5.4galUS

2969 MG

Six Sports
1929 UK
78.0mph 125.5kmh
20.0mpg 16.7mpgUS 14.1L/100km
Petrol 4-stroke piston
2468cc 150.6cu in
In-line 6 2 Carburettor
Compression ratio: 5.8:1
Bore: 69.0mm 2.7in
Stroke: 110.0mm 4.3in
Valve type/No: Overhead 12
Transmission: Manual
No. of forward speeds: 3
Wheels driven: Rear
Brakes F/R: Drum/Drum
Wheelbase: 289.6cm 114.0in
Track F: 121.9cm 48.0in
Track R: 121.9cm 48.0in
Length: 401.3cm 158.0in
Width: 154.9cm 61.0in
Height: 162.6cm 64.0in
Kerb weight: 1169.5kg 2576.0lb
Fuel: 54.6L 12.0gal 14.4galUS

2970 MG

Mk II Montlhery Supercharged
1931 UK
87.8mph 141.3kmh
27.0mpg 22.5mpgUS 10.5L/100km
Petrol 4-stroke piston
746cc 45.5cu in supercharged
In-line 4
Bore: 53.0mm 2.1in
Stroke: 73.0mm 2.9in
Valve type/No: Overhead 8
Transmission: Manual
No. of forward speeds: 4
Wheels driven: Rear
Brakes F/R: Drum/Drum
Wheelbase: 205.7cm 81.0in
Track F: 106.7cm 42.0in
Track R: 106.7cm 42.0in
Length: 350.5cm 138.0in
Width: 132.1cm 52.0in
Height: 124.5cm 49.0in
Kerb weight: 661.0kg 1456.0lb
Fuel: 68.2L 15.0gal 18.0galUS

2971 MG
Magna Continental Coupe
1934 UK
72.5mph 116.7kmh
0-50mph 80.5kmh: 19.0secs
41.0bhp 30.6kW 41.6PS
@ 5500rpm
48.2bhp/ton 47.4bhp/tonne
37.7bhp/L 28.1kW/L 38.2PS/L
42.8ft/sec 13.0m/sec
26.0mpg 21.6mpgUS 10.9L/100km
Petrol 4-stroke piston
1087cc 66.3cu in
In-line 6 2 Carburettor
Compression ratio: 6.4:1
Bore: 57.0mm 2.2in
Stroke: 71.0mm 2.8in
Valve type/No: Overhead 12
Transmission: Manual
No. of forward speeds: 4
Wheels driven: Rear
Brakes F/R: Drum/Drum
Kerb weight: 864.4kg 1904.0lb
Fuel: 59.1L 13.0gal 15.6galUS

2972 MG
Magnette N Two-seater
1934 UK
80.7mph 129.8kmh
0-50mph 80.5kmh: 16.4secs
0-60mph 96.5kmh: 22.8secs
24.0mpg 20.0mpgUS 11.8L/100km
Petrol 4-stroke piston
1287cc 78.5cu in
In-line 6
Bore: 57.0mm 2.2in
Stroke: 84.0mm 3.3in
Transmission: Manual
No. of forward speeds: 4
Wheels driven: Rear
Brakes F/R: Drum/Drum
Kerb weight: 940.7kg 2072.0lb
Fuel: 45.5L 10.0gal 12.0galUS

2973 MG
Midget P Type
1934 UK
74.3mph 119.5kmh
0-50mph 80.5kmh: 20.8secs
0-60mph 96.5kmh: 32.2secs
36.0bhp 26.8kW 36.5PS
@ 5500rpm
53.3bhp/ton 52.4bhp/tonne
42.5bhp/L 31.7kW/L 43.1PS/L
50.0ft/sec 15.2m/sec
35.0mpg 29.1mpgUS 8.1L/100km
Petrol 4-stroke piston
846cc 51.6cu in
In-line 4 2 Carburettor
Compression ratio: 6.1:1
Bore: 57.0mm 2.2in
Stroke: 83.0mm 3.3in
Valve type/No: Overhead 8
Transmission: Manual
No. of forward speeds: 4
Wheels driven: Rear
Brakes F/R: Drum/Drum
Kerb weight: 686.4kg 1512.0lb
Fuel: 54.6L 12.0gal 14.4galUS

2974 MG
Magnette KN Saloon
1935 UK
75.3mph 121.2kmh
0-50mph 80.5kmh: 18.4secs
0-60mph 96.5kmh: 28.6secs
25.0mpg 20.8mpgUS 11.3L/100km
Petrol 4-stroke piston
1287cc 78.5cu in
In-line 6
Bore: 57.0mm 2.2in
Stroke: 84.0mm 3.3in
Transmission: Manual
No. of forward speeds: 4
Wheels driven: Rear
Brakes F/R: Drum/Drum
Kerb weight: 1067.8kg 2352.0lb
Fuel: 45.5L 10.0gal 12.0galUS

2975 MG
Midget PB
1936 UK
75.0mph 120.7kmh
0-50mph 80.5kmh: 16.4secs
0-60mph 96.5kmh: 27.4secs
43.0bhp 32.1kW 43.6PS
@ 5500rpm
55.0bhp/ton 54.1bhp/tonne
51.2bhp/L 38.2kW/L 52.0PS/L
50.0ft/sec 15.2m/sec
35.0mpg 29.1mpgUS 8.1L/100km
Petrol 4-stroke piston
839cc 51.2cu in
In-line 4 2 Carburettor
Compression ratio: 6.8:1
Bore: 60.0mm 2.4in
Stroke: 83.0mm 3.3in
Valve type/No: Overhead 8
Transmission: Manual
No. of forward speeds: 4
Wheels driven: Rear
Brakes F/R: Drum/Drum
Kerb weight: 795.4kg 1752.0lb
Fuel: 54.6L 12.0gal 14.4galUS

2976 MG
Midget Series T
1936 UK
79.6mph 128.1kmh
0-50mph 80.5kmh: 15.4secs
0-60mph 96.5kmh: 23.1secs
50.0bhp 37.3kW 50.7PS
@ 4500rpm
57.9bhp/ton 56.9bhp/tonne
38.7bhp/L 28.9kW/L 39.2PS/L
50.2ft/sec 15.3m/sec
27.0mpg 22.5mpgUS 10.5L/100km
Petrol 4-stroke piston
1292cc 78.8cu in
In-line 4 2 Carburettor
Compression ratio: 6.5:1
Bore: 63.5mm 2.5in
Stroke: 102.0mm 4.0in
Valve type/No: Overhead 8
Transmission: Manual
No. of forward speeds: 4
Wheels driven: Rear
Brakes F/R: Drum/Drum
Kerb weight: 878.5kg 1935.0lb
Fuel: 68.2L 15.0gal 18.0galUS

2977 MG
TC Midget
1947 UK
78.0mph 125.5kmh
0-50mph 80.5kmh: 14.7secs
0-60mph 96.5kmh: 22.7secs
54.4bhp 40.6kW 55.1PS
@ 5200rpm
67.3bhp/ton 66.2bhp/tonne
43.5bhp/L 32.5kW/L 44.1PS/L
51.1ft/sec 15.6m/sec
28.0mpg 23.3mpgUS 10.1L/100km
Petrol 4-stroke piston
1250cc 76.3cu in
In-line 4
Compression ratio: 7.2:1
Bore: 66.5mm 2.6in
Stroke: 90.0mm 3.5in
Valve type/No: Overhead 8
Transmission: Manual
No. of forward speeds: 4
Wheels driven: Rear
Brakes F/R: Drum/Drum
Wheelbase: 238.8cm 94.0in
Track F: 114.3cm 45.0in
Track R: 114.3cm 45.0in
Length: 354.3cm 139.5in
Width: 142.2cm 56.0in
Height: 134.6cm 53.0in
Ground clearance: 15.2cm 6.0in
Kerb weight: 822.2kg 1811.0lb
Fuel: 61.4L 13.5gal 16.2galUS

2978 MG
TC
1949 UK
73.0mph 117.5kmh
0-50mph 80.5kmh: 13.8secs
0-60mph 96.5kmh: 21.2secs
0-1/4 mile: 21.8secs
54.4bhp 40.6kW 55.1PS
@ 5200rpm
64.0lbft 86.7Nm @ 2700rpm
66.0bhp/ton 64.9bhp/tonne
43.5bhp/L 32.5kW/L 44.1PS/L
51.1ft/sec 15.6m/sec
15.5mph 24.9kmh/1000rpm
26.4mpg 22.0mpgUS 10.7L/100km
Petrol 4-stroke piston
1250cc 76.3cu in
In-line 4 1 Carburettor
Compression ratio: 7.3:1
Bore: 66.5mm 2.6in
Stroke: 90.0mm 3.5in
Valve type/No: Overhead 8
Transmission: Manual
No. of forward speeds: 4
Wheels driven: Rear
Springs F/R: Leaf/Leaf
Brakes F/R: Drum/Drum
Steering: Bishop cam
Wheelbase: 238.8cm 94.0in
Track F: 114.3cm 45.0in
Track R: 114.3cm 45.0in
Length: 367.0cm 144.5in
Width: 142.2cm 56.0in
Height: 135.1cm 53.2in
Ground clearance: 15.0cm 5.9in
Kerb weight: 837.6kg 1845.0lb
Fuel: 61.3L 13.5gal 16.2galUS

2979 MG
TD
1950 UK
78.9mph 127.0kmh
0-50mph 80.5kmh: 13.8secs
0-60mph 96.5kmh: 19.4secs
0-1/4 mile: 21.3secs
54.0bhp 40.3kW 54.7PS
@ 5200rpm
63.8lbft 86.4Nm @ 2600rpm
60.3bhp/ton 59.3bhp/tonne
43.2bhp/L 32.2kW/L 43.8PS/L
51.1ft/sec 15.6m/sec
14.9mph 24.0kmh/1000rpm
Petrol 4-stroke piston
1250cc 76.3cu in
In-line 4
Compression ratio: 7.3:1
Bore: 66.5mm 2.6in
Stroke: 89.9mm 3.5in
Valve type/No: Overhead 8
Transmission: Manual
No. of forward speeds: 4
Wheels driven: Rear
Wheelbase: 238.8cm 94.0in
Track F: 120.4cm 47.4in
Track R: 127.0cm 50.0in
Length: 365.8cm 144.0in
Width: 148.8cm 58.6in
Height: 134.4cm 52.9in
Ground clearance: 15.0cm 5.9in
Kerb weight: 910.3kg 2005.0lb

2980 MG
TD
1951 UK
81.0mph 130.3kmh
0-50mph 80.5kmh: 13.0secs
0-1/4 mile: 20.8secs
54.4bhp 40.6kW 55.1PS
@ 5200rpm
60.4bhp/ton 59.4bhp/tonne
43.5bhp/L 32.5kW/L 44.1PS/L
51.1ft/sec 15.6m/sec
Petrol 4-stroke piston
1250cc 76.3cu in
In-line 4 2 Carburettor
Compression ratio: 7.3:1
Bore: 65.0mm 2.6in
Stroke: 89.9mm 3.5in
Valve type/No: Overhead 8
Transmission: Manual
No. of forward speeds: 4
Wheels driven: Rear
Brakes F/R: Drum/Drum
Wheelbase: 238.8cm 94.0in
Track F: 120.4cm 47.4in
Track R: 127.0cm 50.0in
Length: 368.3cm 145.0in
Width: 149.1cm 58.7in
Height: 134.6cm 53.0in
Ground clearance: 15.2cm 6.0in
Kerb weight: 915.3kg 2016.0lb

2981 MG
1.25-litre Saloon
1952 UK
75.0mph 120.7kmh
0-50mph 80.5kmh: 18.4secs
0-60mph 96.5kmh: 30.4secs
0-1/4 mile: 24.5secs
46.0bhp 34.3kW 46.6PS
@ 4800rpm
58.5lbft 79.3Nm @ 2400rpm
44.0bhp/ton 43.3bhp/tonne
36.8bhp/L 27.4kW/L 37.3PS/L
47.2ft/sec 14.4m/sec
14.4mph 23.2kmh/1000rpm
26.5mpg 22.1mpgUS 10.7L/100km
Petrol 4-stroke piston
1250cc 76.3cu in
In-line 4
Compression ratio: 7.2:1
Bore: 66.5mm 2.6in
Stroke: 90.0mm 3.5in
Valve type/No: Overhead 8
Transmission: Manual
No. of forward speeds: 4
Wheels driven: Rear
Springs F/R: Coil/Leaf
Brakes F/R: Drum/Drum
Wheelbase: 251.5cm 99.0in
Track F: 120.4cm 47.4in
Track R: 127.0cm 50.0in
Length: 416.6cm 164.0in
Width: 149.9cm 59.0in
Height: 144.8cm 57.0in
Ground clearance: 14.0cm 5.5in
Kerb weight: 1062.8kg 2341.0lb
Fuel: 36.4L 8.0gal 9.6galUS

2982 MG
Midget
1953 UK
75.0mph 120.7kmh
0-50mph 80.5kmh: 15.6secs
0-60mph 96.5kmh: 23.9secs
0-1/4 mile: 23.4secs
54.4bhp 40.6kW 55.1PS
@ 5200rpm
63.5lbft 86.0Nm @ 2600rpm
61.1bhp/ton 60.1bhp/tonne
43.5bhp/L 32.5kW/L 44.1PS/L
51.1ft/sec 15.6m/sec
14.5mph 23.3kmh/1000rpm
25.0mpg 20.8mpgUS 11.3L/100km
Petrol 4-stroke piston
1250cc 76.3cu in
In-line 4
Compression ratio: 7.2:1
Bore: 66.5mm 2.6in
Stroke: 90.0mm 3.5in
Valve type/No: Overhead 8
Transmission: Manual
No. of forward speeds: 4
Wheels driven: Rear
Springs F/R: Coil/Leaf
Brakes F/R: Drum/Drum
Wheelbase: 238.8cm 94.0in
Track F: 120.4cm 47.4in
Track R: 127.0cm 50.0in
Length: 368.3cm 145.0in
Width: 148.8cm 58.6in
Height: 142.2cm 56.0in
Ground clearance: 15.2cm 6.0in
Kerb weight: 905.7kg 1995.0lb
Fuel: 56.9L 12.5gal 15.0galUS

2983 MG
TD
1953 UK
78.9mph 127.0kmh
0-50mph 80.5kmh: 13.8secs
0-60mph 96.5kmh: 19.4secs
0-1/4 mile: 21.3secs
54.0bhp 40.3kW 54.7PS
@ 5200rpm
60.3bhp/ton 59.3bhp/tonne
43.2bhp/L 32.2kW/L 43.8PS/L
51.1ft/sec 15.6m/sec
14.4mph 23.2kmh/1000rpm
Petrol 4-stroke piston
1250cc 76.3cu in
In-line 4
Compression ratio: 7.3:1
Bore: 66.5mm 2.6in
Stroke: 90.0mm 3.5in
Valve type/No: Overhead 8
Transmission: Manual
No. of forward speeds: 4
Wheels driven: Rear
Wheelbase: 238.8cm 94.0in
Track F: 120.4cm 47.4in
Track R: 127.0cm 50.0in
Kerb weight: 910.3kg 2005.0lb

2984 MG
TDC Mk II
1953 UK

81.3mph 130.8kmh
0-50mph 80.5kmh: 11.1secs
0-60mph 96.5kmh: 16.5secs
0-1/4 mile: 20.9secs
60.0bhp 44.7kW 60.8PS
@ 5500rpm
66.7bhp/ton 65.6bhp/tonne
48.0bhp/L 35.8kW/L 48.7PS/L
54.1ft/sec 16.5m/sec
15.2mph 24.5kmh/1000rpm
Petrol 4-stroke piston
1250cc 76.3cu in
In-line 4
Compression ratio: 8.1:1
Bore: 66.5mm 2.6in
Stroke: 90.0mm 3.5in
Valve type/No: Overhead 8
Transmission: Manual
No. of forward speeds: 4
Wheels driven: Rear
Wheelbase: 238.8cm 94.0in
Track F: 120.4cm 47.4in
Track R: 127.0cm 50.0in
Kerb weight: 914.8kg 2015.0lb

2985 MG

Magnette
1954 UK
83.0mph 133.5kmh
0-50mph 80.5kmh: 13.9secs
0-60mph 96.5kmh: 22.0secs
0-1/4 mile: 22.2secs
60.0bhp 44.7kW 60.8PS
@ 4600rpm
54.0bhp/ton 53.1bhp/tonne
40.3bhp/L 30.0kW/L 40.8PS/L
44.7ft/sec 13.6m/sec
Petrol 4-stroke piston
1489cc 90.8cu in
In-line 4
Bore: 73.0mm 2.9in
Stroke: 88.9mm 3.5in
Valve type/No: Overhead 8
Transmission: Manual
No. of forward speeds: 4
Wheels driven: Rear
Wheelbase: 259.1cm 102.0in
Track F: 129.5cm 51.0in
Track R: 129.5cm 51.0in
Kerb weight: 1130.5kg 2490.0lb

2986 MG

TD Laystall
1954 UK
87.9mph 141.4kmh
0-50mph 80.5kmh: 12.5secs
0-60mph 96.5kmh: 18.0secs
0-1/4 mile: 20.9secs
54.4bhp 40.6kW 55.1PS
@ 5200rpm
63.5lbft 86.0Nm @ 2600rpm
60.5bhp/ton 59.5bhp/tonne
43.5bhp/L 32.5kW/L 44.1PS/L
51.1ft/sec 15.6m/sec
14.4mph 23.2kmh/1000rpm
Petrol 4-stroke piston
1250cc 76.3cu in
In-line 4
Compression ratio: 7.3:1
Bore: 66.5mm 2.6in
Stroke: 89.9mm 3.5in
Valve type/No: Overhead 8
Transmission: Manual
No. of forward speeds: 4
Wheels driven: Rear
Wheelbase: 238.8cm 94.0in
Track F: 120.4cm 47.4in
Track R: 127.0cm 50.0in
Kerb weight: 914.8kg 2015.0lb

2987 MG

TF
1954 UK
80.1mph 128.9kmh
0-50mph 80.5kmh: 13.0secs
0-60mph 96.5kmh: 18.9secs
0-1/4 mile: 21.6secs
57.5bhp 42.9kW 58.3PS
@ 5500rpm
65.0lbft 88.1Nm @ 3000rpm
63.8bhp/ton 62.7bhp/tonne
46.0bhp/L 34.3kW/L 46.6PS/L
54.1ft/sec 16.5m/sec
15.6mph 25.1kmh/1000rpm
Petrol 4-stroke piston
1250cc 76.3cu in
In-line 4
Compression ratio: 8.0:1
Bore: 66.5mm 2.6in
Stroke: 89.9mm 3.5in
Valve type/No: Overhead 8
Transmission: Manual
No. of forward speeds: 4
Wheels driven: Rear
Wheelbase: 238.8cm 94.0in
Track F: 122.4cm 48.2in
Track R: 129.0cm 50.8in
Length: 373.4cm 147.0in
Width: 158.0cm 62.2in
Height: 133.1cm 52.4in
Ground clearance: 15.0cm 5.9in
Kerb weight: 917.1kg 2020.0lb

2988 MG

TF 1500
1954 UK
85.4mph 137.4kmh
0-50mph 80.5kmh: 11.0secs
0-60mph 96.5kmh: 16.3secs
0-1/4 mile: 20.7secs
65.0bhp 48.5kW 65.9PS
@ 5500rpm
76.0lbft 103.0Nm @ 3000rpm
72.3bhp/ton 71.0bhp/tonne
44.3bhp/L 33.1kW/L 44.9PS/L
54.1ft/sec 16.5m/sec
15.3mph 24.6kmh/1000rpm
Petrol 4-stroke piston
1466cc 89.4cu in
In-line 4
Compression ratio: 8.0:1
Bore: 72.0mm 2.8in
Stroke: 89.9mm 3.5in
Valve type/No: Overhead 8
Transmission: Manual
No. of forward speeds: 4
Wheels driven: Rear
Wheelbase: 238.8cm 94.0in
Track F: 122.4cm 48.2in
Track R: 129.0cm 50.8in
Kerb weight: 914.8kg 2015.0lb

2989 MG

TF Supercharged
1954 UK
87.0mph 140.0kmh
0-50mph 80.5kmh: 11.2secs
0-60mph 96.5kmh: 15.5secs
0-1/4 mile: 19.5secs
57.5bhp 42.9kW 58.3PS
@ 5500rpm
62.8bhp/ton 61.8bhp/tonne
46.0bhp/L 34.3kW/L 46.6PS/L
54.1ft/sec 16.5m/sec
Petrol 4-stroke piston
1250cc 76.3cu in supercharged
In-line 4
Bore: 66.5mm 2.6in
Stroke: 89.9mm 3.5in
Valve type/No: Overhead 8
Transmission: Manual
No. of forward speeds: 4
Wheels driven: Rear
Wheelbase: 238.8cm 94.0in
Track F: 129.0cm 50.8in
Track R: 129.0cm 50.8in
Kerb weight: 930.7kg 2050.0lb

2990 MG

A
1955 UK
95.1mph 153.0kmh
0-50mph 80.5kmh: 10.2secs
0-60mph 96.5kmh: 14.5secs
0-1/4 mile: 19.6secs
68.0bhp 50.7kW 68.9PS
@ 5500rpm
77.4lbft 104.9Nm @ 3500rpm
75.4bhp/ton 74.1bhp/tonne
45.7bhp/L 34.1kW/L 46.3PS/L
53.5ft/sec 16.3m/sec
17.0mph 27.4kmh/1000rpm
Petrol 4-stroke piston
1488cc 90.8cu in
In-line 4
Compression ratio: 8.3:1
Bore: 73.0mm 2.9in
Stroke: 88.9mm 3.5in
Valve type/No: Overhead 8
Transmission: Manual
No. of forward speeds: 4
Wheels driven: Rear
Wheelbase: 238.8cm 94.0in
Track F: 120.4cm 47.4in
Track R: 124.0cm 48.8in
Kerb weight: 917.1kg 2020.0lb

2991 MG

Magnette
1955 UK
81.0mph 130.3kmh
0-50mph 80.5kmh: 15.3secs
0-60mph 96.5kmh: 22.6secs
0-1/4 mile: 22.4secs
60.0bhp 44.7kW 60.8PS
@ 4600rpm
76.1lbft 103.1Nm @ 3000rpm
54.2bhp/ton 53.3bhp/tonne
40.3bhp/L 30.0kW/L 40.8PS/L
44.7ft/sec 13.6m/sec
15.2mph 24.5kmh/1000rpm
25.3mpg 21.1mpgUS 11.2L/100km
Petrol 4-stroke piston
1489cc 90.8cu in
In-line 4
Compression ratio: 7.1:1
Bore: 73.0mm 2.9in
Stroke: 89.0mm 3.5in
Valve type/No: Overhead 8
Transmission: Manual
No. of forward speeds: 4
Wheels driven: Rear
Springs F/R: Coil/Leaf
Brakes F/R: Drum/Drum
Wheelbase: 259.1cm 102.0in
Track F: 129.5cm 51.0in
Track R: 129.5cm 51.0in
Length: 429.3cm 169.0in
Width: 160.0cm 63.0in
Height: 147.3cm 58.0in
Ground clearance: 16.5cm 6.5in
Kerb weight: 1125.0kg 2478.0lb
Fuel: 40.9L 9.0gal 10.8galUS

2992 MG

A
1956 UK
99.0mph 159.3kmh
0-50mph 80.5kmh: 11.0secs
0-60mph 96.5kmh: 15.6secs
0-1/4 mile: 20.2secs
68.0bhp 50.7kW 68.9PS
@ 5500rpm
77.4lbft 104.9Nm @ 3500rpm
80.0bhp/ton 78.7bhp/tonne
45.7bhp/L 34.1kW/L 46.3PS/L
53.5ft/sec 16.3m/sec
17.0mph 27.4kmh/1000rpm
27.0mpg 22.5mpgUS 10.5L/100km
Petrol 4-stroke piston
1489cc 90.8cu in
In-line 4
Compression ratio: 8.3:1
Bore: 73.0mm 2.9in
Stroke: 89.0mm 3.5in
Valve type/No: Overhead 8
Transmission: Manual
No. of forward speeds: 4
Wheels driven: Rear
Springs F/R: Coil/Leaf
Brakes F/R: Drum/Drum
Wheelbase: 238.8cm 94.0in
Track F: 120.7cm 47.5in
Track R: 123.7cm 48.7in
Length: 396.2cm 156.0in
Width: 147.3cm 58.0in
Height: 127.0cm 50.0in
Ground clearance: 15.2cm 6.0in
Kerb weight: 864.4kg 1904.0lb
Fuel: 45.5L 10.0gal 12.0galUS

2993 MG

A Coupe
1957 UK
102.0mph 164.1kmh
0-50mph 80.5kmh: 10.8secs
0-60mph 96.5kmh: 15.0secs
0-1/4 mile: 19.3secs
72.0bhp 53.7kW 73.0PS
@ 5500rpm
76.4lbft 103.5Nm @ 3500rpm
76.5bhp/ton 75.3bhp/tonne
48.3bhp/L 36.1kW/L 49.0PS/L
53.5ft/sec 16.3m/sec
17.0mph 27.4kmh/1000rpm
28.0mpg 23.3mpgUS 10.1L/100km
Petrol 4-stroke piston
1489cc 90.8cu in
In-line 4
Compression ratio: 8.3:1
Bore: 73.0mm 2.9in
Stroke: 88.9mm 3.5in
Valve type/No: Overhead 8
Transmission: Manual
No. of forward speeds: 4
Wheels driven: Rear
Springs F/R: Coil/Leaf
Brakes F/R: Drum/Drum
Wheelbase: 238.8cm 94.0in
Track F: 124.0cm 48.8in
Track R: 123.7cm 48.7in
Length: 396.2cm 156.0in
Width: 145.3cm 57.2in
Height: 127.0cm 50.0in
Ground clearance: 15.2cm 6.0in
Kerb weight: 956.6kg 2107.0lb
Fuel: 45.5L 10.0gal 12.0galUS

2994 MG

A Judson
1958 UK
105.0mph 168.9kmh
0-50mph 80.5kmh: 8.6secs
0-60mph 96.5kmh: 12.5secs
0-1/4 mile: 18.1secs
90.0bhp 67.1kW 91.2PS
@ 5500rpm
95.0lbft 128.7Nm @ 3500rpm
95.5bhp/ton 93.9bhp/tonne
60.4bhp/L 45.1kW/L 61.3PS/L
53.5ft/sec 16.3m/sec
Petrol 4-stroke piston
1489cc 90.8cu in
In-line 4
Compression ratio: 8.3:1
Bore: 73.0mm 2.9in
Stroke: 88.9mm 3.5in
Valve type/No: Overhead 8
Transmission: Manual
No. of forward speeds: 4
Wheels driven: Rear
Wheelbase: 238.8cm 94.0in
Track F: 120.4cm 47.4in
Track R: 124.0cm 48.8in
Kerb weight: 957.9kg 2110.0lb

2995 MG

A Twin Cam
1958 UK
113.0mph 181.8kmh
0-50mph 80.5kmh: 7.3secs
0-60mph 96.5kmh: 9.9secs
0-1/4 mile: 18.1secs
108.0bhp 80.5kW 109.5PS
@ 6700rpm
104.0lbft 140.9Nm @ 4500rpm
110.0bhp/ton 108.1bhp/tonne
68.0bhp/L 50.7kW/L 68.9PS/L
65.1ft/sec 19.8m/sec
17.6mph 28.3kmh/1000rpm
Petrol 4-stroke piston
1588cc 96.9cu in
In-line 4
Compression ratio: 9.9:1
Bore: 75.4mm 3.0in
Stroke: 88.9mm 3.5in
Valve type/No: Overhead 8
Transmission: Manual
No. of forward speeds: 4
Wheels driven: Rear
Wheelbase: 238.8cm 94.0in
Track F: 121.7cm 47.9in
Track R: 124.2cm 48.9in
Length: 396.2cm 156.0in
Width: 147.3cm 58.0in
Height: 127.0cm 50.0in
Kerb weight: 998.8kg 2200.0lb

2996 MG

Magnette
1958 UK
88.0mph 141.6kmh
0-50mph 80.5kmh: 12.6secs
0-60mph 96.5kmh: 18.5secs
0-1/4 mile: 21.2secs
68.0bhp 50.7kW 68.9PS
@ 5400rpm
83.0lbft 112.5Nm @ 3000rpm
61.8bhp/ton 60.8bhp/tonne
45.7bhp/L 34.1kW/L 46.3PS/L
52.5ft/sec 16.0m/sec
16.3mph 26.2kmh/1000rpm
25.1mpg 20.9mpgUS 11.3L/100km
Petrol 4-stroke piston

1489cc 90.8cu in
In-line 4
Compression ratio: 8.3:1
Bore: 73.0mm 2.9in
Stroke: 88.9mm 3.5in
Valve type/No: Overhead 8
Transmission: Manual
No. of forward speeds: 4
Wheels driven: Rear
Springs F/R: Coil/Leaf
Brakes F/R: Drum/Drum
Wheelbase: 259.1cm 102.0in
Track F: 129.5cm 51.0in
Track R: 129.5cm 51.0in
Length: 429.3cm 169.0in
Width: 160.0cm 63.0in
Height: 147.3cm 58.0in
Ground clearance: 15.2cm 6.0in
Kerb weight: 1118.7kg 2464.0lb
Fuel: 42.1L 9.2gal 11.1galUS

2997 MG
Twin Cam MGA
1958 UK
114.0mph 183.4kmh
0-50mph 80.5kmh: 9.4secs
0-60mph 96.5kmh: 13.3secs
0-1/4 mile: 18.6secs
108.0bhp 80.5kW 109.5PS
@ 6700rpm
104.0lbft 140.9Nm @ 4500rpm
96.5bhp/ton 94.9bhp/tonne
68.0bhp/L 50.7kW/L 68.9PS/L
65.1ft/sec 19.8m/sec
17.3mph 27.8kmh/1000rpm
21.8mpg 18.2mpgUS 13.0L/100km
Petrol 4-stroke piston
1588cc 96.9cu in
In-line 4 2 Carburettor
Compression ratio: 9.9:1
Bore: 75.4mm 3.0in
Stroke: 88.9mm 3.5in
Valve type/No: Overhead 8
Transmission: Manual
No. of forward speeds: 4
Wheels driven: Rear
Springs F/R: Coil/Leaf
Brakes F/R: Disc/Disc
Steering: Rack & pinion
Wheelbase: 238.8cm 94.0in
Track F: 121.7cm 47.9in
Track R: 124.0cm 48.8in
Length: 396.2cm 156.0in
Width: 147.3cm 58.0in
Height: 127.0cm 50.0in
Ground clearance: 15.2cm 6.0in
Kerb weight: 1137.7kg 2506.0lb
Fuel: 45.5L 10.0gal 12.0galUS

2998 MG
A 1600
1959 UK
101.4mph 163.2kmh
0-50mph 80.5kmh: 10.3secs
0-60mph 96.5kmh: 14.2secs
0-1/4 mile: 19.3secs
79.5bhp 59.3kW 80.6PS
@ 5600rpm
87.0lbft 117.9Nm @ 3800rpm
87.7bhp/ton 86.3bhp/tonne
50.1bhp/L 37.3kW/L 50.8PS/L
54.4ft/sec 16.6m/sec
17.1mph 27.5kmh/1000rpm
24.1mpg 20.1mpgUS 11.7L/100km
Petrol 4-stroke piston
1588cc 96.9cu in
In-line 4
Compression ratio: 8.3:1
Bore: 75.4mm 3.0in
Stroke: 88.9mm 3.5in
Valve type/No: Overhead 8
Transmission: Manual
No. of forward speeds: 4
Wheels driven: Rear
Springs F/R: Coil/Leaf
Brakes F/R: Disc/Drum
Wheelbase: 238.8cm 94.0in
Track F: 120.7cm 47.5in
Track R: 123.7cm 48.7in
Length: 396.2cm 156.0in
Width: 147.3cm 58.0in
Height: 127.0cm 50.0in
Ground clearance: 15.2cm 6.0in
Kerb weight: 921.6kg 2030.0lb
Fuel: 45.5L 10.0gal 12.0galUS

2999 MG
Magnette Mk III
1959 UK
86.0mph 138.4kmh
0-50mph 80.5kmh: 14.3secs
0-60mph 96.5kmh: 20.6secs
0-1/4 mile: 21.9secs
66.5bhp 49.6kW 67.4PS
@ 5200rpm
85.0lbft 115.2Nm @ 3300rpm
60.3bhp/ton 59.2bhp/tonne
44.7bhp/L 33.3kW/L 45.3PS/L
50.6ft/sec 15.4m/sec
16.5mph 26.5kmh/1000rpm
26.6mpg 22.1mpgUS 10.6L/100km
Petrol 4-stroke piston
1489cc 90.8cu in
In-line 4
Compression ratio: 8.3:1
Bore: 73.0mm 2.9in
Stroke: 88.9mm 3.5in
Valve type/No: Overhead 8
Transmission: Manual
No. of forward speeds: 4
Wheels driven: Rear
Springs F/R: Coil/Leaf
Brakes F/R: Drum/Drum
Wheelbase: 252.0cm 99.2in
Track F: 124.0cm 48.8in
Track R: 126.5cm 49.8in
Length: 452.1cm 178.0in
Width: 161.3cm 63.5in
Height: 151.6cm 59.7in
Ground clearance: 16.5cm 6.5in
Kerb weight: 1122.3kg 2472.0lb
Fuel: 45.5L 10.0gal 12.0galUS

3000 MG
A 1600 Mk II
1961 UK
102.3mph 164.6kmh
0-50mph 80.5kmh: 9.7secs
0-60mph 96.5kmh: 13.7secs
0-1/4 mile: 19.1secs
90.0bhp 67.1kW 91.2PS
@ 5500rpm
97.0lbft 131.4Nm @ 4000rpm
100.0bhp/ton 98.3bhp/tonne
55.5bhp/L 41.4kW/L 56.3PS/L
53.5ft/sec 16.3m/sec
17.7mph 28.5kmh/1000rpm
22.3mpg 18.6mpgUS 12.7L/100km
Petrol 4-stroke piston
1622cc 99.0cu in
In-line 4
Compression ratio: 8.9:1
Bore: 76.2mm 3.0in
Stroke: 88.9mm 3.5in
Valve type/No: Overhead 8
Transmission: Manual
No. of forward speeds: 4
Wheels driven: Rear
Springs F/R: Coil/Leaf
Brakes F/R: Disc/Drum
Wheelbase: 238.8cm 94.0in
Track F: 120.7cm 47.5in
Track R: 123.7cm 48.7in
Length: 396.2cm 156.0in
Width: 147.3cm 58.0in
Height: 127.0cm 50.0in
Ground clearance: 15.2cm 6.0in
Kerb weight: 915.3kg 2016.0lb
Fuel: 45.5L 10.0gal 12.0galUS

3001 MG
A Mk II
1961 UK
105.0mph 168.9kmh
0-50mph 80.5kmh: 9.3secs
0-60mph 96.5kmh: 12.8secs
0-1/4 mile: 18.7secs
90.0bhp 67.1kW 91.2PS
@ 5500rpm
100.0lbft 135.5Nm @ 3500rpm
98.3bhp/ton 96.7bhp/tonne
55.4bhp/L 41.3kW/L 56.2PS/L
53.5ft/sec 16.3m/sec
18.1mph 29.1kmh/1000rpm
Petrol 4-stroke piston
1624cc 99.1cu in
In-line 4
Compression ratio: 8.9:1
Bore: 76.2mm 3.0in
Stroke: 88.9mm 3.5in
Valve type/No: Overhead 8
Transmission: Manual
No. of forward speeds: 4
Wheels driven: Rear
Wheelbase: 238.8cm 94.0in
Track F: 120.7cm 47.5in
Track R: 124.0cm 48.8in
Length: 401.3cm 158.0in
Width: 147.3cm 58.0in
Height: 127.0cm 50.0in
Ground clearance: 15.2cm 6.0in
Kerb weight: 930.7kg 2050.0lb

3002 MG
Midget
1961 UK
86.0mph 138.4kmh
0-50mph 80.5kmh: 14.4secs
0-60mph 96.5kmh: 20.2secs
0-1/4 mile: 21.9secs
41.6bhp 31.0kW 42.2PS
@ 5500rpm
53.0lbft 71.8Nm @ 3000rpm
60.0bhp/ton 59.0bhp/tonne
43.9bhp/L 32.7kW/L 44.5PS/L
45.8ft/sec 14.0m/sec
15.4mph 24.8kmh/1000rpm
33.4mpg 27.8mpgUS 8.5L/100km
Petrol 4-stroke piston
948cc 57.8cu in
In-line 4
Compression ratio: 9.0:1
Bore: 62.9mm 2.5in
Stroke: 76.2mm 3.0in
Valve type/No: Overhead 8
Transmission: Manual
No. of forward speeds: 4
Wheels driven: Rear
Springs F/R: Coil/Leaf
Brakes F/R: Drum/Drum
Wheelbase: 203.2cm 80.0in
Track F: 116.1cm 45.7in
Track R: 113.5cm 44.7in
Length: 346.7cm 136.5in
Width: 134.6cm 53.0in
Height: 126.2cm 49.7in
Ground clearance: 12.7cm 5.0in
Kerb weight: 705.5kg 1554.0lb
Fuel: 27.3L 6.0gal 7.2galUS

3003 MG
1100
1962 UK
89.0mph 143.2kmh
0-50mph 80.5kmh: 12.7secs
0-60mph 96.5kmh: 18.4secs
0-1/4 mile: 21.3secs
55.0bhp 41.0kW 55.8PS
@ 5500rpm
61.0lbft 82.7Nm @ 2500rpm
66.7bhp/ton 65.6bhp/tonne
50.1bhp/L 37.3kW/L 50.8PS/L
50.4ft/sec 15.3m/sec
14.9mph 24.0kmh/1000rpm
29.1mpg 24.2mpgUS 9.7L/100km
Petrol 4-stroke piston
1098cc 67.0cu in
In-line 4 2 Carburettor
Compression ratio: 8.9:1
Bore: 64.6mm 2.5in
Stroke: 83.7mm 3.3in
Valve type/No: Overhead 8
Transmission: Manual
No. of forward speeds: 4
Wheels driven: Front
Springs F/R: Gas/Gas
Brakes F/R: Disc/Drum
Steering: Rack & pinion
Wheelbase: 237.5cm 93.5in
Track F: 130.8cm 51.5in
Track R: 129.3cm 50.9in
Length: 372.6cm 146.7in
Width: 153.4cm 60.4in
Height: 133.9cm 52.7in
Ground clearance: 15.2cm 6.0in
Kerb weight: 839.0kg 1848.0lb
Fuel: 38.7L 8.5gal 10.2galUS

3004 MG
B 1800
1962 UK
105.0mph 168.9kmh
0-50mph 80.5kmh: 8.5secs
0-60mph 96.5kmh: 12.2secs
0-1/4 mile: 18.7secs
95.0bhp 70.8kW 96.3PS
@ 5400rpm
110.0lbft 149.1Nm @ 3000rpm
102.7bhp/ton 101.0bhp/tonne
52.8bhp/L 39.4kW/L 53.6PS/L
52.5ft/sec 16.0m/sec
17.9mph 28.8kmh/1000rpm
21.4mpg 17.8mpgUS 13.2L/100km
Petrol 4-stroke piston
1798cc 109.7cu in
In-line 4 2 Carburettor
Compression ratio: 8.8:1
Bore: 80.3mm 3.2in
Stroke: 89.0mm 3.5in
Valve type/No: Overhead 8
Transmission: Manual
No. of forward speeds: 4
Wheels driven: Rear
Springs F/R: Coil/Leaf
Brakes F/R: Disc/Drum
Steering: Rack & pinion
Wheelbase: 231.1cm 91.0in
Track F: 124.5cm 49.0in
Track R: 125.0cm 49.2in
Length: 389.1cm 153.2in
Width: 152.1cm 59.9in
Height: 125.5cm 49.4in
Ground clearance: 12.7cm 5.0in
Kerb weight: 940.7kg 2072.0lb
Fuel: 45.5L 10.0gal 12.0galUS

3005 MG
1100
1963 UK
80.0mph 128.7kmh
0-50mph 80.5kmh: 14.3secs
0-60mph 96.5kmh: 22.8secs
0-1/4 mile: 22.2secs
55.0bhp 41.0kW 55.8PS
@ 5500rpm
61.0lbft 82.7Nm @ 2500rpm
67.6bhp/ton 66.5bhp/tonne
50.1bhp/L 37.3kW/L 50.8PS/L
50.4ft/sec 15.4m/sec
15.0mph 24.1kmh/1000rpm
Petrol 4-stroke piston
1098cc 67.0cu in
In-line 4 2 Carburettor
Compression ratio: 8.9:1
Bore: 64.5mm 2.5in
Stroke: 83.8mm 3.3in
Valve type/No: Overhead 8
Transmission: Manual
No. of forward speeds: 4
Wheels driven: Front
Wheelbase: 237.5cm 93.5in
Track F: 130.8cm 51.5in
Track R: 129.3cm 50.9in
Length: 372.6cm 146.7in
Width: 153.4cm 60.4in
Height: 133.9cm 52.7in
Ground clearance: 15.2cm 6.0in
Kerb weight: 827.2kg 1822.0lb
Fuel: 37.8L 8.3gal 10.0galUS

3006 MG
Magnette Mk IV
1963 UK
86.5mph 139.2kmh
0-50mph 80.5kmh: 13.5secs
0-60mph 96.5kmh: 19.5secs
0-1/4 mile: 21.5secs
68.0bhp 50.7kW 68.9PS
@ 5000rpm
89.0lbft 120.6Nm @ 2500rpm
60.1bhp/ton 59.1bhp/tonne
41.9bhp/L 31.3kW/L 42.5PS/L
48.6ft/sec 14.8m/sec
16.5mph 26.5kmh/1000rpm
25.2mpg 21.0mpgUS 11.2L/100km
Petrol 4-stroke piston
1622cc 99.0cu in
In-line 4 2 Carburettor
Compression ratio: 8.3:1
Bore: 76.2mm 3.0in
Stroke: 88.9mm 3.5in
Valve type/No: Overhead 8
Transmission: Manual
No. of forward speeds: 4
Wheels driven: Rear
Springs F/R: Coil/Leaf
Brakes F/R: Drum/Drum
Steering: Cam & peg
Wheelbase: 254.5cm 100.2in
Track F: 128.5cm 50.6in
Track R: 130.6cm 51.4in
Length: 452.1cm 178.0in
Width: 161.3cm 63.5in
Height: 149.4cm 58.8in
Ground clearance: 15.0cm 5.9in
Kerb weight: 1150.4kg 2534.0lb
Fuel: 45.5L 10.0gal 12.0galUS

3007 MG
Midget
1963 UK
90.0mph 144.8kmh
0-50mph 80.5kmh: 12.0secs
0-60mph 96.5kmh: 17.2secs
0-1/4 mile: 21.1secs
56.0bhp 41.8kW 56.8PS
@ 5750rpm
62.0lbft 84.0Nm @ 3250rpm
78.6bhp/ton 77.3bhp/tonne
51.0bhp/L 38.0kW/L 51.7PS/L
52.7ft/sec 16.0m/sec
15.3mph 24.6kmh/1000rpm
29.1mpg 24.2mpgUS 9.7L/100km
Petrol 4-stroke piston
1098cc 67.0cu in
In-line 4 2 Carburettor
Compression ratio: 8.9:1
Bore: 64.6mm 2.5in
Stroke: 83.7mm 3.3in
Valve type/No: Overhead 8
Transmission: Manual
No. of forward speeds: 4
Wheels driven: Rear
Springs F/R: Coil/Leaf
Brakes F/R: Disc/Drum
Steering: Rack & pinion
Wheelbase: 203.2cm 80.0in
Track F: 116.1cm 45.7in
Track R: 113.5cm 44.7in
Length: 348.5cm 137.2in
Width: 134.6cm 53.0in
Height: 126.2cm 49.7in
Ground clearance: 12.7cm 5.0in
Kerb weight: 724.6kg 1596.0lb
Fuel: 27.3L 6.0gal 7.2galUS

3008 MG
B
1965 UK
106.0mph 170.6kmh
0-50mph 80.5kmh: 9.0secs
0-60mph 96.5kmh: 12.9secs
0-1/4 mile: 18.9secs
95.0bhp 70.8kW 96.3PS
@ 5400rpm
100.0lbft 135.5Nm @ 3000rpm
100.0bhp/ton 98.3bhp/tonne
52.8bhp/L 39.4kW/L 53.6PS/L
52.5ft/sec 16.0m/sec
22.4mph 36.0kmh/1000rpm
22.0mpg 18.3mpgUS 12.8L/100km
Petrol 4-stroke piston
1798cc 109.7cu in
In-line 4 2 Carburettor
Compression ratio: 8.8:1
Bore: 80.0mm 3.1in
Stroke: 89.0mm 3.5in
Valve type/No: Overhead 8
Transmission: Manual with overdrive
No. of forward speeds: 6
Wheels driven: Rear
Springs F/R: Coil/Leaf
Brakes F/R: Disc/Drum
Steering: Rack & pinion
Wheelbase: 231.1cm 91.0in
Track F: 124.5cm 49.0in
Track R: 125.0cm 49.2in
Length: 389.1cm 153.2in
Width: 152.1cm 59.9in
Height: 125.5cm 49.4in
Ground clearance: 12.7cm 5.0in
Kerb weight: 966.1kg 2128.0lb
Fuel: 45.5L 10.0gal 12.0galUS

3009 MG
B GT
1966 UK
105.0mph 168.9kmh
0-50mph 80.5kmh: 9.9secs
0-60mph 96.5kmh: 13.6secs
0-1/4 mile: 19.6secs
98.0bhp 73.1kW 99.4PS
@ 5400rpm
107.0lbft 145.0Nm @ 3500rpm
95.1bhp/ton 93.5bhp/tonne
54.5bhp/L 40.6kW/L 55.3PS/L
52.5ft/sec 16.0m/sec
17.5mph 28.2kmh/1000rpm
Petrol 4-stroke piston
1798cc 109.7cu in
In-line 4 2 Carburettor
Compression ratio: 8.8:1
Bore: 80.3mm 3.2in
Stroke: 89.0mm 3.5in
Valve type/No: Overhead 8
Transmission: Manual
No. of forward speeds: 4
Wheels driven: Rear
Springs F/R: Coil/Leaf
Brakes F/R: Disc/Drum
Steering: Rack & pinion
Wheelbase: 231.1cm 91.0in
Track F: 125.0cm 49.2in
Track R: 125.0cm 49.2in
Length: 389.1cm 153.2in
Width: 152.1cm 59.9in
Height: 126.5cm 49.8in
Ground clearance: 11.4cm 4.5in
Kerb weight: 1047.8kg 2308.0lb
Fuel: 45.4L 10.0gal 12.0galUS

3010 MG
B GT Coupe
1966 UK
102.0mph 164.1kmh
0-50mph 80.5kmh: 9.3secs
0-60mph 96.5kmh: 13.6secs
0-1/4 mile: 19.1secs
0-1km: 35.5secs
95.0bhp 70.8kW 96.3PS
@ 5400rpm
110.0lbft 149.1Nm @ 3000rpm
89.4bhp/ton 88.0bhp/tonne
52.8bhp/L 39.4kW/L 53.6PS/L
52.5ft/sec 16.0m/sec
22.3mph 35.9kmh/1000rpm
22.8mpg 19.0mpgUS 12.4L/100km
Petrol 4-stroke piston
1798cc 109.7cu in
In-line 4 2 Carburettor
Compression ratio: 8.8:1
Bore: 80.3mm 3.2in
Stroke: 89.0mm 3.5in
Valve type/No: Overhead 8
Transmission: Manual with overdrive
No. of forward speeds: 6
Wheels driven: Rear
Springs F/R: Coil/Leaf
Brakes F/R: Disc/Drum
Steering: Rack & pinion
Wheelbase: 231.1cm 91.0in
Track F: 124.5cm 49.0in
Track R: 125.0cm 49.2in
Length: 389.1cm 153.2in
Width: 152.1cm 59.9in
Height: 125.5cm 49.4in
Ground clearance: 12.7cm 5.0in
Kerb weight: 1080.1kg 2379.0lb
Fuel: 54.6L 12.0gal 14.4galUS

3011 MG
C
1967 UK
121.0mph 194.7kmh
0-50mph 80.5kmh: 7.6secs
0-60mph 96.5kmh: 10.0secs
0-1/4 mile: 17.7secs
0-1km: 32.0secs
145.0bhp 108.1kW 147.0PS
@ 5250rpm
170.0lbft 230.4Nm @ 3400rpm
131.1bhp/ton 128.9bhp/tonne
49.8bhp/L 37.1kW/L 50.5PS/L
51.0ft/sec 15.6m/sec
26.9mph 43.3kmh/1000rpm
17.5mpg 14.6mpgUS 16.1L/100km
Petrol 4-stroke piston
2912cc 177.7cu in
In-line 6 2 Carburettor
Compression ratio: 9.0:1
Bore: 83.4mm 3.3in
Stroke: 88.9mm 3.5in
Valve type/No: Overhead 12
Transmission: Manual with overdrive
No. of forward speeds: 6
Wheels driven: Rear
Springs F/R: Coil/Leaf
Brake system: PA
Brakes F/R: Disc/Drum
Steering: Rack & pinion
Wheelbase: 231.1cm 91.0in
Track F: 127.0cm 50.0in
Track R: 125.0cm 49.2in
Length: 389.1cm 153.2in
Width: 152.1cm 59.9in
Height: 127.5cm 50.2in
Ground clearance: 11.4cm 4.5in
Kerb weight: 1124.6kg 2477.0lb
Fuel: 54.6L 12.0gal 14.4galUS

3012 MG
Midget Mk III
1967 UK
95.0mph 152.9kmh
0-50mph 80.5kmh: 9.9secs
0-60mph 96.5kmh: 14.6secs
0-1/4 mile: 19.7secs
0-1km: 37.4secs
65.0bhp 48.5kW 65.9PS
@ 6000rpm
72.0lbft 97.6Nm @ 3000rpm
91.6bhp/ton 90.1bhp/tonne
51.0bhp/L 38.0kW/L 51.7PS/L
53.3ft/sec 16.3m/sec
15.4mph 24.8kmh/1000rpm
28.4mpg 23.6mpgUS 9.9L/100km
Petrol 4-stroke piston
1275cc 77.8cu in
In-line 4 2 Carburettor
Compression ratio: 8.8:1
Bore: 70.6mm 2.8in
Stroke: 81.3mm 3.2in
Valve type/No: Overhead 8
Transmission: Manual
No. of forward speeds: 4
Wheels driven: Rear
Springs F/R: Coil/Leaf
Brakes F/R: Disc/Drum
Steering: Rack & pinion
Wheelbase: 203.2cm 80.0in
Track F: 116.1cm 45.7in
Track R: 113.5cm 44.7in
Length: 348.5cm 137.2in
Width: 134.6cm 53.0in
Height: 124.5cm 49.0in
Ground clearance: 12.7cm 5.0in
Kerb weight: 721.4kg 1589.0lb
Fuel: 27.3L 6.0gal 7.2galUS

3013 MG
1300 Mk II
1968 UK
101.0mph 162.5kmh
0-50mph 80.5kmh: 9.4secs
0-60mph 96.5kmh: 14.1secs
0-1/4 mile: 19.6secs
0-1km: 36.4secs
70.0bhp 52.2kW 71.0PS
@ 6000rpm
77.0lbft 104.3Nm @ 3000rpm
84.9bhp/ton 83.5bhp/tonne
54.9bhp/L 40.9kW/L 55.7PS/L
53.3ft/sec 16.3m/sec
16.8mph 27.0kmh/1000rpm
26.8mpg 22.3mpgUS 10.5L/100km
Petrol 4-stroke piston
1275cc 77.8cu in
In-line 4 2 Carburettor
Compression ratio: 9.7:1
Bore: 70.6mm 2.8in
Stroke: 81.3mm 3.2in
Valve type/No: Overhead 8
Transmission: Manual
No. of forward speeds: 4
Wheels driven: Front
Springs F/R: Gas/Gas
Brakes F/R: Disc/Drum
Steering: Rack & pinion
Wheelbase: 237.5cm 93.5in
Track F: 130.8cm 51.5in
Track R: 129.5cm 51.0in
Length: 372.6cm 146.7in
Width: 153.7cm 60.5in
Height: 134.6cm 53.0in
Ground clearance: 15.2cm 6.0in
Kerb weight: 838.5kg 1847.0lb
Fuel: 36.4L 8.0gal 9.6galUS

3014 MG
1300 Mk II Auto
1968 UK
95.0mph 152.9kmh
0-50mph 80.5kmh: 10.3secs
0-60mph 96.5kmh: 14.3secs
0-1/4 mile: 20.3secs
0-1km: 38.4secs
70.0bhp 52.2kW 71.0PS
@ 6000rpm
77.0lbft 104.3Nm @ 3000rpm
81.0bhp/ton 79.6bhp/tonne
54.9bhp/L 40.9kW/L 55.7PS/L
53.3ft/sec 16.3m/sec
16.3mph 26.2kmh/1000rpm
25.4mpg 21.1mpgUS 11.1L/100km
Petrol 4-stroke piston
1275cc 77.8cu in
In-line 4 2 Carburettor
Compression ratio: 9.7:1
Bore: 70.6mm 2.8in
Stroke: 81.3mm 3.2in
Valve type/No: Overhead 8
Transmission: Automatic
No. of forward speeds: 4
Wheels driven: Front
Springs F/R: Gas/Gas
Brakes F/R: Disc/Drum
Steering: Rack & pinion
Wheelbase: 242.6cm 95.5in
Track F: 130.8cm 51.5in
Track R: 129.5cm 51.0in
Length: 372.6cm 146.7in
Width: 153.7cm 60.5in
Height: 134.6cm 53.0in
Ground clearance: 15.2cm 6.0in
Kerb weight: 878.9kg 1936.0lb
Fuel: 36.4L 8.0gal 9.6galUS

3015 MG
B All-Synchro
1968 UK
104.0mph 167.3kmh
0-50mph 80.5kmh: 8.4secs
0-60mph 96.5kmh: 12.1secs
0-1/4 mile: 18.7secs
92.0bhp 68.6kW 93.3PS
@ 5400rpm
110.0lbft 149.1Nm @ 3000rpm
92.8bhp/ton 91.3bhp/tonne
51.2bhp/L 38.1kW/L 51.9PS/L
52.5ft/sec 16.0m/sec
17.6mph 28.3kmh/1000rpm
Petrol 4-stroke piston
1798cc 109.7cu in
In-line 4 2 Carburettor
Compression ratio: 8.8:1
Bore: 80.3mm 3.2in
Stroke: 89.0mm 3.5in
Valve type/No: Overhead 8
Transmission: Manual
No. of forward speeds: 4
Wheels driven: Rear
Springs F/R: Coil/Leaf
Brakes F/R: Disc/Drum
Steering: Rack & pinion
Wheelbase: 231.1cm 91.0in
Track F: 125.0cm 49.2in
Track R: 125.0cm 49.2in
Length: 389.1cm 153.2in
Width: 152.1cm 59.9in
Height: 126.5cm 49.8in
Ground clearance: 11.4cm 4.5in
Kerb weight: 1007.9kg 2220.0lb
Fuel: 45.4L 10.0gal 12.0galUS

3016 MG
C GT Automatic
1968 UK
117.0mph 188.3kmh
0-50mph 80.5kmh: 8.2secs
0-60mph 96.5kmh: 10.9secs
0-1/4 mile: 18.2secs
0-1km: 33.2secs
145.0bhp 108.1kW 147.0PS
@ 5250rpm
170.0lbft 230.4Nm @ 3400rpm
124.2bhp/ton 122.1bhp/tonne
49.8bhp/L 37.1kW/L 50.5PS/L
51.0ft/sec 15.6m/sec
22.1mph 35.6kmh/1000rpm
19.0mpg 15.8mpgUS 14.9L/100km
Petrol 4-stroke piston
2912cc 177.7cu in
In-line 6 2 Carburettor
Compression ratio: 9.0:1
Bore: 83.4mm 3.3in
Stroke: 88.9mm 3.5in
Valve type/No: Overhead 12
Transmission: Automatic
No. of forward speeds: 3
Wheels driven: Rear
Springs F/R: Torsion bar/Leaf
Brake system: PA
Brakes F/R: Disc/Drum
Steering: Rack & pinion
Wheelbase: 231.1cm 91.0in
Track F: 127.0cm 50.0in
Track R: 125.0cm 49.2in
Length: 389.1cm 153.2in
Width: 152.1cm 59.9in
Height: 127.0cm 50.0in
Ground clearance: 14.0cm 5.5in
Kerb weight: 1187.2kg 2615.0lb
Fuel: 54.6L 12.0gal 14.4galUS

3017 MG
C
1969 UK
118.0mph 189.9kmh
0-50mph 80.5kmh: 7.2secs
0-60mph 96.5kmh: 10.1secs
0-1/4 mile: 17.7secs
145.0bhp 108.1kW 147.0PS
@ 5250rpm
170.0lbft 230.4Nm @ 3500rpm
124.9bhp/ton 122.8bhp/tonne
49.8bhp/L 37.1kW/L 50.5PS/L
51.0ft/sec 15.6m/sec
24.7mph 39.7kmh/1000rpm
21.4mpg 17.8mpgUS 13.2L/100km
Petrol 4-stroke piston
2912cc 177.7cu in
In-line 6 2 Carburettor
Compression ratio: 9.0:1
Bore: 83.3mm 3.3in
Stroke: 88.9mm 3.5in
Valve type/No: Overhead 12
Transmission: Manual with overdrive
Wheels driven: Rear
Springs F/R: Torsion bar/Leaf
Brakes F/R: Disc/Drum
Steering: Rack & pinion
Wheelbase: 231.1cm 91.0in
Track F: 127.0cm 50.0in
Track R: 125.0cm 49.2in
Length: 389.1cm 153.2in
Width: 152.1cm 59.9in
Height: 126.5cm 49.8in
Ground clearance: 11.2cm 4.4in
Kerb weight: 1180.4kg 2600.0lb
Fuel: 53.0L 11.6gal 14.0galUS

3018 MG
B Automatic
1970 UK
106.0mph 170.6kmh
0-50mph 80.5kmh: 10.0secs
0-60mph 96.5kmh: 13.6secs
0-1/4 mile: 19.5secs
0-1km: 35.7secs
95.0bhp 70.8kW 96.3PS
@ 5400rpm
100.0lbft 135.5Nm @ 3000rpm
99.3bhp/ton 97.6bhp/tonne
52.8bhp/L 39.4kW/L 53.6PS/L
52.5ft/sec 16.0m/sec
19.0mph 30.6kmh/1000rpm
25.5mpg 21.2mpgUS 11.1L/100km
Petrol 4-stroke piston
1798cc 109.7cu in
In-line 4 2 Carburettor
Compression ratio: 8.8:1
Bore: 80.0mm 3.1in
Stroke: 89.0mm 3.5in
Valve type/No: Overhead 8
Transmission: Automatic
No. of forward speeds: 3
Wheels driven: Rear
Springs F/R: Coil/Leaf
Brakes F/R: Disc/Drum
Steering: Rack & pinion
Wheelbase: 231.1cm 91.0in
Track F: 124.5cm 49.0in
Track R: 125.0cm 49.2in
Length: 389.1cm 153.2in
Width: 152.1cm 59.9in
Height: 125.5cm 49.4in
Ground clearance: 12.7cm 5.0in
Kerb weight: 972.9kg 2143.0lb
Fuel: 54.6L 12.0gal 14.4galUS

3019 MG
B Mk II
1970 UK
104.0mph 167.3kmh
0-60mph 96.5kmh: 12.1secs
0-1/4 mile: 18.7secs
92.0bhp 68.6kW 93.3PS
@ 5400rpm
110.0lbft 149.1Nm @ 3000rpm
92.8bhp/ton 91.3bhp/tonne
51.2bhp/L 38.1kW/L 51.9PS/L
52.5ft/sec 16.0m/sec
28.2mpg 23.5mpgUS 10.0L/100km
Petrol 4-stroke piston
1798cc 109.7cu in
In-line 4
Bore: 80.3mm 3.2in
Stroke: 89.0mm 3.5in
Valve type/No: Overhead 8
Transmission: Manual
No. of forward speeds: 4
Wheels driven: Rear
Brakes F/R: Disc/Drum
Wheelbase: 231.1cm 91.0in
Track F: 124.5cm 49.0in
Track R: 125.2cm 49.3in
Length: 387.9cm 152.7in
Width: 152.1cm 59.9in
Height: 125.5cm 49.4in
Kerb weight: 1007.9kg 2220.0lb
Fuel: 45.4L 10.0gal 12.0galUS

3020 MG
B GT
1971 UK
105.0mph 168.9kmh
0-50mph 80.5kmh: 8.7secs
0-60mph 96.5kmh: 13.0secs
0-1/4 mile: 18.5secs
0-1km: 34.7secs
95.0bhp 70.8kW 96.3PS
@ 5400rpm
110.0lbft 149.1Nm @ 3000rpm
89.4bhp/ton 88.0bhp/tonne
52.8bhp/L 39.4kW/L 53.6PS/L
52.5ft/sec 16.0m/sec
22.1mph 35.6kmh/1000rpm
23.7mpg 19.7mpgUS 11.9L/100km
Petrol 4-stroke piston
1798cc 109.7cu in
In-line 4 2 Carburettor
Compression ratio: 8.8:1
Bore: 80.3mm 3.2in
Stroke: 89.0mm 3.5in
Valve type/No: Overhead 8
Transmission: Manual with overdrive
No. of forward speeds: 6
Wheels driven: Rear
Springs F/R: Coil/Leaf
Brakes F/R: Disc/Drum
Steering: Rack & pinion
Wheelbase: 231.1cm 91.0in
Track F: 124.5cm 49.0in
Track R: 125.0cm 49.2in
Length: 389.1cm 153.2in
Width: 152.4cm 60.0in
Height: 125.5cm 49.4in
Ground clearance: 12.7cm 5.0in
Kerb weight: 1080.1kg 2379.0lb
Fuel: 54.6L 12.0gal 14.4galUS

3021 MG
Midget Mk III
1971 UK
96.0mph 154.5kmh
0-50mph 80.5kmh: 9.6secs
0-60mph 96.5kmh: 14.1secs
0-1/4 mile: 19.6secs
0-1km: 36.6secs
64.0bhp 47.7kW 64.9PS
@ 5800rpm
72.0lbft 97.6Nm @ 3000rpm
92.7bhp/ton 91.2bhp/tonne
50.2bhp/L 37.4kW/L 50.9PS/L
51.6ft/sec 15.7m/sec
16.5mph 26.5kmh/1000rpm
29.6mpg 24.6mpgUS 9.5L/100km
Petrol 4-stroke piston
1275cc 77.8cu in
In-line 4 2 Carburettor
Compression ratio: 8.8:1
Bore: 70.6mm 2.8in
Stroke: 81.3mm 3.2in
Valve type/No: Overhead 8
Transmission: Manual
No. of forward speeds: 4
Wheels driven: Rear
Springs F/R: Coil/Leaf
Brakes F/R: Disc/Drum
Steering: Rack & pinion
Wheelbase: 203.2cm 80.0in
Track F: 117.6cm 46.3in
Track R: 113.5cm 44.7in
Length: 349.0cm 137.4in
Width: 139.4cm 54.9in
Height: 123.4cm 48.6in
Ground clearance: 12.7cm 5.0in
Kerb weight: 701.9kg 1546.0lb
Fuel: 27.3L 6.0gal 7.2galUS

3022 MG
Costello B GT V8
1972 UK
130.0mph 209.2kmh
0-50mph 80.5kmh: 5.9secs
0-60mph 96.5kmh: 7.8secs
0-1/4 mile: 15.8secs
0-1km: 28.9secs
150.0bhp 111.9kW 152.1PS
@ 5000rpm
201.0lbft 272.4Nm @ 2750rpm
146.6bhp/ton 144.1bhp/tonne
42.5bhp/L 31.7kW/L 43.1PS/L
38.9ft/sec 11.8m/sec
27.9mph 44.9kmh/1000rpm
18.8mpg 15.7mpgUS 15.0L/100km
Petrol 4-stroke piston
3528cc 215.2cu in
Vee 8 2 Carburettor
Compression ratio: 10.5:1
Bore: 88.9mm 3.5in
Stroke: 71.1mm 2.8in
Valve type/No: Overhead 16
Transmission: Manual with overdrive
No. of forward speeds: 6
Wheels driven: Rear
Springs F/R: Coil/Leaf
Brakes F/R: Disc/Drum
Steering: Rack & pinion
Wheelbase: 231.1cm 91.0in
Track F: 124.5cm 49.0in
Track R: 125.0cm 49.2in
Length: 389.1cm 153.2in
Width: 152.4cm 60.0in
Height: 125.5cm 49.4in
Ground clearance: 12.7cm 5.0in
Kerb weight: 1040.6kg 2292.0lb
Fuel: 54.6L 12.0gal 14.4galUS

3023 MG
B
1973 UK
100.0mph 160.9kmh
0-50mph 80.5kmh: 10.0secs
0-60mph 96.5kmh: 13.7secs
0-1/4 mile: 19.5secs
79.0bhp 58.9kW 80.1PS
@ 5350rpm
94.0lbft 127.4Nm @ 3000rpm
78.3bhp/ton 77.0bhp/tonne
43.9bhp/L 32.8kW/L 44.5PS/L
52.0ft/sec 15.9m/sec
17.6mph 28.3kmh/1000rpm
26.4mpg 22.0mpgUS 10.7L/100km
Petrol 4-stroke piston
1798cc 109.7cu in
In-line 4 2 Carburettor
Compression ratio: 8.0:1
Bore: 80.3mm 3.2in
Stroke: 89.0mm 3.5in
Valve type/No: Overhead 8
Transmission: Manual
No. of forward speeds: 4
Wheels driven: Rear
Springs F/R: Coil/Leaf
Brakes F/R: Disc/Drum
Steering: Rack & pinion
Wheelbase: 231.1cm 91.0in
Track F: 125.2cm 49.3in
Track R: 125.2cm 49.3in
Length: 387.9cm 152.7in
Width: 152.1cm 59.9in
Height: 125.5cm 49.4in
Ground clearance: 12.7cm 5.0in
Kerb weight: 1026.0kg 2260.0lb
Fuel: 53.0L 11.6gal 14.0galUS

3024 MG
B GT
1973 UK
96.0mph 154.5kmh
0-50mph 80.5kmh: 10.7secs
0-60mph 96.5kmh: 14.6secs
0-1/4 mile: 20.0secs
79.0bhp 58.9kW 80.1PS
@ 5350rpm
94.0lbft 127.4Nm @ 3000rpm
74.3bhp/ton 73.1bhp/tonne
43.9bhp/L 32.8kW/L 44.5PS/L
Petrol 4-stroke piston
1798cc 109.7cu in
In-line 4
Transmission: Manual
No. of forward speeds: 4
Wheels driven: Rear
Springs F/R: Coil/Leaf
Brakes F/R: Disc/Drum
Wheelbase: 231.1cm 91.0in
Track F: 125.2cm 49.3in
Track R: 125.2cm 49.3in
Length: 387.9cm 152.7in
Width: 152.1cm 59.9in
Height: 125.5cm 49.4in
Kerb weight: 1080.5kg 2380.0lb

3025 MG
B GT V8
1973 UK
125.4mph 201.8kmh
0-50mph 80.5kmh: 6.4secs
0-60mph 96.5kmh: 8.6secs
0-1/4 mile: 16.4secs
0-1km: 30.4secs
137.0bhp 102.2kW 138.9PS
@ 5000rpm
193.0lbft 261.5Nm @ 2900rpm
128.6bhp/ton 126.4bhp/tonne
38.8bhp/L 29.0kW/L 39.4PS/L
38.9ft/sec 11.8m/sec
28.5mph 45.9kmh/1000rpm
23.4mpg 19.5mpgUS 12.1L/100km
Petrol 4-stroke piston
3528cc 215.2cu in
Vee 8 2 Carburettor
Compression ratio: 8.2:1
Bore: 88.9mm 3.5in
Stroke: 71.1mm 2.8in
Valve type/No: Overhead 16
Transmission: Manual with overdrive
No. of forward speeds: 5
Wheels driven: Rear
Springs F/R: Coil/Leaf
Brakes F/R: Disc/Drum
Steering: Rack & pinion
Wheelbase: 231.1cm 91.0in
Track F: 124.5cm 49.0in
Track R: 125.0cm 49.2in
Length: 392.9cm 154.7in
Width: 152.4cm 60.0in
Height: 127.0cm 50.0in
Ground clearance: 11.4cm 4.5in
Kerb weight: 1083.7kg 2387.0lb
Fuel: 54.6L 12.0gal 14.4galUS

3026 MG
Midget
1973 UK
90.0mph 144.8kmh
0-50mph 80.5kmh: 10.7secs
0-60mph 96.5kmh: 15.5secs
0-1/4 mile: 20.3secs
55.0bhp 41.0kW 55.8PS
@ 5500rpm
67.0lbft 90.8Nm @ 3250rpm
75.6bhp/ton 74.3bhp/tonne
43.1bhp/L 32.2kW/L 43.7PS/L
48.7ft/sec 14.8m/sec
16.3mph 26.2kmh/1000rpm
28.8mpg 24.0mpgUS 9.8L/100km
Petrol 4-stroke piston
1275cc 77.8cu in
In-line 4 2 Carburettor
Compression ratio: 8.0:1
Bore: 71.0mm 2.8in
Stroke: 81.0mm 3.2in
Valve type/No: Overhead 8
Transmission: Manual
No. of forward speeds: 4
Wheels driven: Rear
Springs F/R: Coil/Leaf
Brakes F/R: Disc/Drum
Steering: Rack & pinion
Wheelbase: 203.2cm 80.0in
Track F: 117.6cm 46.3in
Track R: 113.8cm 44.8in
Length: 349.5cm 137.6in
Width: 139.4cm 54.9in
Height: 126.5cm 49.8in
Ground clearance: 12.7cm 5.0in
Kerb weight: 740.0kg 1630.0lb
Fuel: 27.6L 6.1gal 7.3galUS

3027 MG
B
1975 UK
111.0mph 178.6kmh
0-50mph 80.5kmh: 8.2secs
0-60mph 96.5kmh: 12.1secs
0-1/4 mile: 18.3secs
0-1km: 34.3secs
84.0bhp 62.6kW 85.2PS
@ 5250rpm
102.0lbft 138.2Nm @ 2500rpm
82.2bhp/ton 80.8bhp/tonne
46.7bhp/L 34.8kW/L 47.4PS/L
51.0ft/sec 15.6m/sec
21.8mph 35.1kmh/1000rpm
26.1mpg 21.7mpgUS 10.8L/100km
Petrol 4-stroke piston
1798cc 109.7cu in
In-line 4 2 Carburettor
Compression ratio: 9.0:1

Bore: 80.3mm 3.2in
Stroke: 89.0mm 3.5in
Valve type/No: Overhead 8
Transmission: Manual with overdrive
No. of forward speeds: 6
Wheels driven: Rear
Springs F/R: Coil/Leaf
Brake system: PA
Brakes F/R: Disc/Drum
Steering: Rack & pinion
Wheelbase: 231.1cm 91.0in
Track F: 124.5cm 49.0in
Track R: 125.0cm 49.2in
Length: 401.8cm 158.2in
Width: 152.4cm 60.0in
Height: 129.5cm 51.0in
Ground clearance: 12.7cm 5.0in
Kerb weight: 1039.2kg 2289.0lb
Fuel: 54.6L 12.0gal 14.4galUS

3028 MG

Midget 1500
1975 UK
102.0mph 164.1kmh
0-50mph 80.5kmh: 8.5secs
0-60mph 96.5kmh: 12.3secs
0-1/4 mile: 18.5secs
0-1km: 34.9secs
66.0bhp 49.2kW 66.9PS
@ 5500rpm
77.0lbft 104.3Nm @ 3000rpm
85.9bhp/ton 84.5bhp/tonne
44.2bhp/L 33.0kW/L 44.8PS/L
52.6ft/sec 16.0m/sec
16.4mph 26.4kmh/1000rpm
27.9mpg 23.2mpgUS 10.1L/100km
Petrol 4-stroke piston
1493cc 91.1cu in
In-line 4 2 Carburettor
Compression ratio: 9.0:1
Bore: 73.7mm 2.9in
Stroke: 87.5mm 3.4in
Valve type/No: Overhead 8
Transmission: Manual
No. of forward speeds: 4
Wheels driven: Rear
Springs F/R: Coil/Leaf
Brakes F/R: Disc/Drum
Steering: Rack & pinion
Wheelbase: 203.2cm 80.0in
Track F: 117.6cm 46.3in
Track R: 113.5cm 44.7in
Length: 358.1cm 141.0in
Width: 139.4cm 54.9in
Height: 123.4cm 48.6in
Ground clearance: 12.7cm 5.0in
Kerb weight: 780.9kg 1720.0lb
Fuel: 31.8L 7.0gal 8.4galUS

3029 MG

B
1976 UK
90.0mph 144.8kmh
0-50mph 80.5kmh: 12.8secs
0-60mph 96.5kmh: 18.3secs
0-1/4 mile: 21.5secs
62.5bhp 46.6kW 63.4PS
@ 5000rpm
72.0lbft 97.6Nm @ 5000rpm
60.3bhp/ton 59.3bhp/tonne
34.8bhp/L 25.9kW/L 35.2PS/L
48.6ft/sec 14.8m/sec
26.4mpg 22.0mpgUS 10.7L/100km
Petrol 4-stroke piston
1798cc 109.7cu in
In-line 4 1 Carburettor
Compression ratio: 8.0:1
Bore: 80.3mm 3.2in
Stroke: 89.0mm 3.5in
Valve type/No: Overhead 8
Transmission: Manual
No. of forward speeds: 4
Wheels driven: Rear
Springs F/R: Coil/Leaf
Brakes F/R: Disc/Drum
Steering: Rack & pinion
Wheelbase: 231.4cm 91.1in
Track F: 124.5cm 49.0in
Track R: 125.2cm 49.3in
Length: 402.1cm 158.3in
Width: 139.4cm 54.9in
Height: 129.3cm 50.9in
Ground clearance: 10.7cm 4.2in
Kerb weight: 1053.3kg 2320.0lb
Fuel: 53.0L 11.6gal 14.0galUS

3030 MG

Midget
1976 UK
83.0mph 133.5kmh
0-60mph 96.5kmh: 15.5secs
0-1/4 mile: 20.1secs
55.5bhp 41.4kW 56.3PS
@ 5000rpm
73.0lbft 98.9Nm @ 2500rpm
70.8bhp/ton 69.7bhp/tonne
37.2bhp/L 27.7kW/L 37.7PS/L
47.8ft/sec 14.6m/sec
34.8mpg 29.0mpgUS 8.1L/100km
Petrol 4-stroke piston
1493cc 91.1cu in
In-line 4 1 Carburettor
Compression ratio: 9.0:1
Bore: 73.7mm 2.9in
Stroke: 87.4mm 3.4in
Valve type/No: Overhead 8
Transmission: Manual
No. of forward speeds: 4
Wheels driven: Rear
Wheelbase: 203.2cm 80.0in
Track F: 117.6cm 46.3in
Track R: 113.8cm 44.8in
Length: 358.1cm 141.0in
Width: 137.2cm 54.0in
Height: 122.7cm 48.3in
Kerb weight: 796.8kg 1755.0lb
Fuel: 28.4L 6.2gal 7.5galUS

3031 MG

Midget Mk IV
1976 UK
83.0mph 133.5kmh
0-50mph 80.5kmh: 10.7secs
0-60mph 96.5kmh: 15.5secs
0-1/4 mile: 20.1secs
55.5bhp 41.4kW 56.3PS
@ 5000rpm
73.0lbft 98.9Nm @ 2500rpm
70.0bhp/ton 68.9bhp/tonne
37.2bhp/L 27.7kW/L 37.7PS/L
47.8ft/sec 14.6m/sec
16.2mph 26.1kmh/1000rpm
33.0mpg 27.5mpgUS 8.6L/100km
Petrol 4-stroke piston
1493cc 91.1cu in
In-line 4
Compression ratio: 9.0:1
Bore: 73.7mm 2.9in
Stroke: 87.4mm 3.4in
Valve type/No: Overhead 8
Transmission: Manual
No. of forward speeds: 4
Wheels driven: Rear
Springs F/R: Coil/Leaf
Brakes F/R: Disc/Drum
Steering: Rack & pinion
Wheelbase: 203.2cm 80.0in
Track F: 117.6cm 46.3in
Track R: 113.8cm 44.8in
Length: 358.1cm 141.0in
Width: 137.2cm 54.0in
Height: 122.7cm 48.3in
Kerb weight: 805.8kg 1775.0lb
Fuel: 28.4L 6.2gal 7.5galUS

3032 MG

B GT
1977 UK
104.0mph 167.3kmh
0-50mph 80.5kmh: 9.3secs
0-60mph 96.5kmh: 14.0secs
0-1/4 mile: 19.1secs
0-1km: 36.4secs
84.0bhp 62.6kW 85.2PS
@ 5500rpm
105.0lbft 142.3Nm @ 2500rpm
77.0bhp/ton 75.8bhp/tonne
46.7bhp/L 34.8kW/L 47.4PS/L
53.5ft/sec 16.3m/sec
21.8mph 35.1kmh/1000rpm
25.7mpg 21.4mpgUS 11.0L/100km
Petrol 4-stroke piston
1798cc 109.7cu in
In-line 4 2 Carburettor
Compression ratio: 9.0:1
Bore: 80.3mm 3.2in
Stroke: 88.9mm 3.5in
Valve type/No: Overhead 8
Transmission: Manual with overdrive
No. of forward speeds: 6
Wheels driven: Rear
Springs F/R: Coil/Leaf
Brake system: PA
Brakes F/R: Disc/Drum
Steering: Rack & pinion
Wheelbase: 231.1cm 91.0in
Track F: 124.5cm 49.0in
Track R: 125.0cm 49.2in
Length: 401.8cm 158.2in
Width: 156.7cm 61.7in
Height: 129.5cm 51.0in
Ground clearance: 12.7cm 5.0in
Kerb weight: 1108.7kg 2442.0lb
Fuel: 50.0L 11.0gal 13.2galUS

3033 MG

B
1979 UK
93.0mph 149.6kmh
0-50mph 80.5kmh: 9.4secs
0-60mph 96.5kmh: 13.9secs
0-1/4 mile: 19.8secs
62.5bhp 46.6kW 63.4PS
@ 4600rpm
88.0lbft 119.2Nm @ 2500rpm
60.0bhp/ton 59.0bhp/tonne
34.8bhp/L 25.9kW/L 35.2PS/L
44.7ft/sec 13.6m/sec
18.4mph 29.6kmh/1000rpm
22.2mpg 18.5mpgUS 12.7L/100km
Petrol 4-stroke piston
1798cc 109.7cu in
In-line 4
Compression ratio: 8.0:1
Bore: 80.3mm 3.2in
Stroke: 89.0mm 3.5in
Valve type/No: Overhead 8
Transmission: Manual with overdrive
Wheels driven: Rear
Springs F/R: Coil/Leaf
Brake system: PA
Brakes F/R: Disc/Drum
Steering: Rack & pinion
Wheelbase: 231.4cm 91.1in
Track F: 124.5cm 49.0in
Track R: 125.0cm 49.2in
Length: 401.8cm 158.2in
Width: 152.1cm 59.9in
Height: 129.5cm 51.0in
Kerb weight: 1060.1kg 2335.0lb
Fuel: 49.2L 10.8gal 13.0galUS

3034 MG

Midget
1979 UK
85.0mph 136.8kmh
0-50mph 80.5kmh: 10.2secs
0-60mph 96.5kmh: 14.3secs
0-1/4 mile: 20.3secs
50.0bhp 37.3kW 50.7PS
@ 5000rpm
67.0lbft 90.8Nm @ 2500rpm
61.0bhp/ton 60.0bhp/tonne
33.5bhp/L 25.0kW/L 33.9PS/L
47.8ft/sec 14.6m/sec
17.9mph 28.8kmh/1000rpm
34.2mpg 28.5mpgUS 8.3L/100km
Petrol 4-stroke piston
1493cc 91.1cu in
In-line 4
Compression ratio: 7.5:1
Bore: 73.7mm 2.9in
Stroke: 87.4mm 3.4in
Valve type/No: Overhead 8
Transmission: Manual
No. of forward speeds: 4
Wheels driven: Rear
Springs F/R: Coil/Leaf
Brakes F/R: Disc/Drum
Steering: Rack & pinion
Wheelbase: 203.2cm 80.0in
Track F: 117.6cm 46.3in
Track R: 113.8cm 44.8in
Length: 363.2cm 143.0in
Width: 137.2cm 54.0in
Height: 122.7cm 48.3in
Kerb weight: 833.1kg 1835.0lb
Fuel: 28.4L 6.2gal 7.5galUS

3035 MG

B
1980 UK
94.0mph 151.2kmh
0-50mph 80.5kmh: 9.3secs
0-60mph 96.5kmh: 13.6secs
0-1/4 mile: 19.6secs
67.0bhp 50.0kW 67.9PS
@ 4900rpm
94.0lbft 127.4Nm @ 2500rpm
64.3bhp/ton 63.2bhp/tonne
37.3bhp/L 27.8kW/L 37.8PS/L
47.6ft/sec 14.5m/sec
18.6mph 29.9kmh/1000rpm
22.2mpg 18.5mpgUS 12.7L/100km
Petrol 4-stroke piston
1798cc 109.7cu in
In-line 4 1 Carburettor
Compression ratio: 8.0:1
Bore: 80.3mm 3.2in
Stroke: 89.0mm 3.5in
Valve type/No: Overhead 8
Transmission: Manual
No. of forward speeds: 4
Wheels driven: Rear
Springs F/R: Coil/Leaf
Brake system: PA
Brakes F/R: Disc/Drum
Steering: Rack & pinion
Wheelbase: 231.4cm 91.1in
Track F: 124.5cm 49.0in
Track R: 125.0cm 49.2in
Length: 401.8cm 158.2in
Width: 152.1cm 59.9in
Height: 129.5cm 51.0in
Kerb weight: 1060.1kg 2335.0lb
Fuel: 49.2L 10.8gal 13.0galUS

3036 MG

Metro 1300
1982 UK
103.0mph 165.7kmh
0-50mph 80.5kmh: 8.2secs
0-60mph 96.5kmh: 12.2secs
0-1/4 mile: 18.6secs
0-1km: 36.7secs
72.0bhp 53.7kW 73.0PS
@ 6000rpm
73.0lbft 98.9Nm @ 4000rpm
90.3bhp/ton 88.8bhp/tonne
56.5bhp/L 42.1kW/L 57.2PS/L
53.3ft/sec 16.3m/sec
17.2mph 27.7kmh/1000rpm
38.8mpg 32.3mpgUS 7.3L/100km
Petrol 4-stroke piston
1275cc 77.8cu in
In-line 4 1 Carburettor
Compression ratio: 10.5:1
Bore: 70.6mm 2.8in
Stroke: 81.3mm 3.2in
Valve type/No: Overhead 8
Transmission: Manual
No. of forward speeds: 4
Wheels driven: Front
Springs F/R: Gas/Gas
Brake system: PA
Brakes F/R: Disc/Drum
Steering: Rack & pinion
Wheelbase: 225.0cm 88.6in
Track F: 127.3cm 50.1in
Track R: 127.3cm 50.1in
Length: 340.6cm 134.1in
Width: 154.7cm 60.9in
Height: 136.1cm 53.6in
Ground clearance: 16.5cm 6.5in
Kerb weight: 810.4kg 1785.0lb
Fuel: 30.0L 6.6gal 7.9galUS

3037 MG

Metro Turbo
1983 UK
111.0mph 178.6kmh
0-50mph 80.5kmh: 6.5secs
0-60mph 96.5kmh: 9.4secs
0-1/4 mile: 17.0secs
0-1km: 32.1secs
93.0bhp 69.3kW 94.3PS
@ 6130rpm
85.0lbft 115.2Nm @ 2650rpm
114.1bhp/ton 112.2bhp/tonne
72.9bhp/L 54.4kW/L 73.9PS/L
54.5ft/sec 16.6m/sec
18.6mph 29.9kmh/1000rpm
30.3mpg 25.2mpgUS 9.3L/100km
Petrol 4-stroke piston
1275cc 77.8cu in turbocharged
In-line 4 1 Carburettor
Compression ratio: 9.4:1
Bore: 70.6mm 2.8in
Stroke: 81.3mm 3.2in
Valve type/No: Overhead 8
Transmission: Manual
No. of forward speeds: 4
Wheels driven: Front
Springs F/R: Gas/Gas
Brake system: PA
Brakes F/R: Disc/Drum

Steering: Rack & pinion
Wheelbase: 225.0cm 88.6in
Track F: 131.3cm 51.7in
Track R: 128.8cm 50.7in
Length: 340.6cm 134.1in
Width: 156.0cm 61.4in
Height: 132.8cm 52.3in
Ground clearance: 16.5cm 6.5in
Kerb weight: 829.0kg 1826.0lb
Fuel: 30.0L 6.6gal 7.9galUS

3038 MG

Montego EFi
1984 UK
116.0mph 186.6kmh
0-50mph 80.5kmh: 6.8secs
0-60mph 96.5kmh: 9.6secs
0-1/4 mile: 17.0secs
0-1km: 31.6secs
117.0bhp 87.2kW 118.6PS
@ 5500rpm
134.0lbft 181.6Nm @ 2800rpm
113.9bhp/ton 112.0bhp/tonne
58.7bhp/L 43.8kW/L 59.5PS/L
53.5ft/sec 16.3m/sec
20.6mph 33.1kmh/1000rpm
29.3mpg 24.4mpgUS 9.6L/100km
Petrol 4-stroke piston
1994cc 121.7cu in
In-line 4 fuel injection
Compression ratio: 9.0:1
Bore: 84.5mm 3.3in
Stroke: 89.0mm 3.5in
Valve type/No: Overhead 8
Transmission: Manual
No. of forward speeds: 5
Wheels driven: Front
Springs F/R: Coil/Coil
Brake system: PA
Brakes F/R: Disc/Drum
Steering: Rack & pinion
Wheelbase: 256.5cm 101.0in
Track F: 144.0cm 56.7in
Track R: 145.8cm 57.4in
Length: 446.8cm 175.9in
Width: 170.9cm 67.3in
Height: 142.0cm 55.9in
Ground clearance: 15.7cm 6.2in
Kerb weight: 1044.2kg 2300.0lb
Fuel: 51.0L 11.2gal 13.5galUS

3039 MG

Montego Turbo
1985 UK
127.0mph 204.3kmh
0-50mph 80.5kmh: 5.7secs
0-60mph 96.5kmh: 7.5secs
0-1/4 mile: 15.9secs
0-1km: 29.2secs
150.0bhp 111.9kW 152.1PS
@ 5100rpm
169.0lbft 229.0Nm @ 3500rpm
141.2bhp/ton 138.8bhp/tonne
75.2bhp/L 56.1kW/L 76.3PS/L
49.6ft/sec 15.1m/sec
25.0mph 40.2kmh/1000rpm
23.0mpg 19.2mpgUS 12.3L/100km
Petrol 4-stroke piston
1994cc 121.7cu in turbocharged
In-line 4 1 Carburettor
Compression ratio: 8.5:1
Bore: 84.5mm 3.3in
Stroke: 89.0mm 3.5in
Valve type/No: Overhead 8
Transmission: Manual
No. of forward speeds: 5
Wheels driven: Front
Springs F/R: Coil/Coil
Brake system: PA
Brakes F/R: Disc/Drum
Steering: Rack & pinion PA
Wheelbase: 256.5cm 101.0in
Track F: 144.0cm 56.7in
Track R: 145.8cm 57.4in
Length: 446.8cm 175.9in
Width: 170.9cm 67.3in
Height: 142.0cm 55.9in
Ground clearance: 15.7cm 6.2in
Kerb weight: 1080.5kg 2380.0lb
Fuel: 50.0L 11.0gal 13.2galUS

3040 MG

Maestro Turbo
1989 UK
131.0mph 210.8kmh
0-50mph 80.5kmh: 5.2secs
0-60mph 96.5kmh: 6.9secs
0-1/4 mile: 15.4secs
0-1km: 28.4secs
152.0bhp 113.3kW 154.1PS
@ 5100rpm
169.0lbft 229.0Nm @ 3500rpm
143.1bhp/ton 140.7bhp/tonne
76.2bhp/L 56.8kW/L 77.3PS/L
49.6ft/sec 15.1m/sec
25.0mph 40.2kmh/1000rpm
20.9mpg 17.4mpgUS 13.5L/100km
Petrol 4-stroke piston
1994cc 122.0cu in turbocharged
In-line 4 1 Carburettor
Compression ratio: 8.5:1
Bore: 84.5mm 3.3in
Stroke: 89.0mm 3.5in
Valve type/No: Overhead 8
Transmission: Manual
No. of forward speeds: 5
Wheels driven: Front
Springs F/R: Coil/Coil
Brake system: PA
Brakes F/R: Disc/Drum
Steering: Rack & pinion PA
Wheelbase: 250.6cm 98.7in
Track F: 148.1cm 58.3in
Track R: 145.5cm 57.3in
Length: 400.3cm 157.6in
Width: 193.0cm 76.0in
Height: 142.0cm 55.9in
Ground clearance: 17.9cm 7.0in
Kerb weight: 1080.0kg 2378.8lb
Fuel: 50.0L 11.0gal 13.2galUS

3041 MG

B British Motor Heritage
1990 UK
105.0mph 168.9kmh
0-60mph 96.5kmh: 12.8secs
0-1/4 mile: 19.0secs
92.0bhp 68.6kW 93.3PS
@ 5400rpm
110.0lbft 149.1Nm @ 3000rpm
89.4bhp/ton 87.9bhp/tonne
51.2bhp/L 38.1kW/L 51.9PS/L
52.5ft/sec 16.0m/sec
30.0mpg 25.0mpgUS 9.4L/100km
Petrol 4-stroke piston
1798cc 109.7cu in
In-line 4 2 Carburettor
Compression ratio: 8.8:1
Bore: 80.3mm 3.2in
Stroke: 89.0mm 3.5in
Valve type/No: Overhead 8
Transmission: Manual with overdrive
Wheels driven: Rear
Springs F/R: Coil/Leaf
Brake system: PA
Brakes F/R: Disc/Drum
Steering: Rack & pinion
Wheelbase: 231.1cm 91.0in
Track F: 125.2cm 49.3in
Track R: 125.2cm 49.3in
Length: 387.9cm 152.7in
Width: 152.1cm 59.9in
Height: 126.5cm 49.8in
Kerb weight: 1046.5kg 2305.0lb
Fuel: 45.4L 10.0gal 12.0galUS

3042 Minerva

22/28hp Limousine
1930 Nederlands
72.0mph 115.8kmh
26.0mpg 21.6mpgUS 10.9L/100km
Petrol 4-stroke piston
3962cc 241.7cu in
In-line 8
Bore: 75.0mm 2.9in
Stroke: 112.0mm 4.4in
Transmission: Manual
No. of forward speeds: 4
Wheels driven: Rear
Brakes F/R: Drum/Drum
Wheelbase: 365.8cm 144.0in
Track F: 149.9cm 59.0in
Track R: 149.9cm 59.0in
Length: 533.4cm 210.0in
Width: 182.9cm 72.0in
Height: 182.9cm 72.0in
Kerb weight: 1983.1kg 4368.0lb
Fuel: 91.0L 20.0gal 24.0galUS

3043 Mini

Minor de Luxe
1959 UK
74.5mph 119.9kmh
0-50mph 80.5kmh: 16.9secs
0-60mph 96.5kmh: 26.5secs
0-1/4 mile: 23.3secs
37.0bhp 27.6kW 37.5PS
@ 5500rpm
44.0lbft 59.6Nm @ 2900rpm
62.0bhp/ton 61.0bhp/tonne
43.6bhp/L 32.5kW/L 44.2PS/L
41.1ft/sec 12.5m/sec
14.8mph 23.8kmh/1000rpm
40.1mpg 33.4mpgUS 7.0L/100km
Petrol 4-stroke piston
848cc 51.7cu in
In-line 4 1 Carburettor
Compression ratio: 8.3:1
Bore: 62.9mm 2.5in
Stroke: 68.2mm 2.7in
Valve type/No: Overhead 8
Transmission: Manual
No. of forward speeds: 4
Wheels driven: Front
Springs F/R: Rubber/Rubber
Brakes F/R: Drum/Drum
Steering: Rack & pinion
Wheelbase: 203.2cm 80.0in
Track F: 121.2cm 47.7in
Track R: 116.3cm 45.8in
Length: 304.8cm 120.0in
Width: 141.0cm 55.5in
Height: 134.6cm 53.0in
Ground clearance: 18.0cm 7.1in
Kerb weight: 607.0kg 1337.0lb
Fuel: 25.0L 5.5gal 6.6galUS

3044 Mini

Minor
1960 UK
75.0mph 120.7kmh
0-50mph 80.5kmh: 16.9secs
0-60mph 96.5kmh: 27.0secs
0-1/4 mile: 23.5secs
37.0bhp 27.6kW 37.5PS
@ 5500rpm
44.0lbft 59.6Nm @ 2900rpm
61.8bhp/ton 60.8bhp/tonne
43.6bhp/L 32.5kW/L 44.2PS/L
41.1ft/sec 12.5m/sec
15.0mph 24.1kmh/1000rpm
Petrol 4-stroke piston
848cc 51.7cu in
In-line 4 1 Carburettor
Compression ratio: 8.3:1
Bore: 63.0mm 2.5in
Stroke: 68.3mm 2.7in
Valve type/No: Overhead 8
Transmission: Manual
No. of forward speeds: 4
Wheels driven: Front
Wheelbase: 203.2cm 80.0in
Track F: 122.4cm 48.2in
Track R: 117.3cm 46.2in
Length: 304.8cm 120.0in
Width: 141.0cm 55.5in
Height: 134.6cm 53.0in
Kerb weight: 608.4kg 1340.0lb

3045 Mini

Traveller
1960 UK
68.5mph 110.2kmh
0-50mph 80.5kmh: 21.1secs
0-60mph 96.5kmh: 33.8secs
0-1/4 mile: 24.3secs
34.0bhp 25.3kW 34.5PS
@ 5500rpm
44.0lbft 59.6Nm @ 2900rpm
51.3bhp/ton 50.5bhp/tonne
40.1bhp/L 29.9kW/L 40.6PS/L
41.1ft/sec 12.5m/sec
14.8mph 23.8kmh/1000rpm
38.4mpg 32.0mpgUS 7.4L/100km
Petrol 4-stroke piston
848cc 51.7cu in
In-line 4 1 Carburettor
Compression ratio: 8.3:1
Bore: 62.9mm 2.5in
Stroke: 68.2mm 2.7in
Valve type/No: Overhead 8
Transmission: Manual
No. of forward speeds: 4
Wheels driven: Front
Springs F/R: Rubber/Rubber
Brakes F/R: Drum/Drum
Steering: Rack & pinion
Wheelbase: 213.6cm 84.1in
Track F: 121.2cm 47.7in
Track R: 116.3cm 45.8in
Length: 329.7cm 129.8in
Width: 141.0cm 55.5in
Height: 135.9cm 53.5in
Ground clearance: 16.3cm 6.4in
Kerb weight: 673.7kg 1484.0lb
Fuel: 29.6L 6.5gal 7.8galUS

3046 Mini

Cooper
1961 UK
87.4mph 140.6kmh
0-50mph 80.5kmh: 12.6secs
0-60mph 96.5kmh: 18.0secs
0-1/4 mile: 20.9secs
55.0bhp 41.0kW 55.8PS
@ 6000rpm
54.5lbft 73.8Nm @ 3600rpm
85.8bhp/ton 84.4bhp/tonne
55.2bhp/L 41.1kW/L 55.9PS/L
53.3ft/sec 16.2m/sec
14.9mph 24.0kmh/1000rpm
26.8mpg 22.3mpgUS 10.5L/100km
Petrol 4-stroke piston
997cc 60.8cu in
In-line 4 2 Carburettor
Compression ratio: 9.0:1
Bore: 62.4mm 2.5in
Stroke: 81.2mm 3.2in
Valve type/No: Overhead 8
Transmission: Manual
No. of forward speeds: 4
Wheels driven: Front
Springs F/R: Gas/Gas
Brakes F/R: Disc/Drum
Steering: Rack & pinion
Wheelbase: 203.2cm 80.0in
Track F: 121.2cm 47.7in
Track R: 116.6cm 45.9in
Length: 304.8cm 120.0in
Width: 139.7cm 55.0in
Height: 134.6cm 53.0in
Ground clearance: 16.3cm 6.4in
Kerb weight: 651.5kg 1435.0lb
Fuel: 25.0L 5.5gal 6.6galUS

3047 Mini

Cooper S
1963 UK
91.0mph 146.4kmh
0-50mph 80.5kmh: 9.6secs
0-60mph 96.5kmh: 13.5secs
0-1/4 mile: 19.2secs
70.0bhp 52.2kW 71.0PS
@ 6200rpm
62.0lbft 84.0Nm @ 4500rpm
108.0bhp/ton 106.2bhp/tonne
65.4bhp/L 48.7kW/L 66.3PS/L
46.3ft/sec 14.1m/sec
14.6mph 23.5kmh/1000rpm
29.4mpg 24.5mpgUS 9.6L/100km
Petrol 4-stroke piston
1071cc 65.3cu in
In-line 4 2 Carburettor
Compression ratio: 9.0:1
Bore: 70.6mm 2.8in
Stroke: 68.3mm 2.7in
Valve type/No: Overhead 8
Transmission: Manual
No. of forward speeds: 4
Wheels driven: Front
Springs F/R: Gas/Gas
Brake system: PA
Brakes F/R: Disc/Drum
Steering: Rack & pinion
Wheelbase: 203.2cm 80.0in
Track F: 122.9cm 48.4in
Track R: 116.6cm 45.9in
Length: 305.3cm 120.2in
Width: 141.0cm 55.5in
Height: 134.6cm 53.0in
Ground clearance: 15.2cm 6.0in
Kerb weight: 659.2kg 1452.0lb
Fuel: 25.0L 5.5gal 6.6galUS

3048 Mini

Super de Luxe
1963 UK
74.0mph 119.1kmh
0-50mph 80.5kmh: 18.3secs
0-60mph 96.5kmh: 29.7secs
0-1/4 mile: 23.6secs
34.0bhp 25.3kW 34.5PS
@ 5500rpm
44.0lbft 59.6Nm @ 2900rpm
54.4bhp/ton 53.5bhp/tonne

40.1bhp/L 29.9kW/L 40.6PS/L
41.1ft/sec 12.5m/sec
14.8mph 23.8kmh/1000rpm
36.6mpg 30.5mpgUS 7.7L/100km
Petrol 4-stroke piston
848cc 51.7cu in
In-line 4 1 Carburettor
Compression ratio: 8.3:1
Bore: 62.9mm 2.5in
Stroke: 68.2mm 2.7in
Valve type/No: Overhead 8
Transmission: Manual
No. of forward speeds: 4
Wheels driven: Front
Springs F/R: Rubber/Rubber
Brakes F/R: Drum/Drum
Steering: Rack & pinion
Wheelbase: 203.7cm 80.2in
Track F: 120.4cm 47.4in
Track R: 116.6cm 45.9in
Length: 305.3cm 120.2in
Width: 141.0cm 55.5in
Height: 134.6cm 53.0in
Ground clearance: 15.2cm 6.0in
Kerb weight: 635.6kg 1400.0lb
Fuel: 25.0L 5.5gal 6.6galUS

3049 Mini
Cooper 1275S
1964 UK
97.5mph 156.9kmh
0-50mph 80.5kmh: 8.2secs
0-60mph 96.5kmh: 11.2secs
0-1/4 mile: 18.4secs
76.0bhp 56.7kW 77.0PS
@ 5900rpm
79.0lbft 107.0Nm @ 3000rpm
118.6bhp/ton 116.7bhp/tonne
59.6bhp/L 44.4kW/L 60.4PS/L
52.4ft/sec 16.0m/sec
16.1mph 25.9kmh/1000rpm
28.5mpg 23.7mpgUS 9.9L/100km
Petrol 4-stroke piston
1275cc 77.8cu in
In-line 4 2 Carburettor
Compression ratio: 9.7:1
Bore: 70.6mm 2.8in
Stroke: 81.3mm 3.2in
Valve type/No: Overhead 8
Transmission: Manual
No. of forward speeds: 4
Wheels driven: Front
Springs F/R: Rubber/Rubber
Brake system: PA
Brakes F/R: Disc/Drum
Steering: Rack & pinion
Wheelbase: 203.2cm 80.0in
Track F: 122.9cm 48.4in
Track R: 119.1cm 46.9in
Length: 305.3cm 120.2in
Width: 141.0cm 55.5in
Height: 134.6cm 53.0in
Ground clearance: 15.2cm 6.0in
Kerb weight: 651.5kg 1435.0lb
Fuel: 25.0L 5.5gal 6.6galUS

3050 Mini
Cooper
1965 UK
90.0mph 144.8kmh
0-50mph 80.5kmh: 11.9secs
0-60mph 96.5kmh: 16.8secs
0-1/4 mile: 20.1secs
55.0bhp 41.0kW 55.8PS
@ 5800rpm
57.0lbft 77.2Nm @ 3000rpm
88.0bhp/ton 86.5bhp/tonne
55.1bhp/L 41.1kW/L 55.9PS/L
48.3ft/sec 14.7m/sec
14.8mph 23.8kmh/1000rpm
32.5mpg 27.1mpgUS 8.7L/100km
Petrol 4-stroke piston
998cc 60.9cu in
In-line 4 2 Carburettor
Compression ratio: 9.0:1
Bore: 64.6mm 2.5in
Stroke: 76.2mm 3.0in
Valve type/No: Overhead 8
Transmission: Manual
No. of forward speeds: 4
Wheels driven: Front
Springs F/R: Gas/Gas
Brakes F/R: Disc/Drum
Steering: Rack & pinion
Wheelbase: 203.2cm 80.0in
Track F: 120.4cm 47.4in
Track R: 116.6cm 45.9in
Length: 305.3cm 120.2in
Width: 141.0cm 55.5in
Height: 134.6cm 53.0in
Ground clearance: 15.2cm 6.0in
Kerb weight: 635.6kg 1400.0lb
Fuel: 25.0L 5.5gal 6.6galUS

3051 Mini
Cooper 1275S
1965 UK
98.0mph 157.7kmh
0-50mph 80.5kmh: 7.5secs
0-60mph 96.5kmh: 10.5secs
0-1/4 mile: 18.1secs
75.0bhp 55.9kW 76.0PS
@ 5800rpm
80.0lbft 108.4Nm @ 3000rpm
113.5bhp/ton 111.6bhp/tonne
58.8bhp/L 43.9kW/L 59.6PS/L
51.6ft/sec 15.7m/sec
16.1mph 25.9kmh/1000rpm
Petrol 4-stroke piston
1275cc 77.8cu in
In-line 4 2 Carburettor
Compression ratio: 9.8:1
Bore: 70.6mm 2.8in
Stroke: 81.3mm 3.2in
Valve type/No: Overhead 8
Transmission: Manual
No. of forward speeds: 4
Wheels driven: Front
Springs F/R: Gas/Gas
Brakes F/R: Disc/Drum
Steering: Rack & pinion
Wheelbase: 203.2cm 80.0in
Track F: 123.2cm 48.5in
Track R: 119.4cm 47.0in
Length: 306.8cm 120.8in
Width: 141.0cm 55.5in
Height: 135.4cm 53.3in
Ground clearance: 14.0cm 5.5in
Kerb weight: 671.9kg 1480.0lb
Fuel: 24.6L 5.4gal 6.5galUS

3052 Mini
Super de Luxe Mk II
1967 UK
79.0mph 127.1kmh
0-50mph 80.5kmh: 17.2secs
0-60mph 96.5kmh: 26.2secs
0-1/4 mile: 22.7secs
0-1km: 44.0secs
38.0bhp 28.3kW 38.5PS
@ 5250rpm
52.0lbft 70.5Nm @ 2700rpm
61.7bhp/ton 60.7bhp/tonne
38.1bhp/L 28.4kW/L 38.6PS/L
43.8ft/sec 13.3m/sec
16.2mph 26.1kmh/1000rpm
34.0mpg 28.3mpgUS 8.3L/100km
Petrol 4-stroke piston
998cc 60.9cu in
In-line 4 1 Carburettor
Compression ratio: 8.3:1
Bore: 64.6mm 2.5in
Stroke: 76.2mm 3.0in
Valve type/No: Overhead 8
Transmission: Manual
No. of forward speeds: 4
Wheels driven: Front
Springs F/R: Gas/Gas
Brakes F/R: Drum/Drum
Steering: Rack & pinion
Wheelbase: 203.2cm 80.0in
Track F: 120.4cm 47.4in
Track R: 116.6cm 45.9in
Length: 305.3cm 120.2in
Width: 141.0cm 55.5in
Height: 134.6cm 53.0in
Ground clearance: 15.2cm 6.0in
Kerb weight: 626.1kg 1379.0lb
Fuel: 25.0L 5.5gal 6.6galUS

3053 Mini
1275GT
1969 UK
88.0mph 141.6kmh
0-50mph 80.5kmh: 10.2secs
0-60mph 96.5kmh: 14.7secs
0-1/4 mile: 19.8secs
0-1km: 37.6secs
59.0bhp 44.0kW 59.8PS
@ 5300rpm
65.5lbft 88.8Nm @ 2550rpm
89.5bhp/ton 88.0bhp/tonne
46.3bhp/L 34.5kW/L 46.9PS/L
47.1ft/sec 14.4m/sec
15.0mph 24.1kmh/1000rpm
30.2mpg 25.1mpgUS 9.4L/100km
Petrol 4-stroke piston
1275cc 77.8cu in
In-line 4 1 Carburettor
Compression ratio: 8.0:1
Bore: 70.6mm 2.8in
Stroke: 81.3mm 3.2in
Valve type/No: Overhead 8
Transmission: Manual
No. of forward speeds: 4
Wheels driven: Front
Springs F/R: Gas/Gas
Brake system: PA
Brakes F/R: Disc/Drum
Steering: Rack & pinion
Wheelbase: 203.2cm 80.0in
Track F: 121.9cm 48.0in
Track R: 119.9cm 47.2in
Length: 318.0cm 125.2in
Width: 141.0cm 55.5in
Height: 134.6cm 53.0in
Ground clearance: 15.2cm 6.0in
Kerb weight: 670.1kg 1476.0lb
Fuel: 25.0L 5.5gal 6.6galUS

3054 Mini
1275GT
1971 UK
91.0mph 146.4kmh
0-50mph 80.5kmh: 9.3secs
0-60mph 96.5kmh: 13.3secs
0-1/4 mile: 19.0secs
0-1km: 36.2secs
59.0bhp 44.0kW 59.8PS
@ 5300rpm
65.5lbft 88.8Nm @ 2550rpm
89.5bhp/ton 88.0bhp/tonne
46.3bhp/L 34.5kW/L 46.9PS/L
47.1ft/sec 14.4m/sec
15.9mph 25.6kmh/1000rpm
30.5mpg 25.4mpgUS 9.3L/100km
Petrol 4-stroke piston
1275cc 77.8cu in
In-line 4 1 Carburettor
Compression ratio: 8.0:1
Bore: 70.6mm 2.8in
Stroke: 81.3mm 3.2in
Valve type/No: Overhead 8
Transmission: Manual
No. of forward speeds: 4
Wheels driven: Front
Springs F/R: Rubber/Rubber
Brake system: PA
Brakes F/R: Disc/Drum
Steering: Rack & pinion
Wheelbase: 203.2cm 80.0in
Track F: 121.9cm 48.0in
Track R: 119.9cm 47.2in
Length: 318.0cm 125.2in
Width: 141.0cm 55.5in
Height: 134.6cm 53.0in
Ground clearance: 15.2cm 6.0in
Kerb weight: 670.1kg 1476.0lb
Fuel: 25.0L 5.5gal 6.6galUS

3055 Mini
850
1973 UK
83.0mph 133.5kmh
0-50mph 80.5kmh: 16.6secs
0-60mph 96.5kmh: 27.5secs
0-1/4 mile: 22.9secs
0-1km: 44.3secs
34.0bhp 25.3kW 34.5PS
@ 5500rpm
44.0lbft 59.6Nm @ 2900rpm
58.8bhp/ton 57.8bhp/tonne
40.1bhp/L 29.9kW/L 40.6PS/L
41.1ft/sec 12.5m/sec
14.6mph 23.5kmh/1000rpm
35.6mpg 29.6mpgUS 7.9L/100km
Petrol 4-stroke piston
848cc 51.7cu in
In-line 4 1 Carburettor
Compression ratio: 8.3:1
Bore: 62.9mm 2.5in
Stroke: 68.2mm 2.7in
Valve type/No: Overhead 8
Transmission: Manual
No. of forward speeds: 4
Wheels driven: Front
Springs F/R: Rubber/Rubber
Brakes F/R: Drum/Drum
Steering: Rack & pinion
Wheelbase: 203.7cm 80.2in
Track F: 120.4cm 47.4in
Track R: 116.3cm 45.8in
Length: 306.1cm 120.5in
Width: 141.0cm 55.5in
Height: 134.6cm 53.0in
Ground clearance: 15.2cm 6.0in
Kerb weight: 587.9kg 1295.0lb
Fuel: 25.0L 5.5gal 6.6galUS

3056 Mini
1275GT
1974 UK
90.0mph 144.8kmh
0-50mph 80.5kmh: 10.0secs
0-60mph 96.5kmh: 14.6secs
0-1/4 mile: 19.7secs
0-1km: 37.6secs
54.0bhp 40.3kW 54.7PS
@ 5250rpm
67.0lbft 90.8Nm @ 2500rpm
83.8bhp/ton 82.4bhp/tonne
42.3bhp/L 31.6kW/L 42.9PS/L
46.7ft/sec 14.2m/sec
16.8mph 27.0kmh/1000rpm
30.8mpg 25.6mpgUS 9.2L/100km
Petrol 4-stroke piston
1275cc 77.8cu in
In-line 4 1 Carburettor
Compression ratio: 8.8:1
Bore: 70.6mm 2.8in
Stroke: 81.3mm 3.2in
Valve type/No: Overhead 8
Transmission: Manual
No. of forward speeds: 4
Wheels driven: Front
Springs F/R: Rubber/Rubber
Brakes F/R: Disc/Drum
Steering: Rack & pinion
Wheelbase: 203.2cm 80.0in
Track F: 121.9cm 48.0in
Track R: 119.9cm 47.2in
Length: 318.0cm 125.2in
Width: 141.0cm 55.5in
Height: 134.6cm 53.0in
Ground clearance: 15.2cm 6.0in
Kerb weight: 655.6kg 1444.0lb
Fuel: 34.1L 7.5gal 9.0galUS

3057 Mini
1000
1975 UK
82.0mph 131.9kmh
0-50mph 80.5kmh: 12.5secs
0-60mph 96.5kmh: 18.7secs
0-1/4 mile: 21.1secs
0-1km: 39.9secs
39.0bhp 29.1kW 39.5PS
@ 4750rpm
51.6lbft 69.9Nm @ 2000rpm
65.9bhp/ton 64.8bhp/tonne
39.1bhp/L 29.1kW/L 39.6PS/L
39.6ft/sec 12.1m/sec
15.9mph 25.6kmh/1000rpm
34.2mpg 28.5mpgUS 8.3L/100km
Petrol 4-stroke piston
998cc 60.9cu in
In-line 4 1 Carburettor
Compression ratio: 8.3:1
Bore: 64.6mm 2.5in
Stroke: 76.2mm 3.0in
Valve type/No: Overhead 8
Transmission: Manual
No. of forward speeds: 4
Wheels driven: Front
Springs F/R: Rubber/Rubber
Brakes F/R: Drum/Drum
Steering: Rack & pinion
Wheelbase: 203.2cm 80.0in
Track F: 120.4cm 47.4in
Track R: 116.3cm 45.8in
Length: 306.1cm 120.5in
Width: 141.0cm 55.5in
Height: 134.6cm 53.0in
Ground clearance: 15.2cm 6.0in
Kerb weight: 602.0kg 1326.0lb
Fuel: 24.6L 5.4gal 6.5galUS

3058 Mini
Automatic
1975 UK
72.0mph 115.8kmh
0-50mph 80.5kmh: 18.3secs
0-60mph 96.5kmh: 32.0secs
0-1/4 mile: 24.3secs
34.0bhp 25.3kW 34.5PS
@ 5500rpm

44.0lbft 59.6Nm @ 2900rpm
54.8bhp/ton 53.9bhp/tonne
40.1bhp/L 29.9kW/L 40.6PS/L
41.1ft/sec 12.5m/sec
14.9mph 24.0kmh/1000rpm
33.1mpg 27.6mpgUS 8.5L/100km
Petrol 4-stroke piston
848cc 51.7cu in
In-line 4 1 Carburettor
Compression ratio: 8.3:1
Bore: 62.9mm 2.5in
Stroke: 68.2mm 2.7in
Valve type/No: Overhead 8
Transmission: Automatic
No. of forward speeds: 4
Wheels driven: Front
Springs F/R: Gas/Gas
Brakes F/R: Drum/Drum
Steering: Rack & pinion
Wheelbase: 203.7cm 80.2in
Track F: 120.4cm 47.4in
Track R: 116.6cm 45.9in
Length: 305.3cm 120.2in
Width: 141.0cm 55.5in
Height: 134.6cm 53.0in
Ground clearance: 15.2cm 6.0in
Kerb weight: 630.6kg 1389.0lb
Fuel: 25.0L 5.5gal 6.6galUS

3059 Mini

Clubman 1100
1976 UK
83.0mph 133.5kmh
0-50mph 80.5kmh: 12.4secs
0-60mph 96.5kmh: 17.9secs
0-1/4 mile: 20.7secs
0-1km: 39.6secs
45.0bhp 33.6kW 45.6PS
@ 5250rpm
56.0lbft 75.9Nm @ 2700rpm
73.0bhp/ton 71.8bhp/tonne
41.0bhp/L 30.6kW/L 41.5PS/L
48.3ft/sec 14.7m/sec
15.9mph 25.6kmh/1000rpm
37.2mpg 31.0mpgUS 7.6L/100km
Petrol 4-stroke piston
1098cc 67.0cu in
In-line 4 1 Carburettor
Compression ratio: 8.5:1
Bore: 65.0mm 2.6in
Stroke: 84.0mm 3.3in
Valve type/No: Overhead 8
Transmission: Manual
No. of forward speeds: 4
Wheels driven: Front
Springs F/R: Rubber/Rubber
Brakes F/R: Drum/Drum
Steering: Rack & pinion
Wheelbase: 203.2cm 80.0in
Track F: 121.9cm 48.0in
Track R: 119.9cm 47.2in
Length: 318.0cm 125.2in
Width: 141.0cm 55.5in
Height: 134.6cm 53.0in
Ground clearance: 15.2cm 6.0in
Kerb weight: 627.0kg 1381.0lb
Fuel: 24.6L 5.4gal 6.5galUS

3060 Mini

850 Super de Luxe
1979 UK
80.0mph 128.7kmh
0-50mph 80.5kmh: 13.0secs
0-60mph 96.5kmh: 20.3secs
0-1/4 mile: 21.9secs
0-1km: 42.0secs
34.0bhp 25.3kW 34.5PS
@ 5300rpm
44.0lbft 59.6Nm @ 2900rpm
56.4bhp/ton 55.4bhp/tonne
40.1bhp/L 29.9kW/L 40.6PS/L
39.6ft/sec 12.1m/sec
14.7mph 23.7kmh/1000rpm
38.1mpg 31.7mpgUS 7.4L/100km
Petrol 4-stroke piston
848cc 51.7cu in
In-line 4 1 Carburettor
Compression ratio: 8.8:1
Bore: 62.9mm 2.5in
Stroke: 68.2mm 2.7in
Valve type/No: Overhead 8
Transmission: Manual
No. of forward speeds: 4
Wheels driven: Front
Springs F/R: Rubber/Rubber
Brakes F/R: Drum/Drum
Steering: Rack & pinion
Wheelbase: 203.7cm 80.2in
Track F: 121.4cm 47.8in
Track R: 117.9cm 46.4in
Length: 305.6cm 120.3in
Width: 141.0cm 55.5in
Height: 134.6cm 53.0in
Ground clearance: 15.2cm 6.0in
Kerb weight: 613.3kg 1351.0lb
Fuel: 25.0L 5.5gal 6.6galUS

3061 Mitsubishi

Colt 1100F
1968 Japan
83.0mph 133.5kmh
0-50mph 80.5kmh: 12.3secs
0-60mph 96.5kmh: 17.5secs
0-1/4 mile: 20.8secs
0-1km: 39.8secs
58.0bhp 43.2kW 58.8PS
@ 6000rpm
59.3lbft 80.4Nm @ 3800rpm
78.2bhp/ton 76.9bhp/tonne
53.3bhp/L 39.7kW/L 54.0PS/L
42.7ft/sec 13.0m/sec
14.0mph 22.5kmh/1000rpm
29.3mpg 24.4mpgUS 9.6L/100km
Petrol 4-stroke piston
1088cc 66.4cu in
In-line 4 1 Carburettor
Compression ratio: 8.5:1
Bore: 73.0mm 2.9in
Stroke: 65.0mm 2.6in
Valve type/No: Overhead 8
Transmission: Manual
No. of forward speeds: 4
Wheels driven: Rear
Springs F/R: Leaf/Leaf
Brakes F/R: Drum/Drum
Steering: Recirculating ball
Wheelbase: 220.0cm 86.6in
Track F: 121.9cm 48.0in
Track R: 118.6cm 46.7in
Length: 354.8cm 139.7in
Width: 144.8cm 57.0in
Height: 138.9cm 54.7in
Ground clearance: 16.5cm 6.5in
Kerb weight: 754.5kg 1662.0lb
Fuel: 40.0L 8.8gal 10.6galUS

3062 Mitsubishi

Colt Galant 2000
1975 Japan
102.0mph 164.1kmh
0-50mph 80.5kmh: 8.4secs
0-60mph 96.5kmh: 11.9secs
0-1/4 mile: 18.5secs
0-1km: 34.7secs
102.0bhp 76.1kW 103.4PS
@ 6000rpm
123.0lbft 166.7Nm @ 4000rpm
102.6bhp/ton 100.9bhp/tonne
51.1bhp/L 38.1kW/L 51.8PS/L
59.0ft/sec 18.0m/sec
20.2mph 32.5kmh/1000rpm
24.0mpg 20.0mpgUS 11.8L/100km
Petrol 4-stroke piston
1995cc 121.7cu in
In-line 4 1 Carburettor
Compression ratio: 8.5:1
Bore: 84.0mm 3.3in
Stroke: 90.0mm 3.5in
Valve type/No: Overhead 8
Transmission: Manual
No. of forward speeds: 5
Wheels driven: Rear
Springs F/R: Coil/Leaf
Brake system: PA
Brakes F/R: Disc/Drum
Steering: Recirculating ball
Wheelbase: 242.1cm 95.3in
Track F: 131.6cm 51.8in
Track R: 130.0cm 51.2in
Length: 420.1cm 165.4in
Width: 161.5cm 63.6in
Height: 137.9cm 54.3in
Ground clearance: 17.5cm 6.9in
Kerb weight: 1010.6kg 2226.0lb
Fuel: 51.0L 11.2gal 13.5galUS

3063 Mitsubishi

Colt Celeste 2000
1976 Japan
109.0mph 175.4kmh
0-50mph 80.5kmh: 7.9secs
0-60mph 96.5kmh: 11.2secs
0-1/4 mile: 19.1secs
0-1km: 36.8secs
98.0bhp 73.1kW 99.4PS
@ 6000rpm
123.0lbft 166.7Nm @ 4000rpm
100.2bhp/ton 98.6bhp/tonne
49.1bhp/L 36.6kW/L 49.8PS/L
59.0ft/sec 18.0m/sec
20.1mph 32.3kmh/1000rpm
24.9mpg 20.7mpgUS 11.3L/100km
Petrol 4-stroke piston
1995cc 121.7cu in
In-line 4 1 Carburettor
Compression ratio: 9.0:1
Bore: 84.0mm 3.3in
Stroke: 90.0mm 3.5in
Valve type/No: Overhead 8
Transmission: Manual
No. of forward speeds: 5
Wheels driven: Rear
Springs F/R: Coil/Leaf
Brake system: PA
Brakes F/R: Disc/Drum
Steering: Recirculating ball
Wheelbase: 233.9cm 92.1in
Track F: 130.0cm 51.2in
Track R: 127.0cm 50.0in
Length: 411.5cm 162.0in
Width: 160.0cm 63.0in
Height: 133.1cm 52.4in
Ground clearance: 20.3cm 8.0in
Kerb weight: 994.3kg 2190.0lb
Fuel: 45.0L 9.9gal 11.9galUS

3064 Mitsubishi

Colt Sigma 2000
1977 Japan
99.0mph 159.3kmh
0-50mph 80.5kmh: 9.5secs
0-60mph 96.5kmh: 13.4secs
0-1/4 mile: 19.2secs
0-1km: 36.1secs
98.0bhp 73.1kW 99.4PS
@ 6000rpm
123.0lbft 166.7Nm @ 4000rpm
94.8bhp/ton 93.2bhp/tonne
49.1bhp/L 36.6kW/L 49.8PS/L
59.0ft/sec 18.0m/sec
20.2mph 32.5kmh/1000rpm
23.0mpg 19.2mpgUS 12.3L/100km
Petrol 4-stroke piston
1995cc 121.7cu in
In-line 4 1 Carburettor
Compression ratio: 9.0:1
Bore: 84.0mm 3.3in
Stroke: 90.0mm 3.5in
Valve type/No: Overhead 8
Transmission: Manual
No. of forward speeds: 5
Wheels driven: Rear
Springs F/R: Coil/Coil
Brake system: PA
Brakes F/R: Disc/Drum
Steering: Recirculating ball
Wheelbase: 251.7cm 99.1in
Track F: 135.1cm 53.2in
Track R: 134.1cm 52.8in
Length: 433.3cm 170.6in
Width: 165.6cm 65.2in
Height: 136.1cm 53.6in
Ground clearance: 16.5cm 6.5in
Kerb weight: 1051.5kg 2316.0lb
Fuel: 60.1L 13.2gal 15.9galUS

3065 Mitsubishi

Colt Lancer Estate
1978 Japan
94.0mph 151.2kmh
0-50mph 80.5kmh: 8.9secs
0-60mph 96.5kmh: 13.2secs
0-1/4 mile: 19.3secs
0-1km: 36.4secs
68.0bhp 50.7kW 68.9PS
@ 5000rpm
77.0lbft 104.3Nm @ 3000rpm
74.4bhp/ton 73.1bhp/tonne
47.3bhp/L 35.2kW/L 47.9PS/L
47.1ft/sec 14.3m/sec
16.8mph 27.0kmh/1000rpm
24.4mpg 20.3mpgUS 11.6L/100km
Petrol 4-stroke piston
1439cc 87.8cu in
In-line 4 1 Carburettor
Compression ratio: 9.0:1
Bore: 73.0mm 2.9in
Stroke: 86.0mm 3.4in
Valve type/No: Overhead 8
Transmission: Manual
No. of forward speeds: 4
Wheels driven: Rear
Springs F/R: Coil/Leaf
Brake system: PA
Brakes F/R: Disc/Drum
Steering: Recirculating ball
Wheelbase: 233.9cm 92.1in
Track F: 128.5cm 50.6in
Track R: 125.5cm 49.4in
Length: 399.8cm 157.4in
Width: 152.4cm 60.0in
Height: 135.9cm 53.5in
Ground clearance: 16.5cm 6.5in
Kerb weight: 929.8kg 2048.0lb
Fuel: 40.0L 8.8gal 10.6galUS

3066 Mitsubishi

Colt Sappore 2000 GSR
1978 Japan
106.0mph 170.6kmh
0-50mph 80.5kmh: 8.7secs
0-60mph 96.5kmh: 12.7secs
0-1/4 mile: 18.8secs
0-1km: 35.1secs
98.0bhp 73.1kW 99.4PS
@ 5500rpm
105.0lbft 142.3Nm @ 3500rpm
86.9bhp/ton 85.5bhp/tonne
49.1bhp/L 36.6kW/L 49.8PS/L
54.1ft/sec 16.5m/sec
20.1mph 32.3kmh/1000rpm
20.8mpg 17.3mpgUS 13.6L/100km
Petrol 4-stroke piston
1995cc 121.7cu in
In-line 4 2 Carburettor
Compression ratio: 9.5:1
Bore: 84.0mm 3.3in
Stroke: 90.0mm 3.5in
Valve type/No: Overhead 8
Transmission: Manual
No. of forward speeds: 5
Wheels driven: Rear
Springs F/R: Coil/Coil
Brake system: PA
Brakes F/R: Disc/Disc
Steering: Recirculating ball PA
Wheelbase: 251.5cm 99.0in
Track F: 136.9cm 53.9in
Track R: 135.4cm 53.3in
Length: 437.9cm 172.4in
Width: 167.4cm 65.9in
Height: 133.1cm 52.4in
Ground clearance: 16.0cm 6.3in
Kerb weight: 1146.3kg 2525.0lb
Fuel: 60.1L 13.2gal 15.9galUS

3067 Mitsubishi

Colt 1400 GLX
1979 Japan
96.0mph 154.5kmh
0-50mph 80.5kmh: 9.4secs
0-60mph 96.5kmh: 13.8secs
0-1/4 mile: 19.3secs
0-1km: 36.2secs
70.0bhp 52.2kW 71.0PS
@ 5000rpm
78.1lbft 105.8Nm @ 3500rpm
88.5bhp/ton 87.0bhp/tonne
49.6bhp/L 37.0kW/L 50.3PS/L
44.9ft/sec 13.7m/sec
17.1mph 27.5kmh/1000rpm
34.4mpg 28.6mpgUS 8.2L/100km
Petrol 4-stroke piston
1410cc 86.0cu in
In-line 4 1 Carburettor
Compression ratio: 9.0:1
Bore: 74.0mm 2.9in
Stroke: 82.0mm 3.2in
Valve type/No: Overhead 8
Transmission: Manual
No. of forward speeds: 4
Wheels driven: Front
Springs F/R: Coil/Coil
Brake system: PA
Brakes F/R: Disc/Drum
Steering: Rack & pinion
Wheelbase: 230.1cm 90.6in
Track F: 136.9cm 53.9in
Track R: 134.1cm 52.8in
Length: 417.1cm 164.2in
Width: 158.5cm 62.4in
Height: 134.6cm 53.0in
Ground clearance: 15.2cm 6.0in
Kerb weight: 804.5kg 1772.0lb
Fuel: 40.0L 8.8gal 10.6galUS

3068 Mitsubishi
Colt Lancer 2000 Turbo
1981 Japan
132.0mph 212.4kmh
0-50mph 80.5kmh: 6.2secs
0-60mph 96.5kmh: 8.6secs
0-1/4 mile: 16.1secs
0-1km: 29.1secs
168.0bhp 125.3kW 170.3PS
@ 5500rpm
181.0lbft 245.3Nm @ 3500rpm
161.1bhp/ton 158.4bhp/tonne
84.1bhp/L 62.7kW/L 85.3PS/L
52.9ft/sec 16.1m/sec
23.2mph 37.3kmh/1000rpm
26.0mpg 21.6mpgUS 10.9L/100km
Petrol 4-stroke piston
1997cc 121.8cu in turbocharged
In-line 4 fuel injection
Compression ratio: 7.6:1
Bore: 85.0mm 3.3in
Stroke: 88.0mm 3.5in
Valve type/No: Overhead 8
Transmission: Manual
No. of forward speeds: 5
Wheels driven: Rear
Springs F/R: Coil/Coil
Brake system: PA
Brakes F/R: Disc/Disc
Steering: Recirculating ball
Wheelbase: 243.8cm 96.0in
Track F: 136.7cm 53.8in
Track R: 135.6cm 53.4in
Length: 422.4cm 166.3in
Width: 162.1cm 63.8in
Height: 138.4cm 54.5in
Ground clearance: 16.5cm 6.5in
Kerb weight: 1060.5kg 2336.0lb
Fuel: 50.0L 11.0gal 13.2galUS

3069 Mitsubishi
Colt Cordia Turbo
1982 Japan
116.0mph 186.6kmh
0-50mph 80.5kmh: 6.9secs
0-60mph 96.5kmh: 9.2secs
0-1/4 mile: 17.2secs
0-1km: 32.6secs
112.0bhp 83.5kW 113.5PS
@ 5500rpm
125.0lbft 169.4Nm @ 3500rpm
116.7bhp/ton 114.8bhp/tonne
70.1bhp/L 52.3kW/L 71.1PS/L
51.8ft/sec 15.8m/sec
22.8mph 36.7kmh/1000rpm
25.2mpg 21.0mpgUS 11.2L/100km
Petrol 4-stroke piston
1597cc 97.4cu in turbocharged
In-line 4 1 Carburettor
Compression ratio: 8.5:1
Bore: 76.9mm 3.0in
Stroke: 86.0mm 3.4in
Valve type/No: Overhead 8
Transmission: Manual
No. of forward speeds: 8
Wheels driven: Front
Springs F/R: Coil/Coil
Brake system: PA
Brakes F/R: Disc/Drum
Steering: Rack & pinion
Wheelbase: 244.6cm 96.3in
Track F: 141.0cm 55.5in
Track R: 137.4cm 54.1in
Length: 427.5cm 168.3in
Width: 166.1cm 65.4in
Height: 132.1cm 52.0in
Ground clearance: 16.5cm 6.5in
Kerb weight: 975.6kg 2149.0lb
Fuel: 50.0L 11.0gal 13.2galUS

3070 Mitsubishi
Colt Hatchback Turbo
1982 Japan
105.0mph 168.9kmh
0-50mph 80.5kmh: 6.1secs
0-60mph 96.5kmh: 9.9secs
0-1/4 mile: 17.2secs
0-1km: 32.3secs
103.5bhp 77.2kW 104.9PS
@ 5000rpm
114.0lbft 154.5Nm @ 3500rpm
123.3bhp/ton 121.3bhp/tonne
73.4bhp/L 54.7kW/L 74.4PS/L
44.9ft/sec 13.7m/sec
22.6mph 36.4kmh/1000rpm
29.0mpg 24.1mpgUS 9.7L/100km
Petrol 4-stroke piston
1410cc 86.0cu in turbocharged
In-line 4 1 Carburettor
Compression ratio: 8.7:1
Bore: 74.0mm 2.9in
Stroke: 82.0mm 3.2in
Valve type/No: Overhead 8
Transmission: Manual
No. of forward speeds: 8
Wheels driven: Front
Springs F/R: Coil/Coil
Brake system: PA
Brakes F/R: Disc/Drum
Steering: Rack & pinion
Wheelbase: 230.1cm 90.6in
Track F: 136.9cm 53.9in
Track R: 134.1cm 52.8in
Length: 379.0cm 149.2in
Width: 158.5cm 62.4in
Height: 134.6cm 53.0in
Ground clearance: 17.0cm 6.7in
Kerb weight: 853.5kg 1880.0lb
Fuel: 40.0L 8.8gal 10.6galUS

3071 Mitsubishi
Colt Starion Turbo
1982 Japan
134.0mph 215.6kmh
0-50mph 80.5kmh: 5.8secs
0-60mph 96.5kmh: 7.5secs
0-1/4 mile: 16.1secs
0-1km: 29.4secs
168.0bhp 125.3kW 170.3PS
@ 5500rpm
181.0lbft 245.3Nm @ 3500rpm
139.5bhp/ton 137.2bhp/tonne
84.1bhp/L 62.7kW/L 85.3PS/L
52.9ft/sec 16.1m/sec
24.4mph 39.3kmh/1000rpm
22.1mpg 18.4mpgUS 12.8L/100km
Petrol 4-stroke piston
1997cc 121.8cu in turbocharged
In-line 4 fuel injection
Compression ratio: 7.6:1
Bore: 85.0mm 3.3in
Stroke: 88.0mm 3.5in
Valve type/No: Overhead 8
Transmission: Manual
No. of forward speeds: 5
Wheels driven: Rear
Springs F/R: Coil/Coil
Brake system: PA
Brakes F/R: Disc/Disc
Steering: Recirculating ball PA
Wheelbase: 243.6cm 95.9in
Track F: 139.4cm 54.9in
Track R: 140.0cm 55.1in
Length: 442.5cm 174.2in
Width: 170.4cm 67.1in
Height: 131.6cm 51.8in
Ground clearance: 15.5cm 6.1in
Kerb weight: 1224.9kg 2698.0lb
Fuel: 75.1L 16.5gal 19.8galUS

3072 Mitsubishi
Cordia LS
1982 Japan
101.0mph 162.5kmh
0-50mph 80.5kmh: 9.4secs
0-60mph 96.5kmh: 13.2secs
0-1/4 mile: 19.1secs
82.0bhp 61.1kW 83.1PS
@ 5000rpm
93.0lbft 126.0Nm @ 3000rpm
79.7bhp/ton 78.4bhp/tonne
45.7bhp/L 34.1kW/L 46.3PS/L
48.1ft/sec 14.7m/sec
21.8mph 35.1kmh/1000rpm
32.4mpg 27.0mpgUS 8.7L/100km
Petrol 4-stroke piston
1795cc 109.5cu in
In-line 4 1 Carburettor
Compression ratio: 8.5:1
Bore: 80.6mm 3.2in
Stroke: 88.0mm 3.5in
Valve type/No: Overhead 8
Transmission: Manual
No. of forward speeds: 4
Wheels driven: Front
Springs F/R: Coil/Coil
Brake system: PA
Brakes F/R: Disc/Drum
Steering: Rack & pinion PA
Wheelbase: 244.6cm 96.3in
Track F: 141.0cm 55.5in
Track R: 137.4cm 54.1in
Length: 439.4cm 173.0in
Width: 166.1cm 65.4in
Height: 122.4cm 48.2in
Ground clearance: 14.5cm 5.7in
Kerb weight: 1046.5kg 2305.0lb
Fuel: 50.0L 11.0gal 13.2galUS

3073 Mitsubishi
Colt Shogun
1983 Japan
90.0mph 144.8kmh
0-50mph 80.5kmh: 9.9secs
0-60mph 96.5kmh: 14.5secs
0-1/4 mile: 19.8secs
0-1km: 37.7secs
102.0bhp 76.1kW 103.4PS
@ 4500rpm
143.0lbft 193.8Nm @ 2500rpm
72.0bhp/ton 70.8bhp/tonne
39.9bhp/L 29.8kW/L 40.5PS/L
48.2ft/sec 14.7m/sec
19.7mph 31.7kmh/1000rpm
18.8mpg 15.7mpgUS 15.0L/100km
Petrol 4-stroke piston
2555cc 155.9cu in
In-line 4 1 Carburettor
Compression ratio: 8.2:1
Bore: 91.1mm 3.6in
Stroke: 98.0mm 3.9in
Valve type/No: Overhead 8
Transmission: Manual
No. of forward speeds: 5
Wheels driven: 4-wheel drive
Springs F/R: Torsion bar/Leaf
Brake system: PA
Brakes F/R: Disc/Drum
Steering: Recirculating ball PA
Wheelbase: 235.0cm 92.5in
Track F: 140.0cm 55.1in
Track R: 137.4cm 54.1in
Length: 393.4cm 154.9in
Width: 167.9cm 66.1in
Height: 184.4cm 72.6in
Ground clearance: 21.1cm 8.3in
Kerb weight: 1439.6kg 3171.0lb
Fuel: 59.1L 13.0gal 15.6galUS

3074 Mitsubishi
Starion
1983 Japan
120.0mph 193.1kmh
0-60mph 96.5kmh: 9.2secs
0-1/4 mile: 17.0secs
145.0bhp 108.1kW 147.0PS
@ 5000rpm
185.0lbft 250.7Nm @ 2500rpm
111.6bhp/ton 109.7bhp/tonne
56.7bhp/L 42.3kW/L 57.5PS/L
53.6ft/sec 16.3m/sec
24.6mpg 20.5mpgUS 11.5L/100km
Petrol 4-stroke piston
2555cc 155.9cu in turbocharged
In-line 4 fuel injection
Compression ratio: 7.0:1
Bore: 91.1mm 3.6in
Stroke: 98.0mm 3.9in
Valve type/No: Overhead 8
Transmission: Manual
No. of forward speeds: 5
Wheels driven: Rear
Springs F/R: Coil/Coil
Brakes F/R: Disc/Disc
Wheelbase: 243.6cm 95.9in
Track F: 139.4cm 54.9in
Track R: 140.0cm 55.1in
Length: 439.9cm 173.2in
Width: 168.4cm 66.3in
Height: 131.6cm 51.8in
Kerb weight: 1321.1kg 2910.0lb
Fuel: 74.9L 16.5gal 19.8galUS

3075 Mitsubishi
Starion Turbo
1983 Japan
120.0mph 193.1kmh
0-50mph 80.5kmh: 6.4secs
0-60mph 96.5kmh: 9.2secs
0-1/4 mile: 17.0secs
145.0bhp 108.1kW 147.0PS
@ 5000rpm
185.0lbft 250.7Nm @ 2500rpm
111.6bhp/ton 109.7bhp/tonne
56.7bhp/L 42.3kW/L 57.5PS/L
53.6ft/sec 16.3m/sec
23.3mph 37.5kmh/1000rpm
21.6mpg 18.0mpgUS 13.1L/100km
Petrol 4-stroke piston
2555cc 155.9cu in turbocharged
In-line 4 fuel injection
Compression ratio: 7.0:1
Bore: 91.1mm 3.6in
Stroke: 98.0mm 3.9in
Valve type/No: Overhead 8
Transmission: Manual
No. of forward speeds: 5
Wheels driven: Rear
Springs F/R: Coil/Coil
Brake system: PA ABS
Brakes F/R: Disc/Drum
Steering: Recirculating ball PA
Wheelbase: 243.6cm 95.9in
Track F: 139.4cm 54.9in
Track R: 140.0cm 55.1in
Length: 439.9cm 173.2in
Width: 168.4cm 66.3in
Height: 131.6cm 51.8in
Ground clearance: 15.0cm 5.9in
Kerb weight: 1321.1kg 2910.0lb
Fuel: 74.9L 16.5gal 19.8galUS

3076 Mitsubishi
Tredia Turbo
1983 Japan
113.0mph 181.8kmh
0-60mph 96.5kmh: 9.0secs
0-1/4 mile: 16.7secs
116.0bhp 86.5kW 117.6PS
@ 5500rpm
129.0lbft 174.8Nm @ 3000rpm
105.8bhp/ton 104.1bhp/tonne
64.6bhp/L 48.2kW/L 65.5PS/L
52.9ft/sec 16.1m/sec
21.9mph 35.2kmh/1000rpm
26.4mpg 22.0mpgUS 10.7L/100km
Petrol 4-stroke piston
1795cc 109.5cu in turbocharged
In-line 4 fuel injection
Compression ratio: 7.5:1
Bore: 80.6mm 3.2in
Stroke: 88.0mm 3.5in
Valve type/No: Overhead 8
Transmission: Manual
No. of forward speeds: 5
Wheels driven: Front
Springs F/R: Coil/Coil
Brake system: PA
Brakes F/R: Disc/Drum
Steering: Rack & pinion PA
Wheelbase: 244.6cm 96.3in
Track F: 141.0cm 55.5in
Track R: 137.4cm 54.1in
Length: 437.9cm 172.4in
Width: 166.1cm 65.4in
Height: 131.1cm 51.6in
Ground clearance: 10.9cm 4.3in
Kerb weight: 1114.6kg 2455.0lb
Fuel: 48.4L 10.6gal 12.8galUS

3077 Mitsubishi
Colt 1600 Turbo
1984 Japan
115.0mph 185.0kmh
0-50mph 80.5kmh: 6.2secs
0-60mph 96.5kmh: 8.7secs
0-1/4 mile: 16.8secs
0-1km: 31.0secs
120.0bhp 89.5kW 121.7PS
@ 5500rpm
127.0lbft 172.1Nm @ 3000rpm
124.7bhp/ton 122.6bhp/tonne
75.1bhp/L 56.0kW/L 76.1PS/L
51.8ft/sec 15.8m/sec
23.6mph 38.0kmh/1000rpm
23.0mpg 19.2mpgUS 12.3L/100km
Petrol 4-stroke piston
1598cc 97.5cu in turbocharged
In-line 4 fuel injection
Compression ratio: 7.8:1
Bore: 76.9mm 3.0in
Stroke: 86.0mm 3.4in
Valve type/No: Overhead 8
Transmission: Manual
No. of forward speeds: 5
Wheels driven: Front
Springs F/R: Coil/Coil
Brake system: PA
Brakes F/R: Disc/Drum
Steering: Rack & pinion
Wheelbase: 238.0cm 93.7in
Track F: 138.9cm 54.7in
Track R: 133.9cm 52.7in
Length: 387.1cm 152.4in
Width: 163.6cm 64.4in
Height: 135.9cm 53.5in
Ground clearance: 15.0cm 5.9in

Kerb weight: 978.8kg 2156.0lb
Fuel: 45.0L 9.9gal 11.9galUS

3078 Mitsubishi

Cordia Turbo 1.8
1984 Japan
115.0mph 185.0kmh
0-50mph 80.5kmh: 6.5secs
0-60mph 96.5kmh: 9.5secs
0-1/4 mile: 17.0secs
116.0bhp 86.5kW 117 6PS
@ 5500rpm
129.0lbft 174.8Nm @ 3000rpm
105.4bhp/ton 103.6bhp/tonne
64.6bhp/L 48.2kW/L 65.5PS/L
52.9ft/sec 16.1m/sec
22.8mph 36.7kmh/1000rpm
26.4mpg 22.0mpgUS 10.7L/100km
Petrol 4-stroke piston
1795cc 109.5cu in turbocharged
In-line 4 fuel injection
Compression ratio: 7.5:1
Bore: 80.6mm 3.2in
Stroke: 88.0mm 3.5in
Valve type/No: Overhead 8
Transmission: Manual
No. of forward speeds: 5
Wheels driven: Front
Springs F/R: Coil/Coil
Brake system: PA
Brakes F/R: Disc/Drum
Steering: Rack & pinion PA
Wheelbase: 244.6cm 96.3in
Track F: 141.0cm 55.5in
Track R: 137.4cm 54.1in
Length: 439.4cm 173.0in
Width: 166.1cm 65.4in
Height: 125.5cm 49.4in
Kerb weight: 1119.1kg 2465.0lb
Fuel: 48.4L 10.6gal 12.8galUS

3079 Mitsubishi

Galant 1600 GL
1984 Japan
103.0mph 165.7kmh
0-50mph 80.5kmh: 8.9secs
0-60mph 96.5kmh: 12.8secs
0-1/4 mile: 18.7secs
0-1km: 35.1secs
75.0bhp 55.9kW 76.0PS
@ 5500rpm
90.0lbft 122.0Nm @ 3500rpm
70.6bhp/ton 69.4bhp/tonne
47.0bhp/L 35.0kW/L 47.6PS/L
51.8ft/sec 15.8m/sec
22.7mph 36.5kmh/1000rpm
27.7mpg 23.1mpgUS 10.2L/100km
Petrol 4-stroke piston
1597cc 97.4cu in
In-line 4 1 Carburettor
Compression ratio: 9.0:1
Bore: 76.9mm 3.0in
Stroke: 86.0mm 3.4in
Valve type/No: Overhead 8
Transmission: Manual
No. of forward speeds: 5
Wheels driven: Front
Springs F/R: Coil/Coil
Brake system: PA
Brakes F/R: Disc/Drum
Steering: Rack & pinion
Wheelbase: 260.1cm 102.4in
Track F: 144.5cm 56.9in
Track R: 140.5cm 55.3in
Length: 455.9cm 179.5in
Width: 169.4cm 66.7in
Height: 138.4cm 54.5in
Ground clearance: 16.5cm 6.5in
Kerb weight: 1081.0kg 2381.0lb
Fuel: 60.1L 13.2gal 15.9galUS

3080 Mitsubishi

Mirage Turbo
1984 Japan
108.0mph 173.8kmh
0-50mph 80.5kmh: 7.2secs
0-60mph 96.5kmh: 10.4secs
0-1/4 mile: 18.1secs
102.0bhp 76.1kW 103.4PS
@ 5500rpm
122.0lbft 165.3Nm @ 3000rpm
103.6bhp/ton 101.9bhp/tonne
63.9bhp/L 47.6kW/L 64.7PS/L
51.8ft/sec 15.8m/sec
22.2mph 35.7kmh/1000rpm
34.8mpg 29.0mpgUS 8.1L/100km
Petrol 4-stroke piston
1597cc 97.4cu in turbocharged
In-line 4 fuel injection
Compression ratio: 7.6:1
Bore: 76.9mm 3.0in
Stroke: 86.0mm 3.4in
Valve type/No: Overhead 8
Transmission: Manual
No. of forward speeds: 5
Wheels driven: Front
Springs F/R: Coil/Coil
Brake system: PA
Brakes F/R: Disc/Drum
Steering: Rack & pinion
Wheelbase: 238.0cm 93.7in
Track F: 138.9cm 54.7in
Track R: 134.1cm 52.8in
Length: 399.5cm 157.3in
Width: 163.6cm 64.4in
Height: 129.0cm 50.8in
Ground clearance: 15.2cm 6.0in
Kerb weight: 1001.1kg 2205.0lb
Fuel: 45.0L 9.9gal 11.9galUS

3081 Mitsubishi

Colt Starion Turbo
1985 Japan
140.0mph 225.3kmh
0-50mph 80.5kmh: 5.5secs
0-60mph 96.5kmh: 6.6secs
0-1/4 mile: 15.5secs
0-1km: 28.8secs
177.0bhp 132.0kW 179.4PS
@ 6000rpm
214.0lbft 290.0Nm @ 3500rpm
146.3bhp/ton 143.9bhp/tonne
88.6bhp/L 66.1kW/L 89.9PS/L
57.7ft/sec 17.6m/sec
23.9mph 38.5kmh/1000rpm
20.6mpg 17.2mpgUS 13.7L/100km
Petrol 4-stroke piston
1997cc 121.8cu in turbocharged
In-line 4 fuel injection
Compression ratio: 7.6:1
Bore: 85.0mm 3.3in
Stroke: 88.0mm 3.5in
Valve type/No: Overhead 8
Transmission: Manual
No. of forward speeds: 5
Wheels driven: Rear
Springs F/R: Coil/Coil
Brake system: PA
Brakes F/R: Disc/Disc
Steering: Recirculating ball PA
Wheelbase: 243.6cm 95.9in
Track F: 139.4cm 54.9in
Track R: 140.0cm 55.1in
Length: 442.5cm 174.2in
Width: 170.4cm 67.1in
Height: 131.6cm 51.8in
Ground clearance: 15.5cm 6.1in
Kerb weight: 1230.3kg 2710.0lb
Fuel: 75.1L 16.5gal 19.8galUS

3082 Mitsubishi

Galant
1985 Japan
163.0mph 262.3kmh
0-50mph 80.5kmh: 10.3secs
0-60mph 96.5kmh: 14.4secs
0-1/4 mile: 20.3secs
101.0bhp 75.3kW 102.4PS
@ 5000rpm
131.0lbft 177.5Nm @ 2500rpm
76.6bhp/ton 75.3bhp/tonne
43.0bhp/L 32.0kW/L 43.6PS/L
54.7ft/sec 16.7m/sec
26.7mph 43.0kmh/1000rpm
25.2mpg 21.0mpgUS 11.2L/100km
Petrol 4-stroke piston
2350cc 143.4cu in
In-line 4 fuel injection
Compression ratio: 8.5:1
Bore: 86.5mm 3.4in
Stroke: 100.0mm 3.9in
Valve type/No: Overhead 8
Transmission: Automatic
No. of forward speeds: 4
Wheels driven: Front
Springs F/R: Coil/Coil
Brake system: PA
Brakes F/R: Disc/Disc
Steering: Rack & pinion PA
Wheelbase: 260.1cm 102.4in
Track F: 144.5cm 56.9in
Track R: 140.5cm 55.3in
Length: 465.1cm 183.1in
Width: 169.4cm 66.7in
Height: 131.1cm 51.6in
Ground clearance: 16.5cm 6.5in
Kerb weight: 1341.6kg 2955.0lb
Fuel: 60.2L 13.2gal 15.9galUS

3083 Mitsubishi

Galant Turbo
1985 Japan
126.0mph 202.7kmh
0-50mph 80.5kmh: 6.3secs
0-60mph 96.5kmh: 8.6secs
0-1/4 mile: 16.5secs
0-1km: 30.4secs
147.0bhp 109.6kW 149.0PS
@ 5500rpm
180.0lbft 243.9Nm @ 3500rpm
123.3bhp/ton 121.3bhp/tonne
73.6bhp/L 54.9kW/L 74.6PS/L
52.9ft/sec 16.1m/sec
24.6mph 39.6kmh/1000rpm
22.1mpg 18.4mpgUS 12.8L/100km
Petrol 4-stroke piston
1997cc 121.8cu in turbocharged
In-line 4 fuel injection
Compression ratio: 7.6:1
Bore: 85.0mm 3.3in
Stroke: 88.0mm 3.5in
Valve type/No: Overhead 8
Transmission: Manual
No. of forward speeds: 5
Wheels driven: Front
Springs F/R: Coil/Coil
Brake system: PA
Brakes F/R: Disc/Disc
Steering: Rack & pinion PA
Wheelbase: 260.1cm 102.4in
Track F: 144.5cm 56.9in
Track R: 140.5cm 55.3in
Length: 455.9cm 179.5in
Width: 169.4cm 66.7in
Height: 138.4cm 54.5in
Ground clearance: 16.5cm 6.5in
Kerb weight: 1212.2kg 2670.0lb
Fuel: 60.1L 13.2gal 15.9galUS

3084 Mitsubishi

Space Wagon 1800GLX
1985 Japan
99.0mph 159.3kmh
0-50mph 80.5kmh: 8.4secs
0-60mph 96.5kmh: 12.5secs
0-1/4 mile: 19.2secs
0-1km: 35.9secs
90.0bhp 67.1kW 91.2PS
@ 5500rpm
97.3lbft 131.8Nm @ 4000rpm
83.0bhp/ton 81.6bhp/tonne
51.3bhp/L 38.2kW/L 52.0PS/L
51.8ft/sec 15.8m/sec
22.7mph 36.5kmh/1000rpm
27.1mpg 22.6mpgUS 10.4L/100km
Petrol 4-stroke piston
1755cc 107.1cu in
In-line 4 1 Carburettor
Compression ratio: 9.0:1
Bore: 80.6mm 3.2in
Stroke: 86.0mm 3.4in
Valve type/No: Overhead 8
Transmission: Manual
No. of forward speeds: 5
Wheels driven: Front
Springs F/R: Coil/Coil
Brake system: PA
Brakes F/R: Disc/Drum
Steering: Rack & pinion PA
Wheelbase: 262.4cm 103.3in
Track F: 141.0cm 55.5in
Track R: 137.4cm 54.1in
Length: 429.5cm 169.1in
Width: 164.1cm 64.6in
Height: 152.4cm 60.0in
Ground clearance: 15.0cm 5.9in
Kerb weight: 1103.2kg 2430.0lb
Fuel: 50.0L 11.0gal 13.2galUS

3085 Mitsubishi

Starion
1985 Japan
120.0mph 193.1kmh
0-60mph 96.5kmh: 9.2secs
0-1/4 mile: 17.0secs
145.0bhp 108.1kW 147.0PS
@ 5000rpm
185.0lbft 250.7Nm @ 2500rpm
111.0bhp/ton 109.2bhp/tonne
56.7bhp/L 42.3kW/L 57.5PS/L
Petrol 4-stroke piston
2555cc 155.9cu in turbocharged
In-line 4 fuel injection
Valve type/No: Overhead 8
Transmission: Manual
No. of forward speeds: 5
Wheels driven: Rear
Springs F/R: Coil/Coil
Brakes F/R: Disc/Disc
Steering: Recirculating ball PA
Wheelbase: 243.6cm 95.9in
Length: 439.9cm 173.2in
Width: 168.4cm 66.3in
Height: 127.5cm 50.2in
Kerb weight: 1327.9kg 2925.0lb
Fuel: 74.9L 16.5gal 19.8galUS

3086 Mitsubishi

Starion ESI
1985 Japan
127.0mph 204.3kmh
0-50mph 80.5kmh: 5.7secs
0-60mph 96.5kmh: 7.5secs
0-1/4 mile: 16.0secs
170.0bhp 126.8kW 172.4PS
@ 5000rpm
220.0lbft 298.1Nm @ 2500rpm
126.3bhp/ton 124.2bhp/tonne
66.7bhp/L 49.7kW/L 67.6PS/L
53.6ft/sec 16.3m/sec
23.5mph 37.8kmh/1000rpm
22.8mpg 19.0mpgUS 12.4L/100km
Petrol 4-stroke piston
2550cc 155.6cu in turbocharged
In-line 4 fuel injection
Compression ratio: 7.1:1
Bore: 91.1mm 3.6in
Stroke: 98.0mm 3.9in
Valve type/No: Overhead 8
Transmission: Manual
No. of forward speeds: 5
Wheels driven: Rear
Springs F/R: Coil/Coil
Brake system: PA
Brakes F/R: Disc/Disc
Steering: Recirculating ball PA
Wheelbase: 242.6cm 95.5in
Track F: 139.4cm 54.9in
Track R: 140.0cm 55.1in
Length: 439.9cm 173.2in
Width: 168.4cm 66.3in
Height: 127.5cm 50.2in
Kerb weight: 1368.8kg 3015.0lb
Fuel: 74.9L 16.5gal 19.8galUS

3087 Mitsubishi

Cordia Turbo
1986 Japan
115.0mph 185.0kmh
0-60mph 96.5kmh: 8.5secs
0-1/4 mile: 16.5secs
116.0bhp 86.5kW 117.6PS
@ 5500rpm
129.0lbft 174.8Nm @ 3000rpm
103.1bhp/ton 101.4bhp/tonne
64.6bhp/L 48.2kW/L 65.5PS/L
52.9ft/sec 16.1m/sec
24.6mpg 20.5mpgUS 11.5L/100km
Petrol 4-stroke piston
1795cc 109.5cu in turbocharged
In-line 4 fuel injection
Compression ratio: 7.5:1
Bore: 80.6mm 3.2in
Stroke: 88.0mm 3.5in
Valve type/No: Overhead 8
Transmission: Manual
No. of forward speeds: 5
Wheels driven: Front
Springs F/R: Coil/Coil
Brake system: PA
Brakes F/R: Disc/Drum
Steering: Rack & pinion PA
Wheelbase: 244.6cm 96.3in
Track F: 141.0cm 55.5in
Track R: 137.4cm 54.1in
Length: 439.4cm 173.0in
Width: 166.1cm 65.4in
Height: 125.5cm 49.4in
Kerb weight: 1144.1kg 2520.0lb
Fuel: 48.4L 10.6gal 12.8galUS

3088 Mitsubishi

Lancer 1.5 GLX Estate
1986 Japan
97.0mph 156.1kmh

0-50mph 80.5kmh: 10.1secs
0-60mph 96.5kmh: 14.0secs
0-1/4 mile: 19.7secs
0-1km: 38.6secs
74.0bhp 55.2kW 75.0PS
@ 5500rpm
87.0lbft 117.9Nm @ 4000rpm
76.6bhp/ton 75.3bhp/tonne
50.4bhp/L 37.6kW/L 51.1PS/L
49.3ft/sec 15.0m/sec
20.8mph 33.5kmh/1000rpm
27.8mpg 23.1mpgUS 10.2L/100km
Petrol 4-stroke piston
1468cc 89.6cu in
In-line 4 1 Carburettor
Compression ratio: 9.5:1
Bore: 75.5mm 3.0in
Stroke: 82.0mm 3.2in
Valve type/No: Overhead 8
Transmission: Manual
No. of forward speeds: 5
Wheels driven: Front
Springs F/R: Coil/Coil
Brake system: PA
Brakes F/R: Disc/Drum
Steering: Rack & pinion PA
Wheelbase: 238.0cm 93.7in
Track F: 138.9cm 54.7in
Track R: 133.9cm 52.7in
Length: 413.3cm 162.7in
Width: 163.3cm 64.3in
Height: 142.0cm 55.9in
Ground clearance: 15.0cm 5.9in
Kerb weight: 982.5kg 2164.0lb
Fuel: 46.9L 10.3gal 12.4galUS

3089 Mitsubishi

Mirage
1986 Japan
0-60mph 96.5kmh: 12.0secs
0-1/4 mile: 18.6secs
68.0bhp 50.7kW 68.9PS
@ 5500rpm
82.0lbft 111.1Nm @ 3500rpm
76.3bhp/ton 75.1bhp/tonne
46.3bhp/L 34.5kW/L 47.0PS/L
49.3ft/sec 15.0m/sec
24.0mph 38.6kmh/1000rpm
35.2mpg 29.3mpgUS 8.0L/100km
Petrol 4-stroke piston
1468cc 89.6cu in
In-line 4 1 Carburettor
Compression ratio: 9.4:1
Bore: 75.5mm 3.0in
Stroke: 82.0mm 3.2in
Valve type/No: Overhead 8
Transmission: Manual
No. of forward speeds: 4
Wheels driven: Front
Springs F/R: Torsion bar/Coil
Brake system: PA
Brakes F/R: Disc/Drum
Steering: Rack & pinion
Wheelbase: 238.0cm 93.7in
Track F: 138.9cm 54.7in
Track R: 134.1cm 52.8in
Length: 399.5cm 157.3in
Width: 163.6cm 64.4in
Height: 129.0cm 50.8in
Kerb weight: 905.7kg 1995.0lb
Fuel: 45.0L 9.9gal 11.9galUS

3090 Mitsubishi

Starion ESI-R
1986 Japan
0-60mph 96.5kmh: 8.3secs
0-1/4 mile: 16.2secs
176.0bhp 131.2kW 178.4PS
@ 5000rpm
223.0lbft 302.2Nm @ 2500rpm
129.3bhp/ton 127.1bhp/tonne
68.9bhp/L 51.4kW/L 69.8PS/L
53.6ft/sec 16.3m/sec
22.2mpg 18.5mpgUS 12.7L/100km
Petrol 4-stroke piston
2555cc 155.9cu in turbocharged
In-line 4 fuel injection
Compression ratio: 7.1:1
Bore: 91.1mm 3.6in
Stroke: 98.0mm 3.9in
Valve type/No: Overhead 8
Transmission: Manual
No. of forward speeds: 5
Wheels driven: Rear
Brakes F/R: Disc/Disc
Steering: Recirculating ball PA
Wheelbase: 243.6cm 95.9in
Length: 439.9cm 173.2in
Width: 169.7cm 66.8in
Height: 127.5cm 50.2in
Kerb weight: 1384.7kg 3050.0lb

3091 Mitsubishi

Colt 1500 GLX 5-door
1987 Japan
95.0mph 152.9kmh
0-50mph 80.5kmh: 8.5secs
0-60mph 96.5kmh: 12.2secs
0-1/4 mile: 18.9secs
0-1km: 35.4secs
74.0bhp 55.2kW 75.0PS
@ 5500rpm
87.0lbft 117.9Nm @ 4000rpm
85.5bhp/ton 84.1bhp/tonne
50.4bhp/L 37.6kW/L 51.1PS/L
49.3ft/sec 15.0m/sec
21.1mph 33.9kmh/1000rpm
29.2mpg 24.3mpgUS 9.7L/100km
Petrol 4-stroke piston
1468cc 90.0cu in
In-line 4 1 Carburettor
Compression ratio: 9.5:1
Bore: 75.5mm 3.0in
Stroke: 82.0mm 3.2in
Valve type/No: Overhead 8
Transmission: Manual
No. of forward speeds: 5
Wheels driven: Front
Springs F/R: Coil/Coil
Brake system: PA
Brakes F/R: Disc/Drum
Steering: Rack & pinion PA
Wheelbase: 238.0cm 93.7in
Track F: 141.0cm 55.5in
Track R: 134.0cm 52.8in
Length: 396.5cm 156.1in
Width: 163.5cm 64.4in
Height: 136.0cm 53.5in
Ground clearance: 15.5cm 6.1in
Kerb weight: 880.0kg 1938.3lb
Fuel: 45.0L 9.9gal 11.9galUS

3092 Mitsubishi

Galant 2000 GLS Automatic
1987 Japan
105.0mph 168.9kmh
0-50mph 80.5kmh: 9.7secs
0-60mph 96.5kmh: 13.1secs
0-1/4 mile: 19.6secs
0-1km: 36.0secs
101.0bhp 75.3kW 102.4PS
@ 6000rpm
114.0lbft 154.5Nm @ 3500rpm
90.1bhp/ton 88.6bhp/tonne
50.6bhp/L 37.7kW/L 51.3PS/L
57.7ft/sec 17.6m/sec
27.7mph 44.6kmh/1000rpm
25.3mpg 21.1mpgUS 11.2L/100km
Petrol 4-stroke piston
1997cc 122.0cu in
In-line 4 1 Carburettor
Compression ratio: 9.5:1
Bore: 85.0mm 3.3in
Stroke: 88.0mm 3.5in
Valve type/No: Overhead 8
Transmission: Automatic
No. of forward speeds: 4
Wheels driven: Front
Springs F/R: Coil/Coil
Brake system: PA
Brakes F/R: Disc/Disc
Steering: Rack & pinion PA
Wheelbase: 259.0cm 102.0in
Track F: 144.5cm 56.9in
Track R: 140.5cm 55.3in
Length: 456.0cm 179.5in
Width: 195.5cm 77.0in
Height: 139.9cm 55.1in
Ground clearance: 15.6cm 6.1in
Kerb weight: 1140.0kg 2511.0lb
Fuel: 59.6L 13.1gal 15.7galUS

3093 Mitsubishi

Galant Sapporo
1987 Japan
115.0mph 185.0kmh
0-50mph 80.5kmh: 7.7secs
0-60mph 96.5kmh: 10.4secs
0-1/4 mile: 18.0secs
0-1km: 33.0secs
127.0bhp 94.7kW 128.8PS
@ 5000rpm
142.0lbft 192.4Nm @ 4000rpm
104.9bhp/ton 103.2bhp/tonne
54.0bhp/L 40.3kW/L 54.8PS/L
54.7ft/sec 16.7m/sec
26.1mph 42.0kmh/1000rpm
24.8mpg 20.7mpgUS 11.4L/100km
Petrol 4-stroke piston
2351cc 143.0cu in
In-line 4 fuel injection
Compression ratio: 9.5:1
Bore: 86.5mm 3.4in
Stroke: 100.0mm 3.9in
Valve type/No: Overhead 8
Transmission: Automatic
No. of forward speeds: 4
Wheels driven: Front
Springs F/R: Coil/Coil
Brake system: PA ABS
Brakes F/R: Disc/Disc
Steering: Rack & pinion PA
Wheelbase: 260.0cm 102.4in
Track F: 144.5cm 56.9in
Track R: 141.5cm 55.7in
Length: 466.0cm 183.5in
Width: 195.5cm 77.0in
Height: 137.0cm 53.9in
Ground clearance: 15.4cm 6.1in
Kerb weight: 1231.0kg 2711.4lb
Fuel: 60.1L 13.2gal 15.9galUS

3094 Mitsubishi

Shogun Turbo Diesel 5-door
1987 Japan
83.0mph 133.5kmh
0-50mph 80.5kmh: 11.7secs
0-60mph 96.5kmh: 17.8secs
0-1/4 mile: 20.6secs
0-1km: 40.0secs
84.0bhp 62.6kW 85.2PS
@ 4200rpm
148.0lbft 200.5Nm @ 2000rpm
48.5bhp/ton 47.7bhp/tonne
33.9bhp/L 25.3kW/L 34.4PS/L
43.6ft/sec 13.3m/sec
20.1mph 32.3kmh/1000rpm
22.1mpg 18.4mpgUS 12.8L/100km
Diesel 4-stroke piston
2477cc 151.0cu in turbocharged
In-line 4 fuel injection
Compression ratio: 21.0:1
Bore: 91.0mm 3.6in
Stroke: 95.0mm 3.7in
Valve type/No: Overhead 8
Transmission: Manual
No. of forward speeds: 5
Wheels driven: 4-wheel engageable
Springs F/R: Torsion bar/Leaf
Brake system: PA
Brakes F/R: Disc/Drum
Steering: Recirculating ball PA
Wheelbase: 269.5cm 106.1in
Track F: 140.0cm 55.1in
Track R: 137.5cm 54.1in
Length: 460.0cm 181.1in
Width: 168.0cm 66.1in
Height: 188.0cm 74.0in
Ground clearance: 20.5cm 8.1in
Kerb weight: 1760.0kg 3876.6lb
Fuel: 91.9L 20.2gal 24.3galUS

3095 Mitsubishi

Starion 2000 Turbo
1987 Japan
136.0mph 218.8kmh
0-50mph 80.5kmh: 5.3secs
0-60mph 96.5kmh: 6.9secs
0-1/4 mile: 16.0secs
0-1km: 28.6secs
177.0bhp 132.0kW 179.4PS
@ 6000rpm
214.0lbft 290.0Nm @ 3500rpm
137.6bhp/ton 135.3bhp/tonne
88.6bhp/L 66.1kW/L 89.9PS/L
57.7ft/sec 17.6m/sec
23.9mph 38.5kmh/1000rpm
19.0mpg 15.8mpgUS 14.9L/100km
Petrol 4-stroke piston
1997cc 122.0cu in turbocharged
In-line 4 fuel injection
Compression ratio: 7.6:1
Bore: 85.0mm 3.3in
Stroke: 88.0mm 3.5in
Valve type/No: Overhead 8
Transmission: Manual
No. of forward speeds: 5
Wheels driven: Rear
Springs F/R: Coil/Coil
Brake system: PA ABS
Brakes F/R: Disc/Disc
Steering: Recirculating ball PA
Wheelbase: 243.5cm 95.9in
Track F: 146.5cm 57.7in
Track R: 145.5cm 57.3in
Length: 443.0cm 174.4in
Width: 174.5cm 68.7in
Height: 131.5cm 51.8in
Ground clearance: 15.5cm 6.1in
Kerb weight: 1308.0kg 2881.1lb
Fuel: 75.1L 16.5gal 19.8galUS

3096 Mitsubishi

Starion ESI-R
1987 Japan
0-60mph 96.5kmh: 8.3secs
0-1/4 mile: 16.2secs
176.0bhp 131.2kW 178.4PS
@ 5000rpm
223.0lbft 302.2Nm @ 2500rpm
129.3bhp/ton 127.1bhp/tonne
68.9bhp/L 51.4kW/L 69.8PS/L
23.8mpg 19.8mpgUS 11.9L/100km
Petrol 4-stroke piston
2555cc 155.9cu in turbocharged
In-line 4
Valve type/No: Overhead 8
Transmission: Manual
No. of forward speeds: 5
Wheels driven: Rear
Brake system: ABS
Brakes F/R: Disc/Disc
Steering: Recirculating ball PA
Length: 439.9cm 173.2in
Kerb weight: 1384.7kg 3050.0lb

3097 Mitsubishi

Cordia Turbo
1988 Japan
115.0mph 185.0kmh
0-50mph 80.5kmh: 5.8secs
0-60mph 96.5kmh: 8.4secs
0-1/4 mile: 16.4secs
116.0bhp 86.5kW 117.6PS
@ 5500rpm
129.0lbft 174.8Nm @ 3000rpm
105.6bhp/ton 103.9bhp/tonne
64.6bhp/L 48.2kW/L 65.5PS/L
52.9ft/sec 16.1m/sec
25.2mpg 21.0mpgUS 11.2L/100km
Petrol 4-stroke piston
1795cc 109.5cu in turbocharged
In-line 4 fuel injection
Compression ratio: 7.5:1
Bore: 80.6mm 3.2in
Stroke: 88.0mm 3.5in
Valve type/No: Overhead 8
Transmission: Manual
No. of forward speeds: 5
Wheels driven: Front
Springs F/R: Coil/Coil
Brake system: PA
Brakes F/R: Disc/Drum
Steering: Rack & pinion PA
Wheelbase: 244.6cm 96.3in
Track F: 141.0cm 55.5in
Track R: 137.4cm 54.1in
Length: 439.4cm 173.0in
Width: 166.1cm 65.4in
Height: 125.5cm 49.4in
Kerb weight: 1116.8kg 2460.0lb
Fuel: 48.4L 10.6gal 12.8galUS

3098 Mitsubishi

Galant 2000 GLSi
1988 Japan
112.0mph 180.2kmh
0-50mph 80.5kmh: 7.7secs
0-60mph 96.5kmh: 10.9secs
0-1/4 mile: 17.4secs
0-1km: 32.7secs
110.0bhp 82.0kW 111.5PS
@ 5500rpm
118.1lbft 160.0Nm @ 4500rpm
93.8bhp/ton 92.2bhp/tonne
55.1bhp/L 41.1kW/L 55.8PS/L
52.9ft/sec 16.1m/sec
21.6mph 34.8kmh/1000rpm
21.2mpg 17.7mpgUS 13.3L/100km
Petrol 4-stroke piston
1997cc 122.0cu in
In-line 4 fuel injection
Compression ratio: 9.0:1
Bore: 85.0mm 3.3in
Stroke: 88.0mm 3.5in
Valve type/No: Overhead 8

Transmission: Manual
No. of forward speeds: 5
Wheels driven: Front
Springs F/R: Coil/Coil
Brake system: PA ABS
Brakes F/R: Disc/Disc
Steering: Rack & pinion PA
Wheelbase: 260.0cm 102.4in
Track F: 146.0cm 57.5in
Track R: 145.0cm 57.1in
Length: 454.0cm 178.7in
Width: 169.5cm 66.7in
Height: 141.5cm 55.7in
Ground clearance: 17.9cm 7.0in
Kerb weight: 1193.0kg 2627.7lb
Fuel: 60.1L 13.2gal 15.9galUS

3099 Mitsubishi

Galant GTi-16v
1988 Japan
122.0mph 196.3kmh
0-50mph 80.5kmh: 6.2secs
0-60mph 96.5kmh: 8.7secs
0-1/4 mile: 16.6secs
0-1km: 30.4secs
144.0bhp 107.4kW 146.0PS
@ 6500rpm
125.5lbft 170.0Nm @ 5000rpm
119.2bhp/ton 117.2bhp/tonne
72.1bhp/L 53.8kW/L 73.1PS/L
62.5ft/sec 19.1m/sec
19.8mph 31.9kmh/1000rpm
24.4mpg 20.3mpgUS 11.6L/100km
Petrol 4-stroke piston
1997cc 122.0cu in
In-line 4 fuel injection
Compression ratio: 9.8:1
Bore: 85.0mm 3.3in
Stroke: 88.0mm 3.5in
Valve type/No: Overhead 16
Transmission: Manual
No. of forward speeds: 5
Wheels driven: Front
Springs F/R: Coil/Coil
Brake system: PA ABS
Brakes F/R: Disc/Disc
Steering: Rack & pinion PA
Wheelbase: 260.0cm 102.4in
Track F: 146.0cm 57.5in
Track R: 145.0cm 57.1in
Length: 454.0cm 178.7in
Width: 169.5cm 66.7in
Height: 141.5cm 55.7in
Ground clearance: 17.9cm 7.0in
Kerb weight: 1229.0kg 2707.0lb
Fuel: 60.1L 13.2gal 15.9galUS

3100 Mitsubishi

Lancer GTi 16v
1988 Japan
116.0mph 186.6kmh
0-50mph 80.5kmh: 6.4secs
0-60mph 96.5kmh: 9.0secs
0-1/4 mile: 17.1secs
0-1km: 31.2secs
123.0bhp 91.7kW 124.7PS
@ 6500rpm
104.8lbft 142.0Nm @ 5000rpm
116.4bhp/ton 114.4bhp/tonne
77.1bhp/L 57.5kW/L 78.1PS/L
53.3ft/sec 16.2m/sec
19.3mph 31.1kmh/1000rpm
25.9mpg 21.6mpgUS 10.9L/100km
Petrol 4-stroke piston
1596cc 97.0cu in
In-line 4 fuel injection
Compression ratio: 10.0:1
Bore: 82.3mm 3.2in
Stroke: 75.0mm 2.9in
Valve type/No: Overhead 16
Transmission: Manual
No. of forward speeds: 5
Wheels driven: Front
Springs F/R: Coil/Coil
Brake system: PA
Brakes F/R: Disc/Disc
Steering: Rack & pinion PA
Wheelbase: 245.5cm 96.7in
Track F: 143.0cm 56.3in
Track R: 143.0cm 56.3in
Length: 423.5cm 166.7in
Width: 167.0cm 65.7in
Height: 167.0cm 65.7in
Ground clearance: 15.5cm 6.1in
Kerb weight: 1075.0kg 2367.8lb
Fuel: 50.0L 11.0gal 13.2galUS

3101 Mitsubishi

Mirage Turbo
1988 Japan
118.0mph 189.9kmh
0-50mph 80.5kmh: 5.8secs
0-60mph 96.5kmh: 8.2secs
0-1/4 mile: 16.3secs
105.0bhp 78.3kW 106.5PS
@ 5500rpm
122.0lbft 165.3Nm @ 3500rpm
106.7bhp/ton 104.9bhp/tonne
65.7bhp/L 49.0kW/L 66.7PS/L
51.8ft/sec 15.8m/sec
30.0mpg 25.0mpgUS 9.4L/100km
Petrol 4-stroke piston
1597cc 97.4cu in turbocharged
In-line 4 fuel injection
Compression ratio: 7.6:1
Bore: 76.9mm 3.0in
Stroke: 86.0mm 3.4in
Valve type/No: Overhead 8
Transmission: Manual
No. of forward speeds: 5
Wheels driven: Front
Springs F/R: Coil/Coil
Brake system: PA
Brakes F/R: Disc/Drum
Steering: Rack & pinion PA
Wheelbase: 238.0cm 93.7in
Track F: 138.9cm 54.7in
Track R: 134.1cm 52.8in
Length: 399.5cm 157.3in
Width: 163.6cm 64.4in
Height: 129.0cm 50.8in
Kerb weight: 1001.1kg 2205.0lb
Fuel: 45.0L 9.9gal 11.9galUS

3102 Mitsubishi

Eclipse
1989 Japan
143.0mph 230.1kmh
0-50mph 80.5kmh: 5.5secs
0-60mph 96.5kmh: 7.2secs
0-1/4 mile: 15.8secs
190.0bhp 141.7kW 192.6PS
@ 6000rpm
203.0lbft 275.1Nm @ 3000rpm
149.6bhp/ton 147.1bhp/tonne
96.1bhp/L 71.7kW/L 97.4PS/L
57.7ft/sec 17.6m/sec
27.6mpg 23.0mpgUS 10.2L/100km
Petrol 4-stroke piston
1977cc 120.6cu in turbocharged
In-line 4 fuel injection
Compression ratio: 7.8:1
Bore: 85.0mm 3.3in
Stroke: 88.0mm 3.5in
Valve type/No: Overhead 16
Transmission: Manual
No. of forward speeds: 5
Wheels driven: Front
Springs F/R: Coil/Coil
Brake system: PA
Brakes F/R: Disc/Disc
Steering: Rack & pinion PA
Wheelbase: 246.9cm 97.2in
Track F: 146.6cm 57.7in
Track R: 145.0cm 57.1in
Length: 433.1cm 170.5in
Width: 168.9cm 66.5in
Height: 130.6cm 51.4in
Ground clearance: 16.5cm 6.5in
Kerb weight: 1291.6kg 2845.0lb
Fuel: 60.2L 13.2gal 15.9galUS

3103 Mitsubishi

Eclipse GSX
1989 Japan
0-60mph 96.5kmh: 6.8secs
0-1/4 mile: 15.3secs
195.0bhp 145.4kW 197.7PS
@ 6000rpm
203.0lbft 275.1Nm @ 3000rpm
138.9bhp/ton 136.6bhp/tonne
97.6bhp/L 72.8kW/L 99.0PS/L
57.7ft/sec 17.6m/sec
19.8mpg 16.5mpgUS 14.3L/100km
Petrol 4-stroke piston
1997cc 121.8cu in turbocharged
In-line 4 fuel injection
Compression ratio: 7.8:1
Bore: 85.0mm 3.3in
Stroke: 88.0mm 3.5in
Valve type/No: Overhead 16
Transmission: Manual
No. of forward speeds: 5
Wheels driven: 4-wheel drive
Springs F/R: Coil/Coil
Brake system: PA
Brakes F/R: Disc/Disc
Steering: Rack & pinion PA
Wheelbase: 246.9cm 97.2in
Track F: 146.6cm 57.7in
Track R: 145.5cm 57.3in
Length: 437.9cm 172.4in
Width: 168.9cm 66.5in
Height: 132.1cm 52.0in
Kerb weight: 1427.8kg 3145.0lb
Fuel: 60.2L 13.2gal 15.9galUS

3104 Mitsubishi

Galant GS
1989 Japan
120.0mph 193.1kmh
0-50mph 80.5kmh: 6.8secs
0-60mph 96.5kmh: 9.7secs
0-1/4 mile: 18.2secs
135.0bhp 100.7kW 136.9PS
@ 6000rpm
125.0lbft 169.4Nm @ 5000rpm
105.0bhp/ton 103.2bhp/tonne
67.6bhp/L 50.4kW/L 68.5PS/L
57.7ft/sec 17.6m/sec
27.5mpg 22.9mpgUS 10.3L/100km
Petrol 4-stroke piston
1997cc 121.8cu in
In-line 4 fuel injection
Compression ratio: 9.0:1
Bore: 85.0mm 3.3in
Stroke: 88.0mm 3.5in
Valve type/No: Overhead 16
Transmission: Manual
No. of forward speeds: 5
Wheels driven: Front
Springs F/R: Coil/Coil
Brake system: PA ABS
Brakes F/R: Disc/Disc
Steering: Rack & pinion PA
Wheelbase: 260.1cm 102.4in
Track F: 146.1cm 57.5in
Track R: 145.0cm 57.1in
Length: 467.1cm 183.9in
Width: 169.4cm 66.7in
Height: 141.0cm 55.5in
Kerb weight: 1307.5kg 2880.0lb
Fuel: 60.2L 13.2gal 15.9galUS

3105 Mitsubishi

Shogun V6 5-door
1989 Japan
102.0mph 164.1kmh
0-50mph 80.5kmh: 9.0secs
0-60mph 96.5kmh: 12.8secs
0-1/4 mile: 18.8secs
0-1km: 35.2secs
141.0bhp 105.1kW 143.0PS
@ 5000rpm
166.1lbft 225.0Nm @ 3000rpm
75.5bhp/ton 74.2bhp/tonne
47.4bhp/L 35.4kW/L 48.1PS/L
41.5ft/sec 12.7m/sec
20.9mph 33.6kmh/1000rpm
19.7mpg 16.4mpgUS 14.3L/100km
Petrol 4-stroke piston
2972cc 181.0cu in
Vee 6 fuel injection
Compression ratio: 8.9:1
Bore: 91.1mm 3.6in
Stroke: 76.0mm 3.0in
Valve type/No: Overhead 12
Transmission: Manual
No. of forward speeds: 5
Wheels driven: 4-wheel drive
Springs F/R: Torsion bar/Leaf
Brake system: PA
Brakes F/R: Disc/Drum
Steering: Recirculating ball PA
Wheelbase: 269.5cm 106.1in
Track F: 140.0cm 55.1in
Track R: 137.5cm 54.1in
Length: 460.0cm 181.1in
Width: 168.0cm 66.1in
Height: 188.0cm 74.0in
Ground clearance: 20.5cm 8.1in
Kerb weight: 1900.0kg 4185.0lb
Fuel: 91.9L 20.2gal 24.3galUS

3106 Mitsubishi

Starion 2.6 Turbo
1989 Japan
130.0mph 209.2kmh
0-50mph 80.5kmh: 5.6secs
0-60mph 96.5kmh: 7.8secs
0-1/4 mile: 15.9secs
0-1km: 29.4secs
153.0bhp 114.1kW 155.1PS
@ 5000rpm
207.4lbft 281.0Nm @ 2500rpm
113.2bhp/ton 111.3bhp/tonne
59.9bhp/L 44.6kW/L 60.7PS/L
53.6ft/sec 16.3m/sec
23.7mph 38.1kmh/1000rpm
18.8mpg 15.7mpgUS 15.0L/100km
Petrol 4-stroke piston
2555cc 156.0cu in turbocharged
In-line 4 fuel injection
Compression ratio: 7.0:1
Bore: 91.1mm 3.6in
Stroke: 98.0mm 3.9in
Valve type/No: Overhead 12
Transmission: Manual
No. of forward speeds: 5
Wheels driven: Rear
Springs F/R: Coil/Coil
Brake system: PA
Brakes F/R: Disc/Disc
Steering: Recirculating ball PA
Wheelbase: 243.5cm 95.9in
Track F: 146.5cm 57.7in
Track R: 145.5cm 57.3in
Length: 443.0cm 174.4in
Width: 174.5cm 68.7in
Height: 131.5cm 51.8in
Ground clearance: 15.5cm 6.1in
Kerb weight: 1375.0kg 3028.6lb
Fuel: 75.1L 16.5gal 19.8galUS

3107 Mitsubishi

Starion ESI-R
1989 Japan
127.0mph 204.3kmh
0-50mph 80.5kmh: 5.9secs
0-60mph 96.5kmh: 8.0secs
0-1/4 mile: 16.3secs
188.0bhp 140.2kW 190.6PS
@ 5000rpm
234.0lbft 317.1Nm @ 2500rpm
135.8bhp/ton 133.6bhp/tonne
73.6bhp/L 54.9kW/L 74.6PS/L
53.6ft/sec 16.3m/sec
24.0mpg 20.0mpgUS 11.8L/100km
Petrol 4-stroke piston
2555cc 155.9cu in turbocharged
In-line 4 fuel injection
Compression ratio: 7.0:1
Bore: 91.5mm 3.6in
Stroke: 98.0mm 3.9in
Valve type/No: Overhead 8
Transmission: Manual
No. of forward speeds: 5
Wheels driven: Rear
Springs F/R: Coil/Coil
Brake system: PA ABS
Brakes F/R: Disc/Disc
Steering: Recirculating ball PA
Wheelbase: 243.6cm 95.9in
Track F: 146.6cm 57.7in
Track R: 145.5cm 57.3in
Length: 439.9cm 173.2in
Width: 173.5cm 68.3in
Height: 127.5cm 50.2in
Kerb weight: 1407.4kg 3100.0lb
Fuel: 74.9L 16.5gal 19.8galUS

3108 Mitsubishi

Galant 2000 GLSi Coupe
1990 Japan
113.0mph 181.8kmh
0-50mph 80.5kmh: 7.4secs
0-60mph 96.5kmh: 10.4secs
0-1/4 mile: 17.9secs
0-1km: 33.1secs
111.0bhp 82.8kW 112.5PS
@ 5500rpm
118.1lbft 160.0Nm @ 4500rpm
90.4bhp/ton 88.9bhp/tonne
55.6bhp/L 41.5kW/L 56.4PS/L
52.9ft/sec 16.1m/sec
23.4mph 37.7kmh/1000rpm
23.0mpg 19.2mpgUS 12.3L/100km
Petrol 4-stroke piston
1996cc 122.0cu in
In-line 4 fuel injection
Compression ratio: 9.0:1
Bore: 85.0mm 3.3in
Stroke: 88.0mm 3.5in
Valve type/No: Overhead 8
Transmission: Manual
No. of forward speeds: 5
Wheels driven: Front

ɔrings F/R: Coil/Coil
'ake system: PA ABS
'akes F/R: Disc/Disc
:eering: Rack & pinion PA
'heelbase: 259.8cm 102.3in
rack F: 145.8cm 57.4in
rack R: 144.8cm 57.0in
ength: 453.9cm 178.7in
'idth: 169.4cm 66.7in
eight: 140.0cm 55.1in
round clearance: 16.8cm 6.6in
erb weight: 1248.0kg 2748.9lb
uel: 60.1L 13.2gal 15.9galUS

109 Mitsubishi

ancer GLXi 4WD Liftback
990 Japan
05.0mph 168.9kmh
-50mph 80.5kmh: 8.2secs
-60mph 96.5kmh: 11.7secs
-1/4 mile: 18.3secs
-1km: 34.4secs
5.0bhp 70.8kW 96.3PS
5500rpm
04.1lbft 141.0Nm @ 4000rpm
9.8bhp/ton 78.5bhp/tonne
4.1bhp/L 40.4kW/L 54.9PS/L
1.8ft/sec 15.8m/sec
9.8mph 31.9kmh/1000rpm
4.6mpg 20.5mpgUS 11.5L/100km
etrol 4-stroke piston
755cc 107.0cu in
ı-line 4 fuel injection
ompression ratio: 9.5:1
ore: 81.0mm 3.2in
troke: 86.0mm 3.4in
'alve type/No: Overhead 8
'ransmission: Manual
o. of forward speeds: 5
Vheels driven: 4-wheel drive
prings F/R: Coil/Coil
rake system: PA
rakes F/R: Disc/Drum
teering: Rack & pinion PA
Vheelbase: 245.5cm 96.7in
'rack F: 142.5cm 56.1in
'rack R: 142.0cm 55.9in
ength: 423.5cm 166.7in
Vidth: 167.0cm 65.7in
leight: 142.5cm 56.1in
round clearance: 15.5cm 6.1in
erb weight: 1210.0kg 2665.2lb
uel: 50.0L 11.0gal 13.2galUS

110 Mitsubishi

ancer Liftback 1800 GTi-16v
990 Japan
22.0mph 196.3kmh
-50mph 80.5kmh: 6.2secs
-60mph 96.5kmh: 8.5secs
-1/4 mile: 16.7secs
-1km: 30.0secs
34.0bhp 99.9kW 135.9PS
@ 6500rpm
19.6lbft 162.0Nm @ 4500rpm
17.1bhp/ton 115.1bhp/tonne
'3.0bhp/L 54.4kW/L 74.0PS/L
2.5ft/sec 19.1m/sec
9.1mph 30.7kmh/1000rpm
2.9mpg 19.1mpgUS 12.3L/100km
'etrol 4-stroke piston
836cc 112.0cu in
ı-line 4 fuel injection
ompression ratio: 10.5:1
ore: 81.5mm 3.2in
troke: 88.0mm 3.5in
'alve type/No: Overhead 16
'ransmission: Manual
lo. of forward speeds: 5
Vheels driven: Front
prings F/R: Coil/Coil
rake system: PA
rakes F/R: Disc/Disc
teering: Rack & pinion PA
Vheelbase: 245.5cm 96.7in
'rack F: 143.0cm 56.3in
'rack R: 143.0cm 56.3in
ength: 424.5cm 167.1in
Vidth: 167.0cm 65.7in
leight: 140.5cm 55.3in
round clearance: 15.3cm 6.0in
erb weight: 1164.0kg 2563.9lb
uel: 50.0L 11.0gal 13.2galUS

3111 Mitsubishi

000GT VR-4
1991 Japan
159.0mph 255.8kmh
0-50mph 80.5kmh: 4.8secs
0-60mph 96.5kmh: 6.3secs
0-1/4 mile: 14.7secs
300.0bhp 223.7kW 304.2PS
@ 6000rpm
307.0lbft 416.0Nm @ 2500rpm
173.4bhp/ton 170.5bhp/tonne
100.9bhp/L 75.3kW/L 102.3PS/L
49.8ft/sec 15.2m/sec
21.6mpg 18.0mpgUS 13.1L/100km
Petrol 4-stroke piston
2972cc 181.3cu in turbocharged
Vee 6 fuel injection
Compression ratio: 8.0:1
Bore: 91.1mm 3.6in
Stroke: 76.0mm 3.0in
Valve type/No: Overhead 24
Transmission: Manual
No. of forward speeds: 5
Wheels driven: 4-wheel drive
Springs F/R: Coil/Coil
Brake system: PA ABS
Brakes F/R: Disc/Disc
Steering: Rack & pinion PA
Wheelbase: 246.9cm 97.2in
Track F: 156.0cm 61.4in
Track R: 158.0cm 62.2in
Length: 458.5cm 180.5in
Width: 183.9cm 72.4in
Height: 128.5cm 50.6in
Ground clearance: 14.5cm 5.7in
Kerb weight: 1759.2kg 3875.0lb
Fuel: 74.9L 16.5gal 19.8galUS

3112 Mitsubishi

Colt 1800 GTI-16v
1991 Japan
121.0mph 194.7kmh
0-50mph 80.5kmh: 6.0secs
0-60mph 96.5kmh: 8.3secs
0-1/4 mile: 16.5secs
0-1km: 30.3secs
134.0bhp 99.9kW 135.9PS
@ 6500rpm
119.6lbft 162.0Nm @ 4500rpm
127.2bhp/ton 125.1bhp/tonne
73.0bhp/L 54.4kW/L 74.0PS/L
62.5ft/sec 19.1m/sec
19.3mph 31.1kmh/1000rpm
26.9mpg 22.4mpgUS 10.5L/100km
Petrol 4-stroke piston
1836cc 112.0cu in
In-line 4 fuel injection
Compression ratio: 10.5:1
Bore: 81.5mm 3.2in
Stroke: 88.0mm 3.5in
Valve type/No: Overhead 16
Transmission: Manual
No. of forward speeds: 5
Wheels driven: Front
Springs F/R: Coil/Coil
Brake system: PA
Brakes F/R: Disc/Disc
Steering: Rack & pinion PA
Wheelbase: 238.5cm 93.9in
Track F: 143.0cm 56.3in
Track R: 143.0cm 56.3in
Length: 396.0cm 155.9in
Width: 166.9cm 65.7in
Height: 137.9cm 54.3in
Ground clearance: 12.4cm 4.9in
Kerb weight: 1071.0kg 2359.0lb
Fuel: 50.0L 11.0gal 13.2galUS

3113 Mitsubishi

Diamante LS
1991 Japan
130.0mph 209.2kmh
0-50mph 80.5kmh: 6.6secs
0-60mph 96.5kmh: 9.0secs
0-1/4 mile: 16.7secs
202.0bhp 150.6kW 204.8PS
@ 6000rpm
199.0lbft 269.6Nm @ 3000rpm
120.7bhp/ton 118.6bhp/tonne
68.0bhp/L 50.7kW/L 68.9PS/L
49.8ft/sec 15.2m/sec
22.8mpg 19.0mpgUS 12.4L/100km
Petrol 4-stroke piston
2972cc 181.3cu in
Vee 6 fuel injection
Compression ratio: 10.0:1
Bore: 91.0mm 3.6in
Stroke: 76.0mm 3.0in
Valve type/No: Overhead 24
Transmission: Automatic
No. of forward speeds: 4
Wheels driven: Front
Springs F/R: Coil/Coil
Brake system: PA ABS
Brakes F/R: Disc/Disc
Steering: Rack & pinion PA
Wheelbase: 272.0cm 107.1in
Track F: 153.4cm 60.4in
Track R: 152.9cm 60.2in
Length: 483.1cm 190.2in
Width: 177.5cm 69.9in
Height: 141.0cm 55.5in
Ground clearance: 15.2cm 6.0in
Kerb weight: 1702.5kg 3750.0lb
Fuel: 71.9L 15.8gal 19.0galUS

3114 Mitsubishi

Galant VR-4
1991 Japan
130.0mph 209.2kmh
0-60mph 96.5kmh: 7.9secs
0-1/4 mile: 15.8secs
195.0bhp 145.4kW 197.7PS
@ 6000rpm
203.0lbft 275.1Nm @ 3000rpm
127.7bhp/ton 125.6bhp/tonne
97.6bhp/L 72.8kW/L 99.0PS/L
57.7ft/sec 17.6m/sec
25.2mpg 21.0mpgUS 11.2L/100km
Petrol 4-stroke piston
1997cc 121.8cu in turbocharged
In-line 4 fuel injection
Compression ratio: 7.8:1
Bore: 85.0mm 3.3in
Stroke: 88.0mm 3.5in
Valve type/No: Overhead 16
Transmission: Manual
No. of forward speeds: 5
Wheels driven: 4-wheel drive
Springs F/R: Coil/Coil
Brake system: PA ABS
Brakes F/R: Disc/Disc
Steering: Rack & pinion PA
Wheelbase: 260.1cm 102.4in
Track F: 146.1cm 57.5in
Track R: 145.0cm 57.1in
Length: 467.1cm 183.9in
Width: 169.4cm 66.7in
Height: 141.0cm 55.5in
Kerb weight: 1552.7kg 3420.0lb
Fuel: 60.2L 13.2gal 15.9galUS

3115 Mitsubishi

Shogun V6 LWB
1991 Japan
105.0mph 168.9kmh
0-50mph 80.5kmh: 9.4secs
0-60mph 96.5kmh: 13.1secs
0-1/4 mile: 19.7secs
0-1km: 30.6secs
147.0bhp 109.6kW 149.0PS
@ 5000rpm
174.2lbft 236.0Nm @ 4000rpm
72.7bhp/ton 71.5bhp/tonne
49.5bhp/L 36.9kW/L 50.1PS/L
41.5ft/sec 12.7m/sec
20.9mph 33.6kmh/1000rpm
16.1mpg 13.4mpgUS 17.5L/100km
Petrol 4-stroke piston
2972cc 181.0cu in
Vee 6 fuel injection
Compression ratio: 8.9:1
Bore: 91.1mm 3.6in
Stroke: 76.0mm 3.0in
Valve type/No: Overhead 12
Transmission: Manual
No. of forward speeds: 5
Wheels driven: 4-wheel engageable
Springs F/R: Coil/Torsion bar
Brake system: PA ABS
Brakes F/R: Disc/Disc
Steering: Rack & pinion PA
Wheelbase: 272.5cm 107.3in
Track F: 148.6cm 58.5in
Track R: 148.6cm 58.5in
Length: 472.4cm 186.0in
Width: 178.6cm 70.3in
Height: 186.9cm 73.6in
Ground clearance: 21.6cm 8.5in
Kerb weight: 2055.0kg 4526.4lb
Fuel: 92.0L 20.2gal 24.3galUS

3116 Mitsubishi

Sigma
1991 Japan
130.0mph 209.2kmh
0-50mph 80.5kmh: 7.2secs
0-60mph 96.5kmh: 9.3secs
0-1/4 mile: 17.2secs
0-1km: 30.8secs
202.0bhp 150.6kW 204.8PS
@ 6000rpm
200.0lbft 271.0Nm @ 3000rpm
126.3bhp/ton 124.2bhp/tonne
68.0bhp/L 50.7kW/L 68.9PS/L
49.8ft/sec 15.2m/sec
24.6mph 39.6kmh/1000rpm
18.3mpg 15.2mpgUS 15.4L/100km
Petrol 4-stroke piston
2972cc 181.0cu in
Vee 6 fuel injection
Compression ratio: 10.0:1
Bore: 91.0mm 3.6in
Stroke: 76.0mm 3.0in
Valve type/No: Overhead 24
Transmission: Automatic
No. of forward speeds: 4
Wheels driven: Front
Springs F/R: Coil/Coil
Brake system: PA ABS
Brakes F/R: Disc/Disc
Steering: Rack & pinion PA
Wheelbase: 272.0cm 107.1in
Track F: 153.4cm 60.4in
Track R: 152.9cm 60.2in
Length: 475.0cm 187.0in
Width: 177.5cm 69.9in
Height: 143.5cm 56.5in
Ground clearance: 15.5cm 6.1in
Kerb weight: 1626.0kg 3581.5lb
Fuel: 72.8L 16.0gal 19.2galUS

3117 Mitsubishi

Space Runner 1800-16v GLXi
1991 Japan
115.0mph 185.0kmh
0-50mph 80.5kmh: 7.5secs
0-60mph 96.5kmh: 10.0secs
0-1/4 mile: 18.1secs
0-1km: 33.4secs
121.0bhp 90.2kW 122.7PS
@ 6000rpm
119.0lbft 161.2Nm @ 4500rpm
97.7bhp/ton 96.0bhp/tonne
66.0bhp/L 49.2kW/L 66.9PS/L
58.3ft/sec 17.8m/sec
20.3mph 32.7kmh/1000rpm
27.2mpg 22.6mpgUS 10.4L/100km
Petrol 4-stroke piston
1834cc 111.9cu in
In-line 4 fuel injection
Compression ratio: 10.0:1
Bore: 81.0mm 3.2in
Stroke: 89.0mm 3.5in
Valve type/No: Overhead 16
Transmission: Manual
No. of forward speeds: 5
Wheels driven: Front
Springs F/R: Coil/Coil
Brake system: PA
Brakes F/R: Disc/Drum
Steering: Rack & pinion PA
Wheelbase: 252.0cm 99.2in
Track F: 146.1cm 57.5in
Track R: 146.1cm 57.5in
Length: 429.0cm 168.9in
Width: 169.4cm 66.7in
Height: 162.6cm 64.0in
Ground clearance: 16.0cm 6.3in
Kerb weight: 1259.8kg 2775.0lb
Fuel: 55.1L 12.1gal 14.5galUS

3118 Monteverdi

375L
1969 Switzerland
152.0mph 244.6kmh
0-50mph 80.5kmh: 4.9secs
0-60mph 96.5kmh: 6.3secs
0-1/4 mile: 14.6secs
0-1km: 26.3secs
380.0bhp 283.4kW 385.3PS
@ 4600rpm
480.0lbft 650.4Nm @ 3200rpm
216.0bhp/ton 212.4bhp/tonne
52.7bhp/L 39.3kW/L 53.5PS/L
47.9ft/sec 14.6m/sec
28.0mph 45.1kmh/1000rpm
11.6mpg 9.7mpgUS 24.4L/100km
Petrol 4-stroke piston
7206cc 439.7cu in
Vee 8 1 Carburettor
Compression ratio: 10.0:1

Bore: 109.7mm 4.3in
Stroke: 95.3mm 3.8in
Valve type/No: Overhead 16
Transmission: Automatic
No. of forward speeds: 3
Wheels driven: Rear
Springs F/R: Coil/Coil
Brake system: PA
Brakes F/R: Disc/Disc
Steering: Worm & roller PA
Wheelbase: 265.9cm 104.7in
Track F: 149.9cm 59.0in
Track R: 146.1cm 57.5in
Length: 480.1cm 189.0in
Width: 179.1cm 70.5in
Height: 127.0cm 50.0in
Ground clearance: 11.4cm 4.5in
Kerb weight: 1788.8kg 3940.0lb
Fuel: 131.9L 29.0gal 34.9galUS

3119 Moretti

750 Grand Sport Berlinetta Coupe
1954 Italy
100.0mph 160.9kmh
0-50mph 80.5kmh: 11.4secs
0-60mph 96.5kmh: 15.5secs
0-1/4 mile: 20.0secs
51.0bhp 38.0kW 51.7PS
@ 6000rpm
102.0bhp/ton 100.3bhp/tonne
68.2bhp/L 50.8kW/L 69.1PS/L
43.3ft/sec 13.2m/sec
14.3mph 23.0kmh/1000rpm
Petrol 4-stroke piston
748cc 45.6cu in
In-line 4
Bore: 59.9mm 2.4in
Stroke: 66.0mm 2.6in
Valve type/No: Overhead 8
Transmission: Manual
No. of forward speeds: 4
Wheels driven: Rear
Wheelbase: 198.1cm 78.0in
Track F: 122.4cm 48.2in
Track R: 115.6cm 45.5in
Kerb weight: 508.5kg 1120.0lb

3120 Morgan

4/4
1936 UK
77.5mph 124.7kmh
0-50mph 80.5kmh: 15.9secs
0-60mph 96.5kmh: 28.4secs
35.0bhp 26.1kW 35.5PS
@ 4500rpm
49.6bhp/ton 48.7bhp/tonne
31.2bhp/L 23.3kW/L 31.6PS/L
44.2ft/sec 13.5m/sec
35.0mpg 29.1mpgUS 8.1L/100km
Petrol 4-stroke piston
1122cc 68.5cu in
In-line 4
Compression ratio: 6.8:1
Bore: 63.0mm 2.5in
Stroke: 90.0mm 3.5in
Valve type/No: IOE 8
Transmission: Manual
No. of forward speeds: 4
Wheels driven: Rear
Brakes F/R: Drum/Drum
Kerb weight: 718.2kg 1582.0lb
Fuel: 40.9L 9.0gal 10.8galUS

3121 Morgan

4/4
1938 UK
78.2mph 125.8kmh
0-50mph 80.5kmh: 17.3secs
0-60mph 96.5kmh: 28.3secs
35.0bhp 26.1kW 35.5PS
@ 4500rpm
48.6bhp/ton 47.8bhp/tonne
31.9bhp/L 23.8kW/L 32.3PS/L
44.2ft/sec 13.5m/sec
35.0mpg 29.1mpgUS 8.1L/100km
Petrol 4-stroke piston
1098cc 67.0cu in
In-line 4
Compression ratio: 6.8:1
Bore: 63.0mm 2.5in
Stroke: 90.0mm 3.5in
Valve type/No: IOE 8
Transmission: Manual
No. of forward speeds: 4
Wheels driven: Rear
Brakes F/R: Drum/Drum
Kerb weight: 732.8kg 1614.0lb
Fuel: 36.4L 8.0gal 9.6galUS

3122 Morgan

SS
1939 UK
85.0mph 136.8kmh
0-50mph 80.5kmh: 9.6secs
0-60mph 96.5kmh: 14.0secs
0-1/4 mile: 18.5secs
39.0bhp 29.1kW 39.5PS
@ 4200rpm
50.0lbft 67.8Nm @ 2400rpm
97.5bhp/ton 95.9bhp/tonne
39.4bhp/L 29.4kW/L 39.9PS/L
39.3ft/sec 12.0m/sec
Petrol 4-stroke piston
990cc 60.4cu in
Vee 2
Compression ratio: 7.5:1
Bore: 85.6mm 3.4in
Stroke: 85.6mm 3.4in
Valve type/No: Overhead 4
Transmission: Manual
No. of forward speeds: 3
Wheels driven: Rear
Wheelbase: 215.9cm 85.0in
Track F: 125.7cm 49.5in
Kerb weight: 406.8kg 896.0lb

3123 Morgan

Plus 4
1952 UK
81.4mph 131.0kmh
0-50mph 80.5kmh: 11.4secs
0-60mph 96.5kmh: 17.1secs
0-1/4 mile: 21.2secs
68.0bhp 50.7kW 68.9PS
@ 4200rpm
81.0bhp/ton 79.7bhp/tonne
32.6bhp/L 24.3kW/L 33.0PS/L
42.2ft/sec 12.9m/sec
Petrol 4-stroke piston
2088cc 127.4cu in
In-line 4
Compression ratio: 6.7:1
Bore: 85.1mm 3.3in
Stroke: 91.9mm 3.6in
Valve type/No: Overhead 8
Transmission: Manual
No. of forward speeds: 4
Wheels driven: Rear
Wheelbase: 243.8cm 96.0in
Track F: 119.4cm 47.0in
Track R: 119.4cm 47.0in
Length: 355.6cm 140.0in
Width: 142.2cm 56.0in
Height: 132.1cm 52.0in
Ground clearance: 15.2cm 6.0in
Kerb weight: 853.5kg 1880.0lb

3124 Morgan

Plus 4
1954 UK
102.0mph 164.1kmh
0-50mph 80.5kmh: 9.0secs
0-60mph 96.5kmh: 13.3secs
0-1/4 mile: 18.5secs
90.0bhp 67.1kW 91.2PS
@ 4800rpm
130.0lbft 176.2Nm @ 2600rpm
107.5bhp/ton 105.7bhp/tonne
45.2bhp/L 33.7kW/L 45.8PS/L
48.3ft/sec 14.7m/sec
21.0mph 33.8kmh/1000rpm
30.0mpg 25.0mpgUS 9.4L/100km
Petrol 4-stroke piston
1991cc 121.5cu in
In-line 4
Compression ratio: 8.5:1
Bore: 83.0mm 3.3in
Stroke: 92.0mm 3.6in
Valve type/No: Overhead 8
Transmission: Manual
No. of forward speeds: 4
Wheels driven: Rear
Springs F/R: Coil/Leaf
Brakes F/R: Drum/Drum
Wheelbase: 243.8cm 96.0in
Track F: 119.4cm 47.0in
Track R: 119.4cm 47.0in
Length: 355.6cm 140.0in
Width: 142.2cm 56.0in
Height: 133.4cm 52.5in
Ground clearance: 17.8cm 7.0in
Kerb weight: 851.7kg 1876.0lb
Fuel: 50.0L 11.0gal 13.2galUS

3125 Morgan

Plus 4
1955 UK
98.4mph 158.3kmh
0-50mph 80.5kmh: 7.9secs
0-60mph 96.5kmh: 10.8secs
0-1/4 mile: 18.3secs
90.0bhp 67.1kW 91.2PS
@ 4800rpm
116.5lbft 157.9Nm @ 3000rpm
103.9bhp/ton 102.2bhp/tonne
45.2bhp/L 33.7kW/L 45.8PS/L
48.3ft/sec 14.7m/sec
20.9mph 33.6kmh/1000rpm
Petrol 4-stroke piston
1991cc 121.5cu in
In-line 4
Compression ratio: 8.5:1
Bore: 83.1mm 3.3in
Stroke: 91.9mm 3.6in
Valve type/No: Overhead 8
Transmission: Manual
No. of forward speeds: 4
Wheels driven: Rear
Wheelbase: 243.8cm 96.0in
Track F: 119.4cm 47.0in
Track R: 119.4cm 47.0in
Kerb weight: 880.8kg 1940.0lb

3126 Morgan

4/4 Modified
1957 UK
80.0mph 128.7kmh
0-50mph 80.5kmh: 13.4secs
0-60mph 96.5kmh: 20.5secs
0-1/4 mile: 21.4secs
44.0bhp 32.8kW 44.6PS
@ 4800rpm
60.0lbft 81.3Nm @ 2400rpm
63.6bhp/ton 62.5bhp/tonne
37.5bhp/L 28.0kW/L 38.1PS/L
48.5ft/sec 14.8m/sec
Petrol 4-stroke piston
1172cc 71.5cu in
In-line 4
Compression ratio: 8.0:1
Bore: 63.5mm 2.5in
Stroke: 92.5mm 3.6in
Valve type/No: Side 8
Transmission: Manual
No. of forward speeds: 3
Wheels driven: Rear
Wheelbase: 243.8cm 96.0in
Track F: 119.4cm 47.0in
Track R: 119.4cm 47.0in
Kerb weight: 703.7kg 1550.0lb

3127 Morgan

Plus 4
1959 UK
102.1mph 164.3kmh
0-50mph 80.5kmh: 6.8secs
0-60mph 96.5kmh: 9.9secs
0-1/4 mile: 17.5secs
106.0bhp 79.0kW 107.5PS
@ 5500rpm
117.0lbft 158.5Nm @ 3000rpm
126.3bhp/ton 124.2bhp/tonne
53.2bhp/L 39.7kW/L 54.0PS/L
55.3ft/sec 16.8m/sec
18.6mph 29.9kmh/1000rpm
Petrol 4-stroke piston
1991cc 121.5cu in
In-line 4
Compression ratio: 9.2:1
Bore: 83.1mm 3.3in
Stroke: 91.9mm 3.6in
Valve type/No: Overhead 8
Transmission: Manual
No. of forward speeds: 4
Wheels driven: Rear
Wheelbase: 243.8cm 96.0in
Track F: 117.3cm 46.2in
Track R: 122.4cm 48.2in
Length: 381.0cm 150.0in
Width: 142.2cm 56.0in
Height: 129.5cm 51.0in
Kerb weight: 853.5kg 1880.0lb

3128 Morgan

4/4
1963 UK
80.0mph 128.7kmh
0-50mph 80.5kmh: 10.7secs
0-60mph 96.5kmh: 16.5secs
0-1/4 mile: 20.6secs
64.0bhp 47.7kW 64.9PS
@ 4800rpm
81.5lbft 110.4Nm @ 2300rpm
93.0bhp/ton 91.4bhp/tonne
42.7bhp/L 31.8kW/L 43.3PS/L
38.1ft/sec 11.6m/sec
16.1mph 25.9kmh/1000rpm
Petrol 4-stroke piston
1499cc 91.5cu in
In-line 4 1 Carburettor
Compression ratio: 8.3:1
Bore: 81.0mm 3.2in
Stroke: 72.6mm 2.9in
Valve type/No: Overhead 8
Transmission: Manual
No. of forward speeds: 4
Wheels driven: Rear
Wheelbase: 243.8cm 96.0in
Track F: 119.4cm 47.0in
Track R: 119.4cm 47.0in
Length: 381.0cm 150.0in
Width: 142.2cm 56.0in
Height: 129.5cm 51.0in
Ground clearance: 14.5cm 5.7in
Kerb weight: 700.1kg 1542.0lb

3129 Morgan

Plus 8
1968 UK
125.0mph 201.1kmh
0-50mph 80.5kmh: 5.2secs
0-60mph 96.5kmh: 6.7secs
0-1/4 mile: 15.1secs
0-1km: 27.9secs
160.5bhp 119.7kW 162.7PS
@ 5200rpm
210.0lbft 284.6Nm @ 3000rpm
181.7bhp/ton 178.6bhp/tonne
45.5bhp/L 33.9kW/L 46.1PS/L
40.4ft/sec 12.3m/sec
22.0mph 35.4kmh/1000rpm
18.3mpg 15.2mpgUS 15.4L/100km
Petrol 4-stroke piston
3529cc 215.3cu in
Vee 8 2 Carburettor
Compression ratio: 10.5:1
Bore: 88.9mm 3.5in
Stroke: 71.1mm 2.8in
Valve type/No: Overhead 16
Transmission: Manual
No. of forward speeds: 4
Wheels driven: Rear
Springs F/R: Coil/Leaf
Brake system: PA
Brakes F/R: Disc/Drum
Steering: Worm & nut
Wheelbase: 248.9cm 98.0in
Track F: 124.5cm 49.0in
Track R: 129.5cm 51.0in
Length: 386.1cm 152.0in
Width: 144.8cm 57.0in
Height: 127.0cm 50.0in
Ground clearance: 17.8cm 7.0in
Kerb weight: 898.5kg 1979.0lb
Fuel: 61.4L 13.5gal 16.2galUS

3130 Morgan

Plus 8
1970 UK
105.0mph 168.9kmh
0-50mph 80.5kmh: 6.7secs
0-60mph 96.5kmh: 8.5secs
0-1/4 mile: 16.6secs
184.0bhp 137.2kW 186.5PS
@ 5200rpm
226.0lbft 306.2Nm @ 3000rpm
205.6bhp/ton 202.1bhp/tonne
52.1bhp/L 38.9kW/L 52.9PS/L
40.4ft/sec 12.3m/sec
19.7mph 31.7kmh/1000rpm
19.2mpg 16.0mpgUS 14.7L/100km
Petrol 4-stroke piston
3528cc 215.2cu in
Vee 8 2 Carburettor
Compression ratio: 10.5:1
Bore: 88.9mm 3.5in
Stroke: 71.1mm 2.8in
Valve type/No: Overhead 16
Transmission: Manual
No. of forward speeds: 4
Wheels driven: Rear
Springs F/R: Coil/Leaf
Brake system: PA
Brakes F/R: Disc/Drum
Steering: Cam & peg
Wheelbase: 248.9cm 98.0in

Track F: 124.5cm 49.0in
Track R: 129.5cm 51.0in
Length: 386.1cm 152.0in
Width: 147.3cm 58.0in
Height: 124.5cm 49.0in
Ground clearance: 16.5cm 6.5in
Kerb weight: 910.3kg 2005.0lb
Fuel: 60.9L 13.4gal 16.1galUS

3131 Morgan

Plus 8
1978 UK
124.0mph 199.5kmh
0-50mph 80.5kmh: 4.6secs
0-60mph 96.5kmh: 6.5secs
0-1/4 mile: 15.1secs
0-1km: 28.4secs
155.0bhp 115.6kW 157.1PS
@ 5250rpm
198.0lbft 268.3Nm @ 2500rpm
163.2bhp/ton 160.4bhp/tonne
43.9bhp/L 32.7kW/L 44.5PS/L
40.8ft/sec 12.4m/sec
26.2mph 42.2kmh/1000rpm
20.5mpg 17.1mpgUS 13.8L/100km
Petrol 4-stroke piston
3532cc 215.5cu in
Vee 8 2 Carburettor
Compression ratio: 9.3:1
Bore: 88.9mm 3.5in
Stroke: 71.1mm 2.8in
Valve type/No: Overhead 16
Transmission: Manual
No. of forward speeds: 5
Wheels driven: Rear
Springs F/R: Coil/Leaf
Brake system: PA
Brakes F/R: Disc/Drum
Steering: Worm & nut
Wheelbase: 248.9cm 98.0in
Track F: 132.1cm 52.0in
Track R: 134.6cm 53.0in
Length: 373.4cm 147.0in
Width: 157.5cm 62.0in
Height: 132.1cm 52.0in
Ground clearance: 17.8cm 7.0in
Kerb weight: 966.1kg 2128.0lb
Fuel: 63.7L 14.0gal 16.8galUS

3132 Morgan

Plus 8 Turbo
1980 UK
128.0mph 206.0kmh
0-60mph 96.5kmh: 6.8secs
0-1/4 mile: 15.1secs
225.0bhp 167.8kW 228.1PS
@ 5000rpm
240.0lbft 325.2Nm @ 3000rpm
220.6bhp/ton 216.9bhp/tonne
63.8bhp/L 47.6kW/L 64.7PS/L
38.9ft/sec 11.8m/sec
25.5mph 41.0kmh/1000rpm
19.2mpg 16.0mpgUS 14.7L/100km
Petrol 4-stroke piston
3528cc 215.2cu in turbocharged
Vee 8 1 Carburettor
Compression ratio: 9.4:1
Bore: 88.9mm 3.5in
Stroke: 71.1mm 2.8in
Valve type/No: Overhead 16
Transmission: Manual
No. of forward speeds: 5
Wheels driven: Rear
Springs F/R: Coil/Leaf
Brakes F/R: Disc/Drum
Steering: Cam & peg
Wheelbase: 251.5cm 99.0in
Track F: 132.1cm 52.0in
Track R: 134.6cm 53.0in
Length: 398.8cm 157.0in
Width: 157.5cm 62.0in
Height: 132.1cm 52.0in
Ground clearance: 15.2cm 6.0in
Kerb weight: 1037.4kg 2285.0lb
Fuel: 58.3L 12.8gal 15.4galUS

3133 Morgan

4/4
1984 UK
103.0mph 165.7kmh
0-60mph 96.5kmh: 10.4secs
0-1/4 mile: 17.6secs
112.0bhp 83.5kW 113.5PS
@ 5500rpm
123.0lbft 166.7Nm @ 3600rpm
124.5bhp/ton 122.4bhp/tonne
56.1bhp/L 41.9kW/L 56.9PS/L
54.1ft/sec 16.5m/sec
23.4mpg 19.5mpgUS 12.1L/100km
Petrol 4-stroke piston
1995cc 121.7cu in
In-line 4 1 Carburettor
Compression ratio: 8.9:1
Bore: 84.0mm 3.3in
Stroke: 90.0mm 3.5in
Valve type/No: Overhead 16
Transmission: Manual
No. of forward speeds: 5
Wheels driven: Rear
Springs F/R: Coil/Leaf
Brakes F/R: Disc/Drum
Steering: Cam & peg
Wheelbase: 243.8cm 96.0in
Track F: 128.3cm 50.5in
Track R: 130.8cm 51.5in
Length: 383.5cm 151.0in
Width: 142.2cm 56.0in
Height: 129.5cm 51.0in
Kerb weight: 914.8kg 2015.0lb
Fuel: 54.9L 12.1gal 14.5galUS

3134 Morgan

Plus 8
1987 UK
126.0mph 202.7kmh
0-50mph 80.5kmh: 4.3secs
0-60mph 96.5kmh: 5.6secs
0-1/4 mile: 14.4secs
0-1km: 26.7secs
190.0bhp 141.7kW 192.6PS
@ 5280rpm
220.0lbft 298.1Nm @ 4000rpm
211.2bhp/ton 207.6bhp/tonne
53.8bhp/L 40.2kW/L 54.6PS/L
41.1ft/sec 12.5m/sec
27.5mph 44.2kmh/1000rpm
20.9mpg 17.4mpgUS 13.5L/100km
Petrol 4-stroke piston
3528cc 215.0cu in
Vee 8 fuel injection
Compression ratio: 9.7:1
Bore: 88.9mm 3.5in
Stroke: 71.1mm 2.8in
Valve type/No: Overhead 16
Transmission: Manual
No. of forward speeds: 5
Wheels driven: Rear
Springs F/R: Coil/Leaf
Brake system: PA
Brakes F/R: Disc/Drum
Steering: Rack & pinion
Wheelbase: 248.9cm 98.0in
Track F: 134.6cm 53.0in
Track R: 137.2cm 54.0in
Length: 396.2cm 156.0in
Width: 160.0cm 63.0in
Height: 132.1cm 52.0in
Ground clearance: 15.2cm 6.0in
Kerb weight: 915.0kg 2015.4lb
Fuel: 63.7L 14.0gal 16.8galUS

3135 Morgan

Plus 8
1988 UK
125.0mph 201.1kmh
0-50mph 80.5kmh: 5.3secs
0-60mph 96.5kmh: 7.4secs
0-1/4 mile: 15.6secs
190.0bhp 141.7kW 192.6PS
@ 5280rpm
220.0lbft 298.1Nm @ 4000rpm
198.9bhp/ton 195.6bhp/tonne
53.8bhp/L 40.2kW/L 54.6PS/L
41.1ft/sec 12.5m/sec
23.4mpg 19.5mpgUS 12.1L/100km
Petrol 4-stroke piston
3528cc 215.2cu in
Vee 8 1 Carburettor
Compression ratio: 9.8:1
Bore: 89.0mm 3.5in
Stroke: 71.0mm 2.8in
Valve type/No: Overhead 16
Transmission: Manual
No. of forward speeds: 5
Wheels driven: Rear
Springs F/R: Coil/Leaf
Brakes F/R: Disc/Drum
Steering: Rack & pinion
Wheelbase: 248.9cm 98.0in
Track F: 132.1cm 52.0in
Track R: 134.6cm 53.0in
Length: 398.8cm 157.0in
Width: 157.5cm 62.0in
Height: 132.1cm 52.0in
Kerb weight: 971.6kg 2140.0lb
Fuel: 66.2L 14.6gal 17.5galUS

3136 Morgan

Plus 4 Mk III
1990 UK
0-60mph 96.5kmh: 7.7secs
0-1/4 mile: 15.2secs
138.0bhp 102.9kW 139.9PS
@ 6000rpm
131.0lbft 177.5Nm @ 4500rpm
155.7bhp/ton 153.1bhp/tonne
69.2bhp/L 51.6kW/L 70.2PS/L
58.3ft/sec 17.8m/sec
Petrol 4-stroke piston
1994cc 121.7cu in
In-line 4 fuel injection
Compression ratio: 10.0:1
Bore: 84.5mm 3.3in
Stroke: 89.0mm 3.5in
Valve type/No: Overhead 16
Transmission: Manual
No. of forward speeds: 5
Wheels driven: Rear
Springs F/R: Coil/Leaf
Brakes F/R: Disc/Drum
Steering: Recirculating ball
Wheelbase: 248.9cm 98.0in
Track F: 132.1cm 52.0in
Track R: 134.6cm 53.0in
Length: 398.8cm 157.0in
Width: 157.5cm 62.0in
Height: 132.1cm 52.0in
Kerb weight: 901.2kg 1985.0lb
Fuel: 56.8L 12.5gal 15.0galUS

3137 Morgan

Plus 8
1991 UK
122.0mph 196.3kmh
0-50mph 80.5kmh: 4.7secs
0-60mph 96.5kmh: 6.1secs
0-1/4 mile: 15.1secs
0-1km: 27.8secs
190.0bhp 141.7kW 192.6PS
@ 4750rpm
230.3lbft 312.0Nm @ 2600rpm
206.7bhp/ton 203.2bhp/tonne
48.1bhp/L 35.9kW/L 48.8PS/L
36.9ft/sec 11.3m/sec
27.6mph 44.4kmh/1000rpm
20.1mpg 16.7mpgUS 14.1L/100km
Petrol 4-stroke piston
3946cc 241.0cu in
Vee 8 fuel injection
Compression ratio: 9.3:1
Bore: 94.0mm 3.7in
Stroke: 71.1mm 2.8in
Valve type/No: Overhead 16
Transmission: Manual
No. of forward speeds: 5
Wheels driven: Rear
Springs F/R: Coil/Leaf
Brake system: PA
Brakes F/R: Disc/Drum
Steering: Rack & pinion
Wheelbase: 248.9cm 98.0in
Track F: 137.1cm 54.0in
Track R: 137.1cm 54.0in
Length: 396.2cm 156.0in
Width: 160.0cm 63.0in
Height: 121.9cm 48.0in
Kerb weight: 935.0kg 2059.5lb
Fuel: 54.6L 12.0gal 14.4galUS

3138 Morris

Minor Saloon
1928 UK
55.0mph 88.5kmh
43.0mpg 35.8mpgUS 6.6L/100km
Petrol 4-stroke piston
847cc 51.7cu in
In-line 4 1 Carburettor
Bore: 57.0mm 2.2in
Stroke: 83.0mm 3.3in
Valve type/No: Overhead 8
Transmission: Manual
No. of forward speeds: 3
Wheels driven: Rear
Brakes F/R: Drum/Drum
Wheelbase: 198.1cm 78.0in
Track F: 106.7cm 42.0in
Track R: 106.7cm 42.0in
Length: 304.8cm 120.0in
Width: 125.7cm 49.5in
Fuel: 25.0L 5.5gal 6.6galUS

3139 Morris

Isis
1929 UK
60.0mph 96.5kmh
22.0mpg 18.3mpgUS 12.8L/100km
Petrol 4-stroke piston
2468cc 150.6cu in
In-line 6 1 Carburettor
Bore: 69.0mm 2.7in
Stroke: 110.0mm 4.3in
Valve type/No: Overhead 12
Transmission: Manual
No. of forward speeds: 3
Wheels driven: Rear
Brakes F/R: Drum/Drum
Wheelbase: 289.6cm 114.0in
Track F: 142.2cm 56.0in
Track R: 142.2cm 56.0in
Length: 429.8cm 169.2in
Width: 168.9cm 66.5in
Height: 179.1cm 70.5in
Kerb weight: 1436.5kg 3164.0lb
Fuel: 68.2L 15.0gal 18.0galUS

3140 Morris

8 Minor
1930 UK
55.2mph 88.8kmh
45.0mpg 37.5mpgUS 6.3L/100km
Petrol 4-stroke piston
847cc 51.7cu in
In-line 4 1 Carburettor
Bore: 57.0mm 2.2in
Stroke: 83.0mm 3.3in
Valve type/No: Overhead 8
Transmission: Manual
No. of forward speeds: 3
Wheels driven: Rear
Brakes F/R: Drum/Drum
Wheelbase: 198.1cm 78.0in
Track F: 106.7cm 42.0in
Track R: 106.7cm 42.0in
Length: 322.6cm 127.0in
Width: 127.0cm 50.0in
Height: 149.9cm 59.0in
Kerb weight: 562.0kg 1238.0lb
Fuel: 22.7L 5.0gal 6.0galUS

3141 Morris

Major Six Saloon
1931 UK
58.0mph 93.3kmh
27.0mpg 22.5mpgUS 10.5L/100km
Petrol 4-stroke piston
1803cc 110.0cu in
In-line 6 1 Carburettor
Bore: 61.2mm 2.4in
Stroke: 102.0mm 4.0in
Valve type/No: Side 12
Transmission: Manual
No. of forward speeds: 4
Wheels driven: Rear
Brakes F/R: Drum/Drum
Wheelbase: 269.2cm 106.0in
Track F: 132.1cm 52.0in
Track R: 132.1cm 52.0in
Length: 414.0cm 163.0in
Width: 162.6cm 64.0in
Height: 175.3cm 69.0in
Kerb weight: 1217.6kg 2682.0lb
Fuel: 40.9L 9.0gal 10.8galUS

3142 Morris

10/4
1933 UK
57.3mph 92.2kmh
0-50mph 80.5kmh: 33.6secs
35.0mpg 29.1mpgUS 8.1L/100km
Petrol 4-stroke piston
1292cc 78.8cu in
In-line 4
Bore: 63.5mm 2.5in
Stroke: 102.0mm 4.0in
Transmission: Manual
No. of forward speeds: 4
Wheels driven: Rear
Brakes F/R: Drum/Drum
Kerb weight: 1042.4kg 2296.0lb
Fuel: 29.6L 6.5gal 7.8galUS

3143 Morris

10/6
1933 UK

59.2mph 95.3kmh
0-50mph 80.5kmh: 33.4secs
30.0mpg 25.0mpgUS 9.4L/100km
Petrol 4-stroke piston
1378cc 84.1cu in
In-line 6 1 Carburettor
Bore: 57.0mm 2.2in
Stroke: 90.0mm 3.5in
Valve type/No: Side 12
Transmission: Manual
No. of forward speeds: 4
Wheels driven: Rear
Brakes F/R: Drum/Drum
Kerb weight: 1082.3kg 2384.0lb
Fuel: 29.6L 6.5gal 7.8galUS

3144 Morris
Cowley Saloon
1933 UK
56.9mph 91.6kmh
27.0bhp 20.1kW 27.4PS
@ 3400rpm
24.0bhp/ton 23.6bhp/tonne
17.4bhp/L 13.0kW/L 17.7PS/L
38.0ft/sec 11.6m/sec
30.0mpg 25.0mpgUS 9.4L/100km
Petrol 4-stroke piston
1550cc 94.6cu in
In-line 4 1 Carburettor
Bore: 69.5mm 2.7in
Stroke: 102.0mm 4.0in
Valve type/No: Side 8
Transmission: Manual
No. of forward speeds: 4
Wheels driven: Rear
Brakes F/R: Drum/Drum
Kerb weight: 1144.1kg 2520.0lb
Fuel: 34.1L 7.5gal 9.0galUS

3145 Morris
Cowley Six
1933 UK
61.2mph 98.5kmh
0-50mph 80.5kmh: 36.4secs
25.0mpg 20.8mpgUS 11.3L/100km
Petrol 4-stroke piston
1938cc 118.2cu in
In-line 6 1 Carburettor
Bore: 63.5mm 2.5in
Stroke: 102.0mm 4.0in
Valve type/No: Side 12
Transmission: Manual
No. of forward speeds: 4
Wheels driven: Rear
Brakes F/R: Drum/Drum
Kerb weight: 1233.1kg 2716.0lb
Fuel: 45.5L 10.0gal 12.0galUS

3146 Morris
15/6 Saloon
1934 UK
59.3mph 95.4kmh
0-50mph 80.5kmh: 32.8secs
25.0mpg 20.8mpgUS 11.3L/100km
Petrol 4-stroke piston
1938cc 118.2cu in
In-line 6
Bore: 63.5mm 2.5in
Stroke: 102.0mm 4.0in
Transmission: Manual
No. of forward speeds: 4
Wheels driven: Rear
Brakes F/R: Drum/Drum
Kerb weight: 1220.3kg 2688.0lb
Fuel: 45.5L 10.0gal 12.0galUS

3147 Morris
8 Saloon
1934 UK
58.0mph 93.3kmh
0-50mph 80.5kmh: 37.4secs
42.0mpg 35.0mpgUS 6.7L/100km
Petrol 4-stroke piston
918cc 56.0cu in
In-line 4 1 Carburettor
Bore: 57.0mm 2.2in
Stroke: 90.0mm 3.5in
Valve type/No: Side 8
Transmission: Manual
No. of forward speeds: 3
Wheels driven: Rear
Brakes F/R: Drum/Drum
Kerb weight: 750.0kg 1652.0lb
Fuel: 25.0L 5.5gal 6.6galUS

3148 Morris
10/6 Sports Tourer
1935 UK
66.6mph 107.2kmh
0-50mph 80.5kmh: 22.8secs
0-60mph 96.5kmh: 42.8secs
22.0mpg 18.3mpgUS 12.8L/100km
Petrol 4-stroke piston
1378cc 84.1cu in
In-line 6
Bore: 57.0mm 2.2in
Stroke: 90.0mm 3.5in
Valve type/No: Side 12
Transmission: Manual
No. of forward speeds: 4
Wheels driven: Rear
Brakes F/R: Drum/Drum
Kerb weight: 1046.9kg 2306.0lb
Fuel: 29.6L 6.5gal 7.8galUS

3149 Morris
16 Series II Saloon
1935 UK
69.2mph 111.3kmh
0-50mph 80.5kmh: 24.8secs
22.0mpg 18.3mpgUS 12.8L/100km
Petrol 4-stroke piston
2062cc 125.8cu in
In-line 6
Bore: 65.5mm 2.6in
Stroke: 102.0mm 4.0in
Valve type/No: Side 12
Transmission: Manual
No. of forward speeds: 3
Wheels driven: Rear
Brakes F/R: Drum/Drum
Kerb weight: 1436.9kg 3165.0lb
Fuel: 45.5L 10.0gal 12.0galUS

3150 Morris
21 Series II Saloon
1935 UK
73.7mph 118.6kmh
0-50mph 80.5kmh: 24.4secs
0-60mph 96.5kmh: 39.4secs
19.0mpg 15.8mpgUS 14.9L/100km
Petrol 4-stroke piston
2916cc 177.9cu in
In-line 6
Bore: 75.0mm 2.9in
Stroke: 110.0mm 4.3in
Valve type/No: Side 12
Transmission: Manual
No. of forward speeds: 3
Wheels driven: Rear
Brakes F/R: Drum/Drum
Kerb weight: 1554.0kg 3423.0lb
Fuel: 59.1L 13.0gal 15.6galUS

3151 Morris
10 Series II
1937 UK
59.2mph 95.3kmh
0-50mph 80.5kmh: 40.4secs
32.0mpg 26.6mpgUS 8.8L/100km
Petrol 4-stroke piston
1292cc 78.8cu in
In-line 4 1 Carburettor
Bore: 63.5mm 2.5in
Stroke: 102.0mm 4.0in
Valve type/No: Side 8
Transmission: Manual
No. of forward speeds: 4
Wheels driven: Rear
Brakes F/R: Drum/Drum
Kerb weight: 1080.1kg 2379.0lb
Fuel: 31.8L 7.0gal 8.4galUS

3152 Morris
10 Series III
1938 UK
65.2mph 104.9kmh
0-50mph 80.5kmh: 24.5secs
28.0mpg 23.3mpgUS 10.1L/100km
Petrol 4-stroke piston
1292cc 78.8cu in
In-line 4 1 Carburettor
Bore: 63.5mm 2.5in
Stroke: 102.0mm 4.0in
Valve type/No: Overhead 8
Transmission: Manual
No. of forward speeds: 4
Wheels driven: Rear
Brakes F/R: Drum/Drum
Kerb weight: 1105.9kg 2436.0lb
Fuel: 31.8L 7.0gal 8.4galUS

3153 Morris
8 Tourer
1938 UK
59.2mph 95.3kmh
0-50mph 80.5kmh: 41.9secs
37.0mpg 30.8mpgUS 7.6L/100km
Petrol 4-stroke piston
918cc 56.0cu in
In-line 4 1 Carburettor
Bore: 57.0mm 2.2in
Stroke: 90.0mm 3.5in
Valve type/No: Side 8
Transmission: Manual
No. of forward speeds: 3
Wheels driven: Rear
Brakes F/R: Drum/Drum
Kerb weight: 710.5kg 1565.0lb
Fuel: 25.0L 5.5gal 6.6galUS

3154 Morris
8hp Tourer
1938 UK
59.2mph 95.3kmh
0-50mph 80.5kmh: 41.9secs
Petrol 4-stroke piston
918cc 56.0cu in
In-line 4 1 Carburettor
Bore: 57.0mm 2.2in
Stroke: 90.0mm 3.5in
Valve type/No: Side 8
Transmission: Manual
No. of forward speeds: 3
Wheels driven: Rear
Brakes F/R: Drum/Drum
Kerb weight: 710.5kg 1565.0lb
Fuel: 25.0L 5.5gal 6.6galUS

3155 Morris
8 Series E Tourer
1939 UK
63.8mph 102.7kmh
0-50mph 80.5kmh: 32.0secs
29.6bhp 22.1kW 30.0PS
@ 4400rpm
42.1bhp/ton 41.4bhp/tonne
32.2bhp/L 24.0kW/L 32.7PS/L
43.3ft/sec 13.2m/sec
36.0mpg 30.0mpgUS 7.8L/100km
Petrol 4-stroke piston
918cc 56.0cu in
In-line 4 1 Carburettor
Compression ratio: 6.5:1
Bore: 57.0mm 2.2in
Stroke: 90.0mm 3.5in
Valve type/No: Side 8
Transmission: Manual
No. of forward speeds: 4
Wheels driven: Rear
Brakes F/R: Drum/Drum
Kerb weight: 714.1kg 1573.0lb
Fuel: 25.0L 5.5gal 6.6galUS

3156 Morris
8hp Series E Tourer
1939 UK
63.8mph 102.7kmh
0-50mph 80.5kmh: 32.0secs
Petrol 4-stroke piston
918cc 56.0cu in
In-line 4 1 Carburettor
Bore: 57.0mm 2.2in
Stroke: 90.0mm 3.5in
Valve type/No: Side 8
Transmission: Manual
No. of forward speeds: 4
Wheels driven: Rear
Brakes F/R: Drum/Drum
Kerb weight: 714.1kg 1573.0lb
Fuel: 25.0L 5.5gal 6.6galUS

3157 Morris
Minor
1948 UK
62.0mph 99.8kmh
0-50mph 80.5kmh: 36.5secs
29.5bhp 22.0kW 29.9PS
@ 4400rpm
37.9bhp/ton 37.3bhp/tonne
32.1bhp/L 24.0kW/L 32.6PS/L
43.3ft/sec 13.2m/sec
36.0mpg 30.0mpgUS 7.8L/100km
Petrol 4-stroke piston
918cc 56.0cu in
In-line 4
Compression ratio: 6.6:1
Bore: 57.0mm 2.2in
Stroke: 90.0mm 3.5in
Valve type/No: Side 8
Transmission: Manual
No. of forward speeds: 4
Wheels driven: Rear
Brakes F/R: Drum/Drum
Wheelbase: 218.4cm 86.0in
Track F: 127.8cm 50.3in
Track R: 127.8cm 50.3in
Length: 375.9cm 148.0in
Width: 154.9cm 61.0in
Height: 152.4cm 60.0in
Ground clearance: 17.0cm 6.7in
Kerb weight: 791.3kg 1743.0lb
Fuel: 22.7L 5.0gal 6.0galUS

3158 Morris
Oxford
1948 UK
70.0mph 112.6kmh
0-50mph 80.5kmh: 24.0secs
0-60mph 96.5kmh: 41.4secs
40.5bhp 30.2kW 41.1PS
@ 4200rpm
37.7bhp/ton 37.0bhp/tonne
27.4bhp/L 20.5kW/L 27.8PS/L
40.0ft/sec 12.2m/sec
26.0mpg 21.6mpgUS 10.9L/100km
Petrol 4-stroke piston
1476cc 90.0cu in
In-line 4
Compression ratio: 7.0:1
Bore: 73.5mm 2.9in
Stroke: 87.0mm 3.4in
Valve type/No: Side 8
Transmission: Manual
No. of forward speeds: 4
Wheels driven: Rear
Brakes F/R: Drum/Drum
Wheelbase: 271.8cm 107.0in
Track F: 134.6cm 53.0in
Track R: 134.6cm 53.0in
Length: 424.2cm 167.0in
Width: 165.1cm 65.0in
Height: 160.0cm 63.0in
Ground clearance: 17.0cm 6.7in
Kerb weight: 1093.2kg 2408.0lb
Fuel: 43.2L 9.5gal 11.4galUS

3159 Morris
Minor Tourer
1950 UK
61.0mph 98.1kmh
0-50mph 80.5kmh: 44.4secs
27.5bhp 20.5kW 27.9PS
@ 4400rpm
39.0lbft 52.8Nm @ 2400rpm
37.4bhp/ton 36.8bhp/tonne
30.0bhp/L 22.3kW/L 30.4PS/L
43.3ft/sec 13.2m/sec
15.0mph 24.1kmh/1000rpm
Petrol 4-stroke piston
918cc 56.0cu in
In-line 4 1 Carburettor
Compression ratio: 6.6:1
Bore: 57.0mm 2.2in
Stroke: 90.0mm 3.5in
Valve type/No: Side 8
Transmission: Manual
No. of forward speeds: 4
Wheels driven: Rear
Springs F/R: Torsion bar
Brakes F/R: Drum/Drum
Steering: Rack & pinion
Wheelbase: 218.4cm 86.0in
Track F: 128.3cm 50.5in
Track R: 127.8cm 50.3in
Length: 375.9cm 148.0in
Width: 154.9cm 61.0in
Height: 144.8cm 57.0in
Ground clearance: 17.0cm 6.7in
Kerb weight: 747.7kg 1647.0lb
Fuel: 22.7L 5.0gal 6.0galUS

3160 Morris
Oxford Saloon
1950 UK
67.0mph 107.8kmh

0-50mph 80.5kmh: 27.4secs
0-60mph 96.5kmh: 46.7secs
41.7bhp 31.1kW 42.3PS
@ 4000rpm
65.0lbft 88.1Nm @ 1800rpm
39.1bhp/ton 38.5bhp/tonne
28.2bhp/L 21.1kW/L 28.6PS/L
38.1ft/sec 11.6m/sec
15.0mph 24.1kmh/1000rpm
27.0mpg 22.5mpgUS 10.5L/100km
Petrol 4-stroke piston
1476cc 90.0cu in
In-line 4 1 Carburettor
Compression ratio: 6.5:1
Bore: 73.5mm 2.9in
Stroke: 87.0mm 3.4in
Valve type/No: Side 8
Transmission: Manual
No. of forward speeds: 4
Wheels driven: Rear
Brakes F/R: Drum/Drum
Wheelbase: 246.4cm 97.0in
Track F: 134.6cm 53.0in
Track R: 134.6cm 53.0in
Length: 424.2cm 167.0in
Width: 165.1cm 65.0in
Height: 129.5cm 51.0in
Ground clearance: 17.0cm 6.7in
Kerb weight: 1084.1kg 2388.0lb
Fuel: 40.9L 9.0gal 10.8galUS

3161 Morris
Minor Series II
1953 UK
62.0mph 99.8kmh
0-50mph 80.5kmh: 25.7secs
0-1/4 mile: 26.9secs
30.0bhp 22.4kW 30.4PS
@ 4800rpm
40.0lbft 54.2Nm @ 2400rpm
37.8bhp/ton 37.2bhp/tonne
37.5bhp/L 28.0kW/L 38.0PS/L
39.9ft/sec 12.2m/sec
13.0mph 20.9kmh/1000rpm
36.2mpg 30.1mpgUS 7.8L/100km
Petrol 4-stroke piston
800cc 48.8cu in
In-line 4
Compression ratio: 7.2:1
Bore: 58.0mm 2.3in
Stroke: 76.0mm 3.0in
Valve type/No: Overhead 8
Transmission: Manual
No. of forward speeds: 4
Wheels driven: Rear
Springs F/R: Torsion bar/Leaf
Brakes F/R: Drum/Drum
Wheelbase: 218.4cm 86.0in
Track F: 128.3cm 50.5in
Track R: 128.3cm 50.5in
Length: 375.9cm 148.0in
Width: 154.9cm 61.0in
Height: 152.4cm 60.0in
Ground clearance: 17.0cm 6.7in
Kerb weight: 807.2kg 1778.0lb
Fuel: 22.7L 5.0gal 6.0galUS

3162 Morris
Oxford Travellers' Car
1953 UK
66.0mph 106.2kmh
0-50mph 80.5kmh: 23.7secs
0-60mph 96.5kmh: 45.8secs
0-1/4 mile: 26.7secs
41.0bhp 30.6kW 41.6PS
@ 4000rpm
65.0lbft 88.1Nm @ 2000rpm
37.3bhp/ton 36.6bhp/tonne
27.8bhp/L 20.7kW/L 28.2PS/L
38.1ft/sec 11.6m/sec
15.0mph 24.1kmh/1000rpm
23.2mpg 19.3mpgUS 12.2L/100km
Petrol 4-stroke piston
1476cc 90.0cu in
In-line 4 1 Carburettor
Compression ratio: 6.6:1
Bore: 73.0mm 2.9in
Stroke: 87.0mm 3.4in
Valve type/No: Side 8
Transmission: Manual
No. of forward speeds: 4
Wheels driven: Rear
Springs F/R: Torsion bar/Leaf
Brakes F/R: Drum/Drum
Wheelbase: 246.4cm 97.0in
Track F: 135.9cm 53.5in
Track R: 134.6cm 53.0in
Length: 420.4cm 165.5in
Width: 165.1cm 65.0in
Height: 129.5cm 51.0in
Ground clearance: 17.0cm 6.7in
Kerb weight: 1118.7kg 2464.0lb
Fuel: 40.9L 9.0gal 10.8galUS

3163 Morris
Minor
1954 UK
62.7mph 100.9kmh
0-50mph 80.5kmh: 29.2secs
0-60mph 96.5kmh: 52.5secs
0-1/4 mile: 27.1secs
30.0bhp 22.4kW 30.4PS
@ 4800rpm
40.0lbft 54.2Nm @ 2400rpm
38.6bhp/ton 38.0bhp/tonne
37.4bhp/L 27.9kW/L 37.9PS/L
39.9ft/sec 12.1m/sec
13.1mph 21.1kmh/1000rpm
Petrol 4-stroke piston
803cc 49.0cu in
In-line 4
Compression ratio: 7.2:1
Bore: 57.9mm 2.3in
Stroke: 75.9mm 3.0in
Valve type/No: Overhead 8
Transmission: Manual
No. of forward speeds: 4
Wheels driven: Rear
Wheelbase: 218.4cm 86.0in
Track F: 128.3cm 50.5in
Track R: 128.3cm 50.5in
Kerb weight: 790.0kg 1740.0lb

3164 Morris
Oxford Saloon
1954 UK
76.0mph 122.3kmh
0-50mph 80.5kmh: 18.2secs
0-60mph 96.5kmh: 29.0secs
0-1/4 mile: 24.2secs
50.0bhp 37.3kW 50.7PS
@ 4200rpm
78.0lbft 105.7Nm @ 2400rpm
46.5bhp/ton 45.7bhp/tonne
33.6bhp/L 25.0kW/L 34.0PS/L
40.8ft/sec 12.5m/sec
15.2mph 24.5kmh/1000rpm
26.0mpg 21.6mpgUS 10.9L/100km
Petrol 4-stroke piston
1489cc 90.8cu in
In-line 4 1 Carburettor
Compression ratio: 7.4:1
Bore: 73.0mm 2.9in
Stroke: 89.0mm 3.5in
Valve type/No: Overhead 8
Transmission: Manual
No. of forward speeds: 4
Wheels driven: Rear
Springs F/R: Torsion bar/Leaf
Brakes F/R: Drum/Drum
Wheelbase: 246.4cm 97.0in
Track F: 135.9cm 53.5in
Track R: 134.6cm 53.0in
Length: 431.8cm 170.0in
Width: 165.1cm 65.0in
Height: 129.5cm 51.0in
Ground clearance: 15.7cm 6.2in
Kerb weight: 1093.2kg 2408.0lb
Fuel: 54.6L 12.0gal 14.4galUS

3165 Morris
Cowley
1955 UK
67.0mph 107.8kmh
0-50mph 80.5kmh: 22.0secs
0-60mph 96.5kmh: 37.5secs
0-1/4 mile: 25.7secs
42.0bhp 31.3kW 42.6PS
@ 4500rpm
58.0lbft 78.6Nm @ 2400rpm
39.1bhp/ton 38.4bhp/tonne
35.0bhp/L 26.1kW/L 35.5PS/L
43.8ft/sec 13.3m/sec
14.3mph 23.0kmh/1000rpm
29.0mpg 24.1mpgUS 9.7L/100km
Petrol 4-stroke piston
1200cc 73.2cu in
In-line 4
Compression ratio: 7.2:1
Bore: 65.5mm 2.6in
Stroke: 89.0mm 3.5in
Valve type/No: Overhead 8
Transmission: Manual
No. of forward speeds: 4
Wheels driven: Rear
Springs F/R: Torsion bar/Leaf
Brakes F/R: Drum/Drum
Wheelbase: 246.4cm 97.0in
Track F: 135.9cm 53.5in
Track R: 134.6cm 53.0in
Length: 434.3cm 171.0in
Width: 165.1cm 65.0in
Height: 160.0cm 63.0in
Ground clearance: 15.7cm 6.2in
Kerb weight: 1093.2kg 2408.0lb
Fuel: 54.6L 12.0gal 14.4galUS

3166 Morris
Isis
1956 UK
88.0mph 141.6kmh
0-50mph 80.5kmh: 12.8secs
0-60mph 96.5kmh: 17.8secs
0-1/4 mile: 21.1secs
86.0bhp 64.1kW 87.2PS
@ 4250rpm
124.0lbft 168.0Nm @ 2000rpm
63.7bhp/ton 62.6bhp/tonne
32.6bhp/L 24.3kW/L 33.0PS/L
41.3ft/sec 12.6m/sec
19.1mph 30.7kmh/1000rpm
23.0mpg 19.2mpgUS 12.3L/100km
Petrol 4-stroke piston
2639cc 161.0cu in
In-line 6
Compression ratio: 7.2:1
Bore: 79.3mm 3.1in
Stroke: 88.9mm 3.5in
Valve type/No: Overhead 12
Transmission: Manual with overdrive
No. of forward speeds: 7
Wheels driven: Rear
Springs F/R: Torsion bar/Leaf
Brakes F/R: Drum/Drum
Wheelbase: 273.1cm 107.5in
Track F: 136.1cm 53.6in
Track R: 134.6cm 53.0in
Length: 452.1cm 178.0in
Width: 165.1cm 65.0in
Height: 161.8cm 63.7in
Ground clearance: 17.8cm 7.0in
Kerb weight: 1372.9kg 3024.0lb
Fuel: 54.6L 12.0gal 14.4galUS

3167 Morris
Minor 1000
1957 UK
75.2mph 121.0kmh
0-50mph 80.5kmh: 18.8secs
0-60mph 96.5kmh: 31.3secs
0-1/4 mile: 24.2secs
37.0bhp 27.6kW 37.5PS
@ 4750rpm
48.0lbft 65.0Nm @ 3000rpm
47.0bhp/ton 46.2bhp/tonne
39.0bhp/L 29.1kW/L 39.6PS/L
39.6ft/sec 12.1m/sec
15.2mph 24.5kmh/1000rpm
39.4mpg 32.8mpgUS 7.2L/100km
Petrol 4-stroke piston
948cc 57.8cu in
In-line 4 1 Carburettor
Compression ratio: 8.3:1
Bore: 62.9mm 2.5in
Stroke: 76.2mm 3.0in
Valve type/No: Overhead 8
Transmission: Manual
No. of forward speeds: 4
Wheels driven: Rear
Springs F/R: Torsion bar/Leaf
Brakes F/R: Drum/Drum
Steering: Rack & pinion
Wheelbase: 218.4cm 86.0in
Track F: 128.3cm 50.5in
Track R: 127.3cm 50.1in
Length: 375.9cm 148.0in
Width: 154.9cm 61.0in
Height: 152.4cm 60.0in
Ground clearance: 17.0cm 6.7in
Kerb weight: 800.9kg 1764.0lb
Fuel: 22.7L 5.0gal 6.0galUS

3168 Morris
Minor 1100
1957 UK
73.2mph 117.8kmh
0-50mph 80.5kmh: 18.3secs
0-60mph 96.5kmh: 31.2secs
0-1/4 mile: 24.0secs
37.0bhp 27.6kW 37.5PS
@ 4750rpm
48.0lbft 65.0Nm @ 3000rpm
48.7bhp/ton 47.9bhp/tonne
39.0bhp/L 29.1kW/L 39.6PS/L
39.6ft/sec 12.1m/sec
Petrol 4-stroke piston
948cc 57.8cu in
In-line 4
Compression ratio: 8.3:1
Bore: 63.0mm 2.5in
Stroke: 76.2mm 3.0in
Valve type/No: Overhead 8
Transmission: Manual
No. of forward speeds: 4
Wheels driven: Rear
Wheelbase: 218.4cm 86.0in
Track F: 128.5cm 50.6in
Track R: 127.8cm 50.3in
Kerb weight: 771.8kg 1700.0lb

3169 Morris
Oxford Series III
1957 UK
75.5mph 121.5kmh
0-50mph 80.5kmh: 17.9secs
0-60mph 96.5kmh: 27.1secs
0-1/4 mile: 23.9secs
55.0bhp 41.0kW 55.8PS
@ 4400rpm
78.0lbft 105.7Nm @ 2400rpm
50.7bhp/ton 49.8bhp/tonne
36.9bhp/L 27.5kW/L 37.4PS/L
42.8ft/sec 13.0m/sec
15.0mph 24.1kmh/1000rpm
29.2mpg 24.3mpgUS 9.7L/100km
Petrol 4-stroke piston
1489cc 90.8cu in
In-line 4 1 Carburettor
Compression ratio: 8.3:1
Bore: 73.0mm 2.9in
Stroke: 88.9mm 3.5in
Valve type/No: Overhead 8
Transmission: Manual
No. of forward speeds: 4
Wheels driven: Rear
Springs F/R: Torsion bar/Leaf
Brakes F/R: Drum/Drum
Wheelbase: 246.4cm 97.0in
Track F: 135.9cm 53.5in
Track R: 134.6cm 53.0in
Length: 434.3cm 171.0in
Width: 165.1cm 65.0in
Height: 129.5cm 51.0in
Ground clearance: 15.7cm 6.2in
Kerb weight: 1103.7kg 2431.0lb
Fuel: 54.6L 12.0gal 14.4galUS

3170 Morris
Minor 1000 Traveller
1958 UK
70.0mph 112.6kmh
0-50mph 80.5kmh: 19.3secs
0-60mph 96.5kmh: 34.1secs
0-1/4 mile: 23.9secs
37.0bhp 27.6kW 37.5PS
@ 4800rpm
50.0lbft 67.8Nm @ 2500rpm
45.4bhp/ton 44.6bhp/tonne
39.0bhp/L 29.1kW/L 39.6PS/L
40.0ft/sec 12.2m/sec
15.2mph 24.5kmh/1000rpm
38.0mpg 31.6mpgUS 7.4L/100km
Petrol 4-stroke piston
948cc 57.8cu in
In-line 4 1 Carburettor
Compression ratio: 8.3:1
Bore: 62.9mm 2.5in
Stroke: 76.2mm 3.0in
Valve type/No: Overhead 8
Transmission: Manual
No. of forward speeds: 4
Wheels driven: Rear
Springs F/R: Torsion bar/Leaf
Brakes F/R: Drum/Drum
Steering: Rack & pinion
Wheelbase: 218.4cm 86.0in
Track F: 128.3cm 50.5in
Track R: 127.8cm 50.3in
Length: 375.9cm 148.0in
Width: 154.9cm 61.0in
Height: 152.4cm 60.0in
Ground clearance: 17.0cm 6.7in
Kerb weight: 829.5kg 1827.0lb
Fuel: 29.6L 6.5gal 7.8galUS

3171 Morris
Oxford Traveller Series III
1958 UK
78.0mph 125.5kmh
0-50mph 80.5kmh: 18.5secs
0-60mph 96.5kmh: 29.9secs
0-1/4 mile: 24.2secs
55.0bhp 41.0kW 55.8PS
@ 4400rpm
78.0lbft 105.7Nm @ 2400rpm
46.8bhp/ton 46.0bhp/tonne
36.9bhp/L 27.5kW/L 37.4PS/L
42.8ft/sec 13.0m/sec
15.3mph 24.6kmh/1000rpm
26.2mpg 21.8mpgUS 10.8L/100km
Petrol 4-stroke piston
1489cc 90.8cu in
In-line 4 1 Carburettor
Compression ratio: 8.3:1
Bore: 73.0mm 2.9in
Stroke: 88.9mm 3.5in
Valve type/No: Overhead 8
Transmission: Manual
No. of forward speeds: 4
Wheels driven: Rear
Springs F/R: Torsion bar/Leaf
Brakes F/R: Drum/Drum
Wheelbase: 246.4cm 97.0in
Track F: 135.9cm 53.5in
Track R: 134.6cm 53.0in
Length: 429.3cm 169.0in
Width: 165.1cm 65.0in
Height: 129.5cm 51.0in
Ground clearance: 15.7cm 6.2in
Kerb weight: 1194.9kg 2632.0lb
Fuel: 50.0L 11.0gal 13.2galUS

3172 Morris
Minor 1000
1961 UK
76.0mph 122.3kmh
0-50mph 80.5kmh: 18.8secs
0-60mph 96.5kmh: 32.6secs
0-1/4 mile: 23.5secs
37.0bhp 27.6kW 37.5PS
@ 4750rpm
50.0lbft 67.8Nm @ 2500rpm
46.4bhp/ton 45.7bhp/tonne
39.0bhp/L 29.1kW/L 39.6PS/L
39.6ft/sec 12.1m/sec
15.2mph 24.5kmh/1000rpm
34.7mpg 28.9mpgUS 8.1L/100km
Petrol 4-stroke piston
948cc 57.8cu in
In-line 4
Compression ratio: 8.3:1
Bore: 63.0mm 2.5in
Stroke: 76.2mm 3.0in
Valve type/No: Overhead 8
Transmission: Manual
No. of forward speeds: 4
Wheels driven: Rear
Springs F/R: Torsion bar/Leaf
Brakes F/R: Drum/Drum
Wheelbase: 218.4cm 86.0in
Track F: 128.5cm 50.6in
Track R: 128.5cm 50.6in
Length: 375.9cm 148.0in
Width: 154.9cm 61.0in
Height: 152.4cm 60.0in
Ground clearance: 17.0cm 6.7in
Kerb weight: 810.4kg 1785.0lb
Fuel: 29.6L 6.5gal 7.8galUS

3173 Morris
1100
1963 UK
78.5mph 126.3kmh
0-50mph 80.5kmh: 15.2secs
0-60mph 96.5kmh: 22.2secs
0-1/4 mile: 22.7secs
48.0bhp 35.8kW 48.7PS
@ 5100rpm
60.0lbft 81.3Nm @ 2500rpm
59.1bhp/ton 58.1bhp/tonne
43.7bhp/L 32.6kW/L 44.3PS/L
46.7ft/sec 14.2m/sec
14.9mph 24.0kmh/1000rpm
32.7mpg 27.2mpgUS 8.6L/100km
Petrol 4-stroke piston
1098cc 67.0cu in
In-line 4 1 Carburettor
Compression ratio: 8.5:1
Bore: 64.6mm 2.5in
Stroke: 83.7mm 3.3in
Valve type/No: Overhead 8
Transmission: Manual
No. of forward speeds: 4
Wheels driven: Front
Springs F/R: Gas/Gas
Brakes F/R: Disc/Drum
Steering: Rack & pinion
Wheelbase: 237.5cm 93.5in
Track F: 130.8cm 51.5in
Track R: 129.3cm 50.9in
Length: 372.6cm 146.7in
Width: 153.4cm 60.4in
Height: 133.9cm 52.7in
Ground clearance: 15.2cm 6.0in
Kerb weight: 826.3kg 1820.0lb
Fuel: 38.7L 8.5gal 10.2galUS

3174 Morris
Minor 1000 de Luxe
1964 UK
77.0mph 123.9kmh
0-50mph 80.5kmh: 16.1secs
0-60mph 96.5kmh: 24.8secs
0-1/4 mile: 22.8secs
48.0bhp 35.8kW 48.7PS
@ 5100rpm
60.0lbft 81.3Nm @ 2500rpm
62.9bhp/ton 61.9bhp/tonne
43.7bhp/L 32.6kW/L 44.3PS/L
46.7ft/sec 14.2m/sec
16.2mph 26.1kmh/1000rpm
31.2mpg 26.0mpgUS 9.1L/100km
Petrol 4-stroke piston
1098cc 67.0cu in
In-line 4 1 Carburettor
Compression ratio: 8.5:1
Bore: 64.6mm 2.5in
Stroke: 83.7mm 3.3in
Valve type/No: Overhead 8
Transmission: Manual
No. of forward speeds: 4
Wheels driven: Rear
Springs F/R: Torsion bar/Leaf
Brakes F/R: Drum/Drum
Steering: Rack & pinion
Wheelbase: 218.4cm 86.0in
Track F: 128.5cm 50.6in
Track R: 127.5cm 50.2in
Length: 379.7cm 149.5in
Width: 152.4cm 60.0in
Height: 147.3cm 58.0in
Ground clearance: 17.0cm 6.7in
Kerb weight: 775.4kg 1708.0lb
Fuel: 29.6L 6.5gal 7.8galUS

3175 Morris
Oxford VI Traveller
1964 UK
80.5mph 129.5kmh
0-50mph 80.5kmh: 17.0secs
0-60mph 96.5kmh: 25.1secs
0-1/4 mile: 22.9secs
61.0bhp 45.5kW 61.8PS
@ 4500rpm
90.0lbft 122.0Nm @ 2100rpm
52.6bhp/ton 51.7bhp/tonne
37.6bhp/L 28.0kW/L 38.1PS/L
43.8ft/sec 13.3m/sec
16.0mph 25.7kmh/1000rpm
26.0mpg 21.6mpgUS 10.9L/100km
Petrol 4-stroke piston
1622cc 99.0cu in
In-line 4 1 Carburettor
Compression ratio: 8.3:1
Bore: 76.2mm 3.0in
Stroke: 88.9mm 3.5in
Valve type/No: Overhead 8
Transmission: Manual
No. of forward speeds: 4
Wheels driven: Rear
Springs F/R: Coil/Leaf
Brakes F/R: Drum/Drum
Steering: Cam & lever
Wheelbase: 254.5cm 100.2in
Track F: 128.5cm 50.6in
Track R: 130.6cm 51.4in
Length: 443.2cm 174.5in
Width: 161.3cm 63.5in
Height: 149.6cm 58.9in
Ground clearance: 15.0cm 5.9in
Kerb weight: 1179.9kg 2599.0lb
Fuel: 45.5L 10.0gal 12.0galUS

3176 Morris
1800
1966 UK
92.0mph 148.0kmh
0-50mph 80.5kmh: 12.3secs
0-60mph 96.5kmh: 17.4secs
0-1/4 mile: 20.9secs
0-1km: 39.2secs
80.0bhp 59.7kW 81.1PS
@ 5000rpm
100.0lbft 135.5Nm @ 2100rpm
68.2bhp/ton 67.1bhp/tonne
44.5bhp/L 33.2kW/L 45.1PS/L
48.6ft/sec 14.8m/sec
17.7mph 28.5kmh/1000rpm
23.2mpg 19.3mpgUS 12.2L/100km
Petrol 4-stroke piston
1798cc 109.7cu in
In-line 4 1 Carburettor
Compression ratio: 8.2:1
Bore: 80.3mm 3.2in
Stroke: 89.0mm 3.5in
Valve type/No: Overhead 8
Transmission: Manual
No. of forward speeds: 4
Wheels driven: Front
Springs F/R: Gas/Gas
Brake system: PA
Brakes F/R: Disc/Drum
Steering: Rack & pinion
Wheelbase: 269.2cm 106.0in
Track F: 142.5cm 56.1in
Track R: 141.0cm 55.5in
Length: 417.3cm 164.3in
Width: 170.2cm 67.0in
Height: 141.0cm 55.5in
Ground clearance: 16.5cm 6.5in
Kerb weight: 1192.7kg 2627.0lb
Fuel: 47.8L 10.5gal 12.6galUS

3177 Morris
1800S
1969 UK
101.0mph 162.5kmh
0-50mph 80.5kmh: 9.2secs
0-60mph 96.5kmh: 13.7secs
0-1/4 mile: 19.4secs
0-1km: 36.5secs
97.0bhp 72.3kW 98.3PS
@ 5700rpm
106.0lbft 143.6Nm @ 3000rpm
83.8bhp/ton 82.4bhp/tonne
53.9bhp/L 40.2kW/L 54.7PS/L
55.4ft/sec 16.9m/sec
18.0mph 29.0kmh/1000rpm
22.3mpg 18.6mpgUS 12.7L/100km
Petrol 4-stroke piston
1798cc 109.7cu in
In-line 4 2 Carburettor
Compression ratio: 9.5:1
Bore: 80.3mm 3.2in
Stroke: 89.0mm 3.5in
Valve type/No: Overhead 8
Transmission: Manual
No. of forward speeds: 4
Wheels driven: Front
Springs F/R: Gas/Gas
Brake system: PA
Brakes F/R: Disc/Drum
Steering: Rack & pinion
Wheelbase: 269.2cm 106.0in
Track F: 142.5cm 56.1in
Track R: 141.0cm 55.5in
Length: 423.4cm 166.7in
Width: 170.2cm 67.0in
Height: 141.0cm 55.5in
Ground clearance: 16.5cm 6.5in
Kerb weight: 1176.8kg 2592.0lb
Fuel: 47.8L 10.5gal 12.6galUS

3178 Morris
1100 Mk II
1970 UK
80.0mph 128.7kmh
0-50mph 80.5kmh: 15.2secs
0-60mph 96.5kmh: 24.0secs
0-1/4 mile: 22.9secs
0-1km: 43.5secs
48.0bhp 35.8kW 48.7PS
@ 5100rpm
60.0lbft 81.3Nm @ 2500rpm
57.9bhp/ton 57.0bhp/tonne
43.7bhp/L 32.6kW/L 44.3PS/L
46.7ft/sec 14.2m/sec
14.9mph 24.0kmh/1000rpm
27.1mpg 22.6mpgUS 10.4L/100km
Petrol 4-stroke piston
1098cc 67.0cu in
In-line 4 1 Carburettor
Compression ratio: 8.5:1
Bore: 64.6mm 2.5in
Stroke: 83.7mm 3.3in
Valve type/No: Overhead 8
Transmission: Manual
No. of forward speeds: 4
Wheels driven: Front
Springs F/R: Gas/Gas
Brakes F/R: Disc/Drum
Steering: Rack & pinion
Wheelbase: 237.5cm 93.5in
Track F: 130.8cm 51.5in
Track R: 129.3cm 50.9in
Length: 372.6cm 146.7in
Width: 153.4cm 60.4in
Height: 133.9cm 52.7in
Ground clearance: 15.2cm 6.0in
Kerb weight: 842.6kg 1856.0lb
Fuel: 36.4L 8.0gal 9.6galUS

3179 Morris
Marina 1.3 Super Coupe
1971 UK
88.0mph 141.6kmh
0-50mph 80.5kmh: 11.7secs
0-60mph 96.5kmh: 17.3secs
0-1/4 mile: 20.7secs
0-1km: 39.4secs
60.0bhp 44.7kW 60.8PS
@ 5250rpm
69.0lbft 93.5Nm @ 2500rpm
72.3bhp/ton 71.1bhp/tonne
47.1bhp/L 35.1kW/L 47.7PS/L
46.7ft/sec 14.2m/sec
15.6mph 25.1kmh/1000rpm
28.9mpg 24.1mpgUS 9.8L/100km
Petrol 4-stroke piston
1275cc 77.8cu in
In-line 4 1 Carburettor
Compression ratio: 8.8:1
Bore: 70.6mm 2.8in
Stroke: 81.3mm 3.2in
Valve type/No: Overhead 8
Transmission: Manual
No. of forward speeds: 4
Wheels driven: Rear
Springs F/R: Torsion bar/Leaf
Brakes F/R: Drum/Drum
Steering: Rack & pinion
Wheelbase: 243.8cm 96.0in
Track F: 129.5cm 51.0in
Track R: 132.1cm 52.0in
Length: 414.0cm 163.0in
Width: 162.6cm 64.0in
Height: 139.7cm 55.0in
Ground clearance: 14.5cm 5.7in
Kerb weight: 844.0kg 1859.0lb
Fuel: 52.3L 11.5gal 13.8galUS

3180 Morris
Marina 1.8TC
1971 UK
100.0mph 160.9kmh
0-50mph 80.5kmh: 8.4secs
0-60mph 96.5kmh: 12.3secs
0-1/4 mile: 19.0secs
95.0bhp 70.8kW 96.3PS
@ 5500rpm
105.0lbft 142.3Nm @ 2500rpm
101.3bhp/ton 99.6bhp/tonne
52.8bhp/L 39.4kW/L 53.6PS/L
53.5ft/sec 16.3m/sec
25.2mpg 21.0mpgUS 11.2L/100km
Petrol 4-stroke piston
1798cc 109.7cu in
In-line 4 2 Carburettor
Compression ratio: 9.0:1
Bore: 80.3mm 3.2in
Stroke: 88.9mm 3.5in
Valve type/No: Overhead 8
Transmission: Manual
No. of forward speeds: 4
Wheels driven: Rear
Springs F/R: Torsion bar/Leaf
Brake system: PA
Brakes F/R: Disc/Drum
Steering: Rack & pinion
Wheelbase: 243.8cm 96.0in
Length: 414.3cm 163.1in
Width: 164.6cm 64.8in
Height: 142.2cm 56.0in
Ground clearance: 13.7cm 5.4in
Kerb weight: 953.4kg 2100.0lb
Fuel: 52.2L 11.5gal 13.8galUS

3181 Morris
Marina TC
1971 UK
103.0mph 165.7kmh

0-50mph 80.5kmh: 8.3secs
0-60mph 96.5kmh: 12.1secs
0-1/4 mile: 18.7secs
0-1km: 34.6secs
94.5bhp 70.5kW 95.8PS
@ 5500rpm
105.0lbft 142.3Nm @ 2500rpm
99.9bhp/ton 98.3bhp/tonne
52.6bhp/L 39.2kW/L 53.3PS/L
53.5ft/sec 16.3m/sec
17.6mph 28.3kmh/1000rpm
21.5mpg 17.9mpgUS 13.1L/100km
Petrol 4-stroke piston
1798cc 109.7cu in
In-line 4 2 Carburettor
Compression ratio: 9.0:1
Bore: 80.2mm 3.2in
Stroke: 88.9mm 3.5in
Valve type/No: Overhead 8
Transmission: Manual
No. of forward speeds: 4
Wheels driven: Rear
Springs F/R: Torsion bar/Leaf
Brakes F/R: Disc/Drum
Steering: Rack & pinion
Wheelbase: 243.8cm 96.0in
Track F: 129.5cm 51.0in
Track R: 132.1cm 52.0in
Length: 421.6cm 166.0in
Width: 162.6cm 64.0in
Height: 142.2cm 56.0in
Ground clearance: 13.7cm 5.4in
Kerb weight: 961.6kg 2118.0lb
Fuel: 52.3L 11.5gal 13.8galUS

3182 Morris

Marina Estate
1972 UK
96.0mph 154.5kmh
0-50mph 80.5kmh: 9.3secs
0-60mph 96.5kmh: 13.5secs
0-1/4 mile: 19.1secs
0-1km: 36.1secs
82.5bhp 61.5kW 83.6PS
@ 5100rpm
99.4lbft 134.7Nm @ 2900rpm
84.4bhp/ton 83.0bhp/tonne
45.9bhp/L 34.2kW/L 46.5PS/L
49.6ft/sec 15.1m/sec
18.0mph 29.0kmh/1000rpm
25.2mpg 21.0mpgUS 11.2L/100km
Petrol 4-stroke piston
1798cc 109.7cu in
In-line 4 1 Carburettor
Compression ratio: 9.0:1
Bore: 80.2mm 3.2in
Stroke: 88.9mm 3.5in
Valve type/No: Overhead 8
Transmission: Manual
No. of forward speeds: 4
Wheels driven: Rear
Springs F/R: Torsion bar/Leaf
Brakes F/R: Disc/Drum
Steering: Rack & pinion
Wheelbase: 243.8cm 96.0in
Track F: 132.1cm 52.0in
Track R: 132.1cm 52.0in
Length: 421.6cm 166.0in
Width: 163.8cm 64.5in
Height: 142.2cm 56.0in
Ground clearance: 14.5cm 5.7in
Kerb weight: 993.8kg 2189.0lb
Fuel: 52.3L 11.5gal 13.8galUS

3183 Morris

Marina 1.8 HL
1976 UK
104.0mph 167.3kmh
0-50mph 80.5kmh: 7.8secs
0-60mph 96.5kmh: 11.4secs
0-1/4 mile: 18.3secs
0-1km: 34.2secs
85.0bhp 63.4kW 86.2PS
@ 5500rpm
100.0lbft 135.5Nm @ 3000rpm
89.2bhp/ton 87.7bhp/tonne
47.3bhp/L 35.2kW/L 47.9PS/L
53.5ft/sec 16.3m/sec
18.0mph 29.0kmh/1000rpm
27.2mpg 22.6mpgUS 10.4L/100km
Petrol 4-stroke piston
1798cc 109.7cu in
In-line 4 2 Carburettor
Compression ratio: 9.0:1
Bore: 80.2mm 3.2in
Stroke: 88.9mm 3.5in
Valve type/No: Overhead 8
Transmission: Manual
No. of forward speeds: 4
Wheels driven: Rear
Springs F/R: Torsion bar/Leaf
Brake system: PA
Brakes F/R: Disc/Drum
Steering: Rack & pinion
Wheelbase: 243.8cm 96.0in
Track F: 132.1cm 52.0in
Track R: 132.1cm 52.0in
Length: 431.0cm 169.7in
Width: 163.8cm 64.5in
Height: 142.2cm 56.0in
Ground clearance: 11.9cm 4.7in
Kerb weight: 969.3kg 2135.0lb
Fuel: 52.3L 11.5gal 13.8galUS

3184 Morris

Marina 1.3 Super Coupe
1977 UK
88.0mph 141.6kmh
0-50mph 80.5kmh: 12.5secs
0-60mph 96.5kmh: 18.2secs
0-1/4 mile: 21.1secs
0-1km: 40.1secs
57.0bhp 42.5kW 57.8PS
@ 5500rpm
69.0lbft 93.5Nm @ 2450rpm
65.1bhp/ton 64.1bhp/tonne
44.7bhp/L 33.3kW/L 45.3PS/L
48.9ft/sec 14.9m/sec
15.6mph 25.1kmh/1000rpm
28.0mpg 23.3mpgUS 10.1L/100km
Petrol 4-stroke piston
1275cc 77.8cu in
In-line 4 1 Carburettor
Compression ratio: 8.8:1
Bore: 70.6mm 2.8in
Stroke: 81.3mm 3.2in
Valve type/No: Overhead 8
Transmission: Manual
No. of forward speeds: 4
Wheels driven: Rear
Springs F/R: Torsion bar/Leaf
Brake system: PA
Brakes F/R: Disc/Drum
Steering: Rack & pinion
Wheelbase: 243.8cm 96.0in
Track F: 132.1cm 52.0in
Track R: 132.1cm 52.0in
Length: 414.0cm 163.0in
Width: 162.6cm 64.0in
Height: 139.7cm 55.0in
Ground clearance: 14.5cm 5.7in
Kerb weight: 889.8kg 1960.0lb
Fuel: 52.3L 11.5gal 13.8galUS

3185 Morris

Marina 1700HL
1978 UK
101.0mph 162.5kmh
0-50mph 80.5kmh: 8.5secs
0-60mph 96.5kmh: 12.5secs
0-1/4 mile: 18.7secs
0-1km: 35.4secs
78.0bhp 58.2kW 79.1PS
@ 5150rpm
93.0lbft 126.0Nm @ 3400rpm
82.5bhp/ton 81.2bhp/tonne
45.9bhp/L 34.2kW/L 46.6PS/L
42.6ft/sec 13.0m/sec
17.9mph 28.8kmh/1000rpm
27.5mpg 22.9mpgUS 10.3L/100km
Petrol 4-stroke piston
1698cc 103.6cu in
In-line 4 1 Carburettor
Compression ratio: 9.0:1
Bore: 84.4mm 3.3in
Stroke: 75.8mm 3.0in
Valve type/No: Overhead 8
Transmission: Manual
No. of forward speeds: 4
Wheels driven: Rear
Springs F/R: Torsion bar/Leaf
Brake system: PA
Brakes F/R: Disc/Drum
Steering: Rack & pinion
Wheelbase: 243.8cm 96.0in
Track F: 132.1cm 52.0in
Track R: 132.1cm 52.0in
Length: 429.0cm 168.9in
Width: 163.8cm 64.5in
Height: 142.0cm 55.9in
Ground clearance: 15.2cm 6.0in
Kerb weight: 961.1kg 2117.0lb
Fuel: 52.3L 11.5gal 13.8galUS

3186 Morris

Ital 2.0 HLS Automatic
1981 UK
102.0mph 164.1kmh
0-50mph 80.5kmh: 8.5secs
0-60mph 96.5kmh: 11.7secs
0-1/4 mile: 18.8secs
0-1km: 34.7secs
90.0bhp 67.1kW 91.2PS
@ 4750rpm
114.0lbft 154.5Nm @ 3250rpm
93.2bhp/ton 91.6bhp/tonne
45.1bhp/L 33.7kW/L 45.8PS/L
46.2ft/sec 14.1m/sec
20.2mph 32.5kmh/1000rpm
27.1mpg 22.6mpgUS 10.4L/100km
Petrol 4-stroke piston
1994cc 121.7cu in
In-line 4 1 Carburettor
Compression ratio: 9.0:1
Bore: 85.0mm 3.3in
Stroke: 89.0mm 3.5in
Valve type/No: Overhead 8
Transmission: Automatic
No. of forward speeds: 3
Wheels driven: Rear
Springs F/R: Torsion bar/Leaf
Brake system: PA
Brakes F/R: Disc/Drum
Steering: Rack & pinion
Wheelbase: 243.8cm 96.0in
Track F: 132.1cm 52.0in
Track R: 132.1cm 52.0in
Length: 434.3cm 171.0in
Width: 163.8cm 64.5in
Height: 142.0cm 55.9in
Ground clearance: 15.2cm 6.0in
Kerb weight: 982.0kg 2163.0lb
Fuel: 52.3L 11.5gal 13.8galUS

3187 Moskvich

De Luxe
1967 USSR
81.0mph 130.3kmh
0-50mph 80.5kmh: 19.2secs
0-60mph 96.5kmh: 27.5secs
0-1/4 mile: 24.4secs
0-1km: 46.2secs
55.0bhp 41.0kW 55.8PS
@ 4750rpm
80.0lbft 108.4Nm @ 2750rpm
54.3bhp/ton 53.4bhp/tonne
40.4bhp/L 30.1kW/L 41.0PS/L
38.9ft/sec 11.9m/sec
16.5mph 26.5kmh/1000rpm
23.4mpg 19.5mpgUS 12.1L/100km
Petrol 4-stroke piston
1360cc 83.0cu in
In-line 4 1 Carburettor
Compression ratio: 7.0:1
Bore: 76.0mm 3.0in
Stroke: 75.0mm 2.9in
Valve type/No: Overhead 8
Transmission: Manual
No. of forward speeds: 4
Wheels driven: Rear
Springs F/R: Coil/Leaf
Brakes F/R: Drum/Drum
Steering: Worm & roller
Wheelbase: 240.0cm 94.5in
Track F: 123.7cm 48.7in
Track R: 123.2cm 48.5in
Length: 408.9cm 161.0in
Width: 154.9cm 61.0in
Height: 147.3cm 58.0in
Ground clearance: 20.3cm 8.0in
Kerb weight: 1029.2kg 2267.0lb
Fuel: 45.5L 10.0gal 12.0galUS

3188 Moskvich

1500
1975 USSR
95.0mph 152.9kmh
0-50mph 80.5kmh: 9.9secs
0-60mph 96.5kmh: 14.5secs
0-1/4 mile: 19.7secs
0-1km: 37.0secs
80.0bhp 59.7kW 81.1PS
@ 5800rpm
85.0lbft 115.2Nm @ 3400rpm
59.3bhp/ton 58.3bhp/tonne
54.1bhp/L 40.3kW/L 54.8PS/L
44.5ft/sec 13.5m/sec
16.5mph 26.5kmh/1000rpm
24.7mpg 20.6mpgUS 11.4L/100km
Petrol 4-stroke piston
1479cc 90.2cu in
In-line 4 1 Carburettor
Compression ratio: 8.8:1
Bore: 82.0mm 3.2in
Stroke: 70.0mm 2.8in
Valve type/No: Overhead 8
Transmission: Manual
No. of forward speeds: 4
Wheels driven: Rear
Springs F/R: Coil/Leaf
Brake system: PA
Brakes F/R: Drum/Drum
Steering: Worm & roller
Wheelbase: 240.0cm 94.5in
Track F: 123.2cm 48.5in
Track R: 123.2cm 48.5in
Length: 417.8cm 164.5in
Width: 154.9cm 61.0in
Height: 148.6cm 58.5in
Ground clearance: 16.5cm 6.5in
Kerb weight: 1372.9kg 3024.0lb
Fuel: 45.5L 10.0gal 12.0galUS

3189 Muntz

Jet
1951 USA
108.0mph 173.8kmh
0-50mph 80.5kmh: 9.0secs
0-60mph 96.5kmh: 12.3secs
0-1/4 mile: 18.8secs
152.0bhp 113.3kW 154.1PS
@ 3600rpm
90.1bhp/ton 88.6bhp/tonne
27.5bhp/L 20.5kW/L 27.9PS/L
43.8ft/sec 13.4m/sec
Petrol 4-stroke piston
5520cc 336.8cu in
Vee 8
Bore: 88.9mm 3.5in
Stroke: 111.3mm 4.4in
Valve type/No: Overhead 16
Transmission: Automatic
Wheels driven: Rear
Wheelbase: 294.6cm 116.0in
Track F: 142.2cm 56.0in
Track R: 142.2cm 56.0in
Length: 472.4cm 186.0in
Width: 180.3cm 71.0in
Height: 142.2cm 56.0in
Ground clearance: 15.2cm 6.0in
Kerb weight: 1716.1kg 3780.0lb

3190 MVS

Venturi GT
1987 France
153.0mph 246.2kmh
0-60mph 96.5kmh: 6.0secs
0-1/4 mile: 14.8secs
200.0bhp 149.1kW 202.8PS
@ 5750rpm
195.0lbft 264.2Nm @ 2500rpm
172.6bhp/ton 169.8bhp/tonne
81.4bhp/L 60.7kW/L 82.5PS/L
39.6ft/sec 12.1m/sec
Petrol 4-stroke piston
2458cc 150.0cu in turbocharged
Vee 6 fuel injection
Compression ratio: 8.6:1
Bore: 91.0mm 3.6in
Stroke: 63.0mm 2.5in
Valve type/No: Overhead 12
Transmission: Manual
No. of forward speeds: 5
Wheels driven: Rear
Springs F/R: Coil/Coil
Brake system: PA
Brakes F/R: Disc/Disc
Steering: Rack & pinion PA
Wheelbase: 240.0cm 94.5in
Track F: 146.6cm 57.7in
Track R: 147.1cm 57.9in
Length: 408.9cm 161.0in
Width: 170.2cm 67.0in
Height: 116.8cm 46.0in
Kerb weight: 1178.1kg 2595.0lb
Fuel: 68.9L 15.1gal 18.2galUS

3191 MVS

Venturi
1990 France
0-60mph 96.5kmh: 6.5secs
0-1/4 mile: 14.5secs
200.0bhp 149.1kW 202.8PS
@ 5750rpm
210.0lbft 284.6Nm @ 2500rpm
158.9bhp/ton 156.2bhp/tonne
81.4bhp/L 60.7kW/L 82.5PS/L

39.6ft/sec 12.1m/sec
Petrol 4-stroke piston
2458cc 150.0cu in turbocharged
Vee 6 fuel injection
Compression ratio: 8.0:1
Bore: 91.0mm 3.6in
Stroke: 63.0mm 2.5in
Valve type/No: Overhead 12
Transmission: Manual
No. of forward speeds: 5
Wheels driven: Rear
Springs F/R: Coil/Coil
Brakes F/R: Disc/Disc
Steering: Rack & pinion PA
Wheelbase: 240.0cm 94.5in
Track F: 146.6cm 57.7in
Track R: 147.1cm 57.9in
Length: 408.9cm 161.0in
Width: 170.2cm 67.0in
Height: 116.8cm 46.0in
Kerb weight: 1280.3kg 2820.0lb
Fuel: 87.8L 19.3gal 23.2galUS

3192 Nardi

Blue Ray 1
1955 Italy
140.0mph 225.3kmh
190.0bhp 141.7kW 192.6PS
@ 5500rpm
224.0bhp/ton 220.3bhp/tonne
76.0bhp/L 56.7kW/L 77.1PS/L
51.5ft/sec 15.7m/sec
Petrol 4-stroke piston
2500cc 152.5cu in
Vee 6 3 Carburettor
Compression ratio: 9.5:1
Bore: 78.0mm 3.1in
Stroke: 85.5mm 3.4in
Valve type/No: Overhead 12
Transmission: Manual
No. of forward speeds: 4
Wheels driven: Rear
Springs F/R: Coil/Coil
Brakes F/R: Drum/Drum
Steering: Worm & sector
Wheelbase: 254.0cm 100.0in
Track F: 144.8cm 57.0in
Track R: 144.8cm 57.0in
Length: 429.3cm 169.0in
Width: 166.4cm 65.5in
Height: 121.9cm 48.0in
Kerb weight: 862.6kg 1900.0lb

3193 Nardi

Blue Ray 2
1958 Italy
125.0mph 201.1kmh
140.0bhp 104.4kW 141.9PS
@ 5500rpm
136.3bhp/ton 134.1bhp/tonne
56.0bhp/L 41.8kW/L 56.8PS/L
51.5ft/sec 15.7m/sec
Petrol 4-stroke piston
2500cc 152.5cu in
Vee 6 1 Carburettor
Compression ratio: 9.5:1
Bore: 78.0mm 3.1in
Stroke: 85.5mm 3.4in
Valve type/No: Overhead 12
Transmission: Manual
No. of forward speeds: 4
Wheels driven: Rear
Springs F/R: Coil/Coil
Brakes F/R: Drum/Drum
Steering: Worm & sector
Wheelbase: 260.4cm 102.5in
Track F: 143.5cm 56.5in
Track R: 143.5cm 56.5in
Length: 448.3cm 176.5in
Width: 162.6cm 64.0in
Height: 127.0cm 50.0in
Kerb weight: 1044.2kg 2300.0lb

3194 Nash

Straight Eight Saloon
1930 USA
72.5mph 116.7kmh
12.0mpg 10.0mpgUS 23.5L/100km
Petrol 4-stroke piston
4934cc 301.0cu in
In-line 8
Bore: 82.5mm 3.2in
Stroke: 114.3mm 4.5in
Transmission: Manual
No. of forward speeds: 3
Wheels driven: Rear
Brakes F/R: Drum/Drum
Wheelbase: 337.8cm 133.0in
Track F: 146.1cm 57.5in
Track R: 146.1cm 57.5in
Length: 502.9cm 198.0in
Width: 188.0cm 74.0in
Height: 182.9cm 72.0in
Kerb weight: 1957.6kg 4312.0lb
Fuel: 71.9L 15.8gal 19.0galUS

3195 Nash

Ambassador Six Saloon
1938 USA
87.3mph 140.5kmh
0-50mph 80.5kmh: 13.6secs
0-60mph 96.5kmh: 20.2secs
17.0mpg 14.2mpgUS 16.6L/100km
Petrol 4-stroke piston
3820cc 233.1cu in
In-line 6
Bore: 85.8mm 3.4in
Stroke: 112.0mm 4.4in
Valve type/No: Overhead 12
Transmission: Manual
No. of forward speeds: 3
Wheels driven: Rear
Brakes F/R: Drum/Drum
Kerb weight: 1632.6kg 3596.0lb
Fuel: 75.1L 16.5gal 19.8galUS

3196 Nash

Rambler Station Wagon
1952 USA
79.0mph 127.1kmh
0-50mph 80.5kmh: 14.5secs
0-60mph 96.5kmh: 21.9secs
0-1/4 mile: 22.7secs
82.0bhp 61.1kW 83.1PS
@ 3800rpm
138.0lbft 187.0Nm @ 1600rpm
69.8bhp/ton 68.7bhp/tonne
29.0bhp/L 21.6kW/L 29.4PS/L
39.6ft/sec 12.1m/sec
24.7mph 39.7kmh/1000rpm
22.0mpg 18.3mpgUS 12.8L/100km
Petrol 4-stroke piston
2830cc 172.7cu in
In-line 6
Compression ratio: 7.2:1
Bore: 79.4mm 3.1in
Stroke: 95.2mm 3.8in
Valve type/No: Side 12
Transmission: Manual with overdrive
No. of forward speeds: 4
Wheels driven: Rear
Springs F/R: Coil/Leaf
Brakes F/R: Drum/Drum
Wheelbase: 254.0cm 100.0in
Track F: 135.1cm 53.2in
Track R: 134.6cm 53.0in
Length: 447.0cm 176.0in
Width: 186.7cm 73.5in
Height: 157.5cm 62.0in
Ground clearance: 20.3cm 8.0in
Kerb weight: 1194.0kg 2630.0lb
Fuel: 75.1L 16.5gal 19.8galUS

3197 Nash

Metropolitan
1954 UK
74.0mph 119.1kmh
0-50mph 80.5kmh: 15.2secs
0-60mph 96.5kmh: 22.4secs
0-1/4 mile: 23.4secs
42.0bhp 31.3kW 42.6PS
@ 4500rpm
62.0lbft 84.0Nm @ 2400rpm
52.4bhp/ton 51.5bhp/tonne
35.0bhp/L 26.1kW/L 35.5PS/L
43.8ft/sec 13.3m/sec
14.0mph 22.5kmh/1000rpm
Petrol 4-stroke piston
1200cc 73.2cu in
In-line 4
Bore: 65.5mm 2.6in
Stroke: 88.9mm 3.5in
Valve type/No: Overhead 8
Transmission: Manual
No. of forward speeds: 3
Wheels driven: Rear
Wheelbase: 215.9cm 85.0in
Track F: 115.1cm 45.3in
Track R: 113.8cm 44.8in
Kerb weight: 814.9kg 1795.0lb

3198 Nash

Nash-Healey Roadster
1954 UK
104.6mph 168.3kmh
0-50mph 80.5kmh: 7.9secs
0-60mph 96.5kmh: 11.5secs
0-1/4 mile: 18.0secs
140.0bhp 104.4kW 141.9PS
@ 4000rpm
230.0lbft 311.7Nm @ 2000rpm
106.3bhp/ton 104.5bhp/tonne
33.8bhp/L 25.2kW/L 34.3PS/L
48.7ft/sec 14.8m/sec
27.1mph 43.6kmh/1000rpm
Petrol 4-stroke piston
4140cc 252.6cu in
In-line 6
Compression ratio: 8.0:1
Bore: 88.9mm 3.5in
Stroke: 111.3mm 4.4in
Valve type/No: Overhead 12
Transmission: Manual
No. of forward speeds: 3
Wheels driven: Rear
Wheelbase: 259.1cm 102.0in
Track F: 134.6cm 53.0in
Track R: 139.4cm 54.9in
Kerb weight: 1339.3kg 2950.0lb

3199 Nash

Metropolitan
1955 UK
76.0mph 122.3kmh
0-50mph 80.5kmh: 18.0secs
0-60mph 96.5kmh: 27.0secs
0-1/4 mile: 23.8secs
42.0bhp 31.3kW 42.6PS
@ 4500rpm
62.0lbft 84.0Nm @ 2400rpm
50.3bhp/ton 49.5bhp/tonne
35.0bhp/L 26.1kW/L 35.5PS/L
43.8ft/sec 13.3m/sec
14.0mph 22.5kmh/1000rpm
34.0mpg 28.3mpgUS 8.3L/100km
Petrol 4-stroke piston
1200cc 73.2cu in
In-line 4
Compression ratio: 7.2:1
Bore: 65.5mm 2.6in
Stroke: 89.0mm 3.5in
Valve type/No: Overhead 8
Transmission: Manual
No. of forward speeds: 3
Wheels driven: Rear
Springs F/R: Coil/Leaf
Brakes F/R: Drum/Drum
Wheelbase: 215.9cm 85.0in
Track F: 115.1cm 45.3in
Track R: 113.8cm 44.8in
Length: 379.7cm 149.5in
Width: 156.2cm 61.5in
Height: 137.2cm 54.0in
Ground clearance: 16.3cm 6.4in
Kerb weight: 848.5kg 1869.0lb
Fuel: 47.8L 10.5gal 12.6galUS

3200 Nash

Nash-Healey Roadster Supercharged
1955 UK
112.8mph 181.5kmh
0-50mph 80.5kmh: 7.6secs
0-60mph 96.5kmh: 9.8secs
0-1/4 mile: 17.1secs
140.0bhp 104.4kW 141.9PS
@ 4000rpm
230.0lbft 311.7Nm @ 2000rpm
106.3bhp/ton 104.5bhp/tonne
33.8bhp/L 25.2kW/L 34.3PS/L
48.7ft/sec 14.8m/sec
27.1mph 43.6kmh/1000rpm
Petrol 4-stroke piston
4140cc 252.6cu in supercharged
In-line 6
Compression ratio: 8.0:1
Bore: 88.9mm 3.5in
Stroke: 111.3mm 4.4in
Valve type/No: Overhead 12
Transmission: Manual
No. of forward speeds: 3
Wheels driven: Rear
Wheelbase: 259.1cm 102.0in
Track F: 134.6cm 53.0in
Track R: 139.4cm 54.9in
Kerb weight: 1339.3kg 2950.0lb

3201 Nash

Rambler Station Wagon
1956 USA
78.0mph 125.5kmh
0-50mph 80.5kmh: 13.2secs
0-60mph 96.5kmh: 20.7secs
0-1/4 mile: 22.0secs
120.0bhp 89.5kW 121.7PS
@ 4200rpm
170.0lbft 230.4Nm @ 1600rpm
82.8bhp/ton 81.4bhp/tonne
37.4bhp/L 27.9kW/L 38.0PS/L
49.6ft/sec 15.1m/sec
25.0mph 40.2kmh/1000rpm
22.5mpg 18.7mpgUS 12.6L/100km
Petrol 4-stroke piston
3205cc 195.5cu in
In-line 6
Compression ratio: 7.4:1
Bore: 79.4mm 3.1in
Stroke: 107.9mm 4.2in
Valve type/No: Overhead 12
Transmission: Manual with overdrive
No. of forward speeds: 4
Wheels driven: Rear
Springs F/R: Coil/Coil
Brakes F/R: Drum/Drum
Wheelbase: 274.3cm 108.0in
Track F: 146.6cm 57.7in
Track R: 147.3cm 58.0in
Length: 504.7cm 198.7in
Width: 180.3cm 71.0in
Height: 147.3cm 58.0in
Ground clearance: 20.3cm 8.0in
Kerb weight: 1474.6kg 3248.0lb
Fuel: 72.8L 16.0gal 19.2galUS

3202 Nash

Metropolitan 1500
1958 UK
75.5mph 121.5kmh
0-50mph 80.5kmh: 14.8secs
0-60mph 96.5kmh: 22.9secs
0-1/4 mile: 22.1secs
47.0bhp 35.0kW 47.6PS
@ 4100rpm
74.0lbft 100.3Nm @ 2100rpm
56.1bhp/ton 55.2bhp/tonne
31.6bhp/L 23.5kW/L 32.0PS/L
39.9ft/sec 12.2m/sec
15.4mph 24.8kmh/1000rpm
31.0mpg 25.8mpgUS 9.1L/100km
Petrol 4-stroke piston
1489cc 90.8cu in
In-line 4 1 Carburettor
Compression ratio: 7.2:1
Bore: 73.1mm 2.9in
Stroke: 89.0mm 3.5in
Valve type/No: Overhead 8
Transmission: Manual
No. of forward speeds: 3
Wheels driven: Rear
Springs F/R: Coil/Leaf
Brakes F/R: Drum/Drum
Wheelbase: 215.9cm 85.0in
Track F: 115.3cm 45.4in
Track R: 113.8cm 44.8in
Length: 379.7cm 149.5in
Width: 156.2cm 61.5in
Height: 143.5cm 56.5in
Ground clearance: 16.3cm 6.4in
Kerb weight: 851.7kg 1876.0lb
Fuel: 39.8L 8.8gal 10.5galUS

3203 Naylor

TF 1700
1985 UK
93.0mph 149.6kmh
0-50mph 80.5kmh: 8.6secs
0-60mph 96.5kmh: 12.5secs
0-1/4 mile: 19.5secs
0-1km: 35.9secs
77.0bhp 57.4kW 78.1PS
@ 5180rpm
99.0lbft 134.1Nm @ 3700rpm
89.3bhp/ton 87.8bhp/tonne
45.3bhp/L 33.8kW/L 45.9PS/L
42.9ft/sec 13.1m/sec
19.3mph 31.1kmh/1000rpm
25.9mpg 21.6mpgUS 10.9L/100km
Petrol 4-stroke piston
1700cc 103.7cu in
In-line 4 1 Carburettor
Compression ratio: 9.0:1
Bore: 85.4mm 3.4in
Stroke: 75.8mm 3.0in
Valve type/No: Overhead 8

Transmission: Manual
No. of forward speeds: 4
Wheels driven: Rear
Springs F/R: Coil/Coil
Brake system: PA
Brakes F/R: Disc/Drum
Steering: Rack & pinion
Wheelbase: 240.0cm 94.5in
Track F: 132.6cm 52.2in
Track R: 133.6cm 52.6in
Length: 373.4cm 147.0in
Width: 151.6cm 59.7in
Height: 133.4cm 52.5in
Kerb weight: 877.1kg 1932.0lb
Fuel: 54.6L 12.0gal 14.4galUS

3204 Nissan

Sentra
1982 Japan
90.0mph 144.8kmh
0-60mph 96.5kmh: 15.0secs
0-1/4 mile: 19.9secs
67.0bhp 50.0kW 67.9PS
@ 5200rpm
85.0lbft 115.2Nm @ 3200rpm
71.5bhp/ton 70.3bhp/tonne
45.0bhp/L 33.6kW/L 45.6PS/L
46.7ft/sec 14.2m/sec
23.3mph 37.5kmh/1000rpm
39.6mpg 33.0mpgUS 7.1L/100km
Petrol 4-stroke piston
1488cc 90.8cu in
In-line 4 1 Carburettor
Compression ratio: 9.3:1
Bore: 76.0mm 3.0in
Stroke: 82.0mm 3.2in
Valve type/No: Overhead 8
Transmission: Manual
No. of forward speeds: 5
Wheels driven: Front
Springs F/R: Coil/Coil
Brake system: PA
Brakes F/R: Disc/Drum
Steering: Rack & pinion PA
Wheelbase: 240.0cm 94.5in
Track F: 139.4cm 54.9in
Track R: 137.4cm 54.1in
Length: 424.9cm 167.3in
Width: 162.1cm 63.8in
Height: 135.4cm 53.3in
Ground clearance: 17.0cm 6.7in
Kerb weight: 953.4kg 2100.0lb
Fuel: 50.0L 11.0gal 13.2galUS

3205 Nissan

Stanza XE
1982 Japan
105.0mph 168.9kmh
0-50mph 80.5kmh: 8.0secs
0-60mph 96.5kmh: 11.3secs
0-1/4 mile: 18.2secs
88.0bhp 65.6kW 89.2PS
@ 5200rpm
112.0lbft 151.8Nm @ 2800rpm
79.3bhp/ton 78.0bhp/tonne
44.6bhp/L 33.2kW/L 45.2PS/L
50.0ft/sec 15.2m/sec
26.7mph 43.0kmh/1000rpm
34.2mpg 28.5mpgUS 8.3L/100km
Petrol 4-stroke piston
1974cc 120.4cu in
In-line 4 1 Carburettor
Compression ratio: 8.5:1
Bore: 84.5mm 3.3in
Stroke: 88.0mm 3.5in
Valve type/No: Overhead 8
Transmission: Manual
No. of forward speeds: 5
Wheels driven: Front
Springs F/R: Coil/Coil
Brake system: PA
Brakes F/R: Disc/Drum
Steering: Rack & pinion PA
Wheelbase: 246.9cm 97.2in
Track F: 143.0cm 56.3in
Track R: 141.0cm 55.5in
Length: 440.4cm 173.4in
Width: 166.6cm 65.6in
Height: 138.9cm 54.7in
Ground clearance: 16.5cm 6.5in
Kerb weight: 1128.2kg 2485.0lb
Fuel: 54.1L 11.9gal 14.3galUS

3206 Nissan

Pulsar NX
1983 Japan
101.0mph 162.5kmh
0-50mph 80.5kmh: 8.7secs
0-60mph 96.5kmh: 12.8secs
0-1/4 mile: 18.8secs
69.0bhp 51.4kW 70.0PS
@ 5200rpm
92.0lbft 124.7Nm @ 3200rpm
75.4bhp/ton 74.1bhp/tonne
43.2bhp/L 32.2kW/L 43.8PS/L
50.0ft/sec 15.2m/sec
25.0mph 40.2kmh/1000rpm
31.8mpg 26.5mpgUS 8.9L/100km
Petrol 4-stroke piston
1597cc 97.4cu in
In-line 4 1 Carburettor
Compression ratio: 9.4:1
Bore: 76.0mm 3.0in
Stroke: 88.0mm 3.5in
Valve type/No: Overhead 8
Transmission: Manual
No. of forward speeds: 5
Wheels driven: Front
Springs F/R: Coil/Coil
Brake system: PA
Brakes F/R: Disc/Drum
Steering: Rack & pinion PA
Wheelbase: 241.6cm 95.1in
Track F: 139.4cm 54.9in
Track R: 137.4cm 54.1in
Length: 412.5cm 162.4in
Width: 161.8cm 63.7in
Height: 137.4cm 54.1in
Ground clearance: 15.0cm 5.9in
Kerb weight: 930.7kg 2050.0lb
Fuel: 50.0L 11.0gal 13.2galUS

3207 Nissan

200SX Turbo
1984 Japan
116.0mph 186.6kmh
0-50mph 80.5kmh: 6.6secs
0-60mph 96.5kmh: 9.5secs
0-1/4 mile: 16.9secs
120.0bhp 89.5kW 121.7PS
@ 5200rpm
134.0lbft 181.6Nm @ 3200rpm
95.0bhp/ton 93.4bhp/tonne
66.3bhp/L 49.5kW/L 67.2PS/L
47.5ft/sec 14.5m/sec
21.1mph 33.9kmh/1000rpm
24.6mpg 20.5mpgUS 11.5L/100km
Petrol 4-stroke piston
1809cc 110.4cu in turbocharged
In-line 4 fuel injection
Compression ratio: 8.0:1
Bore: 83.0mm 3.3in
Stroke: 83.6mm 3.3in
Valve type/No: Overhead 8
Transmission: Manual
No. of forward speeds: 5
Wheels driven: Rear
Springs F/R: Coil/Coil
Brake system: PA
Brakes F/R: Disc/Disc
Steering: Rack & pinion PA
Wheelbase: 242.6cm 95.5in
Track F: 137.9cm 54.3in
Track R: 135.9cm 53.5in
Length: 443.0cm 174.4in
Width: 166.1cm 65.4in
Height: 133.1cm 52.4in
Ground clearance: 13.5cm 5.3in
Kerb weight: 1284.8kg 2830.0lb
Fuel: 54.9L 12.1gal 14.5galUS

3208 Nissan

300ZX
1984 Japan
128.0mph 206.0kmh
0-60mph 96.5kmh: 8.2secs
0-1/4 mile: 16.4secs
160.0bhp 119.3kW 162.2PS
@ 5200rpm
173.0lbft 234.4Nm @ 3600rpm
119.9bhp/ton 117.9bhp/tonne
54.0bhp/L 40.3kW/L 54.8PS/L
47.2ft/sec 14.4m/sec
21.6mpg 18.0mpgUS 13.1L/100km
Petrol 4-stroke piston
2960cc 180.6cu in
Vee 6 fuel injection
Compression ratio: 9.2:1
Bore: 87.0mm 3.4in
Stroke: 83.0mm 3.3in
Valve type/No: Overhead 12
Transmission: Manual
No. of forward speeds: 5
Wheels driven: Rear
Springs F/R: Coil/Coil
Brakes F/R: Disc/Disc
Steering: Rack & pinion PA
Wheelbase: 231.9cm 91.3in
Track F: 141.5cm 55.7in
Track R: 143.5cm 56.5in
Length: 433.6cm 170.7in
Width: 172.5cm 67.9in
Height: 129.5cm 51.0in
Kerb weight: 1357.5kg 2990.0lb
Fuel: 74.2L 16.3gal 19.6galUS

3209 Nissan

300ZX Turbo
1984 Japan
138.0mph 222.0kmh
0-50mph 80.5kmh: 5.5secs
0-60mph 96.5kmh: 7.2secs
0-1/4 mile: 15.4secs
0-1km: 28.3secs
228.0bhp 170.0kW 231.2PS
@ 5400rpm
242.0lbft 327.9Nm @ 4400rpm
158.3bhp/ton 155.6bhp/tonne
77.0bhp/L 57.4kW/L 78.1PS/L
49.3ft/sec 15.0m/sec
27.3mph 43.9kmh/1000rpm
21.5mpg 17.9mpgUS 13.1L/100km
Petrol 4-stroke piston
2960cc 180.6cu in turbocharged
Vee 6 1 Carburettor
Compression ratio: 7.4:1
Bore: 87.0mm 3.4in
Stroke: 83.6mm 3.3in
Valve type/No: Overhead 12
Transmission: Manual
No. of forward speeds: 5
Wheels driven: Rear
Springs F/R: Coil/Coil
Brake system: PA
Brakes F/R: Disc/Disc
Steering: Rack & pinion PA
Wheelbase: 247.9cm 97.6in
Track F: 141.5cm 55.7in
Track R: 143.5cm 56.5in
Length: 453.4cm 178.5in
Width: 172.5cm 67.9in
Height: 131.1cm 51.6in
Ground clearance: 15.0cm 5.9in
Kerb weight: 1465.1kg 3227.0lb
Fuel: 71.9L 15.8gal 19.0galUS

3210 Nissan

Pulsar NX Turbo
1984 Japan
0-50mph 80.5kmh: 7.7secs
0-60mph 96.5kmh: 10.6secs
0-1/4 mile: 17.8secs
100.0bhp 74.6kW 101.4PS
@ 5200rpm
112.0lbft 151.8Nm @ 3200rpm
104.2bhp/ton 102.4bhp/tonne
67.2bhp/L 50.1kW/L 68.2PS/L
46.7ft/sec 14.2m/sec
27.6mpg 23.0mpgUS 10.2L/100km
Petrol 4-stroke piston
1487cc 90.7cu in turbocharged
In-line 4 fuel injection
Compression ratio: 8.0:1
Bore: 75.9mm 3.0in
Stroke: 82.0mm 3.2in
Valve type/No: Overhead 8
Transmission: Automatic
No. of forward speeds: 3
Wheels driven: Front
Wheelbase: 241.6cm 95.1in
Track F: 139.4cm 54.9in
Track R: 137.4cm 54.1in
Length: 412.5cm 162.4in
Width: 161.8cm 63.7in
Height: 137.4cm 54.1in
Kerb weight: 976.1kg 2150.0lb

3211 Nissan

Silvia Turbo ZX
1984 Japan
126.0mph 202.7kmh
0-50mph 80.5kmh: 6.2secs
0-60mph 96.5kmh: 8.9secs
0-1/4 mile: 16.5secs
0-1km: 30.1secs
137.0bhp 102.2kW 138.9PS
@ 6000rpm
191.0lbft 258.8Nm @ 4000rpm
118.9bhp/ton 116.9bhp/tonne
75.7bhp/L 56.5kW/L 76.8PS/L
54.8ft/sec 16.7m/sec
23.0mph 37.0kmh/1000rpm
23.0mpg 19.2mpgUS 12.3L/100km
Petrol 4-stroke piston
1809cc 110.4cu in turbocharged
In-line 4 fuel injection
Compression ratio: 8.0:1
Bore: 83.0mm 3.3in
Stroke: 83.6mm 3.3in
Valve type/No: Overhead 8
Transmission: Manual
No. of forward speeds: 5
Wheels driven: Rear
Springs F/R: Coil/Coil
Brake system: PA
Brakes F/R: Disc/Disc
Steering: Rack & pinion PA
Wheelbase: 242.6cm 95.5in
Track F: 137.9cm 54.3in
Track R: 135.9cm 53.5in
Length: 435.1cm 171.3in
Width: 166.1cm 65.4in
Height: 133.1cm 52.4in
Ground clearance: 15.5cm 6.1in
Kerb weight: 1171.8kg 2581.0lb
Fuel: 52.8L 11.6gal 13.9galUS

3212 Nissan

Bluebird Turbo ZX
1985 Japan
120.0mph 193.1kmh
0-50mph 80.5kmh: 6.3secs
0-60mph 96.5kmh: 8.8secs
0-1/4 mile: 16.3secs
0-1km: 31.0secs
135.0bhp 100.7kW 136.9PS
@ 6000rpm
121.0lbft 164.0Nm @ 3600rpm
113.1bhp/ton 111.2bhp/tonne
74.6bhp/L 55.6kW/L 75.7PS/L
54.8ft/sec 16.7m/sec
24.0mph 38.6kmh/1000rpm
27.7mpg 23.1mpgUS 10.2L/100km
Petrol 4-stroke piston
1809cc 110.4cu in turbocharged
In-line 4 fuel injection
Compression ratio: 8.0:1
Bore: 83.0mm 3.3in
Stroke: 83.6mm 3.3in
Valve type/No: Overhead 8
Transmission: Manual
No. of forward speeds: 5
Wheels driven: Front
Springs F/R: Coil/Coil
Brake system: PA
Brakes F/R: Disc/Disc
Steering: Rack & pinion PA
Wheelbase: 255.0cm 100.4in
Track F: 146.1cm 57.5in
Track R: 145.0cm 57.1in
Length: 436.1cm 171.7in
Width: 168.9cm 66.5in
Height: 140.0cm 55.1in
Ground clearance: 18.5cm 7.3in
Kerb weight: 1214.0kg 2674.0lb
Fuel: 60.1L 13.2gal 15.9galUS

3213 Nissan

Cherry 1.3 SGT
1985 Japan
94.0mph 151.2kmh
0-50mph 80.5kmh: 8.7secs
0-60mph 96.5kmh: 12.8secs
0-1/4 mile: 19.0secs
0-1km: 35.9secs
60.0bhp 44.7kW 60.8PS
@ 5600rpm
74.0lbft 100.3Nm @ 3600rpm
76.5bhp/ton 75.2bhp/tonne
47.2bhp/L 35.2kW/L 47.9PS/L
42.9ft/sec 13.1m/sec
22.8mph 36.7kmh/1000rpm
32.3mpg 26.9mpgUS 8.7L/100km
Petrol 4-stroke piston
1270cc 77.5cu in
In-line 4 1 Carburettor
Compression ratio: 9.0:1
Bore: 76.0mm 3.0in
Stroke: 70.0mm 2.8in
Valve type/No: Overhead 8
Transmission: Manual
No. of forward speeds: 5
Wheels driven: Front
Springs F/R: Coil/Coil
Brake system: PA
Brakes F/R: Disc/Drum

Steering: Rack & pinion
Wheelbase: 241.6cm 95.1in
Track F: 139.4cm 54.9in
Track R: 138.4cm 54.5in
Length: 399.5cm 157.3in
Width: 162.1cm 63.8in
Height: 138.4cm 54.5in
Ground clearance: 16.5cm 6.5in
Kerb weight: 797.7kg 1757.0lb
Fuel: 50.0L 11.0gal 13.2galUS

3214 Nissan

Maxima SE
1985 Japan
120.0mph 193.1kmh
0-50mph 80.5kmh: 5.4secs
0-60mph 96.5kmh: 8.6secs
0-1/4 mile: 16.7secs
152.0bhp 113.3kW 154.1PS
@ 5200rpm
167.0lbft 226.3Nm @ 3600rpm
109.1bhp/ton 107.3bhp/tonne
51.3bhp/L 38.3kW/L 52.1PS/L
47.2ft/sec 14.4m/sec
28.6mph 46.0kmh/1000rpm
24.0mpg 20.0mpgUS 11.8L/100km
Petrol 4-stroke piston
2960cc 180.6cu in
Vee 6 fuel injection
Compression ratio: 9.0:1
Bore: 87.0mm 3.4in
Stroke: 83.0mm 3.3in
Valve type/No: Overhead 12
Transmission: Manual
No. of forward speeds: 5
Wheels driven: Front
Springs F/R: Coil/Coil
Brake system: PA
Brakes F/R: Disc/Disc
Steering: Rack & pinion PA
Wheelbase: 255.0cm 100.4in
Track F: 146.1cm 57.5in
Track R: 145.0cm 57.1in
Length: 461.5cm 181.7in
Width: 168.9cm 66.5in
Height: 140.0cm 55.1in
Ground clearance: 14.7cm 5.8in
Kerb weight: 1416.5kg 3120.0lb
Fuel: 60.2L 13.2gal 15.9galUS

3215 Nissan

300ZX
1986 Japan
128.0mph 206.0kmh
0-50mph 80.5kmh: 6.5secs
0-60mph 96.5kmh: 9.1secs
0-1/4 mile: 16.9secs
160.0bhp 119.3kW 162.2PS
@ 5200rpm
174.0lbft 235.8Nm @ 4000rpm
110.6bhp/ton 108.8bhp/tonne
54.0bhp/L 40.3kW/L 54.8PS/L
47.2ft/sec 14.4m/sec
25.9mph 41.7kmh/1000rpm
21.6mpg 18.0mpgUS 13.1L/100km
Petrol 4-stroke piston
2960cc 180.6cu in
Vee 6 fuel injection
Compression ratio: 9.0:1
Bore: 87.0mm 3.4in
Stroke: 83.0mm 3.3in
Valve type/No: Overhead 12
Transmission: Manual
No. of forward speeds: 5
Wheels driven: Rear
Springs F/R: Coil/Coil
Brake system: PA
Brakes F/R: Disc/Disc
Steering: Rack & pinion PA
Wheelbase: 231.9cm 91.3in
Track F: 145.5cm 57.3in
Track R: 147.6cm 58.1in
Length: 433.6cm 170.7in
Width: 172.5cm 67.9in
Height: 129.5cm 51.0in
Kerb weight: 1471.0kg 3240.0lb
Fuel: 71.9L 15.8gal 19.0galUS

3216 Nissan

300ZX Turbo
1986 Japan
133.0mph 214.0kmh
0-50mph 80.5kmh: 5.3secs
0-60mph 96.5kmh: 7.2secs
0-1/4 mile: 15.7secs
200.0bhp 149.1kW 202.8PS
@ 5200rpm
227.0lbft 307.6Nm @ 3600rpm
134.7bhp/ton 132.5bhp/tonne
67.6bhp/L 50.4kW/L 68.5PS/L
47.2ft/sec 14.4m/sec
26.9mph 43.3kmh/1000rpm
20.4mpg 17.0mpgUS 13.8L/100km
Petrol 4-stroke piston
2960cc 180.6cu in turbocharged
Vee 6 fuel injection
Compression ratio: 9.0:1
Bore: 87.0mm 3.4in
Stroke: 83.0mm 3.3in
Valve type/No: Overhead 12
Transmission: Manual
No. of forward speeds: 5
Wheels driven: Rear
Springs F/R: Coil/Coil
Brake system: PA
Brakes F/R: Disc/Disc
Steering: Rack & pinion PA
Wheelbase: 231.9cm 91.3in
Track F: 143.5cm 56.5in
Track R: 145.5cm 57.3in
Length: 433.6cm 170.7in
Width: 172.5cm 67.9in
Height: 129.5cm 51.0in
Kerb weight: 1509.5kg 3325.0lb
Fuel: 71.9L 15.8gal 19.0galUS

3217 Nissan

Bluebird 1.8 ZX
1986 Japan
118.0mph 189.9kmh
0-50mph 80.5kmh: 6.3secs
0-60mph 96.5kmh: 8.6secs
0-1/4 mile: 16.5secs
0-1km: 30.6secs
135.0bhp 100.7kW 136.9PS
@ 6000rpm
141.0lbft 191.1Nm @ 4000rpm
108.5bhp/ton 106.7bhp/tonne
74.6bhp/L 55.6kW/L 75.7PS/L
54.8ft/sec 16.7m/sec
24.2mph 38.9kmh/1000rpm
23.8mpg 19.8mpgUS 11.9L/100km
Petrol 4-stroke piston
1809cc 110.0cu in turbocharged
In-line 4 fuel injection
Compression ratio: 8.0:1
Bore: 83.0mm 3.3in
Stroke: 83.6mm 3.3in
Valve type/No: Overhead 8
Transmission: Manual
No. of forward speeds: 5
Wheels driven: Front
Springs F/R: Coil/Coil
Brake system: PA
Brakes F/R: Disc/Disc
Steering: Rack & pinion PA
Wheelbase: 255.0cm 100.4in
Track F: 146.0cm 57.5in
Track R: 146.0cm 57.5in
Length: 440.5cm 173.4in
Width: 169.0cm 66.5in
Height: 139.5cm 54.9in
Ground clearance: 15.0cm 5.9in
Kerb weight: 1265.0kg 2786.3lb
Fuel: 60.1L 13.2gal 15.9galUS

3218 Nissan

Laurel 2.4 SGL Automatic
1986 Japan
105.0mph 168.9kmh
0-50mph 80.5kmh: 8.6secs
0-60mph 96.5kmh: 11.6secs
0-1/4 mile: 18.4secs
0-1km: 33.6secs
128.0bhp 95.4kW 129.8PS
@ 5600rpm
135.0lbft 182.9Nm @ 4400rpm
98.5bhp/ton 96.8bhp/tonne
53.5bhp/L 39.9kW/L 54.2PS/L
45.1ft/sec 13.8m/sec
25.1mph 40.4kmh/1000rpm
20.0mpg 16.7mpgUS 14.1L/100km
Petrol 4-stroke piston
2393cc 146.0cu in
In-line 6 fuel injection
Compression ratio: 8.9:1
Bore: 83.0mm 3.3in
Stroke: 73.7mm 2.9in
Valve type/No: Overhead 12
Transmission: Automatic
No. of forward speeds: 4
Wheels driven: Rear
Springs F/R: Coil/Coil
Brake system: PA
Brakes F/R: Disc/Drum
Steering: Rack & pinion PA
Wheelbase: 267.0cm 105.1in
Track F: 142.0cm 55.9in
Track R: 140.7cm 55.4in
Length: 464.8cm 183.0in
Width: 168.9cm 66.5in
Height: 142.5cm 56.1in
Ground clearance: 17.8cm 7.0in
Kerb weight: 1321.6kg 2911.0lb
Fuel: 65.1L 14.3gal 17.2galUS

3219 Nissan

Sentra
1986 Japan
0-60mph 96.5kmh: 11.8secs
0-1/4 mile: 18.6secs
70.0bhp 52.2kW 71.0PS
@ 5000rpm
94.0lbft 127.4Nm @ 2800rpm
70.8bhp/ton 69.6bhp/tonne
43.8bhp/L 32.7kW/L 44.4PS/L
48.1ft/sec 14.7m/sec
22.2mph 35.7kmh/1000rpm
35.9mpg 29.9mpgUS 7.9L/100km
Petrol 4-stroke piston
1597cc 97.4cu in
In-line 4 1 Carburettor
Compression ratio: 9.4:1
Bore: 76.0mm 3.0in
Stroke: 88.0mm 3.5in
Valve type/No: Overhead 8
Transmission: Manual
No. of forward speeds: 5
Wheels driven: Front
Springs F/R: Coil/Coil
Brake system: PA
Brakes F/R: Disc/Drum
Steering: Rack & pinion
Wheelbase: 243.1cm 95.7in
Track F: 143.0cm 56.3in
Track R: 143.0cm 56.3in
Length: 428.5cm 168.7in
Width: 164.1cm 64.6in
Height: 137.9cm 54.3in
Kerb weight: 1005.6kg 2215.0lb
Fuel: 50.0L 11.0gal 13.2galUS

3220 Nissan

Sentra Sport Coupe SE
1986 Japan
100.0mph 160.9kmh
0-50mph 80.5kmh: 9.6secs
0-60mph 96.5kmh: 13.3secs
0-1/4 mile: 19.0secs
70.0bhp 52.2kW 71.0PS
@ 5000rpm
94.0lbft 127.4Nm @ 2800rpm
65.7bhp/ton 64.6bhp/tonne
43.8bhp/L 32.7kW/L 44.4PS/L
48.1ft/sec 14.7m/sec
32.4mpg 27.0mpgUS 8.7L/100km
Petrol 4-stroke piston
1597cc 97.4cu in
In-line 4 1 Carburettor
Compression ratio: 9.4:1
Bore: 76.0mm 3.0in
Stroke: 88.0mm 3.5in
Valve type/No: Overhead 8
Transmission: Manual
No. of forward speeds: 5
Wheels driven: Front
Springs F/R: Coil/Coil
Brake system: PA
Brakes F/R: Disc/Drum
Steering: Rack & pinion PA
Wheelbase: 243.1cm 95.7in
Track F: 143.5cm 56.5in
Track R: 143.5cm 56.5in
Length: 422.9cm 166.5in
Width: 166.6cm 65.6in
Height: 132.6cm 52.2in
Ground clearance: 14.0cm 5.5in
Kerb weight: 1082.8kg 2385.0lb
Fuel: 50.0L 11.0gal 13.2galUS

3221 Nissan

Sunny 1.3 LX 5-door
1986 Japan
93.0mph 149.6kmh
0-50mph 80.5kmh: 9.7secs
0-60mph 96.5kmh: 13.7secs
0-1/4 mile: 19.7secs
0-1km: 37.1secs
60.0bhp 44.7kW 60.8PS
@ 5600rpm
74.0lbft 100.3Nm @ 3600rpm
64.9bhp/ton 63.8bhp/tonne
47.2bhp/L 35.2kW/L 47.9PS/L
42.9ft/sec 13.1m/sec
18.4mph 29.6kmh/1000rpm
31.0mpg 25.8mpgUS 9.1L/100km
Petrol 4-stroke piston
1270cc 77.0cu in
In-line 4 1 Carburettor
Compression ratio: 9.0:1
Bore: 76.0mm 3.0in
Stroke: 70.0mm 2.8in
Valve type/No: Overhead 8
Transmission: Manual
No. of forward speeds: 5
Wheels driven: Front
Springs F/R: Coil/Coil
Brake system: PA
Brakes F/R: Disc/Drum
Steering: Rack & pinion
Wheelbase: 243.0cm 95.7in
Track F: 143.5cm 56.5in
Track R: 143.0cm 56.3in
Length: 403.0cm 158.7in
Width: 164.0cm 64.6in
Height: 138.0cm 54.3in
Ground clearance: 14.9cm 5.9in
Kerb weight: 940.0kg 2070.5lb
Fuel: 50.0L 11.0gal 13.2galUS

3222 Nissan

200SX SE V6
1987 Japan
0-60mph 96.5kmh: 7.9secs
0-1/4 mile: 16.1secs
160.0bhp 119.3kW 162.2PS
@ 5200rpm
174.0lbft 235.8Nm @ 4000rpm
120.5bhp/ton 118.5bhp/tonne
54.0bhp/L 40.3kW/L 54.8PS/L
24.0mpg 20.0mpgUS 11.8L/100km
Petrol 4-stroke piston
2960cc 180.6cu in
Vee 6
Valve type/No: Overhead 12
Transmission: Manual
No. of forward speeds: 5
Wheels driven: Rear
Brakes F/R: Disc/Disc
Steering: Rack & pinion PA
Length: 443.0cm 174.4in
Kerb weight: 1350.6kg 2975.0lb

3223 Nissan

300ZX
1987 Japan
125.0mph 201.1kmh
0-60mph 96.5kmh: 8.8secs
0-1/4 mile: 16.5secs
160.0bhp 119.3kW 162.2PS
@ 5200rpm
174.0lbft 235.8Nm @ 4000rpm
108.3bhp/ton 106.5bhp/tonne
54.0bhp/L 40.3kW/L 54.8PS/L
47.2ft/sec 14.4m/sec
23.8mpg 19.8mpgUS 11.9L/100km
Petrol 4-stroke piston
2960cc 180.6cu in
Vee 6 fuel injection
Compression ratio: 9.0:1
Bore: 87.0mm 3.4in
Stroke: 83.0mm 3.3in
Valve type/No: Overhead 24
Transmission: Manual
No. of forward speeds: 5
Wheels driven: Rear
Springs F/R: Coil/Coil
Brakes F/R: Disc/Disc
Steering: Rack & pinion PA
Wheelbase: 252.0cm 99.2in
Track F: 141.5cm 55.7in
Track R: 143.5cm 56.5in
Length: 453.4cm 178.5in
Width: 172.5cm 67.9in
Height: 126.5cm 49.8in
Kerb weight: 1502.7kg 3310.0lb
Fuel: 71.9L 15.8gal 19.0galUS

3224 Nissan

300ZX Turbo
1987 Japan
144.0mph 231.7kmh
0-50mph 80.5kmh: 5.2secs
0-60mph 96.5kmh: 7.0secs
0-1/4 mile: 15.5secs

0-1km: 28.1secs
225.0bhp 167.8kW 228.1PS
@ 5400rpm
240.0lbft 325.2Nm @ 4400rpm
154.8bhp/ton 152.2bhp/tonne
76.0bhp/L 56.7kW/L 77.1PS/L
49.0ft/sec 14.9m/sec
28.1mph 45.2kmh/1000rpm
19.2mpg 16.0mpgUS 14.7L/100km
Petrol 4-stroke piston
2960cc 181.0cu in turbocharged
Vee 6 fuel injection
Compression ratio: 7.8:1
Bore: 87.0mm 3.4in
Stroke: 83.0mm 3.3in
Valve type/No: Overhead 12
Transmission: Manual
No. of forward speeds: 5
Wheels driven: Rear
Springs F/R: Coil/Coil
Brake system: PA
Brakes F/R: Disc/Disc
Steering: Rack & pinion PA
Wheelbase: 252.0cm 99.2in
Track F: 145.5cm 57.3in
Track R: 147.3cm 58.0in
Length: 460.5cm 181.3in
Width: 172.5cm 67.9in
Height: 131.0cm 51.6in
Ground clearance: 15.0cm 5.9in
Kerb weight: 1478.0kg 3255.5lb
Fuel: 77.3L 17.0gal 20.4galUS

3225 Nissan
Micra SGL 5-DR
1987 Japan
89.0mph 143.2kmh
0-50mph 80.5kmh: 9.8secs
0-60mph 96.5kmh: 14.5secs
0-1/4 mile: 19.6secs
0-1km: 37.4secs
55.0bhp 41.0kW 55.8PS
@ 6000rpm
56.0lbft 75.9Nm @ 3600rpm
80.5bhp/ton 79.1bhp/tonne
55.7bhp/L 41.5kW/L 56.4PS/L
44.7ft/sec 13.6m/sec
17.8mph 28.6kmh/1000rpm
40.9mpg 34.1mpgUS 6.9L/100km
Petrol 4-stroke piston
988cc 60.0cu in
In-line 4 1 Carburettor
Compression ratio: 10.3:1
Bore: 68.0mm 2.7in
Stroke: 68.0mm 2.7in
Valve type/No: Overhead 8
Transmission: Manual
No. of forward speeds: 5
Wheels driven: Front
Springs F/R: Coil/Coil
Brake system: PA
Brakes F/R: Disc/Drum
Steering: Rack & pinion
Wheelbase: 230.0cm 90.6in
Track F: 134.6cm 53.0in
Track R: 133.1cm 52.4in
Length: 364.5cm 143.5in
Width: 156.0cm 61.4in
Height: 139.5cm 54.9in
Ground clearance: 15.2cm 6.0in
Kerb weight: 695.0kg 1530.8lb
Fuel: 40.0L 8.8gal 10.6galUS

3226 Nissan
Pulsar NX SE
1987 Japan
115.0mph 185.0kmh
0-50mph 80.5kmh: 7.2secs
0-60mph 96.5kmh: 10.3secs
0-1/4 mile: 17.8secs
113.0bhp 84.3kW 114.6PS
@ 6400rpm
99.0lbft 134.1Nm @ 4800rpm
97.3bhp/ton 95.7bhp/tonne
70.8bhp/L 52.8kW/L 71.7PS/L
58.5ft/sec 17.8m/sec
28.8mpg 24.0mpgUS 9.8L/100km
Petrol 4-stroke piston
1597cc 97.4cu in
In-line 4 fuel injection
Compression ratio: 9.0:1
Bore: 78.0mm 3.1in
Stroke: 83.6mm 3.3in
Valve type/No: Overhead 16
Transmission: Manual
No. of forward speeds: 5
Wheels driven: Front
Springs F/R: Coil/Coil
Brake system: PA
Brakes F/R: Disc/Drum
Steering: Rack & pinion PA
Wheelbase: 243.1cm 95.7in
Track F: 144.0cm 56.7in
Track R: 144.0cm 56.7in
Length: 422.9cm 166.5in
Width: 166.9cm 65.7in
Height: 129.0cm 50.8in
Ground clearance: 14.7cm 5.8in
Kerb weight: 1180.4kg 2600.0lb
Fuel: 50.0L 11.0gal 13.2galUS

3227 Nissan
Sunny ZX Coupe
1987 Japan
118.0mph 189.9kmh
0-50mph 80.5kmh: 6.6secs
0-60mph 96.5kmh: 9.2secs
0-1/4 mile: 17.2secs
0-1km: 31.5secs
120.0bhp 89.5kW 121.7PS
@ 6600rpm
102.0lbft 138.2Nm @ 5200rpm
112.3bhp/ton 110.4bhp/tonne
75.1bhp/L 56.0kW/L 76.1PS/L
60.3ft/sec 18.4m/sec
18.1mph 29.1kmh/1000rpm
27.2mpg 22.6mpgUS 10.4L/100km
Petrol 4-stroke piston
1598cc 97.0cu in
In-line 4 fuel injection
Compression ratio: 10.0:1
Bore: 78.0mm 3.1in
Stroke: 83.6mm 3.3in
Valve type/No: Overhead 16
Transmission: Manual
No. of forward speeds: 5
Wheels driven: Front
Springs F/R: Coil/Coil
Brake system: PA
Brakes F/R: Disc/Disc
Steering: Rack & pinion PA
Wheelbase: 243.0cm 95.7in
Track F: 143.5cm 56.5in
Track R: 143.5cm 56.5in
Length: 423.5cm 166.7in
Width: 166.5cm 65.6in
Height: 132.5cm 52.2in
Ground clearance: 14.0cm 5.5in
Kerb weight: 1087.0kg 2394.3lb
Fuel: 50.0L 11.0gal 13.2galUS

3228 Nissan
Sunny 1.6 SLX Coupe
1987 Japan
105.0mph 168.9kmh
0-50mph 80.5kmh: 8.1secs
0-60mph 96.5kmh: 11.6secs
0-1/4 mile: 18.2secs
0-1km: 34.0secs
84.0bhp 62.6kW 85.2PS
@ 5600rpm
97.0lbft 131.4Nm @ 3200rpm
86.7bhp/ton 85.3bhp/tonne
52.6bhp/L 39.2kW/L 53.3PS/L
50.2ft/sec 15.3m/sec
20.9mph 33.6kmh/1000rpm
28.7mpg 23.9mpgUS 9.8L/100km
Petrol 4-stroke piston
1597cc 97.0cu in
In-line 4 1 Carburettor
Compression ratio: 9.6:1
Bore: 76.0mm 3.0in
Stroke: 82.0mm 3.2in
Valve type/No: Overhead 8
Transmission: Manual
No. of forward speeds: 5
Wheels driven: Front
Springs F/R: Coil/Coil
Brake system: PA
Brakes F/R: Disc/Drum
Steering: Rack & pinion PA
Wheelbase: 243.0cm 95.7in
Track F: 143.5cm 56.5in
Track R: 143.5cm 56.5in
Length: 423.5cm 166.7in
Width: 166.5cm 65.6in
Height: 132.5cm 52.2in
Ground clearance: 14.0cm 5.5in
Kerb weight: 985.0kg 2169.6lb
Fuel: 50.0L 11.0gal 13.2galUS

3229 Nissan
200SX SE V6
1988 Japan
119.0mph 191.5kmh
0-50mph 80.5kmh: 6.1secs
0-60mph 96.5kmh: 8.4secs
0-1/4 mile: 16.4secs
165.0bhp 123.0kW 167.3PS
@ 5200rpm
168.0lbft 227.6Nm @ 3200rpm
123.0bhp/ton 120.9bhp/tonne
55.7bhp/L 41.6kW/L 56.5PS/L
47.2ft/sec 14.4m/sec
23.4mpg 19.5mpgUS 12.1L/100km
Petrol 4-stroke piston
2960cc 180.6cu in
Vee 6 fuel injection
Compression ratio: 9.0:1
Bore: 87.0mm 3.4in
Stroke: 83.0mm 3.3in
Valve type/No: Overhead 12
Transmission: Manual
No. of forward speeds: 5
Wheels driven: Rear
Springs F/R: Coil/Coil
Brake system: PA
Brakes F/R: Disc/Disc
Steering: Rack & pinion PA
Wheelbase: 242.6cm 95.5in
Track F: 138.9cm 54.7in
Track R: 142.5cm 56.1in
Length: 446.0cm 175.6in
Width: 166.9cm 65.7in
Height: 128.0cm 50.4in
Kerb weight: 1364.3kg 3005.0lb
Fuel: 53.0L 11.6gal 14.0galUS

3230 Nissan
240SX
1988 Japan
125.0mph 201.1kmh
0-50mph 80.5kmh: 6.3secs
0-60mph 96.5kmh: 8.8secs
0-1/4 mile: 16.5secs
140.0bhp 104.4kW 141.9PS
@ 5600rpm
152.0lbft 206.0Nm @ 4400rpm
112.0bhp/ton 110.1bhp/tonne
58.6bhp/L 43.7kW/L 59.4PS/L
58.8ft/sec 17.9m/sec
30.0mpg 25.0mpgUS 9.4L/100km
Petrol 4-stroke piston
2389cc 145.8cu in
In-line 4 fuel injection
Compression ratio: 8.7:1
Bore: 89.0mm 3.5in
Stroke: 96.0mm 3.8in
Valve type/No: Overhead 12
Transmission: Manual
No. of forward speeds: 5
Wheels driven: Rear
Springs F/R: Coil/Coil
Brake system: PA
Brakes F/R: Disc/Disc
Steering: Rack & pinion PA
Wheelbase: 247.4cm 97.4in
Track F: 146.1cm 57.5in
Track R: 146.1cm 57.5in
Length: 452.1cm 178.0in
Width: 168.9cm 66.5in
Height: 129.0cm 50.8in
Ground clearance: 14.5cm 5.7in
Kerb weight: 1271.2kg 2800.0lb
Fuel: 60.2L 13.2gal 15.9galUS

3231 Nissan
300ZX
1988 Japan
125.0mph 201.1kmh
0-50mph 80.5kmh: 5.2secs
0-60mph 96.5kmh: 7.4secs
0-1/4 mile: 16.4secs
205.0bhp 152.9kW 207.8PS
@ 5200rpm
227.0lbft 307.6Nm @ 3600rpm
140.6bhp/ton 138.3bhp/tonne
69.3bhp/L 51.6kW/L 70.2PS/L
47.2ft/sec 14.4m/sec
25.2mpg 21.0mpgUS 11.2L/100km
Petrol 4-stroke piston
2960cc 180.6cu in turbocharged
Vee 6 fuel injection
Compression ratio: 8.3:1
Bore: 87.0mm 3.4in
Stroke: 83.0mm 3.3in
Valve type/No: Overhead 12
Transmission: Manual
No. of forward speeds: 5
Wheels driven: Rear
Springs F/R: Coil/Coil
Brake system: PA
Brakes F/R: Disc/Disc
Steering: Rack & pinion PA
Wheelbase: 231.9cm 91.3in
Track F: 143.5cm 56.5in
Track R: 145.5cm 57.3in
Length: 440.4cm 173.4in
Width: 172.5cm 67.9in
Height: 126.2cm 49.7in
Kerb weight: 1482.3kg 3265.0lb
Fuel: 71.9L 15.8gal 19.0galUS

3232 Nissan
200SX
1989 Japan
141.0mph 226.9kmh
0-50mph 80.5kmh: 5.2secs
0-60mph 96.5kmh: 7.2secs
0-1/4 mile: 15.3secs
0-1km: 28.0secs
171.0bhp 127.5kW 173.4PS
@ 6400rpm
168.3lbft 228.0Nm @ 4000rpm
141.7bhp/ton 139.4bhp/tonne
94.5bhp/L 70.5kW/L 95.8PS/L
58.5ft/sec 17.8m/sec
21.4mph 34.4kmh/1000rpm
19.5mpg 16.2mpgUS 14.5L/100km
Petrol 4-stroke piston
1809cc 110.0cu in turbocharged
In-line 4 fuel injection
Compression ratio: 8.5:1
Bore: 83.0mm 3.3in
Stroke: 83.6mm 3.3in
Valve type/No: Overhead 16
Transmission: Manual
No. of forward speeds: 5
Wheels driven: Rear
Springs F/R: Coil/Coil
Brake system: PA ABS
Brakes F/R: Disc/Disc
Steering: Rack & pinion PA
Wheelbase: 247.5cm 97.4in
Track F: 146.5cm 57.7in
Track R: 146.5cm 57.7in
Length: 453.5cm 178.5in
Width: 169.0cm 66.5in
Height: 129.0cm 50.8in
Ground clearance: 14.5cm 5.7in
Kerb weight: 1227.0kg 2702.6lb
Fuel: 60.1L 13.2gal 15.9galUS

3233 Nissan
240SX Turbo Tokico/Cartech
1989 Japan
0-50mph 80.5kmh: 4.7secs
0-60mph 96.5kmh: 6.3secs
0-1/4 mile: 15.1secs
200.0bhp 149.1kW 202.8PS
@ 5300rpm
200.0lbft 271.0Nm @ 4600rpm
155.6bhp/ton 153.0bhp/tonne
83.7bhp/L 62.4kW/L 84.9PS/L
55.6ft/sec 17.0m/sec
Petrol 4-stroke piston
2389cc 145.8cu in turbocharged
In-line 4 fuel injection
Compression ratio: 8.7:1
Bore: 89.0mm 3.5in
Stroke: 96.0mm 3.8in
Valve type/No: Overhead 12
Transmission: Manual
No. of forward speeds: 5
Wheels driven: Rear
Springs F/R: Coil/Coil
Brake system: PA
Brakes F/R: Disc/Disc
Steering: Rack & pinion PA
Wheelbase: 247.4cm 97.4in
Track F: 146.1cm 57.5in
Track R: 146.1cm 57.5in
Length: 452.1cm 178.0in
Width: 168.9cm 66.5in
Height: 129.0cm 50.8in
Kerb weight: 1307.5kg 2880.0lb

3234 Nissan
300ZX
1989 Japan
148.0mph 238.1kmh
0-50mph 80.5kmh: 5.4secs
0-60mph 96.5kmh: 7.1secs
0-1/4 mile: 15.5secs
222.0bhp 165.5kW 225.1PS
@ 6400rpm

198.0lbft 268.3Nm @ 4800rpm
154.4bhp/ton 151.9bhp/tonne
75.0bhp/L 55.9kW/L 76.0PS/L
58.1ft/sec 17.7m/sec
28.2mpg 23.5mpgUS 10.0L/100km
Petrol 4-stroke piston
2960cc 180.6cu in
Vee 6 fuel injection
Compression ratio: 10.1:1
Bore: 87.0mm 3.4in
Stroke: 83.0mm 3.3in
Valve type/No: Overhead 24
Transmission: Manual
No. of forward speeds: 5
Wheels driven: Rear
Springs F/R: Coil/Coil
Brake system: PA ABS
Brakes F/R: Disc/Disc
Steering: Rack & pinion PA
Wheelbase: 245.1cm 96.5in
Track F: 149.6cm 58.9in
Track R: 153.4cm 60.4in
Length: 430.5cm 169.5in
Width: 179.1cm 70.5in
Height: 125.5cm 49.4in
Ground clearance: 12.7cm 5.0in
Kerb weight: 1461.9kg 3220.0lb
Fuel: 70.8L 15.6gal 18.7galUS

3235 Nissan

Maxima
1989 Japan
122.0mph 196.3kmh
0-50mph 80.5kmh: 7.0secs
0-60mph 96.5kmh: 9.4secs
0-1/4 mile: 16.8secs
0-1km: 31.1secs
172.0bhp 128.3kW 174.4PS
@ 5600rpm
134.3lbft 182.0Nm @ 2800rpm
123.0bhp/ton 121.0bhp/tonne
58.1bhp/L 43.3kW/L 58.9PS/L
50.9ft/sec 15.5m/sec
29.2mph 47.0kmh/1000rpm
16.8mpg 14.0mpgUS 16.8L/100km
Petrol 4-stroke piston
2960cc 181.0cu in
Vee 6 fuel injection
Compression ratio: 10.0:1
Bore: 87.0mm 3.4in
Stroke: 83.0mm 3.3in
Valve type/No: Overhead 12
Transmission: Automatic
No. of forward speeds: 4
Wheels driven: Front
Springs F/R: Coil/Coil
Brake system: PA
Brakes F/R: Disc/Disc
Steering: Rack & pinion PA
Wheelbase: 264.9cm 104.3in
Track F: 150.9cm 59.4in
Track R: 149.1cm 58.7in
Length: 478.0cm 188.2in
Width: 162.3cm 63.9in
Height: 140.5cm 55.3in
Kerb weight: 1421.5kg 3131.0lb
Fuel: 70.1L 15.4gal 18.5galUS

3236 Nissan

Maxima SE
1989 Japan
120.0mph 193.1kmh
0-50mph 80.5kmh: 6.3secs
0-60mph 96.5kmh: 8.5secs
0-1/4 mile: 16.6secs
160.0bhp 119.3kW 162.2PS
@ 5200rpm
182.0lbft 246.6Nm @ 2800rpm
114.0bhp/ton 112.1bhp/tonne
54.0bhp/L 40.3kW/L 54.8PS/L
47.2ft/sec 14.4m/sec
24.6mpg 20.5mpgUS 11.5L/100km
Petrol 4-stroke piston
2960cc 180.6cu in
Vee 6 fuel injection
Compression ratio: 9.0:1
Bore: 87.0mm 3.4in
Stroke: 83.0mm 3.3in
Valve type/No: Overhead 12
Transmission: Manual
No. of forward speeds: 5
Wheels driven: Front
Springs F/R: Coil/Coil
Brake system: PA ABS
Brakes F/R: Disc/Disc
Steering: Rack & pinion PA
Wheelbase: 264.9cm 104.3in
Track F: 150.9cm 59.4in
Track R: 149.1cm 58.7in
Length: 476.5cm 187.6in
Width: 176.0cm 69.3in
Height: 140.0cm 55.1in
Ground clearance: 12.7cm 5.0in
Kerb weight: 1427.8kg 3145.0lb
Fuel: 70.0L 15.4gal 18.5galUS

3237 Nissan

Micra 1.2 GSX
1989 Japan
93.0mph 149.6kmh
0-50mph 80.5kmh: 9.6secs
0-60mph 96.5kmh: 14.0secs
0-1/4 mile: 19.6secs
0-1km: 36.5secs
60.0bhp 44.7kW 60.8PS
@ 5600rpm
69.4lbft 94.0Nm @ 3200rpm
76.7bhp/ton 75.4bhp/tonne
48.6bhp/L 36.2kW/L 49.3PS/L
47.8ft/sec 14.6m/sec
22.8mph 36.7kmh/1000rpm
32.3mpg 26.9mpgUS 8.7L/100km
Petrol 4-stroke piston
1235cc 75.0cu in
In-line 4 1 Carburettor
Compression ratio: 9.0:1
Bore: 71.0mm 2.8in
Stroke: 78.0mm 3.1in
Valve type/No: Overhead 8
Transmission: Manual
No. of forward speeds: 5
Wheels driven: Front
Springs F/R: Coil/Coil
Brake system: PA
Brakes F/R: Disc/Drum
Steering: Rack & pinion
Wheelbase: 230.0cm 90.6in
Track F: 134.6cm 53.0in
Track R: 133.1cm 52.4in
Length: 364.5cm 143.5in
Width: 156.0cm 61.4in
Height: 139.5cm 54.9in
Ground clearance: 15.2cm 6.0in
Kerb weight: 796.0kg 1753.3lb
Fuel: 40.0L 8.8gal 10.6galUS

3238 Nissan

Prairie
1989 Japan
98.0mph 157.7kmh
0-50mph 80.5kmh: 10.3secs
0-60mph 96.5kmh: 14.4secs
0-1/4 mile: 19.4secs
0-1km: 36.1secs
98.0bhp 73.1kW 99.4PS
@ 5600rpm
118.8lbft 161.0Nm @ 3200rpm
76.0bhp/ton 74.7bhp/tonne
49.6bhp/L 37.0kW/L 50.3PS/L
53.8ft/sec 16.4m/sec
25.7mph 41.4kmh/1000rpm
20.6mpg 17.2mpgUS 13.7L/100km
Petrol 4-stroke piston
1974cc 120.0cu in
In-line 4 1 Carburettor
Compression ratio: 9.4:1
Bore: 84.5mm 3.3in
Stroke: 88.0mm 3.5in
Valve type/No: Overhead 8
Transmission: Automatic
No. of forward speeds: 4
Wheels driven: Front
Springs F/R: Coil/Coil
Brake system: PA ABS
Brakes F/R: Disc/Drum
Steering: Rack & pinion PA
Wheelbase: 261.0cm 102.8in
Track F: 146.0cm 57.5in
Track R: 143.0cm 56.3in
Length: 436.0cm 171.7in
Width: 169.0cm 66.5in
Height: 163.0cm 64.2in
Ground clearance: 19.5cm 7.7in
Kerb weight: 1312.0kg 2889.9lb
Fuel: 65.1L 14.3gal 17.2galUS

3239 Nissan

Sunny 1.4 LS
1989 Japan
105.0mph 168.9kmh
0-50mph 80.5kmh: 8.0secs
0-60mph 96.5kmh: 12.0secs
0-1/4 mile: 18.5secs
0-1km: 34.4secs
83.0bhp 61.9kW 84.1PS
@ 6200rpm
81.9lbft 111.0Nm @ 4000rpm
87.2bhp/ton 85.7bhp/tonne
59.6bhp/L 44.5kW/L 60.4PS/L
55.5ft/sec 16.9m/sec
21.5mph 34.6kmh/1000rpm
28.9mpg 24.1mpgUS 9.8L/100km
Petrol 4-stroke piston
1392cc 85.0cu in
In-line 4 1 Carburettor
Compression ratio: 9.4:1
Bore: 73.6mm 2.9in
Stroke: 81.8mm 3.2in
Valve type/No: Overhead 12
Transmission: Manual
No. of forward speeds: 5
Wheels driven: Front
Springs F/R: Coil/Coil
Brake system: PA
Brakes F/R: Disc/Drum
Steering: Rack & pinion
Wheelbase: 243.0cm 95.7in
Track F: 143.5cm 56.5in
Track R: 143.0cm 56.3in
Length: 403.0cm 158.7in
Width: 164.0cm 64.6in
Height: 138.0cm 54.3in
Ground clearance: 14.9cm 5.9in
Kerb weight: 968.0kg 2132.2lb
Fuel: 50.0L 11.0gal 13.2galUS

3240 Nissan

300ZX
1990 Japan
158.0mph 254.2kmh
0-50mph 80.5kmh: 4.3secs
0-60mph 96.5kmh: 5.6secs
0-1/4 mile: 14.4secs
0-1km: 25.6secs
280.0bhp 208.8kW 283.9PS
@ 6400rpm
274.5lbft 372.0Nm @ 3600rpm
180.2bhp/ton 177.2bhp/tonne
94.6bhp/L 70.5kW/L 95.9PS/L
58.1ft/sec 17.7m/sec
25.7mph 41.4kmh/1000rpm
17.0mpg 14.2mpgUS 16.6L/100km
Petrol 4-stroke piston
2960cc 181.0cu in turbocharged
Vee 6 fuel injection
Compression ratio: 8.5:1
Bore: 87.0mm 3.4in
Stroke: 83.0mm 3.3in
Valve type/No: Overhead 24
Transmission: Manual
No. of forward speeds: 5
Wheels driven: Rear
Springs F/R: Coil/Coil
Brake system: PA ABS
Brakes F/R: Disc/Disc
Steering: Rack & pinion PA
Wheelbase: 257.0cm 101.2in
Track F: 149.5cm 58.9in
Track R: 153.5cm 60.4in
Length: 452.5cm 178.1in
Width: 180.0cm 70.9in
Height: 125.5cm 49.4in
Kerb weight: 1580.0kg 3480.2lb
Fuel: 71.9L 15.8gal 19.0galUS

3241 Nissan

300ZX Turbo
1990 Japan
155.0mph 249.4kmh
0-50mph 80.5kmh: 5.0secs
0-60mph 96.5kmh: 6.5secs
0-1/4 mile: 15.0secs
300.0bhp 223.7kW 304.2PS
@ 6400rpm
283.0lbft 383.5Nm @ 3600rpm
193.1bhp/ton 189.9bhp/tonne
101.3bhp/L 75.6kW/L 102.8PS/L
58.1ft/sec 17.7m/sec
Petrol 4-stroke piston
2960cc 180.6cu in turbocharged
Vee 6 fuel injection
Compression ratio: 8.5:1
Bore: 87.0mm 3.4in
Stroke: 83.0mm 3.3in
Valve type/No: Overhead 24
Transmission: Manual
No. of forward speeds: 5
Wheels driven: Rear
Springs F/R: Coil/Coil
Brake system: PA ABS
Brakes F/R: Disc/Disc
Steering: Rack & pinion PA
Wheelbase: 245.1cm 96.5in
Track F: 149.6cm 58.9in
Track R: 155.4cm 61.2in
Length: 430.5cm 169.5in
Width: 179.1cm 70.5in
Height: 125.0cm 49.2in
Kerb weight: 1579.9kg 3480.0lb
Fuel: 70.8L 15.6gal 18.7galUS

3242 Nissan

Primera 1.6 LS
1990 UK
112.8mph 181.5kmh
0-50mph 80.5kmh: 8.7secs
0-60mph 96.5kmh: 12.4secs
0-1/4 mile: 18.3secs
0-1km: 34.2secs
95.0bhp 70.8kW 96.3PS
@ 6000rpm
98.9lbft 134.0Nm @ 4000rpm
84.7bhp/ton 83.3bhp/tonne
59.5bhp/L 44.4kW/L 60.3PS/L
56.5ft/sec 17.2m/sec
22.7mph 36.5kmh/1000rpm
29.2mpg 24.3mpgUS 9.7L/100km
Petrol 4-stroke piston
1597cc 97.0cu in
In-line 4 1 Carburettor
Compression ratio: 9.8:1
Bore: 76.0mm 3.0in
Stroke: 86.0mm 3.4in
Valve type/No: Overhead 16
Transmission: Manual
No. of forward speeds: 5
Wheels driven: Front
Springs F/R: Coil/Coil
Brake system: PA
Brakes F/R: Disc/Drum
Steering: Rack & pinion PA
Wheelbase: 255.0cm 100.4in
Track F: 147.0cm 57.9in
Track R: 146.0cm 57.5in
Length: 440.0cm 173.2in
Width: 170.0cm 66.9in
Height: 139.0cm 54.7in
Ground clearance: 17.9cm 7.0in
Kerb weight: 1140.0kg 2511.0lb
Fuel: 60.1L 13.2gal 15.9galUS

3243 Nissan

Skyline GT-R
1990 Japan
156.0mph 251.0kmh
0-60mph 96.5kmh: 5.6secs
0-1/4 mile: 13.6secs
276.0bhp 205.8kW 279.8PS
@ 6800rpm
260.0lbft 352.3Nm @ 4400rpm
196.3bhp/ton 193.0bhp/tonne
107.5bhp/L 80.1kW/L 109.0PS/L
54.8ft/sec 16.7m/sec
Petrol 4-stroke piston
2568cc 156.7cu in turbocharged
In-line 6 fuel injection
Compression ratio: 8.5:1
Bore: 86.0mm 3.4in
Stroke: 73.7mm 2.9in
Valve type/No: Overhead 24
Transmission: Manual
No. of forward speeds: 5
Wheels driven: 4-wheel drive
Springs F/R: Coil/Coil
Brake system: PA ABS
Brakes F/R: Disc/Disc
Steering: Rack & pinion PA
Wheelbase: 261.6cm 103.0in
Track F: 148.1cm 58.3in
Track R: 148.1cm 58.3in
Length: 454.7cm 179.0in
Width: 175.5cm 69.1in
Height: 134.1cm 52.8in
Kerb weight: 1430.1kg 3150.0lb
Fuel: 71.9L 15.8gal 19.0galUS

3244 Nissan

100NX
1991 Japan
116.0mph 186.6kmh
0-50mph 80.5kmh: 7.3secs
0-60mph 96.5kmh: 10.1secs
0-1/4 mile: 17.7secs
0-1km: 32.6secs
95.0bhp 70.8kW 96.3PS
@ 6000rpm

98.9lbft 134.0Nm @ 4000rpm
93.8bhp/ton 92.2bhp/tonne
59.5bhp/L 44.4kW/L 60.3PS/L
57.7ft/sec 17.6m/sec
21.1mph 33.9kmh/1000rpm
27.2mpg 22.6mpgUS 10.4L/100km
Petrol 4-stroke piston
1597cc 97.0cu in
In-line 4 1 Carburettor
Compression ratio: 9.5:1
Bore: 76.0mm 3.0in
Stroke: 88.0mm 3.5in
Valve type/No: Overhead 16
Transmission: Manual
No. of forward speeds: 5
Wheels driven: Front
Springs F/R: Coil/Coil
Brake system: PA
Brakes F/R: Disc/Drum
Steering: Rack & pinion PA
Wheelbase: 243.1cm 95.7in
Track F: 143.5cm 56.5in
Track R: 143.5cm 56.5in
Length: 414.0cm 163.0in
Width: 167.9cm 66.1in
Height: 131.1cm 51.6in
Kerb weight: 1030.0kg 2268.7lb
Fuel: 50.0L 11.0gal 13.2galUS

3245 Nissan

240SX
1991 Japan
115.0mph 185.0kmh
0-50mph 80.5kmh: 6.4secs
0-60mph 96.5kmh: 8.8secs
0-1/4 mile: 16.7secs
155.0bhp 115.6kW 157.1PS
@ 5600rpm
160.0lbft 216.8Nm @ 4400rpm
124.0bhp/ton 121.9bhp/tonne
64.9bhp/L 48.4kW/L 65.8PS/L
58.8ft/sec 17.9m/sec
28.6mpg 23.8mpgUS 9.9L/100km
Petrol 4-stroke piston
2389cc 145.8cu in
In-line 4 fuel injection
Compression ratio: 8.6:1
Bore: 89.0mm 3.5in
Stroke: 96.0mm 3.8in
Valve type/No: Overhead 16
Transmission: Manual
No. of forward speeds: 5
Wheels driven: Rear
Springs F/R: Coil/Coil
Brake system: PA ABS
Brakes F/R: Disc/Disc
Steering: Rack & pinion PA
Wheelbase: 247.4cm 97.4in
Track F: 146.6cm 57.7in
Track R: 146.1cm 57.5in
Length: 452.1cm 178.0in
Width: 168.9cm 66.5in
Height: 129.0cm 50.8in
Kerb weight: 1271.2kg 2800.0lb
Fuel: 60.2L 13.2gal 15.9galUS

3246 Nissan

300ZX Motor Sports International SR-71
1991 Japan
0-60mph 96.5kmh: 5.6secs
0-1/4 mile: 13.9secs
428.0bhp 319.2kW 433.9PS
@ 6700rpm
406.0lbft 550.1Nm @ 4750rpm
270.1bhp/ton 265.6bhp/tonne
144.6bhp/L 107.8kW/L 146.6PS/L
60.9ft/sec 18.5m/sec
Petrol 4-stroke piston
2960cc 180.6cu in turbocharged
Vee 6 fuel injection
Compression ratio: 8.5:1
Bore: 87.0mm 3.4in
Stroke: 83.0mm 3.3in
Valve type/No: Overhead 24
Transmission: Manual
No. of forward speeds: 5
Wheels driven: Rear
Springs F/R: Coil/Coil
Brake system: PA ABS
Brakes F/R: Disc/Disc
Steering: Rack & pinion PA
Wheelbase: 245.1cm 96.5in
Track F: 149.6cm 58.9in
Track R: 155.4cm 61.2in
Length: 430.5cm 169.5in
Width: 179.1cm 70.5in
Height: 125.0cm 49.2in
Kerb weight: 1611.7kg 3550.0lb

3247 Nissan

300ZX Turbo Millen Super GTZ
1991 Japan
166.0mph 267.1kmh
0-50mph 80.5kmh: 4.0secs
0-60mph 96.5kmh: 5.0secs
0-1/4 mile: 13.5secs
460.0bhp 343.0kW 466.4PS
@ 6500rpm
430.0lbft 582.7Nm @ 4750rpm
295.2bhp/ton 290.3bhp/tonne
155.4bhp/L 115.9kW/L 157.6PS/L
59.0ft/sec 18.0m/sec
19.2mpg 16.0mpgUS 14.7L/100km
Petrol 4-stroke piston
2960cc 180.6cu in turbocharged
Vee 6 fuel injection
Compression ratio: 10.1:1
Bore: 87.0mm 3.4in
Stroke: 83.0mm 3.3in
Valve type/No: Overhead 24
Transmission: Manual
No. of forward speeds: 5
Wheels driven: Rear
Springs F/R: Coil/Coil
Brake system: PA ABS
Brakes F/R: Disc/Disc
Steering: Rack & pinion PA
Wheelbase: 245.1cm 96.5in
Track F: 149.6cm 58.9in
Track R: 153.4cm 60.4in
Length: 430.5cm 169.5in
Width: 179.1cm 70.5in
Height: 125.5cm 49.4in
Ground clearance: 12.7cm 5.0in
Kerb weight: 1584.5kg 3490.0lb
Fuel: 70.8L 15.6gal 18.7galUS

3248 Nissan

300ZX Twin Turbo
1991 Japan
155.0mph 249.4kmh
0-50mph 80.5kmh: 5.0secs
0-60mph 96.5kmh: 6.5secs
0-1/4 mile: 15.0secs
300.0bhp 223.7kW 304.2PS
@ 6400rpm
283.0lbft 383.5Nm @ 3600rpm
193.4bhp/ton 190.2bhp/tonne
101.3bhp/L 75.6kW/L 102.8PS/L
58.1ft/sec 17.7m/sec
23.5mpg 19.6mpgUS 12.0L/100km
Petrol 4-stroke piston
2960cc 180.6cu in turbocharged
Vee 6 fuel injection
Compression ratio: 8.5:1
Bore: 87.0mm 3.4in
Stroke: 83.0mm 3.3in
Valve type/No: Overhead 24
Transmission: Manual
No. of forward speeds: 5
Wheels driven: Rear
Springs F/R: Coil/Coil
Brake system: PA ABS
Brakes F/R: Disc/Disc
Steering: Rack & pinion PA
Wheelbase: 245.1cm 96.5in
Track F: 149.6cm 58.9in
Track R: 155.4cm 61.2in
Length: 430.5cm 169.5in
Width: 179.1cm 70.5in
Height: 125.0cm 49.2in
Kerb weight: 1577.6kg 3475.0lb
Fuel: 70.8L 15.6gal 18.7galUS

3249 Nissan

NX2000
1991 Japan
130.0mph 209.2kmh
0-60mph 96.5kmh: 8.1secs
0-1/4 mile: 16.6secs
140.0bhp 104.4kW 141.9PS
@ 6400rpm
130.0lbft 176.2Nm @ 4800rpm
119.5bhp/ton 117.5bhp/tonne
70.1bhp/L 52.2kW/L 71.0PS/L
60.3ft/sec 18.3m/sec
36.0mpg 30.0mpgUS 7.8L/100km
Petrol 4-stroke piston
1998cc 121.9cu in
In-line 4 fuel injection
Compression ratio: 9.5:1
Bore: 86.0mm 3.4in
Stroke: 86.0mm 3.4in
Valve type/No: Overhead 16
Transmission: Manual
No. of forward speeds: 5
Wheels driven: Front
Springs F/R: Coil/Coil
Brake system: PA ABS
Brakes F/R: Disc/Disc
Steering: Rack & pinion PA
Wheelbase: 243.1cm 95.7in
Track F: 144.5cm 56.9in
Track R: 142.5cm 56.1in
Length: 412.5cm 162.4in
Width: 167.9cm 66.1in
Height: 131.6cm 51.8in
Kerb weight: 1191.7kg 2625.0lb
Fuel: 50.0L 11.0gal 13.2galUS

3250 Nissan

Primera 2.0 GSX
1991 UK
125.0mph 201.1kmh
0-50mph 80.5kmh: 6.4secs
0-60mph 96.5kmh: 8.9secs
0-1/4 mile: 16.9secs
0-1km: 31.1secs
121.0bhp 90.2kW 122.7PS
@ 6000rpm
124.7lbft 169.0Nm @ 6000rpm
100.4bhp/ton 98.8bhp/tonne
60.6bhp/L 45.2kW/L 61.4PS/L
56.5ft/sec 17.2m/sec
22.6mph 36.4kmh/1000rpm
26.0mpg 21.6mpgUS 10.9L/100km
Petrol 4-stroke piston
1998cc 122.0cu in
In-line 4 fuel injection
Compression ratio: 9.5:1
Bore: 86.0mm 3.4in
Stroke: 86.0mm 3.4in
Valve type/No: Overhead 16
Transmission: Manual
No. of forward speeds: 5
Wheels driven: Front
Springs F/R: Coil/Coil
Brake system: PA
Brakes F/R: Disc/Disc
Steering: Rack & pinion PA
Wheelbase: 254.8cm 100.3in
Track F: 146.8cm 57.8in
Track R: 145.8cm 57.4in
Length: 439.9cm 173.2in
Width: 169.9cm 66.9in
Height: 139.4cm 54.9in
Ground clearance: 14.0cm 5.5in
Kerb weight: 1225.0kg 2698.2lb
Fuel: 60.1L 13.2gal 15.9galUS

3251 Nissan

Primera 2.0E ZX
1991 UK
132.0mph 212.4kmh
0-50mph 80.5kmh: 6.5secs
0-60mph 96.5kmh: 8.7secs
0-1/4 mile: 17.9secs
0-1km: 30.7secs
150.0bhp 111.9kW 152.1PS
@ 6400rpm
133.6lbft 181.0Nm @ 4800rpm
120.1bhp/ton 118.1bhp/tonne
75.1bhp/L 56.0kW/L 76.1PS/L
60.3ft/sec 18.3m/sec
21.1mph 33.9kmh/1000rpm
26.8mpg 22.3mpgUS 10.5L/100km
Petrol 4-stroke piston
1998cc 122.0cu in
In-line 4 fuel injection
Compression ratio: 10.0:1
Bore: 86.0mm 3.4in
Stroke: 86.0mm 3.4in
Valve type/No: Overhead 16
Transmission: Manual
No. of forward speeds: 5
Wheels driven: Front
Springs F/R: Coil/Coil
Brake system: PA ABS
Brakes F/R: Disc/Disc
Steering: Rack & pinion PA
Wheelbase: 255.0cm 100.4in
Track F: 147.0cm 57.9in
Track R: 146.0cm 57.5in
Length: 440.0cm 173.2in
Width: 170.0cm 66.9in
Height: 139.5cm 54.9in
Ground clearance: 14.0cm 5.5in
Kerb weight: 1270.0kg 2797.4lb
Fuel: 60.1L 13.2gal 15.9galUS

3252 Nissan

Sentra SE-R
1991 Japan
125.0mph 201.1kmh
0-50mph 80.5kmh: 5.9secs
0-60mph 96.5kmh: 8.1secs
0-1/4 mile: 16.2secs
140.0bhp 104.4kW 141.9PS
@ 6400rpm
132.0lbft 178.9Nm @ 4800rpm
120.6bhp/ton 118.6bhp/tonne
70.1bhp/L 52.2kW/L 71.0PS/L
60.3ft/sec 18.3m/sec
19.2mpg 16.0mpgUS 14.7L/100km
Petrol 4-stroke piston
1998cc 121.9cu in
In-line 4 fuel injection
Compression ratio: 9.5:1
Bore: 86.0mm 3.4in
Stroke: 86.0mm 3.4in
Valve type/No: Overhead 16
Transmission: Manual
No. of forward speeds: 5
Wheels driven: Front
Springs F/R: Coil/Coil
Brake system: PA ABS
Brakes F/R: Disc/Disc
Steering: Rack & pinion PA
Wheelbase: 243.1cm 95.7in
Track F: 144.5cm 56.9in
Track R: 143.0cm 56.3in
Length: 432.6cm 170.3in
Width: 166.6cm 65.6in
Height: 136.9cm 53.9in
Ground clearance: 15.2cm 6.0in
Kerb weight: 1180.4kg 2600.0lb
Fuel: 50.0L 11.0gal 13.2galUS

3253 Nissan

Sunny 1.6 GS 5-door
1991 Japan
112.0mph 180.2kmh
0-50mph 80.5kmh: 7.5secs
0-60mph 96.5kmh: 10.5secs
0-1/4 mile: 17.9secs
0-1km: 32.9secs
95.0bhp 70.8kW 96.3PS
@ 6000rpm
98.9lbft 134.0Nm @ 4000rpm
91.1bhp/ton 89.6bhp/tonne
59.5bhp/L 44.4kW/L 60.3PS/L
53.8ft/sec 16.4m/sec
23.6mph 38.0kmh/1000rpm
31.6mpg 26.3mpgUS 8.9L/100km
Petrol 4-stroke piston
1597cc 97.0cu in
In-line 4 1 Carburettor
Compression ratio: 9.5:1
Bore: 74.0mm 2.9in
Stroke: 82.0mm 3.2in
Valve type/No: Overhead 16
Transmission: Manual
No. of forward speeds: 5
Wheels driven: Front
Springs F/R: Coil/Coil
Brake system: PA
Brakes F/R: Disc/Drum
Steering: Rack & pinion PA
Wheelbase: 242.8cm 95.6in
Length: 414.3cm 163.1in
Width: 166.9cm 65.7in
Height: 139.4cm 54.9in
Kerb weight: 1060.0kg 2334.8lb
Fuel: 50.0L 11.0gal 13.2galUS

3254 Nissan

200SX
1992 Japan
140.0mph 225.3kmh
0-50mph 80.5kmh: 5.1secs
0-60mph 96.5kmh: 6.8secs
0-1/4 mile: 15.3secs
0-1km: 27.8secs
164.0bhp 122.3kW 166.3PS
@ 6400rpm
163.0lbft 220.9Nm @ 4000rpm
133.6bhp/ton 131.4bhp/tonne
90.7bhp/L 67.6kW/L 91.9PS/L
58.8ft/sec 17.9m/sec
21.4mph 34.4kmh/1000rpm
19.7mpg 16.4mpgUS 14.3L/100km
Petrol 4-stroke piston
1809cc 110.4cu in turbocharged
In-line 4 fuel injection
Compression ratio: 8.5:1
Bore: 83.0mm 3.3in
Stroke: 84.0mm 3.3in

Valve type/No: Overhead 16
Transmission: Manual
No. of forward speeds: 5
Wheels driven: Rear
Springs F/R: Coil/Coil
Brake system: PA ABS
Brakes F/R: Disc/Disc
Steering: Rack & pinion PA
Wheelbase: 247.5cm 97.4in
Track F: 146.5cm 57.7in
Track R: 146.5cm 57.7in
Length: 453.5cm 178.5in
Width: 169.0cm 66.5in
Height: 129.0cm 50.8in
Kerb weight: 1248.0kg 2748.9lb
Fuel: 60.1L 13.2gal 15.9galUS

3255 Nissan

Sunny 2.0 GTi
1992 Japan
132.0mph 212.4kmh
0-50mph 80.5kmh: 5.7secs
0-60mph 96.5kmh: 7.5secs
0-1/4 mile: 16.0secs
0-1km: 29.1secs
143.0bhp 106.6kW 145.0PS
@ 6400rpm
131.0lbft 177.5Nm @ 4800rpm
130.9bhp/ton 128.7bhp/tonne
71.6bhp/L 53.4kW/L 72.6PS/L
60.3ft/sec 18.3m/sec
19.8mph 31.9kmh/1000rpm
27.8mpg 23.1mpgUS 10.2L/100km
Petrol 4-stroke piston
1998cc 121.9cu in
In-line 4 fuel injection
Compression ratio: 10.0:1
Bore: 86.0mm 3.4in
Stroke: 86.0mm 3.4in
Valve type/No: Overhead 16
Transmission: Manual
No. of forward speeds: 5
Wheels driven: Front
Springs F/R: Coil/Coil
Brake system: PA ABS
Brakes F/R: Disc/Disc
Steering: Rack & pinion PA
Wheelbase: 243.1cm 95.7in
Track F: 144.5cm 56.9in
Track R: 142.0cm 55.9in
Length: 397.5cm 156.5in
Width: 168.9cm 66.5in
Height: 139.4cm 54.9in
Ground clearance: 12.4cm 4.9in
Kerb weight: 1110.9kg 2447.0lb
Fuel: 50.0L 11.0gal 13.2galUS

3256 NSU

Prinz 34hp
1959 Germany
70.4mph 113.3kmh
0-50mph 80.5kmh: 16.5secs
0-60mph 96.5kmh: 26.5secs
0-1/4 mile: 22.5secs
34.0bhp 25.3kW 34.5PS
@ 5800rpm
30.4lbft 41.2Nm @ 3000rpm
69.2bhp/ton 68.1bhp/tonne
58.3bhp/L 43.5kW/L 59.1PS/L
41.9ft/sec 12.8m/sec
13.3mph 21.4kmh/1000rpm
Petrol 4-stroke piston
583cc 35.6cu in
In-line 2
Compression ratio: 7.5:1
Bore: 74.9mm 2.9in
Stroke: 66.0mm 2.6in
Valve type/No: Overhead 4
Transmission: Manual
No. of forward speeds: 4
Wheels driven: Rear
Wheelbase: 199.9cm 78.7in
Track F: 119.9cm 47.2in
Track R: 119.9cm 47.2in
Length: 315.0cm 124.0in
Width: 142.0cm 55.9in
Height: 135.1cm 53.2in
Kerb weight: 499.4kg 1100.0lb

3257 NSU

Prinz II
1959 Germany
64.0mph 103.0kmh
0-50mph 80.5kmh: 27.2secs
0-1/4 mile: 25.6secs
24.0bhp 17.9kW 24.3PS
@ 4800rpm
33.5lbft 45.4Nm @ 2300rpm
48.3bhp/ton 47.5bhp/tonne
41.2bhp/L 30.7kW/L 41.7PS/L
34.7ft/sec 10.6m/sec
13.1mph 21.1kmh/1000rpm
46.1mpg 38.4mpgUS 6.1L/100km
Petrol 4-stroke piston
583cc 35.6cu in
In-line 2
Compression ratio: 6.8:1
Bore: 75.0mm 2.9in
Stroke: 66.0mm 2.6in
Valve type/No: Overhead 4
Transmission: Manual
No. of forward speeds: 4
Wheels driven: Rear
Springs F/R: Coil/Coil
Brakes F/R: Drum/Drum
Wheelbase: 199.9cm 78.7in
Track F: 119.9cm 47.2in
Track R: 119.9cm 47.2in
Length: 312.4cm 123.0in
Width: 142.2cm 56.0in
Height: 137.2cm 54.0in
Ground clearance: 17.8cm 7.0in
Kerb weight: 505.3kg 1113.0lb
Fuel: 25.0L 5.5gal 6.6galUS

3258 NSU

Sport-Prinz
1960 Germany
76.0mph 122.3kmh
0-50mph 80.5kmh: 16.9secs
0-60mph 96.5kmh: 27.7secs
0-1/4 mile: 23.5secs
30.0bhp 22.4kW 30.4PS
@ 5500rpm
31.0lbft 42.0Nm @ 3000rpm
55.9bhp/ton 55.0bhp/tonne
51.5bhp/L 38.4kW/L 52.2PS/L
39.7ft/sec 12.1m/sec
12.8mph 20.6kmh/1000rpm
37.4mpg 31.1mpgUS 7.6L/100km
Petrol 4-stroke piston
583cc 35.6cu in
In-line 2
Compression ratio: 7.6:1
Bore: 75.0mm 2.9in
Stroke: 66.0mm 2.6in
Valve type/No: Overhead 4
Transmission: Manual
No. of forward speeds: 4
Wheels driven: Rear
Springs F/R: Coil/Coil
Brakes F/R: Drum/Drum
Wheelbase: 199.6cm 78.6in
Track F: 119.4cm 47.0in
Track R: 119.4cm 47.0in
Length: 356.9cm 140.5in
Width: 144.8cm 57.0in
Height: 124.5cm 49.0in
Ground clearance: 17.8cm 7.0in
Kerb weight: 545.7kg 1202.0lb
Fuel: 25.0L 5.5gal 6.6galUS

3259 NSU

Prinz 4
1962 Germany
73.5mph 118.3kmh
0-50mph 80.5kmh: 17.3secs
0-60mph 96.5kmh: 27.7secs
0-1/4 mile: 23.6secs
30.0bhp 22.4kW 30.4PS
@ 5500rpm
32.5lbft 44.0Nm @ 3250rpm
54.5bhp/ton 53.6bhp/tonne
50.2bhp/L 37.4kW/L 50.9PS/L
39.7ft/sec 12.1m/sec
12.2mph 19.6kmh/1000rpm
37.4mpg 31.1mpgUS 7.6L/100km
Petrol 4-stroke piston
598cc 36.5cu in
In-line 2 1 Carburettor
Compression ratio: 7.5:1
Bore: 76.0mm 3.0in
Stroke: 66.0mm 2.6in
Valve type/No: Overhead 4
Transmission: Manual
No. of forward speeds: 4
Wheels driven: Rear
Springs F/R: Coil/Gas
Brakes F/R: Drum/Drum
Steering: Rack & pinion
Wheelbase: 204.0cm 80.3in
Track F: 122.9cm 48.4in
Track R: 120.7cm 47.5in
Length: 344.2cm 135.5in
Width: 148.6cm 58.5in
Height: 135.9cm 53.5in
Ground clearance: 17.8cm 7.0in
Kerb weight: 559.3kg 1232.0lb
Fuel: 36.4L 8.0gal 9.6galUS

3260 NSU

Prinz 1000L
1965 Germany
80.0mph 128.7kmh
0-50mph 80.5kmh: 13.2secs
0-60mph 96.5kmh: 20.5secs
0-1/4 mile: 21.2secs
43.0bhp 32.1kW 43.6PS
@ 5500rpm
53.0lbft 71.8Nm @ 2000rpm
67.9bhp/ton 66.7bhp/tonne
43.2bhp/L 32.2kW/L 43.8PS/L
40.0ft/sec 12.2m/sec
15.5mph 24.9kmh/1000rpm
33.1mpg 27.6mpgUS 8.5L/100km
Petrol 4-stroke piston
996cc 60.8cu in
In-line 4 1 Carburettor
Compression ratio: 7.7:1
Bore: 69.0mm 2.7in
Stroke: 66.6mm 2.6in
Valve type/No: Overhead 8
Transmission: Manual
No. of forward speeds: 4
Wheels driven: Rear
Springs F/R: Coil/Coil
Brakes F/R: Disc/Drum
Steering: Rack & pinion
Wheelbase: 224.8cm 88.5in
Track F: 124.7cm 49.1in
Track R: 123.4cm 48.6in
Length: 379.2cm 149.3in
Width: 149.6cm 58.9in
Height: 136.4cm 53.7in
Ground clearance: 19.1cm 7.5in
Kerb weight: 644.2kg 1419.0lb
Fuel: 36.9L 8.1gal 9.7galUS

3261 NSU

Spider
1965 Germany
96.0mph 154.5kmh
0-60mph 96.5kmh: 14.2secs
0-1/4 mile: 21.8secs
58.0bhp 43.2kW 58.8PS
@ 5000rpm
52.0lbft 70.5Nm @ 2500rpm
83.8bhp/ton 82.4bhp/tonne
116.0bhp/L 86.5kW/L 117.6PS/L
27.0mpg 22.5mpgUS 10.5L/100km
Petrol Wankel rotary
500cc 30.5cu in
Rotary 1 1 Carburettor
Compression ratio: 8.6:1
Transmission: Manual
No. of forward speeds: 4
Wheels driven: Rear
Brakes F/R: Disc/Drum
Steering: Rack & pinion
Wheelbase: 201.9cm 79.5in
Length: 358.1cm 141.0in
Width: 152.4cm 60.0in
Height: 124.5cm 49.0in
Kerb weight: 703.7kg 1550.0lb
Fuel: 31.0L 6.8gal 8.2galUS

3262 NSU

Wankel Spider
1965 Germany
98.0mph 157.7kmh
0-50mph 80.5kmh: 12.2secs
0-60mph 96.5kmh: 16.7secs
0-1/4 mile: 20.5secs
50.0bhp 37.3kW 50.7PS
@ 5000rpm
52.0lbft 70.5Nm @ 2500rpm
72.7bhp/ton 71.5bhp/tonne
100.0bhp/L 74.6kW/L 101.4PS/L
16.2mph 26.1kmh/1000rpm
26.2mpg 21.8mpgUS 10.8L/100km
Petrol Wankel rotary
500cc 30.5cu in
Rotary 1 1 Carburettor
Compression ratio: 8.6:1
Valve type/No: Ports
Transmission: Manual
No. of forward speeds: 4
Wheels driven: Rear
Springs F/R: Coil/Coil
Brakes F/R: Disc/Drum
Steering: Rack & pinion
Wheelbase: 203.2cm 80.0in
Track F: 124.5cm 49.0in
Track R: 122.4cm 48.2in
Length: 357.4cm 140.7in
Width: 151.6cm 59.7in
Height: 126.2cm 49.7in
Ground clearance: 14.5cm 5.7in
Kerb weight: 699.2kg 1540.0lb
Fuel: 35.0L 7.7gal 9.2galUS

3263 NSU

Typ 110
1966 Germany
87.0mph 140.0kmh
0-50mph 80.5kmh: 12.3secs
0-60mph 96.5kmh: 18.4secs
0-1/4 mile: 21.0secs
0-1km: 40.1secs
53.0bhp 39.5kW 53.7PS
@ 5000rpm
58.0lbft 78.6Nm @ 2500rpm
77.1bhp/ton 75.8bhp/tonne
48.8bhp/L 36.4kW/L 49.5PS/L
36.1ft/sec 11.0m/sec
16.0mph 25.7kmh/1000rpm
26.9mpg 22.4mpgUS 10.5L/100km
Petrol 4-stroke piston
1085cc 66.2cu in
In-line 4 1 Carburettor
Compression ratio: 8.0:1
Bore: 72.0mm 2.8in
Stroke: 66.0mm 2.6in
Valve type/No: Overhead 8
Transmission: Manual
No. of forward speeds: 4
Wheels driven: Rear
Springs F/R: Coil/Coil
Brakes F/R: Disc/Drum
Steering: Rack & pinion
Wheelbase: 243.8cm 96.0in
Track F: 128.3cm 50.5in
Track R: 124.5cm 49.0in
Length: 400.1cm 157.5in
Width: 149.9cm 59.0in
Height: 138.4cm 54.5in
Ground clearance: 21.6cm 8.5in
Kerb weight: 699.2kg 1540.0lb
Fuel: 45.5L 10.0gal 12.0galUS

3264 NSU

Ro80
1968 Germany
108.0mph 173.8kmh
0-50mph 80.5kmh: 10.1secs
0-60mph 96.5kmh: 13.9secs
0-1/4 mile: 19.2secs
0-1km: 36.1secs
113.5bhp 84.6kW 115.1PS
@ 5500rpm
117.2lbft 158.8Nm @ 4500rpm
95.3bhp/ton 93.7bhp/tonne
114.1bhp/L 85.1kW/L 115.6PS/L
18.6mph 29.9kmh/1000rpm
18.2mpg 15.2mpgUS 15.5L/100km
Petrol Wankel rotary
995cc 60.7cu in
Rotary 2 2 Carburettor
Compression ratio: 9.0:1
Valve type/No: Ports
Transmission: Pre-selector
No. of forward speeds: 3
Wheels driven: Front
Brake system: PA
Brakes F/R: Disc/Disc
Steering: Rack & pinion PA
Wheelbase: 286.3cm 112.7in
Track F: 148.6cm 58.5in
Track R: 143.5cm 56.5in
Length: 482.6cm 190.0in
Width: 176.5cm 69.5in
Height: 141.0cm 55.5in
Ground clearance: 11.4cm 4.5in
Kerb weight: 1211.3kg 2668.0lb
Fuel: 81.9L 18.0gal 21.6galUS

3265 NSU

Super Prinz
1968 Germany
74.0mph 119.1kmh
0-50mph 80.5kmh: 21.1secs
0-60mph 96.5kmh: 35.7secs
0-1/4 mile: 24.9secs
0-1km: 47.5secs
30.0bhp 22.4kW 30.4PS

@ 5500rpm
32.5lbft 44.0Nm @ 3250rpm
54.0bhp/ton 53.1bhp/tonne
50.2bhp/L 37.4kW/L 50.9PS/L
39.7ft/sec 12.1m/sec
13.0mph 20.9kmh/1000rpm
34.6mpg 28.8mpgUS 8.2L/100km
Petrol 4-stroke piston
598cc 36.5cu in
In-line 2 1 Carburettor
Compression ratio: 7.5:1
Bore: 76.0mm 3.0in
Stroke: 66.0mm 2.6in
Valve type/No: Overhead 4
Transmission: Manual
No. of forward speeds: 4
Wheels driven: Rear
Springs F/R: Coil/Coil
Brakes F/R: Drum/Drum
Steering: Rack & pinion
Wheelbase: 204.0cm 80.3in
Track F: 122.9cm 48.4in
Track R: 119.9cm 47.2in
Length: 350.5cm 138.0in
Width: 148.8cm 58.6in
Height: 135.9cm 53.5in
Ground clearance: 17.8cm 7.0in
Kerb weight: 565.2kg 1245.0lb
Fuel: 36.9L 8.1gal 9.7galUS

3266 NSU

Ro80
1974 Germany
112.0mph 180.2kmh
0-50mph 80.5kmh: 9.6secs
0-60mph 96.5kmh: 13.1secs
0-1/4 mile: 19.1secs
0-1km: 35.0secs
115.0bhp 85.8kW 116.6PS
@ 5500rpm
121.0lbft 164.0Nm @ 4500rpm
95.8bhp/ton 94.2bhp/tonne
115.6bhp/L 86.2kW/L 117.2PS/L
18.6mph 29.9kmh/1000rpm
16.0mpg 13.3mpgUS 17.7L/100km
Petrol Wankel rotary
995cc 60.7cu in
Rotary 2 1 Carburettor
Compression ratio: 9.0:1
Valve type/No: Ports
Transmission: Pre-selector
No. of forward speeds: 3
Wheels driven: Front
Springs F/R: Coil/Coil
Brake system: PA
Brakes F/R: Disc/Disc
Steering: Rack & pinion PA
Wheelbase: 286.3cm 112.7in
Track F: 148.6cm 58.5in
Track R: 143.5cm 56.5in
Length: 482.6cm 190.0in
Width: 176.5cm 69.5in
Height: 141.0cm 55.5in
Ground clearance: 11.4cm 4.5in
Kerb weight: 1220.3kg 2688.0lb
Fuel: 81.9L 18.0gal 21.6galUS

3267 Ogle

1.5
1961 UK
93.0mph 149.6kmh
0-50mph 80.5kmh: 13.8secs
0-60mph 96.5kmh: 20.1secs
0-1/4 mile: 21.3secs
60.0bhp 44.7kW 60.8PS
@ 4800rpm
81.0lbft 109.8Nm @ 2400rpm
68.0bhp/ton 66.9bhp/tonne
40.3bhp/L 30.0kW/L 40.8PS/L
46.7ft/sec 14.2m/sec
18.0mph 29.0kmh/1000rpm
28.2mpg 23.5mpgUS 10.0L/100km
Petrol 4-stroke piston
1489cc 90.8cu in
In-line 4
Compression ratio: 8.3:1
Bore: 73.0mm 2.9in
Stroke: 88.9mm 3.5in
Valve type/No: Overhead 8
Transmission: Manual
No. of forward speeds: 4
Wheels driven: Rear
Springs F/R: Torsion bar/Coil
Brakes F/R: Drum/Drum
Wheelbase: 218.4cm 86.0in
Track F: 129.3cm 50.9in
Track R: 127.8cm 50.3in
Length: 419.1cm 165.0in
Width: 153.7cm 60.5in
Height: 134.6cm 53.0in
Ground clearance: 12.7cm 5.0in
Kerb weight: 896.6kg 1975.0lb
Fuel: 31.8L 7.0gal 8.4galUS

3268 Ogle

Austin Mini Cooper GT
1962 UK
99.0mph 159.3kmh
0-50mph 80.5kmh: 9.7secs
0-60mph 96.5kmh: 16.2secs
0-1/4 mile: 19.7secs
68.0bhp 50.7kW 68.9PS
@ 6000rpm
54.5lbft 73.8Nm @ 3600rpm
101.1bhp/ton 99.4bhp/tonne
68.2bhp/L 50.9kW/L 69.1PS/L
53.3ft/sec 16.3m/sec
14.9mph 24.0kmh/1000rpm
29.4mpg 24.5mpgUS 9.6L/100km
Petrol 4-stroke piston
997cc 60.8cu in
In-line 4 2 Carburettor
Compression ratio: 9.5:1
Bore: 62.4mm 2.5in
Stroke: 81.3mm 3.2in
Valve type/No: Overhead 8
Transmission: Manual
No. of forward speeds: 4
Wheels driven: Front
Springs F/R: Rubber/Rubber
Brakes F/R: Disc/Drum
Steering: Rack & pinion
Wheelbase: 203.2cm 80.0in
Track F: 118.1cm 46.5in
Track R: 116.6cm 45.9in
Length: 342.9cm 135.0in
Width: 147.3cm 58.0in
Height: 118.1cm 46.5in
Ground clearance: 15.2cm 6.0in
Kerb weight: 684.2kg 1507.0lb
Fuel: 47.8L 10.5gal 12.6galUS

3269 Oldsmobile

26.3hp Saloon
1935 USA
79.6mph 128.1kmh
0-50mph 80.5kmh: 16.2secs
0-60mph 96.5kmh: 22.4secs
20.0mpg 16.7mpgUS 14.1L/100km
Petrol 4-stroke piston
3496cc 213.3cu in
In-line 6
Bore: 85.8mm 3.4in
Stroke: 104.8mm 4.1in
Valve type/No: Side 12
Transmission: Manual
No. of forward speeds: 3
Wheels driven: Rear
Brakes F/R: Drum/Drum
Kerb weight: 1569.5kg 3457.0lb
Fuel: 54.6L 12.0gal 14.4galUS

3270 Oldsmobile

28.8hp Saloon
1936 USA
80.3mph 129.2kmh
0-50mph 80.5kmh: 15.4secs
0-60mph 96.5kmh: 21.7secs
15.0mpg 12.5mpgUS 18.8L/100km
Petrol 4-stroke piston
3940cc 240.4cu in
In-line 8
Bore: 76.2mm 3.0in
Stroke: 107.9mm 4.2in
Valve type/No: Side 16
Transmission: Manual
No. of forward speeds: 3
Wheels driven: Rear
Brakes F/R: Drum/Drum
Kerb weight: 1699.8kg 3744.0lb
Fuel: 66.0L 14.5gal 17.4galUS

3271 Oldsmobile

Super 88
1955 USA
101.0mph 162.5kmh
0-50mph 80.5kmh: 8.7secs
0-60mph 96.5kmh: 12.1secs
0-1/4 mile: 18.3secs
202.0bhp 150.6kW 204.8PS
@ 4000rpm
332.0lbft 449.9Nm @ 2400rpm
112.6bhp/ton 110.7bhp/tonne
38.0bhp/L 28.4kW/L 38.5PS/L
38.2ft/sec 11.6m/sec
15.0mph 24.1kmh/1000rpm
19.0mpg 15.8mpgUS 14.9L/100km
Petrol 4-stroke piston
5312cc 324.1cu in
Vee 8
Compression ratio: 8.5:1
Bore: 98.4mm 3.9in
Stroke: 87.3mm 3.4in
Valve type/No: Overhead 16
Transmission: Manual
No. of forward speeds: 4
Wheels driven: Rear
Springs F/R: Coil/Leaf
Brake system: PA
Brakes F/R: Drum/Drum
Wheelbase: 309.9cm 122.0in
Track F: 149.9cm 59.0in
Track R: 147.3cm 58.0in
Length: 515.6cm 203.0in
Width: 195.6cm 77.0in
Height: 152.4cm 60.0in
Ground clearance: 16.5cm 6.5in
Kerb weight: 1824.2kg 4018.0lb
Fuel: 77.3L 17.0gal 20.4galUS

3272 Oldsmobile

Super 88
1958 USA
115.0mph 185.0kmh
0-50mph 80.5kmh: 7.5secs
0-60mph 96.5kmh: 10.2secs
0-1/4 mile: 17.1secs
305.0bhp 227.4kW 309.2PS
@ 4600rpm
410.0lbft 555.6Nm @ 2800rpm
152.4bhp/ton 149.9bhp/tonne
50.2bhp/L 37.4kW/L 50.9PS/L
47.1ft/sec 14.4m/sec
24.6mph 39.6kmh/1000rpm
16.0mpg 13.3mpgUS 17.7L/100km
Petrol 4-stroke piston
6077cc 370.8cu in
Vee 8
Compression ratio: 8.4:1
Bore: 101.6mm 4.0in
Stroke: 93.7mm 3.7in
Valve type/No: Overhead 16
Transmission: Automatic
No. of forward speeds: 3
Wheels driven: Rear
Springs F/R: Coil/Leaf
Brake system: PA
Brakes F/R: Drum/Drum
Wheelbase: 309.9cm 122.0in
Track F: 149.9cm 59.0in
Track R: 147.3cm 58.0in
Length: 528.8cm 208.2in
Width: 199.9cm 78.7in
Height: 149.9cm 59.0in
Ground clearance: 17.0cm 6.7in
Kerb weight: 2034.8kg 4482.0lb
Fuel: 77.3L 17.0gal 20.4galUS

3273 Oldsmobile

F-85
1961 USA
102.0mph 164.1kmh
0-50mph 80.5kmh: 10.0secs
0-60mph 96.5kmh: 14.5secs
0-1/4 mile: 19.7secs
155.0bhp 115.6kW 157.1PS
@ 4800rpm
210.0lbft 284.6Nm @ 2800rpm
125.3bhp/ton 123.2bhp/tonne
43.9bhp/L 32.7kW/L 44.5PS/L
37.3ft/sec 11.4m/sec
21.8mph 35.1kmh/1000rpm
Petrol 4-stroke piston
3533cc 215.6cu in
Vee 8 1 Carburettor
Compression ratio: 8.8:1
Bore: 88.9mm 3.5in
Stroke: 71.1mm 2.8in
Valve type/No: Overhead 16
Transmission: Automatic
No. of forward speeds: 3
Wheels driven: Rear
Brakes F/R: Drum/Drum
Wheelbase: 284.5cm 112.0in
Track F: 142.2cm 56.0in
Track R: 142.2cm 56.0in
Length: 478.0cm 188.2in
Width: 181.9cm 71.6in
Height: 133.6cm 52.6in
Ground clearance: 14.0cm 5.5in
Kerb weight: 1257.6kg 2770.0lb

3274 Oldsmobile

F-85 Station Wagon
1961 USA
102.0mph 164.1kmh
0-50mph 80.5kmh: 10.3secs
0-60mph 96.5kmh: 14.2secs
0-1/4 mile: 19.5secs
155.0bhp 115.6kW 157.1PS
@ 4800rpm
210.0lbft 284.6Nm @ 3200rpm
119.8bhp/ton 117.8bhp/tonne
44.0bhp/L 32.8kW/L 44.6PS/L
37.3ft/sec 11.4m/sec
19.7mph 31.7kmh/1000rpm
20.8mpg 17.3mpgUS 13.6L/100km
Petrol 4-stroke piston
3525cc 215.1cu in
Vee 8 1 Carburettor
Compression ratio: 8.7:1
Bore: 88.9mm 3.5in
Stroke: 71.1mm 2.8in
Valve type/No: Overhead 16
Transmission: Manual
No. of forward speeds: 3
Wheels driven: Rear
Springs F/R: Coil/Coil
Brake system: PA
Brakes F/R: Drum/Drum
Wheelbase: 284.5cm 112.0in
Track F: 142.2cm 56.0in
Track R: 142.2cm 56.0in
Length: 478.0cm 188.2in
Width: 181.6cm 71.5in
Height: 137.9cm 54.3in
Ground clearance: 16.5cm 6.5in
Kerb weight: 1315.7kg 2898.0lb
Fuel: 61.4L 13.5gal 16.2galUS

3275 Oldsmobile

98 Holiday Sports Sedan
1962 USA
122.0mph 196.3kmh
0-50mph 80.5kmh: 7.1secs
0-60mph 96.5kmh: 9.4secs
0-1/4 mile: 17.2secs
330.0bhp 246.1kW 334.6PS
@ 4600rpm
440.0lbft 596.2Nm @ 2800rpm
159.6bhp/ton 157.0bhp/tonne
51.1bhp/L 38.1kW/L 51.8PS/L
47.1ft/sec 14.4m/sec
26.5mph 42.6kmh/1000rpm
Petrol 4-stroke piston
6457cc 394.0cu in
Vee 8
Compression ratio: 10.3:1
Bore: 104.6mm 4.1in
Stroke: 93.7mm 3.7in
Valve type/No: Overhead 16
Transmission: Manual
No. of forward speeds: 4
Wheels driven: Rear
Brake system: PA
Steering: PA
Wheelbase: 320.0cm 126.0in
Track F: 154.9cm 61.0in
Track R: 154.9cm 61.0in
Length: 558.8cm 220.0in
Width: 197.9cm 77.9in
Height: 143.8cm 56.6in
Ground clearance: 15.7cm 6.2in
Kerb weight: 2102.0kg 4630.0lb
Fuel: 75.7L 16.6gal 20.0galUS

3276 Oldsmobile

Dynamic 88 Celebrity Sedan
1962 USA
115.0mph 185.0kmh
0-50mph 80.5kmh: 8.9secs
0-60mph 96.5kmh: 12.8secs
0-1/4 mile: 17.8secs
280.0bhp 208.8kW 283.9PS
@ 4400rpm
430.0lbft 582.7Nm @ 2400rpm
148.6bhp/ton 146.1bhp/tonne
43.4bhp/L 32.3kW/L 44.0PS/L
45.1ft/sec 13.7m/sec
31.0mph 49.9kmh/1000rpm
Petrol 4-stroke piston
6457cc 394.0cu in
Vee 8 1 Carburettor
Compression ratio: 10.3:1

Bore: 104.9mm 4.1in
Stroke: 93.7mm 3.7in
Valve type/No: Overhead 16
Transmission: Automatic
No. of forward speeds: 3
Wheels driven: Rear
Brake system: PA
Steering: PA
Wheelbase: 312.4cm 123.0in
Track F: 154.9cm 61.0in
Track R: 154.9cm 61.0in
Length: 543.3cm 213.9in
Width: 197.9cm 77.9in
Height: 141.7cm 55.8in
Ground clearance: 15.0cm 5.9in
Kerb weight: 1915.9kg 4220.0lb
Fuel: 75.7L 16.6gal 20.0galUS

3277 Oldsmobile

F-85 Jetfire Sports Coupe
1962 USA
107.0mph 172.2kmh
0-50mph 80.5kmh: 6.1secs
0-60mph 96.5kmh: 8.5secs
0-1/4 mile: 16.5secs
215.0bhp 160.3kW 218.0PS
@ 4600rpm
300.0lbft 406.5Nm @ 3200rpm
168.4bhp/ton 165.6bhp/tonne
60.9bhp/L 45.4kW/L 61.7PS/L
35.8ft/sec 10.9m/sec
21.0mph 33.8kmh/1000rpm
Petrol 4-stroke piston
3531cc 215.4cu in turbocharged
Vee 8 1 Carburettor
Compression ratio: 10.2:1
Bore: 88.9mm 3.5in
Stroke: 71.1mm 2.8in
Valve type/No: Overhead 16
Transmission: Automatic
No. of forward speeds: 3
Wheels driven: Rear
Brake system: PA
Steering: PA
Wheelbase: 284.5cm 112.0in
Track F: 142.2cm 56.0in
Track R: 142.2cm 56.0in
Length: 478.0cm 188.2in
Width: 181.9cm 71.6in
Height: 132.8cm 52.3in
Ground clearance: 14.0cm 5.5in
Kerb weight: 1298.4kg 2860.0lb
Fuel: 60.6L 13.3gal 16.0galUS

3278 Oldsmobile

F-85 V8
1962 USA
102.0mph 164.1kmh
0-50mph 80.5kmh: 10.0secs
0-60mph 96.5kmh: 14.0secs
0-1/4 mile: 19.4secs
155.0bhp 115.6kW 157.1PS
@ 4800rpm
210.0lbft 284.6Nm @ 3200rpm
126.2bhp/ton 124.1bhp/tonne
43.9bhp/L 32.7kW/L 44.5PS/L
37.3ft/sec 11.4m/sec
21.8mph 35.1kmh/1000rpm
Petrol 4-stroke piston
3533cc 215.6cu in
Vee 8 1 Carburettor
Compression ratio: 8.8:1
Bore: 88.9mm 3.5in
Stroke: 71.1mm 2.8in
Valve type/No: Overhead 16
Transmission: Automatic
No. of forward speeds: 3
Wheels driven: Rear
Brakes F/R: Drum/Drum
Wheelbase: 284.5cm 112.0in
Track F: 142.2cm 56.0in
Track R: 142.2cm 56.0in
Length: 478.0cm 188.2in
Width: 181.9cm 71.6in
Height: 133.9cm 52.7in
Ground clearance: 14.0cm 5.5in
Kerb weight: 1248.5kg 2750.0lb

3279 Oldsmobile

F-85 Jetfire
1963 USA
100.0mph 160.9kmh
0-50mph 80.5kmh: 7.0secs
0-60mph 96.5kmh: 9.8secs
0-1/4 mile: 17.1secs
215.0bhp 160.3kW 218.0PS
@ 4600rpm
300.0lbft 406.5Nm @ 3200rpm
164.4bhp/ton 161.6bhp/tonne
60.9bhp/L 45.4kW/L 61.7PS/L
35.8ft/sec 10.9m/sec
21.0mph 33.8kmh/1000rpm
Petrol 4-stroke piston
3531cc 215.4cu in supercharged
Vee 8 1 Carburettor
Compression ratio: 10.3:1
Bore: 88.9mm 3.5in
Stroke: 71.1mm 2.8in
Valve type/No: Overhead 16
Transmission: Manual
No. of forward speeds: 4
Wheels driven: Rear
Brake system: PA
Brakes F/R: Drum/Drum
Steering: PA
Wheelbase: 284.5cm 112.0in
Track F: 142.2cm 56.0in
Track R: 142.2cm 56.0in
Length: 488.2cm 192.2in
Width: 187.2cm 73.7in
Height: 133.6cm 52.6in
Ground clearance: 13.7cm 5.4in
Kerb weight: 1330.2kg 2930.0lb
Fuel: 60.6L 13.3gal 16.0galUS

3280 Oldsmobile

Starfire
1963 USA
112.0mph 180.2kmh
0-50mph 80.5kmh: 6.7secs
0-60mph 96.5kmh: 8.5secs
0-1/4 mile: 17.2secs
345.0bhp 257.3kW 349.8PS
@ 4800rpm
440.0lbft 596.2Nm @ 3200rpm
178.5bhp/ton 175.5bhp/tonne
53.4bhp/L 39.8kW/L 54.2PS/L
49.2ft/sec 15.0m/sec
23.2mph 37.3kmh/1000rpm
Petrol 4-stroke piston
6457cc 394.0cu in
Vee 8 1 Carburettor
Compression ratio: 10.5:1
Bore: 104.6mm 4.1in
Stroke: 93.7mm 3.7in
Valve type/No: Overhead 16
Transmission: Automatic
No. of forward speeds: 3
Wheels driven: Rear
Brake system: PA
Steering: PA
Wheelbase: 312.4cm 123.0in
Track F: 158.0cm 62.2in
Track R: 154.9cm 61.0in
Length: 544.8cm 214.5in
Width: 197.9cm 77.9in
Height: 139.7cm 55.0in
Ground clearance: 15.0cm 5.9in
Kerb weight: 1965.8kg 4330.0lb
Fuel: 79.5L 17.5gal 21.0galUS

3281 Oldsmobile

Cutlass 442
1964 USA
120.0mph 193.1kmh
0-50mph 80.5kmh: 5.7secs
0-60mph 96.5kmh: 7.4secs
0-1/4 mile: 15.6secs
310.0bhp 231.2kW 314.3PS
@ 5200rpm
355.0lbft 481.0Nm @ 3600rpm
57.3bhp/L 42.7kW/L 58.1PS/L
24.0mph 38.6kmh/1000rpm
Petrol 4-stroke piston
5408cc 330.0cu in
Vee 8
Valve type/No: Overhead 16
Transmission: Manual
No. of forward speeds: 4
Wheels driven: Rear
Wheelbase: 292.1cm 115.0in
Track F: 147.3cm 58.0in
Track R: 147.3cm 58.0in
Length: 515.6cm 203.0in

3282 Oldsmobile

F-85 Cutlass Holiday
1964 USA
111.0mph 178.6kmh
0-50mph 80.5kmh: 7.2secs
0-60mph 96.5kmh: 9.4secs
0-1/4 mile: 16.9secs
290.0bhp 216.2kW 294.0PS
@ 4800rpm
355.0lbft 481.0Nm @ 2800rpm
196.9bhp/ton 193.6bhp/tonne
53.6bhp/L 40.0kW/L 54.4PS/L
45.2ft/sec 13.8m/sec
24.1mph 38.8kmh/1000rpm
Petrol 4-stroke piston
5408cc 330.0cu in
Vee 8 1 Carburettor
Compression ratio: 10.3:1
Bore: 100.0mm 3.9in
Stroke: 86.0mm 3.4in
Valve type/No: Overhead 16
Transmission: Automatic
No. of forward speeds: 2
Wheels driven: Rear
Brake system: PA
Steering: PA
Wheelbase: 292.1cm 115.0in
Track F: 147.3cm 58.0in
Track R: 147.3cm 58.0in
Length: 515.6cm 203.0in
Width: 187.5cm 73.8in
Height: 136.4cm 53.7in
Ground clearance: 14.7cm 5.8in
Kerb weight: 1497.7kg 3299.0lb
Fuel: 75.7L 16.6gal 20.0galUS

3283 Oldsmobile

Jetstar I
1964 USA
117.0mph 188.3kmh
0-50mph 80.5kmh: 5.8secs
0-60mph 96.5kmh: 7.5secs
0-1/4 mile: 16.3secs
345.0bhp 257.3kW 349.8PS
@ 4800rpm
440.0lbft 596.2Nm @ 3200rpm
174.0bhp/ton 171.1bhp/tonne
53.4bhp/L 39.8kW/L 54.2PS/L
49.2ft/sec 15.0m/sec
23.4mph 37.7kmh/1000rpm
Petrol 4-stroke piston
6457cc 394.0cu in
Vee 8 1 Carburettor
Compression ratio: 10.5:1
Bore: 104.8mm 4.1in
Stroke: 93.7mm 3.7in
Valve type/No: Overhead 16
Transmission: Automatic
No. of forward speeds: 3
Wheels driven: Rear
Brake system: PA
Steering: PA
Wheelbase: 312.4cm 123.0in
Track F: 158.0cm 62.2in
Track R: 155.2cm 61.1in
Length: 546.9cm 215.3in
Width: 197.6cm 77.8in
Height: 137.7cm 54.2in
Ground clearance: 12.4cm 4.9in
Kerb weight: 2015.8kg 4440.0lb
Fuel: 79.5L 17.5gal 21.0galUS

3284 Oldsmobile

Cutlass Holiday 442
1965 USA
118.0mph 189.9kmh
0-50mph 80.5kmh: 6.2secs
0-60mph 96.5kmh: 7.8secs
0-1/4 mile: 15.5secs
345.0bhp 257.3kW 349.8PS
@ 4800rpm
440.0lbft 596.2Nm @ 3200rpm
217.1bhp/ton 213.5bhp/tonne
52.6bhp/L 39.2kW/L 53.4PS/L
53.1ft/sec 16.2m/sec
23.5mph 37.8kmh/1000rpm
Petrol 4-stroke piston
6555cc 399.9cu in
Vee 8 1 Carburettor
Compression ratio: 10.3:1
Bore: 101.6mm 4.0in
Stroke: 101.0mm 4.0in
Valve type/No: Overhead 16
Transmission: Automatic
No. of forward speeds: 2
Wheels driven: Rear
Brakes F/R: Drum/Drum
Wheelbase: 292.1cm 115.0in
Track F: 147.3cm 58.0in
Track R: 147.3cm 58.0in
Length: 518.9cm 204.3in
Width: 189.0cm 74.4in
Height: 137.2cm 54.0in
Ground clearance: 14.7cm 5.8in
Kerb weight: 1616.2kg 3560.0lb
Fuel: 75.7L 16.6gal 20.0galUS

3285 Oldsmobile

Dynamic Delta 88 Holiday
1965 USA
110.0mph 177.0kmh
0-50mph 80.5kmh: 7.8secs
0-60mph 96.5kmh: 9.8secs
0-1/4 mile: 17.1secs
310.0bhp 231.2kW 314.3PS
@ 4400rpm
450.0lbft 609.8Nm @ 2400rpm
167.3bhp/ton 164.5bhp/tonne
44.5bhp/L 33.2kW/L 45.1PS/L
48.6ft/sec 14.8m/sec
26.1mph 42.0kmh/1000rpm
Petrol 4-stroke piston
6965cc 424.9cu in
Vee 8 1 Carburettor
Compression ratio: 10.3:1
Bore: 104.8mm 4.1in
Stroke: 101.0mm 4.0in
Valve type/No: Overhead 16
Transmission: Automatic
No. of forward speeds: 3
Wheels driven: Rear
Brake system: PA
Brakes F/R: Drum/Drum
Steering: PA
Wheelbase: 312.4cm 123.0in
Track F: 158.8cm 62.5in
Track R: 160.0cm 63.0in
Length: 550.9cm 216.9in
Width: 203.2cm 80.0in
Height: 141.0cm 55.5in
Ground clearance: 14.7cm 5.8in
Kerb weight: 1884.1kg 4150.0lb
Fuel: 94.6L 20.8gal 25.0galUS

3286 Oldsmobile

Toronado
1965 USA
124.0mph 199.5kmh
0-50mph 80.5kmh: 7.1secs
0-60mph 96.5kmh: 9.9secs
0-1/4 mile: 17.8secs
385.0bhp 287.1kW 390.3PS
@ 4800rpm
475.0lbft 643.6Nm @ 3200rpm
185.3bhp/ton 182.2bhp/tonne
55.3bhp/L 41.2kW/L 56.0PS/L
53.1ft/sec 16.2m/sec
25.8mph 41.5kmh/1000rpm
Petrol 4-stroke piston
6965cc 424.9cu in
Vee 8 1 Carburettor
Compression ratio: 10.5:1
Bore: 105.0mm 4.1in
Stroke: 101.0mm 4.0in
Valve type/No: Overhead 16
Transmission: Automatic
No. of forward speeds: 3
Wheels driven: Front
Springs F/R: Torsion bar/Leaf
Brakes F/R: Drum/Drum
Steering: PA
Wheelbase: 302.3cm 119.0in
Track F: 161.3cm 63.5in
Track R: 160.0cm 63.0in
Length: 535.9cm 211.0in
Width: 199.4cm 78.5in
Height: 134.1cm 52.8in
Ground clearance: 11.9cm 4.7in
Kerb weight: 2113.4kg 4655.0lb
Fuel: 90.8L 20.0gal 24.0galUS

3287 Oldsmobile

Cutlass 442
1966 USA
121.0mph 194.7kmh
0-50mph 80.5kmh: 4.7secs
0-60mph 96.5kmh: 6.3secs
0-1/4 mile: 14.8secs
360.0bhp 268.4kW 365.0PS
@ 5000rpm
440.0lbft 596.2Nm @ 3600rpm
222.8bhp/ton 219.0bhp/tonne
54.9bhp/L 40.9kW/L 55.7PS/L
55.3ft/sec 16.8m/sec
21.6mph 34.8kmh/1000rpm
Petrol 4-stroke piston
6555cc 399.9cu in
Vee 8 3 Carburettor
Compression ratio: 10.3:1
Bore: 101.6mm 4.0in

Stroke: 101.0mm 4.0in
Valve type/No: Overhead 16
Transmission: Manual
No. of forward speeds: 4
Wheels driven: Rear
Springs F/R: Coil/Coil
Brake system: PA
Brakes F/R: Drum/Drum
Steering: Recirculating ball PA
Wheelbase: 292.1cm 115.0in
Track F: 147.3cm 58.0in
Track R: 147.3cm 58.0in
Length: 518.7cm 204.2in
Width: 191.5cm 75.4in
Height: 136.1cm 53.6in
Ground clearance: 18.3cm 7.2in
Kerb weight: 1643.5kg 3620.0lb
Fuel: 75.7L 16.6gal 20.0galUS

3288 Oldsmobile

Toronado
1966 USA
127.0mph 204.3kmh
0-50mph 80.5kmh: 6.7secs
0-60mph 96.5kmh: 8.7secs
0-1/4 mile: 16.9secs
0-1km: 30.0secs
385.0bhp 287.1kW 390.3PS
@ 4800rpm
475.0lbft 643.6Nm @ 3200rpm
188.7bhp/ton 185.6bhp/tonne
55.3bhp/L 41.2kW/L 56.0PS/L
53.1ft/sec 16.2m/sec
25.8mph 41.5kmh/1000rpm
11.8mpg 9.8mpgUS 23.9L/100km
Petrol 4-stroke piston
6965cc 424.9cu in
Vee 8 1 Carburettor
Compression ratio: 10.5:1
Bore: 104.8mm 4.1in
Stroke: 101.0mm 4.0in
Valve type/No: Overhead 16
Transmission: Automatic
No. of forward speeds: 3
Wheels driven: Rear
Springs F/R: Torsion bar/Leaf
Brake system: PA
Brakes F/R: Drum/Drum
Steering: Recirculating ball PA
Wheelbase: 302.3cm 119.0in
Track F: 161.3cm 63.5in
Track R: 160.0cm 63.0in
Length: 535.9cm 211.0in
Width: 194.3cm 76.5in
Height: 134.6cm 53.0in
Ground clearance: 17.8cm 7.0in
Kerb weight: 2074.8kg 4570.0lb
Fuel: 91.0L 20.0gal 24.0galUS

3289 Oldsmobile

F-85 Cutlass Cruiser
1967 USA
130.0mph 209.2kmh
0-50mph 80.5kmh: 6.3secs
0-60mph 96.5kmh: 8.2secs
0-1/4 mile: 16.0secs
300.0bhp 223.7kW 304.2PS
@ 4600rpm
425.0lbft 575.9Nm @ 3000rpm
180.2bhp/ton 177.2bhp/tonne
45.8bhp/L 34.2kW/L 46.5PS/L
50.9ft/sec 15.5m/sec
31.5mph 50.7kmh/1000rpm
Petrol 4-stroke piston
6545cc 399.3cu in
Vee 8 1 Carburettor
Compression ratio: 10.5:1
Bore: 101.6mm 4.0in
Stroke: 101.0mm 4.0in
Valve type/No: Overhead 16
Transmission: Automatic
No. of forward speeds: 3
Wheels driven: Rear
Springs F/R: Coil/Coil
Brake system: PA
Brakes F/R: Drum/Drum
Steering: Recirculating ball PA
Wheelbase: 292.1cm 115.0in
Track F: 147.3cm 58.0in
Track R: 147.3cm 58.0in
Length: 518.7cm 204.2in
Width: 193.0cm 76.0in
Height: 138.2cm 54.4in
Ground clearance: 12.2cm 4.8in
Kerb weight: 1693.4kg 3730.0lb
Fuel: 75.7L 16.6gal 20.0galUS

3290 Oldsmobile

4-4-2
1968 USA
115.0mph 185.0kmh
0-50mph 80.5kmh: 5.5secs
0-60mph 96.5kmh: 7.0secs
0-1/4 mile: 15.1secs
350.0bhp 261.0kW 354.8PS
@ 4800rpm
440.0lbft 596.2Nm @ 3200rpm
210.7bhp/ton 207.2bhp/tonne
53.4bhp/L 39.8kW/L 54.1PS/L
56.7ft/sec 17.3m/sec
22.6mph 36.4kmh/1000rpm
Petrol 4-stroke piston
6555cc 399.9cu in
Vee 8 1 Carburettor
Compression ratio: 10.5:1
Bore: 98.3mm 3.9in
Stroke: 108.0mm 4.2in
Valve type/No: Overhead 16
Transmission: Automatic
No. of forward speeds: 3
Wheels driven: Rear
Springs F/R: Coil/Coil
Brake system: PA
Brakes F/R: Disc/Drum
Steering: Recirculating ball PA
Wheelbase: 284.5cm 112.0in
Track F: 149.9cm 59.0in
Track R: 149.9cm 59.0in
Length: 512.1cm 201.6in
Width: 194.6cm 76.6in
Height: 134.1cm 52.8in
Kerb weight: 1688.9kg 3720.0lb
Fuel: 75.7L 16.6gal 20.0galUS

3291 Oldsmobile

Delmont
1968 USA
120.0mph 193.1kmh
0-50mph 80.5kmh: 7.3secs
0-60mph 96.5kmh: 9.7secs
0-1/4 mile: 17.2secs
310.0bhp 231.2kW 314.3PS
@ 4200rpm
490.0lbft 664.0Nm @ 2400rpm
167.1bhp/ton 164.3bhp/tonne
41.6bhp/L 31.0kW/L 42.1PS/L
49.6ft/sec 15.1m/sec
32.1mph 51.6kmh/1000rpm
Petrol 4-stroke piston
7456cc 454.9cu in
Vee 8 1 Carburettor
Compression ratio: 9.0:1
Bore: 104.8mm 4.1in
Stroke: 108.0mm 4.2in
Valve type/No: Overhead 16
Transmission: Automatic
No. of forward speeds: 3
Wheels driven: Rear
Springs F/R: Coil/Coil
Brake system: PA
Brakes F/R: Drum/Drum
Steering: Recirculating ball PA
Wheelbase: 312.4cm 123.0in
Track F: 158.8cm 62.5in
Track R: 160.0cm 63.0in
Length: 553.2cm 217.8in
Width: 201.4cm 79.3in
Height: 141.0cm 55.5in
Kerb weight: 1886.8kg 4156.0lb
Fuel: 75.7L 16.6gal 20.0galUS

3292 Oldsmobile

Toronado
1968 USA
123.0mph 197.9kmh
0-50mph 80.5kmh: 6.3secs
0-60mph 96.5kmh: 8.0secs
0-1/4 mile: 16.3secs
400.0bhp 298.3kW 405.5PS
@ 4800rpm
500.0lbft 677.5Nm @ 3200rpm
192.3bhp/ton 189.1bhp/tonne
53.6bhp/L 40.0kW/L 54.4PS/L
56.7ft/sec 17.3m/sec
24.6mph 39.6kmh/1000rpm
Petrol 4-stroke piston
7456cc 454.9cu in
Vee 8 1 Carburettor
Compression ratio: 10.3:1
Bore: 104.8mm 4.1in
Stroke: 108.0mm 4.2in
Valve type/No: Overhead 16
Transmission: Automatic
No. of forward speeds: 3
Wheels driven: Front
Springs F/R: Torsion bar/Leaf
Brake system: PA
Brakes F/R: Disc/Drum
Steering: Recirculating ball PA
Wheelbase: 302.3cm 119.0in
Track F: 161.3cm 63.5in
Track R: 160.0cm 63.0in
Length: 537.0cm 211.4in
Width: 194.1cm 76.4in
Height: 134.1cm 52.8in
Kerb weight: 2115.6kg 4660.0lb
Fuel: 90.8L 20.0gal 24.0galUS

3293 Oldsmobile

442 Hurst
1969 USA
132.0mph 212.4kmh
0-50mph 80.5kmh: 5.0secs
0-60mph 96.5kmh: 6.2secs
0-1/4 mile: 14.1secs
380.0bhp 283.4kW 385.3PS
@ 5000rpm
500.0lbft 677.5Nm @ 3200rpm
219.1bhp/ton 215.4bhp/tonne
51.0bhp/L 38.0kW/L 51.7PS/L
59.0ft/sec 18.0m/sec
21.7mph 34.9kmh/1000rpm
Petrol 4-stroke piston
7456cc 454.9cu in
Vee 8 1 Carburettor
Compression ratio: 10.5:1
Bore: 104.8mm 4.1in
Stroke: 108.0mm 4.2in
Valve type/No: Overhead 16
Transmission: Automatic
No. of forward speeds: 3
Wheels driven: Rear
Springs F/R: Coil/Coil
Brake system: PA
Brakes F/R: Disc/Drum
Steering: Recirculating ball PA
Wheelbase: 284.5cm 112.0in
Track F: 154.9cm 61.0in
Track R: 152.4cm 60.0in
Length: 513.1cm 202.0in
Width: 193.0cm 76.0in
Height: 134.6cm 53.0in
Kerb weight: 1763.8kg 3885.0lb
Fuel: 75.7L 16.6gal 20.0galUS

3294 Oldsmobile

88 Delta Royale
1969 USA
118.0mph 189.9kmh
0-50mph 80.5kmh: 7.4secs
0-60mph 96.5kmh: 9.4secs
0-1/4 mile: 16.6secs
365.0bhp 272.2kW 370.1PS
@ 4600rpm
510.0lbft 691.1Nm @ 3000rpm
187.1bhp/ton 184.0bhp/tonne
48.9bhp/L 36.5kW/L 49.6PS/L
54.3ft/sec 16.6m/sec
28.9mph 46.5kmh/1000rpm
Petrol 4-stroke piston
7456cc 454.9cu in
Vee 8 1 Carburettor
Compression ratio: 10.3:1
Bore: 104.8mm 4.1in
Stroke: 108.0mm 4.2in
Valve type/No: Overhead 16
Transmission: Automatic
No. of forward speeds: 3
Wheels driven: Rear
Springs F/R: Coil/Coil
Brake system: PA
Brakes F/R: Drum/Drum
Steering: Recirculating ball PA
Wheelbase: 315.0cm 124.0in
Track F: 160.0cm 63.0in
Track R: 160.0cm 63.0in
Length: 556.3cm 219.0in
Width: 203.2cm 80.0in
Height: 139.7cm 55.0in
Kerb weight: 1984.0kg 4370.0lb
Fuel: 94.6L 20.8gal 25.0galUS

3295 Oldsmobile

Cutlass W-31
1969 USA
128.0mph 206.0kmh
0-50mph 80.5kmh: 5.2secs
0-60mph 96.5kmh: 6.6secs
0-1/4 mile: 14.9secs
325.0bhp 242.3kW 329.5PS
@ 5400rpm
360.0lbft 487.8Nm @ 3600rpm
200.0bhp/ton 196.7bhp/tonne
56.7bhp/L 42.3kW/L 57.5PS/L
50.8ft/sec 15.5m/sec
19.3mph 31.1kmh/1000rpm
Petrol 4-stroke piston
5735cc 349.9cu in
Vee 8 1 Carburettor
Compression ratio: 10.5:1
Bore: 103.1mm 4.1in
Stroke: 86.1mm 3.4in
Valve type/No: Overhead 16
Transmission: Automatic
No. of forward speeds: 3
Wheels driven: Rear
Springs F/R: Coil/Coil
Brakes F/R: Disc/Drum
Steering: Recirculating ball PA
Wheelbase: 284.5cm 112.0in
Track F: 149.9cm 59.0in
Track R: 149.9cm 59.0in
Length: 512.8cm 201.9in
Width: 193.5cm 76.2in
Height: 134.1cm 52.8in
Kerb weight: 1652.6kg 3640.0lb
Fuel: 75.7L 16.6gal 20.0galUS

3296 Oldsmobile

4-4-2 W30
1970 USA
116.0mph 186.6kmh
0-50mph 80.5kmh: 4.5secs
0-60mph 96.5kmh: 5.7secs
0-1/4 mile: 14.4secs
370.0bhp 275.9kW 375.1PS
@ 5200rpm
500.0lbft 677.5Nm @ 3600rpm
220.7bhp/ton 217.0bhp/tonne
49.6bhp/L 37.0kW/L 50.3PS/L
61.4ft/sec 18.7m/sec
21.7mph 34.9kmh/1000rpm
14.7mpg 12.2mpgUS 19.3L/100km
Petrol 4-stroke piston
7456cc 454.9cu in
Vee 8 1 Carburettor
Compression ratio: 10.5:1
Bore: 104.8mm 4.1in
Stroke: 108.0mm 4.2in
Valve type/No: Overhead 16
Transmission: Automatic
No. of forward speeds: 3
Wheels driven: Rear
Springs F/R: Coil/Coil
Brake system: PA
Brakes F/R: Disc/Drum
Steering: Recirculating ball PA
Wheelbase: 284.5cm 112.0in
Track F: 149.9cm 59.0in
Track R: 149.9cm 59.0in
Length: 516.1cm 203.2in
Width: 193.5cm 76.2in
Height: 134.1cm 52.8in
Kerb weight: 1704.8kg 3755.0lb
Fuel: 75.7L 16.6gal 20.0galUS

3297 Oldsmobile

Rallye 350
1970 USA
122.0mph 196.3kmh
0-50mph 80.5kmh: 5.2secs
0-60mph 96.5kmh: 7.0secs
0-1/4 mile: 15.3secs
310.0bhp 231.2kW 314.3PS
@ 4800rpm
390.0lbft 528.5Nm @ 3200rpm
185.4bhp/ton 182.3bhp/tonne
54.0bhp/L 40.3kW/L 54.8PS/L
45.2ft/sec 13.8m/sec
22.2mph 35.7kmh/1000rpm
16.1mpg 13.4mpgUS 17.6L/100km
Petrol 4-stroke piston
5735cc 349.9cu in
Vee 8 1 Carburettor
Compression ratio: 10.3:1
Bore: 103.0mm 4.1in
Stroke: 86.0mm 3.4in
Valve type/No: Overhead 16
Transmission: Manual
No. of forward speeds: 4
Wheels driven: Rear
Springs F/R: Coil/Coil
Brake system: PA
Brakes F/R: Disc/Drum
Steering: Recirculating ball PA
Wheelbase: 284.5cm 112.0in
Track F: 149.9cm 59.0in

Track R: 149.9cm 59.0in
Length: 516.1cm 203.2in
Width: 193.5cm 76.2in
Height: 134.1cm 52.8in
Kerb weight: 1700.2kg 3745.0lb
Fuel: 75.7L 16.6gal 20.0galUS

3298 Oldsmobile

Cutlass Salon
1973 USA
110.0mph 177.0kmh
0-50mph 80.5kmh: 8.0secs
0-60mph 96.5kmh: 11.1secs
0-1/4 mile: 18.1secs
180.0bhp 134.2kW 182.5PS
@ 3800rpm
275.0lbft 372.6Nm @ 2800rpm
93.7bhp/ton 92.1bhp/tonne
31.5bhp/L 23.5kW/L 31.9PS/L
35.7ft/sec 10.9m/sec
25.6mph 41.2kmh/1000rpm
13.8mpg 11.5mpgUS 20.5L/100km
Petrol 4-stroke piston
5719cc 348.9cu in
Vee 8 1 Carburettor
Compression ratio: 8.5:1
Bore: 103.0mm 4.1in
Stroke: 85.8mm 3.4in
Valve type/No: Overhead 16
Transmission: Automatic
No. of forward speeds: 3
Wheels driven: Rear
Springs F/R: Coil/Coil
Brake system: PA
Brakes F/R: Disc/Drum
Steering: Recirculating ball PA
Wheelbase: 294.6cm 116.0in
Track F: 156.0cm 61.4in
Track R: 154.2cm 60.7in
Length: 540.8cm 212.9in
Width: 194.3cm 76.5in
Height: 137.2cm 54.0in
Ground clearance: 13.7cm 5.4in
Kerb weight: 1954.5kg 4305.0lb
Fuel: 83.3L 18.3gal 22.0galUS

3299 Oldsmobile

Starfire
1976 USA
87.0mph 140.0kmh
0-50mph 80.5kmh: 12.2secs
0-60mph 96.5kmh: 17.2secs
0-1/4 mile: 21.0secs
84.0bhp 62.6kW 85.2PS
@ 4400rpm
113.0lbft 153.1Nm @ 3200rpm
60.0bhp/ton 59.0bhp/tonne
36.7bhp/L 27.4kW/L 37.2PS/L
44.2ft/sec 13.5m/sec
26.4mpg 22.0mpgUS 10.7L/100km
Petrol 4-stroke piston
2287cc 139.5cu in
In-line 4 1 Carburettor
Compression ratio: 8.0:1
Bore: 88.9mm 3.5in
Stroke: 92.0mm 3.6in
Valve type/No: Overhead 8
Transmission: Manual
No. of forward speeds: 5
Wheels driven: Rear
Springs F/R: Coil/Coil
Brake system: PA
Brakes F/R: Disc/Drum
Steering: Recirculating ball PA
Wheelbase: 246.4cm 97.0in
Track F: 138.9cm 54.7in
Track R: 136.1cm 53.6in
Length: 455.4cm 179.3in
Width: 166.1cm 65.4in
Height: 127.5cm 50.2in
Ground clearance: 12.4cm 4.9in
Kerb weight: 1423.3kg 3135.0lb
Fuel: 70.0L 15.4gal 18.5galUS

3300 Oldsmobile

Cutlass Diesel
1980 USA
0-60mph 96.5kmh: 18.2secs
0-1/4 mile: 21.3secs
105.0bhp 78.3kW 106.5PS
@ 3200rpm
205.0lbft 277.8Nm @ 1600rpm
62.5bhp/ton 61.4bhp/tonne
18.3bhp/L 13.6kW/L 18.6PS/L
30.1ft/sec 9.2m/sec
24.0mpg 20.0mpgUS 11.8L/100km
Diesel 4-stroke piston
5735cc 349.9cu in
Vee 8 fuel injection
Compression ratio: 22.5:1
Bore: 103.1mm 4.1in
Stroke: 86.0mm 3.4in
Valve type/No: Overhead 16
Transmission: Automatic
No. of forward speeds: 3
Wheels driven: Rear
Brakes F/R: Disc/Drum
Wheelbase: 274.6cm 108.1in
Track F: 148.6cm 58.5in
Track R: 146.8cm 57.8in
Length: 505.7cm 199.1in
Width: 181.6cm 71.5in
Height: 137.7cm 54.2in
Kerb weight: 1709.3kg 3765.0lb
Fuel: 74.9L 16.5gal 19.8galUS

3301 Oldsmobile

Cutlass Calais International Series
1988 USA
120.0mph 193.1kmh
0-50mph 80.5kmh: 5.7secs
0-60mph 96.5kmh: 8.2secs
0-1/4 mile: 16.2secs
150.0bhp 111.9kW 152.1PS
@ 5200rpm
160.0lbft 216.8Nm @ 4000rpm
131.8bhp/ton 129.6bhp/tonne
66.4bhp/L 49.5kW/L 67.3PS/L
48.4ft/sec 14.7m/sec
27.6mpg 23.0mpgUS 10.2L/100km
Petrol 4-stroke piston
2260cc 137.9cu in
In-line 4 fuel injection
Compression ratio: 9.5:1
Bore: 92.0mm 3.6in
Stroke: 85.0mm 3.3in
Valve type/No: Overhead 16
Transmission: Manual
No. of forward speeds: 5
Wheels driven: Front
Springs F/R: Coil/Coil
Brake system: PA
Brakes F/R: Disc/Drum
Steering: Rack & pinion PA
Wheelbase: 262.6cm 103.4in
Track F: 141.0cm 55.5in
Track R: 140.2cm 55.2in
Length: 454.2cm 178.8in
Width: 169.9cm 66.9in
Height: 133.1cm 52.4in
Kerb weight: 1157.7kg 2550.0lb
Fuel: 51.5L 11.3gal 13.6galUS

3302 Oldsmobile

Cutlass International Series
1988 USA
0-60mph 96.5kmh: 11.4secs
0-1/4 mile: 18.3secs
130.0bhp 96.9kW 131.8PS
@ 4500rpm
170.0lbft 230.4Nm @ 3600rpm
88.5bhp/ton 87.0bhp/tonne
45.8bhp/L 34.2kW/L 46.5PS/L
37.4ft/sec 11.4m/sec
24.6mpg 20.5mpgUS 11.5L/100km
Petrol 4-stroke piston
2837cc 173.1cu in
Vee 6 fuel injection
Compression ratio: 8.9:1
Bore: 89.0mm 3.5in
Stroke: 76.0mm 3.0in
Valve type/No: Overhead 12
Transmission: Automatic
No. of forward speeds: 4
Wheels driven: Front
Springs F/R: Coil/Leaf
Brake system: PA
Brakes F/R: Disc/Disc
Steering: Rack & pinion PA
Wheelbase: 273.1cm 107.5in
Track F: 151.1cm 59.5in
Track R: 147.3cm 58.0in
Length: 487.9cm 192.1in
Width: 180.3cm 71.0in
Height: 134.1cm 52.8in
Kerb weight: 1493.7kg 3290.0lb
Fuel: 61.7L 13.6gal 16.3galUS

3303 Oldsmobile

Calais HO Quad 4
1989 USA
125.0mph 201.1kmh
0-50mph 80.5kmh: 5.9secs
0-60mph 96.5kmh: 7.6secs
0-1/4 mile: 16.5secs
180.0bhp 134.2kW 182.5PS
@ 6200rpm
160.0lbft 216.8Nm @ 5200rpm
147.1bhp/ton 144.7bhp/tonne
79.6bhp/L 59.4kW/L 80.7PS/L
57.7ft/sec 17.6m/sec
32.4mpg 27.0mpgUS 8.7L/100km
Petrol 4-stroke piston
2260cc 137.9cu in
In-line 4 fuel injection
Compression ratio: 10.0:1
Bore: 92.0mm 3.6in
Stroke: 85.0mm 3.3in
Valve type/No: Overhead 16
Transmission: Manual
No. of forward speeds: 5
Wheels driven: Front
Springs F/R: Coil/Coil
Brake system: PA
Brakes F/R: Disc/Drum
Steering: Rack & pinion PA
Wheelbase: 262.6cm 103.4in
Track F: 141.2cm 55.6in
Track R: 140.2cm 55.2in
Length: 454.2cm 178.8in
Width: 169.4cm 66.7in
Height: 133.1cm 52.4in
Ground clearance: 14.7cm 5.8in
Kerb weight: 1244.0kg 2740.0lb
Fuel: 51.5L 11.3gal 13.6galUS

3304 Oldsmobile

Cutlass Calais International Series HO
1989 USA
125.0mph 201.1kmh
0-50mph 80.5kmh: 5.9secs
0-60mph 96.5kmh: 7.6secs
0-1/4 mile: 16.5secs
180.0bhp 134.2kW 182.5PS
@ 6200rpm
160.0lbft 216.8Nm @ 5200rpm
147.1bhp/ton 144.7bhp/tonne
79.6bhp/L 59.4kW/L 80.7PS/L
57.7ft/sec 17.6m/sec
32.4mpg 27.0mpgUS 8.7L/100km
Petrol 4-stroke piston
2260cc 137.9cu in
In-line 4 fuel injection
Compression ratio: 10.0:1
Bore: 92.0mm 3.6in
Stroke: 85.0mm 3.3in
Valve type/No: Overhead 16
Transmission: Manual
No. of forward speeds: 5
Wheels driven: Front
Springs F/R: Coil/Coil
Brake system: PA
Brakes F/R: Disc/Drum
Steering: Rack & pinion PA
Wheelbase: 262.6cm 103.4in
Track F: 141.2cm 55.6in
Track R: 140.2cm 55.2in
Length: 454.2cm 178.8in
Width: 169.4cm 66.7in
Height: 133.1cm 52.4in
Kerb weight: 1244.0kg 2740.0lb
Fuel: 51.5L 11.3gal 13.6galUS

3305 Oldsmobile

Toronado Trofeo
1990 USA
125.0mph 201.1kmh
0-50mph 80.5kmh: 7.3secs
0-60mph 96.5kmh: 10.4secs
0-1/4 mile: 17.6secs
170.0bhp 126.8kW 172.4PS
@ 4800rpm
220.0lbft 298.1Nm @ 3200rpm
107.1bhp/ton 105.3bhp/tonne
44.8bhp/L 33.4kW/L 45.5PS/L
45.3ft/sec 13.8m/sec
21.4mpg 17.8mpgUS 13.2L/100km
Petrol 4-stroke piston
3791cc 231.3cu in
Vee 6 fuel injection
Compression ratio: 8.5:1
Bore: 96.5mm 3.8in
Stroke: 86.4mm 3.4in
Valve type/No: Overhead 12
Transmission: Automatic
No. of forward speeds: 4
Wheels driven: Front
Springs F/R: Coil/Leaf
Brake system: PA ABS
Brakes F/R: Disc/Disc
Steering: Rack & pinion PA
Wheelbase: 274.3cm 108.0in
Track F: 152.1cm 59.9in
Track R: 152.1cm 59.9in
Length: 508.8cm 200.3in
Width: 184.9cm 72.8in
Height: 134.6cm 53.0in
Kerb weight: 1614.0kg 3555.0lb
Fuel: 69.3L 15.2gal 18.3galUS

3306 Opel

Kadet Saloon
1937 Germany
59.2mph 95.3kmh
0-50mph 80.5kmh: 37.9secs
36.0mpg 30.0mpgUS 7.8L/100km
Petrol 4-stroke piston
1066cc 65.0cu in
In-line 4
Bore: 67.5mm 2.7in
Stroke: 75.0mm 2.9in
Valve type/No: Side 8
Transmission: Manual
No. of forward speeds: 3
Wheels driven: Rear
Brakes F/R: Drum/Drum
Kerb weight: 771.8kg 1700.0lb
Fuel: 26.2L 5.7gal 6.9galUS

3307 Opel

Olympia Saloon
1938 Germany
69.2mph 111.3kmh
0-50mph 80.5kmh: 20.9secs
0-60mph 96.5kmh: 34.2secs
27.0mpg 22.5mpgUS 10.5L/100km
Petrol 4-stroke piston
1488cc 90.8cu in
In-line 4
Bore: 80.0mm 3.1in
Stroke: 74.0mm 2.9in
Valve type/No: Overhead 8
Transmission: Manual
No. of forward speeds: 4
Wheels driven: Rear
Brakes F/R: Drum/Drum
Kerb weight: 901.2kg 1985.0lb
Fuel: 27.3L 6.0gal 7.2galUS

3308 Opel

Rekord
1958 Germany
78.2mph 125.8kmh
0-50mph 80.5kmh: 12.5secs
0-60mph 96.5kmh: 19.6secs
0-1/4 mile: 21.0secs
55.0bhp 41.0kW 55.8PS
@ 4200rpm
78.8lbft 106.8Nm @ 2000rpm
61.9bhp/ton 60.9bhp/tonne
37.0bhp/L 27.6kW/L 37.5PS/L
33.9ft/sec 10.3m/sec
17.5mph 28.2kmh/1000rpm
Petrol 4-stroke piston
1488cc 90.8cu in
In-line 4
Compression ratio: 7.5:1
Bore: 80.0mm 3.1in
Stroke: 73.9mm 2.9in
Valve type/No: Overhead 8
Transmission: Manual
No. of forward speeds: 3
Wheels driven: Rear
Wheelbase: 254.0cm 100.0in
Track F: 126.0cm 49.6in
Track R: 127.0cm 50.0in
Length: 444.5cm 175.0in
Width: 161.5cm 63.6in
Height: 149.1cm 58.7in
Kerb weight: 903.5kg 1990.0lb

3309 Opel

Kadett
1964 Germany
76.0mph 122.3kmh
0-50mph 80.5kmh: 14.0secs
0-60mph 96.5kmh: 23.0secs
0-1/4 mile: 22.0secs
46.0bhp 34.3kW 46.6PS
@ 5200rpm
54.0lbft 73.2Nm @ 2600rpm
69.6bhp/ton 68.5bhp/tonne
46.6bhp/L 34.7kW/L 47.2PS/L

34.7ft/sec 10.6m/sec
16.4mph 26.4kmh/1000rpm
Petrol 4-stroke piston
987cc 60.2cu in
In-line 4 1 Carburettor
Compression ratio: 7.8:1
Bore: 72.1mm 2.8in
Stroke: 61.0mm 2.4in
Valve type/No: Overhead 8
Transmission: Manual
No. of forward speeds: 4
Wheels driven: Rear
Wheelbase: 232.4cm 91.5in
Track F: 119.9cm 47.2in
Track R: 120.4cm 47.4in
Length: 392.4cm 154.5in
Width: 147.1cm 57.9in
Height: 141.0cm 55.5in
Ground clearance: 14.7cm 5.8in
Kerb weight: 671.9kg 1480.0lb
Fuel: 32.9L 7.2gal 8.7galUS

3310 Opel

Diplomat
1965 Germany
123.0mph 197.9kmh
0-50mph 80.5kmh: 8.3secs
0-60mph 96.5kmh: 10.8secs
0-1/4 mile: 17.6secs
190.0bhp 141.7kW 192.6PS
@ 4600rpm
253.0lbft 342.8Nm @ 2400rpm
127.6bhp/ton 125.5bhp/tonne
41.0bhp/L 30.5kW/L 41.5PS/L
38.3ft/sec 11.7m/sec
25.1mph 40.4kmh/1000rpm
16.4mpg 13.7mpgUS 17.2L/100km
Petrol 4-stroke piston
4638cc 283.0cu in
Vee 8 1 Carburettor
Compression ratio: 9.2:1
Bore: 98.4mm 3.9in
Stroke: 76.2mm 3.0in
Valve type/No: Overhead 16
Transmission: Automatic
No. of forward speeds: 2
Wheels driven: Rear
Springs F/R: Coil/Leaf
Brake system: PA
Brakes F/R: Disc/Drum
Steering: Recirculating ball PA
Wheelbase: 284.5cm 112.0in
Track F: 149.4cm 58.8in
Track R: 150.9cm 59.4in
Length: 494.8cm 194.8in
Width: 190.2cm 74.9in
Height: 129.3cm 50.9in
Ground clearance: 14.5cm 5.7in
Kerb weight: 1514.1kg 3335.0lb
Fuel: 81.9L 18.0gal 21.6galUS

3311 Opel

Kadett S
1966 Germany
85.0mph 136.8kmh
0-50mph 80.5kmh: 11.6secs
0-60mph 96.5kmh: 17.8secs
0-1/4 mile: 20.7secs
59.0bhp 44.0kW 59.8PS
@ 5600rpm
63.0lbft 85.4Nm @ 3000rpm
81.6bhp/ton 80.2bhp/tonne
54.7bhp/L 40.8kW/L 55.5PS/L
37.3ft/sec 11.4m/sec
16.4mph 26.4kmh/1000rpm
Petrol 4-stroke piston
1078cc 65.8cu in
In-line 4 1 Carburettor
Compression ratio: 8.8:1
Bore: 74.9mm 2.9in
Stroke: 61.0mm 2.4in
Valve type/No: Overhead 8
Transmission: Manual
No. of forward speeds: 4
Wheels driven: Rear
Springs F/R: Leaf/Leaf
Brakes F/R: Disc/Drum
Steering: Rack & pinion
Wheelbase: 241.3cm 95.0in
Track F: 125.0cm 49.2in
Track R: 128.0cm 50.4in
Length: 418.3cm 164.7in
Width: 157.2cm 61.9in
Height: 138.7cm 54.6in
Ground clearance: 17.3cm 6.8in
Kerb weight: 735.5kg 1620.0lb
Fuel: 40.1L 8.8gal 10.6galUS

3312 Opel

Kadett Rallye
1967 Germany
91.0mph 146.4kmh
0-50mph 80.5kmh: 11.3secs
0-60mph 96.5kmh: 15.9secs
0-1/4 mile: 19.9secs
67.0bhp 50.0kW 67.9PS
@ 6000rpm
62.0lbft 84.0Nm @ 4600rpm
84.8bhp/ton 83.4bhp/tonne
62.1bhp/L 46.3kW/L 63.0PS/L
40.0ft/sec 12.2m/sec
15.5mph 24.9kmh/1000rpm
Petrol 4-stroke piston
1078cc 65.8cu in
In-line 4
Compression ratio: 9.2:1
Bore: 75.0mm 2.9in
Stroke: 61.0mm 2.4in
Valve type/No: Overhead 8
Transmission: Manual
No. of forward speeds: 4
Wheels driven: Rear
Brakes F/R: Disc/Drum
Steering: Recirculating ball
Wheelbase: 241.6cm 95.1in
Track F: 125.0cm 49.2in
Track R: 128.0cm 50.4in
Length: 418.1cm 164.6in
Width: 157.2cm 61.9in
Height: 136.9cm 53.9in
Kerb weight: 803.6kg 1770.0lb
Fuel: 39.7L 8.7gal 10.5galUS

3313 Opel

Rekord Coupe
1967 Germany
102.0mph 164.1kmh
0-50mph 80.5kmh: 9.3secs
0-60mph 96.5kmh: 12.7secs
0-1/4 mile: 18.6secs
0-1km: 34.6secs
90.0bhp 67.1kW 91.2PS
@ 5100rpm
108.0lbft 146.3Nm @ 2800rpm
81.7bhp/ton 80.3bhp/tonne
47.4bhp/L 35.4kW/L 48.1PS/L
39.0ft/sec 11.9m/sec
16.9mph 27.2kmh/1000rpm
27.4mpg 22.8mpgUS 10.3L/100km
Petrol 4-stroke piston
1897cc 115.7cu in
In-line 4 1 Carburettor
Compression ratio: 9.0:1
Bore: 93.0mm 3.7in
Stroke: 69.8mm 2.7in
Valve type/No: Overhead 8
Transmission: Manual
No. of forward speeds: 4
Wheels driven: Rear
Springs F/R: Coil/Coil
Brake system: PA
Brakes F/R: Disc/Drum
Steering: Recirculating ball
Wheelbase: 266.7cm 105.0in
Track F: 139.7cm 55.0in
Track R: 139.7cm 55.0in
Length: 459.7cm 181.0in
Width: 175.8cm 69.2in
Height: 142.5cm 56.1in
Ground clearance: 12.7cm 5.0in
Kerb weight: 1120.5kg 2468.0lb
Fuel: 66.0L 14.5gal 17.4galUS

3314 Opel

Kadette Rallye 1.9
1968 Germany
101.0mph 162.5kmh
0-50mph 80.5kmh: 8.7secs
0-60mph 96.5kmh: 12.1secs
0-1/4 mile: 18.3secs
102.0bhp 76.1kW 103.4PS
@ 5400rpm
115.0lbft 155.8Nm @ 3100rpm
114.8bhp/ton 112.9bhp/tonne
53.8bhp/L 40.1kW/L 54.5PS/L
41.2ft/sec 12.6m/sec
17.0mph 27.4kmh/1000rpm
Petrol 4-stroke piston
1897cc 115.7cu in
In-line 4 1 Carburettor
Compression ratio: 9.0:1
Bore: 93.0mm 3.7in
Stroke: 69.8mm 2.7in
Valve type/No: Overhead 8
Transmission: Manual
No. of forward speeds: 4
Wheels driven: Rear
Springs F/R: Leaf/Coil
Brake system: PA
Brakes F/R: Disc/Drum
Steering: Recirculating ball
Wheelbase: 241.6cm 95.1in
Track F: 125.0cm 49.2in
Track R: 127.5cm 50.2in
Length: 418.1cm 164.6in
Width: 157.2cm 61.9in
Height: 140.5cm 55.3in
Ground clearance: 11.4cm 4.5in
Kerb weight: 903.5kg 1990.0lb
Fuel: 40.1L 8.8gal 10.6galUS

3315 Opel

Station Wagon 1.1
1968 Germany
75.0mph 120.7kmh
0-1/4 mile: 22.5secs
55.0bhp 41.0kW 55.8PS
50.0bhp/L 37.3kW/L 50.7PS/L
Petrol 4-stroke piston
1100cc 67.1cu in
In-line 4
Valve type/No: Overhead 8
Wheels driven: Rear
Wheelbase: 241.6cm 95.1in
Length: 417.6cm 164.4in

3316 Opel

Station Wagon 1.5
1968 Germany
90.0mph 144.8kmh
0-1/4 mile: 19.5secs
80.0bhp 59.7kW 81.1PS
53.3bhp/L 39.8kW/L 54.1PS/L
27.6mpg 23.0mpgUS 10.2L/100km
Petrol 4-stroke piston
1500cc 91.5cu in
In-line 4
Valve type/No: Overhead 8
Wheels driven: Rear
Wheelbase: 241.6cm 95.1in
Length: 417.6cm 164.4in

3317 Opel

Station Wagon 1.9
1968 Germany
100.0mph 160.9kmh
0-1/4 mile: 18.5secs
102.0bhp 76.1kW 103.4PS
53.7bhp/L 40.0kW/L 54.4PS/L
Petrol 4-stroke piston
1900cc 115.9cu in
In-line 4
Valve type/No: Overhead 8
Wheels driven: Rear
Wheelbase: 241.6cm 95.1in
Length: 417.6cm 164.4in

3318 Opel

Commodore GS Coupe
1969 Germany
116.0mph 186.6kmh
0-50mph 80.5kmh: 8.8secs
0-60mph 96.5kmh: 12.8secs
0-1/4 mile: 18.6secs
0-1km: 34.5secs
130.0bhp 96.9kW 131.8PS
@ 5300rpm
138.0lbft 187.0Nm @ 4000rpm
108.9bhp/ton 107.1bhp/tonne
52.2bhp/L 38.9kW/L 52.9PS/L
40.5ft/sec 12.3m/sec
19.6mph 31.5kmh/1000rpm
20.3mpg 16.9mpgUS 13.9L/100km
Petrol 4-stroke piston
2490cc 151.9cu in
In-line 6 2 Carburettor
Compression ratio: 9.5:1
Bore: 87.0mm 3.4in
Stroke: 69.8mm 2.7in
Valve type/No: Overhead 12
Transmission: Manual
No. of forward speeds: 4
Wheels driven: Rear
Springs F/R: Coil/Coil
Brake system: PA
Brakes F/R: Disc/Drum
Steering: Recirculating ball
Wheelbase: 241.3cm 95.0in
Track F: 141.0cm 55.5in
Track R: 141.0cm 55.5in
Length: 459.7cm 181.0in
Width: 175.8cm 69.2in
Height: 141.5cm 55.7in
Ground clearance: 12.7cm 5.0in
Kerb weight: 1213.5kg 2673.0lb
Fuel: 54.6L 12.0gal 14.4galUS

3319 Opel

GT
1969 Germany
111.0mph 178.6kmh
0-50mph 80.5kmh: 7.4secs
0-60mph 96.5kmh: 10.2secs
0-1/4 mile: 17.4secs
102.0bhp 76.1kW 103.4PS
@ 5400rpm
115.0lbft 155.8Nm @ 3100rpm
110.4bhp/ton 108.5bhp/tonne
53.7bhp/L 40.1kW/L 54.5PS/L
41.2ft/sec 12.6m/sec
19.3mph 31.1kmh/1000rpm
Petrol 4-stroke piston
1898cc 115.8cu in
In-line 4 1 Carburettor
Compression ratio: 9.0:1
Bore: 93.0mm 3.7in
Stroke: 69.9mm 2.7in
Valve type/No: Overhead 8
Transmission: Manual
No. of forward speeds: 4
Wheels driven: Rear
Springs F/R: Leaf/Coil
Brake system: PA
Brakes F/R: Disc/Drum
Steering: Rack & pinion
Wheelbase: 241.6cm 95.1in
Track F: 124.5cm 49.0in
Track R: 127.0cm 50.0in
Length: 411.5cm 162.0in
Width: 157.5cm 62.0in
Height: 121.9cm 48.0in
Kerb weight: 939.8kg 2070.0lb
Fuel: 39.7L 8.7gal 10.5galUS

3320 Opel

GT 1.9
1969 Germany
113.0mph 181.8kmh
0-50mph 80.5kmh: 7.4secs
0-60mph 96.5kmh: 10.8secs
0-1/4 mile: 17.7secs
102.0bhp 76.1kW 103.4PS
@ 5400rpm
115.0lbft 155.8Nm @ 3100rpm
108.5bhp/ton 106.7bhp/tonne
53.8bhp/L 40.1kW/L 54.5PS/L
41.2ft/sec 12.6m/sec
19.8mph 31.9kmh/1000rpm
33.0mpg 27.5mpgUS 8.6L/100km
Petrol 4-stroke piston
1897cc 115.7cu in
In-line 4 1 Carburettor
Compression ratio: 9.0:1
Bore: 93.0mm 3.7in
Stroke: 69.8mm 2.7in
Valve type/No: Overhead 8
Transmission: Manual
No. of forward speeds: 4
Wheels driven: Rear
Springs F/R: Leaf/Coil
Brake system: PA
Brakes F/R: Disc/Drum
Steering: Rack & pinion
Wheelbase: 243.1cm 95.7in
Track F: 125.5cm 49.4in
Track R: 128.5cm 50.6in
Length: 411.2cm 161.9in
Width: 158.0cm 62.2in
Height: 122.4cm 48.2in
Ground clearance: 13.0cm 5.1in
Kerb weight: 955.7kg 2105.0lb
Fuel: 50.0L 11.0gal 13.2galUS

3321 Opel

GT 1900
1969 Germany
116.0mph 186.6kmh
0-50mph 80.5kmh: 8.3secs
0-60mph 96.5kmh: 12.0secs
0-1/4 mile: 18.6secs
0-1km: 34.0secs
90.0bhp 67.1kW 91.2PS
@ 5100rpm
108.0lbft 146.3Nm @ 2800rpm
95.7bhp/ton 94.1bhp/tonne

47.4bhp/L 35.4kW/L 48.1PS/L
39.0ft/sec 11.9m/sec
19.8mph 31.9kmh/1000rpm
28.7mpg 23.9mpgUS 9.8L/100km
Petrol 4-stroke piston
1897cc 115.7cu in
In-line 4 1 Carburettor
Compression ratio: 9.5:1
Bore: 93.0mm 3.7in
Stroke: 69.8mm 2.7in
Valve type/No: Overhead 8
Transmission: Manual
No. of forward speeds: 4
Wheels driven: Rear
Springs F/R: Leaf/Coil
Brake system: PA
Brakes F/R: Disc/Drum
Steering: Rack & pinion
Wheelbase: 242.8cm 95.6in
Track F: 125.5cm 49.4in
Track R: 127.8cm 50.3in
Length: 411.5cm 162.0in
Width: 157.5cm 62.0in
Height: 122.4cm 48.2in
Ground clearance: 15.2cm 6.0in
Kerb weight: 956.6kg 2107.0lb
Fuel: 55.1L 12.1gal 14.5galUS

3322 Opel

Kadett Rallye 1.9
1969 Germany
101.0mph 162.5kmh
0-50mph 80.5kmh: 9.2secs
0-60mph 96.5kmh: 12.3secs
0-1/4 mile: 18.2secs
102.0bhp 76.1kW 103.4PS
@ 5400rpm
115.0lbft 155.8Nm @ 3100rpm
113.7bhp/ton 111.8bhp/tonne
53.7bhp/L 40.1kW/L 54.5PS/L
41.2ft/sec 12.6m/sec
17.2mph 27.7kmh/1000rpm
Petrol 4-stroke piston
1898cc 115.8cu in
In-line 4 1 Carburettor
Compression ratio: 9.0:1
Bore: 93.0mm 3.7in
Stroke: 69.9mm 2.7in
Valve type/No: Overhead 8
Transmission: Manual
No. of forward speeds: 4
Wheels driven: Rear
Springs F/R: Leaf/Coil
Brake system: PA
Brakes F/R: Disc/Drum
Steering: Recirculating ball
Wheelbase: 241.6cm 95.1in
Track F: 125.2cm 49.3in
Track R: 127.5cm 50.2in
Length: 418.1cm 164.6in
Width: 157.2cm 61.9in
Height: 140.5cm 55.3in
Kerb weight: 912.5kg 2010.0lb
Fuel: 39.7L 8.7gal 10.5galUS

3323 Opel

Diplomat
1970 Germany
114.0mph 183.4kmh
0-50mph 80.5kmh: 8.2secs
0-60mph 96.5kmh: 11.1secs
0-1/4 mile: 18.1secs
165.0bhp 123.0kW 167.3PS
@ 5600rpm
187.0lbft 253.4Nm @ 4200rpm
106.3bhp/ton 106.5bhp/tonne
59.3bhp/L 44.2kW/L 60.1PS/L
42.8ft/sec 13.0m/sec
20.4mph 32.8kmh/1000rpm
14.3mpg 11.9mpgUS 19.8L/100km
Petrol 4-stroke piston
2784cc 169.9cu in
In-line 6 fuel injection
Compression ratio: 9.5:1
Bore: 92.0mm 3.6in
Stroke: 69.8mm 2.7in
Valve type/No: Overhead 12
Transmission: Automatic
No. of forward speeds: 3
Wheels driven: Rear
Springs F/R: Coil/Coil
Brake system: PA
Brakes F/R: Disc/Disc
Steering: Recirculating ball PA
Wheelbase: 284.5cm 112.0in
Track F: 150.6cm 59.3in
Track R: 150.6cm 59.3in
Length: 495.3cm 195.0in
Width: 190.5cm 75.0in
Height: 147.3cm 58.0in
Ground clearance: 20.3cm 8.0in
Kerb weight: 1549.0kg 3412.0lb
Fuel: 79.6L 17.5gal 21.0galUS

3324 Opel

Manta Rallye 1.9
1970 Germany
109.0mph 175.4kmh
0-50mph 80.5kmh: 8.5secs
0-60mph 96.5kmh: 12.2secs
0-1/4 mile: 18.2secs
0-1km: 34.1secs
90.0bhp 67.1kW 91.2PS
@ 5100rpm
108.0lbft 146.3Nm @ 2800rpm
95.5bhp/ton 93.9bhp/tonne
47.4bhp/L 35.4kW/L 48.1PS/L
39.0ft/sec 11.9m/sec
18.5mph 29.8kmh/1000rpm
25.3mpg 21.1mpgUS 11.2L/100km
Petrol 4-stroke piston
1897cc 115.7cu in
In-line 4 1 Carburettor
Compression ratio: 9.0:1
Bore: 93.0mm 3.7in
Stroke: 69.8mm 2.7in
Valve type/No: Overhead 8
Transmission: Manual
No. of forward speeds: 4
Wheels driven: Rear
Springs F/R: Coil/Coil
Brake system: PA
Brakes F/R: Disc/Drum
Steering: Rack & pinion
Wheelbase: 243.1cm 95.7in
Track F: 133.4cm 52.5in
Track R: 132.1cm 52.0in
Length: 429.3cm 169.0in
Width: 162.6cm 64.0in
Height: 135.9cm 53.5in
Ground clearance: 17.8cm 7.0in
Kerb weight: 958.4kg 2111.0lb
Fuel: 47.8L 10.5gal 12.6galUS

3325 Opel

Senator
1970 Germany
120.0mph 193.1kmh
0-50mph 80.5kmh: 6.8secs
0-60mph 96.5kmh: 9.2secs
0-1/4 mile: 17.0secs
0-1km: 31.2secs
180.0bhp 134.2kW 182.5PS
@ 5800rpm
179.0lbft 242.5Nm @ 4800rpm
130.9bhp/ton 128.7bhp/tonne
60.6bhp/L 45.2kW/L 61.5PS/L
44.3ft/sec 13.5m/sec
20.9mph 33.6kmh/1000rpm
18.6mpg 15.5mpgUS 15.2L/100km
Petrol 4-stroke piston
2968cc 181.1cu in
In-line 6 fuel injection
Compression ratio: 9.4:1
Bore: 95.0mm 3.7in
Stroke: 69.8mm 2.7in
Valve type/No: Overhead 12
Transmission: Automatic
No. of forward speeds: 3
Wheels driven: Rear
Springs F/R: Coil/Coil
Brake system: PA
Brakes F/R: Disc/Drum
Steering: Recirculating ball PA
Wheelbase: 268.2cm 105.6in
Track F: 144.3cm 56.8in
Track R: 147.3cm 58.0in
Length: 481.1cm 189.4in
Width: 172.7cm 68.0in
Height: 141.5cm 55.7in
Ground clearance: 14.0cm 5.5in
Kerb weight: 1398.3kg 3080.0lb
Fuel: 75.1L 16.5gal 19.8galUS

3326 Opel

Ascona Voyage
1971 Germany
96.0mph 154.5kmh
0-50mph 80.5kmh: 9.8secs
0-60mph 96.5kmh: 14.5secs
0-1/4 mile: 19.5secs
0-1km: 36.2secs
80.0bhp 59.7kW 81.1PS
@ 5200rpm
95.0lbft 128.7Nm @ 4200rpm
82.2bhp/ton 80.8bhp/tonne
50.5bhp/L 37.7kW/L 51.2PS/L
39.7ft/sec 12.1m/sec
18.5mph 29.8kmh/1000rpm
24.9mpg 20.7mpgUS 11.3L/100km
Petrol 4-stroke piston
1584cc 96.6cu in
In-line 4 1 Carburettor
Compression ratio: 9.5:1
Bore: 85.0mm 3.3in
Stroke: 69.8mm 2.7in
Valve type/No: Overhead 8
Transmission: Manual
No. of forward speeds: 4
Wheels driven: Rear
Springs F/R: Coil/Coil
Brake system: PA
Brakes F/R: Disc/Drum
Steering: Rack & pinion
Wheelbase: 243.8cm 96.0in
Track F: 133.4cm 52.5in
Track R: 132.1cm 52.0in
Length: 419.1cm 165.0in
Width: 162.6cm 64.0in
Height: 139.7cm 55.0in
Ground clearance: 17.8cm 7.0in
Kerb weight: 989.7kg 2180.0lb
Fuel: 45.0L 9.9gal 11.9galUS

3327 Opel

GT
1971 Germany
110.0mph 177.0kmh
0-60mph 96.5kmh: 11.9secs
0-1/4 mile: 18.4secs
90.0bhp 67.1kW 91.2PS
@ 5200rpm
111.0lbft 150.4Nm @ 3400rpm
95.5bhp/ton 93.9bhp/tonne
47.4bhp/L 35.4kW/L 48.1PS/L
39.7ft/sec 12.1m/sec
31.1mpg 25.9mpgUS 9.1L/100km
Petrol 4-stroke piston
1897cc 115.7cu in
In-line 4
Bore: 93.0mm 3.7in
Stroke: 69.8mm 2.7in
Valve type/No: Overhead 8
Transmission: Manual
No. of forward speeds: 4
Wheels driven: Rear
Springs F/R: Leaf/Coil
Brakes F/R: Disc/Drum
Wheelbase: 243.1cm 95.7in
Track F: 125.5cm 49.4in
Track R: 128.5cm 50.6in
Length: 411.2cm 161.9in
Width: 158.0cm 62.2in
Height: 122.4cm 48.2in
Kerb weight: 957.9kg 2110.0lb
Fuel: 50.0L 11.0gal 13.2galUS

3328 Opel

Rallye 1900
1971 Germany
93.0mph 149.6kmh
0-50mph 80.5kmh: 9.7secs
0-60mph 96.5kmh: 13.6secs
0-1/4 mile: 18.9secs
90.0bhp 67.1kW 91.2PS
@ 5200rpm
108.0lbft 146.3Nm @ 2800rpm
94.3bhp/ton 92.8bhp/tonne
47.4bhp/L 35.4kW/L 48.1PS/L
39.1ft/sec 11.9m/sec
17.7mph 28.5kmh/1000rpm
30.6mpg 25.5mpgUS 9.2L/100km
Petrol 4-stroke piston
1897cc 115.7cu in
In-line 4 1 Carburettor
Compression ratio: 7.6:1
Bore: 93.0mm 3.7in
Stroke: 68.8mm 2.7in
Valve type/No: Overhead 8
Transmission: Manual
No. of forward speeds: 4
Wheels driven: Rear
Springs F/R: Coil/Coil
Brake system: PA
Brakes F/R: Disc/Drum
Steering: Rack & pinion
Wheelbase: 243.1cm 95.7in
Track F: 133.1cm 52.4in
Track R: 132.1cm 52.0in
Length: 434.3cm 171.0in
Width: 163.3cm 64.3in
Height: 135.4cm 53.3in
Ground clearance: 15.2cm 6.0in
Kerb weight: 970.2kg 2137.0lb
Fuel: 45.4L 10.0gal 12.0galUS

3329 Opel

Rekord 1900
1972 Germany
103.0mph 165.7kmh
0-50mph 80.5kmh: 8.7secs
0-60mph 96.5kmh: 12.3secs
0-1/4 mile: 18.6secs
0-1km: 34.5secs
97.0bhp 72.3kW 98.3PS
@ 5200rpm
109.0lbft 147.7Nm @ 3800rpm
91.3bhp/ton 89.7bhp/tonne
51.1bhp/L 38.1kW/L 51.8PS/L
39.7ft/sec 12.1m/sec
18.5mph 29.8kmh/1000rpm
24.1mpg 20.1mpgUS 11.7L/100km
Petrol 4-stroke piston
1897cc 115.7cu in
In-line 4 1 Carburettor
Compression ratio: 9.8:1
Bore: 93.0mm 3.7in
Stroke: 69.8mm 2.7in
Valve type/No: Overhead 8
Transmission: Manual
No. of forward speeds: 4
Wheels driven: Rear
Springs F/R: Coil/Coil
Brake system: PA
Brakes F/R: Disc/Drum
Steering: Recirculating ball
Wheelbase: 266.7cm 105.0in
Track F: 142.5cm 56.1in
Track R: 141.2cm 55.6in
Length: 456.7cm 179.8in
Width: 171.7cm 67.6in
Height: 140.5cm 55.3in
Ground clearance: 20.3cm 8.0in
Kerb weight: 1081.0kg 2381.0lb
Fuel: 70.1L 15.4gal 18.5galUS

3330 Opel

1900 Station Wagon
1973 Germany
0-60mph 96.5kmh: 14.2secs
0-1/4 mile: 19.4secs
75.0bhp 55.9kW 76.0PS
@ 4800rpm
92.0lbft 124.7Nm @ 2800rpm
76.2bhp/ton 74.9bhp/tonne
39.5bhp/L 29.5kW/L 40.1PS/L
29.4mpg 24.5mpgUS 9.6L/100km
Petrol 4-stroke piston
1897cc 115.7cu in
In-line 4
Valve type/No: Overhead 8
Transmission: Manual
No. of forward speeds: 4
Wheels driven: Rear
Brake system: PA
Brakes F/R: Disc/Drum
Wheelbase: 243.1cm 95.7in
Length: 418.1cm 164.6in
Width: 163.3cm 64.3in
Height: 135.4cm 53.3in
Kerb weight: 1001.1kg 2205.0lb

3331 Opel

Ascona 1900SR
1973 Germany
101.0mph 162.5kmh
0-50mph 80.5kmh: 8.5secs
0-60mph 96.5kmh: 12.5secs
0-1/4 mile: 18.3secs
0-1km: 34.7secs
90.0bhp 67.1kW 91.2PS
@ 5100rpm
108.0lbft 146.3Nm @ 2800rpm
94.4bhp/ton 92.8bhp/tonne
47.4bhp/L 35.4kW/L 48.1PS/L
39.0ft/sec 11.9m/sec
19.6mph 31.5kmh/1000rpm
23.5mpg 19.6mpgUS 12.0L/100km
Petrol 4-stroke piston
1897cc 115.7cu in
In-line 4 1 Carburettor
Compression ratio: 9.0:1
Bore: 93.0mm 3.7in
Stroke: 69.8mm 2.7in
Valve type/No: Overhead 8
Transmission: Manual

No. of forward speeds: 4
Wheels driven: Rear
Springs F/R: Coil/Coil
Brake system: PA
Brakes F/R: Disc/Drum
Steering: Rack & pinion
Wheelbase: 243.8cm 96.0in
Track F: 132.1cm 52.0in
Track R: 132.1cm 52.0in
Length: 417.8cm 164.5in
Width: 162.6cm 64.0in
Height: 139.7cm 55.0in
Ground clearance: 15.2cm 6.0in
Kerb weight: 969.3kg 2135.0lb
Fuel: 47.8L 10.5gal 12.6galUS

3332 Opel

Commodore GS Coupe
1973 Germany
114.0mph 183.4kmh
0-50mph 80.5kmh: 8.2secs
0-60mph 96.5kmh: 11.4secs
0-1/4 mile: 18.3secs
0-1km: 33.9secs
130.0bhp 96.9kW 131.8PS
@ 5300rpm
137.0lbft 185.6Nm @ 4000rpm
103.3bhp/ton 101.5bhp/tonne
52.2bhp/L 38.9kW/L 52.9PS/L
40.5ft/sec 12.3m/sec
20.2mph 32.5kmh/1000rpm
18.2mpg 15.2mpgUS 15.5L/100km
Petrol 4-stroke piston
2490cc 151.9cu in
In-line 6 2 Carburettor
Compression ratio: 9.0:1
Bore: 87.0mm 3.4in
Stroke: 69.8mm 2.7in
Valve type/No: Overhead 12
Transmission: Automatic
No. of forward speeds: 3
Wheels driven: Rear
Springs F/R: Coil/Coil
Brake system: PA
Brakes F/R: Disc/Drum
Steering: Recirculating ball PA
Wheelbase: 241.3cm 95.0in
Track F: 142.5cm 56.1in
Track R: 141.2cm 55.6in
Length: 456.7cm 179.8in
Width: 171.7cm 67.6in
Height: 139.7cm 55.0in
Ground clearance: 20.3cm 8.0in
Kerb weight: 1280.3kg 2820.0lb
Fuel: 70.1L 15.4gal 18.5galUS

3333 Opel

GT
1973 Germany
100.0mph 160.9kmh
0-50mph 80.5kmh: 9.1secs
0-60mph 96.5kmh: 13.2secs
0-1/4 mile: 19.7secs
75.0bhp 55.9kW 76.0PS
@ 4800rpm
92.0lbft 124.7Nm @ 2800rpm
82.6bhp/ton 81.2bhp/tonne
39.5bhp/L 29.5kW/L 40.1PS/L
36.7ft/sec 11.2m/sec
19.2mph 30.9kmh/1000rpm
28.8mpg 24.0mpgUS 9.8L/100km
Petrol 4-stroke piston
1897cc 115.7cu in
In-line 4 1 Carburettor
Compression ratio: 7.6:1
Bore: 93.0mm 3.7in
Stroke: 69.8mm 2.7in
Valve type/No: Overhead 8
Transmission: Manual
No. of forward speeds: 4
Wheels driven: Rear
Springs F/R: Leaf/Coil
Brake system: PA
Brakes F/R: Disc/Drum
Steering: Rack & pinion
Wheelbase: 243.1cm 95.7in
Track F: 125.5cm 49.4in
Track R: 128.5cm 50.6in
Length: 411.2cm 161.9in
Width: 158.0cm 62.2in
Height: 120.4cm 47.4in
Ground clearance: 13.0cm 5.1in
Kerb weight: 923.9kg 2035.0lb
Fuel: 54.9L 12.1gal 14.5galUS

3334 Opel

Manta
1973 Germany
93.0mph 149.6kmh
0-50mph 80.5kmh: 9.7secs
0-60mph 96.5kmh: 13.3secs
0-1/4 mile: 19.5secs
75.0bhp 55.9kW 76.0PS
@ 4800rpm
92.0lbft 124.7Nm @ 2800rpm
78.5bhp/ton 77.2bhp/tonne
39.5bhp/L 29.5kW/L 40.1PS/L
36.1ft/sec 11.0m/sec
18.9mph 30.4kmh/1000rpm
27.0mpg 22.5mpgUS 10.5L/100km
Petrol 4-stroke piston
1897cc 115.7cu in
In-line 4 1 Carburettor
Compression ratio: 7.6:1
Bore: 93.0mm 3.7in
Stroke: 68.8mm 2.7in
Valve type/No: Overhead 8
Transmission: Manual
No. of forward speeds: 4
Wheels driven: Rear
Springs F/R: Coil/Coil
Brake system: PA
Brakes F/R: Disc/Drum
Steering: Rack & pinion
Wheelbase: 243.1cm 95.7in
Track F: 133.1cm 52.4in
Track R: 132.1cm 52.0in
Length: 434.3cm 171.0in
Width: 163.3cm 64.3in
Height: 135.4cm 53.3in
Ground clearance: 15.2cm 6.0in
Kerb weight: 971.6kg 2140.0lb
Fuel: 45.0L 9.9gal 11.9galUS

3335 Opel

Manta Berlinetta Auto
1973 Germany
100.0mph 160.9kmh
0-50mph 80.5kmh: 9.4secs
0-60mph 96.5kmh: 13.2secs
0-1/4 mile: 19.3secs
0-1km: 35.7secs
90.0bhp 67.1kW 91.2PS
@ 5100rpm
108.0lbft 146.3Nm @ 2800rpm
95.1bhp/ton 93.5bhp/tonne
47.4bhp/L 35.4kW/L 48.1PS/L
39.0ft/sec 11.9m/sec
19.6mph 31.5kmh/1000rpm
25.2mpg 21.0mpgUS 11.2L/100km
Petrol 4-stroke piston
1897cc 115.7cu in
In-line 4 1 Carburettor
Compression ratio: 9.0:1
Bore: 93.0mm 3.7in
Stroke: 69.8mm 2.7in
Valve type/No: Overhead 8
Transmission: Automatic
No. of forward speeds: 3
Wheels driven: Rear
Springs F/R: Coil/Coil
Brake system: PA
Brakes F/R: Disc/Drum
Steering: Rack & pinion
Wheelbase: 243.1cm 95.7in
Track F: 133.4cm 52.5in
Track R: 132.1cm 52.0in
Length: 434.3cm 171.0in
Width: 162.6cm 64.0in
Height: 135.9cm 53.5in
Ground clearance: 17.8cm 7.0in
Kerb weight: 962.0kg 2119.0lb
Fuel: 45.0L 9.9gal 11.9galUS

3336 Opel

Commodore GS 2.8
1974 Germany
115.0mph 185.0kmh
0-50mph 80.5kmh: 8.0secs
0-60mph 96.5kmh: 10.7secs
142.0bhp 105.9kW 144.0PS
@ 5200rpm
216.0lbft 292.7Nm @ 4200rpm
112.4bhp/ton 110.5bhp/tonne
51.0bhp/L 38.0kW/L 51.7PS/L
39.7ft/sec 12.1m/sec
20.8mph 33.5kmh/1000rpm
18.0mpg 15.0mpgUS 15.7L/100km
Petrol 4-stroke piston
2784cc 169.9cu in
In-line 6
Compression ratio: 9.5:1
Bore: 92.0mm 3.6in
Stroke: 69.8mm 2.7in
Valve type/No: Overhead 12
Transmission: Automatic
No. of forward speeds: 3
Wheels driven: Rear
Springs F/R: Coil/Coil
Brake system: PA
Brakes F/R: Disc/Drum
Steering: Recirculating ball PA
Wheelbase: 266.7cm 105.0in
Track F: 143.0cm 56.3in
Track R: 140.0cm 55.1in
Length: 459.7cm 181.0in
Width: 173.0cm 68.1in
Height: 140.2cm 55.2in
Kerb weight: 1284.8kg 2830.0lb
Fuel: 69.6L 15.3gal 18.4galUS

3337 Opel

Commodore GSE
1974 Germany
118.0mph 189.9kmh
0-50mph 80.5kmh: 7.7secs
0-60mph 96.5kmh: 10.7secs
0-1/4 mile: 17.6secs
0-1km: 32.8secs
160.0bhp 119.3kW 162.2PS
@ 5400rpm
168.0lbft 227.6Nm @ 4200rpm
123.0bhp/ton 120.9bhp/tonne
57.5bhp/L 42.9kW/L 58.3PS/L
41.2ft/sec 12.6m/sec
20.8mph 33.5kmh/1000rpm
18.1mpg 15.1mpgUS 15.6L/100km
Petrol 4-stroke piston
2784cc 169.9cu in
In-line 6 fuel injection
Compression ratio: 9.5:1
Bore: 92.0mm 3.6in
Stroke: 69.8mm 2.7in
Valve type/No: Overhead 12
Transmission: Automatic
No. of forward speeds: 3
Wheels driven: Rear
Springs F/R: Coil/Coil
Brake system: PA
Brakes F/R: Disc/Disc
Steering: Ball & nut PA
Wheelbase: 266.7cm 105.0in
Track F: 142.5cm 56.1in
Track R: 141.2cm 55.6in
Length: 456.7cm 179.8in
Width: 172.2cm 67.8in
Height: 141.0cm 55.5in
Ground clearance: 20.3cm 8.0in
Kerb weight: 1323.0kg 2914.0lb
Fuel: 70.1L 15.4gal 18.5galUS

3338 Opel

Kadett Coupe
1974 Germany
96.0mph 154.5kmh
0-50mph 80.5kmh: 10.3secs
0-60mph 96.5kmh: 15.5secs
0-1/4 mile: 20.1secs
0-1km: 37.0secs
60.0bhp 44.7kW 60.8PS
@ 5400rpm
70.0lbft 94.9Nm @ 3800rpm
76.0bhp/ton 74.7bhp/tonne
50.2bhp/L 37.4kW/L 50.9PS/L
36.4ft/sec 11.1m/sec
15.9mph 25.6kmh/1000rpm
32.0mpg 26.6mpgUS 8.8L/100km
Petrol 4-stroke piston
1196cc 73.0cu in
In-line 4 1 Carburettor
Compression ratio: 9.2:1
Bore: 79.0mm 3.1in
Stroke: 61.8mm 2.4in
Valve type/No: Overhead 8
Transmission: Manual
No. of forward speeds: 4
Wheels driven: Rear
Springs F/R: Coil/Coil
Brake system: PA
Brakes F/R: Disc/Drum
Steering: Rack & pinion
Wheelbase: 241.6cm 95.1in
Track F: 130.6cm 51.4in
Track R: 130.6cm 51.4in
Length: 412.5cm 162.4in
Width: 157.0cm 61.8in
Height: 133.6cm 52.6in
Ground clearance: 12.7cm 5.0in
Kerb weight: 803.1kg 1769.0lb
Fuel: 44.1L 9.7gal 11.7galUS

3339 Opel

1900
1975 Germany
96.0mph 154.5kmh
0-50mph 80.5kmh: 9.6secs
0-60mph 96.5kmh: 14.0secs
0-1/4 mile: 19.5secs
75.0bhp 55.9kW 76.0PS
@ 4800rpm
92.0lbft 124.7Nm @ 2800rpm
78.1bhp/ton 76.8bhp/tonne
39.5bhp/L 29.5kW/L 40.1PS/L
Petrol 4-stroke piston
1897cc 115.7cu in
In-line 4
Transmission: Manual
No. of forward speeds: 4
Wheels driven: Rear
Springs F/R: Coil/Coil
Brakes F/R: Disc/Drum
Wheelbase: 243.1cm 95.7in
Track F: 133.1cm 52.4in
Track R: 132.1cm 52.0in
Length: 432.3cm 170.2in
Width: 163.3cm 64.3in
Height: 136.1cm 53.6in
Kerb weight: 976.1kg 2150.0lb

3340 Opel

Ascona 1900SR
1975 Germany
103.0mph 165.7kmh
0-50mph 80.5kmh: 8.0secs
0-60mph 96.5kmh: 11.6secs
0-1/4 mile: 18.3secs
0-1km: 34.2secs
90.0bhp 67.1kW 91.2PS
@ 4800rpm
105.0lbft 142.3Nm @ 3800rpm
92.7bhp/ton 91.2bhp/tonne
47.4bhp/L 35.4kW/L 48.1PS/L
36.7ft/sec 11.2m/sec
18.2mph 29.3kmh/1000rpm
25.7mpg 21.4mpgUS 11.0L/100km
Petrol 4-stroke piston
1897cc 115.7cu in
In-line 4 1 Carburettor
Compression ratio: 8.8:1
Bore: 93.0mm 3.7in
Stroke: 69.8mm 2.7in
Valve type/No: Overhead 8
Transmission: Manual
No. of forward speeds: 4
Wheels driven: Rear
Springs F/R: Coil/Coil
Brake system: PA
Brakes F/R: Disc/Drum
Steering: Rack & pinion
Wheelbase: 251.5cm 99.0in
Track F: 137.2cm 54.0in
Track R: 137.2cm 54.0in
Length: 439.4cm 173.0in
Width: 175.3cm 69.0in
Height: 137.2cm 54.0in
Ground clearance: 21.6cm 8.5in
Kerb weight: 987.0kg 2174.0lb
Fuel: 50.0L 11.0gal 13.2galUS

3341 Opel

Manta
1975 Germany
104.0mph 167.3kmh
0-50mph 80.5kmh: 9.2secs
0-60mph 96.5kmh: 12.7secs
0-1/4 mile: 19.0secs
77.0bhp 57.4kW 78.1PS
@ 5000rpm
95.0lbft 128.7Nm @ 2200rpm
74.2bhp/ton 72.9bhp/tonne
40.6bhp/L 30.3kW/L 41.1PS/L
38.2ft/sec 11.6m/sec
19.5mph 31.4kmh/1000rpm
22.8mpg 19.0mpgUS 12.4L/100km
Petrol 4-stroke piston
1897cc 115.7cu in
In-line 4 fuel injection
Compression ratio: 7.6:1
Bore: 92.9mm 3.7in
Stroke: 69.8mm 2.7in
Valve type/No: Overhead 8
Transmission: Manual
No. of forward speeds: 4
Wheels driven: Rear
Springs F/R: Coil/Coil
Brake system: PA
Brakes F/R: Disc/Drum
Steering: Rack & pinion

Wheelbase: 243.1cm 95.7in
Track F: 133.1cm 52.4in
Track R: 132.1cm 52.0in
Length: 447.3cm 176.1in
Width: 163.3cm 64.3in
Height: 135.4cm 53.3in
Ground clearance: 12.7cm 5.0in
Kerb weight: 1055.5kg 2325.0lb
Fuel: 45.0L 9.9gal 11.9galUS

3342 Opel

Rekord 2100D
1976 Germany
82.0mph 131.9kmh
0-50mph 80.5kmh: 17.8secs
0-60mph 96.5kmh: 27.4secs
0-1/4 mile: 24.0secs
0-1km: 44.9secs
60.0bhp 44.7kW 60.8PS
@ 4400rpm
87.0lbft 117.9Nm @ 2500rpm
48.5bhp/ton 47.7bhp/tonne
29.0bhp/L 21.6kW/L 29.4PS/L
40.9ft/sec 12.5m/sec
18.4mph 29.6kmh/1000rpm
27.0mpg 22.5mpgUS 10.5L/100km
Diesel 4-stroke piston
2068cc 126.2cu in
In-line 4 fuel injection
Compression ratio: 22.0:1
Bore: 88.0mm 3.5in
Stroke: 85.0mm 3.3in
Valve type/No: Overhead 8
Transmission: Automatic
No. of forward speeds: 3
Wheels driven: Rear
Springs F/R: Coil/Coil
Brake system: PA
Brakes F/R: Disc/Drum
Steering: Recirculating ball PA
Wheelbase: 266.7cm 105.0in
Track F: 142.5cm 56.1in
Track R: 141.2cm 55.6in
Length: 456.7cm 179.8in
Width: 172.2cm 67.8in
Height: 141.0cm 55.5in
Ground clearance: 20.3cm 8.0in
Kerb weight: 1258.9kg 2773.0lb
Fuel: 70.1L 15.4gal 18.5galUS

3343 Opel

Rekord Berlina Pacesetter
1976 Germany
102.0mph 164.1kmh
0-50mph 80.5kmh: 10.2secs
0-60mph 96.5kmh: 13.9secs
0-1/4 mile: 20.0secs
0-1km: 36.7secs
100.0bhp 74.6kW 101.4PS
@ 5200rpm
109.0lbft 147.7Nm @ 3800rpm
87.3bhp/ton 85.9bhp/tonne
50.5bhp/L 37.7kW/L 51.2PS/L
39.7ft/sec 12.1m/sec
18.1mph 29.1kmh/1000rpm
22.6mpg 18.8mpgUS 12.5L/100km
Petrol 4-stroke piston
1979cc 120.7cu in
In-line 4 1 Carburettor
Compression ratio: 9.0:1
Bore: 95.0mm 3.7in
Stroke: 69.8mm 2.7in
Valve type/No: Overhead 8
Transmission: Automatic
No. of forward speeds: 3
Wheels driven: Rear
Springs F/R: Coil/Coil
Brake system: PA
Brakes F/R: Disc/Drum
Steering: Recirculating ball
Wheelbase: 266.7cm 105.0in
Track F: 142.5cm 56.1in
Track R: 141.2cm 55.6in
Length: 456.7cm 179.8in
Width: 172.2cm 67.8in
Height: 141.0cm 55.5in
Ground clearance: 20.3cm 8.0in
Kerb weight: 1164.5kg 2565.0lb
Fuel: 70.1L 15.4gal 18.5galUS

3344 Opel

Rekord 2.0S
1978 Germany
105.0mph 168.9kmh
0-50mph 80.5kmh: 8.1secs
0-60mph 96.5kmh: 11.0secs
0-1/4 mile: 18.2secs
0-1km: 33.7secs
100.0bhp 74.6kW 101.4PS
@ 5200rpm
117.0lbft 158.5Nm @ 3800rpm
92.8bhp/ton 91.2bhp/tonne
50.5bhp/L 37.7kW/L 51.2PS/L
39.7ft/sec 12.1m/sec
19.6mph 31.5kmh/1000rpm
23.2mpg 19.3mpgUS 12.2L/100km
Petrol 4-stroke piston
1979cc 120.7cu in
In-line 4 1 Carburettor
Compression ratio: 9.0:1
Bore: 95.0mm 3.7in
Stroke: 69.8mm 2.7in
Valve type/No: Overhead 8
Transmission: Manual
No. of forward speeds: 4
Wheels driven: Rear
Springs F/R: Coil/Coil
Brake system: PA
Brakes F/R: Disc/Drum
Steering: Recirculating ball PA
Wheelbase: 266.7cm 105.0in
Track F: 143.5cm 56.5in
Track R: 141.2cm 55.6in
Length: 457.2cm 180.0in
Width: 177.8cm 70.0in
Height: 142.2cm 56.0in
Ground clearance: 20.3cm 8.0in
Kerb weight: 1096.0kg 2414.0lb
Fuel: 65.1L 14.3gal 17.2galUS

3345 Opel

Kadett 1.3S Berlina
1979 Germany
104.0mph 167.3kmh
0-50mph 80.5kmh: 9.8secs
0-60mph 96.5kmh: 14.2secs
0-1/4 mile: 19.6secs
0-1km: 36.4secs
75.0bhp 55.9kW 76.0PS
@ 5800rpm
74.5lbft 100.9Nm @ 4600rpm
88.6bhp/ton 87.2bhp/tonne
57.8bhp/L 43.1kW/L 58.6PS/L
46.6ft/sec 14.2m/sec
16.0mph 25.7kmh/1000rpm
30.2mpg 25.1mpgUS 9.4L/100km
Petrol 4-stroke piston
1297cc 79.1cu in
In-line 4 1 Carburettor
Compression ratio: 9.2:1
Bore: 75.0mm 2.9in
Stroke: 73.4mm 2.9in
Valve type/No: Overhead 8
Transmission: Manual
No. of forward speeds: 4
Wheels driven: Front
Springs F/R: Coil/Coil
Brake system: PA
Brakes F/R: Disc/Drum
Steering: Rack & pinion
Wheelbase: 251.5cm 99.0in
Track F: 140.0cm 55.1in
Track R: 140.7cm 55.4in
Length: 399.8cm 157.4in
Width: 163.6cm 64.4in
Height: 137.9cm 54.3in
Ground clearance: 15.2cm 6.0in
Kerb weight: 860.3kg 1895.0lb
Fuel: 45.0L 9.9gal 11.9galUS

3346 Opel

Manta GTJ
1981 Germany
109.0mph 175.4kmh
0-50mph 80.5kmh: 7.6secs
0-60mph 96.5kmh: 11.0secs
0-1/4 mile: 17.4secs
0-1km: 32.9secs
100.0bhp 74.6kW 101.4PS
@ 5400rpm
105.0lbft 142.3Nm @ 3400rpm
99.7bhp/ton 98.0bhp/tonne
50.5bhp/L 37.7kW/L 51.2PS/L
41.2ft/sec 12.6m/sec
19.1mph 30.7kmh/1000rpm
22.3mpg 18.6mpgUS 12.7L/100km
Petrol 4-stroke piston
1979cc 120.7cu in
In-line 4 1 Carburettor
Compression ratio: 9.0:1
Bore: 95.0mm 3.7in
Stroke: 69.8mm 2.7in
Valve type/No: Overhead 8
Transmission: Manual
No. of forward speeds: 4
Wheels driven: Rear
Springs F/R: Coil/Coil
Brake system: PA
Brakes F/R: Disc/Drum
Steering: Rack & pinion
Wheelbase: 248.9cm 98.0in
Track F: 137.2cm 54.0in
Track R: 137.2cm 54.0in
Length: 442.0cm 174.0in
Width: 167.6cm 66.0in
Height: 132.1cm 52.0in
Ground clearance: 15.2cm 6.0in
Kerb weight: 1020.1kg 2247.0lb
Fuel: 50.0L 11.0gal 13.2galUS

3347 Opel

Manta Monza S3.0E
1981 Germany
135.0mph 217.2kmh
0-50mph 80.5kmh: 6.3secs
0-60mph 96.5kmh: 8.5secs
0-1/4 mile: 16.5secs
0-1km: 30.2secs
180.0bhp 134.2kW 182.5PS
@ 5800rpm
182.0lbft 246.6Nm @ 4200rpm
123.4bhp/ton 121.3bhp/tonne
60.6bhp/L 45.2kW/L 61.5PS/L
44.3ft/sec 13.5m/sec
23.5mph 37.8kmh/1000rpm
23.0mpg 19.2mpgUS 12.3L/100km
Petrol 4-stroke piston
2968cc 181.1cu in
In-line 6 fuel injection
Compression ratio: 9.4:1
Bore: 95.0mm 3.7in
Stroke: 69.8mm 2.7in
Valve type/No: Overhead 12
Transmission: Manual
No. of forward speeds: 5
Wheels driven: Rear
Springs F/R: Coil/Coil
Brake system: PA
Brakes F/R: Disc/Disc
Steering: Recirculating ball PA
Wheelbase: 266.7cm 105.0in
Track F: 144.3cm 56.8in
Track R: 146.6cm 57.7in
Length: 475.7cm 187.3in
Width: 173.5cm 68.3in
Height: 133.4cm 52.5in
Ground clearance: 15.2cm 6.0in
Kerb weight: 1483.7kg 3268.0lb
Fuel: 70.1L 15.4gal 18.5galUS

3348 Opel

Manta Berlinetta 1.8S
1983 Germany
110.0mph 177.0kmh
0-50mph 80.5kmh: 8.1secs
0-60mph 96.5kmh: 11.1secs
0-1/4 mile: 18.2secs
0-1km: 33.9secs
90.0bhp 67.1kW 91.2PS
@ 5400rpm
105.0lbft 142.3Nm @ 3000rpm
85.7bhp/ton 84.3bhp/tonne
50.1bhp/L 37.4kW/L 50.8PS/L
46.9ft/sec 14.3m/sec
24.3mph 39.1kmh/1000rpm
27.8mpg 23.1mpgUS 10.2L/100km
Petrol 4-stroke piston
1796cc 109.6cu in
In-line 4 1 Carburettor
Compression ratio: 9.2:1
Bore: 84.8mm 3.3in
Stroke: 79.5mm 3.1in
Valve type/No: Overhead 8
Transmission: Manual
No. of forward speeds: 5
Wheels driven: Rear
Springs F/R: Coil/Coil
Brake system: PA
Brakes F/R: Disc/Drum
Steering: Rack & pinion
Wheelbase: 248.9cm 98.0in
Track F: 137.9cm 54.3in
Track R: 137.4cm 54.1in
Length: 444.2cm 174.9in
Width: 168.7cm 66.4in
Height: 133.1cm 52.4in
Ground clearance: 15.2cm 6.0in
Kerb weight: 1067.8kg 2352.0lb
Fuel: 50.0L 11.0gal 13.2galUS

3349 Opel

Manta GTE
1983 Germany
122.0mph 196.3kmh
0-50mph 80.5kmh: 6.6secs
0-60mph 96.5kmh: 9.0secs
0-1/4 mile: 16.8secs
0-1km: 31.0secs
110.0bhp 82.0kW 111.5PS
@ 5400rpm
119.5lbft 161.9Nm @ 3400rpm
106.9bhp/ton 105.1bhp/tonne
55.6bhp/L 41.4kW/L 56.4PS/L
41.2ft/sec 12.6m/sec
24.4mph 39.3kmh/1000rpm
29.1mpg 24.2mpgUS 9.7L/100km
Petrol 4-stroke piston
1979cc 120.7cu in
In-line 4 fuel injection
Compression ratio: 9.4:1
Bore: 95.0mm 3.7in
Stroke: 69.8mm 2.7in
Valve type/No: Overhead 8
Transmission: Manual
No. of forward speeds: 5
Wheels driven: Rear
Springs F/R: Coil/Coil
Brake system: PA
Brakes F/R: Disc/Drum
Steering: Rack & pinion
Wheelbase: 248.9cm 98.0in
Track F: 137.9cm 54.3in
Track R: 137.4cm 54.1in
Length: 444.2cm 174.9in
Width: 168.7cm 66.4in
Height: 133.1cm 52.4in
Ground clearance: 15.2cm 6.0in
Kerb weight: 1046.5kg 2305.0lb
Fuel: 50.0L 11.0gal 13.2galUS

3350 Opel

Manta Monza GSE
1984 Germany
134.0mph 215.6kmh
0-50mph 80.5kmh: 6.1secs
0-60mph 96.5kmh: 8.7secs
0-1/4 mile: 16.4secs
0-1km: 30.1secs
180.0bhp 134.2kW 182.5PS
@ 5800rpm
182.0lbft 246.6Nm @ 4200rpm
122.5bhp/ton 120.5bhp/tonne
60.6bhp/L 45.2kW/L 61.5PS/L
44.3ft/sec 13.5m/sec
25.8mph 41.5kmh/1000rpm
20.5mpg 17.1mpgUS 13.8L/100km
Petrol 4-stroke piston
2969cc 181.1cu in
In-line 6 fuel injection
Compression ratio: 9.4:1
Bore: 95.0mm 3.7in
Stroke: 69.8mm 2.7in
Valve type/No: Overhead 12
Transmission: Manual
No. of forward speeds: 5
Wheels driven: Rear
Springs F/R: Coil/Coil
Brake system: PA
Brakes F/R: Disc/Disc
Steering: Recirculating ball PA
Wheelbase: 266.7cm 105.0in
Track F: 144.3cm 56.8in
Track R: 146.6cm 57.7in
Length: 471.9cm 185.8in
Width: 172.2cm 67.8in
Height: 135.6cm 53.4in
Ground clearance: 15.0cm 5.9in
Kerb weight: 1493.7kg 3290.0lb
Fuel: 70.1L 15.4gal 18.5galUS

3351 Opel

Calibra 2.0i 16v
1991 Germany
137.0mph 220.4kmh
0-50mph 80.5kmh: 5.8secs
0-60mph 96.5kmh: 7.6secs
0-1/4 mile: 15.9secs
150.0bhp 111.9kW 152.1PS
@ 6000rpm
145.0lbft 196.5Nm @ 4800rpm
125.4bhp/ton 123.3bhp/tonne
75.1bhp/L 56.0kW/L 76.1PS/L
56.5ft/sec 17.2m/sec
30.0mpg 25.0mpgUS 9.4L/100km
Petrol 4-stroke piston
1998cc 121.9cu in

In-line 4 fuel injection
Compression ratio: 10.5:1
Bore: 86.0mm 3.4in
Stroke: 86.0mm 3.4in
Valve type/No: Overhead 16
Transmission: Manual
No. of forward speeds: 5
Wheels driven: Front
Springs F/R: Coil/Coil
Brake system: PA ABS
Brakes F/R: Disc/Disc
Steering: Rack & pinion PA
Wheelbase: 260.1cm 102.4in
Track F: 142.5cm 56.1in
Track R: 144.5cm 56.9in
Length: 449.3cm 176.9in
Width: 167.6cm 66.0in
Height: 128.8cm 50.7in
Kerb weight: 1216.7kg 2680.0lb
Fuel: 65.1L 14.3gal 17.2galUS

3352 Opel

Omega Lotus
1991 Germany
174.0mph 280.0kmh
0-60mph 96.5kmh: 4.9secs
0-1/4 mile: 13.5secs
377.0bhp 281.1kW 382.2PS
@ 5200rpm
409.0lbft 554.2Nm @ 4200rpm
227.0bhp/ton 223.2bhp/tonne
103.7bhp/L 77.3kW/L 105.1PS/L
48.4ft/sec 14.7m/sec
Petrol 4-stroke piston
3637cc 221.9cu in turbocharged
In-line 6 fuel injection
Compression ratio: 8.2:1
Bore: 95.3mm 3.8in
Stroke: 85.0mm 3.3in
Valve type/No: Overhead 24
Transmission: Manual
No. of forward speeds: 6
Wheels driven: Rear
Springs F/R: Coil/Coil
Brake system: PA ABS
Brakes F/R: Disc/Disc
Steering: Rack & pinion
Wheelbase: 273.1cm 107.5in
Track F: 148.8cm 58.6in
Track R: 153.4cm 60.4in
Length: 476.8cm 187.7in
Width: 181.1cm 71.3in
Height: 143.3cm 56.4in
Kerb weight: 1688.9kg 3720.0lb

3353 Osca

1490cc Spyder
1955 Italy
0-50mph 80.5kmh: 5.4secs
0-60mph 96.5kmh: 7.0secs
0-1/4 mile: 15.7secs
110.0bhp 82.0kW 111.5PS
@ 6200rpm
192.5bhp/ton 189.3bhp/tonne
73.8bhp/L 55.0kW/L 74.8PS/L
52.9ft/sec 16.1m/sec
17.1mph 27.5kmh/1000rpm
Petrol 4-stroke piston
1490cc 90.9cu in
In-line 4
Compression ratio: 8.8:1
Bore: 78.0mm 3.1in
Stroke: 78.0mm 3.1in
Valve type/No: Overhead 8
Transmission: Manual
No. of forward speeds: 4
Wheels driven: Rear
Wheelbase: 220.0cm 86.6in
Track F: 119.9cm 47.2in
Track R: 115.1cm 45.3in
Kerb weight: 581.1kg 1280.0lb

3354 Packard

32.5hp Saloon
1929 USA
70.0mph 112.6kmh
14.0mpg 11.7mpgUS 20.2L/100km
Petrol 4-stroke piston
5342cc 325.9cu in
In-line 8
Bore: 81.0mm 3.2in
Stroke: 127.0mm 5.0in
Transmission: Manual
No. of forward speeds: 3
Wheels driven: Rear
Brakes F/R: Drum/Drum
Wheelbase: 320.0cm 126.0in
Track F: 142.2cm 56.0in
Track R: 142.2cm 56.0in
Length: 480.1cm 189.0in
Width: 175.3cm 69.0in
Height: 188.0cm 74.0in
Kerb weight: 1900.0kg 4185.0lb
Fuel: 81.9L 18.0gal 21.6galUS

3355 Packard

7-34 Phaeton
1930 USA
92.5mph 148.8kmh
0-50mph 80.5kmh: 12.3secs
0-60mph 96.5kmh: 17.2secs
0-1/4 mile: 20.5secs
145.0bhp 108.1kW 147.0PS
@ 3400rpm
290.0lbft 393.0Nm @ 1600rpm
75.5bhp/ton 74.3bhp/tonne
23.0bhp/L 17.1kW/L 23.3PS/L
47.2ft/sec 14.4m/sec
Petrol 4-stroke piston
6308cc 384.9cu in
In-line 8
Compression ratio: 6.3:1
Bore: 88.9mm 3.5in
Stroke: 127.0mm 5.0in
Valve type/No: Side 16
Transmission: Manual
No. of forward speeds: 4
Wheels driven: Rear
Wheelbase: 341.6cm 134.5in
Track F: 146.1cm 57.5in
Track R: 149.9cm 59.0in
Kerb weight: 1952.2kg 4300.0lb

3356 Packard

Super 8 Phaeton
1932 USA
85.0mph 136.8kmh
0-50mph 80.5kmh: 13.2secs
0-60mph 96.5kmh: 18.8secs
0-1/4 mile: 21.2secs
135.0bhp 100.7kW 136.9PS
@ 3200rpm
290.0lbft 393.0Nm @ 1600rpm
60.7bhp/ton 59.7bhp/tonne
21.4bhp/L 16.0kW/L 21.7PS/L
44.4ft/sec 13.5m/sec
20.5mph 33.0kmh/1000rpm
Petrol 4-stroke piston
6308cc 384.9cu in
In-line 8 1 Carburettor
Compression ratio: 6.0:1
Bore: 88.9mm 3.5in
Stroke: 127.0mm 5.0in
Valve type/No: Side 16
Transmission: Manual
No. of forward speeds: 3
Wheels driven: Rear
Wheelbase: 360.7cm 142.0in
Track F: 146.1cm 57.5in
Track R: 149.9cm 59.0in
Length: 520.7cm 205.0in
Width: 182.9cm 72.0in
Height: 177.8cm 70.0in
Kerb weight: 2260.9kg 4980.0lb

3357 Packard

Straight Eight Saloon
1933 USA
80.3mph 129.2kmh
0-50mph 80.5kmh: 15.6secs
0-60mph 96.5kmh: 23.0secs
13.5mpg 11.2mpgUS 20.9L/100km
Petrol 4-stroke piston
5342cc 325.9cu in
In-line 8
Bore: 81.0mm 3.2in
Stroke: 127.0mm 5.0in
Transmission: Manual
No. of forward speeds: 3
Wheels driven: Rear
Brakes F/R: Drum/Drum
Kerb weight: 2091.1kg 4606.0lb
Fuel: 72.8L 16.0gal 19.2galUS

3358 Packard

32.5hp Saloon
1934 USA
86.1mph 138.5kmh
0-50mph 80.5kmh: 14.0secs
0-60mph 96.5kmh: 21.2secs
14.0mpg 11.7mpgUS 20.2L/100km
Petrol 4-stroke piston
5342cc 325.9cu in
In-line 8
Bore: 81.0mm 3.2in
Stroke: 127.0mm 5.0in
Transmission: Manual
No. of forward speeds: 3
Wheels driven: Rear
Brakes F/R: Drum/Drum
Kerb weight: 2135.6kg 4704.0lb
Fuel: 91.0L 20.0gal 24.0galUS

3359 Packard

Twelve Victoria
1934 USA
88.0mph 141.6kmh
0-50mph 80.5kmh: 14.1secs
0-60mph 96.5kmh: 19.2secs
0-1/4 mile: 21.5secs
160.0bhp 119.3kW 162.2PS
@ 3200rpm
310.0lbft 420.1Nm @ 1800rpm
64.0bhp/ton 62.9bhp/tonne
21.4bhp/L 16.0kW/L 21.7PS/L
35.6ft/sec 10.8m/sec
19.7mph 31.7kmh/1000rpm
Petrol 4-stroke piston
7467cc 455.6cu in
Vee 12 1 Carburettor
Compression ratio: 6.0:1
Bore: 87.4mm 3.4in
Stroke: 101.6mm 4.0in
Valve type/No: Side 24
Transmission: Manual
No. of forward speeds: 3
Wheels driven: Rear
Brakes F/R: Drum/Drum
Wheelbase: 373.4cm 147.0in
Track F: 146.1cm 57.5in
Track R: 149.9cm 59.0in
Length: 533.4cm 210.0in
Width: 182.9cm 72.0in
Height: 153.2cm 60.3in
Kerb weight: 2542.4kg 5600.0lb

3360 Packard

120 Saloon
1935 USA
84.9mph 136.6kmh
0-50mph 80.5kmh: 13.6secs
0-60mph 96.5kmh: 20.2secs
17.0mpg 14.2mpgUS 16.6L/100km
Petrol 4-stroke piston
3668cc 223.8cu in
In-line 6
Bore: 73.0mm 2.9in
Stroke: 114.3mm 4.5in
Valve type/No: Side 12
Transmission: Manual
No. of forward speeds: 3
Wheels driven: Rear
Brakes F/R: Drum/Drum
Ground clearance: 20.3cm 8.0in
Kerb weight: 1665.3kg 3668.0lb
Fuel: 72.8L 16.0gal 19.2galUS

3361 Packard

32.5hp Standard Eight Saloon
1936 USA
84.9mph 136.6kmh
0-50mph 80.5kmh: 15.0secs
0-60mph 96.5kmh: 20.4secs
12.0mpg 10.0mpgUS 23.5L/100km
Petrol 4-stroke piston
5342cc 325.9cu in
In-line 8
Bore: 81.0mm 3.2in
Stroke: 127.0mm 5.0in
Valve type/No: Side 16
Transmission: Manual
No. of forward speeds: 3
Wheels driven: Rear
Brakes F/R: Drum/Drum
Kerb weight: 2321.3kg 5113.0lb
Fuel: 91.0L 20.0gal 24.0galUS

3362 Packard

120 Saloon
1937 USA
84.9mph 136.6kmh
0-50mph 80.5kmh: 13.5secs
0-60mph 96.5kmh: 19.9secs
16.0mpg 13.3mpgUS 17.7L/100km
Petrol 4-stroke piston
4621cc 281.9cu in
In-line 8
Bore: 82.6mm 3.2in
Stroke: 108.0mm 4.2in
Valve type/No: Side 16
Transmission: Manual
No. of forward speeds: 3
Wheels driven: Rear
Brakes F/R: Drum/Drum
Kerb weight: 1680.7kg 3702.0lb
Fuel: 72.8L 16.0gal 19.2galUS

3363 Packard

30hp Six Saloon
1938 USA
77.5mph 124.7kmh
0-50mph 80.5kmh: 15.8secs
0-60mph 96.5kmh: 23.3secs
16.0mpg 13.3mpgUS 17.7L/100km
Petrol 4-stroke piston
4020cc 245.3cu in
In-line 6
Bore: 88.9mm 3.5in
Stroke: 107.9mm 4.2in
Valve type/No: Side 12
Transmission: Manual
No. of forward speeds: 3
Wheels driven: Rear
Brakes F/R: Drum/Drum
Kerb weight: 1683.0kg 3707.0lb
Fuel: 61.4L 13.5gal 16.2galUS

3364 Panhard

18hp Saloon
1930 France
66.1mph 106.4kmh
21.0mpg 17.5mpgUS 13.5L/100km
Petrol 4-stroke piston
2300cc 140.3cu in
In-line 6
Bore: 69.5mm 2.7in
Stroke: 103.0mm 4.1in
Valve type/No: Ports
Transmission: Manual
No. of forward speeds: 4
Wheels driven: Rear
Brakes F/R: Drum/Drum
Wheelbase: 317.5cm 125.0in
Track F: 135.9cm 53.5in
Track R: 135.9cm 53.5in
Length: 436.9cm 172.0in
Width: 172.7cm 68.0in
Height: 182.9cm 72.0in
Kerb weight: 1627.1kg 3584.0lb
Fuel: 68.2L 15.0gal 18.0galUS

3365 Panhard

Dyna
1954 France
75.5mph 121.5kmh
0-50mph 80.5kmh: 16.7secs
0-60mph 96.5kmh: 26.1secs
0-1/4 mile: 23.2secs
42.0bhp 31.3kW 42.6PS
@ 5000rpm
47.0lbft 63.7Nm @ 3500rpm
59.8bhp/ton 58.8bhp/tonne
49.4bhp/L 36.8kW/L 50.1PS/L
41.0ft/sec 12.5m/sec
15.0mph 24.1kmh/1000rpm
34.0mpg 28.3mpgUS 8.3L/100km
Petrol 4-stroke piston
850cc 51.9cu in
Flat 2
Compression ratio: 7.2:1
Bore: 85.0mm 3.3in
Stroke: 75.0mm 2.9in
Valve type/No: Overhead 4
Transmission: Manual
No. of forward speeds: 4
Wheels driven: Front
Springs F/R: Leaf/Torsion bar
Brakes F/R: Drum/Drum
Wheelbase: 257.0cm 101.2in
Track F: 130.0cm 51.2in
Track R: 130.0cm 51.2in
Length: 457.7cm 180.2in
Width: 158.0cm 62.2in
Height: 145.3cm 57.2in
Ground clearance: 20.1cm 7.9in
Kerb weight: 714.1kg 1573.0lb
Fuel: 39.6L 8.7gal 10.5galUS

3366 Panhard
Dyna Junior Sports
1954 France
76.9mph 123.7kmh
0-50mph 80.5kmh: 15.7secs
0-60mph 96.5kmh: 26.2secs
0-1/4 mile: 23.3secs
40.0bhp 29.8kW 40.5PS
@ 5000rpm
47.0lbft 63.7Nm @ 4000rpm
55.3bhp/ton 54.4bhp/tonne
47.0bhp/L 35.0kW/L 47.6PS/L
41.0ft/sec 12.5m/sec
15.2mph 24.5kmh/1000rpm
53.8mpg 44.8mpgUS 5.3L/100km
Petrol 4-stroke piston
851cc 51.9cu in
Flat 2
Compression ratio: 7.3:1
Bore: 85.1mm 3.3in
Stroke: 74.9mm 2.9in
Valve type/No: Overhead 4
Transmission: Manual
No. of forward speeds: 4
Wheels driven: Front
Wheelbase: 226.8cm 89.3in
Track F: 121.9cm 48.0in
Track R: 121.9cm 48.0in
Kerb weight: 735.5kg 1620.0lb

3367 Panhard
Dyna Sedan
1956 France
80.2mph 129.0kmh
0-50mph 80.5kmh: 15.0secs
0-60mph 96.5kmh: 23.7secs
0-1/4 mile: 23.0secs
50.0bhp 37.3kW 50.7PS
@ 5000rpm
47.0lbft 63.7Nm @ 3500rpm
62.9bhp/ton 61.9bhp/tonne
58.8bhp/L 43.9kW/L 59.6PS/L
41.0ft/sec 12.5m/sec
Petrol 4-stroke piston
850cc 51.9cu in
Flat 2
Compression ratio: 7.3:1
Bore: 85.1mm 3.3in
Stroke: 74.9mm 2.9in
Valve type/No: Overhead 4
Transmission: Manual
No. of forward speeds: 4
Wheels driven: Front
Wheelbase: 257.0cm 101.2in
Track F: 130.0cm 51.2in
Track R: 130.0cm 51.2in
Kerb weight: 808.1kg 1780.0lb

3368 Panhard
Dyna
1959 France
79.0mph 127.1kmh
0-50mph 80.5kmh: 16.8secs
0-60mph 96.5kmh: 24.0secs
0-1/4 mile: 23.7secs
42.0bhp 31.3kW 42.6PS
@ 5000rpm
51.0lbft 69.1Nm @ 2250rpm
50.0bhp/ton 49.2bhp/tonne
49.4bhp/L 36.8kW/L 50.1PS/L
41.0ft/sec 12.5m/sec
15.1mph 24.3kmh/1000rpm
Petrol 4-stroke piston
850cc 51.9cu in
Flat 2
Compression ratio: 7.3:1
Bore: 85.1mm 3.3in
Stroke: 74.9mm 2.9in
Valve type/No: Overhead 4
Transmission: Manual
No. of forward speeds: 4
Wheels driven: Front
Wheelbase: 257.0cm 101.2in
Track F: 130.0cm 51.2in
Track R: 130.0cm 51.2in
Length: 457.2cm 180.0in
Width: 166.1cm 65.4in
Height: 154.9cm 61.0in
Kerb weight: 853.5kg 1880.0lb

3369 Panhard
PL17
1959 France
79.0mph 127.1kmh
0-50mph 80.5kmh: 19.0secs
0-60mph 96.5kmh: 28.6secs
0-1/4 mile: 24.1secs
42.0bhp 31.3kW 42.6PS
@ 5300rpm
50.6lbft 68.6Nm @ 2500rpm
50.9bhp/ton 50.1bhp/tonne
49.3bhp/L 36.8kW/L 50.0PS/L
43.4ft/sec 13.2m/sec
15.2mph 24.5kmh/1000rpm
32.1mpg 26.7mpgUS 8.8L/100km
Petrol 4-stroke piston
851cc 51.9cu in
Flat 2 1 Carburettor
Compression ratio: 7.2:1
Bore: 85.0mm 3.3in
Stroke: 75.0mm 2.9in
Valve type/No: Overhead 4
Transmission: Manual
No. of forward speeds: 4
Wheels driven: Front
Springs F/R: Leaf/Torsion bar
Brakes F/R: Drum/Drum
Wheelbase: 270.0cm 106.3in
Track F: 129.8cm 51.1in
Track R: 129.8cm 51.1in
Length: 458.2cm 180.4in
Width: 165.9cm 65.3in
Height: 146.1cm 57.5in
Ground clearance: 16.3cm 6.4in
Kerb weight: 839.0kg 1848.0lb
Fuel: 43.2L 9.5gal 11.4galUS

3370 Panhard
PL17 Tiger
1962 France
81.0mph 130.3kmh
0-50mph 80.5kmh: 15.8secs
0-60mph 96.5kmh: 22.8secs
0-1/4 mile: 22.6secs
50.0bhp 37.3kW 50.7PS
@ 5800rpm
50.6lbft 68.6Nm @ 3600rpm
59.7bhp/ton 58.7bhp/tonne
59.0bhp/L 44.0kW/L 59.8PS/L
47.5ft/sec 14.5m/sec
15.8mph 25.4kmh/1000rpm
28.7mpg 23.9mpgUS 9.8L/100km
Petrol 4-stroke piston
848cc 51.7cu in
Flat 2 1 Carburettor
Compression ratio: 8.3:1
Bore: 85.0mm 3.3in
Stroke: 75.0mm 2.9in
Valve type/No: Overhead 4
Transmission: Manual
No. of forward speeds: 4
Wheels driven: Front
Springs F/R: Leaf
Brakes F/R: Drum/Drum
Steering: Rack & pinion
Wheelbase: 256.5cm 101.0in
Track F: 129.5cm 51.0in
Track R: 129.5cm 51.0in
Length: 458.2cm 180.4in
Width: 165.1cm 65.0in
Height: 146.1cm 57.5in
Ground clearance: 15.2cm 6.0in
Kerb weight: 851.7kg 1876.0lb
Fuel: 40.9L 9.0gal 10.8galUS

3371 Panhard
24CT Sports Coupe
1964 France
92.0mph 148.0kmh
0-50mph 80.5kmh: 15.1secs
0-60mph 96.5kmh: 22.3secs
0-1/4 mile: 22.5secs
60.0bhp 44.7kW 60.8PS
@ 6000rpm
54.0lbft 73.2Nm @ 3500rpm
73.3bhp/ton 72.1bhp/tonne
70.7bhp/L 52.8kW/L 71.7PS/L
49.2ft/sec 15.0m/sec
15.2mph 24.5kmh/1000rpm
33.3mpg 27.7mpgUS 8.5L/100km
Petrol 4-stroke piston
848cc 51.7cu in
Flat 2 1 Carburettor
Compression ratio: 8.0:1
Bore: 84.8mm 3.3in
Stroke: 75.0mm 2.9in
Valve type/No: Overhead 4
Transmission: Manual
No. of forward speeds: 4
Wheels driven: Front
Springs F/R: Leaf/Torsion bar
Brakes F/R: Drum/Drum
Steering: Rack & pinion
Wheelbase: 228.6cm 90.0in
Track F: 129.5cm 51.0in
Track R: 129.5cm 51.0in
Length: 426.7cm 168.0in
Width: 162.6cm 64.0in
Height: 125.7cm 49.5in
Ground clearance: 15.7cm 6.2in
Kerb weight: 832.6kg 1834.0lb
Fuel: 42.1L 9.2gal 11.1galUS

3372 Panther
J72
1972 UK
115.0mph 185.0kmh
0-50mph 80.5kmh: 5.0secs
0-60mph 96.5kmh: 6.4secs
0-1/4 mile: 15.3secs
0-1km: 29.0secs
190.0bhp 141.7kW 192.6PS
@ 5000rpm
200.0lbft 271.0Nm @ 3000rpm
170.0bhp/ton 167.1bhp/tonne
50.2bhp/L 37.5kW/L 50.9PS/L
57.9ft/sec 17.7m/sec
28.2mph 45.4kmh/1000rpm
14.3mpg 11.9mpgUS 19.8L/100km
Petrol 4-stroke piston
3781cc 230.7cu in
In-line 6 2 Carburettor
Compression ratio: 8.0:1
Bore: 87.0mm 3.4in
Stroke: 106.0mm 4.2in
Valve type/No: Overhead 12
Transmission: Manual with overdrive
No. of forward speeds: 5
Wheels driven: Rear
Springs F/R: Coil/Coil
Brake system: PA
Brakes F/R: Disc/Disc
Steering: Recirculating ball
Wheelbase: 276.9cm 109.0in
Track F: 138.4cm 54.5in
Track R: 138.4cm 54.5in
Length: 406.4cm 160.0in
Width: 166.4cm 65.5in
Height: 134.6cm 53.0in
Ground clearance: 12.7cm 5.0in
Kerb weight: 1136.8kg 2504.0lb
Fuel: 127.4L 28.0gal 33.6galUS

3373 Panther
De Ville
1975 UK
0-60mph 96.5kmh: 12.0secs
0-1/4 mile: 18.4secs
244.0bhp 181.9kW 247.4PS
@ 5750rpm
331.0lbft 448.5Nm @ 4000rpm
123.7bhp/ton 121.6bhp/tonne
45.7bhp/L 34.0kW/L 46.3PS/L
44.1ft/sec 13.4m/sec
13.2mpg 11.0mpgUS 21.4L/100km
Petrol 4-stroke piston
5343cc 326.0cu in
Vee 12
Compression ratio: 7.8:1
Bore: 90.0mm 3.5in
Stroke: 70.0mm 2.8in
Valve type/No: Overhead 24
Transmission: Automatic
No. of forward speeds: 3
Wheels driven: Rear
Springs F/R: Coil/Coil
Brake system: PA
Brakes F/R: Disc/Disc
Steering: Rack & pinion PA
Wheelbase: 360.7cm 142.0in
Track F: 167.6cm 66.0in
Track R: 167.6cm 66.0in
Length: 518.2cm 204.0in
Width: 180.3cm 71.0in
Height: 154.9cm 61.0in
Kerb weight: 2006.7kg 4420.0lb
Fuel: 118.1L 26.0gal 31.2galUS

3374 Panther
J72
1975 UK
108.0mph 173.8kmh
0-50mph 80.5kmh: 7.3secs
0-60mph 96.5kmh: 10.7secs
0-1/4 mile: 18.2secs
186.0bhp 138.7kW 188.6PS
@ 4500rpm
240.0lbft 325.2Nm @ 3750rpm
140.8bhp/ton 138.4bhp/tonne
44.6bhp/L 33.2kW/L 45.2PS/L
52.1ft/sec 15.9m/sec
26.4mph 42.5kmh/1000rpm
16.2mpg 13.5mpgUS 17.4L/100km
Petrol 4-stroke piston
4173cc 254.6cu in
In-line 6
Compression ratio: 8.0:1
Bore: 92.1mm 3.6in
Stroke: 106.0mm 4.2in
Valve type/No: Overhead 12
Transmission: Manual with overdrive
Wheels driven: Rear
Springs F/R: Coil/Coil
Brake system: PA
Brakes F/R: Disc/Disc
Steering: Recirculating ball
Wheelbase: 276.9cm 109.0in
Track F: 137.7cm 54.2in
Track R: 137.7cm 54.2in
Length: 408.9cm 161.0in
Width: 168.9cm 66.5in
Height: 124.5cm 49.0in
Kerb weight: 1343.8kg 2960.0lb
Fuel: 118.1L 26.0gal 31.2galUS

3375 Panther
Lima
1977 UK
120.0mph 193.1kmh
0-50mph 80.5kmh: 4.9secs
0-60mph 96.5kmh: 6.7secs
0-1/4 mile: 15.1secs
0-1km: 28.6secs
108.0bhp 80.5kW 109.5PS
@ 5000rpm
138.0lbft 187.0Nm @ 3000rpm
124.1bhp/ton 122.0bhp/tonne
47.4bhp/L 35.3kW/L 48.0PS/L
53.3ft/sec 16.2m/sec
19.5mph 31.4kmh/1000rpm
21.8mpg 18.2mpgUS 13.0L/100km
Petrol 4-stroke piston
2279cc 139.0cu in
In-line 4 1 Carburettor
Compression ratio: 8.5:1
Bore: 76.2mm 3.0in
Stroke: 97.5mm 3.8in
Valve type/No: Overhead 8
Transmission: Manual
No. of forward speeds: 4
Wheels driven: Rear
Springs F/R: Coil/Coil
Brake system: PA
Brakes F/R: Disc/Drum
Steering: Rack & pinion
Wheelbase: 246.4cm 97.0in
Track F: 132.8cm 52.3in
Track R: 132.1cm 52.0in
Length: 360.7cm 142.0in
Width: 161.0cm 63.4in
Height: 122.7cm 48.3in
Ground clearance: 11.4cm 4.5in
Kerb weight: 885.3kg 1950.0lb
Fuel: 45.5L 10.0gal 12.0galUS

3376 Panther
Kallista 2.8
1983 UK
112.0mph 180.2kmh
0-50mph 80.5kmh: 6.0secs
0-60mph 96.5kmh: 7.8secs
0-1/4 mile: 16.1secs
0-1km: 30.6secs
135.0bhp 100.7kW 136.9PS
@ 5200rpm
162.0lbft 219.5Nm @ 3000rpm
148.6bhp/ton 146.1bhp/tonne
48.3bhp/L 36.1kW/L 49.0PS/L
39.0ft/sec 11.9m/sec
26.2mph 42.2kmh/1000rpm
24.1mpg 20.1mpgUS 11.7L/100km
Petrol 4-stroke piston
2792cc 170.3cu in
Vee 6 1 Carburettor
Compression ratio: 9.2:1
Bore: 93.0mm 3.7in
Stroke: 68.5mm 2.7in
Valve type/No: Overhead 12
Transmission: Manual
No. of forward speeds: 5
Wheels driven: Rear
Springs F/R: Coil/Coil
Brake system: PA
Brakes F/R: Disc/Drum
Steering: Rack & pinion

Wheelbase: 255.3cm 100.5in
Track F: 147.6cm 58.1in
Track R: 139.7cm 55.0in
Length: 385.1cm 151.6in
Width: 169.4cm 66.7in
Height: 127.0cm 50.0in
Ground clearance: 9.9cm 3.9in
Kerb weight: 923.9kg 2035.0lb
Fuel: 49.1L 10.8gal 13.0galUS

3377 Panther

Kallista 2.8
1984 UK
112.0mph 180.2kmh
0-50mph 80.5kmh: 6.2secs
0-60mph 96.5kmh: 7.7secs
0-1/4 mile: 16.3secs
0-1km: 30.6secs
150.0bhp 111.9kW 152.1PS
@ 5700rpm
159.0lbft 215.4Nm @ 4000rpm
163.0bhp/ton 160.3bhp/tonne
53.7bhp/L 40.1kW/L 54.5PS/L
42.7ft/sec 13.0m/sec
26.7mph 43.0kmh/1000rpm
24.4mpg 20.3mpgUS 11.6L/100km
Petrol 4-stroke piston
2792cc 170.3cu in
Vee 6 fuel injection
Compression ratio: 9.2:1
Bore: 93.0mm 3.7in
Stroke: 68.5mm 2.7in
Valve type/No: Overhead 12
Transmission: Manual
No. of forward speeds: 5
Wheels driven: Rear
Springs F/R: Coil/Coil
Brake system: PA
Brakes F/R: Disc/Drum
Steering: Rack & pinion
Wheelbase: 255.3cm 100.5in
Track F: 147.6cm 58.1in
Track R: 139.7cm 55.0in
Length: 385.1cm 151.6in
Width: 169.4cm 66.7in
Height: 127.0cm 50.0in
Ground clearance: 9.9cm 3.9in
Kerb weight: 935.7kg 2061.0lb
Fuel: 49.1L 10.8gal 13.0galUS

3378 Panther

Kallista 1.6L
1985 UK
92.0mph 148.0kmh
0-50mph 80.5kmh: 8.3secs
0-60mph 96.5kmh: 12.6secs
0-1/4 mile: 18.0secs
0-1km: 35.8secs
96.0bhp 71.6kW 97.3PS
@ 6000rpm
98.0lbft 132.8Nm @ 4000rpm
105.9bhp/ton 104.2bhp/tonne
60.1bhp/L 44.8kW/L 60.9PS/L
52.2ft/sec 15.9m/sec
22.0mph 35.4kmh/1000rpm
23.7mpg 19.7mpgUS 11.9L/100km
Petrol 4-stroke piston
1597cc 97.4cu in
In-line 4 1 Carburettor
Compression ratio: 9.5:1
Bore: 80.0mm 3.1in
Stroke: 79.5mm 3.1in
Valve type/No: Overhead 8
Transmission: Manual
No. of forward speeds: 5
Wheels driven: Rear
Springs F/R: Coil/Coil
Brake system: PA
Brakes F/R: Disc/Drum
Steering: Rack & pinion
Wheelbase: 255.3cm 100.5in
Track F: 147.6cm 58.1in
Track R: 139.7cm 55.0in
Length: 385.1cm 151.6in
Width: 169.4cm 66.7in
Height: 127.0cm 50.0in
Ground clearance: 9.9cm 3.9in
Kerb weight: 921.6kg 2030.0lb
Fuel: 50.0L 11.0gal 13.2galUS

3379 Panther

Kallista
1990 UK
0-60mph 96.5kmh: 8.9secs
95.0bhp 70.8kW 96.3PS
@ 6000rpm
98.0lbft 132.8Nm @ 4000rpm
107.2bhp/ton 105.4bhp/tonne
59.5bhp/L 44.4kW/L 60.3PS/L
52.2ft/sec 15.9m/sec
Petrol 4-stroke piston
1597cc 97.4cu in
In-line 4 1 Carburettor
Compression ratio: 9.5:1
Bore: 80.0mm 3.1in
Stroke: 79.5mm 3.1in
Valve type/No: Overhead 8
Transmission: Manual
No. of forward speeds: 5
Wheels driven: Rear
Springs F/R: Coil/Coil
Brakes F/R: Disc/Drum
Steering: Rack & pinion
Wheelbase: 255.0cm 100.4in
Track F: 146.6cm 57.7in
Track R: 138.4cm 54.5in
Length: 388.9cm 153.1in
Width: 169.4cm 66.7in
Height: 127.0cm 50.0in
Kerb weight: 901.2kg 1985.0lb
Fuel: 50.0L 11.0gal 13.2galUS

3380 Panther

Solo
1990 UK
146.0mph 234.9kmh
0-50mph 80.5kmh: 5.3secs
0-60mph 96.5kmh: 6.8secs
0-1/4 mile: 15.3secs
0-1km: 27.4secs
204.0bhp 152.1kW 206.8PS
@ 6000rpm
203.7lbft 276.0Nm @ 4500rpm
154.8bhp/ton 152.2bhp/tonne
102.4bhp/L 76.3kW/L 103.8PS/L
50.5ft/sec 15.4m/sec
23.5mph 37.8kmh/1000rpm
19.4mpg 16.2mpgUS 14.6L/100km
Petrol 4-stroke piston
1993cc 122.0cu in turbocharged
In-line 4 fuel injection
Compression ratio: 8.0:1
Bore: 91.0mm 3.6in
Stroke: 77.0mm 3.0in
Valve type/No: Overhead 16
Transmission: Manual
No. of forward speeds: 5
Wheels driven: 4-wheel drive
Springs F/R: Coil/Coil
Brake system: PA ABS
Brakes F/R: Disc/Disc
Steering: Rack & pinion
Wheelbase: 254.0cm 100.0in
Track F: 152.9cm 60.2in
Track R: 151.4cm 59.6in
Length: 433.4cm 170.6in
Width: 179.0cm 70.5in
Height: 118.0cm 46.5in
Ground clearance: 12.7cm 5.0in
Kerb weight: 1340.0kg 2951.5lb
Fuel: 54.6L 12.0gal 14.4galUS

3381 Paramount

Roadster
1956 UK
72.0mph 115.8kmh
0-50mph 80.5kmh: 20.0secs
0-60mph 96.5kmh: 30.6secs
0-1/4 mile: 24.4secs
47.0bhp 35.0kW 47.6PS
@ 4400rpm
72.0lbft 97.6Nm @ 2000rpm
42.7bhp/ton 42.0bhp/tonne
31.2bhp/L 23.2kW/L 31.6PS/L
36.7ft/sec 11.2m/sec
17.0mph 27.4kmh/1000rpm
26.0mpg 21.6mpgUS 10.9L/100km
Petrol 4-stroke piston
1508cc 92.0cu in
In-line 4
Compression ratio: 6.8:1
Bore: 79.4mm 3.1in
Stroke: 76.2mm 3.0in
Valve type/No: Overhead 8
Transmission: Manual
No. of forward speeds: 3
Wheels driven: Rear
Springs F/R: Leaf/Leaf
Brakes F/R: Drum/Drum
Wheelbase: 259.1cm 102.0in
Track F: 128.3cm 50.5in
Track R: 129.5cm 51.0in
Length: 426.7cm 168.0in
Width: 167.6cm 66.0in
Height: 142.2cm 56.0in
Ground clearance: 15.2cm 6.0in
Kerb weight: 1118.7kg 2464.0lb
Fuel: 68.2L 15.0gal 18.0galUS

3382 Parradine V-12

1991 UK
170.0mph 273.5kmh
0-60mph 96.5kmh: 5.4secs
277.0bhp 206.6kW 280.8PS
@ 5150rpm
397.0lbft 537.9Nm @ 2800rpm
225.6bhp/ton 221.9bhp/tonne
51.8bhp/L 38.7kW/L 52.6PS/L
39.5ft/sec 12.0m/sec
Petrol 4-stroke piston
5343cc 326.0cu in
Vee 12 fuel injection
Compression ratio: 11.5:1
Bore: 90.0mm 3.5in
Stroke: 70.0mm 2.8in
Valve type/No: Overhead 24
Transmission: Manual
No. of forward speeds: 5
Wheels driven: Rear
Springs F/R: Coil/Coil
Brake system: ABS
Brakes F/R: Disc/Disc
Steering: Rack & pinion PA
Wheelbase: 236.2cm 93.0in
Length: 418.6cm 164.8in
Width: 187.2cm 73.7in
Height: 134.4cm 52.9in
Kerb weight: 1248.5kg 2750.0lb

3383 Peerless

GT Coupe
1959 UK
110.0mph 177.0kmh
0-50mph 80.5kmh: 8.4secs
0-60mph 96.5kmh: 12.4secs
0-1/4 mile: 18.1secs
100.0bhp 74.6kW 101.4PS
@ 5000rpm
117.5lbft 159.2Nm @ 3000rpm
93.3bhp/ton 91.8bhp/tonne
50.2bhp/L 37.4kW/L 50.9PS/L
50.3ft/sec 15.3m/sec
20.1mph 32.3kmh/1000rpm
Petrol 4-stroke piston
1991cc 121.5cu in
In-line 4
Compression ratio: 8.5:1
Bore: 83.1mm 3.3in
Stroke: 91.9mm 3.6in
Valve type/No: Overhead 8
Transmission: Manual with overdrive
Wheels driven: Rear
Wheelbase: 240.0cm 94.5in
Track F: 129.5cm 51.0in
Track R: 129.5cm 51.0in
Length: 388.6cm 153.0in
Width: 160.0cm 63.0in
Height: 127.0cm 50.0in
Kerb weight: 1089.6kg 2400.0lb

3384 Peugeot

203
1955 France
70.5mph 113.4kmh
0-50mph 80.5kmh: 21.2secs
0-60mph 96.5kmh: 34.5secs
0-1/4 mile: 23.9secs
45.0bhp 33.6kW 45.6PS
@ 4500rpm
46.0bhp/ton 45.3bhp/tonne
34.9bhp/L 26.0kW/L 35.4PS/L
35.9ft/sec 10.9m/sec
16.5mph 26.5kmh/1000rpm
Petrol 4-stroke piston
1290cc 78.7cu in
In-line 4
Bore: 74.9mm 2.9in
Stroke: 72.9mm 2.9in
Valve type/No: Overhead 8
Transmission: Manual
No. of forward speeds: 4
Wheels driven: Rear
Wheelbase: 258.1cm 101.6in
Track F: 132.1cm 52.0in
Track R: 132.1cm 52.0in
Kerb weight: 994.3kg 2190.0lb

3385 Peugeot

403
1955 France
77.0mph 123.9kmh
0-50mph 80.5kmh: 16.1secs
0-60mph 96.5kmh: 24.0secs
0-1/4 mile: 23.0secs
58.0bhp 43.2kW 58.8PS
@ 4900rpm
75.0lbft 101.6Nm @ 2500rpm
54.9bhp/ton 54.0bhp/tonne
39.5bhp/L 29.5kW/L 40.0PS/L
39.1ft/sec 11.9m/sec
17.0mph 27.4kmh/1000rpm
29.8mpg 24.8mpgUS 9.5L/100km
Petrol 4-stroke piston
1468cc 89.6cu in
In-line 4 1 Carburettor
Compression ratio: 7.0:1
Bore: 80.0mm 3.1in
Stroke: 73.0mm 2.9in
Valve type/No: Overhead 8
Transmission: Manual with overdrive
No. of forward speeds: 4
Wheels driven: Rear
Springs F/R: Leaf/Coil
Brakes F/R: Drum/Drum
Wheelbase: 265.4cm 104.5in
Track F: 133.9cm 52.7in
Track R: 132.1cm 52.0in
Length: 445.8cm 175.5in
Width: 167.6cm 66.0in
Height: 150.4cm 59.2in
Ground clearance: 17.8cm 7.0in
Kerb weight: 1074.2kg 2366.0lb
Fuel: 47.8L 10.5gal 12.6galUS

3386 Peugeot

403
1960 France
80.8mph 130.0kmh
0-50mph 80.5kmh: 14.1secs
0-60mph 96.5kmh: 20.5secs
0-1/4 mile: 21.7secs
66.0bhp 49.2kW 66.9PS
@ 4750rpm
85.0lbft 115.2Nm @ 3000rpm
61.1bhp/ton 60.1bhp/tonne
45.0bhp/L 33.5kW/L 45.6PS/L
37.9ft/sec 11.5m/sec
16.8mph 27.0kmh/1000rpm
Petrol 4-stroke piston
1468cc 89.6cu in
In-line 4 1 Carburettor
Compression ratio: 7.5:1
Bore: 80.0mm 3.1in
Stroke: 72.9mm 2.9in
Valve type/No: Overhead 8
Transmission: Manual
No. of forward speeds: 3
Wheels driven: Rear
Wheelbase: 265.9cm 104.7in
Track F: 134.1cm 52.8in
Track R: 132.1cm 52.0in
Length: 447.0cm 176.0in
Width: 167.1cm 65.8in
Height: 151.1cm 59.5in
Kerb weight: 1098.7kg 2420.0lb

3387 Peugeot

404
1960 France
92.0mph 148.0kmh
0-50mph 80.5kmh: 13.9secs
0-60mph 96.5kmh: 19.9secs
0-1/4 mile: 22.2secs
72.0bhp 53.7kW 73.0PS
@ 5400rpm
94.0lbft 127.4Nm @ 2250rpm
68.3bhp/ton 67.2bhp/tonne
44.5bhp/L 33.2kW/L 45.1PS/L
43.0ft/sec 13.1m/sec
17.6mph 28.3kmh/1000rpm
25.9mpg 21.6mpgUS 10.9L/100km
Petrol 4-stroke piston
1618cc 98.7cu in
In-line 4 1 Carburettor
Compression ratio: 7.3:1
Bore: 84.0mm 3.3in
Stroke: 73.0mm 2.9in
Valve type/No: Overhead 8
Transmission: Manual
No. of forward speeds: 4
Wheels driven: Rear
Springs F/R: Coil/Coil
Brakes F/R: Drum/Drum
Wheelbase: 264.9cm 104.3in

Track F: 134.4cm 52.9in
Track R: 128.0cm 50.4in
Length: 441.7cm 173.9in
Width: 162.6cm 64.0in
Height: 145.0cm 57.1in
Ground clearance: 15.0cm 5.9in
Kerb weight: 1071.4kg 2360.0lb
Fuel: 50.0L 11.0gal 13.2galUS

3388 Peugeot
404
1961 France
88.4mph 142.2kmh
0-50mph 80.5kmh: 12.5secs
0-60mph 96.5kmh: 18.4secs
0-1/4 mile: 21.0secs
72.0bhp 53.7kW 73.0PS
@ 5400rpm
94.0lbft 127.4Nm @ 2250rpm
67.8bhp/ton 66.6bhp/tonne
44.5bhp/L 33.2kW/L 45.1PS/L
43.0ft/sec 13.1m/sec
18.5mph 29.8kmh/1000rpm
Petrol 4-stroke piston
1618cc 98.7cu in
In-line 4 1 Carburettor
Compression ratio: 7.4:1
Bore: 84.1mm 3.3in
Stroke: 72.9mm 2.9in
Valve type/No: Overhead 8
Transmission: Manual
No. of forward speeds: 4
Wheels driven: Rear
Brakes F/R: Drum/Drum
Wheelbase: 264.9cm 104.3in
Track F: 134.4cm 52.9in
Track R: 128.0cm 50.4in
Length: 442.0cm 174.0in
Width: 162.6cm 64.0in
Height: 145.0cm 57.1in
Ground clearance: 15.0cm 5.9in
Kerb weight: 1080.5kg 2380.0lb

3389 Peugeot
403 B Estate Car
1962 France
83.0mph 133.5kmh
0-50mph 80.5kmh: 16.6secs
0-60mph 96.5kmh: 25.2secs
0-1/4 mile: 23.1secs
65.0bhp 48.5kW 65.9PS
@ 4900rpm
74.5lbft 100.9Nm @ 2500rpm
55.3bhp/ton 54.4bhp/tonne
44.3bhp/L 33.0kW/L 44.9PS/L
39.1ft/sec 11.9m/sec
16.5mph 26.5kmh/1000rpm
24.7mpg 20.6mpgUS 11.4L/100km
Petrol 4-stroke piston
1468cc 89.6cu in
In-line 4 1 Carburettor
Compression ratio: 7.2:1
Bore: 80.0mm 3.1in
Stroke: 73.0mm 2.9in
Valve type/No: Overhead 8
Transmission: Manual
No. of forward speeds: 4
Wheels driven: Rear
Springs F/R: Leaf/Leaf
Brakes F/R: Drum/Drum
Steering: Rack & pinion
Wheelbase: 289.6cm 114.0in
Track F: 132.6cm 52.2in
Track R: 132.1cm 52.0in
Length: 461.0cm 181.5in
Width: 166.4cm 65.5in
Height: 161.8cm 63.7in
Ground clearance: 15.2cm 6.0in
Kerb weight: 1194.9kg 2632.0lb
Fuel: 50.0L 11.0gal 13.2galUS

3390 Peugeot
404 U6 Estate Car
1962 France
85.0mph 136.8kmh
0-50mph 80.5kmh: 14.5secs
0-60mph 96.5kmh: 20.5secs
0-1/4 mile: 22.1secs
66.0bhp 49.2kW 66.9PS
@ 5000rpm
83.0lbft 112.5Nm @ 2500rpm
58.7bhp/ton 57.7bhp/tonne
45.0bhp/L 33.5kW/L 45.6PS/L
39.9ft/sec 12.2m/sec
16.5mph 26.5kmh/1000rpm
26.8mpg 22.3mpgUS 10.5L/100km
Petrol 4-stroke piston
1468cc 89.6cu in
In-line 4 1 Carburettor
Compression ratio: 7.5:1
Bore: 80.0mm 3.1in
Stroke: 73.0mm 2.9in
Valve type/No: Overhead 8
Transmission: Manual
No. of forward speeds: 4
Wheels driven: Rear
Springs F/R: Coil/Coil
Brakes F/R: Drum/Drum
Steering: Rack & pinion
Wheelbase: 284.5cm 112.0in
Track F: 134.6cm 53.0in
Track R: 129.5cm 51.0in
Length: 458.5cm 180.5in
Width: 165.6cm 65.2in
Height: 157.5cm 62.0in
Ground clearance: 15.2cm 6.0in
Kerb weight: 1144.1kg 2520.0lb
Fuel: 50.0L 11.0gal 13.2galUS

3391 Peugeot
404
1965 France
90.0mph 144.8kmh
0-50mph 80.5kmh: 11.9secs
0-60mph 96.5kmh: 18.1secs
0-1/4 mile: 21.0secs
76.0bhp 56.7kW 77.0PS
@ 5500rpm
96.0lbft 130.1Nm @ 2500rpm
68.9bhp/ton 67.8bhp/tonne
47.0bhp/L 35.0kW/L 47.6PS/L
43.8ft/sec 13.4m/sec
17.9mph 28.8kmh/1000rpm
Petrol 4-stroke piston
1618cc 98.7cu in
In-line 4 1 Carburettor
Compression ratio: 7.6:1
Bore: 84.1mm 3.3in
Stroke: 72.9mm 2.9in
Valve type/No: Overhead 8
Transmission: Manual
No. of forward speeds: 4
Wheels driven: Rear
Springs F/R: Coil/Coil
Brakes F/R: Drum/Drum
Steering: Rack & pinion
Wheelbase: 264.9cm 104.3in
Track F: 134.4cm 52.9in
Track R: 128.0cm 50.4in
Length: 442.0cm 174.0in
Width: 162.6cm 64.0in
Height: 145.0cm 57.1in
Ground clearance: 15.2cm 6.0in
Kerb weight: 1121.4kg 2470.0lb
Fuel: 49.2L 10.8gal 13.0galUS

3392 Peugeot
404 Diesel
1965 France
82.0mph 131.9kmh
0-50mph 80.5kmh: 16.3secs
0-60mph 96.5kmh: 25.4secs
0-1/4 mile: 23.1secs
55.0bhp 41.0kW 55.8PS
@ 4500rpm
87.5lbft 118.6Nm @ 2250rpm
50.9bhp/ton 50.1bhp/tonne
28.2bhp/L 21.0kW/L 28.6PS/L
39.4ft/sec 12.0m/sec
17.7mph 28.5kmh/1000rpm
32.3mpg 26.9mpgUS 8.7L/100km
Diesel 4-stroke piston
1948cc 118.8cu in
In-line 4 fuel injection
Compression ratio: 22.0:1
Bore: 88.0mm 3.5in
Stroke: 80.0mm 3.1in
Valve type/No: Overhead 8
Transmission: Manual
No. of forward speeds: 4
Wheels driven: Rear
Springs F/R: Coil/Coil
Brakes F/R: Drum/Drum
Steering: Rack & pinion
Wheelbase: 264.7cm 104.2in
Track F: 133.9cm 52.7in
Track R: 127.5cm 50.2in
Length: 442.0cm 174.0in
Width: 165.6cm 65.2in
Height: 145.3cm 57.2in
Ground clearance: 15.2cm 6.0in
Kerb weight: 1098.7kg 2420.0lb
Fuel: 50.0L 11.0gal 13.2galUS

3393 Peugeot
404 KF2
1965 France
101.0mph 162.5kmh
0-50mph 80.5kmh: 9.9secs
0-60mph 96.5kmh: 13.9secs
0-1/4 mile: 18.8secs
88.0bhp 65.6kW 89.2PS
@ 5500rpm
101.0lbft 136.9Nm @ 2800rpm
81.6bhp/ton 80.3bhp/tonne
54.4bhp/L 40.6kW/L 55.1PS/L
43.8ft/sec 13.4m/sec
17.7mph 28.5kmh/1000rpm
25.1mpg 20.9mpgUS 11.3L/100km
Petrol 4-stroke piston
1618cc 98.7cu in
In-line 4 fuel injection
Compression ratio: 8.8:1
Bore: 84.0mm 3.3in
Stroke: 73.0mm 2.9in
Valve type/No: Overhead 8
Transmission: Manual
No. of forward speeds: 4
Wheels driven: Rear
Springs F/R: Coil/Coil
Brake system: PA
Brakes F/R: Drum/Drum
Steering: Rack & pinion
Wheelbase: 264.7cm 104.2in
Track F: 133.9cm 52.7in
Track R: 128.0cm 50.4in
Length: 442.0cm 174.0in
Width: 165.6cm 65.2in
Height: 145.3cm 57.2in
Ground clearance: 15.2cm 6.0in
Kerb weight: 1096.4kg 2415.0lb
Fuel: 50.0L 11.0gal 13.2galUS

3394 Peugeot
204
1966 France
91.0mph 146.4kmh
0-50mph 80.5kmh: 12.3secs
0-60mph 96.5kmh: 18.3secs
0-1/4 mile: 21.1secs
0-1km: 39.8secs
53.0bhp 39.5kW 53.7PS
@ 5800rpm
60.5lbft 82.0Nm @ 3000rpm
63.3bhp/ton 62.3bhp/tonne
46.9bhp/L 35.0kW/L 47.6PS/L
40.6ft/sec 12.4m/sec
15.6mph 25.1kmh/1000rpm
32.1mpg 26.7mpgUS 8.8L/100km
Petrol 4-stroke piston
1130cc 68.9cu in
In-line 4 1 Carburettor
Compression ratio: 8.8:1
Bore: 75.0mm 2.9in
Stroke: 64.0mm 2.5in
Valve type/No: Overhead 8
Transmission: Manual
No. of forward speeds: 4
Wheels driven: Front
Springs F/R: Coil/Coil
Brakes F/R: Disc/Drum
Steering: Rack & pinion
Wheelbase: 256.5cm 101.0in
Track F: 129.5cm 51.0in
Track R: 124.5cm 49.0in
Length: 396.2cm 156.0in
Width: 154.9cm 61.0in
Height: 139.7cm 55.0in
Ground clearance: 24.1cm 9.5in
Kerb weight: 851.2kg 1875.0lb
Fuel: 41.9L 9.2gal 11.1galUS

3395 Peugeot
404 Automatique
1967 France
87.0mph 140.0kmh
0-50mph 80.5kmh: 13.5secs
0-60mph 96.5kmh: 20.0secs
0-1/4 mile: 21.5secs
80.0bhp 59.7kW 81.1PS
@ 5600rpm
97.5lbft 132.1Nm @ 2500rpm
72.3bhp/ton 71.0bhp/tonne
49.4bhp/L 36.9kW/L 50.1PS/L
44.6ft/sec 13.6m/sec
16.8mph 27.0kmh/1000rpm
Petrol 4-stroke piston
1618cc 98.7cu in
In-line 4
Compression ratio: 8.3:1
Bore: 84.2mm 3.3in
Stroke: 73.0mm 2.9in
Valve type/No: Overhead 8
Transmission: Automatic
No. of forward speeds: 3
Wheels driven: Rear
Brake system: PA
Brakes F/R: Drum/Drum
Steering: Rack & pinion
Wheelbase: 264.9cm 104.3in
Track F: 134.4cm 52.9in
Track R: 128.0cm 50.4in
Length: 442.0cm 174.0in
Width: 162.6cm 64.0in
Height: 145.0cm 57.1in
Kerb weight: 1125.9kg 2480.0lb
Fuel: 54.9L 12.1gal 14.5galUS

3396 Peugeot
404 L Estate
1967 France
90.0mph 144.8kmh
0-50mph 80.5kmh: 12.5secs
0-60mph 96.5kmh: 19.2secs
0-1/4 mile: 21.1secs
0-1km: 40.4secs
74.0bhp 55.2kW 75.0PS
@ 5600rpm
98.0lbft 132.8Nm @ 2500rpm
62.2bhp/ton 61.2bhp/tonne
45.7bhp/L 34.1kW/L 46.4PS/L
44.6ft/sec 13.6m/sec
16.1mph 25.9kmh/1000rpm
22.2mpg 18.5mpgUS 12.7L/100km
Petrol 4-stroke piston
1618cc 98.7cu in
In-line 4 1 Carburettor
Compression ratio: 8.3:1
Bore: 84.0mm 3.3in
Stroke: 73.0mm 2.9in
Valve type/No: Overhead 8
Transmission: Manual
No. of forward speeds: 4
Wheels driven: Rear
Springs F/R: Coil/Coil
Brake system: PA
Brakes F/R: Drum/Drum
Steering: Rack & pinion
Wheelbase: 284.5cm 112.0in
Track F: 134.6cm 53.0in
Track R: 129.5cm 51.0in
Length: 458.5cm 180.5in
Width: 165.6cm 65.2in
Height: 157.5cm 62.0in
Ground clearance: 15.2cm 6.0in
Kerb weight: 1209.0kg 2663.0lb
Fuel: 50.0L 11.0gal 13.2galUS

3397 Peugeot
204 Coupe
1968 France
89.0mph 143.2kmh
0-50mph 80.5kmh: 13.9secs
0-60mph 96.5kmh: 19.9secs
0-1/4 mile: 21.5secs
0-1km: 40.0secs
53.0bhp 39.5kW 53.7PS
@ 5800rpm
60.5lbft 82.0Nm @ 3000rpm
60.6bhp/ton 59.6bhp/tonne
46.9bhp/L 35.0kW/L 47.6PS/L
40.6ft/sec 12.4m/sec
15.9mph 25.6kmh/1000rpm
27.5mpg 22.9mpgUS 10.3L/100km
Petrol 4-stroke piston
1130cc 68.9cu in
In-line 4 1 Carburettor
Compression ratio: 8.8:1
Bore: 75.0mm 2.9in
Stroke: 64.0mm 2.5in
Valve type/No: Overhead 8
Transmission: Manual
No. of forward speeds: 4
Wheels driven: Front
Springs F/R: Coil/Coil
Brake system: PA
Brakes F/R: Disc/Drum
Steering: Rack & pinion
Wheelbase: 228.6cm 90.0in
Track F: 132.1cm 52.0in
Track R: 125.0cm 49.2in
Length: 373.4cm 147.0in
Width: 156.0cm 61.4in
Height: 129.5cm 51.0in
Ground clearance: 15.2cm 6.0in
Kerb weight: 889.8kg 1960.0lb
Fuel: 42.1L 9.2gal 11.1galUS

3398 Peugeot
404 Station Wagon
1968 France
85.0mph 136.8kmh
0-1/4 mile: 21.0secs
80.0bhp 59.7kW 81.1PS
49.4bhp/L 36.9kW/L 50.1PS/L
28.8mpg 24.0mpgUS 9.8L/100km
Petrol 4-stroke piston
1618cc 98.7cu in
In-line 4
Valve type/No: Overhead 8
Wheels driven: Rear
Wheelbase: 284.0cm 111.8in
Length: 457.2cm 180.0in

3399 Peugeot
504 Injection
1968 France
107.0mph 172.2kmh
0-50mph 80.5kmh: 8.8secs
0-60mph 96.5kmh: 12.6secs
0-1/4 mile: 18.7secs
0-1km: 35.1secs
97.0bhp 72.3kW 98.3PS
@ 5600rpm
113.0lbft 153.1Nm @ 3000rpm
83.6bhp/ton 82.2bhp/tonne
54.0bhp/L 40.3kW/L 54.8PS/L
49.6ft/sec 15.1m/sec
18.9mph 30.4kmh/1000rpm
25.3mpg 21.1mpgUS 11.2L/100km
Petrol 4-stroke piston
1796cc 109.6cu in
In-line 4 fuel injection
Compression ratio: 8.3:1
Bore: 84.0mm 3.3in
Stroke: 81.0mm 3.2in
Valve type/No: Overhead 8
Transmission: Manual
No. of forward speeds: 4
Wheels driven: Rear
Springs F/R: Coil/Coil
Brake system: PA
Brakes F/R: Disc/Disc
Steering: Rack & pinion
Wheelbase: 274.1cm 107.9in
Track F: 142.0cm 55.9in
Track R: 135.9cm 53.5in
Length: 448.8cm 176.7in
Width: 168.9cm 66.5in
Height: 146.1cm 57.5in
Ground clearance: 17.8cm 7.0in
Kerb weight: 1180.4kg 2600.0lb
Fuel: 56.0L 12.3gal 14.8galUS

3400 Peugeot
404 Automatic
1969 France
91.0mph 146.4kmh
0-50mph 80.5kmh: 13.3secs
0-60mph 96.5kmh: 19.3secs
0-1/4 mile: 21.2secs
0-1km: 40.6secs
74.0bhp 55.2kW 75.0PS
@ 5600rpm
98.0lbft 132.8Nm @ 2500rpm
69.3bhp/ton 68.1bhp/tonne
45.7bhp/L 34.1kW/L 46.4PS/L
44.6ft/sec 13.6m/sec
17.6mph 28.3kmh/1000rpm
23.4mpg 19.5mpgUS 12.1L/100km
Petrol 4-stroke piston
1618cc 98.7cu in
In-line 4 1 Carburettor
Compression ratio: 8.3:1
Bore: 84.0mm 3.3in
Stroke: 73.0mm 2.9in
Valve type/No: Overhead 8
Transmission: Automatic
No. of forward speeds: 3
Wheels driven: Rear
Springs F/R: Coil/Coil
Brake system: PA
Brakes F/R: Disc/Drum
Steering: Rack & pinion
Wheelbase: 264.2cm 104.0in
Track F: 134.1cm 52.8in
Track R: 128.0cm 50.4in
Length: 445.0cm 175.2in
Width: 166.4cm 65.5in
Height: 145.5cm 57.3in
Ground clearance: 15.2cm 6.0in
Kerb weight: 1086.4kg 2393.0lb
Fuel: 54.6L 12.0gal 14.4galUS

3401 Peugeot
504
1970 France
98.0mph 157.7kmh
0-50mph 80.5kmh: 11.2secs
0-60mph 96.5kmh: 15.9secs
0-1/4 mile: 19.7secs
87.0bhp 64.9kW 88.2PS
@ 5500rpm
108.0lbft 146.3Nm @ 3000rpm
72.3bhp/ton 71.1bhp/tonne
48.4bhp/L 36.1kW/L 49.1PS/L
48.7ft/sec 14.8m/sec
17.9mph 28.8kmh/1000rpm
25.8mpg 21.5mpgUS 10.9L/100km
Petrol 4-stroke piston
1796cc 109.6cu in
In-line 4 2 Carburettor
Compression ratio: 8.4:1
Bore: 84.0mm 3.3in
Stroke: 81.0mm 3.2in
Valve type/No: Overhead 8
Transmission: Manual
No. of forward speeds: 4
Wheels driven: Rear
Springs F/R: Coil/Coil
Brake system: PA
Brakes F/R: Disc/Disc
Steering: Rack & pinion
Wheelbase: 274.3cm 108.0in
Track F: 143.5cm 56.5in
Track R: 135.9cm 53.5in
Length: 449.6cm 177.0in
Width: 168.9cm 66.5in
Height: 146.1cm 57.5in
Ground clearance: 16.5cm 6.5in
Kerb weight: 1223.5kg 2695.0lb
Fuel: 56.0L 12.3gal 14.8galUS

3402 Peugeot
304
1971 France
88.0mph 141.6kmh
0-50mph 80.5kmh: 10.9secs
0-60mph 96.5kmh: 16.5secs
0-1/4 mile: 21.2secs
70.0bhp 52.2kW 71.0PS
@ 6100rpm
74.0lbft 100.3Nm @ 3750rpm
74.8bhp/ton 73.6bhp/tonne
54.3bhp/L 40.5kW/L 55.1PS/L
47.4ft/sec 14.4m/sec
16.5mph 26.5kmh/1000rpm
36.5mpg 30.4mpgUS 7.7L/100km
Petrol 4-stroke piston
1288cc 78.6cu in
In-line 4 1 Carburettor
Compression ratio: 8.8:1
Bore: 76.0mm 3.0in
Stroke: 71.0mm 2.8in
Valve type/No: Overhead 8
Transmission: Manual
No. of forward speeds: 4
Wheels driven: Front
Springs F/R: Coil/Coil
Brake system: PA
Brakes F/R: Disc/Drum
Steering: Rack & pinion
Wheelbase: 258.8cm 101.9in
Track F: 131.8cm 51.9in
Track R: 126.0cm 49.6in
Length: 413.8cm 162.9in
Width: 157.0cm 61.8in
Height: 141.0cm 55.5in
Ground clearance: 14.0cm 5.5in
Kerb weight: 951.1kg 2095.0lb
Fuel: 42.0L 9.2gal 11.1galUS

3403 Peugeot
504 Automatic
1971 France
100.0mph 160.9kmh
0-50mph 80.5kmh: 10.9secs
0-60mph 96.5kmh: 14.8secs
0-1/4 mile: 20.4secs
0-1km: 37.6secs
97.0bhp 72.3kW 98.3PS
@ 5600rpm
122.0lbft 165.3Nm @ 3000rpm
81.4bhp/ton 80.0bhp/tonne
49.2bhp/L 36.7kW/L 49.9PS/L
49.6ft/sec 15.1m/sec
18.9mph 30.4kmh/1000rpm
19.9mpg 16.6mpgUS 14.2L/100km
Petrol 4-stroke piston
1971cc 120.3cu in
In-line 4 fuel injection
Compression ratio: 8.4:1
Bore: 88.0mm 3.5in
Stroke: 81.0mm 3.2in
Valve type/No: Overhead 8
Transmission: Automatic
No. of forward speeds: 3
Wheels driven: Rear
Springs F/R: Coil/Coil
Brake system: PA
Brakes F/R: Disc/Disc
Steering: Rack & pinion
Wheelbase: 274.1cm 107.9in
Track F: 142.0cm 55.9in
Track R: 135.9cm 53.5in
Length: 448.8cm 176.7in
Width: 168.9cm 66.5in
Height: 146.1cm 57.5in
Ground clearance: 17.8cm 7.0in
Kerb weight: 1212.2kg 2670.0lb
Fuel: 56.0L 12.3gal 14.8galUS

3404 Peugeot
204
1972 France
84.0mph 135.2kmh
0-50mph 80.5kmh: 11.7secs
0-60mph 96.5kmh: 17.4secs
0-1/4 mile: 20.3secs
0-1km: 39.1secs
50.0bhp 37.3kW 50.7PS
@ 5600rpm
61.0lbft 82.7Nm @ 3000rpm
57.6bhp/ton 56.6bhp/tonne
44.2bhp/L 33.0kW/L 44.9PS/L
39.2ft/sec 11.9m/sec
16.4mph 26.4kmh/1000rpm
28.2mpg 23.5mpgUS 10.0L/100km
Petrol 4-stroke piston
1130cc 68.9cu in
In-line 4 1 Carburettor
Compression ratio: 8.8:1
Bore: 75.0mm 2.9in
Stroke: 64.0mm 2.5in
Valve type/No: Overhead 8
Transmission: Manual
No. of forward speeds: 4
Wheels driven: Front
Springs F/R: Coil/Coil
Brake system: PA
Brakes F/R: Disc/Drum
Steering: Rack & pinion
Wheelbase: 259.1cm 102.0in
Track F: 132.1cm 52.0in
Track R: 125.7cm 49.5in
Length: 396.2cm 156.0in
Width: 156.2cm 61.5in
Height: 139.7cm 55.0in
Ground clearance: 16.5cm 6.5in
Kerb weight: 883.0kg 1945.0lb
Fuel: 42.1L 9.2gal 11.1galUS

3405 Peugeot
304 Estate Car
1972 France
92.0mph 148.0kmh
0-50mph 80.5kmh: 10.1secs
0-60mph 96.5kmh: 14.6secs
0-1/4 mile: 19.8secs
0-1km: 36.8secs
65.0bhp 48.5kW 65.9PS
@ 5750rpm
69.0lbft 93.5Nm @ 3750rpm
70.3bhp/ton 69.1bhp/tonne
50.5bhp/L 37.6kW/L 51.2PS/L
44.7ft/sec 13.6m/sec
16.7mph 26.9kmh/1000rpm
25.0mpg 20.8mpgUS 11.3L/100km
Petrol 4-stroke piston
1288cc 78.6cu in
In-line 4 1 Carburettor
Compression ratio: 8.8:1
Bore: 76.0mm 3.0in
Stroke: 71.0mm 2.8in
Valve type/No: Overhead 8
Transmission: Manual
No. of forward speeds: 4
Wheels driven: Front
Springs F/R: Coil/Coil
Brake system: PA
Brakes F/R: Disc/Drum
Steering: Rack & pinion
Wheelbase: 259.1cm 102.0in
Track F: 132.1cm 52.0in
Track R: 125.7cm 49.5in
Length: 414.0cm 163.0in
Width: 156.7cm 61.7in
Height: 139.7cm 55.0in
Ground clearance: 16.5cm 6.5in
Kerb weight: 940.7kg 2072.0lb
Fuel: 42.1L 9.2gal 11.1galUS

3406 Peugeot
504 Family Estate
1972 France
100.0mph 160.9kmh
0-50mph 80.5kmh: 9.7secs
0-60mph 96.5kmh: 14.1secs
0-1/4 mile: 19.2secs
0-1km: 35.8secs
93.0bhp 69.3kW 94.3PS
@ 5200rpm
118.0lbft 159.9Nm @ 3000rpm
71.8bhp/ton 70.6bhp/tonne
47.2bhp/L 35.2kW/L 47.8PS/L
46.1ft/sec 14.0m/sec
17.9mph 28.8kmh/1000rpm
20.9mpg 17.4mpgUS 13.5L/100km
Petrol 4-stroke piston
1971cc 120.3cu in
In-line 4 1 Carburettor
Compression ratio: 8.3:1
Bore: 88.0mm 3.5in
Stroke: 81.0mm 3.2in
Valve type/No: Overhead 8
Transmission: Manual
No. of forward speeds: 4
Wheels driven: Rear
Springs F/R: Coil/Coil
Brake system: PA
Brakes F/R: Disc/Drum
Steering: Rack & pinion
Wheelbase: 289.6cm 114.0in
Track F: 142.0cm 55.9in
Track R: 135.9cm 53.5in
Length: 480.1cm 189.0in
Width: 168.9cm 66.5in
Height: 154.9cm 61.0in
Ground clearance: 17.8cm 7.0in
Kerb weight: 1316.6kg 2900.0lb
Fuel: 60.1L 13.2gal 15.9galUS

3407 Peugeot
104
1973 France
86.0mph 138.4kmh
0-50mph 80.5kmh: 13.1secs
0-60mph 96.5kmh: 18.5secs
0-1/4 mile: 20.3secs
0-1km: 38.9secs
50.0bhp 37.3kW 50.7PS
@ 6250rpm
54.0lbft 73.2Nm @ 3000rpm
67.2bhp/ton 66.1bhp/tonne
52.4bhp/L 39.1kW/L 53.1PS/L
42.4ft/sec 12.9m/sec
14.6mph 23.5kmh/1000rpm
31.2mpg 26.0mpgUS 9.1L/100km
Petrol 4-stroke piston
954cc 58.2cu in
In-line 4 1 Carburettor
Compression ratio: 8.8:1
Bore: 70.0mm 2.8in
Stroke: 62.0mm 2.4in
Valve type/No: Overhead 8
Transmission: Manual
No. of forward speeds: 4
Wheels driven: Front
Springs F/R: Coil/Coil
Brakes F/R: Disc/Drum
Steering: Rack & pinion
Wheelbase: 241.3cm 95.0in
Track F: 127.0cm 50.0in
Track R: 127.0cm 50.0in
Length: 358.1cm 141.0in
Width: 147.3cm 58.0in
Height: 139.7cm 55.0in
Ground clearance: 20.3cm 8.0in
Kerb weight: 756.8kg 1667.0lb
Fuel: 40.0L 8.8gal 10.6galUS

3408 Peugeot
504
1973 France
0-60mph 96.5kmh: 15.9secs
0-1/4 mile: 20.4secs
92.0bhp 68.6kW 93.3PS
@ 5500rpm
120.0lbft 162.6Nm @ 3000rpm
76.6bhp/ton 75.3bhp/tonne
46.7bhp/L 34.8kW/L 47.3PS/L
48.7ft/sec 14.8m/sec
24.0mpg 20.0mpgUS 11.8L/100km
Petrol 4-stroke piston

1971cc 120.3cu in
In-line 4 1 Carburettor
Compression ratio: 7.5:1
Bore: 88.0mm 3.5in
Stroke: 81.0mm 3.2in
Valve type/No: Overhead 8
Transmission: Manual
No. of forward speeds: 4
Wheels driven: Rear
Brake system: PA
Brakes F/R: Disc/Disc
Wheelbase: 274.3cm 108.0in
Length: 449.6cm 177.0in
Width: 168.9cm 66.5in
Height: 146.1cm 57.5in
Ground clearance: 16.5cm 6.5in
Kerb weight: 1221.3kg 2690.0lb
Fuel: 55.6L 12.2gal 14.7galUS

3409 Peugeot

504 Diesel
1973 France
83.0mph 133.5kmh
0-50mph 80.5kmh: 18.6secs
0-60mph 96.5kmh: 28.1secs
0-1/4 mile: 23.8secs
62.0bhp 46.2kW 62.9PS
@ 4500rpm
88.0lbft 119.2Nm @ 2000rpm
49.8bhp/ton 48.9bhp/tonne
29.4bhp/L 21.9kW/L 29.8PS/L
40.9ft/sec 12.4m/sec
18.9mph 30.4kmh/1000rpm
35.4mpg 29.5mpgUS 8.0L/100km
Diesel 4-stroke piston
2112cc 128.9cu in
In-line 4
Compression ratio: 22.2:1
Bore: 90.0mm 3.5in
Stroke: 83.0mm 3.3in
Valve type/No: Overhead 8
Transmission: Manual
No. of forward speeds: 4
Wheels driven: Rear
Springs F/R: Coil/Coil
Brake system: PA
Brakes F/R: Disc/Disc
Steering: Rack & pinion
Wheelbase: 274.3cm 108.0in
Track F: 143.5cm 56.5in
Track R: 135.9cm 53.5in
Length: 449.6cm 177.0in
Width: 168.9cm 66.5in
Height: 146.1cm 57.5in
Kerb weight: 1266.7kg 2790.0lb
Fuel: 56.0L 12.3gal 14.8galUS

3410 Peugeot

504 L Diesel
1974 France
85.0mph 136.8kmh
0-50mph 80.5kmh: 14.8secs
0-60mph 96.5kmh: 21.7secs
0-1/4 mile: 22.4secs
0-1km: 42.4secs
56.0bhp 41.8kW 56.8PS
@ 4500rpm
79.6lbft 107.9Nm @ 2000rpm
48.1bhp/ton 47.3bhp/tonne
28.7bhp/L 21.4kW/L 29.1PS/L
39.4ft/sec 12.0m/sec
18.1mph 29.1kmh/1000rpm
31.1mpg 25.9mpgUS 9.1L/100km
Diesel 4-stroke piston
1948cc 118.8cu in
In-line 4 fuel injection
Compression ratio: 21.8:1
Bore: 88.0mm 3.5in
Stroke: 80.0mm 3.1in
Valve type/No: Overhead 8
Transmission: Manual
No. of forward speeds: 4
Wheels driven: Rear
Springs F/R: Coil/Coil
Brake system: PA
Brakes F/R: Disc/Drum
Steering: Rack & pinion
Wheelbase: 274.1cm 107.9in
Track F: 142.0cm 55.9in
Track R: 135.9cm 53.5in
Length: 448.8cm 176.7in
Width: 168.9cm 66.5in
Height: 146.1cm 57.5in
Ground clearance: 17.8cm 7.0in
Kerb weight: 1183.6kg 2607.0lb
Fuel: 56.0L 12.3gal 14.8galUS

3411 Peugeot

504 Station Wagon
1974 France
0-60mph 96.5kmh: 18.1secs
0-1/4 mile: 21.1secs
82.0bhp 61.1kW 83.1PS
@ 5200rpm
105.0lbft 142.3Nm @ 3000rpm
57.5bhp/ton 56.5bhp/tonne
41.6bhp/L 31.0kW/L 42.2PS/L
22.2mpg 18.5mpgUS 12.7L/100km
Petrol 4-stroke piston
1971cc 120.3cu in
In-line 4
Valve type/No: Overhead 8
Transmission: Automatic
No. of forward speeds: 3
Wheels driven: Rear
Brakes F/R: Disc/Disc
Wheelbase: 287.0cm 113.0in
Length: 492.8cm 194.0in
Width: 165.1cm 65.0in
Height: 152.4cm 60.0in
Kerb weight: 1450.5kg 3195.0lb

3412 Peugeot

504
1975 France
96.0mph 154.5kmh
0-50mph 80.5kmh: 11.4secs
0-60mph 96.5kmh: 16.7secs
0-1/4 mile: 20.1secs
87.0bhp 64.9kW 88.2PS
@ 5500rpm
110.0lbft 149.1Nm @ 2900rpm
65.7bhp/ton 64.6bhp/tonne
44.1bhp/L 32.9kW/L 44.7PS/L
48.9ft/sec 14.9m/sec
19.4mph 31.2kmh/1000rpm
25.2mpg 21.0mpgUS 11.2L/100km
Petrol 4-stroke piston
1971cc 120.3cu in
In-line 4
Compression ratio: 8.4:1
Bore: 87.9mm 3.5in
Stroke: 81.3mm 3.2in
Valve type/No: Overhead 8
Transmission: Manual
No. of forward speeds: 4
Wheels driven: Rear
Springs F/R: Coil/Coil
Brake system: PA
Brakes F/R: Disc/Disc
Steering: Rack & pinion
Wheelbase: 274.3cm 108.0in
Track F: 142.2cm 56.0in
Track R: 135.9cm 53.5in
Length: 464.3cm 182.8in
Width: 169.4cm 66.7in
Height: 140.5cm 55.3in
Kerb weight: 1346.1kg 2965.0lb
Fuel: 56.0L 12.3gal 14.8galUS

3413 Peugeot

604
1975 France
113.0mph 181.8kmh
0-50mph 80.5kmh: 6.7secs
0-60mph 96.5kmh: 9.4secs
0-1/4 mile: 17.1secs
0-1km: 31.9secs
136.0bhp 101.4kW 137.9PS
@ 5750rpm
153.0lbft 207.3Nm @ 3500rpm
97.9bhp/ton 96.3bhp/tonne
51.0bhp/L 38.1kW/L 51.8PS/L
45.8ft/sec 14.0m/sec
19.4mph 31.2kmh/1000rpm
19.6mpg 16.3mpgUS 14.4L/100km
Petrol 4-stroke piston
2664cc 162.5cu in
Vee 6 1 Carburettor
Compression ratio: 8.6:1
Bore: 88.0mm 3.5in
Stroke: 73.0mm 2.9in
Valve type/No: Overhead 12
Transmission: Manual
No. of forward speeds: 4
Wheels driven: Rear
Springs F/R: Coil/Coil
Brake system: PA
Brakes F/R: Disc/Disc
Steering: Rack & pinion PA
Wheelbase: 279.4cm 110.0in
Track F: 148.6cm 58.5in
Track R: 142.2cm 56.0in
Length: 471.2cm 185.5in
Width: 176.5cm 69.5in
Height: 138.4cm 54.5in
Ground clearance: 15.2cm 6.0in
Kerb weight: 1412.4kg 3111.0lb
Fuel: 70.1L 15.4gal 18.5galUS

3414 Peugeot

104
1976 France
85.0mph 136.8kmh
0-50mph 80.5kmh: 13.0secs
0-60mph 96.5kmh: 19.0secs
0-1/4 mile: 21.0secs
0-1km: 40.3secs
46.0bhp 34.3kW 46.6PS
@ 6000rpm
50.0lbft 67.8Nm @ 3000rpm
59.8bhp/ton 58.8bhp/tonne
48.2bhp/L 35.9kW/L 48.9PS/L
40.7ft/sec 12.4m/sec
14.6mph 23.5kmh/1000rpm
35.0mpg 29.1mpgUS 8.1L/100km
Petrol 4-stroke piston
954cc 58.2cu in
In-line 4 1 Carburettor
Compression ratio: 8.8:1
Bore: 70.0mm 2.8in
Stroke: 62.0mm 2.4in
Valve type/No: Overhead 8
Transmission: Manual
No. of forward speeds: 4
Wheels driven: Front
Springs F/R: Coil/Coil
Brakes F/R: Disc/Drum
Steering: Rack & pinion
Wheelbase: 241.3cm 95.0in
Track F: 127.0cm 50.0in
Track R: 127.0cm 50.0in
Length: 358.1cm 141.0in
Width: 147.3cm 58.0in
Height: 138.9cm 54.7in
Ground clearance: 20.3cm 8.0in
Kerb weight: 782.2kg 1723.0lb
Fuel: 40.0L 8.8gal 10.6galUS

3415 Peugeot

104 ZS
1976 France
100.0mph 160.9kmh
0-50mph 80.5kmh: 9.3secs
0-60mph 96.5kmh: 13.6secs
0-1/4 mile: 19.2secs
0-1km: 36.2secs
66.0bhp 49.2kW 66.9PS
@ 6200rpm
61.5lbft 83.3Nm @ 4000rpm
86.5bhp/ton 85.1bhp/tonne
58.7bhp/L 43.8kW/L 59.5PS/L
46.8ft/sec 14.3m/sec
15.9mph 25.6kmh/1000rpm
29.5mpg 24.6mpgUS 9.6L/100km
Petrol 4-stroke piston
1124cc 68.6cu in
In-line 4 1 Carburettor
Compression ratio: 9.2:1
Bore: 72.0mm 2.8in
Stroke: 69.0mm 2.7in
Valve type/No: Overhead 8
Transmission: Manual
No. of forward speeds: 4
Wheels driven: Front
Springs F/R: Coil/Coil
Brake system: PA
Brakes F/R: Disc/Drum
Steering: Rack & pinion
Wheelbase: 223.0cm 87.8in
Track F: 129.0cm 50.8in
Track R: 124.0cm 48.8in
Length: 330.5cm 130.1in
Width: 151.9cm 59.8in
Height: 134.1cm 52.8in
Ground clearance: 12.7cm 5.0in
Kerb weight: 775.9kg 1709.0lb
Fuel: 40.0L 8.8gal 10.6galUS

3416 Peugeot

504 Diesel Automatique
1977 France
86.0mph 138.4kmh
0-50mph 80.5kmh: 14.9secs
0-60mph 96.5kmh: 21.7secs
0-1/4 mile: 22.8secs
71.0bhp 52.9kW 72.0PS
@ 4500rpm
99.0lbft 134.1Nm @ 2500rpm
50.2bhp/ton 49.4bhp/tonne
30.8bhp/L 23.0kW/L 31.2PS/L
40.7ft/sec 12.4m/sec
30.0mpg 25.0mpgUS 9.4L/100km
Diesel 4-stroke piston
2304cc 140.6cu in
In-line 4
Compression ratio: 22.4:1
Bore: 94.0mm 3.7in
Stroke: 82.8mm 3.3in
Valve type/No: Overhead 8
Transmission: Automatic
No. of forward speeds: 3
Wheels driven: Rear
Springs F/R: Coil/Coil
Brake system: PA
Brakes F/R: Disc/Disc
Steering: Rack & pinion PA
Wheelbase: 274.3cm 108.0in
Track F: 141.7cm 55.8in
Track R: 133.1cm 52.4in
Length: 463.3cm 182.4in
Width: 169.4cm 66.7in
Height: 144.8cm 57.0in
Kerb weight: 1436.9kg 3165.0lb
Fuel: 70.0L 15.4gal 18.5galUS

3417 Peugeot

604 SLV-6
1977 France
111.0mph 178.6kmh
0-50mph 80.5kmh: 8.6secs
0-60mph 96.5kmh: 12.2secs
0-1/4 mile: 18.8secs
133.0bhp 99.2kW 134.8PS
@ 5750rpm
147.0lbft 199.2Nm @ 3500rpm
88.9bhp/ton 87.4bhp/tonne
49.9bhp/L 37.2kW/L 50.6PS/L
45.8ft/sec 14.0m/sec
21.6mph 34.8kmh/1000rpm
18.0mpg 15.0mpgUS 15.7L/100km
Petrol 4-stroke piston
2664cc 162.5cu in
Vee 6 1 Carburettor
Compression ratio: 8.2:1
Bore: 87.8mm 3.5in
Stroke: 72.9mm 2.9in
Valve type/No: Overhead 12
Transmission: Manual
No. of forward speeds: 4
Wheels driven: Rear
Springs F/R: Coil/Coil
Brake system: PA
Brakes F/R: Disc/Disc
Steering: Rack & pinion PA
Wheelbase: 279.9cm 110.2in
Track F: 151.6cm 59.7in
Track R: 143.0cm 56.3in
Length: 488.4cm 192.3in
Width: 177.0cm 69.7in
Height: 143.0cm 56.3in
Ground clearance: 13.2cm 5.2in
Kerb weight: 1520.9kg 3350.0lb
Fuel: 70.0L 15.4gal 18.5galUS

3418 Peugeot

305 SR
1978 France
96.0mph 154.5kmh
0-50mph 80.5kmh: 9.0secs
0-60mph 96.5kmh: 13.0secs
0-1/4 mile: 19.3secs
0-1km: 36.0secs
74.0bhp 55.2kW 75.0PS
@ 6000rpm
69.0lbft 93.5Nm @ 3750rpm
78.9bhp/ton 77.6bhp/tonne
50.3bhp/L 37.5kW/L 51.0PS/L
50.5ft/sec 15.4m/sec
17.8mph 28.6kmh/1000rpm
26.1mpg 21.7mpgUS 10.8L/100km
Petrol 4-stroke piston
1472cc 89.8cu in
In-line 4 1 Carburettor
Compression ratio: 8.8:1
Bore: 78.0mm 3.1in
Stroke: 77.0mm 3.0in
Valve type/No: Overhead 8
Transmission: Manual
No. of forward speeds: 4
Wheels driven: Front
Springs F/R: Coil/Coil
Brake system: PA
Brakes F/R: Disc/Drum
Steering: Rack & pinion
Wheelbase: 261.9cm 103.1in
Track F: 136.9cm 53.9in

Track R: 132.1cm 52.0in
Length: 423.7cm 166.8in
Width: 164.1cm 64.6in
Height: 140.0cm 55.1in
Ground clearance: 12.2cm 4.8in
Kerb weight: 953.4kg 2100.0lb
Fuel: 42.8L 9.4gal 11.3galUS

3419 Peugeot
504
1979 France
99.0mph 159.3kmh
0-50mph 80.5kmh: 9.1secs
0-60mph 96.5kmh: 13.4secs
0-1/4 mile: 18.9secs
0-1km: 36.0secs
79.0bhp 58.9kW 80.1PS
@ 5100rpm
105.0lbft 142.3Nm @ 2500rpm
71.7bhp/ton 70.5bhp/tonne
44.0bhp/L 32.8kW/L 44.6PS/L
45.2ft/sec 13.8m/sec
18.2mph 29.3kmh/1000rpm
24.1mpg 20.1mpgUS 11.7L/100km
Petrol 4-stroke piston
1796cc 109.6cu in
In-line 4 1 Carburettor
Compression ratio: 7.5:1
Bore: 84.0mm 3.3in
Stroke: 81.0mm 3.2in
Valve type/No: Overhead 8
Transmission: Manual
No. of forward speeds: 4
Wheels driven: Rear
Springs F/R: Coil/Coil
Brake system: PA
Brakes F/R: Disc/Drum
Steering: Rack & pinion
Wheelbase: 274.1cm 107.9in
Track F: 142.0cm 55.9in
Track R: 135.9cm 53.5in
Length: 448.8cm 176.7in
Width: 168.9cm 66.5in
Height: 146.1cm 57.5in
Ground clearance: 17.8cm 7.0in
Kerb weight: 1120.9kg 2469.0lb
Fuel: 56.0L 12.3gal 14.8galUS

3420 Peugeot
505 STI
1979 France
103.0mph 165.7kmh
0-50mph 80.5kmh: 9.1secs
0-60mph 96.5kmh: 12.3secs
0-1/4 mile: 18.7secs
0-1km: 34.4secs
110.0bhp 82.0kW 111.5PS
@ 5250rpm
126.0lbft 170.7Nm @ 4000rpm
90.0bhp/ton 88.5bhp/tonne
55.1bhp/L 41.1kW/L 55.9PS/L
47.1ft/sec 14.3m/sec
18.4mph 29.6kmh/1000rpm
22.6mpg 18.8mpgUS 12.5L/100km
Petrol 4-stroke piston
1995cc 121.7cu in
In-line 4 fuel injection
Compression ratio: 9.2:1
Bore: 88.0mm 3.5in
Stroke: 82.0mm 3.2in
Valve type/No: Overhead 8
Transmission: Manual
No. of forward speeds: 4
Wheels driven: Rear
Springs F/R: Coil/Coil
Brake system: PA
Brakes F/R: Disc/Disc
Steering: Rack & pinion PA
Wheelbase: 274.3cm 108.0in
Track F: 146.1cm 57.5in
Track R: 143.0cm 56.3in
Length: 458.0cm 180.3in
Width: 169.4cm 66.7in
Height: 145.0cm 57.1in
Ground clearance: 20.1cm 7.9in
Kerb weight: 1242.6kg 2737.0lb
Fuel: 56.0L 12.3gal 14.8galUS

3421 Peugeot
604
1979 France
112.0mph 180.2kmh
0-50mph 80.5kmh: 7.3secs
0-60mph 96.5kmh: 10.7secs
0-1/4 mile: 17.8secs
133.0bhp 99.2kW 134.8PS
@ 5250rpm
162.0lbft 219.5Nm @ 3000rpm
86.7bhp/ton 85.3bhp/tonne
46.7bhp/L 34.8kW/L 47.3PS/L
41.8ft/sec 12.8m/sec
23.3mph 37.5kmh/1000rpm
19.2mpg 16.0mpgUS 14.7L/100km
Petrol 4-stroke piston
2849cc 173.8cu in
Vee 6 2 Carburettor
Compression ratio: 8.2:1
Bore: 90.9mm 3.6in
Stroke: 72.9mm 2.9in
Valve type/No: Overhead 12
Transmission: Manual
No. of forward speeds: 5
Wheels driven: Rear
Springs F/R: Coil/Coil
Brake system: PA
Brakes F/R: Disc/Disc
Steering: Rack & pinion PA
Wheelbase: 279.9cm 110.2in
Track F: 151.6cm 59.7in
Track R: 143.0cm 56.3in
Length: 488.4cm 192.3in
Width: 177.0cm 69.7in
Height: 143.0cm 56.3in
Kerb weight: 1559.5kg 3435.0lb
Fuel: 68.1L 15.0gal 18.0galUS

3422 Peugeot
505 S
1980 France
103.0mph 165.7kmh
0-60mph 96.5kmh: 13.0secs
0-1/4 mile: 18.7secs
96.0bhp 71.6kW 97.3PS
@ 4900rpm
116.0lbft 157.2Nm @ 3300rpm
70.8bhp/ton 69.7bhp/tonne
48.7bhp/L 36.3kW/L 49.4PS/L
43.4ft/sec 13.2m/sec
20.7mph 33.3kmh/1000rpm
22.8mpg 19.0mpgUS 12.4L/100km
Petrol 4-stroke piston
1971cc 120.3cu in
In-line 4 fuel injection
Compression ratio: 8.4:1
Bore: 88.0mm 3.5in
Stroke: 81.0mm 3.2in
Valve type/No: Overhead 8
Transmission: Manual
No. of forward speeds: 5
Wheels driven: Rear
Springs F/R: Coil/Coil
Brake system: PA
Brakes F/R: Disc/Disc
Steering: Rack & pinion PA
Wheelbase: 274.3cm 108.0in
Track F: 146.1cm 57.5in
Track R: 143.5cm 56.5in
Length: 474.2cm 186.7in
Width: 173.5cm 68.3in
Height: 144.0cm 56.7in
Ground clearance: 11.2cm 4.4in
Kerb weight: 1377.9kg 3035.0lb
Fuel: 68.1L 15.0gal 18.0galUS

3423 Peugeot
505 SD
1980 France
0-60mph 96.5kmh: 23.1secs
0-1/4 mile: 22.9secs
71.0bhp 52.9kW 72.0PS
@ 4500rpm
99.0lbft 134.1Nm @ 2500rpm
50.4bhp/ton 49.6bhp/tonne
30.8bhp/L 23.0kW/L 31.2PS/L
40.7ft/sec 12.4m/sec
32.4mpg 27.0mpgUS 8.7L/100km
Diesel 4-stroke piston
2304cc 140.6cu in
In-line 4 fuel injection
Compression ratio: 22.4:1
Bore: 94.0mm 3.7in
Stroke: 82.8mm 3.3in
Valve type/No: Overhead 8
Transmission: Manual
No. of forward speeds: 4
Wheels driven: Rear
Brakes F/R: Disc/Disc
Wheelbase: 274.3cm 108.0in
Track F: 146.1cm 57.5in
Track R: 143.5cm 56.5in
Length: 474.2cm 186.7in
Width: 173.5cm 68.3in
Height: 144.0cm 56.7in
Kerb weight: 1432.4kg 3155.0lb
Fuel: 68.1L 15.0gal 18.0galUS

3424 Peugeot
604 D Turbo
1980 France
96.0mph 154.5kmh
0-50mph 80.5kmh: 12.9secs
0-60mph 96.5kmh: 17.0secs
0-1/4 mile: 20.9secs
0-1km: 38.5secs
80.0bhp 59.7kW 81.1PS
@ 4150rpm
136.0lbft 184.3Nm @ 2000rpm
53.0bhp/ton 52.1bhp/tonne
34.7bhp/L 25.9kW/L 35.2PS/L
37.7ft/sec 11.5m/sec
23.9mph 38.5kmh/1000rpm
27.7mpg 23.1mpgUS 10.2L/100km
Diesel 4-stroke piston
2304cc 140.6cu in turbocharged
In-line 4 fuel injection
Compression ratio: 21.0:1
Bore: 94.0mm 3.7in
Stroke: 83.0mm 3.3in
Valve type/No: Overhead 8
Transmission: Manual
No. of forward speeds: 5
Wheels driven: Rear
Springs F/R: Coil/Coil
Brake system: PA
Brakes F/R: Disc/Disc
Steering: Rack & pinion PA
Wheelbase: 279.4cm 110.0in
Track F: 148.6cm 58.5in
Track R: 142.2cm 56.0in
Length: 471.2cm 185.5in
Width: 176.5cm 69.5in
Height: 138.4cm 54.5in
Ground clearance: 15.2cm 6.0in
Kerb weight: 1535.0kg 3381.0lb
Fuel: 70.1L 15.4gal 18.5galUS

3425 Peugeot
305 S
1981 France
97.0mph 156.1kmh
0-50mph 80.5kmh: 8.8secs
0-60mph 96.5kmh: 12.8secs
0-1/4 mile: 18.5secs
0-1km: 35.0secs
89.0bhp 66.4kW 90.2PS
@ 6000rpm
92.0lbft 124.7Nm @ 3000rpm
92.5bhp/ton 90.9bhp/tonne
60.5bhp/L 45.1kW/L 61.3PS/L
50.5ft/sec 15.4m/sec
17.8mph 28.6kmh/1000rpm
29.9mpg 24.9mpgUS 9.4L/100km
Petrol 4-stroke piston
1472cc 89.8cu in
In-line 4 1 Carburettor
Compression ratio: 9.2:1
Bore: 68.0mm 2.7in
Stroke: 77.0mm 3.0in
Valve type/No: Overhead 8
Transmission: Manual
No. of forward speeds: 4
Wheels driven: Front
Springs F/R: Coil/Coil
Brake system: PA
Brakes F/R: Disc/Drum
Steering: Rack & pinion
Wheelbase: 261.9cm 103.1in
Track F: 136.9cm 53.9in
Track R: 132.1cm 52.0in
Length: 423.7cm 166.8in
Width: 164.1cm 64.6in
Height: 140.0cm 55.1in
Ground clearance: 12.2cm 4.8in
Kerb weight: 978.8kg 2156.0lb
Fuel: 43.2L 9.5gal 11.4galUS

3426 Peugeot
505 S Turbodiesel
1981 France
90.0mph 144.8kmh
0-50mph 80.5kmh: 11.9secs
0-60mph 96.5kmh: 17.6secs
0-1/4 mile: 20.8secs
80.0bhp 59.7kW 81.1PS
@ 4150rpm
136.0lbft 184.3Nm @ 2000rpm
55.3bhp/ton 54.4bhp/tonne
34.7bhp/L 25.9kW/L 35.2PS/L
37.6ft/sec 11.4m/sec
23.9mph 38.5kmh/1000rpm
32.4mpg 27.0mpgUS 8.7L/100km
Diesel 4-stroke piston
2304cc 140.6cu in turbocharged
In-line 4 fuel injection
Compression ratio: 21.0:1
Bore: 94.0mm 3.7in
Stroke: 82.8mm 3.3in
Valve type/No: Overhead 8
Transmission: Manual
No. of forward speeds: 5
Wheels driven: Rear
Springs F/R: Coil/Coil
Brake system: PA
Brakes F/R: Disc/Disc
Steering: Rack & pinion PA
Wheelbase: 274.3cm 108.0in
Track F: 146.1cm 57.5in
Track R: 143.5cm 56.5in
Length: 474.2cm 186.7in
Width: 173.5cm 68.3in
Height: 144.0cm 56.7in
Kerb weight: 1471.0kg 3240.0lb
Fuel: 68.1L 15.0gal 18.0galUS

3427 Peugeot
505 GR Estate
1982 France
102.0mph 164.1kmh
0-50mph 80.5kmh: 8.3secs
0-60mph 96.5kmh: 12.4secs
0-1/4 mile: 19.1secs
0-1km: 35.9secs
96.0bhp 71.6kW 97.3PS
@ 5200rpm
116.0lbft 157.2Nm @ 3000rpm
76.7bhp/ton 75.4bhp/tonne
48.7bhp/L 36.3kW/L 49.4PS/L
46.1ft/sec 14.0m/sec
18.9mph 30.4kmh/1000rpm
26.2mpg 21.8mpgUS 10.8L/100km
Petrol 4-stroke piston
1971cc 120.3cu in
In-line 4 1 Carburettor
Compression ratio: 8.8:1
Bore: 88.0mm 3.5in
Stroke: 81.0mm 3.2in
Valve type/No: Overhead 8
Transmission: Manual
No. of forward speeds: 4
Wheels driven: Rear
Springs F/R: Coil/Coil
Brake system: PA
Brakes F/R: Disc/Drum
Steering: Rack & pinion PA
Wheelbase: 290.1cm 114.2in
Track F: 146.8cm 57.8in
Track R: 144.0cm 56.7in
Length: 488.2cm 192.2in
Width: 173.0cm 68.1in
Height: 153.9cm 60.6in
Ground clearance: 13.0cm 5.1in
Kerb weight: 1272.6kg 2803.0lb
Fuel: 56.9L 12.5gal 15.0galUS

3428 Peugeot
505 STI
1982 France
101.0mph 162.5kmh
0-50mph 80.5kmh: 9.6secs
0-60mph 96.5kmh: 14.3secs
0-1/4 mile: 19.4secs
97.0bhp 72.3kW 98.3PS
@ 5000rpm
116.0lbft 157.2Nm @ 3500rpm
70.7bhp/ton 69.5bhp/tonne
49.2bhp/L 36.7kW/L 49.9PS/L
44.3ft/sec 13.5m/sec
23.6mph 38.0kmh/1000rpm
27.6mpg 23.0mpgUS 10.2L/100km
Petrol 4-stroke piston
1971cc 120.3cu in
In-line 4 fuel injection
Compression ratio: 8.3:1
Bore: 87.8mm 3.5in
Stroke: 81.0mm 3.2in
Valve type/No: Overhead 8
Transmission: Manual
No. of forward speeds: 5
Wheels driven: Rear
Springs F/R: Coil/Coil
Brake system: PA
Brakes F/R: Disc/Disc
Steering: Rack & pinion PA
Wheelbase: 274.3cm 108.0in
Track F: 146.1cm 57.5in
Track R: 143.5cm 56.5in

Length: 474.2cm 186.7in
Width: 173.5cm 68.3in
Height: 144.0cm 56.7in
Kerb weight: 1396.0kg 3075.0lb
Fuel: 68.1L 15.0gal 18.0galUS

3429 Peugeot

205 GR
1983 France
100.0mph 160.9kmh
0-50mph 80.5kmh: 8.2secs
0-60mph 96.5kmh: 12.5secs
0-1/4 mile: 19.0secs
0-1km: 36.1secs
59.0bhp 44.0kW 59.8PS
@ 5000rpm
78.0lbft 105.7Nm @ 2500rpm
75.1bhp/ton 73.9bhp/tonne
43.4bhp/L 32.3kW/L 44.0PS/L
42.1ft/sec 12.8m/sec
22.6mph 36.4kmh/1000rpm
37.4mpg 31.1mpgUS 7.6L/100km
Petrol 4-stroke piston
1360cc 83.0cu in
In-line 4 1 Carburettor
Compression ratio: 9.3:1
Bore: 75.0mm 2.9in
Stroke: 77.0mm 3.0in
Valve type/No: Overhead 8
Transmission: Manual
No. of forward speeds: 5
Wheels driven: Front
Springs F/R: Coil/Torsion bar
Brake system: PA
Brakes F/R: Disc/Drum
Steering: Rack & pinion
Wheelbase: 242.1cm 95.3in
Track F: 135.1cm 53.2in
Track R: 130.0cm 51.2in
Length: 370.6cm 145.9in
Width: 156.2cm 61.5in
Height: 137.7cm 54.2in
Ground clearance: 11.9cm 4.7in
Kerb weight: 798.6kg 1759.0lb
Fuel: 50.0L 11.0gal 13.2galUS

3430 Peugeot

305 SR
1983 France
103.0mph 165.7kmh
0-50mph 80.5kmh: 8.7secs
0-60mph 96.5kmh: 12.7secs
0-1/4 mile: 18.8secs
0-1km: 35.5secs
73.0bhp 54.4kW 74.0PS
@ 5500rpm
87.5lbft 118.6Nm @ 2500rpm
77.1bhp/ton 75.8bhp/tonne
49.6bhp/L 37.0kW/L 50.3PS/L
46.3ft/sec 14.1m/sec
19.1mph 30.7kmh/1000rpm
32.6mpg 27.1mpgUS 8.7L/100km
Petrol 4-stroke piston
1472cc 89.8cu in
In-line 4 1 Carburettor
Compression ratio: 9.2:1
Bore: 78.0mm 3.1in
Stroke: 77.0mm 3.0in
Valve type/No: Overhead 8
Transmission: Manual
No. of forward speeds: 4
Wheels driven: Front
Springs F/R: Coil/Coil
Brake system: PA
Brakes F/R: Disc/Drum
Steering: Rack & pinion
Wheelbase: 261.9cm 103.1in
Track F: 136.9cm 53.9in
Track R: 132.1cm 52.0in
Length: 423.7cm 166.8in
Width: 164.1cm 64.6in
Height: 140.0cm 55.1in
Ground clearance: 12.2cm 4.8in
Kerb weight: 963.4kg 2122.0lb
Fuel: 56.0L 12.3gal 14.8galUS

3431 Peugeot

205 GTi
1984 France
120.0mph 193.1kmh
0-50mph 80.5kmh: 6.2secs
0-60mph 96.5kmh: 8.6secs
0-1/4 mile: 16.6secs
0-1km: 30.9secs
105.0bhp 78.3kW 106.5PS
@ 6250rpm
99.0lbft 134.1Nm @ 4000rpm
117.4bhp/ton 115.4bhp/tonne
66.5bhp/L 49.6kW/L 67.4PS/L
49.8ft/sec 15.2m/sec
18.7mph 30.1kmh/1000rpm
29.5mpg 24.6mpgUS 9.6L/100km
Petrol 4-stroke piston
1580cc 96.4cu in
In-line 4 fuel injection
Compression ratio: 10.2:1
Bore: 83.0mm 3.3in
Stroke: 73.0mm 2.9in
Valve type/No: Overhead 8
Transmission: Manual
No. of forward speeds: 5
Wheels driven: Front
Springs F/R: Coil/Torsion bar
Brake system: PA
Brakes F/R: Disc/Drum
Steering: Rack & pinion
Wheelbase: 242.1cm 95.3in
Track F: 139.2cm 54.8in
Track R: 133.1cm 52.4in
Length: 370.6cm 145.9in
Width: 157.2cm 61.9in
Height: 135.4cm 53.3in
Ground clearance: 11.9cm 4.7in
Kerb weight: 909.8kg 2004.0lb
Fuel: 50.0L 11.0gal 13.2galUS

3432 Peugeot

505 GRi
1984 France
108.0mph 173.8kmh
0-50mph 80.5kmh: 7.2secs
0-60mph 96.5kmh: 10.1secs
0-1/4 mile: 17.8secs
0-1km: 32.7secs
125.0bhp 93.2kW 126.7PS
@ 5750rpm
139.0lbft 188.3Nm @ 4250rpm
96.4bhp/ton 94.8bhp/tonne
57.7bhp/L 43.0kW/L 58.5PS/L
55.9ft/sec 17.1m/sec
22.3mph 35.9kmh/1000rpm
27.4mpg 22.8mpgUS 10.3L/100km
Petrol 4-stroke piston
2165cc 132.1cu in
In-line 4 fuel injection
Compression ratio: 9.8:1
Bore: 88.0mm 3.5in
Stroke: 89.0mm 3.5in
Valve type/No: Overhead 8
Transmission: Manual
No. of forward speeds: 5
Wheels driven: Rear
Springs F/R: Coil/Coil
Brake system: PA
Brakes F/R: Disc/Disc
Steering: Rack & pinion PA
Wheelbase: 274.3cm 108.0in
Track F: 149.1cm 58.7in
Track R: 145.8cm 57.4in
Length: 457.2cm 180.0in
Width: 173.7cm 68.4in
Height: 143.3cm 56.4in
Ground clearance: 20.1cm 7.9in
Kerb weight: 1318.9kg 2905.0lb
Fuel: 70.1L 15.4gal 18.5galUS

3433 Peugeot

505 S Wagon
1984 France
97.0mph 156.1kmh
0-60mph 96.5kmh: 16.2secs
0-1/4 mile: 20.3secs
97.0bhp 72.3kW 98.3PS
@ 5000rpm
116.0lbft 157.2Nm @ 3500rpm
67.7bhp/ton 66.6bhp/tonne
49.2bhp/L 36.7kW/L 49.9PS/L
44.3ft/sec 13.5m/sec
22.2mpg 18.5mpgUS 12.7L/100km
Petrol 4-stroke piston
1971cc 120.3cu in
In-line 4 fuel injection
Compression ratio: 8.4:1
Bore: 88.0mm 3.5in
Stroke: 81.0mm 3.2in
Valve type/No: Overhead 8
Transmission: Manual
No. of forward speeds: 5
Wheels driven: Rear
Springs F/R: Coil/Coil
Brakes F/R: Disc/Drum
Steering: Rack & pinion PA
Wheelbase: 290.1cm 114.2in
Track F: 148.1cm 58.3in
Track R: 145.0cm 57.1in
Length: 505.2cm 198.9in
Width: 173.7cm 68.4in
Height: 155.2cm 61.1in
Kerb weight: 1457.3kg 3210.0lb
Fuel: 68.1L 15.0gal 18.0galUS

3434 Peugeot

205 XL
1985 France
88.0mph 141.6kmh
0-50mph 80.5kmh: 10.7secs
0-60mph 96.5kmh: 16.1secs
0-1/4 mile: 20.3secs
50.0bhp 37.3kW 50.7PS
@ 4800rpm
63.0lbft 85.4Nm @ 2800rpm
68.3bhp/ton 67.2bhp/tonne
44.5bhp/L 33.2kW/L 45.1PS/L
36.3ft/sec 11.0m/sec
20.3mph 32.7kmh/1000rpm
36.5mpg 30.4mpgUS 7.7L/100km
Petrol 4-stroke piston
1124cc 68.6cu in
In-line 4 1 Carburettor
Compression ratio: 9.7:1
Bore: 72.0mm 2.8in
Stroke: 69.0mm 2.7in
Valve type/No: Overhead 8
Transmission: Manual
No. of forward speeds: 4
Wheels driven: Front
Springs F/R: Coil/Torsion bar
Brake system: PA
Brakes F/R: Disc/Drum
Steering: Rack & pinion
Wheelbase: 242.1cm 95.3in
Track F: 139.2cm 54.8in
Track R: 133.1cm 52.4in
Length: 370.6cm 145.9in
Width: 157.2cm 61.9in
Height: 135.4cm 53.3in
Ground clearance: 11.9cm 4.7in
Kerb weight: 744.1kg 1639.0lb
Fuel: 50.0L 11.0gal 13.2galUS

3435 Peugeot

305 GRD Estate
1985 France
93.0mph 149.6kmh
0-50mph 80.5kmh: 11.7secs
0-60mph 96.5kmh: 16.8secs
0-1/4 mile: 20.9secs
0-1km: 39.4secs
65.0bhp 48.5kW 65.9PS
@ 4600rpm
88.0lbft 119.2Nm @ 2000rpm
60.6bhp/ton 59.6bhp/tonne
34.1bhp/L 25.4kW/L 34.6PS/L
44.2ft/sec 13.5m/sec
20.7mph 33.3kmh/1000rpm
35.5mpg 29.6mpgUS 8.0L/100km
Diesel 4-stroke piston
1905cc 116.2cu in
In-line 4 fuel injection
Compression ratio: 23.5:1
Bore: 83.0mm 3.3in
Stroke: 88.0mm 3.5in
Valve type/No: Overhead 8
Transmission: Manual
No. of forward speeds: 5
Wheels driven: Front
Springs F/R: Coil/Coil
Brake system: PA
Brakes F/R: Disc/Drum
Steering: Rack & pinion PA
Wheelbase: 262.1cm 103.2in
Track F: 142.0cm 55.9in
Track R: 134.9cm 53.1in
Length: 428.2cm 168.6in
Width: 163.6cm 64.4in
Height: 142.5cm 56.1in
Ground clearance: 12.2cm 4.8in
Kerb weight: 1090.0kg 2401.0lb
Fuel: 50.0L 11.0gal 13.2galUS

3436 Peugeot

309 1.3 GL
1985 France
98.0mph 157.7kmh
0-50mph 80.5kmh: 9.5secs
0-60mph 96.5kmh: 13.2secs
0-1/4 mile: 19.4secs
0-1km: 36.1secs
65.0bhp 48.5kW 65.9PS
@ 5600rpm
76.0lbft 103.0Nm @ 2800rpm
71.7bhp/ton 70.5bhp/tonne
50.2bhp/L 37.5kW/L 50.9PS/L
42.9ft/sec 13.1m/sec
20.2mph 32.5kmh/1000rpm
29.7mpg 24.7mpgUS 9.5L/100km
Petrol 4-stroke piston
1294cc 78.9cu in
In-line 4 1 Carburettor
Compression ratio: 9.5:1
Bore: 76.7mm 3.0in
Stroke: 70.0mm 2.8in
Valve type/No: Overhead 8
Transmission: Manual
No. of forward speeds: 5
Wheels driven: Front
Springs F/R: Coil/Torsion bar
Brake system: PA
Brakes F/R: Disc/Drum
Steering: Rack & pinion
Wheelbase: 246.9cm 97.2in
Track F: 140.7cm 55.4in
Track R: 137.4cm 54.1in
Length: 404.9cm 159.4in
Width: 162.6cm 64.0in
Height: 137.9cm 54.3in
Ground clearance: 16.5cm 6.5in
Kerb weight: 921.6kg 2030.0lb
Fuel: 55.1L 12.1gal 14.5galUS

3437 Peugeot

505 Turbo
1985 France
119.0mph 191.5kmh
0-50mph 80.5kmh: 7.1secs
0-60mph 96.5kmh: 10.1secs
0-1/4 mile: 18.3secs
142.0bhp 105.9kW 144.0PS
@ 5600rpm
163.0lbft 220.9Nm @ 3800rpm
101.6bhp/ton 99.9bhp/tonne
65.9bhp/L 49.2kW/L 66.9PS/L
49.9ft/sec 15.2m/sec
23.5mph 37.8kmh/1000rpm
22.2mpg 18.5mpgUS 12.7L/100km
Petrol 4-stroke piston
2153cc 131.4cu in turbocharged
In-line 4 fuel injection
Compression ratio: 7.0:1
Bore: 91.7mm 3.6in
Stroke: 81.5mm 3.2in
Valve type/No: Overhead 8
Transmission: Manual
No. of forward speeds: 5
Wheels driven: Rear
Springs F/R: Coil/Coil
Brake system: PA
Brakes F/R: Disc/Disc
Steering: Rack & pinion PA
Wheelbase: 274.3cm 108.0in
Track F: 149.1cm 58.7in
Track R: 145.8cm 57.4in
Length: 474.2cm 186.7in
Width: 173.5cm 68.3in
Height: 142.2cm 56.0in
Kerb weight: 1421.0kg 3130.0lb
Fuel: 68.1L 15.0gal 18.0galUS

3438 Peugeot

205 GTi
1986 France
122.0mph 196.3kmh
0-50mph 80.5kmh: 6.5secs
0-60mph 96.5kmh: 8.7secs
0-1/4 mile: 17.4secs
0-1km: 31.1secs
115.0bhp 85.8kW 116.6PS
@ 6250rpm
98.4lbft 133.3Nm @ 4000rpm
132.3bhp/ton 130.1bhp/tonne
72.8bhp/L 54.3kW/L 73.8PS/L
49.8ft/sec 15.2m/sec
18.6mph 29.9kmh/1000rpm
29.9mpg 24.9mpgUS 9.4L/100km
Petrol 4-stroke piston
1580cc 96.0cu in
In-line 4 fuel injection
Compression ratio: 9.8:1
Bore: 83.0mm 3.3in
Stroke: 73.0mm 2.9in
Valve type/No: Overhead 8
Transmission: Manual
No. of forward speeds: 5
Wheels driven: Front
Springs F/R: Coil/Torsion bar
Brake system: PA

Brakes F/R: Disc/Drum
Steering: Rack & pinion
Wheelbase: 242.0cm 95.3in
Track F: 139.3cm 54.8in
Track R: 133.2cm 52.4in
Length: 370.5cm 145.9in
Width: 157.2cm 61.9in
Height: 135.5cm 53.3in
Ground clearance: 12.0cm 4.7in
Kerb weight: 883.7kg 1946.5lb
Fuel: 50.0L 11.0gal 13.2galUS

3439 Peugeot

309 1.6 GR
1986 France
99.0mph 159.3kmh
0-50mph 80.5kmh: 8.9secs
0-60mph 96.5kmh: 12.9secs
0-1/4 mile: 19.0secs
0-1km: 35.7secs
80.0bhp 59.7kW 81.1PS
@ 5600rpm
97.7lbft 132.4Nm @ 2800rpm
90.5bhp/ton 89.0bhp/tonne
50.6bhp/L 37.8kW/L 51.3PS/L
44.6ft/sec 13.6m/sec
22.2mph 35.7kmh/1000rpm
29.8mpg 24.8mpgUS 9.5L/100km
Petrol 4-stroke piston
1580cc 96.4cu in
In-line 4 1 Carburettor
Compression ratio: 9.4:1
Bore: 83.0mm 3.3in
Stroke: 73.0mm 2.9in
Valve type/No: Overhead 8
Transmission: Manual
No. of forward speeds: 5
Wheels driven: Front
Springs F/R: Coil/Torsion bar
Brake system: PA
Brakes F/R: Disc/Drum
Steering: Rack & pinion
Wheelbase: 246.9cm 97.2in
Track F: 140.7cm 55.4in
Track R: 137.4cm 54.1in
Length: 404.9cm 159.4in
Width: 162.6cm 64.0in
Height: 137.9cm 54.3in
Ground clearance: 16.5cm 6.5in
Kerb weight: 898.9kg 1980.0lb
Fuel: 55.1L 12.1gal 14.5galUS

3440 Peugeot

309 SR Injection
1986 France
122.0mph 196.3kmh
0-50mph 80.5kmh: 7.1secs
0-60mph 96.5kmh: 9.7secs
0-1/4 mile: 17.9secs
0-1km: 32.1secs
115.0bhp 85.8kW 116.6PS
@ 6250rpm
98.4lbft 133.3Nm @ 4000rpm
127.5bhp/ton 125.4bhp/tonne
72.8bhp/L 54.3kW/L 73.8PS/L
49.8ft/sec 15.2m/sec
18.7mph 30.1kmh/1000rpm
30.9mpg 25.7mpgUS 9.1L/100km
Petrol 4-stroke piston
1580cc 96.0cu in
In-line 4 fuel injection
Compression ratio: 9.8:1
Bore: 83.0mm 3.3in
Stroke: 73.0mm 2.9in
Valve type/No: Overhead 8
Transmission: Manual
No. of forward speeds: 5
Wheels driven: Front
Springs F/R: Coil/Coil
Brake system: PA
Brakes F/R: Disc/Drum
Steering: Rack & pinion
Wheelbase: 246.9cm 97.2in
Track F: 140.8cm 55.4in
Track R: 137.6cm 54.2in
Length: 405.1cm 159.5in
Width: 162.8cm 64.1in
Height: 138.0cm 54.3in
Ground clearance: 16.5cm 6.5in
Kerb weight: 917.0kg 2019.8lb
Fuel: 55.1L 12.1gal 14.5galUS

3441 Peugeot

505 GTi Family Estate
1986 France
109.0mph 175.4kmh
0-50mph 80.5kmh: 6.3secs
0-60mph 96.5kmh: 10.5secs
0-1/4 mile: 17.6secs
0-1km: 33.0secs
130.0bhp 96.9kW 131.8PS
@ 5750rpm
139.0lbft 188.3Nm @ 4250rpm
94.2bhp/ton 92.7bhp/tonne
60.0bhp/L 44.8kW/L 60.9PS/L
55.9ft/sec 17.1m/sec
21.2mph 34.1kmh/1000rpm
20.6mpg 17.2mpgUS 13.7L/100km
Petrol 4-stroke piston
2165cc 132.0cu in
In-line 4 fuel injection
Compression ratio: 9.8:1
Bore: 88.0mm 3.5in
Stroke: 89.0mm 3.5in
Valve type/No: Overhead 8
Transmission: Manual
No. of forward speeds: 5
Wheels driven: Rear
Springs F/R: Coil/Coil
Brake system: PA
Brakes F/R: Disc/Drum
Steering: Rack & pinion PA
Wheelbase: 290.0cm 114.2in
Track F: 149.6cm 58.9in
Track R: 145.0cm 57.1in
Length: 490.1cm 193.0in
Width: 173.7cm 68.4in
Height: 154.4cm 60.8in
Ground clearance: 13.0cm 5.1in
Kerb weight: 1403.0kg 3090.3lb
Fuel: 70.1L 15.4gal 18.5galUS

3442 Peugeot

505 Turbo
1986 France
0-60mph 96.5kmh: 8.9secs
0-1/4 mile: 16.8secs
150.0bhp 111.9kW 152.1PS
@ 5000rpm
181.0lbft 245.3Nm @ 2750rpm
107.2bhp/ton 105.4bhp/tonne
69.7bhp/L 52.0kW/L 70.6PS/L
44.6ft/sec 13.6m/sec
22.2mpg 18.5mpgUS 12.7L/100km
Petrol 4-stroke piston
2153cc 131.4cu in turbocharged
In-line 4 fuel injection
Compression ratio: 7.5:1
Bore: 91.7mm 3.6in
Stroke: 81.5mm 3.2in
Valve type/No: Overhead 8
Transmission: Manual
No. of forward speeds: 5
Wheels driven: Rear
Springs F/R: Coil/Coil
Brakes F/R: Disc/Disc
Steering: Rack & pinion PA
Wheelbase: 274.3cm 108.0in
Length: 474.2cm 186.7in
Width: 173.5cm 68.3in
Height: 141.0cm 55.5in
Kerb weight: 1423.3kg 3135.0lb

3443 Peugeot

205 GTi 1.9
1987 France
123.0mph 197.9kmh
0-50mph 80.5kmh: 5.9secs
0-60mph 96.5kmh: 7.8secs
0-1/4 mile: 16.3secs
0-1km: 30.2secs
130.0bhp 96.9kW 131.8PS
@ 6000rpm
118.7lbft 160.8Nm @ 4750rpm
145.3bhp/ton 142.9bhp/tonne
68.2bhp/L 50.9kW/L 69.2PS/L
57.7ft/sec 17.6m/sec
20.8mph 33.5kmh/1000rpm
28.1mpg 23.4mpgUS 10.1L/100km
Petrol 4-stroke piston
1905cc 116.0cu in
In-line 4 fuel injection
Compression ratio: 9.6:1
Bore: 83.0mm 3.3in
Stroke: 88.0mm 3.5in
Valve type/No: Overhead 8
Transmission: Manual
No. of forward speeds: 5
Wheels driven: Front
Springs F/R: Coil/Coil
Brake system: PA
Brakes F/R: Disc/Disc
Steering: Rack & pinion
Wheelbase: 242.0cm 95.3in
Track F: 139.3cm 54.8in
Track R: 133.2cm 52.4in
Length: 370.5cm 145.9in
Width: 157.2cm 61.9in
Height: 135.5cm 53.3in
Ground clearance: 12.0cm 4.7in
Kerb weight: 910.0kg 2004.4lb
Fuel: 50.0L 11.0gal 13.2galUS

3444 Peugeot

309 GTi
1987 France
122.0mph 196.3kmh
0-50mph 80.5kmh: 6.4secs
0-60mph 96.5kmh: 8.7secs
0-1/4 mile: 17.0secs
0-1km: 31.2secs
130.0bhp 96.9kW 131.8PS
@ 6000rpm
119.0lbft 161.2Nm @ 4750rpm
134.6bhp/ton 132.4bhp/tonne
68.2bhp/L 50.9kW/L 69.2PS/L
57.7ft/sec 17.6m/sec
20.9mph 33.6kmh/1000rpm
28.3mpg 23.6mpgUS 10.0L/100km
Petrol 4-stroke piston
1905cc 116.0cu in
In-line 4 fuel injection
Compression ratio: 9.6:1
Bore: 83.0mm 3.3in
Stroke: 88.0mm 3.5in
Valve type/No: Overhead 8
Transmission: Manual
No. of forward speeds: 5
Wheels driven: Front
Springs F/R: Coil/Torsion bar
Brake system: PA
Brakes F/R: Disc/Disc
Steering: Rack & pinion PA
Wheelbase: 246.9cm 97.2in
Track F: 140.8cm 55.4in
Track R: 137.6cm 54.2in
Length: 405.1cm 159.5in
Width: 162.8cm 64.1in
Height: 138.0cm 54.3in
Ground clearance: 16.5cm 6.5in
Kerb weight: 982.0kg 2163.0lb
Fuel: 55.1L 12.1gal 14.5galUS

3445 Peugeot

505 STX
1987 France
125.0mph 201.1kmh
0-50mph 80.5kmh: 6.8secs
0-60mph 96.5kmh: 9.8secs
0-1/4 mile: 17.2secs
145.0bhp 108.1kW 147.0PS
@ 5000rpm
173.0lbft 234.4Nm @ 3750rpm
102.5bhp/ton 100.7bhp/tonne
50.9bhp/L 37.9kW/L 51.6PS/L
39.9ft/sec 12.1m/sec
28.8mpg 24.0mpgUS 9.8L/100km
Petrol 4-stroke piston
2849cc 173.8cu in
Vee 6 fuel injection
Compression ratio: 9.5:1
Bore: 91.0mm 3.6in
Stroke: 72.9mm 2.9in
Valve type/No: Overhead 12
Transmission: Manual
No. of forward speeds: 5
Wheels driven: Rear
Springs F/R: Coil/Coil
Brake system: PA ABS
Brakes F/R: Disc/Disc
Steering: Rack & pinion PA
Wheelbase: 274.3cm 108.0in
Track F: 150.1cm 59.1in
Track R: 145.5cm 57.3in
Length: 474.2cm 186.7in
Width: 173.5cm 68.3in
Height: 141.2cm 55.6in
Kerb weight: 1439.2kg 3170.0lb
Fuel: 68.1L 15.0gal 18.0galUS

3446 Peugeot

405 1.6 GL
1988 France
108.0mph 173.8kmh
0-50mph 80.5kmh: 7.9secs
0-60mph 96.5kmh: 10.9secs
0-1/4 mile: 18.1secs
0-1km: 33.7secs
92.0bhp 68.6kW 93.3PS
@ 6000rpm
99.0lbft 134.1Nm @ 2600rpm
91.0bhp/ton 89.5bhp/tonne
58.2bhp/L 43.4kW/L 59.0PS/L
47.8ft/sec 14.6m/sec
21.2mph 34.1kmh/1000rpm
27.9mpg 23.2mpgUS 10.1L/100km
Petrol 4-stroke piston
1580cc 96.0cu in
In-line 4 1 Carburettor
Compression ratio: 8.9:1
Bore: 83.0mm 3.3in
Stroke: 73.0mm 2.9in
Valve type/No: Overhead 8
Transmission: Manual
No. of forward speeds: 5
Wheels driven: Front
Springs F/R: Coil/Torsion bar
Brake system: PA
Brakes F/R: Disc/Drum
Steering: Rack & pinion
Wheelbase: 266.9cm 105.1in
Track F: 145.0cm 57.1in
Track R: 143.6cm 56.5in
Length: 440.8cm 173.5in
Width: 169.4cm 66.7in
Height: 140.6cm 55.4in
Ground clearance: 15.3cm 6.0in
Kerb weight: 1028.0kg 2264.3lb
Fuel: 70.1L 15.4gal 18.5galUS

3447 Peugeot

405 GRD
1988 France
102.0mph 164.1kmh
0-50mph 80.5kmh: 10.9secs
0-60mph 96.5kmh: 15.4secs
0-1/4 mile: 20.8secs
0-1km: 38.7secs
70.0bhp 52.2kW 71.0PS
@ 4600rpm
88.6lbft 120.0Nm @ 2000rpm
63.3bhp/ton 62.2bhp/tonne
36.7bhp/L 27.4kW/L 37.2PS/L
44.2ft/sec 13.5m/sec
22.2mph 35.7kmh/1000rpm
38.2mpg 31.8mpgUS 7.4L/100km
Diesel 4-stroke piston
1905cc 116.0cu in
In-line 4 fuel injection
Compression ratio: 22.5:1
Bore: 83.0mm 3.3in
Stroke: 88.0mm 3.5in
Valve type/No: Overhead 8
Transmission: Manual
No. of forward speeds: 5
Wheels driven: Front
Springs F/R: Coil/Torsion bar
Brake system: PA
Brakes F/R: Disc/Drum
Steering: Rack & pinion PA
Wheelbase: 266.9cm 105.1in
Track F: 145.0cm 57.1in
Track R: 143.6cm 56.5in
Length: 440.8cm 173.5in
Width: 169.4cm 66.7in
Height: 140.6cm 55.4in
Ground clearance: 15.3cm 6.0in
Kerb weight: 1125.0kg 2478.0lb
Fuel: 70.1L 15.4gal 18.5galUS

3448 Peugeot

405 Mi16
1988 France
134.0mph 215.6kmh
0-50mph 80.5kmh: 5.9secs
0-60mph 96.5kmh: 8.0secs
0-1/4 mile: 16.3secs
0-1km: 29.7secs
160.0bhp 119.3kW 162.2PS
@ 6500rpm
133.6lbft 181.0Nm @ 5000rpm
142.0bhp/ton 139.6bhp/tonne
84.0bhp/L 62.6kW/L 85.1PS/L
62.5ft/sec 19.1m/sec
19.9mph 32.0kmh/1000rpm
26.6mpg 22.1mpgUS 10.6L/100km
Petrol 4-stroke piston
1905cc 116.0cu in
In-line 4 fuel injection
Compression ratio: 10.4:1
Bore: 83.0mm 3.3in
Stroke: 88.0mm 3.5in
Valve type/No: Overhead 16
Transmission: Manual
No. of forward speeds: 5
Wheels driven: Front

Springs F/R: Coil/Torsion bar
Brake system: PA ABS
Brakes F/R: Disc/Disc
Steering: Rack & pinion PA
Wheelbase: 266.9cm 105.1in
Track F: 145.0cm 57.1in
Track R: 143.6cm 56.5in
Length: 440.8cm 173.5in
Width: 169.4cm 66.7in
Height: 140.6cm 55.4in
Ground clearance: 15.3cm 6.0in
Kerb weight: 1146.0kg 2524.2lb
Fuel: 70.1L 15.4gal 18.5galUS

3449 Peugeot

405 SRi
1988 France
118.0mph 189.9kmh
0-50mph 80.5kmh: 7.4secs
0-60mph 96.5kmh: 10.3secs
0-1/4 mile: 17.9secs
0-1km: 33.2secs
125.0bhp 93.2kW 126.7PS
@ 5500rpm
130.6lbft 177.0Nm @ 4500rpm
122.2bhp/ton 120.2bhp/tonne
65.6bhp/L 48.9kW/L 66.5PS/L
52.9ft/sec 16.1m/sec
22.0mph 35.4kmh/1000rpm
23.8mpg 19.8mpgUS 11.9L/100km
Petrol 4-stroke piston
1905cc 116.0cu in
In-line 4 fuel injection
Compression ratio: 9.3:1
Bore: 83.0mm 3.3in
Stroke: 88.0mm 3.5in
Valve type/No: Overhead 8
Transmission: Manual
No. of forward speeds: 5
Wheels driven: Front
Springs F/R: Coil/Torsion bar
Brake system: PA
Brakes F/R: Disc/Disc
Steering: Rack & pinion PA
Wheelbase: 266.9cm 105.1in
Track F: 145.0cm 57.1in
Track R: 143.6cm 56.5in
Length: 440.8cm 173.5in
Width: 169.4cm 66.7in
Height: 140.6cm 55.4in
Ground clearance: 15.3cm 6.0in
Kerb weight: 1040.0kg 2290.7lb
Fuel: 70.1L 15.4gal 18.5galUS

3450 Peugeot

205 1.1GL
1989 France
99.0mph 159.3kmh
0-50mph 80.5kmh: 9.3secs
0-60mph 96.5kmh: 13.3secs
0-1/4 mile: 19.4secs
0-1km: 32.6secs
55.0bhp 41.0kW 55.8PS
@ 5800rpm
63.5lbft 86.0Nm @ 3200rpm
70.8bhp/ton 69.6bhp/tonne
48.9bhp/L 36.5kW/L 49.6PS/L
43.8ft/sec 13.3m/sec
21.0mph 33.8kmh/1000rpm
39.5mpg 32.9mpgUS 7.2L/100km
Petrol 4-stroke piston
1124cc 69.0cu in
In-line 4 1 Carburettor
Compression ratio: 9.4:1
Bore: 72.0mm 2.8in
Stroke: 69.0mm 2.7in
Valve type/No: Overhead 8
Transmission: Manual
No. of forward speeds: 4
Wheels driven: Front
Springs F/R: Coil/Torsion bar
Brake system: PA
Brakes F/R: Disc/Drum
Steering: Rack & pinion
Wheelbase: 242.0cm 95.3in
Track F: 139.3cm 54.8in
Track R: 133.2cm 52.4in
Length: 370.5cm 145.9in
Width: 157.2cm 61.9in
Height: 137.0cm 53.9in
Ground clearance: 12.0cm 4.7in
Kerb weight: 790.0kg 1740.1lb
Fuel: 50.0L 11.0gal 13.2galUS

3451 Peugeot

205 CJ
1989 France
101.0mph 162.5kmh
0-50mph 80.5kmh: 7.3secs
0-60mph 96.5kmh: 11.7secs
0-1/4 mile: 18.4secs
0-1km: 45.4secs
65.0bhp 48.5kW 65.9PS
@ 5400rpm
83.4lbft 113.0Nm @ 3000rpm
76.0bhp/ton 74.7bhp/tonne
47.8bhp/L 35.6kW/L 48.5PS/L
45.4ft/sec 13.9m/sec
17.6mph 28.3kmh/1000rpm
37.2mpg 31.0mpgUS 7.6L/100km
Petrol 4-stroke piston
1360cc 83.0cu in
In-line 4 1 Carburettor
Compression ratio: 9.3:1
Bore: 75.0mm 2.9in
Stroke: 77.0mm 3.0in
Valve type/No: Overhead 8
Transmission: Manual
No. of forward speeds: 5
Wheels driven: Front
Springs F/R: Coil/Torsion bar
Brake system: PA
Brakes F/R: Disc/Drum
Steering: Rack & pinion
Wheelbase: 242.0cm 95.3in
Track F: 139.3cm 54.8in
Track R: 133.2cm 52.4in
Length: 370.5cm 145.9in
Width: 157.2cm 61.9in
Height: 135.5cm 53.3in
Ground clearance: 12.0cm 4.7in
Kerb weight: 870.0kg 1916.3lb
Fuel: 50.0L 11.0gal 13.2galUS

3452 Peugeot

309 GLX
1989 France
95.0mph 152.9kmh
0-50mph 80.5kmh: 11.3secs
0-60mph 96.5kmh: 16.5secs
0-1/4 mile: 20.6secs
0-1km: 38.7secs
65.0bhp 48.5kW 65.9PS
@ 5600rpm
76.0lbft 103.0Nm @ 2800rpm
75.1bhp/ton 73.9bhp/tonne
50.2bhp/L 37.5kW/L 50.9PS/L
42.9ft/sec 13.1m/sec
20.2mph 32.5kmh/1000rpm
28.2mpg 23.5mpgUS 10.0L/100km
Petrol 4-stroke piston
1294cc 79.0cu in
In-line 4 1 Carburettor
Compression ratio: 9.4:1
Bore: 76.7mm 3.0in
Stroke: 70.0mm 2.8in
Valve type/No: Overhead 8
Transmission: Manual
No. of forward speeds: 5
Wheels driven: Front
Springs F/R: Coil/Torsion bar
Brake system: PA
Brakes F/R: Disc/Drum
Steering: Rack & pinion
Wheelbase: 246.9cm 97.2in
Track F: 140.8cm 55.4in
Track R: 137.6cm 54.2in
Length: 405.1cm 159.5in
Width: 162.8cm 64.1in
Height: 138.0cm 54.3in
Ground clearance: 16.5cm 6.5in
Kerb weight: 880.0kg 1938.3lb
Fuel: 55.1L 12.1gal 14.5galUS

3453 Peugeot

309 GTi
1989 France
125.0mph 201.1kmh
0-50mph 80.5kmh: 6.6secs
0-60mph 96.5kmh: 8.8secs
0-1/4 mile: 16.5secs
0-1km: 29.7secs
130.0bhp 96.9kW 131.8PS
@ 6000rpm
118.8lbft 161.0Nm @ 4750rpm
133.8bhp/ton 131.6bhp/tonne
68.2bhp/L 50.9kW/L 69.2PS/L
57.7ft/sec 17.6m/sec
20.9mph 33.6kmh/1000rpm
25.2mpg 21.0mpgUS 11.2L/100km
Petrol 4-stroke piston
1905cc 116.0cu in
In-line 4 fuel injection
Compression ratio: 9.6:1
Bore: 83.0mm 3.3in
Stroke: 88.0mm 3.5in
Valve type/No: Overhead 8
Transmission: Manual
No. of forward speeds: 5
Wheels driven: Front
Springs F/R: Coil/Torsion bar
Brake system: PA
Brakes F/R: Disc/Disc
Steering: Rack & pinion PA
Wheelbase: 246.9cm 97.2in
Track F: 140.8cm 55.4in
Track R: 136.6cm 53.8in
Length: 405.1cm 159.5in
Width: 162.8cm 64.1in
Height: 138.0cm 54.3in
Ground clearance: 16.5cm 6.5in
Kerb weight: 988.0kg 2176.2lb
Fuel: 55.1L 12.1gal 14.5galUS

3454 Peugeot

405 GTD Turbo
1989 France
109.0mph 175.4kmh
0-50mph 80.5kmh: 8.8secs
0-60mph 96.5kmh: 12.2secs
0-1/4 mile: 18.6secs
0-1km: 33.9secs
92.0bhp 68.6kW 93.3PS
@ 4300rpm
132.8lbft 180.0Nm @ 2200rpm
82.7bhp/ton 81.3bhp/tonne
52.0bhp/L 38.8kW/L 52.7PS/L
41.3ft/sec 12.6m/sec
25.3mph 40.7kmh/1000rpm
31.3mpg 26.1mpgUS 9.0L/100km
Diesel 4-stroke piston
1769cc 108.0cu in turbocharged
In-line 4 fuel injection
Compression ratio: 22.5:1
Bore: 80.0mm 3.1in
Stroke: 88.0mm 3.5in
Valve type/No: Overhead 8
Transmission: Manual
No. of forward speeds: 5
Wheels driven: Front
Springs F/R: Coil/Torsion bar
Brake system: PA
Brakes F/R: Disc/Drum
Steering: Rack & pinion PA
Wheelbase: 266.9cm 105.1in
Track F: 145.0cm 57.1in
Track R: 143.6cm 56.5in
Length: 440.8cm 173.5in
Width: 169.4cm 66.7in
Height: 140.6cm 55.4in
Ground clearance: 15.3cm 6.0in
Kerb weight: 1131.0kg 2491.2lb
Fuel: 70.1L 15.4gal 18.5galUS

3455 Peugeot

405 Mi16
1989 France
130.0mph 209.2kmh
0-50mph 80.5kmh: 6.6secs
0-60mph 96.5kmh: 9.0secs
0-1/4 mile: 16.8secs
150.0bhp 111.9kW 152.1PS
@ 6400rpm
128.0lbft 173.4Nm @ 5000rpm
124.7bhp/ton 122.6bhp/tonne
78.7bhp/L 58.7kW/L 79.8PS/L
61.5ft/sec 18.8m/sec
26.4mpg 22.0mpgUS 10.7L/100km
Petrol 4-stroke piston
1905cc 116.2cu in
In-line 4 fuel injection
Compression ratio: 9.5:1
Bore: 83.0mm 3.3in
Stroke: 88.0mm 3.5in
Valve type/No: Overhead 16
Transmission: Manual
No. of forward speeds: 5
Wheels driven: Front
Springs F/R: Coil/Torsion bar
Brake system: PA
Brakes F/R: Disc/Disc
Steering: Rack & pinion PA
Wheelbase: 267.0cm 105.1in
Track F: 144.0cm 56.7in
Track R: 143.3cm 56.4in
Length: 451.4cm 177.7in
Width: 171.7cm 67.6in
Height: 140.7cm 55.4in
Ground clearance: 14.5cm 5.7in
Kerb weight: 1223.5kg 2695.0lb
Fuel: 65.1L 14.3gal 17.2galUS

3456 Peugeot

309 Style 5-door
1990 France
96.0mph 154.5kmh
0-50mph 80.5kmh: 10.1secs
0-60mph 96.5kmh: 14.7secs
0-1/4 mile: 20.0secs
0-1km: 37.3secs
65.0bhp 48.5kW 65.9PS
@ 5600rpm
76.0lbft 103.0Nm @ 2800rpm
76.4bhp/ton 75.1bhp/tonne
50.2bhp/L 37.5kW/L 50.9PS/L
42.9ft/sec 13.1m/sec
21.0mph 33.8kmh/1000rpm
30.4mpg 25.3mpgUS 9.3L/100km
Petrol 4-stroke piston
1294cc 79.0cu in
In-line 4 1 Carburettor
Compression ratio: 9.4:1
Bore: 77.0mm 3.0in
Stroke: 70.0mm 2.8in
Valve type/No: Overhead 8
Transmission: Manual
No. of forward speeds: 5
Wheels driven: Front
Springs F/R: Coil/Coil
Brake system: PA
Brakes F/R: Disc/Drum
Steering: Rack & pinion
Wheelbase: 246.9cm 97.2in
Track F: 140.8cm 55.4in
Track R: 137.6cm 54.2in
Length: 405.1cm 159.5in
Width: 162.8cm 64.1in
Height: 138.0cm 54.3in
Ground clearance: 16.5cm 6.5in
Kerb weight: 865.0kg 1905.3lb
Fuel: 55.1L 12.1gal 14.5galUS

3457 Peugeot

405 GLx4
1990 France
117.0mph 188.3kmh
0-50mph 80.5kmh: 7.7secs
0-60mph 96.5kmh: 10.9secs
0-1/4 mile: 18.0secs
0-1km: 33.5secs
110.0bhp 82.0kW 111.5PS
@ 6000rpm
118.1lbft 160.0Nm @ 3000rpm
88.6bhp/ton 87.2bhp/tonne
57.7bhp/L 43.1kW/L 58.5PS/L
57.7ft/sec 17.6m/sec
20.3mph 32.7kmh/1000rpm
24.4mpg 20.3mpgUS 11.6L/100km
Petrol 4-stroke piston
1905cc 116.0cu in
In-line 4 1 Carburettor
Compression ratio: 9.3:1
Bore: 83.0mm 3.3in
Stroke: 88.0mm 3.5in
Valve type/No: Overhead 8
Transmission: Manual
No. of forward speeds: 5
Wheels driven: 4-wheel drive
Springs F/R: Coil/Coil
Brake system: PA ABS
Brakes F/R: Disc/Disc
Steering: Rack & pinion PA
Wheelbase: 266.9cm 105.1in
Track F: 145.0cm 57.1in
Track R: 143.6cm 56.5in
Length: 440.8cm 173.5in
Width: 169.4cm 66.7in
Height: 140.6cm 55.4in
Ground clearance: 15.3cm 6.0in
Kerb weight: 1262.0kg 2779.7lb
Fuel: 70.5L 15.5gal 18.6galUS

3458 Peugeot

405 GR Injection Auto
1990 France
121.0mph 194.7kmh
0-50mph 80.5kmh: 9.0secs
0-60mph 96.5kmh: 11.9secs
0-1/4 mile: 18.8secs
0-1km: 34.0secs
125.0bhp 93.2kW 126.7PS
@ 5500rpm
129.2lbft 175.0Nm @ 4500rpm
110.5bhp/ton 108.7bhp/tonne
65.6bhp/L 48.9kW/L 66.5PS/L
52.9ft/sec 16.1m/sec
23.0mph 37.0kmh/1000rpm
27.3mpg 22.7mpgUS 10.3L/100km
Petrol 4-stroke piston

1905cc 116.0cu in
In-line 4 fuel injection
Compression ratio: 9.3:1
Bore: 83.0mm 3.3in
Stroke: 88.0mm 3.5in
Valve type/No: Overhead 8
Transmission: Automatic
No. of forward speeds: 4
Wheels driven: Front
Springs F/R: Coil/Coil
Brake system: PA ABS
Brakes F/R: Disc/Disc
Steering: Rack & pinion PA
Wheelbase: 266.9cm 105.1in
Track F: 145.0cm 57.1in
Track R: 143.6cm 56.5in
Length: 440.8cm 173.5in
Width: 169.4cm 66.7in
Height: 140.6cm 55.4in
Ground clearance: 15.3cm 6.0in
Kerb weight: 1150.0kg 2533.0lb
Fuel: 70.1L 15.4gal 18.5galUS

3459 Peugeot

405 Mi16x4
1990 France
127.0mph 204.3kmh
0-50mph 80.5kmh: 6.8secs
0-60mph 96.5kmh: 9.5secs
0-1/4 mile: 17.1secs
0-1km: 30.6secs
160.0bhp 119.3kW 162.2PS
@ 6500rpm
132.8lbft 180.0Nm @ 5000rpm
126.1bhp/ton 124.0bhp/tonne
84.0bhp/L 62.6kW/L 85.1PS/L
62.5ft/sec 19.1m/sec
19.1mph 30.7kmh/1000rpm
26.0mpg 21.6mpgUS 10.9L/100km
Petrol 4-stroke piston
1905cc 116.0cu in
In-line 4 fuel injection
Compression ratio: 10.4:1
Bore: 83.0mm 3.3in
Stroke: 88.0mm 3.5in
Valve type/No: Overhead 16
Transmission: Manual
No. of forward speeds: 5
Wheels driven: 4-wheel drive
Springs F/R: Coil/Gas
Brake system: PA ABS
Brakes F/R: Disc/Disc
Steering: Rack & pinion PA
Wheelbase: 266.9cm 105.1in
Track F: 145.0cm 57.1in
Track R: 143.6cm 56.5in
Length: 440.8cm 173.5in
Width: 169.4cm 66.7in
Height: 140.8cm 55.4in
Ground clearance: 15.3cm 6.0in
Kerb weight: 1290.0kg 2841.4lb
Fuel: 70.1L 15.4gal 18.5galUS

3460 Peugeot

405 Turbo 16 Pike's Peak
1990 France
125.0mph 201.1kmh
0-60mph 96.5kmh: 6.2secs
640.0bhp 477.2kW 648.9PS
@ 7000rpm
542.0lbft 734.4Nm @ 6000rpm
764.6bhp/ton 751.8bhp/tonne
336.0bhp/L 250.5kW/L 340.6PS/L
67.3ft/sec 20.5m/sec
Petrol 4-stroke piston
1905cc 116.2cu in turbocharged
In-line 4 fuel injection
Compression ratio: 7.0:1
Bore: 83.0mm 3.3in
Stroke: 88.0mm 3.5in
Valve type/No: Overhead 16
Transmission: Manual
No. of forward speeds: 6
Wheels driven: 4-wheel drive
Springs F/R: Coil/Coil
Brakes F/R: Disc/Disc
Steering: Rack & pinion PA
Wheelbase: 288.8cm 113.7in
Track F: 151.9cm 59.8in
Track R: 151.9cm 59.8in
Length: 424.9cm 167.3in
Width: 176.0cm 69.3in
Height: 119.9cm 47.2in
Kerb weight: 851.2kg 1875.0lb
Fuel: 60.2L 13.2gal 15.9galUS

3461 Peugeot

605 SRi
1990 France
123.0mph 197.9kmh
0-50mph 80.5kmh: 8.5secs
0-60mph 96.5kmh: 11.8secs
0-1/4 mile: 18.2secs
0-1km: 33.4secs
122.0bhp 91.0kW 123.7PS
@ 5600rpm
126.0lbft 170.7Nm @ 4000rpm
88.8bhp/ton 87.3bhp/tonne
61.1bhp/L 45.5kW/L 61.9PS/L
52.7ft/sec 16.0m/sec
22.2mph 35.7kmh/1000rpm
24.7mpg 20.6mpgUS 11.4L/100km
Petrol 4-stroke piston
1998cc 121.9cu in
In-line 4 fuel injection
Compression ratio: 8.8:1
Bore: 86.0mm 3.4in
Stroke: 86.0mm 3.4in
Valve type/No: Overhead 8
Transmission: Manual
No. of forward speeds: 5
Wheels driven: Front
Springs F/R: Coil/Coil
Brake system: PA ABS
Brakes F/R: Disc/Disc
Steering: Rack & pinion PA
Wheelbase: 279.9cm 110.2in
Track F: 152.7cm 60.1in
Track R: 152.7cm 60.1in
Length: 472.2cm 185.9in
Width: 179.8cm 70.8in
Height: 141.5cm 55.7in
Kerb weight: 1397.0kg 3077.0lb
Fuel: 79.6L 17.5gal 21.0galUS

3462 Peugeot

106 XR
1991 France
97.0mph 156.1kmh
0-50mph 80.5kmh: 9.5secs
0-60mph 96.5kmh: 13.8secs
0-1/4 mile: 19.5secs
0-1km: 36.4secs
60.0bhp 44.7kW 60.8PS
@ 5800rpm
66.4lbft 90.0Nm @ 3200rpm
77.2bhp/ton 75.9bhp/tonne
53.4bhp/L 39.8kW/L 54.1PS/L
43.8ft/sec 13.3m/sec
20.2mph 32.5kmh/1000rpm
32.1mpg 26.7mpgUS 8.8L/100km
Petrol 4-stroke piston
1124cc 69.0cu in
In-line 4 fuel injection
Compression ratio: 9.4:1
Bore: 72.0mm 2.8in
Stroke: 69.0mm 2.7in
Valve type/No: Overhead 8
Transmission: Manual
No. of forward speeds: 5
Wheels driven: Front
Springs F/R: Coil/Torsion bar
Brake system: PA
Brakes F/R: Disc/Drum
Steering: Rack & pinion
Wheelbase: 238.3cm 93.8in
Track F: 135.6cm 53.4in
Track R: 132.3cm 52.1in
Length: 356.4cm 140.3in
Width: 158.8cm 62.5in
Height: 136.7cm 53.8in
Kerb weight: 790.0kg 1740.1lb
Fuel: 45.0L 9.9gal 11.9galUS

3463 Peugeot

106 XSi
1991 France
118.0mph 189.9kmh
0-50mph 80.5kmh: 6.9secs
0-60mph 96.5kmh: 9.7secs
0-1/4 mile: 17.5secs
0-1km: 31.8secs
100.0bhp 74.6kW 101.4PS
@ 6800rpm
89.0lbft 120.6Nm @ 4200rpm
113.8bhp/ton 111.9bhp/tonne
73.5bhp/L 54.8kW/L 74.5PS/L
57.2ft/sec 17.4m/sec
17.7mph 28.5kmh/1000rpm
26.9mpg 22.4mpgUS 10.5L/100km
Petrol 4-stroke piston
1360cc 83.0cu in
In-line 4 fuel injection
Compression ratio: 9.6:1
Bore: 75.0mm 2.9in
Stroke: 77.0mm 3.0in
Valve type/No: Overhead 8
Transmission: Manual
No. of forward speeds: 5
Wheels driven: Front
Springs F/R: Coil/Torsion bar
Brake system: PA
Brakes F/R: Disc/Drum
Steering: Rack & pinion
Wheelbase: 238.3cm 93.8in
Track F: 135.6cm 53.4in
Track R: 132.3cm 52.1in
Length: 356.4cm 140.3in
Width: 158.8cm 62.5in
Height: 136.7cm 53.8in
Kerb weight: 893.9kg 1969.0lb
Fuel: 45.0L 9.9gal 11.9galUS

3464 Peugeot

205 D Turbo
1991 France
103.0mph 165.7kmh
0-50mph 80.5kmh: 8.9secs
0-60mph 96.5kmh: 12.3secs
0-1/4 mile: 18.9secs
0-1km: 35.1secs
78.0bhp 58.2kW 79.1PS
@ 4300rpm
115.9lbft 157.0Nm @ 2100rpm
83.5bhp/ton 82.1bhp/tonne
44.1bhp/L 32.9kW/L 44.7PS/L
41.3ft/sec 12.6m/sec
24.3mph 39.1kmh/1000rpm
34.4mpg 28.6mpgUS 8.2L/100km
Diesel 4-stroke piston
1769cc 108.0cu in turbocharged
In-line 4 fuel injection
Compression ratio: 22.0:1
Bore: 80.0mm 3.1in
Stroke: 88.0mm 3.5in
Valve type/No: Overhead 8
Transmission: Manual
No. of forward speeds: 5
Wheels driven: Front
Springs F/R: Coil/Torsion bar
Brake system: PA
Brakes F/R: Disc/Drum
Steering: Rack & pinion PA
Wheelbase: 241.3cm 95.0in
Track F: 136.4cm 53.7in
Track R: 131.3cm 51.7in
Length: 370.6cm 145.9in
Width: 154.9cm 61.0in
Height: 137.2cm 54.0in
Ground clearance: 11.9cm 4.7in
Kerb weight: 950.0kg 2092.5lb
Fuel: 50.0L 11.0gal 13.2galUS

3465 Peugeot

605 SR TD
1991 France
116.0mph 186.6kmh
0-50mph 80.5kmh: 9.5secs
0-60mph 96.5kmh: 12.8secs
0-1/4 mile: 19.3secs
0-1km: 35.1secs
110.0bhp 82.0kW 111.5PS
@ 4300rpm
183.0lbft 248.0Nm @ 2000rpm
74.8bhp/ton 73.6bhp/tonne
52.7bhp/L 39.3kW/L 53.4PS/L
43.2ft/sec 13.2m/sec
27.4mph 44.1kmh/1000rpm
33.3mpg 27.7mpgUS 8.5L/100km
Diesel 4-stroke piston
2088cc 127.0cu in turbocharged
In-line 4 fuel injection
Compression ratio: 21.5:1
Bore: 85.0mm 3.3in
Stroke: 92.0mm 3.6in
Valve type/No: Overhead 8
Transmission: Manual
No. of forward speeds: 5
Wheels driven: Front
Springs F/R: Coil/Coil
Brake system: PA ABS
Brakes F/R: Disc/Disc
Steering: Rack & pinion PA
Wheelbase: 279.9cm 110.2in
Track F: 152.7cm 60.1in
Track R: 152.7cm 60.1in
Length: 472.2cm 185.9in
Width: 179.8cm 70.8in
Height: 141.5cm 55.7in
Kerb weight: 1495.0kg 3292.9lb
Fuel: 79.6L 17.5gal 21.0galUS

3466 Peugeot

605 SV 3.0 Auto
1991 France
133.0mph 214.0kmh
0-50mph 80.5kmh: 7.8secs
0-60mph 96.5kmh: 10.6secs
0-1/4 mile: 17.5secs
0-1km: 31.8secs
170.0bhp 126.8kW 172.4PS
@ 6000rpm
177.1lbft 240.0Nm @ 6400rpm
112.3bhp/ton 110.4bhp/tonne
57.1bhp/L 42.6kW/L 57.9PS/L
47.8ft/sec 14.6m/sec
25.1mph 40.4kmh/1000rpm
19.8mpg 16.5mpgUS 14.3L/100km
Petrol 4-stroke piston
2975cc 182.0cu in
Vee 6 fuel injection
Compression ratio: 9.5:1
Bore: 93.0mm 3.7in
Stroke: 73.0mm 2.9in
Valve type/No: Overhead 12
Transmission: Automatic
No. of forward speeds: 4
Wheels driven: Front
Springs F/R: Coil/Coil
Brake system: PA ABS
Brakes F/R: Disc/Disc
Steering: Rack & pinion PA
Wheelbase: 279.9cm 110.2in
Track F: 152.7cm 60.1in
Track R: 152.7cm 60.1in
Length: 472.2cm 185.9in
Width: 179.8cm 70.8in
Height: 141.5cm 55.7in
Kerb weight: 1540.0kg 3392.1lb
Fuel: 80.1L 17.6gal 21.1galUS

3467 Peugeot

605 SVE 24
1991 France
144.0mph 231.7kmh
0-50mph 80.5kmh: 6.1secs
0-60mph 96.5kmh: 7.9secs
0-1/4 mile: 16.3secs
0-1km: 29.5secs
200.0bhp 149.1kW 202.8PS
@ 6000rpm
191.9lbft 260.0Nm @ 3600rpm
128.3bhp/ton 126.2bhp/tonne
67.2bhp/L 50.1kW/L 68.2PS/L
47.8ft/sec 14.6m/sec
23.1mph 37.2kmh/1000rpm
20.4mpg 17.0mpgUS 13.8L/100km
Petrol 4-stroke piston
2975cc 182.0cu in
Vee 6 fuel injection
Compression ratio: 9.5:1
Bore: 93.0mm 3.7in
Stroke: 73.0mm 2.9in
Valve type/No: Overhead 24
Transmission: Manual
No. of forward speeds: 5
Wheels driven: Front
Springs F/R: Coil/Coil
Brake system: PA ABS
Brakes F/R: Disc/Disc
Steering: Rack & pinion PA
Wheelbase: 280.0cm 110.2in
Track F: 152.7cm 60.1in
Track R: 153.6cm 60.5in
Length: 472.3cm 185.9in
Width: 179.9cm 70.8in
Height: 141.7cm 55.8in
Kerb weight: 1585.0kg 3491.2lb
Fuel: 79.5L 17.5gal 21.0galUS

3468 Peugeot

106 XT
1992 France
109.0mph 175.4kmh
0-50mph 80.5kmh: 8.1secs
0-60mph 96.5kmh: 11.0secs
0-1/4 mile: 18.5secs
0-1km: 31.4secs
75.0bhp 55.9kW 76.0PS
@ 5800rpm
84.0lbft 113.8Nm @ 3800rpm
93.2bhp/ton 91.7bhp/tonne
55.1bhp/L 41.1kW/L 55.9PS/L
48.8ft/sec 14.9m/sec
21.3mph 34.3kmh/1000rpm
32.7mpg 27.2mpgUS 8.6L/100km
Petrol 4-stroke piston
1360cc 83.0cu in
In-line 4 1 Carburettor

Compression ratio: 9.3:1
Bore: 75.0mm 2.9in
Stroke: 77.0mm 3.0in
Valve type/No: Overhead 8
Transmission: Manual
No. of forward speeds: 5
Wheels driven: Front
Springs F/R: Coil/Torsion bar
Brake system: PA
Brakes F/R: Disc/Drum
Steering: Rack & pinion
Wheelbase: 238.5cm 93.9in
Track F: 135.6cm 53.4in
Track R: 132.3cm 52.1in
Length: 356.4cm 140.3in
Width: 159.0cm 62.6in
Height: 136.7cm 53.8in
Kerb weight: 818.0kg 1801.8lb
Fuel: 45.0L 9.9gal 11.9galUS

3469 Pininfarina

Azzurra
1984 Italy
106.0mph 170.6kmh
0-50mph 80.5kmh: 8.1secs
0-60mph 96.5kmh: 11.2secs
0-1/4 mile: 18.1secs
102.0bhp 76.1kW 103.4PS
@ 5500rpm
110.0lbft 149.1Nm @ 3000rpm
95.8bhp/ton 94.2bhp/tonne
51.1bhp/L 38.1kW/L 51.8PS/L
54.1ft/sec 16.5m/sec
17.6mph 28.3kmh/1000rpm
28.8mpg 24.0mpgUS 9.8L/100km
Petrol 4-stroke piston
1995cc 121.7cu in
In-line 4 fuel injection
Compression ratio: 8.2:1
Bore: 84.0mm 3.3in
Stroke: 90.0mm 3.5in
Valve type/No: Overhead 16
Transmission: Manual
No. of forward speeds: 5
Wheels driven: Rear
Springs F/R: Coil/Coil
Brake system: PA
Brakes F/R: Disc/Disc
Steering: Worm & roller
Wheelbase: 228.1cm 89.8in
Track F: 135.4cm 53.3in
Track R: 135.4cm 53.3in
Length: 413.8cm 162.9in
Width: 161.3cm 63.5in
Height: 127.0cm 50.0in
Kerb weight: 1082.8kg 2385.0lb
Fuel: 40.1L 8.8gal 10.6galUS

3470 Pininfarina

Spider
1984 Italy
0-60mph 96.5kmh: 10.9secs
102.0bhp 76.1kW 103.4PS
@ 5500rpm
110.0lbft 149.1Nm @ 3000rpm
96.0bhp/ton 94.4bhp/tonne
51.1bhp/L 38.1kW/L 51.8PS/L
30.0mpg 25.0mpgUS 9.4L/100km
Petrol 4-stroke piston
1995cc 121.7cu in
In-line 4 fuel injection
Valve type/No: Overhead 8
Transmission: Manual
No. of forward speeds: 5
Wheels driven: Rear
Springs F/R: Coil/Coil
Brakes F/R: Disc/Disc
Steering: Worm & roller
Wheelbase: 227.8cm 89.7in
Length: 414.0cm 163.0in
Width: 161.3cm 63.5in
Height: 125.0cm 49.2in
Kerb weight: 1080.5kg 2380.0lb
Fuel: 43.1L 9.5gal 11.4galUS

3471 Plymouth

Cambridge
1952 USA
86.5mph 139.2kmh
0-1/4 mile: 21.6secs
97.0bhp 72.3kW 98.3PS
@ 3600rpm
71.3bhp/ton 70.1bhp/tonne
27.2bhp/L 20.3kW/L 27.6PS/L
43.7ft/sec 13.3m/sec
26.8mpg 22.3mpgUS 10.5L/100km
Petrol 4-stroke piston
3569cc 217.7cu in
In-line 6
Compression ratio: 7.0:1
Bore: 82.6mm 3.2in
Stroke: 111.1mm 4.4in
Valve type/No: Side 12
Transmission: Manual
No. of forward speeds: 3
Wheels driven: Rear
Wheelbase: 301.0cm 118.5in
Track F: 142.0cm 55.9in
Track R: 148.3cm 58.4in
Length: 492.8cm 194.0in
Width: 188.0cm 74.0in
Height: 164.8cm 64.9in
Ground clearance: 17.3cm 6.8in
Kerb weight: 1382.9kg 3046.0lb

3472 Plymouth

Fury
1956 USA
114.8mph 184.7kmh
0-50mph 80.5kmh: 6.8secs
0-60mph 96.5kmh: 9.0secs
0-1/4 mile: 16.6secs
240.0bhp 179.0kW 243.3PS
@ 4800rpm
310.0lbft 420.1Nm @ 2800rpm
148.5bhp/ton 146.0bhp/tonne
48.3bhp/L 36.0kW/L 49.0PS/L
44.1ft/sec 13.5m/sec
Petrol 4-stroke piston
4967cc 303.0cu in
Vee 8
Compression ratio: 9.3:1
Bore: 96.8mm 3.8in
Stroke: 84.1mm 3.3in
Valve type/No: Overhead 16
Transmission: Manual
No. of forward speeds: 3
Wheels driven: Rear
Wheelbase: 292.1cm 115.0in
Track F: 149.4cm 58.8in
Track R: 149.4cm 58.8in
Kerb weight: 1643.5kg 3620.0lb

3473 Plymouth

Savoy
1956 USA
95.0mph 152.9kmh
0-50mph 80.5kmh: 9.9secs
0-60mph 96.5kmh: 13.7secs
0-1/4 mile: 19.4secs
187.0bhp 139.4kW 189.6PS
@ 4440rpm
265.0lbft 359.1Nm @ 2400rpm
116.0bhp/ton 114.0bhp/tonne
41.6bhp/L 31.0kW/L 42.1PS/L
38.6ft/sec 11.8m/sec
22.8mph 36.7kmh/1000rpm
16.4mpg 13.7mpgUS 17.2L/100km
Petrol 4-stroke piston
4500cc 274.6cu in
Vee 8
Compression ratio: 8.0:1
Bore: 95.2mm 3.8in
Stroke: 79.5mm 3.1in
Valve type/No: Overhead 16
Transmission: Automatic
No. of forward speeds: 2
Wheels driven: Rear
Springs F/R: Coil/Leaf
Brake system: PA
Brakes F/R: Drum/Drum
Wheelbase: 292.1cm 115.0in
Track F: 148.3cm 58.4in
Track R: 148.6cm 58.5in
Length: 520.2cm 204.8in
Width: 189.5cm 74.6in
Height: 152.7cm 60.1in
Ground clearance: 19.1cm 7.5in
Kerb weight: 1639.8kg 3612.0lb
Fuel: 64.6L 14.2gal 17.1galUS

3474 Plymouth

Fury
1958 USA
120.6mph 194.0kmh
0-50mph 80.5kmh: 5.3secs
0-60mph 96.5kmh: 8.0secs
0-1/4 mile: 15.6secs
305.0bhp 227.4kW 309.2PS
@ 5000rpm
370.0lbft 501.4Nm @ 3600rpm
174.5bhp/ton 171.6bhp/tonne
53.1bhp/L 39.6kW/L 53.9PS/L
46.9ft/sec 14.3m/sec
Petrol 4-stroke piston
5738cc 350.1cu in
Vee 8
Compression ratio: 10.0:1
Bore: 103.1mm 4.1in
Stroke: 85.9mm 3.4in
Valve type/No: Overhead 16
Transmission: Manual
No. of forward speeds: 3
Wheels driven: Rear
Wheelbase: 299.7cm 118.0in
Track F: 154.7cm 60.9in
Track R: 151.4cm 59.6in
Kerb weight: 1777.4kg 3915.0lb

3475 Plymouth

Fury
1959 USA
106.0mph 170.6kmh
0-50mph 80.5kmh: 7.9secs
0-60mph 96.5kmh: 10.8secs
0-1/4 mile: 17.8secs
225.0bhp 167.8kW 228.1PS
@ 4400rpm
340.0lbft 460.7Nm @ 2400rpm
128.1bhp/ton 126.0bhp/tonne
43.2bhp/L 32.2kW/L 43.8PS/L
40.5ft/sec 12.3m/sec
26.6mph 42.8kmh/1000rpm
16.2mpg 13.5mpgUS 17.4L/100km
Petrol 4-stroke piston
5212cc 318.0cu in
Vee 8 1 Carburettor
Compression ratio: 9.0:1
Bore: 99.3mm 3.9in
Stroke: 84.0mm 3.3in
Valve type/No: Overhead 16
Transmission: Automatic
No. of forward speeds: 3
Wheels driven: Rear
Springs F/R: Torsion bar/Leaf
Brake system: PA
Brakes F/R: Drum/Drum
Wheelbase: 299.7cm 118.0in
Track F: 154.7cm 60.9in
Track R: 151.9cm 59.8in
Length: 528.8cm 208.2in
Width: 198.1cm 78.0in
Height: 143.8cm 56.6in
Ground clearance: 13.7cm 5.4in
Kerb weight: 1786.0kg 3934.0lb
Fuel: 77.3L 17.0gal 20.4galUS

3476 Plymouth

Valiant
1960 USA
95.2mph 153.2kmh
0-50mph 80.5kmh: 10.3secs
0-60mph 96.5kmh: 13.9secs
0-1/4 mile: 19.5secs
101.0bhp 75.3kW 102.4PS
@ 4400rpm
155.0lbft 210.0Nm @ 2400rpm
82.3bhp/ton 80.9bhp/tonne
36.2bhp/L 27.0kW/L 36.7PS/L
38.1ft/sec 11.6m/sec
19.9mph 32.0kmh/1000rpm
Petrol 4-stroke piston
2791cc 170.3cu in
In-line 6 1 Carburettor
Compression ratio: 8.5:1
Bore: 86.4mm 3.4in
Stroke: 79.2mm 3.1in
Valve type/No: Overhead 12
Transmission: Manual
No. of forward speeds: 3
Wheels driven: Rear
Wheelbase: 270.5cm 106.5in
Track F: 142.2cm 56.0in
Track R: 141.0cm 55.5in
Length: 467.4cm 184.0in
Width: 178.8cm 70.4in
Height: 135.4cm 53.3in
Kerb weight: 1248.5kg 2750.0lb

3477 Plymouth

Valiant Automatic
1960 USA
95.0mph 152.9kmh
0-50mph 80.5kmh: 11.0secs
0-60mph 96.5kmh: 16.0secs
0-1/4 mile: 20.0secs
101.0bhp 75.3kW 102.4PS
@ 4400rpm
155.0lbft 210.0Nm @ 2400rpm
82.0bhp/ton 80.6bhp/tonne
36.2bhp/L 27.0kW/L 36.7PS/L
38.1ft/sec 11.6m/sec
19.9mph 32.0kmh/1000rpm
Petrol 4-stroke piston
2791cc 170.3cu in
In-line 6 1 Carburettor
Compression ratio: 8.5:1
Bore: 86.4mm 3.4in
Stroke: 79.2mm 3.1in
Valve type/No: Overhead 12
Transmission: Automatic
No. of forward speeds: 3
Wheels driven: Rear
Wheelbase: 270.5cm 106.5in
Track F: 142.2cm 56.0in
Track R: 141.0cm 55.5in
Length: 467.4cm 184.0in
Width: 178.8cm 70.4in
Height: 135.4cm 53.3in
Kerb weight: 1253.0kg 2760.0lb

3478 Plymouth

Savoy 6
1961 USA
93.5mph 150.4kmh
0-50mph 80.5kmh: 10.7secs
0-60mph 96.5kmh: 15.3secs
0-1/4 mile: 20.0secs
145.0bhp 108.1kW 147.0PS
@ 4000rpm
215.0lbft 291.3Nm @ 2800rpm
92.7bhp/ton 91.1bhp/tonne
39.3bhp/L 29.3kW/L 39.9PS/L
45.9ft/sec 14.0m/sec
23.4mph 37.7kmh/1000rpm
Petrol 4-stroke piston
3688cc 225.0cu in
In-line 6 1 Carburettor
Compression ratio: 8.2:1
Bore: 86.4mm 3.4in
Stroke: 104.8mm 4.1in
Valve type/No: Overhead 12
Transmission: Automatic
No. of forward speeds: 3
Wheels driven: Rear
Brakes F/R: Drum/Drum
Wheelbase: 299.7cm 118.0in
Track F: 154.7cm 60.9in
Track R: 151.4cm 59.6in
Length: 532.1cm 209.5in
Width: 203.2cm 80.0in
Height: 138.2cm 54.4in
Ground clearance: 11.9cm 4.7in
Kerb weight: 1591.3kg 3505.0lb

3479 Plymouth

Savoy Station Wagon
1962 USA
102.0mph 164.1kmh
0-50mph 80.5kmh: 8.8secs
0-60mph 96.5kmh: 12.0secs
0-1/4 mile: 17.6secs
230.0bhp 171.5kW 233.2PS
@ 4400rpm
340.0lbft 460.7Nm @ 2400rpm
142.1bhp/ton 139.7bhp/tonne
44.1bhp/L 32.9kW/L 44.7PS/L
40.5ft/sec 12.3m/sec
23.2mph 37.3kmh/1000rpm
Petrol 4-stroke piston
5211cc 317.9cu in
Vee 8 1 Carburettor
Compression ratio: 9.0:1
Bore: 99.3mm 3.9in
Stroke: 84.1mm 3.3in
Valve type/No: Overhead 16
Transmission: Manual
No. of forward speeds: 3
Wheels driven: Rear
Wheelbase: 294.6cm 116.0in
Track F: 150.9cm 59.4in
Track R: 146.1cm 57.5in
Length: 533.4cm 210.0in
Width: 192.0cm 75.6in
Height: 136.7cm 53.8in
Ground clearance: 11.7cm 4.6in
Kerb weight: 1645.7kg 3625.0lb
Fuel: 81.4L 17.9gal 21.5galUS

3480 Plymouth

Savoy V8
1962 USA
110.0mph 177.0kmh
0-50mph 80.5kmh: 7.7secs

0-60mph 96.5kmh: 10.5secs
0-1/4 mile: 17.2secs
230.0bhp 171.5kW 233.2PS
@ 4400rpm
340.0lbft 460.7Nm @ 2400rpm
154.5bhp/ton 151.9bhp/tonne
44.1bhp/L 32.9kW/L 44.7PS/L
40.5ft/sec 12.3m/sec
23.9mph 38.5kmh/1000rpm
Petrol 4-stroke piston
5213cc 318.1cu in
Vee 8 1 Carburettor
Compression ratio: 9.0:1
Bore: 99.3mm 3.9in
Stroke: 84.1mm 3.3in
Valve type/No: Overhead 16
Transmission: Manual
No. of forward speeds: 3
Wheels driven: Rear
Brakes F/R: Drum/Drum
Wheelbase: 294.6cm 116.0in
Track F: 150.9cm 59.4in
Track R: 146.1cm 57.5in
Length: 513.1cm 202.0in
Width: 191.5cm 75.4in
Height: 137.2cm 54.0in
Ground clearance: 12.7cm 5.0in
Kerb weight: 1514.1kg 3335.0lb

3481 Plymouth

Sport Fury
1962 USA
120.0mph 193.1kmh
0-50mph 80.5kmh: 6.3secs
0-60mph 96.5kmh: 8.2secs
0-1/4 mile: 15.5secs
305.0bhp 227.4kW 309.2PS
@ 4800rpm
395.0lbft 535.2Nm @ 3000rpm
185.6bhp/ton 182.6bhp/tonne
51.6bhp/L 38.4kW/L 52.3PS/L
45.1ft/sec 13.7m/sec
28.0mph 45.1kmh/1000rpm
Petrol 4-stroke piston
5916cc 360.9cu in
Vee 8 1 Carburettor
Compression ratio: 9.0:1
Bore: 104.6mm 4.1in
Stroke: 85.9mm 3.4in
Valve type/No: Overhead 16
Transmission: Automatic
No. of forward speeds: 3
Wheels driven: Rear
Brake system: PA
Steering: PA
Wheelbase: 294.6cm 116.0in
Track F: 150.9cm 59.4in
Track R: 146.1cm 57.5in
Length: 513.1cm 202.0in
Width: 192.0cm 75.6in
Height: 137.2cm 54.0in
Ground clearance: 11.9cm 4.7in
Kerb weight: 1670.7kg 3680.0lb
Fuel: 75.7L 16.6gal 20.0galUS

3482 Plymouth

Fury
1963 USA
109.5mph 176.2kmh
0-50mph 80.5kmh: 8.5secs
0-60mph 96.5kmh: 11.5secs
0-1/4 mile: 18.1secs
225.0bhp 167.8kW 228.1PS
@ 4400rpm
330.0lbft 447.2Nm @ 2800rpm
141.7bhp/ton 139.4bhp/tonne
43.9bhp/L 32.7kW/L 44.5PS/L
40.5ft/sec 12.3m/sec
28.5mph 45.9kmh/1000rpm
15.5mpg 12.9mpgUS 18.2L/100km
Petrol 4-stroke piston
5130cc 313.0cu in
Vee 8 1 Carburettor
Compression ratio: 9.0:1
Bore: 98.4mm 3.9in
Stroke: 84.1mm 3.3in
Valve type/No: Overhead 16
Transmission: Automatic
No. of forward speeds: 2
Wheels driven: Rear
Springs F/R: Torsion bar/Leaf
Brakes F/R: Drum/Drum
Steering: Worm & nut
Wheelbase: 287.0cm 113.0in
Track F: 150.9cm 59.4in
Track R: 147.1cm 57.9in
Length: 520.7cm 205.0in
Width: 193.0cm 76.0in
Height: 142.2cm 56.0in
Ground clearance: 16.5cm 6.5in
Kerb weight: 1614.4kg 3556.0lb
Fuel: 76.0L 16.7gal 20.1galUS

3483 Plymouth

Sport Fury
1963 USA
119.0mph 191.5kmh
0-50mph 80.5kmh: 6.2secs
0-60mph 96.5kmh: 8.0secs
0-1/4 mile: 15.5secs
330.0bhp 246.1kW 334.6PS
@ 4600rpm
425.0lbft 575.9Nm @ 2800rpm
202.5bhp/ton 199.1bhp/tonne
52.6bhp/L 39.2kW/L 53.3PS/L
43.2ft/sec 13.2m/sec
23.6mph 38.0kmh/1000rpm
Petrol 4-stroke piston
6276cc 382.9cu in
Vee 8 1 Carburettor
Compression ratio: 10.0:1
Bore: 108.0mm 4.2in
Stroke: 85.9mm 3.4in
Valve type/No: Overhead 16
Transmission: Automatic
No. of forward speeds: 3
Wheels driven: Rear
Brake system: PA
Steering: PA
Wheelbase: 294.6cm 116.0in
Track F: 151.1cm 59.5in
Track R: 146.1cm 57.5in
Length: 520.7cm 205.0in
Width: 192.0cm 75.6in
Height: 136.9cm 53.9in
Ground clearance: 11.9cm 4.7in
Kerb weight: 1657.1kg 3650.0lb
Fuel: 75.7L 16.6gal 20.0galUS

3484 Plymouth

Valiant V-100
1963 USA
98.0mph 157.7kmh
0-50mph 80.5kmh: 9.3secs
0-60mph 96.5kmh: 12.7secs
0-1/4 mile: 19.3secs
101.0bhp 75.3kW 102.4PS
@ 4400rpm
155.0lbft 210.0Nm @ 2400rpm
84.6bhp/ton 83.2bhp/tonne
36.2bhp/L 27.0kW/L 36.8PS/L
38.3ft/sec 11.6m/sec
21.7mph 34.9kmh/1000rpm
Petrol 4-stroke piston
2786cc 170.0cu in
In-line 4 1 Carburettor
Compression ratio: 8.2:1
Bore: 86.4mm 3.4in
Stroke: 79.4mm 3.1in
Valve type/No: Overhead 8
Transmission: Manual
No. of forward speeds: 3
Wheels driven: Rear
Brakes F/R: Drum/Drum
Wheelbase: 269.2cm 106.0in
Track F: 142.0cm 55.9in
Track R: 141.2cm 55.6in
Length: 472.9cm 186.2in
Width: 174.8cm 68.8in
Height: 135.6cm 53.4in
Ground clearance: 13.5cm 5.3in
Kerb weight: 1214.4kg 2675.0lb
Fuel: 53.0L 11.6gal 14.0galUS

3485 Plymouth

Barracuda
1964 USA
105.0mph 168.9kmh
0-50mph 80.5kmh: 9.5secs
0-60mph 96.5kmh: 12.9secs
0-1/4 mile: 17.8secs
180.0bhp 134.2kW 182.5PS
@ 4200rpm
260.0lbft 352.3Nm @ 1600rpm
128.0bhp/ton 125.9bhp/tonne
40.2bhp/L 30.0kW/L 40.8PS/L
38.6ft/sec 11.8m/sec
24.5mph 39.4kmh/1000rpm
Petrol 4-stroke piston
4474cc 273.0cu in
Vee 8 1 Carburettor
Compression ratio: 8.8:1
Bore: 92.2mm 3.6in
Stroke: 84.1mm 3.3in
Valve type/No: Overhead 16
Transmission: Automatic
No. of forward speeds: 3
Wheels driven: Rear
Steering: PA
Wheelbase: 269.2cm 106.0in
Track F: 142.0cm 55.9in
Track R: 141.2cm 55.6in
Length: 478.0cm 188.2in
Width: 178.1cm 70.1in
Height: 136.7cm 53.8in
Ground clearance: 13.5cm 5.3in
Kerb weight: 1430.1kg 3150.0lb
Fuel: 68.1L 15.0gal 18.0galUS

3486 Plymouth

Barracuda S
1965 USA
118.0mph 189.9kmh
0-50mph 80.5kmh: 6.5secs
0-60mph 96.5kmh: 8.2secs
0-1/4 mile: 15.9secs
235.0bhp 175.2kW 238.3PS
@ 5200rpm
280.0lbft 379.4Nm @ 4000rpm
164.5bhp/ton 161.8bhp/tonne
52.5bhp/L 39.2kW/L 53.2PS/L
47.8ft/sec 14.6m/sec
22.6mph 36.4kmh/1000rpm
Petrol 4-stroke piston
4474cc 273.0cu in
Vee 8 1 Carburettor
Compression ratio: 10.5:1
Bore: 92.2mm 3.6in
Stroke: 84.1mm 3.3in
Valve type/No: Overhead 16
Transmission: Manual
No. of forward speeds: 4
Wheels driven: Rear
Springs F/R: Torsion bar/Leaf
Brakes F/R: Drum/Drum
Steering: PA
Wheelbase: 269.2cm 106.0in
Track F: 143.8cm 56.6in
Track R: 143.0cm 56.3in
Length: 478.0cm 188.2in
Width: 178.1cm 70.1in
Height: 142.2cm 56.0in
Ground clearance: 17.3cm 6.8in
Kerb weight: 1452.8kg 3200.0lb
Fuel: 68.1L 15.0gal 18.0galUS

3487 Plymouth

Belvedere Satellite
1965 USA
115.0mph 185.0kmh
0-50mph 80.5kmh: 6.7secs
0-60mph 96.5kmh: 8.7secs
0-1/4 mile: 16.2secs
330.0bhp 246.1kW 334.6PS
@ 4600rpm
425.0lbft 575.9Nm @ 2800rpm
198.7bhp/ton 195.4bhp/tonne
52.6bhp/L 39.2kW/L 53.3PS/L
43.2ft/sec 13.2m/sec
27.3mph 43.9kmh/1000rpm
Petrol 4-stroke piston
6276cc 382.9cu in
Vee 8 1 Carburettor
Compression ratio: 10.0:1
Bore: 108.0mm 4.2in
Stroke: 85.9mm 3.4in
Valve type/No: Overhead 16
Transmission: Automatic
No. of forward speeds: 3
Wheels driven: Rear
Brake system: PA
Steering: PA
Wheelbase: 294.6cm 116.0in
Track F: 151.1cm 59.5in
Track R: 148.6cm 58.5in
Length: 516.6cm 203.4in
Width: 192.0cm 75.6in
Height: 140.2cm 55.2in
Ground clearance: 13.0cm 5.1in
Kerb weight: 1688.9kg 3720.0lb
Fuel: 75.7L 16.6gal 20.0galUS

3488 Plymouth

Fury Station Wagon
1965 USA
113.0mph 181.8kmh
0-50mph 80.5kmh: 8.4secs
0-60mph 96.5kmh: 11.1secs
0-1/4 mile: 17.5secs
330.0bhp 246.1kW 334.6PS
@ 4600rpm
425.0lbft 575.9Nm @ 2800rpm
154.8bhp/ton 152.2bhp/tonne
52.6bhp/L 39.2kW/L 53.3PS/L
43.2ft/sec 13.2m/sec
24.6mph 39.6kmh/1000rpm
Petrol 4-stroke piston
6276cc 382.9cu in
Vee 8 1 Carburettor
Compression ratio: 10.0:1
Bore: 108.0mm 4.2in
Stroke: 85.9mm 3.4in
Valve type/No: Overhead 16
Transmission: Automatic
No. of forward speeds: 3
Wheels driven: Rear
Brake system: PA
Brakes F/R: Drum/Drum
Steering: PA
Wheelbase: 307.3cm 121.0in
Track F: 157.5cm 62.0in
Track R: 154.2cm 60.7in
Length: 548.9cm 216.1in
Width: 198.4cm 78.1in
Height: 144.8cm 57.0in
Ground clearance: 16.8cm 6.6in
Kerb weight: 2167.8kg 4775.0lb
Fuel: 83.3L 18.3gal 22.0galUS

3489 Plymouth

Barracuda S
1966 USA
115.0mph 185.0kmh
0-50mph 80.5kmh: 7.6secs
0-60mph 96.5kmh: 10.3secs
0-1/4 mile: 17.7secs
235.0bhp 175.2kW 238.3PS
@ 5200rpm
280.0lbft 379.4Nm @ 4000rpm
160.5bhp/ton 157.8bhp/tonne
52.5bhp/L 39.2kW/L 53.2PS/L
47.8ft/sec 14.6m/sec
21.4mph 34.4kmh/1000rpm
Petrol 4-stroke piston
4474cc 273.0cu in
Vee 8 1 Carburettor
Compression ratio: 10.5:1
Bore: 92.2mm 3.6in
Stroke: 84.1mm 3.3in
Valve type/No: Overhead 16
Transmission: Automatic
No. of forward speeds: 3
Wheels driven: Rear
Brakes F/R: Disc/Drum
Steering: Recirculating ball PA
Wheelbase: 269.2cm 106.0in
Track F: 142.0cm 55.9in
Track R: 141.2cm 55.6in
Length: 478.3cm 188.3in
Width: 178.3cm 70.2in
Height: 134.6cm 53.0in
Kerb weight: 1489.1kg 3280.0lb
Fuel: 68.1L 15.0gal 18.0galUS

3490 Plymouth

Satellite
1966 USA
120.0mph 193.1kmh
0-50mph 80.5kmh: 5.5secs
0-60mph 96.5kmh: 7.1secs
0-1/4 mile: 15.6secs
325.0bhp 242.3kW 329.5PS
@ 4800rpm
425.0lbft 575.9Nm @ 2800rpm
192.6bhp/ton 189.4bhp/tonne
51.8bhp/L 38.6kW/L 52.5PS/L
45.1ft/sec 13.7m/sec
24.8mph 39.9kmh/1000rpm
Petrol 4-stroke piston
6276cc 382.9cu in
Vee 8 1 Carburettor
Compression ratio: 10.0:1
Bore: 108.0mm 4.2in
Stroke: 85.9mm 3.4in
Valve type/No: Overhead 16
Transmission: Manual
No. of forward speeds: 4
Wheels driven: Rear
Springs F/R: Torsion bar/Leaf
Brakes F/R: Drum/Drum
Steering: Rack & sector PA
Wheelbase: 294.6cm 116.0in
Track F: 151.1cm 59.5in
Track R: 148.6cm 58.5in
Length: 509.3cm 200.5in
Width: 191.8cm 75.5in

Height: 135.1cm 53.2in
Ground clearance: 15.2cm 6.0in
Kerb weight: 1716.1kg 3780.0lb
Fuel: 71.9L 15.8gal 19.0galUS

3491 Plymouth

Satellite Street Hemi
1966 USA
130.0mph 209.2kmh
0-50mph 80.5kmh: 5.4secs
0-60mph 96.5kmh: 7.1secs
0-1/4 mile: 14.5secs
425.0bhp 316.9kW 430.9PS
@ 5000rpm
490.0lbft 664.0Nm @ 4500rpm
241.6bhp/ton 237.6bhp/tonne
60.9bhp/L 45.4kW/L 61.7PS/L
52.1ft/sec 15.9m/sec
23.7mph 38.1kmh/1000rpm
Petrol 4-stroke piston
6981cc 425.9cu in
Vee 8 2 Carburettor
Compression ratio: 10.3:1
Bore: 108.0mm 4.2in
Stroke: 95.3mm 3.8in
Valve type/No: Overhead 16
Transmission: Automatic
No. of forward speeds: 3
Wheels driven: Rear
Springs F/R: Torsion bar/Leaf
Brake system: PA
Brakes F/R: Drum/Drum
Steering: Rack & sector PA
Wheelbase: 294.6cm 116.0in
Track F: 151.1cm 59.5in
Track R: 148.6cm 58.5in
Length: 509.3cm 200.5in
Width: 191.8cm 75.5in
Height: 135.1cm 53.2in
Ground clearance: 15.2cm 6.0in
Kerb weight: 1788.8kg 3940.0lb
Fuel: 71.9L 15.8gal 19.0galUS

3492 Plymouth

VIP
1966 USA
104.0mph 167.3kmh
0-50mph 80.5kmh: 6.8secs
0-60mph 96.5kmh: 8.9secs
0-1/4 mile: 16.8secs
325.0bhp 242.3kW 329.5PS
@ 4800rpm
425.0lbft 575.9Nm @ 2800rpm
168.2bhp/ton 165.4bhp/tonne
51.8bhp/L 38.6kW/L 52.5PS/L
45.1ft/sec 13.7m/sec
25.0mph 40.2kmh/1000rpm
Petrol 4-stroke piston
6276cc 382.9cu in
Vee 8 1 Carburettor
Compression ratio: 10.0:1
Bore: 108.0mm 4.2in
Stroke: 85.9mm 3.4in
Valve type/No: Overhead 16
Transmission: Automatic
No. of forward speeds: 3
Wheels driven: Rear
Springs F/R: Torsion bar/Leaf
Brake system: PA
Brakes F/R: Drum/Drum
Steering: Rack & sector PA
Wheelbase: 302.3cm 119.0in
Track F: 157.5cm 62.0in
Track R: 154.2cm 60.7in
Length: 532.9cm 209.8in
Width: 199.9cm 78.7in
Height: 140.5cm 55.3in
Kerb weight: 1964.5kg 4327.0lb
Fuel: 94.6L 20.8gal 25.0galUS

3493 Plymouth

Barracuda
1967 USA
108.0mph 173.8kmh
0-50mph 80.5kmh: 7.7secs
0-60mph 96.5kmh: 10.9secs
0-1/4 mile: 17.8secs
0-1km: 33.0secs
180.0bhp 134.2kW 182.5PS
@ 4200rpm
260.0lbft 352.3Nm @ 1600rpm
125.3bhp/ton 123.2bhp/tonne
40.2bhp/L 30.0kW/L 40.8PS/L
38.6ft/sec 11.8m/sec
22.0mph 35.4kmh/1000rpm
16.9mpg 14.1mpgUS 16.7L/100km
Petrol 4-stroke piston
4473cc 272.9cu in
Vee 8 1 Carburettor
Compression ratio: 8.8:1
Bore: 92.2mm 3.6in
Stroke: 84.0mm 3.3in
Valve type/No: Overhead 16
Transmission: Automatic
No. of forward speeds: 3
Wheels driven: Rear
Springs F/R: Torsion bar/Leaf
Brake system: PA
Brakes F/R: Disc/Drum
Steering: Recirculating ball
Wheelbase: 274.3cm 108.0in
Track F: 146.1cm 57.5in
Track R: 141.0cm 55.5in
Length: 490.2cm 193.0in
Width: 181.6cm 71.5in
Height: 135.9cm 53.5in
Ground clearance: 16.5cm 6.5in
Kerb weight: 1461.4kg 3219.0lb
Fuel: 65.1L 14.3gal 17.2galUS

3494 Plymouth

Barracuda 6
1967 USA
97.0mph 156.1kmh
0-50mph 80.5kmh: 9.8secs
0-60mph 96.5kmh: 13.6secs
0-1/4 mile: 19.4secs
145.0bhp 108.1kW 147.0PS
@ 4000rpm
215.0lbft 291.3Nm @ 2400rpm
99.0bhp/ton 97.4bhp/tonne
39.4bhp/L 29.4kW/L 39.9PS/L
45.9ft/sec 14.0m/sec
24.4mph 39.3kmh/1000rpm
Petrol 4-stroke piston
3680cc 224.5cu in
In-line 6 1 Carburettor
Compression ratio: 8.4:1
Bore: 86.4mm 3.4in
Stroke: 104.8mm 4.1in
Valve type/No: Overhead 12
Transmission: Automatic
No. of forward speeds: 3
Wheels driven: Rear
Springs F/R: Torsion bar/Leaf
Brake system: PA
Brakes F/R: Disc/Drum
Steering: Recirculating ball PA
Wheelbase: 274.3cm 108.0in
Track F: 145.8cm 57.4in
Track R: 141.2cm 55.6in
Length: 489.7cm 192.8in
Width: 181.9cm 71.6in
Height: 134.6cm 53.0in
Ground clearance: 14.2cm 5.6in
Kerb weight: 1489.1kg 3280.0lb
Fuel: 68.1L 15.0gal 18.0galUS

3495 Plymouth

Barracuda Fastback V8
1967 USA
118.0mph 189.9kmh
0-50mph 80.5kmh: 6.9secs
0-60mph 96.5kmh: 9.2secs
0-1/4 mile: 16.9secs
235.0bhp 175.2kW 238.3PS
@ 5200rpm
280.0lbft 379.4Nm @ 4000rpm
159.0bhp/ton 156.4bhp/tonne
52.4bhp/L 39.0kW/L 53.1PS/L
47.8ft/sec 14.6m/sec
22.6mph 36.4kmh/1000rpm
Petrol 4-stroke piston
4488cc 273.8cu in
Vee 8 1 Carburettor
Compression ratio: 10.5:1
Bore: 92.2mm 3.6in
Stroke: 84.1mm 3.3in
Valve type/No: Overhead 16
Transmission: Automatic
No. of forward speeds: 3
Wheels driven: Rear
Springs F/R: Torsion bar/Leaf
Brake system: PA
Brakes F/R: Disc/Drum
Steering: Recirculating ball PA
Wheelbase: 274.3cm 108.0in
Track F: 145.8cm 57.4in
Track R: 141.2cm 55.6in
Length: 489.7cm 192.8in
Width: 181.9cm 71.6in
Height: 134.6cm 53.0in
Ground clearance: 14.5cm 5.7in
Kerb weight: 1502.7kg 3310.0lb
Fuel: 68.1L 15.0gal 18.0galUS

3496 Plymouth

Fury III
1967 USA
115.0mph 185.0kmh
0-50mph 80.5kmh: 6.5secs
0-60mph 96.5kmh: 8.7secs
0-1/4 mile: 16.6secs
325.0bhp 242.3kW 329.5PS
@ 4800rpm
425.0lbft 575.9Nm @ 2800rpm
170.1bhp/ton 167.3bhp/tonne
51.7bhp/L 38.5kW/L 52.4PS/L
45.1ft/sec 13.7m/sec
24.2mph 38.9kmh/1000rpm
Petrol 4-stroke piston
6287cc 383.6cu in
Vee 8 1 Carburettor
Compression ratio: 10.0:1
Bore: 108.0mm 4.2in
Stroke: 85.9mm 3.4in
Valve type/No: Overhead 16
Transmission: Automatic
No. of forward speeds: 3
Wheels driven: Rear
Springs F/R: Coil/Leaf
Brake system: PA
Brakes F/R: Disc/Drum
Steering: Recirculating ball PA
Wheelbase: 302.3cm 119.0in
Track F: 157.5cm 62.0in
Track R: 154.2cm 60.7in
Length: 541.3cm 213.1in
Width: 197.4cm 77.7in
Height: 141.0cm 55.5in
Ground clearance: 16.0cm 6.3in
Kerb weight: 1943.1kg 4280.0lb
Fuel: 94.6L 20.8gal 25.0galUS

3497 Plymouth

GTX
1967 USA
120.0mph 193.1kmh
0-50mph 80.5kmh: 5.2secs
0-60mph 96.5kmh: 6.6secs
0-1/4 mile: 15.2secs
375.0bhp 279.6kW 380.2PS
@ 4600rpm
480.0lbft 650.4Nm @ 3200rpm
219.3bhp/ton 215.7bhp/tonne
52.1bhp/L 38.8kW/L 52.8PS/L
47.9ft/sec 14.6m/sec
23.6mph 38.0kmh/1000rpm
Petrol 4-stroke piston
7202cc 439.4cu in
Vee 8 1 Carburettor
Compression ratio: 10.1:1
Bore: 109.7mm 4.3in
Stroke: 95.3mm 3.8in
Valve type/No: Overhead 16
Transmission: Automatic
No. of forward speeds: 3
Wheels driven: Rear
Springs F/R: Torsion bar/Leaf
Brake system: PA
Brakes F/R: Disc/Drum
Steering: Recirculating ball PA
Wheelbase: 294.6cm 116.0in
Track F: 151.1cm 59.5in
Track R: 148.6cm 58.5in
Length: 509.3cm 200.5in
Width: 194.1cm 76.4in
Height: 137.2cm 54.0in
Ground clearance: 16.3cm 6.4in
Kerb weight: 1738.8kg 3830.0lb
Fuel: 71.9L 15.8gal 19.0galUS

3498 Plymouth

Barracuda 340-S
1968 USA
127.0mph 204.3kmh
0-50mph 80.5kmh: 5.5secs
0-60mph 96.5kmh: 7.0secs
0-1/4 mile: 15.0secs
275.0bhp 205.1kW 278.8PS
@ 5000rpm
340.0lbft 460.7Nm @ 3200rpm
177.5bhp/ton 174.6bhp/tonne
49.4bhp/L 36.9kW/L 50.1PS/L
46.0ft/sec 14.0m/sec
23.2mph 37.3kmh/1000rpm
Petrol 4-stroke piston
5563cc 339.4cu in
Vee 8 1 Carburettor
Compression ratio: 10.5:1
Bore: 102.6mm 4.0in
Stroke: 84.1mm 3.3in
Valve type/No: Overhead 16
Transmission: Automatic
No. of forward speeds: 3
Wheels driven: Rear
Springs F/R: Torsion bar/Leaf
Brakes F/R: Disc/Drum
Steering: Recirculating ball PA
Wheelbase: 274.3cm 108.0in
Track F: 145.8cm 57.4in
Track R: 141.2cm 55.6in
Length: 489.7cm 192.8in
Width: 181.9cm 71.6in
Height: 134.1cm 52.8in
Ground clearance: 15.7cm 6.2in
Kerb weight: 1575.4kg 3470.0lb
Fuel: 68.1L 15.0gal 18.0galUS

3499 Plymouth

Barracuda Fastback
1968 USA
118.0mph 189.9kmh
0-50mph 80.5kmh: 7.0secs
0-60mph 96.5kmh: 9.4secs
0-1/4 mile: 16.5secs
230.0bhp 171.5kW 233.2PS
@ 4400rpm
340.0lbft 460.7Nm @ 2400rpm
149.8bhp/ton 147.3bhp/tonne
44.1bhp/L 32.9kW/L 44.7PS/L
40.5ft/sec 12.3m/sec
27.2mph 43.8kmh/1000rpm
Petrol 4-stroke piston
5211cc 317.9cu in
Vee 8 1 Carburettor
Compression ratio: 9.2:1
Bore: 99.3mm 3.9in
Stroke: 84.1mm 3.3in
Valve type/No: Overhead 16
Transmission: Automatic
No. of forward speeds: 3
Wheels driven: Rear
Springs F/R: Torsion bar/Leaf
Brakes F/R: Drum/Drum
Steering: Recirculating ball PA
Wheelbase: 274.3cm 108.0in
Track F: 145.8cm 57.4in
Track R: 141.2cm 55.6in
Length: 489.7cm 192.8in
Width: 181.9cm 71.6in
Height: 134.1cm 52.8in
Kerb weight: 1561.8kg 3440.0lb
Fuel: 68.1L 15.0gal 18.0galUS

3500 Plymouth

Fury III
1968 USA
110.0mph 177.0kmh
0-50mph 80.5kmh: 7.7secs
0-60mph 96.5kmh: 10.7secs
0-1/4 mile: 17.6secs
0-1km: 32.4secs
294.0bhp 219.2kW 298.1PS
@ 4400rpm
390.0lbft 528.5Nm @ 2800rpm
161.9bhp/ton 159.2bhp/tonne
46.8bhp/L 34.9kW/L 47.5PS/L
41.3ft/sec 12.6m/sec
28.5mph 45.9kmh/1000rpm
11.7mpg 9.7mpgUS 24.1L/100km
Petrol 4-stroke piston
6276cc 382.9cu in
Vee 8 1 Carburettor
Compression ratio: 9.2:1
Bore: 107.9mm 4.2in
Stroke: 85.8mm 3.4in
Valve type/No: Overhead 16
Transmission: Automatic
No. of forward speeds: 3
Wheels driven: Rear
Springs F/R: Torsion bar/Leaf
Brake system: PA
Brakes F/R: Drum/Drum
Steering: Recirculating ball
Wheelbase: 302.3cm 119.0in
Track F: 157.5cm 62.0in
Track R: 170.2cm 67.0in
Length: 541.0cm 213.0in
Width: 197.4cm 77.7in
Height: 143.3cm 56.4in
Ground clearance: 16.5cm 6.5in
Kerb weight: 1846.4kg 4067.0lb
Fuel: 72.8L 16.0gal 19.2galUS

3501 Plymouth

GTX
1968 USA
121.0mph 194.7kmh
0-50mph 80.5kmh: 5.3secs
0-60mph 96.5kmh: 6.8secs
0-1/4 mile: 14.6secs
375.0bhp 279.6kW 380.2PS
@ 4600rpm
480.0lbft 650.4Nm @ 3200rpm
217.0bhp/ton 213.4bhp/tonne
52.0bhp/L 38.8kW/L 52.8PS/L
46.5ft/sec 14.2m/sec
23.5mph 37.8kmh/1000rpm
Petrol 4-stroke piston
7206cc 439.7cu in
Vee 8 1 Carburettor
Compression ratio: 10.1:1
Bore: 109.7mm 4.3in
Stroke: 92.5mm 3.6in
Valve type/No: Overhead 16
Transmission: Automatic
No. of forward speeds: 3
Wheels driven: Rear
Springs F/R: Torsion bar/Leaf
Brake system: PA
Brakes F/R: Disc/Drum
Steering: Recirculating ball PA
Wheelbase: 294.6cm 116.0in
Track F: 151.1cm 59.5in
Track R: 150.4cm 59.2in
Length: 514.9cm 202.7in
Width: 194.1cm 76.4in
Height: 138.9cm 54.7in
Ground clearance: 16.5cm 6.5in
Kerb weight: 1757.0kg 3870.0lb
Fuel: 71.9L 15.8gal 19.0galUS

3502 Plymouth

GTX Hemi
1968 USA
144.0mph 231.7kmh
0-50mph 80.5kmh: 5.1secs
0-60mph 96.5kmh: 6.3secs
0-1/4 mile: 14.0secs
425.0bhp 316.9kW 430.9PS
@ 5000rpm
490.0lbft 664.0Nm @ 4000rpm
241.0bhp/ton 237.0bhp/tonne
60.9bhp/L 45.4kW/L 61.8PS/L
52.1ft/sec 15.9m/sec
24.3mph 39.1kmh/1000rpm
Petrol 4-stroke piston
6974cc 425.5cu in
Vee 8 2 Carburettor
Compression ratio: 10.3:1
Bore: 108.0mm 4.2in
Stroke: 95.3mm 3.8in
Valve type/No: Overhead 16
Transmission: Automatic
No. of forward speeds: 3
Wheels driven: Rear
Springs F/R: Torsion bar/Leaf
Brake system: PA
Brakes F/R: Disc/Drum
Steering: Recirculating ball PA
Wheelbase: 294.6cm 116.0in
Track F: 151.1cm 59.5in
Track R: 150.4cm 59.2in
Length: 514.9cm 202.7in
Width: 194.1cm 76.4in
Height: 138.9cm 54.7in
Ground clearance: 16.3cm 6.4in
Kerb weight: 1793.3kg 3950.0lb
Fuel: 71.9L 15.8gal 19.0galUS

3503 Plymouth

Road Runner
1968 USA
122.0mph 196.3kmh
0-50mph 80.5kmh: 5.7secs
0-60mph 96.5kmh: 7.3secs
0-1/4 mile: 15.4secs
335.0bhp 249.8kW 339.6PS
@ 5200rpm
425.0lbft 575.9Nm @ 3400rpm
205.6bhp/ton 202.2bhp/tonne
53.4bhp/L 39.8kW/L 54.1PS/L
48.8ft/sec 14.9m/sec
23.5mph 37.8kmh/1000rpm
Petrol 4-stroke piston
6276cc 382.9cu in
Vee 8 1 Carburettor
Compression ratio: 10.0:1
Bore: 108.0mm 4.2in
Stroke: 85.9mm 3.4in
Valve type/No: Overhead 16
Transmission: Automatic
No. of forward speeds: 3
Wheels driven: Rear
Springs F/R: Torsion bar/Leaf
Brake system: PA
Brakes F/R: Drum/Drum
Steering: Recirculating ball PA
Wheelbase: 294.6cm 116.0in
Track F: 151.1cm 59.5in
Track R: 150.4cm 59.2in
Length: 514.9cm 202.7in
Width: 194.1cm 76.4in
Height: 138.9cm 54.7in
Kerb weight: 1657.1kg 3650.0lb
Fuel: 71.9L 15.8gal 19.0galUS

3504 Plymouth

Cuda 340
1969 USA
119.6mph 192.4kmh
0-50mph 80.5kmh: 5.6secs
0-60mph 96.5kmh: 7.1secs
0-1/4 mile: 14.9secs
275.0bhp 205.1kW 278.8PS
@ 5000rpm
340.0lbft 460.7Nm @ 3200rpm
177.5bhp/ton 174.6bhp/tonne
49.3bhp/L 36.8kW/L 50.0PS/L
46.0ft/sec 14.0m/sec
19.3mph 31.1kmh/1000rpm
Petrol 4-stroke piston
5572cc 340.0cu in
Vee 8 1 Carburettor
Compression ratio: 10.5:1
Bore: 102.6mm 4.0in
Stroke: 84.1mm 3.3in
Valve type/No: Overhead 16
Transmission: Manual
No. of forward speeds: 4
Wheels driven: Rear
Springs F/R: Coil/Leaf
Brake system: PA
Brakes F/R: Disc/Drum
Steering: Recirculating ball PA
Wheelbase: 274.3cm 108.0in
Track F: 146.6cm 57.7in
Track R: 141.2cm 55.6in
Length: 489.7cm 192.8in
Width: 176.8cm 69.6in
Height: 133.9cm 52.7in
Kerb weight: 1575.4kg 3470.0lb
Fuel: 68.1L 15.0gal 18.0galUS

3505 Plymouth

Cuda 440
1969 USA
118.0mph 189.9kmh
0-50mph 80.5kmh: 4.4secs
0-60mph 96.5kmh: 5.6secs
0-1/4 mile: 14.0secs
375.0bhp 279.6kW 380.2PS
@ 4600rpm
480.0lbft 650.4Nm @ 3200rpm
246.7bhp/ton 242.6bhp/tonne
52.0bhp/L 38.8kW/L 52.7PS/L
47.9ft/sec 14.6m/sec
24.1mph 38.8kmh/1000rpm
Petrol 4-stroke piston
7210cc 439.9cu in
Vee 8 1 Carburettor
Compression ratio: 10.1:1
Bore: 109.7mm 4.3in
Stroke: 95.3mm 3.8in
Valve type/No: Overhead 16
Transmission: Automatic
No. of forward speeds: 3
Wheels driven: Rear
Springs F/R: Torsion bar/Leaf
Brakes F/R: Drum/Drum
Steering: Recirculating ball
Wheelbase: 274.3cm 108.0in
Track F: 147.3cm 58.0in
Track R: 142.2cm 56.0in
Length: 490.2cm 193.0in
Width: 177.8cm 70.0in
Height: 134.6cm 53.0in
Kerb weight: 1545.9kg 3405.0lb
Fuel: 68.1L 15.0gal 18.0galUS

3506 Plymouth

Fury III
1969 USA
115.0mph 185.0kmh
0-50mph 80.5kmh: 7.3secs
0-60mph 96.5kmh: 9.7secs
0-1/4 mile: 16.7secs
290.0bhp 216.2kW 294.0PS
@ 4000rpm
390.0lbft 528.5Nm @ 2800rpm
153.0bhp/ton 150.5bhp/tonne
46.2bhp/L 34.5kW/L 46.8PS/L
37.6ft/sec 11.4m/sec
28.0mph 45.1kmh/1000rpm
Petrol 4-stroke piston
6276cc 382.9cu in
Vee 8 1 Carburettor
Compression ratio: 9.2:1
Bore: 108.0mm 4.2in
Stroke: 85.9mm 3.4in
Valve type/No: Overhead 16
Transmission: Automatic
No. of forward speeds: 3
Wheels driven: Rear
Springs F/R: Torsion bar/Leaf
Brake system: PA
Brakes F/R: Disc/Drum
Steering: Recirculating ball PA
Wheelbase: 304.8cm 120.0in
Track F: 157.5cm 62.0in
Track R: 154.9cm 61.0in
Length: 546.1cm 215.0in
Width: 203.2cm 80.0in
Height: 139.7cm 55.0in
Kerb weight: 1927.2kg 4245.0lb
Fuel: 90.8L 20.0gal 24.0galUS

3507 Plymouth

Road Runner
1969 USA
113.0mph 181.8kmh
0-50mph 80.5kmh: 4.0secs
0-60mph 96.5kmh: 5.1secs
0-1/4 mile: 14.7secs
335.0bhp 249.8kW 339.6PS
@ 5200rpm
425.0lbft 575.9Nm @ 3200rpm
205.9bhp/ton 202.4bhp/tonne
53.4bhp/L 39.8kW/L 54.1PS/L
48.8ft/sec 14.9m/sec
19.5mph 31.4kmh/1000rpm
14.4mpg 12.0mpgUS 19.6L/100km
Petrol 4-stroke piston
6276cc 382.9cu in
Vee 8 1 Carburettor
Compression ratio: 10.0:1
Bore: 108.0mm 4.2in
Stroke: 85.9mm 3.4in
Valve type/No: Overhead 16
Transmission: Manual
No. of forward speeds: 4
Wheels driven: Rear
Springs F/R: Torsion bar/Leaf
Brake system: PA
Brakes F/R: Drum/Drum
Steering: Recirculating ball PA
Wheelbase: 294.6cm 116.0in
Track F: 151.1cm 59.5in
Track R: 150.4cm 59.2in
Length: 514.9cm 202.7in
Width: 194.1cm 76.4in
Height: 134.9cm 53.1in
Kerb weight: 1654.8kg 3645.0lb
Fuel: 71.9L 15.8gal 19.0galUS

3508 Plymouth

Satellite Sport
1969 USA
113.0mph 181.8kmh
0-50mph 80.5kmh: 6.2secs
0-60mph 96.5kmh: 8.6secs
0-1/4 mile: 17.2secs
230.0bhp 171.5kW 233.2PS
@ 4400rpm
340.0lbft 460.7Nm @ 2400rpm
159.3bhp/ton 156.6bhp/tonne
44.1bhp/L 32.9kW/L 44.7PS/L
40.5ft/sec 12.3m/sec
28.9mph 46.5kmh/1000rpm
Petrol 4-stroke piston
5211cc 317.9cu in
Vee 8 1 Carburettor
Compression ratio: 9.2:1
Bore: 99.3mm 3.9in
Stroke: 84.1mm 3.3in
Valve type/No: Overhead 16
Transmission: Automatic
No. of forward speeds: 3
Wheels driven: Rear
Springs F/R: Torsion bar/Leaf
Brake system: PA
Brakes F/R: Drum/Drum
Steering: Recirculating ball PA
Wheelbase: 294.6cm 116.0in
Track F: 151.1cm 59.5in
Track R: 150.4cm 59.2in
Length: 514.9cm 202.7in
Width: 194.1cm 76.4in
Height: 134.6cm 53.0in
Kerb weight: 1468.7kg 3235.0lb
Fuel: 71.9L 15.8gal 19.0galUS

3509 Plymouth

Barracuda
1970 USA
125.4mph 201.8kmh
0-50mph 80.5kmh: 5.5secs
0-60mph 96.5kmh: 7.5secs
0-1/4 mile: 15.0secs
275.0bhp 205.1kW 278.8PS
@ 5000rpm
340.0lbft 460.7Nm @ 3200rpm
169.7bhp/ton 166.9bhp/tonne
49.3bhp/L 36.8kW/L 50.0PS/L
46.0ft/sec 14.0m/sec
20.9mph 33.6kmh/1000rpm
16.7mpg 13.9mpgUS 16.9L/100km
Petrol 4-stroke piston
5572cc 340.0cu in
Vee 8 1 Carburettor
Compression ratio: 10.5:1
Bore: 102.6mm 4.0in
Stroke: 84.1mm 3.3in
Valve type/No: Overhead 16
Transmission: Automatic
No. of forward speeds: 3
Wheels driven: Rear
Springs F/R: Torsion bar/Leaf
Brake system: PA
Brakes F/R: Drum/Drum
Steering: Recirculating ball PA
Wheelbase: 274.3cm 108.0in
Track F: 151.6cm 59.7in
Track R: 154.2cm 60.7in
Length: 474.2cm 186.7in
Width: 190.2cm 74.9in
Height: 129.3cm 50.9in
Kerb weight: 1648.0kg 3630.0lb
Fuel: 71.9L 15.8gal 19.0galUS

3510 Plymouth

Duster 340
1970 USA
120.0mph 193.1kmh
0-50mph 80.5kmh: 4.8secs
0-60mph 96.5kmh: 6.2secs
0-1/4 mile: 14.7secs
275.0bhp 205.1kW 278.8PS
@ 5000rpm
340.0lbft 460.7Nm @ 3200rpm
198.4bhp/ton 195.1bhp/tonne
49.3bhp/L 36.8kW/L 50.0PS/L
46.0ft/sec 14.0m/sec
23.0mph 37.0kmh/1000rpm
17.8mpg 14.8mpgUS 15.9L/100km
Petrol 4-stroke piston
5572cc 340.0cu in
Vee 8 1 Carburettor
Compression ratio: 10.5:1
Bore: 102.6mm 4.0in
Stroke: 84.1mm 3.3in
Valve type/No: Overhead 16
Transmission: Automatic
No. of forward speeds: 3
Wheels driven: Rear
Springs F/R: Torsion bar/Leaf
Brake system: PA
Brakes F/R: Disc/Drum
Steering: Recirculating ball
Wheelbase: 274.3cm 108.0in
Track F: 145.8cm 57.4in
Track R: 145.8cm 57.4in
Length: 478.5cm 188.4in
Width: 181.9cm 71.6in
Height: 133.6cm 52.6in
Kerb weight: 1409.7kg 3105.0lb
Fuel: 68.1L 15.0gal 18.0galUS

3511 Plymouth

Cricket
1971 UK
85.0mph 136.8kmh
0-50mph 80.5kmh: 12.0secs
0-60mph 96.5kmh: 18.5secs
0-1/4 mile: 20.7secs
80.0bhp 59.7kW 81.1PS
@ 5000rpm
95.0lbft 128.7Nm @ 3000rpm
89.4bhp/ton 87.9bhp/tonne
53.4bhp/L 39.8kW/L 54.1PS/L

35.1ft/sec 10.7m/sec
18.5mph 29.8kmh/1000rpm
26.4mpg 22.0mpgUS 10.7L/100km
Petrol 4-stroke piston
1498cc 91.4cu in
In-line 4 1 Carburettor
Compression ratio: 8.0:1
Bore: 86.1mm 3.4in
Stroke: 64.3mm 2.5in
Valve type/No: Overhead 8
Transmission: Manual
No. of forward speeds: 4
Wheels driven: Rear
Springs F/R: Coil/Coil
Brake system: PA
Brakes F/R: Disc/Drum
Steering: Rack & pinion
Wheelbase: 248.9cm 98.0in
Track F: 129.5cm 51.0in
Track R: 129.5cm 51.0in
Length: 411.5cm 162.0in
Width: 158.8cm 62.5in
Height: 138.7cm 54.6in
Ground clearance: 16.5cm 6.5in
Kerb weight: 910.3kg 2005.0lb
Fuel: 34.1L 7.5gal 9.0galUS

3512 Plymouth

Arrow GT
1976 Japan
102.0mph 164.1kmh
0-50mph 80.5kmh: 9.8secs
0-60mph 96.5kmh: 14.0secs
0-1/4 mile: 19.4secs
96.0bhp 71.6kW 97.3PS
@ 5500rpm
109.0lbft 147.7Nm @ 3500rpm
91.5bhp/ton 90.0bhp/tonne
48.1bhp/L 35.9kW/L 48.8PS/L
54.1ft/sec 16.5m/sec
20.0mph 32.2kmh/1000rpm
27.6mpg 23.0mpgUS 10.2L/100km
Petrol 4-stroke piston
1995cc 121.7cu in
In-line 4 1 Carburettor
Compression ratio: 8.5:1
Bore: 84.0mm 3.3in
Stroke: 90.0mm 3.5in
Valve type/No: Overhead 8
Transmission: Manual
No. of forward speeds: 5
Wheels driven: Rear
Springs F/R: Coil/Leaf
Brake system: PA
Brakes F/R: Disc/Drum
Steering: Recirculating ball
Wheelbase: 233.9cm 92.1in
Track F: 130.0cm 51.2in
Track R: 127.0cm 50.0in
Length: 424.9cm 167.3in
Width: 161.0cm 63.4in
Height: 132.6cm 52.2in
Ground clearance: 15.0cm 5.9in
Kerb weight: 1066.9kg 2350.0lb
Fuel: 45.0L 9.9gal 11.9galUS

3513 Plymouth

Volare Station Wagon
1976 USA
99.0mph 159.3kmh
0-50mph 80.5kmh: 10.3secs
0-60mph 96.5kmh: 14.6secs
0-1/4 mile: 19.7secs
150.0bhp 111.9kW 152.1PS
@ 4000rpm
250.0lbft 338.8Nm @ 2000rpm
84.8bhp/ton 83.4bhp/tonne
28.8bhp/L 21.5kW/L 29.2PS/L
36.8ft/sec 11.2m/sec
26.3mph 42.3kmh/1000rpm
15.0mpg 12.5mpgUS 18.8L/100km
Petrol 4-stroke piston
5212cc 318.0cu in
Vee 8 1 Carburettor
Compression ratio: 8.5:1
Bore: 99.3mm 3.9in
Stroke: 84.1mm 3.3in
Valve type/No: Overhead 16
Transmission: Automatic
No. of forward speeds: 3
Wheels driven: Rear
Springs F/R: Torsion bar/Leaf
Brake system: PA
Brakes F/R: Disc/Drum
Steering: Recirculating ball PA
Wheelbase: 285.8cm 112.5in
Track F: 152.4cm 60.0in
Track R: 148.6cm 58.5in
Length: 511.0cm 201.2in
Width: 184.9cm 72.8in
Height: 139.2cm 54.8in
Ground clearance: 13.5cm 5.3in
Kerb weight: 1797.8kg 3960.0lb
Fuel: 68.1L 15.0gal 18.0galUS

3514 Plymouth

Horizon
1978 USA
96.0mph 154.5kmh
0-50mph 80.5kmh: 9.5secs
0-60mph 96.5kmh: 14.0secs
0-1/4 mile: 19.6secs
70.0bhp 52.2kW 71.0PS
@ 5600rpm
85.0lbft 115.2Nm @ 3200rpm
66.7bhp/ton 65.6bhp/tonne
40.8bhp/L 30.4kW/L 41.4PS/L
52.9ft/sec 16.1m/sec
19.7mph 31.7kmh/1000rpm
33.6mpg 28.0mpgUS 8.4L/100km
Petrol 4-stroke piston
1716cc 104.7cu in
In-line 4 1 Carburettor
Compression ratio: 8.2:1
Bore: 79.5mm 3.1in
Stroke: 86.4mm 3.4in
Valve type/No: Overhead 8
Transmission: Manual
No. of forward speeds: 4
Wheels driven: Front
Springs F/R: Coil/Coil
Brake system: PA
Brakes F/R: Disc/Drum
Steering: Rack & pinion PA
Wheelbase: 252.0cm 99.2in
Track F: 141.0cm 55.5in
Track R: 140.0cm 55.1in
Length: 418.6cm 164.8in
Width: 168.1cm 66.2in
Height: 135.6cm 53.4in
Ground clearance: 13.0cm 5.1in
Kerb weight: 1066.9kg 2350.0lb
Fuel: 49.2L 10.8gal 13.0galUS

3515 Plymouth

Sapporo
1978 Japan
108.0mph 173.8kmh
0-60mph 96.5kmh: 12.1secs
0-1/4 mile: 18.7secs
105.0bhp 78.3kW 106.5PS
@ 5000rpm
139.0lbft 188.3Nm @ 2500rpm
85.8bhp/ton 84.4bhp/tonne
41.1bhp/L 30.6kW/L 41.7PS/L
53.6ft/sec 16.3m/sec
28.2mpg 23.5mpgUS 10.0L/100km
Petrol 4-stroke piston
2555cc 155.9cu in
In-line 4 1 Carburettor
Compression ratio: 8.2:1
Bore: 91.1mm 3.6in
Stroke: 98.0mm 3.9in
Valve type/No: Overhead 8
Transmission: Manual
No. of forward speeds: 5
Wheels driven: Rear
Brakes F/R: Disc/Disc
Wheelbase: 251.5cm 99.0in
Track F: 136.9cm 53.9in
Track R: 135.4cm 53.3in
Length: 465.1cm 183.1in
Width: 167.4cm 65.9in
Height: 131.6cm 51.8in
Kerb weight: 1244.0kg 2740.0lb
Fuel: 60.2L 13.2gal 15.9galUS

3516 Plymouth

Fire Arrow
1979 Japan
108.0mph 173.8kmh
0-50mph 80.5kmh: 6.8secs
0-60mph 96.5kmh: 9.6secs
0-1/4 mile: 17.7secs
105.0bhp 78.3kW 106.5PS
@ 5000rpm
139.0lbft 188.3Nm @ 2500rpm
97.4bhp/ton 95.8bhp/tonne
41.1bhp/L 30.6kW/L 41.7PS/L
53.6ft/sec 16.3m/sec
23.1mph 37.2kmh/1000rpm
30.0mpg 25.0mpgUS 9.4L/100km
Petrol 4-stroke piston
2555cc 155.9cu in
In-line 4 1 Carburettor
Compression ratio: 8.2:1
Bore: 91.1mm 3.6in
Stroke: 98.0mm 3.9in
Valve type/No: Overhead 8
Transmission: Manual
No. of forward speeds: 5
Wheels driven: Rear
Springs F/R: Coil/Leaf
Brake system: PA
Brakes F/R: Disc/Disc
Steering: Recirculating ball
Wheelbase: 233.9cm 92.1in
Track F: 130.0cm 51.2in
Track R: 136.9cm 53.9in
Length: 424.9cm 167.3in
Width: 161.0cm 63.4in
Height: 129.5cm 51.0in
Kerb weight: 1096.4kg 2415.0lb
Fuel: 50.0L 11.0gal 13.2galUS

3517 Plymouth

Champ
1980 Japan
0-60mph 96.5kmh: 10.4secs
0-1/4 mile: 18.0secs
80.0bhp 59.7kW 81.1PS
@ 5200rpm
87.0lbft 117.9Nm @ 3000rpm
91.9bhp/ton 90.4bhp/tonne
50.1bhp/L 37.4kW/L 50.8PS/L
49.0ft/sec 14.9m/sec
32.4mpg 27.0mpgUS 8.7L/100km
Petrol 4-stroke piston
1597cc 97.4cu in
In-line 4 1 Carburettor
Compression ratio: 8.5:1
Bore: 76.9mm 3.0in
Stroke: 86.0mm 3.4in
Valve type/No: Overhead 8
Transmission: Manual with overdrive
Wheels driven: Front
Brakes F/R: Disc/Drum
Wheelbase: 230.1cm 90.6in
Track F: 136.9cm 53.9in
Track R: 134.1cm 52.8in
Length: 398.5cm 156.9in
Width: 158.5cm 62.4in
Height: 128.5cm 50.6in
Kerb weight: 885.3kg 1950.0lb
Fuel: 37.8L 8.3gal 10.0galUS

3518 Plymouth

Colt GTS Turbo
1984 Japan
106.0mph 170.6kmh
0-50mph 80.5kmh: 7.0secs
0-60mph 96.5kmh: 9.4secs
0-1/4 mile: 17.2secs
102.0bhp 76.1kW 103.4PS
@ 5500rpm
122.0lbft 165.3Nm @ 3000rpm
111.4bhp/ton 109.6bhp/tonne
63.9bhp/L 47.6kW/L 64.7PS/L
51.8ft/sec 15.8m/sec
21.4mph 34.4kmh/1000rpm
36.6mpg 30.5mpgUS 7.7L/100km
Petrol 4-stroke piston
1597cc 97.4cu in turbocharged
In-line 4 fuel injection
Compression ratio: 7.6:1
Bore: 76.9mm 3.0in
Stroke: 86.0mm 3.4in
Valve type/No: Overhead 8
Transmission: Manual
No. of forward speeds: 4
Wheels driven: Front
Springs F/R: Coil/Coil
Brake system: PA
Brakes F/R: Disc/Drum
Steering: Rack & pinion
Wheelbase: 230.1cm 90.6in
Track F: 137.4cm 54.1in
Track R: 134.1cm 52.8in
Length: 398.5cm 156.9in
Width: 158.5cm 62.4in
Height: 127.0cm 50.0in
Ground clearance: 10.9cm 4.3in
Kerb weight: 930.7kg 2050.0lb
Fuel: 37.8L 8.3gal 10.0galUS

3519 Plymouth

Voyager
1984 USA
102.0mph 164.1kmh
0-50mph 80.5kmh: 10.3secs
0-60mph 96.5kmh: 14.7secs
0-1/4 mile: 20.1secs
104.0bhp 77.5kW 105.4PS
@ 4800rpm
142.0lbft 192.4Nm @ 2800rpm
67.3bhp/ton 66.2bhp/tonne
40.7bhp/L 30.3kW/L 41.3PS/L
51.5ft/sec 15.7m/sec
22.6mph 36.4kmh/1000rpm
21.0mpg 17.5mpgUS 13.4L/100km
Petrol 4-stroke piston
2555cc 155.9cu in
In-line 4 1 Carburettor
Compression ratio: 8.7:1
Bore: 91.1mm 3.6in
Stroke: 98.0mm 3.9in
Valve type/No: Overhead 8
Transmission: Automatic
No. of forward speeds: 3
Wheels driven: Front
Springs F/R: Coil/Leaf
Brake system: PA
Brakes F/R: Disc/Drum
Steering: Rack & pinion PA
Wheelbase: 284.5cm 112.0in
Track F: 152.1cm 59.9in
Track R: 157.7cm 62.1in
Length: 446.8cm 175.9in
Width: 176.8cm 69.6in
Height: 163.1cm 64.2in
Ground clearance: 13.7cm 5.4in
Kerb weight: 1570.8kg 3460.0lb
Fuel: 75.7L 16.6gal 20.0galUS

3520 Plymouth

Horizon America
1986 USA
0-60mph 96.5kmh: 10.2secs
0-1/4 mile: 17.7secs
96.0bhp 71.6kW 97.3PS
@ 5200rpm
119.0lbft 161.2Nm @ 3200rpm
90.9bhp/ton 89.4bhp/tonne
43.4bhp/L 32.3kW/L 44.0PS/L
52.3ft/sec 15.9m/sec
30.8mph 49.6kmh/1000rpm
29.4mpg 24.5mpgUS 9.6L/100km
Petrol 4-stroke piston
2213cc 135.0cu in
In-line 4 1 Carburettor
Compression ratio: 9.5:1
Bore: 87.5mm 3.4in
Stroke: 92.0mm 3.6in
Valve type/No: Overhead 8
Transmission: Manual
No. of forward speeds: 5
Wheels driven: Front
Springs F/R: Torsion bar/Coil
Brake system: PA
Brakes F/R: Disc/Drum
Steering: Rack & pinion PA
Wheelbase: 251.7cm 99.1in
Track F: 142.5cm 56.1in
Track R: 141.5cm 55.7in
Length: 414.5cm 163.2in
Width: 162.1cm 63.8in
Height: 134.6cm 53.0in
Kerb weight: 1073.7kg 2365.0lb
Fuel: 49.2L 10.8gal 13.0galUS

3521 Plymouth

Laser RS
1989 Japan
143.0mph 230.1kmh
0-50mph 80.5kmh: 5.5secs
0-60mph 96.5kmh: 7.2secs
0-1/4 mile: 15.8secs
190.0bhp 141.7kW 192.6PS
@ 6000rpm
203.0lbft 275.1Nm @ 3000rpm
149.6bhp/ton 147.1bhp/tonne
96.1bhp/L 71.7kW/L 97.4PS/L
57.7ft/sec 17.6m/sec
27.6mpg 23.0mpgUS 10.2L/100km
Petrol 4-stroke piston
1977cc 120.6cu in turbocharged
In-line 4 fuel injection
Compression ratio: 7.8:1
Bore: 85.0mm 3.3in
Stroke: 88.0mm 3.5in
Valve type/No: Overhead 16
Transmission: Manual
No. of forward speeds: 5
Wheels driven: Front
Springs F/R: Coil/Coil
Brake system: PA

Brakes F/R: Disc/Disc
Steering: Rack & pinion PA
Wheelbase: 246.9cm 97.2in
Track F: 146.6cm 57.7in
Track R: 145.0cm 57.1in
Length: 433.1cm 170.5in
Width: 168.9cm 66.5in
Height: 130.6cm 51.4in
Kerb weight: 1291.6kg 2845.0lb
Fuel: 60.2L 13.2gal 15.9galUS

3522 Plymouth

Laser RS Turbo
1990 USA
143.0mph 230.1kmh
0-60mph 96.5kmh: 6.9secs
0-1/4 mile: 15.4secs
190.0bhp 141.7kW 192.6PS
@ 6000rpm
203.0lbft 275.1Nm @ 4400rpm
149.6bhp/ton 147.1bhp/tonne
95.1bhp/L 70.9kW/L 96.5PS/L
57.7ft/sec 17.6m/sec
29.5mpg 24.6mpgUS 9.6L/100km
Petrol 4-stroke piston
1997cc 121.8cu in turbocharged
In-line 4 fuel injection
Compression ratio: 7.8:1
Bore: 85.0mm 3.3in
Stroke: 88.0mm 3.5in
Valve type/No: Overhead 16
Transmission: Manual
No. of forward speeds: 5
Wheels driven: Front
Springs F/R: Coil/Coil
Brake system: PA
Brakes F/R: Disc/Disc
Steering: Rack & pinion PA
Wheelbase: 246.9cm 97.2in
Track F: 146.6cm 57.7in
Track R: 145.0cm 57.1in
Length: 433.1cm 170.5in
Width: 168.9cm 66.5in
Height: 126.5cm 49.8in
Kerb weight: 1291.6kg 2845.0lb
Fuel: 60.2L 13.2gal 15.9galUS

3523 Plymouth

Laser RS Turbo
1991 USA
125.0mph 201.1kmh
0-60mph 96.5kmh: 8.0secs
0-1/4 mile: 16.2secs
190.0bhp 141.7kW 192.6PS
@ 6000rpm
203.0lbft 275.1Nm @ 3000rpm
149.3bhp/ton 146.8bhp/tonne
95.1bhp/L 70.9kW/L 96.5PS/L
57.7ft/sec 17.6m/sec
24.0mpg 20.0mpgUS 11.8L/100km
Petrol 4-stroke piston
1997cc 121.8cu in turbocharged
In-line 4 fuel injection
Compression ratio: 7.8:1
Bore: 85.0mm 3.3in
Stroke: 88.0mm 3.5in
Valve type/No: Overhead 16
Transmission: Automatic
No. of forward speeds: 4
Wheels driven: Front
Springs F/R: Coil/Coil
Brake system: PA ABS
Brakes F/R: Disc/Disc
Steering: Rack & pinion PA
Wheelbase: 246.9cm 97.2in
Track F: 146.6cm 57.7in
Track R: 145.0cm 57.1in
Length: 433.1cm 170.5in
Width: 168.9cm 66.5in
Height: 126.5cm 49.8in
Kerb weight: 1293.9kg 2850.0lb
Fuel: 60.2L 13.2gal 15.9galUS

3524 Polonez

1500
1979 Poland
92.0mph 148.0kmh
0-50mph 80.5kmh: 11.7secs
0-60mph 96.5kmh: 17.0secs
0-1/4 mile: 20.8secs
0-1km: 38.9secs
76.0bhp 56.7kW 77.0PS
@ 5250rpm
85.0lbft 115.2Nm @ 3300rpm
75.7bhp/ton 74.4bhp/tonne
51.3bhp/L 38.3kW/L 52.0PS/L
45.6ft/sec 13.9m/sec
16.6mph 26.7kmh/1000rpm
21.9mpg 18.2mpgUS 12.9L/100km
Petrol 4-stroke piston
1481cc 90.4cu in
In-line 4 1 Carburettor
Compression ratio: 9.0:1
Bore: 77.0mm 3.0in
Stroke: 79.5mm 3.1in
Valve type/No: Overhead 8
Transmission: Manual
No. of forward speeds: 4
Wheels driven: Rear
Springs F/R: Coil/Leaf
Brake system: PA
Brakes F/R: Disc/Disc
Steering: Worm & roller
Wheelbase: 251.0cm 98.8in
Track F: 131.3cm 51.7in
Track R: 129.3cm 50.9in
Length: 427.2cm 168.2in
Width: 165.1cm 65.0in
Height: 137.9cm 54.3in
Ground clearance: 15.2cm 6.0in
Kerb weight: 1021.5kg 2250.0lb
Fuel: 45.0L 9.9gal 11.9galUS

3525 Polski Fiat

125P
1975 Poland
93.0mph 149.6kmh
0-50mph 80.5kmh: 11.1secs
0-60mph 96.5kmh: 15.6secs
0-1/4 mile: 20.1secs
0-1km: 37.9secs
70.0bhp 52.2kW 71.0PS
@ 5400rpm
88.9lbft 120.5Nm @ 3200rpm
68.7bhp/ton 67.5bhp/tonne
47.3bhp/L 35.2kW/L 47.9PS/L
46.9ft/sec 14.3m/sec
16.4mph 26.4kmh/1000rpm
29.0mpg 24.1mpgUS 9.7L/100km
Petrol 4-stroke piston
1481cc 90.4cu in
In-line 4 1 Carburettor
Compression ratio: 9.0:1
Bore: 77.0mm 3.0in
Stroke: 79.5mm 3.1in
Valve type/No: Overhead 8
Transmission: Manual
No. of forward speeds: 4
Wheels driven: Rear
Springs F/R: Coil/Leaf
Brake system: PA
Brakes F/R: Disc/Disc
Steering: Worm & roller
Wheelbase: 250.4cm 98.6in
Track F: 131.3cm 51.7in
Track R: 129.0cm 50.8in
Length: 422.1cm 166.2in
Width: 161.0cm 63.4in
Height: 139.4cm 54.9in
Ground clearance: 17.5cm 6.9in
Kerb weight: 1036.5kg 2283.0lb
Fuel: 45.5L 10.0gal 12.0galUS

3526 Pontiac

Touring Saloon de Luxe
1936 USA
80.3mph 129.2kmh
0-50mph 80.5kmh: 17.6secs
0-60mph 96.5kmh: 24.4secs
20.0mpg 16.7mpgUS 14.1L/100km
Petrol 4-stroke piston
3409cc 208.0cu in
In-line 6
Bore: 85.7mm 3.4in
Stroke: 98.4mm 3.9in
Valve type/No: Side 12
Transmission: Manual
No. of forward speeds: 3
Wheels driven: Rear
Brakes F/R: Drum/Drum
Kerb weight: 1603.1kg 3531.0lb
Fuel: 54.6L 12.0gal 14.4galUS

3527 Pontiac

Eight Fixed-head Coupe
1937 USA
85.7mph 137.9kmh
0-50mph 80.5kmh: 13.3secs
0-60mph 96.5kmh: 19.3secs
16.0mpg 13.3mpgUS 17.7L/100km
Petrol 4-stroke piston
4112cc 250.9cu in
In-line 8
Bore: 82.6mm 3.2in
Stroke: 95.3mm 3.8in
Valve type/No: Side 16
Transmission: Manual
No. of forward speeds: 3
Wheels driven: Rear
Brakes F/R: Drum/Drum
Kerb weight: 1630.8kg 3592.0lb
Fuel: 68.2L 15.0gal 18.0galUS

3528 Pontiac

Bonneville
1959 USA
114.0mph 183.4kmh
0-50mph 80.5kmh: 7.3secs
0-60mph 96.5kmh: 9.7secs
0-1/4 mile: 17.4secs
300.0bhp 223.7kW 304.2PS
@ 4600rpm
420.0lbft 569.1Nm @ 2800rpm
153.8bhp/ton 151.3bhp/tonne
47.0bhp/L 35.1kW/L 47.7PS/L
47.9ft/sec 14.6m/sec
11.8mpg 9.8mpgUS 23.9L/100km
Petrol 4-stroke piston
6377cc 389.1cu in
Vee 8 1 Carburettor
Compression ratio: 10.0:1
Bore: 103.1mm 4.1in
Stroke: 95.2mm 3.8in
Valve type/No: Overhead 16
Transmission: Automatic
No. of forward speeds: 4
Wheels driven: Rear
Springs F/R: Coil/Coil
Brakes F/R: Drum/Drum
Wheelbase: 315.0cm 124.0in
Track F: 149.4cm 58.8in
Track R: 150.9cm 59.4in
Length: 560.6cm 220.7in
Width: 205.0cm 80.7in
Height: 144.3cm 56.8in
Ground clearance: 16.5cm 6.5in
Kerb weight: 1983.1kg 4368.0lb
Fuel: 81.9L 18.0gal 21.6galUS

3529 Pontiac

Catalina Super Stock
1961 USA
114.0mph 183.4kmh
0-50mph 80.5kmh: 3.8secs
0-60mph 96.5kmh: 4.6secs
0-1/4 mile: 13.7secs
348.0bhp 259.5kW 352.8PS
@ 4800rpm
430.0lbft 582.7Nm @ 3200rpm
200.9bhp/ton 197.6bhp/tonne
54.6bhp/L 40.7kW/L 55.3PS/L
50.0ft/sec 15.2m/sec
17.8mph 28.6kmh/1000rpm
Petrol 4-stroke piston
6377cc 389.1cu in
Vee 8 2 Carburettor
Compression ratio: 10.8:1
Bore: 103.1mm 4.1in
Stroke: 95.3mm 3.8in
Valve type/No: Overhead 16
Transmission: Manual
No. of forward speeds: 3
Wheels driven: Rear
Brakes F/R: Drum/Drum
Wheelbase: 312.4cm 123.0in
Track F: 158.8cm 62.5in
Track R: 158.8cm 62.5in
Length: 551.2cm 217.0in
Width: 198.6cm 78.2in
Height: 141.5cm 55.7in
Ground clearance: 15.2cm 6.0in
Kerb weight: 1761.5kg 3880.0lb

3530 Pontiac

Tempest
1961 USA
85.0mph 136.8kmh
0-50mph 80.5kmh: 10.5secs
0-60mph 96.5kmh: 15.0secs
0-1/4 mile: 19.9secs
110.0bhp 82.0kW 111.5PS
@ 3800rpm
190.0lbft 257.5Nm @ 2000rpm
84.4bhp/ton 83.0bhp/tonne
34.5bhp/L 25.7kW/L 35.0PS/L
39.6ft/sec 12.1m/sec
21.2mph 34.1kmh/1000rpm
Petrol 4-stroke piston
3188cc 194.5cu in
In-line 4 1 Carburettor
Compression ratio: 8.6:1
Bore: 103.1mm 4.1in
Stroke: 95.3mm 3.8in
Valve type/No: Overhead 8
Transmission: Manual
No. of forward speeds: 3
Wheels driven: Rear
Wheelbase: 284.5cm 112.0in
Track F: 144.3cm 56.8in
Track R: 144.3cm 56.8in
Length: 480.8cm 189.3in
Width: 183.4cm 72.2in
Height: 135.9cm 53.5in
Ground clearance: 15.2cm 6.0in
Kerb weight: 1325.7kg 2920.0lb

3531 Pontiac

Tempest Automatic
1961 USA
102.0mph 164.1kmh
0-50mph 80.5kmh: 11.0secs
0-60mph 96.5kmh: 14.6secs
0-1/4 mile: 20.0secs
155.0bhp 115.6kW 157.1PS
@ 4800rpm
215.0lbft 291.3Nm @ 2800rpm
116.1bhp/ton 114.2bhp/tonne
48.6bhp/L 36.2kW/L 49.3PS/L
50.0ft/sec 15.2m/sec
21.3mph 34.3kmh/1000rpm
Petrol 4-stroke piston
3189cc 194.6cu in
In-line 4 1 Carburettor
Compression ratio: 10.3:1
Bore: 103.2mm 4.1in
Stroke: 95.3mm 3.8in
Valve type/No: Overhead 8
Transmission: Automatic
No. of forward speeds: 2
Wheels driven: Rear
Wheelbase: 284.5cm 112.0in
Track F: 144.3cm 56.8in
Track R: 144.3cm 56.8in
Length: 480.8cm 189.3in
Width: 183.4cm 72.2in
Height: 135.9cm 53.5in
Ground clearance: 15.2cm 6.0in
Kerb weight: 1357.5kg 2990.0lb

3532 Pontiac

Tempest Supercharged
1961 USA
127.0mph 204.3kmh
0-50mph 80.5kmh: 5.6secs
0-60mph 96.5kmh: 7.0secs
0-1/4 mile: 15.5secs
250.0bhp 186.4kW 253.5PS
@ 5600rpm
255.0lbft 345.5Nm @ 3200rpm
187.9bhp/ton 184.8bhp/tonne
78.4bhp/L 58.5kW/L 79.5PS/L
58.3ft/sec 17.8m/sec
20.5mph 33.0kmh/1000rpm
Petrol 4-stroke piston
3189cc 194.6cu in supercharged
In-line 4 1 Carburettor
Compression ratio: 5.0:1
Bore: 103.2mm 4.1in
Stroke: 95.3mm 3.8in
Valve type/No: Overhead 8
Transmission: Manual
No. of forward speeds: 3
Wheels driven: Rear
Brakes F/R: Drum/Drum
Wheelbase: 284.5cm 112.0in
Track F: 144.3cm 56.8in
Track R: 144.3cm 56.8in
Length: 480.8cm 189.3in
Width: 183.4cm 72.2in
Height: 135.9cm 53.5in
Ground clearance: 15.2cm 6.0in
Kerb weight: 1352.9kg 2980.0lb

3533 Pontiac

Grand Prix 421
1962 USA
135.0mph 217.2kmh
0-50mph 80.5kmh: 4.5secs
0-60mph 96.5kmh: 6.0secs
0-1/4 mile: 14.3secs
405.0bhp 302.0kW 410.6PS
@ 5600rpm
425.0lbft 575.9Nm @ 4400rpm
227.4bhp/ton 223.6bhp/tonne

58.7bhp/L 43.8kW/L 59.5PS/L
62.2ft/sec 19.0m/sec
23.4mph 37.7kmh/1000rpm
Petrol 4-stroke piston
6899cc 420.9cu in
Vee 8 1 Carburettor
Compression ratio: 11.0:1
Bore: 104.9mm 4.1in
Stroke: 101.6mm 4.0in
Valve type/No: Overhead 16
Transmission: Manual
No. of forward speeds: 3
Wheels driven: Rear
Brake system: PA
Steering: PA
Wheelbase: 304.8cm 120.0in
Track F: 158.8cm 62.5in
Track R: 158.8cm 62.5in
Length: 537.5cm 211.6in
Width: 199.6cm 78.6in
Height: 138.4cm 54.5in
Ground clearance: 15.2cm 6.0in
Kerb weight: 1811.5kg 3990.0lb
Fuel: 94.6L 20.8gal 25.0galUS

3534 Pontiac

Parisienne
1962 USA
100.0mph 160.9kmh
0-50mph 80.5kmh: 10.5secs
0-60mph 96.5kmh: 14.8secs
0-1/4 mile: 19.8secs
170.0bhp 126.8kW 172.4PS
@ 4100rpm
275.0lbft 372.6Nm @ 2200rpm
99.3bhp/ton 97.6bhp/tonne
36.6bhp/L 27.3kW/L 37.1PS/L
34.2ft/sec 10.4m/sec
22.7mph 36.5kmh/1000rpm
15.2mpg 12.7mpgUS 18.6L/100km
Petrol 4-stroke piston
4640cc 283.1cu in
Vee 8 1 Carburettor
Compression ratio: 8.5:1
Bore: 98.4mm 3.9in
Stroke: 76.2mm 3.0in
Valve type/No: Overhead 16
Transmission: Automatic
No. of forward speeds: 2
Wheels driven: Rear
Springs F/R: Coil/Coil
Brake system: PA
Brakes F/R: Drum/Drum
Steering: Recirculating ball PA
Wheelbase: 302.3cm 119.0in
Track F: 153.2cm 60.3in
Track R: 150.6cm 59.3in
Length: 537.5cm 211.6in
Width: 199.6cm 78.6in
Height: 141.0cm 55.5in
Ground clearance: 16.5cm 6.5in
Kerb weight: 1741.5kg 3836.0lb
Fuel: 75.5L 16.6gal 19.9galUS

3535 Pontiac

Royal Bobcat
1962 USA
117.0mph 188.3kmh
0-50mph 80.5kmh: 4.6secs
0-60mph 96.5kmh: 6.5secs
0-1/4 mile: 14.5secs
370.0bhp 275.9kW 375.1PS
@ 4800rpm
460.0lbft 623.3Nm @ 2800rpm
209.3bhp/ton 205.8bhp/tonne
58.0bhp/L 43.3kW/L 58.8PS/L
50.0ft/sec 15.2m/sec
20.5mph 33.0kmh/1000rpm
Petrol 4-stroke piston
6375cc 389.0cu in
Vee 8 3 Carburettor
Compression ratio: 10.8:1
Bore: 103.1mm 4.1in
Stroke: 95.3mm 3.8in
Valve type/No: Overhead 16
Transmission: Manual
No. of forward speeds: 4
Wheels driven: Rear
Wheelbase: 304.8cm 120.0in
Track F: 158.8cm 62.5in
Track R: 158.8cm 62.5in
Length: 537.5cm 211.6in
Width: 199.6cm 78.6in
Height: 142.0cm 55.9in
Ground clearance: 15.0cm 5.9in
Kerb weight: 1797.8kg 3960.0lb
Fuel: 94.6L 20.8gal 25.0galUS

3536 Pontiac

Tempest 4
1962 USA
92.0mph 148.0kmh
0-50mph 80.5kmh: 11.3secs
0-60mph 96.5kmh: 15.9secs
0-1/4 mile: 21.2secs
140.0bhp 104.4kW 141.9PS
@ 4400rpm
207.0lbft 280.5Nm @ 2200rpm
104.9bhp/ton 103.1bhp/tonne
43.9bhp/L 32.7kW/L 44.5PS/L
45.8ft/sec 14.0m/sec
24.2mph 38.9kmh/1000rpm
Petrol 4-stroke piston
3188cc 194.5cu in
In-line 4 1 Carburettor
Compression ratio: 10.3:1
Bore: 103.1mm 4.1in
Stroke: 95.3mm 3.8in
Valve type/No: Overhead 8
Transmission: Automatic
No. of forward speeds: 2
Wheels driven: Rear
Brakes F/R: Drum/Drum
Wheelbase: 284.5cm 112.0in
Track F: 144.3cm 56.8in
Track R: 144.3cm 56.8in
Length: 480.8cm 189.3in
Width: 183.4cm 72.2in
Height: 136.1cm 53.6in
Ground clearance: 15.2cm 6.0in
Kerb weight: 1357.5kg 2990.0lb

3537 Pontiac

Catalina
1963 USA
117.0mph 188.3kmh
0-50mph 80.5kmh: 7.9secs
0-60mph 96.5kmh: 10.1secs
0-1/4 mile: 17.9secs
267.0bhp 199.1kW 270.7PS
@ 4200rpm
410.0lbft 555.6Nm @ 2400rpm
150.1bhp/ton 147.6bhp/tonne
41.9bhp/L 31.2kW/L 42.5PS/L
43.8ft/sec 13.3m/sec
29.2mph 47.0kmh/1000rpm
Petrol 4-stroke piston
6375cc 389.0cu in
Vee 8 1 Carburettor
Compression ratio: 10.3:1
Bore: 103.2mm 4.1in
Stroke: 95.3mm 3.8in
Valve type/No: Overhead 16
Transmission: Automatic
No. of forward speeds: 3
Wheels driven: Rear
Brake system: PA
Brakes F/R: Drum/Drum
Steering: PA
Wheelbase: 304.8cm 120.0in
Track F: 158.8cm 62.5in
Track R: 162.6cm 64.0in
Length: 538.2cm 211.9in
Width: 199.9cm 78.7in
Height: 137.7cm 54.2in
Ground clearance: 15.2cm 6.0in
Kerb weight: 1809.2kg 3985.0lb
Fuel: 94.6L 20.8gal 25.0galUS

3538 Pontiac

Grand Prix
1963 USA
114.0mph 183.4kmh
0-50mph 80.5kmh: 7.2secs
0-60mph 96.5kmh: 9.5secs
0-1/4 mile: 17.3secs
313.0bhp 233.4kW 317.3PS
@ 4600rpm
430.0lbft 582.7Nm @ 3200rpm
161.4bhp/ton 158.7bhp/tonne
49.1bhp/L 36.6kW/L 49.8PS/L
47.9ft/sec 14.6m/sec
24.8mph 39.9kmh/1000rpm
Petrol 4-stroke piston
6375cc 389.0cu in
Vee 8 3 Carburettor
Compression ratio: 10.3:1
Bore: 103.1mm 4.1in
Stroke: 95.3mm 3.8in
Valve type/No: Overhead 16
Transmission: Automatic
No. of forward speeds: 3
Wheels driven: Rear
Brake system: PA
Steering: PA
Wheelbase: 304.8cm 120.0in
Track F: 158.8cm 62.5in
Track R: 162.6cm 64.0in
Length: 538.2cm 211.9in
Width: 199.9cm 78.7in
Height: 137.4cm 54.1in
Ground clearance: 15.2cm 6.0in
Kerb weight: 1972.6kg 4345.0lb
Fuel: 94.6L 20.8gal 25.0galUS

3539 Pontiac

Tempest Le Mans V8
1963 USA
115.0mph 185.0kmh
0-50mph 80.5kmh: 7.1secs
0-60mph 96.5kmh: 9.5secs
0-1/4 mile: 17.0secs
260.0bhp 193.9kW 263.6PS
@ 4800rpm
352.0lbft 477.0Nm @ 2800rpm
178.6bhp/ton 175.7bhp/tonne
48.7bhp/L 36.3kW/L 49.3PS/L
50.0ft/sec 15.2m/sec
25.1mph 40.4kmh/1000rpm
Petrol 4-stroke piston
5342cc 325.9cu in
Vee 8 1 Carburettor
Compression ratio: 10.3:1
Bore: 94.5mm 3.7in
Stroke: 95.3mm 3.8in
Valve type/No: Overhead 16
Transmission: Automatic
No. of forward speeds: 2
Wheels driven: Rear
Steering: PA
Wheelbase: 284.5cm 112.0in
Track F: 145.5cm 57.3in
Track R: 147.3cm 58.0in
Length: 493.5cm 194.3in
Width: 188.5cm 74.2in
Height: 137.7cm 54.2in
Ground clearance: 15.2cm 6.0in
Kerb weight: 1480.0kg 3260.0lb
Fuel: 75.7L 16.6gal 20.0galUS

3540 Pontiac

Tempest GTO
1964 USA
122.0mph 196.3kmh
0-50mph 80.5kmh: 5.4secs
0-60mph 96.5kmh: 6.9secs
0-1/4 mile: 15.0secs
325.0bhp 242.3kW 329.5PS
@ 4800rpm
428.0lbft 579.9Nm @ 3200rpm
214.1bhp/ton 210.5bhp/tonne
51.0bhp/L 38.0kW/L 51.7PS/L
50.0ft/sec 15.2m/sec
23.7mph 38.1kmh/1000rpm
Petrol 4-stroke piston
6377cc 389.1cu in
Vee 8 1 Carburettor
Compression ratio: 10.8:1
Bore: 103.1mm 4.1in
Stroke: 95.2mm 3.8in
Valve type/No: Overhead 16
Transmission: Manual
No. of forward speeds: 4
Wheels driven: Rear
Springs F/R: Coil/Coil
Brakes F/R: Drum/Drum
Steering: Recirculating ball
Wheelbase: 292.1cm 115.0in
Track F: 147.3cm 58.0in
Track R: 147.3cm 58.0in
Length: 515.6cm 203.0in
Width: 186.2cm 73.3in
Height: 137.2cm 54.0in
Ground clearance: 15.2cm 6.0in
Kerb weight: 1543.6kg 3400.0lb
Fuel: 81.4L 17.9gal 21.5galUS

3541 Pontiac

Bonneville Vista
1965 USA
119.0mph 191.5kmh
0-50mph 80.5kmh: 6.7secs
0-60mph 96.5kmh: 8.8secs
0-1/4 mile: 16.6secs
325.0bhp 242.3kW 329.5PS
@ 4800rpm
429.0lbft 581.3Nm @ 2800rpm
166.6bhp/ton 163.8bhp/tonne
51.0bhp/L 38.0kW/L 51.7PS/L
50.0ft/sec 15.2m/sec
29.6mph 47.6kmh/1000rpm
Petrol 4-stroke piston
6375cc 389.0cu in
Vee 8 1 Carburettor
Compression ratio: 10.5:1
Bore: 103.1mm 4.1in
Stroke: 95.3mm 3.8in
Valve type/No: Overhead 16
Transmission: Automatic
No. of forward speeds: 3
Wheels driven: Rear
Brake system: PA
Brakes F/R: Drum/Drum
Steering: PA
Wheelbase: 315.0cm 124.0in
Track F: 160.0cm 63.0in
Track R: 162.6cm 64.0in
Length: 563.1cm 221.7in
Width: 202.2cm 79.6in
Height: 137.9cm 54.3in
Ground clearance: 14.2cm 5.6in
Kerb weight: 1984.0kg 4370.0lb
Fuel: 100.3L 22.0gal 26.5galUS

3542 Pontiac

Catalina 2+2
1965 USA
120.0mph 193.1kmh
0-50mph 80.5kmh: 5.5secs
0-60mph 96.5kmh: 7.4secs
0-1/4 mile: 15.8secs
338.0bhp 252.0kW 342.7PS
@ 4600rpm
459.0lbft 622.0Nm @ 2800rpm
183.3bhp/ton 180.3bhp/tonne
49.0bhp/L 36.5kW/L 49.7PS/L
51.1ft/sec 15.6m/sec
23.2mph 37.3kmh/1000rpm
Petrol 4-stroke piston
6899cc 420.9cu in
Vee 8 1 Carburettor
Compression ratio: 10.5:1
Bore: 103.9mm 4.1in
Stroke: 101.6mm 4.0in
Valve type/No: Overhead 16
Transmission: Manual
No. of forward speeds: 4
Wheels driven: Rear
Brake system: PA
Steering: PA
Wheelbase: 307.3cm 121.0in
Track F: 160.0cm 63.0in
Track R: 162.6cm 64.0in
Length: 545.1cm 214.6in
Width: 202.2cm 79.6in
Height: 140.2cm 55.2in
Ground clearance: 14.2cm 5.6in
Kerb weight: 1875.0kg 4130.0lb
Fuel: 100.3L 22.0gal 26.5galUS

3543 Pontiac

Tempest GTO
1965 USA
114.0mph 183.4kmh
0-50mph 80.5kmh: 4.7secs
0-60mph 96.5kmh: 5.8secs
0-1/4 mile: 14.5secs
360.0bhp 268.4kW 365.0PS
@ 5200rpm
424.0lbft 574.5Nm @ 3600rpm
224.6bhp/ton 220.9bhp/tonne
56.5bhp/L 42.1kW/L 57.2PS/L
54.2ft/sec 16.5m/sec
18.9mph 30.4kmh/1000rpm
Petrol 4-stroke piston
6375cc 389.0cu in
Vee 8 3 Carburettor
Compression ratio: 10.8:1
Bore: 103.1mm 4.1in
Stroke: 95.3mm 3.8in
Valve type/No: Overhead 16
Transmission: Manual
No. of forward speeds: 4
Wheels driven: Rear
Brake system: PA
Steering: PA
Wheelbase: 292.1cm 115.0in
Track F: 147.3cm 58.0in
Track R: 147.3cm 58.0in
Length: 523.5cm 206.1in
Width: 186.4cm 73.4in
Height: 135.9cm 53.5in
Ground clearance: 14.0cm 5.5in
Kerb weight: 1629.9kg 3590.0lb
Fuel: 81.4L 17.9gal 21.5galUS

3544 Pontiac
GTO
1966 USA
121.0mph 194.7kmh
0-50mph 80.5kmh: 6.5secs
0-60mph 96.5kmh: 7.9secs
0-1/4 mile: 15.3secs
0-1km: 27.7secs
365.0bhp 272.2kW 370.1PS
@ 5200rpm
424.0lbft 574.5Nm @ 3600rpm
224.6bhp/ton 220.9bhp/tonne
57.2bhp/L 42.7kW/L 58.0PS/L
54.2ft/sec 16.5m/sec
23.1mph 37.2kmh/1000rpm
12.7mpg 10.6mpgUS 22.2L/100km
Petrol 4-stroke piston
6375cc 389.0cu in
Vee 8 3 Carburettor
Compression ratio: 10.7:1
Bore: 103.1mm 4.1in
Stroke: 95.3mm 3.8in
Valve type/No: Overhead 16
Transmission: Automatic
No. of forward speeds: 2
Wheels driven: Rear
Springs F/R: Coil/Coil
Brake system: PA
Brakes F/R: Drum/Drum
Steering: Recirculating ball PA
Wheelbase: 292.1cm 115.0in
Track F: 147.3cm 58.0in
Track R: 149.9cm 59.0in
Length: 524.5cm 206.5in
Width: 189.2cm 74.5in
Height: 136.4cm 53.7in
Ground clearance: 12.7cm 5.0in
Kerb weight: 1652.6kg 3640.0lb
Fuel: 81.4L 17.9gal 21.5galUS

3545 Pontiac
Le Mans OHC
1966 USA
113.0mph 181.8kmh
0-50mph 80.5kmh: 7.3secs
0-60mph 96.5kmh: 10.0secs
0-1/4 mile: 17.2secs
207.0bhp 154.4kW 209.9PS
@ 5200rpm
228.0lbft 308.9Nm @ 3800rpm
135.6bhp/ton 133.3bhp/tonne
54.9bhp/L 40.9kW/L 55.7PS/L
46.9ft/sec 14.3m/sec
21.7mph 34.9kmh/1000rpm
Petrol 4-stroke piston
3770cc 230.0cu in
In-line 6 1 Carburettor
Compression ratio: 10.5:1
Bore: 98.7mm 3.9in
Stroke: 82.5mm 3.2in
Valve type/No: Overhead 12
Transmission: Manual
No. of forward speeds: 4
Wheels driven: Rear
Springs F/R: Coil/Coil
Brakes F/R: Drum/Drum
Steering: Recirculating ball PA
Wheelbase: 292.1cm 115.0in
Track F: 147.3cm 58.0in
Track R: 149.9cm 59.0in
Length: 524.3cm 206.4in
Width: 189.0cm 74.4in
Height: 137.2cm 54.0in
Ground clearance: 16.0cm 6.3in
Kerb weight: 1552.7kg 3420.0lb
Fuel: 81.4L 17.9gal 21.5galUS

3546 Pontiac
Tempest GTO
1966 USA
125.0mph 201.1kmh
0-50mph 80.5kmh: 4.8secs
0-60mph 96.5kmh: 6.8secs
0-1/4 mile: 15.4secs
335.0bhp 249.8kW 339.6PS
@ 5000rpm
431.0lbft 584.0Nm @ 3200rpm
207.3bhp/ton 203.8bhp/tonne
52.5bhp/L 39.2kW/L 53.3PS/L
52.1ft/sec 15.9m/sec
25.1mph 40.4kmh/1000rpm
Petrol 4-stroke piston
6375cc 389.0cu in
Vee 8 1 Carburettor
Compression ratio: 10.8:1
Bore: 103.2mm 4.1in
Stroke: 95.3mm 3.8in
Valve type/No: Overhead 16
Transmission: Manual
No. of forward speeds: 4
Wheels driven: Rear
Springs F/R: Coil/Coil
Brakes F/R: Drum/Drum
Steering: Recirculating ball
Wheelbase: 292.1cm 115.0in
Track F: 147.3cm 58.0in
Track R: 149.9cm 59.0in
Length: 524.3cm 206.4in
Width: 189.0cm 74.4in
Height: 135.1cm 53.2in
Ground clearance: 18.8cm 7.4in
Kerb weight: 1643.5kg 3620.0lb
Fuel: 81.4L 17.9gal 21.5galUS

3547 Pontiac
Tempest Sprint
1966 USA
113.0mph 181.8kmh
0-50mph 80.5kmh: 5.9secs
0-60mph 96.5kmh: 8.2secs
0-1/4 mile: 16.7secs
207.0bhp 154.4kW 209.9PS
@ 5200rpm
228.0lbft 308.9Nm @ 3800rpm
135.2bhp/ton 132.9bhp/tonne
54.9bhp/L 41.0kW/L 55.7PS/L
46.9ft/sec 14.3m/sec
21.7mph 34.9kmh/1000rpm
Petrol 4-stroke piston
3769cc 230.0cu in
In-line 6 1 Carburettor
Compression ratio: 10.5:1
Bore: 98.4mm 3.9in
Stroke: 82.6mm 3.2in
Valve type/No: Overhead 12
Transmission: Manual
No. of forward speeds: 4
Wheels driven: Rear
Springs F/R: Coil/Coil
Brake system: PA
Brakes F/R: Drum/Drum
Steering: Recirculating ball PA
Wheelbase: 292.1cm 115.0in
Track F: 147.3cm 58.0in
Track R: 149.9cm 59.0in
Length: 524.3cm 206.4in
Width: 189.0cm 74.4in
Height: 137.2cm 54.0in
Ground clearance: 18.8cm 7.4in
Kerb weight: 1557.2kg 3430.0lb
Fuel: 81.4L 17.9gal 21.5galUS

3548 Pontiac
Tempest Sprint Automatic
1966 USA
100.0mph 160.9kmh
0-50mph 80.5kmh: 9.8secs
0-60mph 96.5kmh: 12.7secs
0-1/4 mile: 19.7secs
207.0bhp 154.4kW 209.9PS
@ 5200rpm
228.0lbft 308.9Nm @ 3800rpm
133.6bhp/ton 131.4bhp/tonne
54.9bhp/L 41.0kW/L 55.7PS/L
46.9ft/sec 14.3m/sec
23.1mph 37.2kmh/1000rpm
Petrol 4-stroke piston
3769cc 230.0cu in
In-line 6 1 Carburettor
Compression ratio: 10.5:1
Bore: 98.4mm 3.9in
Stroke: 82.6mm 3.2in
Valve type/No: Overhead 12
Transmission: Automatic
No. of forward speeds: 2
Wheels driven: Rear
Springs F/R: Coil/Coil
Brake system: PA
Brakes F/R: Drum/Drum
Steering: Recirculating ball PA
Wheelbase: 292.1cm 115.0in
Track F: 147.3cm 58.0in
Track R: 149.9cm 59.0in
Length: 524.3cm 206.4in
Width: 189.0cm 74.4in
Height: 137.2cm 54.0in
Ground clearance: 16.5cm 6.5in
Kerb weight: 1575.4kg 3470.0lb
Fuel: 81.4L 17.9gal 21.5galUS

3549 Pontiac
Firebird 440
1967 USA
115.0mph 185.0kmh
0-50mph 80.5kmh: 5.2secs
0-60mph 96.5kmh: 6.5secs
0-1/4 mile: 14.7secs
325.0bhp 242.3kW 329.5PS
@ 4800rpm
410.0lbft 555.6Nm @ 3400rpm
203.3bhp/ton 200.0bhp/tonne
49.6bhp/L 37.0kW/L 50.3PS/L
50.0ft/sec 15.2m/sec
22.4mph 36.0kmh/1000rpm
Petrol 4-stroke piston
6555cc 399.9cu in
Vee 8 1 Carburettor
Compression ratio: 10.8:1
Bore: 104.6mm 4.1in
Stroke: 95.3mm 3.8in
Valve type/No: Overhead 16
Transmission: Manual
No. of forward speeds: 4
Wheels driven: Rear
Springs F/R: Coil/Leaf
Brake system: PA
Brakes F/R: Disc/Drum
Steering: Recirculating ball PA
Wheelbase: 274.3cm 108.0in
Track F: 149.9cm 59.0in
Track R: 152.4cm 60.0in
Length: 479.6cm 188.8in
Width: 184.4cm 72.6in
Height: 130.8cm 51.5in
Ground clearance: 18.0cm 7.1in
Kerb weight: 1625.3kg 3580.0lb
Fuel: 70.0L 15.4gal 18.5galUS

3550 Pontiac
Firebird Sprint
1967 USA
114.0mph 183.4kmh
0-50mph 80.5kmh: 7.3secs
0-60mph 96.5kmh: 10.1secs
0-1/4 mile: 17.2secs
215.0bhp 160.3kW 218.0PS
@ 5200rpm
240.0lbft 325.2Nm @ 3800rpm
146.8bhp/ton 144.4bhp/tonne
57.0bhp/L 42.5kW/L 57.8PS/L
46.8ft/sec 14.3m/sec
21.2mph 34.1kmh/1000rpm
Petrol 4-stroke piston
3770cc 230.0cu in
In-line 6 1 Carburettor
Compression ratio: 10.5:1
Bore: 98.2mm 3.9in
Stroke: 82.3mm 3.2in
Valve type/No: Overhead 12
Transmission: Manual
No. of forward speeds: 4
Wheels driven: Rear
Springs F/R: Coil/Leaf
Brake system: PA
Brakes F/R: Disc/Drum
Steering: Recirculating ball PA
Wheelbase: 274.6cm 108.1in
Track F: 149.9cm 59.0in
Track R: 152.4cm 60.0in
Length: 479.6cm 188.8in
Width: 184.4cm 72.6in
Height: 130.8cm 51.5in
Ground clearance: 17.8cm 7.0in
Kerb weight: 1489.1kg 3280.0lb
Fuel: 70.0L 15.4gal 18.5galUS

3551 Pontiac
Grand Prix
1967 USA
110.0mph 177.0kmh
0-50mph 80.5kmh: 7.2secs
0-60mph 96.5kmh: 9.4secs
0-1/4 mile: 17.1secs
350.0bhp 261.0kW 354.8PS
@ 5000rpm
440.0lbft 596.2Nm @ 3200rpm
188.5bhp/ton 185.3bhp/tonne
53.4bhp/L 39.8kW/L 54.1PS/L
52.1ft/sec 15.9m/sec
28.9mph 46.5kmh/1000rpm
Petrol 4-stroke piston
6555cc 399.9cu in
Vee 8 1 Carburettor
Compression ratio: 10.5:1
Bore: 104.6mm 4.1in
Stroke: 95.3mm 3.8in
Valve type/No: Overhead 16
Transmission: Automatic
No. of forward speeds: 3
Wheels driven: Rear
Springs F/R: Coil/Coil
Brake system: PA
Brakes F/R: Drum/Drum
Steering: Recirculating ball PA
Wheelbase: 307.3cm 121.0in
Track F: 160.0cm 63.0in
Track R: 162.6cm 64.0in
Length: 547.6cm 215.6in
Width: 201.7cm 79.4in
Height: 137.7cm 54.2in
Ground clearance: 16.0cm 6.3in
Kerb weight: 1888.6kg 4160.0lb
Fuel: 100.3L 22.0gal 26.5galUS

3552 Pontiac
GTO Ram Air
1967 USA
107.0mph 172.2kmh
0-50mph 80.5kmh: 4.8secs
0-60mph 96.5kmh: 6.1secs
0-1/4 mile: 14.5secs
360.0bhp 268.4kW 365.0PS
@ 5400rpm
438.0lbft 593.5Nm @ 3800rpm
213.3bhp/ton 209.8bhp/tonne
54.9bhp/L 40.9kW/L 55.7PS/L
56.3ft/sec 17.1m/sec
19.1mph 30.7kmh/1000rpm
Petrol 4-stroke piston
6555cc 399.9cu in
Vee 8 1 Carburettor
Compression ratio: 10.8:1
Bore: 104.6mm 4.1in
Stroke: 95.3mm 3.8in
Valve type/No: Overhead 16
Transmission: Automatic
No. of forward speeds: 3
Wheels driven: Rear
Springs F/R: Coil/Coil
Brake system: PA
Brakes F/R: Disc/Drum
Steering: Recirculating ball PA
Wheelbase: 292.1cm 115.0in
Track F: 147.3cm 58.0in
Track R: 150.4cm 59.2in
Length: 524.8cm 206.6in
Width: 189.7cm 74.7in
Height: 136.4cm 53.7in
Ground clearance: 15.5cm 6.1in
Kerb weight: 1716.1kg 3780.0lb
Fuel: 81.4L 17.9gal 21.5galUS

3553 Pontiac
Firebird RA400
1968 USA
107.0mph 172.2kmh
0-50mph 80.5kmh: 5.5secs
0-60mph 96.5kmh: 6.7secs
0-1/4 mile: 14.1secs
335.0bhp 249.8kW 339.6PS
@ 5300rpm
430.0lbft 582.7Nm @ 3600rpm
217.5bhp/ton 213.9bhp/tonne
51.1bhp/L 38.1kW/L 51.8PS/L
55.2ft/sec 16.8m/sec
19.5mph 31.4kmh/1000rpm
Petrol 4-stroke piston
6554cc 399.9cu in
Vee 8 1 Carburettor
Compression ratio: 10.8:1
Bore: 104.6mm 4.1in
Stroke: 95.3mm 3.8in
Valve type/No: Overhead 16
Transmission: Manual
No. of forward speeds: 4
Wheels driven: Rear
Springs F/R: Coil/Leaf
Brake system: PA
Brakes F/R: Disc/Drum
Steering: Recirculating ball PA
Wheelbase: 274.6cm 108.1in
Track F: 152.4cm 60.0in
Track R: 152.4cm 60.0in
Length: 479.6cm 188.8in
Width: 184.9cm 72.8in
Height: 127.0cm 50.0in
Kerb weight: 1566.3kg 3450.0lb
Fuel: 70.0L 15.4gal 18.5galUS

3554 Pontiac
GTO
1968 USA
112.0mph 180.2kmh
0-50mph 80.5kmh: 5.2secs
0-60mph 96.5kmh: 6.6secs
0-1/4 mile: 14.5secs

360.0bhp 268.4kW 365.0PS
@ 5400rpm
445.0lbft 603.0Nm @ 3800rpm
214.7bhp/ton 211.2bhp/tonne
54.9bhp/L 40.9kW/L 55.7PS/L
56.3ft/sec 17.1m/sec
19.4mph 31.2kmh/1000rpm
Petrol 4-stroke piston
6555cc 399.9cu in
Vee 8 1 Carburettor
Compression ratio: 10.8:1
Bore: 104.6mm 4.1in
Stroke: 95.3mm 3.8in
Valve type/No: Overhead 16
Transmission: Manual
No. of forward speeds: 4
Wheels driven: Rear
Springs F/R: Coil/Coil
Brake system: PA
Brakes F/R: Disc/Drum
Steering: Recirculating ball PA
Wheelbase: 284.5cm 112.0in
Track F: 152.4cm 60.0in
Track R: 152.4cm 60.0in
Length: 509.8cm 200.7in
Width: 190.0cm 74.8in
Height: 132.6cm 52.2in
Kerb weight: 1704.8kg 3755.0lb
Fuel: 81.4L 17.9gal 21.5galUS

3555 Pontiac

Firebird TransAm
1969 USA
0-50mph 80.5kmh: 4.3secs
0-60mph 96.5kmh: 5.8secs
0-1/4 mile: 14.4secs
335.0bhp 249.8kW 339.6PS
@ 5000rpm
430.0lbft 582.7Nm @ 3400rpm
199.3bhp/ton 196.0bhp/tonne
51.1bhp/L 38.1kW/L 51.8PS/L
51.9ft/sec 15.8m/sec
10.8mpg 9.0mpgUS 26.1L/100km
Petrol 4-stroke piston
6550cc 399.6cu in
Vee 8 1 Carburettor
Compression ratio: 10.7:1
Bore: 105.0mm 4.1in
Stroke: 95.0mm 3.7in
Valve type/No: Overhead 16
Transmission: Automatic
No. of forward speeds: 3
Wheels driven: Rear
Springs F/R: Coil/Leaf
Brakes F/R: Disc/Disc
Steering: Recirculating ball PA
Wheelbase: 274.6cm 108.1in
Track F: 152.4cm 60.0in
Track R: 152.4cm 60.0in
Length: 485.4cm 191.1in
Width: 187.7cm 73.9in
Height: 126.0cm 49.6in
Kerb weight: 1709.3kg 3765.0lb
Fuel: 70.0L 15.4gal 18.5galUS

3556 Pontiac

Grand Prix
1969 USA
129.0mph 207.6kmh
0-50mph 80.5kmh: 5.3secs
0-60mph 96.5kmh: 6.8secs
0-1/4 mile: 15.0secs
390.0bhp 290.8kW 395.4PS
@ 5200rpm
472.0lbft 639.6Nm @ 3400rpm
215.6bhp/ton 212.0bhp/tonne
55.6bhp/L 41.5kW/L 56.4PS/L
54.2ft/sec 16.5m/sec
21.0mph 33.8kmh/1000rpm
13.2mpg 11.0mpgUS 21.4L/100km
Petrol 4-stroke piston
7014cc 427.9cu in
Vee 8 1 Carburettor
Compression ratio: 10.5:1
Bore: 104.8mm 4.1in
Stroke: 95.3mm 3.8in
Valve type/No: Overhead 16
Transmission: Automatic
No. of forward speeds: 3
Wheels driven: Rear
Springs F/R: Coil/Leaf
Brake system: PA
Brakes F/R: Disc/Drum
Steering: Recirculating ball PA
Wheelbase: 299.7cm 118.0in
Track F: 157.5cm 62.0in
Track R: 152.4cm 60.0in
Length: 533.9cm 210.2in
Width: 192.3cm 75.7in
Height: 132.3cm 52.1in
Ground clearance: 10.9cm 4.3in
Kerb weight: 1839.6kg 4052.0lb
Fuel: 81.4L 17.9gal 21.5galUS

3557 Pontiac

GTO Judge
1969 USA
124.0mph 199.5kmh
0-50mph 80.5kmh: 5.6secs
0-60mph 96.5kmh: 6.2secs
0-1/4 mile: 14.5secs
370.0bhp 275.9kW 375.1PS
@ 5500rpm
445.0lbft 603.0Nm @ 3900rpm
221.9bhp/ton 218.2bhp/tonne
56.4bhp/L 42.1kW/L 57.2PS/L
57.3ft/sec 17.5m/sec
21.5mph 34.6kmh/1000rpm
Petrol 4-stroke piston
6555cc 399.9cu in
Vee 8 1 Carburettor
Compression ratio: 10.8:1
Bore: 104.6mm 4.1in
Stroke: 95.3mm 3.8in
Valve type/No: Overhead 16
Transmission: Manual
No. of forward speeds: 4
Wheels driven: Rear
Springs F/R: Coil/Coil
Brake system: PA
Brakes F/R: Disc/Drum
Steering: Recirculating ball PA
Wheelbase: 284.5cm 112.0in
Track F: 152.4cm 60.0in
Track R: 152.4cm 60.0in
Length: 513.1cm 202.0in
Width: 190.5cm 75.0in
Height: 132.1cm 52.0in
Kerb weight: 1695.7kg 3735.0lb
Fuel: 83.3L 18.3gal 22.0galUS

3558 Pontiac

Tempest
1969 USA
105.0mph 168.9kmh
0-50mph 80.5kmh: 8.5secs
0-60mph 96.5kmh: 11.4secs
0-1/4 mile: 18.6secs
265.0bhp 197.6kW 268.7PS
@ 4600rpm
355.0lbft 481.0Nm @ 2800rpm
152.6bhp/ton 150.0bhp/tonne
46.2bhp/L 34.5kW/L 46.8PS/L
47.9ft/sec 14.6m/sec
24.9mph 40.1kmh/1000rpm
Petrol 4-stroke piston
5735cc 349.9cu in
Vee 8 1 Carburettor
Compression ratio: 9.2:1
Bore: 98.6mm 3.9in
Stroke: 95.3mm 3.8in
Valve type/No: Overhead 16
Transmission: Automatic
No. of forward speeds: 3
Wheels driven: Rear
Springs F/R: Coil/Coil
Brake system: PA
Brakes F/R: Disc/Drum
Steering: Recirculating ball PA
Wheelbase: 294.6cm 116.0in
Track F: 154.9cm 61.0in
Track R: 152.4cm 60.0in
Length: 522.0cm 205.5in
Width: 192.5cm 75.8in
Height: 133.9cm 52.7in
Kerb weight: 1766.1kg 3890.0lb
Fuel: 83.3L 18.3gal 22.0galUS

3559 Pontiac

Formula 400
1970 USA
123.0mph 197.9kmh
0-50mph 80.5kmh: 5.1secs
0-60mph 96.5kmh: 6.4secs
0-1/4 mile: 14.9secs
330.0bhp 246.1kW 334.6PS
@ 4800rpm
430.0lbft 582.7Nm @ 3000rpm
196.6bhp/ton 193.3bhp/tonne
50.3bhp/L 37.5kW/L 51.0PS/L
50.0ft/sec 15.2m/sec
24.6mph 39.6kmh/1000rpm
15.0mpg 12.5mpgUS 18.8L/100km
Petrol 4-stroke piston
6555cc 399.9cu in
Vee 8 1 Carburettor
Compression ratio: 10.3:1
Bore: 104.6mm 4.1in
Stroke: 95.3mm 3.8in
Valve type/No: Overhead 16
Transmission: Automatic
No. of forward speeds: 3
Wheels driven: Rear
Springs F/R: Coil/Leaf
Brake system: PA
Brakes F/R: Disc/Drum
Steering: Recirculating ball PA
Wheelbase: 274.3cm 108.0in
Track F: 156.5cm 61.6in
Track R: 153.2cm 60.3in
Length: 486.7cm 191.6in
Width: 186.4cm 73.4in
Height: 128.0cm 50.4in
Kerb weight: 1707.0kg 3760.0lb
Fuel: 73.8L 16.2gal 19.5galUS

3560 Pontiac

GTO 400
1970 USA
121.0mph 194.7kmh
0-50mph 80.5kmh: 4.5secs
0-60mph 96.5kmh: 6.0secs
0-1/4 mile: 14.6secs
366.0bhp 272.9kW 371.1PS
@ 5100rpm
445.0lbft 603.0Nm @ 3600rpm
214.1bhp/ton 210.5bhp/tonne
55.8bhp/L 41.6kW/L 56.6PS/L
53.0ft/sec 16.2m/sec
19.8mph 31.9kmh/1000rpm
10.7mpg 8.9mpgUS 26.4L/100km
Petrol 4-stroke piston
6555cc 399.9cu in
Vee 8 1 Carburettor
Compression ratio: 10.5:1
Bore: 104.6mm 4.1in
Stroke: 95.1mm 3.7in
Valve type/No: Overhead 16
Transmission: Manual
No. of forward speeds: 4
Wheels driven: Rear
Springs F/R: Coil/Coil
Brake system: PA
Brakes F/R: Disc/Drum
Steering: Recirculating ball PA
Wheelbase: 284.5cm 112.0in
Track F: 154.9cm 61.0in
Track R: 152.4cm 60.0in
Length: 515.4cm 202.9in
Width: 194.8cm 76.7in
Height: 132.8cm 52.3in
Kerb weight: 1738.8kg 3830.0lb
Fuel: 80.6L 17.7gal 21.3galUS

3561 Pontiac

GTO 455
1970 USA
118.0mph 189.9kmh
0-50mph 80.5kmh: 5.3secs
0-60mph 96.5kmh: 6.6secs
0-1/4 mile: 14.8secs
360.0bhp 268.4kW 365.0PS
@ 4300rpm
500.0lbft 677.5Nm @ 2700rpm
198.9bhp/ton 195.5bhp/tonne
48.3bhp/L 36.0kW/L 48.9PS/L
50.3ft/sec 15.3m/sec
21.8mph 35.1kmh/1000rpm
14.2mpg 11.8mpgUS 19.9L/100km
Petrol 4-stroke piston
7456cc 454.9cu in
Vee 8 1 Carburettor
Compression ratio: 10.3:1
Bore: 105.4mm 4.1in
Stroke: 106.9mm 4.2in
Valve type/No: Overhead 16
Transmission: Automatic
No. of forward speeds: 3
Wheels driven: Rear
Springs F/R: Coil/Coil
Brake system: PA
Brakes F/R: Disc/Drum
Steering: Recirculating ball PA
Wheelbase: 284.5cm 112.0in
Track F: 154.9cm 61.0in
Track R: 152.4cm 60.0in
Length: 515.4cm 202.9in
Width: 194.8cm 76.7in
Height: 132.8cm 52.3in
Kerb weight: 1841.0kg 4055.0lb
Fuel: 81.4L 17.9gal 21.5galUS

3562 Pontiac

Grand Am
1973 USA
110.0mph 177.0kmh
0-50mph 80.5kmh: 7.4secs
0-60mph 96.5kmh: 10.3secs
0-1/4 mile: 17.5secs
170.0bhp 126.8kW 172.4PS
@ 3600rpm
320.0lbft 433.6Nm @ 2000rpm
88.6bhp/ton 87.1bhp/tonne
25.9bhp/L 19.3kW/L 26.3PS/L
37.5ft/sec 11.4m/sec
24.5mph 39.4kmh/1000rpm
13.2mpg 11.0mpgUS 21.4L/100km
Petrol 4-stroke piston
6556cc 400.0cu in
Vee 8 1 Carburettor
Compression ratio: 8.0:1
Bore: 104.6mm 4.1in
Stroke: 95.3mm 3.8in
Valve type/No: Overhead 16
Transmission: Automatic
No. of forward speeds: 3
Wheels driven: Rear
Springs F/R: Coil/Coil
Brake system: PA
Brakes F/R: Disc/Drum
Steering: Recirculating ball PA
Wheelbase: 284.5cm 112.0in
Track F: 157.2cm 61.9in
Track R: 155.2cm 61.1in
Length: 529.8cm 208.6in
Width: 197.4cm 77.7in
Height: 134.4cm 52.9in
Ground clearance: 10.7cm 4.2in
Kerb weight: 1952.2kg 4300.0lb
Fuel: 94.6L 20.8gal 25.0galUS

3563 Pontiac

Firebird TransAm
1976 USA
110.0mph 177.0kmh
0-50mph 80.5kmh: 6.5secs
0-60mph 96.5kmh: 8.4secs
0-1/4 mile: 15.9secs
200.0bhp 149.1kW 202.8PS
@ 3500rpm
330.0lbft 447.2Nm @ 2000rpm
119.5bhp/ton 117.5bhp/tonne
26.8bhp/L 20.0kW/L 27.2PS/L
40.9ft/sec 12.5m/sec
23.0mph 37.0kmh/1000rpm
17.4mpg 14.5mpgUS 16.2L/100km
Petrol 4-stroke piston
7458cc 455.0cu in
Vee 8 1 Carburettor
Compression ratio: 7.6:1
Bore: 105.4mm 4.1in
Stroke: 106.9mm 4.2in
Valve type/No: Overhead 16
Transmission: Manual
No. of forward speeds: 4
Wheels driven: Rear
Springs F/R: Coil/Leaf
Brake system: PA
Brakes F/R: Disc/Drum
Steering: Recirculating ball PA
Wheelbase: 274.6cm 108.1in
Track F: 155.4cm 61.2in
Track R: 153.2cm 60.3in
Length: 499.9cm 196.8in
Width: 185.4cm 73.0in
Height: 126.0cm 49.6in
Ground clearance: 13.5cm 5.3in
Kerb weight: 1702.5kg 3750.0lb
Fuel: 76.5L 16.8gal 20.2galUS

3564 Pontiac

Bonneville
1977 USA
103.0mph 165.7kmh
0-50mph 80.5kmh: 10.6secs
0-60mph 96.5kmh: 14.8secs
0-1/4 mile: 20.0secs
135.0bhp 100.7kW 136.9PS
@ 4000rpm
245.0lbft 332.0Nm @ 2000rpm
74.8bhp/ton 73.6bhp/tonne
27.0bhp/L 20.1kW/L 27.4PS/L
37.7ft/sec 11.5m/sec
18.2mph 29.3kmh/1000rpm
16.2mpg 13.5mpgUS 17.4L/100km
Petrol 4-stroke piston
5000cc 305.1cu in
Vee 8 1 Carburettor
Compression ratio: 8.2:1

Bore: 103.0mm 4.1in
Stroke: 86.0mm 3.4in
Valve type/No: Overhead 16
Transmission: Automatic
No. of forward speeds: 3
Wheels driven: Rear
Springs F/R: Coil/Coil
Brake system: PA
Brakes F/R: Disc/Drum
Steering: Recirculating ball PA
Wheelbase: 294.4cm 115.9in
Track F: 156.7cm 61.7in
Track R: 154.2cm 60.7in
Length: 543.1cm 213.8in
Width: 191.5cm 75.4in
Height: 150.6cm 59.3in
Ground clearance: 14.2cm 5.6in
Kerb weight: 1834.2kg 4040.0lb
Fuel: 75.7L 16.6gal 20.0galUS

3565 Pontiac

Firebird TransAm
1978 USA
0-60mph 96.5kmh: 6.5secs
0-1/4 mile: 15.3secs
220.0bhp 164.0kW 223.0PS
@ 4000rpm
320.0lbft 433.6Nm @ 2800rpm
133.7bhp/ton 131.5bhp/tonne
33.6bhp/L 25.0kW/L 34.0PS/L
41.7ft/sec 12.7m/sec
23.0mph 37.0kmh/1000rpm
18.6mpg 15.5mpgUS 15.2L/100km
Petrol 4-stroke piston
6555cc 399.9cu in
Vee 8 1 Carburettor
Compression ratio: 8.1:1
Bore: 104.7mm 4.1in
Stroke: 95.3mm 3.8in
Valve type/No: Overhead 16
Transmission: Manual
No. of forward speeds: 4
Wheels driven: Rear
Springs F/R: Coil/Leaf
Brake system: PA
Brakes F/R: Disc/Drum
Steering: Recirculating ball PA
Track F: 156.5cm 61.6in
Track R: 153.2cm 60.3in
Length: 499.9cm 196.8in
Width: 185.4cm 73.0in
Height: 125.7cm 49.5in
Ground clearance: 13.5cm 5.3in
Kerb weight: 1673.0kg 3685.0lb
Fuel: 79.5L 17.5gal 21.0galUS

3566 Pontiac

Firebird TransAm Silverbird
1978 USA
144.0mph 231.7kmh
0-50mph 80.5kmh: 3.2secs
0-60mph 96.5kmh: 4.0secs
0-1/4 mile: 12.3secs
590.0bhp 440.0kW 598.2PS
@ 7500rpm
460.0lbft 623.3Nm @ 5000rpm
455.7bhp/ton 448.1bhp/tonne
98.4bhp/L 73.3kW/L 99.7PS/L
70.4ft/sec 21.5m/sec
20.7mph 33.3kmh/1000rpm
4.8mpg 4.0mpgUS 58.8L/100km
Petrol 4-stroke piston
5998cc 365.9cu in
Vee 8 fuel injection
Compression ratio: 12.0:1
Bore: 105.4mm 4.1in
Stroke: 85.9mm 3.4in
Valve type/No: Overhead 16
Transmission: Manual
No. of forward speeds: 5
Wheels driven: Rear
Springs F/R: Coil/Leaf
Brakes F/R: Disc/Disc
Steering: Rack & pinion
Wheelbase: 274.3cm 108.0in
Track F: 152.4cm 60.0in
Track R: 147.3cm 58.0in
Length: 515.1cm 202.8in
Width: 199.4cm 78.5in
Height: 111.8cm 44.0in
Ground clearance: 7.6cm 3.0in
Kerb weight: 1316.6kg 2900.0lb
Fuel: 121.1L 26.6gal 32.0galUS

3567 Pontiac

Firebird TransAm Turbo
1980 USA
106.0mph 170.6kmh
0-50mph 80.5kmh: 7.3secs
0-60mph 96.5kmh: 9.8secs
0-1/4 mile: 17.5secs
210.0bhp 156.6kW 212.9PS
@ 4000rpm
345.0lbft 467.5Nm @ 2000rpm
126.1bhp/ton 124.0bhp/tonne
42.6bhp/L 31.7kW/L 43.2PS/L
33.3ft/sec 10.2m/sec
24.2mph 38.9kmh/1000rpm
15.6mpg 13.0mpgUS 18.1L/100km
Petrol 4-stroke piston
4932cc 300.9cu in turbocharged
Vee 8 1 Carburettor
Compression ratio: 7.6:1
Bore: 101.6mm 4.0in
Stroke: 76.2mm 3.0in
Valve type/No: Overhead 16
Transmission: Automatic
No. of forward speeds: 3
Wheels driven: Rear
Springs F/R: Coil/Leaf
Brake system: PA
Brakes F/R: Disc/Disc
Steering: Recirculating ball PA
Wheelbase: 274.8cm 108.2in
Track F: 155.7cm 61.3in
Track R: 152.4cm 60.0in
Length: 503.2cm 198.1in
Width: 185.4cm 73.0in
Height: 125.2cm 49.3in
Kerb weight: 1693.4kg 3730.0lb
Fuel: 79.5L 17.5gal 21.0galUS

3568 Pontiac

Phoenix
1980 USA
99.0mph 159.3kmh
0-50mph 80.5kmh: 8.3secs
0-60mph 96.5kmh: 12.1secs
0-1/4 mile: 19.1secs
90.0bhp 67.1kW 91.2PS
@ 4000rpm
134.0lbft 181.6Nm @ 2400rpm
74.7bhp/ton 73.4bhp/tonne
36.4bhp/L 27.1kW/L 36.9PS/L
33.3ft/sec 10.2m/sec
26.1mph 42.0kmh/1000rpm
26.4mpg 22.0mpgUS 10.7L/100km
Petrol 4-stroke piston
2474cc 150.9cu in
In-line 4 1 Carburettor
Compression ratio: 8.2:1
Bore: 101.6mm 4.0in
Stroke: 76.2mm 3.0in
Valve type/No: Overhead 8
Transmission: Automatic
No. of forward speeds: 3
Wheels driven: Front
Springs F/R: Coil/Coil
Brake system: PA
Brakes F/R: Disc/Drum
Steering: Rack & pinion PA
Wheelbase: 266.4cm 104.9in
Track F: 149.1cm 58.7in
Track R: 144.8cm 57.0in
Length: 462.5cm 182.1in
Width: 175.3cm 69.0in
Height: 138.9cm 54.7in
Kerb weight: 1225.8kg 2700.0lb
Fuel: 53.0L 11.6gal 14.0galUS

3569 Pontiac

J2000
1981 USA
85.0mph 136.8kmh
0-50mph 80.5kmh: 11.6secs
0-60mph 96.5kmh: 16.3secs
0-1/4 mile: 20.6secs
85.0bhp 63.4kW 86.2PS
@ 5100rpm
100.0lbft 135.5Nm @ 2800rpm
72.4bhp/ton 71.2bhp/tonne
46.3bhp/L 34.5kW/L 46.9PS/L
41.2ft/sec 12.6m/sec
24.0mph 38.6kmh/1000rpm
26.4mpg 22.0mpgUS 10.7L/100km
Petrol 4-stroke piston
1836cc 112.0cu in
In-line 4 1 Carburettor
Compression ratio: 8.9:1
Bore: 89.0mm 3.5in
Stroke: 74.0mm 2.9in
Valve type/No: Overhead 8
Transmission: Automatic
No. of forward speeds: 3
Wheels driven: Front
Springs F/R: Coil/Coil
Brake system: PA
Brakes F/R: Disc/Drum
Steering: Rack & pinion PA
Wheelbase: 257.0cm 101.2in
Track F: 140.7cm 55.4in
Track R: 140.2cm 55.2in
Length: 440.7cm 173.5in
Width: 165.1cm 65.0in
Height: 131.8cm 51.9in
Ground clearance: 15.2cm 6.0in
Kerb weight: 1194.0kg 2630.0lb
Fuel: 53.0L 11.6gal 14.0galUS

3570 Pontiac

Firebird TransAm
1982 USA
106.0mph 170.6kmh
0-60mph 96.5kmh: 9.2secs
0-1/4 mile: 17.0secs
165.0bhp 123.0kW 167.3PS
@ 4200rpm
240.0lbft 325.2Nm @ 2400rpm
109.2bhp/ton 107.4bhp/tonne
33.0bhp/L 24.6kW/L 33.5PS/L
40.6ft/sec 12.4m/sec
21.2mph 34.1kmh/1000rpm
17.4mpg 14.5mpgUS 16.2L/100km
Petrol 4-stroke piston
4998cc 304.9cu in
Vee 8 fuel injection
Compression ratio: 9.5:1
Bore: 94.9mm 3.7in
Stroke: 88.4mm 3.5in
Valve type/No: Overhead 16
Transmission: Automatic
No. of forward speeds: 3
Wheels driven: Rear
Springs F/R: Coil/Coil
Brake system: PA
Brakes F/R: Disc/Disc
Steering: Recirculating ball PA
Wheelbase: 256.5cm 101.0in
Track F: 154.2cm 60.7in
Track R: 156.5cm 61.6in
Length: 482.1cm 189.8in
Width: 182.9cm 72.0in
Height: 126.5cm 49.8in
Kerb weight: 1536.8kg 3385.0lb
Fuel: 60.6L 13.3gal 16.0galUS

3571 Pontiac

Petty Grand National
1982 USA
183.0mph 294.4kmh
0-50mph 80.5kmh: 4.2secs
0-60mph 96.5kmh: 5.2secs
0-1/4 mile: 13.5secs
590.0bhp 440.0kW 598.2PS
@ 7500rpm
356.7bhp/ton 350.8bhp/tonne
100.2bhp/L 74.7kW/L 101.6PS/L
72.9ft/sec 22.2m/sec
22.9mph 36.8kmh/1000rpm
5.4mpg 4.5mpgUS 52.3L/100km
Petrol 4-stroke piston
5888cc 359.2cu in
Vee 8 1 Carburettor
Compression ratio: 13.0:1
Bore: 102.4mm 4.0in
Stroke: 88.9mm 3.5in
Valve type/No: Overhead 16
Transmission: Manual
No. of forward speeds: 4
Wheels driven: Rear
Springs F/R: Coil/Coil
Brakes F/R: Disc/Disc
Steering: Recirculating ball
Wheelbase: 279.4cm 110.0in
Track F: 156.2cm 61.5in
Track R: 153.7cm 60.5in
Length: 512.6cm 201.8in
Width: 183.6cm 72.3in
Height: 129.5cm 51.0in
Ground clearance: 10.2cm 4.0in
Kerb weight: 1682.1kg 3705.0lb
Fuel: 83.3L 18.3gal 22.0galUS

3572 Pontiac

6000STE
1983 USA
105.0mph 168.9kmh
0-60mph 96.5kmh: 11.2secs
0-1/4 mile: 18.2secs
135.0bhp 100.7kW 136.9PS
@ 5400rpm
145.0lbft 196.5Nm @ 2400rpm
100.8bhp/ton 99.1bhp/tonne
47.6bhp/L 35.5kW/L 48.2PS/L
45.0ft/sec 13.7m/sec
20.3mph 32.7kmh/1000rpm
21.7mpg 18.1mpgUS 13.0L/100km
Petrol 4-stroke piston
2837cc 173.1cu in
Vee 6 1 Carburettor
Compression ratio: 8.9:1
Bore: 89.0mm 3.5in
Stroke: 76.2mm 3.0in
Valve type/No: Overhead 12
Transmission: Automatic
No. of forward speeds: 3
Wheels driven: Front
Springs F/R: Coil/Coil
Brakes F/R: Disc/Drum
Wheelbase: 266.4cm 104.9in
Track F: 149.1cm 58.7in
Track R: 144.8cm 57.0in
Length: 479.6cm 188.8in
Width: 182.9cm 72.0in
Height: 136.4cm 53.7in
Kerb weight: 1362.0kg 3000.0lb
Fuel: 62.1L 13.6gal 16.4galUS

3573 Pontiac

Fiero
1984 USA
103.0mph 165.7kmh
0-60mph 96.5kmh: 10.9secs
0-1/4 mile: 17.8secs
92.0bhp 68.6kW 93.3PS
@ 4000rpm
134.0lbft 181.6Nm @ 2800rpm
79.0bhp/ton 77.6bhp/tonne
37.2bhp/L 27.8kW/L 37.7PS/L
33.3ft/sec 10.2m/sec
26.4mph 22.0mpgUS 10.7L/100km
Petrol 4-stroke piston
2471cc 150.8cu in
In-line 4 fuel injection
Compression ratio: 9.0:1
Bore: 101.6mm 4.0in
Stroke: 76.2mm 3.0in
Valve type/No: Overhead 8
Transmission: Manual
No. of forward speeds: 4
Wheels driven: Rear
Springs F/R: Coil/Coil
Brakes F/R: Disc/Disc
Steering: Rack & pinion
Wheelbase: 237.2cm 93.4in
Track F: 146.8cm 57.8in
Track R: 149.1cm 58.7in
Length: 407.2cm 160.3in
Width: 175.0cm 68.9in
Height: 119.1cm 46.9in
Kerb weight: 1184.9kg 2610.0lb
Fuel: 38.6L 8.5gal 10.2galUS

3574 Pontiac

Fiero SE
1984 USA
103.0mph 165.7kmh
0-50mph 80.5kmh: 8.0secs
0-60mph 96.5kmh: 11.6secs
0-1/4 mile: 18.2secs
92.0bhp 68.6kW 93.3PS
@ 4000rpm
134.0lbft 181.6Nm @ 2800rpm
79.6bhp/ton 78.2bhp/tonne
37.2bhp/L 27.8kW/L 37.7PS/L
33.3ft/sec 10.2m/sec
20.7mph 33.3kmh/1000rpm
30.0mpg 25.0mpgUS 9.4L/100km
Petrol 4-stroke piston
2471cc 150.8cu in
In-line 4 fuel injection
Compression ratio: 9.0:1
Bore: 101.6mm 4.0in
Stroke: 76.2mm 3.0in
Valve type/No: Overhead 8
Transmission: Manual
No. of forward speeds: 4
Wheels driven: Rear
Springs F/R: Coil/Coil
Brake system: PA
Brakes F/R: Disc/Disc
Steering: Rack & pinion
Wheelbase: 237.2cm 93.4in
Track F: 146.8cm 57.8in
Track R: 149.1cm 58.7in
Length: 407.2cm 160.3in

Width: 175.0cm 68.9in
Height: 119.1cm 46.9in
Ground clearance: 15.2cm 6.0in
Kerb weight: 1175.9kg 2590.0lb
Fuel: 38.6L 8.5gal 10.2galUS

3575 Pontiac

Firebird TransAm
1984 USA
108.0mph 173.8kmh
0-50mph 80.5kmh: 6.3secs
0-60mph 96.5kmh: 8.6secs
0-1/4 mile: 17.5secs
190.0bhp 141.7kW 192.6PS
@ 4800rpm
240.0lbft 325.2Nm @ 3200rpm
123.7bhp/ton 121.7bhp/tonne
38.0bhp/L 28.3kW/L 38.5PS/L
46.4ft/sec 14.1m/sec
Petrol 4-stroke piston
4998cc 304.9cu in
Vee 8
Compression ratio: 9.5:1
Bore: 94.9mm 3.7in
Stroke: 88.4mm 3.5in
Valve type/No: Overhead 16
Transmission: Manual
No. of forward speeds: 5
Wheels driven: Rear
Springs F/R: Coil/Coil
Brakes F/R: Disc/Disc
Steering: Recirculating ball PA
Wheelbase: 256.5cm 101.0in
Track F: 154.2cm 60.7in
Track R: 156.5cm 61.6in
Length: 482.1cm 189.8in
Width: 182.9cm 72.0in
Height: 127.0cm 50.0in
Kerb weight: 1561.8kg 3440.0lb

3576 Pontiac

Firebird TransAm HO
1984 USA
0-50mph 80.5kmh: 5.8secs
0-60mph 96.5kmh: 7.9secs
0-1/4 mile: 16.1secs
190.0bhp 141.7kW 192.6PS
@ 4800rpm
240.0lbft 325.2Nm @ 3200rpm
130.9bhp/ton 128.8bhp/tonne
38.0bhp/L 28.3kW/L 38.5PS/L
46.4ft/sec 14.1m/sec
Petrol 4-stroke piston
5002cc 305.2cu in
Vee 8 1 Carburettor
Compression ratio: 9.5:1
Bore: 94.9mm 3.7in
Stroke: 88.4mm 3.5in
Valve type/No: Overhead 16
Transmission: Manual
No. of forward speeds: 5
Wheels driven: Rear
Wheelbase: 256.5cm 101.0in
Track F: 154.2cm 60.7in
Track R: 156.5cm 61.6in
Length: 482.3cm 189.9in
Width: 183.9cm 72.4in
Height: 126.2cm 49.7in
Kerb weight: 1475.5kg 3250.0lb
Fuel: 60.9L 13.4gal 16.1galUS

3577 Pontiac

Fiero GT
1985 USA
125.0mph 201.1kmh
0-50mph 80.5kmh: 5.8secs
0-60mph 96.5kmh: 8.4secs
0-1/4 mile: 16.5secs
140.0bhp 104.4kW 141.9PS
@ 5200rpm
170.0lbft 230.4Nm @ 3600rpm
114.4bhp/ton 112.5bhp/tonne
49.3bhp/L 36.8kW/L 50.0PS/L
43.2ft/sec 13.2m/sec
23.3mph 37.5kmh/1000rpm
26.4mpg 22.0mpgUS 10.7L/100km
Petrol 4-stroke piston
2837cc 173.1cu in
Vee 6 fuel injection
Compression ratio: 8.9:1
Bore: 89.0mm 3.5in
Stroke: 76.0mm 3.0in
Valve type/No: Overhead 12
Transmission: Manual
No. of forward speeds: 4
Wheels driven: Rear
Springs F/R: Coil/Coil
Brake system: PA
Brakes F/R: Disc/Disc
Steering: Rack & pinion
Wheelbase: 237.2cm 93.4in
Track F: 146.8cm 57.8in
Track R: 149.1cm 58.7in
Length: 419.4cm 165.1in
Width: 175.0cm 68.9in
Height: 119.1cm 46.9in
Ground clearance: 15.2cm 6.0in
Kerb weight: 1244.0kg 2740.0lb
Fuel: 38.6L 8.5gal 10.2galUS

3578 Pontiac

Fiero GT
1986 USA
125.0mph 201.1kmh
0-50mph 80.5kmh: 5.5secs
0-60mph 96.5kmh: 7.7secs
0-1/4 mile: 15.9secs
140.0bhp 104.4kW 141.9PS
@ 5200rpm
170.0lbft 230.4Nm @ 3600rpm
109.6bhp/ton 107.8bhp/tonne
49.3bhp/L 36.8kW/L 50.0PS/L
43.2ft/sec 13.2m/sec
27.0mpg 22.5mpgUS 10.5L/100km
Petrol 4-stroke piston
2837cc 173.1cu in
Vee 6 fuel injection
Compression ratio: 8.9:1
Bore: 89.0mm 3.5in
Stroke: 76.0mm 3.0in
Valve type/No: Overhead 12
Transmission: Manual
No. of forward speeds: 4
Wheels driven: Rear
Springs F/R: Coil/Coil
Brake system: PA
Brakes F/R: Disc/Disc
Steering: Rack & pinion
Wheelbase: 237.2cm 93.4in
Track F: 146.8cm 57.8in
Track R: 149.1cm 58.7in
Length: 419.4cm 165.1in
Width: 175.0cm 68.9in
Height: 119.1cm 46.9in
Kerb weight: 1298.4kg 2860.0lb
Fuel: 38.6L 8.5gal 10.2galUS

3579 Pontiac

Bonneville SE
1987 USA
120.0mph 193.1kmh
0-50mph 80.5kmh: 6.8secs
0-60mph 96.5kmh: 9.7secs
0-1/4 mile: 17.3secs
150.0bhp 111.9kW 152.1PS
@ 4400rpm
200.0lbft 271.0Nm @ 2000rpm
98.1bhp/ton 96.5bhp/tonne
39.6bhp/L 29.5kW/L 40.1PS/L
41.6ft/sec 12.7m/sec
22.2mpg 18.5mpgUS 12.7L/100km
Petrol 4-stroke piston
3791cc 231.3cu in
Vee 6 fuel injection
Compression ratio: 8.5:1
Bore: 96.5mm 3.8in
Stroke: 86.4mm 3.4in
Valve type/No: Overhead 12
Transmission: Automatic
No. of forward speeds: 4
Wheels driven: Front
Springs F/R: Coil/Coil
Brake system: PA
Brakes F/R: Disc/Drum
Steering: Rack & pinion PA
Wheelbase: 281.4cm 110.8in
Track F: 153.2cm 60.3in
Track R: 151.9cm 59.8in
Length: 504.7cm 198.7in
Width: 183.1cm 72.1in
Height: 141.0cm 55.5in
Ground clearance: 16.5cm 6.5in
Kerb weight: 1554.9kg 3425.0lb
Fuel: 68.1L 15.0gal 18.0galUS

3580 Pontiac

Fiero Formula
1987 USA
125.0mph 201.1kmh
0-50mph 80.5kmh: 5.5secs
0-60mph 96.5kmh: 8.0secs
0-1/4 mile: 16.0secs
135.0bhp 100.7kW 136.9PS
@ 4500rpm
165.0lbft 223.6Nm @ 3600rpm
109.0bhp/ton 107.2bhp/tonne
47.6bhp/L 35.5kW/L 48.2PS/L
37.4ft/sec 11.4m/sec
20.7mpg 17.2mpgUS 13.7L/100km
Petrol 4-stroke piston
2837cc 173.1cu in
Vee 6 fuel injection
Compression ratio: 8.5:1
Bore: 89.0mm 3.5in
Stroke: 76.0mm 3.0in
Valve type/No: Overhead 12
Transmission: Manual
No. of forward speeds: 5
Wheels driven: Rear
Springs F/R: Coil/Coil
Brakes F/R: Disc/Disc
Steering: Rack & pinion
Wheelbase: 237.2cm 93.4in
Track F: 151.6cm 59.7in
Track R: 153.4cm 60.4in
Length: 414.3cm 163.1in
Width: 175.0cm 68.9in
Height: 119.1cm 46.9in
Kerb weight: 1259.8kg 2775.0lb
Fuel: 45.0L 9.9gal 11.9galUS

3581 Pontiac

Fiero GT
1987 USA
0-60mph 96.5kmh: 7.7secs
0-1/4 mile: 16.0secs
135.0bhp 100.7kW 136.9PS
@ 4900rpm
160.0lbft 216.8Nm @ 3900rpm
111.6bhp/ton 109.7bhp/tonne
47.6bhp/L 35.5kW/L 48.2PS/L
23.4mpg 19.5mpgUS 12.1L/100km
Petrol 4-stroke piston
2837cc 173.1cu in
Vee 6
Valve type/No: Overhead 12
Transmission: Manual
No. of forward speeds: 5
Wheels driven: Rear
Brakes F/R: Disc/Disc
Steering: Rack & pinion
Length: 419.4cm 165.1in
Kerb weight: 1230.3kg 2710.0lb

3582 Pontiac

Firebird Formula 5.0
1987 USA
0-50mph 80.5kmh: 4.5secs
0-60mph 96.5kmh: 6.3secs
0-1/4 mile: 14.9secs
205.0bhp 152.9kW 207.8PS
@ 4400rpm
285.0lbft 386.2Nm @ 3200rpm
137.7bhp/ton 135.4bhp/tonne
41.0bhp/L 30.6kW/L 41.6PS/L
42.5ft/sec 13.0m/sec
18.3mpg 15.2mpgUS 15.5L/100km
Petrol 4-stroke piston
5001cc 305.1cu in
Vee 8 fuel injection
Compression ratio: 9.3:1
Bore: 94.9mm 3.7in
Stroke: 88.4mm 3.5in
Valve type/No: Overhead 16
Transmission: Manual
No. of forward speeds: 5
Wheels driven: Rear
Springs F/R: Coil/Coil
Brakes F/R: Disc/Disc
Steering: Rack & pinion PA
Wheelbase: 256.5cm 101.0in
Track F: 154.2cm 60.7in
Track R: 156.5cm 61.6in
Length: 486.7cm 191.6in
Width: 183.9cm 72.4in
Height: 126.2cm 49.7in
Kerb weight: 1514.1kg 3335.0lb
Fuel: 58.7L 12.9gal 15.5galUS

3583 Pontiac

Le Mans
1987 Korea
100.0mph 160.9kmh
0-60mph 96.5kmh: 12.1secs
0-1/4 mile: 18.7secs
74.0bhp 55.2kW 75.0PS
@ 5200rpm
88.0lbft 119.2Nm @ 3400rpm
72.1bhp/ton 70.9bhp/tonne
46.3bhp/L 34.5kW/L 46.9PS/L
46.4ft/sec 14.1m/sec
36.6mpg 30.5mpgUS 7.7L/100km
Petrol 4-stroke piston
1598cc 97.5cu in
In-line 4 fuel injection
Compression ratio: 8.6:1
Bore: 79.0mm 3.1in
Stroke: 81.5mm 3.2in
Valve type/No: Overhead 8
Transmission: Manual
No. of forward speeds: 5
Wheels driven: Front
Springs F/R: Coil/Coil
Brake system: PA
Brakes F/R: Disc/Drum
Steering: Rack & pinion PA
Wheelbase: 252.0cm 99.2in
Track F: 140.7cm 55.4in
Track R: 140.7cm 55.4in
Length: 436.6cm 171.9in
Width: 166.4cm 65.5in
Height: 138.9cm 54.7in
Kerb weight: 1044.2kg 2300.0lb
Fuel: 49.2L 10.8gal 13.0galUS

3584 Pontiac

6000STE AWD
1988 USA
135.0bhp 100.7kW 136.9PS
@ 4800rpm
180.0lbft 243.9Nm @ 3600rpm
88.9bhp/ton 87.5bhp/tonne
43.2bhp/L 32.2kW/L 43.8PS/L
44.0ft/sec 13.4m/sec
Petrol 4-stroke piston
3122cc 190.5cu in
Vee 6 fuel injection
Compression ratio: 8.8:1
Bore: 88.9mm 3.5in
Stroke: 83.8mm 3.3in
Valve type/No: Overhead 12
Transmission: Automatic
No. of forward speeds: 3
Wheels driven: 4-wheel drive
Springs F/R: Coil/Leaf
Brake system: PA ABS
Brakes F/R: Disc/Disc
Steering: Rack & pinion PA
Wheelbase: 266.4cm 104.9in
Track F: 149.1cm 58.7in
Track R: 144.8cm 57.0in
Length: 479.6cm 188.8in
Width: 182.9cm 72.0in
Height: 136.4cm 53.7in
Kerb weight: 1543.6kg 3400.0lb
Fuel: 68.1L 15.0gal 18.0galUS

3585 Pontiac

Bonneville SE
1988 USA
115.0mph 185.0kmh
0-60mph 96.5kmh: 9.5secs
0-1/4 mile: 17.2secs
165.0bhp 123.0kW 167.3PS
@ 5200rpm
210.0lbft 284.6Nm @ 2000rpm
105.0bhp/ton 103.2bhp/tonne
43.5bhp/L 32.5kW/L 44.1PS/L
49.1ft/sec 15.0m/sec
21.6mpg 18.0mpgUS 13.1L/100km
Petrol 4-stroke piston
3791cc 231.3cu in
Vee 6 fuel injection
Compression ratio: 8.5:1
Bore: 96.5mm 3.8in
Stroke: 86.4mm 3.4in
Valve type/No: Overhead 12
Transmission: Automatic
No. of forward speeds: 4
Wheels driven: Front
Springs F/R: Coil/Coil
Brake system: PA
Brakes F/R: Disc/Drum
Steering: Rack & pinion PA
Wheelbase: 281.4cm 110.8in
Track F: 153.2cm 60.3in
Track R: 151.9cm 59.8in
Length: 503.7cm 198.3in
Width: 183.9cm 72.4in
Height: 141.0cm 55.5in
Kerb weight: 1598.1kg 3520.0lb
Fuel: 68.1L 15.0gal 18.0galUS

3586 Pontiac
Grand Prix SE
1988 USA
0-60mph 96.5kmh: 9.7secs
0-1/4 mile: 17.1secs
130.0bhp 96.9kW 131.8PS
@ 4500rpm
170.0lbft 230.4Nm @ 3600rpm
90.7bhp/ton 89.2bhp/tonne
45.8bhp/L 34.2kW/L 46.5PS/L
37.4ft/sec 11.4m/sec
25.8mpg 21.5mpgUS 10.9L/100km
Petrol 4-stroke piston
2837cc 173.1cu in
Vee 6 fuel injection
Compression ratio: 8.9:1
Bore: 89.0mm 3.5in
Stroke: 76.0mm 3.0in
Valve type/No: Overhead 12
Transmission: Manual
No. of forward speeds: 5
Wheels driven: Front
Springs F/R: Coil/Leaf
Brake system: PA
Brakes F/R: Disc/Disc
Steering: Rack & pinion PA
Wheelbase: 273.1cm 107.5in
Track F: 151.1cm 59.5in
Track R: 147.3cm 58.0in
Length: 492.5cm 193.9in
Width: 182.6cm 71.9in
Height: 134.1cm 52.8in
Kerb weight: 1457.3kg 3210.0lb
Fuel: 60.6L 13.3gal 16.0galUS

3587 Pontiac
Sunbird GT
1988 USA
125.0mph 201.1kmh
0-50mph 80.5kmh: 5.6secs
0-60mph 96.5kmh: 7.8secs
0-1/4 mile: 15.9secs
165.0bhp 123.0kW 167.3PS
@ 5600rpm
175.0lbft 237.1Nm @ 4000rpm
146.1bhp/ton 143.6bhp/tonne
82.3bhp/L 61.4kW/L 83.4PS/L
52.7ft/sec 16.0m/sec
31.2mpg 26.0mpgUS 9.0L/100km
Petrol 4-stroke piston
2005cc 122.3cu in turbocharged
In-line 4 fuel injection
Compression ratio: 8.0:1
Bore: 86.0mm 3.4in
Stroke: 86.0mm 3.4in
Valve type/No: Overhead 8
Transmission: Manual
No. of forward speeds: 5
Wheels driven: Front
Springs F/R: Coil/Coil
Brake system: PA
Brakes F/R: Disc/Drum
Steering: Rack & pinion PA
Wheelbase: 257.0cm 101.2in
Track F: 141.2cm 55.6in
Track R: 140.2cm 55.2in
Length: 452.6cm 178.2in
Width: 165.1cm 65.0in
Height: 128.0cm 50.4in
Kerb weight: 1148.6kg 2530.0lb
Fuel: 51.5L 11.3gal 13.6galUS

3588 Pontiac
Firebird T/A Turbo Pontiac Engineering
1989 USA
178.0mph 286.4kmh
0-50mph 80.5kmh: 5.1secs
0-60mph 96.5kmh: 6.5secs
0-1/4 mile: 14.8secs
380.0bhp 283.4kW 385.3PS
@ 5000rpm
425.0lbft 575.9Nm @ 4500rpm
238.1bhp/ton 234.1bhp/tonne
100.2bhp/L 74.7kW/L 101.6PS/L
47.2ft/sec 14.4m/sec
Petrol 4-stroke piston
3791cc 231.3cu in turbocharged
Vee 6 fuel injection
Compression ratio: 8.6:1
Bore: 96.5mm 3.8in
Stroke: 86.4mm 3.4in
Valve type/No: Overhead 12
Transmission: Manual
No. of forward speeds: 6
Wheels driven: Rear
Springs F/R: Coil/Coil
Brake system: PA
Brakes F/R: Disc/Disc
Steering: Recirculating ball PA
Wheelbase: 256.5cm 101.0in
Track F: 154.2cm 60.7in
Track R: 156.5cm 61.6in
Length: 486.7cm 191.6in
Width: 183.9cm 72.4in
Height: 127.0cm 50.0in
Kerb weight: 1623.0kg 3575.0lb

3589 Pontiac
Firebird TransAm 20th Anniversary
1989 USA
155.0mph 249.4kmh
0-50mph 80.5kmh: 3.8secs
0-60mph 96.5kmh: 5.1secs
0-1/4 mile: 13.7secs
250.0bhp 186.4kW 253.5PS
@ 4000rpm
340.0lbft 460.7Nm @ 2800rpm
164.7bhp/ton 162.0bhp/tonne
65.9bhp/L 49.2kW/L 66.9PS/L
37.8ft/sec 11.5m/sec
Petrol 4-stroke piston
3791cc 231.3cu in turbocharged
Vee 6 fuel injection
Compression ratio: 8.0:1
Bore: 96.5mm 3.8in
Stroke: 86.4mm 3.4in
Valve type/No: Overhead 12
Transmission: Automatic
No. of forward speeds: 4
Wheels driven: Rear
Springs F/R: Coil/Coil
Brake system: PA
Brakes F/R: Disc/Disc
Steering: Recirculating ball PA
Wheelbase: 256.5cm 101.0in
Track F: 154.2cm 60.7in
Track R: 156.5cm 61.6in
Length: 483.4cm 190.3in
Width: 183.9cm 72.4in
Height: 126.5cm 49.8in
Kerb weight: 1543.6kg 3400.0lb
Fuel: 58.7L 12.9gal 15.5galUS

3590 Pontiac
Firebird TransAm Turbo
1989 USA
150.0mph 241.4kmh
0-60mph 96.5kmh: 5.3secs
0-1/4 mile: 13.9secs
250.0bhp 186.4kW 253.5PS
@ 4000rpm
340.0lbft 460.7Nm @ 2800rpm
163.0bhp/ton 160.3bhp/tonne
65.9bhp/L 49.2kW/L 66.9PS/L
37.8ft/sec 11.5m/sec
16.8mpg 14.0mpgUS 16.8L/100km
Petrol 4-stroke piston
3791cc 231.3cu in turbocharged
Vee 6 fuel injection
Compression ratio: 8.0:1
Bore: 96.5mm 3.8in
Stroke: 86.4mm 3.4in
Valve type/No: Overhead 12
Transmission: Automatic
No. of forward speeds: 4
Wheels driven: Rear
Springs F/R: Coil/Coil
Brake system: PA
Brakes F/R: Disc/Disc
Steering: Recirculating ball PA
Wheelbase: 256.5cm 101.0in
Track F: 154.2cm 60.7in
Track R: 156.5cm 61.6in
Length: 483.4cm 190.3in
Width: 183.9cm 72.4in
Height: 126.5cm 49.8in
Kerb weight: 1559.5kg 3435.0lb
Fuel: 58.7L 12.9gal 15.5galUS

3591 Pontiac
Grand Am Turbo
1989 USA
120.0mph 193.1kmh
0-50mph 80.5kmh: 5.7secs
0-60mph 96.5kmh: 7.9secs
0-1/4 mile: 16.1secs
165.0bhp 123.0kW 167.3PS
@ 5600rpm
175.0lbft 237.1Nm @ 4000rpm
123.4bhp/ton 121.3bhp/tonne
82.6bhp/L 61.6kW/L 83.7PS/L
52.7ft/sec 16.0m/sec
Petrol 4-stroke piston
1998cc 121.9cu in turbocharged
In-line 4 fuel injection
Compression ratio: 8.0:1
Bore: 86.0mm 3.4in
Stroke: 86.0mm 3.4in
Valve type/No: Overhead 8
Transmission: Automatic
No. of forward speeds: 3
Wheels driven: Front
Springs F/R: Coil/Coil
Brake system: PA
Brakes F/R: Disc/Drum
Steering: Rack & pinion PA
Wheelbase: 262.6cm 103.4in
Track F: 141.2cm 55.6in
Track R: 140.2cm 55.2in
Length: 457.5cm 180.1in
Width: 168.9cm 66.5in
Height: 133.4cm 52.5in
Kerb weight: 1359.7kg 2995.0lb
Fuel: 51.5L 11.3gal 13.6galUS

3592 Pontiac
Grand Prix McLaren Turbo
1989 USA
128.0mph 206.0kmh
0-50mph 80.5kmh: 5.2secs
0-60mph 96.5kmh: 7.0secs
0-1/4 mile: 15.3secs
205.0bhp 152.9kW 207.8PS
@ 5200rpm
225.0lbft 304.9Nm @ 2400rpm
133.1bhp/ton 130.9bhp/tonne
65.5bhp/L 48.9kW/L 66.4PS/L
47.8ft/sec 14.6m/sec
25.2mpg 21.0mpgUS 11.2L/100km
Petrol 4-stroke piston
3128cc 190.8cu in turbocharged
Vee 6 fuel injection
Compression ratio: 8.7:1
Bore: 88.9mm 3.5in
Stroke: 84.0mm 3.3in
Valve type/No: Overhead 12
Transmission: Automatic
No. of forward speeds: 4
Wheels driven: Front
Springs F/R: Coil/Coil
Brake system: PA ABS
Brakes F/R: Disc/Disc
Steering: Rack & pinion PA
Wheelbase: 273.1cm 107.5in
Track F: 151.1cm 59.5in
Track R: 147.3cm 58.0in
Length: 492.5cm 193.9in
Width: 182.6cm 71.9in
Height: 134.1cm 52.8in
Kerb weight: 1566.3kg 3450.0lb
Fuel: 60.6L 13.3gal 16.0galUS

3593 Pontiac
Firebird Formula
1990 USA
135.0mph 217.2kmh
0-50mph 80.5kmh: 5.0secs
0-60mph 96.5kmh: 6.6secs
0-1/4 mile: 15.2secs
225.0bhp 167.8kW 228.1PS
@ 4400rpm
300.0lbft 406.5Nm @ 3200rpm
151.8bhp/ton 149.3bhp/tonne
44.9bhp/L 33.5kW/L 45.5PS/L
42.5ft/sec 13.0m/sec
Petrol 4-stroke piston
5012cc 305.8cu in
Vee 8 fuel injection
Compression ratio: 9.3:1
Bore: 95.0mm 3.7in
Stroke: 88.4mm 3.5in
Valve type/No: Overhead 16
Transmission: Manual
No. of forward speeds: 5
Wheels driven: Rear
Springs F/R: Coil/Coil
Brake system: PA
Brakes F/R: Disc/Disc
Steering: Recirculating ball PA
Wheelbase: 256.5cm 101.0in
Track F: 154.2cm 60.7in
Track R: 156.5cm 61.6in
Length: 486.7cm 191.6in
Width: 182.9cm 72.0in
Height: 126.2cm 49.7in
Kerb weight: 1507.3kg 3320.0lb
Fuel: 58.7L 12.9gal 15.5galUS

3594 Pontiac
Firebird TransAm GTA
1990 USA
136.0mph 218.8kmh
0-50mph 80.5kmh: 5.3secs
0-60mph 96.5kmh: 7.1secs
0-1/4 mile: 15.5secs
235.0bhp 175.2kW 238.3PS
@ 4400rpm
340.0lbft 460.7Nm @ 3200rpm
149.1bhp/ton 146.6bhp/tonne
41.0bhp/L 30.6kW/L 41.5PS/L
42.5ft/sec 13.0m/sec
21.3mpg 17.7mpgUS 13.3L/100km
Petrol 4-stroke piston
5735cc 349.9cu in
Vee 8 fuel injection
Compression ratio: 9.3:1
Bore: 101.6mm 4.0in
Stroke: 88.4mm 3.5in
Valve type/No: Overhead 16
Transmission: Automatic
No. of forward speeds: 4
Wheels driven: Rear
Springs F/R: Coil/Coil
Brake system: PA
Brakes F/R: Disc/Disc
Steering: Recirculating ball PA
Wheelbase: 256.5cm 101.0in
Track F: 154.2cm 60.7in
Track R: 156.5cm 61.6in
Length: 486.7cm 191.6in
Width: 182.9cm 72.0in
Height: 126.2cm 49.7in
Kerb weight: 1602.6kg 3530.0lb
Fuel: 58.7L 12.9gal 15.5galUS

3595 Pontiac
Grand Prix STE Turbo
1990 USA
124.0mph 199.5kmh
0-50mph 80.5kmh: 5.6secs
0-60mph 96.5kmh: 7.7secs
0-1/4 mile: 15.8secs
205.0bhp 152.9kW 207.8PS
@ 4800rpm
220.0lbft 298.1Nm @ 3200rpm
132.3bhp/ton 130.1bhp/tonne
65.5bhp/L 48.9kW/L 66.4PS/L
44.1ft/sec 13.4m/sec
24.5mpg 20.4mpgUS 11.5L/100km
Petrol 4-stroke piston
3128cc 190.8cu in turbocharged
Vee 6 fuel injection
Compression ratio: 8.8:1
Bore: 88.9mm 3.5in
Stroke: 84.0mm 3.3in
Valve type/No: Overhead 12
Transmission: Automatic
No. of forward speeds: 4
Wheels driven: Front
Springs F/R: Coil/Leaf
Brake system: PA ABS
Brakes F/R: Disc/Disc
Steering: Rack & pinion PA
Wheelbase: 273.1cm 107.5in
Track F: 151.1cm 59.5in
Track R: 147.3cm 58.0in
Length: 494.8cm 194.8in
Width: 180.1cm 70.9in
Height: 137.9cm 54.3in
Kerb weight: 1575.4kg 3470.0lb
Fuel: 60.6L 13.3gal 16.0galUS

3596 Pontiac
Firebird GTA
1991 USA
150.0mph 241.4kmh
0-50mph 80.5kmh: 5.1secs
0-60mph 96.5kmh: 6.6secs
0-1/4 mile: 15.2secs
240.0bhp 179.0kW 243.3PS
@ 4400rpm
340.0lbft 460.7Nm @ 3200rpm
155.6bhp/ton 153.0bhp/tonne
41.9bhp/L 31.2kW/L 42.4PS/L
42.5ft/sec 13.0m/sec
21.3mpg 17.7mpgUS 13.3L/100km
Petrol 4-stroke piston
5733cc 349.8cu in
Vee 8 fuel injection
Compression ratio: 9.3:1
Bore: 101.6mm 4.0in
Stroke: 88.4mm 3.5in
Valve type/No: Overhead 16
Transmission: Automatic
No. of forward speeds: 4

Wheels driven: Rear
Springs F/R: Coil/Coil
Brake system: PA
Brakes F/R: Disc/Disc
Steering: Recirculating ball PA
Wheelbase: 256.5cm 101.0in
Track F: 154.2cm 60.7in
Track R: 156.5cm 61.6in
Length: 495.6cm 195.1in
Width: 182.9cm 72.0in
Height: 125.7cm 49.5in
Kerb weight: 1568.6kg 3455.0lb
Fuel: 58.7L 12.9gal 15.5galUS

3597 Pontiac

Firebird TDM Technologies
1991 USA
192.0mph 308.9kmh
0-60mph 96.5kmh: 4.1secs
0-1/4 mile: 12.7secs
685.0bhp 510.8kW 694.5PS
@ 4500rpm
785.0lbft 1063.7Nm @ 4500rpm
426.2bhp/ton 419.1bhp/tonne
119.5bhp/L 89.1kW/L 121.1PS/L
43.5ft/sec 13.3m/sec
Petrol 4-stroke piston
5733cc 349.8cu in turbocharged
Vee 8
Compression ratio: 9.0:1
Bore: 101.6mm 4.0in
Stroke: 88.4mm 3.5in
Valve type/No: Overhead 16
Transmission: Manual
No. of forward speeds: 6
Wheels driven: Rear
Springs F/R: Coil/Leaf
Brakes F/R: Disc/Disc
Steering: Recirculating ball PA
Wheelbase: 256.5cm 101.0in
Track F: 154.2cm 60.7in
Track R: 157.2cm 61.9in
Length: 486.7cm 191.6in
Width: 182.9cm 72.0in
Height: 126.2cm 49.7in
Kerb weight: 1634.4kg 3600.0lb

3598 Pontiac

Firebird TransAm Convertible
1991 USA
130.0mph 209.2kmh
0-50mph 80.5kmh: 6.0secs
0-60mph 96.5kmh: 7.8secs
0-1/4 mile: 16.2secs
205.0bhp 152.9kW 207.8PS
@ 4200rpm
285.0lbft 386.2Nm @ 3200rpm
133.5bhp/ton 131.3bhp/tonne
41.0bhp/L 30.6kW/L 41.5PS/L
40.6ft/sec 12.4m/sec
22.8mpg 19.0mpgUS 12.4L/100km
Petrol 4-stroke piston
5002cc 305.2cu in
Vee 8 fuel injection
Compression ratio: 9.3:1
Bore: 94.9mm 3.7in
Stroke: 88.4mm 3.5in
Valve type/No: Overhead 16
Transmission: Manual
No. of forward speeds: 5
Wheels driven: Rear
Springs F/R: Coil/Coil
Brake system: PA
Brakes F/R: Disc/Drum
Steering: Recirculating ball PA
Wheelbase: 256.5cm 101.0in
Track F: 154.2cm 60.7in
Track R: 156.5cm 61.6in
Length: 495.6cm 195.1in
Width: 183.9cm 72.4in
Height: 126.2cm 49.7in
Kerb weight: 1561.8kg 3440.0lb
Fuel: 58.7L 12.9gal 15.5galUS

3599 Pontiac

Grand Prix GTP
1991 USA
125.0mph 201.1kmh
0-60mph 96.5kmh: 8.4secs
0-1/4 mile: 16.3secs
200.0bhp 149.1kW 202.8PS
@ 5000rpm
215.0lbft 291.3Nm @ 4000rpm
129.1bhp/ton 126.9bhp/tonne
59.7bhp/L 44.5kW/L 60.5PS/L
46.0ft/sec 14.0m/sec
25.2mpg 21.0mpgUS 11.2L/100km
Petrol 4-stroke piston
3352cc 204.5cu in
Vee 6 fuel injection
Compression ratio: 9.3:1
Bore: 92.0mm 3.6in
Stroke: 84.0mm 3.3in
Valve type/No: Overhead 24
Transmission: Automatic
No. of forward speeds: 4
Wheels driven: Front
Springs F/R: Coil/Leaf
Brake system: PA ABS
Brakes F/R: Disc/Disc
Steering: Rack & pinion PA
Wheelbase: 273.1cm 107.5in
Track F: 151.1cm 59.5in
Track R: 147.3cm 58.0in
Length: 494.8cm 194.8in
Width: 180.1cm 70.9in
Height: 137.9cm 54.3in
Kerb weight: 1575.4kg 3470.0lb
Fuel: 62.4L 13.7gal 16.5galUS

3600 Pontiac

Bonneville SSEi
1992 USA
128.0mph 206.0kmh
0-50mph 80.5kmh: 6.3secs
0-60mph 96.5kmh: 9.0secs
0-1/4 mile: 16.7secs
205.0bhp 152.9kW 207.8PS
@ 4600rpm
260.0lbft 352.3Nm @ 2800rpm
127.7bhp/ton 125.6bhp/tonne
54.1bhp/L 40.3kW/L 54.8PS/L
43.4ft/sec 13.2m/sec
24.0mpg 20.0mpgUS 11.8L/100km
Petrol 4-stroke piston
3791cc 231.3cu in supercharged
Vee 6 fuel injection
Compression ratio: 8.5:1
Bore: 96.5mm 3.8in
Stroke: 86.4mm 3.4in
Valve type/No: Overhead 12
Transmission: Automatic
No. of forward speeds: 4
Wheels driven: Front
Springs F/R: Coil/Coil
Brake system: PA ABS
Brakes F/R: Disc/Drum
Steering: Rack & pinion PA
Wheelbase: 281.4cm 110.8in
Track F: 153.7cm 60.5in
Track R: 152.9cm 60.2in
Length: 511.0cm 201.2in
Width: 186.9cm 73.6in
Height: 141.0cm 55.5in
Ground clearance: 13.5cm 5.3in
Kerb weight: 1632.1kg 3595.0lb
Fuel: 68.1L 15.0gal 18.0galUS

3601 Porsche

356 4
1952 Germany
103.0mph 165.7kmh
0-50mph 80.5kmh: 8.7secs
0-60mph 96.5kmh: 13.8secs
0-1/4 mile: 18.4secs
65.0bhp 48.5kW 65.9PS
@ 4800rpm
78.7bhp/ton 77.4bhp/tonne
43.7bhp/L 32.6kW/L 44.3PS/L
38.8ft/sec 11.8m/sec
20.7mph 33.3kmh/1000rpm
Petrol 4-stroke piston
1488cc 90.8cu in
Flat 4
Compression ratio: 7.2:1
Bore: 80.0mm 3.1in
Stroke: 74.0mm 2.9in
Valve type/No: Overhead 8
Transmission: Manual
No. of forward speeds: 4
Wheels driven: Rear
Wheelbase: 210.8cm 83.0in
Track F: 129.0cm 50.8in
Track R: 125.2cm 49.3in
Length: 387.4cm 152.5in
Width: 160.8cm 63.3in
Height: 129.5cm 51.0in
Ground clearance: 17.8cm 7.0in
Kerb weight: 839.9kg 1850.0lb
Fuel: 54.1L 11.9gal 14.3galUS

3602 Porsche

356
1954 Germany
91.0mph 146.4kmh
0-50mph 80.5kmh: 10.6secs
0-60mph 96.5kmh: 17.0secs
0-1/4 mile: 20.1secs
55.0bhp 41.0kW 55.8PS
@ 4000rpm
78.0lbft 105.7Nm @ 3200rpm
68.8bhp/ton 67.6bhp/tonne
37.0bhp/L 27.6kW/L 37.5PS/L
32.3ft/sec 9.9m/sec
23.0mph 37.0kmh/1000rpm
28.0mpg 23.3mpgUS 10.1L/100km
Petrol 4-stroke piston
1488cc 90.8cu in
Flat 4
Compression ratio: 7.0:1
Bore: 80.0mm 3.1in
Stroke: 74.0mm 2.9in
Valve type/No: Overhead 8
Transmission: Manual
No. of forward speeds: 4
Wheels driven: Rear
Springs F/R: Torsion bar/Torsion bar
Brakes F/R: Drum/Drum
Wheelbase: 210.8cm 83.0in
Track F: 128.8cm 50.7in
Track R: 125.0cm 49.2in
Length: 384.8cm 151.5in
Width: 166.1cm 65.4in
Height: 130.0cm 51.2in
Ground clearance: 15.7cm 6.2in
Kerb weight: 813.6kg 1792.0lb
Fuel: 54.6L 12.0gal 14.4galUS

3603 Porsche

Super Coupe
1954 Germany
107.6mph 173.1kmh
0-50mph 80.5kmh: 8.7secs
0-60mph 96.5kmh: 12.4secs
0-1/4 mile: 18.9secs
70.0bhp 52.2kW 71.0PS
@ 5000rpm
79.0lbft 107.0Nm @ 3600rpm
84.3bhp/ton 82.9bhp/tonne
47.0bhp/L 35.1kW/L 47.7PS/L
40.4ft/sec 12.3m/sec
21.1mph 33.9kmh/1000rpm
Petrol 4-stroke piston
1488cc 90.8cu in
Flat 4
Compression ratio: 8.2:1
Bore: 80.0mm 3.1in
Stroke: 73.9mm 2.9in
Valve type/No: Overhead 8
Transmission: Manual
No. of forward speeds: 4
Wheels driven: Rear
Wheelbase: 210.8cm 83.0in
Track F: 129.0cm 50.8in
Track R: 125.2cm 49.3in
Kerb weight: 844.4kg 1860.0lb

3604 Porsche

1500 S Speedster
1955 Germany
100.5mph 161.7kmh
0-50mph 80.5kmh: 7.4secs
0-60mph 96.5kmh: 10.3secs
0-1/4 mile: 17.4secs
84.0bhp 62.6kW 85.2PS
@ 5000rpm
79.0lbft 107.0Nm @ 3600rpm
105.1bhp/ton 103.4bhp/tonne
56.4bhp/L 42.1kW/L 57.2PS/L
40.4ft/sec 12.3m/sec
19.2mph 30.9kmh/1000rpm
Petrol 4-stroke piston
1488cc 90.8cu in
Flat 4
Compression ratio: 8.2:1
Bore: 80.0mm 3.1in
Stroke: 73.9mm 2.9in
Valve type/No: Overhead 8
Transmission: Manual
No. of forward speeds: 4
Wheels driven: Rear
Wheelbase: 210.1cm 82.7in
Track F: 129.0cm 50.8in
Track R: 125.0cm 49.2in
Kerb weight: 812.7kg 1790.0lb

3605 Porsche

1600
1956 Germany
102.0mph 164.1kmh
0-50mph 80.5kmh: 10.6secs
0-60mph 96.5kmh: 15.3secs
0-1/4 mile: 19.5secs
70.0bhp 52.2kW 71.0PS
@ 4500rpm
81.2lbft 110.0Nm @ 2800rpm
86.2bhp/ton 84.8bhp/tonne
44.2bhp/L 33.0kW/L 44.9PS/L
36.4ft/sec 11.1m/sec
20.0mph 32.2kmh/1000rpm
31.0mpg 25.8mpgUS 9.1L/100km
Petrol 4-stroke piston
1582cc 96.5cu in
Flat 4
Compression ratio: 7.5:1
Bore: 82.5mm 3.2in
Stroke: 74.0mm 2.9in
Valve type/No: Overhead 8
Transmission: Manual
No. of forward speeds: 4
Wheels driven: Rear
Springs F/R: Torsion bar/Torsion bar
Brakes F/R: Drum/Drum
Wheelbase: 210.8cm 83.0in
Track F: 130.6cm 51.4in
Track R: 127.3cm 50.1in
Length: 394.5cm 155.3in
Width: 166.6cm 65.6in
Height: 130.8cm 51.5in
Ground clearance: 16.0cm 6.3in
Kerb weight: 825.8kg 1819.0lb
Fuel: 52.3L 11.5gal 13.8galUS

3606 Porsche

Carrera Coupe
1956 Germany
120.0mph 193.1kmh
0-50mph 80.5kmh: 9.0secs
0-60mph 96.5kmh: 11.5secs
0-1/4 mile: 17.7secs
110.0bhp 82.0kW 111.5PS
@ 6200rpm
87.5lbft 118.6Nm @ 5200rpm
121.1bhp/ton 119.1bhp/tonne
73.4bhp/L 54.8kW/L 74.4PS/L
44.8ft/sec 13.6m/sec
Petrol 4-stroke piston
1498cc 91.4cu in
Flat 4
Compression ratio: 8.7:1
Bore: 85.1mm 3.3in
Stroke: 66.0mm 2.6in
Valve type/No: Overhead 8
Transmission: Manual
No. of forward speeds: 4
Wheels driven: Rear
Wheelbase: 210.1cm 82.7in
Track F: 130.6cm 51.4in
Track R: 127.3cm 50.1in
Kerb weight: 923.9kg 2035.0lb

3607 Porsche

Continental Coupe
1956 Germany
98.1mph 157.8kmh
0-50mph 80.5kmh: 11.6secs
0-60mph 96.5kmh: 15.0secs
0-1/4 mile: 19.8secs
66.0bhp 49.2kW 66.9PS
@ 4400rpm
78.0lbft 105.7Nm @ 3200rpm
77.0bhp/ton 75.7bhp/tonne
44.3bhp/L 33.1kW/L 45.0PS/L
35.6ft/sec 10.8m/sec
20.9mph 33.6kmh/1000rpm
42.3mpg 35.2mpgUS 6.7L/100km
Petrol 4-stroke piston
1488cc 90.8cu in
Flat 4
Compression ratio: 7.0:1
Bore: 80.0mm 3.1in
Stroke: 73.9mm 2.9in
Valve type/No: Overhead 8
Transmission: Manual
No. of forward speeds: 4
Wheels driven: Rear
Wheelbase: 210.1cm 82.7in
Track F: 129.0cm 50.8in
Track R: 125.0cm 49.2in
Kerb weight: 871.7kg 1920.0lb

3608 Porsche
Continental Speedster
1956 Germany
95.4mph 153.5kmh
0-50mph 80.5kmh: 9.3secs
0-60mph 96.5kmh: 13.9secs
0-1/4 mile: 19.2secs
66.0bhp 49.2kW 66.9PS
@ 4400rpm
78.0lbft 105.7Nm @ 3200rpm
84.5bhp/ton 83.1bhp/tonne
44.3bhp/L 33.1kW/L 45.0PS/L
35.6ft/sec 10.8m/sec
19.2mph 30.9kmh/1000rpm
38.0mpg 31.6mpgUS 7.4L/100km
Petrol 4-stroke piston
1488cc 90.8cu in
Flat 4
Compression ratio: 7.0:1
Bore: 80.0mm 3.1in
Stroke: 73.9mm 2.9in
Valve type/No: Overhead 8
Transmission: Manual
No. of forward speeds: 4
Wheels driven: Rear
Wheelbase: 210.1cm 82.7in
Track F: 129.0cm 50.8in
Track R: 125.0cm 49.2in
Kerb weight: 794.5kg 1750.0lb

3609 Porsche
1600 Coupe
1957 Germany
101.4mph 163.2kmh
0-50mph 80.5kmh: 10.9secs
0-60mph 96.5kmh: 14.4secs
0-1/4 mile: 19.3secs
70.0bhp 52.2kW 71.0PS
@ 4500rpm
81.0lbft 109.8Nm @ 2800rpm
81.2bhp/ton 79.9bhp/tonne
44.2bhp/L 33.0kW/L 44.9PS/L
36.4ft/sec 11.1m/sec
Petrol 4-stroke piston
1582cc 96.5cu in
Flat 4
Compression ratio: 7.5:1
Bore: 82.6mm 3.2in
Stroke: 73.9mm 2.9in
Valve type/No: Overhead 8
Transmission: Manual
No. of forward speeds: 4
Wheels driven: Rear
Wheelbase: 210.1cm 82.7in
Track F: 130.6cm 51.4in
Track R: 127.3cm 50.1in
Kerb weight: 876.2kg 1930.0lb

3610 Porsche
550 Spyder
1957 Germany
121.6mph 195.7kmh
0-50mph 80.5kmh: 6.2secs
0-60mph 96.5kmh: 8.2secs
0-1/4 mile: 16.1secs
137.0bhp 102.2kW 138.9PS
@ 6200rpm
95.5lbft 129.4Nm @ 5500rpm
203.2bhp/ton 199.8bhp/tonne
91.5bhp/L 68.2kW/L 92.7PS/L
44.8ft/sec 13.6m/sec
Petrol 4-stroke piston
1498cc 91.4cu in
Flat 4
Compression ratio: 9.5:1
Bore: 85.0mm 3.3in
Stroke: 66.0mm 2.6in
Valve type/No: Overhead 8
Transmission: Manual
No. of forward speeds: 4
Wheels driven: Rear
Wheelbase: 210.1cm 82.7in
Track F: 129.0cm 50.8in
Track R: 125.0cm 49.2in
Kerb weight: 685.5kg 1510.0lb

3611 Porsche
1600
1958 Germany
103.0mph 165.7kmh
0-50mph 80.5kmh: 9.5secs
0-60mph 96.5kmh: 14.1secs
0-1/4 mile: 19.1secs
70.0bhp 52.2kW 71.0PS
@ 5500rpm
82.2lbft 111.4Nm @ 2800rpm
83.3bhp/ton 81.9bhp/tonne
44.2bhp/L 33.0kW/L 44.9PS/L
44.5ft/sec 13.6m/sec
22.0mph 35.4kmh/1000rpm
32.1mpg 26.7mpgUS 8.8L/100km
Petrol 4-stroke piston
1582cc 96.5cu in
Flat 4
Compression ratio: 7.5:1
Bore: 82.5mm 3.2in
Stroke: 74.0mm 2.9in
Valve type/No: Overhead 8
Transmission: Manual
No. of forward speeds: 4
Wheels driven: Rear
Springs F/R: Torsion bar/Torsion bar
Brakes F/R: Drum/Drum
Wheelbase: 210.1cm 82.7in
Track F: 130.8cm 51.5in
Track R: 127.0cm 50.0in
Length: 395.7cm 155.8in
Width: 166.4cm 65.5in
Height: 130.8cm 51.5in
Ground clearance: 16.5cm 6.5in
Kerb weight: 854.9kg 1883.0lb
Fuel: 52.3L 11.5gal 13.8galUS

3612 Porsche
1600 Super Speedster
1958 Germany
105.2mph 169.3kmh
0-50mph 80.5kmh: 7.2secs
0-60mph 96.5kmh: 10.5secs
0-1/4 mile: 17.1secs
88.0bhp 65.6kW 89.2PS
@ 5000rpm
86.0lbft 116.5Nm @ 3700rpm
110.1bhp/ton 108.3bhp/tonne
55.6bhp/L 41.5kW/L 56.4PS/L
40.4ft/sec 12.3m/sec
Petrol 4-stroke piston
1582cc 96.5cu in
Flat 4
Compression ratio: 8.5:1
Bore: 82.6mm 3.2in
Stroke: 73.9mm 2.9in
Valve type/No: Overhead 8
Transmission: Manual
No. of forward speeds: 4
Wheels driven: Rear
Wheelbase: 210.1cm 82.7in
Track F: 130.6cm 51.4in
Track R: 127.3cm 50.1in
Kerb weight: 812.7kg 1790.0lb

3613 Porsche
RSK
1958 Germany
155.0mph 249.4kmh
0-60mph 96.5kmh: 5.0secs
0-1/4 mile: 14.0secs
170.0bhp 126.8kW 172.4PS
@ 8000rpm
120.0lbft 162.6Nm @ 6300rpm
287.4bhp/ton 282.6bhp/tonne
101.3bhp/L 75.5kW/L 102.7PS/L
57.8ft/sec 17.6m/sec
Petrol 4-stroke piston
1678cc 102.4cu in
Flat 4 2 Carburettor
Bore: 90.0mm 3.5in
Stroke: 66.0mm 2.6in
Valve type/No: Overhead 16
Transmission: Manual
No. of forward speeds: 5
Wheels driven: Rear
Springs F/R: Torsion bar/Torsion bar
Brakes F/R: Drum/Drum
Steering: Worm & peg
Wheelbase: 210.1cm 82.7in
Track F: 129.0cm 50.8in
Track R: 125.0cm 49.2in
Length: 359.9cm 141.7in
Width: 150.9cm 59.4in
Height: 87.9cm 34.6in
Kerb weight: 601.5kg 1325.0lb

3614 Porsche
1600 Convertible D
1959 Germany
98.0mph 157.7kmh
0-50mph 80.5kmh: 10.6secs
0-60mph 96.5kmh: 14.0secs
0-1/4 mile: 19.4secs
70.0bhp 52.2kW 71.0PS
@ 4500rpm
86.2lbft 116.8Nm @ 2800rpm
82.5bhp/ton 81.1bhp/tonne
44.2bhp/L 33.0kW/L 44.9PS/L
36.4ft/sec 11.1m/sec
19.1mph 30.7kmh/1000rpm
Petrol 4-stroke piston
1582cc 96.5cu in
Flat 4
Compression ratio: 7.5:1
Bore: 82.6mm 3.2in
Stroke: 73.9mm 2.9in
Valve type/No: Overhead 8
Transmission: Manual
No. of forward speeds: 4
Wheels driven: Rear
Wheelbase: 210.1cm 82.7in
Track F: 130.6cm 51.4in
Track R: 127.3cm 50.1in
Length: 396.2cm 156.0in
Width: 166.6cm 65.6in
Height: 130.8cm 51.5in
Kerb weight: 862.6kg 1900.0lb

3615 Porsche
Super 75
1960 Germany
110.0mph 177.0kmh
0-50mph 80.5kmh: 7.8secs
0-60mph 96.5kmh: 11.4secs
0-1/4 mile: 18.1secs
75.0bhp 55.9kW 76.0PS
@ 5000rpm
88.0lbft 119.2Nm @ 3700rpm
87.0bhp/ton 85.5bhp/tonne
47.4bhp/L 35.3kW/L 48.1PS/L
40.4ft/sec 12.3m/sec
20.0mph 32.2kmh/1000rpm
29.2mpg 24.3mpgUS 9.7L/100km
Petrol 4-stroke piston
1582cc 96.5cu in
Flat 4
Compression ratio: 8.5:1
Bore: 82.5mm 3.2in
Stroke: 74.0mm 2.9in
Valve type/No: Overhead 8
Transmission: Manual
No. of forward speeds: 4
Wheels driven: Rear
Springs F/R: Torsion bar/Torsion bar
Brakes F/R: Drum/Drum
Wheelbase: 210.1cm 82.7in
Track F: 130.6cm 51.4in
Track R: 127.5cm 50.2in
Length: 400.6cm 157.7in
Width: 166.6cm 65.6in
Height: 133.1cm 52.4in
Ground clearance: 15.0cm 5.9in
Kerb weight: 877.1kg 1932.0lb
Fuel: 52.3L 11.5gal 13.8galUS

3616 Porsche
Super 90 Cabriolet
1960 Germany
117.0mph 188.3kmh
0-50mph 80.5kmh: 9.0secs
0-60mph 96.5kmh: 12.5secs
0-1/4 mile: 17.7secs
102.0bhp 76.1kW 103.4PS
@ 5500rpm
89.0lbft 120.6Nm @ 4300rpm
118.1bhp/ton 116.1bhp/tonne
64.5bhp/L 48.1kW/L 65.4PS/L
44.5ft/sec 13.5m/sec
19.9mph 32.0kmh/1000rpm
Petrol 4-stroke piston
1582cc 96.5cu in
Flat 4 1 Carburettor
Compression ratio: 9.0:1
Bore: 82.6mm 3.2in
Stroke: 73.9mm 2.9in
Valve type/No: Overhead 8
Transmission: Manual
No. of forward speeds: 4
Wheels driven: Rear
Wheelbase: 210.1cm 82.7in
Track F: 130.6cm 51.4in
Track R: 127.3cm 50.1in
Length: 401.3cm 158.0in
Width: 166.4cm 65.5in
Height: 130.8cm 51.5in
Kerb weight: 878.5kg 1935.0lb

3617 Porsche
1600 N
1961 Germany
100.0mph 160.9kmh
0-50mph 80.5kmh: 10.8secs
0-60mph 96.5kmh: 14.4secs
0-1/4 mile: 19.4secs
70.0bhp 52.2kW 71.0PS
@ 4500rpm
81.0lbft 109.8Nm @ 2800rpm
79.2bhp/ton 77.9bhp/tonne
44.2bhp/L 33.0kW/L 44.9PS/L
36.4ft/sec 11.1m/sec
20.5mph 33.0kmh/1000rpm
Petrol 4-stroke piston
1582cc 96.5cu in
Flat 4 1 Carburettor
Compression ratio: 7.5:1
Bore: 82.6mm 3.2in
Stroke: 73.9mm 2.9in
Valve type/No: Overhead 8
Transmission: Manual
No. of forward speeds: 4
Wheels driven: Rear
Wheelbase: 210.1cm 82.7in
Track F: 130.6cm 51.4in
Track R: 127.3cm 50.1in
Length: 401.3cm 158.0in
Width: 166.6cm 65.6in
Height: 133.1cm 52.4in
Ground clearance: 15.0cm 5.9in
Kerb weight: 898.9kg 1980.0lb

3618 Porsche
Carrera 2-litre
1962 Germany
122.7mph 197.4kmh
0-50mph 80.5kmh: 6.9secs
0-60mph 96.5kmh: 9.2secs
0-1/4 mile: 16.9secs
152.0bhp 113.3kW 154.1PS
@ 6200rpm
131.0lbft 177.5Nm @ 4600rpm
153.4bhp/ton 150.8bhp/tonne
77.3bhp/L 57.7kW/L 78.4PS/L
50.1ft/sec 15.3m/sec
19.6mph 31.5kmh/1000rpm
Petrol 4-stroke piston
1966cc 119.9cu in
Flat 4 2 Carburettor
Compression ratio: 9.5:1
Bore: 91.9mm 3.6in
Stroke: 73.9mm 2.9in
Valve type/No: Overhead 8
Transmission: Manual
No. of forward speeds: 4
Wheels driven: Rear
Wheelbase: 210.1cm 82.7in
Track F: 130.6cm 51.4in
Track R: 127.3cm 50.1in
Length: 401.3cm 158.0in
Width: 167.1cm 65.8in
Height: 132.8cm 52.3in
Ground clearance: 15.2cm 6.0in
Kerb weight: 1007.9kg 2220.0lb

3619 Porsche
Super 90 Cabriolet
1962 Germany
112.5mph 181.0kmh
0-50mph 80.5kmh: 8.2secs
0-60mph 96.5kmh: 11.5secs
0-1/4 mile: 18.3secs
90.0bhp 67.1kW 91.2PS
@ 5500rpm
89.0lbft 120.6Nm @ 4300rpm
104.0bhp/ton 102.2bhp/tonne
56.9bhp/L 42.4kW/L 57.7PS/L
44.5ft/sec 13.6m/sec
19.8mph 31.9kmh/1000rpm
24.4mpg 20.3mpgUS 11.6L/100km
Petrol 4-stroke piston
1582cc 96.5cu in
Flat 4 2 Carburettor
Compression ratio: 9.0:1
Bore: 82.5mm 3.2in
Stroke: 74.0mm 2.9in
Valve type/No: Overhead 8
Transmission: Manual
No. of forward speeds: 4
Wheels driven: Rear
Springs F/R: Torsion bar/Torsion bar
Brakes F/R: Drum/Drum
Steering: Worm & peg
Wheelbase: 209.6cm 82.5in
Track F: 130.8cm 51.5in
Track R: 127.0cm 50.0in
Length: 401.3cm 158.0in
Width: 166.4cm 65.5in
Height: 133.4cm 52.5in

Ground clearance: 15.2cm 6.0in
Kerb weight: 880.3kg 1939.0lb
Fuel: 52.3L 11.5gal 13.8galUS

3620 Porsche

356 C
1964 Germany
100.0mph 160.9kmh
0-50mph 80.5kmh: 9.9secs
0-60mph 96.5kmh: 13.5secs
0-1/4 mile: 18.9secs
88.0bhp 65.6kW 89.2PS
@ 5200rpm
90.0lbft 122.0Nm @ 3600rpm
100.1bhp/ton 98.4bhp/tonne
55.6bhp/L 41.5kW/L 56.4PS/L
42.2ft/sec 12.9m/sec
19.2mph 30.9kmh/1000rpm
Petrol 4-stroke piston
1582cc 96.5cu in
Flat 4 2 Carburettor
Compression ratio: 8.5:1
Bore: 82.6mm 3.2in
Stroke: 74.2mm 2.9in
Valve type/No: Overhead 8
Transmission: Manual
No. of forward speeds: 4
Wheels driven: Rear
Springs F/R: Torsion bar/Coil
Brakes F/R: Disc/Disc
Steering: Worm & sector
Wheelbase: 210.8cm 83.0in
Track F: 130.6cm 51.4in
Track R: 127.0cm 50.0in
Length: 401.3cm 158.0in
Width: 167.1cm 65.8in
Height: 131.3cm 51.7in
Ground clearance: 15.0cm 5.9in
Kerb weight: 894.4kg 1970.0lb
Fuel: 47.3L 10.4gal 12.5galUS

3621 Porsche

904 Carrera GTS
1964 Germany
150.0mph 241.4kmh
0-50mph 80.5kmh: 5.2secs
0-60mph 96.5kmh: 6.4secs
0-1/4 mile: 14.5secs
198.0bhp 147.6kW 200.7PS
@ 7200rpm
144.5lbft 195.8Nm @ 5000rpm
328.5bhp/ton 323.0bhp/tonne
100.7bhp/L 75.1kW/L 102.1PS/L
58.2ft/sec 17.7m/sec
19.4mph 31.2kmh/1000rpm
Petrol 4-stroke piston
1966cc 119.9cu in
Flat 4 2 Carburettor
Compression ratio: 9.8:1
Bore: 91.9mm 3.6in
Stroke: 73.9mm 2.9in
Valve type/No: Overhead 8
Transmission: Manual
No. of forward speeds: 5
Wheels driven: Rear
Springs F/R: Coil/Coil
Brakes F/R: Disc/Disc
Steering: Rack & pinion
Wheelbase: 230.1cm 90.6in
Track F: 131.3cm 51.7in
Track R: 131.3cm 51.7in
Length: 408.9cm 161.0in
Width: 153.9cm 60.6in
Height: 106.4cm 41.9in
Ground clearance: 11.9cm 4.7in
Kerb weight: 612.9kg 1350.0lb
Fuel: 109.8L 24.1gal 29.0galUS

3622 Porsche

911
1965 Germany
132.0mph 212.4kmh
0-50mph 80.5kmh: 6.9secs
0-60mph 96.5kmh: 9.0secs
0-1/4 mile: 16.5secs
145.0bhp 108.1kW 147.0PS
@ 6100rpm
143.0lbft 193.8Nm @ 4200rpm
137.6bhp/ton 135.3bhp/tonne
72.8bhp/L 54.3kW/L 73.8PS/L
44.1ft/sec 13.4m/sec
20.5mph 33.0kmh/1000rpm
Petrol 4-stroke piston
1991cc 121.5cu in
Flat 6 2 Carburettor
Compression ratio: 9.0:1
Bore: 80.0mm 3.1in
Stroke: 66.0mm 2.6in
Valve type/No: Overhead 12
Transmission: Manual
No. of forward speeds: 5
Wheels driven: Rear
Springs F/R: Torsion bar/Torsion bar
Brakes F/R: Disc/Disc
Steering: Rack & pinion
Wheelbase: 221.0cm 87.0in
Track F: 137.4cm 54.1in
Track R: 131.6cm 51.8in
Length: 417.8cm 164.5in
Width: 161.5cm 63.6in
Height: 132.1cm 52.0in
Ground clearance: 15.2cm 6.0in
Kerb weight: 1071.4kg 2360.0lb
Fuel: 62.1L 13.6gal 16.4galUS

3623 Porsche

912
1965 Germany
121.0mph 194.7kmh
0-50mph 80.5kmh: 8.6secs
0-60mph 96.5kmh: 11.9secs
0-1/4 mile: 18.2secs
90.0bhp 67.1kW 91.2PS
@ 5800rpm
90.0lbft 122.0Nm @ 3500rpm
94.5bhp/ton 92.9bhp/tonne
56.9bhp/L 42.4kW/L 57.7PS/L
46.9ft/sec 14.3m/sec
19.8mph 31.9kmh/1000rpm
23.6mpg 19.7mpgUS 12.0L/100km
Petrol 4-stroke piston
1582cc 96.5cu in
Flat 4 2 Carburettor
Compression ratio: 9.3:1
Bore: 82.5mm 3.2in
Stroke: 74.0mm 2.9in
Valve type/No: Overhead 8
Transmission: Manual
No. of forward speeds: 5
Wheels driven: Rear
Springs F/R: Torsion bar/Torsion bar
Brakes F/R: Disc/Disc
Steering: Rack & pinion
Wheelbase: 221.0cm 87.0in
Track F: 133.4cm 52.5in
Track R: 131.3cm 51.7in
Length: 416.6cm 164.0in
Width: 161.3cm 63.5in
Height: 132.1cm 52.0in
Ground clearance: 15.2cm 6.0in
Kerb weight: 968.8kg 2134.0lb
Fuel: 61.9L 13.6gal 16.3galUS

3624 Porsche

911 S
1966 Germany
137.0mph 220.4kmh
0-50mph 80.5kmh: 6.1secs
0-60mph 96.5kmh: 8.0secs
0-1/4 mile: 15.8secs
0-1km: 28.7secs
160.0bhp 119.3kW 162.2PS
@ 6600rpm
132.0lbft 178.9Nm @ 5200rpm
152.8bhp/ton 150.3bhp/tonne
80.4bhp/L 59.9kW/L 81.5PS/L
47.7ft/sec 14.5m/sec
20.4mph 32.8kmh/1000rpm
15.7mpg 13.1mpgUS 18.0L/100km
Petrol 4-stroke piston
1991cc 121.5cu in
Flat 6 2 Carburettor
Compression ratio: 9.8:1
Bore: 80.0mm 3.1in
Stroke: 66.0mm 2.6in
Valve type/No: Overhead 12
Transmission: Manual
No. of forward speeds: 5
Wheels driven: Rear
Springs F/R: Torsion bar/Torsion bar
Brakes F/R: Disc/Disc
Steering: Rack & pinion
Wheelbase: 221.0cm 87.0in
Track F: 133.4cm 52.5in
Track R: 131.3cm 51.7in
Length: 416.6cm 164.0in
Width: 161.3cm 63.5in
Height: 132.1cm 52.0in
Ground clearance: 15.2cm 6.0in
Kerb weight: 1064.6kg 2345.0lb
Fuel: 62.3L 13.7gal 16.5galUS

3625 Porsche

912
1966 Germany
119.0mph 191.5kmh
0-50mph 80.5kmh: 8.4secs
0-60mph 96.5kmh: 11.6secs
0-1/4 mile: 18.1secs
102.0bhp 76.1kW 103.4PS
@ 5800rpm
90.0lbft 122.0Nm @ 3500rpm
108.8bhp/ton 107.0bhp/tonne
64.5bhp/L 48.1kW/L 65.4PS/L
46.9ft/sec 14.3m/sec
19.2mph 30.9kmh/1000rpm
Petrol 4-stroke piston
1582cc 96.5cu in
Flat 4 2 Carburettor
Compression ratio: 9.3:1
Bore: 82.5mm 3.2in
Stroke: 74.0mm 2.9in
Valve type/No: Overhead 8
Transmission: Manual
No. of forward speeds: 5
Wheels driven: Rear
Springs F/R: Torsion bar/Torsion bar
Brakes F/R: Disc/Disc
Steering: Rack & pinion
Wheelbase: 221.0cm 87.0in
Track F: 133.6cm 52.6in
Track R: 131.6cm 51.8in
Length: 416.3cm 163.9in
Width: 161.0cm 63.4in
Height: 132.1cm 52.0in
Ground clearance: 16.8cm 6.6in
Kerb weight: 953.4kg 2100.0lb
Fuel: 62.1L 13.6gal 16.4galUS

3626 Porsche

911 S
1967 Germany
141.0mph 226.9kmh
0-50mph 80.5kmh: 6.0secs
0-60mph 96.5kmh: 8.1secs
0-1/4 mile: 15.7secs
180.0bhp 134.2kW 182.5PS
@ 6600rpm
144.0lbft 195.1Nm @ 5200rpm
170.5bhp/ton 167.6bhp/tonne
90.4bhp/L 67.4kW/L 91.7PS/L
47.7ft/sec 14.5m/sec
20.5mph 33.0kmh/1000rpm
Petrol 4-stroke piston
1991cc 121.5cu in
Flat 6 2 Carburettor
Compression ratio: 9.8:1
Bore: 80.0mm 3.1in
Stroke: 66.0mm 2.6in
Valve type/No: Overhead 12
Transmission: Manual
No. of forward speeds: 5
Wheels driven: Rear
Springs F/R: Torsion bar/Torsion bar
Brakes F/R: Disc/Disc
Steering: Rack & pinion
Wheelbase: 221.0cm 87.0in
Track F: 135.6cm 53.4in
Track R: 132.6cm 52.2in
Length: 416.3cm 163.9in
Width: 161.0cm 63.4in
Height: 132.1cm 52.0in
Ground clearance: 15.0cm 5.9in
Kerb weight: 1073.7kg 2365.0lb
Fuel: 62.1L 13.6gal 16.4galUS

3627 Porsche

911 E Sportomatic
1968 Germany
134.0mph 215.6kmh
0-50mph 80.5kmh: 7.1secs
0-60mph 96.5kmh: 9.8secs
0-1/4 mile: 17.0secs
0-1km: 30.8secs
140.0bhp 104.4kW 141.9PS
@ 6500rpm
129.0lbft 174.8Nm @ 4500rpm
134.1bhp/ton 131.9bhp/tonne
70.3bhp/L 52.4kW/L 71.3PS/L
46.9ft/sec 14.3m/sec
20.1mph 32.3kmh/1000rpm
19.0mpg 15.8mpgUS 14.9L/100km
Petrol 4-stroke piston
1991cc 121.5cu in
Flat 6 fuel injection
Compression ratio: 9.1:1
Bore: 80.0mm 3.1in
Stroke: 66.0mm 2.6in
Valve type/No: Overhead 12
Transmission: Automatic
No. of forward speeds: 4
Wheels driven: Rear
Springs F/R: Torsion bar/Torsion bar
Brakes F/R: Disc/Disc
Steering: Rack & pinion
Wheelbase: 227.3cm 89.5in
Track F: 133.4cm 52.5in
Track R: 131.3cm 51.7in
Length: 416.6cm 164.0in
Width: 161.3cm 63.5in
Height: 132.1cm 52.0in
Ground clearance: 15.2cm 6.0in
Kerb weight: 1061.4kg 2338.0lb
Fuel: 62.3L 13.7gal 16.5galUS

3628 Porsche

911 Sportomatic
1968 Germany
117.0mph 188.3kmh
0-50mph 80.5kmh: 7.3secs
0-60mph 96.5kmh: 10.3secs
0-1/4 mile: 17.3secs
148.0bhp 110.4kW 150.0PS
@ 6100rpm
145.0lbft 196.5Nm @ 4200rpm
137.0bhp/ton 134.7bhp/tonne
74.3bhp/L 55.4kW/L 75.4PS/L
44.1ft/sec 13.4m/sec
18.1mph 29.1kmh/1000rpm
Petrol 4-stroke piston
1991cc 121.5cu in
Flat 6 2 Carburettor
Compression ratio: 9.0:1
Bore: 80.0mm 3.1in
Stroke: 66.0mm 2.6in
Valve type/No: Overhead 12
No. of forward speeds: 4
Wheels driven: Rear
Springs F/R: Torsion bar/Torsion bar
Brakes F/R: Disc/Disc
Steering: Rack & pinion
Wheelbase: 221.0cm 87.0in
Track F: 136.7cm 53.8in
Track R: 133.6cm 52.6in
Length: 416.3cm 163.9in
Width: 161.0cm 63.4in
Height: 132.1cm 52.0in
Ground clearance: 15.0cm 5.9in
Kerb weight: 1098.7kg 2420.0lb
Fuel: 62.1L 13.6gal 16.4galUS

3629 Porsche

911 E
1969 Germany
130.0mph 209.2kmh
0-50mph 80.5kmh: 6.5secs
0-60mph 96.5kmh: 8.4secs
0-1/4 mile: 16.0secs
160.0bhp 119.3kW 162.2PS
@ 6500rpm
145.0lbft 196.5Nm @ 4500rpm
151.8bhp/ton 149.3bhp/tonne
80.4bhp/L 59.9kW/L 81.5PS/L
46.9ft/sec 14.3m/sec
20.1mph 32.3kmh/1000rpm
22.1mpg 18.4mpgUS 12.8L/100km
Petrol 4-stroke piston
1991cc 121.5cu in
Flat 6
Compression ratio: 9.1:1
Bore: 80.0mm 3.1in
Stroke: 66.0mm 2.6in
Valve type/No: Overhead 12
Transmission: Manual
No. of forward speeds: 4
Wheels driven: Rear
Brakes F/R: Disc/Disc
Steering: Rack & pinion
Wheelbase: 226.6cm 89.2in
Track F: 136.1cm 53.6in
Track R: 134.1cm 52.8in
Length: 416.3cm 163.9in
Width: 161.0cm 63.4in
Height: 132.1cm 52.0in
Kerb weight: 1071.9kg 2361.0lb
Fuel: 62.1L 13.6gal 16.4galUS

3630 Porsche

911 T
1969 Germany
122.0mph 196.3kmh
0-60mph 96.5kmh: 8.8secs
0-1/4 mile: 16.2secs
125.0bhp 93.2kW 126.7PS
@ 5800rpm

131.0lbft 177.5Nm @ 4200rpm
116.9bhp/ton 115.0bhp/tonne
62.8bhp/L 46.8kW/L 63.6PS/L
41.9ft/sec 12.8m/sec
25.6mpg 21.3mpgUS 11.0L/100km
Petrol 4-stroke piston
1991cc 121.5cu in
Flat 6
Bore: 80.0mm 3.1in
Stroke: 66.0mm 2.6in
Valve type/No: Overhead 12
Transmission: Manual
No. of forward speeds: 4
Wheels driven: Rear
Brakes F/R: Disc/Disc
Wheelbase: 226.6cm 89.2in
Track F: 136.1cm 53.6in
Track R: 134.1cm 52.8in
Length: 416.3cm 163.9in
Width: 161.0cm 63.4in
Height: 132.1cm 52.0in
Kerb weight: 1087.3kg 2395.0lb

3631 Porsche

911 S 2.2-litre
1970 Germany
144.0mph 231.7kmh
0-50mph 80.5kmh: 5.6secs
0-60mph 96.5kmh: 7.3secs
0-1/4 mile: 14.9secs
200.0bhp 149.1kW 202.8PS
@ 6500rpm
164.0lbft 222.2Nm @ 5200rpm
187.4bhp/ton 184.3bhp/tonne
91.1bhp/L 67.9kW/L 92.4PS/L
46.9ft/sec 14.3m/sec
21.6mph 34.8kmh/1000rpm
18.0mpg 15.0mpgUS 15.7L/100km
Petrol 4-stroke piston
2195cc 133.9cu in
Flat 6 fuel injection
Compression ratio: 9.8:1
Bore: 84.0mm 3.3in
Stroke: 66.0mm 2.6in
Valve type/No: Overhead 12
Transmission: Manual
No. of forward speeds: 5
Wheels driven: Rear
Springs F/R: Torsion bar/Torsion bar
Brake system: PA
Brakes F/R: Disc/Disc
Steering: Rack & pinion
Wheelbase: 227.3cm 89.5in
Track F: 136.7cm 53.8in
Track R: 134.6cm 53.0in
Length: 416.3cm 163.9in
Width: 161.0cm 63.4in
Height: 132.1cm 52.0in
Ground clearance: 15.0cm 5.9in
Kerb weight: 1085.1kg 2390.0lb
Fuel: 62.1L 13.6gal 16.4galUS

3632 Porsche

911 T
1970 Germany
131.0mph 210.8kmh
0-50mph 80.5kmh: 6.0secs
0-60mph 96.5kmh: 8.1secs
0-1/4 mile: 16.0secs
0-1km: 29.3secs
125.0bhp 93.2kW 126.7PS
@ 5800rpm
130.0lbft 176.2Nm @ 4200rpm
120.7bhp/ton 118.7bhp/tonne
56.9bhp/L 42.5kW/L 57.7PS/L
41.9ft/sec 12.8m/sec
21.7mph 34.9kmh/1000rpm
17.9mpg 14.9mpgUS 15.8L/100km
Petrol 4-stroke piston
2195cc 133.9cu in
Flat 6 2 Carburettor
Compression ratio: 8.6:1
Bore: 84.0mm 3.3in
Stroke: 66.0mm 2.6in
Valve type/No: Overhead 12
Transmission: Manual
No. of forward speeds: 5
Wheels driven: Rear
Springs F/R: Torsion bar/Torsion bar
Brakes F/R: Disc/Disc
Steering: Rack & pinion
Wheelbase: 226.1cm 89.0in
Track F: 137.2cm 54.0in
Track R: 135.9cm 53.5in
Length: 416.6cm 164.0in
Width: 161.3cm 63.5in
Height: 132.1cm 52.0in
Ground clearance: 14.0cm 5.5in
Kerb weight: 1052.8kg 2319.0lb
Fuel: 61.9L 13.6gal 16.3galUS

3633 Porsche

914
1970 Germany
109.0mph 175.4kmh
0-50mph 80.5kmh: 10.0secs
0-60mph 96.5kmh: 13.9secs
0-1/4 mile: 19.2secs
85.0bhp 63.4kW 86.2PS
@ 4900rpm
103.0lbft 139.6Nm @ 2800rpm
91.3bhp/ton 89.8bhp/tonne
50.6bhp/L 37.7kW/L 51.3PS/L
35.4ft/sec 10.8m/sec
22.4mph 36.0kmh/1000rpm
30.6mpg 25.5mpgUS 9.2L/100km
Petrol 4-stroke piston
1679cc 102.4cu in
Flat 4 fuel injection
Compression ratio: 8.2:1
Bore: 90.0mm 3.5in
Stroke: 66.0mm 2.6in
Valve type/No: Overhead 8
Transmission: Manual
No. of forward speeds: 5
Wheels driven: Rear
Springs F/R: Torsion bar/Coil
Brakes F/R: Disc/Disc
Steering: Rack & pinion
Wheelbase: 244.9cm 96.4in
Track F: 133.6cm 52.6in
Track R: 137.4cm 54.1in
Length: 398.5cm 156.9in
Width: 165.1cm 65.0in
Height: 121.9cm 48.0in
Ground clearance: 11.9cm 4.7in
Kerb weight: 946.6kg 2085.0lb
Fuel: 62.1L 13.6gal 16.4galUS

3634 Porsche

914 6
1970 Germany
123.0mph 197.9kmh
0-50mph 80.5kmh: 6.3secs
0-60mph 96.5kmh: 8.7secs
0-1/4 mile: 16.3secs
125.0bhp 93.2kW 126.7PS
@ 5800rpm
131.0lbft 177.5Nm @ 4200rpm
127.6bhp/ton 125.4bhp/tonne
62.8bhp/L 46.8kW/L 63.6PS/L
41.9ft/sec 12.8m/sec
21.1mph 33.9kmh/1000rpm
25.6mpg 21.3mpgUS 11.0L/100km
Petrol 4-stroke piston
1991cc 121.5cu in
Flat 6 2 Carburettor
Compression ratio: 8.6:1
Bore: 80.0mm 3.1in
Stroke: 66.0mm 2.6in
Valve type/No: Overhead 12
Transmission: Manual
No. of forward speeds: 5
Wheels driven: Rear
Springs F/R: Torsion bar/Coil
Brakes F/R: Disc/Disc
Steering: Rack & pinion
Wheelbase: 244.9cm 96.4in
Track F: 136.1cm 53.6in
Track R: 138.2cm 54.4in
Length: 398.5cm 156.9in
Width: 165.1cm 65.0in
Height: 121.9cm 48.0in
Ground clearance: 13.0cm 5.1in
Kerb weight: 996.5kg 2195.0lb
Fuel: 62.1L 13.6gal 16.4galUS

3635 Porsche

911 E 2.4-litre
1971 Germany
140.0mph 225.3kmh
0-50mph 80.5kmh: 5.1secs
0-60mph 96.5kmh: 6.4secs
0-1/4 mile: 14.4secs
0-1km: 26.9secs
165.0bhp 123.0kW 167.3PS
@ 6200rpm
152.0lbft 206.0Nm @ 4500rpm
154.4bhp/ton 151.8bhp/tonne
70.5bhp/L 52.6kW/L 71.5PS/L
47.7ft/sec 14.5m/sec
22.2mph 35.7kmh/1000rpm
15.6mpg 13.0mpgUS 18.1L/100km
Petrol 4-stroke piston
2341cc 142.8cu in
Flat 6 fuel injection
Compression ratio: 8.0:1
Bore: 84.0mm 3.3in
Stroke: 70.4mm 2.8in
Valve type/No: Overhead 12
Transmission: Manual
No. of forward speeds: 5
Wheels driven: Rear
Springs F/R: Torsion bar/Torsion bar
Brakes F/R: Disc/Disc
Steering: Rack & pinion
Wheelbase: 226.1cm 89.0in
Track F: 137.2cm 54.0in
Track R: 135.9cm 53.5in
Length: 416.6cm 164.0in
Width: 161.3cm 63.5in
Height: 132.1cm 52.0in
Ground clearance: 14.0cm 5.5in
Kerb weight: 1086.9kg 2394.0lb
Fuel: 61.9L 13.6gal 16.3galUS

3636 Porsche

911 T Sportomatic
1971 Germany
122.0mph 196.3kmh
0-50mph 80.5kmh: 6.8secs
0-60mph 96.5kmh: 9.1secs
0-1/4 mile: 17.2secs
142.0bhp 105.9kW 144.0PS
@ 5800rpm
148.0lbft 200.5Nm @ 4200rpm
133.1bhp/ton 130.9bhp/tonne
64.7bhp/L 48.2kW/L 65.6PS/L
41.9ft/sec 12.8m/sec
20.3mph 32.7kmh/1000rpm
23.8mpg 19.8mpgUS 11.9L/100km
Petrol 4-stroke piston
2195cc 133.9cu in
In-line 6 2 Carburettor
Compression ratio: 9.8:1
Bore: 84.0mm 3.3in
Stroke: 66.0mm 2.6in
Valve type/No: Overhead 12
No. of forward speeds: 4
Wheels driven: Rear
Springs F/R: Torsion bar/Torsion bar
Brakes F/R: Disc/Disc
Steering: Rack & pinion
Wheelbase: 227.3cm 89.5in
Track F: 136.7cm 53.8in
Track R: 134.6cm 53.0in
Length: 416.3cm 163.9in
Width: 161.0cm 63.4in
Height: 132.1cm 52.0in
Ground clearance: 15.0cm 5.9in
Kerb weight: 1085.1kg 2390.0lb
Fuel: 62.1L 13.6gal 16.4galUS

3637 Porsche

911 E
1972 Germany
138.0mph 222.0kmh
0-50mph 80.5kmh: 5.1secs
0-60mph 96.5kmh: 6.6secs
0-1/4 mile: 15.4secs
165.0bhp 123.0kW 167.3PS
@ 6200rpm
152.0lbft 206.0Nm @ 4500rpm
148.7bhp/ton 146.2bhp/tonne
70.5bhp/L 52.6kW/L 71.5PS/L
47.7ft/sec 14.5m/sec
21.1mph 33.9kmh/1000rpm
22.3mpg 18.6mpgUS 12.6L/100km
Petrol 4-stroke piston
2341cc 142.8cu in
In-line 6 fuel injection
Compression ratio: 8.0:1
Bore: 84.0mm 3.3in
Stroke: 70.4mm 2.8in
Valve type/No: Overhead 12
Transmission: Manual
No. of forward speeds: 5
Wheels driven: Rear
Springs F/R: Torsion bar/Torsion bar
Brakes F/R: Disc/Disc
Steering: Rack & pinion
Wheelbase: 227.3cm 89.5in
Track F: 137.4cm 54.1in
Track R: 135.4cm 53.3in
Length: 416.3cm 163.9in
Width: 161.0cm 63.4in
Height: 132.1cm 52.0in
Ground clearance: 15.0cm 5.9in
Kerb weight: 1128.2kg 2485.0lb
Fuel: 62.1L 13.6gal 16.4galUS

3638 Porsche

911 S
1973 Germany
142.0mph 228.5kmh
0-50mph 80.5kmh: 6.1secs
0-60mph 96.5kmh: 7.8secs
0-1/4 mile: 16.3secs
181.0bhp 135.0kW 183.5PS
@ 6500rpm
154.0lbft 208.7Nm @ 5200rpm
157.8bhp/ton 155.1bhp/tonne
77.3bhp/L 57.6kW/L 78.4PS/L
50.0ft/sec 15.2m/sec
20.8mph 33.5kmh/1000rpm
15.0mpg 12.5mpgUS 18.8L/100km
Petrol 4-stroke piston
2341cc 142.8cu in
Flat 6 fuel injection
Compression ratio: 8.5:1
Bore: 84.0mm 3.3in
Stroke: 70.4mm 2.8in
Valve type/No: Overhead 12
Transmission: Manual
No. of forward speeds: 5
Wheels driven: Rear
Springs F/R: Torsion bar/Torsion bar
Brakes F/R: Disc/Disc
Steering: Rack & pinion
Wheelbase: 227.1cm 89.4in
Track F: 137.4cm 54.1in
Track R: 135.4cm 53.3in
Length: 427.7cm 168.4in
Width: 161.0cm 63.4in
Height: 132.1cm 52.0in
Ground clearance: 15.0cm 5.9in
Kerb weight: 1166.8kg 2570.0lb
Fuel: 62.1L 13.6gal 16.4galUS

3639 Porsche

914 1.7-litre
1973 Germany
96.0mph 154.5kmh
0-50mph 80.5kmh: 9.2secs
0-60mph 96.5kmh: 12.7secs
0-1/4 mile: 19.4secs
76.0bhp 56.7kW 77.0PS
@ 4900rpm
95.0lbft 128.7Nm @ 2700rpm
79.2bhp/ton 77.9bhp/tonne
45.3bhp/L 33.7kW/L 45.9PS/L
Petrol 4-stroke piston
1679cc 102.4cu in
Flat 4
Transmission: Manual
No. of forward speeds: 5
Wheels driven: Rear
Springs F/R: Torsion bar/Coil
Brakes F/R: Disc/Disc
Wheelbase: 245.1cm 96.5in
Track F: 133.1cm 52.4in
Track R: 137.2cm 54.0in
Length: 404.9cm 159.4in
Width: 165.1cm 65.0in
Height: 122.9cm 48.4in
Kerb weight: 976.1kg 2150.0lb

3640 Porsche

914 2-litre
1973 Germany
119.0mph 191.5kmh
0-50mph 80.5kmh: 7.6secs
0-60mph 96.5kmh: 10.3secs
0-1/4 mile: 17.8secs
91.0bhp 67.9kW 92.3PS
@ 4900rpm
109.0lbft 147.7Nm @ 3000rpm
95.0bhp/ton 93.4bhp/tonne
46.2bhp/L 34.4kW/L 46.8PS/L
38.1ft/sec 11.6m/sec
23.3mph 37.5kmh/1000rpm
29.4mpg 24.5mpgUS 9.6L/100km
Petrol 4-stroke piston
1971cc 120.3cu in
Flat 4 fuel injection
Compression ratio: 7.6:1
Bore: 94.0mm 3.7in
Stroke: 71.0mm 2.8in
Valve type/No: Overhead 8
Transmission: Manual
No. of forward speeds: 5
Wheels driven: Rear
Springs F/R: Torsion bar/Coil
Brakes F/R: Disc/Disc
Steering: Rack & pinion
Wheelbase: 245.1cm 96.5in
Track F: 134.4cm 52.9in
Track R: 138.2cm 54.4in

Length: 404.9cm 159.4in
Width: 165.1cm 65.0in
Height: 122.9cm 48.4in
Ground clearance: 11.9cm 4.7in
Kerb weight: 973.8kg 2145.0lb
Fuel: 62.1L 13.6gal 16.4galUS

3641 Porsche

Carrera RS Touring
1973 Germany
149.0mph 239.7kmh
0-50mph 80.5kmh: 4.6secs
0-60mph 96.5kmh: 5.5secs
0-1/4 mile: 14.1secs
0-1km: 25.4secs
210.0bhp 156.6kW 212.9PS
@ 6300rpm
188.0lbft 254.7Nm @ 5100rpm
196.2bhp/ton 192.9bhp/tonne
78.1bhp/L 58.3kW/L 79.2PS/L
48.5ft/sec 14.8m/sec
24.0mph 38.6kmh/1000rpm
16.7mpg 13.9mpgUS 16.9L/100km
Petrol 4-stroke piston
2687cc 163.9cu in
Flat 6 fuel injection
Compression ratio: 8.5:1
Bore: 90.0mm 3.5in
Stroke: 70.4mm 2.8in
Valve type/No: Overhead 12
Transmission: Manual
No. of forward speeds: 5
Wheels driven: Rear
Springs F/R: Torsion bar/Torsion bar
Brake system: PA
Brakes F/R: Disc/Disc
Steering: Rack & pinion
Wheelbase: 226.1cm 89.0in
Track F: 137.2cm 54.0in
Track R: 135.9cm 53.5in
Length: 416.6cm 164.0in
Width: 161.3cm 63.5in
Height: 132.1cm 52.0in
Ground clearance: 14.0cm 5.5in
Kerb weight: 1088.7kg 2398.0lb
Fuel: 61.9L 13.6gal 16.3galUS

3642 Porsche

Carrera RSR
1973 Germany
178.0mph 286.4kmh
0-60mph 96.5kmh: 5.6secs
0-1/4 mile: 13.2secs
280.0bhp 208.8kW 283.9PS
@ 8000rpm
215.0lbft 291.3Nm @ 6300rpm
339.0bhp/ton 333.4bhp/tonne
99.8bhp/L 74.4kW/L 101.2PS/L
61.6ft/sec 18.8m/sec
23.3mph 37.5kmh/1000rpm
7.2mpg 6.0mpgUS 39.2L/100km
Petrol 4-stroke piston
2806cc 171.2cu in
Flat 6 fuel injection
Compression ratio: 10.3:1
Bore: 92.0mm 3.6in
Stroke: 70.4mm 2.8in
Valve type/No: Overhead 12
Transmission: Manual
No. of forward speeds: 5
Wheels driven: Rear
Springs F/R: Torsion bar/Torsion bar
Brakes F/R: Disc/Disc
Steering: Rack & pinion
Wheelbase: 227.1cm 89.4in
Track F: 140.2cm 55.2in
Track R: 142.2cm 56.0in
Length: 412.8cm 162.5in
Width: 165.1cm 65.0in
Height: 132.1cm 52.0in
Ground clearance: 15.0cm 5.9in
Kerb weight: 839.9kg 1850.0lb
Fuel: 109.8L 24.1gal 29.0galUS

3643 Porsche

911 Carrera
1974 Germany
144.0mph 231.7kmh
0-50mph 80.5kmh: 5.2secs
0-60mph 96.5kmh: 7.5secs
0-1/4 mile: 15.1secs
167.0bhp 124.5kW 169.3PS
@ 5800rpm
168.0lbft 227.6Nm @ 5200rpm
150.2bhp/ton 147.7bhp/tonne
62.1bhp/L 46.3kW/L 63.0PS/L
44.6ft/sec 13.6m/sec
22.2mph 35.7kmh/1000rpm
19.2mpg 16.0mpgUS 14.7L/100km
Petrol 4-stroke piston
2687cc 163.9cu in
Flat 6 fuel injection
Compression ratio: 8.5:1
Bore: 90.0mm 3.5in
Stroke: 70.4mm 2.8in
Valve type/No: Overhead 12
Transmission: Manual
No. of forward speeds: 5
Wheels driven: Rear
Springs F/R: Torsion bar/Torsion bar
Brakes F/R: Disc/Disc
Steering: Rack & pinion
Wheelbase: 227.1cm 89.4in
Track F: 137.2cm 54.0in
Track R: 139.4cm 54.9in
Length: 429.0cm 168.9in
Width: 165.1cm 65.0in
Height: 132.1cm 52.0in
Ground clearance: 15.0cm 5.9in
Kerb weight: 1130.5kg 2490.0lb
Fuel: 79.9L 17.6gal 21.1galUS

3644 Porsche

911 Targa
1974 Germany
127.0mph 204.3kmh
0-60mph 96.5kmh: 8.5secs
0-1/4 mile: 16.4secs
143.0bhp 106.6kW 145.0PS
@ 5700rpm
168.0lbft 227.6Nm @ 3800rpm
125.6bhp/ton 123.5bhp/tonne
53.2bhp/L 39.7kW/L 54.0PS/L
43.9ft/sec 13.4m/sec
18.6mpg 15.5mpgUS 15.2L/100km
Petrol 4-stroke piston
2687cc 163.9cu in
Flat 6 fuel injection
Compression ratio: 8.0:1
Bore: 90.0mm 3.5in
Stroke: 70.4mm 2.8in
Valve type/No: Overhead 12
Transmission: Manual
No. of forward speeds: 4
Wheels driven: Rear
Brakes F/R: Disc/Disc
Wheelbase: 227.1cm 89.4in
Track F: 137.2cm 54.0in
Track R: 135.4cm 53.3in
Length: 429.0cm 168.9in
Width: 161.0cm 63.4in
Height: 132.1cm 52.0in
Ground clearance: 15.0cm 5.9in
Kerb weight: 1157.7kg 2550.0lb
Fuel: 79.9L 17.6gal 21.1galUS

3645 Porsche

911S 2.7-litre
1974 Germany
142.0mph 228.5kmh
0-50mph 80.5kmh: 4.7secs
0-60mph 96.5kmh: 6.1secs
0-1/4 mile: 15.0secs
0-1km: 27.4secs
175.0bhp 130.5kW 177.4PS
@ 5800rpm
174.0lbft 235.8Nm @ 4000rpm
160.5bhp/ton 157.8bhp/tonne
65.1bhp/L 48.6kW/L 66.0PS/L
44.6ft/sec 13.6m/sec
22.9mph 36.8kmh/1000rpm
23.2mpg 19.3mpgUS 12.2L/100km
Petrol 4-stroke piston
2687cc 163.9cu in
Flat 6 fuel injection
Compression ratio: 8.5:1
Bore: 90.0mm 3.5in
Stroke: 70.4mm 2.8in
Valve type/No: Overhead 12
Transmission: Manual
No. of forward speeds: 5
Wheels driven: Rear
Springs F/R: Torsion bar/Torsion bar
Brakes F/R: Disc/Disc
Steering: Rack & pinion
Wheelbase: 227.3cm 89.5in
Track F: 137.2cm 54.0in
Track R: 135.9cm 53.5in
Length: 429.3cm 169.0in
Width: 161.3cm 63.5in
Height: 132.1cm 52.0in
Ground clearance: 14.0cm 5.5in
Kerb weight: 1109.1kg 2443.0lb
Fuel: 80.1L 17.6gal 21.1galUS

3646 Porsche

911 Carrera
1975 Germany
134.0mph 215.6kmh
0-50mph 80.5kmh: 6.4secs
0-60mph 96.5kmh: 8.2secs
0-1/4 mile: 16.5secs
152.0bhp 113.3kW 154.1PS
@ 5800rpm
166.0lbft 224.9Nm @ 4000rpm
134.8bhp/ton 132.6bhp/tonne
56.6bhp/L 42.2kW/L 57.3PS/L
44.6ft/sec 13.6m/sec
22.5mph 36.2kmh/1000rpm
21.0mpg 17.5mpgUS 13.4L/100km
Petrol 4-stroke piston
2687cc 163.9cu in
Flat 6
Compression ratio: 8.5:1
Bore: 90.0mm 3.5in
Stroke: 70.4mm 2.8in
Valve type/No: Overhead 12
Transmission: Manual
No. of forward speeds: 5
Wheels driven: Rear
Springs F/R: Torsion bar/Torsion bar
Brakes F/R: Disc/Disc
Steering: Rack & pinion
Wheelbase: 227.1cm 89.4in
Track F: 137.2cm 54.0in
Track R: 137.9cm 54.3in
Length: 429.0cm 168.9in
Width: 165.1cm 65.0in
Height: 131.8cm 51.9in
Kerb weight: 1146.3kg 2525.0lb

3647 Porsche

Carrera RS 3-litre
1975 Germany
149.0mph 239.7kmh
0-50mph 80.5kmh: 4.2secs
0-60mph 96.5kmh: 5.2secs
0-1/4 mile: 14.0secs
220.0bhp 164.0kW 223.0PS
@ 6200rpm
202.0lbft 273.7Nm @ 5000rpm
204.5bhp/ton 201.1bhp/tonne
73.5bhp/L 54.8kW/L 74.5PS/L
47.7ft/sec 14.5m/sec
23.6mph 38.0kmh/1000rpm
13.8mpg 11.5mpgUS 20.5L/100km
Petrol 4-stroke piston
2993cc 182.6cu in
Flat 6
Compression ratio: 9.8:1
Bore: 95.0mm 3.7in
Stroke: 70.4mm 2.8in
Valve type/No: Overhead 12
Transmission: Manual
No. of forward speeds: 5
Wheels driven: Rear
Springs F/R: Torsion bar/Torsion bar
Brakes F/R: Disc/Disc
Steering: Rack & pinion
Wheelbase: 227.1cm 89.4in
Track F: 144.3cm 56.8in
Track R: 147.3cm 58.0in
Length: 424.2cm 167.0in
Width: 177.8cm 70.0in
Height: 132.1cm 52.0in
Kerb weight: 1094.1kg 2410.0lb
Fuel: 81.4L 17.9gal 21.5galUS

3648 Porsche

Turbo 3-litre
1975 Germany
153.0mph 246.2kmh
0-50mph 80.5kmh: 4.3secs
0-60mph 96.5kmh: 6.1secs
0-1/4 mile: 14.7secs
0-1km: 26.0secs
260.0bhp 193.9kW 263.6PS
@ 5500rpm
253.0lbft 342.8Nm @ 4000rpm
215.5bhp/ton 211.9bhp/tonne
86.8bhp/L 64.8kW/L 88.0PS/L
42.3ft/sec 12.9m/sec
26.0mph 41.8kmh/1000rpm
18.5mpg 15.4mpgUS 15.3L/100km
Petrol 4-stroke piston
2994cc 182.7cu in turbocharged
Flat 6 fuel injection
Compression ratio: 6.5:1
Bore: 95.0mm 3.7in
Stroke: 70.4mm 2.8in
Valve type/No: Overhead 12
Transmission: Manual
No. of forward speeds: 4
Wheels driven: Rear
Springs F/R: Torsion bar/Torsion bar
Brake system: PA
Brakes F/R: Disc/Disc
Steering: Rack & pinion
Wheelbase: 226.1cm 89.0in
Track F: 143.5cm 56.5in
Track R: 154.9cm 61.0in
Length: 431.8cm 170.0in
Width: 182.9cm 72.0in
Height: 132.1cm 52.0in
Ground clearance: 14.0cm 5.5in
Kerb weight: 1227.2kg 2703.0lb
Fuel: 80.1L 17.6gal 21.1galUS

3649 Porsche

911 S
1976 Germany
138.0mph 222.0kmh
0-50mph 80.5kmh: 5.7secs
0-60mph 96.5kmh: 7.5secs
0-1/4 mile: 15.8secs
157.0bhp 117.1kW 159.2PS
@ 5800rpm
168.0lbft 227.6Nm @ 4000rpm
142.1bhp/ton 139.7bhp/tonne
58.4bhp/L 43.6kW/L 59.2PS/L
44.6ft/sec 13.6m/sec
23.3mph 37.5kmh/1000rpm
24.0mpg 20.0mpgUS 11.8L/100km
Petrol 4-stroke piston
2687cc 163.9cu in
Flat 6 fuel injection
Compression ratio: 8.5:1
Bore: 90.0mm 3.5in
Stroke: 70.4mm 2.8in
Valve type/No: Overhead 12
Transmission: Manual
No. of forward speeds: 5
Wheels driven: Rear
Springs F/R: Torsion bar/Torsion bar
Brakes F/R: Disc/Disc
Steering: Rack & pinion
Track F: 137.2cm 54.0in
Track R: 135.1cm 53.2in
Length: 429.0cm 168.9in
Width: 161.0cm 63.4in
Height: 132.1cm 52.0in
Ground clearance: 18.0cm 7.1in
Kerb weight: 1123.6kg 2475.0lb
Fuel: 79.9L 17.6gal 21.1galUS

3650 Porsche

911 Turbo Carrera
1976 Germany
156.0mph 251.0kmh
0-50mph 80.5kmh: 5.2secs
0-60mph 96.5kmh: 6.7secs
0-1/4 mile: 15.2secs
234.0bhp 174.5kW 237.2PS
@ 5500rpm
246.0lbft 333.3Nm @ 4500rpm
188.2bhp/ton 185.1bhp/tonne
78.2bhp/L 58.3kW/L 79.3PS/L
42.3ft/sec 12.9m/sec
26.0mph 41.8kmh/1000rpm
20.4mpg 17.0mpgUS 13.8L/100km
Petrol 4-stroke piston
2993cc 182.6cu in turbocharged
Flat 6 fuel injection
Compression ratio: 6.5:1
Bore: 95.0mm 3.7in
Stroke: 70.4mm 2.8in
Valve type/No: Overhead 12
Transmission: Manual
No. of forward speeds: 4
Wheels driven: Rear
Springs F/R: Torsion bar/Torsion bar
Brakes F/R: Disc/Disc
Steering: Rack & pinion
Wheelbase: 227.1cm 89.4in
Track F: 143.3cm 56.4in
Track R: 150.1cm 59.1in
Length: 429.0cm 168.9in
Width: 177.5cm 69.9in
Height: 132.1cm 52.0in
Ground clearance: 15.0cm 5.9in
Kerb weight: 1264.4kg 2785.0lb
Fuel: 79.9L 17.6gal 21.1galUS

3651 Porsche

912 E
1976 Germany
115.0mph 185.0kmh
0-50mph 80.5kmh: 8.0secs

0-60mph 96.5kmh: 11.3secs
0-1/4 mile: 18.2secs
86.0bhp 64.1kW 87.2PS
@ 4900rpm
98.0lbft 132.8Nm @ 4000rpm
80.4bhp/ton 79.1bhp/tonne
43.6bhp/L 32.5kW/L 44.2PS/L
41.2ft/sec 12.6m/sec
22.9mph 36.8kmh/1000rpm
27.6mpg 23.0mpgUS 10.2L/100km
Petrol 4-stroke piston
1971cc 120.3cu in
Flat 4 fuel injection
Compression ratio: 7.6:1
Bore: 94.0mm 3.7in
Stroke: 77.0mm 3.0in
Valve type/No: Overhead 8
Transmission: Manual
No. of forward speeds: 5
Wheels driven: Rear
Springs F/R: Torsion bar/Torsion bar
Brakes F/R: Disc/Disc
Steering: Rack & pinion
Track F: 135.9cm 53.5in
Track R: 133.1cm 52.4in
Length: 429.0cm 168.9in
Width: 161.0cm 63.4in
Height: 134.1cm 52.8in
Ground clearance: 18.0cm 7.1in
Kerb weight: 1087.3kg 2395.0lb
Fuel: 79.9L 17.6gal 21.1galUS

3652 Porsche

914 2.0-litre
1976 Germany
107.0mph 172.2kmh
0-50mph 80.5kmh: 9.3secs
0-60mph 96.5kmh: 12.7secs
0-1/4 mile: 19.2secs
84.0bhp 62.6kW 85.2PS
@ 4900rpm
97.0lbft 131.4Nm @ 4000rpm
83.6bhp/ton 82.2bhp/tonne
42.6bhp/L 31.8kW/L 43.2PS/L
38.1ft/sec 11.6m/sec
31.8mpg 26.5mpgUS 8.9L/100km
Petrol 4-stroke piston
1971cc 120.3cu in
Flat 4 fuel injection
Compression ratio: 7.6:1
Bore: 94.0mm 3.7in
Stroke: 71.0mm 2.8in
Valve type/No: Overhead 8
Transmission: Manual
No. of forward speeds: 5
Wheels driven: Rear
Springs F/R: Torsion bar/Coil
Brakes F/R: Disc/Disc
Steering: Rack & pinion
Wheelbase: 245.1cm 96.5in
Track F: 134.1cm 52.8in
Track R: 138.2cm 54.4in
Length: 417.6cm 164.4in
Width: 165.1cm 65.0in
Height: 122.9cm 48.4in
Ground clearance: 13.0cm 5.1in
Kerb weight: 1021.5kg 2250.0lb
Fuel: 62.1L 13.6gal 16.4galUS

3653 Porsche

924
1976 Germany
111.0mph 178.6kmh
0-60mph 96.5kmh: 11.9secs
0-1/4 mile: 18.3secs
95.0bhp 70.8kW 96.3PS
@ 5500rpm
109.0lbft 147.7Nm @ 3000rpm
88.1bhp/ton 86.6bhp/tonne
47.9bhp/L 35.7kW/L 48.5PS/L
50.7ft/sec 15.5m/sec
29.4mpg 24.5mpgUS 9.6L/100km
Petrol 4-stroke piston
1984cc 121.0cu in
In-line 4 fuel injection
Compression ratio: 8.0:1
Bore: 86.5mm 3.4in
Stroke: 84.4mm 3.3in
Valve type/No: Overhead 8
Transmission: Manual
No. of forward speeds: 4
Wheels driven: Rear
Springs F/R: Coil/Torsion bar
Brake system: PA
Brakes F/R: Disc/Drum
Steering: Rack & pinion
Wheelbase: 240.0cm 94.5in
Track F: 142.0cm 55.9in
Track R: 137.2cm 54.0in
Length: 432.1cm 170.1in
Width: 168.4cm 66.3in
Height: 127.0cm 50.0in
Kerb weight: 1096.4kg 2415.0lb
Fuel: 62.1L 13.6gal 16.4galUS

3654 Porsche

911 SC
1977 Germany
141.0mph 226.9kmh
0-50mph 80.5kmh: 5.1secs
0-60mph 96.5kmh: 6.5secs
0-1/4 mile: 15.1secs
0-1km: 27.5secs
180.0bhp 134.2kW 182.5PS
@ 5800rpm
195.2lbft 264.5Nm @ 4100rpm
148.4bhp/ton 146.0bhp/tonne
60.1bhp/L 44.8kW/L 61.0PS/L
44.6ft/sec 13.6m/sec
22.9mph 36.8kmh/1000rpm
17.9mpg 14.9mpgUS 15.8L/100km
Petrol 4-stroke piston
2993cc 182.6cu in
Flat 6 fuel injection
Compression ratio: 8.5:1
Bore: 90.5mm 3.6in
Stroke: 70.4mm 2.8in
Valve type/No: Overhead 12
Transmission: Manual
No. of forward speeds: 5
Wheels driven: Rear
Springs F/R: Torsion bar/Torsion bar
Brake system: PA
Brakes F/R: Disc/Disc
Steering: Rack & pinion
Wheelbase: 227.3cm 89.5in
Track F: 137.7cm 54.2in
Track R: 136.4cm 53.7in
Length: 429.3cm 169.0in
Width: 165.1cm 65.0in
Height: 132.1cm 52.0in
Ground clearance: 11.9cm 4.7in
Kerb weight: 1233.1kg 2716.0lb
Fuel: 80.1L 17.6gal 21.1galUS

3655 Porsche

911 Turbo
1977 Germany
0-60mph 96.5kmh: 6.7secs
0-1/4 mile: 15.2secs
234.0bhp 174.5kW 237.2PS
@ 5500rpm
246.0lbft 333.3Nm @ 4500rpm
188.2bhp/ton 185.1bhp/tonne
78.2bhp/L 58.3kW/L 79.3PS/L
42.3ft/sec 12.9m/sec
26.0mph 41.8kmh/1000rpm
20.4mpg 17.0mpgUS 13.8L/100km
Petrol 4-stroke piston
2993cc 182.6cu in turbocharged
Flat 6 fuel injection
Compression ratio: 6.5:1
Bore: 95.0mm 3.7in
Stroke: 70.4mm 2.8in
Valve type/No: Overhead 12
Transmission: Manual
No. of forward speeds: 4
Wheels driven: Rear
Springs F/R: Torsion bar/Torsion bar
Brakes F/R: Disc/Disc
Track F: 143.3cm 56.4in
Track R: 150.1cm 59.1in
Length: 429.0cm 168.9in
Width: 177.5cm 69.9in
Height: 132.1cm 52.0in
Ground clearance: 15.0cm 5.9in
Kerb weight: 1264.4kg 2785.0lb
Fuel: 79.9L 17.6gal 21.1galUS

3656 Porsche

924
1977 Germany
126.0mph 202.7kmh
0-50mph 80.5kmh: 7.4secs
0-60mph 96.5kmh: 9.7secs
0-1/4 mile: 17.2secs
0-1km: 31.7secs
125.0bhp 93.2kW 126.7PS
@ 5800rpm
122.0lbft 165.3Nm @ 3500rpm
121.7bhp/ton 119.7bhp/tonne
63.0bhp/L 47.0kW/L 63.9PS/L
53.5ft/sec 16.3m/sec
21.1mph 33.9kmh/1000rpm
27.8mpg 23.1mpgUS 10.2L/100km
Petrol 4-stroke piston
1984cc 121.0cu in
In-line 4 fuel injection
Compression ratio: 9.3:1
Bore: 86.5mm 3.4in
Stroke: 84.4mm 3.3in
Valve type/No: Overhead 8
Transmission: Manual
No. of forward speeds: 4
Wheels driven: Rear
Springs F/R: Coil/Torsion bar
Brake system: PA
Brakes F/R: Disc/Drum
Steering: Rack & pinion
Wheelbase: 235.5cm 92.7in
Track F: 142.0cm 55.9in
Track R: 137.2cm 54.0in
Length: 419.9cm 165.3in
Width: 165.6cm 65.2in
Height: 127.0cm 50.0in
Ground clearance: 15.2cm 6.0in
Kerb weight: 1044.2kg 2300.0lb
Fuel: 61.9L 13.6gal 16.3galUS

3657 Porsche

935 Group 4 Holbert
1977 Germany
163.0mph 262.3kmh
0-50mph 80.5kmh: 5.1secs
0-60mph 96.5kmh: 5.8secs
0-1/4 mile: 14.2secs
485.0bhp 361.7kW 491.7PS
@ 7000rpm
434.0lbft 588.1Nm @ 5400rpm
409.2bhp/ton 402.4bhp/tonne
162.0bhp/L 120.8kW/L 164.3PS/L
53.9ft/sec 16.4m/sec
22.7mph 36.5kmh/1000rpm
4.8mpg 4.0mpgUS 58.8L/100km
Petrol 4-stroke piston
2993cc 182.6cu in turbocharged
Flat 6 fuel injection
Compression ratio: 6.5:1
Bore: 95.0mm 3.7in
Stroke: 70.4mm 2.8in
Valve type/No: Overhead 12
Transmission: Manual
No. of forward speeds: 4
Wheels driven: Rear
Springs F/R: Torsion bar
Brakes F/R: Disc/Disc
Steering: Rack & pinion
Wheelbase: 227.1cm 89.4in
Track F: 147.3cm 58.0in
Track R: 149.6cm 58.9in
Length: 429.0cm 168.9in
Width: 187.5cm 73.8in
Height: 130.3cm 51.3in
Ground clearance: 7.9cm 3.1in
Kerb weight: 1205.4kg 2655.0lb
Fuel: 120.0L 26.4gal 31.7galUS

3658 Porsche

911 SC
1978 Germany
126.0mph 202.7kmh
0-50mph 80.5kmh: 4.8secs
0-60mph 96.5kmh: 6.3secs
0-1/4 mile: 15.3secs
172.0bhp 128.3kW 174.4PS
@ 5500rpm
189.0lbft 256.1Nm @ 4200rpm
140.6bhp/ton 138.3bhp/tonne
57.4bhp/L 42.8kW/L 58.2PS/L
42.3ft/sec 12.9m/sec
23.2mph 37.3kmh/1000rpm
21.6mpg 18.0mpgUS 13.1L/100km
Petrol 4-stroke piston
2994cc 182.7cu in
Flat 6
Compression ratio: 8.5:1
Bore: 95.0mm 3.7in
Stroke: 70.4mm 2.8in
Valve type/No: Overhead 12
Transmission: Manual
No. of forward speeds: 5
Wheels driven: Rear
Springs F/R: Torsion bar/Torsion bar
Brake system: PA
Brakes F/R: Disc/Disc
Steering: Rack & pinion
Wheelbase: 227.1cm 89.4in
Track F: 136.1cm 53.6in
Track R: 136.7cm 53.8in
Length: 429.0cm 168.9in
Width: 161.0cm 63.4in
Height: 134.1cm 52.8in
Kerb weight: 1244.0kg 2740.0lb
Fuel: 79.9L 17.6gal 21.1galUS

3659 Porsche

911 Turbo
1978 Germany
156.0mph 251.0kmh
0-50mph 80.5kmh: 3.6secs
0-60mph 96.5kmh: 5.0secs
0-1/4 mile: 13.7secs
253.0bhp 188.7kW 256.5PS
@ 5500rpm
282.0lbft 382.1Nm @ 4000rpm
191.5bhp/ton 188.3bhp/tonne
76.7bhp/L 57.2kW/L 77.7PS/L
44.8ft/sec 13.6m/sec
27.9mph 44.9kmh/1000rpm
19.2mpg 16.0mpgUS 14.7L/100km
Petrol 4-stroke piston
3299cc 201.3cu in turbocharged
Flat 6
Compression ratio: 7.0:1
Bore: 97.0mm 3.8in
Stroke: 74.4mm 2.9in
Valve type/No: Overhead 12
Transmission: Manual
No. of forward speeds: 4
Wheels driven: Rear
Springs F/R: Torsion bar/Torsion bar
Brake system: PA
Brakes F/R: Disc/Disc
Steering: Rack & pinion
Wheelbase: 227.1cm 89.4in
Track F: 143.3cm 56.4in
Track R: 150.1cm 59.1in
Length: 429.0cm 168.9in
Width: 177.5cm 69.9in
Height: 131.1cm 51.6in
Kerb weight: 1343.8kg 2960.0lb
Fuel: 79.9L 17.6gal 21.1galUS

3660 Porsche

924 Lux
1978 Germany
127.0mph 204.3kmh
0-50mph 80.5kmh: 6.8secs
0-60mph 96.5kmh: 9.5secs
0-1/4 mile: 17.1secs
0-1km: 32.4secs
125.0bhp 93.2kW 126.7PS
@ 5800rpm
122.0lbft 165.3Nm @ 3500rpm
114.3bhp/ton 112.4bhp/tonne
63.0bhp/L 47.0kW/L 63.9PS/L
53.5ft/sec 16.3m/sec
21.1mph 33.9kmh/1000rpm
25.0mpg 20.8mpgUS 11.3L/100km
Petrol 4-stroke piston
1984cc 121.0cu in
In-line 4 fuel injection
Compression ratio: 9.3:1
Bore: 86.5mm 3.4in
Stroke: 84.4mm 3.3in
Valve type/No: Overhead 8
Transmission: Manual
No. of forward speeds: 5
Wheels driven: Rear
Springs F/R: Coil/Coil
Brake system: PA
Brakes F/R: Disc/Drum
Steering: Rack & pinion
Wheelbase: 235.5cm 92.7in
Track F: 142.0cm 55.9in
Track R: 137.2cm 54.0in
Length: 419.9cm 165.3in
Width: 165.6cm 65.2in
Height: 127.0cm 50.0in
Ground clearance: 15.2cm 6.0in
Kerb weight: 1112.3kg 2450.0lb
Fuel: 61.9L 13.6gal 16.3galUS

3661 Porsche

928
1978 Germany
143.0mph 230.1kmh
0-50mph 80.5kmh: 5.7secs
0-60mph 96.5kmh: 7.5secs
0-1/4 mile: 15.7secs
0-1km: 28.9secs
240.0bhp 179.0kW 243.3PS
@ 5500rpm
257.0lbft 348.2Nm @ 3600rpm
160.5bhp/ton 157.8bhp/tonne
53.6bhp/L 40.0kW/L 54.4PS/L

47.5ft/sec 14.5m/sec
25.6mph 41.2kmh/1000rpm
17.1mpg 14.2mpgUS 16.5L/100km
Petrol 4-stroke piston
4474cc 273.0cu in
Vee 8 fuel injection
Compression ratio: 8.5:1
Bore: 95.0mm 3.7in
Stroke: 78.9mm 3.1in
Valve type/No: Overhead 16
Transmission: Manual
No. of forward speeds: 5
Wheels driven: Rear
Springs F/R: Coil/Coil
Brake system: PA
Brakes F/R: Disc/Disc
Steering: Rack & pinion PA
Wheelbase: 249.9cm 98.4in
Track F: 154.4cm 60.8in
Track R: 151.4cm 59.6in
Length: 444.8cm 175.1in
Width: 183.6cm 72.3in
Height: 131.8cm 51.9in
Ground clearance: 16.5cm 6.5in
Kerb weight: 1520.9kg 3350.0lb
Fuel: 86.9L 19.1gal 23.0galUS

3662 Porsche

928 Automatic
1978 Germany
138.0mph 222.0kmh
0-50mph 80.5kmh: 6.3secs
0-60mph 96.5kmh: 8.0secs
0-1/4 mile: 16.2secs
0-1km: 29.3secs
240.0bhp 179.0kW 243.3PS
@ 5500rpm
257.0lbft 348.2Nm @ 3600rpm
160.6bhp/ton 157.9bhp/tonne
53.6bhp/L 40.0kW/L 54.4PS/L
47.5ft/sec 14.5m/sec
25.6mph 41.2kmh/1000rpm
14.6mpg 12.2mpgUS 19.3L/100km
Petrol 4-stroke piston
4474cc 273.0cu in
Vee 8 fuel injection
Compression ratio: 8.5:1
Bore: 95.0mm 3.7in
Stroke: 78.9mm 3.1in
Valve type/No: Overhead 16
Transmission: Automatic
No. of forward speeds: 3
Wheels driven: Rear
Springs F/R: Coil/Coil
Brake system: PA
Brakes F/R: Disc/Disc
Steering: Rack & pinion PA
Wheelbase: 249.9cm 98.4in
Track F: 154.4cm 60.8in
Track R: 151.4cm 59.6in
Length: 444.8cm 175.1in
Width: 183.6cm 72.3in
Height: 131.8cm 51.9in
Ground clearance: 16.5cm 6.5in
Kerb weight: 1519.5kg 3347.0lb
Fuel: 86.9L 19.1gal 23.0galUS

3663 Porsche

924
1979 Germany
117.0mph 188.3kmh
0-50mph 80.5kmh: 7.7secs
0-60mph 96.5kmh: 11.0secs
0-1/4 mile: 18.0secs
110.0bhp 82.0kW 111.5PS
@ 5750rpm
111.0lbft 150.4Nm @ 3500rpm
95.7bhp/ton 94.1bhp/tonne
55.4bhp/L 41.3kW/L 56.2PS/L
53.0ft/sec 16.2m/sec
18.9mph 30.4kmh/1000rpm
22.2mpg 18.5mpgUS 12.7L/100km
Petrol 4-stroke piston
1984cc 121.0cu in
In-line 4 fuel injection
Compression ratio: 8.5:1
Bore: 86.5mm 3.4in
Stroke: 84.4mm 3.3in
Valve type/No: Overhead 8
Transmission: Manual
No. of forward speeds: 4
Wheels driven: Rear
Springs F/R: Coil/Torsion bar
Brake system: PA
Brakes F/R: Disc/Drum
Steering: Rack & pinion
Wheelbase: 240.0cm 94.5in
Track F: 142.0cm 55.9in
Track R: 137.2cm 54.0in
Length: 432.1cm 170.1in
Width: 168.4cm 66.3in
Height: 127.0cm 50.0in
Ground clearance: 15.0cm 5.9in
Kerb weight: 1169.0kg 2575.0lb
Fuel: 62.1L 13.6gal 16.4galUS

3664 Porsche

924 Turbo
1979 Germany
144.0mph 231.7kmh
0-50mph 80.5kmh: 5.3secs
0-60mph 96.5kmh: 6.9secs
0-1/4 mile: 15.0secs
0-1km: 27.5secs
170.0bhp 126.8kW 172.4PS
@ 5500rpm
181.0lbft 245.3Nm @ 3500rpm
146.3bhp/ton 143.9bhp/tonne
85.7bhp/L 63.9kW/L 86.9PS/L
50.7ft/sec 15.5m/sec
25.4mph 40.9kmh/1000rpm
19.8mpg 16.5mpgUS 14.3L/100km
Petrol 4-stroke piston
1984cc 121.0cu in turbocharged
In-line 4 fuel injection
Compression ratio: 7.5:1
Bore: 86.5mm 3.4in
Stroke: 84.4mm 3.3in
Valve type/No: Overhead 8
Transmission: Manual
No. of forward speeds: 5
Wheels driven: Rear
Springs F/R: Coil/Torsion bar
Brake system: PA
Brakes F/R: Disc/Disc
Steering: Rack & pinion
Wheelbase: 235.5cm 92.7in
Track F: 142.0cm 55.9in
Track R: 137.2cm 54.0in
Length: 419.9cm 165.3in
Width: 165.6cm 65.2in
Height: 127.0cm 50.0in
Ground clearance: 15.2cm 6.0in
Kerb weight: 1181.3kg 2602.0lb
Fuel: 68.2L 15.0gal 18.0galUS

3665 Porsche

928 Automatic
1979 Germany
133.0mph 214.0kmh
0-50mph 80.5kmh: 6.7secs
0-60mph 96.5kmh: 8.3secs
0-1/4 mile: 16.6secs
219.0bhp 163.3kW 222.0PS
@ 5250rpm
254.0lbft 344.2Nm @ 3600rpm
134.4bhp/ton 132.2bhp/tonne
48.9bhp/L 36.5kW/L 49.6PS/L
45.3ft/sec 13.8m/sec
27.9mph 44.9kmh/1000rpm
18.0mpg 15.0mpgUS 15.7L/100km
Petrol 4-stroke piston
4474cc 273.0cu in
Vee 8
Compression ratio: 8.5:1
Bore: 95.0mm 3.7in
Stroke: 78.9mm 3.1in
Valve type/No: Overhead 16
Transmission: Automatic
No. of forward speeds: 3
Wheels driven: Rear
Springs F/R: Coil/Coil
Brake system: PA
Brakes F/R: Disc/Disc
Steering: Rack & pinion PA
Wheelbase: 249.9cm 98.4in
Track F: 154.4cm 60.8in
Track R: 151.4cm 59.6in
Length: 446.3cm 175.7in
Width: 183.6cm 72.3in
Height: 131.3cm 51.7in
Kerb weight: 1657.1kg 3650.0lb
Fuel: 84.8L 18.6gal 22.4galUS

3666 Porsche

911 SC
1980 Germany
138.0mph 222.0kmh
0-50mph 80.5kmh: 4.9secs
0-60mph 96.5kmh: 6.7secs
0-1/4 mile: 15.3secs
172.0bhp 128.3kW 174.4PS
@ 5500rpm
189.0lbft 256.1Nm @ 4200rpm
137.3bhp/ton 135.1bhp/tonne
57.4bhp/L 42.8kW/L 58.2PS/L
42.3ft/sec 12.9m/sec
23.2mph 37.3kmh/1000rpm
22.2mpg 18.5mpgUS 12.7L/100km
Petrol 4-stroke piston
2994cc 182.7cu in
Flat 6 fuel injection
Compression ratio: 9.3:1
Bore: 95.0mm 3.7in
Stroke: 70.4mm 2.8in
Valve type/No: Overhead 12
Transmission: Manual
No. of forward speeds: 5
Wheels driven: Rear
Springs F/R: Torsion bar/Torsion bar
Brake system: PA
Brakes F/R: Disc/Disc
Steering: Rack & pinion
Wheelbase: 227.1cm 89.4in
Track F: 136.1cm 53.6in
Track R: 134.1cm 52.8in
Length: 429.0cm 168.9in
Width: 165.1cm 65.0in
Height: 132.1cm 52.0in
Kerb weight: 1273.5kg 2805.0lb
Fuel: 79.9L 17.6gal 21.1galUS

3667 Porsche

924
1980 Germany
123.0mph 197.9kmh
0-50mph 80.5kmh: 7.4secs
0-60mph 96.5kmh: 10.6secs
0-1/4 mile: 17.6secs
115.0bhp 85.8kW 116.6PS
@ 5750rpm
111.0lbft 150.4Nm @ 3500rpm
96.1bhp/ton 94.5bhp/tonne
58.0bhp/L 43.2kW/L 58.8PS/L
53.0ft/sec 16.2m/sec
25.0mph 40.2kmh/1000rpm
27.6mpg 23.0mpgUS 10.2L/100km
Petrol 4-stroke piston
1984cc 121.0cu in
In-line 4 fuel injection
Compression ratio: 9.0:1
Bore: 86.5mm 3.4in
Stroke: 84.4mm 3.3in
Valve type/No: Overhead 8
Transmission: Manual
No. of forward speeds: 5
Wheels driven: Rear
Springs F/R: Coil/Torsion bar
Brake system: PA
Brakes F/R: Disc/Drum
Steering: Rack & pinion
Wheelbase: 240.0cm 94.5in
Track F: 142.0cm 55.9in
Track R: 137.2cm 54.0in
Length: 432.1cm 170.1in
Width: 168.4cm 66.3in
Height: 127.0cm 50.0in
Kerb weight: 1216.7kg 2680.0lb
Fuel: 62.1L 13.6gal 16.4galUS

3668 Porsche

924 S Turbo
1980 Germany
129.0mph 207.6kmh
0-50mph 80.5kmh: 6.4secs
0-60mph 96.5kmh: 9.3secs
0-1/4 mile: 17.0secs
143.0bhp 106.6kW 145.0PS
@ 5500rpm
147.0lbft 199.2Nm @ 3000rpm
112.4bhp/ton 110.5bhp/tonne
72.1bhp/L 53.7kW/L 73.1PS/L
50.7ft/sec 15.5m/sec
27.3mph 43.9kmh/1000rpm
24.0mpg 20.0mpgUS 11.8L/100km
Petrol 4-stroke piston
1984cc 121.0cu in turbocharged
In-line 4 fuel injection
Compression ratio: 7.5:1
Bore: 86.5mm 3.4in
Stroke: 84.4mm 3.3in
Valve type/No: Overhead 8
Transmission: Manual
No. of forward speeds: 5
Wheels driven: Rear
Springs F/R: Coil/Torsion bar
Brake system: PA
Brakes F/R: Disc/Disc
Steering: Rack & pinion
Wheelbase: 240.0cm 94.5in
Track F: 142.0cm 55.9in
Track R: 139.2cm 54.8in
Length: 429.0cm 168.9in
Width: 168.4cm 66.3in
Height: 127.5cm 50.2in
Kerb weight: 1293.9kg 2850.0lb
Fuel: 62.1L 13.6gal 16.4galUS

3669 Porsche

928
1980 Germany
140.0mph 225.3kmh
0-50mph 80.5kmh: 6.3secs
0-60mph 96.5kmh: 8.1secs
0-1/4 mile: 16.2secs
220.0bhp 164.0kW 223.0PS
@ 5500rpm
265.0lbft 359.1Nm @ 4000rpm
146.2bhp/ton 143.8bhp/tonne
49.2bhp/L 36.7kW/L 49.8PS/L
47.5ft/sec 14.5m/sec
26.0mph 41.8kmh/1000rpm
21.6mpg 18.0mpgUS 13.1L/100km
Petrol 4-stroke piston
4474cc 273.0cu in
Vee 8 fuel injection
Compression ratio: 9.0:1
Bore: 95.0mm 3.7in
Stroke: 78.9mm 3.1in
Valve type/No: Overhead 16
Transmission: Automatic
No. of forward speeds: 3
Wheels driven: Rear
Springs F/R: Coil/Coil
Brake system: PA
Brakes F/R: Disc/Disc
Steering: Rack & pinion PA
Wheelbase: 249.7cm 98.3in
Track F: 154.4cm 60.8in
Track R: 151.4cm 59.6in
Length: 446.3cm 175.7in
Width: 183.6cm 72.3in
Height: 131.1cm 51.6in
Ground clearance: 11.9cm 4.7in
Kerb weight: 1530.0kg 3370.0lb
Fuel: 53.7L 11.8gal 14.2galUS

3670 Porsche

911 SC
1981 Germany
146.0mph 234.9kmh
0-50mph 80.5kmh: 4.4secs
0-60mph 96.5kmh: 5.8secs
0-1/4 mile: 14.2secs
0-1km: 26.2secs
204.0bhp 152.1kW 206.8PS
@ 5900rpm
195.0lbft 264.2Nm @ 4300rpm
170.0bhp/ton 167.2bhp/tonne
68.1bhp/L 50.8kW/L 69.1PS/L
48.0ft/sec 14.6m/sec
23.6mph 38.0kmh/1000rpm
19.7mpg 16.4mpgUS 14.3L/100km
Petrol 4-stroke piston
2994cc 182.7cu in
Flat 6 fuel injection
Compression ratio: 9.8:1
Bore: 95.0mm 3.7in
Stroke: 74.4mm 2.9in
Valve type/No: Overhead 12
Transmission: Manual
No. of forward speeds: 5
Wheels driven: Rear
Springs F/R: Torsion bar/Torsion bar
Brake system: PA
Brakes F/R: Disc/Disc
Steering: Rack & pinion
Wheelbase: 227.1cm 89.4in
Track F: 138.2cm 54.4in
Track R: 136.4cm 53.7in
Length: 429.0cm 168.9in
Width: 165.1cm 65.0in
Height: 132.1cm 52.0in
Ground clearance: 11.9cm 4.7in
Kerb weight: 1220.3kg 2688.0lb
Fuel: 80.1L 17.6gal 21.1galUS

3671 Porsche

924 Turbo
1981 Germany
127.0mph 204.3kmh
0-60mph 96.5kmh: 9.2secs
0-1/4 mile: 16.7secs
154.0bhp 114.8kW 156.1PS
@ 5500rpm
155.0lbft 210.0Nm @ 3300rpm

121.0bhp/ton 119.0bhp/tonne
77.6bhp/L 57.9kW/L 78.7PS/L
50.7ft/sec 15.5m/sec
22.8mpg 19.0mpgUS 12.4L/100km
Petrol 4-stroke piston
1984cc 121.0cu in turbocharged
In-line 4 fuel injection
Compression ratio: 8.0:1
Bore: 86.5mm 3.4in
Stroke: 84.4mm 3.3in
Valve type/No: Overhead 8
Transmission: Manual
No. of forward speeds: 5
Wheels driven: Rear
Springs F/R: Coil/Coil
Brakes F/R: Disc/Disc
Wheelbase: 240.0cm 94.5in
Track F: 142.0cm 55.9in
Track R: 139.2cm 54.8in
Length: 429.0cm 168.9in
Width: 168.4cm 66.3in
Height: 127.5cm 50.2in
Kerb weight: 1293.9kg 2850.0lb
Fuel: 62.1L 13.6gal 16.4galUS

3672 Porsche

924 Weissach
1982 Germany
123.0mph 197.9kmh
0-60mph 96.5kmh: 10.6secs
0-1/4 mile: 17.6secs
110.0bhp 82.0kW 111.5PS
@ 5750rpm
111.0lbft 150.4Nm @ 3500rpm
93.0bhp/ton 91.4bhp/tonne
55.4bhp/L 41.3kW/L 56.2PS/L
53.0ft/sec 16.2m/sec
25.0mph 40.2kmh/1000rpm
27.0mpg 22.5mpgUS 10.5L/100km
Petrol 4-stroke piston
1984cc 121.0cu in
In-line 4 fuel injection
Compression ratio: 9.0:1
Bore: 86.5mm 3.4in
Stroke: 84.4mm 3.3in
Valve type/No: Overhead 8
Transmission: Manual
No. of forward speeds: 5
Wheels driven: Rear
Springs F/R: Coil/Torsion bar
Brake system: PA
Brakes F/R: Disc/Drum
Steering: Rack & pinion
Wheelbase: 240.0cm 94.5in
Track F: 141.7cm 55.8in
Track R: 139.2cm 54.8in
Length: 432.1cm 170.1in
Width: 168.4cm 66.3in
Height: 127.0cm 50.0in
Ground clearance: 15.0cm 5.9in
Kerb weight: 1203.1kg 2650.0lb
Fuel: 62.1L 13.6gal 16.4galUS

3673 Porsche

944
1982 Germany
132.0mph 212.4kmh
0-60mph 96.5kmh: 8.3secs
0-1/4 mile: 16.3secs
143.0bhp 106.6kW 145.0PS
@ 5500rpm
137.0lbft 185.6Nm @ 3000rpm
114.8bhp/ton 112.9bhp/tonne
57.7bhp/L 43.0kW/L 58.5PS/L
47.5ft/sec 14.5m/sec
25.0mph 40.2kmh/1000rpm
26.4mpg 22.0mpgUS 10.7L/100km
Petrol 4-stroke piston
2479cc 151.2cu in
In-line 4 fuel injection
Compression ratio: 9.5:1
Bore: 100.0mm 3.9in
Stroke: 78.9mm 3.1in
Valve type/No: Overhead 8
Transmission: Manual
No. of forward speeds: 5
Wheels driven: Rear
Springs F/R: Coil/Torsion bar
Brake system: PA
Brakes F/R: Disc/Disc
Steering: Rack & pinion
Wheelbase: 240.0cm 94.5in
Track F: 147.8cm 58.2in
Track R: 145.0cm 57.1in
Length: 431.8cm 170.0in
Width: 173.5cm 68.3in
Height: 127.5cm 50.2in
Ground clearance: 12.4cm 4.9in
Kerb weight: 1266.7kg 2790.0lb
Fuel: 62.1L 13.6gal 16.4galUS

3674 Porsche

944 Lux
1982 Germany
137.0mph 220.4kmh
0-50mph 80.5kmh: 5.3secs
0-60mph 96.5kmh: 7.4secs
0-1/4 mile: 15.6secs
0-1km: 28.7secs
163.0bhp 121.5kW 165.3PS
@ 5800rpm
151.6lbft 205.4Nm @ 3000rpm
138.7bhp/ton 136.4bhp/tonne
65.7bhp/L 49.0kW/L 66.7PS/L
50.1ft/sec 15.2m/sec
22.8mph 36.7kmh/1000rpm
26.2mpg 21.8mpgUS 10.8L/100km
Petrol 4-stroke piston
2479cc 151.2cu in
In-line 4 fuel injection
Compression ratio: 10.6:1
Bore: 100.0mm 3.9in
Stroke: 78.9mm 3.1in
Valve type/No: Overhead 8
Transmission: Manual
No. of forward speeds: 5
Wheels driven: Rear
Springs F/R: Coil/Torsion bar
Brake system: PA
Brakes F/R: Disc/Disc
Steering: Rack & pinion
Wheelbase: 240.0cm 94.5in
Track F: 147.8cm 58.2in
Track R: 145.0cm 57.1in
Length: 419.9cm 165.3in
Width: 173.5cm 68.3in
Height: 127.5cm 50.2in
Ground clearance: 12.4cm 4.9in
Kerb weight: 1194.9kg 2632.0lb
Fuel: 66.0L 14.5gal 17.4galUS

3675 Porsche

911 Cabriolet
1983 Germany
124.0mph 199.5kmh
0-60mph 96.5kmh: 7.0secs
0-1/4 mile: 15.5secs
172.0bhp 128.3kW 174.4PS
@ 5500rpm
175.0lbft 237.1Nm @ 4200rpm
140.1bhp/ton 137.8bhp/tonne
57.4bhp/L 42.8kW/L 58.2PS/L
42.3ft/sec 12.9m/sec
23.2mph 37.3kmh/1000rpm
28.2mpg 23.5mpgUS 10.0L/100km
Petrol 4-stroke piston
2994cc 182.7cu in
Flat 6 fuel injection
Compression ratio: 9.3:1
Bore: 95.0mm 3.7in
Stroke: 70.4mm 2.8in
Valve type/No: Overhead 12
Transmission: Manual
No. of forward speeds: 5
Wheels driven: Rear
Springs F/R: Torsion bar/Torsion bar
Brake system: PA
Brakes F/R: Disc/Disc
Steering: Rack & pinion
Wheelbase: 227.3cm 89.5in
Track F: 136.9cm 53.9in
Track R: 137.9cm 54.3in
Length: 429.0cm 168.9in
Width: 165.1cm 65.0in
Height: 131.1cm 51.6in
Ground clearance: 11.9cm 4.7in
Kerb weight: 1248.5kg 2750.0lb
Fuel: 79.5L 17.5gal 21.0galUS

3676 Porsche

911 Turbo
1983 Germany
165.0mph 265.5kmh
0-50mph 80.5kmh: 3.6secs
0-60mph 96.5kmh: 5.1secs
0-1/4 mile: 13.4secs
0-1km: 24.5secs
300.0bhp 223.7kW 304.2PS
@ 5500rpm
318.0lbft 430.9Nm @ 4000rpm
226.4bhp/ton 222.6bhp/tonne
90.9bhp/L 67.8kW/L 92.2PS/L
44.8ft/sec 13.6m/sec
27.4mph 44.1kmh/1000rpm
16.4mpg 13.7mpgUS 17.2L/100km
Petrol 4-stroke piston
3299cc 201.3cu in turbocharged
Flat 6 fuel injection
Compression ratio: 7.0:1
Bore: 97.0mm 3.8in
Stroke: 74.4mm 2.9in
Valve type/No: Overhead 12
Transmission: Manual
No. of forward speeds: 4
Wheels driven: Rear
Springs F/R: Torsion bar/Torsion bar
Brake system: PA
Brakes F/R: Disc/Disc
Steering: Rack & pinion
Wheelbase: 227.3cm 89.5in
Track F: 143.3cm 56.4in
Track R: 150.1cm 59.1in
Length: 429.0cm 168.9in
Width: 177.5cm 69.9in
Height: 131.1cm 51.6in
Ground clearance: 11.9cm 4.7in
Kerb weight: 1347.5kg 2968.0lb
Fuel: 80.1L 17.6gal 21.1galUS

3677 Porsche

928 S
1983 Germany
136.0mph 218.8kmh
0-50mph 80.5kmh: 5.5secs
0-60mph 96.5kmh: 7.0secs
0-1/4 mile: 15.4secs
234.0bhp 174.5kW 237.2PS
@ 5500rpm
263.0lbft 356.4Nm @ 4000rpm
155.8bhp/ton 153.2bhp/tonne
50.4bhp/L 37.6kW/L 51.1PS/L
47.5ft/sec 14.5m/sec
32.4mph 52.1kmh/1000rpm
19.2mpg 16.0mpgUS 14.7L/100km
Petrol 4-stroke piston
4644cc 283.3cu in
Vee 8 fuel injection
Compression ratio: 9.3:1
Bore: 97.0mm 3.8in
Stroke: 78.9mm 3.1in
Valve type/No: Overhead 16
Transmission: Manual
No. of forward speeds: 5
Wheels driven: Rear
Springs F/R: Coil/Coil
Brake system: PA
Brakes F/R: Disc/Disc
Steering: Rack & pinion PA
Wheelbase: 249.9cm 98.4in
Track F: 155.2cm 61.1in
Track R: 152.9cm 60.2in
Length: 446.3cm 175.7in
Width: 183.6cm 72.3in
Height: 128.3cm 50.5in
Kerb weight: 1527.7kg 3365.0lb
Fuel: 85.9L 18.9gal 22.7galUS

3678 Porsche

944
1983 Germany
125.0mph 201.1kmh
0-60mph 96.5kmh: 9.0secs
0-1/4 mile: 16.4secs
143.0bhp 106.6kW 145.0PS
@ 5500rpm
137.0lbft 185.6Nm @ 3000rpm
114.2bhp/ton 112.3bhp/tonne
57.7bhp/L 43.0kW/L 58.5PS/L
47.5ft/sec 14.5m/sec
25.8mpg 21.5mpgUS 10.9L/100km
Petrol 4-stroke piston
2479cc 151.2cu in
In-line 4 fuel injection
Compression ratio: 9.5:1
Bore: 100.0mm 3.9in
Stroke: 78.9mm 3.1in
Valve type/No: Overhead 8
Transmission: Manual
No. of forward speeds: 5
Wheels driven: Rear
Springs F/R: Coil/Torsion bar
Brakes F/R: Disc/Disc
Wheelbase: 240.0cm 94.5in
Track F: 147.8cm 58.2in
Track R: 145.0cm 57.1in
Length: 431.8cm 170.0in
Width: 173.5cm 68.3in
Height: 127.5cm 50.2in
Kerb weight: 1273.5kg 2805.0lb
Fuel: 62.1L 13.6gal 16.4galUS

3679 Porsche

911 Carrera
1984 Germany
146.0mph 234.9kmh
0-50mph 80.5kmh: 4.8secs
0-60mph 96.5kmh: 6.2secs
0-1/4 mile: 14.6secs
200.0bhp 149.1kW 202.8PS
@ 5900rpm
185.0lbft 250.7Nm @ 4800rpm
160.0bhp/ton 157.3bhp/tonne
63.2bhp/L 47.1kW/L 64.1PS/L
48.0ft/sec 14.6m/sec
24.6mph 39.6kmh/1000rpm
24.6mpg 20.5mpgUS 11.5L/100km
Petrol 4-stroke piston
3164cc 193.0cu in
Flat 6 fuel injection
Compression ratio: 9.5:1
Bore: 95.0mm 3.7in
Stroke: 74.4mm 2.9in
Valve type/No: Overhead 12
Transmission: Manual
No. of forward speeds: 5
Wheels driven: Rear
Springs F/R: Torsion bar/Torsion bar
Brake system: PA
Brakes F/R: Disc/Disc
Steering: Rack & pinion
Wheelbase: 227.3cm 89.5in
Track F: 136.9cm 53.9in
Track R: 137.9cm 54.3in
Length: 429.0cm 168.9in
Width: 165.1cm 65.0in
Height: 131.1cm 51.6in
Kerb weight: 1271.2kg 2800.0lb
Fuel: 79.5L 17.5gal 21.0galUS

3680 Porsche

911 Turbo Cabriolet Ruf
1984 Germany
160.0mph 257.4kmh
0-50mph 80.5kmh: 4.1secs
0-60mph 96.5kmh: 5.3secs
0-1/4 mile: 14.2secs
300.0bhp 223.7kW 304.2PS
@ 5500rpm
304.0lbft 411.9Nm @ 4000rpm
225.5bhp/ton 221.7bhp/tonne
91.0bhp/L 67.8kW/L 92.2PS/L
44.8ft/sec 13.6m/sec
27.5mph 44.2kmh/1000rpm
19.2mpg 16.0mpgUS 14.7L/100km
Petrol 4-stroke piston
3297cc 201.2cu in turbocharged
In-line 6 fuel injection
Compression ratio: 7.0:1
Bore: 97.0mm 3.8in
Stroke: 74.4mm 2.9in
Valve type/No: Overhead 12
Transmission: Manual
No. of forward speeds: 5
Wheels driven: Rear
Springs F/R: Torsion bar/Torsion bar
Brake system: PA
Brakes F/R: Disc/Disc
Steering: Rack & pinion
Wheelbase: 227.1cm 89.4in
Track F: 144.5cm 56.9in
Track R: 151.4cm 59.6in
Length: 429.0cm 168.9in
Width: 177.5cm 69.9in
Height: 127.0cm 50.0in
Kerb weight: 1352.9kg 2980.0lb
Fuel: 79.9L 17.6gal 21.1galUS

3681 Porsche

944
1984 Germany
110.0mph 177.0kmh
0-50mph 80.5kmh: 5.9secs
0-60mph 96.5kmh: 8.3secs
0-1/4 mile: 16.3secs
143.0bhp 106.6kW 145.0PS
@ 5500rpm
137.0lbft 185.6Nm @ 3000rpm
114.8bhp/ton 112.9bhp/tonne
57.7bhp/L 43.0kW/L 58.5PS/L
47.5ft/sec 14.5m/sec
Petrol 4-stroke piston
2479cc 151.2cu in
In-line 4
Compression ratio: 9.5:1
Bore: 100.0mm 3.9in
Stroke: 78.9mm 3.1in
Valve type/No: Overhead 8
Transmission: Manual

No. of forward speeds: 5
Wheels driven: Rear
Springs F/R: Coil/Torsion bar
Brakes F/R: Disc/Disc
Steering: Rack & pinion
Wheelbase: 240.0cm 94.5in
Track F: 147.8cm 58.2in
Track R: 145.0cm 57.1in
Length: 431.8cm 170.0in
Width: 173.5cm 68.3in
Height: 127.5cm 50.2in
Ground clearance: 12.4cm 4.9in
Kerb weight: 1266.7kg 2790.0lb

3682 Porsche

911 Carrera
1985 Germany
151.0mph 243.0kmh
0-60mph 96.5kmh: 5.5secs
0-1/4 mile: 14.0secs
231.0bhp 172.3kW 234.2PS
@ 5900rpm
209.0lbft 283.2Nm @ 4800rpm
193.8bhp/ton 190.6bhp/tonne
73.0bhp/L 54.4kW/L 74.0PS/L
48.0ft/sec 14.6m/sec
24.0mph 38.6kmh/1000rpm
22.8mpg 19.0mpgUS 12.4L/100km
Petrol 4-stroke piston
3164cc 193.0cu in
Flat 6 fuel injection
Compression ratio: 10.3:1
Bore: 95.0mm 3.7in
Stroke: 74.4mm 2.9in
Valve type/No: Overhead 12
Transmission: Manual
No. of forward speeds: 5
Wheels driven: Rear
Springs F/R: Torsion bar/Torsion bar
Brakes F/R: Disc/Disc
Steering: Rack & pinion
Wheelbase: 227.3cm 89.5in
Track F: 136.9cm 53.9in
Track R: 137.9cm 54.3in
Length: 429.0cm 168.9in
Width: 165.1cm 65.0in
Height: 132.1cm 52.0in
Kerb weight: 1212.2kg 2670.0lb
Fuel: 79.5L 17.5gal 21.0galUS

3683 Porsche

928 S
1985 Germany
143.0mph 230.1kmh
0-50mph 80.5kmh: 4.3secs
0-60mph 96.5kmh: 5.9secs
0-1/4 mile: 14.2secs
288.0bhp 214.8kW 292.0PS
@ 5750rpm
302.0lbft 409.2Nm @ 2700rpm
188.4bhp/ton 185.2bhp/tonne
58.1bhp/L 43.3kW/L 58.9PS/L
49.7ft/sec 15.1m/sec
31.3mph 50.4kmh/1000rpm
20.4mpg 17.0mpgUS 13.8L/100km
Petrol 4-stroke piston
4957cc 302.4cu in
Vee 8 fuel injection
Compression ratio: 10.0:1
Bore: 100.0mm 3.9in
Stroke: 78.9mm 3.1in
Valve type/No: Overhead 32
Transmission: Manual
No. of forward speeds: 5
Wheels driven: Rear
Springs F/R: Coil/Coil
Brake system: PA
Brakes F/R: Disc/Disc
Steering: Rack & pinion PA
Wheelbase: 249.9cm 98.4in
Track F: 155.2cm 61.1in
Track R: 152.9cm 60.2in
Length: 446.3cm 175.7in
Width: 183.6cm 72.3in
Height: 128.3cm 50.5in
Kerb weight: 1554.9kg 3425.0lb
Fuel: 85.9L 18.9gal 22.7galUS

3684 Porsche

928 S Series II
1985 Germany
151.0mph 243.0kmh
0-50mph 80.5kmh: 5.1secs
0-60mph 96.5kmh: 6.7secs
0-1/4 mile: 14.9secs
0-1km: 27.2secs
310.0bhp 231.2kW 314.3PS
@ 5900rpm
295.6lbft 400.5Nm @ 4500rpm
196.6bhp/ton 193.3bhp/tonne
66.5bhp/L 49.6kW/L 67.4PS/L
50.8ft/sec 15.5m/sec
31.2mph 50.2kmh/1000rpm
18.0mpg 15.0mpgUS 15.7L/100km
Petrol 4-stroke piston
4664cc 284.6cu in
Vee 8 fuel injection
Compression ratio: 10.4:1
Bore: 97.0mm 3.8in
Stroke: 78.8mm 3.1in
Valve type/No: Overhead 16
Transmission: Automatic
No. of forward speeds: 4
Wheels driven: Rear
Springs F/R: Coil/Coil
Brake system: PA ABS
Brakes F/R: Disc/Disc
Steering: Rack & pinion PA
Wheelbase: 249.9cm 98.4in
Track F: 154.4cm 60.8in
Track R: 151.4cm 59.6in
Length: 444.8cm 175.1in
Width: 183.6cm 72.3in
Height: 131.8cm 51.9in
Ground clearance: 16.5cm 6.5in
Kerb weight: 1603.5kg 3532.0lb
Fuel: 86.0L 18.9gal 22.7galUS

3685 Porsche

944 Lux
1985 Germany
137.0mph 220.4kmh
0-50mph 80.5kmh: 5.8secs
0-60mph 96.5kmh: 8.2secs
0-1/4 mile: 15.9secs
0-1km: 29.3secs
163.0bhp 121.5kW 165.3PS
@ 5800rpm
151.2lbft 204.9Nm @ 3000rpm
129.7bhp/ton 127.5bhp/tonne
65.7bhp/L 49.0kW/L 66.7PS/L
50.1ft/sec 15.2m/sec
28.2mph 45.4kmh/1000rpm
21.4mpg 17.8mpgUS 13.2L/100km
Petrol 4-stroke piston
2479cc 151.2cu in
In-line 4 fuel injection
Compression ratio: 10.6:1
Bore: 100.0mm 3.9in
Stroke: 78.9mm 3.1in
Valve type/No: Overhead 8
Transmission: Manual
No. of forward speeds: 5
Wheels driven: Rear
Springs F/R: Coil/Torsion bar
Brake system: PA
Brakes F/R: Disc/Disc
Steering: Rack & pinion PA
Wheelbase: 240.0cm 94.5in
Track F: 147.8cm 58.2in
Track R: 145.0cm 57.1in
Length: 419.9cm 165.3in
Width: 173.5cm 68.3in
Height: 127.5cm 50.2in
Ground clearance: 12.4cm 4.9in
Kerb weight: 1278.0kg 2815.0lb
Fuel: 80.1L 17.6gal 21.1galUS

3686 Porsche

944 Turbo
1985 Germany
153.0mph 246.2kmh
0-60mph 96.5kmh: 6.3secs
0-1/4 mile: 14.8secs
220.0bhp 164.0kW 223.0PS
@ 5800rpm
243.0lbft 329.3Nm @ 3500rpm
174.7bhp/ton 171.8bhp/tonne
88.7bhp/L 66.2kW/L 90.0PS/L
50.1ft/sec 15.2m/sec
25.0mph 40.2kmh/1000rpm
23.4mpg 19.5mpgUS 12.1L/100km
Petrol 4-stroke piston
2479cc 151.2cu in turbocharged
In-line 4 fuel injection
Compression ratio: 8.0:1
Bore: 100.0mm 3.9in
Stroke: 78.9mm 3.1in
Valve type/No: Overhead 8
Transmission: Manual
No. of forward speeds: 5
Wheels driven: Rear
Springs F/R: Coil/Torsion bar
Brakes F/R: Disc/Disc
Steering: Rack & pinion PA
Wheelbase: 240.0cm 94.5in
Track F: 147.8cm 58.2in
Track R: 145.0cm 57.1in
Length: 422.9cm 166.5in
Width: 173.5cm 68.3in
Height: 127.5cm 50.2in
Kerb weight: 1280.3kg 2820.0lb
Fuel: 62.1L 13.6gal 16.4galUS

3687 Porsche

911 Cabriolet
1986 Germany
130.0mph 209.2kmh
0-60mph 96.5kmh: 5.7secs
0-1/4 mile: 14.3secs
200.0bhp 149.1kW 202.8PS
@ 5900rpm
185.0lbft 250.7Nm @ 4800rpm
162.9bhp/ton 160.2bhp/tonne
63.2bhp/L 47.1kW/L 64.1PS/L
48.0ft/sec 14.6m/sec
23.2mph 37.3kmh/1000rpm
22.3mpg 18.6mpgUS 12.6L/100km
Petrol 4-stroke piston
3164cc 193.0cu in
Flat 6 fuel injection
Compression ratio: 9.5:1
Bore: 95.0mm 3.7in
Stroke: 74.4mm 2.9in
Valve type/No: Overhead 12
Transmission: Manual
No. of forward speeds: 5
Wheels driven: Rear
Springs F/R: Torsion bar/Torsion bar
Brake system: PA
Brakes F/R: Disc/Disc
Steering: Rack & pinion
Wheelbase: 227.3cm 89.5in
Track F: 136.9cm 53.9in
Track R: 137.9cm 54.3in
Length: 429.0cm 168.9in
Width: 165.1cm 65.0in
Height: 131.1cm 51.6in
Kerb weight: 1248.5kg 2750.0lb

3688 Porsche

911 Carrera SE
1986 Germany
149.0mph 239.7kmh
0-50mph 80.5kmh: 4.3secs
0-60mph 96.5kmh: 5.6secs
0-1/4 mile: 14.4secs
0-1km: 26.4secs
231.0bhp 172.3kW 234.2PS
@ 5900rpm
209.6lbft 284.0Nm @ 4800rpm
186.1bhp/ton 183.0bhp/tonne
73.0bhp/L 54.4kW/L 74.0PS/L
48.0ft/sec 14.6m/sec
24.0mph 38.6kmh/1000rpm
19.2mpg 16.0mpgUS 14.7L/100km
Petrol 4-stroke piston
3164cc 193.0cu in
Flat 6 fuel injection
Compression ratio: 10.3:1
Bore: 95.0mm 3.7in
Stroke: 74.4mm 2.9in
Valve type/No: Overhead 12
Transmission: Manual
No. of forward speeds: 5
Wheels driven: Rear
Springs F/R: Torsion bar/Torsion bar
Brake system: PA
Brakes F/R: Disc/Disc
Steering: Rack & pinion
Wheelbase: 227.3cm 89.5in
Track F: 143.3cm 56.4in
Track R: 150.1cm 59.1in
Length: 429.0cm 168.9in
Width: 177.5cm 69.9in
Height: 131.1cm 51.6in
Ground clearance: 11.9cm 4.7in
Kerb weight: 1262.1kg 2780.0lb
Fuel: 85.1L 18.7gal 22.5galUS

3689 Porsche

911 Turbo
1986 Germany
153.0mph 246.2kmh
0-60mph 96.5kmh: 5.0secs
0-1/4 mile: 13.4secs
282.0bhp 210.3kW 285.9PS
@ 5500rpm
278.0lbft 376.7Nm @ 4000rpm
206.4bhp/ton 203.0bhp/tonne
85.5bhp/L 63.7kW/L 86.7PS/L
44.8ft/sec 13.6m/sec
28.6mph 46.0kmh/1000rpm
20.4mpg 17.0mpgUS 13.8L/100km
Petrol 4-stroke piston
3299cc 201.3cu in turbocharged
Flat 6 fuel injection
Compression ratio: 7.0:1
Bore: 97.0mm 3.8in
Stroke: 74.4mm 2.9in
Valve type/No: Overhead 12
Transmission: Manual
No. of forward speeds: 4
Wheels driven: Rear
Springs F/R: Torsion bar/Torsion bar
Brake system: PA
Brakes F/R: Disc/Disc
Steering: Rack & pinion
Wheelbase: 227.3cm 89.5in
Track F: 143.3cm 56.4in
Track R: 149.1cm 58.7in
Length: 429.0cm 168.9in
Width: 177.5cm 69.9in
Height: 131.1cm 51.6in
Kerb weight: 1389.2kg 3060.0lb

3690 Porsche

924 S
1986 Germany
132.0mph 212.4kmh
0-60mph 96.5kmh: 7.8secs
0-1/4 mile: 15.8secs
147.0bhp 109.6kW 149.0PS
@ 5800rpm
140.0lbft 189.7Nm @ 3000rpm
119.1bhp/ton 117.1bhp/tonne
59.3bhp/L 44.2kW/L 60.1PS/L
50.1ft/sec 15.2m/sec
26.4mpg 22.0mpgUS 10.7L/100km
Petrol 4-stroke piston
2479cc 151.2cu in
In-line 4 fuel injection
Compression ratio: 9.7:1
Bore: 100.0mm 3.9in
Stroke: 78.9mm 3.1in
Valve type/No: Overhead 8
Transmission: Manual
No. of forward speeds: 5
Wheels driven: Rear
Springs F/R: Coil/Torsion bar
Brake system: PA
Brakes F/R: Disc/Disc
Steering: Rack & pinion PA
Wheelbase: 240.0cm 94.5in
Track F: 142.0cm 55.9in
Track R: 139.2cm 54.8in
Length: 429.0cm 168.9in
Width: 168.4cm 66.3in
Height: 127.5cm 50.2in
Kerb weight: 1255.3kg 2765.0lb
Fuel: 65.9L 14.5gal 17.4galUS

3691 Porsche

928 S
1986 Germany
152.0mph 244.6kmh
0-60mph 96.5kmh: 6.3secs
0-1/4 mile: 14.7secs
288.0bhp 214.8kW 292.0PS
@ 5750rpm
302.0lbft 409.2Nm @ 2700rpm
182.2bhp/ton 179.2bhp/tonne
58.1bhp/L 43.3kW/L 58.9PS/L
49.7ft/sec 15.1m/sec
32.9mph 52.9kmh/1000rpm
19.6mpg 16.3mpgUS 14.4L/100km
Petrol 4-stroke piston
4957cc 302.4cu in
Vee 8 fuel injection
Compression ratio: 10.0:1
Bore: 100.0mm 3.9in
Stroke: 78.9mm 3.1in
Valve type/No: Overhead 16
Transmission: Automatic
No. of forward speeds: 4
Wheels driven: Rear
Springs F/R: Coil/Coil
Brake system: PA ABS
Brakes F/R: Disc/Disc
Steering: Rack & pinion PA
Wheelbase: 249.9cm 98.4in
Track F: 154.9cm 61.0in
Track R: 152.1cm 59.9in
Length: 446.3cm 175.7in
Width: 183.6cm 72.3in
Height: 128.3cm 50.5in
Kerb weight: 1607.2kg 3540.0lb

3692 Porsche
928 S4 Automatic
1986 Germany
161.0mph 259.0kmh
0-50mph 80.5kmh: 4.7secs
0-60mph 96.5kmh: 6.2secs
0-1/4 mile: 14.5secs
0-1km: 26.2secs
320.0bhp 238.6kW 324.4PS
@ 6000rpm
317.0lbft 429.5Nm @ 3000rpm
205.2bhp/ton 201.8bhp/tonne
64.6bhp/L 48.1kW/L 65.4PS/L
51.8ft/sec 15.8m/sec
28.0mph 45.1kmh/1000rpm
17.0mpg 14.2mpgUS 16.6L/100km
Petrol 4-stroke piston
4957cc 302.0cu in
Vee 8 fuel injection
Compression ratio: 10.0:1
Bore: 100.0mm 3.9in
Stroke: 78.9mm 3.1in
Valve type/No: Overhead 32
Transmission: Automatic
No. of forward speeds: 4
Wheels driven: Rear
Springs F/R: Coil/Coil
Brake system: PA ABS
Brakes F/R: Disc/Disc
Steering: Rack & pinion PA
Wheelbase: 250.0cm 98.4in
Track F: 155.1cm 61.1in
Track R: 154.6cm 60.9in
Length: 452.0cm 178.0in
Width: 183.6cm 72.3in
Height: 128.2cm 50.5in
Ground clearance: 16.5cm 6.5in
Kerb weight: 1586.0kg 3493.4lb
Fuel: 86.4L 19.0gal 22.8galUS

3693 Porsche
944
1986 Germany
123.0mph 197.9kmh
0-60mph 96.5kmh: 8.9secs
0-1/4 mile: 16.6secs
147.0bhp 109.6kW 149.0PS
@ 5800rpm
144.0lbft 195.1Nm @ 3000rpm
113.5bhp/ton 111.6bhp/tonne
59.3bhp/L 44.2kW/L 60.1PS/L
50.1ft/sec 15.2m/sec
26.7mph 43.0kmh/1000rpm
26.5mpg 22.1mpgUS 10.6L/100km
Petrol 4-stroke piston
2479cc 151.2cu in
In-line 4 fuel injection
Compression ratio: 9.7:1
Bore: 100.0mm 3.9in
Stroke: 78.9mm 3.1in
Valve type/No: Overhead 8
Transmission: Manual
No. of forward speeds: 5
Wheels driven: Rear
Springs F/R: Coil/Torsion bar
Brake system: PA
Brakes F/R: Disc/Disc
Steering: Rack & pinion PA
Wheelbase: 240.0cm 94.5in
Track F: 147.8cm 58.2in
Track R: 145.0cm 57.1in
Length: 429.0cm 168.9in
Width: 173.5cm 68.3in
Height: 127.5cm 50.2in
Kerb weight: 1316.6kg 2900.0lb

3694 Porsche
944 S
1986 Germany
141.0mph 226.9kmh
0-50mph 80.5kmh: 5.1secs
0-60mph 96.5kmh: 6.7secs
0-1/4 mile: 15.1secs
0-1km: 27.8secs
190.0bhp 141.7kW 192.6PS
@ 6000rpm
170.0lbft 230.4Nm @ 4300rpm
151.0bhp/ton 148.4bhp/tonne
76.6bhp/L 57.1kW/L 77.7PS/L
51.8ft/sec 15.8m/sec
22.3mph 35.9kmh/1000rpm
23.5mpg 19.6mpgUS 12.0L/100km
Petrol 4-stroke piston
2479cc 151.0cu in
In-line 4 fuel injection
Compression ratio: 10.9:1
Bore: 100.0mm 3.9in
Stroke: 78.9mm 3.1in
Valve type/No: Overhead 16
Transmission: Manual
No. of forward speeds: 5
Wheels driven: Rear
Springs F/R: Coil/Torsion bar
Brake system: PA
Brakes F/R: Disc/Disc
Steering: Rack & pinion PA
Wheelbase: 240.0cm 94.5in
Track F: 147.7cm 58.1in
Track R: 145.1cm 57.1in
Length: 420.0cm 165.4in
Width: 173.5cm 68.3in
Height: 127.5cm 50.2in
Ground clearance: 13.8cm 5.4in
Kerb weight: 1280.0kg 2819.4lb
Fuel: 80.1L 17.6gal 21.1galUS

3695 Porsche
944 Turbo
1986 Germany
158.0mph 254.2kmh
0-50mph 80.5kmh: 4.5secs
0-60mph 96.5kmh: 6.0secs
0-1/4 mile: 14.8secs
0-1km: 27.0secs
220.0bhp 164.0kW 223.0PS
@ 5800rpm
243.0lbft 329.3Nm @ 3500rpm
165.6bhp/ton 162.9bhp/tonne
88.7bhp/L 66.2kW/L 90.0PS/L
50.1ft/sec 15.2m/sec
25.6mph 41.2kmh/1000rpm
22.9mpg 19.1mpgUS 12.3L/100km
Petrol 4-stroke piston
2479cc 151.2cu in turbocharged
In-line 4 fuel injection
Compression ratio: 8.0:1
Bore: 100.0mm 3.9in
Stroke: 78.9mm 3.1in
Valve type/No: Overhead 8
Transmission: Manual
No. of forward speeds: 5
Wheels driven: Rear
Springs F/R: Coil/Torsion bar
Brake system: PA
Brakes F/R: Disc/Disc
Steering: Rack & pinion PA
Wheelbase: 240.0cm 94.5in
Track F: 147.8cm 58.2in
Track R: 145.0cm 57.1in
Length: 419.9cm 165.3in
Width: 173.5cm 68.3in
Height: 127.5cm 50.2in
Ground clearance: 11.9cm 4.7in
Kerb weight: 1350.6kg 2975.0lb
Fuel: 80.1L 17.6gal 21.1galUS

3696 Porsche
911 Carrera
1987 Germany
0-60mph 96.5kmh: 5.7secs
0-1/4 mile: 14.3secs
214.0bhp 159.6kW 217.0PS
@ 5900rpm
195.0lbft 264.2Nm @ 4800rpm
174.0bhp/ton 171.1bhp/tonne
67.6bhp/L 50.4kW/L 68.6PS/L
22.2mpg 18.5mpgUS 12.7L/100km
Petrol 4-stroke piston
3164cc 193.0cu in
Flat 6
Valve type/No: Overhead 12
Transmission: Manual
No. of forward speeds: 5
Wheels driven: Rear
Brakes F/R: Disc/Disc
Steering: Rack & pinion
Length: 429.0cm 168.9in
Kerb weight: 1250.8kg 2755.0lb

3697 Porsche
911 Turbo Gemballa Avalanche
1987 Germany
165.0mph 265.5kmh
0-60mph 96.5kmh: 4.9secs
0-1/4 mile: 13.0secs
282.0bhp 210.3kW 285.9PS
@ 5500rpm
278.0lbft 376.7Nm @ 4000rpm
191.1bhp/ton 187.9bhp/tonne
85.5bhp/L 63.7kW/L 86.7PS/L
44.8ft/sec 13.6m/sec
Petrol 4-stroke piston
3299cc 201.3cu in turbocharged
Flat 6 fuel injection
Compression ratio: 7.0:1
Bore: 97.0mm 3.8in
Stroke: 74.4mm 2.9in
Valve type/No: Overhead 12
Transmission: Manual
No. of forward speeds: 4
Wheels driven: Rear
Springs F/R: Torsion bar/Torsion bar
Brake system: PA
Brakes F/R: Disc/Disc
Steering: Rack & pinion
Wheelbase: 227.3cm 89.5in
Track F: 144.8cm 57.0in
Track R: 151.9cm 59.8in
Length: 428.0cm 168.5in
Width: 192.8cm 75.9in
Height: 131.1cm 51.6in
Kerb weight: 1500.5kg 3305.0lb
Fuel: 85.2L 18.7gal 22.5galUS

3698 Porsche
911 Turbo Ruf 3.4
1987 Germany
158.0mph 254.2kmh
0-60mph 96.5kmh: 4.5secs
0-1/4 mile: 13.0secs
374.0bhp 278.9kW 379.2PS
@ 6000rpm
354.0lbft 479.7Nm @ 4800rpm
299.2bhp/ton 294.2bhp/tonne
111.1bhp/L 82.9kW/L 112.6PS/L
28.4mph 45.7kmh/1000rpm
Petrol 4-stroke piston
3366cc 205.4cu in turbocharged
Flat 6 fuel injection
Compression ratio: 7.0:1
Valve type/No: Overhead 12
Transmission: Manual
No. of forward speeds: 5
Wheels driven: Rear
Springs F/R: Torsion bar/Torsion bar
Brake system: PA
Brakes F/R: Disc/Disc
Steering: Rack & pinion
Wheelbase: 227.3cm 89.5in
Track F: 146.6cm 57.7in
Track R: 150.1cm 59.1in
Length: 429.0cm 168.9in
Width: 177.5cm 69.9in
Height: 128.0cm 50.4in
Kerb weight: 1271.2kg 2800.0lb

3699 Porsche
911 Turbo Slant-Nose
1987 Germany
157.0mph 252.6kmh
0-60mph 96.5kmh: 5.0secs
0-1/4 mile: 13.4secs
282.0bhp 210.3kW 285.9PS
@ 5500rpm
278.0lbft 376.7Nm @ 4000rpm
212.3bhp/ton 208.8bhp/tonne
85.5bhp/L 63.7kW/L 86.7PS/L
44.8ft/sec 13.6m/sec
Petrol 4-stroke piston
3299cc 201.3cu in turbocharged
Flat 6 fuel injection
Compression ratio: 7.0:1
Bore: 97.0mm 3.8in
Stroke: 74.4mm 2.9in
Valve type/No: Overhead 12
Transmission: Manual
No. of forward speeds: 4
Wheels driven: Rear
Springs F/R: Torsion bar/Torsion bar
Brake system: PA
Brakes F/R: Disc/Disc
Steering: Rack & pinion
Wheelbase: 227.3cm 89.5in
Track F: 143.3cm 56.4in
Track R: 149.1cm 58.7in
Length: 429.0cm 168.9in
Width: 177.5cm 69.9in
Height: 131.1cm 51.6in
Kerb weight: 1350.6kg 2975.0lb
Fuel: 85.2L 18.7gal 22.5galUS

3700 Porsche
924 S
1987 Germany
136.0mph 218.8kmh
0-50mph 80.5kmh: 5.6secs
0-60mph 96.5kmh: 8.0secs
0-1/4 mile: 16.3secs
0-1km: 29.2secs
160.0bhp 119.3kW 162.2PS
@ 5900rpm
155.0lbft 210.0Nm @ 4500rpm
136.2bhp/ton 133.9bhp/tonne
64.5bhp/L 48.1kW/L 65.4PS/L
51.0ft/sec 15.5m/sec
22.2mph 35.7kmh/1000rpm
22.6mpg 18.8mpgUS 12.5L/100km
Petrol 4-stroke piston
2479cc 151.0cu in
In-line 4 fuel injection
Compression ratio: 10.2:1
Bore: 100.0mm 3.9in
Stroke: 78.9mm 3.1in
Valve type/No: Overhead 8
Transmission: Manual
No. of forward speeds: 5
Wheels driven: Rear
Springs F/R: Coil/Coil
Brake system: PA
Brakes F/R: Disc/Disc
Steering: Rack & pinion PA
Wheelbase: 235.5cm 92.7in
Track F: 142.0cm 55.9in
Track R: 137.2cm 54.0in
Length: 419.9cm 165.3in
Width: 165.6cm 65.2in
Height: 127.0cm 50.0in
Ground clearance: 15.2cm 6.0in
Kerb weight: 1195.0kg 2632.2lb
Fuel: 66.0L 14.5gal 17.4galUS

3701 Porsche
944 S
1987 Germany
0-60mph 96.5kmh: 7.2secs
0-1/4 mile: 15.6secs
188.0bhp 140.2kW 190.6PS
@ 6000rpm
170.0lbft 230.4Nm @ 4300rpm
147.0bhp/ton 144.5bhp/tonne
75.8bhp/L 56.5kW/L 76.9PS/L
25.2mpg 21.0mpgUS 11.2L/100km
Petrol 4-stroke piston
2479cc 151.2cu in
In-line 4
Valve type/No: Overhead 16
Transmission: Manual
No. of forward speeds: 5
Wheels driven: Rear
Brakes F/R: Disc/Disc
Steering: Rack & pinion PA
Length: 429.0cm 168.9in
Kerb weight: 1300.7kg 2865.0lb

3702 Porsche
959 S
1987 Germany
201.0mph 323.4kmh
0-60mph 96.5kmh: 4.7secs
0-1/4 mile: 11.9secs
600.0bhp 447.4kW 608.3PS
@ 6500rpm
369.0lbft 500.0Nm @ 5500rpm
451.0bhp/ton 443.5bhp/tonne
210.6bhp/L 157.0kW/L 213.5PS/L
47.7ft/sec 14.5m/sec
Petrol 4-stroke piston
2849cc 173.8cu in turbocharged
Flat 6 fuel injection
Compression ratio: 8.0:1
Bore: 95.0mm 3.7in
Stroke: 67.0mm 2.6in
Valve type/No: Overhead 24
Transmission: Manual
No. of forward speeds: 6
Wheels driven: 4-wheel drive
Springs F/R: Coil/Coil
Brake system: PA ABS
Brakes F/R: Disc/Disc
Steering: Rack & pinion PA
Wheelbase: 229.9cm 90.5in
Track F: 150.4cm 59.2in
Track R: 154.9cm 61.0in
Length: 426.0cm 167.7in
Width: 183.9cm 72.4in
Height: 128.0cm 50.4in
Kerb weight: 1352.9kg 2980.0lb

3703 Porsche
911 Cabriolet
1988 Germany
149.0mph 239.7kmh
0-60mph 96.5kmh: 6.5secs
0-1/4 mile: 15.0secs
214.0bhp 159.6kW 217.0PS

@ 5900rpm
195.0lbft 264.2Nm @ 4800rpm
163.0bhp/ton 160.3bhp/tonne
67.6bhp/L 50.4kW/L 68.6PS/L
48.0ft/sec 14.6m/sec
27.0mpg 22.5mpgUS 10.5L/100km
Petrol 4-stroke piston
3164cc 193.0cu in
Flat 6 fuel injection
Compression ratio: 9.5:1
Bore: 95.0mm 3.7in
Stroke: 74.4mm 2.9in
Valve type/No: Overhead 12
Transmission: Manual
No. of forward speeds: 5
Wheels driven: Rear
Springs F/R: Coil/Torsion bar
Brake system: PA
Brakes F/R: Disc/Disc
Steering: Rack & pinion
Wheelbase: 227.3cm 89.5in
Track F: 136.9cm 53.9in
Track R: 137.9cm 54.3in
Length: 429.0cm 168.9in
Width: 165.1cm 65.0in
Height: 131.1cm 51.6in
Kerb weight: 1334.8kg 2940.0lb
Fuel: 85.2L 18.7gal 22.5galUS

3704 Porsche

911 Carrera
1988 Germany
149.0mph 239.7kmh
0-50mph 80.5kmh: 5.4secs
0-60mph 96.5kmh: 7.0secs
0-1/4 mile: 15.1secs
214.0bhp 159.6kW 217.0PS
@ 5900rpm
195.0lbft 264.2Nm @ 4800rpm
173.0bhp/ton 170.2bhp/tonne
67.6bhp/L 50.4kW/L 68.6PS/L
48.0ft/sec 14.6m/sec
24.6mph 39.6kmh/1000rpm
21.6mpg 18.0mpgUS 13.1L/100km
Petrol 4-stroke piston
3164cc 193.0cu in
Flat 6 fuel injection
Compression ratio: 9.5:1
Bore: 95.0mm 3.7in
Stroke: 74.4mm 2.9in
Valve type/No: Overhead 12
Transmission: Manual
No. of forward speeds: 5
Wheels driven: Rear
Springs F/R: Torsion bar/Torsion bar
Brake system: PA
Brakes F/R: Disc/Disc
Steering: Rack & pinion
Wheelbase: 227.3cm 89.5in
Track F: 136.9cm 53.9in
Track R: 137.9cm 54.3in
Length: 429.0cm 168.9in
Width: 165.1cm 65.0in
Height: 132.1cm 52.0in
Ground clearance: 13.0cm 5.1in
Kerb weight: 1257.6kg 2770.0lb
Fuel: 85.2L 18.7gal 22.5galUS

3705 Porsche

911 Carrera Club Sport
1988 Germany
152.0mph 244.6kmh
0-50mph 80.5kmh: 4.0secs
0-60mph 96.5kmh: 5.2secs
0-1/4 mile: 13.9secs
0-1km: 25.3secs
231.0bhp 172.3kW 234.2PS
@ 5900rpm
210.0lbft 284.6Nm @ 4800rpm
198.4bhp/ton 195.1bhp/tonne
73.0bhp/L 54.4kW/L 74.0PS/L
48.0ft/sec 14.6m/sec
24.3mph 39.1kmh/1000rpm
20.6mpg 17.2mpgUS 13.7L/100km
Petrol 4-stroke piston
3164cc 193.0cu in
Flat 6 fuel injection
Compression ratio: 10.3:1
Bore: 95.0mm 3.7in
Stroke: 74.4mm 2.9in
Valve type/No: Overhead 12
Transmission: Manual
No. of forward speeds: 5
Wheels driven: Rear
Springs F/R: Torsion bar/Torsion bar
Brake system: PA
Brakes F/R: Disc/Disc
Steering: Rack & pinion
Wheelbase: 227.2cm 89.4in
Track F: 143.2cm 56.4in
Track R: 150.1cm 59.1in
Length: 429.0cm 168.9in
Width: 177.5cm 69.9in
Height: 131.0cm 51.6in
Ground clearance: 12.0cm 4.7in
Kerb weight: 1184.0kg 2608.0lb
Fuel: 85.1L 18.7gal 22.5galUS

3706 Porsche

911 Club Sport
1988 Germany
149.0mph 239.7kmh
0-50mph 80.5kmh: 4.5secs
0-60mph 96.5kmh: 5.7secs
0-1/4 mile: 14.3secs
214.0bhp 159.6kW 217.0PS
@ 5900rpm
195.0lbft 264.2Nm @ 4800rpm
184.4bhp/ton 181.3bhp/tonne
67.6bhp/L 50.4kW/L 68.6PS/L
48.0ft/sec 14.6m/sec
21.6mpg 18.0mpgUS 13.1L/100km
Petrol 4-stroke piston
3164cc 193.0cu in
Flat 6 fuel injection
Compression ratio: 9.5:1
Bore: 95.0mm 3.7in
Stroke: 74.4mm 2.9in
Valve type/No: Overhead 12
Transmission: Manual
No. of forward speeds: 5
Wheels driven: Rear
Springs F/R: Torsion bar/Torsion bar
Brake system: PA
Brakes F/R: Disc/Disc
Steering: Rack & pinion
Wheelbase: 227.3cm 89.5in
Track F: 140.0cm 55.1in
Track R: 140.7cm 55.4in
Length: 429.0cm 168.9in
Width: 165.1cm 65.0in
Height: 132.1cm 52.0in
Ground clearance: 13.0cm 5.1in
Kerb weight: 1180.4kg 2600.0lb
Fuel: 85.2L 18.7gal 22.5galUS

3707 Porsche

911 Speedster
1988 Germany
155.0mph 249.4kmh
0-60mph 96.5kmh: 6.5secs
0-1/4 mile: 14.5secs
231.0bhp 172.3kW 234.2PS
@ 5900rpm
209.0lbft 283.2Nm @ 4800rpm
200.6bhp/ton 197.2bhp/tonne
73.0bhp/L 54.4kW/L 74.0PS/L
48.0ft/sec 14.6m/sec
Petrol 4-stroke piston
3164cc 193.0cu in
Flat 6 fuel injection
Compression ratio: 9.5:1
Bore: 95.0mm 3.7in
Stroke: 74.4mm 2.9in
Valve type/No: Overhead 12
Transmission: Manual
No. of forward speeds: 5
Wheels driven: Rear
Springs F/R: Torsion bar/Torsion bar
Brake system: PA
Brakes F/R: Disc/Disc
Steering: Rack & pinion
Wheelbase: 227.3cm 89.5in
Track F: 139.7cm 55.0in
Track R: 140.5cm 55.3in
Length: 429.0cm 168.9in
Width: 165.1cm 65.0in
Height: 130.0cm 51.2in
Kerb weight: 1171.3kg 2580.0lb
Fuel: 79.5L 17.5gal 21.0galUS

3708 Porsche

911 Turbo
1988 Germany
155.0mph 249.4kmh
0-50mph 80.5kmh: 3.4secs
0-60mph 96.5kmh: 5.0secs
0-1/4 mile: 13.4secs
282.0bhp 210.3kW 285.9PS
@ 5500rpm
278.0lbft 376.7Nm @ 4000rpm
206.8bhp/ton 203.3bhp/tonne
85.5bhp/L 63.7kW/L 86.7PS/L
44.8ft/sec 13.6m/sec
28.6mph 46.0kmh/1000rpm
19.2mpg 16.0mpgUS 14.7L/100km
Petrol 4-stroke piston
3299cc 201.3cu in turbocharged
Flat 6 fuel injection
Compression ratio: 7.0:1
Bore: 97.0mm 3.8in
Stroke: 74.4mm 2.9in
Valve type/No: Overhead 12
Transmission: Manual
No. of forward speeds: 4
Wheels driven: Rear
Springs F/R: Torsion bar/Torsion bar
Brake system: PA
Brakes F/R: Disc/Disc
Steering: Rack & pinion
Wheelbase: 227.3cm 89.5in
Track F: 143.3cm 56.4in
Track R: 150.1cm 59.1in
Length: 429.0cm 168.9in
Width: 177.5cm 69.9in
Height: 131.1cm 51.6in
Ground clearance: 11.9cm 4.7in
Kerb weight: 1387.0kg 3055.0lb
Fuel: 85.2L 18.7gal 22.5galUS

3709 Porsche

911 Turbo Koenig RS
1988 Germany
201.0mph 323.4kmh
0-60mph 96.5kmh: 4.0secs
0-1/4 mile: 11.6secs
520.0bhp 387.8kW 527.2PS
@ 6300rpm
490.0lbft 664.0Nm @ 5500rpm
416.0bhp/ton 409.1bhp/tonne
154.5bhp/L 115.2kW/L 156.6PS/L
51.3ft/sec 15.6m/sec
Petrol 4-stroke piston
3366cc 205.4cu in turbocharged
Flat 6 fuel injection
Compression ratio: 7.5:1
Bore: 98.0mm 3.9in
Stroke: 74.4mm 2.9in
Valve type/No: Overhead 12
Transmission: Manual
No. of forward speeds: 5
Wheels driven: Rear
Springs F/R: Torsion bar/Torsion bar
Brake system: PA
Brakes F/R: Disc/Disc
Steering: Rack & pinion
Wheelbase: 227.3cm 89.5in
Track F: 143.3cm 56.4in
Track R: 150.1cm 59.1in
Length: 429.0cm 168.9in
Width: 177.5cm 69.9in
Height: 131.1cm 51.6in
Kerb weight: 1271.2kg 2800.0lb
Fuel: 85.2L 18.7gal 22.5galUS

3710 Porsche

911 Turbo Ruf Twin Turbo
1988 Germany
211.0mph 339.5kmh
0-60mph 96.5kmh: 4.0secs
0-1/4 mile: 11.7secs
469.0bhp 349.7kW 475.5PS
@ 5950rpm
457.0lbft 619.2Nm @ 5100rpm
415.2bhp/ton 408.3bhp/tonne
139.3bhp/L 103.9kW/L 141.3PS/L
48.4ft/sec 14.8m/sec
Petrol 4-stroke piston
3366cc 205.4cu in turbocharged
Flat 6 fuel injection
Compression ratio: 7.5:1
Bore: 98.0mm 3.9in
Stroke: 74.4mm 2.9in
Valve type/No: Overhead 12
Transmission: Manual
No. of forward speeds: 5
Wheels driven: Rear
Springs F/R: Torsion bar/Torsion bar
Brake system: PA
Brakes F/R: Disc/Disc
Steering: Rack & pinion
Wheelbase: 227.3cm 89.5in
Track F: 143.3cm 56.4in
Track R: 150.1cm 59.1in
Length: 429.0cm 168.9in
Width: 177.5cm 69.9in
Height: 131.1cm 51.6in
Kerb weight: 1148.6kg 2530.0lb
Fuel: 85.2L 18.7gal 22.5galUS

3711 Porsche

924 S
1988 Germany
138.0mph 222.0kmh
0-50mph 80.5kmh: 5.3secs
0-60mph 96.5kmh: 7.5secs
0-1/4 mile: 15.8secs
147.0bhp 109.6kW 149.0PS
@ 5800rpm
140.0lbft 189.7Nm @ 3000rpm
117.0bhp/ton 115.0bhp/tonne
59.3bhp/L 44.2kW/L 60.1PS/L
50.1ft/sec 15.2m/sec
26.7mph 43.0kmh/1000rpm
26.4mpg 22.0mpgUS 10.7L/100km
Petrol 4-stroke piston
2479cc 151.2cu in
In-line 4 fuel injection
Compression ratio: 9.7:1
Bore: 100.0mm 3.9in
Stroke: 78.9mm 3.1in
Valve type/No: Overhead 8
Transmission: Manual
No. of forward speeds: 5
Wheels driven: Rear
Springs F/R: Coil/Torsion bar
Brake system: PA
Brakes F/R: Disc/Disc
Steering: Rack & pinion PA
Wheelbase: 240.0cm 94.5in
Track F: 142.0cm 55.9in
Track R: 139.2cm 54.8in
Length: 429.0cm 168.9in
Width: 168.4cm 66.3in
Height: 127.5cm 50.2in
Ground clearance: 11.9cm 4.7in
Kerb weight: 1278.0kg 2815.0lb
Fuel: 65.9L 14.5gal 17.4galUS

3712 Porsche

928 S4
1988 Germany
165.0mph 265.5kmh
0-50mph 80.5kmh: 4.4secs
0-60mph 96.5kmh: 5.5secs
0-1/4 mile: 13.9secs
316.0bhp 235.6kW 320.4PS
@ 6000rpm
317.0lbft 429.5Nm @ 3000rpm
200.8bhp/ton 197.5bhp/tonne
63.7bhp/L 47.5kW/L 64.6PS/L
51.8ft/sec 15.8m/sec
33.0mph 53.1kmh/1000rpm
19.8mpg 16.5mpgUS 14.3L/100km
Petrol 4-stroke piston
4957cc 302.4cu in
Vee 8 fuel injection
Compression ratio: 10.0:1
Bore: 100.0mm 3.9in
Stroke: 78.9mm 3.1in
Valve type/No: Overhead 32
Transmission: Manual
No. of forward speeds: 5
Wheels driven: Rear
Springs F/R: Coil/Coil
Brake system: PA ABS
Brakes F/R: Disc/Disc
Steering: Rack & pinion PA
Wheelbase: 249.9cm 98.4in
Track F: 154.9cm 61.0in
Track R: 154.7cm 60.9in
Length: 452.4cm 178.1in
Width: 183.6cm 72.3in
Height: 128.3cm 50.5in
Ground clearance: 11.9cm 4.7in
Kerb weight: 1600.3kg 3525.0lb
Fuel: 85.9L 18.9gal 22.7galUS

3713 Porsche

944
1988 Germany
132.0mph 212.4kmh
0-50mph 80.5kmh: 6.4secs
0-60mph 96.5kmh: 8.7secs
0-1/4 mile: 16.4secs
147.0bhp 109.6kW 149.0PS
@ 5800rpm
140.0lbft 189.7Nm @ 3000rpm
111.1bhp/ton 109.2bhp/tonne
59.3bhp/L 44.2kW/L 60.1PS/L
50.1ft/sec 15.2m/sec
26.7mph 43.0kmh/1000rpm
25.2mpg 21.0mpgUS 11.2L/100km
Petrol 4-stroke piston
2479cc 151.2cu in
In-line 4 fuel injection
Compression ratio: 9.7:1

Bore: 100.0mm 3.9in
Stroke: 78.9mm 3.1in
Valve type/No: Overhead 8
Transmission: Manual
No. of forward speeds: 5
Wheels driven: Rear
Springs F/R: Coil/Torsion bar
Brake system: PA
Brakes F/R: Disc/Disc
Steering: Rack & pinion PA
Wheelbase: 240.0cm 94.5in
Track F: 147.8cm 58.2in
Track R: 145.0cm 57.1in
Length: 429.0cm 168.9in
Width: 173.5cm 68.3in
Height: 127.5cm 50.2in
Ground clearance: 11.9cm 4.7in
Kerb weight: 1346.1kg 2965.0lb
Fuel: 79.9L 17.6gal 21.1galUS

3714 Porsche

944 S
1988 Germany
140.0mph 225.3kmh
0-50mph 80.5kmh: 5.0secs
0-60mph 96.5kmh: 7.5secs
0-1/4 mile: 15.8secs
188.0bhp 140.2kW 190.6PS
@ 6000rpm
170.0lbft 230.4Nm @ 4300rpm
141.5bhp/ton 139.2bhp/tonne
75.8bhp/L 56.5kW/L 76.9PS/L
51.8ft/sec 15.8m/sec
20.7mph 33.3kmh/1000rpm
23.4mpg 19.5mpgUS 12.1L/100km
Petrol 4-stroke piston
2479cc 151.2cu in
In-line 4 fuel injection
Compression ratio: 10.9:1
Bore: 100.0mm 3.9in
Stroke: 78.9mm 3.1in
Valve type/No: Overhead 16
Transmission: Manual
No. of forward speeds: 5
Wheels driven: Rear
Springs F/R: Coil/Torsion bar
Brake system: PA
Brakes F/R: Disc/Disc
Steering: Rack & pinion PA
Wheelbase: 240.0cm 94.5in
Track F: 147.8cm 58.2in
Track R: 145.0cm 57.1in
Length: 429.0cm 168.9in
Width: 173.5cm 68.3in
Height: 127.5cm 50.2in
Ground clearance: 11.9cm 4.7in
Kerb weight: 1350.6kg 2975.0lb
Fuel: 79.9L 17.6gal 21.1galUS

3715 Porsche

944 Turbo
1988 Germany
155.0mph 249.4kmh
0-50mph 80.5kmh: 4.7secs
0-60mph 96.5kmh: 6.0secs
0-1/4 mile: 14.6secs
217.0bhp 161.8kW 220.0PS
@ 5800rpm
243.0lbft 329.3Nm @ 3500rpm
156.0bhp/ton 153.4bhp/tonne
87.5bhp/L 65.3kW/L 88.7PS/L
50.1ft/sec 15.2m/sec
26.7mph 43.0kmh/1000rpm
22.8mpg 19.0mpgUS 12.4L/100km
Petrol 4-stroke piston
2479cc 151.2cu in turbocharged
In-line 4 fuel injection
Compression ratio: 8.0:1
Bore: 100.0mm 3.9in
Stroke: 78.9mm 3.1in
Valve type/No: Overhead 8
Transmission: Manual
No. of forward speeds: 5
Wheels driven: Rear
Springs F/R: Coil/Torsion bar
Brake system: PA
Brakes F/R: Disc/Disc
Steering: Rack & pinion PA
Wheelbase: 240.0cm 94.5in
Track F: 147.8cm 58.2in
Track R: 145.0cm 57.1in
Length: 429.0cm 168.9in
Width: 173.5cm 68.3in
Height: 127.5cm 50.2in
Ground clearance: 11.9cm 4.7in
Kerb weight: 1414.2kg 3115.0lb
Fuel: 79.9L 17.6gal 21.1galUS

3716 Porsche

944 Turbo SE
1988 Germany
154.0mph 247.8kmh
0-50mph 80.5kmh: 4.6secs
0-60mph 96.5kmh: 5.7secs
0-1/4 mile: 14.2secs
0-1km: 25.8secs
250.0bhp 186.4kW 253.5PS
@ 6000rpm
258.3lbft 350.0Nm @ 4000rpm
208.2bhp/ton 204.7bhp/tonne
100.8bhp/L 75.2kW/L 102.2PS/L
51.8ft/sec 15.8m/sec
25.3mph 40.7kmh/1000rpm
19.1mpg 15.9mpgUS 14.8L/100km
Petrol 4-stroke piston
2479cc 151.0cu in turbocharged
In-line 4 fuel injection
Compression ratio: 8.0:1
Bore: 100.0mm 3.9in
Stroke: 78.9mm 3.1in
Valve type/No: Overhead 8
Transmission: Manual
No. of forward speeds: 5
Wheels driven: Rear
Springs F/R: Coil/Torsion bar
Brake system: PA ABS
Brakes F/R: Disc/Disc
Steering: Rack & pinion PA
Wheelbase: 240.0cm 94.5in
Track F: 147.7cm 58.1in
Track R: 145.1cm 57.1in
Length: 420.0cm 165.4in
Width: 173.5cm 68.3in
Height: 127.5cm 50.2in
Ground clearance: 12.0cm 4.7in
Kerb weight: 1221.0kg 2689.4lb
Fuel: 80.1L 17.6gal 21.1galUS

3717 Porsche

959 Comfort
1988 Germany
198.0mph 318.6kmh
0-60mph 96.5kmh: 4.0secs
0-1/4 mile: 12.4secs
450.0bhp 335.6kW 456.2PS
@ 6500rpm
370.0lbft 501.4Nm @ 5500rpm
316.0bhp/ton 310.7bhp/tonne
157.9bhp/L 117.8kW/L 160.1PS/L
47.7ft/sec 14.5m/sec
Petrol 4-stroke piston
2849cc 173.8cu in turbocharged
Flat 6 fuel injection
Compression ratio: 8.3:1
Bore: 95.0mm 3.7in
Stroke: 67.0mm 2.6in
Valve type/No: Overhead 24
Transmission: Manual
No. of forward speeds: 6
Wheels driven: 4-wheel drive
Springs F/R: Coil/Coil
Brake system: ABS
Brakes F/R: Disc/Disc
Steering: Rack & pinion PA
Wheelbase: 227.3cm 89.5in
Track F: 150.4cm 59.2in
Track R: 154.9cm 61.0in
Length: 426.0cm 167.7in
Width: 183.9cm 72.4in
Height: 128.0cm 50.4in
Kerb weight: 1448.3kg 3190.0lb
Fuel: 90.1L 19.8gal 23.8galUS

3718 Porsche

959 Sport
1988 Germany
198.0mph 318.6kmh
0-60mph 96.5kmh: 3.6secs
0-1/4 mile: 11.9secs
450.0bhp 335.6kW 456.2PS
@ 6500rpm
370.0lbft 501.4Nm @ 5500rpm
339.4bhp/ton 333.7bhp/tonne
157.9bhp/L 117.8kW/L 160.1PS/L
47.7ft/sec 14.5m/sec
Petrol 4-stroke piston
2849cc 173.8cu in turbocharged
Flat 6 fuel injection
Compression ratio: 8.3:1
Bore: 95.0mm 3.7in
Stroke: 67.0mm 2.6in
Valve type/No: Overhead 24
Transmission: Manual
No. of forward speeds: 6
Wheels driven: 4-wheel drive
Springs F/R: Coil/Coil
Brake system: ABS
Brakes F/R: Disc/Disc
Steering: Rack & pinion PA
Wheelbase: 227.3cm 89.5in
Track F: 150.4cm 59.2in
Track R: 154.9cm 61.0in
Length: 426.0cm 167.7in
Width: 183.9cm 72.4in
Height: 128.0cm 50.4in
Kerb weight: 1348.4kg 2970.0lb
Fuel: 90.1L 19.8gal 23.8galUS

3719 Porsche

911 3.3 Turbo
1989 Germany
158.0mph 254.2kmh
0-50mph 80.5kmh: 3.8secs
0-60mph 96.5kmh: 4.9secs
0-1/4 mile: 13.1secs
0-1km: 24.1secs
300.0bhp 223.7kW 304.2PS
@ 5500rpm
317.3lbft 430.0Nm @ 4000rpm
220.3bhp/ton 216.6bhp/tonne
90.9bhp/L 67.8kW/L 92.2PS/L
44.8ft/sec 13.6m/sec
27.4mph 44.1kmh/1000rpm
16.6mpg 13.8mpgUS 17.0L/100km
Petrol 4-stroke piston
3299cc 201.0cu in turbocharged
Flat 6 fuel injection
Compression ratio: 7.0:1
Bore: 97.0mm 3.8in
Stroke: 74.4mm 2.9in
Valve type/No: Overhead 12
Transmission: Manual
No. of forward speeds: 5
Wheels driven: Rear
Springs F/R: Torsion bar/Torsion bar
Brake system: PA
Brakes F/R: Disc/Disc
Steering: Rack & pinion
Wheelbase: 227.2cm 89.4in
Track F: 143.2cm 56.4in
Track R: 150.1cm 59.1in
Length: 429.0cm 168.9in
Width: 177.5cm 69.9in
Height: 131.0cm 51.6in
Ground clearance: 12.0cm 4.7in
Kerb weight: 1385.0kg 3050.7lb
Fuel: 85.1L 18.7gal 22.5galUS

3720 Porsche

911 Carrera 4
1989 Germany
161.0mph 259.0kmh
0-50mph 80.5kmh: 3.8secs
0-60mph 96.5kmh: 4.9secs
0-1/4 mile: 13.5secs
250.0bhp 186.4kW 253.5PS
@ 6100rpm
229.0lbft 310.3Nm @ 4800rpm
168.7bhp/ton 165.9bhp/tonne
69.4bhp/L 51.8kW/L 70.4PS/L
51.0ft/sec 15.5m/sec
20.4mpg 17.0mpgUS 13.8L/100km
Petrol 4-stroke piston
3600cc 219.6cu in
Flat 6 fuel injection
Compression ratio: 11.3:1
Bore: 100.0mm 3.9in
Stroke: 76.4mm 3.0in
Valve type/No: Overhead 12
Transmission: Manual
No. of forward speeds: 5
Wheels driven: 4-wheel drive
Springs F/R: Coil/Coil
Brake system: PA ABS
Brakes F/R: Disc/Disc
Steering: Rack & pinion PA
Wheelbase: 227.1cm 89.4in
Track F: 137.9cm 54.3in
Track R: 137.4cm 54.1in
Length: 424.9cm 167.3in
Width: 165.1cm 65.0in
Height: 132.1cm 52.0in
Ground clearance: 16.0cm 6.3in
Kerb weight: 1507.3kg 3320.0lb
Fuel: 76.8L 16.9gal 20.3galUS

3721 Porsche

911 Carrera Cabriolet
1989 Germany
149.0mph 239.7kmh
0-50mph 80.5kmh: 4.7secs
0-60mph 96.5kmh: 6.1secs
0-1/4 mile: 14.8secs
214.0bhp 159.6kW 217.0PS
@ 5900rpm
195.0lbft 264.2Nm @ 4800rpm
173.0bhp/ton 170.2bhp/tonne
67.6bhp/L 50.4kW/L 68.6PS/L
48.0ft/sec 14.6m/sec
24.6mph 39.6kmh/1000rpm
24.0mpg 20.0mpgUS 11.8L/100km
Petrol 4-stroke piston
3164cc 193.0cu in
Flat 6 fuel injection
Compression ratio: 9.5:1
Bore: 95.0mm 3.7in
Stroke: 74.4mm 2.9in
Valve type/No: Overhead 12
Transmission: Manual
No. of forward speeds: 5
Wheels driven: Rear
Springs F/R: Torsion bar/Torsion bar
Brake system: PA
Brakes F/R: Disc/Disc
Steering: Rack & pinion
Wheelbase: 227.3cm 89.5in
Track F: 136.9cm 53.9in
Track R: 137.9cm 54.3in
Length: 429.0cm 168.9in
Width: 165.1cm 65.0in
Height: 132.1cm 52.0in
Ground clearance: 13.0cm 5.1in
Kerb weight: 1257.6kg 2770.0lb
Fuel: 85.2L 18.7gal 22.5galUS

3722 Porsche

911 Club Sport
1989 Germany
154.0mph 247.8kmh
0-60mph 96.5kmh: 5.3secs
0-1/4 mile: 13.9secs
214.0bhp 159.6kW 217.0PS
@ 5900rpm
195.0lbft 264.2Nm @ 4800rpm
184.4bhp/ton 181.3bhp/tonne
67.6bhp/L 50.4kW/L 68.6PS/L
48.0ft/sec 14.6m/sec
Petrol 4-stroke piston
3164cc 193.0cu in
Flat 6 fuel injection
Compression ratio: 9.5:1
Bore: 95.0mm 3.7in
Stroke: 74.4mm 2.9in
Valve type/No: Overhead 12
Transmission: Manual
No. of forward speeds: 5
Wheels driven: Rear
Springs F/R: Torsion bar/Torsion bar
Brake system: PA
Brakes F/R: Disc/Disc
Steering: Rack & pinion
Wheelbase: 227.3cm 89.5in
Track F: 140.0cm 55.1in
Track R: 140.7cm 55.4in
Length: 429.0cm 168.9in
Width: 165.1cm 65.0in
Height: 132.1cm 52.0in
Kerb weight: 1180.4kg 2600.0lb
Fuel: 85.2L 18.7gal 22.5galUS

3723 Porsche

911 Turbo
1989 Germany
159.0mph 255.8kmh
0-50mph 80.5kmh: 3.8secs
0-60mph 96.5kmh: 4.8secs
0-1/4 mile: 13.6secs
282.0bhp 210.3kW 285.9PS
@ 5500rpm
288.0lbft 390.2Nm @ 4000rpm
206.8bhp/ton 203.3bhp/tonne
85.5bhp/L 63.7kW/L 86.7PS/L
44.8ft/sec 13.6m/sec
27.6mph 44.4kmh/1000rpm
19.2mpg 16.0mpgUS 14.7L/100km
Petrol 4-stroke piston
3299cc 201.3cu in turbocharged
Flat 6 fuel injection
Compression ratio: 7.0:1
Bore: 97.0mm 3.8in
Stroke: 74.4mm 2.9in
Valve type/No: Overhead 12
Transmission: Manual
No. of forward speeds: 5
Wheels driven: Rear
Springs F/R: Torsion bar/Torsion bar
Brake system: PA
Brakes F/R: Disc/Disc

Steering: Rack & pinion
Wheelbase: 227.3cm 89.5in
Track F: 143.3cm 56.4in
Track R: 150.1cm 59.1in
Length: 429.0cm 168.9in
Width: 177.5cm 69.9in
Height: 131.1cm 51.6in
Ground clearance: 11.9cm 4.7in
Kerb weight: 1387.0kg 3055.0lb
Fuel: 85.2L 18.7gal 22.5galUS

3724 Porsche

911 Turbo Motorsport Design
1989 Germany
183.0mph 294.4kmh
0-50mph 80.5kmh: 3.1secs
0-60mph 96.5kmh: 4.0secs
0-1/4 mile: 12.4secs
488.0bhp 363.9kW 494.8PS
@ 6250rpm
490.0lbft 664.0Nm @ 5000rpm
366.8bhp/ton 360.7bhp/tonne
147.9bhp/L 110.3kW/L 150.0PS/L
50.9ft/sec 15.5m/sec
Petrol 4-stroke piston
3299cc 201.3cu in turbocharged
Flat 6 fuel injection
Compression ratio: 7.0:1
Bore: 97.0mm 3.8in
Stroke: 74.4mm 2.9in
Valve type/No: Overhead 12
Transmission: Manual
No. of forward speeds: 4
Wheels driven: Rear
Springs F/R: Torsion bar/Torsion bar
Brake system: PA
Brakes F/R: Disc/Disc
Steering: Rack & pinion PA
Wheelbase: 227.1cm 89.4in
Track F: 143.3cm 56.4in
Track R: 150.1cm 59.1in
Length: 429.0cm 168.9in
Width: 177.5cm 69.9in
Height: 129.8cm 51.1in
Kerb weight: 1352.9kg 2980.0lb

3725 Porsche

928 Cabrio Strosek
1989 Germany
155.0mph 249.4kmh
0-60mph 96.5kmh: 5.5secs
0-1/4 mile: 13.9secs
325.0bhp 242.3kW 329.5PS
@ 6000rpm
317.0lbft 429.5Nm @ 3000rpm
206.5bhp/ton 203.1bhp/tonne
65.6bhp/L 48.9kW/L 66.5PS/L
51.8ft/sec 15.8m/sec
Petrol 4-stroke piston
4957cc 302.4cu in
Vee 8 fuel injection
Compression ratio: 10.0:1
Bore: 100.0mm 3.9in
Stroke: 78.9mm 3.1in
Valve type/No: Overhead 32
Transmission: Manual
No. of forward speeds: 5
Wheels driven: Rear
Springs F/R: Coil/Coil
Brake system: PA ABS
Brakes F/R: Disc/Disc
Steering: Rack & pinion PA
Wheelbase: 249.9cm 98.4in
Track F: 160.0cm 63.0in
Track R: 159.8cm 62.9in
Length: 452.4cm 178.1in
Width: 195.6cm 77.0in
Height: 125.7cm 49.5in
Kerb weight: 1600.3kg 3525.0lb
Fuel: 85.9L 18.9gal 22.7galUS

3726 Porsche

928 S4 Koenig
1989 Germany
186.0mph 299.3kmh
0-60mph 96.5kmh: 4.8secs
430.0bhp 320.6kW 436.0PS
@ 6000rpm
470.0lbft 636.9Nm @ 3000rpm
253.5bhp/ton 249.2bhp/tonne
86.7bhp/L 64.7kW/L 87.9PS/L
51.8ft/sec 15.8m/sec
Petrol 4-stroke piston
4957cc 302.4cu in supercharged
Vee 8 fuel injection
Compression ratio: 10.1:1
Bore: 100.0mm 3.9in
Stroke: 78.9mm 3.1in
Valve type/No: Overhead 32
Transmission: Manual
No. of forward speeds: 5
Wheels driven: Rear
Springs F/R: Coil/Coil
Brake system: PA ABS
Brakes F/R: Disc/Disc
Steering: Rack & pinion PA
Wheelbase: 249.9cm 98.4in
Track F: 154.9cm 61.0in
Track R: 154.7cm 60.9in
Length: 452.4cm 178.1in
Width: 183.6cm 72.3in
Height: 127.0cm 50.0in
Kerb weight: 1725.2kg 3800.0lb
Fuel: 85.9L 18.9gal 22.7galUS

3727 Porsche

928 S4 SE
1989 Germany
162.0mph 260.7kmh
0-50mph 80.5kmh: 4.3secs
0-60mph 96.5kmh: 5.5secs
0-1/4 mile: 13.8secs
0-1km: 25.1secs
320.0bhp 238.6kW 324.4PS
@ 6000rpm
317.3lbft 430.0Nm @ 3000rpm
206.0bhp/ton 202.5bhp/tonne
64.6bhp/L 48.1kW/L 65.4PS/L
51.8ft/sec 15.8m/sec
26.1mph 42.0kmh/1000rpm
18.6mpg 15.5mpgUS 15.2L/100km
Petrol 4-stroke piston
4957cc 302.0cu in
Vee 8 fuel injection
Compression ratio: 10.0:1
Bore: 100.0mm 3.9in
Stroke: 78.9mm 3.1in
Valve type/No: Overhead 32
Transmission: Manual
No. of forward speeds: 5
Wheels driven: Rear
Springs F/R: Coil/Coil
Brake system: PA ABS
Brakes F/R: Disc/Disc
Steering: Rack & pinion PA
Wheelbase: 250.0cm 98.4in
Track F: 151.1cm 59.5in
Track R: 154.6cm 60.9in
Length: 452.0cm 178.0in
Width: 183.6cm 72.3in
Height: 128.2cm 50.5in
Ground clearance: 16.5cm 6.5in
Kerb weight: 1580.0kg 3480.2lb
Fuel: 93.7L 20.6gal 24.8galUS

3728 Porsche

944
1989 Germany
139.0mph 223.7kmh
0-50mph 80.5kmh: 5.1secs
0-60mph 96.5kmh: 7.0secs
0-1/4 mile: 15.7secs
0-1km: 28.5secs
165.0bhp 123.0kW 167.3PS
@ 5800rpm
166.1lbft 225.0Nm @ 4200rpm
127.1bhp/ton 125.0bhp/tonne
61.5bhp/L 45.9kW/L 62.4PS/L
50.1ft/sec 15.3m/sec
22.3mph 35.9kmh/1000rpm
20.7mpg 17.2mpgUS 13.6L/100km
Petrol 4-stroke piston
2681cc 164.0cu in
In-line 4 fuel injection
Compression ratio: 10.9:1
Bore: 104.0mm 4.1in
Stroke: 79.0mm 3.1in
Valve type/No: Overhead 8
Transmission: Manual
No. of forward speeds: 5
Wheels driven: Rear
Springs F/R: Coil/Torsion bar
Brake system: PA ABS
Brakes F/R: Disc/Disc
Steering: Rack & pinion PA
Wheelbase: 240.0cm 94.5in
Track F: 147.7cm 58.1in
Track R: 145.1cm 57.1in
Length: 420.0cm 165.4in
Width: 173.5cm 68.3in
Height: 127.5cm 50.2in
Ground clearance: 12.0cm 4.7in
Kerb weight: 1320.0kg 2907.5lb
Fuel: 80.1L 17.6gal 21.1galUS

3729 Porsche

944 S2
1989 Germany
147.0mph 236.5kmh
0-50mph 80.5kmh: 4.5secs
0-60mph 96.5kmh: 6.0secs
0-1/4 mile: 14.4secs
0-1km: 26.1secs
211.0bhp 157.3kW 213.9PS
@ 5800rpm
206.6lbft 280.0Nm @ 4000rpm
158.9bhp/ton 156.3bhp/tonne
70.6bhp/L 52.6kW/L 71.5PS/L
55.7ft/sec 17.0m/sec
23.7mph 38.1kmh/1000rpm
20.7mpg 17.2mpgUS 13.6L/100km
Petrol 4-stroke piston
2990cc 182.0cu in
In-line 4 fuel injection
Compression ratio: 10.9:1
Bore: 104.0mm 4.1in
Stroke: 88.0mm 3.5in
Valve type/No: Overhead 16
Transmission: Manual
No. of forward speeds: 5
Wheels driven: Rear
Springs F/R: Coil/Torsion bar
Brake system: PA ABS
Brakes F/R: Disc/Disc
Steering: Rack & pinion PA
Wheelbase: 240.0cm 94.5in
Track F: 147.7cm 58.1in
Track R: 145.1cm 57.1in
Length: 420.0cm 165.4in
Width: 173.5cm 68.3in
Height: 127.5cm 50.2in
Ground clearance: 12.0cm 4.7in
Kerb weight: 1350.0kg 2973.6lb
Fuel: 80.1L 17.6gal 21.1galUS

3730 Porsche

944 Turbo
1989 Germany
162.0mph 260.7kmh
0-50mph 80.5kmh: 4.3secs
0-60mph 96.5kmh: 5.5secs
0-1/4 mile: 14.2secs
250.0bhp 186.4kW 253.5PS
@ 6000rpm
258.0lbft 349.6Nm @ 4000rpm
175.3bhp/ton 172.3bhp/tonne
100.8bhp/L 75.2kW/L 102.2PS/L
51.8ft/sec 15.8m/sec
26.7mph 43.0kmh/1000rpm
22.2mpg 18.5mpgUS 12.7L/100km
Petrol 4-stroke piston
2479cc 151.2cu in turbocharged
In-line 4 fuel injection
Compression ratio: 8.0:1
Bore: 100.0mm 3.9in
Stroke: 78.9mm 3.1in
Valve type/No: Overhead 8
Transmission: Manual
No. of forward speeds: 5
Wheels driven: Rear
Springs F/R: Coil/Coil
Brake system: PA ABS
Brakes F/R: Disc/Disc
Steering: Rack & pinion PA
Wheelbase: 240.0cm 94.5in
Track F: 147.8cm 58.2in
Track R: 144.3cm 56.8in
Length: 429.0cm 168.9in
Width: 173.5cm 68.3in
Height: 127.5cm 50.2in
Ground clearance: 11.9cm 4.7in
Kerb weight: 1450.5kg 3195.0lb
Fuel: 79.9L 17.6gal 21.1galUS

3731 Porsche

959
1989 Germany
198.0mph 318.6kmh
0-50mph 80.5kmh: 2.8secs
0-60mph 96.5kmh: 3.6secs
0-1/4 mile: 11.9secs
450.0bhp 335.6kW 456.2PS
@ 6500rpm
370.0lbft 501.4Nm @ 5500rpm
316.0bhp/ton 310.7bhp/tonne
157.9bhp/L 117.8kW/L 160.1PS/L
47.7ft/sec 14.5m/sec
Petrol 4-stroke piston
2849cc 173.8cu in turbocharged
Flat 6 fuel injection
Compression ratio: 8.3:1
Bore: 95.0mm 3.7in
Stroke: 67.0mm 2.6in
Valve type/No: Overhead 24
Transmission: Manual
No. of forward speeds: 6
Wheels driven: 4-wheel drive
Springs F/R: Coil/Coil
Brake system: ABS
Brakes F/R: Disc/Disc
Steering: Rack & pinion PA
Wheelbase: 227.1cm 89.4in
Track F: 150.4cm 59.2in
Track R: 154.9cm 61.0in
Length: 426.0cm 167.7in
Width: 183.9cm 72.4in
Height: 128.0cm 50.4in
Kerb weight: 1448.3kg 3190.0lb
Fuel: 90.1L 19.8gal 23.8galUS

3732 Porsche

911 Carrera 2
1990 Germany
160.0mph 257.4kmh
0-50mph 80.5kmh: 4.0secs
0-60mph 96.5kmh: 5.1secs
0-1/4 mile: 13.6secs
0-1km: 24.6secs
250.0bhp 186.4kW 253.5PS
@ 6100rpm
228.8lbft 310.0Nm @ 4800rpm
184.2bhp/ton 181.2bhp/tonne
69.4bhp/L 51.8kW/L 70.4PS/L
51.0ft/sec 15.5m/sec
24.2mph 38.9kmh/1000rpm
20.4mpg 17.0mpgUS 13.8L/100km
Petrol 4-stroke piston
3600cc 220.0cu in
Flat 6 fuel injection
Compression ratio: 11.3:1
Bore: 100.0mm 3.9in
Stroke: 76.4mm 3.0in
Valve type/No: Overhead 12
Transmission: Manual
No. of forward speeds: 5
Wheels driven: Rear
Springs F/R: Coil/Coil
Brake system: PA ABS
Brakes F/R: Disc/Disc
Steering: Rack & pinion PA
Wheelbase: 227.2cm 89.4in
Track F: 138.0cm 54.3in
Track R: 137.4cm 54.1in
Length: 425.0cm 167.3in
Width: 165.2cm 65.0in
Height: 132.0cm 52.0in
Ground clearance: 12.0cm 4.7in
Kerb weight: 1380.0kg 3039.6lb
Fuel: 76.9L 16.9gal 20.3galUS

3733 Porsche

911 Carrera 2 Tiptronic
1990 Germany
159.0mph 255.8kmh
0-60mph 96.5kmh: 6.9secs
0-1/4 mile: 15.0secs
247.0bhp 184.2kW 250.4PS
@ 6100rpm
228.0lbft 308.9Nm @ 4800rpm
174.3bhp/ton 171.4bhp/tonne
68.5bhp/L 51.1kW/L 69.5PS/L
51.0ft/sec 15.6m/sec
21.0mpg 17.5mpgUS 13.4L/100km
Petrol 4-stroke piston
3605cc 219.9cu in
Flat 6 fuel injection
Compression ratio: 11.3:1
Bore: 100.0mm 3.9in
Stroke: 76.5mm 3.0in
Valve type/No: Overhead 12
Transmission: Automatic
No. of forward speeds: 4
Wheels driven: Rear
Springs F/R: Coil/Coil
Brake system: PA ABS
Brakes F/R: Disc/Disc
Steering: Rack & pinion PA
Wheelbase: 227.1cm 89.4in
Track F: 137.9cm 54.3in
Track R: 137.4cm 54.1in
Length: 427.5cm 168.3in
Width: 165.1cm 65.0in
Height: 132.1cm 52.0in
Kerb weight: 1441.4kg 3175.0lb
Fuel: 76.8L 16.9gal 20.3galUS

3734 Porsche

911 Carrera 4

1990 Germany
161.0mph 259.0kmh
0-50mph 80.5kmh: 4.5secs
0-60mph 96.5kmh: 5.8secs
0-1/4 mile: 14.4secs
250.0bhp 186.4kW 253.5PS
@ 6100rpm
229.0lbft 310.3Nm @ 4800rpm
168.7bhp/ton 165.9bhp/tonne
69.4bhp/L 51.8kW/L 70.4PS/L
51.0ft/sec 15.5m/sec
20.4mpg 17.0mpgUS 13.8L/100km
Petrol 4-stroke piston
3600cc 219.6cu in
Flat 6 fuel injection
Compression ratio: 11.3:1
Bore: 100.0mm 3.9in
Stroke: 76.4mm 3.0in
Valve type/No: Overhead 12
Transmission: Manual
No. of forward speeds: 5
Wheels driven: 4-wheel drive
Springs F/R: Coil/Coil
Brake system: PA ABS
Brakes F/R: Disc/Disc
Steering: Rack & pinion PA
Wheelbase: 227.3cm 89.5in
Track F: 137.9cm 54.3in
Track R: 137.4cm 54.1in
Length: 424.9cm 167.3in
Width: 165.1cm 65.0in
Height: 132.1cm 52.0in
Kerb weight: 1507.3kg 3320.0lb
Fuel: 76.8L 16.9gal 20.3galUS

3735 Porsche

911 Speedster
1990 Germany
149.0mph 239.7kmh
0-60mph 96.5kmh: 6.0secs
0-1/4 mile: 14.5secs
214.0bhp 159.6kW 217.0PS
@ 5900rpm
195.0lbft 264.2Nm @ 4800rpm
163.9bhp/ton 161.1bhp/tonne
67.6bhp/L 50.4kW/L 68.6PS/L
48.3ft/sec 14.7m/sec
24.0mpg 20.0mpgUS 11.8L/100km
Petrol 4-stroke piston
3164cc 193.0cu in
Flat 6 fuel injection
Compression ratio: 9.5:1
Bore: 87.0mm 3.4in
Stroke: 75.0mm 2.9in
Valve type/No: Overhead 12
Transmission: Manual
No. of forward speeds: 5
Wheels driven: Rear
Springs F/R: Torsion bar/Torsion bar
Brake system: PA
Brakes F/R: Disc/Disc
Steering: Rack & pinion
Wheelbase: 227.3cm 89.5in
Track F: 143.3cm 56.4in
Track R: 149.1cm 58.7in
Length: 429.0cm 168.9in
Width: 177.5cm 69.9in
Height: 128.0cm 50.4in
Kerb weight: 1327.9kg 2925.0lb
Fuel: 85.2L 18.7gal 22.5galUS

3736 Porsche

911 Turbo
1990 Germany
159.0mph 255.8kmh
0-60mph 96.5kmh: 5.1secs
0-1/4 mile: 13.6secs
300.0bhp 223.7kW 304.2PS
@ 5500rpm
317.0lbft 429.5Nm @ 4000rpm
220.0bhp/ton 216.3bhp/tonne
90.9bhp/L 67.8kW/L 92.2PS/L
44.8ft/sec 13.6m/sec
19.8mpg 16.5mpgUS 14.3L/100km
Petrol 4-stroke piston
3299cc 201.3cu in turbocharged
Flat 6 fuel injection
Compression ratio: 7.0:1
Bore: 97.0mm 3.8in
Stroke: 74.4mm 2.9in
Valve type/No: Overhead 12
Transmission: Manual
No. of forward speeds: 5
Wheels driven: Rear
Springs F/R: Torsion bar/Torsion bar
Brake system: PA
Brakes F/R: Disc/Disc
Steering: Rack & pinion
Wheelbase: 227.3cm 89.5in
Track F: 143.3cm 56.4in
Track R: 150.1cm 59.1in
Length: 429.0cm 168.9in
Width: 177.5cm 69.9in
Height: 131.1cm 51.6in
Kerb weight: 1387.0kg 3055.0lb
Fuel: 85.2L 18.7gal 22.5galUS

3737 Porsche

911 Turbo RS Tuning
1990 Germany
216.0mph 347.5kmh
0-60mph 96.5kmh: 4.6secs
580.0bhp 432.5kW 588.0PS
@ 6900rpm
465.0lbft 630.1Nm @ 5500rpm
172.2bhp/L 128.4kW/L 174.6PS/L
56.2ft/sec 17.1m/sec
Petrol 4-stroke piston
3368cc 205.5cu in turbocharged
Flat 6 fuel injection
Bore: 98.0mm 3.9in
Stroke: 74.4mm 2.9in
Valve type/No: Overhead 12
Transmission: Manual
No. of forward speeds: 6
Wheels driven: Rear
Springs F/R: Coil/Coil
Brake system: PA
Brakes F/R: Disc/Disc
Steering: Rack & pinion
Wheelbase: 227.1cm 89.4in
Track F: 143.3cm 56.4in
Track R: 149.1cm 58.7in
Length: 429.0cm 168.9in
Width: 177.5cm 69.9in
Height: 131.1cm 51.6in
Fuel: 85.2L 18.7gal 22.5galUS

3738 Porsche

928
1990 Germany
0-60mph 96.5kmh: 6.1secs
0-1/4 mile: 14.8secs
326.0bhp 243.1kW 330.5PS
@ 6200rpm
317.0lbft 429.5Nm @ 4100rpm
206.9bhp/ton 203.4bhp/tonne
65.5bhp/L 48.9kW/L 66.4PS/L
53.6ft/sec 16.3m/sec
Petrol 4-stroke piston
4974cc 303.5cu in
Vee 8 fuel injection
Compression ratio: 10.0:1
Bore: 100.1mm 3.9in
Stroke: 79.0mm 3.1in
Valve type/No: Overhead 32
Transmission: Manual
No. of forward speeds: 5
Wheels driven: Rear
Springs F/R: Coil/Coil
Brake system: PA ABS
Brakes F/R: Disc/Disc
Steering: Rack & pinion PA
Wheelbase: 249.9cm 98.4in
Track F: 155.2cm 61.1in
Track R: 154.7cm 60.9in
Length: 452.4cm 178.1in
Width: 183.6cm 72.3in
Height: 128.3cm 50.5in
Kerb weight: 1602.6kg 3530.0lb
Fuel: 85.9L 18.9gal 22.7galUS

3739 Porsche

928 Automatic
1990 Germany
0-50mph 80.5kmh: 4.8secs
0-60mph 96.5kmh: 6.3secs
0-1/4 mile: 14.6secs
316.0bhp 235.6kW 320.4PS
@ 6000rpm
317.0lbft 429.5Nm @ 3000rpm
200.5bhp/ton 197.2bhp/tonne
63.5bhp/L 47.4kW/L 64.4PS/L
51.8ft/sec 15.8m/sec
Petrol 4-stroke piston
4974cc 303.5cu in
Vee 8 fuel injection
Compression ratio: 10.0:1
Bore: 100.1mm 3.9in
Stroke: 79.0mm 3.1in
Valve type/No: Overhead 32
Transmission: Automatic
No. of forward speeds: 4
Wheels driven: Rear
Springs F/R: Coil/Coil
Brake system: PA ABS
Brakes F/R: Disc/Disc
Steering: Rack & pinion PA
Wheelbase: 249.9cm 98.4in
Track F: 155.2cm 61.1in
Track R: 154.7cm 60.9in
Length: 452.4cm 178.1in
Width: 183.6cm 72.3in
Height: 128.3cm 50.5in
Kerb weight: 1602.6kg 3530.0lb
Fuel: 85.9L 18.9gal 22.7galUS

3740 Porsche

928 Gemballa
1990 Germany
0-60mph 96.5kmh: 6.1secs
0-1/4 mile: 14.8secs
326.0bhp 243.1kW 330.5PS
@ 6200rpm
317.0lbft 429.5Nm @ 4100rpm
198.4bhp/ton 195.1bhp/tonne
65.5bhp/L 48.9kW/L 66.4PS/L
53.6ft/sec 16.3m/sec
Petrol 4-stroke piston
4974cc 303.5cu in
Vee 8 fuel injection
Compression ratio: 10.0:1
Bore: 100.1mm 3.9in
Stroke: 79.0mm 3.1in
Valve type/No: Overhead 32
Transmission: Manual
No. of forward speeds: 5
Wheels driven: Rear
Springs F/R: Coil/Coil
Brake system: PA ABS
Brakes F/R: Disc/Disc
Steering: Rack & pinion PA
Wheelbase: 249.9cm 98.4in
Track F: 155.2cm 61.1in
Track R: 154.7cm 60.9in
Length: 452.4cm 178.1in
Width: 200.2cm 78.8in
Height: 128.3cm 50.5in
Kerb weight: 1670.7kg 3680.0lb
Fuel: 85.9L 18.9gal 22.7galUS

3741 Porsche

944 Cabriolet
1990 Germany
0-60mph 96.5kmh: 7.1secs
0-1/4 mile: 15.3secs
208.0bhp 155.1kW 210.9PS
@ 5800rpm
207.0lbft 280.5Nm @ 4100rpm
150.5bhp/ton 148.0bhp/tonne
69.6bhp/L 51.9kW/L 70.5PS/L
55.7ft/sec 17.0m/sec
27.6mpg 23.0mpgUS 10.2L/100km
Petrol 4-stroke piston
2990cc 182.4cu in
In-line 4
Bore: 104.0mm 4.1in
Stroke: 88.0mm 3.5in
Valve type/No: Overhead 16
Transmission: Manual
No. of forward speeds: 5
Wheels driven: Rear
Springs F/R: Coil/Torsion bar
Brake system: ABS
Brakes F/R: Disc/Disc
Steering: Rack & pinion PA
Wheelbase: 240.0cm 94.5in
Track F: 147.8cm 58.2in
Track R: 145.0cm 57.1in
Length: 429.0cm 168.9in
Width: 173.5cm 68.3in
Height: 127.5cm 50.2in
Kerb weight: 1405.1kg 3095.0lb

3742 Porsche

944 S2
1990 Germany
149.0mph 239.7kmh
0-60mph 96.5kmh: 6.7secs
0-1/4 mile: 14.7secs
208.0bhp 155.1kW 210.9PS
@ 5800rpm
207.0lbft 280.5Nm @ 4100rpm
156.1bhp/ton 153.5bhp/tonne
69.6bhp/L 51.9kW/L 70.5PS/L
55.7ft/sec 17.0m/sec
22.2mpg 18.5mpgUS 12.7L/100km
Petrol 4-stroke piston
2990cc 182.4cu in
In-line 4 fuel injection
Compression ratio: 10.9:1
Bore: 104.0mm 4.1in
Stroke: 88.0mm 3.5in
Valve type/No: Overhead 16
Transmission: Manual
No. of forward speeds: 5
Wheels driven: Rear
Springs F/R: Coil/Torsion bar
Brake system: PA ABS
Brakes F/R: Disc/Disc
Steering: Rack & pinion PA
Wheelbase: 240.0cm 94.5in
Track F: 147.8cm 58.2in
Track R: 145.0cm 57.1in
Length: 429.0cm 168.9in
Width: 173.5cm 68.3in
Height: 127.5cm 50.2in
Kerb weight: 1355.2kg 2985.0lb
Fuel: 79.9L 17.6gal 21.1galUS

3743 Porsche

944 S2 Cabriolet
1990 Germany
149.0mph 239.7kmh
0-50mph 80.5kmh: 5.2secs
0-60mph 96.5kmh: 7.1secs
0-1/4 mile: 15.3secs
208.0bhp 155.1kW 210.9PS
@ 5800rpm
207.0lbft 280.5Nm @ 4100rpm
150.5bhp/ton 148.0bhp/tonne
69.6bhp/L 51.9kW/L 70.5PS/L
55.7ft/sec 17.0m/sec
22.2mpg 18.5mpgUS 12.7L/100km
Petrol 4-stroke piston
2990cc 182.4cu in
In-line 4 fuel injection
Compression ratio: 10.9:1
Bore: 104.0mm 4.1in
Stroke: 88.0mm 3.5in
Valve type/No: Overhead 16
Transmission: Manual
No. of forward speeds: 5
Wheels driven: Rear
Springs F/R: Coil/Torsion bar
Brake system: PA ABS
Brakes F/R: Disc/Disc
Steering: Rack & pinion PA
Wheelbase: 240.0cm 94.5in
Track F: 147.8cm 58.2in
Track R: 145.0cm 57.1in
Length: 429.0cm 168.9in
Width: 173.5cm 68.3in
Height: 127.5cm 50.2in
Kerb weight: 1405.1kg 3095.0lb
Fuel: 79.9L 17.6gal 21.1galUS

3744 Porsche

Carrera 2 Cabriolet Tiptronic
1990 Germany
159.0mph 255.8kmh
0-50mph 80.5kmh: 4.8secs
0-60mph 96.5kmh: 6.2secs
0-1/4 mile: 14.6secs
0-1km: 26.1secs
250.0bhp 186.4kW 253.5PS
@ 6100rpm
228.8lbft 310.0Nm @ 4800rpm
211.9bhp/ton 208.3bhp/tonne
69.4bhp/L 51.8kW/L 70.4PS/L
51.0ft/sec 15.5m/sec
26.8mph 43.1kmh/1000rpm
17.4mpg 14.5mpgUS 16.2L/100km
Petrol 4-stroke piston
3600cc 220.0cu in
Flat 6 fuel injection
Compression ratio: 11.3:1
Bore: 100.0mm 3.9in
Stroke: 76.4mm 3.0in
Valve type/No: Overhead 24
Transmission: Automatic
No. of forward speeds: 4
Wheels driven: Rear
Springs F/R: Coil/Coil
Brake system: PA ABS
Brakes F/R: Disc/Disc
Steering: Rack & pinion PA
Wheelbase: 227.2cm 89.4in
Track F: 138.0cm 54.3in
Track R: 137.4cm 54.1in
Length: 425.0cm 167.3in
Width: 165.2cm 65.0in
Height: 132.0cm 52.0in
Ground clearance: 12.0cm 4.7in
Kerb weight: 1200.0kg 2643.2lb
Fuel: 76.9L 16.9gal 20.3galUS

3745 Porsche
Panamericana
1990 Germany
0-60mph 96.5kmh: 5.8secs
0-1/4 mile: 14.4secs
250.0bhp 186.4kW 253.5PS
@ 6100rpm
229.0lbft 310.3Nm @ 4800rpm
172.3bhp/ton 169.4bhp/tonne
69.4bhp/L 51.8kW/L 70.4PS/L
51.0ft/sec 15.5m/sec
Petrol 4-stroke piston
3600cc 219.6cu in
Flat 6 fuel injection
Compression ratio: 11.3:1
Bore: 100.0mm 3.9in
Stroke: 76.4mm 3.0in
Valve type/No: Overhead 12
Transmission: Manual
No. of forward speeds: 5
Wheels driven: 4-wheel drive
Springs F/R: Coil/Coil
Brake system: PA ABS
Brakes F/R: Disc/Disc
Steering: Rack & pinion PA
Wheelbase: 227.3cm 89.5in
Track F: 137.9cm 54.3in
Track R: 137.4cm 54.1in
Length: 420.1cm 165.4in
Width: 185.9cm 73.2in
Height: 130.0cm 51.2in
Kerb weight: 1475.5kg 3250.0lb
Fuel: 76.8L 16.9gal 20.3galUS

3746 Porsche
911 Carrera Turbo
1991 Germany
168.0mph 270.3kmh
0-60mph 96.5kmh: 4.6secs
0-1/4 mile: 12.9secs
320.0bhp 238.6kW 324.4PS
@ 5750rpm
332.0lbft 449.9Nm @ 4500rpm
218.9bhp/ton 215.2bhp/tonne
97.0bhp/L 72.3kW/L 98.3PS/L
46.8ft/sec 14.3m/sec
18.0mpg 15.0mpgUS 15.7L/100km
Petrol 4-stroke piston
3299cc 201.3cu in turbocharged
Flat 6 fuel injection
Compression ratio: 7.0:1
Bore: 97.0mm 3.8in
Stroke: 74.4mm 2.9in
Valve type/No: Overhead 12
Transmission: Manual
No. of forward speeds: 5
Wheels driven: Rear
Springs F/R: Coil/Coil
Brake system: PA ABS
Brakes F/R: Disc/Disc
Steering: Rack & pinion PA
Wheelbase: 227.1cm 89.4in
Track F: 143.5cm 56.5in
Track R: 149.4cm 58.8in
Length: 427.5cm 168.3in
Width: 177.8cm 70.0in
Height: 131.1cm 51.6in
Kerb weight: 1486.8kg 3275.0lb
Fuel: 76.8L 16.9gal 20.3galUS

3747 Porsche
911 Ruf
1991 Germany
196.0mph 315.4kmh
0-60mph 96.5kmh: 3.8secs
0-1/4 mile: 12.0secs
455.0bhp 339.3kW 461.3PS
@ 5800rpm
482.0lbft 653.1Nm @ 4500rpm
335.8bhp/ton 330.2bhp/tonne
129.8bhp/L 96.8kW/L 131.6PS/L
47.2ft/sec 14.4m/sec
Petrol 4-stroke piston
3504cc 213.8cu in turbocharged
Flat 6 fuel injection
Compression ratio: 7.6:1
Bore: 100.0mm 3.9in
Stroke: 74.4mm 2.9in
Valve type/No: Overhead 12
Transmission: Manual
No. of forward speeds: 6
Wheels driven: Rear
Springs F/R: Coil/Coil
Brake system: ABS
Brakes F/R: Disc/Disc
Steering: Rack & pinion
Wheelbase: 227.1cm 89.4in
Track F: 136.9cm 53.9in
Track R: 137.9cm 54.3in
Length: 427.5cm 168.3in
Width: 165.1cm 65.0in
Height: 127.3cm 50.1in
Kerb weight: 1377.9kg 3035.0lb

3748 Porsche
911 Ruf CTR
1991 Germany
208.0mph 334.7kmh
0-60mph 96.5kmh: 3.9secs
0-1/4 mile: 11.9secs
469.0bhp 349.7kW 475.5PS
@ 5950rpm
408.0lbft 552.8Nm @ 5100rpm
345.6bhp/ton 339.8bhp/tonne
139.3bhp/L 103.9kW/L 141.2PS/L
48.4ft/sec 14.8m/sec
16.8mpg 14.0mpgUS 16.8L/100km
Petrol 4-stroke piston
3367cc 205.4cu in turbocharged
Flat 6 fuel injection
Compression ratio: 7.5:1
Bore: 98.0mm 3.9in
Stroke: 74.4mm 2.9in
Valve type/No: Overhead 12
Transmission: Manual
No. of forward speeds: 6
Wheels driven: Rear
Springs F/R: Coil/Coil
Brake system: PA
Brakes F/R: Disc/Disc
Steering: Rack & pinion
Wheelbase: 227.3cm 89.5in
Track F: 143.3cm 56.4in
Track R: 149.1cm 58.7in
Length: 429.0cm 168.9in
Width: 177.5cm 69.9in
Height: 131.1cm 51.6in
Kerb weight: 1380.2kg 3040.0lb
Fuel: 85.2L 18.7gal 22.5galUS

3749 Porsche
911 Ruf TR2
1991 Germany
196.1mph 315.5kmh
0-60mph 96.5kmh: 3.8secs
0-1/4 mile: 12.0secs
455.0bhp 339.3kW 461.3PS
@ 5800rpm
483.0lbft 654.5Nm @ 4500rpm
335.3bhp/ton 329.7bhp/tonne
129.8bhp/L 96.8kW/L 131.6PS/L
Petrol 4-stroke piston
3504cc 213.8cu in
Flat 6
Valve type/No: Overhead 12
Transmission: Manual
No. of forward speeds: 6
Wheels driven: Rear
Wheelbase: 227.1cm 89.4in
Length: 427.5cm 168.3in
Width: 177.8cm 70.0in
Height: 129.5cm 51.0in
Kerb weight: 1380.2kg 3040.0lb

3750 Porsche
911 Turbo
1991 Germany
171.0mph 275.1kmh
0-50mph 80.5kmh: 3.7secs
0-60mph 96.5kmh: 4.7secs
0-1/4 mile: 13.3secs
0-1km: 24.0secs
320.0bhp 238.6kW 324.4PS
@ 5750rpm
332.1lbft 450.0Nm @ 4500rpm
222.9bhp/ton 219.2bhp/tonne
97.0bhp/L 72.3kW/L 98.3PS/L
46.5ft/sec 14.2m/sec
27.8mph 44.7kmh/1000rpm
15.1mpg 12.6mpgUS 18.7L/100km
Petrol 4-stroke piston
3299cc 201.0cu in turbocharged
Flat 6 fuel injection
Compression ratio: 7.0:1
Bore: 97.0mm 3.8in
Stroke: 74.0mm 2.9in
Valve type/No: Overhead 12
Transmission: Manual
No. of forward speeds: 5
Wheels driven: Rear
Springs F/R: Coil/Coil
Brake system: PA ABS
Brakes F/R: Disc/Disc
Steering: Rack & pinion PA
Wheelbase: 227.1cm 89.4in
Track F: 143.3cm 56.4in
Track R: 149.1cm 58.7in
Length: 424.9cm 167.3in
Width: 177.3cm 69.8in
Height: 130.8cm 51.5in
Ground clearance: 11.9cm 4.7in
Kerb weight: 1460.0kg 3215.9lb
Fuel: 77.3L 17.0gal 20.4galUS

3751 Porsche
911 Turbo Gemballa Mirage
1991 Germany
205.0mph 329.8kmh
0-60mph 96.5kmh: 4.1secs
0-1/4 mile: 12.3secs
490.0bhp 365.4kW 496.8PS
@ 5900rpm
420.0lbft 569.1Nm
368.3bhp/ton 362.2bhp/tonne
145.5bhp/L 108.5kW/L 147.5PS/L
48.0ft/sec 14.6m/sec
Petrol 4-stroke piston
3367cc 205.4cu in turbocharged
Flat 6 fuel injection
Compression ratio: 7.5:1
Bore: 98.0mm 3.9in
Stroke: 74.4mm 2.9in
Valve type/No: Overhead 12
Transmission: Manual
No. of forward speeds: 6
Wheels driven: Rear
Springs F/R: Torsion bar/Torsion bar
Brakes F/R: Disc/Disc
Steering: Rack & pinion
Wheelbase: 227.3cm 89.5in
Track F: 143.3cm 56.4in
Track R: 150.1cm 59.1in
Length: 435.1cm 171.3in
Width: 210.1cm 82.7in
Height: 115.1cm 45.3in
Kerb weight: 1352.9kg 2980.0lb
Fuel: 85.2L 18.7gal 22.5galUS

3752 Porsche
928
1991 Germany
0-50mph 80.5kmh: 4.8secs
0-60mph 96.5kmh: 6.3secs
0-1/4 mile: 14.6secs
326.0bhp 243.1kW 330.5PS
@ 6200rpm
317.0lbft 429.5Nm @ 4100rpm
208.3bhp/ton 204.9bhp/tonne
65.5bhp/L 48.9kW/L 66.4PS/L
53.6ft/sec 16.3m/sec
Petrol 4-stroke piston
4974cc 303.5cu in
Vee 8 fuel injection
Compression ratio: 10.0:1
Bore: 100.1mm 3.9in
Stroke: 79.0mm 3.1in
Valve type/No: Overhead 32
Transmission: Automatic
No. of forward speeds: 4
Wheels driven: Rear
Springs F/R: Coil/Coil
Brake system: PA ABS
Brakes F/R: Disc/Disc
Steering: Rack & pinion PA
Wheelbase: 249.9cm 98.4in
Track F: 155.2cm 61.1in
Track R: 154.7cm 60.9in
Length: 452.4cm 178.1in
Width: 183.6cm 72.3in
Height: 128.3cm 50.5in
Kerb weight: 1591.3kg 3505.0lb
Fuel: 85.9L 18.9gal 22.7galUS

3753 Porsche
911 Carrera RS
1992 Germany
161.0mph 259.0kmh
0-50mph 80.5kmh: 3.8secs
0-60mph 96.5kmh: 4.9secs
0-1/4 mile: 13.4secs
0-1km: 24.3secs
260.0bhp 193.9kW 263.6PS
@ 6100rpm
239.9lbft 325.0Nm @ 4800rpm
221.3bhp/ton 217.6bhp/tonne
72.2bhp/L 53.9kW/L 73.2PS/L
51.0ft/sec 15.5m/sec
24.2mph 38.9kmh/1000rpm
Petrol 4-stroke piston
3600cc 220.0cu in
Flat 6 fuel injection
Compression ratio: 11.3:1
Bore: 100.0mm 3.9in
Stroke: 76.4mm 3.0in
Valve type/No: Overhead 12
Transmission: Manual
No. of forward speeds: 5
Wheels driven: Rear
Springs F/R: Coil/Coil
Brake system: PA ABS
Brakes F/R: Disc/Disc
Steering: Rack & pinion PA
Wheelbase: 227.2cm 89.4in
Track F: 143.4cm 56.5in
Track R: 149.3cm 58.8in
Length: 425.0cm 167.3in
Width: 177.5cm 69.9in
Height: 131.0cm 51.6in
Ground clearance: 12.0cm 4.7in
Kerb weight: 1195.0kg 2632.2lb
Fuel: 77.0L 16.9gal 20.3galUS

3754 Proton
1.5 SE Aeroback
1989 Malaysia
99.0mph 159.3kmh
0-50mph 80.5kmh: 10.1secs
0-60mph 96.5kmh: 14.4secs
0-1/4 mile: 19.8secs
0-1km: 37.0secs
75.0bhp 55.9kW 76.0PS
@ 5500rpm
87.1lbft 118.0Nm @ 3500rpm
82.2bhp/ton 80.8bhp/tonne
51.1bhp/L 38.1kW/L 51.8PS/L
49.3ft/sec 15.0m/sec
23.2mph 37.3kmh/1000rpm
28.0mpg 23.3mpgUS 10.1L/100km
Petrol 4-stroke piston
1468cc 90.0cu in
In-line 4 1 Carburettor
Compression ratio: 9.5:1
Bore: 75.5mm 3.0in
Stroke: 82.0mm 3.2in
Valve type/No: Overhead 8
Transmission: Manual
No. of forward speeds: 5
Wheels driven: Front
Springs F/R: Coil/Coil
Brakes F/R: Disc/Drum
Steering: Rack & pinion PA
Wheelbase: 238.0cm 93.7in
Track F: 139.0cm 54.7in
Track R: 134.2cm 52.8in
Length: 413.5cm 162.8in
Width: 163.0cm 64.2in
Height: 136.0cm 53.5in
Ground clearance: 18.5cm 7.3in
Kerb weight: 928.0kg 2044.0lb
Fuel: 45.5L 10.0gal 12.0galUS

3755 Proton
1.5 SE Triple Valve Aeroback
1991 Malaysia
100.0mph 160.9kmh
0-50mph 80.5kmh: 8.7secs
0-60mph 96.5kmh: 12.4secs
0-1/4 mile: 17.9secs
0-1km: 33.0secs
86.0bhp 64.1kW 87.2PS
@ 6000rpm
87.1lbft 118.0Nm @ 4000rpm
88.3bhp/ton 86.9bhp/tonne
58.6bhp/L 43.7kW/L 59.4PS/L
53.8ft/sec 16.4m/sec
20.9mph 33.6kmh/1000rpm
28.5mpg 23.7mpgUS 9.9L/100km
Petrol 4-stroke piston
1468cc 90.0cu in
In-line 4 1 Carburettor
Compression ratio: 9.2:1
Bore: 76.0mm 3.0in
Stroke: 82.0mm 3.2in
Valve type/No: Overhead 12
Transmission: Manual
No. of forward speeds: 5
Wheels driven: Front
Springs F/R: Coil/Coil
Brake system: PA
Brakes F/R: Disc/Drum
Steering: Rack & pinion PA
Wheelbase: 238.0cm 93.7in
Track F: 138.9cm 54.7in
Track R: 134.1cm 52.8in
Length: 414.0cm 163.0in
Width: 163.6cm 64.4in

Height: 135.9cm 53.5in
Ground clearance: 15.0cm 5.9in
Kerb weight: 990.0kg 2180.6lb
Fuel: 45.5L 10.0gal 12.0galUS

3756 Railton
Terraplane
1934 UK
88.2mph 141.9kmh
0-50mph 80.5kmh: 7.2secs
0-60mph 96.5kmh: 9.2secs
113.0bhp 84.3kW 114.6PS
@ 3800rpm
104.3bhp/ton 102.6bhp/tonne
27.1bhp/L 20.2kW/L 27.5PS/L
47.4ft/sec 14.4m/sec
18.0mpg 15.0mpgUS 15.7L/100km
Petrol 4-stroke piston
4168cc 254.3cu in
In-line 8 1 Carburettor
Compression ratio: 6.5:1
Bore: 76.0mm 3.0in
Stroke: 114.0mm 4.5in
Valve type/No: Side 16
Transmission: Manual
No. of forward speeds: 3
Wheels driven: Rear
Brakes F/R: Drum/Drum
Kerb weight: 1101.4kg 2426.0lb
Fuel: 59.1L 13.0gal 15.6galUS

3757 Railton
Light Sports Tourer
1935 UK
100.5mph 161.7kmh
0-50mph 80.5kmh: 7.0secs
0-60mph 96.5kmh: 9.8secs
113.0bhp 84.3kW 114.6PS
@ 3800rpm
114.9bhp/ton 113.0bhp/tonne
27.1bhp/L 20.2kW/L 27.5PS/L
47.4ft/sec 14.4m/sec
14.0mpg 11.7mpgUS 20.2L/100km
Petrol 4-stroke piston
4168cc 254.3cu in
In-line 8 1 Carburettor
Compression ratio: 6.5:1
Bore: 76.0mm 3.0in
Stroke: 114.0mm 4.5in
Valve type/No: Side 16
Transmission: Manual
No. of forward speeds: 3
Wheels driven: Rear
Brakes F/R: Drum/Drum
Ground clearance: 17.8cm 7.0in
Kerb weight: 1000.2kg 2203.0lb
Fuel: 59.1L 13.0gal 15.6galUS

3758 Railton
Straight Eight Saloon
1936 UK
91.8mph 147.7kmh
0-50mph 80.5kmh: 8.6secs
0-60mph 96.5kmh: 11.2secs
124.0bhp 92.5kW 125.7PS
@ 4200rpm
102.9bhp/ton 101.2bhp/tonne
29.7bhp/L 22.2kW/L 30.2PS/L
52.4ft/sec 16.0m/sec
15.0mpg 12.5mpgUS 18.8L/100km
Petrol 4-stroke piston
4168cc 254.3cu in
In-line 8 1 Carburettor
Compression ratio: 6.5:1
Bore: 76.0mm 3.0in
Stroke: 114.0mm 4.5in
Valve type/No: Side 16
Transmission: Manual
No. of forward speeds: 3
Wheels driven: Rear
Brakes F/R: Drum/Drum
Kerb weight: 1225.3kg 2699.0lb
Fuel: 59.1L 13.0gal 15.6galUS

3759 Railton
Cobham Saloon
1937 UK
88.2mph 141.9kmh
0-50mph 80.5kmh: 10.9secs
0-60mph 96.5kmh: 15.6secs
124.0bhp 92.5kW 125.7PS
@ 4200rpm
90.7bhp/ton 89.2bhp/tonne
29.7bhp/L 22.2kW/L 30.2PS/L
52.4ft/sec 16.0m/sec
17.0mpg 14.2mpgUS 16.6L/100km
Petrol 4-stroke piston
4168cc 254.3cu in
In-line 8 1 Carburettor
Compression ratio: 6.5:1
Bore: 76.0mm 3.0in
Stroke: 114.0mm 4.5in
Valve type/No: Side 16
Transmission: Manual
No. of forward speeds: 3
Wheels driven: Rear
Brakes F/R: Drum/Drum
Kerb weight: 1390.6kg 3063.0lb
Fuel: 61.4L 13.5gal 16.2galUS

3760 Railton
10 Drop-head Coupe
1938 UK
68.7mph 110.5kmh
0-50mph 80.5kmh: 21.6secs
0-60mph 96.5kmh: 35.6secs
33.0bhp 24.6kW 33.5PS
@ 4000rpm
37.2bhp/ton 36.6bhp/tonne
26.0bhp/L 19.4kW/L 26.4PS/L
43.8ft/sec 13.3m/sec
31.0mpg 25.8mpgUS 9.1L/100km
Petrol 4-stroke piston
1267cc 77.3cu in
In-line 4 1 Carburettor
Compression ratio: 6.5:1
Bore: 68.5mm 2.7in
Stroke: 100.0mm 3.9in
Valve type/No: Side 8
Transmission: Manual
No. of forward speeds: 4
Wheels driven: Rear
Brakes F/R: Drum/Drum
Kerb weight: 902.5kg 1988.0lb
Fuel: 31.8L 7.0gal 8.4galUS

3761 Rambler
American
1959 USA
84.0mph 135.2kmh
0-50mph 80.5kmh: 11.7secs
0-60mph 96.5kmh: 17.7secs
0-1/4 mile: 20.6secs
90.0bhp 67.1kW 91.2PS
@ 3800rpm
150.0lbft 203.3Nm @ 1600rpm
78.7bhp/ton 77.4bhp/tonne
28.1bhp/L 20.9kW/L 28.5PS/L
44.9ft/sec 13.7m/sec
20.1mph 32.3kmh/1000rpm
24.3mpg 20.2mpgUS 11.6L/100km
Petrol 4-stroke piston
3205cc 195.5cu in
In-line 6 1 Carburettor
Compression ratio: 8.0:1
Bore: 79.3mm 3.1in
Stroke: 107.9mm 4.2in
Valve type/No: Overhead 12
Transmission: Manual
No. of forward speeds: 3
Wheels driven: Rear
Springs F/R: Coil/Leaf
Brakes F/R: Drum/Drum
Wheelbase: 254.0cm 100.0in
Track F: 138.7cm 54.6in
Track R: 139.7cm 55.0in
Length: 452.9cm 178.3in
Width: 185.4cm 73.0in
Height: 145.5cm 57.3in
Ground clearance: 19.6cm 7.7in
Kerb weight: 1163.1kg 2562.0lb
Fuel: 76.0L 16.7gal 20.1galUS

3762 Rambler
Rebel V8
1960 USA
110.0mph 177.0kmh
0-50mph 80.5kmh: 8.1secs
0-60mph 96.5kmh: 11.0secs
0-1/4 mile: 18.0secs
200.0bhp 149.1kW 202.8PS
@ 4900rpm
245.0lbft 332.0Nm @ 2500rpm
129.9bhp/ton 127.7bhp/tonne
48.8bhp/L 36.4kW/L 49.5PS/L
44.2ft/sec 13.5m/sec
24.6mph 39.6kmh/1000rpm
Petrol 4-stroke piston
4100cc 250.1cu in
Vee 8 1 Carburettor
Compression ratio: 8.7:1
Bore: 88.9mm 3.5in
Stroke: 82.6mm 3.2in
Valve type/No: Overhead 16
Transmission: Automatic
No. of forward speeds: 3
Wheels driven: Rear
Wheelbase: 274.3cm 108.0in
Track F: 149.4cm 58.8in
Track R: 150.1cm 59.1in
Length: 481.3cm 189.5in
Width: 183.4cm 72.2in
Height: 145.0cm 57.1in
Kerb weight: 1566.3kg 3450.0lb

3763 Rambler
Six
1960 USA
88.2mph 141.9kmh
0-50mph 80.5kmh: 11.7secs
0-60mph 96.5kmh: 14.9secs
0-1/4 mile: 19.3secs
127.0bhp 94.7kW 128.8PS
@ 4200rpm
180.0lbft 243.9Nm @ 1600rpm
92.7bhp/ton 91.1bhp/tonne
39.6bhp/L 29.5kW/L 40.1PS/L
49.6ft/sec 15.1m/sec
20.8mph 33.5kmh/1000rpm
Petrol 4-stroke piston
3207cc 195.7cu in
In-line 6 1 Carburettor
Compression ratio: 8.7:1
Bore: 79.5mm 3.1in
Stroke: 108.0mm 4.2in
Valve type/No: Overhead 12
Transmission: Automatic
No. of forward speeds: 3
Wheels driven: Rear
Wheelbase: 274.3cm 108.0in
Track F: 146.8cm 57.8in
Track R: 147.3cm 58.0in
Length: 481.3cm 189.5in
Width: 183.4cm 72.2in
Height: 145.5cm 57.3in
Kerb weight: 1393.8kg 3070.0lb

3764 Rambler
Super 6 Station Wagon
1960 USA
91.0mph 146.4kmh
0-50mph 80.5kmh: 11.8secs
0-60mph 96.5kmh: 17.3secs
0-1/4 mile: 20.6secs
127.0bhp 94.7kW 128.8PS
@ 4200rpm
180.0lbft 243.9Nm @ 1600rpm
87.6bhp/ton 86.1bhp/tonne
39.6bhp/L 29.5kW/L 40.2PS/L
49.6ft/sec 15.1m/sec
27.2mph 43.8kmh/1000rpm
18.7mpg 15.6mpgUS 15.1L/100km
Petrol 4-stroke piston
3205cc 195.5cu in
In-line 6 1 Carburettor
Compression ratio: 8.7:1
Bore: 79.3mm 3.1in
Stroke: 107.9mm 4.2in
Valve type/No: Overhead 12
Transmission: Manual with overdrive
No. of forward speeds: 5
Wheels driven: Rear
Springs F/R: Coil/Coil
Brakes F/R: Drum/Drum
Wheelbase: 297.2cm 117.0in
Track F: 146.6cm 57.7in
Track R: 147.3cm 58.0in
Length: 481.3cm 189.5in
Width: 188.0cm 74.0in
Height: 146.1cm 57.5in
Ground clearance: 17.0cm 6.7in
Kerb weight: 1474.6kg 3248.0lb
Fuel: 69.6L 15.3gal 18.4galUS

3765 Rambler
American
1961 USA
85.0mph 136.8kmh
0-50mph 80.5kmh: 13.5secs
0-60mph 96.5kmh: 19.6secs
0-1/4 mile: 21.3secs
125.0bhp 93.2kW 126.7PS
@ 4200rpm
180.0lbft 243.9Nm @ 1600rpm
97.6bhp/ton 95.9bhp/tonne
39.0bhp/L 29.1kW/L 39.5PS/L
49.6ft/sec 15.1m/sec
32.1mph 51.6kmh/1000rpm
Petrol 4-stroke piston
3206cc 195.6cu in
In-line 6 1 Carburettor
Compression ratio: 8.7:1
Bore: 79.4mm 3.1in
Stroke: 108.0mm 4.2in
Valve type/No: Overhead 12
Transmission: Manual
No. of forward speeds: 3
Wheels driven: Rear
Wheelbase: 254.0cm 100.0in
Track F: 138.7cm 54.6in
Track R: 139.7cm 55.0in
Length: 439.7cm 173.1in
Width: 177.8cm 70.0in
Height: 142.7cm 56.2in
Ground clearance: 16.5cm 6.5in
Kerb weight: 1303.0kg 2870.0lb

3766 Rambler
Estate
1961 USA
91.5mph 147.2kmh
0-50mph 80.5kmh: 13.2secs
0-60mph 96.5kmh: 18.4secs
0-1/4 mile: 21.4secs
127.0bhp 94.7kW 128.8PS
@ 4200rpm
180.0lbft 243.9Nm @ 1600rpm
89.9bhp/ton 88.4bhp/tonne
39.6bhp/L 29.5kW/L 40.2PS/L
49.6ft/sec 15.1m/sec
23.7mph 38.1kmh/1000rpm
19.4mpg 16.2mpgUS 14.6L/100km
Petrol 4-stroke piston
3205cc 195.5cu in
In-line 6 1 Carburettor
Compression ratio: 8.7:1
Bore: 79.3mm 3.1in
Stroke: 107.9mm 4.2in
Valve type/No: Overhead 12
Transmission: Automatic
No. of forward speeds: 3
Wheels driven: Rear
Springs F/R: Coil/Coil
Brakes F/R: Drum/Drum
Wheelbase: 274.3cm 108.0in
Track F: 145.3cm 57.2in
Track R: 147.3cm 58.0in
Length: 480.1cm 189.0in
Width: 184.2cm 72.5in
Height: 147.3cm 58.0in
Ground clearance: 14.2cm 5.6in
Kerb weight: 1436.0kg 3163.0lb
Fuel: 76.0L 16.7gal 20.1galUS

3767 Rambler
770 Six
1964 USA
95.0mph 152.9kmh
0-50mph 80.5kmh: 10.3secs
0-60mph 96.5kmh: 14.7secs
0-1/4 mile: 19.9secs
138.0bhp 102.9kW 139.9PS
@ 4500rpm
185.0lbft 250.7Nm @ 1800rpm
105.0bhp/ton 103.3bhp/tonne
43.0bhp/L 32.1kW/L 43.6PS/L
53.1ft/sec 16.2m/sec
22.4mph 36.0kmh/1000rpm
18.3mpg 15.2mpgUS 15.4L/100km
Petrol 4-stroke piston
3206cc 195.6cu in
In-line 6 1 Carburettor
Compression ratio: 8.7:1
Bore: 79.4mm 3.1in
Stroke: 108.0mm 4.2in
Valve type/No: Overhead 12
Transmission: Automatic
No. of forward speeds: 3
Wheels driven: Rear
Springs F/R: Coil/Coil
Brakes F/R: Drum/Drum
Steering: Recirculating ball
Wheelbase: 285.8cm 112.5in
Track F: 148.8cm 58.6in
Track R: 146.1cm 57.5in
Length: 482.6cm 190.0in
Width: 188.0cm 74.0in
Height: 142.2cm 56.0in
Ground clearance: 15.2cm 6.0in
Kerb weight: 1336.1kg 2943.0lb
Fuel: 72.8L 16.0gal 19.2galUS

3768 Rambler

770 V8 Convertible
1966 USA
107.0mph 172.2kmh
0-50mph 80.5kmh: 9.3secs
0-60mph 96.5kmh: 12.6secs
0-1/4 mile: 18.8secs
198.0bhp 147.6kW 200.7PS
@ 4700rpm
280.0lbft 379.4Nm @ 2600rpm
124.9bhp/ton 122.8bhp/tonne
42.1bhp/L 31.4kW/L 42.7PS/L
42.4ft/sec 12.9m/sec
24.3mph 39.1kmh/1000rpm
15.1mpg 12.6mpgUS 18.7L/100km
Petrol 4-stroke piston
4704cc 287.0cu in
Vee 8 1 Carburettor
Compression ratio: 8.7:1
Bore: 93.5mm 3.7in
Stroke: 82.6mm 3.2in
Valve type/No: Overhead 16
Transmission: Automatic
No. of forward speeds: 3
Wheels driven: Rear
Springs F/R: Coil/Coil
Brake system: PA
Brakes F/R: Disc/Drum
Steering: Recirculating ball
Wheelbase: 284.5cm 112.0in
Track F: 148.6cm 58.5in
Track R: 146.1cm 57.5in
Length: 495.3cm 195.0in
Width: 189.2cm 74.5in
Height: 137.7cm 54.2in
Ground clearance: 15.2cm 6.0in
Kerb weight: 1611.7kg 3550.0lb
Fuel: 71.9L 15.8gal 19.0galUS

3769 Rambler

Rebel 6 Estate Car
1967 USA
99.0mph 159.3kmh
0-50mph 80.5kmh: 10.0secs
0-60mph 96.5kmh: 14.2secs
0-1/4 mile: 19.4secs
0-1km: 36.3secs
155.0bhp 115.6kW 157.1PS
@ 4400rpm
222.0lbft 300.8Nm @ 1600rpm
101.0bhp/ton 99.4bhp/tonne
40.8bhp/L 30.4kW/L 41.3PS/L
42.8ft/sec 13.0m/sec
24.8mph 39.9kmh/1000rpm
17.4mpg 14.5mpgUS 16.2L/100km
Petrol 4-stroke piston
3802cc 232.0cu in
In-line 6 1 Carburettor
Compression ratio: 8.5:1
Bore: 95.3mm 3.8in
Stroke: 88.9mm 3.5in
Valve type/No: Overhead 12
Transmission: Automatic
No. of forward speeds: 3
Wheels driven: Rear
Springs F/R: Coil/Coil
Brake system: PA
Brakes F/R: Disc/Drum
Steering: Recirculating ball
Wheelbase: 289.6cm 114.0in
Track F: 147.3cm 58.0in
Track R: 147.3cm 58.0in
Length: 513.1cm 202.0in
Width: 198.1cm 78.0in
Height: 152.4cm 60.0in
Ground clearance: 22.9cm 9.0in
Kerb weight: 1559.9kg 3436.0lb
Fuel: 81.4L 17.9gal 21.5galUS

3770 Rambler

Javelin Hardtop SST
1968 USA
120.0mph 193.1kmh
0-50mph 80.5kmh: 7.2secs
0-60mph 96.5kmh: 9.4secs
0-1/4 mile: 16.9secs
0-1km: 31.4secs
284.0bhp 211.8kW 287.9PS
@ 4800rpm
365.0lbft 494.6Nm @ 3000rpm
187.4bhp/ton 184.3bhp/tonne
50.5bhp/L 37.7kW/L 51.2PS/L
43.7ft/sec 13.3m/sec
26.7mph 43.0kmh/1000rpm
15.5mpg 12.9mpgUS 18.2L/100km
Petrol 4-stroke piston
5622cc 343.0cu in
Vee 8 1 Carburettor
Compression ratio: 10.2:1
Bore: 103.5mm 4.1in
Stroke: 83.2mm 3.3in
Valve type/No: Overhead 16
Transmission: Automatic
No. of forward speeds: 3
Wheels driven: Rear
Springs F/R: Coil/Leaf
Brake system: PA
Brakes F/R: Disc/Drum
Steering: Recirculating ball PA
Wheelbase: 276.9cm 109.0in
Track F: 147.3cm 58.0in
Track R: 148.6cm 58.5in
Length: 480.1cm 189.0in
Width: 182.9cm 72.0in
Height: 139.7cm 55.0in
Ground clearance: 15.2cm 6.0in
Kerb weight: 1541.3kg 3395.0lb
Fuel: 71.9L 15.8gal 19.0galUS

3771 Range Rover

V8
1970 UK
92.0mph 148.0kmh
0-50mph 80.5kmh: 10.0secs
0-60mph 96.5kmh: 13.9secs
0-1/4 mile: 19.1secs
0-1km: 35.5secs
135.0bhp 100.7kW 136.9PS
@ 4750rpm
205.0lbft 277.8Nm @ 3000rpm
77.9bhp/ton 76.6bhp/tonne
38.3bhp/L 28.5kW/L 38.8PS/L
36.9ft/sec 11.3m/sec
20.0mph 32.2kmh/1000rpm
14.4mpg 12.0mpgUS 19.6L/100km
Petrol 4-stroke piston
3528cc 215.2cu in
Vee 8 2 Carburettor
Compression ratio: 8.5:1
Bore: 88.9mm 3.5in
Stroke: 71.1mm 2.8in
Valve type/No: Overhead 16
Transmission: Manual
No. of forward speeds: 4
Wheels driven: 4-wheel drive
Springs F/R: Coil/Coil
Brake system: PA
Brakes F/R: Disc/Disc
Steering: Recirculating ball
Wheelbase: 254.0cm 100.0in
Track F: 148.6cm 58.5in
Track R: 148.6cm 58.5in
Length: 447.0cm 176.0in
Width: 177.8cm 70.0in
Height: 177.8cm 70.0in
Ground clearance: 19.1cm 7.5in
Kerb weight: 1761.5kg 3880.0lb
Fuel: 86.4L 19.0gal 22.8galUS

3772 Range Rover

V8
1975 UK
105.0mph 168.9kmh
0-50mph 80.5kmh: 10.8secs
0-60mph 96.5kmh: 14.6secs
0-1/4 mile: 20.1secs
0-1km: 37.2secs
130.0bhp 96.9kW 131.8PS
@ 5000rpm
185.0lbft 250.7Nm @ 2500rpm
73.4bhp/ton 72.2bhp/tonne
36.8bhp/L 27.5kW/L 37.4PS/L
38.9ft/sec 11.8m/sec
20.1mph 32.3kmh/1000rpm
14.1mpg 11.7mpgUS 20.0L/100km
Petrol 4-stroke piston
3528cc 215.2cu in
Vee 8 2 Carburettor
Compression ratio: 8.2:1
Bore: 88.9mm 3.5in
Stroke: 71.1mm 2.8in
Valve type/No: Overhead 16
Transmission: Manual
No. of forward speeds: 4
Wheels driven: 4-wheel drive
Springs F/R: Coil/Coil
Brake system: PA
Brakes F/R: Disc/Disc
Steering: Recirculating ball
Wheelbase: 254.0cm 100.0in
Track F: 148.6cm 58.5in
Track R: 148.6cm 58.5in
Length: 447.0cm 176.0in
Width: 177.8cm 70.0in
Height: 177.8cm 70.0in
Ground clearance: 19.1cm 7.5in
Kerb weight: 1800.1kg 3965.0lb
Fuel: 86.4L 19.0gal 22.8galUS

3773 Range Rover

V8
1978 UK
100.0mph 160.9kmh
0-50mph 80.5kmh: 10.1secs
0-60mph 96.5kmh: 14.3secs
0-1/4 mile: 19.7secs
0-1km: 37.4secs
130.0bhp 96.9kW 131.8PS
@ 5000rpm
185.0lbft 250.7Nm @ 2500rpm
72.6bhp/ton 71.4bhp/tonne
36.8bhp/L 27.5kW/L 37.4PS/L
38.9ft/sec 11.8m/sec
27.0mph 43.4kmh/1000rpm
14.2mpg 11.8mpgUS 19.9L/100km
Petrol 4-stroke piston
3528cc 215.2cu in
Vee 8 2 Carburettor
Compression ratio: 8.2:1
Bore: 88.9mm 3.5in
Stroke: 71.1mm 2.8in
Valve type/No: Overhead 16
Transmission: Manual with overdrive
No. of forward speeds: 5
Wheels driven: 4-wheel drive
Springs F/R: Coil/Coil
Brake system: PA
Brakes F/R: Disc/Disc
Steering: Recirculating ball
Wheelbase: 254.0cm 100.0in
Track F: 148.6cm 58.5in
Track R: 148.6cm 58.5in
Length: 447.0cm 176.0in
Width: 177.8cm 70.0in
Height: 177.8cm 70.0in
Ground clearance: 19.1cm 7.5in
Kerb weight: 1820.1kg 4009.0lb
Fuel: 81.9L 18.0gal 21.6galUS

3774 Range Rover

Vogue
1986 UK
106.0mph 170.6kmh
0-50mph 80.5kmh: 8.2secs
0-60mph 96.5kmh: 11.9secs
0-1/4 mile: 18.4secs
0-1km: 34.3secs
165.0bhp 123.0kW 167.3PS
@ 4750rpm
207.4lbft 281.0Nm @ 3200rpm
85.1bhp/ton 83.7bhp/tonne
46.8bhp/L 34.9kW/L 47.4PS/L
36.9ft/sec 11.3m/sec
25.8mph 41.5kmh/1000rpm
15.0mpg 12.5mpgUS 18.8L/100km
Petrol 4-stroke piston
3528cc 215.2cu in
Vee 8 fuel injection
Compression ratio: 9.3:1
Bore: 88.9mm 3.5in
Stroke: 71.1mm 2.8in
Valve type/No: Overhead 16
Transmission: Manual
No. of forward speeds: 5
Wheels driven: 4-wheel drive
Springs F/R: Coil/Coil
Brake system: PA
Brakes F/R: Disc/Disc
Steering: Recirculating ball PA
Wheelbase: 259.1cm 102.0in
Track F: 148.6cm 58.5in
Track R: 148.6cm 58.5in
Length: 447.0cm 176.0in
Width: 177.8cm 70.0in
Height: 177.8cm 70.0in
Ground clearance: 19.1cm 7.5in
Kerb weight: 1972.2kg 4344.0lb
Fuel: 79.6L 17.5gal 21.0galUS

3775 Range Rover

V8
1987 UK
90.0mph 144.8kmh
0-50mph 80.5kmh: 9.2secs
0-60mph 96.5kmh: 12.6secs
0-1/4 mile: 19.0secs
150.0bhp 111.9kW 152.1PS
@ 4750rpm
195.0lbft 264.2Nm @ 3000rpm
77.9bhp/ton 76.6bhp/tonne
42.5bhp/L 31.7kW/L 43.1PS/L
36.9ft/sec 11.3m/sec
16.2mpg 13.5mpgUS 17.4L/100km
Petrol 4-stroke piston
3532cc 215.5cu in
Vee 8 fuel injection
Compression ratio: 8.1:1
Bore: 88.9mm 3.5in
Stroke: 71.1mm 2.8in
Valve type/No: Overhead 16
Transmission: Automatic
No. of forward speeds: 4
Wheels driven: 4-wheel drive
Springs F/R: Coil/Coil
Brake system: PA
Brakes F/R: Disc/Disc
Steering: Recirculating ball PA
Wheelbase: 254.0cm 100.0in
Track F: 148.6cm 58.5in
Track R: 148.6cm 58.5in
Length: 444.5cm 175.0in
Width: 181.9cm 71.6in
Height: 179.8cm 70.8in
Kerb weight: 1959.0kg 4315.0lb
Fuel: 75.7L 16.6gal 20.0galUS

3776 Range Rover

Vogue Turbo D
1988 UK
93.0mph 149.6kmh
0-50mph 80.5kmh: 11.6secs
0-60mph 96.5kmh: 16.5secs
0-1/4 mile: 20.6secs
0-1km: 38.6secs
112.0bhp 83.5kW 113.5PS
@ 4200rpm
183.0lbft 248.0Nm @ 2400rpm
56.5bhp/ton 55.6bhp/tonne
46.8bhp/L 34.9kW/L 47.5PS/L
41.3ft/sec 12.6m/sec
25.2mph 40.5kmh/1000rpm
21.4mpg 17.8mpgUS 13.2L/100km
Diesel 4-stroke piston
2392cc 146.0cu in turbocharged
In-line 4 fuel injection
Compression ratio: 22.0:1
Bore: 92.0mm 3.6in
Stroke: 90.0mm 3.5in
Valve type/No: Overhead 8
Transmission: Manual
No. of forward speeds: 5
Wheels driven: 4-wheel drive
Springs F/R: Coil/Coil
Brake system: PA
Brakes F/R: Disc/Disc
Steering: Recirculating ball PA
Wheelbase: 259.1cm 102.0in
Track F: 148.6cm 58.5in
Track R: 148.6cm 58.5in
Length: 447.0cm 176.0in
Width: 177.8cm 70.0in
Height: 177.8cm 70.0in
Ground clearance: 19.1cm 7.5in
Kerb weight: 2016.0kg 4440.5lb
Fuel: 81.9L 18.0gal 21.6galUS

3777 Range Rover

Vogue
1989 UK
106.0mph 170.6kmh
0-50mph 80.5kmh: 8.4secs
0-60mph 96.5kmh: 12.1secs
0-1/4 mile: 18.3secs
0-1km: 34.3secs
168.0bhp 125.3kW 170.3PS
@ 4750rpm
207.4lbft 281.0Nm @ 3200rpm
90.4bhp/ton 88.9bhp/tonne
47.6bhp/L 35.5kW/L 48.3PS/L
36.9ft/sec 11.3m/sec
25.4mph 40.9kmh/1000rpm
18.7mpg 15.6mpgUS 15.1L/100km
Petrol 4-stroke piston
3528cc 215.0cu in
Vee 8 fuel injection
Compression ratio: 9.3:1
Bore: 88.9mm 3.5in
Stroke: 71.1mm 2.8in
Valve type/No: Overhead 16
Transmission: Manual
No. of forward speeds: 5
Wheels driven: 4-wheel drive
Springs F/R: Coil/Coil
Brake system: PA
Brakes F/R: Disc/Disc
Steering: Recirculating ball PA
Wheelbase: 254.0cm 100.0in
Track F: 148.6cm 58.5in

Track R: 148.6cm 58.5in
Length: 447.0cm 176.0in
Width: 177.8cm 70.0in
Height: 177.8cm 70.0in
Ground clearance: 19.1cm 7.5in
Kerb weight: 1890.0kg 4163.0lb
Fuel: 76.4L 16.8gal 20.2galUS

3778 Range Rover

Vogue SE
1989 UK
102.0mph 164.1kmh
0-50mph 80.5kmh: 8.4secs
0-60mph 96.5kmh: 11.7secs
0-1/4 mile: 18.9secs
0-1km: 35.0secs
165.0bhp 123.0kW 167.3PS
@ 4750rpm
207.4lbft 281.0Nm @ 3200rpm
88.2bhp/ton 86.7bhp/tonne
46.1bhp/L 34.3kW/L 46.7PS/L
36.9ft/sec 11.3m/sec
26.6mph 42.8kmh/1000rpm
15.8mpg 13.2mpgUS 17.9L/100km
Petrol 4-stroke piston
3582cc 219.0cu in
Vee 8 fuel injection
Compression ratio: 9.3:1
Bore: 88.9mm 3.5in
Stroke: 71.1mm 2.8in
Valve type/No: Overhead 16
Transmission: Automatic
No. of forward speeds: 4
Wheels driven: 4-wheel drive
Springs F/R: Coil/Coil
Brake system: PA
Brakes F/R: Disc/Disc
Steering: Recirculating ball PA
Wheelbase: 259.1cm 102.0in
Track F: 148.6cm 58.5in
Track R: 148.6cm 58.5in
Length: 447.0cm 176.0in
Width: 177.8cm 70.0in
Height: 177.8cm 70.0in
Ground clearance: 19.1cm 7.5in
Kerb weight: 1903.0kg 4191.6lb
Fuel: 79.6L 17.5gal 21.0galUS

3779 Range Rover

County
1990 UK
109.0mph 175.4kmh
0-60mph 96.5kmh: 12.3secs
0-1/4 mile: 18.7secs
178.0bhp 132.7kW 180.5PS
@ 4750rpm
220.0lbft 298.1Nm @ 3250rpm
88.9bhp/ton 87.4bhp/tonne
45.1bhp/L 33.6kW/L 45.7PS/L
36.9ft/sec 11.3m/sec
16.2mpg 13.5mpgUS 17.4L/100km
Petrol 4-stroke piston
3947cc 240.8cu in
Vee 8 fuel injection
Compression ratio: 8.1:1
Bore: 94.0mm 3.7in
Stroke: 71.1mm 2.8in
Valve type/No: Overhead 16
Transmission: Automatic
No. of forward speeds: 4
Wheels driven: 4-wheel drive
Springs F/R: Coil/Coil
Brake system: PA ABS
Brakes F/R: Disc/Disc
Steering: Worm & roller PA
Wheelbase: 254.0cm 100.0in
Track F: 148.6cm 58.5in
Track R: 148.6cm 58.5in
Length: 444.5cm 175.0in
Width: 181.4cm 71.4in
Height: 179.8cm 70.8in
Kerb weight: 2036.2kg 4485.0lb
Fuel: 75.7L 16.6gal 20.0galUS

3780 Range Rover

Vogue SE
1990 UK
110.0mph 177.0kmh
0-50mph 80.5kmh: 8.2secs
0-60mph 96.5kmh: 11.3secs
0-1/4 mile: 18.5secs
0-1km: 34.7secs
185.0bhp 137.9kW 187.6PS
@ 4650rpm
235.4lbft 319.0Nm @ 2600rpm
94.6bhp/ton 93.1bhp/tonne
46.9bhp/L 34.9kW/L 47.5PS/L
36.2ft/sec 11.0m/sec
26.9mph 43.3kmh/1000rpm
14.6mpg 12.2mpgUS 19.3L/100km
Petrol 4-stroke piston
3947cc 241.0cu in
Vee 8 fuel injection
Compression ratio: 9.3:1
Bore: 94.0mm 3.7in
Stroke: 71.1mm 2.8in
Valve type/No: Overhead 16
Transmission: Automatic
No. of forward speeds: 4
Wheels driven: 4-wheel drive
Springs F/R: Coil/Coil
Brake system: PA ABS
Brakes F/R: Disc/Disc
Steering: Recirculating ball PA
Wheelbase: 254.0cm 100.0in
Track F: 148.6cm 58.5in
Track R: 148.6cm 58.5in
Length: 447.0cm 176.0in
Width: 177.8cm 70.0in
Height: 177.8cm 70.0in
Ground clearance: 19.1cm 7.5in
Kerb weight: 1988.0kg 4378.8lb
Fuel: 79.6L 17.5gal 21.0galUS

3781 Range Rover

Vogue SE
1992 UK
108.0mph 173.8kmh
0-50mph 80.5kmh: 7.9secs
0-60mph 96.5kmh: 10.8secs
0-1/4 mile: 18.2secs
0-1km: 33.6secs
178.0bhp 132.7kW 180.5PS
@ 4750rpm
220.0lbft 298.1Nm @ 3250rpm
90.1bhp/ton 88.6bhp/tonne
45.1bhp/L 33.6kW/L 45.7PS/L
36.9ft/sec 11.2m/sec
26.9mph 43.3kmh/1000rpm
14.2mpg 11.8mpgUS 19.9L/100km
Petrol 4-stroke piston
3947cc 240.8cu in
Vee 8 fuel injection
Compression ratio: 9.3:1
Bore: 94.0mm 3.7in
Stroke: 71.0mm 2.8in
Valve type/No: Overhead 16
Transmission: Automatic
No. of forward speeds: 4
Wheels driven: 4-wheel drive
Springs F/R: Coil/Coil
Brake system: PA
Brakes F/R: Disc/Disc
Steering: Recirculating ball PA
Wheelbase: 254.0cm 100.0in
Track F: 148.6cm 58.5in
Track R: 148.6cm 58.5in
Length: 447.0cm 176.0in
Width: 177.8cm 70.0in
Height: 177.8cm 70.0in
Ground clearance: 19.1cm 7.5in
Kerb weight: 2009.9kg 4427.0lb
Fuel: 81.9L 18.0gal 21.6galUS

3782 Reliant

Sabre Sports
1962 UK
90.8mph 146.1kmh
0-50mph 80.5kmh: 11.4secs
0-60mph 96.5kmh: 16.6secs
0-1/4 mile: 20.3secs
71.5bhp 53.3kW 72.5PS
@ 4400rpm
91.0lbft 123.3Nm @ 2300rpm
87.7bhp/ton 86.2bhp/tonne
42.0bhp/L 31.3kW/L 42.6PS/L
38.3ft/sec 11.7m/sec
19.4mph 31.2kmh/1000rpm
28.8mpg 24.0mpgUS 9.8L/100km
Petrol 4-stroke piston
1703cc 103.9cu in
In-line 4 1 Carburettor
Compression ratio: 8.8:1
Bore: 82.6mm 3.2in
Stroke: 79.6mm 3.1in
Valve type/No: Overhead 8
Transmission: Manual
No. of forward speeds: 4
Wheels driven: Rear
Springs F/R: Coil/Coil
Brakes F/R: Disc/Drum
Steering: Rack & pinion
Wheelbase: 228.6cm 90.0in
Track F: 129.5cm 51.0in
Track R: 127.0cm 50.0in
Length: 419.1cm 165.0in
Width: 154.9cm 61.0in
Height: 127.0cm 50.0in
Ground clearance: 12.7cm 5.0in
Kerb weight: 829.5kg 1827.0lb
Fuel: 54.6L 12.0gal 14.4galUS

3783 Reliant

Sabre Six GT
1964 UK
110.5mph 177.8kmh
0-50mph 80.5kmh: 9.2secs
0-60mph 96.5kmh: 12.2secs
0-1/4 mile: 18.3secs
109.0bhp 81.3kW 110.5PS
@ 4800rpm
137.0lbft 185.6Nm @ 2400rpm
110.0bhp/ton 108.2bhp/tonne
42.7bhp/L 31.8kW/L 43.3PS/L
41.7ft/sec 12.7m/sec
26.1mph 42.0kmh/1000rpm
20.3mpg 16.9mpgUS 13.9L/100km
Petrol 4-stroke piston
2553cc 155.8cu in
In-line 6 1 Carburettor
Compression ratio: 8.3:1
Bore: 82.6mm 3.2in
Stroke: 79.5mm 3.1in
Valve type/No: Overhead 12
Transmission: Manual with overdrive
No. of forward speeds: 8
Wheels driven: Rear
Springs F/R: Coil/Coil
Brakes F/R: Disc/Drum
Steering: Rack & pinion
Wheelbase: 228.6cm 90.0in
Track F: 121.9cm 48.0in
Track R: 121.9cm 48.0in
Length: 406.4cm 160.0in
Width: 154.9cm 61.0in
Height: 129.5cm 51.0in
Ground clearance: 12.7cm 5.0in
Kerb weight: 1007.4kg 2219.0lb
Fuel: 54.6L 12.0gal 14.4galUS

3784 Reliant

Scimitar
1965 UK
118.0mph 189.9kmh
0-50mph 80.5kmh: 8.5secs
0-60mph 96.5kmh: 11.4secs
0-1/4 mile: 18.0secs
120.0bhp 89.5kW 121.7PS
@ 5000rpm
140.0lbft 189.7Nm @ 2600rpm
111.3bhp/ton 109.5bhp/tonne
47.0bhp/L 35.0kW/L 47.6PS/L
43.5ft/sec 13.2m/sec
23.9mph 38.5kmh/1000rpm
19.8mpg 16.5mpgUS 14.3L/100km
Petrol 4-stroke piston
2553cc 155.8cu in
In-line 6 3 Carburettor
Compression ratio: 8.3:1
Bore: 82.5mm 3.2in
Stroke: 79.5mm 3.1in
Valve type/No: Overhead 12
Transmission: Manual with overdrive
No. of forward speeds: 6
Wheels driven: Rear
Springs F/R: Coil/Coil
Brake system: PA
Brakes F/R: Disc/Drum
Steering: Rack & pinion
Wheelbase: 235.0cm 92.5in
Track F: 127.0cm 50.0in
Track R: 127.0cm 50.0in
Length: 424.2cm 167.0in
Width: 162.6cm 64.0in
Height: 130.8cm 51.5in
Ground clearance: 14.0cm 5.5in
Kerb weight: 1096.0kg 2414.0lb
Fuel: 91.0L 20.0gal 24.0galUS

3785 Reliant

Scimitar GT
1967 UK
122.0mph 196.3kmh
0-50mph 80.5kmh: 7.2secs
0-60mph 96.5kmh: 10.0secs
0-1/4 mile: 17.1secs
0-1km: 32.3secs
136.0bhp 101.4kW 137.9PS
@ 4750rpm
192.0lbft 260.2Nm @ 3000rpm
123.3bhp/ton 121.2bhp/tonne
45.4bhp/L 33.9kW/L 46.1PS/L
37.6ft/sec 11.5m/sec
24.6mph 39.6kmh/1000rpm
22.1mpg 18.4mpgUS 12.8L/100km
Petrol 4-stroke piston
2994cc 182.7cu in
Vee 6 1 Carburettor
Compression ratio: 8.9:1
Bore: 93.7mm 3.7in
Stroke: 72.4mm 2.8in
Valve type/No: Overhead 12
Transmission: Manual with overdrive
No. of forward speeds: 6
Wheels driven: Rear
Springs F/R: Coil/Coil
Brake system: PA
Brakes F/R: Disc/Drum
Steering: Rack & pinion
Wheelbase: 235.0cm 92.5in
Track F: 127.0cm 50.0in
Track R: 127.0cm 50.0in
Length: 424.2cm 167.0in
Width: 162.6cm 64.0in
Height: 130.8cm 51.5in
Ground clearance: 14.0cm 5.5in
Kerb weight: 1121.8kg 2471.0lb
Fuel: 96.9L 21.3gal 25.6galUS

3786 Reliant

Rebel 700 Estate
1968 UK
70.0mph 112.6kmh
0-50mph 80.5kmh: 18.5secs
0-60mph 96.5kmh: 35.9secs
0-1/4 mile: 23.7secs
0-1km: 46.0secs
31.0bhp 23.1kW 31.4PS
@ 5000rpm
38.0lbft 51.5Nm @ 2500rpm
51.8bhp/ton 51.0bhp/tonne
44.2bhp/L 33.0kW/L 44.8PS/L
33.3ft/sec 10.2m/sec
14.0mph 22.5kmh/1000rpm
38.1mpg 31.7mpgUS 7.4L/100km
Petrol 4-stroke piston
701cc 42.8cu in
In-line 4 1 Carburettor
Compression ratio: 8.8:1
Bore: 60.5mm 2.4in
Stroke: 61.0mm 2.4in
Valve type/No: Overhead 8
Transmission: Manual
No. of forward speeds: 4
Wheels driven: Rear
Springs F/R: Coil/Leaf
Brakes F/R: Drum/Drum
Steering: Worm & peg
Wheelbase: 226.1cm 89.0in
Track F: 121.9cm 48.0in
Track R: 118.1cm 46.5in
Length: 370.8cm 146.0in
Width: 147.3cm 58.0in
Height: 139.7cm 55.0in
Ground clearance: 14.0cm 5.5in
Kerb weight: 608.4kg 1340.0lb
Fuel: 27.3L 6.0gal 7.2galUS

3787 Reliant

Scimitar GTE Automatic
1970 UK
116.0mph 186.6kmh
0-50mph 80.5kmh: 8.0secs
0-60mph 96.5kmh: 10.7secs
0-1/4 mile: 18.0secs
0-1km: 33.0secs
128.0bhp 95.4kW 129.8PS
@ 4750rpm
173.0lbft 234.4Nm @ 3000rpm
108.1bhp/ton 106.3bhp/tonne
42.7bhp/L 31.9kW/L 43.3PS/L
37.6ft/sec 11.5m/sec
23.5mph 37.8kmh/1000rpm
20.4mpg 17.0mpgUS 13.8L/100km
Petrol 4-stroke piston
2994cc 182.7cu in
Vee 6 1 Carburettor
Compression ratio: 8.9:1
Bore: 93.7mm 3.7in
Stroke: 72.4mm 2.8in
Valve type/No: Overhead 12
Transmission: Automatic
No. of forward speeds: 3
Wheels driven: Rear
Springs F/R: Coil/Coil
Brake system: PA

Brakes F/R: Disc/Drum
Steering: Rack & pinion
Wheelbase: 251.5cm 99.0in
Track F: 141.2cm 55.6in
Track R: 135.4cm 53.3in
Length: 431.8cm 170.0in
Width: 167.6cm 66.0in
Height: 133.4cm 52.5in
Ground clearance: 12.7cm 5.0in
Kerb weight: 1204.0kg 2652.0lb
Fuel: 77.3L 17.0gal 20.4galUS

3788 Reliant

Scimitar GTE
1973 UK
123.0mph 197.9kmh
0-50mph 80.5kmh: 6.4secs
0-60mph 96.5kmh: 8.9secs
0-1/4 mile: 16.9secs
0-1km: 31.1secs
138.0bhp 102.9kW 139.9PS
@ 5000rpm
172.0lbft 233.1Nm @ 3000rpm
126.7bhp/ton 124.6bhp/tonne
46.1bhp/L 34.4kW/L 46.7PS/L
39.6ft/sec 12.1m/sec
23.7mph 38.1kmh/1000rpm
20.8mpg 17.3mpgUS 13.6L/100km
Petrol 4-stroke piston
2994cc 182.7cu in
Vee 6 1 Carburettor
Compression ratio: 8.9:1
Bore: 93.7mm 3.7in
Stroke: 72.4mm 2.8in
Valve type/No: Overhead 12
Transmission: Manual
No. of forward speeds: 4
Wheels driven: Rear
Springs F/R: Coil/Coil
Brake system: PA
Brakes F/R: Disc/Drum
Steering: Rack & pinion
Wheelbase: 251.5cm 99.0in
Track F: 141.2cm 55.6in
Track R: 135.4cm 53.3in
Length: 431.8cm 170.0in
Width: 167.6cm 66.0in
Height: 133.4cm 52.5in
Ground clearance: 12.7cm 5.0in
Kerb weight: 1107.8kg 2440.0lb
Fuel: 77.3L 17.0gal 20.4galUS

3789 Reliant

Kitten
1975 UK
80.0mph 128.7kmh
0-50mph 80.5kmh: 11.8secs
0-60mph 96.5kmh: 19.6secs
0-1/4 mile: 21.2secs
0-1km: 40.9secs
40.0bhp 29.8kW 40.5PS
@ 5500rpm
46.0lbft 62.3Nm @ 3500rpm
77.3bhp/ton 76.0bhp/tonne
47.2bhp/L 35.2kW/L 47.8PS/L
41.6ft/sec 12.7m/sec
16.9mph 27.2kmh/1000rpm
41.5mpg 34.6mpgUS 6.8L/100km
Petrol 4-stroke piston
848cc 51.7cu in
In-line 4 1 Carburettor
Compression ratio: 9.5:1
Bore: 62.5mm 2.5in
Stroke: 69.1mm 2.7in
Valve type/No: Overhead 8
Transmission: Manual
No. of forward speeds: 4
Wheels driven: Rear
Springs F/R: Coil/Leaf
Brakes F/R: Drum/Drum
Steering: Rack & pinion
Wheelbase: 213.9cm 84.2in
Track F: 123.2cm 48.5in
Track R: 124.5cm 49.0in
Length: 337.8cm 133.0in
Width: 142.2cm 56.0in
Height: 139.7cm 55.0in
Ground clearance: 20.3cm 8.0in
Kerb weight: 526.2kg 1159.0lb
Fuel: 27.3L 6.0gal 7.2galUS

3790 Reliant

Kitten DL Estate
1976 UK
80.0mph 128.7kmh
0-50mph 80.5kmh: 12.8secs
0-60mph 96.5kmh: 20.2secs
0-1/4 mile: 21.3secs
0-1km: 40.5secs
40.0bhp 29.8kW 40.5PS
@ 5500rpm
46.0lbft 62.3Nm @ 3500rpm
75.4bhp/ton 74.2bhp/tonne
47.2bhp/L 35.2kW/L 47.8PS/L
41.6ft/sec 12.7m/sec
16.9mph 27.2kmh/1000rpm
41.5mpg 34.6mpgUS 6.8L/100km
Petrol 4-stroke piston
848cc 51.7cu in
In-line 4 1 Carburettor
Compression ratio: 9.5:1
Bore: 62.5mm 2.5in
Stroke: 69.1mm 2.7in
Valve type/No: Overhead 8
Transmission: Manual
No. of forward speeds: 4
Wheels driven: Rear
Springs F/R: Coil/Leaf
Brakes F/R: Drum/Drum
Steering: Rack & pinion
Wheelbase: 213.9cm 84.2in
Track F: 123.2cm 48.5in
Track R: 124.5cm 49.0in
Length: 337.8cm 133.0in
Width: 142.2cm 56.0in
Height: 139.7cm 55.0in
Ground clearance: 20.3cm 8.0in
Kerb weight: 539.3kg 1188.0lb
Fuel: 27.3L 6.0gal 7.2galUS

3791 Reliant

Scimitar GTE
1976 UK
119.0mph 191.5kmh
0-50mph 80.5kmh: 7.4secs
0-60mph 96.5kmh: 10.0secs
0-1/4 mile: 17.6secs
0-1km: 32.0secs
135.0bhp 100.7kW 136.9PS
@ 5500rpm
172.0lbft 233.1Nm @ 3000rpm
109.2bhp/ton 107.3bhp/tonne
45.1bhp/L 33.6kW/L 45.7PS/L
43.5ft/sec 13.3m/sec
21.9mph 35.2kmh/1000rpm
20.3mpg 16.9mpgUS 13.9L/100km
Petrol 4-stroke piston
2994cc 182.7cu in
Vee 6 1 Carburettor
Compression ratio: 8.9:1
Bore: 93.7mm 3.7in
Stroke: 72.4mm 2.8in
Valve type/No: Overhead 12
Transmission: Automatic
No. of forward speeds: 3
Wheels driven: Rear
Springs F/R: Coil/Coil
Brake system: PA
Brakes F/R: Disc/Drum
Steering: Rack & pinion
Wheelbase: 263.7cm 103.8in
Track F: 147.6cm 58.1in
Track R: 142.5cm 56.1in
Length: 443.2cm 174.5in
Width: 170.7cm 67.2in
Height: 132.1cm 52.0in
Ground clearance: 14.0cm 5.5in
Kerb weight: 1257.6kg 2770.0lb
Fuel: 91.0L 20.0gal 24.0galUS

3792 Reliant

Scimitar GTE
1977 UK
119.0mph 191.5kmh
0-50mph 80.5kmh: 6.9secs
0-60mph 96.5kmh: 9.4secs
0-1/4 mile: 17.2secs
0-1km: 31.8secs
135.0bhp 100.7kW 136.9PS
@ 5500rpm
172.0lbft 233.1Nm @ 3000rpm
109.2bhp/ton 107.3bhp/tonne
45.1bhp/L 33.6kW/L 45.7PS/L
43.5ft/sec 13.3m/sec
28.3mph 45.5kmh/1000rpm
21.1mpg 17.6mpgUS 13.4L/100km
Petrol 4-stroke piston
2994cc 182.7cu in
Vee 6 1 Carburettor
Compression ratio: 8.9:1
Bore: 93.7mm 3.7in
Stroke: 72.4mm 2.8in
Valve type/No: Overhead 12
Transmission: Manual with overdrive
No. of forward speeds: 6
Wheels driven: Rear
Springs F/R: Coil/Coil
Brake system: PA
Brakes F/R: Disc/Drum
Steering: Rack & pinion
Wheelbase: 263.7cm 103.8in
Track F: 147.6cm 58.1in
Track R: 142.5cm 56.1in
Length: 443.2cm 174.5in
Width: 170.7cm 67.2in
Height: 132.1cm 52.0in
Ground clearance: 14.0cm 5.5in
Kerb weight: 1257.6kg 2770.0lb
Fuel: 91.0L 20.0gal 24.0galUS

3793 Reliant

Scimitar GTE
1981 UK
117.0mph 188.3kmh
0-50mph 80.5kmh: 8.0secs
0-60mph 96.5kmh: 10.8secs
0-1/4 mile: 17.8secs
0-1km: 33.0secs
135.0bhp 100.7kW 136.9PS
@ 5200rpm
159.0lbft 215.4Nm @ 3000rpm
111.0bhp/ton 109.2bhp/tonne
48.3bhp/L 36.1kW/L 49.0PS/L
39.0ft/sec 11.9m/sec
20.9mph 33.6kmh/1000rpm
20.5mpg 17.1mpgUS 13.8L/100km
Petrol 4-stroke piston
2792cc 170.3cu in
Vee 6 1 Carburettor
Compression ratio: 9.2:1
Bore: 93.0mm 3.7in
Stroke: 68.5mm 2.7in
Valve type/No: Overhead 12
Transmission: Automatic
No. of forward speeds: 3
Wheels driven: Rear
Springs F/R: Coil/Coil
Brake system: PA
Brakes F/R: Disc/Drum
Steering: Rack & pinion
Wheelbase: 263.7cm 103.8in
Track F: 147.6cm 58.1in
Track R: 142.5cm 56.1in
Length: 443.2cm 174.5in
Width: 172.2cm 67.8in
Height: 132.1cm 52.0in
Ground clearance: 14.0cm 5.5in
Kerb weight: 1236.2kg 2723.0lb
Fuel: 91.0L 20.0gal 24.0galUS

3794 Reliant

Scimitar SS1 1600
1985 UK
110.0mph 177.0kmh
0-50mph 80.5kmh: 8.1secs
0-60mph 96.5kmh: 11.5secs
0-1/4 mile: 18.1secs
0-1km: 33.6secs
96.0bhp 71.6kW 97.3PS
@ 6000rpm
98.0lbft 132.8Nm @ 4000rpm
110.9bhp/ton 109.0bhp/tonne
60.1bhp/L 44.9kW/L 61.0PS/L
52.2ft/sec 15.9m/sec
20.4mph 32.8kmh/1000rpm
32.8mpg 27.3mpgUS 8.6L/100km
Petrol 4-stroke piston
1596cc 97.4cu in
In-line 4 1 Carburettor
Compression ratio: 9.5:1
Bore: 80.0mm 3.1in
Stroke: 79.5mm 3.1in
Valve type/No: Overhead 8
Transmission: Manual
No. of forward speeds: 5
Wheels driven: Rear
Springs F/R: Coil/Coil
Brake system: PA
Brakes F/R: Disc/Drum
Steering: Rack & pinion
Wheelbase: 213.4cm 84.0in
Track F: 130.0cm 51.2in
Track R: 132.1cm 52.0in
Length: 388.6cm 153.0in
Width: 158.2cm 62.3in
Height: 124.0cm 48.8in
Ground clearance: 15.2cm 6.0in
Kerb weight: 880.3kg 1939.0lb
Fuel: 45.5L 10.0gal 12.0galUS

3795 Reliant

Scimitar Ti
1986 UK
124.0mph 199.5kmh
0-50mph 80.5kmh: 5.4secs
0-60mph 96.5kmh: 7.2secs
0-1/4 mile: 15.5secs
0-1km: 28.4secs
135.0bhp 100.7kW 136.9PS
@ 6000rpm
143.0lbft 193.8Nm @ 4000rpm
154.4bhp/ton 151.9bhp/tonne
74.6bhp/L 55.6kW/L 75.7PS/L
54.8ft/sec 16.7m/sec
20.6mph 33.1kmh/1000rpm
21.7mpg 18.1mpgUS 13.0L/100km
Petrol 4-stroke piston
1809cc 110.0cu in turbocharged
In-line 4 fuel injection
Compression ratio: 8.0:1
Bore: 83.0mm 3.3in
Stroke: 83.6mm 3.3in
Valve type/No: Overhead 8
Transmission: Manual
No. of forward speeds: 5
Wheels driven: Rear
Springs F/R: Coil/Coil
Brake system: PA
Brakes F/R: Disc/Drum
Steering: Rack & pinion
Wheelbase: 213.3cm 84.0in
Track F: 130.1cm 51.2in
Track R: 132.0cm 52.0in
Length: 388.6cm 153.0in
Width: 158.2cm 62.3in
Height: 123.9cm 48.8in
Ground clearance: 15.2cm 6.0in
Kerb weight: 889.0kg 1958.1lb
Fuel: 45.5L 10.0gal 12.0galUS

3796 Reliant

Scimitar SST 1800Ti
1990 UK
132.0mph 212.4kmh
0-50mph 80.5kmh: 5.2secs
0-60mph 96.5kmh: 7.0secs
0-1/4 mile: 15.5secs
0-1km: 28.3secs
135.0bhp 100.7kW 136.9PS
@ 6000rpm
141.0lbft 191.0Nm @ 4000rpm
147.6bhp/ton 145.2bhp/tonne
74.6bhp/L 55.6kW/L 75.7PS/L
54.8ft/sec 16.7m/sec
20.7mph 33.3kmh/1000rpm
21.7mpg 18.1mpgUS 13.0L/100km
Petrol 4-stroke piston
1809cc 110.0cu in turbocharged
In-line 4 fuel injection
Compression ratio: 8.1:1
Bore: 83.0mm 3.3in
Stroke: 83.6mm 3.3in
Valve type/No: Overhead 8
Transmission: Manual
No. of forward speeds: 5
Wheels driven: Rear
Springs F/R: Coil/Coil
Brake system: PA
Brakes F/R: Disc/Drum
Steering: Rack & pinion
Wheelbase: 213.4cm 84.0in
Length: 388.6cm 153.0in
Width: 177.8cm 70.0in
Height: 127.0cm 50.0in
Kerb weight: 930.0kg 2048.5lb
Fuel: 45.5L 10.0gal 12.0galUS

3797 Renault

Vivasix Saloon
1930 France
60.0mph 96.5kmh
23.0mpg 19.2mpgUS 12.3L/100km
Petrol 4-stroke piston
3180cc 194.0cu in
In-line 6
Bore: 75.0mm 2.9in
Stroke: 120.0mm 4.7in
Transmission: Manual
No. of forward speeds: 3
Wheels driven: Rear
Brakes F/R: Drum/Drum
Wheelbase: 316.2cm 124.5in
Track F: 144.0cm 56.7in
Track R: 144.0cm 56.7in
Length: 468.1cm 184.3in
Width: 171.5cm 67.5in
Height: 185.4cm 73.0in

Kerb weight: 1932.2kg 4256.0lb
Fuel: 70.5L 15.5gal 18.6galUS

3798 Renault
12.1hp Airline Saloon
1935 France
58.0mph 93.3kmh
0-50mph 80.5kmh: 33.2secs
27.0mpg 22.5mpgUS 10.5L/100km
Petrol 4-stroke piston
1463cc 89.3cu in
In-line 4
Bore: 70.0mm 2.8in
Stroke: 95.0mm 3.7in
Transmission: Manual
No. of forward speeds: 3
Wheels driven: Rear
Brakes F/R: Drum/Drum
Kerb weight: 1156.8kg 2548.0lb
Fuel: 45.5L 10.0gal 12.0galUS

3799 Renault
24hp Big Six Saloon
1935 France
76.9mph 123.7kmh
0-50mph 80.5kmh: 21.2secs
0-60mph 96.5kmh: 31.6secs
18.0mpg 15.0mpgUS 15.7L/100km
Petrol 4-stroke piston
3620cc 220.9cu in
In-line 6
Bore: 80.0mm 3.1in
Stroke: 120.0mm 4.7in
Valve type/No: Side 12
Transmission: Manual
No. of forward speeds: 3
Wheels driven: Rear
Brakes F/R: Drum/Drum
Kerb weight: 1786.0kg 3934.0lb
Fuel: 95.5L 21.0gal 25.2galUS

3800 Renault
17.9hp Touring Saloon
1937 France
70.3mph 113.1kmh
0-50mph 80.5kmh: 25.3secs
0-60mph 96.5kmh: 45.5secs
24.0mpg 20.0mpgUS 11.8L/100km
Petrol 4-stroke piston
2383cc 145.4cu in
In-line 4
Bore: 85.0mm 3.3in
Stroke: 105.0mm 4.1in
Valve type/No: Side 8
Transmission: Manual
No. of forward speeds: 3
Wheels driven: Rear
Brakes F/R: Drum/Drum
Kerb weight: 1281.6kg 2823.0lb
Fuel: 45.5L 10.0gal 12.0galUS

3801 Renault
4CV
1948 France
60.0mph 96.5kmh
19.0bhp 14.2kW 19.3PS
@ 4000rpm
37.0bhp/ton 36.4bhp/tonne
25.0bhp/L 18.6kW/L 25.3PS/L
35.0ft/sec 10.7m/sec
45.6mpg 38.0mpgUS 6.2L/100km
Petrol 4-stroke piston
760cc 46.4cu in
In-line 4 1 Carburettor
Compression ratio: 6.7:1
Bore: 50.0mm 2.0in
Stroke: 80.0mm 3.1in
Valve type/No: Overhead 8
Transmission: Manual
No. of forward speeds: 3
Wheels driven: Rear
Springs F/R: Coil/Coil
Brakes F/R: Drum/Drum
Steering: Rack & pinion
Wheelbase: 210.1cm 82.7in
Track F: 118.9cm 46.8in
Track R: 118.9cm 46.8in
Length: 360.2cm 141.8in
Width: 143.0cm 56.3in
Height: 144.8cm 57.0in
Ground clearance: 17.8cm 7.0in
Kerb weight: 522.1kg 1150.0lb

3802 Renault
750
1953 France
60.0mph 96.5kmh
0-50mph 80.5kmh: 29.3secs
0-1/4 mile: 26.6secs
21.0bhp 15.7kW 21.3PS
@ 5000rpm
29.0lbft 39.3Nm @ 2000rpm
34.6bhp/ton 34.1bhp/tonne
28.1bhp/L 20.9kW/L 28.5PS/L
43.8ft/sec 13.3m/sec
13.5mph 21.7kmh/1000rpm
44.0mpg 36.6mpgUS 6.4L/100km
Petrol 4-stroke piston
748cc 45.6cu in
In-line 4
Compression ratio: 7.2:1
Bore: 54.5mm 2.1in
Stroke: 80.0mm 3.1in
Valve type/No: Overhead 8
Transmission: Manual
No. of forward speeds: 3
Wheels driven: Rear
Springs F/R: Coil/Coil
Brakes F/R: Drum/Drum
Wheelbase: 209.6cm 82.5in
Track F: 120.7cm 47.5in
Track R: 120.7cm 47.5in
Length: 360.7cm 142.0in
Width: 142.7cm 56.2in
Height: 147.1cm 57.9in
Ground clearance: 18.3cm 7.2in
Kerb weight: 616.5kg 1358.0lb
Fuel: 27.3L 6.0gal 7.2galUS

3803 Renault
4CV
1955 France
65.3mph 105.1kmh
0-50mph 80.5kmh: 21.2secs
0-60mph 96.5kmh: 31.9secs
0-1/4 mile: 24.7secs
28.0bhp 20.9kW 28.4PS
@ 4500rpm
46.5bhp/ton 45.7bhp/tonne
37.5bhp/L 27.9kW/L 38.0PS/L
39.5ft/sec 12.0m/sec
Petrol 4-stroke piston
747cc 45.6cu in
In-line 4
Bore: 54.6mm 2.1in
Stroke: 80.3mm 3.2in
Valve type/No: Overhead 8
Transmission: Manual
No. of forward speeds: 3
Wheels driven: Rear
Wheelbase: 209.6cm 82.5in
Track F: 120.7cm 47.5in
Track R: 120.7cm 47.5in
Kerb weight: 612.9kg 1350.0lb

3804 Renault
750
1955 France
64.0mph 103.0kmh
0-50mph 80.5kmh: 26.3secs
0-1/4 mile: 25.9secs
21.0bhp 15.7kW 21.3PS
@ 4100rpm
33.2lbft 45.0Nm @ 2000rpm
33.8bhp/ton 33.2bhp/tonne
28.1bhp/L 20.9kW/L 28.5PS/L
35.9ft/sec 10.9m/sec
14.0mph 22.5kmh/1000rpm
50.0mpg 41.6mpgUS 5.6L/100km
Petrol 4-stroke piston
748cc 45.6cu in
In-line 4
Compression ratio: 7.2:1
Bore: 54.5mm 2.1in
Stroke: 80.0mm 3.1in
Valve type/No: Overhead 8
Transmission: Manual
No. of forward speeds: 3
Wheels driven: Rear
Springs F/R: Coil/Coil
Brakes F/R: Drum/Drum
Wheelbase: 209.6cm 82.5in
Track F: 120.7cm 47.5in
Track R: 120.7cm 47.5in
Length: 360.7cm 142.0in
Width: 142.7cm 56.2in
Height: 144.8cm 57.0in
Ground clearance: 18.3cm 7.2in
Kerb weight: 632.4kg 1393.0lb
Fuel: 27.3L 6.0gal 7.2galUS

3805 Renault
Dauphine
1956 France
72.1mph 116.0kmh
0-50mph 80.5kmh: 18.1secs
0-60mph 96.5kmh: 30.8secs
0-1/4 mile: 24.2secs
35.0bhp 26.1kW 35.5PS
@ 4500rpm
48.5lbft 65.7Nm @ 2000rpm
54.8bhp/ton 53.9bhp/tonne
41.4bhp/L 30.9kW/L 42.0PS/L
39.4ft/sec 12.0m/sec
Petrol 4-stroke piston
845cc 51.6cu in
In-line 4
Compression ratio: 7.3:1
Bore: 57.9mm 2.3in
Stroke: 80.0mm 3.1in
Valve type/No: Overhead 8
Transmission: Manual
No. of forward speeds: 3
Wheels driven: Rear
Wheelbase: 227.1cm 89.4in
Track F: 125.0cm 49.2in
Track R: 121.9cm 48.0in
Kerb weight: 649.2kg 1430.0lb

3806 Renault
Dauphine
1957 France
67.5mph 108.6kmh
0-50mph 80.5kmh: 24.8secs
0-60mph 96.5kmh: 45.7secs
0-1/4 mile: 25.4secs
26.5bhp 19.8kW 26.9PS
@ 4200rpm
48.4lbft 65.6Nm @ 2000rpm
41.6bhp/ton 40.9bhp/tonne
31.4bhp/L 23.4kW/L 31.8PS/L
36.7ft/sec 11.2m/sec
14.8mph 23.8kmh/1000rpm
42.0mpg 35.0mpgUS 6.7L/100km
Petrol 4-stroke piston
845cc 51.6cu in
In-line 4 1 Carburettor
Compression ratio: 7.2:1
Bore: 58.0mm 2.3in
Stroke: 80.0mm 3.1in
Valve type/No: Overhead 8
Transmission: Manual
No. of forward speeds: 3
Wheels driven: Rear
Springs F/R: Coil/Coil
Brakes F/R: Drum/Drum
Wheelbase: 226.8cm 89.3in
Track F: 125.7cm 49.5in
Track R: 121.9cm 48.0in
Length: 368.3cm 145.0in
Width: 152.4cm 60.0in
Height: 144.8cm 57.0in
Ground clearance: 17.8cm 7.0in
Kerb weight: 648.3kg 1428.0lb
Fuel: 31.8L 7.0gal 8.4galUS

3807 Renault
Dauphine Ferry
1958 France
79.2mph 127.4kmh
0-50mph 80.5kmh: 14.2secs
0-60mph 96.5kmh: 21.5secs
0-1/4 mile: 22.0secs
45.0bhp 33.6kW 45.6PS
@ 5000rpm
55.0lbft 74.5Nm @ 3000rpm
70.5bhp/ton 69.3bhp/tonne
53.2bhp/L 39.7kW/L 54.0PS/L
43.8ft/sec 13.3m/sec
Petrol 4-stroke piston
845cc 51.6cu in
In-line 4
Compression ratio: 8.1:1
Bore: 57.9mm 2.3in
Stroke: 80.0mm 3.1in
Valve type/No: Overhead 8
Transmission: Manual
No. of forward speeds: 3
Wheels driven: Rear
Wheelbase: 227.1cm 89.4in
Track F: 125.0cm 49.2in
Track R: 121.9cm 48.0in
Kerb weight: 649.2kg 1430.0lb

3808 Renault
Fregate Transfluide
1958 France
82.0mph 131.9kmh
0-50mph 80.5kmh: 20.6secs
0-60mph 96.5kmh: 31.5secs
0-1/4 mile: 25.2secs
80.0bhp 59.7kW 81.1PS
@ 4000rpm
124.0lbft 168.0Nm @ 4000rpm
58.4bhp/ton 57.5bhp/tonne
37.4bhp/L 27.9kW/L 37.9PS/L
38.4ft/sec 11.7m/sec
19.8mph 31.9kmh/1000rpm
20.8mpg 17.3mpgUS 13.6L/100km
Petrol 4-stroke piston
2141cc 130.6cu in
In-line 4
Compression ratio: 7.5:1
Bore: 88.0mm 3.5in
Stroke: 88.0mm 3.5in
Valve type/No: Overhead 8
Transmission: Automatic
No. of forward speeds: 3
Springs F/R: Coil/Coil
Brakes F/R: Disc/Disc
Wheelbase: 279.9cm 110.2in
Track F: 140.2cm 55.2in
Track R: 140.2cm 55.2in
Length: 469.9cm 185.0in
Width: 172.0cm 67.7in
Height: 122.4cm 48.2in
Ground clearance: 17.8cm 7.0in
Kerb weight: 1392.0kg 3066.0lb
Fuel: 59.1L 13.0gal 15.6galUS

3809 Renault
Caravelle
1959 France
75.6mph 121.6kmh
0-50mph 80.5kmh: 16.1secs
0-60mph 96.5kmh: 22.4secs
0-1/4 mile: 22.4secs
40.0bhp 29.8kW 40.5PS
@ 5000rpm
48.0lbft 65.0Nm @ 3300rpm
53.5bhp/ton 52.6bhp/tonne
47.3bhp/L 35.3kW/L 48.0PS/L
43.8ft/sec 13.3m/sec
15.3mph 24.6kmh/1000rpm
Petrol 4-stroke piston
845cc 51.6cu in
In-line 4
Compression ratio: 8.0:1
Bore: 57.9mm 2.3in
Stroke: 80.0mm 3.1in
Valve type/No: Overhead 8
Transmission: Manual
No. of forward speeds: 4
Wheels driven: Rear
Wheelbase: 227.1cm 89.4in
Track F: 125.0cm 49.2in
Track R: 121.9cm 48.0in
Length: 416.6cm 164.0in
Width: 152.4cm 60.0in
Height: 139.7cm 55.0in
Kerb weight: 760.4kg 1675.0lb

3810 Renault
Dauphine
1959 France
69.0mph 111.0kmh
0-50mph 80.5kmh: 25.1secs
0-60mph 96.5kmh: 43.9secs
0-1/4 mile: 25.2secs
31.0bhp 23.1kW 31.4PS
@ 4200rpm
48.4lbft 65.6Nm @ 2000rpm
47.2bhp/ton 46.4bhp/tonne
36.7bhp/L 27.4kW/L 37.2PS/L
36.7ft/sec 11.2m/sec
14.7mph 23.7kmh/1000rpm
40.9mpg 34.1mpgUS 6.9L/100km
Petrol 4-stroke piston
845cc 51.6cu in
In-line 4 1 Carburettor
Compression ratio: 7.7:1
Bore: 58.0mm 2.3in
Stroke: 80.0mm 3.1in
Valve type/No: Overhead 8
Transmission: Manual
No. of forward speeds: 3
Wheels driven: Rear
Springs F/R: Coil/Coil
Brakes F/R: Drum/Drum
Wheelbase: 226.8cm 89.3in
Track F: 124.7cm 49.1in
Track R: 121.9cm 48.0in
Length: 394.5cm 155.3in

Width: 152.4cm 60.0in
Height: 144.0cm 56.7in
Ground clearance: 17.8cm 7.0in
Kerb weight: 667.4kg 1470.0lb
Fuel: 31.8L 7.0gal 8.4galUS

3811 Renault
Dauphine Gordini
1959 France
73.4mph 118.1kmh
0-50mph 80.5kmh: 19.0secs
0-60mph 96.5kmh: 31.4secs
0-1/4 mile: 24.6secs
37.8bhp 28.2kW 38.3PS
@ 5000rpm
48.4lbft 65.6Nm @ 2000rpm
56.8bhp/ton 55.9bhp/tonne
44.7bhp/L 33.4kW/L 45.3PS/L
43.8ft/sec 13.3m/sec
14.7mph 23.7kmh/1000rpm
42.1mpg 35.1mpgUS 6.7L/100km
Petrol 4-stroke piston
845cc 51.6cu in
In-line 4 1 Carburettor
Compression ratio: 7.7:1
Bore: 58.0mm 2.3in
Stroke: 80.0mm 3.1in
Valve type/No: Overhead 8
Transmission: Manual
No. of forward speeds: 3
Wheels driven: Rear
Springs F/R: Coil/Coil
Brakes F/R: Drum/Drum
Wheelbase: 226.8cm 89.3in
Track F: 124.7cm 49.1in
Track R: 121.9cm 48.0in
Length: 394.5cm 155.3in
Width: 152.4cm 60.0in
Height: 144.0cm 56.7in
Ground clearance: 17.8cm 7.0in
Kerb weight: 676.5kg 1490.0lb
Fuel: 31.8L 7.0gal 8.4galUS

3812 Renault
Caravelle
1960 France
77.5mph 124.7kmh
0-50mph 80.5kmh: 16.0secs
0-60mph 96.5kmh: 22.5secs
0-1/4 mile: 22.5secs
40.0bhp 29.8kW 40.5PS
@ 5000rpm
48.0lbft 65.0Nm @ 3300rpm
52.2bhp/ton 51.4bhp/tonne
47.3bhp/L 35.3kW/L 48.0PS/L
43.8ft/sec 13.3m/sec
15.3mph 24.6kmh/1000rpm
Petrol 4-stroke piston
845cc 51.6cu in
In-line 4 1 Carburettor
Compression ratio: 8.0:1
Bore: 57.9mm 2.3in
Stroke: 80.0mm 3.1in
Valve type/No: Overhead 8
Transmission: Manual
No. of forward speeds: 4
Wheels driven: Rear
Wheelbase: 227.1cm 89.4in
Track F: 125.0cm 49.2in
Track R: 121.9cm 48.0in
Length: 416.6cm 164.0in
Width: 152.4cm 60.0in
Height: 139.7cm 55.0in
Kerb weight: 778.6kg 1715.0lb

3813 Renault
Floride
1960 France
83.0mph 133.5kmh
0-50mph 80.5kmh: 15.9secs
0-60mph 96.5kmh: 23.8secs
0-1/4 mile: 22.7secs
40.0bhp 29.8kW 40.5PS
@ 5000rpm
48.0lbft 65.0Nm @ 3300rpm
51.2bhp/ton 50.3bhp/tonne
47.3bhp/L 35.3kW/L 48.0PS/L
43.8ft/sec 13.3m/sec
15.3mph 24.6kmh/1000rpm
35.3mpg 29.4mpgUS 8.0L/100km
Petrol 4-stroke piston
845cc 51.6cu in
In-line 4 1 Carburettor
Compression ratio: 8.0:1
Bore: 58.0mm 2.3in
Stroke: 80.0mm 3.1in
Valve type/No: Overhead 8
Transmission: Manual
No. of forward speeds: 4
Wheels driven: Rear
Springs F/R: Coil/Coil
Brakes F/R: Drum/Drum
Wheelbase: 227.3cm 89.5in
Track F: 125.2cm 49.3in
Track R: 121.9cm 48.0in
Length: 425.5cm 167.5in
Width: 157.0cm 61.8in
Height: 130.8cm 51.5in
Ground clearance: 17.8cm 7.0in
Kerb weight: 794.5kg 1750.0lb
Fuel: 31.8L 7.0gal 8.4galUS

3814 Renault
Dauphine Gordini
1961 France
80.0mph 128.7kmh
0-50mph 80.5kmh: 15.0secs
0-60mph 96.5kmh: 22.3secs
0-1/4 mile: 22.4secs
40.0bhp 29.8kW 40.5PS
@ 5000rpm
48.0lbft 65.0Nm @ 3300rpm
57.8bhp/ton 56.8bhp/tonne
47.3bhp/L 35.3kW/L 48.0PS/L
43.8ft/sec 13.3m/sec
15.1mph 24.3kmh/1000rpm
Petrol 4-stroke piston
845cc 51.6cu in
In-line 4 1 Carburettor
Compression ratio: 8.0:1
Bore: 57.9mm 2.3in
Stroke: 80.0mm 3.1in
Valve type/No: Overhead 8
Transmission: Manual
No. of forward speeds: 4
Wheels driven: Rear
Wheelbase: 227.1cm 89.4in
Track F: 125.0cm 49.2in
Track R: 121.9cm 48.0in
Length: 394.5cm 155.3in
Width: 152.4cm 60.0in
Height: 144.0cm 56.7in
Ground clearance: 15.2cm 6.0in
Kerb weight: 703.7kg 1550.0lb

3815 Renault
Caravelle S
1962 France
85.0mph 136.8kmh
0-50mph 80.5kmh: 13.5secs
0-60mph 96.5kmh: 19.4secs
0-1/4 mile: 21.5secs
51.0bhp 38.0kW 51.7PS
@ 5500rpm
54.0lbft 73.2Nm @ 3500rpm
66.6bhp/ton 65.5bhp/tonne
53.3bhp/L 39.8kW/L 54.1PS/L
43.4ft/sec 13.2m/sec
15.3mph 24.6kmh/1000rpm
Petrol 4-stroke piston
956cc 58.3cu in
In-line 4
Compression ratio: 9.5:1
Bore: 65.0mm 2.6in
Stroke: 72.1mm 2.8in
Valve type/No: Overhead 8
Transmission: Manual
No. of forward speeds: 4
Wheels driven: Rear
Wheelbase: 227.1cm 89.4in
Track F: 125.2cm 49.3in
Track R: 121.9cm 48.0in
Length: 426.5cm 167.9in
Width: 157.5cm 62.0in
Height: 134.1cm 52.8in
Ground clearance: 14.7cm 5.8in
Kerb weight: 778.6kg 1715.0lb

3816 Renault
Dauphine
1962 France
69.5mph 111.8kmh
0-50mph 80.5kmh: 19.0secs
0-60mph 96.5kmh: 34.5secs
0-1/4 mile: 24.0secs
32.0bhp 23.9kW 32.4PS
@ 4350rpm
50.0lbft 67.8Nm @ 2000rpm
47.6bhp/ton 46.8bhp/tonne
37.9bhp/L 28.2kW/L 38.4PS/L
38.1ft/sec 11.6m/sec
15.1mph 24.3kmh/1000rpm
Petrol 4-stroke piston
845cc 51.6cu in
In-line 4
Compression ratio: 8.0:1
Bore: 57.9mm 2.3in
Stroke: 80.0mm 3.1in
Valve type/No: Overhead 8
Transmission: Manual
No. of forward speeds: 3
Wheels driven: Rear
Wheelbase: 227.1cm 89.4in
Track F: 125.0cm 49.2in
Track R: 121.9cm 48.0in
Length: 394.5cm 155.3in
Width: 152.4cm 60.0in
Height: 144.0cm 56.7in
Ground clearance: 15.2cm 6.0in
Kerb weight: 683.3kg 1505.0lb

3817 Renault
Dauphine Gordini de Luxe
1962 France
79.0mph 127.1kmh
0-50mph 80.5kmh: 15.3secs
0-60mph 96.5kmh: 22.8secs
0-1/4 mile: 22.6secs
35.5bhp 26.5kW 36.0PS
@ 5000rpm
48.0lbft 65.0Nm @ 3300rpm
53.1bhp/ton 52.2bhp/tonne
42.0bhp/L 31.3kW/L 42.6PS/L
43.8ft/sec 13.3m/sec
15.3mph 24.6kmh/1000rpm
34.7mpg 28.9mpgUS 8.1L/100km
Petrol 4-stroke piston
845cc 51.6cu in
In-line 4 1 Carburettor
Compression ratio: 8.0:1
Bore: 58.0mm 2.3in
Stroke: 80.0mm 3.1in
Valve type/No: Overhead 8
Transmission: Manual
No. of forward speeds: 4
Wheels driven: Rear
Springs F/R: Coil/Coil
Brakes F/R: Drum/Drum
Steering: Rack & pinion
Wheelbase: 226.8cm 89.3in
Track F: 124.7cm 49.1in
Track R: 121.9cm 48.0in
Length: 393.7cm 155.0in
Width: 152.4cm 60.0in
Height: 144.3cm 56.8in
Ground clearance: 15.2cm 6.0in
Kerb weight: 680.1kg 1498.0lb
Fuel: 31.8L 7.0gal 8.4galUS

3818 Renault
R8
1962 France
83.5mph 134.4kmh
0-50mph 80.5kmh: 14.1secs
0-60mph 96.5kmh: 22.0secs
0-1/4 mile: 22.3secs
48.0bhp 35.8kW 48.7PS
@ 5200rpm
53.3lbft 72.2Nm @ 2500rpm
68.3bhp/ton 67.1bhp/tonne
50.2bhp/L 37.4kW/L 50.9PS/L
40.9ft/sec 12.5m/sec
15.0mph 24.1kmh/1000rpm
33.7mpg 28.1mpgUS 8.4L/100km
Petrol 4-stroke piston
956cc 58.3cu in
In-line 4 1 Carburettor
Compression ratio: 8.5:1
Bore: 65.0mm 2.6in
Stroke: 72.0mm 2.8in
Valve type/No: Overhead 8
Transmission: Manual
No. of forward speeds: 4
Wheels driven: Rear
Springs F/R: Coil/Coil
Brakes F/R: Disc/Disc
Steering: Rack & pinion
Wheelbase: 227.1cm 89.4in
Track F: 124.7cm 49.1in
Track R: 121.9cm 48.0in
Length: 398.8cm 157.0in
Width: 148.8cm 58.6in
Height: 141.0cm 55.5in
Ground clearance: 14.5cm 5.7in
Kerb weight: 715.0kg 1575.0lb
Fuel: 30.9L 6.8gal 8.2galUS

3819 Renault
4 L Estate Car
1963 France
70.0mph 112.6kmh
0-50mph 80.5kmh: 21.3secs
0-60mph 96.5kmh: 40.5secs
0-1/4 mile: 24.3secs
28.0bhp 20.9kW 28.4PS
@ 4700rpm
49.0lbft 66.4Nm @ 2300rpm
47.4bhp/ton 46.6bhp/tonne
33.1bhp/L 24.7kW/L 33.6PS/L
41.1ft/sec 12.5m/sec
14.5mph 23.3kmh/1000rpm
35.3mpg 29.4mpgUS 8.0L/100km
Petrol 4-stroke piston
845cc 51.6cu in
In-line 4 1 Carburettor
Compression ratio: 8.0:1
Bore: 58.0mm 2.3in
Stroke: 80.0mm 3.1in
Valve type/No: Overhead 8
Transmission: Manual
No. of forward speeds: 3
Wheels driven: Front
Springs F/R: Torsion bar/Torsion bar
Brakes F/R: Drum/Drum
Steering: Rack & pinion
Wheelbase: 244.3cm 96.2in
Track F: 122.2cm 48.1in
Track R: 120.4cm 47.4in
Length: 365.5cm 143.9in
Width: 148.6cm 58.5in
Height: 153.7cm 60.5in
Ground clearance: 20.1cm 7.9in
Kerb weight: 600.6kg 1323.0lb
Fuel: 26.2L 5.7gal 6.9galUS

3820 Renault
Dauphine Automatic
1963 France
72.2mph 116.2kmh
0-50mph 80.5kmh: 26.4secs
0-60mph 96.5kmh: 39.9secs
0-1/4 mile: 26.0secs
32.0bhp 23.9kW 32.4PS
@ 4200rpm
50.0lbft 67.8Nm @ 2000rpm
47.9bhp/ton 47.1bhp/tonne
37.9bhp/L 28.2kW/L 38.4PS/L
36.7ft/sec 11.2m/sec
15.4mph 24.8kmh/1000rpm
Petrol 4-stroke piston
845cc 51.6cu in
In-line 4 1 Carburettor
Compression ratio: 8.1:1
Bore: 58.0mm 2.3in
Stroke: 80.0mm 3.1in
Valve type/No: Overhead 8
Transmission: Automatic
No. of forward speeds: 3
Wheels driven: Rear
Wheelbase: 226.1cm 89.0in
Track F: 124.5cm 49.0in
Track R: 121.9cm 48.0in
Length: 398.8cm 157.0in
Width: 152.4cm 60.0in
Height: 144.8cm 57.0in
Ground clearance: 15.2cm 6.0in
Kerb weight: 678.7kg 1495.0lb

3821 Renault
Floride Caravelle
1963 France
81.0mph 130.3kmh
0-50mph 80.5kmh: 16.6secs
0-60mph 96.5kmh: 25.4secs
0-1/4 mile: 22.5secs
45.0bhp 33.6kW 45.6PS
@ 5500rpm
54.0lbft 73.2Nm @ 3500rpm
56.6bhp/ton 55.7bhp/tonne
47.1bhp/L 35.1kW/L 47.7PS/L
43.2ft/sec 13.2m/sec
15.2mph 24.5kmh/1000rpm
31.2mpg 26.0mpgUS 9.1L/100km
Petrol 4-stroke piston
956cc 58.3cu in
In-line 4 1 Carburettor
Compression ratio: 9.5:1
Bore: 65.0mm 2.6in
Stroke: 72.0mm 2.8in
Valve type/No: Overhead 8
Transmission: Manual
No. of forward speeds: 4
Wheels driven: Rear
Springs F/R: Coil/Coil

Brakes F/R: Disc/Disc
Steering: Rack & pinion
Wheelbase: 226.6cm 89.2in
Track F: 125.0cm 49.2in
Track R: 121.9cm 48.0in
Length: 426.7cm 168.0in
Width: 157.5cm 62.0in
Height: 132.1cm 52.0in
Ground clearance: 14.5cm 5.7in
Kerb weight: 808.1kg 1780.0lb
Fuel: 30.9L 6.8gal 8.2galUS

3822 Renault
R8
1963 France
79.0mph 127.1kmh
0-50mph 80.5kmh: 15.0secs
0-60mph 96.5kmh: 21.4secs
0-1/4 mile: 22.5secs
48.0bhp 35.8kW 48.7PS
@ 5200rpm
55.0lbft 74.5Nm @ 2500rpm
67.2bhp/ton 66.1bhp/tonne
50.2bhp/L 37.4kW/L 50.9PS/L
40.9ft/sec 12.5m/sec
15.2mph 24.5kmh/1000rpm
Petrol 4-stroke piston
956cc 58.3cu in
In-line 4 1 Carburettor
Compression ratio: 8.5:1
Bore: 65.0mm 2.6in
Stroke: 71.9mm 2.8in
Valve type/No: Overhead 8
Transmission: Manual
No. of forward speeds: 4
Wheels driven: Rear
Wheelbase: 227.1cm 89.4in
Track F: 125.5cm 49.4in
Track R: 122.7cm 48.3in
Length: 400.1cm 157.5in
Width: 149.1cm 58.7in
Height: 141.0cm 55.5in
Ground clearance: 14.5cm 5.7in
Kerb weight: 726.4kg 1600.0lb

3823 Renault
R8 1100
1964 France
84.0mph 135.2kmh
0-50mph 80.5kmh: 13.8secs
0-60mph 96.5kmh: 20.6secs
0-1/4 mile: 21.9secs
44.5bhp 33.2kW 45.1PS
@ 4900rpm
65.1lbft 88.2Nm @ 2500rpm
60.3bhp/ton 59.3bhp/tonne
40.2bhp/L 29.9kW/L 40.7PS/L
38.5ft/sec 11.8m/sec
16.3mph 26.2kmh/1000rpm
36.4mpg 30.3mpgUS 7.8L/100km
Petrol 4-stroke piston
1108cc 67.6cu in
In-line 4 1 Carburettor
Compression ratio: 8.5:1
Bore: 70.0mm 2.8in
Stroke: 72.0mm 2.8in
Valve type/No: Overhead 8
Transmission: Manual
No. of forward speeds: 4
Wheels driven: Rear
Springs F/R: Coil/Coil
Brakes F/R: Disc/Disc
Steering: Rack & pinion
Wheelbase: 227.1cm 89.4in
Track F: 124.7cm 49.1in
Track R: 121.9cm 48.0in
Length: 398.8cm 157.0in
Width: 149.9cm 59.0in
Height: 138.4cm 54.5in
Ground clearance: 14.5cm 5.7in
Kerb weight: 750.0kg 1652.0lb
Fuel: 38.7L 8.5gal 10.2galUS

3824 Renault
8 Gordini
1965 France
110.0mph 177.0kmh
0-50mph 80.5kmh: 8.6secs
0-60mph 96.5kmh: 12.3secs
0-1/4 mile: 18.8secs
95.0bhp 70.8kW 96.3PS
@ 6500rpm
76.0lbft 103.0Nm @ 5000rpm
124.0bhp/ton 121.9bhp/tonne
85.7bhp/L 63.9kW/L 86.9PS/L
51.1ft/sec 15.6m/sec
15.8mph 25.4kmh/1000rpm
25.0mpg 20.8mpgUS 11.3L/100km
Petrol 4-stroke piston
1108cc 67.6cu in
In-line 4 2 Carburettor
Compression ratio: 10.4:1
Bore: 70.0mm 2.8in
Stroke: 72.0mm 2.8in
Valve type/No: Overhead 8
Transmission: Manual
No. of forward speeds: 4
Wheels driven: Rear
Springs F/R: Coil/Coil
Brake system: PA
Brakes F/R: Disc/Disc
Steering: Rack & pinion
Wheelbase: 227.1cm 89.4in
Track F: 124.7cm 49.1in
Track R: 121.9cm 48.0in
Length: 398.8cm 157.0in
Width: 147.3cm 58.0in
Height: 134.6cm 53.0in
Ground clearance: 14.5cm 5.7in
Kerb weight: 779.1kg 1716.0lb
Fuel: 38.7L 8.5gal 10.2galUS

3825 Renault
Caravelle
1965 France
90.0mph 144.8kmh
0-50mph 80.5kmh: 12.4secs
0-60mph 96.5kmh: 17.6secs
0-1/4 mile: 20.9secs
54.0bhp 40.3kW 54.7PS
@ 5400rpm
58.0lbft 78.6Nm @ 3300rpm
66.9bhp/ton 65.8bhp/tonne
48.7bhp/L 36.3kW/L 49.4PS/L
42.4ft/sec 13.0m/sec
16.3mph 26.2kmh/1000rpm
30.4mpg 25.3mpgUS 9.3L/100km
Petrol 4-stroke piston
1108cc 67.6cu in
In-line 4 1 Carburettor
Compression ratio: 8.5:1
Bore: 70.0mm 2.8in
Stroke: 72.0mm 2.8in
Valve type/No: Overhead 8
Transmission: Manual
No. of forward speeds: 4
Wheels driven: Rear
Springs F/R: Coil/Coil
Brakes F/R: Disc/Disc
Steering: Rack & pinion
Wheelbase: 226.6cm 89.2in
Track F: 122.4cm 48.2in
Track R: 121.9cm 48.0in
Length: 426.7cm 168.0in
Width: 157.5cm 62.0in
Height: 132.1cm 52.0in
Ground clearance: 14.5cm 5.7in
Kerb weight: 820.8kg 1808.0lb
Fuel: 38.7L 8.5gal 10.2galUS

3826 Renault
R8 Rally
1965 France
98.0mph 157.7kmh
0-50mph 80.5kmh: 8.7secs
0-60mph 96.5kmh: 12.2secs
0-1/4 mile: 18.0secs
95.0bhp 70.8kW 96.3PS
@ 6500rpm
72.0lbft 97.6Nm @ 5500rpm
117.9bhp/ton 115.9bhp/tonne
85.7bhp/L 63.9kW/L 86.9PS/L
51.3ft/sec 15.6m/sec
15.6mph 25.1kmh/1000rpm
Petrol 4-stroke piston
1108cc 67.6cu in
In-line 4 2 Carburettor
Compression ratio: 10.5:1
Bore: 70.1mm 2.8in
Stroke: 72.1mm 2.8in
Valve type/No: Overhead 8
Transmission: Manual
No. of forward speeds: 4
Wheels driven: Rear
Springs F/R: Coil/Coil
Brakes F/R: Disc/Disc
Steering: Rack & pinion
Wheelbase: 227.1cm 89.4in
Track F: 124.5cm 49.0in
Track R: 121.9cm 48.0in
Length: 399.3cm 157.2in
Width: 149.1cm 58.7in
Height: 137.9cm 54.3in
Ground clearance: 9.7cm 3.8in
Kerb weight: 819.5kg 1805.0lb
Fuel: 37.8L 8.3gal 10.0galUS

3827 Renault
1100 Automatic
1966 France
82.0mph 131.9kmh
0-50mph 80.5kmh: 15.6secs
0-60mph 96.5kmh: 24.8secs
0-1/4 mile: 23.0secs
0-1km: 43.3secs
46.0bhp 34.3kW 46.6PS
@ 4600rpm
62.2lbft 84.3Nm @ 2800rpm
58.8bhp/ton 57.8bhp/tonne
41.5bhp/L 31.0kW/L 42.1PS/L
36.2ft/sec 11.0m/sec
16.3mph 26.2kmh/1000rpm
34.6mpg 28.8mpgUS 8.2L/100km
Petrol 4-stroke piston
1108cc 67.6cu in
In-line 4 1 Carburettor
Compression ratio: 8.5:1
Bore: 70.0mm 2.8in
Stroke: 72.0mm 2.8in
Valve type/No: Overhead 8
Transmission: Automatic
No. of forward speeds: 3
Wheels driven: Rear
Springs F/R: Coil/Coil
Brakes F/R: Disc/Disc
Steering: Rack & pinion
Wheelbase: 226.8cm 89.3in
Track F: 122.4cm 48.2in
Track R: 121.9cm 48.0in
Length: 420.4cm 165.5in
Width: 148.6cm 58.5in
Height: 141.0cm 55.5in
Ground clearance: 14.0cm 5.5in
Kerb weight: 795.4kg 1752.0lb
Fuel: 38.7L 8.5gal 10.2galUS

3828 Renault
16 GL
1966 France
90.0mph 144.8kmh
0-50mph 80.5kmh: 11.7secs
0-60mph 96.5kmh: 16.7secs
0-1/4 mile: 20.8secs
0-1km: 39.0secs
62.6bhp 46.7kW 63.5PS
@ 5000rpm
77.7lbft 105.3Nm @ 2800rpm
64.6bhp/ton 63.6bhp/tonne
42.6bhp/L 31.8kW/L 43.2PS/L
44.3ft/sec 13.5m/sec
17.2mph 27.7kmh/1000rpm
26.9mpg 22.4mpgUS 10.5L/100km
Petrol 4-stroke piston
1470cc 89.7cu in
In-line 4 1 Carburettor
Compression ratio: 8.5:1
Bore: 76.0mm 3.0in
Stroke: 81.0mm 3.2in
Valve type/No: Overhead 8
Transmission: Manual
No. of forward speeds: 4
Wheels driven: Front
Springs F/R: Torsion bar/Torsion bar
Brakes F/R: Disc/Drum
Steering: Rack & pinion
Wheelbase: 271.8cm 107.0in
Track F: 134.1cm 52.8in
Track R: 129.3cm 50.9in
Length: 422.9cm 166.5in
Width: 164.8cm 64.9in
Height: 145.3cm 57.2in
Ground clearance: 19.1cm 7.5in
Kerb weight: 984.7kg 2169.0lb
Fuel: 54.6L 12.0gal 14.4galUS

3829 Renault
4 Estate Car
1966 France
68.0mph 109.4kmh
0-50mph 80.5kmh: 21.6secs
0-60mph 96.5kmh: 38.1secs
0-1/4 mile: 24.6secs
0-1km: 48.1secs
30.0bhp 22.4kW 30.4PS
@ 4700rpm
48.0lbft 65.0Nm @ 2300rpm
48.2bhp/ton 47.4bhp/tonne
35.5bhp/L 26.5kW/L 36.0PS/L
41.1ft/sec 12.5m/sec
14.5mph 23.3kmh/1000rpm
37.0mpg 30.8mpgUS 7.6L/100km
Petrol 4-stroke piston
845cc 51.6cu in
In-line 4 1 Carburettor
Compression ratio: 8.0:1
Bore: 58.0mm 2.3in
Stroke: 80.0mm 3.1in
Valve type/No: Overhead 8
Transmission: Manual
No. of forward speeds: 3
Wheels driven: Front
Springs F/R: Torsion bar/Torsion bar
Brakes F/R: Drum/Drum
Steering: Rack & pinion
Wheelbase: 244.3cm 96.2in
Track F: 122.2cm 48.1in
Track R: 120.4cm 47.4in
Length: 365.8cm 144.0in
Width: 148.6cm 58.5in
Height: 153.7cm 60.5in
Ground clearance: 20.1cm 7.9in
Kerb weight: 632.4kg 1393.0lb
Fuel: 26.2L 5.7gal 6.9galUS

3830 Renault
10
1967 France
79.0mph 127.1kmh
0-50mph 80.5kmh: 13.3secs
0-60mph 96.5kmh: 19.0secs
0-1/4 mile: 21.7secs
50.0bhp 37.3kW 50.7PS
@ 4600rpm
57.0lbft 77.2Nm @ 3000rpm
64.0bhp/ton 62.9bhp/tonne
45.1bhp/L 33.7kW/L 45.7PS/L
36.2ft/sec 11.0m/sec
16.6mph 26.7kmh/1000rpm
Petrol 4-stroke piston
1108cc 67.6cu in
In-line 4 1 Carburettor
Compression ratio: 8.5:1
Bore: 70.0mm 2.8in
Stroke: 72.0mm 2.8in
Valve type/No: Overhead 8
Transmission: Manual
No. of forward speeds: 4
Wheels driven: Rear
Springs F/R: Coil/Coil
Brakes F/R: Disc/Disc
Steering: Rack & pinion
Wheelbase: 226.1cm 89.0in
Track F: 124.5cm 49.0in
Track R: 121.9cm 48.0in
Length: 425.5cm 167.5in
Width: 152.4cm 60.0in
Height: 141.0cm 55.5in
Ground clearance: 20.3cm 8.0in
Kerb weight: 794.5kg 1750.0lb
Fuel: 37.8L 8.3gal 10.0galUS

3831 Renault
8 Gordini 1300
1967 France
108.0mph 173.8kmh
0-50mph 80.5kmh: 7.6secs
0-60mph 96.5kmh: 10.9secs
0-1/4 mile: 17.7secs
0-1km: 33.3secs
103.0bhp 76.8kW 104.4PS
@ 6750rpm
85.6lbft 116.0Nm @ 5000rpm
122.7bhp/ton 120.6bhp/tonne
82.1bhp/L 61.2kW/L 83.2PS/L
53.1ft/sec 16.2m/sec
16.1mph 25.9kmh/1000rpm
22.5mpg 18.7mpgUS 12.6L/100km
Petrol 4-stroke piston
1255cc 76.6cu in
In-line 4 2 Carburettor
Compression ratio: 10.5:1
Bore: 74.5mm 2.9in
Stroke: 72.0mm 2.8in
Valve type/No: Overhead 8
Transmission: Manual
No. of forward speeds: 5
Wheels driven: Rear
Springs F/R: Coil/Coil
Brake system: PA
Brakes F/R: Disc/Disc
Steering: Rack & pinion
Wheelbase: 227.1cm 89.4in
Track F: 124.7cm 49.1in
Track R: 121.9cm 48.0in
Length: 398.8cm 157.0in
Width: 147.3cm 58.0in

Height: 134.6cm 53.0in
Ground clearance: 14.5cm 5.7in
Kerb weight: 854.0kg 1881.0lb
Fuel: 38.7L 8.5gal 10.2galUS

3832 Renault

16
1968 France
93.0mph 149.6kmh
0-50mph 80.5kmh: 11.7secs
0-60mph 96.5kmh: 16.2secs
0-1/4 mile: 20.2secs
70.0bhp 52.2kW 71.0PS
@ 5200rpm
86.0lbft 116.5Nm @ 2500rpm
69.4bhp/ton 68.2bhp/tonne
44.7bhp/L 33.3kW/L 45.3PS/L
47.8ft/sec 14.6m/sec
17.8mph 28.6kmh/1000rpm
34.8mpg 29.0mpgUS 8.1L/100km
Petrol 4-stroke piston
1565cc 95.5cu in
In-line 4 1 Carburettor
Compression ratio: 8.6:1
Bore: 77.0mm 3.0in
Stroke: 84.0mm 3.3in
Valve type/No: Overhead 8
Transmission: Manual
No. of forward speeds: 4
Wheels driven: Front
Springs F/R: Torsion bar/Torsion bar
Brakes F/R: Disc/Drum
Steering: Rack & pinion
Wheelbase: 270.8cm 106.6in
Track F: 133.6cm 52.6in
Track R: 127.8cm 50.3in
Length: 423.7cm 166.8in
Width: 165.1cm 65.0in
Height: 144.8cm 57.0in
Ground clearance: 15.2cm 6.0in
Kerb weight: 1026.0kg 2260.0lb
Fuel: 50.0L 11.0gal 13.2galUS

3833 Renault

16 TS
1969 France
104.0mph 167.3kmh
0-50mph 80.5kmh: 9.0secs
0-60mph 96.5kmh: 12.4secs
0-1/4 mile: 18.8secs
0-1km: 35.3secs
83.0bhp 61.9kW 84.1PS
@ 5750rpm
87.0lbft 117.9Nm @ 3500rpm
81.6bhp/ton 80.2bhp/tonne
53.0bhp/L 39.5kW/L 53.8PS/L
52.9ft/sec 16.1m/sec
17.8mph 28.6kmh/1000rpm
23.3mpg 19.4mpgUS 12.1L/100km
Petrol 4-stroke piston
1565cc 95.5cu in
In-line 4 1 Carburettor
Compression ratio: 8.6:1
Bore: 77.0mm 3.0in
Stroke: 84.0mm 3.3in
Valve type/No: Overhead 8
Transmission: Manual
No. of forward speeds: 4
Wheels driven: Front
Springs F/R: Torsion bar/Torsion bar
Brake system: PA
Brakes F/R: Disc/Drum
Steering: Rack & pinion
Wheelbase: 271.8cm 107.0in
Track F: 134.1cm 52.8in
Track R: 129.3cm 50.9in
Length: 422.9cm 166.5in
Width: 164.8cm 64.9in
Height: 145.3cm 57.2in
Ground clearance: 19.1cm 7.5in
Kerb weight: 1034.7kg 2279.0lb
Fuel: 54.6L 12.0gal 14.4galUS

3834 Renault

6
1969 France
75.0mph 120.7kmh
0-50mph 80.5kmh: 18.3secs
0-60mph 96.5kmh: 29.8secs
0-1/4 mile: 23.8secs
0-1km: 45.6secs
34.0bhp 25.3kW 34.5PS
@ 5000rpm
42.0lbft 56.9Nm @ 3000rpm
47.3bhp/ton 46.5bhp/tonne
40.2bhp/L 30.0kW/L 40.8PS/L
43.8ft/sec 13.3m/sec
14.6mph 23.5kmh/1000rpm
32.1mpg 26.7mpgUS 8.8L/100km
Petrol 4-stroke piston
845cc 51.6cu in
In-line 4 1 Carburettor
Compression ratio: 8.0:1
Bore: 58.0mm 2.3in
Stroke: 80.0mm 3.1in
Valve type/No: Overhead 8
Transmission: Manual
No. of forward speeds: 4
Wheels driven: Front
Springs F/R: Torsion bar/Torsion bar
Brakes F/R: Drum/Drum
Steering: Rack & pinion
Wheelbase: 245.1cm 96.5in
Track F: 129.5cm 51.0in
Track R: 124.5cm 49.0in
Length: 386.1cm 152.0in
Width: 152.4cm 60.0in
Height: 146.1cm 57.5in
Ground clearance: 22.9cm 9.0in
Kerb weight: 730.9kg 1610.0lb
Fuel: 31.8L 7.0gal 8.4galUS

3835 Renault

10
1970 France
88.0mph 141.6kmh
0-50mph 80.5kmh: 12.6secs
0-60mph 96.5kmh: 18.9secs
0-1/4 mile: 21.3secs
0-1km: 40.5secs
48.0bhp 35.8kW 48.7PS
@ 4800rpm
71.0lbft 96.2Nm @ 2500rpm
59.2bhp/ton 58.2bhp/tonne
37.2bhp/L 27.8kW/L 37.8PS/L
40.4ft/sec 12.3m/sec
16.3mph 26.2kmh/1000rpm
30.9mpg 25.7mpgUS 9.1L/100km
Petrol 4-stroke piston
1289cc 78.6cu in
In-line 4 1 Carburettor
Compression ratio: 8.0:1
Bore: 73.0mm 2.9in
Stroke: 77.0mm 3.0in
Valve type/No: Overhead 8
Transmission: Manual
No. of forward speeds: 4
Wheels driven: Rear
Springs F/R: Coil/Coil
Brakes F/R: Disc/Disc
Steering: Rack & pinion
Wheelbase: 227.3cm 89.5in
Track F: 124.5cm 49.0in
Track R: 121.9cm 48.0in
Length: 420.4cm 165.5in
Width: 152.4cm 60.0in
Height: 137.2cm 54.0in
Ground clearance: 15.2cm 6.0in
Kerb weight: 824.9kg 1817.0lb
Fuel: 38.7L 8.5gal 10.2galUS

3836 Renault

12 TL
1970 France
90.0mph 144.8kmh
0-50mph 80.5kmh: 11.5secs
0-60mph 96.5kmh: 16.5secs
0-1/4 mile: 20.6secs
0-1km: 39.0secs
54.0bhp 40.3kW 54.7PS
@ 5250rpm
69.0lbft 93.5Nm @ 3000rpm
63.1bhp/ton 62.1bhp/tonne
41.9bhp/L 31.2kW/L 42.5PS/L
44.2ft/sec 13.5m/sec
16.5mph 26.5kmh/1000rpm
27.9mpg 23.2mpgUS 10.1L/100km
Petrol 4-stroke piston
1289cc 78.6cu in
In-line 4 1 Carburettor
Compression ratio: 8.5:1
Bore: 73.0mm 2.9in
Stroke: 77.0mm 3.0in
Valve type/No: Overhead 8
Transmission: Manual
No. of forward speeds: 4
Wheels driven: Front
Springs F/R: Coil/Coil
Brakes F/R: Disc/Drum
Steering: Rack & pinion
Wheelbase: 242.6cm 95.5in
Track F: 130.8cm 51.5in
Track R: 130.8cm 51.5in
Length: 445.0cm 175.2in
Width: 168.9cm 66.5in
Height: 143.5cm 56.5in
Ground clearance: 14.0cm 5.5in
Kerb weight: 869.9kg 1916.0lb
Fuel: 50.0L 11.0gal 13.2galUS

3837 Renault

16 TL Automatic
1971 France
92.0mph 148.0kmh
0-50mph 80.5kmh: 11.9secs
0-60mph 96.5kmh: 16.8secs
0-1/4 mile: 20.9secs
0-1km: 38.7secs
67.0bhp 50.0kW 67.9PS
@ 5000rpm
84.0lbft 113.8Nm @ 3000rpm
69.1bhp/ton 67.9bhp/tonne
42.8bhp/L 31.9kW/L 43.4PS/L
46.0ft/sec 14.0m/sec
17.2mph 27.7kmh/1000rpm
28.0mpg 23.3mpgUS 10.1L/100km
Petrol 4-stroke piston
1565cc 95.5cu in
In-line 4 1 Carburettor
Compression ratio: 8.5:1
Bore: 77.0mm 3.0in
Stroke: 84.0mm 3.3in
Valve type/No: Overhead 8
Transmission: Automatic
No. of forward speeds: 3
Wheels driven: Front
Springs F/R: Torsion bar/Torsion bar
Brake system: PA
Brakes F/R: Disc/Drum
Steering: Rack & pinion
Wheelbase: 271.8cm 107.0in
Track F: 134.1cm 52.8in
Track R: 129.3cm 50.9in
Length: 422.9cm 166.5in
Width: 164.8cm 64.9in
Height: 145.3cm 57.2in
Ground clearance: 19.1cm 7.5in
Kerb weight: 986.1kg 2172.0lb
Fuel: 50.0L 11.0gal 13.2galUS

3838 Renault

6 1100
1971 France
81.0mph 130.3kmh
0-50mph 80.5kmh: 14.1secs
0-60mph 96.5kmh: 20.7secs
0-1/4 mile: 22.0secs
0-1km: 41.7secs
45.0bhp 33.6kW 45.6PS
@ 5300rpm
58.0lbft 78.6Nm @ 3000rpm
62.1bhp/ton 61.1bhp/tonne
40.6bhp/L 30.3kW/L 41.2PS/L
41.7ft/sec 12.7m/sec
15.4mph 24.8kmh/1000rpm
31.3mpg 26.1mpgUS 9.0L/100km
Petrol 4-stroke piston
1108cc 67.6cu in
In-line 4 1 Carburettor
Compression ratio: 8.0:1
Bore: 70.0mm 2.8in
Stroke: 72.0mm 2.8in
Valve type/No: Overhead 8
Transmission: Manual
No. of forward speeds: 4
Wheels driven: Front
Springs F/R: Torsion bar/Torsion bar
Brakes F/R: Disc/Drum
Steering: Rack & pinion
Wheelbase: 245.1cm 96.5in
Track F: 129.5cm 51.0in
Track R: 124.5cm 49.0in
Length: 386.1cm 152.0in
Width: 152.4cm 60.0in
Height: 146.1cm 57.5in
Ground clearance: 22.9cm 9.0in
Kerb weight: 736.4kg 1622.0lb
Fuel: 38.7L 8.5gal 10.2galUS

3839 Renault

12 Estate
1972 France
89.0mph 143.2kmh
0-50mph 80.5kmh: 11.4secs
0-60mph 96.5kmh: 16.5secs
0-1/4 mile: 20.1secs
0-1km: 38.2secs
54.0bhp 40.3kW 54.7PS
@ 5250rpm
69.0lbft 93.5Nm @ 3000rpm
59.0bhp/ton 58.0bhp/tonne
41.9bhp/L 31.2kW/L 42.5PS/L
44.2ft/sec 13.5m/sec
16.3mph 26.2kmh/1000rpm
29.8mpg 24.8mpgUS 9.5L/100km
Petrol 4-stroke piston
1289cc 78.6cu in
In-line 4 1 Carburettor
Compression ratio: 8.5:1
Bore: 73.0mm 2.9in
Stroke: 77.0mm 3.0in
Valve type/No: Overhead 8
Transmission: Manual
No. of forward speeds: 4
Wheels driven: Front
Springs F/R: Coil/Coil
Brakes F/R: Disc/Drum
Steering: Rack & pinion
Wheelbase: 242.6cm 95.5in
Track F: 130.8cm 51.5in
Track R: 130.8cm 51.5in
Length: 445.0cm 175.2in
Width: 168.9cm 66.5in
Height: 143.5cm 56.5in
Ground clearance: 14.0cm 5.5in
Kerb weight: 930.2kg 2049.0lb
Fuel: 50.0L 11.0gal 13.2galUS

3840 Renault

12 TL
1972 France
89.0mph 143.2kmh
0-50mph 80.5kmh: 11.1secs
0-60mph 96.5kmh: 15.9secs
0-1/4 mile: 20.4secs
73.0bhp 54.4kW 74.0PS
@ 5000rpm
88.0lbft 119.2Nm @ 3000rpm
75.7bhp/ton 74.4bhp/tonne
46.6bhp/L 34.8kW/L 47.3PS/L
46.0ft/sec 14.0m/sec
16.9mph 27.2kmh/1000rpm
28.6mpg 23.8mpgUS 9.9L/100km
Petrol 4-stroke piston
1565cc 95.5cu in
In-line 4 1 Carburettor
Compression ratio: 8.6:1
Bore: 77.0mm 3.0in
Stroke: 84.0mm 3.3in
Valve type/No: Overhead 8
Transmission: Manual
No. of forward speeds: 4
Wheels driven: Front
Springs F/R: Coil/Coil
Brakes F/R: Disc/Drum
Steering: Rack & pinion
Wheelbase: 243.8cm 96.0in
Track F: 130.8cm 51.5in
Track R: 130.8cm 51.5in
Length: 434.3cm 171.0in
Width: 163.8cm 64.5in
Height: 143.5cm 56.5in
Ground clearance: 14.0cm 5.5in
Kerb weight: 980.6kg 2160.0lb
Fuel: 50.0L 11.0gal 13.2galUS

3841 Renault

15 Coupe
1972 France
92.0mph 148.0kmh
0-50mph 80.5kmh: 11.1secs
0-60mph 96.5kmh: 15.7secs
0-1/4 mile: 20.2secs
68.0bhp 50.7kW 68.9PS
@ 5000rpm
86.0lbft 116.5Nm @ 3000rpm
67.5bhp/ton 66.4bhp/tonne
43.4bhp/L 32.4kW/L 44.0PS/L
46.0ft/sec 14.0m/sec
16.7mph 26.9kmh/1000rpm
28.2mpg 23.5mpgUS 10.0L/100km
Petrol 4-stroke piston
1565cc 95.5cu in
In-line 4 1 Carburettor
Compression ratio: 8.6:1
Bore: 77.0mm 3.0in
Stroke: 84.0mm 3.3in
Valve type/No: Overhead 8
Transmission: Manual
No. of forward speeds: 4
Wheels driven: Front
Springs F/R: Coil/Coil
Brake system: PA
Brakes F/R: Disc/Drum
Steering: Rack & pinion
Wheelbase: 243.8cm 96.0in

Track F: 130.8cm 51.5in
Track R: 130.8cm 51.5in
Length: 426.0cm 167.7in
Width: 162.6cm 64.0in
Height: 130.8cm 51.5in
Ground clearance: 11.9cm 4.7in
Kerb weight: 1023.8kg 2255.0lb
Fuel: 54.9L 12.1gal 14.5galUS

3842 Renault
15 TL
1972 France
96.0mph 154.5kmh
0-50mph 80.5kmh: 9.4secs
0-60mph 96.5kmh: 13.6secs
0-1/4 mile: 19.3secs
0-1km: 36.1secs
60.0bhp 44.7kW 60.8PS
@ 5500rpm
72.0lbft 97.6Nm @ 3500rpm
63.0bhp/ton 61.9bhp/tonne
46.5bhp/L 34.7kW/L 47.2PS/L
43.3ft/sec 14.1m/sec
16.5mph 26.5kmh/1000rpm
31.8mpg 26.5mpgUS 8.9L/100km
Petrol 4-stroke piston
1289cc 78.6cu in
In-line 4 1 Carburettor
Compression ratio: 9.5:1
Bore: 73.0mm 2.9in
Stroke: 77.0mm 3.0in
Valve type/No: Overhead 8
Transmission: Manual
No. of forward speeds: 4
Wheels driven: Front
Springs F/R: Coil/Coil
Brake system: PA
Brakes F/R: Disc/Drum
Steering: Rack & pinion
Wheelbase: 243.8cm 96.0in
Track F: 130.8cm 51.5in
Track R: 130.8cm 51.5in
Length: 426.7cm 168.0in
Width: 163.8cm 64.5in
Height: 130.8cm 51.5in
Ground clearance: 14.0cm 5.5in
Kerb weight: 968.8kg 2134.0lb
Fuel: 54.6L 12.0gal 14.4galUS

3843 Renault
16 TS
1972 France
100.0mph 160.9kmh
0-50mph 80.5kmh: 10.6secs
0-60mph 96.5kmh: 14.9secs
0-1/4 mile: 20.0secs
0-1km: 36.7secs
83.0bhp 61.9kW 84.1PS
@ 5750rpm
90.0lbft 122.0Nm @ 3500rpm
84.0bhp/ton 82.6bhp/tonne
53.0bhp/L 39.5kW/L 53.8PS/L
52.9ft/sec 16.1m/sec
17.2mph 27.7kmh/1000rpm
24.7mpg 20.6mpgUS 11.4L/100km
Petrol 4-stroke piston
1565cc 95.5cu in
In-line 4 1 Carburettor
Compression ratio: 8.6:1
Bore: 77.0mm 3.0in
Stroke: 84.0mm 3.3in
Valve type/No: Overhead 8
Transmission: Automatic
No. of forward speeds: 3
Wheels driven: Front
Springs F/R: Torsion bar/Torsion bar
Brake system: PA
Brakes F/R: Disc/Drum
Steering: Rack & pinion
Wheelbase: 271.8cm 107.0in
Track F: 134.1cm 52.8in
Track R: 129.3cm 50.9in
Length: 422.9cm 166.5in
Width: 164.8cm 64.9in
Height: 145.3cm 57.2in
Ground clearance: 19.1cm 7.5in
Kerb weight: 1004.2kg 2212.0lb
Fuel: 50.0L 11.0gal 13.2galUS

3844 Renault
17
1973 France
103.0mph 165.7kmh
0-50mph 80.5kmh: 9.3secs
0-60mph 96.5kmh: 12.5secs
0-1/4 mile: 18.9secs
107.0bhp 79.8kW 108.5PS
@ 6000rpm
96.0lbft 130.1Nm @ 4500rpm
103.1bhp/ton 101.4bhp/tonne
68.4bhp/L 51.0kW/L 69.3PS/L
55.2ft/sec 16.8m/sec
17.2mph 27.7kmh/1000rpm
33.6mpg 28.0mpgUS 8.4L/100km
Petrol 4-stroke piston
1565cc 95.5cu in
In-line 4 fuel injection
Compression ratio: 9.0:1
Bore: 77.0mm 3.0in
Stroke: 84.0mm 3.3in
Valve type/No: Overhead 8
Transmission: Manual
No. of forward speeds: 4
Wheels driven: Front
Springs F/R: Coil/Coil
Brake system: PA
Brakes F/R: Disc/Disc
Steering: Rack & pinion
Wheelbase: 243.8cm 96.0in
Track F: 133.9cm 52.7in
Track R: 133.9cm 52.7in
Length: 426.0cm 167.7in
Width: 162.6cm 64.0in
Height: 130.8cm 51.5in
Ground clearance: 12.7cm 5.0in
Kerb weight: 1055.5kg 2325.0lb
Fuel: 54.9L 12.1gal 14.5galUS

3845 Renault
5 TL
1973 France
87.0mph 140.0kmh
0-50mph 80.5kmh: 13.8secs
0-60mph 96.5kmh: 20.6secs
0-1/4 mile: 21.8secs
0-1km: 41.3secs
43.0bhp 32.1kW 43.6PS
@ 5500rpm
45.0lbft 61.0Nm @ 3500rpm
59.2bhp/ton 58.2bhp/tonne
45.0bhp/L 33.5kW/L 45.6PS/L
43.2ft/sec 13.2m/sec
15.1mph 24.3kmh/1000rpm
26.8mpg 22.3mpgUS 10.5L/100km
Petrol 4-stroke piston
956cc 58.3cu in
In-line 4 1 Carburettor
Compression ratio: 9.2:1
Bore: 65.0mm 2.6in
Stroke: 72.0mm 2.8in
Valve type/No: Overhead 8
Transmission: Manual
No. of forward speeds: 4
Wheels driven: Front
Springs F/R: Torsion bar/Torsion bar
Brake system: PA
Brakes F/R: Disc/Drum
Steering: Rack & pinion
Wheelbase: 240.0cm 94.5in
Track F: 127.5cm 50.2in
Track R: 124.5cm 49.0in
Length: 349.3cm 137.5in
Width: 152.4cm 60.0in
Height: 139.7cm 55.0in
Ground clearance: 17.0cm 6.7in
Kerb weight: 738.7kg 1627.0lb
Fuel: 40.9L 9.0gal 10.8galUS

3846 Renault
6 TL
1974 France
87.0mph 140.0kmh
0-50mph 80.5kmh: 11.6secs
0-60mph 96.5kmh: 17.2secs
0-1/4 mile: 21.0secs
0-1km: 40.1secs
47.0bhp 35.0kW 47.6PS
@ 5500rpm
55.7lbft 75.5Nm @ 3000rpm
64.3bhp/ton 63.3bhp/tonne
42.4bhp/L 31.6kW/L 43.0PS/L
43.2ft/sec 13.2m/sec
15.0mph 24.1kmh/1000rpm
34.6mpg 28.8mpgUS 8.2L/100km
Petrol 4-stroke piston
1108cc 67.6cu in
In-line 4 1 Carburettor
Compression ratio: 9.5:1
Bore: 70.0mm 2.8in
Stroke: 72.0mm 2.8in
Valve type/No: Overhead 8
Transmission: Manual
No. of forward speeds: 4
Wheels driven: Front
Springs F/R: Torsion bar/Torsion bar
Brakes F/R: Disc/Drum
Steering: Rack & pinion
Wheelbase: 238.8cm 94.0in
Track F: 129.5cm 51.0in
Track R: 124.5cm 49.0in
Length: 386.1cm 152.0in
Width: 152.4cm 60.0in
Height: 146.1cm 57.5in
Ground clearance: 22.9cm 9.0in
Kerb weight: 742.7kg 1636.0lb
Fuel: 38.7L 8.5gal 10.2galUS

3847 Renault
12
1975 France
0-60mph 96.5kmh: 17.5secs
0-1/4 mile: 21.2secs
65.0bhp 48.5kW 65.9PS
@ 5000rpm
84.0lbft 113.8Nm @ 3500rpm
65.1bhp/ton 64.1bhp/tonne
39.5bhp/L 29.4kW/L 40.0PS/L
46.0ft/sec 14.0m/sec
27.6mpg 23.0mpgUS 10.2L/100km
Petrol 4-stroke piston
1647cc 100.5cu in
In-line 4 1 Carburettor
Compression ratio: 8.0:1
Bore: 79.0mm 3.1in
Stroke: 84.0mm 3.3in
Valve type/No: Overhead 8
Transmission: Manual
No. of forward speeds: 4
Wheels driven: Front
Brake system: PA
Wheelbase: 243.8cm 96.0in
Track F: 130.8cm 51.5in
Track R: 130.8cm 51.5in
Length: 442.0cm 174.0in
Width: 163.8cm 64.5in
Height: 143.8cm 56.6in
Ground clearance: 14.0cm 5.5in
Kerb weight: 1014.7kg 2235.0lb
Fuel: 54.9L 12.1gal 14.5galUS

3848 Renault
17 Gordini
1975 France
120.0mph 193.1kmh
0-50mph 80.5kmh: 6.9secs
0-60mph 96.5kmh: 9.8secs
0-1/4 mile: 17.4secs
0-1km: 32.3secs
108.0bhp 80.5kW 109.5PS
@ 6000rpm
100.0lbft 135.5Nm @ 5500rpm
101.9bhp/ton 100.2bhp/tonne
67.3bhp/L 50.2kW/L 68.2PS/L
55.2ft/sec 16.8m/sec
19.1mph 30.7kmh/1000rpm
25.2mpg 21.0mpgUS 11.2L/100km
Petrol 4-stroke piston
1605cc 97.9cu in
In-line 4 fuel injection
Compression ratio: 10.2:1
Bore: 78.0mm 3.1in
Stroke: 84.0mm 3.3in
Valve type/No: Overhead 8
Transmission: Manual
No. of forward speeds: 5
Wheels driven: Front
Springs F/R: Coil/Coil
Brake system: PA
Brakes F/R: Disc/Disc
Steering: Rack & pinion
Wheelbase: 243.8cm 96.0in
Track F: 130.8cm 51.5in
Track R: 130.8cm 51.5in
Length: 426.7cm 168.0in
Width: 163.1cm 64.2in
Height: 131.1cm 51.6in
Ground clearance: 16.5cm 6.5in
Kerb weight: 1077.3kg 2373.0lb
Fuel: 54.6L 12.0gal 14.4galUS

3849 Renault
5 TS
1975 France
102.0mph 164.1kmh
0-50mph 80.5kmh: 9.4secs
0-60mph 96.5kmh: 13.4secs
0-1/4 mile: 19.2secs
0-1km: 36.4secs
64.0bhp 47.7kW 64.9PS
@ 6000rpm
69.0lbft 93.5Nm @ 3500rpm
80.0bhp/ton 78.6bhp/tonne
49.6bhp/L 37.0kW/L 50.3PS/L
50.5ft/sec 15.4m/sec
17.1mph 27.5kmh/1000rpm
31.9mpg 26.6mpgUS 8.9L/100km
Petrol 4-stroke piston
1289cc 78.6cu in
In-line 4 1 Carburettor
Compression ratio: 9.5:1
Bore: 73.0mm 2.9in
Stroke: 77.0mm 3.0in
Valve type/No: Overhead 8
Transmission: Manual
No. of forward speeds: 4
Wheels driven: Front
Springs F/R: Torsion bar/Torsion bar
Brake system: PA
Brakes F/R: Disc/Drum
Steering: Rack & pinion
Wheelbase: 240.0cm 94.5in
Track F: 127.5cm 50.2in
Track R: 124.5cm 49.0in
Length: 349.3cm 137.5in
Width: 152.4cm 60.0in
Height: 139.7cm 55.0in
Ground clearance: 17.0cm 6.7in
Kerb weight: 814.0kg 1793.0lb
Fuel: 40.9L 9.0gal 10.8galUS

3850 Renault
15 GTL
1976 France
102.0mph 164.1kmh
0-50mph 80.5kmh: 10.4secs
0-60mph 96.5kmh: 15.1secs
0-1/4 mile: 20.0secs
0-1km: 36.9secs
60.0bhp 44.7kW 60.8PS
@ 5500rpm
67.2lbft 91.1Nm @ 3500rpm
64.4bhp/ton 63.4bhp/tonne
46.5bhp/L 34.7kW/L 47.2PS/L
46.3ft/sec 14.1m/sec
16.8mph 27.0kmh/1000rpm
30.9mpg 25.7mpgUS 9.1L/100km
Petrol 4-stroke piston
1289cc 78.6cu in
In-line 4 1 Carburettor
Compression ratio: 9.5:1
Bore: 73.0mm 2.9in
Stroke: 77.0mm 3.0in
Valve type/No: Overhead 8
Transmission: Manual
No. of forward speeds: 4
Wheels driven: Front
Springs F/R: Coil/Coil
Brake system: PA
Brakes F/R: Disc/Drum
Steering: Rack & pinion
Wheelbase: 243.8cm 96.0in
Track F: 130.8cm 51.5in
Track R: 130.8cm 51.5in
Length: 426.7cm 168.0in
Width: 163.1cm 64.2in
Height: 130.8cm 51.5in
Ground clearance: 14.0cm 5.5in
Kerb weight: 947.0kg 2086.0lb
Fuel: 54.6L 12.0gal 14.4galUS

3851 Renault
17 Gordini
1976 France
108.0mph 173.8kmh
0-50mph 80.5kmh: 9.5secs
0-60mph 96.5kmh: 13.2secs
0-1/4 mile: 19.5secs
93.5bhp 69.7kW 94.8PS
@ 6250rpm
90.0lbft 122.0Nm @ 3500rpm
84.6bhp/ton 83.2bhp/tonne
56.8bhp/L 42.3kW/L 57.6PS/L
57.5ft/sec 17.5m/sec
19.4mph 31.2kmh/1000rpm
31.2mpg 26.0mpgUS 9.0L/100km
Petrol 4-stroke piston
1647cc 100.5cu in
In-line 4 fuel injection
Compression ratio: 8.6:1
Bore: 79.0mm 3.1in
Stroke: 84.0mm 3.3in
Valve type/No: Overhead 8
Transmission: Manual
No. of forward speeds: 5
Wheels driven: Front
Springs F/R: Coil/Coil
Brake system: PA
Brakes F/R: Disc/Drum

Steering: Rack & pinion
Wheelbase: 243.8cm 96.0in
Track F: 133.9cm 52.7in
Track R: 133.4cm 52.5in
Length: 436.9cm 172.0in
Width: 162.6cm 64.0in
Height: 133.4cm 52.5in
Ground clearance: 12.7cm 5.0in
Kerb weight: 1123.6kg 2475.0lb
Fuel: 54.9L 12.1gal 14.5galUS

3852 Renault

20 TL
1976 France
101.0mph 162.5kmh
0-50mph 80.5kmh: 8.4secs
0-60mph 96.5kmh: 12.6secs
0-1/4 mile: 18.5secs
0-1km: 35.2secs
90.0bhp 67.1kW 91.2PS
@ 5750rpm
97.0lbft 131.4Nm @ 3500rpm
80.3bhp/ton 79.0bhp/tonne
54.6bhp/L 40.7kW/L 55.4PS/L
52.9ft/sec 16.1m/sec
17.1mph 27.5kmh/1000rpm
25.4mpg 21.1mpgUS 11.1L/100km
Petrol 4-stroke piston
1647cc 100.5cu in
In-line 4 1 Carburettor
Compression ratio: 9.3:1
Bore: 79.0mm 3.1in
Stroke: 84.0mm 3.3in
Valve type/No: Overhead 8
Transmission: Manual
No. of forward speeds: 4
Wheels driven: Front
Springs F/R: Coil/Coil
Brake system: PA
Brakes F/R: Disc/Drum
Steering: Rack & pinion
Wheelbase: 266.7cm 105.0in
Track F: 144.8cm 57.0in
Track R: 143.5cm 56.5in
Length: 452.1cm 178.0in
Width: 172.7cm 68.0in
Height: 142.2cm 56.0in
Ground clearance: 17.8cm 7.0in
Kerb weight: 1139.5kg 2510.0lb
Fuel: 59.1L 13.0gal 15.6galUS

3853 Renault

30 TS
1976 France
116.0mph 186.6kmh
0-50mph 80.5kmh: 8.6secs
0-60mph 96.5kmh: 11.7secs
0-1/4 mile: 18.4secs
0-1km: 33.9secs
131.0bhp 97.7kW 132.8PS
@ 5500rpm
148.3lbft 200.9Nm @ 2500rpm
102.8bhp/ton 101.1bhp/tonne
49.2bhp/L 36.7kW/L 49.9PS/L
43.8ft/sec 13.4m/sec
19.2mph 30.9kmh/1000rpm
20.2mpg 16.8mpgUS 14.0L/100km
Petrol 4-stroke piston
2664cc 162.5cu in
Vee 6 2 Carburettor
Compression ratio: 8.6:1
Bore: 88.0mm 3.5in
Stroke: 73.0mm 2.9in
Valve type/No: Overhead 12
Transmission: Automatic
No. of forward speeds: 3
Wheels driven: Front
Springs F/R: Coil/Coil
Brake system: PA
Brakes F/R: Disc/Disc
Steering: Rack & pinion PA
Wheelbase: 266.7cm 105.0in
Track F: 144.8cm 57.0in
Track R: 143.5cm 56.5in
Length: 452.1cm 178.0in
Width: 172.7cm 68.0in
Height: 142.2cm 56.0in
Ground clearance: 17.8cm 7.0in
Kerb weight: 1295.3kg 2853.0lb
Fuel: 67.1L 14.7gal 17.7galUS

3854 Renault

5 GTL
1976 France
90.0mph 144.8kmh
0-50mph 80.5kmh: 11.6secs
0-60mph 96.5kmh: 17.6secs
0-1/4 mile: 20.7secs
0-1km: 39.6secs
44.0bhp 32.8kW 44.6PS
@ 5000rpm
62.0lbft 84.0Nm @ 2000rpm
59.1bhp/ton 58.1bhp/tonne
34.1bhp/L 25.4kW/L 34.6PS/L
42.1ft/sec 12.8m/sec
20.0mph 32.2kmh/1000rpm
42.0mpg 35.0mpgUS 6.7L/100km
Petrol 4-stroke piston
1289cc 78.6cu in
In-line 4 1 Carburettor
Compression ratio: 9.5:1
Bore: 73.0mm 2.9in
Stroke: 77.0mm 3.0in
Valve type/No: Overhead 8
Transmission: Manual
No. of forward speeds: 4
Wheels driven: Front
Springs F/R: Torsion bar/Torsion bar
Brakes F/R: Disc/Drum
Steering: Rack & pinion
Wheelbase: 240.0cm 94.5in
Track F: 127.5cm 50.2in
Track R: 124.5cm 49.0in
Length: 349.3cm 137.5in
Width: 152.4cm 60.0in
Height: 139.7cm 55.0in
Ground clearance: 17.0cm 6.7in
Kerb weight: 757.3kg 1668.0lb
Fuel: 40.9L 9.0gal 10.8galUS

3855 Renault

12 TL
1977 France
88.0mph 141.6kmh
0-50mph 80.5kmh: 11.0secs
0-60mph 96.5kmh: 16.7secs
0-1/4 mile: 20.7secs
0-1km: 39.2secs
54.0bhp 40.3kW 54.7PS
@ 5250rpm
65.1lbft 88.2Nm @ 3500rpm
62.2bhp/ton 61.2bhp/tonne
41.9bhp/L 31.2kW/L 42.5PS/L
44.2ft/sec 13.5m/sec
16.3mph 26.2kmh/1000rpm
26.8mpg 22.3mpgUS 10.5L/100km
Petrol 4-stroke piston
1289cc 78.6cu in
In-line 4 1 Carburettor
Compression ratio: 9.5:1
Bore: 73.0mm 2.9in
Stroke: 77.0mm 3.0in
Valve type/No: Overhead 8
Transmission: Manual
No. of forward speeds: 4
Wheels driven: Front
Springs F/R: Coil/Coil
Brake system: PA
Brakes F/R: Disc/Drum
Steering: Rack & pinion
Wheelbase: 242.6cm 95.5in
Track F: 130.8cm 51.5in
Track R: 130.8cm 51.5in
Length: 445.0cm 175.2in
Width: 168.9cm 66.5in
Height: 143.5cm 56.5in
Ground clearance: 14.0cm 5.5in
Kerb weight: 882.6kg 1944.0lb
Fuel: 46.6L 10.2gal 12.3galUS

3856 Renault

14
1977 France
93.0mph 149.6kmh
0-50mph 80.5kmh: 9.9secs
0-60mph 96.5kmh: 15.3secs
0-1/4 mile: 19.9secs
0-1km: 37.6secs
57.0bhp 42.5kW 57.8PS
@ 6000rpm
68.0lbft 92.1Nm @ 3000rpm
70.7bhp/ton 69.5bhp/tonne
46.8bhp/L 34.9kW/L 47.4PS/L
45.3ft/sec 13.8m/sec
15.9mph 25.6kmh/1000rpm
32.5mpg 27.1mpgUS 8.7L/100km
Petrol 4-stroke piston
1219cc 74.4cu in
In-line 4 1 Carburettor
Compression ratio: 9.3:1
Bore: 75.0mm 2.9in
Stroke: 69.0mm 2.7in
Valve type/No: Overhead 8
Transmission: Manual
No. of forward speeds: 4
Wheels driven: Front
Springs F/R: Coil/Torsion bar
Brake system: PA
Brakes F/R: Disc/Drum
Steering: Rack & pinion
Wheelbase: 252.7cm 99.5in
Track F: 135.1cm 53.2in
Track R: 138.4cm 54.5in
Length: 402.6cm 158.5in
Width: 162.6cm 64.0in
Height: 140.2cm 55.2in
Ground clearance: 15.2cm 6.0in
Kerb weight: 819.9kg 1806.0lb
Fuel: 38.2L 8.4gal 10.1galUS

3857 Renault

17 TS
1977 France
102.0mph 164.1kmh
0-50mph 80.5kmh: 7.8secs
0-60mph 96.5kmh: 11.4secs
0-1/4 mile: 18.2secs
0-1km: 33.9secs
98.0bhp 73.1kW 99.4PS
@ 5750rpm
97.6lbft 132.2Nm @ 3500rpm
99.2bhp/ton 97.6bhp/tonne
59.5bhp/L 44.4kW/L 60.3PS/L
52.9ft/sec 16.1m/sec
20.2mph 32.5kmh/1000rpm
26.1mpg 21.7mpgUS 10.8L/100km
Petrol 4-stroke piston
1647cc 100.5cu in
In-line 4 1 Carburettor
Compression ratio: 9.3:1
Bore: 79.0mm 3.1in
Stroke: 84.0mm 3.3in
Valve type/No: Overhead 8
Transmission: Manual
No. of forward speeds: 5
Wheels driven: Front
Springs F/R: Coil/Coil
Brake system: PA
Brakes F/R: Disc/Drum
Steering: Rack & pinion
Wheelbase: 243.8cm 96.0in
Track F: 133.4cm 52.5in
Track R: 133.4cm 52.5in
Length: 425.5cm 167.5in
Width: 162.6cm 64.0in
Height: 132.1cm 52.0in
Ground clearance: 16.5cm 6.5in
Kerb weight: 1004.2kg 2212.0lb
Fuel: 54.6L 12.0gal 14.4galUS

3858 Renault

20 TS
1977 France
100.0mph 160.9kmh
0-50mph 80.5kmh: 10.6secs
0-60mph 96.5kmh: 14.8secs
0-1/4 mile: 20.4secs
0-1km: 37.3secs
110.0bhp 82.0kW 111.5PS
@ 5500rpm
127.5lbft 172.8Nm @ 3000rpm
89.5bhp/ton 88.0bhp/tonne
55.1bhp/L 41.1kW/L 55.9PS/L
49.3ft/sec 15.0m/sec
17.7mph 28.5kmh/1000rpm
22.9mpg 19.1mpgUS 12.3L/100km
Petrol 4-stroke piston
1995cc 121.7cu in
In-line 4 1 Carburettor
Compression ratio: 9.2:1
Bore: 88.0mm 3.5in
Stroke: 82.0mm 3.2in
Valve type/No: Overhead 8
Transmission: Automatic
No. of forward speeds: 3
Wheels driven: Front
Springs F/R: Coil/Coil
Brake system: PA
Brakes F/R: Disc/Drum
Steering: Rack & pinion
Wheelbase: 266.7cm 105.0in
Track F: 144.8cm 57.0in
Track R: 143.5cm 56.5in
Length: 452.1cm 178.0in
Width: 172.7cm 68.0in
Height: 142.2cm 56.0in
Ground clearance: 17.8cm 7.0in
Kerb weight: 1250.3kg 2754.0lb
Fuel: 67.1L 14.7gal 17.7galUS

3859 Renault

30 TS
1978 France
119.0mph 191.5kmh
0-50mph 80.5kmh: 6.9secs
0-60mph 96.5kmh: 9.8secs
0-1/4 mile: 17.6secs
0-1km: 32.7secs
125.0bhp 93.2kW 126.7PS
@ 5000rpm
150.0lbft 203.3Nm @ 2500rpm
98.4bhp/ton 96.8bhp/tonne
46.9bhp/L 35.0kW/L 47.6PS/L
39.9ft/sec 12.2m/sec
19.8mph 31.9kmh/1000rpm
18.5mpg 15.4mpgUS 15.3L/100km
Petrol 4-stroke piston
2664cc 162.5cu in
Vee 6 1 Carburettor
Compression ratio: 8.6:1
Bore: 88.0mm 3.5in
Stroke: 73.0mm 2.9in
Valve type/No: Overhead 12
Transmission: Manual
No. of forward speeds: 4
Wheels driven: Front
Springs F/R: Coil/Coil
Brake system: PA
Brakes F/R: Disc/Disc
Steering: Rack & pinion PA
Wheelbase: 266.7cm 105.0in
Track F: 144.8cm 57.0in
Track R: 143.5cm 56.5in
Length: 452.1cm 178.0in
Width: 172.7cm 68.0in
Height: 142.2cm 56.0in
Ground clearance: 17.8cm 7.0in
Kerb weight: 1291.2kg 2844.0lb
Fuel: 63.7L 14.0gal 16.8galUS

3860 Renault

5 Automatic
1978 France
90.0mph 144.8kmh
0-50mph 80.5kmh: 13.8secs
0-60mph 96.5kmh: 20.1secs
0-1/4 mile: 22.1secs
0-1km: 41.2secs
55.0bhp 41.0kW 55.8PS
@ 5750rpm
69.0lbft 93.5Nm @ 2500rpm
69.3bhp/ton 68.1bhp/tonne
42.7bhp/L 31.8kW/L 43.3PS/L
48.4ft/sec 14.8m/sec
19.1mph 30.7kmh/1000rpm
28.4mpg 23.6mpgUS 9.9L/100km
Petrol 4-stroke piston
1289cc 78.6cu in
In-line 4 1 Carburettor
Compression ratio: 9.5:1
Bore: 72.0mm 2.8in
Stroke: 77.0mm 3.0in
Valve type/No: Overhead 8
Transmission: Automatic
No. of forward speeds: 3
Wheels driven: Front
Springs F/R: Torsion bar/Torsion bar
Brake system: PA
Brakes F/R: Disc/Drum
Steering: Rack & pinion
Wheelbase: 240.0cm 94.5in
Track F: 127.5cm 50.2in
Track R: 124.5cm 49.0in
Length: 349.3cm 137.5in
Width: 152.4cm 60.0in
Height: 139.7cm 55.0in
Ground clearance: 17.0cm 6.7in
Kerb weight: 807.2kg 1778.0lb
Fuel: 37.8L 8.3gal 10.0galUS

3861 Renault

18 GTS
1979 France
100.0mph 160.9kmh
0-50mph 80.5kmh: 9.4secs
0-60mph 96.5kmh: 13.4secs
0-1/4 mile: 19.1secs
0-1km: 35.8secs
79.0bhp 58.9kW 80.1PS
@ 5500rpm
89.0lbft 120.6Nm @ 3000rpm
83.2bhp/ton 81.8bhp/tonne
48.0bhp/L 35.8kW/L 48.6PS/L
50.6ft/sec 15.4m/sec
20.2mph 32.5kmh/1000rpm
28.8mpg 24.0mpgUS 9.8L/100km
Petrol 4-stroke piston

1647cc 100.5cu in
In-line 4 1 Carburettor
Compression ratio: 9.3:1
Bore: 79.0mm 3.1in
Stroke: 84.0mm 3.3in
Valve type/No: Overhead 8
Transmission: Manual
No. of forward speeds: 5
Wheels driven: Front
Springs F/R: Coil/Coil
Brake system: PA
Brakes F/R: Disc/Drum
Steering: Rack & pinion
Wheelbase: 244.1cm 96.1in
Track F: 141.7cm 55.8in
Track R: 135.6cm 53.4in
Length: 436.9cm 172.0in
Width: 168.9cm 66.5in
Height: 140.5cm 55.3in
Ground clearance: 11.9cm 4.7in
Kerb weight: 966.1kg 2128.0lb
Fuel: 53.2L 11.7gal 14.1galUS

3862 Renault

18 TS Estate
1979 France
97.0mph 156.1kmh
0-50mph 80.5kmh: 10.2secs
0-60mph 96.5kmh: 14.3secs
0-1/4 mile: 19.6secs
0-1km: 36.6secs
79.0bhp 58.9kW 80.1PS
@ 5500rpm
90.0lbft 122.0Nm @ 3000rpm
80.4bhp/ton 79.1bhp/tonne
48.0bhp/L 35.8kW/L 48.6PS/L
50.6ft/sec 15.4m/sec
17.9mph 28.8kmh/1000rpm
31.7mpg 26.4mpgUS 8.9L/100km
Petrol 4-stroke piston
1647cc 100.5cu in
In-line 4 1 Carburettor
Compression ratio: 9.3:1
Bore: 79.0mm 3.1in
Stroke: 84.0mm 3.3in
Valve type/No: Overhead 8
Transmission: Manual
No. of forward speeds: 4
Wheels driven: Front
Springs F/R: Coil/Coil
Brake system: PA
Brakes F/R: Disc/Drum
Steering: Rack & pinion
Wheelbase: 244.1cm 96.1in
Track F: 141.7cm 55.8in
Track R: 135.6cm 53.4in
Length: 445.5cm 175.4in
Width: 168.1cm 66.2in
Height: 140.5cm 55.3in
Ground clearance: 11.9cm 4.7in
Kerb weight: 998.8kg 2200.0lb
Fuel: 56.9L 12.5gal 15.0galUS

3863 Renault

30 TX
1979 France
117.0mph 188.3kmh
0-50mph 80.5kmh: 7.2secs
0-60mph 96.5kmh: 10.3secs
0-1/4 mile: 17.1secs
0-1km: 31.7secs
142.0bhp 105.9kW 144.0PS
@ 5500rpm
161.0lbft 218.2Nm @ 3000rpm
112.0bhp/ton 110.1bhp/tonne
53.3bhp/L 39.7kW/L 54.0PS/L
43.8ft/sec 13.4m/sec
22.8mph 36.7kmh/1000rpm
19.5mpg 16.2mpgUS 14.5L/100km
Petrol 4-stroke piston
2664cc 162.5cu in
Vee 6 fuel injection
Compression ratio: 9.2:1
Bore: 88.0mm 3.5in
Stroke: 73.0mm 2.9in
Valve type/No: Overhead 12
Transmission: Manual
No. of forward speeds: 5
Wheels driven: Front
Springs F/R: Coil/Coil
Brake system: PA
Brakes F/R: Disc/Disc
Steering: Rack & pinion PA
Wheelbase: 266.7cm 105.0in
Track F: 144.8cm 57.0in
Track R: 143.5cm 56.5in
Length: 452.1cm 178.0in
Width: 172.7cm 68.0in
Height: 142.2cm 56.0in
Ground clearance: 17.8cm 7.0in
Kerb weight: 1289.4kg 2840.0lb
Fuel: 63.7L 14.0gal 16.8galUS

3864 Renault

5 Gordini
1979 France
112.0mph 180.2kmh
0-50mph 80.5kmh: 8.3secs
0-60mph 96.5kmh: 10.7secs
0-1/4 mile: 17.8secs
0-1km: 33.3secs
93.0bhp 69.3kW 94.3PS
@ 6400rpm
85.4lbft 115.7Nm @ 4000rpm
114.9bhp/ton 113.0bhp/tonne
66.6bhp/L 49.6kW/L 67.5PS/L
53.9ft/sec 16.4m/sec
18.7mph 30.1kmh/1000rpm
30.0mpg 25.0mpgUS 9.4L/100km
Petrol 4-stroke piston
1397cc 85.2cu in
In-line 4 1 Carburettor
Compression ratio: 10.0:1
Bore: 76.0mm 3.0in
Stroke: 77.0mm 3.0in
Valve type/No: Overhead 8
Transmission: Manual
No. of forward speeds: 5
Wheels driven: Front
Springs F/R: Torsion bar/Torsion bar
Brake system: PA
Brakes F/R: Disc/Drum
Steering: Rack & pinion
Wheelbase: 244.1cm 96.1in
Track F: 129.5cm 51.0in
Track R: 125.2cm 49.3in
Length: 355.6cm 140.0in
Width: 152.4cm 60.0in
Height: 139.7cm 55.0in
Ground clearance: 11.9cm 4.7in
Kerb weight: 823.1kg 1813.0lb
Fuel: 38.2L 8.4gal 10.1galUS

3865 Renault

5 Racer
1979 France
109.0mph 175.4kmh
0-50mph 80.5kmh: 5.7secs
0-60mph 96.5kmh: 7.4secs
0-1/4 mile: 16.3secs
143.0bhp 106.6kW 145.0PS
@ 8000rpm
103.0lbft 139.6Nm @ 6500rpm
190.1bhp/ton 186.9bhp/tonne
108.7bhp/L 81.0kW/L 110.2PS/L
67.3ft/sec 20.5m/sec
12.8mph 20.6kmh/1000rpm
13.3mpg 11.1mpgUS 21.2L/100km
Petrol 4-stroke piston
1316cc 80.3cu in
In-line 4 2 Carburettor
Compression ratio: 12.0:1
Bore: 73.8mm 2.9in
Stroke: 77.0mm 3.0in
Valve type/No: Overhead 8
Transmission: Manual
No. of forward speeds: 4
Wheels driven: Front
Springs F/R: Torsion bar/Torsion bar
Brakes F/R: Disc/Drum
Steering: Rack & pinion
Wheelbase: 243.3cm 95.8in
Track F: 130.0cm 51.2in
Track R: 126.5cm 49.8in
Length: 359.4cm 141.5in
Width: 152.4cm 60.0in
Height: 132.8cm 52.3in
Ground clearance: 5.1cm 2.0in
Kerb weight: 765.0kg 1685.0lb
Fuel: 83.3L 18.3gal 22.0galUS

3866 Renault

5 TL
1979 France
84.0mph 135.2kmh
0-50mph 80.5kmh: 10.9secs
0-60mph 96.5kmh: 15.7secs
0-1/4 mile: 21.2secs
0-1km: 39.9secs
45.0bhp 33.6kW 45.6PS
@ 4400rpm
63.0lbft 85.4Nm @ 2000rpm
61.3bhp/ton 60.3bhp/tonne
40.6bhp/L 30.3kW/L 41.2PS/L
34.6ft/sec 10.6m/sec
19.5mph 31.4kmh/1000rpm
41.3mpg 34.4mpgUS 6.8L/100km
Petrol 4-stroke piston
1108cc 67.6cu in
In-line 4 1 Carburettor
Compression ratio: 9.5:1
Bore: 70.0mm 2.8in
Stroke: 72.0mm 2.8in
Valve type/No: Overhead 8
Transmission: Manual
No. of forward speeds: 4
Wheels driven: Front
Springs F/R: Torsion bar/Torsion bar
Brake system: PA
Brakes F/R: Disc/Drum
Steering: Rack & pinion
Wheelbase: 240.0cm 94.5in
Track F: 127.5cm 50.2in
Track R: 124.5cm 49.0in
Length: 349.3cm 137.5in
Width: 152.4cm 60.0in
Height: 139.7cm 55.0in
Ground clearance: 17.0cm 6.7in
Kerb weight: 746.4kg 1644.0lb
Fuel: 37.8L 8.3gal 10.0galUS

3867 Renault

Gordini
1979 France
100.0mph 160.9kmh
0-50mph 80.5kmh: 8.2secs
0-60mph 96.5kmh: 11.9secs
0-1/4 mile: 18.8secs
95.0bhp 70.8kW 96.3PS
@ 6250rpm
90.0lbft 122.0Nm @ 3500rpm
87.2bhp/ton 85.8bhp/tonne
57.7bhp/L 43.0kW/L 58.5PS/L
57.5ft/sec 17.5m/sec
20.6mph 33.1kmh/1000rpm
24.0mpg 20.0mpgUS 11.8L/100km
Petrol 4-stroke piston
1647cc 100.5cu in
In-line 4 fuel injection
Compression ratio: 9.3:1
Bore: 79.0mm 3.1in
Stroke: 84.0mm 3.3in
Valve type/No: Overhead 8
Transmission: Manual
No. of forward speeds: 5
Wheels driven: Front
Springs F/R: Coil/Coil
Brake system: PA
Brakes F/R: Disc/Drum
Steering: Rack & pinion
Wheelbase: 243.8cm 96.0in
Track F: 132.1cm 52.0in
Track R: 132.1cm 52.0in
Length: 436.9cm 172.0in
Width: 162.6cm 64.0in
Height: 130.8cm 51.5in
Ground clearance: 11.9cm 4.7in
Kerb weight: 1107.8kg 2440.0lb
Fuel: 47.3L 10.4gal 12.5galUS

3868 Renault

Le Car
1979 France
0-60mph 96.5kmh: 12.6secs
0-1/4 mile: 19.2secs
58.0bhp 43.2kW 58.8PS
@ 6000rpm
70.0lbft 94.9Nm @ 3500rpm
71.6bhp/ton 70.4bhp/tonne
45.0bhp/L 33.5kW/L 45.6PS/L
50.5ft/sec 15.4m/sec
17.2mph 27.7kmh/1000rpm
36.0mpg 30.0mpgUS 7.8L/100km
Petrol 4-stroke piston
1289cc 78.6cu in
In-line 4 1 Carburettor
Compression ratio: 8.5:1
Bore: 73.0mm 2.9in
Stroke: 77.0mm 3.0in
Valve type/No: Overhead 8
Transmission: Manual
No. of forward speeds: 4
Wheels driven: Front
Springs F/R: Torsion bar/Torsion bar
Brakes F/R: Disc/Drum
Steering: Rack & pinion
Track F: 128.8cm 50.7in
Track R: 124.5cm 49.0in
Height: 139.7cm 55.0in
Ground clearance: 12.7cm 5.0in
Kerb weight: 824.0kg 1815.0lb
Fuel: 37.8L 8.3gal 10.0galUS

3869 Renault

14 TS
1981 France
101.0mph 162.5kmh
0-50mph 80.5kmh: 8.7secs
0-60mph 96.5kmh: 12.5secs
0-1/4 mile: 19.0secs
0-1km: 36.4secs
70.0bhp 52.2kW 71.0PS
@ 6000rpm
78.0lbft 105.7Nm @ 3000rpm
83.6bhp/ton 82.2bhp/tonne
51.5bhp/L 38.4kW/L 52.2PS/L
50.5ft/sec 15.4m/sec
18.8mph 30.2kmh/1000rpm
30.7mpg 25.6mpgUS 9.2L/100km
Petrol 4-stroke piston
1360cc 83.0cu in
In-line 4 1 Carburettor
Compression ratio: 9.3:1
Bore: 75.0mm 2.9in
Stroke: 77.0mm 3.0in
Valve type/No: Overhead 8
Transmission: Manual
No. of forward speeds: 5
Wheels driven: Front
Springs F/R: Coil/Torsion bar
Brake system: PA
Brakes F/R: Disc/Drum
Steering: Rack & pinion
Wheelbase: 252.7cm 99.5in
Track F: 135.1cm 53.2in
Track R: 138.4cm 54.5in
Length: 402.6cm 158.5in
Width: 162.6cm 64.0in
Height: 140.2cm 55.2in
Ground clearance: 15.2cm 6.0in
Kerb weight: 851.7kg 1876.0lb
Fuel: 48.2L 10.6gal 12.7galUS

3870 Renault

18 Turbo
1981 France
114.0mph 183.4kmh
0-50mph 80.5kmh: 8.1secs
0-60mph 96.5kmh: 10.8secs
0-1/4 mile: 17.5secs
0-1km: 32.4secs
110.0bhp 82.0kW 111.5PS
@ 5000rpm
133.8lbft 181.3Nm @ 2250rpm
104.6bhp/ton 102.9bhp/tonne
70.3bhp/L 52.4kW/L 71.3PS/L
46.0ft/sec 14.0m/sec
20.9mph 33.6kmh/1000rpm
25.9mpg 21.6mpgUS 10.9L/100km
Petrol 4-stroke piston
1565cc 95.5cu in turbocharged
In-line 4 1 Carburettor
Compression ratio: 8.6:1
Bore: 77.0mm 3.0in
Stroke: 84.0mm 3.3in
Valve type/No: Overhead 8
Transmission: Manual
No. of forward speeds: 5
Wheels driven: Front
Springs F/R: Coil/Coil
Brake system: PA
Brakes F/R: Disc/Drum
Steering: Rack & pinion PA
Wheelbase: 244.1cm 96.1in
Track F: 141.7cm 55.8in
Track R: 135.6cm 53.4in
Length: 436.9cm 172.0in
Width: 168.9cm 66.5in
Height: 140.5cm 55.3in
Ground clearance: 11.9cm 4.7in
Kerb weight: 1069.2kg 2355.0lb
Fuel: 53.2L 11.7gal 14.1galUS

3871 Renault

18i
1981 France
108.0mph 173.8kmh
0-60mph 96.5kmh: 13.0secs
0-1/4 mile: 19.0secs
82.0bhp 61.1kW 83.1PS
@ 5500rpm
86.0lbft 116.5Nm @ 2500rpm
74.4bhp/ton 73.1bhp/tonne
49.8bhp/L 37.1kW/L 50.5PS/L
50.6ft/sec 15.4m/sec
20.0mph 32.2kmh/1000rpm

31.8mpg 26.5mpgUS 8.9L/100km
Petrol 4-stroke piston
1647cc 100.5cu in
In-line 4 fuel injection
Compression ratio: 8.6:1
Bore: 79.0mm 3.1in
Stroke: 84.0mm 3.3in
Valve type/No: Overhead 8
Transmission: Manual
No. of forward speeds: 5
Wheels driven: Front
Springs F/R: Coil/Coil
Brake system: PA
Brakes F/R: Disc/Drum
Steering: Rack & pinion PA
Wheelbase: 244.1cm 96.1in
Track F: 141.0cm 55.5in
Track R: 134.9cm 53.1in
Length: 455.7cm 179.4in
Width: 168.9cm 66.5in
Height: 140.0cm 55.1in
Ground clearance: 11.9cm 4.7in
Kerb weight: 1121.4kg 2470.0lb
Fuel: 53.0L 11.6gal 14.0galUS

3872 Renault

20 TX
1981 France
107.0mph 172.2kmh
0-50mph 80.5kmh: 7.3secs
0-60mph 96.5kmh: 10.5secs
0-1/4 mile: 18.0secs
0-1km: 32.5secs
115.0bhp 85.8kW 116.6PS
@ 5500rpm
133.0lbft 180.2Nm @ 3000rpm
90.0bhp/ton 88.5bhp/tonne
53.1bhp/L 39.6kW/L 53.9PS/L
53.5ft/sec 16.3m/sec
21.2mph 34.1kmh/1000rpm
23.1mpg 19.2mpgUS 12.2L/100km
Petrol 4-stroke piston
2165cc 132.1cu in
In-line 4 1 Carburettor
Compression ratio: 9.2:1
Bore: 88.0mm 3.5in
Stroke: 89.0mm 3.5in
Valve type/No: Overhead 8
Transmission: Manual
No. of forward speeds: 5
Wheels driven: Front
Springs F/R: Coil/Coil
Brake system: PA
Brakes F/R: Disc/Drum
Steering: Rack & pinion PA
Wheelbase: 266.7cm 105.0in
Track F: 144.8cm 57.0in
Track R: 143.5cm 56.5in
Length: 452.1cm 178.0in
Width: 172.7cm 68.0in
Height: 142.2cm 56.0in
Ground clearance: 17.8cm 7.0in
Kerb weight: 1299.8kg 2863.0lb
Fuel: 67.1L 14.7gal 17.7galUS

3873 Renault

5 Turbo
1981 France
122.0mph 196.3kmh
0-50mph 80.5kmh: 5.5secs
0-60mph 96.5kmh: 7.7secs
0-1/4 mile: 16.0secs
160.0bhp 119.3kW 162.2PS
@ 6000rpm
155.0lbft 210.0Nm @ 3250rpm
164.4bhp/ton 161.7bhp/tonne
114.5bhp/L 85.4kW/L 116.1PS/L
50.5ft/sec 15.4m/sec
20.3mph 32.7kmh/1000rpm
18.0mpg 15.0mpgUS 15.7L/100km
Petrol 4-stroke piston
1397cc 85.2cu in turbocharged
In-line 4 fuel injection
Compression ratio: 7.0:1
Bore: 76.0mm 3.0in
Stroke: 77.0mm 3.0in
Valve type/No: Overhead 8
Transmission: Manual
No. of forward speeds: 5
Wheels driven: Rear
Springs F/R: Torsion bar/Coil
Brake system: PA
Brakes F/R: Disc/Disc
Steering: Rack & pinion
Wheelbase: 243.1cm 95.7in
Track F: 134.6cm 53.0in
Track R: 147.6cm 58.1in
Length: 372.4cm 146.6in
Width: 177.8cm 70.0in
Height: 134.4cm 52.9in
Ground clearance: 11.4cm 4.5in
Kerb weight: 989.7kg 2180.0lb
Fuel: 93.1L 20.5gal 24.6galUS

3874 Renault

Le Car Turbo
1981 France
158.0mph 254.2kmh
0-50mph 80.5kmh: 3.8secs
0-60mph 96.5kmh: 4.8secs
0-1/4 mile: 13.3secs
260.0bhp 193.9kW 263.6PS
@ 7000rpm
220.0lbft 298.1Nm @ 4500rpm
353.0bhp/ton 347.1bhp/tonne
181.8bhp/L 135.6kW/L 184.3PS/L
58.9ft/sec 18.0m/sec
20.5mph 33.0kmh/1000rpm
6.0mpg 5.0mpgUS 47.0L/100km
Petrol 4-stroke piston
1430cc 87.2cu in turbocharged
In-line 4 fuel injection
Compression ratio: 6.5:1
Bore: 76.9mm 3.0in
Stroke: 77.0mm 3.0in
Valve type/No: Overhead 8
Transmission: Manual
No. of forward speeds: 5
Wheels driven: Rear
Springs F/R: Coil/Coil
Brakes F/R: Disc/Disc
Steering: Rack & pinion
Wheelbase: 243.1cm 95.7in
Track F: 135.9cm 53.5in
Track R: 144.8cm 57.0in
Length: 365.8cm 144.0in
Width: 185.4cm 73.0in
Height: 124.5cm 49.0in
Ground clearance: 5.1cm 2.0in
Kerb weight: 749.1kg 1650.0lb
Fuel: 109.8L 24.1gal 29.0galUS

3875 Renault

18 GTX Estate
1982 France
110.0mph 177.0kmh
0-50mph 80.5kmh: 7.5secs
0-60mph 96.5kmh: 10.6secs
0-1/4 mile: 17.7secs
0-1km: 33.2secs
104.0bhp 77.5kW 105.4PS
@ 5500rpm
136.0lbft 184.3Nm @ 3250rpm
101.8bhp/ton 100.1bhp/tonne
52.1bhp/L 38.9kW/L 52.8PS/L
49.3ft/sec 15.0m/sec
22.8mph 36.7kmh/1000rpm
28.1mpg 23.4mpgUS 10.1L/100km
Petrol 4-stroke piston
1995cc 121.7cu in
In-line 4 1 Carburettor
Compression ratio: 9.2:1
Bore: 88.0mm 3.5in
Stroke: 82.0mm 3.2in
Valve type/No: Overhead 8
Transmission: Manual
No. of forward speeds: 5
Wheels driven: Front
Springs F/R: Coil/Coil
Brake system: PA
Brakes F/R: Disc/Drum
Steering: Rack & pinion PA
Wheelbase: 243.8cm 96.0in
Track F: 142.0cm 55.9in
Track R: 134.6cm 53.0in
Length: 448.8cm 176.7in
Width: 168.9cm 66.5in
Height: 140.2cm 55.2in
Ground clearance: 11.9cm 4.7in
Kerb weight: 1039.2kg 2289.0lb
Fuel: 57.3L 12.6gal 15.1galUS

3876 Renault

5 Gordini Turbo
1982 France
115.0mph 185.0kmh
0-50mph 80.5kmh: 7.1secs
0-60mph 96.5kmh: 9.8secs
0-1/4 mile: 16.9secs
0-1km: 29.5secs
110.0bhp 82.0kW 111.5PS
@ 6000rpm
108.5lbft 147.0Nm @ 4000rpm
131.3bhp/ton 129.1bhp/tonne
78.7bhp/L 58.7kW/L 79.8PS/L
50.5ft/sec 15.4m/sec
19.1mph 30.7kmh/1000rpm
30.1mpg 25.1mpgUS 9.4L/100km
Petrol 4-stroke piston
1397cc 85.2cu in turbocharged
In-line 4 1 Carburettor
Compression ratio: 8.6:1
Bore: 76.0mm 3.0in
Stroke: 77.0mm 3.0in
Valve type/No: Overhead 8
Transmission: Manual
No. of forward speeds: 5
Wheels driven: Front
Springs F/R: Torsion bar/Torsion bar
Brake system: PA
Brakes F/R: Disc/Disc
Steering: Rack & pinion
Wheelbase: 244.1cm 96.1in
Track F: 129.3cm 50.9in
Track R: 127.0cm 50.0in
Length: 355.6cm 140.0in
Width: 152.4cm 60.0in
Height: 141.0cm 55.5in
Ground clearance: 11.9cm 4.7in
Kerb weight: 851.7kg 1876.0lb
Fuel: 38.2L 8.4gal 10.1galUS

3877 Renault

9 GLT
1982 France
96.0mph 154.5kmh
0-50mph 80.5kmh: 9.6secs
0-60mph 96.5kmh: 14.2secs
0-1/4 mile: 19.2secs
0-1km: 36.9secs
60.0bhp 44.7kW 60.8PS
@ 5250rpm
74.0lbft 100.3Nm @ 3000rpm
76.0bhp/ton 74.7bhp/tonne
42.9bhp/L 32.0kW/L 43.5PS/L
44.2ft/sec 13.5m/sec
20.5mph 33.0kmh/1000rpm
32.4mpg 27.0mpgUS 8.7L/100km
Petrol 4-stroke piston
1397cc 85.2cu in
In-line 4 1 Carburettor
Compression ratio: 9.2:1
Bore: 76.0mm 3.0in
Stroke: 77.0mm 3.0in
Valve type/No: Overhead 8
Transmission: Manual
No. of forward speeds: 5
Wheels driven: Front
Springs F/R: Coil/Torsion bar
Brake system: PA
Brakes F/R: Disc/Drum
Steering: Rack & pinion
Wheelbase: 247.7cm 97.5in
Track F: 138.4cm 54.5in
Track R: 134.6cm 53.0in
Length: 406.4cm 160.0in
Width: 163.3cm 64.3in
Height: 133.1cm 52.4in
Ground clearance: 11.9cm 4.7in
Kerb weight: 802.7kg 1768.0lb
Fuel: 46.9L 10.3gal 12.4galUS

3878 Renault

9 TC
1982 France
93.0mph 149.6kmh
0-50mph 80.5kmh: 12.0secs
0-60mph 96.5kmh: 18.3secs
0-1/4 mile: 21.1secs
0-1km: 40.0secs
47.5bhp 35.4kW 48.2PS
@ 5250rpm
59.0lbft 79.9Nm @ 2500rpm
62.3bhp/ton 61.2bhp/tonne
42.9bhp/L 32.0kW/L 43.5PS/L
41.3ft/sec 12.6m/sec
18.4mph 29.6kmh/1000rpm
35.4mpg 29.5mpgUS 8.0L/100km
Petrol 4-stroke piston
1108cc 67.6cu in
In-line 4 1 Carburettor
Compression ratio: 9.2:1
Bore: 70.0mm 2.8in
Stroke: 72.0mm 2.8in
Valve type/No: Overhead 8
Transmission: Manual
No. of forward speeds: 4
Wheels driven: Front
Springs F/R: Coil/Torsion bar
Brake system: PA
Brakes F/R: Disc/Drum
Steering: Rack & pinion
Wheelbase: 247.7cm 97.5in
Track F: 138.4cm 54.5in
Track R: 134.6cm 53.0in
Length: 406.4cm 160.0in
Width: 163.3cm 64.3in
Height: 133.1cm 52.4in
Ground clearance: 11.9cm 4.7in
Kerb weight: 775.9kg 1709.0lb
Fuel: 46.9L 10.3gal 12.4galUS

3879 Renault

9 TSE
1982 France
96.0mph 154.5kmh
0-50mph 80.5kmh: 8.6secs
0-60mph 96.5kmh: 12.6secs
0-1/4 mile: 18.5secs
0-1km: 35.2secs
72.0bhp 53.7kW 73.0PS
@ 5250rpm
78.0lbft 105.7Nm @ 3500rpm
85.0bhp/ton 83.6bhp/tonne
51.5bhp/L 38.4kW/L 52.2PS/L
44.2ft/sec 13.5m/sec
20.5mph 33.0kmh/1000rpm
34.3mpg 28.6mpgUS 8.2L/100km
Petrol 4-stroke piston
1397cc 85.2cu in
In-line 4 1 Carburettor
Compression ratio: 9.2:1
Bore: 76.0mm 3.0in
Stroke: 77.0mm 3.0in
Valve type/No: Overhead 8
Transmission: Manual
No. of forward speeds: 5
Wheels driven: Front
Springs F/R: Coil/Torsion bar
Brake system: PA
Brakes F/R: Disc/Drum
Steering: Rack & pinion
Wheelbase: 247.7cm 97.5in
Track F: 138.4cm 54.5in
Track R: 134.6cm 53.0in
Length: 406.4cm 160.0in
Width: 163.3cm 64.3in
Height: 133.1cm 52.4in
Ground clearance: 11.9cm 4.7in
Kerb weight: 861.7kg 1898.0lb
Fuel: 46.9L 10.3gal 12.4galUS

3880 Renault

Alliance DL
1982 France
90.0mph 144.8kmh
0-50mph 80.5kmh: 10.7secs
0-60mph 96.5kmh: 15.4secs
0-1/4 mile: 19.9secs
64.0bhp 47.7kW 64.9PS
@ 4500rpm
77.0lbft 104.3Nm @ 3000rpm
67.3bhp/ton 66.2bhp/tonne
45.8bhp/L 34.2kW/L 46.4PS/L
37.9ft/sec 11.5m/sec
22.0mph 35.4kmh/1000rpm
38.4mpg 32.0mpgUS 7.4L/100km
Petrol 4-stroke piston
1397cc 85.2cu in
In-line 4 fuel injection
Compression ratio: 8.8:1
Bore: 76.0mm 3.0in
Stroke: 77.0mm 3.0in
Valve type/No: Overhead 8
Transmission: Manual
No. of forward speeds: 5
Wheels driven: Front
Springs F/R: Coil/Torsion bar
Brake system: PA
Brakes F/R: Disc/Drum
Steering: Rack & pinion
Wheelbase: 246.9cm 97.2in
Track F: 140.2cm 55.2in
Track R: 134.1cm 52.8in
Length: 416.1cm 163.8in
Width: 165.1cm 65.0in
Height: 138.4cm 54.5in
Ground clearance: 15.2cm 6.0in
Kerb weight: 967.0kg 2130.0lb
Fuel: 47.3L 10.4gal 12.5galUS

3881 Renault

Fuego GTS
1982 France
112.0mph 180.2kmh
0-50mph 80.5kmh: 7.6secs

0-60mph 96.5kmh: 11.2secs
0-1/4 mile: 18.1secs
0-1km: 33.8secs
96.0bhp 71.6kW 97.3PS
@ 5750rpm
98.2lbft 133.1Nm @ 3500rpm
97.2bhp/ton 95.6bhp/tonne
58.3bhp/L 43.5kW/L 59.1PS/L
52.9ft/sec 16.1m/sec
20.8mph 33.5kmh/1000rpm
31.2mpg 26.0mpgUS 9.1L/100km
Petrol 4-stroke piston
1647cc 100.5cu in
In-line 4 1 Carburettor
Compression ratio: 9.3:1
Bore: 79.0mm 3.1in
Stroke: 84.0mm 3.3in
Valve type/No: Overhead 8
Transmission: Manual
No. of forward speeds: 5
Wheels driven: Front
Springs F/R: Coil/Coil
Brake system: PA
Brakes F/R: Disc/Drum
Steering: Rack & pinion
Wheelbase: 243.8cm 96.0in
Track F: 142.5cm 56.1in
Track R: 134.6cm 53.0in
Length: 435.6cm 171.5in
Width: 169.2cm 66.6in
Height: 131.3cm 51.7in
Ground clearance: 12.7cm 5.0in
Kerb weight: 1004.2kg 2212.0lb
Fuel: 56.9L 12.5gal 15.0galUS

3882 Renault

Fuego Turbo
1982 France
102.0mph 164.1kmh
0-50mph 80.5kmh: 8.1secs
0-60mph 96.5kmh: 10.7secs
0-1/4 mile: 17.9secs
107.0bhp 79.8kW 108.5PS
@ 5500rpm
120.0lbft 162.6Nm @ 2500rpm
94.5bhp/ton 93.0bhp/tonne
68.4bhp/L 51.0kW/L 69.4PS/L
50.6ft/sec 15.4m/sec
21.1mph 33.9kmh/1000rpm
33.0mpg 27.5mpgUS 8.6L/100km
Petrol 4-stroke piston
1564cc 95.4cu in turbocharged
In-line 4 fuel injection
Compression ratio: 8.0:1
Bore: 77.0mm 3.0in
Stroke: 84.0mm 3.3in
Valve type/No: Overhead 8
Transmission: Manual
No. of forward speeds: 5
Wheels driven: Front
Springs F/R: Coil/Coil
Brake system: PA
Brakes F/R: Disc/Drum
Steering: Rack & pinion PA
Wheelbase: 244.1cm 96.1in
Track F: 143.3cm 56.4in
Track R: 134.6cm 53.0in
Length: 449.1cm 176.8in
Width: 169.2cm 66.6in
Height: 128.3cm 50.5in
Ground clearance: 11.9cm 4.7in
Kerb weight: 1150.9kg 2535.0lb
Fuel: 56.0L 12.3gal 14.8galUS

3883 Renault

11 TSE
1983 France
96.0mph 154.5kmh
0-50mph 80.5kmh: 9.5secs
0-60mph 96.5kmh: 12.8secs
0-1/4 mile: 18.8secs
0-1km: 35.4secs
72.0bhp 53.7kW 73.0PS
@ 5750rpm
78.0lbft 105.7Nm @ 3500rpm
84.6bhp/ton 83.2bhp/tonne
51.5bhp/L 38.4kW/L 52.2PS/L
48.4ft/sec 14.8m/sec
20.4mph 32.8kmh/1000rpm
34.1mpg 28.4mpgUS 8.3L/100km
Petrol 4-stroke piston
1397cc 85.2cu in
In-line 4 1 Carburettor
Compression ratio: 9.2:1
Bore: 76.0mm 3.0in
Stroke: 77.0mm 3.0in
Valve type/No: Overhead 8
Transmission: Manual
No. of forward speeds: 5
Wheels driven: Front
Springs F/R: Coil/Torsion bar
Brake system: PA
Brakes F/R: Disc/Drum
Steering: Rack & pinion
Wheelbase: 246.9cm 97.2in
Track F: 147.1cm 57.9in
Track R: 134.9cm 53.1in
Length: 398.5cm 156.9in
Width: 168.9cm 66.5in
Height: 140.0cm 55.1in
Ground clearance: 11.9cm 4.7in
Kerb weight: 865.8kg 1907.0lb
Fuel: 46.9L 10.3gal 12.4galUS

3884 Renault

Fuego Turbo
1983 France
116.0mph 186.6kmh
0-60mph 96.5kmh: 10.7secs
0-1/4 mile: 16.8secs
107.0bhp 79.8kW 108.5PS
@ 5500rpm
120.0lbft 162.6Nm @ 2500rpm
94.5bhp/ton 93.0bhp/tonne
68.4bhp/L 51.0kW/L 69.4PS/L
50.6ft/sec 15.4m/sec
32.4mpg 27.0mpgUS 8.7L/100km
Petrol 4-stroke piston
1564cc 95.4cu in turbocharged
In-line 4 fuel injection
Compression ratio: 8.0:1
Bore: 77.0mm 3.0in
Stroke: 84.0mm 3.3in
Valve type/No: Overhead 8
Transmission: Manual
No. of forward speeds: 5
Wheels driven: Front
Springs F/R: Coil/Coil
Brakes F/R: Disc/Drum
Wheelbase: 244.1cm 96.1in
Track F: 143.3cm 56.4in
Track R: 134.6cm 53.0in
Length: 449.1cm 176.8in
Width: 169.2cm 66.6in
Height: 128.3cm 50.5in
Kerb weight: 1150.9kg 2535.0lb
Fuel: 56.0L 12.3gal 14.8galUS

3885 Renault

25 V6
1984 France
130.0mph 209.2kmh
0-50mph 80.5kmh: 6.4secs
0-60mph 96.5kmh: 9.0secs
0-1/4 mile: 16.5secs
0-1km: 30.3secs
142.0bhp 105.9kW 144.0PS
@ 5500rpm
162.0lbft 219.5Nm @ 3000rpm
111.2bhp/ton 109.3bhp/tonne
53.3bhp/L 39.7kW/L 54.0PS/L
43.8ft/sec 13.4m/sec
23.8mph 38.3kmh/1000rpm
19.9mpg 16.6mpgUS 14.2L/100km
Petrol 4-stroke piston
2664cc 162.5cu in
Vee 6 fuel injection
Compression ratio: 9.2:1
Bore: 88.0mm 3.5in
Stroke: 73.0mm 2.9in
Valve type/No: Overhead 12
Transmission: Manual
No. of forward speeds: 5
Wheels driven: Front
Springs F/R: Coil/Coil
Brake system: PA
Brakes F/R: Disc/Disc
Steering: Rack & pinion PA
Wheelbase: 272.3cm 107.2in
Track F: 144.8cm 57.0in
Track R: 139.7cm 55.0in
Length: 464.8cm 183.0in
Width: 177.3cm 69.8in
Height: 140.5cm 55.3in
Ground clearance: 11.9cm 4.7in
Kerb weight: 1298.9kg 2861.0lb
Fuel: 71.9L 15.8gal 19.0galUS

3886 Renault

5 Turbo 2
1984 France
126.0mph 202.7kmh
0-50mph 80.5kmh: 4.7secs
0-60mph 96.5kmh: 6.7secs
0-1/4 mile: 15.0secs
185.0bhp 137.9kW 187.6PS
@ 6000rpm
159.0lbft 215.4Nm @ 3250rpm
185.8bhp/ton 182.7bhp/tonne
132.4bhp/L 98.7kW/L 134.3PS/L
50.5ft/sec 15.4m/sec
21.0mph 33.8kmh/1000rpm
21.6mpg 18.0mpgUS 13.1L/100km
Petrol 4-stroke piston
1397cc 85.2cu in turbocharged
In-line 4 fuel injection
Compression ratio: 7.0:1
Bore: 76.0mm 3.0in
Stroke: 77.0mm 3.0in
Valve type/No: Overhead 8
Transmission: Manual
No. of forward speeds: 5
Wheels driven: Rear
Springs F/R: Torsion bar/Coil
Brake system: PA
Brakes F/R: Disc/Disc
Steering: Rack & pinion
Wheelbase: 243.1cm 95.7in
Track F: 134.6cm 53.0in
Track R: 147.3cm 58.0in
Length: 366.8cm 144.4in
Width: 175.3cm 69.0in
Height: 132.1cm 52.0in
Kerb weight: 1012.4kg 2230.0lb
Fuel: 87.8L 19.3gal 23.2galUS

3887 Renault

Fuego
1984 France
0-60mph 96.5kmh: 11.0secs
0-1/4 mile: 17.8secs
91.0bhp 67.9kW 92.3PS
@ 4000rpm
120.0lbft 162.6Nm @ 2500rpm
79.3bhp/ton 78.0bhp/tonne
42.0bhp/L 31.3kW/L 42.6PS/L
43.3ft/sec 13.2m/sec
28.2mpg 23.5mpgUS 10.0L/100km
Petrol 4-stroke piston
2165cc 132.1cu in
In-line 4
Compression ratio: 8.7:1
Bore: 88.0mm 3.5in
Stroke: 99.0mm 3.9in
Valve type/No: Overhead 8
Transmission: Manual
No. of forward speeds: 5
Wheels driven: Front
Kerb weight: 1166.8kg 2570.0lb

3888 Renault

Fuego 2.2
1984 France
0-60mph 96.5kmh: 11.0secs
110.0bhp 82.0kW 111.5PS
@ 5500rpm
125.0lbft 169.4Nm @ 3000rpm
99.3bhp/ton 97.7bhp/tonne
50.8bhp/L 37.9kW/L 51.5PS/L
30.0mpg 25.0mpgUS 9.4L/100km
Petrol 4-stroke piston
2165cc 132.1cu in
In-line 4 fuel injection
Valve type/No: Overhead 8
Transmission: Manual
No. of forward speeds: 5
Wheels driven: Front
Springs F/R: Coil/Coil
Brakes F/R: Disc/Drum
Steering: Rack & pinion PA
Wheelbase: 244.1cm 96.1in
Length: 449.1cm 176.8in
Width: 169.2cm 66.6in
Height: 128.3cm 50.5in
Kerb weight: 1125.9kg 2480.0lb
Fuel: 56.0L 12.3gal 14.8galUS

3889 Renault

25 V6 Turbo
1985 France
139.0mph 223.7kmh
0-50mph 80.5kmh: 5.7secs
0-60mph 96.5kmh: 8.1secs
0-1/4 mile: 15.9secs
0-1km: 29.3secs
182.0bhp 135.7kW 184.5PS
@ 5500rpm
207.0lbft 280.5Nm @ 3000rpm
137.5bhp/ton 135.2bhp/tonne
74.0bhp/L 55.2kW/L 75.1PS/L
37.9ft/sec 11.5m/sec
24.3mph 39.1kmh/1000rpm
18.5mpg 15.4mpgUS 15.3L/100km
Petrol 4-stroke piston
2458cc 150.0cu in turbocharged
Vee 6 fuel injection
Compression ratio: 8.6:1
Bore: 91.0mm 3.6in
Stroke: 63.0mm 2.5in
Valve type/No: Overhead 12
Transmission: Manual
No. of forward speeds: 5
Wheels driven: Front
Springs F/R: Coil/Coil
Brake system: PA
Brakes F/R: Disc/Disc
Steering: Rack & pinion PA
Wheelbase: 272.3cm 107.2in
Track F: 144.8cm 57.0in
Track R: 139.7cm 55.0in
Length: 464.8cm 183.0in
Width: 177.3cm 69.8in
Height: 140.5cm 55.3in
Ground clearance: 11.9cm 4.7in
Kerb weight: 1346.1kg 2965.0lb
Fuel: 71.9L 15.8gal 19.0galUS

3890 Renault

5 TSE
1985 France
106.0mph 170.6kmh
0-50mph 80.5kmh: 7.7secs
0-60mph 96.5kmh: 11.4secs
0-1/4 mile: 18.2secs
0-1km: 34.2secs
72.0bhp 53.7kW 73.0PS
@ 5750rpm
78.0lbft 105.7Nm @ 3500rpm
93.2bhp/ton 91.6bhp/tonne
51.5bhp/L 38.4kW/L 52.2PS/L
48.4ft/sec 14.8m/sec
19.9mph 32.0kmh/1000rpm
29.5mpg 24.6mpgUS 9.6L/100km
Petrol 4-stroke piston
1397cc 85.2cu in
In-line 4 1 Carburettor
Compression ratio: 9.2:1
Bore: 76.0mm 3.0in
Stroke: 77.0mm 3.0in
Valve type/No: Overhead 8
Transmission: Manual
No. of forward speeds: 5
Wheels driven: Front
Springs F/R: Coil/Torsion bar
Brake system: PA
Brakes F/R: Disc/Drum
Steering: Rack & pinion
Wheelbase: 240.8cm 94.8in
Track F: 132.3cm 52.1in
Track R: 128.0cm 50.4in
Length: 359.2cm 141.4in
Width: 158.5cm 62.4in
Height: 139.7cm 55.0in
Ground clearance: 20.3cm 8.0in
Kerb weight: 785.9kg 1731.0lb
Fuel: 42.8L 9.4gal 11.3galUS

3891 Renault

Encore GS
1985 France
100.0mph 160.9kmh
0-50mph 80.5kmh: 7.9secs
0-60mph 96.5kmh: 11.5secs
0-1/4 mile: 19.3secs
78.0bhp 58.2kW 79.1PS
@ 5000rpm
95.0lbft 128.7Nm @ 3000rpm
78.0bhp/ton 76.7bhp/tonne
45.3bhp/L 33.8kW/L 45.9PS/L
45.7ft/sec 13.9m/sec
23.4mph 37.7kmh/1000rpm
36.6mpg 30.5mpgUS 7.7L/100km
Petrol 4-stroke piston
1721cc 105.0cu in
In-line 4 fuel injection
Compression ratio: 9.5:1
Bore: 81.0mm 3.2in
Stroke: 83.5mm 3.3in
Valve type/No: Overhead 8
Transmission: Manual
No. of forward speeds: 5
Wheels driven: Front
Springs F/R: Coil/Torsion bar
Brakes F/R: Disc/Drum
Steering: Rack & pinion PA
Wheelbase: 248.4cm 97.8in

Track F: 140.2cm 55.2in
Track R: 134.1cm 52.8in
Length: 407.9cm 160.6in
Width: 165.1cm 65.0in
Height: 138.4cm 54.5in
Kerb weight: 1017.0kg 2240.0lb
Fuel: 47.3L 10.4gal 12.5galUS

3892 Renault

Espace 2000 TSE
1985 France
113.0mph 181.8kmh
0-50mph 80.5kmh: 8.3secs
0-60mph 96.5kmh: 12.1secs
0-1/4 mile: 18.2secs
0-1km: 34.0secs
110.0bhp 82.0kW 111.5PS
@ 5500rpm
120.0lbft 162.6Nm @ 3000rpm
94.7bhp/ton 93.1bhp/tonne
55.1bhp/L 41.1kW/L 55.9PS/L
49.3ft/sec 15.0m/sec
22.8mph 36.7kmh/1000rpm
24.3mpg 20.2mpgUS 11.6L/100km
Petrol 4-stroke piston
1995cc 121.7cu in
In-line 4 1 Carburettor
Compression ratio: 9.2:1
Bore: 88.0mm 3.5in
Stroke: 82.0mm 3.2in
Valve type/No: Overhead 8
Transmission: Manual
No. of forward speeds: 5
Wheels driven: Front
Springs F/R: Coil/Coil
Brake system: PA
Brakes F/R: Disc/Drum
Steering: Rack & pinion PA
Wheelbase: 258.1cm 101.6in
Track F: 142.5cm 56.1in
Track R: 148.8cm 58.6in
Length: 424.9cm 167.3in
Width: 177.8cm 70.0in
Height: 166.1cm 65.4in
Ground clearance: 15.0cm 5.9in
Kerb weight: 1181.3kg 2602.0lb
Fuel: 63.7L 14.0gal 16.8galUS

3893 Renault

21 GTS
1986 France
114.0mph 183.4kmh
0-50mph 80.5kmh: 7.6secs
0-60mph 96.5kmh: 10.9secs
0-1/4 mile: 17.8secs
0-1km: 33.1secs
90.0bhp 67.1kW 91.2PS
@ 5500rpm
102.0lbft 138.2Nm @ 3500rpm
92.3bhp/ton 90.7bhp/tonne
52.3bhp/L 39.0kW/L 53.0PS/L
50.3ft/sec 15.3m/sec
23.9mph 38.5kmh/1000rpm
29.7mpg 24.7mpgUS 9.5L/100km
Petrol 4-stroke piston
1721cc 105.0cu in
In-line 4 1 Carburettor
Compression ratio: 10.0:1
Bore: 81.0mm 3.2in
Stroke: 83.5mm 3.3in
Valve type/No: Overhead 8
Transmission: Manual
No. of forward speeds: 5
Wheels driven: Front
Springs F/R: Coil/Torsion bar
Brake system: PA
Brakes F/R: Disc/Drum
Steering: Rack & pinion
Wheelbase: 265.9cm 104.7in
Track F: 143.0cm 56.3in
Track R: 140.2cm 55.2in
Length: 446.2cm 175.7in
Width: 171.4cm 67.5in
Height: 141.4cm 55.7in
Ground clearance: 15.3cm 6.0in
Kerb weight: 992.0kg 2185.0lb
Fuel: 66.0L 14.5gal 17.4galUS

3894 Renault

21 Savanna GTX
1986 France
122.0mph 196.3kmh
0-50mph 80.5kmh: 6.8secs
0-60mph 96.5kmh: 9.8secs
0-1/4 mile: 17.6secs
0-1km: 32.1secs
120.0bhp 89.5kW 121.7PS
@ 5500rpm
124.0lbft 168.0Nm @ 4500rpm
107.0bhp/ton 105.3bhp/tonne
60.1bhp/L 44.8kW/L 61.0PS/L
49.3ft/sec 15.0m/sec
22.8mph 36.7kmh/1000rpm
27.8mpg 23.1mpgUS 10.2L/100km
Petrol 4-stroke piston
1995cc 122.0cu in
In-line 4 fuel injection
Compression ratio: 10.0:1
Bore: 88.0mm 3.5in
Stroke: 82.0mm 3.2in
Valve type/No: Overhead 8
Transmission: Manual
No. of forward speeds: 5
Wheels driven: Front
Springs F/R: Coil/Torsion bar
Brake system: PA
Brakes F/R: Disc/Drum
Steering: Rack & pinion
Wheelbase: 280.9cm 110.6in
Track F: 142.9cm 56.3in
Track R: 140.6cm 55.4in
Length: 464.4cm 182.8in
Width: 171.5cm 67.5in
Height: 142.7cm 56.2in
Ground clearance: 15.3cm 6.0in
Kerb weight: 1140.0kg 2511.0lb
Fuel: 66.0L 14.5gal 17.4galUS

3895 Renault

5 GT Turbo
1986 France
126.0mph 202.7kmh
0-50mph 80.5kmh: 5.3secs
0-60mph 96.5kmh: 7.1secs
0-1/4 mile: 15.7secs
0-1km: 29.1secs
115.0bhp 85.8kW 116.6PS
@ 5750rpm
121.0lbft 164.0Nm @ 3000rpm
147.3bhp/ton 144.8bhp/tonne
82.3bhp/L 61.4kW/L 83.5PS/L
48.4ft/sec 14.8m/sec
21.7mph 34.9kmh/1000rpm
22.0mpg 18.3mpgUS 12.8L/100km
Petrol 4-stroke piston
1397cc 85.2cu in turbocharged
In-line 4 1 Carburettor
Compression ratio: 7.9:1
Bore: 76.0mm 3.0in
Stroke: 77.0mm 3.0in
Valve type/No: Overhead 8
Transmission: Manual
No. of forward speeds: 5
Wheels driven: Front
Springs F/R: Coil/Torsion bar
Brake system: PA
Brakes F/R: Disc/Disc
Steering: Rack & pinion
Wheelbase: 240.8cm 94.8in
Track F: 132.3cm 52.1in
Track R: 131.1cm 51.6in
Length: 358.9cm 141.3in
Width: 159.5cm 62.8in
Height: 136.7cm 53.8in
Ground clearance: 20.3cm 8.0in
Kerb weight: 794.0kg 1749.0lb
Fuel: 50.0L 11.0gal 13.2galUS

3896 Renault

5 GTL 5-door
1986 France
99.0mph 159.3kmh
0-50mph 80.5kmh: 9.6secs
0-60mph 96.5kmh: 14.8secs
0-1/4 mile: 19.5secs
0-1km: 37.1secs
60.0bhp 44.7kW 60.8PS
@ 5250rpm
77.0lbft 104.3Nm @ 2500rpm
79.5bhp/ton 78.2bhp/tonne
42.9bhp/L 32.0kW/L 43.5PS/L
44.2ft/sec 13.5m/sec
23.1mph 37.2kmh/1000rpm
35.5mpg 29.6mpgUS 8.0L/100km
Petrol 4-stroke piston
1397cc 85.0cu in
In-line 4 1 Carburettor
Compression ratio: 9.2:1
Bore: 76.0mm 3.0in
Stroke: 77.0mm 3.0in
Valve type/No: Overhead 8
Transmission: Manual
No. of forward speeds: 5
Wheels driven: Front
Springs F/R: Coil/Torsion bar
Brake system: PA
Brakes F/R: Disc/Drum
Steering: Rack & pinion
Wheelbase: 240.7cm 94.8in
Track F: 132.3cm 52.1in
Track R: 128.0cm 50.4in
Length: 359.1cm 141.4in
Width: 158.4cm 62.4in
Height: 139.7cm 55.0in
Ground clearance: 12.0cm 4.7in
Kerb weight: 767.0kg 1689.4lb
Fuel: 43.2L 9.5gal 11.4galUS

3897 Renault

9 Turbo
1986 France
116.0mph 186.6kmh
0-50mph 80.5kmh: 6.4secs
0-60mph 96.5kmh: 9.0secs
0-1/4 mile: 16.6secs
0-1km: 31.7secs
105.0bhp 78.3kW 106.5PS
@ 5500rpm
119.0lbft 161.2Nm @ 2500rpm
115.3bhp/ton 113.4bhp/tonne
75.2bhp/L 56.0kW/L 76.2PS/L
46.3ft/sec 14.1m/sec
21.3mph 34.3kmh/1000rpm
29.4mpg 24.5mpgUS 9.6L/100km
Petrol 4-stroke piston
1397cc 85.0cu in turbocharged
In-line 4 1 Carburettor
Compression ratio: 8.0:1
Bore: 76.0mm 3.0in
Stroke: 77.0mm 3.0in
Valve type/No: Overhead 8
Transmission: Manual
No. of forward speeds: 5
Wheels driven: Front
Springs F/R: Coil/Torsion bar
Brake system: PA
Brakes F/R: Disc/Drum
Steering: Rack & pinion
Wheelbase: 247.7cm 97.5in
Track F: 138.5cm 54.5in
Track R: 134.7cm 53.0in
Length: 406.3cm 160.0in
Width: 166.8cm 65.7in
Height: 140.5cm 55.3in
Ground clearance: 12.0cm 4.7in
Kerb weight: 926.0kg 2039.6lb
Fuel: 46.9L 10.3gal 12.4galUS

3898 Renault

Alliance 1.7L
1986 France
0-60mph 96.5kmh: 11.4secs
0-1/4 mile: 18.2secs
82.0bhp 61.1kW 83.1PS
@ 5000rpm
101.0lbft 136.9Nm @ 3250rpm
88.1bhp/ton 86.6bhp/tonne
47.6bhp/L 35.5kW/L 48.3PS/L
45.7ft/sec 13.9m/sec
24.0mph 38.6kmh/1000rpm
37.0mpg 30.8mpgUS 7.6L/100km
Petrol 4-stroke piston
1721cc 105.0cu in
In-line 4 fuel injection
Compression ratio: 9.5:1
Bore: 81.0mm 3.2in
Stroke: 83.5mm 3.3in
Valve type/No: Overhead 8
Transmission: Manual
No. of forward speeds: 5
Wheels driven: Front
Springs F/R: Torsion bar/Torsion bar
Brake system: PA
Brakes F/R: Disc/Drum
Steering: Rack & pinion PA
Wheelbase: 246.9cm 97.2in
Track F: 140.2cm 55.2in
Track R: 134.1cm 52.8in
Length: 416.1cm 163.8in
Width: 165.1cm 65.0in
Height: 138.4cm 54.5in
Kerb weight: 946.6kg 2085.0lb
Fuel: 47.3L 10.4gal 12.5galUS

3899 Renault

GTA V6 Turbo
1986 France
152.0mph 244.6kmh
0-50mph 80.5kmh: 4.8secs
0-60mph 96.5kmh: 6.3secs
0-1/4 mile: 15.3secs
0-1km: 27.4secs
200.0bhp 149.1kW 202.8PS
@ 5750rpm
214.0lbft 290.0Nm @ 2500rpm
171.3bhp/ton 168.5bhp/tonne
81.4bhp/L 60.7kW/L 82.5PS/L
39.6ft/sec 12.1m/sec
26.4mph 42.5kmh/1000rpm
20.5mpg 17.1mpgUS 13.8L/100km
Petrol 4-stroke piston
2458cc 150.0cu in turbocharged
Vee 6 fuel injection
Compression ratio: 8.6:1
Bore: 91.0mm 3.6in
Stroke: 63.0mm 2.5in
Valve type/No: Overhead 12
Transmission: Manual
No. of forward speeds: 5
Wheels driven: Rear
Springs F/R: Coil/Coil
Brake system: PA
Brakes F/R: Disc/Disc
Steering: Rack & pinion
Wheelbase: 233.9cm 92.1in
Track F: 149.3cm 58.8in
Track R: 146.2cm 57.6in
Length: 433.0cm 170.5in
Width: 175.5cm 69.1in
Height: 119.7cm 47.1in
Ground clearance: 14.0cm 5.5in
Kerb weight: 1187.0kg 2614.5lb
Fuel: 71.9L 15.8gal 19.0galUS

3900 Renault

11 Turbo
1987 France
123.0mph 197.9kmh
0-50mph 80.5kmh: 5.8secs
0-60mph 96.5kmh: 7.9secs
0-1/4 mile: 16.4secs
0-1km: 30.4secs
115.0bhp 85.8kW 116.6PS
@ 5750rpm
121.0lbft 164.0Nm @ 3000rpm
124.7bhp/ton 122.6bhp/tonne
82.3bhp/L 61.4kW/L 83.5PS/L
48.4ft/sec 14.8m/sec
20.3mph 32.7kmh/1000rpm
27.3mpg 22.7mpgUS 10.3L/100km
Petrol 4-stroke piston
1397cc 85.0cu in turbocharged
In-line 4 1 Carburettor
Compression ratio: 7.9:1
Bore: 76.0mm 3.0in
Stroke: 77.0mm 3.0in
Valve type/No: Overhead 8
Transmission: Manual
No. of forward speeds: 5
Wheels driven: Front
Springs F/R: Coil/Torsion bar
Brake system: PA
Brakes F/R: Disc/Disc
Steering: Rack & pinion
Wheelbase: 248.4cm 97.8in
Track F: 149.0cm 58.7in
Track R: 135.0cm 53.1in
Length: 397.3cm 156.4in
Width: 163.1cm 64.2in
Height: 141.0cm 55.5in
Ground clearance: 12.0cm 4.7in
Kerb weight: 938.0kg 2066.1lb
Fuel: 46.9L 10.3gal 12.4galUS

3901 Renault

5 GT Turbo
1987 France
122.0mph 196.3kmh
0-50mph 80.5kmh: 5.5secs
0-60mph 96.5kmh: 7.3secs
0-1/4 mile: 16.0secs
0-1km: 29.6secs
120.0bhp 89.5kW 121.7PS
@ 5750rpm
121.0lbft 164.0Nm @ 3750rpm
142.7bhp/ton 140.3bhp/tonne
85.9bhp/L 64.0kW/L 87.1PS/L
48.4ft/sec 14.8m/sec
21.9mph 35.2kmh/1000rpm
28.4mpg 23.6mpgUS 9.9L/100km
Petrol 4-stroke piston
1397cc 85.0cu in turbocharged
In-line 4 1 Carburettor
Compression ratio: 7.9:1
Bore: 76.0mm 3.0in
Stroke: 77.0mm 3.0in

Valve type/No: Overhead 8
Transmission: Manual
No. of forward speeds: 5
Wheels driven: Front
Springs F/R: Coil/Torsion bar
Brake system: PA
Brakes F/R: Disc/Disc
Steering: Rack & pinion
Wheelbase: 240.7cm 94.8in
Track F: 132.3cm 52.1in
Track R: 131.0cm 51.6in
Length: 358.9cm 141.3in
Width: 159.5cm 62.8in
Height: 136.6cm 53.8in
Ground clearance: 20.3cm 8.0in
Kerb weight: 855.0kg 1883.3lb
Fuel: 50.0L 11.0gal 13.2galUS

3902 Renault

5 GTX 3-DR
1987 France
112.0mph 180.2kmh
0-50mph 80.5kmh: 6.8secs
0-60mph 96.5kmh: 9.5secs
0-1/4 mile: 17.0secs
0-1km: 31.6secs
90.0bhp 67.1kW 91.2PS
@ 5500rpm
102.0lbft 138.2Nm @ 3500rpm
110.9bhp/ton 109.1bhp/tonne
52.3bhp/L 39.0kW/L 53.0PS/L
50.3ft/sec 15.3m/sec
21.8mph 35.1kmh/1000rpm
30.0mpg 25.0mpgUS 9.4L/100km
Petrol 4-stroke piston
1721cc 105.0cu in
In-line 4 1 Carburettor
Compression ratio: 10.0:1
Bore: 81.0mm 3.2in
Stroke: 83.5mm 3.3in
Valve type/No: Overhead 8
Transmission: Manual
No. of forward speeds: 5
Wheels driven: Front
Springs F/R: Coil/Torsion bar
Brake system: PA
Brakes F/R: Disc/Drum
Steering: Rack & pinion
Wheelbase: 240.7cm 94.8in
Track F: 132.3cm 52.1in
Track R: 131.0cm 51.6in
Length: 358.9cm 141.3in
Width: 159.5cm 62.8in
Height: 136.6cm 53.8in
Ground clearance: 20.3cm 8.0in
Kerb weight: 825.0kg 1817.2lb
Fuel: 43.2L 9.5gal 11.4galUS

3903 Renault

Alliance GTA
1987 France
110.0mph 177.0kmh
0-50mph 80.5kmh: 8.6secs
0-60mph 96.5kmh: 11.1secs
0-1/4 mile: 18.0secs
95.0bhp 70.8kW 96.3PS
@ 5250rpm
114.0lbft 154.5Nm @ 2750rpm
88.5bhp/ton 87.0bhp/tonne
48.3bhp/L 36.0kW/L 49.0PS/L
53.4ft/sec 16.3m/sec
30.6mpg 25.5mpgUS 9.2L/100km
Petrol 4-stroke piston
1965cc 119.9cu in
In-line 4 fuel injection
Compression ratio: 9.5:1
Bore: 82.0mm 3.2in
Stroke: 93.0mm 3.7in
Valve type/No: Overhead 8
Transmission: Manual
No. of forward speeds: 5
Wheels driven: Front
Springs F/R: Coil/Torsion bar
Brake system: PA
Brakes F/R: Disc/Drum
Steering: Rack & pinion PA
Wheelbase: 248.4cm 97.8in
Track F: 140.2cm 55.2in
Track R: 134.1cm 52.8in
Length: 416.1cm 163.8in
Width: 165.1cm 65.0in
Height: 134.9cm 53.1in
Kerb weight: 1091.9kg 2405.0lb
Fuel: 47.3L 10.4gal 12.5galUS

3904 Renault

21 Ti
1988 France
122.0mph 196.3kmh
0-50mph 80.5kmh: 7.3secs
0-60mph 96.5kmh: 10.3secs
0-1/4 mile: 17.7secs
0-1km: 32.3secs
120.0bhp 89.5kW 121.7PS
@ 5500rpm
121.0lbft 164.0Nm @ 4500rpm
110.4bhp/ton 108.6bhp/tonne
60.1bhp/L 44.8kW/L 61.0PS/L
55.3ft/sec 16.9m/sec
22.8mph 36.7kmh/1000rpm
25.7mpg 21.4mpgUS 11.0L/100km
Petrol 4-stroke piston
1995cc 122.0cu in
In-line 4 fuel injection
Compression ratio: 10.0:1
Bore: 88.0mm 3.5in
Stroke: 92.0mm 3.6in
Valve type/No: Overhead 8
Transmission: Manual
No. of forward speeds: 5
Wheels driven: Front
Springs F/R: Coil/Torsion bar
Brake system: PA
Brakes F/R: Disc/Drum
Steering: Rack & pinion PA
Wheelbase: 265.9cm 104.7in
Track F: 143.0cm 56.3in
Track R: 140.2cm 55.2in
Length: 446.2cm 175.7in
Width: 171.4cm 67.5in
Height: 141.4cm 55.7in
Ground clearance: 15.3cm 6.0in
Kerb weight: 1105.0kg 2433.9lb
Fuel: 66.0L 14.5gal 17.4galUS

3905 Renault

21 Turbo
1988 France
139.0mph 223.7kmh
0-50mph 80.5kmh: 5.8secs
0-60mph 96.5kmh: 7.9secs
0-1/4 mile: 15.5secs
0-1km: 28.1secs
175.0bhp 130.5kW 177.4PS
@ 5200rpm
199.3lbft 270.0Nm @ 3000rpm
145.2bhp/ton 142.7bhp/tonne
87.7bhp/L 65.4kW/L 88.9PS/L
46.7ft/sec 14.2m/sec
23.9mph 38.5kmh/1000rpm
18.3mpg 15.2mpgUS 15.4L/100km
Petrol 4-stroke piston
1995cc 122.0cu in turbocharged
In-line 4 fuel injection
Compression ratio: 8.0:1
Bore: 88.0mm 3.5in
Stroke: 82.0mm 3.2in
Valve type/No: Overhead 8
Transmission: Manual
No. of forward speeds: 5
Wheels driven: Front
Springs F/R: Coil/Coil
Brake system: PA ABS
Brakes F/R: Disc/Disc
Steering: Rack & pinion PA
Wheelbase: 259.8cm 102.3in
Track F: 145.3cm 57.2in
Track R: 140.5cm 55.3in
Length: 446.3cm 175.7in
Width: 169.4cm 66.7in
Height: 141.5cm 55.7in
Ground clearance: 15.2cm 6.0in
Kerb weight: 1226.0kg 2700.4lb
Fuel: 66.0L 14.5gal 17.4galUS

3906 Renault

GTA V6
1988 France
141.0mph 226.9kmh
0-50mph 80.5kmh: 5.6secs
0-60mph 96.5kmh: 7.5secs
0-1/4 mile: 16.0secs
0-1km: 29.4secs
160.0bhp 119.3kW 162.2PS
@ 5750rpm
163.1lbft 221.0Nm @ 3500rpm
141.9bhp/ton 139.5bhp/tonne
56.2bhp/L 41.9kW/L 56.9PS/L
45.8ft/sec 14.0m/sec
24.4mph 39.3kmh/1000rpm
19.1mpg 15.9mpgUS 14.8L/100km
Petrol 4-stroke piston
2849cc 174.0cu in
Vee 6 2 Carburettor
Compression ratio: 9.5:1
Bore: 91.0mm 3.6in
Stroke: 73.0mm 2.9in
Valve type/No: Overhead 12
Transmission: Manual
No. of forward speeds: 5
Wheels driven: Rear
Springs F/R: Coil/Coil
Brake system: PA
Brakes F/R: Disc/Disc
Steering: Rack & pinion
Wheelbase: 233.0cm 91.7in
Track F: 149.3cm 58.8in
Track R: 146.2cm 57.6in
Length: 433.0cm 170.5in
Width: 175.5cm 69.1in
Height: 119.7cm 47.1in
Ground clearance: 14.0cm 5.5in
Kerb weight: 1147.0kg 2526.4lb
Fuel: 71.9L 15.8gal 19.0galUS

3907 Renault

19 TSE
1989 France
108.0mph 173.8kmh
0-50mph 80.5kmh: 9.0secs
0-60mph 96.5kmh: 12.8secs
0-1/4 mile: 18.7secs
0-1km: 34.0secs
80.0bhp 59.7kW 81.1PS
@ 5750rpm
81.2lbft 110.0Nm @ 2750rpm
82.6bhp/ton 81.2bhp/tonne
57.5bhp/L 42.9kW/L 58.3PS/L
48.4ft/sec 14.8m/sec
19.9mph 32.0kmh/1000rpm
34.9mpg 29.1mpgUS 8.1L/100km
Petrol 4-stroke piston
1390cc 85.0cu in
In-line 4 1 Carburettor
Compression ratio: 9.5:1
Bore: 75.8mm 3.0in
Stroke: 77.0mm 3.0in
Valve type/No: Overhead 8
Transmission: Manual
No. of forward speeds: 5
Wheels driven: Front
Springs F/R: Coil/Torsion bar
Brake system: PA
Brakes F/R: Disc/Drum
Steering: Rack & pinion
Wheelbase: 254.5cm 100.2in
Track F: 141.8cm 55.8in
Track R: 141.7cm 55.8in
Length: 415.5cm 163.6in
Width: 167.6cm 66.0in
Height: 141.2cm 55.6in
Ground clearance: 12.0cm 4.7in
Kerb weight: 985.0kg 2169.6lb
Fuel: 55.1L 12.1gal 14.5galUS

3908 Renault

19 TXE
1989 France
112.0mph 180.2kmh
0-50mph 80.5kmh: 8.2secs
0-60mph 96.5kmh: 11.7secs
0-1/4 mile: 18.4secs
0-1km: 33.7secs
92.0bhp 68.6kW 93.3PS
@ 5750rpm
98.9lbft 134.0Nm @ 3000rpm
90.0bhp/ton 88.5bhp/tonne
53.5bhp/L 39.9kW/L 54.2PS/L
52.5ft/sec 16.0m/sec
21.3mph 34.3kmh/1000rpm
26.1mpg 21.7mpgUS 10.8L/100km
Petrol 4-stroke piston
1721cc 105.0cu in
In-line 4 1 Carburettor
Compression ratio: 9.5:1
Bore: 81.0mm 3.2in
Stroke: 83.5mm 3.3in
Valve type/No: Overhead 8
Transmission: Manual
No. of forward speeds: 5
Wheels driven: Front
Springs F/R: Coil/Torsion bar
Brake system: PA
Brakes F/R: Disc/Drum
Steering: Rack & pinion PA
Wheelbase: 254.5cm 100.2in
Track F: 141.8cm 55.8in
Track R: 141.7cm 55.8in
Length: 415.5cm 163.6in
Width: 167.6cm 66.0in
Height: 141.2cm 55.6in
Ground clearance: 12.0cm 4.7in
Kerb weight: 1040.0kg 2290.7lb
Fuel: 55.0L 12.1gal 14.5galUS

3909 Renault

21 GTS Hatchback
1989 France
112.0mph 180.2kmh
0-50mph 80.5kmh: 8.3secs
0-60mph 96.5kmh: 11.6secs
0-1/4 mile: 18.3secs
0-1km: 34.0secs
92.0bhp 68.6kW 93.3PS
@ 5750rpm
99.6lbft 135.0Nm @ 3000rpm
86.3bhp/ton 84.9bhp/tonne
53.5bhp/L 39.9kW/L 54.2PS/L
52.5ft/sec 16.0m/sec
23.1mph 37.2kmh/1000rpm
28.1mpg 23.4mpgUS 10.1L/100km
Petrol 4-stroke piston
1721cc 105.0cu in
In-line 4 1 Carburettor
Compression ratio: 9.5:1
Bore: 81.0mm 3.2in
Stroke: 83.5mm 3.3in
Valve type/No: Overhead 8
Transmission: Manual
No. of forward speeds: 5
Wheels driven: Front
Springs F/R: Coil/Torsion bar
Brake system: PA
Brakes F/R: Disc/Drum
Steering: Rack & pinion
Wheelbase: 265.9cm 104.7in
Track F: 143.5cm 56.5in
Track R: 139.9cm 55.1in
Length: 446.0cm 175.6in
Width: 172.4cm 67.9in
Height: 139.9cm 55.1in
Ground clearance: 17.9cm 7.0in
Kerb weight: 1084.0kg 2387.7lb
Fuel: 66.0L 14.5gal 17.4galUS

3910 Renault

25 TXi
1989 France
128.0mph 206.0kmh
0-50mph 80.5kmh: 7.4secs
0-60mph 96.5kmh: 10.0secs
0-1/4 mile: 17.3secs
0-1km: 31.8secs
140.0bhp 104.4kW 141.9PS
@ 6000rpm
129.9lbft 176.0Nm @ 4300rpm
103.6bhp/ton 101.9bhp/tonne
70.2bhp/L 52.3kW/L 71.1PS/L
53.8ft/sec 16.4m/sec
21.1mph 33.9kmh/1000rpm
22.5mpg 18.7mpgUS 12.6L/100km
Petrol 4-stroke piston
1995cc 122.0cu in
In-line 4 fuel injection
Compression ratio: 9.3:1
Bore: 88.0mm 3.5in
Stroke: 82.0mm 3.2in
Valve type/No: Overhead 12
Transmission: Manual
No. of forward speeds: 5
Wheels driven: Front
Springs F/R: Coil/Coil
Brake system: PA
Brakes F/R: Disc/Disc
Steering: Rack & pinion PA
Wheelbase: 272.3cm 107.2in
Track F: 150.2cm 59.1in
Track R: 147.9cm 58.2in
Length: 471.3cm 185.6in
Width: 180.6cm 71.1in
Height: 141.5cm 55.7in
Ground clearance: 12.0cm 4.7in
Kerb weight: 1374.0kg 3026.4lb
Fuel: 71.9L 15.8gal 19.0galUS

3911 Renault

5 Campus
1989 France
92.0mph 148.0kmh
0-50mph 80.5kmh: 10.8secs
0-60mph 96.5kmh: 16.3secs
0-1/4 mile: 19.5secs
0-1km: 38.0secs
47.0bhp 35.0kW 47.6PS
@ 5250rpm

58.3lbft 79.0Nm @ 2500rpm
63.8bhp/ton 62.7bhp/tonne
42.4bhp/L 31.6kW/L 43.0PS/L
41.3ft/sec 12.6m/sec
18.3mph 29.4kmh/1000rpm
41.0mpg 34.1mpgUS 6.9L/100km
Petrol 4-stroke piston
1108cc 68.0cu in
In-line 4 1 Carburettor
Compression ratio: 9.5:1
Bore: 70.0mm 2.8in
Stroke: 72.0mm 2.8in
Valve type/No: Overhead 8
Transmission: Manual
No. of forward speeds: 4
Wheels driven: Front
Springs F/R: Coil/Coil
Brake system: PA
Brakes F/R: Disc/Drum
Steering: Rack & pinion
Wheelbase: 246.9cm 97.2in
Track F: 132.3cm 52.1in
Track R: 129.0cm 50.8in
Length: 365.0cm 143.7in
Width: 159.0cm 62.6in
Height: 139.0cm 54.7in
Ground clearance: 12.0cm 4.7in
Kerb weight: 749.0kg 1649.8lb
Fuel: 43.2L 9.5gal 11.4galUS

3912 Renault

Espace TXE
1989 France
109.0mph 175.4kmh
0-50mph 80.5kmh: 7.7secs
0-60mph 96.5kmh: 10.8secs
0-1/4 mile: 18.0secs
0-1km: 33.5secs
120.0bhp 89.5kW 121.7PS
@ 5500rpm
124.0lbft 168.0Nm @ 4500rpm
97.8bhp/ton 96.1bhp/tonne
60.1bhp/L 44.8kW/L 61.0PS/L
49.3ft/sec 15.0m/sec
21.2mph 34.1kmh/1000rpm
26.7mpg 22.2mpgUS 10.6L/100km
Petrol 4-stroke piston
1995cc 122.0cu in
In-line 4 fuel injection
Compression ratio: 10.0:1
Bore: 88.0mm 3.5in
Stroke: 82.0mm 3.2in
Valve type/No: Overhead 8
Transmission: Manual
No. of forward speeds: 5
Wheels driven: Front
Springs F/R: Coil/Torsion bar
Brake system: PA
Brakes F/R: Disc/Disc
Steering: Rack & pinion PA
Wheelbase: 258.0cm 101.6in
Track F: 146.7cm 57.8in
Track R: 148.9cm 58.6in
Length: 436.5cm 171.9in
Width: 177.7cm 70.0in
Height: 166.0cm 65.4in
Ground clearance: 15.0cm 5.9in
Kerb weight: 1248.0kg 2748.9lb
Fuel: 63.2L 13.9gal 16.7galUS

3913 Renault

19 TXE Chamade
1990 France
111.0mph 178.6kmh
0-50mph 80.5kmh: 8.2secs
0-60mph 96.5kmh: 11.4secs
0-1/4 mile: 18.1secs
0-1km: 30.3secs
92.0bhp 68.6kW 93.3PS
@ 5750rpm
98.9lbft 134.0Nm @ 3000rpm
91.7bhp/ton 90.2bhp/tonne
53.5bhp/L 39.9kW/L 54.2PS/L
52.9ft/sec 16.1m/sec
21.3mph 34.3kmh/1000rpm
30.9mpg 25.7mpgUS 9.1L/100km
Petrol 4-stroke piston
1721cc 105.0cu in
In-line 4 1 Carburettor
Compression ratio: 9.5:1
Bore: 81.0mm 3.2in
Stroke: 84.0mm 3.3in
Valve type/No: Overhead 8
Transmission: Manual
No. of forward speeds: 5
Wheels driven: Front
Springs F/R: Coil/Torsion bar
Brake system: PA
Brakes F/R: Disc/Drum
Steering: Rack & pinion
Wheelbase: 254.0cm 100.0in
Track F: 141.8cm 55.8in
Track R: 140.6cm 55.4in
Length: 426.2cm 167.8in
Width: 168.4cm 66.3in
Height: 141.2cm 55.6in
Ground clearance: 12.0cm 4.7in
Kerb weight: 1020.0kg 2246.7lb
Fuel: 55.1L 12.1gal 14.5galUS

3914 Renault

21 Turbo Quadra
1990 France
140.0mph 225.3kmh
0-50mph 80.5kmh: 5.5secs
0-60mph 96.5kmh: 7.8secs
0-1/4 mile: 15.4secs
0-1km: 28.9secs
175.0bhp 130.5kW 177.4PS
@ 5200rpm
199.0lbft 269.6Nm @ 3000rpm
124.0bhp/ton 122.0bhp/tonne
87.7bhp/L 65.4kW/L 88.9PS/L
46.7ft/sec 14.2m/sec
23.9mph 38.5kmh/1000rpm
22.1mpg 18.4mpgUS 12.8L/100km
Petrol 4-stroke piston
1995cc 122.0cu in turbocharged
In-line 4 fuel injection
Compression ratio: 8.0:1
Bore: 88.0mm 3.5in
Stroke: 82.0mm 3.2in
Valve type/No: Overhead 8
Transmission: Manual
No. of forward speeds: 5
Wheels driven: Front
Springs F/R: Coil/Coil
Brake system: PA ABS
Brakes F/R: Disc/Disc
Steering: Rack & pinion PA
Wheelbase: 259.8cm 102.3in
Track F: 145.3cm 57.2in
Track R: 140.0cm 55.1in
Length: 452.6cm 178.2in
Width: 176.0cm 69.3in
Height: 140.0cm 55.1in
Ground clearance: 15.2cm 6.0in
Kerb weight: 1434.6kg 3160.0lb
Fuel: 61.9L 13.6gal 16.3galUS

3915 Renault

21 TXi
1990 France
126.0mph 202.7kmh
0-50mph 80.5kmh: 6.9secs
0-60mph 96.5kmh: 9.8secs
0-1/4 mile: 17.1secs
0-1km: 31.5secs
140.0bhp 104.4kW 141.9PS
@ 6000rpm
129.9lbft 176.0Nm @ 4300rpm
114.8bhp/ton 112.9bhp/tonne
70.2bhp/L 52.3kW/L 71.1PS/L
53.8ft/sec 16.4m/sec
21.1mph 33.9kmh/1000rpm
25.5mpg 21.2mpgUS 11.1L/100km
Petrol 4-stroke piston
1995cc 122.0cu in
In-line 4 fuel injection
Compression ratio: 9.3:1
Bore: 88.0mm 3.5in
Stroke: 82.0mm 3.2in
Valve type/No: Overhead 12
Transmission: Manual
No. of forward speeds: 5
Wheels driven: Front
Springs F/R: Coil/Coil
Brake system: PA ABS
Brakes F/R: Disc/Disc
Steering: Rack & pinion PA
Wheelbase: 265.9cm 104.7in
Track F: 143.5cm 56.5in
Track R: 139.9cm 55.1in
Length: 446.0cm 175.6in
Width: 172.4cm 67.9in
Height: 139.9cm 55.1in
Ground clearance: 17.9cm 7.0in
Kerb weight: 1240.0kg 2731.3lb
Fuel: 66.0L 14.5gal 17.4galUS

3916 Renault

25 V6 2.9 Auto
1990 France
129.0mph 207.6kmh
0-50mph 80.5kmh: 7.2secs
0-60mph 96.5kmh: 9.5secs
0-1/4 mile: 17.4secs
0-1km: 31.4secs
160.0bhp 119.3kW 162.2PS
@ 5400rpm
169.7lbft 230.0Nm @ 2500rpm
115.8bhp/ton 113.9bhp/tonne
56.2bhp/L 41.9kW/L 56.9PS/L
43.0ft/sec 13.1m/sec
21.2mph 34.1kmh/1000rpm
21.2mpg 17.7mpgUS 13.3L/100km
Petrol 4-stroke piston
2849cc 174.0cu in
Vee 6 fuel injection
Compression ratio: 9.5:1
Bore: 91.0mm 3.6in
Stroke: 73.0mm 2.9in
Valve type/No: Overhead 24
Transmission: Automatic
No. of forward speeds: 4
Wheels driven: Front
Springs F/R: Coil/Coil
Brake system: PA
Brakes F/R: Disc/Disc
Steering: Rack & pinion PA
Wheelbase: 272.3cm 107.2in
Track F: 150.2cm 59.1in
Track R: 147.9cm 58.2in
Length: 471.3cm 185.6in
Width: 180.6cm 71.1in
Height: 141.5cm 55.7in
Ground clearance: 12.0cm 4.7in
Kerb weight: 1405.0kg 3094.7lb
Fuel: 71.9L 15.8gal 19.0galUS

3917 Renault

19 16v
1991 France
130.0mph 209.2kmh
0-50mph 80.5kmh: 7.1secs
0-60mph 96.5kmh: 9.5secs
0-1/4 mile: 17.3secs
0-1km: 31.4secs
137.0bhp 102.2kW 138.9PS
@ 6500rpm
118.8lbft 161.0Nm @ 4250rpm
123.3bhp/ton 121.2bhp/tonne
77.7bhp/L 57.9kW/L 78.7PS/L
59.8ft/sec 18.2m/sec
20.3mph 32.7kmh/1000rpm
28.2mpg 23.5mpgUS 10.0L/100km
Petrol 4-stroke piston
1764cc 108.0cu in
In-line 4 fuel injection
Compression ratio: 10.0:1
Bore: 82.0mm 3.2in
Stroke: 84.0mm 3.3in
Valve type/No: Overhead 16
Transmission: Manual
No. of forward speeds: 5
Wheels driven: Front
Springs F/R: Coil/Torsion bar
Brake system: PA ABS
Brakes F/R: Disc/Disc
Steering: Rack & pinion PA
Wheelbase: 254.0cm 100.0in
Track F: 141.7cm 55.8in
Track R: 141.5cm 55.7in
Length: 415.3cm 163.5in
Width: 167.4cm 65.9in
Height: 141.5cm 55.7in
Ground clearance: 11.9cm 4.7in
Kerb weight: 1130.0kg 2489.0lb
Fuel: 55.1L 12.1gal 14.5galUS

3918 Renault

Alpine A610 Turbo
1991 France
165.0mph 265.5kmh
0-60mph 96.5kmh: 5.7secs
250.0bhp 186.4kW 253.5PS
@ 5750rpm
258.0lbft 349.6Nm @ 2900rpm
179.2bhp/ton 176.2bhp/tonne
84.0bhp/L 62.7kW/L 85.2PS/L
45.8ft/sec 14.0m/sec
Petrol 4-stroke piston
2975cc 181.5cu in turbocharged
Vee 6 fuel injection
Compression ratio: 7.6:1
Bore: 91.0mm 3.6in
Stroke: 73.0mm 2.9in
Valve type/No: Overhead 12
Transmission: Manual
No. of forward speeds: 5
Wheels driven: Rear
Brake system: PA ABS
Brakes F/R: Disc/Disc
Steering: Rack & pinion
Wheelbase: 233.9cm 92.1in
Length: 444.5cm 175.0in
Width: 175.5cm 69.1in
Height: 119.6cm 47.1in
Kerb weight: 1418.7kg 3125.0lb
Fuel: 75.7L 16.6gal 20.0galUS

3919 Renault

Clio 1.2 RN
1991 France
100.1mph 161.0kmh
0-50mph 80.5kmh: 9.8secs
0-60mph 96.5kmh: 14.0secs
0-1/4 mile: 19.7secs
0-1km: 36.5secs
60.0bhp 44.7kW 60.8PS
@ 6000rpm
62.7lbft 85.0Nm @ 3500rpm
72.0bhp/ton 70.8bhp/tonne
51.2bhp/L 38.2kW/L 51.9PS/L
42.7ft/sec 13.0m/sec
18.8mph 30.2kmh/1000rpm
36.8mpg 30.6mpgUS 7.7L/100km
Petrol 4-stroke piston
1171cc 71.0cu in
In-line 4 fuel injection
Compression ratio: 9.2:1
Bore: 75.8mm 3.0in
Stroke: 64.9mm 2.6in
Valve type/No: Overhead 8
Transmission: Manual
No. of forward speeds: 5
Wheels driven: Front
Springs F/R: Coil/Torsion bar
Brakes F/R: Disc/Drum
Steering: Rack & pinion
Wheelbase: 247.2cm 97.3in
Track F: 135.8cm 53.5in
Track R: 132.4cm 52.1in
Length: 370.9cm 146.0in
Width: 162.5cm 64.0in
Height: 139.5cm 54.9in
Kerb weight: 847.0kg 1865.6lb
Fuel: 43.0L 9.4gal 11.4galUS

3920 Renault

Clio 1.4RT
1991 France
107.0mph 172.2kmh
0-50mph 80.5kmh: 8.2secs
0-60mph 96.5kmh: 12.0secs
0-1/4 mile: 18.7secs
0-1km: 34.5secs
80.0bhp 59.7kW 81.1PS
@ 5750rpm
79.0lbft 107.0Nm @ 3500rpm
91.9bhp/ton 90.4bhp/tonne
57.5bhp/L 42.9kW/L 58.3PS/L
48.4ft/sec 14.8m/sec
22.0mph 35.4kmh/1000rpm
38.3mpg 31.9mpgUS 7.4L/100km
Petrol 4-stroke piston
1390cc 85.0cu in
In-line 4 fuel injection
Compression ratio: 9.5:1
Bore: 76.0mm 3.0in
Stroke: 77.0mm 3.0in
Valve type/No: Overhead 8
Transmission: Manual
No. of forward speeds: 5
Wheels driven: Front
Springs F/R: Coil/Coil
Brake system: PA
Brakes F/R: Disc/Drum
Steering: Rack & pinion PA
Wheelbase: 247.1cm 97.3in
Track F: 135.6cm 53.4in
Track R: 132.3cm 52.1in
Length: 370.8cm 146.0in
Width: 187.7cm 73.9in
Height: 139.4cm 54.9in
Kerb weight: 885.0kg 1949.3lb
Fuel: 43.2L 9.5gal 11.4galUS

3921 Renault

Espace V6
1991 France
118.0mph 189.9kmh
0-50mph 80.5kmh: 6.6secs
0-60mph 96.5kmh: 9.4secs
0-1/4 mile: 17.2secs
0-1km: 31.7secs

153.0bhp 114.1kW 155.1PS
@ 5400rpm
166.1lbft 225.0Nm @ 2500rpm
105.8bhp/ton 104.1bhp/tonne
53.7bhp/L 40.0kW/L 54.4PS/L
43.0ft/sec 13.1m/sec
22.6mph 36.4kmh/1000rpm
19.9mpg 16.6mpgUS 14.2L/100km
Petrol 4-stroke piston
2849cc 174.0cu in
Vee 6 fuel injection
Compression ratio: 9.5:1
Bore: 91.0mm 3.6in
Stroke: 73.0mm 2.9in
Valve type/No: Overhead 12
Transmission: Manual
No. of forward speeds: 5
Wheels driven: Front
Springs F/R: Coil/Torsion bar
Brake system: PA ABS
Brakes F/R: Disc/Disc
Steering: Rack & pinion PA
Wheelbase: 258.0cm 101.6in
Track F: 151.7cm 59.7in
Track R: 150.8cm 59.4in
Length: 442.9cm 174.4in
Width: 179.5cm 70.7in
Height: 180.5cm 71.1in
Ground clearance: 15.0cm 5.9in
Kerb weight: 1470.0kg 3237.9lb
Fuel: 77.0L 16.9gal 20.3galUS

3922 Renault

19 16v Cabriolet
1992 France
129.0mph 207.6kmh
0-50mph 80.5kmh: 6.6secs
0-60mph 96.5kmh: 8.8secs
0-1/4 mile: 16.9secs
0-1km: 30.8secs
137.0bhp 102.2kW 138.9PS
@ 6500rpm
119.0lbft 161.2Nm @ 4250rpm
118.1bhp/ton 116.1bhp/tonne
77.7bhp/L 57.9kW/L 78.7PS/L
59.8ft/sec 18.2m/sec
20.3mph 32.7kmh/1000rpm
24.9mpg 20.7mpgUS 11.3L/100km
Petrol 4-stroke piston
1764cc 107.6cu in
In-line 4 fuel injection
Compression ratio: 10.0:1
Bore: 82.0mm 3.2in
Stroke: 84.0mm 3.3in
Valve type/No: Overhead 16
Transmission: Manual
No. of forward speeds: 5
Wheels driven: Front
Springs F/R: Coil/Torsion bar
Brake system: PA
Brakes F/R: Disc/Disc
Steering: Rack & pinion
Wheelbase: 254.0cm 100.0in
Track F: 142.7cm 56.2in
Track R: 140.5cm 55.3in
Length: 415.0cm 163.4in
Width: 168.1cm 66.2in
Height: 136.4cm 53.7in
Ground clearance: 11.9cm 4.7in
Kerb weight: 1179.9kg 2599.0lb
Fuel: 55.1L 12.1gal 14.5galUS

3923 Renault

Cleo 16v
1992 France
126.8mph 204.0kmh
0-50mph 80.5kmh: 6.3secs
0-60mph 96.5kmh: 8.6secs
0-1/4 mile: 16.7secs
0-1km: 30.4secs
137.0bhp 102.2kW 138.9PS
@ 6500rpm
118.8lbft 161.0Nm @ 4250rpm
136.6bhp/ton 134.3bhp/tonne
77.7bhp/L 57.9kW/L 78.7PS/L
59.4ft/sec 18.1m/sec
19.4mph 31.2kmh/1000rpm
26.0mpg 21.6mpgUS 10.9L/100km
Petrol 4-stroke piston
1764cc 108.0cu in
In-line 4 fuel injection
Compression ratio: 10.0:1
Bore: 82.0mm 3.2in
Stroke: 83.5mm 3.3in
Valve type/No: Overhead 16
Transmission: Manual
No. of forward speeds: 5
Wheels driven: Front
Springs F/R: Coil/Torsion bar
Brake system: PA ABS
Brakes F/R: Disc/Disc
Steering: Rack & pinion PA
Wheelbase: 247.2cm 97.3in
Track F: 135.8cm 53.5in
Track R: 132.4cm 52.1in
Length: 370.9cm 146.0in
Width: 162.5cm 64.0in
Height: 139.5cm 54.9in
Kerb weight: 1020.0kg 2246.7lb
Fuel: 50.0L 11.0gal 13.2galUS

3924 Riley

12 Mentone Saloon
1934 UK
67.1mph 108.0kmh
0-50mph 80.5kmh: 21.4secs
23.0mpg 19.2mpgUS 12.3L/100km
Petrol 4-stroke piston
1458cc 89.0cu in
In-line 6 2 Carburettor
Compression ratio: 7.0:1
Bore: 57.0mm 2.2in
Stroke: 95.2mm 3.8in
Valve type/No: Overhead 12
Transmission: Manual
No. of forward speeds: 4
Wheels driven: Rear
Brakes F/R: Drum/Drum
Kerb weight: 1182.2kg 2604.0lb
Fuel: 52.3L 11.5gal 13.8galUS

3925 Riley

1.5 Kestrel Special
1935 UK
81.8mph 131.6kmh
0-50mph 80.5kmh: 14.2secs
0-60mph 96.5kmh: 21.8secs
25.0mpg 20.8mpgUS 11.3L/100km
Petrol 4-stroke piston
1495cc 91.2cu in
In-line 4
Bore: 69.0mm 2.7in
Stroke: 100.0mm 3.9in
Valve type/No: Overhead 8
Transmission: Manual
No. of forward speeds: 4
Wheels driven: Rear
Brakes F/R: Drum/Drum
Kerb weight: 1194.9kg 2632.0lb
Fuel: 34.1L 7.5gal 9.0galUS

3926 Riley

1.5 Falcon Saloon
1936 UK
73.1mph 117.6kmh
0-50mph 80.5kmh: 23.1secs
27.0mpg 22.5mpgUS 10.5L/100km
Petrol 4-stroke piston
1496cc 91.3cu in
In-line 4
Bore: 69.0mm 2.7in
Stroke: 100.0mm 3.9in
Valve type/No: Overhead 8
Transmission: Manual
No. of forward speeds: 4
Wheels driven: Rear
Brakes F/R: Drum/Drum
Kerb weight: 1276.2kg 2811.0lb
Fuel: 45.5L 10.0gal 12.0galUS

3927 Riley

8/90 Adelphi Saloon
1937 UK
81.8mph 131.6kmh
0-50mph 80.5kmh: 15.7secs
0-60mph 96.5kmh: 23.8secs
17.0mpg 14.2mpgUS 16.6L/100km
Petrol 4-stroke piston
2178cc 132.9cu in
In-line 8
Bore: 60.3mm 2.4in
Stroke: 95.2mm 3.8in
Valve type/No: Overhead 16
Transmission: Pre-selector
No. of forward speeds: 4
Wheels driven: Rear
Brakes F/R: Drum/Drum
Kerb weight: 1592.2kg 3507.0lb
Fuel: 52.3L 11.5gal 13.8galUS

3928 Riley

9 Monaco
1937 UK
63.8mph 102.7kmh
0-50mph 80.5kmh: 32.6secs
29.0bhp 21.6kW 29.4PS
@ 4500rpm
25.7bhp/ton 25.3bhp/tonne
26.6bhp/L 19.9kW/L 27.0PS/L
46.9ft/sec 14.3m/sec
26.0mpg 21.6mpgUS 10.9L/100km
Petrol 4-stroke piston
1089cc 66.4cu in
In-line 4 1 Carburettor
Compression ratio: 5.5:1
Bore: 60.3mm 2.4in
Stroke: 95.2mm 3.8in
Valve type/No: Overhead 8
Transmission: Manual
No. of forward speeds: 4
Wheels driven: Rear
Brakes F/R: Drum/Drum
Kerb weight: 1146.8kg 2526.0lb
Fuel: 43.2L 9.5gal 11.4galUS

3929 Riley

Kestrel Sprite
1937 UK
78.9mph 127.0kmh
0-50mph 80.5kmh: 17.4secs
0-60mph 96.5kmh: 29.4secs
51.0bhp 38.0kW 51.7PS
@ 4800rpm
40.0bhp/ton 39.3bhp/tonne
34.1bhp/L 25.4kW/L 34.6PS/L
52.5ft/sec 16.0m/sec
20.0mpg 16.7mpgUS 14.1L/100km
Petrol 4-stroke piston
1496cc 91.3cu in
In-line 4 1 Carburettor
Bore: 69.0mm 2.7in
Stroke: 100.0mm 3.9in
Valve type/No: Overhead 8
Transmission: Manual
No. of forward speeds: 4
Wheels driven: Rear
Brakes F/R: Drum/Drum
Kerb weight: 1296.6kg 2856.0lb
Fuel: 52.3L 11.5gal 13.8galUS

3930 Riley

Sprite
1937 UK
86.5mph 139.2kmh
0-50mph 80.5kmh: 13.1secs
0-60mph 96.5kmh: 18.8secs
61.0bhp 45.5kW 61.8PS
@ 5500rpm
61.8bhp/ton 60.8bhp/tonne
40.8bhp/L 30.4kW/L 41.3PS/L
60.2ft/sec 18.3m/sec
21.0mpg 17.5mpgUS 13.5L/100km
Petrol 4-stroke piston
1496cc 91.3cu in
In-line 4 2 Carburettor
Bore: 69.0mm 2.7in
Stroke: 100.0mm 3.9in
Valve type/No: Overhead 8
Transmission: Manual
No. of forward speeds: 4
Wheels driven: Rear
Brakes F/R: Drum/Drum
Kerb weight: 1003.8kg 2211.0lb
Fuel: 68.2L 15.0gal 18.0galUS

3931 Riley

16 2.5
1938 UK
84.1mph 135.3kmh
0-50mph 80.5kmh: 13.1secs
0-60mph 96.5kmh: 18.8secs
82.0bhp 61.1kW 83.1PS
@ 4300rpm
53.1bhp/ton 52.2bhp/tonne
33.6bhp/L 25.0kW/L 34.0PS/L
56.4ft/sec 17.2m/sec
18.0mpg 15.0mpgUS 15.7L/100km
Petrol 4-stroke piston
2443cc 149.0cu in
In-line 4 1 Carburettor
Bore: 80.5mm 3.2in
Stroke: 120.0mm 4.7in
Valve type/No: Overhead 8
Transmission: Manual
No. of forward speeds: 3
Wheels driven: Rear
Brakes F/R: Drum/Drum
Kerb weight: 1571.3kg 3461.0lb
Fuel: 52.3L 11.5gal 13.8galUS

3932 Riley

1.5
1947 UK
81.0mph 130.3kmh
0-50mph 80.5kmh: 19.0secs
0-60mph 96.5kmh: 31.2secs
55.0bhp 41.0kW 55.8PS
@ 4500rpm
45.4bhp/ton 44.6bhp/tonne
36.8bhp/L 27.4kW/L 37.3PS/L
49.2ft/sec 15.0m/sec
25.0mpg 20.8mpgUS 11.3L/100km
Petrol 4-stroke piston
1496cc 91.3cu in
In-line 4
Compression ratio: 6.7:1
Bore: 69.0mm 2.7in
Stroke: 100.0mm 3.9in
Valve type/No: Overhead 8
Transmission: Manual
No. of forward speeds: 4
Wheels driven: Rear
Brakes F/R: Drum/Drum
Wheelbase: 285.8cm 112.5in
Track F: 132.6cm 52.2in
Track R: 132.6cm 52.2in
Length: 454.7cm 179.0in
Width: 161.3cm 63.5in
Height: 149.9cm 59.0in
Ground clearance: 19.1cm 7.5in
Kerb weight: 1233.1kg 2716.0lb
Fuel: 56.9L 12.5gal 15.0galUS

3933 Riley

2.5 Saloon
1947 UK
90.0mph 144.8kmh
0-50mph 80.5kmh: 13.3secs
0-60mph 96.5kmh: 18.8secs
90.0bhp 67.1kW 91.2PS
@ 4300rpm
62.1bhp/ton 61.0bhp/tonne
36.8bhp/L 27.5kW/L 37.3PS/L
56.4ft/sec 17.2m/sec
20.0mpg 16.7mpgUS 14.1L/100km
Petrol 4-stroke piston
2443cc 149.0cu in
In-line 4
Compression ratio: 6.8:1
Bore: 80.5mm 3.2in
Stroke: 120.0mm 4.7in
Valve type/No: Overhead 8
Transmission: Manual
No. of forward speeds: 4
Wheels driven: Rear
Brakes F/R: Drum/Drum
Wheelbase: 302.3cm 119.0in
Track F: 132.6cm 52.2in
Track R: 132.6cm 52.2in
Length: 472.4cm 186.0in
Width: 160.0cm 63.0in
Height: 149.9cm 59.0in
Ground clearance: 17.5cm 6.9in
Kerb weight: 1474.6kg 3248.0lb
Fuel: 56.9L 12.5gal 15.0galUS

3934 Riley

2.5 Sports
1948 UK
90.0mph 144.8kmh
0-50mph 80.5kmh: 14.0secs
0-60mph 96.5kmh: 19.0secs
100.0bhp 74.6kW 101.4PS
@ 4500rpm
72.7bhp/ton 71.5bhp/tonne
40.9bhp/L 30.5kW/L 41.5PS/L
59.0ft/sec 18.0m/sec
20.0mpg 16.7mpgUS 14.1L/100km
Petrol 4-stroke piston
2443cc 149.0cu in
In-line 4
Compression ratio: 6.8:1
Bore: 80.5mm 3.2in
Stroke: 120.0mm 4.7in
Valve type/No: Overhead 8
Transmission: Manual
No. of forward speeds: 4
Wheels driven: Rear
Brakes F/R: Drum/Drum
Wheelbase: 302.3cm 119.0in
Track F: 132.6cm 52.2in

Track R: 132.6cm 52.2in
Length: 472.4cm 186.0in
Width: 167.6cm 66.0in
Height: 139.7cm 55.0in
Ground clearance: 17.8cm 7.0in
Kerb weight: 1398.3kg 3080.0lb
Fuel: 91.0L 20.0gal 24.0galUS

3935 Riley

2.5 Saloon
1949 UK
92.0mph 148.0kmh
0-50mph 80.5kmh: 13.0secs
0-60mph 96.5kmh: 18.4secs
100.0bhp 74.6kW 101.4PS
@ 4400rpm
70.0bhp/ton 68.8bhp/tonne
40.9bhp/L 30.5kW/L 41.5PS/L
57.7ft/sec 17.6m/sec
18.0mpg 15.0mpgUS 15.7L/100km
Petrol 4-stroke piston
2443cc 149.0cu in
In-line 4
Compression ratio: 6.9:1
Bore: 80.5mm 3.2in
Stroke: 120.0mm 4.7in
Valve type/No: Overhead 8
Transmission: Manual
No. of forward speeds: 4
Wheels driven: Rear
Brakes F/R: Drum/Drum
Wheelbase: 302.3cm 119.0in
Track F: 132.6cm 52.2in
Track R: 132.6cm 52.2in
Length: 472.4cm 186.0in
Width: 161.3cm 63.5in
Height: 151.1cm 59.5in
Ground clearance: 17.8cm 7.0in
Kerb weight: 1452.3kg 3199.0lb
Fuel: 56.9L 12.5gal 15.0galUS

3936 Riley

2.5
1952 UK
94.5mph 152.1kmh
0-1/4 mile: 19.6secs
100.0bhp 74.6kW 101.4PS
@ 4500rpm
69.6bhp/ton 68.4bhp/tonne
40.9bhp/L 30.5kW/L 41.5PS/L
59.0ft/sec 18.0m/sec
Petrol 4-stroke piston
2443cc 149.0cu in
In-line 4 2 Carburettor
Compression ratio: 6.8:1
Bore: 80.5mm 3.2in
Stroke: 120.0mm 4.7in
Valve type/No: Overhead 8
Transmission: Manual
No. of forward speeds: 4
Wheels driven: Rear
Springs F/R: /Leaf
Brakes F/R: Drum/Drum
Wheelbase: 302.3cm 119.0in
Track F: 133.4cm 52.5in
Track R: 133.4cm 52.5in
Length: 472.4cm 186.0in
Width: 161.3cm 63.5in
Height: 151.1cm 59.5in
Ground clearance: 17.8cm 7.0in
Kerb weight: 1461.9kg 3220.0lb

3937 Riley

1.5
1953 UK
75.5mph 121.5kmh
0-50mph 80.5kmh: 15.9secs
0-60mph 96.5kmh: 25.1secs
0-1/4 mile: 22.8secs
54.0bhp 40.3kW 54.7PS
@ 4500rpm
76.0lbft 103.0Nm @ 2500rpm
42.1bhp/ton 41.4bhp/tonne
36.1bhp/L 26.9kW/L 36.6PS/L
49.2ft/sec 15.0m/sec
15.2mph 24.5kmh/1000rpm
24.0mpg 20.0mpgUS 11.8L/100km
Petrol 4-stroke piston
1496cc 91.3cu in
In-line 4
Compression ratio: 6.8:1
Bore: 69.0mm 2.7in
Stroke: 100.0mm 3.9in
Valve type/No: Overhead 8
Transmission: Manual
No. of forward speeds: 4
Wheels driven: Rear
Springs F/R: Torsion bar/Leaf
Brakes F/R: Drum/Drum
Wheelbase: 285.8cm 112.5in
Track F: 132.6cm 52.2in
Track R: 132.6cm 52.2in
Length: 454.7cm 179.0in
Width: 161.3cm 63.5in
Height: 153.7cm 60.5in
Ground clearance: 19.1cm 7.5in
Kerb weight: 1303.0kg 2870.0lb
Fuel: 56.9L 12.5gal 15.0galUS

3938 Riley

2.5
1953 UK
94.0mph 151.2kmh
0-50mph 80.5kmh: 12.0secs
0-60mph 96.5kmh: 16.4secs
0-1/4 mile: 20.8secs
100.0bhp 74.6kW 101.4PS
@ 4400rpm
134.0lbft 181.6Nm @ 3000rpm
66.7bhp/ton 65.6bhp/tonne
40.9bhp/L 30.5kW/L 41.5PS/L
57.7ft/sec 17.6m/sec
19.5mph 31.4kmh/1000rpm
20.8mpg 17.3mpgUS 13.6L/100km
Petrol 4-stroke piston
2443cc 149.0cu in
In-line 4
Compression ratio: 6.6:1
Bore: 80.5mm 3.2in
Stroke: 120.0mm 4.7in
Valve type/No: Overhead 8
Transmission: Manual
No. of forward speeds: 4
Wheels driven: Rear
Springs F/R: Torsion bar/Leaf
Brakes F/R: Drum/Drum
Wheelbase: 302.3cm 119.0in
Track F: 132.6cm 52.2in
Track R: 132.6cm 52.2in
Length: 472.4cm 186.0in
Width: 161.3cm 63.5in
Height: 151.1cm 59.5in
Ground clearance: 17.8cm 7.0in
Kerb weight: 1523.6kg 3356.0lb
Fuel: 56.9L 12.5gal 15.0galUS

3939 Riley

Pathfinder
1955 UK
102.0mph 164.1kmh
0-50mph 80.5kmh: 11.9secs
0-60mph 96.5kmh: 16.7secs
0-1/4 mile: 20.6secs
110.0bhp 82.0kW 111.5PS
@ 4400rpm
134.0lbft 181.6Nm @ 3000rpm
70.7bhp/ton 69.5bhp/tonne
45.0bhp/L 33.6kW/L 45.6PS/L
57.7ft/sec 17.6m/sec
20.1mph 32.3kmh/1000rpm
21.0mpg 17.5mpgUS 13.5L/100km
Petrol 4-stroke piston
2443cc 149.0cu in
In-line 4
Compression ratio: 7.2:1
Bore: 80.5mm 3.2in
Stroke: 120.0mm 4.7in
Valve type/No: Overhead 8
Transmission: Manual
No. of forward speeds: 4
Wheels driven: Rear
Springs F/R: Torsion bar/Coil
Brake system: PA
Brakes F/R: Drum/Drum
Wheelbase: 288.3cm 113.5in
Track F: 137.2cm 54.0in
Track R: 138.4cm 54.5in
Length: 464.8cm 183.0in
Width: 170.2cm 67.0in
Height: 152.4cm 60.0in
Ground clearance: 17.8cm 7.0in
Kerb weight: 1582.6kg 3486.0lb
Fuel: 59.1L 13.0gal 15.6galUS

3940 Riley

Pathfinder
1956 UK
100.2mph 161.2kmh
0-50mph 80.5kmh: 13.1secs
0-60mph 96.5kmh: 18.8secs
0-1/4 mile: 21.0secs
110.0bhp 82.0kW 111.5PS
@ 4400rpm
134.0lbft 181.6Nm @ 3000rpm
70.3bhp/ton 69.1bhp/tonne
45.0bhp/L 33.6kW/L 45.6PS/L
57.7ft/sec 17.6m/sec
28.7mph 46.2kmh/1000rpm
23.7mpg 19.7mpgUS 11.9L/100km
Petrol 4-stroke piston
2443cc 149.0cu in
In-line 4
Compression ratio: 7.2:1
Bore: 80.5mm 3.2in
Stroke: 120.0mm 4.7in
Valve type/No: Overhead 8
Transmission: Manual with overdrive
No. of forward speeds: 7
Wheels driven: Rear
Springs F/R: Torsion bar/Coil
Brakes F/R: Drum/Drum
Wheelbase: 288.3cm 113.5in
Track F: 137.2cm 54.0in
Track R: 138.4cm 54.5in
Length: 464.8cm 183.0in
Width: 170.2cm 67.0in
Height: 152.4cm 60.0in
Ground clearance: 17.8cm 7.0in
Kerb weight: 1591.7kg 3506.0lb
Fuel: 59.1L 13.0gal 15.6galUS

3941 Riley

1.5
1958 UK
85.0mph 136.8kmh
0-50mph 80.5kmh: 11.7secs
0-60mph 96.5kmh: 17.4secs
0-1/4 mile: 20.5secs
68.0bhp 50.7kW 68.9PS
@ 5400rpm
83.0lbft 112.5Nm @ 3200rpm
72.8bhp/ton 71.6bhp/tonne
45.4bhp/L 33.8kW/L 46.0PS/L
52.5ft/sec 16.0m/sec
18.5mph 29.8kmh/1000rpm
27.6mpg 23.0mpgUS 10.2L/100km
Petrol 4-stroke piston
1498cc 91.4cu in
In-line 4 1 Carburettor
Compression ratio: 8.3:1
Bore: 73.0mm 2.9in
Stroke: 88.9mm 3.5in
Valve type/No: Overhead 8
Transmission: Manual
No. of forward speeds: 4
Wheels driven: Rear
Springs F/R: Torsion bar/Leaf
Brakes F/R: Drum/Drum
Wheelbase: 218.4cm 86.0in
Track F: 129.3cm 50.9in
Track R: 127.8cm 50.3in
Length: 388.6cm 153.0in
Width: 154.9cm 61.0in
Height: 152.4cm 60.0in
Ground clearance: 15.2cm 6.0in
Kerb weight: 950.2kg 2093.0lb
Fuel: 31.8L 7.0gal 8.4galUS

3942 Riley

4/68
1960 UK
91.0mph 146.4kmh
0-50mph 80.5kmh: 13.9secs
0-60mph 96.5kmh: 20.5secs
0-1/4 mile: 22.0secs
66.5bhp 49.6kW 67.4PS
@ 5200rpm
82.0lbft 111.1Nm @ 2500rpm
58.4bhp/ton 57.4bhp/tonne
44.4bhp/L 33.1kW/L 45.0PS/L
50.6ft/sec 15.4m/sec
16.5mph 26.5kmh/1000rpm
23.3mpg 19.4mpgUS 12.1L/100km
Petrol 4-stroke piston
1498cc 91.4cu in
In-line 4
Compression ratio: 8.3:1
Bore: 73.0mm 2.9in
Stroke: 88.9mm 3.5in
Valve type/No: Overhead 8
Transmission: Manual
No. of forward speeds: 4
Wheels driven: Rear
Springs F/R: Coil/Leaf
Brakes F/R: Drum/Drum
Wheelbase: 252.0cm 99.2in
Track F: 124.0cm 48.8in
Track R: 126.5cm 49.8in
Length: 452.1cm 178.0in
Width: 161.3cm 63.5in
Height: 151.6cm 59.7in
Ground clearance: 16.5cm 6.5in
Kerb weight: 1158.6kg 2552.0lb
Fuel: 45.5L 10.0gal 12.0galUS

3943 Riley

1.5
1961 UK
86.0mph 138.4kmh
0-50mph 80.5kmh: 13.4secs
0-60mph 96.5kmh: 19.8secs
0-1/4 mile: 21.2secs
60.0bhp 44.7kW 60.8PS
@ 4800rpm
81.0lbft 109.8Nm @ 2400rpm
65.1bhp/ton 64.0bhp/tonne
40.0bhp/L 29.9kW/L 40.6PS/L
46.7ft/sec 14.2m/sec
18.6mph 29.9kmh/1000rpm
25.2mpg 21.0mpgUS 11.2L/100km
Petrol 4-stroke piston
1498cc 91.4cu in
In-line 4
Compression ratio: 8.3:1
Bore: 73.0mm 2.9in
Stroke: 88.9mm 3.5in
Valve type/No: Overhead 8
Transmission: Manual
No. of forward speeds: 4
Wheels driven: Rear
Springs F/R: Torsion bar/Leaf
Brakes F/R: Drum/Drum
Wheelbase: 218.4cm 86.0in
Track F: 129.3cm 50.9in
Track R: 127.8cm 50.3in
Length: 389.1cm 153.2in
Width: 154.9cm 61.0in
Height: 151.9cm 59.8in
Ground clearance: 16.5cm 6.5in
Kerb weight: 937.5kg 2065.0lb
Fuel: 31.8L 7.0gal 8.4galUS

3944 Riley

Elf
1962 UK
73.5mph 118.3kmh
0-50mph 80.5kmh: 18.3secs
0-60mph 96.5kmh: 32.3secs
0-1/4 mile: 23.7secs
34.0bhp 25.3kW 34.5PS
@ 5500rpm
44.0lbft 59.6Nm @ 2900rpm
53.1bhp/ton 52.2bhp/tonne
40.1bhp/L 29.9kW/L 40.6PS/L
41.1ft/sec 12.5m/sec
14.8mph 23.8kmh/1000rpm
32.9mpg 27.4mpgUS 8.6L/100km
Petrol 4-stroke piston
848cc 51.7cu in
In-line 4 1 Carburettor
Compression ratio: 8.3:1
Bore: 62.9mm 2.5in
Stroke: 68.3mm 2.7in
Valve type/No: Overhead 8
Transmission: Manual
No. of forward speeds: 4
Wheels driven: Front
Springs F/R: Rubber/Rubber
Brakes F/R: Drum/Drum
Steering: Rack & pinion
Wheelbase: 203.7cm 80.2in
Track F: 120.4cm 47.4in
Track R: 116.6cm 45.9in
Length: 327.2cm 128.8in
Width: 141.0cm 55.5in
Height: 134.6cm 53.0in
Ground clearance: 15.2cm 6.0in
Kerb weight: 651.0kg 1434.0lb
Fuel: 25.0L 5.5gal 6.6galUS

3945 Riley

Kestrel
1967 UK
91.0mph 146.4kmh
0-50mph 80.5kmh: 12.2secs
0-60mph 96.5kmh: 17.3secs
0-1/4 mile: 20.7secs
0-1km: 39.2secs
58.0bhp 43.2kW 58.8PS
@ 5250rpm
69.0lbft 93.5Nm @ 3500rpm
69.5bhp/ton 68.3bhp/tonne
45.5bhp/L 33.9kW/L 46.1PS/L
46.7ft/sec 14.2m/sec
15.0mph 24.1kmh/1000rpm

29.6mpg 24.6mpgUS 9.5L/100km
Petrol 4-stroke piston
1275cc 77.8cu in
In-line 4 1 Carburettor
Compression ratio: 8.8:1
Bore: 70.6mm 2.8in
Stroke: 81.3mm 3.2in
Valve type/No: Overhead 8
Transmission: Manual
No. of forward speeds: 4
Wheels driven: Front
Springs F/R: Gas/Gas
Brakes F/R: Disc/Drum
Steering: Rack & pinion
Wheelbase: 237.5cm 93.5in
Track F: 130.8cm 51.5in
Track R: 129.3cm 50.9in
Length: 372.6cm 146.7in
Width: 153.4cm 60.4in
Height: 133.9cm 52.7in
Ground clearance: 15.2cm 6.0in
Kerb weight: 848.5kg 1869.0lb
Fuel: 36.4L 8.0gal 9.6galUS

3946 Rolls-Royce

Phantom I Phaeton
1927 UK
80.0mph 128.7kmh
0-50mph 80.5kmh: 16.8secs
0-60mph 96.5kmh: 24.0secs
0-1/4 mile: 24.0secs
107.0bhp 79.8kW 108.5PS
@ 2750rpm
320.0lbft 433.6Nm @ 1200rpm
50.7bhp/ton 49.8bhp/tonne
13.9bhp/L 10.4kW/L 14.1PS/L
42.0ft/sec 12.8m/sec
27.5mph 44.2kmh/1000rpm
Petrol 4-stroke piston
7668cc 467.8cu in
In-line 6
Compression ratio: 4.5:1
Bore: 108.0mm 4.2in
Stroke: 139.7mm 5.5in
Valve type/No: Overhead 12
Transmission: Manual
No. of forward speeds: 4
Wheels driven: Rear
Wheelbase: 365.8cm 144.0in
Track F: 142.2cm 56.0in
Track R: 142.2cm 56.0in
Length: 485.1cm 191.0in
Width: 182.9cm 72.0in
Height: 152.4cm 60.0in
Kerb weight: 2147.4kg 4730.0lb

3947 Rolls-Royce

20 Saloon
1929 UK
65.0mph 104.6kmh
50.0bhp 37.3kW 50.7PS
@ 3000rpm
33.2bhp/ton 32.7bhp/tonne
16.0bhp/L 11.9kW/L 16.2PS/L
37.5ft/sec 11.4m/sec
20.0mpg 16.7mpgUS 14.1L/100km
Petrol 4-stroke piston
3127cc 190.8cu in
In-line 6 1 Carburettor
Compression ratio: 4.8:1
Bore: 76.2mm 3.0in
Stroke: 114.3mm 4.5in
Valve type/No: Overhead 12
Transmission: Manual
No. of forward speeds: 4
Wheels driven: Rear
Brakes F/R: Drum/Drum
Wheelbase: 327.7cm 129.0in
Track F: 142.2cm 56.0in
Track R: 142.2cm 56.0in
Length: 452.1cm 178.0in
Width: 177.8cm 70.0in
Height: 185.4cm 73.0in
Kerb weight: 1529.1kg 3368.0lb
Fuel: 63.7L 14.0gal 16.8galUS

3948 Rolls-Royce

25 Saloon
1931 UK
67.6mph 108.8kmh
18.0mpg 15.0mpgUS 15.7L/100km
Petrol 4-stroke piston
3680cc 224.5cu in
In-line 6 1 Carburettor
Compression ratio: 5.7:1
Bore: 82.6mm 3.2in
Stroke: 114.3mm 4.5in
Valve type/No: Overhead 12
Transmission: Manual
No. of forward speeds: 4
Wheels driven: Rear
Brakes F/R: Drum/Drum
Wheelbase: 335.3cm 132.0in
Track F: 142.2cm 56.0in
Track R: 142.2cm 56.0in
Length: 459.7cm 181.0in
Width: 177.8cm 70.0in
Height: 182.9cm 72.0in
Kerb weight: 1712.9kg 3773.0lb
Fuel: 63.7L 14.0gal 16.8galUS

3949 Rolls-Royce

Phantom II
1932 UK
88.0mph 141.6kmh
0-50mph 80.5kmh: 15.2secs
0-60mph 96.5kmh: 21.0secs
0-1/4 mile: 22.0secs
135.0bhp 100.7kW 136.9PS
@ 3000rpm
340.0lbft 460.7Nm @ 1500rpm
55.1bhp/ton 54.2bhp/tonne
17.6bhp/L 13.1kW/L 17.8PS/L
45.8ft/sec 14.0m/sec
26.3mph 42.3kmh/1000rpm
Petrol 4-stroke piston
7668cc 467.8cu in
In-line 6 1 Carburettor
Compression ratio: 4.6:1
Bore: 108.0mm 4.2in
Stroke: 139.7mm 5.5in
Valve type/No: Overhead 12
Transmission: Manual
No. of forward speeds: 4
Wheels driven: Rear
Wheelbase: 381.0cm 150.0in
Track F: 149.1cm 58.7in
Track R: 152.9cm 60.2in
Length: 563.9cm 222.0in
Width: 182.9cm 72.0in
Height: 162.6cm 64.0in
Kerb weight: 2492.5kg 5490.0lb

3950 Rolls-Royce

Phantom II
1933 UK
92.3mph 148.5kmh
0-50mph 80.5kmh: 14.4secs
0-60mph 96.5kmh: 19.6secs
120.0bhp 89.5kW 121.7PS
@ 3500rpm
49.0bhp/ton 48.2bhp/tonne
15.6bhp/L 11.7kW/L 15.9PS/L
53.6ft/sec 16.3m/sec
10.0mpg 8.3mpgUS 28.2L/100km
Petrol 4-stroke piston
7668cc 467.8cu in
In-line 6 1 Carburettor
Compression ratio: 5.2:1
Bore: 108.0mm 4.2in
Stroke: 140.0mm 5.5in
Valve type/No: Overhead 12
Transmission: Manual
No. of forward speeds: 4
Wheels driven: Rear
Brakes F/R: Drum/Drum
Kerb weight: 2491.5kg 5488.0lb
Fuel: 91.0L 20.0gal 24.0galUS

3951 Rolls-Royce

20/25 Touring Saloon
1935 UK
76.2mph 122.6kmh
0-50mph 80.5kmh: 21.0secs
0-60mph 96.5kmh: 31.4secs
15.0mpg 12.5mpgUS 18.8L/100km
Petrol 4-stroke piston
3669cc 223.9cu in
In-line 6 1 Carburettor
Bore: 82.0mm 3.2in
Stroke: 114.0mm 4.5in
Valve type/No: Overhead 12
Transmission: Manual
No. of forward speeds: 4
Wheels driven: Rear
Brakes F/R: Drum/Drum
Ground clearance: 21.6cm 8.5in
Kerb weight: 1928.6kg 4248.0lb
Fuel: 81.9L 18.0gal 21.6galUS

3952 Rolls-Royce

Phantom III
1936 UK
92.5mph 148.8kmh
0-50mph 80.5kmh: 12.3secs
0-60mph 96.5kmh: 16.5secs
0-1/4 mile: 21.0secs
160.0bhp 119.3kW 162.2PS
@ 4000rpm
350.0lbft 474.3Nm @ 2000rpm
61.3bhp/ton 60.2bhp/tonne
21.8bhp/L 16.3kW/L 22.1PS/L
50.0ft/sec 15.2m/sec
Petrol 4-stroke piston
7338cc 447.7cu in
Vee 12
Compression ratio: 6.0:1
Bore: 82.6mm 3.2in
Stroke: 114.3mm 4.5in
Valve type/No: Overhead 24
Transmission: Manual
No. of forward speeds: 4
Wheels driven: Rear
Wheelbase: 360.7cm 142.0in
Track F: 153.2cm 60.3in
Track R: 154.9cm 61.0in
Kerb weight: 2655.9kg 5850.0lb

3953 Rolls-Royce

Silver Wraith
1949 UK
69.5mph 111.8kmh
0-50mph 80.5kmh: 17.2secs
0-60mph 96.5kmh: 24.0secs
23.0mph 37.0kmh/1000rpm
15.0mpg 12.5mpgUS 18.8L/100km
Petrol 4-stroke piston
4256cc 259.7cu in
In-line 6
Compression ratio: 6.4:1
Bore: 89.0mm 3.5in
Stroke: 114.0mm 4.5in
Valve type/No: IOE 12
Transmission: Manual
No. of forward speeds: 3
Wheels driven: Rear
Brakes F/R: Drum/Drum
Wheelbase: 322.6cm 127.0in
Track F: 148.6cm 58.5in
Track R: 152.4cm 60.0in
Length: 523.2cm 206.0in
Width: 185.4cm 73.0in
Height: 180.3cm 71.0in
Ground clearance: 20.6cm 8.1in
Kerb weight: 2148.3kg 4732.0lb
Fuel: 81.9L 18.0gal 21.6galUS

3954 Rolls-Royce

Silver Dawn
1953 UK
87.8mph 141.3kmh
0-50mph 80.5kmh: 11.4secs
0-60mph 96.5kmh: 17.0secs
0-1/4 mile: 20.9secs
126.0bhp 94.0kW 127.7PS
@ 3750rpm
237.0lbft 321.1Nm @ 2000rpm
67.2bhp/ton 66.1bhp/tonne
27.6bhp/L 20.6kW/L 28.0PS/L
46.9ft/sec 14.3m/sec
22.4mph 36.0kmh/1000rpm
Petrol 4-stroke piston
4566cc 278.6cu in
In-line 6
Compression ratio: 6.4:1
Bore: 91.9mm 3.6in
Stroke: 114.3mm 4.5in
Valve type/No: Side 12
Transmission: Manual
No. of forward speeds: 4
Wheels driven: Rear
Wheelbase: 304.8cm 120.0in
Track F: 143.5cm 56.5in
Track R: 148.6cm 58.5in
Kerb weight: 1906.8kg 4200.0lb

3955 Rolls-Royce

Silver Dawn
1954 UK
87.5mph 140.8kmh
0-50mph 80.5kmh: 11.4secs
0-60mph 96.5kmh: 16.2secs
0-1/4 mile: 20.4secs
22.0mph 35.4kmh/1000rpm
14.2mpg 11.8mpgUS 19.9L/100km
Petrol 4-stroke piston
4566cc 278.6cu in
In-line 6
Compression ratio: 6.7:1
Bore: 92.0mm 3.6in
Stroke: 114.3mm 4.5in
Valve type/No: IOE 12
Transmission: Manual
No. of forward speeds: 4
Wheels driven: Rear
Springs F/R: Coil/Leaf
Brake system: PA
Brakes F/R: Drum/Drum
Wheelbase: 304.8cm 120.0in
Track F: 144.0cm 56.7in
Track R: 148.8cm 58.6in
Length: 510.5cm 201.0in
Width: 177.8cm 70.0in
Height: 167.6cm 66.0in
Kerb weight: 1875.9kg 4132.0lb
Fuel: 81.9L 18.0gal 21.6galUS

3956 Rolls-Royce

Silver Cloud
1958 UK
106.0mph 170.6kmh
0-50mph 80.5kmh: 9.4secs
0-60mph 96.5kmh: 13.0secs
0-1/4 mile: 18.8secs
25.0mph 40.2kmh/1000rpm
12.0mpg 10.0mpgUS 23.5L/100km
Petrol 4-stroke piston
4887cc 298.2cu in
In-line 6
Compression ratio: 8.0:1
Bore: 95.2mm 3.8in
Stroke: 114.3mm 4.5in
Valve type/No: Overhead 12
Transmission: Manual
No. of forward speeds: 4
Wheels driven: Rear
Springs F/R: Coil/Leaf
Brake system: PA
Brakes F/R: Drum/Drum
Wheelbase: 312.4cm 123.0in
Track F: 147.3cm 58.0in
Track R: 152.4cm 60.0in
Length: 537.7cm 211.7in
Width: 189.7cm 74.7in
Height: 162.6cm 64.0in
Ground clearance: 17.8cm 7.0in
Kerb weight: 1881.4kg 4144.0lb
Fuel: 81.9L 18.0gal 21.6galUS

3957 Rolls-Royce

Silver Cloud "S"
1958 UK
102.5mph 164.9kmh
0-50mph 80.5kmh: 8.5secs
0-60mph 96.5kmh: 12.1secs
0-1/4 mile: 18.4secs
180.0bhp 134.2kW 182.5PS
@ 4000rpm
280.0lbft 379.4Nm @ 2000rpm
89.8bhp/ton 88.3bhp/tonne
36.8bhp/L 27.5kW/L 37.3PS/L
50.0ft/sec 15.2m/sec
Petrol 4-stroke piston
4887cc 298.2cu in
In-line 6
Compression ratio: 8.0:1
Bore: 95.3mm 3.8in
Stroke: 114.3mm 4.5in
Valve type/No: Overhead 12
Transmission: Manual
No. of forward speeds: 4
Wheels driven: Rear
Wheelbase: 312.4cm 123.0in
Track F: 147.3cm 58.0in
Track R: 152.4cm 60.0in
Kerb weight: 2038.5kg 4490.0lb

3958 Rolls-Royce

Silver Cloud II
1960 UK
115.0mph 185.0kmh
0-50mph 80.5kmh: 8.3secs
0-60mph 96.5kmh: 11.5secs
0-1/4 mile: 18.2secs
27.8mph 44.7kmh/1000rpm
11.8mpg 9.8mpgUS 23.9L/100km
Petrol 4-stroke piston
6230cc 380.1cu in
Vee 8
Compression ratio: 8.0:1
Bore: 104.4mm 4.1in

Stroke: 91.4mm 3.6in
Valve type/No: Overhead 16
Transmission: Manual
No. of forward speeds: 4
Wheels driven: Rear
Springs F/R: Coil/Leaf
Brake system: PA
Brakes F/R: Drum/Drum
Wheelbase: 312.4cm 123.0in
Track F: 148.6cm 58.5in
Track R: 152.4cm 60.0in
Length: 537.7cm 211.7in
Width: 189.7cm 74.7in
Height: 162.6cm 64.0in
Ground clearance: 17.8cm 7.0in
Kerb weight: 2053.0kg 4522.0lb
Fuel: 81.9L 18.0gal 21.6galUS

3959 Rolls-Royce

Silver Cloud II V8
1960 UK
112.0mph 180.2kmh
0-50mph 80.5kmh: 8.0secs
0-60mph 96.5kmh: 11.4secs
0-1/4 mile: 18.0secs
220.0bhp 164.0kW 223.0PS
@ 4000rpm
340.0lbft 460.7Nm @ 2200rpm
105.3bhp/ton 103.5bhp/tonne
35.3bhp/L 26.3kW/L 35.8PS/L
40.0ft/sec 12.2m/sec
27.8mph 44.7kmh/1000rpm
Petrol 4-stroke piston
6230cc 380.1cu in
Vee 8 1 Carburettor
Compression ratio: 8.0:1
Bore: 104.1mm 4.1in
Stroke: 91.4mm 3.6in
Valve type/No: Overhead 16
Transmission: Automatic
No. of forward speeds: 4
Wheels driven: Rear
Wheelbase: 312.4cm 123.0in
Track F: 148.6cm 58.5in
Track R: 152.1cm 59.9in
Length: 538.5cm 212.0in
Width: 190.0cm 74.8in
Height: 162.6cm 64.0in
Kerb weight: 2124.7kg 4680.0lb

3960 Rolls-Royce

Silver Cloud III
1963 UK
117.0mph 188.3kmh
0-50mph 80.5kmh: 7.7secs
0-60mph 96.5kmh: 10.8secs
0-1/4 mile: 17.7secs
27.8mph 44.7kmh/1000rpm
12.3mpg 10.2mpgUS 23.0L/100km
Petrol 4-stroke piston
6230cc 380.1cu in
Vee 8 2 Carburettor
Compression ratio: 9.0:1
Bore: 104.0mm 4.1in
Stroke: 91.5mm 3.6in
Valve type/No: Overhead 16
Transmission: Automatic
No. of forward speeds: 4
Wheels driven: Rear
Springs F/R: Coil/Leaf
Brake system: PA
Brakes F/R: Drum/Drum
Steering: Cam & roller PA
Wheelbase: 312.4cm 123.0in
Track F: 148.6cm 58.5in
Track R: 152.4cm 60.0in
Length: 533.9cm 210.2in
Width: 188.0cm 74.0in
Height: 161.3cm 63.5in
Ground clearance: 17.8cm 7.0in
Kerb weight: 2078.4kg 4578.0lb
Fuel: 81.9L 18.0gal 21.6galUS

3961 Rolls-Royce

Silver Shadow
1966 UK
118.0mph 189.9kmh
0-50mph 80.5kmh: 7.8secs
0-60mph 96.5kmh: 10.9secs
0-1/4 mile: 17.6secs
0-1km: 33.0secs
26.2mph 42.2kmh/1000rpm
12.2mpg 10.2mpgUS 23.2L/100km
Petrol 4-stroke piston
6230cc 380.1cu in
Vee 8 2 Carburettor
Compression ratio: 9.0:1
Bore: 104.0mm 4.1in
Stroke: 91.4mm 3.6in
Valve type/No: Overhead 16
Transmission: Automatic
No. of forward speeds: 4
Wheels driven: Rear
Springs F/R: Coil/Coil
Brake system: PA
Brakes F/R: Disc/Disc
Steering: Recirculating ball PA
Wheelbase: 303.5cm 119.5in
Track F: 146.1cm 57.5in
Track R: 146.1cm 57.5in
Length: 516.9cm 203.5in
Width: 180.3cm 71.0in
Height: 151.6cm 59.7in
Ground clearance: 16.5cm 6.5in
Kerb weight: 2115.6kg 4660.0lb
Fuel: 109.2L 24.0gal 28.8galUS

3962 Rolls-Royce

Silver Shadow
1969 UK
114.0mph 183.4kmh
0-50mph 80.5kmh: 8.1secs
0-60mph 96.5kmh: 11.0secs
0-1/4 mile: 17.4secs
300.0bhp 223.7kW 304.2PS
@ 4000rpm
400.0lbft 542.0Nm @ 2500rpm
143.3bhp/ton 140.9bhp/tonne
48.1bhp/L 35.9kW/L 48.8PS/L
40.0ft/sec 12.2m/sec
26.2mph 42.2kmh/1000rpm
11.6mpg 9.7mpgUS 24.2L/100km
Petrol 4-stroke piston
6230cc 380.1cu in
Vee 8 2 Carburettor
Compression ratio: 9.0:1
Bore: 104.1mm 4.1in
Stroke: 91.4mm 3.6in
Valve type/No: Overhead 16
Transmission: Automatic
No. of forward speeds: 3
Wheels driven: Rear
Springs F/R: Coil/Coil
Brake system: PA
Brakes F/R: Disc/Disc
Steering: Recirculating ball PA
Wheelbase: 303.5cm 119.5in
Track F: 146.1cm 57.5in
Track R: 146.1cm 57.5in
Length: 516.9cm 203.5in
Width: 180.3cm 71.0in
Height: 151.9cm 59.8in
Ground clearance: 16.5cm 6.5in
Kerb weight: 2129.3kg 4690.0lb
Fuel: 106.0L 23.3gal 28.0galUS

3963 Rolls-Royce

Silver Shadow
1972 UK
119.0mph 191.5kmh
0-50mph 80.5kmh: 7.4secs
0-60mph 96.5kmh: 10.2secs
0-1/4 mile: 17.5secs
0-1km: 32.5secs
26.2mph 42.2kmh/1000rpm
12.4mpg 10.3mpgUS 22.8L/100km
Petrol 4-stroke piston
6750cc 411.8cu in
Vee 8 2 Carburettor
Compression ratio: 9.0:1
Bore: 104.1mm 4.1in
Stroke: 99.0mm 3.9in
Valve type/No: Overhead 16
Transmission: Automatic
No. of forward speeds: 3
Wheels driven: Rear
Springs F/R: Coil/Coil
Brake system: PA
Brakes F/R: Disc/Disc
Steering: Recirculating ball PA
Wheelbase: 303.5cm 119.5in
Track F: 146.1cm 57.5in
Track R: 146.1cm 57.5in
Length: 516.9cm 203.5in
Width: 180.3cm 71.0in
Height: 151.6cm 59.7in
Ground clearance: 15.2cm 6.0in
Kerb weight: 2120.2kg 4670.0lb
Fuel: 106.9L 23.5gal 28.2galUS

3964 Rolls-Royce

Corniche
1974 UK
122.0mph 196.3kmh
0-50mph 80.5kmh: 6.8secs
0-60mph 96.5kmh: 9.6secs
0-1/4 mile: 17.1secs
0-1km: 31.8secs
26.2mph 42.2kmh/1000rpm
11.9mpg 9.9mpgUS 23.7L/100km
Petrol 4-stroke piston
6750cc 411.8cu in
Vee 8 2 Carburettor
Compression ratio: 9.0:1
Bore: 104.1mm 4.1in
Stroke: 99.1mm 3.9in
Valve type/No: Overhead 16
Transmission: Automatic
No. of forward speeds: 3
Wheels driven: Rear
Springs F/R: Coil/Coil
Brake system: PA
Brakes F/R: Disc/Disc
Steering: Recirculating ball PA
Wheelbase: 304.0cm 119.7in
Track F: 151.1cm 59.5in
Track R: 146.6cm 57.7in
Length: 516.9cm 203.5in
Width: 182.9cm 72.0in
Height: 149.1cm 58.7in
Ground clearance: 16.5cm 6.5in
Kerb weight: 2186.5kg 4816.0lb
Fuel: 106.9L 23.5gal 28.2galUS

3965 Rolls-Royce

Silver Shadow
1976 UK
120.0mph 193.1kmh
0-50mph 80.5kmh: 7.6secs
0-60mph 96.5kmh: 10.6secs
0-1/4 mile: 18.1secs
0-1km: 33.3secs
25.8mph 41.5kmh/1000rpm
13.6mpg 11.3mpgUS 20.8L/100km
Petrol 4-stroke piston
6750cc 411.8cu in
Vee 8 2 Carburettor
Compression ratio: 8.0:1
Bore: 104.1mm 4.1in
Stroke: 99.0mm 3.9in
Valve type/No: Overhead 16
Transmission: Automatic
No. of forward speeds: 3
Wheels driven: Rear
Springs F/R: Coil/Coil
Brake system: PA
Brakes F/R: Disc/Disc
Steering: Recirculating ball PA
Wheelbase: 304.8cm 120.0in
Track F: 146.1cm 57.5in
Track R: 146.1cm 57.5in
Length: 516.9cm 203.5in
Width: 180.3cm 71.0in
Height: 151.6cm 59.7in
Ground clearance: 15.2cm 6.0in
Kerb weight: 2157.4kg 4752.0lb
Fuel: 106.9L 23.5gal 28.2galUS

3966 Rolls-Royce

Silver Shadow
1977 UK
106.0mph 170.6kmh
0-50mph 80.5kmh: 8.4secs
0-60mph 96.5kmh: 11.8secs
0-1/4 mile: 18.7secs
190.0bhp 141.7kW 192.6PS
@ 4000rpm
290.0lbft 393.0Nm @ 2500rpm
85.0bhp/ton 83.6bhp/tonne
28.1bhp/L 21.0kW/L 28.5PS/L
43.3ft/sec 13.2m/sec
25.5mph 41.0kmh/1000rpm
12.6mpg 10.5mpgUS 22.4L/100km
Petrol 4-stroke piston
6750cc 411.8cu in
Vee 8 2 Carburettor
Compression ratio: 7.3:1
Bore: 104.0mm 4.1in
Stroke: 99.1mm 3.9in
Valve type/No: Overhead 16
Transmission: Automatic
No. of forward speeds: 3
Wheels driven: Rear
Springs F/R: Coil/Coil
Brake system: PA
Brakes F/R: Disc/Disc
Steering: Recirculating ball PA
Wheelbase: 313.7cm 123.5in
Track F: 146.1cm 57.5in
Track R: 146.1cm 57.5in
Length: 537.2cm 211.5in
Width: 182.4cm 71.8in
Height: 151.9cm 59.8in
Ground clearance: 16.5cm 6.5in
Kerb weight: 2272.3kg 5005.0lb
Fuel: 98.4L 21.6gal 26.0galUS

3967 Rolls-Royce

Silver Wraith II
1978 UK
120.0mph 193.1kmh
0-50mph 80.5kmh: 7.4secs
0-60mph 96.5kmh: 10.1secs
0-1/4 mile: 17.3secs
0-1km: 32.1secs
26.2mph 42.2kmh/1000rpm
13.2mpg 11.0mpgUS 21.4L/100km
Petrol 4-stroke piston
6748cc 411.7cu in
Vee 8 2 Carburettor
Compression ratio: 8.0:1
Bore: 104.1mm 4.1in
Stroke: 99.1mm 3.9in
Valve type/No: Overhead 16
Transmission: Automatic
No. of forward speeds: 3
Wheels driven: Rear
Springs F/R: Coil/Coil
Brake system: PA
Brakes F/R: Disc/Disc
Steering: Rack & pinion PA
Wheelbase: 315.0cm 124.0in
Track F: 152.4cm 60.0in
Track R: 151.1cm 59.5in
Length: 529.6cm 208.5in
Width: 182.9cm 72.0in
Height: 151.6cm 59.7in
Ground clearance: 16.5cm 6.5in
Kerb weight: 2051.6kg 4519.0lb
Fuel: 106.9L 23.5gal 28.2galUS

3968 Rolls-Royce

Silver Shadow II
1980 UK
114.0mph 183.4kmh
0-50mph 80.5kmh: 8.1secs
0-60mph 96.5kmh: 11.3secs
0-1/4 mile: 18.4secs
190.0bhp 141.7kW 192.6PS
@ 4000rpm
290.0lbft 393.0Nm @ 2500rpm
85.6bhp/ton 84.2bhp/tonne
28.1bhp/L 21.0kW/L 28.5PS/L
43.3ft/sec 13.2m/sec
25.5mph 41.0kmh/1000rpm
11.4mpg 9.5mpgUS 24.8L/100km
Petrol 4-stroke piston
6750cc 411.8cu in
Vee 8 2 Carburettor
Compression ratio: 7.3:1
Bore: 104.0mm 4.1in
Stroke: 99.1mm 3.9in
Valve type/No: Overhead 16
Transmission: Automatic
No. of forward speeds: 3
Wheels driven: Rear
Springs F/R: Coil/Coil
Brakes F/R: Disc/Disc
Steering: Rack & pinion PA
Wheelbase: 315.2cm 124.1in
Track F: 146.1cm 57.5in
Track R: 146.1cm 57.5in
Length: 537.2cm 211.5in
Width: 182.4cm 71.8in
Height: 151.9cm 59.8in
Kerb weight: 2256.4kg 4970.0lb
Fuel: 85.2L 18.7gal 22.5galUS

3969 Rolls-Royce

Silver Spirit
1981 UK
119.0mph 191.5kmh
0-50mph 80.5kmh: 7.3secs
0-60mph 96.5kmh: 10.0secs
0-1/4 mile: 17.1secs
0-1km: 31.9secs
26.2mph 42.2kmh/1000rpm
14.0mpg 11.7mpgUS 20.2L/100km
Petrol 4-stroke piston
6750cc 411.8cu in
Vee 8 2 Carburettor
Compression ratio: 9.0:1
Bore: 104.1mm 4.1in
Stroke: 99.1mm 3.9in
Valve type/No: Overhead 16

Transmission: Automatic
No. of forward speeds: 3
Wheels driven: Rear
Springs F/R: Coil/Coil
Brake system: PA
Brakes F/R: Disc/Disc
Steering: Rack & pinion PA
Wheelbase: 306.1cm 120.5in
Track F: 153.7cm 60.5in
Track R: 153.7cm 60.5in
Length: 526.8cm 207.4in
Width: 188.7cm 74.3in
Height: 148.6cm 58.5in
Ground clearance: 16.5cm 6.5in
Kerb weight: 2227.8kg 4907.0lb
Fuel: 106.9L 23.5gal 28.2galUS

3970 Rolls-Royce

Corniche
1982 UK
129.0mph 207.6kmh
0-50mph 80.5kmh: 7.0secs
0-60mph 96.5kmh: 9.7secs
0-1/4 mile: 17.1secs
0-1km: 31.5secs
26.2mph 42.2kmh/1000rpm
12.3mpg 10.2mpgUS 23.0L/100km
Petrol 4-stroke piston
6750cc 411.8cu in
Vee 8 1 Carburettor
Compression ratio: 9.0:1
Bore: 104.1mm 4.1in
Stroke: 99.1mm 3.9in
Valve type/No: Overhead 16
Transmission: Automatic
No. of forward speeds: 3
Wheels driven: Rear
Springs F/R: Coil/Coil
Brake system: PA
Brakes F/R: Disc/Disc
Steering: Rack & pinion PA
Wheelbase: 304.8cm 120.0in
Track F: 152.4cm 60.0in
Track R: 153.9cm 60.6in
Length: 519.4cm 204.5in
Width: 182.9cm 72.0in
Height: 151.6cm 59.7in
Ground clearance: 15.2cm 6.0in
Kerb weight: 2300.0kg 5066.0lb
Fuel: 106.9L 23.5gal 28.2galUS

3971 Rolls-Royce

Silver Spur
1982 UK
108.0mph 173.8kmh
0-50mph 80.5kmh: 9.0secs
0-60mph 96.5kmh: 12.6secs
0-1/4 mile: 18.8secs
260.0bhp 193.9kW 263.6PS
@ 4000rpm
380.0lbft 514.9Nm @ 2500rpm
117.1bhp/ton 115.1bhp/tonne
38.5bhp/L 28.7kW/L 39.0PS/L
43.3ft/sec 13.2m/sec
25.0mph 40.2kmh/1000rpm
12.0mpg 10.0mpgUS 23.5L/100km
Petrol 4-stroke piston
6750cc 411.8cu in
Vee 8 fuel injection
Compression ratio: 8.0:1
Bore: 104.0mm 4.1in
Stroke: 99.1mm 3.9in
Valve type/No: Overhead 16
Transmission: Automatic
No. of forward speeds: 3
Wheels driven: Rear
Springs F/R: Coil/Coil
Brakes F/R: Disc/Disc
Steering: Rack & pinion PA
Wheelbase: 316.2cm 124.5in
Track F: 153.9cm 60.6in
Track R: 153.9cm 60.6in
Length: 538.0cm 211.8in
Width: 189.0cm 74.4in
Height: 148.6cm 58.5in
Ground clearance: 14.0cm 5.5in
Kerb weight: 2258.6kg 4975.0lb
Fuel: 107.9L 23.7gal 28.5galUS

3972 Rolls-Royce

Silver Spirit II
1991 UK
128.0mph 206.0kmh
0-50mph 80.5kmh: 7.6secs
0-60mph 96.5kmh: 10.4secs
0-1/4 mile: 17.4secs
0-1km: 32.0secs
226.0bhp 168.5kW 229.1PS
@ 4300rpm
339.5lbft 460.0Nm @ 1500rpm
100.4bhp/ton 98.7bhp/tonne
33.5bhp/L 25.0kW/L 33.9PS/L
46.6ft/sec 14.2m/sec
30.0mph 48.3kmh/1000rpm
13.8mpg 11.5mpgUS 20.5L/100km
Petrol 4-stroke piston
6750cc 412.0cu in
Vee 8 fuel injection
Compression ratio: 8.0:1
Bore: 104.0mm 4.1in
Stroke: 99.0mm 3.9in
Valve type/No: Overhead 16
Transmission: Automatic
No. of forward speeds: 3
Wheels driven: Rear
Springs F/R: Coil/Coil
Brake system: PA ABS
Brakes F/R: Disc/Disc
Steering: Rack & pinion PA
Wheelbase: 306.1cm 120.5in
Track F: 153.7cm 60.5in
Track R: 153.7cm 60.5in
Length: 526.8cm 207.4in
Width: 188.7cm 74.3in
Height: 148.6cm 58.5in
Ground clearance: 13.5cm 5.3in
Kerb weight: 2290.0kg 5044.0lb
Fuel: 107.8L 23.7gal 28.5galUS

3973 Rover

Light Six Speed Model
1931 UK
81.8mph 131.6kmh
60.0bhp 44.7kW 60.8PS
52.2bhp/ton 51.3bhp/tonne
23.4bhp/L 17.4kW/L 23.7PS/L
27.0mpg 22.5mpgUS 10.5L/100km
Petrol 4-stroke piston
2565cc 156.5cu in
In-line 6
Bore: 72.0mm 2.8in
Stroke: 105.0mm 4.1in
Valve type/No: Overhead 12
Transmission: Manual
No. of forward speeds: 4
Wheels driven: Rear
Brakes F/R: Drum/Drum
Wheelbase: 269.2cm 106.0in
Track F: 127.0cm 50.0in
Track R: 127.0cm 50.0in
Length: 398.8cm 157.0in
Width: 152.4cm 60.0in
Height: 137.2cm 54.0in
Kerb weight: 1169.5kg 2576.0lb
Fuel: 54.6L 12.0gal 14.4galUS

3974 Rover

Pilot
1932 UK
60.8mph 97.8kmh
35.0bhp 26.1kW 35.5PS
@ 3800rpm
30.4bhp/ton 29.9bhp/tonne
22.2bhp/L 16.5kW/L 22.5PS/L
37.4ft/sec 11.4m/sec
25.0mpg 20.8mpgUS 11.3L/100km
Petrol 4-stroke piston
1577cc 96.2cu in
In-line 6
Bore: 61.0mm 2.4in
Stroke: 90.0mm 3.5in
Valve type/No: Overhead 12
Transmission: Manual
No. of forward speeds: 4
Wheels driven: Rear
Brakes F/R: Drum/Drum
Wheelbase: 264.2cm 104.0in
Track F: 129.5cm 51.0in
Track R: 129.5cm 51.0in
Length: 396.2cm 156.0in
Width: 154.9cm 61.0in
Height: 170.2cm 67.0in
Kerb weight: 1169.5kg 2576.0lb
Fuel: 40.9L 9.0gal 10.8galUS

3975 Rover

12 Saloon
1934 UK
69.7mph 112.1kmh
0-50mph 80.5kmh: 18.4secs
0-60mph 96.5kmh: 29.8secs
26.0mpg 21.6mpgUS 10.9L/100km
Petrol 4-stroke piston
1495cc 91.2cu in
In-line 4
Bore: 69.0mm 2.7in
Stroke: 100.0mm 3.9in
Transmission: Manual
No. of forward speeds: 4
Wheels driven: Rear
Brakes F/R: Drum/Drum
Kerb weight: 1245.8kg 2744.0lb
Fuel: 43.2L 9.5gal 11.4galUS

3976 Rover

Speed 14 Streamline Coupe
1935 UK
82.5mph 132.7kmh
0-50mph 80.5kmh: 14.4secs
0-60mph 96.5kmh: 21.4secs
22.0mpg 18.3mpgUS 12.8L/100km
Petrol 4-stroke piston
1577cc 96.2cu in
In-line 6
Bore: 61.0mm 2.4in
Stroke: 90.0mm 3.5in
Valve type/No: Overhead 12
Transmission: Manual
No. of forward speeds: 4
Wheels driven: Rear
Brakes F/R: Drum/Drum
Kerb weight: 1299.3kg 2862.0lb
Fuel: 50.0L 11.0gal 13.2galUS

3977 Rover

16 Sports Saloon
1937 UK
77.5mph 124.7kmh
0-50mph 80.5kmh: 17.0secs
0-60mph 96.5kmh: 28.0secs
22.0mpg 18.3mpgUS 12.8L/100km
Petrol 4-stroke piston
2147cc 131.0cu in
In-line 6
Bore: 67.5mm 2.7in
Stroke: 100.0mm 3.9in
Valve type/No: Overhead 12
Transmission: Manual
No. of forward speeds: 4
Wheels driven: Rear
Brakes F/R: Drum/Drum
Kerb weight: 1441.0kg 3174.0lb
Fuel: 47.8L 10.5gal 12.6galUS

3978 Rover

14
1938 UK
72.0mph 115.8kmh
0-50mph 80.5kmh: 22.2secs
0-60mph 96.5kmh: 41.3secs
22.0mpg 18.3mpgUS 12.8L/100km
Petrol 4-stroke piston
1901cc 116.0cu in
In-line 6
Bore: 63.5mm 2.5in
Stroke: 100.0mm 3.9in
Valve type/No: Overhead 12
Transmission: Manual
No. of forward speeds: 4
Wheels driven: Rear
Brakes F/R: Drum/Drum
Kerb weight: 1456.9kg 3209.0lb
Fuel: 53.5L 11.7gal 14.1galUS

3979 Rover

16 Saloon
1938 UK
75.6mph 121.6kmh
0-50mph 80.5kmh: 17.8secs
0-60mph 96.5kmh: 28.3secs
22.0mpg 18.3mpgUS 12.8L/100km
Petrol 4-stroke piston
2147cc 131.0cu in
In-line 6
Bore: 67.5mm 2.7in
Stroke: 100.0mm 3.9in
Valve type/No: Overhead 12
Transmission: Manual
No. of forward speeds: 4
Wheels driven: Rear
Brakes F/R: Drum/Drum
Kerb weight: 1463.7kg 3224.0lb
Fuel: 52.3L 11.5gal 13.8galUS

3980 Rover

75
1949 UK
75.0mph 120.7kmh
0-50mph 80.5kmh: 18.2secs
0-60mph 96.5kmh: 29.4secs
72.0bhp 53.7kW 73.0PS
@ 4000rpm
52.3bhp/ton 51.4bhp/tonne
34.3bhp/L 25.6kW/L 34.8PS/L
45.9ft/sec 14.0m/sec
24.5mpg 20.4mpgUS 11.5L/100km
Petrol 4-stroke piston
2100cc 128.1cu in
In-line 6 1 Carburettor
Compression ratio: 7.2:1
Bore: 65.2mm 2.6in
Stroke: 105.0mm 4.1in
Valve type/No: IOE 12
Transmission: Manual
No. of forward speeds: 4
Wheels driven: Rear
Brakes F/R: Drum/Drum
Wheelbase: 280.7cm 110.5in
Track F: 129.8cm 51.1in
Track R: 139.2cm 54.8in
Length: 434.8cm 171.2in
Width: 160.0cm 63.0in
Height: 157.5cm 62.0in
Ground clearance: 19.1cm 7.5in
Kerb weight: 1400.1kg 3084.0lb
Fuel: 50.0L 11.0gal 13.2galUS

3981 Rover

75 Saloon
1949 UK
75.0mph 120.7kmh
0-50mph 80.5kmh: 18.2secs
0-60mph 96.5kmh: 29.4secs
72.0bhp 53.7kW 73.0PS
@ 4000rpm
52.3bhp/ton 51.4bhp/tonne
34.3bhp/L 25.6kW/L 34.8PS/L
45.9ft/sec 14.0m/sec
23.0mpg 19.2mpgUS 12.3L/100km
Petrol 4-stroke piston
2100cc 128.1cu in
In-line 6
Compression ratio: 7.2:1
Bore: 65.2mm 2.6in
Stroke: 105.0mm 4.1in
Valve type/No: IOE 12
Transmission: Manual
No. of forward speeds: 4
Wheels driven: Rear
Brakes F/R: Drum/Drum
Wheelbase: 280.7cm 110.5in
Track F: 130.0cm 51.2in
Track R: 139.2cm 54.8in
Length: 434.8cm 171.2in
Width: 160.0cm 63.0in
Height: 157.5cm 62.0in
Ground clearance: 19.1cm 7.5in
Kerb weight: 1400.1kg 3084.0lb
Fuel: 50.0L 11.0gal 13.2galUS

3982 Rover

75
1950 UK
82.0mph 131.9kmh
0-50mph 80.5kmh: 16.2secs
0-60mph 96.5kmh: 23.1secs
75.0bhp 55.9kW 76.0PS
@ 4200rpm
111.0lbft 150.4Nm @ 2500rpm
52.5bhp/ton 51.7bhp/tonne
35.7bhp/L 26.6kW/L 36.2PS/L
48.2ft/sec 14.7m/sec
18.0mph 29.0kmh/1000rpm
23.0mpg 19.2mpgUS 12.3L/100km
Petrol 4-stroke piston
2103cc 128.3cu in
In-line 6 1 Carburettor
Compression ratio: 7.2:1
Bore: 65.2mm 2.6in
Stroke: 105.0mm 4.1in
Valve type/No: IOE 12
Transmission: Manual
No. of forward speeds: 4
Wheels driven: Rear
Brakes F/R: Drum/Drum
Wheelbase: 281.9cm 111.0in
Track F: 132.1cm 52.0in
Track R: 130.8cm 51.5in
Length: 452.6cm 178.2in
Width: 166.1cm 65.4in
Height: 160.5cm 63.2in

Ground clearance: 18.3cm 7.2in
Kerb weight: 1451.9kg 3198.0lb
Fuel: 52.3L 11.5gal 13.8galUS

3983 Rover

75
1952 UK
80.5mph 129.5kmh
0-50mph 80.5kmh: 16.3secs
0-60mph 96.5kmh: 24.7secs
0-1/4 mile: 22.7secs
75.0bhp 55.9kW 76.0PS
@ 4200rpm
111.0lbft 150.4Nm @ 2500rpm
51.8bhp/ton 51.0bhp/tonne
35.7bhp/L 26.6kW/L 36.2PS/L
48.2ft/sec 14.7m/sec
18.0mph 29.0kmh/1000rpm
23.7mpg 19.7mpgUS 11.9L/100km
Petrol 4-stroke piston
2103cc 128.3cu in
In-line 6
Compression ratio: 7.2:1
Bore: 65.2mm 2.6in
Stroke: 105.0mm 4.1in
Valve type/No: IOE 12
Transmission: Manual
No. of forward speeds: 4
Wheels driven: Rear
Springs F/R: Coil/Leaf
Brakes F/R: Drum/Drum
Wheelbase: 281.9cm 111.0in
Track F: 132.1cm 52.0in
Track R: 130.8cm 51.5in
Length: 452.9cm 178.3in
Width: 166.9cm 65.7in
Height: 161.8cm 63.7in
Ground clearance: 18.0cm 7.1in
Kerb weight: 1471.4kg 3241.0lb
Fuel: 52.3L 11.5gal 13.8galUS

3984 Rover

Jet
1953 UK
151.0mph 243.0kmh
0-50mph 80.5kmh: 5.9secs
0-60mph 96.5kmh: 6.5secs
0-1/4 mile: 12.1secs
240.0bhp 179.0kW 243.3PS
@ 45000rpm
192.0bhp/ton 188.8bhp/tonne
Gas turbine
Wheels driven: Rear
Wheelbase: 281.9cm 111.0in
Track F: 132.1cm 52.0in
Track R: 130.8cm 51.5in
Kerb weight: 1271.2kg 2800.0lb

3985 Rover

60
1954 UK
79.0mph 127.1kmh
0-50mph 80.5kmh: 15.5secs
0-60mph 96.5kmh: 23.2secs
0-1/4 mile: 23.1secs
60.0bhp 44.7kW 60.8PS
@ 4000rpm
101.0lbft 136.9Nm @ 2000rpm
44.4bhp/ton 43.7bhp/tonne
30.0bhp/L 22.4kW/L 30.5PS/L
45.9ft/sec 14.0m/sec
18.0mph 29.0kmh/1000rpm
28.7mpg 23.9mpgUS 9.8L/100km
Petrol 4-stroke piston
1997cc 121.8cu in
In-line 4
Compression ratio: 6.7:1
Bore: 77.8mm 3.1in
Stroke: 105.0mm 4.1in
Valve type/No: IOE 8
Transmission: Manual
No. of forward speeds: 4
Wheels driven: Rear
Springs F/R: Coil/Leaf
Brakes F/R: Drum/Drum
Wheelbase: 281.9cm 111.0in
Track F: 132.1cm 52.0in
Track R: 130.8cm 51.5in
Length: 452.6cm 178.2in
Width: 166.6cm 65.6in
Height: 161.8cm 63.7in
Ground clearance: 17.8cm 7.0in
Kerb weight: 1372.9kg 3024.0lb
Fuel: 52.3L 11.5gal 13.8galUS

3986 Rover

90
1954 UK
90.0mph 144.8kmh
0-50mph 80.5kmh: 13.3secs
0-60mph 96.5kmh: 19.8secs
0-1/4 mile: 21.6secs
90.0bhp 67.1kW 91.2PS
@ 4500rpm
130.0lbft 176.2Nm @ 1500rpm
63.1bhp/ton 62.0bhp/tonne
34.1bhp/L 25.4kW/L 34.6PS/L
51.6ft/sec 15.7m/sec
19.8mph 31.9kmh/1000rpm
22.3mpg 18.6mpgUS 12.7L/100km
Petrol 4-stroke piston
2638cc 160.9cu in
In-line 6
Compression ratio: 6.7:1
Bore: 73.0mm 2.9in
Stroke: 105.0mm 4.1in
Valve type/No: IOE 12
Transmission: Manual
No. of forward speeds: 4
Wheels driven: Rear
Springs F/R: Coil/Leaf
Brakes F/R: Drum/Drum
Wheelbase: 281.9cm 111.0in
Track F: 132.1cm 52.0in
Track R: 130.8cm 51.5in
Length: 452.6cm 178.2in
Width: 166.9cm 65.7in
Height: 161.8cm 63.7in
Ground clearance: 17.8cm 7.0in
Kerb weight: 1451.0kg 3196.0lb
Fuel: 52.3L 11.5gal 13.8galUS

3987 Rover

75
1955 UK
87.0mph 140.0kmh
0-50mph 80.5kmh: 13.8secs
0-60mph 96.5kmh: 20.8secs
0-1/4 mile: 21.9secs
80.0bhp 59.7kW 81.1PS
@ 4500rpm
113.0lbft 153.1Nm @ 1750rpm
55.2bhp/ton 54.2bhp/tonne
35.9bhp/L 26.7kW/L 36.4PS/L
43.8ft/sec 13.3m/sec
18.0mph 29.0kmh/1000rpm
21.9mpg 18.2mpgUS 12.9L/100km
Petrol 4-stroke piston
2230cc 136.1cu in
In-line 6 1 Carburettor
Compression ratio: 6.9:1
Bore: 73.0mm 2.9in
Stroke: 88.9mm 3.5in
Valve type/No: IOE 12
Transmission: Manual
No. of forward speeds: 4
Wheels driven: Rear
Springs F/R: Coil/Leaf
Brakes F/R: Drum/Drum
Wheelbase: 281.9cm 111.0in
Track F: 132.1cm 52.0in
Track R: 130.8cm 51.5in
Length: 452.6cm 178.2in
Width: 166.1cm 65.4in
Height: 161.8cm 63.7in
Ground clearance: 19.1cm 7.5in
Kerb weight: 1474.6kg 3248.0lb
Fuel: 52.3L 11.5gal 13.8galUS

3988 Rover

60
1956 UK
78.0mph 125.5kmh
0-50mph 80.5kmh: 18.6secs
0-60mph 96.5kmh: 27.9secs
0-1/4 mile: 23.6secs
60.0bhp 44.7kW 60.8PS
@ 4000rpm
101.0lbft 136.9Nm @ 2000rpm
43.8bhp/ton 43.1bhp/tonne
30.0bhp/L 22.4kW/L 30.5PS/L
45.9ft/sec 14.0m/sec
18.0mph 29.0kmh/1000rpm
29.0mpg 24.1mpgUS 9.7L/100km
Petrol 4-stroke piston
1997cc 121.8cu in
In-line 4
Compression ratio: 6.9:1
Bore: 77.8mm 3.1in
Stroke: 105.0mm 4.1in
Valve type/No: IOE 8
Transmission: Manual
No. of forward speeds: 4
Wheels driven: Rear
Springs F/R: Coil/Leaf
Brakes F/R: Drum/Drum
Wheelbase: 281.9cm 111.0in
Track F: 132.1cm 52.0in
Track R: 130.8cm 51.5in
Length: 452.6cm 178.2in
Width: 166.6cm 65.6in
Height: 161.8cm 63.7in
Ground clearance: 18.0cm 7.1in
Kerb weight: 1392.0kg 3066.0lb
Fuel: 52.3L 11.5gal 13.8galUS

3989 Rover

90
1956 UK
91.0mph 146.4kmh
0-50mph 80.5kmh: 13.7secs
0-60mph 96.5kmh: 19.3secs
0-1/4 mile: 21.6secs
93.0bhp 69.3kW 94.3PS
@ 4500rpm
138.0lbft 187.0Nm @ 1750rpm
62.0bhp/ton 61.0bhp/tonne
35.2bhp/L 26.3kW/L 35.7PS/L
51.6ft/sec 15.7m/sec
23.3mph 37.5kmh/1000rpm
23.4mpg 19.5mpgUS 12.1L/100km
Petrol 4-stroke piston
2638cc 160.9cu in
In-line 6
Compression ratio: 7.5:1
Bore: 73.0mm 2.9in
Stroke: 105.0mm 4.1in
Valve type/No: IOE 12
Transmission: Manual with overdrive
No. of forward speeds: 5
Wheels driven: Rear
Springs F/R: Coil/Leaf
Brake system: PA
Brakes F/R: Drum/Drum
Wheelbase: 281.9cm 111.0in
Track F: 132.1cm 52.0in
Track R: 130.8cm 51.5in
Length: 452.6cm 178.2in
Width: 166.9cm 65.7in
Height: 161.8cm 63.7in
Ground clearance: 19.1cm 7.5in
Kerb weight: 1525.4kg 3360.0lb
Fuel: 52.3L 11.5gal 13.8galUS

3990 Rover

105S
1957 UK
96.0mph 154.5kmh
0-50mph 80.5kmh: 12.8secs
0-60mph 96.5kmh: 17.9secs
0-1/4 mile: 20.4secs
108.0bhp 80.5kW 109.5PS
@ 4250rpm
152.0lbft 206.0Nm @ 2500rpm
70.2bhp/ton 69.1bhp/tonne
40.9bhp/L 30.5kW/L 41.5PS/L
48.8ft/sec 14.9m/sec
23.4mph 37.7kmh/1000rpm
18.5mpg 15.4mpgUS 15.3L/100km
Petrol 4-stroke piston
2638cc 160.9cu in
In-line 6
Compression ratio: 8.5:1
Bore: 73.0mm 2.9in
Stroke: 105.0mm 4.1in
Valve type/No: IOE 12
Transmission: Manual with overdrive
No. of forward speeds: 5
Wheels driven: Rear
Springs F/R: Coil/Leaf
Brake system: PA
Brakes F/R: Drum/Drum
Wheelbase: 281.9cm 111.0in
Track F: 132.1cm 52.0in
Track R: 130.8cm 51.5in
Length: 452.6cm 178.2in
Width: 166.1cm 65.4in
Height: 161.8cm 63.7in
Ground clearance: 18.3cm 7.2in
Kerb weight: 1563.6kg 3444.0lb
Fuel: 52.3L 11.5gal 13.8galUS

3991 Rover

105R de Luxe
1958 UK
91.0mph 146.4kmh
0-50mph 80.5kmh: 19.5secs
0-60mph 96.5kmh: 25.2secs
0-1/4 mile: 24.5secs
108.0bhp 80.5kW 109.5PS
@ 4250rpm
152.0lbft 206.0Nm @ 2500rpm
69.1bhp/ton 68.0bhp/tonne
40.9bhp/L 30.5kW/L 41.5PS/L
48.8ft/sec 14.9m/sec
21.7mph 34.9kmh/1000rpm
21.4mpg 17.8mpgUS 13.2L/100km
Petrol 4-stroke piston
2638cc 160.9cu in
In-line 6 1 Carburettor
Compression ratio: 8.5:1
Bore: 73.0mm 2.9in
Stroke: 105.0mm 4.1in
Valve type/No: IOE 12
Transmission: Automatic
No. of forward speeds: 3
Wheels driven: Rear
Springs F/R: Coil/Leaf
Brake system: PA
Brakes F/R: Drum/Drum
Wheelbase: 281.9cm 111.0in
Track F: 132.1cm 52.0in
Track R: 130.8cm 51.5in
Length: 452.6cm 178.2in
Width: 166.6cm 65.6in
Height: 161.8cm 63.7in
Ground clearance: 18.0cm 7.1in
Kerb weight: 1589.0kg 3500.0lb
Fuel: 52.3L 11.5gal 13.8galUS

3992 Rover

3-litre
1959 UK
97.5mph 156.9kmh
0-50mph 80.5kmh: 11.7secs
0-60mph 96.5kmh: 16.2secs
0-1/4 mile: 20.3secs
115.0bhp 85.8kW 116.6PS
@ 4500rpm
164.0lbft 222.2Nm @ 1500rpm
70.9bhp/ton 69.7bhp/tonne
38.4bhp/L 28.6kW/L 38.9PS/L
51.6ft/sec 15.7m/sec
23.4mph 37.7kmh/1000rpm
19.2mpg 16.0mpgUS 14.7L/100km
Petrol 4-stroke piston
2995cc 182.7cu in
In-line 6 1 Carburettor
Compression ratio: 8.7:1
Bore: 77.8mm 3.1in
Stroke: 105.0mm 4.1in
Valve type/No: IOE 12
Transmission: Manual with overdrive
No. of forward speeds: 5
Wheels driven: Rear
Springs F/R: Torsion bar/Leaf
Brake system: PA
Brakes F/R: Disc/Drum
Wheelbase: 280.7cm 110.5in
Track F: 139.7cm 55.0in
Track R: 142.2cm 56.0in
Length: 473.7cm 186.5in
Width: 177.8cm 70.0in
Height: 152.9cm 60.2in
Ground clearance: 19.8cm 7.8in
Kerb weight: 1649.4kg 3633.0lb
Fuel: 56.9L 12.5gal 15.0galUS

3993 Rover

80
1959 UK
87.0mph 140.0kmh
0-50mph 80.5kmh: 17.4secs
0-60mph 96.5kmh: 22.8secs
0-1/4 mile: 23.4secs
77.0bhp 57.4kW 78.1PS
@ 4250rpm
124.0lbft 168.0Nm @ 2500rpm
52.2bhp/ton 51.3bhp/tonne
33.7bhp/L 25.1kW/L 34.1PS/L
41.3ft/sec 12.6m/sec
22.8mph 36.7kmh/1000rpm
19.8mpg 16.5mpgUS 14.3L/100km
Petrol 4-stroke piston
2286cc 139.5cu in
In-line 4 1 Carburettor
Compression ratio: 7.0:1
Bore: 90.5mm 3.6in
Stroke: 88.9mm 3.5in
Valve type/No: Overhead 8
Transmission: Manual with overdrive
No. of forward speeds: 5
Wheels driven: Rear
Springs F/R: Coil/Leaf
Brakes F/R: Drum/Drum

Wheelbase: 281.9cm 111.0in
Track F: 133.4cm 52.5in
Track R: 130.8cm 51.5in
Length: 452.6cm 178.2in
Width: 166.6cm 65.6in
Height: 161.8cm 63.7in
Ground clearance: 22.1cm 8.7in
Kerb weight: 1500.0kg 3304.0lb
Fuel: 52.3L 11.5gal 13.8galUS

3994 Rover
100
1960 UK
95.0mph 152.9kmh
0-50mph 80.5kmh: 12.9secs
0-60mph 96.5kmh: 17.9secs
0-1/4 mile: 21.0secs
104.0bhp 77.5kW 105.4PS
@ 4750rpm
138.0lbft 187.0Nm @ 1500rpm
67.6bhp/ton 66.5bhp/tonne
39.6bhp/L 29.5kW/L 40.2PS/L
47.9ft/sec 14.6m/sec
22.8mph 36.7kmh/1000rpm
19.5mpg 16.2mpgUS 14.5L/100km
Petrol 4-stroke piston
2625cc 160.2cu in
In-line 6 1 Carburettor
Compression ratio: 7.8:1
Bore: 77.8mm 3.1in
Stroke: 92.1mm 3.6in
Valve type/No: IOE 12
Transmission: Manual with overdrive
No. of forward speeds: 5
Wheels driven: Rear
Springs F/R: Coil/Leaf
Brake system: PA
Brakes F/R: Disc/Drum
Wheelbase: 281.9cm 111.0in
Track F: 133.4cm 52.5in
Track R: 130.8cm 51.5in
Length: 452.6cm 178.2in
Width: 166.6cm 65.6in
Height: 161.8cm 63.7in
Ground clearance: 18.0cm 7.1in
Kerb weight: 1563.6kg 3444.0lb
Fuel: 52.3L 11.5gal 13.8galUS

3995 Rover
3-litre
1960 UK
100.0mph 160.9kmh
0-50mph 80.5kmh: 13.0secs
0-60mph 96.5kmh: 17.7secs
0-1/4 mile: 21.6secs
115.0bhp 85.8kW 116.6PS
@ 4500rpm
164.0lbft 222.2Nm @ 1500rpm
68.3bhp/ton 67.2bhp/tonne
38.4bhp/L 28.6kW/L 38.9PS/L
51.7ft/sec 15.8m/sec
20.4mph 32.8kmh/1000rpm
Petrol 4-stroke piston
2995cc 182.7cu in
In-line 6
Compression ratio: 8.8:1
Bore: 77.7mm 3.1in
Stroke: 105.2mm 4.1in
Valve type/No: Side 12
Transmission: Automatic
No. of forward speeds: 3
Wheels driven: Rear
Wheelbase: 280.7cm 110.5in
Track F: 139.7cm 55.0in
Track R: 142.2cm 56.0in
Length: 475.0cm 187.0in
Width: 177.8cm 70.0in
Height: 153.2cm 60.3in
Kerb weight: 1711.6kg 3770.0lb

3996 Rover
100
1961 UK
95.0mph 152.9kmh
0-50mph 80.5kmh: 12.8secs
0-60mph 96.5kmh: 18.1secs
0-1/4 mile: 21.2secs
104.0bhp 77.5kW 105.4PS
@ 4750rpm
138.0lbft 187.0Nm @ 1500rpm
70.1bhp/ton 68.9bhp/tonne
39.6bhp/L 29.5kW/L 40.2PS/L
47.8ft/sec 14.5m/sec
22.8mph 36.7kmh/1000rpm
Petrol 4-stroke piston
2625cc 160.2cu in
In-line 6 1 Carburettor
Compression ratio: 7.8:1
Bore: 77.7mm 3.1in
Stroke: 91.9mm 3.6in
Valve type/No: Side 12
Transmission: Manual with overdrive
Wheels driven: Rear
Wheelbase: 281.9cm 111.0in
Track F: 134.6cm 53.0in
Track R: 130.8cm 51.5in
Length: 452.6cm 178.2in
Width: 166.4cm 65.5in
Height: 158.0cm 62.2in
Ground clearance: 17.8cm 7.0in
Kerb weight: 1509.5kg 3325.0lb

3997 Rover
3-litre Automatic
1961 UK
103.0mph 165.7kmh
0-50mph 80.5kmh: 12.5secs
0-60mph 96.5kmh: 17.1secs
0-1/4 mile: 20.8secs
119.0bhp 88.7kW 120.6PS
@ 4600rpm
161.0lbft 218.2Nm @ 2500rpm
70.5bhp/ton 69.3bhp/tonne
39.7bhp/L 29.6kW/L 40.3PS/L
52.8ft/sec 16.1m/sec
20.6mph 33.1kmh/1000rpm
15.6mpg 13.0mpgUS 18.1L/100km
Petrol 4-stroke piston
2995cc 182.7cu in
In-line 6 1 Carburettor
Compression ratio: 8.0:1
Bore: 77.8mm 3.1in
Stroke: 105.0mm 4.1in
Valve type/No: IOE 12
Transmission: Automatic
No. of forward speeds: 3
Wheels driven: Rear
Springs F/R: Torsion bar/Leaf
Brake system: PA
Brakes F/R: Disc/Drum
Steering: Worm & peg PA
Wheelbase: 280.7cm 110.5in
Track F: 140.5cm 55.3in
Track R: 142.2cm 56.0in
Length: 473.7cm 186.5in
Width: 178.6cm 70.3in
Height: 149.9cm 59.0in
Ground clearance: 20.1cm 7.9in
Kerb weight: 1716.1kg 3780.0lb
Fuel: 63.7L 14.0gal 16.8galUS

3998 Rover
3-litre
1962 UK
100.0mph 160.9kmh
0-50mph 80.5kmh: 13.0secs
0-60mph 96.5kmh: 18.6secs
0-1/4 mile: 21.6secs
115.0bhp 85.8kW 116.6PS
@ 4500rpm
164.0lbft 222.2Nm @ 1500rpm
70.2bhp/ton 69.0bhp/tonne
38.4bhp/L 28.6kW/L 38.9PS/L
51.6ft/sec 15.7m/sec
20.2mph 32.5kmh/1000rpm
Petrol 4-stroke piston
2995cc 182.7cu in
In-line 6
Compression ratio: 8.8:1
Bore: 77.7mm 3.1in
Stroke: 104.9mm 4.1in
Valve type/No: Side 12
Transmission: Automatic
No. of forward speeds: 3
Wheels driven: Rear
Wheelbase: 280.7cm 110.5in
Track F: 141.2cm 55.6in
Track R: 142.2cm 56.0in
Length: 473.7cm 186.5in
Width: 177.8cm 70.0in
Height: 152.9cm 60.2in
Ground clearance: 19.8cm 7.8in
Kerb weight: 1666.2kg 3670.0lb

3999 Rover
2000
1963 UK
104.5mph 168.1kmh
0-50mph 80.5kmh: 10.0secs
0-60mph 96.5kmh: 15.1secs
0-1/4 mile: 19.9secs
90.0bhp 67.1kW 91.2PS
@ 5000rpm
113.5lbft 153.8Nm @ 2750rpm
71.9bhp/ton 70.7bhp/tonne
45.5bhp/L 33.9kW/L 46.1PS/L
46.8ft/sec 14.3m/sec
19.1mph 30.7kmh/1000rpm
24.0mpg 20.0mpgUS 11.8L/100km
Petrol 4-stroke piston
1978cc 120.7cu in
In-line 4 1 Carburettor
Compression ratio: 9.0:1
Bore: 85.7mm 3.4in
Stroke: 85.7mm 3.4in
Valve type/No: Overhead 8
Transmission: Manual
No. of forward speeds: 4
Wheels driven: Rear
Springs F/R: Coil/Coil
Brake system: PA
Brakes F/R: Disc/Disc
Steering: Worm & roller
Wheelbase: 262.9cm 103.5in
Track F: 135.6cm 53.4in
Track R: 135.6cm 53.4in
Length: 448.3cm 176.5in
Width: 167.6cm 66.0in
Height: 147.8cm 58.2in
Ground clearance: 13.2cm 5.2in
Kerb weight: 1273.0kg 2804.0lb
Fuel: 54.6L 12.0gal 14.4galUS

4000 Rover
3-litre Coupe
1963 UK
110.3mph 177.5kmh
0-50mph 80.5kmh: 10.3secs
0-60mph 96.5kmh: 15.0secs
0-1/4 mile: 19.6secs
121.0bhp 90.2kW 122.7PS
@ 5000rpm
169.0lbft 229.0Nm @ 1750rpm
72.2bhp/ton 71.0bhp/tonne
40.4bhp/L 30.1kW/L 41.0PS/L
57.4ft/sec 17.5m/sec
23.8mph 38.3kmh/1000rpm
17.6mpg 14.7mpgUS 16.1L/100km
Petrol 4-stroke piston
2995cc 182.7cu in
In-line 6 1 Carburettor
Compression ratio: 8.7:1
Bore: 77.8mm 3.1in
Stroke: 105.0mm 4.1in
Valve type/No: IOE 12
Transmission: Manual with overdrive
No. of forward speeds: 5
Wheels driven: Rear
Springs F/R: Torsion bar/Leaf
Brake system: PA
Brakes F/R: Disc/Drum
Steering: Worm & peg PA
Wheelbase: 280.7cm 110.5in
Track F: 140.5cm 55.3in
Track R: 142.2cm 56.0in
Length: 473.7cm 186.5in
Width: 178.6cm 70.3in
Height: 149.9cm 59.0in
Ground clearance: 20.1cm 7.9in
Kerb weight: 1703.4kg 3752.0lb
Fuel: 63.7L 14.0gal 16.8galUS

4001 Rover
Coupe
1963 UK
105.0mph 168.9kmh
0-50mph 80.5kmh: 11.6secs
0-60mph 96.5kmh: 15.5secs
0-1/4 mile: 19.7secs
134.0bhp 99.9kW 135.9PS
@ 5000rpm
169.0lbft 229.0Nm @ 1750rpm
82.5bhp/ton 81.1bhp/tonne
44.7bhp/L 33.4kW/L 45.4PS/L
57.4ft/sec 17.5m/sec
24.4mph 39.3kmh/1000rpm
Petrol 4-stroke piston
2995cc 182.7cu in
In-line 6 1 Carburettor
Compression ratio: 8.8:1
Bore: 78.2mm 3.1in
Stroke: 104.9mm 4.1in
Valve type/No: Side 12
Transmission: Manual with overdrive
Wheels driven: Rear
Wheelbase: 280.7cm 110.5in
Track F: 140.5cm 55.3in
Track R: 142.2cm 56.0in
Length: 471.2cm 185.5in
Width: 177.8cm 70.0in
Height: 145.3cm 57.2in
Ground clearance: 19.8cm 7.8in
Kerb weight: 1652.6kg 3640.0lb

4002 Rover
2000
1964 UK
101.0mph 162.5kmh
0-50mph 80.5kmh: 10.8secs
0-60mph 96.5kmh: 15.3secs
0-1/4 mile: 20.2secs
90.0bhp 67.1kW 91.2PS
@ 5000rpm
113.5lbft 153.8Nm @ 3600rpm
70.7bhp/ton 69.6bhp/tonne
45.5bhp/L 33.9kW/L 46.1PS/L
46.8ft/sec 14.3m/sec
19.7mph 31.7kmh/1000rpm
Petrol 4-stroke piston
1978cc 120.7cu in
In-line 4 1 Carburettor
Compression ratio: 9.0:1
Bore: 85.7mm 3.4in
Stroke: 85.7mm 3.4in
Valve type/No: Overhead 8
Transmission: Manual
No. of forward speeds: 4
Wheels driven: Rear
Springs F/R: Coil/Coil
Brakes F/R: Disc/Disc
Steering: Worm & roller
Wheelbase: 262.6cm 103.4in
Track F: 135.6cm 53.4in
Track R: 133.4cm 52.5in
Length: 453.4cm 178.5in
Width: 168.9cm 66.5in
Height: 139.2cm 54.8in
Ground clearance: 21.6cm 8.5in
Kerb weight: 1293.9kg 2850.0lb
Fuel: 54.5L 12.0gal 14.4galUS

4003 Rover
2000 Automatic
1966 UK
94.0mph 151.2kmh
0-50mph 80.5kmh: 12.8secs
0-60mph 96.5kmh: 18.0secs
0-1/4 mile: 21.5secs
0-1km: 39.2secs
90.0bhp 67.1kW 91.2PS
@ 5000rpm
113.5lbft 153.8Nm @ 2750rpm
69.9bhp/ton 68.7bhp/tonne
45.5bhp/L 33.9kW/L 46.1PS/L
46.8ft/sec 14.3m/sec
19.5mph 31.4kmh/1000rpm
21.8mpg 18.2mpgUS 13.0L/100km
Petrol 4-stroke piston
1978cc 120.7cu in
In-line 4 1 Carburettor
Compression ratio: 9.0:1
Bore: 85.7mm 3.4in
Stroke: 85.7mm 3.4in
Valve type/No: Overhead 8
Transmission: Automatic
No. of forward speeds: 3
Wheels driven: Rear
Springs F/R: Coil/Coil
Brake system: PA
Brakes F/R: Disc/Disc
Steering: Worm & roller
Wheelbase: 262.9cm 103.5in
Track F: 135.6cm 53.4in
Track R: 135.6cm 53.4in
Length: 453.4cm 178.5in
Width: 167.6cm 66.0in
Height: 141.0cm 55.5in
Ground clearance: 19.1cm 7.5in
Kerb weight: 1309.8kg 2885.0lb
Fuel: 54.6L 12.0gal 14.4galUS

4004 Rover
2000TC
1966 UK
116.0mph 186.6kmh
0-50mph 80.5kmh: 9.3secs
0-60mph 96.5kmh: 12.6secs
0-1/4 mile: 18.9secs
114.0bhp 85.0kW 115.6PS
@ 5000rpm
126.0lbft 170.7Nm @ 3500rpm
88.1bhp/ton 86.6bhp/tonne
57.6bhp/L 42.9kW/L 58.4PS/L
46.8ft/sec 14.3m/sec
19.3mph 31.1kmh/1000rpm
Petrol 4-stroke piston

1980cc 120.8cu in
In-line 4 2 Carburettor
Compression ratio: 10.0:1
Bore: 85.7mm 3.4in
Stroke: 85.7mm 3.4in
Valve type/No: Overhead 8
Transmission: Manual
No. of forward speeds: 4
Wheels driven: Rear
Springs F/R: Coil/Coil
Brakes F/R: Disc/Disc
Steering: Worm & roller
Wheelbase: 262.6cm 103.4in
Track F: 135.6cm 53.4in
Track R: 133.4cm 52.5in
Length: 453.4cm 178.5in
Width: 167.6cm 66.0in
Height: 139.2cm 54.8in
Ground clearance: 13.5cm 5.3in
Kerb weight: 1316.6kg 2900.0lb
Fuel: 54.5L 12.0gal 14.4galUS

4005 Rover

3-litre Coupe Mk III
1966 UK
112.0mph 180.2kmh
0-50mph 80.5kmh: 10.7secs
0-60mph 96.5kmh: 15.0secs
0-1/4 mile: 19.6secs
0-1km: 36.1secs
121.0bhp 90.2kW 122.7PS
@ 4800rpm
160.0lbft 216.8Nm @ 2650rpm
70.7bhp/ton 69.5bhp/tonne
40.4bhp/L 30.1kW/L 41.0PS/L
55.1ft/sec 16.8m/sec
23.8mph 38.3kmh/1000rpm
18.2mpg 15.2mpgUS 15.5L/100km
Petrol 4-stroke piston
2995cc 182.7cu in
In-line 6 1 Carburettor
Compression ratio: 8.7:1
Bore: 77.8mm 3.1in
Stroke: 105.0mm 4.1in
Valve type/No: IOE 12
Transmission: Manual with overdrive
No. of forward speeds: 5
Wheels driven: Rear
Springs F/R: Torsion bar/Leaf
Brake system: PA
Brakes F/R: Disc/Drum
Steering: Worm & peg PA
Wheelbase: 280.7cm 110.5in
Track F: 140.5cm 55.3in
Track R: 142.2cm 56.0in
Length: 473.7cm 186.5in
Width: 178.6cm 70.3in
Height: 149.9cm 59.0in
Ground clearance: 20.1cm 7.9in
Kerb weight: 1741.5kg 3836.0lb
Fuel: 63.7L 14.0gal 16.8galUS

4006 Rover

Rover-BRM Turbine
1966 UK
142.0mph 228.5kmh
0-50mph 80.5kmh: 9.0secs
0-60mph 96.5kmh: 11.3secs
0-1/4 mile: 18.9secs
126.0bhp 94.0kW 127.7PS
@ 39000rpm
267.0lbft 361.8Nm
169.0bhp/ton 166.2bhp/tonne
78.7bhp/L 58.7kW/L 79.8PS/L
3.5mph 5.6kmh/1000rpm
14.2mpg 11.8mpgUS 19.9L/100km
Gas turbine
1600cc 97.6cu in
Gas turbine fuel injection
Compression ratio: 4.0:1
Wheels driven: Rear
Springs F/R: Coil/Coil
Brakes F/R: Disc/Disc
Steering: Rack & pinion
Wheelbase: 237.5cm 93.5in
Track F: 133.4cm 52.5in
Track R: 130.8cm 51.5in
Length: 423.7cm 166.8in
Width: 162.6cm 64.0in
Height: 108.0cm 42.5in
Ground clearance: 12.2cm 4.8in
Kerb weight: 758.2kg 1670.0lb
Fuel: 109.8L 24.1gal 29.0galUS

4007 Rover

3.5-litre
1967 UK
109.0mph 175.4kmh
0-50mph 80.5kmh: 8.9secs
0-60mph 96.5kmh: 12.4secs
0-1/4 mile: 18.3secs
0-1km: 34.1secs
160.5bhp 119.7kW 162.7PS
@ 5200rpm
210.0lbft 284.6Nm @ 2600rpm
102.3bhp/ton 100.6bhp/tonne
45.5bhp/L 33.9kW/L 46.1PS/L
40.4ft/sec 12.3m/sec
22.7mph 36.5kmh/1000rpm
19.2mpg 16.0mpgUS 14.7L/100km
Petrol 4-stroke piston
3528cc 215.2cu in
Vee 8 2 Carburettor
Compression ratio: 10.5:1
Bore: 88.9mm 3.5in
Stroke: 71.2mm 2.8in
Valve type/No: Overhead 16
Transmission: Automatic
No. of forward speeds: 3
Wheels driven: Rear
Springs F/R: Torsion bar/Leaf
Brake system: PA
Brakes F/R: Disc/Drum
Steering: Worm & peg PA
Wheelbase: 280.7cm 110.5in
Track F: 140.5cm 55.3in
Track R: 142.2cm 56.0in
Length: 473.7cm 186.5in
Width: 178.6cm 70.3in
Height: 149.9cm 59.0in
Ground clearance: 20.1cm 7.9in
Kerb weight: 1595.4kg 3514.0lb
Fuel: 63.7L 14.0gal 16.8galUS

4008 Rover

2000TC
1969 UK
106.0mph 170.6kmh
0-50mph 80.5kmh: 9.2secs
0-60mph 96.5kmh: 13.2secs
0-1/4 mile: 18.8secs
124.0bhp 92.5kW 125.7PS
@ 5500rpm
132.0lbft 178.9Nm @ 4000rpm
96.1bhp/ton 94.5bhp/tonne
62.7bhp/L 46.7kW/L 63.6PS/L
51.5ft/sec 15.7m/sec
18.8mph 30.2kmh/1000rpm
24.7mpg 20.6mpgUS 11.4L/100km
Petrol 4-stroke piston
1978cc 120.7cu in
In-line 4 2 Carburettor
Compression ratio: 10.0:1
Bore: 85.7mm 3.4in
Stroke: 85.7mm 3.4in
Valve type/No: Overhead 8
Transmission: Manual
No. of forward speeds: 4
Wheels driven: Rear
Springs F/R: Coil/Coil
Brake system: PA
Brakes F/R: Disc/Disc
Steering: Worm & roller
Wheelbase: 262.6cm 103.4in
Track F: 135.6cm 53.4in
Track R: 133.4cm 52.5in
Length: 453.4cm 178.5in
Width: 168.9cm 66.5in
Height: 140.2cm 55.2in
Ground clearance: 21.6cm 8.5in
Kerb weight: 1312.1kg 2890.0lb
Fuel: 54.5L 12.0gal 14.4galUS

4009 Rover

3500
1970 UK
113.0mph 181.8kmh
0-50mph 80.5kmh: 7.9secs
0-60mph 96.5kmh: 10.8secs
0-1/4 mile: 17.9secs
0-1km: 33.2secs
160.5bhp 119.7kW 162.7PS
@ 5200rpm
210.0lbft 284.6Nm @ 2600rpm
120.6bhp/ton 118.6bhp/tonne
45.5bhp/L 33.9kW/L 46.1PS/L
40.4ft/sec 12.3m/sec
23.5mph 37.8kmh/1000rpm
18.0mpg 15.0mpgUS 15.7L/100km
Petrol 4-stroke piston
3528cc 215.2cu in
Vee 8 2 Carburettor
Compression ratio: 10.0:1
Bore: 88.9mm 3.5in
Stroke: 71.1mm 2.8in
Valve type/No: Overhead 16
Transmission: Automatic
No. of forward speeds: 3
Wheels driven: Rear
Springs F/R: Coil/Coil
Brake system: PA
Brakes F/R: Disc/Disc
Steering: Cam & roller PA
Wheelbase: 262.9cm 103.5in
Track F: 135.6cm 53.4in
Track R: 135.6cm 53.4in
Length: 454.7cm 179.0in
Width: 167.6cm 66.0in
Height: 142.2cm 56.0in
Ground clearance: 19.1cm 7.5in
Kerb weight: 1352.9kg 2980.0lb
Fuel: 68.2L 15.0gal 18.0galUS

4010 Rover

3500S
1970 UK
117.0mph 188.3kmh
0-50mph 80.5kmh: 8.4secs
0-60mph 96.5kmh: 11.9secs
0-1/4 mile: 17.7secs
184.0bhp 137.2kW 186.5PS
@ 5200rpm
226.0lbft 306.2Nm @ 3000rpm
129.0bhp/ton 126.8bhp/tonne
52.1bhp/L 38.9kW/L 52.9PS/L
40.4ft/sec 12.3m/sec
22.2mph 35.7kmh/1000rpm
21.0mpg 17.5mpgUS 13.4L/100km
Petrol 4-stroke piston
3528cc 215.2cu in
Vee 8 2 Carburettor
Compression ratio: 10.5:1
Bore: 88.9mm 3.5in
Stroke: 71.1mm 2.8in
Valve type/No: Overhead 16
Transmission: Automatic
No. of forward speeds: 3
Wheels driven: Rear
Springs F/R: Coil/Coil
Brake system: PA
Brakes F/R: Disc/Drum
Steering: Cam & follower PA
Wheelbase: 262.6cm 103.4in
Track F: 135.6cm 53.4in
Track R: 131.3cm 51.7in
Length: 459.7cm 181.0in
Width: 165.1cm 65.0in
Height: 142.7cm 56.2in
Ground clearance: 17.8cm 7.0in
Kerb weight: 1450.5kg 3195.0lb
Fuel: 68.1L 15.0gal 18.0galUS

4011 Rover

2000TC
1971 UK
108.0mph 173.8kmh
0-50mph 80.5kmh: 8.6secs
0-60mph 96.5kmh: 12.2secs
0-1/4 mile: 18.5secs
0-1km: 34.2secs
114.0bhp 85.0kW 115.6PS
@ 5500rpm
126.0lbft 170.7Nm @ 3500rpm
89.6bhp/ton 88.1bhp/tonne
57.6bhp/L 43.0kW/L 58.4PS/L
51.5ft/sec 15.7m/sec
19.1mph 30.7kmh/1000rpm
22.4mpg 18.7mpgUS 12.6L/100km
Petrol 4-stroke piston
1978cc 120.7cu in
In-line 4 2 Carburettor
Compression ratio: 10.0:1
Bore: 85.7mm 3.4in
Stroke: 85.7mm 3.4in
Valve type/No: Overhead 8
Transmission: Manual
No. of forward speeds: 4
Wheels driven: Rear
Springs F/R: Coil/Coil
Brake system: PA
Brakes F/R: Disc/Disc
Steering: Worm & roller
Wheelbase: 262.9cm 103.5in
Track F: 135.6cm 53.4in
Track R: 135.6cm 53.4in
Length: 454.7cm 179.0in
Width: 167.6cm 66.0in
Height: 142.2cm 56.0in
Ground clearance: 19.1cm 7.5in
Kerb weight: 1293.4kg 2849.0lb
Fuel: 54.6L 12.0gal 14.4galUS

4012 Rover

3500S
1971 UK
125.0mph 201.1kmh
0-50mph 80.5kmh: 6.9secs
0-60mph 96.5kmh: 9.1secs
0-1/4 mile: 16.8secs
0-1km: 31.2secs
152.5bhp 113.7kW 154.6PS
@ 5000rpm
203.0lbft 275.1Nm @ 2750rpm
114.8bhp/ton 112.9bhp/tonne
43.2bhp/L 32.2kW/L 43.8PS/L
38.9ft/sec 11.8m/sec
24.0mph 38.6kmh/1000rpm
20.1mpg 16.7mpgUS 14.1L/100km
Petrol 4-stroke piston
3528cc 215.2cu in
Vee 8 2 Carburettor
Compression ratio: 10.5:1
Bore: 88.9mm 3.5in
Stroke: 71.1mm 2.8in
Valve type/No: Overhead 16
Transmission: Manual
No. of forward speeds: 4
Wheels driven: Rear
Springs F/R: Coil/Coil
Brake system: PA
Brakes F/R: Disc/Disc
Steering: Cam & roller PA
Wheelbase: 262.9cm 103.5in
Track F: 135.6cm 53.4in
Track R: 135.6cm 53.4in
Length: 454.7cm 179.0in
Width: 167.6cm 66.0in
Height: 142.2cm 56.0in
Ground clearance: 19.1cm 7.5in
Kerb weight: 1350.6kg 2975.0lb
Fuel: 68.2L 15.0gal 18.0galUS

4013 Rover

2000SC
1973 UK
104.0mph 167.3kmh
0-50mph 80.5kmh: 10.5secs
0-60mph 96.5kmh: 14.7secs
0-1/4 mile: 20.0secs
0-1km: 36.8secs
89.0bhp 66.4kW 90.2PS
@ 5000rpm
108.0lbft 146.3Nm @ 2500rpm
71.1bhp/ton 69.9bhp/tonne
45.0bhp/L 33.5kW/L 45.6PS/L
46.8ft/sec 14.3m/sec
19.1mph 30.7kmh/1000rpm
25.3mpg 21.1mpgUS 11.2L/100km
Petrol 4-stroke piston
1978cc 120.7cu in
In-line 4 1 Carburettor
Compression ratio: 9.0:1
Bore: 85.7mm 3.4in
Stroke: 85.7mm 3.4in
Valve type/No: Overhead 8
Transmission: Manual
No. of forward speeds: 4
Wheels driven: Rear
Springs F/R: Coil/Coil
Brake system: PA
Brakes F/R: Disc/Disc
Steering: Worm & roller
Wheelbase: 262.9cm 103.5in
Track F: 135.6cm 53.4in
Track R: 135.6cm 53.4in
Length: 454.7cm 179.0in
Width: 167.6cm 66.0in
Height: 142.2cm 56.0in
Ground clearance: 19.1cm 7.5in
Kerb weight: 1273.0kg 2804.0lb
Fuel: 54.6L 12.0gal 14.4galUS

4014 Rover

2200SC Automatic
1973 UK
103.0mph 165.7kmh
0-50mph 80.5kmh: 10.4secs
0-60mph 96.5kmh: 14.5secs
0-1/4 mile: 19.7secs
0-1km: 36.9secs
98.0bhp 73.1kW 99.4PS
@ 5000rpm
126.0lbft 170.7Nm @ 2500rpm
76.5bhp/ton 75.2bhp/tonne
44.4bhp/L 33.1kW/L 45.1PS/L
46.8ft/sec 14.3m/sec
19.7mph 31.7kmh/1000rpm
20.5mpg 17.1mpgUS 13.8L/100km
Petrol 4-stroke piston

2205cc 134.5cu in
In-line 4 1 Carburettor
Compression ratio: 9.0:1
Bore: 90.5mm 3.6in
Stroke: 85.7mm 3.4in
Valve type/No: Overhead 8
Transmission: Automatic
No. of forward speeds: 3
Wheels driven: Rear
Springs F/R: Coil/Coil
Brake system: PA
Brakes F/R: Disc/Disc
Steering: Worm & roller
Wheelbase: 262.9cm 103.5in
Track F: 135.6cm 53.4in
Track R: 135.6cm 53.4in
Length: 454.7cm 179.0in
Width: 167.6cm 66.0in
Height: 142.2cm 56.0in
Ground clearance: 19.1cm 7.5in
Kerb weight: 1303.0kg 2870.0lb
Fuel: 68.2L 15.0gal 18.0galUS

4015 Rover

2200TC
1974 UK
112.0mph 180.2kmh
0-50mph 80.5kmh: 8.0secs
0-60mph 96.5kmh: 11.4secs
0-1/4 mile: 18.3secs
0-1km: 34.2secs
115.0bhp 85.8kW 116.6PS
@ 5000rpm
135.0lbft 182.9Nm @ 3000rpm
89.2bhp/ton 87.7bhp/tonne
52.1bhp/L 38.9kW/L 52.9PS/L
46.8ft/sec 14.3m/sec
19.7mph 31.7kmh/1000rpm
20.9mpg 17.4mpgUS 13.5L/100km
Petrol 4-stroke piston
2205cc 134.5cu in
In-line 4 2 Carburettor
Compression ratio: 9.0:1
Bore: 90.5mm 3.6in
Stroke: 85.7mm 3.4in
Valve type/No: Overhead 8
Transmission: Manual
No. of forward speeds: 4
Wheels driven: Rear
Springs F/R: Coil/Coil
Brake system: PA
Brakes F/R: Disc/Disc
Steering: Worm & roller
Wheelbase: 262.9cm 103.5in
Track F: 135.6cm 53.4in
Track R: 135.6cm 53.4in
Length: 454.7cm 179.0in
Width: 167.6cm 66.0in
Height: 142.2cm 56.0in
Ground clearance: 19.1cm 7.5in
Kerb weight: 1310.7kg 2887.0lb
Fuel: 68.2L 15.0gal 18.0galUS

4016 Rover

3500
1976 UK
126.0mph 202.7kmh
0-50mph 80.5kmh: 6.3secs
0-60mph 96.5kmh: 8.4secs
0-1/4 mile: 16.6secs
0-1km: 30.7secs
155.0bhp 115.6kW 157.1PS
@ 5250rpm
198.0lbft 268.3Nm @ 2500rpm
116.2bhp/ton 114.2bhp/tonne
43.9bhp/L 32.8kW/L 44.5PS/L
40.8ft/sec 12.4m/sec
28.6mph 46.0kmh/1000rpm
20.5mpg 17.1mpgUS 13.8L/100km
Petrol 4-stroke piston
3528cc 215.2cu in
Vee 8 2 Carburettor
Compression ratio: 9.3:1
Bore: 88.9mm 3.5in
Stroke: 71.1mm 2.8in
Valve type/No: Overhead 16
Transmission: Manual
No. of forward speeds: 5
Wheels driven: Rear
Springs F/R: Coil/Coil
Brake system: PA
Brakes F/R: Disc/Drum
Steering: Rack & pinion PA
Wheelbase: 281.4cm 110.8in
Track F: 150.1cm 59.1in
Track R: 150.1cm 59.1in
Length: 469.9cm 185.0in
Width: 176.8cm 69.6in
Height: 135.4cm 53.3in
Ground clearance: 15.5cm 6.1in
Kerb weight: 1357.0kg 2989.0lb
Fuel: 66.0L 14.5gal 17.4galUS

4017 Rover

3500 Automatic
1976 UK
119.0mph 191.5kmh
0-50mph 80.5kmh: 7.8secs
0-60mph 96.5kmh: 10.3secs
0-1/4 mile: 17.9secs
0-1km: 32.6secs
155.0bhp 115.6kW 157.1PS
@ 5250rpm
198.0lbft 268.3Nm @ 2500rpm
114.0bhp/ton 112.1bhp/tonne
43.9bhp/L 32.8kW/L 44.5PS/L
40.8ft/sec 12.4m/sec
23.8mph 38.3kmh/1000rpm
18.0mpg 15.0mpgUS 15.7L/100km
Petrol 4-stroke piston
3528cc 215.2cu in
Vee 8 2 Carburettor
Compression ratio: 9.3:1
Bore: 88.9mm 3.5in
Stroke: 71.1mm 2.8in
Valve type/No: Overhead 16
Transmission: Automatic
No. of forward speeds: 3
Wheels driven: Rear
Springs F/R: Coil/Coil
Brake system: PA
Brakes F/R: Disc/Drum
Steering: Rack & pinion PA
Wheelbase: 281.4cm 110.8in
Track F: 150.1cm 59.1in
Track R: 150.1cm 59.1in
Length: 469.9cm 185.0in
Width: 176.8cm 69.6in
Height: 135.4cm 53.3in
Ground clearance: 15.5cm 6.1in
Kerb weight: 1382.4kg 3045.0lb
Fuel: 66.0L 14.5gal 17.4galUS

4018 Rover

2600
1977 UK
118.0mph 189.9kmh
0-50mph 80.5kmh: 7.8secs
0-60mph 96.5kmh: 10.7secs
0-1/4 mile: 17.7secs
0-1km: 32.6secs
136.0bhp 101.4kW 137.9PS
@ 5000rpm
152.0lbft 206.0Nm @ 3750rpm
103.1bhp/ton 101.4bhp/tonne
52.4bhp/L 39.0kW/L 53.1PS/L
46.0ft/sec 14.0m/sec
25.0mph 40.2kmh/1000rpm
22.4mpg 18.7mpgUS 12.6L/100km
Petrol 4-stroke piston
2597cc 158.4cu in
In-line 6 2 Carburettor
Compression ratio: 9.2:1
Bore: 81.0mm 3.2in
Stroke: 84.0mm 3.3in
Valve type/No: Overhead 12
Transmission: Manual
No. of forward speeds: 5
Wheels driven: Rear
Springs F/R: Coil/Coil
Brake system: PA
Brakes F/R: Disc/Drum
Steering: Rack & pinion PA
Wheelbase: 281.4cm 110.8in
Track F: 150.1cm 59.1in
Track R: 150.1cm 59.1in
Length: 469.9cm 185.0in
Width: 176.8cm 69.6in
Height: 135.4cm 53.3in
Ground clearance: 15.5cm 6.1in
Kerb weight: 1341.1kg 2954.0lb
Fuel: 66.0L 14.5gal 17.4galUS

4019 Rover

2300
1978 UK
111.0mph 178.6kmh
0-50mph 80.5kmh: 8.7secs
0-60mph 96.5kmh: 11.9secs
0-1/4 mile: 18.7secs
0-1km: 34.3secs
123.0bhp 91.7kW 124.7PS
@ 5000rpm
134.0lbft 181.6Nm @ 4000rpm
93.3bhp/ton 91.7bhp/tonne
52.3bhp/L 39.0kW/L 53.1PS/L
41.5ft/sec 12.7m/sec
24.9mph 40.1kmh/1000rpm
22.0mpg 18.3mpgUS 12.8L/100km
Petrol 4-stroke piston
2350cc 143.4cu in
In-line 6 2 Carburettor
Compression ratio: 9.2:1
Bore: 81.0mm 3.2in
Stroke: 76.0mm 3.0in
Valve type/No: Overhead 12
Transmission: Manual
No. of forward speeds: 5
Wheels driven: Rear
Springs F/R: Coil/Coil
Brake system: PA
Brakes F/R: Disc/Drum
Steering: Rack & pinion PA
Wheelbase: 281.4cm 110.8in
Track F: 150.1cm 59.1in
Track R: 150.1cm 59.1in
Length: 469.9cm 185.0in
Width: 176.8cm 69.6in
Height: 135.4cm 53.3in
Ground clearance: 15.5cm 6.1in
Kerb weight: 1341.1kg 2954.0lb
Fuel: 66.0L 14.5gal 17.4galUS

4020 Rover

3500
1980 UK
116.0mph 186.6kmh
0-60mph 96.5kmh: 10.0secs
0-1/4 mile: 17.6secs
133.0bhp 99.2kW 134.8PS
@ 5000rpm
165.0lbft 223.6Nm @ 3250rpm
92.9bhp/ton 91.4bhp/tonne
37.7bhp/L 28.1kW/L 38.2PS/L
38.9ft/sec 11.8m/sec
28.6mph 46.0kmh/1000rpm
24.6mpg 20.5mpgUS 11.5L/100km
Petrol 4-stroke piston
3528cc 215.2cu in
Vee 8 fuel injection
Compression ratio: 8.1:1
Bore: 88.9mm 3.5in
Stroke: 71.1mm 2.8in
Valve type/No: Overhead 16
Transmission: Manual
No. of forward speeds: 5
Wheels driven: Rear
Springs F/R: Coil/Coil
Brake system: PA
Brakes F/R: Disc/Drum
Steering: Rack & pinion PA
Wheelbase: 281.4cm 110.8in
Track F: 150.6cm 59.3in
Track R: 150.6cm 59.3in
Length: 485.1cm 191.0in
Width: 176.8cm 69.6in
Height: 138.2cm 54.4in
Ground clearance: 13.7cm 5.4in
Kerb weight: 1455.1kg 3205.0lb
Fuel: 63.6L 14.0gal 16.8galUS

4021 Rover

Vanden Plas
1981 UK
126.0mph 202.7kmh
0-50mph 80.5kmh: 7.4secs
0-60mph 96.5kmh: 9.7secs
0-1/4 mile: 17.3secs
0-1km: 32.0secs
155.0bhp 115.6kW 157.1PS
@ 5250rpm
198.0lbft 268.3Nm @ 5000rpm
104.3bhp/ton 102.5bhp/tonne
43.9bhp/L 32.8kW/L 44.5PS/L
40.8ft/sec 12.4m/sec
29.7mph 47.8kmh/1000rpm
20.7mpg 17.2mpgUS 13.6L/100km
Petrol 4-stroke piston
3528cc 215.2cu in
Vee 8 2 Carburettor
Compression ratio: 9.3:1
Bore: 88.9mm 3.5in
Stroke: 71.1mm 2.8in
Valve type/No: Overhead 16
Transmission: Manual
No. of forward speeds: 5
Wheels driven: Rear
Springs F/R: Coil/Coil
Brake system: PA
Brakes F/R: Disc/Drum
Steering: Rack & pinion PA
Wheelbase: 281.4cm 110.8in
Track F: 150.1cm 59.1in
Track R: 150.1cm 59.1in
Length: 469.9cm 185.0in
Width: 176.8cm 69.6in
Height: 138.4cm 54.5in
Ground clearance: 15.5cm 6.1in
Kerb weight: 1511.8kg 3330.0lb
Fuel: 66.0L 14.5gal 17.4galUS

4022 Rover

2000
1982 UK
105.0mph 168.9kmh
0-50mph 80.5kmh: 8.6secs
0-60mph 96.5kmh: 12.4secs
0-1/4 mile: 18.6secs
0-1km: 34.8secs
101.0bhp 75.3kW 102.4PS
@ 5250rpm
120.0lbft 162.6Nm @ 3250rpm
76.8bhp/ton 75.5bhp/tonne
50.6bhp/L 37.8kW/L 51.3PS/L
51.0ft/sec 15.6m/sec
23.3mph 37.5kmh/1000rpm
22.8mpg 19.0mpgUS 12.4L/100km
Petrol 4-stroke piston
1994cc 121.7cu in
In-line 4 2 Carburettor
Compression ratio: 9.0:1
Bore: 84.4mm 3.3in
Stroke: 89.0mm 3.5in
Valve type/No: Overhead 8
Transmission: Manual
No. of forward speeds: 5
Wheels driven: Rear
Springs F/R: Coil/Coil
Brake system: PA
Brakes F/R: Disc/Drum
Steering: Rack & pinion PA
Wheelbase: 281.4cm 110.8in
Track F: 150.1cm 59.1in
Track R: 150.1cm 59.1in
Length: 469.9cm 185.0in
Width: 176.8cm 69.6in
Height: 138.4cm 54.5in
Ground clearance: 12.7cm 5.0in
Kerb weight: 1337.9kg 2947.0lb
Fuel: 66.0L 14.5gal 17.4galUS

4023 Rover

SD Turbo
1982 UK
106.0mph 170.6kmh
0-50mph 80.5kmh: 10.3secs
0-60mph 96.5kmh: 14.3secs
0-1/4 mile: 19.7secs
0-1km: 37.5secs
90.0bhp 67.1kW 91.2PS
@ 4280rpm
142.0lbft 192.4Nm @ 2350rpm
62.2bhp/ton 61.2bhp/tonne
37.6bhp/L 28.0kW/L 38.1PS/L
42.1ft/sec 12.8m/sec
23.9mph 38.5kmh/1000rpm
29.6mpg 24.6mpgUS 9.5L/100km
Diesel 4-stroke piston
2393cc 146.0cu in turbocharged
In-line 4 fuel injection
Compression ratio: 20.5:1
Bore: 92.0mm 3.6in
Stroke: 90.0mm 3.5in
Valve type/No: Overhead 8
Transmission: Manual
No. of forward speeds: 5
Wheels driven: Rear
Springs F/R: Coil/Coil
Brake system: PA
Brakes F/R: Disc/Drum
Steering: Rack & pinion PA
Wheelbase: 281.4cm 110.8in
Track F: 150.1cm 59.1in
Track R: 150.1cm 59.1in
Length: 469.9cm 185.0in
Width: 176.8cm 69.6in
Height: 138.4cm 54.5in
Ground clearance: 12.7cm 5.0in
Kerb weight: 1471.4kg 3241.0lb
Fuel: 66.0L 14.5gal 17.4galUS

4024 Rover

Vitesse
1983 UK
133.0mph 214.0kmh
0-50mph 80.5kmh: 5.9secs

0-60mph 96.5kmh: 7.6secs
0-1/4 mile: 15.9secs
0-1km: 29.3secs
190.0bhp 141.7kW 192.6PS
@ 5280rpm
220.0lbft 298.1Nm @ 4000rpm
135.7bhp/ton 133.4bhp/tonne
53.8bhp/L 40.2kW/L 54.6PS/L
41.1ft/sec 12.5m/sec
29.4mph 47.3kmh/1000rpm
21.8mpg 18.2mpgUS 13.0L/100km
Petrol 4-stroke piston
3528cc 215.2cu in
Vee 8 fuel injection
Compression ratio: 9.7:1
Bore: 88.9mm 3.5in
Stroke: 71.1mm 2.8in
Valve type/No: Overhead 16
Transmission: Manual
No. of forward speeds: 5
Wheels driven: Rear
Springs F/R: Coil/Coil
Brake system: PA
Brakes F/R: Disc/Drum
Steering: Rack & pinion PA
Wheelbase: 281.4cm 110.8in
Track F: 150.1cm 59.1in
Track R: 150.1cm 59.1in
Length: 469.9cm 185.0in
Width: 176.8cm 69.6in
Height: 138.4cm 54.5in
Ground clearance: 12.7cm 5.0in
Kerb weight: 1423.7kg 3136.0lb
Fuel: 66.0L 14.5gal 17.4galUS

4025 Rover
213 Vanden Plas
1984 UK
98.0mph 157.7kmh
0-50mph 80.5kmh: 8.9secs
0-60mph 96.5kmh: 13.0secs
0-1/4 mile: 18.7secs
0-1km: 32.2secs
70.0bhp 52.2kW 71.0PS
@ 6000rpm
77.0lbft 104.3Nm @ 3500rpm
81.0bhp/ton 79.6bhp/tonne
52.2bhp/L 38.9kW/L 52.9PS/L
51.2ft/sec 15.6m/sec
21.2mph 34.1kmh/1000rpm
30.9mpg 25.7mpgUS 9.1L/100km
Petrol 4-stroke piston
1342cc 81.9cu in
In-line 4 1 Carburettor
Compression ratio: 8.7:1
Bore: 74.0mm 2.9in
Stroke: 78.0mm 3.1in
Valve type/No: Overhead 12
Transmission: Manual
No. of forward speeds: 5
Wheels driven: Front
Springs F/R: Torsion bar/Coil
Brake system: PA
Brakes F/R: Disc/Drum
Steering: Rack & pinion
Wheelbase: 245.1cm 96.5in
Track F: 140.0cm 55.1in
Track R: 144.0cm 56.7in
Length: 416.1cm 163.8in
Width: 162.1cm 63.8in
Height: 137.9cm 54.3in
Ground clearance: 16.0cm 6.3in
Kerb weight: 878.9kg 1936.0lb
Fuel: 46.0L 10.1gal 12.1galUS

4026 Rover
216 Vitesse
1985 UK
108.0mph 173.8kmh
0-50mph 80.5kmh: 6.8secs
0-60mph 96.5kmh: 9.4secs
0-1/4 mile: 17.4secs
0-1km: 32.1secs
104.0bhp 77.5kW 105.4PS
@ 6080rpm
102.0lbft 138.2Nm @ 3500rpm
111.8bhp/ton 109.9bhp/tonne
65.1bhp/L 48.5kW/L 66.0PS/L
58.1ft/sec 17.7m/sec
19.9mph 32.0kmh/1000rpm
32.0mpg 26.6mpgUS 8.8L/100km
Petrol 4-stroke piston
1598cc 97.5cu in
In-line 4 fuel injection
Compression ratio: 9.6:1
Bore: 76.2mm 3.0in
Stroke: 87.4mm 3.4in
Valve type/No: Overhead 8
Transmission: Manual
No. of forward speeds: 5
Wheels driven: Front
Springs F/R: Torsion bar/Coil
Brake system: PA
Brakes F/R: Disc/Drum
Steering: Rack & pinion
Wheelbase: 245.1cm 96.5in
Track F: 140.0cm 55.1in
Track R: 144.0cm 56.7in
Length: 416.1cm 163.8in
Width: 162.1cm 63.8in
Height: 137.9cm 54.3in
Ground clearance: 16.5cm 6.5in
Kerb weight: 946.1kg 2084.0lb
Fuel: 46.0L 10.1gal 12.1galUS

4027 Rover
825i
1986 UK
130.0mph 209.2kmh
0-50mph 80.5kmh: 6.1secs
0-60mph 96.5kmh: 8.0secs
0-1/4 mile: 16.3secs
0-1km: 29.8secs
173.0bhp 129.0kW 175.4PS
@ 6000rpm
160.0lbft 216.8Nm @ 5000rpm
132.9bhp/ton 130.7bhp/tonne
69.4bhp/L 51.7kW/L 70.3PS/L
49.2ft/sec 15.0m/sec
24.5mph 39.4kmh/1000rpm
26.3mpg 21.9mpgUS 10.7L/100km
Petrol 4-stroke piston
2494cc 152.0cu in
Vee 6 fuel injection
Compression ratio: 9.6:1
Bore: 84.0mm 3.3in
Stroke: 75.0mm 2.9in
Valve type/No: Overhead 24
Transmission: Manual
No. of forward speeds: 5
Wheels driven: Front
Springs F/R: Coil/Coil
Brake system: PA
Brakes F/R: Disc/Disc
Steering: Rack & pinion PA
Wheelbase: 275.9cm 108.6in
Track F: 149.0cm 58.7in
Track R: 145.0cm 57.1in
Length: 469.4cm 184.8in
Width: 194.6cm 76.6in
Height: 139.8cm 55.0in
Ground clearance: 14.5cm 5.7in
Kerb weight: 1324.0kg 2916.3lb
Fuel: 68.2L 15.0gal 18.0galUS

4028 Rover
820SE
1987 UK
118.0mph 189.9kmh
0-50mph 80.5kmh: 7.5secs
0-60mph 96.5kmh: 10.2secs
0-1/4 mile: 18.5secs
0-1km: 32.1secs
118.0bhp 88.0kW 119.6PS
@ 5600rpm
119.0lbft 161.2Nm @ 3500rpm
94.3bhp/ton 92.7bhp/tonne
59.2bhp/L 44.1kW/L 60.0PS/L
54.4ft/sec 16.6m/sec
21.7mph 34.9kmh/1000rpm
26.6mpg 22.1mpgUS 10.6L/100km
Petrol 4-stroke piston
1994cc 122.0cu in
In-line 4 fuel injection
Compression ratio: 10.0:1
Bore: 84.2mm 3.3in
Stroke: 89.0mm 3.5in
Valve type/No: Overhead 16
Transmission: Manual
No. of forward speeds: 5
Wheels driven: Front
Springs F/R: Coil/Coil
Brake system: PA
Brakes F/R: Disc/Disc
Steering: Rack & pinion PA
Wheelbase: 275.9cm 108.6in
Track F: 149.0cm 58.7in
Track R: 145.0cm 57.1in
Length: 469.4cm 184.8in
Width: 194.6cm 76.6in
Height: 139.8cm 55.0in
Ground clearance: 14.5cm 5.7in
Kerb weight: 1273.0kg 2804.0lb
Fuel: 68.2L 15.0gal 18.0galUS

4029 Rover
Montego 1.6L
1987 UK
106.0mph 170.6kmh
0-50mph 80.5kmh: 8.0secs
0-60mph 96.5kmh: 11.5secs
0-1/4 mile: 18.2secs
0-1km: 33.9secs
86.0bhp 64.1kW 87.2PS
@ 5600rpm
97.0lbft 131.4Nm @ 3500rpm
85.7bhp/ton 84.3bhp/tonne
53.8bhp/L 40.1kW/L 54.6PS/L
53.4ft/sec 16.3m/sec
22.2mph 35.7kmh/1000rpm
29.5mpg 24.6mpgUS 9.6L/100km
Petrol 4-stroke piston
1598cc 97.0cu in
In-line 4 1 Carburettor
Compression ratio: 9.7:1
Bore: 76.2mm 3.0in
Stroke: 87.2mm 3.4in
Valve type/No: Overhead 8
Transmission: Manual
No. of forward speeds: 5
Wheels driven: Front
Springs F/R: Coil/Coil
Brake system: PA
Brakes F/R: Disc/Drum
Steering: Rack & pinion
Wheelbase: 256.5cm 101.0in
Track F: 144.0cm 56.7in
Track R: 145.8cm 57.4in
Length: 446.8cm 175.9in
Width: 171.0cm 67.3in
Height: 142.0cm 55.9in
Ground clearance: 15.7cm 6.2in
Kerb weight: 1020.0kg 2246.7lb
Fuel: 51.0L 11.2gal 13.5galUS

4030 Rover
Sterling Automatic
1987 UK
127.0mph 204.3kmh
0-50mph 80.5kmh: 7.6secs
0-60mph 96.5kmh: 10.1secs
0-1/4 mile: 17.7secs
0-1km: 32.0secs
165.0bhp 123.0kW 167.3PS
@ 6000rpm
163.0lbft 220.9Nm @ 4000rpm
124.6bhp/ton 122.5bhp/tonne
66.2bhp/L 49.3kW/L 67.1PS/L
49.2ft/sec 15.0m/sec
25.0mph 40.2kmh/1000rpm
21.0mpg 17.5mpgUS 13.5L/100km
Petrol 4-stroke piston
2494cc 152.0cu in
Vee 6 fuel injection
Compression ratio: 9.6:1
Bore: 84.0mm 3.3in
Stroke: 75.0mm 2.9in
Valve type/No: Overhead 24
Transmission: Automatic
No. of forward speeds: 4
Wheels driven: Front
Springs F/R: Coil/Coil
Brake system: PA
Brakes F/R: Disc/Disc
Steering: Rack & pinion PA
Wheelbase: 275.9cm 108.6in
Track F: 149.0cm 58.7in
Track R: 145.0cm 57.1in
Length: 469.4cm 184.8in
Width: 194.6cm 76.6in
Height: 139.8cm 55.0in
Ground clearance: 14.5cm 5.7in
Kerb weight: 1347.0kg 2967.0lb
Fuel: 68.2L 15.0gal 18.0galUS

4031 Rover
820 Fastback
1988 UK
115.0mph 185.0kmh
0-50mph 80.5kmh: 8.3secs
0-60mph 96.5kmh: 11.6secs
0-1/4 mile: 18.4secs
0-1km: 33.8secs
100.0bhp 74.6kW 101.4PS
@ 5400rpm
120.3lbft 163.0Nm @ 3000rpm
76.6bhp/ton 75.4bhp/tonne
50.1bhp/L 37.4kW/L 50.8PS/L
52.5ft/sec 16.0m/sec
22.6mph 36.4kmh/1000rpm
24.4mpg 20.3mpgUS 11.6L/100km
Petrol 4-stroke piston
1994cc 122.0cu in
In-line 4 1 Carburettor
Compression ratio: 10.0:1
Bore: 84.5mm 3.3in
Stroke: 89.0mm 3.5in
Valve type/No: Overhead 8
Transmission: Manual
No. of forward speeds: 5
Wheels driven: Front
Springs F/R: Coil/Coil
Brake system: PA
Brakes F/R: Disc/Disc
Steering: Rack & pinion PA
Wheelbase: 275.9cm 108.6in
Track F: 149.0cm 58.7in
Track R: 145.0cm 57.1in
Length: 469.4cm 184.8in
Width: 194.6cm 76.6in
Height: 139.8cm 55.0in
Ground clearance: 14.5cm 5.7in
Kerb weight: 1327.0kg 2922.9lb
Fuel: 68.2L 15.0gal 18.0galUS

4032 Rover
827 SLi Auto
1988 UK
132.0mph 212.4kmh
0-50mph 80.5kmh: 6.4secs
0-60mph 96.5kmh: 8.4secs
0-1/4 mile: 16.5secs
0-1km: 29.8secs
177.0bhp 132.0kW 179.4PS
@ 6000rpm
168.3lbft 228.0Nm @ 4500rpm
127.8bhp/ton 125.7bhp/tonne
66.2bhp/L 49.3kW/L 67.1PS/L
49.2ft/sec 15.0m/sec
21.3mph 34.3kmh/1000rpm
17.9mpg 14.9mpgUS 15.8L/100km
Petrol 4-stroke piston
2675cc 163.0cu in
Vee 6 fuel injection
Compression ratio: 9.4:1
Bore: 87.0mm 3.4in
Stroke: 75.0mm 2.9in
Valve type/No: Overhead 24
Transmission: Automatic
No. of forward speeds: 4
Wheels driven: Front
Springs F/R: Coil/Coil
Brake system: PA ABS
Brakes F/R: Disc/Disc
Steering: Rack & pinion PA
Wheelbase: 275.9cm 108.6in
Track F: 149.0cm 58.7in
Track R: 145.0cm 57.1in
Length: 469.4cm 184.8in
Width: 194.6cm 76.6in
Height: 139.8cm 55.0in
Ground clearance: 14.5cm 5.7in
Kerb weight: 1408.0kg 3101.3lb
Fuel: 68.2L 15.0gal 18.0galUS

4033 Rover
Vitesse
1988 UK
134.0mph 215.6kmh
0-50mph 80.5kmh: 7.3secs
0-60mph 96.5kmh: 9.7secs
0-1/4 mile: 17.0secs
0-1km: 30.7secs
177.0bhp 132.0kW 179.4PS
@ 6000rpm
168.3lbft 228.0Nm @ 4500rpm
125.6bhp/ton 123.5bhp/tonne
66.2bhp/L 49.3kW/L 67.1PS/L
49.2ft/sec 15.0m/sec
22.3mph 35.9kmh/1000rpm
19.9mpg 16.6mpgUS 14.2L/100km
Petrol 4-stroke piston
2675cc 163.0cu in
Vee 6 fuel injection
Compression ratio: 9.4:1
Bore: 87.0mm 3.4in
Stroke: 75.0mm 2.9in
Valve type/No: Overhead 24
Transmission: Automatic
No. of forward speeds: 4
Wheels driven: Front
Springs F/R: Coil/Coil
Brake system: PA ABS
Brakes F/R: Disc/Disc
Steering: Rack & pinion PA
Wheelbase: 275.9cm 108.6in
Track F: 149.0cm 58.7in
Track R: 145.0cm 57.1in
Length: 469.4cm 184.8in

Width: 194.6cm 76.6in
Height: 139.8cm 55.0in
Ground clearance: 14.5cm 5.7in
Kerb weight: 1433.0kg 3156.4lb
Fuel: 68.2L 15.0gal 18.0galUS

4034 Rover

Montego 2.0 DSL Turbo
1989 UK
102.0mph 164.1kmh
0-50mph 80.5kmh: 9.2secs
0-60mph 96.5kmh: 13.2secs
0-1/4 mile: 19.1secs
0-1km: 35.1secs
81.0bhp 60.4kW 82.1PS
@ 4500rpm
116.6lbft 158.0Nm @ 2500rpm
74.9bhp/ton 73.6bhp/tonne
40.6bhp/L 30.3kW/L 41.2PS/L
43.8ft/sec 13.3m/sec
28.7mph 46.2kmh/1000rpm
39.7mpg 33.1mpgUS 7.1L/100km
Diesel 4-stroke piston
1994cc 122.0cu in turbocharged
In-line 4 fuel injection
Compression ratio: 17.2:1
Bore: 84.5mm 3.3in
Stroke: 89.0mm 3.5in
Valve type/No: Overhead 8
Transmission: Manual
No. of forward speeds: 5
Wheels driven: Front
Springs F/R: Coil/Coil
Brake system: PA
Brakes F/R: Disc/Drum
Steering: Rack & pinion PA
Wheelbase: 257.1cm 101.2in
Track F: 144.0cm 56.7in
Track R: 145.8cm 57.4in
Length: 446.6cm 175.8in
Width: 171.0cm 67.3in
Height: 142.0cm 55.9in
Ground clearance: 15.3cm 6.0in
Kerb weight: 1100.0kg 2422.9lb
Fuel: 50.0L 11.0gal 13.2galUS

4035 Rover

Sterling Catalyst
1989 UK
132.0mph 212.4kmh
0-50mph 80.5kmh: 7.0secs
0-60mph 96.5kmh: 9.3secs
0-1/4 mile: 16.9secs
0-1km: 30.7secs
171.0bhp 127.5kW 173.4PS
@ 6000rpm
162.4lbft 220.0Nm @ 4500rpm
118.5bhp/ton 116.6bhp/tonne
63.9bhp/L 47.7kW/L 64.8PS/L
49.2ft/sec 15.0m/sec
21.3mph 34.3kmh/1000rpm
21.3mpg 17.7mpgUS 13.3L/100km
Petrol 4-stroke piston
2675cc 163.0cu in
Vee 6 fuel injection
Compression ratio: 9.0:1
Bore: 87.0mm 3.4in
Stroke: 75.0mm 2.9in
Valve type/No: Overhead 24
Transmission: Automatic
No. of forward speeds: 4
Wheels driven: Front
Springs F/R: Coil/Coil
Brake system: PA ABS
Brakes F/R: Disc/Disc
Steering: Rack & pinion PA
Wheelbase: 275.9cm 108.6in
Track F: 149.0cm 58.7in
Track R: 145.0cm 57.1in
Length: 469.4cm 184.8in
Width: 194.6cm 76.6in
Height: 139.8cm 55.0in
Ground clearance: 14.5cm 5.7in
Kerb weight: 1467.0kg 3231.3lb
Fuel: 68.2L 15.0gal 18.0galUS

4036 Rover

Vitesse
1989 UK
138.0mph 222.0kmh
0-50mph 80.5kmh: 6.2secs
0-60mph 96.5kmh: 8.0secs
0-1/4 mile: 16.6secs
0-1km: 29.5secs
177.0bhp 132.0kW 179.4PS
@ 6000rpm
168.3lbft 228.0Nm @ 4500rpm
126.3bhp/ton 124.2bhp/tonne
66.2bhp/L 49.3kW/L 67.1PS/L
49.2ft/sec 15.0m/sec
22.6mph 36.4kmh/1000rpm
22.1mpg 18.4mpgUS 12.8L/100km
Petrol 4-stroke piston
2675cc 163.0cu in
Vee 6 fuel injection
Compression ratio: 9.4:1
Bore: 87.0mm 3.4in
Stroke: 75.0mm 2.9in
Valve type/No: Overhead 24
Transmission: Manual
No. of forward speeds: 5
Wheels driven: Front
Springs F/R: Coil/Coil
Brake system: PA ABS
Brakes F/R: Disc/Disc
Steering: Rack & pinion PA
Wheelbase: 275.9cm 108.6in
Track F: 149.0cm 58.7in
Track R: 145.0cm 57.1in
Length: 469.4cm 184.8in
Width: 194.6cm 76.6in
Height: 139.8cm 55.0in
Ground clearance: 14.5cm 5.7in
Kerb weight: 1425.0kg 3138.8lb
Fuel: 68.2L 15.0gal 18.0galUS

4037 Rover

214 GSi
1990 UK
108.0mph 173.8kmh
0-50mph 80.5kmh: 8.3secs
0-60mph 96.5kmh: 11.7secs
0-1/4 mile: 18.3secs
0-1km: 33.9secs
95.0bhp 70.8kW 96.3PS
@ 6250rpm
91.5lbft 124.0Nm @ 4000rpm
87.8bhp/ton 86.4bhp/tonne
68.0bhp/L 50.7kW/L 69.0PS/L
54.0ft/sec 16.5m/sec
19.8mph 31.9kmh/1000rpm
28.9mpg 24.1mpgUS 9.8L/100km
Petrol 4-stroke piston
1396cc 85.0cu in
In-line 4 fuel injection
Compression ratio: 9.5:1
Bore: 75.0mm 2.9in
Stroke: 79.0mm 3.1in
Valve type/No: Overhead 16
Transmission: Manual
No. of forward speeds: 5
Wheels driven: Front
Springs F/R: Coil/Coil
Brake system: PA ABS
Brakes F/R: Disc/Disc
Steering: Rack & pinion PA
Wheelbase: 255.0cm 100.4in
Length: 422.0cm 166 1in
Width: 194.0cm 76.4in
Height: 140.0cm 55.1in
Ground clearance: 15.0cm 5.9in
Kerb weight: 1100.0kg 2422.9lb
Fuel: 55.1L 12.1gal 14.5galUS

4038 Rover

216 GSi
1990 UK
117.0mph 188.3kmh
0-50mph 80.5kmh: 7.6secs
0-60mph 96.5kmh: 10.9secs
0-1/4 mile: 18.2secs
0-1km: 33.4secs
114.0bhp 85.0kW 115.6PS
@ 6300rpm
104.1lbft 141.0Nm @ 5200rpm
99.9bhp/ton 98.3bhp/tonne
71.7bhp/L 53.5kW/L 72.7PS/L
61.9ft/sec 18.9m/sec
19.4mph 31.2kmh/1000rpm
26.0mpg 21.6mpgUS 10.9L/100km
Petrol 4-stroke piston
1590cc 97.0cu in
In-line 4 fuel injection
Compression ratio: 9.1:1
Bore: 75.0mm 2.9in
Stroke: 90.0mm 3.5in
Valve type/No: Overhead 16
Transmission: Manual
No. of forward speeds: 5
Wheels driven: Front
Springs F/R: Coil/Coil
Brake system: PA ABS
Brakes F/R: Disc/Disc
Steering: Rack & pinion PA
Wheelbase: 255.0cm 100.4in
Length: 421.6cm 166.0in
Width: 194.3cm 76.5in
Height: 139.7cm 55.0in
Ground clearance: 15.2cm 6.0in
Kerb weight: 1160.0kg 2555.1lb
Fuel: 55.1L 12.1gal 14.5galUS

4039 Rover

414 Si
1990 UK
105.0mph 168.9kmh
0-50mph 80.5kmh: 8.2secs
0-60mph 96.5kmh: 11.5secs
0-1/4 mile: 18.5secs
0-1km: 34.2secs
95.0bhp 70.8kW 96.3PS
@ 6250rpm
91.5lbft 124.0Nm @ 4000rpm
92.4bhp/ton 90.9bhp/tonne
68.0bhp/L 50.7kW/L 69.0PS/L
54.0ft/sec 16.5m/sec
19.8mph 31.9kmh/1000rpm
32.7mpg 27.2mpgUS 8.6L/100km
Petrol 4-stroke piston
1396cc 85.0cu in
In-line 4 fuel injection
Compression ratio: 9.5:1
Bore: 75.0mm 2.9in
Stroke: 79.0mm 3.1in
Valve type/No: Overhead 16
Transmission: Manual
No. of forward speeds: 5
Wheels driven: Front
Springs F/R: Coil/Coil
Brake system: PA ABS
Brakes F/R: Disc/Drum
Steering: Rack & pinion
Wheelbase: 254.0cm 100.0in
Length: 421.6cm 166.0in
Width: 194.1cm 76.4in
Height: 140.0cm 55.1in
Ground clearance: 15.2cm 6.0in
Kerb weight: 1045.0kg 2301.8lb
Fuel: 55.1L 12.1gal 14.5galUS

4040 Rover

416 GTi
1990 UK
121.0mph 194.7kmh
0-50mph 80.5kmh: 7.2secs
0-60mph 96.5kmh: 10.0secs
0-1/4 mile: 17.2secs
0-1km: 31.6secs
130.0bhp 96.9kW 131.8PS
@ 6800rpm
105.5lbft 143.0Nm @ 5700rpm
117.0bhp/ton 115.0bhp/tonne
81.8bhp/L 61.0kW/L 82.9PS/L
66.9ft/sec 20.4m/sec
18.2mph 29.3kmh/1000rpm
25.1mpg 20.9mpgUS 11.3L/100km
Petrol 4-stroke piston
1590cc 97.0cu in
In-line 4 fuel injection
Compression ratio: 9.5:1
Bore: 75.0mm 2.9in
Stroke: 90.0mm 3.5in
Valve type/No: Overhead 16
Transmission: Manual
No. of forward speeds: 5
Wheels driven: Front
Springs F/R: Coil/Coil
Brake system: PA ABS
Brakes F/R: Disc/Disc
Steering: Rack & pinion PA
Wheelbase: 254.0cm 100.0in
Length: 421.6cm 166.0in
Width: 194.3cm 76.5in
Height: 139.7cm 55.0in
Ground clearance: 15.2cm 6.0in
Kerb weight: 1130.0kg 2489.0lb
Fuel: 55.1L 12.1gal 14.5galUS

4041 Rover

Metro 1.4SL
1990 UK
106.0mph 170.6kmh
0-50mph 80.5kmh: 8.5secs
0-60mph 96.5kmh: 12.0secs
0-1/4 mile: 18.2secs
0-1km: 31.4secs
75.0bhp 55.9kW 76.0PS
@ 5500rpm
86.3lbft 117.0Nm @ 3500rpm
89.7bhp/ton 88.2bhp/tonne
53.7bhp/L 40.1kW/L 54.5PS/L
47.5ft/sec 14.5m/sec
19.9mph 32.0kmh/1000rpm
33.7mpg 28.1mpgUS 8.4L/100km
Petrol 4-stroke piston
1396cc 85.0cu in
In-line 4 1 Carburettor
Compression ratio: 9.7:1
Bore: 75.0mm 2.9in
Stroke: 79.0mm 3.1in
Valve type/No: Overhead 8
Transmission: Manual
No. of forward speeds: 5
Wheels driven: Front
Springs F/R: Gas/Gas
Brake system: PA
Brakes F/R: Disc/Disc
Steering: Rack & pinion
Wheelbase: 226.8cm 89.3in
Track F: 134.1cm 52.8in
Track R: 129.3cm 50.9in
Length: 352.0cm 138.6in
Width: 177.3cm 69.8in
Height: 137.7cm 54.2in
Ground clearance: 15.0cm 5.9in
Kerb weight: 850.0kg 1872.2lb
Fuel: 35.5L 7.8gal 9.4galUS

4042 Rover

Metro GTi 16v
1990 UK
115.0mph 185.0kmh
0-50mph 80.5kmh: 7.1secs
0-60mph 96.5kmh: 9.8secs
0-1/4 mile: 17.4secs
0-1km: 31.7secs
95.0bhp 70.8kW 96.3PS
@ 6250rpm
91.5lbft 124.0Nm @ 4000rpm
109.2bhp/ton 107.3bhp/tonne
68.0bhp/L 50.7kW/L 69.0PS/L
54.0ft/sec 16.5m/sec
18.9mph 30.4kmh/1000rpm
31.6mpg 26.3mpgUS 8.9L/100km
Petrol 4-stroke piston
1396cc 85.0cu in
In-line 4 fuel injection
Compression ratio: 9.5:1
Bore: 75.0mm 2.9in
Stroke: 79.0mm 3.1in
Valve type/No: Overhead 16
Transmission: Manual
No. of forward speeds: 5
Wheels driven: Front
Springs F/R: Gas/Gas
Brake system: PA
Brakes F/R: Disc/Drum
Steering: Rack & pinion
Wheelbase: 226.9cm 89.3in
Track F: 134.0cm 52.8in
Track R: 129.4cm 50.9in
Length: 352.1cm 138.6in
Width: 177.5cm 69.9in
Height: 137.7cm 54.2in
Ground clearance: 14.9cm 5.9in
Kerb weight: 885.0kg 1949.3lb
Fuel: 35.5L 7.8gal 9.4galUS

4043 Rover

214S
1991 UK
102.0mph 164.1kmh
0-50mph 80.5kmh: 9.2secs
0-60mph 96.5kmh: 13.3secs
0-1/4 mile: 19.3secs
0-1km: 35.9secs
75.0bhp 55.9kW 76.0PS
@ 5700rpm
84.1lbft 114.0Nm @ 3500rpm
74.4bhp/ton 73.2bhp/tonne
53.8bhp/L 40.1kW/L 54.5PS/L
49.2ft/sec 15.0m/sec
19.6mph 31.5kmh/1000rpm
30.0mpg 25.0mpgUS 9.4L/100km
Petrol 4-stroke piston
1394cc 85.0cu in
In-line 4 1 Carburettor
Compression ratio: 9.8:1
Bore: 75.0mm 2.9in
Stroke: 79.0mm 3.1in
Valve type/No: Overhead 8
Transmission: Manual
No. of forward speeds: 5
Wheels driven: Front
Springs F/R: Coil/Coil
Brake system: PA

Brakes F/R: Disc/Drum
Steering: Rack & pinion
Wheelbase: 255.0cm 100.4in
Length: 421.6cm 166.0in
Width: 194.3cm 76.5in
Height: 139.7cm 55.0in
Ground clearance: 15.2cm 6.0in
Kerb weight: 1025.0kg 2257.7lb
Fuel: 55.1L 12.1gal 14.5galUS

4044 Rover

216 GTi
1991 UK
126.0mph 202.7kmh
0-50mph 80.5kmh: 6.5secs
0-60mph 96.5kmh: 8.8secs
0-1/4 mile: 16.8secs
0-1km: 30.9secs
130.0bhp 96.9kW 131.8PS
@ 6800rpm
105.5lbft 143.0Nm @ 5700rpm
115.0bhp/ton 113.0bhp/tonne
81.8bhp/L 61.0kW/L 82.9PS/L
66.9ft/sec 20.4m/sec
18.4mph 29.6kmh/1000rpm
24.5mpg 20.4mpgUS 11.5L/100km
Petrol 4-stroke piston
1590cc 97.0cu in
In-line 4 fuel injection
Compression ratio: 9.5:1
Bore: 75.0mm 2.9in
Stroke: 90.0mm 3.5in
Valve type/No: Overhead 16
Transmission: Manual
No. of forward speeds: 5
Wheels driven: Front
Springs F/R: Coil/Coil
Brake system: PA ABS
Brakes F/R: Disc/Disc
Steering: Rack & pinion PA
Wheelbase: 255.0cm 100.4in
Length: 421.9cm 166.1in
Width: 194.1cm 76.4in
Height: 140.0cm 55.1in
Kerb weight: 1150.0kg 2533.0lb
Fuel: 55.1L 12.1gal 14.5galUS

4045 Rover

218 SD
1991 UK
97.0mph 156.1kmh
0-50mph 80.5kmh: 12.0secs
0-60mph 96.5kmh: 16.9secs
0-1/4 mile: 20.9secs
0-1km: 38.9secs
66.0bhp 49.2kW 66.9PS
@ 4600rpm
89.3lbft 121.0Nm @ 2500rpm
55.9bhp/ton 55.0bhp/tonne
34.6bhp/L 25.8kW/L 35.1PS/L
44.2ft/sec 13.5m/sec
22.8mph 36.7kmh/1000rpm
35.3mpg 29.4mpgUS 8.0L/100km
Diesel 4-stroke piston
1905cc 116.0cu in
In-line 4 fuel injection
Compression ratio: 23.0:1
Bore: 83.0mm 3.3in
Stroke: 88.0mm 3.5in
Valve type/No: Overhead 8
Transmission: Manual
No. of forward speeds: 5
Wheels driven: Front
Springs F/R: Coil/Coil
Brake system: PA ABS
Brakes F/R: Disc/Drum
Steering: Rack & pinion PA
Wheelbase: 255.0cm 100.4in
Length: 422.0cm 166.1in
Width: 194.0cm 76.4in
Height: 140.0cm 55.1in
Kerb weight: 1200.0kg 2643.2lb
Fuel: 55.1L 12.1gal 14.5galUS

4046 Rover

220 GTi
1991 UK
128.0mph 206.0kmh
0-50mph 80.5kmh: 6.5secs
0-60mph 96.5kmh: 8.8secs
0-1/4 mile: 16.9secs
0-1km: 30.8secs
140.0bhp 104.4kW 141.9PS
@ 6000rpm
132.8lbft 180.0Nm @ 4500rpm
121.7bhp/ton 119.7bhp/tonne
70.2bhp/L 52.4kW/L 71.2PS/L
58.3ft/sec 17.8m/sec
20.7mph 33.3kmh/1000rpm
27.1mpg 22.6mpgUS 10.4L/100km
Petrol 4-stroke piston
1994cc 122.0cu in
In-line 4 fuel injection
Compression ratio: 10.0:1
Bore: 84.5mm 3.3in
Stroke: 89.0mm 3.5in
Valve type/No: Overhead 16
Transmission: Manual
No. of forward speeds: 5
Wheels driven: Front
Springs F/R: Coil/Coil
Brake system: PA ABS
Brakes F/R: Disc/Disc
Steering: Rack & pinion PA
Wheelbase: 255.0cm 100.4in
Length: 422.0cm 166.1in
Width: 194.0cm 76.4in
Height: 140.0cm 55.1in
Kerb weight: 1170.0kg 2577.1lb
Fuel: 55.1L 12.1gal 14.5galUS

4047 Rover

825 TD
1991 UK
117.0mph 188.3kmh
0-50mph 80.5kmh: 8.4secs
0-60mph 96.5kmh: 11.7secs
0-1/4 mile: 18.5secs
0-1km: 34.1secs
118.0bhp 88.0kW 119.6PS
@ 4200rpm
197.8lbft 268.0Nm @ 2100rpm
82.5bhp/ton 81.1bhp/tonne
47.2bhp/L 35.2kW/L 47.9PS/L
43.2ft/sec 13.2m/sec
28.8mph 46.3kmh/1000rpm
36.2mpg 30.1mpgUS 7.8L/100km
Diesel 4-stroke piston
2500cc 153.0cu in turbocharged
In-line 4 fuel injection
Compression ratio: 22.1:1
Bore: 92.0mm 3.6in
Stroke: 94.0mm 3.7in
Valve type/No: Overhead 8
Transmission: Manual
No. of forward speeds: 5
Wheels driven: Front
Springs F/R: Coil/Coil
Brake system: PA
Brakes F/R: Disc/Disc
Steering: Rack & pinion PA
Wheelbase: 275.8cm 108.6in
Track F: 149.1cm 58.7in
Track R: 145.0cm 57.1in
Length: 481.1cm 189.4in
Width: 189.0cm 74.4in
Height: 139.7cm 55.0in
Ground clearance: 14.5cm 5.7in
Kerb weight: 1455.0kg 3204.8lb
Fuel: 68.2L 15.0gal 18.0galUS

4048 Rover

Mini Cooper S
1991 UK
98.0mph 157.7kmh
0-50mph 80.5kmh: 7.6secs
0-60mph 96.5kmh: 11.0secs
0-1/4 mile: 18.1secs
0-1km: 29.3secs
78.0bhp 58.2kW 79.1PS
@ 6000rpm
78.2lbft 106.0Nm @ 3250rpm
112.4bhp/ton 110.5bhp/tonne
61.2bhp/L 45.6kW/L 62.0PS/L
53.3ft/sec 16.3m/sec
18.6mph 29.9kmh/1000rpm
26.5mpg 22.1mpgUS 10.7L/100km
Petrol 4-stroke piston
1275cc 78.0cu in
In-line 4 2 Carburettor
Compression ratio: 10.2:1
Bore: 70.6mm 2.8in
Stroke: 81.3mm 3.2in
Valve type/No: Overhead 8
Transmission: Manual
No. of forward speeds: 4
Wheels driven: Front
Springs F/R: Coil/Coil
Brake system: PA
Brakes F/R: Disc/Drum
Steering: Rack & pinion
Wheelbase: 203.5cm 80.1in
Track F: 120.7cm 47.5in
Track R: 116.8cm 46.0in
Length: 310.4cm 122.2in
Width: 141.0cm 55.5in
Height: 135.1cm 53.2in
Ground clearance: 15.2cm 6.0in
Kerb weight: 706.0kg 1555.1lb
Fuel: 34.1L 7.5gal 9.0galUS

4049 Rover

Sterling 827SL
1991 UK
0-60mph 96.5kmh: 9.4secs
0-1/4 mile: 17.1secs
160.0bhp 119.3kW 162.2PS
@ 5900rpm
162.0lbft 219.5Nm @ 4500rpm
112.5bhp/ton 110.6bhp/tonne
59.8bhp/L 44.6kW/L 60.6PS/L
48.3ft/sec 14.7m/sec
25.6mpg 21.3mpgUS 11.0L/100km
Petrol 4-stroke piston
2675cc 163.2cu in
Vee 6
Bore: 87.0mm 3.4in
Stroke: 75.0mm 2.9in
Valve type/No: Overhead 24
Transmission: Manual
No. of forward speeds: 5
Wheels driven: Front
Springs F/R: Coil/Coil
Brake system: ABS
Brakes F/R: Disc/Disc
Steering: Rack & pinion PA
Wheelbase: 275.8cm 108.6in
Track F: 149.1cm 58.7in
Track R: 145.0cm 57.1in
Length: 479.6cm 188.8in
Width: 173.0cm 68.1in
Height: 139.2cm 54.8in
Kerb weight: 1446.0kg 3185.0lb

4050 Rover

820i
1992 UK
126.0mph 202.7kmh
0-50mph 80.5kmh: 6.9secs
0-60mph 96.5kmh: 9.2secs
0-1/4 mile: 17.2secs
0-1km: 31.2secs
136.0bhp 101.4kW 137.9PS
@ 6000rpm
136.0lbft 184.3Nm @ 2500rpm
102.1bhp/ton 100.4bhp/tonne
68.2bhp/L 50.9kW/L 69.1PS/L
58.3ft/sec 17.8m/sec
22.5mph 36.2kmh/1000rpm
27.4mpg 22.8mpgUS 10.3L/100km
Petrol 4-stroke piston
1994cc 122.0cu in
In-line 4 fuel injection
Compression ratio: 10.0:1
Bore: 84.5mm 3.3in
Stroke: 89.0mm 3.5in
Valve type/No: Overhead 16
Transmission: Manual
No. of forward speeds: 5
Wheels driven: Front
Springs F/R: Coil/Coil
Brake system: PA ABS
Brakes F/R: Disc/Disc
Steering: Rack & pinion PA
Wheelbase: 276.6cm 108.9in
Track F: 148.3cm 58.4in
Track R: 145.0cm 57.1in
Length: 488.2cm 192.2in
Width: 195.5cm 77.0in
Height: 139.3cm 54.8in
Ground clearance: 14.2cm 5.6in
Kerb weight: 1355.0kg 2984.6lb
Fuel: 68.0L 14.9gal 18.0galUS

4051 Rover

Sterling Automatic
1992 UK
131.0mph 210.8kmh
0-50mph 80.5kmh: 7.2secs
0-60mph 96.5kmh: 9.4secs
0-1/4 mile: 17.4secs
0-1km: 31.4secs
169.0bhp 126.0kW 171.3PS
@ 5900rpm
165.0lbft 223.6Nm @ 4500rpm
118.9bhp/ton 117.0bhp/tonne
63.2bhp/L 47.1kW/L 64.0PS/L
48.3ft/sec 14.7m/sec
21.3mph 34.3kmh/1000rpm
19.6mpg 16.3mpgUS 14.4L/100km
Petrol 4-stroke piston
2675cc 163.2cu in
Vee 6 fuel injection
Compression ratio: 9.0:1
Bore: 87.0mm 3.4in
Stroke: 75.0mm 2.9in
Valve type/No: Overhead 24
Transmission: Automatic
No. of forward speeds: 4
Wheels driven: Front
Springs F/R: Coil/Coil
Brake system: PA ABS
Brakes F/R: Disc/Disc
Steering: Rack & pinion PA
Wheelbase: 277.0cm 109.1in
Track F: 160.0cm 63.0in
Track R: 157.2cm 61.9in
Length: 488.0cm 192.1in
Width: 188.5cm 74.2in
Height: 139.0cm 54.7in
Kerb weight: 1445.0kg 3182.8lb
Fuel: 68.2L 15.0gal 18.0galUS

4052 Ruger

Bentley Clone
1970 USA
116.0mph 186.6kmh
0-50mph 80.5kmh: 6.1secs
0-60mph 96.5kmh: 7.7secs
0-1/4 mile: 15.3secs
0-1km: 28.2secs
425.0bhp 316.9kW 430.9PS
@ 6000rpm
490.0lbft 664.0Nm @ 3700rpm
269.4bhp/ton 264.9bhp/tonne
60.8bhp/L 45.3kW/L 61.6PS/L
66.3ft/sec 20.2m/sec
25.8mph 41.5kmh/1000rpm
10.0mpg 8.3mpgUS 28.2L/100km
Petrol 4-stroke piston
6989cc 426.4cu in
Vee 8 2 Carburettor
Compression ratio: 11.0:1
Bore: 104.9mm 4.1in
Stroke: 101.1mm 4.0in
Valve type/No: Overhead 16
Transmission: Manual
No. of forward speeds: 4
Wheels driven: Rear
Springs F/R: Leaf/Leaf
Brake system: PA
Brakes F/R: Drum/Drum
Steering: Worm & roller
Wheelbase: 332.7cm 131.0in
Track F: 149.9cm 59.0in
Track R: 147.3cm 58.0in
Length: 472.4cm 186.0in
Width: 171.5cm 67.5in
Height: 170.2cm 67.0in
Ground clearance: 20.3cm 8.0in
Kerb weight: 1604.4kg 3534.0lb
Fuel: 83.3L 18.3gal 22.0galUS

4053 Saab

93
1956 Sweden
76.0mph 122.3kmh
0-50mph 80.5kmh: 18.0secs
0-1/4 mile: 23.5secs
38.0bhp 28.3kW 38.5PS
@ 5000rpm
52.1lbft 70.6Nm @ 2000rpm
47.5bhp/ton 46.7bhp/tonne
50.8bhp/L 37.9kW/L 51.5PS/L
39.9ft/sec 12.1m/sec
13.5mph 21.7kmh/1000rpm
35.0mpg 29.1mpgUS 8.1L/100km
Petrol 2-stroke piston
748cc 45.6cu in
In-line 3 1 Carburettor
Compression ratio: 7.3:1
Bore: 66.0mm 2.6in
Stroke: 72.9mm 2.9in
Valve type/No: Ports
Transmission: Manual
No. of forward speeds: 3
Wheels driven: Front
Springs F/R: Coil/Coil
Brakes F/R: Drum/Drum
Wheelbase: 248.9cm 98.0in
Track F: 121.9cm 48.0in
Track R: 121.9cm 48.0in
Length: 399.3cm 157.2in
Width: 156.2cm 61.5in
Height: 145.3cm 57.2in
Ground clearance: 19.1cm 7.5in

Kerb weight: 813.6kg 1792.0lb
Fuel: 36.4L 8.0gal 9.6galUS

4054 Saab

93
1957 Sweden
74.8mph 120.4kmh
0-50mph 80.5kmh: 17.7secs
0-60mph 96.5kmh: 27.2secs
0-1/4 mile: 23.0secs
38.0bhp 28.3kW 38.5PS
@ 5000rpm
52.0lbft 70.5Nm @ 2000rpm
47.9bhp/ton 47.2bhp/tonne
50.8bhp/L 37.9kW/L 51.5PS/L
39.9ft/sec 12.1m/sec
Petrol 2-stroke piston
748cc 45.6cu in
In-line 3
Compression ratio: 7.3:1
Bore: 66.0mm 2.6in
Stroke: 72.9mm 2.9in
Transmission: Manual
No. of forward speeds: 3
Wheels driven: Front
Wheelbase: 248.7cm 97.9in
Track F: 121.9cm 48.0in
Track R: 121.9cm 48.0in
Kerb weight: 805.8kg 1775.0lb

4055 Saab

Gran Turismo
1958 Sweden
88.0mph 141.6kmh
0-50mph 80.5kmh: 11.0secs
0-60mph 96.5kmh: 15.2secs
0-1/4 mile: 18.5secs
50.0bhp 37.3kW 50.7PS
@ 5000rpm
56.0lbft 75.9Nm @ 3500rpm
61.0bhp/ton 60.0bhp/tonne
66.8bhp/L 49.8kW/L 67.8PS/L
39.9ft/sec 12.1m/sec
15.8mph 25.4kmh/1000rpm
Petrol 2-stroke piston
748cc 45.6cu in
In-line 3
Compression ratio: 9.0:1
Bore: 66.0mm 2.6in
Stroke: 72.9mm 2.9in
Transmission: Manual
No. of forward speeds: 3
Wheels driven: Front
Wheelbase: 248.7cm 97.9in
Track F: 121.9cm 48.0in
Track R: 121.9cm 48.0in
Length: 401.3cm 158.0in
Width: 157.0cm 61.8in
Height: 147.1cm 57.9in
Kerb weight: 833.1kg 1835.0lb

4056 Saab

96
1960 Sweden
74.0mph 119.1kmh
0-50mph 80.5kmh: 16.6secs
0-60mph 96.5kmh: 26.6secs
0-1/4 mile: 23.5secs
38.0bhp 28.3kW 38.5PS
@ 4250rpm
59.0lbft 79.9Nm @ 3000rpm
48.1bhp/ton 47.3bhp/tonne
45.2bhp/L 33.7kW/L 45.8PS/L
33.9ft/sec 10.3m/sec
13.6mph 21.9kmh/1000rpm
28.7mpg 23.9mpgUS 9.8L/100km
Petrol 2-stroke piston
841cc 51.3cu in
In-line 3 1 Carburettor
Compression ratio: 7.3:1
Bore: 70.0mm 2.8in
Stroke: 72.9mm 2.9in
Valve type/No: Ports
Transmission: Manual
No. of forward speeds: 3
Wheels driven: Front
Springs F/R: Coil/Coil
Brakes F/R: Drum/Drum
Wheelbase: 248.9cm 98.0in
Track F: 121.9cm 48.0in
Track R: 121.9cm 48.0in
Length: 401.3cm 158.0in
Width: 157.5cm 62.0in
Height: 147.3cm 58.0in
Ground clearance: 19.1cm 7.5in
Kerb weight: 804.0kg 1771.0lb
Fuel: 38.7L 8.5gal 10.2galUS

4057 Saab

96 Sedan
1961 Sweden
80.0mph 128.7kmh
0-50mph 80.5kmh: 14.9secs
0-60mph 96.5kmh: 24.5secs
0-1/4 mile: 22.0secs
42.0bhp 31.3kW 42.6PS
@ 5000rpm
59.0lbft 79.9Nm @ 3000rpm
52.3bhp/ton 51.4bhp/tonne
49.8bhp/L 37.1kW/L 50.5PS/L
39.9ft/sec 12.1m/sec
13.6mph 21.9kmh/1000rpm
Petrol 2-stroke piston
843cc 51.4cu in
In-line 3 1 Carburettor
Compression ratio: 7.3:1
Bore: 70.1mm 2.8in
Stroke: 72.9mm 2.9in
Transmission: Manual
No. of forward speeds: 3
Wheels driven: Front
Wheelbase: 248.9cm 98.0in
Track F: 121.9cm 48.0in
Track R: 121.9cm 48.0in
Length: 401.3cm 158.0in
Width: 157.0cm 61.8in
Height: 147.3cm 58.0in
Ground clearance: 19.1cm 7.5in
Kerb weight: 817.2kg 1800.0lb

4058 Saab

95
1963 Sweden
68.0mph 109.4kmh
0-50mph 80.5kmh: 23.0secs
0-60mph 96.5kmh: 44.0secs
0-1/4 mile: 24.8secs
38.0bhp 28.3kW 38.5PS
@ 4250rpm
59.0lbft 79.9Nm @ 3000rpm
42.7bhp/ton 42.0bhp/tonne
45.2bhp/L 33.7kW/L 45.8PS/L
33.9ft/sec 10.3m/sec
15.8mph 25.4kmh/1000rpm
27.8mpg 23.1mpgUS 10.2L/100km
Petrol 2-stroke piston
841cc 51.3cu in
In-line 3 1 Carburettor
Compression ratio: 7.3:1
Bore: 70.0mm 2.8in
Stroke: 73.0mm 2.9in
Valve type/No: Ports
Transmission: Manual
No. of forward speeds: 4
Wheels driven: Front
Springs F/R: Coil/Coil
Brakes F/R: Drum/Drum
Steering: Rack & pinion
Wheelbase: 248.9cm 98.0in
Track F: 121.9cm 48.0in
Track R: 121.9cm 48.0in
Length: 411.5cm 162.0in
Width: 157.5cm 62.0in
Height: 147.3cm 58.0in
Ground clearance: 19.1cm 7.5in
Kerb weight: 905.7kg 1995.0lb
Fuel: 38.7L 8.5gal 10.2galUS

4059 Saab

850GT
1964 Sweden
87.0mph 140.0kmh
0-50mph 80.5kmh: 14.6secs
0-60mph 96.5kmh: 21.2secs
0-1/4 mile: 21.9secs
57.0bhp 42.5kW 57.8PS
@ 5000rpm
68.0lbft 92.1Nm @ 3500rpm
68.6bhp/ton 67.5bhp/tonne
67.8bhp/L 50.5kW/L 68.7PS/L
39.9ft/sec 12.1m/sec
16.4mph 26.4kmh/1000rpm
Petrol 2-stroke piston
841cc 51.3cu in
In-line 3 3 Carburettor
Compression ratio: 9.0:1
Bore: 70.1mm 2.8in
Stroke: 72.9mm 2.9in
Transmission: Manual
No. of forward speeds: 4
Wheels driven: Front
Springs F/R: Coil/Coil
Brakes F/R: Disc/Drum
Steering: Rack & pinion
Wheelbase: 248.9cm 98.0in
Track F: 121.9cm 48.0in
Track R: 121.9cm 48.0in
Length: 403.9cm 159.0in
Width: 157.5cm 62.0in
Height: 147.3cm 58.0in
Ground clearance: 14.0cm 5.5in
Kerb weight: 844.4kg 1860.0lb
Fuel: 37.8L 8.3gal 10.0galUS

4060 Saab

96
1966 Sweden
79.0mph 127.1kmh
0-50mph 80.5kmh: 15.7secs
0-60mph 96.5kmh: 24.1secs
0-1/4 mile: 22.3secs
0-1km: 39.7secs
42.0bhp 31.3kW 42.6PS
@ 4250rpm
60.0lbft 81.3Nm @ 3000rpm
53.1bhp/ton 52.2bhp/tonne
49.9bhp/L 37.2kW/L 50.6PS/L
33.9ft/sec 10.3m/sec
15.6mph 25.1kmh/1000rpm
22.0mpg 18.3mpgUS 12.8L/100km
Petrol 2-stroke piston
841cc 51.3cu in
In-line 3 1 Carburettor
Compression ratio: 8.5:1
Bore: 70.0mm 2.8in
Stroke: 73.0mm 2.9in
Valve type/No: Ports
Transmission: Manual
No. of forward speeds: 4
Wheels driven: Front
Springs F/R: Coil/Coil
Brakes F/R: Drum/Drum
Steering: Rack & pinion
Wheelbase: 248.9cm 98.0in
Track F: 121.9cm 48.0in
Track R: 121.9cm 48.0in
Length: 411.5cm 162.0in
Width: 157.5cm 62.0in
Height: 146.1cm 57.5in
Ground clearance: 19.1cm 7.5in
Kerb weight: 804.5kg 1772.0lb
Fuel: 40.0L 8.8gal 10.6galUS

4061 Saab

96 V4
1967 Sweden
93.0mph 149.6kmh
0-50mph 80.5kmh: 11.4secs
0-60mph 96.5kmh: 16.5secs
0-1/4 mile: 20.0secs
0-1km: 39.2secs
65.0bhp 48.5kW 65.9PS
@ 4700rpm
85.0lbft 115.2Nm @ 2500rpm
64.0bhp/ton 62.9bhp/tonne
43.4bhp/L 32.4kW/L 44.0PS/L
30.3ft/sec 9.2m/sec
17.2mph 27.7kmh/1000rpm
29.4mpg 24.5mpgUS 9.6L/100km
Petrol 4-stroke piston
1498cc 91.4cu in
Vee 4 1 Carburettor
Compression ratio: 9.0:1
Bore: 90.0mm 3.5in
Stroke: 58.9mm 2.3in
Valve type/No: Overhead 8
Transmission: Manual
No. of forward speeds: 4
Wheels driven: Front
Springs F/R: Coil/Coil
Brakes F/R: Disc/Drum
Steering: Rack & pinion
Wheelbase: 248.9cm 98.0in
Track F: 121.9cm 48.0in
Track R: 121.9cm 48.0in
Length: 416.6cm 164.0in
Width: 157.5cm 62.0in
Height: 146.1cm 57.5in
Ground clearance: 19.1cm 7.5in
Kerb weight: 1032.8kg 2275.0lb
Fuel: 40.0L 8.8gal 10.6galUS

4062 Saab

V4
1967 Sweden
93.0mph 149.6kmh
0-50mph 80.5kmh: 12.2secs
0-60mph 96.5kmh: 17.5secs
0-1/4 mile: 21.2secs
73.0bhp 54.4kW 74.0PS
@ 5000rpm
87.0lbft 117.9Nm @ 2700rpm
85.6bhp/ton 84.2bhp/tonne
48.7bhp/L 36.3kW/L 49.4PS/L
32.2ft/sec 9.8m/sec
17.5mph 28.2kmh/1000rpm
Petrol 4-stroke piston
1498cc 91.4cu in
Vee 4 1 Carburettor
Compression ratio: 9.0:1
Bore: 90.0mm 3.5in
Stroke: 58.9mm 2.3in
Valve type/No: Overhead 8
Transmission: Manual
No. of forward speeds: 4
Wheels driven: Front
Springs F/R: Coil/Coil
Brakes F/R: Disc/Drum
Steering: Rack & pinion
Wheelbase: 249.7cm 98.3in
Track F: 121.9cm 48.0in
Track R: 121.9cm 48.0in
Length: 416.6cm 164.0in
Width: 160.0cm 63.0in
Height: 147.3cm 58.0in
Ground clearance: 17.8cm 7.0in
Kerb weight: 867.1kg 1910.0lb
Fuel: 39.7L 8.7gal 10.5galUS

4063 Saab

Sonnet V4
1968 Sweden
97.0mph 156.1kmh
0-50mph 80.5kmh: 9.8secs
0-60mph 96.5kmh: 13.7secs
0-1/4 mile: 18.7secs
73.0bhp 54.4kW 74.0PS
@ 5000rpm
87.0lbft 117.9Nm @ 2700rpm
95.1bhp/ton 93.5bhp/tonne
48.7bhp/L 36.3kW/L 49.4PS/L
32.2ft/sec 9.8m/sec
18.1mph 29.1kmh/1000rpm
Petrol 4-stroke piston
1498cc 91.4cu in
Vee 4 1 Carburettor
Compression ratio: 9.0:1
Bore: 90.0mm 3.5in
Stroke: 58.9mm 2.3in
Valve type/No: Overhead 8
Transmission: Manual
No. of forward speeds: 4
Wheels driven: Front
Springs F/R: Coil/Coil
Brakes F/R: Disc/Drum
Steering: Rack & pinion
Wheelbase: 215.9cm 85.0in
Track F: 121.9cm 48.0in
Track R: 121.9cm 48.0in
Length: 375.9cm 148.0in
Width: 149.9cm 59.0in
Height: 116.8cm 46.0in
Ground clearance: 12.7cm 5.0in
Kerb weight: 780.9kg 1720.0lb
Fuel: 59.8L 13.1gal 15.8galUS

4064 Saab

Station Wagon V4
1968 Sweden
90.0mph 144.8kmh
0-1/4 mile: 20.5secs
73.0bhp 54.4kW 74.0PS
48.7bhp/L 36.3kW/L 49.4PS/L
31.2mpg 26.0mpgUS 9.0L/100km
Petrol 4-stroke piston
1498cc 91.4cu in
Vee 4
Valve type/No: Overhead 8
Wheels driven: Front
Wheelbase: 249.9cm 98.4in
Length: 427.0cm 168.1in

4065 Saab

99
1969 Sweden
91.0mph 146.4kmh
0-50mph 80.5kmh: 11.5secs
0-60mph 96.5kmh: 15.7secs
0-1/4 mile: 20.2secs
87.0bhp 64.9kW 88.2PS
@ 5200rpm
98.0lbft 132.8Nm @ 3000rpm
82.6bhp/ton 81.2bhp/tonne

50.9bhp/L 38.0kW/L 51.6PS/L
44.3ft/sec 13.5m/sec
17.7mph 28.5kmh/1000rpm
28.0mpg 23.3mpgUS 10.1L/100km
Petrol 4-stroke piston
1709cc 104.3cu in
In-line 4 1 Carburettor
Compression ratio: 9.0:1
Bore: 83.5mm 3.3in
Stroke: 78.0mm 3.1in
Valve type/No: Overhead 8
Transmission: Manual
No. of forward speeds: 4
Wheels driven: Front
Springs F/R: Coil/Coil
Brake system: PA
Brakes F/R: Disc/Disc
Steering: Rack & pinion
Wheelbase: 247.4cm 97.4in
Track F: 138.9cm 54.7in
Track R: 140.0cm 55.1in
Length: 435.4cm 171.4in
Width: 167.6cm 66.0in
Height: 145.0cm 57.1in
Ground clearance: 17.0cm 6.7in
Kerb weight: 1071.4kg 2360.0lb
Fuel: 47.7L 10.5gal 12.6galUS

4066 Saab

Sport
1969 Sweden
88.0mph 141.6kmh
0-50mph 80.5kmh: 13.4secs
0-60mph 96.5kmh: 19.1secs
0-1/4 mile: 21.2secs
55.0bhp 41.0kW 55.8PS
@ 5000rpm
67.0lbft 90.8Nm @ 3800rpm
64.7bhp/ton 63.6bhp/tonne
65.4bhp/L 48.8kW/L 66.3PS/L
39.9ft/sec 12.2m/sec
16.2mph 26.1kmh/1000rpm
20.7mpg 17.2mpgUS 13.6L/100km
Petrol 2-stroke piston
841cc 51.3cu in
In-line 3 3 Carburettor
Compression ratio: 9.0:1
Bore: 70.0mm 2.8in
Stroke: 73.0mm 2.9in
Valve type/No: Ports
Transmission: Manual
No. of forward speeds: 4
Wheels driven: Front
Springs F/R: Coil/Coil
Brakes F/R: Disc/Drum
Steering: Rack & pinion
Wheelbase: 248.9cm 98.0in
Track F: 121.9cm 48.0in
Track R: 121.9cm 48.0in
Length: 416.6cm 164.0in
Width: 157.5cm 62.0in
Height: 146.1cm 57.5in
Ground clearance: 19.1cm 7.5in
Kerb weight: 864.4kg 1904.0lb
Fuel: 40.0L 8.8gal 10.6galUS

4067 Saab

99
1970 Sweden
92.0mph 148.0kmh
0-50mph 80.5kmh: 11.5secs
0-60mph 96.5kmh: 17.4secs
0-1/4 mile: 20.8secs
0-1km: 39.2secs
80.0bhp 59.7kW 81.1PS
@ 5300rpm
95.0lbft 128.7Nm @ 3200rpm
77.0bhp/ton 75.7bhp/tonne
46.8bhp/L 34.9kW/L 47.5PS/L
45.2ft/sec 13.8m/sec
17.7mph 28.5kmh/1000rpm
24.0mpg 20.0mpgUS 11.8L/100km
Petrol 4-stroke piston
1709cc 104.3cu in
In-line 4 1 Carburettor
Compression ratio: 8.8:1
Bore: 83.5mm 3.3in
Stroke: 78.0mm 3.1in
Valve type/No: Overhead 8
Transmission: Manual
No. of forward speeds: 4
Wheels driven: Front
Springs F/R: Coil/Coil
Brake system: PA
Brakes F/R: Disc/Disc
Steering: Rack & pinion
Wheelbase: 247.7cm 97.5in
Track F: 138.4cm 54.5in
Track R: 139.7cm 55.0in
Length: 434.3cm 171.0in
Width: 163.8cm 64.5in
Height: 143.5cm 56.5in
Ground clearance: 15.2cm 6.0in
Kerb weight: 1056.5kg 2327.0lb
Fuel: 47.8L 10.5gal 12.6galUS

4068 Saab

99E
1970 Sweden
92.0mph 148.0kmh
0-50mph 80.5kmh: 10.9secs
0-60mph 96.5kmh: 14.8secs
0-1/4 mile: 20.0secs
95.0bhp 70.8kW 96.3PS
@ 5500rpm
98.0lbft 132.8Nm @ 3000rpm
89.4bhp/ton 87.9bhp/tonne
55.6bhp/L 41.4kW/L 56.4PS/L
46.9ft/sec 14.3m/sec
17.7mph 28.5kmh/1000rpm
28.8mpg 24.0mpgUS 9.8L/100km
Petrol 4-stroke piston
1709cc 104.3cu in
In-line 4
Compression ratio: 9.0:1
Bore: 83.5mm 3.3in
Stroke: 78.0mm 3.1in
Valve type/No: Overhead 8
Transmission: Manual
No. of forward speeds: 4
Wheels driven: Front
Brake system: PA
Brakes F/R: Disc/Disc
Steering: Rack & pinion
Wheelbase: 247.4cm 97.4in
Track F: 138.9cm 54.7in
Track R: 140.0cm 55.1in
Length: 435.4cm 171.4in
Width: 167.6cm 66.0in
Height: 145.0cm 57.1in
Kerb weight: 1080.5kg 2380.0lb
Fuel: 47.7L 10.5gal 12.6galUS

4069 Saab

Sonnet III
1970 Sweden
100.0mph 160.9kmh
0-50mph 80.5kmh: 11.1secs
0-60mph 96.5kmh: 14.4secs
0-1/4 mile: 19.0secs
73.0bhp 54.4kW 74.0PS
@ 5000rpm
87.0lbft 117.9Nm @ 2700rpm
92.6bhp/ton 91.1bhp/tonne
43.0bhp/L 32.0kW/L 43.6PS/L
36.5ft/sec 11.1m/sec
18.1mph 29.1kmh/1000rpm
27.6mpg 23.0mpgUS 10.2L/100km
Petrol 4-stroke piston
1699cc 103.7cu in
Vee 4 1 Carburettor
Compression ratio: 9.0:1
Bore: 90.0mm 3.5in
Stroke: 66.8mm 2.6in
Valve type/No: Overhead 8
Transmission: Manual
No. of forward speeds: 4
Wheels driven: Front
Springs F/R: Coil/Coil
Brakes F/R: Disc/Drum
Steering: Rack & pinion
Wheelbase: 212.3cm 83.6in
Track F: 123.4cm 48.6in
Track R: 123.4cm 48.6in
Length: 389.9cm 153.5in
Width: 150.1cm 59.1in
Height: 119.1cm 46.9in
Ground clearance: 15.2cm 6.0in
Kerb weight: 801.3kg 1765.0lb
Fuel: 60.2L 13.2gal 15.9galUS

4070 Saab

99
1971 Sweden
97.0mph 156.1kmh
0-50mph 80.5kmh: 9.0secs
0-60mph 96.5kmh: 12.8secs
0-1/4 mile: 18.7secs
0-1km: 35.6secs
86.0bhp 64.1kW 87.2PS
@ 5200rpm
108.0lbft 146.3Nm @ 3000rpm
79.6bhp/ton 78.2bhp/tonne
46.4bhp/L 34.6kW/L 47.0PS/L
44.3ft/sec 13.5m/sec
17.7mph 28.5kmh/1000rpm
26.5mpg 22.1mpgUS 10.7L/100km
Petrol 4-stroke piston
1854cc 113.1cu in
In-line 4 1 Carburettor
Compression ratio: 9.0:1
Bore: 87.0mm 3.4in
Stroke: 78.0mm 3.1in
Valve type/No: Overhead 8
Transmission: Manual
No. of forward speeds: 4
Wheels driven: Front
Springs F/R: Coil/Coil
Brake system: PA
Brakes F/R: Disc/Disc
Steering: Rack & pinion
Wheelbase: 247.7cm 97.5in
Track F: 138.4cm 54.5in
Track R: 139.7cm 55.0in
Length: 434.3cm 171.0in
Width: 163.8cm 64.5in
Height: 143.5cm 56.5in
Ground clearance: 15.2cm 6.0in
Kerb weight: 1099.1kg 2421.0lb
Fuel: 47.8L 10.5gal 12.6galUS

4071 Saab

99CM4 2.0
1972 Sweden
103.0mph 165.7kmh
0-50mph 80.5kmh: 8.6secs
0-60mph 96.5kmh: 12.0secs
0-1/4 mile: 18.5secs
0-1km: 34.5secs
95.0bhp 70.8kW 96.3PS
@ 5200rpm
116.0lbft 157.2Nm @ 3500rpm
86.0bhp/ton 84.6bhp/tonne
47.9bhp/L 35.7kW/L 48.5PS/L
44.3ft/sec 13.5m/sec
17.9mph 28.8kmh/1000rpm
25.8mpg 21.5mpgUS 10.9L/100km
Petrol 4-stroke piston
1985cc 121.1cu in
In-line 4 1 Carburettor
Compression ratio: 8.7:1
Bore: 90.0mm 3.5in
Stroke: 78.0mm 3.1in
Valve type/No: Overhead 8
Transmission: Manual
No. of forward speeds: 4
Wheels driven: Front
Springs F/R: Coil/Coil
Brake system: PA
Brakes F/R: Disc/Disc
Steering: Rack & pinion
Wheelbase: 247.7cm 97.5in
Track F: 138.4cm 54.5in
Track R: 139.7cm 55.0in
Length: 434.3cm 171.0in
Width: 163.8cm 64.5in
Height: 143.5cm 56.5in
Ground clearance: 15.2cm 6.0in
Kerb weight: 1122.7kg 2473.0lb
Fuel: 47.8L 10.5gal 12.6galUS

4072 Saab

99E 1.85
1972 Sweden
98.0mph 157.7kmh
0-50mph 80.5kmh: 9.1secs
0-60mph 96.5kmh: 12.7secs
0-1/4 mile: 18.4secs
95.0bhp 70.8kW 96.3PS
@ 5200rpm
106.0lbft 143.6Nm @ 3200rpm
86.6bhp/ton 85.2bhp/tonne
51.2bhp/L 38.2kW/L 51.9PS/L
44.3ft/sec 13.5m/sec
17.4mph 28.0kmh/1000rpm
28.8mpg 24.0mpgUS 9.8L/100km
Petrol 4-stroke piston
1854cc 113.1cu in
In-line 4
Compression ratio: 9.0:1
Bore: 87.0mm 3.4in
Stroke: 78.0mm 3.1in
Valve type/No: Overhead 8
Transmission: Manual
No. of forward speeds: 4
Wheels driven: Front
Brake system: PA
Brakes F/R: Disc/Disc
Steering: Rack & pinion
Wheelbase: 247.4cm 97.4in
Track F: 138.9cm 54.7in
Track R: 140.0cm 55.1in
Length: 436.9cm 172.0in
Width: 168.9cm 66.5in
Height: 144.0cm 56.7in
Kerb weight: 1115.5kg 2457.0lb
Fuel: 45.0L 9.9gal 11.9galUS

4073 Saab

99EA
1972 Sweden
97.0mph 156.1kmh
0-50mph 80.5kmh: 10.3secs
0-60mph 96.5kmh: 14.3secs
0-1/4 mile: 20.0secs
0-1km: 37.1secs
97.0bhp 72.3kW 98.3PS
@ 5200rpm
105.0lbft 142.3Nm @ 3000rpm
88.8bhp/ton 87.3bhp/tonne
52.3bhp/L 39.0kW/L 53.0PS/L
44.3ft/sec 13.5m/sec
18.0mph 29.0kmh/1000rpm
25.0mpg 20.8mpgUS 11.3L/100km
Petrol 4-stroke piston
1854cc 113.1cu in
In-line 4 fuel injection
Compression ratio: 9.0:1
Bore: 87.0mm 3.4in
Stroke: 78.0mm 3.1in
Valve type/No: Overhead 8
Transmission: Automatic
No. of forward speeds: 3
Wheels driven: Front
Springs F/R: Coil/Coil
Brake system: PA
Brakes F/R: Disc/Disc
Steering: Rack & pinion
Wheelbase: 247.7cm 97.5in
Track F: 138.4cm 54.5in
Track R: 139.7cm 55.0in
Length: 434.3cm 171.0in
Width: 163.8cm 64.5in
Height: 143.5cm 56.5in
Ground clearance: 15.2cm 6.0in
Kerb weight: 1110.5kg 2446.0lb
Fuel: 45.5L 10.0gal 12.0galUS

4074 Saab

Sonnet III
1972 Sweden
95.0mph 152.9kmh
0-50mph 80.5kmh: 9.7secs
0-60mph 96.5kmh: 13.4secs
0-1/4 mile: 18.6secs
65.0bhp 48.5kW 65.9PS
@ 4700rpm
85.0lbft 115.2Nm @ 2500rpm
79.6bhp/ton 78.2bhp/tonne
38.3bhp/L 28.5kW/L 38.8PS/L
34.3ft/sec 10.5m/sec
17.2mph 27.7kmh/1000rpm
31.7mpg 26.4mpgUS 8.9L/100km
Petrol 4-stroke piston
1699cc 103.7cu in
Vee 4 1 Carburettor
Compression ratio: 8.0:1
Bore: 90.0mm 3.5in
Stroke: 66.8mm 2.6in
Valve type/No: Overhead 8
Transmission: Manual
No. of forward speeds: 4
Wheels driven: Front
Springs F/R: Coil/Coil
Brakes F/R: Disc/Drum
Steering: Rack & pinion
Wheelbase: 214.9cm 84.6in
Track F: 123.2cm 48.5in
Track R: 123.2cm 48.5in
Length: 384.8cm 151.5in
Width: 149.9cm 59.0in
Height: 119.4cm 47.0in
Ground clearance: 12.4cm 4.9in
Kerb weight: 830.8kg 1830.0lb
Fuel: 59.8L 13.1gal 15.8galUS

4075 Saab

99E
1973 Sweden
0-60mph 96.5kmh: 12.7secs
0-1/4 mile: 18.4secs
97.0bhp 72.3kW 98.3PS
@ 5200rpm
105.0lbft 142.3Nm @ 3200rpm
86.2bhp/ton 84.8bhp/tonne
52.3bhp/L 39.0kW/L 53.0PS/L

44.3ft/sec 13.5m/sec
26.4mpg 22.0mpgUS 10.7L/100km
Petrol 4-stroke piston
1854cc 113.1cu in
In-line 4 fuel injection
Compression ratio: 9.0:1
Bore: 87.0mm 3.4in
Stroke: 78.0mm 3.1in
Valve type/No: Overhead 8
Transmission: Manual
No. of forward speeds: 4
Wheels driven: Front
Brake system: PA
Brakes F/R: Disc/Disc
Wheelbase: 247.4cm 97.4in
Length: 436.9cm 172.0in
Width: 168.9cm 66.5in
Height: 144.0cm 56.7in
Ground clearance: 17.3cm 6.8in
Kerb weight: 1144.1kg 2520.0lb
Fuel: 45.0L 9.9gal 11.9galUS

4076 Saab

Sonnet
1973 Sweden
65.0bhp 48.5kW 65.9PS
@ 4700rpm
85.0lbft 115.2Nm @ 2500rpm
79.6bhp/ton 78.2bhp/tonne
38.3bhp/L 28.5kW/L 38.8PS/L
Petrol 4-stroke piston
1698cc 103.6cu in
In-line 4
Valve type/No: Overhead 8
Wheels driven: Front
Springs F/R: Coil/Coil
Wheelbase: 214.9cm 84.6in
Track F: 123.2cm 48.5in
Track R: 123.2cm 48.5in
Length: 406.4cm 160.0in
Width: 150.1cm 59.1in
Height: 119.4cm 47.0in
Kerb weight: 830.8kg 1830.0lb

4077 Saab

99LE Wagonback
1974 Sweden
108.0mph 173.8kmh
0-50mph 80.5kmh: 8.5secs
0-60mph 96.5kmh: 12.0secs
0-1/4 mile: 19.0secs
110.0bhp 82.0kW 111.5PS
@ 5500rpm
123.0lbft 166.7Nm @ 3700rpm
97.6bhp/ton 96.0bhp/tonne
55.4bhp/L 41.3kW/L 56.2PS/L
46.9ft/sec 14.3m/sec
18.8mph 30.2kmh/1000rpm
24.0mpg 20.0mpgUS 11.8L/100km
Petrol 4-stroke piston
1985cc 121.1cu in
In-line 4 fuel injection
Compression ratio: 8.7:1
Bore: 90.0mm 3.5in
Stroke: 78.0mm 3.1in
Valve type/No: Overhead 8
Transmission: Manual
No. of forward speeds: 4
Wheels driven: Front
Springs F/R: Coil/Coil
Brake system: PA
Brakes F/R: Disc/Disc
Steering: Rack & pinion
Wheelbase: 247.4cm 97.4in
Track F: 139.2cm 54.8in
Track R: 140.5cm 55.3in
Length: 452.1cm 178.0in
Width: 168.9cm 66.5in
Height: 143.8cm 56.6in
Ground clearance: 17.3cm 6.8in
Kerb weight: 1146.3kg 2525.0lb
Fuel: 54.9L 12.1gal 14.5galUS

4078 Saab

99EMS
1975 Sweden
110.0mph 177.0kmh
0-50mph 80.5kmh: 7.3secs
0-60mph 96.5kmh: 10.3secs
0-1/4 mile: 17.7secs
0-1km: 33.0secs
110.0bhp 82.0kW 111.5PS
@ 5500rpm
123.0lbft 166.7Nm @ 3700rpm
98.3bhp/ton 96.7bhp/tonne
55.4bhp/L 41.3kW/L 56.2PS/L
46.9ft/sec 14.3m/sec
18.7mph 30.1kmh/1000rpm
23.2mpg 19.3mpgUS 12.2L/100km
Petrol 4-stroke piston
1985cc 121.1cu in
In-line 4 fuel injection
Compression ratio: 8.7:1
Bore: 90.0mm 3.5in
Stroke: 78.0mm 3.1in
Valve type/No: Overhead 8
Transmission: Manual
No. of forward speeds: 4
Wheels driven: Front
Springs F/R: Coil/Coil
Brake system: PA
Brakes F/R: Disc/Disc
Steering: Rack & pinion
Wheelbase: 247.7cm 97.5in
Track F: 138.4cm 54.5in
Track R: 139.7cm 55.0in
Length: 434.3cm 171.0in
Width: 166.4cm 65.5in
Height: 144.0cm 56.7in
Ground clearance: 15.2cm 6.0in
Kerb weight: 1137.7kg 2506.0lb
Fuel: 45.5L 10.0gal 12.0galUS

4079 Saab

99GL Super Combi
1976 Sweden
105.0mph 168.9kmh
0-50mph 80.5kmh: 10.3secs
0-60mph 96.5kmh: 14.4secs
0-1/4 mile: 19.7secs
0-1km: 37.4secs
108.0bhp 80.5kW 109.5PS
@ 5300rpm
121.0lbft 164.0Nm @ 3300rpm
94.7bhp/ton 93.1bhp/tonne
54.4bhp/L 40.6kW/L 55.2PS/L
45.2ft/sec 13.8m/sec
18.7mph 30.1kmh/1000rpm
22.5mpg 18.7mpgUS 12.6L/100km
Petrol 4-stroke piston
1985cc 121.1cu in
In-line 4 2 Carburettor
Compression ratio: 9.2:1
Bore: 90.0mm 3.5in
Stroke: 78.0mm 3.1in
Valve type/No: Overhead 8
Transmission: Automatic
No. of forward speeds: 3
Wheels driven: Front
Springs F/R: Coil/Coil
Brake system: PA
Brakes F/R: Disc/Disc
Steering: Rack & pinion
Wheelbase: 247.7cm 97.5in
Track F: 140.0cm 55.1in
Track R: 142.0cm 55.9in
Length: 452.9cm 178.3in
Width: 168.9cm 66.5in
Height: 144.0cm 56.7in
Ground clearance: 15.2cm 6.0in
Kerb weight: 1160.0kg 2555.0lb
Fuel: 45.5L 10.0gal 12.0galUS

4080 Saab

99EMS
1977 Sweden
102.0mph 164.1kmh
0-60mph 96.5kmh: 11.8secs
0-1/4 mile: 18.6secs
115.0bhp 85.8kW 116.6PS
@ 5500rpm
123.0lbft 166.7Nm @ 3500rpm
100.6bhp/ton 98.9bhp/tonne
57.9bhp/L 43.2kW/L 58.7PS/L
46.9ft/sec 14.3m/sec
Petrol 4-stroke piston
1985cc 121.1cu in
In-line 4 fuel injection
Compression ratio: 8.7:1
Bore: 90.0mm 3.5in
Stroke: 78.0mm 3.1in
Valve type/No: Overhead 8
Transmission: Manual
No. of forward speeds: 4
Wheels driven: Front
Brakes F/R: Disc/Disc
Wheelbase: 247.4cm 97.4in
Track F: 140.0cm 55.1in
Track R: 142.0cm 55.9in
Length: 442.0cm 174.0in
Width: 168.9cm 66.5in
Height: 144.0cm 56.7in
Kerb weight: 1162.2kg 2560.0lb
Fuel: 54.9L 12.1gal 14.5galUS

4081 Saab

Turbo
1978 Sweden
123.0mph 197.9kmh
0-50mph 80.5kmh: 6.7secs
0-60mph 96.5kmh: 8.9secs
0-1/4 mile: 16.9secs
0-1km: 31.0secs
145.0bhp 108.1kW 147.0PS
@ 5000rpm
174.0lbft 235.8Nm @ 3000rpm
119.6bhp/ton 117.6bhp/tonne
72.7bhp/L 54.2kW/L 73.7PS/L
42.6ft/sec 13.0m/sec
20.5mph 33.0kmh/1000rpm
21.4mpg 17.8mpgUS 13.2L/100km
Petrol 4-stroke piston
1995cc 121.7cu in turbocharged
In-line 4 fuel injection
Compression ratio: 7.2:1
Bore: 90.0mm 3.5in
Stroke: 78.0mm 3.1in
Valve type/No: Overhead 8
Transmission: Manual
No. of forward speeds: 4
Wheels driven: Front
Springs F/R: Coil/Coil
Brake system: PA
Brakes F/R: Disc/Disc
Steering: Rack & pinion
Wheelbase: 247.7cm 97.5in
Track F: 140.0cm 55.1in
Track R: 142.0cm 55.9in
Length: 452.9cm 178.3in
Width: 168.9cm 66.5in
Height: 144.0cm 56.7in
Ground clearance: 15.2cm 6.0in
Kerb weight: 1233.1kg 2716.0lb
Fuel: 55.1L 12.1gal 14.5galUS

4082 Saab

900 Turbo
1979 Sweden
119.0mph 191.5kmh
0-50mph 80.5kmh: 7.2secs
0-60mph 96.5kmh: 9.6secs
0-1/4 mile: 17.2secs
0-1km: 31.5secs
145.0bhp 108.1kW 147.0PS
@ 5000rpm
174.0lbft 235.8Nm @ 3000rpm
112.5bhp/ton 110.6bhp/tonne
73.0bhp/L 54.5kW/L 74.1PS/L
42.6ft/sec 13.0m/sec
21.3mph 34.3kmh/1000rpm
22.2mpg 18.5mpgUS 12.7L/100km
Petrol 4-stroke piston
1985cc 121.1cu in turbocharged
In-line 4 fuel injection
Compression ratio: 7.2:1
Bore: 90.0mm 3.5in
Stroke: 78.0mm 3.1in
Valve type/No: Overhead 8
Transmission: Manual
No. of forward speeds: 4
Wheels driven: Front
Springs F/R: Coil/Coil
Brake system: PA
Brakes F/R: Disc/Disc
Steering: Rack & pinion PA
Wheelbase: 252.5cm 99.4in
Track F: 142.0cm 55.9in
Track R: 143.0cm 56.3in
Length: 473.9cm 186.6in
Width: 169.0cm 66.5in
Height: 142.0cm 55.9in
Ground clearance: 15.0cm 5.9in
Kerb weight: 1311.1kg 2888.0lb
Fuel: 55.1L 12.1gal 14.5galUS

4083 Saab

900GL
1979 Sweden
105.0mph 168.9kmh
0-50mph 80.5kmh: 10.4secs
0-60mph 96.5kmh: 13.3secs
0-1/4 mile: 18.2secs
0-1km: 34.4secs
100.0bhp 74.6kW 101.4PS
@ 5200rpm
111.5lbft 151.1Nm @ 3500rpm
86.7bhp/ton 85.3bhp/tonne
50.4bhp/L 37.6kW/L 51.1PS/L
44.3ft/sec 13.5m/sec
19.4mph 31.2kmh/1000rpm
24.5mpg 20.4mpgUS 11.5L/100km
Petrol 4-stroke piston
1985cc 121.1cu in
In-line 4 1 Carburettor
Compression ratio: 9.2:1
Bore: 90.0mm 3.5in
Stroke: 78.0mm 3.1in
Valve type/No: Overhead 8
Transmission: Manual
No. of forward speeds: 4
Wheels driven: Front
Springs F/R: Coil/Coil
Brake system: PA
Brakes F/R: Disc/Disc
Steering: Rack & pinion
Wheelbase: 252.5cm 99.4in
Track F: 142.0cm 55.9in
Track R: 142.0cm 55.9in
Length: 472.4cm 186.0in
Width: 168.9cm 66.5in
Height: 142.7cm 56.2in
Ground clearance: 15.0cm 5.9in
Kerb weight: 1172.7kg 2583.0lb
Fuel: 58.2L 12.8gal 15.4galUS

4084 Saab

900GLE
1980 Sweden
0-60mph 96.5kmh: 13.2secs
0-1/4 mile: 19.1secs
110.0bhp 82.0kW 111.5PS
@ 5250rpm
119.0lbft 161.2Nm @ 3500rpm
86.8bhp/ton 85.3bhp/tonne
55.4bhp/L 41.3kW/L 56.2PS/L
44.8ft/sec 13.6m/sec
27.0mpg 22.5mpgUS 10.5L/100km
Petrol 4-stroke piston
1985cc 121.1cu in
In-line 4 fuel injection
Compression ratio: 9.3:1
Bore: 90.0mm 3.5in
Stroke: 78.0mm 3.1in
Valve type/No: Overhead 8
Transmission: Manual
No. of forward speeds: 4
Wheels driven: Front
Brakes F/R: Disc/Disc
Wheelbase: 252.5cm 99.4in
Track F: 142.0cm 55.9in
Track R: 143.0cm 56.3in
Length: 476.5cm 187.6in
Width: 168.9cm 66.5in
Height: 142.0cm 55.9in
Kerb weight: 1289.4kg 2840.0lb
Fuel: 54.9L 12.1gal 14.5galUS

4085 Saab

900 Turbo
1981 Sweden
107.0mph 172.2kmh
0-50mph 80.5kmh: 8.3secs
0-60mph 96.5kmh: 11.4secs
0-1/4 mile: 18.3secs
135.0bhp 100.7kW 136.9PS
@ 4800rpm
160.0lbft 216.8Nm @ 3500rpm
105.9bhp/ton 104.1bhp/tonne
68.0bhp/L 50.7kW/L 68.9PS/L
40.9ft/sec 12.5m/sec
20.0mph 32.2kmh/1000rpm
27.6mpg 23.0mpgUS 10.2L/100km
Petrol 4-stroke piston
1985cc 121.1cu in turbocharged
In-line 4 fuel injection
Compression ratio: 7.2:1
Bore: 89.9mm 3.5in
Stroke: 78.0mm 3.1in
Valve type/No: Overhead 8
Transmission: Automatic
No. of forward speeds: 3
Wheels driven: Front
Springs F/R: Coil/Coil
Brake system: PA
Brakes F/R: Disc/Disc
Steering: Rack & pinion PA
Wheelbase: 252.5cm 99.4in
Track F: 142.0cm 55.9in
Track R: 143.0cm 56.3in
Length: 474.0cm 186.6in
Width: 168.9cm 66.5in
Height: 142.0cm 55.9in
Kerb weight: 1296.2kg 2855.0lb
Fuel: 62.8L 13.8gal 16.6galUS

4086 Saab

900GLS
1981 Sweden

106.0mph 170.6kmh
0-50mph 80.5kmh: 9.3secs
0-60mph 96.5kmh: 13.9secs
0-1/4 mile: 19.0secs
0-1km: 35.8secs
108.0bhp 80.5kW 109.5PS
@ 5200rpm
121.0lbft 164.0Nm @ 3300rpm
91.8bhp/ton 90.3bhp/tonne
54.4bhp/L 40.6kW/L 55.2PS/L
44.3ft/sec 13.5m/sec
20.9mph 33.6kmh/1000rpm
28.3mpg 23.6mpgUS 10.0L/100km
Petrol 4-stroke piston
1985cc 121.1cu in
In-line 4 2 Carburettor
Compression ratio: 9.5:1
Bore: 90.0mm 3.5in
Stroke: 78.0mm 3.1in
Valve type/No: Overhead 8
Transmission: Manual
No. of forward speeds: 4
Wheels driven: Front
Springs F/R: Coil/Coil
Brake system: PA
Brakes F/R: Disc/Disc
Steering: Rack & pinion PA
Wheelbase: 252.5cm 99.4in
Track F: 142.0cm 55.9in
Track R: 143.0cm 56.3in
Length: 473.7cm 186.5in
Width: 168.9cm 66.5in
Height: 142.7cm 56.2in
Ground clearance: 15.0cm 5.9in
Kerb weight: 1195.8kg 2634.0lb
Fuel: 66.0L 14.5gal 17.4galUS

4087 Saab

900
1982 Sweden
105.0mph 168.9kmh
0-50mph 80.5kmh: 9.5secs
0-60mph 96.5kmh: 13.8secs
0-1/4 mile: 19.3secs
110.0bhp 82.0kW 111.5PS
@ 5250rpm
119.0lbft 161.2Nm @ 3500rpm
95.1bhp/ton 93.5bhp/tonne
55.5bhp/L 41.4kW/L 56.2PS/L
44.8ft/sec 13.6m/sec
24.0mph 38.6kmh/1000rpm
26.4mpg 22.0mpgUS 10.7L/100km
Petrol 4-stroke piston
1983cc 121.0cu in
In-line 4 fuel injection
Compression ratio: 9.3:1
Bore: 90.0mm 3.5in
Stroke: 78.0mm 3.1in
Valve type/No: Overhead 8
Transmission: Manual
No. of forward speeds: 5
Wheels driven: Front
Springs F/R: Coil/Coil
Brake system: PA
Brakes F/R: Disc/Disc
Steering: Rack & pinion PA
Wheelbase: 252.5cm 99.4in
Track F: 142.0cm 55.9in
Track R: 143.0cm 56.3in
Length: 476.5cm 187.6in
Width: 168.9cm 66.5in
Height: 142.0cm 55.9in
Kerb weight: 1175.9kg 2590.0lb
Fuel: 54.9L 12.1gal 14.5galUS

4088 Saab

900 Turbo
1982 Sweden
116.0mph 186.6kmh
0-50mph 80.5kmh: 7.0secs
0-60mph 96.5kmh: 10.0secs
0-1/4 mile: 17.3secs
135.0bhp 100.7kW 136.9PS
@ 4800rpm
170.0lbft 230.4Nm @ 3500rpm
107.2bhp/ton 105.4bhp/tonne
68.1bhp/L 50.8kW/L 69.0PS/L
40.9ft/sec 12.5m/sec
23.3mph 37.5kmh/1000rpm
27.0mpg 22.5mpgUS 10.5L/100km
Petrol 4-stroke piston
1983cc 121.0cu in turbocharged
In-line 4 fuel injection
Compression ratio: 8.5:1
Bore: 90.0mm 3.5in
Stroke: 78.0mm 3.1in
Valve type/No: Overhead 8
Transmission: Manual
No. of forward speeds: 5
Wheels driven: Front
Springs F/R: Coil/Coil
Brake system: PA
Brakes F/R: Disc/Disc
Steering: Rack & pinion PA
Wheelbase: 252.5cm 99.4in
Track F: 142.0cm 55.9in
Track R: 143.0cm 56.3in
Length: 476.5cm 187.6in
Width: 168.9cm 66.5in
Height: 142.0cm 55.9in
Kerb weight: 1280.3kg 2820.0lb
Fuel: 54.9L 12.1gal 14.5galUS

4089 Saab

900 Turbo
1985 Sweden
124.0mph 199.5kmh
0-50mph 80.5kmh: 6.3secs
0-60mph 96.5kmh: 8.6secs
0-1/4 mile: 16.5secs
160.0bhp 119.3kW 162.2PS
@ 5500rpm
188.0lbft 254.7Nm @ 3000rpm
123.2bhp/ton 121.1bhp/tonne
80.6bhp/L 60.1kW/L 81.7PS/L
46.9ft/sec 14.3m/sec
22.4mph 36.0kmh/1000rpm
27.0mpg 22.5mpgUS 10.5L/100km
Petrol 4-stroke piston
1985cc 121.1cu in turbocharged
In-line 4 fuel injection
Compression ratio: 9.0:1
Bore: 90.0mm 3.5in
Stroke: 78.0mm 3.1in
Valve type/No: Overhead 16
Transmission: Manual
No. of forward speeds: 5
Wheels driven: Front
Springs F/R: Coil/Coil
Brake system: PA
Brakes F/R: Disc/Disc
Steering: Rack & pinion PA
Wheelbase: 251.7cm 99.1in
Track F: 143.0cm 56.3in
Track R: 144.0cm 56.7in
Length: 474.0cm 186.6in
Width: 168.9cm 66.5in
Height: 142.5cm 56.1in
Kerb weight: 1321.1kg 2910.0lb
Fuel: 62.8L 13.8gal 16.6galUS

4090 Saab

9000 Turbo 16v
1985 Sweden
139.0mph 223.7kmh
0-50mph 80.5kmh: 5.6secs
0-60mph 96.5kmh: 8.3secs
0-1/4 mile: 15.9secs
0-1km: 28.7secs
175.0bhp 130.5kW 177.4PS
@ 5300rpm
201.0lbft 272.4Nm @ 3000rpm
136.6bhp/ton 134.3bhp/tonne
88.2bhp/L 65.7kW/L 89.4PS/L
45.2ft/sec 13.8m/sec
24.1mph 38.8kmh/1000rpm
22.7mpg 18.9mpgUS 12.4L/100km
Petrol 4-stroke piston
1985cc 121.1cu in turbocharged
In-line 4 fuel injection
Compression ratio: 9.5:1
Bore: 90.0mm 3.5in
Stroke: 78.0mm 3.1in
Valve type/No: Overhead 16
Transmission: Manual
No. of forward speeds: 5
Wheels driven: Front
Springs F/R: Coil/Coil
Brake system: PA
Brakes F/R: Disc/Disc
Steering: Rack & pinion PA
Wheelbase: 266.7cm 105.0in
Track F: 152.1cm 59.9in
Track R: 149.1cm 58.7in
Length: 462.0cm 181.9in
Width: 177.5cm 69.9in
Height: 142.0cm 55.9in
Ground clearance: 15.2cm 6.0in
Kerb weight: 1303.0kg 2870.0lb
Fuel: 68.2L 15.0gal 18.0galUS

4091 Saab

900i
1985 Sweden
106.0mph 170.6kmh
0-50mph 80.5kmh: 8.6secs
0-60mph 96.5kmh: 12.7secs
0-1/4 mile: 18.6secs
0-1km: 33.9secs
118.0bhp 88.0kW 119.6PS
@ 5500rpm
123.0lbft 166.7Nm @ 3700rpm
99.7bhp/ton 98.1bhp/tonne
59.4bhp/L 44.3kW/L 60.3PS/L
46.9ft/sec 14.3m/sec
22.9mph 36.8kmh/1000rpm
24.4mpg 20.3mpgUS 11.6L/100km
Petrol 4-stroke piston
1985cc 121.1cu in
In-line 4 fuel injection
Compression ratio: 9.5:1
Bore: 90.0mm 3.5in
Stroke: 78.0mm 3.1in
Valve type/No: Overhead 8
Transmission: Manual
No. of forward speeds: 5
Wheels driven: Front
Springs F/R: Coil/Coil
Brake system: PA
Brakes F/R: Disc/Disc
Steering: Rack & pinion PA
Wheelbase: 252.5cm 99.4in
Track F: 143.0cm 56.3in
Track R: 144.0cm 56.7in
Length: 474.0cm 186.6in
Width: 168.9cm 66.5in
Height: 142.0cm 55.9in
Ground clearance: 15.0cm 5.9in
Kerb weight: 1203.1kg 2650.0lb
Fuel: 63.2L 13.9gal 16.7galUS

4092 Saab

9000
1986 Sweden
124.0mph 199.5kmh
0-60mph 96.5kmh: 8.6secs
0-1/4 mile: 15.6secs
160.0bhp 119.3kW 162.2PS
@ 5500rpm
188.0lbft 254.7Nm @ 3000rpm
119.3bhp/ton 117.3bhp/tonne
80.6bhp/L 60.1kW/L 81.7PS/L
46.9ft/sec 14.3m/sec
25.2mpg 21.0mpgUS 11.2L/100km
Petrol 4-stroke piston
1985cc 121.1cu in
In-line 4 fuel injection
Compression ratio: 9.0:1
Bore: 90.0mm 3.5in
Stroke: 78.0mm 3.1in
Valve type/No: Overhead 16
Transmission: Manual
No. of forward speeds: 5
Wheels driven: Front
Springs F/R: Coil/Coil
Brake system: PA
Brakes F/R: Disc/Disc
Steering: Rack & pinion PA
Wheelbase: 267.2cm 105.2in
Track F: 152.1cm 59.9in
Track R: 149.1cm 58.7in
Length: 462.0cm 181.9in
Width: 176.3cm 69.4in
Height: 142.0cm 55.9in
Ground clearance: 16.5cm 6.5in
Kerb weight: 1364.3kg 3005.0lb
Fuel: 67.7L 14.9gal 17.9galUS

4093 Saab

9000i
1986 Sweden
121.0mph 194.7kmh
0-50mph 80.5kmh: 7.0secs
0-60mph 96.5kmh: 9.6secs
0-1/4 mile: 17.9secs
0-1km: 32.7secs
130.0bhp 96.9kW 131.8PS
@ 5500rpm
127.0lbft 172.1Nm @ 3000rpm
100.8bhp/ton 99.2bhp/tonne
65.5bhp/L 48.8kW/L 66.4PS/L
46.9ft/sec 14.3m/sec
23.0mph 37.0kmh/1000rpm
25.7mpg 21.4mpgUS 11.0L/100km
Petrol 4-stroke piston
1985cc 121.0cu in
In-line 4 fuel injection
Compression ratio: 10.0:1
Bore: 90.0mm 3.5in
Stroke: 78.0mm 3.1in
Valve type/No: Overhead 16
Transmission: Manual
No. of forward speeds: 5
Wheels driven: Front
Springs F/R: Coil/Coil
Brake system: PA
Brakes F/R: Disc/Disc
Steering: Rack & pinion PA
Wheelbase: 267.2cm 105.2in
Track F: 152.2cm 59.9in
Track R: 149.2cm 58.7in
Length: 462.0cm 181.9in
Width: 176.4cm 69.4in
Height: 142.0cm 55.9in
Ground clearance: 15.0cm 5.9in
Kerb weight: 1311.0kg 2887.7lb
Fuel: 68.2L 15.0gal 18.0galUS

4094 Saab

9000CD
1988 Sweden
140.0mph 225.3kmh
0-50mph 80.5kmh: 5.5secs
0-60mph 96.5kmh: 6.9secs
0-1/4 mile: 15.8secs
0-1km: 28.7secs
175.0bhp 130.5kW 177.4PS
@ 5300rpm
201.5lbft 273.0Nm @ 3000rpm
133.5bhp/ton 131.3bhp/tonne
87.7bhp/L 65.4kW/L 88.9PS/L
45.2ft/sec 13.8m/sec
25.3mph 40.7kmh/1000rpm
20.3mpg 16.9mpgUS 13.9L/100km
Petrol 4-stroke piston
1995cc 122.0cu in turbocharged
In-line 4 fuel injection
Compression ratio: 9.0:1
Bore: 90.0mm 3.5in
Stroke: 78.0mm 3.1in
Valve type/No: Overhead 16
Transmission: Manual
No. of forward speeds: 5
Wheels driven: Front
Springs F/R: Coil/Coil
Brake system: PA ABS
Brakes F/R: Disc/Disc
Steering: Rack & pinion PA
Wheelbase: 267.2cm 105.2in
Track F: 152.2cm 59.9in
Track R: 149.2cm 58.7in
Length: 478.0cm 188.2in
Width: 176.4cm 69.4in
Height: 142.0cm 55.9in
Ground clearance: 15.0cm 5.9in
Kerb weight: 1333.0kg 2936.1lb
Fuel: 67.8L 14.9gal 17.9galUS

4095 Saab

900 Turbo S
1989 Sweden
124.0mph 199.5kmh
0-50mph 80.5kmh: 6.1secs
0-60mph 96.5kmh: 8.9secs
155.0bhp 115.6kW 157.1PS
@ 5000rpm
177.1lbft 240.0Nm @ 3000rpm
125.8bhp/ton 123.7bhp/tonne
78.1bhp/L 58.2kW/L 79.2PS/L
42.6ft/sec 13.0m/sec
22.6mph 36.4kmh/1000rpm
19.1mpg 15.9mpgUS 14.8L/100km
Petrol 4-stroke piston
1985cc 121.0cu in turbocharged
In-line 4 fuel injection
Compression ratio: 8.5:1
Bore: 90.0mm 3.5in
Stroke: 78.0mm 3.1in
Valve type/No: Overhead 8
Transmission: Manual
No. of forward speeds: 5
Wheels driven: Front
Springs F/R: Coil/Coil
Brake system: PA
Brakes F/R: Disc/Disc
Steering: Rack & pinion PA
Wheelbase: 251.7cm 99.1in
Track F: 142.0cm 55.9in
Track R: 143.0cm 56.3in
Length: 468.7cm 184.5in
Width: 169.0cm 66.5in
Height: 142.0cm 55.9in
Ground clearance: 15.0cm 5.9in
Kerb weight: 1253.0kg 2759.9lb
Fuel: 63.2L 13.9gal 16.7galUS

4096 Saab
9000 Turbo
1989 Sweden
135.0mph 217.2kmh
0-50mph 80.5kmh: 6.0secs
0-60mph 96.5kmh: 7.7secs
0-1/4 mile: 16.2secs
160.0bhp 119.3kW 162.2PS
@ 5500rpm
188.0lbft 254.7Nm @ 3000rpm
114.9bhp/ton 113.0bhp/tonne
80.6bhp/L 60.1kW/L 81.7PS/L
46.9ft/sec 14.3m/sec
25.2mpg 21.0mpgUS 11.2L/100km
Petrol 4-stroke piston
1985cc 121.1cu in turbocharged
In-line 4 fuel injection
Compression ratio: 9.0:1
Bore: 90.0mm 3.5in
Stroke: 78.0mm 3.1in
Valve type/No: Overhead 16
Transmission: Manual
No. of forward speeds: 5
Wheels driven: Front
Springs F/R: Coil/Coil
Brake system: PA ABS
Brakes F/R: Disc/Disc
Steering: Rack & pinion PA
Wheelbase: 267.0cm 105.1in
Track F: 152.1cm 59.9in
Track R: 149.1cm 58.7in
Length: 462.0cm 181.9in
Width: 176.3cm 69.4in
Height: 142.7cm 56.2in
Kerb weight: 1416.5kg 3120.0lb
Fuel: 67.7L 14.9gal 17.9galUS

4097 Saab
Carlsson
1989 Sweden
148.0mph 238.1kmh
0-50mph 80.5kmh: 5.5secs
0-60mph 96.5kmh: 7.3secs
0-1/4 mile: 15.8secs
0-1km: 28.1secs
204.0bhp 152.1kW 206.8PS
@ 6000rpm
214.0lbft 290.0Nm @ 3000rpm
152.5bhp/ton 150.0bhp/tonne
102.8bhp/L 76.6kW/L 104.2PS/L
51.2ft/sec 15.6m/sec
24.2mph 38.9kmh/1000rpm
21.6mpg 18.0mpgUS 13.1L/100km
Petrol 4-stroke piston
1985cc 121.0cu in turbocharged
In-line 4 fuel injection
Compression ratio: 9.0:1
Bore: 90.0mm 3.5in
Stroke: 78.0mm 3.1in
Valve type/No: Overhead 16
Transmission: Manual
No. of forward speeds: 5
Wheels driven: Front
Springs F/R: Coil/Coil
Brake system: PA ABS
Brakes F/R: Disc/Disc
Steering: Rack & pinion PA
Wheelbase: 267.2cm 105.2in
Track F: 152.2cm 59.9in
Track R: 149.2cm 58.7in
Length: 462.0cm 181.9in
Width: 176.4cm 69.4in
Height: 142.0cm 55.9in
Ground clearance: 15.0cm 5.9in
Kerb weight: 1360.0kg 2995.6lb
Fuel: 67.8L 14.9gal 17.9galUS

4098 Saab
9000CD
1990 Sweden
125.0mph 201.1kmh
0-60mph 96.5kmh: 9.7secs
0-1/4 mile: 17.1secs
150.0bhp 111.9kW 152.1PS
@ 5500rpm
156.0lbft 211.4Nm @ 3800rpm
108.9bhp/ton 107.1bhp/tonne
65.5bhp/L 48.8kW/L 66.4PS/L
54.1ft/sec 16.5m/sec
25.2mpg 21.0mpgUS 11.2L/100km
Petrol 4-stroke piston
2290cc 139.7cu in
In-line 4 fuel injection
Compression ratio: 10.0:1
Bore: 90.0mm 3.5in
Stroke: 90.0mm 3.5in
Valve type/No: Overhead 16
Transmission: Manual
No. of forward speeds: 5
Wheels driven: Front
Springs F/R: Coil/Coil
Brake system: PA ABS
Brakes F/R: Disc/Disc
Steering: Rack & pinion PA
Wheelbase: 267.2cm 105.2in
Track F: 152.1cm 59.9in
Track R: 149.1cm 58.7in
Length: 478.0cm 188.2in
Width: 176.3cm 69.4in
Height: 142.0cm 55.9in
Kerb weight: 1400.6kg 3085.0lb
Fuel: 65.9L 14.5gal 17.4galUS

4099 Saab
900SPG
1990 Sweden
125.0mph 201.1kmh
0-50mph 80.5kmh: 6.4secs
0-60mph 96.5kmh: 9.1secs
0-1/4 mile: 16.7secs
175.0bhp 130.5kW 177.4PS
@ 5500rpm
195.0lbft 264.2Nm @ 3000rpm
132.9bhp/ton 130.7bhp/tonne
88.2bhp/L 65.7kW/L 89.4PS/L
46.9ft/sec 14.3m/sec
25.7mpg 21.4mpgUS 11.0L/100km
Petrol 4-stroke piston
1985cc 121.1cu in turbocharged
In-line 4 fuel injection
Compression ratio: 9.0:1
Bore: 89.9mm 3.5in
Stroke: 77.9mm 3.1in
Valve type/No: Overhead 16
Transmission: Manual
No. of forward speeds: 5
Wheels driven: Front
Springs F/R: Coil/Coil
Brake system: PA ABS
Brakes F/R: Disc/Disc
Steering: Rack & pinion PA
Wheelbase: 251.7cm 99.1in
Track F: 145.5cm 57.3in
Track R: 146.6cm 57.7in
Length: 468.6cm 184.5in
Width: 169.4cm 66.7in
Height: 140.5cm 55.3in
Kerb weight: 1339.3kg 2950.0lb
Fuel: 68.1L 15.0gal 18.0galUS

4100 Saab
CDS 2.3
1990 Sweden
127.0mph 204.3kmh
0-50mph 80.5kmh: 6.8secs
0-60mph 96.5kmh: 9.3secs
0-1/4 mile: 16.9secs
0-1km: 30.9secs
150.0bhp 111.9kW 152.1PS
@ 5500rpm
156.5lbft 212.0Nm @ 3800rpm
109.7bhp/ton 107.9bhp/tonne
65.5bhp/L 48.8kW/L 66.4PS/L
54.1ft/sec 16.5m/sec
22.8mph 36.7kmh/1000rpm
22.0mpg 18.3mpgUS 12.8L/100km
Petrol 4-stroke piston
2290cc 140.0cu in
In-line 4 fuel injection
Compression ratio: 10.0:1
Bore: 90.0mm 3.5in
Stroke: 90.0mm 3.5in
Valve type/No: Overhead 16
Transmission: Manual
No. of forward speeds: 5
Wheels driven: Front
Springs F/R: Coil/Coil
Brake system: PA ABS
Brakes F/R: Disc/Disc
Steering: Rack & pinion PA
Wheelbase: 267.2cm 105.2in
Track F: 152.2cm 59.9in
Track R: 149.2cm 58.7in
Length: 478.0cm 188.2in
Width: 176.4cm 69.4in
Height: 142.0cm 55.9in
Ground clearance: 15.0cm 5.9in
Kerb weight: 1390.0kg 3061.7lb
Fuel: 66.0L 14.5gal 17.4galUS

4101 Saab
9000 2.3 Turbo TCS
1991 Sweden
142.0mph 228.5kmh
0-50mph 80.5kmh: 5.5secs
0-60mph 96.5kmh: 7.5secs
0-1/4 mile: 15.5secs
0-1km: 27.7secs
200.0bhp 149.1kW 202.8PS
@ 5000rpm
243.5lbft 330.0Nm @ 2000rpm
146.8bhp/ton 144.4bhp/tonne
87.3bhp/L 65.1kW/L 88.5PS/L
49.2ft/sec 15.0m/sec
24.0mph 38.6kmh/1000rpm
19.7mpg 16.4mpgUS 14.3L/100km
Petrol 4-stroke piston
2290cc 140.0cu in turbocharged
In-line 4 fuel injection
Compression ratio: 8.5:1
Bore: 90.0mm 3.5in
Stroke: 90.0mm 3.5in
Valve type/No: Overhead 16
Transmission: Manual
No. of forward speeds: 5
Wheels driven: Front
Springs F/R: Coil/Coil
Brake system: PA ABS
Brakes F/R: Disc/Disc
Steering: Rack & pinion PA
Wheelbase: 266.7cm 105.0in
Track F: 152.1cm 59.9in
Track R: 149.1cm 58.7in
Length: 477.8cm 188.1in
Width: 176.3cm 69.4in
Height: 142.0cm 55.9in
Ground clearance: 15.2cm 6.0in
Kerb weight: 1385.0kg 3050.7lb
Fuel: 62.3L 13.7gal 16.5galUS

4102 Saab
9000 Turbo
1991 Sweden
135.0mph 217.2kmh
0-60mph 96.5kmh: 6.8secs
0-1/4 mile: 15.4secs
200.0bhp 149.1kW 202.8PS
@ 5000rpm
244.0lbft 330.6Nm @ 2000rpm
141.1bhp/ton 138.7bhp/tonne
87.3bhp/L 65.1kW/L 88.5PS/L
49.2ft/sec 15.0m/sec
27.6mpg 23.0mpgUS 10.2L/100km
Petrol 4-stroke piston
2290cc 139.7cu in turbocharged
In-line 4 fuel injection
Compression ratio: 8.5:1
Bore: 90.0mm 3.5in
Stroke: 90.0mm 3.5in
Valve type/No: Overhead 16
Transmission: Manual
No. of forward speeds: 5
Wheels driven: Front
Springs F/R: Coil/Coil
Brake system: PA ABS
Brakes F/R: Disc/Disc
Steering: Rack & pinion PA
Wheelbase: 267.2cm 105.2in
Track F: 149.6cm 58.9in
Track R: 149.1cm 58.7in
Length: 466.6cm 183.7in
Width: 176.3cm 69.4in
Height: 142.0cm 55.9in
Kerb weight: 1441.4kg 3175.0lb
Fuel: 62.1L 13.6gal 16.4galUS

4103 Saab
9000CS Turbo S
1991 Sweden
138.6mph 223.0kmh
0-50mph 80.5kmh: 6.2secs
0-60mph 96.5kmh: 8.0secs
0-1/4 mile: 16.3secs
0-1km: 29.2secs
200.0bhp 149.1kW 202.8PS
@ 5000rpm
245.0lbft 332.0Nm @ 2000rpm
143.2bhp/ton 140.8bhp/tonne
87.3bhp/L 65.1kW/L 88.5PS/L
49.2ft/sec 15.0m/sec
21.6mph 34.8kmh/1000rpm
22.2mpg 18.5mpgUS 12.7L/100km
Petrol 4-stroke piston
2290cc 140.0cu in turbocharged
In-line 4 fuel injection
Compression ratio: 8.5:1
Bore: 90.0mm 3.5in
Stroke: 90.0mm 3.5in
Valve type/No: Overhead 16
Transmission: Manual
No. of forward speeds: 5
Wheels driven: Front
Springs F/R: Coil/Coil
Brake system: PA ABS
Brakes F/R: Disc/Disc
Steering: Rack & pinion PA
Wheelbase: 266.2cm 104.8in
Track F: 152.2cm 59.9in
Track R: 149.2cm 58.7in
Length: 476.1cm 187.4in
Width: 176.4cm 69.4in
Height: 142.0cm 55.9in
Ground clearance: 15.0cm 5.9in
Kerb weight: 1420.0kg 3127.7lb
Fuel: 66.0L 14.5gal 17.4galUS

4104 Saab
9000S
1991 Sweden
0-60mph 96.5kmh: 10.0secs
0-1/4 mile: 17.4secs
150.0bhp 111.9kW 152.1PS
@ 5500rpm
157.0lbft 212.7Nm @ 3800rpm
108.6bhp/ton 106.7bhp/tonne
65.5bhp/L 48.8kW/L 66.4PS/L
54.1ft/sec 16.5m/sec
28.0mpg 23.3mpgUS 10.1L/100km
Petrol 4-stroke piston
2290cc 139.7cu in
In-line 4
Bore: 90.0mm 3.5in
Stroke: 90.0mm 3.5in
Valve type/No: Overhead 16
Transmission: Manual
No. of forward speeds: 5
Wheels driven: Front
Springs F/R: Coil/Coil
Brake system: ABS
Brakes F/R: Disc/Disc
Steering: Rack & pinion PA
Wheelbase: 267.2cm 105.2in
Track F: 144.5cm 56.9in
Track R: 149.1cm 58.7in
Length: 466.6cm 183.7in
Width: 176.3cm 69.4in
Height: 142.0cm 55.9in
Kerb weight: 1405.1kg 3095.0lb

4105 Saab
9000 2.3CS
1992 Sweden
129.0mph 207.6kmh
0-50mph 80.5kmh: 7.0secs
0-60mph 96.5kmh: 9.5secs
0-1/4 mile: 17.4secs
0-1km: 31.4secs
150.0bhp 111.9kW 152.1PS
@ 5500rpm
156.0lbft 211.4Nm @ 3800rpm
109.7bhp/ton 107.9bhp/tonne
65.5bhp/L 48.8kW/L 66.4PS/L
54.1ft/sec 16.5m/sec
23.1mph 37.2kmh/1000rpm
23.6mpg 19.7mpgUS 12.0L/100km
Petrol 4-stroke piston
2290cc 139.7cu in
In-line 4 fuel injection
Compression ratio: 10.0:1
Bore: 90.0mm 3.5in
Stroke: 90.0mm 3.5in
Valve type/No: Overhead 16
Transmission: Manual
No. of forward speeds: 5
Wheels driven: Front
Springs F/R: Coil/Coil
Brake system: PA
Brakes F/R: Disc/Disc
Steering: Rack & pinion PA
Wheelbase: 266.7cm 105.0in
Track F: 152.1cm 59.9in
Track R: 149.1cm 58.7in
Length: 476.3cm 187.5in
Width: 177.8cm 70.0in
Height: 142.0cm 55.9in
Ground clearance: 15.2cm 6.0in
Kerb weight: 1390.1kg 3062.0lb
Fuel: 66.0L 14.5gal 17.4galUS

4106 Safir
GT40
1991 UK
193.0mph 310.5kmh
0-60mph 96.5kmh: 4.0secs
0-1/4 mile: 11.9secs
600.0bhp 447.4kW 608.3PS

@ 6000rpm
603.0lbft 817.1Nm @ 4200rpm
564.7bhp/ton 555.3bhp/tonne
74.3bhp/L 55.4kW/L 75.4PS/L
72.8ft/sec 22.2m/sec
Petrol 4-stroke piston
8071cc 492.4cu in
Vee 8 1 Carburettor
Compression ratio: 12.0:1
Bore: 107.5mm 4.2in
Stroke: 111.1mm 4.4in
Valve type/No: Overhead 16
Transmission: Manual
No. of forward speeds: 5
Wheels driven: Rear
Springs F/R: Coil/Coil
Brakes F/R: Disc/Disc
Steering: Rack & pinion
Wheelbase: 241.3cm 95.0in
Track F: 144.8cm 57.0in
Track R: 142.2cm 56.0in
Length: 420.4cm 165.5in
Width: 188.0cm 74.0in
Height: 104.1cm 41.0in
Kerb weight: 1080.5kg 2380.0lb

4107 Saturn

Sports Coupe
1991 USA
124.0mph 199.5kmh
0-50mph 80.5kmh: 6.2secs
0-60mph 96.5kmh: 8.6secs
0-1/4 mile: 16.6secs
123.0bhp 91.7kW 124.7PS
@ 6000rpm
121.0lbft 164.0Nm @ 4800rpm
116.0bhp/ton 114.1bhp/tonne
64.7bhp/L 48.2kW/L 65.6PS/L
59.0ft/sec 18.0m/sec
31.2mpg 26.0mpgUS 9.0L/100km
Petrol 4-stroke piston
1901cc 116.0cu in
In-line 4 fuel injection
Compression ratio: 9.5:1
Bore: 82.0mm 3.2in
Stroke: 90.0mm 3.5in
Valve type/No: Overhead 16
Transmission: Manual
No. of forward speeds: 5
Wheels driven: Front
Springs F/R: Coil/Coil
Brake system: PA ABS
Brakes F/R: Disc/Disc
Steering: Rack & pinion PA
Wheelbase: 252.0cm 99.2in
Track F: 144.3cm 56.8in
Track R: 141.7cm 55.8in
Length: 446.5cm 175.8in
Width: 171.5cm 67.5in
Height: 128.5cm 50.6in
Ground clearance: 14.2cm 5.6in
Kerb weight: 1078.2kg 2375.0lb
Fuel: 50.0L 11.0gal 13.2galUS

4108 Sbarro

Chrono 3.5
1990 Switzerland
124.0mph 199.5kmh
0-60mph 96.5kmh: 3.5secs
500.0bhp 372.8kW 506.9PS
@ 9200rpm
347.0lbft 470.2Nm @ 6500rpm
780.5bhp/ton 767.5bhp/tonne
142.9bhp/L 106.6kW/L 144.9PS/L
84.6ft/sec 25.8m/sec
Petrol 4-stroke piston
3498cc 213.4cu in
In-line 6 fuel injection
Bore: 94.0mm 3.7in
Stroke: 84.0mm 3.3in
Valve type/No: Overhead 24
Transmission: Manual
No. of forward speeds: 5
Wheels driven: Rear
Brakes F/R: Disc/Disc
Wheelbase: 225.0cm 88.6in
Track F: 134.9cm 53.1in
Track R: 150.1cm 59.1in
Length: 305.1cm 120.1in
Width: 186.9cm 73.6in
Height: 100.1cm 39.4in
Kerb weight: 651.5kg 1435.0lb
Fuel: 59.8L 13.1gal 15.8galUS

4109 Scarab

Mk II
1959 USA
161.0mph 259.0kmh
0-50mph 80.5kmh: 3.5secs
0-60mph 96.5kmh: 4.2secs
0-1/4 mile: 12.2secs
360.0bhp 268.4kW 365.0PS
@ 6000rpm
380.0lbft 514.9Nm @ 4000rpm
424.4bhp/ton 417.3bhp/tonne
64.7bhp/L 48.3kW/L 65.6PS/L
56.3ft/sec 17.2m/sec
24.8mph 39.9kmh/1000rpm
Petrol 4-stroke piston
5562cc 339.3cu in
Vee 8
Compression ratio: 10.0:1
Bore: 101.6mm 4.0in
Stroke: 85.9mm 3.4in
Valve type/No: Overhead 16
Transmission: Manual
No. of forward speeds: 4
Wheels driven: Rear
Wheelbase: 233.7cm 92.0in
Track F: 132.1cm 52.0in
Track R: 127.0cm 50.0in
Length: 426.7cm 168.0in
Width: 167.6cm 66.0in
Height: 106.7cm 42.0in
Kerb weight: 862.6kg 1900.0lb

4110 Seat

1200 Sport
1976 Spain
99.0mph 159.3kmh
0-50mph 80.5kmh: 8.6secs
0-60mph 96.5kmh: 13.0secs
0-1/4 mile: 18.5secs
0-1km: 35.6secs
67.0bhp 50.0kW 67.9PS
@ 5600rpm
67.0lbft 90.8Nm @ 3700rpm
84.6bhp/ton 83.2bhp/tonne
56.0bhp/L 41.7kW/L 56.7PS/L
43.7ft/sec 13.3m/sec
16.3mph 26.2kmh/1000rpm
29.9mpg 24.9mpgUS 9.4L/100km
Petrol 4-stroke piston
1197cc 73.0cu in
In-line 4 1 Carburettor
Compression ratio: 8.8:1
Bore: 73.0mm 2.9in
Stroke: 71.5mm 2.8in
Valve type/No: Overhead 8
Transmission: Manual
No. of forward speeds: 4
Wheels driven: Front
Springs F/R: Coil/Leaf
Brakes F/R: Disc/Drum
Steering: Rack & pinion
Wheelbase: 222.3cm 87.5in
Track F: 129.5cm 51.0in
Track R: 132.1cm 52.0in
Length: 367.0cm 144.5in
Width: 155.4cm 61.2in
Height: 126.5cm 49.8in
Ground clearance: 15.2cm 6.0in
Kerb weight: 805.4kg 1774.0lb
Fuel: 30.0L 6.6gal 7.9galUS

4111 Seat

1.5 GLX
1985 Spain
109.0mph 175.4kmh
0-50mph 80.5kmh: 7.3secs
0-60mph 96.5kmh: 10.9secs
0-1/4 mile: 17.7secs
0-1km: 33.1secs
85.0bhp 63.4kW 86.2PS
@ 5600rpm
86.0lbft 116.5Nm @ 3500rpm
97.3bhp/ton 95.7bhp/tonne
58.2bhp/L 43.4kW/L 59.0PS/L
41.4ft/sec 12.6m/sec
22.4mph 36.0kmh/1000rpm
30.3mpg 25.2mpgUS 9.3L/100km
Petrol 4-stroke piston
1461cc 89.1cu in
In-line 4 1 Carburettor
Compression ratio: 10.5:1
Bore: 83.0mm 3.3in
Stroke: 67.5mm 2.7in
Valve type/No: Overhead 8
Transmission: Manual
No. of forward speeds: 5
Wheels driven: Front
Springs F/R: Coil/Leaf
Brake system: PA
Brakes F/R: Disc/Drum
Steering: Rack & pinion
Wheelbase: 244.6cm 96.3in
Track F: 129.8cm 51.1in
Track R: 141.0cm 55.5in
Length: 363.7cm 143.2in
Width: 174.8cm 68.8in
Height: 133.9cm 52.7in
Ground clearance: 15.2cm 6.0in
Kerb weight: 888.5kg 1957.0lb
Fuel: 46.9L 10.3gal 12.4galUS

4112 Seat

Malaga 1.2L
1986 Spain
94.0mph 151.2kmh
0-50mph 80.5kmh: 10.9secs
0-60mph 96.5kmh: 15.7secs
0-1/4 mile: 20.4secs
0-1km: 37.9secs
63.0bhp 47.0kW 63.9PS
@ 5800rpm
65.0lbft 88.1Nm @ 3500rpm
68.5bhp/ton 67.4bhp/tonne
52.8bhp/L 39.4kW/L 53.5PS/L
42.9ft/sec 13.0m/sec
19.9mph 32.0kmh/1000rpm
31.3mpg 26.1mpgUS 9.0L/100km
Petrol 4-stroke piston
1193cc 73.0cu in
In-line 4 1 Carburettor
Compression ratio: 9.5:1
Bore: 73.0mm 2.9in
Stroke: 67.5mm 2.7in
Valve type/No: Overhead 8
Transmission: Manual
No. of forward speeds: 5
Wheels driven: Front
Springs F/R: Coil/Leaf
Brake system: PA
Brakes F/R: Disc/Drum
Steering: Rack & pinion
Wheelbase: 244.7cm 96.3in
Track F: 140.0cm 55.1in
Track R: 141.0cm 55.5in
Length: 408.9cm 161.0in
Width: 165.0cm 65.0in
Height: 140.0cm 55.1in
Ground clearance: 15.3cm 6.0in
Kerb weight: 935.0kg 2059.5lb
Fuel: 50.0L 11.0gal 13.2galUS

4113 Seat

Ibiza SXi
1989 Spain
108.0mph 173.8kmh
0-50mph 80.5kmh: 7.4secs
0-60mph 96.5kmh: 10.3secs
0-1/4 mile: 17.4secs
0-1km: 33.3secs
100.0bhp 74.6kW 101.4PS
@ 5900rpm
94.5lbft 128.0Nm @ 4700rpm
109.8bhp/ton 108.0bhp/tonne
68.4bhp/L 51.0kW/L 69.4PS/L
42.9ft/sec 13.1m/sec
19.9mph 32.0kmh/1000rpm
34.9mpg 29.1mpgUS 8.1L/100km
Petrol 4-stroke piston
1461cc 89.0cu in
In-line 4 fuel injection
Compression ratio: 11.0:1
Bore: 83.0mm 3.3in
Stroke: 66.5mm 2.6in
Valve type/No: Overhead 8
Transmission: Manual
No. of forward speeds: 5
Wheels driven: Front
Springs F/R: Coil/Coil
Brake system: PA
Brakes F/R: Disc/Drum
Steering: Rack & pinion
Wheelbase: 244.3cm 96.2in
Track F: 142.1cm 55.9in
Track R: 138.7cm 54.6in
Length: 363.8cm 143.2in
Width: 161.0cm 63.4in
Height: 134.0cm 52.8in
Ground clearance: 15.3cm 6.0in
Kerb weight: 926.0kg 2039.6lb
Fuel: 50.0L 11.0gal 13.2galUS

4114 Seat

Toledo 1.9 CL Diesel
1992 Spain
103.0mph 165.7kmh
0-50mph 80.5kmh: 11.0secs
0-60mph 96.5kmh: 15.6secs
0-1/4 mile: 20.4secs
0-1km: 37.7secs
68.0bhp 50.7kW 68.9PS
@ 4400rpm
94.0lbft 127.4Nm @ 2400rpm
65.4bhp/ton 64.3bhp/tonne
35.9bhp/L 26.7kW/L 36.4PS/L
46.0ft/sec 14.0m/sec
24.1mph 38.8kmh/1000rpm
37.6mpg 31.3mpgUS 7.5L/100km
Diesel 4-stroke piston
1896cc 115.7cu in
In-line 4 fuel injection
Compression ratio: 23.0:1
Bore: 79.5mm 3.1in
Stroke: 95.5mm 3.8in
Valve type/No: Overhead 8
Transmission: Manual
No. of forward speeds: 5
Wheels driven: Front
Springs F/R: Coil/Coil
Brake system: PA
Brakes F/R: Disc/Drum
Steering: Rack & pinion PA
Wheelbase: 246.9cm 97.2in
Track F: 142.7cm 56.2in
Track R: 142.0cm 55.9in
Length: 432.1cm 170.1in
Width: 166.1cm 65.4in
Height: 142.2cm 56.0in
Kerb weight: 1057.8kg 2330.0lb
Fuel: 60.1L 13.2gal 15.9galUS

4115 Seat

Toledo 2.0 GTi
1992 Spain
124.0mph 199.5kmh
0-50mph 80.5kmh: 7.6secs
0-60mph 96.5kmh: 10.6secs
0-1/4 mile: 17.9secs
0-1km: 32.5secs
115.0bhp 85.8kW 116.6PS
@ 5400rpm
122.5lbft 166.0Nm @ 3200rpm
101.3bhp/ton 99.6bhp/tonne
58.0bhp/L 43.2kW/L 58.8PS/L
54.7ft/sec 16.7m/sec
22.2mph 35.7kmh/1000rpm
31.8mpg 26.5mpgUS 8.9L/100km
Petrol 4-stroke piston
1984cc 121.0cu in
In-line 4 fuel injection
Compression ratio: 10.0:1
Bore: 82.5mm 3.2in
Stroke: 92.8mm 3.6in
Valve type/No: Overhead 8
Transmission: Manual
No. of forward speeds: 5
Wheels driven: Front
Springs F/R: Coil/Coil
Brake system: PA ABS
Brakes F/R: Disc/Disc
Steering: Rack & pinion PA
Wheelbase: 247.1cm 97.3in
Track F: 142.9cm 56.3in
Track R: 142.2cm 56.0in
Length: 432.1cm 170.1in
Width: 166.2cm 65.4in
Height: 142.4cm 56.1in
Kerb weight: 1155.0kg 2544.0lb
Fuel: 50.0L 11.0gal 13.2galUS

4116 Shelby

AC Ford Cobra
1962 USA
153.0mph 246.2kmh
0-50mph 80.5kmh: 3.3secs
0-60mph 96.5kmh: 4.2secs
0-1/4 mile: 13.8secs
260.0bhp 193.9kW 263.6PS
@ 5800rpm
269.0lbft 364.5Nm @ 4500rpm
288.3bhp/ton 283.5bhp/tonne
61.0bhp/L 45.5kW/L 61.9PS/L
46.2ft/sec 14.1m/sec
21.8mph 35.1kmh/1000rpm
Petrol 4-stroke piston
4261cc 260.0cu in
Vee 8
Compression ratio: 9.2:1
Bore: 96.5mm 3.8in
Stroke: 72.9mm 2.9in
Valve type/No: Overhead 16
Transmission: Manual
No. of forward speeds: 4

Wheels driven: Rear
Wheelbase: 228.6cm 90.0in
Track F: 130.8cm 51.5in
Track R: 133.4cm 52.5in
Length: 384.8cm 151.5in
Width: 154.9cm 61.0in
Height: 124.5cm 49.0in
Ground clearance: 17.8cm 7.0in
Kerb weight: 917.1kg 2020.0lb

4117 Shelby

AC Ford Cobra
1964 USA
139.0mph 223.7kmh
0-50mph 80.5kmh: 5.0secs
0-60mph 96.5kmh: 6.6secs
0-1/4 mile: 14.0secs
271.0bhp 202.1kW 274.8PS
@ 6000rpm
314.0lbft 425.5Nm @ 3400rpm
279.7bhp/ton 275.1bhp/tonne
57.3bhp/L 42.7kW/L 58.1PS/L
47.8ft/sec 14.6m/sec
20.2mph 32.5kmh/1000rpm
Petrol 4-stroke piston
4730cc 288.6cu in
Vee 8 1 Carburettor
Compression ratio: 11.6:1
Bore: 101.6mm 4.0in
Stroke: 72.9mm 2.9in
Valve type/No: Overhead 16
Transmission: Manual
No. of forward speeds: 4
Wheels driven: Rear
Springs F/R: Leaf/Leaf
Brakes F/R: Disc/Disc
Steering: Rack & pinion
Wheelbase: 228.6cm 90.0in
Track F: 130.8cm 51.5in
Track R: 133.4cm 52.5in
Length: 384.8cm 151.5in
Width: 154.9cm 61.0in
Height: 124.5cm 49.0in
Ground clearance: 12.7cm 5.0in
Kerb weight: 985.2kg 2170.0lb
Fuel: 68.1L 15.0gal 18.0galUS

4118 Shelby

Cobra USRRC
1964 USA
0-60mph 96.5kmh: 5.1secs
0-1/4 mile: 13.2secs
318.0bhp 237.1kW 322.4PS
@ 6000rpm
300.0lbft 406.5Nm @ 4000rpm
347.5bhp/ton 341.7bhp/tonne
67.2bhp/L 50.1kW/L 68.1PS/L
Petrol 4-stroke piston
4734cc 288.8cu in
Vee 8 4 Carburettor
Valve type/No: Overhead 16
Transmission: Manual
No. of forward speeds: 4
Wheels driven: Rear
Springs F/R: Leaf/Leaf
Brakes F/R: Disc/Disc
Steering: Rack & pinion
Wheelbase: 228.6cm 90.0in
Track F: 132.1cm 52.0in
Track R: 135.9cm 53.5in
Length: 384.8cm 151.5in
Width: 170.2cm 67.0in
Height: 124.5cm 49.0in
Kerb weight: 930.7kg 2050.0lb

4119 Shelby

Cobra Daytona Coupe
1965 USA
190.0mph 305.7kmh
385.0bhp 287.1kW 390.3PS
@ 6750rpm
340.0lbft 460.7Nm @ 4000rpm
375.0bhp/ton 368.7bhp/tonne
81.4bhp/L 60.7kW/L 82.6PS/L
53.8ft/sec 16.4m/sec
Petrol 4-stroke piston
4728cc 288.5cu in
Vee 8 4 Carburettor
Compression ratio: 10.0:1
Bore: 101.6mm 4.0in
Stroke: 72.9mm 2.9in
Valve type/No: Overhead 16
Transmission: Manual
No. of forward speeds: 4
Wheels driven: Rear
Springs F/R: Leaf/Leaf
Brakes F/R: Disc/Disc
Steering: Rack & pinion
Wheelbase: 228.6cm 90.0in
Track F: 135.4cm 53.3in
Track R: 134.1cm 52.8in
Length: 461.0cm 181.5in
Width: 175.3cm 69.0in
Height: 142.2cm 56.0in
Kerb weight: 1044.2kg 2300.0lb
Fuel: 98.4L 21.6gal 26.0galUS

4120 Shelby

GT 350
1965 USA
124.0mph 199.5kmh
0-50mph 80.5kmh: 5.2secs
0-60mph 96.5kmh: 6.8secs
0-1/4 mile: 14.7secs
306.0bhp 228.2kW 310.2PS
@ 6000rpm
329.0lbft 445.8Nm @ 4200rpm
245.7bhp/ton 241.6bhp/tonne
64.6bhp/L 48.2kW/L 65.5PS/L
47.8ft/sec 14.6m/sec
20.3mph 32.7kmh/1000rpm
Petrol 4-stroke piston
4736cc 289.0cu in
Vee 8 1 Carburettor
Compression ratio: 11.5:1
Bore: 101.6mm 4.0in
Stroke: 72.9mm 2.9in
Valve type/No: Overhead 16
Transmission: Manual
No. of forward speeds: 4
Wheels driven: Rear
Springs F/R: Coil/Leaf
Brakes F/R: Disc/Drum
Steering: Recirculating ball
Wheelbase: 274.3cm 108.0in
Track F: 143.5cm 56.5in
Track R: 144.8cm 57.0in
Length: 461.3cm 181.6in
Width: 173.2cm 68.2in
Height: 130.0cm 51.2in
Ground clearance: 14.0cm 5.5in
Kerb weight: 1266.7kg 2790.0lb
Fuel: 60.6L 13.3gal 16.0galUS

4121 Shelby

GT 350-S
1966 USA
127.0mph 204.3kmh
0-50mph 80.5kmh: 4.8secs
0-60mph 96.5kmh: 6.2secs
0-1/4 mile: 14.0secs
390.0bhp 290.8kW 395.4PS
@ 6000rpm
329.0lbft 445.8Nm @ 4200rpm
296.1bhp/ton 291.2bhp/tonne
82.3bhp/L 61.4kW/L 83.5PS/L
47.8ft/sec 14.6m/sec
18.1mph 29.1kmh/1000rpm
Petrol 4-stroke piston
4736cc 289.0cu in supercharged
Vee 8 1 Carburettor
Compression ratio: 10.5:1
Bore: 101.7mm 4.0in
Stroke: 72.9mm 2.9in
Valve type/No: Overhead 16
Transmission: Automatic
No. of forward speeds: 3
Wheels driven: Rear
Springs F/R: Coil/Leaf
Brakes F/R: Disc/Drum
Steering: Recirculating ball
Wheelbase: 274.3cm 108.0in
Track F: 144.8cm 57.0in
Track R: 144.8cm 57.0in
Length: 461.3cm 181.6in
Width: 173.2cm 68.2in
Height: 139.7cm 55.0in
Ground clearance: 14.0cm 5.5in
Kerb weight: 1339.3kg 2950.0lb
Fuel: 60.6L 13.3gal 16.0galUS

4122 Shelby

GT 500
1967 USA
132.0mph 212.4kmh
0-50mph 80.5kmh: 5.7secs
0-60mph 96.5kmh: 7.2secs
0-1/4 mile: 15.5secs
355.0bhp 264.7kW 359.9PS
@ 5400rpm
420.0lbft 569.1Nm @ 3200rpm
225.9bhp/ton 222.1bhp/tonne
50.6bhp/L 37.7kW/L 51.3PS/L
59.7ft/sec 18.2m/sec
23.8mph 38.3kmh/1000rpm
Petrol 4-stroke piston
7014cc 427.9cu in
Vee 8 2 Carburettor
Compression ratio: 10.5:1
Bore: 115.0mm 4.5in
Stroke: 101.0mm 4.0in
Valve type/No: Overhead 16
Transmission: Automatic
No. of forward speeds: 3
Wheels driven: Rear
Springs F/R: Coil/Leaf
Brake system: PA
Brakes F/R: Disc/Drum
Steering: Recirculating ball PA
Wheelbase: 274.3cm 108.0in
Track F: 147.3cm 58.0in
Track R: 147.3cm 58.0in
Length: 474.0cm 186.6in
Width: 180.1cm 70.9in
Height: 124.5cm 49.0in
Ground clearance: 13.0cm 5.1in
Kerb weight: 1598.1kg 3520.0lb
Fuel: 64.3L 14.1gal 17.0galUS

4123 Shelby

GT 350
1968 USA
119.0mph 191.5kmh
0-50mph 80.5kmh: 4.9secs
0-60mph 96.5kmh: 6.3secs
0-1/4 mile: 14.9secs
315.0bhp 234.9kW 319.4PS
@ 5000rpm
333.0lbft 451.2Nm @ 3800rpm
211.6bhp/ton 208.0bhp/tonne
63.6bhp/L 47.5kW/L 64.5PS/L
41.7ft/sec 12.7m/sec
18.4mph 29.6kmh/1000rpm
Petrol 4-stroke piston
4949cc 301.9cu in
Vee 8 2 Carburettor
Compression ratio: 11.0:1
Bore: 101.6mm 4.0in
Stroke: 76.3mm 3.0in
Valve type/No: Overhead 16
Transmission: Manual
No. of forward speeds: 4
Wheels driven: Rear
Springs F/R: Coil/Leaf
Brake system: PA
Brakes F/R: Disc/Drum
Steering: Recirculating ball PA
Wheelbase: 274.3cm 108.0in
Track F: 147.6cm 58.1in
Track R: 147.6cm 58.1in
Length: 474.5cm 186.8in
Width: 180.1cm 70.9in
Height: 131.6cm 51.8in
Ground clearance: 12.4cm 4.9in
Kerb weight: 1514.1kg 3335.0lb
Fuel: 60.6L 13.3gal 16.0galUS

4124 Shelby

GT 500-KR
1968 USA
130.0mph 209.2kmh
0-50mph 80.5kmh: 4.8secs
0-60mph 96.5kmh: 6.9secs
0-1/4 mile: 14.6secs
335.0bhp 249.8kW 339.6PS
@ 5200rpm
440.0lbft 596.2Nm @ 3400rpm
214.4bhp/ton 210.8bhp/tonne
47.8bhp/L 35.6kW/L 48.4PS/L
57.5ft/sec 17.5m/sec
21.3mph 34.3kmh/1000rpm
Petrol 4-stroke piston
7014cc 427.9cu in
Vee 8 1 Carburettor
Compression ratio: 10.6:1
Bore: 104.9mm 4.1in
Stroke: 101.1mm 4.0in
Valve type/No: Overhead 16
Transmission: Manual
No. of forward speeds: 4
Wheels driven: Rear
Springs F/R: Coil/Leaf
Brake system: PA
Brakes F/R: Disc/Drum
Steering: Recirculating ball PA
Wheelbase: 274.3cm 108.0in
Track F: 148.6cm 58.5in
Track R: 148.6cm 58.5in
Length: 466.3cm 183.6in
Width: 180.1cm 70.9in
Height: 130.6cm 51.4in
Kerb weight: 1589.0kg 3500.0lb
Fuel: 60.6L 13.3gal 16.0galUS

4125 Shelby

GT 500
1969 USA
130.0mph 209.2kmh
0-60mph 96.5kmh: 6.9secs
0-1/4 mile: 14.5secs
335.0bhp 249.8kW 339.6PS
@ 5200rpm
440.0lbft 596.2Nm @ 3400rpm
194.9bhp/ton 191.7bhp/tonne
47.7bhp/L 35.6kW/L 48.4PS/L
57.5ft/sec 17.5m/sec
Petrol 4-stroke piston
7015cc 428.0cu in
Vee 8 1 Carburettor
Compression ratio: 10.6:1
Bore: 104.9mm 4.1in
Stroke: 101.1mm 4.0in
Valve type/No: Overhead 16
Transmission: Manual
No. of forward speeds: 4
Wheels driven: Rear
Springs F/R: Coil/Leaf
Brake system: PA
Brakes F/R: Disc/Drum
Steering: Recirculating ball PA
Wheelbase: 274.3cm 108.0in
Track F: 148.6cm 58.5in
Track R: 148.6cm 58.5in
Length: 484.1cm 190.6in
Width: 182.6cm 71.9in
Height: 128.5cm 50.6in
Kerb weight: 1747.9kg 3850.0lb
Fuel: 75.7L 16.6gal 20.0galUS

4126 Shelby

Cobra 427
1974 USA
162.0mph 260.7kmh
0-50mph 80.5kmh: 4.3secs
0-60mph 96.5kmh: 5.3secs
0-1/4 mile: 13.8secs
425.0bhp 316.9kW 430.9PS
@ 6000rpm
480.0lbft 650.4Nm @ 3700rpm
376.3bhp/ton 370.0bhp/tonne
60.7bhp/L 45.3kW/L 61.6PS/L
63.2ft/sec 19.2m/sec
25.0mph 40.2kmh/1000rpm
14.4mpg 12.0mpgUS 19.6L/100km
Petrol 4-stroke piston
6998cc 427.0cu in
Vee 8 2 Carburettor
Compression ratio: 11.5:1
Bore: 108.0mm 4.2in
Stroke: 96.2mm 3.8in
Valve type/No: Overhead 16
Transmission: Manual
No. of forward speeds: 4
Wheels driven: Rear
Springs F/R: Coil/Coil
Brake system: PA
Brakes F/R: Disc/Disc
Steering: Rack & pinion
Wheelbase: 228.6cm 90.0in
Track F: 142.2cm 56.0in
Track R: 142.2cm 56.0in
Length: 396.2cm 156.0in
Width: 172.7cm 68.0in
Height: 124.5cm 49.0in
Ground clearance: 11.2cm 4.4in
Kerb weight: 1148.6kg 2530.0lb
Fuel: 68.1L 15.0gal 18.0galUS

4127 Siata

Spyder V8
1953 Italy
104.8mph 168.6kmh
0-50mph 80.5kmh: 8.4secs
0-60mph 96.5kmh: 12.4secs
0-1/4 mile: 17.9secs
105.0bhp 78.3kW 106.5PS
@ 5800rpm
120.0bhp/ton 118.0bhp/tonne
52.6bhp/L 39.2kW/L 53.3PS/L
39.0ft/sec 11.9m/sec
18.5mph 29.8kmh/1000rpm
Petrol 4-stroke piston
1996cc 121.8cu in
Vee 8
Compression ratio: 8.5:1

Bore: 63.0mm 2.5in
Stroke: 61.5mm 2.4in
Valve type/No: Overhead 16
Transmission: Manual
No. of forward speeds: 4
Wheels driven: Rear
Wheelbase: 229.9cm 90.5in
Track F: 130.0cm 51.2in
Track R: 130.0cm 51.2in
Kerb weight: 889.8kg 1960.0lb

4128 Siata

Spring 850
1969 Italy
73.0mph 117.5kmh
0-50mph 80.5kmh: 14.2secs
0-60mph 96.5kmh: 25.0secs
0-1/4 mile: 21.5secs
42.0bhp 31.3kW 42.6PS
@ 5300rpm
44.0lbft 59.6Nm @ 3600rpm
66.2bhp/ton 65.1bhp/tonne
49.8bhp/L 37.1kW/L 50.5PS/L
36.8ft/sec 11.2m/sec
13.6mph 21.9kmh/1000rpm
36.0mpg 30.0mpgUS 7.8L/100km
Petrol 4-stroke piston
843cc 51.4cu in
In-line 4 1 Carburettor
Compression ratio: 8.8:1
Bore: 65.0mm 2.6in
Stroke: 63.5mm 2.5in
Valve type/No: Overhead 8
Transmission: Manual
No. of forward speeds: 4
Wheels driven: Rear
Springs F/R: Leaf/Coil
Brakes F/R: Drum/Drum
Steering: Worm & sector
Wheelbase: 204.5cm 80.5in
Track F: 116.8cm 46.0in
Track R: 123.2cm 48.5in
Length: 354.8cm 139.7in
Width: 140.0cm 55.1in
Height: 121.9cm 48.0in
Ground clearance: 15.2cm 6.0in
Kerb weight: 644.7kg 1420.0lb
Fuel: 29.9L 6.6gal 7.9galUS

4129 Simca

8 Sport
1951 France
82.3mph 132.4kmh
0-60mph 96.5kmh: 24.0secs
50.0bhp 37.3kW 50.7PS
@ 4800rpm
56.4bhp/ton 55.5bhp/tonne
40.9bhp/L 30.5kW/L 41.5PS/L
39.3ft/sec 12.0m/sec
Petrol 4-stroke piston
1221cc 74.5cu in
In-line 4
Bore: 71.9mm 2.8in
Stroke: 75.0mm 2.9in
Valve type/No: Overhead 8
Transmission: Manual
No. of forward speeds: 4
Wheels driven: Rear
Wheelbase: 242.1cm 95.3in
Track F: 122.9cm 48.4in
Track R: 122.9cm 48.4in
Length: 410.0cm 161.4in
Width: 154.9cm 61.0in
Height: 130.0cm 51.2in
Ground clearance: 17.0cm 6.7in
Kerb weight: 900.7kg 1984.0lb

4130 Simca

Aronde
1952 France
73.5mph 118.3kmh
0-50mph 80.5kmh: 16.7secs
45.0bhp 33.6kW 45.6PS
@ 4500rpm
61.0lbft 82.7Nm @ 2600rpm
47.8bhp/ton 47.0bhp/tonne
36.9bhp/L 27.5kW/L 37.4PS/L
36.9ft/sec 11.2m/sec
15.8mph 25.4kmh/1000rpm
30.0mpg 25.0mpgUS 9.4L/100km
Petrol 4-stroke piston
1221cc 74.5cu in
In-line 4
Compression ratio: 6.8:1
Bore: 72.0mm 2.8in
Stroke: 75.0mm 2.9in
Valve type/No: Overhead 8
Transmission: Manual
No. of forward speeds: 4
Wheels driven: Rear
Wheelbase: 244.3cm 96.2in
Track F: 123.2cm 48.5in
Track R: 123.2cm 48.5in
Length: 406.4cm 160.0in
Width: 155.4cm 61.2in
Height: 152.1cm 59.9in
Ground clearance: 16.0cm 6.3in
Kerb weight: 956.6kg 2107.0lb
Fuel: 40.0L 8.8gal 10.6galUS

4131 Simca

Aronde
1954 France
76.0mph 122.3kmh
0-50mph 80.5kmh: 19.0secs
0-60mph 96.5kmh: 29.4secs
0-1/4 mile: 23.6secs
45.0bhp 33.6kW 45.6PS
@ 4500rpm
61.0lbft 82.7Nm @ 2600rpm
47.7bhp/ton 46.9bhp/tonne
36.9bhp/L 27.5kW/L 37.4PS/L
36.9ft/sec 11.2m/sec
15.8mph 25.4kmh/1000rpm
35.0mpg 29.1mpgUS 8.1L/100km
Petrol 4-stroke piston
1221cc 74.5cu in
In-line 4
Compression ratio: 6.8:1
Bore: 72.0mm 2.8in
Stroke: 75.0mm 2.9in
Valve type/No: Overhead 8
Transmission: Manual
No. of forward speeds: 4
Wheels driven: Rear
Springs F/R: Coil/Leaf
Brakes F/R: Drum/Drum
Wheelbase: 243.8cm 96.0in
Track F: 123.2cm 48.5in
Track R: 123.2cm 48.5in
Length: 406.4cm 160.0in
Width: 154.9cm 61.0in
Height: 152.4cm 60.0in
Ground clearance: 15.7cm 6.2in
Kerb weight: 959.8kg 2114.0lb
Fuel: 40.0L 8.8gal 10.6galUS

4132 Simca

Aronde
1955 France
76.5mph 123.1kmh
0-50mph 80.5kmh: 17.8secs
0-60mph 96.5kmh: 27.9secs
0-1/4 mile: 23.1secs
45.0bhp 33.6kW 45.6PS
@ 4500rpm
61.0lbft 82.7Nm @ 2600rpm
50.7bhp/ton 49.9bhp/tonne
36.9bhp/L 27.5kW/L 37.4PS/L
36.9ft/sec 11.2m/sec
15.8mph 25.4kmh/1000rpm
34.0mpg 28.3mpgUS 8.3L/100km
Petrol 4-stroke piston
1221cc 74.5cu in
In-line 4
Compression ratio: 6.8:1
Bore: 72.0mm 2.8in
Stroke: 75.0mm 2.9in
Valve type/No: Overhead 8
Transmission: Manual
No. of forward speeds: 4
Wheels driven: Rear
Springs F/R: Coil/Leaf
Brakes F/R: Drum/Drum
Wheelbase: 244.3cm 96.2in
Track F: 123.2cm 48.5in
Track R: 123.2cm 48.5in
Length: 406.4cm 160.0in
Width: 154.9cm 61.0in
Height: 143.5cm 56.5in
Ground clearance: 13.2cm 5.2in
Kerb weight: 902.5kg 1988.0lb
Fuel: 40.0L 8.8gal 10.6galUS

4133 Simca

Elysee
1956 France
76.0mph 122.3kmh
0-50mph 80.5kmh: 16.8secs
0-60mph 96.5kmh: 24.7secs
0-1/4 mile: 23.3secs
48.0bhp 35.8kW 48.7PS
@ 4500rpm
65.0lbft 88.1Nm @ 2800rpm
51.9bhp/ton 51.0bhp/tonne
37.2bhp/L 27.7kW/L 37.7PS/L
36.9ft/sec 11.2m/sec
16.3mph 26.2kmh/1000rpm
31.0mpg 25.8mpgUS 9.1L/100km
Petrol 4-stroke piston
1290cc 78.7cu in
In-line 4
Compression ratio: 6.8:1
Bore: 74.0mm 2.9in
Stroke: 75.0mm 2.9in
Valve type/No: Overhead 8
Transmission: Manual
No. of forward speeds: 4
Wheels driven: Rear
Springs F/R: Coil/Leaf
Brakes F/R: Drum/Drum
Wheelbase: 244.3cm 96.2in
Track F: 122.4cm 48.2in
Track R: 125.0cm 49.2in
Length: 411.5cm 162.0in
Width: 156.7cm 61.7in
Height: 151.6cm 59.7in
Ground clearance: 14.0cm 5.5in
Kerb weight: 940.7kg 2072.0lb
Fuel: 43.2L 9.5gal 11.4galUS

4134 Simca

Sports Coupe
1956 France
84.3mph 135.6kmh
0-50mph 80.5kmh: 13.7secs
0-60mph 96.5kmh: 19.3secs
0-1/4 mile: 21.5secs
57.0bhp 42.5kW 57.8PS
@ 4800rpm
66.5lbft 90.1Nm @ 3100rpm
59.7bhp/ton 58.7bhp/tonne
44.2bhp/L 32.9kW/L 44.8PS/L
39.3ft/sec 12.0m/sec
16.3mph 26.2kmh/1000rpm
Petrol 4-stroke piston
1290cc 78.7cu in
In-line 4
Compression ratio: 7.8:1
Bore: 73.9mm 2.9in
Stroke: 74.9mm 2.9in
Valve type/No: Overhead 8
Transmission: Manual
No. of forward speeds: 4
Wheels driven: Rear
Wheelbase: 244.3cm 96.2in
Track F: 125.5cm 49.4in
Track R: 125.0cm 49.2in
Kerb weight: 971.6kg 2140.0lb

4135 Simca

Versailles V8
1957 France
87.4mph 140.6kmh
0-50mph 80.5kmh: 11.2secs
0-60mph 96.5kmh: 17.2secs
0-1/4 mile: 20.6secs
79.0bhp 58.9kW 80.1PS
@ 4600rpm
106.0lbft 143.6Nm @ 2600rpm
69.7bhp/ton 68.5bhp/tonne
33.6bhp/L 25.1kW/L 34.1PS/L
43.1ft/sec 13.1m/sec
Petrol 4-stroke piston
2351cc 143.4cu in
Vee 8
Compression ratio: 7.2:1
Bore: 66.0mm 2.6in
Stroke: 85.7mm 3.4in
Valve type/No: Side 16
Transmission: Manual
No. of forward speeds: 3
Wheels driven: Rear
Wheelbase: 269.0cm 105.9in
Track F: 136.9cm 53.9in
Track R: 134.1cm 52.8in
Kerb weight: 1153.2kg 2540.0lb

4136 Simca

Aronde Montlhery
1958 France
84.6mph 136.1kmh
0-50mph 80.5kmh: 14.4secs
0-60mph 96.5kmh: 20.6secs
0-1/4 mile: 21.7secs
57.0bhp 42.5kW 57.8PS
@ 5200rpm
66.5lbft 90.1Nm @ 3100rpm
62.5bhp/ton 61.4bhp/tonne
44.2bhp/L 32.9kW/L 44.8PS/L
42.6ft/sec 13.0m/sec
15.8mph 25.4kmh/1000rpm
28.8mpg 24.0mpgUS 9.8L/100km
Petrol 4-stroke piston
1290cc 78.7cu in
In-line 4
Compression ratio: 7.8:1
Bore: 74.0mm 2.9in
Stroke: 75.0mm 2.9in
Valve type/No: Overhead 8
Transmission: Manual
No. of forward speeds: 4
Wheels driven: Rear
Springs F/R: Coil/Leaf
Brakes F/R: Drum/Drum
Wheelbase: 244.3cm 96.2in
Track F: 125.0cm 49.2in
Track R: 125.0cm 49.2in
Length: 411.5cm 162.0in
Width: 157.5cm 62.0in
Height: 147.3cm 58.0in
Ground clearance: 14.0cm 5.5in
Kerb weight: 928.0kg 2044.0lb
Fuel: 42.1L 9.2gal 11.1galUS

4137 Simca

Vedette Beaulieu
1958 France
92.0mph 148.0kmh
0-50mph 80.5kmh: 12.1secs
0-60mph 96.5kmh: 18.4secs
0-1/4 mile: 21.0secs
84.0bhp 62.6kW 85.2PS
@ 4800rpm
112.0lbft 151.8Nm @ 2750rpm
69.3bhp/ton 68.1bhp/tonne
35.7bhp/L 26.6kW/L 36.2PS/L
44.9ft/sec 13.7m/sec
20.2mph 32.5kmh/1000rpm
22.0mpg 18.3mpgUS 12.8L/100km
Petrol 4-stroke piston
2351cc 143.4cu in
Vee 8
Compression ratio: 7.5:1
Bore: 66.0mm 2.6in
Stroke: 85.7mm 3.4in
Valve type/No: Side 16
Transmission: Manual
No. of forward speeds: 3
Wheels driven: Rear
Springs F/R: Coil/Leaf
Brakes F/R: Drum/Drum
Wheelbase: 269.2cm 106.0in
Track F: 137.2cm 54.0in
Track R: 133.9cm 52.7in
Length: 475.0cm 187.0in
Width: 177.0cm 69.7in
Height: 146.1cm 57.5in
Ground clearance: 17.3cm 6.8in
Kerb weight: 1233.1kg 2716.0lb
Fuel: 60.3L 13.2gal 15.9galUS

4138 Simca

Elysee
1959 France
76.0mph 122.3kmh
0-50mph 80.5kmh: 13.9secs
0-60mph 96.5kmh: 21.1secs
0-1/4 mile: 22.8secs
48.0bhp 35.8kW 48.7PS
@ 4800rpm
64.7lbft 87.7Nm @ 2800rpm
53.5bhp/ton 52.6bhp/tonne
37.2bhp/L 27.7kW/L 37.7PS/L
39.3ft/sec 12.0m/sec
16.3mph 26.2kmh/1000rpm
Petrol 4-stroke piston
1290cc 78.7cu in
In-line 4
Compression ratio: 6.8:1
Bore: 73.9mm 2.9in
Stroke: 74.9mm 2.9in
Valve type/No: Overhead 8
Transmission: Manual
No. of forward speeds: 4
Wheels driven: Rear
Wheelbase: 243.8cm 96.0in
Track F: 125.0cm 49.2in
Track R: 125.0cm 49.2in
Length: 408.9cm 161.0in
Width: 157.5cm 62.0in
Height: 147.3cm 58.0in
Kerb weight: 912.5kg 2010.0lb

4139 Simca
Etoile
1960 France
80.0mph 128.7kmh
0-50mph 80.5kmh: 16.6secs
0-60mph 96.5kmh: 25.7secs
0-1/4 mile: 22.8secs
51.5bhp 38.4kW 52.2PS
@ 4900rpm
69.4lbft 94.0Nm @ 2700rpm
56.9bhp/ton 56.0bhp/tonne
39.9bhp/L 29.8kW/L 40.5PS/L
40.1ft/sec 12.2m/sec
15.9mph 25.6kmh/1000rpm
27.8mpg 23.1mpgUS 10.2L/100km
Petrol 4-stroke piston
1290cc 78.7cu in
In-line 4
Compression ratio: 7.2:1
Bore: 74.0mm 2.9in
Stroke: 75.0mm 2.9in
Valve type/No: Overhead 8
Transmission: Manual
No. of forward speeds: 4
Wheels driven: Rear
Springs F/R: Coil/Leaf
Brakes F/R: Drum/Drum
Wheelbase: 243.8cm 96.0in
Track F: 125.5cm 49.4in
Track R: 125.0cm 49.2in
Length: 414.0cm 163.0in
Width: 157.5cm 62.0in
Height: 142.2cm 56.0in
Ground clearance: 13.7cm 5.4in
Kerb weight: 920.3kg 2027.0lb
Fuel: 43.7L 9.6gal 11.5galUS

4140 Simca
Oceane
1960 France
79.5mph 127.9kmh
0-50mph 80.5kmh: 14.2secs
0-60mph 96.5kmh: 20.7secs
0-1/4 mile: 21.8secs
57.0bhp 42.5kW 57.8PS
@ 5200rpm
68.5lbft 92.8Nm @ 3000rpm
54.6bhp/ton 53.6bhp/tonne
44.2bhp/L 32.9kW/L 44.8PS/L
42.6ft/sec 13.0m/sec
16.3mph 26.2kmh/1000rpm
Petrol 4-stroke piston
1290cc 78.7cu in
In-line 4 1 Carburettor
Compression ratio: 7.8:1
Bore: 73.9mm 2.9in
Stroke: 74.9mm 2.9in
Valve type/No: Overhead 8
Transmission: Manual
No. of forward speeds: 4
Wheels driven: Rear
Wheelbase: 244.3cm 96.2in
Track F: 125.5cm 49.4in
Track R: 125.0cm 49.2in
Length: 421.6cm 166.0in
Width: 160.0cm 63.0in
Height: 133.4cm 52.5in
Kerb weight: 1062.4kg 2340.0lb

4141 Simca
Vedette V8
1960 France
91.0mph 146.4kmh
0-50mph 80.5kmh: 12.1secs
0-60mph 96.5kmh: 18.4secs
0-1/4 mile: 20.2secs
84.0bhp 62.6kW 85.2PS
@ 4800rpm
112.0lbft 151.8Nm @ 2750rpm
74.1bhp/ton 72.8bhp/tonne
35.7bhp/L 26.6kW/L 36.2PS/L
44.9ft/sec 13.7m/sec
18.7mph 30.1kmh/1000rpm
Petrol 4-stroke piston
2351cc 143.4cu in
Vee 8 1 Carburettor
Compression ratio: 7.5:1
Bore: 66.0mm 2.6in
Stroke: 85.6mm 3.4in
Valve type/No: Side 16
Transmission: Manual
No. of forward speeds: 3
Wheels driven: Rear
Wheelbase: 269.0cm 105.9in
Track F: 136.9cm 53.9in
Track R: 134.1cm 52.8in
Length: 475.0cm 187.0in
Width: 177.0cm 69.7in
Height: 145.8cm 57.4in
Kerb weight: 1153.2kg 2540.0lb

4142 Simca
Aronde Montlhery
1961 France
85.0mph 136.8kmh
0-50mph 80.5kmh: 14.6secs
0-60mph 96.5kmh: 21.9secs
0-1/4 mile: 22.5secs
60.5bhp 45.1kW 61.3PS
@ 5200rpm
73.8lbft 100.0Nm @ 2600rpm
66.5bhp/ton 65.4bhp/tonne
46.9bhp/L 35.0kW/L 47.5PS/L
42.6ft/sec 13.0m/sec
16.0mph 25.7kmh/1000rpm
29.3mpg 24.4mpgUS 9.6L/100km
Petrol 4-stroke piston
1290cc 78.7cu in
In-line 4
Compression ratio: 8.5:1
Bore: 74.0mm 2.9in
Stroke: 75.0mm 2.9in
Valve type/No: Overhead 8
Transmission: Manual
No. of forward speeds: 4
Wheels driven: Rear
Springs F/R: Coil/Leaf
Brakes F/R: Drum/Drum
Wheelbase: 244.6cm 96.3in
Track F: 125.5cm 49.4in
Track R: 125.0cm 49.2in
Length: 419.1cm 165.0in
Width: 156.7cm 61.7in
Height: 142.7cm 56.2in
Ground clearance: 14.0cm 5.5in
Kerb weight: 924.8kg 2037.0lb
Fuel: 43.7L 9.6gal 11.5galUS

4143 Simca
1000
1962 France
73.0mph 117.5kmh
0-50mph 80.5kmh: 15.7secs
0-60mph 96.5kmh: 26.6secs
0-1/4 mile: 23.0secs
45.0bhp 33.6kW 45.6PS
@ 5000rpm
54.2lbft 73.4Nm @ 2750rpm
64.3bhp/ton 63.2bhp/tonne
47.7bhp/L 35.5kW/L 48.3PS/L
35.6ft/sec 10.8m/sec
15.5mph 24.9kmh/1000rpm
36.5mpg 30.4mpgUS 7.7L/100km
Petrol 4-stroke piston
944cc 57.6cu in
In-line 4 1 Carburettor
Compression ratio: 7.8:1
Bore: 68.0mm 2.7in
Stroke: 65.0mm 2.6in
Valve type/No: Overhead 8
Transmission: Manual
No. of forward speeds: 4
Wheels driven: Rear
Springs F/R: Leaf/Coil
Brakes F/R: Drum/Drum
Steering: Worm & roller
Wheelbase: 222.3cm 87.5in
Track F: 125.7cm 49.5in
Track R: 123.4cm 48.6in
Length: 379.7cm 149.5in
Width: 148.6cm 58.5in
Height: 133.4cm 52.5in
Ground clearance: 14.0cm 5.5in
Kerb weight: 711.9kg 1568.0lb
Fuel: 30.0L 6.6gal 7.9galUS

4144 Simca
5
1962 France
80.0mph 128.7kmh
0-50mph 80.5kmh: 12.9secs
0-60mph 96.5kmh: 20.0secs
0-1/4 mile: 21.6secs
65.0bhp 48.5kW 65.9PS
@ 5200rpm
72.8lbft 98.6Nm @ 2500rpm
73.0bhp/ton 71.8bhp/tonne
50.4bhp/L 37.6kW/L 51.1PS/L
42.6ft/sec 13.0m/sec
16.3mph 26.2kmh/1000rpm
Petrol 4-stroke piston
1290cc 78.7cu in
In-line 4
Compression ratio: 8.5:1
Bore: 73.9mm 2.9in
Stroke: 74.9mm 2.9in
Valve type/No: Overhead 8
Transmission: Manual
No. of forward speeds: 4
Wheels driven: Rear
Wheelbase: 244.6cm 96.3in
Track F: 125.5cm 49.4in
Track R: 125.0cm 49.2in
Length: 418.8cm 164.9in
Width: 156.7cm 61.7in
Height: 143.5cm 56.5in
Ground clearance: 15.2cm 6.0in
Kerb weight: 905.7kg 1995.0lb

4145 Simca
1000
1963 France
75.0mph 120.7kmh
0-50mph 80.5kmh: 16.2secs
0-60mph 96.5kmh: 22.3secs
0-1/4 mile: 22.3secs
45.0bhp 33.6kW 45.6PS
@ 5000rpm
50.4lbft 68.3Nm @ 2800rpm
62.6bhp/ton 61.5bhp/tonne
47.7bhp/L 35.5kW/L 48.3PS/L
35.6ft/sec 10.8m/sec
15.0mph 24.1kmh/1000rpm
Petrol 4-stroke piston
944cc 57.6cu in
In-line 4 1 Carburettor
Compression ratio: 7.8:1
Bore: 68.1mm 2.7in
Stroke: 65.0mm 2.6in
Valve type/No: Overhead 8
Transmission: Manual
No. of forward speeds: 4
Wheels driven: Rear
Wheelbase: 222.3cm 87.5in
Track F: 125.0cm 49.2in
Track R: 123.7cm 48.7in
Length: 380.0cm 149.6in
Width: 148.6cm 58.5in
Height: 139.2cm 54.8in
Ground clearance: 15.2cm 6.0in
Kerb weight: 731.4kg 1611.0lb

4146 Simca
1000 Special
1963 France
81.0mph 130.3kmh
0-50mph 80.5kmh: 14.5secs
0-60mph 96.5kmh: 22.5secs
0-1/4 mile: 21.8secs
50.0bhp 37.3kW 50.7PS
@ 5200rpm
54.2lbft 73.4Nm @ 2800rpm
68.7bhp/ton 67.5bhp/tonne
53.0bhp/L 39.5kW/L 53.7PS/L
37.0ft/sec 11.3m/sec
15.5mph 24.9kmh/1000rpm
31.6mpg 26.3mpgUS 8.9L/100km
Petrol 4-stroke piston
944cc 57.6cu in
In-line 4 1 Carburettor
Compression ratio: 8.2:1
Bore: 68.0mm 2.7in
Stroke: 65.0mm 2.6in
Valve type/No: Overhead 8
Transmission: Manual
No. of forward speeds: 4
Wheels driven: Rear
Springs F/R: Leaf/Coil
Brakes F/R: Drum/Drum
Steering: Worm & roller
Wheelbase: 222.3cm 87.5in
Track F: 125.7cm 49.5in
Track R: 123.4cm 48.6in
Length: 379.7cm 149.5in
Width: 148.6cm 58.5in
Height: 133.4cm 52.5in
Ground clearance: 14.0cm 5.5in
Kerb weight: 740.5kg 1631.0lb
Fuel: 35.9L 7.9gal 9.5galUS

4147 Simca
1300GL
1963 France
84.5mph 136.0kmh
0-50mph 80.5kmh: 16.4secs
0-60mph 96.5kmh: 23.3secs
0-1/4 mile: 22.9secs
62.0bhp 46.2kW 62.9PS
@ 5200rpm
74.0lbft 100.3Nm @ 2600rpm
65.6bhp/ton 64.5bhp/tonne
48.1bhp/L 35.8kW/L 48.7PS/L
42.6ft/sec 13.0m/sec
15.3mph 24.6kmh/1000rpm
29.1mpg 24.2mpgUS 9.7L/100km
Petrol 4-stroke piston
1290cc 78.7cu in
In-line 4 1 Carburettor
Compression ratio: 8.5:1
Bore: 74.0mm 2.9in
Stroke: 75.0mm 2.9in
Valve type/No: Overhead 8
Transmission: Manual
No. of forward speeds: 4
Wheels driven: Rear
Springs F/R: Coil/Coil
Brakes F/R: Drum/Drum
Steering: Cam & roller
Wheelbase: 252.7cm 99.5in
Track F: 132.1cm 52.0in
Track R: 129.5cm 51.0in
Length: 424.2cm 167.0in
Width: 157.5cm 62.0in
Height: 142.2cm 56.0in
Ground clearance: 19.1cm 7.5in
Kerb weight: 960.7kg 2116.0lb
Fuel: 54.6L 12.0gal 14.4galUS

4148 Simca
1500
1964 France
94.0mph 151.2kmh
0-50mph 80.5kmh: 10.7secs
0-60mph 96.5kmh: 15.1secs
0-1/4 mile: 19.7secs
81.0bhp 60.4kW 82.1PS
@ 5400rpm
90.4lbft 122.5Nm @ 3500rpm
84.1bhp/ton 82.7bhp/tonne
54.9bhp/L 40.9kW/L 55.7PS/L
49.0ft/sec 14.9m/sec
15.5mph 24.9kmh/1000rpm
27.7mpg 23.1mpgUS 10.2L/100km
Petrol 4-stroke piston
1475cc 90.0cu in
In-line 4 1 Carburettor
Compression ratio: 9.3:1
Bore: 75.2mm 3.0in
Stroke: 83.0mm 3.3in
Valve type/No: Overhead 8
Transmission: Manual
No. of forward speeds: 4
Wheels driven: Rear
Springs F/R: Coil/Coil
Brakes F/R: Disc/Drum
Steering: Cam & roller
Wheelbase: 252.7cm 99.5in
Track F: 132.1cm 52.0in
Track R: 129.5cm 51.0in
Length: 424.2cm 167.0in
Width: 157.5cm 62.0in
Height: 142.2cm 56.0in
Ground clearance: 19.1cm 7.5in
Kerb weight: 979.7kg 2158.0lb
Fuel: 54.6L 12.0gal 14.4galUS

4149 Simca
1500GL Estate
1965 France
94.0mph 151.2kmh
0-50mph 80.5kmh: 11.6secs
0-60mph 96.5kmh: 16.7secs
0-1/4 mile: 20.4secs
81.0bhp 60.4kW 82.1PS
@ 5400rpm
90.4lbft 122.5Nm @ 3500rpm
75.8bhp/ton 74.5bhp/tonne
54.9bhp/L 40.9kW/L 55.7PS/L
49.0ft/sec 14.9m/sec
15.5mph 24.9kmh/1000rpm
24.8mpg 20.7mpgUS 11.4L/100km
Petrol 4-stroke piston
1475cc 90.0cu in
In-line 4 1 Carburettor
Compression ratio: 9.3:1
Bore: 75.2mm 3.0in
Stroke: 83.0mm 3.3in
Valve type/No: Overhead 8
Transmission: Manual
No. of forward speeds: 4
Wheels driven: Rear
Springs F/R: Coil/Coil
Brakes F/R: Disc/Drum
Steering: Cam & roller
Wheelbase: 252.7cm 99.5in
Track F: 132.1cm 52.0in

Track R: 129.5cm 51.0in
Length: 424.2cm 167.0in
Width: 157.5cm 62.0in
Height: 142.2cm 56.0in
Ground clearance: 19.1cm 7.5in
Kerb weight: 1086.9kg 2394.0lb
Fuel: 54.6L 12.0gal 14.4galUS

4150 Simca

1000GLS
1966 France
82.0mph 131.9kmh
0-50mph 80.5kmh: 16.5secs
0-60mph 96.5kmh: 24.6secs
0-1/4 mile: 23.6secs
0-1km: 43.5secs
52.0bhp 38.8kW 52.7PS
@ 5400rpm
55.0lbft 74.5Nm @ 3400rpm
70.2bhp/ton 69.0bhp/tonne
55.1bhp/L 41.1kW/L 55.8PS/L
38.4ft/sec 11.7m/sec
15.5mph 24.9kmh/1000rpm
31.4mpg 26.1mpgUS 9.0L/100km
Petrol 4-stroke piston
944cc 57.6cu in
In-line 4 1 Carburettor
Compression ratio: 9.2:1
Bore: 68.0mm 2.7in
Stroke: 65.0mm 2.6in
Valve type/No: Overhead 8
Transmission: Automatic
No. of forward speeds: 3
Wheels driven: Rear
Springs F/R: Leaf/Coil
Brakes F/R: Drum/Drum
Steering: Worm & roller
Wheelbase: 222.3cm 87.5in
Track F: 125.7cm 49.5in
Track R: 123.4cm 48.6in
Length: 379.7cm 149.5in
Width: 148.6cm 58.5in
Height: 133.4cm 52.5in
Ground clearance: 14.0cm 5.5in
Kerb weight: 753.6kg 1660.0lb
Fuel: 35.9L 7.9gal 9.5galUS

4151 Simca

1000GLS
1967 France
81.0mph 130.3kmh
0-50mph 80.5kmh: 13.8secs
0-60mph 96.5kmh: 21.7secs
0-1/4 mile: 22.2secs
52.0bhp 38.8kW 52.7PS
@ 5400rpm
55.0lbft 74.5Nm @ 3500rpm
70.6bhp/ton 69.4bhp/tonne
55.1bhp/L 41.1kW/L 55.8PS/L
38.2ft/sec 11.7m/sec
15.0mph 24.1kmh/1000rpm
34.8mpg 29.0mpgUS 8.1L/100km
Petrol 4-stroke piston
944cc 57.6cu in
In-line 4 1 Carburettor
Compression ratio: 9.0:1
Bore: 67.1mm 2.6in
Stroke: 64.8mm 2.5in
Valve type/No: Overhead 8
Transmission: Manual
No. of forward speeds: 4
Wheels driven: Rear
Springs F/R: Leaf/Coil
Brakes F/R: Drum/Drum
Steering: Worm & roller
Wheelbase: 222.0cm 87.4in
Track F: 125.0cm 49.2in
Track R: 123.4cm 48.6in
Length: 379.7cm 149.5in
Width: 148.6cm 58.5in
Height: 138.9cm 54.7in
Ground clearance: 14.0cm 5.5in
Kerb weight: 749.1kg 1650.0lb
Fuel: 36.0L 7.9gal 9.5galUS

4152 Simca

1301
1967 France
82.0mph 131.9kmh
0-50mph 80.5kmh: 14.3secs
0-60mph 96.5kmh: 21.5secs
0-1/4 mile: 21.9secs
0-1km: 41.5secs
62.0bhp 46.2kW 62.9PS
@ 5200rpm
74.0lbft 100.3Nm @ 2600rpm
62.6bhp/ton 61.6bhp/tonne
48.1bhp/L 35.8kW/L 48.7PS/L
42.6ft/sec 13.0m/sec
15.3mph 24.6kmh/1000rpm
28.6mpg 23.8mpgUS 9.9L/100km
Petrol 4-stroke piston
1290cc 78.7cu in
In-line 4 1 Carburettor
Compression ratio: 8.8:1
Bore: 74.0mm 2.9in
Stroke: 75.0mm 2.9in
Valve type/No: Overhead 8
Transmission: Manual
No. of forward speeds: 4
Wheels driven: Rear
Springs F/R: Coil/Coil
Brakes F/R: Disc/Drum
Steering: Cam & roller
Wheelbase: 251.5cm 99.0in
Track F: 134.6cm 53.0in
Track R: 132.1cm 52.0in
Length: 447.0cm 176.0in
Width: 157.5cm 62.0in
Height: 142.2cm 56.0in
Ground clearance: 20.3cm 8.0in
Kerb weight: 1007.0kg 2218.0lb
Fuel: 54.6L 12.0gal 14.4galUS

4153 Simca

1100GLS
1968 France
85.0mph 136.8kmh
0-50mph 80.5kmh: 13.2secs
0-60mph 96.5kmh: 19.0secs
0-1/4 mile: 21.3secs
0-1km: 40.5secs
56.0bhp 41.8kW 56.8PS
@ 5800rpm
60.0lbft 81.3Nm @ 3600rpm
60.9bhp/ton 59.9bhp/tonne
50.1bhp/L 37.3kW/L 50.8PS/L
41.2ft/sec 12.6m/sec
15.0mph 24.1kmh/1000rpm
28.0mpg 23.3mpgUS 10.1L/100km
Petrol 4-stroke piston
1118cc 68.2cu in
In-line 4 1 Carburettor
Compression ratio: 9.6:1
Bore: 74.0mm 2.9in
Stroke: 65.0mm 2.6in
Valve type/No: Overhead 8
Transmission: Manual
No. of forward speeds: 4
Wheels driven: Front
Springs F/R: Torsion bar/Torsion bar
Brakes F/R: Disc/Drum
Steering: Rack & pinion
Wheelbase: 252.0cm 99.2in
Track F: 135.6cm 53.4in
Track R: 131.1cm 51.6in
Length: 394.5cm 155.3in
Width: 158.0cm 62.2in
Height: 144.8cm 57.0in
Ground clearance: 14.0cm 5.5in
Kerb weight: 934.3kg 2058.0lb
Fuel: 41.9L 9.2gal 11.1galUS

4154 Simca

1204
1969 France
87.0mph 140.0kmh
0-50mph 80.5kmh: 11.7secs
0-60mph 96.5kmh: 16.6secs
0-1/4 mile: 20.5secs
62.0bhp 46.2kW 62.9PS
@ 5800rpm
65.0lbft 88.1Nm @ 3400rpm
66.4bhp/ton 65.3bhp/tonne
51.5bhp/L 38.4kW/L 52.2PS/L
44.5ft/sec 13.5m/sec
15.0mph 24.1kmh/1000rpm
32.4mpg 27.0mpgUS 8.7L/100km
Petrol 4-stroke piston
1204cc 73.5cu in
In-line 4 1 Carburettor
Compression ratio: 8.8:1
Bore: 74.0mm 2.9in
Stroke: 70.0mm 2.8in
Valve type/No: Overhead 8
Transmission: Manual
No. of forward speeds: 4
Wheels driven: Front
Springs F/R: Torsion bar/Torsion bar
Brakes F/R: Disc/Drum
Steering: Rack & pinion
Wheelbase: 252.0cm 99.2in
Track F: 136.7cm 53.8in
Track R: 131.1cm 51.6in
Length: 394.5cm 155.3in
Width: 158.8cm 62.5in
Height: 145.8cm 57.4in
Ground clearance: 14.0cm 5.5in
Kerb weight: 949.3kg 2091.0lb
Fuel: 41.6L 9.1gal 11.0galUS

4155 Simca

1501 Special Estate
1969 France
93.0mph 149.6kmh
0-50mph 80.5kmh: 12.6secs
0-60mph 96.5kmh: 19.2secs
0-1/4 mile: 21.8secs
0-1km: 40.3secs
74.0bhp 55.2kW 75.0PS
@ 5200rpm
86.0lbft 116.5Nm @ 4000rpm
69.0bhp/ton 67.8bhp/tonne
50.2bhp/L 37.4kW/L 50.9PS/L
47.2ft/sec 14.4m/sec
18.2mph 29.3kmh/1000rpm
22.5mpg 18.7mpgUS 12.6L/100km
Petrol 4-stroke piston
1475cc 90.0cu in
In-line 4 1 Carburettor
Compression ratio: 9.3:1
Bore: 75.2mm 3.0in
Stroke: 83.0mm 3.3in
Valve type/No: Overhead 8
Transmission: Manual
No. of forward speeds: 4
Wheels driven: Rear
Springs F/R: Coil/Coil
Brake system: PA
Brakes F/R: Disc/Drum
Steering: Cam & peg
Wheelbase: 251.5cm 99.0in
Track F: 134.6cm 53.0in
Track R: 132.1cm 52.0in
Length: 430.5cm 169.5in
Width: 157.5cm 62.0in
Height: 142.2cm 56.0in
Ground clearance: 20.3cm 8.0in
Kerb weight: 1091.0kg 2403.0lb
Fuel: 54.6L 12.0gal 14.4galUS

4156 Simca

1204 Special
1970 France
97.0mph 156.1kmh
0-50mph 80.5kmh: 9.4secs
0-60mph 96.5kmh: 13.6secs
0-1/4 mile: 19.3secs
0-1km: 36.5secs
75.0bhp 55.9kW 76.0PS
@ 6000rpm
70.0lbft 94.9Nm @ 3600rpm
81.2bhp/ton 79.8bhp/tonne
62.3bhp/L 46.4kW/L 63.2PS/L
46.0ft/sec 14.0m/sec
16.1mph 25.9kmh/1000rpm
30.3mpg 25.2mpgUS 9.3L/100km
Petrol 4-stroke piston
1204cc 73.5cu in
In-line 4 2 Carburettor
Compression ratio: 9.5:1
Bore: 74.0mm 2.9in
Stroke: 70.0mm 2.8in
Valve type/No: Overhead 8
Transmission: Manual
No. of forward speeds: 4
Wheels driven: Front
Springs F/R: Torsion bar/Torsion bar
Brake system: PA
Brakes F/R: Disc/Drum
Steering: Rack & pinion
Wheelbase: 252.0cm 99.2in
Track F: 130.6cm 51.4in
Track R: 130.0cm 51.2in
Length: 394.5cm 155.3in
Width: 158.0cm 62.2in
Height: 144.8cm 57.0in
Ground clearance: 14.0cm 5.5in
Kerb weight: 939.8kg 2070.0lb
Fuel: 41.9L 9.2gal 11.1galUS

4157 Simca

1100 Special
1974 France
92.0mph 148.0kmh
0-50mph 80.5kmh: 8.9secs
0-60mph 96.5kmh: 13.1secs
0-1/4 mile: 19.1secs
0-1km: 36.2secs
75.0bhp 55.9kW 76.0PS
@ 5800rpm
72.0lbft 97.6Nm @ 3400rpm
80.6bhp/ton 79.3bhp/tonne
58.0bhp/L 43.2kW/L 58.8PS/L
44.5ft/sec 13.5m/sec
16.1mph 25.9kmh/1000rpm
28.4mpg 23.6mpgUS 9.9L/100km
Petrol 4-stroke piston
1294cc 78.9cu in
In-line 4 1 Carburettor
Compression ratio: 9.6:1
Bore: 76.7mm 3.0in
Stroke: 70.0mm 2.8in
Valve type/No: Overhead 8
Transmission: Manual
No. of forward speeds: 4
Wheels driven: Front
Springs F/R: Torsion bar/Torsion bar
Brake system: PA
Brakes F/R: Disc/Drum
Steering: Rack & pinion
Wheelbase: 252.0cm 99.2in
Track F: 130.6cm 51.4in
Track R: 130.0cm 51.2in
Length: 394.5cm 155.3in
Width: 158.0cm 62.2in
Height: 144.8cm 57.0in
Ground clearance: 14.0cm 5.5in
Kerb weight: 945.7kg 2083.0lb
Fuel: 42.1L 9.2gal 11.1galUS

4158 Simca

1000LS
1977 France
82.0mph 131.9kmh
0-50mph 80.5kmh: 13.4secs
0-60mph 96.5kmh: 21.7secs
0-1/4 mile: 22.1secs
0-1km: 42.0secs
40.0bhp 29.8kW 40.5PS
@ 5800rpm
47.0lbft 63.7Nm @ 2200rpm
56.4bhp/ton 55.4bhp/tonne
42.4bhp/L 31.6kW/L 43.0PS/L
41.2ft/sec 12.6m/sec
15.2mph 24.5kmh/1000rpm
33.7mpg 28.1mpgUS 8.4L/100km
Petrol 4-stroke piston
944cc 57.6cu in
In-line 4 1 Carburettor
Compression ratio: 9.4:1
Bore: 68.0mm 2.7in
Stroke: 65.0mm 2.6in
Valve type/No: Overhead 8
Transmission: Manual
No. of forward speeds: 4
Wheels driven: Rear
Springs F/R: Leaf/Coil
Brakes F/R: Drum/Drum
Steering: Rack & pinion
Wheelbase: 222.3cm 87.5in
Track F: 125.0cm 49.2in
Track R: 123.2cm 48.5in
Length: 379.7cm 149.5in
Width: 148.6cm 58.5in
Height: 138.9cm 54.7in
Ground clearance: 14.0cm 5.5in
Kerb weight: 721.4kg 1589.0lb
Fuel: 36.4L 8.0gal 9.6galUS

4159 Singer

14/6 Saloon
1932 UK
60.8mph 97.8kmh
26.0mpg 21.6mpgUS 10.9L/100km
Petrol 4-stroke piston
1611cc 98.3cu in
In-line 6
Bore: 60.0mm 2.4in
Stroke: 95.0mm 3.7in
Valve type/No: Overhead 12
Transmission: Manual
No. of forward speeds: 4
Wheels driven: Rear
Brakes F/R: Drum/Drum
Wheelbase: 275.6cm 108.5in
Track F: 132.1cm 52.0in
Track R: 132.1cm 52.0in
Length: 411.5cm 162.0in
Width: 165.1cm 65.0in
Height: 172.7cm 68.0in
Kerb weight: 1194.9kg 2632.0lb
Fuel: 45.5L 10.0gal 12.0galUS

4160 Singer
9 Sports
1933 UK
66.1mph 106.4kmh
0-50mph 80.5kmh: 23.8secs
35.0bhp 26.1kW 35.5PS
@ 4500rpm
45.9bhp/ton 45.1bhp/tonne
36.0bhp/L 26.8kW/L 36.5PS/L
42.4ft/sec 12.9m/sec
30.0mpg 25.0mpgUS 9.4L/100km
Petrol 4-stroke piston
972cc 59.3cu in
In-line 4 2 Carburettor
Bore: 60.0mm 2.4in
Stroke: 86.0mm 3.4in
Valve type/No: Overhead 8
Transmission: Manual
No. of forward speeds: 4
Wheels driven: Rear
Brakes F/R: Drum/Drum
Kerb weight: 775.4kg 1708.0lb
Fuel: 31.8L 7.0gal 8.4galUS

4161 Singer
Le Mans Special Speed Model
1935 UK
75.6mph 121.6kmh
0-50mph 80.5kmh: 17.0secs
0-60mph 96.5kmh: 34.8secs
35.0bhp 26.1kW 35.5PS
@ 4500rpm
44.4bhp/ton 43.6bhp/tonne
36.0bhp/L 26.8kW/L 36.5PS/L
42.4ft/sec 12.9m/sec
28.0mpg 23.3mpgUS 10.1L/100km
Petrol 4-stroke piston
972cc 59.3cu in
In-line 4 2 Carburettor
Bore: 60.0mm 2.4in
Stroke: 86.0mm 3.4in
Valve type/No: Overhead 8
Transmission: Manual
No. of forward speeds: 4
Wheels driven: Rear
Brakes F/R: Drum/Drum
Ground clearance: 16.5cm 6.5in
Kerb weight: 801.8kg 1766.0lb
Fuel: 60.3L 13.2gal 15.9galUS

4162 Singer
Super 10 Saloon
1940 UK
62.5mph 100.6kmh
0-50mph 80.5kmh: 24.0secs
37.0bhp 27.6kW 37.5PS
@ 5000rpm
38.1bhp/ton 37.4bhp/tonne
31.2bhp/L 23.3kW/L 31.6PS/L
51.9ft/sec 15.8m/sec
34.0mpg 28.3mpgUS 8.3L/100km
Petrol 4-stroke piston
1185cc 72.3cu in
In-line 4
Compression ratio: 6.5:1
Bore: 63.0mm 2.5in
Stroke: 95.0mm 3.7in
Valve type/No: Overhead 8
Transmission: Manual
No. of forward speeds: 4
Wheels driven: Rear
Brakes F/R: Drum/Drum
Kerb weight: 987.9kg 2176.0lb
Fuel: 40.9L 9.0gal 10.8galUS

4163 Singer
9 Roadster
1949 UK
70.0mph 112.6kmh
0-50mph 80.5kmh: 25.2secs
36.0bhp 26.8kW 36.5PS
@ 5000rpm
47.0lbft 63.7Nm @ 2800rpm
45.9bhp/ton 45.1bhp/tonne
33.5bhp/L 25.0kW/L 34.0PS/L
51.9ft/sec 15.8m/sec
13.9mph 22.4kmh/1000rpm
32.0mpg 26.6mpgUS 8.8L/100km
Petrol 4-stroke piston
1074cc 65.5cu in
In-line 4
Compression ratio: 7.0:1
Bore: 60.0mm 2.4in
Stroke: 95.0mm 3.7in
Valve type/No: Overhead 8
Transmission: Manual
No. of forward speeds: 4
Wheels driven: Rear
Brakes F/R: Drum/Drum
Wheelbase: 231.1cm 91.0in
Track F: 114.3cm 45.0in
Track R: 114.3cm 45.0in
Length: 385.3cm 151.7in
Width: 141.5cm 55.7in
Height: 148.6cm 58.5in
Ground clearance: 15.2cm 6.0in
Kerb weight: 797.7kg 1757.0lb
Fuel: 31.8L 7.0gal 8.4galUS

4164 Singer
SM1500 Saloon
1949 UK
72.0mph 115.8kmh
0-50mph 80.5kmh: 23.9secs
0-60mph 96.5kmh: 36.7secs
50.0bhp 37.3kW 50.7PS
@ 4500rpm
79.0lbft 107.0Nm @ 2400rpm
41.6bhp/ton 40.9bhp/tonne
33.2bhp/L 24.8kW/L 33.7PS/L
44.2ft/sec 13.5m/sec
15.2mph 24.5kmh/1000rpm
26.0mpg 21.6mpgUS 10.9L/100km
Petrol 4-stroke piston
1506cc 91.9cu in
In-line 4 1 Carburettor
Compression ratio: 7.0:1
Bore: 73.0mm 2.9in
Stroke: 90.0mm 3.5in
Valve type/No: Overhead 8
Transmission: Manual
No. of forward speeds: 4
Wheels driven: Rear
Springs F/R: Coil/Leaf
Brakes F/R: Drum/Drum
Wheelbase: 273.1cm 107.5in
Track F: 128.3cm 50.5in
Track R: 129.5cm 51.0in
Length: 442.0cm 174.0in
Width: 160.0cm 63.0in
Height: 162.6cm 64.0in
Ground clearance: 17.8cm 7.0in
Kerb weight: 1223.5kg 2695.0lb
Fuel: 45.5L 10.0gal 12.0galUS

4165 Singer
SM Roadster
1952 UK
75.0mph 120.7kmh
0-50mph 80.5kmh: 13.7secs
0-60mph 96.5kmh: 20.8secs
48.0bhp 35.8kW 48.7PS
@ 4200rpm
72.0lbft 97.6Nm @ 2200rpm
59.3bhp/ton 58.3bhp/tonne
32.1bhp/L 23.9kW/L 32.5PS/L
41.1ft/sec 12.5m/sec
15.5mph 24.9kmh/1000rpm
28.0mpg 23.3mpgUS 10.1L/100km
Petrol 4-stroke piston
1497cc 91.3cu in
In-line 4
Compression ratio: 7.0:1
Bore: 73.0mm 2.9in
Stroke: 89.4mm 3.5in
Valve type/No: Overhead 8
Transmission: Manual
No. of forward speeds: 4
Wheels driven: Rear
Brakes F/R: Drum/Drum
Wheelbase: 231.1cm 91.0in
Track F: 118.6cm 46.7in
Track R: 118.6cm 46.7in
Length: 383.5cm 151.0in
Width: 147.3cm 58.0in
Height: 148.6cm 58.5in
Ground clearance: 16.5cm 6.5in
Kerb weight: 823.1kg 1813.0lb
Fuel: 31.8L 7.0gal 8.4galUS

4166 Singer
SM1500 Saloon
1952 UK
75.0mph 120.7kmh
0-50mph 80.5kmh: 17.8secs
0-60mph 96.5kmh: 27.9secs
0-1/4 mile: 24.1secs
48.0bhp 35.8kW 48.7PS
@ 4200rpm
72.0lbft 97.6Nm @ 2200rpm
41.1bhp/ton 40.4bhp/tonne
32.1bhp/L 23.9kW/L 32.5PS/L
41.1ft/sec 12.5m/sec
15.2mph 24.5kmh/1000rpm
29.0mpg 24.1mpgUS 9.7L/100km
Petrol 4-stroke piston
1497cc 91.3cu in
In-line 4
Compression ratio: 7.0:1
Bore: 73.0mm 2.9in
Stroke: 89.4mm 3.5in
Valve type/No: Overhead 8
Transmission: Manual
No. of forward speeds: 4
Wheels driven: Rear
Springs F/R: Coil/Leaf
Brakes F/R: Drum/Drum
Wheelbase: 273.1cm 107.5in
Track F: 128.3cm 50.5in
Track R: 129.5cm 51.0in
Length: 442.0cm 174.0in
Width: 160.0cm 63.0in
Height: 162.6cm 64.0in
Ground clearance: 17.8cm 7.0in
Kerb weight: 1188.6kg 2618.0lb
Fuel: 45.5L 10.0gal 12.0galUS

4167 Singer
Roadster
1953 UK
83.3mph 134.0kmh
0-50mph 80.5kmh: 11.8secs
0-60mph 96.5kmh: 17.0secs
0-1/4 mile: 20.6secs
58.0bhp 43.2kW 58.8PS
@ 4600rpm
79.0lbft 107.0Nm @ 2500rpm
69.3bhp/ton 68.1bhp/tonne
38.7bhp/L 28.9kW/L 39.3PS/L
45.0ft/sec 13.7m/sec
17.1mph 27.5kmh/1000rpm
Petrol 4-stroke piston
1497cc 91.3cu in
In-line 4
Compression ratio: 8.2:1
Bore: 73.0mm 2.9in
Stroke: 89.4mm 3.5in
Valve type/No: Overhead 8
Transmission: Manual
No. of forward speeds: 4
Wheels driven: Rear
Wheelbase: 231.1cm 91.0in
Track F: 118.9cm 46.8in
Track R: 118.9cm 46.8in
Kerb weight: 851.2kg 1875.0lb

4168 Singer
SM1500 Saloon
1953 UK
79.5mph 127.9kmh
0-50mph 80.5kmh: 14.8secs
0-60mph 96.5kmh: 23.1secs
0-1/4 mile: 22.5secs
58.0bhp 43.2kW 58.8PS
@ 4600rpm
77.0lbft 104.3Nm @ 2600rpm
48.5bhp/ton 47.7bhp/tonne
38.7bhp/L 28.9kW/L 39.3PS/L
45.0ft/sec 13.7m/sec
15.2mph 24.5kmh/1000rpm
20.6mpg 17.2mpgUS 13.7L/100km
Petrol 4-stroke piston
1497cc 91.3cu in
In-line 4
Compression ratio: 7.4:1
Bore: 73.0mm 2.9in
Stroke: 89.4mm 3.5in
Valve type/No: Overhead 8
Transmission: Manual
No. of forward speeds: 4
Wheels driven: Rear
Springs F/R: Coil/Leaf
Brakes F/R: Drum/Drum
Wheelbase: 273.1cm 107.5in
Track F: 129.5cm 51.0in
Track R: 129.5cm 51.0in
Length: 449.6cm 177.0in
Width: 160.0cm 63.0in
Height: 162.6cm 64.0in
Ground clearance: 17.8cm 7.0in
Kerb weight: 1214.9kg 2676.0lb
Fuel: 45.5L 10.0gal 12.0galUS

4169 Singer
SM Roadster
1954 UK
75.0mph 120.7kmh
0-50mph 80.5kmh: 18.4secs
0-60mph 96.5kmh: 29.1secs
0-1/4 mile: 23.6secs
48.0bhp 35.8kW 48.7PS
@ 4200rpm
72.0lbft 97.6Nm @ 2200rpm
58.4bhp/ton 57.4bhp/tonne
32.1bhp/L 23.9kW/L 32.5PS/L
41.1ft/sec 12.5m/sec
15.5mph 24.9kmh/1000rpm
27.0mpg 22.5mpgUS 10.5L/100km
Petrol 4-stroke piston
1497cc 91.3cu in
In-line 4
Compression ratio: 7.0:1
Bore: 73.0mm 2.9in
Stroke: 89.4mm 3.5in
Valve type/No: Overhead 8
Transmission: Manual
No. of forward speeds: 4
Wheels driven: Rear
Springs F/R: Coil/Leaf
Brakes F/R: Drum/Drum
Wheelbase: 231.1cm 91.0in
Track F: 118.6cm 46.7in
Track R: 118.6cm 46.7in
Length: 386.1cm 152.0in
Width: 147.3cm 58.0in
Height: 148.6cm 58.5in
Ground clearance: 16.5cm 6.5in
Kerb weight: 835.8kg 1841.0lb
Fuel: 31.8L 7.0gal 8.4galUS

4170 Singer
Hunter
1955 UK
76.0mph 122.3kmh
0-50mph 80.5kmh: 17.0secs
0-60mph 96.5kmh: 26.3secs
0-1/4 mile: 23.4secs
58.0bhp 43.2kW 58.8PS
@ 4600rpm
48.0lbft 65.0Nm @ 4200rpm
48.1bhp/ton 47.3bhp/tonne
38.7bhp/L 28.9kW/L 39.3PS/L
45.0ft/sec 13.7m/sec
15.2mph 24.5kmh/1000rpm
21.5mpg 17.9mpgUS 13.1L/100km
Petrol 4-stroke piston
1497cc 91.3cu in
In-line 4
Compression ratio: 7.5:1
Bore: 73.0mm 2.9in
Stroke: 89.4mm 3.5in
Valve type/No: Overhead 8
Transmission: Manual
No. of forward speeds: 4
Wheels driven: Rear
Springs F/R: Coil/Leaf
Brakes F/R: Drum/Drum
Wheelbase: 273.1cm 107.5in
Track F: 128.3cm 50.5in
Track R: 129.5cm 51.0in
Length: 449.6cm 177.0in
Width: 160.0cm 63.0in
Height: 162.6cm 64.0in
Ground clearance: 17.8cm 7.0in
Kerb weight: 1226.7kg 2702.0lb
Fuel: 45.5L 10.0gal 12.0galUS

4171 Singer
Gazelle IIA Convertible
1958 UK
84.0mph 135.2kmh
0-50mph 80.5kmh: 14.3secs
0-60mph 96.5kmh: 21.4secs
0-1/4 mile: 22.4secs
60.0bhp 44.7kW 60.8PS
@ 4500rpm
82.8lbft 112.2Nm @ 2300rpm
55.6bhp/ton 54.7bhp/tonne
40.2bhp/L 29.9kW/L 40.7PS/L
37.5ft/sec 11.4m/sec
20.5mph 33.0kmh/1000rpm
31.2mpg 26.0mpgUS 9.1L/100km
Petrol 4-stroke piston
1494cc 91.1cu in
In-line 4
Compression ratio: 8.5:1
Bore: 79.0mm 3.1in
Stroke: 76.2mm 3.0in
Valve type/No: Overhead 8
Transmission: Manual with overdrive
No. of forward speeds: 6
Wheels driven: Rear
Springs F/R: Coil/Leaf
Brakes F/R: Drum/Drum

Wheelbase: 243.8cm 96.0in
Track F: 124.5cm 49.0in
Track R: 123.2cm 48.5in
Length: 415.3cm 163.5in
Width: 154.2cm 60.7in
Height: 147.3cm 58.0in
Ground clearance: 17.8cm 7.0in
Kerb weight: 1096.4kg 2415.0lb
Fuel: 45.5L 10.0gal 12.0galUS

4172 Singer

Gazelle Series IIIB
1961 UK
85.0mph 136.8kmh
0-50mph 80.5kmh: 16.5secs
0-60mph 96.5kmh: 23.9secs
0-1/4 mile: 22.2secs
60.0bhp 44.7kW 60.8PS
@ 4500rpm
82.8lbft 112.2Nm @ 2300rpm
56.6bhp/ton 55.7bhp/tonne
40.2bhp/L 29.9kW/L 40.7PS/L
37.5ft/sec 11.4m/sec
18.7mph 30.1kmh/1000rpm
25.3mpg 21.1mpgUS 11.2L/100km
Petrol 4-stroke piston
1494cc 91.1cu in
In-line 4
Compression ratio: 8.5:1
Bore: 79.0mm 3.1in
Stroke: 76.2mm 3.0in
Valve type/No: Overhead 8
Transmission: Manual with overdrive
No. of forward speeds: 6
Wheels driven: Rear
Springs F/R: Coil/Leaf
Brakes F/R: Drum/Drum
Wheelbase: 243.8cm 96.0in
Track F: 124.5cm 49.0in
Track R: 123.2cm 48.5in
Length: 415.3cm 163.5in
Width: 154.2cm 60.7in
Height: 151.1cm 59.5in
Ground clearance: 17.8cm 7.0in
Kerb weight: 1077.3kg 2373.0lb
Fuel: 45.5L 10.0gal 12.0galUS

4173 Singer

Vogue
1961 UK
85.0mph 136.8kmh
0-50mph 80.5kmh: 14.1secs
0-60mph 96.5kmh: 20.9secs
0-1/4 mile: 21.5secs
62.0bhp 46.2kW 62.9PS
@ 4800rpm
85.8lbft 116.3Nm @ 3000rpm
57.2bhp/ton 56.2bhp/tonne
38.9bhp/L 29.0kW/L 39.5PS/L
40.0ft/sec 12.2m/sec
19.1mph 30.7kmh/1000rpm
23.4mpg 19.5mpgUS 12.1L/100km
Petrol 4-stroke piston
1592cc 97.1cu in
In-line 4 1 Carburettor
Compression ratio: 8.3:1
Bore: 81.5mm 3.2in
Stroke: 76.2mm 3.0in
Valve type/No: Overhead 8
Transmission: Manual with overdrive
No. of forward speeds: 6
Wheels driven: Rear
Springs F/R: Coil/Leaf
Brakes F/R: Drum/Drum
Wheelbase: 256.5cm 101.0in
Track F: 130.8cm 51.5in
Track R: 123.2cm 48.5in
Length: 419.9cm 165.3in
Width: 158.2cm 62.3in
Height: 148.1cm 58.3in
Ground clearance: 16.5cm 6.5in
Kerb weight: 1102.8kg 2429.0lb
Fuel: 50.0L 11.0gal 13.2galUS

4174 Singer

Vogue Mk II
1963 UK
85.0mph 136.8kmh
0-50mph 80.5kmh: 16.3secs
0-60mph 96.5kmh: 23.3secs
0-1/4 mile: 22.8secs
58.0bhp 43.2kW 58.8PS
@ 4400rpm
86.3lbft 116.9Nm @ 2500rpm
53.3bhp/ton 52.4bhp/tonne
36.4bhp/L 27.2kW/L 36.9PS/L
36.7ft/sec 11.2m/sec
20.2mph 32.5kmh/1000rpm
22.8mpg 19.0mpgUS 12.4L/100km
Petrol 4-stroke piston
1592cc 97.1cu in
In-line 4 1 Carburettor
Compression ratio: 8.3:1
Bore: 81.5mm 3.2in
Stroke: 76.2mm 3.0in
Valve type/No: Overhead 8
Transmission: Manual with overdrive
No. of forward speeds: 6
Wheels driven: Rear
Springs F/R: Coil/Leaf
Brakes F/R: Disc/Drum
Steering: Recirculating ball
Wheelbase: 256.5cm 101.0in
Track F: 130.8cm 51.5in
Track R: 123.2cm 48.5in
Length: 419.9cm 165.3in
Width: 158.0cm 62.2in
Height: 147.8cm 58.2in
Ground clearance: 16.5cm 6.5in
Kerb weight: 1106.4kg 2437.0lb
Fuel: 47.8L 10.5gal 12.6galUS

4175 Singer

Chamois
1964 UK
84.0mph 135.2kmh
0-50mph 80.5kmh: 14.7secs
0-60mph 96.5kmh: 22.9secs
0-1/4 mile: 22.0secs
39.0bhp 29.1kW 39.5PS
@ 5000rpm
52.0lbft 70.5Nm @ 2800rpm
54.6bhp/ton 53.7bhp/tonne
44.6bhp/L 33.2kW/L 45.2PS/L
33.1ft/sec 10.1m/sec
15.0mph 24.1kmh/1000rpm
35.4mpg 29.5mpgUS 8.0L/100km
Petrol 4-stroke piston
875cc 53.4cu in
In-line 4 1 Carburettor
Compression ratio: 10.0:1
Bore: 68.0mm 2.7in
Stroke: 60.4mm 2.4in
Valve type/No: Overhead 8
Transmission: Manual
No. of forward speeds: 4
Wheels driven: Rear
Springs F/R: Coil/Coil
Brakes F/R: Drum/Drum
Steering: Rack & pinion
Wheelbase: 208.3cm 82.0in
Track F: 124.7cm 49.1in
Track R: 121.7cm 47.9in
Length: 358.1cm 141.0in
Width: 152.9cm 60.2in
Height: 138.4cm 54.5in
Ground clearance: 15.7cm 6.2in
Kerb weight: 726.8kg 1601.0lb
Fuel: 27.3L 6.0gal 7.2galUS

4176 Singer

Gazelle Series V
1964 UK
80.0mph 128.7kmh
0-50mph 80.5kmh: 16.3secs
0-60mph 96.5kmh: 24.9secs
0-1/4 mile: 22.5secs
52.8bhp 39.4kW 53.5PS
@ 4100rpm
86.8lbft 117.6Nm @ 2100rpm
52.6bhp/ton 51.7bhp/tonne
33.2bhp/L 24.7kW/L 33.6PS/L
34.2ft/sec 10.4m/sec
20.0mph 32.2kmh/1000rpm
27.6mpg 23.0mpgUS 10.2L/100km
Petrol 4-stroke piston
1592cc 97.1cu in
In-line 4 1 Carburettor
Compression ratio: 8.3:1
Bore: 81.5mm 3.2in
Stroke: 76.2mm 3.0in
Valve type/No: Overhead 8
Transmission: Manual with overdrive
No. of forward speeds: 6
Wheels driven: Rear
Springs F/R: Coil/Leaf
Brakes F/R: Disc/Drum
Steering: Recirculating ball
Wheelbase: 243.8cm 96.0in
Track F: 131.3cm 51.7in
Track R: 123.2cm 48.5in
Length: 417.8cm 164.5in
Width: 154.2cm 60.7in
Height: 147.3cm 58.0in
Ground clearance: 15.2cm 6.0in
Kerb weight: 1021.5kg 2250.0lb
Fuel: 45.5L 10.0gal 12.0galUS

4177 Singer

Vogue Mk III Estate
1965 UK
90.0mph 144.8kmh
0-50mph 80.5kmh: 12.4secs
0-60mph 96.5kmh: 17.7secs
0-1/4 mile: 20.8secs
78.5bhp 58.5kW 79.6PS
@ 5000rpm
91.0lbft 123.3Nm @ 3500rpm
68.6bhp/ton 67.4bhp/tonne
49.3bhp/L 36.8kW/L 50.0PS/L
41.7ft/sec 12.7m/sec
20.7mph 33.3kmh/1000rpm
22.9mpg 19.1mpgUS 12.3L/100km
Petrol 4-stroke piston
1592cc 97.1cu in
In-line 4 1 Carburettor
Compression ratio: 9.0:1
Bore: 81.5mm 3.2in
Stroke: 76.2mm 3.0in
Valve type/No: Overhead 8
Transmission: Manual with overdrive
No. of forward speeds: 6
Wheels driven: Rear
Springs F/R: Coil/Leaf
Brakes F/R: Disc/Drum
Steering: Recirculating ball
Wheelbase: 256.5cm 101.0in
Track F: 129.8cm 51.1in
Track R: 123.2cm 48.5in
Length: 420.4cm 165.5in
Width: 160.0cm 63.0in
Height: 148.6cm 58.5in
Ground clearance: 16.5cm 6.5in
Kerb weight: 1164.1kg 2564.0lb
Fuel: 47.8L 10.5gal 12.6galUS

4178 Singer

Vogue
1966 UK
95.0mph 152.9kmh
0-50mph 80.5kmh: 11.2secs
0-60mph 96.5kmh: 15.4secs
0-1/4 mile: 20.4secs
0-1km: 37.7secs
85.0bhp 63.4kW 86.2PS
@ 5500rpm
99.0lbft 134.1Nm @ 3500rpm
80.0bhp/ton 78.7bhp/tonne
49.3bhp/L 36.7kW/L 50.0PS/L
49.6ft/sec 15.1m/sec
20.2mph 32.5kmh/1000rpm
21.9mpg 18.2mpgUS 12.9L/100km
Petrol 4-stroke piston
1725cc 105.2cu in
In-line 4 1 Carburettor
Compression ratio: 9.2:1
Bore: 81.5mm 3.2in
Stroke: 82.6mm 3.2in
Valve type/No: Overhead 8
Transmission: Manual with overdrive
No. of forward speeds: 6
Wheels driven: Rear
Springs F/R: Coil/Leaf
Brakes F/R: Disc/Drum
Steering: Recirculating ball
Wheelbase: 256.5cm 101.0in
Track F: 130.8cm 51.5in
Track R: 123.2cm 48.5in
Length: 425.5cm 167.5in
Width: 158.0cm 62.2in
Height: 146.1cm 57.5in
Ground clearance: 16.5cm 6.5in
Kerb weight: 1080.5kg 2380.0lb
Fuel: 47.8L 10.5gal 12.6galUS

4179 Singer

Vogue Automatic
1966 UK
86.0mph 138.4kmh
0-50mph 80.5kmh: 12.0secs
0-60mph 96.5kmh: 17.4secs
0-1/4 mile: 20.9secs
0-1km: 39.9secs
74.0bhp 55.2kW 75.0PS
@ 5000rpm
96.0lbft 130.1Nm @ 3000rpm
80.0bhp/ton 78.7bhp/tonne
42.9bhp/L 32.0kW/L 43.5PS/L
45.1ft/sec 13.8m/sec
18.3mph 29.4kmh/1000rpm
24.1mpg 20.1mpgUS 11.7L/100km
Petrol 4-stroke piston
1725cc 105.2cu in
In-line 4 1 Carburettor
Compression ratio: 9.2:1
Bore: 81.5mm 3.2in
Stroke: 82.5mm 3.2in
Valve type/No: Overhead 8
Transmission: Automatic
No. of forward speeds: 3
Wheels driven: Rear
Springs F/R: Coil/Leaf
Brakes F/R: Disc/Drum
Steering: Recirculating ball
Wheelbase: 250.2cm 98.5in
Track F: 132.1cm 52.0in
Track R: 132.1cm 52.0in
Length: 435.6cm 171.5in
Width: 161.3cm 63.5in
Height: 142.2cm 56.0in
Ground clearance: 19.1cm 7.5in
Kerb weight: 940.7kg 2072.0lb
Fuel: 45.5L 10.0gal 12.0galUS

4180 Singer

Gazelle
1967 UK
87.0mph 140.0kmh
0-50mph 80.5kmh: 12.9secs
0-60mph 96.5kmh: 18.5secs
0-1/4 mile: 21.4secs
0-1km: 40.5secs
60.0bhp 44.7kW 60.8PS
@ 4800rpm
80.5lbft 109.1Nm @ 2600rpm
65.6bhp/ton 64.5bhp/tonne
40.1bhp/L 29.9kW/L 40.7PS/L
37.6ft/sec 11.5m/sec
17.4mph 28.0kmh/1000rpm
26.2mpg 21.8mpgUS 10.8L/100km
Petrol 4-stroke piston
1496cc 91.3cu in
In-line 4 1 Carburettor
Compression ratio: 8.4:1
Bore: 81.5mm 3.2in
Stroke: 71.6mm 2.8in
Valve type/No: Overhead 8
Transmission: Manual
No. of forward speeds: 4
Wheels driven: Rear
Springs F/R: Coil/Leaf
Brakes F/R: Disc/Drum
Steering: Recirculating ball
Wheelbase: 250.2cm 98.5in
Track F: 132.1cm 52.0in
Track R: 132.1cm 52.0in
Length: 435.6cm 171.5in
Width: 161.3cm 63.5in
Height: 142.2cm 56.0in
Ground clearance: 15.2cm 6.0in
Kerb weight: 930.7kg 2050.0lb
Fuel: 45.5L 10.0gal 12.0galUS

4181 Singer

Chamois
1969 UK
78.0mph 125.5kmh
0-50mph 80.5kmh: 16.9secs
0-60mph 96.5kmh: 26.2secs
0-1/4 mile: 20.3secs
0-1km: 43.9secs
39.0bhp 29.1kW 39.5PS
@ 5000rpm
52.0lbft 70.5Nm @ 2800rpm
57.5bhp/ton 56.6bhp/tonne
44.6bhp/L 33.2kW/L 45.2PS/L
33.1ft/sec 10.1m/sec
15.1mph 24.3kmh/1000rpm
35.7mpg 29.7mpgUS 7.9L/100km
Petrol 4-stroke piston
875cc 53.4cu in
In-line 4 1 Carburettor
Compression ratio: 10.0:1
Bore: 68.0mm 2.7in
Stroke: 60.4mm 2.4in
Valve type/No: Overhead 8
Transmission: Manual
No. of forward speeds: 4
Wheels driven: Rear
Springs F/R: Coil/Coil
Brakes F/R: Drum/Drum
Steering: Rack & pinion
Wheelbase: 208.3cm 82.0in
Track F: 128.3cm 50.5in
Track R: 121.9cm 48.0in
Length: 358.1cm 141.0in

Width: 152.4cm 60.0in
Height: 143.5cm 56.5in
Ground clearance: 15.7cm 6.2in
Kerb weight: 689.2kg 1518.0lb
Fuel: 27.3L 6.0gal 7.2galUS

4182 Skoda

Octavia
1960 Czechoslovakia
76.0mph 122.3kmh
0-50mph 80.5kmh: 18.7secs
0-60mph 96.5kmh: 33.1secs
0-1/4 mile: 24.0secs
40.0bhp 29.8kW 40.5PS
@ 4200rpm
50.6lbft 68.6Nm @ 2800rpm
44.7bhp/ton 43.9bhp/tonne
36.7bhp/L 27.4kW/L 37.2PS/L
34.4ft/sec 10.5m/sec
14.9mph 24.0kmh/1000rpm
28.3mpg 23.6mpgUS 10.0L/100km
Petrol 4-stroke piston
1089cc 66.4cu in
In-line 4
Compression ratio: 7.0:1
Bore: 68.0mm 2.7in
Stroke: 75.0mm 2.9in
Valve type/No: Overhead 8
Transmission: Manual
No. of forward speeds: 4
Wheels driven: Rear
Springs F/R: Coil/Leaf
Brakes F/R: Drum/Drum
Wheelbase: 240.0cm 94.5in
Track F: 120.9cm 47.6in
Track R: 124.5cm 49.0in
Length: 403.9cm 159.0in
Width: 160.0cm 63.0in
Height: 142.2cm 56.0in
Ground clearance: 21.8cm 8.6in
Kerb weight: 910.3kg 2005.0lb
Fuel: 30.0L 6.6gal 7.9galUS

4183 Skoda

Felicia
1961 Czechoslovakia
83.0mph 133.5kmh
0-50mph 80.5kmh: 15.6secs
0-60mph 96.5kmh: 24.5secs
0-1/4 mile: 22.2secs
53.0bhp 39.5kW 53.7PS
@ 5000rpm
55.0lbft 74.5Nm @ 3500rpm
59.1bhp/ton 58.1bhp/tonne
48.7bhp/L 36.3kW/L 49.3PS/L
41.0ft/sec 12.5m/sec
15.5mph 24.9kmh/1000rpm
25.8mpg 21.5mpgUS 10.9L/100km
Petrol 4-stroke piston
1089cc 66.4cu in
In-line 4
Compression ratio: 8.4:1
Bore: 68.0mm 2.7in
Stroke: 75.0mm 2.9in
Valve type/No: Overhead 8
Transmission: Manual
No. of forward speeds: 4
Wheels driven: Rear
Springs F/R: Coil/Leaf
Brakes F/R: Drum/Drum
Wheelbase: 240.0cm 94.5in
Track F: 120.9cm 47.6in
Track R: 124.7cm 49.1in
Length: 406.4cm 160.0in
Width: 160.0cm 63.0in
Height: 143.0cm 56.3in
Ground clearance: 21.8cm 8.6in
Kerb weight: 912.1kg 2009.0lb
Fuel: 30.0L 6.6gal 7.9galUS

4184 Skoda

1000MB
1965 Czechoslovakia
76.0mph 122.3kmh
0-50mph 80.5kmh: 17.6secs
0-60mph 96.5kmh: 30.8secs
0-1/4 mile: 23.6secs
45.0bhp 33.6kW 45.6PS
@ 4650rpm
50.6lbft 68.6Nm @ 3200rpm
58.1bhp/ton 57.1bhp/tonne
45.5bhp/L 34.0kW/L 46.2PS/L
34.6ft/sec 10.5m/sec
15.5mph 24.9kmh/1000rpm
31.4mpg 26.1mpgUS 9.0L/100km
Petrol 4-stroke piston
988cc 60.3cu in
In-line 4 1 Carburettor
Compression ratio: 8.3:1
Bore: 68.0mm 2.7in
Stroke: 68.0mm 2.7in
Valve type/No: Overhead 8
Transmission: Manual
No. of forward speeds: 4
Wheels driven: Rear
Springs F/R: Coil/Coil
Brakes F/R: Drum/Drum
Steering: Worm & peg
Wheelbase: 240.0cm 94.5in
Track F: 128.0cm 50.4in
Track R: 125.0cm 49.2in
Length: 418.3cm 164.7in
Width: 162.6cm 64.0in
Height: 142.2cm 56.0in
Ground clearance: 17.5cm 6.9in
Kerb weight: 788.1kg 1736.0lb
Fuel: 31.8L 7.0gal 8.4galUS

4185 Skoda

S100L
1970 Czechoslovakia
80.0mph 128.7kmh
0-50mph 80.5kmh: 17.5secs
0-60mph 96.5kmh: 29.0secs
0-1/4 mile: 23.4secs
0-1km: 45.3secs
43.0bhp 32.1kW 43.6PS
@ 4650rpm
54.0lbft 73.2Nm @ 3000rpm
54.0bhp/ton 53.1bhp/tonne
43.5bhp/L 32.5kW/L 44.1PS/L
34.6ft/sec 10.5m/sec
16.1mph 25.9kmh/1000rpm
32.6mpg 27.1mpgUS 8.7L/100km
Petrol 4-stroke piston
988cc 60.3cu in
In-line 4 1 Carburettor
Compression ratio: 8.3:1
Bore: 68.0mm 2.7in
Stroke: 68.0mm 2.7in
Valve type/No: Overhead 8
Transmission: Manual
No. of forward speeds: 4
Wheels driven: Rear
Springs F/R: Coil/Coil
Brakes F/R: Disc/Drum
Steering: Worm & peg
Wheelbase: 240.0cm 94.5in
Track F: 128.0cm 50.4in
Track R: 125.0cm 49.2in
Length: 414.0cm 163.0in
Width: 162.6cm 64.0in
Height: 142.2cm 56.0in
Ground clearance: 17.8cm 7.0in
Kerb weight: 810.4kg 1785.0lb
Fuel: 31.8L 7.0gal 8.4galUS

4186 Skoda

S110LS
1972 Czechoslovakia
86.0mph 138.4kmh
0-50mph 80.5kmh: 13.7secs
0-60mph 96.5kmh: 19.6secs
0-1/4 mile: 21.6secs
0-1km: 41.0secs
52.0bhp 38.8kW 52.7PS
@ 4750rpm
64.0lbft 86.7Nm @ 3500rpm
63.2bhp/ton 62.1bhp/tonne
47.0bhp/L 35.0kW/L 47.6PS/L
35.4ft/sec 10.8m/sec
16.1mph 25.9kmh/1000rpm
34.4mpg 28.6mpgUS 8.2L/100km
Petrol 4-stroke piston
1107cc 67.5cu in
In-line 4 1 Carburettor
Compression ratio: 9.5:1
Bore: 72.0mm 2.8in
Stroke: 68.0mm 2.7in
Valve type/No: Overhead 8
Transmission: Manual
No. of forward speeds: 4
Wheels driven: Rear
Springs F/R: Coil/Coil
Brakes F/R: Disc/Drum
Steering: Worm & peg
Wheelbase: 240.0cm 94.5in
Track F: 128.0cm 50.4in
Track R: 125.0cm 49.2in
Length: 414.0cm 163.0in
Width: 162.6cm 64.0in
Height: 142.2cm 56.0in
Ground clearance: 17.8cm 7.0in
Kerb weight: 837.2kg 1844.0lb
Fuel: 31.8L 7.0gal 8.4galUS

4187 Skoda

120L
1977 Czechoslovakia
86.0mph 138.4kmh
0-50mph 80.5kmh: 13.1secs
0-60mph 96.5kmh: 18.9secs
0-1/4 mile: 21.5secs
0-1km: 40.7secs
52.0bhp 38.8kW 52.7PS
@ 5000rpm
63.0lbft 85.4Nm @ 3000rpm
60.0bhp/ton 59.0bhp/tonne
44.3bhp/L 33.0kW/L 44.9PS/L
39.3ft/sec 12.0m/sec
15.5mph 24.9kmh/1000rpm
30.4mpg 25.3mpgUS 9.3L/100km
Petrol 4-stroke piston
1174cc 71.6cu in
In-line 4 1 Carburettor
Compression ratio: 8.5:1
Bore: 72.0mm 2.8in
Stroke: 72.0mm 2.8in
Valve type/No: Overhead 8
Transmission: Manual
No. of forward speeds: 4
Wheels driven: Rear
Springs F/R: Coil/Coil
Brakes F/R: Disc/Drum
Steering: Worm & nut
Wheelbase: 240.0cm 94.5in
Track F: 128.0cm 50.4in
Track R: 125.0cm 49.2in
Length: 416.1cm 163.8in
Width: 159.5cm 62.8in
Height: 140.0cm 55.1in
Ground clearance: 17.0cm 6.7in
Kerb weight: 880.8kg 1940.0lb
Fuel: 38.2L 8.4gal 10.1galUS

4188 Skoda

Estelle 120 LSE
1986 Czechoslovakia
88.0mph 141.6kmh
0-50mph 80.5kmh: 14.0secs
0-60mph 96.5kmh: 19.9secs
0-1/4 mile: 21.9secs
0-1km: 41.3secs
54.3bhp 40.5kW 55.0PS
@ 5200rpm
66.3lbft 89.8Nm @ 3250rpm
62.4bhp/ton 61.4bhp/tonne
46.2bhp/L 34.5kW/L 46.9PS/L
40.9ft/sec 12.5m/sec
19.4mph 31.2kmh/1000rpm
30.1mpg 25.1mpgUS 9.4L/100km
Petrol 4-stroke piston
1174cc 72.0cu in
In-line 4 1 Carburettor
Compression ratio: 9.5:1
Bore: 72.0mm 2.8in
Stroke: 72.0mm 2.8in
Valve type/No: Overhead 8
Transmission: Manual
No. of forward speeds: 5
Wheels driven: Rear
Springs F/R: Coil/Coil
Brake system: PA
Brakes F/R: Disc/Drum
Steering: Rack & pinion
Wheelbase: 240.0cm 94.5in
Track F: 139.0cm 54.7in
Track R: 135.0cm 53.1in
Length: 420.0cm 165.4in
Width: 161.0cm 63.4in
Height: 140.0cm 55.1in
Ground clearance: 14.5cm 5.7in
Kerb weight: 885.0kg 1949.3lb
Fuel: 35.9L 7.9gal 9.5galUS

4189 Skoda

136 Rapide Coupe
1989 Czechoslovakia
92.0mph 148.0kmh
0-50mph 80.5kmh: 10.3secs
0-60mph 96.5kmh: 14.9secs
0-1/4 mile: 19.5secs
0-1km: 36.5secs
62.0bhp 46.2kW 62.9PS
@ 5000rpm
73.8lbft 100.0Nm @ 3000rpm
68.5bhp/ton 67.4bhp/tonne
47.7bhp/L 35.6kW/L 48.4PS/L
39.3ft/sec 12.0m/sec
20.9mph 33.6kmh/1000rpm
30.6mpg 25.5mpgUS 9.2L/100km
Petrol 4-stroke piston
1299cc 79.0cu in
In-line 4 1 Carburettor
Compression ratio: 9.7:1
Bore: 75.5mm 3.0in
Stroke: 72.0mm 2.8in
Valve type/No: Overhead 8
Transmission: Manual
No. of forward speeds: 5
Wheels driven: Rear
Springs F/R: Coil/Coil
Brake system: PA
Brakes F/R: Disc/Drum
Steering: Rack & pinion
Wheelbase: 240.0cm 94.5in
Track F: 139.5cm 54.9in
Track R: 135.5cm 53.3in
Length: 420.0cm 165.4in
Width: 161.0cm 63.4in
Height: 138.0cm 54.3in
Ground clearance: 12.0cm 4.7in
Kerb weight: 920.0kg 2026.4lb
Fuel: 35.9L 7.9gal 9.5galUS

4190 Squire

X101
1935 UK
105.0mph 168.9kmh
0-60mph 96.5kmh: 10.9secs
110.0bhp 82.0kW 111.5PS
@ 5000rpm
107.1bhp/ton 105.3bhp/tonne
73.5bhp/L 54.8kW/L 74.5PS/L
54.7ft/sec 16.7m/sec
Petrol 4-stroke piston
1496cc 91.3cu in supercharged
In-line 4 1 Carburettor
Bore: 69.0mm 2.7in
Stroke: 100.0mm 3.9in
Valve type/No: Overhead 8
Transmission: Manual
No. of forward speeds: 4
Wheels driven: Rear
Springs F/R: Leaf/Leaf
Brakes F/R: Drum/Drum
Steering: Worm & sector
Wheelbase: 264.2cm 104.0in
Track F: 137.2cm 54.0in
Track R: 137.2cm 54.0in
Kerb weight: 1044.2kg 2300.0lb

4191 Standard

16 Special Saloon
1933 UK
61.6mph 99.1kmh
0-50mph 80.5kmh: 24.6secs
20.0mpg 16.7mpgUS 14.1L/100km
Petrol 4-stroke piston
2054cc 125.3cu in
In-line 6
Bore: 65.5mm 2.6in
Stroke: 101.6mm 4.0in
Transmission: Manual
No. of forward speeds: 4
Wheels driven: Rear
Brakes F/R: Drum/Drum
Kerb weight: 1194.9kg 2632.0lb
Fuel: 40.9L 9.0gal 10.8galUS

4192 Standard

Avon 16 Open Four-Seater
1933 UK
73.7mph 118.6kmh
0-50mph 80.5kmh: 16.8secs
29.0mpg 24.1mpgUS 9.7L/100km
Petrol 4-stroke piston
2054cc 125.3cu in
In-line 6
Bore: 65.5mm 2.6in
Stroke: 101.6mm 4.0in
Valve type/No: Side 12
Transmission: Manual
No. of forward speeds: 4
Wheels driven: Rear
Brakes F/R: Drum/Drum
Kerb weight: 1080.5kg 2380.0lb
Fuel: 40.9L 9.0gal 10.8galUS

4193 Standard

Avon Coupe
1933 UK
75.0mph 120.7kmh

20.0mpg 16.7mpgUS 14.1L/100km
Petrol 4-stroke piston
2054cc 125.3cu in
In-line 6
Bore: 65.5mm 2.6in
Stroke: 101.6mm 4.0in
Valve type/No: Side 12
Transmission: Manual
No. of forward speeds: 4
Wheels driven: Rear
Brakes F/R: Drum/Drum
Kerb weight: 1131.4kg 2492.0lb
Fuel: 40.9L 9.0gal 10.8galUS

4194 Standard

Flying 10
1937 UK
63.8mph 102.7kmh
0-50mph 80.5kmh: 24.7secs
0-60mph 96.5kmh: 49.7secs
33.0bhp 24.6kW 33.5PS
@ 4000rpm
35.6bhp/ton 35.0bhp/tonne
26.0bhp/L 19.4kW/L 26.4PS/L
43.8ft/sec 13.3m/sec
33.0mpg 27.5mpgUS 8.6L/100km
Petrol 4-stroke piston
1267cc 77.3cu in
In-line 4 1 Carburettor
Compression ratio: 6.5:1
Bore: 63.5mm 2.5in
Stroke: 100.0mm 3.9in
Valve type/No: Side 8
Transmission: Manual
No. of forward speeds: 4
Wheels driven: Rear
Brakes F/R: Drum/Drum
Kerb weight: 942.0kg 2075.0lb
Fuel: 31.8L 7.0gal 8.4galUS

4195 Standard

Flying 20
1938 UK
76.9mph 123.7kmh
0-50mph 80.5kmh: 16.7secs
0-60mph 96.5kmh: 25.6secs
65.0bhp 48.5kW 65.9PS
@ 3800rpm
46.5bhp/ton 45.8bhp/tonne
24.4bhp/L 18.2kW/L 24.7PS/L
44.0ft/sec 13.4m/sec
18.0mpg 15.0mpgUS 15.7L/100km
Petrol 4-stroke piston
2664cc 162.5cu in
In-line 6 1 Carburettor
Compression ratio: 6.5:1
Bore: 73.0mm 2.9in
Stroke: 106.0mm 4.2in
Valve type/No: Side 12
Transmission: Manual
No. of forward speeds: 4
Wheels driven: Rear
Brakes F/R: Drum/Drum
Kerb weight: 1420.6kg 3129.0lb
Fuel: 54.6L 12.0gal 14.4galUS

4196 Standard

12 Saloon
1947 UK
72.0mph 115.8kmh
0-50mph 80.5kmh: 20.7secs
0-60mph 96.5kmh: 36.0secs
44.0bhp 32.8kW 44.6PS
@ 4000rpm
39.1bhp/ton 38.5bhp/tonne
27.3bhp/L 20.4kW/L 27.7PS/L
46.3ft/sec 14.1m/sec
27.0mpg 22.5mpgUS 10.5L/100km
Petrol 4-stroke piston
1609cc 98.2cu in
In-line 4
Compression ratio: 6.5:1
Bore: 69.5mm 2.7in
Stroke: 106.0mm 4.2in
Valve type/No: Side 8
Transmission: Manual
No. of forward speeds: 4
Wheels driven: Rear
Brakes F/R: Drum/Drum
Wheelbase: 254.0cm 100.0in
Track F: 124.5cm 49.0in
Track R: 138.4cm 54.5in
Length: 419.1cm 165.0in
Width: 160.0cm 63.0in
Height: 160.0cm 63.0in
Ground clearance: 17.8cm 7.0in
Kerb weight: 1144.1kg 2520.0lb
Fuel: 45.5L 10.0gal 12.0galUS

4197 Standard

8
1948 UK
61.0mph 98.1kmh
0-50mph 80.5kmh: 25.1secs
28.0bhp 20.9kW 28.4PS
@ 4000rpm
35.0bhp/ton 34.4bhp/tonne
27.7bhp/L 20.7kW/L 28.1PS/L
43.8ft/sec 13.3m/sec
40.0mpg 33.3mpgUS 7.1L/100km
Petrol 4-stroke piston
1009cc 61.6cu in
In-line 4
Compression ratio: 6.7:1
Bore: 56.7mm 2.2in
Stroke: 100.0mm 3.9in
Valve type/No: Side 8
Transmission: Manual
No. of forward speeds: 4
Wheels driven: Rear
Brakes F/R: Drum/Drum
Wheelbase: 210.8cm 83.0in
Track F: 114.3cm 45.0in
Track R: 114.3cm 45.0in
Length: 353.1cm 139.0in
Width: 142.2cm 56.0in
Height: 154.9cm 61.0in
Ground clearance: 17.8cm 7.0in
Kerb weight: 813.6kg 1792.0lb
Fuel: 27.3L 6.0gal 7.2galUS

4198 Standard

Vanguard
1948 UK
78.0mph 125.5kmh
0-50mph 80.5kmh: 16.3secs
0-60mph 96.5kmh: 24.8secs
68.0bhp 50.7kW 68.9PS
@ 4200rpm
56.8bhp/ton 55.9bhp/tonne
32.6bhp/L 24.3kW/L 33.0PS/L
42.2ft/sec 12.9m/sec
22.0mpg 18.3mpgUS 12.8L/100km
Petrol 4-stroke piston
2088cc 127.4cu in
In-line 4
Compression ratio: 6.7:1
Bore: 85.0mm 3.3in
Stroke: 92.0mm 3.6in
Valve type/No: Overhead 8
Transmission: Manual
No. of forward speeds: 3
Wheels driven: Rear
Brakes F/R: Drum/Drum
Wheelbase: 238.8cm 94.0in
Track F: 129.5cm 51.0in
Track R: 137.2cm 54.0in
Length: 416.6cm 164.0in
Width: 175.3cm 69.0in
Height: 162.6cm 64.0in
Ground clearance: 20.3cm 8.0in
Kerb weight: 1216.7kg 2680.0lb
Fuel: 68.2L 15.0gal 18.0galUS

4199 Standard

Vanguard
1952 UK
81.5mph 131.1kmh
0-50mph 80.5kmh: 15.8secs
0-60mph 96.5kmh: 24.5secs
0-1/4 mile: 22.4secs
68.0bhp 50.7kW 68.9PS
@ 4200rpm
108.0lbft 146.3Nm @ 2000rpm
54.0bhp/ton 53.1bhp/tonne
32.6bhp/L 24.3kW/L 33.0PS/L
42.2ft/sec 12.9m/sec
21.7mph 34.9kmh/1000rpm
27.6mpg 23.0mpgUS 10.2L/100km
Petrol 4-stroke piston
2088cc 127.4cu in
In-line 4
Compression ratio: 6.7:1
Bore: 85.0mm 3.3in
Stroke: 92.0mm 3.6in
Valve type/No: Overhead 8
Transmission: Manual with overdrive
No. of forward speeds: 4
Wheels driven: Rear
Springs F/R: Coil/Leaf
Brakes F/R: Drum/Drum
Wheelbase: 238.8cm 94.0in
Track F: 129.5cm 51.0in
Track R: 137.2cm 54.0in
Length: 421.6cm 166.0in
Width: 175.3cm 69.0in
Height: 162.6cm 64.0in
Ground clearance: 20.3cm 8.0in
Kerb weight: 1281.6kg 2823.0lb
Fuel: 68.2L 15.0gal 18.0galUS

4200 Standard

8
1953 UK
63.0mph 101.4kmh
0-50mph 80.5kmh: 24.4secs
0-60mph 96.5kmh: 52.0secs
0-1/4 mile: 25.7secs
26.0bhp 19.4kW 26.4PS
@ 4500rpm
39.2lbft 53.1Nm @ 2800rpm
37.1bhp/ton 36.5bhp/tonne
32.4bhp/L 24.1kW/L 32.8PS/L
37.4ft/sec 11.4m/sec
13.5mph 21.7kmh/1000rpm
44.0mpg 36.6mpgUS 6.4L/100km
Petrol 4-stroke piston
803cc 49.0cu in
In-line 4
Compression ratio: 7.2:1
Bore: 58.0mm 2.3in
Stroke: 76.0mm 3.0in
Valve type/No: Overhead 8
Transmission: Manual
No. of forward speeds: 4
Wheels driven: Rear
Springs F/R: Coil/Leaf
Brakes F/R: Drum/Drum
Wheelbase: 213.4cm 84.0in
Track F: 123.2cm 48.5in
Track R: 123.2cm 48.5in
Length: 360.7cm 142.0in
Width: 147.3cm 58.0in
Height: 152.4cm 60.0in
Ground clearance: 17.8cm 7.0in
Kerb weight: 711.9kg 1568.0lb
Fuel: 31.8L 7.0gal 8.4galUS

4201 Standard

Vanguard Estate
1953 UK
80.0mph 128.7kmh
0-50mph 80.5kmh: 15.1secs
0-60mph 96.5kmh: 22.0secs
0-1/4 mile: 22.4secs
68.0bhp 50.7kW 68.9PS
@ 4200rpm
108.3lbft 146.7Nm @ 2000rpm
53.3bhp/ton 52.4bhp/tonne
32.6bhp/L 24.3kW/L 33.0PS/L
42.2ft/sec 12.9m/sec
21.6mph 34.8kmh/1000rpm
21.7mpg 18.1mpgUS 13.0L/100km
Petrol 4-stroke piston
2088cc 127.4cu in
In-line 4
Compression ratio: 7.0:1
Bore: 85.0mm 3.3in
Stroke: 92.0mm 3.6in
Valve type/No: Overhead 8
Transmission: Manual with overdrive
No. of forward speeds: 4
Wheels driven: Rear
Springs F/R: Coil/Leaf
Brakes F/R: Drum/Drum
Wheelbase: 238.8cm 94.0in
Track F: 129.5cm 51.0in
Track R: 137.2cm 54.0in
Length: 443.7cm 174.7in
Width: 175.3cm 69.0in
Height: 167.6cm 66.0in
Ground clearance: 20.3cm 8.0in
Kerb weight: 1296.6kg 2856.0lb
Fuel: 68.2L 15.0gal 18.0galUS

4202 Standard

Vanguard Phase II
1953 UK
81.0mph 130.3kmh
0-50mph 80.5kmh: 13.8secs
0-60mph 96.5kmh: 20.8secs
0-1/4 mile: 21.9secs
68.0bhp 50.7kW 68.9PS
@ 4200rpm
108.0lbft 146.3Nm @ 2000rpm
53.9bhp/ton 53.0bhp/tonne
32.6bhp/L 24.3kW/L 33.0PS/L
42.2ft/sec 12.9m/sec
17.2mph 27.7kmh/1000rpm
21.5mpg 17.9mpgUS 13.1L/100km
Petrol 4-stroke piston
2088cc 127.4cu in
In-line 4
Compression ratio: 7.2:1
Bore: 85.0mm 3.3in
Stroke: 92.0mm 3.6in
Valve type/No: Overhead 8
Transmission: Manual
No. of forward speeds: 3
Wheels driven: Rear
Springs F/R: Coil/Leaf
Brakes F/R: Drum/Drum
Wheelbase: 238.8cm 94.0in
Track F: 129.5cm 51.0in
Track R: 137.2cm 54.0in
Length: 426.7cm 168.0in
Width: 175.3cm 69.0in
Height: 165.1cm 65.0in
Ground clearance: 20.3cm 8.0in
Kerb weight: 1283.9kg 2828.0lb
Fuel: 54.6L 12.0gal 14.4galUS

4203 Standard

10
1955 UK
67.0mph 107.8kmh
0-50mph 80.5kmh: 19.2secs
0-60mph 96.5kmh: 33.8secs
0-1/4 mile: 24.1secs
33.0bhp 24.6kW 33.5PS
@ 4500rpm
46.0lbft 62.3Nm @ 2500rpm
43.6bhp/ton 42.9bhp/tonne
34.8bhp/L 26.0kW/L 35.3PS/L
37.4ft/sec 11.4m/sec
15.0mph 24.1kmh/1000rpm
35.5mpg 29.6mpgUS 8.0L/100km
Petrol 4-stroke piston
948cc 57.8cu in
In-line 4
Compression ratio: 7.0:1
Bore: 63.0mm 2.5in
Stroke: 76.0mm 3.0in
Valve type/No: Overhead 8
Transmission: Manual
No. of forward speeds: 4
Wheels driven: Rear
Springs F/R: Coil/Leaf
Brakes F/R: Drum/Drum
Wheelbase: 213.4cm 84.0in
Track F: 123.2cm 48.5in
Track R: 123.2cm 48.5in
Length: 368.3cm 145.0in
Width: 147.3cm 58.0in
Height: 152.4cm 60.0in
Ground clearance: 17.8cm 7.0in
Kerb weight: 769.1kg 1694.0lb
Fuel: 31.8L 7.0gal 8.4galUS

4204 Standard

Vanguard III
1956 UK
80.0mph 128.7kmh
0-50mph 80.5kmh: 14.6secs
0-60mph 96.5kmh: 22.2secs
0-1/4 mile: 22.2secs
68.0bhp 50.7kW 68.9PS
@ 4200rpm
108.0lbft 146.3Nm @ 2000rpm
55.5bhp/ton 54.6bhp/tonne
32.6bhp/L 24.3kW/L 33.0PS/L
42.2ft/sec 12.9m/sec
23.0mph 37.0kmh/1000rpm
30.8mpg 25.6mpgUS 9.2L/100km
Petrol 4-stroke piston
2088cc 127.4cu in
In-line 4
Compression ratio: 7.0:1
Bore: 85.0mm 3.3in
Stroke: 92.0mm 3.6in
Valve type/No: Overhead 8
Transmission: Manual with overdrive
No. of forward speeds: 5
Wheels driven: Rear
Springs F/R: Coil/Leaf
Brakes F/R: Drum/Drum
Wheelbase: 259.1cm 102.0in
Track F: 129.5cm 51.0in
Track R: 129.5cm 51.0in
Length: 436.9cm 172.0in
Width: 171.5cm 67.5in
Height: 156.2cm 61.5in
Ground clearance: 18.3cm 7.2in
Kerb weight: 1245.8kg 2744.0lb
Fuel: 56.9L 12.5gal 15.0galUS

4205 Standard
Vanguard Sportsman
1956 UK
90.0mph 144.8kmh
0-50mph 80.5kmh: 12.2secs
0-60mph 96.5kmh: 17.6secs
0-1/4 mile: 21.7secs
90.0bhp 67.1kW 91.2PS
@ 4500rpm
122.0lbft 165.3Nm @ 2500rpm
72.9bhp/ton 71.7bhp/tonne
43.1bhp/L 32.1kW/L 43.7PS/L
45.2ft/sec 13.8m/sec
22.0mph 35.4kmh/1000rpm
25.8mpg 21.5mpgUS 10.9L/100km
Petrol 4-stroke piston
2088cc 127.4cu in
In-line 4
Compression ratio: 8.0:1
Bore: 85.0mm 3.3in
Stroke: 92.0mm 3.6in
Valve type/No: Overhead 8
Transmission: Manual with overdrive
No. of forward speeds: 5
Wheels driven: Rear
Springs F/R: Coil/Leaf
Brakes F/R: Drum/Drum
Wheelbase: 259.1cm 102.0in
Track F: 129.5cm 51.0in
Track R: 129.5cm 51.0in
Length: 440.7cm 173.5in
Width: 168.9cm 66.5in
Height: 125.7cm 49.5in
Ground clearance: 15.7cm 6.2in
Kerb weight: 1255.8kg 2766.0lb
Fuel: 54.6L 12.0gal 14.4galUS

4206 Standard
Vanguard III
1957 UK
81.5mph 131.1kmh
0-50mph 80.5kmh: 16.5secs
0-60mph 96.5kmh: 25.9secs
0-1/4 mile: 24.9secs
68.0bhp 50.7kW 68.9PS
@ 4200rpm
113.3lbft 153.5Nm @ 2000rpm
52.3bhp/ton 51.4bhp/tonne
32.6bhp/L 24.3kW/L 33.0PS/L
42.2ft/sec 12.9m/sec
23.0mph 37.0kmh/1000rpm
31.2mpg 26.0mpgUS 9.1L/100km
Petrol 4-stroke piston
2088cc 127.4cu in
In-line 4 1 Carburettor
Compression ratio: 7.5:1
Bore: 85.0mm 3.3in
Stroke: 92.0mm 3.6in
Valve type/No: Overhead 8
Transmission: Manual with overdrive
No. of forward speeds: 5
Wheels driven: Rear
Springs F/R: Coil/Leaf
Brakes F/R: Drum/Drum
Wheelbase: 259.1cm 102.0in
Track F: 129.5cm 51.0in
Track R: 129.5cm 51.0in
Length: 433.1cm 170.5in
Width: 171.5cm 67.5in
Height: 156.2cm 61.5in
Ground clearance: 18.3cm 7.2in
Kerb weight: 1322.0kg 2912.0lb
Fuel: 63.7L 14.0gal 16.8galUS

4207 Standard
8
1958 UK
65.0mph 104.6kmh
0-50mph 80.5kmh: 24.5secs
0-60mph 96.5kmh: 54.4secs
0-1/4 mile: 25.9secs
33.0bhp 24.6kW 33.5PS
@ 5000rpm
42.5lbft 57.6Nm @ 2700rpm
47.1bhp/ton 46.4bhp/tonne
41.1bhp/L 30.6kW/L 41.7PS/L
41.5ft/sec 12.7m/sec
17.5mph 28.2kmh/1000rpm
44.0mpg 36.6mpgUS 6.4L/100km
Petrol 4-stroke piston
803cc 49.0cu in
In-line 4 1 Carburettor
Compression ratio: 8.2:1
Bore: 58.0mm 2.3in
Stroke: 76.0mm 3.0in
Valve type/No: Overhead 8
Transmission: Manual with overdrive
No. of forward speeds: 7
Wheels driven: Rear
Springs F/R: Coil/Leaf
Brakes F/R: Drum/Drum
Wheelbase: 213.4cm 84.0in
Track F: 123.2cm 48.5in
Track R: 123.2cm 48.5in
Length: 360.7cm 142.0in
Width: 147.3cm 58.0in
Height: 152.4cm 60.0in
Ground clearance: 16.5cm 6.5in
Kerb weight: 711.9kg 1568.0lb
Fuel: 31.8L 7.0gal 8.4galUS

4208 Standard
Ensign
1958 UK
79.0mph 127.1kmh
0-50mph 80.5kmh: 16.4secs
0-60mph 96.5kmh: 25.4secs
0-1/4 mile: 22.9secs
60.0bhp 44.7kW 60.8PS
@ 4000rpm
91.7lbft 124.3Nm @ 2200rpm
51.6bhp/ton 50.7bhp/tonne
35.9bhp/L 26.8kW/L 36.4PS/L
40.2ft/sec 12.3m/sec
18.0mph 29.0kmh/1000rpm
28.2mpg 23.5mpgUS 10.0L/100km
Petrol 4-stroke piston
1670cc 101.9cu in
In-line 4 1 Carburettor
Compression ratio: 8.0:1
Bore: 76.0mm 3.0in
Stroke: 92.0mm 3.6in
Valve type/No: Overhead 8
Transmission: Manual
No. of forward speeds: 4
Wheels driven: Rear
Springs F/R: Coil/Leaf
Brakes F/R: Drum/Drum
Steering: Recirculating ball
Wheelbase: 259.1cm 102.0in
Track F: 130.8cm 51.5in
Track R: 130.8cm 51.5in
Length: 435.6cm 171.5in
Width: 171.5cm 67.5in
Height: 152.4cm 60.0in
Ground clearance: 17.8cm 7.0in
Kerb weight: 1182.2kg 2604.0lb
Fuel: 54.6L 12.0gal 14.4galUS

4209 Standard
Pennant
1958 UK
67.0mph 107.8kmh
0-50mph 80.5kmh: 19.5secs
0-60mph 96.5kmh: 34.9secs
0-1/4 mile: 25.0secs
37.0bhp 27.6kW 37.5PS
@ 5000rpm
50.0lbft 67.8Nm @ 2750rpm
47.5bhp/ton 46.7bhp/tonne
39.0bhp/L 29.1kW/L 39.6PS/L
41.5ft/sec 12.7m/sec
15.0mph 24.1kmh/1000rpm
39.6mpg 33.0mpgUS 7.1L/100km
Petrol 4-stroke piston
948cc 57.8cu in
In-line 4 1 Carburettor
Compression ratio: 8.0:1
Bore: 63.0mm 2.5in
Stroke: 76.0mm 3.0in
Valve type/No: Overhead 8
Transmission: Manual with overdrive
No. of forward speeds: 7
Wheels driven: Rear
Springs F/R: Coil/Leaf
Brakes F/R: Drum/Drum
Wheelbase: 213.4cm 84.0in
Track F: 123.2cm 48.5in
Track R: 123.2cm 48.5in
Length: 360.7cm 142.0in
Width: 147.3cm 58.0in
Height: 149.9cm 59.0in
Ground clearance: 15.2cm 6.0in
Kerb weight: 792.2kg 1745.0lb
Fuel: 31.8L 7.0gal 8.4galUS

4210 Standard
Super 10
1958 UK
65.5mph 105.4kmh
0-50mph 80.5kmh: 23.3secs
0-60mph 96.5kmh: 38.1secs
0-1/4 mile: 26.0secs
35.0bhp 26.1kW 35.5PS
@ 4500rpm
47.9lbft 64.9Nm @ 2500rpm
44.4bhp/ton 43.7bhp/tonne
36.9bhp/L 27.5kW/L 37.4PS/L
37.4ft/sec 11.4m/sec
20.0mph 32.2kmh/1000rpm
40.5mpg 33.7mpgUS 7.0L/100km
Petrol 4-stroke piston
948cc 57.8cu in
In-line 4 1 Carburettor
Compression ratio: 7.5:1
Bore: 63.0mm 2.5in
Stroke: 76.0mm 3.0in
Valve type/No: Overhead 8
Transmission: Manual with overdrive
No. of forward speeds: 7
Wheels driven: Rear
Springs F/R: Coil/Leaf
Brakes F/R: Drum/Drum
Wheelbase: 213.4cm 84.0in
Track F: 123.2cm 48.5in
Track R: 123.2cm 48.5in
Length: 365.8cm 144.0in
Width: 152.4cm 60.0in
Height: 152.4cm 60.0in
Ground clearance: 17.8cm 7.0in
Kerb weight: 800.9kg 1764.0lb
Fuel: 31.8L 7.0gal 8.4galUS

4211 Standard
Vanguard III Automatic
1958 UK
82.6mph 132.9kmh
0-50mph 80.5kmh: 17.3secs
0-60mph 96.5kmh: 27.5secs
0-1/4 mile: 23.9secs
68.0bhp 50.7kW 68.9PS
@ 4200rpm
113.3lbft 153.5Nm @ 2000rpm
54.1bhp/ton 53.2bhp/tonne
32.6bhp/L 24.3kW/L 33.0PS/L
42.2ft/sec 12.9m/sec
17.3mph 27.8kmh/1000rpm
25.4mpg 21.1mpgUS 11.1L/100km
Petrol 4-stroke piston
2088cc 127.4cu in
In-line 4 1 Carburettor
Compression ratio: 7.5:1
Bore: 85.0mm 3.3in
Stroke: 92.0mm 3.6in
Valve type/No: Overhead 8
Transmission: Automatic
No. of forward speeds: 3
Wheels driven: Rear
Springs F/R: Coil/Leaf
Brakes F/R: Drum/Drum
Wheelbase: 259.1cm 102.0in
Track F: 130.8cm 51.5in
Track R: 130.8cm 51.5in
Length: 436.9cm 172.0in
Width: 171.5cm 67.5in
Height: 152.4cm 60.0in
Ground clearance: 18.3cm 7.2in
Kerb weight: 1277.6kg 2814.0lb
Fuel: 54.6L 12.0gal 14.4galUS

4212 Standard
Vanguard
1961 UK
85.0mph 136.8kmh
0-50mph 80.5kmh: 13.0secs
0-60mph 96.5kmh: 19.7secs
0-1/4 mile: 21.5secs
85.0bhp 63.4kW 86.2PS
@ 4500rpm
113.0lbft 153.1Nm @ 2500rpm
72.3bhp/ton 71.1bhp/tonne
42.5bhp/L 31.7kW/L 43.1PS/L
37.4ft/sec 11.4m/sec
19.8mph 31.9kmh/1000rpm
20.0mpg 16.7mpgUS 14.1L/100km
Petrol 4-stroke piston
1998cc 121.9cu in
In-line 6 1 Carburettor
Compression ratio: 8.0:1
Bore: 74.7mm 2.9in
Stroke: 76.0mm 3.0in
Valve type/No: Overhead 12
Transmission: Manual with overdrive
No. of forward speeds: 5
Wheels driven: Rear
Springs F/R: Coil/Leaf
Brakes F/R: Drum/Drum
Wheelbase: 259.1cm 102.0in
Track F: 130.8cm 51.5in
Track R: 130.8cm 51.5in
Length: 434.3cm 171.0in
Width: 171.5cm 67.5in
Height: 152.4cm 60.0in
Ground clearance: 18.3cm 7.2in
Kerb weight: 1194.9kg 2632.0lb
Fuel: 54.6L 12.0gal 14.4galUS

4213 Standard
Ensign de Luxe Estate
1962 UK
94.0mph 151.2kmh
0-50mph 80.5kmh: 13.2secs
0-60mph 96.5kmh: 18.7secs
0-1/4 mile: 21.4secs
75.0bhp 55.9kW 76.0PS
@ 4100rpm
125.0lbft 169.4Nm @ 2050rpm
59.8bhp/ton 58.8bhp/tonne
35.1bhp/L 26.2kW/L 35.6PS/L
41.2ft/sec 12.6m/sec
19.0mph 30.6kmh/1000rpm
24.8mpg 20.7mpgUS 11.4L/100km
Petrol 4-stroke piston
2138cc 130.4cu in
In-line 4 1 Carburettor
Compression ratio: 8.5:1
Bore: 86.0mm 3.4in
Stroke: 92.0mm 3.6in
Valve type/No: Overhead 8
Transmission: Manual
No. of forward speeds: 4
Wheels driven: Rear
Springs F/R: Coil/Leaf
Brakes F/R: Drum/Drum
Steering: Recirculating ball
Wheelbase: 259.1cm 102.0in
Track F: 129.5cm 51.0in
Track R: 129.5cm 51.0in
Length: 435.6cm 171.5in
Width: 171.5cm 67.5in
Height: 152.4cm 60.0in
Ground clearance: 17.8cm 7.0in
Kerb weight: 1274.4kg 2807.0lb
Fuel: 63.7L 14.0gal 16.8galUS

4214 Studebaker
Double-twelve Open Tourer
1929 USA
91.0mph 146.4kmh
15.0mpg 12.5mpgUS 18.8L/100km
Petrol 4-stroke piston
5517cc 336.6cu in
In-line 8
Bore: 88.9mm 3.5in
Stroke: 111.1mm 4.4in
Transmission: Manual
No. of forward speeds: 3
Wheels driven: Rear
Brakes F/R: Drum/Drum
Wheelbase: 317.5cm 125.0in
Track F: 146.1cm 57.5in
Track R: 146.1cm 57.5in
Length: 490.2cm 193.0in
Width: 175.3cm 69.0in
Height: 177.8cm 70.0in
Kerb weight: 1728.8kg 3808.0lb
Fuel: 136.5L 30.0gal 36.1galUS

4215 Studebaker
Commander Brougham
1930 USA
70.3mph 113.1kmh
18.0mpg 15.0mpgUS 15.7L/100km
Petrol 4-stroke piston
4104cc 250.4cu in
In-line 8
Bore: 77.8mm 3.1in
Stroke: 107.9mm 4.2in
Transmission: Manual
No. of forward speeds: 3
Wheels driven: Rear
Brakes F/R: Drum/Drum
Wheelbase: 315.0cm 124.0in
Track F: 147.3cm 58.0in
Track R: 147.3cm 58.0in
Length: 485.1cm 191.0in
Width: 182.9cm 72.0in
Height: 182.9cm 72.0in
Kerb weight: 1634.4kg 3600.0lb
Fuel: 66.0L 14.5gal 17.4galUS

4216 Studebaker
Erskine Saloon

1930 USA
62.5mph 100.6kmh
20.0mpg 16.7mpgUS 14.1L/100km
Petrol 4-stroke piston
3364cc 205.2cu in
In-line 6
Bore: 82.5mm 3.2in
Stroke: 104.7mm 4.1in
Transmission: Manual
No. of forward speeds: 3
Wheels driven: Rear
Brakes F/R: Drum/Drum
Wheelbase: 289.6cm 114.0in
Track F: 146.1cm 57.5in
Track R: 146.1cm 57.5in
Length: 449.6cm 177.0in
Width: 177.8cm 70.0in
Height: 177.8cm 70.0in
Kerb weight: 1398.3kg 3080.0lb
Fuel: 54.6L 12.0gal 14.4galUS

4217 Studebaker

President Limousine
1931 USA
72.0mph 115.8kmh
15.0mpg 12.5mpgUS 18.8L/100km
Petrol 4-stroke piston
5522cc 336.9cu in
In-line 8
Bore: 88.9mm 3.5in
Stroke: 111.1mm 4.4in
Transmission: Manual
No. of forward speeds: 3
Wheels driven: Rear
Brakes F/R: Drum/Drum
Wheelbase: 345.4cm 136.0in
Track F: 147.3cm 58.0in
Track R: 147.3cm 58.0in
Length: 508.0cm 200.0in
Width: 182.9cm 72.0in
Height: 188.0cm 74.0in
Kerb weight: 1983.1kg 4368.0lb
Fuel: 66.0L 14.5gal 17.4galUS

4218 Studebaker

Dictator Saloon de Luxe
1935 USA
77.5mph 124.7kmh
0-50mph 80.5kmh: 16.6secs
0-60mph 96.5kmh: 24.4secs
20.0mpg 16.7mpgUS 14.1L/100km
Petrol 4-stroke piston
3364cc 205.2cu in
In-line 6
Bore: 82.5mm 3.2in
Stroke: 104.7mm 4.1in
Valve type/No: Side 12
Transmission: Manual
No. of forward speeds: 3
Wheels driven: Rear
Brakes F/R: Drum/Drum
Kerb weight: 1529.1kg 3368.0lb
Fuel: 54.6L 12.0gal 14.4galUS

4219 Studebaker

President Saloon
1935 USA
87.3mph 140.5kmh
0-50mph 80.5kmh: 14.0secs
0-60mph 96.5kmh: 20.4secs
18.0mpg 15.0mpgUS 15.7L/100km
Petrol 4-stroke piston
4103cc 250.3cu in
In-line 8
Bore: 77.8mm 3.1in
Stroke: 107.9mm 4.2in
Valve type/No: Side 16
Transmission: Manual
No. of forward speeds: 3
Wheels driven: Rear
Brakes F/R: Drum/Drum
Ground clearance: 20.8cm 8.2in
Kerb weight: 1823.7kg 4017.0lb
Fuel: 63.7L 14.0gal 16.8galUS

4220 Studebaker

De Luxe Saloon
1936 USA
81.0mph 130.3kmh
0-50mph 80.5kmh: 13.0secs
0-60mph 96.5kmh: 19.6secs
20.0mpg 16.7mpgUS 14.1L/100km
Petrol 4-stroke piston
3569cc 217.7cu in
In-line 6
Bore: 82.5mm 3.2in
Stroke: 111.1mm 4.4in
Valve type/No: Side 12
Transmission: Manual
No. of forward speeds: 3
Wheels driven: Rear
Brakes F/R: Drum/Drum
Kerb weight: 1540.0kg 3392.0lb
Fuel: 63.7L 14.0gal 16.8galUS

4221 Studebaker

Dictator de Luxe Saloon
1937 USA
78.2mph 125.8kmh
0-50mph 80.5kmh: 15.1secs
0-60mph 96.5kmh: 22.4secs
18.0mpg 15.0mpgUS 15.7L/100km
Petrol 4-stroke piston
3569cc 217.7cu in
In-line 6
Bore: 82.6mm 3.2in
Stroke: 111.1mm 4.4in
Valve type/No: Side 12
Transmission: Manual
No. of forward speeds: 3
Wheels driven: Rear
Brakes F/R: Drum/Drum
Kerb weight: 1585.8kg 3493.0lb
Fuel: 68.2L 15.0gal 18.0galUS

4222 Studebaker

Champion
1949 USA
77.5mph 124.7kmh
0-50mph 80.5kmh: 17.7secs
0-60mph 96.5kmh: 25.9secs
85.0bhp 63.4kW 86.2PS
@ 4000rpm
138.0lbft 187.0Nm @ 2400rpm
63.4bhp/ton 62.3bhp/tonne
30.6bhp/L 22.8kW/L 31.0PS/L
44.4ft/sec 13.5m/sec
16.9mph 27.2kmh/1000rpm
18.0mpg 15.0mpgUS 15.7L/100km
Petrol 4-stroke piston
2779cc 169.5cu in
In-line 6
Compression ratio: 7.0:1
Bore: 76.2mm 3.0in
Stroke: 101.6mm 4.0in
Valve type/No: Side 12
Transmission: Manual with overdrive
No. of forward speeds: 4
Wheels driven: Rear
Brakes F/R: Drum/Drum
Wheelbase: 287.0cm 113.0in
Track F: 143.5cm 56.5in
Track R: 137.2cm 54.0in
Length: 501.7cm 197.5in
Width: 177.5cm 69.9in
Height: 156.2cm 61.5in
Ground clearance: 20.3cm 8.0in
Kerb weight: 1363.4kg 3003.0lb
Fuel: 67.8L 14.9gal 17.9galUS

4223 Studebaker

Land Cruiser
1951 USA
92.8mph 149.3kmh
0-50mph 80.5kmh: 11.8secs
0-60mph 96.5kmh: 15.4secs
0-1/4 mile: 21.1secs
120.0bhp 89.5kW 121.7PS
@ 4000rpm
81.6bhp/ton 80.3bhp/tonne
31.5bhp/L 23.5kW/L 31.9PS/L
36.1ft/sec 11.0m/sec
24.0mpg 20.0mpgUS 11.8L/100km
Petrol 4-stroke piston
3812cc 232.6cu in
Vee 8
Bore: 85.7mm 3.4in
Stroke: 82.6mm 3.2in
Transmission: Automatic
Wheels driven: Rear
Wheelbase: 302.3cm 119.0in
Track F: 143.5cm 56.5in
Track R: 137.2cm 54.0in
Length: 511.8cm 201.5in
Width: 179.6cm 70.7in
Height: 157.0cm 61.8in
Ground clearance: 20.3cm 8.0in
Kerb weight: 1495.0kg 3293.0lb

4224 Studebaker

Commander Coupe
1953 USA
95.3mph 153.3kmh
0-50mph 80.5kmh: 10.8secs
0-60mph 96.5kmh: 14.9secs
0-1/4 mile: 20.1secs
120.0bhp 89.5kW 121.7PS
@ 4000rpm
190.0lbft 257.5Nm @ 2000rpm
80.5bhp/ton 79.1bhp/tonne
31.5bhp/L 23.5kW/L 31.9PS/L
36.1ft/sec 11.0m/sec
25.5mph 41.0kmh/1000rpm
Petrol 4-stroke piston
3813cc 232.6cu in
Vee 8
Compression ratio: 7.0:1
Bore: 85.9mm 3.4in
Stroke: 82.6mm 3.2in
Valve type/No: Overhead 16
Transmission: Manual
No. of forward speeds: 3
Wheels driven: Rear
Wheelbase: 306.1cm 120.5in
Track F: 143.5cm 56.5in
Track R: 141.0cm 55.5in
Kerb weight: 1516.4kg 3340.0lb

4225 Studebaker

Commander Supercharged
1953 USA
107.1mph 172.3kmh
0-50mph 80.5kmh: 8.5secs
0-60mph 96.5kmh: 11.9secs
0-1/4 mile: 18.6secs
25.5mph 41.0kmh/1000rpm
Petrol 4-stroke piston
3813cc 232.6cu in supercharged
Vee 8
Bore: 85.9mm 3.4in
Stroke: 82.6mm 3.2in
Valve type/No: Overhead 16
Transmission: Manual
No. of forward speeds: 3
Wheels driven: Rear
Wheelbase: 306.1cm 120.5in
Track F: 143.5cm 56.5in
Track R: 141.0cm 55.5in
Kerb weight: 1516.4kg 3340.0lb

4226 Studebaker

Commander Coupe
1954 USA
94.0mph 151.2kmh
0-50mph 80.5kmh: 12.1secs
0-60mph 96.5kmh: 16.9secs
0-1/4 mile: 20.4secs
120.0bhp 89.5kW 121.7PS
@ 4000rpm
190.0lbft 257.5Nm @ 2000rpm
79.5bhp/ton 78.2bhp/tonne
31.5bhp/L 23.5kW/L 31.9PS/L
36.1ft/sec 11.0m/sec
22.9mph 36.8kmh/1000rpm
19.0mpg 15.8mpgUS 14.9L/100km
Petrol 4-stroke piston
3812cc 232.6cu in
Vee 8
Compression ratio: 7.0:1
Bore: 85.7mm 3.4in
Stroke: 82.5mm 3.2in
Valve type/No: Overhead 16
Transmission: Automatic
No. of forward speeds: 2
Wheels driven: Rear
Springs F/R: Coil/Leaf
Brakes F/R: Drum/Drum
Wheelbase: 306.1cm 120.5in
Track F: 143.5cm 56.5in
Track R: 141.0cm 55.5in
Length: 512.8cm 201.9in
Width: 180.3cm 71.0in
Height: 143.3cm 56.4in
Ground clearance: 20.8cm 8.2in
Kerb weight: 1534.5kg 3380.0lb
Fuel: 68.2L 15.0gal 18.0galUS

4227 Studebaker

Lark 6
1959 USA
80.0mph 128.7kmh
0-50mph 80.5kmh: 13.1secs
0-60mph 96.5kmh: 21.0secs
0-1/4 mile: 21.4secs
90.0bhp 67.1kW 91.2PS
@ 4000rpm
145.0lbft 196.5Nm @ 2000rpm
73.3bhp/ton 72.1bhp/tonne
32.4bhp/L 24.1kW/L 32.8PS/L
44.4ft/sec 13.5m/sec
21.4mph 34.4kmh/1000rpm
Petrol 4-stroke piston
2780cc 169.6cu in
In-line 6
Compression ratio: 8.3:1
Bore: 76.2mm 3.0in
Stroke: 101.6mm 4.0in
Valve type/No: Side 12
Transmission: Manual
No. of forward speeds: 3
Wheels driven: Rear
Wheelbase: 275.6cm 108.5in
Track F: 145.8cm 57.4in
Track R: 143.8cm 56.6in
Length: 444.5cm 175.0in
Width: 181.4cm 71.4in
Height: 146.1cm 57.5in
Kerb weight: 1248.5kg 2750.0lb

4228 Studebaker

Lark 6
1960 USA
82.0mph 131.9kmh
0-50mph 80.5kmh: 12.0secs
0-60mph 96.5kmh: 17.9secs
0-1/4 mile: 21.0secs
90.0bhp 67.1kW 91.2PS
@ 4000rpm
145.0lbft 196.5Nm @ 2000rpm
69.5bhp/ton 68.4bhp/tonne
32.4bhp/L 24.1kW/L 32.8PS/L
44.4ft/sec 13.5m/sec
18.5mph 29.8kmh/1000rpm
Petrol 4-stroke piston
2780cc 169.6cu in
In-line 6 1 Carburettor
Compression ratio: 8.3:1
Bore: 76.2mm 3.0in
Stroke: 101.6mm 4.0in
Valve type/No: Side 12
Transmission: Manual
No. of forward speeds: 3
Wheels driven: Rear
Wheelbase: 275.6cm 108.5in
Track F: 145.8cm 57.4in
Track R: 143.8cm 56.6in
Length: 444.5cm 175.0in
Width: 181.4cm 71.4in
Height: 146.1cm 57.5in
Kerb weight: 1316.6kg 2900.0lb

4229 Studebaker

Lark V8
1960 USA
105.0mph 168.9kmh
0-50mph 80.5kmh: 7.8secs
0-60mph 96.5kmh: 10.5secs
0-1/4 mile: 17.8secs
180.0bhp 134.2kW 182.5PS
@ 4500rpm
260.0lbft 352.3Nm @ 2800rpm
128.0bhp/ton 125.9bhp/tonne
42.4bhp/L 31.6kW/L 43.0PS/L
40.6ft/sec 12.4m/sec
24.4mph 39.3kmh/1000rpm
Petrol 4-stroke piston
4248cc 259.2cu in
Vee 8 1 Carburettor
Compression ratio: 8.8:1
Bore: 90.4mm 3.6in
Stroke: 82.6mm 3.2in
Valve type/No: Overhead 16
Transmission: Automatic
No. of forward speeds: 3
Wheels driven: Rear
Wheelbase: 275.6cm 108.5in
Track F: 145.8cm 57.4in
Track R: 143.8cm 56.6in
Length: 444.5cm 175.0in
Width: 181.4cm 71.4in
Height: 146.1cm 57.5in
Kerb weight: 1430.1kg 3150.0lb

4230 Studebaker

Hawk 4-speed
1961 USA
115.0mph 185.0kmh
0-50mph 80.5kmh: 7.1secs
0-60mph 96.5kmh: 10.2secs
0-1/4 mile: 17.3secs

210.0bhp 156.6kW 212.9PS
@ 4500rpm
300.0lbft 406.5Nm @ 2800rpm
140.4bhp/ton 138.1bhp/tonne
44.3bhp/L 33.0kW/L 44.9PS/L
45.2ft/sec 13.8m/sec
26.8mph 43.1kmh/1000rpm
Petrol 4-stroke piston
4738cc 289.1cu in
Vee 8 1 Carburettor
Compression ratio: 8.8:1
Bore: 90.4mm 3.6in
Stroke: 91.9mm 3.6in
Valve type/No: Overhead 16
Transmission: Manual
No. of forward speeds: 4
Wheels driven: Rear
Wheelbase: 306.1cm 120.5in
Track F: 145.8cm 57.4in
Track R: 143.8cm 56.6in
Length: 518.2cm 204.0in
Width: 181.1cm 71.3in
Height: 141.0cm 55.5in
Ground clearance: 17.5cm 6.9in
Kerb weight: 1520.9kg 3350.0lb

4231 Studebaker

Lark 6
1961 USA
90.0mph 144.8kmh
0-50mph 80.5kmh: 10.2secs
0-60mph 96.5kmh: 14.0secs
0-1/4 mile: 19.2secs
112.0bhp 83.5kW 113.5PS
@ 4500rpm
154.0lbft 208.7Nm @ 2000rpm
86.2bhp/ton 84.8bhp/tonne
40.3bhp/L 30.0kW/L 40.8PS/L
50.0ft/sec 15.2m/sec
20.5mph 33.0kmh/1000rpm
Petrol 4-stroke piston
2780cc 169.6cu in
In-line 6 1 Carburettor
Compression ratio: 8.5:1
Bore: 76.2mm 3.0in
Stroke: 101.6mm 4.0in
Valve type/No: Overhead 12
Transmission: Manual
No. of forward speeds: 3
Wheels driven: Rear
Brakes F/R: Drum/Drum
Wheelbase: 275.6cm 108.5in
Track F: 145.8cm 57.4in
Track R: 143.8cm 56.6in
Length: 444.5cm 175.0in
Width: 181.4cm 71.4in
Height: 143.5cm 56.5in
Ground clearance: 15.5cm 6.1in
Kerb weight: 1321.1kg 2910.0lb

4232 Studebaker

Lark Cruiser
1961 USA
105.0mph 168.9kmh
0-50mph 80.5kmh: 7.4secs
0-60mph 96.5kmh: 10.0secs
0-1/4 mile: 17.2secs
210.0bhp 156.6kW 212.9PS
@ 4500rpm
300.0lbft 406.5Nm @ 2800rpm
139.8bhp/ton 137.5bhp/tonne
44.3bhp/L 33.0kW/L 44.9PS/L
45.2ft/sec 13.8m/sec
25.7mph 41.4kmh/1000rpm
Petrol 4-stroke piston
4738cc 289.1cu in
Vee 8 1 Carburettor
Compression ratio: 8.8:1
Bore: 90.5mm 3.6in
Stroke: 91.9mm 3.6in
Valve type/No: Overhead 16
Transmission: Automatic
No. of forward speeds: 3
Wheels driven: Rear
Brake system: PA
Wheelbase: 287.0cm 113.0in
Track F: 145.8cm 57.4in
Track R: 143.8cm 56.6in
Length: 454.7cm 179.0in
Width: 181.4cm 71.4in
Height: 143.5cm 56.5in
Ground clearance: 16.3cm 6.4in
Kerb weight: 1527.7kg 3365.0lb

4233 Studebaker

Avanti
1962 USA
117.0mph 188.3kmh
0-50mph 80.5kmh: 5.6secs
0-60mph 96.5kmh: 7.3secs
0-1/4 mile: 16.2secs
275.0bhp 205.1kW 278.8PS
@ 5200rpm
330.0lbft 447.2Nm @ 3500rpm
181.2bhp/ton 178.1bhp/tonne
64.7bhp/L 48.3kW/L 65.6PS/L
46.9ft/sec 14.3m/sec
19.5mph 31.4kmh/1000rpm
Petrol 4-stroke piston
4249cc 259.2cu in
Vee 8
Compression ratio: 9.0:1
Bore: 90.4mm 3.6in
Stroke: 82.6mm 3.2in
Valve type/No: Overhead 16
Transmission: Manual
No. of forward speeds: 4
Wheels driven: Rear
Wheelbase: 276.9cm 109.0in
Track F: 145.8cm 57.4in
Track R: 143.8cm 56.6in
Length: 488.7cm 192.4in
Width: 178.8cm 70.4in
Height: 136.9cm 53.9in
Ground clearance: 16.5cm 6.5in
Kerb weight: 1543.6kg 3400.0lb

4234 Studebaker

Hawk Gran Turismo
1962 USA
103.0mph 165.7kmh
0-50mph 80.5kmh: 8.5secs
0-60mph 96.5kmh: 11.4secs
0-1/4 mile: 18.2secs
225.0bhp 167.8kW 228.1PS
@ 4500rpm
305.0lbft 413.3Nm @ 3000rpm
142.8bhp/ton 140.4bhp/tonne
47.5bhp/L 35.4kW/L 48.2PS/L
45.2ft/sec 13.8m/sec
21.4mph 34.4kmh/1000rpm
Petrol 4-stroke piston
4736cc 289.0cu in
Vee 8 1 Carburettor
Compression ratio: 8.5:1
Bore: 90.4mm 3.6in
Stroke: 91.9mm 3.6in
Valve type/No: Overhead 16
Transmission: Manual
No. of forward speeds: 4
Wheels driven: Rear
Brake system: PA
Steering: PA
Wheelbase: 306.1cm 120.5in
Track F: 145.8cm 57.4in
Track R: 143.8cm 56.6in
Length: 518.2cm 204.0in
Width: 180.3cm 71.0in
Height: 138.9cm 54.7in
Ground clearance: 19.1cm 7.5in
Kerb weight: 1602.6kg 3530.0lb
Fuel: 68.1L 15.0gal 18.0galUS

4235 Studebaker

Lark Daytona
1962 USA
100.0mph 160.9kmh
0-50mph 80.5kmh: 9.4secs
0-60mph 96.5kmh: 12.9secs
0-1/4 mile: 18.9secs
180.0bhp 134.2kW 182.5PS
@ 4500rpm
260.0lbft 352.3Nm @ 2800rpm
114.2bhp/ton 112.3bhp/tonne
42.4bhp/L 31.6kW/L 43.0PS/L
40.6ft/sec 12.4m/sec
24.1mph 38.8kmh/1000rpm
Petrol 4-stroke piston
4248cc 259.2cu in
Vee 8 1 Carburettor
Compression ratio: 8.5:1
Bore: 90.4mm 3.6in
Stroke: 82.6mm 3.2in
Valve type/No: Overhead 16
Transmission: Automatic
No. of forward speeds: 3
Wheels driven: Rear
Wheelbase: 276.9cm 109.0in
Track F: 145.8cm 57.4in
Track R: 143.8cm 56.6in
Length: 467.4cm 184.0in
Width: 180.8cm 71.2in
Height: 147.6cm 58.1in
Ground clearance: 17.8cm 7.0in
Kerb weight: 1602.6kg 3530.0lb
Fuel: 68.1L 15.0gal 18.0galUS

4236 Studebaker

Avanti
1963 USA
120.0mph 193.1kmh
0-50mph 80.5kmh: 6.4secs
0-60mph 96.5kmh: 9.1secs
0-1/4 mile: 17.2secs
24.1mph 38.8kmh/1000rpm
Petrol 4-stroke piston
4739cc 289.1cu in
Vee 8 1 Carburettor
Compression ratio: 10.3:1
Bore: 90.4mm 3.6in
Stroke: 92.2mm 3.6in
Valve type/No: Overhead 16
Transmission: Automatic
No. of forward speeds: 3
Wheels driven: Rear
Brake system: PA
Brakes F/R: Disc/Drum
Steering: PA
Wheelbase: 276.9cm 109.0in
Track F: 145.8cm 57.4in
Track R: 143.8cm 56.6in
Length: 488.7cm 192.4in
Width: 178.8cm 70.4in
Height: 136.9cm 53.9in
Ground clearance: 16.5cm 6.5in
Kerb weight: 1584.5kg 3490.0lb
Fuel: 79.5L 17.5gal 21.0galUS

4237 Studebaker

Regal Wagonaire Supercharged
1963 USA
121.0mph 194.7kmh
0-50mph 80.5kmh: 5.6secs
0-60mph 96.5kmh: 7.8secs
0-1/4 mile: 16.2secs
280.0bhp 208.8kW 283.9PS
@ 5200rpm
330.0lbft 447.2Nm @ 3600rpm
157.0bhp/ton 154.4bhp/tonne
59.1bhp/L 44.1kW/L 59.9PS/L
50.6ft/sec 15.4m/sec
20.9mph 33.6kmh/1000rpm
Petrol 4-stroke piston
4736cc 289.0cu in supercharged
Vee 8 1 Carburettor
Compression ratio: 9.0:1
Bore: 90.4mm 3.6in
Stroke: 88.9mm 3.5in
Valve type/No: Overhead 16
Transmission: Automatic
No. of forward speeds: 3
Wheels driven: Rear
Brake system: PA
Brakes F/R: Disc/Drum
Steering: PA
Wheelbase: 287.0cm 113.0in
Track F: 145.8cm 57.4in
Track R: 143.8cm 56.6in
Length: 475.0cm 187.0in
Width: 180.8cm 71.2in
Height: 144.8cm 57.0in
Ground clearance: 15.0cm 5.9in
Kerb weight: 1813.7kg 3995.0lb
Fuel: 68.1L 15.0gal 18.0galUS

4238 Studebaker

Daytona R-4
1964 USA
132.0mph 212.4kmh
0-50mph 80.5kmh: 6.1secs
0-60mph 96.5kmh: 7.8secs
0-1/4 mile: 15.8secs
280.0bhp 208.8kW 283.9PS
@ 5000rpm
171.4bhp/ton 168.5bhp/tonne
56.1bhp/L 41.8kW/L 56.9PS/L
50.4ft/sec 15.3m/sec
22.0mph 35.4kmh/1000rpm
Petrol 4-stroke piston
4990cc 304.4cu in
Vee 8 2 Carburettor
Compression ratio: 12.0:1
Bore: 92.8mm 3.6in
Stroke: 92.1mm 3.6in
Valve type/No: Overhead 16
Transmission: Manual
No. of forward speeds: 4
Wheels driven: Rear
Steering: PA
Wheelbase: 276.9cm 109.0in
Track F: 145.8cm 57.4in
Track R: 143.8cm 56.6in
Length: 492.8cm 194.0in
Width: 181.6cm 71.5in
Height: 139.2cm 54.8in
Ground clearance: 13.5cm 5.3in
Kerb weight: 1661.6kg 3660.0lb
Fuel: 75.7L 16.6gal 20.0galUS

4239 Stutz

Roadster
1928 USA
80.0mph 128.7kmh
0-50mph 80.5kmh: 14.5secs
0-60mph 96.5kmh: 20.5secs
0-1/4 mile: 22.6secs
115.0bhp 85.8kW 116.6PS
@ 3600rpm
210.0lbft 284.6Nm @ 1500rpm
58.9bhp/ton 58.0bhp/tonne
23.5bhp/L 17.5kW/L 23.8PS/L
45.0ft/sec 13.7m/sec
19.9mph 32.0kmh/1000rpm
Petrol 4-stroke piston
4895cc 298.7cu in
In-line 8 1 Carburettor
Compression ratio: 5.0:1
Bore: 82.6mm 3.2in
Stroke: 114.3mm 4.5in
Valve type/No: Overhead 16
Transmission: Manual
No. of forward speeds: 3
Wheels driven: Rear
Brakes F/R: Drum/Drum
Wheelbase: 332.7cm 131.0in
Track F: 143.3cm 56.4in
Track R: 148.8cm 58.6in
Length: 482.6cm 190.0in
Width: 182.9cm 72.0in
Height: 182.9cm 72.0in
Ground clearance: 21.6cm 8.5in
Kerb weight: 1984.0kg 4370.0lb

4240 Stutz

36.4hp Saloon
1929 USA
72.0mph 115.8kmh
12.0mpg 10.0mpgUS 23.5L/100km
Petrol 4-stroke piston
5274cc 321.8cu in
In-line 8
Bore: 85.7mm 3.4in
Stroke: 114.3mm 4.5in
Transmission: Manual
No. of forward speeds: 4
Wheels driven: Rear
Brakes F/R: Drum/Drum
Wheelbase: 368.3cm 145.0in
Track F: 148.8cm 58.6in
Track R: 148.8cm 58.6in
Length: 520.7cm 205.0in
Width: 172.7cm 68.0in
Height: 175.3cm 69.0in
Kerb weight: 2288.2kg 5040.0lb
Fuel: 72.8L 16.0gal 19.2galUS

4241 Stutz

Straight Eight Saloon
1931 USA
77.5mph 124.7kmh
10.0mpg 8.3mpgUS 28.2L/100km
Petrol 4-stroke piston
5277cc 322.0cu in
In-line 8
Bore: 85.7mm 3.4in
Stroke: 114.3mm 4.5in
Transmission: Manual
No. of forward speeds: 4
Wheels driven: Rear
Brakes F/R: Drum/Drum
Wheelbase: 341.6cm 134.5in
Track F: 143.3cm 56.4in
Track R: 148.6cm 58.5in
Length: 510.5cm 201.0in
Width: 182.9cm 72.0in
Height: 172.7cm 68.0in
Kerb weight: 2237.3kg 4928.0lb
Fuel: 72.8L 16.0gal 19.2galUS

4242 Stutz

DV32 Sports Saloon
1932 USA
90.0mph 144.8kmh
10.0mpg 8.3mpgUS 28.2L/100km

Petrol 4-stroke piston
5277cc 322.0cu in
In-line 8
Bore: 85.7mm 3.4in
Stroke: 114.3mm 4.5in
Transmission: Manual
No. of forward speeds: 4
Wheels driven: Rear
Brakes F/R: Drum/Drum
Wheelbase: 341.6cm 134.5in
Track F: 143.3cm 56.4in
Track R: 148.6cm 58.5in
Length: 487.7cm 192.0in
Width: 182.9cm 72.0in
Height: 142.2cm 56.0in
Kerb weight: 2186.5kg 4816.0lb
Fuel: 72.8L 16.0gal 19.2galUS

4243 Subaru

360
1969 Japan
56.0mph 90.1kmh
0-50mph 80.5kmh: 36.7secs
0-1/4 mile: 27.4secs
25.0bhp 18.6kW 25.3PS
@ 5500rpm
25.0lbft 33.9Nm @ 4500rpm
57.1bhp/ton 56.2bhp/tonne
70.2bhp/L 52.4kW/L 71.2PS/L
36.1ft/sec 11.0m/sec
11.0mph 17.7kmh/1000rpm
33.6mpg 28.0mpgUS 8.4L/100km
Petrol 2-stroke piston
356cc 21.7cu in
In-line 2
Compression ratio: 6.5:1
Bore: 61.5mm 2.4in
Stroke: 60.0mm 2.4in
Transmission: Manual
No. of forward speeds: 4
Wheels driven: Rear
Brakes F/R: Drum/Drum
Steering: Rack & pinion
Wheelbase: 180.1cm 70.9in
Track F: 114.0cm 44.9in
Track R: 106.9cm 42.1in
Length: 299.5cm 117.9in
Width: 130.0cm 51.2in
Height: 134.9cm 53.1in
Kerb weight: 444.9kg 980.0lb
Fuel: 25.0L 5.5gal 6.6galUS

4244 Subaru

Star
1969 Japan
83.0mph 133.5kmh
0-50mph 80.5kmh: 12.5secs
0-60mph 96.5kmh: 18.8secs
0-1/4 mile: 21.2secs
62.0bhp 46.2kW 62.9PS
@ 6000rpm
62.9lbft 85.2Nm @ 3200rpm
87.3bhp/ton 85.9bhp/tonne
57.0bhp/L 42.5kW/L 57.8PS/L
39.3ft/sec 12.0m/sec
15.1mph 24.3kmh/1000rpm
33.4mpg 27.8mpgUS 8.5L/100km
Petrol 4-stroke piston
1088cc 66.4cu in
Flat 4 1 Carburettor
Compression ratio: 9.0:1
Bore: 76.0mm 3.0in
Stroke: 60.0mm 2.4in
Valve type/No: Overhead 8
Transmission: Manual
No. of forward speeds: 4
Wheels driven: Front
Springs F/R: Torsion bar/Torsion bar
Brake system: PA
Brakes F/R: Drum/Drum
Steering: Rack & pinion
Wheelbase: 241.8cm 95.2in
Track F: 122.4cm 48.2in
Track R: 120.9cm 47.6in
Length: 393.7cm 155.0in
Width: 148.1cm 58.3in
Height: 138.9cm 54.7in
Ground clearance: 18.0cm 7.1in
Kerb weight: 721.9kg 1590.0lb
Fuel: 36.0L 7.9gal 9.5galUS

4245 Subaru

Hapi Van 360
1971 Japan
25.0bhp 18.6kW 25.3PS
@ 5500rpm
25.0lbft 33.9Nm @ 4500rpm
46.7bhp/ton 45.9bhp/tonne
70.2bhp/L 52.4kW/L 71.2PS/L
36.1ft/sec 11.0m/sec
50.4mpg 42.0mpgUS 5.6L/100km
Petrol 2-stroke piston
356cc 21.7cu in
In-line 2
Compression ratio: 6.7:1
Bore: 61.5mm 2.4in
Stroke: 59.9mm 2.4in
Transmission: Manual
No. of forward speeds: 4
Wheels driven: Rear
Wheelbase: 175.0cm 68.9in
Track F: 112.0cm 44.1in
Track R: 108.0cm 42.5in
Length: 299.5cm 117.9in
Width: 129.5cm 51.0in
Height: 153.4cm 60.4in
Ground clearance: 18.5cm 7.3in
Kerb weight: 544.8kg 1200.0lb

4246 Subaru

FF-1 1300
1972 Japan
93.0mph 149.6kmh
0-50mph 80.5kmh: 10.4secs
0-60mph 96.5kmh: 14.7secs
0-1/4 mile: 19.7secs
80.0bhp 59.7kW 81.1PS
@ 6400rpm
73.0lbft 98.9Nm @ 4000rpm
108.6bhp/ton 106.8bhp/tonne
63.1bhp/L 47.1kW/L 64.0PS/L
42.0ft/sec 12.8m/sec
15.4mph 24.8kmh/1000rpm
34.8mpg 29.0mpgUS 8.1L/100km
Petrol 4-stroke piston
1267cc 77.3cu in
Flat 4
Compression ratio: 9.0:1
Bore: 82.0mm 3.2in
Stroke: 60.0mm 2.4in
Valve type/No: Overhead 8
Transmission: Manual
No. of forward speeds: 4
Wheels driven: Front
Brakes F/R: Drum/Drum
Steering: Rack & pinion
Wheelbase: 242.1cm 95.3in
Track F: 122.4cm 48.2in
Track R: 120.4cm 47.4in
Length: 392.9cm 154.7in
Width: 148.1cm 58.3in
Height: 138.9cm 54.7in
Kerb weight: 749.1kg 1650.0lb
Fuel: 36.0L 7.9gal 9.5galUS

4247 Subaru

1300 GL Coupe
1973 Japan
93.0mph 149.6kmh
0-50mph 80.5kmh: 11.1secs
0-60mph 96.5kmh: 15.6secs
0-1/4 mile: 20.4secs
80.0bhp 59.7kW 81.1PS
@ 6400rpm
70.0lbft 94.9Nm @ 4000rpm
100.1bhp/ton 98.4bhp/tonne
63.1bhp/L 47.1kW/L 64.0PS/L
42.0ft/sec 12.8m/sec
16.1mph 25.9kmh/1000rpm
32.4mpg 27.0mpgUS 8.7L/100km
Petrol 4-stroke piston
1267cc 77.3cu in
Flat 4 1 Carburettor
Compression ratio: 9.0:1
Bore: 82.0mm 3.2in
Stroke: 60.0mm 2.4in
Valve type/No: Overhead 8
Transmission: Manual
No. of forward speeds: 4
Wheels driven: Front
Springs F/R: Coil/Torsion bar
Brakes F/R: Disc/Drum
Steering: Rack & pinion
Wheelbase: 245.4cm 96.6in
Track F: 126.0cm 49.6in
Track R: 120.4cm 47.4in
Length: 404.1cm 159.1in
Width: 150.4cm 59.2in
Height: 134.1cm 52.8in
Ground clearance: 16.5cm 6.5in
Kerb weight: 812.7kg 1790.0lb
Fuel: 50.0L 11.0gal 13.2galUS

4248 Subaru

1400 DL
1973 Japan
0-60mph 96.5kmh: 16.2secs
0-1/4 mile: 20.5secs
61.0bhp 45.5kW 61.8PS
@ 5600rpm
69.0lbft 93.5Nm @ 3600rpm
69.2bhp/ton 68.0bhp/tonne
44.8bhp/L 33.4kW/L 45.4PS/L
31.8mpg 26.5mpgUS 8.9L/100km
Petrol 4-stroke piston
1361cc 83.0cu in
Flat 4
Valve type/No: Overhead 8
Transmission: Manual
No. of forward speeds: 4
Wheels driven: Front
Brakes F/R: Disc/Drum
Wheelbase: 245.4cm 96.6in
Length: 404.6cm 159.3in
Width: 150.4cm 59.2in
Height: 141.0cm 55.5in
Kerb weight: 896.6kg 1975.0lb

4249 Subaru

DL
1975 Japan
0-60mph 96.5kmh: 16.0secs
0-1/4 mile: 20.6secs
80.0bhp 59.7kW 81.1PS
@ 6400rpm
70.0lbft 94.9Nm @ 4000rpm
90.0bhp/ton 88.5bhp/tonne
58.8bhp/L 43.8kW/L 59.6PS/L
42.0ft/sec 12.8m/sec
31.8mpg 26.5mpgUS 8.9L/100km
Petrol 4-stroke piston
1361cc 83.0cu in
Flat 4 1 Carburettor
Compression ratio: 9.0:1
Bore: 85.0mm 3.3in
Stroke: 60.0mm 2.4in
Valve type/No: Overhead 8
Transmission: Manual
No. of forward speeds: 4
Wheels driven: Front
Wheelbase: 245.4cm 96.6in
Track F: 127.5cm 50.2in
Track R: 121.9cm 48.0in
Length: 417.6cm 164.4in
Width: 150.4cm 59.2in
Height: 138.4cm 54.5in
Ground clearance: 17.0cm 6.7in
Kerb weight: 903.5kg 1990.0lb
Fuel: 50.0L 11.0gal 13.2galUS

4250 Subaru

4WD Station Wagon
1976 Japan
83.0mph 133.5kmh
0-50mph 80.5kmh: 15.3secs
0-60mph 96.5kmh: 23.3secs
0-1/4 mile: 22.6secs
56.0bhp 41.8kW 56.8PS
@ 5200rpm
68.0lbft 92.1Nm @ 2400rpm
55.0bhp/ton 54.1bhp/tonne
41.1bhp/L 30.7kW/L 41.7PS/L
34.1ft/sec 10.4m/sec
20.9mph 33.6kmh/1000rpm
25.8mpg 21.5mpgUS 10.9L/100km
Petrol 4-stroke piston
1361cc 83.0cu in
Flat 4 1 Carburettor
Compression ratio: 8.5:1
Bore: 85.0mm 3.3in
Stroke: 60.0mm 2.4in
Valve type/No: Overhead 8
Transmission: Manual
No. of forward speeds: 4
Wheels driven: 4-wheel drive
Springs F/R: Coil/Torsion bar
Brake system: PA
Brakes F/R: Disc/Drum
Steering: Rack & pinion
Wheelbase: 244.1cm 96.1in
Track F: 125.5cm 49.4in
Track R: 120.4cm 47.4in
Length: 403.1cm 158.7in
Width: 150.1cm 59.1in
Height: 146.1cm 57.5in
Ground clearance: 19.1cm 7.5in
Kerb weight: 1035.1kg 2280.0lb
Fuel: 45.0L 9.9gal 11.9galUS

4251 Subaru

1600 4WD Estate
1977 Japan
88.0mph 141.6kmh
0-50mph 80.5kmh: 11.4secs
0-60mph 96.5kmh: 16.7secs
0-1/4 mile: 20.7secs
0-1km: 39.5secs
68.0bhp 50.7kW 68.9PS
@ 5200rpm
82.5lbft 111.8Nm @ 2400rpm
69.7bhp/ton 68.6bhp/tonne
42.6bhp/L 31.8kW/L 43.2PS/L
34.1ft/sec 10.4m/sec
16.3mph 26.2kmh/1000rpm
28.8mpg 24.0mpgUS 9.8L/100km
Petrol 4-stroke piston
1595cc 97.3cu in
Flat 4 1 Carburettor
Compression ratio: 8.5:1
Bore: 92.0mm 3.6in
Stroke: 60.0mm 2.4in
Valve type/No: Overhead 8
Transmission: Manual
No. of forward speeds: 4
Wheels driven: 4-wheel engageable
Springs F/R: Coil/Torsion bar
Brake system: PA
Brakes F/R: Disc/Drum
Steering: Rack & pinion
Wheelbase: 245.1cm 96.5in
Track F: 126.5cm 49.8in
Track R: 121.4cm 47.8in
Length: 402.6cm 158.5in
Width: 154.9cm 61.0in
Height: 144.0cm 56.7in
Ground clearance: 20.1cm 7.9in
Kerb weight: 991.5kg 2184.0lb
Fuel: 45.0L 9.9gal 11.9galUS

4252 Subaru

1600 Coupe
1978 Japan
101.0mph 162.5kmh
0-50mph 80.5kmh: 9.1secs
0-60mph 96.5kmh: 13.4secs
0-1/4 mile: 19.3secs
0-1km: 36.4secs
70.0bhp 52.2kW 71.0PS
@ 5200rpm
83.2lbft 112.7Nm @ 2400rpm
84.1bhp/ton 82.7bhp/tonne
43.9bhp/L 32.7kW/L 44.5PS/L
34.1ft/sec 10.4m/sec
16.8mph 27.0kmh/1000rpm
32.2mpg 26.8mpgUS 8.8L/100km
Petrol 4-stroke piston
1595cc 97.3cu in
Flat 4 1 Carburettor
Compression ratio: 8.5:1
Bore: 92.0mm 3.6in
Stroke: 60.0mm 2.4in
Valve type/No: Overhead 8
Transmission: Manual
No. of forward speeds: 4
Wheels driven: Front
Springs F/R: Coil/Torsion bar
Brake system: PA
Brakes F/R: Disc/Drum
Steering: Rack & pinion
Wheelbase: 246.1cm 96.9in
Track F: 127.5cm 50.2in
Track R: 126.0cm 49.6in
Length: 400.6cm 157.7in
Width: 154.9cm 61.0in
Height: 134.9cm 53.1in
Ground clearance: 16.5cm 6.5in
Kerb weight: 846.3kg 1864.0lb
Fuel: 50.0L 11.0gal 13.2galUS

4253 Subaru

DL
1978 Japan
93.0mph 149.6kmh
0-50mph 80.5kmh: 8.5secs
0-60mph 96.5kmh: 12.3secs
0-1/4 mile: 19.2secs
67.0bhp 50.0kW 67.9PS
@ 5200rpm
81.0lbft 109.8Nm @ 2400rpm
72.0bhp/ton 70.8bhp/tonne
42.0bhp/L 31.3kW/L 42.6PS/L
34.1ft/sec 10.4m/sec
23.2mph 37.3kmh/1000rpm
36.0mpg 30.0mpgUS 7.8L/100km
Petrol 4-stroke piston
1595cc 97.3cu in

Flat 4
Compression ratio: 8.5:1
Bore: 91.9mm 3.6in
Stroke: 59.9mm 2.4in
Valve type/No: Overhead 8
Transmission: Manual
No. of forward speeds: 5
Wheels driven: Front
Springs F/R: Coil/Torsion bar
Brake system: PA
Brakes F/R: Disc/Drum
Steering: Rack & pinion
Wheelbase: 246.1cm 96.9in
Track F: 127.5cm 50.2in
Track R: 126.0cm 49.6in
Length: 417.1cm 164.2in
Width: 154.9cm 61.0in
Height: 113.5cm 44.7in
Kerb weight: 946.6kg 2085.0lb
Fuel: 50.0L 11.0gal 13.2galUS

4254 Subaru

DL-5
1980 Japan
91.0mph 146.4kmh
0-60mph 96.5kmh: 13.4secs
0-1/4 mile: 19.2secs
67.0bhp 50.0kW 67.9PS
@ 4800rpm
81.0lbft 109.8Nm @ 2800rpm
72.1bhp/ton 70.9bhp/tonne
42.0bhp/L 31.3kW/L 42.6PS/L
31.5ft/sec 9.6m/sec
24.5mph 39.4kmh/1000rpm
31.8mpg 26.5mpgUS 8.9L/100km
Petrol 4-stroke piston
1595cc 97.3cu in
Flat 4 1 Carburettor
Compression ratio: 8.5:1
Bore: 91.9mm 3.6in
Stroke: 59.9mm 2.4in
Valve type/No: Overhead 8
Transmission: Manual
No. of forward speeds: 5
Wheels driven: Front
Springs F/R: Coil/Torsion bar
Brake system: PA
Brakes F/R: Disc/Drum
Steering: Rack & pinion
Wheelbase: 246.1cm 96.9in
Track F: 133.1cm 52.4in
Track R: 134.6cm 53.0in
Length: 424.9cm 167.3in
Width: 161.0cm 63.4in
Height: 135.1cm 53.2in
Ground clearance: 16.5cm 6.5in
Kerb weight: 944.3kg 2080.0lb
Fuel: 50.0L 11.0gal 13.2galUS

4255 Subaru

1800 4WD Estate
1981 Japan
91.0mph 146.4kmh
0-50mph 80.5kmh: 11.0secs
0-60mph 96.5kmh: 16.3secs
0-1/4 mile: 20.5secs
0-1km: 38.9secs
78.9bhp 58.8kW 80.0PS
@ 5200rpm
97.6lbft 132.2Nm @ 2400rpm
72.1bhp/ton 70.9bhp/tonne
44.3bhp/L 33.0kW/L 44.9PS/L
38.1ft/sec 11.6m/sec
19.1mph 30.7kmh/1000rpm
28.1mpg 23.4mpgUS 10.1L/100km
Petrol 4-stroke piston
1781cc 108.7cu in
Flat 4 1 Carburettor
Compression ratio: 8.7:1
Bore: 92.0mm 3.6in
Stroke: 67.0mm 2.6in
Valve type/No: Overhead 8
Transmission: Manual
No. of forward speeds: 4
Wheels driven: 4-wheel engageable
Springs F/R: Coil/Torsion bar
Brake system: PA
Brakes F/R: Disc/Disc
Steering: Rack & pinion
Wheelbase: 244.3cm 96.2in
Track F: 133.4cm 52.5in
Track R: 136.4cm 53.7in
Length: 427.5cm 168.3in
Width: 162.1cm 63.8in
Height: 144.5cm 56.9in
Ground clearance: 20.8cm 8.2in
Kerb weight: 1112.3kg 2450.0lb
Fuel: 45.0L 9.9gal 11.9galUS

4256 Subaru

GL
1982 Japan
95.0mph 152.9kmh
0-50mph 80.5kmh: 10.0secs
0-60mph 96.5kmh: 14.8secs
0-1/4 mile: 19.7secs
71.0bhp 52.9kW 72.0PS
@ 4400rpm
94.0lbft 127.4Nm @ 2400rpm
71.6bhp/ton 70.4bhp/tonne
39.9bhp/L 29.7kW/L 40.4PS/L
32.3ft/sec 9.8m/sec
24.0mph 38.6kmh/1000rpm
31.2mpg 26.0mpgUS 9.0L/100km
Petrol 4-stroke piston
1781cc 108.7cu in
Flat 4 1 Carburettor
Compression ratio: 8.7:1
Bore: 91.9mm 3.6in
Stroke: 67.0mm 2.6in
Valve type/No: Overhead 8
Transmission: Manual
No. of forward speeds: 5
Wheels driven: Front
Springs F/R: Coil/Torsion bar
Brake system: PA
Brakes F/R: Disc/Drum
Steering: Rack & pinion
Wheelbase: 246.1cm 96.9in
Track F: 133.1cm 52.4in
Track R: 134.6cm 53.0in
Length: 427.0cm 168.1in
Width: 161.5cm 63.6in
Height: 138.9cm 54.7in
Kerb weight: 1007.9kg 2220.0lb
Fuel: 50.0L 11.0gal 13.2galUS

4257 Subaru

GL Turbo Traction Wagon
1983 Japan
96.0mph 154.5kmh
0-50mph 80.5kmh: 8.9secs
0-60mph 96.5kmh: 13.0secs
0-1/4 mile: 19.0secs
95.0bhp 70.8kW 96.3PS
@ 4800rpm
123.0lbft 166.7Nm @ 2000rpm
80.9bhp/ton 79.6bhp/tonne
53.3bhp/L 39.8kW/L 54.1PS/L
35.2ft/sec 10.7m/sec
21.4mph 34.4kmh/1000rpm
24.0mpg 20.0mpgUS 11.8L/100km
Petrol 4-stroke piston
1781cc 108.7cu in turbocharged
Flat 4 fuel injection
Compression ratio: 7.7:1
Bore: 92.0mm 3.6in
Stroke: 67.0mm 2.6in
Valve type/No: Overhead 8
Transmission: Automatic
No. of forward speeds: 3
Wheels driven: 4-wheel drive
Springs F/R: Coil/Torsion bar
Brake system: PA
Brakes F/R: Disc/Drum
Steering: Rack & pinion PA
Wheelbase: 245.6cm 96.7in
Track F: 134.9cm 53.1in
Track R: 136.9cm 53.9in
Length: 428.0cm 168.5in
Width: 162.1cm 63.8in
Height: 143.5cm 56.5in
Ground clearance: 20.6cm 8.1in
Kerb weight: 1194.0kg 2630.0lb
Fuel: 54.9L 12.1gal 14.5galUS

4258 Subaru

1.8 GTi
1985 Japan
105.0mph 168.9kmh
0-50mph 80.5kmh: 7.4secs
0-60mph 96.5kmh: 10.1secs
0-1/4 mile: 18.0secs
0-1km: 32.0secs
108.0bhp 80.5kW 109.5PS
@ 6000rpm
104.0lbft 140.9Nm @ 3600rpm
110.8bhp/ton 108.9bhp/tonne
60.6bhp/L 45.2kW/L 61.5PS/L
44.0ft/sec 13.4m/sec
21.7mph 34.9kmh/1000rpm
25.2mpg 21.0mpgUS 11.2L/100km
Petrol 4-stroke piston
1781cc 108.7cu in
Flat 4 fuel injection
Compression ratio: 10.0:1
Bore: 92.0mm 3.6in
Stroke: 67.0mm 2.6in
Valve type/No: Overhead 8
Transmission: Manual
No. of forward speeds: 5
Wheels driven: Front
Springs F/R: Coil/Coil
Brake system: PA
Brakes F/R: Disc/Drum
Steering: Rack & pinion PA
Wheelbase: 246.9cm 97.2in
Track F: 142.5cm 56.1in
Track R: 142.5cm 56.1in
Length: 436.9cm 172.0in
Width: 166.1cm 65.4in
Height: 138.4cm 54.5in
Ground clearance: 16.5cm 6.5in
Kerb weight: 991.5kg 2184.0lb
Fuel: 60.1L 13.2gal 15.9galUS

4259 Subaru

1.8 RX Turbo
1985 Japan
120.0mph 193.1kmh
0-50mph 80.5kmh: 7.1secs
0-60mph 96.5kmh: 9.9secs
0-1/4 mile: 18.1secs
0-1km: 31.3secs
134.0bhp 99.9kW 135.9PS
@ 5600rpm
144.0lbft 195.1Nm @ 2800rpm
122.7bhp/ton 120.6bhp/tonne
75.2bhp/L 56.1kW/L 76.3PS/L
41.1ft/sec 12.5m/sec
23.5mph 37.8kmh/1000rpm
22.6mpg 18.8mpgUS 12.5L/100km
Petrol 4-stroke piston
1781cc 108.7cu in turbocharged
Flat 4 fuel injection
Compression ratio: 7.7:1
Bore: 92.0mm 3.6in
Stroke: 67.0mm 2.6in
Valve type/No: Overhead 8
Transmission: Manual
No. of forward speeds: 5
Wheels driven: 4-wheel engageable
Springs F/R: Coil/Coil
Brake system: PA
Brakes F/R: Disc/Disc
Steering: Rack & pinion
Wheelbase: 246.9cm 97.2in
Track F: 142.5cm 56.1in
Track R: 142.5cm 56.1in
Length: 436.9cm 172.0in
Width: 166.1cm 65.4in
Height: 138.4cm 54.5in
Ground clearance: 16.5cm 6.5in
Kerb weight: 1110.9kg 2447.0lb
Fuel: 60.1L 13.2gal 15.9galUS

4260 Subaru

4WD Turbo
1985 Japan
101.0mph 162.5kmh
0-50mph 80.5kmh: 6.9secs
0-60mph 96.5kmh: 10.1secs
0-1/4 mile: 17.3secs
111.0bhp 82.8kW 112.5PS
@ 4800rpm
134.0lbft 181.6Nm @ 2800rpm
94.2bhp/ton 92.6bhp/tonne
62.3bhp/L 46.5kW/L 63.2PS/L
35.2ft/sec 10.7m/sec
24.0mph 38.6kmh/1000rpm
27.6mpg 23.0mpgUS 10.2L/100km
Petrol 4-stroke piston
1781cc 108.7cu in turbocharged
Flat 4 fuel injection
Compression ratio: 7.7:1
Bore: 92.0mm 3.6in
Stroke: 67.0mm 2.6in
Valve type/No: Overhead 8
Transmission: Manual
No. of forward speeds: 5
Wheels driven: 4-wheel engageable
Springs F/R: Gas/Gas
Brake system: PA
Brakes F/R: Disc/Disc
Steering: Rack & pinion PA
Wheelbase: 246.9cm 97.2in
Track F: 142.5cm 56.1in
Track R: 142.5cm 56.1in
Length: 436.9cm 172.0in
Width: 166.1cm 65.4in
Height: 133.4cm 52.5in
Ground clearance: 18.3cm 7.2in
Kerb weight: 1198.6kg 2640.0lb
Fuel: 59.8L 13.1gal 15.8galUS

4261 Subaru

4WD Turbo XT Coupe
1985 Japan
120.0mph 193.1kmh
0-50mph 80.5kmh: 6.9secs
0-60mph 96.5kmh: 9.7secs
0-1/4 mile: 17.2secs
111.0bhp 82.8kW 112.5PS
@ 4800rpm
134.0lbft 181.6Nm @ 2800rpm
94.7bhp/ton 93.1bhp/tonne
62.3bhp/L 46.5kW/L 63.2PS/L
35.2ft/sec 10.7m/sec
24.5mph 39.4kmh/1000rpm
25.2mpg 21.0mpgUS 11.2L/100km
Petrol 4-stroke piston
1781cc 108.7cu in turbocharged
Flat 4 fuel injection
Compression ratio: 7.7:1
Bore: 92.0mm 3.6in
Stroke: 67.0mm 2.6in
Valve type/No: Overhead 8
Transmission: Manual
No. of forward speeds: 5
Wheels driven: 4-wheel engageable
Springs F/R: Gas/Gas
Brake system: PA
Brakes F/R: Disc/Disc
Steering: Rack & pinion PA
Wheelbase: 246.6cm 97.1in
Track F: 143.5cm 56.5in
Track R: 142.5cm 56.1in
Length: 445.0cm 175.2in
Width: 168.9cm 66.5in
Height: 133.6cm 52.6in
Ground clearance: 18.0cm 7.1in
Kerb weight: 1191.7kg 2625.0lb
Fuel: 60.2L 13.2gal 15.9galUS

4262 Subaru

Turbo 4WD Estate
1985 Japan
112.0mph 180.2kmh
0-50mph 80.5kmh: 7.4secs
0-60mph 96.5kmh: 10.7secs
0-1/4 mile: 17.8secs
0-1km: 33.4secs
134.0bhp 99.9kW 135.9PS
@ 5600rpm
144.0lbft 195.1Nm @ 2800rpm
129.0bhp/ton 126.9bhp/tonne
75.2bhp/L 56.1kW/L 76.3PS/L
41.1ft/sec 12.5m/sec
22.9mph 36.8kmh/1000rpm
19.9mpg 16.6mpgUS 14.2L/100km
Petrol 4-stroke piston
1781cc 108.7cu in turbocharged
Flat 4 fuel injection
Compression ratio: 7.7:1
Bore: 92.0mm 3.6in
Stroke: 67.0mm 2.6in
Valve type/No: Overhead 8
Transmission: Manual
No. of forward speeds: 5
Wheels driven: 4-wheel engageable
Springs F/R: Gas/Gas
Brake system: PA
Brakes F/R: Disc/Disc
Steering: Rack & pinion PA
Wheelbase: 246.9cm 97.2in
Track F: 144.5cm 56.9in
Track R: 142.5cm 56.1in
Length: 440.9cm 173.6in
Width: 166.1cm 65.4in
Height: 149.1cm 58.7in
Ground clearance: 16.5cm 6.5in
Kerb weight: 1056.0kg 2326.0lb
Fuel: 60.1L 13.2gal 15.9galUS

4263 Subaru

XT Coupe DL
1985 Japan
115.0mph 185.0kmh
0-50mph 80.5kmh: 7.2secs
0-60mph 96.5kmh: 10.3secs
0-1/4 mile: 17.9secs
94.0bhp 70.1kW 95.3PS
@ 5200rpm
101.0lbft 136.9Nm @ 2800rpm
92.5bhp/ton 91.0bhp/tonne
20.7mph 33.3kmh/1000rpm
31.8mpg 26.5mpgUS 8.9L/100km
Petrol 4-stroke piston
Flat 4
Valve type/No: Overhead 8
Transmission: Manual
No. of forward speeds: 5

Wheels driven: Front
Brake system: PA
Brakes F/R: Disc/Drum
Steering: Rack & pinion
Wheelbase: 246.4cm 97.0in
Height: 125.5cm 49.4in
Ground clearance: 12.2cm 4.8in
Kerb weight: 1032.8kg 2275.0lb

4264 Subaru

XT Turbo Coupe
1985 Japan
120.0mph 193.1kmh
0-50mph 80.5kmh: 6.6secs
0-60mph 96.5kmh: 9.5secs
0-1/4 mile: 17.0secs
0-1km: 31.7secs
134.0bhp 99.9kW 135.9PS
@ 5600rpm
145.0lbft 196.5Nm @ 2800rpm
119.0bhp/ton 117.0bhp/tonne
75.2bhp/L 56.1kW/L 76.3PS/L
41.1ft/sec 12.5m/sec
23.3mph 37.5kmh/1000rpm
20.0mpg 16.7mpgUS 14.1L/100km
Petrol 4-stroke piston
1781cc 108.7cu in turbocharged
Flat 4 fuel injection
Compression ratio: 7.7:1
Bore: 92.0mm 3.6in
Stroke: 67.0mm 2.6in
Valve type/No: Overhead 8
Transmission: Manual
No. of forward speeds: 5
Wheels driven: 4-wheel engageable
Springs F/R: Gas/Gas
Brake system: PA
Brakes F/R: Disc/Disc
Steering: Rack & pinion PA
Wheelbase: 246.4cm 97.0in
Track F: 143.5cm 56.5in
Track R: 144.0cm 56.7in
Length: 445.0cm 175.2in
Width: 169.2cm 66.6in
Height: 129.3cm 50.9in
Kerb weight: 1145.4kg 2523.0lb
Fuel: 60.1L 13.2gal 15.9galUS

4265 Subaru

4WD 3-door Turbo Coupe
1986 Japan
114.0mph 183.4kmh
0-50mph 80.5kmh: 7.4secs
0-60mph 96.5kmh: 10.1secs
0-1/4 mile: 17.4secs
0-1km: 32.6secs
134.0bhp 99.9kW 135.9PS
@ 5600rpm
144.6lbft 195.9Nm @ 2800rpm
118.8bhp/ton 116.9bhp/tonne
75.2bhp/L 56.1kW/L 76.3PS/L
41.1ft/sec 12.5m/sec
19.3mph 31.1kmh/1000rpm
22.6mpg 18.8mpgUS 12.5L/100km
Petrol 4-stroke piston
1781cc 109.0cu in turbocharged
Flat 4 fuel injection
Compression ratio: 7.7:1
Bore: 92.0mm 3.6in
Stroke: 67.0mm 2.6in
Valve type/No: Overhead 8
Transmission: Automatic
No. of forward speeds: 3
Wheels driven: 4-wheel engageable
Springs F/R: Coil/Coil
Brake system: PA
Brakes F/R: Disc/Disc
Steering: Rack & pinion PA
Wheelbase: 246.5cm 97.0in
Length: 437.0cm 172.0in
Width: 166.0cm 65.4in
Height: 140.5cm 55.3in
Ground clearance: 17.8cm 7.0in
Kerb weight: 1146.6kg 2525.5lb
Fuel: 60.1L 13.2gal 15.9galUS

4266 Subaru

Hatchback
1986 Japan
0-60mph 96.5kmh: 13.2secs
0-1/4 mile: 19.0secs
69.0bhp 51.4kW 70.0PS
@ 4800rpm
86.0lbft 116.5Nm @ 2800rpm
74.1bhp/ton 72.9bhp/tonne
43.3bhp/L 32.3kW/L 43.9PS/L
31.5ft/sec 9.6m/sec
25.0mph 40.2kmh/1000rpm
34.3mpg 28.6mpgUS 8.2L/100km
Petrol 4-stroke piston
1595cc 97.3cu in
Flat 4 1 Carburettor
Compression ratio: 9.0:1
Bore: 92.0mm 3.6in
Stroke: 60.0mm 2.4in
Valve type/No: Overhead 8
Transmission: Manual
No. of forward speeds: 4
Wheels driven: Front
Springs F/R: Coil/Torsion bar
Brake system: PA
Brakes F/R: Disc/Drum
Steering: Rack & pinion
Wheelbase: 238.0cm 93.7in
Track F: 134.1cm 52.8in
Track R: 134.6cm 53.0in
Length: 398.5cm 156.9in
Width: 161.0cm 63.4in
Height: 136.4cm 53.7in
Kerb weight: 946.6kg 2085.0lb
Fuel: 50.0L 11.0gal 13.2galUS

4267 Subaru

Justy
1987 Japan
91.0mph 146.4kmh
0-50mph 80.5kmh: 9.2secs
0-60mph 96.5kmh: 13.0secs
0-1/4 mile: 19.1secs
0-1km: 34.0secs
67.0bhp 50.0kW 67.9PS
@ 5600rpm
70.8lbft 95.9Nm @ 3600rpm
87.0bhp/ton 85.6bhp/tonne
56.3bhp/L 42.0kW/L 57.1PS/L
50.9ft/sec 15.5m/sec
18.5mph 29.8kmh/1000rpm
32.9mpg 27.4mpgUS 8.6L/100km
Petrol 4-stroke piston
1189cc 73.0cu in
In-line 3 1 Carburettor
Compression ratio: 9.1:1
Bore: 78.0mm 3.1in
Stroke: 83.0mm 3.3in
Valve type/No: Overhead 9
Transmission: Manual
No. of forward speeds: 5
Wheels driven: 4-wheel engageable
Springs F/R: Coil/Coil
Brake system: PA
Brakes F/R: Disc/Drum
Steering: Rack & pinion
Wheelbase: 228.5cm 90.0in
Track F: 133.0cm 52.4in
Track R: 129.0cm 50.8in
Length: 353.5cm 139.2in
Width: 153.5cm 60.4in
Height: 139.0cm 54.7in
Ground clearance: 15.0cm 5.9in
Kerb weight: 783.0kg 1724.7lb
Fuel: 35.0L 7.7gal 9.2galUS

4268 Subaru

XT Turbo 4WD
1987 Japan
121.0mph 194.7kmh
0-50mph 80.5kmh: 6.2secs
0-60mph 96.5kmh: 8.7secs
0-1/4 mile: 16.9secs
0-1km: 31.0secs
134.0bhp 99.9kW 135.9PS
@ 5600rpm
145.0lbft 196.5Nm @ 2800rpm
119.6bhp/ton 117.6bhp/tonne
75.2bhp/L 56.1kW/L 76.3PS/L
41.1ft/sec 12.5m/sec
25.1mph 40.4kmh/1000rpm
25.8mpg 21.5mpgUS 10.9L/100km
Petrol 4-stroke piston
1781cc 109.0cu in turbocharged
Flat 4 fuel injection
Compression ratio: 7.7:1
Bore: 92.0mm 3.6in
Stroke: 67.0mm 2.6in
Valve type/No: Overhead 8
Transmission: Manual
No. of forward speeds: 5
Wheels driven: 4-wheel drive
Springs F/R: Gas/Gas
Brake system: PA
Brakes F/R: Disc/Disc
Steering: Rack & pinion PA
Wheelbase: 246.5cm 97.0in
Track F: 142.0cm 55.9in
Track R: 142.0cm 55.9in
Length: 449.0cm 176.8in
Width: 168.9cm 66.5in
Height: 133.0cm 52.4in
Ground clearance: 15.5cm 6.1in
Kerb weight: 1139.0kg 2508.8lb
Fuel: 60.1L 13.2gal 15.9galUS

4269 Subaru

4WD Turbo Estate
1988 Japan
116.0mph 186.6kmh
0-50mph 80.5kmh: 6.2secs
0-60mph 96.5kmh: 8.5secs
0-1/4 mile: 16.5secs
0-1km: 31.1secs
134.0bhp 99.9kW 135.9PS
@ 5600rpm
134.3lbft 182.0Nm @ 2800rpm
117.1bhp/ton 115.1bhp/tonne
75.2bhp/L 56.1kW/L 76.3PS/L
41.1ft/sec 12.5m/sec
23.6mph 38.0kmh/1000rpm
19.9mpg 16.6mpgUS 14.2L/100km
Petrol 4-stroke piston
1781cc 109.0cu in turbocharged
Flat 4 fuel injection
Compression ratio: 7.7:1
Bore: 92.0mm 3.6in
Stroke: 67.0mm 2.6in
Valve type/No: Overhead 8
Transmission: Manual
No. of forward speeds: 5
Wheels driven: 4-wheel drive
Springs F/R: Gas/Gas
Brake system: PA
Brakes F/R: Disc/Disc
Steering: Rack & pinion PA
Wheelbase: 246.0cm 96.9in
Track F: 141.0cm 55.5in
Track R: 142.5cm 56.1in
Length: 441.0cm 173.6in
Width: 166.0cm 65.4in
Height: 149.0cm 58.7in
Ground clearance: 16.5cm 6.5in
Kerb weight: 1164.0kg 2563.9lb
Fuel: 60.1L 13.2gal 15.9galUS

4270 Subaru

Justy 4WD GL
1988 Japan
0-60mph 96.5kmh: 12.0secs
68.0bhp 50.7kW 68.9PS
@ 5200rpm
70.0lbft 94.9Nm @ 3600rpm
84.9bhp/ton 83.4bhp/tonne
57.2bhp/L 42.6kW/L 58.0PS/L
47.2ft/sec 14.4m/sec
35.9mpg 29.9mpgUS 7.9L/100km
Petrol 4-stroke piston
1189cc 72.5cu in
In-line 3 1 Carburettor
Compression ratio: 9.1:1
Bore: 78.0mm 3.1in
Stroke: 83.0mm 3.3in
Valve type/No: Overhead 9
Transmission: Manual
No. of forward speeds: 5
Wheels driven: 4-wheel engageable
Springs F/R: Coil/Coil
Brakes F/R: Disc/Disc
Steering: Rack & pinion
Wheelbase: 228.6cm 90.0in
Track F: 133.1cm 52.4in
Track R: 129.0cm 50.8in
Length: 353.6cm 139.2in
Width: 153.4cm 60.4in
Height: 138.9cm 54.7in
Kerb weight: 814.9kg 1795.0lb
Fuel: 34.8L 7.6gal 9.2galUS

4271 Subaru

Justy GL
1988 Japan
0-60mph 96.5kmh: 11.1secs
0-1/4 mile: 18.2secs
66.0bhp 49.2kW 66.9PS
@ 5200rpm
70.0lbft 94.9Nm @ 3600rpm
88.0bhp/ton 86.5bhp/tonne
55.5bhp/L 41.4kW/L 56.3PS/L
47.2ft/sec 14.4m/sec
35.4mpg 29.5mpgUS 8.0L/100km
Petrol 4-stroke piston
1189cc 72.5cu in
In-line 3 1 Carburettor
Compression ratio: 9.1:1
Bore: 78.0mm 3.1in
Stroke: 83.0mm 3.3in
Valve type/No: Overhead 6
Transmission: Manual
No. of forward speeds: 5
Wheels driven: Front
Springs F/R: Coil/Coil
Brake system: PA
Brakes F/R: Disc/Drum
Steering: Rack & pinion
Wheelbase: 228.6cm 90.0in
Track F: 133.1cm 52.4in
Track R: 129.0cm 50.8in
Length: 353.6cm 139.2in
Width: 153.4cm 60.4in
Height: 138.9cm 54.7in
Kerb weight: 762.7kg 1680.0lb
Fuel: 34.8L 7.6gal 9.2galUS

4272 Subaru

XT6 4WD
1988 Japan
0-60mph 96.5kmh: 9.2secs
145.0bhp 108.1kW 147.0PS
@ 5200rpm
156.0lbft 211.4Nm @ 4000rpm
112.2bhp/ton 110.3bhp/tonne
54.3bhp/L 40.5kW/L 55.0PS/L
38.1ft/sec 11.6m/sec
29.3mpg 24.4mpgUS 9.6L/100km
Petrol 4-stroke piston
2672cc 163.0cu in
Flat 6 fuel injection
Compression ratio: 9.5:1
Bore: 92.0mm 3.6in
Stroke: 67.0mm 2.6in
Valve type/No: Overhead 12
Transmission: Manual
No. of forward speeds: 5
Wheels driven: 4-wheel drive
Springs F/R: Gas/Gas
Brake system: PA
Brakes F/R: Disc/Disc
Steering: Rack & pinion PA
Wheelbase: 246.4cm 97.0in
Track F: 143.5cm 56.5in
Track R: 144.0cm 56.7in
Length: 451.1cm 177.6in
Width: 168.9cm 66.5in
Height: 133.6cm 52.6in
Kerb weight: 1314.3kg 2895.0lb
Fuel: 60.2L 13.2gal 15.9galUS

4273 Subaru

Justy GL II 5-door 4WD
1989 Japan
93.0mph 149.6kmh
0-50mph 80.5kmh: 10.1secs
0-60mph 96.5kmh: 14.4secs
0-1/4 mile: 16.9secs
0-1km: 37.1secs
67.0bhp 50.0kW 67.9PS
@ 5600rpm
71.6lbft 97.0Nm @ 3600rpm
78.7bhp/ton 77.4bhp/tonne
56.3bhp/L 42.0kW/L 57.1PS/L
50.9ft/sec 15.5m/sec
17.6mph 28.3kmh/1000rpm
31.0mpg 25.8mpgUS 9.1L/100km
Petrol 4-stroke piston
1189cc 73.0cu in
In-line 3 1 Carburettor
Compression ratio: 9.1:1
Bore: 78.0mm 3.1in
Stroke: 83.0mm 3.3in
Valve type/No: Overhead 6
Transmission: Manual
No. of forward speeds: 5
Wheels driven: 4-wheel engageable
Springs F/R: Coil/Coil
Brake system: PA
Brakes F/R: Disc/Drum
Steering: Rack & pinion
Wheelbase: 228.5cm 90.0in
Track F: 133.0cm 52.4in
Track R: 129.0cm 50.8in
Length: 369.5cm 145.5in
Width: 153.5cm 60.4in
Height: 142.0cm 55.9in
Ground clearance: 17.5cm 6.9in
Kerb weight: 866.0kg 1907.5lb
Fuel: 35.0L 7.7gal 9.2galUS

4274 Subaru

Legacy FIA Record
1989 Japan
161.0mph 259.0kmh
0-50mph 80.5kmh: 4.5secs
0-60mph 96.5kmh: 6.2secs
0-1/4 mile: 14.6secs
235.0bhp 175.2kW 238.3PS
@ 6400rpm
190.4bhp/ton 187.2bhp/tonne
117.8bhp/L 87.9kW/L 119.5PS/L
52.4ft/sec 16.0m/sec
Petrol 4-stroke piston
1994cc 121.7cu in turbocharged
Flat 4 fuel injection
Compression ratio: 8.5:1
Bore: 92.0mm 3.6in
Stroke: 75.0mm 2.9in
Valve type/No: Overhead 16
Transmission: Manual
No. of forward speeds: 5
Wheels driven: 4-wheel drive
Springs F/R: Coil/Coil
Brake system: PA
Brakes F/R: Disc/Disc
Steering: Rack & pinion PA
Wheelbase: 258.1cm 101.6in
Track F: 146.1cm 57.5in
Track R: 145.0cm 57.1in
Length: 451.1cm 177.6in
Width: 168.9cm 66.5in
Height: 132.3cm 52.1in
Kerb weight: 1255.3kg 2765.0lb

4275 Subaru

XT6
1989 Japan
115.0mph 185.0kmh
0-50mph 80.5kmh: 7.0secs
0-60mph 96.5kmh: 9.7secs
0-1/4 mile: 17.2secs
145.0bhp 108.1kW 147.0PS
@ 5200rpm
156.0lbft 211.4Nm @ 4000rpm
112.2bhp/ton 110.3bhp/tonne
54.3bhp/L 40.5kW/L 55.0PS/L
38.1ft/sec 11.6m/sec
29.3mpg 24.4mpgUS 9.6L/100km
Petrol 4-stroke piston
2672cc 163.0cu in
Flat 6 fuel injection
Compression ratio: 9.5:1
Bore: 92.0mm 3.6in
Stroke: 67.0mm 2.6in
Valve type/No: Overhead 12
Transmission: Automatic
No. of forward speeds: 4
Wheels driven: 4-wheel drive
Springs F/R: Gas/Gas
Brake system: PA
Brakes F/R: Disc/Disc
Steering: Rack & pinion PA
Wheelbase: 246.4cm 97.0in
Track F: 143.5cm 56.5in
Track R: 144.0cm 56.7in
Length: 451.1cm 177.6in
Width: 168.9cm 66.5in
Height: 133.6cm 52.6in
Kerb weight: 1314.3kg 2895.0lb
Fuel: 60.2L 13.2gal 15.9galUS

4276 Subaru

Legacy 2.2 GX 4WD
1990 Japan
119.0mph 191.5kmh
0-50mph 80.5kmh: 7.8secs
0-60mph 96.5kmh: 10.8secs
0-1/4 mile: 18.0secs
0-1km: 33.3secs
134.0bhp 99.9kW 135.9PS
@ 6000rpm
139.5lbft 189.0Nm @ 4800rpm
106.5bhp/ton 104.7bhp/tonne
60.6bhp/L 45.2kW/L 61.4PS/L
49.2ft/sec 15.0m/sec
20.7mph 33.3kmh/1000rpm
25.0mpg 20.8mpgUS 11.3L/100km
Petrol 4-stroke piston
2212cc 135.0cu in
Flat 4 fuel injection
Compression ratio: 9.5:1
Bore: 96.9mm 3.8in
Stroke: 75.0mm 2.9in
Valve type/No: Overhead 16
Transmission: Manual
No. of forward speeds: 5
Wheels driven: 4-wheel drive
Springs F/R: Coil/Coil
Brake system: PA ABS
Brakes F/R: Disc/Disc
Steering: Rack & pinion PA
Wheelbase: 258.0cm 101.6in
Track F: 146.5cm 57.7in
Track R: 146.0cm 57.5in
Length: 451.0cm 177.6in
Width: 169.0cm 66.5in
Height: 140.0cm 55.1in
Ground clearance: 17.4cm 6.9in
Kerb weight: 1280.0kg 2819.4lb
Fuel: 60.1L 13.2gal 15.9galUS

4277 Subaru

Legacy 2.0 4Cam Turbo Estate
1991 Japan
134.0mph 215.6kmh
0-50mph 80.5kmh: 5.3secs
0-60mph 96.5kmh: 7.0secs
0-1/4 mile: 15.6secs
0-1km: 28.6secs
197.0bhp 146.9kW 199.7PS
@ 6000rpm
193.4lbft 262.0Nm @ 3600rpm
138.2bhp/ton 135.9bhp/tonne
98.8bhp/L 73.7kW/L 100.2PS/L
49.2ft/sec 15.0m/sec
23.4mph 37.7kmh/1000rpm
21.8mpg 18.2mpgUS 13.0L/100km
Petrol 4-stroke piston
1994cc 122.0cu in turbocharged
Flat 4 fuel injection
Compression ratio: 8.0:1
Bore: 92.0mm 3.6in
Stroke: 75.0mm 2.9in
Valve type/No: Overhead 32
Transmission: Manual
No. of forward speeds: 5
Wheels driven: 4-wheel drive
Springs F/R: Coil/Coil
Brake system: PA ABS
Brakes F/R: Disc/Disc
Steering: Rack & pinion PA
Wheelbase: 258.1cm 101.6in
Track F: 146.1cm 57.5in
Track R: 145.0cm 57.1in
Length: 462.0cm 181.9in
Width: 168.9cm 66.5in
Height: 138.9cm 54.7in
Ground clearance: 17.5cm 6.9in
Kerb weight: 1450.0kg 3193.8lb
Fuel: 60.1L 13.2gal 15.9galUS

4278 Subaru

Legacy Sports Sedan
1991 Japan
129.0mph 207.6kmh
0-50mph 80.5kmh: 6.0secs
0-60mph 96.5kmh: 8.1secs
0-1/4 mile: 16.2secs
160.0bhp 119.3kW 162.2PS
@ 5600rpm
181.0lbft 245.3Nm @ 2800rpm
113.8bhp/ton 111.9bhp/tonne
72.3bhp/L 53.9kW/L 73.3PS/L
45.9ft/sec 14.0m/sec
24.0mpg 20.0mpgUS 11.8L/100km
Petrol 4-stroke piston
2212cc 135.0cu in
Flat 4 fuel injection
Compression ratio: 8.0:1
Bore: 96.9mm 3.8in
Stroke: 75.0mm 2.9in
Valve type/No: Overhead 16
Transmission: Manual
No. of forward speeds: 5
Wheels driven: 4-wheel drive
Springs F/R: Coil/Coil
Brake system: PA ABS
Brakes F/R: Disc/Disc
Steering: Rack & pinion PA
Wheelbase: 258.1cm 101.6in
Track F: 146.6cm 57.7in
Track R: 146.6cm 57.7in
Length: 451.1cm 177.6in
Width: 168.9cm 66.5in
Height: 135.9cm 53.5in
Ground clearance: 11.4cm 4.5in
Kerb weight: 1430.1kg 3150.0lb
Fuel: 60.2L 13.2gal 15.9galUS

4279 Subaru

SVX
1992 Japan
143.0mph 230.1kmh
0-50mph 80.5kmh: 5.3secs
0-60mph 96.5kmh: 7.3secs
0-1/4 mile: 15.4secs
230.0bhp 171.5kW 233.2PS
@ 5400rpm
224.0lbft 303.5Nm @ 4400rpm
143.9bhp/ton 141.5bhp/tonne
69.3bhp/L 51.7kW/L 70.3PS/L
44.2ft/sec 13.5m/sec
21.0mpg 17.5mpgUS 13.4L/100km
Petrol 4-stroke piston
3318cc 202.4cu in
Flat 6 fuel injection
Compression ratio: 10.0:1
Bore: 96.9mm 3.8in
Stroke: 75.0mm 2.9in
Valve type/No: Overhead 24
Transmission: Automatic
No. of forward speeds: 4
Wheels driven: 4-wheel drive
Springs F/R: Coil/Coil
Brake system: PA ABS
Brakes F/R: Disc/Disc
Steering: Rack & pinion PA
Wheelbase: 261.1cm 102.8in
Track F: 149.9cm 59.0in
Track R: 148.1cm 58.3in
Length: 462.5cm 182.1in
Width: 177.0cm 69.7in
Height: 130.0cm 51.2in
Ground clearance: 13.5cm 5.3in
Kerb weight: 1625.3kg 3580.0lb
Fuel: 70.0L 15.4gal 18.5galUS

4280 Sunbeam

Weymann Saloon
1929 UK
70.0mph 112.6kmh
55.0bhp 41.0kW 55.8PS
@ 3600rpm
33.8bhp/ton 33.3bhp/tonne
18.9bhp/L 14.1kW/L 19.1PS/L
43.3ft/sec 13.2m/sec
16.0mpg 13.3mpgUS 17.7L/100km
Petrol 4-stroke piston
2916cc 177.9cu in
In-line 6 1 Carburettor
Compression ratio: 5.5:1
Bore: 75.0mm 2.9in
Stroke: 110.0mm 4.3in
Valve type/No: Overhead 12
Transmission: Manual
No. of forward speeds: 4
Wheels driven: Rear
Brakes F/R: Drum/Drum
Wheelbase: 316.2cm 124.5in
Track F: 139.7cm 55.0in
Track R: 139.7cm 55.0in
Length: 439.9cm 173.2in
Width: 176.5cm 69.5in
Height: 185.4cm 73.0in
Kerb weight: 1652.6kg 3640.0lb
Fuel: 61.4L 13.5gal 16.2galUS

4281 Sunbeam

20 Saloon
1935 UK
66.6mph 107.2kmh
0-50mph 80.5kmh: 24.0secs
0-60mph 96.5kmh: 37.0secs
17.0mpg 14.2mpgUS 16.6L/100km
Petrol 4-stroke piston
2762cc 168.5cu in
In-line 6
Bore: 73.0mm 2.9in
Stroke: 110.0mm 4.3in
Transmission: Manual
No. of forward speeds: 4
Wheels driven: Rear
Brakes F/R: Drum/Drum
Kerb weight: 1754.3kg 3864.0lb
Fuel: 63.7L 14.0gal 16.8galUS

4282 Sunbeam

Talbot 90
1951 UK
87.0mph 140.0kmh
0-50mph 80.5kmh: 13.6secs
0-60mph 96.5kmh: 20.2secs
0-1/4 mile: 21.4secs
70.0bhp 52.2kW 71.0PS
@ 4000rpm
57.6bhp/ton 56.6bhp/tonne
30.9bhp/L 23.0kW/L 31.3PS/L
48.1ft/sec 14.7m/sec
Petrol 4-stroke piston
2267cc 138.3cu in
In-line 4
Compression ratio: 7.5:1
Bore: 73.7mm 2.9in
Stroke: 110.0mm 4.3in
Transmission: Manual
No. of forward speeds: 4
Wheels driven: Rear
Wheelbase: 247.7cm 97.5in
Track F: 120.7cm 47.5in
Track R: 128.3cm 50.5in
Length: 425.5cm 167.5in
Width: 158.8cm 62.5in
Height: 158.8cm 62.5in
Ground clearance: 15.2cm 6.0in
Kerb weight: 1236.2kg 2723.0lb

4283 Sunbeam

Alpine
1954 UK
96.0mph 154.5kmh
0-50mph 80.5kmh: 12.9secs
0-60mph 96.5kmh: 18.9secs
0-1/4 mile: 21.1secs
80.0bhp 59.7kW 81.1PS
@ 4200rpm
124.0lbft 168.0Nm @ 1800rpm
60.4bhp/ton 59.4bhp/tonne
35.3bhp/L 26.3kW/L 35.8PS/L
50.5ft/sec 15.4m/sec
20.1mph 32.3kmh/1000rpm
24.6mpg 20.5mpgUS 11.5L/100km
Petrol 4-stroke piston
2267cc 138.3cu in
In-line 4
Compression ratio: 7.4:1
Bore: 81.0mm 3.2in
Stroke: 110.0mm 4.3in
Valve type/No: Overhead 8
Transmission: Manual
No. of forward speeds: 4
Wheels driven: Rear
Springs F/R: Coil/Leaf
Brakes F/R: Drum/Drum
Wheelbase: 247.7cm 97.5in
Track F: 120.7cm 47.5in
Track R: 128.3cm 50.5in
Length: 432.3cm 170.2in
Width: 158.8cm 62.5in
Height: 146.6cm 57.7in
Ground clearance: 17.0cm 6.7in
Kerb weight: 1347.5kg 2968.0lb
Fuel: 45.5L 10.0gal 12.0galUS

4284 Sunbeam

Alpine II
1954 UK
98.0mph 157.7kmh
0-50mph 80.5kmh: 10.3secs
0-60mph 96.5kmh: 14.8secs
0-1/4 mile: 19.7secs
80.0bhp 59.7kW 81.1PS
@ 5000rpm
94.0lbft 127.4Nm @ 3800rpm
80.8bhp/ton 79.4bhp/tonne
50.2bhp/L 37.5kW/L 50.9PS/L
41.7ft/sec 12.7m/sec
19.8mph 31.9kmh/1000rpm
20.6mpg 17.2mpgUS 13.7L/100km
Petrol 4-stroke piston
1592cc 97.1cu in
In-line 4
Compression ratio: 9.1:1
Bore: 81.5mm 3.2in
Stroke: 76.2mm 3.0in
Valve type/No: Overhead 8
Transmission: Manual with overdrive
No. of forward speeds: 6
Wheels driven: Rear
Springs F/R: Coil/Leaf
Brakes F/R: Disc/Drum
Wheelbase: 218.4cm 86.0in
Track F: 129.5cm 51.0in
Track R: 123.2cm 48.5in
Length: 394.5cm 155.3in
Width: 153.7cm 60.5in
Height: 135.9cm 53.5in
Ground clearance: 13.2cm 5.2in
Kerb weight: 1007.4kg 2219.0lb
Fuel: 40.9L 9.0gal 10.8galUS

4285 Sunbeam

Mk III
1955 UK
95.0mph 152.9kmh
0-50mph 80.5kmh: 12.6secs

0-60mph 96.5kmh: 18.4secs
0-1/4 mile: 21.4secs
80.0bhp 59.7kW 81.1PS
@ 4400rpm
122.0lbft 165.3Nm @ 2400rpm
57.4bhp/ton 56.4bhp/tonne
35.3bhp/L 26.3kW/L 35.8PS/L
52.9ft/sec 16.1m/sec
23.8mph 38.3kmh/1000rpm
20.8mpg 17.3mpgUS 13.6L/100km
Petrol 4-stroke piston
2267cc 138.3cu in
In-line 4
Compression ratio: 7.5:1
Bore: 81.0mm 3.2in
Stroke: 110.0mm 4.3in
Valve type/No: Overhead 8
Transmission: Manual with overdrive
No. of forward speeds: 5
Wheels driven: Rear
Springs F/R: Coil/Leaf
Brakes F/R: Drum/Drum
Wheelbase: 247.7cm 97.5in
Track F: 120.7cm 47.5in
Track R: 128.3cm 50.5in
Length: 428.0cm 168.5in
Width: 158.8cm 62.5in
Height: 154.2cm 60.7in
Ground clearance: 17.0cm 6.7in
Kerb weight: 1417.4kg 3122.0lb
Fuel: 45.5L 10.0gal 12.0galUS

4286 Sunbeam

Rapier
1956 UK
85.0mph 136.8kmh
0-50mph 80.5kmh: 14.9secs
0-60mph 96.5kmh: 21.7secs
0-1/4 mile: 22.4secs
62.0bhp 46.2kW 62.9PS
@ 5000rpm
87.8lbft 119.0Nm @ 3000rpm
58.3bhp/ton 57.4bhp/tonne
44.6bhp/L 33.3kW/L 45.2PS/L
41.7ft/sec 12.7m/sec
18.5mph 29.8kmh/1000rpm
34.0mpg 28.3mpgUS 8.3L/100km
Petrol 4-stroke piston
1390cc 84.8cu in
In-line 4
Compression ratio: 8.0:1
Bore: 76.2mm 3.0in
Stroke: 76.2mm 3.0in
Valve type/No: Overhead 8
Transmission: Manual with overdrive
No. of forward speeds: 6
Wheels driven: Rear
Springs F/R: Coil/Leaf
Brakes F/R: Drum/Drum
Wheelbase: 243.8cm 96.0in
Track F: 124.5cm 49.0in
Track R: 123.2cm 48.5in
Length: 407.7cm 160.5in
Width: 154.2cm 60.7in
Height: 147.3cm 58.0in
Ground clearance: 17.8cm 7.0in
Kerb weight: 1080.5kg 2380.0lb
Fuel: 45.5L 10.0gal 12.0galUS

4287 Sunbeam

Rapier
1957 UK
85.7mph 137.9kmh
0-50mph 80.5kmh: 13.8secs
0-60mph 96.5kmh: 20.6secs
0-1/4 mile: 21.3secs
67.0bhp 50.0kW 67.9PS
@ 5400rpm
74.0lbft 100.3Nm @ 3000rpm
62.4bhp/ton 61.4bhp/tonne
48.2bhp/L 35.9kW/L 48.9PS/L
45.0ft/sec 13.7m/sec
Petrol 4-stroke piston
1390cc 84.8cu in
In-line 4
Compression ratio: 8.0:1
Bore: 76.2mm 3.0in
Stroke: 76.2mm 3.0in
Valve type/No: Overhead 8
Transmission: Manual with overdrive
Wheels driven: Rear
Wheelbase: 243.8cm 96.0in
Track F: 124.5cm 49.0in
Track R: 123.2cm 48.5in
Kerb weight: 1091.9kg 2405.0lb

4288 Sunbeam

Rapier
1958 UK
87.0mph 140.0kmh
0-50mph 80.5kmh: 13.0secs
0-60mph 96.5kmh: 19.4secs
0-1/4 mile: 21.5secs
67.0bhp 50.0kW 67.9PS
@ 5400rpm
74.2lbft 100.5Nm @ 3000rpm
61.6bhp/ton 60.6bhp/tonne
48.2bhp/L 35.9kW/L 48.9PS/L
45.0ft/sec 13.7m/sec
18.5mph 29.8kmh/1000rpm
30.2mpg 25.1mpgUS 9.4L/100km
Petrol 4-stroke piston
1390cc 84.8cu in
In-line 4
Compression ratio: 8.0:1
Bore: 76.2mm 3.0in
Stroke: 76.2mm 3.0in
Valve type/No: Overhead 8
Transmission: Manual with overdrive
No. of forward speeds: 6
Wheels driven: Rear
Springs F/R: Coil/Leaf
Brakes F/R: Drum/Drum
Wheelbase: 243.8cm 96.0in
Track F: 124.5cm 49.0in
Track R: 123.2cm 48.5in
Length: 405.1cm 159.5in
Width: 154.9cm 61.0in
Height: 148.6cm 58.5in
Ground clearance: 17.8cm 7.0in
Kerb weight: 1105.9kg 2436.0lb
Fuel: 45.5L 10.0gal 12.0galUS

4289 Sunbeam

Rapier Series II
1958 UK
91.0mph 146.4kmh
0-50mph 80.5kmh: 13.1secs
0-60mph 96.5kmh: 20.2secs
0-1/4 mile: 21.1secs
73.0bhp 54.4kW 74.0PS
@ 5200rpm
81.2lbft 110.0Nm @ 3000rpm
68.1bhp/ton 67.0bhp/tonne
48.9bhp/L 36.4kW/L 49.5PS/L
43.3ft/sec 13.2m/sec
20.2mph 32.5kmh/1000rpm
31.5mpg 26.2mpgUS 9.0L/100km
Petrol 4-stroke piston
1494cc 91.1cu in
In-line 4
Compression ratio: 8.5:1
Bore: 79.0mm 3.1in
Stroke: 76.2mm 3.0in
Valve type/No: Overhead 8
Transmission: Manual with overdrive
No. of forward speeds: 6
Wheels driven: Rear
Springs F/R: Coil/Leaf
Brakes F/R: Drum/Drum
Wheelbase: 243.8cm 96.0in
Track F: 124.5cm 49.0in
Track R: 123.2cm 48.5in
Length: 412.8cm 162.5in
Width: 154.2cm 60.7in
Height: 147.3cm 58.0in
Ground clearance: 14.5cm 5.7in
Kerb weight: 1090.0kg 2401.0lb
Fuel: 45.5L 10.0gal 12.0galUS

4290 Sunbeam

Alpine
1959 UK
101.0mph 162.5kmh
0-50mph 80.5kmh: 10.6secs
0-60mph 96.5kmh: 14.0secs
0-1/4 mile: 19.8secs
78.0bhp 58.2kW 79.1PS
@ 5300rpm
89.5lbft 121.3Nm @ 3400rpm
78.4bhp/ton 77.1bhp/tonne
52.2bhp/L 38.9kW/L 52.9PS/L
44.2ft/sec 13.5m/sec
19.8mph 31.9kmh/1000rpm
25.5mpg 21.2mpgUS 11.1L/100km
Petrol 4-stroke piston
1494cc 91.1cu in
In-line 4
Compression ratio: 9.2:1
Bore: 79.0mm 3.1in
Stroke: 76.2mm 3.0in
Valve type/No: Overhead 8
Transmission: Manual with overdrive
No. of forward speeds: 6
Wheels driven: Rear
Springs F/R: Coil/Leaf
Brakes F/R: Disc/Drum
Steering: Recirculating ball
Wheelbase: 218.4cm 86.0in
Track F: 129.5cm 51.0in
Track R: 123.2cm 48.5in
Length: 394.2cm 155.2in
Width: 153.7cm 60.5in
Height: 130.8cm 51.5in
Ground clearance: 13.0cm 5.1in
Kerb weight: 1012.0kg 2229.0lb
Fuel: 40.9L 9.0gal 10.8galUS

4291 Sunbeam

Rapier III
1959 UK
93.0mph 149.6kmh
0-50mph 80.5kmh: 16.5secs
0-60mph 96.5kmh: 24.9secs
0-1/4 mile: 20.7secs
73.0bhp 54.4kW 74.0PS
@ 5400rpm
83.0lbft 112.5Nm @ 3500rpm
67.9bhp/ton 66.8bhp/tonne
48.9bhp/L 36.4kW/L 49.5PS/L
45.0ft/sec 13.7m/sec
19.1mph 30.7kmh/1000rpm
29.2mpg 24.3mpgUS 9.7L/100km
Petrol 4-stroke piston
1494cc 91.1cu in
In-line 4
Compression ratio: 9.2:1
Bore: 79.0mm 3.1in
Stroke: 76.2mm 3.0in
Valve type/No: Overhead 8
Transmission: Manual with overdrive
No. of forward speeds: 6
Wheels driven: Rear
Springs F/R: Coil/Leaf
Brakes F/R: Disc/Drum
Wheelbase: 243.8cm 96.0in
Track F: 131.3cm 51.7in
Track R: 123.2cm 48.5in
Length: 412.8cm 162.5in
Width: 154.2cm 60.7in
Height: 146.1cm 57.5in
Ground clearance: 14.5cm 5.7in
Kerb weight: 1093.2kg 2408.0lb
Fuel: 45.5L 10.0gal 12.0galUS

4292 Sunbeam

Alpine
1960 UK
95.0mph 152.9kmh
0-50mph 80.5kmh: 10.6secs
0-60mph 96.5kmh: 15.2secs
0-1/4 mile: 20.6secs
83.5bhp 62.3kW 84.7PS
@ 5300rpm
89.6lbft 121.4Nm @ 3600rpm
85.0bhp/ton 83.6bhp/tonne
55.9bhp/L 41.7kW/L 56.7PS/L
44.2ft/sec 13.5m/sec
17.9mph 28.8kmh/1000rpm
Petrol 4-stroke piston
1494cc 91.1cu in
In-line 4 1 Carburettor
Compression ratio: 9.2:1
Bore: 79.0mm 3.1in
Stroke: 76.2mm 3.0in
Valve type/No: Overhead 8
Transmission: Manual
No. of forward speeds: 4
Wheels driven: Rear
Wheelbase: 218.4cm 86.0in
Track F: 130.0cm 51.2in
Track R: 123.7cm 48.7in
Length: 393.7cm 155.0in
Width: 153.7cm 60.5in
Height: 131.3cm 51.7in
Kerb weight: 998.8kg 2200.0lb

4293 Sunbeam

Alpine Mk II
1961 UK
100.0mph 160.9kmh
0-50mph 80.5kmh: 9.9secs
0-60mph 96.5kmh: 14.0secs
0-1/4 mile: 19.3secs
85.5bhp 63.8kW 86.7PS
@ 5000rpm
94.0lbft 127.4Nm @ 3800rpm
89.1bhp/ton 87.6bhp/tonne
53.7bhp/L 40.0kW/L 54.4PS/L
41.7ft/sec 12.7m/sec
17.9mph 28.8kmh/1000rpm
Petrol 4-stroke piston
1592cc 97.1cu in
In-line 4 1 Carburettor
Compression ratio: 9.1:1
Bore: 81.5mm 3.2in
Stroke: 76.2mm 3.0in
Valve type/No: Overhead 8
Transmission: Manual
No. of forward speeds: 4
Wheels driven: Rear
Wheelbase: 218.4cm 86.0in
Track F: 130.0cm 51.2in
Track R: 123.7cm 48.7in
Length: 394.2cm 155.2in
Width: 153.7cm 60.5in
Height: 131.3cm 51.7in
Ground clearance: 13.2cm 5.2in
Kerb weight: 976.1kg 2150.0lb

4294 Sunbeam

Harrington Le Mans
1962 UK
105.8mph 170.2kmh
0-50mph 80.5kmh: 9.0secs
0-60mph 96.5kmh: 13.0secs
0-1/4 mile: 19.3secs
96.0bhp 71.6kW 97.3PS
@ 6000rpm
105.0lbft 142.3Nm @ 4500rpm
94.5bhp/ton 92.9bhp/tonne
60.3bhp/L 45.0kW/L 61.1PS/L
50.0ft/sec 15.2m/sec
19.7mph 31.7kmh/1000rpm
20.1mpg 16.7mpgUS 14.1L/100km
Petrol 4-stroke piston
1592cc 97.1cu in
In-line 4 2 Carburettor
Compression ratio: 9.0:1
Bore: 81.5mm 3.2in
Stroke: 76.2mm 3.0in
Valve type/No: Overhead 8
Transmission: Manual with overdrive
No. of forward speeds: 7
Wheels driven: Rear
Springs F/R: Coil/Leaf
Brake system: PA
Brakes F/R: Disc/Drum
Steering: Recirculating ball
Wheelbase: 218.4cm 86.0in
Track F: 129.5cm 51.0in
Track R: 123.2cm 48.5in
Length: 401.3cm 158.0in
Width: 153.7cm 60.5in
Height: 135.9cm 53.5in
Ground clearance: 13.0cm 5.1in
Kerb weight: 1032.8kg 2275.0lb
Fuel: 40.9L 9.0gal 10.8galUS

4295 Sunbeam

Le Mans
1962 UK
100.0mph 160.9kmh
0-50mph 80.5kmh: 9.3secs
0-60mph 96.5kmh: 12.2secs
0-1/4 mile: 19.0secs
103.0bhp 76.8kW 104.4PS
@ 6000rpm
105.0lbft 142.3Nm @ 4500rpm
103.5bhp/ton 101.7bhp/tonne
64.7bhp/L 48.2kW/L 65.6PS/L
50.0ft/sec 15.2m/sec
17.3mph 27.8kmh/1000rpm
Petrol 4-stroke piston
1592cc 97.1cu in
In-line 4
Compression ratio: 9.5:1
Bore: 81.5mm 3.2in
Stroke: 76.2mm 3.0in
Valve type/No: Overhead 8
Transmission: Manual
No. of forward speeds: 4
Wheels driven: Rear
Wheelbase: 218.4cm 86.0in
Track F: 130.0cm 51.2in
Track R: 123.7cm 48.7in
Length: 394.2cm 155.2in
Width: 153.7cm 60.5in
Height: 134.6cm 53.0in
Ground clearance: 13.2cm 5.2in
Kerb weight: 1012.4kg 2230.0lb

4296 Sunbeam

Alpine GT
1963 UK

98.0mph 157.7kmh
0-50mph 80.5kmh: 10.1secs
0-60mph 96.5kmh: 14.9secs
0-1/4 mile: 19.8secs
77.0bhp 57.4kW 78.1PS
@ 5000rpm
91.0lbft 123.3Nm @ 3500rpm
75.6bhp/ton 74.3bhp/tonne
48.4bhp/L 36.1kW/L 49.0PS/L
41.7ft/sec 12.7m/sec
21.9mph 35.2kmh/1000rpm
24.9mpg 20.7mpgUS 11.3L/100km
Petrol 4-stroke piston
1592cc 97.1cu in
In-line 4 1 Carburettor
Compression ratio: 9.0:1
Bore: 81.5mm 3.2in
Stroke: 76.2mm 3.0in
Valve type/No: Overhead 8
Transmission: Manual with overdrive
No. of forward speeds: 6
Wheels driven: Rear
Springs F/R: Coil/Leaf
Brake system: PA
Brakes F/R: Disc/Drum
Steering: Recirculating ball
Wheelbase: 218.4cm 86.0in
Track F: 130.0cm 51.2in
Track R: 130.8cm 51.5in
Length: 394.2cm 155.2in
Width: 153.7cm 60.5in
Height: 132.1cm 52.0in
Ground clearance: 11.7cm 4.6in
Kerb weight: 1036.0kg 2282.0lb
Fuel: 51.0L 11.2gal 13.5galUS

4297 Sunbeam

Alpine Series III
1963 UK
100.0mph 160.9kmh
0-50mph 80.5kmh: 12.0secs
0-60mph 96.5kmh: 18.1secs
0-1/4 mile: 22.2secs
80.2bhp 59.8kW 81.3PS
@ 5000rpm
92.0lbft 124.7Nm @ 3600rpm
82.2bhp/ton 80.8bhp/tonne
50.4bhp/L 37.6kW/L 51.1PS/L
41.7ft/sec 12.7m/sec
17.3mph 27.8kmh/1000rpm
Petrol 4-stroke piston
1592cc 97.1cu in
In-line 4 1 Carburettor
Compression ratio: 9.1:1
Bore: 81.5mm 3.2in
Stroke: 76.2mm 3.0in
Valve type/No: Overhead 8
Transmission: Manual
No. of forward speeds: 4
Wheels driven: Rear
Wheelbase: 218.4cm 86.0in
Track F: 130.0cm 51.2in
Track R: 123.7cm 48.7in
Length: 394.2cm 155.2in
Width: 153.7cm 60.5in
Height: 133.4cm 52.5in
Ground clearance: 13.2cm 5.2in
Kerb weight: 992.0kg 2185.0lb

4298 Sunbeam

Alpine GT Series IV Automatic
1964 UK
92.0mph 148.0kmh
0-50mph 80.5kmh: 13.3secs
0-60mph 96.5kmh: 18.8secs
0-1/4 mile: 22.5secs
82.0bhp 61.1kW 83.1PS
@ 5000rpm
93.4lbft 126.6Nm @ 3500rpm
81.5bhp/ton 80.2bhp/tonne
51.5bhp/L 38.4kW/L 52.2PS/L
41.7ft/sec 12.7m/sec
17.8mph 28.6kmh/1000rpm
20.9mpg 17.4mpgUS 13.5L/100km
Petrol 4-stroke piston
1592cc 97.1cu in
In-line 4 1 Carburettor
Compression ratio: 9.1:1
Bore: 81.5mm 3.2in
Stroke: 76.2mm 3.0in
Valve type/No: Overhead 8
Transmission: Automatic
No. of forward speeds: 3
Wheels driven: Rear
Springs F/R: Coil/Leaf
Brake system: PA
Brakes F/R: Disc/Drum
Steering: Recirculating ball
Wheelbase: 218.4cm 86.0in
Track F: 130.0cm 51.2in
Track R: 130.8cm 51.5in
Length: 396.7cm 156.2in
Width: 153.7cm 60.5in
Height: 137.2cm 54.0in
Ground clearance: 11.7cm 4.6in
Kerb weight: 1022.9kg 2253.0lb
Fuel: 51.2L 11.3gal 13.5galUS

4299 Sunbeam

Alpine Series IV
1964 UK
90.0mph 144.8kmh
0-50mph 80.5kmh: 12.3secs
0-60mph 96.5kmh: 16.5secs
0-1/4 mile: 21.0secs
90.0bhp 67.1kW 91.2PS
@ 5000rpm
93.0lbft 126.0Nm @ 3500rpm
88.4bhp/ton 86.9bhp/tonne
56.5bhp/L 42.1kW/L 57.3PS/L
41.7ft/sec 12.7m/sec
Petrol 4-stroke piston
1592cc 97.1cu in
In-line 4 1 Carburettor
Compression ratio: 9.1:1
Bore: 81.5mm 3.2in
Stroke: 76.2mm 3.0in
Valve type/No: Overhead 8
Transmission: Automatic
No. of forward speeds: 3
Wheels driven: Rear
Brakes F/R: Disc/Drum
Steering: Recirculating ball
Wheelbase: 218.4cm 86.0in
Track F: 129.5cm 51.0in
Track R: 123.2cm 48.5in
Length: 393.7cm 155.0in
Width: 153.7cm 60.5in
Height: 130.8cm 51.5in
Kerb weight: 1035.1kg 2280.0lb
Fuel: 51.1L 11.2gal 13.5galUS

4300 Sunbeam

Imp
1964 UK
76.0mph 122.3kmh
0-50mph 80.5kmh: 17.0secs
0-60mph 96.5kmh: 25.2secs
0-1/4 mile: 22.8secs
42.0bhp 31.3kW 42.6PS
@ 5000rpm
52.0lbft 70.5Nm @ 2800rpm
57.4bhp/ton 56.4bhp/tonne
48.0bhp/L 35.8kW/L 48.7PS/L
33.1ft/sec 10.1m/sec
15.0mph 24.1kmh/1000rpm
Petrol 4-stroke piston
875cc 53.4cu in
In-line 4 1 Carburettor
Compression ratio: 10.0:1
Bore: 68.1mm 2.7in
Stroke: 60.5mm 2.4in
Valve type/No: Overhead 8
Transmission: Manual
No. of forward speeds: 4
Wheels driven: Rear
Springs F/R: Coil/Coil
Brakes F/R: Drum/Drum
Steering: Rack & pinion
Wheelbase: 208.3cm 82.0in
Track F: 124.5cm 49.0in
Track R: 121.9cm 48.0in
Length: 353.1cm 139.0in
Width: 152.4cm 60.0in
Height: 137.2cm 54.0in
Ground clearance: 14.0cm 5.5in
Kerb weight: 744.6kg 1640.0lb
Fuel: 27.2L 6.0gal 7.2galUS

4301 Sunbeam

Tiger
1964 UK
118.0mph 189.9kmh
0-50mph 80.5kmh: 5.8secs
0-60mph 96.5kmh: 7.8secs
0-1/4 mile: 16.0secs
164.0bhp 122.3kW 166.3PS
@ 4400rpm
258.0lbft 349.6Nm @ 2200rpm
143.2bhp/ton 140.8bhp/tonne
38.5bhp/L 28.7kW/L 39.0PS/L
35.1ft/sec 10.7m/sec
24.3mph 39.1kmh/1000rpm
Petrol 4-stroke piston
4262cc 260.0cu in
Vee 8 1 Carburettor
Compression ratio: 8.8:1
Bore: 96.5mm 3.8in
Stroke: 72.9mm 2.9in
Valve type/No: Overhead 16
Transmission: Manual
No. of forward speeds: 4
Wheels driven: Rear
Springs F/R: Coil/Leaf
Brakes F/R: Disc/Drum
Steering: Rack & pinion
Wheelbase: 218.4cm 86.0in
Track F: 129.5cm 51.0in
Track R: 123.2cm 48.5in
Length: 396.2cm 156.0in
Width: 153.7cm 60.5in
Height: 130.8cm 51.5in
Ground clearance: 11.4cm 4.5in
Kerb weight: 1164.5kg 2565.0lb
Fuel: 51.1L 11.2gal 13.5galUS

4302 Sunbeam

Tiger 260
1965 UK
118.0mph 189.9kmh
0-50mph 80.5kmh: 6.8secs
0-60mph 96.5kmh: 9.5secs
0-1/4 mile: 17.0secs
164.0bhp 122.3kW 166.3PS
@ 4400rpm
258.0lbft 349.6Nm @ 2200rpm
138.9bhp/ton 136.6bhp/tonne
38.5bhp/L 28.7kW/L 39.0PS/L
35.1ft/sec 10.7m/sec
23.9mph 38.5kmh/1000rpm
16.9mpg 14.1mpgUS 16.7L/100km
Petrol 4-stroke piston
4261cc 260.0cu in
Vee 8 1 Carburettor
Compression ratio: 8.8:1
Bore: 96.5mm 3.8in
Stroke: 73.0mm 2.9in
Valve type/No: Overhead 16
Transmission: Manual
No. of forward speeds: 4
Wheels driven: Rear
Springs F/R: Coil/Leaf
Brake system: PA
Brakes F/R: Disc/Drum
Steering: Rack & pinion
Wheelbase: 218.4cm 86.0in
Track F: 131.3cm 51.7in
Track R: 123.2cm 48.5in
Length: 401.8cm 158.2in
Width: 153.7cm 60.5in
Height: 130.8cm 51.5in
Ground clearance: 12.7cm 5.0in
Kerb weight: 1200.4kg 2644.0lb
Fuel: 51.2L 11.2gal 13.5galUS

4303 Sunbeam

Alpine 1.7
1966 UK
96.0mph 154.5kmh
0-50mph 80.5kmh: 9.8secs
0-60mph 96.5kmh: 14.0secs
0-1/4 mile: 19.3secs
99.0bhp 73.8kW 100.4PS
@ 5500rpm
103.0lbft 139.6Nm @ 3700rpm
99.9bhp/ton 98.2bhp/tonne
57.4bhp/L 42.8kW/L 58.2PS/L
49.6ft/sec 15.1m/sec
16.1mph 25.9kmh/1000rpm
Petrol 4-stroke piston
1724cc 105.2cu in
In-line 4 2 Carburettor
Compression ratio: 9.1:1
Bore: 81.5mm 3.2in
Stroke: 82.6mm 3.2in
Valve type/No: Overhead 8
Transmission: Manual
No. of forward speeds: 4
Wheels driven: Rear
Springs F/R: Coil/Leaf
Brakes F/R: Disc/Drum
Steering: Recirculating ball
Wheelbase: 218.4cm 86.0in
Track F: 129.5cm 51.0in
Track R: 123.2cm 48.5in
Length: 394.5cm 155.3in
Width: 153.7cm 60.5in
Height: 130.8cm 51.5in
Ground clearance: 10.9cm 4.3in
Kerb weight: 1007.9kg 2220.0lb
Fuel: 50.0L 11.0gal 13.2galUS

4304 Sunbeam

Alpine Series V
1966 UK
100.0mph 160.9kmh
0-50mph 80.5kmh: 9.8secs
0-60mph 96.5kmh: 13.6secs
0-1/4 mile: 19.1secs
0-1km: 35.8secs
92.5bhp 69.0kW 93.8PS
@ 5500rpm
110.0lbft 149.1Nm @ 3700rpm
92.2bhp/ton 90.7bhp/tonne
53.6bhp/L 40.0kW/L 54.4PS/L
49.6ft/sec 15.1m/sec
20.3mph 32.7kmh/1000rpm
25.5mpg 21.2mpgUS 11.1L/100km
Petrol 4-stroke piston
1725cc 105.2cu in
In-line 4 2 Carburettor
Compression ratio: 9.2:1
Bore: 81.5mm 3.2in
Stroke: 82.5mm 3.2in
Valve type/No: Overhead 8
Transmission: Manual with overdrive
No. of forward speeds: 6
Wheels driven: Rear
Springs F/R: Coil/Leaf
Brake system: PA
Brakes F/R: Disc/Drum
Steering: Recirculating ball
Wheelbase: 218.4cm 86.0in
Track F: 131.3cm 51.7in
Track R: 123.2cm 48.5in
Length: 396.2cm 156.0in
Width: 153.7cm 60.5in
Height: 130.8cm 51.5in
Ground clearance: 11.7cm 4.6in
Kerb weight: 1019.7kg 2246.0lb
Fuel: 51.2L 11.2gal 13.5galUS

4305 Sunbeam

Imp Sport
1966 UK
90.0mph 144.8kmh
0-50mph 80.5kmh: 11.1secs
0-60mph 96.5kmh: 16.3secs
0-1/4 mile: 20.2secs
0-1km: 38.5secs
51.0bhp 38.0kW 51.7PS
@ 6100rpm
52.0lbft 70.5Nm @ 4300rpm
69.7bhp/ton 68.6bhp/tonne
58.3bhp/L 43.5kW/L 59.1PS/L
40.3ft/sec 12.3m/sec
15.1mph 24.3kmh/1000rpm
33.1mpg 27.6mpgUS 8.5L/100km
Petrol 4-stroke piston
875cc 53.4cu in
In-line 4 2 Carburettor
Compression ratio: 10.0:1
Bore: 68.0mm 2.7in
Stroke: 60.4mm 2.4in
Valve type/No: Overhead 8
Transmission: Manual
No. of forward speeds: 4
Wheels driven: Rear
Springs F/R: Coil/Coil
Brake system: PA
Brakes F/R: Drum/Drum
Steering: Rack & pinion
Wheelbase: 208.3cm 82.0in
Track F: 124.7cm 49.1in
Track R: 121.7cm 47.9in
Length: 358.1cm 141.0in
Width: 152.9cm 60.2in
Height: 138.4cm 54.5in
Ground clearance: 15.7cm 6.2in
Kerb weight: 743.6kg 1638.0lb
Fuel: 27.3L 6.0gal 7.2galUS

4306 Sunbeam

Stiletto
1967 UK
89.0mph 143.2kmh
0-50mph 80.5kmh: 12.0secs
0-60mph 96.5kmh: 17.6secs
0-1/4 mile: 20.5secs
0-1km: 38.8secs
51.0bhp 38.0kW 51.7PS
@ 6100rpm
52.0lbft 70.5Nm @ 4300rpm
69.1bhp/ton 68.0bhp/tonne
58.3bhp/L 43.5kW/L 59.1PS/L
40.3ft/sec 12.3m/sec
15.1mph 24.3kmh/1000rpm
32.4mpg 27.0mpgUS 8.7L/100km
Petrol 4-stroke piston

875cc 53.4cu in
In-line 4 2 Carburettor
Compression ratio: 10.0:1
Bore: 68.0mm 2.7in
Stroke: 60.4mm 2.4in
Valve type/No: Overhead 8
Transmission: Manual
No. of forward speeds: 4
Wheels driven: Rear
Springs F/R: Coil/Coil
Brake system: PA
Brakes F/R: Drum/Drum
Steering: Rack & pinion
Wheelbase: 208.3cm 82.0in
Track F: 124.7cm 49.1in
Track R: 121.7cm 47.9in
Length: 342.9cm 135.0in
Width: 152.9cm 60.2in
Height: 129.5cm 51.0in
Ground clearance: 15.7cm 6.2in
Kerb weight: 750.0kg 1652.0lb
Fuel: 27.3L 6.0gal 7.2galUS

4307 Sunbeam

Tiger II
1967 UK
122.0mph 196.3kmh
0-50mph 80.5kmh: 5.6secs
0-60mph 96.5kmh: 7.5secs
0-1/4 mile: 16.0secs
200.0bhp 149.1kW 202.8PS
@ 4400rpm
282.0lbft 382.1Nm @ 2400rpm
175.0bhp/ton 172.1bhp/tonne
42.2bhp/L 31.5kW/L 42.8PS/L
35.1ft/sec 10.7m/sec
23.9mph 38.5kmh/1000rpm
Petrol 4-stroke piston
4737cc 289.0cu in
Vee 8
Compression ratio: 9.3:1
Bore: 101.6mm 4.0in
Stroke: 73.0mm 2.9in
Valve type/No: Overhead 16
Transmission: Manual
No. of forward speeds: 4
Wheels driven: Rear
Brakes F/R: Disc/Drum
Steering: Rack & pinion
Wheelbase: 218.4cm 86.0in
Track F: 131.6cm 51.8in
Track R: 123.4cm 48.6in
Length: 396.2cm 156.0in
Width: 153.7cm 60.5in
Height: 130.8cm 51.5in
Kerb weight: 1162.2kg 2560.0lb
Fuel: 51.1L 11.2gal 13.5galUS

4308 Sunbeam

Arrow Station Wagon
1968 UK
90.0mph 144.8kmh
0-1/4 mile: 20.0secs
80.0bhp 59.7kW 81.1PS
46.4bhp/L 34.6kW/L 47.0PS/L
26.4mpg 22.0mpgUS 10.7L/100km
Petrol 4-stroke piston
1725cc 105.2cu in
In-line 4
Valve type/No: Overhead 8
Wheels driven: Rear
Wheelbase: 249.9cm 98.4in
Length: 432.3cm 170.2in

4309 Sunbeam

Rapier
1968 UK
106.0mph 170.6kmh
0-50mph 80.5kmh: 9.0secs
0-60mph 96.5kmh: 12.8secs
0-1/4 mile: 18.7secs
0-1km: 34.7secs
88.0bhp 65.6kW 89.2PS
@ 5200rpm
100.0lbft 135.5Nm @ 4000rpm
86.5bhp/ton 85.0bhp/tonne
51.0bhp/L 38.0kW/L 51.7PS/L
46.9ft/sec 14.3m/sec
19.3mph 31.1kmh/1000rpm
26.6mpg 22.1mpgUS 10.6L/100km
Petrol 4-stroke piston
1725cc 105.2cu in
In-line 4 2 Carburettor
Compression ratio: 9.2:1
Bore: 81.5mm 3.2in
Stroke: 82.6mm 3.2in
Valve type/No: Overhead 8
Transmission: Manual with overdrive
No. of forward speeds: 6
Wheels driven: Rear
Springs F/R: Coil/Leaf
Brake system: PA
Brakes F/R: Disc/Drum
Steering: Recirculating ball
Wheelbase: 250.2cm 98.5in
Track F: 132.1cm 52.0in
Track R: 132.1cm 52.0in
Length: 444.0cm 174.8in
Width: 164.3cm 64.7in
Height: 139.7cm 55.0in
Ground clearance: 12.7cm 5.0in
Kerb weight: 1034.7kg 2279.0lb
Fuel: 68.2L 15.0gal 18.0galUS

4310 Sunbeam

Alpine
1969 UK
92.0mph 148.0kmh
0-50mph 80.5kmh: 10.2secs
0-60mph 96.5kmh: 14.6secs
0-1/4 mile: 19.9secs
0-1km: 37.5secs
74.0bhp 55.2kW 75.0PS
@ 5000rpm
96.0lbft 130.1Nm @ 3000rpm
76.6bhp/ton 75.4bhp/tonne
42.9bhp/L 32.0kW/L 43.5PS/L
45.1ft/sec 13.8m/sec
21.6mph 34.8kmh/1000rpm
25.8mpg 21.5mpgUS 10.9L/100km
Petrol 4-stroke piston
1725cc 105.2cu in
In-line 4 1 Carburettor
Compression ratio: 9.2:1
Bore: 81.5mm 3.2in
Stroke: 82.5mm 3.2in
Valve type/No: Overhead 8
Transmission: Manual with overdrive
No. of forward speeds: 6
Wheels driven: Rear
Springs F/R: Coil/Leaf
Brake system: PA
Brakes F/R: Disc/Drum
Steering: Recirculating ball
Wheelbase: 250.2cm 98.5in
Track F: 132.1cm 52.0in
Track R: 132.1cm 52.0in
Length: 443.5cm 174.6in
Width: 164.3cm 64.7in
Height: 139.7cm 55.0in
Ground clearance: 12.7cm 5.0in
Kerb weight: 982.0kg 2163.0lb
Fuel: 68.2L 15.0gal 18.0galUS

4311 Sunbeam

Alpine GT
1969 UK
94.0mph 151.2kmh
0-50mph 80.5kmh: 8.7secs
0-60mph 96.5kmh: 12.3secs
0-1/4 mile: 19.1secs
94.0bhp 70.1kW 95.3PS
@ 5300rpm
105.0lbft 142.3Nm @ 3100rpm
89.2bhp/ton 87.7bhp/tonne
54.5bhp/L 40.7kW/L 55.3PS/L
47.8ft/sec 14.6m/sec
16.2mph 26.1kmh/1000rpm
27.3mpg 22.7mpgUS 10.4L/100km
Petrol 4-stroke piston
1724cc 105.2cu in
In-line 4 2 Carburettor
Compression ratio: 9.2:1
Bore: 81.5mm 3.2in
Stroke: 82.5mm 3.2in
Valve type/No: Overhead 8
Transmission: Manual
No. of forward speeds: 4
Wheels driven: Rear
Springs F/R: Coil/Leaf
Brake system: PA
Brakes F/R: Disc/Drum
Steering: Recirculating ball
Wheelbase: 250.2cm 98.5in
Track F: 132.1cm 52.0in
Track R: 132.1cm 52.0in
Length: 443.2cm 174.5in
Width: 164.6cm 64.8in
Height: 135.9cm 53.5in
Ground clearance: 12.7cm 5.0in
Kerb weight: 1071.4kg 2360.0lb
Fuel: 68.1L 15.0gal 18.0galUS

4312 Sunbeam

Rapier H120
1969 UK
106.0mph 170.6kmh
0-50mph 80.5kmh: 7.8secs
0-60mph 96.5kmh: 11.1secs
0-1/4 mile: 17.7secs
0-1km: 33.0secs
105.0bhp 78.3kW 106.5PS
@ 5200rpm
120.0lbft 162.6Nm @ 4000rpm
102.0bhp/ton 100.3bhp/tonne
60.9bhp/L 45.4kW/L 61.7PS/L
46.9ft/sec 14.3m/sec
21.5mph 34.6kmh/1000rpm
21.9mpg 18.2mpgUS 12.9L/100km
Petrol 4-stroke piston
1725cc 105.2cu in
In-line 4 2 Carburettor
Compression ratio: 9.6:1
Bore: 81.5mm 3.2in
Stroke: 82.5mm 3.2in
Valve type/No: Overhead 8
Transmission: Manual with overdrive
No. of forward speeds: 6
Wheels driven: Rear
Springs F/R: Coil/Leaf
Brake system: PA
Brakes F/R: Disc/Drum
Steering: Recirculating ball
Wheelbase: 250.2cm 98.5in
Track F: 132.1cm 52.0in
Track R: 132.1cm 52.0in
Length: 443.2cm 174.5in
Width: 164.3cm 64.7in
Height: 139.7cm 55.0in
Ground clearance: 12.7cm 5.0in
Kerb weight: 1046.5kg 2305.0lb
Fuel: 68.2L 15.0gal 18.0galUS

4313 Sunbeam

Rapier
1975 UK
102.0mph 164.1kmh
0-50mph 80.5kmh: 9.2secs
0-60mph 96.5kmh: 12.8secs
0-1/4 mile: 18.8secs
0-1km: 35.6secs
82.0bhp 61.1kW 83.1PS
@ 5200rpm
93.0lbft 126.0Nm @ 3300rpm
80.0bhp/ton 78.7bhp/tonne
47.5bhp/L 35.4kW/L 48.2PS/L
46.9ft/sec 14.3m/sec
19.3mph 31.1kmh/1000rpm
24.3mpg 20.2mpgUS 11.6L/100km
Petrol 4-stroke piston
1725cc 105.2cu in
In-line 4 2 Carburettor
Compression ratio: 9.2:1
Bore: 81.5mm 3.2in
Stroke: 82.5mm 3.2in
Valve type/No: Overhead 8
Transmission: Manual with overdrive
No. of forward speeds: 6
Wheels driven: Rear
Springs F/R: Coil/Leaf
Brake system: PA
Brakes F/R: Disc/Drum
Steering: Recirculating ball
Wheelbase: 250.2cm 98.5in
Track F: 131.6cm 51.8in
Track R: 131.6cm 51.8in
Length: 444.5cm 175.0in
Width: 164.3cm 64.7in
Height: 139.7cm 55.0in
Ground clearance: 16.5cm 6.5in
Kerb weight: 1041.9kg 2295.0lb
Fuel: 68.2L 15.0gal 18.0galUS

4314 Sunbeam-Talbot

2-litre Sports Tourer
1939 UK
80.0mph 128.7kmh
0-50mph 80.5kmh: 14.3secs
0-60mph 96.5kmh: 22.1secs
56.0bhp 41.8kW 56.8PS
@ 3800rpm
55.7bhp/ton 54.7bhp/tonne
28.8bhp/L 21.5kW/L 29.2PS/L
45.7ft/sec 13.9m/sec
28.0mpg 23.3mpgUS 10.1L/100km
Petrol 4-stroke piston
1944cc 118.6cu in
In-line 4 1 Carburettor
Compression ratio: 6.4:1
Bore: 75.0mm 2.9in
Stroke: 110.0mm 4.3in
Valve type/No: Side 8
Transmission: Manual
No. of forward speeds: 4
Wheels driven: Rear
Brakes F/R: Drum/Drum
Kerb weight: 1022.9kg 2253.0lb
Fuel: 38.7L 8.5gal 10.2galUS

4315 Sunbeam-Talbot

10 Sports Saloon
1947 UK
68.0mph 109.4kmh
0-50mph 80.5kmh: 23.4secs
0-60mph 96.5kmh: 35.2secs
39.0bhp 29.1kW 39.5PS
@ 4400rpm
38.6bhp/ton 38.0bhp/tonne
32.9bhp/L 24.6kW/L 33.4PS/L
45.7ft/sec 13.9m/sec
30.0mpg 25.0mpgUS 9.4L/100km
Petrol 4-stroke piston
1184cc 72.2cu in
In-line 4
Compression ratio: 6.4:1
Bore: 63.0mm 2.5in
Stroke: 95.0mm 3.7in
Valve type/No: Side 8
Transmission: Manual
No. of forward speeds: 4
Wheels driven: Rear
Brakes F/R: Drum/Drum
Wheelbase: 238.8cm 94.0in
Track F: 120.7cm 47.5in
Track R: 123.2cm 48.5in
Length: 396.2cm 156.0in
Width: 152.4cm 60.0in
Height: 148.6cm 58.5in
Ground clearance: 15.2cm 6.0in
Kerb weight: 1026.5kg 2261.0lb
Fuel: 38.7L 8.5gal 10.2galUS

4316 Sunbeam-Talbot

2-litre Sports Saloon
1947 UK
72.0mph 115.8kmh
0-50mph 80.5kmh: 18.8secs
56.0bhp 41.8kW 56.8PS
@ 3800rpm
48.6bhp/ton 47.7bhp/tonne
28.8bhp/L 21.5kW/L 29.2PS/L
45.7ft/sec 13.9m/sec
25.0mpg 20.8mpgUS 11.3L/100km
Petrol 4-stroke piston
1944cc 118.6cu in
In-line 4
Bore: 75.0mm 2.9in
Stroke: 110.0mm 4.3in
Valve type/No: Side 8
Transmission: Manual
No. of forward speeds: 4
Wheels driven: Rear
Brakes F/R: Drum/Drum
Wheelbase: 248.2cm 97.7in
Track F: 120.7cm 47.5in
Track R: 123.2cm 48.5in
Length: 402.6cm 158.5in
Width: 152.4cm 60.0in
Height: 148.6cm 58.5in
Ground clearance: 15.2cm 6.0in
Kerb weight: 1172.7kg 2583.0lb
Fuel: 38.7L 8.5gal 10.2galUS

4317 Sunbeam-Talbot

90 Sports Saloon
1948 UK
80.0mph 128.7kmh
0-50mph 80.5kmh: 17.6secs
0-60mph 96.5kmh: 26.8secs
64.0bhp 47.7kW 64.9PS
@ 4100rpm
50.7bhp/ton 49.8bhp/tonne
32.9bhp/L 24.5kW/L 33.4PS/L
49.3ft/sec 15.0m/sec
22.0mpg 18.3mpgUS 12.8L/100km
Petrol 4-stroke piston
1944cc 118.6cu in
In-line 4
Compression ratio: 6.6:1
Bore: 75.0mm 2.9in

Stroke: 110.0mm 4.3in
Valve type/No: Overhead 8
Transmission: Manual
No. of forward speeds: 4
Wheels driven: Rear
Brakes F/R: Drum/Drum
Wheelbase: 247.7cm 97.5in
Track F: 120.7cm 47.5in
Track R: 128.3cm 50.5in
Length: 425.5cm 167.5in
Width: 158.8cm 62.5in
Height: 154.2cm 60.7in
Ground clearance: 14.0cm 5.5in
Kerb weight: 1283.9kg 2828.0lb
Fuel: 45.5L 10.0gal 12.0galUS

4318 Sunbeam-Talbot

80 Saloon
1949 UK
74.0mph 119.1kmh
0-50mph 80.5kmh: 22.2secs
0-60mph 96.5kmh: 36.4secs
47.0bhp 35.0kW 47.6PS
@ 4800rpm
42.4bhp/ton 41.7bhp/tonne
39.7bhp/L 29.6kW/L 40.2PS/L
49.9ft/sec 15.2m/sec
26.0mpg 21.6mpgUS 10.9L/100km
Petrol 4-stroke piston
1184cc 72.2cu in
In-line 4
Compression ratio: 6.8:1
Bore: 63.0mm 2.5in
Stroke: 95.0mm 3.7in
Valve type/No: Overhead 8
Transmission: Manual
No. of forward speeds: 4
Wheels driven: Rear
Brakes F/R: Drum/Drum
Wheelbase: 247.7cm 97.5in
Track F: 120.7cm 47.5in
Track R: 128.3cm 50.5in
Length: 425.5cm 167.5in
Width: 158.8cm 62.5in
Height: 154.2cm 60.7in
Ground clearance: 14.0cm 5.5in
Kerb weight: 1128.2kg 2485.0lb
Fuel: 45.5L 10.0gal 12.0galUS

4319 Sunbeam-Talbot

90 Mk IIA
1953 UK
83.0mph 133.5kmh
0-50mph 80.5kmh: 14.4secs
0-60mph 96.5kmh: 20.8secs
0-1/4 mile: 22.2secs
70.0bhp 52.2kW 71.0PS
@ 4000rpm
113.0lbft 153.1Nm @ 2400rpm
50.2bhp/ton 49.4bhp/tonne
30.9bhp/L 23.0kW/L 31.3PS/L
48.1ft/sec 14.7m/sec
19.9mph 32.0kmh/1000rpm
28.1mpg 23.4mpgUS 10.1L/100km
Petrol 4-stroke piston
2267cc 138.3cu in
In-line 4
Compression ratio: 6.4:1
Bore: 81.0mm 3.2in
Stroke: 110.0mm 4.3in
Valve type/No: Overhead 8
Transmission: Manual
No. of forward speeds: 4
Wheels driven: Rear
Springs F/R: Coil/Leaf
Brakes F/R: Drum/Drum
Wheelbase: 247.7cm 97.5in
Track F: 120.7cm 47.5in
Track R: 128.3cm 50.5in
Length: 425.5cm 167.5in
Width: 158.8cm 62.5in
Height: 154.2cm 60.7in
Ground clearance: 16.8cm 6.6in
Kerb weight: 1417.4kg 3122.0lb
Fuel: 45.5L 10.0gal 12.0galUS

4320 Suzuki

Brute
1971 Japan
48.0mph 77.2kmh
32.0bhp 23.9kW 32.4PS
@ 6000rpm
27.0lbft 36.6Nm @ 5000rpm
53.1bhp/ton 52.2bhp/tonne
88.9bhp/L 66.3kW/L 90.1PS/L
40.3ft/sec 12.3m/sec
33.6mpg 28.0mpgUS 8.4L/100km
Petrol 2-stroke piston
360cc 22.0cu in
In-line 2
Compression ratio: 7.3:1
Bore: 61.0mm 2.4in
Stroke: 61.5mm 2.4in
Transmission: Manual
No. of forward speeds: 4
Wheels driven: 4-wheel drive
Brakes F/R: Drum/Drum
Wheelbase: 193.0cm 76.0in
Track F: 109.2cm 43.0in
Track R: 110.0cm 43.3in
Length: 299.5cm 117.9in
Width: 129.5cm 51.0in
Height: 164.6cm 64.8in
Ground clearance: 24.1cm 9.5in
Kerb weight: 612.9kg 1350.0lb
Fuel: 26.5L 5.8gal 7.0galUS

4321 Suzuki

SC 100
1980 Japan
78.0mph 125.5kmh
0-50mph 80.5kmh: 13.7secs
0-60mph 96.5kmh: 21.2secs
0-1/4 mile: 21.7secs
0-1km: 41.8secs
47.0bhp 35.0kW 47.6PS
@ 5000rpm
61.0lbft 82.7Nm @ 3000rpm
71.8bhp/ton 70.6bhp/tonne
48.4bhp/L 36.1kW/L 49.1PS/L
39.3ft/sec 12.0m/sec
17.8mph 28.6kmh/1000rpm
38.9mpg 32.4mpgUS 7.3L/100km
Petrol 4-stroke piston
970cc 59.2cu in
In-line 4 1 Carburettor
Compression ratio: 9.0:1
Bore: 65.5mm 2.6in
Stroke: 72.0mm 2.8in
Valve type/No: Overhead 8
Transmission: Manual
No. of forward speeds: 4
Wheels driven: Rear
Springs F/R: Coil/Coil
Brakes F/R: Disc/Drum
Steering: Rack & pinion
Wheelbase: 202.9cm 79.9in
Track F: 121.9cm 48.0in
Track R: 119.4cm 47.0in
Length: 320.0cm 126.0in
Width: 139.4cm 54.9in
Height: 122.4cm 48.2in
Ground clearance: 16.0cm 6.3in
Kerb weight: 665.6kg 1466.0lb
Fuel: 25.9L 5.7gal 6.8galUS

4322 Suzuki

Alto FX
1981 Japan
84.0mph 135.2kmh
0-50mph 80.5kmh: 10.8secs
0-60mph 96.5kmh: 15.8secs
0-1/4 mile: 20.5secs
0-1km: 39.1secs
40.0bhp 29.8kW 40.5PS
@ 5500rpm
43.4lbft 58.8Nm @ 3000rpm
61.5bhp/ton 60.5bhp/tonne
50.2bhp/L 37.5kW/L 50.9PS/L
43.2ft/sec 13.2m/sec
14.7mph 23.7kmh/1000rpm
40.1mpg 33.4mpgUS 7.0L/100km
Petrol 4-stroke piston
796cc 48.6cu in
In-line 3 1 Carburettor
Compression ratio: 8.7:1
Bore: 68.5mm 2.7in
Stroke: 72.0mm 2.8in
Valve type/No: Overhead 6
Transmission: Manual
No. of forward speeds: 4
Wheels driven: Front
Springs F/R: Coil/Leaf
Brakes F/R: Disc/Drum
Steering: Rack & pinion
Wheelbase: 214.9cm 84.6in
Track F: 121.4cm 47.8in
Track R: 117.1cm 46.1in
Length: 330.2cm 130.0in
Width: 139.4cm 54.9in
Height: 133.6cm 52.6in
Ground clearance: 15.2cm 6.0in
Kerb weight: 661.0kg 1456.0lb
Fuel: 26.8L 5.9gal 7.1galUS

4323 Suzuki

Alto FX Automatic
1983 Japan
78.0mph 125.5kmh
0-50mph 80.5kmh: 14.7secs
0-60mph 96.5kmh: 22.5secs
0-1/4 mile: 23.3secs
0-1km: 42.9secs
40.0bhp 29.8kW 40.5PS
@ 5500rpm
43.4lbft 58.8Nm @ 3000rpm
67.6bhp/ton 66.4bhp/tonne
50.2bhp/L 37.5kW/L 50.9PS/L
43.2ft/sec 13.2m/sec
13.5mph 21.7kmh/1000rpm
34.9mpg 29.1mpgUS 8.1L/100km
Petrol 4-stroke piston
796cc 48.6cu in
In-line 3 1 Carburettor
Compression ratio: 8.7:1
Bore: 68.5mm 2.7in
Stroke: 72.0mm 2.8in
Valve type/No: Overhead 6
Transmission: Automatic
No. of forward speeds: 2
Wheels driven: Front
Springs F/R: Coil/Leaf
Brakes F/R: Disc/Drum
Steering: Rack & pinion
Wheelbase: 214.9cm 84.6in
Track F: 121.4cm 47.8in
Track R: 117.1cm 46.1in
Length: 330.2cm 130.0in
Width: 139.4cm 54.9in
Height: 133.6cm 52.6in
Ground clearance: 15.2cm 6.0in
Kerb weight: 602.0kg 1326.0lb
Fuel: 26.8L 5.9gal 7.1galUS

4324 Suzuki

Swift 1.3GS
1985 Japan
103.0mph 165.7kmh
0-50mph 80.5kmh: 7.5secs
0-60mph 96.5kmh: 10.3secs
0-1/4 mile: 17.6secs
0-1km: 33.5secs
73.0bhp 54.4kW 74.0PS
@ 5800rpm
77.0lbft 104.3Nm @ 4000rpm
99.9bhp/ton 98.3bhp/tonne
55.1bhp/L 41.1kW/L 55.9PS/L
48.8ft/sec 14.9m/sec
22.8mph 36.7kmh/1000rpm
33.3mpg 27.7mpgUS 8.5L/100km
Petrol 4-stroke piston
1324cc 80.8cu in
In-line 4 1 Carburettor
Compression ratio: 9.5:1
Bore: 74.0mm 2.9in
Stroke: 77.0mm 3.0in
Valve type/No: Overhead 8
Transmission: Manual
No. of forward speeds: 5
Wheels driven: Front
Springs F/R: Coil/Leaf
Brake system: PA
Brakes F/R: Disc/Drum
Steering: Rack & pinion
Wheelbase: 224.5cm 88.4in
Track F: 133.1cm 52.4in
Track R: 130.0cm 51.2in
Length: 358.4cm 141.1in
Width: 152.9cm 60.2in
Height: 134.9cm 53.1in
Ground clearance: 18.0cm 7.1in
Kerb weight: 742.7kg 1636.0lb
Fuel: 30.9L 6.8gal 8.2galUS

4325 Suzuki

Alto GLA
1986 Japan
80.0mph 128.7kmh
0-50mph 80.5kmh: 16.2secs
0-60mph 96.5kmh: 24.4secs
0-1/4 mile: 22.9secs
0-1km: 43.3secs
40.0bhp 29.8kW 40.5PS
@ 5500rpm
43.0lbft 58.3Nm @ 3000rpm
63.1bhp/ton 62.0bhp/tonne
50.2bhp/L 37.5kW/L 50.9PS/L
43.2ft/sec 13.2m/sec
13.6mph 21.9kmh/1000rpm
35.0mpg 29.1mpgUS 8.1L/100km
Petrol 4-stroke piston
796cc 49.0cu in
In-line 3 1 Carburettor
Compression ratio: 8.7:1
Bore: 68.5mm 2.7in
Stroke: 72.0mm 2.8in
Valve type/No: Overhead 6
Transmission: Automatic
No. of forward speeds: 2
Wheels driven: Front
Springs F/R: Coil/Leaf
Brakes F/R: Disc/Drum
Steering: Rack & pinion
Wheelbase: 215.0cm 84.6in
Track F: 121.5cm 47.8in
Track R: 120.0cm 47.2in
Length: 330.0cm 129.9in
Width: 140.5cm 55.3in
Height: 141.0cm 55.5in
Ground clearance: 17.0cm 6.7in
Kerb weight: 645.0kg 1420.7lb
Fuel: 30.0L 6.6gal 7.9galUS

4326 Suzuki

Swift 1.3 GTi
1986 Japan
112.0mph 180.2kmh
0-50mph 80.5kmh: 6.5secs
0-60mph 96.5kmh: 9.1secs
0-1/4 mile: 16.8secs
0-1km: 31.8secs
101.0bhp 75.3kW 102.4PS
@ 6600rpm
79.7lbft 108.0Nm @ 5500rpm
134.3bhp/ton 132.0bhp/tonne
77.8bhp/L 58.0kW/L 78.9PS/L
54.4ft/sec 16.6m/sec
17.2mph 27.7kmh/1000rpm
30.9mpg 25.7mpgUS 9.1L/100km
Petrol 4-stroke piston
1298cc 79.2cu in
In-line 4 fuel injection
Compression ratio: 10.0:1
Bore: 74.0mm 2.9in
Stroke: 75.5mm 3.0in
Valve type/No: Overhead 16
Transmission: Manual
No. of forward speeds: 5
Wheels driven: Front
Springs F/R: Coil/Coil
Brake system: PA
Brakes F/R: Disc/Drum
Steering: Rack & pinion
Wheelbase: 224.5cm 88.4in
Track F: 133.1cm 52.4in
Track R: 130.0cm 51.2in
Length: 358.4cm 141.1in
Width: 152.9cm 60.2in
Height: 134.9cm 53.1in
Ground clearance: 18.0cm 7.1in
Kerb weight: 765.0kg 1685.0lb
Fuel: 33.2L 7.3gal 8.8galUS

4327 Suzuki

SJ413V JX
1987 Japan
76.0mph 122.3kmh
0-50mph 80.5kmh: 12.2secs
0-60mph 96.5kmh: 19.4secs
0-1/4 mile: 20.5secs
0-1km: 40.9secs
63.0bhp 47.0kW 63.9PS
@ 6000rpm
73.3lbft 99.3Nm @ 3500rpm
75.9bhp/ton 74.6bhp/tonne
47.6bhp/L 35.5kW/L 48.2PS/L
50.5ft/sec 15.4m/sec
17.6mph 28.3kmh/1000rpm
24.8mpg 20.7mpgUS 11.4L/100km
Petrol 4-stroke piston
1324cc 81.0cu in
In-line 4 1 Carburettor
Compression ratio: 8.9:1
Bore: 74.0mm 2.9in
Stroke: 77.0mm 3.0in
Valve type/No: Overhead 8
Transmission: Manual
No. of forward speeds: 5
Wheels driven: 4-wheel engageable
Springs F/R: Leaf/Leaf
Brake system: PA
Brakes F/R: Disc/Drum

Steering: Recirculating ball
Wheelbase: 203.0cm 79.9in
Track F: 121.0cm 47.6in
Track R: 122.0cm 48.0in
Length: 343.0cm 135.0in
Width: 146.0cm 57.5in
Height: 168.0cm 66.1in
Ground clearance: 22.5cm 8.9in
Kerb weight: 844.0kg 1859.0lb
Fuel: 40.0L 8.8gal 10.6galUS

4328 Suzuki

Swift 1.3 GLX
1987 Japan
102.0mph 164.1kmh
0-50mph 80.5kmh: 7.8secs
0-60mph 96.5kmh: 11.3secs
0-1/4 mile: 18.3secs
0-1km: 34.1secs
67.0bhp 50.0kW 67.9PS
@ 5300rpm
76.3lbft 103.4Nm @ 3700rpm
93.0bhp/ton 91.4bhp/tonne
50.6bhp/L 37.7kW/L 51.3PS/L
44.6ft/sec 13.6m/sec
22.8mph 36.7kmh/1000rpm
37.0mpg 30.8mpgUS 7.6L/100km
Petrol 4-stroke piston
1324cc 81.0cu in
In-line 4 1 Carburettor
Compression ratio: 8.9:1
Bore: 74.0mm 2.9in
Stroke: 77.0mm 3.0in
Valve type/No: Overhead 8
Transmission: Manual
No. of forward speeds: 5
Wheels driven: Front
Springs F/R: Coil/Coil
Brake system: PA
Brakes F/R: Disc/Drum
Steering: Rack & pinion
Wheelbase: 234.5cm 92.3in
Track F: 133.5cm 52.6in
Track R: 130.0cm 51.2in
Length: 377.0cm 148.4in
Width: 154.5cm 60.8in
Height: 135.0cm 53.1in
Ground clearance: 18.0cm 7.1in
Kerb weight: 733.0kg 1614.5lb
Fuel: 33.2L 7.3gal 8.8galUS

4329 Suzuki

Swift 1.3 GLX Executive
1987 Japan
97.0mph 156.1kmh
0-50mph 80.5kmh: 10.1secs
0-60mph 96.5kmh: 14.5secs
0-1/4 mile: 19.9secs
0-1km: 37.1secs
67.0bhp 50.0kW 67.9PS
@ 5300rpm
76.0lbft 103.0Nm @ 3700rpm
93.3bhp/ton 91.8bhp/tonne
50.6bhp/L 37.7kW/L 51.3PS/L
44.6ft/sec 13.6m/sec
17.3mph 27.8kmh/1000rpm
36.0mpg 30.0mpgUS 7.8L/100km
Petrol 4-stroke piston
1324cc 81.0cu in
In-line 4 1 Carburettor
Compression ratio: 8.9:1
Bore: 74.0mm 2.9in
Stroke: 77.0mm 3.0in
Valve type/No: Overhead 8
Transmission: Automatic
No. of forward speeds: 3
Wheels driven: Front
Springs F/R: Coil/Coil
Brake system: PA
Brakes F/R: Disc/Drum
Steering: Rack & pinion
Wheelbase: 234.5cm 92.3in
Track F: 133.5cm 52.6in
Track R: 130.0cm 51.2in
Length: 377.0cm 148.4in
Width: 154.5cm 60.8in
Height: 135.0cm 53.1in
Ground clearance: 18.0cm 7.1in
Kerb weight: 730.0kg 1607.9lb
Fuel: 33.2L 7.3gal 8.8galUS

4330 Suzuki

Swift 1.3 GLX
1989 Japan
103.0mph 165.7kmh
0-50mph 80.5kmh: 8.2secs
0-60mph 96.5kmh: 11.6secs
0-1/4 mile: 18.5secs
0-1km: 34.8secs
67.0bhp 50.0kW 67.9PS
@ 6000rpm
74.5lbft 101.0Nm @ 4950rpm
89.2bhp/ton 87.7bhp/tonne
51.6bhp/L 38.5kW/L 52.3PS/L
49.5ft/sec 15.1m/sec
23.3mph 37.5kmh/1000rpm
35.7mpg 29.7mpgUS 7.9L/100km
Petrol 4-stroke piston
1298cc 79.0cu in
In-line 4 1 Carburettor
Compression ratio: 9.5:1
Bore: 74.0mm 2.9in
Stroke: 75.5mm 3.0in
Valve type/No: Overhead 8
Transmission: Manual
No. of forward speeds: 5
Wheels driven: Front
Springs F/R: Coil/Coil
Brake system: PA
Brakes F/R: Disc/Drum
Steering: Rack & pinion
Wheelbase: 245.0cm 96.5in
Track F: 136.5cm 53.7in
Track R: 134.0cm 52.8in
Length: 381.0cm 150.0in
Width: 159.0cm 62.6in
Height: 138.0cm 54.3in
Ground clearance: 17.0cm 6.7in
Kerb weight: 764.0kg 1682.8lb
Fuel: 40.0L 8.8gal 10.6galUS

4331 Suzuki

Swift 1.3 GTi
1989 Japan
116.0mph 186.6kmh
0-50mph 80.5kmh: 6.4secs
0-60mph 96.5kmh: 8.7secs
0-1/4 mile: 16.8secs
0-1km: 30.1secs
101.0bhp 75.3kW 102.4PS
@ 6450rpm
83.4lbft 113.0Nm @ 4950rpm
126.8bhp/ton 124.7bhp/tonne
77.8bhp/L 58.0kW/L 78.9PS/L
53.2ft/sec 16.2m/sec
17.9mph 28.8kmh/1000rpm
29.2mpg 24.3mpgUS 9.7L/100km
Petrol 4-stroke piston
1298cc 79.0cu in
In-line 4 fuel injection
Compression ratio: 10.0:1
Bore: 74.0mm 2.9in
Stroke: 75.5mm 3.0in
Valve type/No: Overhead 16
Transmission: Manual
No. of forward speeds: 5
Wheels driven: Front
Springs F/R: Coil/Coil
Brake system: PA
Brakes F/R: Disc/Disc
Steering: Rack & pinion
Wheelbase: 226.5cm 89.2in
Track F: 136.5cm 53.7in
Track R: 134.0cm 52.8in
Length: 371.0cm 146.1in
Width: 159.0cm 62.6in
Height: 135.0cm 53.1in
Ground clearance: 17.0cm 6.7in
Kerb weight: 810.0kg 1784.1lb
Fuel: 40.0L 8.8gal 10.6galUS

4332 Suzuki

Vitara JLX
1989 Japan
90.0mph 144.8kmh
0-50mph 80.5kmh: 10.0secs
0-60mph 96.5kmh: 14.5secs
0-1/4 mile: 19.5secs
0-1km: 37.1secs
75.0bhp 55.9kW 76.0PS
@ 5250rpm
90.8lbft 123.0Nm @ 3100rpm
74.6bhp/ton 73.3bhp/tonne
47.2bhp/L 35.2kW/L 47.8PS/L
51.6ft/sec 15.7m/sec
17.8mph 28.6kmh/1000rpm
24.2mpg 20.2mpgUS 11.7L/100km
Petrol 4-stroke piston
1590cc 97.0cu in
In-line 4 1 Carburettor
Compression ratio: 8.9:1
Bore: 75.0mm 2.9in
Stroke: 90.0mm 3.5in
Valve type/No: Overhead 8
Transmission: Manual
No. of forward speeds: 5
Wheels driven: 4-wheel engageable
Springs F/R: Coil/Coil
Brake system: PA
Brakes F/R: Disc/Drum
Steering: Recirculating ball
Wheelbase: 220.0cm 86.6in
Track F: 139.5cm 54.9in
Track R: 140.0cm 55.1in
Length: 362.0cm 142.5in
Width: 163.0cm 64.2in
Height: 166.5cm 65.6in
Ground clearance: 20.0cm 7.9in
Kerb weight: 1023.0kg 2253.3lb
Fuel: 43.2L 9.5gal 11.4galUS

4333 Suzuki

Swift GT
1990 Japan
105.0mph 168.9kmh
0-60mph 96.5kmh: 9.5secs
0-1/4 mile: 17.0secs
100.0bhp 74.6kW 101.4PS
@ 6500rpm
83.0lbft 112.5Nm @ 5000rpm
119.5bhp/ton 117.5bhp/tonne
77.0bhp/L 57.4kW/L 78.0PS/L
53.6ft/sec 16.4m/sec
37.8mpg 31.5mpgUS 7.5L/100km
Petrol 4-stroke piston
1299cc 79.3cu in
In-line 4 fuel injection
Compression ratio: 10.0:1
Bore: 74.0mm 2.9in
Stroke: 75.5mm 3.0in
Valve type/No: Overhead 16
Transmission: Manual
No. of forward speeds: 5
Wheels driven: Front
Springs F/R: Coil/Coil
Brake system: PA
Brakes F/R: Disc/Disc
Steering: Rack & pinion
Wheelbase: 226.6cm 89.2in
Track F: 136.4cm 53.7in
Track R: 134.1cm 52.8in
Length: 371.1cm 146.1in
Width: 158.5cm 62.4in
Height: 134.9cm 53.1in
Kerb weight: 851.2kg 1875.0lb
Fuel: 40.1L 8.8gal 10.6galUS

4334 Swallow

Doretti
1955 UK
101.0mph 162.5kmh
0-50mph 80.5kmh: 9.4secs
0-60mph 96.5kmh: 13.4secs
0-1/4 mile: 18.8secs
90.0bhp 67.1kW 91.2PS
@ 4800rpm
116.6lbft 158.0Nm @ 3000rpm
93.5bhp/ton 91.9bhp/tonne
45.2bhp/L 33.7kW/L 45.8PS/L
48.3ft/sec 14.7m/sec
24.5mph 39.4kmh/1000rpm
28.0mpg 23.3mpgUS 10.1L/100km
Petrol 4-stroke piston
1991cc 121.5cu in
In-line 4
Compression ratio: 8.5:1
Bore: 83.0mm 3.3in
Stroke: 92.0mm 3.6in
Valve type/No: Overhead 8
Transmission: Manual with overdrive
No. of forward speeds: 5
Wheels driven: Rear
Springs F/R: Coil/Leaf
Brakes F/R: Drum/Drum
Wheelbase: 241.3cm 95.0in
Track F: 121.9cm 48.0in
Track R: 115.6cm 45.5in
Length: 396.2cm 156.0in
Width: 154.9cm 61.0in
Height: 129.5cm 51.0in
Ground clearance: 15.2cm 6.0in
Kerb weight: 978.8kg 2156.0lb
Fuel: 56.9L 12.5gal 15.0galUS

4335 Talbot

65 Saloon
1932 UK
65.6mph 105.6kmh
46.0bhp 34.3kW 46.6PS
@ 4500rpm
32.0bhp/ton 31.5bhp/tonne
27.6bhp/L 20.6kW/L 28.0PS/L
46.7ft/sec 14.2m/sec
22.0mpg 18.3mpgUS 12.8L/100km
Petrol 4-stroke piston
1665cc 101.6cu in
In-line 6 1 Carburettor
Bore: 61.0mm 2.4in
Stroke: 95.0mm 3.7in
Valve type/No: Overhead 12
Transmission: Manual
No. of forward speeds: 4
Wheels driven: Rear
Brakes F/R: Drum/Drum
Wheelbase: 289.6cm 114.0in
Track F: 142.2cm 56.0in
Track R: 142.2cm 56.0in
Length: 408.9cm 161.0in
Width: 175.3cm 69.0in
Height: 168.9cm 66.5in
Kerb weight: 1461.9kg 3220.0lb
Fuel: 72.8L 16.0gal 19.2galUS

4336 Talbot

105 Speed Model
1933 UK
88.2mph 141.9kmh
0-50mph 80.5kmh: 14.6secs
0-60mph 96.5kmh: 19.4secs
100.0bhp 74.6kW 101.4PS
@ 4500rpm
57.1bhp/ton 56.2bhp/tonne
33.7bhp/L 25.1kW/L 34.1PS/L
55.1ft/sec 16.8m/sec
16.0mpg 13.3mpgUS 17.7L/100km
Petrol 4-stroke piston
2969cc 181.1cu in
In-line 6 1 Carburettor
Compression ratio: 6.5:1
Bore: 75.0mm 2.9in
Stroke: 112.0mm 4.4in
Valve type/No: Overhead 12
Transmission: Manual
No. of forward speeds: 4
Wheels driven: Rear
Brakes F/R: Drum/Drum
Kerb weight: 1779.7kg 3920.0lb
Fuel: 88.7L 19.5gal 23.4galUS

4337 Talbot

75 Saloon
1934 UK
70.3mph 113.1kmh
0-50mph 80.5kmh: 21.2secs
20.0mpg 16.7mpgUS 14.1L/100km
Petrol 4-stroke piston
2276cc 138.9cu in
In-line 6
Bore: 69.5mm 2.7in
Stroke: 100.0mm 3.9in
Transmission: Manual
No. of forward speeds: 4
Wheels driven: Rear
Brakes F/R: Drum/Drum
Kerb weight: 1652.6kg 3640.0lb
Fuel: 72.8L 16.0gal 19.2galUS

4338 Talbot

75 Drop-frame Sports Saloon
1935 UK
73.7mph 118.6kmh
0-50mph 80.5kmh: 20.8secs
0-60mph 96.5kmh: 34.4secs
20.0mpg 16.7mpgUS 14.1L/100km
Petrol 4-stroke piston
2276cc 138.9cu in
In-line 6
Bore: 69.5mm 2.7in
Stroke: 100.0mm 3.9in
Valve type/No: Overhead 12
Transmission: Manual
No. of forward speeds: 4
Wheels driven: Rear
Brakes F/R: Drum/Drum
Kerb weight: 1748.8kg 3852.0lb
Fuel: 72.8L 16.0gal 19.2galUS

4339 Talbot

105 Airline Saloon
1936 UK
89.1mph 143.4kmh
0-50mph 80.5kmh: 13.7secs
0-60mph 96.5kmh: 19.8secs

16.0mpg 13.3mpgUS 17.7L/100km
Petrol 4-stroke piston
2969cc 181.1cu in
In-line 6
Bore: 75.0mm 2.9in
Stroke: 112.0mm 4.4in
Valve type/No: Overhead 12
Transmission: Manual
No. of forward speeds: 4
Wheels driven: Rear
Brakes F/R: Drum/Drum
Kerb weight: 1836.4kg 4045.0lb
Fuel: 86.4L 19.0gal 22.8galUS

4340 Talbot

3.5-litre Speed Saloon
1936 UK
92.7mph 149.2kmh
0-50mph 80.5kmh: 11.8secs
0-60mph 96.5kmh: 16.8secs
123.0bhp 91.7kW 124.7PS
@ 4500rpm
69.1bhp/ton 68.0bhp/tonne
36.4bhp/L 27.2kW/L 36.9PS/L
55.1ft/sec 16.8m/sec
15.0mpg 12.5mpgUS 18.8L/100km
Petrol 4-stroke piston
3377cc 206.0cu in
In-line 6
Bore: 80.0mm 3.1in
Stroke: 112.0mm 4.4in
Valve type/No: Overhead 12
Transmission: Manual
No. of forward speeds: 4
Wheels driven: Rear
Brakes F/R: Drum/Drum
Kerb weight: 1809.2kg 3985.0lb
Fuel: 86.4L 19.0gal 22.8galUS

4341 Talbot

10hp Drop-head Coupe
1938 UK
69.2mph 111.3kmh
0-50mph 80.5kmh: 21.9secs
30.0mpg 25.0mpgUS 9.4L/100km
Petrol 4-stroke piston
1185cc 72.3cu in
In-line 4
Bore: 63.0mm 2.5in
Stroke: 95.0mm 3.7in
Valve type/No: Side 8
Transmission: Manual
No. of forward speeds: 4
Wheels driven: Rear
Brakes F/R: Drum/Drum
Kerb weight: 947.0kg 2086.0lb
Fuel: 38.7L 8.5gal 10.2galUS

4342 Talbot

3-litre Saloon
1938 UK
84.9mph 136.6kmh
0-50mph 80.5kmh: 13.7secs
0-60mph 96.5kmh: 20.1secs
17.0mpg 14.2mpgUS 16.6L/100km
Petrol 4-stroke piston
3181cc 194.1cu in
In-line 6
Bore: 75.0mm 2.9in
Stroke: 120.0mm 4.7in
Valve type/No: Overhead 12
Transmission: Manual
No. of forward speeds: 4
Wheels driven: Rear
Brakes F/R: Drum/Drum
Kerb weight: 1614.0kg 3555.0lb
Fuel: 59.1L 13.0gal 15.6galUS

4343 Talbot

Figoni et Falaschi
1938 France
115.0mph 185.0kmh
140.0bhp 104.4kW 141.9PS
@ 4000rpm
95.0bhp/ton 93.4bhp/tonne
35.1bhp/L 26.2kW/L 35.6PS/L
45.7ft/sec 13.9m/sec
Petrol 4-stroke piston
3988cc 243.3cu in
In-line 6 3 Carburettor
Compression ratio: 7.4:1
Bore: 90.0mm 3.5in
Stroke: 104.5mm 4.1in
Valve type/No: Overhead 12
Transmission: Manual
No. of forward speeds: 4
Wheels driven: Rear
Springs F/R: Leaf/Leaf
Brakes F/R: Drum/Drum
Steering: Worm & nut
Wheelbase: 264.2cm 104.0in
Track F: 137.2cm 54.0in
Track R: 146.1cm 57.5in
Kerb weight: 1498.2kg 3300.0lb

4344 Talbot

Solara GLS
1981 UK
98.0mph 157.7kmh
0-50mph 80.5kmh: 8.1secs
0-60mph 96.5kmh: 12.0secs
0-1/4 mile: 18.5secs
0-1km: 34.9secs
87.0bhp 64.9kW 88.2PS
@ 5400rpm
101.0lbft 136.9Nm @ 3000rpm
86.6bhp/ton 85.1bhp/tonne
54.6bhp/L 40.7kW/L 55.4PS/L
46.0ft/sec 14.0m/sec
20.9mph 33.6kmh/1000rpm
29.0mpg 24.1mpgUS 9.7L/100km
Petrol 4-stroke piston
1592cc 97.1cu in
In-line 4 1 Carburettor
Compression ratio: 9.3:1
Bore: 80.6mm 3.2in
Stroke: 78.0mm 3.1in
Valve type/No: Overhead 8
Transmission: Manual
No. of forward speeds: 5
Wheels driven: Front
Springs F/R: Torsion bar/Coil
Brake system: PA
Brakes F/R: Disc/Drum
Steering: Rack & pinion
Wheelbase: 260.4cm 102.5in
Track F: 142.2cm 56.0in
Track R: 139.7cm 55.0in
Length: 439.4cm 173.0in
Width: 167.6cm 66.0in
Height: 139.7cm 55.0in
Ground clearance: 12.7cm 5.0in
Kerb weight: 1021.9kg 2251.0lb
Fuel: 58.2L 12.8gal 15.4galUS

4345 Talbot

Tagora 2.2GLS
1981 UK
107.0mph 172.2kmh
0-50mph 80.5kmh: 7.4secs
0-60mph 96.5kmh: 11.3secs
0-1/4 mile: 18.2secs
0-1km: 34.1secs
113.0bhp 84.3kW 114.6PS
@ 5400rpm
133.0lbft 180.2Nm @ 3200rpm
90.5bhp/ton 89.0bhp/tonne
52.4bhp/L 39.1kW/L 53.2PS/L
48.1ft/sec 14.7m/sec
22.5mph 36.2kmh/1000rpm
23.9mpg 19.9mpgUS 11.8L/100km
Petrol 4-stroke piston
2155cc 131.5cu in
In-line 4 1 Carburettor
Compression ratio: 9.4:1
Bore: 91.7mm 3.6in
Stroke: 81.6mm 3.2in
Valve type/No: Overhead 8
Transmission: Manual
No. of forward speeds: 5
Wheels driven: Rear
Springs F/R: Coil/Coil
Brake system: PA
Brakes F/R: Disc/Drum
Steering: Rack & pinion PA
Wheelbase: 280.9cm 110.6in
Track F: 151.1cm 59.5in
Track R: 147.6cm 58.1in
Length: 462.8cm 182.2in
Width: 180.8cm 71.2in
Height: 144.5cm 56.9in
Ground clearance: 16.5cm 6.5in
Kerb weight: 1269.8kg 2797.0lb
Fuel: 70.1L 15.4gal 18.5galUS

4346 Talbot

Samba Cabriolet
1982 UK
96.0mph 154.5kmh
0-50mph 80.5kmh: 8.8secs
0-60mph 96.5kmh: 12.5secs
0-1/4 mile: 18.9secs
0-1km: 35.7secs
71.0bhp 52.9kW 72.0PS
@ 6000rpm
79.0lbft 107.0Nm @ 3000rpm
85.5bhp/ton 84.1bhp/tonne
52.2bhp/L 38.9kW/L 52.9PS/L
50.5ft/sec 15.4m/sec
20.0mph 32.2kmh/1000rpm
35.3mpg 29.4mpgUS 8.0L/100km
Petrol 4-stroke piston
1360cc 83.0cu in
In-line 4 1 Carburettor
Compression ratio: 9.3:1
Bore: 75.0mm 2.9in
Stroke: 77.0mm 3.0in
Valve type/No: Overhead 8
Transmission: Manual
No. of forward speeds: 5
Wheels driven: Front
Springs F/R: Coil/Coil
Brake system: PA
Brakes F/R: Disc/Drum
Steering: Rack & pinion
Wheelbase: 233.9cm 92.1in
Track F: 129.0cm 50.8in
Track R: 127.0cm 50.0in
Length: 350.5cm 138.0in
Width: 152.9cm 60.2in
Height: 136.1cm 53.6in
Ground clearance: 11.9cm 4.7in
Kerb weight: 844.4kg 1860.0lb
Fuel: 40.0L 8.8gal 10.6galUS

4347 Talbot

Samba GL
1982 UK
95.0mph 152.9kmh
0-50mph 80.5kmh: 10.3secs
0-60mph 96.5kmh: 16.0secs
0-1/4 mile: 20.2secs
0-1km: 38.4secs
49.0bhp 36.5kW 49.7PS
@ 4800rpm
63.0lbft 85.4Nm @ 2800rpm
66.8bhp/ton 65.7bhp/tonne
43.6bhp/L 32.5kW/L 44.2PS/L
36.3ft/sec 11.0m/sec
20.3mph 32.7kmh/1000rpm
37.3mpg 31.1mpgUS 7.6L/100km
Petrol 4-stroke piston
1124cc 68.6cu in
In-line 4 1 Carburettor
Compression ratio: 9.7:1
Bore: 72.0mm 2.8in
Stroke: 69.0mm 2.7in
Valve type/No: Overhead 8
Transmission: Manual
No. of forward speeds: 4
Wheels driven: Front
Springs F/R: Coil/Coil
Brake system: PA
Brakes F/R: Disc/Drum
Steering: Rack & pinion
Wheelbase: 233.9cm 92.1in
Track F: 129.0cm 50.8in
Track R: 127.0cm 50.0in
Length: 350.5cm 138.0in
Width: 152.9cm 60.2in
Height: 136.1cm 53.6in
Ground clearance: 11.9cm 4.7in
Kerb weight: 745.5kg 1642.0lb
Fuel: 40.0L 8.8gal 10.6galUS

4348 Talbot

Horizon 1.9LD
1983 UK
98.0mph 157.7kmh
0-50mph 80.5kmh: 9.9secs
0-60mph 96.5kmh: 13.8secs
0-1/4 mile: 19.5secs
0-1km: 36.9secs
64.0bhp 47.7kW 64.9PS
@ 4600rpm
88.0lbft 119.2Nm @ 2000rpm
65.0bhp/ton 63.9bhp/tonne
33.6bhp/L 25.0kW/L 34.1PS/L
44.2ft/sec 13.5m/sec
21.5mph 34.6kmh/1000rpm
37.6mpg 31.3mpgUS 7.5L/100km
Diesel 4-stroke piston
1905cc 116.2cu in
In-line 4 fuel injection
Compression ratio: 23.5:1
Bore: 83.0mm 3.3in
Stroke: 88.0mm 3.5in
Valve type/No: Overhead 8
Transmission: Manual
No. of forward speeds: 5
Wheels driven: Front
Springs F/R: Torsion bar/Coil
Brake system: PA
Brakes F/R: Disc/Drum
Steering: Rack & pinion
Wheelbase: 252.0cm 99.2in
Track F: 141.7cm 55.8in
Track R: 136.9cm 53.9in
Length: 396.0cm 155.9in
Width: 167.9cm 66.1in
Height: 141.0cm 55.5in
Ground clearance: 12.7cm 5.0in
Kerb weight: 1001.1kg 2205.0lb
Fuel: 45.0L 9.9gal 11.9galUS

4349 Tatra

12hp Drop-head Coupe
1932 Czechoslovakia
57.6mph 92.7kmh
33.0mpg 27.5mpgUS 8.6L/100km
Petrol 4-stroke piston
1154cc 70.4cu in
Flat 4
Bore: 70.0mm 2.8in
Stroke: 75.0mm 2.9in
Transmission: Manual
No. of forward speeds: 4
Wheels driven: Rear
Brakes F/R: Drum/Drum
Steering: Rack & pinion
Wheelbase: 251.5cm 99.0in
Track F: 119.4cm 47.0in
Track R: 119.4cm 47.0in
Length: 345.4cm 136.0in
Width: 149.9cm 59.0in
Height: 149.9cm 59.0in
Kerb weight: 762.7kg 1680.0lb
Fuel: 25.0L 5.5gal 6.6galUS

4350 Toyota

Toyopet Crown de Luxe
1958 Japan
72.0mph 115.8kmh
0-50mph 80.5kmh: 18.0secs
0-60mph 96.5kmh: 26.0secs
0-1/4 mile: 23.4secs
60.0bhp 44.7kW 60.8PS
@ 4400rpm
79.5lbft 107.7Nm @ 2600rpm
48.7bhp/ton 47.9bhp/tonne
41.3bhp/L 30.8kW/L 41.9PS/L
37.5ft/sec 11.4m/sec
Petrol 4-stroke piston
1453cc 88.6cu in
In-line 4
Compression ratio: 8.0:1
Bore: 77.0mm 3.0in
Stroke: 78.0mm 3.1in
Valve type/No: Overhead 8
Transmission: Manual
No. of forward speeds: 3
Wheels driven: Rear
Wheelbase: 253.0cm 99.6in
Track F: 132.6cm 52.2in
Track R: 136.9cm 53.9in
Kerb weight: 1253.0kg 2760.0lb

4351 Toyota

Toyopet Tiara
1960 Japan
80.3mph 129.2kmh
0-50mph 80.5kmh: 14.0secs
0-60mph 96.5kmh: 20.7secs
0-1/4 mile: 21.6secs
75.0bhp 55.9kW 76.0PS
@ 5000rpm
83.6lbft 113.3Nm @ 3000rpm
76.5bhp/ton 75.3bhp/tonne
51.6bhp/L 38.5kW/L 52.3PS/L
42.6ft/sec 13.0m/sec
15.4mph 24.8kmh/1000rpm
Petrol 4-stroke piston
1453cc 88.6cu in
In-line 4 1 Carburettor
Compression ratio: 8.4:1
Bore: 77.0mm 3.0in
Stroke: 78.0mm 3.1in
Valve type/No: Overhead 8
Transmission: Manual
No. of forward speeds: 3
Wheels driven: Rear
Wheelbase: 240.0cm 94.5in
Track F: 122.9cm 48.4in

Track R: 122.9cm 48.4in
Length: 398.8cm 157.0in
Width: 149.9cm 59.0in
Height: 144.8cm 57.0in
Kerb weight: 996.5kg 2195.0lb

4352 Toyota

1900
1964 Japan
92.0mph 148.0kmh
0-50mph 80.5kmh: 11.3secs
0-60mph 96.5kmh: 16.9secs
0-1/4 mile: 20.2secs
85.0bhp 63.4kW 86.2PS
@ 4600rpm
110.0lbft 149.1Nm @ 2600rpm
86.1bhp/ton 84.7bhp/tonne
44.8bhp/L 33.4kW/L 45.4PS/L
39.2ft/sec 12.0m/sec
Petrol 4-stroke piston
1896cc 115.7cu in
In-line 4 1 Carburettor
Compression ratio: 7.7:1
Bore: 87.9mm 3.5in
Stroke: 78.0mm 3.1in
Valve type/No: Overhead 8
Transmission: Manual
No. of forward speeds: 3
Wheels driven: Rear
Brakes F/R: Drum/Drum
Steering: Worm & sector
Wheelbase: 240.0cm 94.5in
Track F: 123.2cm 48.5in
Track R: 123.2cm 48.5in
Length: 403.1cm 158.7in
Width: 149.1cm 58.7in
Height: 144.5cm 56.9in
Kerb weight: 1003.3kg 2210.0lb
Fuel: 40.1L 8.8gal 10.6galUS

4353 Toyota

Corona
1966 Japan
87.0mph 140.0kmh
0-50mph 80.5kmh: 11.6secs
0-60mph 96.5kmh: 17.2secs
0-1/4 mile: 20.3secs
0-1km: 39.0secs
74.0bhp 55.2kW 75.0PS
@ 5000rpm
85.0lbft 115.2Nm @ 2600rpm
76.9bhp/ton 75.6bhp/tonne
49.7bhp/L 37.0kW/L 50.4PS/L
42.6ft/sec 13.0m/sec
16.0mph 25.7kmh/1000rpm
26.8mpg 22.3mpgUS 10.5L/100km
Petrol 4-stroke piston
1490cc 90.9cu in
In-line 4 1 Carburettor
Compression ratio: 8.0:1
Bore: 78.0mm 3.1in
Stroke: 78.0mm 3.1in
Valve type/No: Overhead 8
Transmission: Manual
No. of forward speeds: 4
Wheels driven: Rear
Springs F/R: Coil/Leaf
Brakes F/R: Drum/Drum
Steering: Worm & sector
Wheelbase: 215.9cm 85.0in
Track F: 127.0cm 50.0in
Track R: 127.0cm 50.0in
Length: 408.9cm 161.0in
Width: 154.9cm 61.0in
Height: 142.2cm 56.0in
Ground clearance: 19.1cm 7.5in
Kerb weight: 978.8kg 2156.0lb
Fuel: 45.0L 9.9gal 11.9galUS

4354 Toyota

Corona 1900
1966 Japan
90.0mph 144.8kmh
0-50mph 80.5kmh: 14.3secs
0-60mph 96.5kmh: 18.8secs
0-1/4 mile: 21.8secs
90.0bhp 67.1kW 91.2PS
@ 4600rpm
110.0lbft 149.1Nm @ 2600rpm
92.9bhp/ton 91.3bhp/tonne
47.5bhp/L 35.4kW/L 48.1PS/L
39.2ft/sec 12.0m/sec
17.5mph 28.2kmh/1000rpm
Petrol 4-stroke piston
1896cc 115.7cu in
In-line 4 1 Carburettor
Compression ratio: 8.0:1
Bore: 87.9mm 3.5in
Stroke: 78.0mm 3.1in
Valve type/No: Overhead 8
Transmission: Automatic
No. of forward speeds: 2
Wheels driven: Rear
Springs F/R: Coil/Leaf
Brakes F/R: Drum/Drum
Steering: Recirculating ball
Wheelbase: 242.1cm 95.3in
Track F: 127.0cm 50.0in
Track R: 127.0cm 50.0in
Length: 411.0cm 161.8in
Width: 154.9cm 61.0in
Height: 142.0cm 55.9in
Ground clearance: 18.0cm 7.1in
Kerb weight: 985.2kg 2170.0lb
Fuel: 45.4L 10.0gal 12.0galUS

4355 Toyota

Crown Custom
1966 Japan
92.0mph 148.0kmh
0-50mph 80.5kmh: 11.2secs
0-60mph 96.5kmh: 15.9secs
0-1/4 mile: 21.0secs
110.0bhp 82.0kW 111.5PS
@ 5200rpm
118.0lbft 159.9Nm @ 3600rpm
81.0bhp/ton 79.7bhp/tonne
55.3bhp/L 41.3kW/L 56.1PS/L
42.6ft/sec 13.0m/sec
21.6mph 34.8kmh/1000rpm
Petrol 4-stroke piston
1988cc 121.3cu in
In-line 6 1 Carburettor
Compression ratio: 8.8:1
Bore: 74.9mm 2.9in
Stroke: 74.9mm 2.9in
Valve type/No: Overhead 12
Transmission: Manual
No. of forward speeds: 3
Wheels driven: Rear
Brakes F/R: Drum/Drum
Steering: Recirculating ball
Wheelbase: 269.0cm 105.9in
Track F: 135.9cm 53.5in
Track R: 137.9cm 54.3in
Length: 468.9cm 184.6in
Width: 169.4cm 66.7in
Height: 147.1cm 57.9in
Kerb weight: 1380.2kg 3040.0lb
Fuel: 50.0L 11.0gal 13.2galUS

4356 Toyota

2000GT
1967 Japan
128.0mph 206.0kmh
0-50mph 80.5kmh: 7.7secs
0-60mph 96.5kmh: 10.0secs
0-1/4 mile: 16.6secs
150.0bhp 111.9kW 152.1PS
@ 6600rpm
130.0lbft 176.2Nm @ 5000rpm
135.5bhp/ton 133.2bhp/tonne
75.4bhp/L 56.3kW/L 76.5PS/L
54.1ft/sec 16.5m/sec
19.8mph 31.9kmh/1000rpm
Petrol 4-stroke piston
1988cc 121.3cu in
In-line 6 3 Carburettor
Compression ratio: 8.4:1
Bore: 75.0mm 2.9in
Stroke: 75.0mm 2.9in
Valve type/No: Overhead 12
Transmission: Manual
No. of forward speeds: 5
Wheels driven: Rear
Springs F/R: Coil/Coil
Brake system: PA
Brakes F/R: Disc/Disc
Steering: Rack & pinion PA
Wheelbase: 232.9cm 91.7in
Track F: 130.0cm 51.2in
Track R: 130.0cm 51.2in
Length: 417.6cm 164.4in
Width: 160.0cm 63.0in
Height: 116.1cm 45.7in
Ground clearance: 15.5cm 6.1in
Kerb weight: 1125.9kg 2480.0lb
Fuel: 59.8L 13.1gal 15.8galUS

4357 Toyota

Corona Coupe
1967 Japan
90.0mph 144.8kmh
0-50mph 80.5kmh: 12.2secs
0-60mph 96.5kmh: 18.3secs
0-1/4 mile: 21.1secs
90.0bhp 67.1kW 91.2PS
@ 4600rpm
110.0lbft 149.1Nm @ 2600rpm
92.0bhp/ton 90.5bhp/tonne
47.4bhp/L 35.4kW/L 48.1PS/L
39.2ft/sec 12.0m/sec
17.8mph 28.6kmh/1000rpm
Petrol 4-stroke piston
1897cc 115.7cu in
In-line 4 1 Carburettor
Compression ratio: 8.0:1
Bore: 88.0mm 3.5in
Stroke: 78.0mm 3.1in
Valve type/No: Overhead 8
Transmission: Automatic
No. of forward speeds: 2
Wheels driven: Rear
Springs F/R: Coil/Leaf
Brakes F/R: Drum/Drum
Steering: Recirculating ball
Wheelbase: 242.1cm 95.3in
Track F: 127.0cm 50.0in
Track R: 127.0cm 50.0in
Length: 411.0cm 161.8in
Width: 156.5cm 61.6in
Height: 137.4cm 54.1in
Ground clearance: 15.7cm 6.2in
Kerb weight: 994.3kg 2190.0lb
Fuel: 45.4L 10.0gal 12.0galUS

4358 Toyota

Land Cruiser
1967 Japan
77.0mph 123.9kmh
0-50mph 80.5kmh: 13.9secs
0-60mph 96.5kmh: 20.6secs
0-1/4 mile: 21.4secs
134.0bhp 99.9kW 135.9PS
@ 3800rpm
217.0lbft 294.0Nm @ 2000rpm
73.8bhp/ton 72.6bhp/tonne
34.6bhp/L 25.8kW/L 35.1PS/L
42.2ft/sec 12.9m/sec
20.4mph 32.8kmh/1000rpm
Petrol 4-stroke piston
3869cc 236.1cu in
In-line 6 1 Carburettor
Compression ratio: 7.7:1
Bore: 89.9mm 3.5in
Stroke: 101.6mm 4.0in
Valve type/No: Overhead 12
Transmission: Manual
No. of forward speeds: 3
Wheels driven: 4-wheel drive
Springs F/R: Leaf/Leaf
Brakes F/R: Drum/Drum
Steering: Worm & sector
Wheelbase: 264.9cm 104.3in
Track F: 140.5cm 55.3in
Track R: 140.0cm 55.1in
Length: 470.7cm 185.3in
Width: 172.0cm 67.7in
Height: 177.0cm 69.7in
Ground clearance: 22.1cm 8.7in
Kerb weight: 1845.5kg 4065.0lb
Fuel: 70.0L 15.4gal 18.5galUS

4359 Toyota

Corolla
1968 Japan
83.0mph 133.5kmh
0-50mph 80.5kmh: 11.2secs
0-60mph 96.5kmh: 17.0secs
0-1/4 mile: 20.5secs
60.0bhp 44.7kW 60.8PS
@ 6000rpm
62.0lbft 84.0Nm @ 3800rpm
81.9bhp/ton 80.6bhp/tonne
55.7bhp/L 41.5kW/L 56.5PS/L
40.0ft/sec 12.2m/sec
15.1mph 24.3kmh/1000rpm
Petrol 4-stroke piston
1077cc 65.7cu in
In-line 4 2 Carburettor
Compression ratio: 9.0:1
Bore: 74.9mm 2.9in
Stroke: 61.0mm 2.4in
Valve type/No: Overhead 8
Transmission: Manual
No. of forward speeds: 4
Wheels driven: Rear
Springs F/R: Coil/Leaf
Brakes F/R: Drum/Drum
Steering: Worm & roller
Wheelbase: 228.6cm 90.0in
Track F: 122.9cm 48.4in
Track R: 121.9cm 48.0in
Length: 384.6cm 151.4in
Width: 148.6cm 58.5in
Height: 137.9cm 54.3in
Kerb weight: 744.6kg 1640.0lb
Fuel: 36.0L 7.9gal 9.5galUS

4360 Toyota

Corolla de Luxe
1968 Japan
86.0mph 138.4kmh
0-50mph 80.5kmh: 11.4secs
0-60mph 96.5kmh: 16.3secs
0-1/4 mile: 20.4secs
0-1km: 39.1secs
60.0bhp 44.7kW 60.8PS
@ 6000rpm
61.5lbft 83.3Nm @ 3800rpm
82.8bhp/ton 81.4bhp/tonne
55.7bhp/L 41.5kW/L 56.5PS/L
40.0ft/sec 12.2m/sec
14.6mph 23.5kmh/1000rpm
32.3mpg 26.9mpgUS 8.7L/100km
Petrol 4-stroke piston
1077cc 65.7cu in
In-line 4 1 Carburettor
Compression ratio: 9.0:1
Bore: 75.0mm 2.9in
Stroke: 61.0mm 2.4in
Valve type/No: Overhead 8
Transmission: Manual
No. of forward speeds: 4
Wheels driven: Rear
Springs F/R: Leaf/Leaf
Brakes F/R: Drum/Drum
Steering: Worm & sector
Wheelbase: 228.6cm 90.0in
Track F: 122.9cm 48.4in
Track R: 121.9cm 48.0in
Length: 384.6cm 151.4in
Width: 148.6cm 58.5in
Height: 137.9cm 54.3in
Ground clearance: 17.0cm 6.7in
Kerb weight: 737.3kg 1624.0lb
Fuel: 35.9L 7.9gal 9.5galUS

4361 Toyota

Corona
1968 Japan
91.0mph 146.4kmh
0-50mph 80.5kmh: 10.2secs
0-60mph 96.5kmh: 14.0secs
0-1/4 mile: 19.7secs
90.0bhp 67.1kW 91.2PS
@ 4600rpm
110.0lbft 149.1Nm @ 2600rpm
94.2bhp/ton 92.6bhp/tonne
47.4bhp/L 35.4kW/L 48.1PS/L
39.2ft/sec 12.0m/sec
17.8mph 28.6kmh/1000rpm
Petrol 4-stroke piston
1898cc 115.8cu in
In-line 4 1 Carburettor
Compression ratio: 8.0:1
Bore: 87.9mm 3.5in
Stroke: 78.0mm 3.1in
Valve type/No: Overhead 8
Transmission: Manual
No. of forward speeds: 4
Wheels driven: Rear
Springs F/R: Coil/Leaf
Brakes F/R: Drum/Drum
Steering: Recirculating ball
Wheelbase: 242.1cm 95.3in
Track F: 127.8cm 50.3in
Track R: 126.7cm 49.9in
Length: 412.5cm 162.4in
Width: 154.9cm 61.0in
Height: 142.0cm 55.9in
Ground clearance: 16.8cm 6.6in
Kerb weight: 971.6kg 2140.0lb
Fuel: 45.4L 10.0gal 12.0galUS

4362 Toyota

Crown Toyoglide
1969 Japan
100.0mph 160.9kmh
0-50mph 80.5kmh: 11.3secs
0-60mph 96.5kmh: 16.0secs
0-1/4 mile: 20.1secs
0-1km: 37.6secs
115.0bhp 85.8kW 116.6PS
@ 5200rpm

127.0lbft 172.1Nm @ 3600rpm
89.2bhp/ton 87.7bhp/tonne
51.0bhp/L 38.1kW/L 51.7PS/L
48.4ft/sec 14.7m/sec
16.4mph 26.4kmh/1000rpm
17.3mpg 14.4mpgUS 16.3L/100km
Petrol 4-stroke piston
2253cc 137.5cu in
In-line 6 1 Carburettor
Compression ratio: 8.8:1
Bore: 75.0mm 2.9in
Stroke: 85.0mm 3.3in
Valve type/No: Overhead 12
Transmission: Automatic
No. of forward speeds: 3
Wheels driven: Rear
Springs F/R: Coil/Coil
Brake system: PA
Brakes F/R: Disc/Drum
Steering: Recirculating ball
Wheelbase: 269.0cm 105.9in
Track F: 135.9cm 53.5in
Track R: 137.9cm 54.3in
Length: 466.6cm 183.7in
Width: 168.9cm 66.5in
Height: 144.5cm 56.9in
Ground clearance: 15.2cm 6.0in
Kerb weight: 1311.1kg 2888.0lb
Fuel: 65.1L 14.3gal 17.2galUS

4363 Toyota
Corona Mk II
1970 Japan
98.0mph 157.7kmh
0-50mph 80.5kmh: 10.3secs
0-60mph 96.5kmh: 14.5secs
0-1/4 mile: 19.6secs
108.0bhp 80.5kW 109.5PS
@ 5500rpm
117.0lbft 158.5Nm @ 3600rpm
100.4bhp/ton 98.7bhp/tonne
58.1bhp/L 43.3kW/L 58.9PS/L
48.1ft/sec 14.7m/sec
17.6mph 28.3kmh/1000rpm
29.3mpg 24.4mpgUS 9.6L/100km
Petrol 4-stroke piston
1858cc 113.4cu in
In-line 4 1 Carburettor
Compression ratio: 9.0:1
Bore: 86.0mm 3.4in
Stroke: 80.0mm 3.1in
Valve type/No: Overhead 8
Transmission: Manual
No. of forward speeds: 4
Wheels driven: Rear
Springs F/R: Coil/Leaf
Brakes F/R: Disc/Drum
Steering: Recirculating ball
Wheelbase: 251.0cm 98.8in
Track F: 132.6cm 52.2in
Track R: 132.1cm 52.0in
Length: 433.1cm 170.5in
Width: 161.0cm 63.4in
Height: 140.5cm 55.3in
Ground clearance: 18.0cm 7.1in
Kerb weight: 1094.1kg 2410.0lb
Fuel: 51.8L 11.4gal 13.7galUS

4364 Toyota
Corona Mk II 1900
1970 Japan
102.0mph 164.1kmh
0-50mph 80.5kmh: 9.2secs
0-60mph 96.5kmh: 13.5secs
0-1/4 mile: 19.2secs
0-1km: 36.1secs
100.0bhp 74.6kW 101.4PS
@ 5500rpm
108.0lbft 146.3Nm @ 3600rpm
96.5bhp/ton 94.9bhp/tonne
53.8bhp/L 40.1kW/L 54.6PS/L
48.1ft/sec 14.7m/sec
18.2mph 29.3kmh/1000rpm
22.9mpg 19.1mpgUS 12.3L/100km
Petrol 4-stroke piston
1858cc 113.4cu in
In-line 4 1 Carburettor
Compression ratio: 9.0:1
Bore: 86.0mm 3.4in
Stroke: 80.0mm 3.1in
Valve type/No: Overhead 8
Transmission: Manual
No. of forward speeds: 4
Wheels driven: Rear
Springs F/R: Coil/Leaf
Brake system: PA
Brakes F/R: Disc/Drum
Steering: Recirculating ball
Wheelbase: 250.2cm 98.5in
Track F: 133.4cm 52.5in
Track R: 134.6cm 53.0in
Length: 431.8cm 170.0in
Width: 167.6cm 66.0in
Height: 138.4cm 54.5in
Ground clearance: 15.2cm 6.0in
Kerb weight: 1053.3kg 2320.0lb
Fuel: 52.3L 11.5gal 13.8galUS

4365 Toyota
Crown
1970 Japan
93.0mph 149.6kmh
0-50mph 80.5kmh: 10.9secs
0-60mph 96.5kmh: 15.3secs
0-1/4 mile: 19.9secs
115.0bhp 85.8kW 116.6PS
@ 5200rpm
127.0lbft 172.1Nm @ 3000rpm
87.9bhp/ton 86.4bhp/tonne
51.0bhp/L 38.1kW/L 51.7PS/L
48.4ft/sec 14.7m/sec
17.1mph 27.5kmh/1000rpm
24.9mpg 20.7mpgUS 11.4L/100km
Petrol 4-stroke piston
2253cc 137.5cu in
In-line 6 1 Carburettor
Compression ratio: 8.8:1
Bore: 75.0mm 2.9in
Stroke: 85.0mm 3.3in
Valve type/No: Overhead 12
Transmission: Manual
No. of forward speeds: 4
Wheels driven: Rear
Springs F/R: Coil/Coil
Brake system: PA
Brakes F/R: Disc/Drum
Steering: Recirculating ball
Wheelbase: 269.0cm 105.9in
Track F: 136.9cm 53.9in
Track R: 136.9cm 53.9in
Length: 468.9cm 184.6in
Width: 168.9cm 66.5in
Height: 146.6cm 57.7in
Ground clearance: 18.5cm 7.3in
Kerb weight: 1330.2kg 2930.0lb
Fuel: 65.1L 14.3gal 17.2galUS

4366 Toyota
1900SL
1971 Japan
104.0mph 167.3kmh
0-50mph 80.5kmh: 9.2secs
0-60mph 96.5kmh: 12.9secs
0-1/4 mile: 19.0secs
0-1km: 35.2secs
124.0bhp 92.5kW 125.7PS
@ 6000rpm
121.0lbft 164.0Nm @ 4000rpm
121.3bhp/ton 119.3bhp/tonne
66.7bhp/L 49.8kW/L 67.7PS/L
52.5ft/sec 16.0m/sec
18.2mph 29.3kmh/1000rpm
23.8mpg 19.8mpgUS 11.9L/100km
Petrol 4-stroke piston
1858cc 113.4cu in
In-line 4 2 Carburettor
Compression ratio: 10.2:1
Bore: 86.0mm 3.4in
Stroke: 80.0mm 3.1in
Valve type/No: Overhead 8
Transmission: Manual
No. of forward speeds: 4
Wheels driven: Rear
Springs F/R: Coil/Leaf
Brake system: PA
Brakes F/R: Disc/Drum
Steering: Recirculating ball
Wheelbase: 250.2cm 98.5in
Track F: 133.4cm 52.5in
Track R: 134.6cm 53.0in
Length: 432.8cm 170.4in
Width: 167.6cm 66.0in
Height: 138.4cm 54.5in
Ground clearance: 15.2cm 6.0in
Kerb weight: 1039.7kg 2290.0lb
Fuel: 52.3L 11.5gal 13.8galUS

4367 Toyota
Celica
1971 Japan
108.0mph 173.8kmh
0-50mph 80.5kmh: 8.3secs
0-60mph 96.5kmh: 11.5secs
0-1/4 mile: 18.2secs
0-1km: 34.1secs
113.0bhp 84.3kW 114.6PS
@ 6000rpm
109.0lbft 147.7Nm @ 4200rpm
118.9bhp/ton 117.0bhp/tonne
71.2bhp/L 53.1kW/L 72.1PS/L
46.0ft/sec 14.0m/sec
17.1mph 27.5kmh/1000rpm
28.0mpg 23.3mpgUS 10.1L/100km
Petrol 4-stroke piston
1588cc 96.9cu in
In-line 4 2 Carburettor
Compression ratio: 9.4:1
Bore: 85.0mm 3.3in
Stroke: 70.0mm 2.8in
Valve type/No: Overhead 8
Transmission: Manual
No. of forward speeds: 4
Wheels driven: Rear
Springs F/R: Coil/Coil
Brake system: PA
Brakes F/R: Disc/Drum
Steering: Recirculating ball
Wheelbase: 242.6cm 95.5in
Track F: 128.0cm 50.4in
Track R: 128.5cm 50.6in
Length: 406.4cm 160.0in
Width: 160.0cm 63.0in
Height: 132.1cm 52.0in
Ground clearance: 17.5cm 6.9in
Kerb weight: 966.1kg 2128.0lb
Fuel: 50.0L 11.0gal 13.2galUS

4368 Toyota
Corolla
1971 Japan
89.0mph 143.2kmh
0-50mph 80.5kmh: 12.9secs
0-60mph 96.5kmh: 19.0secs
0-1/4 mile: 21.2secs
73.0bhp 54.4kW 74.0PS
@ 6000rpm
74.2lbft 100.5Nm @ 3800rpm
93.7bhp/ton 92.1bhp/tonne
62.6bhp/L 46.7kW/L 63.5PS/L
43.3ft/sec 13.2m/sec
15.5mph 24.9kmh/1000rpm
36.3mpg 30.2mpgUS 7.8L/100km
Petrol 4-stroke piston
1166cc 71.1cu in
In-line 4 1 Carburettor
Compression ratio: 9.0:1
Bore: 75.0mm 2.9in
Stroke: 66.0mm 2.6in
Valve type/No: Overhead 8
Transmission: Manual
No. of forward speeds: 4
Wheels driven: Rear
Springs F/R: Coil/Leaf
Brakes F/R: Disc/Drum
Steering: Recirculating ball
Wheelbase: 233.4cm 91.9in
Track F: 125.5cm 49.4in
Track R: 124.5cm 49.0in
Length: 394.5cm 155.3in
Width: 150.6cm 59.3in
Height: 137.4cm 54.1in
Ground clearance: 17.0cm 6.7in
Kerb weight: 792.2kg 1745.0lb
Fuel: 45.0L 9.9gal 11.9galUS

4369 Toyota
Corolla 1200SL
1971 Japan
97.0mph 156.1kmh
0-50mph 80.5kmh: 10.0secs
0-60mph 96.5kmh: 14.3secs
0-1/4 mile: 19.7secs
0-1km: 37.0secs
83.0bhp 61.9kW 84.1PS
@ 6600rpm
69.4lbft 94.0Nm @ 4600rpm
108.5bhp/ton 106.7bhp/tonne
71.2bhp/L 53.1kW/L 72.2PS/L
47.7ft/sec 14.5m/sec
14.8mph 23.8kmh/1000rpm
30.4mpg 25.3mpgUS 9.3L/100km
Petrol 4-stroke piston
1166cc 71.1cu in
In-line 4 2 Carburettor
Compression ratio: 10.0:1
Bore: 75.0mm 2.9in
Stroke: 66.0mm 2.6in
Valve type/No: Overhead 8
Transmission: Manual
No. of forward speeds: 4
Wheels driven: Rear
Springs F/R: Coil/Leaf
Brakes F/R: Disc/Drum
Steering: Recirculating ball
Wheelbase: 263.9cm 103.9in
Track F: 125.5cm 49.4in
Track R: 124.5cm 49.0in
Length: 394.5cm 155.3in
Width: 150.6cm 59.3in
Height: 134.6cm 53.0in
Ground clearance: 17.0cm 6.7in
Kerb weight: 778.0kg 1713.7lb
Fuel: 45.0L 9.9gal 11.9galUS

4370 Toyota
Corolla 1600
1971 Japan
95.0mph 152.9kmh
0-50mph 80.5kmh: 8.6secs
0-60mph 96.5kmh: 12.0secs
0-1/4 mile: 18.5secs
102.0bhp 76.1kW 103.4PS
@ 6000rpm
101.0lbft 136.9Nm @ 3800rpm
117.8bhp/ton 115.8bhp/tonne
64.2bhp/L 47.9kW/L 65.1PS/L
46.0ft/sec 14.0m/sec
17.0mph 27.4kmh/1000rpm
35.5mpg 29.6mpgUS 7.9L/100km
Petrol 4-stroke piston
1588cc 96.9cu in
In-line 4 1 Carburettor
Compression ratio: 8.5:1
Bore: 85.0mm 3.3in
Stroke: 70.0mm 2.8in
Valve type/No: Overhead 8
Transmission: Manual
No. of forward speeds: 4
Wheels driven: Rear
Springs F/R: Coil/Leaf
Brake system: PA
Brakes F/R: Disc/Drum
Steering: Recirculating ball
Wheelbase: 233.4cm 91.9in
Track F: 125.5cm 49.4in
Track R: 124.5cm 49.0in
Length: 400.1cm 157.5in
Width: 150.6cm 59.3in
Height: 134.6cm 53.0in
Ground clearance: 15.5cm 6.1in
Kerb weight: 880.8kg 1940.0lb
Fuel: 45.4L 10.0gal 12.0galUS

4371 Toyota
Corona de Luxe
1971 Japan
98.0mph 157.7kmh
0-50mph 80.5kmh: 9.5secs
0-60mph 96.5kmh: 13.5secs
0-1/4 mile: 19.0secs
108.0bhp 80.5kW 109.5PS
@ 5500rpm
117.0lbft 158.5Nm @ 3600rpm
109.2bhp/ton 107.4bhp/tonne
58.1bhp/L 43.3kW/L 58.9PS/L
48.1ft/sec 14.7m/sec
17.6mph 28.3kmh/1000rpm
22.9mpg 19.1mpgUS 12.3L/100km
Petrol 4-stroke piston
1858cc 113.4cu in
In-line 4 1 Carburettor
Compression ratio: 9.0:1
Bore: 86.0mm 3.4in
Stroke: 80.0mm 3.1in
Valve type/No: Overhead 8
Transmission: Manual
No. of forward speeds: 4
Wheels driven: Rear
Springs F/R: Coil/Leaf
Brake system: PA
Brakes F/R: Disc/Drum
Steering: Recirculating ball
Wheelbase: 242.6cm 95.5in
Track F: 129.0cm 50.8in
Track R: 127.8cm 50.3in
Length: 416.6cm 164.0in
Width: 157.0cm 61.8in
Height: 140.0cm 55.1in
Ground clearance: 17.8cm 7.0in
Kerb weight: 1005.6kg 2215.0lb
Fuel: 50.0L 11.0gal 13.2galUS

4372 Toyota
Land Cruiser
1971 Japan
82.0mph 131.9kmh

0-60mph 96.5kmh: 18.0secs
155.0bhp 115.6kW 157.1PS
@ 4000rpm
225.0lbft 304.9Nm @ 2200rpm
94.1bhp/ton 92.5bhp/tonne
40.0bhp/L 29.8kW/L 40.5PS/L
44.4ft/sec 13.5m/sec
18.0mpg 15.0mpgUS 15.7L/100km
Petrol 4-stroke piston
3879cc 236.7cu in
In-line 6
Compression ratio: 7.8:1
Bore: 89.9mm 3.5in
Stroke: 101.6mm 4.0in
Valve type/No: Overhead 12
Transmission: Manual
No. of forward speeds: 3
Wheels driven: 4-wheel drive
Brakes F/R: Drum/Drum
Steering: Worm & roller
Wheelbase: 228.6cm 90.0in
Track F: 140.5cm 55.3in
Track R: 140.0cm 55.1in
Length: 387.1cm 152.4in
Width: 166.6cm 65.6in
Height: 193.0cm 76.0in
Ground clearance: 20.3cm 8.0in
Kerb weight: 1675.3kg 3690.0lb
Fuel: 70.0L 15.4gal 18.5galUS

4373 Toyota

Land Cruiser Wagon
1971 Japan
82.0mph 131.9kmh
0-60mph 96.5kmh: 19.6secs
155.0bhp 115.6kW 157.1PS
@ 4000rpm
225.0lbft 304.9Nm @ 2200rpm
83.9bhp/ton 82.5bhp/tonne
40.0bhp/L 29.8kW/L 40.5PS/L
44.4ft/sec 13.5m/sec
14.4mpg 12.0mpgUS 19.6L/100km
Petrol 4-stroke piston
3879cc 236.7cu in
In-line 6
Compression ratio: 7.8:1
Bore: 89.9mm 3.5in
Stroke: 101.6mm 4.0in
Valve type/No: Overhead 12
Transmission: Manual
No. of forward speeds: 3
Wheels driven: 4-wheel drive
Brakes F/R: Drum/Drum
Steering: Worm & roller
Wheelbase: 270.0cm 106.3in
Track F: 140.5cm 55.3in
Track R: 140.0cm 55.1in
Length: 467.4cm 184.0in
Width: 173.5cm 68.3in
Height: 186.4cm 73.4in
Ground clearance: 20.3cm 8.0in
Kerb weight: 1879.6kg 4140.0lb
Fuel: 90.1L 19.8gal 23.8galUS

4374 Toyota

Carina
1972 Japan
94.0mph 151.2kmh
0-50mph 80.5kmh: 9.6secs
0-60mph 96.5kmh: 13.5secs
0-1/4 mile: 19.2secs
88.0bhp 65.6kW 89.2PS
@ 6000rpm
91.0lbft 123.3Nm @ 3800rpm
92.3bhp/ton 90.8bhp/tonne
55.4bhp/L 41.3kW/L 56.2PS/L
46.0ft/sec 14.0m/sec
16.7mph 26.9kmh/1000rpm
31.6mpg 26.3mpgUS 8.9L/100km
Petrol 4-stroke piston
1588cc 96.9cu in
In-line 4 1 Carburettor
Compression ratio: 8.5:1
Bore: 85.0mm 3.3in
Stroke: 70.0mm 2.8in
Valve type/No: Overhead 8
Transmission: Manual
No. of forward speeds: 4
Wheels driven: Rear
Springs F/R: Coil/Coil
Brake system: PA
Brakes F/R: Disc/Drum
Steering: Recirculating ball
Wheelbase: 242.6cm 95.5in
Track F: 128.0cm 50.4in
Track R: 128.5cm 50.6in
Length: 413.5cm 162.8in
Width: 157.0cm 61.8in
Height: 138.4cm 54.5in
Ground clearance: 17.5cm 6.9in
Kerb weight: 969.3kg 2135.0lb
Fuel: 50.0L 11.0gal 13.2galUS

4375 Toyota

Crown 2600
1972 Japan
90.0mph 144.8kmh
0-50mph 80.5kmh: 10.2secs
0-60mph 96.5kmh: 14.1secs
0-1/4 mile: 19.7secs
122.0bhp 91.0kW 123.7PS
@ 5200rpm
141.0lbft 191.1Nm @ 3600rpm
86.8bhp/ton 85.3bhp/tonne
47.6bhp/L 35.5kW/L 48.3PS/L
48.4ft/sec 14.7m/sec
17.1mph 27.5kmh/1000rpm
19.2mpg 16.0mpgUS 14.7L/100km
Petrol 4-stroke piston
2563cc 156.4cu in
In-line 6 1 Carburettor
Compression ratio: 8.5:1
Bore: 80.0mm 3.1in
Stroke: 85.0mm 3.3in
Valve type/No: Overhead 12
Transmission: Automatic
No. of forward speeds: 3
Wheels driven: Rear
Springs F/R: Coil/Coil
Brake system: PA
Brakes F/R: Disc/Drum
Steering: Recirculating ball PA
Wheelbase: 269.0cm 105.9in
Track F: 139.2cm 54.8in
Track R: 138.2cm 54.4in
Length: 468.4cm 184.4in
Width: 168.9cm 66.5in
Height: 142.0cm 55.9in
Ground clearance: 17.5cm 6.9in
Kerb weight: 1430.1kg 3150.0lb
Fuel: 70.0L 15.4gal 18.5galUS

4376 Toyota

Custom Crown Estate
1972 Japan
102.0mph 164.1kmh
0-50mph 80.5kmh: 8.9secs
0-60mph 96.5kmh: 12.1secs
0-1/4 mile: 19.1secs
0-1km: 35.2secs
140.0bhp 104.4kW 141.9PS
@ 5200rpm
156.0lbft 211.4Nm @ 3600rpm
101.8bhp/ton 100.1bhp/tonne
54.6bhp/L 40.7kW/L 55.4PS/L
48.4ft/sec 14.7m/sec
17.5mph 28.2kmh/1000rpm
18.5mpg 15.4mpgUS 15.3L/100km
Petrol 4-stroke piston
2563cc 156.4cu in
In-line 6 1 Carburettor
Compression ratio: 8.5:1
Bore: 80.0mm 3.1in
Stroke: 85.0mm 3.3in
Valve type/No: Overhead 12
Transmission: Automatic
No. of forward speeds: 3
Wheels driven: Rear
Springs F/R: Coil/Coil
Brake system: PA
Brakes F/R: Disc/Drum
Steering: Recirculating ball
Wheelbase: 269.0cm 105.9in
Track F: 139.2cm 54.8in
Track R: 138.2cm 54.4in
Length: 468.4cm 184.4in
Width: 168.9cm 66.5in
Height: 142.0cm 55.9in
Ground clearance: 20.3cm 8.0in
Kerb weight: 1398.3kg 3080.0lb
Fuel: 60.1L 13.2gal 15.9galUS

4377 Toyota

Celica
1973 Japan
97.0mph 156.1kmh
0-50mph 80.5kmh: 9.4secs
0-60mph 96.5kmh: 13.6secs
0-1/4 mile: 19.6secs
97.0bhp 72.3kW 98.3PS
@ 5500rpm
106.0lbft 143.6Nm @ 3600rpm
92.5bhp/ton 90.9bhp/tonne
49.3bhp/L 36.7kW/L 50.0PS/L
48.1ft/sec 14.7m/sec
17.2mph 27.7kmh/1000rpm
26.4mpg 22.0mpgUS 10.7L/100km
Petrol 4-stroke piston
1968cc 120.1cu in
In-line 4 1 Carburettor
Compression ratio: 8.5:1
Bore: 88.5mm 3.5in
Stroke: 80.0mm 3.1in
Valve type/No: Overhead 8
Transmission: Manual
No. of forward speeds: 4
Wheels driven: Rear
Springs F/R: Coil/Coil
Brake system: PA
Brakes F/R: Disc/Drum
Steering: Recirculating ball
Wheelbase: 242.6cm 95.5in
Track F: 128.0cm 50.4in
Track R: 128.5cm 50.6in
Length: 416.3cm 163.9in
Width: 160.0cm 63.0in
Height: 131.1cm 51.6in
Ground clearance: 17.5cm 6.9in
Kerb weight: 1066.9kg 2350.0lb
Fuel: 50.0L 11.0gal 13.2galUS

4378 Toyota

Corolla
1973 Japan
0-60mph 96.5kmh: 13.9secs
0-1/4 mile: 19.4secs
88.0bhp 65.6kW 89.2PS
@ 6000rpm
91.0lbft 123.3Nm @ 3800rpm
94.8bhp/ton 93.2bhp/tonne
55.4bhp/L 41.3kW/L 56.2PS/L
31.2mpg 26.0mpgUS 9.0L/100km
Petrol 4-stroke piston
1588cc 96.9cu in
In-line 4
Valve type/No: Overhead 8
Transmission: Manual
No. of forward speeds: 4
Wheels driven: Rear
Brake system: PA
Brakes F/R: Disc/Drum
Wheelbase: 233.4cm 91.9in
Length: 406.9cm 160.2in
Width: 150.6cm 59.3in
Height: 140.5cm 55.3in
Kerb weight: 944.3kg 2080.0lb

4379 Toyota

Corolla SR5
1973 Japan
86.0mph 138.4kmh
0-50mph 80.5kmh: 9.9secs
0-60mph 96.5kmh: 13.7secs
0-1/4 mile: 20.0secs
88.0bhp 65.6kW 89.2PS
@ 6000rpm
91.0lbft 123.3Nm @ 3800rpm
95.5bhp/ton 93.9bhp/tonne
55.4bhp/L 41.3kW/L 56.2PS/L
46.0ft/sec 14.0m/sec
18.5mph 29.8kmh/1000rpm
27.6mpg 23.0mpgUS 10.2L/100km
Petrol 4-stroke piston
1588cc 96.9cu in
In-line 4
Compression ratio: 8.5:1
Bore: 85.0mm 3.3in
Stroke: 70.0mm 2.8in
Valve type/No: Overhead 8
Transmission: Manual
No. of forward speeds: 5
Wheels driven: Rear
Springs F/R: Coil/Leaf
Brake system: PA
Brakes F/R: Disc/Drum
Steering: Recirculating ball
Wheelbase: 233.4cm 91.9in
Track F: 127.0cm 50.0in
Track R: 129.5cm 51.0in
Length: 404.9cm 159.4in
Width: 159.5cm 62.8in
Height: 133.6cm 52.6in
Kerb weight: 937.5kg 2065.0lb
Fuel: 45.0L 9.9gal 11.9galUS

4380 Toyota

Corona
1973 Japan
0-60mph 96.5kmh: 13.0secs
0-1/4 mile: 19.0secs
97.0bhp 72.3kW 98.3PS
@ 5500rpm
106.0lbft 143.6Nm @ 3600rpm
89.0bhp/ton 87.6bhp/tonne
49.3bhp/L 36.7kW/L 50.0PS/L
25.8mpg 21.5mpgUS 10.9L/100km
Petrol 4-stroke piston
1968cc 120.1cu in
In-line 4
Valve type/No: Overhead 8
Transmission: Manual
No. of forward speeds: 4
Wheels driven: Rear
Brake system: PA
Brakes F/R: Disc/Drum
Wheelbase: 246.1cm 96.9in
Length: 435.1cm 171.3in
Width: 157.0cm 61.8in
Height: 142.0cm 55.9in
Kerb weight: 1107.8kg 2440.0lb

4381 Toyota

Mk II
1973 Japan
96.0mph 154.5kmh
0-50mph 80.5kmh: 10.4secs
0-60mph 96.5kmh: 14.2secs
0-1/4 mile: 19.7secs
109.0bhp 81.3kW 110.5PS
@ 5200rpm
120.0lbft 162.6Nm @ 3600rpm
89.0bhp/ton 87.5bhp/tonne
48.4bhp/L 36.1kW/L 49.0PS/L
48.4ft/sec 14.7m/sec
18.2mph 29.3kmh/1000rpm
24.0mpg 20.0mpgUS 11.8L/100km
Petrol 4-stroke piston
2253cc 137.5cu in
In-line 6 1 Carburettor
Compression ratio: 8.5:1
Bore: 75.0mm 2.9in
Stroke: 85.0mm 3.3in
Valve type/No: Overhead 12
Transmission: Manual
No. of forward speeds: 4
Wheels driven: Rear
Springs F/R: Coil/Coil
Brake system: PA
Brakes F/R: Disc/Drum
Steering: Recirculating ball
Wheelbase: 258.6cm 101.8in
Track F: 136.1cm 53.6in
Track R: 134.6cm 53.0in
Length: 442.0cm 174.0in
Width: 162.6cm 64.0in
Height: 140.0cm 55.1in
Ground clearance: 17.5cm 6.9in
Kerb weight: 1245.8kg 2744.0lb
Fuel: 60.2L 13.2gal 15.9galUS

4382 Toyota

Mk II 2.6
1973 Japan
101.0mph 162.5kmh
0-50mph 80.5kmh: 9.2secs
0-60mph 96.5kmh: 12.4secs
0-1/4 mile: 19.0secs
122.0bhp 91.0kW 123.7PS
@ 5200rpm
141.0lbft 191.1Nm @ 3600rpm
97.4bhp/ton 95.8bhp/tonne
47.6bhp/L 35.5kW/L 48.3PS/L
48.4ft/sec 14.7m/sec
17.9mph 28.8kmh/1000rpm
21.0mpg 17.5mpgUS 13.4L/100km
Petrol 4-stroke piston
2563cc 156.4cu in
In-line 6
Compression ratio: 8.5:1
Bore: 80.0mm 3.1in
Stroke: 85.0mm 3.3in
Valve type/No: Overhead 12
Transmission: Automatic
No. of forward speeds: 3
Wheels driven: Rear
Springs F/R: Coil/Coil
Brake system: PA
Brakes F/R: Disc/Drum
Steering: Recirculating ball PA
Wheelbase: 258.6cm 101.8in
Track F: 136.1cm 53.6in
Track R: 134.6cm 53.0in
Length: 445.5cm 175.4in
Width: 162.6cm 64.0in
Height: 138.9cm 54.7in
Kerb weight: 1273.5kg 2805.0lb
Fuel: 60.2L 13.2gal 15.9galUS

4383 Toyota
Celica GT
1974 Japan
104.0mph 167.3kmh
0-50mph 80.5kmh: 9.3secs
0-60mph 96.5kmh: 13.3secs
0-1/4 mile: 19.3secs
97.0bhp 72.3kW 98.3PS
@ 5500rpm
106.0lbft 143.6Nm @ 3600rpm
89.4bhp/ton 87.9bhp/tonne
49.3bhp/L 36.7kW/L 50.0PS/L
48.1ft/sec 14.7m/sec
20.2mph 32.5kmh/1000rpm
29.4mpg 24.5mpgUS 9.6L/100km
Petrol 4-stroke piston
1968cc 120.1cu in
In-line 4
Compression ratio: 8.5:1
Bore: 88.5mm 3.5in
Stroke: 80.0mm 3.1in
Valve type/No: Overhead 8
Transmission: Manual
No. of forward speeds: 5
Wheels driven: Rear
Springs F/R: Coil/Coil
Brake system: PA
Brakes F/R: Disc/Drum
Steering: Recirculating ball
Wheelbase: 242.6cm 95.5in
Track F: 130.0cm 51.2in
Track R: 130.6cm 51.4in
Length: 429.8cm 169.2in
Width: 160.0cm 63.0in
Height: 131.1cm 51.6in
Kerb weight: 1103.2kg 2430.0lb
Fuel: 50.0L 11.0gal 13.2galUS

4384 Toyota
Corona 2000 Mk II Automatic
1974 Japan
97.0mph 156.1kmh
0-50mph 80.5kmh: 11.5secs
0-60mph 96.5kmh: 16.4secs
0-1/4 mile: 20.5secs
0-1km: 38.1secs
119.0bhp 88.7kW 120.6PS
@ 5500rpm
129.0lbft 174.8Nm @ 3600rpm
104.9bhp/ton 103.2bhp/tonne
60.5bhp/L 45.1kW/L 61.3PS/L
48.1ft/sec 14.7m/sec
18.0mph 29.0kmh/1000rpm
24.2mpg 20.2mpgUS 11.7L/100km
Petrol 4-stroke piston
1968cc 120.1cu in
In-line 4 1 Carburettor
Compression ratio: 8.5:1
Bore: 88.5mm 3.5in
Stroke: 80.0mm 3.1in
Valve type/No: Overhead 8
Transmission: Automatic
No. of forward speeds: 3
Wheels driven: Rear
Springs F/R: Coil/Coil
Brake system: PA
Brakes F/R: Disc/Drum
Steering: Recirculating ball
Wheelbase: 258.6cm 101.8in
Track F: 135.9cm 53.5in
Track R: 134.6cm 53.0in
Length: 432.6cm 170.3in
Width: 162.6cm 64.0in
Height: 138.9cm 54.7in
Ground clearance: 17.5cm 6.9in
Kerb weight: 1153.2kg 2540.0lb
Fuel: 60.1L 13.2gal 15.9galUS

4385 Toyota
Corona SR
1974 Japan
96.0mph 154.5kmh
0-50mph 80.5kmh: 11.1secs
0-60mph 96.5kmh: 16.0secs
0-1/4 mile: 20.4secs
97.0bhp 72.3kW 98.3PS
@ 5500rpm
106.0lbft 143.6Nm @ 3600rpm
82.8bhp/ton 81.4bhp/tonne
49.3bhp/L 36.7kW/L 50.0PS/L
48.1ft/sec 14.7m/sec
21.1mph 33.9kmh/1000rpm
27.6mpg 23.0mpgUS 10.2L/100km
Petrol 4-stroke piston
1968cc 120.1cu in
In-line 4 1 Carburettor
Compression ratio: 8.5:1
Bore: 88.5mm 3.5in
Stroke: 80.0mm 3.1in
Valve type/No: Overhead 8
Transmission: Manual
No. of forward speeds: 5
Wheels driven: Rear
Springs F/R: Coil/Leaf
Brake system: PA
Brakes F/R: Disc/Drum
Steering: Recirculating ball
Wheelbase: 249.9cm 98.4in
Track F: 134.4cm 52.9in
Track R: 132.1cm 52.0in
Length: 436.6cm 171.9in
Width: 161.0cm 63.4in
Height: 140.0cm 55.1in
Ground clearance: 17.8cm 7.0in
Kerb weight: 1191.7kg 2625.0lb
Fuel: 54.9L 12.1gal 14.5galUS

4386 Toyota
Mk II Station Wagon
1974 Japan
0-60mph 96.5kmh: 14.4secs
0-1/4 mile: 19.4secs
122.0bhp 91.0kW 123.7PS
@ 5200rpm
141.0lbft 191.1Nm @ 3600rpm
93.1bhp/ton 91.6bhp/tonne
47.6bhp/L 35.5kW/L 48.3PS/L
20.4mpg 17.0mpgUS 13.8L/100km
Petrol 4-stroke piston
2563cc 156.4cu in
In-line 6
Valve type/No: Overhead 12
Transmission: Automatic
No. of forward speeds: 3
Wheels driven: Rear
Brakes F/R: Disc/Drum
Wheelbase: 258.6cm 101.8in
Length: 464.6cm 182.9in
Width: 162.6cm 64.0in
Height: 144.0cm 56.7in
Kerb weight: 1332.5kg 2935.0lb

4387 Toyota
Celica GT
1975 Japan
120.0mph 193.1kmh
0-50mph 80.5kmh: 6.8secs
0-60mph 96.5kmh: 9.3secs
0-1/4 mile: 17.1secs
0-1km: 31.9secs
124.0bhp 92.5kW 125.7PS
@ 6400rpm
113.0lbft 153.1Nm @ 5200rpm
125.4bhp/ton 123.3bhp/tonne
78.1bhp/L 58.2kW/L 79.2PS/L
49.1ft/sec 14.9m/sec
19.0mph 30.6kmh/1000rpm
29.8mpg 24.8mpgUS 9.5L/100km
Petrol 4-stroke piston
1588cc 96.9cu in
In-line 4 2 Carburettor
Compression ratio: 9.8:1
Bore: 85.0mm 3.3in
Stroke: 70.0mm 2.8in
Valve type/No: Overhead 8
Transmission: Manual
No. of forward speeds: 5
Wheels driven: Rear
Springs F/R: Coil/Coil
Brake system: PA
Brakes F/R: Disc/Drum
Steering: Recirculating ball
Wheelbase: 242.6cm 95.5in
Track F: 128.0cm 50.4in
Track R: 128.5cm 50.6in
Length: 416.6cm 164.0in
Width: 160.0cm 63.0in
Height: 131.1cm 51.6in
Ground clearance: 17.5cm 6.9in
Kerb weight: 1005.6kg 2215.0lb
Fuel: 50.0L 11.0gal 13.2galUS

4388 Toyota
Corolla
1975 Japan
0-60mph 96.5kmh: 14.3secs
0-1/4 mile: 19.4secs
75.0bhp 55.9kW 76.0PS
@ 5800rpm
83.0lbft 112.5Nm @ 3800rpm
77.2bhp/ton 75.9bhp/tonne
47.2bhp/L 35.2kW/L 47.9PS/L
44.5ft/sec 13.5m/sec
29.4mpg 24.5mpgUS 9.6L/100km
Petrol 4-stroke piston
1588cc 96.9cu in
In-line 4 1 Carburettor
Compression ratio: 9.0:1
Bore: 85.0mm 3.3in
Stroke: 70.0mm 2.8in
Valve type/No: Overhead 8
Transmission: Manual
No. of forward speeds: 4
Wheels driven: Rear
Brake system: PA
Wheelbase: 237.0cm 93.3in
Track F: 130.0cm 51.2in
Track R: 128.5cm 50.6in
Length: 419.6cm 165.2in
Width: 157.0cm 61.8in
Height: 138.4cm 54.5in
Ground clearance: 14.0cm 5.5in
Kerb weight: 987.4kg 2175.0lb
Fuel: 50.0L 11.0gal 13.2galUS

4389 Toyota
Corolla 30
1975 Japan
90.0mph 144.8kmh
0-50mph 80.5kmh: 11.6secs
0-60mph 96.5kmh: 16.9secs
0-1/4 mile: 20.6secs
0-1km: 39.3secs
73.0bhp 54.4kW 74.0PS
@ 6000rpm
74.0lbft 100.3Nm @ 3800rpm
86.0bhp/ton 84.5bhp/tonne
62.6bhp/L 46.7kW/L 63.5PS/L
43.3ft/sec 13.2m/sec
15.2mph 24.5kmh/1000rpm
31.1mpg 25.9mpgUS 9.1L/100km
Petrol 4-stroke piston
1166cc 71.1cu in
In-line 4 1 Carburettor
Compression ratio: 9.0:1
Bore: 75.0mm 2.9in
Stroke: 66.0mm 2.6in
Valve type/No: Overhead 8
Transmission: Manual
No. of forward speeds: 4
Wheels driven: Rear
Springs F/R: Coil/Leaf
Brake system: PA
Brakes F/R: Disc/Drum
Steering: Recirculating ball
Wheelbase: 237.0cm 93.3in
Track F: 129.5cm 51.0in
Track R: 128.5cm 50.6in
Length: 399.5cm 157.3in
Width: 157.0cm 61.8in
Height: 137.4cm 54.1in
Ground clearance: 17.0cm 6.7in
Kerb weight: 863.5kg 1902.0lb
Fuel: 50.0L 11.0gal 13.2galUS

4390 Toyota
Corolla SR5
1975 Japan
98.0mph 157.7kmh
0-50mph 80.5kmh: 11.3secs
0-60mph 96.5kmh: 15.9secs
0-1/4 mile: 20.5secs
75.0bhp 55.9kW 76.0PS
@ 5800rpm
83.0lbft 112.5Nm @ 3800rpm
71.9bhp/ton 70.7bhp/tonne
47.2bhp/L 35.2kW/L 47.9PS/L
44.5ft/sec 13.5m/sec
18.4mph 29.6kmh/1000rpm
29.4mpg 24.5mpgUS 9.6L/100km
Petrol 4-stroke piston
1588cc 96.9cu in
In-line 4 1 Carburettor
Compression ratio: 9.0:1
Bore: 85.0mm 3.3in
Stroke: 70.0mm 2.8in
Valve type/No: Overhead 8
Transmission: Manual
No. of forward speeds: 5
Wheels driven: Rear
Springs F/R: Coil/Leaf
Brake system: PA
Brakes F/R: Disc/Drum
Steering: Recirculating ball
Wheelbase: 237.0cm 93.3in
Track F: 132.1cm 52.0in
Track R: 133.6cm 52.6in
Length: 419.6cm 165.2in
Width: 165.1cm 65.0in
Height: 135.9cm 53.5in
Ground clearance: 15.5cm 6.1in
Kerb weight: 1060.1kg 2335.0lb
Fuel: 50.0L 11.0gal 13.2galUS

4391 Toyota
Crown Super
1975 Japan
101.0mph 162.5kmh
0-50mph 80.5kmh: 9.7secs
0-60mph 96.5kmh: 13.3secs
0-1/4 mile: 19.4secs
0-1km: 35.9secs
150.0bhp 111.9kW 152.1PS
@ 5400rpm
164.0lbft 222.2Nm @ 3800rpm
103.6bhp/ton 101.9bhp/tonne
58.5bhp/L 43.6kW/L 59.3PS/L
50.2ft/sec 15.3m/sec
17.7mph 28.5kmh/1000rpm
19.0mpg 15.8mpgUS 14.9L/100km
Petrol 4-stroke piston
2563cc 156.4cu in
In-line 6 1 Carburettor
Compression ratio: 8.5:1
Bore: 80.8mm 3.2in
Stroke: 85.0mm 3.3in
Valve type/No: Overhead 12
Transmission: Automatic
No. of forward speeds: 3
Wheels driven: Rear
Springs F/R: Coil/Coil
Brake system: PA
Brakes F/R: Disc/Drum
Steering: Recirculating ball PA
Wheelbase: 269.0cm 105.9in
Track F: 141.5cm 55.7in
Track R: 138.2cm 54.4in
Length: 459.0cm 180.7in
Width: 169.2cm 66.6in
Height: 143.5cm 56.5in
Ground clearance: 20.3cm 8.0in
Kerb weight: 1472.3kg 3243.0lb
Fuel: 71.9L 15.8gal 19.0galUS

4392 Toyota
Pickup SR5
1975 Japan
94.0mph 151.2kmh
0-50mph 80.5kmh: 9.8secs
0-60mph 96.5kmh: 13.9secs
0-1/4 mile: 19.5secs
96.0bhp 71.6kW 97.3PS
@ 4800rpm
120.0lbft 162.6Nm @ 2800rpm
80.7bhp/ton 79.3bhp/tonne
43.9bhp/L 32.7kW/L 44.5PS/L
46.7ft/sec 14.2m/sec
19.7mph 31.7kmh/1000rpm
24.0mpg 20.0mpgUS 11.8L/100km
Petrol 4-stroke piston
2189cc 133.6cu in
In-line 4 1 Carburettor
Compression ratio: 8.4:1
Bore: 88.4mm 3.5in
Stroke: 88.9mm 3.5in
Valve type/No: Overhead 8
Transmission: Manual
No. of forward speeds: 5
Wheels driven: Rear
Springs F/R: Coil/Leaf
Brake system: PA
Brakes F/R: Disc/Drum
Steering: Recirculating ball
Wheelbase: 258.1cm 101.6in
Track F: 132.6cm 52.2in
Track R: 129.0cm 50.8in
Length: 428.5cm 168.7in
Width: 158.0cm 62.2in
Height: 155.4cm 61.2in
Ground clearance: 19.1cm 7.5in
Kerb weight: 1209.9kg 2665.0lb
Fuel: 45.8L 10.1gal 12.1galUS

4393 Toyota
1000
1976 Japan
88.0mph 141.6kmh
0-50mph 80.5kmh: 10.9secs
0-60mph 96.5kmh: 16.9secs
0-1/4 mile: 20.7secs
0-1km: 39.6secs
47.0bhp 35.0kW 47.6PS
@ 5800rpm
48.5lbft 65.7Nm @ 3800rpm
66.5bhp/ton 65.4bhp/tonne
47.3bhp/L 35.3kW/L 48.0PS/L

38.7ft/sec 11.8m/sec
14.8mph 23.8kmh/1000rpm
35.9mpg 29.9mpgUS 7.9L/100km
Petrol 4-stroke piston
993cc 60.6cu in
In-line 4 1 Carburettor
Compression ratio: 9.0:1
Bore: 72.0mm 2.8in
Stroke: 61.0mm 2.4in
Valve type/No: Overhead 8
Transmission: Manual
No. of forward speeds: 4
Wheels driven: Rear
Springs F/R: Coil/Leaf
Brakes F/R: Drum/Drum
Steering: Recirculating ball
Wheelbase: 215.9cm 85.0in
Track F: 123.2cm 48.5in
Track R: 119.9cm 47.2in
Length: 369.3cm 145.4in
Width: 145.0cm 57.1in
Height: 137.9cm 54.3in
Ground clearance: 17.0cm 6.7in
Kerb weight: 718.2kg 1582.0lb
Fuel: 40.0L 8.8gal 10.6galUS

4394 Toyota

Carina
1976 Japan
97.0mph 156.1kmh
0-50mph 80.5kmh: 9.7secs
0-60mph 96.5kmh: 14.3secs
0-1/4 mile: 19.6secs
0-1km: 38.0secs
75.0bhp 55.9kW 76.0PS
@ 5200rpm
85.0lbft 115.2Nm @ 3800rpm
76.7bhp/ton 75.4bhp/tonne
47.2bhp/L 35.2kW/L 47.9PS/L
39.9ft/sec 12.1m/sec
17.2mph 27.7kmh/1000rpm
27.0mpg 22.5mpgUS 10.5L/100km
Petrol 4-stroke piston
1588cc 96.9cu in
In-line 4 1 Carburettor
Compression ratio: 9.0:1
Bore: 85.0mm 3.3in
Stroke: 70.0mm 2.8in
Valve type/No: Overhead 8
Transmission: Manual
No. of forward speeds: 4
Wheels driven: Rear
Springs F/R: Coil/Coil
Brake system: PA
Brakes F/R: Disc/Drum
Steering: Recirculating ball
Wheelbase: 249.4cm 98.2in
Track F: 133.4cm 52.5in
Track R: 129.5cm 51.0in
Length: 420.4cm 165.5in
Width: 159.3cm 62.7in
Height: 138.9cm 54.7in
Ground clearance: 15.2cm 6.0in
Kerb weight: 994.7kg 2191.0lb
Fuel: 58.2L 12.8gal 15.4galUS

4395 Toyota

Celica Liftback
1976 Japan
105.0mph 168.9kmh
0-50mph 80.5kmh: 8.7secs
0-60mph 96.5kmh: 12.7secs
0-1/4 mile: 18.8secs
0-1km: 35.0secs
95.0bhp 70.8kW 96.3PS
@ 5000rpm
104.0lbft 140.9Nm @ 3600rpm
90.3bhp/ton 88.8bhp/tonne
48.3bhp/L 36.0kW/L 48.9PS/L
43.8ft/sec 13.3m/sec
20.0mph 32.2kmh/1000rpm
27.6mpg 23.0mpgUS 10.2L/100km
Petrol 4-stroke piston
1968cc 120.1cu in
In-line 4 1 Carburettor
Compression ratio: 8.5:1
Bore: 88.5mm 3.5in
Stroke: 80.0mm 3.1in
Valve type/No: Overhead 8
Transmission: Manual
No. of forward speeds: 5
Wheels driven: Rear
Springs F/R: Coil/Coil
Brake system: PA
Brakes F/R: Disc/Drum
Steering: Recirculating ball
Wheelbase: 249.4cm 98.2in
Track F: 134.9cm 53.1in
Track R: 131.1cm 51.6in
Length: 423.9cm 166.9in
Width: 162.1cm 63.8in
Height: 129.5cm 51.0in
Ground clearance: 17.0cm 6.7in
Kerb weight: 1069.6kg 2356.0lb
Fuel: 58.2L 12.8gal 15.4galUS

4396 Toyota

Corolla Liftback
1976 Japan
93.0mph 149.6kmh
0-50mph 80.5kmh: 10.1secs
0-60mph 96.5kmh: 14.8secs
0-1/4 mile: 19.7secs
75.0bhp 55.9kW 76.0PS
@ 5800rpm
83.0lbft 112.5Nm @ 3800rpm
73.5bhp/ton 72.3bhp/tonne
47.2bhp/L 35.2kW/L 47.9PS/L
44.5ft/sec 13.5m/sec
18.3mph 29.4kmh/1000rpm
33.0mpg 27.5mpgUS 8.6L/100km
Petrol 4-stroke piston
1588cc 96.9cu in
In-line 4
Compression ratio: 9.0:1
Bore: 85.0mm 3.3in
Stroke: 70.0mm 2.8in
Valve type/No: Overhead 8
Transmission: Manual
No. of forward speeds: 5
Wheels driven: Rear
Springs F/R: Coil/Leaf
Brake system: PA
Brakes F/R: Disc/Drum
Steering: Recirculating ball
Wheelbase: 237.0cm 93.3in
Track F: 132.1cm 52.0in
Track R: 133.6cm 52.6in
Length: 427.5cm 168.3in
Width: 161.5cm 63.6in
Height: 132.1cm 52.0in
Kerb weight: 1037.4kg 2285.0lb
Fuel: 50.0L 11.0gal 13.2galUS

4397 Toyota

Corolla 1200
1977 Japan
85.0mph 136.8kmh
0-50mph 80.5kmh: 11.7secs
0-60mph 96.5kmh: 17.1secs
0-1/4 mile: 20.9secs
58.0bhp 43.2kW 58.8PS
@ 5800rpm
63.0lbft 85.4Nm @ 3800rpm
65.8bhp/ton 64.7bhp/tonne
49.7bhp/L 37.1kW/L 50.4PS/L
41.9ft/sec 12.8m/sec
15.8mph 25.4kmh/1000rpm
42.0mpg 35.0mpgUS 6.7L/100km
Petrol 4-stroke piston
1166cc 71.1cu in
In-line 4
Compression ratio: 9.0:1
Bore: 74.9mm 2.9in
Stroke: 66.0mm 2.6in
Valve type/No: Overhead 8
Transmission: Manual
No. of forward speeds: 4
Wheels driven: Rear
Springs F/R: Coil/Leaf
Brake system: PA
Brakes F/R: Disc/Drum
Steering: Recirculating ball
Wheelbase: 237.0cm 93.3in
Track F: 129.5cm 51.0in
Track R: 128.5cm 50.6in
Length: 418.1cm 164.6in
Width: 157.0cm 61.8in
Height: 138.4cm 54.5in
Kerb weight: 896.6kg 1975.0lb
Fuel: 50.0L 11.0gal 13.2galUS

4398 Toyota

Corona Cressida
1977 Japan
97.0mph 156.1kmh
0-50mph 80.5kmh: 9.0secs
0-60mph 96.5kmh: 12.9secs
0-1/4 mile: 19.3secs
0-1km: 36.2secs
89.0bhp 66.4kW 90.2PS
@ 5000rpm
103.0lbft 139.6Nm @ 3600rpm
83.5bhp/ton 82.2bhp/tonne
45.2bhp/L 33.7kW/L 45.8PS/L
43.8ft/sec 13.3m/sec
18.3mph 29.4kmh/1000rpm
23.6mpg 19.7mpgUS 12.0L/100km
Petrol 4-stroke piston
1968cc 120.1cu in
In-line 4 1 Carburettor
Compression ratio: 8.5:1
Bore: 88.5mm 3.5in
Stroke: 80.0mm 3.1in
Valve type/No: Overhead 8
Transmission: Automatic
No. of forward speeds: 3
Wheels driven: Rear
Springs F/R: Coil/Coil
Brake system: PA
Brakes F/R: Disc/Drum
Steering: Recirculating ball
Wheelbase: 264.4cm 104.1in
Track F: 137.4cm 54.1in
Track R: 134.9cm 53.1in
Length: 452.9cm 178.3in
Width: 167.9cm 66.1in
Height: 144.5cm 56.9in
Ground clearance: 17.5cm 6.9in
Kerb weight: 1083.2kg 2386.0lb
Fuel: 65.1L 14.3gal 17.2galUS

4399 Toyota

Celica
1978 Japan
113.0mph 181.8kmh
0-60mph 96.5kmh: 10.4secs
0-1/4 mile: 18.1secs
95.0bhp 70.8kW 96.3PS
@ 4800rpm
122.0lbft 165.3Nm @ 2400rpm
84.9bhp/ton 83.5bhp/tonne
43.4bhp/L 32.4kW/L 44.0PS/L
46.7ft/sec 14.2m/sec
27.0mpg 22.5mpgUS 10.5L/100km
Petrol 4-stroke piston
2189cc 133.6cu in
In-line 4 1 Carburettor
Compression ratio: 8.4:1
Bore: 88.4mm 3.5in
Stroke: 88.9mm 3.5in
Valve type/No: Overhead 8
Transmission: Manual
No. of forward speeds: 5
Wheels driven: Rear
Brakes F/R: Disc/Drum
Wheelbase: 249.9cm 98.4in
Track F: 136.4cm 53.7in
Track R: 136.7cm 53.8in
Length: 440.9cm 173.6in
Width: 163.6cm 64.4in
Height: 131.1cm 51.6in
Kerb weight: 1137.3kg 2505.0lb
Fuel: 60.9L 13.4gal 16.1galUS

4400 Toyota

Celica 2000GT
1978 Japan
113.0mph 181.8kmh
0-50mph 80.5kmh: 6.3secs
0-60mph 96.5kmh: 8.8secs
0-1/4 mile: 16.8secs
0-1km: 31.2secs
118.0bhp 88.0kW 119.6PS
@ 5800rpm
112.0lbft 151.8Nm @ 5200rpm
113.3bhp/ton 111.4bhp/tonne
60.0bhp/L 44.7kW/L 60.8PS/L
50.7ft/sec 15.5m/sec
20.9mph 33.6kmh/1000rpm
23.9mpg 19.9mpgUS 11.8L/100km
Petrol 4-stroke piston
1968cc 120.1cu in
In-line 4 2 Carburettor
Compression ratio: 9.7:1
Bore: 88.5mm 3.5in
Stroke: 80.0mm 3.1in
Valve type/No: Overhead 8
Transmission: Manual
No. of forward speeds: 5
Wheels driven: Rear
Springs F/R: Coil/Coil
Brake system: PA
Brakes F/R: Disc/Drum
Steering: Recirculating ball
Wheelbase: 249.9cm 98.4in
Track F: 134.9cm 53.1in
Track R: 136.4cm 53.7in
Length: 433.1cm 170.5in
Width: 164.1cm 64.6in
Height: 131.6cm 51.8in
Ground clearance: 16.5cm 6.5in
Kerb weight: 1059.2kg 2333.0lb
Fuel: 61.4L 13.5gal 16.2galUS

4401 Toyota

Celica GT Liftback
1978 Japan
113.0mph 181.8kmh
0-50mph 80.5kmh: 7.3secs
0-60mph 96.5kmh: 10.4secs
0-1/4 mile: 18.1secs
95.0bhp 70.8kW 96.3PS
@ 4800rpm
122.0lbft 165.3Nm @ 2400rpm
84.9bhp/ton 83.5bhp/tonne
43.4bhp/L 32.4kW/L 44.0PS/L
46.7ft/sec 14.2m/sec
25.0mph 40.2kmh/1000rpm
31.2mpg 26.0mpgUS 9.0L/100km
Petrol 4-stroke piston
2189cc 133.6cu in
In-line 4 1 Carburettor
Compression ratio: 8.4:1
Bore: 88.4mm 3.5in
Stroke: 88.9mm 3.5in
Valve type/No: Overhead 8
Transmission: Manual
No. of forward speeds: 5
Wheels driven: Rear
Springs F/R: Coil/Coil
Brake system: PA
Brakes F/R: Disc/Drum
Steering: Recirculating ball
Wheelbase: 249.9cm 98.4in
Track F: 136.4cm 53.7in
Track R: 136.7cm 53.8in
Length: 440.9cm 173.6in
Width: 163.6cm 64.4in
Height: 131.1cm 51.6in
Ground clearance: 17.0cm 6.7in
Kerb weight: 1137.3kg 2505.0lb
Fuel: 60.9L 13.4gal 16.1galUS

4402 Toyota

Cressida
1978 Japan
93.0mph 149.6kmh
0-50mph 80.5kmh: 8.3secs
0-60mph 96.5kmh: 11.4secs
0-1/4 mile: 18.7secs
108.0bhp 80.5kW 109.5PS
@ 5000rpm
134.0lbft 181.6Nm @ 2400rpm
86.7bhp/ton 85.3bhp/tonne
42.1bhp/L 31.4kW/L 42.7PS/L
45.8ft/sec 14.0m/sec
25.0mph 40.2kmh/1000rpm
24.0mpg 20.0mpgUS 11.8L/100km
Petrol 4-stroke piston
2563cc 156.4cu in
In-line 6 1 Carburettor
Compression ratio: 8.5:1
Bore: 81.3mm 3.2in
Stroke: 83.8mm 3.3in
Valve type/No: Overhead 12
Transmission: Automatic
No. of forward speeds: 4
Wheels driven: Rear
Springs F/R: Coil/Coil
Brake system: PA
Brakes F/R: Disc/Drum
Steering: Recirculating ball PA
Wheelbase: 264.4cm 104.1in
Track F: 137.4cm 54.1in
Track R: 134.9cm 53.1in
Length: 469.9cm 185.0in
Width: 167.9cm 66.1in
Height: 141.5cm 55.7in
Ground clearance: 17.0cm 6.7in
Kerb weight: 1266.7kg 2790.0lb
Fuel: 65.1L 14.3gal 17.2galUS

4403 Toyota

Celica Supra
1979 Japan
112.0mph 180.2kmh
0-50mph 80.5kmh: 7.2secs
0-60mph 96.5kmh: 10.2secs
0-1/4 mile: 18.0secs
110.0bhp 82.0kW 111.5PS
@ 4800rpm
136.0lbft 184.3Nm @ 2400rpm
85.1bhp/ton 83.7bhp/tonne
42.9bhp/L 32.0kW/L 43.5PS/L
44.7ft/sec 13.6m/sec

21.9mph 35.2kmh/1000rpm
24.0mpg 20.0mpgUS 11.8L/100km
Petrol 4-stroke piston
2563cc 156.4cu in
In-line 6 fuel injection
Compression ratio: 8.5:1
Bore: 80.0mm 3.1in
Stroke: 85.0mm 3.3in
Valve type/No: Overhead 12
Transmission: Manual
No. of forward speeds: 5
Wheels driven: Rear
Springs F/R: Coil/Coil
Brake system: PA
Brakes F/R: Disc/Disc
Steering: Recirculating ball
Wheelbase: 262.9cm 103.5in
Track F: 136.4cm 53.7in
Track R: 136.4cm 53.7in
Length: 461.5cm 181.7in
Width: 165.1cm 65.0in
Height: 131.6cm 51.8in
Kerb weight: 1314.3kg 2895.0lb
Fuel: 60.9L 13.4gal 16.1galUS

4404 Toyota
Corona 5-door
1979 Japan
100.0mph 160.9kmh
0-60mph 96.5kmh: 12.0secs
0-1/4 mile: 18.9secs
90.0bhp 67.1kW 91.2PS
@ 4800rpm
122.0lbft 165.3Nm @ 2400rpm
74.1bhp/ton 72.9bhp/tonne
41.1bhp/L 30.7kW/L 41.7PS/L
46.7ft/sec 14.2m/sec
23.1mph 37.2kmh/1000rpm
25.2mpg 21.0mpgUS 11.2L/100km
Petrol 4-stroke piston
2189cc 133.6cu in
In-line 4 1 Carburettor
Compression ratio: 8.4:1
Bore: 88.4mm 3.5in
Stroke: 88.9mm 3.5in
Valve type/No: Overhead 8
Transmission: Manual
No. of forward speeds: 5
Wheels driven: Rear
Springs F/R: Coil/Coil
Brake system: PA
Brakes F/R: Disc/Drum
Steering: Recirculating ball PA
Wheelbase: 252.5cm 99.4in
Track F: 136.4cm 53.7in
Track R: 136.4cm 53.7in
Length: 444.5cm 175.0in
Width: 165.6cm 65.2in
Height: 134.6cm 53.0in
Ground clearance: 13.0cm 5.1in
Kerb weight: 1234.9kg 2720.0lb
Fuel: 60.9L 13.4gal 16.1galUS

4405 Toyota
Corona Liftback
1979 Japan
104.0mph 167.3kmh
0-50mph 80.5kmh: 9.2secs
0-60mph 96.5kmh: 13.2secs
0-1/4 mile: 19.1secs
0-1km: 34.7secs
86.0bhp 64.1kW 87.2PS
@ 5400rpm
102.0lbft 138.2Nm @ 3400rpm
78.8bhp/ton 77.5bhp/tonne
48.6bhp/L 36.2kW/L 49.3PS/L
46.0ft/sec 14.0m/sec
20.5mph 33.0kmh/1000rpm
28.0mpg 23.3mpgUS 10.1L/100km
Petrol 4-stroke piston
1770cc 108.0cu in
In-line 4 1 Carburettor
Compression ratio: 9.0:1
Bore: 85.0mm 3.3in
Stroke: 78.0mm 3.1in
Valve type/No: Overhead 8
Transmission: Manual
No. of forward speeds: 5
Wheels driven: Rear
Springs F/R: Coil/Coil
Brake system: PA
Brakes F/R: Disc/Drum
Steering: Recirculating ball
Wheelbase: 252.5cm 99.4in
Track F: 134.9cm 53.1in
Track R: 134.9cm 53.1in
Length: 429.0cm 168.9in
Width: 165.6cm 65.2in
Height: 141.0cm 55.5in
Ground clearance: 15.2cm 6.0in
Kerb weight: 1110.0kg 2445.0lb
Fuel: 61.0L 13.4gal 16.1galUS

4406 Toyota
Celica GT
1980 Japan
110.0mph 177.0kmh
0-60mph 96.5kmh: 10.6secs
0-1/4 mile: 18.3secs
90.0bhp 67.1kW 91.2PS
@ 4800rpm
122.0lbft 165.3Nm @ 2400rpm
80.6bhp/ton 79.3bhp/tonne
41.1bhp/L 30.7kW/L 41.7PS/L
46.7ft/sec 14.2m/sec
26.0mph 41.8kmh/1000rpm
32.4mpg 27.0mpgUS 8.7L/100km
Petrol 4-stroke piston
2189cc 133.6cu in
In-line 4 1 Carburettor
Compression ratio: 8.4:1
Bore: 88.4mm 3.5in
Stroke: 88.9mm 3.5in
Valve type/No: Overhead 8
Transmission: Manual
No. of forward speeds: 5
Wheels driven: Rear
Springs F/R: Coil/Coil
Brake system: PA
Brakes F/R: Disc/Drum
Steering: Recirculating ball PA
Wheelbase: 249.9cm 98.4in
Track F: 136.4cm 53.7in
Track R: 136.7cm 53.8in
Length: 445.8cm 175.5in
Width: 164.1cm 64.6in
Height: 129.0cm 50.8in
Ground clearance: 17.0cm 6.7in
Kerb weight: 1135.0kg 2500.0lb
Fuel: 60.9L 13.4gal 16.1galUS

4407 Toyota
Corolla Sport Coupe
1980 Japan
98.0mph 157.7kmh
0-60mph 96.5kmh: 12.0secs
0-1/4 mile: 19.0secs
75.0bhp 55.9kW 76.0PS
@ 5000rpm
95.0lbft 128.7Nm @ 2600rpm
73.2bhp/ton 72.0bhp/tonne
42.4bhp/L 31.6kW/L 43.0PS/L
42.6ft/sec 13.0m/sec
21.8mph 35.1kmh/1000rpm
30.0mpg 25.0mpgUS 9.4L/100km
Petrol 4-stroke piston
1770cc 108.0cu in
In-line 4 1 Carburettor
Compression ratio: 9.0:1
Bore: 85.1mm 3.3in
Stroke: 78.0mm 3.1in
Valve type/No: Overhead 8
Transmission: Manual
No. of forward speeds: 5
Wheels driven: Rear
Springs F/R: Coil/Coil
Brake system: PA
Brakes F/R: Disc/Drum
Steering: Recirculating ball
Wheelbase: 240.0cm 94.5in
Track F: 132.6cm 52.2in
Track R: 133.6cm 52.6in
Length: 427.5cm 168.3in
Width: 162.6cm 64.0in
Height: 129.0cm 50.8in
Ground clearance: 15.5cm 6.1in
Kerb weight: 1041.9kg 2295.0lb
Fuel: 50.0L 11.0gal 13.2galUS

4408 Toyota
Corolla Tercel SR5
1980 Japan
91.0mph 146.4kmh
0-60mph 96.5kmh: 14.8secs
0-1/4 mile: 20.4secs
60.0bhp 44.7kW 60.8PS
@ 4800rpm
72.0lbft 97.6Nm @ 2800rpm
66.2bhp/ton 65.1bhp/tonne
41.3bhp/L 30.8kW/L 41.9PS/L
40.4ft/sec 12.3m/sec
21.4mph 34.4kmh/1000rpm
33.6mpg 28.0mpgUS 8.4L/100km
Petrol 4-stroke piston
1452cc 88.6cu in
In-line 4 1 Carburettor
Compression ratio: 8.7:1
Bore: 77.5mm 3.0in
Stroke: 77.0mm 3.0in
Valve type/No: Overhead 8
Transmission: Manual
No. of forward speeds: 5
Wheels driven: Front
Springs F/R: Coil/Coil
Brake system: PA
Brakes F/R: Disc/Drum
Steering: Rack & pinion
Wheelbase: 249.9cm 98.4in
Track F: 133.1cm 52.4in
Track R: 131.6cm 51.8in
Length: 406.4cm 160.0in
Width: 155.4cm 61.2in
Height: 134.1cm 52.8in
Ground clearance: 17.5cm 6.9in
Kerb weight: 921.6kg 2030.0lb
Fuel: 45.0L 9.9gal 11.9galUS

4409 Toyota
Cressida
1981 Japan
100.0mph 160.9kmh
0-60mph 96.5kmh: 12.1secs
0-1/4 mile: 18.6secs
116.0bhp 86.5kW 117.6PS
@ 4800rpm
145.0lbft 196.5Nm @ 3600rpm
87.5bhp/ton 86.0bhp/tonne
42.0bhp/L 31.3kW/L 42.6PS/L
44.7ft/sec 13.6m/sec
25.0mph 40.2kmh/1000rpm
23.4mpg 19.5mpgUS 12.1L/100km
Petrol 4-stroke piston
2759cc 168.3cu in
In-line 6 fuel injection
Compression ratio: 8.0:1
Bore: 83.1mm 3.3in
Stroke: 85.0mm 3.3in
Valve type/No: Overhead 12
Transmission: Automatic
No. of forward speeds: 4
Wheels driven: Rear
Springs F/R: Coil/Coil
Brake system: PA
Brakes F/R: Disc/Drum
Steering: Recirculating ball PA
Wheelbase: 264.4cm 104.1in
Track F: 138.9cm 54.7in
Track R: 138.4cm 54.5in
Length: 469.4cm 184.8in
Width: 168.9cm 66.5in
Height: 141.5cm 55.7in
Ground clearance: 17.0cm 6.7in
Kerb weight: 1348.4kg 2970.0lb
Fuel: 65.1L 14.3gal 17.2galUS

4410 Toyota
Cressida DX Estate
1981 Japan
106.0mph 170.6kmh
0-50mph 80.5kmh: 7.7secs
0-60mph 96.5kmh: 11.3secs
0-1/4 mile: 18.1secs
0-1km: 34.0secs
105.0bhp 78.3kW 106.5PS
@ 5200rpm
116.0lbft 157.2Nm @ 3600rpm
92.4bhp/ton 90.9bhp/tonne
53.2bhp/L 39.7kW/L 54.0PS/L
50.6ft/sec 15.4m/sec
21.5mph 34.6kmh/1000rpm
26.0mpg 21.6mpgUS 10.9L/100km
Petrol 4-stroke piston
1972cc 120.3cu in
In-line 4 1 Carburettor
Compression ratio: 9.0:1
Bore: 84.0mm 3.3in
Stroke: 89.0mm 3.5in
Valve type/No: Overhead 8
Transmission: Manual
No. of forward speeds: 5
Wheels driven: Rear
Springs F/R: Coil/Coil
Brake system: PA
Brakes F/R: Disc/Drum
Steering: Rack & pinion
Wheelbase: 264.4cm 104.1in
Track F: 138.9cm 54.7in
Track R: 138.4cm 54.5in
Length: 464.6cm 182.9in
Width: 168.9cm 66.5in
Height: 147.6cm 58.1in
Ground clearance: 16.5cm 6.5in
Kerb weight: 1155.0kg 2544.0lb
Fuel: 65.1L 14.3gal 17.2galUS

4411 Toyota
Starlet
1981 Japan
93.0mph 149.6kmh
0-60mph 96.5kmh: 14.2secs
0-1/4 mile: 19.5secs
58.0bhp 43.2kW 58.8PS
@ 5200rpm
67.0lbft 90.8Nm @ 3600rpm
71.8bhp/ton 70.6bhp/tonne
45.0bhp/L 33.5kW/L 45.6PS/L
41.5ft/sec 12.6m/sec
22.2mph 35.7kmh/1000rpm
44.4mpg 37.0mpgUS 6.4L/100km
Petrol 4-stroke piston
1290cc 78.7cu in
In-line 4 1 Carburettor
Compression ratio: 9.0:1
Bore: 75.0mm 2.9in
Stroke: 73.0mm 2.9in
Valve type/No: Overhead 8
Transmission: Manual
No. of forward speeds: 5
Wheels driven: Rear
Springs F/R: Coil/Coil
Brake system: PA
Brakes F/R: Disc/Drum
Steering: Rack & pinion
Wheelbase: 230.1cm 90.6in
Track F: 129.0cm 50.8in
Track R: 127.5cm 50.2in
Length: 386.6cm 152.2in
Width: 152.4cm 60.0in
Height: 137.9cm 54.3in
Ground clearance: 15.2cm 6.0in
Kerb weight: 821.7kg 1810.0lb
Fuel: 40.1L 8.8gal 10.6galUS

4412 Toyota
Celica
1982 Japan
111.0mph 178.6kmh
0-60mph 96.5kmh: 12.2secs
0-1/4 mile: 18.6secs
96.0bhp 71.6kW 97.3PS
@ 4800rpm
129.0lbft 174.8Nm @ 2800rpm
79.9bhp/ton 78.6bhp/tonne
40.6bhp/L 30.3kW/L 41.1PS/L
46.7ft/sec 14.2m/sec
29.4mpg 24.5mpgUS 9.6L/100km
Petrol 4-stroke piston
2366cc 144.4cu in
In-line 4 1 Carburettor
Compression ratio: 9.0:1
Bore: 92.0mm 3.6in
Stroke: 89.0mm 3.5in
Valve type/No: Overhead 8
Transmission: Manual
No. of forward speeds: 5
Wheels driven: Rear
Springs F/R: Coil/Coil
Brakes F/R: Disc/Drum
Wheelbase: 249.9cm 98.4in
Track F: 139.4cm 54.9in
Track R: 136.4cm 53.7in
Length: 447.5cm 176.2in
Width: 166.6cm 65.6in
Height: 132.1cm 52.0in
Kerb weight: 1221.3kg 2690.0lb
Fuel: 60.9L 13.4gal 16.1galUS

4413 Toyota
Celica 2.0ST
1982 Japan
110.0mph 177.0kmh
0-50mph 80.5kmh: 7.4secs
0-60mph 96.5kmh: 10.5secs
0-1/4 mile: 17.7secs
0-1km: 33.0secs
103.0bhp 76.8kW 104.4PS
@ 5000rpm
116.0lbft 157.2Nm @ 4000rpm
89.6bhp/ton 88.1bhp/tonne
52.2bhp/L 38.9kW/L 53.0PS/L
48.6ft/sec 14.8m/sec
20.9mph 33.6kmh/1000rpm
25.2mpg 21.0mpgUS 11.2L/100km
Petrol 4-stroke piston
1972cc 120.3cu in
In-line 4 1 Carburettor

Compression ratio: 9.0:1
Bore: 84.0mm 3.3in
Stroke: 89.0mm 3.5in
Valve type/No: Overhead 8
Transmission: Manual
No. of forward speeds: 5
Wheels driven: Rear
Springs F/R: Coil/Coil
Brake system: PA
Brakes F/R: Disc/Drum
Steering: Rack & pinion PA
Wheelbase: 249.9cm 98.4in
Track F: 139.4cm 54.9in
Track R: 138.4cm 54.5in
Length: 433.3cm 170.6in
Width: 166.6cm 65.6in
Height: 132.1cm 52.0in
Ground clearance: 17.0cm 6.7in
Kerb weight: 1169.5kg 2576.0lb
Fuel: 61.0L 13.4gal 16.1galUS

4414 Toyota

Celica GTA
1982 Japan
103.0mph 165.7kmh
0-50mph 80.5kmh: 9.5secs
0-60mph 96.5kmh: 13.5secs
0-1/4 mile: 19.3secs
96.0bhp 71.6kW 97.3PS
@ 4800rpm
129.0lbft 174.8Nm @ 2800rpm
86.0bhp/ton 84.6bhp/tonne
40.6bhp/L 30.2kW/L 41.1PS/L
46.7ft/sec 14.2m/sec
26.1mph 42.0kmh/1000rpm
28.8mpg 24.0mpgUS 9.8L/100km
Petrol 4-stroke piston
2367cc 144.4cu in
In-line 4 1 Carburettor
Compression ratio: 9.0:1
Bore: 91.9mm 3.6in
Stroke: 88.9mm 3.5in
Valve type/No: Overhead 8
Transmission: Automatic
No. of forward speeds: 4
Wheels driven: Rear
Springs F/R: Coil/Coil
Brake system: PA
Brakes F/R: Disc/Drum
Steering: Recirculating ball PA
Wheelbase: 249.9cm 98.4in
Track F: 134.9cm 53.1in
Track R: 136.4cm 53.7in
Length: 446.0cm 175.6in
Width: 164.1cm 64.6in
Height: 129.0cm 50.8in
Ground clearance: 17.0cm 6.7in
Kerb weight: 1135.0kg 2500.0lb
Fuel: 60.9L 13.4gal 16.1galUS

4415 Toyota

Celica Supra
1982 Japan
132.0mph 212.4kmh
0-50mph 80.5kmh: 6.6secs
0-60mph 96.5kmh: 8.7secs
0-1/4 mile: 16.7secs
0-1km: 30.6secs
168.0bhp 125.3kW 170.3PS
@ 5600rpm
169.0lbft 229.0Nm @ 4600rpm
131.1bhp/ton 128.9bhp/tonne
60.9bhp/L 45.4kW/L 61.7PS/L
52.1ft/sec 15.9m/sec
22.6mph 36.4kmh/1000rpm
23.0mpg 19.2mpgUS 12.3L/100km
Petrol 4-stroke piston
2759cc 168.3cu in
In-line 6 fuel injection
Compression ratio: 9.2:1
Bore: 83.0mm 3.3in
Stroke: 85.0mm 3.3in
Valve type/No: Overhead 12
Transmission: Manual
No. of forward speeds: 5
Wheels driven: Rear
Springs F/R: Coil/Coil
Brake system: PA
Brakes F/R: Disc/Disc
Steering: Rack & pinion PA
Wheelbase: 261.6cm 103.0in
Track F: 142.5cm 56.1in
Track R: 138.4cm 54.5in
Length: 462.0cm 181.9in
Width: 168.4cm 66.3in
Height: 131.6cm 51.8in
Ground clearance: 16.0cm 6.3in
Kerb weight: 1303.0kg 2870.0lb
Fuel: 61.0L 13.4gal 16.1galUS

4416 Toyota

Camry LE
1983 Japan
104.0mph 167.3kmh
0-50mph 80.5kmh: 9.0secs
0-60mph 96.5kmh: 12.6secs
0-1/4 mile: 18.9secs
92.0bhp 68.6kW 93.3PS
@ 4200rpm
113.0lbft 153.1Nm @ 2400rpm
81.1bhp/ton 79.8bhp/tonne
46.1bhp/L 34.4kW/L 46.8PS/L
41.3ft/sec 12.6m/sec
29.3mph 47.1kmh/1000rpm
Petrol 4-stroke piston
1995cc 121.7cu in
In-line 4 fuel injection
Compression ratio: 8.7:1
Bore: 84.0mm 3.3in
Stroke: 90.0mm 3.5in
Valve type/No: Overhead 8
Transmission: Automatic
No. of forward speeds: 4
Wheels driven: Front
Springs F/R: Coil/Coil
Brake system: PA
Brakes F/R: Disc/Drum
Steering: Rack & pinion PA
Wheelbase: 260.1cm 102.4in
Track F: 146.6cm 57.7in
Track R: 142.0cm 55.9in
Length: 446.0cm 175.6in
Width: 168.9cm 66.5in
Height: 136.9cm 53.9in
Ground clearance: 14.7cm 5.8in
Kerb weight: 1153.2kg 2540.0lb
Fuel: 52.2L 11.5gal 13.8galUS

4417 Toyota

Celica GTS
1983 Japan
105.0mph 168.9kmh
0-60mph 96.5kmh: 11.8secs
0-1/4 mile: 18.3secs
105.0bhp 78.3kW 106.5PS
@ 4800rpm
137.0lbft 185.6Nm @ 2800rpm
84.8bhp/ton 83.3bhp/tonne
44.4bhp/L 33.1kW/L 45.0PS/L
46.7ft/sec 14.2m/sec
25.6mph 41.2kmh/1000rpm
27.6mpg 23.0mpgUS 10.2L/100km
Petrol 4-stroke piston
2367cc 144.4cu in
In-line 4 fuel injection
Compression ratio: 9.0:1
Bore: 91.9mm 3.6in
Stroke: 88.9mm 3.5in
Valve type/No: Overhead 8
Transmission: Manual
No. of forward speeds: 5
Wheels driven: Rear
Springs F/R: Coil/Coil
Brake system: PA
Brakes F/R: Disc/Drum
Steering: Rack & pinion PA
Wheelbase: 249.9cm 98.4in
Track F: 143.5cm 56.5in
Track R: 143.5cm 56.5in
Length: 447.5cm 176.2in
Width: 172.0cm 67.7in
Height: 132.1cm 52.0in
Ground clearance: 15.5cm 6.1in
Kerb weight: 1259.8kg 2775.0lb
Fuel: 60.9L 13.4gal 16.1galUS

4418 Toyota

Corolla GL
1983 Japan
98.0mph 157.7kmh
0-50mph 80.5kmh: 8.8secs
0-60mph 96.5kmh: 14.2secs
0-1/4 mile: 19.0secs
0-1km: 35.8secs
63.0bhp 47.0kW 63.9PS
@ 6000rpm
75.0lbft 101.6Nm @ 3800rpm
71.9bhp/ton 70.7bhp/tonne
48.7bhp/L 36.3kW/L 49.4PS/L
46.8ft/sec 14.3m/sec
19.7mph 31.7kmh/1000rpm
30.2mpg 25.1mpgUS 9.4L/100km
Petrol 4-stroke piston
1294cc 78.9cu in
In-line 4 1 Carburettor
Compression ratio: 9.3:1
Bore: 76.0mm 3.0in
Stroke: 71.4mm 2.8in
Valve type/No: Overhead 8
Transmission: Manual
No. of forward speeds: 5
Wheels driven: Front
Springs F/R: Coil/Coil
Brake system: PA
Brakes F/R: Disc/Drum
Steering: Rack & pinion
Wheelbase: 243.1cm 95.7in
Track F: 142.5cm 56.1in
Track R: 140.5cm 55.3in
Length: 413.3cm 162.7in
Width: 163.6cm 64.4in
Height: 138.4cm 54.5in
Ground clearance: 16.0cm 6.3in
Kerb weight: 890.7kg 1962.0lb
Fuel: 50.0L 11.0gal 13.2galUS

4419 Toyota

Corolla SR5 Hardtop
1983 Japan
99.0mph 159.3kmh
0-50mph 80.5kmh: 9.8secs
0-60mph 96.5kmh: 13.7secs
0-1/4 mile: 19.3secs
70.0bhp 52.2kW 71.0PS
@ 4800rpm
85.0lbft 115.2Nm @ 2800rpm
69.7bhp/ton 68.5bhp/tonne
44.1bhp/L 32.9kW/L 44.7PS/L
40.4ft/sec 12.3m/sec
20.0mph 32.2kmh/1000rpm
34.8mpg 29.0mpgUS 8.1L/100km
Petrol 4-stroke piston
1587cc 96.8cu in
In-line 4 1 Carburettor
Compression ratio: 9.0:1
Bore: 100.0mm 3.9in
Stroke: 77.0mm 3.0in
Valve type/No: Overhead 8
Transmission: Manual
No. of forward speeds: 5
Wheels driven: Rear
Springs F/R: Coil/Coil
Brake system: PA
Brakes F/R: Disc/Drum
Steering: Rack & pinion PA
Wheelbase: 240.0cm 94.5in
Track F: 134.1cm 52.8in
Track R: 134.6cm 53.0in
Length: 427.5cm 168.3in
Width: 162.6cm 64.0in
Height: 129.0cm 50.8in
Ground clearance: 13.5cm 5.3in
Kerb weight: 1021.5kg 2250.0lb
Fuel: 50.0L 11.0gal 13.2galUS

4420 Toyota

Cressida
1983 Japan
113.0mph 181.8kmh
0-50mph 80.5kmh: 7.9secs
0-60mph 96.5kmh: 10.2secs
0-1/4 mile: 17.8secs
143.0bhp 106.6kW 145.0PS
@ 5200rpm
154.0lbft 208.7Nm @ 4400rpm
106.4bhp/ton 104.6bhp/tonne
51.8bhp/L 38.6kW/L 52.5PS/L
48.4ft/sec 14.7m/sec
25.0mph 40.2kmh/1000rpm
22.2mpg 18.5mpgUS 12.7L/100km
Petrol 4-stroke piston
2759cc 168.3cu in
In-line 6 fuel injection
Compression ratio: 8.8:1
Bore: 83.0mm 3.3in
Stroke: 85.0mm 3.3in
Valve type/No: Overhead 24
Transmission: Automatic
No. of forward speeds: 4
Wheels driven: Rear
Springs F/R: Coil/Coil
Brake system: PA
Brakes F/R: Disc/Disc
Steering: Recirculating ball PA
Wheelbase: 264.4cm 104.1in
Track F: 138.9cm 54.7in
Track R: 139.4cm 54.9in
Length: 472.9cm 186.2in
Width: 168.9cm 66.5in
Height: 137.9cm 54.3in
Kerb weight: 1366.5kg 3010.0lb
Fuel: 65.1L 14.3gal 17.2galUS

4421 Toyota

Supra
1983 Japan
127.0mph 204.3kmh
0-60mph 96.5kmh: 8.9secs
0-1/4 mile: 16.8secs
150.0bhp 111.9kW 152.1PS
@ 5200rpm
159.0lbft 215.4Nm @ 4400rpm
110.3bhp/ton 108.5bhp/tonne
54.4bhp/L 40.5kW/L 55.1PS/L
48.4ft/sec 14.7m/sec
25.2mpg 21.0mpgUS 11.2L/100km
Petrol 4-stroke piston
2759cc 168.3cu in
In-line 6 fuel injection
Compression ratio: 8.8:1
Bore: 83.0mm 3.3in
Stroke: 85.0mm 3.3in
Valve type/No: Overhead 24
Transmission: Manual
No. of forward speeds: 5
Wheels driven: Rear
Springs F/R: Coil/Coil
Brakes F/R: Disc/Disc
Wheelbase: 261.4cm 102.9in
Track F: 147.1cm 57.9in
Track R: 144.0cm 56.7in
Length: 466.1cm 183.5in
Width: 172.0cm 67.7in
Height: 132.1cm 52.0in
Kerb weight: 1382.4kg 3045.0lb
Fuel: 60.9L 13.4gal 16.1galUS

4422 Toyota

Tercel 4WD Wagon
1983 Japan
85.0mph 136.8kmh
0-60mph 96.5kmh: 16.5secs
0-1/4 mile: 20.4secs
62.0bhp 46.2kW 62.9PS
@ 4800rpm
76.0lbft 103.0Nm @ 2800rpm
57.3bhp/ton 56.3bhp/tonne
42.7bhp/L 31.8kW/L 43.3PS/L
40.4ft/sec 12.3m/sec
21.7mph 34.9kmh/1000rpm
34.2mpg 28.5mpgUS 8.3L/100km
Petrol 4-stroke piston
1452cc 88.6cu in
In-line 4 1 Carburettor
Compression ratio: 9.0:1
Bore: 77.5mm 3.0in
Stroke: 77.0mm 3.0in
Valve type/No: Overhead 8
Transmission: Manual
No. of forward speeds: 5
Wheels driven: 4-wheel engageable
Springs F/R: Coil/Coil
Brake system: PA
Brakes F/R: Disc/Drum
Steering: Rack & pinion PA
Wheelbase: 243.1cm 95.7in
Track F: 137.9cm 54.3in
Track R: 134.9cm 53.1in
Length: 431.0cm 169.7in
Width: 161.5cm 63.6in
Height: 149.9cm 59.0in
Ground clearance: 13.5cm 5.3in
Kerb weight: 1100.9kg 2425.0lb
Fuel: 50.0L 11.0gal 13.2galUS

4423 Toyota

Tercel GL
1983 Japan
99.0mph 159.3kmh
0-50mph 80.5kmh: 9.3secs
0-60mph 96.5kmh: 13.5secs
0-1/4 mile: 19.9secs
0-1km: 36.6secs
64.3bhp 47.9kW 65.2PS
@ 6000rpm
73.0lbft 98.9Nm @ 3800rpm
73.4bhp/ton 72.1bhp/tonne
49.6bhp/L 37.0kW/L 50.3PS/L
46.8ft/sec 14.3m/sec
20.8mph 33.5kmh/1000rpm
34.2mpg 28.5mpgUS 8.3L/100km
Petrol 4-stroke piston
1295cc 79.0cu in
In-line 4 1 Carburettor
Compression ratio: 9.3:1
Bore: 76.0mm 3.0in
Stroke: 71.4mm 2.8in

Valve type/No: Overhead 8
Transmission: Manual
No. of forward speeds: 5
Wheels driven: Front
Springs F/R: Coil/Coil
Brake system: PA
Brakes F/R: Disc/Drum
Steering: Rack & pinion
Wheelbase: 243.1cm 95.7in
Track F: 138.4cm 54.5in
Track R: 136.9cm 53.9in
Length: 388.1cm 152.8in
Width: 161.5cm 63.6in
Height: 138.9cm 54.7in
Ground clearance: 17.0cm 6.7in
Kerb weight: 891.2kg 1963.0lb
Fuel: 45.0L 9.9gal 11.9galUS

4424 Toyota

Carina II 116GL
1984 Japan
104.0mph 167.3kmh
0-50mph 80.5kmh: 8.8secs
0-60mph 96.5kmh: 12.6secs
0-1/4 mile: 18.7secs
0-1km: 34.9secs
83.0bhp 61.9kW 84.1PS
@ 5600rpm
96.0lbft 130.1Nm @ 3600rpm
86.5bhp/ton 85.1bhp/tonne
52.3bhp/L 39.0kW/L 53.0PS/L
43.6ft/sec 13.2m/sec
20.5mph 33.0kmh/1000rpm
35.6mpg 29.6mpgUS 7.9L/100km
Petrol 4-stroke piston
1587cc 96.8cu in
In-line 4 1 Carburettor
Compression ratio: 9.3:1
Bore: 81.0mm 3.2in
Stroke: 71.0mm 2.8in
Valve type/No: Overhead 8
Transmission: Manual
No. of forward speeds: 5
Wheels driven: Front
Springs F/R: Coil/Coil
Brake system: PA
Brakes F/R: Disc/Drum
Steering: Rack & pinion PA
Wheelbase: 251.5cm 99.0in
Track F: 142.5cm 56.1in
Track R: 143.5cm 56.5in
Length: 431.8cm 170.0in
Width: 166.9cm 65.7in
Height: 136.4cm 53.7in
Ground clearance: 16.0cm 6.3in
Kerb weight: 975.6kg 2149.0lb
Fuel: 55.1L 12.1gal 14.5galUS

4425 Toyota

Celica 2.8i Supra
1984 Japan
128.0mph 206.0kmh
0-50mph 80.5kmh: 6.1secs
0-60mph 96.5kmh: 8.1secs
0-1/4 mile: 16.8secs
0-1km: 30.7secs
168.0bhp 125.3kW 170.3PS
@ 5600rpm
169.0lbft 229.0Nm @ 4600rpm
129.7bhp/ton 127.6bhp/tonne
60.9bhp/L 45.4kW/L 61.7PS/L
52.1ft/sec 15.9m/sec
22.1mph 35.6kmh/1000rpm
24.4mpg 20.3mpgUS 11.6L/100km
Petrol 4-stroke piston
2759cc 168.3cu in
In-line 6 fuel injection
Compression ratio: 9.2:1
Bore: 83.0mm 3.3in
Stroke: 85.0mm 3.3in
Valve type/No: Overhead 12
Transmission: Manual
No. of forward speeds: 5
Wheels driven: Rear
Springs F/R: Coil/Coil
Brake system: PA
Brakes F/R: Disc/Disc
Steering: Rack & pinion PA
Wheelbase: 261.6cm 103.0in
Track F: 142.5cm 56.1in
Track R: 138.4cm 54.5in
Length: 462.0cm 181.9in
Width: 168.4cm 66.3in
Height: 131.6cm 51.8in
Ground clearance: 16.0cm 6.3in
Kerb weight: 1317.0kg 2901.0lb
Fuel: 61.0L 13.4gal 16.1galUS

4426 Toyota

Corolla GT Coupe
1984 Japan
120.0mph 193.1kmh
0-50mph 80.5kmh: 6.2secs
0-60mph 96.5kmh: 8.6secs
0-1/4 mile: 16.4secs
0-1km: 30.5secs
124.0bhp 92.5kW 125.7PS
@ 6600rpm
105.0lbft 142.3Nm @ 5200rpm
128.8bhp/ton 126.7bhp/tonne
78.1bhp/L 58.3kW/L 79.2PS/L
55.5ft/sec 16.9m/sec
18.3mph 29.4kmh/1000rpm
27.0mpg 22.5mpgUS 10.5L/100km
Petrol 4-stroke piston
1587cc 96.8cu in
In-line 4 fuel injection
Compression ratio: 10.0:1
Bore: 81.0mm 3.2in
Stroke: 77.0mm 3.0in
Valve type/No: Overhead 16
Transmission: Manual
No. of forward speeds: 5
Wheels driven: Rear
Springs F/R: Coil/Coil
Brake system: PA
Brakes F/R: Disc/Drum
Steering: Rack & pinion
Wheelbase: 240.0cm 94.5in
Track F: 135.4cm 53.3in
Track R: 134.4cm 52.9in
Length: 418.1cm 164.6in
Width: 162.6cm 64.0in
Height: 133.6cm 52.6in
Ground clearance: 15.0cm 5.9in
Kerb weight: 978.8kg 2156.0lb
Fuel: 50.0L 11.0gal 13.2galUS

4427 Toyota

Corolla GTS
1984 Japan
115.0mph 185.0kmh
0-50mph 80.5kmh: 7.3secs
0-60mph 96.5kmh: 10.5secs
0-1/4 mile: 18.6secs
112.0bhp 83.5kW 113.5PS
@ 6600rpm
97.0lbft 131.4Nm @ 4800rpm
102.4bhp/ton 100.7bhp/tonne
70.6bhp/L 52.6kW/L 71.5PS/L
55.5ft/sec 16.9m/sec
17.1mph 27.5kmh/1000rpm
30.0mpg 25.0mpgUS 9.4L/100km
Petrol 4-stroke piston
1587cc 96.8cu in
In-line 4 fuel injection
Compression ratio: 9.4:1
Bore: 81.0mm 3.2in
Stroke: 77.0mm 3.0in
Valve type/No: Overhead 16
Transmission: Manual
No. of forward speeds: 5
Wheels driven: Rear
Springs F/R: Coil/Coil
Brake system: PA
Brakes F/R: Disc/Disc
Steering: Rack & pinion PA
Wheelbase: 240.0cm 94.5in
Track F: 133.6cm 52.6in
Track R: 134.6cm 53.0in
Length: 428.5cm 168.7in
Width: 162.6cm 64.0in
Height: 133.6cm 52.6in
Ground clearance: 13.5cm 5.3in
Kerb weight: 1112.3kg 2450.0lb
Fuel: 50.0L 11.0gal 13.2galUS

4428 Toyota

Corolla LE
1984 Japan
97.0mph 156.1kmh
0-50mph 80.5kmh: 8.9secs
0-60mph 96.5kmh: 13.1secs
0-1/4 mile: 18.9secs
70.0bhp 52.2kW 71.0PS
@ 4800rpm
85.0lbft 115.2Nm @ 2800rpm
70.6bhp/ton 69.4bhp/tonne
44.1bhp/L 32.9kW/L 44.7PS/L
40.4ft/sec 12.3m/sec
24.0mph 38.6kmh/1000rpm
37.2mpg 31.0mpgUS 7.6L/100km
Petrol 4-stroke piston
1587cc 96.8cu in
In-line 4 1 Carburettor
Compression ratio: 9.0:1
Bore: 81.0mm 3.2in
Stroke: 77.0mm 3.0in
Valve type/No: Overhead 8
Transmission: Manual
No. of forward speeds: 5
Wheels driven: Front
Springs F/R: Coil/Coil
Brake system: PA
Brakes F/R: Disc/Drum
Steering: Rack & pinion PA
Wheelbase: 243.1cm 95.7in
Track F: 142.5cm 56.1in
Track R: 140.5cm 55.3in
Length: 422.4cm 166.3in
Width: 163.6cm 64.4in
Height: 134.6cm 53.0in
Ground clearance: 14.0cm 5.5in
Kerb weight: 1007.9kg 2220.0lb
Fuel: 50.0L 11.0gal 13.2galUS

4429 Toyota

Supra
1984 Japan
130.0mph 209.2kmh
0-50mph 80.5kmh: 6.5secs
0-60mph 96.5kmh: 8.7secs
0-1/4 mile: 26.8secs
160.0bhp 119.3kW 162.2PS
@ 5600rpm
163.0lbft 220.9Nm @ 4400rpm
117.7bhp/ton 115.7bhp/tonne
58.0bhp/L 43.2kW/L 58.8PS/L
52.1ft/sec 15.9m/sec
21.2mph 34.1kmh/1000rpm
24.6mpg 20.5mpgUS 11.5L/100km
Petrol 4-stroke piston
2759cc 168.3cu in
In-line 6 fuel injection
Compression ratio: 9.2:1
Bore: 83.0mm 3.3in
Stroke: 85.0mm 3.3in
Valve type/No: Overhead 12
Transmission: Manual
No. of forward speeds: 5
Wheels driven: Rear
Springs F/R: Coil/Coil
Brake system: PA
Brakes F/R: Disc/Disc
Steering: Rack & pinion PA
Wheelbase: 261.4cm 102.9in
Track F: 147.1cm 57.9in
Track R: 144.0cm 56.7in
Length: 466.1cm 183.5in
Width: 172.0cm 67.7in
Height: 132.1cm 52.0in
Kerb weight: 1382.4kg 3045.0lb
Fuel: 60.9L 13.4gal 16.1galUS

4430 Toyota

Van LE
1984 Japan
93.0mph 149.6kmh
0-60mph 96.5kmh: 15.3secs
0-1/4 mile: 20.0secs
90.0bhp 67.1kW 91.2PS
@ 4400rpm
120.0lbft 162.6Nm @ 3000rpm
61.7bhp/ton 60.7bhp/tonne
45.0bhp/L 33.6kW/L 45.7PS/L
41.4ft/sec 12.6m/sec
22.6mph 36.4kmh/1000rpm
30.0mpg 25.0mpgUS 9.4L/100km
Petrol 4-stroke piston
1998cc 121.9cu in
In-line 4 fuel injection
Compression ratio: 8.8:1
Bore: 86.0mm 3.4in
Stroke: 86.0mm 3.4in
Valve type/No: Overhead 8
Transmission: Manual
No. of forward speeds: 5
Wheels driven: Rear
Springs F/R: Torsion bar/Coil
Brake system: PA
Brakes F/R: Disc/Drum
Steering: Recirculating ball PA
Wheelbase: 223.5cm 88.0in
Track F: 142.5cm 56.1in
Track R: 137.9cm 54.3in
Length: 445.5cm 175.4in
Width: 166.9cm 65.7in
Height: 178.1cm 70.1in
Ground clearance: 15.7cm 6.2in
Kerb weight: 1482.3kg 3265.0lb
Fuel: 60.2L 13.2gal 15.9galUS

4431 Toyota

Celica GTS
1985 Japan
110.0mph 177.0kmh
0-60mph 96.5kmh: 11.5secs
0-1/4 mile: 18.0secs
116.0bhp 86.5kW 117.6PS
@ 4800rpm
140.0lbft 189.7Nm @ 2800rpm
93.6bhp/ton 92.1bhp/tonne
49.0bhp/L 36.5kW/L 49.7PS/L
Petrol 4-stroke piston
2367cc 144.4cu in
In-line 4 fuel injection
Valve type/No: Overhead 8
Transmission: Manual
No. of forward speeds: 5
Wheels driven: Rear
Springs F/R: Coil/Coil
Brakes F/R: Disc/Disc
Steering: Rack & pinion PA
Wheelbase: 249.9cm 98.4in
Length: 419.6cm 165.2in
Width: 172.0cm 67.7in
Height: 132.1cm 52.0in
Kerb weight: 1259.8kg 2775.0lb
Fuel: 60.9L 13.4gal 16.1galUS

4432 Toyota

Corolla GT Hatchback
1985 Japan
121.0mph 194.7kmh
0-50mph 80.5kmh: 6.2secs
0-60mph 96.5kmh: 8.5secs
0-1/4 mile: 16.2secs
0-1km: 30.3secs
119.0bhp 88.7kW 120.6PS
@ 6600rpm
103.0lbft 139.6Nm @ 5000rpm
127.5bhp/ton 125.3bhp/tonne
75.0bhp/L 55.9kW/L 76.0PS/L
55.5ft/sec 16.9m/sec
18.6mph 29.9kmh/1000rpm
28.8mpg 24.0mpgUS 9.8L/100km
Petrol 4-stroke piston
1587cc 96.8cu in
In-line 4 fuel injection
Compression ratio: 10.0:1
Bore: 81.0mm 3.2in
Stroke: 77.0mm 3.0in
Valve type/No: Overhead 16
Transmission: Manual
No. of forward speeds: 5
Wheels driven: Front
Springs F/R: Coil/Coil
Brake system: PA
Brakes F/R: Disc/Disc
Steering: Rack & pinion
Wheelbase: 243.1cm 95.7in
Track F: 142.5cm 56.1in
Track R: 140.5cm 55.3in
Length: 397.0cm 156.3in
Width: 165.6cm 65.2in
Height: 137.9cm 54.3in
Ground clearance: 16.0cm 6.3in
Kerb weight: 949.3kg 2091.0lb
Fuel: 50.0L 11.0gal 13.2galUS

4433 Toyota

MR2
1985 Japan
124.0mph 199.5kmh
0-50mph 80.5kmh: 5.7secs
0-60mph 96.5kmh: 7.7secs
0-1/4 mile: 16.0secs
0-1km: 30.5secs
121.9bhp 90.9kW 123.6PS
@ 6600rpm
104.8lbft 142.0Nm @ 5000rpm
117.7bhp/ton 115.8bhp/tonne
76.8bhp/L 57.3kW/L 77.9PS/L
55.5ft/sec 16.9m/sec
18.6mph 29.9kmh/1000rpm
29.1mpg 24.2mpgUS 9.7L/100km
Petrol 4-stroke piston
1587cc 96.8cu in
In-line 4 fuel injection
Compression ratio: 10.0:1
Bore: 81.0mm 3.2in
Stroke: 77.0mm 3.0in
Valve type/No: Overhead 16
Transmission: Manual
No. of forward speeds: 5
Wheels driven: Rear
Springs F/R: Coil/Coil
Brake system: PA
Brakes F/R: Disc/Disc

Steering: Rack & pinion
Wheelbase: 228.6cm 90.0in
Track F: 137.2cm 54.0in
Track R: 137.2cm 54.0in
Length: 386.1cm 152.0in
Width: 165.1cm 65.0in
Height: 132.1cm 52.0in
Ground clearance: 17.8cm 7.0in
Kerb weight: 1052.8kg 2319.0lb
Fuel: 40.9L 9.0gal 10.8galUS

4434 Toyota

Space Cruiser
1985 Japan
90.0mph 144.8kmh
0-50mph 80.5kmh: 11.2secs
0-60mph 96.5kmh: 16.1secs
0-1/4 mile: 19.9secs
0-1km: 39.9secs
87.0bhp 64.9kW 88.2PS
@ 4600rpm
119.5lbft 161.9Nm @ 2600rpm
66.4bhp/ton 65.3bhp/tonne
43.5bhp/L 32.5kW/L 44.1PS/L
43.3ft/sec 13.2m/sec
20.8mph 33.5kmh/1000rpm
23.0mpg 19.2mpgUS 12.3L/100km
Petrol 4-stroke piston
1998cc 121.9cu in
In-line 4 1 Carburettor
Compression ratio: 8.8:1
Bore: 86.0mm 3.4in
Stroke: 86.0mm 3.4in
Valve type/No: Overhead 8
Transmission: Manual
No. of forward speeds: 5
Wheels driven: Rear
Springs F/R: Torsion bar/Coil
Brake system: PA
Brakes F/R: Disc/Drum
Steering: Recirculating ball PA
Wheelbase: 221.5cm 87.2in
Track F: 141.2cm 55.6in
Track R: 136.7cm 53.8in
Length: 424.4cm 167.1in
Width: 165.4cm 65.1in
Height: 179.8cm 70.8in
Ground clearance: 20.3cm 8.0in
Kerb weight: 1331.6kg 2933.0lb
Fuel: 54.6L 12.0gal 14.4galUS

4435 Toyota

Starlet 1.0GL
1985 Japan
88.0mph 141.6kmh
0-50mph 80.5kmh: 10.4secs
0-60mph 96.5kmh: 14.8secs
0-1/4 mile: 19.7secs
0-1km: 37.8secs
54.0bhp 40.3kW 54.7PS
@ 6000rpm
55.0lbft 74.5Nm @ 3800rpm
74.5bhp/ton 73.2bhp/tonne
54.0bhp/L 40.3kW/L 54.8PS/L
42.0ft/sec 12.8m/sec
19.4mph 31.2kmh/1000rpm
33.5mpg 27.9mpgUS 8.4L/100km
Petrol 4-stroke piston
999cc 60.9cu in
In-line 4 1 Carburettor
Compression ratio: 9.0:1
Bore: 70.5mm 2.8in
Stroke: 64.0mm 2.5in
Valve type/No: Overhead 12
Transmission: Manual
No. of forward speeds: 5
Wheels driven: Front
Springs F/R: Coil/Coil
Brake system: PA
Brakes F/R: Disc/Drum
Steering: Rack & pinion
Wheelbase: 228.6cm 90.0in
Track F: 138.4cm 54.5in
Track R: 134.4cm 52.9in
Length: 370.1cm 145.7in
Width: 159.0cm 62.6in
Height: 139.4cm 54.9in
Ground clearance: 16.5cm 6.5in
Kerb weight: 737.3kg 1624.0lb
Fuel: 40.0L 8.8gal 10.6galUS

4436 Toyota

Supra
1985 Japan
127.0mph 204.3kmh
0-60mph 96.5kmh: 8.4secs
0-1/4 mile: 16.5secs
161.0bhp 120.1kW 163.2PS
@ 5200rpm
169.0lbft 229.0Nm @ 4500rpm
118.4bhp/ton 116.5bhp/tonne
58.3bhp/L 43.5kW/L 59.2PS/L
Petrol 4-stroke piston
2759cc 168.3cu in
In-line 6 fuel injection
Valve type/No: Overhead 24
Transmission: Manual
No. of forward speeds: 5
Wheels driven: Rear
Springs F/R: Coil/Coil
Brakes F/R: Disc/Disc
Steering: Rack & pinion PA
Wheelbase: 261.4cm 102.9in
Length: 466.1cm 183.5in
Width: 172.0cm 67.7in
Height: 132.1cm 52.0in
Kerb weight: 1382.4kg 3045.0lb
Fuel: 60.9L 13.4gal 16.1galUS

4437 Toyota

Tercel 4WD Estate
1985 Japan
94.0mph 151.2kmh
0-50mph 80.5kmh: 10.4secs
0-60mph 96.5kmh: 14.9secs
0-1/4 mile: 19.9secs
0-1km: 37.6secs
71.0bhp 52.9kW 72.0PS
@ 5600rpm
82.7lbft 112.1Nm @ 2400rpm
71.3bhp/ton 70.1bhp/tonne
48.9bhp/L 36.5kW/L 49.6PS/L
47.1ft/sec 14.4m/sec
19.4mph 31.2kmh/1000rpm
31.2mpg 26.0mpgUS 9.1L/100km
Petrol 4-stroke piston
1452cc 88.6cu in
In-line 4 1 Carburettor
Compression ratio: 9.0:1
Bore: 77.5mm 3.0in
Stroke: 77.0mm 3.0in
Valve type/No: Overhead 8
Transmission: Manual
No. of forward speeds: 5
Wheels driven: 4-wheel engageable
Springs F/R: Coil/Leaf
Brake system: PA
Brakes F/R: Disc/Drum
Steering: Rack & pinion
Wheelbase: 243.1cm 95.7in
Track F: 139.4cm 54.9in
Track R: 135.9cm 53.5in
Length: 436.1cm 171.7in
Width: 161.5cm 63.6in
Height: 149.6cm 58.9in
Ground clearance: 17.0cm 6.7in
Kerb weight: 1012.4kg 2230.0lb
Fuel: 50.0L 11.0gal 13.2galUS

4438 Toyota

Celica 2.0GT
1986 Japan
133.0mph 214.0kmh
0-50mph 80.5kmh: 6.1secs
0-60mph 96.5kmh: 8.2secs
0-1/4 mile: 16.7secs
0-1km: 30.4secs
147.0bhp 109.6kW 149.0PS
@ 6400rpm
130.0lbft 176.2Nm @ 4800rpm
117.4bhp/ton 115.4bhp/tonne
73.6bhp/L 54.9kW/L 74.6PS/L
60.3ft/sec 18.3m/sec
21.0mph 33.8kmh/1000rpm
25.0mpg 20.8mpgUS 11.3L/100km
Petrol 4-stroke piston
1998cc 121.9cu in
In-line 4 fuel injection
Compression ratio: 9.8:1
Bore: 86.0mm 3.4in
Stroke: 86.0mm 3.4in
Valve type/No: Overhead 16
Transmission: Manual
No. of forward speeds: 5
Wheels driven: Front
Springs F/R: Coil/Coil
Brake system: PA
Brakes F/R: Disc/Disc
Steering: Rack & pinion PA
Wheelbase: 252.5cm 99.4in
Track F: 146.3cm 57.6in
Track R: 142.7cm 56.2in
Length: 436.4cm 171.8in
Width: 170.9cm 67.3in
Ground clearance: 17.8cm 7.0in
Kerb weight: 1273.5kg 2805.0lb
Fuel: 60.1L 13.2gal 15.9galUS

4439 Toyota

Celica GTS
1986 Japan
123.0mph 197.9kmh
0-60mph 96.5kmh: 8.6secs
0-1/4 mile: 16.5secs
135.0bhp 100.7kW 136.9PS
@ 6000rpm
125.0lbft 169.4Nm @ 4800rpm
111.2bhp/ton 109.3bhp/tonne
67.6bhp/L 50.4kW/L 68.5PS/L
56.5ft/sec 17.2m/sec
24.3mpg 20.2mpgUS 11.6L/100km
Petrol 4-stroke piston
1998cc 121.9cu in
In-line 4 fuel injection
Compression ratio: 9.2:1
Bore: 86.0mm 3.4in
Stroke: 86.0mm 3.4in
Valve type/No: Overhead 16
Transmission: Manual
No. of forward speeds: 5
Wheels driven: Front
Springs F/R: Coil/Coil
Brake system: PA
Brakes F/R: Disc/Disc
Steering: Rack & pinion PA
Wheelbase: 252.5cm 99.4in
Track F: 147.1cm 57.9in
Track R: 143.5cm 56.5in
Length: 440.9cm 173.6in
Width: 170.9cm 67.3in
Height: 126.5cm 49.8in
Ground clearance: 14.0cm 5.5in
Kerb weight: 1234.9kg 2720.0lb
Fuel: 60.2L 13.2gal 15.9galUS

4440 Toyota

MR2
1986 Japan
121.0mph 194.7kmh
0-60mph 96.5kmh: 8.4secs
0-1/4 mile: 16.5secs
112.0bhp 83.5kW 113.5PS
@ 6600rpm
97.0lbft 131.4Nm @ 4800rpm
105.0bhp/ton 103.2bhp/tonne
70.6bhp/L 52.6kW/L 71.5PS/L
55.5ft/sec 16.9m/sec
30.0mpg 25.0mpgUS 9.4L/100km
Petrol 4-stroke piston
1587cc 96.8cu in
In-line 4 fuel injection
Compression ratio: 9.4:1
Bore: 81.0mm 3.2in
Stroke: 77.0mm 3.0in
Valve type/No: Overhead 16
Transmission: Manual
No. of forward speeds: 5
Wheels driven: Rear
Springs F/R: Coil/Coil
Brake system: PA
Brakes F/R: Disc/Disc
Steering: Rack & pinion
Wheelbase: 231.9cm 91.3in
Track F: 144.0cm 56.7in
Track R: 144.5cm 56.9in
Length: 392.4cm 154.5in
Width: 166.6cm 65.6in
Height: 125.0cm 49.2in
Kerb weight: 1085.1kg 2390.0lb
Fuel: 40.9L 9.0gal 10.8galUS

4441 Toyota

MR2 T-Bar
1986 Japan
122.0mph 196.3kmh
0-50mph 80.5kmh: 5.7secs
0-60mph 96.5kmh: 7.7secs
0-1/4 mile: 16.5secs
0-1km: 30.7secs
122.0bhp 91.0kW 123.7PS
@ 6600rpm
105.0lbft 142.3Nm @ 5000rpm
116.4bhp/ton 114.4bhp/tonne
76.9bhp/L 57.3kW/L 77.9PS/L
55.5ft/sec 16.9m/sec
18.6mph 29.9kmh/1000rpm
28.6mpg 23.8mpgUS 9.9L/100km
Petrol 4-stroke piston
1587cc 97.0cu in
In-line 4 fuel injection
Compression ratio: 10.0:1
Bore: 81.0mm 3.2in
Stroke: 77.0mm 3.0in
Valve type/No: Overhead 16
Transmission: Manual
No. of forward speeds: 5
Wheels driven: Rear
Springs F/R: Coil/Coil
Brake system: PA
Brakes F/R: Disc/Disc
Steering: Rack & pinion
Wheelbase: 232.0cm 91.3in
Track F: 144.0cm 56.7in
Track R: 144.0cm 56.7in
Length: 392.5cm 154.5in
Width: 166.6cm 65.6in
Height: 124.9cm 49.2in
Ground clearance: 17.9cm 7.0in
Kerb weight: 1066.0kg 2348.0lb
Fuel: 40.9L 9.0gal 10.8galUS

4442 Toyota

Supra
1986 Japan
133.0mph 214.0kmh
0-50mph 80.5kmh: 5.1secs
0-60mph 96.5kmh: 7.0secs
0-1/4 mile: 15.4secs
200.0bhp 149.1kW 202.8PS
@ 6000rpm
185.0lbft 250.7Nm @ 4800rpm
131.4bhp/ton 129.2bhp/tonne
67.7bhp/L 50.5kW/L 68.6PS/L
59.7ft/sec 18.2m/sec
21.6mpg 18.0mpgUS 13.1L/100km
Petrol 4-stroke piston
2954cc 180.2cu in
In-line 6 fuel injection
Compression ratio: 9.2:1
Bore: 83.0mm 3.3in
Stroke: 91.0mm 3.6in
Valve type/No: Overhead 24
Transmission: Manual
No. of forward speeds: 5
Wheels driven: Rear
Springs F/R: Coil/Coil
Brake system: PA
Brakes F/R: Disc/Disc
Steering: Rack & pinion PA
Wheelbase: 259.6cm 102.2in
Track F: 148.6cm 58.5in
Track R: 148.6cm 58.5in
Length: 462.0cm 181.9in
Width: 174.5cm 68.7in
Height: 131.1cm 51.6in
Ground clearance: 14.0cm 5.5in
Kerb weight: 1548.1kg 3410.0lb
Fuel: 70.0L 15.4gal 18.5galUS

4443 Toyota

Supra 3.0i
1986 Japan
138.0mph 222.0kmh
0-50mph 80.5kmh: 5.6secs
0-60mph 96.5kmh: 7.7secs
0-1/4 mile: 16.0secs
0-1km: 29.4secs
201.0bhp 149.9kW 203.8PS
@ 6000rpm
187.4lbft 253.9Nm @ 4000rpm
131.9bhp/ton 129.7bhp/tonne
68.0bhp/L 50.7kW/L 69.0PS/L
59.7ft/sec 18.2m/sec
23.8mph 38.3kmh/1000rpm
19.4mpg 16.2mpgUS 14.6L/100km
Petrol 4-stroke piston
2954cc 180.0cu in
In-line 6 fuel injection
Compression ratio: 9.2:1
Bore: 83.0mm 3.3in
Stroke: 91.0mm 3.6in
Valve type/No: Overhead 24
Transmission: Manual
No. of forward speeds: 5
Wheels driven: Rear
Springs F/R: Coil/Coil
Brake system: PA ABS
Brakes F/R: Disc/Disc
Steering: Rack & pinion PA
Wheelbase: 259.5cm 102.2in
Track F: 148.5cm 58.5in
Track R: 148.0cm 58.3in
Length: 462.0cm 181.9in
Width: 174.5cm 68.7in
Height: 131.0cm 51.6in
Kerb weight: 1550.0kg 3414.1lb
Fuel: 70.1L 15.4gal 18.5galUS

4444 Toyota
Tercel DX
1986 Japan
0-60mph 96.5kmh: 11.4secs
0-1/4 mile: 18.3secs
78.0bhp 58.2kW 79.1PS
@ 6000rpm
87.0lbft 117.9Nm @ 4000rpm
81.8bhp/ton 80.5bhp/tonne
53.6bhp/L 39.9kW/L 54.3PS/L
57.2ft/sec 17.4m/sec
23.5mph 37.8kmh/1000rpm
33.9mpg 28.2mpgUS 8.3L/100km
Petrol 4-stroke piston
1456cc 88.8cu in
In-line 4 1 Carburettor
Compression ratio: 9.5:1
Bore: 73.0mm 2.9in
Stroke: 87.0mm 3.4in
Valve type/No: Overhead 8
Transmission: Manual
No. of forward speeds: 5
Wheels driven: Front
Springs F/R: Torsion bar/Coil
Brake system: PA
Brakes F/R: Disc/Drum
Steering: Rack & pinion PA
Wheelbase: 238.0cm 93.7in
Track F: 137.9cm 54.3in
Track R: 137.4cm 54.1in
Length: 399.5cm 157.3in
Width: 162.6cm 64.0in
Height: 133.6cm 52.6in
Kerb weight: 969.3kg 2135.0lb
Fuel: 45.0L 9.9gal 11.9galUS

4445 Toyota
Camry 2.0 GLi
1987 Japan
118.0mph 189.9kmh
0-50mph 80.5kmh: 6.4secs
0-60mph 96.5kmh: 9.0secs
0-1/4 mile: 16.9secs
0-1km: 31.2secs
126.0bhp 94.0kW 127.7PS
@ 5600rpm
132.0lbft 178.9Nm @ 4400rpm
107.4bhp/ton 105.6bhp/tonne
63.1bhp/L 47.0kW/L 63.9PS/L
52.7ft/sec 16.0m/sec
23.1mph 37.2kmh/1000rpm
30.5mpg 25.4mpgUS 9.3L/100km
Petrol 4-stroke piston
1998cc 122.0cu in
In-line 4 fuel injection
Compression ratio: 9.8:1
Bore: 86.0mm 3.4in
Stroke: 86.0mm 3.4in
Valve type/No: Overhead 16
Transmission: Manual
No. of forward speeds: 5
Wheels driven: Front
Springs F/R: Coil/Coil
Brake system: PA
Brakes F/R: Disc/Drum
Steering: Rack & pinion PA
Wheelbase: 260.0cm 102.4in
Track F: 147.5cm 58.1in
Track R: 144.5cm 56.9in
Length: 452.0cm 178.0in
Width: 171.0cm 67.3in
Height: 140.0cm 55.1in
Ground clearance: 17.0cm 6.7in
Kerb weight: 1193.0kg 2627.7lb
Fuel: 60.1L 13.2gal 15.9galUS

4446 Toyota
Camry 2.0 GLi Estate
1987 Japan
112.0mph 180.2kmh
0-50mph 80.5kmh: 7.1secs
0-60mph 96.5kmh: 10.1secs
0-1/4 mile: 17.7secs
0-1km: 32.5secs
126.0bhp 94.0kW 127.7PS
@ 5600rpm
132.0lbft 178.9Nm @ 4400rpm
99.2bhp/ton 97.6bhp/tonne
63.1bhp/L 47.0kW/L 63.9PS/L
52.7ft/sec 16.0m/sec
23.1mph 37.2kmh/1000rpm
28.7mpg 23.9mpgUS 9.8L/100km
Petrol 4-stroke piston
1998cc 122.0cu in
In-line 4 fuel injection
Compression ratio: 9.8:1
Bore: 86.0mm 3.4in
Stroke: 86.0mm 3.4in
Valve type/No: Overhead 16
Transmission: Manual
No. of forward speeds: 5
Wheels driven: Front
Springs F/R: Coil/Coil
Brake system: PA
Brakes F/R: Disc/Drum
Steering: Rack & pinion PA
Wheelbase: 260.0cm 102.4in
Track F: 147.5cm 58.1in
Track R: 144.5cm 56.9in
Length: 461.0cm 181.5in
Width: 171.0cm 67.3in
Height: 140.0cm 55.1in
Ground clearance: 17.0cm 6.7in
Kerb weight: 1291.0kg 2843.6lb
Fuel: 60.1L 13.2gal 15.9galUS

4447 Toyota
Celica GT Cabriolet
1987 Japan
127.0mph 204.3kmh
0-50mph 80.5kmh: 6.3secs
0-60mph 96.5kmh: 8.6secs
0-1/4 mile: 16.9secs
0-1km: 31.2secs
147.0bhp 109.6kW 149.0PS
@ 6400rpm
133.0lbft 180.2Nm @ 4800rpm
125.1bhp/ton 123.0bhp/tonne
73.6bhp/L 54.9kW/L 74.6PS/L
60.3ft/sec 18.3m/sec
21.4mph 34.4kmh/1000rpm
28.7mpg 23.9mpgUS 9.8L/100km
Petrol 4-stroke piston
1998cc 122.0cu in
In-line 4 fuel injection
Compression ratio: 9.8:1
Bore: 86.0mm 3.4in
Stroke: 86.0mm 3.4in
Valve type/No: Overhead 16
Transmission: Manual
No. of forward speeds: 5
Wheels driven: Front
Springs F/R: Coil/Coil
Brakes F/R: Disc/Disc
Steering: Rack & pinion PA
Wheelbase: 252.5cm 99.4in
Track F: 146.5cm 57.7in
Track R: 143.0cm 56.3in
Length: 436.5cm 171.9in
Width: 171.0cm 67.3in
Ground clearance: 17.9cm 7.0in
Kerb weight: 1195.0kg 2632.2lb
Fuel: 60.1L 13.2gal 15.9galUS

4448 Toyota
Corolla Executive
1987 Japan
104.0mph 167.3kmh
0-50mph 80.5kmh: 7.9secs
0-60mph 96.5kmh: 11.1secs
0-1/4 mile: 18.0secs
0-1km: 33.4secs
94.0bhp 70.1kW 95.3PS
@ 6000rpm
100.0lbft 135.5Nm @ 3600rpm
93.7bhp/ton 92.2bhp/tonne
59.2bhp/L 44.2kW/L 60.0PS/L
50.5ft/sec 15.4m/sec
19.9mph 32.0kmh/1000rpm
29.6mpg 24.6mpgUS 9.5L/100km
Petrol 4-stroke piston
1587cc 97.0cu in
In-line 4 1 Carburettor
Compression ratio: 9.5:1
Bore: 81.0mm 3.2in
Stroke: 77.0mm 3.0in
Valve type/No: Overhead 16
Transmission: Manual
No. of forward speeds: 5
Wheels driven: Front
Springs F/R: Coil/Coil
Brake system: PA
Brakes F/R: Disc/Drum
Steering: Rack & pinion PA
Wheelbase: 243.0cm 95.7in
Track F: 143.0cm 56.3in
Track R: 141.0cm 55.5in
Length: 421.5cm 165.9in
Width: 165.5cm 65.2in
Height: 136.5cm 53.7in
Ground clearance: 15.5cm 6.1in
Kerb weight: 1020.0kg 2246.7lb
Fuel: 50.0L 11.0gal 13.2galUS

4449 Toyota
Corolla FX-16 GTS
1987 Japan
105.0mph 168.9kmh
0-50mph 80.5kmh: 6.7secs
0-60mph 96.5kmh: 9.2secs
0-1/4 mile: 17.0secs
108.0bhp 80.5kW 109.5PS
@ 6600rpm
96.0lbft 130.1Nm @ 4800rpm
98.1bhp/ton 96.5bhp/tonne
68.0bhp/L 50.7kW/L 69.0PS/L
55.5ft/sec 16.9m/sec
30.6mpg 25.5mpgUS 9.2L/100km
Petrol 4-stroke piston
1587cc 96.8cu in
In-line 4 fuel injection
Compression ratio: 9.4:1
Bore: 81.0mm 3.2in
Stroke: 77.0mm 3.0in
Valve type/No: Overhead 16
Transmission: Manual
No. of forward speeds: 5
Wheels driven: Front
Springs F/R: Coil/Coil
Brake system: PA
Brakes F/R: Disc/Disc
Steering: Rack & pinion PA
Wheelbase: 243.1cm 95.7in
Track F: 143.5cm 56.5in
Track R: 141.5cm 55.7in
Length: 406.4cm 160.0in
Width: 165.6cm 65.2in
Height: 134.1cm 52.8in
Ground clearance: 13.5cm 5.3in
Kerb weight: 1119.1kg 2465.0lb
Fuel: 50.0L 11.0gal 13.2galUS

4450 Toyota
Landcruiser
1987 Japan
87.0mph 140.0kmh
0-50mph 80.5kmh: 14.2secs
0-60mph 96.5kmh: 21.6secs
0-1/4 mile: 22.0secs
0-1km: 45.9secs
102.0bhp 76.1kW 103.4PS
@ 3500rpm
178.0lbft 241.2Nm @ 1800rpm
47.8bhp/ton 47.0bhp/tonne
25.6bhp/L 19.1kW/L 26.0PS/L
39.1ft/sec 11.9m/sec
26.8mph 43.1kmh/1000rpm
17.9mpg 14.9mpgUS 15.8L/100km
Diesel 4-stroke piston
3980cc 243.0cu in
In-line 6 fuel injection
Compression ratio: 22.7:1
Bore: 91.0mm 3.6in
Stroke: 102.0mm 4.0in
Valve type/No: Overhead 12
Transmission: Manual
No. of forward speeds: 5
Wheels driven: 4-wheel engageable
Springs F/R: Leaf/Leaf
Brake system: PA
Brakes F/R: Disc/Drum
Steering: Recirculating ball PA
Wheelbase: 273.0cm 107.5in
Track F: 147.5cm 58.1in
Track R: 146.0cm 57.5in
Length: 467.5cm 184.1in
Width: 180.0cm 70.9in
Height: 180.0cm 70.9in
Ground clearance: 18.0cm 7.1in
Kerb weight: 2170.0kg 4779.7lb
Fuel: 90.1L 19.8gal 23.8galUS

4451 Toyota
MR2 Supercharged
1987 Japan
135.0mph 217.2kmh
0-50mph 80.5kmh: 5.0secs
0-60mph 96.5kmh: 7.0secs
0-1/4 mile: 15.3secs
145.0bhp 108.1kW 147.0PS
@ 6400rpm
140.0lbft 189.7Nm @ 4000rpm
124.0bhp/ton 121.9bhp/tonne
91.4bhp/L 68.1kW/L 92.6PS/L
53.9ft/sec 16.4m/sec
25.3mpg 21.1mpgUS 11.1L/100km
Petrol 4-stroke piston
1587cc 96.8cu in supercharged
In-line 4 fuel injection
Compression ratio: 8.0:1
Bore: 81.0mm 3.2in
Stroke: 77.0mm 3.0in
Valve type/No: Overhead 16
Transmission: Manual
No. of forward speeds: 5
Wheels driven: Rear
Springs F/R: Coil/Coil
Brakes F/R: Disc/Disc
Steering: Rack & pinion
Wheelbase: 231.9cm 91.3in
Track F: 144.0cm 56.7in
Track R: 144.0cm 56.7in
Length: 395.0cm 155.5in
Width: 166.6cm 65.6in
Height: 123.4cm 48.6in
Kerb weight: 1189.5kg 2620.0lb
Fuel: 40.9L 9.0gal 10.8galUS

4452 Toyota
Supra
1987 Japan
130.0mph 209.2kmh
0-60mph 96.5kmh: 7.9secs
0-1/4 mile: 16.0secs
200.0bhp 149.1kW 202.8PS
@ 6000rpm
185.0lbft 250.7Nm @ 4800rpm
126.9bhp/ton 124.8bhp/tonne
67.7bhp/L 50.5kW/L 68.6PS/L
59.7ft/sec 18.2m/sec
22.8mpg 19.0mpgUS 12.4L/100km
Petrol 4-stroke piston
2954cc 180.2cu in
In-line 6 fuel injection
Compression ratio: 9.2:1
Bore: 83.0mm 3.3in
Stroke: 91.0mm 3.6in
Valve type/No: Overhead 24
Transmission: Manual
No. of forward speeds: 5
Wheels driven: Rear
Springs F/R: Coil/Coil
Brake system: ABS
Brakes F/R: Disc/Disc
Steering: Rack & pinion PA
Wheelbase: 259.6cm 102.2in
Track F: 148.6cm 58.5in
Track R: 148.6cm 58.5in
Length: 462.0cm 181.9in
Width: 174.5cm 68.7in
Height: 131.1cm 51.6in
Kerb weight: 1602.6kg 3530.0lb
Fuel: 70.0L 15.4gal 18.5galUS

4453 Toyota
Carina 1.6 GL
1988 Japan
109.0mph 175.4kmh
0-50mph 80.5kmh: 7.6secs
0-60mph 96.5kmh: 10.5secs
0-1/4 mile: 17.9secs
0-1km: 33.3secs
94.0bhp 70.1kW 95.3PS
@ 6000rpm
100.4lbft 136.0Nm @ 3600rpm
88.5bhp/ton 87.0bhp/tonne
59.2bhp/L 44.2kW/L 60.0PS/L
51.0ft/sec 15.6m/sec
20.5mph 33.0kmh/1000rpm
28.5mpg 23.7mpgUS 9.9L/100km
Petrol 4-stroke piston
1587cc 97.0cu in
In-line 4 1 Carburettor
Compression ratio: 9.5:1
Bore: 81.0mm 3.2in
Stroke: 77.8mm 3.1in
Valve type/No: Overhead 16
Transmission: Manual
No. of forward speeds: 5
Wheels driven: Front
Springs F/R: Coil/Coil
Brakes F/R: Disc/Drum
Steering: Rack & pinion PA
Wheelbase: 252.5cm 99.4in
Track F: 145.5cm 57.3in
Track R: 142.5cm 56.1in
Length: 440.0cm 173.2in
Width: 169.0cm 66.5in
Height: 137.0cm 53.9in
Ground clearance: 16.0cm 6.3in
Kerb weight: 1080.0kg 2378.8lb
Fuel: 60.1L 13.2gal 15.9galUS

4454 Toyota
Celica All-Trac Turbo
1988 Japan
134.0mph 215.6kmh

0-50mph 80.5kmh: 5.5secs
0-60mph 96.5kmh: 7.7secs
0-1/4 mile: 15.6secs
190.0bhp 141.7kW 192.6PS
@ 6000rpm
190.0lbft 257.5Nm @ 3200rpm
130.1bhp/ton 128.0bhp/tonne
95.1bhp/L 70.9kW/L 96.4PS/L
56.5ft/sec 17.2m/sec
24.0mpg 20.0mpgUS 11.8L/100km
Petrol 4-stroke piston
1998cc 121.9cu in turbocharged
In-line 4 fuel injection
Compression ratio: 8.5:1
Bore: 86.0mm 3.4in
Stroke: 86.0mm 3.4in
Valve type/No: Overhead 16
Transmission: Manual
No. of forward speeds: 5
Wheels driven: 4-wheel drive
Springs F/R: Coil/Coil
Brake system: PA ABS
Brakes F/R: Disc/Disc
Steering: Rack & pinion PA
Wheelbase: 252.5cm 99.4in
Track F: 147.1cm 57.9in
Track R: 144.5cm 56.9in
Length: 436.6cm 171.9in
Width: 170.9cm 67.3in
Height: 126.5cm 49.8in
Kerb weight: 1484.6kg 3270.0lb
Fuel: 60.2L 13.2gal 15.9galUS

4455 Toyota
Celica GT4
1988 Japan
137.0mph 220.4kmh
0-50mph 80.5kmh: 5.6secs
0-60mph 96.5kmh: 7.6secs
0-1/4 mile: 15.7secs
0-1km: 28.9secs
182.0bhp 135.7kW 184.5PS
@ 6000rpm
184.5lbft 250.0Nm @ 3600rpm
125.5bhp/ton 123.4bhp/tonne
91.1bhp/L 67.9kW/L 92.3PS/L
56.5ft/sec 17.2m/sec
23.6mph 38.0kmh/1000rpm
19.2mpg 16.0mpgUS 14.7L/100km
Petrol 4-stroke piston
1998cc 122.0cu in turbocharged
In-line 4 fuel injection
Compression ratio: 8.5:1
Bore: 86.0mm 3.4in
Stroke: 86.0mm 3.4in
Valve type/No: Overhead 16
Transmission: Manual
No. of forward speeds: 5
Wheels driven: 4-wheel drive
Springs F/R: Coil/Coil
Brake system: PA ABS
Brakes F/R: Disc/Disc
Steering: Rack & pinion PA
Wheelbase: 252.5cm 99.4in
Track F: 146.5cm 57.7in
Track R: 143.0cm 56.3in
Length: 436.5cm 171.9in
Width: 171.0cm 67.3in
Height: 127.0cm 50.0in
Ground clearance: 17.9cm 7.0in
Kerb weight: 1475.0kg 3248.9lb
Fuel: 62.6L 13.7gal 16.5galUS

4456 Toyota
Corolla 1.3 GL
1988 Japan
97.0mph 156.1kmh
0-50mph 80.5kmh: 8.7secs
0-60mph 96.5kmh: 12.8secs
0-1/4 mile: 19.0secs
0-1km: 35.9secs
74.0bhp 55.2kW 75.0PS
@ 6200rpm
76.0lbft 103.0Nm @ 4200rpm
76.8bhp/ton 75.5bhp/tonne
57.1bhp/L 42.6kW/L 57.9PS/L
52.5ft/sec 16.0m/sec
19.8mph 31.9kmh/1000rpm
31.2mpg 26.0mpgUS 9.1L/100km
Petrol 4-stroke piston
1295cc 79.0cu in
In-line 4 1 Carburettor
Compression ratio: 9.5:1
Bore: 73.0mm 2.9in
Stroke: 77.4mm 3.0in
Valve type/No: Overhead 8
Transmission: Manual
No. of forward speeds: 5
Wheels driven: Front
Springs F/R: Coil/Coil
Brake system: PA
Brakes F/R: Disc/Drum
Steering: Rack & pinion
Wheelbase: 243.0cm 95.7in
Track F: 143.0cm 56.3in
Track R: 141.0cm 55.5in
Length: 399.5cm 157.3in
Width: 165.5cm 65.2in
Height: 136.5cm 53.7in
Ground clearance: 19.0cm 7.5in
Kerb weight: 980.0kg 2158.6lb
Fuel: 50.0L 11.0gal 13.2galUS

4457 Toyota
Corolla 4WD Estate
1988 Japan
97.0mph 156.1kmh
0-50mph 80.5kmh: 8.4secs
0-60mph 96.5kmh: 12.1secs
0-1/4 mile: 18.6secs
0-1km: 35.0secs
94.0bhp 70.1kW 95.3PS
@ 6000rpm
100.4lbft 136.0Nm @ 3600rpm
82.1bhp/ton 80.7bhp/tonne
59.2bhp/L 44.2kW/L 60.0PS/L
51.0ft/sec 15.6m/sec
19.8mph 31.9kmh/1000rpm
21.3mpg 17.7mpgUS 13.3L/100km
Petrol 4-stroke piston
1587cc 97.0cu in
In-line 4 1 Carburettor
Compression ratio: 9.5:1
Bore: 81.0mm 3.2in
Stroke: 77.8mm 3.1in
Valve type/No: Overhead 16
Transmission: Manual
No. of forward speeds: 5
Wheels driven: 4-wheel drive
Springs F/R: Coil/Coil
Brake system: PA
Brakes F/R: Disc/Drum
Steering: Rack & pinion PA
Wheelbase: 243.0cm 95.7in
Track F: 144.0cm 56.7in
Track R: 138.0cm 54.3in
Length: 425.0cm 167.3in
Width: 165.5cm 65.2in
Height: 145.0cm 57.1in
Ground clearance: 21.5cm 8.5in
Kerb weight: 1165.0kg 2566.1lb
Fuel: 50.0L 11.0gal 13.2galUS

4458 Toyota
Landcruiser II TD
1988 Japan
81.0mph 130.3kmh
0-50mph 80.5kmh: 14.9secs
0-60mph 96.5kmh: 23.5secs
0-1/4 mile: 22.3secs
0-1km: 42.4secs
84.0bhp 62.6kW 85.2PS
@ 4000rpm
138.0lbft 187.0Nm @ 2400rpm
47.9bhp/ton 47.1bhp/tonne
34.3bhp/L 25.6kW/L 34.8PS/L
40.2ft/sec 12.3m/sec
20.4mph 32.8kmh/1000rpm
20.2mpg 16.8mpgUS 14.0L/100km
Diesel 4-stroke piston
2446cc 149.0cu in turbocharged
In-line 4 fuel injection
Compression ratio: 20.0:1
Bore: 92.0mm 3.6in
Stroke: 92.0mm 3.6in
Valve type/No: Overhead 8
Transmission: Manual
No. of forward speeds: 5
Wheels driven: 4-wheel engageable
Springs F/R: Coil/Coil
Brake system: PA
Brakes F/R: Disc/Drum
Steering: Recirculating ball PA
Wheelbase: 231.0cm 90.9in
Track F: 141.5cm 55.7in
Track R: 146.0cm 57.5in
Length: 406.0cm 159.8in
Width: 179.0cm 70.5in
Height: 187.5cm 73.8in
Ground clearance: 18.0cm 7.1in
Kerb weight: 1784.0kg 3929.5lb
Fuel: 90.1L 19.8gal 23.8galUS

4459 Toyota
Supra
1988 Japan
133.0mph 214.0kmh
0-50mph 80.5kmh: 5.0secs
0-60mph 96.5kmh: 7.5secs
0-1/4 mile: 15.9secs
200.0bhp 149.1kW 202.8PS
@ 6000rpm
188.0lbft 254.7Nm @ 3600rpm
129.9bhp/ton 127.7bhp/tonne
67.7bhp/L 50.5kW/L 68.6PS/L
59.7ft/sec 18.2m/sec
21.6mpg 18.0mpgUS 13.1L/100km
Petrol 4-stroke piston
2954cc 180.2cu in
In-line 6 fuel injection
Compression ratio: 9.2:1
Bore: 83.0mm 3.3in
Stroke: 91.0mm 3.6in
Valve type/No: Overhead 24
Transmission: Manual
No. of forward speeds: 5
Wheels driven: Rear
Springs F/R: Coil/Coil
Brake system: PA
Brakes F/R: Disc/Disc
Steering: Rack & pinion PA
Wheelbase: 259.6cm 102.2in
Track F: 148.6cm 58.5in
Track R: 148.6cm 58.5in
Length: 462.0cm 181.9in
Width: 174.5cm 68.7in
Height: 131.1cm 51.6in
Kerb weight: 1566.3kg 3450.0lb
Fuel: 70.0L 15.4gal 18.5galUS

4460 Toyota
Supra Turbo
1988 Japan
140.0mph 225.3kmh
0-50mph 80.5kmh: 5.1secs
0-60mph 96.5kmh: 7.0secs
0-1/4 mile: 15.2secs
230.0bhp 171.5kW 233.2PS
@ 5600rpm
246.0lbft 333.3Nm @ 4000rpm
142.5bhp/ton 140.1bhp/tonne
77.9bhp/L 58.1kW/L 78.9PS/L
55.7ft/sec 17.0m/sec
24.0mpg 20.0mpgUS 11.8L/100km
Petrol 4-stroke piston
2954cc 180.2cu in turbocharged
In-line 6 fuel injection
Compression ratio: 8.4:1
Bore: 83.0mm 3.3in
Stroke: 90.9mm 3.6in
Valve type/No: Overhead 24
Transmission: Manual
No. of forward speeds: 5
Wheels driven: Rear
Springs F/R: Coil/Coil
Brake system: PA ABS
Brakes F/R: Disc/Disc
Steering: Rack & pinion PA
Wheelbase: 259.6cm 102.2in
Track F: 148.6cm 58.5in
Track R: 148.6cm 58.5in
Length: 462.0cm 181.9in
Width: 174.5cm 68.7in
Height: 131.1cm 51.6in
Kerb weight: 1641.2kg 3615.0lb
Fuel: 70.0L 15.4gal 18.5galUS

4461 Toyota
Camry V6 GXi
1989 Japan
119.0mph 191.5kmh
0-50mph 80.5kmh: 8.2secs
0-60mph 96.5kmh: 11.1secs
0-1/4 mile: 25.0secs
0-1km: 34.2secs
158.0bhp 117.8kW 160.2PS
@ 5800rpm
152.0lbft 206.0Nm @ 4600rpm
112.8bhp/ton 110.9bhp/tonne
63.0bhp/L 47.0kW/L 63.9PS/L
44.1ft/sec 13.4m/sec
24.2mph 38.9kmh/1000rpm
20.6mpg 17.2mpgUS 13.7L/100km
Petrol 4-stroke piston
2507cc 153.0cu in
Vee 6 fuel injection
Compression ratio: 9.0:1
Bore: 87.5mm 3.4in
Stroke: 69.5mm 2.7in
Valve type/No: Overhead 24
Transmission: Automatic
No. of forward speeds: 4
Wheels driven: Front
Springs F/R: Coil/Coil
Brake system: PA ABS
Brakes F/R: Disc/Disc
Steering: Rack & pinion PA
Wheelbase: 260.0cm 102.4in
Track F: 147.5cm 58.1in
Track R: 144.5cm 56.9in
Length: 452.0cm 178.0in
Width: 171.0cm 67.3in
Height: 140.0cm 55.1in
Ground clearance: 17.0cm 6.7in
Kerb weight: 1425.0kg 3138.8lb
Fuel: 60.1L 13.2gal 15.9galUS

4462 Toyota
Carina II 1.6 GL Liftback
1989 Japan
110.0mph 177.0kmh
0-50mph 80.5kmh: 8.7secs
0-60mph 96.5kmh: 12.2secs
0-1/4 mile: 18.6secs
0-1km: 34.0secs
94.0bhp 70.1kW 95.3PS
@ 6000rpm
100.4lbft 136.0Nm @ 3600rpm
87.3bhp/ton 85.8bhp/tonne
59.2bhp/L 44.2kW/L 60.0PS/L
51.0ft/sec 15.6m/sec
20.5mph 33.0kmh/1000rpm
30.0mpg 25.0mpgUS 9.4L/100km
Petrol 4-stroke piston
1587cc 97.0cu in
In-line 4 1 Carburettor
Compression ratio: 9.5:1
Bore: 81.0mm 3.2in
Stroke: 77.8mm 3.1in
Valve type/No: Overhead 16
Transmission: Manual
No. of forward speeds: 5
Wheels driven: Front
Springs F/R: Coil/Coil
Brake system: PA
Brakes F/R: Disc/Disc
Steering: Rack & pinion PA
Wheelbase: 252.5cm 99.4in
Track F: 145.5cm 57.3in
Track R: 142.5cm 56.1in
Length: 440.0cm 173.2in
Width: 169.0cm 66.5in
Height: 137.0cm 53.9in
Ground clearance: 16.0cm 6.3in
Kerb weight: 1095.0kg 2411.9lb
Fuel: 60.1L 13.2gal 15.9galUS

4463 Toyota
Corolla GTS
1989 Japan
115.0mph 185.0kmh
0-50mph 80.5kmh: 7.0secs
0-60mph 96.5kmh: 9.3secs
0-1/4 mile: 17.1secs
115.0bhp 85.8kW 116.6PS
@ 6600rpm
100.0lbft 135.5Nm @ 4800rpm
103.2bhp/ton 101.5bhp/tonne
72.5bhp/L 54.0kW/L 73.5PS/L
55.5ft/sec 16.9m/sec
33.6mpg 28.0mpgUS 8.4L/100km
Petrol 4-stroke piston
1587cc 96.8cu in
In-line 4 fuel injection
Compression ratio: 9.4:1
Bore: 81.0mm 3.2in
Stroke: 77.0mm 3.0in
Valve type/No: Overhead 16
Transmission: Manual
No. of forward speeds: 5
Wheels driven: Front
Springs F/R: Coil/Coil
Brake system: PA
Brakes F/R: Disc/Disc
Steering: Rack & pinion PA
Wheelbase: 243.1cm 95.7in
Track F: 144.3cm 56.8in
Track R: 142.5cm 56.1in
Length: 437.6cm 172.3in
Width: 166.6cm 65.6in
Height: 126.0cm 49.6in
Kerb weight: 1132.7kg 2495.0lb
Fuel: 50.0L 11.0gal 13.2galUS

4464 Toyota
MR2 Supercharged

1989 Japan
135.0mph 217.2kmh
0-50mph 80.5kmh: 5.3secs
0-60mph 96.5kmh: 7.7secs
0-1/4 mile: 16.0secs
145.0bhp 108.1kW 147.0PS
@ 6400rpm
140.0lbft 189.7Nm @ 4000rpm
124.0bhp/ton 121.9bhp/tonne
91.4bhp/L 68.1kW/L 92.6PS/L
53.9ft/sec 16.4m/sec
27.6mpg 23.0mpgUS 10.2L/100km
Petrol 4-stroke piston
1587cc 96.8cu in supercharged
In-line 4 fuel injection
Compression ratio: 8.0:1
Bore: 81.0mm 3.2in
Stroke: 77.0mm 3.0in
Valve type/No: Overhead 16
Transmission: Manual
No. of forward speeds: 5
Wheels driven: Rear
Springs F/R: Coil/Coil
Brake system: PA
Brakes F/R: Disc/Disc
Steering: Rack & pinion
Wheelbase: 231.9cm 91.3in
Track F: 144.0cm 56.7in
Track R: 144.0cm 56.7in
Length: 395.0cm 155.5in
Width: 166.6cm 65.6in
Height: 123.4cm 48.6in
Kerb weight: 1189.5kg 2620.0lb
Fuel: 40.9L 9.0gal 10.8galUS

4465 Toyota

Supra 3.0i Turbo
1989 Japan
146.0mph 234.9kmh
0-50mph 80.5kmh: 5.3secs
0-60mph 96.5kmh: 6.9secs
0-1/4 mile: 15.9secs
0-1km: 28.0secs
232.0bhp 173.0kW 235.2PS
@ 5600rpm
254.6lbft 345.0Nm @ 3200rpm
149.8bhp/ton 147.3bhp/tonne
78.5bhp/L 58.6kW/L 79.6PS/L
55.7ft/sec 17.0m/sec
25.7mph 41.4kmh/1000rpm
18.8mpg 15.7mpgUS 15.0L/100km
Petrol 4-stroke piston
2954cc 180.0cu in turbocharged
In-line 6 fuel injection
Compression ratio: 8.4:1
Bore: 83.0mm 3.3in
Stroke: 91.0mm 3.6in
Valve type/No: Overhead 24
Transmission: Manual
No. of forward speeds: 5
Wheels driven: Rear
Springs F/R: Coil/Coil
Brake system: PA ABS
Brakes F/R: Disc/Disc
Steering: Rack & pinion PA
Wheelbase: 259.5cm 102.2in
Track F: 148.5cm 58.5in
Track R: 148.0cm 58.3in
Length: 462.0cm 181.9in
Width: 174.5cm 68.7in
Height: 131.0cm 51.6in
Kerb weight: 1575.0kg 3469.2lb
Fuel: 70.1L 15.4gal 18.5galUS

4466 Toyota

Supra Turbo
1989 Japan
140.0mph 225.3kmh
0-50mph 80.5kmh: 5.0secs
0-60mph 96.5kmh: 6.6secs
0-1/4 mile: 15.2secs
233.0bhp 173.7kW 236.2PS
@ 5600rpm
254.0lbft 344.2Nm @ 3200rpm
144.2bhp/ton 141.8bhp/tonne
78.9bhp/L 58.8kW/L 80.0PS/L
55.7ft/sec 17.0m/sec
26.4mpg 22.0mpgUS 10.7L/100km
Petrol 4-stroke piston
2954cc 180.2cu in turbocharged
In-line 6 fuel injection
Compression ratio: 8.4:1
Bore: 83.0mm 3.3in
Stroke: 90.9mm 3.6in
Valve type/No: Overhead 24
Transmission: Manual
No. of forward speeds: 5
Wheels driven: Rear
Springs F/R: Coil/Coil
Brake system: PA ABS
Brakes F/R: Disc/Disc
Steering: Rack & pinion PA
Wheelbase: 259.6cm 102.2in
Track F: 148.6cm 58.5in
Track R: 148.6cm 58.5in
Length: 462.0cm 181.9in
Width: 174.5cm 68.7in
Height: 131.1cm 51.6in
Kerb weight: 1643.5kg 3620.0lb
Fuel: 70.0L 15.4gal 18.5galUS

4467 Toyota

Supra Turbo TRD
1989 Japan
0-60mph 96.5kmh: 5.8secs
0-1/4 mile: 14.2secs
430.0bhp 320.6kW 436.0PS
@ 6500rpm
382.0lbft 517.6Nm @ 5500rpm
258.2bhp/ton 253.9bhp/tonne
145.6bhp/L 108.5kW/L 147.6PS/L
63.9ft/sec 19.5m/sec
Petrol 4-stroke piston
2954cc 180.2cu in turbocharged
In-line 6 fuel injection
Compression ratio: 8.4:1
Bore: 83.0mm 3.3in
Stroke: 90.0mm 3.5in
Valve type/No: Overhead 24
Transmission: Manual
No. of forward speeds: 5
Wheels driven: Rear
Springs F/R: Coil/Coil
Brake system: PA ABS
Brakes F/R: Disc/Disc
Steering: Rack & pinion PA
Wheelbase: 259.6cm 102.2in
Track F: 148.6cm 58.5in
Track R: 148.6cm 58.5in
Length: 462.0cm 181.9in
Width: 174.5cm 68.7in
Height: 126.0cm 49.6in
Kerb weight: 1693.4kg 3730.0lb

4468 Toyota

Celica 2.0 GT
1990 Japan
134.0mph 215.6kmh
0-50mph 80.5kmh: 6.2secs
0-60mph 96.5kmh: 8.1secs
0-1/4 mile: 16.5secs
0-1km: 29.7secs
158.0bhp 117.8kW 160.2PS
@ 6600rpm
141.0lbft 191.0Nm @ 4800rpm
131.5bhp/ton 129.3bhp/tonne
79.1bhp/L 59.0kW/L 80.2PS/L
62.1ft/sec 18.9m/sec
21.2mph 34.1kmh/1000rpm
22.5mpg 18.7mpgUS 12.6L/100km
Petrol 4-stroke piston
1998cc 122.0cu in
In-line 4 fuel injection
Compression ratio: 10.0:1
Bore: 86.0mm 3.4in
Stroke: 86.0mm 3.4in
Valve type/No: Overhead 16
Transmission: Manual
No. of forward speeds: 5
Wheels driven: Front
Springs F/R: Coil/Coil
Brake system: PA ABS
Brakes F/R: Disc/Disc
Steering: Rack & pinion PA
Wheelbase: 252.5cm 99.4in
Track F: 146.5cm 57.7in
Track R: 143.0cm 56.3in
Length: 442.0cm 174.0in
Width: 170.5cm 67.1in
Height: 130.0cm 51.2in
Ground clearance: 17.4cm 6.9in
Kerb weight: 1222.0kg 2691.6lb
Fuel: 60.1L 13.2gal 15.9galUS

4469 Toyota

Celica All-Trac Turbo
1990 Japan
125.0mph 201.1kmh
0-50mph 80.5kmh: 6.6secs
0-60mph 96.5kmh: 9.5secs
0-1/4 mile: 16.8secs
200.0bhp 149.1kW 202.8PS
@ 6000rpm
200.0lbft 271.0Nm @ 3200rpm
137.0bhp/ton 134.7bhp/tonne
100.1bhp/L 74.6kW/L 101.5PS/L
56.5ft/sec 17.2m/sec
Petrol 4-stroke piston
1998cc 121.9cu in turbocharged
In-line 4 fuel injection
Compression ratio: 8.8:1
Bore: 86.1mm 3.4in
Stroke: 86.1mm 3.4in
Valve type/No: Overhead 16
Transmission: Manual
No. of forward speeds: 5
Wheels driven: 4-wheel drive
Springs F/R: Coil/Coil
Brake system: PA ABS
Brakes F/R: Disc/Disc
Steering: Rack & pinion PA
Wheelbase: 252.5cm 99.4in
Track F: 148.1cm 58.3in
Track R: 144.5cm 56.9in
Length: 442.0cm 174.0in
Width: 174.5cm 68.7in
Height: 128.0cm 50.4in
Kerb weight: 1484.6kg 3270.0lb
Fuel: 60.2L 13.2gal 15.9galUS

4470 Toyota

Celica GTS
1990 Japan
125.0mph 201.1kmh
0-60mph 96.5kmh: 10.5secs
0-1/4 mile: 17.6secs
130.0bhp 96.9kW 131.8PS
@ 5400rpm
140.0lbft 189.7Nm @ 4400rpm
97.9bhp/ton 96.2bhp/tonne
60.1bhp/L 44.8kW/L 60.9PS/L
53.7ft/sec 16.4m/sec
29.8mpg 24.8mpgUS 9.5L/100km
Petrol 4-stroke piston
2164cc 132.0cu in
In-line 4 fuel injection
Compression ratio: 9.5:1
Bore: 87.1mm 3.4in
Stroke: 90.9mm 3.6in
Valve type/No: Overhead 16
Transmission: Manual
No. of forward speeds: 5
Wheels driven: Front
Springs F/R: Coil/Coil
Brake system: PA ABS
Brakes F/R: Disc/Disc
Steering: Rack & pinion PA
Wheelbase: 252.5cm 99.4in
Track F: 148.1cm 58.3in
Track R: 144.5cm 56.9in
Length: 442.0cm 174.0in
Width: 174.5cm 68.7in
Height: 128.0cm 50.4in
Kerb weight: 1350.6kg 2975.0lb
Fuel: 60.2L 13.2gal 15.9galUS

4471 Toyota

MR2
1990 Japan
0-60mph 96.5kmh: 8.5secs
0-1/4 mile: 16.3secs
130.0bhp 96.9kW 131.8PS
@ 5400rpm
140.0lbft 189.7Nm @ 4400rpm
109.1bhp/ton 107.2bhp/tonne
60.1bhp/L 44.8kW/L 60.9PS/L
53.7ft/sec 16.4m/sec
28.8mpg 24.0mpgUS 9.8L/100km
Petrol 4-stroke piston
2164cc 132.0cu in
In-line 4
Bore: 87.0mm 3.4in
Stroke: 91.0mm 3.6in
Valve type/No: Overhead 16
Transmission: Manual
No. of forward speeds: 5
Wheels driven: Rear
Springs F/R: Coil/Coil
Brakes F/R: Disc/Disc
Steering: Rack & pinion
Wheelbase: 240.0cm 94.5in
Track F: 147.1cm 57.9in
Track R: 145.0cm 57.1in
Length: 417.1cm 164.2in
Width: 169.9cm 66.9in
Height: 124.0cm 48.8in
Kerb weight: 1212.2kg 2670.0lb

4472 Toyota

MR2 GT
1990 Japan
139.0mph 223.7kmh
0-50mph 80.5kmh: 5.1secs
0-60mph 96.5kmh: 6.7secs
0-1/4 mile: 15.2secs
0-1km: 27.5secs
158.0bhp 117.8kW 160.2PS
@ 6600rpm
140.2lbft 190.0Nm @ 4800rpm
132.2bhp/ton 130.0bhp/tonne
79.1bhp/L 59.0kW/L 80.2PS/L
62.1ft/sec 18.9m/sec
21.2mph 34.1kmh/1000rpm
27.2mpg 22.6mpgUS 10.4L/100km
Petrol 4-stroke piston
1998cc 122.0cu in
In-line 4 fuel injection
Compression ratio: 10.0:1
Bore: 86.0mm 3.4in
Stroke: 86.0mm 3.4in
Valve type/No: Overhead 16
Transmission: Manual
No. of forward speeds: 5
Wheels driven: Rear
Springs F/R: Coil/Coil
Brake system: PA
Brakes F/R: Disc/Disc
Steering: Rack & pinion
Wheelbase: 240.0cm 94.5in
Track F: 147.0cm 57.9in
Track R: 145.0cm 57.1in
Length: 418.0cm 164.6in
Width: 170.0cm 66.9in
Height: 124.0cm 48.8in
Kerb weight: 1215.0kg 2676.2lb
Fuel: 54.6L 12.0gal 14.4galUS

4473 Toyota

MR2 Turbo
1990 Japan
145.0mph 233.3kmh
0-50mph 80.5kmh: 4.6secs
0-60mph 96.5kmh: 6.2secs
0-1/4 mile: 14.7secs
200.0bhp 149.1kW 202.8PS
@ 6000rpm
200.0lbft 271.0Nm @ 3200rpm
158.6bhp/ton 155.9bhp/tonne
100.1bhp/L 74.6kW/L 101.5PS/L
56.5ft/sec 17.2m/sec
22.2mpg 18.5mpgUS 12.7L/100km
Petrol 4-stroke piston
1998cc 121.9cu in turbocharged
In-line 4 fuel injection
Compression ratio: 8.8:1
Bore: 86.0mm 3.4in
Stroke: 86.0mm 3.4in
Valve type/No: Overhead 16
Transmission: Manual
No. of forward speeds: 5
Wheels driven: Rear
Springs F/R: Coil/Coil
Brake system: PA ABS
Brakes F/R: Disc/Disc
Steering: Rack & pinion
Wheelbase: 240.0cm 94.5in
Track F: 147.1cm 57.9in
Track R: 145.0cm 57.1in
Length: 417.1cm 164.2in
Width: 169.9cm 66.9in
Height: 124.0cm 48.8in
Ground clearance: 14.0cm 5.5in
Kerb weight: 1282.5kg 2825.0lb
Fuel: 54.1L 11.9gal 14.3galUS

4474 Toyota

Previa LE
1990 Japan
107.0mph 172.2kmh
0-60mph 96.5kmh: 12.5secs
0-1/4 mile: 18.8secs
138.0bhp 102.9kW 139.9PS
@ 5000rpm
154.0lbft 208.7Nm @ 4000rpm
80.3bhp/ton 78.9bhp/tonne
56.6bhp/L 42.2kW/L 57.4PS/L
47.1ft/sec 14.3m/sec
22.8mpg 19.0mpgUS 12.4L/100km
Petrol 4-stroke piston
2438cc 148.7cu in
In-line 4 fuel injection
Compression ratio: 9.3:1
Bore: 95.0mm 3.7in
Stroke: 86.0mm 3.4in
Valve type/No: Overhead 16

Transmission: Automatic
No. of forward speeds: 4
Wheels driven: Rear
Springs F/R: Coil/Coil
Brake system: PA
Brakes F/R: Disc/Disc
Steering: Rack & pinion PA
Wheelbase: 286.5cm 112.8in
Track F: 156.5cm 61.6in
Track R: 155.4cm 61.2in
Length: 475.0cm 187.0in
Width: 180.1cm 70.9in
Height: 174.5cm 68.7in
Kerb weight: 1747.9kg 3850.0lb
Fuel: 74.9L 16.5gal 19.8galUS

4475 Toyota
Starlet GL
1990 Japan
91.0mph 146.4kmh
0-50mph 80.5kmh: 10.3secs
0-60mph 96.5kmh: 14.7secs
0-1/4 mile: 20.1secs
0-1km: 37.4secs
54.0bhp 40.3kW 54.7PS
@ 6000rpm
55.4lbft 75.0Nm @ 3800rpm
70.4bhp/ton 69.2bhp/tonne
54.0bhp/L 40.3kW/L 54.8PS/L
42.0ft/sec 12.8m/sec
19.5mph 31.4kmh/1000rpm
38.1mpg 31.7mpgUS 7.4L/100km
Petrol 4-stroke piston
999cc 61.0cu in
In-line 4 1 Carburettor
Compression ratio: 9.0:1
Bore: 70.5mm 2.8in
Stroke: 64.0mm 2.5in
Valve type/No: Overhead 12
Transmission: Manual
No. of forward speeds: 5
Wheels driven: Front
Springs F/R: Coil/Coil
Brake system: PA
Brakes F/R: Disc/Drum
Steering: Rack & pinion
Wheelbase: 230.1cm 90.6in
Track F: 138.9cm 54.7in
Track R: 136.9cm 53.9in
Length: 372.1cm 146.5in
Width: 160.0cm 63.0in
Height: 138.4cm 54.5in
Ground clearance: 15.2cm 6.0in
Kerb weight: 780.0kg 1718.1lb
Fuel: 40.0L 8.8gal 10.6galUS

4476 Toyota
Camry 2.2 GL
1991 Japan
126.0mph 202.7kmh
0-50mph 80.5kmh: 7.0secs
0-60mph 96.5kmh: 9.7secs
0-1/4 mile: 17.4secs
0-1km: 31.7secs
134.0bhp 99.9kW 135.9PS
@ 5400rpm
145.0lbft 196.5Nm @ 4000rpm
103.2bhp/ton 101.5bhp/tonne
61.9bhp/L 46.2kW/L 62.8PS/L
53.7ft/sec 16.4m/sec
23.3mph 37.5kmh/1000rpm
24.5mpg 20.4mpgUS 11.5L/100km
Petrol 4-stroke piston
2164cc 132.0cu in
In-line 4 fuel injection
Compression ratio: 9.8:1
Bore: 87.0mm 3.4in
Stroke: 91.0mm 3.6in
Valve type/No: Overhead 16
Transmission: Manual
No. of forward speeds: 5
Wheels driven: Front
Springs F/R: Coil/Coil
Brake system: PA ABS
Brakes F/R: Disc/Disc
Steering: Rack & pinion PA
Wheelbase: 262.0cm 103.1in
Track F: 154.5cm 60.8in
Track R: 150.0cm 59.1in
Length: 472.5cm 186.0in
Width: 177.0cm 69.7in
Height: 140.0cm 55.1in
Ground clearance: 15.0cm 5.9in
Kerb weight: 1320.0kg 2907.5lb
Fuel: 70.0L 15.4gal 18.5galUS

4477 Toyota
Celica GT Convertible
1991 Japan
120.0mph 193.1kmh
0-50mph 80.5kmh: 7.4secs
0-60mph 96.5kmh: 10.8secs
0-1/4 mile: 17.8secs
130.0bhp 96.9kW 131.8PS
@ 5400rpm
140.0lbft 189.7Nm @ 4400rpm
97.2bhp/ton 95.6bhp/tonne
60.1bhp/L 44.8kW/L 60.9PS/L
53.7ft/sec 16.4m/sec
27.6mpg 23.0mpgUS 10.2L/100km
Petrol 4-stroke piston
2164cc 132.0cu in
In-line 4 fuel injection
Compression ratio: 9.5:1
Bore: 87.0mm 3.4in
Stroke: 91.0mm 3.6in
Valve type/No: Overhead 16
Transmission: Manual
No. of forward speeds: 5
Wheels driven: Front
Springs F/R: Coil/Coil
Brake system: PA
Brakes F/R: Disc/Drum
Steering: Rack & pinion PA
Wheelbase: 252.5cm 99.4in
Track F: 147.1cm 57.9in
Track R: 143.5cm 56.5in
Length: 447.0cm 176.0in
Width: 170.4cm 67.1in
Height: 128.5cm 50.6in
Ground clearance: 13.0cm 5.1in
Kerb weight: 1359.7kg 2995.0lb
Fuel: 60.2L 13.2gal 15.9galUS

4478 Toyota
Landcruiser VX
1991 Japan
104.0mph 167.3kmh
0-50mph 80.5kmh: 9.2secs
0-60mph 96.5kmh: 12.6secs
0-1/4 mile: 19.2secs
0-1km: 35.0secs
165.0bhp 123.0kW 167.3PS
@ 3600rpm
143.9lbft 195.0Nm @ 1800rpm
74.3bhp/ton 73.1bhp/tonne
39.6bhp/L 29.5kW/L 40.2PS/L
39.4ft/sec 12.0m/sec
26.6mph 42.8kmh/1000rpm
19.8mpg 16.5mpgUS 14.3L/100km
Diesel 4-stroke piston
4164cc 254.0cu in turbocharged
In-line 6 fuel injection
Compression ratio: 18.6:1
Bore: 94.0mm 3.7in
Stroke: 100.0mm 3.9in
Valve type/No: Overhead 12
Transmission: Manual
No. of forward speeds: 5
Wheels driven: 4-wheel drive
Springs F/R: Coil/Coil
Brake system: PA
Brakes F/R: Disc/Disc
Steering: Recirculating ball PA
Wheelbase: 285.0cm 112.2in
Track F: 157.5cm 62.0in
Track R: 157.5cm 62.0in
Length: 462.8cm 182.2in
Width: 190.0cm 74.8in
Height: 190.0cm 74.8in
Ground clearance: 21.8cm 8.6in
Kerb weight: 2257.0kg 4971.4lb
Fuel: 95.5L 21.0gal 25.2galUS

4479 Toyota
MR2
1991 Japan
123.0mph 197.9kmh
0-50mph 80.5kmh: 6.6secs
0-60mph 96.5kmh: 9.3secs
0-1/4 mile: 17.0secs
0-1km: 31.4secs
119.0bhp 88.7kW 120.6PS
@ 5600rpm
93.0lbft 126.0Nm @ 4000rpm
102.6bhp/ton 100.8bhp/tonne
59.6bhp/L 44.4kW/L 60.4PS/L
52.7ft/sec 16.0m/sec
21.3mph 34.3kmh/1000rpm
26.7mpg 22.2mpgUS 10.6L/100km
Petrol 4-stroke piston
1998cc 122.0cu in
In-line 4 fuel injection
Compression ratio: 9.8:1
Bore: 86.0mm 3.4in
Stroke: 86.0mm 3.4in
Valve type/No: Overhead 16
Transmission: Manual
No. of forward speeds: 5
Wheels driven: Rear
Springs F/R: Coil/Coil
Brake system: PA
Brakes F/R: Disc/Disc
Steering: Rack & pinion
Wheelbase: 239.8cm 94.4in
Track F: 146.8cm 57.8in
Track R: 144.8cm 57.0in
Length: 417.8cm 164.5in
Width: 169.9cm 66.9in
Height: 124.0cm 48.8in
Kerb weight: 1180.0kg 2599.1lb
Fuel: 55.1L 12.1gal 14.5galUS

4480 Toyota
MR2 HKS
1991 Japan
0-60mph 96.5kmh: 5.8secs
0-1/4 mile: 14.4secs
245.0bhp 182.7kW 248.4PS
@ 6200rpm
251.0lbft 340.1Nm @ 3450rpm
194.3bhp/ton 191.0bhp/tonne
122.6bhp/L 91.4kW/L 124.3PS/L
58.4ft/sec 17.8m/sec
Petrol 4-stroke piston
1998cc 121.9cu in turbocharged
In-line 4 fuel injection
Compression ratio: 8.8:1
Bore: 86.0mm 3.4in
Stroke: 86.0mm 3.4in
Valve type/No: Overhead 16
Transmission: Manual
No. of forward speeds: 5
Wheels driven: Rear
Springs F/R: Coil/Coil
Brake system: PA
Brakes F/R: Disc/Disc
Steering: Rack & pinion PA
Wheelbase: 240.0cm 94.5in
Track F: 151.6cm 59.7in
Track R: 145.0cm 57.1in
Length: 417.1cm 164.2in
Width: 169.9cm 66.9in
Height: 124.0cm 48.8in
Kerb weight: 1282.5kg 2825.0lb

4481 Toyota
Previa
1991 Japan
110.0mph 177.0kmh
0-50mph 80.5kmh: 8.8secs
0-60mph 96.5kmh: 12.9secs
0-1/4 mile: 19.1secs
0-1km: 34.7secs
133.0bhp 99.2kW 134.8PS
@ 5000rpm
152.0lbft 206.0Nm @ 4000rpm
78.6bhp/ton 77.3bhp/tonne
54.5bhp/L 40.7kW/L 55.3PS/L
47.1ft/sec 14.3m/sec
22.1mph 35.6kmh/1000rpm
21.6mpg 18.0mpgUS 13.1L/100km
Petrol 4-stroke piston
2438cc 149.0cu in
In-line 4 fuel injection
Compression ratio: 9.3:1
Bore: 95.0mm 3.7in
Stroke: 86.0mm 3.4in
Valve type/No: Overhead 16
Transmission: Manual
No. of forward speeds: 5
Wheels driven: Rear
Springs F/R: Coil/Coil
Brake system: PA
Brakes F/R: Disc/Disc
Steering: Rack & pinion PA
Wheelbase: 286.0cm 112.6in
Track F: 156.0cm 61.4in
Track R: 155.0cm 61.0in
Length: 475.0cm 187.0in
Width: 180.0cm 70.9in
Height: 179.0cm 70.5in
Kerb weight: 1720.0kg 3788.5lb
Fuel: 75.1L 16.5gal 19.8galUS

4482 Toyota
Tercel LE
1991 Japan
105.0mph 168.9kmh
0-50mph 80.5kmh: 8.3secs
0-60mph 96.5kmh: 12.2secs
0-1/4 mile: 18.4secs
82.0bhp 61.1kW 83.1PS
@ 5200rpm
90.0lbft 122.0Nm @ 4400rpm
85.8bhp/ton 84.4bhp/tonne
56.3bhp/L 42.0kW/L 57.1PS/L
49.5ft/sec 15.1m/sec
36.0mpg 30.0mpgUS 7.8L/100km
Petrol 4-stroke piston
1457cc 88.9cu in
In-line 4 fuel injection
Compression ratio: 9.3:1
Bore: 73.0mm 2.9in
Stroke: 87.0mm 3.4in
Valve type/No: Overhead 12
Transmission: Manual
No. of forward speeds: 5
Wheels driven: Front
Springs F/R: Coil/Coil
Brake system: PA
Brakes F/R: Disc/Drum
Steering: Rack & pinion PA
Wheelbase: 238.0cm 93.7in
Track F: 140.0cm 55.1in
Track R: 143.0cm 56.3in
Length: 411.0cm 161.8in
Width: 166.1cm 65.4in
Height: 135.1cm 53.2in
Ground clearance: 14.0cm 5.5in
Kerb weight: 971.6kg 2140.0lb
Fuel: 45.0L 9.9gal 11.9galUS

4483 Toyota
Paseo
1992 Japan
125.0mph 201.1kmh
0-60mph 96.5kmh: 10.3secs
0-1/4 mile: 17.6secs
100.0bhp 74.6kW 101.4PS
@ 6400rpm
91.0lbft 123.3Nm @ 3200rpm
102.5bhp/ton 100.8bhp/tonne
66.8bhp/L 49.8kW/L 67.7PS/L
61.0ft/sec 18.6m/sec
36.0mpg 30.0mpgUS 7.8L/100km
Petrol 4-stroke piston
1497cc 91.3cu in
In-line 4 fuel injection
Compression ratio: 9.4:1
Bore: 74.0mm 2.9in
Stroke: 87.0mm 3.4in
Valve type/No: Overhead 16
Transmission: Manual
No. of forward speeds: 5
Wheels driven: Front
Springs F/R: Coil/Coil
Brake system: PA
Brakes F/R: Disc/Drum
Steering: Rack & pinion PA
Wheelbase: 238.0cm 93.7in
Track F: 140.5cm 55.3in
Track R: 139.4cm 54.9in
Length: 414.5cm 163.2in
Width: 165.6cm 65.2in
Height: 127.5cm 50.2in
Kerb weight: 992.0kg 2185.0lb
Fuel: 45.0L 9.9gal 11.9galUS

4484 Tracta
Sports Two-seater
1930 France
71.4mph 114.9kmh
20.0mpg 16.7mpgUS 14.1L/100km
Petrol 4-stroke piston
1498cc 91.4cu in
In-line 4
Bore: 67.0mm 2.6in
Stroke: 105.0mm 4.1in
Transmission: Manual
No. of forward speeds: 4
Wheels driven: Front
Brakes F/R: Drum/Drum
Wheelbase: 259.1cm 102.0in
Track F: 129.5cm 51.0in
Track R: 129.5cm 51.0in
Length: 403.9cm 159.0in
Width: 160.0cm 63.0in
Height: 96.5cm 38.0in
Kerb weight: 940.7kg 2072.0lb
Fuel: 45.5L 10.0gal 12.0galUS

4485 Treser
T1
1989 Germany

130.0mph 209.2kmh
0-60mph 96.5kmh: 8.5secs
130.0bhp 96.9kW 131.8PS
@ 5800rpm
168.0lbft 227.6Nm @ 4600rpm
128.6bhp/ton 126.4bhp/tonne
73.0bhp/L 54.4kW/L 74.0PS/L
54.8ft/sec 16.7m/sec
Petrol 4-stroke piston
1781cc 108.7cu in
In-line 4 fuel injection
Compression ratio: 10.0:1
Bore: 81.0mm 3.2in
Stroke: 86.4mm 3.4in
Valve type/No: Overhead 16
Transmission: Manual
No. of forward speeds: 5
Wheels driven: Rear
Springs F/R: Coil/Coil
Brake system: PA
Brakes F/R: Disc/Disc
Steering: Rack & pinion PA
Wheelbase: 249.9cm 98.4in
Track F: 145.5cm 57.3in
Track R: 148.8cm 58.6in
Length: 404.4cm 159.2in
Width: 173.0cm 68.1in
Height: 125.0cm 49.2in
Kerb weight: 1028.3kg 2265.0lb
Fuel: 71.9L 15.8gal 19.0galUS

4486 Trihawk

304
1982 USA
94.0mph 151.2kmh
0-50mph 80.5kmh: 7.1secs
0-60mph 96.5kmh: 10.2secs
0-1/4 mile: 17.6secs
69.0bhp 51.4kW 70.0PS
@ 5500rpm
72.0lbft 97.6Nm @ 3500rpm
112.0bhp/ton 110.1bhp/tonne
53.1bhp/L 39.6kW/L 53.9PS/L
39.4ft/sec 12.0m/sec
17.4mph 28.0kmh/1000rpm
31.2mpg 26.0mpgUS 9.0L/100km
Petrol 4-stroke piston
1299cc 79.3cu in
Flat 4 1 Carburettor
Compression ratio: 8.7:1
Bore: 79.4mm 3.1in
Stroke: 65.6mm 2.6in
Valve type/No: Overhead 8
Transmission: Manual
No. of forward speeds: 5
Wheels driven: Front
Springs F/R: Coil/Coil
Brakes F/R: Disc/Drum
Steering: Rack & pinion
Wheelbase: 248.9cm 98.0in
Track F: 167.6cm 66.0in
Length: 392.4cm 154.5in
Width: 185.9cm 73.2in
Height: 111.8cm 44.0in
Ground clearance: 12.7cm 5.0in
Kerb weight: 626.5kg 1380.0lb
Fuel: 41.6L 9.1gal 11.0galUS

4487 Triumph

Super 7 Saloon
1930 UK
52.9mph 85.1kmh
21.0bhp 15.7kW 21.3PS
@ 4000rpm
36.5bhp/ton 35.9bhp/tonne
25.2bhp/L 18.8kW/L 25.6PS/L
36.3ft/sec 11.1m/sec
35.0mpg 29.1mpgUS 8.1L/100km
Petrol 4-stroke piston
832cc 50.8cu in
In-line 4 1 Carburettor
Bore: 56.5mm 2.2in
Stroke: 83.0mm 3.3in
Valve type/No: Side 8
Transmission: Manual
No. of forward speeds: 3
Wheels driven: Rear
Brakes F/R: Drum/Drum
Wheelbase: 205.7cm 81.0in
Track F: 106.7cm 42.0in
Track R: 106.7cm 42.0in
Length: 299.7cm 118.0in
Width: 129.5cm 51.0in
Height: 160.0cm 63.0in
Kerb weight: 584.7kg 1288.0lb
Fuel: 20.5L 4.5gal 5.4galUS

4488 Triumph

Supercharged 7
1930 UK
67.6mph 108.8kmh
26.0mpg 21.6mpgUS 10.9L/100km
Petrol 4-stroke piston
832cc 50.8cu in supercharged
In-line 4
Bore: 56.5mm 2.2in
Stroke: 83.0mm 3.3in
Valve type/No: Side 8
Transmission: Manual
No. of forward speeds: 3
Wheels driven: Rear
Brakes F/R: Drum/Drum
Wheelbase: 205.7cm 81.0in
Track F: 106.7cm 42.0in
Track R: 106.7cm 42.0in
Length: 327.7cm 129.0in
Width: 129.5cm 51.0in
Height: 146.1cm 57.5in
Kerb weight: 622.9kg 1372.0lb
Fuel: 27.3L 6.0gal 7.2galUS

4489 Triumph

Gloria 6 Vitesse
1934 UK
75.0mph 120.7kmh
0-50mph 80.5kmh: 14.6secs
0-60mph 96.5kmh: 22.0secs
55.0bhp 41.0kW 55.8PS
@ 4500rpm
46.8bhp/ton 46.0bhp/tonne
27.6bhp/L 20.6kW/L 28.0PS/L
49.2ft/sec 15.0m/sec
23.0mpg 19.2mpgUS 12.3L/100km
Petrol 4-stroke piston
1991cc 121.5cu in
In-line 6 2 Carburettor
Bore: 65.0mm 2.6in
Stroke: 100.0mm 3.9in
Valve type/No: IOE 12
Transmission: Manual
No. of forward speeds: 4
Wheels driven: Rear
Brakes F/R: Drum/Drum
Kerb weight: 1194.9kg 2632.0lb
Fuel: 54.6L 12.0gal 14.4galUS

4490 Triumph

2-litre Southern Cross
1935 UK
83.3mph 134.0kmh
0-50mph 80.5kmh: 13.4secs
0-60mph 96.5kmh: 19.0secs
65.0bhp 48.5kW 65.9PS
@ 4750rpm
59.8bhp/ton 58.8bhp/tonne
32.6bhp/L 24.3kW/L 33.1PS/L
52.0ft/sec 15.8m/sec
21.0mpg 17.5mpgUS 13.5L/100km
Petrol 4-stroke piston
1991cc 121.5cu in
In-line 6
Bore: 65.0mm 2.6in
Stroke: 100.0mm 3.9in
Valve type/No: IOE 12
Transmission: Manual
No. of forward speeds: 4
Wheels driven: Rear
Brakes F/R: Drum/Drum
Ground clearance: 17.0cm 6.7in
Kerb weight: 1105.9kg 2436.0lb
Fuel: 59.1L 13.0gal 15.6galUS

4491 Triumph

14/60 Dolomite Saloon
1936 UK
72.5mph 116.7kmh
0-50mph 80.5kmh: 19.8secs
0-60mph 96.5kmh: 32.2secs
26.0mpg 21.6mpgUS 10.9L/100km
Petrol 4-stroke piston
1767cc 107.8cu in
In-line 4
Bore: 75.0mm 2.9in
Stroke: 100.0mm 3.9in
Valve type/No: Overhead 8
Transmission: Manual
No. of forward speeds: 4
Wheels driven: Rear
Brakes F/R: Drum/Drum
Kerb weight: 1362.9kg 3002.0lb
Fuel: 59.1L 13.0gal 15.6galUS

4492 Triumph

Gloria 6 Vitesse
1936 UK
78.2mph 125.8kmh
0-50mph 80.5kmh: 16.0secs
0-60mph 96.5kmh: 26.6secs
55.0bhp 41.0kW 55.8PS
@ 4500rpm
40.6bhp/ton 39.9bhp/tonne
27.6bhp/L 20.6kW/L 28.0PS/L
49.2ft/sec 15.0m/sec
22.0mpg 18.3mpgUS 12.8L/100km
Petrol 4-stroke piston
1991cc 121.5cu in
In-line 6 2 Carburettor
Bore: 65.0mm 2.6in
Stroke: 100.0mm 3.9in
Valve type/No: IOE 12
Transmission: Manual
No. of forward speeds: 4
Wheels driven: Rear
Brakes F/R: Drum/Drum
Kerb weight: 1378.8kg 3037.0lb
Fuel: 54.6L 12.0gal 14.4galUS

4493 Triumph

Vitesse
1936 UK
78.2mph 125.8kmh
0-50mph 80.5kmh: 15.9secs
0-60mph 96.5kmh: 25.4secs
26.0mpg 21.6mpgUS 10.9L/100km
Petrol 4-stroke piston
1767cc 107.8cu in
In-line 4
Bore: 75.0mm 2.9in
Stroke: 100.0mm 3.9in
Valve type/No: Overhead 8
Transmission: Manual
No. of forward speeds: 4
Wheels driven: Rear
Brakes F/R: Drum/Drum
Kerb weight: 1248.9kg 2751.0lb
Fuel: 54.6L 12.0gal 14.4galUS

4494 Triumph

Gloria 12
1937 UK
69.7mph 112.1kmh
0-50mph 80.5kmh: 22.9secs
0-60mph 96.5kmh: 40.7secs
50.0bhp 37.3kW 50.7PS
@ 5000rpm
39.9bhp/ton 39.2bhp/tonne
33.4bhp/L 24.9kW/L 33.9PS/L
54.7ft/sec 16.7m/sec
28.0mpg 23.3mpgUS 10.1L/100km
Petrol 4-stroke piston
1496cc 91.3cu in
In-line 4
Bore: 69.0mm 2.7in
Stroke: 100.0mm 3.9in
Valve type/No: IOE 8
Transmission: Manual
No. of forward speeds: 4
Wheels driven: Rear
Brakes F/R: Drum/Drum
Kerb weight: 1273.9kg 2806.0lb
Fuel: 54.6L 12.0gal 14.4galUS

4495 Triumph

2-litre Dolomite
1939 UK
81.0mph 130.3kmh
0-50mph 80.5kmh: 15.0secs
0-60mph 96.5kmh: 23.0secs
65.0bhp 48.5kW 65.9PS
@ 4750rpm
46.2bhp/ton 45.5bhp/tonne
32.6bhp/L 24.3kW/L 33.1PS/L
52.0ft/sec 15.8m/sec
22.0mpg 18.3mpgUS 12.8L/100km
Petrol 4-stroke piston
1991cc 121.5cu in
In-line 6 3 Carburettor
Bore: 65.0mm 2.6in
Stroke: 100.0mm 3.9in
Valve type/No: Overhead 12
Transmission: Manual
No. of forward speeds: 4
Wheels driven: Rear
Brakes F/R: Drum/Drum
Kerb weight: 1429.6kg 3149.0lb
Fuel: 50.0L 11.0gal 13.2galUS

4496 Triumph

1800 Roadster
1947 UK
80.0mph 128.7kmh
0-50mph 80.5kmh: 20.9secs
0-60mph 96.5kmh: 34.4secs
65.0bhp 48.5kW 65.9PS
@ 4500rpm
57.3bhp/ton 56.3bhp/tonne
36.6bhp/L 27.3kW/L 37.1PS/L
52.1ft/sec 15.9m/sec
23.0mpg 19.2mpgUS 12.3L/100km
Petrol 4-stroke piston
1776cc 108.4cu in
In-line 4
Compression ratio: 7.5:1
Bore: 73.0mm 2.9in
Stroke: 106.0mm 4.2in
Valve type/No: Overhead 8
Transmission: Manual
No. of forward speeds: 4
Wheels driven: Rear
Brakes F/R: Drum/Drum
Wheelbase: 254.0cm 100.0in
Track F: 126.2cm 49.7in
Track R: 138.9cm 54.7in
Length: 427.7cm 168.4in
Width: 162.6cm 64.0in
Height: 142.2cm 56.0in
Ground clearance: 16.5cm 6.5in
Kerb weight: 1153.6kg 2541.0lb
Fuel: 45.5L 10.0gal 12.0galUS

4497 Triumph

1800 Saloon
1947 UK
75.0mph 120.7kmh
0-50mph 80.5kmh: 18.7secs
0-60mph 96.5kmh: 29.1secs
65.0bhp 48.5kW 65.9PS
@ 4500rpm
51.5bhp/ton 50.6bhp/tonne
36.6bhp/L 27.3kW/L 37.1PS/L
52.1ft/sec 15.9m/sec
26.0mpg 21.6mpgUS 10.9L/100km
Petrol 4-stroke piston
1776cc 108.4cu in
In-line 4
Compression ratio: 7.5:1
Bore: 73.0mm 2.9in
Stroke: 106.0mm 4.2in
Valve type/No: Overhead 8
Transmission: Manual
No. of forward speeds: 4
Wheels driven: Rear
Brakes F/R: Drum/Drum
Wheelbase: 274.3cm 108.0in
Track F: 126.2cm 49.7in
Track R: 138.9cm 54.7in
Length: 447.0cm 176.0in
Width: 161.3cm 63.5in
Height: 161.3cm 63.5in
Ground clearance: 17.8cm 7.0in
Kerb weight: 1283.9kg 2828.0lb
Fuel: 45.5L 10.0gal 12.0galUS

4498 Triumph

2000 Saloon
1949 UK
75.0mph 120.7kmh
0-50mph 80.5kmh: 17.9secs
0-60mph 96.5kmh: 28.4secs
68.0bhp 50.7kW 68.9PS
@ 4200rpm
108.3lbft 146.7Nm @ 2000rpm
54.0bhp/ton 53.1bhp/tonne
32.6bhp/L 24.3kW/L 33.0PS/L
42.2ft/sec 12.9m/sec
17.0mph 27.4kmh/1000rpm
23.0mpg 19.2mpgUS 12.3L/100km
Petrol 4-stroke piston
2088cc 127.0cu in
In-line 4 1 Carburettor
Compression ratio: 6.7:1
Bore: 85.0mm 3.3in
Stroke: 92.0mm 3.6in
Valve type/No: Overhead 8
Transmission: Manual
No. of forward speeds: 3
Wheels driven: Rear
Springs F/R: Leaf/Leaf
Brakes F/R: Drum/Drum
Steering: Worm & peg
Wheelbase: 274.3cm 108.0in
Track F: 128.3cm 50.5in
Track R: 138.9cm 54.7in
Length: 444.5cm 175.0in

Width: 161.3cm 63.5in
Height: 160.0cm 63.0in
Ground clearance: 17.8cm 7.0in
Kerb weight: 1280.7kg 2821.0lb
Fuel: 45.5L 10.0gal 12.0galUS

4499 Triumph

Roadster
1949 UK
77.0mph 123.9kmh
0-50mph 80.5kmh: 17.7secs
0-60mph 96.5kmh: 27.9secs
68.0bhp 50.7kW 68.9PS
@ 4200rpm
61.9bhp/ton 60.9bhp/tonne
32.6bhp/L 24.3kW/L 33.0PS/L
42.2ft/sec 12.9m/sec
23.0mpg 19.2mpgUS 12.3L/100km
Petrol 4-stroke piston
2088cc 127.4cu in
In-line 4
Compression ratio: 6.7:1
Bore: 85.0mm 3.3in
Stroke: 92.0mm 3.6in
Valve type/No: Overhead 8
Transmission: Manual
No. of forward speeds: 3
Wheels driven: Rear
Brakes F/R: Drum/Drum
Wheelbase: 254.0cm 100.0in
Track F: 128.3cm 50.5in
Track R: 138.9cm 54.7in
Length: 436.9cm 172.0in
Width: 162.6cm 64.0in
Height: 142.2cm 56.0in
Ground clearance: 16.5cm 6.5in
Kerb weight: 1116.8kg 2460.0lb
Fuel: 45.5L 10.0gal 12.0galUS

4500 Triumph

TR2
1954 UK
103.0mph 165.7kmh
0-50mph 80.5kmh: 8.3secs
0-60mph 96.5kmh: 12.2secs
0-1/4 mile: 18.4secs
90.0bhp 67.1kW 91.2PS
@ 4800rpm
116.5lbft 157.9Nm @ 3000rpm
97.4bhp/ton 95.8bhp/tonne
45.2bhp/L 33.7kW/L 45.8PS/L
48.3ft/sec 14.7m/sec
20.0mph 32.2kmh/1000rpm
Petrol 4-stroke piston
1991cc 121.5cu in
In-line 4
Compression ratio: 8.5:1
Bore: 83.1mm 3.3in
Stroke: 91.9mm 3.6in
Valve type/No: Overhead 8
Transmission: Manual with overdrive
Wheels driven: Rear
Wheelbase: 223.5cm 88.0in
Track F: 114.3cm 45.0in
Track R: 115.6cm 45.5in
Kerb weight: 939.8kg 2070.0lb

4501 Triumph
TR2 Sports
1954 UK
105.0mph 168.9kmh
0-50mph 80.5kmh: 8.2secs
0-60mph 96.5kmh: 11.9secs
0-1/4 mile: 18.7secs
90.0bhp 67.1kW 91.2PS
@ 4800rpm
116.6lbft 158.0Nm @ 3000rpm
96.0bhp/ton 94.4bhp/tonne
45.2bhp/L 33.7kW/L 45.8PS/L
48.3ft/sec 14.7m/sec
24.5mph 39.4kmh/1000rpm
32.0mpg 26.6mpgUS 8.8L/100km
Petrol 4-stroke piston
1991cc 121.5cu in
In-line 4
Compression ratio: 8.5:1
Bore: 83.0mm 3.3in
Stroke: 92.0mm 3.6in
Valve type/No: Overhead 8
Transmission: Manual with overdrive
No. of forward speeds: 5
Wheels driven: Rear
Springs F/R: Coil/Leaf
Brakes F/R: Drum/Drum
Wheelbase: 223.5cm 88.0in
Track F: 114.3cm 45.0in
Track R: 115.6cm 45.5in
Length: 383.5cm 151.0in
Width: 141.0cm 55.5in
Height: 127.0cm 50.0in
Ground clearance: 15.2cm 6.0in
Kerb weight: 953.4kg 2100.0lb
Fuel: 56.9L 12.5gal 15.0galUS

4502 Triumph

TR2 Hardtop
1955 UK
107.0mph 172.2kmh
0-50mph 80.5kmh: 8.8secs
0-60mph 96.5kmh: 12.6secs
0-1/4 mile: 18.8secs
90.0bhp 67.1kW 91.2PS
@ 4800rpm
117.0lbft 158.5Nm @ 3000rpm
92.3bhp/ton 90.8bhp/tonne
45.2bhp/L 33.7kW/L 45.8PS/L
48.3ft/sec 14.7m/sec
24.4mph 39.3kmh/1000rpm
31.0mpg 25.8mpgUS 9.1L/100km
Petrol 4-stroke piston
1991cc 121.5cu in
In-line 4
Compression ratio: 8.5:1
Bore: 83.0mm 3.3in
Stroke: 92.0mm 3.6in
Valve type/No: Overhead 8
Transmission: Manual with overdrive
No. of forward speeds: 5
Wheels driven: Rear
Springs F/R: Coil/Leaf
Brakes F/R: Drum/Drum
Wheelbase: 223.5cm 88.0in
Track F: 114.3cm 45.0in
Track R: 115.6cm 45.5in
Length: 383.5cm 151.0in
Width: 141.0cm 55.5in
Height: 127.0cm 50.0in
Ground clearance: 15.2cm 6.0in
Kerb weight: 991.5kg 2184.0lb
Fuel: 56.9L 12.5gal 15.0galUS

4503 Triumph

TR3
1956 UK
104.7mph 168.5kmh
0-50mph 80.5kmh: 8.3secs
0-60mph 96.5kmh: 12.0secs
0-1/4 mile: 18.4secs
100.0bhp 74.6kW 101.4PS
@ 4800rpm
117.5lbft 159.2Nm @ 3000rpm
107.2bhp/ton 105.4bhp/tonne
50.2bhp/L 37.4kW/L 50.9PS/L
48.3ft/sec 14.7m/sec
20.1mph 32.3kmh/1000rpm
Petrol 4-stroke piston
1991cc 121.5cu in
In-line 4
Compression ratio: 8.5:1
Bore: 83.1mm 3.3in
Stroke: 91.9mm 3.6in
Valve type/No: Overhead 8
Transmission: Manual
No. of forward speeds: 4
Wheels driven: Rear
Wheelbase: 223.5cm 88.0in
Track F: 114.3cm 45.0in
Track R: 115.6cm 45.5in
Kerb weight: 948.9kg 2090.0lb

4504 Triumph

TR2 Hardtop
1957 UK
103.0mph 165.7kmh
0-50mph 80.5kmh: 8.8secs
0-60mph 96.5kmh: 12.5secs
0-1/4 mile: 18.7secs
100.0bhp 74.6kW 101.4PS
@ 5000rpm
117.5lbft 159.2Nm @ 3000rpm
90.9bhp/ton 89.4bhp/tonne
50.2bhp/L 37.4kW/L 50.9PS/L
50.3ft/sec 15.3m/sec
24.4mph 39.3kmh/1000rpm
24.9mpg 20.7mpgUS 11.3L/100km
Petrol 4-stroke piston
1991cc 121.5cu in
In-line 4
Compression ratio: 8.5:1
Bore: 83.0mm 3.3in
Stroke: 92.0mm 3.6in
Valve type/No: Overhead 8
Transmission: Manual with overdrive
No. of forward speeds: 7
Wheels driven: Rear
Springs F/R: Coil/Leaf
Brakes F/R: Disc/Drum
Wheelbase: 223.5cm 88.0in
Track F: 114.3cm 45.0in
Track R: 115.6cm 45.5in
Length: 383.5cm 151.0in
Width: 141.0cm 55.5in
Height: 127.0cm 50.0in
Ground clearance: 15.2cm 6.0in
Kerb weight: 1118.7kg 2464.0lb
Fuel: 54.6L 12.0gal 14.4galUS

4505 Triumph

TR3
1957 UK
106.0mph 170.6kmh
0-50mph 80.5kmh: 7.8secs
0-60mph 96.5kmh: 11.4secs
0-1/4 mile: 17.9secs
100.0bhp 74.6kW 101.4PS
@ 5000rpm
117.5lbft 159.2Nm @ 3000rpm
98.7bhp/ton 97.0bhp/tonne
50.2bhp/L 37.4kW/L 50.9PS/L
51.9ft/sec 15.8m/sec
Petrol 4-stroke piston
1991cc 121.5cu in
In-line 4
Compression ratio: 8.5:1
Bore: 83.1mm 3.3in
Stroke: 94.9mm 3.7in
Valve type/No: Overhead 8
Transmission: Manual with overdrive
Wheels driven: Rear
Wheelbase: 223.5cm 88.0in
Track F: 114.3cm 45.0in
Track R: 115.6cm 45.5in
Kerb weight: 1030.6kg 2270.0lb

4506 Triumph

Station Wagon
1958 UK
72.8mph 117.1kmh
0-50mph 80.5kmh: 18.6secs
0-60mph 96.5kmh: 29.2secs
0-1/4 mile: 23.9secs
40.0bhp 29.8kW 40.5PS
@ 5000rpm
50.0lbft 67.8Nm @ 2700rpm
49.5bhp/ton 48.7bhp/tonne
42.2bhp/L 31.5kW/L 42.8PS/L
41.5ft/sec 12.6m/sec
14.7mph 23.7kmh/1000rpm
Petrol 4-stroke piston
948cc 57.8cu in
In-line 4
Compression ratio: 8.0:1
Bore: 63.0mm 2.5in
Stroke: 75.9mm 3.0in
Valve type/No: Overhead 8
Transmission: Manual
No. of forward speeds: 4
Wheels driven: Rear
Wheelbase: 213.4cm 84.0in
Track F: 123.2cm 48.5in
Track R: 123.2cm 48.5in
Length: 365.8cm 144.0in
Width: 152.4cm 60.0in
Height: 149.9cm 59.0in
Kerb weight: 821.7kg 1810.0lb

4507 Triumph

Herald Coupe
1959 UK
80.0mph 128.7kmh
0-50mph 80.5kmh: 15.5secs
0-60mph 96.5kmh: 23.2secs
0-1/4 mile: 22.4secs
42.5bhp 31.7kW 43.1PS
@ 5500rpm
48.7lbft 66.0Nm @ 3000rpm
54.0bhp/ton 53.1bhp/tonne
44.8bhp/L 33.4kW/L 45.4PS/L
45.7ft/sec 13.9m/sec
14.0mph 22.5kmh/1000rpm
33.2mpg 27.6mpgUS 8.5L/100km
Petrol 4-stroke piston
948cc 57.8cu in
In-line 4
Compression ratio: 8.5:1
Bore: 63.0mm 2.5in
Stroke: 76.0mm 3.0in
Valve type/No: Overhead 8
Transmission: Manual
No. of forward speeds: 4
Wheels driven: Rear
Springs F/R: Coil/Leaf
Brakes F/R: Drum/Drum
Wheelbase: 232.4cm 91.5in
Track F: 121.9cm 48.0in
Track R: 121.9cm 48.0in
Length: 388.6cm 153.0in
Width: 152.4cm 60.0in
Height: 130.0cm 51.2in
Ground clearance: 17.0cm 6.7in
Kerb weight: 800.9kg 1764.0lb
Fuel: 31.8L 7.0gal 8.4galUS

4508 Triumph

Herald Saloon
1959 UK
71.5mph 115.0kmh
0-50mph 80.5kmh: 19.3secs
0-60mph 96.5kmh: 30.4secs
0-1/4 mile: 24.3secs
34.5bhp 25.7kW 35.0PS
@ 4500rpm
48.0lbft 65.0Nm @ 2750rpm
44.3bhp/ton 43.6bhp/tonne
36.4bhp/L 27.1kW/L 36.9PS/L
37.4ft/sec 11.4m/sec
13.3mph 21.4kmh/1000rpm
32.4mpg 27.0mpgUS 8.7L/100km
Petrol 4-stroke piston
948cc 57.8cu in
In-line 4
Compression ratio: 8.0:1
Bore: 63.0mm 2.5in
Stroke: 76.0mm 3.0in
Valve type/No: Overhead 8
Transmission: Manual
No. of forward speeds: 4
Wheels driven: Rear
Springs F/R: Coil/Leaf
Brakes F/R: Drum/Drum
Wheelbase: 232.4cm 91.5in
Track F: 121.9cm 48.0in
Track R: 121.9cm 48.0in
Length: 388.6cm 153.0in
Width: 152.4cm 60.0in
Height: 130.0cm 51.2in
Ground clearance: 17.0cm 6.7in
Kerb weight: 791.8kg 1744.0lb
Fuel: 31.8L 7.0gal 8.4galUS

4509 Triumph

Herald Convertible
1960 UK
79.0mph 127.1kmh
0-50mph 80.5kmh: 16.9secs
0-60mph 96.5kmh: 26.5secs
0-1/4 mile: 23.0secs
45.0bhp 33.6kW 45.6PS
@ 5800rpm
48.7lbft 66.0Nm @ 3000rpm
57.9bhp/ton 57.0bhp/tonne
47.5bhp/L 35.4kW/L 48.1PS/L
48.2ft/sec 14.7m/sec
14.0mph 22.5kmh/1000rpm
27.6mpg 23.0mpgUS 10.2L/100km
Petrol 4-stroke piston
948cc 57.8cu in
In-line 4
Compression ratio: 8.5:1
Bore: 63.0mm 2.5in
Stroke: 76.0mm 3.0in
Valve type/No: Overhead 8
Transmission: Manual
No. of forward speeds: 4
Wheels driven: Rear
Springs F/R: Coil/Leaf
Brakes F/R: Drum/Drum
Wheelbase: 232.4cm 91.5in
Track F: 121.9cm 48.0in
Track R: 121.9cm 48.0in
Length: 388.6cm 153.0in
Width: 152.4cm 60.0in
Height: 132.1cm 52.0in
Ground clearance: 17.0cm 6.7in
Kerb weight: 790.0kg 1740.0lb
Fuel: 31.8L 7.0gal 8.4galUS

4510 Triumph

Herald Coupe
1960 UK
80.0mph 128.7kmh
0-50mph 80.5kmh: 16.2secs
0-60mph 96.5kmh: 24.0secs
0-1/4 mile: 22.8secs

50.5bhp 37.7kW 51.2PS
@ 6000rpm
50.8lbft 68.8Nm @ 3200rpm
62.8bhp/ton 61.8bhp/tonne
53.3bhp/L 39.7kW/L 54.0PS/L
48.3ft/sec 14.7m/sec
14.6mph 23.5kmh/1000rpm
Petrol 4-stroke piston
948cc 57.8cu in
In-line 4 1 Carburettor
Compression ratio: 8.5:1
Bore: 63.0mm 2.5in
Stroke: 73.7mm 2.9in
Valve type/No: Overhead 8
Transmission: Manual
No. of forward speeds: 4
Wheels driven: Rear
Wheelbase: 232.4cm 91.5in
Track F: 121.9cm 48.0in
Track R: 121.9cm 48.0in
Length: 388.6cm 153.0in
Width: 152.4cm 60.0in
Height: 130.3cm 51.3in
Kerb weight: 817.2kg 1800.0lb

4511 Triumph

Herald 1200
1961 UK
76.0mph 122.3kmh
0-50mph 80.5kmh: 18.4secs
0-60mph 96.5kmh: 28.6secs
0-1/4 mile: 23.4secs
39.0bhp 29.1kW 39.5PS
@ 4500rpm
60.8lbft 82.4Nm @ 2250rpm
49.3bhp/ton 48.5bhp/tonne
34.0bhp/L 25.3kW/L 34.5PS/L
37.4ft/sec 11.4m/sec
15.7mph 25.3kmh/1000rpm
31.7mpg 26.4mpgUS 8.9L/100km
Petrol 4-stroke piston
1147cc 70.0cu in
In-line 4
Compression ratio: 8.0:1
Bore: 69.3mm 2.7in
Stroke: 76.0mm 3.0in
Valve type/No: Overhead 8
Transmission: Manual
No. of forward speeds: 4
Wheels driven: Rear
Springs F/R: Coil/Leaf
Brakes F/R: Drum/Drum
Wheelbase: 232.4cm 91.5in
Track F: 121.9cm 48.0in
Track R: 121.9cm 48.0in
Length: 388.6cm 153.0in
Width: 152.4cm 60.0in
Height: 132.1cm 52.0in
Ground clearance: 17.0cm 6.7in
Kerb weight: 804.0kg 1771.0lb
Fuel: 31.8L 7.0gal 8.4galUS

4512 Triumph

Herald
1962 UK
72.0mph 115.8kmh
0-50mph 80.5kmh: 15.5secs
0-60mph 96.5kmh: 22.6secs
0-1/4 mile: 22.6secs
43.0bhp 32.1kW 43.6PS
@ 4500rpm
65.0lbft 88.1Nm @ 2250rpm
54.6bhp/ton 53.7bhp/tonne
37.5bhp/L 28.0kW/L 38.0PS/L
37.4ft/sec 11.4m/sec
16.3mph 26.2kmh/1000rpm
Petrol 4-stroke piston
1147cc 70.0cu in
In-line 4
Compression ratio: 8.0:1
Bore: 63.9mm 2.5in
Stroke: 75.9mm 3.0in
Valve type/No: Overhead 8
Transmission: Manual
No. of forward speeds: 4
Wheels driven: Rear
Wheelbase: 232.4cm 91.5in
Track F: 121.9cm 48.0in
Track R: 121.9cm 48.0in
Length: 388.6cm 153.0in
Width: 152.4cm 60.0in
Height: 132.1cm 52.0in
Ground clearance: 17.0cm 6.7in
Kerb weight: 801.3kg 1765.0lb

4513 Triumph

Herald 1200 Estate
1962 UK
74.5mph 119.9kmh
0-50mph 80.5kmh: 17.3secs
0-60mph 96.5kmh: 28.7secs
0-1/4 mile: 23.4secs
39.0bhp 29.1kW 39.5PS
@ 4500rpm
60.8lbft 82.4Nm @ 2250rpm
44.6bhp/ton 43.8bhp/tonne
34.0bhp/L 25.3kW/L 34.5PS/L
37.4ft/sec 11.4m/sec
16.3mph 26.2kmh/1000rpm
32.1mpg 26.7mpgUS 8.8L/100km
Petrol 4-stroke piston
1147cc 70.0cu in
In-line 4
Compression ratio: 8.0:1
Bore: 69.3mm 2.7in
Stroke: 76.0mm 3.0in
Valve type/No: Overhead 8
Transmission: Manual
No. of forward speeds: 4
Wheels driven: Rear
Springs F/R: Coil/Leaf
Brakes F/R: Drum/Drum
Steering: Rack & pinion
Wheelbase: 232.4cm 91.5in
Track F: 121.9cm 48.0in
Track R: 121.9cm 48.0in
Length: 388.6cm 153.0in
Width: 152.4cm 60.0in
Height: 132.1cm 52.0in
Ground clearance: 17.0cm 6.7in
Kerb weight: 889.8kg 1960.0lb
Fuel: 40.9L 9.0gal 10.8galUS

4514 Triumph

Spitfire 4
1962 UK
94.0mph 151.2kmh
0-50mph 80.5kmh: 11.9secs
0-60mph 96.5kmh: 17.3secs
0-1/4 mile: 20.9secs
63.0bhp 47.0kW 63.9PS
@ 5750rpm
77.0lbft 104.3Nm @ 3500rpm
88.8bhp/ton 87.3bhp/tonne
54.9bhp/L 41.0kW/L 55.7PS/L
47.8ft/sec 14.6m/sec
15.7mph 25.3kmh/1000rpm
31.2mpg 26.0mpgUS 9.1L/100km
Petrol 4-stroke piston
1147cc 70.0cu in
In-line 4 2 Carburettor
Compression ratio: 9.0:1
Bore: 69.3mm 2.7in
Stroke: 76.0mm 3.0in
Valve type/No: Overhead 8
Transmission: Manual
No. of forward speeds: 4
Wheels driven: Rear
Springs F/R: Coil/Leaf
Brakes F/R: Disc/Drum
Steering: Rack & pinion
Wheelbase: 210.8cm 83.0in
Track F: 124.5cm 49.0in
Track R: 121.9cm 48.0in
Length: 368.3cm 145.0in
Width: 147.3cm 58.0in
Height: 120.7cm 47.5in
Ground clearance: 12.7cm 5.0in
Kerb weight: 721.4kg 1589.0lb
Fuel: 37.5L 8.2gal 9.9galUS

4515 Triumph

Sports 6
1962 UK
82.0mph 131.9kmh
0-50mph 80.5kmh: 12.0secs
0-60mph 96.5kmh: 17.7secs
0-1/4 mile: 21.0secs
70.0bhp 52.2kW 71.0PS
@ 5000rpm
92.5lbft 125.3Nm @ 2800rpm
77.4bhp/ton 76.1bhp/tonne
43.9bhp/L 32.7kW/L 44.5PS/L
41.5ft/sec 12.6m/sec
16.4mph 26.4kmh/1000rpm
Petrol 4-stroke piston
1596cc 97.4cu in
In-line 6
Compression ratio: 8.8:1
Bore: 66.8mm 2.6in
Stroke: 75.9mm 3.0in
Valve type/No: Overhead 12
Transmission: Manual
No. of forward speeds: 4
Wheels driven: Rear
Wheelbase: 232.4cm 91.5in
Track F: 124.5cm 49.0in
Track R: 121.9cm 48.0in
Length: 388.6cm 153.0in
Width: 152.4cm 60.0in
Height: 133.4cm 52.5in
Ground clearance: 17.0cm 6.7in
Kerb weight: 919.3kg 2025.0lb

4516 Triumph

TR4
1962 UK
104.0mph 167.3kmh
0-50mph 80.5kmh: 8.3secs
0-60mph 96.5kmh: 10.9secs
0-1/4 mile: 17.8secs
100.0bhp 74.6kW 101.4PS
@ 4600rpm
127.0lbft 172.1Nm @ 3350rpm
102.6bhp/ton 100.8bhp/tonne
46.8bhp/L 34.9kW/L 47.4PS/L
46.3ft/sec 14.1m/sec
20.0mph 32.2kmh/1000rpm
22.5mpg 18.7mpgUS 12.6L/100km
Petrol 4-stroke piston
2138cc 130.4cu in
In-line 4 2 Carburettor
Compression ratio: 9.0:1
Bore: 86.0mm 3.4in
Stroke: 92.0mm 3.6in
Valve type/No: Overhead 8
Transmission: Manual
No. of forward speeds: 4
Wheels driven: Rear
Springs F/R: Coil/Leaf
Brakes F/R: Disc/Drum
Steering: Rack & pinion
Wheelbase: 223.5cm 88.0in
Track F: 127.0cm 50.0in
Track R: 124.5cm 49.0in
Length: 383.5cm 151.0in
Width: 146.1cm 57.5in
Height: 127.0cm 50.0in
Ground clearance: 15.2cm 6.0in
Kerb weight: 991.5kg 2184.0lb
Fuel: 53.5L 11.7gal 14.1galUS

4517 Triumph

Herald 12/50
1963 UK
78.0mph 125.5kmh
0-50mph 80.5kmh: 15.2secs
0-60mph 96.5kmh: 25.2secs
0-1/4 mile: 22.1secs
51.0bhp 38.0kW 51.7PS
@ 5200rpm
63.0lbft 85.4Nm @ 2600rpm
61.6bhp/ton 60.6bhp/tonne
44.5bhp/L 33.2kW/L 45.1PS/L
43.2ft/sec 13.2m/sec
15.7mph 25.3kmh/1000rpm
31.3mpg 26.1mpgUS 9.0L/100km
Petrol 4-stroke piston
1147cc 70.0cu in
In-line 4 1 Carburettor
Compression ratio: 8.5:1
Bore: 69.3mm 2.7in
Stroke: 76.0mm 3.0in
Valve type/No: Overhead 8
Transmission: Manual
No. of forward speeds: 4
Wheels driven: Rear
Springs F/R: Coil/Leaf
Brakes F/R: Disc/Drum
Steering: Rack & pinion
Wheelbase: 232.4cm 91.5in
Track F: 121.9cm 48.0in
Track R: 121.9cm 48.0in
Length: 388.6cm 153.0in
Width: 152.4cm 60.0in
Height: 132.1cm 52.0in
Ground clearance: 17.0cm 6.7in
Kerb weight: 842.2kg 1855.0lb
Fuel: 29.6L 6.5gal 7.8galUS

4518 Triumph

Spitfire 4
1963 UK
90.0mph 144.8kmh
0-50mph 80.5kmh: 11.0secs
0-60mph 96.5kmh: 15.5secs
0-1/4 mile: 20.8secs
63.0bhp 47.0kW 63.9PS
@ 5750rpm
67.0lbft 90.8Nm @ 3500rpm
90.7bhp/ton 89.2bhp/tonne
54.9bhp/L 41.0kW/L 55.7PS/L
47.8ft/sec 14.5m/sec
16.0mph 25.7kmh/1000rpm
Petrol 4-stroke piston
1147cc 70.0cu in
In-line 4 1 Carburettor
Compression ratio: 9.0:1
Bore: 69.3mm 2.7in
Stroke: 75.9mm 3.0in
Valve type/No: Overhead 8
Transmission: Manual
No. of forward speeds: 4
Wheels driven: Rear
Wheelbase: 210.8cm 83.0in
Track F: 124.5cm 49.0in
Track R: 121.9cm 48.0in
Length: 368.3cm 145.0in
Width: 144.8cm 57.0in
Height: 120.7cm 47.5in
Ground clearance: 12.7cm 5.0in
Kerb weight: 706.0kg 1555.0lb

4519 Triumph

Vitesse 6
1963 UK
88.0mph 141.6kmh
0-50mph 80.5kmh: 12.2secs
0-60mph 96.5kmh: 17.8secs
0-1/4 mile: 20.7secs
70.0bhp 52.2kW 71.0PS
@ 5000rpm
92.0lbft 124.7Nm @ 2800rpm
77.2bhp/ton 75.9bhp/tonne
43.9bhp/L 32.7kW/L 44.5PS/L
41.5ft/sec 12.7m/sec
20.4mph 32.8kmh/1000rpm
24.6mpg 20.5mpgUS 11.5L/100km
Petrol 4-stroke piston
1596cc 97.4cu in
In-line 6 2 Carburettor
Compression ratio: 8.7:1
Bore: 66.7mm 2.6in
Stroke: 76.0mm 3.0in
Valve type/No: Overhead 12
Transmission: Manual with overdrive
No. of forward speeds: 6
Wheels driven: Rear
Springs F/R: Coil/Leaf
Brakes F/R: Disc/Drum
Steering: Rack & pinion
Wheelbase: 232.4cm 91.5in
Track F: 121.9cm 48.0in
Track R: 121.9cm 48.0in
Length: 388.6cm 153.0in
Width: 152.4cm 60.0in
Height: 135.9cm 53.5in
Ground clearance: 17.0cm 6.7in
Kerb weight: 921.6kg 2030.0lb
Fuel: 39.8L 8.8gal 10.5galUS

4520 Triumph

2000
1964 UK
94.0mph 151.2kmh
0-50mph 80.5kmh: 9.9secs
0-60mph 96.5kmh: 14.1secs
0-1/4 mile: 19.4secs
90.0bhp 67.1kW 91.2PS
@ 5000rpm
117.0lbft 158.5Nm @ 2900rpm
78.7bhp/ton 77.4bhp/tonne
45.0bhp/L 33.6kW/L 45.7PS/L
41.5ft/sec 12.7m/sec
20.6mph 33.1kmh/1000rpm
24.5mpg 20.4mpgUS 11.5L/100km
Petrol 4-stroke piston
1998cc 121.9cu in
In-line 6 2 Carburettor
Compression ratio: 8.0:1
Bore: 74.7mm 2.9in
Stroke: 76.0mm 3.0in
Valve type/No: Overhead 12
Transmission: Manual with overdrive
No. of forward speeds: 6
Wheels driven: Rear
Springs F/R: Coil/Coil
Brake system: PA
Brakes F/R: Disc/Drum
Steering: Rack & pinion
Wheelbase: 269.2cm 106.0in
Track F: 132.1cm 52.0in
Track R: 133.1cm 52.4in
Length: 444.5cm 175.0in
Width: 165.1cm 65.0in

Height: 142.2cm 56.0in
Ground clearance: 14.0cm 5.5in
Kerb weight: 1163.1kg 2562.0lb
Fuel: 63.7L 14.0gal 16.8galUS

4521 Triumph

TR4
1964 UK
101.0mph 162.5kmh
0-50mph 80.5kmh: 7.6secs
0-60mph 96.5kmh: 10.7secs
0-1/4 mile: 18.1secs
100.0bhp 74.6kW 101.4PS
@ 4600rpm
128.0lbft 173.4Nm @ 3350rpm
101.8bhp/ton 100.1bhp/tonne
46.8bhp/L 34.9kW/L 47.4PS/L
46.3ft/sec 14.1m/sec
20.4mph 32.8kmh/1000rpm
Petrol 4-stroke piston
2138cc 130.4cu in
In-line 4 2 Carburettor
Compression ratio: 9.0:1
Bore: 86.1mm 3.4in
Stroke: 91.9mm 3.6in
Valve type/No: Overhead 8
Transmission: Manual
No. of forward speeds: 4
Wheels driven: Rear
Springs F/R: /Leaf
Brakes F/R: Disc/Drum
Steering: Rack & pinion
Wheelbase: 223.5cm 88.0in
Track F: 124.5cm 49.0in
Track R: 121.9cm 48.0in
Length: 393.7cm 155.0in
Width: 146.1cm 57.5in
Height: 127.0cm 50.0in
Ground clearance: 14.0cm 5.5in
Kerb weight: 998.8kg 2200.0lb
Fuel: 53.0L 11.6gal 14.0galUS

4522 Triumph

2000
1965 UK
93.0mph 149.6kmh
0-50mph 80.5kmh: 9.8secs
0-60mph 96.5kmh: 13.5secs
0-1/4 mile: 19.2secs
90.0bhp 67.1kW 91.2PS
@ 5000rpm
117.0lbft 158.5Nm @ 2900rpm
80.5bhp/ton 79.1bhp/tonne
45.0bhp/L 33.6kW/L 45.7PS/L
41.5ft/sec 12.6m/sec
16.9mph 27.2kmh/1000rpm
Petrol 4-stroke piston
1998cc 121.9cu in
In-line 6 2 Carburettor
Compression ratio: 9.0:1
Bore: 74.7mm 2.9in
Stroke: 75.9mm 3.0in
Valve type/No: Overhead 12
Transmission: Manual
No. of forward speeds: 4
Wheels driven: Rear
Springs F/R: Coil/Coil
Brakes F/R: Disc/Drum
Steering: Rack & pinion
Wheelbase: 269.2cm 106.0in
Track F: 132.1cm 52.0in
Track R: 128.0cm 50.4in
Length: 441.5cm 173.8in
Width: 165.1cm 65.0in
Height: 142.2cm 56.0in
Ground clearance: 17.8cm 7.0in
Kerb weight: 1137.3kg 2505.0lb
Fuel: 63.6L 14.0gal 16.8galUS

4523 Triumph

Spitfire Mk II
1965 UK
92.0mph 148.0kmh
0-50mph 80.5kmh: 10.4secs
0-60mph 96.5kmh: 15.0secs
0-1/4 mile: 20.4secs
67.0bhp 50.0kW 67.9PS
@ 6000rpm
67.0lbft 90.8Nm @ 3750rpm
92.1bhp/ton 90.5bhp/tonne
58.4bhp/L 43.6kW/L 59.2PS/L
49.8ft/sec 15.2m/sec
15.8mph 25.4kmh/1000rpm
Petrol 4-stroke piston
1147cc 70.0cu in
In-line 4 2 Carburettor
Compression ratio: 9.0:1
Bore: 69.3mm 2.7in
Stroke: 75.9mm 3.0in
Valve type/No: Overhead 8
Transmission: Manual
No. of forward speeds: 4
Wheels driven: Rear
Springs F/R: Coil/Leaf
Brakes F/R: Disc/Drum
Steering: Rack & pinion
Wheelbase: 210.8cm 83.0in
Track F: 124.5cm 49.0in
Track R: 121.9cm 48.0in
Length: 368.3cm 145.0in
Width: 144.8cm 57.0in
Height: 120.7cm 47.5in
Ground clearance: 12.7cm 5.0in
Kerb weight: 740.0kg 1630.0lb
Fuel: 38.6L 8.5gal 10.2galUS

4524 Triumph

TR4A
1965 UK
107.0mph 172.2kmh
0-50mph 80.5kmh: 7.3secs
0-60mph 96.5kmh: 10.5secs
0-1/4 mile: 17.5secs
105.0bhp 78.3kW 106.5PS
@ 4650rpm
128.0lbft 173.4Nm @ 3350rpm
100.9bhp/ton 99.3bhp/tonne
49.1bhp/L 36.6kW/L 49.8PS/L
46.8ft/sec 14.2m/sec
20.4mph 32.8kmh/1000rpm
Petrol 4-stroke piston
2138cc 130.4cu in
In-line 4 2 Carburettor
Compression ratio: 9.0:1
Bore: 86.1mm 3.4in
Stroke: 91.9mm 3.6in
Valve type/No: Overhead 8
Transmission: Manual with overdrive
Wheels driven: Rear
Springs F/R: Coil/Coil
Brakes F/R: Disc/Drum
Steering: Rack & pinion
Wheelbase: 223.5cm 88.0in
Track F: 124.5cm 49.0in
Track R: 121.9cm 48.0in
Length: 393.7cm 155.0in
Width: 146.1cm 57.5in
Height: 125.7cm 49.5in
Ground clearance: 14.0cm 5.5in
Kerb weight: 1057.8kg 2330.0lb
Fuel: 53.0L 11.6gal 14.0galUS

4525 Triumph

TR4A IRS
1965 UK
111.0mph 178.6kmh
0-50mph 80.5kmh: 8.3secs
0-60mph 96.5kmh: 11.4secs
0-1/4 mile: 18.5secs
104.0bhp 77.5kW 105.4PS
@ 4700rpm
132.5lbft 179.5Nm @ 3000rpm
98.8bhp/ton 97.1bhp/tonne
48.6bhp/L 36.3kW/L 49.3PS/L
47.3ft/sec 14.4m/sec
24.4mph 39.3kmh/1000rpm
25.4mpg 21.1mpgUS 11.1L/100km
Petrol 4-stroke piston
2138cc 130.4cu in
In-line 4 2 Carburettor
Compression ratio: 9.0:1
Bore: 86.0mm 3.4in
Stroke: 92.0mm 3.6in
Valve type/No: Overhead 8
Transmission: Manual with overdrive
No. of forward speeds: 7
Wheels driven: Rear
Springs F/R: Coil/Coil
Brakes F/R: Disc/Drum
Steering: Rack & pinion
Wheelbase: 223.5cm 88.0in
Track F: 127.0cm 50.0in
Track R: 124.5cm 49.0in
Length: 383.5cm 151.0in
Width: 146.1cm 57.5in
Height: 127.0cm 50.0in
Ground clearance: 15.2cm 6.0in
Kerb weight: 1070.5kg 2358.0lb
Fuel: 53.5L 11.7gal 14.1galUS

4526 Triumph

Vitesse Convertible
1965 UK
91.0mph 146.4kmh
0-50mph 80.5kmh: 10.4secs
0-60mph 96.5kmh: 15.5secs
0-1/4 mile: 20.3secs
70.0bhp 52.2kW 71.0PS
@ 5000rpm
110.0lbft 149.1Nm @ 2800rpm
76.2bhp/ton 74.9bhp/tonne
43.9bhp/L 32.7kW/L 44.5PS/L
41.5ft/sec 12.7m/sec
20.4mph 32.8kmh/1000rpm
25.8mpg 21.5mpgUS 10.9L/100km
Petrol 4-stroke piston
1596cc 97.4cu in
In-line 6 2 Carburettor
Compression ratio: 8.7:1
Bore: 66.8mm 2.6in
Stroke: 76.0mm 3.0in
Valve type/No: Overhead 12
Transmission: Manual with overdrive
No. of forward speeds: 6
Wheels driven: Rear
Springs F/R: Coil/Leaf
Brakes F/R: Disc/Drum
Steering: Rack & pinion
Wheelbase: 232.4cm 91.5in
Track F: 121.9cm 48.0in
Track R: 121.9cm 48.0in
Length: 388.6cm 153.0in
Width: 152.4cm 60.0in
Height: 135.9cm 53.5in
Ground clearance: 17.0cm 6.7in
Kerb weight: 934.3kg 2058.0lb
Fuel: 39.8L 8.8gal 10.5galUS

4527 Triumph

1300
1966 UK
86.0mph 138.4kmh
0-50mph 80.5kmh: 12.8secs
0-60mph 96.5kmh: 19.0secs
0-1/4 mile: 21.3secs
0-1km: 40.2secs
61.0bhp 45.5kW 61.8PS
@ 5000rpm
73.0lbft 98.9Nm @ 3000rpm
69.7bhp/ton 68.5bhp/tonne
47.1bhp/L 35.1kW/L 47.7PS/L
41.5ft/sec 12.7m/sec
15.4mph 24.8kmh/1000rpm
28.0mpg 23.3mpgUS 10.1L/100km
Petrol 4-stroke piston
1296cc 79.1cu in
In-line 4 1 Carburettor
Compression ratio: 8.5:1
Bore: 73.7mm 2.9in
Stroke: 76.0mm 3.0in
Valve type/No: Overhead 8
Transmission: Manual
No. of forward speeds: 4
Wheels driven: Front
Springs F/R: Coil/Coil
Brakes F/R: Disc/Drum
Steering: Rack & pinion
Wheelbase: 245.4cm 96.6in
Track F: 134.6cm 53.0in
Track R: 133.6cm 52.6in
Length: 393.7cm 155.0in
Width: 156.7cm 61.7in
Height: 137.2cm 54.0in
Ground clearance: 14.0cm 5.5in
Kerb weight: 889.8kg 1960.0lb
Fuel: 53.7L 11.8gal 14.2galUS

4528 Triumph

2000 Estate Car
1966 UK
94.0mph 151.2kmh
0-50mph 80.5kmh: 11.0secs
0-60mph 96.5kmh: 15.6secs
0-1/4 mile: 20.0secs
0-1km: 38.1secs
90.0bhp 67.1kW 91.2PS
@ 5000rpm
117.0lbft 158.5Nm @ 2900rpm
74.4bhp/ton 73.2bhp/tonne
45.0bhp/L 33.6kW/L 45.7PS/L
41.5ft/sec 12.7m/sec
20.4mph 32.8kmh/1000rpm
21.8mpg 18.2mpgUS 13.0L/100km
Petrol 4-stroke piston
1998cc 121.9cu in
In-line 6 2 Carburettor
Compression ratio: 9.0:1
Bore: 74.7mm 2.9in
Stroke: 76.0mm 3.0in
Valve type/No: Overhead 12
Transmission: Manual with overdrive
No. of forward speeds: 6
Wheels driven: Rear
Springs F/R: Coil/Coil
Brake system: PA
Brakes F/R: Disc/Drum
Steering: Rack & pinion
Wheelbase: 269.2cm 106.0in
Track F: 132.1cm 52.0in
Track R: 133.1cm 52.4in
Length: 444.5cm 175.0in
Width: 165.1cm 65.0in
Height: 142.2cm 56.0in
Ground clearance: 14.0cm 5.5in
Kerb weight: 1229.9kg 2709.0lb
Fuel: 52.3L 11.5gal 13.8galUS

4529 Triumph

Spitfire Mk II
1966 UK
94.0mph 151.2kmh
0-50mph 80.5kmh: 11.0secs
0-60mph 96.5kmh: 15.5secs
0-1/4 mile: 20.0secs
0-1km: 37.3secs
67.0bhp 50.0kW 67.9PS
@ 6000rpm
67.0lbft 90.8Nm @ 3750rpm
91.8bhp/ton 90.3bhp/tonne
58.4bhp/L 43.6kW/L 59.2PS/L
49.8ft/sec 15.2m/sec
19.0mph 30.6kmh/1000rpm
29.8mpg 24.8mpgUS 9.5L/100km
Petrol 4-stroke piston
1147cc 70.0cu in
In-line 4 2 Carburettor
Compression ratio: 9.0:1
Bore: 69.4mm 2.7in
Stroke: 76.0mm 3.0in
Valve type/No: Overhead 8
Transmission: Manual with overdrive
No. of forward speeds: 6
Wheels driven: Rear
Springs F/R: Coil/Leaf
Brakes F/R: Disc/Drum
Steering: Rack & pinion
Wheelbase: 210.8cm 83.0in
Track F: 124.5cm 49.0in
Track R: 121.9cm 48.0in
Length: 368.3cm 145.0in
Width: 147.3cm 58.0in
Height: 120.7cm 47.5in
Ground clearance: 12.7cm 5.0in
Kerb weight: 742.3kg 1635.0lb
Fuel: 37.5L 8.2gal 9.9galUS

4530 Triumph

GT6
1967 UK
108.0mph 173.8kmh
0-50mph 80.5kmh: 8.5secs
0-60mph 96.5kmh: 12.0secs
0-1/4 mile: 18.5secs
0-1km: 34.3secs
95.0bhp 70.8kW 96.3PS
@ 5000rpm
117.0lbft 158.5Nm @ 3000rpm
108.3bhp/ton 106.5bhp/tonne
47.5bhp/L 35.5kW/L 48.2PS/L
41.5ft/sec 12.7m/sec
21.1mph 33.9kmh/1000rpm
20.2mpg 16.8mpgUS 14.0L/100km
Petrol 4-stroke piston
1998cc 121.9cu in
In-line 6 2 Carburettor
Compression ratio: 9.5:1
Bore: 74.7mm 2.9in
Stroke: 76.0mm 3.0in
Valve type/No: Overhead 12
Transmission: Manual with overdrive
No. of forward speeds: 6
Wheels driven: Rear
Springs F/R: Disc/Leaf
Brakes F/R: Disc/Drum
Steering: Rack & pinion
Wheelbase: 210.8cm 83.0in
Track F: 124.5cm 49.0in
Track R: 121.9cm 48.0in
Length: 368.3cm 145.0in
Width: 144.8cm 57.0in
Height: 119.4cm 47.0in
Ground clearance: 15.2cm 6.0in
Kerb weight: 891.7kg 1964.0lb
Fuel: 44.4L 9.7gal 11.7galUS

4531 Triumph
Herald 1200
1967 UK
80.0mph 128.7kmh
0-50mph 80.5kmh: 16.0secs
0-60mph 96.5kmh: 25.8secs
0-1/4 mile: 22.3secs
0-1km: 42.6secs
48.0bhp 35.8kW 48.7PS
@ 5200rpm
61.5lbft 83.3Nm @ 2500rpm
58.4bhp/ton 57.4bhp/tonne
41.8bhp/L 31.2kW/L 42.4PS/L
43.2ft/sec 13.2m/sec
15.7mph 25.3kmh/1000rpm
28.1mpg 23.4mpgUS 10.1L/100km
Petrol 4-stroke piston
1147cc 70.0cu in
In-line 4 1 Carburettor
Compression ratio: 8.5:1
Bore: 69.3mm 2.7in
Stroke: 76.0mm 3.0in
Valve type/No: Overhead 8
Transmission: Manual
No. of forward speeds: 4
Wheels driven: Rear
Springs F/R: Coil/Leaf
Brakes F/R: Disc/Drum
Steering: Rack & pinion
Wheelbase: 232.4cm 91.5in
Track F: 121.9cm 48.0in
Track R: 121.9cm 48.0in
Length: 388.6cm 153.0in
Width: 152.4cm 60.0in
Height: 132.1cm 52.0in
Ground clearance: 17.0cm 6.7in
Kerb weight: 835.8kg 1841.0lb
Fuel: 31.8L 7.0gal 8.4galUS

4532 Triumph
Spitfire Mk III
1967 UK
100.0mph 160.9kmh
0-50mph 80.5kmh: 9.3secs
0-60mph 96.5kmh: 13.6secs
0-1/4 mile: 19.3secs
75.0bhp 55.9kW 76.0PS
@ 6000rpm
75.0lbft 101.6Nm @ 4000rpm
100.0bhp/ton 98.3bhp/tonne
57.9bhp/L 43.2kW/L 58.7PS/L
49.8ft/sec 15.2m/sec
15.9mph 25.6kmh/1000rpm
Petrol 4-stroke piston
1296cc 79.1cu in
In-line 4
Compression ratio: 9.0:1
Bore: 73.7mm 2.9in
Stroke: 76.0mm 3.0in
Valve type/No: Overhead 8
Transmission: Manual
No. of forward speeds: 4
Wheels driven: Rear
Brakes F/R: Disc/Drum
Steering: Rack & pinion
Wheelbase: 210.8cm 83.0in
Track F: 124.5cm 49.0in
Track R: 121.9cm 48.0in
Length: 373.4cm 147.0in
Width: 144.8cm 57.0in
Height: 120.7cm 47.5in
Kerb weight: 762.7kg 1680.0lb
Fuel: 37.5L 8.2gal 9.9galUS

4533 Triumph
Herald 13/60 Convertible
1968 UK
85.0mph 136.8kmh
0-50mph 80.5kmh: 12.5secs
0-60mph 96.5kmh: 17.7secs
0-1/4 mile: 20.9secs
0-1km: 39.9secs
61.0bhp 45.5kW 61.8PS
@ 5000rpm
73.0lbft 98.9Nm @ 3000rpm
74.0bhp/ton 72.8bhp/tonne
47.1bhp/L 35.1kW/L 47.7PS/L
41.5ft/sec 12.7m/sec
15.7mph 25.3kmh/1000rpm
28.3mpg 23.6mpgUS 10.0L/100km
Petrol 4-stroke piston
1296cc 79.1cu in
In-line 4 1 Carburettor
Compression ratio: 8.5:1
Bore: 73.7mm 2.9in
Stroke: 76.0mm 3.0in
Valve type/No: Overhead 8
Transmission: Manual
No. of forward speeds: 4
Wheels driven: Rear
Springs F/R: Coil/Leaf
Brakes F/R: Disc/Drum
Steering: Rack & pinion
Wheelbase: 232.4cm 91.5in
Track F: 121.9cm 48.0in
Track R: 121.9cm 48.0in
Length: 388.6cm 153.0in
Width: 152.4cm 60.0in
Height: 132.1cm 52.0in
Ground clearance: 17.0cm 6.7in
Kerb weight: 838.1kg 1846.0lb
Fuel: 29.6L 6.5gal 7.8galUS

4534 Triumph
Spitfire
1968 UK
100.0mph 160.9kmh
0-60mph 96.5kmh: 13.6secs
0-1/4 mile: 19.3secs
75.0bhp 55.9kW 76.0PS
@ 6000rpm
75.0lbft 101.6Nm @ 4000rpm
100.0bhp/ton 98.3bhp/tonne
57.9bhp/L 43.2kW/L 58.7PS/L
49.8ft/sec 15.2m/sec
15.9mph 25.6kmh/1000rpm
Petrol 4-stroke piston
1296cc 79.1cu in
In-line 4
Bore: 73.7mm 2.9in
Stroke: 76.0mm 3.0in
Valve type/No: Overhead 8
Transmission: Manual
No. of forward speeds: 4
Wheels driven: Rear
Springs F/R: /Coil
Brakes F/R: Disc/Drum
Wheelbase: 210.8cm 83.0in
Track F: 124.5cm 49.0in
Track R: 121.9cm 48.0in
Length: 373.4cm 147.0in
Width: 144.8cm 57.0in
Height: 120.7cm 47.5in
Kerb weight: 762.7kg 1680.0lb

4535 Triumph
TR250
1968 UK
107.0mph 172.2kmh
0-50mph 80.5kmh: 8.6secs
0-60mph 96.5kmh: 10.6secs
0-1/4 mile: 17.8secs
111.0bhp 82.8kW 112.5PS
@ 4500rpm
152.0lbft 206.0Nm @ 3000rpm
105.8bhp/ton 104.0bhp/tonne
44.4bhp/L 33.1kW/L 45.0PS/L
46.7ft/sec 14.2m/sec
25.3mph 40.7kmh/1000rpm
Petrol 4-stroke piston
2498cc 152.4cu in
In-line 6
Compression ratio: 8.5:1
Bore: 74.7mm 2.9in
Stroke: 95.0mm 3.7in
Valve type/No: Overhead 12
Transmission: Manual with overdrive
Wheels driven: Rear
Brakes F/R: Disc/Drum
Steering: Rack & pinion
Wheelbase: 223.5cm 88.0in
Track F: 126.5cm 49.8in
Track R: 125.0cm 49.2in
Length: 390.1cm 153.6in
Width: 147.3cm 58.0in
Height: 127.0cm 50.0in
Kerb weight: 1066.9kg 2350.0lb
Fuel: 51.1L 11.2gal 13.5galUS

4536 Triumph
TR5 PI
1968 UK
121.0mph 194.7kmh
0-50mph 80.5kmh: 6.5secs
0-60mph 96.5kmh: 8.8secs
0-1/4 mile: 16.8secs
0-1km: 31.3secs
150.0bhp 111.9kW 152.1PS
@ 5500rpm
164.0lbft 222.2Nm @ 3000rpm
144.9bhp/ton 142.5bhp/tonne
60.0bhp/L 44.8kW/L 60.9PS/L
57.1ft/sec 17.4m/sec
21.2mph 34.1kmh/1000rpm
19.6mpg 16.3mpgUS 14.4L/100km
Petrol 4-stroke piston
2498cc 152.4cu in
In-line 6 fuel injection
Compression ratio: 9.5:1
Bore: 74.7mm 2.9in
Stroke: 95.0mm 3.7in
Valve type/No: Overhead 12
Transmission: Manual
No. of forward speeds: 4
Wheels driven: Rear
Springs F/R: Coil/Coil
Brake system: PA
Brakes F/R: Disc/Drum
Steering: Rack & pinion
Wheelbase: 223.5cm 88.0in
Track F: 127.0cm 50.0in
Track R: 124.5cm 49.0in
Length: 383.5cm 151.0in
Width: 146.1cm 57.5in
Height: 127.0cm 50.0in
Ground clearance: 12.7cm 5.0in
Kerb weight: 1052.8kg 2319.0lb
Fuel: 51.2L 11.2gal 13.5galUS

4537 Triumph
2.5PI
1969 UK
107.0mph 172.2kmh
0-50mph 80.5kmh: 7.4secs
0-60mph 96.5kmh: 10.4secs
0-1/4 mile: 17.4secs
0-1km: 32.7secs
132.0bhp 98.4kW 133.8PS
@ 5450rpm
152.0lbft 206.0Nm @ 2000rpm
110.7bhp/ton 108.8bhp/tonne
52.8bhp/L 39.4kW/L 53.6PS/L
56.6ft/sec 17.3m/sec
24.6mph 39.6kmh/1000rpm
21.6mpg 18.0mpgUS 13.1L/100km
Petrol 4-stroke piston
2498cc 152.4cu in
In-line 6 fuel injection
Compression ratio: 9.5:1
Bore: 74.7mm 2.9in
Stroke: 95.0mm 3.7in
Valve type/No: Overhead 12
Transmission: Manual with overdrive
No. of forward speeds: 6
Wheels driven: Rear
Springs F/R: Coil/Coil
Brake system: PA
Brakes F/R: Disc/Drum
Steering: Rack & pinion
Wheelbase: 269.2cm 106.0in
Track F: 132.1cm 52.0in
Track R: 133.1cm 52.4in
Length: 441.2cm 173.7in
Width: 165.1cm 65.0in
Height: 142.2cm 56.0in
Ground clearance: 15.2cm 6.0in
Kerb weight: 1212.6kg 2671.0lb
Fuel: 63.7L 14.0gal 16.8galUS

4538 Triumph
2000 Mk II
1969 UK
98.0mph 157.7kmh
0-50mph 80.5kmh: 10.6secs
0-60mph 96.5kmh: 14.9secs
0-1/4 mile: 19.7secs
0-1km: 36.5secs
90.0bhp 67.1kW 91.2PS
@ 5000rpm
117.0lbft 158.5Nm @ 2900rpm
76.3bhp/ton 75.0bhp/tonne
45.0bhp/L 33.6kW/L 45.7PS/L
41.5ft/sec 12.7m/sec
20.4mph 32.8kmh/1000rpm
20.1mpg 16.7mpgUS 14.1L/100km
Petrol 4-stroke piston
1998cc 121.9cu in
In-line 6 2 Carburettor
Compression ratio: 9.2:1
Bore: 74.7mm 2.9in
Stroke: 76.0mm 3.0in
Valve type/No: Overhead 12
Transmission: Manual with overdrive
No. of forward speeds: 6
Wheels driven: Rear
Springs F/R: Coil/Coil
Brake system: PA
Brakes F/R: Disc/Drum
Steering: Rack & pinion
Wheelbase: 269.2cm 106.0in
Track F: 133.4cm 52.5in
Track R: 134.4cm 52.9in
Length: 463.0cm 182.3in
Width: 165.1cm 65.0in
Height: 142.2cm 56.0in
Ground clearance: 15.2cm 6.0in
Kerb weight: 1199.9kg 2643.0lb
Fuel: 63.7L 14.0gal 16.8galUS

4539 Triumph
GT6
1969 UK
109.0mph 175.4kmh
0-50mph 80.5kmh: 8.0secs
0-60mph 96.5kmh: 11.0secs
0-1/4 mile: 18.0secs
95.0bhp 70.8kW 96.3PS
@ 4700rpm
117.0lbft 158.5Nm @ 3400rpm
107.7bhp/ton 105.9bhp/tonne
47.5bhp/L 35.5kW/L 48.2PS/L
39.0ft/sec 11.9m/sec
20.9mph 33.6kmh/1000rpm
28.7mpg 23.9mpgUS 9.8L/100km
Petrol 4-stroke piston
1998cc 121.9cu in
In-line 6
Compression ratio: 9.3:1
Bore: 74.7mm 2.9in
Stroke: 76.0mm 3.0in
Valve type/No: Overhead 12
Transmission: Manual with overdrive
Wheels driven: Rear
Brakes F/R: Disc/Drum
Steering: Rack & pinion
Wheelbase: 210.8cm 83.0in
Track F: 124.5cm 49.0in
Track R: 124.5cm 49.0in
Length: 373.4cm 147.0in
Width: 144.8cm 57.0in
Height: 119.4cm 47.0in
Kerb weight: 896.6kg 1975.0lb
Fuel: 44.3L 9.7gal 11.7galUS

4540 Triumph
GT6 Mk II
1969 UK
107.0mph 172.2kmh
0-50mph 80.5kmh: 7.2secs
0-60mph 96.5kmh: 10.0secs
0-1/4 mile: 17.3secs
0-1km: 32.4secs
104.0bhp 77.5kW 105.4PS
@ 5300rpm
117.0lbft 158.5Nm @ 3000rpm
117.2bhp/ton 115.2bhp/tonne
52.0bhp/L 38.8kW/L 52.8PS/L
44.0ft/sec 13.4m/sec
21.1mph 33.9kmh/1000rpm
25.2mpg 21.0mpgUS 11.2L/100km
Petrol 4-stroke piston
1998cc 121.9cu in
In-line 6 2 Carburettor
Compression ratio: 9.2:1
Bore: 74.7mm 2.9in
Stroke: 76.0mm 3.0in
Valve type/No: Overhead 12
Transmission: Manual with overdrive
No. of forward speeds: 6
Wheels driven: Rear
Springs F/R: Coil/Leaf
Brakes F/R: Disc/Drum
Steering: Rack & pinion
Wheelbase: 210.8cm 83.0in
Track F: 124.5cm 49.0in
Track R: 121.9cm 48.0in
Length: 373.4cm 147.0in
Width: 144.8cm 57.0in
Height: 119.4cm 47.0in
Ground clearance: 14.0cm 5.5in
Kerb weight: 902.5kg 1988.0lb
Fuel: 44.4L 9.7gal 11.7galUS

4541 Triumph
TR6
1969 UK
121.0mph 194.7kmh
0-50mph 80.5kmh: 6.3secs
0-60mph 96.5kmh: 8.2secs
0-1/4 mile: 16.3secs
0-1km: 30.6secs
142.0bhp 105.9kW 144.0PS
@ 5700rpm
149.0lbft 201.9Nm @ 3000rpm
128.6bhp/ton 126.5bhp/tonne
56.8bhp/L 42.4kW/L 57.6PS/L

59.2ft/sec 18.0m/sec
25.9mph 41.7kmh/1000rpm
19.8mpg 16.5mpgUS 14.3L/100km
Petrol 4-stroke piston
2498cc 152.4cu in
In-line 6 fuel injection
Compression ratio: 9.5:1
Bore: 74.7mm 2.9in
Stroke: 95.0mm 3.7in
Valve type/No: Overhead 12
Transmission: Manual with overdrive
No. of forward speeds: 7
Wheels driven: Rear
Springs F/R: Coil/Coil
Brake system: PA
Brakes F/R: Disc/Drum
Steering: Rack & pinion
Wheelbase: 223.5cm 88.0in
Track F: 125.0cm 49.2in
Track R: 123.7cm 48.7in
Length: 384.8cm 151.5in
Width: 154.9cm 61.0in
Height: 127.0cm 50.0in
Ground clearance: 15.2cm 6.0in
Kerb weight: 1122.7kg 2473.0lb
Fuel: 51.2L 11.2gal 13.5galUS

4542 Triumph

Vitesse 2-litre Mk II
1969 UK
102.0mph 164.1kmh
0-50mph 80.5kmh: 7.7secs
0-60mph 96.5kmh: 11.9secs
0-1/4 mile: 18.4secs
0-1km: 34.3secs
104.0bhp 77.5kW 105.4PS
@ 5300rpm
117.0lbft 158.5Nm @ 3000rpm
107.3bhp/ton 105.6bhp/tonne
52.0bhp/L 38.8kW/L 52.8PS/L
44.0ft/sec 13.4m/sec
21.3mph 34.3kmh/1000rpm
23.5mpg 19.6mpgUS 12.0L/100km
Petrol 4-stroke piston
1998cc 121.9cu in
In-line 6 2 Carburettor
Compression ratio: 9.2:1
Bore: 74.7mm 2.9in
Stroke: 76.0mm 3.0in
Valve type/No: Overhead 12
Transmission: Manual with overdrive
No. of forward speeds: 6
Wheels driven: Rear
Springs F/R: Coil/Leaf
Brakes F/R: Disc/Drum
Steering: Rack & pinion
Wheelbase: 232.4cm 91.5in
Track F: 124.5cm 49.0in
Track R: 123.2cm 48.5in
Length: 388.6cm 153.0in
Width: 152.4cm 60.0in
Height: 133.4cm 52.5in
Ground clearance: 17.0cm 6.7in
Kerb weight: 985.2kg 2170.0lb
Fuel: 39.8L 8.8gal 10.5galUS

4543 Triumph

1500
1970 UK
88.0mph 141.6kmh
0-50mph 80.5kmh: 11.7secs
0-60mph 96.5kmh: 17.1secs
0-1/4 mile: 20.7secs
0-1km: 39.0secs
61.0bhp 45.5kW 61.8PS
@ 5000rpm
81.0lbft 109.8Nm @ 2700rpm
65.4bhp/ton 64.3bhp/tonne
40.9bhp/L 30.5kW/L 41.4PS/L
47.8ft/sec 14.6m/sec
16.1mph 25.9kmh/1000rpm
26.6mpg 22.1mpgUS 10.6L/100km
Petrol 4-stroke piston
1493cc 91.1cu in
In-line 4 1 Carburettor
Compression ratio: 8.5:1
Bore: 73.7mm 2.9in
Stroke: 87.5mm 3.4in
Valve type/No: Overhead 8
Transmission: Manual
No. of forward speeds: 4
Wheels driven: Front
Springs F/R: Coil/Coil
Brake system: PA
Brakes F/R: Disc/Drum
Steering: Rack & pinion
Wheelbase: 245.4cm 96.6in
Track F: 135.9cm 53.5in
Track R: 128.3cm 50.5in
Length: 411.5cm 162.0in
Width: 157.5cm 62.0in
Height: 137.2cm 54.0in
Ground clearance: 15.2cm 6.0in
Kerb weight: 948.4kg 2089.0lb
Fuel: 56.9L 12.5gal 15.0galUS

4544 Triumph

Stag
1970 UK
117.0mph 188.3kmh
0-50mph 80.5kmh: 8.1secs
0-60mph 96.5kmh: 11.6secs
0-1/4 mile: 18.2secs
0-1km: 33.4secs
145.0bhp 108.1kW 147.0PS
@ 5500rpm
170.0lbft 230.4Nm @ 3500rpm
115.8bhp/ton 113.9bhp/tonne
48.4bhp/L 36.1kW/L 49.0PS/L
38.8ft/sec 11.8m/sec
24.1mph 38.8kmh/1000rpm
20.6mpg 17.2mpgUS 13.7L/100km
Petrol 4-stroke piston
2997cc 182.9cu in
Vee 8 2 Carburettor
Compression ratio: 8.8:1
Bore: 86.0mm 3.4in
Stroke: 64.5mm 2.5in
Valve type/No: Overhead 16
Transmission: Manual with overdrive
No. of forward speeds: 6
Wheels driven: Rear
Springs F/R: Coil/Coil
Brake system: PA
Brakes F/R: Disc/Drum
Steering: Rack & pinion PA
Wheelbase: 254.0cm 100.0in
Track F: 133.4cm 52.5in
Track R: 134.1cm 52.8in
Length: 441.2cm 173.7in
Width: 161.3cm 63.5in
Height: 130.8cm 51.5in
Ground clearance: 15.2cm 6.0in
Kerb weight: 1273.5kg 2805.0lb
Fuel: 63.7L 14.0gal 16.8galUS

4545 Triumph

Toledo
1970 UK
86.0mph 138.4kmh
0-50mph 80.5kmh: 12.1secs
0-60mph 96.5kmh: 17.6secs
0-1/4 mile: 21.1secs
0-1km: 40.2secs
58.0bhp 43.2kW 58.8PS
@ 5300rpm
70.0lbft 94.9Nm @ 3000rpm
70.3bhp/ton 69.1bhp/tonne
44.7bhp/L 33.4kW/L 45.4PS/L
44.0ft/sec 13.4m/sec
15.4mph 24.8kmh/1000rpm
30.3mpg 25.2mpgUS 9.3L/100km
Petrol 4-stroke piston
1296cc 79.1cu in
In-line 4 1 Carburettor
Compression ratio: 8.5:1
Bore: 73.7mm 2.9in
Stroke: 76.0mm 3.0in
Valve type/No: Overhead 8
Transmission: Manual
No. of forward speeds: 4
Wheels driven: Rear
Springs F/R: Coil/Coil
Brakes F/R: Drum/Drum
Steering: Rack & pinion
Wheelbase: 245.4cm 96.6in
Track F: 134.6cm 53.0in
Track R: 127.0cm 50.0in
Length: 397.8cm 156.6in
Width: 156.7cm 61.7in
Height: 137.2cm 54.0in
Ground clearance: 14.0cm 5.5in
Kerb weight: 839.0kg 1848.0lb
Fuel: 47.8L 10.5gal 12.6galUS

4546 Triumph

TR6
1970 UK
109.0mph 175.4kmh
0-60mph 96.5kmh: 10.7secs
0-1/4 mile: 17.9secs
104.0bhp 77.5kW 105.4PS
@ 4500rpm
142.0lbft 192.4Nm @ 3000rpm
98.7bhp/ton 97.1bhp/tonne
41.6bhp/L 31.0kW/L 42.2PS/L
46.7ft/sec 14.2m/sec
28.8mpg 24.0mpgUS 9.8L/100km
Petrol 4-stroke piston
2498cc 152.4cu in
In-line 6
Bore: 74.7mm 2.9in
Stroke: 95.0mm 3.7in
Valve type/No: Overhead 12
Transmission: Manual
No. of forward speeds: 4
Wheels driven: Rear
Brakes F/R: Disc/Drum
Wheelbase: 223.5cm 88.0in
Track F: 127.5cm 50.2in
Track R: 126.5cm 49.8in
Length: 396.2cm 156.0in
Width: 147.3cm 58.0in
Height: 127.0cm 50.0in
Kerb weight: 1071.4kg 2360.0lb
Fuel: 51.1L 11.2gal 13.5galUS

4547 Triumph

GT6 Mk III
1971 UK
112.0mph 180.2kmh
0-50mph 80.5kmh: 7.7secs
0-60mph 96.5kmh: 10.1secs
0-1/4 mile: 17.4secs
0-1km: 32.5secs
98.0bhp 73.1kW 99.4PS
@ 5300rpm
108.3lbft 146.7Nm @ 3000rpm
108.5bhp/ton 106.7bhp/tonne
49.0bhp/L 36.6kW/L 49.7PS/L
44.0ft/sec 13.4m/sec
20.1mph 32.3kmh/1000rpm
27.6mpg 23.0mpgUS 10.2L/100km
Petrol 4-stroke piston
1998cc 121.9cu in
In-line 6 2 Carburettor
Compression ratio: 9.2:1
Bore: 74.7mm 2.9in
Stroke: 76.0mm 3.0in
Valve type/No: Overhead 12
Transmission: Manual
No. of forward speeds: 4
Wheels driven: Rear
Springs F/R: Coil/Leaf
Brakes F/R: Disc/Drum
Steering: Rack & pinion
Wheelbase: 210.8cm 83.0in
Track F: 127.0cm 50.0in
Track R: 121.9cm 48.0in
Length: 383.5cm 151.0in
Width: 144.8cm 57.0in
Height: 119.4cm 47.0in
Ground clearance: 14.0cm 5.5in
Kerb weight: 918.4kg 2023.0lb
Fuel: 44.4L 9.7gal 11.7galUS

4548 Triumph

Spitfire 4
1971 UK
93.0mph 149.6kmh
0-50mph 80.5kmh: 11.0secs
0-60mph 96.5kmh: 16.2secs
0-1/4 mile: 20.6secs
0-1km: 37.9secs
63.0bhp 47.0kW 63.9PS
@ 6000rpm
69.0lbft 93.5Nm @ 3500rpm
82.2bhp/ton 80.8bhp/tonne
48.6bhp/L 36.2kW/L 49.3PS/L
49.8ft/sec 15.2m/sec
20.8mph 33.5kmh/1000rpm
32.1mpg 26.7mpgUS 8.8L/100km
Petrol 4-stroke piston
1296cc 79.1cu in
In-line 4 2 Carburettor
Compression ratio: 9.0:1
Bore: 73.7mm 2.9in
Stroke: 76.0mm 3.0in
Valve type/No: Overhead 8
Transmission: Manual with overdrive
No. of forward speeds: 6
Wheels driven: Rear
Springs F/R: Coil/Leaf
Brakes F/R: Disc/Drum
Steering: Rack & pinion
Wheelbase: 210.8cm 83.0in
Track F: 124.5cm 49.0in
Track R: 121.9cm 48.0in
Length: 381.0cm 150.0in
Width: 147.3cm 58.0in
Height: 114.3cm 45.0in
Ground clearance: 12.7cm 5.0in
Kerb weight: 779.5kg 1717.0lb
Fuel: 39.8L 8.8gal 10.5galUS

4549 Triumph

Spitfire Mk IV
1971 UK
86.0mph 138.4kmh
0-50mph 80.5kmh: 11.3secs
0-60mph 96.5kmh: 15.9secs
0-1/4 mile: 21.0secs
68.0bhp 50.7kW 68.9PS
@ 5500rpm
73.0lbft 98.9Nm @ 3000rpm
84.9bhp/ton 83.4bhp/tonne
52.5bhp/L 39.1kW/L 53.2PS/L
45.7ft/sec 13.9m/sec
17.5mph 28.2kmh/1000rpm
36.4mpg 30.3mpgUS 7.8L/100km
Petrol 4-stroke piston
1296cc 79.1cu in
In-line 4
Compression ratio: 9.0:1
Bore: 73.7mm 2.9in
Stroke: 76.0mm 3.0in
Valve type/No: Overhead 8
Transmission: Manual
No. of forward speeds: 4
Wheels driven: Rear
Brakes F/R: Disc/Drum
Steering: Rack & pinion
Wheelbase: 210.8cm 83.0in
Track F: 124.5cm 49.0in
Track R: 121.9cm 48.0in
Length: 378.5cm 149.0in
Width: 148.6cm 58.5in
Height: 120.7cm 47.5in
Kerb weight: 814.9kg 1795.0lb
Fuel: 37.5L 8.2gal 9.9galUS

4550 Triumph

Stag
1971 UK
112.0mph 180.2kmh
0-50mph 80.5kmh: 8.5secs
0-60mph 96.5kmh: 11.5secs
0-1/4 mile: 18.5secs
145.0bhp 108.1kW 147.0PS
@ 5500rpm
170.0lbft 230.4Nm @ 3500rpm
116.2bhp/ton 114.3bhp/tonne
48.4bhp/L 36.1kW/L 49.0PS/L
38.8ft/sec 11.8m/sec
20.1mph 32.3kmh/1000rpm
21.5mpg 17.9mpgUS 13.1L/100km
Petrol 4-stroke piston
2997cc 182.9cu in
Vee 8 2 Carburettor
Compression ratio: 8.8:1
Bore: 86.0mm 3.4in
Stroke: 64.5mm 2.5in
Valve type/No: Overhead 16
Transmission: Automatic
No. of forward speeds: 3
Wheels driven: Rear
Springs F/R: Coil/Coil
Brake system: PA
Brakes F/R: Disc/Drum
Steering: Rack & pinion PA
Wheelbase: 254.0cm 100.0in
Track F: 133.4cm 52.5in
Track R: 134.4cm 52.9in
Length: 441.5cm 173.8in
Width: 161.3cm 63.5in
Height: 125.7cm 49.5in
Ground clearance: 15.7cm 6.2in
Kerb weight: 1268.9kg 2795.0lb
Fuel: 63.6L 14.0gal 16.8galUS

4551 Triumph

Stag Automatic
1971 UK
113.0mph 181.8kmh
0-50mph 80.5kmh: 7.9secs
0-60mph 96.5kmh: 10.4secs
0-1/4 mile: 17.9secs
0-1km: 32.6secs
145.0bhp 108.1kW 147.0PS
@ 5500rpm
170.0lbft 230.4Nm @ 3500rpm
114.6bhp/ton 112.7bhp/tonne
48.4bhp/L 36.1kW/L 49.0PS/L
38.8ft/sec 11.8m/sec
19.8mph 31.9kmh/1000rpm
17.2mpg 14.3mpgUS 16.4L/100km

Petrol 4-stroke piston
2997cc 182.9cu in
Vee 8 2 Carburettor
Compression ratio: 8.8:1
Bore: 86.0mm 3.4in
Stroke: 64.5mm 2.5in
Valve type/No: Overhead 16
Transmission: Automatic
No. of forward speeds: 3
Wheels driven: Rear
Springs F/R: Coil/Coil
Brake system: PA
Brakes F/R: Disc/Drum
Steering: Rack & pinion PA
Wheelbase: 254.0cm 100.0in
Track F: 133.4cm 52.5in
Track R: 134.1cm 52.8in
Length: 441.2cm 173.7in
Width: 161.3cm 63.5in
Height: 130.8cm 51.5in
Ground clearance: 15.2cm 6.0in
Kerb weight: 1287.1kg 2835.0lb
Fuel: 63.7L 14.0gal 16.8galUS

4552 Triumph

2.5PI Mk II
1972 UK
107.0mph 172.2kmh
0-50mph 80.5kmh: 7.9secs
0-60mph 96.5kmh: 11.4secs
0-1/4 mile: 18.0secs
0-1km: 33.6secs
132.0bhp 98.4kW 133.8PS
@ 5450rpm
153.0lbft 207.3Nm @ 2000rpm
105.9bhp/ton 104.1bhp/tonne
52.8bhp/L 39.4kW/L 53.6PS/L
56.6ft/sec 17.3m/sec
24.6mph 39.6kmh/1000rpm
20.2mpg 16.8mpgUS 14.0L/100km
Petrol 4-stroke piston
2498cc 152.4cu in
In-line 6 fuel injection
Compression ratio: 9.5:1
Bore: 74.7mm 2.9in
Stroke: 95.0mm 3.7in
Valve type/No: Overhead 12
Transmission: Manual with overdrive
No. of forward speeds: 6
Wheels driven: Rear
Springs F/R: Coil/Coil
Brake system: PA
Brakes F/R: Disc/Drum
Steering: Rack & pinion
Wheelbase: 269.2cm 106.0in
Track F: 133.4cm 52.5in
Track R: 134.4cm 52.9in
Length: 447.0cm 176.0in
Width: 165.1cm 65.0in
Height: 142.2cm 56.0in
Ground clearance: 15.2cm 6.0in
Kerb weight: 1268.0kg 2793.0lb
Fuel: 63.7L 14.0gal 16.8galUS

4553 Triumph

Dolomite
1972 UK
103.0mph 165.7kmh
0-50mph 80.5kmh: 8.3secs
0-60mph 96.5kmh: 11.6secs
0-1/4 mile: 18.4secs
0-1km: 34.5secs
91.0bhp 67.9kW 92.3PS
@ 5200rpm
105.0lbft 142.3Nm @ 3500rpm
95.8bhp/ton 94.2bhp/tonne
49.1bhp/L 36.6kW/L 49.8PS/L
44.3ft/sec 13.5m/sec
18.0mph 29.0kmh/1000rpm
27.0mpg 22.5mpgUS 10.5L/100km
Petrol 4-stroke piston
1854cc 113.1cu in
In-line 4 2 Carburettor
Compression ratio: 9.0:1
Bore: 87.0mm 3.4in
Stroke: 78.0mm 3.1in
Valve type/No: Overhead 8
Transmission: Manual
No. of forward speeds: 4
Wheels driven: Rear
Springs F/R: Coil/Coil
Brake system: PA
Brakes F/R: Disc/Drum
Steering: Rack & pinion
Wheelbase: 245.4cm 96.6in
Track F: 135.9cm 53.5in
Track R: 128.3cm 50.5in
Length: 411.5cm 162.0in
Width: 157.5cm 62.0in
Height: 137.2cm 54.0in
Ground clearance: 15.2cm 6.0in
Kerb weight: 965.7kg 2127.0lb
Fuel: 56.9L 12.5gal 15.0galUS

4554 Triumph

1500TC
1973 UK
93.0mph 149.6kmh
0-50mph 80.5kmh: 8.8secs
0-60mph 96.5kmh: 13.2secs
0-1/4 mile: 19.4secs
0-1km: 36.6secs
64.0bhp 47.7kW 64.9PS
@ 5000rpm
77.5lbft 105.0Nm @ 3000rpm
67.4bhp/ton 66.2bhp/tonne
42.9bhp/L 32.0kW/L 43.5PS/L
47.8ft/sec 14.6m/sec
16.9mph 27.2kmh/1000rpm
27.0mpg 22.5mpgUS 10.5L/100km
Petrol 4-stroke piston
1493cc 91.1cu in
In-line 4 2 Carburettor
Compression ratio: 9.0:1
Bore: 73.7mm 2.9in
Stroke: 87.5mm 3.4in
Valve type/No: Overhead 8
Transmission: Manual
No. of forward speeds: 4
Wheels driven: Rear
Springs F/R: Coil/Coil
Brake system: PA
Brakes F/R: Disc/Drum
Steering: Rack & pinion
Wheelbase: 245.4cm 96.6in
Track F: 135.6cm 53.4in
Track R: 128.0cm 50.4in
Length: 411.5cm 162.0in
Width: 156.7cm 61.7in
Height: 137.2cm 54.0in
Ground clearance: 15.2cm 6.0in
Kerb weight: 966.1kg 2128.0lb
Fuel: 56.9L 12.5gal 15.0galUS

4555 Triumph

Dolomite Automatic
1973 UK
97.0mph 156.1kmh
0-50mph 80.5kmh: 9.6secs
0-60mph 96.5kmh: 13.5secs
0-1/4 mile: 18.5secs
0-1km: 35.7secs
91.0bhp 67.9kW 92.3PS
@ 5200rpm
105.0lbft 142.3Nm @ 3500rpm
93.6bhp/ton 92.0bhp/tonne
49.1bhp/L 36.6kW/L 49.8PS/L
44.3ft/sec 13.5m/sec
20.0mph 32.2kmh/1000rpm
25.9mpg 21.6mpgUS 10.9L/100km
Petrol 4-stroke piston
1854cc 113.1cu in
In-line 4 2 Carburettor
Compression ratio: 9.0:1
Bore: 87.0mm 3.4in
Stroke: 78.0mm 3.1in
Valve type/No: Overhead 8
Transmission: Automatic
No. of forward speeds: 3
Wheels driven: Rear
Springs F/R: Coil/Coil
Brake system: PA
Brakes F/R: Disc/Drum
Steering: Rack & pinion
Wheelbase: 245.4cm 96.6in
Track F: 135.1cm 53.2in
Track R: 127.0cm 50.0in
Length: 411.5cm 162.0in
Width: 156.7cm 61.7in
Height: 137.2cm 54.0in
Ground clearance: 15.2cm 6.0in
Kerb weight: 988.8kg 2178.0lb
Fuel: 56.9L 12.5gal 15.0galUS

4556 Triumph

GT6
1973 UK
104.0mph 167.3kmh
0-50mph 80.5kmh: 9.3secs
0-60mph 96.5kmh: 12.6secs
0-1/4 mile: 19.6secs
79.0bhp 58.9kW 80.1PS
@ 4900rpm
97.0lbft 131.4Nm @ 2700rpm
87.4bhp/ton 85.9bhp/tonne
39.5bhp/L 29.5kW/L 40.1PS/L
40.7ft/sec 12.4m/sec
20.2mph 32.5kmh/1000rpm
25.2mpg 21.0mpgUS 11.2L/100km
Petrol 4-stroke piston
1998cc 121.9cu in
In-line 6
Compression ratio: 8.0:1
Bore: 74.7mm 2.9in
Stroke: 76.0mm 3.0in
Valve type/No: Overhead 12
Transmission: Manual
No. of forward speeds: 4
Wheels driven: Rear
Springs F/R: Coil/Leaf
Brakes F/R: Disc/Drum
Steering: Rack & pinion
Wheelbase: 210.8cm 83.0in
Track F: 124.5cm 49.0in
Track R: 129.5cm 51.0in
Length: 378.5cm 149.0in
Width: 148.6cm 58.5in
Height: 120.7cm 47.5in
Kerb weight: 919.3kg 2025.0lb
Fuel: 44.3L 9.7gal 11.7galUS

4557 Triumph

Spitfire
1973 UK
86.0mph 138.4kmh
0-50mph 80.5kmh: 11.2secs
0-60mph 96.5kmh: 16.0secs
0-1/4 mile: 20.2secs
57.0bhp 42.5kW 57.8PS
@ 5000rpm
73.0lbft 98.9Nm @ 3000rpm
73.6bhp/ton 72.4bhp/tonne
38.2bhp/L 28.5kW/L 38.7PS/L
Petrol 4-stroke piston
1493cc 91.1cu in
In-line 4
Transmission: Manual
No. of forward speeds: 4
Wheels driven: Rear
Springs F/R: Coil/Leaf
Brakes F/R: Disc/Drum
Wheelbase: 210.8cm 83.0in
Track F: 124.5cm 49.0in
Track R: 127.0cm 50.0in
Length: 378.5cm 149.0in
Width: 148.6cm 58.5in
Height: 120.7cm 47.5in
Kerb weight: 787.7kg 1735.0lb

4558 Triumph

Spitfire 1500
1973 UK
94.0mph 151.2kmh
0-50mph 80.5kmh: 10.9secs
0-60mph 96.5kmh: 15.4secs
0-1/4 mile: 20.2secs
57.0bhp 42.5kW 57.8PS
@ 5000rpm
73.0lbft 98.9Nm @ 3000rpm
73.6bhp/ton 72.4bhp/tonne
38.2bhp/L 28.5kW/L 38.7PS/L
47.8ft/sec 14.6m/sec
17.4mph 28.0kmh/1000rpm
30.0mpg 25.0mpgUS 9.4L/100km
Petrol 4-stroke piston
1493cc 91.1cu in
In-line 4 1 Carburettor
Compression ratio: 8.0:1
Bore: 73.7mm 2.9in
Stroke: 87.5mm 3.4in
Valve type/No: Overhead 8
Transmission: Manual
No. of forward speeds: 4
Wheels driven: Rear
Springs F/R: Coil/Leaf
Brakes F/R: Disc/Drum
Steering: Rack & pinion
Wheelbase: 210.8cm 83.0in
Track F: 124.5cm 49.0in
Track R: 127.0cm 50.0in
Length: 378.5cm 149.0in
Width: 148.6cm 58.5in
Height: 120.7cm 47.5in
Ground clearance: 10.2cm 4.0in
Kerb weight: 787.7kg 1735.0lb
Fuel: 37.5L 8.2gal 9.9galUS

4559 Triumph

TR6
1973 UK
106.0mph 170.6kmh
0-50mph 80.5kmh: 7.8secs
0-60mph 96.5kmh: 11.6secs
0-1/4 mile: 18.2secs
106.0bhp 79.0kW 107.5PS
@ 4900rpm
133.0lbft 180.2Nm @ 3000rpm
100.6bhp/ton 98.9bhp/tonne
42.4bhp/L 31.6kW/L 43.0PS/L
50.9ft/sec 15.5m/sec
20.9mph 33.6kmh/1000rpm
21.6mpg 18.0mpgUS 13.1L/100km
Petrol 4-stroke piston
2498cc 152.4cu in
In-line 6 2 Carburettor
Compression ratio: 7.7:1
Bore: 74.7mm 2.9in
Stroke: 95.0mm 3.7in
Valve type/No: Overhead 12
Transmission: Manual
No. of forward speeds: 4
Wheels driven: Rear
Springs F/R: Coil/Coil
Brakes F/R: Disc/Drum
Steering: Rack & pinion
Wheelbase: 223.5cm 88.0in
Track F: 127.5cm 50.2in
Track R: 126.5cm 49.8in
Length: 396.2cm 156.0in
Width: 147.3cm 58.0in
Height: 127.0cm 50.0in
Ground clearance: 15.2cm 6.0in
Kerb weight: 1071.4kg 2360.0lb
Fuel: 54.9L 12.1gal 14.5galUS

4560 Triumph

2500TC
1974 UK
108.0mph 173.8kmh
0-50mph 80.5kmh: 8.2secs
0-60mph 96.5kmh: 11.8secs
0-1/4 mile: 18.7secs
0-1km: 34.7secs
99.0bhp 73.8kW 100.4PS
@ 4700rpm
133.0lbft 180.2Nm @ 3000rpm
82.7bhp/ton 81.3bhp/tonne
39.6bhp/L 29.5kW/L 40.2PS/L
48.8ft/sec 14.9m/sec
25.0mph 40.2kmh/1000rpm
24.1mpg 20.1mpgUS 11.7L/100km
Petrol 4-stroke piston
2498cc 152.4cu in
In-line 6 2 Carburettor
Compression ratio: 8.5:1
Bore: 74.7mm 2.9in
Stroke: 95.0mm 3.7in
Valve type/No: Overhead 12
Transmission: Manual with overdrive
No. of forward speeds: 6
Wheels driven: Rear
Springs F/R: Coil/Coil
Brake system: PA
Brakes F/R: Disc/Drum
Steering: Rack & pinion
Wheelbase: 269.2cm 106.0in
Track F: 133.4cm 52.5in
Track R: 134.4cm 52.9in
Length: 463.0cm 182.3in
Width: 165.1cm 65.0in
Height: 142.2cm 56.0in
Ground clearance: 15.2cm 6.0in
Kerb weight: 1217.2kg 2681.0lb
Fuel: 63.7L 14.0gal 16.8galUS

4561 Triumph

Spitfire
1974 UK
94.0mph 151.2kmh
0-60mph 96.5kmh: 15.4secs
0-1/4 mile: 20.2secs
57.0bhp 42.5kW 57.8PS
@ 5000rpm
73.0lbft 98.9Nm @ 3000rpm
70.9bhp/ton 69.7bhp/tonne
38.2bhp/L 28.5kW/L 38.7PS/L
17.4mph 28.0kmh/1000rpm
30.0mpg 25.0mpgUS 9.4L/100km
Petrol 4-stroke piston
1493cc 91.1cu in
In-line 4
Valve type/No: Overhead 8
Transmission: Manual
No. of forward speeds: 4
Wheels driven: Rear
Springs F/R: Coil/Leaf

Brakes F/R: Disc/Drum
Steering: Rack & pinion
Wheelbase: 210.8cm 83.0in
Track F: 124.5cm 49.0in
Track R: 127.0cm 50.0in
Length: 394.2cm 155.2in
Width: 148.6cm 58.5in
Height: 120.7cm 47.5in
Kerb weight: 817.2kg 1800.0lb
Fuel: 37.5L 8.2gal 9.9galUS

4562 Triumph

Toledo
1974 UK
90.0mph 144.8kmh
0-50mph 80.5kmh: 11.6secs
0-60mph 96.5kmh: 17.1secs
0-1/4 mile: 20.9secs
0-1km: 39.6secs
58.0bhp 43.2kW 58.8PS
@ 5500rpm
68.0lbft 92.1Nm @ 3300rpm
68.0bhp/ton 66.8bhp/tonne
44.7bhp/L 33.4kW/L 45.4PS/L
45.7ft/sec 13.9m/sec
15.9mph 25.6kmh/1000rpm
28.8mpg 24.0mpgUS 9.8L/100km
Petrol 4-stroke piston
1296cc 79.1cu in
In-line 4 1 Carburettor
Compression ratio: 8.5:1
Bore: 73.7mm 2.9in
Stroke: 76.0mm 3.0in
Valve type/No: Overhead 8
Transmission: Manual
No. of forward speeds: 4
Wheels driven: Rear
Springs F/R: Coil/Coil
Brake system: PA
Brakes F/R: Disc/Drum
Steering: Rack & pinion
Wheelbase: 245.4cm 96.6in
Track F: 134.6cm 53.0in
Track R: 127.0cm 50.0in
Length: 397.8cm 156.6in
Width: 156.7cm 61.7in
Height: 137.2cm 54.0in
Ground clearance: 14.0cm 5.5in
Kerb weight: 867.6kg 1911.0lb
Fuel: 47.8L 10.5gal 12.6galUS

4563 Triumph

2500S
1975 UK
108.0mph 173.8kmh
0-50mph 80.5kmh: 7.4secs
0-60mph 96.5kmh: 10.4secs
0-1/4 mile: 17.8secs
0-1km: 33.3secs
106.0bhp 79.0kW 107.5PS
@ 4700rpm
139.0lbft 188.3Nm @ 2750rpm
91.0bhp/ton 89.5bhp/tonne
42.4bhp/L 31.6kW/L 43.0PS/L
48.8ft/sec 14.9m/sec
26.7mph 43.0kmh/1000rpm
24.8mpg 20.7mpgUS 11.4L/100km
Petrol 4-stroke piston
2498cc 152.4cu in
In-line 6 2 Carburettor
Compression ratio: 8.5:1
Bore: 74.7mm 2.9in
Stroke: 95.0mm 3.7in
Valve type/No: Overhead 12
Transmission: Manual with overdrive
No. of forward speeds: 6
Wheels driven: Rear
Springs F/R: Coil/Coil
Brake system: PA
Brakes F/R: Disc/Drum
Steering: Rack & pinion
Wheelbase: 269.2cm 106.0in
Track F: 133.4cm 52.5in
Track R: 134.4cm 52.9in
Length: 463.0cm 182.3in
Width: 165.1cm 65.0in
Height: 142.2cm 56.0in
Ground clearance: 15.2cm 6.0in
Kerb weight: 1184.5kg 2609.0lb
Fuel: 63.7L 14.0gal 16.8galUS

4564 Triumph

Dolomite
1975 UK
102.0mph 164.1kmh
0-50mph 80.5kmh: 8.5secs
0-60mph 96.5kmh: 11.8secs
0-1/4 mile: 18.7secs
0-1km: 34.5secs
91.0bhp 67.9kW 92.3PS
@ 5200rpm
105.0lbft 142.3Nm @ 3500rpm
96.6bhp/ton 95.0bhp/tonne
49.1bhp/L 36.6kW/L 49.8PS/L
44.3ft/sec 13.5m/sec
22.6mph 36.4kmh/1000rpm
27.7mpg 23.1mpgUS 10.2L/100km
Petrol 4-stroke piston
1854cc 113.1cu in
In-line 4 2 Carburettor
Compression ratio: 9.0:1
Bore: 87.0mm 3.4in
Stroke: 78.0mm 3.1in
Valve type/No: Overhead 8
Transmission: Manual with overdrive
No. of forward speeds: 6
Wheels driven: Rear
Springs F/R: Coil/Coil
Brake system: PA
Brakes F/R: Disc/Drum
Steering: Rack & pinion
Wheelbase: 245.4cm 96.6in
Track F: 135.1cm 53.2in
Track R: 127.0cm 50.0in
Length: 411.5cm 162.0in
Width: 158.8cm 62.5in
Height: 137.2cm 54.0in
Ground clearance: 11.9cm 4.7in
Kerb weight: 957.9kg 2110.0lb
Fuel: 56.9L 12.5gal 15.0galUS

4565 Triumph

Dolomite Sprint
1975 UK
117.0mph 188.3kmh
0-50mph 80.5kmh: 6.3secs
0-60mph 96.5kmh: 8.7secs
0-1/4 mile: 16.7secs
0-1km: 31.0secs
127.0bhp 94.7kW 128.8PS
@ 5700rpm
124.0lbft 168.0Nm @ 4500rpm
128.5bhp/ton 126.3bhp/tonne
63.6bhp/L 47.4kW/L 64.4PS/L
48.6ft/sec 14.8m/sec
23.7mph 38.1kmh/1000rpm
23.6mpg 19.7mpgUS 12.0L/100km
Petrol 4-stroke piston
1998cc 121.9cu in
In-line 4 2 Carburettor
Compression ratio: 9.5:1
Bore: 90.3mm 3.6in
Stroke: 78.0mm 3.1in
Valve type/No: Overhead 16
Transmission: Manual with overdrive
No. of forward speeds: 6
Wheels driven: Rear
Springs F/R: Coil/Coil
Brake system: PA
Brakes F/R: Disc/Drum
Steering: Rack & pinion
Wheelbase: 245.4cm 96.6in
Track F: 135.6cm 53.4in
Track R: 128.0cm 50.4in
Length: 411.5cm 162.0in
Width: 156.7cm 61.7in
Height: 137.2cm 54.0in
Ground clearance: 15.2cm 6.0in
Kerb weight: 1005.2kg 2214.0lb
Fuel: 56.9L 12.5gal 15.0galUS

4566 Triumph

Spitfire 1500
1975 UK
101.0mph 162.5kmh
0-50mph 80.5kmh: 8.8secs
0-60mph 96.5kmh: 13.2secs
0-1/4 mile: 19.1secs
0-1km: 35.8secs
71.0bhp 52.9kW 72.0PS
@ 5500rpm
82.0lbft 111.1Nm @ 3000rpm
89.3bhp/ton 87.9bhp/tonne
47.6bhp/L 35.5kW/L 48.2PS/L
52.6ft/sec 16.0m/sec
22.6mph 36.4kmh/1000rpm
29.2mpg 24.3mpgUS 9.7L/100km
Petrol 4-stroke piston
1493cc 91.1cu in
In-line 4 2 Carburettor
Compression ratio: 9.0:1
Bore: 73.7mm 2.9in
Stroke: 87.5mm 3.4in
Valve type/No: Overhead 8
Transmission: Manual with overdrive
No. of forward speeds: 6
Wheels driven: Rear
Springs F/R: Coil/Leaf
Brakes F/R: Disc/Drum
Steering: Rack & pinion
Wheelbase: 210.8cm 83.0in
Track F: 124.5cm 49.0in
Track R: 121.9cm 48.0in
Length: 378.5cm 149.0in
Width: 147.3cm 58.0in
Height: 114.3cm 45.0in
Ground clearance: 12.7cm 5.0in
Kerb weight: 808.1kg 1780.0lb
Fuel: 33.0L 7.2gal 8.7galUS

4567 Triumph

TR7
1975 UK
108.0mph 173.8kmh
0-50mph 80.5kmh: 8.6secs
0-60mph 96.5kmh: 11.3secs
0-1/4 mile: 18.5secs
90.0bhp 67.1kW 91.2PS
@ 5000rpm
105.0lbft 142.3Nm @ 3000rpm
85.6bhp/ton 84.2bhp/tonne
45.0bhp/L 33.6kW/L 45.7PS/L
42.6ft/sec 13.0m/sec
18.2mph 29.3kmh/1000rpm
33.0mpg 27.5mpgUS 8.6L/100km
Petrol 4-stroke piston
1998cc 121.9cu in
In-line 4 2 Carburettor
Compression ratio: 8.0:1
Bore: 90.3mm 3.6in
Stroke: 78.0mm 3.1in
Valve type/No: Overhead 8
Transmission: Manual
No. of forward speeds: 4
Wheels driven: Rear
Springs F/R: Coil/Coil
Brake system: PA
Brakes F/R: Disc/Drum
Steering: Rack & pinion
Wheelbase: 215.9cm 85.0in
Track F: 141.0cm 55.5in
Track R: 140.5cm 55.3in
Length: 417.8cm 164.5in
Width: 168.1cm 66.2in
Height: 126.7cm 49.9in
Ground clearance: 11.4cm 4.5in
Kerb weight: 1069.2kg 2355.0lb
Fuel: 54.9L 12.1gal 14.5galUS

4568 Triumph

Dolomite 1500HL
1976 UK
95.0mph 152.9kmh
0-50mph 80.5kmh: 9.4secs
0-60mph 96.5kmh: 14.2secs
0-1/4 mile: 19.2secs
0-1km: 36.8secs
71.0bhp 52.9kW 72.0PS
@ 5500rpm
82.0lbft 111.1Nm @ 3000rpm
73.6bhp/ton 72.4bhp/tonne
47.6bhp/L 35.5kW/L 48.2PS/L
52.6ft/sec 16.0m/sec
21.1mph 33.9kmh/1000rpm
27.1mpg 22.6mpgUS 10.4L/100km
Petrol 4-stroke piston
1493cc 91.1cu in
In-line 4 2 Carburettor
Compression ratio: 9.0:1
Bore: 73.7mm 2.9in
Stroke: 87.5mm 3.4in
Valve type/No: Overhead 8
Transmission: Manual with overdrive
No. of forward speeds: 6
Wheels driven: Rear
Springs F/R: Coil/Coil
Brake system: PA
Brakes F/R: Disc/Drum
Steering: Rack & pinion
Wheelbase: 245.4cm 96.6in
Track F: 135.1cm 53.2in
Track R: 127.0cm 50.0in
Length: 411.5cm 162.0in
Width: 156.7cm 61.7in
Height: 137.2cm 54.0in
Ground clearance: 15.2cm 6.0in
Kerb weight: 981.1kg 2161.0lb
Fuel: 56.9L 12.5gal 15.0galUS

4569 Triumph

Spitfire
1976 UK
86.0mph 138.4kmh
0-50mph 80.5kmh: 10.8secs
0-60mph 96.5kmh: 15.3secs
0-1/4 mile: 20.2secs
57.5bhp 42.9kW 58.3PS
@ 5000rpm
75.0lbft 101.6Nm @ 2500rpm
73.2bhp/ton 72.0bhp/tonne
38.5bhp/L 28.7kW/L 39.0PS/L
47.8ft/sec 14.6m/sec
30.0mpg 25.0mpgUS 9.4L/100km
Petrol 4-stroke piston
1493cc 91.1cu in
In-line 4 1 Carburettor
Compression ratio: 9.0:1
Bore: 73.7mm 2.9in
Stroke: 87.5mm 3.4in
Valve type/No: Overhead 8
Transmission: Manual
No. of forward speeds: 4
Wheels driven: Rear
Springs F/R: Coil/Leaf
Brakes F/R: Disc/Drum
Steering: Rack & pinion
Wheelbase: 210.8cm 83.0in
Track F: 124.5cm 49.0in
Track R: 127.0cm 50.0in
Length: 397.0cm 156.3in
Width: 148.6cm 58.5in
Height: 120.7cm 47.5in
Ground clearance: 12.7cm 5.0in
Kerb weight: 799.0kg 1760.0lb
Fuel: 37.5L 8.2gal 9.9galUS

4570 Triumph

TR7
1976 UK
110.0mph 177.0kmh
0-50mph 80.5kmh: 6.7secs
0-60mph 96.5kmh: 9.1secs
0-1/4 mile: 17.0secs
0-1km: 31.5secs
105.0bhp 78.3kW 106.5PS
@ 5500rpm
119.0lbft 161.2Nm @ 3500rpm
110.5bhp/ton 108.7bhp/tonne
52.5bhp/L 39.2kW/L 53.3PS/L
46.9ft/sec 14.3m/sec
17.9mph 28.8kmh/1000rpm
26.4mpg 22.0mpgUS 10.7L/100km
Petrol 4-stroke piston
1998cc 121.9cu in
In-line 4 2 Carburettor
Compression ratio: 9.2:1
Bore: 90.3mm 3.6in
Stroke: 78.0mm 3.1in
Valve type/No: Overhead 8
Transmission: Manual
No. of forward speeds: 4
Wheels driven: Rear
Springs F/R: Coil/Coil
Brake system: PA
Brakes F/R: Disc/Drum
Steering: Rack & pinion
Wheelbase: 215.9cm 85.0in
Track F: 141.0cm 55.5in
Track R: 140.5cm 55.3in
Length: 417.3cm 164.3in
Width: 168.1cm 66.2in
Height: 126.7cm 49.9in
Ground clearance: 11.4cm 4.5in
Kerb weight: 966.1kg 2128.0lb
Fuel: 54.6L 12.0gal 14.4galUS

4571 Triumph

TR7
1977 UK
110.0mph 177.0kmh
0-50mph 80.5kmh: 7.8secs
0-60mph 96.5kmh: 11.2secs
0-1/4 mile: 18.2secs
86.0bhp 64.1kW 87.2PS
@ 5500rpm
103.0lbft 139.6Nm @ 3250rpm
78.0bhp/ton 76.7bhp/tonne
43.0bhp/L 32.1kW/L 43.6PS/L
46.9ft/sec 14.3m/sec
20.8mph 33.5kmh/1000rpm
33.0mpg 27.5mpgUS 8.6L/100km
Petrol 4-stroke piston
1998cc 121.9cu in
In-line 4 2 Carburettor
Compression ratio: 8.0:1
Bore: 90.3mm 3.6in

Stroke: 78.0mm 3.1in
Valve type/No: Overhead 8
Transmission: Manual
No. of forward speeds: 5
Wheels driven: Rear
Springs F/R: Coil/Coil
Brake system: PA
Brakes F/R: Disc/Drum
Steering: Rack & pinion
Wheelbase: 215.9cm 85.0in
Track F: 141.0cm 55.5in
Track R: 140.5cm 55.3in
Length: 417.8cm 164.5in
Width: 168.1cm 66.2in
Height: 126.7cm 49.9in
Ground clearance: 11.4cm 4.5in
Kerb weight: 1121.4kg 2470.0lb
Fuel: 54.5L 12.0gal 14.4galUS

4572 Triumph

TR7 Tullius
1977 UK
132.0mph 212.4kmh
0-50mph 80.5kmh: 5.4secs
0-60mph 96.5kmh: 6.9secs
0-1/4 mile: 15.5secs
175.0bhp 130.5kW 177.4PS
@ 6800rpm
146.0lbft 197.8Nm @ 4600rpm
199.0bhp/ton 195.7bhp/tonne
85.5bhp/L 63.7kW/L 86.7PS/L
58.0ft/sec 17.7m/sec
17.4mph 28.0kmh/1000rpm
7.8mpg 6.5mpgUS 36.2L/100km
Petrol 4-stroke piston
2047cc 124.9cu in
In-line 4 2 Carburettor
Compression ratio: 11.5:1
Bore: 91.4mm 3.6in
Stroke: 78.0mm 3.1in
Valve type/No: Overhead 8
Transmission: Manual
No. of forward speeds: 4
Wheels driven: Rear
Springs F/R: Coil/Coil
Brakes F/R: Disc/Drum
Steering: Rack & pinion
Wheelbase: 215.9cm 85.0in
Track F: 146.1cm 57.5in
Track R: 145.5cm 57.3in
Length: 417.8cm 164.5in
Width: 176.5cm 69.5in
Height: 121.4cm 47.8in
Ground clearance: 7.6cm 3.0in
Kerb weight: 894.4kg 1970.0lb
Fuel: 53.0L 11.6gal 14.0galUS

4573 Triumph

Dolomite 1850HL
1979 UK
99.0mph 159.3kmh
0-50mph 80.5kmh: 9.3secs
0-60mph 96.5kmh: 12.9secs
0-1/4 mile: 18.6secs
0-1km: 35.5secs
91.0bhp 67.9kW 92.3PS
@ 5200rpm
105.0lbft 142.3Nm @ 3500rpm
95.8bhp/ton 94.2bhp/tonne
49.1bhp/L 36.6kW/L 49.8PS/L
44.3ft/sec 13.5m/sec
22.6mph 36.4kmh/1000rpm
29.9mpg 24.9mpgUS 9.4L/100km
Petrol 4-stroke piston
1854cc 113.1cu in
In-line 4 2 Carburettor
Compression ratio: 9.0:1
Bore: 87.0mm 3.4in
Stroke: 78.0mm 3.1in
Valve type/No: Overhead 8
Transmission: Manual with overdrive
No. of forward speeds: 6
Wheels driven: Rear
Springs F/R: Coil/Coil
Brake system: PA
Brakes F/R: Disc/Drum
Steering: Rack & pinion
Wheelbase: 245.4cm 96.6in
Track F: 134.9cm 53.1in
Track R: 126.7cm 49.9in
Length: 412.5cm 162.4in
Width: 158.8cm 62.5in
Height: 137.2cm 54.0in
Ground clearance: 15.2cm 6.0in
Kerb weight: 966.1kg 2128.0lb
Fuel: 56.9L 12.5gal 15.0galUS

4574 Triumph

Spitfire
1979 UK
89.0mph 143.2kmh
0-50mph 80.5kmh: 9.8secs
0-60mph 96.5kmh: 14.3secs
0-1/4 mile: 19.7secs
52.5bhp 39.1kW 53.2PS
@ 5000rpm
68.8lbft 93.2Nm @ 2500rpm
64.1bhp/ton 63.0bhp/tonne
35.2bhp/L 26.2kW/L 35.6PS/L
47.8ft/sec 14.6m/sec
17.3mph 27.8kmh/1000rpm
31.8mpg 26.5mpgUS 8.9L/100km
Petrol 4-stroke piston
1493cc 91.1cu in
In-line 4
Compression ratio: 7.5:1
Bore: 73.7mm 2.9in
Stroke: 87.5mm 3.4in
Valve type/No: Overhead 8
Transmission: Manual
No. of forward speeds: 4
Wheels driven: Rear
Springs F/R: Coil/Leaf
Brakes F/R: Disc/Drum
Steering: Rack & pinion
Wheelbase: 210.8cm 83.0in
Track F: 124.5cm 49.0in
Track R: 127.0cm 50.0in
Length: 397.0cm 156.3in
Width: 148.6cm 58.5in
Height: 115.8cm 45.6in
Kerb weight: 833.1kg 1835.0lb
Fuel: 32.9L 7.2gal 8.7galUS

4575 Triumph

TR7
1979 UK
110.0mph 177.0kmh
0-50mph 80.5kmh: 7.8secs
0-60mph 96.5kmh: 11.2secs
0-1/4 mile: 18.2secs
88.5bhp 66.0kW 89.7PS
@ 5500rpm
102.0lbft 138.2Nm @ 3250rpm
80.3bhp/ton 78.9bhp/tonne
44.3bhp/L 33.0kW/L 44.9PS/L
46.9ft/sec 14.3m/sec
20.7mph 33.3kmh/1000rpm
33.0mpg 27.5mpgUS 8.6L/100km
Petrol 4-stroke piston
1998cc 121.9cu in
In-line 4 2 Carburettor
Compression ratio: 8.0:1
Bore: 90.3mm 3.6in
Stroke: 78.0mm 3.1in
Valve type/No: Overhead 8
Transmission: Manual
No. of forward speeds: 5
Wheels driven: Rear
Springs F/R: Coil/Coil
Brake system: PA
Brakes F/R: Disc/Drum
Steering: Rack & pinion
Wheelbase: 215.9cm 85.0in
Track F: 141.0cm 55.5in
Track R: 140.5cm 55.3in
Length: 417.8cm 164.5in
Width: 168.1cm 66.2in
Height: 126.7cm 49.9in
Ground clearance: 11.4cm 4.5in
Kerb weight: 1121.4kg 2470.0lb
Fuel: 55.3L 12.1gal 14.6galUS

4576 Triumph

Spitfire
1980 UK
90.0mph 144.8kmh
0-50mph 80.5kmh: 9.8secs
0-60mph 96.5kmh: 14.3secs
0-1/4 mile: 19.7secs
53.0bhp 39.5kW 53.7PS
@ 5000rpm
69.0lbft 93.5Nm @ 2500rpm
64.7bhp/ton 63.6bhp/tonne
35.5bhp/L 26.5kW/L 36.0PS/L
47.8ft/sec 14.6m/sec
17.3mph 27.8kmh/1000rpm
28.8mpg 24.0mpgUS 9.8L/100km
Petrol 4-stroke piston
1493cc 91.1cu in
In-line 4 1 Carburettor
Compression ratio: 7.5:1
Bore: 73.7mm 2.9in
Stroke: 87.5mm 3.4in
Valve type/No: Overhead 8
Transmission: Manual with overdrive
Wheels driven: Rear
Springs F/R: Coil/Leaf
Brakes F/R: Disc/Drum
Steering: Rack & pinion
Wheelbase: 210.8cm 83.0in
Track F: 124.5cm 49.0in
Track R: 127.0cm 50.0in
Length: 400.1cm 157.5in
Width: 148.6cm 58.5in
Height: 115.8cm 45.6in
Ground clearance: 17.5cm 6.9in
Kerb weight: 833.1kg 1835.0lb
Fuel: 33.3L 7.3gal 8.8galUS

4577 Triumph

TR8
1980 UK
120.0mph 193.1kmh
0-60mph 96.5kmh: 8.4secs
0-1/4 mile: 16.3secs
137.0bhp 102.2kW 138.9PS
@ 5000rpm
165.0lbft 223.6Nm @ 3200rpm
115.6bhp/ton 113.7bhp/tonne
38.8bhp/L 29.0kW/L 39.4PS/L
38.9ft/sec 11.8m/sec
26.1mph 42.0kmh/1000rpm
18.0mpg 15.0mpgUS 15.7L/100km
Petrol 4-stroke piston
3528cc 215.2cu in
Vee 8 fuel injection
Compression ratio: 8.1:1
Bore: 88.9mm 3.5in
Stroke: 71.1mm 2.8in
Valve type/No: Overhead 16
Transmission: Manual
No. of forward speeds: 5
Wheels driven: Rear
Springs F/R: Coil/Coil
Brake system: PA
Brakes F/R: Disc/Drum
Steering: Rack & pinion PA
Wheelbase: 215.9cm 85.0in
Track F: 141.0cm 55.5in
Track R: 140.5cm 55.3in
Length: 420.1cm 165.4in
Width: 168.1cm 66.2in
Height: 125.7cm 49.5in
Ground clearance: 8.9cm 3.5in
Kerb weight: 1205.4kg 2655.0lb
Fuel: 63.6L 14.0gal 16.8galUS

4578 Triumph

TR8 Group 44
1980 UK
150.0mph 241.4kmh
0-50mph 80.5kmh: 3.6secs
0-60mph 96.5kmh: 4.3secs
0-1/4 mile: 12.7secs
360.0bhp 268.4kW 365.0PS
@ 8000rpm
310.0lbft 420.1Nm @ 5500rpm
315.0bhp/ton 309.7bhp/tonne
90.2bhp/L 67.3kW/L 91.5PS/L
68.9ft/sec 21.0m/sec
18.0mph 29.0kmh/1000rpm
3.6mpg 3.0mpgUS 78.4L/100km
Petrol 4-stroke piston
3989cc 243.4cu in
Vee 8 fuel injection
Compression ratio: 12.5:1
Bore: 89.9mm 3.5in
Stroke: 78.7mm 3.1in
Valve type/No: Overhead 16
Transmission: Manual
No. of forward speeds: 4
Wheels driven: Rear
Springs F/R: Coil/Coil
Brake system: PA
Brakes F/R: Disc/Disc
Steering: Rack & pinion
Wheelbase: 215.9cm 85.0in
Track F: 147.3cm 58.0in
Track R: 154.9cm 61.0in
Length: 420.1cm 165.4in
Width: 170.2cm 67.0in
Height: 121.9cm 48.0in
Ground clearance: 7.6cm 3.0in
Kerb weight: 1162.2kg 2560.0lb
Fuel: 120.4L 26.5gal 31.8galUS

4579 Triumph

TR8 Libra Rally
1980 UK
107.0mph 172.2kmh
0-50mph 80.5kmh: 4.4secs
0-60mph 96.5kmh: 5.3secs
0-1/4 mile: 13.9secs
280.0bhp 208.8kW 283.9PS
@ 7000rpm
245.0lbft 332.0Nm @ 5000rpm
262.4bhp/ton 258.0bhp/tonne
79.4bhp/L 59.2kW/L 80.5PS/L
54.4ft/sec 16.6m/sec
14.3mph 23.0kmh/1000rpm
Petrol 4-stroke piston
3528cc 215.2cu in
Vee 8 1 Carburettor
Compression ratio: 10.5:1
Bore: 88.9mm 3.5in
Stroke: 71.1mm 2.8in
Valve type/No: Overhead 16
Transmission: Manual
No. of forward speeds: 4
Wheels driven: Rear
Springs F/R: Coil/Coil
Brake system: PA
Brakes F/R: Disc/Disc
Steering: Rack & pinion
Wheelbase: 215.9cm 85.0in
Track F: 141.0cm 55.5in
Track R: 144.3cm 56.8in
Length: 420.1cm 165.4in
Width: 168.1cm 66.2in
Height: 135.9cm 53.5in
Ground clearance: 19.1cm 7.5in
Kerb weight: 1085.1kg 2390.0lb
Fuel: 56.8L 12.5gal 15.0galUS

4580 Triumph

Acclaim HL
1981 UK
92.0mph 148.0kmh
0-50mph 80.5kmh: 9.3secs
0-60mph 96.5kmh: 12.9secs
0-1/4 mile: 18.6secs
0-1km: 35.8secs
70.0bhp 52.2kW 71.0PS
@ 5750rpm
74.0lbft 100.3Nm @ 3500rpm
86.6bhp/ton 85.2bhp/tonne
52.4bhp/L 39.1kW/L 53.2PS/L
51.6ft/sec 15.7m/sec
19.8mph 31.9kmh/1000rpm
31.8mpg 26.5mpgUS 8.9L/100km
Petrol 4-stroke piston
1335cc 81.4cu in
In-line 4 2 Carburettor
Compression ratio: 8.4:1
Bore: 72.0mm 2.8in
Stroke: 82.0mm 3.2in
Valve type/No: Overhead 8
Transmission: Manual
No. of forward speeds: 5
Wheels driven: Front
Springs F/R: Coil/Coil
Brake system: PA
Brakes F/R: Disc/Drum
Steering: Rack & pinion
Wheelbase: 231.9cm 91.3in
Track F: 135.9cm 53.5in
Track R: 137.9cm 54.3in
Length: 409.4cm 161.2in
Width: 160.0cm 63.0in
Height: 133.9cm 52.7in
Ground clearance: 15.2cm 6.0in
Kerb weight: 821.7kg 1810.0lb
Fuel: 45.5L 10.0gal 12.0galUS

4581 Triumph

TR7 Convertible
1982 UK
109.0mph 175.4kmh
0-50mph 80.5kmh: 7.9secs
0-60mph 96.5kmh: 11.5secs
0-1/4 mile: 18.5secs
85.5bhp 63.8kW 86.7PS
@ 5500rpm
102.0lbft 138.2Nm @ 3250rpm
77.5bhp/ton 76.2bhp/tonne
42.8bhp/L 31.9kW/L 43.4PS/L
46.9ft/sec 14.3m/sec
21.4mph 34.4kmh/1000rpm
33.0mpg 27.5mpgUS 8.6L/100km
Petrol 4-stroke piston
1998cc 121.9cu in
In-line 4 2 Carburettor
Compression ratio: 8.0:1
Bore: 90.3mm 3.6in
Stroke: 78.0mm 3.1in
Valve type/No: Overhead 8
Transmission: Manual

No. of forward speeds: 5
Wheels driven: Rear
Springs F/R: Coil/Coil
Brake system: PA
Brakes F/R: Disc/Drum
Steering: Rack & pinion
Wheelbase: 215.9cm 85.0in
Track F: 141.0cm 55.5in
Track R: 140.5cm 55.3in
Length: 420.4cm 165.5in
Width: 168.1cm 66.2in
Height: 125.7cm 49.5in
Kerb weight: 1121.4kg 2470.0lb
Fuel: 54.5L 12.0gal 14.4galUS

4582 Turner

Turner-Climax
1960 UK
104.0mph 167.3kmh
0-50mph 80.5kmh: 9.5secs
0-60mph 96.5kmh: 12.8secs
0-1/4 mile: 19.3secs
75.0bhp 55.9kW 76.0PS
@ 6000rpm
69.0lbft 93.5Nm @ 5000rpm
122.4bhp/ton 120.4bhp/tonne
68.3bhp/L 50.9kW/L 69.2PS/L
43.7ft/sec 13.3m/sec
16.5mph 26.5kmh/1000rpm
25.5mpg 21.2mpgUS 11.1L/100km
Petrol 4-stroke piston
1098cc 67.0cu in
In-line 4
Compression ratio: 9.8:1
Bore: 72.4mm 2.8in
Stroke: 66.6mm 2.6in
Valve type/No: Overhead 8
Transmission: Manual
No. of forward speeds: 4
Wheels driven: Rear
Springs F/R: Coil/Torsion bar
Brakes F/R: Disc/Drum
Wheelbase: 204.5cm 80.5in
Track F: 115.6cm 45.5in
Track R: 113.5cm 44.7in
Length: 350.5cm 138.0in
Width: 137.2cm 54.0in
Height: 119.4cm 47.0in
Ground clearance: 15.2cm 6.0in
Kerb weight: 622.9kg 1372.0lb
Fuel: 26.2L 5.7gal 6.9galUS

4583 Turner

Sports
1961 UK
80.0mph 128.7kmh
0-50mph 80.5kmh: 14.2secs
0-60mph 96.5kmh: 21.3secs
0-1/4 mile: 21.8secs
43.0bhp 32.1kW 43.6PS
@ 4750rpm
50.0lbft 67.8Nm @ 2000rpm
74.7bhp/ton 73.4bhp/tonne
45.4bhp/L 33.8kW/L 46.0PS/L
39.6ft/sec 12.1m/sec
14.9mph 24.0kmh/1000rpm
Petrol 4-stroke piston
948cc 57.8cu in
In-line 4 1 Carburettor
Compression ratio: 8.3:1
Bore: 63.0mm 2.5in
Stroke: 76.2mm 3.0in
Valve type/No: Overhead 8
Transmission: Manual
No. of forward speeds: 4
Wheels driven: Rear
Wheelbase: 205.7cm 81.0in
Track F: 118.1cm 46.5in
Track R: 119.4cm 47.0in
Length: 355.6cm 140.0in
Width: 144.0cm 56.7in
Height: 125.0cm 49.2in
Ground clearance: 8.9cm 3.5in
Kerb weight: 585.7kg 1290.0lb

4584 TVR

Grantura
1961 UK
101.0mph 162.5kmh
0-50mph 80.5kmh: 8.2secs
0-60mph 96.5kmh: 10.8secs
0-1/4 mile: 18.3secs
83.0bhp 61.9kW 84.1PS
@ 6300rpm
75.0lbft 101.6Nm @ 4750rpm
120.7bhp/ton 118.7bhp/tonne
68.3bhp/L 50.9kW/L 69.2PS/L
45.8ft/sec 14.0m/sec
16.0mph 25.7kmh/1000rpm
25.8mpg 21.5mpgUS 10.9L/100km
Petrol 4-stroke piston
1216cc 74.2cu in
In-line 4
Compression ratio: 10.0:1
Bore: 76.2mm 3.0in
Stroke: 66.6mm 2.6in
Valve type/No: Overhead 8
Transmission: Manual
No. of forward speeds: 4
Wheels driven: Rear
Springs F/R: Torsion bar/Torsion bar
Brakes F/R: Disc/Drum
Steering: Rack & pinion
Wheelbase: 213.4cm 84.0in
Track F: 132.1cm 52.0in
Track R: 132.1cm 52.0in
Length: 350.5cm 138.0in
Width: 162.6cm 64.0in
Height: 121.9cm 48.0in
Ground clearance: 12.7cm 5.0in
Kerb weight: 699.2kg 1540.0lb
Fuel: 39.8L 8.8gal 10.5galUS

4585 TVR

Vixen S2
1969 UK
111.0mph 178.6kmh
0-50mph 80.5kmh: 7.4secs
0-60mph 96.5kmh: 10.5secs
0-1/4 mile: 17.2secs
0-1km: 32.4secs
88.0bhp 65.6kW 89.2PS
@ 5400rpm
96.0lbft 130.1Nm @ 3000rpm
121.4bhp/ton 119.3bhp/tonne
33.9bhp/L 25.2kW/L 34.3PS/L
45.9ft/sec 14.0m/sec
18.8mph 30.2kmh/1000rpm
26.5mpg 22.1mpgUS 10.7L/100km
Petrol 4-stroke piston
2599cc 158.6cu in
In-line 4 1 Carburettor
Compression ratio: 9.0:1
Bore: 81.0mm 3.2in
Stroke: 77.6mm 3.1in
Valve type/No: Overhead 8
Transmission: Manual
No. of forward speeds: 4
Wheels driven: Rear
Springs F/R: Coil/Coil
Brake system: PA
Brakes F/R: Disc/Drum
Steering: Rack & pinion
Wheelbase: 228.6cm 90.0in
Track F: 132.1cm 52.0in
Track R: 134.6cm 53.0in
Length: 368.3cm 145.0in
Width: 162.6cm 64.0in
Height: 121.9cm 48.0in
Ground clearance: 12.7cm 5.0in
Kerb weight: 737.3kg 1624.0lb
Fuel: 68.2L 15.0gal 18.0galUS

4586 TVR

Tuscan
1970 UK
119.0mph 191.5kmh
0-50mph 80.5kmh: 4.8secs
0-60mph 96.5kmh: 7.2secs
0-1/4 mile: 15.4secs
220.0bhp 164.0kW 223.0PS
@ 4600rpm
300.0lbft 406.5Nm @ 2600rpm
220.0bhp/ton 216.3bhp/tonne
44.4bhp/L 33.1kW/L 45.1PS/L
38.3ft/sec 11.7m/sec
24.7mph 39.7kmh/1000rpm
18.7mpg 15.6mpgUS 15.1L/100km
Petrol 4-stroke piston
4949cc 301.9cu in
Vee 8 1 Carburettor
Compression ratio: 9.5:1
Bore: 101.6mm 4.0in
Stroke: 76.2mm 3.0in
Valve type/No: Overhead 16
Transmission: Manual
No. of forward speeds: 4
Wheels driven: Rear
Springs F/R: Coil/Coil
Brake system: PA
Brakes F/R: Disc/Drum
Steering: Rack & pinion
Wheelbase: 228.6cm 90.0in
Track F: 133.4cm 52.5in
Track R: 135.9cm 53.5in
Length: 388.6cm 153.0in
Width: 165.6cm 65.2in
Height: 125.2cm 49.3in
Ground clearance: 12.7cm 5.0in
Kerb weight: 1017.0kg 2240.0lb
Fuel: 68.1L 15.0gal 18.0galUS

4587 TVR

Vixen
1970 UK
100.0mph 160.9kmh
0-50mph 80.5kmh: 8.1secs
0-60mph 96.5kmh: 11.4secs
0-1/4 mile: 18.0secs
89.5bhp 66.7kW 90.7PS
@ 5400rpm
98.0lbft 132.8Nm @ 3600rpm
115.9bhp/ton 113.9bhp/tonne
56.0bhp/L 41.7kW/L 56.7PS/L
45.9ft/sec 14.0m/sec
17.8mph 28.6kmh/1000rpm
30.6mpg 25.5mpgUS 9.2L/100km
Petrol 4-stroke piston
1599cc 97.6cu in
In-line 4 1 Carburettor
Compression ratio: 9.0:1
Bore: 81.0mm 3.2in
Stroke: 77.6mm 3.1in
Valve type/No: Overhead 8
Transmission: Manual
No. of forward speeds: 4
Wheels driven: Rear
Springs F/R: Coil/Coil
Brake system: PA
Brakes F/R: Disc/Drum
Steering: Rack & pinion
Wheelbase: 228.6cm 90.0in
Track F: 133.4cm 52.5in
Track R: 135.9cm 53.5in
Length: 365.8cm 144.0in
Width: 162.6cm 64.0in
Height: 121.9cm 48.0in
Ground clearance: 12.7cm 5.0in
Kerb weight: 785.4kg 1730.0lb
Fuel: 68.1L 15.0gal 18.0galUS

4588 TVR

Vixen 2500M
1973 UK
111.0mph 178.6kmh
0-50mph 80.5kmh: 7.5secs
0-60mph 96.5kmh: 10.6secs
0-1/4 mile: 17.7secs
104.0bhp 77.5kW 105.4PS
@ 5000rpm
142.0lbft 192.4Nm @ 3000rpm
108.3bhp/ton 106.5bhp/tonne
41.6bhp/L 31.0kW/L 42.2PS/L
51.9ft/sec 15.8m/sec
20.8mph 33.5kmh/1000rpm
31.2mpg 26.0mpgUS 9.0L/100km
Petrol 4-stroke piston
2498cc 152.4cu in
In-line 6 2 Carburettor
Compression ratio: 8.5:1
Bore: 74.7mm 2.9in
Stroke: 95.0mm 3.7in
Valve type/No: Overhead 12
Transmission: Manual
No. of forward speeds: 4
Wheels driven: Rear
Springs F/R: Coil/Coil
Brake system: PA
Brakes F/R: Disc/Drum
Steering: Rack & pinion
Wheelbase: 228.6cm 90.0in
Track F: 134.6cm 53.0in
Track R: 137.2cm 54.0in
Length: 365.8cm 144.0in
Width: 162.6cm 64.0in
Height: 121.9cm 48.0in
Ground clearance: 12.7cm 5.0in
Kerb weight: 976.1kg 2150.0lb
Fuel: 51.1L 11.2gal 13.5galUS

4589 TVR

3000M
1974 UK
124.0mph 199.5kmh
0-50mph 80.5kmh: 5.8secs
0-60mph 96.5kmh: 7.7secs
0-1/4 mile: 16.0secs
0-1km: 30.1secs
142.0bhp 105.9kW 144.0PS
@ 5300rpm
172.0lbft 233.1Nm @ 3000rpm
142.0bhp/ton 139.6bhp/tonne
47.4bhp/L 35.4kW/L 48.1PS/L
42.0ft/sec 12.8m/sec
21.6mph 34.8kmh/1000rpm
21.4mpg 17.8mpgUS 13.2L/100km
Petrol 4-stroke piston
2994cc 182.7cu in
Vee 6 1 Carburettor
Compression ratio: 8.9:1
Bore: 94.1mm 3.7in
Stroke: 72.3mm 2.8in
Valve type/No: Overhead 12
Transmission: Manual
No. of forward speeds: 4
Wheels driven: Rear
Springs F/R: Coil/Coil
Brake system: PA
Brakes F/R: Disc/Drum
Steering: Rack & pinion
Wheelbase: 228.6cm 90.0in
Track F: 136.4cm 53.7in
Track R: 136.4cm 53.7in
Length: 401.3cm 158.0in
Width: 162.6cm 64.0in
Height: 119.4cm 47.0in
Ground clearance: 12.7cm 5.0in
Kerb weight: 1017.0kg 2240.0lb
Fuel: 54.6L 12.0gal 14.4galUS

4590 TVR

1600M
1976 UK
106.0mph 170.6kmh
0-50mph 80.5kmh: 7.2secs
0-60mph 96.5kmh: 10.4secs
0-1/4 mile: 17.6secs
0-1km: 33.1secs
84.0bhp 62.6kW 85.2PS
@ 5500rpm
92.0lbft 124.7Nm @ 3500rpm
95.3bhp/ton 93.7bhp/tonne
52.5bhp/L 39.2kW/L 53.3PS/L
46.7ft/sec 14.2m/sec
18.7mph 30.1kmh/1000rpm
25.2mpg 21.0mpgUS 11.2L/100km
Petrol 4-stroke piston
1599cc 97.6cu in
In-line 4 1 Carburettor
Compression ratio: 9.0:1
Bore: 81.0mm 3.2in
Stroke: 77.6mm 3.1in
Valve type/No: Overhead 8
Transmission: Manual
No. of forward speeds: 4
Wheels driven: Rear
Springs F/R: Coil/Coil
Brake system: PA
Brakes F/R: Disc/Drum
Steering: Rack & pinion
Wheelbase: 228.6cm 90.0in
Track F: 136.4cm 53.7in
Track R: 136.4cm 53.7in
Length: 401.3cm 158.0in
Width: 162.6cm 64.0in
Height: 119.4cm 47.0in
Ground clearance: 12.7cm 5.0in
Kerb weight: 896.2kg 1974.0lb
Fuel: 54.6L 12.0gal 14.4galUS

4591 TVR

2500M
1977 UK
109.0mph 175.4kmh
0-50mph 80.5kmh: 6.6secs
0-60mph 96.5kmh: 9.3secs
0-1/4 mile: 17.3secs
106.0bhp 79.0kW 107.5PS
@ 4900rpm
117.0lbft 158.5Nm @ 3000rpm
104.4bhp/ton 102.6bhp/tonne
42.4bhp/L 31.6kW/L 43.0PS/L
50.9ft/sec 15.5m/sec
21.8mph 35.1kmh/1000rpm
27.6mpg 23.0mpgUS 10.2L/100km
Petrol 4-stroke piston
2498cc 152.4cu in
In-line 6 2 Carburettor
Compression ratio: 8.5:1
Bore: 74.7mm 2.9in
Stroke: 95.0mm 3.7in
Valve type/No: Overhead 12
Transmission: Manual
No. of forward speeds: 4
Wheels driven: Rear
Springs F/R: Coil/Coil

Brake system: PA
Brakes F/R: Disc/Drum
Steering: Rack & pinion
Wheelbase: 228.6cm 90.0in
Track F: 136.7cm 53.8in
Track R: 136.7cm 53.8in
Length: 391.2cm 154.0in
Width: 162.6cm 64.0in
Height: 119.4cm 47.0in
Ground clearance: 12.7cm 5.0in
Kerb weight: 1032.8kg 2275.0lb
Fuel: 45.4L 10.0gal 12.0galUS

4592 TVR

Taimar
1977 UK
119.0mph 191.5kmh
0-50mph 80.5kmh: 5.8secs
0-60mph 96.5kmh: 7.8secs
0-1/4 mile: 16.3secs
0-1km: 30.1secs
142.0bhp 105.9kW 144.0PS
@ 5000rpm
172.0lbft 233.1Nm @ 3000rpm
140.7bhp/ton 138.4bhp/tonne
47.4bhp/L 35.4kW/L 48.1PS/L
39.6ft/sec 12.1m/sec
21.3mph 34.3kmh/1000rpm
21.1mpg 17.6mpgUS 13.4L/100km
Petrol 4-stroke piston
2994cc 182.7cu in
Vee 6 1 Carburettor
Compression ratio: 8.9:1
Bore: 93.4mm 3.7in
Stroke: 72.4mm 2.8in
Valve type/No: Overhead 12
Transmission: Manual
No. of forward speeds: 4
Wheels driven: Rear
Springs F/R: Coil/Coil
Brake system: PA
Brakes F/R: Disc/Drum
Steering: Rack & pinion
Wheelbase: 228.6cm 90.0in
Track F: 136.4cm 53.7in
Track R: 136.4cm 53.7in
Length: 401.3cm 158.0in
Width: 162.6cm 64.0in
Height: 119.4cm 47.0in
Ground clearance: 12.7cm 5.0in
Kerb weight: 1026.0kg 2260.0lb
Fuel: 54.6L 12.0gal 14.4galUS

4593 TVR

Convertible Turbo
1979 UK
140.0mph 225.3kmh
0-50mph 80.5kmh: 4.5secs
0-60mph 96.5kmh: 5.8secs
0-1/4 mile: 14.5secs
0-1km: 26.3secs
230.0bhp 171.5kW 233.2PS
@ 5500rpm
273.0lbft 369.9Nm @ 3500rpm
211.5bhp/ton 208.0bhp/tonne
76.8bhp/L 57.3kW/L 77.9PS/L
43.5ft/sec 13.3m/sec
21.7mph 34.9kmh/1000rpm
17.7mpg 14.7mpgUS 16.0L/100km
Petrol 4-stroke piston
2994cc 182.7cu in turbocharged
In-line 6 1 Carburettor
Compression ratio: 8.0:1
Bore: 93.9mm 3.7in
Stroke: 72.4mm 2.8in
Valve type/No: Overhead 12
Transmission: Manual
No. of forward speeds: 4
Wheels driven: Rear
Springs F/R: Coil/Coil
Brake system: PA
Brakes F/R: Disc/Drum
Steering: Rack & pinion
Wheelbase: 228.6cm 90.0in
Track F: 136.4cm 53.7in
Track R: 136.4cm 53.7in
Length: 388.6cm 153.0in
Width: 162.6cm 64.0in
Height: 111.8cm 44.0in
Ground clearance: 14.2cm 5.6in
Kerb weight: 1105.9kg 2436.0lb
Fuel: 54.6L 12.0gal 14.4galUS

4594 TVR

Taimar Roadster
1979 UK
125.0mph 201.1kmh
0-50mph 80.5kmh: 5.7secs
0-60mph 96.5kmh: 7.7secs
0-1/4 mile: 16.6secs
142.0bhp 105.9kW 144.0PS
@ 5000rpm
172.0lbft 233.1Nm @ 3000rpm
136.2bhp/ton 133.9bhp/tonne
47.4bhp/L 35.4kW/L 48.1PS/L
39.6ft/sec 12.1m/sec
21.4mph 34.4kmh/1000rpm
24.0mpg 20.0mpgUS 11.8L/100km
Petrol 4-stroke piston
2994cc 182.7cu in
Vee 6 1 Carburettor
Compression ratio: 8.9:1
Bore: 94.0mm 3.7in
Stroke: 72.4mm 2.8in
Valve type/No: Overhead 12
Transmission: Manual
No. of forward speeds: 4
Wheels driven: Rear
Springs F/R: Coil/Coil
Brake system: PA
Brakes F/R: Disc/Drum
Steering: Rack & pinion
Wheelbase: 228.6cm 90.0in
Track F: 136.7cm 53.8in
Track R: 136.7cm 53.8in
Length: 393.7cm 155.0in
Width: 162.6cm 64.0in
Height: 119.4cm 47.0in
Ground clearance: 12.7cm 5.0in
Kerb weight: 1060.1kg 2335.0lb
Fuel: 45.4L 10.0gal 12.0galUS

4595 TVR

3000S Roadster
1980 UK
125.0mph 201.1kmh
0-60mph 96.5kmh: 7.7secs
0-1/4 mile: 16.6secs
142.0bhp 105.9kW 144.0PS
@ 5000rpm
172.0lbft 233.1Nm @ 3000rpm
136.2bhp/ton 133.9bhp/tonne
47.4bhp/L 35.4kW/L 48.1PS/L
39.6ft/sec 12.1m/sec
22.5mph 36.2kmh/1000rpm
24.0mpg 20.0mpgUS 11.8L/100km
Petrol 4-stroke piston
2994cc 182.7cu in
Vee 6 1 Carburettor
Compression ratio: 8.9:1
Bore: 94.0mm 3.7in
Stroke: 72.4mm 2.8in
Valve type/No: Overhead 12
Transmission: Manual
No. of forward speeds: 4
Wheels driven: Rear
Springs F/R: Coil/Coil
Brake system: PA
Brakes F/R: Disc/Drum
Steering: Rack & pinion
Wheelbase: 228.6cm 90.0in
Track F: 136.7cm 53.8in
Track R: 136.7cm 53.8in
Length: 393.7cm 155.0in
Width: 162.6cm 64.0in
Height: 119.4cm 47.0in
Ground clearance: 12.7cm 5.0in
Kerb weight: 1060.1kg 2335.0lb
Fuel: 45.4L 10.0gal 12.0galUS

4596 TVR

Tasmin
1981 UK
126.0mph 202.7kmh
0-50mph 80.5kmh: 5.8secs
0-60mph 96.5kmh: 7.8secs
0-1/4 mile: 16.2secs
0-1km: 30.2secs
160.0bhp 119.3kW 162.2PS
@ 5700rpm
162.0lbft 219.5Nm @ 4200rpm
142.8bhp/ton 140.4bhp/tonne
57.3bhp/L 42.7kW/L 58.1PS/L
42.7ft/sec 13.0m/sec
22.2mph 35.7kmh/1000rpm
20.7mpg 17.2mpgUS 13.6L/100km
Petrol 4-stroke piston
2792cc 170.3cu in
Vee 6 fuel injection
Compression ratio: 9.2:1
Bore: 93.0mm 3.7in
Stroke: 68.5mm 2.7in
Valve type/No: Overhead 12
Transmission: Manual
No. of forward speeds: 4
Wheels driven: Rear
Springs F/R: Coil/Coil
Brake system: PA
Brakes F/R: Disc/Disc
Steering: Rack & pinion
Wheelbase: 238.8cm 94.0in
Track F: 143.5cm 56.5in
Track R: 144.0cm 56.7in
Length: 401.3cm 158.0in
Width: 172.7cm 68.0in
Height: 119.4cm 47.0in
Ground clearance: 14.0cm 5.5in
Kerb weight: 1139.5kg 2510.0lb
Fuel: 63.7L 14.0gal 16.8galUS

4597 TVR

Tasmin Convertible
1983 UK
108.0mph 173.8kmh
0-50mph 80.5kmh: 8.6secs
0-60mph 96.5kmh: 11.8secs
0-1/4 mile: 18.5secs
145.0bhp 108.1kW 147.0PS
@ 5700rpm
150.0lbft 203.3Nm @ 4300rpm
122.6bhp/ton 120.5bhp/tonne
51.9bhp/L 38.7kW/L 52.6PS/L
42.7ft/sec 13.0m/sec
21.6mph 34.8kmh/1000rpm
24.0mpg 20.0mpgUS 11.8L/100km
Petrol 4-stroke piston
2792cc 170.3cu in
Vee 6 fuel injection
Compression ratio: 9.2:1
Bore: 93.0mm 3.7in
Stroke: 68.5mm 2.7in
Valve type/No: Overhead 12
Transmission: Manual
No. of forward speeds: 4
Wheels driven: Rear
Springs F/R: Coil/Coil
Brake system: PA
Brakes F/R: Disc/Disc
Steering: Rack & pinion
Wheelbase: 238.8cm 94.0in
Track F: 143.5cm 56.5in
Track R: 144.0cm 56.7in
Length: 406.4cm 160.0in
Width: 172.7cm 68.0in
Height: 119.4cm 47.0in
Ground clearance: 14.0cm 5.5in
Kerb weight: 1203.1kg 2650.0lb
Fuel: 62.8L 13.8gal 16.6galUS

4598 TVR

350i Series II
1985 UK
138.0mph 222.0kmh
0-50mph 80.5kmh: 5.0secs
0-60mph 96.5kmh: 6.6secs
0-1/4 mile: 14.8secs
0-1km: 27.2secs
197.0bhp 146.9kW 199.7PS
@ 5280rpm
220.0lbft 298.1Nm @ 4000rpm
175.1bhp/ton 172.2bhp/tonne
55.8bhp/L 41.6kW/L 56.6PS/L
41.1ft/sec 12.5m/sec
25.4mph 40.9kmh/1000rpm
19.6mpg 16.3mpgUS 14.4L/100km
Petrol 4-stroke piston
3528cc 215.2cu in
Vee 6 fuel injection
Compression ratio: 9.7:1
Bore: 88.9mm 3.5in
Stroke: 71.1mm 2.8in
Valve type/No: Overhead 12
Transmission: Manual
No. of forward speeds: 5
Wheels driven: Rear
Springs F/R: Coil/Coil
Brake system: PA
Brakes F/R: Disc/Disc
Steering: Rack & pinion
Wheelbase: 238.8cm 94.0in
Track F: 143.5cm 56.5in
Track R: 144.0cm 56.7in
Length: 401.3cm 158.0in
Width: 172.7cm 68.0in
Height: 119.4cm 47.0in
Ground clearance: 14.0cm 5.5in
Kerb weight: 1144.1kg 2520.0lb
Fuel: 59.1L 13.0gal 15.6galUS

4599 TVR

390 SE
1987 UK
144.0mph 231.7kmh
0-50mph 80.5kmh: 4.4secs
0-60mph 96.5kmh: 5.7secs
0-1/4 mile: 14.2secs
0-1km: 25.6secs
275.0bhp 205.1kW 278.8PS
@ 5500rpm
270.0lbft 365.9Nm @ 3500rpm
230.7bhp/ton 226.9bhp/tonne
70.4bhp/L 52.5kW/L 71.4PS/L
46.4ft/sec 14.1m/sec
25.9mph 41.7kmh/1000rpm
16.6mpg 13.8mpgUS 17.0L/100km
Petrol 4-stroke piston
3905cc 238.0cu in
Vee 8 fuel injection
Compression ratio: 10.5:1
Bore: 93.5mm 3.7in
Stroke: 77.1mm 3.0in
Valve type/No: Overhead 16
Transmission: Manual
No. of forward speeds: 5
Wheels driven: Rear
Springs F/R: Coil/Coil
Brake system: PA
Brakes F/R: Disc/Disc
Steering: Rack & pinion PA
Wheelbase: 288.7cm 113.7in
Track F: 145.0cm 57.1in
Track R: 148.0cm 58.3in
Length: 401.3cm 158.0in
Width: 172.8cm 68.0in
Height: 120.5cm 47.4in
Ground clearance: 15.2cm 6.0in
Kerb weight: 1212.0kg 2669.6lb
Fuel: 61.4L 13.5gal 16.2galUS

4600 TVR

S Convertible
1987 UK
130.0mph 209.2kmh
0-50mph 80.5kmh: 5.6secs
0-60mph 96.5kmh: 7.6secs
0-1/4 mile: 15.9secs
0-1km: 29.9secs
160.0bhp 119.3kW 162.2PS
@ 6000rpm
162.0lbft 219.5Nm @ 4300rpm
164.7bhp/ton 161.9bhp/tonne
57.3bhp/L 42.7kW/L 58.1PS/L
45.0ft/sec 13.7m/sec
23.3mph 37.5kmh/1000rpm
27.3mpg 22.7mpgUS 10.3L/100km
Petrol 4-stroke piston
2792cc 170.0cu in
Vee 6 fuel injection
Compression ratio: 9.2:1
Bore: 93.0mm 3.7in
Stroke: 68.5mm 2.7in
Valve type/No: Overhead 12
Transmission: Manual
No. of forward speeds: 5
Wheels driven: Rear
Springs F/R: Coil/Coil
Brake system: PA
Brakes F/R: Disc/Drum
Steering: Rack & pinion
Wheelbase: 228.6cm 90.0in
Track F: 139.8cm 55.0in
Track R: 139.8cm 55.0in
Length: 400.0cm 157.5in
Width: 145.0cm 57.1in
Height: 111.7cm 44.0in
Ground clearance: 14.3cm 5.6in
Kerb weight: 988.0kg 2176.2lb
Fuel: 54.6L 12.0gal 14.4galUS

4601 TVR

420 SEAC
1989 UK
165.0mph 265.5kmh
0-60mph 96.5kmh: 5.0secs
300.0bhp 223.7kW 304.2PS
@ 5500rpm
290.0lbft 393.0Nm @ 4500rpm
305.4bhp/ton 300.4bhp/tonne
71.0bhp/L 52.9kW/L 71.9PS/L
46.3ft/sec 14.1m/sec
Petrol 4-stroke piston
4228cc 258.0cu in
Vee 8 fuel injection
Compression ratio: 10.5:1
Bore: 93.5mm 3.7in
Stroke: 77.0mm 3.0in

Valve type/No: Overhead 16
Transmission: Manual
No. of forward speeds: 5
Wheels driven: Rear
Springs F/R: Coil/Coil
Brake system: PA
Brakes F/R: Disc/Disc
Steering: Rack & pinion PA
Wheelbase: 238.8cm 94.0in
Track F: 145.0cm 57.1in
Track R: 148.1cm 58.3in
Length: 401.3cm 158.0in
Width: 172.7cm 68.0in
Height: 120.4cm 47.4in
Kerb weight: 998.8kg 2200.0lb
Fuel: 60.9L 13.4gal 16.1galUS

4602 TVR

S Convertible
1989 UK
140.0mph 225.3kmh
0-60mph 96.5kmh: 7.0secs
0-1/4 mile: 14.5secs
160.0bhp 119.3kW 162.2PS
@ 6000rpm
162.0lbft 219.5Nm @ 4300rpm
164.8bhp/ton 162.0bhp/tonne
57.3bhp/L 42.7kW/L 58.1PS/L
45.0ft/sec 13.7m/sec
Petrol 4-stroke piston
2792cc 170.3cu in
Vee 6 fuel injection
Compression ratio: 9.2:1
Bore: 93.0mm 3.7in
Stroke: 68.5mm 2.7in
Valve type/No: Overhead 12
Transmission: Manual
No. of forward speeds: 5
Wheels driven: Rear
Springs F/R: Coil/Coil
Brake system: PA
Brakes F/R: Disc/Drum
Steering: Rack & pinion
Wheelbase: 228.6cm 90.0in
Track F: 139.7cm 55.0in
Track R: 139.7cm 55.0in
Length: 400.1cm 157.5in
Width: 145.0cm 57.1in
Height: 111.8cm 44.0in
Kerb weight: 987.4kg 2175.0lb
Fuel: 54.5L 12.0gal 14.4galUS

4603 TVR

V8 S
1991 UK
150.0mph 241.4kmh
0-50mph 80.5kmh: 4.1secs
0-60mph 96.5kmh: 5.2secs
0-1/4 mile: 14.0secs
0-1km: 25.3secs
240.0bhp 179.0kW 243.3PS
@ 5750rpm
275.3lbft 373.0Nm @ 4200rpm
239.3bhp/ton 235.3bhp/tonne
60.8bhp/L 45.3kW/L 61.6PS/L
44.7ft/sec 13.6m/sec
26.9mph 43.3kmh/1000rpm
20.1mpg 16.7mpgUS 14.1L/100km
Petrol 4-stroke piston
3950cc 241.0cu in
Vee 8 fuel injection
Compression ratio: 10.5:1
Bore: 94.0mm 3.7in
Stroke: 71.0mm 2.8in
Valve type/No: Overhead 16
Transmission: Manual
No. of forward speeds: 5
Wheels driven: Rear
Springs F/R: Coil/Coil
Brake system: PA
Brakes F/R: Disc/Disc
Steering: Rack & pinion
Wheelbase: 228.6cm 90.0in
Track F: 143.8cm 56.6in
Track R: 143.8cm 56.6in
Length: 395.7cm 155.8in
Width: 166.4cm 65.5in
Height: 122.2cm 48.1in
Ground clearance: 14.0cm 5.5in
Kerb weight: 1020.0kg 2246.7lb
Fuel: 54.6L 12.0gal 14.4galUS

4604 Vanden Plas

Princess
1960 UK
98.0mph 157.7kmh
0-50mph 80.5kmh: 12.8secs
0-60mph 96.5kmh: 17.9secs
0-1/4 mile: 21.4secs
108.0bhp 80.5kW 109.5PS
@ 4750rpm
157.0lbft 212.7Nm @ 2300rpm
69.8bhp/ton 68.6bhp/tonne
37.1bhp/L 27.7kW/L 37.6PS/L
46.2ft/sec 14.1m/sec
20.8mph 33.5kmh/1000rpm
17.1mpg 14.2mpgUS 16.5L/100km
Petrol 4-stroke piston
2912cc 177.7cu in
In-line 6
Compression ratio: 8.3:1
Bore: 83.3mm 3.3in
Stroke: 89.0mm 3.5in
Valve type/No: Overhead 12
Transmission: Automatic
No. of forward speeds: 3
Wheels driven: Rear
Springs F/R: Coil/Leaf
Brake system: PA
Brakes F/R: Disc/Drum
Wheelbase: 274.3cm 108.0in
Track F: 137.2cm 54.0in
Track R: 135.1cm 53.2in
Length: 478.8cm 188.5in
Width: 174.0cm 68.5in
Height: 149.9cm 59.0in
Ground clearance: 17.0cm 6.7in
Kerb weight: 1573.1kg 3465.0lb
Fuel: 72.8L 16.0gal 19.2galUS

4605 Vanden Plas

Princess 3-litre Automatic
1963 UK
106.0mph 170.6kmh
0-50mph 80.5kmh: 12.2secs
0-60mph 96.5kmh: 16.9secs
0-1/4 mile: 21.4secs
120.0bhp 89.5kW 121.7PS
@ 4750rpm
163.0lbft 220.9Nm @ 2750rpm
73.4bhp/ton 72.2bhp/tonne
41.2bhp/L 30.7kW/L 41.8PS/L
46.2ft/sec 14.1m/sec
20.9mph 33.6kmh/1000rpm
18.3mpg 15.2mpgUS 15.4L/100km
Petrol 4-stroke piston
2912cc 177.7cu in
In-line 6 2 Carburettor
Compression ratio: 8.3:1
Bore: 83.3mm 3.3in
Stroke: 89.0mm 3.5in
Valve type/No: Overhead 12
Transmission: Automatic
No. of forward speeds: 3
Wheels driven: Rear
Springs F/R: Coil/Leaf
Brake system: PA
Brakes F/R: Disc/Drum
Steering: Cam & lever
Wheelbase: 279.4cm 110.0in
Track F: 136.7cm 53.8in
Track R: 135.1cm 53.2in
Length: 477.5cm 188.0in
Width: 168.9cm 66.5in
Height: 152.4cm 60.0in
Ground clearance: 17.0cm 6.7in
Kerb weight: 1662.1kg 3661.0lb
Fuel: 72.8L 16.0gal 19.2galUS

4606 Vanden Plas

Princess 1100
1965 UK
86.0mph 138.4kmh
0-50mph 80.5kmh: 14.7secs
0-60mph 96.5kmh: 21.1secs
0-1/4 mile: 21.7secs
55.0bhp 41.0kW 55.8PS
@ 5500rpm
61.0lbft 82.7Nm @ 2750rpm
62.4bhp/ton 61.4bhp/tonne
50.1bhp/L 37.3kW/L 50.8PS/L
50.4ft/sec 15.3m/sec
14.9mph 24.0kmh/1000rpm
30.8mpg 25.6mpgUS 9.2L/100km
Petrol 4-stroke piston
1098cc 67.0cu in
In-line 4 2 Carburettor
Compression ratio: 8.9:1
Bore: 64.6mm 2.5in
Stroke: 83.7mm 3.3in
Valve type/No: Overhead 8
Transmission: Manual
No. of forward speeds: 4
Wheels driven: Front
Springs F/R: Gas/Gas
Brakes F/R: Disc/Drum
Steering: Rack & pinion
Wheelbase: 237.5cm 93.5in
Track F: 130.8cm 51.5in
Track R: 129.3cm 50.9in
Length: 372.6cm 146.7in
Width: 153.4cm 60.4in
Height: 133.9cm 52.7in
Ground clearance: 15.2cm 6.0in
Kerb weight: 895.7kg 1973.0lb
Fuel: 36.4L 8.0gal 9.6galUS

4607 Vanden Plas

1500
1974 UK
91.0mph 146.4kmh
0-50mph 80.5kmh: 11.0secs
0-60mph 96.5kmh: 16.7secs
0-1/4 mile: 20.9secs
0-1km: 39.3secs
68.0bhp 50.7kW 68.9PS
@ 5500rpm
80.0lbft 108.4Nm @ 2900rpm
76.2bhp/ton 74.9bhp/tonne
45.8bhp/L 34.1kW/L 46.4PS/L
48.9ft/sec 14.9m/sec
19.4mph 31.2kmh/1000rpm
27.2mpg 22.6mpgUS 10.4L/100km
Petrol 4-stroke piston
1485cc 90.6cu in
In-line 4 1 Carburettor
Compression ratio: 9.0:1
Bore: 76.2mm 3.0in
Stroke: 81.3mm 3.2in
Valve type/No: Overhead 8
Transmission: Manual
No. of forward speeds: 5
Wheels driven: Front
Springs F/R: Gas/Gas
Brake system: PA
Brakes F/R: Disc/Drum
Steering: Rack & pinion
Wheelbase: 244.1cm 96.1in
Track F: 136.1cm 53.6in
Track R: 136.4cm 53.7in
Length: 385.1cm 151.6in
Width: 161.3cm 63.5in
Height: 140.7cm 55.4in
Ground clearance: 17.8cm 7.0in
Kerb weight: 908.0kg 2000.0lb
Fuel: 47.8L 10.5gal 12.6galUS

4608 Vanden Plas

Princess R
1974 UK
107.5mph 173.0kmh
0-50mph 80.5kmh: 9.3secs
0-60mph 96.5kmh: 12.7secs
0-1/4 mile: 18.9secs
175.0bhp 130.5kW 177.4PS
@ 4800rpm
218.0lbft 295.4Nm @ 3000rpm
109.8bhp/ton 108.0bhp/tonne
44.8bhp/L 33.4kW/L 45.4PS/L
48.0ft/sec 14.6m/sec
23.5mph 37.8kmh/1000rpm
14.8mpg 12.3mpgUS 19.1L/100km
Petrol 4-stroke piston
3909cc 238.5cu in
In-line 6 2 Carburettor
Compression ratio: 7.8:1
Bore: 95.2mm 3.8in
Stroke: 91.4mm 3.6in
Valve type/No: IOE 12
Transmission: Automatic
No. of forward speeds: 3
Wheels driven: Rear
Springs F/R: Coil/Leaf
Brake system: PA
Brakes F/R: Disc/Drum
Steering: Recirculating ball
Wheelbase: 279.4cm 110.0in
Track F: 136.7cm 53.8in
Track R: 135.1cm 53.2in
Length: 477.5cm 188.0in
Width: 174.0cm 68.5in
Height: 152.4cm 60.0in
Ground clearance: 17.0cm 6.7in
Kerb weight: 1620.8kg 3570.0lb
Fuel: 72.8L 16.0gal 19.2galUS

4609 Vauxhall

20/60 Limousine
1929 UK
65.0mph 104.6kmh
20.0mpg 16.7mpgUS 14.1L/100km
Petrol 4-stroke piston
2916cc 177.9cu in
In-line 6
Bore: 75.0mm 2.9in
Stroke: 110.0mm 4.3in
Valve type/No: Overhead 12
Transmission: Manual
No. of forward speeds: 4
Wheels driven: Rear
Brakes F/R: Drum/Drum
Wheelbase: 330.2cm 130.0in
Track F: 143.8cm 56.6in
Track R: 143.8cm 56.6in
Length: 436.9cm 172.0in
Width: 182.9cm 72.0in
Height: 190.5cm 75.0in
Kerb weight: 1754.3kg 3864.0lb
Fuel: 63.7L 14.0gal 16.8galUS

4610 Vauxhall

Cadet Saloon
1931 UK
61.2mph 98.5kmh
42.0bhp 31.3kW 42.6PS
@ 3300rpm
33.6bhp/ton 33.0bhp/tonne
20.5bhp/L 15.3kW/L 20.8PS/L
33.5ft/sec 10.2m/sec
22.0mpg 18.3mpgUS 12.8L/100km
Petrol 4-stroke piston
2048cc 124.9cu in
In-line 6 1 Carburettor
Bore: 67.5mm 2.7in
Stroke: 93.0mm 3.7in
Valve type/No: Side 12
Transmission: Manual
No. of forward speeds: 3
Wheels driven: Rear
Brakes F/R: Drum/Drum
Wheelbase: 271.8cm 107.0in
Track F: 142.2cm 56.0in
Track R: 142.2cm 56.0in
Length: 408.9cm 161.0in
Width: 168.9cm 66.5in
Height: 176.5cm 69.5in
Kerb weight: 1271.2kg 2800.0lb
Fuel: 38.7L 8.5gal 10.2galUS

4611 Vauxhall

20 Saloon
1934 UK
69.7mph 112.1kmh
0-50mph 80.5kmh: 23.4secs
19.0mpg 15.8mpgUS 14.9L/100km
Petrol 4-stroke piston
2392cc 145.9cu in
In-line 6
Bore: 73.0mm 2.9in
Stroke: 95.2mm 3.8in
Valve type/No: Overhead 12
Transmission: Manual
No. of forward speeds: 4
Wheels driven: Rear
Brakes F/R: Drum/Drum
Kerb weight: 1398.3kg 3080.0lb
Fuel: 54.6L 12.0gal 14.4galUS

4612 Vauxhall

27 Saloon
1935 UK
71.4mph 114.9kmh
0-50mph 80.5kmh: 20.0secs
0-60mph 96.5kmh: 28.6secs
18.0mpg 15.0mpgUS 15.7L/100km
Petrol 4-stroke piston
3184cc 194.3cu in
In-line 6
Bore: 84.1mm 3.3in
Stroke: 95.2mm 3.8in
Valve type/No: Overhead 12
Transmission: Manual
No. of forward speeds: 4
Wheels driven: Rear
Brakes F/R: Drum/Drum
Kerb weight: 1526.3kg 3362.0lb
Fuel: 54.6L 12.0gal 14.4galUS

4613 Vauxhall

10/4 de Luxe Saloon
1937 UK
60.4mph 97.2kmh
0-50mph 80.5kmh: 25.5secs
34.0bhp 25.3kW 34.5PS

@ 3800rpm
37.6bhp/ton 36.9bhp/tonne
28.3bhp/L 21.1kW/L 28.6PS/L
39.5ft/sec 12.0m/sec
36.0mpg 30.0mpgUS 7.8L/100km
Petrol 4-stroke piston
1203cc 73.4cu in
In-line 4 1 Carburettor
Bore: 63.5mm 2.5in
Stroke: 95.0mm 3.7in
Valve type/No: Overhead 8
Transmission: Manual
No. of forward speeds: 3
Wheels driven: Rear
Brakes F/R: Drum/Drum
Kerb weight: 920.3kg 2027.0lb
Fuel: 30.7L 6.7gal 8.1galUS

4614 Vauxhall

14 de Luxe
1937 UK
68.1mph 109.6kmh
0-50mph 80.5kmh: 22.8secs
0-60mph 96.5kmh: 38.0secs
25.0mpg 20.8mpgUS 11.3L/100km
Petrol 4-stroke piston
1781cc 108.7cu in
In-line 6
Bore: 61.5mm 2.4in
Stroke: 100.0mm 3.9in
Valve type/No: Overhead 12
Transmission: Manual
No. of forward speeds: 4
Wheels driven: Rear
Brakes F/R: Drum/Drum
Kerb weight: 1199.0kg 2641.0lb
Fuel: 40.9L 9.0gal 10.8galUS

4615 Vauxhall

10 Saloon de Luxe
1938 UK
63.3mph 101.8kmh
0-50mph 80.5kmh: 25.1secs
34.0bhp 25.3kW 34.5PS
@ 3800rpm
37.3bhp/ton 36.7bhp/tonne
28.3bhp/L 21.1kW/L 28.6PS/L
39.5ft/sec 12.0m/sec
38.0mpg 31.6mpgUS 7.4L/100km
Petrol 4-stroke piston
1203cc 73.4cu in
In-line 4 1 Carburettor
Bore: 63.5mm 2.5in
Stroke: 95.0mm 3.7in
Valve type/No: Overhead 8
Transmission: Manual
No. of forward speeds: 3
Wheels driven: Rear
Brakes F/R: Drum/Drum
Kerb weight: 925.7kg 2039.0lb
Fuel: 30.7L 6.7gal 8.1galUS

4616 Vauxhall

12/4 de Luxe Saloon
1938 UK
67.1mph 108.0kmh
0-50mph 80.5kmh: 22.2secs
34.0mpg 28.3mpgUS 8.3L/100km
Petrol 4-stroke piston
1442cc 88.0cu in
In-line 4
Bore: 69.5mm 2.7in
Stroke: 95.0mm 3.7in
Valve type/No: Overhead 8
Transmission: Manual
No. of forward speeds: 3
Wheels driven: Rear
Brakes F/R: Drum/Drum
Kerb weight: 969.7kg 2136.0lb
Fuel: 30.7L 6.7gal 8.1galUS

4617 Vauxhall

25 Saloon
1938 UK
81.0mph 130.3kmh
0-50mph 80.5kmh: 14.8secs
0-60mph 96.5kmh: 21.9secs
18.0mpg 15.0mpgUS 15.7L/100km
Petrol 4-stroke piston
3215cc 196.2cu in
In-line 6
Bore: 81.9mm 3.2in
Stroke: 101.6mm 4.0in
Valve type/No: Overhead 12
Transmission: Manual
No. of forward speeds: 3
Wheels driven: Rear
Brakes F/R: Drum/Drum
Kerb weight: 1558.6kg 3433.0lb
Fuel: 54.6L 12.0gal 14.4galUS

4618 Vauxhall

12 Saloon
1940 UK
63.3mph 101.8kmh
0-50mph 80.5kmh: 23.4secs
35.0bhp 26.1kW 35.5PS
@ 3600rpm
36.6bhp/ton 36.0bhp/tonne
24.3bhp/L 18.1kW/L 24.6PS/L
37.4ft/sec 11.4m/sec
32.0mpg 26.6mpgUS 8.8L/100km
Petrol 4-stroke piston
1442cc 88.0cu in
In-line 4
Compression ratio: 6.8:1
Bore: 69.5mm 2.7in
Stroke: 95.0mm 3.7in
Valve type/No: Overhead 8
Transmission: Manual
No. of forward speeds: 3
Wheels driven: Rear
Brakes F/R: Drum/Drum
Wheelbase: 257.0cm 101.2in
Track F: 122.4cm 48.2in
Track R: 125.7cm 49.5in
Length: 414.0cm 163.0in
Width: 153.7cm 60.5in
Ground clearance: 19.6cm 7.7in
Kerb weight: 972.0kg 2141.0lb
Fuel: 30.7L 6.7gal 8.1galUS

4619 Vauxhall

12 Saloon
1947 UK
65.0mph 104.6kmh
0-50mph 80.5kmh: 19.6secs
35.0bhp 26.1kW 35.5PS
@ 3600rpm
37.3bhp/ton 36.7bhp/tonne
24.3bhp/L 18.1kW/L 24.6PS/L
37.4ft/sec 11.4m/sec
32.0mpg 26.6mpgUS 8.8L/100km
Petrol 4-stroke piston
1442cc 88.0cu in
In-line 4
Compression ratio: 6.8:1
Bore: 69.5mm 2.7in
Stroke: 95.0mm 3.7in
Valve type/No: Overhead 8
Transmission: Manual
No. of forward speeds: 3
Wheels driven: Rear
Brakes F/R: Drum/Drum
Wheelbase: 248.2cm 97.7in
Track F: 122.4cm 48.2in
Track R: 126.0cm 49.6in
Length: 403.1cm 158.7in
Width: 154.9cm 61.0in
Height: 165.1cm 65.0in
Ground clearance: 19.6cm 7.7in
Kerb weight: 953.4kg 2100.0lb
Fuel: 30.7L 6.7gal 8.1galUS

4620 Vauxhall

14
1948 UK
71.0mph 114.2kmh
0-50mph 80.5kmh: 22.1secs
47.5bhp 35.4kW 48.2PS
@ 3600rpm
42.7bhp/ton 42.0bhp/tonne
26.7bhp/L 19.9kW/L 27.0PS/L
39.4ft/sec 12.0m/sec
25.0mpg 20.8mpgUS 11.3L/100km
Petrol 4-stroke piston
1781cc 108.7cu in
In-line 6
Compression ratio: 6.7:1
Bore: 61.5mm 2.4in
Stroke: 100.0mm 3.9in
Valve type/No: Overhead 12
Transmission: Manual
No. of forward speeds: 3
Wheels driven: Rear
Brakes F/R: Drum/Drum
Wheelbase: 266.7cm 105.0in
Track F: 128.3cm 50.5in
Track R: 129.5cm 51.0in
Length: 428.8cm 168.8in
Width: 160.0cm 63.0in
Height: 167.6cm 66.0in
Ground clearance: 19.8cm 7.8in
Kerb weight: 1131.4kg 2492.0lb
Fuel: 46.6L 10.2gal 12.3galUS

4621 Vauxhall

Velox
1948 UK
76.0mph 122.3kmh
0-50mph 80.5kmh: 15.5secs
0-60mph 96.5kmh: 23.3secs
54.7bhp 40.8kW 55.5PS
@ 3300rpm
51.5bhp/ton 50.7bhp/tonne
24.1bhp/L 17.9kW/L 24.4PS/L
36.1ft/sec 11.0m/sec
23.0mpg 19.2mpgUS 12.3L/100km
Petrol 4-stroke piston
2275cc 138.8cu in
In-line 6
Compression ratio: 6.7:1
Bore: 69.5mm 2.7in
Stroke: 100.0mm 3.9in
Valve type/No: Overhead 12
Transmission: Manual
No. of forward speeds: 3
Wheels driven: Rear
Brakes F/R: Drum/Drum
Wheelbase: 248.2cm 97.7in
Track F: 128.8cm 50.7in
Track R: 127.0cm 50.0in
Length: 418.1cm 164.6in
Width: 157.5cm 62.0in
Height: 165.6cm 65.2in
Ground clearance: 18.0cm 7.1in
Kerb weight: 1080.5kg 2380.0lb
Fuel: 45.5L 10.0gal 12.0galUS

4622 Vauxhall

Wyvern
1949 UK
62.0mph 99.8kmh
0-50mph 80.5kmh: 28.8secs
35.0bhp 26.1kW 35.5PS
@ 3600rpm
36.1bhp/ton 35.5bhp/tonne
24.3bhp/L 18.1kW/L 24.6PS/L
37.4ft/sec 11.4m/sec
30.0mpg 25.0mpgUS 9.4L/100km
Petrol 4-stroke piston
1442cc 88.0cu in
In-line 4
Compression ratio: 6.4:1
Bore: 69.5mm 2.7in
Stroke: 95.0mm 3.7in
Valve type/No: Overhead 8
Transmission: Manual
No. of forward speeds: 3
Wheels driven: Rear
Brakes F/R: Drum/Drum
Wheelbase: 248.2cm 97.7in
Track F: 125.0cm 49.2in
Track R: 125.5cm 49.4in
Length: 417.6cm 164.4in
Width: 157.5cm 62.0in
Height: 165.1cm 65.0in
Ground clearance: 17.3cm 6.8in
Kerb weight: 985.2kg 2170.0lb
Fuel: 45.5L 10.0gal 12.0galUS

4623 Vauxhall

Velox
1950 UK
75.0mph 120.7kmh
0-50mph 80.5kmh: 19.3secs
0-60mph 96.5kmh: 30.6secs
58.3bhp 43.5kW 59.1PS
@ 3500rpm
106.5lbft 144.3Nm @ 1100rpm
52.9bhp/ton 52.0bhp/tonne
25.6bhp/L 19.1kW/L 26.0PS/L
38.3ft/sec 11.7m/sec
18.2mph 29.3kmh/1000rpm
20.0mpg 16.7mpgUS 14.1L/100km
Petrol 4-stroke piston
2275cc 138.8cu in
In-line 6
Compression ratio: 6.7:1
Bore: 69.5mm 2.7in
Stroke: 100.0mm 3.9in
Valve type/No: Overhead 12
Transmission: Manual
No. of forward speeds: 3
Wheels driven: Rear
Brakes F/R: Drum/Drum
Wheelbase: 248.2cm 97.7in
Track F: 129.0cm 50.8in
Track R: 127.0cm 50.0in
Length: 418.1cm 164.6in
Width: 157.5cm 62.0in
Height: 165.6cm 65.2in
Ground clearance: 17.5cm 6.9in
Kerb weight: 1120.0kg 2467.0lb
Fuel: 45.5L 10.0gal 12.0galUS

4624 Vauxhall

Velox
1951 UK
78.5mph 126.3kmh
0-50mph 80.5kmh: 15.6secs
0-60mph 96.5kmh: 22.4secs
58.3bhp 43.5kW 59.1PS
@ 3500rpm
106.5lbft 144.3Nm @ 1100rpm
52.6bhp/ton 51.7bhp/tonne
25.6bhp/L 19.1kW/L 26.0PS/L
38.3ft/sec 11.7m/sec
18.4mph 29.6kmh/1000rpm
22.0mpg 18.3mpgUS 12.8L/100km
Petrol 4-stroke piston
2275cc 138.8cu in
In-line 6
Compression ratio: 6.7:1
Bore: 69.5mm 2.7in
Stroke: 100.0mm 3.9in
Valve type/No: Overhead 12
Transmission: Manual
No. of forward speeds: 3
Wheels driven: Rear
Brakes F/R: Drum/Drum
Wheelbase: 261.6cm 103.0in
Track F: 134.6cm 53.0in
Track R: 138.4cm 54.5in
Length: 438.2cm 172.5in
Width: 170.2cm 67.0in
Height: 161.3cm 63.5in
Ground clearance: 18.3cm 7.2in
Kerb weight: 1127.3kg 2483.0lb
Fuel: 50.0L 11.0gal 13.2galUS

4625 Vauxhall

Velox
1952 UK
86.0mph 138.4kmh
0-50mph 80.5kmh: 14.1secs
0-60mph 96.5kmh: 20.9secs
0-1/4 mile: 22.0secs
64.0bhp 47.7kW 64.9PS
@ 4000rpm
108.0lbft 146.3Nm @ 1200rpm
57.8bhp/ton 56.9bhp/tonne
28.3bhp/L 21.1kW/L 28.7PS/L
33.3ft/sec 10.2m/sec
18.4mph 29.6kmh/1000rpm
25.7mpg 21.4mpgUS 11.0L/100km
Petrol 4-stroke piston
2262cc 138.0cu in
In-line 6
Compression ratio: 6.4:1
Bore: 79.4mm 3.1in
Stroke: 76.2mm 3.0in
Valve type/No: Overhead 12
Transmission: Manual
No. of forward speeds: 3
Wheels driven: Rear
Springs F/R: Coil/Leaf
Brakes F/R: Drum/Drum
Wheelbase: 261.6cm 103.0in
Track F: 134.6cm 53.0in
Track R: 138.4cm 54.5in
Length: 438.2cm 172.5in
Width: 170.2cm 67.0in
Height: 161.3cm 63.5in
Ground clearance: 17.8cm 7.0in
Kerb weight: 1125.0kg 2478.0lb
Fuel: 50.0L 11.0gal 13.2galUS

4626 Vauxhall

Wyvern
1952 UK
71.0mph 114.2kmh
0-50mph 80.5kmh: 20.0secs
0-60mph 96.5kmh: 31.5secs
0-1/4 mile: 25.3secs
40.0bhp 29.8kW 40.5PS
@ 4000rpm
71.0lbft 96.2Nm @ 2000rpm
38.5bhp/ton 37.9bhp/tonne
26.5bhp/L 19.8kW/L 26.9PS/L
33.3ft/sec 10.2m/sec
16.1mph 25.9kmh/1000rpm

27.8mpg 23.1mpgUS 10.2L/100km
Petrol 4-stroke piston
1507cc 91.9cu in
In-line 4
Compression ratio: 6.4:1
Bore: 79.4mm 3.1in
Stroke: 76.2mm 3.0in
Valve type/No: Overhead 8
Transmission: Manual
No. of forward speeds: 3
Wheels driven: Rear
Springs F/R: Coil/Leaf
Brakes F/R: Drum/Drum
Wheelbase: 261.6cm 103.0in
Track F: 134.6cm 53.0in
Track R: 138.4cm 54.5in
Length: 438.2cm 172.5in
Width: 170.2cm 67.0in
Height: 160.5cm 63.2in
Ground clearance: 17.8cm 7.0in
Kerb weight: 1056.5kg 2327.0lb
Fuel: 50.0L 11.0gal 13.2galUS

4627 Vauxhall

Velox
1954 UK
82.0mph 131.9kmh
0-50mph 80.5kmh: 13.5secs
0-60mph 96.5kmh: 21.2secs
0-1/4 mile: 21.8secs
67.5bhp 50.3kW 68.4PS
@ 4000rpm
114.0lbft 154.5Nm @ 1400rpm
61.2bhp/ton 60.2bhp/tonne
29.8bhp/L 22.2kW/L 30.3PS/L
33.3ft/sec 10.2m/sec
18.4mph 29.6kmh/1000rpm
24.5mpg 20.4mpgUS 11.5L/100km
Petrol 4-stroke piston
2262cc 138.0cu in
In-line 6
Compression ratio: 7.3:1
Bore: 79.4mm 3.1in
Stroke: 76.2mm 3.0in
Valve type/No: Overhead 12
Transmission: Manual
No. of forward speeds: 3
Wheels driven: Rear
Springs F/R: Coil/Leaf
Brakes F/R: Drum/Drum
Wheelbase: 261.6cm 103.0in
Track F: 134.6cm 53.0in
Track R: 138.4cm 54.5in
Length: 438.2cm 172.5in
Width: 170.7cm 67.2in
Height: 161.3cm 63.5in
Ground clearance: 17.8cm 7.0in
Kerb weight: 1121.8kg 2471.0lb
Fuel: 50.0L 11.0gal 13.2galUS

4628 Vauxhall

Cresta
1955 UK
83.5mph 134.4kmh
0-50mph 80.5kmh: 12.8secs
0-60mph 96.5kmh: 19.7secs
0-1/4 mile: 21.2secs
67.5bhp 50.3kW 68.4PS
@ 4000rpm
114.0lbft 154.5Nm @ 2000rpm
59.2bhp/ton 58.2bhp/tonne
29.8bhp/L 22.2kW/L 30.3PS/L
33.3ft/sec 10.2m/sec
18.4mph 29.6kmh/1000rpm
24.1mpg 20.1mpgUS 11.7L/100km
Petrol 4-stroke piston
2262cc 138.0cu in
In-line 6
Compression ratio: 7.3:1
Bore: 79.4mm 3.1in
Stroke: 76.2mm 3.0in
Valve type/No: Overhead 12
Transmission: Manual
No. of forward speeds: 3
Wheels driven: Rear
Springs F/R: Coil/Leaf
Brakes F/R: Drum/Drum
Wheelbase: 261.6cm 103.0in
Track F: 134.6cm 53.0in
Track R: 138.4cm 54.5in
Length: 437.4cm 172.2in
Width: 168.9cm 66.5in
Height: 160.5cm 63.2in
Ground clearance: 17.8cm 7.0in
Kerb weight: 1160.0kg 2555.0lb
Fuel: 50.0L 11.0gal 13.2galUS

4629 Vauxhall

Wyvern
1955 UK
71.0mph 114.2kmh
0-50mph 80.5kmh: 20.2secs
0-60mph 96.5kmh: 31.1secs
0-1/4 mile: 24.3secs
47.7bhp 35.6kW 48.4PS
@ 4000rpm
81.1lbft 109.9Nm @ 2000rpm
44.9bhp/ton 44.1bhp/tonne
31.6bhp/L 23.6kW/L 32.1PS/L
33.3ft/sec 10.2m/sec
16.0mph 25.7kmh/1000rpm
28.6mpg 23.8mpgUS 9.9L/100km
Petrol 4-stroke piston
1507cc 91.9cu in
In-line 4
Compression ratio: 7.3:1
Bore: 79.4mm 3.1in
Stroke: 76.2mm 3.0in
Valve type/No: Overhead 8
Transmission: Manual
No. of forward speeds: 3
Wheels driven: Rear
Springs F/R: Coil/Leaf
Brakes F/R: Drum/Drum
Wheelbase: 261.6cm 103.0in
Track F: 134.6cm 53.0in
Track R: 138.4cm 54.5in
Length: 433.6cm 170.7in
Width: 168.9cm 66.5in
Height: 161.3cm 63.5in
Ground clearance: 17.0cm 6.7in
Kerb weight: 1080.5kg 2380.0lb
Fuel: 50.0L 11.0gal 13.2galUS

4630 Vauxhall

Cresta
1958 UK
90.0mph 144.8kmh
0-50mph 80.5kmh: 11.6secs
0-60mph 96.5kmh: 18.0secs
0-1/4 mile: 20.8secs
78.0bhp 58.2kW 79.1PS
@ 4400rpm
124.0lbft 168.0Nm @ 1800rpm
66.0bhp/ton 64.9bhp/tonne
34.5bhp/L 25.7kW/L 35.0PS/L
36.7ft/sec 11.2m/sec
17.7mph 28.5kmh/1000rpm
23.5mpg 19.6mpgUS 12.0L/100km
Petrol 4-stroke piston
2262cc 138.0cu in
In-line 6
Compression ratio: 7.8:1
Bore: 79.4mm 3.1in
Stroke: 76.2mm 3.0in
Valve type/No: Overhead 12
Transmission: Manual
No. of forward speeds: 3
Wheels driven: Rear
Springs F/R: Coil/Leaf
Brakes F/R: Drum/Drum
Wheelbase: 266.7cm 105.0in
Track F: 137.2cm 54.0in
Track R: 137.2cm 54.0in
Length: 450.9cm 177.5in
Width: 174.0cm 68.5in
Height: 144.8cm 57.0in
Ground clearance: 16.8cm 6.6in
Kerb weight: 1201.3kg 2646.0lb
Fuel: 49.1L 10.8gal 13.0galUS

4631 Vauxhall

Victor
1958 UK
75.2mph 121.0kmh
0-50mph 80.5kmh: 15.2secs
0-60mph 96.5kmh: 25.3secs
0-1/4 mile: 22.6secs
55.0bhp 41.0kW 55.8PS
@ 4200rpm
78.0lbft 105.7Nm @ 2000rpm
56.5bhp/ton 55.6bhp/tonne
36.5bhp/L 27.2kW/L 37.0PS/L
35.0ft/sec 10.7m/sec
Petrol 4-stroke piston
1507cc 91.9cu in
In-line 4
Compression ratio: 7.8:1
Bore: 79.4mm 3.1in
Stroke: 76.2mm 3.0in
Valve type/No: Overhead 8
Transmission: Manual
No. of forward speeds: 3
Wheels driven: Rear
Wheelbase: 248.9cm 98.0in
Track F: 127.0cm 50.0in
Track R: 127.0cm 50.0in
Kerb weight: 989.7kg 2180.0lb

4632 Vauxhall

Victor Estate
1958 UK
73.0mph 117.5kmh
0-50mph 80.5kmh: 17.8secs
0-60mph 96.5kmh: 27.4secs
0-1/4 mile: 23.7secs
55.8bhp 41.6kW 56.6PS
@ 4200rpm
84.5lbft 114.5Nm @ 2400rpm
52.8bhp/ton 51.9bhp/tonne
37.0bhp/L 27.6kW/L 37.5PS/L
35.0ft/sec 10.7m/sec
14.5mph 23.3kmh/1000rpm
30.7mpg 25.6mpgUS 9.2L/100km
Petrol 4-stroke piston
1507cc 91.9cu in
In-line 4
Compression ratio: 7.8:1
Bore: 79.4mm 3.1in
Stroke: 76.2mm 3.0in
Valve type/No: Overhead 8
Transmission: Manual
No. of forward speeds: 3
Wheels driven: Rear
Springs F/R: Coil/Leaf
Brakes F/R: Drum/Drum
Wheelbase: 248.9cm 98.0in
Track F: 127.0cm 50.0in
Track R: 127.0cm 50.0in
Length: 425.5cm 167.5in
Width: 158.8cm 62.5in
Height: 152.4cm 60.0in
Ground clearance: 17.8cm 7.0in
Kerb weight: 1074.2kg 2366.0lb
Fuel: 36.4L 8.0gal 9.6galUS

4633 Vauxhall

Friary Estate Car
1959 UK
91.5mph 147.2kmh
0-50mph 80.5kmh: 12.7secs
0-60mph 96.5kmh: 18.4secs
0-1/4 mile: 21.4secs
82.5bhp 61.5kW 83.6PS
@ 4400rpm
124.0lbft 168.0Nm @ 1800rpm
66.8bhp/ton 65.7bhp/tonne
36.5bhp/L 27.2kW/L 37.0PS/L
36.7ft/sec 11.2m/sec
17.6mph 28.3kmh/1000rpm
21.9mpg 18.2mpgUS 12.9L/100km
Petrol 4-stroke piston
2262cc 138.0cu in
In-line 6
Compression ratio: 7.8:1
Bore: 79.4mm 3.1in
Stroke: 76.2mm 3.0in
Valve type/No: Overhead 12
Transmission: Manual
No. of forward speeds: 3
Wheels driven: Rear
Springs F/R: Coil/Leaf
Brakes F/R: Drum/Drum
Wheelbase: 266.7cm 105.0in
Track F: 137.2cm 54.0in
Track R: 137.2cm 54.0in
Length: 452.1cm 178.0in
Width: 174.0cm 68.5in
Height: 148.6cm 58.5in
Ground clearance: 15.7cm 6.2in
Kerb weight: 1255.3kg 2765.0lb
Fuel: 63.7L 14.0gal 16.8galUS

4634 Vauxhall

Victor de Luxe
1959 UK
80.0mph 128.7kmh
0-50mph 80.5kmh: 15.5secs
0-60mph 96.5kmh: 28.1secs
0-1/4 mile: 22.8secs
54.8bhp 40.9kW 55.6PS
@ 4200rpm
84.5lbft 114.5Nm @ 2400rpm
53.3bhp/ton 52.4bhp/tonne
36.4bhp/L 27.1kW/L 36.9PS/L
35.0ft/sec 10.7m/sec
16.5mph 26.5kmh/1000rpm
28.1mpg 23.4mpgUS 10.1L/100km
Petrol 4-stroke piston
1507cc 91.9cu in
In-line 4
Compression ratio: 7.8:1
Bore: 79.4mm 3.1in
Stroke: 76.2mm 3.0in
Valve type/No: Overhead 8
Transmission: Manual
No. of forward speeds: 3
Wheels driven: Rear
Springs F/R: Coil/Leaf
Brakes F/R: Drum/Drum
Wheelbase: 248.9cm 98.0in
Track F: 127.0cm 50.0in
Track R: 127.0cm 50.0in
Length: 426.7cm 168.0in
Width: 162.8cm 64.1in
Height: 150.4cm 59.2in
Ground clearance: 16.0cm 6.3in
Kerb weight: 1045.6kg 2303.0lb
Fuel: 36.4L 8.0gal 9.6galUS

4635 Vauxhall

Cresta
1960 UK
90.0mph 144.8kmh
0-50mph 80.5kmh: 11.6secs
0-60mph 96.5kmh: 18.0secs
0-1/4 mile: 20.8secs
78.0bhp 58.2kW 79.1PS
@ 4400rpm
124.0lbft 168.0Nm @ 1800rpm
63.2bhp/ton 62.1bhp/tonne
34.5bhp/L 25.7kW/L 35.0PS/L
36.7ft/sec 11.2m/sec
17.7mph 28.5kmh/1000rpm
23.5mpg 19.6mpgUS 12.0L/100km
Petrol 4-stroke piston
2262cc 138.0cu in
In-line 6
Compression ratio: 7.8:1
Bore: 79.4mm 3.1in
Stroke: 76.2mm 3.0in
Valve type/No: Overhead 12
Transmission: Manual
No. of forward speeds: 3
Wheels driven: Rear
Springs F/R: Coil/Leaf
Brakes F/R: Drum/Drum
Wheelbase: 266.7cm 105.0in
Track F: 137.2cm 54.0in
Track R: 137.2cm 54.0in
Length: 450.9cm 177.5in
Width: 174.0cm 68.5in
Height: 144.8cm 57.0in
Ground clearance: 16.8cm 6.6in
Kerb weight: 1255.3kg 2765.0lb
Fuel: 49.1L 10.8gal 13.0galUS

4636 Vauxhall

Cresta Overdrive
1960 UK
97.0mph 156.1kmh
0-50mph 80.5kmh: 11.9secs
0-60mph 96.5kmh: 16.3secs
0-1/4 mile: 20.4secs
94.6bhp 70.5kW 95.9PS
@ 4600rpm
138.0lbft 187.0Nm @ 1600rpm
76.6bhp/ton 75.4bhp/tonne
35.7bhp/L 26.6kW/L 36.2PS/L
41.5ft/sec 12.7m/sec
18.8mph 30.2kmh/1000rpm
20.2mpg 16.8mpgUS 14.0L/100km
Petrol 4-stroke piston
2651cc 161.7cu in
In-line 6
Compression ratio: 8.1:1
Bore: 82.5mm 3.2in
Stroke: 82.5mm 3.2in
Valve type/No: Overhead 12
Transmission: Manual with overdrive
No. of forward speeds: 5
Wheels driven: Rear
Springs F/R: Coil/Leaf
Brakes F/R: Drum/Drum
Wheelbase: 266.7cm 105.0in
Track F: 137.2cm 54.0in
Track R: 137.2cm 54.0in
Length: 450.9cm 177.5in
Width: 174.0cm 68.5in
Height: 144.8cm 57.0in
Ground clearance: 17.8cm 7.0in
Kerb weight: 1255.3kg 2765.0lb
Fuel: 49.1L 10.8gal 13.0galUS

4637 Vauxhall

Velox III

1960 UK
92.0mph 148.0kmh
0-50mph 80.5kmh: 12.7secs
0-60mph 96.5kmh: 17.4secs
0-1/4 mile: 21.1secs
82.5bhp 61.5kW 83.6PS
@ 4400rpm
124.0lbft 168.0Nm @ 1800rpm
69.1bhp/ton 68.0bhp/tonne
36.5bhp/L 27.2kW/L 37.0PS/L
36.7ft/sec 11.2m/sec
22.7mph 36.5kmh/1000rpm
22.1mpg 18.4mpgUS 12.8L/100km
Petrol 4-stroke piston
2262cc 138.0cu in
In-line 6
Compression ratio: 7.8:1
Bore: 79.4mm 3.1in
Stroke: 76.2mm 3.0in
Valve type/No: Overhead 12
Transmission: Manual with overdrive
No. of forward speeds: 5
Wheels driven: Rear
Springs F/R: Coil/Leaf
Brakes F/R: Drum/Drum
Wheelbase: 266.7cm 105.0in
Track F: 137.2cm 54.0in
Track R: 137.2cm 54.0in
Length: 451.1cm 177.6in
Width: 174.0cm 68.5in
Height: 144.8cm 57.0in
Ground clearance: 17.8cm 7.0in
Kerb weight: 1214.0kg 2674.0lb
Fuel: 48.9L 10.7gal 12.9galUS

4638 Vauxhall

Victor Estate
1961 UK
78.0mph 125.5kmh
0-50mph 80.5kmh: 14.9secs
0-60mph 96.5kmh: 23.7secs
0-1/4 mile: 21.8secs
49.5bhp 36.9kW 50.2PS
@ 4600rpm
85.6lbft 116.0Nm @ 2200rpm
49.2bhp/ton 48.4bhp/tonne
32.8bhp/L 24.5kW/L 33.3PS/L
38.3ft/sec 11.7m/sec
16.9mph 27.2kmh/1000rpm
25.9mpg 21.6mpgUS 10.9L/100km
Petrol 4-stroke piston
1507cc 91.9cu in
In-line 4
Compression ratio: 8.1:1
Bore: 79.4mm 3.1in
Stroke: 76.2mm 3.0in
Valve type/No: Overhead 8
Transmission: Manual
No. of forward speeds: 3
Wheels driven: Rear
Springs F/R: Coil/Leaf
Brakes F/R: Drum/Drum
Wheelbase: 254.0cm 100.0in
Track F: 128.8cm 50.7in
Track R: 129.8cm 51.1in
Length: 439.9cm 173.2in
Width: 162.6cm 64.0in
Height: 147.3cm 58.0in
Ground clearance: 16.5cm 6.5in
Kerb weight: 1023.3kg 2254.0lb
Fuel: 45.5L 10.0gal 12.0galUS

4639 Vauxhall

Victor Super
1962 UK
77.0mph 123.9kmh
0-50mph 80.5kmh: 14.9secs
0-60mph 96.5kmh: 23.4secs
0-1/4 mile: 22.4secs
49.5bhp 36.9kW 50.2PS
@ 4600rpm
85.6lbft 116.0Nm @ 2200rpm
51.6bhp/ton 50.7bhp/tonne
32.8bhp/L 24.5kW/L 33.3PS/L
38.3ft/sec 11.7m/sec
17.5mph 28.2kmh/1000rpm
28.0mpg 23.3mpgUS 10.1L/100km
Petrol 4-stroke piston
1508cc 92.0cu in
In-line 4 1 Carburettor
Compression ratio: 8.0:1
Bore: 79.4mm 3.1in
Stroke: 76.2mm 3.0in
Valve type/No: Overhead 8
Transmission: Manual
No. of forward speeds: 4
Wheels driven: Rear
Springs F/R: Coil/Leaf
Brakes F/R: Drum/Drum
Steering: Recirculating ball
Wheelbase: 254.0cm 100.0in
Track F: 128.8cm 50.7in
Track R: 129.8cm 51.1in
Length: 439.9cm 173.2in
Width: 162.6cm 64.0in
Height: 144.8cm 57.0in
Ground clearance: 17.0cm 6.7in
Kerb weight: 975.6kg 2149.0lb
Fuel: 45.5L 10.0gal 12.0galUS

4640 Vauxhall

VX4/90
1962 UK
88.0mph 141.6kmh
0-50mph 80.5kmh: 11.6secs
0-60mph 96.5kmh: 16.9secs
0-1/4 mile: 20.1secs
71.5bhp 53.3kW 72.5PS
@ 5200rpm
91.0lbft 123.3Nm @ 2800rpm
72.4bhp/ton 71.2bhp/tonne
47.4bhp/L 35.4kW/L 48.1PS/L
43.3ft/sec 13.2m/sec
18.2mph 29.3kmh/1000rpm
24.2mpg 20.2mpgUS 11.7L/100km
Petrol 4-stroke piston
1508cc 92.0cu in
In-line 4 2 Carburettor
Compression ratio: 9.3:1
Bore: 79.4mm 3.1in
Stroke: 76.2mm 3.0in
Valve type/No: Overhead 8
Transmission: Manual
No. of forward speeds: 4
Wheels driven: Rear
Springs F/R: Coil/Leaf
Brake system: PA
Brakes F/R: Disc/Drum
Steering: Recirculating ball
Wheelbase: 254.0cm 100.0in
Track F: 130.3cm 51.3in
Track R: 128.5cm 50.6in
Length: 439.9cm 173.2in
Width: 162.6cm 64.0in
Height: 141.7cm 55.8in
Ground clearance: 17.0cm 6.7in
Kerb weight: 1004.2kg 2212.0lb
Fuel: 45.5L 10.0gal 12.0galUS

4641 Vauxhall

Cresta Series PB
1963 UK
93.0mph 149.6kmh
0-50mph 80.5kmh: 11.5secs
0-60mph 96.5kmh: 16.8secs
0-1/4 mile: 20.5secs
94.6bhp 70.5kW 95.9PS
@ 4600rpm
148.0lbft 200.5Nm @ 2400rpm
77.0bhp/ton 75.7bhp/tonne
35.7bhp/L 26.6kW/L 36.2PS/L
41.5ft/sec 12.7m/sec
19.6mph 31.5kmh/1000rpm
18.3mpg 15.2mpgUS 15.4L/100km
Petrol 4-stroke piston
2651cc 161.7cu in
In-line 6 1 Carburettor
Compression ratio: 8.5:1
Bore: 82.6mm 3.2in
Stroke: 82.6mm 3.2in
Valve type/No: Overhead 12
Transmission: Automatic
No. of forward speeds: 3
Wheels driven: Rear
Springs F/R: Coil/Leaf
Brake system: PA
Brakes F/R: Disc/Drum
Steering: Recirculating ball
Wheelbase: 271.8cm 107.0in
Track F: 139.2cm 54.8in
Track R: 142.7cm 56.2in
Length: 459.7cm 181.0in
Width: 177.8cm 70.0in
Height: 147.3cm 58.0in
Ground clearance: 16.5cm 6.5in
Kerb weight: 1248.9kg 2751.0lb
Fuel: 49.1L 10.8gal 13.0galUS

4642 Vauxhall

Viva de Luxe
1963 UK
80.5mph 129.5kmh
0-50mph 80.5kmh: 13.7secs
0-60mph 96.5kmh: 22.1secs
0-1/4 mile: 21.5secs
44.0bhp 32.8kW 44.6PS
@ 5200rpm
56.0lbft 75.9Nm @ 3000rpm
61.5bhp/ton 60.5bhp/tonne
41.6bhp/L 31.0kW/L 42.2PS/L
34.7ft/sec 10.6m/sec
15.0mph 24.1kmh/1000rpm
31.4mpg 26.1mpgUS 9.0L/100km
Petrol 4-stroke piston
1057cc 64.5cu in
In-line 4 1 Carburettor
Compression ratio: 8.5:1
Bore: 74.6mm 2.9in
Stroke: 61.0mm 2.4in
Valve type/No: Overhead 8
Transmission: Manual
No. of forward speeds: 4
Wheels driven: Rear
Springs F/R: Leaf/Leaf
Brakes F/R: Drum/Drum
Steering: Rack & pinion
Wheelbase: 232.4cm 91.5in
Track F: 120.4cm 47.4in
Track R: 122.4cm 48.2in
Length: 394.0cm 155.1in
Width: 150.9cm 59.4in
Height: 135.4cm 53.3in
Ground clearance: 12.7cm 5.0in
Kerb weight: 727.8kg 1603.0lb
Fuel: 31.8L 7.0gal 8.4galUS

4643 Vauxhall

Bedford Beagle
1964 UK
73.0mph 117.5kmh
0-50mph 80.5kmh: 16.7secs
0-60mph 96.5kmh: 29.1secs
0-1/4 mile: 22.6secs
40.3bhp 30.0kW 40.9PS
@ 5200rpm
55.0lbft 74.5Nm @ 2600rpm
53.7bhp/ton 52.8bhp/tonne
38.1bhp/L 28.4kW/L 38.7PS/L
34.7ft/sec 10.6m/sec
15.0mph 24.1kmh/1000rpm
32.1mpg 26.7mpgUS 8.8L/100km
Petrol 4-stroke piston
1057cc 64.5cu in
In-line 4 1 Carburettor
Compression ratio: 7.3:1
Bore: 74.3mm 2.9in
Stroke: 61.0mm 2.4in
Valve type/No: Overhead 8
Transmission: Manual
No. of forward speeds: 4
Wheels driven: Rear
Springs F/R: Leaf/Leaf
Brakes F/R: Drum/Drum
Steering: Rack & pinion
Wheelbase: 232.4cm 91.5in
Track F: 120.4cm 47.4in
Track R: 122.4cm 48.2in
Length: 381.5cm 150.2in
Width: 150.9cm 59.4in
Height: 149.9cm 59.0in
Ground clearance: 12.7cm 5.0in
Kerb weight: 762.7kg 1680.0lb
Fuel: 31.8L 7.0gal 8.4galUS

4644 Vauxhall

Victor Estate
1964 UK
87.0mph 140.0kmh
0-50mph 80.5kmh: 13.1secs
0-60mph 96.5kmh: 19.7secs
0-1/4 mile: 21.2secs
58.5bhp 43.6kW 59.3PS
@ 4800rpm
93.1lbft 126.2Nm @ 2800rpm
55.5bhp/ton 54.6bhp/tonne
36.7bhp/L 27.4kW/L 37.2PS/L
40.0ft/sec 12.2m/sec
18.1mph 29.1kmh/1000rpm
24.0mpg 20.0mpgUS 11.8L/100km
Petrol 4-stroke piston
1594cc 97.2cu in
In-line 4 1 Carburettor
Compression ratio: 8.5:1
Bore: 81.6mm 3.2in
Stroke: 76.2mm 3.0in
Valve type/No: Overhead 8
Transmission: Manual
No. of forward speeds: 4
Wheels driven: Rear
Springs F/R: Coil/Leaf
Brakes F/R: Disc/Drum
Steering: Recirculating ball
Wheelbase: 254.0cm 100.0in
Track F: 128.8cm 50.7in
Track R: 129.8cm 51.1in
Length: 439.4cm 173.0in
Width: 162.6cm 64.0in
Height: 143.5cm 56.5in
Ground clearance: 16.5cm 6.5in
Kerb weight: 1071.4kg 2360.0lb
Fuel: 45.5L 10.0gal 12.0galUS

4645 Vauxhall

VX4/90
1964 UK
94.0mph 151.2kmh
0-50mph 80.5kmh: 11.0secs
0-60mph 96.5kmh: 15.7secs
0-1/4 mile: 20.1secs
73.8bhp 55.0kW 74.8PS
@ 5200rpm
98.7lbft 133.7Nm @ 3200rpm
74.9bhp/ton 73.6bhp/tonne
46.3bhp/L 34.5kW/L 46.9PS/L
43.3ft/sec 13.2m/sec
18.1mph 29.1kmh/1000rpm
24.8mpg 20.7mpgUS 11.4L/100km
Petrol 4-stroke piston
1594cc 97.2cu in
In-line 4 2 Carburettor
Compression ratio: 9.3:1
Bore: 81.6mm 3.2in
Stroke: 76.2mm 3.0in
Valve type/No: Overhead 8
Transmission: Manual
No. of forward speeds: 4
Wheels driven: Rear
Springs F/R: Coil/Leaf
Brakes F/R: Disc/Drum
Steering: Recirculating ball
Wheelbase: 254.0cm 100.0in
Track F: 130.3cm 51.3in
Track R: 128.5cm 50.6in
Length: 439.9cm 173.2in
Width: 162.6cm 64.0in
Height: 141.7cm 55.8in
Ground clearance: 17.0cm 6.7in
Kerb weight: 1002.4kg 2208.0lb
Fuel: 45.5L 10.0gal 12.0galUS

4646 Vauxhall

Cresta de Luxe Powerglide
1965 UK
102.0mph 164.1kmh
0-50mph 80.5kmh: 10.0secs
0-60mph 96.5kmh: 14.0secs
0-1/4 mile: 20.0secs
123.0bhp 91.7kW 124.7PS
@ 4600rpm
176.0lbft 238.5Nm @ 2400rpm
95.2bhp/ton 93.6bhp/tonne
37.3bhp/L 27.8kW/L 37.9PS/L
41.5ft/sec 12.7m/sec
20.9mph 33.6kmh/1000rpm
14.9mpg 12.4mpgUS 19.0L/100km
Petrol 4-stroke piston
3294cc 201.0cu in
In-line 6 1 Carburettor
Compression ratio: 8.5:1
Bore: 92.0mm 3.6in
Stroke: 82.5mm 3.2in
Valve type/No: Overhead 12
Transmission: Automatic
No. of forward speeds: 2
Wheels driven: Rear
Springs F/R: Coil/Leaf
Brake system: PA
Brakes F/R: Disc/Drum
Steering: Recirculating ball PA
Wheelbase: 273.1cm 107.5in
Track F: 138.9cm 54.7in
Track R: 142.7cm 56.2in
Length: 475.0cm 187.0in
Width: 177.8cm 70.0in
Height: 141.0cm 55.5in
Ground clearance: 14.0cm 5.5in
Kerb weight: 1313.9kg 2894.0lb
Fuel: 68.2L 15.0gal 18.0galUS

4647 Vauxhall

Velox
1965 UK
102.0mph 164.1kmh
0-50mph 80.5kmh: 8.2secs
0-60mph 96.5kmh: 11.6secs
0-1/4 mile: 18.2secs
114.8bhp 85.6kW 116.4PS

@ 4200rpm
165.0lbft 223.6Nm @ 2200rpm
94.7bhp/ton 93.1bhp/tonne
34.8bhp/L 26.0kW/L 35.3PS/L
37.9ft/sec 11.6m/sec
20.9mph 33.6kmh/1000rpm
18.7mpg 15.6mpgUS 15.1L/100km
Petrol 4-stroke piston
3294cc 201.0cu in
In-line 6 1 Carburettor
Compression ratio: 8.5:1
Bore: 96.1mm 3.8in
Stroke: 82.5mm 3.2in
Valve type/No: Overhead 12
Transmission: Manual
No. of forward speeds: 4
Wheels driven: Rear
Springs F/R: Coil/Leaf
Brake system: PA
Brakes F/R: Disc/Drum
Steering: Recirculating ball
Wheelbase: 271.8cm 107.0in
Track F: 139.2cm 54.8in
Track R: 142.7cm 56.2in
Length: 459.7cm 181.0in
Width: 177.8cm 70.0in
Height: 147.3cm 58.0in
Ground clearance: 16.5cm 6.5in
Kerb weight: 1233.1kg 2716.0lb
Fuel: 49.1L 10.8gal 13.0galUS

4648 Vauxhall

Victor 101 Estate
1965 UK
85.5mph 137.6kmh
0-50mph 80.5kmh: 12.8secs
0-60mph 96.5kmh: 18.8secs
0-1/4 mile: 21.1secs
60.0bhp 44.7kW 60.8PS
@ 4600rpm
86.0lbft 116.5Nm @ 2400rpm
56.1bhp/ton 55.2bhp/tonne
37.6bhp/L 28.0kW/L 38.1PS/L
38.3ft/sec 11.7m/sec
16.9mph 27.2kmh/1000rpm
21.2mpg 17.7mpgUS 13.3L/100km
Petrol 4-stroke piston
1595cc 97.3cu in
In-line 4 1 Carburettor
Compression ratio: 9.0:1
Bore: 81.6mm 3.2in
Stroke: 76.2mm 3.0in
Valve type/No: Overhead 8
Transmission: Manual
No. of forward speeds: 4
Wheels driven: Rear
Springs F/R: Coil/Leaf
Brake system: PA
Brakes F/R: Disc/Drum
Steering: Recirculating ball
Wheelbase: 243.8cm 96.0in
Track F: 129.5cm 51.0in
Track R: 133.4cm 52.5in
Length: 443.7cm 174.7in
Width: 164.3cm 64.7in
Height: 140.2cm 55.2in
Ground clearance: 17.0cm 6.7in
Kerb weight: 1087.3kg 2395.0lb
Fuel: 45.5L 10.0gal 12.0galUS

4649 Vauxhall

Viva SL90
1965 UK
82.0mph 131.9kmh
0-50mph 80.5kmh: 12.4secs
0-60mph 96.5kmh: 18.2secs
0-1/4 mile: 20.5secs
0-1km: 39.9secs
53.7bhp 40.0kW 54.4PS
@ 5600rpm
60.4lbft 81.8Nm @ 3200rpm
68.7bhp/ton 67.6bhp/tonne
50.8bhp/L 37.9kW/L 51.5PS/L
37.3ft/sec 11.4m/sec
15.0mph 24.1kmh/1000rpm
27.7mpg 23.1mpgUS 10.2L/100km
Petrol 4-stroke piston
1057cc 64.5cu in
In-line 4 1 Carburettor
Compression ratio: 9.0:1
Bore: 74.3mm 2.9in
Stroke: 61.0mm 2.4in
Valve type/No: Overhead 8
Transmission: Manual
No. of forward speeds: 4
Wheels driven: Rear
Springs F/R: Leaf/Leaf
Brake system: PA
Brakes F/R: Disc/Drum
Steering: Rack & pinion
Wheelbase: 232.4cm 91.5in
Track F: 120.4cm 47.4in
Track R: 122.4cm 48.2in
Length: 394.0cm 155.1in
Width: 150.9cm 59.4in
Height: 135.4cm 53.3in
Ground clearance: 12.7cm 5.0in
Kerb weight: 794.5kg 1750.0lb
Fuel: 31.8L 7.0gal 8.4galUS

4650 Vauxhall

VX4/90
1965 UK
96.0mph 154.5kmh
0-50mph 80.5kmh: 11.5secs
0-60mph 96.5kmh: 16.9secs
0-1/4 mile: 20.2secs
73.8bhp 55.0kW 74.8PS
@ 5200rpm
98.7lbft 133.7Nm @ 3200rpm
72.4bhp/ton 71.2bhp/tonne
46.3bhp/L 34.5kW/L 46.9PS/L
43.2ft/sec 13.2m/sec
17.5mph 28.2kmh/1000rpm
23.3mpg 19.4mpgUS 12.1L/100km
Petrol 4-stroke piston
1594cc 97.2cu in
In-line 4 2 Carburettor
Compression ratio: 9.3:1
Bore: 82.0mm 3.2in
Stroke: 76.0mm 3.0in
Valve type/No: Overhead 8
Transmission: Manual
No. of forward speeds: 4
Wheels driven: Rear
Springs F/R: Coil/Leaf
Brake system: PA
Brakes F/R: Disc/Drum
Steering: Recirculating ball
Wheelbase: 254.0cm 100.0in
Track F: 129.5cm 51.0in
Track R: 133.6cm 52.6in
Length: 449.6cm 177.0in
Width: 164.3cm 64.7in
Height: 143.5cm 56.5in
Ground clearance: 15.2cm 6.0in
Kerb weight: 1036.0kg 2282.0lb
Fuel: 45.5L 10.0gal 12.0galUS

4651 Vauxhall

Viscount Automatic
1966 UK
98.0mph 157.7kmh
0-50mph 80.5kmh: 11.5secs
0-60mph 96.5kmh: 15.9secs
0-1/4 mile: 20.5secs
0-1km: 37.9secs
123.0bhp 91.7kW 124.7PS
@ 4600rpm
176.0lbft 238.5Nm @ 2400rpm
89.7bhp/ton 88.2bhp/tonne
37.3bhp/L 27.8kW/L 37.9PS/L
41.5ft/sec 12.6m/sec
21.3mph 34.3kmh/1000rpm
14.3mpg 11.9mpgUS 19.8L/100km
Petrol 4-stroke piston
3294cc 201.0cu in
In-line 6 1 Carburettor
Compression ratio: 8.5:1
Bore: 92.0mm 3.6in
Stroke: 82.5mm 3.2in
Valve type/No: Overhead 12
Transmission: Automatic
No. of forward speeds: 2
Wheels driven: Rear
Springs F/R: Coil/Leaf
Brake system: PA
Brakes F/R: Disc/Drum
Steering: Recirculating ball PA
Wheelbase: 273.1cm 107.5in
Track F: 138.9cm 54.7in
Track R: 142.7cm 56.2in
Length: 475.0cm 187.0in
Width: 177.8cm 70.0in
Height: 141.0cm 55.5in
Ground clearance: 14.0cm 5.5in
Kerb weight: 1393.8kg 3070.0lb
Fuel: 68.2L 15.0gal 18.0galUS

4652 Vauxhall

Viva de Luxe
1966 UK
82.0mph 131.9kmh
0-50mph 80.5kmh: 13.1secs
0-60mph 96.5kmh: 19.7secs
0-1/4 mile: 21.0secs
0-1km: 40.5secs
47.0bhp 35.0kW 47.6PS
@ 5200rpm
61.8lbft 83.7Nm @ 2800rpm
60.7bhp/ton 59.7bhp/tonne
40.5bhp/L 30.2kW/L 41.1PS/L
34.7ft/sec 10.6m/sec
15.8mph 25.4kmh/1000rpm
28.1mpg 23.4mpgUS 10.1L/100km
Petrol 4-stroke piston
1159cc 70.7cu in
In-line 4 1 Carburettor
Compression ratio: 8.5:1
Bore: 77.7mm 3.1in
Stroke: 61.0mm 2.4in
Valve type/No: Overhead 8
Transmission: Manual
No. of forward speeds: 4
Wheels driven: Rear
Springs F/R: Coil/Coil
Brake system: PA
Brakes F/R: Disc/Drum
Steering: Rack & pinion
Wheelbase: 243.3cm 95.8in
Track F: 129.5cm 51.0in
Track R: 129.5cm 51.0in
Length: 410.5cm 161.6in
Width: 160.0cm 63.0in
Height: 134.9cm 53.1in
Ground clearance: 12.7cm 5.0in
Kerb weight: 787.2kg 1734.0lb
Fuel: 36.4L 8.0gal 9.6galUS

4653 Vauxhall

Cresta Estate
1967 UK
103.0mph 165.7kmh
0-50mph 80.5kmh: 10.1secs
0-60mph 96.5kmh: 13.7secs
0-1/4 mile: 19.6secs
0-1km: 35.9secs
123.0bhp 91.7kW 124.7PS
@ 4600rpm
176.0lbft 238.5Nm @ 2400rpm
89.0bhp/ton 87.5bhp/tonne
37.3bhp/L 27.8kW/L 37.9PS/L
41.5ft/sec 12.7m/sec
21.3mph 34.3kmh/1000rpm
18.3mpg 15.2mpgUS 15.4L/100km
Petrol 4-stroke piston
3294cc 201.0cu in
In-line 6 1 Carburettor
Compression ratio: 8.5:1
Bore: 92.1mm 3.6in
Stroke: 82.5mm 3.2in
Valve type/No: Overhead 12
Transmission: Manual
No. of forward speeds: 4
Wheels driven: Rear
Springs F/R: Coil/Leaf
Brake system: PA
Brakes F/R: Disc/Drum
Steering: Recirculating ball
Wheelbase: 273.1cm 107.5in
Track F: 138.9cm 54.7in
Track R: 142.7cm 56.2in
Length: 475.0cm 187.0in
Width: 177.8cm 70.0in
Height: 141.0cm 55.5in
Ground clearance: 14.0cm 5.5in
Kerb weight: 1405.6kg 3096.0lb
Fuel: 68.2L 15.0gal 18.0galUS

4654 Vauxhall

Victor 101 de Luxe
1967 UK
83.0mph 133.5kmh
0-50mph 80.5kmh: 14.5secs
0-60mph 96.5kmh: 20.4secs
0-1/4 mile: 21.6secs
0-1km: 41.2secs
66.0bhp 49.2kW 66.9PS
@ 4800rpm
89.0lbft 120.6Nm @ 2400rpm
63.8bhp/ton 62.8bhp/tonne
41.4bhp/L 30.9kW/L 42.0PS/L
40.0ft/sec 12.2m/sec
16.4mph 26.4kmh/1000rpm
23.1mpg 19.2mpgUS 12.2L/100km
Petrol 4-stroke piston
1595cc 97.3cu in
In-line 4 1 Carburettor
Compression ratio: 9.0:1
Bore: 81.6mm 3.2in
Stroke: 76.2mm 3.0in
Valve type/No: Overhead 8
Transmission: Manual
No. of forward speeds: 4
Wheels driven: Rear
Springs F/R: Coil/Leaf
Brake system: PA
Brakes F/R: Disc/Drum
Steering: Recirculating ball
Wheelbase: 254.0cm 100.0in
Track F: 129.5cm 51.0in
Track R: 133.6cm 52.6in
Length: 449.6cm 177.0in
Width: 164.3cm 64.7in
Height: 143.5cm 56.5in
Ground clearance: 15.2cm 6.0in
Kerb weight: 1051.5kg 2316.0lb
Fuel: 45.5L 10.0gal 12.0galUS

4655 Vauxhall

Victor 2000
1967 UK
98.0mph 157.7kmh
0-50mph 80.5kmh: 10.6secs
0-60mph 96.5kmh: 15.0secs
0-1/4 mile: 19.9secs
0-1km: 37.6secs
88.0bhp 65.6kW 89.2PS
@ 5500rpm
109.0lbft 147.7Nm @ 3000rpm
82.5bhp/ton 81.2bhp/tonne
44.6bhp/L 33.2kW/L 45.2PS/L
41.6ft/sec 12.7m/sec
16.4mph 26.4kmh/1000rpm
23.6mpg 19.7mpgUS 12.0L/100km
Petrol 4-stroke piston
1975cc 120.5cu in
In-line 4 1 Carburettor
Compression ratio: 8.5:1
Bore: 95.3mm 3.8in
Stroke: 69.2mm 2.7in
Valve type/No: Overhead 8
Transmission: Manual
No. of forward speeds: 4
Wheels driven: Rear
Springs F/R: Coil/Coil
Brake system: PA
Brakes F/R: Disc/Drum
Steering: Rack & pinion
Wheelbase: 254.0cm 100.0in
Track F: 138.7cm 54.6in
Track R: 137.2cm 54.0in
Length: 448.8cm 176.7in
Width: 169.9cm 66.9in
Height: 139.7cm 55.0in
Ground clearance: 15.2cm 6.0in
Kerb weight: 1084.1kg 2388.0lb
Fuel: 54.6L 12.0gal 14.4galUS

4656 Vauxhall

Ventora
1968 UK
104.0mph 167.3kmh
0-50mph 80.5kmh: 8.7secs
0-60mph 96.5kmh: 11.8secs
0-1/4 mile: 18.4secs
0-1km: 34.2secs
123.0bhp 91.7kW 124.7PS
@ 4600rpm
176.0lbft 238.5Nm @ 2400rpm
106.4bhp/ton 104.6bhp/tonne
37.3bhp/L 27.8kW/L 37.9PS/L
41.5ft/sec 12.7m/sec
19.5mph 31.4kmh/1000rpm
16.8mpg 14.0mpgUS 16.8L/100km
Petrol 4-stroke piston
3294cc 201.0cu in
In-line 6 1 Carburettor
Compression ratio: 8.5:1
Bore: 92.0mm 3.6in
Stroke: 82.5mm 3.2in
Valve type/No: Overhead 12
Transmission: Manual
No. of forward speeds: 4
Wheels driven: Rear
Springs F/R: Coil/Coil
Brake system: PA
Brakes F/R: Disc/Drum
Steering: Rack & pinion
Wheelbase: 259.1cm 102.0in
Track F: 138.7cm 54.6in
Track R: 137.2cm 54.0in
Length: 448.8cm 176.7in
Width: 169.9cm 66.9in
Height: 139.7cm 55.0in
Ground clearance: 15.2cm 6.0in
Kerb weight: 1175.4kg 2589.0lb
Fuel: 54.6L 12.0gal 14.4galUS

4657 Vauxhall
Victor 2000 Estate Automatic
1968 UK
90.0mph 144.8kmh
0-50mph 80.5kmh: 12.2secs
0-60mph 96.5kmh: 17.1secs
0-1/4 mile: 21.0secs
0-1km: 37.5secs
88.0bhp 65.6kW 89.2PS
@ 5500rpm
109.0lbft 147.7Nm @ 3000rpm
77.6bhp/ton 76.3bhp/tonne
44.6bhp/L 33.2kW/L 45.2PS/L
41.7ft/sec 12.7m/sec
17.4mph 28.0kmh/1000rpm
19.3mpg 16.1mpgUS 14.6L/100km
Petrol 4-stroke piston
1975cc 120.5cu in
In-line 4 1 Carburettor
Compression ratio: 8.5:1
Bore: 95.2mm 3.8in
Stroke: 69.2mm 2.7in
Valve type/No: Overhead 8
Transmission: Automatic
No. of forward speeds: 3
Wheels driven: Rear
Springs F/R: Coil/Coil
Brake system: PA
Brakes F/R: Disc/Drum
Steering: Rack & pinion
Wheelbase: 254.0cm 100.0in
Track F: 138.4cm 54.5in
Track R: 137.2cm 54.0in
Length: 448.3cm 176.5in
Width: 170.2cm 67.0in
Height: 141.0cm 55.5in
Ground clearance: 17.8cm 7.0in
Kerb weight: 1153.2kg 2540.0lb
Fuel: 54.6L 12.0gal 14.4galUS

4658 Vauxhall
Viva GT
1968 UK
102.0mph 164.1kmh
0-50mph 80.5kmh: 8.2secs
0-60mph 96.5kmh: 11.9secs
0-1/4 mile: 18.1secs
0-1km: 34.0secs
104.0bhp 77.5kW 105.4PS
@ 5600rpm
117.0lbft 158.5Nm @ 3400rpm
110.7bhp/ton 108.8bhp/tonne
52.7bhp/L 39.3kW/L 53.4PS/L
42.5ft/sec 12.9m/sec
17.0mph 27.4kmh/1000rpm
22.3mpg 18.6mpgUS 12.7L/100km
Petrol 4-stroke piston
1975cc 120.5cu in
In-line 4 2 Carburettor
Compression ratio: 8.5:1
Bore: 95.2mm 3.8in
Stroke: 69.2mm 2.7in
Valve type/No: Overhead 8
Transmission: Manual
No. of forward speeds: 4
Wheels driven: Rear
Springs F/R: Coil/Coil
Brake system: PA
Brakes F/R: Disc/Drum
Steering: Rack & pinion
Wheelbase: 241.3cm 95.0in
Track F: 129.5cm 51.0in
Track R: 129.5cm 51.0in
Length: 410.5cm 161.6in
Width: 160.0cm 63.0in
Height: 137.2cm 54.0in
Ground clearance: 12.7cm 5.0in
Kerb weight: 955.7kg 2105.0lb
Fuel: 36.4L 8.0gal 9.6galUS

4659 Vauxhall
Viva SL90 Estate
1968 UK
82.0mph 131.9kmh
0-50mph 80.5kmh: 13.1secs
0-60mph 96.5kmh: 19.4secs
0-1/4 mile: 20.8secs
0-1km: 40.1secs
59.5bhp 44.4kW 60.3PS
@ 5600rpm
69.0lbft 93.5Nm @ 4200rpm
70.5bhp/ton 69.3bhp/tonne
51.3bhp/L 38.3kW/L 52.0PS/L
37.3ft/sec 11.4m/sec
14.7mph 23.7kmh/1000rpm
25.8mpg 21.5mpgUS 10.9L/100km
Petrol 4-stroke piston
1159cc 70.7cu in
In-line 4 1 Carburettor
Compression ratio: 9.0:1
Bore: 77.7mm 3.1in
Stroke: 61.0mm 2.4in
Valve type/No: Overhead 8
Transmission: Manual
No. of forward speeds: 4
Wheels driven: Rear
Springs F/R: Coil/Coil
Brake system: PA
Brakes F/R: Disc/Drum
Steering: Rack & pinion
Wheelbase: 241.3cm 95.0in
Track F: 129.5cm 51.0in
Track R: 129.5cm 51.0in
Length: 410.5cm 161.6in
Width: 160.0cm 63.0in
Height: 137.2cm 54.0in
Ground clearance: 12.7cm 5.0in
Kerb weight: 858.5kg 1891.0lb
Fuel: 36.4L 8.0gal 9.6galUS

4660 Vauxhall
Victor
1969 UK
90.0mph 144.8kmh
0-50mph 80.5kmh: 12.7secs
0-60mph 96.5kmh: 19.3secs
0-1/4 mile: 21.2secs
0-1km: 40.0secs
72.0bhp 53.7kW 73.0PS
@ 5600rpm
90.0lbft 122.0Nm @ 3200rpm
68.6bhp/ton 67.5bhp/tonne
45.0bhp/L 33.6kW/L 45.6PS/L
42.3ft/sec 12.9m/sec
16.3mph 26.2kmh/1000rpm
26.5mpg 22.1mpgUS 10.7L/100km
Petrol 4-stroke piston
1599cc 97.6cu in
In-line 4 1 Carburettor
Compression ratio: 8.5:1
Bore: 85.7mm 3.4in
Stroke: 69.2mm 2.7in
Valve type/No: Overhead 8
Transmission: Manual
No. of forward speeds: 4
Wheels driven: Rear
Springs F/R: Coil/Coil
Brake system: PA
Brakes F/R: Disc/Drum
Steering: Rack & pinion
Wheelbase: 254.0cm 100.0in
Track F: 138.7cm 54.6in
Track R: 137.2cm 54.0in
Length: 448.8cm 176.7in
Width: 169.9cm 66.9in
Height: 141.0cm 55.5in
Ground clearance: 15.2cm 6.0in
Kerb weight: 1067.3kg 2351.0lb
Fuel: 54.6L 12.0gal 14.4galUS

4661 Vauxhall
Ventora II
1970 UK
107.0mph 172.2kmh
0-50mph 80.5kmh: 8.4secs
0-60mph 96.5kmh: 12.1secs
0-1/4 mile: 18.7secs
0-1km: 34.6secs
124.0bhp 92.5kW 125.7PS
@ 4600rpm
174.0lbft 235.8Nm @ 2400rpm
105.5bhp/ton 103.7bhp/tonne
37.6bhp/L 28.1kW/L 38.2PS/L
41.5ft/sec 12.7m/sec
21.1mph 33.9kmh/1000rpm
20.6mpg 17.2mpgUS 13.7L/100km
Petrol 4-stroke piston
3294cc 201.0cu in
In-line 6 1 Carburettor
Compression ratio: 8.5:1
Bore: 92.1mm 3.6in
Stroke: 82.6mm 3.2in
Valve type/No: Overhead 12
Transmission: Manual
No. of forward speeds: 4
Wheels driven: Rear
Springs F/R: Coil/Coil
Brake system: PA
Brakes F/R: Disc/Drum
Steering: Rack & pinion
Wheelbase: 259.1cm 102.0in
Track F: 138.7cm 54.6in
Track R: 137.2cm 54.0in
Length: 448.8cm 176.7in
Width: 169.9cm 66.9in
Height: 139.7cm 55.0in
Ground clearance: 15.2cm 6.0in
Kerb weight: 1195.4kg 2633.0lb
Fuel: 54.6L 12.0gal 14.4galUS

4662 Vauxhall
Viva GT
1970 UK
102.0mph 164.1kmh
0-50mph 80.5kmh: 8.2secs
0-60mph 96.5kmh: 12.1secs
0-1/4 mile: 18.5secs
0-1km: 35.0secs
104.0bhp 77.5kW 105.4PS
@ 5600rpm
117.0lbft 158.5Nm @ 3400rpm
109.1bhp/ton 107.2bhp/tonne
52.7bhp/L 39.3kW/L 53.4PS/L
42.5ft/sec 12.9m/sec
18.7mph 30.1kmh/1000rpm
25.2mpg 21.0mpgUS 11.2L/100km
Petrol 4-stroke piston
1975cc 120.5cu in
In-line 4 2 Carburettor
Compression ratio: 8.5:1
Bore: 95.2mm 3.8in
Stroke: 69.2mm 2.7in
Valve type/No: Overhead 8
Transmission: Manual
No. of forward speeds: 4
Wheels driven: Rear
Springs F/R: Coil/Coil
Brake system: PA
Brakes F/R: Disc/Drum
Steering: Rack & pinion
Wheelbase: 241.3cm 95.0in
Track F: 129.5cm 51.0in
Track R: 129.5cm 51.0in
Length: 410.5cm 161.6in
Width: 160.0cm 63.0in
Height: 137.2cm 54.0in
Ground clearance: 12.7cm 5.0in
Kerb weight: 969.7kg 2136.0lb
Fuel: 54.6L 12.0gal 14.4galUS

4663 Vauxhall
Firenza
1971 UK
99.0mph 159.3kmh
0-50mph 80.5kmh: 8.3secs
0-60mph 96.5kmh: 11.8secs
0-1/4 mile: 18.4secs
0-1km: 34.7secs
104.0bhp 77.5kW 105.4PS
@ 5600rpm
117.0lbft 158.5Nm @ 3400rpm
106.4bhp/ton 104.6bhp/tonne
52.7bhp/L 39.3kW/L 53.4PS/L
42.5ft/sec 12.9m/sec
19.2mph 30.9kmh/1000rpm
22.3mpg 18.6mpgUS 12.7L/100km
Petrol 4-stroke piston
1975cc 120.5cu in
In-line 4 2 Carburettor
Compression ratio: 8.5:1
Bore: 95.2mm 3.8in
Stroke: 69.2mm 2.7in
Valve type/No: Overhead 8
Transmission: Manual
No. of forward speeds: 4
Wheels driven: Rear
Springs F/R: Coil/Coil
Brake system: PA
Brakes F/R: Disc/Drum
Steering: Rack & pinion
Wheelbase: 246.4cm 97.0in
Track F: 134.6cm 53.0in
Track R: 134.6cm 53.0in
Length: 411.5cm 162.0in
Width: 162.6cm 64.0in
Height: 139.7cm 55.0in
Ground clearance: 15.2cm 6.0in
Kerb weight: 994.3kg 2190.0lb
Fuel: 54.6L 12.0gal 14.4galUS

4664 Vauxhall
Viva de Luxe
1971 UK
81.0mph 130.3kmh
0-50mph 80.5kmh: 14.3secs
0-60mph 96.5kmh: 21.3secs
0-1/4 mile: 21.8secs
0-1km: 42.1secs
49.0bhp 36.5kW 49.7PS
@ 5300rpm
63.0lbft 85.4Nm @ 2900rpm
57.7bhp/ton 56.7bhp/tonne
42.3bhp/L 31.5kW/L 42.9PS/L
35.3ft/sec 10.8m/sec
16.0mph 25.7kmh/1000rpm
29.3mpg 24.4mpgUS 9.6L/100km
Petrol 4-stroke piston
1159cc 70.7cu in
In-line 4 1 Carburettor
Compression ratio: 8.5:1
Bore: 77.8mm 3.1in
Stroke: 61.0mm 2.4in
Valve type/No: Overhead 8
Transmission: Manual
No. of forward speeds: 4
Wheels driven: Rear
Springs F/R: Coil/Coil
Brake system: PA
Brakes F/R: Disc/Drum
Steering: Rack & pinion
Wheelbase: 246.4cm 97.0in
Track F: 130.8cm 51.5in
Track R: 130.8cm 51.5in
Length: 411.5cm 162.0in
Width: 164.3cm 64.7in
Height: 141.5cm 55.7in
Ground clearance: 13.2cm 5.2in
Kerb weight: 864.0kg 1903.0lb
Fuel: 36.4L 8.0gal 9.6galUS

4665 Vauxhall
Firenza Sport SL
1972 UK
104.0mph 167.3kmh
0-50mph 80.5kmh: 8.3secs
0-60mph 96.5kmh: 11.4secs
0-1/4 mile: 18.0secs
0-1km: 33.6secs
110.0bhp 82.0kW 111.5PS
@ 5200rpm
140.0lbft 189.7Nm @ 3000rpm
112.0bhp/ton 110.1bhp/tonne
48.3bhp/L 36.0kW/L 48.9PS/L
43.3ft/sec 13.2m/sec
19.2mph 30.9kmh/1000rpm
22.2mpg 18.5mpgUS 12.7L/100km
Petrol 4-stroke piston
2279cc 139.0cu in
In-line 4 2 Carburettor
Compression ratio: 8.5:1
Bore: 97.5mm 3.8in
Stroke: 76.2mm 3.0in
Valve type/No: Overhead 8
Transmission: Manual
No. of forward speeds: 4
Wheels driven: Rear
Springs F/R: Coil/Coil
Brake system: PA
Brakes F/R: Disc/Drum
Steering: Rack & pinion
Wheelbase: 246.4cm 97.0in
Track F: 134.6cm 53.0in
Track R: 134.6cm 53.0in
Length: 411.5cm 162.0in
Width: 162.6cm 64.0in
Height: 139.7cm 55.0in
Ground clearance: 15.2cm 6.0in
Kerb weight: 998.8kg 2200.0lb
Fuel: 54.6L 12.0gal 14.4galUS

4666 Vauxhall
Ventora
1972 UK
107.0mph 172.2kmh
0-50mph 80.5kmh: 8.8secs
0-60mph 96.5kmh: 12.6secs
0-1/4 mile: 18.6secs
0-1km: 34.6secs
124.0bhp 92.5kW 125.7PS
@ 4600rpm
174.0lbft 235.8Nm @ 2400rpm
104.8bhp/ton 103.0bhp/tonne
37.6bhp/L 28.1kW/L 38.2PS/L
41.5ft/sec 12.7m/sec
25.9mph 41.7kmh/1000rpm
18.0mpg 15.0mpgUS 15.7L/100km
Petrol 4-stroke piston
3294cc 201.0cu in
In-line 6 1 Carburettor
Compression ratio: 8.5:1
Bore: 92.1mm 3.6in
Stroke: 82.6mm 3.2in
Valve type/No: Overhead 12
Transmission: Manual with overdrive
No. of forward speeds: 6
Wheels driven: Rear
Springs F/R: Coil/Coil

Brake system: PA
Brakes F/R: Disc/Drum
Steering: Rack & pinion
Wheelbase: 266.7cm 105.0in
Track F: 142.7cm 56.2in
Track R: 140.7cm 55.4in
Length: 454.7cm 179.0in
Width: 169.4cm 66.7in
Height: 139.7cm 55.0in
Ground clearance: 15.2cm 6.0in
Kerb weight: 1203.5kg 2651.0lb
Fuel: 64.8L 14.2gal 17.1galUS

4667 Vauxhall

Victor 2300 SL
1972 UK
100.0mph 160.9kmh
0-50mph 80.5kmh: 8.9secs
0-60mph 96.5kmh: 12.4secs
0-1/4 mile: 18.2secs
0-1km: 34.6secs
100.0bhp 74.6kW 101.4PS
@ 5200rpm
138.0lbft 187.0Nm @ 3000rpm
88.9bhp/ton 87.4bhp/tonne
43.9bhp/L 32.7kW/L 44.5PS/L
43.3ft/sec 13.2m/sec
18.9mph 30.4kmh/1000rpm
21.6mpg 18.0mpgUS 13.1L/100km
Petrol 4-stroke piston
2279cc 139.0cu in
In-line 4 1 Carburettor
Compression ratio: 8.5:1
Bore: 97.5mm 3.8in
Stroke: 76.2mm 3.0in
Valve type/No: Overhead 8
Transmission: Manual
No. of forward speeds: 4
Wheels driven: Rear
Springs F/R: Coil/Coil
Brake system: PA
Brakes F/R: Disc/Drum
Steering: Rack & pinion
Wheelbase: 266.7cm 105.0in
Track F: 142.7cm 56.2in
Track R: 140.7cm 55.4in
Length: 454.7cm 179.0in
Width: 169.4cm 66.7in
Height: 139.7cm 55.0in
Ground clearance: 15.2cm 6.0in
Kerb weight: 1143.6kg 2519.0lb
Fuel: 64.8L 14.2gal 17.1galUS

4668 Vauxhall

Viva 1800
1972 UK
100.0mph 160.9kmh
0-50mph 80.5kmh: 9.3secs
0-60mph 96.5kmh: 13.1secs
0-1/4 mile: 18.7secs
0-1km: 35.3secs
78.0bhp 58.2kW 79.1PS
@ 5200rpm
97.0lbft 131.4Nm @ 3000rpm
82.1bhp/ton 80.8bhp/tonne
44.3bhp/L 33.1kW/L 45.0PS/L
43.3ft/sec 13.2m/sec
17.6mph 28.3kmh/1000rpm
23.1mpg 19.2mpgUS 12.2L/100km
Petrol 4-stroke piston
1759cc 107.3cu in
In-line 4 1 Carburettor
Compression ratio: 8.5:1
Bore: 85.7mm 3.4in
Stroke: 76.2mm 3.0in
Valve type/No: Overhead 8
Transmission: Manual
No. of forward speeds: 4
Wheels driven: Rear
Springs F/R: Coil/Coil
Brake system: PA
Brakes F/R: Disc/Drum
Steering: Rack & pinion
Wheelbase: 246.4cm 97.0in
Track F: 130.8cm 51.5in
Track R: 130.8cm 51.5in
Length: 411.5cm 162.0in
Width: 164.3cm 64.7in
Height: 139.7cm 55.0in
Ground clearance: 13.2cm 5.2in
Kerb weight: 965.7kg 2127.0lb
Fuel: 54.6L 12.0gal 14.4galUS

4669 Vauxhall

Viva HC Estate
1972 UK
87.0mph 140.0kmh
0-50mph 80.5kmh: 12.2secs
0-60mph 96.5kmh: 18.1secs
0-1/4 mile: 20.6secs
0-1km: 40.0secs
53.0bhp 39.5kW 53.7PS
@ 5200rpm
65.0lbft 88.1Nm @ 2600rpm
61.5bhp/ton 60.5bhp/tonne
42.2bhp/L 31.5kW/L 42.8PS/L
34.7ft/sec 10.6m/sec
15.9mph 25.6kmh/1000rpm
29.2mpg 24.3mpgUS 9.7L/100km
Petrol 4-stroke piston
1256cc 76.6cu in
In-line 4 1 Carburettor
Compression ratio: 8.5:1
Bore: 81.0mm 3.2in
Stroke: 61.0mm 2.4in
Valve type/No: Overhead 8
Transmission: Manual
No. of forward speeds: 4
Wheels driven: Rear
Springs F/R: Coil/Coil
Brake system: PA
Brakes F/R: Disc/Drum
Steering: Rack & pinion
Wheelbase: 246.4cm 97.0in
Track F: 130.8cm 51.5in
Track R: 130.8cm 51.5in
Length: 411.5cm 162.0in
Width: 164.3cm 64.7in
Height: 139.7cm 55.0in
Ground clearance: 13.2cm 5.2in
Kerb weight: 875.8kg 1929.0lb
Fuel: 36.4L 8.0gal 9.6galUS

4670 Vauxhall

VX4/90
1972 UK
102.0mph 164.1kmh
0-50mph 80.5kmh: 8.9secs
0-60mph 96.5kmh: 12.5secs
0-1/4 mile: 18.4secs
0-1km: 34.8secs
110.0bhp 82.0kW 111.5PS
@ 5200rpm
140.0lbft 189.7Nm @ 3000rpm
95.1bhp/ton 93.5bhp/tonne
48.3bhp/L 36.0kW/L 48.9PS/L
43.3ft/sec 13.2m/sec
24.1mph 38.8kmh/1000rpm
21.5mpg 17.9mpgUS 13.1L/100km
Petrol 4-stroke piston
2279cc 139.0cu in
In-line 4 2 Carburettor
Compression ratio: 8.5:1
Bore: 97.5mm 3.8in
Stroke: 76.2mm 3.0in
Valve type/No: Overhead 8
Transmission: Manual with overdrive
No. of forward speeds: 6
Wheels driven: Rear
Springs F/R: Coil/Coil
Brake system: PA
Brakes F/R: Disc/Drum
Steering: Rack & pinion
Wheelbase: 266.7cm 105.0in
Track F: 142.7cm 56.2in
Track R: 140.7cm 55.4in
Length: 454.7cm 179.0in
Width: 169.4cm 66.7in
Height: 139.7cm 55.0in
Ground clearance: 15.2cm 6.0in
Kerb weight: 1175.9kg 2590.0lb
Fuel: 64.8L 14.2gal 17.1galUS

4671 Vauxhall

Victor Estate
1973 UK
93.0mph 149.6kmh
0-50mph 80.5kmh: 11.7secs
0-60mph 96.5kmh: 17.3secs
0-1/4 mile: 20.6secs
0-1km: 38.7secs
77.0bhp 57.4kW 78.1PS
@ 5200rpm
97.0lbft 131.4Nm @ 3000rpm
67.1bhp/ton 65.9bhp/tonne
43.8bhp/L 32.6kW/L 44.4PS/L
43.3ft/sec 13.2m/sec
17.2mph 27.7kmh/1000rpm
21.2mpg 17.7mpgUS 13.3L/100km
Petrol 4-stroke piston
1759cc 107.3cu in
In-line 4 1 Carburettor
Compression ratio: 8.5:1
Bore: 85.7mm 3.4in
Stroke: 76.2mm 3.0in
Valve type/No: Overhead 8
Transmission: Manual
No. of forward speeds: 4
Wheels driven: Rear
Springs F/R: Coil/Coil
Brake system: PA
Brakes F/R: Disc/Drum
Steering: Rack & pinion
Wheelbase: 266.7cm 105.0in
Track F: 142.7cm 56.2in
Track R: 140.7cm 55.4in
Length: 454.7cm 179.0in
Width: 169.4cm 66.7in
Height: 139.7cm 55.0in
Ground clearance: 15.2cm 6.0in
Kerb weight: 1167.7kg 2572.0lb
Fuel: 64.8L 14.2gal 17.1galUS

4672 Vauxhall

Firenza
1974 UK
119.0mph 191.5kmh
0-50mph 80.5kmh: 7.2secs
0-60mph 96.5kmh: 9.4secs
0-1/4 mile: 16.9secs
0-1km: 31.3secs
131.0bhp 97.7kW 132.8PS
@ 5500rpm
144.0lbft 195.1Nm @ 3500rpm
127.8bhp/ton 125.7bhp/tonne
57.5bhp/L 42.9kW/L 58.3PS/L
45.8ft/sec 14.0m/sec
21.1mph 33.9kmh/1000rpm
20.1mpg 16.7mpgUS 14.1L/100km
Petrol 4-stroke piston
2279cc 139.0cu in
In-line 4 2 Carburettor
Compression ratio: 9.2:1
Bore: 97.5mm 3.8in
Stroke: 76.2mm 3.0in
Valve type/No: Overhead 8
Transmission: Manual
No. of forward speeds: 5
Wheels driven: Rear
Springs F/R: Coil/Coil
Brake system: PA
Brakes F/R: Disc/Drum
Steering: Rack & pinion
Wheelbase: 246.4cm 97.0in
Track F: 137.9cm 54.3in
Track R: 135.9cm 53.5in
Length: 430.3cm 169.4in
Width: 164.3cm 64.7in
Height: 130.3cm 51.3in
Ground clearance: 12.2cm 4.8in
Kerb weight: 1042.4kg 2296.0lb
Fuel: 54.6L 12.0gal 14.4galUS

4673 Vauxhall

Magnum 2300
1974 UK
103.0mph 165.7kmh
0-50mph 80.5kmh: 6.9secs
0-60mph 96.5kmh: 10.0secs
0-1/4 mile: 17.5secs
0-1km: 32.6secs
110.0bhp 82.0kW 111.5PS
@ 5000rpm
140.0lbft 189.7Nm @ 3000rpm
109.3bhp/ton 107.5bhp/tonne
48.3bhp/L 36.0kW/L 48.9PS/L
41.7ft/sec 12.7m/sec
19.2mph 30.9kmh/1000rpm
25.3mpg 21.1mpgUS 11.2L/100km
Petrol 4-stroke piston
2279cc 139.0cu in
In-line 4 2 Carburettor
Compression ratio: 8.5:1
Bore: 97.5mm 3.8in
Stroke: 76.2mm 3.0in
Valve type/No: Overhead 8
Transmission: Manual
No. of forward speeds: 4
Wheels driven: Rear
Springs F/R: Coil/Coil
Brake system: PA
Brakes F/R: Disc/Drum
Steering: Rack & pinion
Wheelbase: 246.4cm 97.0in
Track F: 130.8cm 51.5in
Track R: 130.8cm 51.5in
Length: 411.5cm 162.0in
Width: 164.3cm 64.7in
Height: 139.7cm 55.0in
Ground clearance: 13.2cm 5.2in
Kerb weight: 1023.3kg 2254.0lb
Fuel: 54.6L 12.0gal 14.4galUS

4674 Vauxhall

Viva 1256 DL
1974 UK
88.0mph 141.6kmh
0-50mph 80.5kmh: 12.4secs
0-60mph 96.5kmh: 18.1secs
0-1/4 mile: 21.2secs
0-1km: 39.9secs
68.0bhp 50.7kW 68.9PS
@ 5750rpm
72.0lbft 97.6Nm @ 4000rpm
80.7bhp/ton 79.4bhp/tonne
54.1bhp/L 40.4kW/L 54.9PS/L
38.3ft/sec 11.7m/sec
16.1mph 25.9kmh/1000rpm
33.2mpg 27.6mpgUS 8.5L/100km
Petrol 4-stroke piston
1256cc 76.6cu in
In-line 4 1 Carburettor
Compression ratio: 9.2:1
Bore: 81.0mm 3.2in
Stroke: 61.0mm 2.4in
Valve type/No: Overhead 8
Transmission: Manual
No. of forward speeds: 4
Wheels driven: Rear
Springs F/R: Coil/Coil
Brake system: PA
Brakes F/R: Disc/Drum
Steering: Rack & pinion
Wheelbase: 246.4cm 97.0in
Track F: 130.8cm 51.5in
Track R: 130.8cm 51.5in
Length: 411.5cm 162.0in
Width: 164.3cm 64.7in
Height: 139.7cm 55.0in
Ground clearance: 13.2cm 5.2in
Kerb weight: 856.7kg 1887.0lb
Fuel: 36.4L 8.0gal 9.6galUS

4675 Vauxhall

VX4/90
1974 UK
104.0mph 167.3kmh
0-50mph 80.5kmh: 7.6secs
0-60mph 96.5kmh: 11.1secs
0-1/4 mile: 17.9secs
0-1km: 33.6secs
116.0bhp 86.5kW 117.6PS
@ 5000rpm
145.0lbft 196.5Nm @ 3000rpm
94.0bhp/ton 92.4bhp/tonne
50.9bhp/L 38.0kW/L 51.6PS/L
41.7ft/sec 12.7m/sec
20.1mph 32.3kmh/1000rpm
23.2mpg 19.3mpgUS 12.2L/100km
Petrol 4-stroke piston
2279cc 139.0cu in
In-line 4 2 Carburettor
Compression ratio: 8.5:1
Bore: 97.5mm 3.8in
Stroke: 76.2mm 3.0in
Valve type/No: Overhead 8
Transmission: Manual
No. of forward speeds: 4
Wheels driven: Rear
Springs F/R: Coil/Coil
Brake system: PA
Brakes F/R: Disc/Drum
Steering: Rack & pinion
Wheelbase: 266.7cm 105.0in
Track F: 142.7cm 56.2in
Track R: 140.7cm 55.4in
Length: 454.7cm 179.0in
Width: 169.4cm 66.7in
Height: 139.7cm 55.0in
Ground clearance: 15.2cm 6.0in
Kerb weight: 1255.3kg 2765.0lb
Fuel: 64.8L 14.2gal 17.1galUS

4676 Vauxhall

Chevette L
1975 UK
91.0mph 146.4kmh
0-50mph 80.5kmh: 9.6secs
0-60mph 96.5kmh: 14.5secs
0-1/4 mile: 19.6secs
0-1km: 37.1secs
58.5bhp 43.6kW 59.3PS
@ 5600rpm
68.0lbft 92.1Nm @ 2600rpm
69.7bhp/ton 68.6bhp/tonne
46.6bhp/L 34.7kW/L 47.2PS/L

37.3ft/sec 11.4m/sec
15.9mph 25.6kmh/1000rpm
30.3mpg 25.2mpgUS 9.3L/100km
Petrol 4-stroke piston
1256cc 76.6cu in
In-line 4 1 Carburettor
Compression ratio: 9.2:1
Bore: 81.0mm 3.2in
Stroke: 61.0mm 2.4in
Valve type/No: Overhead 8
Transmission: Manual
No. of forward speeds: 4
Wheels driven: Rear
Springs F/R: Coil/Coil
Brake system: PA
Brakes F/R: Disc/Drum
Steering: Rack & pinion
Wheelbase: 238.8cm 94.0in
Track F: 130.6cm 51.4in
Track R: 130.6cm 51.4in
Length: 399.3cm 157.2in
Width: 158.0cm 62.2in
Height: 137.2cm 54.0in
Ground clearance: 17.8cm 7.0in
Kerb weight: 853.1kg 1879.0lb
Fuel: 36.4L 8.0gal 9.6galUS

4677 Vauxhall

Magnum 1800
1975 UK
94.0mph 151.2kmh
0-50mph 80.5kmh: 10.9secs
0-60mph 96.5kmh: 15.6secs
0-1/4 mile: 20.3secs
0-1km: 38.0secs
77.0bhp 57.4kW 78.1PS
@ 5200rpm
97.0lbft 131.4Nm @ 3000rpm
76.7bhp/ton 75.4bhp/tonne
43.8bhp/L 32.6kW/L 44.4PS/L
43.3ft/sec 13.2m/sec
17.6mph 28.3kmh/1000rpm
26.3mpg 21.9mpgUS 10.7L/100km
Petrol 4-stroke piston
1759cc 107.3cu in
In-line 4 1 Carburettor
Compression ratio: 8.5:1
Bore: 85.7mm 3.4in
Stroke: 76.2mm 3.0in
Valve type/No: Overhead 8
Transmission: Manual
No. of forward speeds: 4
Wheels driven: Rear
Springs F/R: Coil/Coil
Brake system: PA
Brakes F/R: Disc/Drum
Steering: Rack & pinion
Wheelbase: 246.4cm 97.0in
Track F: 130.8cm 51.5in
Track R: 130.8cm 51.5in
Length: 411.5cm 162.0in
Width: 164.3cm 64.7in
Height: 139.7cm 55.0in
Ground clearance: 13.2cm 5.2in
Kerb weight: 1021.5kg 2250.0lb
Fuel: 54.6L 12.0gal 14.4galUS

4678 Vauxhall

Blydenstein Chevette 1500
1976 UK
100.0mph 160.9kmh
0-50mph 80.5kmh: 7.7secs
0-60mph 96.5kmh: 11.4secs
0-1/4 mile: 18.0secs
0-1km: 34.3secs
77.0bhp 57.4kW 78.1PS
@ 5000rpm
92.6bhp/ton 91.0bhp/tonne
51.0bhp/L 38.0kW/L 51.7PS/L
39.3ft/sec 12.0m/sec
15.9mph 25.6kmh/1000rpm
32.9mpg 27.4mpgUS 8.6L/100km
Petrol 4-stroke piston
1511cc 92.2cu in
In-line 4 1 Carburettor
Compression ratio: 10.0:1
Bore: 82.0mm 3.2in
Stroke: 72.0mm 2.8in
Valve type/No: Overhead 8
Transmission: Manual
No. of forward speeds: 4
Wheels driven: Rear
Springs F/R: Coil/Coil
Brake system: PA
Brakes F/R: Disc/Drum
Steering: Rack & pinion
Wheelbase: 238.8cm 94.0in
Track F: 130.8cm 51.5in
Track R: 130.8cm 51.5in
Length: 394.2cm 155.2in
Width: 165.6cm 65.2in
Height: 132.1cm 52.0in
Ground clearance: 17.8cm 7.0in
Kerb weight: 846.0kg 1863.4lb
Fuel: 43.2L 9.5gal 11.4galUS

4679 Vauxhall

Cavalier 1600 GL
1976 UK
100.0mph 160.9kmh
0-50mph 80.5kmh: 10.0secs
0-60mph 96.5kmh: 14.8secs
0-1/4 mile: 19.0secs
0-1km: 36.0secs
75.0bhp 55.9kW 76.0PS
@ 5000rpm
81.0lbft 109.8Nm @ 3800rpm
73.5bhp/ton 72.3bhp/tonne
47.3bhp/L 35.3kW/L 48.0PS/L
38.2ft/sec 11.6m/sec
18.4mph 29.6kmh/1000rpm
27.2mpg 22.6mpgUS 10.4L/100km
Petrol 4-stroke piston
1584cc 96.6cu in
In-line 4 1 Carburettor
Compression ratio: 8.8:1
Bore: 85.0mm 3.3in
Stroke: 69.8mm 2.7in
Valve type/No: Overhead 8
Transmission: Manual
No. of forward speeds: 4
Wheels driven: Rear
Springs F/R: Coil/Coil
Brake system: PA
Brakes F/R: Disc/Drum
Steering: Rack & pinion
Wheelbase: 248.9cm 98.0in
Track F: 137.2cm 54.0in
Track R: 137.2cm 54.0in
Length: 442.0cm 174.0in
Width: 167.6cm 66.0in
Height: 132.1cm 52.0in
Ground clearance: 15.2cm 6.0in
Kerb weight: 1037.8kg 2286.0lb
Fuel: 50.0L 11.0gal 13.2galUS

4680 Vauxhall

Cavalier GL Coupe
1976 UK
110.0mph 177.0kmh
0-50mph 80.5kmh: 7.6secs
0-60mph 96.5kmh: 11.2secs
0-1/4 mile: 18.0secs
0-1km: 33.6secs
89.0bhp 66.4kW 90.2PS
@ 4800rpm
105.0lbft 142.3Nm @ 3800rpm
88.0bhp/ton 86.5bhp/tonne
46.9bhp/L 35.0kW/L 47.6PS/L
36.7ft/sec 11.2m/sec
18.5mph 29.8kmh/1000rpm
23.7mpg 19.7mpgUS 11.9L/100km
Petrol 4-stroke piston
1897cc 115.7cu in
In-line 4 1 Carburettor
Compression ratio: 8.8:1
Bore: 93.0mm 3.7in
Stroke: 69.8mm 2.7in
Valve type/No: Overhead 8
Transmission: Manual
No. of forward speeds: 4
Wheels driven: Rear
Springs F/R: Coil/Coil
Brake system: PA
Brakes F/R: Disc/Drum
Steering: Rack & pinion
Wheelbase: 248.9cm 98.0in
Track F: 137.2cm 54.0in
Track R: 137.2cm 54.0in
Length: 442.0cm 174.0in
Width: 167.6cm 66.0in
Height: 132.1cm 52.0in
Ground clearance: 15.2cm 6.0in
Kerb weight: 1028.3kg 2265.0lb
Fuel: 50.0L 11.0gal 13.2galUS

4681 Vauxhall

Chevette L
1976 UK
91.0mph 146.4kmh
0-50mph 80.5kmh: 12.5secs
0-60mph 96.5kmh: 17.5secs
0-1/4 mile: 20.8secs
0-1km: 39.4secs
58.5bhp 43.6kW 59.3PS
@ 5600rpm
68.0lbft 92.1Nm @ 2600rpm
69.7bhp/ton 68.5bhp/tonne
46.6bhp/L 34.7kW/L 47.2PS/L
37.3ft/sec 11.4m/sec
15.9mph 25.6kmh/1000rpm
31.9mpg 26.6mpgUS 8.9L/100km
Petrol 4-stroke piston
1256cc 76.6cu in
In-line 4 1 Carburettor
Compression ratio: 9.2:1
Bore: 81.0mm 3.2in
Stroke: 61.0mm 2.4in
Valve type/No: Overhead 8
Transmission: Manual
No. of forward speeds: 4
Wheels driven: Rear
Springs F/R: Coil/Coil
Brake system: PA
Brakes F/R: Disc/Drum
Steering: Rack & pinion
Wheelbase: 238.8cm 94.0in
Track F: 130.6cm 51.4in
Track R: 130.6cm 51.4in
Length: 418.8cm 164.9in
Width: 157.0cm 61.8in
Height: 131.3cm 51.7in
Ground clearance: 17.8cm 7.0in
Kerb weight: 854.0kg 1881.0lb
Fuel: 43.2L 9.5gal 11.4galUS

4682 Vauxhall

VX1800
1976 UK
101.0mph 162.5kmh
0-50mph 80.5kmh: 9.6secs
0-60mph 96.5kmh: 13.7secs
0-1/4 mile: 19.2secs
0-1km: 35.7secs
88.0bhp 65.6kW 89.2PS
@ 5800rpm
99.0lbft 134.1Nm @ 3500rpm
83.8bhp/ton 82.4bhp/tonne
50.0bhp/L 37.3kW/L 50.7PS/L
48.3ft/sec 14.7m/sec
18.5mph 29.8kmh/1000rpm
25.1mpg 20.9mpgUS 11.3L/100km
Petrol 4-stroke piston
1759cc 107.3cu in
In-line 4 1 Carburettor
Compression ratio: 8.5:1
Bore: 85.7mm 3.4in
Stroke: 76.2mm 3.0in
Valve type/No: Overhead 8
Transmission: Manual
No. of forward speeds: 4
Wheels driven: Rear
Springs F/R: Coil/Coil
Brake system: PA
Brakes F/R: Disc/Drum
Steering: Rack & pinion
Wheelbase: 266.7cm 105.0in
Track F: 142.7cm 56.2in
Track R: 140.7cm 55.4in
Length: 455.2cm 179.2in
Width: 170.2cm 67.0in
Height: 137.2cm 54.0in
Ground clearance: 15.2cm 6.0in
Kerb weight: 1067.8kg 2352.0lb
Fuel: 64.8L 14.2gal 17.1galUS

4683 Vauxhall

Cavalier 1300L
1977 UK
92.0mph 148.0kmh
0-50mph 80.5kmh: 12.0secs
0-60mph 96.5kmh: 17.8secs
0-1/4 mile: 20.9secs
0-1km: 39.4secs
58.0bhp 43.2kW 58.8PS
@ 5400rpm
66.0lbft 89.4Nm @ 2600rpm
64.8bhp/ton 63.7bhp/tonne
46.2bhp/L 34.4kW/L 46.8PS/L
41.2ft/sec 12.6m/sec
16.4mph 26.4kmh/1000rpm
30.9mpg 25.7mpgUS 9.1L/100km
Petrol 4-stroke piston
1256cc 76.6cu in
In-line 4 1 Carburettor
Compression ratio: 8.7:1
Bore: 81.0mm 3.2in
Stroke: 70.0mm 2.7in
Valve type/No: Overhead 8
Transmission: Manual
No. of forward speeds: 4
Wheels driven: Rear
Springs F/R: Coil/Coil
Brake system: PA
Brakes F/R: Disc/Drum
Steering: Rack & pinion
Wheelbase: 248.9cm 98.0in
Track F: 137.2cm 54.0in
Track R: 137.2cm 54.0in
Length: 442.0cm 174.0in
Width: 167.6cm 66.0in
Height: 132.1cm 52.0in
Ground clearance: 15.2cm 6.0in
Kerb weight: 910.3kg 2005.0lb
Fuel: 50.0L 11.0gal 13.2galUS

4684 Vauxhall

Magnum 1800
1977 UK
103.0mph 165.7kmh
0-50mph 80.5kmh: 8.5secs
0-60mph 96.5kmh: 12.6secs
0-1/4 mile: 18.7secs
0-1km: 35.0secs
88.0bhp 65.6kW 89.2PS
@ 5800rpm
99.0lbft 134.1Nm @ 3500rpm
90.3bhp/ton 88.7bhp/tonne
50.0bhp/L 37.3kW/L 50.7PS/L
48.3ft/sec 14.7m/sec
17.7mph 28.5kmh/1000rpm
25.7mpg 21.4mpgUS 11.0L/100km
Petrol 4-stroke piston
1759cc 107.3cu in
In-line 4 1 Carburettor
Compression ratio: 8.5:1
Bore: 85.7mm 3.4in
Stroke: 76.2mm 3.0in
Valve type/No: Overhead 8
Transmission: Manual
No. of forward speeds: 4
Wheels driven: Rear
Springs F/R: Coil/Coil
Brake system: PA
Brakes F/R: Disc/Drum
Steering: Rack & pinion
Wheelbase: 246.4cm 97.0in
Track F: 130.8cm 51.5in
Track R: 130.8cm 51.5in
Length: 411.5cm 162.0in
Width: 164.3cm 64.7in
Height: 139.7cm 55.0in
Ground clearance: 13.2cm 5.2in
Kerb weight: 991.5kg 2184.0lb
Fuel: 54.6L 12.0gal 14.4galUS

4685 Vauxhall

VX2300 Estate
1977 UK
102.0mph 164.1kmh
0-50mph 80.5kmh: 9.0secs
0-60mph 96.5kmh: 12.9secs
0-1/4 mile: 18.7secs
0-1km: 35.4secs
108.0bhp 80.5kW 109.5PS
@ 5000rpm
138.0lbft 187.0Nm @ 3000rpm
91.7bhp/ton 90.2bhp/tonne
47.4bhp/L 35.3kW/L 48.0PS/L
41.7ft/sec 12.7m/sec
19.9mph 32.0kmh/1000rpm
22.8mpg 19.0mpgUS 12.4L/100km
Petrol 4-stroke piston
2279cc 139.0cu in
In-line 4 1 Carburettor
Compression ratio: 8.5:1
Bore: 97.5mm 3.8in
Stroke: 76.2mm 3.0in
Valve type/No: Overhead 8
Transmission: Manual
No. of forward speeds: 4
Wheels driven: Rear
Springs F/R: Coil/Coil
Brake system: PA
Brakes F/R: Disc/Drum
Steering: Rack & pinion
Wheelbase: 266.7cm 105.0in
Track F: 142.7cm 56.2in
Track R: 140.7cm 55.4in
Length: 454.7cm 179.0in
Width: 169.4cm 66.7in
Height: 139.7cm 55.0in
Ground clearance: 15.2cm 6.0in
Kerb weight: 1197.6kg 2638.0lb
Fuel: 64.8L 14.2gal 17.1galUS

4686 Vauxhall
Carlton
1978 UK
111.0mph 178.6kmh
0-50mph 80.5kmh: 8.2secs
0-60mph 96.5kmh: 11.2secs
0-1/4 mile: 18.5secs
0-1km: 34.1secs
100.0bhp 74.6kW 101.4PS
@ 5200rpm
116.5lbft 157.9Nm @ 3600rpm
87.2bhp/ton 85.8bhp/tonne
50.5bhp/L 37.7kW/L 51.2PS/L
39.7ft/sec 12.1m/sec
19.5mph 31.4kmh/1000rpm
25.0mpg 20.8mpgUS 11.3L/100km
Petrol 4-stroke piston
1979cc 120.7cu in
In-line 4 1 Carburettor
Compression ratio: 9.0:1
Bore: 95.0mm 3.7in
Stroke: 69.8mm 2.7in
Valve type/No: Overhead 8
Transmission: Manual
No. of forward speeds: 4
Wheels driven: Rear
Springs F/R: Coil/Coil
Brake system: PA
Brakes F/R: Disc/Drum
Steering: Recirculating ball
Wheelbase: 266.7cm 105.0in
Track F: 143.5cm 56.5in
Track R: 141.2cm 55.6in
Length: 474.2cm 186.7in
Width: 172.7cm 68.0in
Height: 142.2cm 56.0in
Ground clearance: 18.8cm 7.4in
Kerb weight: 1165.9kg 2568.0lb
Fuel: 65.1L 14.3gal 17.2galUS

4687 Vauxhall
Cavalier 2000 GLS
1978 UK
112.0mph 180.2kmh
0-50mph 80.5kmh: 6.6secs
0-60mph 96.5kmh: 9.2secs
0-1/4 mile: 17.5secs
0-1km: 32.5secs
100.0bhp 74.6kW 101.4PS
@ 5400rpm
113.0lbft 153.1Nm @ 3800rpm
104.5bhp/ton 102.7bhp/tonne
50.5bhp/L 37.7kW/L 51.2PS/L
41.2ft/sec 12.6m/sec
19.0mph 30.6kmh/1000rpm
25.6mpg 21.3mpgUS 11.0L/100km
Petrol 4-stroke piston
1979cc 120.7cu in
In-line 4 1 Carburettor
Compression ratio: 9.0:1
Bore: 95.0mm 3.7in
Stroke: 69.8mm 2.7in
Valve type/No: Overhead 8
Transmission: Manual
No. of forward speeds: 4
Wheels driven: Rear
Springs F/R: Coil/Coil
Brake system: PA
Brakes F/R: Disc/Drum
Steering: Rack & pinion
Wheelbase: 248.9cm 98.0in
Track F: 137.2cm 54.0in
Track R: 137.2cm 54.0in
Length: 442.0cm 174.0in
Width: 167.6cm 66.0in
Height: 132.1cm 52.0in
Ground clearance: 15.2cm 6.0in
Kerb weight: 973.4kg 2144.0lb
Fuel: 50.0L 11.0gal 13.2galUS

4688 Vauxhall
Chevette 2300 HS
1978 UK
117.0mph 188.3kmh
0-50mph 80.5kmh: 6.1secs
0-60mph 96.5kmh: 8.5secs
0-1/4 mile: 16.5secs
0-1km: 30.6secs
135.0bhp 100.7kW 136.9PS
@ 5500rpm
134.0lbft 181.6Nm @ 4500rpm
135.3bhp/ton 133.0bhp/tonne
59.2bhp/L 44.2kW/L 60.1PS/L
45.8ft/sec 14.0m/sec
18.9mph 30.4kmh/1000rpm
21.3mpg 17.7mpgUS 13.3L/100km
Petrol 4-stroke piston
2279cc 139.0cu in
In-line 4 2 Carburettor
Compression ratio: 8.2:1
Bore: 97.5mm 3.8in
Stroke: 76.2mm 3.0in
Valve type/No: Overhead 16
Transmission: Manual
No. of forward speeds: 5
Wheels driven: Rear
Springs F/R: Coil/Coil
Brake system: PA
Brakes F/R: Disc/Drum
Steering: Rack & pinion
Wheelbase: 238.8cm 94.0in
Track F: 130.6cm 51.4in
Track R: 130.6cm 51.4in
Length: 399.3cm 157.2in
Width: 158.0cm 62.2in
Height: 137.2cm 54.0in
Ground clearance: 17.8cm 7.0in
Kerb weight: 1014.7kg 2235.0lb
Fuel: 38.2L 8.4gal 10.1galUS

4689 Vauxhall
Royale Coupe
1979 UK
116.0mph 186.6kmh
0-50mph 80.5kmh: 9.0secs
0-60mph 96.5kmh: 12.1secs
0-1/4 mile: 18.5secs
0-1km: 33.8secs
140.0bhp 104.4kW 141.9PS
@ 5200rpm
161.0lbft 218.2Nm @ 3400rpm
101.6bhp/ton 100.0bhp/tonne
50.3bhp/L 37.5kW/L 51.0PS/L
39.7ft/sec 12.1m/sec
20.8mph 33.5kmh/1000rpm
18.4mpg 15.3mpgUS 15.4L/100km
Petrol 4-stroke piston
2784cc 169.9cu in
In-line 6 1 Carburettor
Compression ratio: 9.0:1
Bore: 92.0mm 3.6in
Stroke: 69.8mm 2.7in
Valve type/No: Overhead 12
Transmission: Automatic
No. of forward speeds: 3
Wheels driven: Rear
Springs F/R: Coil/Coil
Brake system: PA
Brakes F/R: Disc/Disc
Steering: Recirculating ball PA
Wheelbase: 266.7cm 105.0in
Track F: 144.3cm 56.8in
Track R: 146.6cm 57.7in
Length: 475.7cm 187.3in
Width: 173.5cm 68.3in
Height: 133.4cm 52.5in
Ground clearance: 15.2cm 6.0in
Kerb weight: 1400.6kg 3085.0lb
Fuel: 75.1L 16.5gal 19.8galUS

4690 Vauxhall
Cavalier 1.6S GL
1981 UK
108.0mph 173.8kmh
0-50mph 80.5kmh: 8.2secs
0-60mph 96.5kmh: 12.0secs
0-1/4 mile: 18.8secs
0-1km: 32.9secs
90.0bhp 67.1kW 91.2PS
@ 5800rpm
93.0lbft 126.0Nm @ 3800rpm
91.3bhp/ton 89.7bhp/tonne
56.3bhp/L 42.0kW/L 57.1PS/L
50.4ft/sec 15.4m/sec
18.6mph 29.9kmh/1000rpm
30.1mpg 25.1mpgUS 9.4L/100km
Petrol 4-stroke piston
1598cc 97.5cu in
In-line 4 1 Carburettor
Compression ratio: 9.2:1
Bore: 80.0mm 3.1in
Stroke: 79.5mm 3.1in
Valve type/No: Overhead 8
Transmission: Manual
No. of forward speeds: 5
Wheels driven: Front
Springs F/R: Coil/Coil
Brake system: PA
Brakes F/R: Disc/Drum
Steering: Rack & pinion
Wheelbase: 257.3cm 101.3in
Track F: 140.0cm 55.1in
Track R: 140.7cm 55.4in
Length: 436.6cm 171.9in
Width: 166.9cm 65.7in
Height: 139.4cm 54.9in
Ground clearance: 16.5cm 6.5in
Kerb weight: 1002.9kg 2209.0lb
Fuel: 61.0L 13.4gal 16.1galUS

4691 Vauxhall
Astra 1600 GL
1982 UK
108.0mph 173.8kmh
0-50mph 80.5kmh: 7.5secs
0-60mph 96.5kmh: 10.8secs
0-1/4 mile: 18.2secs
0-1km: 34.4secs
90.0bhp 67.1kW 91.2PS
@ 5800rpm
93.0lbft 126.0Nm @ 4000rpm
93.1bhp/ton 91.5bhp/tonne
56.3bhp/L 42.0kW/L 57.1PS/L
50.4ft/sec 15.4m/sec
18.0mph 29.0kmh/1000rpm
23.6mpg 19.7mpgUS 12.0L/100km
Petrol 4-stroke piston
1598cc 97.5cu in
In-line 4 1 Carburettor
Compression ratio: 9.2:1
Bore: 80.0mm 3.1in
Stroke: 79.5mm 3.1in
Valve type/No: Overhead 8
Transmission: Manual
No. of forward speeds: 4
Wheels driven: Front
Springs F/R: Coil/Coil
Brake system: PA
Brakes F/R: Disc/Drum
Steering: Rack & pinion
Wheelbase: 251.5cm 99.0in
Track F: 140.0cm 55.1in
Track R: 140.7cm 55.4in
Length: 399.8cm 157.4in
Width: 163.8cm 64.5in
Height: 132.6cm 52.2in
Ground clearance: 15.2cm 6.0in
Kerb weight: 983.4kg 2166.0lb
Fuel: 41.9L 9.2gal 11.1galUS

4692 Vauxhall
Cavalier GLS
1982 UK
105.0mph 168.9kmh
0-50mph 80.5kmh: 8.0secs
0-60mph 96.5kmh: 10.8secs
0-1/4 mile: 18.1secs
0-1km: 34.0secs
90.0bhp 67.1kW 91.2PS
@ 5800rpm
93.0lbft 126.0Nm @ 3800rpm
87.8bhp/ton 86.3bhp/tonne
56.3bhp/L 42.0kW/L 57.1PS/L
50.4ft/sec 15.4m/sec
24.7mph 39.7kmh/1000rpm
31.9mpg 26.6mpgUS 8.9L/100km
Petrol 4-stroke piston
1598cc 97.5cu in
In-line 4 1 Carburettor
Compression ratio: 9.2:1
Bore: 80.0mm 3.1in
Stroke: 79.5mm 3.1in
Valve type/No: Overhead 8
Transmission: Manual
No. of forward speeds: 5
Wheels driven: Front
Springs F/R: Coil/Coil
Brake system: PA
Brakes F/R: Disc/Drum
Steering: Rack & pinion
Wheelbase: 257.3cm 101.3in
Track F: 140.0cm 55.1in
Track R: 140.7cm 55.4in
Length: 426.2cm 167.8in
Width: 166.9cm 65.7in
Height: 139.4cm 54.9in
Ground clearance: 16.5cm 6.5in
Kerb weight: 1042.4kg 2296.0lb
Fuel: 61.0L 13.4gal 16.1galUS

4693 Vauxhall
Cavalier LD
1982 UK
93.0mph 149.6kmh
0-50mph 80.5kmh: 12.5secs
0-60mph 96.5kmh: 17.8secs
0-1/4 mile: 21.2secs
0-1km: 39.9secs
54.0bhp 40.3kW 54.7PS
@ 4600rpm
71.0lbft 96.2Nm @ 2400rpm
52.6bhp/ton 51.7bhp/tonne
33.8bhp/L 25.2kW/L 34.3PS/L
40.0ft/sec 12.2m/sec
18.5mph 29.8kmh/1000rpm
38.2mpg 31.8mpgUS 7.4L/100km
Diesel 4-stroke piston
1598cc 97.5cu in
In-line 4 fuel injection
Compression ratio: 23.0:1
Bore: 80.0mm 3.1in
Stroke: 79.5mm 3.1in
Valve type/No: Overhead 8
Transmission: Manual
No. of forward speeds: 4
Wheels driven: Front
Springs F/R: Coil/Coil
Brake system: PA
Brakes F/R: Disc/Drum
Steering: Rack & pinion
Wheelbase: 257.3cm 101.3in
Track F: 140.0cm 55.1in
Track R: 140.7cm 55.4in
Length: 436.6cm 171.9in
Width: 166.9cm 65.7in
Height: 139.4cm 54.9in
Ground clearance: 16.5cm 6.5in
Kerb weight: 1043.7kg 2299.0lb
Fuel: 61.0L 13.4gal 16.1galUS

4694 Vauxhall
Astra GTE
1983 UK
118.0mph 189.9kmh
0-50mph 80.5kmh: 6.5secs
0-60mph 96.5kmh: 9.2secs
0-1/4 mile: 16.7secs
0-1km: 31.8secs
113.0bhp 84.3kW 114.6PS
@ 5800rpm
111.0lbft 150.4Nm @ 4800rpm
116.4bhp/ton 114.4bhp/tonne
62.9bhp/L 46.9kW/L 63.8PS/L
50.4ft/sec 15.4m/sec
22.9mph 36.8kmh/1000rpm
29.1mpg 24.2mpgUS 9.7L/100km
Petrol 4-stroke piston
1796cc 109.6cu in
In-line 4 fuel injection
Compression ratio: 9.5:1
Bore: 84.8mm 3.3in
Stroke: 79.5mm 3.1in
Valve type/No: Overhead 8
Transmission: Manual
No. of forward speeds: 5
Wheels driven: Front
Springs F/R: Coil/Coil
Brake system: PA
Brakes F/R: Disc/Drum
Steering: Rack & pinion
Wheelbase: 251.5cm 99.0in
Track F: 140.0cm 55.1in
Track R: 140.7cm 55.4in
Length: 399.8cm 157.4in
Width: 163.8cm 64.5in
Height: 137.9cm 54.3in
Ground clearance: 15.2cm 6.0in
Kerb weight: 987.4kg 2175.0lb
Fuel: 41.9L 9.2gal 11.1galUS

4695 Vauxhall
Carlton 2.0 GL
1983 UK
116.0mph 186.6kmh
0-50mph 80.5kmh: 6.5secs
0-60mph 96.5kmh: 10.0secs
0-1/4 mile: 17.6secs
0-1km: 32.5secs
100.0bhp 74.6kW 101.4PS
@ 5200rpm
115.0lbft 155.8Nm @ 3800rpm
83.8bhp/ton 82.4bhp/tonne
50.5bhp/L 37.7kW/L 51.2PS/L
39.7ft/sec 12.1m/sec
24.1mph 38.8kmh/1000rpm
27.3mpg 22.7mpgUS 10.3L/100km
Petrol 4-stroke piston
1979cc 120.7cu in
In-line 4 1 Carburettor
Compression ratio: 9.0:1
Bore: 95.0mm 3.7in
Stroke: 69.8mm 2.7in
Valve type/No: Overhead 8
Transmission: Manual
No. of forward speeds: 5
Wheels driven: Rear
Springs F/R: Coil/Coil

Brake system: PA
Brakes F/R: Disc/Drum
Steering: Recirculating ball PA
Wheelbase: 266.7cm 105.0in
Track F: 143.5cm 56.5in
Track R: 141.2cm 55.6in
Length: 465.3cm 183.2in
Width: 172.5cm 67.9in
Height: 138.4cm 54.5in
Ground clearance: 18.8cm 7.4in
Kerb weight: 1214.0kg 2674.0lb
Fuel: 65.1L 14.3gal 17.2galUS

4696 Vauxhall

Cavalier CD
1983 UK
116.0mph 186.6kmh
0-50mph 80.5kmh: 6.9secs
0-60mph 96.5kmh: 9.3secs
0-1/4 mile: 17.1secs
0-1km: 31.9secs
115.0bhp 85.8kW 116.6PS
@ 5800rpm
111.4lbft 150.9Nm @ 4800rpm
114.6bhp/ton 112.7bhp/tonne
64.0bhp/L 47.7kW/L 64.9PS/L
50.4ft/sec 15.4m/sec
25.6mph 41.2kmh/1000rpm
29.6mpg 24.6mpgUS 9.5L/100km
Petrol 4-stroke piston
1796cc 109.6cu in
In-line 4 fuel injection
Compression ratio: 9.5:1
Bore: 84.8mm 3.3in
Stroke: 79.5mm 3.1in
Valve type/No: Overhead 8
Transmission: Manual
No. of forward speeds: 5
Wheels driven: Front
Springs F/R: Coil/Coil
Brake system: PA
Brakes F/R: Disc/Drum
Steering: Rack & pinion
Wheelbase: 257.3cm 101.3in
Track F: 140.0cm 55.1in
Track R: 140.7cm 55.4in
Length: 426.2cm 167.8in
Width: 166.9cm 65.7in
Height: 139.4cm 54.9in
Ground clearance: 16.5cm 6.5in
Kerb weight: 1020.1kg 2247.0lb
Fuel: 61.0L 13.4gal 16.1galUS

4697 Vauxhall

Nova 1.2L
1983 UK
98.0mph 157.7kmh
0-50mph 80.5kmh: 9.7secs
0-60mph 96.5kmh: 14.2secs
0-1/4 mile: 19.6secs
0-1km: 37.2secs
55.0bhp 41.0kW 55.8PS
@ 5600rpm
66.0lbft 89.4Nm @ 2200rpm
67.2bhp/ton 66.0bhp/tonne
46.0bhp/L 34.3kW/L 46.6PS/L
38.6ft/sec 11.7m/sec
19.3mph 31.1kmh/1000rpm
36.9mpg 30.7mpgUS 7.7L/100km
Petrol 4-stroke piston
1196cc 73.0cu in
In-line 4 1 Carburettor
Compression ratio: 9.2:1
Bore: 77.8mm 3.1in
Stroke: 62.9mm 2.5in
Valve type/No: Overhead 8
Transmission: Manual
No. of forward speeds: 4
Wheels driven: Front
Springs F/R: Coil/Coil
Brake system: PA
Brakes F/R: Disc/Drum
Steering: Rack & pinion
Wheelbase: 234.2cm 92.2in
Track F: 131.8cm 51.9in
Track R: 133.1cm 52.4in
Length: 362.2cm 142.6in
Width: 153.2cm 60.3in
Height: 136.4cm 53.7in
Ground clearance: 16.5cm 6.5in
Kerb weight: 832.6kg 1834.0lb
Fuel: 41.9L 9.2gal 11.1galUS

4698 Vauxhall

Astra GTE
1984 UK
124.0mph 199.5kmh
0-50mph 80.5kmh: 6.5secs
0-60mph 96.5kmh: 9.0secs
0-1/4 mile: 16.8secs
0-1km: 31.3secs
115.0bhp 85.8kW 116.6PS
@ 5800rpm
111.4lbft 150.9Nm @ 4800rpm
117.1bhp/ton 115.2bhp/tonne
64.0bhp/L 47.7kW/L 64.9PS/L
50.4ft/sec 15.4m/sec
19.7mph 31.7kmh/1000rpm
28.2mpg 23.5mpgUS 10.0L/100km
Petrol 4-stroke piston
1796cc 109.6cu in
In-line 4 fuel injection
Compression ratio: 9.5:1
Bore: 84.8mm 3.3in
Stroke: 79.5mm 3.1in
Valve type/No: Overhead 8
Transmission: Manual
No. of forward speeds: 5
Wheels driven: Front
Springs F/R: Coil/Coil
Brake system: PA
Brakes F/R: Disc/Drum
Steering: Rack & pinion
Wheelbase: 252.0cm 99.2in
Track F: 139.7cm 55.0in
Track R: 138.2cm 54.4in
Length: 399.8cm 157.4in
Width: 166.1cm 65.4in
Height: 139.7cm 55.0in
Ground clearance: 13.2cm 5.2in
Kerb weight: 998.3kg 2199.0lb
Fuel: 41.9L 9.2gal 11.1galUS

4699 Vauxhall

Astra 1.3 GL
1985 UK
105.0mph 168.9kmh
0-50mph 80.5kmh: 8.1secs
0-60mph 96.5kmh: 12.1secs
0-1/4 mile: 19.0secs
0-1km: 35.0secs
75.0bhp 55.9kW 76.0PS
@ 5800rpm
74.5lbft 100.9Nm @ 4200rpm
83.2bhp/ton 81.8bhp/tonne
57.8bhp/L 43.1kW/L 58.6PS/L
46.6ft/sec 14.2m/sec
18.7mph 30.1kmh/1000rpm
32.2mpg 26.8mpgUS 8.8L/100km
Petrol 4-stroke piston
1297cc 79.1cu in
In-line 4 1 Carburettor
Compression ratio: 9.2:1
Bore: 75.0mm 2.9in
Stroke: 73.4mm 2.9in
Valve type/No: Overhead 8
Transmission: Manual
No. of forward speeds: 4
Wheels driven: Front
Springs F/R: Coil/Coil
Brake system: PA
Brakes F/R: Disc/Drum
Steering: Rack & pinion
Wheelbase: 252.0cm 99.2in
Track F: 139.7cm 55.0in
Track R: 138.2cm 54.4in
Length: 399.8cm 157.4in
Width: 166.1cm 65.4in
Height: 139.7cm 55.0in
Ground clearance: 13.2cm 5.2in
Kerb weight: 917.1kg 2020.0lb
Fuel: 41.9L 9.2gal 11.1galUS

4700 Vauxhall

Astra 1.6 SR
1985 UK
105.0mph 168.9kmh
0-50mph 80.5kmh: 8.9secs
0-60mph 96.5kmh: 11.8secs
0-1/4 mile: 18.7secs
0-1km: 32.4secs
90.0bhp 67.1kW 91.2PS
@ 5800rpm
93.0lbft 126.0Nm @ 3800rpm
96.2bhp/ton 94.6bhp/tonne
56.3bhp/L 42.0kW/L 57.1PS/L
50.4ft/sec 15.4m/sec
18.6mph 29.9kmh/1000rpm
27.0mpg 22.5mpgUS 10.5L/100km
Petrol 4-stroke piston
1598cc 97.5cu in
In-line 4 1 Carburettor
Compression ratio: 9.2:1
Bore: 80.0mm 3.1in
Stroke: 79.5mm 3.1in
Valve type/No: Overhead 8
Transmission: Manual
No. of forward speeds: 5
Wheels driven: Front
Springs F/R: Coil/Coil
Brake system: PA
Brakes F/R: Disc/Drum
Steering: Rack & pinion
Wheelbase: 252.0cm 99.2in
Track F: 139.7cm 55.0in
Track R: 138.2cm 54.4in
Length: 399.8cm 157.4in
Width: 166.1cm 65.4in
Height: 139.7cm 55.0in
Ground clearance: 13.2cm 5.2in
Kerb weight: 951.6kg 2096.0lb
Fuel: 41.9L 9.2gal 11.1galUS

4701 Vauxhall

Cavalier SRi
1985 UK
116.0mph 186.6kmh
0-50mph 80.5kmh: 6.7secs
0-60mph 96.5kmh: 9.5secs
0-1/4 mile: 17.1secs
0-1km: 32.4secs
115.0bhp 85.8kW 116.6PS
@ 5800rpm
111.4lbft 150.9Nm @ 4800rpm
109.8bhp/ton 107.9bhp/tonne
64.0bhp/L 47.7kW/L 64.9PS/L
50.4ft/sec 15.4m/sec
19.0mph 30.6kmh/1000rpm
27.1mpg 22.6mpgUS 10.4L/100km
Petrol 4-stroke piston
1796cc 109.6cu in
In-line 4 fuel injection
Compression ratio: 9.2:1
Bore: 84.8mm 3.3in
Stroke: 79.5mm 3.1in
Valve type/No: Overhead 8
Transmission: Manual
No. of forward speeds: 5
Wheels driven: Front
Springs F/R: Coil/Coil
Brake system: PA
Brakes F/R: Disc/Drum
Steering: Rack & pinion
Wheelbase: 257.3cm 101.3in
Track F: 140.0cm 55.1in
Track R: 140.7cm 55.4in
Length: 436.6cm 171.9in
Width: 166.9cm 65.7in
Height: 139.4cm 54.9in
Ground clearance: 16.5cm 6.5in
Kerb weight: 1065.5kg 2347.0lb
Fuel: 61.0L 13.4gal 16.1galUS

4702 Vauxhall

Senator 3.0i CD
1985 UK
125.0mph 201.1kmh
0-50mph 80.5kmh: 7.8secs
0-60mph 96.5kmh: 10.4secs
0-1/4 mile: 18.0secs
0-1km: 32.2secs
180.0bhp 134.2kW 182.5PS
@ 5800rpm
183.0lbft 248.0Nm @ 4800rpm
131.3bhp/ton 129.1bhp/tonne
60.6bhp/L 45.2kW/L 61.5PS/L
44.3ft/sec 13.5m/sec
30.4mph 48.9kmh/1000rpm
22.9mpg 19.1mpgUS 12.3L/100km
Petrol 4-stroke piston
2969cc 181.1cu in
In-line 6 fuel injection
Compression ratio: 9.4:1
Bore: 95.0mm 3.7in
Stroke: 69.8mm 2.7in
Valve type/No: Overhead 12
Transmission: Automatic
No. of forward speeds: 4
Wheels driven: Rear
Springs F/R: Coil/Coil
Brake system: PA
Brakes F/R: Disc/Disc
Steering: Rack & pinion PA
Wheelbase: 268.2cm 105.6in
Track F: 144.3cm 56.8in
Track R: 147.3cm 58.0in
Length: 483.9cm 190.5in
Width: 172.7cm 68.0in
Height: 141.5cm 55.7in
Ground clearance: 14.0cm 5.5in
Kerb weight: 1394.2kg 3071.0lb
Fuel: 75.1L 16.5gal 19.8galUS

4703 Vauxhall

Belmont 1.8 GLSi
1986 UK
120.0mph 193.1kmh
0-50mph 80.5kmh: 6.7secs
0-60mph 96.5kmh: 9.2secs
0-1/4 mile: 17.4secs
0-1km: 31.8secs
115.0bhp 85.8kW 116.6PS
@ 5800rpm
111.4lbft 150.9Nm @ 4800rpm
118.1bhp/ton 116.1bhp/tonne
64.0bhp/L 47.7kW/L 64.9PS/L
50.4ft/sec 15.4m/sec
24.8mph 39.9kmh/1000rpm
32.0mpg 26.6mpgUS 8.8L/100km
Petrol 4-stroke piston
1796cc 109.6cu in
In-line 4 fuel injection
Compression ratio: 9.5:1
Bore: 84.8mm 3.3in
Stroke: 79.5mm 3.1in
Valve type/No: Overhead 8
Transmission: Manual
No. of forward speeds: 5
Wheels driven: Front
Springs F/R: Coil/Coil
Brake system: PA
Brakes F/R: Disc/Drum
Steering: Rack & pinion
Wheelbase: 252.0cm 99.2in
Track F: 139.7cm 55.0in
Track R: 138.2cm 54.4in
Length: 421.9cm 166.1in
Width: 166.4cm 65.5in
Height: 139.7cm 55.0in
Ground clearance: 13.2cm 5.2in
Kerb weight: 990.6kg 2182.0lb
Fuel: 51.9L 11.4gal 13.7galUS

4704 Vauxhall

Carlton CD 2.0i
1986 UK
123.0mph 197.9kmh
0-50mph 80.5kmh: 7.3secs
0-60mph 96.5kmh: 10.4secs
0-1/4 mile: 17.3secs
0-1km: 32.3secs
122.0bhp 91.0kW 123.7PS
@ 5400rpm
129.0lbft 174.8Nm @ 2600rpm
97.3bhp/ton 95.7bhp/tonne
61.1bhp/L 45.5kW/L 61.9PS/L
50.8ft/sec 15.5m/sec
22.5mph 36.2kmh/1000rpm
26.7mpg 22.2mpgUS 10.6L/100km
Petrol 4-stroke piston
1998cc 122.0cu in
In-line 4 fuel injection
Compression ratio: 10.0:1
Bore: 86.0mm 3.4in
Stroke: 86.0mm 3.4in
Valve type/No: Overhead 8
Transmission: Manual
No. of forward speeds: 5
Wheels driven: Rear
Springs F/R: Coil/Coil
Brake system: PA
Brakes F/R: Disc/Disc
Steering: Recirculating ball PA
Wheelbase: 273.0cm 107.5in
Track F: 145.0cm 57.1in
Track R: 146.8cm 57.8in
Length: 468.7cm 184.5in
Width: 177.2cm 69.8in
Height: 144.7cm 57.0in
Ground clearance: 17.9cm 7.0in
Kerb weight: 1275.0kg 2808.4lb
Fuel: 70.1L 15.4gal 18.5galUS

4705 Vauxhall

Nova 1.3 GL 5-door
1986 UK
102.0mph 164.1kmh
0-50mph 80.5kmh: 8.0secs
0-60mph 96.5kmh: 11.8secs
0-1/4 mile: 18.6secs
0-1km: 34.8secs
70.0bhp 52.2kW 71.0PS
@ 5800rpm
74.5lbft 100.9Nm @ 3800rpm
84.4bhp/ton 83.0bhp/tonne
54.0bhp/L 40.2kW/L 54.7PS/L
46.6ft/sec 14.2m/sec
22.6mph 36.4kmh/1000rpm
35.1mpg 29.2mpgUS 8.0L/100km
Petrol 4-stroke piston

1297cc 79.0cu in
In-line 4 1 Carburettor
Compression ratio: 9.2:1
Bore: 75.0mm 2.9in
Stroke: 73.4mm 2.9in
Valve type/No: Overhead 8
Transmission: Manual
No. of forward speeds: 5
Wheels driven: Front
Springs F/R: Coil/Torsion bar
Brake system: PA
Brakes F/R: Disc/Drum
Steering: Rack & pinion
Wheelbase: 234.3cm 92.2in
Track F: 131.8cm 51.9in
Track R: 133.1cm 52.4in
Length: 362.2cm 142.6in
Width: 153.2cm 60.3in
Height: 136.5cm 53.7in
Ground clearance: 16.5cm 6.5in
Kerb weight: 843.0kg 1856.8lb
Fuel: 41.9L 9.2gal 11.1galUS

4706 Vauxhall

Astra GTE 2.0i
1987 UK
125.0mph 201.1kmh
0-50mph 80.5kmh: 6.1secs
0-60mph 96.5kmh: 8.4secs
0-1/4 mile: 16.5secs
0-1km: 30.2secs
124.0bhp 92.5kW 125.7PS
@ 5600rpm
127.6lbft 172.9Nm @ 2600rpm
129.3bhp/ton 127.2bhp/tonne
62.1bhp/L 46.3kW/L 62.9PS/L
52.7ft/sec 16.0m/sec
21.6mph 34.8kmh/1000rpm
33.4mpg 27.8mpgUS 8.5L/100km
Petrol 4-stroke piston
1998cc 122.0cu in
In-line 4 fuel injection
Compression ratio: 10.0:1
Bore: 86.0mm 3.4in
Stroke: 86.0mm 3.4in
Valve type/No: Overhead 8
Transmission: Manual
No. of forward speeds: 5
Wheels driven: Front
Springs F/R: Coil/Coil
Brake system: PA
Brakes F/R: Disc/Drum
Steering: Rack & pinion PA
Wheelbase: 252.0cm 99.2in
Track F: 140.0cm 55.1in
Track R: 140.6cm 55.4in
Length: 399.8cm 157.4in
Width: 166.3cm 65.5in
Height: 139.5cm 54.9in
Ground clearance: 13.3cm 5.2in
Kerb weight: 975.0kg 2147.6lb
Fuel: 51.9L 11.4gal 13.7galUS

4707 Vauxhall

Belmont 1.6 GL
1987 UK
112.0mph 180.2kmh
0-50mph 80.5kmh: 7.5secs
0-60mph 96.5kmh: 10.6secs
0-1/4 mile: 18.3secs
0-1km: 33.6secs
82.0bhp 61.1kW 83.1PS
@ 5400rpm
96.0lbft 130.1Nm @ 2600rpm
86.9bhp/ton 85.4bhp/tonne
51.3bhp/L 38.3kW/L 52.0PS/L
48.1ft/sec 14.7m/sec
23.5mph 37.8kmh/1000rpm
34.0mpg 28.3mpgUS 8.3L/100km
Petrol 4-stroke piston
1598cc 97.0cu in
In-line 4 1 Carburettor
Compression ratio: 10.0:1
Bore: 79.0mm 3.1in
Stroke: 81.5mm 3.2in
Valve type/No: Overhead 8
Transmission: Manual
No. of forward speeds: 5
Wheels driven: Front
Springs F/R: Coil/Coil
Brake system: PA
Brakes F/R: Disc/Drum
Steering: Rack & pinion
Wheelbase: 252.0cm 99.2in
Track F: 140.0cm 55.1in
Track R: 140.6cm 55.4in
Length: 421.8cm 166.1in
Width: 166.3cm 65.5in
Height: 140.0cm 55.1in
Ground clearance: 13.3cm 5.2in
Kerb weight: 960.0kg 2114.5lb
Fuel: 51.9L 11.4gal 13.7galUS

4708 Vauxhall

Carlton 3000 GSi
1987 UK
135.0mph 217.2kmh
0-50mph 80.5kmh: 6.0secs
0-60mph 96.5kmh: 8.2secs
0-1/4 mile: 16.4secs
0-1km: 29.9secs
177.0bhp 132.0kW 179.4PS
@ 5600rpm
177.0lbft 239.8Nm @ 4400rpm
125.9bhp/ton 123.8bhp/tonne
59.6bhp/L 44.5kW/L 60.4PS/L
42.8ft/sec 13.0m/sec
23.2mph 37.3kmh/1000rpm
24.9mpg 20.7mpgUS 11.3L/100km
Petrol 4-stroke piston
2969cc 181.0cu in
In-line 6 fuel injection
Compression ratio: 9.4:1
Bore: 95.0mm 3.7in
Stroke: 69.8mm 2.7in
Valve type/No: Overhead 12
Transmission: Manual
No. of forward speeds: 5
Wheels driven: Rear
Springs F/R: Coil/Coil
Brake system: PA ABS
Brakes F/R: Disc/Disc
Steering: Recirculating ball PA
Wheelbase: 273.0cm 107.5in
Track F: 145.0cm 57.1in
Track R: 146.8cm 57.8in
Length: 468.7cm 184.5in
Width: 177.2cm 69.8in
Height: 144.7cm 57.0in
Ground clearance: 17.9cm 7.0in
Kerb weight: 1430.0kg 3149.8lb
Fuel: 75.1L 16.5gal 19.8galUS

4709 Vauxhall

Cavalier 2.0i CD
1987 UK
115.0mph 185.0kmh
0-50mph 80.5kmh: 6.9secs
0-60mph 96.5kmh: 9.3secs
0-1/4 mile: 17.5secs
0-1km: 32.3secs
115.0bhp 85.8kW 116.6PS
@ 5600rpm
129.1lbft 174.9Nm @ 3000rpm
106.3bhp/ton 104.5bhp/tonne
57.6bhp/L 42.9kW/L 58.4PS/L
52.7ft/sec 16.0m/sec
26.9mph 43.3kmh/1000rpm
26.1mpg 21.7mpgUS 10.8L/100km
Petrol 4-stroke piston
1998cc 122.0cu in
In-line 4 fuel injection
Compression ratio: 9.2:1
Bore: 86.0mm 3.4in
Stroke: 86.0mm 3.4in
Valve type/No: Overhead 8
Transmission: Manual
No. of forward speeds: 5
Wheels driven: Front
Springs F/R: Coil/Coil
Brake system: PA
Brakes F/R: Disc/Drum
Steering: Rack & pinion PA
Wheelbase: 257.4cm 101.3in
Track F: 140.6cm 55.4in
Track R: 140.6cm 55.4in
Length: 426.4cm 167.9in
Width: 166.8cm 65.7in
Height: 138.5cm 54.5in
Ground clearance: 16.5cm 6.5in
Kerb weight: 1100.0kg 2422.9lb
Fuel: 61.0L 13.4gal 16.1galUS

4710 Vauxhall

Cavalier SRi 130 4-door
1987 UK
117.0mph 188.3kmh
0-50mph 80.5kmh: 6.0secs
0-60mph 96.5kmh: 8.2secs
0-1/4 mile: 16.2secs
0-1km: 30.3secs
130.0bhp 96.9kW 131.8PS
@ 5650rpm
133.0lbft 180.2Nm @ 4600rpm
125.3bhp/ton 123.2bhp/tonne
65.1bhp/L 48.5kW/L 66.0PS/L
53.2ft/sec 16.2m/sec
21.3mph 34.3kmh/1000rpm
27.0mpg 22.5mpgUS 10.5L/100km
Petrol 4-stroke piston
1998cc 122.0cu in
In-line 4 fuel injection
Compression ratio: 10.0:1
Bore: 86.0mm 3.4in
Stroke: 86.0mm 3.4in
Valve type/No: Overhead 8
Transmission: Manual
No. of forward speeds: 5
Wheels driven: Front
Springs F/R: Coil/Coil
Brake system: PA
Brakes F/R: Disc/Drum
Steering: Rack & pinion
Wheelbase: 257.4cm 101.3in
Track F: 140.6cm 55.4in
Track R: 140.6cm 55.4in
Length: 436.6cm 171.9in
Width: 166.8cm 65.7in
Height: 139.5cm 54.9in
Ground clearance: 14.8cm 5.8in
Kerb weight: 1055.0kg 2323.8lb
Fuel: 61.0L 13.4gal 16.1galUS

4711 Vauxhall

Senator 3.0i CD
1987 UK
126.0mph 202.7kmh
0-50mph 80.5kmh: 8.2secs
0-60mph 96.5kmh: 10.9secs
0-1/4 mile: 17.9secs
0-1km: 32.5secs
177.0bhp 132.0kW 179.4PS
@ 5600rpm
177.0lbft 239.8Nm @ 4400rpm
117.6bhp/ton 115.7bhp/tonne
59.6bhp/L 44.5kW/L 60.4PS/L
42.8ft/sec 13.0m/sec
30.9mph 49.7kmh/1000rpm
22.7mpg 18.9mpgUS 12.4L/100km
Petrol 4-stroke piston
2969cc 181.0cu in
In-line 6 fuel injection
Compression ratio: 9.4:1
Bore: 95.0mm 3.7in
Stroke: 69.8mm 2.7in
Valve type/No: Overhead 12
Transmission: Automatic
No. of forward speeds: 4
Wheels driven: Rear
Springs F/R: Coil/Coil
Brake system: PA
Brakes F/R: Disc/Disc
Steering: Recirculating ball PA
Wheelbase: 273.0cm 107.5in
Track F: 144.7cm 57.0in
Track R: 146.8cm 57.8in
Length: 484.3cm 190.7in
Width: 176.2cm 69.4in
Height: 144.7cm 57.0in
Ground clearance: 14.5cm 5.7in
Kerb weight: 1530.0kg 3370.0lb
Fuel: 75.1L 16.5gal 19.8galUS

4712 Vauxhall

Carlton L 1.8i
1988 UK
122.0mph 196.3kmh
0-50mph 80.5kmh: 7.5secs
0-60mph 96.5kmh: 10.8secs
0-1/4 mile: 18.1secs
0-1km: 32.9secs
115.0bhp 85.8kW 116.6PS
@ 5600rpm
111.0lbft 150.4Nm @ 4600rpm
97.9bhp/ton 96.2bhp/tonne
64.0bhp/L 47.7kW/L 64.9PS/L
48.7ft/sec 14.8m/sec
22.8mph 36.7kmh/1000rpm
31.4mpg 26.1mpgUS 9.0L/100km
Petrol 4-stroke piston
1796cc 110.0cu in
In-line 4 fuel injection
Compression ratio: 10.0:1
Bore: 84.8mm 3.3in
Stroke: 79.5mm 3.1in
Valve type/No: Overhead 8
Transmission: Manual
No. of forward speeds: 5
Wheels driven: Rear
Springs F/R: Coil/Coil
Brake system: PA ABS
Brakes F/R: Disc/Disc
Steering: Recirculating ball PA
Wheelbase: 273.0cm 107.5in
Track F: 144.7cm 57.0in
Track R: 146.8cm 57.8in
Length: 468.7cm 184.5in
Width: 177.2cm 69.8in
Height: 144.7cm 57.0in
Ground clearance: 17.9cm 7.0in
Kerb weight: 1195.0kg 2632.2lb
Fuel: 75.1L 16.5gal 19.8galUS

4713 Vauxhall

Carlton L 2.3D
1988 UK
105.0mph 168.9kmh
0-50mph 80.5kmh: 11.5secs
0-60mph 96.5kmh: 16.2secs
0-1/4 mile: 21.0secs
0-1km: 38.6secs
73.0bhp 54.4kW 74.0PS
@ 4400rpm
101.8lbft 138.0Nm @ 2400rpm
57.7bhp/ton 56.7bhp/tonne
32.3bhp/L 24.1kW/L 32.7PS/L
40.9ft/sec 12.5m/sec
23.7mph 38.1kmh/1000rpm
31.0mpg 25.8mpgUS 9.1L/100km
Diesel 4-stroke piston
2260cc 138.0cu in
In-line 4 fuel injection
Compression ratio: 23.0:1
Bore: 92.0mm 3.6in
Stroke: 85.0mm 3.3in
Valve type/No: Overhead 8
Transmission: Manual
No. of forward speeds: 5
Wheels driven: Rear
Springs F/R: Coil/Coil
Brake system: PA
Brakes F/R: Disc/Disc
Steering: Recirculating ball PA
Wheelbase: 273.0cm 107.5in
Track F: 144.7cm 57.0in
Track R: 146.8cm 57.8in
Length: 468.7cm 184.5in
Width: 177.2cm 69.8in
Height: 144.7cm 57.0in
Ground clearance: 17.9cm 7.0in
Kerb weight: 1287.0kg 2834.8lb
Fuel: 75.1L 16.5gal 19.8galUS

4714 Vauxhall

Cavalier 4x4
1988 UK
124.0mph 199.5kmh
0-50mph 80.5kmh: 6.1secs
0-60mph 96.5kmh: 8.6secs
0-1/4 mile: 16.5secs
0-1km: 29.7secs
130.0bhp 96.9kW 131.8PS
@ 5600rpm
133.0lbft 180.2Nm @ 4600rpm
104.4bhp/ton 102.7bhp/tonne
65.1bhp/L 48.5kW/L 66.0PS/L
52.7ft/sec 16.0m/sec
20.3mph 32.7kmh/1000rpm
28.3mpg 23.6mpgUS 10.0L/100km
Petrol 4-stroke piston
1998cc 122.0cu in
In-line 4 fuel injection
Compression ratio: 10.0:1
Bore: 86.0mm 3.4in
Stroke: 86.0mm 3.4in
Valve type/No: Overhead 8
Transmission: Manual
No. of forward speeds: 5
Wheels driven: 4-wheel drive
Springs F/R: Coil/Coil
Brake system: PA
Brakes F/R: Disc/Disc
Steering: Rack & pinion PA
Wheelbase: 260.1cm 102.4in
Track F: 142.5cm 56.1in
Track R: 144.5cm 56.9in
Length: 443.0cm 174.4in
Width: 169.9cm 66.9in
Height: 140.0cm 55.1in
Ground clearance: 15.0cm 5.9in
Kerb weight: 1266.2kg 2789.0lb
Fuel: 61.0L 13.4gal 16.1galUS

4715 Vauxhall

Nova GTE
1988 UK

119.0mph 191.5kmh
0-50mph 80.5kmh: 6.5secs
0-60mph 96.5kmh: 9.1secs
0-1/4 mile: 17.0secs
0-1km: 31.5secs
100.0bhp 74.6kW 101.4PS
@ 5600rpm
99.6lbft 135.0Nm @ 3400rpm
116.1bhp/ton 114.2bhp/tonne
62.6bhp/L 46.7kW/L 63.4PS/L
49.9ft/sec 15.2m/sec
19.9mph 32.0kmh/1000rpm
32.5mpg 27.1mpgUS 8.7L/100km
Petrol 4-stroke piston
1598cc 97.0cu in
In-line 4 fuel injection
Compression ratio: 10.0:1
Bore: 79.0mm 3.1in
Stroke: 81.5mm 3.2in
Valve type/No: Overhead 8
Transmission: Manual
No. of forward speeds: 5
Wheels driven: Front
Springs F/R: Coil/Coil
Brake system: PA
Brakes F/R: Disc/Drum
Steering: Rack & pinion
Wheelbase: 234.3cm 92.2in
Track F: 131.8cm 51.9in
Track R: 133.1cm 52.4in
Length: 362.2cm 142.6in
Width: 153.2cm 60.3in
Height: 136.5cm 53.7in
Ground clearance: 16.5cm 6.5in
Kerb weight: 876.0kg 1929.5lb
Fuel: 41.9L 9.2gal 11.1galUS

4716 Vauxhall

Astra 1.7 DL
1989 UK
96.0mph 154.5kmh
0-50mph 80.5kmh: 10.6secs
0-60mph 96.5kmh: 15.1secs
0-1/4 mile: 19.8secs
0-1km: 37.6secs
57.0bhp 42.5kW 57.8PS
@ 4600rpm
77.5lbft 105.0Nm @ 2400rpm
58.3bhp/ton 57.3bhp/tonne
33.5bhp/L 25.0kW/L 34.0PS/L
40.0ft/sec 12.2m/sec
23.5mph 37.8kmh/1000rpm
44.2mpg 36.8mpgUS 6.4L/100km
Diesel 4-stroke piston
1699cc 104.0cu in
In-line 4 fuel injection
Compression ratio: 23.0:1
Bore: 82.5mm 3.2in
Stroke: 79.5mm 3.1in
Valve type/No: Overhead 8
Transmission: Manual
No. of forward speeds: 5
Wheels driven: Front
Springs F/R: Coil/Coil
Brake system: PA
Brakes F/R: Disc/Disc
Steering: Rack & pinion
Wheelbase: 252.0cm 99.2in
Track F: 140.0cm 55.1in
Track R: 140.6cm 55.4in
Length: 399.8cm 157.4in
Width: 166.3cm 65.5in
Height: 140.0cm 55.1in
Ground clearance: 13.5cm 5.3in
Kerb weight: 995.0kg 2191.6lb
Fuel: 51.9L 11.4gal 13.7galUS

4717 Vauxhall

Cavalier 1.4L
1989 UK
107.0mph 172.2kmh
0-50mph 80.5kmh: 8.9secs
0-60mph 96.5kmh: 12.9secs
0-1/4 mile: 19.1secs
0-1km: 35.2secs
75.0bhp 55.9kW 76.0PS
@ 5600rpm
79.7lbft 108.0Nm @ 3000rpm
71.7bhp/ton 70.5bhp/tonne
53.7bhp/L 40.1kW/L 54.5PS/L
45.0ft/sec 13.7m/sec
22.3mph 35.9kmh/1000rpm
34.8mpg 29.0mpgUS 8.1L/100km
Petrol 4-stroke piston
1396cc 85.0cu in
In-line 4 1 Carburettor
Compression ratio: 9.4:1
Bore: 77.8mm 3.1in
Stroke: 73.4mm 2.9in
Valve type/No: Overhead 8
Transmission: Manual
No. of forward speeds: 5
Wheels driven: Front
Springs F/R: Coil/Torsion bar
Brake system: PA
Brakes F/R: Disc/Drum
Steering: Rack & pinion
Wheelbase: 260.0cm 102.4in
Track F: 142.0cm 55.9in
Track R: 142.6cm 56.1in
Length: 435.0cm 171.3in
Width: 170.0cm 66.9in
Height: 140.0cm 55.1in
Ground clearance: 17.9cm 7.0in
Kerb weight: 1064.0kg 2343.6lb
Fuel: 61.0L 13.4gal 16.1galUS

4718 Vauxhall

Cavalier 1.6L
1989 UK
111.0mph 178.6kmh
0-50mph 80.5kmh: 8.7secs
0-60mph 96.5kmh: 12.1secs
0-1/4 mile: 25.0secs
0-1km: 35.0secs
82.0bhp 61.1kW 83.1PS
@ 5200rpm
93.7lbft 127.0Nm @ 2600rpm
78.7bhp/ton 77.4bhp/tonne
51.3bhp/L 38.3kW/L 52.0PS/L
46.4ft/sec 14.1m/sec
24.2mph 38.9kmh/1000rpm
34.1mpg 28.4mpgUS 8.3L/100km
Petrol 4-stroke piston
1598cc 97.0cu in
In-line 4 1 Carburettor
Compression ratio: 10.0:1
Bore: 79.0mm 3.1in
Stroke: 81.5mm 3.2in
Valve type/No: Overhead 8
Transmission: Manual
No. of forward speeds: 5
Wheels driven: Front
Springs F/R: Coil/Coil
Brake system: PA
Brakes F/R: Disc/Drum
Steering: Rack & pinion
Wheelbase: 260.0cm 102.4in
Track F: 142.0cm 55.9in
Track R: 142.6cm 56.1in
Length: 435.0cm 171.3in
Width: 170.0cm 66.9in
Height: 140.0cm 55.1in
Ground clearance: 17.9cm 7.0in
Kerb weight: 1059.0kg 2332.6lb
Fuel: 61.0L 13.4gal 16.1galUS

4719 Vauxhall

Cavalier SRi
1989 UK
126.0mph 202.7kmh
0-50mph 80.5kmh: 6.5secs
0-60mph 96.5kmh: 8.9secs
0-1/4 mile: 16.4secs
0-1km: 30.2secs
130.0bhp 96.9kW 131.8PS
@ 5600rpm
132.8lbft 180.0Nm @ 4600rpm
124.7bhp/ton 122.6bhp/tonne
65.1bhp/L 48.5kW/L 66.0PS/L
52.7ft/sec 16.0m/sec
21.2mph 34.1kmh/1000rpm
25.3mpg 21.1mpgUS 11.2L/100km
Petrol 4-stroke piston
1998cc 122.0cu in
In-line 4 fuel injection
Compression ratio: 10.0:1
Bore: 86.0mm 3.4in
Stroke: 86.0mm 3.4in
Valve type/No: Overhead 8
Transmission: Manual
No. of forward speeds: 5
Wheels driven: Front
Springs F/R: Coil/Torsion bar
Brake system: PA ABS
Brakes F/R: Disc/Disc
Steering: Rack & pinion PA
Wheelbase: 260.0cm 102.4in
Track F: 142.6cm 56.1in
Track R: 144.4cm 56.9in
Length: 443.0cm 174.4in
Width: 170.0cm 66.9in
Height: 140.0cm 55.1in
Ground clearance: 14.9cm 5.9in
Kerb weight: 1060.0kg 2334.8lb
Fuel: 61.0L 13.4gal 16.1galUS

4720 Vauxhall

Senator 2.5i
1989 UK
128.0mph 206.0kmh
0-50mph 80.5kmh: 6.8secs
0-60mph 96.5kmh: 9.3secs
0-1/4 mile: 17.2secs
0-1km: 31.7secs
140.0bhp 104.4kW 141.9PS
@ 5200rpm
151.3lbft 205.0Nm @ 4200rpm
97.2bhp/ton 95.6bhp/tonne
56.2bhp/L 41.9kW/L 57.0PS/L
39.3ft/sec 12.0m/sec
25.3mph 40.7kmh/1000rpm
22.2mpg 18.5mpgUS 12.7L/100km
Petrol 4-stroke piston
2490cc 152.0cu in
In-line 6 fuel injection
Compression ratio: 9.2:1
Bore: 87.0mm 3.4in
Stroke: 69.0mm 2.7in
Valve type/No: Overhead 12
Transmission: Manual
No. of forward speeds: 5
Wheels driven: Rear
Springs F/R: Coil/Coil
Brake system: PA ABS
Brakes F/R: Disc/Disc
Steering: Recirculating ball PA
Wheelbase: 273.0cm 107.5in
Track F: 145.0cm 57.1in
Track R: 146.8cm 57.8in
Length: 484.5cm 190.7in
Width: 176.3cm 69.4in
Height: 145.2cm 57.2in
Ground clearance: 14.6cm 5.7in
Kerb weight: 1465.0kg 3226.9lb
Fuel: 75.1L 16.5gal 19.8galUS

4721 Vauxhall

Senator 3.0i CD
1989 UK
132.0mph 212.4kmh
0-50mph 80.5kmh: 7.0secs
0-60mph 96.5kmh: 9.3secs
0-1/4 mile: 17.2secs
0-1km: 30.2secs
177.0bhp 132.0kW 179.4PS
@ 5600rpm
177.1lbft 240.0Nm @ 4400rpm
117.6bhp/ton 115.7bhp/tonne
59.6bhp/L 44.5kW/L 60.4PS/L
42.9ft/sec 13.1m/sec
28.8mph 46.3kmh/1000rpm
19.3mpg 16.1mpgUS 14.6L/100km
Petrol 4-stroke piston
2969cc 181.0cu in
In-line 6 fuel injection
Compression ratio: 9.4:1
Bore: 95.0mm 3.7in
Stroke: 70.0mm 2.8in
Valve type/No: Overhead 12
Transmission: Automatic
No. of forward speeds: 4
Wheels driven: Rear
Springs F/R: Coil/Coil
Brake system: PA ABS
Brakes F/R: Disc/Disc
Steering: Recirculating ball PA
Wheelbase: 273.0cm 107.5in
Track F: 145.0cm 57.1in
Track R: 146.8cm 57.8in
Length: 484.5cm 190.7in
Width: 176.3cm 69.4in
Height: 145.2cm 57.2in
Ground clearance: 14.6cm 5.7in
Kerb weight: 1530.0kg 3370.0lb
Fuel: 75.1L 16.5gal 19.8galUS

4722 Vauxhall

Calibra 2.0i 16v
1990 UK
139.0mph 223.7kmh
0-50mph 80.5kmh: 6.1secs
0-60mph 96.5kmh: 8.1secs
0-1/4 mile: 16.4secs
0-1km: 29.6secs
150.0bhp 111.9kW 152.1PS
@ 6000rpm
144.6lbft 196.0Nm @ 4800rpm
124.4bhp/ton 122.3bhp/tonne
75.1bhp/L 56.0kW/L 76.1PS/L
56.5ft/sec 17.2m/sec
22.1mph 35.6kmh/1000rpm
25.5mpg 21.2mpgUS 11.1L/100km
Petrol 4-stroke piston
1998cc 122.0cu in
In-line 4 fuel injection
Compression ratio: 10.5:1
Bore: 86.0mm 3.4in
Stroke: 86.0mm 3.4in
Valve type/No: Overhead 16
Transmission: Manual
No. of forward speeds: 5
Wheels driven: Front
Springs F/R: Coil/Coil
Brake system: PA ABS
Brakes F/R: Disc/Disc
Steering: Rack & pinion PA
Wheelbase: 260.1cm 102.4in
Track F: 142.5cm 56.1in
Track R: 144.5cm 56.9in
Length: 449.3cm 176.9in
Width: 168.9cm 66.5in
Height: 132.1cm 52.0in
Kerb weight: 1226.0kg 2700.4lb
Fuel: 63.7L 14.0gal 16.8galUS

4723 Vauxhall

Carlton 3.0i CDX Estate
1990 UK
132.0mph 212.4kmh
0-50mph 80.5kmh: 6.0secs
0-60mph 96.5kmh: 8.4secs
0-1/4 mile: 16.4secs
0-1km: 30.5secs
177.0bhp 132.0kW 179.4PS
@ 5600rpm
177.1lbft 240.0Nm @ 4400rpm
120.0bhp/ton 118.0bhp/tonne
59.6bhp/L 44.5kW/L 60.4PS/L
42.8ft/sec 13.0m/sec
23.2mph 37.3kmh/1000rpm
21.0mpg 17.5mpgUS 13.5L/100km
Petrol 4-stroke piston
2969cc 181.0cu in
In-line 6 fuel injection
Compression ratio: 9.4:1
Bore: 95.0mm 3.7in
Stroke: 69.8mm 2.7in
Valve type/No: Overhead 12
Transmission: Manual
No. of forward speeds: 5
Wheels driven: Rear
Springs F/R: Coil/Coil
Brake system: PA ABS
Brakes F/R: Disc/Disc
Steering: Recirculating ball PA
Wheelbase: 273.1cm 107.5in
Track F: 144.8cm 57.0in
Track R: 147.3cm 58.0in
Length: 472.9cm 186.2in
Width: 193.3cm 76.1in
Height: 152.9cm 60.2in
Ground clearance: 17.8cm 7.0in
Kerb weight: 1500.0kg 3304.0lb
Fuel: 70.1L 15.4gal 18.5galUS

4724 Vauxhall

Carlton GSi 3000 24v
1990 UK
148.0mph 238.1kmh
0-50mph 80.5kmh: 5.3secs
0-60mph 96.5kmh: 7.0secs
0-1/4 mile: 15.4secs
0-1km: 28.1secs
204.0bhp 152.1kW 206.8PS
@ 6000rpm
199.3lbft 270.0Nm @ 3600rpm
139.7bhp/ton 137.4bhp/tonne
68.7bhp/L 51.2kW/L 69.7PS/L
46.0ft/sec 14.0m/sec
24.4mph 39.3kmh/1000rpm
19.5mpg 16.2mpgUS 14.5L/100km
Petrol 4-stroke piston
2969cc 181.0cu in
In-line 6 fuel injection
Compression ratio: 10.1:1
Bore: 95.0mm 3.7in
Stroke: 70.0mm 2.8in
Valve type/No: Overhead 24
Transmission: Manual
No. of forward speeds: 5
Wheels driven: Rear
Springs F/R: Coil/Coil
Brake system: PA ABS
Brakes F/R: Disc/Disc
Steering: Recirculating ball PA
Wheelbase: 273.0cm 107.5in

Track F: 145.0cm 57.1in
Track R: 146.8cm 57.8in
Length: 468.7cm 184.5in
Width: 177.2cm 69.8in
Height: 144.7cm 57.0in
Ground clearance: 17.9cm 7.0in
Kerb weight: 1485.0kg 3270.9lb
Fuel: 75.1L 16.5gal 19.8galUS

4725 Vauxhall

Cavalier GSi 2000 16v
1990 UK
134.0mph 215.6kmh
0-50mph 80.5kmh: 5.9secs
0-60mph 96.5kmh: 7.9secs
0-1/4 mile: 16.2secs
0-1km: 29.6secs
150.0bhp 111.9kW 152.1PS
@ 6000rpm
144.6lbft 196.0Nm @ 4800rpm
124.0bhp/ton 121.9bhp/tonne
75.1bhp/L 56.0kW/L 76.1PS/L
56.5ft/sec 17.2m/sec
21.1mph 33.9kmh/1000rpm
25.0mpg 20.8mpgUS 11.3L/100km
Petrol 4-stroke piston
1998cc 122.0cu in
In-line 4 fuel injection
Compression ratio: 10.5:1
Bore: 86.0mm 3.4in
Stroke: 86.0mm 3.4in
Valve type/No: Overhead 16
Transmission: Manual
No. of forward speeds: 5
Wheels driven: Front
Springs F/R: Coil/Coil
Brake system: PA ABS
Brakes F/R: Disc/Disc
Steering: Rack & pinion PA
Wheelbase: 260.0cm 102.4in
Track F: 142.6cm 56.1in
Track R: 144.4cm 56.9in
Length: 443.0cm 174.4in
Width: 170.0cm 66.9in
Height: 140.0cm 55.1in
Ground clearance: 14.9cm 5.9in
Kerb weight: 1230.0kg 2709.2lb
Fuel: 65.1L 14.3gal 17.2galUS

4726 Vauxhall

Cavalier GSi 2000 16v 4x4
1990 UK
129.0mph 207.6kmh
0-50mph 80.5kmh: 6.1secs
0-60mph 96.5kmh: 8.5secs
0-1/4 mile: 16.2secs
0-1km: 30.2secs
150.0bhp 111.9kW 152.1PS
@ 6000rpm
144.6lbft 196.0Nm @ 4800rpm
113.5bhp/ton 111.6bhp/tonne
75.1bhp/L 56.0kW/L 76.1PS/L
56.5ft/sec 17.2m/sec
21.1mph 33.9kmh/1000rpm
24.0mpg 20.0mpgUS 11.8L/100km
Petrol 4-stroke piston
1998cc 122.0cu in
In-line 4 fuel injection
Compression ratio: 10.5:1
Bore: 86.0mm 3.4in
Stroke: 86.0mm 3.4in
Valve type/No: Overhead 16
Transmission: Manual
No. of forward speeds: 5
Wheels driven: 4-wheel drive
Springs F/R: Coil/Coil
Brake system: PA ABS
Brakes F/R: Disc/Disc
Steering: Rack & pinion PA
Wheelbase: 260.1cm 102.4in
Track F: 142.5cm 56.1in
Track R: 144.5cm 56.9in
Length: 443.0cm 174.4in
Width: 169.9cm 66.9in
Height: 140.0cm 55.1in
Ground clearance: 15.0cm 5.9in
Kerb weight: 1344.0kg 2960.3lb
Fuel: 65.1L 14.3gal 17.2galUS

4727 Vauxhall

Nova 1.5TD Merit
1990 UK
102.0mph 164.1kmh
0-50mph 80.5kmh: 8.9secs
0-60mph 96.5kmh: 12.2secs
0-1/4 mile: 18.9secs
0-1km: 35.1secs
67.0bhp 50.0kW 67.9PS
@ 4600rpm
97.4lbft 132.0Nm @ 2600rpm
83.1bhp/ton 81.7bhp/tonne
45.0bhp/L 33.6kW/L 45.6PS/L
41.3ft/sec 12.6m/sec
24.2mph 38.9kmh/1000rpm
43.8mpg 36.5mpgUS 6.4L/100km
Diesel 4-stroke piston
1488cc 91.0cu in turbocharged
In-line 4 fuel injection
Compression ratio: 22.5:1
Bore: 76.0mm 3.0in
Stroke: 82.0mm 3.2in
Valve type/No: Overhead 8
Transmission: Manual
No. of forward speeds: 5
Wheels driven: Front
Springs F/R: Coil/Coil
Brake system: PA
Brakes F/R: Disc/Drum
Steering: Rack & pinion
Wheelbase: 234.3cm 92.2in
Track F: 132.0cm 52.0in
Track R: 130.7cm 51.5in
Length: 362.2cm 142.6in
Width: 153.2cm 60.3in
Height: 136.5cm 53.7in
Ground clearance: 14.4cm 5.7in
Kerb weight: 820.0kg 1806.2lb
Fuel: 41.9L 9.2gal 11.1galUS

4728 Vauxhall

Calibra 2.0i
1991 UK
128.0mph 206.0kmh
0-50mph 80.5kmh: 6.6secs
0-60mph 96.5kmh: 9.5secs
0-1/4 mile: 17.4secs
0-1km: 31.7secs
115.0bhp 85.8kW 116.6PS
@ 5200rpm
125.5lbft 170.0Nm @ 2600rpm
97.0bhp/ton 95.4bhp/tonne
57.6bhp/L 42.9kW/L 58.4PS/L
49.0ft/sec 14.9m/sec
21.2mph 34.1kmh/1000rpm
29.3mpg 24.4mpgUS 9.6L/100km
Petrol 4-stroke piston
1998cc 122.0cu in
In-line 4 fuel injection
Compression ratio: 9.2:1
Bore: 86.0mm 3.4in
Stroke: 86.0mm 3.4in
Valve type/No: Overhead 8
Transmission: Manual
No. of forward speeds: 5
Wheels driven: Front
Springs F/R: Coil/Coil
Brake system: PA ABS
Brakes F/R: Disc/Disc
Steering: Rack & pinion PA
Wheelbase: 260.1cm 102.4in
Track F: 142.5cm 56.1in
Track R: 144.5cm 56.9in
Length: 449.3cm 176.9in
Width: 168.9cm 66.5in
Height: 132.1cm 52.0in
Kerb weight: 1205.0kg 2654.2lb
Fuel: 63.7L 14.0gal 16.8galUS

4729 Vauxhall

Calibra 4x4
1991 UK
132.0mph 212.4kmh
0-50mph 80.5kmh: 6.4secs
0-60mph 96.5kmh: 9.0secs
0-1/4 mile: 16.8secs
0-1km: 30.7secs
150.0bhp 111.9kW 152.1PS
@ 6000rpm
144.6lbft 196.0Nm @ 4800rpm
112.3bhp/ton 110.5bhp/tonne
75.1bhp/L 56.0kW/L 76.1PS/L
56.5ft/sec 17.2m/sec
22.1mph 35.6kmh/1000rpm
27.3mpg 22.7mpgUS 10.3L/100km
Petrol 4-stroke piston
1998cc 122.0cu in
In-line 4 fuel injection
Compression ratio: 10.5:1
Bore: 86.0mm 3.4in
Stroke: 86.0mm 3.4in
Valve type/No: Overhead 16
Transmission: Manual
No. of forward speeds: 5
Wheels driven: 4-wheel drive
Springs F/R: Coil/Coil
Brake system: PA ABS
Brakes F/R: Disc/Disc
Steering: Rack & pinion PA
Wheelbase: 260.1cm 102.4in
Track F: 142.5cm 56.1in
Track R: 144.5cm 56.9in
Length: 449.3cm 176.9in
Width: 168.9cm 66.5in
Height: 132.1cm 52.0in
Kerb weight: 1358.0kg 2991.2lb
Fuel: 63.7L 14.0gal 16.8galUS

4730 Vauxhall

Nova 1.2 Luxe
1991 UK
94.0mph 151.2kmh
0-50mph 80.5kmh: 9.9secs
0-60mph 96.5kmh: 14.5secs
0-1/4 mile: 19.9secs
0-1km: 43.6secs
55.0bhp 41.0kW 55.8PS
@ 5600rpm
64.9lbft 88.0Nm @ 2200rpm
70.1bhp/ton 68.9bhp/tonne
46.0bhp/L 34.3kW/L 46.6PS/L
38.6ft/sec 11.8m/sec
23.0mph 37.0kmh/1000rpm
35.6mpg 29.6mpgUS 7.9L/100km
Petrol 4-stroke piston
1196cc 73.0cu in
In-line 4 1 Carburettor
Compression ratio: 9.2:1
Bore: 78.0mm 3.1in
Stroke: 63.0mm 2.5in
Valve type/No: Overhead 8
Transmission: Manual
No. of forward speeds: 5
Wheels driven: Front
Springs F/R: Coil/Coil
Brake system: PA
Brakes F/R: Disc/Drum
Steering: Rack & pinion
Wheelbase: 234.2cm 92.2in
Track F: 132.1cm 52.0in
Track R: 131.1cm 51.6in
Length: 362.2cm 142.6in
Width: 160.8cm 63.3in
Height: 136.4cm 53.7in
Ground clearance: 14.5cm 5.7in
Kerb weight: 798.0kg 1757.7lb
Fuel: 41.9L 9.2gal 11.1galUS

4731 Vauxhall

Senator 3.0i 24v
1991 UK
140.0mph 225.3kmh
0-50mph 80.5kmh: 6.9secs
0-60mph 96.5kmh: 9.1secs
0-1/4 mile: 17.0secs
0-1km: 30.2secs
201.2bhp 150.0kW 204.0PS
@ 6000rpm
199.3lbft 270.0Nm @ 3600rpm
130.3bhp/ton 128.2bhp/tonne
67.8bhp/L 50.5kW/L 68.7PS/L
45.8ft/sec 14.0m/sec
27.6mph 44.4kmh/1000rpm
21.4mpg 17.8mpgUS 13.2L/100km
Petrol 4-stroke piston
2969cc 181.0cu in
In-line 6 fuel injection
Compression ratio: 10.0:1
Bore: 95.0mm 3.7in
Stroke: 69.8mm 2.7in
Valve type/No: Overhead 24
Transmission: Automatic
No. of forward speeds: 4
Wheels driven: Rear
Springs F/R: Coil/Coil
Brake system: PA ABS
Brakes F/R: Disc/Disc
Steering: Recirculating ball PA
Wheelbase: 273.0cm 107.5in
Track F: 145.0cm 57.1in
Track R: 146.8cm 57.8in
Length: 484.5cm 190.7in
Width: 176.3cm 69.4in
Height: 143.9cm 56.7in
Ground clearance: 14.6cm 5.7in
Kerb weight: 1570.0kg 3458.1lb
Fuel: 75.1L 16.5gal 19.8galUS

4732 Vauxhall

1.4i GLS
1992 UK
108.0mph 173.8kmh
0-50mph 80.5kmh: 8.7secs
0-60mph 96.5kmh: 12.8secs
0-1/4 mile: 19.0secs
0-1km: 35.3secs
82.0bhp 61.1kW 83.1PS
@ 5800rpm
83.4lbft 113.0Nm @ 3400rpm
80.6bhp/ton 79.2bhp/tonne
58.7bhp/L 43.7kW/L 59.5PS/L
46.6ft/sec 14.2m/sec
22.2mph 35.7kmh/1000rpm
34.7mpg 28.9mpgUS 8.1L/100km
Petrol 4-stroke piston
1398cc 85.0cu in
In-line 4 fuel injection
Compression ratio: 9.8:1
Bore: 77.6mm 3.1in
Stroke: 73.4mm 2.9in
Valve type/No: Overhead 8
Transmission: Manual
No. of forward speeds: 5
Wheels driven: Front
Springs F/R: Coil/Coil
Brake system: PA ABS
Brakes F/R: Disc/Drum
Steering: Rack & pinion PA
Wheelbase: 251.7cm 99.1in
Track F: 142.5cm 56.1in
Track R: 143.0cm 56.3in
Length: 423.9cm 166.9in
Width: 168.9cm 66.5in
Height: 137.9cm 54.3in
Ground clearance: 13.7cm 5.4in
Kerb weight: 1035.0kg 2279.7lb
Fuel: 52.0L 11.4gal 13.7galUS

4733 Vauxhall

Cavalier 1.7 GL TD
1992 UK
111.0mph 178.6kmh
0-50mph 80.5kmh: 9.2secs
0-60mph 96.5kmh: 12.8secs
0-1/4 mile: 19.2secs
0-1km: 35.3secs
82.0bhp 61.1kW 83.1PS
@ 4400rpm
124.0lbft 168.0Nm @ 2400rpm
71.0bhp/ton 69.8bhp/tonne
48.6bhp/L 36.3kW/L 49.3PS/L
41.4ft/sec 12.6m/sec
25.8mph 41.5kmh/1000rpm
37.1mpg 30.9mpgUS 7.6L/100km
Diesel 4-stroke piston
1686cc 102.9cu in
In-line 4 fuel injection
Compression ratio: 22.0:1
Bore: 79.0mm 3.1in
Stroke: 86.0mm 3.4in
Valve type/No: Overhead 8
Transmission: Manual
No. of forward speeds: 5
Wheels driven: Front
Springs F/R: Coil/Coil
Brake system: PA
Brakes F/R: Disc/Drum
Steering: Rack & pinion PA
Wheelbase: 260.0cm 102.4in
Track F: 143.0cm 56.3in
Track R: 143.0cm 56.3in
Length: 443.0cm 174.4in
Width: 170.0cm 66.9in
Height: 140.0cm 55.1in
Ground clearance: 17.9cm 7.0in
Kerb weight: 1175.0kg 2588.1lb
Fuel: 61.0L 13.4gal 16.1galUS

4734 Vauxhall

Frontera 2.3 TD Estate
1992 UK
85.1mph 137.0kmh
0-50mph 80.5kmh: 12.2secs
0-60mph 96.5kmh: 18.1secs
0-1/4 mile: 20.9secs
0-1km: 39.9secs
100.0bhp 74.6kW 101.4PS
@ 4200rpm
158.7lbft 215.0Nm @ 2200rpm
54.1bhp/ton 53.2bhp/tonne
44.2bhp/L 33.0kW/L 44.9PS/L
39.1ft/sec 11.9m/sec
21.8mph 35.1kmh/1000rpm
22.8mpg 19.0mpgUS 12.4L/100km
Diesel 4-stroke piston
2260cc 138.0cu in turbocharged
In-line 4 fuel injection

Compression ratio: 23.0:1
Bore: 92.0mm 3.6in
Stroke: 85.0mm 3.3in
Valve type/No: Overhead 8
Transmission: Manual
No. of forward speeds: 5
Wheels driven: 4-wheel engageable
Springs F/R: Torsion bar/Leaf
Brake system: PA
Brakes F/R: Disc/Disc
Steering: Recirculating ball PA
Wheelbase: 276.0cm 108.7in
Track F: 144.0cm 56.7in
Track R: 144.5cm 56.9in
Length: 470.8cm 185.4in
Width: 172.8cm 68.0in
Height: 171.5cm 67.5in
Kerb weight: 1880.0kg 4141.0lb
Fuel: 80.0L 17.6gal 21.1galUS

4735 Vector

W2
1990 USA
200.0mph 321.8kmh
0-60mph 96.5kmh: 4.0secs
0-1/4 mile: 11.8secs
600.0bhp 447.4kW 608.3PS
@ 5700rpm
580.0lbft 785.9Nm @ 4800rpm
483.4bhp/ton 475.4bhp/tonne
100.0bhp/L 74.6kW/L 101.4PS/L
57.5ft/sec 17.5m/sec
Petrol 4-stroke piston
6000cc 366.1cu in turbocharged
Vee 8 fuel injection
Compression ratio: 8.1:1
Bore: 101.6mm 4.0in
Stroke: 92.2mm 3.6in
Valve type/No: Overhead 16
Transmission: Automatic
No. of forward speeds: 3
Wheels driven: Rear
Springs F/R: Coil/Coil
Brakes F/R: Disc/Disc
Steering: Rack & pinion PA
Wheelbase: 261.6cm 103.0in
Track F: 160.0cm 63.0in
Track R: 165.1cm 65.0in
Length: 436.9cm 172.0in
Width: 193.0cm 76.0in
Height: 108.0cm 42.5in
Kerb weight: 1262.1kg 2780.0lb
Fuel: 106.0L 23.3gal 28.0galUS

4736 Vector

W8 Twin Turbo
1991 USA
218.0mph 350.8kmh
0-50mph 80.5kmh: 3.3secs
0-60mph 96.5kmh: 4.2secs
0-1/4 mile: 12.0secs
625.0bhp 466.1kW 633.7PS
@ 5700rpm
630.0lbft 853.7Nm @ 4900rpm
421.7bhp/ton 414.6bhp/tonne
104.6bhp/L 78.0kW/L 106.1PS/L
57.5ft/sec 17.5m/sec
16.2mpg 13.5mpgUS 17.4L/100km
Petrol 4-stroke piston
5973cc 364.4cu in turbocharged
Vee 8 fuel injection
Compression ratio: 8.0:1
Bore: 101.6mm 4.0in
Stroke: 92.1mm 3.6in
Valve type/No: Overhead 16
Transmission: Automatic
No. of forward speeds: 3
Wheels driven: Rear
Springs F/R: Coil/Coil
Brakes F/R: Disc/Disc
Steering: Rack & pinion PA
Wheelbase: 261.6cm 103.0in
Track F: 160.0cm 63.0in
Track R: 165.1cm 65.0in
Length: 436.9cm 172.0in
Width: 208.3cm 82.0in
Height: 108.0cm 42.5in
Ground clearance: 14.0cm 5.5in
Kerb weight: 1507.3kg 3320.0lb
Fuel: 106.0L 23.3gal 28.0galUS

4737 Volga

M21K
1960 USSR
79.5mph 127.9kmh
0-50mph 80.5kmh: 19.7secs
0-60mph 96.5kmh: 30.3secs
0-1/4 mile: 24.1secs
80.0bhp 59.7kW 81.1PS
@ 4000rpm
130.0lbft 176.2Nm @ 2000rpm
55.6bhp/ton 54.7bhp/tonne
32.7bhp/L 24.4kW/L 33.2PS/L
40.2ft/sec 12.3m/sec
17.2mph 27.7kmh/1000rpm
20.4mpg 17.0mpgUS 13.8L/100km
Petrol 4-stroke piston
2445cc 149.2cu in
In-line 4
Compression ratio: 7.5:1
Bore: 92.0mm 3.6in
Stroke: 92.0mm 3.6in
Valve type/No: Overhead 8
Transmission: Manual
No. of forward speeds: 3
Wheels driven: Rear
Springs F/R: Coil/Leaf
Brakes F/R: Drum/Drum
Wheelbase: 269.7cm 106.2in
Track F: 141.0cm 55.5in
Track R: 142.2cm 56.0in
Length: 482.6cm 190.0in
Width: 185.4cm 73.0in
Height: 163.8cm 64.5in
Ground clearance: 22.9cm 9.0in
Kerb weight: 1463.7kg 3224.0lb
Fuel: 60.1L 13.2gal 15.9galUS

4738 Volkswagen

Sedan de Luxe
1952 Germany
66.1mph 106.4kmh
0-50mph 80.5kmh: 22.5secs
0-60mph 96.5kmh: 37.2secs
0-1/4 mile: 25.2secs
25.0bhp 18.6kW 25.3PS
@ 3300rpm
35.9bhp/ton 35.3bhp/tonne
22.1bhp/L 16.5kW/L 22.4PS/L
23.1ft/sec 7.0m/sec
20.7mph 33.3kmh/1000rpm
Petrol 4-stroke piston
1131cc 69.0cu in
Flat 4
Compression ratio: 5.8:1
Bore: 75.0mm 2.9in
Stroke: 64.0mm 2.5in
Valve type/No: Overhead 8
Transmission: Manual
No. of forward speeds: 4
Wheels driven: Rear
Wheelbase: 240.0cm 94.5in
Track F: 129.5cm 51.0in
Track R: 124.5cm 49.0in
Length: 403.9cm 159.0in
Width: 154.9cm 61.0in
Height: 154.9cm 61.0in
Ground clearance: 21.1cm 8.3in
Kerb weight: 708.2kg 1560.0lb
Fuel: 43.5L 9.6gal 11.5galUS

4739 Volkswagen

Export Saloon
1953 Germany
65.9mph 106.0kmh
0-50mph 80.5kmh: 22.9secs
0-1/4 mile: 24.8secs
24.5bhp 18.3kW 24.8PS
@ 3300rpm
49.0lbft 66.4Nm @ 2000rpm
34.9bhp/ton 34.3bhp/tonne
21.7bhp/L 16.1kW/L 22.0PS/L
23.1ft/sec 7.0m/sec
20.7mph 33.3kmh/1000rpm
37.7mpg 31.4mpgUS 7.5L/100km
Petrol 4-stroke piston
1131cc 69.0cu in
Flat 4
Compression ratio: 5.8:1
Bore: 75.0mm 2.9in
Stroke: 64.0mm 2.5in
Valve type/No: Overhead 8
Transmission: Manual
No. of forward speeds: 4
Wheels driven: Rear
Springs F/R: Torsion bar/Torsion bar
Brakes F/R: Drum/Drum
Steering: Worm & roller
Wheelbase: 240.0cm 94.5in
Track F: 129.5cm 51.0in
Track R: 125.0cm 49.2in
Length: 406.4cm 160.0in
Width: 153.7cm 60.5in
Height: 154.9cm 61.0in
Ground clearance: 16.0cm 6.3in
Kerb weight: 713.2kg 1571.0lb
Fuel: 40.0L 8.8gal 10.6galUS

4740 Volkswagen

De Luxe
1954 Germany
69.0mph 111.0kmh
0-50mph 80.5kmh: 22.2secs
0-1/4 mile: 24.2secs
30.0bhp 22.4kW 30.4PS
@ 3400rpm
56.0lbft 75.9Nm @ 2000rpm
41.2bhp/ton 40.5bhp/tonne
25.2bhp/L 18.8kW/L 25.5PS/L
23.8ft/sec 7.2m/sec
20.0mph 32.2kmh/1000rpm
34.3mpg 28.6mpgUS 8.2L/100km
Petrol 4-stroke piston
1192cc 72.7cu in
Flat 4
Compression ratio: 6.1:1
Bore: 77.0mm 3.0in
Stroke: 64.0mm 2.5in
Valve type/No: Overhead 8
Transmission: Manual
No. of forward speeds: 4
Wheels driven: Rear
Springs F/R: Torsion bar/Torsion bar
Brakes F/R: Drum/Drum
Wheelbase: 240.0cm 94.5in
Track F: 129.5cm 51.0in
Track R: 125.0cm 49.2in
Length: 345.4cm 136.0in
Width: 153.7cm 60.5in
Height: 149.9cm 59.0in
Ground clearance: 17.3cm 6.8in
Kerb weight: 740.5kg 1631.0lb
Fuel: 40.0L 8.8gal 10.6galUS

4741 Volkswagen

Sedan
1954 Germany
65.0mph 104.6kmh
0-50mph 80.5kmh: 22.0secs
0-60mph 96.5kmh: 39.2secs
0-1/4 mile: 24.2secs
30.0bhp 22.4kW 30.4PS
@ 3400rpm
56.0lbft 75.9Nm @ 2100rpm
41.3bhp/ton 40.7bhp/tonne
25.2bhp/L 18.8kW/L 25.5PS/L
23.8ft/sec 7.2m/sec
20.2mph 32.5kmh/1000rpm
Petrol 4-stroke piston
1192cc 72.7cu in
Flat 4
Bore: 77.0mm 3.0in
Stroke: 64.0mm 2.5in
Valve type/No: Overhead 8
Transmission: Manual
No. of forward speeds: 4
Wheels driven: Rear
Wheelbase: 240.0cm 94.5in
Track F: 129.0cm 50.8in
Track R: 125.0cm 49.2in
Kerb weight: 737.7kg 1625.0lb

4742 Volkswagen

Sedan TC
1954 Germany
69.0mph 111.0kmh
0-50mph 80.5kmh: 20.9secs
0-60mph 96.5kmh: 35.0secs
0-1/4 mile: 23.3secs
30.0bhp 22.4kW 30.4PS
@ 3400rpm
41.3bhp/ton 40.7bhp/tonne
25.2bhp/L 18.8kW/L 25.5PS/L
23.8ft/sec 7.2m/sec
Petrol 4-stroke piston
1192cc 72.7cu in
Flat 4 2 Carburettor
Bore: 77.0mm 3.0in
Stroke: 64.0mm 2.5in
Valve type/No: Overhead 8
Transmission: Manual
No. of forward speeds: 4
Wheels driven: Rear
Wheelbase: 240.0cm 94.5in
Track F: 129.0cm 50.8in
Track R: 129.0cm 50.8in
Kerb weight: 737.7kg 1625.0lb

4743 Volkswagen

Sedan Supercharged
1955 Germany
74.5mph 119.9kmh
0-50mph 80.5kmh: 15.1secs
0-60mph 96.5kmh: 22.0secs
0-1/4 mile: 22.4secs
36.0bhp 26.8kW 36.5PS
@ 3700rpm
47.2bhp/ton 46.4bhp/tonne
30.2bhp/L 22.5kW/L 30.6PS/L
25.9ft/sec 7.9m/sec
Petrol 4-stroke piston
1192cc 72.7cu in supercharged
Flat 4
Bore: 77.0mm 3.0in
Stroke: 64.0mm 2.5in
Valve type/No: Overhead 8
Transmission: Manual
No. of forward speeds: 4
Wheels driven: Rear
Wheelbase: 240.0cm 94.5in
Track F: 129.0cm 50.8in
Track R: 129.0cm 50.8in
Kerb weight: 776.3kg 1710.0lb

4744 Volkswagen

Karmann-Ghia
1956 Germany
76.0mph 122.3kmh
0-50mph 80.5kmh: 18.2secs
0-60mph 96.5kmh: 28.8secs
0-1/4 mile: 23.6secs
36.0bhp 26.8kW 36.5PS
@ 3700rpm
56.0lbft 75.9Nm @ 2000rpm
45.8bhp/ton 45.0bhp/tonne
30.2bhp/L 22.5kW/L 30.6PS/L
25.9ft/sec 7.9m/sec
20.2mph 32.5kmh/1000rpm
Petrol 4-stroke piston
1192cc 72.7cu in
Flat 4
Compression ratio: 6.6:1
Bore: 70.0mm 2.8in
Stroke: 64.0mm 2.5in
Valve type/No: Overhead 8
Transmission: Manual
No. of forward speeds: 4
Wheels driven: Rear
Wheelbase: 240.0cm 94.5in
Track F: 129.0cm 50.8in
Track R: 125.0cm 49.2in
Kerb weight: 799.0kg 1760.0lb

4745 Volkswagen

Micro Bus
1956 Germany
59.0mph 94.9kmh
0-50mph 80.5kmh: 30.6secs
0-1/4 mile: 27.0secs
36.0bhp 26.8kW 36.5PS
@ 3700rpm
56.0lbft 75.9Nm @ 2000rpm
33.2bhp/ton 32.6bhp/tonne
30.2bhp/L 22.5kW/L 30.6PS/L
25.9ft/sec 7.9m/sec
Petrol 4-stroke piston
1192cc 72.7cu in
Flat 4
Compression ratio: 6.6:1
Bore: 77.0mm 3.0in
Stroke: 64.0mm 2.5in
Valve type/No: Overhead 8
Transmission: Manual
No. of forward speeds: 4
Wheels driven: Rear
Wheelbase: 240.0cm 94.5in
Track F: 136.9cm 53.9in
Track R: 135.9cm 53.5in
Length: 419.1cm 165.0in
Height: 194.1cm 76.4in
Kerb weight: 1103.2kg 2430.0lb

4746 Volkswagen

Sedan
1956 Germany
70.2mph 113.0kmh
0-50mph 80.5kmh: 18.0secs
0-60mph 96.5kmh: 28.0secs
0-1/4 mile: 23.2secs
36.0bhp 26.8kW 36.5PS
@ 3700rpm
56.0lbft 75.9Nm @ 2000rpm
49.2bhp/ton 48.3bhp/tonne

30.2bhp/L 22.5kW/L 30.6PS/L
25.9ft/sec 7.9m/sec
Petrol 4-stroke piston
1192cc 72.7cu in
Flat 4
Compression ratio: 6.6:1
Bore: 77.0mm 3.0in
Stroke: 64.0mm 2.5in
Valve type/No: Overhead 8
Transmission: Manual
No. of forward speeds: 4
Wheels driven: Rear
Wheelbase: 240.0cm 94.5in
Track F: 129.0cm 50.8in
Track R: 125.0cm 49.2in
Kerb weight: 744.6kg 1640.0lb

4747 Volkswagen
Karmann-Ghia Okrasa
1957 Germany
86.5mph 139.2kmh
0-50mph 80.5kmh: 12.7secs
0-60mph 96.5kmh: 18.4secs
0-1/4 mile: 20.0secs
46.0bhp 34.3kW 46.6PS
@ 4200rpm
66.0lbft 89.4Nm @ 2100rpm
58.5bhp/ton 57.6bhp/tonne
38.6bhp/L 28.8kW/L 39.1PS/L
29.4ft/sec 9.0m/sec
Petrol 4-stroke piston
1192cc 72.7cu in
Flat 4 2 Carburettor
Compression ratio: 7.5:1
Bore: 77.0mm 3.0in
Stroke: 64.0mm 2.5in
Valve type/No: Overhead 8
Transmission: Manual
No. of forward speeds: 4
Wheels driven: Rear
Wheelbase: 240.0cm 94.5in
Track F: 129.0cm 50.8in
Track R: 125.0cm 49.2in
Kerb weight: 799.0kg 1760.0lb

4748 Volkswagen
Sedan Judson
1957 Germany
83.8mph 134.8kmh
0-50mph 80.5kmh: 12.5secs
0-60mph 96.5kmh: 18.0secs
0-1/4 mile: 19.8secs
50.0bhp 37.3kW 50.7PS
@ 4000rpm
70.0lbft 94.9Nm @ 2200rpm
67.5bhp/ton 66.3bhp/tonne
41.9bhp/L 31.3kW/L 42.5PS/L
28.0ft/sec 8.5m/sec
Petrol 4-stroke piston
1192cc 72.7cu in supercharged
Flat 4
Compression ratio: 6.6:1
Bore: 77.0mm 3.0in
Stroke: 64.0mm 2.5in
Valve type/No: Overhead 8
Transmission: Manual
No. of forward speeds: 4
Wheels driven: Rear
Wheelbase: 240.0cm 94.5in
Track F: 129.0cm 50.8in
Track R: 125.0cm 49.2in
Kerb weight: 753.6kg 1660.0lb

4749 Volkswagen
Alken-VW
1958 USA
70.8mph 113.9kmh
0-50mph 80.5kmh: 14.8secs
0-60mph 96.5kmh: 22.3secs
0-1/4 mile: 21.8secs
36.0bhp 26.8kW 36.5PS
@ 3700rpm
56.0lbft 75.9Nm @ 2000rpm
59.5bhp/ton 58.5bhp/tonne
30.2bhp/L 22.5kW/L 30.6PS/L
25.9ft/sec 7.9m/sec
20.5mph 33.0kmh/1000rpm
Petrol 4-stroke piston
1192cc 72.7cu in
Flat 4
Compression ratio: 6.6:1
Bore: 77.0mm 3.0in
Stroke: 64.0mm 2.5in
Valve type/No: Overhead 8
Transmission: Manual
No. of forward speeds: 4
Wheels driven: Rear
Wheelbase: 240.0cm 94.5in
Track F: 129.0cm 50.8in
Track R: 125.0cm 49.2in
Length: 411.5cm 162.0in
Width: 149.9cm 59.0in
Height: 121.9cm 48.0in
Kerb weight: 615.2kg 1355.0lb

4750 Volkswagen
De Luxe Saloon
1958 Germany
65.0mph 104.6kmh
0-50mph 80.5kmh: 22.4secs
0-1/4 mile: 24.6secs
36.0bhp 26.8kW 36.5PS
@ 3400rpm
56.0lbft 75.9Nm @ 2000rpm
50.5bhp/ton 49.7bhp/tonne
30.2bhp/L 22.5kW/L 30.6PS/L
23.8ft/sec 7.2m/sec
20.0mph 32.2kmh/1000rpm
34.0mpg 28.3mpgUS 8.3L/100km
Petrol 4-stroke piston
1192cc 72.7cu in
Flat 4 1 Carburettor
Compression ratio: 6.6:1
Bore: 77.0mm 3.0in
Stroke: 64.0mm 2.5in
Valve type/No: Overhead 8
Transmission: Manual
No. of forward speeds: 4
Wheels driven: Rear
Springs F/R: Torsion bar/Torsion bar
Brakes F/R: Drum/Drum
Wheelbase: 240.0cm 94.5in
Track F: 129.5cm 51.0in
Track R: 125.0cm 49.2in
Length: 406.4cm 160.0in
Width: 153.7cm 60.5in
Height: 149.9cm 59.0in
Ground clearance: 15.2cm 6.0in
Kerb weight: 724.6kg 1596.0lb
Fuel: 40.0L 8.8gal 10.6galUS

4751 Volkswagen
De Luxe
1960 Germany
74.0mph 119.1kmh
0-50mph 80.5kmh: 17.7secs
0-60mph 96.5kmh: 32.1secs
0-1/4 mile: 23.4secs
34.0bhp 25.3kW 34.5PS
@ 3900rpm
61.0lbft 82.7Nm @ 2000rpm
46.3bhp/ton 45.5bhp/tonne
28.5bhp/L 21.3kW/L 28.9PS/L
27.3ft/sec 8.3m/sec
18.6mph 29.9kmh/1000rpm
31.6mpg 26.3mpgUS 8.9L/100km
Petrol 4-stroke piston
1192cc 72.7cu in
Flat 4
Compression ratio: 7.0:1
Bore: 77.0mm 3.0in
Stroke: 64.0mm 2.5in
Valve type/No: Overhead 8
Transmission: Manual
No. of forward speeds: 4
Wheels driven: Rear
Springs F/R: Torsion bar/Torsion bar
Brakes F/R: Drum/Drum
Steering: Worm & roller
Wheelbase: 240.0cm 94.5in
Track F: 129.0cm 50.8in
Track R: 129.0cm 50.8in
Length: 405.1cm 159.5in
Width: 153.7cm 60.5in
Height: 149.9cm 59.0in
Ground clearance: 15.2cm 6.0in
Kerb weight: 746.8kg 1645.0lb
Fuel: 40.0L 8.8gal 10.6galUS

4752 Volkswagen
Sedan
1960 Germany
71.5mph 115.0kmh
0-50mph 80.5kmh: 17.0secs
0-60mph 96.5kmh: 27.8secs
0-1/4 mile: 22.8secs
36.0bhp 26.8kW 36.5PS
@ 3700rpm
56.0lbft 75.9Nm @ 2000rpm
48.9bhp/ton 48.1bhp/tonne
30.2bhp/L 22.5kW/L 30.6PS/L
25.9ft/sec 7.9m/sec
20.2mph 32.5kmh/1000rpm
Petrol 4-stroke piston
1192cc 72.7cu in
Flat 4
Compression ratio: 6.6:1
Bore: 77.0mm 3.0in
Stroke: 64.0mm 2.5in
Valve type/No: Overhead 8
Transmission: Manual
No. of forward speeds: 4
Wheels driven: Rear
Wheelbase: 240.0cm 94.5in
Track F: 130.6cm 51.4in
Track R: 128.8cm 50.7in
Length: 406.4cm 160.0in
Width: 153.9cm 60.6in
Height: 149.9cm 59.0in
Kerb weight: 749.1kg 1650.0lb

4753 Volkswagen
1500
1961 Germany
82.0mph 131.9kmh
0-50mph 80.5kmh: 14.2secs
0-60mph 96.5kmh: 20.7secs
0-1/4 mile: 21.4secs
45.0bhp 33.6kW 45.6PS
@ 3800rpm
83.0lbft 112.5Nm @ 2000rpm
53.2bhp/ton 52.3bhp/tonne
30.1bhp/L 22.5kW/L 30.6PS/L
28.7ft/sec 8.7m/sec
20.6mph 33.1kmh/1000rpm
27.9mpg 23.2mpgUS 10.1L/100km
Petrol 4-stroke piston
1493cc 91.1cu in
Flat 4
Compression ratio: 7.2:1
Bore: 83.0mm 3.3in
Stroke: 69.0mm 2.7in
Valve type/No: Overhead 8
Transmission: Manual
No. of forward speeds: 4
Wheels driven: Rear
Springs F/R: Torsion bar/Torsion bar
Brakes F/R: Drum/Drum
Steering: Worm & roller
Wheelbase: 240.0cm 94.5in
Track F: 130.6cm 51.4in
Track R: 134.6cm 53.0in
Length: 422.9cm 166.5in
Width: 160.8cm 63.3in
Height: 147.3cm 58.0in
Ground clearance: 15.0cm 5.9in
Kerb weight: 860.8kg 1896.0lb
Fuel: 40.0L 8.8gal 10.6galUS

4754 Volkswagen
Karmann Ghia
1961 Germany
78.0mph 125.5kmh
0-50mph 80.5kmh: 17.1secs
0-60mph 96.5kmh: 26.5secs
0-1/4 mile: 23.0secs
34.0bhp 25.3kW 34.5PS
@ 3900rpm
61.0lbft 82.7Nm @ 2000rpm
43.4bhp/ton 42.7bhp/tonne
28.5bhp/L 21.3kW/L 28.9PS/L
27.3ft/sec 8.3m/sec
18.6mph 29.9kmh/1000rpm
31.2mpg 26.0mpgUS 9.1L/100km
Petrol 4-stroke piston
1192cc 72.7cu in
Flat 4 1 Carburettor
Compression ratio: 7.0:1
Bore: 77.0mm 3.0in
Stroke: 64.0mm 2.5in
Valve type/No: Overhead 8
Transmission: Manual
No. of forward speeds: 4
Wheels driven: Rear
Springs F/R: Torsion bar/Torsion bar
Brakes F/R: Drum/Drum
Wheelbase: 240.0cm 94.5in
Track F: 130.6cm 51.4in
Track R: 128.8cm 50.7in
Length: 414.0cm 163.0in
Width: 163.3cm 64.3in
Height: 158.5cm 62.4in
Ground clearance: 15.2cm 6.0in
Kerb weight: 795.9kg 1753.0lb
Fuel: 40.0L 8.8gal 10.6galUS

4755 Volkswagen
Sedan
1961 Germany
71.4mph 114.9kmh
0-50mph 80.5kmh: 16.8secs
0-60mph 96.5kmh: 27.7secs
0-1/4 mile: 22.8secs
40.0bhp 29.8kW 40.5PS
@ 3900rpm
64.0lbft 86.7Nm @ 2400rpm
53.6bhp/ton 52.8bhp/tonne
33.6bhp/L 25.0kW/L 34.0PS/L
27.3ft/sec 8.3m/sec
18.8mph 30.2kmh/1000rpm
Petrol 4-stroke piston
1192cc 72.7cu in
Flat 4 1 Carburettor
Compression ratio: 7.0:1
Bore: 77.0mm 3.0in
Stroke: 64.0mm 2.5in
Valve type/No: Overhead 8
Transmission: Manual
No. of forward speeds: 4
Wheels driven: Rear
Brakes F/R: Drum/Drum
Wheelbase: 240.0cm 94.5in
Track F: 130.6cm 51.4in
Track R: 128.8cm 50.7in
Length: 406.4cm 160.0in
Width: 153.9cm 60.6in
Height: 150.1cm 59.1in
Ground clearance: 15.2cm 6.0in
Kerb weight: 758.2kg 1670.0lb

4756 Volkswagen
Station Wagon
1961 Germany
60.0mph 96.5kmh
0-50mph 80.5kmh: 26.8secs
0-1/4 mile: 25.6secs
40.0bhp 29.8kW 40.5PS
@ 3900rpm
64.0lbft 86.7Nm @ 2400rpm
38.8bhp/ton 38.1bhp/tonne
33.6bhp/L 25.0kW/L 34.0PS/L
27.3ft/sec 8.3m/sec
15.4mph 24.8kmh/1000rpm
Petrol 4-stroke piston
1192cc 72.7cu in
Flat 4 1 Carburettor
Compression ratio: 7.0:1
Bore: 79.5mm 3.1in
Stroke: 64.0mm 2.5in
Valve type/No: Overhead 8
Transmission: Manual
No. of forward speeds: 4
Wheels driven: Rear
Brakes F/R: Drum/Drum
Wheelbase: 240.0cm 94.5in
Track F: 136.9cm 53.9in
Track R: 135.9cm 53.5in
Length: 428.0cm 168.5in
Width: 175.0cm 68.9in
Height: 194.1cm 76.4in
Ground clearance: 23.9cm 9.4in
Kerb weight: 1048.7kg 2310.0lb

4757 Volkswagen
Van
1961 Germany
40.0bhp 29.8kW 40.5PS
@ 3900rpm
64.0lbft 86.7Nm @ 2400rpm
38.8bhp/ton 38.1bhp/tonne
33.6bhp/L 25.0kW/L 34.0PS/L
27.3ft/sec 8.3m/sec
Petrol 4-stroke piston
1191cc 72.7cu in
Flat 4
Compression ratio: 7.0:1
Bore: 77.0mm 3.0in
Stroke: 64.0mm 2.5in
Valve type/No: Overhead 8
Transmission: Manual
No. of forward speeds: 4
Wheels driven: Rear
Wheelbase: 240.0cm 94.5in
Track F: 136.9cm 53.9in
Track R: 135.9cm 53.5in
Length: 429.0cm 168.9in
Width: 175.0cm 68.9in
Height: 194.1cm 76.4in
Ground clearance: 23.9cm 9.4in
Kerb weight: 1048.7kg 2310.0lb

4758 Volkswagen
1200 de Luxe
1962 Germany

73.0mph 117.5kmh
0-50mph 80.5kmh: 15.8secs
0-60mph 96.5kmh: 27.5secs
0-1/4 mile: 22.9secs
34.0bhp 25.3kW 34.5PS
@ 3600rpm
61.0lbft 82.7Nm @ 2000rpm
45.9bhp/ton 45.1bhp/tonne
28.5bhp/L 21.3kW/L 28.9PS/L
25.2ft/sec 7.7m/sec
18.6mph 29.9kmh/1000rpm
30.9mpg 25.7mpgUS 9.1L/100km
Petrol 4-stroke piston
1192cc 72.7cu in
Flat 4 1 Carburettor
Compression ratio: 7.0:1
Bore: 77.0mm 3.0in
Stroke: 64.0mm 2.5in
Valve type/No: Overhead 8
Transmission: Manual
No. of forward speeds: 4
Wheels driven: Rear
Springs F/R: Torsion bar/Torsion bar
Brakes F/R: Drum/Drum
Steering: Worm & roller
Wheelbase: 240.0cm 94.5in
Track F: 130.6cm 51.4in
Track R: 128.8cm 50.7in
Length: 406.9cm 160.2in
Width: 153.9cm 60.6in
Height: 149.9cm 59.0in
Ground clearance: 15.2cm 6.0in
Kerb weight: 753.2kg 1659.0lb
Fuel: 40.0L 8.8gal 10.6galUS

4759 Volkswagen

1500
1962 Germany
82.4mph 132.6kmh
0-50mph 80.5kmh: 16.3secs
0-60mph 96.5kmh: 24.0secs
0-1/4 mile: 22.8secs
53.0bhp 39.5kW 53.7PS
@ 4000rpm
83.0lbft 112.5Nm @ 2000rpm
60.6bhp/ton 59.6bhp/tonne
35.5bhp/L 26.5kW/L 36.0PS/L
30.2ft/sec 9.2m/sec
19.8mph 31.9kmh/1000rpm
Petrol 4-stroke piston
1493cc 91.1cu in
Flat 4
Compression ratio: 7.2:1
Bore: 83.1mm 3.3in
Stroke: 69.1mm 2.7in
Valve type/No: Overhead 8
Transmission: Manual
No. of forward speeds: 4
Wheels driven: Rear
Wheelbase: 240.0cm 94.5in
Track F: 131.1cm 51.6in
Track R: 134.6cm 53.0in
Length: 422.4cm 166.3in
Width: 160.5cm 63.2in
Height: 147.6cm 58.1in
Ground clearance: 15.0cm 5.9in
Kerb weight: 889.8kg 1960.0lb

4760 Volkswagen

Karmann-Ghia
1962 Germany
75.0mph 120.7kmh
0-50mph 80.5kmh: 17.3secs
0-60mph 96.5kmh: 30.0secs
0-1/4 mile: 22.7secs
40.0bhp 29.8kW 40.5PS
@ 3900rpm
64.0lbft 86.7Nm @ 2400rpm
51.2bhp/ton 50.3bhp/tonne
33.6bhp/L 25.0kW/L 34.0PS/L
27.3ft/sec 8.3m/sec
18.8mph 30.2kmh/1000rpm
Petrol 4-stroke piston
1192cc 72.7cu in
Flat 4
Compression ratio: 7.0:1
Bore: 77.0mm 3.0in
Stroke: 64.0mm 2.5in
Valve type/No: Overhead 8
Transmission: Manual
No. of forward speeds: 4
Wheels driven: Rear
Wheelbase: 240.0cm 94.5in
Track F: 130.6cm 51.4in
Track R: 128.8cm 50.7in
Length: 414.0cm 163.0in
Width: 163.1cm 64.2in
Height: 150.4cm 59.2in
Ground clearance: 15.2cm 6.0in
Kerb weight: 794.5kg 1750.0lb

4761 Volkswagen

Sedan EMPI
1962 Germany
80.0mph 128.7kmh
0-50mph 80.5kmh: 13.1secs
0-60mph 96.5kmh: 19.3secs
0-1/4 mile: 20.8secs
48.5bhp 36.2kW 49.2PS
@ 4000rpm
76.0lbft 103.0Nm @ 2700rpm
64.7bhp/ton 63.6bhp/tonne
34.5bhp/L 25.7kW/L 35.0PS/L
30.7ft/sec 9.3m/sec
18.7mph 30.1kmh/1000rpm
Petrol 4-stroke piston
1405cc 85.7cu in
Flat 4 1 Carburettor
Compression ratio: 8.3:1
Bore: 80.0mm 3.1in
Stroke: 70.1mm 2.8in
Valve type/No: Overhead 8
Transmission: Manual
No. of forward speeds: 4
Wheels driven: Rear
Wheelbase: 240.0cm 94.5in
Track F: 130.6cm 51.4in
Track R: 128.8cm 50.7in
Length: 406.4cm 160.0in
Width: 153.9cm 60.6in
Height: 150.1cm 59.1in
Ground clearance: 15.2cm 6.0in
Kerb weight: 762.7kg 1680.0lb

4762 Volkswagen

1500 Estate
1963 Germany
82.0mph 131.9kmh
0-50mph 80.5kmh: 15.2secs
0-60mph 96.5kmh: 22.1secs
0-1/4 mile: 22.1secs
45.0bhp 33.6kW 45.6PS
@ 4000rpm
83.0lbft 112.5Nm @ 2000rpm
49.3bhp/ton 48.5bhp/tonne
30.1bhp/L 22.5kW/L 30.6PS/L
30.2ft/sec 9.2m/sec
20.8mph 33.5kmh/1000rpm
25.2mpg 21.0mpgUS 11.2L/100km
Petrol 4-stroke piston
1493cc 91.1cu in
Flat 4 1 Carburettor
Compression ratio: 7.8:1
Bore: 83.0mm 3.3in
Stroke: 69.0mm 2.7in
Valve type/No: Overhead 8
Transmission: Manual
No. of forward speeds: 4
Wheels driven: Rear
Springs F/R: Torsion bar/Torsion bar
Brakes F/R: Drum/Drum
Steering: Worm & roller
Wheelbase: 240.0cm 94.5in
Track F: 130.8cm 51.5in
Track R: 134.6cm 53.0in
Length: 422.9cm 166.5in
Width: 160.0cm 63.0in
Height: 144.8cm 57.0in
Ground clearance: 12.7cm 5.0in
Kerb weight: 928.0kg 2044.0lb
Fuel: 40.0L 8.8gal 10.6galUS

4763 Volkswagen

Karmann-Ghia 1500
1963 Germany
87.0mph 140.0kmh
0-50mph 80.5kmh: 14.6secs
0-60mph 96.5kmh: 21.7secs
0-1/4 mile: 21.7secs
45.0bhp 33.6kW 45.6PS
@ 3800rpm
83.0lbft 112.5Nm @ 2000rpm
52.2bhp/ton 51.4bhp/tonne
30.1bhp/L 22.5kW/L 30.6PS/L
28.7ft/sec 8.8m/sec
19.8mph 31.9kmh/1000rpm
Petrol 4-stroke piston
1493cc 91.1cu in
Flat 4 1 Carburettor
Compression ratio: 7.2:1
Bore: 83.3mm 3.3in
Stroke: 69.1mm 2.7in
Valve type/No: Overhead 8
Transmission: Manual
No. of forward speeds: 4
Wheels driven: Rear
Wheelbase: 240.0cm 94.5in
Track F: 131.1cm 51.6in
Track R: 134.6cm 53.0in
Length: 429.3cm 169.0in
Width: 162.1cm 63.8in
Height: 132.1cm 52.0in
Ground clearance: 14.2cm 5.6in
Kerb weight: 876.2kg 1930.0lb

4764 Volkswagen

1500S
1964 Germany
86.0mph 138.4kmh
0-50mph 80.5kmh: 13.1secs
0-60mph 96.5kmh: 19.1secs
0-1/4 mile: 21.5secs
54.0bhp 40.3kW 54.7PS
@ 4800rpm
78.0lbft 105.7Nm @ 3000rpm
62.7bhp/ton 61.7bhp/tonne
36.2bhp/L 27.0kW/L 36.7PS/L
36.3ft/sec 11.0m/sec
21.1mph 33.9kmh/1000rpm
26.3mpg 21.9mpgUS 10.7L/100km
Petrol 4-stroke piston
1493cc 91.1cu in
Flat 4 2 Carburettor
Compression ratio: 8.5:1
Bore: 83.0mm 3.3in
Stroke: 69.0mm 2.7in
Valve type/No: Overhead 8
Transmission: Manual
No. of forward speeds: 4
Wheels driven: Rear
Springs F/R: Torsion bar/Torsion bar
Brakes F/R: Drum/Drum
Steering: Worm & roller
Wheelbase: 240.0cm 94.5in
Track F: 130.8cm 51.5in
Track R: 134.6cm 53.0in
Length: 422.9cm 166.5in
Width: 160.0cm 63.0in
Height: 147.3cm 58.0in
Ground clearance: 15.2cm 6.0in
Kerb weight: 875.3kg 1928.0lb
Fuel: 40.0L 8.8gal 10.6galUS

4765 Volkswagen

1200
1965 Germany
72.0mph 115.8kmh
0-50mph 80.5kmh: 18.8secs
0-60mph 96.5kmh: 29.4secs
0-1/4 mile: 22.9secs
40.0bhp 29.8kW 40.5PS
@ 3900rpm
65.0lbft 88.1Nm @ 2400rpm
52.2bhp/ton 51.4bhp/tonne
33.6bhp/L 25.0kW/L 34.0PS/L
27.3ft/sec 8.3m/sec
18.6mph 29.9kmh/1000rpm
Petrol 4-stroke piston
1192cc 72.7cu in
Flat 4 1 Carburettor
Compression ratio: 7.0:1
Bore: 77.0mm 3.0in
Stroke: 64.0mm 2.5in
Valve type/No: Overhead 8
Transmission: Manual
No. of forward speeds: 4
Wheels driven: Rear
Springs F/R: Torsion bar/Torsion bar
Brakes F/R: Drum/Drum
Steering: Worm & sector
Wheelbase: 240.0cm 94.5in
Track F: 130.3cm 51.3in
Track R: 125.7cm 49.5in
Length: 423.7cm 166.8in
Width: 154.4cm 60.8in
Height: 149.9cm 59.0in
Ground clearance: 15.7cm 6.2in
Kerb weight: 778.6kg 1715.0lb
Fuel: 37.8L 8.3gal 10.0galUS

4766 Volkswagen

1300
1965 Germany
75.0mph 120.7kmh
0-50mph 80.5kmh: 16.8secs
0-60mph 96.5kmh: 25.4secs
0-1/4 mile: 22.0secs
50.0bhp 37.3kW 50.7PS
@ 4600rpm
70.0lbft 94.9Nm @ 2000rpm
63.6bhp/ton 62.6bhp/tonne
38.9bhp/L 29.0kW/L 39.4PS/L
34.8ft/sec 10.6m/sec
18.6mph 29.9kmh/1000rpm
Petrol 4-stroke piston
1285cc 78.4cu in
Flat 4 1 Carburettor
Compression ratio: 7.3:1
Bore: 77.0mm 3.0in
Stroke: 69.1mm 2.7in
Valve type/No: Overhead 8
Transmission: Manual
No. of forward speeds: 4
Wheels driven: Rear
Brakes F/R: Drum/Drum
Steering: Worm & sector
Wheelbase: 240.0cm 94.5in
Track F: 130.6cm 51.4in
Track R: 130.0cm 51.2in
Length: 423.7cm 166.8in
Width: 154.4cm 60.8in
Height: 149.9cm 59.0in
Kerb weight: 799.0kg 1760.0lb
Fuel: 37.8L 8.3gal 10.0galUS

4767 Volkswagen

1300
1966 Germany
79.0mph 127.1kmh
0-50mph 80.5kmh: 14.6secs
0-60mph 96.5kmh: 23.0secs
0-1/4 mile: 22.1secs
0-1km: 43.0secs
40.0bhp 29.8kW 40.5PS
@ 4000rpm
64.4lbft 87.3Nm @ 2000rpm
53.6bhp/ton 52.7bhp/tonne
31.1bhp/L 23.2kW/L 31.6PS/L
30.2ft/sec 9.2m/sec
18.7mph 30.1kmh/1000rpm
28.8mpg 24.0mpgUS 9.8L/100km
Petrol 4-stroke piston
1285cc 78.4cu in
Flat 4 1 Carburettor
Compression ratio: 7.3:1
Bore: 77.0mm 3.0in
Stroke: 69.0mm 2.7in
Valve type/No: Overhead 8
Transmission: Manual
No. of forward speeds: 4
Wheels driven: Rear
Springs F/R: Torsion bar/Torsion bar
Brakes F/R: Drum/Drum
Steering: Worm & roller
Wheelbase: 240.0cm 94.5in
Track F: 130.6cm 51.4in
Track R: 128.8cm 50.7in
Length: 406.9cm 160.2in
Width: 153.9cm 60.6in
Height: 149.9cm 59.0in
Ground clearance: 17.0cm 6.7in
Kerb weight: 759.1kg 1672.0lb
Fuel: 40.0L 8.8gal 10.6galUS

4768 Volkswagen

1300 de Luxe
1966 Germany
76.0mph 122.3kmh
0-50mph 80.5kmh: 15.6secs
0-60mph 96.5kmh: 23.7secs
0-1/4 mile: 22.2secs
50.0bhp 37.3kW 50.7PS
@ 4600rpm
69.0lbft 93.5Nm @ 2600rpm
64.0bhp/ton 62.9bhp/tonne
38.9bhp/L 29.0kW/L 39.4PS/L
34.8ft/sec 10.6m/sec
18.8mph 30.2kmh/1000rpm
Petrol 4-stroke piston
1285cc 78.4cu in
Flat 4 1 Carburettor
Compression ratio: 7.3:1
Bore: 77.0mm 3.0in
Stroke: 69.0mm 2.7in
Valve type/No: Overhead 8
Transmission: Manual
No. of forward speeds: 4
Wheels driven: Rear
Springs F/R: Torsion bar/Torsion bar
Brakes F/R: Drum/Drum
Steering: Worm & roller
Wheelbase: 240.0cm 94.5in
Track F: 130.6cm 51.4in
Track R: 130.0cm 51.2in
Length: 406.9cm 160.2in
Width: 153.9cm 60.6in

Height: 149.9cm 59.0in
Ground clearance: 15.2cm 6.0in
Kerb weight: 794.5kg 1750.0lb
Fuel: 40.1L 8.8gal 10.6galUS

4769 Volkswagen

1500
1966 Germany
84.0mph 135.2kmh
0-50mph 80.5kmh: 14.5secs
0-60mph 96.5kmh: 21.9secs
0-1/4 mile: 21.9secs
0-1km: 42.0secs
44.0bhp 32.8kW 44.6PS
@ 4000rpm
74.0lbft 100.3Nm @ 2000rpm
56.8bhp/ton 55.8bhp/tonne
29.5bhp/L 22.0kW/L 29.9PS/L
30.2ft/sec 9.2m/sec
19.8mph 31.9kmh/1000rpm
27.4mpg 22.8mpgUS 10.3L/100km
Petrol 4-stroke piston
1493cc 91.1cu in
Flat 4 1 Carburettor
Compression ratio: 7.5:1
Bore: 83.0mm 3.3in
Stroke: 69.0mm 2.7in
Valve type/No: Overhead 8
Transmission: Manual
No. of forward speeds: 4
Wheels driven: Rear
Springs F/R: Torsion bar/Torsion bar
Brakes F/R: Disc/Drum
Steering: Worm & roller
Wheelbase: 240.0cm 94.5in
Track F: 130.8cm 51.5in
Track R: 134.6cm 53.0in
Length: 406.4cm 160.0in
Width: 153.9cm 60.6in
Height: 149.9cm 59.0in
Ground clearance: 16.5cm 6.5in
Kerb weight: 788.1kg 1736.0lb
Fuel: 40.0L 8.8gal 10.6galUS

4770 Volkswagen

1600 Fastback
1966 Germany
82.0mph 131.9kmh
0-50mph 80.5kmh: 13.3secs
0-60mph 96.5kmh: 18.9secs
0-1/4 mile: 21.7secs
65.0bhp 48.5kW 65.9PS
@ 4600rpm
87.0lbft 117.9Nm @ 2800rpm
72.4bhp/ton 71.2bhp/tonne
41.0bhp/L 30.6kW/L 41.6PS/L
34.8ft/sec 10.6m/sec
19.8mph 31.9kmh/1000rpm
Petrol 4-stroke piston
1584cc 96.6cu in
Flat 4 2 Carburettor
Compression ratio: 7.7:1
Bore: 88.0mm 3.5in
Stroke: 69.0mm 2.7in
Valve type/No: Overhead 8
Transmission: Manual
No. of forward speeds: 4
Wheels driven: Rear
Springs F/R: Torsion bar/Torsion bar
Brakes F/R: Disc/Drum
Steering: Worm & roller
Wheelbase: 240.0cm 94.5in
Track F: 131.1cm 51.6in
Track R: 134.6cm 53.0in
Length: 422.4cm 166.3in
Width: 160.5cm 63.2in
Height: 147.6cm 58.1in
Ground clearance: 15.0cm 5.9in
Kerb weight: 912.5kg 2010.0lb
Fuel: 40.1L 8.8gal 10.6galUS

4771 Volkswagen

1600 TL
1966 Germany
85.0mph 136.8kmh
0-50mph 80.5kmh: 13.7secs
0-60mph 96.5kmh: 20.3secs
0-1/4 mile: 21.3secs
0-1km: 40.8secs
54.0bhp 40.3kW 54.7PS
@ 4000rpm
81.0lbft 109.8Nm @ 2200rpm
59.4bhp/ton 58.4bhp/tonne
34.1bhp/L 25.4kW/L 34.6PS/L
30.2ft/sec 9.2m/sec
21.1mph 33.9kmh/1000rpm
27.0mpg 22.5mpgUS 10.5L/100km
Petrol 4-stroke piston
1584cc 96.6cu in
Flat 4 2 Carburettor
Compression ratio: 7.7:1
Bore: 85.5mm 3.4in
Stroke: 69.0mm 2.7in
Valve type/No: Overhead 8
Transmission: Manual
No. of forward speeds: 4
Wheels driven: Rear
Springs F/R: Coil/Coil
Brakes F/R: Disc/Drum
Steering: Worm & roller
Wheelbase: 240.0cm 94.5in
Track F: 130.8cm 51.5in
Track R: 134.6cm 53.0in
Length: 422.9cm 166.5in
Width: 160.0cm 63.0in
Height: 144.8cm 57.0in
Ground clearance: 15.0cm 5.9in
Kerb weight: 923.9kg 2035.0lb
Fuel: 40.0L 8.8gal 10.6galUS

4772 Volkswagen

1500
1967 Germany
82.0mph 131.9kmh
0-50mph 80.5kmh: 14.2secs
0-60mph 96.5kmh: 20.7secs
0-1/4 mile: 21.4secs
45.0bhp 33.6kW 45.6PS
@ 3800rpm
83.0lbft 112.5Nm @ 2000rpm
53.2bhp/ton 52.3bhp/tonne
30.1bhp/L 22.5kW/L 30.6PS/L
28.7ft/sec 8.7m/sec
20.6mph 33.1kmh/1000rpm
27.9mpg 23.2mpgUS 10.1L/100km
Petrol 4-stroke piston
1493cc 91.1cu in
Flat 4
Compression ratio: 7.2:1
Bore: 83.0mm 3.3in
Stroke: 69.0mm 2.7in
Valve type/No: Overhead 8
Transmission: Manual
No. of forward speeds: 4
Wheels driven: Rear
Springs F/R: Torsion bar/Torsion bar
Brakes F/R: Drum/Drum
Wheelbase: 240.0cm 94.5in
Track F: 130.6cm 51.4in
Track R: 134.6cm 53.0in
Length: 422.9cm 166.5in
Width: 160.8cm 63.3in
Height: 147.3cm 58.0in
Ground clearance: 15.0cm 5.9in
Kerb weight: 860.8kg 1896.0lb
Fuel: 40.0L 8.8gal 10.6galUS

4773 Volkswagen

Beetle 1500
1967 Germany
78.0mph 125.5kmh
0-50mph 80.5kmh: 14.8secs
0-60mph 96.5kmh: 22.5secs
0-1/4 mile: 21.7secs
53.0bhp 39.5kW 53.7PS
@ 4200rpm
78.0lbft 105.7Nm @ 2600rpm
66.3bhp/ton 65.2bhp/tonne
35.5bhp/L 26.5kW/L 36.0PS/L
31.7ft/sec 9.7m/sec
19.8mph 31.9kmh/1000rpm
Petrol 4-stroke piston
1493cc 91.1cu in
Flat 4
Compression ratio: 7.5:1
Bore: 83.0mm 3.3in
Stroke: 69.0mm 2.7in
Valve type/No: Overhead 8
Transmission: Manual
No. of forward speeds: 4
Wheels driven: Rear
Steering: Worm & sector
Wheelbase: 240.0cm 94.5in
Track F: 130.6cm 51.4in
Track R: 135.6cm 53.4in
Length: 407.9cm 160.6in
Width: 153.9cm 60.6in
Height: 150.1cm 59.1in
Kerb weight: 812.7kg 1790.0lb
Fuel: 40.1L 8.8gal 10.6galUS

4774 Volkswagen

1500 Automatic
1968 Germany
75.0mph 120.7kmh
0-50mph 80.5kmh: 15.1secs
0-60mph 96.5kmh: 22.2secs
0-1/4 mile: 22.2secs
53.0bhp 39.5kW 53.7PS
@ 4200rpm
78.1lbft 105.8Nm @ 2600rpm
62.5bhp/ton 61.4bhp/tonne
35.5bhp/L 26.5kW/L 36.0PS/L
31.7ft/sec 9.7m/sec
17.7mph 28.5kmh/1000rpm
Petrol 4-stroke piston
1493cc 91.1cu in
Flat 4 1 Carburettor
Compression ratio: 7.5:1
Bore: 83.0mm 3.3in
Stroke: 69.0mm 2.7in
Valve type/No: Overhead 8
Transmission: Automatic
No. of forward speeds: 3
Wheels driven: Rear
Springs F/R: Torsion bar/Torsion bar
Brakes F/R: Drum/Drum
Steering: Worm & roller
Wheelbase: 240.0cm 94.5in
Track F: 131.1cm 51.6in
Track R: 135.4cm 53.3in
Length: 402.8cm 158.6in
Width: 154.9cm 61.0in
Height: 150.1cm 59.1in
Ground clearance: 15.0cm 5.9in
Kerb weight: 862.6kg 1900.0lb
Fuel: 40.1L 8.8gal 10.6galUS

4775 Volkswagen

1500 Semi-automatic
1968 Germany
80.0mph 128.7kmh
0-50mph 80.5kmh: 17.1secs
0-60mph 96.5kmh: 26.8secs
0-1/4 mile: 22.8secs
0-1km: 43.6secs
44.0bhp 32.8kW 44.6PS
@ 4000rpm
74.0lbft 100.3Nm @ 2000rpm
53.4bhp/ton 52.5bhp/tonne
29.5bhp/L 22.0kW/L 29.9PS/L
30.2ft/sec 9.2m/sec
19.7mph 31.7kmh/1000rpm
25.1mpg 20.9mpgUS 11.3L/100km
Petrol 4-stroke piston
1493cc 91.1cu in
Flat 4 1 Carburettor
Compression ratio: 7.5:1
Bore: 83.0mm 3.3in
Stroke: 69.0mm 2.7in
Valve type/No: Overhead 8
Transmission: Automatic
No. of forward speeds: 3
Wheels driven: Rear
Springs F/R: Torsion bar/Torsion bar
Brakes F/R: Disc/Drum
Steering: Worm & roller
Wheelbase: 240.0cm 94.5in
Track F: 131.6cm 51.8in
Track R: 135.6cm 53.4in
Length: 406.9cm 160.2in
Width: 153.9cm 60.6in
Height: 149.9cm 59.0in
Ground clearance: 15.0cm 5.9in
Kerb weight: 837.6kg 1845.0lb
Fuel: 40.0L 8.8gal 10.6galUS

4776 Volkswagen

1600 Squareback
1968 Germany
85.0mph 136.8kmh
0-1/4 mile: 21.5secs
65.0bhp 48.5kW 65.9PS
41.0bhp/L 30.6kW/L 41.6PS/L
34.8mpg 29.0mpgUS 8.1L/100km
Petrol 4-stroke piston
1584cc 96.6cu in
Flat 4
Valve type/No: Overhead 8
Wheels driven: Rear
Wheelbase: 240.0cm 94.5in
Length: 422.4cm 166.3in

4777 Volkswagen

1600 TL Automatic
1968 Germany
86.0mph 138.4kmh
0-50mph 80.5kmh: 14.7secs
0-60mph 96.5kmh: 22.3secs
0-1/4 mile: 21.8secs
0-1km: 42.3secs
54.0bhp 40.3kW 54.7PS
@ 4000rpm
81.0lbft 109.8Nm @ 2200rpm
57.3bhp/ton 56.3bhp/tonne
34.1bhp/L 25.4kW/L 34.6PS/L
30.2ft/sec 9.2m/sec
19.9mph 32.0kmh/1000rpm
22.4mpg 18.7mpgUS 12.6L/100km
Petrol 4-stroke piston
1584cc 96.6cu in
Flat 4 2 Carburettor
Compression ratio: 7.7:1
Bore: 85.5mm 3.4in
Stroke: 69.0mm 2.7in
Valve type/No: Overhead 8
Transmission: Automatic
No. of forward speeds: 3
Wheels driven: Rear
Springs F/R: Coil/Coil
Brakes F/R: Disc/Drum
Steering: Worm & roller
Wheelbase: 240.0cm 94.5in
Track F: 130.8cm 51.5in
Track R: 134.6cm 53.0in
Length: 422.9cm 166.5in
Width: 160.0cm 63.0in
Height: 147.3cm 58.0in
Ground clearance: 15.0cm 5.9in
Kerb weight: 958.8kg 2112.0lb
Fuel: 40.0L 8.8gal 10.6galUS

4778 Volkswagen

411 L
1968 Germany
87.0mph 140.0kmh
0-50mph 80.5kmh: 10.9secs
0-60mph 96.5kmh: 16.5secs
0-1/4 mile: 20.4secs
0-1km: 38.3secs
68.0bhp 50.7kW 68.9PS
@ 4500rpm
92.0lbft 124.7Nm @ 2800rpm
67.8bhp/ton 66.7bhp/tonne
40.5bhp/L 30.2kW/L 41.1PS/L
32.5ft/sec 9.9m/sec
19.0mph 30.6kmh/1000rpm
22.5mpg 18.7mpgUS 12.6L/100km
Petrol 4-stroke piston
1679cc 102.4cu in
Flat 4 2 Carburettor
Compression ratio: 7.8:1
Bore: 90.0mm 3.5in
Stroke: 66.0mm 2.6in
Valve type/No: Overhead 8
Transmission: Manual
No. of forward speeds: 4
Wheels driven: Rear
Springs F/R: Coil/Coil
Brakes F/R: Disc/Drum
Steering: Recirculating ball
Wheelbase: 249.9cm 98.4in
Track F: 137.7cm 54.2in
Track R: 134.1cm 52.8in
Length: 455.9cm 179.5in
Width: 163.6cm 64.4in
Height: 148.6cm 58.5in
Ground clearance: 13.7cm 5.4in
Kerb weight: 1020.1kg 2247.0lb
Fuel: 50.0L 11.0gal 13.2galUS

4779 Volkswagen

Derby LS
1968 Germany
86.0mph 138.4kmh
0-50mph 80.5kmh: 10.8secs
0-60mph 96.5kmh: 16.1secs
0-1/4 mile: 20.3secs
0-1km: 38.8secs
50.0bhp 37.3kW 50.7PS
@ 6000rpm
57.0lbft 77.2Nm @ 3000rpm
70.9bhp/ton 69.7bhp/tonne
45.7bhp/L 34.1kW/L 46.4PS/L
47.2ft/sec 14.4m/sec
14.4mph 23.2kmh/1000rpm
30.7mpg 25.6mpgUS 9.2L/100km
Petrol 4-stroke piston
1093cc 66.7cu in
In-line 4 1 Carburettor
Compression ratio: 8.0:1
Bore: 69.5mm 2.7in
Stroke: 72.0mm 2.8in

Valve type/No: Overhead 8
Transmission: Manual
No. of forward speeds: 4
Wheels driven: Front
Springs F/R: Coil/Coil
Brakes F/R: Disc/Drum
Steering: Rack & pinion
Wheelbase: 233.7cm 92.0in
Track F: 129.5cm 51.0in
Track R: 130.8cm 51.5in
Length: 376.4cm 148.2in
Width: 156.0cm 61.4in
Height: 135.4cm 53.3in
Ground clearance: 13.5cm 5.3in
Kerb weight: 717.3kg 1580.0lb
Fuel: 36.4L 8.0gal 9.6galUS

4780 Volkswagen

1600 Squareback
1969 Germany
82.0mph 131.9kmh
0-50mph 80.5kmh: 14.4secs
0-60mph 96.5kmh: 20.8secs
0-1/4 mile: 22.3secs
65.0bhp 48.5kW 65.9PS
@ 4600rpm
86.8lbft 117.6Nm @ 2800rpm
64.7bhp/ton 63.6bhp/tonne
41.0bhp/L 30.6kW/L 41.6PS/L
34.8ft/sec 10.6m/sec
19.4mph 31.2kmh/1000rpm
29.4mpg 24.5mpgUS 9.6L/100km
Petrol 4-stroke piston
1584cc 96.6cu in
Flat 4 fuel injection
Compression ratio: 7.7:1
Bore: 85.5mm 3.4in
Stroke: 69.0mm 2.7in
Valve type/No: Overhead 8
Transmission: Automatic
No. of forward speeds: 3
Wheels driven: Rear
Springs F/R: Torsion bar/Torsion bar
Brakes F/R: Disc/Drum
Steering: Worm & roller
Wheelbase: 240.0cm 94.5in
Track F: 131.1cm 51.6in
Track R: 134.6cm 53.0in
Length: 422.4cm 166.3in
Width: 164.1cm 64.6in
Height: 147.1cm 57.9in
Ground clearance: 15.0cm 5.9in
Kerb weight: 1021.5kg 2250.0lb
Fuel: 40.1L 8.8gal 10.6galUS

4781 Volkswagen

411 LE Variant
1970 Germany
99.0mph 159.3kmh
0-50mph 80.5kmh: 10.5secs
0-60mph 96.5kmh: 15.9secs
0-1/4 mile: 19.7secs
0-1km: 37.0secs
80.0bhp 59.7kW 81.1PS
@ 4900rpm
97.5lbft 132.1Nm @ 2700rpm
70.9bhp/ton 69.7bhp/tonne
47.6bhp/L 35.5kW/L 48.3PS/L
35.4ft/sec 10.8m/sec
19.0mph 30.6kmh/1000rpm
22.5mpg 18.7mpgUS 12.6L/100km
Petrol 4-stroke piston
1679cc 102.4cu in
Flat 4 fuel injection
Compression ratio: 8.2:1
Bore: 90.0mm 3.5in
Stroke: 66.0mm 2.6in
Valve type/No: Overhead 8
Transmission: Manual
No. of forward speeds: 4
Wheels driven: Rear
Springs F/R: Coil/Coil
Brakes F/R: Disc/Drum
Steering: Recirculating ball
Wheelbase: 249.9cm 98.4in
Track F: 137.7cm 54.2in
Track R: 134.1cm 52.8in
Length: 455.9cm 179.5in
Width: 163.6cm 64.4in
Height: 148.6cm 58.5in
Ground clearance: 13.7cm 5.4in
Kerb weight: 1147.3kg 2527.0lb
Fuel: 50.0L 11.0gal 13.2galUS

4782 Volkswagen

Porsche 914
1970 Germany
104.0mph 167.3kmh
0-50mph 80.5kmh: 10.9secs
0-60mph 96.5kmh: 14.8secs
0-1/4 mile: 19.9secs
0-1km: 36.9secs
80.0bhp 59.7kW 81.1PS
@ 4900rpm
98.4lbft 133.3Nm @ 2700rpm
94.4bhp/ton 92.8bhp/tonne
47.6bhp/L 35.5kW/L 48.3PS/L
35.4ft/sec 10.8m/sec
22.5mph 36.2kmh/1000rpm
20.5mpg 17.1mpgUS 13.8L/100km
Petrol 4-stroke piston
1679cc 102.4cu in
Flat 4 fuel injection
Compression ratio: 8.2:1
Bore: 90.0mm 3.5in
Stroke: 66.0mm 2.6in
Valve type/No: Overhead 8
Transmission: Manual
No. of forward speeds: 5
Wheels driven: Rear
Springs F/R: Torsion bar/Coil
Brakes F/R: Disc/Disc
Steering: Rack & pinion
Wheelbase: 245.1cm 96.5in
Track F: 135.9cm 53.5in
Track R: 138.2cm 54.4in
Length: 401.3cm 158.0in
Width: 165.1cm 65.0in
Height: 120.7cm 47.5in
Ground clearance: 16.5cm 6.5in
Kerb weight: 861.7kg 1898.0lb
Fuel: 61.9L 13.6gal 16.3galUS

4783 Volkswagen

Super Beetle
1970 Germany
82.0mph 131.9kmh
0-50mph 80.5kmh: 12.1secs
0-60mph 96.5kmh: 18.3secs
0-1/4 mile: 20.7secs
0-1km: 40.0secs
50.0bhp 37.3kW 50.7PS
@ 4000rpm
78.0lbft 105.7Nm @ 2800rpm
60.5bhp/ton 59.5bhp/tonne
31.6bhp/L 23.5kW/L 32.0PS/L
30.2ft/sec 9.2m/sec
19.7mph 31.7kmh/1000rpm
24.0mpg 20.0mpgUS 11.8L/100km
Petrol 4-stroke piston
1584cc 96.6cu in
Flat 4 1 Carburettor
Compression ratio: 7.5:1
Bore: 85.5mm 3.4in
Stroke: 69.0mm 2.7in
Valve type/No: Overhead 8
Transmission: Manual
No. of forward speeds: 4
Wheels driven: Rear
Springs F/R: Torsion bar/Torsion bar
Brakes F/R: Disc/Drum
Steering: Worm & roller
Wheelbase: 242.1cm 95.3in
Track F: 137.9cm 54.3in
Track R: 135.1cm 53.2in
Length: 408.2cm 160.7in
Width: 153.9cm 60.6in
Height: 152.4cm 60.0in
Ground clearance: 15.2cm 6.0in
Kerb weight: 839.9kg 1850.0lb
Fuel: 41.9L 9.2gal 11.1galUS

4784 Volkswagen

411
1971 Germany
84.0mph 135.2kmh
0-50mph 80.5kmh: 11.7secs
0-60mph 96.5kmh: 16.3secs
0-1/4 mile: 20.9secs
85.0bhp 63.4kW 86.2PS
@ 5000rpm
99.0lbft 134.1Nm @ 3500rpm
78.3bhp/ton 77.0bhp/tonne
50.6bhp/L 37.7kW/L 51.3PS/L
36.1ft/sec 11.0m/sec
18.0mph 29.0kmh/1000rpm
27.0mpg 22.5mpgUS 10.5L/100km
Petrol 4-stroke piston
1679cc 102.4cu in
Flat 4 fuel injection
Compression ratio: 8.2:1
Bore: 90.0mm 3.5in
Stroke: 66.0mm 2.6in
Valve type/No: Overhead 8
Transmission: Automatic
No. of forward speeds: 3
Wheels driven: Rear
Springs F/R: Coil/Coil
Brakes F/R: Disc/Drum
Steering: Recirculating ball
Wheelbase: 249.9cm 98.4in
Track F: 137.4cm 54.1in
Track R: 134.6cm 53.0in
Length: 455.2cm 179.2in
Width: 163.3cm 64.3in
Height: 148.3cm 58.4in
Ground clearance: 13.5cm 5.3in
Kerb weight: 1103.2kg 2430.0lb
Fuel: 50.0L 11.0gal 13.2galUS

4785 Volkswagen

Porsche 914/b
1971 Germany
125.0mph 201.1kmh
0-50mph 80.5kmh: 6.2secs
0-60mph 96.5kmh: 8.3secs
0-1/4 mile: 16.2secs
0-1km: 30.0secs
110.0bhp 82.0kW 111.5PS
@ 5800rpm
131.0lbft 177.5Nm @ 4200rpm
116.7bhp/ton 114.7bhp/tonne
55.1bhp/L 41.1kW/L 55.8PS/L
41.9ft/sec 12.8m/sec
21.8mph 35.1kmh/1000rpm
21.3mpg 17.7mpgUS 13.3L/100km
Petrol 4-stroke piston
1998cc 121.9cu in
Flat 6 2 Carburettor
Compression ratio: 8.6:1
Bore: 80.0mm 3.1in
Stroke: 66.0mm 2.6in
Valve type/No: Overhead 12
Transmission: Manual
No. of forward speeds: 5
Wheels driven: Rear
Springs F/R: Torsion bar/Coil
Brakes F/R: Disc/Disc
Steering: Rack & pinion
Wheelbase: 245.1cm 96.5in
Track F: 135.9cm 53.5in
Track R: 138.2cm 54.4in
Length: 401.3cm 158.0in
Width: 165.1cm 65.0in
Height: 120.7cm 47.5in
Ground clearance: 16.5cm 6.5in
Kerb weight: 958.8kg 2112.0lb
Fuel: 61.9L 13.6gal 16.3galUS

4786 Volkswagen

Super Beetle
1971 Germany
79.0mph 127.1kmh
0-50mph 80.5kmh: 12.2secs
0-60mph 96.5kmh: 18.4secs
0-1/4 mile: 21.1secs
60.0bhp 44.7kW 60.8PS
@ 4400rpm
82.0lbft 111.1Nm @ 3000rpm
68.2bhp/ton 67.1bhp/tonne
37.9bhp/L 28.2kW/L 38.4PS/L
33.2ft/sec 10.1m/sec
19.6mph 31.5kmh/1000rpm
34.5mpg 28.7mpgUS 8.2L/100km
Petrol 4-stroke piston
1584cc 96.6cu in
Flat 4
Compression ratio: 7.5:1
Bore: 85.5mm 3.4in
Stroke: 69.0mm 2.7in
Valve type/No: Overhead 8
Transmission: Manual
No. of forward speeds: 4
Wheels driven: Rear
Springs F/R: Coil/Torsion bar
Brakes F/R: Drum/Drum
Steering: Worm & roller
Wheelbase: 242.1cm 95.3in
Track F: 137.9cm 54.3in
Track R: 135.4cm 53.3in
Length: 411.0cm 161.8in
Width: 158.5cm 62.4in
Height: 150.1cm 59.1in
Kerb weight: 894.4kg 1970.0lb
Fuel: 42.0L 9.2gal 11.1galUS

4787 Volkswagen

Van
1971 Germany
0-60mph 96.5kmh: 38.4secs
60.0bhp 44.7kW 60.8PS
@ 4400rpm
82.0lbft 111.1Nm
46.5bhp/ton 45.8bhp/tonne
37.9bhp/L 28.2kW/L 38.4PS/L
33.2ft/sec 10.1m/sec
Petrol 4-stroke piston
1584cc 96.6cu in
Flat 4
Compression ratio: 7.5:1
Bore: 85.3mm 3.4in
Stroke: 69.1mm 2.7in
Valve type/No: Overhead 8
Transmission: Manual
No. of forward speeds: 4
Wheels driven: Rear
Wheelbase: 240.0cm 94.5in
Track F: 138.7cm 54.6in
Track R: 143.8cm 56.6in
Length: 442.0cm 174.0in
Width: 176.5cm 69.5in
Height: 195.6cm 77.0in
Ground clearance: 18.5cm 7.3in
Kerb weight: 1311.1kg 2888.0lb

4788 Volkswagen

K70
1972 Germany
93.0mph 149.6kmh
0-50mph 80.5kmh: 9.7secs
0-60mph 96.5kmh: 12.9secs
0-1/4 mile: 18.8secs
0-1km: 35.9secs
90.0bhp 67.1kW 91.2PS
@ 5200rpm
99.0lbft 134.1Nm @ 4000rpm
85.4bhp/ton 84.0bhp/tonne
56.1bhp/L 41.8kW/L 56.8PS/L
43.2ft/sec 13.2m/sec
18.2mph 29.3kmh/1000rpm
24.1mpg 20.1mpgUS 11.7L/100km
Petrol 4-stroke piston
1605cc 97.9cu in
In-line 4 1 Carburettor
Compression ratio: 9.5:1
Bore: 82.0mm 3.2in
Stroke: 76.0mm 3.0in
Valve type/No: Overhead 8
Transmission: Manual
No. of forward speeds: 4
Wheels driven: Front
Springs F/R: Coil/Coil
Brake system: PA
Brakes F/R: Disc/Drum
Steering: Rack & pinion
Wheelbase: 266.7cm 105.0in
Track F: 139.7cm 55.0in
Track R: 142.2cm 56.0in
Length: 442.0cm 174.0in
Width: 167.6cm 66.0in
Height: 144.8cm 57.0in
Ground clearance: 12.7cm 5.0in
Kerb weight: 1071.4kg 2360.0lb
Fuel: 54.1L 11.9gal 14.3galUS

4789 Volkswagen

Karmann-Ghia
1973 Germany
92.0mph 148.0kmh
0-50mph 80.5kmh: 12.2secs
0-60mph 96.5kmh: 17.5secs
0-1/4 mile: 21.2secs
46.0bhp 34.3kW 46.6PS
@ 4000rpm
72.0lbft 97.6Nm @ 2800rpm
52.6bhp/ton 51.7bhp/tonne
29.0bhp/L 21.6kW/L 29.4PS/L
Petrol 4-stroke piston
1584cc 96.6cu in
Flat 4
Transmission: Manual
No. of forward speeds: 4
Wheels driven: Rear
Springs F/R: Torsion bar/Torsion bar
Brakes F/R: Disc/Drum
Wheelbase: 240.0cm 94.5in
Track F: 130.3cm 51.3in
Track R: 133.9cm 52.7in
Length: 419.1cm 165.0in
Width: 163.3cm 64.3in
Height: 132.1cm 52.0in
Kerb weight: 889.8kg 1960.0lb

4790 Volkswagen

Passat LS
1973 Germany

101.0mph 162.5kmh
0-50mph 80.5kmh: 8.8secs
0-60mph 96.5kmh: 12.4secs
0-1/4 mile: 18.8secs
0-1km: 31.5secs
75.0bhp 55.9kW 76.0PS
@ 5800rpm
81.0lbft 109.8Nm @ 3500rpm
87.8bhp/ton 86.3bhp/tonne
51.0bhp/L 38.0kW/L 51.7PS/L
50.7ft/sec 15.5m/sec
16.5mph 26.5kmh/1000rpm
27.8mpg 23.1mpgUS 10.2L/100km
Petrol 4-stroke piston
1471cc 89.7cu in
In-line 4 1 Carburettor
Compression ratio: 9.7:1
Bore: 76.5mm 3.0in
Stroke: 80.0mm 3.1in
Valve type/No: Overhead 8
Transmission: Manual
No. of forward speeds: 4
Wheels driven: Front
Springs F/R: Coil/Coil
Brake system: PA
Brakes F/R: Disc/Drum
Steering: Rack & pinion
Wheelbase: 248.9cm 98.0in
Track F: 133.9cm 52.7in
Track R: 133.4cm 52.5in
Length: 419.1cm 165.0in
Width: 160.0cm 63.0in
Height: 134.6cm 53.0in
Ground clearance: 14.0cm 5.5in
Kerb weight: 869.0kg 1914.0lb
Fuel: 45.5L 10.0gal 12.0galUS

4791 Volkswagen

SP-2
1973 Brazil
97.0mph 156.1kmh
0-50mph 80.5kmh: 12.1secs
0-60mph 96.5kmh: 16.1secs
65.0bhp 48.5kW 65.9PS
@ 4600rpm
88.0lbft 119.2Nm @ 3000rpm
74.3bhp/ton 73.0bhp/tonne
38.7bhp/L 28.9kW/L 39.3PS/L
34.8ft/sec 10.6m/sec
21.0mph 33.8kmh/1000rpm
32.4mpg 27.0mpgUS 8.7L/100km
Petrol 4-stroke piston
1678cc 102.4cu in
Flat 4
Compression ratio: 7.5:1
Bore: 88.0mm 3.5in
Stroke: 69.0mm 2.7in
Valve type/No: Overhead 8
Transmission: Manual
No. of forward speeds: 4
Wheels driven: Rear
Springs F/R: Torsion bar/Torsion bar
Brakes F/R: Disc/Drum
Steering: Worm & roller
Wheelbase: 240.0cm 94.5in
Track F: 130.6cm 51.4in
Track R: 129.0cm 50.8in
Length: 421.6cm 166.0in
Width: 161.0cm 63.4in
Height: 115.8cm 45.6in
Kerb weight: 889.8kg 1960.0lb
Fuel: 39.7L 8.7gal 10.5galUS

4792 Volkswagen

Sports Bug
1973 Germany
81.0mph 130.3kmh
0-50mph 80.5kmh: 12.6secs
0-60mph 96.5kmh: 18.2secs
0-1/4 mile: 21.2secs
46.0bhp 34.3kW 46.6PS
@ 4000rpm
72.0lbft 97.6Nm @ 2800rpm
52.6bhp/ton 51.7bhp/tonne
29.0bhp/L 21.6kW/L 29.4PS/L
30.2ft/sec 9.2m/sec
20.2mph 32.5kmh/1000rpm
27.6mpg 23.0mpgUS 10.2L/100km
Petrol 4-stroke piston
1584cc 96.6cu in
Flat 4 1 Carburettor
Compression ratio: 7.3:1
Bore: 85.5mm 3.4in
Stroke: 69.0mm 2.7in
Valve type/No: Overhead 8
Transmission: Manual
No. of forward speeds: 4
Wheels driven: Rear
Springs F/R: Coil/Coil
Brakes F/R: Drum/Drum
Steering: Worm & roller
Wheelbase: 242.1cm 95.3in
Track F: 137.9cm 54.3in
Track R: 136.1cm 53.6in
Length: 414.0cm 163.0in
Width: 158.5cm 62.4in
Height: 150.1cm 59.1in
Ground clearance: 15.0cm 5.9in
Kerb weight: 889.8kg 1960.0lb
Fuel: 42.0L 9.2gal 11.1galUS

4793 Volkswagen

Type III
1973 Germany
0-60mph 96.5kmh: 18.2secs
0-1/4 mile: 20.7secs
52.0bhp 38.8kW 52.7PS
@ 4000rpm
77.0lbft 104.3Nm @ 2200rpm
52.5bhp/ton 51.6bhp/tonne
32.8bhp/L 24.5kW/L 33.3PS/L
33.6mpg 28.0mpgUS 8.4L/100km
Petrol 4-stroke piston
1584cc 96.6cu in
Flat 4
Valve type/No: Overhead 8
Transmission: Manual
No. of forward speeds: 4
Wheels driven: Rear
Brakes F/R: Disc/Drum
Wheelbase: 240.0cm 94.5in
Length: 450.6cm 177.4in
Width: 172.0cm 67.7in
Height: 147.1cm 57.9in
Kerb weight: 1007.9kg 2220.0lb

4794 Volkswagen

181
1974 Germany
73.0mph 117.5kmh
0-50mph 80.5kmh: 15.3secs
0-60mph 96.5kmh: 23.2secs
0-1/4 mile: 22.5secs
46.0bhp 34.3kW 46.6PS
@ 4000rpm
72.0lbft 97.6Nm @ 2800rpm
53.7bhp/ton 52.8bhp/tonne
29.0bhp/L 21.6kW/L 29.4PS/L
30.2ft/sec 9.2m/sec
18.8mph 30.2kmh/1000rpm
Petrol 4-stroke piston
1584cc 96.6cu in
Flat 4 1 Carburettor
Compression ratio: 7.3:1
Bore: 85.5mm 3.4in
Stroke: 69.0mm 2.7in
Valve type/No: Overhead 8
Transmission: Manual
No. of forward speeds: 4
Wheels driven: Rear
Springs F/R: Torsion bar/Torsion bar
Brakes F/R: Drum/Drum
Steering: Worm & roller
Wheelbase: 240.0cm 94.5in
Track F: 135.4cm 53.3in
Track R: 144.5cm 56.9in
Length: 378.0cm 148.8in
Width: 164.1cm 64.6in
Height: 162.1cm 63.8in
Ground clearance: 27.9cm 11.0in
Kerb weight: 871.7kg 1920.0lb
Fuel: 40.1L 8.8gal 10.6galUS

4795 Volkswagen

412
1974 Germany
0-60mph 96.5kmh: 16.8secs
0-1/4 mile: 20.5secs
72.0bhp 53.7kW 73.0PS
@ 4800rpm
91.0lbft 123.3Nm @ 3000rpm
62.9bhp/ton 61.8bhp/tonne
40.1bhp/L 29.9kW/L 40.7PS/L
24.6mpg 20.5mpgUS 11.5L/100km
Petrol 4-stroke piston
1795cc 109.5cu in
Flat 4
Valve type/No: Overhead 8
Transmission: Automatic
No. of forward speeds: 3
Wheels driven: Rear
Brakes F/R: Disc/Drum
Wheelbase: 249.9cm 98.4in
Length: 466.6cm 183.7in
Width: 167.4cm 65.9in
Height: 147.6cm 58.1in
Kerb weight: 1164.5kg 2565.0lb

4796 Volkswagen

Dasher
1974 Germany
100.0mph 160.9kmh
0-60mph 96.5kmh: 12.7secs
0-1/4 mile: 19.0secs
75.0bhp 55.9kW 76.0PS
@ 5800rpm
82.0lbft 111.1Nm @ 4000rpm
79.6bhp/ton 78.3bhp/tonne
51.0bhp/L 38.0kW/L 51.7PS/L
17.1mph 27.5kmh/1000rpm
31.8mpg 26.5mpgUS 8.9L/100km
Petrol 4-stroke piston
1471cc 89.7cu in
In-line 4
Valve type/No: Overhead 8
Transmission: Manual
No. of forward speeds: 4
Wheels driven: Front
Springs F/R: Coil/Coil
Brakes F/R: Disc/Drum
Steering: Rack & pinion
Wheelbase: 246.9cm 97.2in
Track F: 133.9cm 52.7in
Track R: 133.6cm 52.6in
Length: 436.6cm 171.9in
Width: 160.0cm 63.0in
Height: 136.9cm 53.9in
Kerb weight: 957.9kg 2110.0lb
Fuel: 45.4L 10.0gal 12.0galUS

4797 Volkswagen

Scirocco TS
1974 Germany
105.0mph 168.9kmh
0-50mph 80.5kmh: 8.0secs
0-60mph 96.5kmh: 11.1secs
0-1/4 mile: 18.3secs
0-1km: 34.1secs
85.0bhp 63.4kW 86.2PS
@ 5800rpm
89.0lbft 120.6Nm @ 3200rpm
102.0bhp/ton 100.3bhp/tonne
57.8bhp/L 43.1kW/L 58.6PS/L
50.7ft/sec 15.5m/sec
17.2mph 27.7kmh/1000rpm
28.5mpg 23.7mpgUS 9.9L/100km
Petrol 4-stroke piston
1471cc 89.7cu in
In-line 4 1 Carburettor
Compression ratio: 9.7:1
Bore: 76.5mm 3.0in
Stroke: 80.0mm 3.1in
Valve type/No: Overhead 8
Transmission: Manual
No. of forward speeds: 4
Wheels driven: Front
Springs F/R: Coil/Coil
Brake system: PA
Brakes F/R: Disc/Drum
Steering: Rack & pinion
Wheelbase: 241.0cm 94.9in
Track F: 138.9cm 54.7in
Track R: 135.9cm 53.5in
Length: 387.6cm 152.6in
Width: 162.6cm 64.0in
Height: 131.1cm 51.6in
Ground clearance: 12.2cm 4.8in
Kerb weight: 847.2kg 1866.0lb
Fuel: 43.2L 9.5gal 11.4galUS

4798 Volkswagen

Beetle
1975 Germany
0-60mph 96.5kmh: 18.1secs
0-1/4 mile: 20.9secs
48.0bhp 35.8kW 48.7PS
@ 4200rpm
73.0lbft 98.9Nm @ 2800rpm
57.8bhp/ton 56.8bhp/tonne
30.3bhp/L 22.6kW/L 30.7PS/L
31.7ft/sec 9.7m/sec
33.0mpg 27.5mpgUS 8.6L/100km
Petrol 4-stroke piston
1584cc 96.6cu in
Flat 4 fuel injection
Compression ratio: 7.3:1
Bore: 85.5mm 3.4in
Stroke: 69.0mm 2.7in
Valve type/No: Overhead 8
Transmission: Manual
No. of forward speeds: 4
Wheels driven: Rear
Wheelbase: 240.0cm 94.5in
Track F: 130.8cm 51.5in
Track R: 134.9cm 53.1in
Length: 415.0cm 163.4in
Width: 154.9cm 61.0in
Height: 150.1cm 59.1in
Ground clearance: 15.0cm 5.9in
Kerb weight: 844.4kg 1860.0lb
Fuel: 40.1L 8.8gal 10.6galUS

4799 Volkswagen

Golf 1100L
1975 Germany
92.0mph 148.0kmh
0-50mph 80.5kmh: 10.4secs
0-60mph 96.5kmh: 15.5secs
0-1/4 mile: 20.0secs
0-1km: 38.6secs
50.0bhp 37.3kW 50.7PS
@ 6000rpm
57.0lbft 77.2Nm @ 3000rpm
61.9bhp/ton 60.9bhp/tonne
45.7bhp/L 34.1kW/L 46.4PS/L
47.2ft/sec 14.4m/sec
14.6mph 23.5kmh/1000rpm
30.1mpg 25.1mpgUS 9.4L/100km
Petrol 4-stroke piston
1093cc 66.7cu in
In-line 4 1 Carburettor
Compression ratio: 8.0:1
Bore: 69.5mm 2.7in
Stroke: 72.0mm 2.8in
Valve type/No: Overhead 8
Transmission: Manual
No. of forward speeds: 4
Wheels driven: Front
Springs F/R: Coil/Coil
Brakes F/R: Disc/Drum
Steering: Rack & pinion
Wheelbase: 240.0cm 94.5in
Track F: 138.9cm 54.7in
Track R: 134.6cm 53.0in
Length: 372.1cm 146.5in
Width: 161.3cm 63.5in
Height: 141.0cm 55.5in
Ground clearance: 13.5cm 5.3in
Kerb weight: 820.8kg 1808.0lb
Fuel: 45.5L 10.0gal 12.0galUS

4800 Volkswagen

Polo
1975 Germany
84.0mph 135.2kmh
0-50mph 80.5kmh: 12.0secs
0-60mph 96.5kmh: 18.0secs
0-1/4 mile: 20.8secs
0-1km: 40.4secs
40.0bhp 29.8kW 40.5PS
@ 5900rpm
45.0lbft 61.0Nm @ 3500rpm
58.9bhp/ton 57.9bhp/tonne
44.7bhp/L 33.3kW/L 45.3PS/L
38.0ft/sec 11.6m/sec
15.1mph 24.3kmh/1000rpm
34.9mpg 29.1mpgUS 8.1L/100km
Petrol 4-stroke piston
895cc 54.6cu in
In-line 4 1 Carburettor
Compression ratio: 8.2:1
Bore: 69.5mm 2.7in
Stroke: 59.0mm 2.3in
Valve type/No: Overhead 8
Transmission: Manual
No. of forward speeds: 4
Wheels driven: Front
Springs F/R: Coil/Coil
Brakes F/R: Disc/Drum
Steering: Rack & pinion
Wheelbase: 233.7cm 92.0in
Track F: 129.5cm 51.0in
Track R: 130.8cm 51.5in
Length: 350.5cm 138.0in
Width: 156.2cm 61.5in
Height: 133.4cm 52.5in
Ground clearance: 20.3cm 8.0in
Kerb weight: 691.0kg 1522.0lb
Fuel: 36.4L 8.0gal 9.6galUS

4801 Volkswagen

Rabbit
1975 Germany
0-60mph 96.5kmh: 12.7secs
0-1/4 mile: 19.0secs

70.0bhp 52.2kW 71.0PS
@ 5800rpm
81.0lbft 109.8Nm @ 3500rpm
82.3bhp/ton 80.9bhp/tonne
47.6bhp/L 35.5kW/L 48.2PS/L
50.7ft/sec 15.5m/sec
36.0mpg 30.0mpgUS 7.8L/100km
Petrol 4-stroke piston
1471cc 89.7cu in
In-line 4 1 Carburettor
Compression ratio: 8.2:1
Bore: 76.5mm 3.0in
Stroke: 80.0mm 3.1in
Valve type/No: Overhead 8
Transmission: Manual
No. of forward speeds: 4
Wheels driven: Front
Wheelbase: 240.0cm 94.5in
Track F: 138.9cm 54.7in
Track R: 134.9cm 53.1in
Length: 394.5cm 155.3in
Width: 161.0cm 63.4in
Height: 141.0cm 55.5in
Ground clearance: 12.4cm 4.9in
Kerb weight: 864.9kg 1905.0lb
Fuel: 45.0L 9.9gal 11.9galUS

4802 Volkswagen

Scirocco
1975 Germany
102.0mph 164.1kmh
0-50mph 80.5kmh: 9.1secs
0-60mph 96.5kmh: 12.7secs
0-1/4 mile: 19.4secs
70.0bhp 52.2kW 71.0PS
@ 6000rpm
81.0lbft 109.8Nm @ 3500rpm
81.2bhp/ton 79.9bhp/tonne
47.6bhp/L 35.5kW/L 48.2PS/L
52.5ft/sec 16.0m/sec
17.1mph 27.5kmh/1000rpm
35.4mpg 29.5mpgUS 8.0L/100km
Petrol 4-stroke piston
1471cc 89.7cu in
In-line 4 1 Carburettor
Compression ratio: 8.2:1
Bore: 76.5mm 3.0in
Stroke: 80.0mm 3.1in
Valve type/No: Overhead 8
Transmission: Manual
No. of forward speeds: 4
Wheels driven: Front
Springs F/R: Coil/Coil
Brakes F/R: Disc/Drum
Steering: Rack & pinion
Wheelbase: 240.0cm 94.5in
Track F: 138.9cm 54.7in
Track R: 134.9cm 53.1in
Length: 395.5cm 155.7in
Width: 162.6cm 64.0in
Height: 130.8cm 51.5in
Ground clearance: 13.5cm 5.3in
Kerb weight: 876.2kg 1930.0lb
Fuel: 45.0L 9.9gal 11.9galUS

4803 Volkswagen

Golf 1600 LS
1976 Germany
99.0mph 159.3kmh
0-50mph 80.5kmh: 7.9secs
0-60mph 96.5kmh: 12.0secs
0-1/4 mile: 18.5secs
0-1km: 34.7secs
75.0bhp 55.9kW 76.0PS
@ 5600rpm
87.5lbft 118.6Nm @ 3200rpm
92.8bhp/ton 91.3bhp/tonne
47.2bhp/L 35.2kW/L 47.9PS/L
49.0ft/sec 14.9m/sec
17.3mph 27.8kmh/1000rpm
27.2mpg 22.6mpgUS 10.4L/100km
Petrol 4-stroke piston
1588cc 96.9cu in
In-line 4 1 Carburettor
Compression ratio: 8.2:1
Bore: 79.5mm 3.1in
Stroke: 80.0mm 3.1in
Valve type/No: Overhead 8
Transmission: Manual
No. of forward speeds: 4
Wheels driven: Front
Springs F/R: Coil/Coil
Brake system: PA
Brakes F/R: Disc/Drum
Steering: Rack & pinion
Wheelbase: 240.0cm 94.5in
Track F: 138.9cm 54.7in
Track R: 134.6cm 53.0in
Length: 372.1cm 146.5in
Width: 161.3cm 63.5in
Height: 141.0cm 55.5in
Ground clearance: 13.5cm 5.3in
Kerb weight: 821.7kg 1810.0lb
Fuel: 45.0L 9.9gal 11.9galUS

4804 Volkswagen

Scirocco TS
1976 Germany
107.0mph 172.2kmh
0-50mph 80.5kmh: 7.4secs
0-60mph 96.5kmh: 10.3secs
0-1/4 mile: 17.6secs
0-1km: 32.2secs
85.0bhp 63.4kW 86.2PS
@ 5600rpm
92.0lbft 124.7Nm @ 3800rpm
105.7bhp/ton 103.9bhp/tonne
53.5bhp/L 39.9kW/L 54.3PS/L
49.0ft/sec 14.9m/sec
17.2mph 27.7kmh/1000rpm
27.6mpg 23.0mpgUS 10.2L/100km
Petrol 4-stroke piston
1588cc 96.9cu in
In-line 4 1 Carburettor
Compression ratio: 8.2:1
Bore: 79.5mm 3.1in
Stroke: 80.0mm 3.1in
Valve type/No: Overhead 8
Transmission: Manual
No. of forward speeds: 4
Wheels driven: Front
Springs F/R: Coil/Coil
Brake system: PA
Brakes F/R: Disc/Drum
Steering: Rack & pinion
Wheelbase: 241.0cm 94.9in
Track F: 138.9cm 54.7in
Track R: 135.9cm 53.5in
Length: 387.6cm 152.6in
Width: 162.6cm 64.0in
Height: 131.1cm 51.6in
Ground clearance: 12.2cm 4.8in
Kerb weight: 818.1kg 1802.0lb
Fuel: 45.0L 9.9gal 11.9galUS

4805 Volkswagen

Dasher
1977 Germany
96.0mph 154.5kmh
0-50mph 80.5kmh: 9.4secs
0-60mph 96.5kmh: 13.2secs
0-1/4 mile: 19.0secs
77.0bhp 57.4kW 78.1PS
@ 5500rpm
86.0lbft 116.5Nm @ 3300rpm
81.0bhp/ton 79.6bhp/tonne
48.5bhp/L 36.2kW/L 49.2PS/L
48.1ft/sec 14.7m/sec
15.6mph 25.1kmh/1000rpm
31.8mpg 26.5mpgUS 8.9L/100km
Petrol 4-stroke piston
1588cc 96.9cu in
In-line 4
Compression ratio: 8.2:1
Bore: 79.5mm 3.1in
Stroke: 80.0mm 3.1in
Valve type/No: Overhead 8
Transmission: Manual
No. of forward speeds: 4
Wheels driven: Front
Springs F/R: Coil/Coil
Brake system: PA
Brakes F/R: Disc/Drum
Steering: Rack & pinion
Wheelbase: 246.9cm 97.2in
Track F: 133.9cm 52.7in
Track R: 133.4cm 52.5in
Length: 437.9cm 172.4in
Width: 160.0cm 63.0in
Height: 135.9cm 53.5in
Kerb weight: 967.0kg 2130.0lb
Fuel: 45.0L 9.9gal 11.9galUS

4806 Volkswagen

Golf GTi
1977 Germany
110.0mph 177.0kmh
0-50mph 80.5kmh: 7.4secs
0-60mph 96.5kmh: 9.8secs
0-1/4 mile: 17.3secs
0-1km: 32.3secs
110.0bhp 82.0kW 111.5PS
@ 6100rpm
101.0lbft 136.9Nm @ 5000rpm
132.3bhp/ton 130.1bhp/tonne
69.3bhp/L 51.7kW/L 70.2PS/L
53.4ft/sec 16.3m/sec
17.3mph 27.8kmh/1000rpm
27.3mpg 22.7mpgUS 10.3L/100km
Petrol 4-stroke piston
1588cc 96.9cu in
In-line 4 fuel injection
Compression ratio: 9.5:1
Bore: 79.5mm 3.1in
Stroke: 80.0mm 3.1in
Valve type/No: Overhead 8
Transmission: Manual
No. of forward speeds: 4
Wheels driven: Front
Springs F/R: Coil/Coil
Brake system: PA
Brakes F/R: Disc/Drum
Steering: Rack & pinion
Wheelbase: 240.0cm 94.5in
Track F: 138.9cm 54.7in
Track R: 134.6cm 53.0in
Length: 372.1cm 146.5in
Width: 161.3cm 63.5in
Height: 141.0cm 55.5in
Ground clearance: 13.5cm 5.3in
Kerb weight: 845.3kg 1862.0lb
Fuel: 45.0L 9.9gal 11.9galUS

4807 Volkswagen

Passat GLS
1977 Germany
104.0mph 167.3kmh
0-50mph 80.5kmh: 8.0secs
0-60mph 96.5kmh: 11.8secs
0-1/4 mile: 18.4secs
0-1km: 34.5secs
85.0bhp 63.4kW 86.2PS
@ 5600rpm
87.5lbft 118.6Nm @ 3200rpm
94.4bhp/ton 92.9bhp/tonne
53.5bhp/L 39.9kW/L 54.3PS/L
49.0ft/sec 14.9m/sec
18.3mph 29.4kmh/1000rpm
29.6mpg 24.6mpgUS 9.5L/100km
Petrol 4-stroke piston
1588cc 96.9cu in
In-line 4 1 Carburettor
Compression ratio: 8.2:1
Bore: 79.5mm 3.1in
Stroke: 80.0mm 3.1in
Valve type/No: Overhead 8
Transmission: Manual
No. of forward speeds: 4
Wheels driven: Front
Springs F/R: Coil/Coil
Brake system: PA
Brakes F/R: Disc/Drum
Steering: Rack & pinion
Wheelbase: 248.9cm 98.0in
Track F: 133.9cm 52.7in
Track R: 133.4cm 52.5in
Length: 419.1cm 165.0in
Width: 160.0cm 63.0in
Height: 134.6cm 53.0in
Ground clearance: 14.0cm 5.5in
Kerb weight: 915.3kg 2016.0lb
Fuel: 45.5L 10.0gal 12.0galUS

4808 Volkswagen

Polo LS
1977 Germany
87.0mph 140.0kmh
0-50mph 80.5kmh: 11.2secs
0-60mph 96.5kmh: 16.0secs
0-1/4 mile: 20.3secs
0-1km: 38.5secs
50.0bhp 37.3kW 50.7PS
@ 6000rpm
53.0lbft 71.8Nm @ 3500rpm
71.4bhp/ton 70.2bhp/tonne
45.7bhp/L 34.1kW/L 46.4PS/L
47.2ft/sec 14.4m/sec
14.5mph 23.3kmh/1000rpm
33.5mpg 27.9mpgUS 8.4L/100km
Petrol 4-stroke piston
1093cc 66.7cu in
In-line 4 1 Carburettor
Compression ratio: 8.0:1
Bore: 69.5mm 2.7in
Stroke: 72.0mm 2.8in
Valve type/No: Overhead 8
Transmission: Manual
No. of forward speeds: 4
Wheels driven: Front
Springs F/R: Coil/Coil
Brakes F/R: Disc/Drum
Steering: Rack & pinion
Wheelbase: 233.7cm 92.0in
Track F: 129.5cm 51.0in
Track R: 130.8cm 51.5in
Length: 350.5cm 138.0in
Width: 156.2cm 61.5in
Height: 133.4cm 52.5in
Ground clearance: 20.3cm 8.0in
Kerb weight: 711.9kg 1568.0lb
Fuel: 36.4L 8.0gal 9.6galUS

4809 Volkswagen

Rabbit Diesel
1977 Germany
90.0mph 144.8kmh
0-50mph 80.5kmh: 10.7secs
0-60mph 96.5kmh: 15.8secs
0-1/4 mile: 20.4secs
48.0bhp 35.8kW 48.7PS
@ 5000rpm
58.0lbft 78.6Nm @ 2500rpm
54.3bhp/ton 53.4bhp/tonne
32.6bhp/L 24.3kW/L 33.1PS/L
43.8ft/sec 13.3m/sec
17.4mph 28.0kmh/1000rpm
51.6mpg 43.0mpgUS 5.5L/100km
Diesel 4-stroke piston
1471cc 89.7cu in
In-line 4
Compression ratio: 23.5:1
Bore: 76.5mm 3.0in
Stroke: 80.0mm 3.1in
Valve type/No: Overhead 8
Transmission: Manual
No. of forward speeds: 4
Wheels driven: Front
Springs F/R: Coil/Coil
Brake system: PA
Brakes F/R: Disc/Drum
Steering: Rack & pinion
Wheelbase: 240.0cm 94.5in
Track F: 138.9cm 54.7in
Track R: 134.9cm 53.1in
Length: 394.5cm 155.3in
Width: 161.0cm 63.4in
Height: 141.0cm 55.5in
Kerb weight: 898.9kg 1980.0lb
Fuel: 41.3L 9.1gal 10.9galUS

4810 Volkswagen

Scirocco Fi
1977 Germany
102.0mph 164.1kmh
0-50mph 80.5kmh: 8.7secs
0-60mph 96.5kmh: 12.2secs
0-1/4 mile: 18.5secs
76.0bhp 56.7kW 77.0PS
@ 5500rpm
83.0lbft 112.5Nm @ 3000rpm
86.0bhp/ton 84.5bhp/tonne
47.9bhp/L 35.7kW/L 48.5PS/L
48.1ft/sec 14.7m/sec
17.1mph 27.5kmh/1000rpm
36.0mpg 30.0mpgUS 7.8L/100km
Petrol 4-stroke piston
1588cc 96.9cu in
In-line 4
Compression ratio: 8.2:1
Bore: 79.5mm 3.1in
Stroke: 80.0mm 3.1in
Valve type/No: Overhead 8
Transmission: Manual
No. of forward speeds: 4
Wheels driven: Front
Springs F/R: Coil/Coil
Brakes F/R: Disc/Drum
Steering: Rack & pinion
Wheelbase: 240.0cm 94.5in
Track F: 138.9cm 54.7in
Track R: 134.9cm 53.1in
Length: 395.5cm 155.7in
Width: 162.6cm 64.0in
Height: 130.8cm 51.5in
Kerb weight: 898.9kg 1980.0lb
Fuel: 41.3L 9.1gal 10.9galUS

4811 Volkswagen

Scirocco GTi
1977 Germany
115.0mph 185.0kmh
0-50mph 80.5kmh: 6.6secs
0-60mph 96.5kmh: 8.8secs
0-1/4 mile: 16.9secs
0-1km: 31.7secs
110.0bhp 82.0kW 111.5PS

@ 6100rpm
101.0lbft 136.9Nm @ 5000rpm
125.7bhp/ton 123.6bhp/tonne
69.3bhp/L 51.7kW/L 70.2PS/L
53.4ft/sec 16.3m/sec
18.4mph 29.6kmh/1000rpm
29.9mpg 24.9mpgUS 9.4L/100km
Petrol 4-stroke piston
1588cc 96.9cu in
In-line 4 fuel injection
Compression ratio: 9.5:1
Bore: 79.5mm 3.1in
Stroke: 80.0mm 3.1in
Valve type/No: Overhead 8
Transmission: Manual
No. of forward speeds: 4
Wheels driven: Front
Springs F/R: Coil/Coil
Brake system: PA
Brakes F/R: Disc/Drum
Steering: Rack & pinion
Wheelbase: 241.0cm 94.9in
Track F: 138.9cm 54.7in
Track R: 135.9cm 53.5in
Length: 387.6cm 152.6in
Width: 162.6cm 64.0in
Height: 131.1cm 51.6in
Ground clearance: 12.2cm 4.8in
Kerb weight: 889.8kg 1960.0lb
Fuel: 40.9L 9.0gal 10.8galUS

4812 Volkswagen
Beetle Convertible
1978 Germany
83.0mph 133.5kmh
0-50mph 80.5kmh: 11.3secs
0-60mph 96.5kmh: 17.0secs
0-1/4 mile: 20.4secs
48.0bhp 35.8kW 48.7PS
@ 4200rpm
73.0lbft 98.9Nm @ 2800rpm
50.7bhp/ton 49.9bhp/tonne
30.3bhp/L 22.6kW/L 30.7PS/L
31.7ft/sec 9.7m/sec
20.9mph 33.6kmh/1000rpm
27.6mpg 23.0mpgUS 10.2L/100km
Petrol 4-stroke piston
1584cc 96.6cu in
Flat 4
Compression ratio: 7.3:1
Bore: 85.5mm 3.4in
Stroke: 69.0mm 2.7in
Valve type/No: Overhead 8
Transmission: Manual
No. of forward speeds: 4
Wheels driven: Rear
Springs F/R: Coil/Torsion bar
Brakes F/R: Drum/Drum
Steering: Rack & pinion
Wheelbase: 242.1cm 95.3in
Track F: 139.4cm 54.9in
Track R: 134.9cm 53.1in
Length: 418.6cm 164.8in
Width: 158.5cm 62.4in
Height: 150.1cm 59.1in
Kerb weight: 962.5kg 2120.0lb
Fuel: 42.0L 9.2gal 11.1galUS

4813 Volkswagen
Golf GLS
1978 Germany
100.0mph 160.9kmh
0-50mph 80.5kmh: 7.7secs
0-60mph 96.5kmh: 11.4secs
0-1/4 mile: 18.4secs
0-1km: 34.6secs
70.0bhp 52.2kW 71.0PS
@ 5600rpm
76.0lbft 103.0Nm @ 3500rpm
88.7bhp/ton 87.2bhp/tonne
48.0bhp/L 35.8kW/L 48.7PS/L
45.0ft/sec 13.7m/sec
17.3mph 27.8kmh/1000rpm
28.2mpg 23.5mpgUS 10.0L/100km
Petrol 4-stroke piston
1457cc 88.9cu in
In-line 4 1 Carburettor
Compression ratio: 8.2:1
Bore: 79.5mm 3.1in
Stroke: 73.4mm 2.9in
Valve type/No: Overhead 8
Transmission: Manual
No. of forward speeds: 4
Wheels driven: Front
Springs F/R: Coil/Coil
Brake system: PA
Brakes F/R: Disc/Drum
Steering: Rack & pinion
Wheelbase: 240.0cm 94.5in
Track F: 138.9cm 54.7in
Track R: 134.6cm 53.0in
Length: 372.1cm 146.5in
Width: 161.3cm 63.5in
Height: 141.0cm 55.5in
Ground clearance: 13.5cm 5.3in
Kerb weight: 802.7kg 1768.0lb
Fuel: 40.9L 9.0gal 10.8galUS

4814 Volkswagen
Golf LD
1978 Germany
85.0mph 136.8kmh
0-50mph 80.5kmh: 12.4secs
0-60mph 96.5kmh: 18.2secs
0-1/4 mile: 21.0secs
0-1km: 40.0secs
50.0bhp 37.3kW 50.7PS
@ 5000rpm
56.5lbft 76.6Nm @ 3000rpm
58.4bhp/ton 57.4bhp/tonne
34.0bhp/L 25.3kW/L 34.5PS/L
41.8ft/sec 12.7m/sec
17.3mph 27.8kmh/1000rpm
46.0mpg 38.3mpgUS 6.1L/100km
Diesel 4-stroke piston
1471cc 89.7cu in
In-line 4 fuel injection
Compression ratio: 23.5:1
Bore: 80.0mm 3.1in
Stroke: 76.5mm 3.0in
Valve type/No: Overhead 8
Transmission: Manual
No. of forward speeds: 4
Wheels driven: Front
Springs F/R: Coil/Coil
Brake system: PA
Brakes F/R: Disc/Drum
Steering: Rack & pinion
Wheelbase: 240.0cm 94.5in
Track F: 138.9cm 54.7in
Track R: 134.6cm 53.0in
Length: 372.1cm 146.5in
Width: 161.3cm 63.5in
Height: 141.0cm 55.5in
Ground clearance: 13.5cm 5.3in
Kerb weight: 870.8kg 1918.0lb
Fuel: 45.5L 10.0gal 12.0galUS

4815 Volkswagen
Scirocco
1979 Germany
104.0mph 167.3kmh
0-50mph 80.5kmh: 7.3secs
0-60mph 96.5kmh: 10.4secs
0-1/4 mile: 18.0secs
71.0bhp 52.9kW 72.0PS
@ 5800rpm
73.0lbft 98.9Nm @ 3500rpm
81.6bhp/ton 80.2bhp/tonne
48.7bhp/L 36.3kW/L 49.4PS/L
46.6ft/sec 14.2m/sec
18.6mph 29.9kmh/1000rpm
33.6mpg 28.0mpgUS 8.4L/100km
Petrol 4-stroke piston
1457cc 88.9cu in
In-line 4 fuel injection
Compression ratio: 8.0:1
Bore: 79.5mm 3.1in
Stroke: 73.4mm 2.9in
Valve type/No: Overhead 8
Transmission: Manual
No. of forward speeds: 4
Wheels driven: Front
Springs F/R: Coil/Coil
Brakes F/R: Disc/Drum
Steering: Rack & pinion
Wheelbase: 240.0cm 94.5in
Track F: 138.9cm 54.7in
Track R: 134.9cm 53.1in
Length: 395.5cm 155.7in
Width: 162.6cm 64.0in
Height: 130.8cm 51.5in
Ground clearance: 12.4cm 4.9in
Kerb weight: 885.3kg 1950.0lb
Fuel: 42.0L 9.2gal 11.1galUS

4816 Volkswagen
Scirocco GLi
1979 Germany
115.0mph 185.0kmh
0-50mph 80.5kmh: 6.8secs
0-60mph 96.5kmh: 8.9secs
0-1/4 mile: 16.8secs
0-1km: 31.5secs
110.0bhp 82.0kW 111.5PS
@ 6100rpm
103.0lbft 139.6Nm @ 5000rpm
129.9bhp/ton 127.7bhp/tonne
69.3bhp/L 51.7kW/L 70.2PS/L
53.4ft/sec 16.3m/sec
17.4mph 28.0kmh/1000rpm
30.5mpg 25.4mpgUS 9.3L/100km
Petrol 4-stroke piston
1588cc 96.9cu in
In-line 4 fuel injection
Compression ratio: 9.5:1
Bore: 79.5mm 3.1in
Stroke: 80.0mm 3.1in
Valve type/No: Overhead 8
Transmission: Manual
No. of forward speeds: 4
Wheels driven: Front
Springs F/R: Coil/Coil
Brake system: PA
Brakes F/R: Disc/Drum
Steering: Rack & pinion
Wheelbase: 241.0cm 94.9in
Track F: 138.9cm 54.7in
Track R: 135.9cm 53.5in
Length: 387.6cm 152.6in
Width: 162.6cm 64.0in
Height: 131.1cm 51.6in
Ground clearance: 12.2cm 4.8in
Kerb weight: 861.2kg 1897.0lb
Fuel: 45.0L 9.9gal 11.9galUS

4817 Volkswagen
Scirocco GLS
1979 Germany
102.0mph 164.1kmh
0-50mph 80.5kmh: 7.3secs
0-60mph 96.5kmh: 10.4secs
0-1/4 mile: 17.5secs
0-1km: 33.0secs
85.0bhp 63.4kW 86.2PS
@ 5600rpm
92.0lbft 124.7Nm @ 3800rpm
105.8bhp/ton 104.0bhp/tonne
53.5bhp/L 39.9kW/L 54.3PS/L
49.0ft/sec 14.9m/sec
17.5mph 28.2kmh/1000rpm
29.4mpg 24.5mpgUS 9.6L/100km
Petrol 4-stroke piston
1588cc 96.9cu in
In-line 4 1 Carburettor
Compression ratio: 8.2:1
Bore: 79.5mm 3.1in
Stroke: 80.0mm 3.1in
Valve type/No: Overhead 8
Transmission: Manual
No. of forward speeds: 4
Wheels driven: Front
Springs F/R: Coil/Coil
Brake system: PA
Brakes F/R: Disc/Drum
Steering: Rack & pinion
Wheelbase: 241.0cm 94.9in
Track F: 138.9cm 54.7in
Track R: 135.9cm 53.5in
Length: 387.6cm 152.6in
Width: 162.6cm 64.0in
Height: 131.1cm 51.6in
Ground clearance: 12.2cm 4.8in
Kerb weight: 817.2kg 1800.0lb
Fuel: 45.0L 9.9gal 11.9galUS

4818 Volkswagen
Dasher Diesel
1980 Germany
94.0mph 151.2kmh
0-50mph 80.5kmh: 8.6secs
0-60mph 96.5kmh: 19.4secs
0-1/4 mile: 22.0secs
48.0bhp 35.8kW 48.7PS
@ 5000rpm
56.0lbft 75.9Nm @ 3000rpm
46.1bhp/ton 45.4bhp/tonne
32.6bhp/L 24.3kW/L 33.1PS/L
43.8ft/sec 13.3m/sec
18.5mph 29.8kmh/1000rpm
48.6mpg 40.5mpgUS 5.8L/100km
Diesel 4-stroke piston
1471cc 89.7cu in
In-line 4 fuel injection
Compression ratio: 23.5:1
Bore: 76.5mm 3.0in
Stroke: 80.0mm 3.1in
Valve type/No: Overhead 8
Transmission: Manual
No. of forward speeds: 4
Wheels driven: Front
Springs F/R: Coil/Coil
Brake system: PA
Brakes F/R: Disc/Drum
Steering: Rack & pinion
Wheelbase: 246.9cm 97.2in
Track F: 133.9cm 52.7in
Track R: 134.9cm 53.1in
Length: 439.7cm 173.1in
Width: 161.5cm 63.6in
Height: 135.9cm 53.5in
Kerb weight: 1057.8kg 2330.0lb
Fuel: 45.0L 9.9gal 11.9galUS

4819 Volkswagen
Jetta
1980 Germany
100.0mph 160.9kmh
0-60mph 96.5kmh: 12.1secs
0-1/4 mile: 18.4secs
76.0bhp 56.7kW 77.0PS
@ 5500rpm
84.0lbft 113.8Nm @ 3200rpm
79.0bhp/ton 77.7bhp/tonne
47.9bhp/L 35.7kW/L 48.5PS/L
48.1ft/sec 14.7m/sec
22.2mph 35.7kmh/1000rpm
33.0mpg 27.5mpgUS 8.6L/100km
Petrol 4-stroke piston
1588cc 96.9cu in
In-line 4 fuel injection
Compression ratio: 8.2:1
Bore: 79.5mm 3.1in
Stroke: 80.0mm 3.1in
Valve type/No: Overhead 8
Transmission: Manual
No. of forward speeds: 5
Wheels driven: Front
Springs F/R: Coil/Coil
Brake system: PA
Brakes F/R: Disc/Drum
Steering: Rack & pinion
Wheelbase: 240.0cm 94.5in
Track F: 138.9cm 54.7in
Track R: 135.9cm 53.5in
Length: 432.6cm 170.3in
Width: 161.0cm 63.4in
Height: 141.0cm 55.5in
Ground clearance: 12.4cm 4.9in
Kerb weight: 978.4kg 2155.0lb
Fuel: 40.1L 8.8gal 10.6galUS

4820 Volkswagen
Jetta GLS
1980 Germany
101.0mph 162.5kmh
0-50mph 80.5kmh: 8.8secs
0-60mph 96.5kmh: 13.0secs
0-1/4 mile: 18.3secs
0-1km: 34.4secs
70.0bhp 52.2kW 71.0PS
@ 5600rpm
81.0lbft 109.8Nm @ 3500rpm
86.1bhp/ton 84.7bhp/tonne
48.0bhp/L 35.8kW/L 48.7PS/L
45.0ft/sec 13.7m/sec
17.1mph 27.5kmh/1000rpm
24.0mpg 20.0mpgUS 11.8L/100km
Petrol 4-stroke piston
1457cc 88.9cu in
In-line 4 1 Carburettor
Compression ratio: 8.2:1
Bore: 79.5mm 3.1in
Stroke: 73.4mm 2.9in
Valve type/No: Overhead 8
Transmission: Manual
No. of forward speeds: 4
Wheels driven: Front
Springs F/R: Coil/Coil
Brake system: PA
Brakes F/R: Disc/Drum
Steering: Rack & pinion
Wheelbase: 239.8cm 94.4in
Track F: 138.9cm 54.7in
Track R: 135.9cm 53.5in
Length: 419.1cm 165.0in
Width: 161.0cm 63.4in
Height: 141.0cm 55.5in
Ground clearance: 13.5cm 5.3in
Kerb weight: 826.3kg 1820.0lb
Fuel: 40.9L 9.0gal 10.8galUS

4821 Volkswagen
Rabbit
1980 Germany
0-60mph 96.5kmh: 12.1secs

0-1/4 mile: 18.9secs
71.0bhp 52.9kW 72.0PS
@ 5800rpm
73.0lbft 98.9Nm @ 3500rpm
76.1bhp/ton 74.8bhp/tonne
48.7bhp/L 36.3kW/L 49.4PS/L
46.6ft/sec 14.2m/sec
30.0mpg 25.0mpgUS 9.4L/100km
Petrol 4-stroke piston
1457cc 88.9cu in
In-line 4 fuel injection
Compression ratio: 8.0:1
Bore: 79.5mm 3.1in
Stroke: 73.4mm 2.9in
Valve type/No: Overhead 8
Transmission: Manual
No. of forward speeds: 4
Wheels driven: Front
Brakes F/R: Disc/Drum
Wheelbase: 239.8cm 94.4in
Track F: 138.9cm 54.7in
Track R: 135.9cm 53.5in
Length: 394.5cm 155.3in
Width: 161.0cm 63.4in
Height: 141.0cm 55.5in
Kerb weight: 948.9kg 2090.0lb
Fuel: 41.3L 9.1gal 10.9galUS

4822 Volkswagen

Scirocco
1980 Germany
108.0mph 173.8kmh
0-50mph 80.5kmh: 7.7secs
0-60mph 96.5kmh: 11.2secs
0-1/4 mile: 18.4secs
76.0bhp 56.7kW 77.0PS
@ 5500rpm
83.0lbft 112.5Nm @ 3200rpm
83.4bhp/ton 82.1bhp/tonne
47.9bhp/L 35.7kW/L 48.5PS/L
48.1ft/sec 14.7m/sec
24.5mph 39.4kmh/1000rpm
29.4mpg 24.5mpgUS 9.6L/100km
Petrol 4-stroke piston
1588cc 96.9cu in
In-line 4 fuel injection
Compression ratio: 8.0:1
Bore: 79.5mm 3.1in
Stroke: 80.0mm 3.1in
Valve type/No: Overhead 8
Transmission: Manual
No. of forward speeds: 5
Wheels driven: Front
Springs F/R: Coil/Coil
Brake system: PA
Brakes F/R: Disc/Drum
Steering: Rack & pinion
Wheelbase: 240.0cm 94.5in
Track F: 138.9cm 54.7in
Track R: 135.9cm 53.5in
Length: 395.5cm 155.7in
Width: 162.3cm 63.9in
Height: 130.8cm 51.5in
Kerb weight: 926.2kg 2040.0lb
Fuel: 40.1L 8.8gal 10.6galUS

4823 Volkswagen

Vanagon
1980 Germany
88.0mph 141.6kmh
0-50mph 80.5kmh: 13.7secs
0-60mph 96.5kmh: 21.2secs
0-1/4 mile: 21.5secs
67.0bhp 50.0kW 67.9PS
@ 4200rpm
101.0lbft 136.9Nm @ 3000rpm
45.6bhp/ton 44.9bhp/tonne
34.0bhp/L 25.4kW/L 34.5PS/L
32.7ft/sec 9.9m/sec
19.0mph 30.6kmh/1000rpm
19.8mpg 16.5mpgUS 14.3L/100km
Petrol 4-stroke piston
1970cc 120.2cu in
Flat 4 fuel injection
Compression ratio: 7.3:1
Bore: 94.0mm 3.7in
Stroke: 71.0mm 2.8in
Valve type/No: Overhead 8
Transmission: Manual
No. of forward speeds: 4
Wheels driven: Rear
Springs F/R: Coil/Coil
Brake system: PA
Brakes F/R: Disc/Drum
Steering: Rack & pinion
Wheelbase: 245.9cm 96.8in
Track F: 157.0cm 61.8in
Track R: 157.0cm 61.8in
Length: 456.9cm 179.9in
Width: 184.4cm 72.6in
Height: 196.1cm 77.2in
Ground clearance: 21.6cm 8.5in
Kerb weight: 1493.7kg 3290.0lb
Fuel: 60.2L 13.2gal 15.9galUS

4824 Volkswagen

Golf 1300 LS
1981 Germany
90.0mph 144.8kmh
0-50mph 80.5kmh: 10.4secs
0-60mph 96.5kmh: 14.7secs
0-1/4 mile: 19.5secs
0-1km: 37.3secs
60.0bhp 44.7kW 60.8PS
@ 5600rpm
69.9lbft 94.7Nm @ 3500rpm
73.4bhp/ton 72.1bhp/tonne
47.2bhp/L 35.2kW/L 47.8PS/L
44.0ft/sec 13.4m/sec
16.1mph 25.9kmh/1000rpm
31.0mpg 25.8mpgUS 9.1L/100km
Petrol 4-stroke piston
1272cc 77.6cu in
In-line 4 1 Carburettor
Compression ratio: 8.2:1
Bore: 75.0mm 2.9in
Stroke: 72.0mm 2.8in
Valve type/No: Overhead 8
Transmission: Manual
No. of forward speeds: 4
Wheels driven: Front
Springs F/R: Coil/Coil
Brake system: PA
Brakes F/R: Disc/Drum
Steering: Rack & pinion
Wheelbase: 239.8cm 94.4in
Track F: 139.7cm 55.0in
Track R: 135.9cm 53.5in
Length: 386.1cm 152.0in
Width: 161.0cm 63.4in
Height: 141.0cm 55.5in
Ground clearance: 13.5cm 5.3in
Kerb weight: 831.7kg 1832.0lb
Fuel: 40.5L 8.9gal 10.7galUS

4825 Volkswagen

Passat CL Formel E
1981 Germany
104.0mph 167.3kmh
0-50mph 80.5kmh: 8.3secs
0-60mph 96.5kmh: 11.9secs
0-1/4 mile: 18.7secs
0-1km: 34.4secs
75.0bhp 55.9kW 76.0PS
@ 5600rpm
89.0lbft 120.6Nm @ 3200rpm
76.9bhp/ton 75.6bhp/tonne
47.2bhp/L 35.2kW/L 47.9PS/L
49.0ft/sec 14.9m/sec
22.4mph 36.0kmh/1000rpm
30.7mpg 25.6mpgUS 9.2L/100km
Petrol 4-stroke piston
1588cc 96.9cu in
In-line 4 1 Carburettor
Compression ratio: 8.2:1
Bore: 79.5mm 3.1in
Stroke: 80.0mm 3.1in
Valve type/No: Overhead 8
Transmission: Manual
No. of forward speeds: 5
Wheels driven: Front
Springs F/R: Coil/Coil
Brake system: PA
Brakes F/R: Disc/Drum
Steering: Rack & pinion
Wheelbase: 255.0cm 100.4in
Track F: 140.0cm 55.1in
Track R: 140.7cm 55.4in
Length: 443.5cm 174.6in
Width: 168.4cm 66.3in
Height: 138.4cm 54.5in
Ground clearance: 15.2cm 6.0in
Kerb weight: 992.0kg 2185.0lb
Fuel: 60.1L 13.2gal 15.9galUS

4826 Volkswagen

Passat GL 5S Estate
1981 Germany
113.0mph 181.8kmh
0-50mph 80.5kmh: 8.2secs
0-60mph 96.5kmh: 11.6secs
0-1/4 mile: 17.9secs
0-1km: 33.1secs
115.0bhp 85.8kW 116.6PS
@ 5900rpm
114.0lbft 154.5Nm @ 3700rpm
108.0bhp/ton 106.2bhp/tonne
59.9bhp/L 44.6kW/L 60.7PS/L
50.0ft/sec 15.2m/sec
25.9mph 41.7kmh/1000rpm
27.8mpg 23.1mpgUS 10.2L/100km
Petrol 4-stroke piston
1921cc 117.2cu in
In-line 5 1 Carburettor
Compression ratio: 10.0:1
Bore: 79.5mm 3.1in
Stroke: 77.4mm 3.0in
Valve type/No: Overhead 10
Transmission: Manual
No. of forward speeds: 5
Wheels driven: Front
Springs F/R: Coil/Coil
Brake system: PA
Brakes F/R: Disc/Drum
Steering: Rack & pinion PA
Wheelbase: 255.0cm 100.4in
Track F: 140.0cm 55.1in
Track R: 140.7cm 55.4in
Length: 453.9cm 178.7in
Width: 168.4cm 66.3in
Height: 136.9cm 53.9in
Ground clearance: 15.2cm 6.0in
Kerb weight: 1082.8kg 2385.0lb
Fuel: 60.1L 13.2gal 15.9galUS

4827 Volkswagen

Rabbit
1981 Germany
0-60mph 96.5kmh: 12.6secs
0-1/4 mile: 18.7secs
74.0bhp 55.2kW 75.0PS
@ 5000rpm
90.0lbft 122.0Nm @ 3000rpm
78.2bhp/ton 76.9bhp/tonne
43.1bhp/L 32.2kW/L 43.8PS/L
47.2ft/sec 14.4m/sec
34.8mpg 29.0mpgUS 8.1L/100km
Petrol 4-stroke piston
1715cc 104.6cu in
In-line 4 fuel injection
Compression ratio: 8.2:1
Bore: 79.5mm 3.1in
Stroke: 86.4mm 3.4in
Valve type/No: Overhead 8
Transmission: Manual
No. of forward speeds: 4
Wheels driven: Front
Brakes F/R: Disc/Drum
Wheelbase: 240.0cm 94.5in
Track F: 138.9cm 54.7in
Track R: 134.9cm 53.1in
Length: 394.5cm 155.3in
Width: 161.0cm 63.4in
Height: 141.0cm 55.5in
Kerb weight: 962.5kg 2120.0lb
Fuel: 40.1L 8.8gal 10.6galUS

4828 Volkswagen

Rabbit Convertible
1981 Germany
95.0mph 152.9kmh
0-50mph 80.5kmh: 9.3secs
0-60mph 96.5kmh: 14.0secs
0-1/4 mile: 19.4secs
76.0bhp 56.7kW 77.0PS
@ 5500rpm
83.0lbft 112.5Nm @ 3200rpm
75.0bhp/ton 73.7bhp/tonne
47.9bhp/L 35.7kW/L 48.5PS/L
48.1ft/sec 14.7m/sec
23.1mph 37.2kmh/1000rpm
32.4mpg 27.0mpgUS 8.7L/100km
Petrol 4-stroke piston
1588cc 96.9cu in
In-line 4 fuel injection
Compression ratio: 8.2:1
Bore: 79.5mm 3.1in
Stroke: 80.0mm 3.1in
Valve type/No: Overhead 8
Transmission: Manual
No. of forward speeds: 5
Wheels driven: Front
Springs F/R: Coil/Coil
Brake system: PA
Brakes F/R: Disc/Drum
Steering: Rack & pinion
Wheelbase: 240.0cm 94.5in
Track F: 138.9cm 54.7in
Track R: 135.9cm 53.5in
Length: 394.5cm 155.3in
Width: 161.0cm 63.4in
Height: 141.2cm 55.6in
Ground clearance: 12.4cm 4.9in
Kerb weight: 1030.6kg 2270.0lb
Fuel: 40.1L 8.8gal 10.6galUS

4829 Volkswagen

Rabbit Diesel
1981 Germany
79.0mph 127.1kmh
0-50mph 80.5kmh: 15.3secs
0-60mph 96.5kmh: 22.9secs
0-1/4 mile: 22.4secs
48.0bhp 35.8kW 48.7PS
@ 5000rpm
57.0lbft 77.2Nm @ 3000rpm
48.0bhp/ton 47.2bhp/tonne
32.6bhp/L 24.3kW/L 33.1PS/L
43.8ft/sec 13.3m/sec
21.7mph 34.9kmh/1000rpm
51.6mpg 43.0mpgUS 5.5L/100km
Diesel 4-stroke piston
1471cc 89.7cu in
In-line 4 fuel injection
Compression ratio: 23.0:1
Bore: 76.5mm 3.0in
Stroke: 80.0mm 3.1in
Valve type/No: Overhead 8
Transmission: Manual
No. of forward speeds: 5
Wheels driven: Front
Springs F/R: Coil/Coil
Brake system: PA
Brakes F/R: Disc/Drum
Steering: Rack & pinion
Wheelbase: 240.0cm 94.5in
Track F: 138.9cm 54.7in
Track R: 134.9cm 53.1in
Length: 394.5cm 155.3in
Width: 161.0cm 63.4in
Height: 141.0cm 55.5in
Kerb weight: 1017.0kg 2240.0lb
Fuel: 40.1L 8.8gal 10.6galUS

4830 Volkswagen

Scirocco GT-3 Davey
1981 Germany
129.0mph 207.6kmh
0-50mph 80.5kmh: 5.2secs
0-60mph 96.5kmh: 6.7secs
0-1/4 mile: 15.1secs
185.0bhp 137.9kW 187.6PS
@ 8500rpm
166.0lbft 224.9Nm @ 6500rpm
212.5bhp/ton 209.0bhp/tonne
116.5bhp/L 86.9kW/L 118.1PS/L
74.4ft/sec 22.7m/sec
14.9mph 24.0kmh/1000rpm
Petrol 4-stroke piston
1588cc 96.9cu in
In-line 4 2 Carburettor
Compression ratio: 12.1:1
Bore: 79.5mm 3.1in
Stroke: 80.0mm 3.1in
Valve type/No: Overhead 8
Transmission: Manual
No. of forward speeds: 5
Wheels driven: Front
Springs F/R: Coil/Coil
Brake system: PA
Brakes F/R: Disc/Disc
Steering: Rack & pinion
Wheelbase: 240.0cm 94.5in
Track F: 146.6cm 57.7in
Track R: 143.5cm 56.5in
Length: 395.5cm 155.7in
Width: 182.9cm 72.0in
Height: 121.9cm 48.0in
Ground clearance: 7.6cm 3.0in
Kerb weight: 885.3kg 1950.0lb
Fuel: 40.1L 8.8gal 10.6galUS

4831 Volkswagen

Scirocco S
1981 Germany
109.0mph 175.4kmh
0-50mph 80.5kmh: 7.9secs
0-60mph 96.5kmh: 11.6secs
0-1/4 mile: 18.2secs
74.0bhp 55.2kW 75.0PS
@ 5000rpm
90.0lbft 122.0Nm @ 3000rpm
79.1bhp/ton 77.8bhp/tonne
43.1bhp/L 32.2kW/L 43.8PS/L
47.2ft/sec 14.4m/sec
23.1mph 37.2kmh/1000rpm

Petrol 4-stroke piston
1715cc 104.6cu in
In-line 4 fuel injection
Compression ratio: 8.2:1
Bore: 79.5mm 3.1in
Stroke: 86.4mm 3.4in
Valve type/No: Overhead 8
Transmission: Manual
No. of forward speeds: 5
Wheels driven: Front
Brake system: PA
Brakes F/R: Disc/Drum
Track F: 138.9cm 54.7in
Track R: 135.9cm 53.5in
Width: 162.3cm 63.9in
Height: 130.8cm 51.5in
Ground clearance: 11.7cm 4.6in
Kerb weight: 951.1kg 2095.0lb

4832 Volkswagen

Golf GTi 1800
1982 Germany
116.0mph 186.6kmh
0-50mph 80.5kmh: 5.6secs
0-60mph 96.5kmh: 8.3secs
0-1/4 mile: 16.2secs
0-1km: 30.2secs
112.0bhp 83.5kW 113.5PS
@ 5800rpm
109.0lbft 147.7Nm @ 3500rpm
130.6bhp/ton 128.4bhp/tonne
62.9bhp/L 46.9kW/L 63.8PS/L
54.8ft/sec 16.7m/sec
19.8mph 31.9kmh/1000rpm
28.5mpg 23.7mpgUS 9.9L/100km
Petrol 4-stroke piston
1781cc 108.7cu in
In-line 4 fuel injection
Compression ratio: 10.0:1
Bore: 81.0mm 3.2in
Stroke: 86.4mm 3.4in
Valve type/No: Overhead 8
Transmission: Manual
No. of forward speeds: 5
Wheels driven: Front
Springs F/R: Coil/Coil
Brake system: PA
Brakes F/R: Disc/Drum
Steering: Rack & pinion
Wheelbase: 239.8cm 94.4in
Track F: 139.7cm 55.0in
Track R: 135.9cm 53.5in
Length: 386.1cm 152.0in
Width: 161.0cm 63.4in
Height: 141.0cm 55.5in
Ground clearance: 13.5cm 5.3in
Kerb weight: 872.1kg 1921.0lb
Fuel: 40.9L 9.0gal 10.8galUS

4833 Volkswagen

Polo C
1982 Germany
86.0mph 138.4kmh
0-50mph 80.5kmh: 11.4secs
0-60mph 96.5kmh: 17.9secs
0-1/4 mile: 20.9secs
0-1km: 39.7secs
40.0bhp 29.8kW 40.5PS
@ 3500rpm
54.4lbft 73.7Nm @ 2700rpm
56.7bhp/ton 55.8bhp/tonne
38.3bhp/L 28.6kW/L 38.9PS/L
22.6ft/sec 6.9m/sec
16.9mph 27.2kmh/1000rpm
35.0mpg 29.1mpgUS 8.1L/100km
Petrol 4-stroke piston
1043cc 63.6cu in
In-line 4 1 Carburettor
Compression ratio: 9.5:1
Bore: 75.0mm 2.9in
Stroke: 59.0mm 2.3in
Valve type/No: Overhead 8
Transmission: Manual
No. of forward speeds: 4
Wheels driven: Front
Springs F/R: Coil/Coil
Brakes F/R: Disc/Drum
Steering: Rack & pinion
Wheelbase: 233.4cm 91.9in
Track F: 130.6cm 51.4in
Track R: 133.1cm 52.4in
Length: 365.5cm 143.9in
Width: 158.0cm 62.2in
Height: 135.4cm 53.3in
Ground clearance: 17.8cm 7.0in
Kerb weight: 717.3kg 1580.0lb
Fuel: 36.4L 8.0gal 9.6galUS

4834 Volkswagen

Polo C Formel E
1982 Germany
91.0mph 146.4kmh
0-50mph 80.5kmh: 10.9secs
0-60mph 96.5kmh: 16.7secs
0-1/4 mile: 20.1secs
0-1km: 38.2secs
50.0bhp 37.3kW 50.7PS
@ 5600rpm
60.2lbft 81.6Nm @ 3200rpm
69.9bhp/ton 68.7bhp/tonne
45.7bhp/L 34.1kW/L 46.4PS/L
44.0ft/sec 13.4m/sec
19.6mph 31.5kmh/1000rpm
37.8mpg 31.5mpgUS 7.5L/100km
Petrol 4-stroke piston
1093cc 66.7cu in
In-line 4 1 Carburettor
Compression ratio: 9.7:1
Bore: 69.5mm 2.7in
Stroke: 72.0mm 2.8in
Valve type/No: Overhead 8
Transmission: Manual
No. of forward speeds: 4
Wheels driven: Front
Springs F/R: Coil/Coil
Brakes F/R: Disc/Drum
Steering: Rack & pinion
Wheelbase: 233.4cm 91.9in
Track F: 130.6cm 51.4in
Track R: 133.1cm 52.4in
Length: 365.5cm 143.9in
Width: 158.0cm 62.2in
Height: 135.4cm 53.3in
Ground clearance: 17.8cm 7.0in
Kerb weight: 727.8kg 1603.0lb
Fuel: 36.4L 8.0gal 9.6galUS

4835 Volkswagen

Quantum
1982 Germany
103.0mph 165.7kmh
0-60mph 96.5kmh: 13.0secs
0-1/4 mile: 19.0secs
74.0bhp 55.2kW 75.0PS
@ 5000rpm
90.0lbft 122.0Nm @ 3000rpm
66.2bhp/ton 65.1bhp/tonne
43.1bhp/L 32.2kW/L 43.8PS/L
47.2ft/sec 14.4m/sec
25.9mph 41.7kmh/1000rpm
34.8mpg 29.0mpgUS 8.1L/100km
Petrol 4-stroke piston
1715cc 104.6cu in
In-line 4 fuel injection
Compression ratio: 8.2:1
Bore: 79.5mm 3.1in
Stroke: 86.4mm 3.4in
Valve type/No: Overhead 8
Transmission: Manual
No. of forward speeds: 5
Wheels driven: Front
Springs F/R: Coil/Coil
Brake system: PA
Brakes F/R: Disc/Drum
Steering: Rack & pinion PA
Wheelbase: 255.0cm 100.4in
Track F: 141.5cm 55.7in
Track R: 142.2cm 56.0in
Length: 452.4cm 178.1in
Width: 169.9cm 66.9in
Height: 140.0cm 55.1in
Ground clearance: 12.7cm 5.0in
Kerb weight: 1137.3kg 2505.0lb
Fuel: 59.8L 13.1gal 15.8galUS

4836 Volkswagen

Santana GX5
1982 Germany
116.0mph 186.6kmh
0-50mph 80.5kmh: 7.9secs
0-60mph 96.5kmh: 10.8secs
0-1/4 mile: 18.0secs
0-1km: 33.8secs
115.0bhp 85.8kW 116.6PS
@ 5900rpm
113.0lbft 153.1Nm @ 3700rpm
105.4bhp/ton 103.7bhp/tonne
59.9bhp/L 44.6kW/L 60.7PS/L
50.0ft/sec 15.2m/sec
25.4mph 40.9kmh/1000rpm
27.6mpg 23.0mpgUS 10.2L/100km
Petrol 4-stroke piston
1921cc 117.2cu in
In-line 5 1 Carburettor
Compression ratio: 10.0:1
Bore: 79.5mm 3.1in
Stroke: 77.4mm 3.0in
Valve type/No: Overhead 10
Transmission: Manual
No. of forward speeds: 5
Wheels driven: Front
Springs F/R: Coil/Coil
Brake system: PA
Brakes F/R: Disc/Drum
Steering: Rack & pinion PA
Wheelbase: 255.0cm 100.4in
Track F: 141.5cm 55.7in
Track R: 142.2cm 56.0in
Length: 454.4cm 178.9in
Width: 169.4cm 66.7in
Height: 137.4cm 54.1in
Ground clearance: 12.4cm 4.9in
Kerb weight: 1109.1kg 2443.0lb
Fuel: 59.1L 13.0gal 15.6galUS

4837 Volkswagen

Scirocco GL
1982 Germany
110.0mph 177.0kmh
0-50mph 80.5kmh: 7.3secs
0-60mph 96.5kmh: 10.3secs
0-1/4 mile: 17.6secs
0-1km: 33.0secs
85.0bhp 63.4kW 86.2PS
@ 5600rpm
93.0lbft 126.0Nm @ 3200rpm
94.8bhp/ton 93.2bhp/tonne
53.5bhp/L 39.9kW/L 54.3PS/L
49.0ft/sec 14.9m/sec
23.6mph 38.0kmh/1000rpm
29.2mpg 24.3mpgUS 9.7L/100km
Petrol 4-stroke piston
1588cc 96.9cu in
In-line 4 1 Carburettor
Compression ratio: 8.2:1
Bore: 79.5mm 3.1in
Stroke: 80.0mm 3.1in
Valve type/No: Overhead 8
Transmission: Manual
No. of forward speeds: 5
Wheels driven: Front
Springs F/R: Coil/Coil
Brake system: PA
Brakes F/R: Disc/Drum
Steering: Rack & pinion
Wheelbase: 239.8cm 94.4in
Track F: 138.9cm 54.7in
Track R: 135.6cm 53.4in
Length: 404.9cm 159.4in
Width: 162.3cm 63.9in
Height: 130.6cm 51.4in
Ground clearance: 10.9cm 4.3in
Kerb weight: 912.1kg 2009.0lb
Fuel: 40.5L 8.9gal 10.7galUS

4838 Volkswagen

Quantum GL5
1983 Germany
105.0mph 168.9kmh
0-50mph 80.5kmh: 8.8secs
0-60mph 96.5kmh: 12.6secs
0-1/4 mile: 18.8secs
100.0bhp 74.6kW 101.4PS
@ 5100rpm
112.0lbft 151.8Nm @ 3000rpm
84.2bhp/ton 82.8bhp/tonne
46.6bhp/L 34.8kW/L 47.3PS/L
48.2ft/sec 14.7m/sec
20.3mph 32.7kmh/1000rpm
25.2mpg 21.0mpgUS 11.2L/100km
Petrol 4-stroke piston
2144cc 130.8cu in
In-line 5 fuel injection
Compression ratio: 8.2:1
Bore: 79.5mm 3.1in
Stroke: 86.4mm 3.4in
Valve type/No: Overhead 10
Transmission: Automatic
No. of forward speeds: 3
Wheels driven: Front
Springs F/R: Coil/Coil
Brake system: PA
Brakes F/R: Disc/Drum
Steering: Rack & pinion PA
Wheelbase: 255.0cm 100.4in
Track F: 141.5cm 55.7in
Track R: 142.2cm 56.0in
Length: 457.7cm 180.2in
Width: 169.9cm 66.9in
Height: 140.0cm 55.1in
Kerb weight: 1207.6kg 2660.0lb
Fuel: 59.8L 13.1gal 15.8galUS

4839 Volkswagen

Rabbit GTi
1983 Germany
107.0mph 172.2kmh
0-50mph 80.5kmh: 7.4secs
0-60mph 96.5kmh: 10.6secs
0-1/4 mile: 17.7secs
90.0bhp 67.1kW 91.2PS
@ 5500rpm
105.0lbft 142.3Nm @ 3250rpm
97.4bhp/ton 95.8bhp/tonne
50.6bhp/L 37.7kW/L 51.3PS/L
51.9ft/sec 15.8m/sec
18.2mph 29.3kmh/1000rpm
34.8mpg 29.0mpgUS 8.1L/100km
Petrol 4-stroke piston
1780cc 108.6cu in
In-line 4 fuel injection
Compression ratio: 8.5:1
Bore: 81.0mm 3.2in
Stroke: 86.4mm 3.4in
Valve type/No: Overhead 8
Transmission: Manual
No. of forward speeds: 5
Wheels driven: Front
Springs F/R: Coil/Coil
Brake system: PA
Brakes F/R: Disc/Drum
Steering: Rack & pinion
Wheelbase: 240.0cm 94.5in
Track F: 138.9cm 54.7in
Track R: 134.9cm 53.1in
Length: 394.5cm 155.3in
Width: 161.0cm 63.4in
Height: 141.0cm 55.5in
Kerb weight: 939.8kg 2070.0lb
Fuel: 37.8L 8.3gal 10.0galUS

4840 Volkswagen

Scirocco
1983 Germany
104.0mph 167.3kmh
0-50mph 80.5kmh: 8.1secs
0-60mph 96.5kmh: 11.7secs
0-1/4 mile: 18.3secs
74.0bhp 55.2kW 75.0PS
@ 5000rpm
90.0lbft 122.0Nm @ 3000rpm
75.9bhp/ton 74.6bhp/tonne
43.1bhp/L 32.2kW/L 43.8PS/L
47.2ft/sec 14.4m/sec
22.6mph 36.4kmh/1000rpm
34.8mpg 29.0mpgUS 8.1L/100km
Petrol 4-stroke piston
1715cc 104.6cu in
In-line 4 fuel injection
Compression ratio: 8.2:1
Bore: 79.5mm 3.1in
Stroke: 86.4mm 3.4in
Valve type/No: Overhead 8
Transmission: Manual
No. of forward speeds: 5
Wheels driven: Front
Springs F/R: Coil/Coil
Brake system: PA
Brakes F/R: Disc/Drum
Steering: Rack & pinion
Wheelbase: 240.0cm 94.5in
Track F: 138.9cm 54.7in
Track R: 135.9cm 53.5in
Length: 426.2cm 167.8in
Width: 161.0cm 63.4in
Height: 130.6cm 51.4in
Kerb weight: 992.0kg 2185.0lb
Fuel: 40.1L 8.8gal 10.6galUS

4841 Volkswagen

Scirocco GTi
1983 Germany
121.0mph 194.7kmh
0-50mph 80.5kmh: 6.3secs
0-60mph 96.5kmh: 9.0secs
0-1/4 mile: 16.9secs
0-1km: 31.4secs
112.0bhp 83.5kW 113.5PS
@ 5800rpm
109.0lbft 147.7Nm @ 3500rpm
119.9bhp/ton 117.9bhp/tonne
62.9bhp/L 46.9kW/L 63.8PS/L
54.6ft/sec 16.6m/sec
18.7mph 30.1kmh/1000rpm
25.5mpg 21.2mpgUS 11.1L/100km
Petrol 4-stroke piston
1781cc 108.7cu in
In-line 4 fuel injection
Compression ratio: 10.0:1
Bore: 81.0mm 3.2in

Stroke: 86.0mm 3.4in
Valve type/No: Overhead 8
Transmission: Manual
No. of forward speeds: 5
Wheels driven: Front
Springs F/R: Coil/Coil
Brake system: PA
Brakes F/R: Disc/Drum
Steering: Rack & pinion
Wheelbase: 239.8cm 94.4in
Track F: 138.9cm 54.7in
Track R: 135.6cm 53.4in
Length: 404.9cm 159.4in
Width: 162.3cm 63.9in
Height: 130.6cm 51.4in
Ground clearance: 10.9cm 4.3in
Kerb weight: 950.2kg 2093.0lb
Fuel: 40.9L 9.0gal 10.8galUS

4842 Volkswagen

Vanagon Wasserboxer
1983 Germany
88.0mph 141.6kmh
0-50mph 80.5kmh: 12.5secs
0-60mph 96.5kmh: 18.3secs
0-1/4 mile: 20.9secs
82.0bhp 61.1kW 83.1PS
@ 4800rpm
106.0lbft 143.6Nm @ 2600rpm
54.0bhp/ton 53.1bhp/tonne
42.8bhp/L 31.9kW/L 43.4PS/L
36.3ft/sec 11.0m/sec
18.2mph 29.3kmh/1000rpm
23.4mpg 19.5mpgUS 12.1L/100km
Petrol 4-stroke piston
1915cc 116.8cu in
Flat 4 fuel injection
Compression ratio: 8.6:1
Bore: 94.0mm 3.7in
Stroke: 69.0mm 2.7in
Valve type/No: Overhead 8
Transmission: Manual
No. of forward speeds: 4
Wheels driven: Rear
Springs F/R: Coil/Coil
Brake system: PA
Brakes F/R: Disc/Drum
Steering: Rack & pinion
Wheelbase: 246.1cm 96.9in
Track F: 158.2cm 62.3in
Track R: 157.0cm 61.8in
Length: 456.9cm 179.9in
Width: 184.4cm 72.6in
Height: 196.1cm 77.2in
Kerb weight: 1543.6kg 3400.0lb
Fuel: 60.2L 13.2gal 15.9galUS

4843 Volkswagen

Jetta GLi
1984 Germany
112.0mph 180.2kmh
0-50mph 80.5kmh: 7.7secs
0-60mph 96.5kmh: 11.2secs
0-1/4 mile: 18.0secs
90.0bhp 67.1kW 91.2PS
@ 5500rpm
100.0lbft 135.5Nm @ 3000rpm
90.0bhp/ton 88.5bhp/tonne
50.6bhp/L 37.7kW/L 51.3PS/L
51.9ft/sec 15.8m/sec
18.5mph 29.8kmh/1000rpm
30.0mpg 25.0mpgUS 9.4L/100km
Petrol 4-stroke piston
1780cc 108.6cu in
In-line 4 fuel injection
Compression ratio: 8.5:1
Bore: 81.0mm 3.2in
Stroke: 86.4mm 3.4in
Valve type/No: Overhead 8
Transmission: Manual
No. of forward speeds: 5
Wheels driven: Front
Springs F/R: Coil/Coil
Brake system: PA
Brakes F/R: Disc/Drum
Steering: Rack & pinion
Wheelbase: 240.0cm 94.5in
Track F: 138.9cm 54.7in
Track R: 135.9cm 53.5in
Length: 426.2cm 167.8in
Width: 163.1cm 64.2in
Height: 141.0cm 55.5in
Kerb weight: 1017.0kg 2240.0lb
Fuel: 40.1L 8.8gal 10.6galUS

4844 Volkswagen

Jetta GLX
1984 Germany
113.0mph 181.8kmh
0-50mph 80.5kmh: 7.4secs
0-60mph 96.5kmh: 10.3secs
0-1/4 mile: 17.8secs
0-1km: 32.9secs
90.0bhp 67.1kW 91.2PS
@ 5200rpm
107.0lbft 145.0Nm @ 3300rpm
91.2bhp/ton 89.7bhp/tonne
50.5bhp/L 37.7kW/L 51.2PS/L
49.1ft/sec 15.0m/sec
24.1mph 38.8kmh/1000rpm
31.7mpg 26.4mpgUS 8.9L/100km
Petrol 4-stroke piston
1781cc 108.7cu in
In-line 4 1 Carburettor
Compression ratio: 10.0:1
Bore: 81.0mm 3.2in
Stroke: 86.4mm 3.4in
Valve type/No: Overhead 8
Transmission: Manual
No. of forward speeds: 5
Wheels driven: Front
Springs F/R: Coil/Coil
Brake system: PA
Brakes F/R: Disc/Drum
Steering: Rack & pinion
Wheelbase: 246.4cm 97.0in
Track F: 142.2cm 56.0in
Track R: 142.2cm 56.0in
Length: 431.8cm 170.0in
Width: 167.6cm 66.0in
Height: 142.2cm 56.0in
Ground clearance: 11.4cm 4.5in
Kerb weight: 1003.3kg 2210.0lb
Fuel: 54.6L 12.0gal 14.4galUS

4845 Volkswagen

Passat CL Turbo Diesel Estate
1984 Germany
104.0mph 167.3kmh
0-50mph 80.5kmh: 9.9secs
0-60mph 96.5kmh: 13.6secs
0-1/4 mile: 19.3secs
0-1km: 36.2secs
70.0bhp 52.2kW 71.0PS
@ 4500rpm
98.0lbft 132.8Nm @ 2600rpm
65.6bhp/ton 64.5bhp/tonne
44.1bhp/L 32.9kW/L 44.7PS/L
42.5ft/sec 13.0m/sec
23.6mph 38.0kmh/1000rpm
40.7mpg 33.9mpgUS 6.9L/100km
Diesel 4-stroke piston
1588cc 96.9cu in turbocharged
In-line 4 fuel injection
Compression ratio: 23.0:1
Bore: 76.5mm 3.0in
Stroke: 86.4mm 3.4in
Valve type/No: Overhead 8
Transmission: Manual
No. of forward speeds: 5
Wheels driven: Front
Springs F/R: Coil/Coil
Brake system: PA
Brakes F/R: Disc/Drum
Steering: Rack & pinion
Wheelbase: 255.0cm 100.4in
Track F: 140.0cm 55.1in
Track R: 140.7cm 55.4in
Length: 453.9cm 178.7in
Width: 168.4cm 66.3in
Height: 136.9cm 53.9in
Ground clearance: 15.2cm 6.0in
Kerb weight: 1084.6kg 2389.0lb
Fuel: 60.1L 13.2gal 15.9galUS

4846 Volkswagen

Scirocco
1984 Germany
109.0mph 175.4kmh
0-60mph 96.5kmh: 10.7secs
0-1/4 mile: 17.8secs
90.0bhp 67.1kW 91.2PS
@ 5500rpm
105.0lbft 142.3Nm @ 3250rpm
92.9bhp/ton 91.3bhp/tonne
50.6bhp/L 37.7kW/L 51.3PS/L
51.9ft/sec 15.8m/sec
18.5mph 29.8kmh/1000rpm
32.4mpg 27.0mpgUS 8.7L/100km
Petrol 4-stroke piston
1780cc 108.6cu in
In-line 4 fuel injection
Compression ratio: 8.5:1
Bore: 81.0mm 3.2in
Stroke: 86.4mm 3.4in
Valve type/No: Overhead 8
Transmission: Manual
No. of forward speeds: 5
Wheels driven: Front
Springs F/R: Coil/Coil
Brakes F/R: Disc/Drum
Steering: Rack & pinion
Wheelbase: 240.0cm 94.5in
Track F: 138.9cm 54.7in
Track R: 135.9cm 53.5in
Length: 426.2cm 167.8in
Width: 161.0cm 63.4in
Height: 130.6cm 51.4in
Kerb weight: 985.2kg 2170.0lb
Fuel: 40.1L 8.8gal 10.6galUS

4847 Volkswagen

Scirocco 16v
1984 Germany
0-60mph 96.5kmh: 7.9secs
139.0bhp 103.6kW 140.9PS
@ 6300rpm
118.0lbft 159.9Nm @ 4500rpm
149.0bhp/ton 146.5bhp/tonne
78.0bhp/L 58.2kW/L 79.1PS/L
24.6mpg 20.5mpgUS 11.5L/100km
Petrol 4-stroke piston
1781cc 108.7cu in
In-line 4 fuel injection
Valve type/No: Overhead 16
Transmission: Manual
No. of forward speeds: 5
Wheels driven: Front
Springs F/R: Coil/Coil
Brakes F/R: Disc/Disc
Steering: Rack & pinion
Wheelbase: 240.0cm 94.5in
Length: 405.1cm 159.5in
Width: 162.1cm 63.8in
Height: 128.0cm 50.4in
Kerb weight: 948.9kg 2090.0lb
Fuel: 54.9L 12.1gal 14.5galUS

4848 Volkswagen

Cabriolet Wolfsburg
1985 Germany
0-60mph 96.5kmh: 11.1secs
0-1/4 mile: 18.0secs
90.0bhp 67.1kW 91.2PS
@ 5500rpm
100.0lbft 135.5Nm @ 3000rpm
86.5bhp/ton 85.1bhp/tonne
50.6bhp/L 37.7kW/L 51.3PS/L
51.9ft/sec 15.8m/sec
26.4mpg 22.0mpgUS 10.7L/100km
Petrol 4-stroke piston
1780cc 108.6cu in
In-line 4 fuel injection
Compression ratio: 8.5:1
Bore: 81.0mm 3.2in
Stroke: 86.4mm 3.4in
Valve type/No: Overhead 8
Transmission: Manual
No. of forward speeds: 5
Wheels driven: Front
Brakes F/R: Disc/Drum
Steering: Rack & pinion
Wheelbase: 240.0cm 94.5in
Length: 404.6cm 159.3in
Width: 163.1cm 64.2in
Height: 141.2cm 55.6in
Kerb weight: 1057.8kg 2330.0lb

4849 Volkswagen

Golf
1985 Germany
107.0mph 172.2kmh
0-50mph 80.5kmh: 7.0secs
0-60mph 96.5kmh: 10.0secs
0-1/4 mile: 17.5secs
85.0bhp 63.4kW 86.2PS
@ 5250rpm
98.0lbft 132.8Nm @ 3000rpm
87.5bhp/ton 86.1bhp/tonne
47.7bhp/L 35.6kW/L 48.4PS/L
49.6ft/sec 15.1m/sec
22.5mph 36.2kmh/1000rpm
31.2mpg 26.0mpgUS 9.0L/100km
Petrol 4-stroke piston
1781cc 108.7cu in
In-line 4 fuel injection
Compression ratio: 8.5:1
Bore: 81.0mm 3.2in
Stroke: 86.4mm 3.4in
Valve type/No: Overhead 8
Transmission: Manual
No. of forward speeds: 5
Wheels driven: Front
Springs F/R: Coil/Coil
Brake system: PA
Brakes F/R: Disc/Drum
Steering: Rack & pinion PA
Wheelbase: 247.4cm 97.4in
Track F: 141.2cm 55.6in
Track R: 140.7cm 55.4in
Length: 401.3cm 158.0in
Width: 166.6cm 65.6in
Height: 141.5cm 55.7in
Ground clearance: 12.4cm 4.9in
Kerb weight: 987.4kg 2175.0lb
Fuel: 54.9L 12.1gal 14.5galUS

4850 Volkswagen

Golf GTi
1985 Germany
107.0mph 172.2kmh
0-50mph 80.5kmh: 6.3secs
0-60mph 96.5kmh: 9.0secs
0-1/4 mile: 16.9secs
100.0bhp 74.6kW 101.4PS
@ 5500rpm
105.0lbft 142.3Nm @ 3000rpm
105.4bhp/ton 103.6bhp/tonne
56.1bhp/L 41.9kW/L 56.9PS/L
51.9ft/sec 15.8m/sec
19.7mph 31.7kmh/1000rpm
32.4mpg 27.0mpgUS 8.7L/100km
Petrol 4-stroke piston
1781cc 108.7cu in
In-line 4 fuel injection
Compression ratio: 10.0:1
Bore: 81.0mm 3.2in
Stroke: 86.4mm 3.4in
Valve type/No: Overhead 8
Transmission: Manual
No. of forward speeds: 5
Wheels driven: Front
Springs F/R: Coil/Coil
Brakes F/R: Disc/Disc
Steering: Rack & pinion PA
Wheelbase: 247.4cm 97.4in
Track F: 141.2cm 55.6in
Track R: 140.7cm 55.4in
Length: 401.3cm 158.0in
Width: 166.6cm 65.6in
Height: 141.5cm 55.7in
Kerb weight: 964.7kg 2125.0lb
Fuel: 54.9L 12.1gal 14.5galUS

4851 Volkswagen

Jetta GLi
1985 Germany
115.0mph 185.0kmh
0-50mph 80.5kmh: 7.4secs
0-60mph 96.5kmh: 10.4secs
0-1/4 mile: 17.8secs
100.0bhp 74.6kW 101.4PS
@ 5500rpm
105.0lbft 142.3Nm @ 3000rpm
91.8bhp/ton 90.3bhp/tonne
56.1bhp/L 41.9kW/L 56.9PS/L
51.9ft/sec 15.8m/sec
19.7mph 31.7kmh/1000rpm
30.6mpg 25.5mpgUS 9.2L/100km
Petrol 4-stroke piston
1781cc 108.7cu in
In-line 4 fuel injection
Compression ratio: 10.0:1
Bore: 81.0mm 3.2in
Stroke: 86.4mm 3.4in
Valve type/No: Overhead 8
Transmission: Manual
No. of forward speeds: 5
Wheels driven: Front
Springs F/R: Coil/Coil
Brake system: PA
Brakes F/R: Disc/Disc
Steering: Rack & pinion PA
Wheelbase: 247.1cm 97.3in
Track F: 143.0cm 56.3in
Track R: 142.2cm 56.0in
Length: 436.1cm 171.7in
Width: 166.4cm 65.5in
Height: 141.5cm 55.7in
Ground clearance: 15.2cm 6.0in
Kerb weight: 1107.8kg 2440.0lb
Fuel: 54.9L 12.1gal 14.5galUS

4852 Volkswagen
Scirocco
1985 Germany
109.0mph 175.4kmh
0-60mph 96.5kmh: 11.6secs
0-1/4 mile: 18.2secs
90.0bhp 67.1kW 91.2PS
@ 5000rpm
100.0lbft 135.5Nm @ 3000rpm
92.4bhp/ton 90.9bhp/tonne
50.6bhp/L 37.7kW/L 51.3PS/L
Petrol 4-stroke piston
1780cc 108.6cu in
In-line 4 fuel injection
Valve type/No: Overhead 8
Transmission: Manual
No. of forward speeds: 5
Wheels driven: Front
Springs F/R: Coil/Coil
Brakes F/R: Disc/Drum
Steering: Rack & pinion
Wheelbase: 240.0cm 94.5in
Length: 420.9cm 165.7in
Width: 162.6cm 64.0in
Height: 130.6cm 51.4in
Kerb weight: 990.2kg 2181.0lb
Fuel: 52.2L 11.5gal 13.8galUS

4853 Volkswagen
Scirocco 16v
1985 Germany
131.0mph 210.8kmh
0-50mph 80.5kmh: 5.8secs
0-60mph 96.5kmh: 8.4secs
0-1/4 mile: 16.3secs
0-1km: 29.7secs
139.0bhp 103.6kW 140.9PS
@ 6300rpm
118.0lbft 159.9Nm @ 4500rpm
143.7bhp/ton 141.3bhp/tonne
78.0bhp/L 58.2kW/L 79.1PS/L
59.5ft/sec 18.1m/sec
20.0mph 32.2kmh/1000rpm
26.4mpg 22.0mpgUS 10.7L/100km
Petrol 4-stroke piston
1781cc 108.7cu in
In-line 4 fuel injection
Compression ratio: 10.0:1
Bore: 81.0mm 3.2in
Stroke: 86.4mm 3.4in
Valve type/No: Overhead 16
Transmission: Manual
No. of forward speeds: 5
Wheels driven: Front
Springs F/R: Coil/Coil
Brake system: PA
Brakes F/R: Disc/Drum
Steering: Rack & pinion PA
Wheelbase: 239.8cm 94.4in
Track F: 138.9cm 54.7in
Track R: 135.6cm 53.4in
Length: 404.9cm 159.4in
Width: 163.3cm 64.3in
Height: 128.0cm 50.4in
Ground clearance: 10.9cm 4.3in
Kerb weight: 983.4kg 2166.0lb
Fuel: 52.3L 11.5gal 13.8galUS

4854 Volkswagen
Scirocco GTX
1985 Germany
122.0mph 196.3kmh
0-50mph 80.5kmh: 6.3secs
0-60mph 96.5kmh: 9.0secs
0-1/4 mile: 16.8secs
0-1km: 31.0secs
112.0bhp 83.5kW 113.5PS
@ 5800rpm
112.5lbft 152.4Nm @ 3500rpm
118.2bhp/ton 116.3bhp/tonne
62.9bhp/L 46.9kW/L 63.8PS/L
54.8ft/sec 16.7m/sec
20.1mph 32.3kmh/1000rpm
26.7mpg 22.2mpgUS 10.6L/100km
Petrol 4-stroke piston
1781cc 108.7cu in
In-line 4 fuel injection
Compression ratio: 10.0:1
Bore: 81.0mm 3.2in
Stroke: 86.4mm 3.4in
Valve type/No: Overhead 8
Transmission: Manual
No. of forward speeds: 5
Wheels driven: Front
Springs F/R: Coil/Coil
Brake system: PA
Brakes F/R: Disc/Drum
Steering: Rack & pinion
Wheelbase: 239.8cm 94.4in
Track F: 138.9cm 54.7in
Track R: 135.6cm 53.4in
Length: 404.9cm 159.4in
Width: 163.3cm 64.3in
Height: 128.0cm 50.4in
Ground clearance: 10.9cm 4.3in
Kerb weight: 963.4kg 2122.0lb
Fuel: 52.3L 11.5gal 13.8galUS

4855 Volkswagen
Caravelle Syncro
1986 Germany
82.0mph 131.9kmh
0-50mph 80.5kmh: 15.8secs
0-60mph 96.5kmh: 24.7secs
0-1/4 mile: 23.0secs
0-1km: 44.7secs
78.0bhp 58.2kW 79.1PS
@ 4600rpm
103.0lbft 139.6Nm @ 2600rpm
47.5bhp/ton 46.7bhp/tonne
40.8bhp/L 30.4kW/L 41.3PS/L
34.6ft/sec 10.6m/sec
18.0mph 29.0kmh/1000rpm
20.7mpg 17.2mpgUS 13.6L/100km
Petrol 4-stroke piston
1913cc 117.0cu in
Flat 4 1 Carburettor
Compression ratio: 8.6:1
Bore: 94.0mm 3.7in
Stroke: 68.9mm 2.7in
Valve type/No: Overhead 8
Transmission: Manual
No. of forward speeds: 4
Wheels driven: 4-wheel drive
Springs F/R: Coil/Coil
Brake system: PA
Brakes F/R: Disc/Drum
Steering: Rack & pinion PA
Wheelbase: 245.5cm 96.7in
Track F: 156.8cm 61.7in
Track R: 156.0cm 61.4in
Length: 457.0cm 179.9in
Width: 184.5cm 72.6in
Height: 199.0cm 78.3in
Ground clearance: 19.0cm 7.5in
Kerb weight: 1669.0kg 3676.2lb
Fuel: 68.2L 15.0gal 18.0galUS

4856 Volkswagen
Golf GTi 16v
1986 Germany
125.0mph 201.1kmh
0-50mph 80.5kmh: 5.9secs
0-60mph 96.5kmh: 8.0secs
0-1/4 mile: 16.2secs
0-1km: 29.8secs
139.0bhp 103.6kW 140.9PS
@ 6100rpm
124.0lbft 168.0Nm @ 4600rpm
140.1bhp/ton 137.8bhp/tonne
78.0bhp/L 58.2kW/L 79.1PS/L
57.6ft/sec 17.6m/sec
19.8mph 31.9kmh/1000rpm
25.3mpg 21.1mpgUS 11.2L/100km
Petrol 4-stroke piston
1781cc 109.0cu in
In-line 4 fuel injection
Compression ratio: 10.0:1
Bore: 81.0mm 3.2in
Stroke: 86.4mm 3.4in
Valve type/No: Overhead 16
Transmission: Manual
No. of forward speeds: 5
Wheels driven: Front
Springs F/R: Coil/Coil
Brake system: PA
Brakes F/R: Disc/Disc
Steering: Rack & pinion PA
Wheelbase: 247.5cm 97.4in
Track F: 142.7cm 56.2in
Track R: 142.2cm 56.0in
Length: 398.8cm 157.0in
Width: 167.6cm 66.0in
Height: 142.2cm 56.0in
Ground clearance: 11.5cm 4.5in
Kerb weight: 1009.0kg 2222.5lb
Fuel: 55.1L 12.1gal 14.5galUS

4857 Volkswagen
Jetta GT
1986 Germany
119.0mph 191.5kmh
0-50mph 80.5kmh: 6.0secs
0-60mph 96.5kmh: 8.5secs
0-1/4 mile: 16.9secs
0-1km: 31.5secs
112.0bhp 83.5kW 113.5PS
@ 5500rpm
114.0lbft 154.5Nm @ 3100rpm
110.0bhp/ton 108.2bhp/tonne
62.9bhp/L 46.9kW/L 63.8PS/L
51.9ft/sec 15.8m/sec
21.2mph 34.1kmh/1000rpm
25.6mpg 21.3mpgUS 11.0L/100km
Petrol 4-stroke piston
1781cc 109.0cu in
In-line 4 fuel injection
Compression ratio: 10.0:1
Bore: 81.0mm 3.2in
Stroke: 86.4mm 3.4in
Valve type/No: Overhead 8
Transmission: Manual
No. of forward speeds: 5
Wheels driven: Front
Springs F/R: Coil/Coil
Brake system: PA
Brakes F/R: Disc/Disc
Steering: Rack & pinion PA
Wheelbase: 246.4cm 97.0in
Track F: 142.2cm 56.0in
Track R: 142.2cm 56.0in
Length: 431.8cm 170.0in
Width: 167.6cm 66.0in
Height: 142.2cm 56.0in
Ground clearance: 11.5cm 4.5in
Kerb weight: 1035.0kg 2279.7lb
Fuel: 54.6L 12.0gal 14.4galUS

4858 Volkswagen
Quantum Synchro Wagon
1986 Germany
113.0mph 181.8kmh
0-50mph 80.5kmh: 7.0secs
0-60mph 96.5kmh: 9.6secs
0-1/4 mile: 17.0secs
115.0bhp 85.8kW 116.6PS
@ 5500rpm
126.0lbft 170.7Nm @ 3000rpm
85.9bhp/ton 84.4bhp/tonne
51.7bhp/L 38.5kW/L 52.4PS/L
51.9ft/sec 15.8m/sec
23.4mpg 19.5mpgUS 12.1L/100km
Petrol 4-stroke piston
2226cc 135.8cu in
In-line 5 fuel injection
Compression ratio: 8.5:1
Bore: 81.0mm 3.2in
Stroke: 86.4mm 3.4in
Valve type/No: Overhead 10
Transmission: Manual
No. of forward speeds: 5
Wheels driven: 4-wheel drive
Springs F/R: Coil/Coil
Brake system: PA
Brakes F/R: Disc/Disc
Steering: Rack & pinion PA
Wheelbase: 255.0cm 100.4in
Track F: 141.2cm 55.6in
Track R: 143.5cm 56.5in
Length: 465.1cm 183.1in
Width: 169.4cm 66.7in
Height: 154.7cm 60.9in
Kerb weight: 1362.0kg 3000.0lb
Fuel: 70.0L 15.4gal 18.5galUS

4859 Volkswagen
Scirocco 16v
1986 Germany
125.0mph 201.1kmh
0-50mph 80.5kmh: 5.8secs
0-60mph 96.5kmh: 7.7secs
0-1/4 mile: 16.1secs
123.0bhp 91.7kW 124.7PS
@ 5800rpm
120.0lbft 162.6Nm @ 4250rpm
116.5bhp/ton 114.6bhp/tonne
69.1bhp/L 51.5kW/L 70.0PS/L
54.8ft/sec 16.7m/sec
30.0mpg 25.0mpgUS 9.4L/100km
Petrol 4-stroke piston
1781cc 108.7cu in
In-line 4 fuel injection
Compression ratio: 10.0:1
Bore: 81.0mm 3.2in
Stroke: 86.4mm 3.4in
Valve type/No: Overhead 16
Transmission: Manual
No. of forward speeds: 5
Wheels driven: Front
Springs F/R: Coil/Coil
Brake system: PA
Brakes F/R: Disc/Disc
Steering: Rack & pinion
Wheelbase: 240.0cm 94.5in
Track F: 138.9cm 54.7in
Track R: 135.9cm 53.5in
Length: 420.9cm 165.7in
Width: 164.6cm 64.8in
Height: 130.6cm 51.4in
Kerb weight: 1073.7kg 2365.0lb
Fuel: 52.2L 11.5gal 13.8galUS

4860 Volkswagen
Scirocco GTX 16v
1986 Germany
120.0mph 193.1kmh
0-60mph 96.5kmh: 8.0secs
120.0bhp 89.5kW 121.7PS
@ 6000rpm
118.0lbft 159.9Nm @ 3500rpm
122.2bhp/ton 120.1bhp/tonne
67.4bhp/L 50.2kW/L 68.3PS/L
Petrol 4-stroke piston
1781cc 108.7cu in
In-line 4 fuel injection
Valve type/No: Overhead 16
Transmission: Manual
No. of forward speeds: 5
Wheels driven: Front
Springs F/R: Coil/Coil
Brakes F/R: Disc/Disc
Steering: Rack & pinion PA
Wheelbase: 240.0cm 94.5in
Length: 420.9cm 165.7in
Width: 162.6cm 64.0in
Height: 130.6cm 51.4in
Kerb weight: 998.8kg 2200.0lb
Fuel: 52.2L 11.5gal 13.8galUS

4861 Volkswagen
Fox GL
1987 Brazil
100.0mph 160.9kmh
0-50mph 80.5kmh: 7.7secs
0-60mph 96.5kmh: 10.8secs
0-1/4 mile: 18.0secs
81.0bhp 60.4kW 82.1PS
@ 5500rpm
93.0lbft 126.0Nm @ 3250rpm
78.7bhp/ton 77.4bhp/tonne
45.5bhp/L 33.9kW/L 46.1PS/L
51.9ft/sec 15.8m/sec
30.0mpg 25.0mpgUS 9.4L/100km
Petrol 4-stroke piston
1780cc 108.6cu in
In-line 4 fuel injection
Compression ratio: 9.0:1
Bore: 81.0mm 3.2in
Stroke: 86.4mm 3.4in
Valve type/No: Overhead 8
Transmission: Manual
No. of forward speeds: 4
Wheels driven: Front
Springs F/R: Coil/Coil
Brake system: PA
Brakes F/R: Disc/Drum
Steering: Rack & pinion
Wheelbase: 235.7cm 92.8in
Track F: 134.9cm 53.1in
Track R: 136.9cm 53.9in
Length: 415.0cm 163.4in
Width: 160.0cm 63.0in
Height: 136.1cm 53.6in
Ground clearance: 15.2cm 6.0in
Kerb weight: 1046.5kg 2305.0lb
Fuel: 48.1L 10.6gal 12.7galUS

4862 Volkswagen
Golf Cabriolet Clipper
1987 Germany
106.0mph 170.6kmh
0-50mph 80.5kmh: 7.4secs
0-60mph 96.5kmh: 10.5secs
0-1/4 mile: 17.8secs
0-1km: 32.8secs
90.0bhp 67.1kW 91.2PS
@ 5200rpm
107.0lbft 145.0Nm @ 3300rpm
96.7bhp/ton 95.1bhp/tonne
50.5bhp/L 37.7kW/L 51.2PS/L
49.1ft/sec 15.0m/sec
20.1mph 32.3kmh/1000rpm
30.0mpg 25.0mpgUS 9.4L/100km
Petrol 4-stroke piston
1781cc 109.0cu in
In-line 4 1 Carburettor

Compression ratio: 10.0:1
Bore: 81.0mm 3.2in
Stroke: 86.4mm 3.4in
Valve type/No: Overhead 8
Transmission: Manual
No. of forward speeds: 5
Wheels driven: Front
Springs F/R: Coil/Torsion bar
Brake system: PA
Brakes F/R: Disc/Drum
Steering: Rack & pinion
Wheelbase: 240.0cm 94.5in
Track F: 140.4cm 55.3in
Track R: 137.2cm 54.0in
Length: 381.5cm 150.2in
Width: 163.0cm 64.2in
Height: 139.5cm 54.9in
Ground clearance: 11.7cm 4.6in
Kerb weight: 946.0kg 2083.7lb
Fuel: 54.6L 12.0gal 14.4galUS

4863 Volkswagen

GTi 16v
1987 Germany
122.0mph 196.3kmh
0-50mph 80.5kmh: 6.0secs
0-60mph 96.5kmh: 8.5secs
0-1/4 mile: 16.5secs
123.0bhp 91.7kW 124.7PS
@ 5800rpm
120.0lbft 162.6Nm @ 4250rpm
114.1bhp/ton 112.2bhp/tonne
69.1bhp/L 51.5kW/L 70.1PS/L
54.8ft/sec 16.7m/sec
28.8mpg 24.0mpgUS 9.8L/100km
Petrol 4-stroke piston
1780cc 108.6cu in
In-line 4 fuel injection
Compression ratio: 10.0:1
Bore: 81.0mm 3.2in
Stroke: 86.4mm 3.4in
Valve type/No: Overhead 16
Transmission: Manual
No. of forward speeds: 5
Wheels driven: Front
Springs F/R: Coil/Coil
Brake system: PA
Brakes F/R: Disc/Disc
Steering: Rack & pinion PA
Wheelbase: 247.1cm 97.3in
Track F: 143.0cm 56.3in
Track R: 142.2cm 56.0in
Length: 401.3cm 158.0in
Width: 167.9cm 66.1in
Height: 141.5cm 55.7in
Kerb weight: 1096.4kg 2415.0lb
Fuel: 54.9L 12.1gal 14.5galUS

4864 Volkswagen

Jetta GTi 16v
1987 Germany
130.0mph 209.2kmh
0-50mph 80.5kmh: 5.4secs
0-60mph 96.5kmh: 7.1secs
0-1/4 mile: 15.9secs
0-1km: 29.5secs
139.0bhp 103.6kW 140.9PS
@ 6100rpm
123.5lbft 167.3Nm @ 4600rpm
140.0bhp/ton 137.6bhp/tonne
78.0bhp/L 58.2kW/L 79.1PS/L
57.6ft/sec 17.6m/sec
19.8mph 31.9kmh/1000rpm
28.8mpg 24.0mpgUS 9.8L/100km
Petrol 4-stroke piston
1781cc 109.0cu in
In-line 4 fuel injection
Compression ratio: 10.0:1
Bore: 81.0mm 3.2in
Stroke: 86.4mm 3.4in
Valve type/No: Overhead 16
Transmission: Manual
No. of forward speeds: 5
Wheels driven: Front
Springs F/R: Coil/Coil
Brake system: PA
Brakes F/R: Disc/Disc
Steering: Rack & pinion
Wheelbase: 246.4cm 97.0in
Track F: 142.2cm 56.0in
Track R: 142.2cm 56.0in
Length: 431.8cm 170.0in
Width: 167.6cm 66.0in
Height: 142.2cm 56.0in
Ground clearance: 11.5cm 4.5in
Kerb weight: 1010.0kg 2224.7lb
Fuel: 55.1L 12.1gal 14.5galUS

4865 Volkswagen

Passat GT 5-door
1987 Germany
104.0mph 167.3kmh
0-50mph 80.5kmh: 7.5secs
0-60mph 96.5kmh: 10.9secs
0-1/4 mile: 18.8secs
0-1km: 34.8secs
90.0bhp 67.1kW 91.2PS
@ 5200rpm
107.0lbft 145.0Nm @ 3300rpm
86.6bhp/ton 85.1bhp/tonne
50.5bhp/L 37.7kW/L 51.2PS/L
49.1ft/sec 15.0m/sec
24.7mph 39.7kmh/1000rpm
30.3mpg 25.2mpgUS 9.3L/100km
Petrol 4-stroke piston
1781cc 109.0cu in
In-line 4 1 Carburettor
Compression ratio: 10.0:1
Bore: 81.0mm 3.2in
Stroke: 86.4mm 3.4in
Valve type/No: Overhead 8
Transmission: Manual
No. of forward speeds: 5
Wheels driven: Front
Springs F/R: Coil/Coil
Brake system: PA
Brakes F/R: Disc/Drum
Steering: Rack & pinion
Wheelbase: 255.0cm 100.4in
Track F: 140.0cm 55.1in
Track R: 140.8cm 55.4in
Length: 443.5cm 174.6in
Width: 168.5cm 66.3in
Height: 138.5cm 54.5in
Ground clearance: 15.2cm 6.0in
Kerb weight: 1057.0kg 2328.2lb
Fuel: 60.1L 13.2gal 15.9galUS

4866 Volkswagen

GTi 16v
1988 Germany
122.0mph 196.3kmh
0-50mph 80.5kmh: 6.0secs
0-60mph 96.5kmh: 8.5secs
0-1/4 mile: 16.5secs
123.0bhp 91.7kW 124.7PS
@ 5800rpm
120.0lbft 162.6Nm @ 4250rpm
114.1bhp/ton 112.2bhp/tonne
69.1bhp/L 51.5kW/L 70.1PS/L
54.8ft/sec 16.7m/sec
28.8mpg 24.0mpgUS 9.8L/100km
Petrol 4-stroke piston
1780cc 108.6cu in
In-line 4 fuel injection
Compression ratio: 10.0:1
Bore: 81.0mm 3.2in
Stroke: 86.4mm 3.4in
Valve type/No: Overhead 16
Transmission: Manual
No. of forward speeds: 5
Wheels driven: Front
Springs F/R: Coil/Coil
Brake system: PA
Brakes F/R: Disc/Disc
Steering: Rack & pinion PA
Wheelbase: 247.1cm 97.3in
Track F: 143.0cm 56.3in
Track R: 142.2cm 56.0in
Length: 401.3cm 158.0in
Width: 167.9cm 66.1in
Height: 141.5cm 55.7in
Kerb weight: 1096.4kg 2415.0lb
Fuel: 54.9L 12.1gal 14.5galUS

4867 Volkswagen

Jetta GLi 16v
1988 Germany
121.0mph 194.7kmh
0-50mph 80.5kmh: 6.2secs
0-60mph 96.5kmh: 8.8secs
0-1/4 mile: 16.6secs
123.0bhp 91.7kW 124.7PS
@ 5800rpm
120.0lbft 162.6Nm @ 4250rpm
109.1bhp/ton 107.3bhp/tonne
69.1bhp/L 51.5kW/L 70.1PS/L
54.8ft/sec 16.7m/sec
28.8mpg 24.0mpgUS 9.8L/100km
Petrol 4-stroke piston
1780cc 108.6cu in
In-line 4 fuel injection
Compression ratio: 10.0:1
Bore: 81.0mm 3.2in
Stroke: 86.4mm 3.4in
Valve type/No: Overhead 16
Transmission: Manual
No. of forward speeds: 5
Wheels driven: Front
Springs F/R: Coil/Coil
Brake system: PA
Brakes F/R: Disc/Disc
Steering: Rack & pinion PA
Wheelbase: 247.1cm 97.3in
Track F: 143.0cm 56.3in
Track R: 142.2cm 56.0in
Length: 436.1cm 171.7in
Width: 167.9cm 66.1in
Height: 141.5cm 55.7in
Kerb weight: 1146.3kg 2525.0lb
Fuel: 54.9L 12.1gal 14.5galUS

4868 Volkswagen

Jetta Turbo Diesel
1988 Germany
104.0mph 167.3kmh
0-50mph 80.5kmh: 9.5secs
0-60mph 96.5kmh: 12.9secs
0-1/4 mile: 19.3secs
0-1km: 35.7secs
70.0bhp 52.2kW 71.0PS
@ 4500rpm
98.2lbft 133.0Nm @ 2600rpm
71.1bhp/ton 69.9bhp/tonne
44.1bhp/L 32.9kW/L 44.7PS/L
42.5ft/sec 13.0m/sec
23.9mph 38.5kmh/1000rpm
39.3mpg 32.7mpgUS 7.2L/100km
Diesel 4-stroke piston
1588cc 97.0cu in turbocharged
In-line 4 fuel injection
Compression ratio: 23.0:1
Bore: 76.5mm 3.0in
Stroke: 86.4mm 3.4in
Valve type/No: Overhead 8
Transmission: Manual
No. of forward speeds: 5
Wheels driven: Front
Springs F/R: Coil/Coil
Brake system: PA
Brakes F/R: Disc/Drum
Steering: Rack & pinion PA
Wheelbase: 246.4cm 97.0in
Track F: 142.2cm 56.0in
Track R: 142.2cm 56.0in
Length: 431.8cm 170.0in
Width: 167.6cm 66.0in
Height: 142.2cm 56.0in
Ground clearance: 11.5cm 4.5in
Kerb weight: 1001.0kg 2204.8lb
Fuel: 54.6L 12.0gal 14.4galUS

4869 Volkswagen

Passat GT
1988 Germany
122.0mph 196.3kmh
0-50mph 80.5kmh: 7.6secs
0-60mph 96.5kmh: 10.3secs
0-1/4 mile: 18.1secs
0-1km: 33.0secs
112.0bhp 83.5kW 113.5PS
@ 5400rpm
117.3lbft 159.0Nm @ 4000rpm
98.5bhp/ton 96.9bhp/tonne
62.9bhp/L 46.9kW/L 63.8PS/L
51.0ft/sec 15.5m/sec
24.6mph 39.6kmh/1000rpm
29.2mpg 24.3mpgUS 9.7L/100km
Petrol 4-stroke piston
1781cc 109.0cu in
In-line 4 fuel injection
Compression ratio: 10.0:1
Bore: 81.0mm 3.2in
Stroke: 86.4mm 3.4in
Valve type/No: Overhead 8
Transmission: Manual
No. of forward speeds: 5
Wheels driven: Front
Springs F/R: Coil/Coil
Brake system: PA
Brakes F/R: Disc/Disc
Steering: Rack & pinion PA
Wheelbase: 262.5cm 103.3in
Track F: 146.0cm 57.5in
Track R: 142.2cm 56.0in
Length: 457.5cm 180.1in
Width: 170.5cm 67.1in
Height: 143.0cm 56.3in
Ground clearance: 10.3cm 4.1in
Kerb weight: 1156.0kg 2546.3lb
Fuel: 70.1L 15.4gal 18.5galUS

4870 Volkswagen

Polo C Saloon
1988 Germany
89.0mph 143.2kmh
0-50mph 80.5kmh: 11.8secs
0-60mph 96.5kmh: 16.9secs
0-1/4 mile: 20.6secs
0-1km: 38.7secs
45.0bhp 33.6kW 45.6PS
@ 5600rpm
55.1lbft 74.6Nm @ 3600rpm
57.4bhp/ton 56.4bhp/tonne
43.1bhp/L 32.2kW/L 43.7PS/L
36.1ft/sec 11.0m/sec
16.3mph 26.2kmh/1000rpm
30.9mpg 25.7mpgUS 9.1L/100km
Petrol 4-stroke piston
1043cc 64.0cu in
In-line 4 1 Carburettor
Compression ratio: 9.5:1
Bore: 75.0mm 2.9in
Stroke: 59.0mm 2.3in
Valve type/No: Overhead 8
Transmission: Manual
No. of forward speeds: 5
Wheels driven: Front
Springs F/R: Coil/Coil
Brake system: PA
Brakes F/R: Disc/Drum
Steering: Rack & pinion
Wheelbase: 233.5cm 91.9in
Track F: 132.0cm 52.0in
Track R: 134.6cm 53.0in
Length: 397.5cm 156.5in
Width: 160.0cm 63.0in
Height: 135.5cm 53.3in
Ground clearance: 11.7cm 4.6in
Kerb weight: 797.4kg 1756.4lb
Fuel: 41.9L 9.2gal 11.1galUS

4871 Volkswagen

Quantum GLS Synchro Wagon
1988 Germany
0-60mph 96.5kmh: 9.8secs
115.0bhp 85.8kW 116.6PS
@ 5500rpm
126.0lbft 170.7Nm @ 3000rpm
84.9bhp/ton 83.5bhp/tonne
51.7bhp/L 38.5kW/L 52.4PS/L
51.9ft/sec 15.8m/sec
25.8mpg 21.5mpgUS 10.9L/100km
Petrol 4-stroke piston
2226cc 135.8cu in
In-line 5 fuel injection
Compression ratio: 8.5:1
Bore: 81.0mm 3.2in
Stroke: 86.4mm 3.4in
Valve type/No: Overhead 10
Transmission: Manual
No. of forward speeds: 5
Wheels driven: 4-wheel drive
Springs F/R: Coil/Coil
Brake system: PA
Brakes F/R: Disc/Disc
Steering: Rack & pinion PA
Wheelbase: 255.0cm 100.4in
Track F: 141.2cm 55.6in
Track R: 143.5cm 56.5in
Length: 459.0cm 180.7in
Width: 169.4cm 66.7in
Height: 147.3cm 58.0in
Kerb weight: 1377.9kg 3035.0lb
Fuel: 70.0L 15.4gal 18.5galUS

4872 Volkswagen

Scirocco 16v
1988 Germany
125.0mph 201.1kmh
0-50mph 80.5kmh: 5.8secs
0-60mph 96.5kmh: 8.3secs
0-1/4 mile: 16.2secs
123.0bhp 91.7kW 124.7PS
@ 5800rpm
120.0lbft 162.6Nm @ 4250rpm
116.5bhp/ton 114.6bhp/tonne
69.1bhp/L 51.5kW/L 70.0PS/L
54.8ft/sec 16.7m/sec
30.0mpg 25.0mpgUS 9.4L/100km
Petrol 4-stroke piston
1781cc 108.7cu in
In-line 4 fuel injection
Compression ratio: 10.0:1
Bore: 81.0mm 3.2in
Stroke: 86.4mm 3.4in
Valve type/No: Overhead 16
Transmission: Manual
No. of forward speeds: 5

Wheels driven: Front
Springs F/R: Coil/Coil
Brake system: PA
Brakes F/R: Disc/Disc
Steering: Rack & pinion
Wheelbase: 240.0cm 94.5in
Track F: 138.9cm 54.7in
Track R: 135.9cm 53.5in
Length: 420.9cm 165.7in
Width: 164.6cm 64.8in
Height: 130.6cm 51.4in
Kerb weight: 1073.7kg 2365.0lb
Fuel: 52.2L 11.5gal 13.8galUS

4873 Volkswagen

Caravelle Carat Automatic
1989 Germany
93.0mph 149.6kmh
0-50mph 80.5kmh: 12.0secs
0-60mph 96.5kmh: 16.9secs
0-1/4 mile: 20.6secs
0-1km: 39.0secs
112.0bhp 83.5kW 113.5PS
@ 4800rpm
128.4lbft 174.0Nm @ 2800rpm
65.8bhp/ton 64.7bhp/tonne
53.1bhp/L 39.6kW/L 53.8PS/L
39.9ft/sec 12.2m/sec
19.5mph 31.4kmh/1000rpm
18.1mpg 15.1mpgUS 15.6L/100km
Petrol 4-stroke piston
2109cc 129.0cu in
Flat 4 fuel injection
Compression ratio: 10.5:1
Bore: 94.0mm 3.7in
Stroke: 76.0mm 3.0in
Valve type/No: Overhead 8
Transmission: Automatic
No. of forward speeds: 3
Wheels driven: Rear
Springs F/R: Coil/Mini blocks
Brake system: PA ABS
Brakes F/R: Disc/Drum
Steering: Rack & pinion PA
Wheelbase: 245.5cm 96.7in
Track F: 156.8cm 61.7in
Track R: 156.0cm 61.4in
Length: 457.0cm 179.9in
Width: 184.5cm 72.6in
Height: 199.0cm 78.3in
Ground clearance: 19.0cm 7.5in
Kerb weight: 1730.0kg 3810.6lb
Fuel: 60.5L 13.3gal 16.0galUS

4874 Volkswagen

Corrado
1989 Germany
140.0mph 225.3kmh
0-60mph 96.5kmh: 7.8secs
158.0bhp 117.8kW 160.2PS
@ 5600rpm
166.0lbft 224.9Nm @ 4000rpm
143.9bhp/ton 141.5bhp/tonne
88.7bhp/L 66.1kW/L 89.9PS/L
52.9ft/sec 16.1m/sec
Petrol 4-stroke piston
1781cc 108.7cu in supercharged
In-line 4
Compression ratio: 8.0:1
Bore: 81.0mm 3.2in
Stroke: 86.4mm 3.4in
Valve type/No: Overhead 8
Transmission: Manual
No. of forward speeds: 5
Wheels driven: Front
Springs F/R: Coil/Coil
Brake system: PA
Brakes F/R: Disc/Disc
Steering: Rack & pinion PA
Wheelbase: 247.1cm 97.3in
Track F: 143.5cm 56.5in
Track R: 142.7cm 56.2in
Length: 404.9cm 159.4in
Width: 167.4cm 65.9in
Height: 131.8cm 51.9in
Kerb weight: 1116.8kg 2460.0lb
Fuel: 54.9L 12.1gal 14.5galUS

4875 Volkswagen

Corrado 16v
1989 Germany
132.0mph 212.4kmh
0-50mph 80.5kmh: 6.4secs
0-60mph 96.5kmh: 8.7secs
0-1/4 mile: 16.5secs
136.0bhp 101.4kW 137.9PS
@ 6300rpm
118.8lbft 161.0Nm @ 4800rpm
119.7bhp/ton 117.7bhp/tonne
76.4bhp/L 56.9kW/L 77.4PS/L
59.3ft/sec 18.1m/sec
19.8mph 31.9kmh/1000rpm
25.9mpg 21.6mpgUS 10.9L/100km
Petrol 4-stroke piston
1781cc 109.0cu in
In-line 4 fuel injection
Compression ratio: 10.0:1
Bore: 81.0mm 3.2in
Stroke: 86.0mm 3.4in
Valve type/No: Overhead 16
Transmission: Manual
No. of forward speeds: 5
Wheels driven: Front
Springs F/R: Coil/Torsion bar
Brake system: PA
Brakes F/R: Disc/Disc
Steering: Rack & pinion PA
Wheelbase: 247.5cm 97.4in
Track F: 142.7cm 56.2in
Track R: 142.2cm 56.0in
Length: 404.8cm 159.4in
Width: 167.4cm 65.9in
Height: 131.8cm 51.9in
Ground clearance: 11.5cm 4.5in
Kerb weight: 1155.0kg 2544.0lb
Fuel: 54.6L 12.0gal 14.4galUS

4876 Volkswagen

Golf CL Catalyst
1989 Germany
99.0mph 159.3kmh
0-50mph 80.5kmh: 8.0secs
0-60mph 96.5kmh: 11.5secs
0-1/4 mile: 18.4secs
0-1km: 34.5secs
72.0bhp 53.7kW 73.0PS
@ 5200rpm
92.0lbft 124.7Nm @ 2700rpm
77.9bhp/ton 76.6bhp/tonne
45.1bhp/L 33.7kW/L 45.8PS/L
44.1ft/sec 13.4m/sec
24.6mph 39.6kmh/1000rpm
38.4mpg 32.0mpgUS 7.4L/100km
Petrol 4-stroke piston
1595cc 97.0cu in
In-line 4 1 Carburettor
Compression ratio: 9.0:1
Bore: 81.0mm 3.2in
Stroke: 77.4mm 3.0in
Valve type/No: Overhead 8
Transmission: Manual
No. of forward speeds: 5
Wheels driven: Front
Springs F/R: Coil/Coil
Brake system: PA
Brakes F/R: Disc/Drum
Steering: Rack & pinion
Wheelbase: 247.5cm 97.4in
Track F: 142.7cm 56.2in
Track R: 142.2cm 56.0in
Length: 398.8cm 157.0in
Width: 167.6cm 66.0in
Height: 142.2cm 56.0in
Ground clearance: 11.5cm 4.5in
Kerb weight: 940.0kg 2070.5lb
Fuel: 54.6L 12.0gal 14.4galUS

4877 Volkswagen

Jetta Syncro
1989 Germany
108.0mph 173.8kmh
0-50mph 80.5kmh: 8.0secs
0-60mph 96.5kmh: 11.3secs
0-1/4 mile: 18.5secs
0-1km: 34.2secs
90.0bhp 67.1kW 91.2PS
@ 5200rpm
107.0lbft 145.0Nm @ 3300rpm
80.3bhp/ton 78.9bhp/tonne
50.5bhp/L 37.7kW/L 51.2PS/L
49.1ft/sec 15.0m/sec
19.6mph 31.5kmh/1000rpm
22.3mpg 18.6mpgUS 12.7L/100km
Petrol 4-stroke piston
1781cc 109.0cu in
In-line 4 1 Carburettor
Compression ratio: 10.0:1
Bore: 81.0mm 3.2in
Stroke: 86.4mm 3.4in
Valve type/No: Overhead 8
Transmission: Manual
No. of forward speeds: 5
Wheels driven: 4-wheel drive
Springs F/R: Coil/Torsion bar
Brake system: PA
Brakes F/R: Disc/Drum
Steering: Rack & pinion PA
Wheelbase: 246.4cm 97.0in
Track F: 142.2cm 56.0in
Track R: 142.2cm 56.0in
Length: 431.8cm 170.0in
Width: 167.6cm 66.0in
Height: 142.2cm 56.0in
Ground clearance: 11.5cm 4.5in
Kerb weight: 1140.0kg 2511.0lb
Fuel: 54.6L 12.0gal 14.4galUS

4878 Volkswagen

Passat GT 16v
1989 Germany
129.0mph 207.6kmh
0-50mph 80.5kmh: 6.4secs
0-60mph 96.5kmh: 8.8secs
0-1/4 mile: 17.3secs
0-1km: 31.7secs
136.0bhp 101.4kW 137.9PS
@ 6300rpm
119.6lbft 162.0Nm @ 4800rpm
108.5bhp/ton 106.7bhp/tonne
76.4bhp/L 56.9kW/L 77.4PS/L
59.5ft/sec 18.1m/sec
25.0mph 40.2kmh/1000rpm
27.4mpg 22.8mpgUS 10.3L/100km
Petrol 4-stroke piston
1781cc 109.0cu in
In-line 4 fuel injection
Compression ratio: 10.0:1
Bore: 81.0mm 3.2in
Stroke: 86.4mm 3.4in
Valve type/No: Overhead 16
Transmission: Manual
No. of forward speeds: 5
Wheels driven: Front
Springs F/R: Coil/Torsion bar
Brake system: PA ABS
Brakes F/R: Disc/Disc
Steering: Rack & pinion PA
Wheelbase: 262.5cm 103.3in
Track F: 146.0cm 57.5in
Track R: 142.2cm 56.0in
Length: 457.5cm 180.1in
Width: 170.5cm 67.1in
Height: 143.0cm 56.3in
Ground clearance: 10.3cm 4.1in
Kerb weight: 1275.0kg 2808.4lb
Fuel: 70.1L 15.4gal 18.5galUS

4879 Volkswagen

Corrado G60
1990 Germany
137.0mph 220.4kmh
0-50mph 80.5kmh: 6.4secs
0-60mph 96.5kmh: 8.9secs
0-1/4 mile: 16.5secs
158.0bhp 117.8kW 160.2PS
@ 5600rpm
166.0lbft 224.9Nm @ 4000rpm
131.3bhp/ton 129.1bhp/tonne
88.7bhp/L 66.1kW/L 89.9PS/L
52.9ft/sec 16.1m/sec
25.8mpg 21.5mpgUS 10.9L/100km
Petrol 4-stroke piston
1781cc 108.7cu in supercharged
In-line 4 fuel injection
Compression ratio: 8.0:1
Bore: 81.0mm 3.2in
Stroke: 86.4mm 3.4in
Valve type/No: Overhead 8
Transmission: Manual
No. of forward speeds: 5
Wheels driven: Front
Springs F/R: Coil/Coil
Brake system: PA ABS
Brakes F/R: Disc/Disc
Steering: Rack & pinion PA
Wheelbase: 247.1cm 97.3in
Track F: 143.5cm 56.5in
Track R: 142.7cm 56.2in
Length: 404.9cm 159.4in
Width: 167.4cm 65.9in
Height: 131.8cm 51.9in
Ground clearance: 12.7cm 5.0in
Kerb weight: 1223.5kg 2695.0lb
Fuel: 54.9L 12.1gal 14.5galUS

4880 Volkswagen

Passat CL TD Estate
1990 Germany
103.0mph 165.7kmh
0-50mph 80.5kmh: 10.7secs
0-60mph 96.5kmh: 15.6secs
0-1/4 mile: 20.1secs
0-1km: 37.5secs
80.0bhp 59.7kW 81.1PS
@ 4500rpm
114.4lbft 155.0Nm @ 2600rpm
65.3bhp/ton 64.3bhp/tonne
50.4bhp/L 37.6kW/L 51.1PS/L
42.5ft/sec 13.0m/sec
24.2mph 38.9kmh/1000rpm
37.0mpg 30.8mpgUS 7.6L/100km
Diesel 4-stroke piston
1588cc 97.0cu in turbocharged
In-line 4 fuel injection
Compression ratio: 23.0:1
Bore: 76.5mm 3.0in
Stroke: 86.4mm 3.4in
Valve type/No: Overhead 8
Transmission: Manual
No. of forward speeds: 5
Wheels driven: Front
Springs F/R: Coil/Coil
Brake system: PA
Brakes F/R: Disc/Disc
Steering: Rack & pinion PA
Wheelbase: 262.5cm 103.3in
Track F: 146.0cm 57.5in
Track R: 142.2cm 56.0in
Length: 457.5cm 180.1in
Width: 170.5cm 67.1in
Height: 143.0cm 56.3in
Ground clearance: 10.3cm 4.1in
Kerb weight: 1245.0kg 2742.3lb
Fuel: 70.1L 15.4gal 18.5galUS

4881 Volkswagen

Passat GL
1990 Germany
125.0mph 201.1kmh
0-50mph 80.5kmh: 7.5secs
0-60mph 96.5kmh: 10.9secs
0-1/4 mile: 17.8secs
134.0bhp 99.9kW 135.9PS
@ 5800rpm
133.0lbft 180.2Nm @ 4400rpm
100.6bhp/ton 98.9bhp/tonne
67.5bhp/L 50.4kW/L 68.5PS/L
58.8ft/sec 17.9m/sec
30.0mpg 25.0mpgUS 9.4L/100km
Petrol 4-stroke piston
1984cc 121.0cu in
In-line 4 fuel injection
Compression ratio: 10.8:1
Bore: 82.5mm 3.2in
Stroke: 92.8mm 3.6in
Valve type/No: Overhead 16
Transmission: Manual
No. of forward speeds: 5
Wheels driven: Front
Springs F/R: Coil/Coil
Brake system: PA ABS
Brakes F/R: Disc/Disc
Steering: Rack & pinion PA
Wheelbase: 262.4cm 103.3in
Track F: 147.8cm 58.2in
Track R: 142.0cm 55.9in
Length: 457.2cm 180.0in
Width: 170.4cm 67.1in
Height: 142.7cm 56.2in
Ground clearance: 15.2cm 6.0in
Kerb weight: 1355.2kg 2985.0lb
Fuel: 70.0L 15.4gal 18.5galUS

4882 Volkswagen

Corrado G60
1991 Germany
139.0mph 223.7kmh
0-50mph 80.5kmh: 6.4secs
0-60mph 96.5kmh: 8.9secs
0-1/4 mile: 16.8secs
0-1km: 30.3secs
160.0bhp 119.3kW 162.2PS
@ 5600rpm
166.1lbft 225.0Nm @ 4000rpm
141.5bhp/ton 139.1bhp/tonne
89.8bhp/L 67.0kW/L 91.1PS/L
52.9ft/sec 16.1m/sec
23.9mph 38.5kmh/1000rpm
22.0mpg 18.3mpgUS 12.8L/100km
Petrol 4-stroke piston
1781cc 109.0cu in supercharged
In-line 4 fuel injection
Compression ratio: 8.0:1
Bore: 81.0mm 3.2in
Stroke: 86.4mm 3.4in
Valve type/No: Overhead 8

Transmission: Manual
No. of forward speeds: 5
Wheels driven: Front
Springs F/R: Coil/Coil
Brake system: PA ABS
Brakes F/R: Disc/Disc
Steering: Rack & pinion PA
Wheelbase: 247.4cm 97.4in
Track F: 147.1cm 57.9in
Track R: 142.0cm 55.9in
Length: 404.6cm 159.3in
Width: 167.4cm 65.9in
Height: 131.6cm 51.8in
Ground clearance: 11.4cm 4.5in
Kerb weight: 1150.0kg 2533.0lb
Fuel: 55.1L 12.1gal 14.5galUS

4883 Volkswagen

Corrado Neuspeed
1991 Germany
0-60mph 96.5kmh: 7.4secs
0-1/4 mile: 15.4secs
215.0bhp 160.3kW 218.0PS
@ 5500rpm
205.0lbft 277.8Nm @ 5000rpm
175.1bhp/ton 172.2bhp/tonne
106.4bhp/L 79.3kW/L 107.9PS/L
56.8ft/sec 17.3m/sec
Petrol 4-stroke piston
2021cc 123.3cu in supercharged
In-line 4 fuel injection
Compression ratio: 8.2:1
Bore: 82.5mm 3.2in
Stroke: 94.5mm 3.7in
Valve type/No: Overhead 8
Transmission: Manual
No. of forward speeds: 5
Wheels driven: Front
Springs F/R: Coil/Coil
Brake system: PA
Brakes F/R: Disc/Disc
Steering: Rack & pinion PA
Wheelbase: 247.1cm 97.3in
Track F: 152.4cm 60.0in
Track R: 131.8cm 51.9in
Length: 404.9cm 159.4in
Width: 167.4cm 65.9in
Height: 128.3cm 50.5in
Kerb weight: 1248.5kg 2750.0lb

4884 Volkswagen

GTi 16v
1991 Germany
122.0mph 196.3kmh
0-60mph 96.5kmh: 8.4secs
0-1/4 mile: 16.8secs
134.0bhp 99.9kW 135.9PS
@ 5800rpm
133.0lbft 180.2Nm @ 4400rpm
119.8bhp/ton 117.8bhp/tonne
67.5bhp/L 50.4kW/L 68.5PS/L
58.8ft/sec 17.9m/sec
30.0mpg 25.0mpgUS 9.4L/100km
Petrol 4-stroke piston
1984cc 121.0cu in
In-line 4 fuel injection
Compression ratio: 10.8:1
Bore: 82.5mm 3.2in
Stroke: 92.8mm 3.6in
Valve type/No: Overhead 16
Transmission: Manual
No. of forward speeds: 5
Wheels driven: Front
Springs F/R: Coil/Coil
Brake system: PA
Brakes F/R: Disc/Disc
Steering: Rack & pinion PA
Wheelbase: 247.1cm 97.3in
Track F: 143.0cm 56.3in
Track R: 142.2cm 56.0in
Length: 404.1cm 159.1in
Width: 167.9cm 66.1in
Height: 141.5cm 55.7in
Kerb weight: 1137.3kg 2505.0lb
Fuel: 54.9L 12.1gal 14.5galUS

4885 Volkswagen

Jetta GLi 16v
1991 Germany
125.0mph 201.1kmh
0-50mph 80.5kmh: 6.5secs
0-60mph 96.5kmh: 9.1secs
0-1/4 mile: 16.8secs
134.0bhp 99.9kW 135.9PS
@ 5800rpm
133.0lbft 180.2Nm @ 4400rpm
123.0bhp/ton 121.0bhp/tonne
67.5bhp/L 50.4kW/L 68.5PS/L
58.8ft/sec 17.9m/sec
28.8mpg 24.0mpgUS 9.8L/100km
Petrol 4-stroke piston
1984cc 121.0cu in
In-line 4 fuel injection
Compression ratio: 10.8:1
Bore: 82.5mm 3.2in
Stroke: 92.8mm 3.6in
Valve type/No: Overhead 16
Transmission: Manual
No. of forward speeds: 5
Wheels driven: Front
Springs F/R: Coil/Coil
Brake system: PA ABS
Brakes F/R: Disc/Disc
Steering: Rack & pinion
Wheelbase: 247.1cm 97.3in
Track F: 143.0cm 56.3in
Track R: 142.2cm 56.0in
Length: 438.4cm 172.6in
Width: 167.9cm 66.1in
Height: 141.5cm 55.7in
Kerb weight: 1107.8kg 2440.0lb
Fuel: 54.9L 12.1gal 14.5galUS

4886 Volkswagen

Polo 1.3 CL Coupe
1991 Germany
99.0mph 159.3kmh
0-50mph 80.5kmh: 9.5secs
0-60mph 96.5kmh: 13.5secs
0-1/4 mile: 19.4secs
0-1km: 32.6secs
55.0bhp 41.0kW 55.8PS
@ 5200rpm
71.6lbft 97.0Nm @ 3000rpm
72.6bhp/ton 71.4bhp/tonne
43.2bhp/L 32.2kW/L 43.8PS/L
40.9ft/sec 12.5m/sec
21.2mph 34.1kmh/1000rpm
35.2mpg 29.3mpgUS 8.0L/100km
Petrol 4-stroke piston
1272cc 78.0cu in
In-line 4 fuel injection
Compression ratio: 10.0:1
Bore: 75.0mm 2.9in
Stroke: 72.0mm 2.8in
Valve type/No: Overhead 8
Transmission: Manual
No. of forward speeds: 5
Wheels driven: Front
Springs F/R: Coil/Coil
Brake system: PA
Brakes F/R: Disc/Drum
Steering: Rack & pinion
Wheelbase: 253.7cm 99.9in
Track F: 130.6cm 51.4in
Track R: 133.1cm 52.4in
Length: 375.9cm 148.0in
Width: 157.0cm 61.8in
Height: 132.1cm 52.0in
Ground clearance: 10.4cm 4.1in
Kerb weight: 770.0kg 1696.0lb
Fuel: 41.9L 9.2gal 11.1galUS

4887 Volkswagen

Polo G40
1991 Germany
120.0mph 193.1kmh
0-50mph 80.5kmh: 6.1secs
0-60mph 96.5kmh: 8.4secs
0-1/4 mile: 16.5secs
0-1km: 26.2secs
113.0bhp 84.3kW 114.6PS
@ 6000rpm
110.7lbft 150.0Nm @ 3600rpm
136.0bhp/ton 133.7bhp/tonne
88.8bhp/L 66.2kW/L 90.1PS/L
47.2ft/sec 14.4m/sec
21.7mph 34.9kmh/1000rpm
30.1mpg 25.1mpgUS 9.4L/100km
Petrol 4-stroke piston
1272cc 78.0cu in supercharged
In-line 4 fuel injection
Compression ratio: 8.0:1
Bore: 75.0mm 2.9in
Stroke: 72.0mm 2.8in
Valve type/No: Overhead 8
Transmission: Manual
No. of forward speeds: 5
Wheels driven: Front
Springs F/R: Coil/Coil
Brake system: PA
Brakes F/R: Disc/Drum
Steering: Rack & pinion
Wheelbase: 233.5cm 91.9in
Track F: 130.6cm 51.4in
Track R: 133.2cm 52.4in
Length: 376.5cm 148.2in
Width: 157.0cm 61.8in
Height: 132.5cm 52.2in
Ground clearance: 10.4cm 4.1in
Kerb weight: 845.0kg 1861.2lb
Fuel: 42.0L 9.2gal 11.1galUS

4888 Volkswagen

Polo GT Coupe
1991 Germany
104.0mph 167.3kmh
0-50mph 80.5kmh: 8.6secs
0-60mph 96.5kmh: 11.7secs
0-1/4 mile: 18.7secs
0-1km: 34.4secs
75.0bhp 55.9kW 76.0PS
@ 5900rpm
73.1lbft 99.0Nm @ 3600rpm
94.7bhp/ton 93.2bhp/tonne
59.0bhp/L 44.0kW/L 59.8PS/L
46.4ft/sec 14.2m/sec
17.8mph 28.6kmh/1000rpm
34.9mpg 29.1mpgUS 8.1L/100km
Petrol 4-stroke piston
1272cc 78.0cu in
In-line 4 fuel injection
Compression ratio: 10.0:1
Bore: 75.0mm 2.9in
Stroke: 72.0mm 2.8in
Valve type/No: Overhead 8
Transmission: Manual
No. of forward speeds: 5
Wheels driven: Front
Springs F/R: Coil/Coil
Brake system: PA
Brakes F/R: Disc/Disc
Steering: Rack & pinion
Wheelbase: 253.7cm 99.9in
Track F: 130.6cm 51.4in
Track R: 133.1cm 52.4in
Length: 375.9cm 148.0in
Width: 157.0cm 61.8in
Height: 132.1cm 52.0in
Ground clearance: 10.4cm 4.1in
Kerb weight: 805.0kg 1773.1lb
Fuel: 41.9L 9.2gal 11.1galUS

4889 Volkswagen

Golf 1.8 GL
1992 Germany
107.0mph 172.2kmh
0-50mph 80.5kmh: 9.0secs
0-60mph 96.5kmh: 12.7secs
0-1/4 mile: 19.2secs
0-1km: 35.1secs
90.0bhp 67.1kW 91.2PS
@ 5500rpm
107.0lbft 145.0Nm @ 2500rpm
84.4bhp/ton 83.0bhp/tonne
50.5bhp/L 37.7kW/L 51.2PS/L
51.9ft/sec 15.8m/sec
21.1mph 33.9kmh/1000rpm
32.2mpg 26.8mpgUS 8.8L/100km
Petrol 4-stroke piston
1781cc 108.7cu in
In-line 4 fuel injection
Compression ratio: 10.0:1
Bore: 81.0mm 3.2in
Stroke: 86.4mm 3.4in
Valve type/No: Overhead 8
Transmission: Manual
No. of forward speeds: 5
Wheels driven: Front
Springs F/R: Coil/Coil
Brake system: PA
Brakes F/R: Disc/Drum
Steering: Rack & pinion PA
Wheelbase: 247.5cm 97.4in
Track F: 147.0cm 57.9in
Track R: 146.0cm 57.5in
Length: 402.0cm 158.3in
Width: 169.0cm 66.5in
Height: 142.5cm 56.1in
Kerb weight: 1084.0kg 2387.7lb
Fuel: 55.1L 12.1gal 14.5galUS

4890 Volkswagen

Golf GTi
1992 Germany
121.0mph 194.7kmh
0-50mph 80.5kmh: 7.2secs
0-60mph 96.5kmh: 9.9secs
0-1/4 mile: 17.5secs
0-1km: 32.1secs
115.0bhp 85.8kW 116.6PS
@ 5400rpm
122.0lbft 165.3Nm @ 3200rpm
58.0bhp/L 43.2kW/L 58.8PS/L
54.7ft/sec 16.7m/sec
22.1mph 35.6kmh/1000rpm
28.8mpg 24.0mpgUS 9.8L/100km
Petrol 4-stroke piston
1984cc 121.0cu in
In-line 4 fuel injection
Compression ratio: 10.4:1
Bore: 82.5mm 3.2in
Stroke: 92.8mm 3.6in
Valve type/No: Overhead 8
Transmission: Manual
No. of forward speeds: 5
Wheels driven: Front
Springs F/R: Coil/Coil
Brake system: PA
Brakes F/R: Disc/Disc
Steering: Rack & pinion PA
Wheelbase: 247.5cm 97.4in
Track F: 146.2cm 57.6in
Track R: 144.4cm 56.9in
Length: 402.0cm 158.3in
Width: 171.0cm 67.3in
Height: 140.5cm 55.3in
Fuel: 55.1L 12.1gal 14.5galUS

4891 Volvo

444
1954 Sweden
78.0mph 125.5kmh
0-50mph 80.5kmh: 17.9secs
0-60mph 96.5kmh: 29.6secs
0-1/4 mile: 23.9secs
44.0bhp 32.8kW 44.6PS
@ 4000rpm
67.0lbft 90.8Nm @ 2200rpm
46.3bhp/ton 45.5bhp/tonne
31.1bhp/L 23.2kW/L 31.5PS/L
35.0ft/sec 10.7m/sec
16.0mph 25.7kmh/1000rpm
28.0mpg 23.3mpgUS 10.1L/100km
Petrol 4-stroke piston
1414cc 86.3cu in
In-line 4
Compression ratio: 6.5:1
Bore: 75.0mm 2.9in
Stroke: 80.0mm 3.1in
Valve type/No: Overhead 8
Transmission: Manual
No. of forward speeds: 3
Wheels driven: Rear
Springs F/R: Coil/Coil
Brakes F/R: Drum/Drum
Wheelbase: 260.4cm 102.5in
Track F: 129.5cm 51.0in
Track R: 132.1cm 52.0in
Length: 449.6cm 177.0in
Width: 157.5cm 62.0in
Height: 156.2cm 61.5in
Ground clearance: 20.3cm 8.0in
Kerb weight: 967.0kg 2130.0lb
Fuel: 35.3L 7.7gal 9.3galUS

4892 Volvo

PV444 California
1956 Sweden
90.0mph 144.8kmh
0-50mph 80.5kmh: 12.7secs
0-60mph 96.5kmh: 19.6secs
0-1/4 mile: 20.9secs
70.0bhp 52.2kW 71.0PS
@ 5500rpm
75.9lbft 102.8Nm @ 3000rpm
73.7bhp/ton 72.5bhp/tonne
49.5bhp/L 36.9kW/L 50.2PS/L
48.1ft/sec 14.7m/sec
16.2mph 26.1kmh/1000rpm
33.0mpg 27.5mpgUS 8.6L/100km
Petrol 4-stroke piston
1414cc 86.3cu in
In-line 4
Compression ratio: 7.8:1
Bore: 75.0mm 2.9in
Stroke: 80.0mm 3.1in
Valve type/No: Overhead 8
Transmission: Manual
No. of forward speeds: 3
Wheels driven: Rear
Springs F/R: Coil/Coil
Brakes F/R: Drum/Drum
Wheelbase: 260.4cm 102.5in
Track F: 129.5cm 51.0in
Track R: 132.1cm 52.0in

Length: 449.6cm 177.0in
Width: 157.5cm 62.0in
Height: 156.2cm 61.5in
Ground clearance: 20.3cm 8.0in
Kerb weight: 966.1kg 2128.0lb
Fuel: 35.0L 7.7gal 9.2galUS

4893 Volvo

PV444
1957 Sweden
90.0mph 144.8kmh
0-50mph 80.5kmh: 10.5secs
0-60mph 96.5kmh: 14.5secs
0-1/4 mile: 20.3secs
70.9bhp 52.9kW 71.9PS
@ 5500rpm
76.0lbft 103.0Nm @ 3000rpm
74.9bhp/ton 73.7bhp/tonne
50.1bhp/L 37.4kW/L 50.8PS/L
48.1ft/sec 14.7m/sec
Petrol 4-stroke piston
1414cc 86.3cu in
In-line 4 2 Carburettor
Compression ratio: 7.8:1
Bore: 74.9mm 2.9in
Stroke: 80.0mm 3.1in
Valve type/No: Overhead 8
Transmission: Manual
No. of forward speeds: 3
Wheels driven: Rear
Wheelbase: 260.1cm 102.4in
Track F: 129.0cm 50.8in
Track R: 131.1cm 51.6in
Kerb weight: 962.5kg 2120.0lb

4894 Volvo

PV444 Sports
1957 Sweden
91.0mph 146.4kmh
0-50mph 80.5kmh: 11.2secs
0-60mph 96.5kmh: 15.9secs
0-1/4 mile: 20.1secs
85.0bhp 63.4kW 86.2PS
@ 5500rpm
86.8lbft 117.6Nm @ 3500rpm
87.5bhp/ton 86.0bhp/tonne
53.8bhp/L 40.1kW/L 54.5PS/L
48.1ft/sec 14.7m/sec
16.2mph 26.1kmh/1000rpm
32.8mpg 27.3mpgUS 8.6L/100km
Petrol 4-stroke piston
1580cc 96.4cu in
In-line 4
Compression ratio: 8.2:1
Bore: 79.3mm 3.1in
Stroke: 80.0mm 3.1in
Valve type/No: Overhead 8
Transmission: Manual
No. of forward speeds: 3
Wheels driven: Rear
Springs F/R: Coil/Coil
Brakes F/R: Drum/Drum
Wheelbase: 259.1cm 102.0in
Track F: 129.5cm 51.0in
Track R: 130.0cm 51.2in
Length: 449.6cm 177.0in
Width: 158.8cm 62.5in
Height: 156.2cm 61.5in
Ground clearance: 19.1cm 7.5in
Kerb weight: 988.4kg 2177.0lb
Fuel: 35.0L 7.7gal 9.2galUS

4895 Volvo

PV444L
1957 Sweden
93.8mph 150.9kmh
0-50mph 80.5kmh: 10.3secs
0-60mph 96.5kmh: 14.3secs
0-1/4 mile: 19.5secs
85.0bhp 63.4kW 86.2PS
@ 5500rpm
87.0lbft 117.9Nm @ 3500rpm
87.7bhp/ton 86.3bhp/tonne
53.9bhp/L 40.2kW/L 54.6PS/L
48.1ft/sec 14.7m/sec
Petrol 4-stroke piston
1577cc 96.2cu in
In-line 4 2 Carburettor
Compression ratio: 8.2:1
Bore: 79.4mm 3.1in
Stroke: 80.0mm 3.1in
Valve type/No: Overhead 8
Transmission: Manual
No. of forward speeds: 3
Wheels driven: Rear
Wheelbase: 260.1cm 102.4in
Track F: 129.0cm 50.8in
Track R: 131.1cm 51.6in
Kerb weight: 985.2kg 2170.0lb

4896 Volvo

4-speed
1958 Sweden
93.5mph 150.4kmh
0-50mph 80.5kmh: 9.9secs
0-60mph 96.5kmh: 13.0secs
0-1/4 mile: 19.1secs
88.0bhp 65.6kW 89.2PS
@ 5500rpm
90.0lbft 122.0Nm @ 3500rpm
91.3bhp/ton 89.7bhp/tonne
55.6bhp/L 41.4kW/L 56.3PS/L
48.1ft/sec 14.7m/sec
16.7mph 26.9kmh/1000rpm
Petrol 4-stroke piston
1584cc 96.6cu in
In-line 4
Compression ratio: 8.2:1
Bore: 79.4mm 3.1in
Stroke: 80.0mm 3.1in
Valve type/No: Overhead 8
Transmission: Manual
No. of forward speeds: 4
Wheels driven: Rear
Wheelbase: 260.1cm 102.4in
Track F: 129.0cm 50.8in
Track R: 131.1cm 51.6in
Length: 449.6cm 177.0in
Width: 158.0cm 62.2in
Height: 156.0cm 61.4in
Kerb weight: 980.6kg 2160.0lb

4897 Volvo

Amazon
1958 Sweden
94.0mph 151.2kmh
0-50mph 80.5kmh: 9.7secs
0-60mph 96.5kmh: 14.0secs
0-1/4 mile: 19.9secs
85.0bhp 63.4kW 86.2PS
@ 5500rpm
87.0lbft 117.9Nm @ 3500rpm
80.9bhp/ton 79.6bhp/tonne
53.7bhp/L 40.0kW/L 54.4PS/L
48.1ft/sec 14.7m/sec
16.2mph 26.1kmh/1000rpm
26.0mpg 21.6mpgUS 10.9L/100km
Petrol 4-stroke piston
1583cc 96.6cu in
In-line 4
Compression ratio: 8.2:1
Bore: 79.4mm 3.1in
Stroke: 80.0mm 3.1in
Valve type/No: Overhead 8
Transmission: Manual
No. of forward speeds: 4
Wheels driven: Rear
Springs F/R: Coil/Coil
Brakes F/R: Drum/Drum
Wheelbase: 260.4cm 102.5in
Track F: 130.8cm 51.5in
Track R: 130.8cm 51.5in
Length: 439.4cm 173.0in
Width: 162.6cm 64.0in
Height: 151.1cm 59.5in
Ground clearance: 18.3cm 7.2in
Kerb weight: 1067.8kg 2352.0lb
Fuel: 45.5L 10.0gal 12.0galUS

4898 Volvo

122S
1959 Sweden
91.9mph 147.9kmh
0-50mph 80.5kmh: 11.4secs
0-60mph 96.5kmh: 16.2secs
0-1/4 mile: 20.0secs
85.0bhp 63.4kW 86.2PS
@ 5500rpm
87.0lbft 117.9Nm @ 3500rpm
85.6bhp/ton 84.1bhp/tonne
53.6bhp/L 40.0kW/L 54.3PS/L
52.9ft/sec 16.1m/sec
16.7mph 26.9kmh/1000rpm
Petrol 4-stroke piston
1586cc 96.8cu in
In-line 4
Compression ratio: 8.2:1
Bore: 79.4mm 3.1in
Stroke: 88.0mm 3.5in
Valve type/No: Overhead 8
Transmission: Manual
No. of forward speeds: 4
Wheels driven: Rear
Wheelbase: 260.1cm 102.4in
Track F: 131.3cm 51.7in
Track R: 131.3cm 51.7in
Length: 439.4cm 173.0in
Width: 161.3cm 63.5in
Height: 150.4cm 59.2in
Kerb weight: 1010.1kg 2225.0lb

4899 Volvo

122S
1961 Sweden
90.0mph 144.8kmh
0-50mph 80.5kmh: 12.0secs
0-60mph 96.5kmh: 16.6secs
0-1/4 mile: 20.4secs
85.0bhp 63.4kW 86.2PS
@ 5500rpm
87.0lbft 117.9Nm @ 3500rpm
79.3bhp/ton 78.0bhp/tonne
53.6bhp/L 40.0kW/L 54.3PS/L
48.1ft/sec 14.7m/sec
16.7mph 26.9kmh/1000rpm
Petrol 4-stroke piston
1586cc 96.8cu in
In-line 4 2 Carburettor
Compression ratio: 8.2:1
Bore: 79.4mm 3.1in
Stroke: 80.0mm 3.1in
Valve type/No: Overhead 8
Transmission: Manual
No. of forward speeds: 4
Wheels driven: Rear
Brakes F/R: Drum/Drum
Wheelbase: 260.1cm 102.4in
Track F: 131.3cm 51.7in
Track R: 131.3cm 51.7in
Length: 444.5cm 175.0in
Width: 160.8cm 63.3in
Height: 150.4cm 59.2in
Ground clearance: 19.6cm 7.7in
Kerb weight: 1089.6kg 2400.0lb

4900 Volvo

P1800
1961 Sweden
105.0mph 168.9kmh
0-50mph 80.5kmh: 9.0secs
0-60mph 96.5kmh: 12.4secs
0-1/4 mile: 18.0secs
100.0bhp 74.6kW 101.4PS
@ 5500rpm
108.0lbft 146.3Nm @ 4000rpm
89.6bhp/ton 88.1bhp/tonne
56.2bhp/L 41.9kW/L 57.0PS/L
48.1ft/sec 14.7m/sec
22.1mph 35.6kmh/1000rpm
Petrol 4-stroke piston
1780cc 108.6cu in
In-line 4 1 Carburettor
Compression ratio: 9.5:1
Bore: 84.1mm 3.3in
Stroke: 80.0mm 3.1in
Valve type/No: Overhead 8
Transmission: Manual with overdrive
Wheels driven: Rear
Wheelbase: 245.1cm 96.5in
Track F: 132.1cm 52.0in
Track R: 132.1cm 52.0in
Length: 439.4cm 173.0in
Width: 170.2cm 67.0in
Height: 129.5cm 51.0in
Ground clearance: 13.5cm 5.3in
Kerb weight: 1135.0kg 2500.0lb

4901 Volvo

122
1962 Sweden
99.5mph 160.1kmh
0-50mph 80.5kmh: 9.8secs
0-60mph 96.5kmh: 14.4secs
0-1/4 mile: 19.8secs
90.0bhp 67.1kW 91.2PS
@ 5000rpm
105.0lbft 142.3Nm @ 3500rpm
84.2bhp/ton 82.8bhp/tonne
50.6bhp/L 37.7kW/L 51.3PS/L
43.8ft/sec 13.3m/sec
21.0mph 33.8kmh/1000rpm
25.3mpg 21.1mpgUS 11.2L/100km
Petrol 4-stroke piston
1780cc 108.6cu in
In-line 4 2 Carburettor
Compression ratio: 8.4:1
Bore: 84.1mm 3.3in
Stroke: 80.0mm 3.1in
Valve type/No: Overhead 8
Transmission: Manual with overdrive
No. of forward speeds: 5
Wheels driven: Rear
Springs F/R: Coil/Coil
Brakes F/R: Disc/Drum
Steering: Cam & roller
Wheelbase: 260.1cm 102.4in
Track F: 131.3cm 51.7in
Track R: 131.3cm 51.7in
Length: 442.5cm 174.2in
Width: 162.1cm 63.8in
Height: 151.1cm 59.5in
Ground clearance: 20.1cm 7.9in
Kerb weight: 1086.9kg 2394.0lb
Fuel: 45.5L 10.0gal 12.0galUS

4902 Volvo

122S B18
1962 Sweden
93.0mph 149.6kmh
0-50mph 80.5kmh: 9.5secs
0-60mph 96.5kmh: 14.5secs
0-1/4 mile: 19.5secs
90.0bhp 67.1kW 91.2PS
@ 5000rpm
105.0lbft 142.3Nm @ 4000rpm
83.6bhp/ton 82.3bhp/tonne
50.6bhp/L 37.7kW/L 51.3PS/L
43.8ft/sec 13.3m/sec
18.4mph 29.6kmh/1000rpm
Petrol 4-stroke piston
1780cc 108.6cu in
In-line 4
Compression ratio: 8.5:1
Bore: 84.1mm 3.3in
Stroke: 80.0mm 3.1in
Valve type/No: Overhead 8
Transmission: Manual
No. of forward speeds: 4
Wheels driven: Rear
Wheelbase: 260.1cm 102.4in
Track F: 131.3cm 51.7in
Track R: 131.3cm 51.7in
Length: 444.5cm 175.0in
Width: 161.3cm 63.5in
Height: 150.4cm 59.2in
Ground clearance: 19.6cm 7.7in
Kerb weight: 1094.1kg 2410.0lb

4903 Volvo

P1800
1962 Sweden
104.0mph 167.3kmh
0-50mph 80.5kmh: 9.6secs
0-60mph 96.5kmh: 13.2secs
0-1/4 mile: 19.1secs
90.0bhp 67.1kW 91.2PS
@ 5500rpm
108.0lbft 146.3Nm @ 4000rpm
81.8bhp/ton 80.4bhp/tonne
50.6bhp/L 37.7kW/L 51.3PS/L
48.1ft/sec 14.7m/sec
21.0mph 33.8kmh/1000rpm
24.9mpg 20.7mpgUS 11.3L/100km
Petrol 4-stroke piston
1780cc 108.6cu in
In-line 4 2 Carburettor
Compression ratio: 9.5:1
Bore: 84.1mm 3.3in
Stroke: 80.0mm 3.1in
Valve type/No: Overhead 8
Transmission: Manual with overdrive
No. of forward speeds: 5
Wheels driven: Rear
Springs F/R: Coil/Coil
Brake system: PA
Brakes F/R: Disc/Drum
Steering: Cam & roller
Wheelbase: 245.1cm 96.5in
Track F: 131.3cm 51.7in
Track R: 131.3cm 51.7in
Length: 439.9cm 173.2in
Width: 170.2cm 67.0in
Height: 129.5cm 51.0in
Ground clearance: 15.2cm 6.0in
Kerb weight: 1118.7kg 2464.0lb
Fuel: 45.5L 10.0gal 12.0galUS

4904 Volvo

121 Estate
1963 Sweden
89.0mph 143.2kmh
0-50mph 80.5kmh: 13.9secs
0-60mph 96.5kmh: 21.1secs
0-1/4 mile: 22.0secs

68.0bhp 50.7kW 68.9PS
@ 4500rpm
101.0lbft 136.9Nm @ 2800rpm
58.9bhp/ton 57.9bhp/tonne
38.2bhp/L 28.5kW/L 38.7PS/L
39.4ft/sec 12.0m/sec
16.2mph 26.1kmh/1000rpm
29.5mpg 24.6mpgUS 9.6L/100km
Petrol 4-stroke piston
1780cc 108.6cu in
In-line 4 1 Carburettor
Compression ratio: 8.5:1
Bore: 84.1mm 3.3in
Stroke: 80.0mm 3.1in
Valve type/No: Overhead 8
Transmission: Manual
No. of forward speeds: 4
Wheels driven: Rear
Springs F/R: Coil/Coil
Brakes F/R: Drum/Drum
Steering: Cam & roller
Wheelbase: 260.1cm 102.4in
Track F: 131.3cm 51.7in
Track R: 131.3cm 51.7in
Length: 442.0cm 174.0in
Width: 162.1cm 63.8in
Height: 156.2cm 61.5in
Ground clearance: 20.1cm 7.9in
Kerb weight: 1174.0kg 2586.0lb
Fuel: 45.5L 10.0gal 12.0galUS

4905 Volvo

PV544
1963 Sweden
92.0mph 148.0kmh
0-50mph 80.5kmh: 9.6secs
0-60mph 96.5kmh: 14.1secs
0-1/4 mile: 19.1secs
90.0bhp 67.1kW 91.2PS
@ 5000rpm
105.0lbft 142.3Nm @ 3500rpm
93.3bhp/ton 91.8bhp/tonne
50.6bhp/L 37.7kW/L 51.3PS/L
43.8ft/sec 13.3m/sec
18.4mph 29.6kmh/1000rpm
Petrol 4-stroke piston
1780cc 108.6cu in
In-line 4 1 Carburettor
Compression ratio: 8.5:1
Bore: 84.1mm 3.3in
Stroke: 80.0mm 3.1in
Valve type/No: Overhead 8
Transmission: Manual
No. of forward speeds: 4
Wheels driven: Rear
Wheelbase: 260.4cm 102.5in
Track F: 129.5cm 51.0in
Track R: 131.3cm 51.7in
Length: 444.5cm 175.0in
Width: 158.8cm 62.5in
Height: 156.2cm 61.5in
Ground clearance: 19.1cm 7.5in
Kerb weight: 980.6kg 2160.0lb

4906 Volvo

122 Automatic
1965 Sweden
90.0mph 144.8kmh
0-50mph 80.5kmh: 11.1secs
0-60mph 96.5kmh: 15.8secs
0-1/4 mile: 20.6secs
90.0bhp 67.1kW 91.2PS
@ 5000rpm
105.0lbft 142.3Nm @ 3500rpm
78.4bhp/ton 77.1bhp/tonne
50.6bhp/L 37.7kW/L 51.3PS/L
43.8ft/sec 13.3m/sec
17.6mph 28.3kmh/1000rpm
Petrol 4-stroke piston
1780cc 108.6cu in
In-line 4 2 Carburettor
Compression ratio: 8.5:1
Bore: 84.1mm 3.3in
Stroke: 80.0mm 3.1in
Valve type/No: Overhead 8
Transmission: Automatic
No. of forward speeds: 3
Wheels driven: Rear
Springs F/R: Coil/Coil
Brakes F/R: Disc/Drum
Steering: Cam & roller
Wheelbase: 260.4cm 102.5in
Track F: 131.3cm 51.7in
Track R: 131.3cm 51.7in
Length: 444.5cm 175.0in
Width: 162.1cm 63.8in
Height: 150.6cm 59.3in
Ground clearance: 17.5cm 6.9in
Kerb weight: 1166.8kg 2570.0lb
Fuel: 45.4L 10.0gal 12.0galUS

4907 Volvo

131
1965 Sweden
92.0mph 148.0kmh
0-50mph 80.5kmh: 11.5secs
0-60mph 96.5kmh: 17.6secs
0-1/4 mile: 20.7secs
75.0bhp 55.9kW 76.0PS
@ 4500rpm
101.0lbft 136.9Nm @ 2800rpm
72.3bhp/ton 71.1bhp/tonne
42.1bhp/L 31.4kW/L 42.7PS/L
39.4ft/sec 12.0m/sec
18.0mph 29.0kmh/1000rpm
26.5mpg 22.1mpgUS 10.7L/100km
Petrol 4-stroke piston
1780cc 108.6cu in
In-line 4 1 Carburettor
Compression ratio: 8.5:1
Bore: 84.1mm 3.3in
Stroke: 80.0mm 3.1in
Valve type/No: Overhead 8
Transmission: Manual
No. of forward speeds: 4
Wheels driven: Rear
Springs F/R: Coil/Coil
Brakes F/R: Disc/Drum
Steering: Cam & roller
Wheelbase: 260.1cm 102.4in
Track F: 131.3cm 51.7in
Track R: 131.3cm 51.7in
Length: 442.5cm 174.2in
Width: 162.1cm 63.8in
Height: 151.1cm 59.5in
Ground clearance: 20.1cm 7.9in
Kerb weight: 1055.1kg 2324.0lb
Fuel: 45.5L 10.0gal 12.0galUS

4908 Volvo

1800S
1966 Sweden
111.0mph 178.6kmh
0-50mph 80.5kmh: 8.7secs
0-60mph 96.5kmh: 11.9secs
0-1/4 mile: 18.6secs
0-1km: 34.0secs
103.0bhp 76.8kW 104.4PS
@ 5600rpm
108.5lbft 147.0Nm @ 3800rpm
96.8bhp/ton 95.2bhp/tonne
57.9bhp/L 43.1kW/L 58.7PS/L
49.0ft/sec 14.9m/sec
21.1mph 33.9kmh/1000rpm
24.0mpg 20.0mpgUS 11.8L/100km
Petrol 4-stroke piston
1780cc 108.6cu in
In-line 4 2 Carburettor
Compression ratio: 10.0:1
Bore: 84.1mm 3.3in
Stroke: 80.0mm 3.1in
Valve type/No: Overhead 8
Transmission: Manual with overdrive
No. of forward speeds: 5
Wheels driven: Rear
Springs F/R: Coil/Coil
Brake system: PA
Brakes F/R: Disc/Drum
Steering: Cam & roller
Wheelbase: 245.1cm 96.5in
Track F: 131.3cm 51.7in
Track R: 131.3cm 51.7in
Length: 439.9cm 173.2in
Width: 170.2cm 67.0in
Height: 129.5cm 51.0in
Ground clearance: 15.2cm 6.0in
Kerb weight: 1081.9kg 2383.0lb
Fuel: 45.5L 10.0gal 12.0galUS

4909 Volvo

144S
1967 Sweden
103.0mph 165.7kmh
0-50mph 80.5kmh: 9.0secs
0-60mph 96.5kmh: 12.6secs
0-1/4 mile: 18.6secs
0-1km: 34.6secs
100.0bhp 74.6kW 101.4PS
@ 5600rpm
107.0lbft 145.0Nm @ 3500rpm
88.3bhp/ton 86.8bhp/tonne
56.2bhp/L 41.9kW/L 57.0PS/L
49.0ft/sec 14.9m/sec
17.7mph 28.5kmh/1000rpm
22.7mpg 18.9mpgUS 12.4L/100km
Petrol 4-stroke piston
1780cc 108.6cu in
In-line 4 2 Carburettor
Compression ratio: 10.0:1
Bore: 84.1mm 3.3in
Stroke: 80.0mm 3.1in
Valve type/No: Overhead 8
Transmission: Manual
No. of forward speeds: 4
Wheels driven: Rear
Springs F/R: Coil/Coil
Brake system: PA
Brakes F/R: Disc/Drum
Steering: Cam & roller
Wheelbase: 260.4cm 102.5in
Track F: 135.1cm 53.2in
Track R: 135.1cm 53.2in
Length: 464.8cm 183.0in
Width: 172.7cm 68.0in
Height: 144.8cm 57.0in
Ground clearance: 19.1cm 7.5in
Kerb weight: 1151.8kg 2537.0lb
Fuel: 59.1L 13.0gal 15.6galUS

4910 Volvo

145S Estate
1968 Sweden
99.0mph 159.3kmh
0-50mph 80.5kmh: 10.0secs
0-60mph 96.5kmh: 14.5secs
0-1/4 mile: 19.6secs
0-1km: 36.0secs
100.0bhp 74.6kW 101.4PS
@ 5600rpm
107.0lbft 145.0Nm @ 3500rpm
83.6bhp/ton 82.2bhp/tonne
56.2bhp/L 41.9kW/L 57.0PS/L
49.0ft/sec 14.9m/sec
15.6mph 25.1kmh/1000rpm
20.7mpg 17.2mpgUS 13.6L/100km
Petrol 4-stroke piston
1778cc 108.5cu in
In-line 4 2 Carburettor
Compression ratio: 10.0:1
Bore: 84.1mm 3.3in
Stroke: 80.0mm 3.1in
Valve type/No: Overhead 8
Transmission: Manual
No. of forward speeds: 4
Wheels driven: Rear
Springs F/R: Coil/Coil
Brake system: PA
Brakes F/R: Disc/Disc
Steering: Cam & roller
Wheelbase: 260.4cm 102.5in
Track F: 135.1cm 53.2in
Track R: 135.1cm 53.2in
Length: 464.8cm 183.0in
Width: 172.7cm 68.0in
Height: 144.8cm 57.0in
Ground clearance: 19.1cm 7.5in
Kerb weight: 1215.8kg 2678.0lb
Fuel: 61.4L 13.5gal 16.2galUS

4911 Volvo

145S Wagon
1968 Sweden
100.0mph 160.9kmh
0-1/4 mile: 19.0secs
115.0bhp 85.8kW 116.6PS
64.7bhp/L 48.2kW/L 65.6PS/L
26.4mpg 22.0mpgUS 10.7L/100km
Petrol 4-stroke piston
1778cc 108.5cu in
In-line 4
Valve type/No: Overhead 8
Wheels driven: Rear
Wheelbase: 260.1cm 102.4in
Length: 464.1cm 182.7in

4912 Volvo

142S 2.0
1969 Sweden
103.0mph 165.7kmh
0-50mph 80.5kmh: 8.5secs
0-60mph 96.5kmh: 12.3secs
0-1/4 mile: 18.5secs
118.0bhp 88.0kW 119.6PS
@ 5800rpm
123.0lbft 166.7Nm @ 3500rpm
105.1bhp/ton 103.3bhp/tonne
59.4bhp/L 44.3kW/L 60.2PS/L
50.7ft/sec 15.5m/sec
17.3mph 27.8kmh/1000rpm
25.2mpg 21.0mpgUS 11.2L/100km
Petrol 4-stroke piston
1986cc 121.2cu in
In-line 4 2 Carburettor
Compression ratio: 9.5:1
Bore: 89.0mm 3.5in
Stroke: 80.0mm 3.1in
Valve type/No: Overhead 8
Transmission: Manual
No. of forward speeds: 4
Wheels driven: Rear
Springs F/R: Coil/Coil
Brakes F/R: Disc/Disc
Steering: Cam & roller
Wheelbase: 260.1cm 102.4in
Track F: 134.9cm 53.1in
Track R: 134.9cm 53.1in
Length: 464.1cm 182.7in
Width: 173.0cm 68.1in
Height: 144.8cm 57.0in
Ground clearance: 18.0cm 7.1in
Kerb weight: 1141.8kg 2515.0lb
Fuel: 57.5L 12.6gal 15.2galUS

4913 Volvo

144S
1969 Sweden
102.0mph 164.1kmh
0-50mph 80.5kmh: 9.0secs
0-60mph 96.5kmh: 12.9secs
0-1/4 mile: 18.8secs
0-1km: 35.1secs
118.0bhp 88.0kW 119.6PS
@ 6000rpm
123.0lbft 166.7Nm @ 3500rpm
103.7bhp/ton 102.0bhp/tonne
59.4bhp/L 44.3kW/L 60.2PS/L
52.5ft/sec 16.0m/sec
17.4mph 28.0kmh/1000rpm
22.3mpg 18.6mpgUS 12.7L/100km
Petrol 4-stroke piston
1986cc 121.2cu in
In-line 4 2 Carburettor
Compression ratio: 9.5:1
Bore: 88.9mm 3.5in
Stroke: 80.0mm 3.1in
Valve type/No: Overhead 8
Transmission: Manual
No. of forward speeds: 4
Wheels driven: Rear
Springs F/R: Coil/Coil
Brake system: PA
Brakes F/R: Disc/Disc
Steering: Cam & roller
Wheelbase: 260.4cm 102.5in
Track F: 134.9cm 53.1in
Track R: 134.9cm 53.1in
Length: 464.8cm 183.0in
Width: 173.0cm 68.1in
Height: 144.0cm 56.7in
Ground clearance: 19.6cm 7.7in
Kerb weight: 1156.8kg 2548.0lb
Fuel: 61.4L 13.5gal 16.2galUS

4914 Volvo

164
1969 Sweden
110.0mph 177.0kmh
0-50mph 80.5kmh: 6.5secs
0-60mph 96.5kmh: 9.5secs
0-1/4 mile: 17.6secs
145.0bhp 108.1kW 147.0PS
@ 5500rpm
163.0lbft 220.9Nm @ 3300rpm
111.2bhp/ton 109.4bhp/tonne
48.7bhp/L 36.3kW/L 49.3PS/L
48.1ft/sec 14.7m/sec
20.1mph 32.3kmh/1000rpm
21.0mpg 17.5mpgUS 13.4L/100km
Petrol 4-stroke piston
2979cc 181.8cu in
In-line 6 2 Carburettor
Compression ratio: 9.2:1
Bore: 89.0mm 3.5in
Stroke: 80.0mm 3.1in
Valve type/No: Overhead 12
Transmission: Manual
No. of forward speeds: 4
Wheels driven: Rear
Springs F/R: Coil/Coil
Brake system: PA
Brakes F/R: Disc/Disc
Steering: Cam & roller PA
Wheelbase: 270.0cm 106.3in
Track F: 134.9cm 53.1in
Track R: 134.9cm 53.1in
Length: 471.4cm 185.6in

Width: 173.5cm 68.3in
Height: 144.0cm 56.7in
Ground clearance: 18.0cm 7.1in
Kerb weight: 1325.7kg 2920.0lb
Fuel: 58.7L 12.9gal 15.5galUS

4915 Volvo

164 Automatic
1970 Sweden
113.0mph 181.8kmh
0-50mph 80.5kmh: 9.6secs
0-60mph 96.5kmh: 12.8secs
0-1/4 mile: 19.0secs
0-1km: 34.7secs
130.0bhp 96.9kW 131.8PS
@ 5000rpm
152.0lbft 206.0Nm @ 2500rpm
97.4bhp/ton 95.8bhp/tonne
43.6bhp/L 32.5kW/L 44.3PS/L
43.8ft/sec 13.3m/sec
21.9mph 35.2kmh/1000rpm
17.9mpg 14.9mpgUS 15.8L/100km
Petrol 4-stroke piston
2978cc 181.7cu in
In-line 6 1 Carburettor
Compression ratio: 9.2:1
Bore: 88.9mm 3.5in
Stroke: 80.0mm 3.1in
Valve type/No: Overhead 12
Transmission: Automatic
No. of forward speeds: 3
Wheels driven: Rear
Springs F/R: Coil/Coil
Brake system: PA
Brakes F/R: Disc/Disc
Steering: Recirculating ball PA
Wheelbase: 270.5cm 106.5in
Track F: 134.6cm 53.0in
Track R: 134.6cm 53.0in
Length: 472.4cm 186.0in
Width: 173.0cm 68.1in
Height: 144.0cm 56.7in
Ground clearance: 17.8cm 7.0in
Kerb weight: 1357.5kg 2990.0lb
Fuel: 57.8L 12.7gal 15.3galUS

4916 Volvo

1800E
1970 Sweden
115.0mph 185.0kmh
0-50mph 80.5kmh: 7.1secs
0-60mph 96.5kmh: 10.1secs
0-1/4 mile: 17.5secs
130.0bhp 96.9kW 131.8PS
@ 6000rpm
130.0lbft 176.2Nm @ 3500rpm
114.9bhp/ton 113.0bhp/tonne
65.5bhp/L 48.8kW/L 66.4PS/L
52.5ft/sec 16.0m/sec
20.8mph 33.5kmh/1000rpm
25.1mpg 20.9mpgUS 11.3L/100km
Petrol 4-stroke piston
1986cc 121.2cu in
In-line 4 fuel injection
Compression ratio: 10.5:1
Bore: 89.0mm 3.5in
Stroke: 80.0mm 3.1in
Valve type/No: Overhead 8
Transmission: Manual with overdrive
Wheels driven: Rear
Springs F/R: Coil/Coil
Brake system: PA
Brakes F/R: Disc/Disc
Steering: Worm & roller
Wheelbase: 245.1cm 96.5in
Track F: 131.1cm 51.6in
Track R: 131.1cm 51.6in
Length: 435.1cm 171.3in
Width: 169.9cm 66.9in
Height: 128.0cm 50.4in
Ground clearance: 15.5cm 6.1in
Kerb weight: 1150.9kg 2535.0lb
Fuel: 44.7L 9.8gal 11.8galUS

4917 Volvo

142E
1971 Sweden
106.0mph 170.6kmh
0-50mph 80.5kmh: 7.2secs
0-60mph 96.5kmh: 10.5secs
0-1/4 mile: 17.5secs
130.0bhp 96.9kW 131.8PS
@ 6000rpm
133.0lbft 180.2Nm @ 3500rpm
108.0bhp/ton 106.2bhp/tonne
65.5bhp/L 48.8kW/L 66.4PS/L
52.5ft/sec 16.0m/sec
17.0mph 27.4kmh/1000rpm
28.5mpg 23.7mpgUS 9.9L/100km
Petrol 4-stroke piston
1986cc 121.2cu in
In-line 4 fuel injection
Compression ratio: 10.5:1
Bore: 89.0mm 3.5in
Stroke: 80.0mm 3.1in
Valve type/No: Overhead 8
Transmission: Manual with overdrive
Wheels driven: Rear
Springs F/R: Coil/Coil
Brake system: PA
Brakes F/R: Disc/Disc
Steering: Cam & roller
Wheelbase: 261.9cm 103.1in
Track F: 134.9cm 53.1in
Track R: 134.9cm 53.1in
Length: 464.1cm 182.7in
Width: 173.5cm 68.3in
Height: 146.6cm 57.7in
Ground clearance: 18.0cm 7.1in
Kerb weight: 1223.5kg 2695.0lb
Fuel: 58.7L 12.9gal 15.5galUS

4918 Volvo

144 Grand Luxe
1971 Sweden
107.0mph 172.2kmh
0-50mph 80.5kmh: 8.7secs
0-60mph 96.5kmh: 11.6secs
0-1/4 mile: 18.3secs
0-1km: 34.3secs
120.0bhp 89.5kW 121.7PS
@ 6000rpm
123.0lbft 166.7Nm @ 3500rpm
101.8bhp/ton 100.1bhp/tonne
60.4bhp/L 45.1kW/L 61.3PS/L
52.5ft/sec 16.0m/sec
17.9mph 28.8kmh/1000rpm
23.8mpg 19.8mpgUS 11.9L/100km
Petrol 4-stroke piston
1986cc 121.2cu in
In-line 4 fuel injection
Compression ratio: 10.5:1
Bore: 88.9mm 3.5in
Stroke: 80.0mm 3.1in
Valve type/No: Overhead 8
Transmission: Manual
No. of forward speeds: 4
Wheels driven: Rear
Springs F/R: Coil/Coil
Brake system: PA
Brakes F/R: Disc/Disc
Steering: Cam & roller
Wheelbase: 260.4cm 102.5in
Track F: 134.9cm 53.1in
Track R: 134.9cm 53.1in
Length: 464.8cm 183.0in
Width: 173.0cm 68.1in
Height: 144.0cm 56.7in
Ground clearance: 19.6cm 7.7in
Kerb weight: 1198.6kg 2640.0lb
Fuel: 58.7L 12.9gal 15.5galUS

4919 Volvo

145E Estate
1971 Sweden
104.0mph 167.3kmh
0-50mph 80.5kmh: 8.4secs
0-60mph 96.5kmh: 11.5secs
0-1/4 mile: 18.1secs
0-1km: 33.6secs
115.0bhp 85.8kW 116.6PS
@ 6000rpm
116.0lbft 157.2Nm @ 3500rpm
91.3bhp/ton 89.8bhp/tonne
57.9bhp/L 43.2kW/L 58.7PS/L
52.5ft/sec 16.0m/sec
17.9mph 28.8kmh/1000rpm
18.9mpg 15.7mpgUS 14.9L/100km
Petrol 4-stroke piston
1986cc 121.2cu in
In-line 4 fuel injection
Compression ratio: 8.7:1
Bore: 88.9mm 3.5in
Stroke: 80.0mm 3.1in
Valve type/No: Overhead 8
Transmission: Manual
No. of forward speeds: 4
Wheels driven: Rear
Springs F/R: Coil/Coil
Brake system: PA
Brakes F/R: Disc/Disc
Steering: Worm & roller
Wheelbase: 260.4cm 102.5in
Track F: 135.1cm 53.2in
Track R: 135.1cm 53.2in
Length: 464.8cm 183.0in
Width: 172.7cm 68.0in
Height: 144.8cm 57.0in
Ground clearance: 19.1cm 7.5in
Kerb weight: 1281.2kg 2822.0lb
Fuel: 58.2L 12.8gal 15.4galUS

4920 Volvo

164E
1972 Sweden
115.0mph 185.0kmh
0-50mph 80.5kmh: 9.0secs
0-60mph 96.5kmh: 12.0secs
0-1/4 mile: 18.8secs
138.0bhp 102.9kW 139.9PS
@ 5800rpm
154.0lbft 208.7Nm @ 2500rpm
101.7bhp/ton 100.0bhp/tonne
46.3bhp/L 34.5kW/L 47.0PS/L
50.7ft/sec 15.5m/sec
20.1mph 32.3kmh/1000rpm
21.3mpg 17.7mpgUS 13.3L/100km
Petrol 4-stroke piston
2979cc 181.8cu in
In-line 6 fuel injection
Compression ratio: 8.7:1
Bore: 89.0mm 3.5in
Stroke: 80.0mm 3.1in
Valve type/No: Overhead 12
Transmission: Automatic
No. of forward speeds: 3
Wheels driven: Rear
Springs F/R: Coil/Coil
Brake system: PA
Brakes F/R: Disc/Disc
Steering: Recirculating ball PA
Wheelbase: 272.0cm 107.1in
Track F: 135.1cm 53.2in
Track R: 135.1cm 53.2in
Length: 471.4cm 185.6in
Width: 173.0cm 68.1in
Height: 144.0cm 56.7in
Ground clearance: 18.0cm 7.1in
Kerb weight: 1380.2kg 3040.0lb
Fuel: 57.9L 12.7gal 15.3galUS

4921 Volvo

1800 ES
1972 Sweden
116.0mph 186.6kmh
0-50mph 80.5kmh: 8.0secs
0-60mph 96.5kmh: 11.3secs
0-1/4 mile: 18.2secs
112.0bhp 83.5kW 113.5PS
@ 6000rpm
115.0lbft 155.8Nm @ 3500rpm
97.6bhp/ton 96.0bhp/tonne
56.4bhp/L 42.0kW/L 57.2PS/L
52.5ft/sec 16.0m/sec
21.4mph 34.4kmh/1000rpm
27.0mpg 22.5mpgUS 10.5L/100km
Petrol 4-stroke piston
1986cc 121.2cu in
In-line 4 fuel injection
Compression ratio: 8.7:1
Bore: 89.0mm 3.5in
Stroke: 80.0mm 3.1in
Valve type/No: Overhead 8
Transmission: Manual with overdrive
Wheels driven: Rear
Springs F/R: Coil/Coil
Brake system: PA
Brakes F/R: Disc/Disc
Steering: Cam & roller
Wheelbase: 245.1cm 96.5in
Track F: 131.1cm 51.6in
Track R: 131.1cm 51.6in
Length: 438.4cm 172.6in
Width: 169.9cm 66.9in
Height: 128.0cm 50.4in
Ground clearance: 15.5cm 6.1in
Kerb weight: 1166.8kg 2570.0lb
Fuel: 45.0L 9.9gal 11.9galUS

4922 Volvo

144 de Luxe
1973 Sweden
94.0mph 151.2kmh
0-50mph 80.5kmh: 9.8secs
0-60mph 96.5kmh: 13.9secs
0-1/4 mile: 19.8secs
0-1km: 37.2secs
82.0bhp 61.1kW 83.1PS
@ 4700rpm
116.0lbft 157.2Nm @ 2300rpm
68.1bhp/ton 67.0bhp/tonne
41.3bhp/L 30.8kW/L 41.9PS/L
41.1ft/sec 12.5m/sec
17.8mph 28.6kmh/1000rpm
23.5mpg 19.6mpgUS 12.0L/100km
Petrol 4-stroke piston
1986cc 121.2cu in
In-line 4 1 Carburettor
Compression ratio: 8.7:1
Bore: 88.9mm 3.5in
Stroke: 80.0mm 3.1in
Valve type/No: Overhead 8
Transmission: Manual
No. of forward speeds: 4
Wheels driven: Rear
Springs F/R: Coil/Coil
Brake system: PA
Brakes F/R: Disc/Disc
Steering: Worm & roller
Wheelbase: 260.4cm 102.5in
Track F: 134.9cm 53.1in
Track R: 134.9cm 53.1in
Length: 464.8cm 183.0in
Width: 173.0cm 68.1in
Height: 144.0cm 56.7in
Ground clearance: 19.6cm 7.7in
Kerb weight: 1224.0kg 2696.0lb
Fuel: 58.2L 12.8gal 15.4galUS

4923 Volvo

144E
1973 Sweden
0-60mph 96.5kmh: 14.5secs
0-1/4 mile: 20.0secs
112.0bhp 83.5kW 113.5PS
@ 6000rpm
115.0lbft 155.8Nm @ 3500rpm
91.7bhp/ton 90.2bhp/tonne
56.4bhp/L 42.0kW/L 57.2PS/L
52.5ft/sec 16.0m/sec
23.4mpg 19.5mpgUS 12.1L/100km
Petrol 4-stroke piston
1986cc 121.2cu in
In-line 4 fuel injection
Compression ratio: 8.7:1
Bore: 88.9mm 3.5in
Stroke: 80.0mm 3.1in
Valve type/No: Overhead 8
Transmission: Manual
No. of forward speeds: 4
Wheels driven: Rear
Brake system: PA
Brakes F/R: Disc/Disc
Wheelbase: 261.6cm 103.0in
Length: 464.1cm 182.7in
Width: 170.4cm 67.1in
Height: 145.5cm 57.3in
Ground clearance: 16.5cm 6.5in
Kerb weight: 1241.7kg 2735.0lb
Fuel: 57.9L 12.7gal 15.3galUS

4924 Volvo

164E
1973 Sweden
120.0mph 193.1kmh
0-50mph 80.5kmh: 6.9secs
0-60mph 96.5kmh: 10.0secs
0-1/4 mile: 17.5secs
0-1km: 32.2secs
160.0bhp 119.3kW 162.2PS
@ 5500rpm
170.0lbft 230.4Nm @ 2500rpm
112.3bhp/ton 110.4bhp/tonne
53.7bhp/L 40.1kW/L 54.5PS/L
48.1ft/sec 14.7m/sec
26.7mph 43.0kmh/1000rpm
17.5mpg 14.6mpgUS 16.1L/100km
Petrol 4-stroke piston
2978cc 181.7cu in
In-line 6 fuel injection
Compression ratio: 10.0:1
Bore: 88.9mm 3.5in
Stroke: 80.0mm 3.1in
Valve type/No: Overhead 12
Transmission: Manual with overdrive
No. of forward speeds: 5
Wheels driven: Rear
Springs F/R: Coil/Coil
Brake system: PA
Brakes F/R: Disc/Disc
Steering: Recirculating ball PA
Wheelbase: 270.5cm 106.5in
Track F: 134.6cm 53.0in
Track R: 134.6cm 53.0in
Length: 472.4cm 186.0in
Width: 173.0cm 68.1in

Height: 144.0cm 56.7in
Ground clearance: 17.8cm 7.0in
Kerb weight: 1449.2kg 3192.0lb
Fuel: 58.2L 12.8gal 15.4galUS

4925 Volvo
142 GL
1974 Sweden
102.0mph 164.1kmh
0-50mph 80.5kmh: 9.0secs
0-60mph 96.5kmh: 12.7secs
0-1/4 mile: 18.7secs
109.0bhp 81.3kW 110.5PS
@ 6000rpm
115.0lbft 155.8Nm @ 3500rpm
85.1bhp/ton 83.6bhp/tonne
54.8bhp/L 40.8kW/L 55.5PS/L
52.5ft/sec 16.0m/sec
21.1mph 33.9kmh/1000rpm
24.0mpg 20.0mpgUS 11.8L/100km
Petrol 4-stroke piston
1990cc 121.4cu in
In-line 4
Compression ratio: 8.7:1
Bore: 88.9mm 3.5in
Stroke: 80.0mm 3.1in
Valve type/No: Overhead 8
Transmission: Manual with overdrive
Wheels driven: Rear
Springs F/R: Coil/Coil
Brake system: PA
Brakes F/R: Disc/Disc
Steering: Cam & roller
Wheelbase: 261.6cm 103.0in
Track F: 134.9cm 53.1in
Track R: 134.9cm 53.1in
Length: 477.5cm 188.0in
Width: 170.4cm 67.1in
Height: 143.5cm 56.5in
Kerb weight: 1303.0kg 2870.0lb
Fuel: 59.8L 13.1gal 15.8galUS

4926 Volvo
145
1974 Sweden
0-60mph 96.5kmh: 16.3secs
0-1/4 mile: 20.1secs
109.0bhp 81.3kW 110.5PS
@ 6000rpm
115.0lbft 155.8Nm @ 3500rpm
80.8bhp/ton 79.5bhp/tonne
54.9bhp/L 40.9kW/L 55.6PS/L
22.8mpg 19.0mpgUS 12.4L/100km
Petrol 4-stroke piston
1986cc 121.2cu in
In-line 4
Valve type/No: Overhead 8
Transmission: Manual
No. of forward speeds: 4
Wheels driven: Rear
Brakes F/R: Disc/Disc
Wheelbase: 261.6cm 103.0in
Length: 477.5cm 188.0in
Width: 170.4cm 67.1in
Height: 145.0cm 57.1in
Kerb weight: 1371.1kg 3020.0lb

4927 Volvo
242 GL
1975 Sweden
95.0mph 152.9kmh
0-50mph 80.5kmh: 10.0secs
0-60mph 96.5kmh: 14.2secs
0-1/4 mile: 20.1secs
94.0bhp 70.1kW 95.3PS
@ 6000rpm
105.0lbft 142.3Nm @ 3500rpm
68.1bhp/ton 67.0bhp/tonne
47.2bhp/L 35.2kW/L 47.9PS/L
52.5ft/sec 16.0m/sec
21.0mph 33.8kmh/1000rpm
22.2mpg 18.5mpgUS 12.7L/100km
Petrol 4-stroke piston
1990cc 121.4cu in
In-line 4 fuel injection
Compression ratio: 8.7:1
Bore: 88.9mm 3.5in
Stroke: 80.0mm 3.1in
Valve type/No: Overhead 8
Transmission: Manual with overdrive
Wheels driven: Rear
Springs F/R: Coil/Coil
Brake system: PA
Brakes F/R: Disc/Disc
Steering: Rack & pinion PA
Wheelbase: 264.2cm 104.0in
Track F: 142.0cm 55.9in
Track R: 134.9cm 53.1in
Length: 489.2cm 192.6in
Width: 170.4cm 67.1in
Height: 143.5cm 56.5in
Ground clearance: 18.0cm 7.1in
Kerb weight: 1402.9kg 3090.0lb
Fuel: 59.8L 13.1gal 15.8galUS

4928 Volvo
244 GL
1975 Sweden
106.0mph 170.6kmh
0-50mph 80.5kmh: 7.7secs
0-60mph 96.5kmh: 11.4secs
0-1/4 mile: 18.0secs
0-1km: 33.7secs
123.0bhp 91.7kW 124.7PS
@ 5500rpm
130.0lbft 176.2Nm @ 3500rpm
93.4bhp/ton 91.8bhp/tonne
57.8bhp/L 43.1kW/L 58.6PS/L
48.1ft/sec 14.7m/sec
22.3mph 35.9kmh/1000rpm
21.3mpg 17.7mpgUS 13.3L/100km
Petrol 4-stroke piston
2127cc 129.8cu in
In-line 4 fuel injection
Compression ratio: 9.3:1
Bore: 92.0mm 3.6in
Stroke: 80.0mm 3.1in
Valve type/No: Overhead 8
Transmission: Manual with overdrive
No. of forward speeds: 5
Wheels driven: Rear
Springs F/R: Coil/Coil
Brake system: PA
Brakes F/R: Disc/Disc
Steering: Recirculating ball
Wheelbase: 264.2cm 104.0in
Track F: 134.9cm 53.1in
Track R: 134.9cm 53.1in
Length: 487.7cm 192.0in
Width: 170.4cm 67.1in
Height: 143.5cm 56.5in
Ground clearance: 19.6cm 7.7in
Kerb weight: 1339.3kg 2950.0lb
Fuel: 60.1L 13.2gal 15.9galUS

4929 Volvo
264 GL
1975 Sweden
108.0mph 173.8kmh
0-50mph 80.5kmh: 9.4secs
0-60mph 96.5kmh: 12.7secs
0-1/4 mile: 19.1secs
0-1km: 35.1secs
140.0bhp 104.4kW 141.9PS
@ 6000rpm
150.0lbft 203.3Nm @ 3000rpm
100.3bhp/ton 98.7bhp/tonne
52.5bhp/L 39.2kW/L 53.3PS/L
47.8ft/sec 14.6m/sec
20.2mph 32.5kmh/1000rpm
18.6mpg 15.5mpgUS 15.2L/100km
Petrol 4-stroke piston
2664cc 162.5cu in
Vee 6 fuel injection
Compression ratio: 8.7:1
Bore: 88.0mm 3.5in
Stroke: 73.0mm 2.9in
Valve type/No: Overhead 12
Transmission: Automatic
No. of forward speeds: 3
Wheels driven: Rear
Springs F/R: Coil/Coil
Brake system: PA
Brakes F/R: Disc/Disc
Steering: Rack & pinion PA
Wheelbase: 264.2cm 104.0in
Track F: 134.9cm 53.1in
Track R: 134.9cm 53.1in
Length: 487.7cm 192.0in
Width: 170.4cm 67.1in
Height: 143.5cm 56.5in
Ground clearance: 19.6cm 7.7in
Kerb weight: 1418.7kg 3125.0lb
Fuel: 60.1L 13.2gal 15.9galUS

4930 Volvo
242 GL
1976 Sweden
98.0mph 157.7kmh
0-50mph 80.5kmh: 9.5secs
0-60mph 96.5kmh: 13.0secs
0-1/4 mile: 18.8secs
99.0bhp 73.8kW 100.4PS
@ 5200rpm
114.0lbft 154.5Nm @ 2500rpm
76.1bhp/ton 74.8bhp/tonne
46.5bhp/L 34.7kW/L 47.2PS/L
45.5ft/sec 13.9m/sec
23.0mph 37.0kmh/1000rpm
25.2mpg 21.0mpgUS 11.2L/100km
Petrol 4-stroke piston
2127cc 129.8cu in
In-line 4
Compression ratio: 8.5:1
Bore: 92.0mm 3.6in
Stroke: 80.0mm 3.1in
Valve type/No: Overhead 8
Transmission: Manual with overdrive
Wheels driven: Rear
Springs F/R: Coil/Coil
Brake system: PA
Brakes F/R: Disc/Disc
Steering: Rack & pinion PA
Wheelbase: 264.2cm 104.0in
Track F: 142.0cm 55.9in
Track R: 134.9cm 53.1in
Length: 489.2cm 192.6in
Width: 170.4cm 67.1in
Height: 143.5cm 56.5in
Kerb weight: 1323.4kg 2915.0lb

4931 Volvo
265 DL
1976 Sweden
108.0mph 173.8kmh
0-50mph 80.5kmh: 9.1secs
0-60mph 96.5kmh: 13.5secs
0-1/4 mile: 18.7secs
121.0bhp 90.2kW 122.7PS
@ 5500rpm
148.0lbft 200.5Nm @ 2750rpm
81.6bhp/ton 80.3bhp/tonne
45.3bhp/L 33.8kW/L 45.9PS/L
43.8ft/sec 13.4m/sec
25.0mph 40.2kmh/1000rpm
19.2mpg 16.0mpgUS 14.7L/100km
Petrol 4-stroke piston
2673cc 163.1cu in
Vee 6 fuel injection
Compression ratio: 8.2:1
Bore: 88.0mm 3.5in
Stroke: 73.0mm 2.9in
Valve type/No: Overhead 12
Transmission: Manual with overdrive
Wheels driven: Rear
Springs F/R: Coil/Coil
Brake system: PA
Brakes F/R: Disc/Disc
Steering: Rack & pinion PA
Wheelbase: 264.2cm 104.0in
Track F: 142.0cm 55.9in
Track R: 134.9cm 53.1in
Length: 489.2cm 192.6in
Width: 170.4cm 67.1in
Height: 146.1cm 57.5in
Ground clearance: 18.0cm 7.1in
Kerb weight: 1507.3kg 3320.0lb
Fuel: 59.8L 13.1gal 15.8galUS

4932 Volvo
244 DL
1977 Sweden
98.0mph 157.7kmh
0-60mph 96.5kmh: 13.6secs
0-1/4 mile: 19.8secs
104.0bhp 77.5kW 105.4PS
@ 5500rpm
114.0lbft 154.5Nm @ 2500rpm
77.8bhp/ton 76.5bhp/tonne
48.9bhp/L 36.5kW/L 49.6PS/L
48.1ft/sec 14.7m/sec
Petrol 4-stroke piston
2127cc 129.8cu in
In-line 4 fuel injection
Compression ratio: 8.5:1
Bore: 92.0mm 3.6in
Stroke: 80.0mm 3.1in
Valve type/No: Overhead 8
Transmission: Manual with overdrive
Wheels driven: Rear
Brakes F/R: Disc/Disc
Wheelbase: 264.2cm 104.0in
Track F: 142.0cm 55.9in
Track R: 134.9cm 53.1in
Length: 489.2cm 192.6in
Width: 170.4cm 67.1in
Height: 143.5cm 56.5in
Kerb weight: 1359.7kg 2995.0lb
Fuel: 59.8L 13.1gal 15.8galUS

4933 Volvo
343
1977 Sweden
88.0mph 141.6kmh
0-50mph 80.5kmh: 11.5secs
0-60mph 96.5kmh: 17.0secs
0-1/4 mile: 20.6secs
0-1km: 38.9secs
70.0bhp 52.2kW 71.0PS
@ 5500rpm
80.0lbft 108.4Nm @ 3500rpm
70.2bhp/ton 69.0bhp/tonne
50.1bhp/L 37.4kW/L 50.8PS/L
46.3ft/sec 14.1m/sec
16.9mph 27.2kmh/1000rpm
26.0mpg 21.6mpgUS 10.9L/100km
Petrol 4-stroke piston
1397cc 85.2cu in
In-line 4 1 Carburettor
Compression ratio: 9.5:1
Bore: 76.0mm 3.0in
Stroke: 77.0mm 3.0in
Valve type/No: Overhead 8
Transmission: Continuously variable
Wheels driven: Rear
Springs F/R: Coil/Leaf
Brake system: PA
Brakes F/R: Disc/Drum
Steering: Rack & pinion
Wheelbase: 239.5cm 94.3in
Track F: 134.9cm 53.1in
Track R: 137.9cm 54.3in
Length: 418.8cm 164.9in
Width: 165.9cm 65.3in
Height: 138.9cm 54.7in
Ground clearance: 13.2cm 5.2in
Kerb weight: 1013.8kg 2233.0lb
Fuel: 45.5L 10.0gal 12.0galUS

4934 Volvo
242 GT
1978 Sweden
109.0mph 175.4kmh
0-50mph 80.5kmh: 7.7secs
0-60mph 96.5kmh: 11.3secs
0-1/4 mile: 18.5secs
101.0bhp 75.3kW 102.4PS
@ 5200rpm
111.0lbft 150.4Nm @ 2500rpm
77.2bhp/ton 75.9bhp/tonne
47.5bhp/L 35.4kW/L 48.1PS/L
45.5ft/sec 13.9m/sec
23.4mph 37.7kmh/1000rpm
24.0mpg 20.0mpgUS 11.8L/100km
Petrol 4-stroke piston
2127cc 129.8cu in
In-line 4
Compression ratio: 8.5:1
Bore: 92.0mm 3.6in
Stroke: 80.0mm 3.1in
Valve type/No: Overhead 8
Transmission: Manual with overdrive
Wheels driven: Rear
Springs F/R: Coil/Coil
Brake system: PA
Brakes F/R: Disc/Disc
Steering: Rack & pinion PA
Wheelbase: 264.2cm 104.0in
Track F: 144.0cm 56.7in
Track R: 134.6cm 53.0in
Length: 489.2cm 192.6in
Width: 170.7cm 67.2in
Height: 142.7cm 56.2in
Kerb weight: 1330.2kg 2930.0lb
Fuel: 59.8L 13.1gal 15.8galUS

4935 Volvo
242 IPD
1978 Sweden
121.0mph 194.7kmh
0-50mph 80.5kmh: 6.3secs
0-60mph 96.5kmh: 8.8secs
0-1/4 mile: 17.0secs
175.0bhp 130.5kW 177.4PS
@ 5000rpm
190.0lbft 257.5Nm @ 2500rpm
125.0bhp/ton 122.9bhp/tonne
82.3bhp/L 61.3kW/L 83.4PS/L
43.8ft/sec 13.3m/sec
23.5mph 37.8kmh/1000rpm
24.0mpg 20.0mpgUS 11.8L/100km
Petrol 4-stroke piston
2127cc 129.8cu in
In-line 4
Compression ratio: 8.5:1
Bore: 92.0mm 3.6in
Stroke: 80.0mm 3.1in

Valve type/No: Overhead 8
Transmission: Manual with overdrive
Wheels driven: Rear
Springs F/R: Coil/Coil
Brake system: PA
Brakes F/R: Disc/Disc
Steering: Rack & pinion
Wheelbase: 264.2cm 104.0in
Track F: 146.1cm 57.5in
Track R: 137.9cm 54.3in
Length: 489.2cm 192.6in
Width: 170.7cm 67.2in
Height: 142.7cm 56.2in
Kerb weight: 1423.3kg 3135.0lb
Fuel: 59.8L 13.1gal 15.8galUS

4936 Volvo

262C
1978 Sweden
109.0mph 175.4kmh
0-50mph 80.5kmh: 7.7secs
0-60mph 96.5kmh: 11.1secs
0-1/4 mile: 18.3secs
125.0bhp 93.2kW 126.7PS
@ 5750rpm
150.0lbft 203.3Nm @ 2750rpm
89.7bhp/ton 88.2bhp/tonne
47.0bhp/L 35.0kW/L 47.6PS/L
45.8ft/sec 14.0m/sec
24.3mph 39.1kmh/1000rpm
19.8mpg 16.5mpgUS 14.3L/100km
Petrol 4-stroke piston
2660cc 162.3cu in
Vee 6 fuel injection
Compression ratio: 8.2:1
Bore: 88.0mm 3.5in
Stroke: 73.0mm 2.9in
Valve type/No: Overhead 12
Transmission: Manual with overdrive
Wheels driven: Rear
Springs F/R: Coil/Coil
Brake system: PA
Brakes F/R: Disc/Disc
Steering: Rack & pinion PA
Wheelbase: 264.2cm 104.0in
Track F: 143.0cm 56.3in
Track R: 135.9cm 53.5in
Length: 489.0cm 192.5in
Width: 170.9cm 67.3in
Height: 136.9cm 53.9in
Ground clearance: 14.0cm 5.5in
Kerb weight: 1416.5kg 3120.0lb
Fuel: 59.8L 13.1gal 15.8galUS

4937 Volvo

265 GLE Estate
1978 Sweden
102.0mph 164.1kmh
0-50mph 80.5kmh: 9.8secs
0-60mph 96.5kmh: 13.5secs
0-1/4 mile: 18.7secs
0-1km: 34.9secs
140.0bhp 104.4kW 141.9PS
@ 6000rpm
153.0lbft 207.3Nm @ 3000rpm
98.0bhp/ton 96.4bhp/tonne
52.5bhp/L 39.2kW/L 53.3PS/L
47.8ft/sec 14.6m/sec
24.7mph 39.7kmh/1000rpm
19.6mpg 16.3mpgUS 14.4L/100km
Petrol 4-stroke piston
2664cc 162.5cu in
Vee 6 fuel injection
Compression ratio: 8.7:1
Bore: 88.0mm 3.5in
Stroke: 73.0mm 2.9in
Valve type/No: Overhead 12
Transmission: Manual with overdrive
No. of forward speeds: 5
Wheels driven: Rear
Springs F/R: Coil/Coil
Brake system: PA
Brakes F/R: Disc/Disc
Steering: Rack & pinion PA
Wheelbase: 264.2cm 104.0in
Track F: 135.1cm 53.2in
Track R: 135.1cm 53.2in
Length: 489.5cm 192.7in
Width: 170.7cm 67.2in
Height: 146.1cm 57.5in
Ground clearance: 14.0cm 5.5in
Kerb weight: 1452.8kg 3200.0lb
Fuel: 60.1L 13.2gal 15.9galUS

4938 Volvo

343
1978 Sweden
96.0mph 154.5kmh
0-50mph 80.5kmh: 10.4secs
0-60mph 96.5kmh: 15.0secs
0-1/4 mile: 19.6secs
0-1km: 37.1secs
70.0bhp 52.2kW 71.0PS
@ 5500rpm
80.0lbft 108.4Nm @ 3500rpm
71.8bhp/ton 70.6bhp/tonne
50.1bhp/L 37.4kW/L 50.8PS/L
46.3ft/sec 14.1m/sec
16.9mph 27.2kmh/1000rpm
26.8mpg 22.3mpgUS 10.5L/100km
Petrol 4-stroke piston
1397cc 85.2cu in
In-line 4 1 Carburettor
Compression ratio: 9.5:1
Bore: 76.0mm 3.0in
Stroke: 77.0mm 3.0in
Valve type/No: Overhead 8
Transmission: Manual
No. of forward speeds: 4
Wheels driven: Rear
Springs F/R: Coil/Leaf
Brake system: PA
Brakes F/R: Disc/Drum
Steering: Rack & pinion
Wheelbase: 239.5cm 94.3in
Track F: 134.9cm 53.1in
Track R: 137.9cm 54.3in
Length: 418.8cm 164.9in
Width: 165.9cm 65.3in
Height: 138.9cm 54.7in
Ground clearance: 13.2cm 5.2in
Kerb weight: 991.5kg 2184.0lb
Fuel: 45.5L 10.0gal 12.0galUS

4939 Volvo

Diesel
1980 Sweden
0-60mph 96.5kmh: 18.5secs
0-1/4 mile: 21.2secs
78.0bhp 58.2kW 79.1PS
@ 4800rpm
102.0lbft 138.2Nm @ 3000rpm
55.5bhp/ton 54.6bhp/tonne
32.7bhp/L 24.4kW/L 33.2PS/L
45.3ft/sec 13.8m/sec
32.4mpg 27.0mpgUS 8.7L/100km
Diesel 4-stroke piston
2383cc 145.4cu in
In-line 6 fuel injection
Compression ratio: 23.5:1
Bore: 76.5mm 3.0in
Stroke: 86.4mm 3.4in
Valve type/No: Overhead 12
Transmission: Manual with overdrive
Wheels driven: Rear
Brakes F/R: Disc/Disc
Wheelbase: 264.2cm 104.0in
Track F: 142.0cm 55.9in
Track R: 134.9cm 53.1in
Length: 489.0cm 192.5in
Width: 170.9cm 67.3in
Height: 143.5cm 56.5in
Kerb weight: 1427.8kg 3145.0lb
Fuel: 59.8L 13.1gal 15.8galUS

4940 Volvo

GL
1980 Sweden
0-60mph 96.5kmh: 14.2secs
0-1/4 mile: 19.6secs
107.0bhp 79.8kW 108.5PS
@ 5250rpm
114.0lbft 154.5Nm @ 2500rpm
79.0bhp/ton 77.6bhp/tonne
50.3bhp/L 37.5kW/L 51.0PS/L
45.9ft/sec 14.0m/sec
24.6mpg 20.5mpgUS 11.5L/100km
Petrol 4-stroke piston
2127cc 129.8cu in
In-line 4 fuel injection
Compression ratio: 9.3:1
Bore: 92.0mm 3.6in
Stroke: 80.0mm 3.1in
Valve type/No: Overhead 8
Transmission: Manual with overdrive
Wheels driven: Rear
Brakes F/R: Disc/Disc
Wheelbase: 264.2cm 104.0in
Track F: 142.0cm 55.9in
Track R: 134.9cm 53.1in
Length: 489.0cm 192.5in
Width: 170.9cm 67.3in
Height: 143.5cm 56.5in
Kerb weight: 1377.9kg 3035.0lb
Fuel: 59.8L 13.1gal 15.8galUS

4941 Volvo

265 GLE
1981 Sweden
112.0mph 180.2kmh
0-50mph 80.5kmh: 7.4secs
0-60mph 96.5kmh: 10.8secs
0-1/4 mile: 17.3secs
0-1km: 32.5secs
155.0bhp 115.6kW 157.1PS
@ 5500rpm
169.0lbft 229.0Nm @ 3000rpm
110.9bhp/ton 109.1bhp/tonne
54.4bhp/L 40.6kW/L 55.2PS/L
43.8ft/sec 13.4m/sec
24.8mph 39.9kmh/1000rpm
18.7mpg 15.6mpgUS 15.1L/100km
Petrol 4-stroke piston
2849cc 173.8cu in
In-line 6 fuel injection
Compression ratio: 9.5:1
Bore: 91.0mm 3.6in
Stroke: 73.0mm 2.9in
Valve type/No: Overhead 12
Transmission: Manual with overdrive
No. of forward speeds: 5
Wheels driven: Rear
Springs F/R: Coil/Coil
Brake system: PA
Brakes F/R: Disc/Disc
Steering: Rack & pinion PA
Wheelbase: 264.2cm 104.0in
Track F: 142.7cm 56.2in
Track R: 135.1cm 53.2in
Length: 489.5cm 192.7in
Width: 170.7cm 67.2in
Height: 146.1cm 57.5in
Ground clearance: 14.0cm 5.5in
Kerb weight: 1421.0kg 3130.0lb
Fuel: 60.1L 13.2gal 15.9galUS

4942 Volvo

240 GL
1982 Sweden
102.0mph 164.1kmh
0-50mph 80.5kmh: 9.0secs
0-60mph 96.5kmh: 13.0secs
0-1/4 mile: 19.4secs
0-1km: 36.2secs
107.0bhp 79.8kW 108.5PS
@ 5000rpm
125.0lbft 169.4Nm @ 2500rpm
84.5bhp/ton 83.1bhp/tonne
50.3bhp/L 37.5kW/L 51.0PS/L
43.8ft/sec 13.3m/sec
25.4mph 40.9kmh/1000rpm
23.1mpg 19.2mpgUS 12.2L/100km
Petrol 4-stroke piston
2127cc 129.8cu in
In-line 4 1 Carburettor
Compression ratio: 9.3:1
Bore: 92.0mm 3.6in
Stroke: 80.0mm 3.1in
Valve type/No: Overhead 8
Transmission: Manual
No. of forward speeds: 4
Wheels driven: Rear
Springs F/R: Coil/Coil
Brake system: PA
Brakes F/R: Disc/Disc
Steering: Rack & pinion PA
Wheelbase: 264.2cm 104.0in
Track F: 142.7cm 56.2in
Track R: 135.1cm 53.2in
Length: 479.0cm 188.6in
Width: 170.9cm 67.3in
Height: 143.0cm 56.3in
Ground clearance: 14.0cm 5.5in
Kerb weight: 1287.1kg 2835.0lb
Fuel: 60.1L 13.2gal 15.9galUS

4943 Volvo

360 GLT
1982 Sweden
112.0mph 180.2kmh
0-50mph 80.5kmh: 7.7secs
0-60mph 96.5kmh: 11.1secs
0-1/4 mile: 18.4secs
0-1km: 30.1secs
115.0bhp 85.8kW 116.6PS
@ 6000rpm
118.0lbft 159.9Nm @ 3600rpm
102.3bhp/ton 100.6bhp/tonne
57.9bhp/L 43.2kW/L 58.7PS/L
52.5ft/sec 16.0m/sec
21.8mph 35.1kmh/1000rpm
23.9mpg 19.9mpgUS 11.8L/100km
Petrol 4-stroke piston
1986cc 121.2cu in
In-line 4 fuel injection
Compression ratio: 10.0:1
Bore: 88.9mm 3.5in
Stroke: 80.0mm 3.1in
Valve type/No: Overhead 8
Transmission: Manual
No. of forward speeds: 5
Wheels driven: Rear
Springs F/R: Coil/Leaf
Brake system: PA
Brakes F/R: Disc/Drum
Steering: Rack & pinion
Wheelbase: 239.5cm 94.3in
Track F: 136.9cm 53.9in
Track R: 140.0cm 55.1in
Length: 430.0cm 169.3in
Width: 165.9cm 65.3in
Height: 139.2cm 54.8in
Ground clearance: 13.2cm 5.2in
Kerb weight: 1142.7kg 2517.0lb
Fuel: 56.9L 12.5gal 15.0galUS

4944 Volvo

760 GLE
1982 Sweden
120.0mph 193.1kmh
0-50mph 80.5kmh: 7.6secs
0-60mph 96.5kmh: 10.1secs
0-1/4 mile: 17.5secs
0-1km: 32.4secs
156.0bhp 116.3kW 158.2PS
@ 5700rpm
173.0lbft 234.4Nm @ 3000rpm
115.6bhp/ton 113.6bhp/tonne
54.8bhp/L 40.8kW/L 55.5PS/L
45.4ft/sec 13.9m/sec
29.4mph 47.3kmh/1000rpm
20.3mpg 16.9mpgUS 13.9L/100km
Petrol 4-stroke piston
2849cc 173.8cu in
In-line 6 fuel injection
Compression ratio: 9.5:1
Bore: 91.0mm 3.6in
Stroke: 73.0mm 2.9in
Valve type/No: Overhead 12
Transmission: Automatic
No. of forward speeds: 4
Wheels driven: Rear
Springs F/R: Coil/Coil
Brake system: PA
Brakes F/R: Disc/Disc
Steering: Rack & pinion PA
Wheelbase: 276.9cm 109.0in
Track F: 144.8cm 57.0in
Track R: 144.8cm 57.0in
Length: 478.8cm 188.5in
Width: 174.5cm 68.7in
Height: 143.5cm 56.5in
Kerb weight: 1372.9kg 3024.0lb
Fuel: 59.1L 13.0gal 15.6galUS

4945 Volvo

GLT Turbo
1982 Sweden
114.0mph 183.4kmh
0-50mph 80.5kmh: 7.0secs
0-60mph 96.5kmh: 10.2secs
0-1/4 mile: 17.4secs
127.0bhp 94.7kW 128.8PS
@ 5400rpm
150.0lbft 203.3Nm @ 3750rpm
92.7bhp/ton 91.1bhp/tonne
59.6bhp/L 44.4kW/L 60.4PS/L
47.2ft/sec 14.4m/sec
24.0mph 38.6kmh/1000rpm
24.6mpg 20.5mpgUS 11.5L/100km
Petrol 4-stroke piston
2131cc 130.0cu in turbocharged
In-line 4 fuel injection
Compression ratio: 7.5:1
Bore: 92.0mm 3.6in
Stroke: 80.0mm 3.1in
Valve type/No: Overhead 8
Transmission: Manual with overdrive
Wheels driven: Rear
Springs F/R: Coil/Coil
Brake system: PA
Brakes F/R: Disc/Disc
Steering: Rack & pinion PA
Wheelbase: 264.9cm 104.3in
Track F: 143.0cm 56.3in
Track R: 135.9cm 53.5in

Length: 489.0cm 192.5in
Width: 170.9cm 67.3in
Height: 142.7cm 56.2in
Kerb weight: 1393.8kg 3070.0lb
Fuel: 59.8L 13.1gal 15.8galUS

4946 Volvo
760 GLE
1983 Sweden
105.0mph 168.9kmh
0-60mph 96.5kmh: 12.3secs
0-1/4 mile: 18.6secs
103.0bhp 76.8kW 104.4PS
@ 4800rpm
139.0lbft 188.3Nm @ 2400rpm
73.7bhp/ton 72.5bhp/tonne
43.2bhp/L 32.2kW/L 43.8PS/L
45.3ft/sec 13.8m/sec
24.3mph 39.1kmh/1000rpm
36.0mpg 30.0mpgUS 7.8L/100km
Diesel 4-stroke piston
2383cc 145.4cu in turbocharged
In-line 6 fuel injection
Compression ratio: 23.0:1
Bore: 76.5mm 3.0in
Stroke: 86.4mm 3.4in
Valve type/No: Overhead 12
Transmission: Manual with overdrive
Wheels driven: Rear
Springs F/R: Coil/Coil
Brake system: PA
Brakes F/R: Disc/Disc
Steering: Rack & pinion PA
Wheelbase: 277.1cm 109.1in
Track F: 146.1cm 57.5in
Track R: 146.1cm 57.5in
Length: 478.5cm 188.4in
Width: 175.0cm 68.9in
Height: 141.0cm 55.5in
Ground clearance: 10.4cm 4.1in
Kerb weight: 1421.0kg 3130.0lb
Fuel: 81.8L 18.0gal 21.6galUS

4947 Volvo
760 Turbo
1983 Sweden
122.0mph 196.3kmh
0-50mph 80.5kmh: 7.8secs
0-60mph 96.5kmh: 9.5secs
0-1/4 mile: 17.0secs
0-1km: 32.1secs
173.0bhp 129.0kW 175.4PS
@ 5700rpm
184.0lbft 249.3Nm @ 3400rpm
120.0bhp/ton 118.0bhp/tonne
74.7bhp/L 55.7kW/L 75.7PS/L
49.9ft/sec 15.2m/sec
25.0mph 40.2kmh/1000rpm
18.5mpg 15.4mpgUS 15.3L/100km
Petrol 4-stroke piston
2316cc 141.3cu in turbocharged
In-line 4 fuel injection
Compression ratio: 9.0:1
Bore: 96.0mm 3.8in
Stroke: 80.0mm 3.1in
Valve type/No: Overhead 8
Transmission: Automatic
No. of forward speeds: 5
Wheels driven: Rear
Springs F/R: Coil/Coil
Brake system: PA
Brakes F/R: Disc/Disc
Steering: Rack & pinion PA
Wheelbase: 276.9cm 109.0in
Track F: 144.8cm 57.0in
Track R: 144.8cm 57.0in
Length: 478.8cm 188.5in
Width: 174.5cm 68.7in
Height: 143.5cm 56.5in
Kerb weight: 1466.4kg 3230.0lb
Fuel: 81.9L 18.0gal 21.6galUS

4948 Volvo
740 GLT
1984 Sweden
114.0mph 183.4kmh
0-50mph 80.5kmh: 6.5secs
0-60mph 96.5kmh: 9.4secs
0-1/4 mile: 16.8secs
0-1km: 31.1secs
131.0bhp 97.7kW 132.8PS
@ 5400rpm
140.0lbft 189.7Nm @ 3600rpm
104.3bhp/ton 102.6bhp/tonne
56.6bhp/L 42.2kW/L 57.3PS/L
47.2ft/sec 14.4m/sec
25.1mph 40.4kmh/1000rpm
25.0mpg 20.8mpgUS 11.3L/100km
Petrol 4-stroke piston
2316cc 141.3cu in
In-line 4 fuel injection
Compression ratio: 10.3:1
Bore: 96.0mm 3.8in
Stroke: 80.0mm 3.1in
Valve type/No: Overhead 8
Transmission: Manual with overdrive
No. of forward speeds: 5
Wheels driven: Rear
Springs F/R: Coil/Coil
Brake system: PA
Brakes F/R: Disc/Disc
Steering: Rack & pinion PA
Wheelbase: 276.9cm 109.0in
Track F: 144.8cm 57.0in
Track R: 144.8cm 57.0in
Length: 478.8cm 188.5in
Width: 174.5cm 68.7in
Height: 143.5cm 56.5in
Kerb weight: 1276.6kg 2812.0lb
Fuel: 60.1L 13.2gal 15.9galUS

4949 Volvo
760 GLE
1984 Sweden
0-50mph 80.5kmh: 5.7secs
0-60mph 96.5kmh: 11.4secs
0-1/4 mile: 18.3secs
130.0bhp 96.9kW 131.8PS
@ 5500rpm
153.0lbft 207.3Nm @ 2750rpm
93.0bhp/ton 91.5bhp/tonne
45.6bhp/L 34.0kW/L 46.3PS/L
43.8ft/sec 13.4m/sec
20.4mpg 17.0mpgUS 13.8L/100km
Petrol 4-stroke piston
2849cc 173.8cu in
Vee 6 fuel injection
Compression ratio: 8.8:1
Bore: 91.0mm 3.6in
Stroke: 73.0mm 2.9in
Valve type/No: Overhead 12
Transmission: Automatic
No. of forward speeds: 3
Wheels driven: Rear
Wheelbase: 277.1cm 109.1in
Track F: 146.1cm 57.5in
Track R: 146.1cm 57.5in
Length: 478.5cm 188.4in
Width: 175.0cm 68.9in
Height: 141.0cm 55.5in
Kerb weight: 1421.0kg 3130.0lb

4950 Volvo
GLT Wagon
1984 Sweden
108.0mph 173.8kmh
0-60mph 96.5kmh: 10.1secs
0-1/4 mile: 17.5secs
162.0bhp 120.8kW 164.2PS
@ 5100rpm
181.0lbft 245.3Nm @ 3900rpm
112.9bhp/ton 111.0bhp/tonne
76.2bhp/L 56.8kW/L 77.2PS/L
44.6ft/sec 13.6m/sec
21.6mpg 18.0mpgUS 13.1L/100km
Petrol 4-stroke piston
2127cc 129.8cu in turbocharged
In-line 4 fuel injection
Compression ratio: 7.5:1
Bore: 92.0mm 3.6in
Stroke: 80.0mm 3.1in
Valve type/No: Overhead 8
Transmission: Automatic
No. of forward speeds: 4
Wheels driven: Rear
Springs F/R: Coil/Coil
Brakes F/R: Disc/Disc
Steering: Rack & pinion PA
Wheelbase: 264.9cm 104.3in
Track F: 143.0cm 56.3in
Track R: 135.9cm 53.5in
Length: 479.6cm 188.8in
Width: 170.7cm 67.2in
Height: 146.1cm 57.5in
Kerb weight: 1459.6kg 3215.0lb
Fuel: 59.8L 13.1gal 15.8galUS

4951 Volvo
740 Turbo Wagon
1985 Sweden
115.0mph 185.0kmh
0-50mph 80.5kmh: 6.2secs
0-60mph 96.5kmh: 8.4secs
0-1/4 mile: 16.6secs
160.0bhp 119.3kW 162.2PS
@ 5300rpm
187.0lbft 253.4Nm @ 2900rpm
115.1bhp/ton 113.1bhp/tonne
69.1bhp/L 51.5kW/L 70.0PS/L
46.4ft/sec 14.1m/sec
24.0mph 38.6kmh/1000rpm
28.8mpg 24.0mpgUS 9.8L/100km
Petrol 4-stroke piston
2316cc 141.3cu in turbocharged
In-line 4 fuel injection
Compression ratio: 8.7:1
Bore: 96.0mm 3.8in
Stroke: 80.0mm 3.1in
Valve type/No: Overhead 8
Transmission: Manual with overdrive
Wheels driven: Rear
Springs F/R: Coil/Coil
Brake system: PA
Brakes F/R: Disc/Disc
Steering: Rack & pinion PA
Wheelbase: 277.1cm 109.1in
Track F: 147.1cm 57.9in
Track R: 146.1cm 57.5in
Length: 478.5cm 188.4in
Width: 176.0cm 69.3in
Height: 143.5cm 56.5in
Ground clearance: 13.5cm 5.3in
Kerb weight: 1414.2kg 3115.0lb
Fuel: 59.8L 13.1gal 15.8galUS

4952 Volvo
760 Turbo Estate
1985 Sweden
128.0mph 206.0kmh
0-50mph 80.5kmh: 5.7secs
0-60mph 96.5kmh: 7.7secs
0-1/4 mile: 15.8secs
0-1km: 29.1secs
180.0bhp 134.2kW 182.5PS
@ 5800rpm
192.0lbft 260.2Nm @ 3400rpm
131.1bhp/ton 128.9bhp/tonne
77.7bhp/L 58.0kW/L 78.8PS/L
50.7ft/sec 15.5m/sec
25.2mph 40.5kmh/1000rpm
19.8mpg 16.5mpgUS 14.3L/100km
Petrol 4-stroke piston
2316cc 141.3cu in turbocharged
In-line 4 fuel injection
Compression ratio: 9.0:1
Bore: 96.0mm 3.8in
Stroke: 80.0mm 3.1in
Valve type/No: Overhead 8
Transmission: Manual with overdrive
No. of forward speeds: 5
Wheels driven: Rear
Springs F/R: Coil/Coil
Brake system: PA
Brakes F/R: Disc/Disc
Steering: Rack & pinion PA
Wheelbase: 277.1cm 109.1in
Track F: 147.1cm 57.9in
Track R: 146.1cm 57.5in
Length: 478.8cm 188.5in
Width: 176.0cm 69.3in
Height: 143.5cm 56.5in
Ground clearance: 17.8cm 7.0in
Kerb weight: 1396.5kg 3076.0lb
Fuel: 60.1L 13.2gal 15.9galUS

4953 Volvo
340 GLE
1986 Sweden
107.0mph 172.2kmh
0-50mph 80.5kmh: 9.5secs
0-60mph 96.5kmh: 13.4secs
0-1/4 mile: 18.8secs
0-1km: 35.5secs
80.0bhp 59.7kW 81.1PS
@ 5400rpm
96.0lbft 130.1Nm @ 3000rpm
79.0bhp/ton 77.7bhp/tonne
46.5bhp/L 34.7kW/L 47.1PS/L
49.3ft/sec 15.0m/sec
21.9mph 35.2kmh/1000rpm
29.1mpg 24.2mpgUS 9.7L/100km
Petrol 4-stroke piston
1721cc 105.0cu in
In-line 4 1 Carburettor
Compression ratio: 10.0:1
Bore: 81.0mm 3.2in
Stroke: 83.5mm 3.3in
Valve type/No: Overhead 8
Transmission: Manual
No. of forward speeds: 5
Wheels driven: Rear
Springs F/R: Coil/Leaf
Brake system: PA
Brakes F/R: Disc/Drum
Steering: Rack & pinion
Wheelbase: 239.5cm 94.3in
Track F: 136.9cm 53.9in
Track R: 139.7cm 55.0in
Length: 443.0cm 174.4in
Width: 165.9cm 65.3in
Height: 143.0cm 56.3in
Ground clearance: 15.2cm 6.0in
Kerb weight: 1029.7kg 2268.0lb
Fuel: 45.0L 9.9gal 11.9galUS

4954 Volvo
480 ES
1987 Sweden
112.0mph 180.2kmh
0-50mph 80.5kmh: 7.3secs
0-60mph 96.5kmh: 10.3secs
0-1/4 mile: 17.7secs
0-1km: 32.8secs
109.0bhp 81.3kW 110.5PS
@ 5800rpm
103.0lbft 139.6Nm @ 4000rpm
108.7bhp/ton 106.9bhp/tonne
63.3bhp/L 47.2kW/L 64.2PS/L
53.0ft/sec 16.1m/sec
21.3mph 34.3kmh/1000rpm
28.8mpg 24.0mpgUS 9.8L/100km
Petrol 4-stroke piston
1721cc 105.0cu in
In-line 4 fuel injection
Compression ratio: 10.5:1
Bore: 81.0mm 3.2in
Stroke: 83.5mm 3.3in
Valve type/No: Overhead 8
Transmission: Manual
No. of forward speeds: 5
Wheels driven: Front
Springs F/R: Coil/Coil
Brake system: PA
Brakes F/R: Disc/Drum
Steering: Rack & pinion PA
Wheelbase: 250.2cm 98.5in
Track F: 141.0cm 55.5in
Track R: 141.0cm 55.5in
Length: 425.8cm 167.6in
Width: 171.0cm 67.3in
Height: 131.8cm 51.9in
Ground clearance: 10.8cm 4.3in
Kerb weight: 1020.0kg 2246.7lb
Fuel: 47.8L 10.5gal 12.6galUS

4955 Volvo
740 Turbo
1987 Sweden
128.0mph 206.0kmh
0-50mph 80.5kmh: 5.9secs
0-60mph 96.5kmh: 8.3secs
0-1/4 mile: 16.4secs
0-1km: 29.8secs
182.0bhp 135.7kW 184.5PS
@ 5800rpm
192.0lbft 260.2Nm @ 3400rpm
135.1bhp/ton 132.8bhp/tonne
78.6bhp/L 58.6kW/L 79.7PS/L
50.7ft/sec 15.5m/sec
25.2mph 40.5kmh/1000rpm
21.8mpg 18.2mpgUS 13.0L/100km
Petrol 4-stroke piston
2316cc 141.0cu in turbocharged
In-line 4 fuel injection
Compression ratio: 9.0:1
Bore: 96.0mm 3.8in
Stroke: 80.0mm 3.1in
Valve type/No: Overhead 8
Transmission: Manual
No. of forward speeds: 5
Wheels driven: Rear
Springs F/R: Coil/Coil
Brake system: PA
Brakes F/R: Disc/Disc
Steering: Rack & pinion PA
Wheelbase: 277.1cm 109.1in
Track F: 146.0cm 57.5in
Track R: 146.0cm 57.5in
Length: 478.7cm 188.5in
Width: 176.0cm 69.3in
Height: 143.0cm 56.3in
Ground clearance: 17.9cm 7.0in
Kerb weight: 1370.0kg 3017.6lb
Fuel: 60.1L 13.2gal 15.9galUS

4956 Volvo
760 GLE
1987 Sweden
114.0mph 183.4kmh
0-50mph 80.5kmh: 7.2secs
0-60mph 96.5kmh: 9.6secs
0-1/4 mile: 17.5secs
0-1km: 32.1secs
170.0bhp 126.8kW 172.4PS
@ 5400rpm
177.0lbft 239.8Nm @ 4500rpm
118.6bhp/ton 116.6bhp/tonne
59.7bhp/L 44.5kW/L 60.5PS/L
43.0ft/sec 13.1m/sec
25.8mph 41.5kmh/1000rpm
19.5mpg 16.2mpgUS 14.5L/100km
Petrol 4-stroke piston
2849cc 174.0cu in
Vee 6 fuel injection
Compression ratio: 10.0:1
Bore: 91.0mm 3.6in
Stroke: 73.0mm 2.9in
Valve type/No: Overhead 12
Transmission: Automatic
No. of forward speeds: 4
Wheels driven: Rear
Springs F/R: Coil/Coil
Brake system: PA ABS
Brakes F/R: Disc/Disc
Steering: Rack & pinion PA
Wheelbase: 277.0cm 109.1in
Track F: 147.0cm 57.9in
Track R: 152.0cm 59.8in
Length: 479.0cm 188.6in
Width: 176.0cm 69.3in
Height: 141.0cm 55.5in
Kerb weight: 1458.0kg 3211.4lb
Fuel: 80.1L 17.6gal 21.1galUS

4957 Volvo
440 Turbo
1989 Sweden
127.0mph 204.3kmh
0-50mph 80.5kmh: 6.8secs
0-60mph 96.5kmh: 9.6secs
0-1/4 mile: 17.1secs
0-1km: 31.5secs
120.0bhp 89.5kW 121.7PS
@ 5400rpm
129.2lbft 175.0Nm @ 1800rpm
114.0bhp/ton 112.1bhp/tonne
69.7bhp/L 52.0kW/L 70.7PS/L
49.3ft/sec 15.0m/sec
23.1mph 37.2kmh/1000rpm
22.5mpg 18.7mpgUS 12.6L/100km
Petrol 4-stroke piston
1721cc 105.0cu in turbocharged
In-line 4 fuel injection
Compression ratio: 8.1:1
Bore: 81.0mm 3.2in
Stroke: 83.5mm 3.3in
Valve type/No: Overhead 8
Transmission: Manual
No. of forward speeds: 5
Wheels driven: Front
Springs F/R: Coil/Coil
Brake system: PA ABS
Brakes F/R: Disc/Disc
Steering: Rack & pinion PA
Wheelbase: 250.5cm 98.6in
Track F: 142.0cm 55.9in
Track R: 143.0cm 56.3in
Length: 431.2cm 169.8in
Width: 171.0cm 67.3in
Height: 140.0cm 55.1in
Ground clearance: 17.9cm 7.0in
Kerb weight: 1070.0kg 2356.8lb
Fuel: 48.2L 10.6gal 12.7galUS

4958 Volvo
740 GLE
1989 Sweden
125.0mph 201.1kmh
0-50mph 80.5kmh: 7.3secs
0-60mph 96.5kmh: 9.6secs
0-1/4 mile: 17.2secs
153.0bhp 114.1kW 155.1PS
@ 5700rpm
150.0lbft 203.3Nm @ 4450rpm
113.7bhp/ton 111.8bhp/tonne
66.1bhp/L 49.3kW/L 67.0PS/L
49.9ft/sec 15.2m/sec
26.7mpg 22.2mpgUS 10.6L/100km
Petrol 4-stroke piston
2316cc 141.3cu in
In-line 4 fuel injection
Compression ratio: 10.0:1
Bore: 96.0mm 3.8in
Stroke: 80.0mm 3.1in
Valve type/No: Overhead 16
Transmission: Automatic
No. of forward speeds: 4
Wheels driven: Rear
Springs F/R: Coil/Coil
Brake system: PA ABS
Brakes F/R: Disc/Disc
Steering: Rack & pinion PA
Wheelbase: 277.1cm 109.1in
Track F: 147.1cm 57.9in
Track R: 146.1cm 57.5in
Length: 478.5cm 188.4in
Width: 176.0cm 69.3in
Height: 141.0cm 55.5in
Kerb weight: 1368.8kg 3015.0lb
Fuel: 59.8L 13.1gal 15.8galUS

4959 Volvo
740 Turbo
1989 Sweden
125.0mph 201.1kmh
0-50mph 80.5kmh: 5.6secs
0-60mph 96.5kmh: 7.8secs
0-1/4 mile: 16.0secs
160.0bhp 119.3kW 162.2PS
@ 5300rpm
187.0lbft 253.4Nm @ 2900rpm
116.5bhp/ton 114.6bhp/tonne
69.1bhp/L 51.5kW/L 70.0PS/L
46.4ft/sec 14.1m/sec
22.6mpg 18.8mpgUS 12.5L/100km
Petrol 4-stroke piston
2316cc 141.3cu in turbocharged
In-line 4 fuel injection
Compression ratio: 8.7:1
Bore: 96.0mm 3.8in
Stroke: 80.0mm 3.1in
Valve type/No: Overhead 8
Transmission: Manual with overdrive
Wheels driven: Rear
Springs F/R: Coil/Coil
Brake system: PA ABS
Brakes F/R: Disc/Disc
Steering: Rack & pinion PA
Wheelbase: 277.1cm 109.1in
Track F: 147.1cm 57.9in
Track R: 146.1cm 57.5in
Length: 478.5cm 188.4in
Width: 176.0cm 69.3in
Height: 141.0cm 55.5in
Kerb weight: 1396.0kg 3075.0lb
Fuel: 59.8L 13.1gal 15.8galUS

4960 Volvo
440 GLE
1990 Sweden
107.0mph 172.2kmh
0-50mph 80.5kmh: 8.6secs
0-60mph 96.5kmh: 12.4secs
0-1/4 mile: 18.9secs
0-1km: 34.8secs
90.0bhp 67.1kW 91.2PS
@ 5800rpm
96.7lbft 131.0Nm @ 3600rpm
89.3bhp/ton 87.8bhp/tonne
52.6bhp/L 39.2kW/L 53.3PS/L
53.0ft/sec 16.1m/sec
22.4mph 36.0kmh/1000rpm
26.9mpg 22.4mpgUS 10.5L/100km
Petrol 4-stroke piston
1712cc 104.0cu in
In-line 4 1 Carburettor
Compression ratio: 9.5:1
Bore: 81.0mm 3.2in
Stroke: 83.5mm 3.3in
Valve type/No: Overhead 8
Transmission: Manual
No. of forward speeds: 5
Wheels driven: Front
Springs F/R: Coil/Coil
Brake system: PA ABS
Brakes F/R: Disc/Drum
Steering: Rack & pinion PA
Wheelbase: 250.5cm 98.6in
Track F: 142.0cm 55.9in
Track R: 143.0cm 56.3in
Length: 431.2cm 169.8in
Width: 171.0cm 67.3in
Height: 140.0cm 55.1in
Ground clearance: 17.9cm 7.0in
Kerb weight: 1025.0kg 2257.7lb
Fuel: 48.2L 10.6gal 12.7galUS

4961 Volvo
460 GLi
1990 Sweden
109.0mph 175.4kmh
0-50mph 80.5kmh: 7.9secs
0-60mph 96.5kmh: 11.1secs
0-1/4 mile: 18.1secs
0-1km: 33.2secs
102.0bhp 76.1kW 103.4PS
@ 5600rpm
104.8lbft 142.0Nm @ 3900rpm
102.2bhp/ton 100.5bhp/tonne
59.3bhp/L 44.2kW/L 60.1PS/L
51.2ft/sec 15.6m/sec
21.5mph 34.6kmh/1000rpm
26.4mpg 22.0mpgUS 10.7L/100km
Petrol 4-stroke piston
1721cc 105.0cu in
In-line 4 fuel injection
Compression ratio: 10.0:1
Bore: 81.0mm 3.2in
Stroke: 83.5mm 3.3in
Valve type/No: Overhead 8
Transmission: Manual
No. of forward speeds: 5
Wheels driven: Front
Springs F/R: Coil/Coil
Brake system: PA ABS
Brakes F/R: Disc/Disc
Steering: Rack & pinion
Wheelbase: 250.2cm 98.5in
Track F: 142.0cm 55.9in
Track R: 142.7cm 56.2in
Length: 440.4cm 173.4in
Width: 168.9cm 66.5in
Height: 137.9cm 54.3in
Ground clearance: 17.8cm 7.0in
Kerb weight: 1015.0kg 2235.7lb
Fuel: 48.2L 10.6gal 12.7galUS

4962 Volvo
460 Turbo
1990 Sweden
126.0mph 202.7kmh
0-50mph 80.5kmh: 6.2secs
0-60mph 96.5kmh: 8.9secs
0-1/4 mile: 16.7secs
0-1km: 30.7secs
122.0bhp 91.0kW 123.7PS
@ 5400rpm
129.2lbft 175.0Nm @ 3500rpm
114.9bhp/ton 113.0bhp/tonne
70.9bhp/L 52.9kW/L 71.9PS/L
49.3ft/sec 15.0m/sec
23.1mph 37.2kmh/1000rpm
26.4mpg 22.0mpgUS 10.7L/100km
Petrol 4-stroke piston
1721cc 105.0cu in turbocharged
In-line 4 fuel injection
Compression ratio: 8.1:1
Bore: 81.0mm 3.2in
Stroke: 83.5mm 3.3in
Valve type/No: Overhead 8
Transmission: Manual
No. of forward speeds: 5
Wheels driven: Front
Springs F/R: Coil/Coil
Brake system: PA ABS
Brakes F/R: Disc/Disc
Steering: Rack & pinion PA
Wheelbase: 250.2cm 98.5in
Track F: 142.0cm 55.9in
Track R: 142.7cm 56.2in
Length: 440.4cm 173.4in
Width: 168.9cm 66.5in
Height: 137.9cm 54.3in
Ground clearance: 17.8cm 7.0in
Kerb weight: 1080.0kg 2378.8lb
Fuel: 48.2L 10.6gal 12.7galUS

4963 Volvo
740 GLT 16v Estate
1990 Sweden
119.0mph 191.5kmh
0-50mph 80.5kmh: 6.6secs
0-60mph 96.5kmh: 9.4secs
0-1/4 mile: 16.9secs
0-1km: 31.5secs
155.0bhp 115.6kW 157.1PS
@ 5800rpm
149.8lbft 203.0Nm @ 4450rpm
111.1bhp/ton 109.2bhp/tonne
66.9bhp/L 49.9kW/L 67.8PS/L
50.7ft/sec 15.5m/sec
24.0mph 38.6kmh/1000rpm
21.1mpg 17.6mpgUS 13.4L/100km
Petrol 4-stroke piston
2316cc 141.0cu in
In-line 4 fuel injection
Compression ratio: 10.0:1
Bore: 96.0mm 3.8in
Stroke: 80.0mm 3.1in
Valve type/No: Overhead 16
Transmission: Manual
No. of forward speeds: 5
Wheels driven: Rear
Springs F/R: Coil/Coil
Brake system: PA ABS
Brakes F/R: Disc/Disc
Steering: Rack & pinion PA
Wheelbase: 277.1cm 109.1in
Track F: 147.0cm 57.9in
Track R: 146.0cm 57.5in
Length: 479.0cm 188.6in
Width: 176.0cm 69.3in
Height: 141.0cm 55.5in
Ground clearance: 17.9cm 7.0in
Kerb weight: 1419.0kg 3125.5lb
Fuel: 60.1L 13.2gal 15.9galUS

4964 Volvo
740 Turbo
1990 Sweden
120.0mph 193.1kmh
0-50mph 80.5kmh: 6.4secs
0-60mph 96.5kmh: 8.8secs
0-1/4 mile: 16.7secs
162.0bhp 120.8kW 164.2PS
@ 4800rpm
195.0lbft 264.2Nm @ 3450rpm
118.0bhp/ton 116.0bhp/tonne
69.9bhp/L 52.2kW/L 70.9PS/L
42.0ft/sec 12.8m/sec
31.8mpg 26.5mpgUS 8.9L/100km
Petrol 4-stroke piston
2316cc 141.3cu in turbocharged
In-line 4 fuel injection
Compression ratio: 8.7:1
Bore: 96.0mm 3.8in
Stroke: 80.0mm 3.1in
Valve type/No: Overhead 8
Transmission: Automatic
No. of forward speeds: 4
Wheels driven: Rear
Springs F/R: Coil/Coil
Brake system: PA ABS
Brakes F/R: Disc/Disc
Steering: Rack & pinion PA
Wheelbase: 277.1cm 109.1in
Track F: 147.1cm 57.9in
Track R: 146.1cm 57.5in
Length: 478.5cm 188.4in
Width: 176.0cm 69.3in
Height: 141.0cm 55.5in
Kerb weight: 1396.0kg 3075.0lb
Fuel: 59.8L 13.1gal 15.8galUS

4965 Volvo
940 SE
1991 Sweden
124.0mph 199.5kmh
0-60mph 96.5kmh: 9.2secs
0-1/4 mile: 17.0secs
162.0bhp 120.8kW 164.2PS
@ 4000rpm
195.0lbft 264.2Nm @ 3450rpm
107.0bhp/ton 105.3bhp/tonne
69.9bhp/L 52.2kW/L 70.9PS/L
35.1ft/sec 10.7m/sec
24.0mpg 20.0mpgUS 11.8L/100km
Petrol 4-stroke piston
2316cc 141.3cu in turbocharged
In-line 4 fuel injection
Compression ratio: 8.7:1
Bore: 96.0mm 3.8in
Stroke: 80.2mm 3.2in
Valve type/No: Overhead 8
Transmission: Automatic
No. of forward speeds: 4
Wheels driven: Rear
Springs F/R: Coil/Coil
Brake system: PA ABS
Brakes F/R: Disc/Disc
Steering: Rack & pinion PA
Wheelbase: 277.1cm 109.1in
Track F: 147.1cm 57.9in
Track R: 151.9cm 59.8in
Length: 486.9cm 191.7in
Width: 176.0cm 69.3in
Height: 141.0cm 55.5in
Kerb weight: 1539.1kg 3390.0lb
Fuel: 79.5L 17.5gal 21.0galUS

4966 Volvo
940 SE Turbo
1991 Sweden
124.0mph 199.5kmh
0-50mph 80.5kmh: 6.7secs
0-60mph 96.5kmh: 9.3secs
0-1/4 mile: 17.2secs
0-1km: 31.4secs
155.0bhp 115.6kW 157.1PS
@ 5600rpm
172.7lbft 234.0Nm @ 3600rpm
113.4bhp/ton 111.5bhp/tonne
78.0bhp/L 58.2kW/L 79.1PS/L
49.0ft/sec 14.9m/sec
25.3mph 40.7kmh/1000rpm
21.2mpg 17.7mpgUS 13.3L/100km
Petrol 4-stroke piston
1986cc 121.0cu in turbocharged
In-line 4 fuel injection
Compression ratio: 8.5:1
Bore: 89.0mm 3.5in
Stroke: 80.0mm 3.1in
Valve type/No: Overhead 8
Transmission: Manual
No. of forward speeds: 5
Wheels driven: Rear
Springs F/R: Coil/Coil
Brake system: PA
Brakes F/R: Disc/Disc
Steering: Rack & pinion PA
Wheelbase: 276.9cm 109.0in
Track F: 146.8cm 57.8in
Track R: 151.9cm 59.8in
Length: 486.9cm 191.7in
Width: 174.8cm 68.8in
Height: 141.0cm 55.5in
Ground clearance: 20.3cm 8.0in
Kerb weight: 1390.0kg 3061.7lb
Fuel: 61.9L 13.6gal 16.3galUS

4967 Volvo
940 Turbo
1991 Sweden
0-60mph 96.5kmh: 8.9secs
0-1/4 mile: 16.8secs
162.0bhp 120.8kW 164.2PS
@ 4800rpm
195.0lbft 264.2Nm @ 3450rpm
118.4bhp/ton 116.4bhp/tonne
69.9bhp/L 52.2kW/L 70.9PS/L
42.0ft/sec 12.8m/sec
25.8mpg 21.5mpgUS 10.9L/100km
Petrol 4-stroke piston
2316cc 141.3cu in turbocharged
In-line 4
Bore: 96.0mm 3.8in
Stroke: 80.0mm 3.1in
Valve type/No: Overhead 8
Transmission: Automatic
No. of forward speeds: 4
Wheels driven: Rear
Springs F/R: Coil/Coil
Brake system: ABS
Brakes F/R: Disc/Disc
Steering: Rack & pinion PA
Wheelbase: 277.1cm 109.1in
Track F: 147.1cm 57.9in
Track R: 146.1cm 57.5in
Length: 486.9cm 191.7in
Width: 176.0cm 69.3in
Height: 141.0cm 55.5in
Kerb weight: 1391.5kg 3065.0lb

4968 Volvo
960 24v
1991 Sweden
129.0mph 207.6kmh
0-50mph 80.5kmh: 7.0secs
0-60mph 96.5kmh: 9.3secs
0-1/4 mile: 16.6secs
0-1km: 30.4secs
204.0bhp 152.1kW 206.8PS
@ 6000rpm
197.0lbft 267.0Nm @ 4300rpm
133.0bhp/ton 130.8bhp/tonne
69.8bhp/L 52.1kW/L 70.8PS/L
59.0ft/sec 18.0m/sec
25.8mph 41.5kmh/1000rpm
18.4mpg 15.3mpgUS 15.4L/100km
Petrol 4-stroke piston
2922cc 178.0cu in
In-line 6 fuel injection
Compression ratio: 10.7:1
Bore: 83.0mm 3.3in
Stroke: 90.0mm 3.5in
Valve type/No: Overhead 24
Transmission: Automatic
No. of forward speeds: 4
Wheels driven: Rear
Springs F/R: Coil/Coil
Brake system: PA ABS
Brakes F/R: Disc/Disc
Steering: Rack & pinion PA
Wheelbase: 276.9cm 109.0in
Track F: 146.8cm 57.8in
Track R: 151.9cm 59.8in
Length: 486.9cm 191.7in
Width: 174.8cm 68.8in
Height: 141.0cm 55.5in
Ground clearance: 20.3cm 8.0in
Kerb weight: 1560.0kg 3436.1lb
Fuel: 80.1L 17.6gal 21.1galUS

4969 Volvo
960
1992 Sweden
135.0mph 217.2kmh
0-60mph 96.5kmh: 10.1secs
0-1/4 mile: 17.4secs
201.0bhp 149.9kW 203.8PS
@ 6000rpm
197.0lbft 266.9Nm @ 4300rpm
128.1bhp/ton 125.9bhp/tonne
68.8bhp/L 51.3kW/L 69.7PS/L
59.0ft/sec 18.0m/sec
24.0mpg 20.0mpgUS 11.8L/100km
Petrol 4-stroke piston
2922cc 178.3cu in
In-line 6 fuel injection
Compression ratio: 10.7:1
Bore: 83.0mm 3.3in
Stroke: 90.0mm 3.5in
Valve type/No: Overhead 24
Transmission: Automatic
No. of forward speeds: 4
Wheels driven: Rear
Springs F/R: Coil/Coil
Brake system: PA ABS
Brakes F/R: Disc/Disc
Steering: Rack & pinion PA
Wheelbase: 277.1cm 109.1in
Track F: 147.1cm 57.9in
Track R: 151.9cm 59.8in
Length: 486.9cm 191.7in
Width: 176.0cm 69.3in
Height: 141.0cm 55.5in
Kerb weight: 1595.8kg 3515.0lb
Fuel: 82.5L 18.1gal 21.8galUS

4970 Wartburg
Knight
1967 E. Germany
73.0mph 117.5kmh
0-50mph 80.5kmh: 12.9secs
0-60mph 96.5kmh: 25.1secs
0-1/4 mile: 22.3secs
0-1km: 42.4secs
45.0bhp 33.6kW 45.6PS
@ 4200rpm
67.0lbft 90.8Nm @ 2200rpm
51.0bhp/ton 50.2bhp/tonne
45.4bhp/L 33.9kW/L 46.0PS/L
35.8ft/sec 10.9m/sec
16.0mph 25.7kmh/1000rpm
24.7mpg 20.6mpgUS 11.4L/100km
Petrol 2-stroke piston
991cc 60.5cu in
In-line 3 1 Carburettor
Compression ratio: 7.5:1
Bore: 63.5mm 2.5in
Stroke: 78.0mm 3.1in
Valve type/No: Ports
Transmission: Manual
No. of forward speeds: 4
Wheels driven: Rear
Springs F/R: Coil/Coil
Brakes F/R: Drum/Drum
Steering: Rack & pinion
Wheelbase: 244.9cm 96.4in
Track F: 125.5cm 49.4in
Track R: 130.0cm 51.2in
Length: 424.2cm 167.0in
Width: 163.8cm 64.5in
Height: 149.4cm 58.8in
Ground clearance: 17.8cm 7.0in
Kerb weight: 897.1kg 1976.0lb
Fuel: 42.3L 9.3gal 11.2galUS

4971 Wartburg
Knight
1973 E. Germany
87.0mph 140.0kmh
0-50mph 80.5kmh: 12.6secs
0-60mph 96.5kmh: 18.7secs
0-1/4 mile: 21.0secs
0-1km: 40.1secs
50.0bhp 37.3kW 50.7PS
@ 4250rpm
69.0lbft 93.5Nm @ 3000rpm
57.4bhp/ton 56.4bhp/tonne
50.4bhp/L 37.6kW/L 51.1PS/L
36.2ft/sec 11.0m/sec
17.6mph 28.3kmh/1000rpm
27.7mpg 23.1mpgUS 10.2L/100km
Petrol 2-stroke piston
992cc 60.5cu in
In-line 3 1 Carburettor
Compression ratio: 7.5:1
Bore: 73.5mm 2.9in
Stroke: 78.0mm 3.1in
Valve type/No: Ports
Transmission: Manual
No. of forward speeds: 4
Wheels driven: Rear
Springs F/R: Coil/Coil
Brakes F/R: Drum/Drum
Steering: Rack & pinion
Wheelbase: 245.1cm 96.5in
Track F: 125.7cm 49.5in
Track R: 130.0cm 51.2in
Length: 424.2cm 167.0in
Width: 163.8cm 64.5in
Height: 147.3cm 58.0in
Ground clearance: 17.8cm 7.0in
Kerb weight: 886.2kg 1952.0lb
Fuel: 43.7L 9.6gal 11.5galUS

4972 Warwick
GT
1961 UK
104.0mph 167.3kmh
0-50mph 80.5kmh: 9.3secs
0-60mph 96.5kmh: 12.8secs
0-1/4 mile: 18.6secs
100.0bhp 74.6kW 101.4PS
@ 5000rpm
117.0lbft 158.5Nm @ 3000rpm
100.0bhp/ton 98.3bhp/tonne
50.2bhp/L 37.4kW/L 50.9PS/L
50.3ft/sec 15.3m/sec
24.4mph 39.3kmh/1000rpm
23.8mpg 19.8mpgUS 11.9L/100km
Petrol 4-stroke piston
1991cc 121.5cu in
In-line 4
Compression ratio: 8.5:1
Bore: 83.0mm 3.3in
Stroke: 92.0mm 3.6in
Valve type/No: Overhead 8
Transmission: Manual with overdrive
No. of forward speeds: 7
Wheels driven: Rear
Springs F/R: Coil/Leaf
Brakes F/R: Disc/Drum
Wheelbase: 240.0cm 94.5in
Track F: 129.5cm 51.0in
Track R: 129.5cm 51.0in
Length: 411.5cm 162.0in
Width: 160.0cm 63.0in
Height: 132.1cm 52.0in
Ground clearance: 15.2cm 6.0in
Kerb weight: 1017.0kg 2240.0lb
Fuel: 63.7L 14.0gal 16.8galUS

4973 Westfield
SEight
1991 UK
140.0mph 225.3kmh
0-50mph 80.5kmh: 3.3secs
0-60mph 96.5kmh: 4.3secs
0-1/4 mile: 13.2secs
273.0bhp 203.6kW 276.8PS
@ 5700rpm
260.0lbft 352.3Nm @ 4200rpm
396.6bhp/ton 390.0bhp/tonne
69.1bhp/L 51.5kW/L 70.1PS/L
44.8ft/sec 13.7m/sec
27.0mph 43.4kmh/1000rpm
20.0mpg 16.7mpgUS 14.1L/100km
Petrol 4-stroke piston
3949cc 241.0cu in
Vee 8 4 Carburettor
Compression ratio: 10.0:1
Bore: 94.0mm 3.7in
Stroke: 71.9mm 2.8in
Valve type/No: Overhead 16
Transmission: Manual
No. of forward speeds: 5
Wheels driven: Rear
Springs F/R: Coil/Coil
Brakes F/R: Disc/Disc
Steering: Rack & pinion
Wheelbase: 236.2cm 93.0in
Track F: 152.4cm 60.0in
Track R: 158.8cm 62.5in
Length: 369.6cm 145.5in
Width: 162.6cm 64.0in
Height: 106.7cm 42.0in
Ground clearance: 10.2cm 4.0in
Kerb weight: 700.0kg 1541.8lb
Fuel: 45.5L 10.0gal 12.0galUS

4974 Wills Sainte Claire
Six
1926 USA
73.0mph 117.5kmh
0-50mph 80.5kmh: 17.7secs
0-60mph 96.5kmh: 26.0secs
0-1/4 mile: 22.8secs
66.0bhp 49.2kW 66.9PS
@ 3000rpm
185.0lbft 250.7Nm @ 1600rpm
41.5bhp/ton 40.8bhp/tonne
14.7bhp/L 11.0kW/L 14.9PS/L
45.8ft/sec 14.0m/sec
21.2mph 34.1kmh/1000rpm
Petrol 4-stroke piston
4487cc 273.8cu in
In-line 6
Compression ratio: 4.5:1
Bore: 82.6mm 3.2in
Stroke: 139.7mm 5.5in
Valve type/No: Overhead 12
Transmission: Manual
No. of forward speeds: 3
Wheels driven: Rear
Wheelbase: 322.6cm 127.0in
Track F: 142.2cm 56.0in
Track R: 142.2cm 56.0in
Length: 457.2cm 180.0in
Width: 175.3cm 69.0in
Height: 177.8cm 70.0in
Kerb weight: 1616.2kg 3560.0lb

4975 Willys
Aero Wing
1952 USA
81.3mph 130.8kmh
0-1/4 mile: 21.3secs
90.0bhp 67.1kW 91.2PS
@ 4000rpm
34.1bhp/L 25.4kW/L 34.6PS/L
38.9ft/sec 11.8m/sec
Petrol 4-stroke piston
2640cc 161.1cu in
In-line 6
Compression ratio: 7.6:1
Bore: 79.4mm 3.1in
Stroke: 88.9mm 3.5in
Valve type/No: Side 12
Transmission: Manual
No. of forward speeds: 3
Wheels driven: Rear
Wheelbase: 274.3cm 108.0in
Track F: 147.3cm 58.0in
Track R: 144.8cm 57.0in
Length: 459.2cm 180.8in
Height: 152.4cm 60.0in
Ground clearance: 17.8cm 7.0in

4976 Willys
Wagoneer 4WD
1963 USA
88.0mph 141.6kmh
0-50mph 80.5kmh: 11.4secs
0-60mph 96.5kmh: 15.9secs
0-1/4 mile: 20.2secs
155.0bhp 115.6kW 157.1PS
@ 4000rpm
230.0lbft 311.7Nm @ 2200rpm
88.8bhp/ton 87.3bhp/tonne
41.1bhp/L 30.7kW/L 41.7PS/L
48.7ft/sec 14.8m/sec
20.9mph 33.6kmh/1000rpm
Petrol 4-stroke piston
3769cc 230.0cu in
In-line 6 1 Carburettor
Compression ratio: 8.5:1
Bore: 84.8mm 3.3in
Stroke: 111.3mm 4.4in
Valve type/No: Overhead 12
Transmission: Automatic
No. of forward speeds: 3
Wheels driven: 4-wheel drive

Brake system: PA
Brakes F/R: Drum/Drum
Steering: PA
Wheelbase: 279.4cm 110.0in
Track F: 144.8cm 57.0in
Track R: 144.8cm 57.0in
Length: 466.6cm 183.7in
Width: 192.0cm 75.6in
Height: 163.1cm 64.2in
Ground clearance: 19.8cm 7.8in
Kerb weight: 1775.1kg 3910.0lb
Fuel: 75.7L 16.6gal 20.0galUS

4977 Wolseley

Hornet
1930 UK
62.2mph 100.1kmh
47.0bhp 35.0kW 47.6PS
@ 5000rpm
64.8bhp/ton 63.7bhp/tonne
37.0bhp/L 27.6kW/L 37.5PS/L
45.4ft/sec 13.8m/sec
35.0mpg 29.1mpgUS 8.1L/100km
Petrol 4-stroke piston
1271cc 77.5cu in
In-line 6 1 Carburettor
Bore: 57.0mm 2.2in
Stroke: 83.0mm 3.3in
Valve type/No: Overhead 12
Transmission: Manual
No. of forward speeds: 3
Wheels driven: Rear
Brakes F/R: Drum/Drum
Wheelbase: 229.9cm 90.5in
Track F: 106.7cm 42.0in
Track R: 106.7cm 42.0in
Length: 337.8cm 133.0in
Width: 129.5cm 51.0in
Height: 160.0cm 63.0in
Kerb weight: 737.3kg 1624.0lb
Fuel: 22.7L 5.0gal 6.0galUS

4978 Wolseley

Viper Saloon
1931 UK
60.0mph 96.5kmh
24.0mpg 20.0mpgUS 11.8L/100km
Petrol 4-stroke piston
2025cc 123.5cu in
In-line 6 2 Carburettor
Bore: 65.0mm 2.6in
Stroke: 101.0mm 4.0in
Valve type/No: Overhead 12
Transmission: Manual
No. of forward speeds: 4
Wheels driven: Rear
Brakes F/R: Drum/Drum
Wheelbase: 297.2cm 117.0in
Track F: 142.2cm 56.0in
Track R: 142.2cm 56.0in
Length: 438.7cm 172.7in
Width: 168.7cm 66.4in
Height: 180.3cm 71.0in
Kerb weight: 1398.3kg 3080.0lb
Fuel: 54.6L 12.0gal 14.4galUS

4979 Wolseley

14 Hornet Special
1935 UK
75.0mph 120.7kmh
0-50mph 80.5kmh: 14.4secs
0-60mph 96.5kmh: 21.0secs
28.0mpg 23.3mpgUS 10.1L/100km
Petrol 4-stroke piston
1604cc 97.9cu in
In-line 6
Bore: 61.5mm 2.4in
Stroke: 90.0mm 3.5in
Valve type/No: Overhead 12
Transmission: Manual
No. of forward speeds: 4
Wheels driven: Rear
Brakes F/R: Drum/Drum
Kerb weight: 877.1kg 1932.0lb
Fuel: 36.4L 8.0gal 9.6galUS

4980 Wolseley

Super 6
1936 UK
81.0mph 130.3kmh
0-50mph 80.5kmh: 14.2secs
0-60mph 96.5kmh: 21.0secs
15.0mpg 12.5mpgUS 18.8L/100km
Petrol 4-stroke piston
3485cc 212.6cu in
In-line 6
Bore: 82.0mm 3.2in
Stroke: 110.0mm 4.3in
Valve type/No: Overhead 12
Transmission: Manual
No. of forward speeds: 4
Wheels driven: Rear
Brakes F/R: Drum/Drum
Kerb weight: 1669.4kg 3677.0lb
Fuel: 61.4L 13.5gal 16.2galUS

4981 Wolseley

Salon de Ville
1937 UK
76.9mph 123.7kmh
0-50mph 80.5kmh: 15.3secs
0-60mph 96.5kmh: 24.4secs
20.0mpg 16.7mpgUS 14.1L/100km
Petrol 4-stroke piston
2322cc 141.7cu in
In-line 6 2 Carburettor
Bore: 69.5mm 2.7in
Stroke: 102.0mm 4.0in
Valve type/No: Overhead 12
Transmission: Manual
No. of forward speeds: 4
Wheels driven: Rear
Brakes F/R: Drum/Drum
Kerb weight: 1490.9kg 3284.0lb
Fuel: 39.8L 8.8gal 10.5galUS

4982 Wolseley

14/56 Salon de Ville
1938 UK
69.2mph 111.3kmh
0-50mph 80.5kmh: 23.0secs
0-60mph 96.5kmh: 35.7secs
22.0mpg 18.3mpgUS 12.8L/100km
Petrol 4-stroke piston
1818cc 110.9cu in
In-line 6
Bore: 61.5mm 2.4in
Stroke: 102.0mm 4.0in
Valve type/No: Overhead 12
Transmission: Manual
No. of forward speeds: 4
Wheels driven: Rear
Brakes F/R: Drum/Drum
Kerb weight: 1464.1kg 3225.0lb
Fuel: 39.8L 8.8gal 10.5galUS

4983 Wolseley

Drop-head Coupe
1938 UK
90.0mph 144.8kmh
0-50mph 80.5kmh: 13.9secs
0-60mph 96.5kmh: 19.1secs
108.0bhp 80.5kW 109.5PS
@ 3600rpm
63.7bhp/ton 62.6bhp/tonne
28.1bhp/L 20.9kW/L 28.5PS/L
43.3ft/sec 13.2m/sec
16.0mpg 13.3mpgUS 17.7L/100km
Petrol 4-stroke piston
3845cc 234.6cu in
In-line 6 2 Carburettor
Bore: 82.0mm 3.2in
Stroke: 110.0mm 4.3in
Valve type/No: Overhead 12
Transmission: Manual
No. of forward speeds: 4
Wheels driven: Rear
Brakes F/R: Drum/Drum
Kerb weight: 1724.7kg 3799.0lb
Fuel: 68.2L 15.0gal 18.0galUS

4984 Wolseley

Super 6
1938 UK
80.0mph 128.7kmh
0-50mph 80.5kmh: 13.5secs
0-60mph 96.5kmh: 20.4secs
108.0bhp 80.5kW 109.5PS
@ 3600rpm
59.7bhp/ton 58.7bhp/tonne
31.0bhp/L 23.1kW/L 31.4PS/L
43.3ft/sec 13.2m/sec
18.0mpg 15.0mpgUS 15.7L/100km
Petrol 4-stroke piston
3485cc 212.6cu in
In-line 6 2 Carburettor
Bore: 82.0mm 3.2in
Stroke: 110.0mm 4.3in
Valve type/No: Overhead 12
Transmission: Manual
No. of forward speeds: 4
Wheels driven: Rear
Brakes F/R: Drum/Drum
Kerb weight: 1839.6kg 4052.0lb
Fuel: 68.2L 15.0gal 18.0galUS

4985 Wolseley

12/48
1939 UK
70.5mph 113.4kmh
0-50mph 80.5kmh: 31.0secs
55.0bhp 41.0kW 55.8PS
@ 4200rpm
42.2bhp/ton 41.5bhp/tonne
35.5bhp/L 26.5kW/L 36.0PS/L
46.9ft/sec 14.3m/sec
23.0mpg 19.2mpgUS 12.3L/100km
Petrol 4-stroke piston
1548cc 94.4cu in
In-line 4
Compression ratio: 6.6:1
Bore: 69.5mm 2.7in
Stroke: 102.0mm 4.0in
Valve type/No: Overhead 8
Transmission: Manual
No. of forward speeds: 4
Wheels driven: Rear
Brakes F/R: Drum/Drum
Kerb weight: 1324.8kg 2918.0lb
Fuel: 45.5L 10.0gal 12.0galUS

4986 Wolseley

4/50
1949 UK
71.0mph 114.2kmh
0-50mph 80.5kmh: 21.0secs
0-60mph 96.5kmh: 36.1secs
50.0bhp 37.3kW 50.7PS
@ 4000rpm
71.7lbft 97.2Nm @ 2900rpm
43.4bhp/ton 42.6bhp/tonne
33.9bhp/L 25.3kW/L 34.3PS/L
38.1ft/sec 11.6m/sec
16.2mph 26.1kmh/1000rpm
25.0mpg 20.8mpgUS 11.3L/100km
Petrol 4-stroke piston
1476cc 90.0cu in
In-line 4 1 Carburettor
Compression ratio: 7.0:1
Bore: 73.5mm 2.9in
Stroke: 87.0mm 3.4in
Valve type/No: Overhead 8
Transmission: Manual
No. of forward speeds: 4
Wheels driven: Rear
Springs F/R: Torsion bar/Leaf
Brakes F/R: Drum/Drum
Wheelbase: 259.1cm 102.0in
Track F: 134.9cm 53.1in
Track R: 134.9cm 53.1in
Length: 431.8cm 170.0in
Width: 167.6cm 66.0in
Height: 160.0cm 63.0in
Ground clearance: 17.8cm 7.0in
Kerb weight: 1172.7kg 2583.0lb
Fuel: 43.2L 9.5gal 11.4galUS

4987 Wolseley

6/80
1950 UK
78.5mph 126.3kmh
0-50mph 80.5kmh: 17.1secs
0-60mph 96.5kmh: 24.4secs
72.0bhp 53.7kW 73.0PS
@ 4600rpm
101.8lbft 137.9Nm @ 2200rpm
55.6bhp/ton 54.7bhp/tonne
32.5bhp/L 24.2kW/L 33.0PS/L
43.8ft/sec 13.3m/sec
18.8mph 30.2kmh/1000rpm
20.0mpg 16.7mpgUS 14.1L/100km
Petrol 4-stroke piston
2214cc 135.1cu in
In-line 6
Compression ratio: 7.0:1
Bore: 73.5mm 2.9in
Stroke: 87.0mm 3.4in
Valve type/No: Overhead 12
Transmission: Manual
No. of forward speeds: 4
Wheels driven: Rear
Brakes F/R: Drum/Drum
Wheelbase: 279.4cm 110.0in
Track F: 137.7cm 54.2in
Track R: 134.6cm 53.0in
Length: 449.6cm 177.0in
Width: 167.6cm 66.0in
Height: 160.0cm 63.0in
Ground clearance: 17.8cm 7.0in
Kerb weight: 1316.6kg 2900.0lb
Fuel: 54.6L 12.0gal 14.4galUS

4988 Wolseley

6/80
1952 UK
84.0mph 135.2kmh
0-50mph 80.5kmh: 13.9secs
0-60mph 96.5kmh: 20.8secs
0-1/4 mile: 22.2secs
72.0bhp 53.7kW 73.0PS
@ 4600rpm
101.0lbft 136.9Nm @ 2200rpm
55.1bhp/ton 54.2bhp/tonne
32.5bhp/L 24.2kW/L 33.0PS/L
43.8ft/sec 13.3m/sec
17.0mph 27.4kmh/1000rpm
18.1mpg 15.1mpgUS 15.6L/100km
Petrol 4-stroke piston
2214cc 135.1cu in
In-line 6
Compression ratio: 6.6:1
Bore: 73.5mm 2.9in
Stroke: 87.0mm 3.4in
Valve type/No: Overhead 12
Transmission: Manual
No. of forward speeds: 4
Wheels driven: Rear
Springs F/R: Torsion bar/Leaf
Brakes F/R: Drum/Drum
Wheelbase: 279.4cm 110.0in
Track F: 137.2cm 54.0in
Track R: 134.6cm 53.0in
Length: 449.6cm 177.0in
Width: 167.6cm 66.0in
Height: 161.0cm 63.4in
Ground clearance: 17.8cm 7.0in
Kerb weight: 1329.3kg 2928.0lb
Fuel: 54.6L 12.0gal 14.4galUS

4989 Wolseley

4/44
1953 UK
72.0mph 115.8kmh
0-50mph 80.5kmh: 19.6secs
0-60mph 96.5kmh: 32.6secs
0-1/4 mile: 24.6secs
46.0bhp 34.3kW 46.6PS
@ 4800rpm
58.5lbft 79.3Nm @ 2400rpm
41.4bhp/ton 40.8bhp/tonne
36.8bhp/L 27.4kW/L 37.3PS/L
47.2ft/sec 14.4m/sec
14.5mph 23.3kmh/1000rpm
24.0mpg 20.0mpgUS 11.8L/100km
Petrol 4-stroke piston
1250cc 76.3cu in
In-line 4
Compression ratio: 7.3:1
Bore: 66.5mm 2.6in
Stroke: 90.0mm 3.5in
Valve type/No: Overhead 8
Transmission: Manual
No. of forward speeds: 4
Wheels driven: Rear
Springs F/R: Coil/Leaf
Brakes F/R: Drum/Drum
Wheelbase: 259.1cm 102.0in
Track F: 129.0cm 50.8in
Track R: 129.5cm 51.0in
Length: 439.4cm 173.0in
Width: 154.9cm 61.0in
Height: 152.4cm 60.0in
Ground clearance: 19.1cm 7.5in
Kerb weight: 1128.6kg 2486.0lb
Fuel: 43.2L 9.5gal 11.4galUS

4990 Wolseley

6/90
1955 UK
94.5mph 152.1kmh
0-50mph 80.5kmh: 13.1secs
0-60mph 96.5kmh: 18.1secs
0-1/4 mile: 21.2secs
95.0bhp 70.8kW 96.3PS
@ 4500rpm
133.0lbft 180.2Nm @ 2000rpm
65.4bhp/ton 64.3bhp/tonne
36.0bhp/L 26.8kW/L 36.5PS/L
43.8ft/sec 13.3m/sec
19.1mph 30.7kmh/1000rpm

21.4mpg 17.8mpgUS 13.2L/100km
Petrol 4-stroke piston
2639cc 161.0cu in
In-line 6
Compression ratio: 7.3:1
Bore: 79.3mm 3.1in
Stroke: 88.9mm 3.5in
Valve type/No: Overhead 12
Transmission: Manual
No. of forward speeds: 4
Wheels driven: Rear
Springs F/R: Torsion bar/Coil
Brakes F/R: Drum/Drum
Wheelbase: 288.3cm 113.5in
Track F: 138.2cm 54.4in
Track R: 138.4cm 54.5in
Length: 477.5cm 188.0in
Width: 170.2cm 67.0in
Height: 157.5cm 62.0in
Ground clearance: 17.8cm 7.0in
Kerb weight: 1477.8kg 3255.0lb
Fuel: 59.1L 13.0gal 15.6galUS

4991 Wolseley

15/50
1957 UK
78.0mph 125.5kmh
0-50mph 80.5kmh: 18.4secs
0-60mph 96.5kmh: 29.8secs
0-1/4 mile: 24.1secs
55.0bhp 41.0kW 55.8PS
@ 4400rpm
78.0lbft 105.7Nm @ 2400rpm
48.7bhp/ton 47.9bhp/tonne
36.9bhp/L 27.5kW/L 37.4PS/L
42.8ft/sec 13.0m/sec
15.0mph 24.1kmh/1000rpm
29.4mpg 24.5mpgUS 9.6L/100km
Petrol 4-stroke piston
1489cc 90.8cu in
In-line 4
Compression ratio: 8.3:1
Bore: 73.0mm 2.9in
Stroke: 88.9mm 3.5in
Valve type/No: Overhead 8
Transmission: Manual
No. of forward speeds: 4
Wheels driven: Rear
Springs F/R: Coil/Leaf
Brakes F/R: Drum/Drum
Wheelbase: 259.1cm 102.0in
Track F: 129.3cm 50.9in
Track R: 129.5cm 51.0in
Length: 439.4cm 173.0in
Width: 154.9cm 61.0in
Height: 152.4cm 60.0in
Ground clearance: 19.1cm 7.5in
Kerb weight: 1147.3kg 2527.0lb
Fuel: 41.9L 9.2gal 11.1galUS

4992 Wolseley

6/90
1957 UK
90.0mph 144.8kmh
0-50mph 80.5kmh: 15.1secs
0-60mph 96.5kmh: 20.3secs
0-1/4 mile: 22.3secs
97.0bhp 72.3kW 98.3PS
@ 4750rpm
135.0lbft 182.9Nm @ 2000rpm
62.3bhp/ton 61.2bhp/tonne
36.8bhp/L 27.4kW/L 37.3PS/L
46.2ft/sec 14.1m/sec
19.9mph 32.0kmh/1000rpm
23.6mpg 19.7mpgUS 12.0L/100km
Petrol 4-stroke piston
2639cc 161.0cu in
In-line 6
Compression ratio: 8.3:1
Bore: 79.3mm 3.1in
Stroke: 88.9mm 3.5in
Valve type/No: Overhead 12
Transmission: Automatic
No. of forward speeds: 3
Wheels driven: Rear
Springs F/R: Torsion bar/Leaf
Brakes F/R: Drum/Drum
Wheelbase: 288.3cm 113.5in
Track F: 138.2cm 54.4in
Track R: 138.4cm 54.5in
Length: 477.5cm 188.0in
Width: 170.2cm 67.0in
Height: 157.5cm 62.0in
Ground clearance: 17.8cm 7.0in
Kerb weight: 1583.5kg 3488.0lb
Fuel: 59.1L 13.0gal 15.6galUS

4993 Wolseley

1500
1958 UK
79.2mph 127.4kmh
0-50mph 80.5kmh: 16.1secs
0-60mph 96.5kmh: 24.4secs
0-1/4 mile: 22.1secs
50.0bhp 37.3kW 50.7PS
@ 4200rpm
74.0lbft 100.3Nm @ 3000rpm
55.6bhp/ton 54.6bhp/tonne
33.6bhp/L 25.0kW/L 34.0PS/L
40.8ft/sec 12.4m/sec
18.5mph 29.8kmh/1000rpm
34.5mpg 28.7mpgUS 8.2L/100km
Petrol 4-stroke piston
1489cc 90.8cu in
In-line 4
Compression ratio: 7.2:1
Bore: 73.0mm 2.9in
Stroke: 88.9mm 3.5in
Valve type/No: Overhead 8
Transmission: Manual
No. of forward speeds: 4
Wheels driven: Rear
Springs F/R: Torsion bar/Leaf
Brakes F/R: Drum/Drum
Wheelbase: 218.4cm 86.0in
Track F: 129.3cm 50.9in
Track R: 127.8cm 50.3in
Length: 385.3cm 151.7in
Width: 154.9cm 61.0in
Height: 151.6cm 59.7in
Ground clearance: 15.2cm 6.0in
Kerb weight: 915.3kg 2016.0lb
Fuel: 31.8L 7.0gal 8.4galUS

4994 Wolseley

15/60
1959 UK
79.0mph 127.1kmh
0-50mph 80.5kmh: 15.1secs
0-60mph 96.5kmh: 24.3secs
0-1/4 mile: 22.6secs
55.0bhp 41.0kW 55.8PS
@ 4400rpm
82.0lbft 111.1Nm @ 2100rpm
51.8bhp/ton 50.9bhp/tonne
36.9bhp/L 27.5kW/L 37.4PS/L
42.8ft/sec 13.0m/sec
15.6mph 25.1kmh/1000rpm
27.9mpg 23.2mpgUS 10.1L/100km
Petrol 4-stroke piston
1489cc 90.8cu in
In-line 4
Compression ratio: 8.3:1
Bore: 73.0mm 2.9in
Stroke: 88.9mm 3.5in
Valve type/No: Overhead 8
Transmission: Manual
No. of forward speeds: 4
Wheels driven: Rear
Springs F/R: Coil/Leaf
Brakes F/R: Drum/Drum
Wheelbase: 252.0cm 99.2in
Track F: 124.0cm 48.8in
Track R: 126.5cm 49.8in
Length: 452.1cm 178.0in
Width: 161.3cm 63.5in
Height: 149.9cm 59.0in
Ground clearance: 15.7cm 6.2in
Kerb weight: 1080.5kg 2380.0lb
Fuel: 45.5L 10.0gal 12.0galUS

4995 Wolseley

6/99
1959 UK
101.6mph 163.5kmh
0-50mph 80.5kmh: 12.4secs
0-60mph 96.5kmh: 17.2secs
0-1/4 mile: 21.1secs
102.5bhp 76.4kW 103.9PS
@ 4500rpm
158.0lbft 214.1Nm @ 2000rpm
67.9bhp/ton 66.8bhp/tonne
35.2bhp/L 26.2kW/L 35.7PS/L
43.8ft/sec 13.3m/sec
20.8mph 33.5kmh/1000rpm
17.2mpg 14.3mpgUS 16.4L/100km
Petrol 4-stroke piston
2912cc 177.7cu in
In-line 6
Compression ratio: 8.2:1
Bore: 83.3mm 3.3in
Stroke: 88.9mm 3.5in
Valve type/No: Overhead 12
Transmission: Automatic
No. of forward speeds: 3
Wheels driven: Rear
Springs F/R: Coil/Leaf
Brake system: PA
Brakes F/R: Disc/Drum
Wheelbase: 274.3cm 108.0in
Track F: 137.2cm 54.0in
Track R: 135.1cm 53.2in
Length: 477.5cm 188.0in
Width: 174.0cm 68.5in
Height: 149.9cm 59.0in
Ground clearance: 16.3cm 6.4in
Kerb weight: 1535.0kg 3381.0lb
Fuel: 72.8L 16.0gal 19.2galUS

4996 Wolseley

16/60 Automatic
1962 UK
79.0mph 127.1kmh
0-50mph 80.5kmh: 17.7secs
0-60mph 96.5kmh: 28.1secs
0-1/4 mile: 24.0secs
61.0bhp 45.5kW 61.8PS
@ 4500rpm
90.0lbft 122.0Nm @ 2100rpm
55.0bhp/ton 54.1bhp/tonne
37.6bhp/L 28.0kW/L 38.1PS/L
43.8ft/sec 13.3m/sec
16.6mph 26.7kmh/1000rpm
24.2mpg 20.2mpgUS 11.7L/100km
Petrol 4-stroke piston
1622cc 99.0cu in
In-line 4 1 Carburettor
Compression ratio: 8.3:1
Bore: 76.2mm 3.0in
Stroke: 88.9mm 3.5in
Valve type/No: Overhead 8
Transmission: Automatic
No. of forward speeds: 3
Wheels driven: Rear
Springs F/R: Coil/Leaf
Brakes F/R: Drum/Drum
Steering: Cam & lever
Wheelbase: 254.5cm 100.2in
Track F: 128.5cm 50.6in
Track R: 130.6cm 51.4in
Length: 443.2cm 174.5in
Width: 161.3cm 63.5in
Height: 149.4cm 58.8in
Ground clearance: 15.0cm 5.9in
Kerb weight: 1128.2kg 2485.0lb
Fuel: 45.5L 10.0gal 12.0galUS

4997 Wolseley

6/110
1962 UK
105.0mph 168.9kmh
0-50mph 80.5kmh: 9.8secs
0-60mph 96.5kmh: 13.3secs
0-1/4 mile: 19.4secs
120.0bhp 89.5kW 121.7PS
@ 4750rpm
163.0lbft 220.9Nm @ 2750rpm
78.5bhp/ton 77.2bhp/tonne
41.2bhp/L 30.7kW/L 41.8PS/L
46.2ft/sec 14.1m/sec
27.0mph 43.4kmh/1000rpm
19.4mpg 16.2mpgUS 14.6L/100km
Petrol 4-stroke piston
2912cc 177.7cu in
In-line 6 2 Carburettor
Compression ratio: 8.3:1
Bore: 83.3mm 3.3in
Stroke: 88.9mm 3.5in
Valve type/No: Overhead 12
Transmission: Manual with overdrive
No. of forward speeds: 6
Wheels driven: Rear
Springs F/R: Coil/Leaf
Brake system: PA
Brakes F/R: Disc/Drum
Steering: Cam & lever
Wheelbase: 279.4cm 110.0in
Track F: 136.7cm 53.8in
Track R: 135.1cm 53.2in
Length: 477.5cm 188.0in
Width: 174.0cm 68.5in
Height: 153.7cm 60.5in
Ground clearance: 15.7cm 6.2in
Kerb weight: 1554.0kg 3423.0lb
Fuel: 72.8L 16.0gal 19.2galUS

4998 Wolseley

Hornet
1963 UK
78.0mph 125.5kmh
0-50mph 80.5kmh: 15.7secs
0-60mph 96.5kmh: 24.1secs
0-1/4 mile: 22.4secs
38.0bhp 28.3kW 38.5PS
@ 5250rpm
52.0lbft 70.5Nm @ 2700rpm
61.1bhp/ton 60.1bhp/tonne
38.1bhp/L 28.4kW/L 38.6PS/L
43.8ft/sec 13.3m/sec
14.8mph 23.8kmh/1000rpm
35.3mpg 29.4mpgUS 8.0L/100km
Petrol 4-stroke piston
998cc 60.9cu in
In-line 4 1 Carburettor
Compression ratio: 8.3:1
Bore: 64.6mm 2.5in
Stroke: 76.2mm 3.0in
Valve type/No: Overhead 8
Transmission: Manual
No. of forward speeds: 4
Wheels driven: Front
Springs F/R: Rubber/Rubber
Brakes F/R: Drum/Drum
Steering: Rack & pinion
Wheelbase: 203.7cm 80.2in
Track F: 120.4cm 47.4in
Track R: 116.6cm 45.9in
Length: 327.2cm 128.8in
Width: 141.0cm 55.5in
Height: 134.6cm 53.0in
Ground clearance: 15.2cm 6.0in
Kerb weight: 632.4kg 1393.0lb
Fuel: 25.0L 5.5gal 6.6galUS

4999 Wolseley

1100
1965 UK
87.0mph 140.0kmh
0-50mph 80.5kmh: 14.4secs
0-60mph 96.5kmh: 20.6secs
0-1/4 mile: 21.6secs
55.0bhp 41.0kW 55.8PS
@ 5500rpm
61.0lbft 82.7Nm @ 2750rpm
68.1bhp/ton 66.9bhp/tonne
50.1bhp/L 37.3kW/L 50.8PS/L
50.4ft/sec 15.3m/sec
14.9mph 24.0kmh/1000rpm
26.5mpg 22.1mpgUS 10.7L/100km
Petrol 4-stroke piston
1098cc 67.0cu in
In-line 4 2 Carburettor
Compression ratio: 8.9:1
Bore: 64.6mm 2.5in
Stroke: 83.7mm 3.3in
Valve type/No: Overhead 8
Transmission: Manual
No. of forward speeds: 4
Wheels driven: Front
Springs F/R: Gas/Gas
Brakes F/R: Disc/Drum
Steering: Rack & pinion
Wheelbase: 237.5cm 93.5in
Track F: 130.8cm 51.5in
Track R: 129.3cm 50.9in
Length: 372.6cm 146.7in
Width: 153.4cm 60.4in
Height: 133.9cm 52.7in
Ground clearance: 15.2cm 6.0in
Kerb weight: 821.7kg 1810.0lb
Fuel: 36.4L 8.0gal 9.6galUS

5000 Wolseley

18/85
1967 UK
91.0mph 146.4kmh
0-50mph 80.5kmh: 12.9secs
0-60mph 96.5kmh: 18.0secs
0-1/4 mile: 21.2secs
0-1km: 39.5secs
85.0bhp 63.4kW 86.2PS
@ 5300rpm
99.0lbft 134.1Nm @ 2100rpm
73.2bhp/ton 72.0bhp/tonne
47.3bhp/L 35.2kW/L 47.9PS/L
51.5ft/sec 15.7m/sec
17.4mph 28.0kmh/1000rpm
21.9mpg 18.2mpgUS 12.9L/100km
Petrol 4-stroke piston
1798cc 109.7cu in
In-line 4 1 Carburettor
Compression ratio: 8.8:1
Bore: 80.3mm 3.2in
Stroke: 89.0mm 3.5in
Valve type/No: Overhead 8
Transmission: Automatic
No. of forward speeds: 3

Wheels driven: Front
Springs F/R: Gas/Gas
Brake system: PA
Brakes F/R: Disc/Drum
Steering: Rack & pinion PA
Wheelbase: 269.2cm 106.0in
Track F: 142.5cm 56.1in
Track R: 141.0cm 55.5in
Length: 424.2cm 167.0in
Width: 170.2cm 67.0in
Height: 141.0cm 55.5in
Ground clearance: 16.5cm 6.5in
Kerb weight: 1180.8kg 2601.0lb
Fuel: 47.8L 10.5gal 12.6galUS

5001 Wolseley

18/85 Mk II
1969 UK
100.0mph 160.9kmh
0-50mph 80.5kmh: 10.3secs
0-60mph 96.5kmh: 15.2secs
0-1/4 mile: 20.4secs
0-1km: 37.3secs
86.0bhp 64.1kW 87.2PS
@ 5300rpm
101.0lbft 136.9Nm @ 3000rpm
73.4bhp/ton 72.1bhp/tonne
47.8bhp/L 35.7kW/L 48.5PS/L
51.5ft/sec 15.7m/sec
18.2mph 29.3kmh/1000rpm
23.5mpg 19.6mpgUS 12.0L/100km
Petrol 4-stroke piston
1798cc 109.7cu in
In-line 4 1 Carburettor
Compression ratio: 9.0:1
Bore: 80.3mm 3.2in
Stroke: 88.9mm 3.5in
Valve type/No: Overhead 8
Transmission: Manual
No. of forward speeds: 4
Wheels driven: Front
Springs F/R: Gas/Gas
Brake system: PA
Brakes F/R: Disc/Drum
Steering: Rack & pinion PA
Wheelbase: 269.2cm 106.0in
Track F: 142.2cm 56.0in
Track R: 141.0cm 55.5in
Length: 421.9cm 166.1in
Width: 170.2cm 67.0in
Height: 141.0cm 55.5in
Ground clearance: 16.5cm 6.5in
Kerb weight: 1192.2kg 2626.0lb
Fuel: 47.8L 10.5gal 12.6galUS

5002 Yugo

GV
1986 Yugoslavia
90.0mph 144.8kmh
0-60mph 96.5kmh: 13.9secs
0-1/4 mile: 19.5secs
55.0bhp 41.0kW 55.8PS
@ 6000rpm
52.0lbft 70.5Nm @ 4600rpm
64.8bhp/ton 63.8bhp/tonne
49.3bhp/L 36.7kW/L 50.0PS/L
36.5ft/sec 11.1m/sec
15.6mph 25.1kmh/1000rpm
36.0mpg 30.0mpgUS 7.8L/100km
Petrol 4-stroke piston
1116cc 68.1cu in
In-line 4 1 Carburettor
Compression ratio: 9.2:1
Bore: 80.0mm 3.1in
Stroke: 55.5mm 2.2in
Valve type/No: Overhead 8
Transmission: Manual
No. of forward speeds: 4
Wheels driven: Front
Springs F/R: Coil/Leaf
Brake system: PA
Brakes F/R: Disc/Drum
Steering: Rack & pinion
Wheelbase: 215.1cm 84.7in
Track F: 130.8cm 51.5in
Track R: 131.3cm 51.7in
Length: 353.1cm 139.0in
Width: 154.2cm 60.7in
Height: 138.9cm 54.7in
Kerb weight: 862.6kg 1900.0lb
Fuel: 32.2L 7.1gal 8.5galUS

5003 Yugo

45 GLS
1987 Yugoslavia
83.0mph 133.5kmh
0-50mph 80.5kmh: 15.0secs
0-60mph 96.5kmh: 21.6secs
0-1/4 mile: 22.1secs
0-1km: 41.9secs
45.0bhp 33.6kW 45.6PS
@ 5800rpm
46.3lbft 62.7Nm @ 3300rpm
55.1bhp/ton 54.2bhp/tonne
49.8bhp/L 37.2kW/L 50.5PS/L
43.2ft/sec 13.1m/sec
14.7mph 23.7kmh/1000rpm
34.7mpg 28.9mpgUS 8.1L/100km
Petrol 4-stroke piston
903cc 55.0cu in
In-line 4 1 Carburettor
Compression ratio: 9.0:1
Bore: 65.0mm 2.6in
Stroke: 68.0mm 2.7in
Valve type/No: Overhead 8
Transmission: Manual
No. of forward speeds: 4
Wheels driven: Front
Springs F/R: Coil/Leaf
Brakes F/R: Disc/Drum
Steering: Rack & pinion
Wheelbase: 215.0cm 84.6in
Track F: 130.8cm 51.5in
Track R: 131.2cm 51.7in
Length: 353.0cm 139.0in
Width: 154.2cm 60.7in
Height: 139.0cm 54.7in
Ground clearance: 17.9cm 7.0in
Kerb weight: 830.0kg 1828.2lb
Fuel: 30.0L 6.6gal 7.9galUS

5004 Yugo

65A GLX
1988 Yugoslavia
97.0mph 156.1kmh
0-50mph 80.5kmh: 8.2secs
0-60mph 96.5kmh: 11.7secs
0-1/4 mile: 18.1secs
0-1km: 36.4secs
65.0bhp 48.5kW 65.9PS
@ 5800rpm
72.3lbft 98.0Nm @ 3500rpm
82.0bhp/ton 80.6bhp/tonne
50.1bhp/L 37.3kW/L 50.8PS/L
35.3ft/sec 10.7m/sec
19.3mph 31.1kmh/1000rpm
31.1mpg 25.9mpgUS 9.1L/100km
Petrol 4-stroke piston
1298cc 79.0cu in
In-line 4 1 Carburettor
Compression ratio: 9.1:1
Bore: 86.4mm 3.4in
Stroke: 55.5mm 2.2in
Valve type/No: Overhead 8
Transmission: Manual
No. of forward speeds: 5
Wheels driven: Front
Springs F/R: Coil/Leaf
Brake system: PA
Brakes F/R: Disc/Drum
Steering: Rack & pinion
Wheelbase: 215.0cm 84.6in
Track F: 130.8cm 51.5in
Track R: 131.2cm 51.7in
Length: 353.0cm 139.0in
Width: 154.2cm 60.7in
Height: 139.0cm 54.7in
Ground clearance: 17.9cm 7.0in
Kerb weight: 806.0kg 1775.3lb
Fuel: 30.0L 6.6gal 7.9galUS

5005 Yugo

Sana 1.4
1990 Yugoslavia
99.0mph 159.3kmh
0-50mph 80.5kmh: 9.4secs
0-60mph 96.5kmh: 13.2secs
0-1/4 mile: 19.2secs
0-1km: 35.9secs
70.0bhp 52.2kW 71.0PS
@ 6000rpm
78.2lbft 106.0Nm @ 2900rpm
76.5bhp/ton 75.3bhp/tonne
51.0bhp/L 38.0kW/L 51.7PS/L
44.5ft/sec 13.5m/sec
19.9mph 32.0kmh/1000rpm
28.1mpg 23.4mpgUS 10.1L/100km
Petrol 4-stroke piston
1372cc 84.0cu in
In-line 4 1 Carburettor
Compression ratio: 9.2:1
Bore: 80.5mm 3.2in
Stroke: 67.7mm 2.7in
Valve type/No: Overhead 8
Transmission: Manual
No. of forward speeds: 5
Wheels driven: Front
Springs F/R: Coil/Coil
Brake system: PA
Brakes F/R: Disc/Drum
Steering: Rack & pinion
Wheelbase: 250.0cm 98.4in
Track F: 140.0cm 55.1in
Track R: 140.0cm 55.1in
Length: 393.2cm 154.8in
Width: 165.8cm 65.3in
Height: 141.0cm 55.5in
Ground clearance: 17.9cm 7.0in
Kerb weight: 930.0kg 2048.5lb
Fuel: 47.8L 10.5gal 12.6galUS

5006 Zastava

1300 ZLX-E
1981 Yugoslavia
92.0mph 148.0kmh
0-50mph 80.5kmh: 10.5secs
0-60mph 96.5kmh: 16.0secs
0-1/4 mile: 20.3secs
0-1km: 38.4secs
65.0bhp 48.5kW 65.9PS
@ 5800rpm
97.1lbft 131.6Nm @ 3900rpm
75.6bhp/ton 74.4bhp/tonne
50.0bhp/L 37.3kW/L 50.6PS/L
35.3ft/sec 10.7m/sec
16.3mph 26.2kmh/1000rpm
31.1mpg 25.9mpgUS 9.1L/100km
Petrol 4-stroke piston
1301cc 79.4cu in
In-line 4 1 Carburettor
Compression ratio: 9.1:1
Bore: 86.5mm 3.4in
Stroke: 55.5mm 2.2in
Valve type/No: Overhead 8
Transmission: Manual
No. of forward speeds: 4
Wheels driven: Front
Springs F/R: Coil/Leaf
Brake system: PA
Brakes F/R: Disc/Drum
Steering: Rack & pinion PA
Wheelbase: 244.9cm 96.4in
Track F: 130.3cm 51.3in
Track R: 130.3cm 51.3in
Length: 379.2cm 149.3in
Width: 159.0cm 62.6in
Height: 137.2cm 54.0in
Ground clearance: 14.5cm 5.7in
Kerb weight: 873.9kg 1925.0lb
Fuel: 42.8L 9.4gal 11.3galUS

5007 Zender

Vision 3
1989 Germany
175.0mph 281.6kmh
0-60mph 96.5kmh: 6.0secs
300.0bhp 223.7kW 304.2PS
@ 5000rpm
335.0lbft 453.9Nm @ 3750rpm
225.9bhp/ton 222.1bhp/tonne
54.1bhp/L 40.3kW/L 54.8PS/L
51.8ft/sec 15.8m/sec
Petrol 4-stroke piston
5547cc 338.4cu in
Vee 8 fuel injection
Compression ratio: 9.0:1
Bore: 96.5mm 3.8in
Stroke: 94.8mm 3.7in
Valve type/No: Overhead 16
Transmission: Manual
No. of forward speeds: 5
Wheels driven: Rear
Springs F/R: Coil/Coil
Brake system: PA
Brakes F/R: Disc/Disc
Steering: Rack & pinion
Wheelbase: 249.9cm 98.4in
Track F: 161.0cm 63.4in
Track R: 164.8cm 64.9in
Length: 406.9cm 160.2in
Width: 197.9cm 77.9in
Height: 111.0cm 43.7in
Kerb weight: 1350.6kg 2975.0lb
Fuel: 86.3L 19.0gal 22.8galUS

5008 Zender

Fact 4
1990 Germany
186.0mph 299.3kmh
0-60mph 96.5kmh: 4.3secs
448.0bhp 334.1kW 454.2PS
@ 6500rpm
390.0lbft 528.5Nm @ 4000rpm
411.3bhp/ton 404.4bhp/tonne
125.8bhp/L 93.8kW/L 127.5PS/L
61.4ft/sec 18.7m/sec
Petrol 4-stroke piston
3562cc 217.3cu in turbocharged
Vee 8 fuel injection
Compression ratio: 9.3:1
Bore: 81.0mm 3.2in
Stroke: 86.4mm 3.4in
Valve type/No: Overhead 32
Transmission: Manual
No. of forward speeds: 5
Wheels driven: Rear
Springs F/R: Coil/Coil
Brakes F/R: Disc/Disc
Steering: Rack & pinion
Wheelbase: 249.9cm 98.4in
Track F: 161.0cm 63.4in
Track R: 164.8cm 64.9in
Length: 407.9cm 160.6in
Width: 199.9cm 78.7in
Height: 112.0cm 44.1in
Kerb weight: 1107.8kg 2440.0lb
Fuel: 99.9L 22.0gal 26.4galUS